THE 2006 ESPN
BASEBALL
ENCYCLOPEDIA

2006 BASEBALL SCHEDULE ON ESPN/ESPN2

Date	Time (EST)	Network	Game(s)	Date	Time (EST)	Network	Game(s)
March 2	1 p.m.	ESPN	CLE vs. HOU Spring Training	March 12	8 p.m.	ESPN2	TBD *MLB World Baseball Classic*
March 3	4 a.m.	ESPN2	CHINA vs. JAPAN	March 12	11 p.m.	ESPN2	TBD *MLB World Baseball Classic*
			MLB World Baseball Classic	March 13	1 p.m.	ESPN	TBD *MLB World Baseball Classic*
March 3	1 p.m.	ESPN	CANADA vs. TBJ Spring Training	March 13	7 p.m.	ESPN2	TBD *MLB World Baseball Classic*
March 4	4 a.m.	ESPN2	CHINESE TAIPEI vs. JAPAN	March 14	1 p.m.	ESPN	STL vs. NYY Spring Training
			MLB World Baseball Classic	March 14	7 p.m.	ESPN2	TBD *MLB World Baseball Classic*
March 5	4 a.m.	ESPN2	KOREA vs. JAPAN	March 15	1 p.m.	ESPN	NYY vs. HOU Spring Training
			MLB World Baseball Classic	March 16	7:30 p.m.	ESPN	TBD *MLB World Baseball Classic*
March 5	2 p.m.	ESPN	PUERTO RICO vs. NYM Spring Training	March 18	3 p.m.	ESPN	TBD *MLB World Baseball Classic*
March 6	1 p.m.	ESPN	CLE vs. NYM Spring Training	March 18	10 p.m.	ESPN	TBD *MLB World Baseball Classic*
March 7	1 p.m.	ESPN	DOMINICAN REPUBLIC vs. VENEZUELA	March 20	1 p.m.	ESPN	ATL vs. STL Spring Training
			MLB World Baseball Classic	March 20	9 p.m.	ESPN	TBD *MLB World Baseball Classic*
March 7	4 p.m.	ESPN2	MEXICO vs. USA	March 21	1 p.m.	ESPN	LAD vs. FLA Spring Training
			MLB World Baseball Classic	March 22	12:30 p.m.	ESPN	PHI vs. ATL Spring Training
March 8	1 p.m.	ESPN2	CUBA vs. PANAMA	March 23	1 p.m.	ESPN2	BOS vs. MIN Spring Training
			MLB World Baseball Classic	March 24	1 p.m.	ESPN2	NYY vs. MIN Spring Training
March 8	4 p.m.	ESPN2	CANADA vs. USA	March 29	1 p.m.	ESPN	PIT vs. BOS Spring Training
			MLB World Baseball Classic	March 30	1 p.m.	ESPN	CIN vs. BOS Spring Training
				March 31	1 p.m.	ESPN	STL vs. NYM Spring Training

Date	Time (EST)	Network	Game(s)	Date	Time (EST)	Network	Game(s)	Date	Time (EST)	Network	Game(s)
Apr 2	8 p.m.	ESPN2	CLE at CWS	June 1	7 p.m.	ESPN	TBD	Aug 10	8 p.m.	ESPN2	TBD
Apr 3	1 p.m.	ESPN	WAS at NYM	June 4	8 p.m.	ESPN	TBD	Aug 13	8 p.m.	ESPN	TBD
Apr 3	2 p.m.	ESPN2	BOS at TEX	June 5	7 p.m.	ESPN	BOS at NYY	Aug 14	10 p.m.	ESPN2	TBD
Apr 3	4 p.m.	ESPN	ATL at LAD	June 7	2 p.m.	ESPN	TBD	Aug 16	2 p.m.	ESPN	TBD
Apr 3	7 p.m.	ESPN2	SF at SD	June 7	7 p.m.	ESPN	TBD	Aug 16	7 p.m.	ESPN	TBD
Apr 3	10 p.m.	ESPN2	NYY at OAK	June 8	7 p.m.	ESPN2	TBD	Aug 17	7 p.m.	ESPN	TBD
Apr 5	12:30 p.m.	ESPN	TBD	June 11	8 p.m.	ESPN	TBD	Aug 20	8 p.m.	ESPN	TBD
Apr 5	7 p.m.	ESPN2	TBD	June 12	7 p.m.	ESPN	CWS at TEX	Aug 21	10 p.m.	ESPN2	TBD
Apr 6	7 p.m.	ESPN	TBD	June 14	12:30 p.m.	ESPN	TBD	Aug 23	12:30 p.m.	ESPN2	TBD
Apr 9	8 p.m.	ESPN	STL at CHC	June 14	7 p.m.	ESPN	TBD	Aug 23	7 p.m.	ESPN2	TBD
Apr 10	7 p.m.	ESPN	PHI at ATL	June 15	8 p.m.	ESPN2	TBD	Aug 24	7 p.m.	ESPN2	TBD
Apr 12	1 p.m.	ESPN	TBD	June 18	8 p.m.	ESPN	TBD	Aug 27	8 p.m.	ESPN	TBD
Apr 12	7 p.m.	ESPN2	TBD	June 19	7 p.m.	ESPN	NYY at PHI	Aug 28	7 p.m.	ESPN2	TBD
Apr 13	7:30 p.m.	ESPN2	TBD	June 21	7 p.m.	ESPN	TBD	Aug 30	12:30 p.m.	ESPN	TBD
Apr 16	8 p.m.	ESPN	SF at LAD	June 21	10 p.m.	ESPN	TBD	Aug 30	7 p.m.	ESPN	TBD
Apr 17	7 p.m.	ESPN	ATL at NYM	June 22	8 p.m.	ESPN	TBD	Aug 31	7 p.m.	ESPN2	TBD
Apr 19	1 p.m.	ESPN	TBD	June 25	8 p.m.	ESPN	TBD	Sept 3	8 p.m.	ESPN2	TBD
Apr 19	7 p.m.	ESPN2	TBD	June 26	7 p.m.	ESPN2	ATL at NYY	Sept 6	1 p.m.	ESPN	TBD
Apr 20	7 p.m.	ESPN2	TBD	June 28	1 p.m.	ESPN2	TBD	Sept 6	7 p.m.	ESPN	TBD
Apr 23	8 p.m.	ESPN	ATL at WAS	June 28	7 p.m.	ESPN	TBD	Sept 7	8 p.m.	ESPN2	TBD
Apr 24	7 p.m.	ESPN	FLA at CHC	June 29	7 p.m.	ESPN2	TBD	Sept 8	7 p.m.	ESPN	TBD
Apr 26	1 p.m.	ESPN	TBD	July 2	8 p.m.	ESPN	TBD	Sept 10	8 p.m.	ESPN	TBD
Apr 26	7 p.m.	ESPN	TBD	July 3	7 p.m.	ESPN	TBD	Sept 13	1 p.m.	ESPN	TBD
Apr 27	7 p.m.	ESPN2	TBD	July 5	7 p.m.	ESPN	TBD	Sept 13	7 p.m.	ESPN	TBD
Apr 30	8 p.m.	ESPN	TEX at CLE	July 5	10 p.m.	ESPN	TBD	Sept 14	7:30 p.m.	ESPN2	TBD
May 1	7 p.m.	ESPN	NYY at BOS	July 6	8 p.m.	ESPN2	TBD	Sept 15	7 p.m.	ESPN	BOS at NYY
May 2	12 p.m.	ESPN	TBD	July 9	8 p.m.	ESPN	STL at HOU	Sept 17	8 p.m.	ESPN	TBD
May 3	7 p.m.	ESPN	TBD	July 13	7 p.m.	ESPN2	TBD	Sept 20	2 p.m.	ESPN	TBD
May 4	8 p.m.	ESPN2	TBD	July 14	2:15 p.m.	ESPN	TBD	Sept 20	7 p.m.	ESPN	TBD
May 7	8 p.m.	ESPN	SF at PHI	July 16	6 p.m.	ESPN	NYM at CHC	Sept 21	7 p.m.	ESPN2	TBD
May 8	7 p.m.	ESPN	MIN at TEX	July 17	7 p.m.	ESPN	ATL at STL	Sept 22	7 p.m.	ESPN	STL at HOU
May 10	1 p.m.	ESPN	TBD	July 19	1 p.m.	ESPN	TBD	Sept 24	8 p.m.	ESPN	TBD
May 10	7 p.m.	ESPN	TBD	July 19	7 p.m.	ESPN	TBD	Sept 27	3:30 p.m.	ESPN2	TBD
May 11	7 p.m.	ESPN2	TBD	July 20	7 p.m.	ESPN2	TBD	Sept 27	7 p.m.	ESPN	TBD
May 14	8 p.m.	ESPN	CWS at MIN	July 23	8 p.m.	ESPN	TBD	Sept 28	7 p.m.	ESPN2	TBD
May 15	7 p.m.	ESPN	BOS at BAL	July 24	7 p.m.	ESPN	TBD	Sept 29	7 p.m.	ESPN	TBD
May 17	3 p.m.	ESPN	TBD	July 26	12 p.m.	ESPN	TBD	Oct 3	1 p.m.	ESPN	Division Series
May 17	7 p.m.	ESPN	TBD	July 26	7 p.m.	ESPN	TBD	Oct 3	4 p.m.	ESPN	Division Series
May 18	7 p.m.	ESPN2	TBD	July 27	8 p.m.	ESPN2	TBD	Oct 4	4 p.m.	ESPN	Division Series
May 21	8 p.m.	ESPN	NYY at NYM	July 30	8 p.m.	ESPN	TBD	Oct 4	7 p.m.	ESPN	Division Series
May 22	7 p.m.	ESPN	NYY at BOS	July 31	7 p.m.	ESPN	CLE at BOS	Oct 4	10 p.m.	ESPN	Division Series
May 24	1 p.m.	ESPN	TBD	Aug 2	1 p.m.	ESPN	TBD	Oct 5	4 p.m.	ESPN	Division Series
May 24	7 p.m.	ESPN	TBD	Aug 2	7 p.m.	ESPN	TBD	Oct 6	4 p.m.	ESPN	Division Series
May 25	7 p.m.	ESPN	TBD	Aug 3	8 p.m.	ESPN2	TBD	Oct 6	8 p.m.	ESPN	Division Series
May 28	8 p.m.	ESPN	OAK at TEX	Aug 6	8 p.m.	ESPN	TBD	Oct 7	1 p.m.	ESPN2	Division Series
May 30	7 p.m.	ESPN	CWS at CLE	Aug 7	7:30 p.m.	ESPN	TBD	Oct 8	1 p.m.	ESPN	Division Series
May 31	1 p.m.	ESPN	TBD	Aug 9	1 p.m.	ESPN	TBD	Oct 8	4 p.m.	ESPN	Division Series
May 31	7 p.m.	ESPN2	TBD	Aug 9	7 p.m.	ESPN	TBD	Oct 8	4 p.m.	ESPN2	Division Series

THE 2006 ESPN BASEBALL ENCYCLOPEDIA

EDITED BY **PETE PALMER** AND **GARY GILLETTE**
FOREWORD BY **PETER GAMMONS**

ASSOCIATE EDITORS **STUART SHEA, MATTHEW SILVERMAN, GREG SPIRA, DOUG WHITE**
CONTRIBUTORS **RICK BENNER, BILL DEANE, SEAN LAHMAN, JAMES A. RILEY**

STERLING PUBLISHING CO.,INC.
NEW YORK

Published by Sterling Publishing Co., Inc.
387 Park Avenue South, New York, NY 10016

© 2006 by 24-7 Baseball, L.L.C.
Foreword copyright © 2006 by ESPN, Inc. All rights reserved.

Distributed in Canada by Sterling Publishing
c/o Canadian Manda Group, 165 Dufferin Street,
Toronto, Ontario, Canada M6K 3H6

Distributed in the United Kingdom by GMC Distribution Services,
Castle Place, 166 High Street, Lewes, East Sussex, England BN7 1XU

Distributed in Australia by Capricorn Link (Australia) Pty. Ltd.
P.O. Box 704, Windsor, NSW 2756, Australia

ISBN-13: 978-1-4027-3625-4
ISBN-10: 1-4027-3625-8

Typesetting by Scribe, Inc. (www.scribenet.com)

Printed in U.S.A. by PA Hutchinson Company
All rights reserved

2 4 6 8 10 9 7 5 3 1

For information about custom editions, special sales, premium and
corporate purchases, please contact Sterling Special Sales
Department at 800-805-5489 or specialsales@sterlingpub.com.

DEDICATION

Dedicated to two veteran baseball scouts and ex-major leaguers whose company I have had the pleasure of sharing: Lenny Yochim—a former pitcher for the Pirates and the epitome of a gracious Southern gentleman—and Deacon Jones—a former first baseman with the White Sox and the 1950 American Legion Player of the Year. Both are incredibly knowledgeable men who have generously shared their experiences as well as their wisdom, for which I am very grateful.

—Gary Gillette

Dedicated to two friends, now gone, who showed me when I was young that there was nothing wrong with maintaining my fascination with baseball as an adult—my English teacher from Mount Hermon, Jack Baldwin, and my fellow engineer at Raytheon, Mason Huse.

—Pete Palmer

ACKNOWLEDGMENTS

No baseball encyclopedia could be prepared without the assistance of many others in the field. The editors hereby extend their appreciation for many different favors—some small, some large—to the honor roll of kind people listed below:

Jim Albright, Jamie Alexander, Stephen Bannen, Carlos Bauer, Evelyn Begley, Alex Belth, Greg Beston, Cliff Blau, Arnie Braunstein, Douglas Brei, Ed Brown, Jeffrey Burk, J.P. Callault, Jim Callis, Bill Carle, Keith Carlson, James Catron, Ryan Chamberlain, Mike Cinoman, Andy Clarke, Clem Comly, Bob Curto, Clay Davenport, Donald M. Davis, Kevin Davis, Merl DeMoll, Dan Dischley, Beth Dowd, Mike Dugan, Steve Elsberry, John Foley, Sean Forman, Marcus Fredericks, Marty Friedrich, Jim Furtado, Steve Geitscher, Ray Gonzalez, John Green, Joe Haardt, Paul Hagen, Gary Hailey, Layton Hall, Hank Hammer, Chris Hand, Paul Hartnett, Ed Hartig, Bill Hickman, Howard Hilton, Bob Hoie, Dan Holmes, Shane Holmes, Sean Holtz, David Horwich, Frederick Ivor-Campbell, Jonathan Jacobs, Jay Jaffe, Bill James, Kevin Johnson, Richard Johnson, Christina Kahrl, Chris Kaminiski, Margaret Kane, Jim Keller, Dave Kirsch, Paul Kisko, Herm Krabbenhoft, David Kronheim, Gary LaFollett, Joseph La Freniere, Leonte Landino, Matt Lemoine, Fred Lenger, Daniel Levine, Michael Lewis, Don Luce, Mike Mackay, Rich Malatzky, Steve Mann, Lou Marinaro, Bruce Markusen, Josh Mathes, Kenneth Matinale, John McCann, Corey McCart, Bob McConnell, Trent McCotter, Wayne McElreavy, Bill McNeil, Andrew Milner, Jim Moore, Bill Moose, Cyril Morong, Peter Morris, Rod Nelson, Rob Neyer, David Nemec, Bill Nowlin, John O'Malley, Marc Okkonen, Rob Olds, Mat Olkin, Phyllis Otto, Doug Pappas, Marvin Peixoto, Fred Percival, Jim Quinlan, John Racano, Bob Richardson, Ken Rosenthal, Bob Rosiek, Bruce Roth, Tom Ruane, Andy Samet, Mike Sandler, Bob Schatzle, Michael Schell, Richard Schrader, John Schwartz, Alan Schwarz, Ron Selter, Ron Shandler, Tom Shieber, Nate Silver, Joe Simenic, Bill Slayback, Dave Smith, Lyle Spatz, Ted Spencer, Dave Statz, Mike Statz, Paul Statz, Marc Stephenson, Chuck Stevens, John Thorn, Bob Tiemann, Tom Tippett, Stephen Tomlinson, Wayne Townsend, Neal Traven, Jules Tygiel, Dixie Tourangeau, David Urban, Frank Vaccaro, John Vaughan, David Vincent, Bill Way, Joe Wayman, Royce Webb, Jim Weigand, Dave Weiner, Paul Wendt, Harold Wexler, Jim Wheeler, Frank Williams, Vic Wilson, Walt Wilson, Keith Woolner, John Zajc, Andy Zimbalist, and Larry Zuckerman. Special thanks go to David Pietrusza, Peter Bird, Kevin Saldana, and Bill Weiss for their assistance and advice.

On the PR front, many thanks to the great community relations managers who promoted the encyclopedia at Barnes & Noble stores, especially Jill Foran, Lynn Payne, Amanda Dahling, Heather Haines, Kelly Langstine, Maria Cellis-Hampton, Kathy Siciliano, Dee Eurs, Mary Anne Diehl, and Anita Johnson.

Every baseball encyclopedia involves a huge amount of complicated design, typesetting, and editorial work. In our case, we are truly blessed to have collaborated with Jeremy C. Ellis, Andy Brown, Heath Missimer, and David Rech of Scribe in Philadelphia. We are indebted to Nathaniel Marunas, our editor at Barnes & Noble and to Jen Boudinot and Devorah Klein, his ace majordomos. We are also very grateful for the support of B&N President and CEO Steve Riggio, B&N Publishing President Alan Kahn, and to Bruce Lubin, B&N Publisher. Kudos to creative director Jeff Batzli; art director Kevin Ullrich; designer Kevin Baier; designer Christine Heun; photo researcher Lori Epstein; and production managers Michael Vagnetti and Charles Ryf. As Yogi might say, we look forward with even greater anticipation to working with everyone for many years to come.

Finally, the editors gratefully thank their patient spouses, who pitched in a pinch for another season: Vicki Gillette, Beth Palmer, Cecilia Garibay, and Anita White.

TABLE OF CONTENTS

DEDICATION v
ACKNOWLEDGMENTS v
FOREWORD ix
INTRODUCTION xi
NO ASTERISKS! 1
THE SCIENCE OF HITTING: THE BATTER REGISTER
    Introduction 5
    Aaron–Duffy 9
    Duffy–Kuntz 192
    Kurowski–Reynolds 381
    Reynolds–Zwilling 570
THE ART OF PITCHING: THE PITCHER REGISTER
    Introduction 756
    Aardsma–Gorman 758
    Gormley–Novoa 937
    Noyes–Zuverink 1118
THE MEN IN THE DUGOUT: THE MANAGERS
    Introduction 1303
    Adair–Goryl 1305
    Gould–McKnight 1310
    McManus–Zimmer 1315
HOMETOWN HEROES: TEAM ROSTERS
    Introduction 1321
    1871–1900 1323
    1901–1940 1329
    1941–1968 1343
    1969–2005 1355
THE LONG SEASON: THE HISTORICAL RECORD
    Introduction 1382
    2005–1969 1384
    1968–1941 1458
    1940–1901 1514
    1900–1871 1596
BLACK BASEBALL AND THE NEGRO LEAGUES
    Introduction 1638
    Leagues and Teams List 1640
    Top 100 Black Baseball/Negro League Players 1641
    Black Baseball/Negro League Season Synopses, 1910–1950 1646
    Standings and Award Winners 1648
    East-West All-Star Games and Postseason Series 1650
    Negro League Home Ballparks by City 1651
MIDSUMMER CLASSICS: THE ALL-STAR GAMES 1653
OCTOBER CLASSICS: POSTSEASON SERIES AND PLAYOFFS
    Introduction 1655
    National League Playoff Series 1657
    Single-Game Playoffs 1657
    American League Division Series 1657
    National League Division Series 1657
    Nineteenth Century National League Championship Series 1657
    American League Championship Series 1657
    National League Championship Series 1657
    Nineteenth Century World Series (American Association vs. National League) 1657
    World Series 1658
THE GLORY OF THEIR TIMES: THE ALL-TIME LEADERS
    Introduction 1659
    Lifetime 1660
    Single-Season 1680
THE NATURALS: THE HALL OF FAME
    Introduction 1697
    Members 1698
    Non-Hall of Famers Who Have Received Votes 1700
    Top Vote-Getters by Year 1703
    Biographical Information for Other Hall of Famers 1705
THE BOYS OF SUMMER: AWARDS AND OTHER HONORS
    Introduction 1707
    Chalmers Award 1707

BBWAA AL & NL MVP Awards 1707
Ex Post Facto MVP Award...1708
BBWAA Cy Young Award...1708
Ex Post Facto Cy Young Award 1708
BBWAA Rookie of the Year Award 1709
Ex Post Facto Rookie of the Year Award..1710
BBWAA Manager of the Year Award 1710
The Sporting News Player and Pitcher of the Year Awards 1710
The Sporting News Rookie Player and Pitcher of the Year Awards 1711
The Sporting News Manager of the Year Award 1712
The Sporting News Comeback Player of the Year Award 1712
The Sporting News Fireman/Reliever of the Year Award 1712
The Sporting News Major League Executive of the Year Award 1713
Rolaids Relief Man of the Year Award 1713
Gold Glove Awards 1713
Baseball America Minor League Player of the Year Award 1716
Baseball America Organization of the Year Award 1716
The Roberto Clemente Award 1716
The Fred Hutchinson Memorial Award 1716
The Lou Gehrig Memorial Award 1716
The J.G. Taylor Spink Award 1717
The Ford C. Frick Award...1717
Retired Uniform Numbers 1718

GREAT PERFORMANCES
Introduction 1719
Most Consecutive Games Batted Safely, Season 1719
DiMaggio's 56-game Hitting Streak 1719
Consecutive Games On-Base Streak 1719
Ichiro's 262-Hit Season 1719
Consecutive Games Played 1720
Games Played Streaks..1720
Four-Homer Games...1720
Career Grand Slam Home Run Leaders 1720
The Single-Season Home Run Record 1720
The Home Run Records of Bonds, McGwire, Maris, and Ruth 1720
On-Base Percentage, Walks, and Intentional Walks 1721
Most Consecutive Hits 1721
Triple Crown Batters..1721
Triple Crown Pitchers..1722
Most Strikeouts in a Game 1722
Most Consecutive Save Opportunities Converted 1722
Gagne's 84-Save Streak...1722
Consecutive Scoreless Inning Streaks 1723
Multiple No-Hitters 1723
Perfect Games...1723
No-Hit Games, Nine or More Innings Pitched..1723
No-Hit Games, Less Than 9 Innings Pitched 1724
No-Hitters Broken Up in Extra Innings...1725

FIELDS OF DREAMS: BIG LEAGUE BALLPARKS
Introduction 1726
Major League Ballparks by City...1727
Spring Training Sites (Since 1901) 1731

THE GLOBAL GAME: INTERNATIONAL BASEBALL
Introduction 1732
Latin America..1732
The Olympics 1733
The Pan American Games...1733
Japan 1733
Taiwan 1734
South Korea 1734
Australia 1735
College Baseball 1735
Little League Baseball...1737
American Legion Baseball..1737

GLOSSARY 1739
EDITORS AND CONTRIBUTORS 1743

Dave Powers was a special assistant to President John F. Kennedy and a major force in collecting many of the late president's artifacts for the JFK Museum in Boston. Whenever a visitor who had some relation to baseball stopped by Powers' office, he would pull out a bound copy of the 1961 *Baseball Register* and proudly show it off.

"This was the president's lucky book," Powers said. "It was his inaugural year, it has a picture of Ted Williams on the inside cover and it was that year's matter of record."

I know someone who keeps two copies of *The Baseball Encyclopedia* readily available in his house, one in his office, one in the bathroom. Which is not all that unusual, as I also know someone who keeps two copies of Bill James' handbook in his house, and someone else who keeps Lee Sinins's *Sabermetric Baseball Encyclopedia* on two laptop computers, just in case one gets infected with a virus and shuts off.

In baseball, statistics and numbers matter. They *really* matter.

Why else would a SABR scholar named Richard "Dixie" Tourangeau spend weeks in the archives of Cooperstown and uncover that a nineteenth-century no-hitter credited to Vic Willis was actually a one-hitter? The historic difference between a no-hitter and one-hitter matters; ask the Mets.

Why else, when the Special Records Committee in 1968 discovered that 37 times prior to 1920 game-ending "home runs" (*walk off pieces*, in twenty-first century jargon) had been credited as singles, doubles, or triples, and that one "triple" hit by Babe Ruth had actually pushed his total to 715, did the SRC make a gut-wrenching reversal of its previous ruling and allow 714 to stand because of its historic significance?

Why else have historians continued for many decades—now with the help of a godsend called Retrosheet—to plow through the numbers of great players, verifying and completing information as well as looking for mistakes? Pete Palmer and others have discovered four mistakes in the batting records of Ty Cobb since 1969, which have changed Cobb's career hits total from 4,191 to 4,189. The original edition of the Macmillan encyclopedia credited Cobb with 4,192 hits, then in subsequent editions listed him with the traditional figure of 4,191. *Total Baseball* later corrected that figure to 4,189. Why else would it be important to get Wee Willie Keeler's 1897 average right (.424, not .432)? As for Cap Anson's hit totals, suffice to say only Pete Palmer and Gary Gillette can explain why they change as much as the president's job approval ratings.

All these figures matter, because so much of baseball is judged by numbers. Everyone understood why *61** was the appropriate title for Billy Crystal's poignant film about Roger Maris. Pitchers are automatically bound for the Hall of Fame with 300 wins, batters with 3,000 hits. There are those Red Sox fans who revere Jim Rice and wonder why he's not in Cooperstown (after all, he finished in the top five in MVP balloting six times in a 12-year span), but look it up in *The ESPN Baseball Encyclopedia*: Rice batted .298 with 382 home runs, while Wade Boggs batted .328, had 3,010 hits and his career OPS was .858, Rice's .854.

They even changed the rules when numbers got askew. In *The Numbers Game*, Alan Schwarz points out how rules were altered in the nineteenth century by statisticians. Then came the aftermath of the 1968 season, which produced league-leading earned run averages of 1.12 by Bob Gibson and 1.60 by Luis Tiant, an American League batting race that nearly had no .300 hitter—Carl Yastrzemski won it at .301. In the offseason, Major League Baseball voted to lower the mound from 15 to 10 inches and restore the strike zone to its pre-1963 dimensions.

No one seems to care much that there are a number of pitchers in the Hall of Fame who either admitted or were known to have doctored baseballs. But corked bats and steroids raise heated, near-hysterical debates because the home run records are "pure" numbers.

Back when Macmillan first published *The Baseball Encyclopedia*, it was essential to the needs of the era. But this library disguised as a book has nearly 40 pages of annual, era, and career leaders in a number of statistics. To an entire generation that has grown up with Pete Palmer, Bill James, Steve Hirdt, and *Baseball Prospectus*, Palmer and Gillette not only provide the core stats—I am still trying to fathom Earl Webb's 67 doubles—but also stats that give a reader hours of pleasure simply turning pages: adjusted earned run average by era, pitchers' batting averages by all-time leaders and by eras, fielding wins, batter-fielder wins, pitcher wins . . . well, start turning, and find your own favorites.

For anyone who takes the Hall of Fame seriously, the rundown of the annual voting is another fascinating exercise. Just how difficult it is to reach Cooperstown is evidenced by the fact that Jeff Burroughs was an American League MVP, and yet got the same vote fraction—0.2 percent—as Jerry Remy on his one and only appearance on the ballot. One can appreciate that Matty Alou was a terrific slap hitter, but his percentage of the vote (1.3 percent) was higher than either of his brothers, Felipe (0.8 percent) or Jesus (0.3 percent). It should be noted that, while Joe Torre now seems a lock for the Hall because of his playing and managerial record, the highest vote that Torre got for his playing skills was only 22.2 percent, Billy Martin 0.3 percent. Torre now also has four World Series rings as a manager, Martin one.

Another fascinating section is the Ex Post Facto awards, where Palmer and Gillette pick who would have won awards before they became functions of the baseball writers. Cy Young would have won five Cy Young Awards, as well as the 1902 MVP in the American League. Babe Ruth would have won four MVPs, including the American League award he actually won in 1923, Ty Cobb five, Honus Wagner six. And Ruth would have won the 1915 Rookie of the Year and the 1916 Cy Young awards.

There is even the listing of retired uniform numbers, which begins with Harold Baines' number 3 with the White Sox, retired while he was an active player for the Texas Rangers. (Is there anything lonelier than being a South Sider in a town of North Siders?) Otherwise, in keeping with the significance of numbers and baseball, there are few frivolous, irrational selections, and when one looks at the retired numbers of the Yankees, Dodgers, and Reds one appreciates how special that retirement ceremony remains.

For many, perusing the encyclopedia means finding gems that slipped through the cracks, like Frank (Moonlight) Graham, who in 1905 did make a defensive appearance for the New York Nationals. Then there is Tom and Jim Paciorek's older brother John, whose career line reads 1 game, 3 AB, 4 R, 3 H, 3 RBI, a 1.000 AVG, 1.000 OBP, 1.000 SLG. He played the final game of the 1963 season for the Houston Colt .45s, hurt his back in the off-season, and never made it back to the show. Or Hall of Famer Robin Yount's older brother Larry, who is listed for one appearance (in 1971) for Houston, but no stats other than playing in 1 game. He pulled a muscle warming up after coming out of the bullpen, never actually threw a pitch in the major leagues, but since he was announced, he is part of Major League Baseball history.

Sometimes we remember individuals too fondly. Bo Jackson is a good example. He was such an electrifying figure, such a decent man, and he not only made some of the greatest commercials and hit unforgettable home runs, but made a throw to nail Harold Reynolds at the plate in the old HO-scaled Seattle Kingdome that might be the single best throw of the era. Granted, Jackson's career was cut short by a hip injury before he fully developed as a baseball player, but the fact remains his career history sits in black and white as a Prince concert, while his career OPS of .783 is exactly the same as Al Martin's.

There are names each one of us bookmark for family reasons. Daff Gammons was a distant cousin from the Rhode Island Gammons who played 28 games for the 1901 Boston Nationals, hitting a rousing .194 with a .242 on-base percentage. (Hey, he almost matched Billy Beane's career OBP of .246.)

What was never quite explained was, Why "Daff?" Nicknames are such a great reason to have an *ESPN Baseball Encyclopedia* at hand. Calvin Coolidge Julius Caesar Tuskahoma "Buster" McLish. Hurricane Hazle, he of the .403 average for the 1957 Braves, only to be sold to the Tigers the next spring. Willie "Puddin' Head" Jones. "Piano Legs" Hickman. "Honest John" Anderson. Charles F. "Alderman" Briody, who also went by the nickname "Fatty." "Glass Arm Eddie" Brown. Three different Careys called "Scoops." Jake "Eagle Eye" Beckley and Max "Camera Eye" Bishop. "Bananas" Benes. Lots of Mooses, Docs, Dukes, Lefties, and Reds, but only one Tuffy (Rhodes).

Baseball encompasses so many of our lives because of its countless layers of fascination, a Mike Cameron catch in the seventh inning of a meaningless September game, a Pokey Reese slide across the outfield grass to snatch away a sure single, Brad Radke's delivery, or Randy Johnson's fiery power. But there is so much more, from debates on the Hall of Fame or the Johnson-Koufax-Carlton-Grove-Spahn argument to remembering a couple of former players—catcher Dave Schmidt of the 1981 Red Sox and pitcher Mark Ciardi of the 1987 Brewers—who are currently successful Hollywood producers of movies (*Racing Stripes* and *Miracle*, respectively).

That's where *The ESPN Baseball Encyclopedia* comes into play, time after time, day after day, the Library of Congress of a very simple game.

You can look it up.

—Peter Gammons

INTRODUCTION

The past is never dead. It's not even past. —William Faulkner

Faulkner penned that memorable line in 1951. Though the titan of American letters was not talking about the National Pastime, his apt turn of phrase would serve well as a requiem for thousands of big-league ballplayers. Most of them are long past playing, but their exploits live on in the pages of this book as well as in the hearts and memories of uncounted millions of baseball fans worldwide.

Baseball in 1951 was in the midst of a postwar boom, though troubling signs had already started to appear. Even then, fifty-five years ago, the Grand Old Game had more than a century of history to brag about, including eighty years of professional play. Other professional team sports in the United States were still in their infancy, though pro football was soon to explode into a formidable rival to the National Game.

Now baseball boasts more than a century and a quarter of carefully documented history. A major part of that documentation is the voluminous amount of baseball statistics that have been compiled and calculated. These statistics record the successes and failures of the more than 16,000 big league players who have worn the uniforms of almost 150 different clubs in half a dozen major leagues.

The value of baseball statistics lies primarily in their completeness and accuracy. Because they are so well designed and so comprehensive, baseball statistics have a magical quality that most mere numbers lack. Because they are so accurate, baseball statistics can be relied upon to form opinions and to make judgments over many decades of play.

Nevertheless, there is a paradox inherent in the historical accuracy of baseball statistics. Too many people mistakenly believe that baseball stats are engraved in stone, like birth and death dates on a granite tombstone. If the Macmillan *Baseball Encyclopedia* showed that Babe Ruth hit 714 career home runs, or that Ty Cobb finished with 4,191 hits and a career batting average of .367, most people believe that these are immutable facts.

Not so. At least four mistakes have been found in the past twenty-five years in the official batting records for Cobb. The net result in correcting these errors in pre-computer record keeping is that "The Georgia Peach" has 4,189 hits and a career .366 average *to the best of our knowledge*. So, when the nation watched as Pete Rose broke the all-time hits record on September 11, 1985 with his 4,192nd base hit, few knew that Rose already had broken Cobb's record three days earlier. By the way, the first edition of the Macmillan encyclopedia showed Ty Cobb with 4,192 official career hits, though that was changed without explanation to 4,191 in subsequent editions.

As for "The Sultan of Swat," how many people are aware that he used to have 715 home runs? His current career total of 714 home runs is accurate *to the best of our knowledge*—provided that one accepts a curious decision of the Special Baseball Records Committee on May 5, 1969. As part of the massive effort to computerize and clean up the game's official statistics and records, this committee was formed and charged with deciding how best to handle certain anomalies and inconsistencies.

In 1968 the Special Records Committee had voted to change the thirty-seven instances prior to 1920 where game-ending home runs were counted only as singles, doubles, or triples (whatever was needed to drive home the winning run). These over-the-fence hits were not home runs according to the scoring practices of their day, but became so with the 1968 ruling. The Special Records Committee also made other changes in previous scoring practices, many of them quite significant: e.g., counting stats in all tie games of five or more innings; not counting walks, wild pitches, passed balls, balks, and hit batsmen as errors at any time; and neither counting walks as outs (as was done in 1876) nor as hits (as was done in 1887).

The committee was logically prepared to count those hits as home runs until a controversy arose because doing so changed Ruth's official career total to 715. Fear of changing one of the game's most important records caused the committee to retract its earlier—and more enlightened—decision. Thus, "The Bambino" lost a home run, and his career total remained at the apparently sacrosanct number of 714.

Regardless of such high-profile examples of historical mistakes or inconsistencies, the level of accuracy of baseball statistics is exceedingly high—so high that it exceeds the standards of accuracy in virtually every other field of endeavor. Twenty-first century Americans make life-changing decisions every day based on evidence supported by underlying statistics not nearly as accurate as baseball stats.

This superlative accuracy is the reason that fans, researchers, and historians can argue about the number of hits compiled by a Hall of Fame player who started his career in 1871 and finished in 1897, more than a century ago. Cap Anson has been dead since 1922, yet his career is still under the contemporary microscope. Good history depends on truly accurate research, not on false allegiance to previously published numbers.

History is process, not perfection. We trust that our effort has contributed to the process of recording and understanding the history of our National Pastime.

BASEBALL ENCYCLOPEDIA ON THE WEB

For the latest news and updates about *The Baseball Encyclopedia*, including extra statistical content that we couldn't squeeze into the book, information on upcoming author appearances, and new articles about baseball history, visit us on the web at http://www.247baseball.com.

To subscribe to our *Baseball Encyclopedia* newsletter, which will include updates, Q&As, and other features, send an e-mail with "Subscribe Newsletter" as the subject to subscribe@247baseball.com and you will be registered to receive the newsletter.

If you have any corrections or suggestions for future editions of the Baseball Encyclopedia please e-mail us at feedback@247baseball.com or send a letter to:

The Baseball Encyclopedia
c/o Barnes & Noble Publishing, Inc.
122 Fifth Avenue, 5th floor
New York, NY 10011

THE PROCESS

Like every reference work that is not created from whole cloth, this encyclopedia builds on the foundation of its predecessors, most importantly the groundbreaking work done by John Thorn and Pete Palmer in *Total Baseball*. When *Total Baseball* made its debut in 1989, all previous baseball encyclopedias were instantly obsolete, including the beloved official *Baseball Encyclopedia* that had been published by Macmillan since 1969.

All of the editors who worked on this book have worked previously on, or contributed to, one or more editions of *Total Baseball*. Furthermore, Palmer, the co-editor of every previous edition of *Total Baseball*, has edited, co-edited, or contributed in one way or another to every complete baseball encyclopedia (i.e., encyclopedias that include year-by-year career registers) published since 1965.

Most of the data underlying the statistics in this encyclopedia comes from a new database compiled by Palmer in the past five years. Much of the remaining data comes from various databases compiled by Gary Gillette in the past six years. Other information has been generously provided by Retrosheet or by members of the Society for American Baseball Research (SABR).

In compiling his new database, Palmer—like everyone before him—has relied on the standard sources of official and unofficial statistics. He has also done new research into historical areas that have heretofore been neglected. After forty years of indefatigable work in the field, there are very few sources of information that Palmer has not examined carefully. Moreover, he has kept detailed records of the mistakes and omissions in each source, so that he can avoid repeating the mistakes of earlier reference books.

While these standard sources are generally accurate, Palmer has made tens of thousands of corrections to the original source material. Many mistakes were simply found by adding up the stats for all players on a team and comparing those totals to the reported team totals. Others were made from the input of various researchers who compared box scores or play-by-play records to the official data. Many of the hardest-to-find mistakes were corrected by comparing statistics in multiple reliable sources and looking for telltale differences. Thousands of hours have been spent compiling, checking, verifying, and correcting this new database.

National Association Statistics. One of the decisions made by the Special Records Committee was to exclude the National Association from major league status. The editors respectfully disagree with that decision and, therefore, have included complete NA records in this encyclopedia. The National Association certainly had its problems—as the Special Records Committee indicated—but it was indisputably the Major League Baseball of its day. To use current standards of reliability as a reason for excluding the NA doesn't make sense.

Despite this, however, we have *not* included NA stats in the totals of the many players who played in both the NA and the NL. Instead, a separate totals line is shown for the NA if a player also later played in the NL. The reason? If the NA and NL totals were combined, they would not match what is in the official records. For most players, that wouldn't be a problem. For some players—like Cap Anson—it would further confuse the picture.

Sources. The primary sources for most of the statistics contained herein are the official National and American League records, starting in 1903 for the NL and 1905 for the AL. The source data for most of the earlier years come from computer printouts at the Hall of Fame originally compiled by Information Concepts, Incorporated, (ICI) for the 1969 *Baseball Encyclopedia*. These ICI printouts were turned over to the Hall in return for access to Lee Allen's biographical data. The primary source for 1876–90 NL statistics are the records compiled by historian John Tattersall and held by SABR. For the National Association (1871–75), records compiled from box scores by Bob Tiemann and Bob Richardson are the primary sources.

Tattersall used the figures from the annual official guides for basic batting and pitching stats for most players, though it should be noted that official pitching stats in those days consisted simply of games, wins, and losses. Tattersall obtained extra-base hits, batter walks, and strikeouts from figures compiled in *The Boston Globe* by Clarence Dow for some years of the 1876–90 period. The unheralded Dow was one of the great early statisticians, though he unfortunately died at the age of 38 in 1893. Dow actually played one game for the Boston Unions in 1884.

Since runs batted in were not officially defined from 1876–90, Tattersall determined RBIs as best he could from newspaper accounts of games. He also retroactively compiled "official" stats from box scores for all players appearing in less than 15 games; those reserve players were not shown in the stats printed in the annual official guides. Tattersall was forced to use box scores for the years when the *Globe* did not publish statistics.

In addition to filling in these gaps in the record, Tattersall counted stats from tie games for 1878–84, which had been excluded at that time. He also counted stats from various other games that had previously been excluded from the official records—for example, for 1877 Cincinnati games, where the team dropped out of the league after 58 games (almost a complete season). Tattersall also wisely standardized the handling of

walks, which were counted as outs in 1876 and as hits in 1887 in the NL; ICI had done this for the 1887 American Association.

For the most part, Tattersall did not make other changes in the official stats as found in the guides. One notable exception was in 1879, when Tattersall was sure that, due to a clerical error, Cap Anson really had only 72 hits (not 90) and batted .317 (not .407). To our knowledge, Tattersall never changed any other official stats from 1871–90 unless he found a clerical or arithmetical error. All of his decisions were endorsed by the Special Records Committee in 1968.

Filling the gaps. Certain other stats were found in box scores. For batters hit-by-pitch, the work was done by John Tattersall, Pete Palmer, John Schwartz, Alex Haas, and others through 1917 in the NL and 1920 in the AL (when the statistic was first kept officially). Likewise, box scores were used for pitcher hit-batsmen before 1903 in the NL and 1908 in the AL.

Runs batted in for years where the totals were not previously complete (1885–87 and 1890 AA) were obtained mostly from incomplete data on the ICI printouts and from newspaper game accounts. Approximately 10 percent of RBIs had to be estimated from other player batting stats, including data on some players for the 1882–84 AA. David Neft supplied some additional RBI data for 1880–84 NL.

Many corrections to home run totals were made by Tattersall and by SABR stalwart Bob McConnell. Over the years, other SABR members also took it upon themselves to research different areas. Frank Williams carefully went over the 1901–19 AL pitching stats and corrected many errors. Joe Wayman did the same for shutouts throughout major league history. Walt Wilson checked games started, which were not kept officially in the AL until 1926 and in the NL until 1938.

Biographical data came originally from research done by Hy Turkin and S.C. Thompson in the 1950s, with additional help later from Bill Haber. Biographical information for current players is collected by the editors and exchanged with the SABR Biographical Committee, which was founded by Cliff Kachline. Richard Topp and the current chairmen, Bill Carle and David Vincent, later made valuable contributions, with yeoman help from Rich Malatsky and Peter Morris.

Manager data was originally compiled by Richard Topp and Bob Tiemann, who made many changes in the previous listings for early managers. They determined that the captain was really what we call the manager today, and that the listed manager was really the club's business manager.

New in 2004 edition. Pitcher run support was obtained from Retrosheet game logs, which were compiled by Tom Ruane from various sources. This data originated with Bob Tiemann's notebook data, which was computerized by Arnie Braunstein. Play-by-plays compiled by Retrosheet, Project Scoresheet, The Baseball Workshop, and by the editors from 1969–2005 were used to calculate blown saves, defensive innings, range, opponents' stolen base and caught stealing stats for catchers, plus throwing for outfielders and DP rates for infielders. Extensive examination and testing of more than thirty years of play-by-plays provided the information needed to refine Palmer's previous estimates of defensive innings before 1969, as well as improve Palmer's defensive evaluations.

There are now more than thirty-five years of play-by-play records available, completely covering the era of divisional play and the careers of almost 6,000 players: more than 40 percent of everyone who has played since 1901 and more than 35 percent of all players in major league history.

Caught stealing for the 1913 NL came from newly discovered data compiled by Ernie Lanigan. Lanigan compiled caught stealing stats from 1912–19 and sold the data to different newspapers, though only about half of it has been found. Since Lanigan sold various features to papers across the country, it is certainly possible that there is more data out there that has not yet been found. We have checked *The Sporting News* and *Sporting Life*, but not individual city papers. If anyone knows of a newspaper that contains caught stealing stats for 1912–19 that are not shown in this book, please contact the editors.

New in 2005 edition. The most important addition to the 2005 edition was a Black Baseball/Negro Leagues section that includes: Top 100 Negro League player list with extensive biographical information, years and teams played for, and capsule biographies; Ex Post Facto MVP, Pitcher of the Year, and Rookie of the Year Awards for black baseball from 1910–1950; Year-by-year standings for all eight Negro major leagues; Details of every East-West All-Star Game; Game scores for Negro League postseason series; and Home ballparks for all Negro League teams.

Other new information included in the 2005 edition: Expanded biographical information for all major league players, including colleges and Negro League service; College World Series champions for NCAA Divisions I, II, and III plus NAIA Baseball champions and CWS Most Outstanding Player awards; Little League and American Legion champions; Spring training sites for all teams from 1901–2004; Complete games at position for every player for every season and for their career, including outfield games by LF-CF-RF; Expanded lists of All-Time Leaders; Expanded Hall of Fame voting data; Biographical information for Hall of Famers who were not players or managers; and home runs hit by pitchers.

Last—but certainly not least—this edition shows Days spent on the DL, year-by-year and career, for every player in major league history. (The Disabled List started in 1941 and was rarely used before the late 1940s.) The editors have compiled this groundbreaking DL data from a variety of historical sources—it has never been published because this is the first time it has ever been compiled.

New in 2006 edition. Continuing our commitment to compile and publish information that has never been included in any previous baseball encyclopedia, this new edition includes three important additions.

First, we have added complete draft information for all major league players selected in the history of the amateur and first-year player drafts (1965–2005). In addition to the drafting team and year, the round and ordinal pick number is also shown along with the type of draft (i.e., Regular or Secondary, January or June). While each year's draft information has been routinely published in many annual reference books, it has never before been compiled in an encyclopedia.

Second, for many players who played in 1950 or later, we have included detailed playing weight information instead of a single nominal weight—often taken from a player's debut season and therefore liable to be inaccurate for those who had long careers. For players whose weight varied by more than 10 pounds from the previously shown weight, we now show a weight range for their career. Given the outcry over the effects of the so-called steroid era, this information is certainly topical.

Finally, we have added more texture to the Black Baseball/Negro Leagues section of the encyclopedia. Jim Riley has written synopses for each year of black baseball from 1910–50, covering both the major Negro Leagues as well as independent black baseball.

SABR and Retrosheet. Any reader who pays careful attention to the explanations and introductions in this work will come across multiple references to both of these eminent nonprofit organizations. For information on the Society for American Baseball Research, please see their page at the very end of the encyclopedia.

Some of the information in this encyclopedia came from the files of Retrosheet, an organization founded for the collection, computerization, and free public distribution of detailed play-by-play information of as many major league games as possible. Much of the information is currently available at www.Retrosheet.org and more is added regularly as additional data files are proofed and readied for release.

Retrosheet has become a standard source of information for many teams, writers, and announcers. It also provides box scores and play-by-play accounts for fans interested in specific games, such as the first one they ever attended. Dozens of ballplayers have received detailed analyses of their careers.

Jayson Stark of ESPN wrote, "Do we even remember life before Retrosheet? I am eternally grateful that Retrosheet pasted every one of them [box scores] into its notebook out there in cyberspace." Peter Gammons calls Retrosheet a "godsend."

Not all the box scores are there yet, but more are on the way all the time as this epic effort continues. The website also includes a "most wanted" list of games for which Retrosheet still needs a scoresheet. If you have scoresheets of any games from 1947–73, or if you think there might still be some scoresheets or an old scorebook in your attic or in your parent's attic, please check out this list!

Slip-Sliding Away: The Ever-Changing Hit Total of Cap Anson. Tattersall's painstaking research was invaluable in creating official records for many players and in supplementing the skimpy official records for those included in the annual guides. Everyone has heretofore accepted Tattersall's numbers without questioning them. However, Pete Palmer has discovered that in 1889, Tattersall—for unknown reasons—changed the official hits totals for most of the White Stockings regulars. In this case, Tattersall apparently believed that the Chicago club (now the Cubs) had erroneously been given an extra 67 hits by either a generous scorer or by a league error, since his box scores did not agree with the league figures published in the official guide.

After poring over the surviving records and after careful reflection, we have decided to undo the changes Tattersall made to the official NL stats for the 1889 Chicago batters. We believe that there is not nearly enough evidence to prove any error that justified those changes. In those days, the teams, not the leagues, employed the official scorers. As one might imagine, there was a lot of favoritism in the selection of official scorers, whose names were kept secret to prevent players or fans from assailing them for controversial decisions.

Since the official scorer's decisions were unknown, virtually every nineteenth century newspaper box score was different. As a consequence, there was no way during the season to tell what the official statistics would later say (i.e., what would be published in the postseason compilations for the annual guides). Even if the official scorer in Chicago in 1889 awarded a somewhat higher number of hits rather than errors for some players—which is pure speculation at this point—it was the duty of those scorers to make judgments based on what they saw.

In 1897 public accusations were made that Baltimore official scorers unfairly aided Orioles outfielder Willie Keeler, who finished the season with a .432 average. One of those casting aspersions on the integrity of the Baltimore scorers was John Heydler, who would later become NL president. (Keeler's average was later revised to .424, based on ICI research.) Corrections due to obvious clerical or arithmetic mistakes were frequently made in the ICI process and in the decades since. In no other case, however, has the judgment of an historian decades later been substituted for the judgment of the scorer of the day about whether a batted ball should have been scored a hit or an error. The White Stockings' anonymous official scorer in the 1890s was later found to have been a female friend of team owner Al Spalding, yet her presumably non-objective decisions have never been overturned.

Why did Tattersall decide to make these changes? We cannot know for sure, as no documentation of Tattersall's reasoning—if, indeed, he recorded any—has survived. It appears that his changes to the White Stockings hit totals in 1889 were an attempt to reconcile the new league pitching stats that Tattersall was compiling with the existing official league batting stats. While that is understandable, the fact remains that there are thousands of differences between the batting and pitching stats in those years, most of which will never be reconciled because the source material (i.e., the official scoresheets) have been lost and only the final totals survive. Attempts to match the official totals for seasons in the 1880s by compiling stats from newspaper box scores have produced large and irreconcilable discrepancies.

Aside from the changes in scoring practices endorsed by the Special Records Committee, no one has ever changed any other official statistic without clear evidence that it was wrong. In fact, in many cases, "official" statistics continue to be published by reputable sources even though it has been documented that they are wrong. For example, there is overwhelming evidence of skullduggery in the final two games played by the St. Louis Browns in 1910, when well-regarded Nap Lajoie was in a tight race for the AL batting title with unpopular Ty Cobb. That malfeasance almost certainly resulted in a number of extra hits for Lajoie—it's theoretically possible, though not very likely, that Lajoie would have gone 8-for-8 had the Browns not played deep at third base and allowed him to lay down seven uncontested bunt hits—yet no one has ever adjusted his hit totals.

If you're still reading at this point, you may enjoy this comparison of the differing career hit totals for Cap Anson in various reference sources. The first entry shows what *The Sporting News* (longtime publisher of the official annual guides and record books) and Elias Sports Bureau list for Anson. The other entries show the wandering totals for Anson in various encyclopedias—most of them official—in the past half-century.

Cap Anson's Hits, by the Books

The Sporting News and Elias Sports Bureau
(official statisticians for MLB)

3,081   Matches official guide data for 1876–97, Anson's entire NL career.

Barnes *Official Encyclopedia of Baseball*, 1951–79
(1st–10th editions)

3,516   Includes 435 hits in the National Association, 1871–75.

Macmillan *Baseball Encyclopedia*, 1969
(1st edition, official)

2,995   Sources Tattersall 1876–90; 72 instead of 90 in 1879 (correcting league error); ICI printouts 1891–97; 86 not 67 in 1877 (includes games vs. Cincinnati that had been thrown out); includes 6 hits in tie games 1878–84 which originally were not counted in the official averages); does not include 60 walks that were counted as hits in 1887; has 161 instead of official 177 in 1889 due to Tattersall change in official stats; has 17 fewer hits from ICI printouts 1891–97.

Macmillan *Baseball Encyclopedia*, 1974–88
(2nd–7th editions, official)

3,041   Restored the 18 hits in 1879 which everyone else had concluded was a league error or an intentional mistake to help his average; also restored the 16 in 1889 that Tattersall had changed; then used official guide figures in 1894 (+5) and 1897 (+7) for a total of +46. They used the ICI figures for 1891–93 and 1895–96 and also used Tattersall's tie games for 1878–84.

Macmillan *Baseball Encyclopedia*, 1990–96
(8th–10th editions; 8th edition official)

3,000   Apparently reverted to 1st edition number, then arbitrarily added 5 hits in 1894 without explanation.

Total Baseball, 1989–99
(1st–6th editions; 4th–6th editions official)

2,995   Same sources and corrections as Macmillan, 1st edition.

Total Baseball, 2001–04
(7th edition, official; 8th edition, unofficial)

3,056   Per edict from Major League Baseball, reversing Special Records Committee decision to count bases on balls as walks for all seasons. Therefore, counts 60 walks in 1887 as hits; it also includes 1 hit in a protested game in 1894 that was not counted by ICI, though it should have been.

Barnes & Noble Baseball Encyclopedia, 2004
(1st edition, unofficial)

ESPN Baseball Encyclopedia
(2005 and 2006 editions, unofficial)

3,012   ICI total with restoration of 16 hits subtracted without explanation by Tattersall in 1889; also counts 1 hit in 1894 protested game.

Historical Standards. Whenever any comprehensive reference work is published, questions arise as to why certain changes were made to previously published works, as well as why other changes *weren't* made. Fair enough.

Because of ongoing research into baseball records by many devoted fans—especially SABR and Retrosheet members—apparent errors in many of baseball's official statistics and records are surfacing. As work continues, even more discrepancies will arise.

In general, the farther back one delves into the past, the less accurate are the official statistics. That is understandable, and there is no shame in admitting that close scrutiny of the records of bygone eras will inevitably produce hundreds of differences.

In the past few years, a few of baseball's most prominent all-time records have been changed: Hack Wilson's major league single-season RBI record, Walter Johnson's AL career strikeout record, and Babe Ruth's career walks record among them. Two decades ago, Ty Cobb's 1910 hits total and batting average were corrected as a result of Pete Palmer's research—and the resulting controversy reached all the way to the commissioner's office.

In most cases, the changes actually were quite small, and usually made when some player had a shot at tying or breaking the record. Yet, because of unrealistic public expectations that hold baseball records as infallible, these changes often provoked cries of outrage from pundits and fans.

As you read this, scores of researchers are poring over the records of baseball's distant past, uncovering valuable new information as well as potential corrections. As an example, SABR member Trent McCotter has checked the official daily logs for a handful of famous players from the American League in the 1920s (Ruth, Cobb, Gehrig, etc.). While doing this, he found a dozen errors just on games where someone hit a home run and was credited with no RBI, plus several entries in the wrong column and other items that don't add up. Based on Ron Liebman's study of Ruth's runs batted in and the Elias corrections to Ruth's walks, it's possible that figures in this period might be off by around one part in 300—a tiny percentage (.00333), really, but still a very meaningful number of hits, runs, or RBIs.

In the past, most of the really big errors in the official records have been found by comparing the sums of the players to their team totals, but many small errors are still uncorrected. Before 1935, the sum of the players usually did not equal the AL team total for at bats, runs or hits, although it was usually off by only a few. Extra base hits were better, but walks and strikeouts were worse. The National League has always been more accurate than the American League. For example, from 1921–30 there are only 75 cases of items not adding up in the NL and 652 in the AL. Most of the NL problems had to do with the batting totals not being equal to the pitching totals, as the NL was not as careful with pitching as they were with batting and fielding. As time went on, accuracy improved gradually, and today the official stats are virtually perfect.

Another example will suffice. In the 2005 edition of this encyclopedia, two new players were added who had fallen into the historical cracks: Bill Ford and Ed Carfrey. Ford started one game for the Boston Braves in 1936, getting no one out but allowing 3 runs in his only big-league appearance. Carfrey played one game at shortstop for Philadelphia in the American Association in 1890; his sole game was erroneously credited to another player when the official stats were computerized.

It is often said that baseball's most important records are sacred. That is thoughtless and silly: baseball records are mere numbers, after all, and should be no more be venerated than census data. Baseball records should be respected for their comprehensiveness and accuracy. The players who accomplish great feats that are recorded by those numbers should be admired for their skill and honored for their endurance. The game itself should be celebrated, not mere numbers.

While we carefully monitor the progress of current research into past records, we have decided to not make any other changes to the statistics in this edition until we have a better grasp of the extent of the discrepancies that are being uncovered. We are also conferring with other experts in the field to establish a set of rigorous, professional, and yet common-sense standards that should be applied to this new research, as well as what level of documentation should be required before more changes are made. As the saga of Cap Anson's career hit totals shows, we aren't afraid to make changes when we are confident they are warranted. We don't believe that the voluminous records of the National Pastime are sacrosanct, and we will be carefully reviewing all future research with an eye toward incorporating it in future editions of our encyclopedia.

Twice-Told Tales: Tales told at the time and retold a century later by reconstructing their statistics. A perfect example of the kind of dedication to the National Pastime that money can't buy is the story of Joe Wayman, an amateur researcher who devoted himself to researching nineteenth-century scoring practices and their impact on pitching records. As with most other advances in documenting the history of the early game, there is little if any economic reward for such work, so it is done by fans who love the game—amateurs in the pure sense of the word.

Here is the saga of Joe Wayman and how he has restored a lost part of baseball's historical tapestry—individual pitching records from the late nineteenth that had been lost for 100 years.

Nineteenth-century scoring practices regarding pitching decisions were well defined, even though they were not formulated in either the Official Playing Rules or the League Constitution. At the same time, because the practices were not expressed in writing, they varied, giving scorers more leeway in their individual interpretations.

Pitching records, inevitably, are influenced by the judgments of official scorers. In the nineteenth century, perforce, since they did not agree amongst themselves, these judgments had more impact than there has ever been since.

Essentially, there were four popular scoring conventions of the day:

- Leaving after pitching 4 ⅔ innings with a lead that lasted thereafter (both reasonable and consistent under the rules of those days as well as today);
- Pitching the most or least effectively (a reasonable practice still in use today for relievers when the starting pitcher doesn't last at least five innings);
- Pitching the bulk of the game before being removed with his team trailing, then having his club rally to win the game (not very common and partly a function of luck);
- Favoritism in borderline situations.

How, then, can these practices be verified? Sadly, of all the official NL records from 1876 through 1902, only the summaries in the annual official guides remain.

One pitching statistic dominates the entire era: *GP* for "Games Played." It was the *sine qua non* of the period and was not at all the same as the modern "games pitched" or "appearances." Unfortunately, the exact meaning—and, therefore, the critical importance—of GP has either been misunderstood, or worse, overlooked, by almost all serious baseball researchers. Until Wayman embarked on his quest.

Here is the key: the Games Played for a club's pitchers, when totaled, equal the number of games that their club played. Ergo, nineteenth-century GP's represent what are today called pitching decisions. (Yes, it's true that Saves have now lumped together by writers and fans along with Wins and Losses as pitching decisions, but a Save by definition, cannot be a decision since it is dependent on a specific relationship to particular kind of decision, the Win.)

When was the GP statistic compiled? With what other records did it share the stage? There were four periods during which the GP stat was used:

1. 1876–1889. A singular GP number was published. Deriving Won-Lost records for pitchers necessitated a day-by-day compilation from newspapers;
2. 1890–1892. The NL published both GPs and Wins for pitchers. With these, Wins, Losses, and Ties (Ties were also decisions) can reliably be determined;
3. 1893–1900. A new wrinkle, WLP (Won-Lost Percentage), was introduced. On the other hand, the NL dropped wins! Even so, Wins, Losses, and Ties could still be deduced for pitchers;
4. 1901–1902. No pitching records were published at all! Fielding records, however, had always agreed with pitchers' GP's, so they could be used.

Where is the mother lode from which this precious treasure of nineteenth-century pitching records can be extracted? Since 1975, Joe Wayman has visited the Hall of Fame Library in Cooperstown, NY; the Library of Congress in Washington, DC; the Amateur Athletic Foundation Library in Los Angeles; and many other libraries to do research in various publications including *Sporting Life*, *The Sporting News*, the *New York Clipper*, the annual *Spalding Guides*, plus numerous local metropolitan daily newspapers from NL cities. He compiled day-by-day and year-by-year pitching statistics such as game appearances, games started, complete games, and games finished from scoring descriptions, for nearly 30,000 games, particularly noting the pitchers' workload.

In addition, Wayman also utilized the Information Concepts, Inc. (ICI) sheets at the Hall of Fame for the game counts from 1891–1902. John Tattersall's summary records from 1876–90, which are the foundation of most nineteenth-century stats included in the *ESPN Baseball Encyclopedia*, *Total Baseball*, and the defunct *Macmillan Baseball Encyclopedia* were compared with Wayman's conclusions and agreed to a whopping 99.9 percent! All three of these encyclopedias, of course, were not compiled until the late twentieth century.

The forebears of the nineteenth-century GP and scoring practices were two giants of the game:

- Henry Chadwick. One of early baseball's greatest minds, the originator of many innovative baseball statistics, and often called the father of baseball, Chadwick devised a newfangled Won-Lost system in 1884 that graced the pages of the 1885 *Spalding Guide*. The National League took notice after a number of minor leagues released W-L records for 1889 and 1890, and the Senior Circuit adopted the new convention by incorporating a Wins column in its official pitching averages in 1890;

- Al Spalding. His 1908 record book recognized the important GP statistic in its own day.

Why does GP matter? Because it was the Rosetta Stone needed to unlock wins, losses, and ties for pitchers in the nineteenth century, adding detailed day-by-day records to what had previously been only season totals.

There are a couple of minor problems, as with almost every historical statistic. Scorers would sometimes award two GPs in a game when a team used more than one pitcher. Sorting these out requires careful analysis, especially to evaluate if there was an offsetting adjustment in the club's season totals.

Another issue is that, to merit inclusion in the official averages published after each season in the nineteenth century, a pitcher had to have been credited with at least six decisions in 1876–78, with 10 decisions in 1879, and with 15 decisions from 1880–1900. In such cases, the missing pitchers' records can be determined from Complete Game statistics and from decisions in their team's multiple-pitcher games.

Joseph M. Wayman spent 30 years investigating nearly 30,000 mostly forgotten baseball games that maybe one fan in a thousand either knows or cares about. Some of these discoveries have been documented in Wayman's *Grandstand Baseball Annual*, which is still being published. He is a prototype of the kind of painstaking researcher who follows his passion to the ends of the earth—or, at least, to the ends of many dusty library shelves all over the country. Wayman welcomes input from others, and future revisions in light of new evidence are certainly possible.

This is just one story of many. There are many other devoted researchers that most baseball fans have never heard of, like Frank Williams, who spent an enormous amount of time and energy filling in missing information and cleaning up problems with early twentieth century statistics. They also walk quietly and humbly among the legions of baseball fans who unknowingly benefit from their devotion to our National Game.

There are many other delicious chestnuts of information buried in the annals of the 135-year history of major league baseball but, without any further ado . . . Let's go on to "The Show."

—Gary Gillette

NO ASTERISKS!

By all accounts, 2005 was a very good year for Major League Baseball. Indeed, according to Commissioner Bud Selig, baseball has never been more popular. The commissioner has been repeating this mantra for years, of course, but people finally started jumping over to his sunny side of the fence in the second half of 2004. The commissioner has also converted much of the media into believing is that competitive balance has been restored due to the synergistic effects the wild-card format, the revised revenue-sharing plan of 2002, and the unprecedented luxury tax instituted after the last collective bargaining agreement.

Among other notable achievements of the past year was the setting of another all-time attendance record in 2005, shattering the record set only a year earlier. Partly as a result, unbelievably large amounts of money flowed into the game from revenue streams both old and new. To underscore it all with a dramatic flourish, the past two years featured exciting and unpredictable postseason play capped by two underdog teams winning World Championships for the first time in more than eight decades.

Most importantly, the majority of baseball fans feel good about the Grand Old Game again. The malaise that had lingered over the National Pastime since the nuclear winter of 1994–95—except for a brief interlude during the great home run race of 1998—finally dissipated in the past two years, and the future looks brighter now than it has since the early 1990s.

With the sun shining brightly, Major League Baseball was busily making plans in 2006 to celebrate another record-breaking performance when the great Barry Bonds is very likely to pass the immortal Babe Ruth with his 715th home run. Only seven home runs away from moving into second-place on the all-time list, Bonds will be climbing ever closer to Hammerin' Hank Aaron's magical lifetime mark of 755 this year. And with only 47 homers to go to tie Aaron, it is possible that the final days of the 2006 season would be filled with the kind of epic drama that will be capture international attention and will be retold for decades: Will Bonds hit No. 755 and No. 756? If so, will he launch these blasts at home? If he doesn't catch Aaron, will Bonds come back for one more season at age 42? Who will catch these million-dollar baseballs? And will whoever snags them get sued?

Uno momento, por favor. No one outside of San Francisco appears to be planning any festivities, and an angry mob of politicians, writers, commentators, broadcasters, fans, and big-league pitchers have embarked on a crusade. With a self-appointed agenda of cleansing the game of the stain of steroids, this populist movement wants to suppress the scoring and home run records of the past 15 years—what has now been widely dubbed by the punditocracry as the "steroid era."

Yes, just when baseball fans thought it was safe to go back into the water and enjoy their favorite game again, a renewed and seemingly interminable focus on steroids in 2005 ripped the scab off of the National Pastime's still festering wound. Retired slugger Jose Canseco, who hit 462 home runs in his career and won a Most Valuable Player trophy, penned a tell-all book in which he admitted using steroids and accused many prominent ballplayers of doing the same. While Canseco's credibility was certainly in question, his charges were front-page news.

Televised Congressional hearings on steroids in March thoroughly embarrassed the ballplayers that were called to testify as well as to the game they played. Acclaimed worldwide as heroes in 1998, sluggers Mark McGwire and Sammy Sosa saw their reputations tarnished when they refused to answer forthrightly questions about possible steroid usage.

After the Major League Baseball Players Association bowed to public and Congressional pressure in spring 2005, accepting suspensions for players testing positive for banned substances for the first time, a dozen players on major league rosters were caught in 2005. Curiously, half of the malefactors suspended were pitchers. Moreover, reports of suspensions in

the minors in the past two years indicate that almost half of minor leaguers suspended were pitchers as well. Where was the outcry against unnaturally pumped-up hurlers taking advantage of unfortunate hitters?

The announcement of every new suspension stirred the controversy a bit more. But the volcanic event that reshaped baseball's landscape occurred in midseason when Rafael Palmeiro, who had slammed 566 home runs in his career and had stroked his 3000th hit only two weeks earlier, was suspended for steroid usage. Widely regarded as a future first-ballot Hall of Famer, the uproar couldn't have been greater unless Palmeiro had waved his finger in front of Congress, testifying that he had "never used steroids. Period." Which, of course, he had only a few months earlier.

In the eyes of the Crusaders, this was proof positive that the game had been corrupted by performance-enhancing drugs and that the offensive records of 1990s and 2000s were tainted. Bolstered by this new evidence, passionate calls were soon heard demanding that recent slugging records be accompanied by a shameful asterisk. Some unthinking zealots went so far as to demand that the career statistics for guilty players be expunged from the record books. The simplicity of this notion, combined with the tsunami of public anger about steroids, has created a perfect storm of righteous indignation about the sullying of some the game's most important records.

If accomplishing things that no one had done previously is accepted as *prima facie* evidence of cheating, where is the sniggering suspicion about fortysomething marvels like the great Roger Clemens and Randy Johnson? Why is it that the Rocket's unreal 1.87 ERA at age 42—more than a run-and-a-half better than the league average, posted in a hitters' park, and the best of his 22-year-career—is to be enthusiastically cheered while the greatest player of the past 50 years crushing home runs in his 40s is to be cynically jeered?

It's hard enough to find anything positive in the steroid scandal that plagues Major League Baseball, although the relentless grandstanding that the media and politicians indulged in last year got completely out of hand. And it's probably going to get worse if scoring and home runs remain below their peak levels of the late 1990s and early 2000s, especially when retired sluggers like Mark McGwire from the so-called steroid era become eligible for the Hall of Fame.

All too often, however, simplicity leads to simplistic solutions, and adding a scarlet asterisk to selected records and to the encyclopedia entries of shamed players is a remedy that is neither right nor necessary. The simple truth is that *all* major league home run records have been controversial—both *when* they were set, *and* for decades afterward. Steroids may have added a different kind of controversial factor, but it is a distinction without a meaningful difference.

The story of the first important home run record imparts a lesson that should have been learned a century ago. The earliest home run record of consequence was set by Ed Williamson, third basemen for the Chicago White Stockings [now the Cubs]. Williamson hit 27 home runs in 107 games in 1884 in Chicago's Lake Front Park, which seems Ruthian given the playing conditions of that age. What was so controversial? Chicago's Lake Front Park had a left-field foul line 180-feet long—or short—that season, turning dozens of easy fly balls into tainted round-trippers. The wooden park, rebuilt in 1883, had power alleys of only 280 and 252 feet, measured only 300 feet to dead center, and was only 196 feet down the right field line. Its capacity was a mere 5,000 souls—cozy enough confines for at a beer-league softball game.

Prior to 1884, balls hit on the fly over that tempting left field fence at Lake Front Park were, quite reasonably, adjudicated to be ground-rule doubles. The whole National League hit a total of 124 homers in 395 games in 1883, for a rate of 1 home run every 6 games, whereas the mighty Cubs "bashed" 142 home runs in 112 games in 1884, more than 8 times the league average a year earlier. In games *not* involving the Cubs, the league's home run rate was slightly less than the previous season.

When the White Stockings moved to West Side Park in 1885, where both foul lines were only 216 feet long, Williamson managed only 3 homers despite playing in 6 more games. Prior to 1884, Williamson had a career total of 8 home runs in 481 games, and he managed to hit only 29 more round-trippers in 615 games before retiring. *Despite the anomalous and controversial circumstances under which it was set, Williamson's mark stood in the record books for 35 years—with no asterisk.*

To be fair, Williamson was somewhat of a slugger before setting the home-run record, and he led the league with 49 doubles in only 99 games in 1883. *Slugging* in days of yore, when the softer baseball was tattered, torn, and discolored for most of the game, was defined mostly by line drives to the gaps that fell in for doubles and triples. The over-the-fence power that is commonly meant by *slugging* since Babe Ruth stood the baseball world on its head in 1920 was unheard of back then.

This nineteenth century story might seem quaintly irrelevant to today's circumstances, but a review of twentieth century home run records reinforces the lesson instead of contravening it.

Babe Ruth set the baseball world agog by hitting a record 54 homers in 1920, then—just for those that didn't immediately understand the revolutionary impact of that event—the Bambino drove the point home by hitting 59 the following year. Finally, capping a decade of dominance with the 1927 Yankees, playing on perhaps the greatest team ever assembled, Ruth smashed his famous 60 home runs. All of Ruth's records were extremely controversial, as dedicated defenders of the dying Deadball-era style of play maintained that Ruth was a mere basher who couldn't or wouldn't play what was then called "scientific baseball."

Somehow, illogically, Ruth's critics thought that their disdain made The Sultan of Swat's titanic accomplishments less impressive. The deep-seated belief in the superiority of the sacrificial one-run, contact-and-baserunning game practiced by Ty Cobb and his colleagues persisted long after the game had irrevocably changed. Evidence can be seen in the vote totals for the first Hall of Fame election in 1936, when The Georgia Peach received more votes than any of the five immortals who were enshrined in the initial class—including Ruth, Honus Wagner, Christy Mathewson, and Walter Johnson.

More than three decades later, Roger Maris' 1961 challenge to Ruth's single-season record was derided as being a product of expansion: both because of the weaker pitching and the new, longer 162-game schedule. The fact that many baseball fans erroneously believe to this day that Maris' record was accompanied by an asterisk speaks to the enduring fallacies of so many of the National Pastime's legends. Its persistence explains the title of Billy Crystal's well-received 2001 HBO movie, *61**, a title that didn't need a word of explanation to anyone older than 50. Ford Frick's acute conflict of interest—the commissioner had been the ghostwriter of Ruth's autobiography in his previous vocation as a sportswriter—was seldom mentioned by those deifying Ruth and demeaning Maris.

A decade later, when indefatigable Hank Aaron was about to eclipse Ruth's career record of 714 homers, the words had changed even though the tune was the same. Defenders of The Sultan of Swat screamed out that Aaron had the benefit of facing expansion pitching for most of his career while getting almost 4,000 more at bats than Ruth. The overtly racist death threats of many of Aaron's assailants was well publicized, but there was an implicit and subtle racism being practiced by the press and the electronic media by ignoring that Ruth had clearly benefited from segregated baseball and never having faced a talented black pitcher.

Fast forward to 1998, when much of the world was transfixed by the great home-run chase that forever entwined the memories of a personable Cubs' slugger and a brooding Cardinals' basher. Mark McGwire launched his 70 moonshots and hammered his name into the record books, pursued closely for most of the season by Sammy Sosa and his 66 bombs. Smaller ballparks, pitching staffs diluted by two more expansion rounds, and supplements like androstendione were cited by the new wave of nattering nabobs that desperately wanted to set up straw sluggers as a way of dismissing McGwire's and Sosa's record-shattering seasons.

Baseball history has now progressed to Barry Bonds, whose intense batting eye, lightning-quick swing, tremendous power, and Prussian-like plate discipline formed a combination that laid waste to enemy pitching as well as to hordes of batting records. As the holder of the single-season record with 73 home runs and the potential future career record holder with 755-plus, Bonds' refusal to kowtow to the media have generated almost as much controversy as his Olympian feats.

When Bonds set his record in 2001; in distinct contrast to the events of just three summers earlier, the national reaction was a giant yawn. Many baseball fans, led on by commentators attempting to foment outrage, refused to acknowledge Bonds as the legitimate owner of the single most important individual record in professional sports. In a poll conducted by ESPN in February 2005, more respondents voted for Roger Maris as the legitimate holder of the record than anyone else, with Bonds finishing a distant fourth after Ruth and McGwire. The idea that Maris' extremely controversial feat would four decades later be hailed as the gold standard surely must have set Ford Frick spinning in his grave.

The long and carefully documented history of the National Pastime should teach thoughtful fans and scholars many lessons. One of the most important is that, whenever a player breaks an important baseball record, it is *always* controversial. Most often, the detractors advance the same timeworn or irrelevant arguments in an attempt to impugn the integrity of both the player and the new record he set. Sometimes, their points are well taken, but merely pointing out that the new record holder has enjoyed substantial—and possibly unique—advantages in no way destroys the validity of the new record.

All record-setting performances are the products of their times and are frequently accomplished in unique circumstances. All players that set important records both enjoyed and exploited whatever significant advantages time and fate gave them. None of that has been changed by Palmeiro's positive steroid test, nor anyone else's steroid usage, real or imagined.

Finally, none of this even scratches the issue of the hypocrisy of the handwringers. Baseball history is replete with pitchers that used spitballs, scuffballs, greaseballs, and other assorted illegal tricks to give them an edge over the hitters. The hallowed Hall of Fame has memorialized in bronze several notorious cheaters who, because they were pitchers, have gotten a free pass. And that doesn't just refer to the notorious Gaylord Perry, who published his autobiography *Me and the Spitter* after he retired but *before* he was elected to the Hall of Fame. Until Pedro Martinez came along, the career record for winning percentage—one of the most important pitching records on the books—was held by Whitey Ford, well-known for his ingenuity in modifying pristine baseballs to his advantage.

The plain truth is that steroid usage is part and parcel of a long and dishonorable tradition in baseball. A brief refresher course in the history of pitcher cheating here will put things in perspective.

Since the very beginning of organized baseball, pitchers and hitters have waged a war for supremacy in their critical individual contest and, therefore, for control of the game itself. Most of that war is, of course, fought on the field, but the battle is also joined in how the rules are written and whether they are strictly enforced.

In 1874, batters were first required to stand in a box rather than run toward the pitch and swing. The number of balls needed for a walk was nine. Pitchers threw from just 45 feet from the plate, but were only allowed to release the ball sidearm or underhand. During the 1880s, pitchers were also, at various times, required to pitch without a windup and from a "pitcher's box." And because the game back then centered on putting the ball in play, hurlers in the first decade of professional ball were mandated to ask batters what kind of pitch they would like and where they wanted it located—high, low, or at the belt.

However, as players looked to gain advantage in what is now erroneously thought of as a gentleman's game, they began to cheat. Pitchers, for their part, were dismayed by the ever-decreasing number of balls needed for a walk as the rules changed from eight to seven to six to the current four errant pitches in just twenty years. Many early moundsmen skirted the rules by putting a "break" on the ball by flicking their wrists in order to make their offerings harder to hit. Pitchers also began changing their arm angles, seeing how much they could get away with by flinging the ball at increasingly high angles. In 1883, the National League responded to this illegitimate practice by passing a rule prohibiting any pitches being thrown from above the shoulder.

Soon, those restrictive rules—which now seem hopelessly quaint—were overhauled or eliminated. Pitchers were finally allowed to legally throw breaking balls, deliver with a long windup, and even throw straight overhand if they wanted to. As pitchers gained more freedom, they gained corresponding tactical advantages that tended to stifle the offense. The official response was to lengthen the distance between the pitcher and the hitter, which was finally set at the contemporary 60 feet, six inches in 1893, which led to a brief boom in scoring.

A succession of rules changes after 1893 chipped away at the batters' superiority, culminating with the adoption of the crucial rules change that counted foul balls as strikes by the NL in 1901, followed by the upstart AL in 1903. The foul-strike rule set the stage for what is now known as the low-scoring Deadball Era, which defined the game until the home run renaissance of the 1920s, which was partly due to rules changes to outlaw the deliberate defacing of the baseball by enterprising pitchers.

Before 1920, pitchers were legally allowed to spit on the ball, rub it with dirt or other substances, and even cut its cover. Such was the ethos of the Deadball Era when pitching, defense, speed, and one-run tactics were judged morally superior to batting in general and slugging in particular. Allowing pitchers to coat baseballs with all kinds of wet, sticky substances was bad enough, but it was combined with a penurious attitude that kept battered and discolored balls in play for the whole game.

Then the roof caved in on the dirty (literally) practices of the first two decades of the century. In August 1920, star Cleveland shortstop Ray Chapman died when his skull was fractured by a high, inside pitch from pitcher Carl Mays. While it is not clear that Chapman's death was caused by a hard-to-see pitch, something had to be done in response to the tragedy since Chapman was as popular in his day as Nomar Garciaparra is today. The major leagues quickly adopted a policy where scuffed or dirty baseballs were removed from play and replaced with clean ones. This decision, combined with the end of the spitter, emery, and shine ball and the strategic revolution wrought by the power hitting of the great Babe Ruth, tremendously increased offense and changed the game forever.

When grandfathered Burleigh Grimes (what a perfect name for a spitballer!) pitched his last big-league game in 1934, the legal spitter breathed its last gasp. That's not to say, though, that the spitball or its outside-the-rules cousins disappeared from the game. Far from it. Furthermore, with the anti-steroid crusade in full swing today, we're sure to see even more of the "wink, wink; nudge, nudge" attitude about pitcher cheating while out-of-bounds sluggers are pilloried.

Ballplayers are, above all else, competitors, and many will do anything to win—including cheating, lying, and taking performance-enhancing drugs. Plenty of pitchers, especially those with fading stuff and those who made it to the majors mostly by their cunning and guile, have been willing to try anything legal or outlawed to help give their pitches an extra break.

Without truly understanding the context, no one can make valid judgments about the integrity of any record-setting feat. It will take more time and a helluva lot of more research before we truly understand what effects steroids have had on the game. The fact is that scoring and home run rates started declining after the controversial 2001 peak. In the past two years, when the wags say that the beefed-up steroid testing program has deterred usage of illegal performance enhancers, offensive levels have been indistinguishable from the preceding two seasons when the program was regarded as ineffectual.

In November 2005, Major League Baseball and the union agreed to a far more stringent policy on steroid testing, with more severe penalties and with provisions for amphetamine testing as well. Whether this new program will help restore the game's reputation or sully it further will be determined by how many players are caught violating the policy.

History is composed of facts. Facts should be accompanied with explanations. Explanations should engender insight. Insight should produce understanding. Well-intentioned but wrongheaded asterisks and ignorant statistical book-burnings add nothing to the historical record and demean the history of our beloved game.

THE SCIENCE OF HITTING: THE BATTER REGISTER

The two most commonly repeated things about hitting are both, not coincidentally, attributed to the late Ted Williams. The first statement was a trifle whose significance is overblown almost as often as it is paraphrased:

"Baseball is the only field of endeavor where a man can succeed three times out of ten and be considered a good performer."—sourced as "widely quoted" in Baseball's Greatest Quotations.

It should not have to be said that Williams was obviously indulging in hyperbole to make a point and not being literal here. After all, it is inconceivable that a player with a lifetime on-base percentage of .482 would think that the success of a batter was measured solely by his batting average.

On the very next page of that same book, the caption next to Williams' picture reads: "Ted Williams, who once termed his 2,019 career bases on balls (the equivalent of four seasons of walking) as my 'proudest record.' " (Williams was second to Babe Ruth in career walks when he retired; that figure has since been corrected to 2,021 walks and has been surpassed by both Rickey Henderson and Barry Bonds.)

No one ever accused "The Splendid Splinter" of being indecisive, so how does one reconcile these two seemingly divergent attitudes? The best way to view Williams' attitude about hitting is to understand that it wasn't reducible to the kind of catchy phrase so loved by the pundits.

The other oft-repeated Williams' comment on hitting—as quoted in Joe Falls' *Sporting News* column of February 8, 1969—is much more substantial and deserves much more scrutiny:

"First of all, the hardest single thing to do in sports is to hit a baseball. If this is true and it is, then it takes more hours of practice, more hours of dedication, more hours of desire to hit a baseball than it does to do anything else."

One reason that Teddy Ballgame is considered by many as the greatest hitter of all time was that he *studied* hitting. He turned it inside out, tested it, and thought constantly about how to improve his approach. For him, hitting *was* baseball. The study of hitting was serious science. Williams honed his bats to perfection, refined his ideas of the strike zone, thought about whether to swing down or up on the ball, and studied pitchers as if they were helpless butterflies he was about to pin to black paper.

Heeding the advice of Rogers Hornsby—often called the best right-handed batter of all time—Williams elected simply not to swing at bad pitches, either taking his walk or forcing the pitcher to come in to him and give him something truly good to swing at. The details are spelled out in *The Science of Hitting*, Williams' classic text (co-authored with John Underwood), which was first published in 1970 and remains in-print today.

Williams' scientific view of batting had little to do with that of the early part of the twentieth century, the era of great hitters like Ty Cobb and Joe Jackson. Players of that time used the term "scientific baseball" to describe things that *managers* told *players* to do. Called "little ball" today, it used stratagems such as sacrifice bunting, squeeze bunting, drag bunting, hitting-and-running, stealing, hitting behind the runner, and the like. Being *scientific* in those days meant employing the right *plays*, rather than how a batter approached his turn at bat.

F.C. Lane's classic work *Batting* was first published in 1925. It was reprinted by SABR in 2001 and is now available from the University of Nebraska Press (www.unp.unl.edu). The book is a treasure trove of insight into attitudes about hitting in the early twentieth century; all of the following quotations come from its pages.

Feared slugger Joe Jackson typified the view of the day, opining that hitters had little choice but to step up to the plate and whale away. "I don't care whether the ball is over the plate or not, so long as it looks good," he said, "Batters can't be choosers. They have to take what the pitcher gives them. And pitchers are not very accommodating."

The greatest hitter of his day, Ty Cobb, disagreed. Cobb believed that hitters controlled their destiny, and that they didn't have to take advantage of their first offering. "Many batters have the mistaken idea that the pitcher is working on them and that there is nothing they can do in self-defense . . . [T]hey reason, 'We have to hit what he gives us.' That's only partially true, however. The batter is seldom compelled to hit any particular ball. He has a choice."

Despite that clear-eyed assessment, Cobb didn't take many more free passes than Jackson on a year-by-year basis. Both of them, though, were smart enough to take a walk when they weren't offered anything to hit.

One of the most patient hitters of the era was Eddie Collins, the great second baseman who, according to Walter Johnson, would "never bite at a bad ball." However, most of the most patient hitters of the day were not stars.

Jack Graney, who twice led the AL in walks, knew what he was trying to accomplish. "Not only does waiting a pitcher out impair his confidence and his control," he said, "But it also makes him work harder . . . I believe the waiting game is the most effective batting system that could possibly be devised."

Another Dead Ball Era player who might be applying for a job as an Oakland or Boston hitting instructor if he were around today was Burt Shotton, who twice topped the AL in walks and later was a successful manager. "The very name baseball is almost the same as base on balls," Shotton noted. "The spectator at the game is likely to look upon the base on balls as a mere incident; a momentary wildness on the part of the pitcher, or a gift to a dangerous batter. This opinion is often justified, but just as often the base on balls is a real tribute to the batter's skill in working the pitcher."

Ted Williams' idea of science was to treat his precious at bats as lab experiments performed under controlled conditions. If he had good equipment, a good idea of the pitcher's strengths and weaknesses, and an eye for the strike zone, Williams believed he could hit anyone at any time. His approach had very little to do with the intricacies of what was—and still is—thought of as "strategic" baseball. Williams himself was the one who made the difference while in the batter's box.

Williams became a truly great hitter by combining a tremendously strong uppercut swing—which he practiced for hours and hours—with discerning strike-zone judgment. Power and plate discipline are still an unbeatable combination.

The science of hitting has certainly changed over time—like everything else in the game—though thoughtful and analytical hitters have followed similar approaches in different eras. When circumstances change dramatically in baseball, failure to make the appropriate adjustments is usually followed by a quick ticket out of the league.

Failure to adjust is a cardinal sin when analyzing baseball statistics. Baseball stats are certainly comparable over time, but they are not *directly* comparable. To take stats from twenty-five years ago and compare them directly to today's numbers is risky; to take stats from 1904 and compare them directly to today's stats is silly. To make judgments based simply on comparing raw stats is sheer folly.

The numbers in this Batter Register provide one with the opportunity to examine the raw stats, the ability to put them into the proper context, and a chance to make informed judgments. Barry Bonds can be compared to Willie Mays, Ted Williams to Joe DiMaggio, Babe Ruth to Ty Cobb. Context is not everything, but it is essential to understanding most things—including the game of baseball and the stats it produces.

BIOGRAPHICAL INFORMATION

There are 16,422 major league players listed in *The Baseball Encyclopedia*: 9,264 in the Batter Register and 7,469 in the Pitcher Register, which means that 311 players are listed in both the Batter and Pitcher Registers.

▲ at the end of the biographical information indicates that the player is also listed in the Pitcher Register. A player whose primary position was not pitcher must have pitched at least 9 innings to appear in the Pitcher Register.

There is a wealth of biographical information in a single line atop each player entry. The biographical information answers questions about a player's life away from the batter's box: When was he born? Did he live to a ripe old age? How tall was he? Was he ever a manager, and for how long? Did he miss time to the military? And was he one of rare few to reach the Hall of Fame? The biographical line is a reminder that a player is more than just a collection of numbers. More details on many of the statistics and formulas shown in this register can be found in the glossary at the end of the encylopedia.

Every player in this register has (at least) a last name and a debut date. If a player has a matronymic name, it is placed in parentheses—for example, Roberto Clemente (Walker). Nicknames are included in the biographical line; if a nickname is what the player is known by during his career, it will be part of his listed name—such as, McInnis, Stuffy. Other features and abbreviations for biographical information follow.

B (mm.dd.yyyy) is the date and place of birth.

D (mm.dd.yyyy) is the date and place of death, if death has occurred.

The side of the plate a player bats from is expressed *BR* (bats right), *BL* (bats left), or *BB* (bats both sides). The arm the player throws with is expressed *TR* (throws right), or *TL* (throws left). If a player changed his batting handedness for a substantial length of time during his career (e.g., from switch-hitting to batting left-handed or vice versa), that change is noted.

Height is shown by feet followed by inches. Weight is expressed in pounds. For many players who played for more than one season after 1949, additional information about their playing weights has been added to this edition. This new, more accurate information is based on extensive research conducted by the editors into year-by-year playing weight information as published in official and quasi-official sources. Those sources include annual team press or media guides, official league publications, and a variety of other reliable annual reference works.

An asterisk after a player's weight indicates that the player's listed weight for every season in his big-league career varied by less than 10 pounds from the weight shown in the encyclopedia.

If a player's weight varied by more than 10 pounds from the weight shown in the encyclopedia, a weight range for that player's career is shown in parentheses. That range represents the lowest and highest weights that he was listed at during his big-league career.

This new information is obviously not perfect, but it is substantially better than anything previous baseball encyclopedias have published. Previously, encyclopedias showed only a single player weight, whether that player played but one game in the majors or played 2,000 games over 15 years. Moreover, that weight was typically what was listed in the player's debut season and never updated. (In earlier editions of *The ESPN Baseball Encyclopedia*, player weights were updated based on research done by Pete Palmer for players whose careers were five years or longer, where Palmer attempted to estimate the midpoint weight for those players' careers.)

Research is ongoing to obtain more accurate player weights pre-1950. However, less information is available from then, so how much weight information will be added in future editions is unclear.

Complete draft information is shown in square brackets in the biographical line for all major league players that were selected in the annual amateur/first-year player drafts that began in 1965. This information has never before been published in a baseball encyclopedia.

The format for each player's draft information is [Team/League/Year Drafted/Round/Pick Number]. Teams and leagues are abbreviated in the same way as in the player registers. The year drafted is shown with two digits (e.g., "89" means 1989; "00" means 2000). The round number shown is the round designated by MLB. Therefore, so-called "sandwich" picks at the end of the first round are shown as first-rounders; ditto for second- and third-round sandwich picks. The pick number is the overall ordinal number of that pick in that draft, *not* the team's pick number. That is because a team's third pick in a particular draft might come in the first round at No. 35 or might come in the fourth round at No. 115.

The defunct Secondary Drafts of players who had been selected by a club in a previous draft but did not sign a professional contract are indicated by a capital *S* before the draft round number. The defunct January drafts (both Regular and Secondary) are indicated by an asterisk after the year; all other drafts were held in June.

The original amateur draft in 1965 had a unique format. From 1966–86, drafts were held in both January and June. After 1986, all four drafts were consolidated into a single June draft. In the late 1990s, MLB officially changed the name of the June amateur draft to the "First-Year Player Draft" after players like J.D. Drew signed pro contracts with independent league teams instead of signing with the major league club that had drafted them.

Team codes are shown as of the year the player was drafted, not the year of that player's major league debut and therefore, a player like Justin Baughman is shown as being drafted by California in 1995 [CalA95] even though he made his debut after the Angels had changed the team name to Anaheim.

Non-drafted players who started their pro careers after 1965, whether because they were ineligible for the draft (like most non-Americans) or because they weren't considered good enough prospects to be drafted, will have no draft information shown.

Debuts are marked *d* followed by the date the player made his first major league appearance. The debut year is the first year listed in the register, so it is not included in the biographical line.

Besides these basic pieces of information available in the biographical line, there are several other designations for players whose career, family, or duty took them beyond the norm.

If a player on a major league roster missed significant parts of any season serving the United States during wartime, the following abbreviations are used to identify how the player served:

Mil indicates military service in the army, navy, air force, or marines;

Mer indicates the merchant marine;

Def indicates defense plant work.

The seasons the player missed at least a part of are listed after the abbreviation for duty. At least one major leaguer missed time during the seasons below as a result of the following wars (dates include post-war service by some veterans):

Spanish-American War, 1898;

World War I, 1917–19;

World War II, 1941–46;

Korean War 1951–59;

Vietnam War 1962–72.

Many major league ballplayers served in the military after their playing days were over. That military service is not shown, which is why former New York Giants player Eddie Grant—who last played in 1915 and died in action World War I three years later—does not have a "Mil" in his bio info. A monument was erected to Grant at the Polo Grounds in 1921.

Negro Lg indicates a player played for a big-league caliber Negro League team prior to playing in the major leagues. The first and last years he played with such a Negro League team are shown. Because of the unstable nature of some Negro Leagues and of many Negro League teams—and because of the often-erratic schedules even in their best years—these dates do not necessarily indicate continuous service in the Negro Leagues. If a former Negro League player also served in the military during wartime, his military service will be shown even if it predates his major league debut.

For a list of all of the Negro Leagues that are considered to be of major league caliber, see the Black Baseball and Negro Leagues section of the encyclopedia.

If the player spent time as a coach, manager, or umpire, that is indicated by the following symbols which are followed by the number of seasons during which he performed those jobs. Abbreviations are:

C: Coach;

M: Manager;

U: Umpire.

HF indicates that the player is a member of the Hall of Fame; the year of election follows *HF*.

If the player had a close family member in the major leagues, the relative's relationship is identified by the codes listed below followed by the relative's first name (and, if it is different, the last name):

b: brother;

twb: twin brother;

f: father;

s: son;

gf: grandfather;

gs: grandson;

ggf: great grandfather;

ggs: great grandson.

Col indicates that the player played collegiate baseball at the university, college, or junior college shown. If a player played collegiate ball at more than one school, only the last school is shown. Typically, players transfer from two-years schools to four-year schools or from one four-years school to another, but a few have reversed that course and transferred from a four-year school to a junior or community college.

If a two-year school does not have *CC* for "Community College," *JC* for "Junior College," or *City* for "City College" as part of its name, we have appended *[JC]* to its name to indicate that. Note that, if a player attended a college but didn't play collegiate baseball there, no college is shown.

Because many colleges and universities have changed their names in the past, and because many of these older names would not be recognizable today, we show the institution's current name, not the name when that player played ball there. North Carolina State University—shown in the player registers as "North Carolina St."—is a good example why this is necessary:

- North Carolina College of Agriculture and Mechanic Arts   1887–1917
- North Carolina College of Agriculture and Engineering   1917–1963
- North Carolina State of the University of North Carolina at Raleigh   1963–1965
- North Carolina State University at Raleigh   1965–present

NC State has had a baseball team every year since 1903, except for 1916. More than a dozen major league players played ball at NCSU prior to 1963, yet almost no one except NC State alumni would recognize the earliest names of that institution if we showed them in a player's bio line.

A few players will have additional information shown in the biographical lines. DL information will be shown in the bio line for those years when that player didn't play in any games. Career games played at the three outfield positions (*LF/CF/RF*) will also be included at the end of the biographical information for some players if there is not enough room to place it in their Games at Position column.

STATISTICAL INFORMATION

Symbols in the first two columns:

† before the team name means he participated in Postseason Play that year;

★ after team name means he participated in All-Star game;

☆ after team name means he was selected to All-Star team but did not play;

✳ after team name means he was selected to All-Star team but replaced due to injury.

Boldface statistics in any category indicates a league-leading total or average.

The columns that appear in the player register after **Year**:

TM: **Team.** Each team is identified by a three-letter code that is usually the first three letters of the city, state, or area where the team is located.

LG: **League.** The leagues in this book include the National League (N), the American League (A), the Federal League (F), the Players League (P), the Union Association (U), the National Association (NA), and the American Association (AA).

G: **Games.** The number of games are boldfaced if the player appeared in all of his team's games for a given year.

AB: At Bats.

R: Runs.

H: Hits.

2B: Doubles.

3B: Triples.

HR: Home Runs.

RBI: Runs Batted In. RBI information is unavailable for 1882–84 American Association and 1884 Union Association. Since 1939, runs scoring on a groundball double play have not been counted as RBIs.

BB: Bases on Balls. Generally referred to today as walks.

IB: Intentional Base on Balls. Walking an opponent on purpose was first counted as a distinct category in 1955.

HP: Hit-by-Pitch. The rule awarding first base to batters hit by pitches was instituted in 1884 by the American Association. It was adopted in 1887 by the National League.

SO: Strikeouts. Strikeouts are available for batters in all years except for 1884 in the Union Association, from 1882–88 and 1890 in the American Association, from 1897–1909 in the National League, and 1901–12 in the American League.

AVG: Batting Average. Hits divided by at bats.

OBP: On-Base Percentage. The official definition of on-base percentage, which was established when OBP was made an official statistic in 1984, is: (hits plus walks plus hit-by-pitches) divided by (at bats plus walks plus hit-by-pitches plus sacrifice flies). This definition is used for 1954 and all later seasons. In the years prior to 1954, the definition depends on the data available.

SLG: Slugging Percentage. Total bases divided by at bats.

AOPS: Adjusted On-Base plus Slugging. On-base percentage and slugging average are added and normalized for the context of the offensive level of the league and the player's home park(s) and then converted to a scale in which 100 is average.

ABR: Adjusted Batting Runs. The linear weights values of the offensive events that the player's plate appearances precipitated are added and then normalized for the context of the offensive level of the league and the player's home park(s). It is then converted to a scale in which 0 is average and the output is the number of runs the player's batting added to or subtracted from his team compared what an average player would have done.

SB: Stolen Bases. Totals are available for all seasons in all leagues from 1886 on, as well as for all the seasons of the National Association.

CS: Caught Stealing. Totals are available for all American League players in 1914–15 and from 1920 on; caught stealing totals are available for all National League players in 1913, 1915, from 1920–26, and from 1951 on. Caught Stealing totals are also available for 1916 for all players who stole at least 20 bases.

FA: Fielding Average. Determined by the formula: (Assists plus Putouts) divided by (Assists plus Putouts plus Errors).

FR: Fielding Runs. This measures how many runs the player saves or loses for his team in the field compared to an average fielder. The formula takes into account assists, putouts, errors, and double plays, as well as passed balls for catchers. All of these defensive statistics are adjusted for context in several different ways. Defensive innings are based on play-by-play from 1969 forward and were estimated for previous years.

RNG: Range. This is calculated different ways for different positions. For infielders, range is based on assists per inning. For outfielders, range is based on putouts per inning. For catchers, range is based on stolen bases allowed per inning. The data is then adjusted in comparison to the league average, with 100 equaling league average—higher is always better. (Thus a 110 rating for a catcher means 10 percent fewer stolen bases allowed than average.) All statistics are adjusted for context, including the number of balls put into play and what direction the balls in play were likely to go in. Innings played data was calculated from play-by-play accounts from 1969 forward and is estimated for previous seasons. Outfielders are rated for their play at all outfield (weighted) positions, while infielders are only rated for their play at their primary position.

THR: Throwing. Throwing is calculated different ways for different positions. For infielders, throwing is based on double plays per inning. For outfielders, throwing is based on assists per inning. For catchers, throwing is based on caught stealing rates per inning. The data is then adjusted in comparison to league average, with 100 equaling league average. All statistics are adjusted for context by various methods. Innings played data was calculated from play-by-play accounts from 1969 forward and is estimated for previous seasons. Outfielders are rated for their play at all outfield positions, while infielders are only rated for their play at their primary position.

Stolen bases and caught stealing off catchers are italicized for both *range and throwing* for years prior to 1969 to indicate data was estimated from player and team data.

GAMES AT POSITION. Positions are listed left to right by decreasing number of games. The number of games played at each position is shown for every player—year-by-year and for his career.

Positions are identified by easily recognizable one- or two-letter abbreviations:

P: Pitcher.
1b: First Base.
2b: Second Base.
3b: Third Base.
S: Shortstop.
O: Outfield.
D: Designated Hitter.
M: Player-Manager (always at end of position codes),
/H: Pinch-Hitter (used only if player had no other position).
/R: Pinch-Runner (used only if player had no other position).

Position codes are followed by the number of games that the player played at that position during a season or in his career. Different positions are normally separated by commas, except when a slash (/) is used to indicate that the player played only one game at positions to the right of the slash. (No commas are used to separate such positions.)

Because the official statistics lump the three outfield positions into only one "outfield" position, the official number of games in the Outfield is always shown first with an *O*. If the player only played one outfield position in that year or in his career, that position will be identified by an *L*, *C*, or *R* after the number of games played.

If the player played two or three outfield positions in a year or in his career, a breakdown of the games in left, center, and right is presented in that order in parentheses, separated by slashes. When a player's career breakdown of games in left, center, and right won't fit in the Games at Position column totals line, that information has been added to the end of the player's biographical information. *If so, the primary outfield position played will be identified by L, C, or R following the number of games played in the outfield in the totals line.*

DL: Disabled List. This new category of information—never-before-published in an encyclopedia—shows the number of days spent on the major league disabled list, year-by-year and for each player's career. All DL assignments from 1941 to the present are shown. If a player was not disabled, his DL column will be blank for that year; if he was never disabled, his DL column will be blank for his career.

The **DL** column in the batter and pitcher registers shows the number of *days* (not *games*) missed by that player during the regular season while he was on the disabled list. If a player was assigned to the DL more than once during a particular season, the lengths of all his DL stints are combined. Time spent on the DL before Opening Day or after the last day of the regular season is not counted, which is why some players will have Days on DL data that is less than the minimum (currently 15 days).

A DL column entry of 166 or greater from 1941–58 indicates that a player spent the whole season on the DL since the length of the regular season in those years was 166–167 days. From 1959–68, the regular season was 171–174 days long, except for the 1960 AL (167 days), which opened almost a week later than the NL.

With expansion to two divisions in 1969, the regular season was stretched to 178–181 days, except in the strike year of 1972 (172 days). From 1982 to the present, the normal season has been 181–183 days long; in the last 20 years, the only seasons that were shorter than 182 days were due to lockouts or strikes in 1990 (178 days), 1994 (131), and 1995 (160). Because of the interruption of the season caused by September 11, the 2001 season went a week longer than its scheduled 183 days. (Note that the early season-opening series in Japan in 2000 and 2004 were not counted as part of the regular-season length.)

If a player spent all or part of any season on the major league DL but did not play in any games that year, his DL information is shown in square brackets at the end of his bio line. The format for these entries is [DL Year Tm Lg Days on DL]. If a player (e.g., Albert Belle) spent time on the DL in more than one season in which he never played, these DL stints will be separated by commas inside a single set of square brackets in his bio line.

In the rare cases when a player was traded while on the DL, the number of days he spent on the DL is shown separately for each team, but no total is shown for that year. There are also a small number of zero-day DL stints where players were put on the DL in the off-season (typically in the spring) but were activated on or before Opening Day and didn't miss any time during the regular season. If such a DL stint is the player's only time on the DL in a given season, we show a zero in the DL column instead of a blank.

The forerunner of the modern DL was instituted in 1941. Aside from a brief experiment by the NL in 1915–16 with a Disabled List (from which no records of disabled players have been found), seriously injured players were simply sent home by major league teams and told to report back when they were healthy enough to play again. If the club wanted to retain future rights to injured players, they simply placed them on the Suspended or Voluntary Retired lists—meaning that injured players were removed from major league rosters and didn't draw a salary, yet these same players still couldn't try to sign on with any other team in Organized Baseball.

The rules for using the DL in the 1940s were quite strict: Only two players from a club could be on the DL at any one time, players had to spend at least 60 days on the DL, and no one could be placed on the DL after August 1. Because of these strict rules and the depletion of top-flight talent during World War II, major league clubs very rarely used the DL before the 1950s. Fewer than a dozen players total ever spent time on the DL before 1946, and the first season that more than 12 players were assigned to the DL was 1950.

After the 1949 season, the rules were liberalized so that players needed to spend only 30 days on the DL. Many other changes to the rules governing disabled players have been made since 1960; 15-day DL stints were allowed for the first time in 1966.

BFW: Batter-Fielder Wins. The sum of a player's batting wins, basestealing wins, and fielding wins, this figure indicates how many games the player won or lost for his team compared to an average player.

For any missing data, such as CS, RBI or SO, the career total is underlined if it is a partial figure.

YEAR	TM LG	G	AB	R	H	2B	3B	HR	RBI	BB-IB	HP	SO	AVG	OBP	SLG	AOPS	ABR	SB-CS	FA	FR	RNG	THR	GAMES AT POSITION	DL	BFW

AARON, HANK Henry Louis "The Hammer" B2.5.1934 Mobile AL BR/TR/6-0/180* d4.13 HF1982 b-Tommie Negro Lg 1952 OF(313/293/2184)

YEAR	TM LG	G	AB	R	H	2B	3B	HR	RBI	BB-IB	HP	SO	AVG	OBP	SLG	AOPS	ABR	SB-CS	FA	FR	RNG	THR	GAMES AT POSITION	DL	BFW
1954	Mil N	122	468	58	131	27	6	13	69	28	3	39	.280	.322	.447	105	1	2-2	.970	-6	93	64	O116(105/0/11)		-1.2
1955	Mil N★	153	602	105	189	37	9	27	106	49-5	3	61	.314	.366	.540	144	37	3-1	.967	1	99	82	O126(26/0/105),2b27		3.4
1956	Mil N★	153	609	106	200	34	14	26	92	37-6	2	54	.328	.365	.558	154	43	2-4	.962	4	105	119	O152R		4.1
1957	†Mil N★	151	615	118	198	27	6	44	132	57-15	0	58	.322	.378	.600	170	58	1-1	.983	-8	94	74	O150(1/69/83)		4.3
1958	†Mil N★	153	601	109	196	34	4	30	95	59-16	1	49	.326	.386	.546	157	48	4-1	.984	-6	94	91	O153(0/39/120)		3.6
1959	Mil N★	154	629	116	223	46	7	39	123	51-17	4	54	.355	.401	.636	188	77	8-0	.982	-4	91	105	O152(0/13/144),3b5		6.8
1960	Mil N★	153	590	102	172	20	11	40	126	60-13	2	63	.292	.352	.566	160	46	16-7	.982	4	108	89	O153(0/3/151),2b2		4.5
1961	Mil N★	155	603	115	197	39	10	34	120	56-20	2	64	.327	.381	.594	165	55	21-9	.982	4	109	93	O154(0/71/88),3b2		5.1
1962	Mil N★	156	592	127	191	28	6	45	128	66-14	3	73	.323	.390	.618	171	58	15-7	.980	1	105	95	O153(0/83/71)/1		5.2
1963	Mil N★	161	631	121	201	29	4	44	130	78-18	0	94	.319	.391	.586	180	66	31-5	.979	-8	92	79	O161R		5.4
1964	Mil N★	145	570	103	187	30	2	24	95	62-9	0	46	.328	.393	.514	152	41	22-4	.983	7	115	133	O139R,2b11		4.5
1965	Mil N★	150	570	109	181	40	1	32	89	60-10	1	81	.318	.379	.560	161	47	24-4	.987	6	111	89	O148R		4.8
1966	Atl N★	158	603	117	168	23	1	44	127	76-15	1	96	.279	.356	.539	144	36	21-3	.988	8	114	109	O158(0/4/158),2b2		3.8
1967	Atl N★	155	600	113	184	37	3	39	109	63-19	0	97	.307	.369	.573	169	53	17-6	.979	6	110	106	O152(0/11/141)/2		5.4
1968	Atl N★	160	606	84	174	33	4	29	86	64-23	1	62	.287	.354	.498	154	40	28-5	.991	11	121	103	O151R,1b14		5.0
1969	†Atl N★	147	547	100	164	30	3	44	97	87-19	2	47	.300	.396	.607	176	57	9-10	.982	2	105	100	O144R,1b4		5.1
1970	Atl N★	150	516	103	154	26	1	38	118	74-15	2	63	.298	.385	.574	146	34	9-0	.977	2	110	74	O125R,1b11		3.0
1971	Atl N★	139	495	95	162	22	3	47	118	71-21	2	58	.327	.410	.669	190	58	1-1	.996	-9	77	92	1b71,O60(1/0/59)		4.2
1972	Atl N★	129	449	75	119	10	0	34	77	92-15	1	55	.265	.390	.514	143	28	4-0	.987	1	101	88	1b109,O15R		2.2
1973	Atl N★	120	392	84	118	12	1	40	96	68-13	1	51	.301	.402	.643	173	39	1-1	.977	1	91	63	O105(87/0/18)		3.5
1974	Atl N★	112	340	47	91	16	0	20	69	39-6	0	29	.268	.341	.491	127	11	1-0	.986	-3	89	54	O89L		0.5
1975	Mil A★	137	465	45	109	16	2	12	60	70-3	1	51	.234	.332	.355	95	-2	0-1	1.000	-1	38	0	D128,O3L		-0.6
1976	Mil A	85	271	22	62	8	0	10	35	35-1	0	38	.229	.315	.369	102	1	0-1	1.000	0	207	0	D74/OL		-0.1
Total	23	3298	12364	2174	3771	624	98	755	2297	1402-293	32	1383	.305	.374	.555	156	932	240-73	.980	14	103	93	O2760R,1b210,D202,2b43,3b7		82.5

AARON, TOMMIE Tommie Lee B8.5.1939 Mobile AL D8.16.1984 Atlanta GA BR/TR/6-1/200* d4.10 C6 b-Hank

YEAR	TM LG	G	AB	R	H	2B	3B	HR	RBI	BB-IB	HP	SO	AVG	OBP	SLG	AOPS	ABR	SB-CS	FA	FR	RNG	THR	GAMES AT POSITION	DL	BFW
1962	Mil N	141	334	54	77	20	2	8	38	41-0	0	58	.231	.312	.374	86	-6	6-0	.989	4	120	121	1b110,O42L/23		-0.6
1963	Mil N	72	135	6	27	6	1	1	15	11-1	0	27	.200	.257	.281	57	-17	0-3	1.000	-3	61	151	1b45,O14(14/1/0),2b6/3		-1.5
1965	Mil N	8	16	1	3	0	0	0	1	1-0	0	2	.188	.235	.188	21	-2	0-0	.961	0	138	85	1b6		-0.2
1968	Atl N	98	283	21	69	10	3	1	25	21-1	0	37	.244	.295	.311	82	-6	3-4	.942	-2	88	87	O62L,1b28/3		-1.5
1969	†Atl N	49	60	13	15	2	0	1	5	6-0	0	6	.250	.318	.333	82	-1	0-1	1.000	0	50	113	1b16,O8L		-0.3
1970	Atl N	44	63	3	13	2	0	2	7	3-0	0	10	.206	.242	.333	50	-5	0-0	.955	-2	48	22	1b16,O12(10/0/2)		-0.7
1971	Atl N	25	53	4	12	2	0	0	3	3-1	0	5	.226	.268	.264	48	-4	0-0	.974	1	103	222	1b11,3b7		-0.3
Total	7	437	944	102	216	42	6	13	94	86-3	0	145	.229	.292	.327	75	-32	9-8	.990	-1	101	120	1b232,O138(136/1/2),3b10,2b7		-5.1

ABAD, ANDY Fausto Andres B8.25.1972 Palm Beach FL BL/TL/6-1/184* [BosA93 16/443] d9.10 Col Middle Georgia JC

YEAR	TM LG	G	AB	R	H	2B	3B	HR	RBI	BB-IB	HP	SO	AVG	OBP	SLG	AOPS	ABR	SB-CS	FA	FR	RNG	THR	GAMES AT POSITION	DL	BFW
2001	Oak A	1	1	0	0	0	0	0	0	0-0	0	0	.000	.000	.000	-99	-0	0-0	1.000	0	0	1175	/1		0.0
2003	Bos A	9	17	1	2	0	0	0	0	2-0	0	5	.118	.211	.118	-10	-3	0-1	.973	-1	32	55	1b7/OR		-0.5
Total	2	10	18	1	2	0	0	0	0	2-0	0	5	.111	.200	.111	-14	-3	0-1	.974	-1	31	84	1b8/OR		-0.5

ABADIE, JOHN John B11.4.1854 Philadelphia PA D5.17.1905 Pemberton NJ BR/TR/6-0/192 d4.26

YEAR	TM LG	G	AB	R	H	2B	3B	HR	RBI	BB-IB	HP	SO	AVG	OBP	SLG	AOPS	ABR	SB-CS	FA	FR	RNG	THR	GAMES AT POSITION	DL	BFW
1875	Cen NA	11	45	3	10	0	0	0	4	0		3	.222	.222	.222	60	-2	1-0	.912	-0	141	18	1b11		-0.1
	Atl NA	1	4	1	1	0	0	0	0	0			.250	.250	.250	85	-0	0-0	.875	-0	0	0	/1		0.0
	Year	12	49	4	11	0	0	0	4	0		3	.224	.224	.224	62	-2	1-0	.910	-0	132	17	1b12		-0.1

ABBATICCHIO, ED Edward James "Batty" B4.15.1877 Latrobe PA D1.6.1957 Ft.Lauderdale FL BR/TR/5-11/170 d9.4

YEAR	TM LG	G	AB	R	H	2B	3B	HR	RBI	BB-IB	HP	SO	AVG	OBP	SLG	AOPS	ABR	SB-CS	FA	FR	RNG	THR	GAMES AT POSITION	DL	BFW
1897	Phi N	3	10	1	3	0	0	0	1	0-0	0		.300	.364	.300	78	-0	1	.875	-1	106	0	2b3		-0.1
1898	Phi N	25	92	9	21	4	0	0	14	7	1		.228	.290	.272	64	-4	4	.818	-10	50	0	3b20,2b4/OR		-1.3
1903	Bos N	136	489	61	111	18	5	1	46	52	4		.227	.306	.290	73	-16	23	.934	3	96	86	2b116,S17		-1.1
1904	Bos N	154	579	76	148	18	10	3	54	40	5		.256	.309	.337	103	-1	24	.915	9	97	77	S154		1.0
1905	Bos N	153	610	70	170	25	12	3	41	35	8		.279	.326	.374	111	7	30	.919	-13	93	84	S152/OC		-0.2
1907	Pit N	147	496	63	130	14	7	2	82	65	8		.262	.357	.331	114	11	35	.951	-22	90	76	2b147		-1.1
1908	Pit N	146	500	43	125	16	4	0	61	58	7		.250	.336	.316	108	7	22	.969	-17	98	108	2b144		-1.0
1909	†Pit N	36	87	13	20	0	0	1	16	19	0		.230	.368	.264	89	-0	2	.966	0	113	101	1b8,2b4/OC		0.1
1910	Pit N	3	3	0	0	0	0	0	0	0	0		.000	.000	.000	-95	-1	0	.500	-0	96	0	/S		-0.1
	Bos N	52	178	20	44	4	2	0	10	12	0	16	.247	.295	.292	68	-8	2	.910	-2	107	97	S46/2		-0.8
	Year	55	181	20	44	4	2	0	10	12	0	16	.243	.290	.287	66	-8	2	.907	-2	107	96	S47/2		-0.9
Total	9	855	3044	355	772	99	43	11	324	289	33	16	.254	.325	.325	98	-3	142	.949	-59	94	88	2b419,S388,3b20,O3(0/2/1)		-4.6

ABBEY, CHARLIE Charles S. B10.14.1866 Falls City NE D4.27.1926 San Francisco CA BL/TL/5-8.5/169 d8.16

YEAR	TM LG	G	AB	R	H	2B	3B	HR	RBI	BB-IB	HP	SO	AVG	OBP	SLG	AOPS	ABR	SB-CS	FA	FR	RNG	THR	GAMES AT POSITION	DL	BFW
1893	Was N	31	116	11	30	1	4	0	12	12	1	6	.259	.333	.336	80	-4	9	.937	3	113	76	O31L		-0.3
1894	Was N	129	523	95	164	26	18	7	101	58	7	38	.314	.389	.472	110	8	31	.909	8	113	99	O129(54/74/0)		0.5
1895	Was N	133	516	102	142	14	10	8	84	43	7	43	.275	.339	.388	88	-11	28	.902	7	166	152	O133(3/99/31)		-1.0
1896	Was N	79	301	47	79	12	6	1	49	27	4	20	.262	.331	.352	80	-9	16	.879	-3	125	112	O78(2/11/65)/P		-1.3
1897	Was N	80	300	52	78	14	8	3	34	27	1		.260	.329	.390	90	-5	9	.946	1	120	47	O80(2/1/77)		-0.7
Total	5	452	1756	307	493	67	46	19	280	167	23	107	.281	.351	.404	93	-21	93	.910	15	132	105	O451(92/185/173)/P		-2.8

ABBOTT, FRED Harry Frederick (b Harry Frederick Winbigler) B10.22.1874 Versailles OH D6.11.1935 Los Angeles CA BR/TR/5-10/180 d4.25

YEAR	TM LG	G	AB	R	H	2B	3B	HR	RBI	BB-IB	HP	SO	AVG	OBP	SLG	AOPS	ABR	SB-CS	FA	FR	RNG	THR	GAMES AT POSITION	DL	BFW
1903	Cle A	77	255	25	60	11	3	1	25	7	5		.235	.270	.374	76	-8	8	.958	5	113	111	C71,1b3		-0.5
1904	Cle A	41	130	14	22	4	2	0	12	6	0		.169	.206	.231	38	-9	2	.953	-1	115	99	C33,1b7		-0.8
1905	Phi N	42	128	9	25	6	0	0	12	6	3		.195	.248	.258	53	-7	4	.954	2	119	88	C34,1b5		-0.3
Total	3	160	513	48	107	21	6	1	49	19	8		.209	.248	.279	61	-24	14	.956	6	115	105	C138,1b15		-0.6

ABBOTT, JEFF Jeffrey William B8.17.1972 Atlanta GA BR/TL/6-2/200* [ChiA94 4/117] d6.10 Col Kentucky

YEAR	TM LG	G	AB	R	H	2B	3B	HR	RBI	BB-IB	HP	SO	AVG	OBP	SLG	AOPS	ABR	SB-CS	FA	FR	RNG	THR	GAMES AT POSITION	DL	BFW
1997	Chi A	19	38	8	10	1	0	1	2	0-0	0	6	.263	.263	.368	52	-2	0-0	1.000	1	136	0	O10(5/1/4),D3		-0.2
1998	Chi A	89	244	33	68	14	1	12	41	9-1	0	28	.279	.298	.492	104	0	3-3	.971	-4	96	0	O76(20/38/27),D2		-0.5
1999	Chi A	17	57	5	9	0	0	2	6	5-0	0	12	.158	.222	.263	24	-7	1-1	.962	-2	81	0	O17L		-0.9
2000	†Chi A	80	215	31	59	15	1	3	29	21-1	2	38	.274	.343	.395	84	-5	2-1	.981	-5	85	67	O65(20/33/16),D7		-1.0
2001	Fla N	28	42	5	11	3	0	0	5	3-0	1	7	.262	.326	.333	74	-2	0-0	.963	0	116	0	O17(1/9/8)	72	-0.2
Total	5	233	596	82	157	33	2	18	83	38-2	3	91	.263	.307	.416	84	-16	6-5	.974	-10	93	39	O185(63/81/55),D12	72	-2.8

ABBOTT, KURT Kurt Thomas B6.2.1969 Zanesville OH BR/TR/6-0/190(170-200) [OakA89 15/400] d9.7 Col St. Petersburg (FL) JC OF(32/4/8)

YEAR	TM LG	G	AB	R	H	2B	3B	HR	RBI	BB-IB	HP	SO	AVG	OBP	SLG	AOPS	ABR	SB-CS	FA	FR	RNG	THR	GAMES AT POSITION	DL	BFW
1993	Oak A	20	61	11	15	1	0	3	9	3-0	0	20	.246	.281	.410	88	-2	2-0	.971	1	129	136	O13L,S6,2b2		-0.2
1994	Fla N	101	345	41	86	17	3	9	33	16-1	5	98	.249	.291	.394	74	-14	3-0	.966	-4	95	99	S99		-1.0
1995	Fla N	120	420	60	107	18	6	17	60	36-4	5	110	.255	.318	.452	100	-2	4-3	.959	-16	89	96	S115		-1.1
1996	Fla N	109	320	37	81	18	7	8	33	22-1	3	99	.253	.307	.428	94	-4	3-3	.969	-3	99	130	S44,3b33,2b20	38	-0.4
1997	†Fla N	94	252	35	69	18	2	6	30	14-3	1	68	.274	.315	.433	97	-2	3-1	.969	0	95	78	2b54,O10L,S7,3b4,D2		0.1
1998	Oak A	35	123	17	33	7	1	2	9	10-0	1	34	.268	.326	.390	82	-2	2-1	.909	-7	90	92	S28,O5(5/0/1)/3D	16	-0.2
	Col N	42	71	9	18	6	0	3	16	2-0	1	19	.254	.276	.465	76	-2	0-0	.929	1	122	0	O9(4/0/5),2b7,S7,3b3/D		-0.2
1999	Col N	96	286	41	78	17	2	8	41	16-0	0	69	.273	.310	.430	68	-14	3-2	.989	-5	94	81	2b66,1b8,O4(0/2/2),S3	30	-1.6
2000	†NY N	79	157	22	34	7	1	6	12	14-2	1	51	.217	.283	.389	72	-8	1-1	.953	-6	89	59	S39,2b23,3b2,O2C	26	-1.1
2001	Atl N	6	9	0	2	0	0	0	0	0-0	0	3	.222	.222	.222	15	-1	1-0	1.000	2	89	0	/2S	177	0.1
Total	9	702	2044	273	523	109	23	62	242	133-11	17	571	.256	.305	.423	84	-51	22-11	.958	-38	93	99	S349,2b173,3b43,O43L,1b8,D6	298	-5.8

ABBOTT, ODY Ody Cleon B9.5.1888 New Eagle PA D4.13.1933 Washington DC BR/TR/6-2/180 d9.10 Col Washington & Jefferson

YEAR	TM LG	G	AB	R	H	2B	3B	HR	RBI	BB-IB	HP	SO	AVG	OBP	SLG	AOPS	ABR	SB-CS	FA	FR	RNG	THR	GAMES AT POSITION	DL	BFW
1910	StL N	22	70	2	13	2	1	0	6	6	0	20	.186	.250	.243	46	-5	3	.982	1	109	70	O21C		-0.6

ABERCROMBIE, FRANCIS Francis Patterson B1.2.1851 Fort Towson OK D11.11.1939 Philadelphia PA d10.21

YEAR	TM LG	G	AB	R	H	2B	3B	HR	RBI	BB-IB	HP	SO	AVG	OBP	SLG	AOPS	ABR	SB-CS	FA	FR	RNG	THR	GAMES AT POSITION	DL	BFW
1871	Tro NA	1	4	0	0	0	0	0	0	0	0		.000	.000	.000	-99	-1	0-0	.667	-0	88	0	/S		-0.1

ABERNATHY, BRENT Michael Brent B9.23.1977 Atlanta GA BR/TR/6-1/185* [TorA96 2/44] d6.25

YEAR	TM LG	G	AB	R	H	2B	3B	HR	RBI	BB-IB	HP	SO	AVG	OBP	SLG	AOPS	ABR	SB-CS	FA	FR	RNG	THR	GAMES AT POSITION	DL	BFW
2001	TB A	79	304	43	82	11	1	5	33	27-1	0	35	.270	.328	.382	88	-5	8-3	.981	-2	93	108	2b79		-0.2
2002	TB A	117	463	46	112	18	4	2	40	25-0	6	46	.242	.288	.311	61	-17	10-4	.979	-4	96	103	2b116/D		-2.4
2003	TB A	2	7	1	0	0	0	0	0	0-0	0	3	.000	.000	.000	-99	-2	1-0	.900	0	156	0	2b2		-0.2
	KC A	10	27	2	2	0	0	0	0	1-0	0	3	.074	.107	.074	-48	-6	0-0	1.000	-1	102	82	2b9		-0.6
	Year	12	34	3	2	0	0	0	0	1-0	0	3	.059	.059	.059	-58	-8	1-0	.976	-0	113	66	2b11		-0.8

YEAR	TM LG	G	AB	R	H	2B	3B	HR	RBI	BB-IB	HP	SO	AVG	OBP	SLG	AOPS	ABR	SB-CS	FA	FR	RNG	THR	GAMES AT POSITION	DL	BFW
2005	Min A	24	67	5	16	1	0	6	7	7-0	1	9	.239	.316	.299	65	-3	2-0	.968	-4	90	106	2b17,O5L,D2	16	-0.6
Total	4	232	868	97	212	36	5	8	79	60-1	7	93	.244	.297	.325	66	-43	21-7	.979	-10	95	104	2b223,O5L,D3	16	-4.0

ABERSON, CLIFF Clifford Alexander "Kif" B8.28.1921 Chicago IL D6.23.1973 Vallejo CA BR/TR/6-0/200 d7.18

YEAR	TM LG	G	AB	R	H	2B	3B	HR	RBI	BB-IB	HP	SO	AVG	OBP	SLG	AOPS	ABR	SB-CS	FA	FR	RNG	THR	GAMES AT POSITION	DL	BFW
1947	Chi N	47	140	24	39	6	3	4	20	20	0	32	.279	.369	.450	121	4	0	.920	-1	78	255	O40L		0.1
1948	Chi N	12	32	1	6	1	0	1	6	5	0	10	.188	.297	.313	68	-1	0	.867	-1	76	168	O8L		-0.3
1949	Chi N	4	7	0	0	0	0	0	0	0	0	0	.000	.000	.000	-99	-2	0	1.000	-0	97	0	/OR		-0.2
Total	3	63	179	25	45	7	3	5	26	25	0	44	.251	.343	.408	103	1	0	.913	-1	78	235	O49(48/0/1)		-0.4

ABNER, SHAWN Shawn Wesley B6.17.1966 Hamilton OH BR/TR/6-1/190* [NYN84 1/1] d9.8

YEAR	TM LG	G	AB	R	H	2B	3B	HR	RBI	BB-IB	HP	SO	AVG	OBP	SLG	AOPS	ABR	SB-CS	FA	FR	RNG	THR	GAMES AT POSITION	DL	BFW
1987	SD N	16	47	5	13	3	1	2	7	2-0	0	8	.277	.306	.511	116	.1	1-0	.926	1	101	257	O14(6/2/6)		0.1
1988	SD N	37	83	6	15	3	0	2	5	4-1	0	19	.181	.225	.289	48	-6	0-1	.982	-0	98	78	O35(10/11/17)		-0.8
1989	SD N	57	102	13	18	4	0	2	14	5-2	0	20	.176	.213	.275	39	-8	1-0	1.000	-0	101	0	O51(23/23/6)		-1.0
1990	SD N	91	184	17	45	9	0	1	15	9-1	2	28	.245	.286	.310	64	-9	2-3	.991	-2	99	36	O62(23/35/6)		-1.3
1991	SD N	53	115	15	19	4	1	1	5	7-4	1	25	.165	.218	.243	29	-11	0-0	1.000	2	117	58	O39(0/36/3)		-1.1
	Cal A	41	101	12	23	6	1	2	9	4-0	0	18	.228	.257	.366	70	-4	1-2	1.000	2	101	205	O38(0/31/7),D3		-0.4
1992	Chi A	97	208	21	58	10	1	1	16	12-2	3	35	.279	.323	.351	91	-3	1-2	1.000	3	115	49	O94(12/14/75)/D		-0.2
Total	6	392	840	89	191	39	4	11	71	43-10	7	153	.227	.269	.323	65	-40	6-8	.993	5	106	75	O333(74/152/120),D4		-4.7

ABRAMS, CAL Calvin Ross B3.2.1924 Philadelphia PA D2.25.1997 Ft.Lauderdale FL BL/TL/6-0/185* d4.20

YEAR	TM LG	G	AB	R	H	2B	3B	HR	RBI	BB-IB	HP	SO	AVG	OBP	SLG	AOPS	ABR	SB-CS	FA	FR	RNG	THR	GAMES AT POSITION	DL	BFW
1949	Bro N	8	24	6	2	1	0	0		7	0	6	.083	.290	.125	15	-3	1	.833	-1	67	197	O7L		-0.4
1950	Bro N	38	44	5	9	1	0	0	4	9	0	4	.205	.340	.227	51	-3	0	1.000	0	114	0	O15(9/1/5)		-0.3
1951	Bro N	67	150	27	42	8	0	3	19	36	0	26	.280	.419	.393	118	6	3-2	.944	-2	89	101	O34L		0.2
1952	Bro N	10	10	1	2	0	0	0	0	2	0	4	.200	.333	.200	51	-1	0-0	—	-0	0	0	/OL		-0.1
	Cin N	71	158	23	44	9	2	2	13	19	0	25	.278	.356	.399	109	2	1-0	1.000	1	110	33	O46(31/18/0)		0.1
	Year	81	168	24	46	9	2	2	13	21	0	29	.274	.354	.387	106	2	1-0	1.000	0	110	33	O47(32/18/0)		0.0
1953	Pit N	119	448	66	128	10	6	15	43	58	0	70	.286	.368	.435	109	6	4-4	.973	3	97	158	O112R		0.5
1954	Pit N	17	42	6	6	1	0	1	2	10	0	9	.143	.308	.214	39	-4	0-0	1.000	1	97	237	O13(5/3/5)		-0.3
	Bal A	115	423	67	124	22	6	6	25	72	4	67	.293	.400	.421	135	24	1-4	.977	1	109	68	O115(0/14/101)		2.0
1955	Bal A	118	309	56	75	12	3	6	32	89-2	3	69	.243	.413	.359	118	15	2-8	.985	-2	94	114	O96(13/58/46),1b4		0.7
1956	Chi A	4	3	0	1	0	0	0	0	2-0	0	1	.333	.600	.333	150	1	0-0	1.000	0	123	0	O2(1/0/1)		0.1
Total	8	567	1611	257	433	64	19	32	138	304-2	7	290	.269	.386	.392	113	43	12-18	.977	1	100	107	O441(101/94/270),1b4		2.5

ABREU, BOBBY Bob Kelly B3.11.1974 Aragua, Venez BL/TR/6-0/186(160-210) d9.1

YEAR	TM LG	G	AB	R	H	2B	3B	HR	RBI	BB-IB	HP	SO	AVG	OBP	SLG	AOPS	ABR	SB-CS	FA	FR	RNG	THR	GAMES AT POSITION	DL	BFW
1996	Hou N	15	22	1	5	1	0	0	1	3	0		.227	.292	.273	54	-1	0-0	1.000	-0	85	0	O7(6/0/1)		-0.2
1997	†Hou N	59	188	22	47	10	2	3	26	21-0	1	48	.250	.329	.372	86	-4	7-2	.978	-1	91	111	O53(10/1/43)	37	-0.6
1998	Phi N	151	497	68	155	29	6	17	74	84-14	0	133	.312	.409	.497	137	30	19-10	.973	6	101	177	O146R		2.8
1999	Phi N	152	546	118	183	35	11	20	93	109-8	3	113	.335	.446	.549	149	47	27-9	.989	-7	90	82	O146R,D5		3.2
2000	Phi N	154	576	103	182	42	10	25	79	100-9	1	116	.316	.416	.554	144	42	28-8	.989	11	111	136	O152R		4.5
2001	Phi N	162	588	118	170	48	4	31	110	106-11	1	137	.289	.393	.543	147	45	36-14	.976	-3	93	101	O162R		3.6
2002	Phi N	157	572	102	176	50	6	20	85	104-9	3	117	.308	.413	.521	159	51	31-12	.983	-6	90	97	O154(0/18/148)		4.0
2003	Phi N	158	577	99	173	35	1	20	101	109-13	2	126	.300	.409	.468	139	40	22-9	.981	-4	100	58	O158R		2.8
2004	Phi N★	159	574	118	173	47	1	30	105	127-10	5	116	.301	.428	.544	145	47	40-5	.982	2	98	127	O158R		4.6
2005	Phi N★	162	588	104	168	37	1	24	102	117-15	6	134	.286	.405	.474	127	29	31-9	.986	-7	92	81	O158R,D3		1.8
Total	10	1329	4728	853	1432	334	42	190	776	879-89	22	1043	.303	.411	.512	141	326	241-78	.982	-10	97	107	O1294(16/19/1272),D8	37	26.5

ABREU, JOE Joseph Lawrence B5.24.1913 Oakland CA D3.17.1993 Hayward CA BR/TR/5-8/160 d4.23

YEAR	TM LG	G	AB	R	H	2B	3B	HR	RBI	BB-IB	HP	SO	AVG	OBP	SLG	AOPS	ABR	SB-CS	FA	FR	RNG	THR	GAMES AT POSITION	DL	BFW
1942	Cin N	9	28	4	6	1	0	1	4	4	0		.214	.313	.357	96	-0	0	.941	-1	85	97	3b6,2b2		0.0

ABSTEIN, BILL William Henry "Big Bill" B2.2.1883 St.Louis MO D4.8.1940 St.Louis MO BR/TR/6-0/185 d9.25

YEAR	TM LG	G	AB	R	H	2B	3B	HR	RBI	BB-IB	HP	SO	AVG	OBP	SLG	AOPS	ABR	SB-CS	FA	FR	RNG	THR	GAMES AT POSITION	DL	BFW
1906	Pit N	8	20	2	4	0	0	0	3	0	0		.200	.200	.200	24	-2	2	.769	-1	91	0	2b3,O2R		-0.3
1909	†Pit N	137	512	51	133	20	10	1	70	27	4		.260	.302	.344	93	-6	16	.982	-6	86	118	1b135		-1.7
1910	StL A	25	87	1	13	2	0	0	3	2	0		.149	.169	.172	7	-10	3	.963	1	148	104	1b23		-1.0
Total	3	170	619	54	150	22	10	1	76	29	4		.242	.281	.315	80	-18	21	.979	-6	95	116	1b158,2b3,O2R		-3.0

ACOSTA, MERITO Baldomero Pedro (Fernandez) B5.19.1896 Bauta, Cuba D11.17.1963 Miami FL BL/TL/5-7/140 d6.15 b-Jose

YEAR	TM LG	G	AB	R	H	2B	3B	HR	RBI	BB-IB	HP	SO	AVG	OBP	SLG	AOPS	ABR	SB-CS	FA	FR	RNG	THR	GAMES AT POSITION	DL	BFW
1913	Was A	12	20	3	6	0	1	0	1	4	0	2	.300	.417	.400	136	1	2	.714	-1	62	0	O9(6/2/1)		-0.1
1914	Was A	39	74	10	19	2	2	0	4	11	0		.257	.353	.338	104	1	3-4	.857	1	79	268	O25(15/5/5)		0.0
1915	Was A	72	163	20	34	4	1	0	18	28	4	15	.209	.338	.245	73	-4	8-4	.963	0	106	78	O53(22/2/29)		-0.6
1916	Was A	5	8	0	1	0	0	0	2	0	0		.125	.300	.125	28	-1	0	1.000	1	148	231	O4L		0.0
1918	Was A	3	2	0	0	0	0	0	0	0	0		.000	.000	.000	-99	0	0	—		0		/H		-0.1
	Phi A	49	169	23	51	3	3	0	14	18	0	10	.302	.369	.355	117	3	4	.944	-2	87	117	O45(5/20/21)		-0.1
	Year	52	171	23	51	3	3	0	14	18	0	10	.298	.365	.351	115	3	4	.944	-2	87	117	O45(5/20/21)		-0.2
Total	5	180	436	56	111	9	7	0	37	63	4	46	.255	.354	.307	97	1	17-8	.933	-1	94	124	O136(52/29/56)		-0.9

ADAIR, JIMMY James Aubrey "Choppy" B1.25.1907 Waxahachie TX D12.9.1982 Dallas TX BR/TR/5-10.5/154 d8.24 C11 Col East Texas Baptist/Marshall

YEAR	TM LG	G	AB	R	H	2B	3B	HR	RBI	BB-IB	HP	SO	AVG	OBP	SLG	AOPS	ABR	SB-CS	FA	FR	RNG	THR	GAMES AT POSITION	DL	BFW
1931	Chi N	18	76	9	21	3	1	0	3	1	0	8	.276	.286	.342	67	-1	1	.948	-1	97	76	S18		-0.4

ADAIR, JERRY Kenneth Jerry B12.17.1936 Sand Springs OK D5.31.1987 Tulsa OK BR/TR/6-0/175* d9.2 C4 Col Oklahoma St.

YEAR	TM LG	G	AB	R	H	2B	3B	HR	RBI	BB-IB	HP	SO	AVG	OBP	SLG	AOPS	ABR	SB-CS	FA	FR	RNG	THR	GAMES AT POSITION	DL	BFW
1958	Bal A	11	19	1	2	0	0	0	0	1-0	0	7	.105	.150	.105	-30	-3	0-0	.967	0	102	80	S10/2		-0.3
1959	Bal A	12	35	3	11	0	1	0	2	1-0	0	5	.314	.333	.371	95	-3	0-0	.932	-3	75	75	2b11/S		-0.3
1960	Bal A	3	5	1	1	0	0	0	0	0-0	0	0	.200	.200	.800	159	0	0-0	1.000	1	123	246	2b3		0.1
1961	Bal A	133	386	41	102	21	1	9	37	35-4	2	51	.264	.326	.394	95	-3	5-2	.987	-6	95	80	2b107,S27,3b2		0.2
1962	Bal A	139	538	67	153	29	4	11	48	27-1	2	77	.284	.319	.414	103	0	7-7	.969	0	95	116	S113,2b34/3		1.1
1963	Bal A	109	382	34	87	21	3	6	32	15-2	2	51	.228	.246	.346	67	-18	3-3	.985	-3	99	109	2b103		-0.7
1964	Bal A	155	569	56	141	20	3	9	47	28-10	1	72	.248	.283	.341	73	-22	3-2	.994	13	101	117	2b153		0.4
1965	Bal A	157	582	51	151	26	3	6	66	35-7	2	65	.259	.303	.351	84	-13	6-4	.986	7	105	103	2b157		0.9
1966	Bal A	17	52	3	15	1	0	0	4	4-0	0	8	.288	.333	.308	89	-1	0-0	.969	-1	93	88	2b13		0.0
	Chi A	105	370	27	90	18	2	4	36	17-0	1	44	.243	.275	.335	81	-10	3-3	.975	8	121	99	S75,2b50		0.7
	Year	122	422	30	105	19	2	4	39	21-0	1	52	.249	.282	.332	82	-11	3-2	.975	7	121	99	S75,2b63		0.6
1967	Chi A	28	98	6	20	4	0	0	9	8-0	0	17	.204	.240	.245	46	-7	0-1	.985	1	96	156	2b27		-0.5
	†Bos A	89	316	41	92	13	1	3	26	13-0	2	35	.291	.321	.367	96	-2	1-4	.952	-7	107	161	3b35,S30,2b23		-0.7
	Year	117	414	47	112	17	1	3	35	17-0	2	52	.271	.302	.338	85	-8	1-5	.976	-8	86	126	2b50,3b35,S30		-1.2
1968	Bos A	74	208	18	45	1	0	2	12	9-2	1	28	.216	.252	.250	50	-13	0-0	.976	-5	92	71	S46,2b12,3b7/1		-1.6
1969	KC A	126	432	29	108	9	1	5	48	20-4	3	36	.250	.285	.310	66	-21	1-3	.984	-21	91	62	2b109,S8/3		-3.7
1970	KC A	7	27	0	4	0	0	0	1	0-0	0	3	.148	.148	.148	22	-3	0-1	1.000	-0	85	109	2b7		-0.3
Total	13	1165	4019	378	1022	163	19	57	366	208-31	17	499	.254	.292	.347	80	-116	29-29	.985	-9	97	100	2b810,S310,3b46/1		-4.7

ADAMS, SPARKY Earl John B8.26.1894 Zerbe PA D2.24.1989 Pottsville PA BR/TR/5-5.5/151 d9.18

YEAR	TM LG	G	AB	R	H	2B	3B	HR	RBI	BB-IB	HP	SO	AVG	OBP	SLG	AOPS	ABR	SB-CS	FA	FR	RNG	THR	GAMES AT POSITION	DL	BFW
1922	Chi N	11	44	5	11	0	1	0	3	4	0	3	.250	.313	.295	56	-3	1-2	.914	-2	98	89	2b11		-0.5
1923	Chi N	95	311	40	90	12	0	4	35	26	1	10	.289	.346	.367	88	-5	20-19	.935	-6	95	103	S79/OR		-0.5
1924	Chi N	117	418	66	117	11	5	1	27	40	0	20	.280	.344	.337	83	-9	15-17	.941	-5	97	117	S88,2b19		-0.8
1925	Chi N	149	627	95	180	29	8	2	48	44	7	15	.287	.341	.368	80	-19	26-12	.983	27	109	105	2b144,S5		1.3
1926	Chi N	154	624	95	193	35	3	0	39	52	5	27	.309	.367	.375	99	1	27	.965	20	105	120	2b136,3b19,S2		2.6
1927	Chi N	146	647	100	189	17	7	0	49	42	0	26	.292	.335	.340	81	-18	26	.994	4	95	97	2b60,3b53,S40		-0.5
1928	Pit N	135	539	91	149	14	6	0	38	64	4	18	.276	.357	.325	76	-17	8	.971	-7	97	79	2b107,S27/OR		-1.7
1929	Pit N	74	196	37	51	8	1	0	11	15	1	5	.260	.316	.311	55	-14	3	.901	-10	85	66	S30,2b20,3b15,O2L		-1.9
1930	†StL N	137	570	98	179	36	6	0	55	45	1	27	.314	.365	.409	84	-14	7	.966	-12	84	101	3b104,2b25,S7		-1.6
1931	†StL N	143	608	97	178	46	5	1	60	42	0	24	.293	.340	.390	92	-5	16	.963	-13	87	122	2b138,S6		-1.2
1932	StL N	31	127	22	35	8	1	0	13	14	1	5	.276	.352	.315	79	-3	0	.931	-2	81	215	3b30		-0.4
1933	StL N	8	30	1	5	0	0	0	0	1	0	5	.167	.219	.200	19	-3	0	.955	-1	101	66	S5,3b3		-0.4
	Cin N	137	538	59	141	21	1	1	22	44	2	30	.262	.325	.310	82	-11	3	.963	1	107	83	3b135,S13		-0.5
	Year	145	568	60	146	21	1	1	22	45	2	33	.257	.315	.305	78	-15	3	.959	0	107	83	3b138,S13		-0.9
1934	Cin N	87	278	38	70	16	1	0	14	20	2	10	.252	.307	.317	69	-12	2	.955	-1	102	175	3b38,2b29		-1.0
Total	13	1424	5557	844	1588	249	48	9	394	453	28	223	.286	.343	.353	82	-132	154-50	.974	-7	102	102	2b551,3b532,S297,O4(2/0/2)		-7.2

YEAR	TM LG	G	AB	R	H	2B	3B	HR	RBI	BB-IB	HP	SO	AVG	OBP	SLG	AOPS	ABR	SB-CS	FA	FR	RNG	THR	GAMES AT POSITION	DL	BFW

ADAMS, BUSTER Elvin Clark B6.24.1915 Trinidad CO D9.1.1990 Rancho Mirage CA BR/TR/6-0/180 d4.27

YEAR	TM LG	G	AB	R	H	2B	3B	HR	RBI	BB-IB	HP	SO	AVG	OBP	SLG	AOPS	ABR	SB-CS	FA	FR	RNG	THR	GAMES AT POSITION	DL	BFW
1939	StL N	2	1	1	0	0	0	0	0	0	0	0	.000	.000	.000	-94	0	0	—	0			/H		0.0
1943	StL N	8	11	1	1	0	0	1	4	0	0	4	.091	.333	.182	48	0	0	1.000	0	111	0	O6C		-0.1
	Phi N	111	418	48	107	14	7	4	38	39	0	67	.256	.319	.352	98	-2	2	.984	0	106	59	O107(1/107/0)		-0.6
	Year	119	429	49	108	15	7	4	39	43	0	71	.252	.320	.347	96	-3	2	.984	0	106	57	O113(1/113/0)		-0.7
1944	Phi N	151	584	86	165	35	3	17	64	74	7	74	.283	.370	.440	132	27	2	.979	3	105	98	O151C		2.5
1945	Phi N	14	56	6	13	3	1	2	8	5	0	5	.232	.295	.429	103	0	0	1.000	-1	93	0	O14L		-0.2
	StL N	140	578	98	169	26	0	20	101	57	3	75	.292	.359	.441	119	14	3	.978	-6	96	74	O140(14/126/0)		0.3
	Year	154	634	104	182	29	1	22	109	62	3	80	.287	.353	.440	117	14	3	.979	-7	96	68	O154(27/126/0)		0.1
1946	StL N	81	173	21	32	6	0	5	22	29	3	27	.185	.312	.306	73	-6	3	.990	-2	97	27	O58(24/35/0)		-1.1
1947	Phi N	69	182	21	45	11	1	2	15	26	0	29	.247	.341	.352	88	-3	2	.954	-1	90	139	O51(6/1/44)		-0.5
Total	6	576	2003	282	532	96	12	50	249	234	13	281	.266	.346	.400	110	30	12	.979	-7	100	77	O527(58/426/44)		0.3

ADAMS, GEORGE George B Grafton MA BR/TR/5-6/175 d6.14

YEAR	TM LG	G	AB	R	H	2B	3B	HR	RBI	BB-IB	HP	SO	AVG	OBP	SLG	AOPS	ABR	SB-CS	FA	FR	RNG	THR	GAMES AT POSITION	DL	BFW
1879	Syr N	4	13	0								1	.231	.286	.231	82	0		1.000	-1	0	0	O2C,1b2		-0.1

ADAMS, GLENN Glenn Charles B10.4.1947 Northbridge MA BL/TR/6-0/185(175-188) [HouN68*1/4] d5.4 Col Springfield

YEAR	TM LG	G	AB	R	H	2B	3B	HR	RBI	BB-IB	HP	SO	AVG	OBP	SLG	AOPS	ABR	SB-CS	FA	FR	RNG	THR	GAMES AT POSITION	DL	BFW
1975	SF N	61	90	10	27	2	1	4	15	11-0	1	25	.300	.379	.478	133	4	1-0	.941	-1	92	77	O25(16/0/9)		0.2
1976	SF N	69	74	2	18	4	0	0	3	1-0	0	12	.243	.253	.297	54	-5	1-0	1.000	-1	44	0	O6(4/0/2)		-0.6
1977	Min A	95	269	32	91	17	0	6	49	18-3	0	30	.338	.376	.468	131	12	0-2	.969	0	96	131	D47,O44(16/0/28)	32	0.8
1978	Min A	116	310	27	80	18	1	7	35	17-0	0	32	.258	.297	.390	89	-5	0-1	1.000	1	289	0	D101,O5(2/0/3)		-0.8
1979	Min A	119	326	34	98	13	1	8	50	25-0	3	27	.301	.350	.420	104	2	2-2	.958	-4	81	67	D55,O53(45/0/8)		-0.6
1980	Min A	99	262	32	75	11	2	6	38	15-1	0	26	.286	.320	.412	94	-3	2-4	.947	-1	86	0	D81,O12L	15	-0.8
1981	Min A	72	220	13	46	10	0	2	24	20-4	0	26	.209	.273	.282	57	-12	0-1	—	0	0	0	D62		-1.5
1982	Tor A	30	66	2	17	4	0	1	11	4-0	0	5	.258	.288	.364	75	-2	0-0	—	0	0	0	D27		-0.3
Total	8	661	1617	152	452	79	5	34	225	111-8	4	183	.280	.324	.398	96	-9	6-10	.959	-7	88	79	D373,O145(95/0/50)	47	-3.6

ADAMS, DOUG Harold Douglas B1.27.1943 Blue River WI BL/TR/6-3/185 d9.8

YEAR	TM LG	G	AB	R	H	2B	3B	HR	RBI	BB-IB	HP	SO	AVG	OBP	SLG	AOPS	ABR	SB-CS	FA	FR	RNG	THR	GAMES AT POSITION	DL	BFW
1969	Chi A	8	14	1	3	0	0	0	0	1-0	0	5	.214	.267	.214	34	-1	0-0	1.000	-1	0	0	C4		-0.2

ADAMS, HERB Herbert Loren B4.14.1928 Hollywood CA BL/TL/5-9/160* d9.17 Mil 1951-52 Col Northern Illinois

YEAR	TM LG	G	AB	R	H	2B	3B	HR	RBI	BB-IB	HP	SO	AVG	OBP	SLG	AOPS	ABR	SB-CS	FA	FR	RNG	THR	GAMES AT POSITION	DL	BFW
1948	Chi A	5	11	1	3	1	0	0	1	0	1	0	.273	.333	.364	88	0	0-0	1.000	2	111	706	O4(0/2/2)		0.1
1949	Chi A	56	208	26	61	5	3	0	16	9	0	16	.293	.323	.346	79	-8	1-2	.975	-1	93	120	O48(14/33/1)		-1.1
1950	Chi A	34	118	12	24	2	3	0	2	12	2	7	.203	.288	.271	45	-10	3-0	.978	-1	104	37	O33C		-1.1
Total	3	95	337	39	88	8	6	0	18	22	2	24	.261	.310	.320	67	-18	4-2	.978	-1	98	113	O85(14/68/3)		-2.1

ADAMS, JIM James J. B1868 E.St.Louis IL TR d4.21

YEAR	TM LG	G	AB	R	H	2B	3B	HR	RBI	BB-IB	HP	SO	AVG	OBP	SLG	AOPS	ABR	SB-CS	FA	FR	RNG	THR	GAMES AT POSITION	DL	BFW
1890	StL AA	1	4	0	1	0	0	0	0	0	0		.250	.250	.250	42	0	0	1.000	-0	99	84	/C		0.0

ADAMS, BERT John Bertram B6.21.1891 Wharton TX D6.24.1940 Los Angeles CA BB/TR/6-1/185 d8.30

YEAR	TM LG	G	AB	R	H	2B	3B	HR	RBI	BB-IB	HP	SO	AVG	OBP	SLG	AOPS	ABR	SB-CS	FA	FR	RNG	THR	GAMES AT POSITION	DL	BFW
1910	Cle A	5	13	1	3	0	0	0	0	0	0		.231	.231	.231	44	-1	0	.964	2	99	250	C5		0.1
1911	Cle A	2	5	0	1	0	0	0	1	0	0		.200	.333	.200	50	0	0	.900	-1	74	111	C2		-0.1
1912	Cle A	20	54	5	11	2	1	0	6	4	0		.204	.259	.278	52	-4	0	.942	1	97	102	C20		-0.1
1915	Phi N	24	27	1	3	0	0	0	2	2	0		.111	.172	.111	-13	-4	0	.974	-2	99	70	C23/1		-0.6
1916	Phi N	11	13	2	3	0	0	0	1	0	0	3	.231	.231	.231	40	-1	0	.929	0	111	116	C11		-0.1
1917	Phi N	43	107	4	22	4	1	1	7	0	0	20	.206	.206	.290	49	-7	0	.994	2	112	111	C38/1		-0.3
1918	Phi N	84	227	10	40	4	0	0	12	10	1	26	.176	.214	.194	23	-21	5	.976	-3	102	83	C76		-2.0
1919	Phi N	78	232	14	54	7	2	1	17	6	0	27	.233	.252	.293	59	-12	4	.966	-7	82	112	C73/1		-1.5
Total	8	267	678	37	137	17	4	2	45	23	1	79	.202	.229	.248	42	-50	9	.970	-9	96	102	C248,1b3		-4.6

ADAMS, DICK Richard Leroy B4.8.1920 Tuolumne CA BR/TL/6-0/185 d5.20 b-Bobby

YEAR	TM LG	G	AB	R	H	2B	3B	HR	RBI	BB-IB	HP	SO	AVG	OBP	SLG	AOPS	ABR	SB-CS	FA	FR	RNG	THR	GAMES AT POSITION	DL	BFW
1947	Phi A	37	89	9	18	2	3	2	11	2	0	18	.202	.220	.360	58	-6	0-0	.995	1	119	114	1b24,O3(1/0/2)		-0.6

ADAMS, RICKY Ricky Lee B1.21.1959 Upland CA BR/TR/6-2/180* [HouN77 1/14] d9.15

YEAR	TM LG	G	AB	R	H	2B	3B	HR	RBI	BB-IB	HP	SO	AVG	OBP	SLG	AOPS	ABR	SB-CS	FA	FR	RNG	THR	GAMES AT POSITION	DL	BFW
1982	Cal A	8	14	1	2	0	0	0	0	0-0	1	2	.143	.200	.143	-4	-2	1-0	.947	-2	81	143	S8		-0.3
1983	Cal A	58	112	22	28	2	0	2	6	5-0	1	12	.250	.300	.321	71	-5	1-1	.960	13	127	135	S38,3b16,2b4		1.1
1985	SF N	54	121	12	23	3	1	2	10	5-3	1	23	.190	.228	.281	44	-10	1-1	.964	2	98	83	S25,3b16,2b6		-0.7
Total	3	120	247	35	53	5	1	4	16	10-3	3	37	.215	.260	.291	54	-17	3-2	.961	13	111	116	S71,3b32,2b10		0.1

ADAMS, BOBBY Robert Henry B12.14.1921 Tuolumne CA D2.13.1997 Gig Harbor WA BR/TR/5-10/170* d4.16 C6 b-Dick s-Mike

YEAR	TM LG	G	AB	R	H	2B	3B	HR	RBI	BB-IB	HP	SO	AVG	OBP	SLG	AOPS	ABR	SB-CS	FA	FR	RNG	THR	GAMES AT POSITION	DL	BFW
1946	Cin N	94	311	35	76	13	3	4	24	18	3	32	.244	.292	.344	83	-8	16	.967	22	123	177	2b74,O2R/3		1.8
1947	Cin N	81	217	39	59	11	2	4	20	25	4	23	.272	.358	.396	101	1	9	.967	6	103	110	2b69		1.0
1948	Cin N	87	262	33	78	20	3	1	21	25	1	23	.298	.361	.408	112	5	6	.965	-7	86	88	2b63,3b7		0.1
1949	Cin N	107	277	32	70	16	2	0	25	26	0	36	.253	.317	.325	72	-11	4	.984	-9	90	74	2b63,3b14		-1.6
1950	Cin N	115	348	50	98	21	8	3	25	43	0	29	.282	.361	.414	103	2	7	.981	-5	98	80	2b53,3b42		0.0
1951	Cin N	125	403	57	107	12	5	5	24	43	1	40	.266	.338	.357	86	-8	4-10	.956	-7	98	59	3b60,2b42/OR		-1.6
1952	Cin N	**154**	637	85	180	25	4	6	48	49	0	67	.283	.334	.363	93	-6	11-9	.962	7	**105**	105	3b154		0.0
1953	Cin N	150	607	99	167	14	6	8	49	58	0	67	.275	.338	.357	81	-17	3-2	.951	2	104	121	3b150		-1.5
1954	Cin N	110	390	69	105	25	6	3	23	55	3	46	.269	.362	.387	93	-2	2-5	.951	1	95	132	3b93,2b2		-0.3
1955	Cin N	64	150	23	41	11	2	2	20	20-1	3	21	.273	.368	.413	102	1	2-0	.969	4	113	158	3b42,2b5		0.5
	Chi A	28	21	8	2	0	1	0	3	4-0	0	4	.095	.240	.190	16	-3	0-0	.933	2	126	0	3b9/2		-0.1
1956	Bal A	41	111	19	25	6	1	0	7	25-0	0	15	.225	.362	.297	84	-1	1-1	.984	-5	94	119	3b24,2b18		-0.5
1957	Chi N	60	187	21	47	10	2	1	10	17-0	2	28	.251	.320	.342	79	-5	0-3	.949	-5	84	58	3b47/2		-1.2
1958	Chi N	62	96	14	27	4	4	0	4	6-0	0	15	.281	.324	.406	93	-1	2-0	.961	-1	118	17	1b11,3b9,2b7		-0.2
1959	Chi N	3	2	0	0	0	0	0	0	0-0	0	1	.000	.000	.000	-99	-1	0-0	.667	-0	0	0	/1		-0.1
Total	14	1281	4019	591	1082	188	49	37	303	414-1	17	447	.269	.340	.368	90	-54	67-30	.955	4	100	103	3b652,2b399,1b12,O3R		-3.7

ADAMS, BOB Robert Melvin B1.6.1952 Pittsburgh PA BR/TR/6-2/200 [DetA73 3/67] d7.10 Col UCLA

YEAR	TM LG	G	AB	R	H	2B	3B	HR	RBI	BB-IB	HP	SO	AVG	OBP	SLG	AOPS	ABR	SB-CS	FA	FR	RNG	THR	GAMES AT POSITION	DL	BFW
1977	Det A	15	24	2	6	1	0	2	2	0-0	0	5	.250	.250	.542	103	0	0-0	1.000	-0	71	59	1b2/C		0.0

ADAMS, MIKE Robert Michael B7.24.1948 Cincinnati OH BR/TR/5-9/180(180-200) [DetA67*S1/2] d9.10 f-Bobby Col Fullerton (CA) JC

YEAR	TM LG	G	AB	R	H	2B	3B	HR	RBI	BB-IB	HP	SO	AVG	OBP	SLG	AOPS	ABR	SB-CS	FA	FR	RNG	THR	GAMES AT POSITION	DL	BFW
1972	Min A	3	6	0	2	0	0	0	0	0-0	0	1	.333	.333	.333	94	0	0-0	1.000	-0	45	0	/OL		0.0
1973	Min A	55	66	21	14	2	0	3	6	17-0	1	18	.212	.381	.379	110	2	2-1	.978	-0	109	0	O24(23/1/0),D2		0.0
1976	Chi N	25	29	1	4	2	0	0	2	8-0	1	7	.138	.342	.207	54	-1	0-0	1.000	-1	60	0	O4(2/0/2),3b3/2		-0.3
1977	Chi N	2	2	0	0	0	0	0	0	0-0	0	1	.000	.000	.000	-90	-1	0-0	—	-0	0	0	O2(1/1/0)		-0.1
1978	Oak A	15	15	5	3	1	0	0	1	7-0	0	2	.200	.455	.267	113	1	0-0	1.000	-0	58	134	2b6,3b3,D3		0.1
Total	5	100	118	27	23	5	0	3	9	32-0	2	29	.195	.375	.314	92	1	2-1	.980	-2	100	0	O31(27/2/2),2b7,3b6,D5		-0.3

ADAMS, RUSS Russ Moore B8.30.1980 Laurinburg NC BL/TR/6-1/180* [TorA02 1/14] d9.3 Col North Carolina

YEAR	TM LG	G	AB	R	H	2B	3B	HR	RBI	BB-IB	HP	SO	AVG	OBP	SLG	AOPS	ABR	SB-CS	FA	FR	RNG	THR	GAMES AT POSITION	DL	BFW
2004	Tor A	22	72	10	22	2	1	4	10	5-0	1	5	.306	.359	.528	120	2	1-0	.936	-4	92	74	S21		-2.2
2005	Tor A	139	481	68	123	27	5	8	63	50-1	3	57	.256	.325	.383	84	-10	11-2	.952	-23	90	87	S132		-2.2
Total	2	161	553	78	145	29	6	12	73	55-1	4	62	.262	.329	.401	89	-8	12-2	.950	-27	90	85	S153		-2.2

ADAMS, SPENCER Spencer Dewey B6.21.1898 Layton UT D11.24.1970 Salt Lake City UT BL/TR/5-9/158 d5.8

YEAR	TM LG	G	AB	R	H	2B	3B	HR	RBI	BB-IB	HP	SO	AVG	OBP	SLG	AOPS	ABR	SB-CS	FA	FR	RNG	THR	GAMES AT POSITION	DL	BFW
1923	Pit N	25	56	11	14	0	1	0	4	6	0	6	.250	.323	.286	60	-3	2-1	.879	-5	85	110	2b11,S6		-0.7
1925	†Was A	39	55	11	15	4	1	0	4	5	1	4	.273	.333	.382	83	-2	1-1	.941	-3	89	85	2b15,S8,3b3		-0.3
1926	†NY A	28	25	7	3	1	0	0	1	3	0	7	.120	.214	.160	-1	-4	1-0	1.000	2	109	163	2b4/3		-0.2
1927	StL A	88	259	32	69	11	3	0	29	24	1	33	.266	.333	.332	71	-11	1-8	.948	2	97	99	2b54,3b28		-0.9
Total	4	180	395	61	101	16	5	0	38	38	2	50	.256	.324	.322	66	-20	5-10	.944	-3	95	101	2b84,3b32,S14		-2.1

ADCOCK, JOE Joseph Wilbur B10.30.1927 Coushatta LA D5.3.1999 Coushatta LA BR/TR/6-4/220(210-232) d4.23 M1 Col Louisiana St.

YEAR	TM LG	G	AB	R	H	2B	3B	HR	RBI	BB-IB	HP	SO	AVG	OBP	SLG	AOPS	ABR	SB-CS	FA	FR	RNG	THR	GAMES AT POSITION	DL	BFW
1950	Cin N	102	372	46	109	16	1	8	55	24	2	24	.293	.336	.406	94	-4	2	.968	2	107	106	O75L,1b24		-0.8
1951	Cin N	113	395	40	96	16	4	10	47	24	1	29	.243	.288	.380	77	-14	1-2	.983	-5	107	94	O107L		-1.9
1952	Cin N	117	378	43	105	22	4	13	52	23	1	38	.278	.321	.460	115	6	1-4	.985	5	122	84	O85L,1b17		0.3
1953	Mil N	**157**	590	71	168	33	6	18	80	42	2	82	.285	.334	.453	110	7	3-2	.991	-3	90	111	1b157		-0.5
1954	Mil N	133	500	73	154	27	6	23	87	44	3	58	.308	.365	.520	137	26	1-4	.995	-11	68	108	1b133		0.3
1955	Mil N	84	288	40	76	14	0	15	45	31-3	2	44	.264	.339	.469	118	7	0-2	.990	-5	80	96	1b78	57	-0.3
1956	Mil N	137	454	76	132	23	1	38	103	32-6	1	86	.291	.337	.597	154	32	1-0	**.995**	-4	87	118	1b129		2.1

YEAR	TM LG	G	AB	R	H	2B	3B	HR	RBI	BB-IB	HP	SO	AVG	OBP	SLG	AOPS	ABR	SB-CS	FA	FR	RNG	THR	GAMES AT POSITION	DL	BFW
1957	†Mil N	65	209	31	60	13	2	12	38	20-3	1	51	.287	.351	.541	146	13	0-0	.996	-3	81	142	1b56	70	0.7
1958	†Mil N	105	320	40	88	15	1	19	54	21-1	1	63	.275	.317	.506	125	10	0-0	.989	-2	93	118	1b71,O22L		0.4
1959	Mil N	115	404	53	118	19	2	25	76	32-6	0	77	.292	.339	.535	141	22	0-0	.998	9	138	102	1b89,O21L		2.4
1960	Mil N★	138	514	55	153	21	4	25	91	46-7	1	86	.298	.354	.500	142	28	2-2	**.993**	3	108	97	1b136		2.3
1961	Mil N	152	562	77	160	20	0	35	108	59-4	2	94	.285	.354	.507	133	26	2-1	**.993**	-6	91	105	1b148		1.1
1962	Mil N	121	391	48	97	12	1	29	78	50-8	1	91	.248	.333	.506	126	13	2-0	**.997**	-2	91	95	1b112		0.6
1963	Cle A	97	283	28	71	7	1	13	49	30-4	0	53	.251	.320	.420	107	2	1-2	.995	-4	73	87	1b78		-0.7
1964	LA A	118	366	39	98	13	0	21	64	48-4	0	61	.268	.352	.475	142	20	0-2	.993	-4	83	125	1b105		1.0
1965	Cal A	122	349	30	84	14	0	14	47	37-3	1	74	.241	.315	.401	104	2	2-2	.996	-2	88	107	1b97		-0.6
1966	Cal A	83	231	33	63	10	3	18	48	31-6	0	48	.273	.355	.576	168	20	2-2	.997	0	100	125	1b71		1.7
Total	17	1959	6606	823	1832	295	35	336	1122	594-55	17	1059	.277	.337	.485	125	216	20-25	.994	-24	90	107	1b1501,O310L	127	8.3

ADDIS, BOB Robert Gordon B11.6.1925 Mineral OH BL/TR/6-0/175* d9.1

YEAR	TM LG	G	AB	R	H	2B	3B	HR	RBI	BB-IB	HP	SO	AVG	OBP	SLG	AOPS	ABR	SB-CS	FA	FR	RNG	THR	GAMES AT POSITION	DL	BFW
1950	Bos N	16	28	7	7	1	0	0	2	3	0	5	.250	.323	.286	66	-1	1	1.000	-1	82	0	O7(2/1/4)		-0.2
1951	Bos N	85	199	23	55	7	0	1	24	9	0	10	.276	.308	.327	76	-7	3-2	.982	-1	108	25	O46(31/10/5)		-1.1
1952	Chi N	93	292	38	86	13	2	1	20	23	0	30	.295	.346	.363	96	-1	4-4	.988	2	103	122	O79(3/42/37)		-0.2
1953	Chi N	10	12	2	2	1	0	0	1	2	0	2	.167	.286	.250	40	-1	0-0	1.000	1	122	475	O3(0/1/2)		-0.1
	Pit N	4	3	0	0	0	0	0	0	0	0	2	.000	.000	.000	-99	-1	0-0	—	0			/H		-0.1
	Year	14	15	2	2	1	0	0	1	2	0	4	.133	.235	.200	15	-2	0-0	1.000	1	122	475	O3(0/1/2)		-0.1
Total	4	208	534	70	150	22	2	2	47	37	0	47	.281	.327	.341	84	-11	8-6	.986	2	105	90	O135(36/54/48)		-1.6

ADDUCI, JIM James David B8.9.1959 Chicago IL BL/TL/6-5/200* [StLN80 7/171] d9.12 Col Southern Illinois

YEAR	TM LG	G	AB	R	H	2B	3B	HR	RBI	BB-IB	HP	SO	AVG	OBP	SLG	AOPS	ABR	SB-CS	FA	FR	RNG	THR	GAMES AT POSITION	DL	BFW
1983	StL N	10	20	0	1	0	0	0	0	1-0	0	6	.050	.095	.050	-58	-4	0-0	1.000	0	105	71	1b6/OL		-0.5
1986	Mil A	3	11	2	1	1	0	0	0	1-0	0	2	.091	.167	.182	-5	-2	0-0	1.000	0	142	42	1b3		-0.1
1988	Mil A	44	94	8	25	6	1	1	15	0-0	0	15	.266	.258	.383	78	-3	0-1	.969	1	100	117	O24(16/0/9),D10,1b3		-0.4
1989	Phi N	13	19	1	7	1	0	0	0	0-0	0	4	.368	.368	.421	125	1	0-0	1.000	1	170	49	1b4/OL		0.1
Total	4	70	144	11	34	8	1	1	15	2-0	0	27	.236	.242	.326	58	-8	0-1	.969	1	98	115	O26(18/0/9),1b16,D10		-0.9

ADDY, BOB Robert Edward "Magnet" B2.1845 Rochester NY D4.9.1910 Pocatello ID BL/TL/5-8/160 d5.6 M2

YEAR	TM LG	G	AB	R	H	2B	3B	HR	RBI	BB-IB	HP	SO	AVG	OBP	SLG	AOPS	ABR	SB-CS	FA	FR	RNG	THR	GAMES AT POSITION	DL	BFW
1871	Rok NA	25	118	30	32	6	0	0	13	4	1		.271	.295	.322	81	-2	8-1	.768	-1	**115**	65	2b22,S3		-0.2
1873	Phi NA	10	51	12	16	1	0	0	10	2	1		.314	.340	.333	97	0	1-1	.855	-2	87	54	2b10		-0.2
	Bos NA	31	152	37	54	6	3	1	32	2	1		.355	.364	.454	131	4	6-5	.702	-3	68	0	O31R		0.2
	Year	41	203	49	70	7	3	1	42	4	1		.345	.357	.424	122	4	7-6	.702	-5	68	0	O31R,2b10		0.0
1874	Har NA	50	213	25	51	9	2	0	22	1	2		.239	.243	.300	70	-8	4-2	.846	2	113	44	2b45,3b5/S		-0.7
1875	Phi NA	69	310	60	80	8	4	0	43	0	2		.258	.258	.310	93	-3	16-8	.761	-1	127	101	O68(0/1/67),2b2,M		0.0
1876	Chi N	32	142	36	40	4	1	0	16	5	0		.282	.306	.324	98	-1		.800	-1	108	0	O32(3/0/29)		-0.2
1877	Cin N	57	245	27	68	2	3	0	31	6	5		.278	.295	.310	102	1		.805	5	165	**229**	O57(0/1/56),M		0.6
Total	4 NA	185	844	164	233	30	9	1	120	9			.276	.284	.336	93	-9	35-17	.746	-5	108	69	O99(0/1/98),2b79,3b5,S4		-0.9
Total	2	89	387	63	108	6	4	0	47	11	5		.279	.299	.315	99	0		.803	4	143	142	O89(3/1/85)		0.4

ADERHOLT, MORRIE Morris Woodroe B9.13.1915 Mt.Olive NC D3.18.1955 Sarasota FL BL/TR/6-1/188 d9.13 Col Wake Forest

YEAR	TM LG	G	AB	R	H	2B	3B	HR	RBI	BB-IB	HP	SO	AVG	OBP	SLG	AOPS	ABR	SB-CS	FA	FR	RNG	THR	GAMES AT POSITION	DL	BFW
1939	Was A	7	25	5	5	0	0	1	4	2	0	6	.200	.259	.320	51	-2	0-1	.872	-1	92	64	2b7		-0.3
1940	Was A	1	2	0	0	0	0	0	0	0	0	0	.000	.000	.000	-99	-1	0-0	1.000	0	59	237	/2		-0.1
1941	Was A	11	14	3	2	0	0	0	1	1	0	3	.143	.200	.143	-8	-2	0-0	.818	-1	45	97	2b2/3		-0.3
1944	Bro N	17	59	9	16	2	3	0	10	4	0	4	.271	.317	.407	105	0	0	.871	-1	92	94	O13(11/0/2)		-0.2
1945	Bro N	39	60	4	13	1	0	0	6	3	0	10	.217	.254	.233	36	-5	0	1.000	-1	66	0	O8(7/0/1)		-0.7
	Bos N	31	102	15	34	4	0	2	11	9	0	6	.333	.387	.431	127	4	3	.984	-0	108	0	O24L/2		0.2
	Year	70	162	19	47	5	0	2	17	12	0	16	.290	.339	.358	94	-1	3	.985	-1	101	0	O32(31/0/1)/2		-0.5
Total	5	106	262	36	70	7	3	3	32	19	0	29	.267	.317	.351	85	-6	3-1	.949	-5	98	29	O45(42/0/3),2b11/3		-1.4

ADKINS, DICK Richard Earl B3.3.1920 Electra TX D9.12.1955 Electra TX BR/TR/5-10/165 d9.19

YEAR	TM LG	G	AB	R	H	2B	3B	HR	RBI	BB-IB	HP	SO	AVG	OBP	SLG	AOPS	ABR	SB-CS	FA	FR	RNG	THR	GAMES AT POSITION	DL	BFW
1942	Phi A	3	7	2	1	0	0	0	0	0	0	3	.143	.333	.143	37	-1		.875	-1	91	81	S3		-0.1

ADKINSON, HENRY Henry Magee B9.1.1874 Chicago IL D5.1.1923 Salt Lake City UT d9.25 Col Chicago

YEAR	TM LG	G	AB	R	H	2B	3B	HR	RBI	BB-IB	HP	SO	AVG	OBP	SLG	AOPS	ABR	SB-CS	FA	FR	RNG	THR	GAMES AT POSITION	DL	BFW
1895	StL N	1	5	1	2	0	0	0	0	0	0	2	.400	.400	.400	108	-0	0	.667	-0	0	0	/OL		0.0

ADLESH, DAVE David George B7.15.1943 Long Beach CA BR/TR/6-0/187* d5.12

YEAR	TM LG	G	AB	R	H	2B	3B	HR	RBI	BB-IB	HP	SO	AVG	OBP	SLG	AOPS	ABR	SB-CS	FA	FR	RNG	THR	GAMES AT POSITION	DL	BFW
1963	Hou N	6	8	0	0	0	0	0	0	0-0	0	4	.000	.000	.000	-99	-2	0-0	.889	-1	74	0	C6		-0.4
1964	Hou N	3	10	0	2	0	0	0	0	0-0	0	5	.200	.200	.200	14	-1	0-0	1.000	-0	48	338	C3		-0.2
1965	Hou N	15	34	2	5	1	0	0	3	2-0	0	12	.147	.216	.176	13	-4	0-0	1.000	-1	102	124	C13		-0.5
1966	Hou N	3	6	0	0	0	0	0	0	0-0	0	4	.000	.000	.000	-99	-2	0-0	1.000	1	0	0	/C		0.0
1967	Hou N	39	94	4	17	1	0	1	4	11-3	0	28	.181	.264	.223	43	-7	0-0	.995	-4	69	67	C31		-1.1
1968	Hou N	40	104	3	19	1	1	0	4	5-2	1	27	.183	.227	.212	33	-9	0-0	.990	-7	49	74	C36		-1.7
Total	6	106	256	9	43	3	1	1	11	18-5	2	80	.168	.227	.199	26	-25	0-0	.992	-13	63	85	C90		-3.9

AFENIR, TROY Michael Troy B9.21.1963 Escondido CA BR/TR/6-4/185(185-210) [HouN83*S1/11] d9.14 Col Palomar (CA) JC

YEAR	TM LG	G	AB	R	H	2B	3B	HR	RBI	BB-IB	HP	SO	AVG	OBP	SLG	AOPS	ABR	SB-CS	FA	FR	RNG	THR	GAMES AT POSITION	DL	BFW
1987	Hou N	10	20	1	6	1	0	0	0	0-0	0	12	.300	.300	.350	74	-1	0-0	.974	-3	49	44	C10		-0.4
1990	Oak A	14	14	0	2	0	0	0	2	0-0	0	6	.143	.133	.143	-21	-2	0-0	1.000	-2	0	78	C12/D		-0.4
1991	Oak A	5	11	0	1	0	0	0	0	0-0	0	2	.091	.091	.091	-52	-2	0-0	1.000	0	188	0	C4/D		-0.2
1992	Cin N	16	34	3	6	1	2	0	4	5-0	0	12	.176	.282	.324	69	-2	0-0	1.000	-3	166	26	C15		-0.5
Total	4	45	79	4	15	2	2	0	7	5-0	0	32	.190	.235	.266	40	-7	0-0	.992	-8	113	35	C41,D2		-1.5

AGBAYANI, BENNY Benny Peter B12.28.1971 Honolulu HI BR/TR/6-0/225* [NYN93 30/836] d6.17 Col Hawaii Pacific

YEAR	TM LG	G	AB	R	H	2B	3B	HR	RBI	BB-IB	HP	SO	AVG	OBP	SLG	AOPS	ABR	SB-CS	FA	FR	RNG	THR	GAMES AT POSITION	DL	BFW
1998	NY N	11	15	1	2	0	0	0	0	1-0	0	5	.133	.188	.133	-14	-3	0-2	1.000	0	80	0	O9(1/2/6)		-0.4
1999	†NY N	101	276	42	79	18	3	14	42	32-4	3	60	.286	.363	.525	128	11	6-4	.984	-4	91	47	O80(47/4/45),D2		0.4
2000	†NY N	119	350	59	101	19	1	15	60	54-2	7	68	.289	.391	.477	126	16	5-5	.975	-3	98	56	O110(102/2/12)/D		0.8
2001	NY N	91	296	28	82	14	2	6	27	36-0	5	73	.277	.364	.399	105	3	4-5	.954	-4	97	21	O84L	35	-0.5
2002	Col N	48	117	10	24	5	0	4	19	10-0	0	35	.205	.266	.350	56	-8	1-0	1.000	0	105	58	O37L/D	24	-0.9
	Bos A	13	37	5	11	1	0	0	8	6-1	0	5	.297	.395	.351	93	0	0-0	.962	1	109	157	O13(11/1/3)		0.0
Total	5	383	1091	145	299	57	6	39	156	139-7	15	246	.274	.362	.445	110	19	16-16	.974	-11	97	48	O333(282/9/66),D4	59	-0.6

AGEE, TOMMIE Tommie Lee B8.9.1942 Magnolia AL D1.22.2001 New York NY BR/TR/5-11/195* d9.14 Col Grambling St.

YEAR	TM LG	G	AB	R	H	2B	3B	HR	RBI	BB-IB	HP	SO	AVG	OBP	SLG	AOPS	ABR	SB-CS	FA	FR	RNG	THR	GAMES AT POSITION	DL	BFW
1962	Cle A	5	14	0	3	0	0	0	0	0-0	0	4	.214	.214	.214	16	-2	0-0	1.000	-1	62	0	O3(2/1/0)		-0.3
1963	Cle A	13	27	3	4	1	0	1	3	2-0	0	9	.148	.207	.296	39	-2	0-0	1.000	0	64	384	O13(4/3/6)		-0.3
1964	Cle A	13	12	0	2	0	0	0	0	0-0	0	3	.167	.167	.167	-7	-2	0-0	1.000	1	56	0	O12(0/3/10)		-0.3
1965	Chi A	10	19	2	3	1	0	0	3	2-0	0	6	.158	.238	.211	30	-2	0-1	1.000	0	114	0	O9(0/5/6)	39	-0.2
1966	Chi A★	160	629	98	172	27	8	22	86	41-3	10	127	.273	.326	.447	129	21	44-18	.982	-3	96	116	O159(8/156/0)		1.7
1967	Chi A★	158	529	73	124	26	2	14	52	44-5	8	129	.234	.302	.371	102	1	28-10	.969	-6	101	65	O152(10/136/9)		-0.8
1968	NY N	132	368	30	80	12	3	5	17	15-3	4	103	.217	.255	.307	68	-15	13-8	.978	-2	96	93	O127(0/116/13)		-2.4
1969	†NY N	149	565	97	153	23	4	26	76	59-2	3	137	.271	.342	.464	121	15	12-9	.986	-1	104	78	O146(0/143/7)		1.0
1970	NY N	153	636	107	182	30	7	24	75	55-3	2	156	.286	.344	.469	124	11	31-15	.967	3	**115**	48	O150(0/149/2)		1.2
1971	†NY N	113	425	58	121	19	0	14	50	50-2	4	85	.285	.362	.428	123	14	28-6	.978	6	114	118	O107(0/94/32)	15	2.2
1972	NY N	114	422	52	96	23	0	13	47	53-6	4	92	.227	.317	.374	98	-4	8-9	.962	4	113	93	O109(6/91/20)		-0.1
1973	Hou N	83	204	30	48	5	2	8	15	16-1	1	55	.235	.294	.397	91	-4	2-5	.983	2	112	56	O67(34/18/17)		-0.6
	StL N	26	62	8	11	3	1	3	7	5-0	0	13	.177	.239	.403	74	-3	1-0	.981	3	147	111	O19(0/19/2)		0.0
	Year	109	266	38	59	8	3	11	22	21-1	1	68	.222	.281	.398	87	-6	3-5	.982	5	120	68	O86(34/37/19)		-0.6
Total	12	1129	3912	558	999	170	27	130	433	342-26	34	918	.255	.320	.412	108	32	167-81	.975	5	106	86	O1073(64/934/124)	54	1.1

AGGANIS, HARRY Harry "The Golden Greek" B4.20.1929 Lynn MA D6.27.1955 Cambridge MA BL/TL/6-2/200* d4.13 Col Boston U.

YEAR	TM LG	G	AB	R	H	2B	3B	HR	RBI	BB-IB	HP	SO	AVG	OBP	SLG	AOPS	ABR	SB-CS	FA	FR	RNG	THR	GAMES AT POSITION	DL	BFW
1954	Bos A	132	434	54	109	13	8	11	57	47	0	57	.251	.321	.394	86	-9	6-3	.990	5	**118**	96	1b119		-1.0
1955	Bos A	25	83	11	26	10	1	0	10	10-0	2	10	.313	.383	.458	116	2	2-0	.987	-1	95	78	1b20		0.1
Total	2	157	517	65	135	23	9	11	67	57-0	2	67	.261	.331	.404	91	-7	8-3	.989	5	114	93	1b139		-0.9

AGLER, JOE Joseph Abram B6.12.1887 Coshocton OH D4.26.1971 Massillon OH BL/TL/5-11/165 d10.1

YEAR	TM LG	G	AB	R	H	2B	3B	HR	RBI	BB-IB	HP	SO	AVG	OBP	SLG	AOPS	ABR	SB-CS	FA	FR	RNG	THR	GAMES AT POSITION	DL	BFW
1912	Was A	2											.000	.000	.000	-99	-1	0	—	0	0	0	/1		0.0
1914	Buf F	135	463	82	126	17	6	0	20	77	0	78	.272	.376	.335	93	-8	21	.985	3	123	114	1b76,O54(44/5/6)		-1.0
1915	Buf F	25	73	11	13	1	2	0	2	20	0	14	.178	.355	.247	69	-3	2	.973	-2	102	0	O20(6/3/11)/1		-0.7

YEAR	TM LG	G	AB	R	H	2B	3B	HR	RBI	BB-IB	HP	SO	AVG	OBP	SLG	AOPS	ABR	SB-CS	FA	FR	RNG	THR	GAMES AT POSITION	DL	BFW
	Bal F	72	214	28	46	4	2	0	14	34	1	38	.215	.325	.252	62	-13	15	.981	4	141	124	1b58,O4(2/1/1),2b3		-1.1
	Year	97	287	39	59	5	4	0	16	54	1	52	.206	.333	.251	64	-16	17	.981	2	140	123	1b59,O24(8/4/12),2b3		-1.8
Total	3	234	751	121	185	22	10	0	36	131	1	130	.246	.359	.302	81	-24	38	.983	5	130	118	1b136,O78(52/9/18),2b3		-2.8

AGNEW, SAM   Samuel Lester "Slam"   B4.12.1887 Farmington MO   D7.19.1951 Sonoma CA   BR/TR/5-11/185   d4.10

YEAR	TM LG	G	AB	R	H	2B	3B	HR	RBI	BB-IB	HP	SO	AVG	OBP	SLG	AOPS	ABR	SB-CS	FA	FR	RNG	THR	GAMES AT POSITION	DL	BFW
1913	StL A	105	307	27	64	9	5	2	24	20	7	49	.208	.272	.290	66	-14	11	.952	5	111	107	C103		0.0
1914	StL A	115	311	22	66	5	4	0	16	24	5	63	.212	.279	.254	63	-15	10-8	.961	0	98	108	C115		-0.7
1915	StL A	104	295	18	60	4	2	0	19	12	5	36	.203	.247	.231	45	-21	5-2	.934	1	94	127	C102		-1.3
1916	Bos A	40	67	4	14	2	1	0	7	6	2	4	.209	.293	.269	69	-3	0	.952	5	155	150	C38		0.5
1917	Bos A	85	260	17	54	6	2	0	16	19	2	30	.208	.267	.246	57	-14	2	.965	-4	118	89	C85		-1.2
1918	†Bos A	72	199	11	33	8	0	0	6	11	3	26	.166	.221	.206	29	-17	0	.965	8	113	115	C72		-0.4
1919	Was A	42	98	6	23	7	0	0	10	10	1	8	.235	.312	.306	74	-3	1	.974	6	97	133	C36		0.6
Total	7	563	1537	105	314	41	14	2	98	102	25	216	.204	.265	.253	56	-87	29-10	.955	21	108	113	C551		-2.5

AGUAYO, LUIS   Luis (Muriel)   B3.13.1959 Vega Baja, PR   BR/TR/5-9/185(173-195)   d4.19

YEAR	TM LG	G	AB	R	H	2B	3B	HR	RBI	BB-IB	HP	SO	AVG	OBP	SLG	AOPS	ABR	SB-CS	FA	FR	RNG	THR	GAMES AT POSITION	DL	BFW
1980	Phi N	20	47	7	13	1	2	1	8	2-0	0	3	.277	.300	.447	101	0	1-1	.962	3	101	121	2b14,S5	15	0.3
1981	†Phi N	45	84	11	18	4	0	1	7	5-0	0	15	.214	.283	.298	61	-4	1-0	.938	-6	79	93	2b21,S21,3b3		-0.3
1982	Phi N	50	56	11	15	1	2	3	7	5-1	1	7	.268	.339	.518	132	2	1-1	.966	-3	98	42	2b21,S15,3b5		0.0
1983	Phi N	2	4	1	1	0	0	0	0	1-0	0	2	.250	.400	.250	84	0	0-0	1.000	-2	0	0	S2	70	-0.2
1984	Phi N	58	72	15	20	4	0	3	11	8-2	0	16	.278	.350	.458	123	2	0-0	.909	4	149	104	3b14,2b12,S10		0.7
1985	Phi N	91	165	27	46	7	3	6	21	22-5	6	26	.279	.378	.467	133	8	1-0	.957	1	92	82	S60,2b17,3b7		1.5
1986	Phi N	62	133	17	28	6	1	4	13	8-0	3	26	.211	.267	.361	70	-6	1-1	.967	-9	99	81	2b31,S20/3		-0.7
1987	Phi N	94	209	25	43	9	1	12	21	15-1	5	56	.206	.273	.431	98	-7	0-0	.971	-2	96	94	S78,2b6,3b2	15	-0.3
1988	Phi N	49	97	9	24	3	0	3	5	13-2	1	17	.247	.336	.371	101	0	2-0	.967	4	104	110	S27,3b13,2b2		0.6
	NY A	50	140	12	35	4	0	3	8	7-1	1	33	.250	.289	.343	77	-5	0-2	.961	-7	97	83	3b33,2b13,S6		-1.2
1989	Cle A	47	97	7	17	4	1	1	8	7-0	2	19	.175	.239	.268	44	-7	0-0	.950	1	99	42	3b19,S15,2b10,D2	24	-0.2
Total	10	568	1104	142	260	43	10	37	109	94-12	20	220	.236	.304	.393	90	-17	7-5	.960	-16	92	90	S259,2b147,3b97,D2	124	-1.4

AGUILA, CHRIS   Christopher Louis   B2.23.1979 Redwood City CA   BR/TR/5-11/180*   [FlaN97 3/96]   d6.28

YEAR	TM LG	G	AB	R	H	2B	3B	HR	RBI	BB-IB	HP	SO	AVG	OBP	SLG	AOPS	ABR	SB-CS	FA	FR	RNG	THR	GAMES AT POSITION	DL	BFW
2004	Fla N	29	45	10	10	2	1	3	5	2-0	0	12	.222	.255	.511	96	-1	0-0	.909	0	99	163	O20(6/0/14)		-0.1
2005	Fla N	65	78	11	19	3	0	0	4	3-0	0	19	.244	.272	.282	48	-6	0-1	1.000	2	128	108	O42(27/2/14)		-0.5
Total	2	94	123	21	29	5	1	3	9	5-0	0	31	.236	.266	.366	66	-7	0-1	.968	2	117	129	O62(33/2/28)		-0.6

AHEARN, CHARLIE   Charles   B Troy NY   d6.19

YEAR	TM LG	G	AB	R	H	2B	3B	HR	RBI	BB-IB	HP	SO	AVG	OBP	SLG	AOPS	ABR	SB-CS	FA	FR	RNG	THR	GAMES AT POSITION	DL	BFW
1880	Tro N	1	4	1	1	0	0	0	0	0		0	.250	.250	.250	67	0		.778	-0			/C		-0.1

AIKENS, WILLIE   Willie Mays   B10.14.1954 Seneca SC   BL/TR/6-3/220*   [AnaA75*1/2]   d5.17   Col South Carolina St.

YEAR	TM LG	G	AB	R	H	2B	3B	HR	RBI	BB-IB	HP	SO	AVG	OBP	SLG	AOPS	ABR	SB-CS	FA	FR	RNG	THR	GAMES AT POSITION	DL	BFW
1977	Cal A	42	91	5	18	4	0	0	6	10-2	0	23	.198	.277	.242	44	-7	1-2	.971	-0	104	105	1b13,D13		-0.9
1979	Cal A	116	379	59	106	18	0	21	81	61-8	1	79	.280	.376	.493	138	22	1-3	.996	-8	73	94	1b55,D51		1.2
1980	†KC A	151	543	70	151	24	0	20	98	64-3	7	88	.278	.356	.433	115	13	0-0	.990	-8	81	85	1b138,D13		-0.3
1981	†KC A	101	349	45	93	16	0	17	53	62-12	3	47	.266	.377	.458	141	21	0-0	.992	-4	89	95	1b99		1.2
1982	KC A	134	466	50	131	29	1	17	74	45-7	3	70	.281	.345	.457	118	12	0-1	.994	1	105	96	1b128	15	0.6
1983	KC A	125	410	49	124	26	1	23	72	45-9	2	75	.302	.373	.539	147	27	0-0	.989	-1	100	111	1b112,D6		1.9
1984	Tor A	93	234	21	48	7	0	11	26	29-1	2	56	.205	.298	.376	82	-6	0-0	1.000	0	98	95	D81,1b2		-0.8
1985	Tor A	12	20	2	4	1	0	1	5	3-0	0	6	.200	.292	.400	88	0	0-0	—	0	0	0	D11		-0.1
Total	8	774	2492	301	675	125	2	110	415	319-42	18	444	.271	.354	.455	122	82	3-6	.991	-15	92	96	1b547,D175	15	2.8

AINGE, DANNY   Daniel Ray   B3.17.1959 Eugene OR   BR/TR (BB 1979p)/6-4/175*   [TorA77 15/389]   d5.21

YEAR	TM LG	G	AB	R	H	2B	3B	HR	RBI	BB-IB	HP	SO	AVG	OBP	SLG	AOPS	ABR	SB-CS	FA	FR	RNG	THR	GAMES AT POSITION	DL	BFW
1979	Tor A	87	308	26	73	7	1	2	19	12-1	2	58	.237	.269	.286	49	-23	1-0	.977	1	102	103	2b86/D		-1.7
1980	Tor A	38	111	11	27	6	1	0	4	2-0	1	29	.243	.263	.315	55	-7	3-0	.986	0	92	152	O29(6/22/1),3b3/2D		-0.6
1981	Tor A	86	246	20	46	6	1	0	14	23-1	1	41	.187	.258	.228	39	-19	8-5	.949	2	103	148	3b77,S6,O4(0/3/1),2b2/D		-1.9
Total	3	211	665	57	146	19	4	2	37	37-2	4	128	.220	.264	.269	47	-49	12-5	.977	3	102	101	2b89,3b80,O33(6/25/2),S6,D4		-4.2

AINSMITH, EDDIE   Edward Wilbur "Dorf" (b Edward Anshmedt)   B2.4.1892 , Russia   D9.6.1981 Ft.Lauderdale FL   BR/TR/5-11/180   d8.9   Mil 1918

YEAR	TM LG	G	AB	R	H	2B	3B	HR	RBI	BB-IB	HP	SO	AVG	OBP	SLG	AOPS	ABR	SB-CS	FA	FR	RNG	THR	GAMES AT POSITION	DL	BFW
1910	Was A	33	104	4	20	1	2	0	9	6	0		.192	.236	.240	52	-6	0	.963	-2	98	110	C30		-0.6
1911	Was A	61	149	12	33	2	3	0	14	10	1		.221	.275	.275	55	-10	5	.952	2	105	104	C47		-0.4
1912	Was A	61	186	22	42	7	2	0	22	14	0		.226	.280	.285	61	-10	4	.958	15	145	83	C59		1.0
1913	Was A	84	229	26	49	4	4	2	20	12	3	41	.214	.262	.293	61	-13	17	.967	6	120	83	C79/P		-0.1
1914	Was A	62	151	11	34	7	0	0	13	9	1	28	.225	.273	.272	61	-7	8-5	.969	5	112	84	C51		0.2
1915	Was A	47	120	13	24	4	0	0	6	10	1	18	.200	.267	.267	59	-6	7-4	.988	6	118	88	C42		0.3
1916	Was A	51	100	11	17	4	0	0	8	8	0	14	.170	.231	.210	33	-8	3	.959	6	113	123	C46		0.1
1917	Was A	125	350	38	67	17	4	0	42	40	3	48	.191	.280	.263	66	-13	16	.971	8	90	116	C119		0.4
1918	Was A	96	292	22	62	10	9	0	20	29	0	44	.212	.283	.308	80	-8	6	.975	3	102	109	C89		0.3
1919	Det A	114	364	42	99	17	12	3	32	45	1	30	.272	.354	.409	117	3	9	.962	-11	88	80	C106		0.6
1920	Det A	69	186	19	43	5	3	1	19	14	0	19	.231	.285	.306	58	-12	4-3	.955	-6	92	95	C61/1		-1.3
1921	Det A	35	98	6	27	5	2	0	12	13	0	7	.276	.360	.367	87	-2	1-0	.947	-4	87	109	C34		-0.3
	StL N	27	62	5	18	0	1	0	5	3	0	4	.290	.323	.323	73	-3	0-0	.956	0	109	87	C23/1		-0.1
1922	StL N	119	379	46	111	14	4	13	59	28	1	43	.293	.343	.454	109	4	2-3	.963	-2	108	98	C116		0.8
1923	StL N	82	263	22	56	11	6	3	34	22	1	19	.213	.276	.335	62	-16	4-0	.980	-7	93	83	C80		-1.6
	Bro N	2	10	0	2	0	0	0	2	0	0	0	.200	.200	.200	6	-1	0-1	1.000	1	94	66	C2		-0.1
	Year	84	273	22	58	11	6	3	36	22	1	19	.212	.274	.330	60	-17	4-1	.981	-7	93	82	C82		-1.7
1924	NY N	10	5	0	3	0	0	0	0	0	0	4	.600	.600	.600	229	1	0-0	1.000	-0	70	0	C9		0.1
Total	15	1078	3048	299	707	108	54	22	317	263	12	315	.232	.296	.324	76	-102	86-16	.966	20	104	96	C993,1b2/P		-0.7

AITON, GEORGE   George Wilson   B12.29.1890 Kingman KS   D8.16.1976 N.Hollywood CA   BB/TR/5-11.5/175   d6.29   Col Friends

YEAR	TM LG	G	AB	R	H	2B	3B	HR	RBI	BB-IB	HP	SO	AVG	OBP	SLG	AOPS	ABR	SB-CS	FA	FR	RNG	THR	GAMES AT POSITION	DL	BFW
1912	StL A	10	17	1	4	0	0	0	1	4	0		.235	.381	.235	80	0	0	.917	0	109	166	O7(5/2/0)		0.0

AKE, JOHN   John Leckie   B8.29.1861 Altoona PA   D5.11.1887 LaCrosse WI   BR/TR/6-1/180   d5.12

YEAR	TM LG	G	AB	R	H	2B	3B	HR	RBI	BB-IB	HP	SO	AVG	OBP	SLG	AOPS	ABR	SB-CS	FA	FR	RNG	THR	GAMES AT POSITION	DL	BFW
1884	Bal AA	13	52	1	10	0	0	0		1	0		.192	.208	.231	41	-4		.677	-3	86	195	3b9,O3(2/0/1)/S		-0.6

AKERS, BILL   William G. "Bump"   B12.25.1904 Chattanooga TN   D4.13.1962 Chattanooga TN   BR/TR/5-11/178   d9.8

YEAR	TM LG	G	AB	R	H	2B	3B	HR	RBI	BB-IB	HP	SO	AVG	OBP	SLG	AOPS	ABR	SB-CS	FA	FR	RNG	THR	GAMES AT POSITION	DL	BFW
1929	Det A	24	83	15	22	4	1	1	9	10	1	9	.265	.351	.373	86	-2	2-0	.935	-6	83	83	S24		-0.5
1930	Det A	85	233	36	65	8	5	9	40	36	0	34	.279	.375	.472	111	4	5-5	.944	6	104	123	S49,3b26		1.4
1931	Det A	29	66	5	13	2	2	0	3	7	0	6	.197	.274	.288	46	-5	0-1	.935	-4	82	79	S21,2b2		-0.8
1932	Bos N	36	93	8	24	3	1	1	17	10	0	15	.258	.330	.344	85	-2	0-0	.927	-5	95	30	3b20,2b5,S5		-0.5
Total	4	174	475	64	124	17	9	11	69	63	1	64	.261	.349	.404	93	-5	7-6	.936	-9	94	106	S99,3b46,2b7		-0.4

ALBERTS, GUS   Augustus Peter   B1861 Reading PA   D5.7.1912 Idaho Springs CO   BR/TR/5-6.5/180   d5.1

YEAR	TM LG	G	AB	R	H	2B	3B	HR	RBI	BB-IB	HP	SO	AVG	OBP	SLG	AOPS	ABR	SB-CS	FA	FR	RNG	THR	GAMES AT POSITION	DL	BFW
1884	Pit AA	2	5	1	1	0	0	0		0	0		.200	.200	.200	31	0		.500	-1	76	0	S2		-0.1
	Was U	4	16	4	4	0	0	0		4			.250	.400	.250	105	0		.870	1	113	132	S4		0.1
1888	Cle AA	102	364	51	75	10	6	1	48	41	7		.206	.299	.275	87	-3	26	.862	8	107	111	S53,3b49		0.6
1891	Mil AA	12	41	6	4	0	0	0	2	7	2	5	.098	.260	.098	2	-5	1	.814	-3	76	106	3b12		-0.8
Total	3	120	426	62	84	10	6	1	50	52	9	5	.197	.298	.256	76	-8	27	.880	5	97	119	3b61,S59		-0.2

ALBERTS, BUTCH   Francis Burt   B5.4.1950 Williamsport PA   BR/TR/6-2/205   [PitN72 28/642]   d9.7   Col Cincinnati

YEAR	TM LG	G	AB	R	H	2B	3B	HR	RBI	BB-IB	HP	SO	AVG	OBP	SLG	AOPS	ABR	SB-CS	FA	FR	RNG	THR	GAMES AT POSITION	DL	BFW
1978	Tor A	6	18	1	5	1	0	0	5	0-0	0	2	.278	.278	.333	70	-1	0-0	—	0			D4		-0.1

ALBRIGHT, JACK   Harold John   B6.30.1921 St.Petersburg FL   D7.22.1991 San Diego CA   BR/TR/5-9/175   d5.19   Col California-Davis

YEAR	TM LG	G	AB	R	H	2B	3B	HR	RBI	BB-IB	HP	SO	AVG	OBP	SLG	AOPS	ABR	SB-CS	FA	FR	RNG	THR	GAMES AT POSITION	DL	BFW
1947	Phi N	41	99	9	23	0	1	0	7	13	1	11	.232	.303	.333	71	-4	1	.943	1	106	96	S33		-0.1

ALCANTARA, ISRAEL   Israel (Cristosomo)   B5.6.1973 Bani, D.R.   BR/TR/6-2/180(180-210)   d6.25

YEAR	TM LG	G	AB	R	H	2B	3B	HR	RBI	BB-IB	HP	SO	AVG	OBP	SLG	AOPS	ABR	SB-CS	FA	FR	RNG	THR	GAMES AT POSITION	DL	BFW
2000	Bos A	21	45	9	13	6	0	4	7	3-0	0	7	.289	.333	.578	121	1	0-0	.889	-1	94	0	O7(1/0/7),1b5,D8	18	0.0
2001	Bos A	14	38	5	10	1	0	3	3	3-0	0	13	.263	.317	.289	61	-2	1-0	.900	-1	64	262	O8(6/0/2),1b4/D		-0.3
2002	Mil N	16	32	3	8	1	0	2	5	0-0	0	6	.250	.256	.469	87	-1	0-1	1.000	-1	76	0	O7(2/0/5),1b2		-0.3
Total	3	51	115	15	31	3	0	6	15	6-0	0	26	.270	.306	.452	88	-2	1-1	.923	-2	76	108	O22(9/0/14),1b11,D9	18	-0.6

YEAR	TM LG	G	AB	R	H	2B	3B	HR	RBI	BB-IB	HP	SO	AVG	OBP	SLG	AOPS	ABR	SB-CS	FA	FR	RNG	THR	GAMES AT POSITION	DL	BFW

ALCARAZ, LUIS Angel Luis (Acosta) B6.20.1941 Humacao, PR BR/TR/5-9/165* d9.13

YEAR	TM LG	G	AB	R	H	2B	3B	HR	RBI	BB-IB	HP	SO	AVG	OBP	SLG	AOPS	ABR	SB-CS	FA	FR	RNG	THR	GAMES AT POSITION	DL	BFW
1967	LA N	17	60	1	14	1	0	0	3	1-0	0	13	.233	.242	.250	46	-4	1-1	.990	3	106	164	2b17		0.0
1968	LA N	41	106	4	16	1	0	2	5	9-2	0	23	.151	.217	.217	33	-9	1-1	.979	9	78	78	2b20,3b13/S		-0.9
1969	KC A	22	79	15	20	2	1	1	7	7-0	0	9	.253	.314	.342	82	-2	0-0	.988	-4	91	44	2b19,3b2/S		-0.5
1970	KC A	35	120	10	20	5	1	1	14	4-0	0	13	.167	.192	.250	21	-13	0-0	.993	-12	76	58	2b31		-2.5
Total 4		115	365	30	70	9	2	4	29	21-2	0	58	.192	.235	.260	43	-28	2-2	.988	-12	90	81	2b87,3b15,S2		-3.9

ALCOCK, SCOTTY John Forbes B11.29.1885 Wooster OH D1.30.1973 Wooster OH BR/TR/5-9.5/160 d4.19

YEAR	TM LG	G	AB	R	H	2B	3B	HR	RBI	BB-IB	HP	SO	AVG	OBP	SLG	AOPS	ABR	SB-CS	FA	FR	RNG	THR	GAMES AT POSITION	DL	BFW
1914	Chi A	54	156	12	27	4	2	0	7	4-1	0	14	.173	.213	.224	32	-14	4-2	.905	1	104	169	3b48/2		-1.2

ALDRETE, MIKE Michael Peter B1.29.1961 Carmel CA BL/TL/5-11/185* [SFN83 7/174] d5.28 C2 Col Stanford

YEAR	TM LG	G	AB	R	H	2B	3B	HR	RBI	BB-IB	HP	SO	AVG	OBP	SLG	AOPS	ABR	SB-CS	FA	FR	RNG	THR	GAMES AT POSITION	DL	BFW
1986	SF N	84	216	27	54	18	3	2	25	33-4	2	34	.250	.353	.389	110	3	1-3	1.000	3	148	149	1b37,O31(30/0/2)		0.4
1987	†SF N	126	357	50	116	18	2	9	51	43-5	0	50	.325	.396	.462	133	18	6-0	.986	1	107	67	O79(43/13/30),1b33		1.7
1988	SF N	139	389	44	104	15	0	3	50	56-13	0	65	.267	.357	.329	103	4	6-5	.982	3	108	89	O115(83/7/40),1b10		0.3
1989	Mon N	76	136	12	30	8	1	1	12	19-0	1	30	.221	.316	.316	81	-3	1-3	.980	1	95	148	O37(16/3/19),1b10	16	-0.4
1990	Mon N	96	161	22	39	7	1	1	18	37-2	1	31	.242	.385	.317	99	2	1-2	.982	1	91	207	O38(26/0/14),1b18		0.1
1991	SD N	12	15	2	0	0	0	0	1	3-0	0	4	.000	.167	.000	-48	-3	0-1	1.000	1	118	593	O5L		-0.3
	Cle A	85	183	22	48	6	1	1	19	36-1	0	37	.262	.380	.322	97	1	1-2	.994	1	92	102	1b47,O16L,D7		-0.4
1993	Oak A	95	255	40	68	13	1	10	33	34-2	0	45	.267	.353	.443	119	7	1-1	.995	-4	74	84	1b59,O20(17/0/3),D6		-0.2
1994	Oak A	76	178	23	43	5	0	4	18	20-1	0	35	.242	.313	.337	75	-7	2-0	1.000	-2	85	0	O35(21/0/15),1b27/D		-1.1
1995	Oak A	60	125	18	34	8	0	4	21	19-1	1	23	.272	.367	.432	114	3	0-0	.989	-3	62	84	1b35,O16(9/1/6)		-0.2
	Cal A	18	24	1	6	0	0	0	3	0-0	0	8	.250	.240	.250	31	-3	0-0	1.000	1	390	0	O2L/1D		-0.2
	Year	78	149	19	40	8	0	4	24	19-1	1	31	.268	.349	.403	101	1	0-0	.989	-2	61	83	1b36,O18(11/1/6),D2		-0.4
1996	Cal A	31	40	5	6	1	0	3	8	5-0	0	4	.150	.239	.400	58	-3	0-0	.750	-1	46	0	O6(4/0/2)/1D		-0.4
	†NY A	32	68	11	17	5	0	3	12	9-0	0	15	.250	.338	.456	98	0	0-1	1.000	-2	70	0	O9(6/0/4),1b8/PD	28	-0.3
	Year	63	108	16	23	6	0	6	20	14-0	0	19	.213	.301	.435	83	-3	0-1	.909	-3	61	0	O15(10/0/6),D15,1b9/P		-0.7
Total 10		930	2147	277	565	104	9	41	271	314-29	5	381	.263	.356	.377	104	20	19-18	.983	-3	100	87	O409(278/24/135),1b286,D31/P	44	-1.0

ALDRIDGE, CORY Cory Jerome B6.13.1979 San Angelo TX BL/TR/6-0/210 [AtlN97 4/142] d9.5 [DL 2002 Atl N 183]

YEAR	TM LG	G	AB	R	H	2B	3B	HR	RBI	BB-IB	HP	SO	AVG	OBP	SLG	AOPS	ABR	SB-CS	FA	FR	RNG	THR	GAMES AT POSITION	DL	BFW
2001	Atl N	8	5	1	0	0	0	0	0	0-0	0	4	.000	.000	.000	-99	-1	0-0	1.000	-0	64	0	O4(1/1/2)		-0.2

ALENO, CHUCK Charles B2.19.1917 St.Louis MO D2.10.2003 DeLand FL BR/TR/6-1.5/215 d5.15

YEAR	TM LG	G	AB	R	H	2B	3B	HR	RBI	BB-IB	HP	SO	AVG	OBP	SLG	AOPS	ABR	SB-CS	FA	FR	RNG	THR	GAMES AT POSITION	DL	BFW
1941	Cin N	54	169	23	41	7	3	1	18	11	0	16	.243	.289	.337	76	-6	3	.975	-1	96	89	3b40,1b2		-0.6
1942	Cin N	7	14	1	2	1	0	0	0	3	0	3	.143	.294	.214	50	-1	0	.727	-2	99	0	3b2/2		-0.1
1943	Cin N	7	10	0	3	0	0	0	1	2	0	1	.300	.417	.300	110	0	0	1.000	-0	69	0	O2L		0.0
1944	Cin N	50	127	10	21	3	0	1	15	15	1	15	.165	.259	.213	35	-11	0	.952	-4	85	102	3b42,1b3,S3		-1.5
Total 4		118	320	34	67	11	3	2	34	31	1	35	.209	.281	.281	60	-18	3	.954	-5	91	91	3b84,1b5,S3,O2L/2		-2.2

ALEXANDER, DALE David Dale "Moose" B4.26.1903 Greeneville TN D3.2.1979 Greeneville TN BR/TR/6-3/210 d4.16 Col Milligan

YEAR	TM LG	G	AB	R	H	2B	3B	HR	RBI	BB-IB	HP	SO	AVG	OBP	SLG	AOPS	ABR	SB-CS	FA	FR	RNG	THR	GAMES AT POSITION	DL	BFW
1929	Det A	155	626	110	215	43	15	25	137	56	0	63	.343	.397	.580	148	42	5-9	.988	-4	92	87	1b155		2.4
1930	Det A	154	602	86	196	33	8	20	135	42	2	56	.326	.372	.507	118	15	6-5	.985	-6	83	106	1b154		-0.1
1931	Det A	135	517	75	168	47	3	3	87	64	2	35	.325	.401	.445	118	17	5-8	.987	-8	75	92	1b126,O4L		-0.4
1932	Det A	23	16	0	4	0	0	0	4	6	0	2	.250	.455	.250	84	0	0-0	1.000	-0	0	0	1b2		0.0
	Bos A	101	376	58	140	27	3	8	56	55	1	19	.372	.454	.524	157	35	4-5	.992	2	107	101	1b101		2.4
	Year	124	392	58	144	27	3	8	60	61	1	21	.367	.454	.513	152	34	4-5	.992	2	107	101	1b103		2.4
1933	Bos A	94	313	40	88	14	1	5	40	25	1	22	.281	.336	.380	90	-5	0-1	.992	3	118	84	1b79		-0.8
Total 5		662	2450	369	811	164	30	61	459	248	6	197	.331	.394	.497	128	104	20-28	.988	-13	92	95	1b617,O4L		3.5

ALEXANDER, GARY Gary Wayne B3.27.1953 Los Angeles CA BR/TR/6-2/200* [SFN72*S2/36] d9.12 Col Los Angeles Harbor (CA) JC

YEAR	TM LG	G	AB	R	H	2B	3B	HR	RBI	BB-IB	HP	SO	AVG	OBP	SLG	AOPS	ABR	SB-CS	FA	FR	RNG	THR	GAMES AT POSITION	DL	BFW
1975	SF N	3	3	1	0	0	0	0	0	1-0	0	2	.000	.250	.000	-25	-2	0-0	1.000	-2	13	0	C2		-0.2
1976	SF N	23	73	12	13	1	1	2	7	10-1	0	16	.178	.274	.301	62	-4	0-0	.964	-6	52	78	C23		-0.9
1977	SF N	51	119	17	36	4	2	5	20	20-2	0	33	.303	.406	.496	142	8	3-1	.968	-10	53	53	C33/OR		0.0
1978	Oak A	58	174	18	36	6	1	10	22	22-2	1	66	.207	.298	.425	107	1	0-3	1.000	1	167	0	D45,O6(3/0/3)/C1		-0.1
	Cle A	90	324	39	76	14	3	17	62	35-3	1	100	.235	.308	.454	114	5	0-2	.983	-3	89	114	C66,D25		0.3
	Year	148	498	57	112	20	4	27	84	57-5	2	166	.225	.304	.444	111	6	0-5	.983	-2	89	114	D70,C67,O6(3/0/3)/1		0.2
1979	Cle A	110	358	54	82	9	2	15	54	46-3	1	100	.229	.313	.391	90	-6	4-2	.961	-22	70	82	C91,D13,O2(1/0/1)		-2.4
1980	Cle A	76	178	22	40	7	1	5	31	17-1	0	52	.225	.288	.360	77	-6	0-4	.971	-2	53	101	D40,C13,O2(1/0/1)		-1.0
1981	Pit N	21	47	6	10	4	1	0	4	1-0	0	12	.213	.255	.404	82	-1	0-0	.964	2	49	86	1b9,O8(7/0/2)		0.0
Total 7		432	1276	169	293	45	11	55	202	154-12	3	381	.230	.311	.411	99	-3	8-12	.969	-42	70	87	C229,D123,O19(12/0/8),1b10		-4.3

ALEXANDER, HUGH Hugh B7.10.1917 Buffalo MO D11.25.2000 Oklahoma City OK BR/TR/6-0/190 d8.15

YEAR	TM LG	G	AB	R	H	2B	3B	HR	RBI	BB-IB	HP	SO	AVG	OBP	SLG	AOPS	ABR	SB-CS	FA	FR	RNG	THR	GAMES AT POSITION	DL	BFW
1937	Cle A	7	11	0	1	0	0	0	0	0-0	0	5	.091	.091	.091	-54	-3	1-0	.667	-1	65	0	O3(1/0/3)		-0.3

ALEXANDER, MANNY Manuel De Jesus (b Manuel De Jesus (Alexander)) B3.20.1971 San Pedro de Macoris, D.R. BR/TR/5-10/150(150-180) d9.18 OF(4/0/2) [DL 1994 Bal A 29]

YEAR	TM LG	G	AB	R	H	2B	3B	HR	RBI	BB-IB	HP	SO	AVG	OBP	SLG	AOPS	ABR	SB-CS	FA	FR	RNG	THR	GAMES AT POSITION	DL	BFW
1992	Bal A	4	5	1	1	0	0	0	0	0-0	0	3	.200	.200	.200	12	-1	0-0	1.000	-0	68	109	S3		-0.1
1993	Bal A	3	0	1	0	0	0	0	0	0-0	0	—	—	—	—	—	0	0-0	—	-0	0		/R		0.0
1995	Bal A	94	242	35	57	9	1	3	23	20-0	2	30	.236	.299	.318	60	-15	11-4	.971	-5	86	122	2b81,S7,3b2/D		-1.4
1996	†Bal A	54	68	6	7	0	0	0	4	3-0	0	27	.103	.141	.103	-37	-15	3-3	.940	-2	111	89	S21,2b7,3b7,O3L/PD		-1.4
1997	NY N	54	149	26	37	9	3	2	15	9-1	1	38	.248	.294	.389	81	-5	11-0	.979	2	112	146	2b31,S26/3	46	0.2
	Chi N	33	99	11	29	3	1	1	7	8-2	2	16	.293	.358	.374	89	-2	2-1	.942	-2	110	71	S28,2b4		-0.1
	Year	87	248	37	66	12	4	3	22	17-3	3	54	.266	.320	.383	85	-6	13-1	.959	0	113	80	S54,2b35/3		0.1
1998	†Chi N	108	264	34	60	10	1	5	25	18-1	1	66	.227	.278	.330	57	-17	4-1	.964	-12	81	80	S50,2b27,3b19/OLD		-2.5
1999	Chi N	90	177	17	48	11	2	0	15	10-0	0	38	.271	.309	.356	68	-9	4-0	.988	1	114	86	S30,3b22,2b17,O2R		-0.5
2000	Bos N	101	194	30	41	4	3	4	19	13-0	0	41	.211	.261	.325	46	-17	2-0	.944	0	95	69	3b63,S20,2b7,D2	2	-1.4
2004	Tex A	21	21	3	5	2	0	0	3	1-0	0	7	.238	.273	.333	55	-1	0-0	.917	-1	124	0	2b11,S7,3b3		-0.2
2005	SD N	10	18	0	2	1	0	0	1	0-0	0	5	.111	.238	.167	9	-2	0-0	1.000	-3	59	0	2b5,S4/13		-0.5
Total 10		572	1237	164	287	49	11	15	111	84-5	7	271	.232	.284	.326	57	-84	37-9	.966	-10	103	82	S196,2b190,3b118,O6L,D6/1P	77	-7.9

ALEXANDER, MATT Matthew B1.30.1947 Shreveport LA BB/TR/5-11/169* [ChiN68 2/35] d8.23 Col Grambling St.

YEAR	TM LG	G	AB	R	H	2B	3B	HR	RBI	BB-IB	HP	SO	AVG	OBP	SLG	AOPS	ABR	SB-CS	FA	FR	RNG	THR	GAMES AT POSITION	DL	BFW
1973	Chi N	12	5	4	1	0	0	0	0	1-0	1	1	.200	.333	.200	47	-0	2-0	1.000	-0	57	0	O3C		0.0
1974	Chi N	45	54	15	11	2	1	0	0	12-1	1	12	.204	.358	.278	76	-1	8-4	.921	-3	79	97	3b19,O4(0/2/1),2b2		-0.4
1975	Oak A	63	10	16	1	0	0	0	0	1-0	0	1	.100	.182	.100	-19	-2	17-10	1.000	-1	102	0	D17,O11(1/3/7),2b3,3b2	28	-0.3
1976	Oak A	61	30	16	1	0	0	0	0	0-0	0	5	.033	.033	.033	-84	-7	20-7	1.000	0	116	0	O23(7/7/11),D19		-0.6
1977	Oak A	90	42	24	10	1	0	0	2	4-0	0	6	.238	.304	.262	57	-2	26-14	1.000	0	93	0	O31(7/17/8),S12,D12,2b4/3		-0.4
1978	Pit N	7	0	2	0	0	0	0	0	0-0	0	0	—	—	—	—	0	4-1	—	0			/R		0.0
1979	†Pit N	44	13	6	7	0	1	0	1	0-0	0	5	.538	.538	.692	221	2	13-1	1.000	0	99	359	O11(6/3/3)/S		0.5
1980	Pit N	37	3	13	1	0	0	0	0	0-0	0	0	.333	.333	.667	167	0	10-3	1.000	0	189	0	O4(2/2/0)/2	15	0.2
1981	Pit N	15	11	5	4	0	0	0	4	0-0	0	1	.364	.364	.364	102	0	3-2	1.000	0	125	0	O6(2/3/1)	95	0.0
Total 9		374	168	111	36	4	2	0		18-1	1	26	.214	.294	.262	56	-10	103-42	1.000	-5	105	41	O93(25/40/31),D48,3b22,S13,2b10	138	-1.0

ALEXANDER, WALT Walter Ernest B3.5.1891 Atlanta GA D12.29.1978 Fort Worth TX BR/TR/5-10.5/165 d6.21

YEAR	TM LG	G	AB	R	H	2B	3B	HR	RBI	BB-IB	HP	SO	AVG	OBP	SLG	AOPS	ABR	SB-CS	FA	FR	RNG	THR	GAMES AT POSITION	DL	BFW
1912	StL A	37	97	5	17	4	0	0	5	8	1		.175	.245	.216	34	-8	1	.969	-3	84	96	C37		-0.9
1913	StL A	43	110	5	15	2	1	0	7	4	1	36	.136	.174	.173	2	-14	1	.947	3	112	127	C43		-0.9
1915	StL A	1	1	0	0	0	0	0	0	0	0		.000	.000	.000	-99	0	0		0	0	0	/C		
	NY A	25	68	7	17	4	0	1	5	13	0	16	.250	.370	.353	117	2	2-1	.967	5	105	118	C24		1.0
	Year	26	69	7	17	4	0	1	5	13	0	16	.246	.366	.348	114	2	2-1	.967	5	105	117	C25		1.0
1916	NY A	36	78	8	20	6	1	0	3	13	0	20	.256	.376	.359	118	3	2-0	.960	2	133	134	C27		0.7
1917	NY A	20	51	1	7	2	1	0	4	4	0	11	.137	.200	.216	27	-5	1	.951	0	140	74	C20		-0.3
Total 5		162	405	26	76	18	3	1	24	42	2	83	.188	.271	.254	59	-25	5-1	.959	7	111	112	C152		-0.4

ALEXANDER, NIN William Henry B11.24.1858 Pana IL D12.22.1933 Pana IL BR/TR/5-4.5/163 d6.7

YEAR	TM LG	G	AB	R	H	2B	3B	HR	RBI	BB-IB	HP	SO	AVG	OBP	SLG	AOPS	ABR	SB-CS	FA	FR	RNG	THR	GAMES AT POSITION	DL	BFW
1884	KC U	19	65	2	9	0	0	0	2	0	0		.138	.152	.138	-13	-11		.907	-1			C17,S2,O2C		-0.9
	StL AA	1	4	0	0	0	0	0	0	0	0		.000	.000	.000	-97	-1		.667	-0			/COC		-0.1
Total 1		20	69	2	9	0	0	0	2	0	0		.130	.143	.130	-19	-12		.895	-1			C18,O3C,S2		-1.0

ALFARO, JASON Jason B11.29.1977 San Antonio TX BR/TR/5-10/185 [HouN97 22/670] d9.9 Col Hill (TX) JC

YEAR	TM LG	G	AB	R	H	2B	3B	HR	RBI	BB-IB	HP	SO	AVG	OBP	SLG	AOPS	ABR	SB-CS	FA	FR	RNG	THR	GAMES AT POSITION	DL	BFW
2004	Hou N	7	11	1	2	0	0	0	0	0-0	0	1	.182	.182	.182	-5	-2	0-0	1.000	-1	54	85	S3		-0.3

ALFONZO, EDGARDO Edgardo Antonio B8.11.1973 Santa Teresa, Venez BR/TR/5-11/187(187-225) d4.26

YEAR	TM LG	G	AB	R	H	2B	3B	HR	RBI	BB-IB	HP	SO	AVG	OBP	SLG	AOPS	ABR	SB-CS	FA	FR	RNG	THR	GAMES AT POSITION	DL	BFW
1995	NY N	101	335	26	93	13	5	4	41	12-1	1	37	.278	.301	.382	82	-10	1-1	.962	-9	100	103	3b58,2b29,S6	21	-1.7
1996	NY N	123	368	36	96	15	2	4	40	25-2	0	56	.261	.304	.345	76	-14	2-0	.974	-5	99	108	2b66,3b36,S15		-1.4
1997	NY N	151	518	84	163	27	2	10	72	63-0	5	56	.315	.391	.432	122	19	11-6	.967	8	113	137	3b143,S12,2b3		2.9
1998	NY N	144	557	94	155	28	2	17	78	65-1	3	77	.278	.355	.427	108	7	8-3	.976	-7	90	83	3b144/S	15	2.8
1999	†NY N	158	628	123	191	41	1	27	108	85-2	3	85	.304	.385	.502	129	30	9-2	.993	-9	95	102	2b158		2.8
2000	†NY N★	150	544	109	176	40	2	25	94	95-1	5	70	.324	.425	.542	151	48	3-2	.985	6	101	96	2b146,D2		5.6
2001	NY N	124	457	64	111	22	0	17	49	51-0	5	62	.243	.322	.403	93	-5	0-0	.987	-6	98	93	2b122	19	-0.4
2002	NY N	135	490	78	151	26	0	16	56	62-8	7	55	.308	.391	.459	135	24	6-0	.969	7	106	85	3b134	20	3.3
2003	†SF N	142	514	56	133	25	2	13	81	58-4	4	41	.259	.334	.391	88	-8	5-2	.966	-17	89	74	3b133,2b6		-2.3
2004	SF N	139	519	66	150	26	1	11	77	46-2	5	40	.289	.350	.407	92	-5	1-1	.965	-6	100	88	3b129,2b5		-1.0
2005	SF N	109	368	36	102	17	1	2	43	27-1	2	34	.277	.327	.345	74	-13	2-0	.967	-14	83	56	3b97,2b2	39	-2.6
Total	11	1476	5298	772	1521	280	18	146	739	589-22	40	613	.287	.359	.429	108	73	53-17	.968	-50	90	90	3b874,2b537,S34,D2	114	5.4

ALICEA, LUIS Luis Rene (De Jesus) B7.29.1965 Santurce, PR BB/TR/5-9/176(165-177) [StLN86 1/23] d4.23 OF(10/0/1)

YEAR	TM LG	G	AB	R	H	2B	3B	HR	RBI	BB-IB	HP	SO	AVG	OBP	SLG	AOPS	ABR	SB-CS	FA	FR	RNG	THR	GAMES AT POSITION	DL	BFW
1988	StL N	93	297	20	63	10	4	1	24	25-4	2	32	.212	.276	.283	60	-15	1-1	.970	0	99	105	2b91		-1.4
1991	StL N	56	68	5	13	3	0	0	0	8-0	0	19	.191	.276	.235	45	-5	0-1	1.000	1	103	83	2b11,3b2/S		-0.4
1992	StL N	85	265	26	65	9	11	3	32	27-1	4	40	.245	.320	.385	103	0	2-5	.989	-7	105	90	2b75,S4		-0.7
1993	StL N	115	362	50	101	19	3	3	46	42-4	4	54	.279	.362	.373	100	2	11-1	.978	8	114	114	2b96,O4L/3		1.6
1994	StL N	88	205	32	57	12	5	5	29	30-4	3	38	.278	.373	.459	117	6	4-5	.986	8	108	120	2b53,O2L		1.5
1995	†Bos A	132	419	64	113	20	3	6	44	63-0	7	61	.270	.367	.375	93	-2	13-10	.977	15	109	117	2b132		1.7
1996	†StL N	129	380	54	98	26	3	5	42	52-10	5	78	.258	.350	.382	94	-1	11-3	.957	-11	93	108	2b125		-0.5
1997	Ana A	128	388	59	96	16	7	5	37	69-3	8	65	.253	.375	.369	95	0	22-8	.978	-5	96	89	2b105,3b12,D6		0.2
1998	†Tex A	101	259	51	71	15	3	6	33	37-0	5	40	.274	.372	.425	102	2	4-3	.970	1	97	101	2b45,3b26,D17,O2L		0.3
1999	Tex A	68	164	33	33	10	0	3	17	28-0	0	32	.201	.316	.317	59	-10	2-1	.980	-4	89	87	2b37,3b10/OLD		-1.2
2000	Tex A	139	540	85	159	25	8	6	63	59-1	5	75	.294	.365	.404	94	-4	1-3	.978	-13	95	91	2b130,3b8,S2,D4		-1.1
2001	KC A	113	387	44	106	16	4	4	32	23-0	4	56	.274	.320	.367	73	-15	8-6	.958	1	109	120	2b67,D22,3b18		-1.2
2002	KC A	94	237	28	54	8	2	1	23	32-1	1	34	.228	.322	.291	58	-14	2-3	.986	8	135	131	2b32,3b32,D16,1b2/SO(1/0/1)		-0.6
Total	13	1341	3971	551	1031	189	53	47	422	500-26	48	624	.260	.346	.369	88	-56	81-50	.975	2	102	105	2b999,3b109,D72,O10L,S8,1b2	51	-1.8

ALLANSON, ANDY Andrew Neal B12.22.1961 Richmond VA BR/TR/6-5/225* [CleA83 2/39] d4.7 Col Richmond [DL 1994 Cal A 41]

YEAR	TM LG	G	AB	R	H	2B	3B	HR	RBI	BB-IB	HP	SO	AVG	OBP	SLG	AOPS	ABR	SB-CS	FA	FR	RNG	THR	GAMES AT POSITION	DL	BFW
1986	Cle A	101	293	30	66	7	3	1	29	14-0	1	36	.225	.260	.280	49	-22	10-1	.960	-12	88	73	C99		-2.8
1987	Cle A	50	154	17	41	6	0	3	16	9-0	0	30	.266	.304	.364	76	-5	1-1	.986	-3	146	57	C50		-0.6
1988	Cle A	133	434	44	114	11	0	5	50	25-2	3	63	.263	.305	.323	74	-15	5-9	.986	4	114	104	C133	20	-0.5
1989	Cle A	111	323	30	75	9	1	3	17	23-2	4	47	.232	.289	.294	64	-16	4-4	.986	5	96	92	C111		-0.5
1991	Det A	60	151	10	35	10	0	1	16	7-0	0	31	.232	.266	.318	60	-8	0-0	.979	-2	143	107	C56,1b2/D		-0.8
1992	Mil A	9	25	6	8	1	0	0	0	1-0	0	2	.320	.346	.360	99	0	3-1	.943	-3	72	0	C9	43	-0.2
1993	SF N	13	24	3	4	1	0	0	2	1-0	0	2	.167	.200	.208	10	-3	0-0	1.000	-1	195	57	C8,1b2		-0.4
1995	Cal A	35	82	5	14	3	0	3	10	7-0	1	12	.171	.244	.317	45	-7	0-0	.994	7	73	139	C35	21	-0.4
Total	8	512	1486	145	357	48	4	16	140	87-4	9	223	.240	.283	.310	64	-76	23-18	.980	-8	109	90	C501,1b4/D	125	-6.2

ALLEN, NICK Artemus Ward B9.14.1888 Norton KS D10.16.1939 Hines IL BR/TR/6-0/180 d5.1 Mil 1918

YEAR	TM LG	G	AB	R	H	2B	3B	HR	RBI	BB-IB	HP	SO	AVG	OBP	SLG	AOPS	ABR	SB-CS	FA	FR	RNG	THR	GAMES AT POSITION	DL	BFW
1914	Buf F	32	63	3	15	1	0	0	4	3	0	12	.238	.273	.254	43	-6	4	.969	2	117	105	C26		-0.3
1915	Buf F	84	215	14	44	7	1	0	17	18	1	34	.205	.269	.247	45	-19	4	.956	-2	80	110	C80		-1.7
1916	Chi N	5	16	1	1	0	0	0	1	0	0	3	.063	.063	.063	-56	-3	0	.958	-0	107	60	C4		-0.4
1918	Cin N	37	96	6	25	2	2	0	5	4	1	7	.260	.297	.323	91	-1	0	.950	5	122	133	C31		0.6
1919	Cin N	15	25	7	8	0	1	0	5	2	1	6	.320	.393	.400	142	1	0	.958	2	134	94	C12		0.4
1920	Cin N	43	85	10	23	3	1	0	4	6	3	11	.271	.340	.329	94	-0	0	.961	3	118	127	C36		0.6
Total	6	216	500	41	116	13	5	0	36	33	6	73	.232	.288	.278	62	-28	8-0	.958	9	102	115	C189		-0.8

ALLEN, BERNIE Bernard Keith B4.16.1939 E.Liverpool OH BL/TR/6-0/185(175-186) d4.10 Col Purdue

YEAR	TM LG	G	AB	R	H	2B	3B	HR	RBI	BB-IB	HP	SO	AVG	OBP	SLG	AOPS	ABR	SB-CS	FA	FR	RNG	THR	GAMES AT POSITION	DL	BFW
1962	Min A	159	573	79	154	27	7	12	64	62-10	0	82	.269	.338	.403	96	-3	0-1	.983	-9	94	110	2b158		0.1
1963	Min A	139	421	52	101	20	1	9	43	38-8	1	52	.240	.302	.356	83	-9	0-0	.976	-24	84	97	2b128		-2.5
1964	Min A	74	243	28	52	8	1	6	20	33-7	1	30	.214	.309	.329	78	-7	1-2	.979	-5	94	89	2b71	52	-0.6
1965	Min A	19	39	2	9	2	0	0	6	6-2	0	8	.231	.326	.282	73	-1	0-0	1.000	-1	91	125	2b10/3	53	-0.1
1966	Min A	101	319	34	76	18	1	5	30	26-5	2	40	.238	.299	.348	80	-7	2-3	.974	-5	92	93	2b89,3b2		-0.6
1967	Was A	87	254	13	49	5	1	3	18	18-1	0	43	.193	.244	.256	51	-16	1-2	.990	14	117	148	2b75		0.3
1968	Was A	120	371	39	90	12	4	6	40	28-5	4	35	.241	.301	.343	98	-2	2-0	.991	6	103	104	2b110,3b2		1.5
1969	Was A	122	365	33	90	17	4	9	45	50-3	0	35	.247	.337	.389	108	4	5-4	.974	9	106	112	2b110,3b6		1.9
1970	Was A	104	261	31	61	7	1	8	29	43-4	0	21	.234	.342	.360	98	0	0-2	.969	8	103	119	2b80,3b12		1.2
1971	Was A	97	229	18	61	11	4	4	22	33-1	0	27	.266	.359	.376	113	5	2-1	.961	-6	100	58	2b41,3b34		0.1
1972	NY A	84	220	26	50	9	0	9	21	23-4	1	42	.227	.296	.391	107	1	0-1	.940	2	104	122	3b44,2b20		0.3
1973	NY A	17	57	5	13	3	0	0	4	5-1	0	5	.228	.290	.281	63	-3	0-0	.985	-0	102	87	2b13,D2		-0.2
	Mon N	16	50	5	9	1	0	2	9	5-1	0	4	.180	.255	.320	56	-3	0-0	.970	-3	80	41	2b9,3b8		-0.6
Total	12	1139	3404	357	815	140	21	73	351	370-52	8	424	.239	.314	.357	90	-41	13-16	.980	-16	98	106	2b914,3b109,D2	105	0.7

ALLEN, JACK Cyrus Alban B10.2.1855 Woodstock IL D4.21.1915 Girard PA BR/TR/?/160 d5.1 Col Case Western Reserve

YEAR	TM LG	G	AB	R	H	2B	3B	HR	RBI	BB-IB	HP	SO	AVG	OBP	SLG	AOPS	ABR	SB-CS	FA	FR	RNG	THR	GAMES AT POSITION	DL	BFW
1879	Syr N	11	48	7	9	2	1	0	3	1		5	.188	.204	.271	62	-2		.655	-5	30	0	3b8,O3R		-0.6
	Cle N	16	60	7	7	1	1	0	4	1		9	.117	.131	.167	-3	-6		.845	2	96	101	3b14,O2C		-0.3
	Year	27	108	14	16	3	2	0	7	2		14	.148	.164	.213	24	-8		.790	-3	73	66	3b22,O5(0/2/3)		-0.9

ALLEN, DUSTY Dustin R. B8.9.1972 Oklahoma City OK BR/TR/6-4/215 [SDN95 30/817] d7.1 Col Stanford

YEAR	TM LG	G	AB	R	H	2B	3B	HR	RBI	BB-IB	HP	SO	AVG	OBP	SLG	AOPS	ABR	SB-CS	FA	FR	RNG	THR	GAMES AT POSITION	DL	BFW
2000	SD N	9	12	0	0	0	0	0	0	2-0	0	5	.143	.143	.000	-64	-3	0-0	1.000	-0	64	0	O2L/1D		-0.3
	Det A	18	16	5	7	2	0	2	2	2-0	0	7	.438	.500	.938	255	4	0-0	1.000	-1	28	111	1b17/3OL		0.2
Total	1	27	28	5	7	2	0	2	2	4-0	0	12	.250	.344	.536	122	1	0-0	1.000	-1	27	109	1b18,O3L/3D		-0.1

ALLEN, ETHAN Ethan Nathan B1.1.1904 Cincinnati OH D9.15.1993 Brookings OR BR/TR/6-1/180 d6.21 Col Cincinnati

YEAR	TM LG	G	AB	R	H	2B	3B	HR	RBI	BB-IB	HP	SO	AVG	OBP	SLG	AOPS	ABR	SB-CS	FA	FR	RNG	THR	GAMES AT POSITION	DL	BFW
1926	Cin N	18	13	4	4	1	0	0	0	0-0	0	3	.308	.308	.385	88	0	0	1.000	1	172	0	O9(5/0/4)		0.0
1927	Cin N	111	359	54	106	26	4	2	20	14	2	29	.295	.325	.407	98	-2	12	.988	-3	100	58	O98(14/72/13)		-0.9
1928	Cin N	129	485	56	148	30	7	1	62	27	1	29	.305	.343	.402	96	-4	6	.981	-1	99	103	O129(1/128/0)		-1.0
1929	Cin N	143	538	69	157	27	11	6	64	20	0	21	.292	.317	.416	84	-17	21	.988	5	107	91	O137(24/134/10)		-1.7
1930	Cin N	21	46	10	10	1	0	3	7	5	0	2	.217	.294	.435	77	-2	1	.969	-0	109	0	O15(1/13/1)		-0.3
	NY N	76	238	48	73	9	2	7	31	12	0	23	.307	.340	.450	91	-4	5	.985	-2	87	130	O62(1/54/7)		-0.8
	Year	97	284	58	83	10	2	10	38	17	0	25	.292	.332	.447	89	-7	6	.981	-3	91	108	O77(2/67/8)		-1.1
1931	NY N	94	298	58	98	18	2	5	43	15	1	15	.329	.363	.453	121	8	6	.975	-2	98	40	O77(40/23/14)		0.2
1932	NY N	54	103	13	18	6	2	1	7	1	2	12	.175	.198	.301	33	-10	0	.957	-1	97	71	O24(11/13/0)		-1.2
1933	StL N	91	261	25	63	7	3	0	36	13	1	22	.241	.280	.291	60	-14	3	.984	7	114	163	O67(0/46/21)		-1.0
1934	Phi N	145	581	87	192	42	4	10	85	33	3	47	.330	.370	.468	108	8	6	.978	11	105	183	O145(87/47/16)		1.1
1935	Phi N	156	645	90	198	46	4	8	63	43	1	54	.307	.351	.419	96	-2	5	.980	13	102	205	O156(19/136/1)		0.6
1936	Phi N	30	125	21	37	3	1	1	9	4	0	8	.296	.318	.360	75	-5	4	.954	-1	108	39	O30(11/16/6)		-0.7
	Chi N	91	373	47	110	18	6	3	39	13	2	30	.295	.322	.399	91	-6	12	.980	-3	99	89	O89(73/16/0)		-1.3
	Year	121	498	68	147	21	7	4	48	17	2	38	.295	.321	.390	87	-11	16	.972	-4	101	33	O119(84/32/6)		-2.0
1937	StL A	103	320	39	101	18	1	0	31	21	1	17	.316	.360	.378	86	-7	3-4	.980	2	101	118	O78(12/54/14)		-0.8
1938	StL A	19	33	4	10	3	1	0	4	2	0	4	.303	.343	.455	98	-0	0-0	1.000	-0	97	0	O7(2/5/0)		-0.1
Total	13	1281	4418	623	1325	255	45	47	501	223	14	310	.300	.336	.410	92	-57	84-4	.981	22	102	115	O1123(301/757/107)		-7.9

ALLEN, SLED Fletcher Manson B8.23.1886 West Plains MO D10.16.1959 Lubbock TX BR/TR/6-1/180 d5.4

YEAR	TM LG	G	AB	R	H	2B	3B	HR	RBI	BB-IB	HP	SO	AVG	OBP	SLG	AOPS	ABR	SB-CS	FA	FR	RNG	THR	GAMES AT POSITION	DL	BFW
1910	StL A	14	23	3	3	1	0	0	1	1	2		.130	.231	.174	29	-2	0	.903	-4	67	77	C12/1		-0.6

ALLEN, HAM Frank Erwin B4.20.1846 Augusta ME D2.6.1881 Natick MA d4.27

YEAR	TM LG	G	AB	R	H	2B	3B	HR	RBI	BB-IB	HP	SO	AVG	OBP	SLG	AOPS	ABR	SB-CS	FA	FR	RNG	THR	GAMES AT POSITION	DL	BFW
1872	Man NA	17	70	9	19	3	0	1		0		1	.271	.271	.314	84	-1	0-0	.778	6	136	110	S9,O9(4/3/2),3b5		0.3

ALLEN, HANK Harold Andrew B7.23.1940 Wampum PA BR/TR/6-0/190* d9.9 b-Dick b-Ron OF(137/95/72)

YEAR	TM LG	G	AB	R	H	2B	3B	HR	RBI	BB-IB	HP	SO	AVG	OBP	SLG	AOPS	ABR	SB-CS	FA	FR	RNG	THR	GAMES AT POSITION	DL	BFW
1966	Was A	9	31	2	12	0	1	0	6	3-0	0	5	.387	.441	.484	167	3	0-0	.917	0	131	0	O9(8/0/3)		0.3
1967	Was A	116	292	34	68	8	4	3	17	13-2	1	53	.233	.264	.318	75	-11	3-4	.980	-6	92	20	O99(59/65/1)		-2.3
1968	Was A	68	128	16	28	2	2	1	9	7-1	1	16	.219	.265	.289	70	-5	0-0	.895	-1	60	0	O25(12/0/13),3b16,2b11		-0.8

YEAR	TM	LG	G	AB	R	H	2B	3B	HR	RBI	BB-IB	HP	SO	AVG	OBP	SLG	AOPS	ABR	SB-CS	FA	FR	RNG	THR	GAMES AT POSITION	DL	BFW
1969	Was	A	109	271	42	75	9	3	1	17	13-1	1	28	.277	.311	.343	88	-6	12-3	.933	0	102	133	O91(48/16/42),3b6,2b3	24	-0.7
1970	Was	A	22	38	3	8	2	0	0	4	5-1	0	5	.211	.295	.263	60	-2	0-0	1.000	-1	79	134	O17(5/3/10)		-0.1
	Mil	A	28	61	4	14	4	0	0	4	7-0	0	5	.230	.309	.295	67	-2	0-1	1.000	2	82	318	O14(1/11/2),2b5,1b4		-0.1
	Year		50	99	7	22	6	0	0	8	12-1	0	14	.222	.304	.283	65	-4	0-1	1.000	2	80	220	O31(6/14/12),2b5,1b4		-0.4
1972	Chi	A	9	21	1	3	0	0	0	0	0-0	0	2	.143	.143	.143	-15	-3	0-0	.905	2	120	443	3b6		-0.2
1973	Chi	A	28	39	2	4	2	0	0	0	1-0	0	9	.103	.125	.154	-21	-6	0-1	1.000	-1	112	0	3b9,1b8,O5(4/0/1)/C2		-0.8
Total	7		389	881	104	212	27	9	6	57	49-5	2	128	.241	.281	.312	74	-32	15-9	.957	-4	93	76	O260L,3b37,2b20,1b12/C	24	-4.9

ALLEN, HEZEKIAH Hezekiah "Ki" B2.25.1863 Westport CT D9.21.1916 Saugatuck CT 5-11/160 d5.16

YEAR	TM	LG	G	AB	R	H	2B	3B	HR	RBI	BB-IB	HP	SO	AVG	OBP	SLG	AOPS	ABR	SB-CS	FA	FR	RNG	THR	GAMES AT POSITION	DL	BFW
1884	Phi	N	1	3	0	2	0	0	0	0	0	0	0	.667	.667	.667	337	1		1.000	-0			/C		0.0

ALLEN, HORACE Horace Tanner "Pug" B6.11.1899 DeLand FL D7.5.1981 Canton NC BL/TR/6-0/187 d6.15 Col Georgia Tech

YEAR	TM	LG	G	AB	R	H	2B	3B	HR	RBI	BB-IB	HP	SO	AVG	OBP	SLG	AOPS	ABR	SB-CS	FA	FR	RNG	THR	GAMES AT POSITION	DL	BFW
1919	Bro	N	4	7	0	0	0	0	0	0	0-0	0	0	.000	.000	.000	-98	-2		1.000	0	62	538	O2(1/1/0)		-0.2

ALLEN, JAMIE James Bradley B5.29.1958 Yakima WA BR/TR/6-0/205 [SeaA79 2/27] d5.1 Col Arizona St.

YEAR	TM	LG	G	AB	R	H	2B	3B	HR	RBI	BB-IB	HP	SO	AVG	OBP	SLG	AOPS	ABR	SB-CS	FA	FR	RNG	THR	GAMES AT POSITION	DL	BFW
1983	Sea	A	86	273	23	61	10	4	0	21	33-0	1	52	.223	.309	.304	67	-12	6-5	.959	-2	92	90	3b82,D2		-1.6

ALLEN, PETE Jesse Hall B5.1.1868 Columbiana OH D4.16.1946 Philadelphia PA BR/TR/5-8.5/185 d8.4 Col Amherst

YEAR	TM	LG	G	AB	R	H	2B	3B	HR	RBI	BB-IB	HP	SO	AVG	OBP	SLG	AOPS	ABR	SB-CS	FA	FR	RNG	THR	GAMES AT POSITION	DL	BFW
1893	Cle	N	1	4	0	0	0	0	0	0	0	0	0	.000	.000	.000	-94	-1	0	1.000	-1	98	0	/C		-0.1

ALLEN, CHAD John Chad B2.6.1975 Dallas TX BR/TR/6-1/195* [MinA96 4/97] d4.6 Col Texas A&M-Commerce

YEAR	TM	LG	G	AB	R	H	2B	3B	HR	RBI	BB-IB	HP	SO	AVG	OBP	SLG	AOPS	ABR	SB-CS	FA	FR	RNG	THR	GAMES AT POSITION	DL	BFW
1999	Min	A	137	481	69	133	21	3	10	46	37-1	2	89	.277	.330	.395	80	-15	14-7	.975	2	105	108	O133(133/0/1),D2		-1.6
2000	Min	A	15	50	2	15	3	0	0	7	3-0	1	14	.300	.345	.360	76	-2	0-2	1.000	1	90	207	O15(2/0/13)		-0.2
2001	Min	A	57	175	20	46	13	2	4	20	19-1	0	37	.263	.333	.429	94	-1	1-2	.968	2	107	176	O27(16/0/15),D23	69	-0.2
2002	Cle	A	5	10	0	1	1	0	0	0	0-0	0	2	.100	.100	.200	-23	-2	0-0	1.000	-1	61	0	O4(3/0/1)		-0.2
2003	Fla	N	12	24	2	5	1	0	0	0	0-0	1	8	.208	.240	.333	49	-2	0-0	1.000	0	141	323	O8(6/1/2)/D		-0.1
2004	Tex	A	20	58	4	14	4	1	0	6	2-0	0	13	.241	.262	.345	55	-4	0-1	1.000	-2	65	0	O13(12/0/1),D5		-0.6
2005	Tex	A	21	53	5	15	1	0	0	5	2-0	0	13	.283	.309	.340	70	-2	0-1	1.000	-0	48	0	D18,O2(1/0/1)		-0.4
Total	7		267	851	102	229	44	8	14	84	63-2	4	173	.269	.321	.389	78	-28	15-13	.978	3	102	122	O202(173/1/34),D49	69	-3.3

ALLEN, KIM Kim Bryant B4.5.1953 Fontana CA BR/TR/5-11/175* d9.2 Col California-Riverside

YEAR	TM	LG	G	AB	R	H	2B	3B	HR	RBI	BB-IB	HP	SO	AVG	OBP	SLG	AOPS	ABR	SB-CS	FA	FR	RNG	THR	GAMES AT POSITION	DL	BFW
1980	Sea	A	23	51	9	12	3	0	0	3	8-2	1	3	.235	.350	.294	77	-1	10-3	.970	-1	115	88	2b15,O4(3/0/2)/S		0.0
1981	Sea	A	19	3	1	0	0	0	0	0	0-0	0	2	.000	.000	.000	-96	-1	2-1	—	-1	0	0	2b2,O2C,D2		-0.2
Total	2		42	54	10	12	3	0	0	3	8-2	1	5	.222	.333	.278	69	-2	12-4	.970	-1	111	85	2b17,O6(3/2/2),D2/S		-0.2

ALLEN, LUKE Lucas Gale B8.4.1978 Covington GA BL/TR/6-2/220(208-220) d9.10

YEAR	TM	LG	G	AB	R	H	2B	3B	HR	RBI	BB-IB	HP	SO	AVG	OBP	SLG	AOPS	ABR	SB-CS	FA	FR	RNG	THR	GAMES AT POSITION	DL	BFW
2002	LA	N	6	7	2	1	1	0	0	0	2-0	0	3	.143	.333	.286	72	0	0-0	1.000	0	110	0	O3R		0.0
2003	Col	N	2	2	0	0	0	0	0	0	0-0	0	0	.000	.000	.000	-88	-1	0-0	—	0			/H		-0.1
Total	2		8	9	2	1	1	0	0	0	2-0	0	3	.111	.273	.222	35	-1	0-0	1.000	0	110	0	O3R		-0.1

ALLEN, MYRON Myron Smith "Zeke" B3.22.1854 Kingston NY D3.8.1924 Kingston NY BR/TR/5-8/150 d7.19 ▲

YEAR	TM	LG	G	AB	R	H	2B	3B	HR	RBI	BB-IB	HP	SO	AVG	OBP	SLG	AOPS	ABR	SB-CS	FA	FR	RNG	THR	GAMES AT POSITION	DL	BFW
1883	NY	N	1	4	0	0	0	0	0	0	1	0	0	.000	.000	.000	-99	-1		1.000	-0	64	0	/P		0.0
1886	Bos	N	1	0	0	0	0	0	0	0	0		1	.000	.000	.000	-99	-1	0	1.000	-0	82	0	/2		-0.1
1887	Cle	AA	117	463	66	128	22	10	4	77	36	5		.276	.335	.393	106	3	26	.894	6	113	119	O115(73/1/41),3b3,S2,P2		0.6
1888	KC	AA	37	136	23	29	6	4	0	10	9	1		.213	.267	.316	81	-3	4	.931	6	144	62	O35(33/2/0),P2		0.1
Total	4		156	606	89	157	28	14	4	88	45	6	3	.259	.317	.371	98	-2	30	.903	12	121	105	O150(106/3/41),P5,3b3,S2/2		0.6

ALLEN, DICK Richard Anthony B3.8.1942 Wampum PA BR/TR/5-11/190* d9.3 b-Hank b-Ron OF(256/1/0)

YEAR	TM	LG	G	AB	R	H	2B	3B	HR	RBI	BB-IB	HP	SO	AVG	OBP	SLG	AOPS	ABR	SB-CS	FA	FR	RNG	THR	GAMES AT POSITION	DL	BFW
1963	Phi	N	10	24	6	7	2	1	0	2	0-0	0	5	.292	.280	.458	114	0	0-0	.833	-1	102	0	O7L/3		-0.1
1964	Phi	N	162	632	125	201	38	13	29	91	67-13	0	138	.318	.382	.557	163	53	3-4	.921	6	103	118	3b162		5.9
1965	Phi	N★	161	619	93	187	31	14	20	85	74-6	2	150	.302	.375	.494	146	39	15-2	.943	0	99	106	3b160,S2		4.2
1966	Phi	N★	141	524	112	166	25	10	40	110	68-13	3	136	.317	.396	.632	181	57	10-6	.967	-6	95	85	3b91,O47L		5.0
1967	Phi	N★	122	463	89	142	31	10	23	77	75-18	1	117	.307	.404	.566	173	46	20-5	.908	-4	99	114	3b121/2S	35	4.7
1968	Phi	N	152	521	87	137	17	9	33	90	74-5	1	161	.263	.352	.520	161	38	7-7	.973	-4	98	59	O139(139/1/0),3b10		2.9
1969	Phi	N	118	438	79	126	23	3	32	89	64-10	1	144	.288	.375	.573	167	39	9-3	.985	-8	77	99	1b117		2.4
1970	StL	N★	122	459	88	128	17	5	34	101	71-16	2	118	.279	.377	.560	144	28	5-4	.993	-12	77	98	1b79,3b38,O3L		0.9
1971	LA	N	155	549	82	162	24	1	23	90	93-13	1	113	.295	.395	.468	152	42	8-1	.918	-6	101	120	3b67,O60L,1b28		3.3
1972	Chi	A★	148	506	90	156	28	5	37	113	99-16	1	126	.308	.420	.603	198	65	19-8	.995	-4	86	83	1b143,3b2		5.8
1973	Chi	A★	72	250	39	79	20	3	16	41	33-3	1	51	.316	.394	.612	175	25	7-2	.994	2	111	95	1b67,2b2/D	69	2.3
1974	Chi	A	128	462	84	139	23	1	32	88	57-9	1	89	.301	.375	.563	164	38	7-1	.986	-7	78	106	1b125/2D		2.4
1975	Phi	N	119	416	54	97	21	3	12	62	58-4	2	109	.233	.327	.385	93	-3	11-2	.982	2	110	96	1b113		-0.9
1976	†Phi	N	85	298	52	80	16	1	15	49	37-2	0	63	.268	.346	.480	129	11	11-4	.989	-1	93	124	1b85	.55	0.5
1977	Oak	A	54	171	19	41	4	0	5	31	24-0	1	36	.240	.330	.351	89	-2	1-3	.984	2	124	94	1b50/D		-0.3
Total	15		1749	6332	1099	1848	320	79	351	1119	894-138	16	1556	.292	.378	.534	156	476	133-52	.989	-42	90	100	1b807,3b652,O256L,2b4,D3,S3	159	39.0

ALLEN, BOB Robert (b Alvah Charles Elliott) B10.13.1894 Muscoda WI D12.18.1975 Naperville IL BR/TR/5-10/180 d8.20 Col Wisconsin-Madison

YEAR	TM	LG	G	AB	R	H	2B	3B	HR	RBI	BB-IB	HP	SO	AVG	OBP	SLG	AOPS	ABR	SB-CS	FA	FR	RNG	THR	GAMES AT POSITION	DL	BFW
1919	Phi	A	9	22	3	4	1	0	0	3	1-0	0	7	.136	.269	.182	27	-2	0	.889	-1	76	0	O6C		-0.4

ALLEN, BOB Robert Gilman B7.10.1867 Marion OH D5.14.1943 Little Rock AR BR/TR/5-11/175 d4.19 M2

YEAR	TM	LG	G	AB	R	H	2B	3B	HR	RBI	BB-IB	HP	SO	AVG	OBP	SLG	AOPS	ABR	SB-CS	FA	FR	RNG	THR	GAMES AT POSITION	DL	BFW
1890	Phi	N	133	456	69	103	15	11	2	57	87	5	54	.226	.356	.320	95	0	13	.924	32	108	138	S133,M		3.2
1891	Phi	N	118	438	46	97	7	4	1	51	43	0	44	.221	.291	.263	60	-23	12	.896	8	106	117	S118		-1.0
1892	Phi	N	152	563	77	128	20	14	2	64	61	1	60	.227	.304	.323	90	-8	15	.919	15	104	129	S152		1.4
1893	Phi	N	124	471	86	126	19	12	8	90	71	5	40	.268	.369	.410	107	5	8	.919	15	103	126	S124		2.2
1894	Phi	N	41	154	27	40	10	4	0	19	17	1	11	.260	.337	.377	73	-7	4	.917	-3	95	85	S41		-0.6
1897	Bos	N	34	119	33	38	5	0	1	24	18	0		.319	.409	.387	104	2	1	.924	5	111	113	S32/OC2		0.7
1900	Cin	N	5	15	0	2	1	0	0	1	0	1		.133	.188	.200	7	-2	0	.864	-1	100	71	S5,M		-0.2
Total	7		607	2216	338	534	77	45	14	306	297	13	209	.241	.334	.335	88	-33	53	.915	72	105	124	S605/2OC		5.7

ALLEN, ROD Roderick Bernet B10.5.1959 Los Angeles CA BR/TR/6-1/185(185-200) [ChiA77 6/131] d4.7

YEAR	TM	LG	G	AB	R	H	2B	3B	HR	RBI	BB-IB	HP	SO	AVG	OBP	SLG	AOPS	ABR	SB-CS	FA	FR	RNG	THR	GAMES AT POSITION	DL	BFW
1983	Sea	A	11	12	1	2	0	0	0	0	0-0	0	1	.167	.167	.167	-2	-2	0-0	1.000	0	133	0	O2R,D3		-0.2
1984	Det	A	15	27	6	8	1	0	0	3	2-0	1	8	.296	.367	.333	95	0	1-0	1.000	0	391	0	D11,O2L		0.0
1988	Cle	A	5	11	1	1	1	0	0	0	0-0	0	2	.091	.091	.182	-25	-2	0-0	—	0			D4		-0.2
Total	3		31	50	8	11	2	0	0	3	2-0	1	11	.220	.264	.260	45	-4	0-0	1.000	0	160	0	D18,O4(2/0/2)		-0.4

ALLEN, RON Ronald Frederick B12.23.1943 Wampum PA BB/TR/6-3/205 d8.11 b-Hank b-Dick Col Youngstown St.

YEAR	TM	LG	G	AB	R	H	2B	3B	HR	RBI	BB-IB	HP	SO	AVG	OBP	SLG	AOPS	ABR	SB-CS	FA	FR	RNG	THR	GAMES AT POSITION	DL	BFW
1972	StL	N	7	11	2	1	0	0	1	3	3-0	0	5	.091	.286	.364	84	0	0-0	.968	-1	52	42	1b5		-0.1

ALLENSON, GARY Gary Martin B2.4.1955 Culver City CA BR/TR/5-11/185* [BosA76 9/214] d4.8 C6 Col Arizona St.

YEAR	TM	LG	G	AB	R	H	2B	3B	HR	RBI	BB-IB	HP	SO	AVG	OBP	SLG	AOPS	ABR	SB-CS	FA	FR	RNG	THR	GAMES AT POSITION	DL	BFW
1979	Bos	A	108	241	27	49	10	2	3	22	20-0	1	42	.203	.264	.299	50	-17	1-1	.980	3	100	93	C104,3b3		-1.1
1980	Bos	A	36	70	9	25	6	0	0	10	13-0	0	11	.357	.452	.443	140	5	2-2	.981	1	111	62	C24,3b5,D6		0.6
1981	Bos	A	47	139	23	31	8	0	5	25	23-0	1	33	.223	.335	.388	102	1	0-0	.969	-3	73	63	C47	25	-0.2
1982	Bos	A	92	264	25	54	11	0	6	33	38-1	1	39	.205	.306	.314	67	-11	0-3	.992	6	130	107	C91		-0.2
1983	Bos	A	84	230	19	53	11	0	3	30	27-0	2	43	.230	.311	.317	70	-9	0-1	.984	-2	83	98	C84		-0.8
1984	Bos	A	35	83	9	19	2	0	2	8	9-2	0	14	.229	.304	.325	71	-3	0-0	.987	-5	70	103	C35		-0.8
1985	Tor	A	14	34	2	4	1	0	0	0	0-0	0	10	.118	.118	.147	-27	-6	0-0	1.000	-3	211	65	C14		-0.8
Total	7		416	1061	114	235	49	2	19	131	130-3	5	192	.221	.307	.325	71	-40	3-7	.982	-3	102	92	C399,3b8,D6	25	-3.1

ALLENSWORTH, JERMAINE Jermaine Lamont B1.11.1972 Anderson IN BR/TR/6-0/190* [PitN93 1/34] d7.23 Col Purdue

YEAR	TM	LG	G	AB	R	H	2B	3B	HR	RBI	BB-IB	HP	SO	AVG	OBP	SLG	AOPS	ABR	SB-CS	FA	FR	RNG	THR	GAMES AT POSITION	DL	BFW
1996	Pit	N	61	229	32	60	9	3	4	31	20-4	4	50	.262	.337	.380	86	-4	11-6	.979	1	101	133	O61C		-0.3
1997	Pit	N	108	369	55	94	18	2	3	43	44-1	7	79	.255	.340	.339	79	-10	14-7	.980	-7	87	109	O104C	38	-1.6
1998	Pit	N	69	233	30	72	13	3	3	24	17-0	7	43	.309	.372	.429	110	4	8-4	.980	-1	98	102	O66C		0.3
	KC	A	30	73	15	15	5	0	0	9	9-0	1	17	.205	.326	.274	56	-4	7-0	.982	-1	105	0	O27(1/24/2)		-0.3
	NY	N	34	54	9	11	2	0	2	7	3-0	1	16	.204	.246	.352	56	-4	0-2	1.000	-2	73	0	O31(4/4/25)		-0.7
1999	NY	N	40	73	14	16	2	0	3	9	9-0	1	23	.219	.310	.370	75	-3	2-1	1.000	2	117	87	O33(10/14/15)		-0.2
Total	4		342	1031	155	268	49	8	15	114	104-1	24	228	.260	.339	.367	84	-21	42-20	.982	-9	95	97	O322(15/273/42)	38	-2.8

ALLEY, GENE Leonard Eugene B7.10.1940 Richmond VA BR/TR/6-0/165* d9.4

YEAR	TM	LG	G	AB	R	H	2B	3B	HR	RBI	BB-IB	HP	SO	AVG	OBP	SLG	AOPS	ABR	SB-CS	FA	FR	RNG	THR	GAMES AT POSITION	DL	BFW
1963	Pit	N	17	51	3	11	1	0	0		2-0	0	12	.216	.245	.235	39	-4	0-1	.947	1	120	230	3b7,2b4,S4		-0.3
1964	Pit	N	81	209	30	44	3	1	6	13	21-2	2	56	.211	.286	.321	72	-8	0-1	.966	15	119	122	S61,3b3/2		1.2

YEAR	TM LG	G	AB	R	H	2B	3B	HR	RBI	BB-IB	HP	SO	AVG	OBP	SLG	AOPS	ABR	SB-CS	FA	FR	RNG	THR	GAMES AT POSITION	DL	BFW
1965	Pit N	153	500	47	126	21	6	5	47	32-9	4	82	.252	.302	.348	82	-12	7-2	.968	24	**115**	**126**	S110,2b40/3		2.6
1966	Pit N	147	579	88	173	28	10	7	43	27-0	5	83	.299	.334	.418	108	5	8-8	.979	15	105	**148**	S143		3.2
1967	Pit N★	152	550	59	158	25	7	6	55	36-5	7	70	.287	.337	.391	108	5	10-5	.967	8	106	112	S146		2.9
1968	Pit N★	133	474	48	116	20	2	4	39	39-6	5	78	.245	.307	.321	91	-5	13-5	.974	26	**118**	**146**	S109,2b24		3.7
1969	Pit N	82	285	29	70	3	2	8	32	19-1	1	48	.246	.293	.354	83	-8	4-0	.977	16	113	128	2b53,S25,3b5	29	1.5
1970	†Pit N	121	426	46	104	16	5	8	41	31-9	3	70	.244	.297	.362	77	-15	7-3	.975	**31**	113	128	S108,2b8,3b2		2.9
1971	†Pit N	114	348	38	79	8	7	6	28	35-14	0	43	.227	.296	.342	80	-10	9-2	.958	-3	98	86	S108/3		-0.5
1972	†Pit N	119	347	30	86	12	2	3	36	38-10	1	52	.248	.321	.320	84	-7	4-3	.970	11	107	**153**	S114,3b4		1.8
1973	Pit N	76	158	25	32	3	2	2	8	20-6	1	28	.203	.292	.285	62	-8	1-0	.981	5	106	80	S49,3b8		0.1
Total	11	1195	3927	447	999	140	44	55	342	300-62	27	622	.254	.310	.354	88	-67	63-30	.970	144	109	127	S977,2b130,3b31	29	19.1

ALLIE, GAIR   Gair Roosevelt   B10.28.1931 Statesville NC   BR/TR/6-1/190   d4.13   Col Wake Forest

YEAR	TM LG	G	AB	R	H	2B	3B	HR	RBI	BB-IB	HP	SO	AVG	OBP	SLG	AOPS	ABR	SB-CS	FA	FR	RNG	THR	GAMES AT POSITION	DL	BFW
1954	Pit N	121	418	38	83	8	6	3	30	56	2	84	.199	.294	.268	49	-32	1-1	.952	-13	91	86	S95,3b19		-3.7

ALLIETTA, BOB   Robert George   B5.1.1952 New Bedford MA   BR/TR/6-0/190   [AnaA71*A1/7]   d5.6

YEAR	TM LG	G	AB	R	H	2B	3B	HR	RBI	BB-IB	HP	SO	AVG	OBP	SLG	AOPS	ABR	SB-CS	FA	FR	RNG	THR	GAMES AT POSITION	DL	BFW
1975	Cal A	21	45	4	8	1	0	1	2	1-1	0	6	.178	.196	.267	32	-4	0-0	1.000	-1	72	73	C21	42	-0.5

ALLISON, ANDY   Andrew K.   B1848 New York NY   5-10/150   d5.7   M1

YEAR	TM LG	G	AB	R	H	2B	3B	HR	RBI	BB-IB	HP	SO	AVG	OBP	SLG	AOPS	ABR	SB-CS	FA	FR	RNG	THR	GAMES AT POSITION	DL	BFW
1872	Eck NA	22	92	9	15	2	0	0	10	1		2	.163	.172	.185	14	-8	0-0	.930	-1	80	53	1b22/ORM		-0.6

ALLISON, ART   Arthur Algernon   B1.29.1849 Philadelphia PA   D2.25.1916 Washington DC   5-8/150   d5.4   b-Doug

YEAR	TM LG	G	AB	R	H	2B	3B	HR	RBI	BB-IB	HP	SO	AVG	OBP	SLG	AOPS	ABR	SB-CS	FA	FR	RNG	THR	GAMES AT POSITION	DL	BFW
1871	Cle NA	**29**	137	28	40	4	5	0	19	2		5	.292	.302	.394	104	1	3-1	.885	1	94	172	O29C,2b2		0.2
1872	Cle NA	19	87	13	23	4	0	0	8	0		2	.264	.264	.310	80	-1	0-0	.804	-1	90	200	O19(0/17/2)		-0.1
1873	Res NA	**23**	100	12	32	2	0	0	11	0		2	.320	.320	.340	104	1	0-0	.816	-3	64	142	O21(8/9/4),1b3/C		0.0
1875	Was NA	26	112	18	24	3	1	0	3	1		2	.214	.221	.259	69	-3	6-0	.924	-3	44	47	1b23,O3(0/1/2)/C		-0.4
	Har NA	40	175	26	42	4	1	1	19	0		4	.240	.240	.291	80	-4	1-2	.785	3	268	212	O37R,2b2/C1		0.1
	Year	66	287	44	66	7	2	1	22	1		5	.230	.233	.279	76	-7	7-2	.800	0	255	202	O40(0/1/39),1b24,C2,2b2		-0.3
1876	Lou N	31	130	9	27	2	1	0	10	2		6	.208	.220	.238	45	-8		.789	3	230	115	O23R,1b8		-0.5
Total	4 NA	137	611	97	161	17	7	1	60	3		14	.264	.267	.319	88	-6	10-3	.827	-1	146	182	O109(8/56/45),1b27,2b4,C3		-0.2

ALLISON, DOUG   Douglas L.   B7.1.1845 Philadelphia PA   D12.19.1916 Washington DC   BR/TR/5-10.5/160   d5.5   M1   b-Art

YEAR	TM LG	G	AB	R	H	2B	3B	HR	RBI	BB-IB	HP	SO	AVG	OBP	SLG	AOPS	ABR	SB-CS	FA	FR	RNG	THR	GAMES AT POSITION	DL	BFW
1871	Oly NA	27	133	28	44	10	2	2	27	0		2	.331	.331	.481	137	9	1-1	.806	-3			C27		0.3
1872	Tro NA	23	114	23	35	4	2	0	20	1		3	.307	.313	.377	110	1	1-1	.897	6			C22/S		0.5
	Eck NA	18	83	18	28	2	1	0	4	1		5	.337	.345	.386	146	6	0-0	.863	-7			C18		-0.1
	Year	41	197	41	63	6	3	0	24	2		8	.320	.327	.381	124	6	1-1	.883	-1			C40/S		0.4
1873	Res NA	19	80	11	24	6	0	0	8	2		1	.300	.317	.375	114	2	0-0	.800	0			C18,O4(0/1/3),M		0.2
	Mut NA	11	48	6	10	0	0	0	3	1		0	.208	.224	.208	30	-4	0-0	.868	2			C11/OR		-0.1
	Year	30	128	17	34	6	0	0	11	3		1	.266	.282	.313	81	-2	0-0	.831	3			C29,O5(0/1/4)		0.1
1874	Mut NA	**65**	318	68	90	7	5	0	28	6		5	.283	.296	.336	99	-1	1-0	.800	1	81	0	O47(0/3/44),C34/2		0.2
1875	Har NA	61	269	38	67	7	0	0	21	6		3	.249	.265	.275	84	-5	2-0	**.896**	17			C59,1b2,O2R		1.1
1876	Har N	44	163	19	43	4	0	0	15	3		9	.264	.287	.288	82	-4		**.881**	10			C40,O6(0/1/5)		0.7
1877	Har N	29	115	14	17	2	0	0	6	3		7	.148	.169	.165	7	-11		.896	1			C29		-0.8
1878	Pro N	19	76	9	22	2	0	0	7	1		8	.289	.299	.316	102	0		.911	0			C19/P		0.1
1879	Pro N	1	5	0	0	0	0	0	0	0			1.000	.000	.000	-99	-1		.833	-0			/C		-0.1
1883	Bal AA	1	3	2	2	0	0	0	0	0			.667	.667	.667	321	1		—	-0	0	0	/OCC		0.1
Total	5 NA	224	1045	192	298	36	10	2	111	17		19	.285	.297	.344	102	6	5-2	.863	18			C189,O54(0/4/50),1b2/2S		2.1
Total	5	94	362	44	84	8	0	0	28	7		25	.232	.247	.254	63	-15		.892	11			C90,O7(0/2/5)/P		-0.0

ALLISON, MILO   Milo Henry   B10.16.1889 Elk Rapids MI   D6.18.1957 Kenosha WI   BL/TR/5-10/155   d9.26

YEAR	TM LG	G	AB	R	H	2B	3B	HR	RBI	BB-IB	HP	SO	AVG	OBP	SLG	AOPS	ABR	SB-CS	FA	FR	RNG	THR	GAMES AT POSITION	DL	BFW
1913	Chi N	2	6	1	2	0	0	0	0	0		0	.333	.333	.333	91	0	1	1.000	-0	92	0	/OC		0.0
1914	Chi N	1	1	0	1	0	0	0	0	0		0	1.000	1.000	1.000	497	0	0	—	0			/H		0.0
1916	Cle A	14	18	10	5	0	0	0	6	0		2	.278	.458	.278	115	1	0	1.000	-0	88	0	O5(1/0/4)		0.0
1917	Cle A	32	35	4	5	0	0	0	9	0		7	.143	.318	.143	38	-2	3	1.000	-1	76	96	O11(4/5/2)		-0.4
Total	4	49	60	15	13	0	0	0	15	0		9	.217	.373	.217	74	-1	4	1.000	-1	81	58	O17(5/6/6)		-0.4

ALLISON, BILL   William Andrew   d5.21

YEAR	TM LG	G	AB	R	H	2B	3B	HR	RBI	BB-IB	HP	SO	AVG	OBP	SLG	AOPS	ABR	SB-CS	FA	FR	RNG	THR	GAMES AT POSITION	DL	BFW
1872	Eck NA	5	19	5	3	0	0	0	1	0		1	.158	.158	.158	-3	-2	0-0	.500	-2	0		O2(0/1/1),1b2/2		-0.2

ALLISON, BOB   William Robert   B7.11.1934 Raytown MO   D4.9.1995 Rio Verde AZ   BR/TR/6-4/220(205-223)   d9.16   Col Kansas

YEAR	TM LG	G	AB	R	H	2B	3B	HR	RBI	BB-IB	HP	SO	AVG	OBP	SLG	AOPS	ABR	SB-CS	FA	FR	RNG	THR	GAMES AT POSITION	DL	BFW
1958	Was A	11	35	1	7	1	0	0	2	2-0		5	.200	.243	.229	31	-3	0-2	1.000	-0	109	0	O11(1/10/0)		-0.5
1959	Was A☆	150	570	83	149	18	**9**	30	85	60-1	2	92	.261	.333	.482	122	15	13-8	.974	-10	90	79	O149(7/134/9)		-0.3
1960	Was A	144	501	79	126	30	3	15	69	92-4	2	94	.251	.367	.413	113	12	11-9	.965	5	112	113	O140(0/4/139),1b4		1.2
1961	Min A	159	556	83	136	21	3	29	105	103-1	5	100	.245	.363	.450	111	11	2-7	.975	4	105	124	O150R,1b18		0.1
1962	Min A	149	519	102	138	24	8	29	102	84-0	4	115	.266	.370	.511	130	23	8-5	.977	4	107	123	O147(2/0/146)		1.7
1963	Min A★	148	527	**99**	143	25	4	35	91	90-2	3	109	.271	.378	.533	**150**	38	6-1	.971	9	115	113	O147(0/8/146)		3.8
1964	Min A★	149	492	90	141	27	4	32	86	92-4	7	99	.287	.404	.553	143	46	10-1	.986	4	99	88	1b93,O61(27/28/16)		4.5
1965	†Min A	135	438	71	102	14	5	23	78	73-4	2	114	.233	.342	.445	118	11	10-2	.972	8	108	151	O122L,1b3		1.5
1966	Min A	70	168	34	37	6	1	8	19	30-2	1	34	.220	.345	.411	110	3	6-0	.967	1	103	105	O56(44/1/11)		1.3
1967	Min A	153	496	73	128	21	6	24	75	74-2	2	114	.258	.356	.470	132	21	6-4	.978	-1	96	68	O145(138/0/9)		1.3
1968	Min A	145	469	63	116	16	8	22	52	52-5	2	98	.247	.324	.456	128	15	9-7	.966	-3	93	61	O117(116/1/1),1b17		0.5
1969	†Min A	81	189	18	43	8	2	8	27	29-5	1	39	.228	.333	.418	106	2	2-4	1.000	-1	94	49	O58L,1b3		-0.4
1970	†Min A	47	72	15	15	5	0	1	7	4-0	1	20	.208	.345	.319	83	-1	1-0	1.000	-0	100	0	O17(12/1/4),1b7		-0.2
Total	13	1541	5032	811	1281	216	53	256	796	795-30	34	1033	.255	.358	.471	126	193	84-50	.975	18	104	101	O1320(527/187/631),1b145		13.5

ALLRED, BEAU   Dale Le Beau   B6.4.1965 Mesa AZ   BL/TL/6-0/193*   [CleA87 25/645]   d9.7   Col Lamar

YEAR	TM LG	G	AB	R	H	2B	3B	HR	RBI	BB-IB	HP	SO	AVG	OBP	SLG	AOPS	ABR	SB-CS	FA	FR	RNG	THR	GAMES AT POSITION	DL	BFW
1989	Cle A	13	24	0	6	3	0	0	1	2-0	0	10	.250	.308	.375	90	0	0-0	1.000	1	122	343	O5(3/0/2),D2		0.1
1990	Cle A	4	16	2	3	1	0	1	2	0-0	0	3	.188	.278	.438	97	0	0-0	.833	-1	64	0	O4(0/3/1)		-0.1
1991	Cle A	48	125	17	29	3	0	3	12	25-2	1	35	.232	.359	.328	92	0	2-2	.972	4	134	39	O42(20/0/27)/D		0.2
Total	3	65	165	19	38	7	0	4	15	29-2	1	48	.230	.345	.345	93	0	2-2	.969	4	128	65	O51(23/3/30),D3		0.2

ALMADA, MEL   Baldomero Melo (Quiros)   B2.7.1913 Huatabampo, Sonora, Mexico   D8.13.1988 Caborca, Sonora, Mexico   BL/TL/6-0/170   d9.8

YEAR	TM LG	G	AB	R	H	2B	3B	HR	RBI	BB-IB	HP	SO	AVG	OBP	SLG	AOPS	ABR	SB-CS	FA	FR	RNG	THR	GAMES AT POSITION	DL	BFW
1933	Bos A	14	44	11	15	0	0	1	3	11	0	3	.341	.473	.409	137	3	3-1	1.000	0	98	-0	O13(7/6/0)		0.3
1934	Bos A	23	90	7	21	2	1	0	10	6	0	8	.233	.281	.278	42	-8	3-2	.985	2	103	207	O23(0/16/7)		-0.7
1935	Bos A	151	607	85	176	27	9	3	59	55	1	34	.290	.350	.379	83	-16	20-9	.968	-1	88	190	O150(0/126/25),1b3		-1.9
1936	Bos A	96	320	40	81	16	4	1	21	24	0	15	.253	.305	.338	55	-24	2-4	.987	6	96	134	O81(11/3/69)		-2.5
1937	Bos A	32	110	17	26	8	2	1	9	15	0	2	.236	.328	.355	69	-5	0-1	.927	-3	88	53	O27(4/2/21),1b4		-1.0
	Was A	100	433	74	134	21	4	4	33	38	0	21	.309	.365	.404	98	-1	12-4	.964	10	109	162	O100(0/97/3)		0.6
	Year	132	543	91	160	27	6	5	42	53	0	27	.295	.357	.394	91	-7	12-5	.960	6	105	134	O127(4/99/24),1b4		-0.4
1938	Was A	47	197	24	48	7	4	1	18	8	1	16	.244	.277	.335	56	-15	4-1	.968	1	105	102	O47C		-1.3
	StL A	102	436	77	149	22	3	5	37	38	3	22	.342	.398	.422	106	5	9-5	.966	-3	96	99	O101C		-0.1
	Year	149	633	101	197	29	7	6	52	46	4	38	.311	.362	.395	92	-9	13-6	.967	-1	99	100	O148C		-1.3
1939	StL A	42	134	17	32	2	1	1	7	10	0	9	.239	.292	.291	48	-11	1-0	.987	-1	93	80	O34(3/31/0)		-1.2
	Bro N	39	112	11	24	4	0	0	3	9	0	17	.214	.273	.250	40	-9	2	.977	1	111	82	O32C		-0.9
Total	7	646	2483	363	706	107	27	15	197	214	5	150	.284	.342	.367	79	-81	56-27	.970	8	98	138	O607(25/461/125),1b7		-8.6

ALMEIDA, RAFAEL   Rafael D. "Mike"   B6.30.1887 Havana, Cuba   D5.18.1969 Havana, Cuba   BR/TR/5-9/164   d7.4

YEAR	TM LG	G	AB	R	H	2B	3B	HR	RBI	BB-IB	HP	SO	AVG	OBP	SLG	AOPS	ABR	SB-CS	FA	FR	RNG	THR	GAMES AT POSITION	DL	BFW
1911	Cin N	36	96	9	30	5	1	0	15	9	2	16	.313	.383	.385	120	3	3	.890	-3	94	27	3b27/2S		0.0
1912	Cin N	16	59	9	13	4	3	0	10	5	0	8	.220	.281	.390	85	-2	0	.891	-1	101	101	3b15		0.2
1913	Cin N	50	130	14	34	4	2	3	21	11	1	16	.262	.324	.392	104	0	4-5	.919	3	113	130	3b37,O3C,S2/2		0.4
Total	3	102	285	32	77	13	6	3	46	25	3	40	.270	.335	.389	106	1	7-5	.904	-1	104	96	3b79,O3C,S3,2b2		0.2

ALMON, BILL   William Francis   B11.21.1952 Providence RI   BR/TR/6-3/190(170-191)   [SDN74 1/1]   d9.2   Col Brown   OF(123/8/35)

YEAR	TM LG	G	AB	R	H	2B	3B	HR	RBI	BB-IB	HP	SO	AVG	OBP	SLG	AOPS	ABR	SB-CS	FA	FR	RNG	THR	GAMES AT POSITION	DL	BFW
1974	SD N	16	38	4	12	1	0	0	3	2-0		9	.316	.350	.342	99	-1		.915	-4	86	53	S14		-0.3
1975	SD N	6	10	0	4	0	0	0	0	0-0		1	.400	.400	.400	131	0		1.000	-1	67	0	S2		0.0
1976	SD N	14	57	6	14	3	0	1	6	2-0		5	.246	.271	.351	82	-2	3-1	.962	4	124	103	S14		0.4
1977	SD N	155	613	75	160	18	11	2	43	37-1		114	.261	.303	.336	79	-21	20-9	.954	15	107	89	S155		1.1
1978	SD N	138	405	39	102	19	2	0	21	33-10		74	.252	.308	.309	78	-12	17-5	.933	-5	99	118	3b114,S15,2b7		-1.6

YEAR	TM LG	G	AB	R	H	2B	3B	HR	RBI	BB-IB	HP	SO	AVG	OBP	SLG	AOPS	ABR	SB-CS	FA	FR	RNG	THR	GAMES AT POSITION	DL	BFW
1979	SD N	100	198	20	45	3	0	1	8	21-7	0	48	.227	.299	.258	57	-12	6-5	.985	5	108	116	2b61,S25/OC		-0.3
1980	Mon N	18	38	2	10	1	1	0	3	1-0	0	5	.263	.275	.342	72	-2	0-0	.911	8	84	19	S12/2		-0.3
	NY N	48	112	13	19	3	2	0	4	8-1	0	27	.170	.225	.232	28	-11	2-0	.967	5	100	131	S22,2b18,3b9		-0.4
	Year	66	150	15	29	4	3	0	7	9-1	0	32	.193	.237	.260	39	-13	2-0	.948	2	95	94	S34,2b19,3b9		-0.7
1981	Chi A	103	349	46	105	10	2	4	41	21-0	2	60	.301	.341	.375	109	3	16-6	.969	15	102	117	S103		3.2
1982	Chi A	111	308	40	79	10	4	4	26	25-0	1	49	.256	.313	.354	83	-8	10-8	.949	20	113	130	S108/D		2.1
1983	Oak A	143	451	45	120	29	1	4	63	26-3	2	67	.266	.302	.361	88	-7	26-8	.941	-17	88	63	S52,3b40,1b38,O23(9/0/15),2b5,D4		-2.0
1984	Oak A	106	211	24	47	11	0	7	16	10-0	0	42	.223	.253	.374	77	-7	5-7	1.000	-4	96	43	O48(33/1/17),1b44,D12,3b4/CS		-1.6
1985	Pit N	88	244	33	66	17	0	6	29	22-0	1	61	.270	.330	.414	109	3	10-7	.987	-7	93	86	S43,O32(26/6/0),1b7,3b7		-0.1
1986	Pit N	102	196	29	43	7	2	7	27	30-2	0	38	.219	.319	.383	91	-2	11-4	.983	-1	89	238	O54(53/0/2),3b28,S19,1b4		-0.5
1987	Pit N	19	20	5	4	1	0	0	1	1-0	0	5	.200	.238	.250	29	-2	0-0	.944	0	92	180	S4,O2L/3		-0.1
	NY N	49	54	8	13	3	0	0	4	8-0	1	16	.241	.339	.296	73	-2	1-0	.972	-2	112	65	S22,2b10,1b2/OR		-0.3
	Year	68	74	13	17	4	0	0	5	9-0	1	21	.230	.313	.284	61	-4	1-0	.963	-2	107	96	S26,2b10,O3(2/0/1),1b2/3		-0.4
1988	Phi N	20	26	1	3	2	0	0	1	3-0	0	11	.115	.207	.192	15	-3	0-0	.944	1	142	0	3b9,S5/1		-0.2
Total	15	1236	3330	390	846	138	25	36	296	250-24	6	636	.254	.305	.343	83	-85	128-60	.956	22	104	101	S616,3b212,O161L,2b102,1b96,D17/C		-0.7

ALMONTE, ERICK Erick R. B2.1.1978 Santo Domingo, D.R. BR/TR/6-2/180* d9.4

YEAR	TM LG	G	AB	R	H	2B	3B	HR	RBI	BB-IB	HP	SO	AVG	OBP	SLG	AOPS	ABR	SB-CS	FA	FR	RNG	THR	GAMES AT POSITION	DL	BFW
2001	NY A	8	4	0	2	1	0	0	0	0-0	1		.500	.500	.750	221	1	2-0	.875	0	93	150	S4,D3		0.2
2003	NY A	31	100	17	26	6	0	1	11	8-0	1	24	.260	.321	.350	78	-3	1-0	.906	-7	81	74	S31		-0.7
Total	2	39	104	17	28	7	0	1	11	8-0	1	25	.269	.327	.365	84	-2	3-0	.904	-6	81	77	S35,D3		-0.5

ALOMAR, ROBERTO Roberto (Velazquez) B2.5.1968 Ponce, PR BB/TR (BL 1997p)/6-0/185(155-190) d4.22 f-Sandy b-Sandy

YEAR	TM LG	G	AB	R	H	2B	3B	HR	RBI	BB-IB	HP	SO	AVG	OBP	SLG	AOPS	ABR	SB-CS	FA	FR	RNG	THR	GAMES AT POSITION	DL	BFW
1988	SD N	143	545	84	145	24	6	9	41	47-5	3	83	.266	.328	.382	105	3	24-6	.980	16	106	111	2b143		2.7
1989	SD N	158	623	82	184	27	1	7	56	53-4	1	76	.295	.347	.376	108	7	42-17	.967	6	104	104	2b157		2.1
1990	SD N★	147	586	80	168	27	5	6	60	48-1	2	72	.287	.340	.381	98	-2	24-7	.976	0	100	99	2b137,S5		0.5
1991	†Tor A★	161	637	88	188	41	11	9	69	57-3	4	86	.295	.354	.436	114	12	53-11	.981	-16	93	78	2b160		0.8
1992	†Tor A★	152	571	105	177	27	8	8	76	87-5	5	52	.310	.405	.427	127	25	49-9	.993	-22	88	70	2b150/D		1.4
1993	†Tor A★	153	589	109	192	35	6	17	93	80-5	5	67	.326	.408	.492	139	35	55-15	.980	-9	97	91	2b150		3.9
1994	Tor A★	107	392	78	120	25	4	8	38	51-2	2	41	.306	.386	.452	114	10	19-8	.991	-2	91	107	2b106		1.3
1995	Tor A★	130	517	71	155	24	7	13	66	47-3	0	45	.300	.354	.449	108	5	30-3	.994	-6	94	90	2b128		1.0
1996	†Bal A★	153	588	132	193	43	4	22	94	90-10	8	65	.328	.411	.527	138	38	17-6	.985	22	113	111	2b141,D10		6.0
1997	†Bal A★	112	412	64	137	23	2	14	60	40-2	3	43	.333	.390	.500	136	22	9-3	.988	10	104	108	2b109,D2	27	3.5
1998	Bal A★	147	588	86	166	36	1	14	56	59-3	2	70	.282	.347	.418	100	1	18-5	.985	21	111	99	2b144,D3	16	2.9
1999	†Cle A★	159	563	138	182	40	3	24	120	99-3	7	96	.323	.422	.533	137	36	37-6	.992	7	102	100	2b156,D2		5.1
2000	Cle A★	155	610	111	189	40	2	19	89	64-4	6	82	.310	.378	.475	111	12	39-4	.980	14	99	103	2b155		3.7
2001	†Cle A★	157	575	113	193	34	12	20	100	80-5	4	71	.336	.415	.541	145	40	30-6	.993	8	99	88	2b157		5.6
2002	NY N	149	590	73	157	24	4	11	53	57-4	1	83	.266	.331	.376	94	-9	16-4	.983	-22	89	99	2b147		-2.2
2003	NY N	73	263	34	69	17	1	2	22	29-2	2	40	.262	.336	.357	86	-5	6-0	.981	-10	92	104	2b72		-1.0
	Chi A	67	253	42	64	11	4	3	17	30-1	1	37	.253	.330	.340	76	-8	6-2	.990	-2	93	94	2b67		-0.7
2004	Ari N	38	110	14	34	5	2	3	16	12-0	1	18	.309	.382	.473	112	2	0-2	.971	-4	84	63	2b28/D	61	-0.2
	Chi A	18	61	4	11	1	0	1	8	2-0	0	13	.180	.203	.246	17	-8	0-0	.982	1	97	190	2b13,D5		-0.6
Total	17	2379	9073	1508	2724	504	80	210	1134	1032-62	50	1140	.300	.371	.443	116	216	474-114	.984	10	99	97	2b2320,D24,S5	104	35.8

ALOMAR, SANDY Santos Jr. (Velazquez) B6.18.1966 Salinas, PR BR/TR/6-5/215(200-235) d9.30 f-Sandy b-Roberto

YEAR	TM LG	G	AB	R	H	2B	3B	HR	RBI	BB-IB	HP	SO	AVG	OBP	SLG	AOPS	ABR	SB-CS	FA	FR	RNG	THR	GAMES AT POSITION	DL	BFW
1988	SD N	1	1	0	0	0	0	0	0	0-0	0	1	.000	.000	.000	-99	0	0-0	—	0			/H		0.0
1989	SD N	7	19	1	4	1	0	1	6	3-1	0	3	.211	.318	.421	110	0	0-0	1.000	1	178	0	C6		0.2
1990	Cle A★	132	445	60	129	26	2	9	66	25-2	2	46	.290	.326	.418	108	4	4-1	.981	-5	102	98	C129		0.6
1991	Cle A★	51	184	10	40	9	0	0	7	8-1	4	24	.217	.264	.266	47	-13	0-4	.987	7	138	82	C46,D4	103	-0.5
1992	Cle A★	89	299	22	75	16	0	2	26	13-3	5	32	.251	.293	.324	74	-11	3-3	.996	3	140	114	C88/D	16	-0.3
1993	Cle A	64	215	24	58	7	1	6	32	11-0	6	28	.270	.318	.395	92	-3	3-1	.984	-4	94	71	C64	98	-0.2
1994	Cle A	80	292	44	84	15	1	14	43	25-2	2	31	.288	.347	.490	112	4	8-4	.996	3	119	93	C78	17	1.2
1995	†Cle A	66	203	32	61	6	0	10	35	7-0	3	26	.300	.332	.478	106	1	3-1	.995	7	93	94	C61	65	1.0
1996	†Cle A★	127	418	53	110	23	0	11	50	19-0	3	42	.263	.299	.397	74	-18	1-0	.988	1	90	114	C124/1		-0.8
1997	†Cle A★	125	451	63	146	37	0	21	83	19-2	3	48	.324	.354	.545	126	16	0-2	.985	-10	90	104	C119/D		1.3
1998	†Cle A★	117	409	45	96	26	2	6	44	18-0	3	45	.235	.270	.352	92	-26	0-3	.992	5	111	82	C111,D3		-1.3
1999	†Cle A	37	137	19	42	13	0	6	25	4-0	2	23	.307	.322	.533	109	1	0-1	.974	-1	77	33	C35/D	118	0.2
2000	Cle A	97	356	44	103	16	2	7	42	16-1	4	41	.289	.324	.404	81	-11	2-2	.989	-12	71	96	C95/D	18	-1.6
2001	Chi A	70	220	17	54	8	1	4	21	12-1	2	17	.245	.288	.345	63	-12	1-2	.990	-0	143	77	C69	40	-0.9
2002	Chi A	51	167	21	48	10	1	7	25	5-0	1	14	.287	.309	.485	104	0	0-0	.994	-2	70	84	C50	18	-0.8
	Col N	38	116	8	31	4	0	0	12	4-0	0	19	.267	.292	.302	52	-8	0-0	1.000	-2	136	61	C38		-0.8
2003	Chi A	75	194	22	52	12	0	5	26	4-0	0	17	.268	.281	.407	76	-7	0-0	.997	-3	162	43	C75	23	-0.6
2004	Chi A	50	146	15	35	4	0	2	14	11-2	2	13	.240	.298	.308	58	-9	0-0	.990	-2	82	179	C49/D	16	-0.8
2005	Tex A	46	128	11	35	7	0	1	14	5-0	1	12	.273	.306	.328	64	-6	0-0	.989	-16	106	90	C46		-0.6
Total	18	1323	4400	511	1203	240	11	115	571	209-15	41	482	.273	.310	.408	86	-98	25-24	.989	-16	106	90	C1283,D12/1	532	-3.7

ALOMAR, SANDY Santos Sr. (Conde) B10.19.1943 Salinas, PR BB/TR (BR 1964p, 65-66)/5-9/155(140-170) d9.15 C11 s-Roberto s-Sandy OF(5/0/3)

YEAR	TM LG	G	AB	R	H	2B	3B	HR	RBI	BB-IB	HP	SO	AVG	OBP	SLG	AOPS	ABR	SB-CS	FA	FR	RNG	THR	GAMES AT POSITION	DL	BFW
1964	Mil N	19	53	3	13	1	0	0	6	0-0	0	11	.245	.245	.264	43	-4	1-0	.967	4	123	89	S19		0.2
1965	Mil N	67	108	16	26	1	1	0	8	4-1	0	12	.241	.268	.269	51	-7	12-5	.964	1	95	77	S39,2b19		-0.2
1966	Atl N	31	44	4	4	1	0	0	2	1-1	0	10	.091	.111	.114	-37	-7	0-0	.981	-3	81	141	2b21,S5		-1.1
1967	NY N	15	22	1	0	0	0	0	0	0-0	0	6	.000	.000	.000	-99	-6	0-0	1.000	1	110	70	S10,3b3,2b2		-0.5
	Chi A	12	15	4	3	0	0	0	0	0-0	0	0	.200	.294	.200	50	-1	2-0	.952	1	106	280	S8,2b2		0.1
1968	Chi A	133	363	41	92	8	2	0	12	20-1	1	42	.253	.292	.287	76	-11	21-8	.958	-14	96	96	2b99,3b27,S9/OL		-1.8
1969	Chi A	22	58	8	13	2	0	0	4	4-0	0	6	.224	.274	.259	47	-4	2-0	.980	3	105	129	2b22		0.0
	Cal A	134	559	60	140	10	2	1	30	36-2	1	48	.250	.296	.281	65	-28	18-3	.969	-6	95	113	2b134		-2.3
	Year	156	617	68	153	12	2	1	34	40-2	1	54	.248	.294	.279	63	-32	20-3	.970	-3	96	115	2b156		-2.3
1970	Cal A★	162	672	82	169	18	2	2	36	31-6	1	65	.251	.302	.293	67	-31	35-12	.979	12	107	125	2b153,S10/3		-0.4
1971	Cal A	162	689	77	179	24	3	4	42	41-4	0	60	.260	.301	.321	82	-19	39-10	.989	7	115	110	2b137,S28		2.3
1972	Cal A	155	610	65	146	20	3	1	25	47-5	0	55	.239	.292	.287	77	-18	20-12	.977	7	98	95	2b154,S4		-0.1
1973	Cal A	136	470	45	112	7	1	0	28	34-1	0	44	.238	.288	.257	59	-26	25-10	.979	5	96	97	2b110,S31		-0.9
1974	Cal A	46	54	12	12	0	1	0	1	2-0	0	8	.222	.250	.259	49	-4	2-0	.977	1	85	135	S19,2b15,3b5/ORD		-0.1
	NY A	76	279	35	75	8	0	1	27	14-0	0	25	.269	.302	.308	77	-9	6-4	.976	-11	89	79	2b76		-1.5
	Year	122	333	47	87	8	1	1	28	16-0	0	33	.261	.293	.300	73	-12	8-4	.976	-10	92	78	2b91,S19,3b5/ORD		-1.5
1975	NY A	151	489	61	117	18	4	2	39	26-0	0	58	.239	.277	.305	65	-24	28-6	.985	-4	93	104	2b150/S		-1.5
1976	†NY A	67	163	20	39	4	0	1	10	13-0	0	12	.239	.295	.282	70	-6	12-7	.970	-3	103	83	2b38,S6,3b3/1ORD		-0.7
1977	Tex A	69	83	21	22	3	0	1	11	8-0	1	13	.265	.333	.337	83	-2	4-3	.973	-6	83	107	D26,2b18,S6,O5(4/0/1),1b4/3		-0.5
1978	Tex A	24	29	3	6	1	0	0	1	1-0	0	7	.207	.233	.241	33	-3	0-0	.975	1	146	128	1b9,2b6,3b3,S2,D3	100	-0.2
Total	15	1481	4760	558	1168	231	18	14	282	302-17	3	482	.245	.294	.285	64	-211	227-80	.977	15	100	107	2b1156,S197,3b43,D39,1b14,O8L	100	-9.2

ALOU, FELIPE Felipe Rojas (b Felipe Rojas (Alou)) B5.12.1935 Haina, D.R. BR/TR/6-0/195(190-205) d6.8 M13/C5 b-Jesus b-Matty s-Moises OF(434/484/736)

YEAR	TM LG	G	AB	R	H	2B	3B	HR	RBI	BB-IB	HP	SO	AVG	OBP	SLG	AOPS	ABR	SB-CS	FA	FR	RNG	THR	GAMES AT POSITION	DL	BFW
1958	SF N	75	182	21	46	9	2	4	16	19-2	1	34	.253	.325	.390	91	-2	4-2	.985	2	118	45	O70(28/3/44)		-0.3
1959	SF N	95	247	38	68	13	2	10	33	17-1	0	38	.275	.318	.466	109	2	5-3	.974	-2	102	48	O69(0/10/64)		-0.1
1960	SF N	106	322	48	85	17	3	8	44	16-1	2	42	.264	.299	.410	99	-2	10-2	.958	-2	99	71	O95(68/7/24)		-0.7
1961	SF N	132	415	59	120	19	0	18	52	26-2	2	41	.289	.333	.465	113	7	11-4	.990	3	104	112	O122(42/6/87)		0.4
1962	†SF N★	154	561	96	177	30	3	25	98	33-3	6	66	.316	.356	.513	133	25	10-7	.971	-2	105	60	O150(11/2/141)		1.2
1963	SF N	157	565	75	159	31	9	20	82	27-3	6	87	.281	.319	.474	127	11	11-2	.986	2	108	82	O153(6/13/144)		1.3
1964	Mil N	121	415	60	105	26	3	9	51	30-5	4	41	.253	.306	.395	96	-2	5-2	.975	1	116	37	O92(14/60/27),1b18	31	-0.5
1965	Mil N	143	555	80	165	29	2	23	78	31-4	5	63	.297	.338	.481	128	19	8-4	.980	1	103	45	O91(66/24/9),1b69,3b2/S		1.4
1966	Atl N☆	154	666	122	218	32	6	31	74	24-6	12	51	.327	.361	.533	143	36	5-7	.988	6	103	95	1b90,O79(47/40/4),3b3/S		3.4
1967	Atl N	140	574	76	157	26	3	15	43	32-7	7	50	.274	.318	.408	108	5	6-5	.993	-12	54	104	1b85,O56(24/30/5)		-1.6
1968	Atl N	160	662	72	210	37	5	11	57	48-14	4	56	.317	.361	.439	140	33	12-11	.989	-0	102	79	O158C		3.0
1969	†Atl N	123	476	54	134	13	1	5	32	23-4	0	23	.282	.319	.345	85	-10	4-6	.989	-0	106	56	O116(3/102/13)		-1.6
1970	Oak A	154	575	70	156	25	3	8	55	32-6	1	31	.271	.308	.387	89	-10	10-5	.977	8	109	110	O145(101/5/81)/1		-1.1
1971	Oak A	2	8	0	2	1	0	0	1	0-0	0	1	.250	.250	.375	76	0	0-0	1.000	1	195	0	O2L		0.0
	NY A	131	461	52	133	20	6	8	69	32-3	2	24	.289	.334	.410	116	8	5-5	.985	-11	79	57	O80(7/20/56),1b42		-1.2
	Year	133	469	52	135	21	6	8	69	32-3	2	25	.288	.333	.409	116	8	5-5	.986	-11	82	56	O82(9/20/56),1b42		-1.2

YEAR	TM LG	G	AB	R	H	2B	3B	HR	RBI	BB-IB	HP	SO	AVG	OBP	SLG	AOPS	ABR	SB-CS	FA	FR	RNG	THR	GAMES AT POSITION	DL	BFW
1972	NY A	120	324	33	90	18	1	6	37	22-1	2	27	.278	.326	.395	117	6	1-0	.990	5	146	120	1b95,O15R		0.6
1973	NY A	93	280	25	66	12	0	4	27	9-5	0	25	.236	.256	.321	64	-14	0-1	.988	-2	90	100	1b67,O22(1/1/21)		-2.3
	Mon N	19	48	4	10	1	0	1	4	2-1	0	4	.208	.240	.292	45	-4	0-1	1.000	3	123	175	O15(14/3/0)/1		-0.1
1974	Mil A	3	3	0	0	0	0	0	0	0-0	0	2	.000	.000	.000	-99	-1	0-0	.000	-0	0	0	/OR		-0.1
Total	17	2082	7339	985	2101	359	49	206	852	423-67	57	706	.286	.328	.433	114	114	107-67	.979	-2	104	82	O1531R,1b468,3b5,S2	31	1.6

ALOU, JESUS — Jesus Maria Rojas (b Jesus Maria Rojas (Alou)) B3.24.1942 Haina, D.R. BR/TR/6-2/195(180-200) d9.10 C1 b-Felipe b-Matty

YEAR	TM LG	G	AB	R	H	2B	3B	HR	RBI	BB-IB	HP	SO	AVG	OBP	SLG	AOPS	ABR	SB-CS	FA	FR	RNG	THR	GAMES AT POSITION	DL	BFW
1963	SF N	16	24	3	6	1	0	0	5	0-0	0	3	.250	.280	.292	66	-1	0-1	.875	-1	73	0	O12(11/0/3)		-0.3
1964	SF N	115	376	42	103	11	0	3	28	13-2	4	35	.274	.305	.327	77	-12	6-6	.973	3	107	120	O108(9/4/99)		-1.7
1965	SF N	143	543	76	162	19	4	9	52	13-0	3	40	.298	.317	.398	98	-3	8-5	.980	1	105	81	O136(6/0/133)		-1.2
1966	SF N	110	370	41	96	13	1	1	20	9-1	2	22	.259	.279	.308	62	-19	5-5	.967	-7	85	61	O100(59/0/42)		-3.4
1967	SF N	129	510	55	149	15	4	5	30	14-2	4	39	.292	.316	.367	96	-4	1-7	.948	-6	94	63	O123(79/0/50)		-2.1
1968	SF N	120	419	26	110	15	4	0	39	9-3	1	23	.263	.278	.317	79	-12	1-4	.989	3	100	132	O105(49/0/65)		-2.0
1969	Hou N	115	452	49	112	19	4	5	34	15-6	4	30	.248	.276	.341	74	-18	4-6	.928	0	100	124	O112(65/0/58)	36	-2.6
1970	Hou N	117	458	59	140	27	3	1	44	21-4	5	15	.306	.335	.402	97	-3	3-2	.962	-5	89	84	O108(30/0/88)		-1.3
1971	Hou N	122	433	41	121	21	4	2	40	13-3	4	17	.279	.305	.360	91	-7	3-7	.983	8	105	87	O109(52/0/63)		-0.7
1972	Hou N	52	93	8	29	4	1	0	11	7-4	1	5	.312	.366	.376	115	2	0-2	.970	-1	108	92	O23(10/0/14)		0.0
1973	Hou N	28	55	7	13	2	0	1	8	1-1	0	6	.236	.276	.327	67	-3	0-0	.941	1	91	0	O14(1/0/13)		-0.4
	†Oak A	36	108	10	33	3	0	1	11	2-1	0	6	.306	.318	.361	95	-1	0-0	1.000	1	109	75	O21(18/1/4),D6		-0.2
1974	†Oak A	96	220	13	59	8	0	2	15	5-1	2	9	.268	.288	.332	83	-6	0-0	1.000	4	132	301	D41,O25(9/0/16)		-0.4
1975	NY N	62	102	8	27	3	0	0	11	4-2	1	5	.265	.299	.294	67	-5	0-1	.963	1	82	279	O20(15/0/5)		-0.6
1978	Hou N	77	139	7	45	5	1	2	19	6-1	0	3	.324	.345	.417	122	3	0-0	.976	-1	88	52	O28(27/0/1)		0.1
1979	Hou N	42	43	3	11	4	0	0	1	6-1	0	1	.256	.347	.349	96	0	0-0	1.000	0	147	0	O6(5/0/1)/1		0.4
Total	15	1380	4345	448	1216	170	26	32	377	138-32	30	267	.280	.305	.353	86	-89	31-46	.968	-1	99	94	O1050(445/5/655),D47/1	36	-16.8

ALOU, MATTY — Mateo Rojas (b Mateo Rojas (Alou)) B12.22.1938 Haina, D.R. BL/TL/5-9/160* d9.26 b-Felipe b-Jesus

YEAR	TM LG	G	AB	R	H	2B	3B	HR	RBI	BB-IB	HP	SO	AVG	OBP	SLG	AOPS	ABR	SB-CS	FA	FR	RNG	THR	GAMES AT POSITION	DL	BFW
1960	SF N	4	3	1	1	0	0	0	0	0-0	0	0	.333	.333	.333	88	0	0-0	1.000	0	239	0	/OL		0.0
1961	SF N	81	200	38	62	7	2	6	24	15-2	0	18	.310	.356	.455	118	5	3-2	.978	-2	100	50	O58(16/3/40)		-0.4
1962	†SF N	78	195	28	57	8	1	3	14	14-0	3	17	.292	.349	.390	100	3	3-1	.976	-2	100	0	O57(35/9/21)		-0.2
1963	SF N	63	76	4	11	1	0	0	2	2-0	1	13	.145	.177	.158	-3	-10	0-1	.952	1	109	151	O20(13/2/7)		-1.2
1964	SF N	110	250	28	66	4	2	1	14	11-3	2	25	.264	.302	.308	71	-10	5-3	.976	2	115	50	O80(42/18/35)	36	-1.2
1965	SF N	117	324	37	75	12	2	2	18	17-2	2	28	.231	.274	.299	60	-17	10-2	.986	2	100	133	O103(72/11/23)/P		-2.0
1966	Pit N	141	535	86	183	18	9	2	27	24-4	4	44	**.342**	.373	.421	121	14	23-15	.972	-5	92	125	O136(1/135/0)		0.6
1967	Pit N	139	550	87	186	21	7	2	28	24-1	6	45	.338	.372	.413	124	16	16-10	.989	-6	85	124	O134C/1		0.6
1968	Pit N★	146	558	59	185	28	4	0	52	27-6	2	26	.332	.362	.396	130	20	18-10	.984	-7	91	89	O144C		1.0
1969	Pit N★	162	698	105	231	41	6	1	48	42-9	2	35	.331	.369	.411	121	20	22-8	.977	-4	96	106	O162(1/162/0)		1.4
1970	†Pit N	155	677	97	201	21	9	1	47	30-3	4	18	.297	.329	.356	84	-17	19-11	.975	-7	86	172	O153(0/152/1)		-2.7
1971	StL N	149	609	85	192	28	6	7	74	34-3	4	27	.315	.350	.411	112	10	19-10	.981	-2	101	158	O94(0/73/21),1b57		0.2
1972	StL N	108	404	46	127	17	2	3	31	24-2	1	23	.314	.353	.389	112	6	11-4	.988	-1	101	100	1b66,O39(1/0/38)		0.2
	†Oak A	32	121	11	34	5	0	1	16	11-1	1	12	.281	.341	.347	112	2	2-1	1.000	-3	78	87	O32(2/0/31)/1		-0.2
1973	NY A	123	497	59	147	22	1	2	28	30-0	3	43	.296	.338	.356	98	-1	5-2	.974	-6	91	109	O85R,1b40/D		-1.4
	StL N	11	11	1	3	0	0	0	1	1-1	0	1	.273	.333	.273	69	0	0-0	1.000	1	0	0	/1OC		0.0
1974	SD N	48	81	8	16	3	0	0	3	5-1	0	6	.198	.241	.235	36	-7	0-0	.947	-2	83	0	O13L,1b2		-1.0
Total	15	1667	5789	780	1777	236	50	31	427	311-38	36	377	.307	.344	.400	104	31	156-80	.979	-37	93	117	O1312(197/844/302),1b168/DP	36	-6.2

ALOU, MOISES — Moises Rojas (b Moises Rojas) B7.3.1966 Atlanta GA BR/TR/6-3/195(175-220) [PitN86*1/2] d7.26 f-Felipe Col Canada (CA) JC [DL 1991 Mon N 182, 1999 Hou N 182]

YEAR	TM LG	G	AB	R	H	2B	3B	HR	RBI	BB-IB	HP	SO	AVG	OBP	SLG	AOPS	ABR	SB-CS	FA	FR	RNG	THR	GAMES AT POSITION	DL	BFW
1990	Pit N	2	5	0	1	0	0	0	0	0-0	0	0	.200	.200	.200	11	-1	0-0	1.000	-0	102	0	O2L		-0.1
	Mon N	14	15	4	3	0	1	0	0	0-0	0	3	.200	.200	.333	46	-1	0-0	1.000	1	106	548	O5(1/2/2)		-0.1
	Year	16	20	4	4	0	1	0	0	0-0	0	3	.200	.200	.300	37	-2	0-0	1.000	1	105	360	O7(3/2/2)		-0.2
1992	Mon N	115	341	53	96	28	2	9	56	25-0	1	46	.282	.328	.455	122	9	16-2	.978	-0	96	138	O100(79/13/15)	20	1.0
1993	Mon N	136	482	70	138	29	6	18	85	38-9	5	53	.286	.340	.483	114	9	17-6	.985	1	99	116	O136(102/12/34)	16	0.7
1994	Mon N★	107	422	81	143	31	5	22	78	42-10	2	63	.339	.397	.592	153	33	7-6	.986	-2	100	97	O106(63/0/45)		2.5
1995	Mon N	93	344	48	94	22	0	14	58	29-6	9	56	.273	.342	.459	106	3	4-3	.981	-3	92	88	O92(61/4/30)	38	-0.4
1996	Mon N	143	540	87	152	28	2	21	96	49-7	2	83	.281	.339	.457	107	5	9-4	.989	2	102	93	O142(33/7/123)	15	0.1
1997	†Fla N★	150	538	88,	157	29	5	23	115	70-9	4	85	.292	.373	.493	131	25	9-5	.988	-11	87	47	O150(89/55/22)		1.1
1998	†Hou N★	159	584	104	182	34	5	38	124	84-11	5	87	.312	.399	.582	159	52	11-3	.980	-8	83	109	O154(152/6/0)/D		3.9
2000	Hou N	126	454	82	161	28	2	30	114	52-4	2	45	.355	.416	.623	148	34	3-3	.970	-8	84	69	O121(59/0/64)/D	16	1.9
2001	†Hou N★	136	513	79	170	31	2	27	108	57-14	3	57	.331	.396	.554	133	27	5-1	.991	-6	83	121	O130R,D4	15	1.5
2002	Chi N	132	484	50	133	23	1	15	61	47-4	0	61	.275	.337	.419	102	-2	8-0	.991	1	98	88	O124(122/1/4),D2	15	-0.4
2003	†Chi N	151	565	83	158	35	1	22	91	63-7	7	67	.280	.357	.462	110	9	3-1	.972	-8	92	89	O142L,D9		-0.4
2004	Chi N★	155	601	106	176	36	3	39	106	68-2	5	80	.293	.361	.557	130	26	3-0	.969	-4	92	89	O154L/D		1.6
2005	SF N★	123	427	67	137	21	3	19	63	56-1	3	43	.321	.400	.518	134	22	5-1	.966	-1	101	75	O117(74/0/53),D3	31	1.7
Total	14	1742	6315	1002	1901	375	37	297	1155	680-84	43	829	.301	.369	.513	127	250	100-35	.981	-46	92	88	O1675(1133/100/522),D21	530	14.6

ALPERMAN, WHITEY — Charles Augustus B11.11.1879 Etna PA D12.25.1942 Pittsburgh PA BR/TR/5-10/180 d4.13

YEAR	TM LG	G	AB	R	H	2B	3B	HR	RBI	BB-IB	HP	SO	AVG	OBP	SLG	AOPS	ABR	SB-CS	FA	FR	RNG	THR	GAMES AT POSITION	DL	BFW
1906	Bro N	128	441	38	111	15	7	3	46	6	14		.252	.284	.338	102	-2	13	.940	-3	102	72	2b103,S24/3		-0.4
1907	Bro N	141	558	44	130	23	**16**	2	39	13	12		.233	.266	.342	98	-6	5	.953	12	112	100	2b115,3b14,S12		0.9
1908	Bro N	70	213	17	42	3	1	1	15	9	7		.197	.253	.235	58	-10	2	.934	-3	102	77	2b42,3b9,O5R,S2		-1.5
1909	Bro N	111	420	35	104	19	12	1	41	2	6		.248	.262	.357	95	-7	7	.931	9	100	84	2b108		0.4
Total	4	450	1632	134	387	60	36	7	141	30	39		.237	.268	.331	90	-25	27	.945	15	105	85	2b368,S38,3b24,O5R		-0.6

ALSTON, TOM — Thomas Edison B1.31.1926 Greensboro NC D12.30.1993 Winston-Salem NC BL/TR/6-5/210(195-210) d4.13 Col North Carolina A&T

YEAR	TM LG	G	AB	R	H	2B	3B	HR	RBI	BB-IB	HP	SO	AVG	OBP	SLG	AOPS	ABR	SB-CS	FA	FR	RNG	THR	GAMES AT POSITION	DL	BFW
1954	StL N	66	244	28	60	14	2	4	34	24	2	41	.246	.317	.369	78	-8	3-5	.989	10	154	97	1b65		-0.3
1955	StL N	13	8	0	1	0	0	0	0	0-0	0	0	.125	.125	.125	-33	-2	0-0	1.000	0	141	109	1b7		-0.1
1956	StL N	3	2	0	0	0	0	0	0	0-0	0	0	.000	.000	.000	-99	-1	0-0	1.000	0	294	264	1b3		0.0
1957	StL N	9	17	2	5	1	0	0	2	1-0	0	5	.294	.333	.353	83	0	0-0	.947	-1	36	135	1b6	103	-0.1
Total	4	91	271	30	66	15	2	4	36	25-0	0	2	46	.244	.311	.358	74	-11	3-5	.987	9	148	100	1b81	103	-0.6

ALSTON, WALTER — Walter Emmons "Smokey" B12.1.1911 Venice OH D10.1.1984 Oxford OH BR/TR/6-2/195 d9.27 M23 HF1983 Col Miami-Ohio

YEAR	TM LG	G	AB	R	H	2B	3B	HR	RBI	BB-IB	HP	SO	AVG	OBP	SLG	AOPS	ABR	SB-CS	FA	FR	RNG	THR	GAMES AT POSITION	DL	BFW
1936	StL N	1	1	0	0	0	0	0	0	0-0	0	1	.000	.000	.000	-99	0	0	.500	-0	0	0	/1		-0.1

ALSTON, DELL — Wendell B9.22.1952 Valhalla NY BL/TR/6-0/175* d5.17 Col Concordia (NY)

YEAR	TM LG	G	AB	R	H	2B	3B	HR	RBI	BB-IB	HP	SO	AVG	OBP	SLG	AOPS	ABR	SB-CS	FA	FR	RNG	THR	GAMES AT POSITION	DL	BFW
1977	NY A	22	40	10	13	4	0	1	4	3-0	0	4	.325	.364	.500	136	2	3-3	1.000	0	58	806	D10,O2R		0.2
1978	NY A	3	3	0	0	0	0	0	0	0-0	0	2	.000	.000	.000	-99	-0	0-0	—	0			/H		-0.1
	Oak A	58	173	17	36	6	0	1	10	10-0	0	21	.208	.250	.237	40	-14	11-10	.956	-3	99	0	O50(22/0/29),1b9,D3		-2.2
	Year	61	176	17	36	6	0	1	10	10-0	0	23	.205	.246	.233	37	-15	11-10	.956	-3	99	0	O50(22/0/29),1b9,D3		-2.3
1979	Cle A	54	62	10	18	0	2	1	12	10-1	0	10	.290	.384	.403	114	1	4-4	.969	0	94	178	O30(18/0/12),D7		0.0
1980	Cle A	52	54	11	12	1	2	0	9	5-2	2	7	.222	.302	.315	71	-2	2-4	.947	0	104	69	O26(12/4/11),D6		-0.4
Total	4	189	332	48	79	7	4	3	35	28-3	2	44	.238	.297	.310	71	-14	20-21	.957	-3	98	74	O108(52/4/54),D26,1b9		-2.5

ALTENBURG, JESSE — Jesse Howard B1.2.1893 Ashley MI D3.12.1973 Lansing MI BL/TR/5-9/158 d9.19

YEAR	TM LG	G	AB	R	H	2B	3B	HR	RBI	BB-IB	HP	SO	AVG	OBP	SLG	AOPS	ABR	SB-CS	FA	FR	RNG	THR	GAMES AT POSITION	DL	BFW
1916	Pit N	8	14	2	6	1	1	0	1	0	1		.429	.467	.643	237	2	0	1.000	-0	85	0	O8(4/2/0)		0.2
1917	Pit N	11	17	1	3	0	0	0	3	0	0		.176	.176	.176	8	-2	0	1.000	-0	99	0	O4(1/0/3)		-0.3
Total	2	19	31	3	9	1	1	0	3	0	1		.290	.313	.387	112	0	0	1.000	-1	91	0	O12(5/2/3)		-0.1

ALTIZER, DAVE — David Tilden "Filipino" B11.6.1876 Pearl IL D5.14.1964 Pleasant Hill IL BL/TR/5-10.5/160 d5.29 OF(4/53/52)

YEAR	TM LG	G	AB	R	H	2B	3B	HR	RBI	BB-IB	HP	SO	AVG	OBP	SLG	AOPS	ABR	SB-CS	FA	FR	RNG	THR	GAMES AT POSITION	DL	BFW
1906	Was A	115	433	56	111	9	5	1	27	35	8		.256	.324	.307	103	-2	37	.931	-15	87	78	S113,O2R		-1.1
1907	Was A	147	540	60	145	15	5	1	42	34	8		.269	.319	.326	115	8	38	.923	-3	99	83	S80,1b50,O17C		0.8
1908	Was A	67	205	19	46	1	1	0	18	13	1		.224	.274	.239	73	-6	8	.959	-2	105	3b16,1b4/S		-0.5
	Cle A	29	89	11	19	1	2	0	5	7	1		.213	.278	.270	78	-2	7	.952	0	165	266	O24(0/20/4),S3		-0.4
	Year	96	294	30	65	2	3	0	23	20	2		.221	.275	.248	75	-8	15	.959	-2	105	105	2b38,O24(0/20/4),3b16,1b4,S4		-1.3
1909	Chi A	116	382	47	89	6	7	1	20	39	**16**		.233	.330	.293	101	2	27	.949	4	103	63	O61(4/14/45),1b46		0.2
1910	Cin N	3	10	3	6	0	0	0	0	0	0		.600	.692	.600	290	3	0	.933	-1	75	77	S3		0.2
1911	Cin N	37	75	8	17	4	1	0	4	9	1		.227	.318	.307	78	-2	2	.907	-0	106	55	S23/12OR		-0.1
Total	6	514	1734	204	433	36	21	4	116	140	33	5	.250	.318	.309	95	1	119	.925	-17	93	76	S223,O105C,1b101,2b39,3b16		-1.3

YEAR	TM LG	G	AB	R	H	2B	3B	HR	RBI	BB-IB	HP	SO	AVG	OBP	SLG	AOPS	ABR	SB-CS	FA	FR	RNG	THR	GAMES AT POSITION	DL	BFW

ALTMAN, GEORGE George Lee B3.20.1933 Goldsboro NC BL/TR/6-4/200* d4.11 Negro Lg 1955 Col Tennessee St.

1959	Chi N	135	420	54	103	14	4	12	47	34-4	7	80	.245	.312	.383	85	-10	1-0	.990	-1	99	105	O121C		-1.6
1960	Chi N	119	334	50	89	16	4	13	51	32-6	1	67	.266	.330	.455	114	6	4-3	.993	-3	98	35	O79(26/32/23),1b21		-0.2
1961	Chi N★	138	518	77	157	28	12	27	96	40-3	4	92	.303	.353	.560	137	26	6-2	.978	-1	100	93	O130(1/25/115),1b3		1.6
1962	Chi N★	147	534	74	170	27	5	22	74	62-14	5	89	.318	.393	.511	136	29	19-7	.972	-4	101	73	O129(0/6/125),1b16		1.7
1963	StL N	135	464	62	127	18	7	9	47	47-2	2	93	.274	.339	.401	104	3	13-4	.979	-3	108	91	O124(12/0/116)		-0.2
1964	NY N	124	422	48	97	14	1	9	47	34-0	1	70	.230	.262	.332	68	-19	4-2	.968	10	110	173	O109(95/0/14)		-1.6
1965	Chi N	90	196	24	46	7	1	4	23	19-2	0	36	.235	.302	.342	79	-5	3-2	.943	-2	98	0	O45(44/0/1),1b2		-1.1
1966	Chi N	88	185	19	41	6	0	5	17	14-3	0	37	.222	.276	.335	68	-8	2-2	.958	-1	72	168	O42(41/0/1),1b4		-1.2
1967	Chi N	15	18	1	2	2	0	0	1	2-0	0	8	.111	.200	.222	20	-2	0-0	1.000	-1	53	0	O4(3/0/1)/1		-0.3
Total	9	991	3091	409	832	132	34	101	403	268-38	20	572	.269	.329	.432	105	20	52-22	.977	-2	101	95	O783(222/184/396),1b47		-2.9

ALTOBELLI, JOE Joseph Salvatore B5.26.1932 Detroit MI BL/TL/6-0/185* d4.14 M7/C7

1955	Cle A	42	75	8	15	3	0	2	5	5-0	1	14	.200	.259	.320	53	-5	0-1	.992	-1	72	72	1b40		-0.9
1957	Cle A	83	87	9	18	3	2	0	9	5-0	1	14	.207	.253	.287	49	-6	3-2	.994	0	90	99	1b56,O7(1/4/2)		-0.8
1961	Min A	41	95	10	21	2	1	3	14	13-0	0	14	.221	.312	.358	75	-3	0-0	.951	-1	104	0	O25L,1b2		-0.5
Total	3	166	257	27	54	8	3	5	28	23-0	2	42	.210	.277	.323	60	-14	3-3	.993	-2	81	81	1b98,O32(26/4/2)		-2.2

ALUSIK, GEORGE George Joseph B2.11.1935 Ashley PA BR/TR/6-3.5/175* d9.11

1958	Det A	2	2	0	0	0	0	0	0	0-0	0	1	.000	.000	.000	-93	-1	0-0	1.000	0	146	0	/OL		-0.1
1961	Det A	15	14	0	2	0	0	0	2	1-0	0	4	.143	.188	.143	-6	-2	0-0	—	-0	0	0	/OR		-0.3
1962	Det A	2	2	0	0	0	0	0	0	0-0	0	0	.000	.000	.000	-97	-1	0-0	—	0			/H		-0.1
	KC A	90	209	29	57	10	1	11	35	16-1	1	29	.273	.326	.488	111	3	1-1	.968	0	99	115	O50(35/0/22)/1		0.0
	Year	92	211	29	57	10	1	11	35	16-1	1	29	.270	.323	.483	109	2	1-1	.968	0	99	115	O50(35/0/22)/1		-0.1
1963	KC A	87	221	28	59	11	0	9	37	26-0	1	33	.267	.345	.439	112	4	0-1	1.000	1	93	133	O63(30/1/36)	.31	0.1
1964	KC A	102	204	18	49	10	1	3	19	30-2	1	36	.240	.342	.343	89	-2	0-0	.984	-1	95	54	O44(43/0/3),1b12		-0.6
Total	5	298	652	75	167	31	2	23	93	73-3	4	103	.256	.333	.416	101	1	1-2	.985	-1	95	105	O159(109/1/62),1b13	31	-1.0

ALVARADO, LUIS Luis Cesar (Martinez) B1.15.1949 Lajas, PR D3.20.2001 Lajas, PR BR/TR/5-9/162* d9.13

1968	Bos A	11	46	3	6	2	0	0	1	1-0	1	11	.130	.167	.174	3	-5	0-0	.976	-4	75	92	S11		-1.1
1969	Bos A	6	5	0	0	0	0	0	0	0-0	0	2	.000	.000	.000	-96	-1	0-1	1.000	1	125	199	S5		-0.1
1970	Bos A	59	183	19	41	11	0	1	10	9-2	0	30	.224	.258	.301	51	-12	1-2	.929	-0	101	34	3b29,S27		-1.1
1971	Chi A	99	264	22	57	14	1	0	8	11-2	0	34	.216	.246	.277	47	-19	1-2	.959	7	99	96	S71,2b16		-0.5
1972	Chi A	103	254	30	54	4	1	4	29	13-5	1	36	.213	.254	.283	58	-14	2-2	.957	-3	98	70	S81,2b16,3b2		-1.0
1973	Chi A	80	203	21	47	7	2	0	20	4-0	1	20	.232	.250	.286	49	-14	6-2	.980	-1	99	83	2b45,S18,3b10/D		-1.2
1974	Chi A	8	10	1	1	0	0	0	0	0-0	0	1	.100	.100	.100	-41	-2	0-0	.667	-1	66	0	S4/23		-0.3
	StL N	17	36	3	5	2	0	0	1	2-0	0	6	.139	.179	.194	6	-5	0-0	.980	-3	86	112	S17		-0.7
	Cle A	61	114	12	25	2	0	0	12	6-0	0	14	.219	.256	.237	43	-8	1-1	.972	-0	102	101	2b46,S7,D3		-0.6
1976	StL N	16	42	5	12	1	0	0	3	3-1	0	6	.286	.333	.310	82	-1	0-0	.936	-8	65	38	2b16		-0.9
1977	NY N	1	2	0	0	0	0	0	0	0-0	0	1	.000	.000	.000	-99	-1	0-0	1.000	0	156	0	/2		-0.1
	Det A	2	1	0	0	0	0	0	0	0-0	0	0	.000	.000	.000	-95	-0	0-0	—	-1	0	0	3b2		-0.1
Total	9	463	1160	116	248	43	4	5	84	49-10	3	160	.214	.247	.271	47	-82	11-10	.957	-13	98	88	S241,2b141,3b44,D4		-7.6

ALVAREZ, TONY Antonio Enrique B5.10.1979 Caracas, Venez BR/TR/6-1/202* d9.4

2002	Pit N	14	26	6	8	2	0	1	2	3-0	0	5	.308	.379	.500	130	1	1-0	1.000	-2	63	0	O8(2/6/1)		0.0
2004	Pit N	24	38	5	8	2	0	1	8	4-0	1	7	.211	.289	.342	66	-2	0-0	1.000	-1	86	0	O16(3/4/9)		-0.3
Total	2	38	64	11	16	4	0	2	10	7-0	1	12	.250	.324	.406	92	-1	1-0	1.000	-2	76	0	O24(5/10/10)		-0.3

ALVAREZ, CLEMENTE Clemente Rafael B5.18.1968 Anzoategui, Venez BR/TR/5-11/180 d9.19

| 2000 | Phi N | 2 | 5 | 1 | 1 | 0 | 0 | 0 | 0 | 0-0 | 0 | 1 | .200 | .200 | .200 | 1 | -1 | 0-0 | 1.000 | 0 | 28 | 0 | C2 | | 0.0 |

ALVAREZ, GABE Gabriel De Jesus B3.6.1974 Navojoa, Sonora, Mexico BR/TR/6-1/205* [SDN95 2/32] d6.22 Col USC

1998	Det A	58	199	16	46	11	0	5	29	18-1	2	65	.231	.299	.362	71	-9	1-3	.873	-3	102	74	3b55,D2		-1.2
1999	Det A	22	53	5	11	3	0	2	4	3-0	0	9	.208	.250	.377	56	-4	0-0	1.000	-1	53	0	D12,O5R,3b2		-0.5
2000	Det A	1	1	0	0	0	0	0	0	2-0	0	1	1.000	.667	.000	90	0	0-1	—	0			/D		0.0
	SD N	11	13	1	2	1	0	0	0	1-0	0	1	.154	.214	.231	13	-2	0-0	1.000	-1	69	0	3b3,O2L		-0.2
Total	3	92	266	22	59	15	0	7	33	24-1	2	76	.222	.289	.357	66	-15	1-4	.875	-5	101	72	3b60,D15,O7(2/0/5)		-1.9

ALVAREZ, ORLANDO Jesus Manuel Orlando (Monge) B2.28.1952 Rio Grande, PR BR/TR/6-0/165* d9.1

1973	LA N	4	4	0	1	1	0	0	0	0-0	0	1	.250	.250	.500	106	0	0-0	—	0			/H		0.0
1974	LA N	2	1	0	0	0	0	0	0	0-0	0	1	.000	.000	.000	-99	0	0-0	1.000	0	230	0	/OL		0.0
1975	LA N	4	4	0	0	0	0	0	0	0-0	0	1	.000	.000	.000	-99	-1	0-0	—	0			/H		-0.1
1976	Cal N	15	42	4	7	1	0	2	8	0-0	0	3	.167	.167	.333	47	-3	0-0	1.000	-1	67	160	O11(10/1/0),D2		-0.5
Total	4	25	51	4	8	2	0	2	8	0-0	0	5	.157	.157	.314	36	-4	0-0	1.000	-1	71	156	O12(11/1/0),D2		-0.6

ALVAREZ, OSSIE Oswaldo (Gonzalez) B10.19.1933 Bolondron, Cuba BR/TR/5-10/165* d4.19

1958	Was A	87	196	20	41	3	0	0	5	16-0	0	26	.209	.269	.224	38	-17	1-1	.968	8	103	90	S64,2b14,3b3		-0.4
1959	Det A	8	2	0	1	0	0	0	0	0-0	0	1	.500	.500	.500	166	0	0-0	—	0					0.0
Total	2	95	198	20	42	3	0	0	5	16-0	0	27	.212	.271	.227	39	-17	1-1	.968	8	103	90	S64,2b14,3b3		-0.4

ALVAREZ, ROGELIO Rogelio (Hernandez) B4.18.1938 Pinar Del Rio, Cuba BR/TR/5-11/185* d9.18

1960	Cin N	3	9	1	1	0	0	0	0	0-0	0	3	.111	.111	.111	-38	-2	0-0	1.000	-1	0	62	1b2		-0.3
1962	Cin N	14	28	1	6	0	0	0	2	1-0	0	10	.214	.241	.214	23	-3	0-0	.973	-1	76	126	1b13		-0.4
Total	2	17	37	2	7	0	0	0	2	1-0	0	13	.189	.211	.189	8	-5	0-0	.979	-1	60	112	1b15		-0.7

ALVIS, MAX Roy Maxwell B2.2.1938 Jasper TX BR/TR/5-11/187* d9.11 Col Texas

1962	Cle A	12	51	1	11	0	0	3	2-0	0	14	.216	.245	.255	36	-5	3-1	.935	-3	69	45	3b12		-0.8
1963	Cle A	158	602	81	165	32	7	22	67	36-2	10	109	.274	.324	.460	118	13	9-7	.942	-6	91	111	3b158		0.6
1964	Cle A	107	381	51	96	14	3	18	53	29-5	6	77	.252	.313	.446	110	4	5-5	.955	-7	91	94	3b105	35	-0.4
1965	Cle A★	159	604	88	149	24	2	21	61	47-4	9	121	.247	.308	.397	99	-2	12-8	.958	-17	80	57	3b156		-2.1
1966	Cle A	157	596	67	146	22	3	17	55	50-6	2	98	.245	.304	.378	95	-4	4-7	.958	-7	86	88	3b157		-1.5
1967	Cle A★	161	637	66	163	23	4	21	70	38-1	4	107	.256	.301	.403	106	2	3-10	.965	-10	86	74	3b161		-1.2
1968	Cle A	131	452	38	101	17	3	8	37	41-5	4	91	.223	.292	.327	90	-6	5-5	.960	-15	80	86	3b128	23	-2.6
1969	Cle A	66	191	-13	43	.6	0	1	15	14-1	0	26	.225	.275	.272	53	-12	1-1	.973	-4	84	88	3b58/S	59	-1.8
1970	Mil A	62	115	16	21	2	0	3	12	5-1	0	20	.183	.217	.278	35	-11	1-2	.909	-0	111	75	3b36		-1.2
Total	9	1013	3629	421	895	142	22	111	373	262-25	35	662	.247	.302	.390	97	-21	43-46	.956	-69	86	84	3b971/S	117	-11.0

ALVORD, BILLY William Charles "Uncle Bill" B8.1863 St.Louis MO 5-10/187 d4.30

1885	StL N	2	5	0	0	0	0	0	1		0	2	.000	.167	.000	-45	-1		.714	-1	27	.0	3b2		-0.2
1889	KC AA	50	186	23	43	8	9	0	18	10	0	35	.231	.270	.371	77	-8	3	.877	3	132	122	3b34,S8,2b8		-0.3
1890	Tol AA	.116	495	69	135	13	16	2	52	22	0		.273	.304	.376	97	-7	21	.872	4	98	76	3b116		0.0
1891	Cle N	13	59	7	17	2	1	1	7	0	1	7	.288	.300	.441	110	0	0	.814	-2	95	50	3b13		-0.1
	Was AA	81	312	28	73	8	3	0	31	11	0	38	.234	.260	.279	57	-19	3	.862	17	117	63	3b81		-0.1
1893	Cle N	3	12	2	2	0	0	0	0	1	0	1	.167	.167	.167	-11	-2	0	.875	-1	38	0	3b3		-0.3
Total	5	265	1069	129	270	31	30	3	109	44	1	83	.253	.283	.346	81	-37	27	.865	20	108	75	3b249,2b8,S8		-1.0

ALYEA, BRANT Garrabrant Ryerson B12.8.1940 Passaic NJ BR/TR/6-3/215* d9.11 Col Hofstra

1965	Was A	8	13	3	3	0	2	6	1-0	0	4	.231	.286	.692	171	1	0-0	1.000	1	0	0	1b3/OL		0.0
1968	Was A	53	150	18	40	11	1	6	23	10-0	1	39	.267	.317	.473	142	7	0-0	1.000	1	120	0	O39(16/0/24)		0.6
1969	Was A	104	237	29	59	4	0	11	40	34-4	1	67	.249	.341	.405	115	5	1-3	.938	-3	82	138	O69(36/0/36),1b3		-0.2
1970	†Min A	94	258	34	75	12	1	16	61	28-0	1	51	.291	.366	.531	142	15	3-3	.980	-1	90	110	O75(73/0/2)		1.0
1971	Min A	79	158	13	28	4	0	2	15	24-3	1	38	.177	.282	.241	50	-10	1-1	.962	-3	74	144	O48(47/0/1)		-1.6
1972	Oak A	10	13	1	3	1	0	0	1	0-0	0	2	.231	.286	.308	80	0	0-0	1.000	-0	104	0	O2L	21	-0.1
	StL N	13	19	0	3	1	0	0	1	0-0	0	6	.158	.158	.211	4	-2	0-0	1.000	1	152	769	O3(1/0/2)		-0.1
	Oak A	10	18	2	3	0	1	2	2-0	0	5	.167	.250	.333	76	-1	0-0	1.000	4	104	0	O6R	21	0.3
Total	6	371	866	100	214	33	2	38	148	100-7	6	210	.247	.326	.421	113	15	5-7	.972	-1	93	127	O243(176/0/71),1b6	42	-0.1

YEAR	TM LG	G	AB	R	H	2B	3B	HR	RBI	BB-IB	HP	SO	AVG	OBP	SLG	AOPS	ABR	SB-CS	FA	FR	RNG	THR	GAMES AT POSITION	DL	BFW

AMALFITANO, JOEY John Joseph B1.23.1934 San Pedro CA BR/TR/5-11/180* d5.2 M3/C31 Col Loyola Marymount

1954	NY N	9	5	2	0	0	0	0	0	0-0	0	4	.000	.000	.000	-99	-1	0-0	1.000	1	192	440	3b4/2		-0.1
1955	NY N	36	22	8	5	1	1	0	1	2-0	0	2	.227	.292	.364	72	-1	0-0	.957	4	194	129	S5,3b2		0.3
1960	SF N	106	328	47	91	15	3	1	27	26-1	3	31	.277	.335	.351	94	-3	2-3	.935	-1	112	93	3b63,2b33,S3/OL		-0.2
1961	SF N	109	384	64	98	11	4	2	23	44-2	0	59	.255	.331	.320	77	-12	7-4	.970	-15	87	79	2b95,3b6		-1.9
1962	Hou N	117	380	44	90	12	5	1	27	45-5	1	43	.237	.317	.303	73	-14	4-4	.967	-5	92	111	2b110,3b5		-1.0
1963	SF N	54	137	11	24	3	0	1	7	12-0	1	18	.175	.245	.219	36	-11	2-6	.980	-5	100	64	2b37,3b7		-1.7
1964	Chi N	100	324	51	78	19	6	4	27	40-1	5	42	.241	.333	.373	95	-1	2-7	.964	4	109	95	2b86/1S		0.9
1965	Chi N	67	96	13	26	4	0	0	8	12-0	2	14	.271	.364	.313	90	0	2-2	.989	5	145	93	2b24,S4		0.6
1966	Chi N	41	38	8	6	2	0	0	3	4-0	0	10	.158	.227	.211	26	-4	0-0	.977	-2	87	93	2b12,3b3,S2		-0.5
1967	Chi N	4	1	0	0	0	0	0	0	0-0	0	1	.000	.000	.000	-96	0	0-0	—	0			/H		0.0
Total	10	643	1715	248	418	67	19	9	123	185-9	12	224	.244	.320	.321	78	-47	19-26	.970	-13	97	92	2b398,3b90,S15/1OL		-3.6

AMARAL, RICH Richard Louis B4.1.1962 Visalia CA BR/TR/6-0/175* [ChiN83 2/34] d5.27 Col UCLA OF(232/101/52)

1991	Sea A	14	16	2	1	0	0	0	0	1-0	1	5	.063	.167	.063	-34	-3	0-0	1.000	1	164	256	2b5,3b2,S2/1D	49	-0.2
1992	Sea A	35	100	9	24	3	0	1	7	5-0	0	16	.240	.276	.300	61	-6	4-2	.955	1	115	121	3b17,S17,O3(3/1/1),1b2/2		-0.4
1993	Sea A	110	373	53	108	24	1	1	44	33-0	3	54	.290	.348	.367	92	-3	19-11	.975	15	104	102	2b77,3b19,S14,1b3,D9	15	1.6
1994	Sea A	77	228	37	60	10	2	4	18	24-1	1	28	.263	.333	.377	82	-6	5-1	.943	2	103	79	2b42,O16(14/2/0),S7,1b2,D6		-0.2
1995	†Sea A	90	238	45	67	14	2	2	19	21-0	1	33	.282	.342	.382	87	-4	21-2	.992	3	102	187	O73(53/29/8)/D		0.1
1996	Sea A	118	312	69	91	11	3	1	29	47-0	5	55	.292	.392	.356	91	-2	25-6	1.000	-5	106	62	O91(63/26/5),2b15,1b10/3D		-0.4
1997	†Sea A	89	190	34	54	5	0	1	21	10-0	3	34	.284	.327	.326	72	-8	12-8	1.000	-3	94	0	O52(39/9/6),1b14,2b11/3SD		-1.2
1998	Sea A	73	134	25	37	6	0	1	4	13-0	1	24	.276	.342	.343	79	-4	11-1	1.000	-3	104	113	O52(43/4/9),2b11,1b7/3D	33	-0.5
1999	Bal A	91	137	21	38	8	1	0	11	15-0	1	20	.277	.348	.350	83	-3	9-6	1.000	1	112	0	O50(14/18/19),D18,1b2,2b2/3		-0.4
2000	Bal A	30	60	10	13	1	1	0	6	7-0	0	8	.217	.299	.267	47	-5	6-2	1.000	4	130	133	O19(3/12/4)/1D	42	-0.1
Total	10	727	1788	305	493	82	10	11	159	176-1	16	277	.276	.344	.351	82	-44	112-39	.996	16	104	89	O356L,2b164,D55,1b42,3b42,S41	139	-1.7

AMARO, RUBEN Ruben Jr. B2.12.1965 Philadelphia PA BB/TR/5-10/175(170-191) [CalA87 11/291] d6.8 f-Ruben Col Stanford

1991	Cal A	10	23	0	5	1	0	0	2	3-1	0	2	.217	.308	.261	59	-1	0-0	1.000	-1	51	578	O5(3/0/2),2b4/D		-0.2
1992	Phi N	126	374	43	82	15	6	7	34	37-1	9	54	.219	.303	.348	84	-8	11-5	.992	5	111	85	O113(27/27/68)		-0.6
1993	Phi N	25	48	7	16	2	2	1	6	6-0	0	5	.333	.400	.521	149	3	0-0	.963	1	107	140	O16(3/8/6)		0.4
1994	Cle A	26	23	5	5	1	0	2	5	2-0	1	3	.217	.280	.522	100	0	2-1	.909	0	146	0	O12(1/10/1),D3		0.0
1995	†Cle A	28	60	5	12	3	0	1	7	4-0	2	6	.200	.273	.300	48	-5	1-3	1.000	-0	103	0	O22(5/14/6),D3	34	-0.6
1996	Phi N	61	117	14	37	10	0	2	15	9-0	3	18	.316	.380	.453	118	4	0-0	1.000	-0	108	0	O35(0/7/28)/1		0.2
1997	Phi N	117	175	18	41	6	1	2	21	21-0	2	24	.234	.320	.314	69	-8	1-1	.987	2	112	107	O72(26/37/15)/1		-0.7
1998	Phi N	92	107	7	20	5	0	1	10	6-0	1	15	.187	.244	.262	29	-11	0-0	1.000	0	76	258	O51(43/3/6)		-1.2
Total	8	485	927	99	218	43	9	16	100	88-2	16	128	.235	.310	.353	80	-26	15-10	.989	6	106	98	O326(108/106/132),D7,2b4,1b2	34	-2.7

AMARO, RUBEN Ruben Sr. (Mora) B1.6.1936 Nueva Laredo, Tamaulipas, Mexico BR/TR/5-11/170* d7.15 C6 s-Ruben

1958	StL N	40	76	8	17	2	1	0	5	5-1	0	8	.224	.272	.276	44	-6	0-1	.948	-1	95	111	S36/2		-0.6
1960	Phi N	92	264	25	61	9	1	0	16	21-2	2	32	.231	.292	.273	56	-16	0-1	.965	-8	95	94	S92		-1.8
1961	Phi N	135	381	34	98	14	9	1	32	53-2	2	59	.257	.351	.349	88	-5	1-0	.970	7	103	109	S132,1b3/2		1.2
1962	Phi N	79	226	24	55	10	0	0	19	30-4	1	28	.243	.330	.288	71	-8	5-2	.968	6	103	107	S78/1		0.5
1963	Phi N	115	217	25	47	9	2	2	19	19-6	0	31	.217	.276	.304	69	-9	0-1	.950	1	94	94	S63,3b45,1b5		-0.9
1964	Phi N	129	299	31	79	11	0	4	34	16-2	1	37	.264	.307	.341	84	-7	1-6	.971	-5	89	109	S79,1b58,2b3,3b3/OL		-0.9
1965	Phi N	118	184	26	39	7	0	0	15	27-3	1	22	.212	.312	.250	63	-8	1-1	.990	-6	162	101	1b60,S60,2b6		-1.1
1966	NY A	14	23	0	5	0	0	0	3	0-0	0	2	.217	.217	.217	26	-2	0-0	.977	2	108	177	S14	133	0.1
1967	NY A	130	417	31	93	12	0	1	17	43-4	1	49	.223	.297	.259	68	-16	3-2	.973	3	107	109	S123,3b3,1b2		0.2
1968	NY A	47	41	3	5	1	0	0	9	9-0	0	6	.122	.280	.146	33	-3	0-0	.962	-4	85	113	S23,1b22		-0.7
1969	Cal A	41	27	4	6	0	0	0	1	4-0	0	6	.222	.323	.222	57	-1	0-0	1.000	-2	0	37	1b18,2b9,S5,3b2		-0.4
Total	11	940	2155	211	505	75	13	8	156	227-24	10	280	.234	.309	.292	70	-81	11-14	.967	-3	99	105	S705,1b169,3b53,2b20/OL	133	-4.0

AMBLER, WAYNE Wayne Harper B11.8.1915 Abington PA D1.3.1998 Ponte Vedra Beach FL BR/TR/5-8.5/165 d6.4 Col Duke

1937	Phi A	56	162	3	35	5	0	0	13	13	0	8	.216	.274	.247	33	-17	1-0	.955	-1	102	102	2b56		-1.4
1938	Phi A	120	393	42	92	21	2	0	38	48	0	31	.234	.317	.298	56	-26	2-1	.942	-16	94	69	S116,2b4		-3.1
1939	Phi A	95	227	15	48	13	0	0	24	22	0	25	.211	.281	.269	42	-20	1-0	.954	-2	104	80	S77,2b19		-1.6
Total	3	271	782	60	175	39	2	0	73	83	0	64	.224	.298	.279	47	-63	4-1	.946	-20	97	73	S193,2b79		-6.1

AMBRES, CHIP Raymond Payne B12.19.1979 Beaumont TX BR/TR/6-1/190 d7.20

2005	KC A	53	145	25	35	8	0	4	9	16-1	2	32	.241	.323	.379	92	-1	3-2	.988	-0	99	104	O47(23/24/0),D2		-0.2

AMELUNG, ED Edward Allen B4.13.1959 Fullerton CA BL/TL/5-11/185* d7.28 Col San Diego St.

1984	LA N	34	46	7	10	0	0	0	4	2-0	0	4	.217	.250	.217	32	-4	3-2	1.000	1	136	0	O23(9/4/11)		-0.4
1986	LA N	8	11	0	1	0	0	0	0	2-0	0	4	.091	.091	.091	-53	-2	0-0	1.000	1	140	0	O4(0/2/2)		-0.2
Total	2	42	57	7	11	0	0	0	4	2-0	0	8	.193	.220	.193	17	-6	3-2	1.000	1	137	0	O27(9/6/13)		-0.6

AMEZAGA, ALFREDO Alfredo (Delgado) B1.16.1978 Ciudad Obregon, Sonora, Mexico BB/TR (BR 2002)/5-10/165* [AnaA99 13/401] d5.24 Col St. Petersburg (FL) JC

2002	Ana A	12	13	3	7	2	0	0	2	0-0	0	1	.538	.538	.692	228	2	1-0	1.000	-0	100	44	S5		0.3
2003	Ana A	37	105	15	22	3	2	2	7	9-0	1	23	.210	.278	.333	63	-6	2-2	.970	-0	93	79	S24,3b13		-0.5
2004	†Ana A	73	93	12	15	2	0	2	11	3-0	3	24	.161	.212	.247	20	-11	3-2	.990	-0	109	43	S32,3b26,2b16		-0.9
2005	Col N	2	3	1	1	0	0	0	0	0-0	0	1	.333	.333	.333	66	0	0-0	—	-0	0	0	/3		0.0
	Pit N	3	3	1	0	0	0	0	0	1-0	0	1	.000	.250	.000	-27	-1	1-0	1.000	0	147	323	/S		0.0
	Year	5	6	2	1	0	0	0	0	1-0	0	2	.167	.286	.167	22	-1	1-0	1.000	0	0	0	/3S		0.0
Total	4	127	217	32	45	7	2	4	20	13-0	4	48	.207	.265	.313	53	-16	7-4	.982	-0	101	63	S62,3b40,2b16		-1.1

AMOROS, SANDY Edmundo (Isasi) B1.30.1930 Havana, Cuba D6.27.1992 Miami FL BL/TL/5-7.5/170* d8.22 Negro Lg 1950

1952	†Bro N	20	44	10	11	3	1	0	3	5	0	14	.250	.327	.364	90	-1	1-0	1.000	-1	95	0	O10(3/4/7)		-0.2
1954	Bro N	79	263	44	72	16	6	9	34	31	1	24	.274	.353	.490	113	5	4-1	.987	1	99	128	O70(68/1/2)		0.1
1955	†Bro N	119	388	59	96	16	7	10	51	55-5	6	45	.247	.347	.402	96	-5	10-5	.972	-1	93	127	O109(102/8/5)		-0.8
1956	†Bro N	114	292	53	76	11	8	16	58	59-6	1	51	.260	.385	.517	130	14	3-4	.955	-7	83	60	O86(79/5/10)		0.2
1957	Bro N	106	238	40	66	7	1	7	26	46-3	3	42	.277	.399	.403	107	-5	3-2	.984	-1	102	68	O66(65/1/2)		0.0
1959	LA N	5	5	1	1	0	0	0	0	0-0	0	1	.200	.200	.200	6	-1	0-0	—	0			/H		-0.1
1960	LA N	9	14	1	2	0	0	0	0	3-1	0	2	.143	.294	.143	23	-1	0-0	1.000	1	107	489	O3(0/1/3)		-0.1
	Det A	65	67	7	10	0	0	1	7	12-1	0	10	.149	.275	.194	29	-7	0-0	1.000	-1	95	0	O10(1/9/0)		-0.8
Total	7	517	1311	215	334	55	23	43	180	211-16	11	189	.255	.361	.430	105	13	18-15	.976	-8	94	94	O354(318/29/29)		-1.7

ANDERSON, ALF Alfred Walton B1.28.1914 Gainesville GA D6.23.1985 Albany GA BR/TR/5-11/165 d4.20 Mil 1944-45 Col Georgia

1941	Pit N	70	223	32	48	7	2	1	10	14	1	30	.215	.265	.278	53	-15	2	.931	-6	100	94	S58		-1.7
1942	Pit N	54	166	24	45	4	1	0	7	18	0	19	.271	.342	.307	89	-2	4	.942	-11	85	73	S48		-1.1
1946	Pit N	2	1	0	0	0	0	0	0	1	0	0	.000	.500	.000	47	0	0	—	0			/H		0.0
Total	3	126	390	56	93	11	3	1	17	33	1	49	.238	.300	.290	68	-17	6	.936	-17	94	85	S106		-2.8

ANDERSON, ANDY Andy Holm B11.13.1922 Bremerton WA D7.18.1982 Seattle WA BR/TR/5-11/172 d5.10

1948	StL A	51	87	13	24	5	1	1	12	8	1	15	.276	.337	.391	91	-1	0-0	.917	-1	118	95	2b21,S10,1b2		-0.1
1949	StL A	71	136	10	17	3	0	1	5	14	0	21	.125	.207	.169	-0	-20	0-1	.957	-3	93	89	S24,2b8,3b8		-2.2
Total	2	122	223	23	41	8	1	2	17	22	1	36	.184	.257	.256	35	-21	0-1	.946	-4	90	93	S54,2b29,3b8,1b2		-2.3

ANDERSON, BRADY Brady Kevin B1.18.1964 Silver Spring MD BL/TL/6-1/185(185-202) [BosA85 10/257] d4.4 Col California-Irvine

1988	Bos A	41	148	14	34	5	3	0	12	15-0	1	35	.230	.315	.304	72	-5	4-2	.989	0	95	141	O41(0/17/25)		-0.6
	Bal A	53	177	17	35	8	1	1	9	8-0	0	40	.198	.232	.271	41	-14	6-4	.981	4	121	46	O49C		-1.1
	Year	94	325	31	69	13	4	1	21	23-0	1	75	.212	.272	.286	56	-19	10-6	.984	4	108	92	O90(0/66/25)		-1.7
1989	Bal A	94	266	44	55	12	2	4	16	43-6	3	45	.207	.324	.312	82	-5	16-4	.985	-2	98	75	O79(3/75/1),D8		-0.5
1990	Bal A	89	234	24	54	5	2	3	24	31-2	5	46	.231	.324	.308	83	-5	15-2	.987	-4	114	86	O63(44/21/1),D11	42	0.0
1991	Bal A	113	256	40	59	12	3	2	27	38-0	5	44	.230	.338	.324	88	-3	12-5	.981	-3	93	74	O101(75/26/9),D2	17	-0.5
1992	Bal A★	159	623	100	169	28	10	21	80	98-14	9	98	.271	.373	.449	127	25	53-16	.986	5	106	89	O158(148/7/3)		3.2
1993	Bal A	142	560	87	147	36	8	13	66	82-4	10	99	.262	.363	.425	107	8	24-12	.993	3	98	81	O140(126/18/3),D2	15	0.1
1994	Bal A	111	453	78	119	25	5	12	48	57-3	10	75	.263	.356	.419	94	-3	31-1	.996	-2	101	55	O109(76/38/5)		-0.1
1995	Bal A	143	554	108	145	33	10	16	64	87-4	10	111	.262	.371	.444	109	9	26-7	.989	-12	91	11	O142(121/40/0)		-0.3

YEAR	TM LG	G	AB	R	H	2B	3B	HR	RBI	BB-IB	HP	SO	AVG	OBP	SLG	AOPS	ABR	SB-CS	FA	FR	RNG	THR	GAMES AT POSITION	DL	BFW
1996	†Bal A★	149	579	117	172	37	5	50	110	76-1	22	106	.297	.396	.637	157	51	21-8	.992	-8	92	113	O143C,D2		4.2
1997	†Bal A★	151	590	97	170	39	7	18	73	84-6	19	105	.288	.393	.469	128	28	18-12	.989	-12	89	32	O124C,D25		1.5
1998	Bal A	133	479	84	113	28	3	18	51	75-1	15	78	.236	.356	.420	103	4	21-7	.985	-14	87	13	O130C	18	-0.6
1999	Bal A	150	564	109	159	28	5	24	81	96-7	24	105	.282	.404	.477	129	30	36-7	.997	-11	91	35	O136(9/129/0),D10		2.3
2000	Bal A	141	506	89	130	26	0	19	50	92-5	8	103	.257	.375	.421	108	10	16-9	.997	-4	102	15	O127(16/88/24),D11		0.5
2001	Bal A	131	430	50	87	12	3	8	45	60-4	1	77	.202	.311	.300	66	-21	12-4	.988	4	105	111	O120(56/6/66),D4		-2.0
2002	Cle A	34	80	4	13	4	0	1	5	18-2	1	23	.162	.327	.250	56	-4	4-0	.981	-2	96	0	O29(14/16/2)/D		-0.5
Total	15	1834	6499	1062	1661	338	67	210	761	960-59	154	1190	.256	.362	.425	108	105	315-100	.989	-54	97	60	O1691(688/927/139),D76	92	5.5

ANDERSON, BRIAN   Brian Nikola   B3.11.1982 Tucson AZ   BR/TR/6-2/205   d8.16 Col Arizona

YEAR	TM LG	G	AB	R	H	2B	3B	HR	RBI	BB-IB	HP	SO	AVG	OBP	SLG	AOPS	ABR	SB-CS	FA	FR	RNG	THR	GAMES AT POSITION	DL	BFW
2005	Chi A	13	34	3	6	1	0	2	3	0-0	0	12	.176	.176	.382	41	-3	1-0	1.000	0	86	193	O12(9/5/1)		-0.3

ANDERSON, DAVE   David Carter   B8.1.1960 Louisville KY   BR/TR/6-2/185*   [LAN81 1/22]   d5.8 Col Memphis

YEAR	TM LG	G	AB	R	H	2B	3B	HR	RBI	BB-IB	HP	SO	AVG	OBP	SLG	AOPS	ABR	SB-CS	FA	FR	RNG	THR	GAMES AT POSITION	DL	BFW
1983	LA N	61	115	12	19	4	2	1	2	12-1	0	15	.165	.244	.261	40	-10	6-3	.969	-5	88	93	S53/3		-1.1
1984	LA N	121	374	51	94	16	2	3	34	45-4	2	55	.251	.331	.329	87	-5	15-5	.965	19	106	109	S111,3b11		2.7
1985	†LA N	77	221	24	44	6	0	4	18	35-3	1	42	.199	.310	.281	68	-9	5-4	.957	9	116	151	3b51,S25,2b2	66	0.2
1986	LA N	92	216	31	53	9	0	1	15	22-1	0	39	.245	.314	.301	76	-7	5-1	.976	0	101	116	3b51,S34,2b5	58	-0.4
1987	LA N	108	265	32	62	12	3	1	13	24-1	1	43	.234	.297	.313	64	-14	9-5	.977	3	99	87	S65,3b35,2b5	20	-0.4
1988	†LA N	116	285	31	71	10	2	2	20	32-4	1	45	.249	.325	.319	89	-4	4-2	.986	9	105	127	S82,3b12,2b11		1.2
1989	LA N	87	140	15	32	2	0	1	14	17-1	0	26	.229	.310	.264	67	-6	2-0	.990	-8	73	114	S33,3b18,2b7		-1.2
1990	SF N	60	100	14	35	5	1	1	6	3-0	0	20	.350	.369	.450	128	3	1-2	1.000	-4	97	65	S29,2b13,1b3,3b2		0.0
1991	SF N	100	226	24	56	5	2	2	13	12-2	0	35	.248	.286	.314	71	-10	2-4	.956	-0	97	133	S63,1b16,3b11,2b6		-0.9
1992	LA N	51	84	10	24	4	0	3	8	4-0	0	11	.286	.311	.440	114	1	0-4	.974	-1	82	106	3b26,S7	31	-0.1
Total	10	873	2026	244	490	73	12	19	143	206-17	5	331	.242	.312	.318	78	-61	49-30	.970	23	100	105	S502,3b218,2b49,1b19	175	0.0

ANDERSON, DWAIN   Dwain Cleaven   B11.23.1947 Oakland CA   BR/TR/5-11/165(165-180)   d9.3

YEAR	TM LG	G	AB	R	H	2B	3B	HR	RBI	BB-IB	HP	SO	AVG	OBP	SLG	AOPS	ABR	SB-CS	FA	FR	RNG	THR	GAMES AT POSITION	DL	BFW
1971	Oak A	16	37	3	10	2	1	0	3	5-1	1	9	.270	.372	.378	115	1	0-1	.968	-2	92	112	S10,2b5/3		-0.1
1972	Oak A	3	7	2	0	0	0	0	0	1-0	0	4	.000	.125	.000	-64	-1	0-0	1.000	-1	60	0	/S3		-0.2
	StL N	57	135	12	36	4	1	1	8	8-1	1	23	.267	.313	.333	84	-3	0-1	.952	1	96	86	S43,3b13/2		0.1
1973	StL N	18	17	5	2	0	0	0	0	4-0	0	4	.118	.286	.118	16	-2	0-0	.500	-2	0	93	S3,O2C		-0.4
	SD N	53	107	11	13	0	0	0	3	14-0	0	29	.121	.223	.121	-2	-15	2-0	.932	2	97	89	S39,3b6		-1.4
	Year	71	124	16	15	0	0	0	3	18-0	0	33	.121	.232	.121	1	-17	2-0	.919	-0	94	86	S42,3b6,O2C		-1.8
1974	Cle A	2	3	0	1	0	0	0	0	0-0	0	1	.333	.333	.333	93	0	0-0	1.000	-1	0	0	/2		-0.1
Total	4	149	306	33	62	6	2	1	14	32-2	2	70	.203	.282	.245	51	-20	2-2	.940	-6	94	87	S96,3b21,2b7,O2C		-2.1

ANDERSON, GOAT   Edward John   B1.13.1880 Cleveland OH   D3.15.1923 South Bend IN   BL/TR   d4.11

YEAR	TM LG	G	AB	R	H	2B	3B	HR	RBI	BB-IB	HP	SO	AVG	OBP	SLG	AOPS	ABR	SB-CS	FA	FR	RNG	THR	GAMES AT POSITION	DL	BFW
1907	Pit N	127	413	73	85	3	1	1	12	80	6		.206	.343	.225	77	-5	27	.953	-0	94	107	O117(2/24/91),2b5		-1.2

ANDERSON, FERRELL   Ferrell Jack "Andy"   B1.9.1918 Maple City KS   D3.12.1978 Joplin MO   BR/TR/6-1/200*   d4.16 Col Kansas

YEAR	TM LG	G	AB	R	H	2B	3B	HR	RBI	BB-IB	HP	SO	AVG	OBP	SLG	AOPS	ABR	SB-CS	FA	FR	RNG	THR	GAMES AT POSITION	DL	BFW
1946	Bro N	79	199	19	51	10	2	0	14	18	4	21	.256	.330	.337	89	-3	1	.964	-2	147	116	C70		0.1
1953	StL N	18	35	1	10	2	0	0	1	0	0	4	.286	.286	.343	63	-5	0-0	1.000	-1	69	80	C12		-0.2
Total	2	97	234	20	61	12	2	0	15	18	4	25	.261	.324	.338	85	-5	1	.968	-0	138	112	C82		-0.1

ANDERSON, GARRET   Garret Joseph   B6.30.1972 Los Angeles CA   BL/TL/6-3/215(190-228)   [CalA90 4/125]   d7.27

YEAR	TM LG	G	AB	R	H	2B	3B	HR	RBI	BB-IB	HP	SO	AVG	OBP	SLG	AOPS	ABR	SB-CS	FA	FR	RNG	THR	GAMES AT POSITION	DL	BFW
1994	Cal A	5	13	0	5	0	0	0	1	0-0	0	2	.385	.385	.385	98	0	0-0	1.000	1	160	0	O4L		0.0
1995	Cal A	106	374	50	120	19	1	16	69	19-4	1	65	.321	.352	.505	122	10	6-2	.978	5	115	109	O100(99/1/1)/D		1.1
1996	Cal A	150	607	79	173	33	2	12	72	27-5	0	84	.285	.314	.405	79	-21	7-9	.979	-2	105	48	O146(140/3/6)/D		-2.7
1997	Ana A	154	624	76	189	36	3	8	92	30-6	1	70	.303	.334	.409	93	-7	10-4	.992	10	111	149	O148(130/27/4),D4		-0.1
1998	Ana A	156	622	62	183	41	7	15	79	29-8	1	80	.294	.325	.455	99	-3	8-3	.983	5	108	104	O155(39/0/122)		-0.4
1999	Ana A	157	620	88	188	36	2	21	80	34-8	0	81	.303	.336	.469	104	2	3-4	.993	2	107	70	O153(32/116/6),D4		0.2
2000	Ana A	159	647	92	185	40	3	35	117	24-5	0	87	.286	.307	.519	102	-1	7-6	.990	-8	95	61	O148(0/137/15),D10		-0.9
2001	Ana A	161	672	83	194	39	2	28	123	27-4	0	100	.289	.314	.478	103	1	13-6	.994	1	100	94	O149(144/12/0),D12		-0.3
2002	†Ana A★	158	638	93	195	56	3	29	123	30-11	0	80	.306	.332	.539	130	25	6-4	.994	-2	97	80	O147(137/14/0),D10		1.7
2003	Ana A★	159	638	80	201	49	4	29	116	31-10	0	83	.315	.345	.541	134	30	6-3	.997	13	112	151	O144L,D15		3.5
2004	Ana A	112	442	57	133	20	1	14	75	29-6	1	75	.301	.343	.446	109	5	2-1	.991	-3	95	92	O94C,D18	49	0.2
2005	†LA A★	142	575	68	163	34	1	17	96	23-8	0	84	.283	.308	.435	97	-4	1-1	.976	-2	96	72	O106L,D36	49	-1.2
Total	12	1619	6472	828	1929	403	29	224	1043	303-75	5	891	.298	.327	.473	106	37	69-43	.988	20	104	93	O1494(975/404/154),D111	49	1.1

ANDERSON, GEORGE   George Jendrus "Andy" (Born George Andrew Jendrus)   B9.26.1889 Cleveland OH   D5.28.1962 Cleveland OH   BL/TR/5-8/160   d5.26

YEAR	TM LG	G	AB	R	H	2B	3B	HR	RBI	BB-IB	HP	SO	AVG	OBP	SLG	AOPS	ABR	SB-CS	FA	FR	RNG	THR	GAMES AT POSITION	DL	BFW
1914	Bro F	98	364	58	115	13	3	3	24	31	4	50	.316	.376	.393	110	0	16	.946	2	104	109	O92(70/21/1)		-0.2
1915	Bro F	136	511	70	135	23	9	3	39	52	8	54	.264	.342	.356	97	-9	20	.956	-4	97	94	O134(40/12/82)		-2.1
1918	StL N	35	132	20	39	4	5	0	6	15	3	7	.295	.380	.402	143	7	0	.956	-3	94	49	O35R		0.2
Total	3	269	1007	148	289	40	17	5	69	98	15	111	.287	.359	.375	108	-2	36	.952	-5	96	94	O261(110/33/118)		-2.1

ANDERSON, SPARKY   George Lee   B2.22.1934 Bridgewater SD   BR/TR/5-9/170   d4.10   M26/C1   HF2000

YEAR	TM LG	G	AB	R	H	2B	3B	HR	RBI	BB-IB	HP	SO	AVG	OBP	SLG	AOPS	ABR	SB-CS	FA	FR	RNG	THR	GAMES AT POSITION	DL	BFW
1959	Phi N	152	477	42	104	9	3	0	34	42-1	1	53	.218	.282	.249	43	-39	6-9	.984	1	98	79	2b152		-3.0

ANDERSON, HAL   Harold   B2.10.1904 St.Louis MO   D5.1.1974 St.Louis MO   BR/TR/5-11/160   d4.12

YEAR	TM LG	G	AB	R	H	2B	3B	HR	RBI	BB-IB	HP	SO	AVG	OBP	SLG	AOPS	ABR	SB-CS	FA	FR	RNG	THR	GAMES AT POSITION	DL	BFW
1932	Chi A	9	32	4	8	0	0	0	2	0-0	0	5	.250	.250	.250	32	-1	0-1	1.000	1	103	162	O9C		-0.3

ANDERSON, HARRY   Harry Walter   B9.10.1931 North East MD   D6.11.1998 Greenville DE   BL/TR/6-3/210*   d4.18 Col West Chester

YEAR	TM LG	G	AB	R	H	2B	3B	HR	RBI	BB-IB	HP	SO	AVG	OBP	SLG	AOPS	ABR	SB-CS	FA	FR	RNG	THR	GAMES AT POSITION	DL	BFW
1957	Phi N	118	400	53	107	15	4	17	61	36-7	6	61	.268	.333	.452	113	7	2-3	.986	5	113	76	O109(107/0/2)		0.5
1958	Phi N	140	515	80	155	34	6	23	97	59-10	3	95	.301	.373	.524	137	28	0-2	.975	-7	93	63	O87L,1b49		1.3
1959	Phi N	142	508	50	122	28	6	14	65	43-14	5	95	.240	.304	.402	85	-11	1-1	.980	10	105	158	O137L		-1.0
1960	Phi N	38	93	10	23	2	0	5	12	10-1	1	19	.247	.333	.430	107	1	0-0	1.000	-4	92	86	O16L,1b12		-0.1
	Cin N	42	66	6	11	3	0	1	9	11-0	0	20	.167	.282	.258	49	-4	0-0	.990	-1	90	69	1b15,O4(2/0/2)		-0.6
	Year	80	159	16	34	5	0	6	21	21-1	1	39	.214	.311	.358	82	-4	0-0	.989	-5	89	57	1b27,O20(18/0/2)		-0.7
1961	Cin N	4	4	0	1	0	0	0	0	0-0	0	1	.250	.250	.250	33	0	0-0	—	0			/H		0.0
Total	5	484	1586	199	419	82	16	60	242	159-32	16	291	.264	.334	.450	109	21	3-6	.982	6	104	105	O353(349/0/4),1b76		0.1

ANDERSON, JIM   James Lea   B2.23.1957 Los Angeles CA   BR/TR/6-0/170*   [AnaA75 2/25]   d7.2

YEAR	TM LG	G	AB	R	H	2B	3B	HR	RBI	BB-IB	HP	SO	AVG	OBP	SLG	AOPS	ABR	SB-CS	FA	FR	RNG	THR	GAMES AT POSITION	DL	BFW
1978	Cal A	48	108	6	21	7	0	0	7	11-1	1	16	.194	.267	.259	51	-7	0-0	.955	-3	87	92	S47/2		-0.6
1979	†Cal A	96	234	33	58	13	1	3	23	17-0	1	31	.248	.298	.350	77	-7	3-2	.949	-2	95	94	S82,3b10,2b6,C3		-0.3
1980	Sea A	116	317	46	72	7	0	8	30	27-1	3	39	.227	.292	.325	68	-14	2-4	.958	7	113	105	S65,3b33,2b2/CD		-0.3
1981	Sea A	70	162	12	33	7	0	2	19	17-0	1	29	.204	.283	.284	61	-8	3-5	.947	1	104	115	S68,3b2		-0.3
1983	Tex A	50	102	8	22	1	1	0	6	5-0	0	8	.216	.252	.245	38	-9	1-2	.962	3	137	84	S27,2b17,3b3,O3(2/0/1)/CD		-0.4
1984	Tex A	39	47	2	5	0	0	0	1	4-0	0	7	.106	.176	.106	-3	-19	0-0	.989	4	107	110	S31,3b6/2		-0.2
Total	6	419	970	107	211	35	2	13	86	81-2	5	130	.218	.280	.298	60	-53	9-13	.955	10	103	103	S320,3b54,2b27,D7,C5,O3(2/0/1)		-2.1

ANDERSON, JOHN   John Joseph "Honest John"   B12.14.1873 Sarpsborg, Norway   D7.23.1949 Worcester MA   BB/TR/6-2/180   d9.8

YEAR	TM LG	G	AB	R	H	2B	3B	HR	RBI	BB-IB	HP	SO	AVG	OBP	SLG	AOPS	ABR	SB-CS	FA	FR	RNG	THR	GAMES AT POSITION	DL	BFW
1894	Bro N	17	63	14	19	1	3	1	19	3	0	3	.302	.333	.460	96	-1	7	.778	3	0	0	O16(15/1/0)/3		-0.4
1895	Bro N	103	423	77	122	11	14	10	89	12	5	29	.288	.316	.452	105	-1	24	.882	-8	68	117	O102(90/0/12)		-1.5
1896	Bro N	108	430	70	135	23	17	1	55	18	2	23	.314	.344	.453	116	7	37	.942	-2	98	174	O68(33/9/26),1b42		0.1
1897	Bro N	117	492	93	160	28	12	4	85	17	7		.325	.357	.451	120	12	29	.936	-2	65	60	O115L,1b3		-0.1
1898	Bro N	6	21	1	3	2	0	0	2	1	1		.143	.217	.238	31	-2	0	1.000	-0	0	0	O5(2/1/2)		-0.2
	Was N	110	430	70	131	28	18	9	71	23	12		.305	.357	.516	150	24	18	.948	7	155	88	O93(13/78/2),1b17		2.3
	Bro N	19	69	11	19	3	4	0	8	5	1		.275	.333	.435	120	1	2	.966	0	0	0	O17L,1b2		0.0
	Year	135	520	82	153	33	22	9	81	29	14		.294	.348	.494	141	24	20	.952	7	145	98	O115(32/79/4),1b19		2.1
1899	Bro N	117	439	65	118	18	7	4	92	27	4		.269	.317	.369	86	-10	25	.933	-3	55	70	O76(7/61/8),1b41		-1.6
1901	Mil A	138	576	90	190	46	7	8	99	24	3		.330	.360	.476	137	28	35	.982	-4	99	106	1b125,O13(12/0/1)		2.5
1902	StL A	126	524	60	149	29	6	4	85	21	0		.284	.316	.385	95	-5	15	.985	-9	67	110	1b126,O3(2/0/1)		-1.5
1903	StL A	138	550	65	156	34	6	2	78	23	0		.284	.312	.385	111	7	16	.986	5	111	113	1b133,O7(2/3/2)		1.0
1904	NY A	143	558	62	155	27	12	3	82	23	6		.278	.313	.385	115	8	20	.956	0	76	35	O112(46/52/13),1b33		0.2
1905	NY A	32	99	12	23	3	1	0	14	8	1		.232	.296	.283	75	-3	9	.900	-1	139	0	O22(1/19/2),1b5		-0.5
	Was A	101	400	50	116	21	6	1	38	22	2		.290	.330	.380	130	13	22	.960	-1	64	38	O97(16/3/78),1b4		0.7
	Year	133	499	62	139	24	7	1	52	30	3		.279	.323	.361	117	9	31	.949	-2	76	32	O119(17/22/80),1b7		0.2
1906	Was A	151	583	62	158	25	4	3	70	19	2		.271	.296	.343	92	1	39	.953	7	100	44	O151L		-0.1

YEAR	TM LG	G	AB	R	H	2B	3B	HR	RBI	BB-IB	HP	SO	AVG	OBP	SLG	AOPS	ABR	SB-CS	FA	FR	RNG	THR	GAMES AT POSITION	DL	BFW
1907	Was A	87	333	33	96	12	4	0	44	34	3		.288	.359	.348	136	15	19	.983	-1	85	45	1b61,O26L		1.3
1908	Chi A	68	355	36	93	17	1	0	47	30	1		.262	.321	.315	109	4	21	.963	-4	97	317	O87(13/2/72),1b9		-0.3
Total	14	1636	6345	871	1843	328	124	50	978	310	53	55	.290	.329	.405	114	98	338	.939	-11	86	87	O1010(561/229/219),1b599/3		1.9

ANDERSON, KENT Kent McKay B8.12.1963 Florence SC BR/TR/6-1/180* [CalA84 4/86] d4.15 b-Mike Col South Carolina-Aiken

YEAR	TM LG	G	AB	R	H	2B	3B	HR	RBI	BB-IB	HP	SO	AVG	OBP	SLG	AOPS	ABR	SB-CS	FA	FR	RNG	THR	GAMES AT POSITION	DL	BFW
1989	Cal A	86	223	27	51	6	1	0	17	17-0	1	42	.229	.285	.265	57	-13	1-2	.972	8	109	134	S70,2b7,3b5,O2R/D		-0.1
1990	Cal A	49	143	16	44	6	1	1	5	13-1	1	19	.308	.369	.385	113	3	0-2	.964	7	97	116	S28,3b16,2b5	38	1.1
Total	2	135	366	43	95	12	2	1	22	30-1	2	61	.260	.318	.311	79	-10	1-4	.969	14	105	129	S98,3b21,2b12,O2R/D	38	1.0

ANDERSON, MARLON Marlon Ordell B1.6.1974 Montgomery AL BL/TR/5-11/198* [PhiN95 2/42] d9.8 Col South Alabama

YEAR	TM LG	G	AB	R	H	2B	3B	HR	RBI	BB-IB	HP	SO	AVG	OBP	SLG	AOPS	ABR	SB-CS	FA	FR	RNG	THR	GAMES AT POSITION	DL	BFW
1998	Phi N	17	43	4	14	3	0	1	4	1-0	0	6	.326	.333	.465	109	0	2-0	.978	1	112	103	2b9		0.2
1999	Phi N	129	452	48	114	26	4	5	54	24-1	2	61	.252	.292	.360	63	-27	13-2	.979	-7	95	86	2b121		-2.5
2000	Phi N	41	162	10	37	8	4	5	15	12-0	0	22	.228	.282	.309	49	-13	2-2	.989	-2	90	121	2b41		-1.3
2001	Phi N	147	522	66	153	30	2	11	61	35-5	2	74	.293	.337	.421	100	-1	8-5	.982	4	106	104	2b140		0.9
2002	Phi N	145	539	64	139	30	6	8	48	42-14	5	71	.258	.315	.380	92	-11	5-1	.970	-6	100	101	2b143		-0.9
2003	TB A	145	482	59	130	27	3	6	67	41-5	3	60	.270	.328	.376	88	-8	19-3	.973	-17	96	108	2b134,O3L,D4		-1.5
2004	†StL N	113	253	31	60	12	0	8	28	12-1	1	38	.237	.269	.379	66	-14	6-2	.969	-1	93	136	2b37,O36(28/0/11),1b2/D		-1.3
2005	NY N	123	235	31	62	9	0	7	19	18-0	1	45	.264	.316	.391	87	-5	6-1	.990	3	143	123	1b23,O23(9/0/14),2b20,D2		-0.3
Total	8	860	2688	316	709	145	16	47	296	185-26	14	377	.264	.312	.382	82	-79	61-16	.977	-25	99	103	2b645,O62(40/0/25),1b25,D7		-6.7

ANDERSON, MIKE Michael Allen B6.22.1951 Florence SC BR/TR/6-2/200(185-205) [PhiN69 1/6] d9.2 b-Kent

YEAR	TM LG	G	AB	R	H	2B	3B	HR	RBI	BB-IB	HP	SO	AVG	OBP	SLG	AOPS	ABR	SB-CS	FA	FR	RNG	THR	GAMES AT POSITION	DL	BFW
1971	Phi N	26	89	11	22	5	1	2	5	13-0	1	28	.247	.343	.393	108	1	0-0	.986	0	107	69	O26C		0.1
1972	Phi N	36	103	8	20	5	1	2	5	19-1	0	36	.194	.317	.320	80	-2	1-0	.987	4	111	257	O35(0/3/34)		0.1
1973	Phi N	87	193	32	49	9	1	8	28	19-4	1	53	.254	.321	.451	109	2	0-3	.981	0	103	96	O67(0/12/57)	24	-0.1
1974	Phi N	145	395	35	99	22	2	5	34	37-13	2	75	.251	.313	.354	83	-9	2-1	.980	10	117	160	O133(1/2/131)/1		-0.5
1975	Phi N	115	247	24	64	10	3	4	28	17-3	2	66	.259	.307	.372	85	-6	1-2	.977	4	109	131	O105(0/24/88),1b3		-0.5
1976	StL N	86	199	17	58	8	1	1	12	26-4	1	30	.291	.371	.357	107	3	1-1	.982	3	108	131	O58(24/2/33),1b5		0.3
1977	StL N	94	154	18	34	4	1	4	17	14-0	1	31	.221	.286	.338	67	-8	2-3	.980	2	113	118	O77(2/1/74)		-0.8
1978	Bal A	53	32	2	3	0	1	0	3	3-0	1	10	.094	.171	.156	-8	-5	0-0	.962	-1	92	0	O47(41/2/6)		-0.7
1979	Phi N	79	78	12	18	4	0	1	2	13-0	0	14	.231	.341	.321	78	-2	1-2	.973	3	118	130	O70(47/6/20)/P		-0.1
Total	9	721	1490	159	367	67	11	28	134	161-25	4	343	.246	.319	.362	88	-26	8-12	.980	26	111	135	O618(115/78/443),1b9/P	24	-2.2

ANDINO, ROBERT Robert Lazaro B4.25.1984 Miami FL BR/TR/6-0/170 d9.4

YEAR	TM LG	G	AB	R	H	2B	3B	HR	RBI	BB-IB	HP	SO	AVG	OBP	SLG	AOPS	ABR	SB-CS	FA	FR	RNG	THR	GAMES AT POSITION	DL	BFW
2005	Fla N	17	44	4	7	4	0	0	1	5-1	0	8	.159	.245	.250	32	-4	1-0	.956	-7	62	76	S17		-1.0

ANDRES, ERNIE Ernest Henry "Junie" B1.11.1918 Jeffersonville IN BR/TR/6-1/200 d4.16 Col Indiana

YEAR	TM LG	G	AB	R	H	2B	3B	HR	RBI	BB-IB	HP	SO	AVG	OBP	SLG	AOPS	ABR	SB-CS	FA	FR	RNG	THR	GAMES AT POSITION	DL	BFW
1946	Bos A	15	41	0	4	2	0	0	3	5-0	0	5	.098	.159	.146	-14	-6	0-0	1.000	1	114	45	3b15		-0.6

ANDREW, KIM Kim Darrell B11.14.1953 Glendale CA BR/TR/5-10/160 d4.16 Col Los Angeles Valley (CA) JC

YEAR	TM LG	G	AB	R	H	2B	3B	HR	RBI	BB-IB	HP	SO	AVG	OBP	SLG	AOPS	ABR	SB-CS	FA	FR	RNG	THR	GAMES AT POSITION	DL	BFW
1975	Bos A	2	2	0	1	0	0	0	0	0-0	0	0	.500	.500	.500	169	0	0-0	1.000	-0	76	0	2b2		0.0

ANDREWS, SHANE Darrell Shane B8.28.1971 Dallas TX BR/TR/6-1/215* [MonN90 1/11] d4.26

YEAR	TM LG	G	AB	R	H	2B	3B	HR	RBI	BB-IB	HP	SO	AVG	OBP	SLG	AOPS	ABR	SB-CS	FA	FR	RNG	THR	GAMES AT POSITION	DL	BFW
1995	Mon N	84	220	27	47	10	1	8	31	17-2	1	68	.214	.271	.377	67	-11	1-1	.973	-1	104	32	3b51,1b29		-1.4
1996	Mon N	127	375	43	85	15	2	19	64	35-8	2	119	.227	.295	.429	86	-9	3-1	.955	16	115	81	3b123		0.8
1997	Mon N	18	64	10	13	3	0	4	9	3-0	0	20	.203	.232	.438	73	-3	0-0	.895	3	121	204	3b18	151	0.0
1998	Mon N	150	492	48	117	30	1	25	69	58-3	0	137	.238	.314	.455	103	1	1-6	.954	18	118	109	3b147		1.8
1999	Mon N	98	281	28	51	8	0	11	37	43-2	0	88	.181	.287	.327	58	-19	1-0	.932	-1	109	79	3b82,1b18/D	21	-1.9
	Chi N	19	67	13	17	4	0	5	14	7-1	1	21	.254	.329	.537	116	1	0-1	.955	-1	98	194	3b19/1		0.0
	Year	117	348	41	68	12	0	16	51	50-3	1	109	.195	.295	.368	70	-18	1-1	.936	-1	107	104	3b101,1b19/D		-1.9
2000	Chi N	66	192	25	44	5	0	14	39	27-1	2	59	.229	.329	.474	101	-1	1-1	.907	4	112	120	3b58,1b6	101	0.3
2002	Bos A	7	13	2	1	1	0	0	1	0-0	0	5	.077	.200	.154	-4	-2	0-0	1.000	1	147	287	3b4,1b2/OLD		-0.1
Total	7	569	1704	196	375	76	4	86	263	191-17	7	515	.220	.299	.421	86	-43	7-10	.946	40	113	100	3b502,1b56,D2/OL	273	-0.5

ANDREWS, FRED Fred B5.4.1952 Lafayette LA BR/TR/5-8/152(152-163) [PhiN70 8/178] d9.26

YEAR	TM LG	G	AB	R	H	2B	3B	HR	RBI	BB-IB	HP	SO	AVG	OBP	SLG	AOPS	ABR	SB-CS	FA	FR	RNG	THR	GAMES AT POSITION	DL	BFW
1976	Phi N	4	6	0	4	0	0	0	0	2-0	1	0	.667	.778	.667	301	2	1-1	1.000	-2	39	62	2b4		0.1
1977	Phi N	12	23	3	4	0	1	0	2	1-0	0	5	.174	.200	.261	24	-3	1-0	1.000	3	127	197	2b7		0.1
Total	2	16	29	4	8	0	1	0	2	3-0	1	5	.276	.353	.345	89	-1	2-1	1.000	1	97	151	2b11		0.2

ANDREWS, ED George Edward B4.5.1859 Painesville OH D8.12.1934 W.Palm Beach FL BR/TR/5-8/160 d5.1 U3 Col Case Western Reserve

YEAR	TM LG	G	AB	R	H	2B	3B	HR	RBI	BB-IB	HP	SO	AVG	OBP	SLG	AOPS	ABR	SB-CS	FA	FR	RNG	THR	GAMES AT POSITION	DL	BFW
1884	Phi N	109	420	74	93	21	2	0	23	9		42	.221	.238	.281	66	-16		.891	-20	95	78	2b109		-2.8
1885	Phi N	103	421	77	112	15	3	2	33	32		25	.266	.318	.316	108	5		.921	1	61	44	O99L,2b5		0.4
1886	Phi N	107	437	93	109	15	4	2	28	31		35	.249	.299	.316	86	-7	56	.903	3	118	73	O104(1/103/0),2b3		-0.6
1887	Phi N	104	464	110	151	19	7	4	67	21	3	21	.325	.359	.422	110	5	57	.902	-7	102	33	O99C,2b7/1		-0.4
1888	Phi N	124	528	75	126	14	4	3	44	21	3	41	.239	.272	.297	77	-14	35	.903	-6	111	129	O124C		-2.4
1889	Phi N	10	39	10	11	1	0	0	7	2		4	.282	.317	.308	89	-2	7	.808	-1	51	0	O9(8/0/1)/2		-0.3
	Ind N	40	173	32	53	11	0	0	22	5	1	10	.306	.330	.370	94	-2	7	.885	-2	140	75	O40C/2		-0.5
	Year	50	212	42	64	12	0	0	29	7	1	14	.302	.327	.358	89	-4	14	.867	-4	121	59	O49(8/40/1),2b2		-0.8
1890	Bro P	94	395	84	100	14	2	0	38	40	1	32	.253	.323	.322	68	-19	21	.912	-3	96	81	O94(1/89/4)		-2.0
1891	Cin AA	83	356	47	75	7	4	0	26	33	1	35	.211	.279	.253	48	-26	22	.961	5	165	118	O83L		-1.1
Total	8	774	3233	602	830	117	26	12	278	194	9	245	.257	.301	.320	82	-76	205	.912	-18	109	79	O652(192/455/5),2b126/1		-9.7

ANDREWS, JIM James Pratt B6.5.1865 Shelburne Falls MA D12.27.1907 Chicago IL d4.19

YEAR	TM LG	G	AB	R	H	2B	3B	HR	RBI	BB-IB	HP	SO	AVG	OBP	SLG	AOPS	ABR	SB-CS	FA	FR	RNG	THR	GAMES AT POSITION	DL	BFW
1890	Chi N	53	202	32	38	4	2	3	17	23	2	41	.188	.278	.272	58	-11	11	.900	1	109	58	O53R		-1.0

ANDREWS, MIKE Michael Jay B7.9.1943 Los Angeles CA BR/TR/6-3/195* d9.18 b-Rob

YEAR	TM LG	G	AB	R	H	2B	3B	HR	RBI	BB-IB	HP	SO	AVG	OBP	SLG	AOPS	ABR	SB-CS	FA	FR	RNG	THR	GAMES AT POSITION	DL	BFW
1966	Bos A	5	18	1	3	0	0	0	0	2-0	0	2	.167	.167	.167	-4	-2	0-0	1.000	2	130	61	2b5		0.0
1967	†Bos A	142	494	79	130	20	6	8	40	62-4	2	72	.263	.346	.352	99	2	7-7	.976	-3	99	87	2b139,S6		1.1
1968	Bos A	147	536	77	145	22	1	7	45	81-1	3	57	.271	.368	.354	113	13	3-8	.976	6	101	113	2b139,S4/3		3.3
1969	Bos A★	121	464	79	136	26	4	15	59	71-0	5	53	.293	.390	.455	130	22	1-1	.972	-0	98	97	2b120		3.0
1970	Bos A	151	589	91	149	28	1	17	65	81-0	3	63	.253	.344	.390	96	-1	2-1	.973	-30	83	73	2b148		-2.2
1971	Chi A	109	330	45	93	16	0	12	44	67-1	1	36	.282	.400	.439	135	19	3-5	.956	-1	100	107	2b76,1b25		2.2
1972	Chi A	148	505	58	111	18	0	7	50	70-3	2	78	.220	.313	.297	82	-9	2-2	.973	-8	90	75	2b145,1b5		-1.0
1973	Chi A	52	159	10	32	9	0	0	23	23-3	0	28	.201	.302	.258	57	-8	0-1	1.000	-1	89	20	D30,1b9,2b6,3b5		-1.1
	†Oak A	18	21	1	4	1	0	0	3	3-0	0	1	.190	.292	.238	53	-1	0-0	.944	-0	76	106	2b9,D2		-0.1
	Year	70	180	11	36	10	0	0	26	26-3	0	29	.200	.301	.256	57	-9	0-1	.974	-1	79	96	D32,2b15,1b9,3b5		-1.2
Total	8	893	3116	441	803	140	4	66	316	458-12	16	390	.258	.353	.369	104	35	18-25	.973	-35	95	91	2b787,1b39,D32,S10,3b6		5.2

ANDREWS, ROB Robert Patrick B12.11.1952 Santa Monica CA BR/TR/6-0/180* [BalA70 10/247] d4.7 b-Mike

YEAR	TM LG	G	AB	R	H	2B	3B	HR	RBI	BB-IB	HP	SO	AVG	OBP	SLG	AOPS	ABR	SB-CS	FA	FR	RNG	THR	GAMES AT POSITION	DL	BFW
1975	Hou N	103	277	29	66	5	4	0	19	31-4	0	34	.238	.310	.285	73	-11	12-5	.982	1	99	117	2b94,S6		-0.3
1976	Hou N	109	410	42	105	8	5	0	23	33-1	0	27	.256	.312	.300	81	-12	7-3	.977	9	109	92	2b107,S3		0.6
1977	SF N	127	436	60	115	11	3	0	25	56-0	0	33	.264	.345	.303	76	-13	5-6	.964	-11	97	94	2b115		-2.0
1978	SF N	79	177	21	39	3	1	1	11	20-1	0	18	.220	.299	.288	67	-8	5-1	.977	-9	83	88	2b62/S		-0.5
1979	SF N	75	154	22	40	3	2	3	13	8-0	0	9	.260	.298	.338	75	-6	4-1	.956	4	105	88	2b53,3b3		0.0
Total	5	493	1454	174	365	30	15	3	91	148-6	0	121	.251	.318	.298	75	-50	33-16	.972	2	96	102	2b431,S10,3b3		-2.2

ANDREWS, STAN Stanley Joseph "Polo" (b Stanley Joseph Andruskewicz) B4.17.1917 Lynn MA D6.10.1995 Bradenton FL BR/TR/5-11/178 d6.11

YEAR	TM LG	G	AB	R	H	2B	3B	HR	RBI	BB-IB	HP	SO	AVG	OBP	SLG	AOPS	ABR	SB-CS	FA	FR	RNG	THR	GAMES AT POSITION	DL	BFW
1939	Bos N	13	26	1	6	2	0	0	2	1	1	5	.231	.259	.231	35	-2	0	.857	-2	190	62	C10		-0.4
1940	Bos N	19	33	1	6	0	0	0	2	0	0	3	.182	.182	.182	1	-5	1	.944	-1	99	87	C14		-0.5
1944	Bro N	4	8	1	1	0	0	0	1	1	0	2	.125	.222	.125	-1	-1	0	1.000	-0	65	0	C4		-0.1
1945	Bro N	21	49	5	8	0	1	0	5	1-0	0	4	.163	.255	.204	29	-5	1	.948	1	99	178	C21		-0.3
	Phi N	13	33	3	11	1	0	1	3	5-0	0	5	.333	.353	.485	135	1	1	.950	-1	75	81	C12		0.2
	Year	34	82	8	19	1	1	1	8	6-0	0	9	.232	.292	.317	70	-4	1	.949	-0	90	142	C33		-0.1
Total	4	70	149	11	32	3	1	1	12	8	1	16	.215	.259	.262	46	-12	2	.938	-3	106	110	C61		-1.2

ANDREWS, WALLY William Walter B9.18.1859 Philadelphia PA D1.20.1940 Indianapolis IN BR/TR/6-3/170 d5.22

YEAR	TM LG	G	AB	R	H	2B	3B	HR	RBI	BB-IB	HP	SO	AVG	OBP	SLG	AOPS	ABR	SB-CS	FA	FR	RNG	THR	GAMES AT POSITION	DL	BFW
1884	Lou AA	14	49	10	10	5	1	0	8	4	0		.204	.264	.347	102	1		.950	-1	138	61	1b9,3b3/OLS		-0.1
1888	Lou AA	26	93	12	18	6	3	0	6	13	0		.194	.292	.323	99	1	5	.997	1	103	128	1b26		-0.1
Total	2	40	142	22	28	11	4	0	14	17	0		.197	.283	.331	100	1	5	.985	0	111	112	1b35,3b3/SOL		-0.2

YEAR	TM LG	G	AB	R	H	2B	3B	HR	RBI	BB-IB	HP	SO	AVG	OBP	SLG	AOPS	ABR	SB-CS	FA	FR	RNG	THR	GAMES AT POSITION	DL	BFW
ANDRUS, FRED Frederick Hotham B8.23.1850 Washington MI D11.10.1937 Detroit MI BR/TR/6-2/185 d7.25 ▲																									
1876	Chi N	8	36	6	11	3	0	0	2	0		5	.306	.306	.389	116	0		.714	-2	0	0	O8(1/3/5)		-0.1
1884	Chi N	1	5	3	1	0	0	0	0	1		0	.200	.333	.200	67	0		1.000	0	163	0	/P		0.0
Total	2	9	41	9	12	3	0	0	2	1		5	.293	.310	.366	110	0		.714	-2	0	0	O8(1/3/5)/P		-0.1
ANDRUS, BILL William Morgan "Andy" B7.25.1907 Beaumont TX D3.12.1982 Washington DC BR/TR/6-0/185 d9.19																									
1931	Was A	3	7	0	0	0	0	0	1	0		0	1.000	.000	.000	-99	-2	0-0	.750	-0	69	422	3b2		-0.2
1937	Phi N	3	2	0	0	0	0	0	0	0		2	.000	.000	.000	-93	-1	0	—	-0	0	0	/3		-0.1
Total	2	6	9	0	0	0	0	0	1	0		3	.000	.000	.000	-98	-3	0-0	.750	-1	64	392	3b3		-0.3
ANDRUS, WIMAN William Wiman B10.14.1858 Orono ON, Can. D6.17.1935 Miles City MT 5-6.5/155 d9.15																									
1885	Pro N	1	4	0	0	0	0	0	0	0			1.000	.000	.000	-99	-1		1.000	1	132	0	/3		0.0
ANGLEY, TOM Thomas Samuel B10.2.1904 Baltimore MD D10.26.1952 Wichita KS BL/TR/5-8/190 d4.23 Col Georgia Tech																									
1929	Chi N	5	16	1	4	1	0	0	6	2		0	.250	.333	.313	61	-1	0	.968	1	157	175	C5		0.0
ANKENMAN, PAT Frederick Norman B12.23.1912 Houston TX D1.13.1989 Houston TX BR/TR/5-4/125 d4.16 Mil 1943 Col Texas																									
1936	StL N	1	3	0	0	0	0	0	0	0		3	.000	.000	.000	-99	-1	0	.600	-1	31	0	/S		-0.2
1943	Bro N	1	2	1	1	0	0	0	0	0		0	.500	.500	.500	189	0	0	1.000	0	91	230	/S		0.1
1944	Bro N	13	24	1	6	1	0	0	3	0		2	.250	.250	.292	53	-2	0	.971	-1	119	48	2b11,S2		-0.1
Total	3	15	29	2	7	1	0	0	3	0		5	.241	.241	.276	46	-3	0	.971	-1	119	48	2b11,S4		-0.2
ANNIS, BILL William Perley B3.8.1857 Stoneham MA D6.10.1923 Kennebunkport ME BR/5-7/150 d5.1																									
1884	Bos N	27	96	17	17	2	0	3				8	.177	.177	.198	18	-9		.900	-1	117	179	O27(4/15/8)		-1.0
ANSON, CAP Adrian Constantine B4.17.1852 Marshalltown IA D4.14.1922 Chicago IL BR/TR/6-0/227 d5.6 M21 HF1939 OF NA(1/5/31) OF(45/3/1)																									
1871	Rok NA	**25**	120	29	39	**11**	3	0	16	2		1	.325	.336	.467	134	6	6-2	.763	1	114	76	3b20,C5,2b2/1OL		0.4
1872	Ath NA	46	217	60	90	10	7	0	48	16		3	.415	**.455**	.525	200	26	6-6	.752	-10	74	99	3b46		1.0
1873	Ath NA	**52**	254	53	101	9	2	0	36	5		2	.398	.409	.449	144	12	1-2	.920	-4	107	120	1b36,3b11,C3,2b3,O3C		0.5
1874	Ath NA	**55**	260	51	87	8	3	0	37	4		1	.335	.345	.388	124	5	6-0	.936	-5	120	138	1b24,3b20,O8R,S6/C		0.1
1875	Ath NA	69	326	84	106	15	3	0	58	4		2	.325	.333	.390	135	9	11-6	.922	11	249	121	1b32,O25(0/2/23),C13,3b5,M		1.9
1876	Chi N	66	309	63	110	9	7	2	59	12		8	.356	.386	.450	157	16		.849	14	113	168	3b66,C2		2.8
1877	Chi N	59	255	52	86	**19**	1	0	32	9		3	.337	.360	.420	129	8		**.883**	7	105	213	3b40,C31		1.5
1878	Chi N	60	261	55	89	12	2	0	40	13		1	.341	.372	.402	145	12		.825	-7	48	0	O48(45/3/0),2b9,3b3,C3		0.3
1879	Chi N	51	227	40	72	20	1	0	34	2		2	**.317**	.323	.414	133	8		.975	0	62	121	1b51,M		0.6
1880	Chi N	**86**	356	54	120	24	1	1	74	14		12	.337	.362	.419	154	20		**.978**	0	72	89	1b81,3b9/S2M		1.9
1881	Chi N	84	343	67	**137**	21	7	1	82	26		4	**.399**	**.442**	.510	**189**	35		**.975**	7	**144**	112	1b84,C2/SM		**3.6**
1882	Chi N	82	348	69	126	29	8	1	83	20		7	.362	.397	.500	177	30		.949	-0	**119**	112	1b82/CM		2.0
1883	Chi N	**98**	413	70	127	36	5	0	68	18		9	.308	.336	.419	118	9		.964	3	**129**	111	1b98,P2/ORCM		0.3
1884	Chi N	112	475	108	159	30	3	21	102	29		13	.335	.373	.543	170	37		.956	-0	-123	**166**	1b112,C3/SPM		2.3
1885	†Chi N	112	464	100	144	**35**	7	7	**108**	34		13	.310	.357	.491	143	21		.958	-4	100	117	1b112/CM		0.6
1886	†Chi N	125	504	117	187	35	11	10	**147**	55		19	.371	.433	.544	170	42	29	.963	9	144	**133**	1b125,C12,M		3.6
1887	Chi N	122	472	107	164	33	13	7	102	60	1	18	**.347**	.422	.517	141	26	27	.973	10	**156**	114	1b122/CM		2.1
1888	Chi N	134	515	101	177	20	12	12	**84**	47	1	24	**.344**	**.400**	.499	172	42	28	**.986**	9	133	**127**	1b434,M		3.8
1889	Chi N	134	518	100	177	32	7	7	117	86	5	19	.342	.440	.471	147	36	27	.982	8	127	98	1b134,M		2.8
1890	Chi N	**139**	504	95	157	14	5	7	107	**113**	6	23	.312	**.443**	.401	141	34	29	.978	1	105	95	1b135,C3,2b2,M		2.0
1891	Chi N	136	540	81	157	24	8	8	**120**	75	1	29	.291	.378	.409	129	22	17	.981	8	129	**123**	1b136,C2,M		1.6
1892	Chi N	146	559	62	152	25	9	1	74	67	4	30	.272	.354	.354	113	10	13	.973	-6	86	78	1b146,M		0.4
1893	Chi N	103	398	70	125	24	2	0	91	68	1	12	.314	.415	.384	115	13	13	.981	-4	79	88	1b101,M		0.8
1894	Chi N	84	343	85	133	29	4	5	100	41	3	15	.388	.457	.539	132	20	17	.990	3	104	94	1b83/2M		1.7
1895	Chi N	122	474	87	159	23	6	2	91	55	3	23	.335	.408	.422	107	6	12	.985	-1	91	110	1b122,M		0.4
1896	Chi N	108	402	72	133	18	2	2	90	49	3	10	.331	.407	.400	109	8	24	.983	-1	103	110	1b98,C10,M		0.6
1897	Chi N	114	424	67	121	17	3	3	75	60	4		.285	.379	.361	92	-2	11	.975	1	112	117	1b103,C11,M		0.0
Total	5 NA	247	1177	277	423	53	18	0	195	31		9	.359	.376	.435	146	58	30-16	.765	-7	83	97	3b102,1b93,O37R,C22,S6,2b5		3.9
Total	22	2277	9104	1722	3012	529	124	97	1880	953		32	**294**	.331	.396	.448	139	453	247	.974	57	114	111	1b2059,3b118,C83,O49L,2b13,P3,S3	35.4
ANTHONY, ERIC Eric Todd B11.8.1967 San Diego CA BL/TL/6-2/195* [HouN86 34/795] d7.28																									
1989	Hou N	25	61	7	11	2	0	4	9-2		0	16	.180	.286	.410	100	0	0-0	1.000	0	102	108	O21(3/0/18)		0.0
1990	Hou N	84	239	26	46	8	0	10	29	29-3	2	78	.192	.279	.351	76	-8	5-0	.970	-3	91	105	O71(13/0/59)		-1.2
1991	Hou N	39	118	11	18	6	0	1	7	12-1	0	41	.153	.227	.229	31	-11	1-0	.986	3	105	210	O37R		-0.9
1992	Hou N	137	440	45	105	15	1	19	80	38-5	1	98	.239	.298	.407	103	-3	5-4	.973	-7	85	85	O115(1/2/113)		-1.2
1993	Hou N	145	486	70	121	19	4	15	66	49-2	2	88	.249	.319	.397	94	-5	3-5	.988	-7	93	67	O131(0/23/121)		-1.8
1994	Sea A	79	262	31	62	14	1	10	30	23-4	0	66	.237	.297	.412	79	-9	6-2	.985	-0	71	108	O71(62/5/10),D4	15	-1.0
1995	†Cin N	47	134	19	36	6	0	5	23	13-2	0	30	.269	.327	.425	97	-1	2-1	1.000	1	102	145	O24(4/1/20),1b17	88	-0.2
1996	Cin N	47	123	22	30	6	0	8	13	22-2	0	36	.244	.359	.488	119	4	0-1	.949	-5	59	99	O37(13/0/24)	44	-0.3
	Col N	32	62	10	15	2	0	4	9	10-0	0	20	.242	.342	.468	91	-1	0-1	1.000	-1	64	233	O19(1/9/10)		-0.3
	Year	79	185	32	45	8	0	12	22	32-2	0	56	.243	.353	.481	107	2	0-2	.967	-6	61	141	O56(14/9/34)		-0.6
1997	LA N	47*	74	8	18	3	2	2	5	12-1	0	18	.243	.349	.419	107	1	2-0	.966	1	98	215	O21(17/0/4)		0.2
Total	9	682	1999	249	462	81	8	78	269	217-22	5	491	.231	.305	.397	90	-30	24-14	.981	-17	91	105	O547(114/40/416),1b17,D4	168	-6.7
ANTOLICK, JOE Joseph B4.11.1916 Hokendauqua PA D6.25.2002 Catasauqua PA BR/TR/6-0/185 d9.20																									
1944	Phi N	4	6	1	2	0	0	0	1	0		0	.333	.429	.333	120	0	0	1.000	1	57	0	C3		0.1
ANTONELLI, JOHN John Lawrence B7.15.1915 Memphis TN D4.18.1990 Memphis TN BR/TR/5-10.5/165 d9.16																									
1944	StL N	8	21	0	4	1	0	0	1	0		4	.190	.190	.238	20	-2	0	1.000	1	177	113	1b3,3b3,2b2		-0.2
1945	StL N	2	3	0	0	0	0	0	0	0		1	.000	.000	.000	-98	-1	0	.667	-1	0	0	/3		-0.1
	Phi N	125	504	50	129	27	2	1	28	24	2	24	.256	.292	.323	73	-20	1	.959	-4	95	109	3b108,2b23/1S		-2.1
	Year	127	507	50	129	27	2	1	28	24	2	25	.254	.291	.321	72	-20	1	.957	-4	94	108	3b109,2b23/1S		-2.2
Total	2	135	528	50	133	28	2	1	29	24	2	29	.252	.287	.318	70	-23	1	.958	-3	95	106	3b112,2b25,1b4/S		-2.4
ANTONELLO, BILL William James B5.19.1927 Brooklyn NY D3.4.1993 Fridley MN BR/TR/5-11/185 d4.30																									
1953	Bro N	40	43	9	7	1	1	1	4	2		12	.163	.200	.302	28	-0	0	.964	1	133	0	O25(20/2/4)		-0.5
APARICIO, LUIS Luis Ernesto (Montiel) B4.29.1934 Maracaibo, Venez BR/TR/5-9/160* d4.17 HF1984																									
1956	Chi A	152	533	69	142	19	6	3	56	34-2	1	63	.266	.311	.341	71	-24	**21**-4	.954	-4	102	97	S152		-1.1
1957	Chi A	143	575	82	148	22	6	3	41	52-1	0	55	.257	.317	.332	78	-18	**28**-8	.972	-10	98	94	S142		-1.3
1958	Chi A★	145	557	76	148	20	9	2	40	35-2	1	38	.266	.309	.345	82	-15	**29**-6	.973	12	105	97	S145		1.3
1959	†Chi A★	152	612	98	157	18	5	6	51	53-1	0	40	.257	.316	.332	80	-17	**56**-13	.970	-6	98	96	S152		-0.2
1960	Chi A★	153	600	86	166	20	7	2	61	43-3	1	39	.277	.323	.343	82	-16	**51**-8	**.979**	34	**114**	118	S153		**3.9**
1961	Chi A★	156	625	90	170	24	4	6	45	38-0	1	33	.272	.313	.352	79	-20	**53**-13	.962	12	**108**	94	S156		1.2
1962	Chi A★	153	581	72	140	23	5	7	40	32-1	1	36	.241	.280	.334	65	-30	**31**-12	.973	18	108	117	S152		0.3
1963	Bal A	146	601	73	150	18	8	5	45	36-2	2	35	.250	.291	.331	78	-20	**40**-6	.983	-2	95	93	S145		-0.3
1964	Bal A★	146	578	93	154	20	3	10	37	49-0	2	51	.266	.324	.363	92	-6	**57**-17	.979	10	104	124	S145		2.4
1965	Bal A	144	564	67	127	20	10	8	40	46-0	1	56	.225	.286	.339	76	-19	26-7	**.971**	3	105	113	S141		-0.1
1966	†Bal A	151	659	97	182	25	8	6	41	33-2	1	42	.276	.311	.366	95	-6	25-11	**.978**	9	96	118	S151		2.0
1967	Bal A	134	546	55	127	22	5	4	31	29-2	1	44	.233	.270	.313	73	-19	18-5	.957	-15	89	96	S131		-2.3
1968	Chi A	155	622	55	164	24	4	4	36	33-3	2	43	.264	.302	.333	90	-17	17-11	.977	21	104	114	S154		3.0
1969	Chi A	156	599	77	168	24	5	5	51	66-1	2	29	.280	.352	.362	96	-2	24-4	.976	33	**119**	102	S154		5.4
1970	Chi A★	146	552	86	173	29	3	5	43	53-1	1	34	.313	.372	.404	111	10	8-3	.976	25	116	108	S146		5.3
1971	Bos A★	125	491	56	114	23	0	4	45	35-0	2	43	.232	.284	.303	62	-24	6-4	.971	-18	91	95	S121		-3.0
1972	Bos A★	110	436	47	112	26	3	3	39	26-0	1	28	.257	.299	.351	88	-6	3-3	.968	-10	91	79	S109	40	-0.4
1973	Bos A	132	499	56	135	17	1	0	49	43-1	0	33	.271	.324	.309	76	-15	13-1	.966	-12	95	87	S132		-1.0
Total	18	2599	10230	1335	2677	394	92	83	791	736-22	27	742	.262	.311	.343	82	-254	506-136	.972	98	103	102	S2581	40	15.1
APPLING, LUKE Lucius Benjamin "Old Aches and Pains" B4.2.1907 High Point NC D1.3.1991 Cumming GA BR/TR/5-10/183* d9.10 Mil 1944-45 M1/C9 HF1964 Col Oglethorpe																									
1930	Chi A	6	26	2	8	2	0	0	2	0		1	.308	.308	.385	77	-1	2-0	.879	-1	92	26	S6		-0.2
1931	Chi A	96	297	36	69	13	4	1	28	29		1	27	.232	.303	.313	66	-15	9-2	.900	-9	102	79	S76/2		-1.6

YEAR	TM	LG	G	AB	R	H	2B	3B	HR	RBI	BB-IB	HP	SO	AVG	OBP	SLG	AOPS	ABR	SB-CS	FA	FR	RNG	THR	GAMES AT POSITION	DL	BFW
1932	Chi	A	139	489	66	134	20	10	3	63	40	0	36	.274	.329	.374	87	-11	9-8	.929	15	112	114	S85,2b30,3b14		1.1
1933	Chi	A	**151**	612	90	197	36	10	6	85	56		29	.322	.379	.443	122	19	6-11	.939	9	**108**	119	S151		3.4
1934	Chi	A	118	452	75	137	28	6	2	61	59		27	.303	.384	.405	100	2	3-1	.945	-7	98	74	S110,2b8		0.3
1935	Chi	A	**153**	525	94	161	28	6	1	71	122	0	40	.307	.437	.389	112	18	12-6	.958	25	113	99	S153		5.1
1936	Chi	A★	138	526	111	204	31	7	6	128	85	1	25	**.388**	.474	.508	137	37	10-6	.951	15	**108**	129	S137		5.4
1937	Chi	A	**154**	574	98	182	42	8	4	77	86	1	28	.317	.407	.439	113	16	18-10	.944	17	**111**	122	S154		4.0
1938	Chi	A	81	294	41	89	14	0	0	44	42	1	17	.303	.392	.350	85	-4	1-3	.953	2	112	72	S78		0.2
1939	Chi	A☆	148	516	82	162	16	6	0	56	105	0	37	.314	.430	.368	103	9	16-9	.951	-1	**102**	95	S148		1.8
1940	Chi	A★	150	566	96	197	27	13	0	79	69	1	35	.348	.420	.442	122	21	3-5	.953	-3	99	101	S150		2.6
1941	Chi	A☆	154	592	93	186	26	8	1	57	82	1	32	.314	.399	.390	111	13	12-8	.948	-4	103	101	S154		1.9
1942	Chi	A	142	543	78	142	26	4	3	53	63	3	23	.262	.342	.341	94	-3	17-5	.948	-3	103	93	S141		0.7
1943	Chi	A☆	**155**	585	63	192	33	2	3	80	90	1	29	**.328**	**.419**	.407	142	37	27-8	.957	8	106	112	S155		6.3
1945	Chi	A	18	57	12	21	2	2	1	10	12	0	7	.368	.478	.526	197	8	1-0	.930	-1	106	64	S17		0.9
1946	Chi	A★	149	582	59	180	27	5	1	55	.71	0	41	.309	.384	.378	118	17	6-4	.951	5	113	107	S149		3.2
1947	Chi	A★	139	503	67	154	29	0	8	49	64	1	28	.306	.386	.412	126	20	8-6	.949	-9	104	91	S129,3b2		1.9
1948	Chi	A	139	497	63	156	16	2	0	47	94	0	35	.314	.423	.354	112	15	10-4	.943	13	124	94	3b72,S64		3.2
1949	Chi	A	142	492	82	148	21	5	5	58	121	0	24	.301	.439	.394	125	27	7-12	.964	-3	**105**	90	S141		2.8
1950	Chi	A	50	128	11	30	3	4	0	13	12	0	8	.234	.300	.320	61	-8	2-0	.967	1	92	96	S20,1b13/2		-0.6
Total	20		2422	8856	1319	2749	440	102	45	1116	1302	11	528	.310	.399	.398	113	217	179-108	.948	68	106	101	S2218,3b88,2b40,1b13		42.4

ARAGON, ANGEL Angel (Valdes) "Pete" B8.2.1890 Havana, Cuba D1.24.1952 New York NY BR/TR/5-5/150 d8.20 s-Jack

YEAR	TM	LG	G	AB	R	H	2B	3B	HR	RBI	BB-IB	HP	SO	AVG	OBP	SLG	AOPS	ABR	SB-CS	FA	FR	RNG	THR	GAMES AT POSITION	DL	BFW
1914	NY	A	6	7	1	1	0	0	0	0	1	1	2	.143	.333	.143	44	0	0	—	-0	0	0	/OC		0.0
1916	NY	A	12	24	1	5	0	0	0	3	2	0	2	.208	.269	.208	43	-2	2	.864	1	143	0	3b8,O2(1/0/1)		-0.1
1917	NY	A	14	45	2	3	1	0	0	2	2	0	2	.067	.106	.089	-40	-7	0	.933	0	92	0	O6(4/2/0),3b4,S2		-0.9
Total	3		32	76	4	9	1	0	0	5	5	1	6	.118	.183	.132	-4	-10	2	.921	1	131	74	3b12,O9(5/3/1),S2		-1.0

ARAGON, JACK Angel Valdes (Reyes) B11.20.1915 Havana, Cuba D4.4.1988 Clearwater FL BR/TR/5-10/176 d8.13 Mil 1942-44 f-Angel

YEAR	TM	LG	G	AB	R	H	2B	3B	HR	RBI	BB-IB	HP	SO	AVG	OBP	SLG	AOPS	ABR	SB-CS	FA	FR	RNG	THR	GAMES AT POSITION	DL	BFW
1941	NY	N	1	0	0	0	0	0	0	0	0	0	0	—	—	—	0	0	0	—	0		0	/R		0.0

ARCHDEACON, MAURICE Maurice John "Flash" B12.14.1897 St.Louis MO D9.5.1954 St.Louis MO BL/TL/5-8/153 d9.17

YEAR	TM	LG	G	AB	R	H	2B	3B	HR	RBI	BB-IB	HP	SO	AVG	OBP	SLG	AOPS	ABR	SB-CS	FA	FR	RNG	THR	GAMES AT POSITION	DL	BFW
1923	Chi	A	22	87	23	35	5	1	0	4	6	0	8	.402	.441	.483	145	6	2-3	.918	-2	93	45	O20(0/18/2)		0.2
1924	Chi	A	95	288	59	92	9	3	0	25	40	4	30	.319	.410	.372	106	-3	11-7	.958	-1	96	126	O77C		0.1
1925	Chi	A	10	9	2	1	0	0	0	0	2	0	1	.111	.273	.111	0	-1	0-0	1.000	0	113	0	/OL		-0.1
Total	3		127	384	84	128	14	4	0	29	48	4	39	.333	.413	.391	112	10	13-10	.950	-3	95	107	O98(1/95/2)		0.2

ARCHER, JIMMY James Patrick B5.13.1883 Dublin, Ireland D3.29.1958 Milwaukee WI BR/TR/5-10/168 d9.6

YEAR	TM	LG	G	AB	R	H	2B	3B	HR	RBI	BB-IB	HP	SO	AVG	OBP	SLG	AOPS	ABR	SB-CS	FA	FR	RNG	THR	GAMES AT POSITION	DL	BFW
1904	Pit	N	7	20	1	3	0	0	0	1	0	0		.150	.150	.150	-7	-3	0	.919	0	127	108	C7/OL		-0.2
1907	†Det	A	18	42	6	5	0	0	0	4	0			.119	.196	.119	1	-5	0	.975	1	113	103	C17/2		-0.2
1909	Chi	N	80	261	31	60	9	2	1	30	12	1		.230	.266	.291	71	-10	5	.960	0	129	89	C80		0.5
1910	†Chi	N	98	313	36	81	17	6	2	41	14	1	49	.259	.293	.371	94	-4	6	.970	5	143	104	C49,1b40		0.9
1911	Chi	N	116	387	41	98	18	5	4	41	18	1	43	.253	.288	.357	80	-13	5	.977	13	160	84	C102,1b10/2		0.9
1912	Chi	N	120	385	35	109	20	2	5	58	22	5	36	.283	.330	.384	95	-3	7	.966	2	131	92	C118		0.9
1913	Chi	N	111	368	38	98	14	7	2	44	19	5	27	.266	.311	.359	91	-5	4-5	.969	-0	112	109	C103,1b8		-0.2
1914	Chi	N	79	248	17	64	9	2	0	19	9	0	9	.258	.284	.310	77	-8	1	.973	-0	93	101	C76		-0.2
1915	Chi	N	97	309	21	75	11	5	1	27	11	2	38	.243	.273	.320	79	-9	5-6	.977	-3	97	104	C88,1b4		-0.6
1916	Chi	N	77	205	11	45	6	2	1	30	12	2	24	.220	.269	.283	63	-9	3	.979	-2	94	91	C61/3		-0.6
1917	Chi	N	2	2	0	0	0	0	0	0	0	0	1	.000	.000	.000	-93	-0	0	—	0			/H		-0.1
1918	Pit	N	24	58	4	9	1	2	0	3	1	2	6	.155	.197	.241	32	-5	0	.989	5	155	133	C21/1		0.2
	Bro	N	9	22	3	6	0	1	0	1	1	0	5	.273	.304	.364	104	0	0	.968	0	93	184	C7		0.1
	Cin	N	9	26	2	7	1	0	0	2	1	0	3	.269	.296	.308	86	0	0	1.000	1	121	127	C7/1		0.1
	Year		42	106	9	22	2	3	0	5	3	2	14	.208	.243	.283	59	-6	0	.987	7	136	142	C35,1b2		0.4
Total	12		847	2646	246	660	106	34	16	296	124	19	241	.249	.288	.333	80	-74	36-11	.971	25	122	98	C736,1b64,2b2/3OL		0.8

ARCHIE, GEORGE George Albert B4.27.1914 Nashville TN D9.20.2001 Nashville TN BR/TR/6-0/170 d9.14 Mil 1942-45

YEAR	TM	LG	G	AB	R	H	2B	3B	HR	RBI	BB-IB	HP	SO	AVG	OBP	SLG	AOPS	ABR	SB-CS	FA	FR	RNG	THR	GAMES AT POSITION	DL	BFW
1938	Det	A	3	1	1	0	0	0	0	0	1	0	0	1.000	.000	.000	-95	-1	0-0	—				/H		-0.1
1941	Was	A	105	379	45	102	20	4	3	48	30	1	42	.269	.324	.367	87	-8	8-4	.936	-4	100	83	3b73,1b23		-1.1
	StL	A	9	29	3	11	3	0	0	5	7	0	3	.379	.500	.483	156	3	2-0	.975	0	120	60	1b8		0.3
	Year		114	408	48	113	23	4	3	53	37	1	45	.277	.339	.375	92	-5	10-4	.936	-3	100	83	3b73,1b31		-0.8
1946	StL	A	4	11	1	2	1	0	0	0	0	0	1	.182	.182	.273	25	-1	0-0	1.000	2	270	195	1b3		0.0
Total	3		121	421	50	115	24	4	3	53	37	1	47	.273	.333	.371	90	-7	10-4	.936	-2	100	83	3b73,1b34		-0.9

ARCIA, JOSE Jose Raimundo (Orta) B8.22.1943 Havana, Cuba BR/TR/6-3/170* d4.10

YEAR	TM	LG	G	AB	R	H	2B	3B	HR	RBI	BB-IB	HP	SO	AVG	OBP	SLG	AOPS	ABR	SB-CS	FA	FR	RNG	THR	GAMES AT POSITION	DL	BFW
1968	Chi	N	59	84	15	16	4	0	1	3	3-0	0	24	.190	.218	.274	44	-6	0-0	1.000	-4	84	0	O17(5/13/0),2b10,S7/3		-1.0
1969	SD	N	120	302	35	65	11	3	0	10	14-0	2	47	.215	.255	.272	49	-21	14-7	.977	2	106	80	2b68,S37,3b8,O4L/1		-1.4
1970	SD	N	114	229	28	51	9	3	0	17	12-1	7	36	.223	.282	.288	55	-15	3-6	.955	1	97	105	S67,2b20,3b9,O7L		-0.9
Total	3		293	615	78	132	24	6	1	35	29-1	9	107	.215	.260	.278	51	-42	17-13	.950	-1	98	91	S111,2b98,O28(16/13/0),3b18/1		-3.3

ARDELL, DAN Daniel Miers B5.27.1941 Seattle WA BL/TL/6-2/190 d9.14 Col USC

YEAR	TM	LG	G	AB	R	H	2B	3B	HR	RBI	BB-IB	HP	SO	AVG	OBP	SLG	AOPS	ABR	SB-CS	FA	FR	RNG	THR	GAMES AT POSITION	DL	BFW
1961	LA	A	7	4	1	1	0	0	0	1-0	0	1	.250	.400	.250	70	0	0-0	1.000	-0		0	107 /1		0.0

ARDNER, JOE Joseph A. "Old Hoss" B2.27.1858 Mt.Vernon OH D9.15.1935 Cleveland OH BR/TR/?/160 d5.1

YEAR	TM	LG	G	AB	R	H	2B	3B	HR	RBI	BB-IB	HP	SO	AVG	OBP	SLG	AOPS	ABR	SB-CS	FA	FR	RNG	THR	GAMES AT POSITION	DL	BFW
1884	Cle	N	26	92	6	16	1	1	0	4	1		24	.174	.183	.207	21	-8		.866	-6	95	61	2b25/3		-1.2
1890	Cle	N	84	323	28	72	13	1	0	35	17	2	40	.223	.266	.269	57	-18	9	.920	-6	98	118	2b84		-1.9
Total	2		110	415	34	88	14	2	0	39	18	2	64	.212	.248	.255	50	-26	9	.908	-12	97	106	2b109/3		-3.1

ARDOIN, DANNY Daniel Wayne B7.8.1974 Mamou LA BR/TR/6-0/218(205-220) [OakA95 5/120] d8.2 Col McNeese St.

YEAR	TM	LG	G	AB	R	H	2B	3B	HR	RBI	BB-IB	HP	SO	AVG	OBP	SLG	AOPS	ABR	SB-CS	FA	FR	RNG	THR	GAMES AT POSITION	DL	BFW
2000	Min	A	15	32	4	4	1	0	1	5	8-0	0	10	.125	.300	.250	39	-3	0-0	.989	4	161	180	C15		0.1
2004	Tex	A	6	8	1	1	0	0	0	1	3-0	0	2	.125	.364	.125	34	-1	0-0	.958	0	37	0	C6		0.0
2005	Col	N	80	210	28	48	10	0	6	22	20-2	9	69	.229	.320	.362	69	-9	1-1	.988	14	153	155	C80		0.9
Total	3		101	250	33	53	11	0	7	28	31-2	9	81	.212	.318	.340	64	-13	1-1	.987	18	150	153	C101		1.0

ARFT, HANK Henry Irven "Bow Wow" B1.28.1922 Manchester MO D12.14.2002 St.Louis MO BL/TL/5-10.5/190* d7.27

YEAR	TM	LG	G	AB	R	H	2B	3B	HR	RBI	BB-IB	HP	SO	AVG	OBP	SLG	AOPS	ABR	SB-CS	FA	FR	RNG	THR	GAMES AT POSITION	DL	BFW
1948	StL	A	69	248	25	59	10	3	5	38	45	0	43	.238	.355	.363	89	-3	1-2	.995	-0	96	111	1b69		-0.6
1949	StL	A	6	5	1	1	0	0	0	2	0	0	1	.200	.200	.400	55	0	0-0	—	0			/H		0.0
1950	StL	A	98	280	45	75	16	4	1	32	46	2	48	.268	.375	.364	87	-4	3-2	.995	-1	96	67	1b84		-0.7
1951	StL	A	112	345	44	90	16	5	7	42	41	1	34	.261	.339	.397	96	-3	4-6	.989	7	124	91	1b97		0.0
1952	StL	A	15	28	1	4	3	1	0	4	5	0	7	.143	.273	.321	63	-1	0-0	.985	-0	81	164	1b10		-0.2
Total	5		300	906	116	229	46	13	13	118	137	2	133	.253	.352	.375	90	-11	8-10	.992	5	106	91	1b260		-1.5

ARIAS, ALEX Alejandro B11.20.1967 New York NY BR/TR/6-3/195(185-202) [ChiN87 3/62] d5.12

YEAR	TM	LG	G	AB	R	H	2B	3B	HR	RBI	BB-IB	HP	SO	AVG	OBP	SLG	AOPS	ABR	SB-CS	FA	FR	RNG	THR	GAMES AT POSITION	DL	BFW
1992	Chi	N	32	99	14	29	6	0	0	7	11-0	2	13	.293	.375	.354	104	1	0-0	.967	-5	94	53	S30		-0.1
1993	Fla	N	96	249	27	67	5	1	2	20	27-0	1	18	.269	.344	.321	76	-8	1-1	.987	-7	101	82	2b30,3b22,S18		-1.2
1994	Fla	N	59	113	4	27	5	0	0	15	9-0	1	19	.239	.298	.283	51	-8	0-1	.985	-4	72	78	S20,3b15		-1.1
1995	Fla	N	94	216	22	58	9	2	3	26	22-1	2	20	.269	.337	.370	86	-4	1-0	.947	-0	98	83	S36,3b21,2b6		-0.1
1996	Fla	N	100	224	27	62	11	2	3	26	17-1	3	28	.277	.335	.384	92	-3	2-0	.956	2	99	144	3b59,S20/12		0.1
1997	†Fla	N	74	93	13	23	2	0	1	11	12-0	3	12	.247	.342	.301	76	-3	0-1	.971	-2	70	116	3b37,S11	18	-0.4
1998	Phi	N	56	133	17	39	8	0	1	16	13-3	4	18	.293	.358	.376	94	-1	2-0	.985	-3	96	54	S38,3b5/2		-0.1
1999	Phi	N	118	347	43	105	20	1	4	48	36-6	4	31	.303	.373	.401	95	-1	2-2	.988	-18	86	81	S95,3b2/2		-1.2
2000	Phi	N	70	155	17	29	9	0	2	15	16-2	3	28	.187	.271	.284	42	-5	1-0	.963	-6	90	90	S39,3b10/2		-1.7
2001	SD	N	70	137	19	31	9	0	2	12	17-1	1	22	.226	.312	.336	74	-5	0-0	.957	-4	137	83	3b18,1b17,2b13,S13	15	-0.8
2002	NY	A	6	7	0	0	0	0	0	2	0-0	0	2	.000	.125	.000	-63	-2	0-0	.750	-0	124	508	3b4/S		-0.2
Total	11		775	1773	203	470	84	6	18	196	181-14	23	211	.265	.338	.350	81	-48	10-5	.973	-47	89	81	S321,3b193,2b53,1b18	33	-6.8

ARIAS, GEORGE George Alberto B3.12.1972 Tucson AZ BR/TR/5-11/190* [CalA93 7/187] d4.2 Col Arizona

YEAR	TM	LG	G	AB	R	H	2B	3B	HR	RBI	BB-IB	HP	SO	AVG	OBP	SLG	AOPS	ABR	SB-CS	FA	FR	RNG	THR	GAMES AT POSITION	DL	BFW
1996	Cal	A	84	252	19	60	8	1	6	28	16-2	2	50	.238	.284	.349	58	-17	2-0	.960	22	136	137	3b83/D		0.5
1997	Ana	A	3	6	1	2	0	0	0	1	0-0	0	1	.333	.333	.333	74	0	0-0	1.000	0	168	0	/3D		0.0
	SD	N	11	22	2	5	1	0	0	2	0-0	0	5	.227	.227	.273	32	-2	0-0	.941	0	116	0	3b8		-0.2

YEAR	TM	LG	G	AB	R	H	2B	3B	HR	RBI	BB-IB	HP	SO	AVG	OBP	SLG	AOPS	ABR	SB-CS	FA	FR	RNG	THR	GAMES AT POSITION	DL	BFW
1998	†SD	N	20	36	4	7	1	1	1	4	3-0	2	16	.194	.293	.361	76	-1	0-0	.933	1	122	121	3b14/1		0.0
1999	SD	N	55	164	20	40	8	0	7	20	6-0	0	54	.244	.271	.421	77	-7	0-0	.941	6	116	58	3b50	29	-0.1
Total 4			173	480	46	114	18	2	14	55	25-2	2	121	.237	.278	.371	65	-27	2-0	.952	29	108	104	3b156,D2/1	29	0.2

ARLETT, BUZZ Russell Loris B1.3.1899 Elmhurst CA D5.16.1964 Minneapolis MN BB/TR/6-2/210 d4.14

YEAR	TM	LG	G	AB	R	H	2B	3B	HR	RBI	BB-IB	HP	SO	AVG	OBP	SLG	AOPS	ABR	SB-CS	FA	FR	RNG	THR	GAMES AT POSITION	DL	BFW
1931	Phi	N	121	418	65	131	26	7	18	72	45	5	39	.313	.387	.538	135	21	3	.955	1	97	122	O94R,1b13		1.5

ARMAS, TONY Antonio Rafael (Machado) B7.2.1953 Anzoategui, Venez BR/TR/6-1/200(182-224) d9.6 b-Marcos s-Tony

YEAR	TM	LG	G	AB	R	H	2B	3B	HR	RBI	BB-IB	HP	SO	AVG	OBP	SLG	AOPS	ABR	SB-CS	FA	FR	RNG	THR	GAMES AT POSITION	DL	BFW
1976	Pit	N	4	6	0	2	0	0	0	1	0-0	0	2	.333	.333	.333	88	0	0-0	1.000	0	101	0	O2(1/1/0)		0.0
1977	Oak	A	118	363	26	87	8	2	13	53	20-2	0	99	.240	.274	.380	79	-12	1-2	.981	9	114	121	O112(3/84/30)/S	27	-0.6
1978	Oak	A	91	239	17	51	6	1	2	13	10-2	2	62	.213	.250	.272	49	-17	1-2	.991	8	129	63	O85(2/40/47),D3	35	-1.2
1979	Oak	A	80	278	29	69	9	3	11	34	16-2	1	67	.248	.290	.421	94	-4	1-0	.976	6	115	154	O80(12/17/53)	51	-0.1
1980	Oak	A	158	628	87	175	18	8	35	109	29-4	2	128	.279	.310	.500	126	17	5-3	.975	11	114	137	O158(0/10/152)		1.9
1981	†Oak	A★	109	440	51	115	24	3	22	76	19-6	2	115	.261	.294	.480	124	11	5-1	.993	5	110	95	O109(0/2/108)		1.0
1982	Oak	A	138	536	58	125	19	2	28	89	33-5	1	128	.233	.275	.433	95	-7	2-2	.983	5	114	87	O135(0/5/133)/D	15	-0.9
1983	Bos	A	145	574	77	125	23	2	36	107	29-0	2	131	.218	.254	.453	85	-15	0-1	.985	-1	103	70	O116C,D27		-1.8
1984	Bos	A☆	157	639	107	171	29	5	43	123	32-9	1	156	.268	.300	.531	120	13	1-3	.974	-9	94	48	O126(0/126/1),D31		0.1
1985	Bos	A	103	385	50	102	17	5	23	64	18-4	2	90	.265	.298	.514	113	5	0-0	.983	-6	88	63	O79(16/69/2),D19	29	-0.3
1986	†Bos	A	121	425	40	112	21	4	11	58	24-1	2	77	.264	.305	.409	92	-6	0-3	.969	-6	93	70	O117(9/108/19)/D	15	-1.4
1987	Cal	A	28	81	8	16	3	1	3	9	1-0	0	11	.198	.205	.370	50	-6	1-0	1.000	-2	87	0	O27(2/0/26)		-0.9
1988	Cal	A	120	368	42	100	20	2	13	49	22-0	0	87	.272	.311	.443	112	4	1-3	.986	-3	92	91	O113(74/36/10),D5		-0.2
1989	Cal	A	60	202	22	52	7	1	11	30	7-2	0	48	.257	.280	.465	109	1	0-0	.990	1	99	115	O47(5/1/42),1b2,D6	69	0.0
Total 14			1432	5164	614	1302	204	39	251	815	260-37	15	1201	.252	.287	.453	102	-16	18-20	.981	17	105	89	O1306(124/615/623),D93,1b2/S	241	-4.4

ARMAS, MARCOS Marcos Rafael (Ruiz) B8.5.1969 Puerto Piritu, Venez BR/TR/6-5/195 d5.25 b-Tony

YEAR	TM	LG	G	AB	R	H	2B	3B	HR	RBI	BB-IB	HP	SO	AVG	OBP	SLG	AOPS	ABR	SB-CS	FA	FR	RNG	THR	GAMES AT POSITION	DL	BFW
1993	Oak	A	15	31	7	6	2	0	1	1	1-0	1	12	.194	.242	.355	62	-2	1-0	1.000	-1	65	53	1b12/ORD		-0.3

ARMBRISTER, ED Edison Rosanda B7.4.1948 Nassau, Bahamas BR/TR/5-11/160* d8.31

YEAR	TM	LG	G	AB	R	H	2B	3B	HR	RBI	BB-IB	HP	SO	AVG	OBP	SLG	AOPS	ABR	SB-CS	FA	FR	RNG	THR	GAMES AT POSITION	DL	BFW
1973	†Cin	N	18	37	5	8	3	1	1	5	2-0	0	8	.216	.250	.432	91	-1	0-0	.917	0	107	143	O14(3/4/7)		-0.1
1974	Cin	N	9	7	0	2	0	0	0	1	0-0	1	1	.286	.375	.286	88	0	0-0	1.000	-0	65	0	O4(2/0/2)		0.0
1975	†Cin	N	59	65	9	12	1	0	0	2	5-0	1	19	.185	.254	.200	27	-6	3-1	.867	-3	57	0	O19(10/4/7)		-1.0
1976	†Cin	N	73	78	20	23	3	2	2	7	6-0	0	22	.295	.341	.462	124	2	7-3	.972	3	100	337	O32(20/0/13)		0.4
1977	Cin	N	65	78	12	20	4	3	1	5	10-0	0	21	.256	.337	.423	101	0	5-6	.903	0	81	272	O27(20/0/6)		-0.1
Total 5			224	265	46	65	11	6	4	19	24-0	1	71	.245	.307	.377	88	-5	15-10	.925	-0	86	209	O96(55/8/36)		-0.8

ARMBRUSTER, CHARLIE Charles A. B8.30.1880 Cincinnati OH D10.7.1964 Grants Pass OR BR/TR/5-9/180 d7.17

YEAR	TM	LG	G	AB	R	H	2B	3B	HR	RBI	BB-IB	HP	SO	AVG	OBP	SLG	AOPS	ABR	SB-CS	FA	FR	RNG	THR	GAMES AT POSITION	DL	BFW
1905	Bos	A	35	91	13	18	4	0	0	6	18	1		.198	.336	.242	83	0	3	.944	-3	123	75	C35		-0.1
1906	Bos	A	72	201	9	29	6	1	0	6	25			.144	.242	.184	34	-14	2	.955	-4	82	112	C66/1		-1.3
1907	Bos	A	23	60	2	6	1	0	0	0	8			.100	.206	.117	3	-6	1	.935	1	119	116	C21		-0.3
	Chi	A	1	3	0	0	0	0	0	0	1			.000	.250	.000	-20	0		1.000	0	153	82	/C		0.0
	Year		24	63	2	6	1	0	0	0	9			.095	.208	.111	2	-7	1	.940	2	121	114	C22		-0.3
Total 3			131	355	24	53	11	1	0	12	52			.149	.262	.186	42	-20	6	.949	-5	101	102	C123/1		-1.7

ARMBRUSTER, HARRY Henry Gregory "Army" B3.20.1882 Liverpool (now Valley City) OH D12.10.1953 Cincinnati OH BL/TL/5-10/190 d4.30

YEAR	TM	LG	G	AB	R	H	2B	3B	HR	RBI	BB-IB	HP	SO	AVG	OBP	SLG	AOPS	ABR	SB-CS	FA	FR	RNG	THR	GAMES AT POSITION	DL	BFW
1906	Phi	A	91	265	40	63	6	3	2	24	43		4	.238	.353	.306	103	3		.971	0	98	51	O74(0/40/34)		0.0

ARMSTRONG, GEORGE Noble George "Dodo" B6.3.1924 Orange NJ D7.24.1993 Orange NJ BR/TR/5-10/190 d4.26

YEAR	TM	LG	G	AB	R	H	2B	3B	HR	RBI	BB-IB	HP	SO	AVG	OBP	SLG	AOPS	ABR	SB-CS	FA	FR	RNG	THR	GAMES AT POSITION	DL	BFW
1946	Phi	A	8	6	0	1	1	0	0	1				.167	.286	.333	73	0	0-0	1.000	0	0	392	C4		0.0

ARMSTRONG, BOB Robert B1850 Baltimore MD 6-2/160 d6.26

YEAR	TM	LG	G	AB	R	H	2B	3B	HR	RBI	BB-IB	HP	SO	AVG	OBP	SLG	AOPS	ABR	SB-CS	FA	FR	RNG	THR	GAMES AT POSITION	DL	BFW
1871	Kek	NA	12	49	9	11	2	1	0	5	0		1	.224	.224	.306	50	-3	0-1	.816	1	132	0	O12(0/11/1)		-0.2

ARNDT, HARRY Harry John B2.12.1879 South Bend IN D3.25.1921 South Bend IN BR/TR/?/165 d7.2

YEAR	TM	LG	G	AB	R	H	2B	3B	HR	RBI	BB-IB	HP	SO	AVG	OBP	SLG	AOPS	ABR	SB-CS	FA	FR	RNG	THR	GAMES AT POSITION	DL	BFW
1902	Det	A	10	34	4	5	0	1	0	7	6		0	.147	.275	.206	34	-3	0	.958	0	0	0	O10(7/0/3)/1		-0.3
	Bal	A	68	248	41	63	7	4	2	28	35		4	.254	.355	.339	89	-3	9	.872	1	121	52	O62(1/0/61),2b4,3b2/S		-0.4
	Year		78	282	45	68	7	5	2	35	41		4	.241	.346	.323	83	-5	9	.885	1	104	45	O72(8/0/64),2b4,3b2/1S		-0.7
1905	StL	N	113	415	40	101	11	6	2	36	24		3	.243	.290	.313	82	-10	13	.951	-10	96	47	2b90,O9R,3b7,S5		-2.0
1906	StL	N	69	256	30	69	7	9	2	26	19			.270	.320	.391	127	6	5	.965	10	106	191	3b65/1OR		2.0
1907	StL	N	11	32	3	6	1	0	0	2	1		0	.188	.212	.219	36	-2	0	1.000	1	129	99	1b4,3b3		-0.2
Total 4			271	985	118	244	26	20	6	99	85		7	.248	.312	.333	91	-12	27	.952	2	97	85	2b94,O82(8/0/74),3b77,S6,1b6		-0.9

ARNDT, LARRY Larry Wayne B2.25.1963 Fremont OH BR/TR/6-1/195 [OakA85 26/663] d6.6 Col Bowling Green

YEAR	TM	LG	G	AB	R	H	2B	3B	HR	RBI	BB-IB	HP	SO	AVG	OBP	SLG	AOPS	ABR	SB-CS	FA	FR	RNG	THR	GAMES AT POSITION	DL	BFW
1989	Oak	A	2	6	1	1	0	0	0	0	0-0	0	1	.167	.167	.167	-6	-1	0-0	1.000	0	132	241	/13		-0.1

ARNOLD, CHRIS Christopher Paul B11.6.1947 Long Beach CA BR/TR/5-10/160(160-175) [SFN65 9/239] d9.7

YEAR	TM	LG	G	AB	R	H	2B	3B	HR	RBI	BB-IB	HP	SO	AVG	OBP	SLG	AOPS	ABR	SB-CS	FA	FR	RNG	THR	GAMES AT POSITION	DL	BFW
1971	SF	N	6	13	2	3	0	0	1	3	1-0	0	2	.231	.286	.462	110	0	0-0	.917	-0	114	0	2b3		0.0
1972	SF	N	51	84	8	19	3	1	1	4	8-1	0	12	.226	.293	.321	73	-3	0-1	.970	-1	119	211	3b17,2b7,S4		-0.3
1973	SF	N	49	54	7	16	2	0	1	13	8-2	0	11	.296	.381	.389	111	1	0-0	.944	-3	48	0	C9/23		-0.1
1974	SF	N	78	174	22	42	7	3	1	26	15-1	1	27	.241	.302	.333	75	-6	1-1	.974	-5	99	83	2b31,3b7/S		-0.9
1975	SF	N	29	41	4	8	0	0	0	4	4-0	0	8	.195	.267	.195	29	-4	0-0	.923	1	93	230	2b4,O4(3/0/1)		-0.4
1976	SF	N	60	69	4	15	0	1	0	5	6-1	0	16	.217	.276	.246	49	-5	0-0	1.000	4	188	67	2b8,3b4/1S		-0.1
Total 6			273	435	47	103	12	5	4	51	42-5	1	76	.237	.303	.315	72	-17	1-2	.971	-4	107	76	2b54,3b29,C9,S6,O4(3/0/1)/1		-1.8

ARNOLD, BILLY Willis S. B3.2.1851 Middletown CT D1.17.1899 Albany NY d4.26

YEAR	TM	LG	G	AB	R	H	2B	3B	HR	RBI	BB-IB	HP	SO	AVG	OBP	SLG	AOPS	ABR	SB-CS	FA	FR	RNG	THR	GAMES AT POSITION	DL	BFW
1872	Man	NA	2	7	2	1	0	0	0	0	0			.143	.143	.143	-13	-1	1-0	1.000	0	0	0	O2R		0.0

ARNOVICH, MORRIE Morris "Snooker" B11.16.1910 Superior WI D7.20.1959 Superior WI BR/TR/5-10/168 d9.14 Mil 1942-45 Col Wisconsin-Superior

YEAR	TM	LG	G	AB	R	H	2B	3B	HR	RBI	BB-IB	HP	SO	AVG	OBP	SLG	AOPS	ABR	SB-CS	FA	FR	RNG	THR	GAMES AT POSITION	DL	BFW
1936	Phi	N	13	48	4	15	3	0	1	7	1	2	3	.313	.353	.438	102	0	0	1.000	1	120	92	O13L		0.1
1937	Phi	N	117	410	60	119	27	4	10	60	34	3	32	.290	.349	.449	107	4	5	.972	7	110	130	O107(97/9/1)		0.5
1938	Phi	N	139	502	47	138	29	0	4	72	42	2	37	.275	.333	.357	92	-4	2	.983	17	118	174	O133(130/1/3)		0.6
1939	Phi	N☆	134	491	68	159	25	2	5	67	58	2	28	.324	.397	.413	122	18	7	.983	14	122	124	O132(131/2/0)		2.4
1940	Phi	N	39	141	13	28	2	1	0	12	14	1	15	.199	.276	.227	42	-11	0	.959	1	105	102	O37(36/0/1)		-1.3
	†Cin	N	62	211	17	60	10	2	0	21	13	0	10	.284	.326	.351	86	-4	1	1.000	3	105	120	O60(57/0/3)		-0.4
	Year		101	352	30	88	12	3	0	33	27	1	25	.250	.305	.301	68	-15	1	.983	4	105	112	O97(93/0/4)		-1.7
1941	NY	N	85	207	25	58	8	3	2	22	23	0	14	.280	.352	.377	103	1	2	.982	1	98	148	O61L		0.0
1946	NY	N	1	3	0	0	0	0	0	0	0	0	0	.000	.000	.000	-99	-1	0	1.000	-0	85	0	/OL		-0.1
Total 7			590	2013	284	577	104	12	22	261	185	10	139	.287	.350	.383	100	3	17	.981	45	113	137	O544(526/12/8)		1.8

ARUNDEL, TUG John Thomas B6.30.1862 Romulus NY D9.5.1912 Auburn NY d5.23

YEAR	TM	LG	G	AB	R	H	2B	3B	HR	RBI	BB-IB	HP	SO	AVG	OBP	SLG	AOPS	ABR	SB-CS	FA	FR	RNG	THR	GAMES AT POSITION	DL	BFW
1882	Phi	AA	1	5	0	0	0	0	0	0	0			.000	.000	.000	-94	-1		.800	-0			/C		-0.1
1884	Tol	AA	15	47	6	4	0	0	0	3	0			.085	.140	.085	-24	-6		.946	5			C15		0.0
1887	Ind	N	43	157	13	31	4	0	0	13	8	1	12	.197	.241	.223	31	-14	8	.865	-8			C42,O2R/1		-1.7
1888	Was	N	17	51	2	10	0	1	0	3	5	0	10	.196	.268	.235	66	-2	1	.840	-6			C17		-0.6
Total 4			76	260	21	45	4	1	0	16	16	1	22	.173	.224	.196	25	-23	9	.882	-9			C75,O2R/1		-2.4

ASADOOR, RANDY Randall Carl B10.20.1962 Fresno CA BR/TR/6-1/185 [TexA83 3/57] d9.14 Col Cal St.-Fresno

YEAR	TM	LG	G	AB	R	H	2B	3B	HR	RBI	BB-IB	HP	SO	AVG	OBP	SLG	AOPS	ABR	SB-CS	FA	FR	RNG	THR	GAMES AT POSITION	DL	BFW
1986	SD	N	15	55	9	22	3	0	0	13				.364	.397	.455	137	3	1-2	.889	-0	103	41	3b15,2b2		0.2

ASBELL, JIM James Marion "Big Train" B6.22.1914 Dallas TX D7.6.1967 San Mateo CA BR/TR/6-0/195 d5.8

YEAR	TM	LG	G	AB	R	H	2B	3B	HR	RBI	BB-IB	HP	SO	AVG	OBP	SLG	AOPS	ABR	SB-CS	FA	FR	RNG	THR	GAMES AT POSITION	DL	BFW
1938	Chi	N	17	33	6	6	2	0	0	3	3	0	9	.182	.250	.242	35	-3	0	1.000	1	94	171	O10(7/0/3)		-0.3

ASBJORNSON, CASPER Robert Anthony (Name Changed To Asby) B6.19.1909 Concord MA D1.21.1970 Williamsport PA BR/TR/6-1/196 d9.17

YEAR	TM	LG	G	AB	R	H	2B	3B	HR	RBI	BB-IB	HP	SO	AVG	OBP	SLG	AOPS	ABR	SB-CS	FA	FR	RNG	THR	GAMES AT POSITION	DL	BFW
1928	Bos	A	6	16	0	3	0	0	0	1	1	0	1	.188	.235	.250	28	-2	0-0	.917	-2	69	134	C6		-0.3
1929	Bos	A	17	29	1	3	0	0	0	1	0	0	6	.103	.133	.103	-39	-6	0-0	.897	-2	90	108	C15		-0.7
1931	Cin	N	45	118	13	36	7	1	0	22	7	1	23	.305	.349	.381	102	0	0-0	.981	-1	83	132	C31		0.1
1932	Cin	N	29	58	5	10	2	0	1	4	0	1	15	.172	.186	.259	19	-7	0-0	.961	-1	94	53	C16		-0.7
Total 4			97	221	19	52	10	1	1	27	9	2	45	.235	.269	.299	56	-15	0-0	.960	-5	86	110	C68		-1.6

YEAR	TM LG	G	AB	R	H	2B	3B	HR	RBI	BB-IB	HP	SO	AVG	OBP	SLG	AOPS	ABR	SB-CS	FA	FR	RNG	THR	GAMES AT POSITION	DL	BFW

ASHBURN, RICHIE Don Richard "Whitey" B3.19.1927 Tilden NE D9.9.1997 New York NY BL/TR/5-10/170* d4.20 HF1995

YEAR	TM LG	G	AB	R	H	2B	3B	HR	RBI	BB-IB	HP	SO	AVG	OBP	SLG	AOPS	ABR	SB-CS	FA	FR	RNG	THR	GAMES AT POSITION	DL	BFW
1948	Phi N★	117	463	78	154	17	4	2	40	60	1	22	.333	.410	.400	122	17	32	.981	9	109	156	O116(15/102/0)		2.2
1949	Phi N	154	662	84	188	18	11	1	37	58	1	38	.284	.343	.349	88	-12	9	.980	10	112	108	O154C		-0.5
1950	†Phi N	151	594	84	180	25	14	2	41	63	2	32	.303	.372	.402	105	5	14	.988	-1	102	64	O147C		0.0
1951	Phi N★	154	643	92	221	31	5	4	63	50	2	37	.344	.393	.426	122	21	29-6	.988	21	125	107	O154C		4.2
1952	Phi N	154	613	93	173	31	6	1	42	75	2	30	.282	.362	.357	101	4	16-11	.980	8	103	147	O154C		0.7
1953	Phi N★	156	622	110	205	25	9	2	57	61	5	35	.330	.394	.408	110	12	14-6	.990	18	115	126	O156C		2.2
1954	Phi N	153	559	111	175	16	8	1	41	125	4	46	.313	.441	.376	116	23	11-8	.984	13	116	102	O153C		2.8
1955	Phi N	140	533	91	180	32	9	3	42	105-5	3	36	.338	.449	.448	142	41	12-10	.983	5	108	94	O140C		3.7
1956	Phi N	154	628	94	190	26	8	3	50	79-3	5	45	.303	.384	.384	110	12	10-1	.983	19	124	97	O154C		2.6
1957	Phi N☆	156	626	93	186	26	8	0	33	94-1	4	44	.297	.390	.364	108	13	13-10	.987	25	124	162	O156(0/156/1)		3.0
1958	Phi N☆	152	615	98	215	24	13	2	33	97-7	4	48	.350	.440	.441	136	39	30-12	.984	12	120	63	O152C		4.5
1959	Phi N	153	564	86	150	16	2	1	20	79-4	6	42	.266	.360	.307	79	-13	9-11	.971	-5	102	48	O149C		-2.8
1960	Chi N	151	547	99	159	16	5	0	40	116-1	1	50	.291	.415	.338	110	16	16-4	.976	-4	94	98	O146(45/106/0)		0.7
1961	Chi N	109	307	49	79	7	4	0	19	55-2	3	27	.257	.373	.306	83	-5	7-6	.978	-8	80	76	O76(14/62/0)		-1.6
1962	NY N★	135	389	60	119	7	3	7	28	81-2	0	39	.306	.424	.393	119	16	12-7	.975	1	97	131	O97(10/56/42),2b2		1.2
Total	15	2189	8365	1322	2574	317	109	29	586	1198-25	43	571	.308	.396	.382	111	189	234-92	.983	121	110	105	O2104(84/1995/43),2b2		22.9

ASHBY, ALAN Alan Dean B7.8.1951 Long Beach CA BB/TR (BL 1976)/6-2/190(170-195) [CleA69 3/63] d7.3 C1

YEAR	TM LG	G	AB	R	H	2B	3B	HR	RBI	BB-IB	HP	SO	AVG	OBP	SLG	AOPS	ABR	SB-CS	FA	FR	RNG	THR	GAMES AT POSITION	DL	BFW
1973	Cle A	11	29	4	5	1	0	1	3	2-0	0	11	.172	.226	.310	49	-2	0-0	.978	-3	150	37	C11		-0.4
1974	Cle A	10	7	1	1	0	0	0	0	1-0	0	2	.143	.250	.143	15	-1	0-0	1.000	0	0	0	C9		-0.1
1975	Cle A	90	254	32	57	10	1	5	32	30-1	1	42	.224	.309	.331	80	-6	3-2	.990	-3	87	110	C87,1b2/3D		-0.6
1976	Cle A	89	247	26	59	5	1	4	30	27-4	0	49	.239	.310	.316	85	-4	0-2	.987	3	82	117	C86,1b2/3		0.1
1977	Tor A	124	396	25	83	16	3	2	29	50-3	2	51	.210	.301	.280	59	-22	0-2	.984	-0	125	117	C124		-1.7
1978	Tor A	81	264	27	69	15	0	9	29	28-4	1	32	.261	.333	.420	109	3	1-1	.986	-6	107	103	C81		0.1
1979	Hou N	108	336	25	68	15	2	2	35	26-10	2	70	.202	.262	.277	51	-24	0-0	.987	1	102	83	C105	18	-1.9
1980	†Hou N	116	352	30	90	19	2	3	48	35-12	0	40	.256	.319	.347	95	-2	0-0	.991	-0	103	62	C114		0.2
1981	†Hou N	83	255	20	69	13	0	4	33	35-6	0	33	.271	.356	.369	113	6	0-2	.982	10	105	130	C81		2.0
1982	Hou N	100	339	40	87	14	2	12	49	27-4	1	53	.257	.311	.416	111	3	2-0	.977	-7	75	69	C95		0.1
1983	Hou N	87	275	31	63	18	1	8	34	31-4	0	38	.229	.303	.389	97	-1	0-0	.974	-8	83	86	C85	27	-0.6
1984	Hou N	66	191	16	50	7	0	4	27	20-2	1	22	.262	.330	.361	102	1	0-0	.986	-4	76	122	C63	34	0.8
1985	Hou N	65	189	20	53	8	0	8	25	24-2	1	27	.280	.363	.450	129	8	0-1	.978	-2	78	108	C60	40	0.8
1986	†Hou N	120	315	24	81	15	0	7	38	39-9	0	56	.257	.333	.371	98	0	1-0	.985	-2	86	76	C103		0.2
1987	Hou N	125	386	53	111	16	0	14	63	50-2	1	52	.288	.367	.438	118	11	0-1	.993	-2	79	74	C110		1.3
1988	Hou N	73	227	19	54	10	0	7	33	29-3	0	36	.238	.319	.374	104	2	0-0	.991	-10	66	67	C66	69	-0.5
1989	Hou N	22	61	4	10	1	1	0	3	7-0	1	8	.164	.257	.213	38	-5	0-0	1.000	-4	87	65	C19		-0.8
Total	17	1370	4123	397	1010	183	13	90	513	461-66	11	622	.245	.320	.361	93	-33	7-10	.986	-36	92	92	C1299,1b4,3b2/D	212	-1.8

ASHFORD, TUCKER Thomas Steven B12.4.1954 Memphis TN BR/TR/6-1/195* [SDN74*1/2] d9.21 Col U. of Mississippi

YEAR	TM LG	G	AB	R	H	2B	3B	HR	RBI	BB-IB	HP	SO	AVG	OBP	SLG	AOPS	ABR	SB-CS	FA	FR	RNG	THR	GAMES AT POSITION	DL	BFW
1976	SD N	4	5	0	3	1	0	0	0	1-0	0	0	.600	.667	.800	341	2	2-0	1.000	-0	90	0	/3		0.2
1977	SD N	81	249	25	54	18	0	3	24	21-4	1	35	.217	.278	.325	69	-11	2-3	.937	-8	102	122	3b74,S10,2b4		-2.1
1978	SD N	75	155	11	38	11	0	3	26	14-1	0	31	.245	.301	.374	97	-1	1-0	.917	-11	47	68	3b32,2b18,1b14		-1.2
1980	Tex A	15	32	2	4	0	0	0	3	3-0	0	3	.125	.200	.125	-9	-5	0-0	.943	2	117	46	3b12,S2		-0.3
1981	NY A	3	0	0	0	0	0	0	0	0-0	0	0	—	—	—	—	-1	0-0	—	-1	0	0	2b2		-0.1
1983	NY N	35	56	3	10	0	1	0	2	7-1	0	4	.179	.270	.214	36	-5	0-0	.957	-0	90	117	3b15,2b13/C		-0.6
1984	KC A	9	13	1	2	1	0	0	1	1-0	0	2	.154	.214	.231	23	-1	0-0	.909	-1	86	125	3b9		-0.2
Total	7	222	510	42	111	31	1	6	55	47-6	1	75	.218	.282	.318	69	-21	5-3	.936	-19	93	105	3b143,2b37,1b14,S12/C		-4.3

ASHLEY, BILLY Billy Manual B7.11.1970 Trenton MI BR/TR/6-7/227(220-242) [LAN88 3/62] d9.1

YEAR	TM LG	G	AB	R	H	2B	3B	HR	RBI	BB-IB	HP	SO	AVG	OBP	SLG	AOPS	ABR	SB-CS	FA	FR	RNG	THR	GAMES AT POSITION	DL	BFW
1992	LA N	29	95	6	21	5	0	2	6	5-0	0	34	.221	.260	.337	69	-4	0-0	.857	-3	72	123	O27(1/0/26)		-0.9
1993	LA N	14	37	0	9	0	0	0	0	2-0	0	11	.243	.282	.243	45	-3	0-0	1.000	1	58	432	O11L		-0.3
1994	LA N	2	6	0	2	1	0	0	0	0-0	0	2	.333	.333	.500	120	0	0-0	1.000	-0	79	0	O2L		0.0
1995	†LA N	81	215	17	51	5	0	8	27	25-4	2	88	.237	.320	.372	89	-4	0-0	.972	-1	103	60	O69L		-0.6
1996	†LA N	71	110	18	22	2	1	9	25	21-1	1	44	.200	.331	.482	119	3	0-0	.952	-1	85	141	O38L	22	0.1
1997	La N	71	131	12	32	7	0	6	19	8-0	1	46	.244	.293	.435	93	-2	0-0	.911	-2	82	121	O35L		-0.5
1998	Bos A	13	24	3	7	3	0	3	7	2-0	0	11	.292	.346	.792	180	3	0-0	.857	0	0	377	1b2,O2L,D5	17	0.3
Total	7	281	618	56	144	23	1	28	84	63-5	4	236	.233	.307	.409	94	-7	0-0	.941	-5	87	130	O184(158/0/26),D5,1b2	39	-1.9

ASMUSSEN, TOM Thomas William B9.26.1876 Chicago IL D8.21.1963 Arlington Heights IL TR d8.10

YEAR	TM LG	G	AB	R	H	2B	3B	HR	RBI	BB-IB	HP	SO	AVG	OBP	SLG	AOPS	ABR	SB-CS	FA	FR	RNG	THR	GAMES AT POSITION	DL	BFW
1907	Bos N	2	5	0	0	0	0	0	0	0-0	0		.000	.000	.000	-99	-1	0	1.000	-1	49	82	C2		-0.2

ASPROMONTE, KEN Kenneth Joseph B9.22.1931 Brooklyn NY BR/TR/6-0/180* d9.2 M3 b-Bob

YEAR	TM LG	G	AB	R	H	2B	3B	HR	RBI	BB-IB	HP	SO	AVG	OBP	SLG	AOPS	ABR	SB-CS	FA	FR	RNG	THR	GAMES AT POSITION	DL	BFW
1957	Bos A	24	78	9	21	5	0	0	4	17-0	0	10	.269	.396	.333	97	1	0-1	.965	-3	102	81	2b24		0.0
1958	Bos A	6	16	0	2	0	0	0	0	3-0	0	1	.125	.263	.125	10	-2	0-0	.952	-2	57	81	2b6		-0.4
	Was A	92	253	15	57	9	1	5	27	25-1	1	28	.225	.296	.328	73	-9	1-1	.964	1	105	93	2b72,3b11/S		-0.4
	Year	98	269	15	59	9	1	5	27	28-1	1	29	.219	.294	.316	69	-11	1-1	.963	-1	102	92	2b78,3b11/S		-0.8
1959	Was A	70	225	31	55	12	0	2	14	26-0	0	39	.244	.321	.324	79	-6	2-1	.960	-6	102	76	2b52,S12/1OL		-0.7
1960	Was A	4	3	0	0	0	0	0	0	0-0	0	1	.000	.000	.000	-99	-1	0-0	—	-0			/H		-0.1
	Cle A	117	459	65	133	20	1	10	48	53-0	2	32	.290	.364	.403	111	8	4-1	.976	-9	95	103	2b80,3b36		0.6
	Year	121	462	65	133	20	1	10	48	53-0	2	33	.288	.362	.400	110	7	4-1	.976	-9	95	103	2b80,3b36		0.5
1961	LA A	66	238	29	53	10	0	2	14	33-1	2	21	.223	.322	.290	58	-13	0-0	.970	20	119	123	2b62		1.2
	Cle A	22	70	5	16	6	1	0	5	6-0	0	3	.229	.295	.343	70	-3	0-0	.963	-3	106	67	2b21		-0.4
	Year	88	308	34	69	16	1	2	19	39-1	2	24	.224	.314	.302	61	-16	0-0	.969	17	116	111	2b83		0.8
1962	Cle A	20	28	4	4	2	0	0	1	6-1	0	5	.143	.286	.214	41	-2	0-0	1.000	-2	53	76	2b6,3b3		-0.3
	Mil N	34	79	11	23	2	0	0	7	6-0	1	5	.291	.341	.316	82	-2	0-1	1.000	0	99	92	2b12,3b6		-0.1
1963	Chi N	20	34	2	5	3	0	0	4	4-1	0	4	.147	.237	.235	35	-3	0-0	.951	2	134	106	2b7,1b2		0.0
Total	7	475	1483	171	369	69	3	19	124	179-4	6	149	.249	.330	.338	82	-32	7-5	.969	-1	104	96	2b342,3b56,S13,1b3/OL		-0.6

ASPROMONTE, BOB Robert Thomas B6.19.1938 Brooklyn NY BR/TR/6-2/185* d9.19 b-Ken OF(60/0/2)

YEAR	TM LG	G	AB	R	H	2B	3B	HR	RBI	BB-IB	HP	SO	AVG	OBP	SLG	AOPS	ABR	SB-CS	FA	FR	RNG	THR	GAMES AT POSITION	DL	BFW
1956	Bro N	1	1	0	0	0	0	0	0	0-0	0	1	.000	.000	.000	-93	-0	0-0	—	0			/H		0.0
1960	LA N	21	55	1	10	1	0	1	6	0-0	1	6	.182	.196	.255	21	-6	1-0	.933	-4	60	77	S15,3b4		-1.0
1961	LA N	47	58	7	14	3	0	2	4	0-0	0	12	.241	.290	.293	51	-4	0-0	.917	1	121	0	3b9,S4,2b2		-0.3
1962	Hou N	149	534	59	142	18	4	11	59	46-4	8	54	.266	.332	.376	97	-2	4-5	.967	-0	92	85	3b142,S11/2		-0.3
1963	Hou N	136	468	42	100	9	5	8	49	40-4	1	57	.214	.276	.306	72	-18	3-1	.938	-8	91	22	3b131/1		-3.0
1964	Hou N	157	553	51	155	20	3	12	69	35-7	8	54	.280	.329	.392	109	6	6-7	.973	-8	95	43	3b155		-0.3
1965	Hou N	152	578	53	152	15	2	5	52	38-5	3	54	.263	.310	.322	85	-13	2-2	.962	8	107	106	3b146,1b6,S4		-0.6
1966	Hou N	152	560	55	141	16	3	8	52	35-7	2	63	.252	.297	.334	81	-16	0-4	.962	-9	90	62	3b149,1b2,S2		-2.8
1967	Hou N	137	486	51	143	24	5	6	58	45-11	2	44	.294	.354	.401	121	14	2-2	.963	-6	86	72	3b133		0.7
1968	Hou N	124	409	25	92	9	2	1	46	35-9	2	57	.225	.285	.264	68	-16	1-0	.973	-0	95	54	3b75,O36(35/0/2)/1S		-2.1
1969	†Atl N	82	198	16	50	8	1	3	24	13-1	2	19	.253	.304	.348	82	-5	0-1	.975	-5	106	88	O24L,3b23,S18,2b2		-1.1
1970	Atl N	62	127	5	27	3	0	0	7	13-0	0	13	.213	.282	.236	39	-11	0-0	.938	-0	102	112	3b30,S4/1OL		-1.1
1971	NY N	104	342	21	77	9	1	5	33	29-4	0	25	.225	.285	.301	66	-15	0-2	.965	-6	81	71	3b97		-2.5
Total	13	1324	4369	386	1103	135	26	60	457	333-52	29	459	.252	.308	.336	85	-86	19-24	.960	-38	93	65	3b1094,O61L,S59,1b11,2b5		-14.4

ASSELSTINE, BRIAN Brian Hanly B9.23.1953 Santa Barbara CA BL/TR/6-1/175(170-190) [AtlN73*S1/15] d9.14 Col Hancock (CA) JC

YEAR	TM LG	G	AB	R	H	2B	3B	HR	RBI	BB-IB	HP	SO	AVG	OBP	SLG	AOPS	ABR	SB-CS	FA	FR	RNG	THR	GAMES AT POSITION	DL	BFW
1976	Atl N	11	33	2	7	0	1	0	3	1-0	0	2	.212	.229	.303	49	-2	0-0	1.000	-1	91	0	O9(0/7/2)		-0.4
1977	Atl N	83	124	12	26	6	0	4	17	9-1	0	10	.210	.263	.355	58	-8	1-0	.983	1	114	64	O35(9/13/13)		-0.7
1978	Atl N	39	103	11	28	3	3	2	13	11-1	2	16	.272	.339	.417	104	0	2-1	.968	-1	100	47	O35(0/11/31)	122	-0.2
1979	Atl N	8	10	1	1	0	0	0	1	1-1	0	2	.100	.182	.100	-20	-2	0-0	1.000	-0	55	0	/OL	116	-0.2
1980	Atl N	87	218	18	62	13	1	3	25	11-3	1	37	.284	.318	.394	98	-1	1-3	.962	-9	79	0	O61(29/32/2)	15	-1.3
1981	Atl N	36	86	8	22	5	0	3	9	7-0	0	7	.256	.297	.384	92	-1	1-3	.958	-0	96	100	O16(4/0/12)	22	-0.2
Total	6	284	574	52	146	27	4	12	68	38-6	3	74	.254	.300	.378	84	-14	5-4	.971	-10	92	31	O157(43/63/60)	275	-3.0

ASTROTH, JOE Joseph Henry B9.1.1922 East Alton IL BR/TR/5-9/187* d8.13 Col Illinois

YEAR	TM LG	G	AB	R	H	2B	3B	HR	RBI	BB-IB	HP	SO	AVG	OBP	SLG	AOPS	ABR	SB-CS	FA	FR	RNG	THR	GAMES AT POSITION	DL	BFW
1945	Phi A	10	17	1	1	0	0	0	1	0	1		.059	.111	.059	-50	-3	0-0	.857	-1	96	137	C8		-0.4
1946	Phi A	4	7	0	1	0	0	0	0	0	0	2	.143	.143	.143	-20	-1	0-0	.889	-0	0	209	C4		-0.1

YEAR	TM LG	G	AB	R	H	2B	3B	HR	RBI	BB-IB	HP	SO	AVG	OBP	SLG	AOPS	ABR	SB-CS	FA	FR	RNG	THR	GAMES AT POSITION	DL	BFW
1949	Phi A	55	148	18	36	4	1	0	12	21	0	13	.243	.337	.284	67	-7	1-0	.979	0	105	115	C44		-0.4
1950	Phi A	39	110	11	36	3	1	1	18	18	0	3	.327	.422	.400	113	2	0-0	.985	-5	87	50	C38		0.0
1951	Phi A	64	187	30	46	10	2	2	19	18	0	13	.246	.312	.353	78	-6	0-1	.992	4	162	67	C57		0.0
1952	Phi A	104	337	24	84	7	2	1	36	25	2	27	.249	.305	.311	62	-17	2-2	.992	-1	121	84	C102		-1.4
1953	Phi A	82	260	28	77	15	2	3	24	27	1	12	.296	.367	.404	104	2	1-0	.987	6	151	130	C79		1.2
1954	Phi A	77	226	22	50	8	1	1	23	21	3	19	.221	.296	.279	58	-13	0-0	.988	-3	95	96	C71		-1.3
1955	KC A	101	274	29	69	4	1	5	23	47-6	6	33	.252	.372	.328	89	-2	2-3	.989	-5	120	82	C100		-0.3
1956	KC A	8	13	0	1	0	0	0	0	0-0	0	1	.077	.077	.077	-59	-3	0-0	1.000	1	108	256	C8		-0.2
Total	10	544	1579	163	401	51	10	13	156	177-6	14	124	.254	.334	.324	77	-47	6-6	.987	-4	122	94	C511		-2.9

ATHERTON, CHARLIE Charles Morgan Herbert "Prexy" B11.19.1874 New Brunswick NJ D12.19.1935 Vienna, Austria BR/TR/5-10/160 d5.30 Col Penn St.

1899	Was N	65	242	28	60	5	6	0	23	21	2		.248	.313	.318	74	-9	2	.890	-5	86	69	3b63/OR		-1.2

ATKINS, GARRETT Garrett Bernard B12.12.1979 Orange CA BR/TR/6-2/190(190-210) [ColN00 5/137] d8.3 Col UCLA

2003	Col N	25	69	6	11	2	0	0	4	3-0	1	14	.159	.205	.188	3	-10	0-0	.850	-5	82	0	3b19		-1.4
2004	Col N	15	28	3	10	2	0	1	8	4-0	0	3	.357	.424	.536	133	2	0-0	1.000	-1	63	152	3b4,1b3,O3L		0.1
2005	Col N	138	519	62	149	31	1	13	89	45-1	5	72	.287	.347	.426	89	-7	0-2	.950	-6	100	81	3b136	23	-1.2
Total	3	178	616	71	170	35	1	14	101	52-1	6	89	.276	.336	.404	81	-15	0-2	.941	-11	97	74	3b159,O3L,1b3	23	-2.5

ATKINSON, ED Edward B1851 Baltimore MD d10.22

1873	Was NA	2	8	2	0	0	0	0	0		0		.000	.000	.000	-99	-2	0-0	1.000	-0	0	0	O2R		-0.1

ATKINSON, LEFTY Hubert Berley B6.2.1906 Chicago IL D2.12.1961 Chicago IL BL/TL/5-6.5/149 d8.5

1927	Was A	1	1	0	0	0	0	0	0		0		.000	.000	.000	-99	-0	0-0	—	0			/H		0.0

ATTREAU, DICK Richard Gilbert B4.8.1897 Chicago IL D7.5.1964 Chicago IL BL/TL/6-0/160 d9.14

1926	Phi N	17	61	9	14	1	1	0	5	6	0	5	.230	.299	.279	53	-4	0	.989	-2	62	77	1b17		-0.7
1927	Phi N	44	83	17	17	1	1	1	11	14	0	18	.205	.320	.277	60	-4	1	.989	-1	70	78	1b26		-0.7
Total	2	61	144	26	31	2	2	1	16	20	0	23	.215	.311	.278	57	-8	1	.989	-3	66	78	1b43		-1.4

ATWELL, TOBY Maurice Dailey B3.8.1924 Leesburg VA D1.25.2003 Purcellville VA BL/TR/5-9.5/185* d4.15 Col VPI

1952	Chi N☆	107	362	36	105	16	3	2	31	40	1	22	.290	.362	.367	102	2	2-1	.977	-9	58	81	C101		-0.1
1953	Chi N	24	74	10	17	2	0	1	8	13	0	7	.230	.345	.297	68	-3	0-0	.940	-1	90	165	C24		-0.3
	Pit N	53	139	11	34	6	0	0	17	20	3	12	.245	.352	.288	70	-5	0-0	.967	-4	69	108	C45		-0.7
	Year	77	213	21	51	8	0	1	25	33	3	19	.239	.349	.291	69	-8	0-0	.957	-5	77	129	C69		-1.0
1954	Pit N	96	287	36	83	8	4	3	26	43	3	21	.289	.384	.376	101	2	2-3	.990	-5	56	109	C88		0.1
1955	Pit N	71	207	21	44	8	0	1	18	40-9	1	16	.213	.337	.266	65	-8	0-1	.992	1	79	91	C67		-0.4
1956	Pit N	12	18	0	2	0	0	0	3	1-0	0	5	.111	.158	.111	-27	-3	0-0	1.000	1	154	109	C9		-0.2
	Mil N	15	30	2	5	1	0	2	7	4-1	0	1	.167	.265	.400	80	-1	0-0	1.000	0	115	135	C10		-0.1
	Year	27	48	2	7	1	0	2	10	5-1	0	6	.146	.226	.292	40	-4	0-0	1.000	1	131	125	C19		-0.3
Total	5	378	1117	116	290	41	7	9	110	161-10	8	84	.260	.355	.333	86	-16	4-5	.980	-16	68	102	C344		-1.7

ATWOOD, BILL William Franklin B9.25.1911 Rome GA D9.14.1993 Snyder TX BR/TR/5-11.5/190 d4.15 Col Hardin-Simmons

1936	Phi N	71	192	21	58	9	2	2	29	11	2	15	.302	.346	.401	92	-2	0	.972	-1	99	77	C53		0.0
1937	Phi N	87	279	27	68	15	1	2	32	30	0	27	.244	.317	.326	69	-11	3	.968	-9	137	93	C80		-1.6
1938	Phi N	102	281	27	55	8	1	3	28	25	0	26	.196	.261	.263	46	-21	0	.969	-7	58	125	C94		-2.3
1939	Phi N	4	6	0	0	0	0	0	1	2	0	3	.000	.250	.000	-29	-1	1	1.000	0	50	0	C2		-0.1
1940	Phi N	78	203	7	39	0	0	4	22	25	1	18	.192	.284	.236	47	-14	0	.989	0	91	105	C69		-1.0
Total	5	342	961	82	220	41	4	7	112	93	3	89	.229	.299	.302	63	-49	4	.974	-17	95	102	C298		-5.0

ATZ, JAKE John Jacob (b Jacob Henry Atz) B7.1.1879 Washington DC D5.22.1945 New Orleans LA BR/TR/5-9/150 d9.24

1902	Was A	3	10	1	1	0	0	0	0		0		.100	.100	.100	-44	-2	0	1.000	1	147	93	2b3		-0.1
1907	Chi A	4	8	0	1	0	0	0	0		0		.125	.125	.125	-21	-1	0	1.000	1	177	469	3b2/OC		0.0
1908	Chi A	83	206	24	40	3	0	0	27	31	4		.194	.311	.209	71	-4	9	.936	-1	104	103	2b46,S18/3		-0.6
1909	Chi A	119	381	39	90	18	3	0	22	38	2		.236	.309	.299	96	-1	14	.954	-5	99	115	2b114,O3R/S		-0.5
Total	4	209	605	64	132	21	3	0	49	69	6		.218	.304	.263	83	-8	23	.949	-5	101	111	2b163,S19,O4(0/1/3),3b3		-1.2

AUBREY, HARRY Harry Herbert "Chub" B7.5.1880 St.Joseph MO D9.18.1953 Baltimore MD BR/TR/5-7/130 d4.22

1903	Bos N	96	325	26	69	8	2	0	27	18	5		.212	.264	.249	49	-22	7	.868	-12	99	56	S94/2OL		-3.1

AUDE, RICH Richard Thomas B7.13.1971 Van Nuys CA BR/TR/6-5/209(180-220) [PitN89 2/48] d9.9

1993	Pit N	13	26	1	3	1	0	0	4	1-0	0	7	.115	.148	.154	-19	-4	0-0	1.000	-1	78	132	1b7/OL		-0.6
1995	Pit N	42	109	10	27	8	0	2	19	6-0	0	20	.248	.287	.376	71	-5	1-2	.996	-3	60	127	1b32		-1.0
1996	Pit N	7	16	0	4	0	0	0	1	0-0	0	8	.250	.250	.250	31	-2	0-0	.969	-0	139	114	1b4		-0.2
Total	3	62	151	11	34	9	0	2	24	7-0	0	35	.225	.259	.325	52	-11	1-2	.994	-3	70	127	1b43/OL		-1.8

AUERBACH, RICK Frederick Steven B2.15.1950 Woodland Hills CA BR/TR/6-0/165* [MilA69*S7/145] d4.13 Col Los Angeles Pierce (CA) JC

1971	Mil A	79	236	22	48	10	0	1	9	20-1	2	40	.203	.271	.258	51	-15	3-2	.963	-11	91	72	S78		-1.9
1972	Mil A	153	554	50	121	16	3	2	30	43-5	2	62	.218	.277	.269	64	-25	24-8	.959	-17	96	97	S153		-2.5
1973	Mil A	6	10	2	1	0	0	0	0	0-0	0	1	.100	.100	.200	-18	-2	0-1	.833	-1	87	0	S2		-0.3
1974	†LA N	45	73	12	25	0	0	1	4	8-0	0	9	.342	.407	.384	127	3	4-2	.950	-2	86	84	S19,2b16,3b3		0.3
1975	LA N	85	170	18	38	9	0	0	12	18-3	0	22	.224	.298	.276	63	-8	3-2	.960	-20	77	62	S81/23	17	-2.3
1976	LA N	36	47	7	6	0	0	0	6	1-0	0	6	.128	.226	.128	2	-6	0-1	.943	1	89	154	S12,3b8,2b7		-0.4
1977	Cin N	33	45	5	7	2	0	0	3	4-0	0	12	.156	.216	.200	15	-5	0-0	.976	0	84	2b19,S12		-0.4
1978	Cin N	63	55	17	18	6	0	2	5	7-0	1	12	.327	.413	.545	165	5	1-0	.971	-0	102	103	S26,2b10,3b3		0.7
1979	†Cin N	62	100	17	21	8	1	1	12	14-1	0	19	.210	.304	.340	76	-3	0-1	.933	-3	112	95	3b18,S16,2b3		-0.5
1980	Cin N	24	33	5	11	1	1	0	4	3-0	0	2	.333	.389	.515	153	2	0-3	1.000	0	167	93	S3,3b3/2		0.2
1981	Sea A	38	84	12	13	3	0	1	6	4-0	1	15	.155	.200	.226	22	-7	1-1	.979	2	106	128	S38	53	-0.4
Total		624	1407	167	309	56	5	9	86	127-10	6	198	.220	.286	.286	65	-63	36-21	.960	-51	93	89	S440,2b57,3b36	70	-7.5

AUGUSTINE, DAVE David Ralph B11.28.1949 Follansbee WV BR/TR/6-2/172* d9.3 Col Miami-Dade Kendall (FL) CC

1973	Pit N	11	7	1	2	1	0	0	0	0-0	0	1	.286	.286	.429	97	0	0		72	578	O9(4/4/1)		0.0
1974	Pit N	18	22	3	4	0	0	0	0-0		0	5	.182	.182	.182	2	-3	0-1	1.000	3	132	483	O11(1/6/4)		-0.1
Total	2	29	29	4	6	1	0	0	0	0-0	0	6	.207	.207	.241	25	-3	0-1	1.000	3	115	511	O20(5/10/5)		-0.1

AULDS, LESLIE Leycester Doyle "Tex" B12.28.1920 Farmerville LA D10.13.1999 Hondo TX BR/TR/6-2/185 d5.25

1947	Bos A	3	4	0	1	0	0	0	0	0	0	1	.250	.250	.250	37	0	0-0	1.000	0	0	0	C3		0.0

AULT, DOUG Douglas Reagan B3.9.1950 Beaumont TX D12.22.2004 Tarpon Springs FL d9.9 Col Texas Tech

1976	Tex A	9	20	0	6	1	0	0	1-0		3	.300	.333	.350	98	0	0-0	1.000	-1	0	57	1b4,D3		-0.1
1977	Tor A	129	445	44	109	22	3	11	64	39-5	4	68	.245	.310	.382	87	-8	4-4	.987	6	120	82	1b122,D4		-1.0
1978	Tor A	54	104	10	25	1	1	3	7	17-1	1	14	.240	.352	.356	90	0	0-0	.979	-2	81	78	1b25,O7(6/0/1),D5		-0.3
1980	Tor A	64	144	12	28	5	1	3	15	14-0	2	23	.194	.273	.306	57	-9	0-1	1.000	2	135	100	1b32,D21/OL		-0.9
Total	4	256	713	66	168	29	5	17	86	71-6	7	108	.236	.309	.362	82	-17	4-5	.988	6	116	84	1b183,D33,O8(7/0/1)		-2.3

AURILIA, RICH Richard Santo B9.2.1971 Brooklyn NY BR/TR/6-1/185(170-190) [TexA92 24/678] d9.6 Col St. Johns

1995	SF N	9	19	4	9	3	0	2	4	1-0	0	2	.474	.476	.947	277	5	0-0	1.000	2	135	165	S6		0.7
1996	SF N	105	318	27	76	7	1	3	26	25-2	1	52	.239	.295	.296	58	-20	4-1	.973	-7	97	87	S93,2b11	6	-1.9
1997	SF N	46	102	16	28	8	0	5	19	8-0	1	15	.275	.321	.500	115	2	1-1	.979	8	119	122	S36		1.1
1998	SF N	122	413	54	110	27	2	9	49	31-3	2	62	.266	.319	.407	94	-4	3-3	.979	2	102	114	S120	16	0.5
1999	SF N	152	558	68	143	25	2	22	80	42-5	5	71	.281	.336	.444	103	0	2-3	.957	-3	99	108	S150		0.7
2000	†SF N	141	509	67	138	24	2	20	79	54-2	0	90	.271	.339	.444	103	1	1-2	.967	10	103	130	S140		2.0
2001	SF N★	156	636	114	206	37	5	37	97	47-2	0	83	.324	.369	.572	147	42	1-3	.975	-5	97	116	S149		4.6
2002	†SF N	133	538	76	138	35	2	15	61	40-3	4	90	.257	.305	.413	94	-9	1-2	.980	-10	90	123	S131	15	-1.0
2003	†SF N	129	505	65	140	26	1	13	58	36-0	1	82	.277	.325	.410	89	-9	2-2	.974	-19	90	109	S123/D	15	-1.8
2004	Sea A	73	261	27	63	13	0	4	28	22-1	2	43	.241	.304	.337	71	-11	1-0	.990	-11	88	85	S73		-1.6
	SD N	51	138	12	38	8	2	2	16	15-0	2	28	.254	.331	.384	90	-2	0-0	.919	-4	82	67	3b29,2b7,S6/1		-0.5

YEAR	TM LG	G	AB	R	H	2B	3B	HR	RBI	BB-IB	HP	SO	AVG	OBP	SLG	AOPS	ABR	SB-CS	FA	FR	RNG	THR	GAMES AT POSITION	DL	BFW
2005	Cin N	114	426	61	120	23	2	14	68	37-2	1	67	.282	.338	.444	107	4	2-0	.981	-2	101	86	2b68,S30,3b18	18	0.7
Total	11	1231	4423	601	1220	234	18	146	585	356-15	18	685	.276	.330	.436	102	-1	19-17	.973	-39	97	111	S1057,2b86,3b47/1D	70	3.5

AUSMUS, BRAD   Bradley David B4.14.1969 New Haven CT BR/TR/5-11/195* [NYA87 48/1152] d7.28

YEAR	TM LG	G	AB	R	H	2B	3B	HR	RBI	BB-IB	HP	SO	AVG	OBP	SLG	AOPS	ABR	SB-CS	FA	FR	RNG	THR	GAMES AT POSITION	DL	BFW
1993	SD N	49	160	18	41	8	1	5	12	6-0	0	28	.256	.283	.412	83	-5	2-0	.975	2	112	119	C49		0.1
1994	SD N	101	327	45	82	12	1	7	24	30-12	1	63	.251	.314	.358	78	-11	5-1	.991	-3	92	104	C99/1		-0.7
1995	SD N	103	328	44	96	16	4	5	34	31-3	2	56	.293	.353	.412	105	3	16-5	.992	5	134	127	C100/1		1.5
1996	SD N	50	149	16	27	4	0	1	13	13-0	3	27	.181	.261	.228	32	-15	1-4	.982	-2	104	116	C46		-1.6
	Det A	75	226	30	56	12	0	4	22	26-1	2	45	.248	.328	.354	73	-9	3-4	.992	-2	92	130	C73		-0.7
1997	†Hou N	130	425	45	113	25	1	4	44	38-4	1	78	.266	.326	.358	83	-10	14-6	.992	13	187	112	C129		1.2
1998	†Hou N	128	412	62	111	10	4	6	45	53-11	3	60	.269	.356	.357	91	-5	10-3	.992	5	128	91	C124		0.9
1999	Det A★	127	458	62	126	25	6	9	54	51-0	14	71	.275	.365	.415	97	-1	12-9	.998	-3	133	94	C127		0.4
2000	Det A	150	523	75	139	25	3	7	51	69-0	6	79	.266	.357	.365	84	-11	11-5	.992	20	196	106	C150/123		1.8
2001	†Hou N	128	422	45	98	23	4	5	34	30-6	1	64	.232	.284	.341	57	-28	4-1	.997	15	151	124	C127		-0.4
2002	Hou N	130	447	57	115	19	3	6	50	38-3	6	71	.257	.322	.353	75	-17	2-3	.997	-5	110	92	C129		-0.2
2003	Hou N	143	450	43	103	12	2	4	47	46-1	4	66	.229	.303	.291	54	-30	5-3	.997	25	97	124	C143		0.3
2004	†Hou N	129	403	38	100	14	1	5	31	33-11	2	56	.248	.306	.325	62	-23	2-2	.995	4	79	115	C128		-1.1
2005	†Hou N	134	387	35	100	19	0	3	47	51-8	5	48	.258	.351	.331	80	-9	5-3	.999	18	157	72	C134/2S		1.7
Total	13	1577	5117	615	1307	224	30	71	508	515-60	52	812	.255	.328	.353	77	-171	92-49	.994	103	131	107	C1558,1b3,2b2/S3		3.2

AUSTIN, HENRY   Henry C. B1844 Brooklyn NY D9.3.1895 Amityville NY d4.28

YEAR	TM LG	G	AB	R	H	2B	3B	HR	RBI	BB-IB	HP	SO	AVG	OBP	SLG	AOPS	ABR	SB-CS	FA	FR	RNG	THR	GAMES AT POSITION	DL	BFW
1873	Res NA	23	101	10	25	3	3	0	11	0		5	.248	.248	.337	78	-2	1-1	.722	-1	114	251	O23(0/14/9)		-0.2

AUSTIN, JIMMY   James Philip "Pepper" B12.8.1879 Swansea, Wales D3.6.1965 Laguna Beach CA BB/TR/5-7.5/155 d4.19 M3/C18

YEAR	TM LG	G	AB	R	H	2B	3B	HR	RBI	BB-IB	HP	SO	AVG	OBP	SLG	AOPS	ABR	SB-CS	FA	FR	RNG	THR	GAMES AT POSITION	DL	BFW
1909	NY A	136	437	37	101	11	5	1	39	32	1		.231	.285	.286	80	-11	30	.928	13	105	134	3b111,S23/2		0.7
1910	NY A	133	432	46	94	11	4	2	36	47	7		.218	.305	.275	77	-10	22	.942	3	98	54	3b133		-0.4
1911	StL A	148	541	84	141	25	11	2	45	69	6		.261	.351	.359	102	3	26	.931	19	116	123	3b148		2.5
1912	StL A	149	536	57	135	14	8	2	44	38	4		.252	.306	.319	82	-14	28	.911	2	98	104	3b149		-0.9
1913	StL A	142	489	56	130	18	6	2	42	45	8	51	.266	.338	.339	101	1	37	.944	6	104	101	3b142,M		1.2
1914	StL A	130	466	55	111	16	4	0	30	40	1	59	.238	.300	.290	80	-12	20-23	.935	-1	99	98	3b127		-1.4
1915	StL A	141	477	61	127	6	6	1	30	64	2	60	.266	.355	.310	103	4	18-15	.917	10	104	143	3b141		1.7
1916	StL A	129	411	55	85	15	6	1	28	74	4	59	.207	.333	.280	89	-2	19	.939	-8	102	91	3b124		-0.8
1917	StL A	127	455	61	109	18	8	0	19	50	3	46	.240	.319	.314	97	-1	13	.947	7	102	118	3b121,S6		1.0
1918	StL A	110	367	42	97	14	4	0	20	53	1	32	.264	.359	.324	109	6	18	.939	-15	88	59	S57,3b48,M		-0.4
1919	StL A	106	396	54	94	9	9	1	21	42	1	31	.237	.314	.313	74	-14	6	.939	6	101	95	3b98		-0.5
1920	StL A	83	280	38	76	11	3	1	32	31	1	15	.271	.352	.343	82	-6	2-4	.943	0	96	106	3b75		-0.5
1921	StL A	27	66	8	18	2	1	0	2	4	1	7	.273	.324	.333	64	-4	2-1	.938	-2	87	0	S14,2b6,3b2		-0.4
1922	StL A	15	31	6	9	3	1	0	1	3	0	2	.290	.353	.452	105	0	0-0	.957	-2	62	0	3b9,2b2		-0.1
1923	StL A	1	0	0	0	0	0	0	0	0	0	0	—	—	—	—	0	0-0		0			/RM		0.0
1925	StL A	1	1	0	0	0	0	0	0	0	0	0	.000	.000	.000	-95	0	0-0	1.000	0	0	0	/3		0.0
1926	StL A	1	2	1	1	1	0	0	1	0	0	0	.500	.500	1.000	272	1	1-0	1.000	0	80	955	/3		0.1
1929	StL A	1	1	0	0	0	0	0	0	0	0	0	.000	.000	.000	-96	0	0-0	1.000	0	236	0	/3		0.0
Total	18	1580	5388	661	1328	174	76	13	390	592	44	363	.246	.326	.314	90	-59	244-43	.933	38	102	105	3b1431,S100,2b9		1.8

AUTRY, CHICK   Martin Gordon B3.5.1903 Martindale TX D1.26.1950 Savannah GA BR/TR/6-0/180 d4.20

YEAR	TM LG	G	AB	R	H	2B	3B	HR	RBI	BB-IB	HP	SO	AVG	OBP	SLG	AOPS	ABR	SB-CS	FA	FR	RNG	THR	GAMES AT POSITION	DL	BFW
1924	NY A	2	1	0	1	0	0	0	0	1	0	0	—	1.000	—	172	0	0-0	1.000	0	0	0	C2		0.0
1926	Cle A	3	7	1	1	0	0	0	0	1	0	0	.143	.250	.143	4	-1	0-0	1.000	-0	97	130	C3		-0.1
1927	Cle A	16	43	5	11	4	1	0	7	0	0	6	.256	.256	.395	66	-2	0-0	.933	1	133	167	C14		0.0
1928	Cle A	22	60	6	18	6	1	1	9	1	0	7	.300	.311	.483	105	0	0-0	.972	0	100	64	C18		0.1
1929	Chi A	43	96	7	20	6	0	1	12	1	1	8	.208	.224	.302	35	-10	0-0	.940	-3	98	78	C30		-1.1
1930	Chi A	34	71	1	18	1	0	0	5	4	0	9	.254	.293	.296	52	-5	0-0	.992	4	108	139	C29		0.0
Total	6	120	277	20	68	17	3	2	33	7	2	29	.245	.269	.350	59	-18	0-0	.965	2	107	109	C96		-1.1

AUTRY, CHICK   William Askew B1.2.1885 Humboldt TN D1.16.1976 Santa Rosa CA BL/TL/5-11/168 d9.18

YEAR	TM LG	G	AB	R	H	2B	3B	HR	RBI	BB-IB	HP	SO	AVG	OBP	SLG	AOPS	ABR	SB-CS	FA	FR	RNG	THR	GAMES AT POSITION	DL	BFW
1907	Cin N	7	25	3	5	0	0	0	4	2	0		.200	.231	.200	34	-2	0	.929	-1	0	0	O7(4/3/0)		-0.4
1909	Cin N	9	33	3	6	2	0	0	4	2	0		.182	.229	.242	46	-2	1	.956	0	152	71	1b9		-0.2
	Bos N	65	199	16	39	4	0	0	13	21	2		.196	.279	.216	51	-11	5	.994	4	125	88	1b61,O4(4/1/0)		-0.9
	Year	74	232	19	45	6	0	0	17	23	2		.194	.272	.220	51	-13	6	.989	5	129	86	1b70,O4(4/1/0)		-1.1
Total	2	81	257	22	50	6	0	0	17	24	2		.195	.269	.218	49	-15	6	.956	4	129	86	1b70,O11(8/4/0)		-1.5

AVEN, BRUCE   David Bruce B3.4.1972 Orange TX BR/TR/5-9/180* [CleA94 30/829] d8.27 Col Lamar

YEAR	TM LG	G	AB	R	H	2B	3B	HR	RBI	BB-IB	HP	SO	AVG	OBP	SLG	AOPS	ABR	SB-CS	FA	FR	RNG	THR	GAMES AT POSITION	DL	BFW
1997	Cle A	13	19	4	4	1	0	0	2	1-0	0	5	.211	.250	.263	33	-2	0-1	1.000	1	125	268	O13(10/1/2)		-0.1
1999	Fla N	137	381	57	110	19	2	12	70	44-1	9	82	.289	.370	.444	113	8	3-0	.984	1	103	73	O102(78/9/24),D6		0.6
2000	Pit N	72	148	18	37	11	0	5	25	5-0	0	31	.250	.275	.426	73	-7	2-3	.980	-3	87	0	O41(17/8/20)	17	-1.1
	LA N	9	20	2	5	0	0	2	4	3-0	0	8	.250	.348	.550	128	1	0-0	1.000	-0	93	0	O9L		0.0
	Year	81	168	20	42	11	0	7	29	8-0	0	39	.250	.284	.440	80	-6	2-3	.984	-3	88	0	O50(26/8/20)		-1.1
2001	LA N	21	24	3	8	2	0	1	2	0-0	2	5	.333	.385	.542	145	2	0-0	1.000	0	78	0	O9(5/0/4)		0.1
2002	Cle A	7	17	1	2	0	0	0	4	4-0	0	4	.118	.286	.118	13	-2	1-0	1.000	-0	106	0	O7(5/1/1)		-0.2
Total	5	259	609	85	166	33	2	20	103	57-1	11	135	.273	.343	.432	99	0	6-4	.986	-1	100	58	O181(124/19/51),D6	17	-0.7

AVERILL, EARL   Earl Douglas B9.9.1931 Cleveland OH BR/TR/5-10/190* d4.19 f-Earl Col Oregon

YEAR	TM LG	G	AB	R	H	2B	3B	HR	RBI	BB-IB	HP	SO	AVG	OBP	SLG	AOPS	ABR	SB-CS	FA	FR	RNG	THR	GAMES AT POSITION	DL	BFW
1956	Cle A	42	93	12	22	6	0	3	14	14-1	1	25	.237	.343	.398	93	-1	0-1	.994	2	83	131	C34		0.3
1958	Cle A	17	55	2	10	1	0	2	7	4-0	1	7	.182	.250	.309	54	-4	1-0	.863	-1	109	94	3b17		-0.5
1959	Chi N	74	186	22	44	10	0	10	34	15-1	2	39	.237	.298	.452	98	-1	0-1	.963	-3	58	70	C32,3b13,O5L,2b2		-0.3
1960	Chi A	52	102	14	24	4	0	1	13	11-1	1	16	.235	.310	.304	71	-4	1-1	.979	-2	58	52	C34/3OL		-0.5
	Chi A	10	14	2	3	0	0	0	2	4-0	0	2	.214	.389	.214	68	0	0-0	1.000	2	80	159	C5		0.2
1961	LA A	115	323	56	86	9	0	21	59	62-1	2	70	.266	.384	.489	119	10	1-0	.991	-1	67	99	C88,O9L/2		1.5
1962	LA A	92	187	21	41	9	0	4	22	43-3	1	47	.219	.366	.332	93	0	0-0	1.000	-2	87	85	O49L,C6		-0.3
1963	Phi N	47	71	8	19	2	0	3	8	9-1	0	14	.268	.341	.423	123	2	0-0	.966	3	81	170	C20,O8L/13		1.0
Total	7	449	1031	137	249	41	0	44	159	162-8	8	220	.242	.346	.409	101	2	3-3	.984	1	68	104	C219,O72L,3b32,2b3/1		1.0

AVERILL, EARL   Howard Earl "Rock","The Earl of Snohomish" B5.21.1902 Snohomish WA D8.16.1983 Everett WA BL/TR/5-9.5/172 d4.16 HF1975 s-Earl

YEAR	TM LG	G	AB	R	H	2B	3B	HR	RBI	BB-IB	HP	SO	AVG	OBP	SLG	AOPS	ABR	SB-CS	FA	FR	RNG	THR	GAMES AT POSITION	DL	BFW
1929	Cle A	152	597	110	198	43	13	18	96	63	3	53	.332	.398	.538	134	30	13-14	.966	-11	89	85	O152C		1.0
1930	Cle A	139	534	102	181	33	8	19	119	56	2	48	.339	.404	.537	131	26	10-7	.949	-4	94	111	O134(0/132/2)		1.4
1931	Cle A	155	627	140	209	36	10	32	143	68	6	38	.333	.404	.576	147	41	9-9	.976	-4	98	76	O155C		3.0
1932	Cle A	153	631	116	198	37	14	32	124	75	6	40	.314	.392	.569	137	33	5-8	.964	-7	94	90	O153C		1.8
1933	Cle A★	151	599	83	180	39	16	11	92	54	5	29	.301	.363	.474	115	12	3-1	.971	-4	100	74	O149C		0.5
1934	Cle A★	154	598	128	187	48	6	31	113	99	4	44	.313	.414	.569	149	46	5-3	.970	3	104	98	O154C		4.1
1935	Cle A★	140	563	109	162	34	13	19	79	70	1	58	.288	.368	.496	119	15	8-4	.982	-7	96	55	O139C		0.5
1936	Cle A	152	614	136	232	39	15	28	126	65	1	35	.378	.438	.627	159	55	3-3	.969	-7	93	86	O150C		3.8
1937	Cle A★	156	609	121	182	33	11	21	92	88	0	65	.299	.387	.493	119	18	5-4	.976	-12	88	77	O156C		0.2
1938	Cle A★	134	482	101	159	27	15	14	93	81	3	48	.330	.429	.535	143	34	5-2	.975	-1	98	115	O131(0/118/13)		2.8
1939	Cle A	24	55	8	15	8	0	1	7	6	0	12	.273	.344	.473	111	-1	0-1	1.000	-1	72	0	O11R		-0.1
	Det A	87	309	58	81	20	6	10	58	43	1	30	.262	.354	.463	100	-1	4-2	.976	-3	94	59	O80(75/5/0)		-0.7
	Year	111	364	66	96	28	6	11	65	49	1	42	.264	.353	.464	102	1	4-3	.977	-2	92	53	O91(75/5/11)		-0.8
1940	†Det A	64	118	10	33	4	1	2	20	5	0	14	.280	.309	.381	71	-5	0-0	.962	-1	69	190	O22(7/11/5)		-0.7
1941	Bos N	8	17	2	2	0	0	0	2	1	1	4	.118	.211	.118	-6	-2	0	1.000	1	70	879	O4(1/3/0)		-0.2
Total	13	1669	6353	1224	2019	401	128	238	1164	774	33	518	.318	.395	.534	132	303	70-58	.970	-57	95	87	O1590(83/1477/31)		17.3

AVILA, BOBBY   Roberto Francisco (Gonzalez) B4.2.1924 Veracruz, Veracruz, Mexico D10.26.2004 Veracruz, Veracruz, Mexico BR/TR/5-10/175* d4.30

YEAR	TM LG	G	AB	R	H	2B	3B	HR	RBI	BB-IB	HP	SO	AVG	OBP	SLG	AOPS	ABR	SB-CS	FA	FR	RNG	THR	GAMES AT POSITION	DL	BFW
1949	Cle A	31	14	3	3	0	0	0	1	3		3	.214	.267	.214	29	-1	0-0	1.000	2	187	110	2b5		0.0
1950	Cle A	80	201	39	60	10	2	1	21	29	1	17	.299	.390	.383	102	2	5-0	.983	-9	80	108	2b62,S2		-0.3
1951	Cle A	141	542	76	165	21	3	10	58	60	1	31	.304	.374	.410	118	14	14-8	.982	-3	97	88	2b136		1.9
1952	Cle A★	150	597	102	179	26	11	7	45	67	1	36	.300	.371	.415	127	21	12-10	.966	-23	94	76	2b149		0.6
1953	Cle A	141	559	85	160	22	3	8	55	58	2	27	.286	.355	.379	101	1	10-8	.986	13	107	108	2b140		2.3
1954	†Cle A★	143	555	112	189	27	2	15	67	59	1	31	.341	.402	.477	139	30	9-7	.976	7	106	114	2b141,S7		4.8

YEAR	TM LG	G	AB	R	H	2B	3B	HR	RBI	BB-IB	HP	SO	AVG	OBP	SLG	AOPS	ABR	SB-CS	FA	FR	RNG	THR	GAMES AT POSITION	DL	BFW
1955	Cle A★	141	537	83	146	22	4	13	61	82-1	2	47	.272	.368	.400	103	5	1-4	.982	-2	91	107	2b141		1.2
1956	Cle A	138	513	71	115	14	2	10	54	70-0	5	68	.224	.323	.318	68	-23	17-4	.977	-2	97	91	2b135		-1.3
1957	Cle A	129	463	60	124	19	3	5	48	46-2	1	47	.268	.334	.354	89	-6	2-4	.983	-10	90	85	2b107,3b16		-1.0
1958	Cle A	113	375	54	95	21	3	5	30	55-0	1	45	.253	.349	.365	100	2	5-7	.986	-10	90	103	2b82,3b33		-0.5
1959	Bal A	20	47	1	8	0	0	0	4	4-0	0	5	.170	.235	.170	14	-6	0-0	1.000	0	85	0	O10(1/0/9),2b8/3		-0.8
	Bos A	22	45	7	11	0	0	3	6	6-0	0	11	.244	.333	.444	107	0	0-0	.975	-1	89	135	2b11		0.0
	Year	42	92	8	19	0	0	3	10	10-0	0	16	.207	.284	.304	61	-5	0-0	.967	-2	96	70	2b19,O10(1/0/9)/3		-0.8
	Mil N	51	172	29	41	3	2	3	19	24-0	1	31	.238	.330	.331	84	-4	3-0	.967	-9	96	70	2b51		-0.8
Total	11	1300	4620	725	1296	185	35	80	467	561-3	14	399	.281	.359	.388	104	35	78-52	.979	-48	96	96	2b1168,3b50,O10(1/0/9),S9		6.1

AVILES, RAMON Ramon Antonio (Miranda) B1.22.1952 Manati, PR BR/TR/5-9/155* d7.10

YEAR	TM LG	G	AB	R	H	2B	3B	HR	RBI	BB-IB	HP	SO	AVG	OBP	SLG	AOPS	ABR	SB-CS	FA	FR	RNG	THR	GAMES AT POSITION	DL	BFW
1977	Bos A	1	0	0	0	0	0	0	0	0-0	0	0	—	—	—	—	0	0-0	1.000	0	137	0	/2		0.0
1979	Phi N	27	61	7	17	2	0	0	12	8-1	1	8	.279	.371	.311	85	-1	0-0	.977	-6	80	66	2b27		-0.6
1980	†Phi N	51	101	12	28	6	0	2	9	10-2	0	9	.277	.336	.396	99	0	0-0	.944	-6	87	112	S29,2b15		-0.4
1981	†Phi N	38	28	2	6	1	0	0	3	3-0	0	5	.214	.290	.250	51	-2	0-0	1.000	1	118	90	2b20,3b13,S5		-0.1
Total	4	117	190	21	51	9	0	2	24	21-3	1	22	.268	.341	.347	88	-3	0-0	.971	-12	83	89	2b63,S34,3b13		-1.1

AYALA, BENNY Benigno (Felix) B2.7.1951 Yauco, PR BR/TR/6-1/185(175-195) d8.27

YEAR	TM LG	G	AB	R	H	2B	3B	HR	RBI	BB-IB	HP	SO	AVG	OBP	SLG	AOPS	ABR	SB-CS	FA	FR	RNG	THR	GAMES AT POSITION	DL	BFW
1974	NY N	23	68	9	16	1	0	2	8	7-0	1	17	.235	.308	.338	83	-2	0-0	.927	-0	105	76	O20(18/0/2)		-0.3
1976	NY N	22	26	2	3	0	0	1	2	2-0	0	6	.115	.179	.231	16	-3	0-1	.889	1	111	410	O7(4/0/3)		-0.3
1977	StL N	1	3	0	1	0	0	0	0	0-0	0	1	.333	.333	.333	80	0	0-0	1.000	2	329	1378	/OR		0.2
1979	†Bal A	42	86	15	22	5	0	6	13	6-1	0	9	.256	.298	.523	123	2	0-0	.974	-0	116	0	O24(23/1/1),D10		0.1
1980	Bal A	76	170	28	45	8	1	10	33	19-3	0	21	.265	.335	.500	129	6	0-0	1.000	0	79	221	D41,O19(16/1/2)		0.5
1981	Bal A	44	86	12	24	2	0	3	13	11-0	1	9	.279	.364	.407	123	3	0-1	1.000	2	109	2196	D27,O4L		0.3
1982	Bal A	64	128	17	39	6	0	6	24	5-2	0	14	.305	.331	.492	123	4	1-1	.972	-1	103	0	O25L,D17,1b3		0.1
1983	†Bal A	47	104	12	23	7	0	4	13	9-0	0	18	.221	.278	.404	88	-2	0-0	.953	-1	101	0	O24(19/0/5),D11		-0.4
1984	Bal A	60	118	9	25	6	0	4	24	8-0	0	24	.212	.258	.364	72	-5	1-1	1.000	0	74	0	D34,O13(11/0/2)		-0.7
1985	Cle A	46	76	10	19	7	0	2	15	4-1	0	17	.250	.284	.421	91	-1	0-0	.917	-1	86	132	O20L,D3		-0.2
Total	10	425	865	114	217	42	1	38	145	71-7	2	136	.251	.305	.434	104	2	2-4	.958	-1	101	106	O157(140/2/16),D143,1b3		-0.7

AYBAR, WILLY Willy Del Jesus B3.8.1983 Bani, D.R. BB/TR/6-0/175 d8.31

YEAR	TM LG	G	AB	R	H	2B	3B	HR	RBI	BB-IB	HP	SO	AVG	OBP	SLG	AOPS	ABR	SB-CS	FA	FR	RNG	THR	GAMES AT POSITION	DL	BFW
2005	LA N	26	86	12	28	8	0	1	10	18-0	1	11	.326	.448	.453	137	6	3-1	.962	-2	94	84	3b20,2b6		0.5

AYLWARD, DICK Richard John "Dandy" B6.4.1925 Baltimore MD D6.11.1983 Spring Valley CA BR/TR/6-0/190 d5.1

YEAR	TM LG	G	AB	R	H	2B	3B	HR	RBI	BB-IB	HP	SO	AVG	OBP	SLG	AOPS	ABR	SB-CS	FA	FR	RNG	THR	GAMES AT POSITION	DL	BFW
1953	Cle A	4	3	0	0	0	0	0	0	0-0	0	1	.000	.000	.000	-99	-1	0-0	1.000	0	0	0	C4		-0.1

AYRAULT, JOE Joseph Allen B10.8.1971 Rochester MI BR/TR/6-3/190 [AtlN90 5/129] d9.1

YEAR	TM LG	G	AB	R	H	2B	3B	HR	RBI	BB-IB	HP	SO	AVG	OBP	SLG	AOPS	ABR	SB-CS	FA	FR	RNG	THR	GAMES AT POSITION	DL	BFW
1996	Atl N	7	5	0	1	0	0	0	0	0-0	1	1	.200	.333	.200	42	0	0-0	1.000	-0	0	0	C7		-0.1

AZCUE, JOE Jose Joaquin (Lopez) B8.18.1939 Cienfuegos, Cuba BR/TR/6-0/200* d8.3

YEAR	TM LG	G	AB	R	H	2B	3B	HR	RBI	BB-IB	HP	SO	AVG	OBP	SLG	AOPS	ABR	SB-CS	FA	FR	RNG	THR	GAMES AT POSITION	DL	BFW
1960	Cin N	14	31	1	3	0	0	0	2	2-0	0	6	.097	.152	.097	-30	-6	0-1	1.000	5	108	132	C14		-0.1
1962	KC A	72	223	18	51	9	1	2	25	17-7	3	27	.229	.287	.305	58	-13	1-0	.985	4	90	126	C70	36	-0.6
1963	KC A	2	4	0	0	0	0	0	0	0-0	0	1	.000	.000	.000	-95	-1	0-0	1.000	0	0	0	/C		-0.1
	Cle A	94	320	26	91	16	0	14	46	15-1	0	46	.284	.314	.466	117	6	1-1	.992	6	110	138	C91		1.7
	Year	96	324	26	91	16	0	14	46	15-1	0	47	.281	.310	.460	114	5	1-1	.992	6	110	137	C92		1.6
1964	Cle A	83	271	20	74	9	1	4	34	16-2	2	38	.273	.314	.358	88	-5	0-2	.993	-4	101	117	C76		-0.6
1965	Cle A	111	335	16	77	7	0	2	35	27-8	3	54	.230	.290	.269	60	-17	2-1	.994	6	132	95	C108		-0.7
1966	Cle A	98	302	22	83	10	1	9	37	20-5	2	22	.275	.319	.404	89	3	0-2	.989	-3	232	120	C97		0.3
1967	Cle A	86	295	33	74	12	5	11	34	22-0	3	35	.251	.307	.437	117	5	0-3	.999	8	184	93	C86		1.8
1968	Cle A★	115	357	23	100	10	0	4	42	28-5	0	33	.280	.331	.342	106	3	1-1	.996	14	177	92	C97		2.4
1969	Cle A	7	24	1	7	0	0	1	1	4-0	0	3	.292	.393	.417	123	1	0-0	.980	1	118	100	C6		0.2
	Bos A	19	51	7	11	2	0	0	3	4-1	0	5	.216	.273	.255	46	-4	0-0	.981	3	205	114	C19		0.0
	Cal A	80	248	15	54	6	0	1	19	27-11	2	28	.218	.295	.254	59	-13	0-1	.992	9	128	111	C80		-0.1
	Year	106	323	23	72	8	0	2	23	35-12	2	36	.223	.299	.266	62	-16	0-1	.989	13	139	111	C105		0.1
1970	Cal A	114	351	19	85	13	1	2	25	24-4	2	40	.242	.292	.302	67	-16	0-0	.991	-4	105	81	C112		-1.6
1972	Cal A	3	2	0	0	0	0	0	0	0-0	0	1	.000	.000	.000	-99	-1	0-0	1.000	1	0	0	C2		0.0
	Mil N	11	14	0	2	0	0	0	0	1-1	0	5	.143	.200	.143	3	-2	0-0	1.000	1	98	250	C9		-0.1
	Year	14	16	0	2	0	0	0	0	1-1	0	6	.125	.176	.125	-9	-2	0-0	1.000	1	93	238	C11		-0.1
Total	11	909	2828	201	712	94	9	50	304	207-45	17	344	.252	.304	.344	85	-60	5-12	.992	46	142	108	C868	36	2.5

AZOCAR, OSCAR Oscar Gregorio (Azocar) B2.21.1965 Soro, Venez BL/TL/6-1/170(170-195) d7.17

YEAR	TM LG	G	AB	R	H	2B	3B	HR	RBI	BB-IB	HP	SO	AVG	OBP	SLG	AOPS	ABR	SB-CS	FA	FR	RNG	THR	GAMES AT POSITION	DL	BFW
1990	NY A	65	214	18	53	8	0	5	19	2-0	1	15	.248	.257	.355	69	-10	7-0	.991	1	99	117	O57(47/0/12)/D		-1.0
1991	SD N	38	57	5	14	2	0	0	5	1-1	1	9	.246	.267	.281	54	-4	2-0	.875	-1	84	0	O13(12/0/1)/1		-0.5
1992	SD N	99	168	15	32	6	0	0	8	9-1	0	12	.190	.230	.226	30	-16	1-0	.942	0	111	68	O37(31/0/6)		-1.8
Total	3	202	439	38	99	16	0	5	36	12-2	2	36	.226	.248	.296	52	-30	10-0	.964	-0	102	90	O107(90/0/19)/1D		-3.3

BABB, CHARLIE Charles Amos B2.20.1873 Milwaukie OR D3.19.1954 Portland OR BB/TR/5-10/165 d4.17

YEAR	TM LG	G	AB	R	H	2B	3B	HR	RBI	BB-IB	HP	SO	AVG	OBP	SLG	AOPS	ABR	SB-CS	FA	FR	RNG	THR	GAMES AT POSITION	DL	BFW
1903	NY N	121	424	68	105	15	8	0	46	45	**22**		.248	.350	.321	88	-4	22	.912	-7	93	93	S113,3b8		-0.7
1904	Bro N	151	521	49	138	18	3	0	53	53	11		.265	.345	.311	106	7	34	.927	-2	97	81	S151		1.0
1905	Bro N	75	235	27	44	8	2	0	17	27	12		.187	.303	.238	67	-7	10	.923	-3	104	51	S36,1b31,3b5,2b2		-1.0
Total	3	347	1180	144	287	41	13	0	116	125	45		.243	.339	.300	92	-4	66	.921	-12	96	82	S300,1b31,3b13,2b2		-0.7

BABE, LOREN Loren Rolland "Bee Bee" B1.11.1928 Pisgah IA D2.14.1984 Omaha NE BL/TR/5-10/180* d8.19 C4

YEAR	TM LG	G	AB	R	H	2B	3B	HR	RBI	BB-IB	HP	SO	AVG	OBP	SLG	AOPS	ABR	SB-CS	FA	FR	RNG	THR	GAMES AT POSITION	DL	BFW
1952	NY A	12	21	1	2	1	0	0	4		0	4	.095	.240	.143	9	-3	1-0	.909	1	132	233	3b9		-0.1
1953	NY A	5	18	2	6	1	0	2	6		0	2	.333	.333	.722	185	2	0-0	.920	2	124	242	3b5		0.3
	Phi A	103	343	34	77	16	2	0	20	35	2	20	.224	.300	.283	56	-21	0-1	.950	0	100	108	3b93/S		-2.1
	Year	108	361	36	83	17	2	2	26	35	2	22	.230	.302	.305	62	-19	0-1	.948	2	101	116	3b98/S		-1.8
Total	2	120	382	37	85	18	2	2	26	39	2	26	.223	.298	.296	59	-22	1-1	.946	3	103	123	3b107/S		-1.9

BABINGTON, CHARLIE Charles Percy B5.4.1895 Cranston RI D3.22.1957 Providence RI BR/TR/6-0/170 d7.20 Col Brown

YEAR	TM LG	G	AB	R	H	2B	3B	HR	RBI	BB-IB	HP	SO	AVG	OBP	SLG	AOPS	ABR	SB-CS	FA	FR	RNG	THR	GAMES AT POSITION	DL	BFW
1915	NY N	28	33	5	8	3	1	0	2	0	1	4	.242	.265	.394	104	0	1	.909	-1	94		O12(2/11/1)/1		-0.1

BABITT, SHOOTY Mack Neal B3.9.1959 Oakland CA BR/TR/5-8/174 [OakA77 25/623] d4.9

YEAR	TM LG	G	AB	R	H	2B	3B	HR	RBI	BB-IB	HP	SO	AVG	OBP	SLG	AOPS	ABR	SB-CS	FA	FR	RNG	THR	GAMES AT POSITION	DL	BFW
1981	Oak A	54	156	10	40	1	3	0	14	13-1	0	31	.256	.314	.301	81	-4	5-4	.972	-21	81	38	2b52		-2.5

BACKMAN, WALLY Walter Wayne B9.22.1959 Hillsboro OR BB/TR/5-9/160* [NYN77 1/16] d9.2

YEAR	TM LG	G	AB	R	H	2B	3B	HR	RBI	BB-IB	HP	SO	AVG	OBP	SLG	AOPS	ABR	SB-CS	FA	FR	RNG	THR	GAMES AT POSITION	DL	BFW
1980	NY N	27	93	12	30	1	1	0	9	11-1	0	14	.323	.396	.355	114	2	2-3	1.000	-9	73	58	2b20,S8		-0.6
1981	NY N	26	36	5	10	2	0	0	0	4-0	0	7	.278	.350	.333	95	0	1-0	.946	-1	102	49	2b11/3		0.0
1982	NY N	96	261	37	71	13	2	3	22	49-1	0	47	.272	.387	.372	113	7	8-7	.964	-4	98	68	2b88,3b6/S	24	0.7
1983	NY N	26	42	6	7	0	1	0	3	2-0	0	8	.167	.205	.214	16	-5	0-0	1.000	-2	75	58	2b14,3b2		-0.8
1984	NY N	128	436	68	122	19	2	1	26	56-2	0	63	.280	.360	.339	99	2	32-9	.981	-6	89	106	2b115,S8		0.7
1985	NY N	145	520	77	142	24	5	1	38	36-1	1	72	.273	.320	.344	98	-9	30-12	.989	-11	93	96	2b140/S		-1.1
1986	†NY N	124	387	67	124	18	2	1	27	36-1	0	32	.320	.376	.385	113	8	13-7	.966	-2	101	103	2b113		1.3
1987	NY N	94	300	43	75	6	1	1	23	25-0	0	43	.250	.307	.287	61	-17	11-3	.983	-9	94	95	2b87	20	-2.1
1988	†NY N	99	294	44	89	12	0	0	17	41-1	1	49	.303	.388	.344	117	9	9-5	.989	-9	92	83	2b92	15	0.2
1989	Min A	87	299	33	69	9	2	1	26	32-0	1	45	.231	.306	.284	63	-14	1-1	.982	-17	87	73	2b84/D	53	-3.0
1990	†Pit N	104	315	62	92	21	3	2	28	42-1	1	53	.292	.374	.397	117	9	6-3	.920	-11	89	63	3b71,2b15		-0.1
1991	Phi N	94	185	20	45	12	0	0	15	30-0	0	30	.243	.344	.308	87	-2	3-2	.981	-11	71	84	2b36,3b20		-1.3
1992	Phi N	42	48	6	13	1	0	0	6	6-1	0	9	.271	.352	.292	84	-1	1-0	.968	4	167	157	2b10,3b2		0.3
1993	Sea A	10	29	2	4	0	0	0	3	1-0	0	8	.138	.167	.138	-17	-5	0-0	.857	-1	100	0	3b9/2	16	-0.6
Total	14	1102	3245	482	893	138	19	10	240	371-9	5	480	.275	.349	.339	94	-16	117-52	.980	-88	92	92	2b826,3b111,S18/D	189	-6.4

BACON, EDDIE Edgar Suter B4.8.1895 Franklin Co. KY D10.2.1963 Louisville KY d8.13

YEAR	TM LG	G	AB	R	H	2B	3B	HR	RBI	BB-IB	HP	SO	AVG	OBP	SLG	AOPS	ABR	SB-CS	FA	FR	RNG	THR	GAMES AT POSITION	DL	BFW
1917	Phi A	4	6	1	3	1	0	0	2	0	0	0	.500	.500	.667	259	1	0	1.000	1	404	0	/P		0.0

BADER, ART Arthur Herman B9.21.1886 St.Louis MO D4.5.1957 St.Louis MO BR/TR/5-9/160 d8.2

YEAR	TM LG	G	AB	R	H	2B	3B	HR	RBI	BB-IB	HP	SO	AVG	OBP	SLG	AOPS	ABR	SB-CS	FA	FR	RNG	THR	GAMES AT POSITION	DL	BFW
1904	StL A	2	3	0	0	0	0	0	0	1	0		.000	.250	.000	-19	0	0	1.000	1	1002	0	/OL		0.0

YEAR	TM LG	G	AB	R	H	2B	3B	HR	RBI	BB-IB	HP	SO	AVG	OBP	SLG	AOPS	ABR	SB-CS	FA	FR	RNG	THR	GAMES AT POSITION	DL	BFW

BADGRO, RED Morris Hiram B12.1.1902 Orillia WA D7.13.1998 Kent WA BL/TR/6-0/190 d6.20 Col USC
1929	StL A	54	148	27	42	12	0	1	18	11	2	15	.284	.342	.385	84	-3	1-0	.983	-2	96	30	O37R		-0.7
1930	StL A	89	234	30	56	18	3	1	27	13	2	27	.239	.285	.355	59	-15	3-5	.952	-0	89	154	O61(4/14/43)		-1.9
Total	2	143	382	57	98	30	3	2	45	24	4	42	.257	.307	.366	69	-18	4-5	.962	-3	91	111	O98(4/14/80)		-2.6

BAERGA, CARLOS Carlos Obed (Ortiz) B11.4.1968 Santurce, PR BB/TR/5-11/200(165-220) d4.14
1990	Cle A	108	312	46	81	17	2	7	47	16-2	4	57	.260	.300	.394	94	-3	0-2	.944	-5	112	108	3b50,S48,2b8		-0.8
1991	Cle A	158	593	80	171	28	2	11	69	48-5	6	74	.288	.346	.398	105	4	3-2	.944	17	114	88	3b89,2b75,S2		2.3
1992	Cle A★	161	657	92	205	32	1	20	105	35-10	13	76	.312	.354	.455	128	23	10-2	.979	8	99	121	2b160/D		3.7
1993	Cle A★	154	624	105	200	28	6	21	114	34-7	6	68	.321	.355	.486	125	20	15-4	.979	8	102	103	2b150,D4		3.5
1994	Cle A	103	442	81	139	32	2	19	80	10-1	6	45	.314	.333	.525	117	9	8-2	.973	4	104	101	2b102/D		1.8
1995	†Cle A★	135	557	87	175	28	2	15	90	35-6	3	31	.314	.355	.452	107	5	11-2	.973	10	107	121	2b134/D		2.1
1996	Cle A	100	424	54	113	25	0	10	55	16-0	7	25	.267	.302	.396	75	-17	1-1	.971	-1	101	96	2b100		-1.2
	NY N	26	83	5	16	3	0	2	11	5-0	2	5	.193	.253	.301	49	-7	0-0	.990	-4	49	72	1b16,3b6/2		-1.1
1997	NY N	133	467	53	131	25	1	9	52	20-1	3	54	.281	.311	.396	89	-9	2-6	.978	1	105	122	2b131		-0.4
1998	NY N	147	511	46	136	27	1	7	53	24-6	6	55	.266	.303	.364	78	-17	0-1	.986	-9	90	118	2b144		-2.0
1999	SD N	33	80	6	20	1	0	2	5	6-0	2	14	.250	.318	.338	71	-4	1-0	1.000	-3	85	136	2b13,3b13,1b2/D		-0.6
	Cle A	22	57	4	13	0	0	1	5	4-1	0	10	.228	.274	.281	41	-5	1-1	.964	-1	88	50	3b15,2b6/D		-0.6
2002	Bos N	73	182	17	52	11	0	2	19	7-1	2	20	.286	.316	.379	83	-4	0-0	.983	2	109	68	D32,2b17/3	24	-0.2
2003	Ari N	105	207	31	71	13	0	4	39	18-1	2	20	.343	.396	.464	115	6	1-1	.985	1	88	110	1b19,2b15,3b5,D6		0.6
2004	Ari N	79	85	6	20	2	0	2	11	6-0	1	3	.235	.309	.329	61	-5	0-0	1.000	-1	155	55	1b6,D2	39	-0.5
2005	Was N	93	158	18	40	7	0	2	19	7-0	8	17	.253	.318	.335	77	-6	0-0	.920	-4	76	46	3b20,1b11,2b7/D		-1.0
Total	14	1630	5439	731	1583	279	17	134	774	291-41	73	580	.291	.332	.423	100	-10	59-24	.976	25	102	113	2b1063,3b199,1b54,D50,S50	63	5.6

BAEZ, JOSE Jose Antonio (b Jose Antonio Mota (Baez)) B12.31.1953 San Cristobal, D.R. BR/TR/5-8/150* d4.6
1977	Sea A	91	305	39	79	14	1	1	17	19-1	1	20	.259	.305	.321	71	-12	6-1	.973	12	112	109	2b77/3D		0.5
1978	Sea A	23	50	8	8	0	1	0	2	6-1	0	7	.160	.250	.200	28	-5	1-0	.978	9	144	209	2b14,3b3/D		0.5
Total	2	114	355	47	87	14	2	1	19	25-2	1	27	.245	.297	.304	65	-17	7-1	.974	21	116	123	2b91,D4,3b4		1.0

BAEZ, KEVIN Kevin Richard B1.10.1967 Brooklyn NY BR/TR/6-0/160* [NYN88 7/182] d9.3 Col Dominican
1990	NY N	5	12	0	2	1	0	0	0	0-0	0	0	.167	.167	.250	13	-1	0-0	1.000	-0	79	66	S4		-0.2
1992	NY N	6	13	0	2	0	0	0	0	0-0	0	5	.154	.154	.154	-13	-2	0-0	.889	-0	98	95	S5	17	-0.2
1993	NY N	52	126	10	23	9	0	0	7	13-1	0	17	.183	.259	.254	33	-11	0-0	.967	-3	98	103	S52		-1.1
Total	3	63	151	10	27	10	0	0	7	13-1	0	17	.179	.244	.245	33	-14	0-0	.962	-3	97	100	S61	17	-1.5

BAGWELL, JEFF Jeffery Robert B5.27.1968 Boston MA BR/TR/6-0/195(195-215) [BosA89 4/110] d4.8 Col Hartford
1991	Hou N	156	554	79	163	26	4	15	82	75-5	13	116	.294	.387	.437	140	33	7-4	.991	-4	89	89	1b155		1.8
1992	Hou N	162	586	87	160	34	6	18	96	84-13	12	97	.273	.368	.444	136	31	10-6	.995	4	107	95	1b159		2.6
1993	Hou N	142	535	76	171	37	4	20	88	62-6	3	73	.320	.388	.516	146	36	13-4	.993	4	106	103	1b140		2.9
1994	Hou N★	110	400	104	147	32	2	39	116	65-14	4	65	.368	.451	.750	219	73	15-4	.991	16	148	108	1b109/OR		7.7
1995	Hou N	114	448	88	130	29	0	21	87	79-12	6	102	.290	.399	.496	145	33	12-5	.994	18	151	84	1b114	32	4.0
1996	Hou N★	162	568	111	179	48	2	31	120	135-20	10	114	.315	.451	.570	182	79	21-7	.989	8	116	84	1b162		7.1
1997	†Hou N★	162	566	109	162	40	2	43	135	127-27	16	122	.286	.425	.592	170	65	31-10	.993	8	118	118	1b158/D		6.0
1998	Hou N	147	540	124	164	33	1	34	111	109-8	7	90	.304	.424	.557	161	53	19-7	.993	5	125	102	1b147	15	5.1
1999	†Hou N★	162	562	143	171	35	0	42	126	149-16	11	127	.304	.454	.591	165	66	30-11	.994	3	102	116	1b161,D2		5.3
2000	Hou N	159	590	152	183	37	1	47	132	107-11	15	116	.310	.424	.615	148	47	9-6	.994	2	103	97	1b158/D		3.2
2001	Hou N	161	600	126	173	43	4	39	130	106-5	10	135	.288	.397	.568	136	36	11-3	.992	15	133	101	1b160		3.6
2002	Hou N	158	571	94	166	33	2	31	98	101-8	10	130	.291	.401	.518	134	30	7-3	.995	6	110	93	1b153,D4		2.3
2003	Hou N	160	605	109	168	28	2	39	100	88-3	6	119	.278	.373	.524	124	23	11-4	.994	5	110	98	1b158		1.4
2004	†Hou N	156	572	104	152	29	2	27	89	96-6	8	131	.266	.377	.465	113	14	6-4	.995	0	93	90	1b152,D2		0.0
2005	†Hou N	39	100	11	25	4	0	3	19	18-1	1	21	.250	.358	.380	97	0	0-0	1.000	9	74	94	1b24	128	-0.2
Total	15	2150	7797	1517	2314	488	32	449	1529	1401-155	128	1558	.297	.408	.540	149	619	202-78	.993	96	114	98	1b2111,D10,OR	175	52.8

BAGWELL, BILL William Mallory "Big Bill" B2.24.1896 Choudrant LA D10.5.1976 Choudrant LA BL/TL/6-1/175 d4.17
1923	Bos N	56	93	8	27	4	2	10	6	0	12	.290	.333	.441	107	0	0-0	1.000	0	105	71	O22L		0.0
1925	Phi A	36	50	4	15	2	1	0	10	2	0	2	.300	.327	.380	74	-2	0-0	.667	-1	34	0	O4L		-0.3
Total	2	92	143	12	42	6	3	2	20	8	0	14	.294	.331	.420	95	-2	0-0	.973	-1	94	60	O26L		-0.3

BAHRET, FRANK Frank F. B1858 Poughkeepsie NY D3.30.1888 Poughkeepsie NY 6-1/184 d4.17
| 1884 | Bal U | 2 | 8 | 0 | 0 | 0 | 0 | 0 | 0 | | 0 | | .000 | .000 | .000 | -91 | -2 | | 1.000 | -0 | 0 | 0 | O2(0/1/1) | | -0.2 |

BAILEY, GENE Arthur Eugene B11.25.1893 Pearsall TX D11.14.1973 Houston TX BR/TR/5-8/160 d9.10 Mil 1918
1917	Phi A	5	12	1	1	0	0	0	1	1	0	1	.083	.154	.083	-28	-2	0	.833	-1	88	0	O4L		-0.3
1919	Bos N	4	6	0	2	0	0	0	1	0	0	2	.333	.333	.333	105	0	1	1.000	0	119	0	O3(0/1/1)		0.0
1920	Bos N	13	24	2	2	0	0	0	0	3	0	3	.083	.185	.083	-22	-4	0-0	.929	0	96	141	O8(5/4/1)		-0.5
	Bos A	46	135	14	31	2	0	0	5	9	1	15	.230	.283	.244	42	-11	2-7	.986	-1	97	70	O40(9/16/15)		-1.6
1923	Bro N	127	411	71	109	11	7	1	42	43	6	34	.265	.343	.333	81	-10	9-7	.959	-1	102	84	O100(25/60/17),1b5		-1.7
1924	Bro N	18	46	7	11	3	0	1	4	7	0	6	.239	.340	.370	93	0	1-0	1.000	1	109	117	O17(0/10/8)		0.0
Total	5	213	634	95	156	16	7	2	52	63	7	61	.246	.321	.303	69	-27	13-15	.965	-1	101	84	O172(43/91/42),1b5		-4.1

BAILEY, FRED Frederick Middleton "Penny" B8.16.1895 Mt.Hope WV D8.16.1972 Huntington WV BL/TL/5-11/150 d8.19 Mil 1918 Col Washington and Lee
1916	Bos N	6	10	0	1	0	0	0	1	0	3	.100	.100	.100	-40	-2	0	1.000	-0	47	0	O2L		-0.2
1917	Bos N	50	110	9	21	2	1	1	5	9		25	.191	.270	.255	65	-4	3	.962	1	94	170	O27(9/15/4)		-0.6
1918	Bos N	4	4	1	1	0	0	0	0				.250	.250	.250	55	0	0	—	0			/H		0.0
Total	3	60	124	10	23	2	1	1	6	9	3	29	.185	.257	.242	57	-6	3	.963	1	92	162	O29(10/15/4)		-0.8

BAILEY, BILL Harry Lewis B11.19.1881 Shawnee OH D10.27.1967 Seattle WA BL/TR/5-10.5/170 d4.21
| 1911 | NY A | 5 | 9 | 1 | 1 | 0 | 0 | 0 | | | | | .111 | .111 | .111 | -36 | -2 | 0 | — | 0 | 0 | 0 | O2/3 | | -0.1 |

BAILEY, MARK John Mark B11.4.1961 Springfield MO BB/TR/6-5/195* [HouN82 6/147] d4.27 C4 Col Missouri St.
1984	Hou N	108	344	38	73	16	1	9	34	53-4	2	71	.212	.318	.343	92	-2	0-1	.983	-4	83	97	C108		-0.2
1985	Hou N	114	332	47	88	14	0	10	45	67-13	1	70	.265	.389	.398	124	14	0-2	.979	-6	116	91	C110,1b2		1.2
1986	Hou N	57	153	9	27	5	0	4	15	28-6	0	45	.176	.302	.288	66	-7	1-1	.989	-0	80	131	C53/1		-0.5
1987	Hou N	35	64	5	13	1	0	0	3	10-0	0	21	.203	.311	.219	45	-5	1-0	.985	-1	84	119	C27		-0.5
1988	Hou N	8	23	1	4	0	0	0	5	0-0	0	6	.130	.286	.130	24	-2	0-1	.981	-0	87	80	C8	24	-0.3
1990	SF N	5	7	1	1	0	0	0	3	0-0	0	1	.143	.143	.571	90	0	0-0	1.000	0	0	0	/C		0.0
1992	SF N	13	26	0	4	1	0	0	1	3-0	0	7	.154	.241	.192	25	-3	0-0	1.000	-0	0	46	C7	31	-0.3
Total	7	340	949	101	209	37	1	24	101	166-23	3	222	.220	.337	.337	92	-5	2-5	.983	-11	93	100	C314,1b3	55	-0.5

BAILEY, ED Lonas Edgar B4.15.1931 Strawberry Plains TN BL/TR/6-2/205* d9.26 b-Jim Col Tennessee
1953	Cin N	2	8	0	3	0	0	1	1	0	3	.375	.444	.500	145	1	0-0	1.000	-1	53	0	C2		0.0
1954	Cin N	73	183	21	36	2	3	9	20	35	0	34	.197	.324	.388	83	-5	1-0	.973	-6	167	84	C61		-0.8
1955	Cin N	21	39	3	8	1	1	1	4	4-0	3	10	.205	.326	.359	77	-1	0-0	.962	2	142	136	C11		0.1
1956	Cin N★	118	383	59	115	8	2	28	75	52-11	3	50	.300	.385	.551	140	22	2-0	.984	1	94	110	C106		2.9
1957	Cin N★	122	391	54	102	15	2	20	48	73-9	2	69	.261	.377	.463	117	12	5-3	.991	-11	111	88	C115		0.7
1958	Cin N	112	360	39	90	23	1	11	59	47-10	1	61	.250	.337	.411	92	-3	2-2	.988	1	125	107	C99		0.3
1959	Cin N	121	379	43	100	13	0	12	40	62-6	2	53	.264	.370	.393	101	3	2-0	.990	5	133	124	C117		1.4
1960	Cin N★	133	441	52	115	19	3	13	67	59-9	2	70	.261	.346	.406	105	4	1-0	.990	-8	128	99	C129		0.5
1961	Cin N	12	43	4	13	4	0	0	2	3-1	0	5	.302	.348	.395	95	0	0-0	.967	-2	401	77	C12		-0.1
	SF N☆	107	340	39	81	9	1	13	51	42-6	4	41	.238	.324	.385	92	-4	1-5	.985	2	89	78	C103/OL		0.2
	Year	119	383	43	94	13	1	13	53	45-7	4	46	.245	.326	.386	93	-4	1-5	.984	1	121	78	C115/OL		0.1
1962	†SF N★	96	254	32	59	9	1	17	45	42-5	6	42	.232	.351	.476	123	9	1-1	.987	-2	125	35	C75		1.0
1963	SF N★	105	308	41	81	8	0	21	68	50-15	1	64	.263	.366	.494	147	20	0-6	.987	-2	91	62	C88		2.2
1964	Mil N	95	271	30	71	10	1	6	34	34-2	1	39	.262	.343	.362	99	1	2-0	.982	-10	112	72	C80		-0.6
1965	SF N	24	28	1	3	0	0	0	3	6-1	0	7	.107	.250	.107	9	-3	0-0	1.000	3	275	127	C12,1b3		0.0
	Chi N	66	150	13	38	6	0	5	23	34-6	1	28	.253	.385	.393	119	6	0-1	.981	-4	71	78	C54,1b3		0.3
	Year	90	178	14	41	6	0	5	26	40-7	1	35	.230	.363	.348	102	2	0-1	.984	-1	98	78	C66,1b5		0.3

YEAR	TM LG	G	AB	R	H	2B	3B	HR	RBI	BB-IB	HP	SO	AVG	OBP	SLG	AOPS	ABR	SB-CS		FA	FR	RNG	THR	GAMES AT POSITION		DL	BFW
1966	Cal A	5	3	0	0	0	0	0	0	1-0	0	1	.000	.250	.000		-22	0-0		—	0			/H			0.0
Total	14	1212	3581	432	915	128	15	155	540	545-77	25	577	.256	.355	.429	110	62	17-18		.986	-30	118	89	C1064,1b5/OL			7.9

BAILEY, BOB Robert Sherwood B10.13.1942 Long Beach CA BR/TR/6-0/188(175-188) d9.14 OF(399/2/3)

YEAR	TM LG	G	AB	R	H	2B	3B	HR	RBI	BB-IB	HP	SO	AVG	OBP	SLG	AOPS	ABR	SB-CS		FA	FR	RNG	THR	GAMES AT POSITION		DL	BFW
1962	Pit N	14	42	6	7	2	1	0	6	6-0	0	10	.167	.271	.262	44	-3	1-1		.921	-0	105	89	3b12			-0.4
1963	Pit N	154	570	60	130	15	3	12	45	58-2	5	98	.228	.303	.328	82	-13	10-9		.933	12	113	162	3b153,S3			-0.3
1964	Pit N	143	530	73	149	26	3	11	51	44-1	1	78	.281	.336	.404	108	6	10-8		.943	8	114	117	3b105,O35(34/2/2),S2			1.2
1965	Pit N	159	626	87	160	28	3	11	49	70-1	1	93	.256	.330	.363	95	-3	10-14		.939	-13	95	118	3b142,O28L			-2.2
1966	Pit N	126	380	51	106	19	3	13	46	47-4	2	65	.279	.360	.447	123	13	5-3		.956	-4	103	109	3b96,O20L			0.9
1967	LA N	116	322	21	73	8	2	4	28	40-4	1	50	.227	.310	.301	84	-6	5-5		.941	-0	112	102	3b65,O27L,1b4/S			-1.0
1968	LA N	105	322	24	73	9	3	8	39	38-4	1	69	.227	.308	.348	105	2	1-2		.953	-5	90	87	3b90/SOL			-0.4
1969	Mon N	111	358	46	95	16	6	9	53	40-3	1	76	.265	.337	.419	111	5	3-3		.992	5	131	106	1b85,O12L/3		29	0.3
1970	Mon N	131	352	77	101	19	3	28	84	72-8	1	70	.287	.407	.597	166	35	5-3		.953	-2	95	62	3b48,O44L,1b18			2.9
1971	Mon N	157	545	65	137	21	4	14	83	97-8	0	105	.251	.359	.382	110	11	13-7		**.960**	-1	102	71	3b120,O51(51/0/1),1b9			0.8
1972	Mon N	143	489	55	114	10	4	16	57	59-7	1	112	.233	.315	.368	92	-5	6-7		.938	-1	103	93	3b134,O5L,1b3			-0.8
1973	Mon N	151	513	77	140	25	4	26	86	88-10	1	99	.273	.379	.489	134	26	5-8		.956	-1	102	88	3b146,O2L			2.4
1974	Mon N	152	507	69	142	20	2	20	73	100-9	1	107	.280	.396	.446	129	24	4-7		.974	-5	72	158	O78L,3b68			1.0
1975	Mon N	106	227	23	62	5	0	5	30	46-3	1	38	.273	.392	.361	106	4	4-4		.979	-1	89	103	O61L,3b3		20	0.0
1976	Cin N	69	124	17	37	6	1	6	23	16-1	0	26	.298	.376	.508	146	8	0-0		.974	-2	79	130	O31L,3b10			0.5
1977	Cin N	49	79	9	20	2	1	2	11	12-2	0	10	.253	.348	.380	94	0	1-1		.975	-0	123	108	1b19,O3L			-0.2
	Bos A	2	2	0	0	0	0	0	0	0-0	0	1	.000	.000	.000	-90	-1	0-0		—	0			/H			-0.1
1978	Bos A	43	94	12	18	3	0	4	9	9-0	1	19	.191	.328	.351	84	-7	2-1		1.000	0	109	0	D34/3OL			-0.2
Total	17	1931	6082	772	1564	234	43	189	773	852-67	17	1126	.257	.347	.403	110	101	83-85		.946	-13	103	104	3b1194,O399L,1b138,D34,S7		49	4.4

BAILOR, BOB Robert Michael B7.10.1951 Connellsville PA BR/TR/5-11/160(159-170) d9.6 C4 OF(79/105/254)

YEAR	TM LG	G	AB	R	H	2B	3B	HR	RBI	BB-IB	HP	SO	AVG	OBP	SLG	AOPS	ABR	SB-CS		FA	FR	RNG	THR	GAMES AT POSITION		DL	BFW
1975	Bal A	5	7	0	1	0	0	0	0	1-0	0	1	.143	.250	.143	14	1	0-0		1.000	1	120	0	S2/2			0.0
1976	Bal A	9	6	2	2	1	0	0	0	0-0	0	0	.333	.333	.667	199	1	0-1		—	-0	0	0	/SD		54	0.0
1977	Tor A	122	496	62	154	21	5	5	32	17-1	2	26	.310	.335	.403	99	-2	15-6		.988	5	102	226	O63(15/47/2),S53,D7			0.9
1978	Tor A	154	621	74	164	29	7	1	52	38-1	5	21	.264	.310	.338	81	-16	5-6		.964	11	109	165	O125(3/25/102),3b28,S4			-1.2
1979	Tor A	130	414	50	95	11	5	1	38	36-2	6	27	.229	.297	.287	59	-24	14-8		.987	9	96	203	O118(4/4/113),3b9/D			-2.3
1980	Tor A	117	347	44	82	14	2	1	16	36-3	2	33	.236	.311	.297	65	-16	12-8		.991	15	108	264	O98(41/28/33),S12,3b11,P3/2D		21	-0.3
1981	NY N	51	81	11	23	3	1	0	8	8-0	1	11	.284	.352	.346	100	0	2-0		.955	-2	99	66	S22,2b13,O13(10/0/3)/3		13	0.1
1982	NY N	110	376	44	104	14	1	0	31	20-0	2	17	.277	.313	.319	78	-11	20-3		.984	1	107	85	S60,2b56,3b21,O4(3/1/0)			-0.1
1983	NY N	118	340	33	85	8	0	1	30	20-2	1	23	.250	.290	.282	61	-18	18-3		.969	6	107	113	S75,2b50,3b11,O3(2/0/1)		16	-0.2
1984	NY N	65	131	11	36	4	0	0	8	8-1	0	23	.275	.317	.305	76	-4	3-1		.944	3	85	68	2b23,3b17,S16		65	0.1
1985	†LA N	74	118	8	29	3	1	0	7	3-0	1	5	.246	.270	.288	58	-7	1-0		.962	7	117	155	3b45,2b16,S5/OL		34	0.1
Total	11	955	2937	339	775	107	23	9	222	187-10	20	164	.264	.310	.325	76	-98	90-36		.980	54	105	207	O425R,S250,2b160,3b143,D10,P3		203	-2.9

BAINES, HAROLD Harold Douglass B3.15.1959 Easton MD BL/TL/6-2/195(175-215) [ChiA77 1/1] d4.10 C2

YEAR	TM LG	G	AB	R	H	2B	3B	HR	RBI	BB-IB	HP	SO	AVG	OBP	SLG	AOPS	ABR	SB-CS		FA	FR	RNG	THR	GAMES AT POSITION		DL	BFW
1980	Chi A	141	491	55	125	23	6	13	49	19-7	1	65	.255	.281	.405	87	-11	2-4		.963	-9	88	62	O137R/D			-2.8
1981	Chi A	82	280	42	80	11	7	10	41	12-4	2	41	.286	.318	.482	130	9	6-2		.985	-0	82	197	O80R/D			0.5
1982	Chi A	161	608	89	165	29	8	25	105	49-10	0	95	.271	.321	.469	115	10	10-3		.980	-4	97	86	O161(1/3/160)			-0.1
1983	†Chi A	156	596	76	167	33	2	20	99	49-1	1	85	.280	.333	.443	108	6	7-5		.973	-4	97	89	O155(1/20/142)			-0.6
1984	Chi A	147	569	72	173	28	10	29	94	54-9	0	75	.304	.361	**.541**	140	29	1-2		.981	-2	100	87	O147(0/7/147)			1.9
1985	Chi A★	160	640	86	198	29	3	22	113	42-8	1	89	.309	.348	.467	117	14	1-1		.994	1	101	78	O159R/D			0.6
1986	Chi A★	145	570	72	169	29	2	21	88	38-9	2	89	.296	.341	.465	113	9	2-1		.984	8	105	153	O141R,D3			0.9
1987	Chi A★	132	505	59	148	26	4	20	93	46-2	1	82	.293	.352	.479	115	10	0-0		1.000	-1	83	0	D117,O8R		31	0.5
1988	Chi A	158	599	55	166	39	1	13	81	67-14	1	109	.277	.347	.411	113	12	0-0		.882	-1	67	167	D147,O9R			0.6
1989	Chi A★	96	333	55	107	20	1	13	56	60-13	1	52	.321	.423	.505	164	32	0-1		.981	-0	112	0	D70,O25R			2.9
	Tex A	50	172	18	49	9	0	3	16	13-0	0	27	.285	.333	.390	102	0	0-2		.667	-0	111	0	D46/OR			-0.2
	Year	146	505	73	156	29	1	16	72	73-13	1	79	.309	.395	.465	143	32	0-3		.964	-0	112	0	D116,O26R			2.7
1990	Tex A	103	321	41	93	10	1	13	44	47-9	1	63	.290	.377	.449	130	14	0-1		.833	0	181	0	D95,O2R			1.1
	†Oak A	32	94	11	25	5	0	3	21	20-1	0	17	.266	.381	.415	131	5	0-2		—	0	0	0	D30			0.4
	Year	135	415	52	118	15	1	16	65	67-10	1	80	.284	.378	.441	131	19	0-3		.831	0	181	0	D125,O2R			1.5
1991	Oak A★	141	488	76	144	25	1	20	90	72-22	1	67	.295	.383	.473	144	32	0-1		.923	-2	77	198	D125,O12(1/0/10)			2.6
1992	†Oak A	140	478	58	121	18	0	16	76	59-6	0	61	.253	.331	.391	108	5	1-3		.964	-2	84	0	D116,O23(6/0/17)			-0.2
1993	Bal A	118	416	64	130	22	0	20	78	57-9	0	52	.313	.390	.510	138	23	0-0		—	0	0	0	D116		22	1.5
1994	Bal A	94	326	44	96	12	1	16	54	30-6	1	49	.294	.356	.485	108	3	0-0		—	0	0	0	D91			-0.2
1995	Bal A	127	385	60	115	19	1	24	63	70-13	1	45	.299	.403	.540	141	25	0-2		—	0	0	0	D122			1.7
1996	Chi A	143	495	80	154	29	0	22	95	73-7	1	62	.311	.399	.503	132	27	3-1		—	0	0	0	D141			1.8
1997	Chi A	93	318	40	97	18	0	12	52	41-10	0	47	.305	.382	.475	127	14	0-1		—	0	0	0	D86			0.8
	†Bal A	44	134	15	39	5	0	4	15	14-1	0	15	.291	.364	.478	105	1	0-0		—	0	0	0	D35/OR			-0.1
	Year	137	452	55	136	23	0	16	67	55-11	0	62	.301	.375	.493	120	15	0-1		.913	-0	0	0	D121/OR			0.7
1998	Bal A	104	293	40	88	17	0	9	57	32-4	1	40	.300	.369	.451	114	7	0-0		—	0	0	0	D80		24	0.2
1999	Bal A★	107	345	57	111	16	1	24	81	43-3	0	38	.322	.395	.583	151	26	1-2		—	0	0	0	D96			1.9
	†Cle A	28	85	5	23	2	0	1	22	11-0	0	10	.271	.354	.329	72	-3	0-0		—	0	0	0	D25			-0.4
	Year	135	430	62	134	18	1	25	103	54-3	0	48	.312	.387	.533	134	22	1-2		—	0	0	0	D121			1.5
2000	Bal A	72	222	24	59	8	0	10	30	29-6	0	35	.266	.349	.437	103	1	0-0		—	0	0	0	D62			-0.2
	†Chi A	24	61	2	13	5	0	1	9	7-1	0	11	.213	.294	.344	59	-4	0-0		—	0	0	0	D16			-0.4
	Year	96	283	26	72	13	0	11	39	36-7	0	50	.254	.338	.417	92	-3	0-0		—	0	0	0	D78			-0.6
2001	Chi A	32	84	3	11	1	0	0	6	8-0	0	16	.131	.202	.143	-5	-13	0-0		—	0	0	0	D22		81	-1.4
Total	22	2830	9908	1299	2866	488	49	384	1628	1062-187	14	1441	.289	.356	.465	120	282	34-34		.978	-16	97	97	D1644,O1061(9/30/1039)		158	13.3

BAIRD, AL Albert Wells B6.2.1895 Cleburne TX D11.27.1976 Shreveport LA BR/TR/5-9/160 d9.10 Mil 1918 Col Louisiana St.

YEAR	TM LG	G	AB	R	H	2B	3B	HR	RBI	BB-IB	HP	SO	AVG	OBP	SLG	AOPS	ABR	SB-CS		FA	FR	RNG	THR	GAMES AT POSITION		DL	BFW
1917	NY N	10	24	1	7	0	0	0	4	2	0	2	.292	.346	.292	100	0	2		1.000	0	92	42	2b7,S3			0.1
1919	NY N	38	83	8	20	1	0	0	5	5	0	9	.241	.284	.253	63	-4	3		.898	6	120	127	2b24,S9,3b5			0.2
Total	2	48	107	9	27	1	0	0	9	7	0	11	.252	.298	.262	71	-4	5		.921	6	113	106	2b31,S12,3b5			0.3

BAIRD, DOUG Howard Douglas B9.27.1891 St.Charles MO D6.13.1967 Thomasville GA BR/TR/5-9.5/148 d4.18 Mil 1918 Col Westminster (MO)

YEAR	TM LG	G	AB	R	H	2B	3B	HR	RBI	BB-IB	HP	SO	AVG	OBP	SLG	AOPS	ABR	SB-CS		FA	FR	RNG	THR	GAMES AT POSITION		DL	BFW
1915	Pit N	145	512	49	112	26	12	1	53	37	4	88	.219	.272	.322	82	-12	29-12		.939	-2	95	83	3b120,O20C,2b3			-1.1
1916	Pit N	128	430	41	93	10	7	1	28	24	3	49	.216	.263	.279	66	-18	20-16		.933	-9	96	108	3b80,2b29,O16(10/5/1)			-3.1
1917	Pit N	43	135	17	35	6	1	0	18	20	0	19	.259	.355	.319	104	2	8		.935	-4	88	44	3b41,2b2			-0.1
	StL N	104	364	38	92	19	12	0	24	23	2	52	.253	.301	.371	108	2	18		.941	14	119	138	3b103,O2C			2.2
	Year	147	499	55	127	25	13	0	42	43	2	71	.255	.316	.357	107	4	26		.940	10	110	112	3b144,2b2,O2C			2.1
1918	StL N	82	316	41	78	12	8	2	25	25	1	42	.247	.304	.354	104	1	25		.967	11	118	81	3b81/SOR			1.6
1919	Phi N	66	242	33	61	13	3	2	30	22	1	28	.252	.317	.355	95	-1	13		.950	9	108	157	3b66			1.1
	StL N	16	33	4	7	0	1	0	4	2	0	3	.212	.257	.273	63	-2	2		.773	-3	64	0	3b8/2OR			-0.5
	Bro N	20	60	6	11	0	1	0	8	4	0	10	.183	.197	.217	24	-6	3		1.000	1	106	84	3b17			-0.5
	Year	102	335	43	79	13	5	2	42	25	1	41	.236	.291	.327	81	-8	18		.946	7	106	132	3b91/2OR			0.1
1920	Bro N	6	6	1	2	0	0	0	1	3	1	0	.333	.556	.333	154	1	0-0		.800	-0	98	0	3b2			0.1
	NY N	7	8	0	1	0	0	0	0	1	0	1	.125	.222	.125	*-1	-1	0-0		1.000	1	120	303	3b4			0.1
	Year	13	14	1	3	0	0	0	1	4	1	1	.214	.389	.214	76	-0	0-0		.929	0	111	174	3b6			0.1
Total	6	617	2106	230	492	86	45	6	191	157	12	295	.234	.291	.326	88	-34	118-28		.944	18	105	104	3b522,O40(10/27/3),2b35/S			-0.3

BAKER, CHARLIE Charles Arthur B1.15.1856 W.Boylston MA D1.15.1937 Manchester NH BR/TR/5-4/140 d8.1

YEAR	TM LG	G	AB	R	H	2B	3B	HR	RBI	BB-IB	HP	SO	AVG	OBP	SLG	AOPS	ABR	SB-CS		FA	FR	RNG	THR	GAMES AT POSITION		DL	BFW
1884	CP U	15	57	5	8	2	0	1		0			.140	.140	.228	10	-8			.722	-1	128	0	O11R,S3/2			-0.8

BAKER, CHUCK Charles Joseph B12.6.1952 Seattle WA BR/TR/5-11/180* [SDN75*S2/43] d4.7 Col Loyola Marymount

YEAR	TM LG	G	AB	R	H	2B	3B	HR	RBI	BB-IB	HP	SO	AVG	OBP	SLG	AOPS	ABR	SB-CS		FA	FR	RNG	THR	GAMES AT POSITION		DL	BFW
1978	SD N	44	58	8	12	1	0	0	3	2-0	0	15	.207	.233	.224	31	-6	0-0		.952	7	121	146	2b24,S12			0.3
1980	SD N	9	22	0	3	0	0	0	0	0-0	0	4	.136	.136	.182	-13	-3	0-0		.963	-0	116	83	S8			-0.3
1981	Min A	40	66	6	12	0	0	0	6	1-0	0	8	.182	.194	.273	31	-6	0-0		.969	4	119	80	S31,2b3/3D			-0.1
Total	3	93	146	14	27	2	0	0	9	3-0	0	27	.185	.201	.240	25	-15	0-0		.962	10	119	95	S51,2b27/D3			-0.1

BAKER, DAVE David Glenn B11.25.1957 Lacona IA BL/TR/6-0/185 [TorA78 11/262] d9.12 b-Doug Col UCLA

YEAR	TM LG	G	AB	R	H	2B	3B	HR	RBI	BB-IB	HP	SO	AVG	OBP	SLG	AOPS	ABR	SB-CS		FA	FR	RNG	THR	GAMES AT POSITION		DL	BFW
1982	Tor A	9	20	3	5	1	0	0	2	3-0	2	3	.250	.400	.300	88	0	0-0		.808	1	127	154	3b8			0.0

YEAR	TM LG	G	AB	R	H	2B	3B	HR	RBI	BB-IB	HP	SO	AVG	OBP	SLG	AOPS	ABR	SB-CS	FA	FR	RNG	THR	GAMES AT POSITION	DL	BFW

BAKER, DEL Delmer David B5.3.1892 Sherwood OR D9.11.1973 San Antonio TX BR/TR/5-11.5/176 d4.16 M9/C20

1914	Det A	44	70	4	15	2	1	0	6		0	9	.214	.276	.271	63	-3	0-2	.920	-5	88	86	C38		-0.8
1915	Det A	68	134	16	33	3	3	0	15	15	1	15	.246	.327	.313	87	-2	3-1	.940	-5	99	93	C61		-0.3
1916	Det A	61	98	7	15	4	0	0	6	11	1	8	.153	.245	.194	31	-8	2	.975	-4	91	59	C59		-1.0
Total 3		173	302	27	63	9	4	0	22	32	2	32	.209	.289	.265	63	-13	5-3	.948	-15	94	80	C158		-2.1

BAKER, DOUG Douglas Lee B4.3.1961 Fullerton CA BB/TR/5-9/165* [DetA82 9/230] d7.2 b-Dave Col Arizona St.

1984 †Det A		43	108	15	20	4	1	0	12	7-0	1	22	.185	.241	.241	34	-10	3-0	.969	-5	93	108	S39,2b5/D		-1.1
1985	Det A	15	27	4	5	1	0	0	1	0-0	0	9	.185	.185	.222	11	-3	0-0	.960	-3	62	50	S12/2		-0.6
1986	Det A	13	24	1	3	1	0	0		2-0	0	7	.125	.192	.167	-1	-3	0-0	.970	-2	87	106	S10,2b2/D		-0.4
1987	Det A	8	1	0	0	0	0	0	0	0-0	0	1	.000	.000	.000	-99	-1	0-0	1.000	5	274	167	S6/23		0.1
1988	Min A	11	7	1	0	0	0	0	0	0-0	0	5	.000	.000	.000	-97	-2	0-0	1.000	-1	63	150	S9/23		-0.3
1989	Min A	43	78	17	23	5	1	0	9	9-0	2	18	.295	.378	.385	109	1	0-0	.982	-5	96	51	2b25,S19/D		-0.3
1990	Min A	3	1	0	0	0	0	0	0	0-0	0	0	.000	.000	.000	-94	0	0-0	1.000	0	120	0	2b3		0.0
Total 7		136	246	38	51	11	2	0	22	18-0	3	62	.207	.269	.268	49	-17	3-0	.973	-14	88	95	S95,2b38,D3,3b2		-2.6

BAKER, GENE Eugene Walter B6.15.1925 Davenport IA D12.1.1999 Davenport IA BR/TR/6-1/170* d9.20 C1 Negro Lg 1948-50 Col St. Ambrose [DL 1959 Pit N 46]

1953	Chi N	7	22	1	5	0	0	0	1		0	4	.227	.261	.273	39	-2	1-0	.917	-2	73	77	2b6,		-0.4
1954	Chi N	135	541	68	149	32	5	13	61	47	2	55	.275	.333	.425	96	-4	4-5	.967	1	101	99	2b134		0.7
1955	Chi N★	154	609	82	163	29	7	11	52	49-1	2	57	.268	.323	.392	89	-10	9-7	.967	6	100	102	2b154		1.2
1956	Chi A	140	546	65	141	23	3	12	57	39-2	3	54	.258	.309	.377	85	-12	4-3	.969	13	104	101	2b140		1.2
1957	Chi N	12	44	4	11	3	1	1	10	6-0	1	3	.250	.353	.432	111	1	0-0	.867	-3	72	45	3b12		-0.2
	Pit N	111	365	36	97	19	4	2	36	29-5	1	29	.266	.318	.356	84	-8	3-2	.955	-2	102	115	3b60,S28,2b13		-0.8
	Year	123	409	40	108	22	5	3	46	35-5	2	32	.264	.322	.364	87	-7	3-2	.942	-5	97	103	3b72,S28,2b13		-1.0
1958	Pit N	29	56	3	14	2	1	0	7	8-0	0	6	.250	.338	.321	80	-1	0-0	1.000	-1	88	0	3b11,2b3	70	-0.2
1960	†Pit N	33	37	5	9	0	0	0	4	2-0	0	9	.243	.275	.243	45	-3	0-0	1.000	-0	82	221	3b7/2		-0.3
1961	Pit N	9	10	1	1	0	0	0	3	1-1	0	2	.100	.308	.100	15	-1	0-0	1.000	0	139	0	3b3		-0.1
Total 8		630	2230	265	590	109	21	39	227	184-9	9	219	.265	.321	.385	88	-40	21-17	.968	12	101	100	2b451,3b93,S28	116	0.5

BAKER, FLOYD Floyd Wilson B10.10.1916 Luray VA D11.17.2004 Youngstown OH BL/TR/5-9/160* d5.4 C4

1943	StL A	22	46	5	8	2	0	0	4	6	0	4	.174	.269	.217	42	-3	0-1	.961	-1	86	105	S10/3		-0.4
1944	†StL A	44	97	10	17	3	0	0	5	11	0	5	.175	.259	.206	32	-8	2-0	.979	-2	88	50	2b17,S16		-0.9
1945	Chi A	82	208	22	52	8	0	0	19	23	0	12	.250	.325	.288	81	-5	3-2	.971	1	104	68	3b58,2b11		-0.3
1946	Chi A	9	24	2	6	1	0	0	3	2	0	3	.250	.308	.292	71	-1	0-0	.962	0	102	68	3b6		-0.1
1947	Chi A	105	371	61	98	12	3	0	22	66	0	28	.264	.375	.313	96	1	9-7	.980	14	121	148	3b101/2S		1.5
1948	Chi A	104	335	47	72	8	3	0	18	73	2	26	.215	.359	.257	68	-12	4-10	.961	16	129	122	3b71,2b18/S		0.2
1949	Chi A	125	388	38	101	15	4	1	40	84	0	32	.260	.392	.327	94	1	3-1	.977	11	115	118	3b122,S3/2		1.2
1950	Chi A	83	186	26	59	7	0	0	11	32	0	10	.317	.417	.355	102	3	1-1	.987	3	105	71	3b53,2b3,O2L		0.5
1951	Chi A	82	133	24	35	6	1	0	14	25	0	17	.263	.380	.323	93	0	0-1	.924	-2	99	87	3b44,2b5,S3		-0.2
1952	Was A	79	263	27	69	8	0	0	33	30	1	17	.262	.342	.293	81	-6	1-0	.994	-15	91	75	2b68,S7/3		-1.7
1953	Was A	9	7	0	0	0	0	0	1		1	0	.000	.222	.000	-37	-1	0-0	.000	-1	0	0	/3		-0.2
	Bos A	81	172	22	47	4	2	0	24	24	1	10	.273	.365	.320	82	-4	0-2	.963	-1	100	97	3b37,2b16		-0.4
	Year	90	179	22	47	4	2	0	24	25	2	10	.263	.359	.307	78	-5	0-2	.952	-1	99	96	3b38,2b16		-0.6
1954	Bos A	21	20	1	4	2	0	0	3	0	0	1	.200	.200	.300	32	-2	0-0	.889	0	94	247	3b7/2		-0.2
	Phi N	23	22	0	5	0	0	0	0	5	0	4	.227	.370	.227	60	-1	0-0	1.000	2	140	0	3b7,2b2		0.1
1955	Phi N	5	8	0	0	0	0	0	0	0-0	0	1	.000	.000	.000	-99	-2	0-0	1.000	1	90	0	/3		-0.2
Total 13		874	2280	285	573	76	13	1	196	382-0	6	165	.251	.360	.297	82	-40	23-25	.971	26	114	111	3b510,2b143,S41,O2L		-1.1

BAKER, FRANK Frank B1.11.1944 Bartow FL BL/TR/5-10/180* d7.27

1969	Cle A	52	172	21	44	5	3	3	15	14-0	1	34	.256	.312	.372	89	-3	2-1	.950	-0	91	152	O46L		-0.6
1971	Cle A	73	181	18	38	12	1	1	23	12-3	1	34	.210	.262	.304	55	-11	1-3	.985	-4	77	72	O51(17/6/30)		-2.0
Total 2		125	353	39	82	17	4	4	38	26-3	2	68	.232	.286	.337	71	-14	3-4	.966	-4	84	112	O97(63/6/30)		-2.6

BAKER, FRANK Frank Watts B10.29.1946 Meridian MS BL/TR/6-2/178* d8.9 Col Southern Mississippi

1970	NY A	35	117	6	27	4	1	0	11	14-0	2	26	.231	.323	.282	71	-3	1-2	.973	5	116	117	S35		0.5
1971	NY A	43	79	9	11	2	0	0	2	16-3	1	22	.139	.281	.165	31	-7	3-0	.949	3	108	171	S38		0.1
1973	†Bal A	44	63	10	12	1	2	1	11	7-0	0	7	.190	.268	.317	65	-3	0-0	.964	-2	89	164	S32,2b7/13		-0.3
1974	†Bal A	24	29	3	5	1	0	0	0	3-0	0	5	.172	.250	.207	33	-2	0-0	.842	-3	101	93	S17,2b3/3		-0.4
Total 4		146	288	28	55	8	3	1	24	40-3	2	60	.191	.292	.250	56	-16	4-2	.953	3	107	142	S122,2b10,3b2/1		-0.1

BAKER, GEORGE George F. B1859 St.Louis MO 5-11/162 d5.24

1883	Bal AA	7	22	0	5	0	0	0		0				.227	.227	.227	45	-1		.667	-2	67	192	S4,C3/OR		-0.3
1884	StL U	80	317	39	52	6	0	0		5				.164	.177	.183	9	-45		.897	15			C68,2b4,O4(2/1/2),3b3,S2		-2.2
1885	StL N	38	131	5	16	0	0	0	5	9			28	.122	.179	.122	-1	-14		.865	-10			C32,3b3,O2(1/1/0)/2		-2.1
1886	KC N	1	4	1	1	0	0	0	0				1	.250	.250	.250	49	-1	0	.889	-0			/C		-0.1
Total 4		126	474	45	74	6	0	0	5	14			29	.156	.180	.169	8	-60		.887	2			C104,O7(3/2/3),3b6,S6,2b5		-4.7

BAKER, HOWARD Howard Francis B3.1.1888 Bridgeport CT D1.16.1964 Bridgeport CT BR/TR/5-11/175 d8.11

1912	Cle A	11	30	1	5	0	0	0	2	5	0		.167	.286	.167	29	-3	0	.964	-1	72	0	3b10		-0.3
1914	Chi A	15	47	4	13	1	1	0	5	3	0	8	.277	.320	.340	100	0	2-1	.879	-2	96	67	3b15		-0.2
1915	Chi A	2	2	0	0	0	0	0	0	0-0	0	2	.000	.000	.000	-97	0	0	—	0			/H		-0.1
	NY N	1	3	0	0	0	0	0	0	0-0	0	0	.000	.000	.000	-99	-1	0	1.000	0	128	0	/3		-0.1
Total 3		29	82	5	18	1	1	0	7	8	0	10	.220	.289	.256	61	-4	2-1	.922	-3	88	38	3b26		-0.7

BAKER, JACK Jack Edward B5.4.1950 Birmingham AL BR/TR/6-5/225* [BosA71 26/604] d9.11 Col Auburn-Montgomery

1976	Bos A	12	23	1	3	0	0	1	2	1-0	0	5	.130	.160	.261	21	-2	0-0	.981	-1	74	134	1b8/D		-0.4
1977	Bos A	2	3	0	0	0	0	0	0	0-0	0	1	.000	.000	.000	-90	-1	0-0	.857	-1	193	0	/1		-0.1
Total 2		14	26	1	3	0	0	1	2	1-0	0	6	.115	.143	.231	8	-3	0-0	.966	-1	87	119	1b9/D		-0.5

BAKER, JEFF Jeffrey Glen B6.21.1981 Bad Kissingen, West Germany BR/TR/6-2/210 d4.4 Col Clemson

| 2005 | Col N | 12 | 38 | 6 | 8 | 4 | 0 | 1 | 4 | 5-0 | 0 | 12 | .211 | .302 | .395 | 70 | -1 | 0-0 | .958 | 0 | 112 | 52 | 3b10 | | -0.1 |

BAKER, JESSE Jesse (b Michael Myron Silverman) B3.4.1895 Cleveland OH D7.29.1976 W.Los Angeles CA BR/TR/5-4/140 d9.14

| 1919 | Was A | 1 | 0 | 0 | 0 | 0 | 0 | 0 | 0 | | 0 | | | | | | | | 1.000 | 0 | 146 | 0 | /S | | 0.0 |

BAKER, FRANK John Franklin "Home Run" B3.13.1886 Trappe MD D6.28.1963 Trappe MD BL/TR/5-11/173 d9.21 HF1955

1908	Phi A	9	31	5	9	0	0	0	2	0	0		.290	.290	.387	112	0	0	1.000	1	108	0	3b9		0.2
1909	Phi A	148	541	73	165	27	19	4	85	26	5		.305	.343	.447	146	25	20	.920	-10	89	95	3b146		2.2
1910	†Phi A	146	561	83	159	25	15	2	74	34	4		.283	.329	.392	127	15	21	.920	2	96	179	3b146		2.3
1911	†Phi A	148	592	96	198	42	14	11	115	40	2		.334	.379	.508	149	36	38	.942	-4	90	125	3b148		3.5
1912	Phi A	149	577	116	200	40	21	10	130	50	6		.347	.404	.541	176	54	40	.941	8	103	119	3b149		6.5
1913	†Phi A	149	564	116	190	34	9	12	117	63	10	31	.337	.413	.493	169	50	34	.921	9	100	95	3b149		6.6
1914	†Phi A	150	570	84	182	23	10	9	89	53	3	37	.319	.380	.442	153	35	19-20	.921	9	99	99	3b149		5.0
1916	NY A	100	360	46	97	23	2	10	52	36	5	30	.269	.344	.428	129	12	15	.940	1	100	90	3b96		1.7
1917	NY A	146	553	57	156	24	2	6	71	48	5	27	.282	.345	.365	116	10	18	.949	9	103	101	3b146		2.6
1918	NY A	126	504	65	154	24	5	6	62	38	2	13	.306	.347	.409	128	16	8	.972	7	103	117	3b126		2.9
1919	NY A	141	567	70	166	22	1	10	83	44	2	18	.293	.346	.388	105	3	13	.955	-5	95	134	3b141		0.3
1921	†NY A	94	330	46	97	16	2	9	71	26	1	9	.294	.353	.436	98	-2	8-5	.959	-5	107	118	3b60		0.8
1922	†NY A	69	234	30	65	12	3	7	36	15	2	14	.278	.327	.444	97	-2	1-3	.962	-10	84	68	3b60		-0.9
Total 13		1575	5984	887	1838	315	103	96	987	473	50	182	.307	.363	.442	136	252	235-28	.943	25	98	114	3b1548		33.7

BAKER, DUSTY Johnnie B B6.15.1949 Riverside CA BR/TR/6-2/187(182-200) [AtlN67 26/504] d9.7 M13/C5

1968	Atl N	6	5	0	2	0	0	0	0-0		0	1	.400	.400	.400	140	0	0-0	—	-1	0	0	O3C		0.0
1969	Atl N	3	7	0	0	0	0	0	0	0-0	0	3	.000	.000	.000	-99	-2	0-0	1.000	-1	42	0	O3C		-0.3
1970	Atl N	13	24	3	7	0	0	0	4	2-0	0	4	.292	.333	.292	69	-1	0-0	.800	-1	87	221	O11(5/4/2)		-0.2
1971	Atl N	29	62	2	14	2	0	1	4	1-1	0	4	.226	.238	.258	38	-5	0-1	1.000	0	89	90	O18(1/4/16)		-0.6
1972	Atl N	127	446	62	143	27	2	17	76	45-2	4	60	.321	.383	.504	139	24	4-7	.989	12	111	104	O123(30/121/3)		3.3

YEAR	TM LG	G	AB	R	H	2B	3B	HR	RBI	BB-IB	HP	SO	AVG	OBP	SLG	AOPS	ABR	SB-CS	FA	FR	RNG	THR	GAMES AT POSITION	DL	BFW
1973	Atl N	159	604	101	174	29	4	21	99	67-8	5	72	.288	.359	.454	116	15	24-3	.983	-4	92	90	O156C		1.1
1974	Atl N	149	574	80	147	35	0	20	69	71-9	1	87	.256	.335	.422	108	7	18-7	.981	0	102	97	O148(0/102/112)		0.3
1975	Atl N	142	494	63	129	18	2	19	72	67-7	0	57	.261	.346	.421	110	7	12-7	.990	4	107	108	O136(0/12/129)		0.5
1976	LA N	112	384	36	93	13	0	4	39	31-3	1	54	.242	.298	.307	73	-14	5-7	.996	-6	97	43	O106(0/83/24)		-2.5
1977	†LA N	153	533	86	155	26	1	30	86	58-6	6	89	.291	.364	.512	132	24	2-6	.987	-8	82	84	O152(150/1/2)		0.8
1978	†LA N	149	522	62	137	24	1	11	66	47-2	3	66	.262	.325	.375	96	-3	12-3	.985	0	95	113	O145L		-0.8
1979	LA N	151	554	86	152	29	1	23	88	56-0	1	70	.274	.340	.455	118	13	11-4	.990	6	99	123	O150L		1.4
1980	LA N	153	579	80	170	26	4	29	97	43-4	3	66	.294	.339	.503	138	27	12-10	.991	-1	102	44	O151(151/1/1)		1.9
1981	†LA N★	103	400	48	128	17	3	9	49	29-1	1	43	.320	.363	.445	135	18	10-7	.990	-3	95	91	O101L		1.1
1982	LA N★	147	570	80	171	19	1	23	88	56-5	3	62	.300	.361	.458	133	25	17-10	.975	-14	81	59	O144(144/0/1)		0.5
1983	†LA N	149	531	71	138	25	1	15	73	72-2	2	59	.260	.346	.395	106	6	7-1	.981	-6	97	39	O143L		-0.5
1984	SF N	100	243	31	71	7	2	3	32	40-1	0	27	.292	.387	.374	120	8	4-1	.974	-2	101	24	O62(29/0/33)		0.4
1985	Oak A	111	343	48	92	15	1	14	52	50-0	1	47	.268	.359	.440	127	14	2-1	.993	-2	72	78	1b58,O35(32/0/5),D13		0.7
1986	Oak A	83	242	25	58	8	0	4	19	27-1	0	37	.240	.314	.322	80	-7	0-1	1.000	-1	86	133	O55(36/0/20),D15,1b3		-1.1
Total	19	2039	7117	964	1981	320	23	242	1013	762-52	30	926	.278	.347	.432	116	156	137-73	.985	-25	96	84	O1842(1117/490/348),1b61,D28		6.0

BAKER, PHIL Philip B9.19.1856 Philadelphia PA D6.4.1940 Washington DC BL/TL/5-8/152 d5.1

YEAR	TM LG	G	AB	R	H	2B	3B	HR	RBI	BB-IB	HP	SO	AVG	OBP	SLG	AOPS	ABR	SB-CS	FA	FR	RNG	THR	GAMES AT POSITION	DL	BFW
1883	Bal AA	28	121	22	33	2	1	1		8				.273	.318	.331	106	1		.883	-5			C19,O14(1/1/12)/S		-0.3
1884	Was U	86	371	75	107	12	5	1		11				.288	.309	.356	104	-9		.955	-3	111	98	1b39,O32C,C27		-1.3
1886	Was N	81	325	37	72	6	5	1	34	20		32		.222	.267	.280	72	-11	16	.967	-5	63	97	1b56,O21(1/7/14),C4		-1.9
Total	3	195	817	134	212	20	11	3	34	39		32		.259	.293	.322	92	-19	16	.963	-13			1b95,O67(2/40/26),C50/S		-3.5

BAKER, TRACE Trace Lee B11.7.1891 Pendleton OR D3.14.1975 Placerville CA BR/TR/6-1/180 d6.19 Col Washington

YEAR	TM LG	G	AB	R	H	2B	3B	HR	RBI	BB-IB	HP	SO	AVG	OBP	SLG	AOPS	ABR	SB-CS	FA	FR	RNG	THR	GAMES AT POSITION	DL	BFW
1911	Bos A	1	0	0	0	0	0	0	0	0-0	0	0	—	—	—	—	0	0	1.000	-0	0	0	/1		0.0

BAKER, BILL William Presley B2.22.1911 Paw Creek NC BR/TR/6-0/200 d5.4 Mil 1944-45 C1

YEAR	TM LG	G	AB	R	H	2B	3B	HR	RBI	BB-IB	HP	SO	AVG	OBP	SLG	AOPS	ABR	SB-CS	FA	FR	RNG	THR	GAMES AT POSITION	DL	BFW
1940	†Cin N	27	69	5	15	1	1	0	7	4	0	8	.217	.260	.261	44	-6	2	1.000	2	114	54	C24		-0.2
1941	Cin N	2	1	0	0	0	0	0	0	1	0	1	.000	.500	.000	49	0	0	1.000	0	0	0	/C		0.0
	Pit N	35	67	5	15	3	0	0	6	11	0	4	.224	.333	.269	71	-2	0	.967	0	113	102	C33		-0.1
	Year	37	68	5	15	3	0	0	6	12	0	1	.221	.338	.265	71	-2	0	.967	0	111	100	C34		-0.1
1942	Pit N	18	17	1	2	0	0	0	2	1	0	0	.118	.167	.118	-16	-3	0	1.000	1	126	0	C11		-0.2
1943	Pit N	63	172	12	47	6	3	1	26	22	3	6	.273	.365	.360	106	2	3	.979	3	138	101	C56		0.8
1946	Pit N	53	113	7	27	4	0	1	8	12	0	6	.239	.312	.301	72	-4	0	.965	-4	71	98	C41/1		-0.7
1948	StL N	45	119	13	35	10	1	0	15	15	0	7	.294	.373	.395	102	1	1	.994	2	311	72	C36		0.5
1949	StL N	20	30	2	4	1	0	0	4	2	0	2	.133	.188	.167	-4	-4	0	1.000	-1	146	0	C10		-0.5
Total	7	263	588	45	145	25	5	2	68	68	3	30	.247	.328	.316	79	-16	6	.983	2	155	83	C212/1		-0.4

BAKO, PAUL Gabor Paul B6.20.1972 Lafayette LA BL/TR/6-2/205* [CinN93 5/148] d4.30 Col Louisiana-Lafayette

YEAR	TM LG	G	AB	R	H	2B	3B	HR	RBI	BB-IB	HP	SO	AVG	OBP	SLG	AOPS	ABR	SB-CS	FA	FR	RNG	THR	GAMES AT POSITION	DL	BFW
1998	Det A	96	305	23	83	12	1	3	30	23-4	0	82	.272	.319	.348	74	-12	1-1	.989	-7	88	130	C94		-1.2
1999	Hou N	73	215	16	55	14	1	2	17	26-3	0	57	.256	.332	.358	77	-7	1-1	.988	7	130	103	C71		0.4
2000	Hou N	1	2	0	0	0	0	0	0	0-0	0	1	.000	.000	.000	-93	-1	0-0	1.000	0	0	0	/C		0.0
	Fla N	56	161	10	39	6	1	0	14	22-7	1	48	.242	.335	.292	64	-8	0-0	.991	-3	87	127	C56		-0.8
	†Atl N	24	58	8	11	4	0	2	6	5-3	0	15	.190	.254	.362	54	-4	0-0	.992	0	116	80	C23/1		-0.3
	Year	81	221	18	50	10	1	2	20	27-10	1	64	.226	.312	.308	60	-14	0-0	.992	-3	94	114	C80/1		-1.1
2001	†Atl N	61	137	19	29	10	1	2	15	20-2	0	34	.212	.312	.343	69	-6	1-0	.991	3	70	153	C60		0.0
2002	Mil N	87	234	24	55	8	1	4	20	20-3	0	46	.235	.295	.329	67	-13	0-2	.991	-10	85	91	C76		-1.9
2003	†Chi N	70	188	19	43	13	3	0	17	22-3	1	47	.229	.311	.330	66	-9	0-1	.987	-8	107	100	C69		-1.3
2004	Chi N	49	138	13	28	8	0	1	10	15-3	2	29	.203	.288	.283	48	-11	1-0	.989	-1	65	166	C47		-0.9
2005	LA N	13	40	1	10	2	0	0	4	7-1	0	12	.250	.362	.300	76	-1	0-0	.985	-3	642	117	C13	129	-0.3
Total	8	530	1478	133	353	77	8	14	133	160-29	4	371	.239	.313	.330	67	-72	4-5	.989	-21	108	119	C510/1	144	-6.3

BALAZ, JOHN John Lawrence B11.24.1950 Toronto ON, Can. BR/TR/6-3/180* [AnaA70 5/108] d9.10 Col San Diego (CA) City

YEAR	TM LG	G	AB	R	H	2B	3B	HR	RBI	BB-IB	HP	SO	AVG	OBP	SLG	AOPS	ABR	SB-CS	FA	FR	RNG	THR	GAMES AT POSITION	DL	BFW
1974	Cal A	14	42	4	10	0	0	1	5	2-0	1	10	.238	.289	.310	76	-1	0-0	1.000	-1	77	0	O12L		-0.4
1975	Cal A	45	120	10	29	8	1	1	10	5-0	0	25	.242	.270	.350	80	-4	0-0	1.000	1	93	188	O27(19/0/8),D11		-0.4
Total	2	59	162	14	39	8	1	2	15	7-0	1	35	.241	.275	.340	79	-5	0-0	1.000	-0	87	123	O39(31/0/8),D11		-0.8

BALBONI, STEVE Stephen Charles B1.16.1957 Brockton MA BR/TR/6-3/225(225-250) [NYA78 2/52] d4.22 Col Eckerd

YEAR	TM LG	G	AB	R	H	2B	3B	HR	RBI	BB-IB	HP	SO	AVG	OBP	SLG	AOPS	ABR	SB-CS	FA	FR	RNG	THR	GAMES AT POSITION	DL	BFW
1981	NY A	4	7	2	2	1	1	0	2	1-0	0	4	.286	.375	.714	210	1	0-0	1.000	0	86	132	1b3/D		0.1
1982	NY A	33	107	8	20	2	1	2	4	6-0	0	34	.187	.228	.280	40	-9	0-0	.990	-0	96	115	1b26,D5		-1.1
1983	NY A	32	86	8	20	2	0	5	17	8-0	0	33	.233	.295	.430	101	0	0-0	.984	-1	82	121	1b23,D4		-0.2
1984	†KC A	126	438	58	107	23	2	28	77	45-5	4	139	.244	.320	.498	121	12	0-0	.987	-2	90	1b125/D		0.2
1985	†KC A	160	600	74	146	28	2	36	88	52-4	5	166	.243	.307	.477	110	7	1-1	.993	-5	90	101	1b160		-0.9
1986	KC A	138	512	54	117	25	1	29	88	43-2	1	146	.229	.286	.451	96	-5	0-0	.987	-4	94	103	1b137		-1.7
1987	KC A	121	386	44	80	11	1	24	60	34-1	2	97	.207	.273	.427	80	-13	0-0	.989	1	112	88	1b55,D52		-1.6
1988	KC A	21	63	2	9	2	0	2	5	1-0	0	20	.143	.156	.270	17	-7	0-0	.980	-1	67	123	1b13,D6		-1.0
	Sea A	97	350	44	88	15	1	21	61	23-2	1	67	.251	.298	.480	109	3	0-1	.994	-1	87	101	D56,1b40		-0.3
	Year	118	413	46	97	17	1	23	66	24-2	1	87	.235	.277	.448	96	-4	0-1	.991	-2	83	106	D62,1b53		-1.3
1989	NY A	110	300	33	71	12	2	17	59	25-5	3	67	.237	.296	.460	113	3	0-0	.994	-0	97	148	D82,1b20		0.0
1990	NY A	116	266	24	51	6	0	17	34	35-2	3	91	.192	.291	.406	93	-4	0-0	.984	-3	49	121	D72,1b28		-1.1
1993	Tex A	2	5	0	3	0	0	0	0	0-0	0	2	.600	.600	.600	231	1	0-0	—	0			D2		0.1
Total	11	960	3120	351	714	127	11	181	495	273-21	19	856	.229	.293	.451	100	-11	1-2	.989	-16	93	105	1b630,D281		-7.5

BALCENA, BOBBY Robert Rudolph B8.1.1925 San Pedro CA D1.5.1990 San Pedro CA BR/TL/5-7/160 d9.16

YEAR	TM LG	G	AB	R	H	2B	3B	HR	RBI	BB-IB	HP	SO	AVG	OBP	SLG	AOPS	ABR	SB-CS	FA	FR	RNG	THR	GAMES AT POSITION	DL	BFW
1956	Cin N	7	2	2	0	0	0	0	0	0-0	0	0	.000	.000	.000	-94	-1	0-0	1.000	0	146	0	O2L		-0.1

BALDELLI, ROCCO Rocco Dan B9.25.1981 Woonsocket RI BR/TR/6-4/190* [TBA00 1/6] d3.31 [DL 2005 TB A 183]

YEAR	TM LG	G	AB	R	H	2B	3B	HR	RBI	BB-IB	HP	SO	AVG	OBP	SLG	AOPS	ABR	SB-CS	FA	FR	RNG	THR	GAMES AT POSITION	DL	BFW
2003	TB A	156	637	89	184	32	8	11	78	30-4	8	128	.289	.326	.416	97	-4	27-10	.989	10	107	197	O154C,D2		1.0
2004	TB A	136	518	79	145	27	3	16	74	30-2	8	88	.280	.326	.436	99	-2	17-4	.978	10	112	183	O124C,D13	18	1.1
Total	2	292	1155	168	329	59	11	27	152	60-6	16	216	.285	.326	.425	98	-6	44-14	.984	20	109	191	O278C,D15	201	2.1

BALDWIN, KID Clarence Geoghan B11.1.1864 Newport KY D7.10.1897 Cincinnati OH BR/TR/5-6/147 d7.27 OF(11/13/8)

YEAR	TM LG	G	AB	R	H	2B	3B	HR	RBI	BB-IB	HP	SO	AVG	OBP	SLG	AOPS	ABR	SB-CS	FA	FR	RNG	THR	GAMES AT POSITION	DL	BFW
1884	KC U	50	191	19	37	6	3	0		4				.194	.210	.257	47	-18		.885	0			C44,O10(8/2/0)/23		-1.3
	CP U	1	1	0	1	0	0	0		0				1.000	1.000	1.000	512	0		1.000	-0			/C		0.0
	Year	51	192	19	38	6	3	0		4				.198	.214	.260	50	-18		.885	-0			C45,O10(8/2/0)/23		-1.3
1885	Cin AA	34	126	9	17	1	0	1	8	3	0			.135	.155	.167	2	-14		.863	-4			C25,O6(0/5/1),2b2,P2/3		-1.4
1886	Cin AA	87	315	41	72	8	7	3	32	8	2			.229	.252	.327	78	-10	12	.891	-7			C71,3b13,O6(0/5/1)		-1.0
1887	Cin AA	96	388	46	98	15	10	1	57	6	4			.253	.271	.351	71	-18	13	.874	-2			C96,O2L		-0.9
1888	Cin AA	67	271	27	59	11	3	1	25	3	3			.218	.235	.292	65	-12	4	.918	-4			C65,O2R/1		-0.9
1889	Cin AA	60	223	34	55	14	2	1	34	5	3	32		.247	.273	.341	72	-9	7	.912	-1			C55,O4(1/1/2)/31		-0.5
1890	Cin N	22	72	5	11	0	0	0	10	3	0	6		.153	.187	.153	-1	-9	2	.902	3	125	119	C20,O2R		-0.4
	Phi AA	24	90	5	21	1	2	0	12	4	1			.233	.247	.289	66	-4	2	.887	-4	83	100	C19,3b5		-0.6
Total	9	441	1677	186	371	56	27	7	178	36	13	38		.221	.243	.299	61	-94	40	.893	-17	103	109	C396,O32C,3b21,2b3,1b2,P2		-7.0

BALDWIN, FRANK Frank De Witt B12.25.1928 High Bridge NJ D11.18.2004 Beaver OH BR/TR/5-11/195 d4.22

YEAR	TM LG	G	AB	R	H	2B	3B	HR	RBI	BB-IB	HP	SO	AVG	OBP	SLG	AOPS	ABR	SB-CS	FA	FR	RNG	THR	GAMES AT POSITION	DL	BFW
1953	Cin N	16	20	0	2	0	0	0	0	1	0	9	.100	.143	.100	-35	-4	0-0	1.000	-1	69	0	C6		-0.5

BALDWIN, HENRY Henry Clay "Ted" B6.13.1894 Chadds Ford PA D2.24.1964 West Chester PA BR/TR/5-11/180 d5.22 Col Swarthmore

YEAR	TM LG	G	AB	R	H	2B	3B	HR	RBI	BB-IB	HP	SO	AVG	OBP	SLG	AOPS	ABR	SB-CS	FA	FR	RNG	THR	GAMES AT POSITION	DL	BFW
1927	Phi N	6	16	1	5	0	0	0		2		3	.313	.353	.313	78	0	0	.857	-1	98	94	S3,3b2		-0.1

BALDWIN, JEFF Jeffrey Allen B9.5.1965 Milford DE BL/TL/6-1/180 [HouN85*14/296] d5.22 Col Camden Co. (NJ) JC

YEAR	TM LG	G	AB	R	H	2B	3B	HR	RBI	BB-IB	HP	SO	AVG	OBP	SLG	AOPS	ABR	SB-CS	FA	FR	RNG	THR	GAMES AT POSITION	DL	BFW
1990	Hou N	7	8	1	0	0	0	0	0	1-0	0	2	.000	.111	.000	-69	-2	0-0	1.000	-0	67	0	O3(2/0/1)		-0.2

BALDWIN, REGGIE Reginald Conrad B8.19.1954 River Rouge MI BR/TR/6-1/195* [HouN76 3/49] d5.25 Col Grambling St.

YEAR	TM LG	G	AB	R	H	2B	3B	HR	RBI	BB-IB	HP	SO	AVG	OBP	SLG	AOPS	ABR	SB-CS	FA	FR	RNG	THR	GAMES AT POSITION	DL	BFW
1978	Hou N	38	67	5	17	5	0	1	11	3-0	0	3	.254	.286	.373	88	-1	0-0	.955	-3	52	83	C17		-0.4
1979	Hou N	14	20	0	4	1	0	0	1	0-0	1	1	.200	.200	.250	23	-2	0-0	1.000	-0	0	0	C3/1		-0.3
Total	2	52	87	5	21	6	0	1	12	3-0	1	4	.241	.240	.345	73	-3	0-0	.956	-4	49	78	C20/1		-0.7

YEAR	TM LG	G	AB	R	H	2B	3B	HR	RBI	BB-IB	HP	SO	AVG	OBP	SLG	AOPS	ABR	SB-CS	FA	FR	RNG	THR	GAMES AT POSITION	DL	BFW

BALDWIN, BILLY Robert Harvey B6.9.1951 Tazewell VA BL/TL/6-0/175* d7.29 Col Southern A&M

1975	Det A	30	95	8	21	3	0	4	8	5-0	0	14	.221	.260	.379	75	-4	2-1	.983	2	100	220	O25(0/13/13)/D		-0.3
1976	NY N	9	22	4	6	1	1	1	5	1-0	0	2	.273	.292	.545	144	1	0-0	.929	1	136	296	O5(3/0/2)		0.2
Total	2	39	117	12	27	4	1	5	13	6-0	0	16	.231	.266	.410	87	-3	2-1	.972	3	106	233	O30(3/13/15)/D		-0.1

BALENTI, MIKE Michael Richard B7.3.1886 Calumet OK D8.4.1955 Altus OK BR/TR/5-11/175 d7.19 Col Texas A&M-Commerce

1911	Cin N	8	8	2	2	0	0	0	0	0-0	0	1	.250	.250	.250	42	-1	3	.857	0	127	248	S2/OC		0.0
1913	StL A	70	211	17	38	2	4	0	11	6	1	32	.180	.206	.227	28	-21	3	.923	-2	103	116	S56,O8L		-2.1
Total	2	78	219	19	40	2	4	0	11	6	1	33	.183	.208	.228	28	-22	6	.922	-2	103	119	S58,O9(8/1/0)		-2.1

BALES, LEE Wesley Owen B12.4.1944 Los Angeles CA BB/TR/5-10.5/165* d8.7

1966	Atl N	12	16	4	1	0	0	0	0-0		0	5	.063	.063	.063	-64	-4	0-0	1.000	2	136	75	2b7,3b3		-0.1
1967	Hou N	19	27	4	3	0	0	0	2	8-0	0	7	.111	.306	.111	28	-2	1-1	.944	-2	69	0	2b6/S		-0.5
Total	2	31	43	8	4	0	0	0	2	8-0	0	12	.093	.231	.093	-3	-6	1-1	.978	-1	98	33	2b13,3b3/S		-0.6

BALL, ART Arthur Clark B4.1876 KY D12.26.1915 Chicago IL TR/?/168 d8.1

1894	StL N	1	3	0	1	0	0	0	0	0-0	0		.333	.333	.333	61	0		.667	-1	0	0	/2		-0.1
1898	Bal N	32	81	7	15	2	0	0	8	7	1		.185	.258	.210	34	-7	2	.906	6	108	182	3b15,S14,2b2/OC		0.0
Total	2	33	84	7	16	2	0	0	8	7	1	1	.190	.261	.214	35	-7	2	.906	5	108	182	3b15,S14,2b3/OC		-0.1

BALL, NEAL Cornelius B4.22.1881 Grand Haven MI D10.15.1957 Bridgeport CT BR/TR/5-7/145 d9.12

1907	NY A	15	44	5	9	1	1	0	4	1	0		.205	.222	.273	53	-3	1	.817	-3	95	68	S11,2b5		-0.6
1908	NY A	132	446	35	110	16	2	0	38	21	2		.247	.284	.291	86	-7	32	.898	-6	100	62	S130/2		-1.1
1909	NY A	8	29	5	6	1	1	0	3	3	0		.207	.281	.310	86	-1	2	.917	-3	77	33	2b8		-0.4
	Cle A	96	324	29	83	13	2	1	25	17	1		.256	.295	.318	90	-4	17	.914	-10	91	129	S95		-1.2
	Year	104	353	34	89	14	3	1	28	20	1		.252	.294	.317	90	-5	19	.914	-13	91	129	S95,2b8		-1.6
1910	Cle A	54	123	13	25	3	1	0	12	9	0		.203	.258	.244	56	-6	4	.927	-3	88	101	S27,2b7,O6(0/5/1),3b3		-1.0
1911	Cle A	116	412	45	122	14	9	3	45	27	0		.296	.339	.396	104	0	21	.945	3	105	111	2b94,3b17/S		0.5
1912	Cle A	40	132	12	30	4	1	0	14	9	0		.227	.277	.273	55	-8	7	.938	0	93	98	2b37		-0.7
	†Bos A	18	45	10	9	2	0	0	6	3	0		.200	.250	.244	40	-4	5	.927	-2	96	35	2b17		-0.6
	Year	58	177	22	39	6	1	0	20	12	0		.220	.270	.266	51	-11	12	.936	-2	94	84	2b54		-1.3
1913	Bos A	23	58	9	10	2	0	0	4	9	1	13	.172	.294	.207	46	-4	3	.902	-3	88	124	2b10,S7/3		-0.6
Total	7	502	1613	163	404	56	17	4	151	99	4	13	.250	.295	.314	83	-37	92	.902	-28	96	89	S271,2b179,3b21,O6(0/5/1)		-5.7

BALL, JIM James Chandler B2.22.1884 Harford Co. MD D4.7.1963 Glendale CA BR/TR/5-11/175 d9.21

1907	Bos N	10	36	3	6	2	0	0	3	2	0		.167	.211	.222	36	-3	0	.963	-2	73	114	C10		-0.5
1908	Bos N	6	15	1	1	0	0	0	0	1	0		.067	.125	.067	-39	-2	0	.917	-1	83	142	C6		-0.3
Total	2	16	51	4	7	2	0	0	3	3	0		.137	.185	.176	14	-5	0	.949	-3	76	123	C16		-0.8

BALL, JEFF Jeffery D. B4.17.1969 Merced CA BR/TR/5-10/185 [HouN90 12/332] d6.10 Col San Jose St.

| 1998 | SF N | 2 | 4 | 0 | 1 | 0 | 0 | 0 | 0 | 0-0 | 0 | 2 | .250 | .250 | .250 | 34 | 0 | 0-0 | 1.000 | -0 | 0 | 158 | /1 | | -0.1 |

BALLENGER, PELHAM Pelham Ashby B2.6.1894 Gilreath Mill SC D12.8.1948 Greenville SC BR/TR/5-11/160 d5.7

| 1928 | Was A | 3 | 9 | 1 | 1 | 0 | 0 | 0 | 0 | 0-0 | 0 | 1 | .111 | .111 | .111 | -42 | -2 | 0-0 | 1.000 | 1 | 161 | 236 | 3b3 | | -0.1 |

BAMBERGER, HAL Harold Earl "Dutch" B10.29.1924 Lebanon PA BL/TR/6-0/173 d9.15

| 1948 | NY N | 7 | 12 | 0 | 1 | 0 | 0 | 0 | 1 | 0 | 0 | 2 | .083 | .154 | .083 | -34 | -2 | 0 | 1.000 | -0 | 102 | 0 | O3(0/1/2) | | -0.3 |

BANCKER, STUD John B Philadelphia PA d4.19

| 1875 | NH NA | 19 | 72 | 3 | 11 | 0 | 0 | 2 | 0 | | | | .153 | .153 | .153 | 7 | -6 | 1-0 | .796 | -4 | | | C14,2b4,3b3/S1 | | -0.8 |

BANCROFT, DAVE David James "Beauty" B4.20.1891 Sioux City IA D10.9.1972 Superior WI BB/TR/5-9.5/160 d4.14 M4/C3 HF1971

1915	†Phi N	**153**	563	85	143	18	2	7	30	77	2	62	.254	.346	.330	104	6	15-27	.928	5	101	105	S153		1.7
1916	Phi N	142	477	53	101	10	0	3	33	74	4	57	.212	.323	.252	75	-10	15	.933	25	110	113	S142		2.8
1917	Phi N	127	478	56	116	22	5	4	43	44	0	42	.243	.307	.335	93	-3	14	.936	28	112	111	S120,2b3,O2L		3.6
1918	Phi N	125	499	69	132	19	4	0	26	54	1	36	.265	.338	.319	94	-1	11	.928	16	104	102	S125		2.6
1919	Phi N	92	335	45	91	13	7	0	25	31	0	30	.272	.333	.352	99	0	8	.951	6	99	96	S88		1.4
1920	Phi N	42	171	23	51	7	2	0	5	9	1	12	.298	.337	.363	96	-1	1-7	.981	9	106	131	S42		1.0
	NY N	108	442	79	132	29	7	0	31	33	1	32	.299	.349	.396	115	9	7-5	.946	28	118	143	S108		4.6
	Year	150	613	102	183	36	9	0	36	42	2	44	.299	.346	.387	109	8	8-12	.955	37	115	140	S150		5.6
1921	†NY N	**153**	606	121	193	26	15	6	67	66	4	23	.318	.389	.441	119	11	17-10	.960	19	104	**141**	S153		5.3
1922	†NY N	**156**	651	117	209	41	5	4	60	79	3	27	.321	.397	.418	109	14	16-11	.941	22	108	114	S156		4.9
1923	†NY N	107	444	80	135	33	3	1	31	62	1	23	.304	.391	.399	110	10	8-7	.936	12	107	94	S96,2b11		3.2
1924	Bos N	79	319	49	89	11	1	2	21	37	1	24	.279	.356	.339	91	-3	4-4	.961	-3	96	107	S79,M		0.3
1925	Bos N	128	479	75	153	29	8	2	49	64	0	29	.319	.400	.426	122	19	7-4	**.945**	10	**108**	101	S125,M		3.9
1926	Bos N	127	453	70	141	18	6	1	44	64	2	29	.311	.399	.384	122	3	8	.956	-5	96	92	S123,3b2,M		2.6
1927	Bos N	111	375	44	91	13	4	1	31	43	1	36	.243	.322	.307	75	-13	5	.939	5	100	100	S104/3M		0.3
1928	Bro N	149	515	47	127	19	5	0	51	59	2	20	.247	.326	.303	66	-24	7	.948	2	98	72	S149		-0.6
1929	Bro N	104	358	35	99	11	3	1	44	29	0	11	.277	.331	.332	66	-19	7	.955	-3	94	69	S102		-1.1
1930	NY N	10	17	0	1	1	0	0	0	2	0	1	.059	.158	.118	-33	-4	0	.966	-0	96	0	S8		-0.3
Total	16	1913	7182	1048	2004	320	77	32	591	827	23	487	.279	.355	.358	98	16	145-75	.944	178	104·	105	S1873,2b14,3b3,O2L		36.2

BANDO, CHRIS Christopher Michael B2.4.1956 Cleveland OH BB/TR/6-0/195* [CleA78 2/36] d8.13 C3 b-Sal Col Arizona St.

1981	Cle A	21	47	3	10	3	0	0	6	2-0	0	5	.213	.240	.277	50	-3	0-0	.967	-2	115	106	C15,D2		-0.5
1982	Cle A	66	184	13	39	6	1	3	16	24-1	0	34	.212	.299	.304	67	-8	0-0	.990	-6	107	108	C63,3b2	46	-1.2
1983	Cle A	48	121	15	31	3	0	4	15	15-0	0	19	.256	.336	.380	94	-1	0-1	.995	0	135	128	C43		0.1
1984	Cle A	75	220	38	64	11	0	12	41	33-5	0	35	.291	.377	.505	141	13	1-2	.982	-1	118	76	C63/13D	18	1.4
1985	Cle A	73	173	11	24	4	1	0	13	22-0	1	41	.139	.234	.173	14	-21	0-1	.986	-8	65	114	C67		-2.7
1986	Cle A	92	254	28	68	9	0	2	26	22-0	1	49	.268	.325	.327	80	-7	0-1	.990	-7	95	77	C86		-1.1
1987	Cle A	89	211	20	46	9	0	5	16	12-0	0	28	.218	.260	.332	55	-14	0-0	.990	-2	100	111	C86		-1.3
1988	Cle A	32	72	6	9	1	0	1	8	8-0	0	12	.125	.217	.181	14	-8	0-0	.979	2	111	128	C32		-0.5
	Det A	1	0	0	0	0	0	0	0	0-0	0	0	—	—	—	—	0	0-0	—	-0	0	0	/C		0.0
	Year	33	72	6	9	1	0	1	8	8-0	0	12	.125	.217	.181	14	-8	0-0	.979	2	110	127	C33		-0.5
1989	Oak A	1	2	0	1	0	0	0	1	0-0	0	1	.500	.500	.500	189	0	0-0	1.000	1	0	0	/C		0.1
Total	9	498	1284	134	292	46	2	27	142	138-6	2	197	.227	.300	.329	73	-49	1-5	.987	-23	102	101	C457,3b3,D3/1	64	-5.7

BANDO, SAL Salvatore Leonard B2.13.1944 Cleveland OH BR/TR/6-0/200* [OakA65 6/119] d9.3 C2 b-Chris Col Arizona St.

1966	KC A	11	24	1	7	1	0	1	0	1-0	0	3	.292	.320	.417	113	0	0-0	.933	4	187	81	3b7		0.4
1967	KC A	47	130	11	25	3	2	0	6	16-0	3	24	.192	.295	.246	64	-6	1-0	.959	9	122	106	3b44		-0.4
1968	Oak A	162	605	67	152	25	5	9	67	51-6	7	78	.251	.314	.354	107	5	13-4	.964	-4	89	97	3b162/OL		0.2
1969	Oak A★	**162**	609	106	171	25	3	31	113	111-5	11	82	.281	.400	.484	152	47	1-4	.958	-8	95	106	3b162		3.8
1970	Oak A	155	502	93	132	20	2	20	75	118-5	6	85	.263	.407	.430	136	32	6-10	.954	-13	88	76	3b152		1.7
1971	†Oak A	153	538	75	146	23	1	24	94	86-11	8	55	.271	.374	.452	137	29	3-7	.971	-20	82	77	3b153		0.8
1972	Oak A★	152	535	64	126	20	3	15	77	78-17	2	55	.236	.341	.368	117	13	3-1	.960	0	102	108	3b151/2		1.5
1973	†Oak A★	**162**	592	97	170	**32**	3	29	98	82-5	4	84	.287	.375	.498	152	42	4-2	.949	-29	80	90	3b159,D3		1.3
1974	†Oak A★	146	498	84	121	21	2	22	103	86-4	5	79	.243	.352	.426	133	24	2-3	.946	-14	89	102	3b141,D3		1.0
1975	†Oak A	160	562	64	129	24	1	15	78	87-2	5	80	.230	.337	.356	98	1	7-1	.967	-20	85	126	3b160		-1.9
1976	Oak A	158	550	75	132	18	2	27	84	76-1	4	74	.240	.335	.422	128	19	20-6	.962	-2	99	108	3b155,S5,D2		2.0
1977	Mil A	159	580	65	145	27	3	17	82	75-3	3	89	.250	.336	.395	99	1	4-2	.966	-1	100	120	3b135,D24/2S		-0.3
1978	Mil A	152	540	85	154	20	4	17	78	72-4	6	52	.285	.371	.439	127	21	3-2	.968	8	113	103	3b134,D12,1b5		2.7
1979	Mil A	130	476	57	117	14	3	9	43	57-3	3	42	.246	.330	.345	82	-11	2-0	.963	-11	94	81	3b109,D19,1b4/P2		-2.4
1980	Mil A	78	254	28	50	12	1	5	31	29-2	1	36	.197	.278	.311	64	-13	5-3	.934	-2	99	114	3b57,D15,1b7		-1.6
1981	†Mil A	32	65	10	13	4	0	2	9	6-1	0	3	.200	.268	.354	81	-2	1-1	.967	-1	94	145	3b15,1b9,D2		-0.4
Total	16	2019	7060	982	1790	289	38	242	1039	1031-69	75	923	.254	.352	.408	119	202	75-46	.959	-103	94	100	3b1896,D80,1b25,S6,2b3/POL		9.2

BANISTER, JEFF Jeffery Todd B1.15.1965 Weatherford OK BR/TR/6-2/200 [PitN86 25/621] d7.23 Col Houston

| 1991 | Pit N | 1 | 1 | 0 | 1 | 0 | 0 | 0 | 0 | 0-0 | 0 | 0 | 1.000 | 1.000 | 1.000 | 469 | 0 | 0-0 | — | 0 | | | /H | | 0.0 |

YEAR	TM	LG	G	AB	R	H	2B	3B	HR	RBI	BB-IB	HP	SO	AVG	OBP	SLG	AOPS	ABR	SB-CS	FA	FR	RNG	THR	GAMES AT POSITION	DL	BFW

BANKS, BRIAN Brian Glen B9.28.1970 Mesa AZ BB/TR/6-3/200* [MilA93 2/43] d9.9 Col Brigham Young

1996	Mil	A	4	7	2	4	2	0	1	2	1-0	0	2	.571	.625	1.286	351	3	0-0	1.000	0	67	0	O3L/1		0.2
1997	Mil	A	28	68	9	14	1	0	1	8	6-0	0	17	.206	.267	.265	40	-6	0-1	.950	-1	71	0	O15(15/0/1),1b5/3D		-0.8
1998	Mil	N	24	24	3	7	2	0	1	5	4-0	0	7	.292	.393	.500	130	1	0-0	1.000	-1	39	0	C5,1b2/3OL		0.0
1999	Mil	N	105	219	34	53	7	1	5	22	25-5	0	59	.242	.317	.352	69	-11	6-1	.992	-5	120	79	1b44,C40,O5(4/0/1)		-1.4
2002	Fla	N	20	28	3	9	1	0	1	4	1-0	0	6	.321	.345	.464	118	0	0-0	1.000	-0	95	0	O8(3/0/5)/13		0.0
2003	†Fla	N	92	149	14	35	6	2	4	23	25-1	2	38	.235	.348	.383	95	-1	2-1	.975	-2	89	69	O33(23/0/10),1b12/D		-0.4
Total	6		273	495	65	122	19	3	13	64	62-6	2	129	.246	.330	.376	83	-14	8-3	.989	-9	111	92	1b65,O65(49/0/17),C45,3b3,D2		-2.4

BANKS, ERNIE Ernest "Mr. Cub" B1.31.1931 Dallas TX BR/TR/6-1/180(170-185) d9.17 C7 HF1977 Negro Lg 1950-53 Mil 1951-52

1953	Chi	N	10	35	3	11	1	1	2	6	4-0	0	5	.314	.385	.571	142	0	2-0	.981	2	112	133	S10		0.5
1954	Chi	N	154	593	70	163	19	7	19	79	40	7	50	.275	.326	.427	94	-7	6-10	.959	-2	99	99	S154		0.2
1955	Chi	N★	154	596	98	176	29	9	44	117	45-6	2	72	.295	.345	.596	145	35	9-3	.972	3	102	100	S154		5.1
1956	Chi	N☆	139	538	82	160	25	8	28	85	52-18	0	62	.297	.358	.530	137	27	6-9	.962	-13	88	100	S139		2.4
1957	Chi	N★	156	594	113	169	34	6	43	102	70-11	3	85	.285	.360	.579	150	41	8-4	.975	-11	91	87	S100,3b58		3.9
1958	Chi	N★	154	617	119	193	23	11	47	129	52-12	4	87	.313	.366	.614	157	47	4-4	.960	-1	99	97	S154		5.9
1959	Chi	N★	155	589	97	179	25	6	45	143	64-20	7	72	.304	.374	.596	156	46	2-4	.985	5	107	102	S154		6.2
1960	Chi	N★	156	597	94	162	32	7	41	117	71-28	2	69	.271	.350	.554	145	36	1-3	.977	12	107	99	S156		6.0
1961	Chi	N★	138	511	75	142	22	4	29	80	54-21	2	75	.278	.346	.507	122	15	1-2	.965	20	118	100	S104,O23L,1b7		4.0
1962	Chi	N★	154	610	87	164	20	6	37	104	30-3	7	71	.269	.306	.503	110	5	5-1	.993	-2	98	98	1b149,3b3		-0.5
1963	Chi	N	130	432	41	98	20	1	18	64	39-16	4	73	.227	.292	.403	94	-3	0-3	.993	-2	95	110	1b125		-1.5
1964	Chi	N	157	591	67	156	29	6	23	95	36-11	3	84	.264	.307	.450	107	4	1-2	.994	10	126	101	1b157		0.4
1965	Chi	N	163	612	79	162	25	3	28	106	55-19	6	64	.265	.328	.403	116	12	3-5	.992	-9	83	108	1b162		-0.8
1966	Chi	N	141	511	52	139	23	7	15	75	29-10	5	59	.272	.315	.432	105	2	0-1	.992	2	110	83	1b130,3b8		-0.4
1967	Chi	N	151	573	68	158	26	4	23	95	27-8	3	93	.276	.310	.455	112	7	2-2	.993	1	102	101	1b147		-0.2
1968	Chi	N	150	552	71	136	27	0	32	83	27-4	15	67	.246	.287	.469	117	9	2-0	.996	-0	97	115	1b147		0.1
1969	Chi	N★	155	565	60	143	19	2	23	106	42-7	7	101	.253	.309	.416	91	-8	0-0	.997	-0	94	103	1b153		-2.1
1970	Chi	N	72	222	25	56	6	2	12	44	20-3	1	33	.252	.313	.459	94	-3	0-0	.993	-2	86	110	1b62	30	-0.9
1971	Chi	N	39	83	4	16	2	0	3	6	6-1	0	14	.193	.247	.325	53	-5	0-0	1.000	0	94	99	1b20	17	-0.7
Total	19		2528	9421	1305	2583	407	90	512	1636	763-198	70	1236	.274	.330	.500	122	262	50-53	.994	15	100	103	1b1259,S1125,3b69,O23L	47	27.6

BANKS, GEORGE George Edward B9.24.1938 Pacolet Mills SC D3.1.1985 Spartanburg SC BR/TR/5-11/185* d4.15

1962	Min	A	63	103	22	26	0	2	4	15	21-0	1	27	.252	.372	.408	109	2	0-0	.962	-2	89	0	O17(7/0/11),3b6		-0.1
1963	Min	A	25	71	5	11	4	0	3	8	9-1	1	21	.155	.259	.338	65	-3	0-0	.910	0	98	120	3b21		-0.3
1964	Min	A	1	1	0	0	0	0	0	0	0-0	0	1	.000	.000	.000	-99	0	0-0	—	0		/H		0.0
	Cle	A	9	17	6	5	1	0	2	3	6-0	0	6	.294	.478	.706	226	3	0-0	1.000	-1	81	0	O3(3/0/1)/23		0.3
	Year		10	18	6	5	1	0	2	3	6-0	0	7	.278	.458	.667	210	3	0-0	1.000	-1	81	0	O3(3/0/1)/23		0.3
1965	Cle	A	4	5	0	1	0	0	0	0	1-0	0	3	.200	.333	.200	107	0	0-1	1.000	0	94	523	/3		0.0
1966	Cle	A	4	4	0	1	0	0	0	1	0-0	0	1	.250	.250	.250	44	0	0-0	—	0		/H		0.0
Total	5		106	201	33	44	6	2	9	27	37-1	2	59	.219	.340	.403	102	2	0-1	.919	-2	98	130	3b29,O20(10/0/12)/2		-0.1

BANKSTON, EVERETT Wilborn Everett B5.25.1893 Barnesville GA D2.26.1970 Griffin GA BL/TR/5-11/180 d8.15

| 1915 | Phi | A | 11 | 36 | 6 | 5 | 1 | 1 | 2 | 1 | 5 | 0 | 5 | .139 | .205 | .306 | 55 | -2 | 1 | .882 | -1 | 85 | 95 | O8(4/4/0) | | -0.4 |

BANNING, JIM James M. B6.11.1865 New York NY D10.14.1952 St.Paul MN BL/TR/5-6/150 d9.27

1888	Was	N	1	0	0	0	0	0	0	0	0	0	0					0	0	1.000	-0		/C		0.0
1889	Was	N	2	1	0	0	0	0	0	0	0	0	0	.000	.000	.000	-99	0	0	1.000	1		C2		0.0
Total	2		3	1	0	0	0	0	0	0	0	0	0	.000	.000	.000	-99	0	0	1.000	1		C3		0.0

BANNISTER, ALAN Alan B9.3.1951 Montebello CA BR/TR/5-11/175* [PhiN73*1/1] d7.13 Col Arizona St. OF(254/72/100)

1974	Phi	N	26	25	4	3	0	0	1	3-0	1	7	.120	.241	.132	3	-3	0-0	1.000	-1	89	0	O8C,S2		-0.4
1975	Phi	N	24	61	10	16	3	1	0	1-0	0	4	.262	.274	.344	67	-3	2-2	1.000	1	134	0	O18(4/14/1)/2S		-0.2
1976	Chi	A	73	145	19	36	6	2	0	8	14-1	1	21	.248	.317	.317	86	-2	12-4	.988	1	120	46	O43(29/13/4),S14,2b4/3D		-2.6
1977	Chi	A	139	560	87	154	20	3	3	57	54-1	2	49	.275	.335	.338	86	-10	4-3	.936	-30	82	62	S133,2b3,O3(2/2/0)		-2.6
1978	Chi	A	49	107	16	24	3	2	0	8	11-1	1	12	.224	.300	.290	66	-5	3-3	1.000	-1	102	0	O15(8/7/0),S8,2b2	65	-0.6
1979	Chi	A	136	506	71	144	28	8	2	55	43-1	3	40	.285	.342	.383	96	-15	22-6	.963	-15	92	68	2b65,O47(47/0/2),3b12/1D		-1.3
1980	Chi	A	45	130	16	25	6	0	0	9	12-5	0	16	.192	.259	.238	38	-11	5-2	1.000	-0	98	0	O23(22/0/1),3b17		-1.2
	Cle	A	81	262	41	86	17	4	1	32	28-1	0	25	.328	.388	.435	125	10	9-2	.968	-4	96	73	2b41,O40(9/9/26),3b3,S2		0.8
	Year		126	392	57	111	23	4	1	41	40-6	0	41	.283	.346	.370	97	-1	14-4	.981	-4	99	56	O63(31/9/27),2b41,3b20,S2		-0.4
1981	Cle	A	68	232	36	61	11	1	1	17	16-2	1	19	.263	.309	.332	86	-4	16-2	.986	-3	108	93	O35(18/6/17),2b30,1b2/S		-0.4
1982	Cle	A	101	348	40	93	16	1	4	41	42-1	1	41	.267	.347	.353	93	-2	18-5	.991	-3	113	35	O55(46/4/9),2b48,S2/3D	31	-0.2
1983	Cle	A	117	377	51	100	25	4	5	45	31-0	1	43	.265	.323	.393	93	-3	6-6	.969	-1	91	123	O91(58/8/34),2b27,1b3,D3		-0.7
1984	Hou	N	9	20	2	4	2	0	0	2-0	0	2	.200	.273	.300	65	-1	0-0	.947	-1	75	51	S4/OL		-0.1
	Tex	A	47	112	20	33	2	1	2	9	21-0	1	17	.295	.407	.384	117	4	3-0	.959	-1	61	38	2b25,O3(1/1/1)/13D	27	-0.5
1985	Tex	A	57	122	17	32	4	1	1	6	14-0	1	17	.262	.338	.336	84	-2	8-2	1.000	-1	92	0	D21,O14(9/0/5),2b10,3b5,1b4	17	-0.3
Total	12		972	3007	430	811	143	28	19	288	292-13	13	318	.270	.334	.355	90	-35	108-37	.983	-65	103	72	O396L,1,2b256,S167,D66,3b40,1b11	140	-7.7

BANNON, JIMMY James Henry "Foxy Grandpa" B5.5.1871 Amesbury MA D3.24.1948 Glen Rock NJ BR/TR/5-5/160 d6.15 b-Tom Col Holy Cross ▲

1893	StL	N	26	107	9	36	3	4	0	15	4	1	5	.336	.366	.439	113	1	8	.795	-5	59	0	O24(1/0/23),S2/P		-0.4
1894	Bos	N	128	494	130	166	29	10	13	114	62	4	42	.336	.414	.514	114	10	47	.873	17	200	242	O128R/P		1.6
1895	Bos	N	124	493	101	171	35	5	6	74	54	5	31	.347	.417	.475	120	6	28	.879	7	161	75	O123(1/0/122)/P		1.3
1896	Bos	N	89	344	53	87	9	5	0	50	32	1	23	.253	.318	.308	62	-20	16	.901	-2	118	76	O76(2/1/73),2b6,S5,3b3		-2.1
Total	4		367	1438	293	460	76	24	19	253	152	11	101	.320	.394	.446	104	7	99	.877	17	160	131	O351(4/1/346),S7,2b6,3b3,P3		0.4

BANNON, TOM Thomas Edward "Ward Six" B5.8.1869 Amesbury MA D1.26.1950 Lynn MA BR/TR/5-8/175 d5.10 b-Jimmy

1895	NY	N	37	159	33	43	6	2	0	8	7	0	8	.270	.301	.333	65	-9	20	.894	1	261	130	O21(13/0/8),1b16		-0.8
1896	NY	N	2	7	1	1	1	0	0	0	1	0	0	.143	.250	.286	42	-1	0	.500	-1	0	0	O2(1/1/0)		-0.1
Total - 2			39	166	34	44	7	2	0	8	8	0	9	.265	.299	.331	64	-10	20	.878	0	246	123	O23(14/1/8),1b16		-0.9

BARAJAS, ROD Rodrigo Richard B9.5.1975 Ontario CA BR/TR/6-2/229* d9.25 Col Cerritos (CA) JC

1999	Ari	N	5	16	3	4	1	0	1	3	1-0	1	5	.250	.294	.500	95	0	0-0	1.000	-2	189	0	C5		-0.2
2000	Ari	N	5	13	1	3	0	0	1	3	0-0	0	4	.231	.231	.462	66	-1	0-0	1.000	-0	0	0	C5		-0.1
2001	†Ari	N	51	106	9	17	3	0	3	9	4-0	0	26	.160	.191	.274	17	-14	0-0	.995	-17	66	91	C50		-2.8
2002	†Ari	N	70	154	12	36	10	0	3	23	10-4	3	25	.234	.288	.357	66	-8	1-0	.997	-15	147	81	C69/1		-2.0
2003	Ari	N	80	220	19	48	15	0	3	28	14-7	1	43	.218	.265	.327	50	-16	0-0	1.000	12	130	113	C79	39	-0.2
2004	Tex	A	108	358	50	89	26	1	15	58	13-0	3	63	.249	.276	.453	83	-10	0-1	.990	2	128	88	C105,1b2		-0.2
2005	Tex	A	120	410	53	104	24	0	21	60	26-0	5	70	.254	.306	.466	98	-2	0-0	.988	-5	142	84	C119/1		0.1
Total	7		439	1277	147	301	79	1	47	184	68-11	13	232	.236	.278	.410	74	-51	1-1	.993	-26	130	89	C432,1b4	39	-5.2

BARBARE, WALTER Walter Lawrence "Dinty" B8.11.1891 Greenville SC D10.28.1965 Greenville SC BR/TR/6-0/162 d9.17

1914	Cle	A	15	52	6	16	2	0	5	2	1	5	.308	.345	.423	126	1	1-4	.933	1	120	148	3b14/S		0.2
1915	Cle	A	77	246	15	47	3	1	0	11	10	4	27	.191	.235	.211	33	-21	6-5	.960	6	104	104	3b68/1		-1.4
1916	Cle	A	13	48	3	11	1	0	0	3	4	0	9	.229	.288	.250	58	-2	0	.977	2	122	88	3b12/1		-0.5
1918	Bos	A	13	29	2	5	3	0	0	2	0	1	.172	.172	.276	36	-2	1	.826	-3	79	73	3b11/S		-0.5
1919	Pit	N	85	293	34	80	11	5	1	34	18	1	18	.273	.317	.355	98	-1	11	.961	-8	82	110	3b80/2		-0.7
1920	Pit	N	57	186	9	51	6	2	0	12	9	0	11	.274	.308	.323	79	-5	5-3	.923	-4	92	102	S34,2b12,3b5		-0.7
1921	Bos	N	134	550	66	166	22	7	0	49	24	0	28	.302	.331	.367	89	-9	11-4	.957	-15	94	89	S121,2b8,3b2		-1.0
1922	Bos	N	106	373	38	86	5	4	0	40	21	0	22	.231	.272	.265	41	-34	2-0	.966	3	103	100	2b45,3b38,1b14		-2.7
Total	8		500	1777	173	462	52	21	1	156	88	6	121	.260	.297	.315	71	-73	37-16	.959	-18	96	105	3b230,S157,2b66,1b15		-6.8

BARBARY, RED Donald Odell B6.20.1920 Simpsonville SC D9.27.2003 Simpsonville SC BR/TR/6-2/195 d5.22

| 1943 | Was | A | 1 | 1 | 0 | 0 | 0 | 0 | 0 | 0 | 0-0 | 0 | 0 | .000 | .000 | .000 | -99 | 0 | 0-0 | — | 0 | | /H | | 0.0 |

BARBEAU, JAP William Joseph B6.10.1882 New York NY D9.10.1969 Milwaukee WI BR/TR/5-5/140 d9.27

1905	Cle	A	11	37	1	10	1	0	0	2	1	0		.270	.289	.351	102	0	1	.905	0	106	213	2b11		0.0
1906	Cle	A	42	129	8	25	5	3	0	12	9	2		.194	.257	.279	69	-5	5	.830	-8	87	204	3b32,S6		-1.3
1909	Pit	N	91	350	60	77	16	3	0	25	37	4		.220	.302	.283	75	-9	19	.891	-18	83	89	3b85		-2.8

YEAR	TM LG	G	AB	R	H	2B	3B	HR	RBI	BB-IB	HP	SO	AVG	OBP	SLG	AOPS	ABR	SB-CS	FA	FR	RNG	THR	GAMES AT POSITION	DL	BFW
	StL N	48	175	23	44	3	0	0	5	28	5		.251	.370	.269	105	3	14	.901	-5	89	126	3b47		0.0
	Year	139	525	83	121	19	3	0	30	65	9		.230	.326	.278	85	-6	33	.895	-22	85	101	3b132		-2.8
1910	StL N	7	21	4	4	0	1	0	2	3	0	3	.190	.292	.286	71	-1	0	.917	2	155	0	3b6/2		0.1
Total	4	199	712	96	160	25	8	0	46	78	11	3	.225	.311	.282	82	-12	39	.884	-29	88	115	3b170,2b12,S6		-4.0

BARBEE, DAVE David Monroe B5.7.1905 Greensboro NC D7.1.1968 Albemarle NC BR/TR/5-11.5/178 d7.29 Col Oglethorpe

YEAR	TM LG	G	AB	R	H	2B	3B	HR	RBI	BB-IB	HP	SO	AVG	OBP	SLG	AOPS	ABR	SB-CS	FA	FR	RNG	THR	GAMES AT POSITION	DL	BFW
1926	Phi A	19	47	7	8	1	1	1	5	2	1	4	.170	.220	.298	32	-5	0-0	1.000	0	101	95	O10R		-0.6
1932	Pit N	97	327	37	84	22	6	5	55	18	2	38	.257	.300	.407	89	-6	1	.975	4	111	103	O78(77/1/0)		-0.6
Total	2	116	374	44	92	23	7	6	60	20	3	42	.246	.290	.393	82	-11	1-0	.977	4	110	102	O88(77/1/10)		-1.2

BARBER, CHARLIE Charles D. B1854 Philadelphia PA D11.23.1910 Philadelphia PA BR/TR d4.17

YEAR	TM LG	G	AB	R	H	2B	3B	HR	RBI	BB-IB	HP	SO	AVG	OBP	SLG	AOPS	ABR	SB-CS	FA	FR	RNG	THR	GAMES AT POSITION	DL	BFW
1884	Cin U	55	204	38	41	1	4	0		11			.201	.242	.245	44	-21		.837	3	111	82	3b55		-1.5

BARBER, TURNER Tyrus Turner B7.9.1893 Lavinia TN D10.20.1968 Milan TN BL/TR/5-11/170 d8.19 Col Union (TN)

YEAR	TM LG	G	AB	R	H	2B	3B	HR	RBI	BB-IB	HP	SO	AVG	OBP	SLG	AOPS	ABR	SB-CS	FA	FR	RNG	THR	GAMES AT POSITION	DL	BFW
1915	Was A	20	53	9	16	1	1	0	6	6	1	7	.302	.383	.358	120	1	0-3	.952	0	78	177	O19(3/0/16)		0.0
1916	Was A	15	33	3	7	0	1	1	5	2	0	3	.212	.257	.364	87	-1	0	.833	-1	90	0	O10(6/0/4)		-0.3
1917	Chi N	7	28	2	6	1	0	0	2	2	0	8	.214	.267	.250	54	-1	1	1.000	1	90	242	O7(1/6/0)		-0.1
1918	†Chi N	55	123	11	29	3	2	0	10	9	1	16	.236	.293	.293	77	-3	3	.940	-2	92	62	O27(4/17/15),1b4		-0.8
1919	Chi N	76	230	26	72	9	4	0	21	14	1	17	.313	.355	.387	122	6	7	.949	-3	95	87	O68(53/13/2)		0.0
1920	Chi N	94	340	27	90	10	5	0	50	9	3	26	.265	.290	.324	74	-12	5-6	.988	-6	73	85	1b69,O17(6/8/3),2b2		-2.3
1921	Chi N	127	452	73	142	14	4	1	54	41	6	24	.314	.379	.369	99	1	5-9	.970	2	90	152	O123(90/20/14)		-0.7
1922	Chi N	84	226	35	70	7	4	0	29	30	1	9	.310	.391	.376	97	0	7-4	.953	-3	93	78	O47(31/0/16),1b16		-0.7
1923	Bro N	13	46	3	10	2	0	0	8	2	0	7	.217	.250	.261	36	-4	0-1	1.000	-1	84	86	O12C		-0.5
Total	9	491	1531	189	442	47	21	2	185	115	12	112	.289	.343	.351	93	-13	28-23	.959	-13	91	114	O330(194/76/70),1b89,2b2		-5.4

BARBERIE, BRET Bret Edward B8.16.1967 Long Beach CA BB/TR/5-11/180* [MonN88 7/180] d6.16 Col USC

YEAR	TM LG	G	AB	R	H	2B	3B	HR	RBI	BB-IB	HP	SO	AVG	OBP	SLG	AOPS	ABR	SB-CS	FA	FR	RNG	THR	GAMES AT POSITION	DL	BFW
1991	Mon N	57	136	16	48	12	2	2	18	20-2	2	22	.353	.435	.515	170	1	0-0	.931	-1	109	93	S19,2b10,3b10/1		1.5
1992	Mon N	111	285	26	66	11	0	1	24	47-3	8	62	.232	.354	.281	83	-3	9-5	.932	5	116	108	3b63,2b26/S	16	0.3
1993	Fla N	99	375	45	104	16	2	5	33	33-2	1	58	.277	.344	.371	87	-6	2-4	.982	7	105	102	2b97	68	0.3
1994	Fla N	107	372	40	112	20	2	5	31	23-3	9	65	.301	.356	.406	94	-2	2-0	.975	7	105	97	2b106		0.9
1995	Bal A	90	237	32	57	14	0	2	25	36-0	6	50	.241	.351	.325	77	-6	3-3	.977	4	101	119	2b74,3b3,D5		0.0
1996	Chi N	15	29	4	1	0	0	1	2	5-0	0	11	.034	.176	.138	-15	-5	0-1	1.000	-1	125	35	2b6,3b2/S		-0.6
Total	6	479	1434	163	388	73	6	16	133	164-10	32	268	.271	.356	.363	92	-8	16-13	.980	21	104	101	2b319,3b78,S21,D5/1	84	2.6

BARBIERI, JIM James Patrick B9.15.1941 Schenectady NY BL/TR/5-7/155 d7.5

YEAR	TM LG	G	AB	R	H	2B	3B	HR	RBI	BB-IB	HP	SO	AVG	OBP	SLG	AOPS	ABR	SB-CS	FA	FR	RNG	THR	GAMES AT POSITION	DL	BFW
1966	†LA N	39	82	9	23	5	0	0	4	8		7	.280	.352	.341	102	1	2-0	.939	1	108	187	O20(9/0/11)		0.1

BARCLAY, GEORGE George Oliver "Deerfoot" B5.16.1876 Millville PA D4.3.1909 Philadelphia PA BR/TR/5-10/162 d4.17 Col Lafayette

YEAR	TM LG	G	AB	R	H	2B	3B	HR	RBI	BB-IB	HP	SO	AVG	OBP	SLG	AOPS	ABR	SB-CS	FA	FR	RNG	THR	GAMES AT POSITION	DL	BFW
1902	StL N	137	543	79	163	14	2	3	53	31	6		.300	.345	.350	119	12	30	.904	-6	87	97	O137L		-0.2
1903	StL N	108	419	37	104	10	8	0	42	15	2		.248	.278	.310	70	-19	12	.901	-7	87	0	O107L		-3.2
1904	StL N	103	375	41	75	7	4	0	28	12	6		.200	.237	.248	52	-22	14	.947	-6	54	55	O103L		-3.7
	Bos N	24	93	5	21	3	1	0	10	2	2		.226	.258	.280	68	-4	3	.935	-2	74	110	O24(6/1/17)		-0.7
	Year	127	468	46	96	10	5	1	38	14	8		.205	.241	.254	55	-26	17	.945	-8	57	64	O127(109/1/17)		-4.4
1905	Bos N	29	108	5	19	1	0	0	7	2	2		.176	.205	.185	17	-11	2	.854	-4	54	109	O28L		-1.8
Total	4	401	1538	167	382	35	15	4	140	62	18		.248	.286	.298	79	-44	61	.911	-25	75	61	O399(381/1/17)		-9.6

BARD, JOSH Joshua David B3.30.1978 Ithaca NY BB/TR/6-3/205* [ColN99 3/100] d8.23 Col Texas Tech

YEAR	TM LG	G	AB	R	H	2B	3B	HR	RBI	BB-IB	HP	SO	AVG	OBP	SLG	AOPS	ABR	SB-CS	FA	FR	RNG	THR	GAMES AT POSITION	DL	BFW
2002	Cle A	24	90	9	20	5	0	3	12	4-0	0	13	.222	.255	.378	64	-5	0-0	.988	0	147	115	C24		-0.3
2003	Cle A	91	303	25	74	13	1	8	36	22-1	0	53	.244	.293	.373	75	-12	0-2	.991	11	110	125	C87/D		0.4
2004	Cle A	7	19	5	8	2	0	1	4	3-0	0	6	.421	.478	.684	212	3	0-0	1.000	1	77	142	C7	92	0.5
2005	Cle A	34	83	6	16	4	0	1	9	9-0	0	11	.193	.266	.277	48	-6	0-0	.983	2	193	71	C31		-0.3
Total	4	156	495	45	118	24	1	13	61	38-1	0	77	.238	.289	.370	74	-20	0-2	.989	14	130	114	C149/D	92	0.3

BARFIELD, JESSE Jesse Lee B10.29.1959 Joliet IL BR/TR/6-1/205(170-206) [TorA77 9/233] d9.3 C3

YEAR	TM LG	G	AB	R	H	2B	3B	HR	RBI	BB-IB	HP	SO	AVG	OBP	SLG	AOPS	ABR	SB-CS	FA	FR	RNG	THR	GAMES AT POSITION	DL	BFW
1981	Tor A	25	95	7	22	3	2	2	9	4-0	1	19	.232	.270	.368	78	-3	4-3	1.000	4	134	105	O25R		-0.1
1982	Tor A	139	394	54	97	13	2	18	58	42-3	3	79	.246	.323	.426	95	-3	1-4	.963	1	95	183	O137(1/3/136)/D		-0.9
1983	Tor A	128	388	58	98	13	3	27	68	22-0	4	110	.253	.296	.510	111	3	2-5	.966	8	107	**209**	O120(0/1/120),D5		0.4
1984	Tor A	110	320	51	91	14	1	14	49	35-5	2	81	.284	.357	.466	121	10	8-2	.952	6	113	178	O88(0/9/79),D9		1.2
1985	†Tor A	155	539	94	156	34	9	27	84	66-5	4	143	.289	.369	.536	141	31	22-8	.989	16	107	**206**	O154(0/8/147)		3.9
1986	Tor A★	158	589	107	170	35	2	**40**	108	69-5	8	146	.289	.368	.559	145	37	8-8	.992	16	112	182	O157(0/18/147)		4.3
1987	Tor A	159	590	89	155	25	3	28	84	58-7	3	141	.263	.331	.458	104	2	3-5	.992	13	112	163	O158(0/13/152)		0.7
1988	Tor A	137	468	62	114	21	5	18	56	41-6	1	108	.244	.302	.425	101	-1	7-3	.988	13	**114**	153	O136(0/13/132)/D	15	0.9
1989	Tor A	21	80	8	16	4	0	5	11	5-0	1	28	.200	.256	.438	93	-1	0-2	.979	2	94	246	O21(1/0/20)		-0.1
	NY A	129	441	71	106	19	1	18	56	82-6	2	122	.240	.360	.410	118	13	5-3	.972	8	106	166	O129(0/18/120)		1.8
	Year	150	521	79	122	23	1	23	67	87-6	3	150	.234	.345	.415	115	12	5-5	.973	10	104	177	O150(1/18/140)		1.7
1990	NY A	153	476	69	117	21	2	25	78	82-4	5	150	.246	.359	.456	126	19	4-3	.973	7	104	158	O151(0/0/151)		2.1
1991	NY A	84	284	57	64	12	0	17	48	36-6	0	80	.225	.312	.447	107	2	1-0	1.000	9	112	177	O81(1/0/81)	70	0.8
1992	NY A	30	95	8	13	2	0	2	7	9-2	0	27	.137	.210	.221	21	-10	1-1	.966	0	95	160	O30R	133	-1.2
Total	12	1428	4759	715	1219	216	30	241	716	551-49	34	1234	.256	.335	.466	116	99	66-47	.980	101	108	176	O1387(3/87/1340),D16	218	13.8

BARKER, AL Alfred L B1.18.1839 Lost Creek Twp. IN D9.15.1912 Rockford IL d6.1

YEAR	TM LG	G	AB	R	H	2B	3B	HR	RBI	BB-IB	HP	SO	AVG	OBP	SLG	AOPS	ABR	SB-CS	FA	FR	RNG	THR	GAMES AT POSITION	DL	BFW
1871	Rok NA	1	4	0	1	0	0	0	2		0		.250	.400	.250	97	0	0-0	1.000	-0	0	0	/OL		0.0

BARKER, GLEN Glen F. B5.10.1971 Albany NY BB/TR/5-10/180* [DetA93 11/305] d4.7 Col St. Rose

YEAR	TM LG	G	AB	R	H	2B	3B	HR	RBI	BB-IB	HP	SO	AVG	OBP	SLG	AOPS	ABR	SB-CS	FA	FR	RNG	THR	GAMES AT POSITION	DL	BFW
1999	†Hou N	81	73	23	21	2	0	1	11	11-0	1	19	.288	.384	.356	91	0	17-6	.981	-0	94	158	O57(3/47/8)/D	15	0.1
2000	Hou N	84	67	18	15	2	1	2	6	7-0	1	21	.224	.307	.373	65	-4	9-6	.985	1	117	72	O69(2/63/4)		-0.3
2001	Hou N	70	24	12	2	0	0	0	1	3-0	2	6	.083	.233	.083	-10	-4	4-6	1.000	-0	112	0	O60C		-0.5
Total	3	235	164	53	38	4	1	3	18	21-0	4	48	.232	.330	.323	65	-8	30-18	.987	1	107	89	O186(5/170/12)/D	15	-0.7

BARKER, KEVIN Kevin Stewart B7.26.1975 Bristol VA BL/TL/6-3/205* [MilA96 3/73] d8.19 Col VPI

YEAR	TM LG	G	AB	R	H	2B	3B	HR	RBI	BB-IB	HP	SO	AVG	OBP	SLG	AOPS	ABR	SB-CS	FA	FR	RNG	THR	GAMES AT POSITION	DL	BFW
1999	Mil N	38	117	13	33	5	0	3	23	9-1	0	19	.282	.331	.385	81	-4	1-0	.996	0	103	80	1b31		-0.6
2000	Mil N	40	100	14	22	5	0	2	9	20-0	1	21	.220	.352	.330	75	-3	1-0	.993	-3	73	96	1b32		-0.8
2002	SD N	7	19	0	3	0	0	0	0	1-0	0	6	.158	.200	.158	-3	-3	1-0	1.000	-1	30	108	1b6		-0.4
Total	3	85	236	27	58	8	0	5	32	30-1	1	46	.246	.331	.343	73	-10	3-0	.995	-3	83	90	1b69		-1.8

BARKER, RAY Raymond Herrell "Buddy" B3.12.1936 Martinsburg WV BL/TR/6-0/192* d9.13

YEAR	TM LG	G	AB	R	H	2B	3B	HR	RBI	BB-IB	HP	SO	AVG	OBP	SLG	AOPS	ABR	SB-CS	FA	FR	RNG	THR	GAMES AT POSITION	DL	BFW
1960	Bal A	5	6	0	0	0	0	0	0	0	0	3	.000	.000	.000	-99	-2	0-0	—	-0	0	0	/OL		-0.2
1965	Cle A	11	6	0	0	0	0	0	0	2-1	0	2	.000	.250	.000	-22	-1	0-0	1.000	-0	0	0	1b3		-0.1
	NY A	98	205	21	52	11	0	7	31	20-5	3	46	.254	.326	.410	109	3	1-0	.991	6	149	110	1b61,3b3		0.6
	Year	109	211	21	52	11	0	7	31	22-6	3	48	.246	.324	.398	105	2	1-0	.991	6	148	109	1b64,3b3		0.5
1966	NY A	61	75	11	14	5	0	3	13	4-0	0	20	.187	.225	.373	72	-3	0-0	.987	4	178	65	1b47		0.0
1967	NY A	17	26	2	2	0	0	0	3	3-0	0	5	.077	.172	.077	-25	-4	0-0	.961	1	163	90	1b13		-0.4
Total	4	192	318	34	68	16	0	10	44	29-6	3	76	.214	.283	.358	84	-7	1-0	.987	11	158	95	1b124,3b3/OL		-1.1

BARKETT, ANDY Andrew Jon B9.5.1974 Miami FL BL/TL/6-1/205 d5.28 Col North Carolina St.

YEAR	TM LG	G	AB	R	H	2B	3B	HR	RBI	BB-IB	HP	SO	AVG	OBP	SLG	AOPS	ABR	SB-CS	FA	FR	RNG	THR	GAMES AT POSITION	DL	BFW
2001	Pit N	17	46	5	14	2	0	1	3	4-1	1	7	.304	.373	.413	100	0	1-0	1.000	1	92	180	O10(9/0/2),1b4/D		0.0

BARKLEY, RED John Duncan B9.19.1913 Childress TX D12.12.2000 Waco TX BR/TR/5-11/160 d9.2 gs-Brian

YEAR	TM LG	G	AB	R	H	2B	3B	HR	RBI	BB-IB	HP	SO	AVG	OBP	SLG	AOPS	ABR	SB-CS	FA	FR	RNG	THR	GAMES AT POSITION	DL	BFW
1937	StL A	31	101	9	27	6	0	0	14	14	0	17	.267	.357	.327	73	-4	1-0	.969	-4	90	88	2b31		-0.5
1939	Bos N	12	11	1	0	0	0	0	0	1	0	2	.000	.083	.000	-82	-3	0	.842	2	158	0	S7,3b4		-0.1
1943	Bro N	20	51	6	16	3	0	0	7	4	0	7	.314	.364	.373	113	1	1	.894	-3	89	109	S18		-0.1
Total	3	63	163	16	43	9	0	0	21	19	0	26	.264	.341	.319	75	-6	1-0	.969	-5	90	88	2b31,S25,3b4		-0.7

BARKLEY, SAM Samuel E B5.24.1858 Wheeling WV D4.20.1912 Wheeling WV BR/TR/5-11.5/180 d5.1 M1

YEAR	TM LG	G	AB	R	H	2B	3B	HR	RBI	BB-IB	HP	SO	AVG	OBP	SLG	AOPS	ABR	SB-CS	FA	FR	RNG	THR	GAMES AT POSITION	DL	BFW
1884	Tol AA	104	435	71	133	**39**	9	1		22	2		.306	.342	.444	149	24		.930	26	111	106	2b103,C2		**4.8**
1885	†StL AA	106	418	67	112	18	10	3	53	25	2		.268	.312	.380	113	5		.921	12	111	106	2b96,1b11		1.7
1886	Pit AA	122	478	77	127	31	8	1	69	58	2		.266	.345	.370	125	16	22	.936	1	94	118	2b112,O8L,1b2		1.8
1887	Pit N	89	340	44	76	10	4	1	35	30	4	24	.224	.282	.285	66	-14	6	.979	-8	76	82	1b53,2b36		-2.2

YEAR	TM LG	G	AB	R	H	2B	3B	HR	RBI	BB-IB	HP	SO	AVG	OBP	SLG	AOPS	ABR	SB-CS	FA	FR	RNG	THR	GAMES AT POSITION	DL	BFW
1888	KC AA	116	482	67	104	21	6	4	51	26	4		.216	.262	.309	78	-14	15	.938	-8	92	89	2b116,M		-1.6
1889	KC AA	45	176	36	50	6	2	0	23	15	0	20	.284	.340	.341	89	-3	8	.923	-10	89	96	2b41,1b4		-1.0
Total	6	582	2329	362	602	125	39	10	231	176	12	44	.258	.314	.359	105	14	51	.929	13	100	103	2b504,1b70,O8L,C2		3.5

BARLOW, TOM Thomas H. B1852 NY d5.2

YEAR	TM LG	G	AB	R	H	2B	3B	HR	RBI	BB-IB	HP	SO	AVG	OBP	SLG	AOPS	ABR	SB-CS	FA	FR	RNG	THR	GAMES AT POSITION	DL	BFW
1872	Atl NA	37	171	34	54	1	0	0	8	3		2	.316	.328	.322	86	-5	7-5	.758	-10			C36,S4/3		-1.1
1873	Atl NA	55	269	48	74	0	2	1	12	5		1	.275	.288	.301	84	-3	3-4	.762	-16			C55/2S		-1.4
1874	Har NA	32	155	37	46	5	1	0	12	2		2	.297	.306	.342	102	0	17-4	.820	8	111	57	S32		0.7
1875	NH NA	1	5	1	1	0	0	0	0	0		0	.200	.200	.200	45	0	0-0	.800	0	109	0	/S		0.0
	Atl NA	1	4	0	0	0	0	0	0	0		0	.000	.000	.000	-99	-1	0-0	.500	-1	0	0	/2		-0.2
	Year	2	9	1	1	0	0	0	0	0		0	.111	.111	.111	-26	-1	0-0	.800	-1	109	0	/S2		-0.2
Total	4 NA	126	604	120	175	6	3	1	32	10		5	.290	.301	.315	88	-9	27-13	.761	-18			C91,S38,2b2/3		-2.0

BARMES, BRUCE Bruce Raymond "Squeaky" B10.23.1929 Vincennes IN BL/TR/5-8/165 d9.13

YEAR	TM LG	G	AB	R	H	2B	3B	HR	RBI	BB-IB	HP	SO	AVG	OBP	SLG	AOPS	ABR	SB-CS	FA	FR	RNG	THR	GAMES AT POSITION	DL	BFW
1953	Was A	5	5	1	1	0	0	0	0	0		0	.200	.200	.200	8	-1	0-0	1.000	0	149	0	/OR		-0.1

BARMES, CLINT Clint Harold B3.6.1979 Vincennes IN BR/TR/6-0/170(170-190) [ColN00 10/287] d9.5 Col Indiana St.

YEAR	TM LG	G	AB	R	H	2B	3B	HR	RBI	BB-IB	HP	SO	AVG	OBP	SLG	AOPS	ABR	SB-CS	FA	FR	RNG	THR	GAMES AT POSITION	DL	BFW
2003	Col N	12	25	2	8	2	0	2	0-0		2	10	.320	.357	.400	89	0	0-0	.958	1	108	99	S12		0.2
2004	Col N	20	71	14	20	3	1	2	10	3-0	1	5	.282	.320	.437	83	-2	0-1	.979	8	135	93	2b9,S9		0.6
2005	Col N	81	350	55	101	19	1	10	46	16-1	6	36	.289	.330	.434	86	-7	6-4	.958	12	110	108	S80	88	1.1
Total	3	113	446	71	129	24	2	12	58	19-1	9	56	.289	.330	.433	85	-9	6-5	.960	21	113	108	S101,2b9	88	1.9

BARNA, BABE Herbert Paul B3.2.1915 Clarksburg WV D5.18.1972 Charleston WV BL/TR/6-2/210 d9.16 Col West Virginia

YEAR	TM LG	G	AB	R	H	2B	3B	HR	RBI	BB-IB	HP	SO	AVG	OBP	SLG	AOPS	ABR	SB-CS	FA	FR	RNG	THR	GAMES AT POSITION	DL	BFW
1937	Phi A	14	36	10	14	2	0	2	9	2	0	1	.389	.421	.611	159	3	1-0	.800	-1	74	0	O9L/1		0.2
1938	Phi A	9	30	4	4	0	0	0	2	3	0	5	.133	.212	.133	-12	-5	0-0	.917	-0	81	205	O7(4/0/3)		-0.6
1941	NY N	10	42	5	9	3	0	1	5	2	0	6	.214	.250	.357	68	-2	0	1.000	0	75	222	O10(2/0/8)		-0.3
1942	NY N	104	331	39	85	8	7	6	58	38	0	48	.257	.333	.378	107	2	3	.983	-4	91	67	O89(88/0/1)		-0.8
1943	NY N	40	113	11	23	5	1	1	12	16	0	9	.204	.302	.292	72	-4	3	.984	1	97	72	O31L		-0.7
	Bos A	30	112	19	19	4	1	2	10	15	0	24	.170	.268	.277	58	-6	2-1	.940	-3	73	140	O29L		-1.1
Total	5	207	664	88	154	22	9	12	96	76	0	98	.232	.311	.346	88	-12	9-1	.969	-9	87	93	O175(163/0/12)/1		-3.3

BARNES, ROSS Charles Roscoe B5.8.1850 Mount Morris NY D2.5.1915 Chicago IL BR/TR/5-8.5/145 d5.5 U1

YEAR	TM LG	G	AB	R	H	2B	3B	HR	RBI	BB-IB	HP	SO	AVG	OBP	SLG	AOPS	ABR	SB-CS	FA	FR	RNG	THR	GAMES AT POSITION	DL	BFW
1871	Bos NA	31	157	66	63	10	9	0	34	13		1	.401	.447	.580	186	17	11-6	.873	12	134	189	2b16,S15		1.8
1872	Bos NA	45	230	81	99	28	2	1	44	9		2	.430	.452	.583	205	28	12-2	.904	26	130	261	2b45		3.5
1873	Bos NA	60	320	125	138	31	11	2	60	20		2	.431	.465	.616	201	38	43-6	.857	19	122	127	2b47,3b13		4.2
1874	Bos NA	51	259	72	88	12	4	0	39	8		2	.340	.360	.417	140	11	8-7	.856	18	117	201	2b51/OL		1.9
1875	Bos NA	78	393	115	143	20	4	1	58	7		1	.364	.375	.443	177	29	29-6	.877	22	110	163	2b76,O3L,S2		4.2
1876	Chi N	66	322	126	138	21	14	1	59	20		8	.429	.462	.590	222	40		.910	7	106	118	2b66/P		4.2
1877	Chi N	22	92	16	25	1	0	0	5	7		4	.272	.323	.283	83	-2		.838	-7	93	60	2b22		-0.7
1879	Cin N	77	323	55	86	9	2	1	30	16		25	.266	.301	.316	109	4		.855	0	104	99	S61,2b16		0.7
1881	Bos N	69	295	42	80	14	1	0	17	16		16	.271	.309	.325	104	3		.854	-3	102	90	S63,2b7		0.3
Total	5 NA	265	1359	459	531	101	30	4	235	57		12	.391	.415	.518	182	123	103-27	.873	97	119	184	2b235,S17,3b13,O4L		15.6
Total	4	234	1032	239	329	45	17	2	111	59		53	.319	.356	.401	143	45		.855	-3	102	90	S124,2b111/P		4.5

BARNES, RED Emile B12.25.1904 Suggsville AL D7.3.1959 Mobile AL BL/TR/5-10.5/158 d9.29 Col Alabama

YEAR	TM LG	G	AB	R	H	2B	3B	HR	RBI	BB-IB	HP	SO	AVG	OBP	SLG	AOPS	ABR	SB-CS	FA	FR	RNG	THR	GAMES AT POSITION	DL	BFW
1927	Was A	3	11	5	4	1	0	0	0	1		0	.364	.417	.455	127	1	0-0	1.000	0	57	383	O3(0/1/2)		0.1
1928	Was A	114	417	82	127	22	15	6	51	55	4	38	.305	.391	.472	127	17	7-3	.978	-4	88	131	O104(8/96/1)		0.8
1929	Was A	72	130	16	26	5	2	1	15	13	0	12	.200	.273	.292	45	-11	1-0	.877	-3	90	85	O30(8/14/9)		-1.4
1930	Was A	12	12	1	2	1	0	0	0	0	0	2	.167	.167	.250	4	-2	0-0	—	0			/H		-0.2
	Chi A	85	266	48	66	12	7	1	31	26	1	20	.248	.317	.357	73	-11	4-2	.939	-1	95	119	O72(1/71/0)		-1.4
	Year	97	278	49	68	13	7	1	31	26	1	23	.245	.311	.353	70	-13	4-2	.939	-1	95	119	O72(1/71/0)		-1.6
Total	4	286	836	152	225	41	24	8	97	95	5	76	.269	.347	.404	95	-6	12-5	.953	-8	90	125	O209(17/182/12)		-2.1

BARNES, EPPIE Everett Duane B12.1.1900 Ossining NY D11.17.1980 Mineola NY BL/TL/5-9/175 d9.25 Col Colgate

YEAR	TM LG	G	AB	R	H	2B	3B	HR	RBI	BB-IB	HP	SO	AVG	OBP	SLG	AOPS	ABR	SB-CS	FA	FR	RNG	THR	GAMES AT POSITION	DL	BFW
1923	Pit N	2	2	0	1	0	0	0	0	0		1	.500	.500	.500	161	0	0-0	1.000	0	568	382	/1		0.0
1924	Pit N	2	5	0	0	0	0	0	0	0		1	.000	.000	.000	-98	-1	0-0	1.000	0	205	0	/1		-0.1
Total	2	4	7	0	1	0	0	0	0	0		2	.143	.143	.143	-23	-1	0-0	1.000	1	304	104	1b2		-0.1

BARNES, JOHN John Delbert B4.24.1976 San Diego CA BR/TR/6-2/205(176-205) [BosA96 4/121] d9.16 Col Grossmont (CA) JC

YEAR	TM LG	G	AB	R	H	2B	3B	HR	RBI	BB-IB	HP	SO	AVG	OBP	SLG	AOPS	ABR	SB-CS	FA	FR	RNG	THR	GAMES AT POSITION	DL	BFW
2000	Min A	11	37	5	13	4	0	0	2	2-0	1	6	.351	.415	.459	113	1	0-1	1.000	2	117	274	O11(2/2/8)		0.2
2001	Min A	9	21	1	1	0	0	0	0	1-0	1	3	.048	.130	.048	-48	-5	0-0	.895	1	119	230	O9(3/0/6)	71	-0.4
Total	2	20	58	6	14	4	0	0	2	3-0	3	9	.241	.313	.310	57	-4	0-1	.959	3	118	258	O20(5/2/14)	71	-0.2

BARNES, HONEY John Francis B1.31.1900 Fulton NY D6.18.1981 Lockport NY BL/TR/5-10/175 d4.20 Col Colgate

YEAR	TM LG	G	AB	R	H	2B	3B	HR	RBI	BB-IB	HP	SO	AVG	OBP	SLG	AOPS	ABR	SB-CS	FA	FR	RNG	THR	GAMES AT POSITION	DL	BFW
1926	NY A	6	0	0	0	0	0	0	0	1		0	—	1.000	—	179	0	0-0	—	0	0	0	/C		0.0

BARNES, LARRY Larry Richard B7.23.1974 Bakersfield CA BL/TL/6-1/195* d4.11 Col Cal St.-Fresno

YEAR	TM LG	G	AB	R	H	2B	3B	HR	RBI	BB-IB	HP	SO	AVG	OBP	SLG	AOPS	ABR	SB-CS	FA	FR	RNG	THR	GAMES AT POSITION	DL	BFW
2001	Ana A	16	40	2	4	0	0	1	2	1-0	0	9	.100	.122	.175	-23	-7	0-0	1.000	-0	93	53	1b16/OL		-0.8
2003	LA N	30	38	2	8	2	0	0	2	1-0	0	9	.211	.231	.263	29	-4	0-0	1.000	-0	57	95	1b8,O2L/D		-0.5
Total	2	46	78	4	12	2	0	1	4	2-0	0	18	.154	.175	.218	2	-11	0-0	1.000	-0	81	67	1b24,O3L/D		-1.3

BARNES, LUTE Luther Owens B4.28.1947 Forest City IA BR/TR/5-10/160* [NYN69 21/482] d8.6 Col Oregon St.

YEAR	TM LG	G	AB	R	H	2B	3B	HR	RBI	BB-IB	HP	SO	AVG	OBP	SLG	AOPS	ABR	SB-CS	FA	FR	RNG	THR	GAMES AT POSITION	DL	BFW
1972	NY N	24	72	5	17	2	2	0	6	6-1	0	4	.236	.291	.319	76	-3	0-1	.959	1	95	140	2b14,S6		-0.1
1973	NY N	3	2	2	1	0	0	0	1	0-0	0	1	.500	.500	.500	179	0	0-0	—	0			/H		0.0
Total	2	27	74	7	18	2	2	0	7	6-1	0	5	.243	.296	.324	78	-3	0-1	.959	1	95	140	2b14,S6		-0.1

BARNES, SAM Samuel Thomas B12.18.1899 Suggsville AL D2.19.1981 Montgomery AL BL/TR/5-8/150 d9.14 Col Auburn-Montgomery

YEAR	TM LG	G	AB	R	H	2B	3B	HR	RBI	BB-IB	HP	SO	AVG	OBP	SLG	AOPS	ABR	SB-CS	FA	FR	RNG	THR	GAMES AT POSITION	DL	BFW
1921	Det A	7	11	2	2	1	0	0	2	1		1	.182	.357	.273	63	0	0-0	.944	1	135	0	2b2		0.0

BARNES, BILL William H. B Indianapolis IN d9.27

YEAR	TM LG	G	AB	R	H	2B	3B	HR	RBI	BB-IB	HP	SO	AVG	OBP	SLG	AOPS	ABR	SB-CS	FA	FR	RNG	THR	GAMES AT POSITION	DL	BFW
1884	StP U	8	30	2	6	1	0	0		0			.200	.200	.233	57	-2		.727	-2	0	290	O8C		-0.4

BARNES, SKEETER William Henry B3.3.1957 Cincinnati OH BR/TR/5-10/180* [CinN78 16/407] d9.6 Col Cincinnati OF(37/11/30)

YEAR	TM LG	G	AB	R	H	2B	3B	HR	RBI	BB-IB	HP	SO	AVG	OBP	SLG	AOPS	ABR	SB-CS	FA	FR	RNG	THR	GAMES AT POSITION	DL	BFW
1983	Cin N	15	34	5	7	0	1	0	4	7-0	2	5	.206	.372	.294	84	0	2-2	1.000	-0	129	103	1b7,3b7		-0.1
1984	Cin N	32	42	5	5	0	0	1	3	4-1	0	6	.119	.196	.190	-4	-5	0-0	1.000	1	108		3b11,O3L		-0.5
1985	Mon N	19	26	0	4	1	0	0	0	0-0	0	2	.154	.154	.192	-4	-4	0-1	1.000	1	118	238	3b4,O3(1/0/2)/1		-0.3
1987	StL N	4	4	1	1	0	0	1	3	0-0	0	0	.250	.250	1.000	207	1	0-0	—	-0	0	/3		0.0
1989	Cin N	5	3	1	0	0	0	0	0	0-0	0	0	.000	.000	.000	-97	-1	0-1	—	0			/H		-0.1
1991	Det A	75	159	28	46	13	2	5	17	9-1	6	24	.289	.325	.491	121	4	10-7	1.000	-0	104	331	O33(13/5/17),3b17,1b9,2b7,D3		0.3
1992	Det A	95	165	27	45	8	1	3	25	10-1	2	18	.273	.318	.388	97	-3	3-1	.919	3	113	126	3b39,1b17,O15(4/6/5),2b7,D7		0.2
1993	Det A	84	160	24	45	8	1	2	27	11-0	0	19	.281	.318	.381	90	-3	5-5	.984	0	107	56	1b27,O18(12/0/6),3b13,D13,2b10,S2		-0.5
1994	Det A	24	21	4	6	0	0	0	4	0-0	0	2	.286	.286	.429	80	-1	0-0	1.000	-0	56	86	1b15,O4L/D		0.2
Total	9	353	614	95	159	30	4	14	83	41-3	4	74	.259	.306	.389	90	-10	20-18	.938	3	108	107	3b92,O76L,1b76,D24,2b24,S2		-1.2

BARNEY, ED Edmund J. B1.23.1890 Amery WI D10.4.1967 Rice Lake WI BL/TR/5-10.5/178 d7.22

YEAR	TM LG	G	AB	R	H	2B	3B	HR	RBI	BB-IB	HP	SO	AVG	OBP	SLG	AOPS	ABR	SB-CS	FA	FR	RNG	THR	GAMES AT POSITION	DL	BFW
1915	NY A	11	36	1	7	0	0	0	8	3		0	.194	.256	.194	35	-3	2-1	1.000	0	96	76	O10(3/7/0)		-0.4
	Pit N	32	99	16	27	1	2	0	5	11		3	.273	.363	.323	110	2	7-3	.972	0	109	61	O26(3/22/1)		0.1
1916	Pit N	45	137	16	27	4	0	0	9	23		0	.197	.313	.226	66	-4	8	.964	3	117	107	O40(20/20/0)		-0.4
Total	2	88	272	33	61	5	2	0	22	37		3	.224	.324	.257	78	-5	17-4	.971	4	112	87	O76(26/49/1)		-0.7

BARNHART, CLYDE Clyde Lee "Pooch" B12.29.1895 Buck Valley PA D1.21.1980 Hagerstown MD BR/TR/5-10/155 d9.22 s-Vic Col Shippensburg

YEAR	TM LG	G	AB	R	H	2B	3B	HR	RBI	BB-IB	HP	SO	AVG	OBP	SLG	AOPS	ABR	SB-CS	FA	FR	RNG	THR	GAMES AT POSITION	DL	BFW
1920	Pit N	12	46	5	15	4	2	0	5	1		0	2	.326	.340	.500	135	2	1-0	.971	0	107	176	3b12		0.3
1921	Pit N	124	449	66	116	15	13	3	62	32	3	36	.258	.312	.370	78	-15	3-3	.956	-19	84	94	3b118		-2.8
1922	Pit N	75	209	30	69	7	5	1	38	25		7	.330	.402	.426	112	5	3-2	.918	-7	64	94	3b30,O26(5/0/21)		-0.3
1923	Pit N	114	327	60	106	25	13	9	72	47		21	.324	.409	.563	151	24	5-7	.985	6	105	144	O92R		2.1
1924	Pit N	102	344	49	95	6	11	3	51	30	2	21	.276	.338	.384	91	-5	8-4	.970	1	108	76	O88R		-1.1
1925	†Pit N	142	539	85	175	32	11	4	114	59		25	.325	.391	.447	106	7	9-5	.962	-1	101	97	O138L		-0.4
1926	Pit N	76	203	26	39	3	0	0	10	23	1	13	.192	.278	.207	30	-20	1	.991	1	100	100	O61(54/0/8)		-2.3
1927	†Pit N	108	360	52	115	23	4	3	54	37	1	19	.319	.384	.431	110	7	2	.978	3	116	58	O94L		0.3

YEAR	TM LG	G	AB	R	H	2B	3B	HR	RBI	BB-IB	HP	SO	AVG	OBP	SLG	AOPS	ABR	SB-CS	FA	FR	RNG	THR	GAMES AT POSITION	DL	BFW
1928	Pit N	61	196	18	58	6	2	4	30	11	0	9	.296	.333	.408	89	-4	3	.971	-0	103	85	O48(45/0/4)/3		-0.7
Total	9	814	2673	404	788	121	61	27	436	265	7	149	.295	.360	.416	100	1	35-21	.973	-17	105	90	O547(336/0/213),3b161		-4.9

BARNHART, VIC   Victor Dee B9.1.1922 Hagerstown MD   BR/TR/6-0/188   d10.1 f-Clyde

YEAR	TM LG	G	AB	R	H	2B	3B	HR	RBI	BB-IB	HP	SO	AVG	OBP	SLG	AOPS	ABR	SB-CS	FA	FR	RNG	THR	GAMES AT POSITION	DL	BFW
1944	Pit N	1	2	0	1	0	0	0	0	1	0	1	.500	.667	.500	222	0	0	.889	0	146	0	/S		0.1
1945	Pit N	71	201	21	54	7	0	0	19	9	0	11	.269	.300	.303	65	-10	2	.928	1	100	111	S60,3b4		-0.5
1946	Pit N	2	1	0	0	0	0	0	0	0	0	0	.000	.000	.000	-98	0	0	—	0			/H		0.0
Total	3	74	204	21	55	7	0	0	19	10	0	12	.270	.304	.304	67	-10	2	.927	1	101	108	S61,3b4		-0.4

BARNIE, BILLY   William Harrison "Bald Billy" B1.26.1853 New York NY   D7.15.1900 Hartford CT   TR/5-7/157   d5.7 M14/U1

YEAR	TM LG	G	AB	R	H	2B	3B	HR	RBI	BB-IB	HP	SO	AVG	OBP	SLG	AOPS	ABR	SB-CS	FA	FR	RNG	THR	GAMES AT POSITION	DL	BFW
1874	Har NA	45	190	21	35	4	2	0	20	1		13	.184	.188	.226	31	-15	2-2	.733	-8			C30,O29(0/4/25)/S		-1.7
1875	Wes NA	10	36	3	4	1	0	0	2	0		3	.111	.111	.139	-13	-4	0-0	.889	0	0	0	O7(0/3/4),C3		-0.3
	Mut NA	9	34	1	5	0	0	0	1	1		0	.147	.171	.147	11	-3	0-0	.750	-5			C6,O3(0/1/2)		-0.5
	Year	19	70	4	9	1	0	0	3	1		3	.129	.141	.143	-1	-7	0-0	.857	-2	0	0	O10(0/4/6),C9		-0.8
1883	Bal AA	17	55	7	11	0	0	0		2			.200	.228	.200	38	-4		.846	-2			C13,O6R/SM		-0.4
1886	Bal AA	2	6	0	0	0	0	0	0	1	0		.000	.143	.000	-55	-1	0	—	-1	0	0	/OCC		-0.2
Total	2 NA	64	260	25	44	5	2	0	23	2		16	.169	.176	.204	23	-22	2-2	.690	-10			O39(0/8/31),C39/S		-2.5
Total	2	19	61	7	11	0	0	0	0	3	0	0	.180	.219	.180	29	-5	0	.848	-3			C14,O7(0/1/6)/S		-0.6

BARONE, DICK   Richard Anthony B10.13.1932 San Jose CA   BR/TR/5-9/165   d9.22

YEAR	TM LG	G	AB	R	H	2B	3B	HR	RBI	BB-IB	HP	SO	AVG	OBP	SLG	AOPS	ABR	SB-CS	FA	FR	RNG	THR	GAMES AT POSITION	DL	BFW
1960	Pit N	3	6	0	0	0	0	0	0	0	0	0	.000	.000	.000	-99	-2	0-0	.875	-1	56	0	S2		-0.3

BARR, SCOTTY   Hyder Edward B10.6.1886 Bristol TN   D12.2.1934 Ft.Worth TX   BR/TR/6-0/175   d8.22 Col Davidson

YEAR	TM LG	G	AB	R	H	2B	3B	HR	RBI	BB-IB	HP	SO	AVG	OBP	SLG	AOPS	ABR	SB-CS	FA	FR	RNG	THR	GAMES AT POSITION	DL	BFW
1908	Phi A	19	56	4	8	2	0	0	1	3	1		.143	.200	.179	22	-5	0	.923	-4	80	0	2b11,3b4,1b2,O2(1/1/0)		-1.0
1909	Phi A	22	51	5	4	1	0	0	1	11	1		.078	.254	.098	12	-5	2	.947	-1	0	0	O15(1/14/0),1b7		-0.7
Total	2	41	107	9	12	3	0	0	2	14	2		.112	.228	.140	17	-10	2	.947	-5	0	0	O17(2/15/0),2b11,1b9,3b4		-1.7

BARRAGAN, CUNO   Facundo Anthony B6.20.1932 Sacramento CA   BR/TR/5-11/180*   d9.1 Col Cal St.-Sacramento

YEAR	TM LG	G	AB	R	H	2B	3B	HR	RBI	BB-IB	HP	SO	AVG	OBP	SLG	AOPS	ABR	SB-CS	FA	FR	RNG	THR	GAMES AT POSITION	DL	BFW
1961	Chi N	10	28	3	6	0	0	1	2	2-0	0	7	.214	.267	.321	54	-1	0-0	1.000	-1	0	102	C10	144	-0.2
1962	Chi N	58	134	11	27	6	1	0	12	21-1	0	28	.201	.306	.261	53	-8	0-2	.971	-6	88	126	C55		-1.3
1963	Chi N	1	1	0	1	0	0	0	0	0-0	0	1	1.000	1.000	1.000	-95	-0	0	1.000	-0	0		/C		-0.1
Total	3	69	163	14	33	6	1	1	14	23-1	0	36	.202	.298	.270	53	-10	0-2	.975	-7	73	121	C66	144	-1.6

BARRANCA, GERMAN   German (Costales) B10.19.1956 Veracruz, Veracruz, Mexico   BL/TR/6-0/160*   d9.2

YEAR	TM LG	G	AB	R	H	2B	3B	HR	RBI	BB-IB	HP	SO	AVG	OBP	SLG	AOPS	ABR	SB-CS	FA	FR	RNG	THR	GAMES AT POSITION	DL	BFW
1979	KC A	5	5	3	3	1	0	0	0	0-0	0	0	.600	.600	.800	268	1	3-1	1.000	2	231	412	/23D		0.4
1980	KC A	7	3	3	0	0	0	0	0	0-0	0	0	—	—	—	—	0	0-0	—	0			/R		0.0
1981	Cin N	9	6	2	2	0	0	1	0	0-0	0	0	.333	.333	.333	90	0	0-0	—	0			/H		0.0
1982	Cin N	46	51	11	13	1	3	0	2	2-0	0	9	.255	.283	.392	87	-1	2-0	.824	-2	80	44	2b6		-0.3
Total	4	67	62	19	18	2	3	0	3	2-0	0	9	.290	.313	.419	102	0	5-1	.893	0	113	125	2b7/D3		0.1

BARRETT, JIMMY   James Erigena B3.28.1875 Athol MA   D10.24.1921 Detroit MI   BL/TR/5-7/170   d9.13

YEAR	TM LG	G	AB	R	H	2B	3B	HR	RBI	BB-IB	HP	SO	AVG	OBP	SLG	AOPS	ABR	SB-CS	FA	FR	RNG	THR	GAMES AT POSITION	DL	BFW
1899	Cin N	26	92	30	34	2	4	0	10	18	1		.370	.477	.478	159	9	4	.936	-2	53	0	O26(3/0/23)		0.5
1900	Cin N	137	545	114	172	11	7	5	42	72	5		.316	.400	.389	121	19	44	.929	2	133	122	O137(0/115/22)		1.2
1901	Det A	135	542	110	159	16	9	4	65	76	5		.293	.385	.378	107	8	26	.940	11	178	175	O135C		1.2
1902	Det A	136	509	93	154	19	6	4	44	74	6		.303	.397	.387	116	15	24	.961	6	126	164	O136C		1.3
1903	Det A	136	517	95	163	13	10	2	31	74	6		.315	.407	.391	144	33	27	.955	7	128	182	O136C		3.4
1904	Det A	162	624	83	167	10	5	0	31	79	3		.268	.353	.300	111	12	15	.971	9	163	121	O162C		1.5
1905	Det A	20	67	2	17	1	0	0	3	6	1		.254	.324	.269	88	-1	0	1.000	-1	0	0	O18C		-0.3
1906	Cin N	5	12	1	0	0	0	0	0	2	0		.000	.143	.000	-53	-2	0	1.000	1	294	1194	O4R		-0.2
1907	Bos N	106	390	52	95	11	6	1	28	38	2		.244	.314	.310	100	1	3	.966	0	100	169	O99(96/3/0)		-0.6
1908	Bos A	3	8	0	1	0	0	0	1	1	0		.125	.222	.125	13	-1	0	1.000	0	0	0	O2C		-0.1
Total	10	866	3306	580	962	83	47	16	255	440	29		.291	.379	.359	117	93	143	.954	32	135	150	O855(99/707/49)		7.9

BARRETT, JOHN   John B Brooklyn NY   d9.18

YEAR	TM LG	G	AB	R	H	2B	3B	HR	RBI	BB-IB	HP	SO	AVG	OBP	SLG	AOPS	ABR	SB-CS	FA	FR	RNG	THR	GAMES AT POSITION	DL	BFW
1872	Atl NA	8	34	6	7	1	0	0	2	0		1	.206	.206	.235	30	-3	1-0	.808	-1	0	0	O8L		-0.2

BARRETT, JOHNNY   John Joseph "Jack" B12.18.1915 Lowell MA   D8.17.1974 Seabrook Beach NH   BL/TL/5-10.5/170   d4.14

YEAR	TM LG	G	AB	R	H	2B	3B	HR	RBI	BB-IB	HP	SO	AVG	OBP	SLG	AOPS	ABR	SB-CS	FA	FR	RNG	THR	GAMES AT POSITION	DL	BFW
1942	Pit N	111	332	56	82	11	6	0	26	48	3	42	.247	.347	.316	92	-2	10	.973	6	109	137	O94(15/5/74)		-0.1
1943	Pit N	130	290	41	67	12	3	1	32	32	4	23	.231	.316	.303	77	-8	5	.988	1	107	76	O99(4/3/92)		-1.3
1944	Pit N	149	568	99	153	24	19	7	83	86	1	56	.269	.366	.415	115	12	28	.972	-2	102	76	O147(1/67/92)		0.3
1945	Pit N	142	507	97	130	29	4	15	67	79	1	68	.256	.357	.418	111	9	25	.976	-6	98	68	O132(0/75/57)		-0.3
1946	Pit N	32	71	7	12	3	0	0	6	8	0	11	.169	.253	.211	32	-6	1	.919	-1	93	69	O21(0/12/9)		-0.9
	Bos A	24	43	3	10	3	0	0	6	12	0	1	.233	.400	.302	100	1	0	.962	-1	92	99	O17(2/11/4)		0.0
	Year	56	114	10	22	6	0	0	12	20	0	12	.193	.313	.246	59	-5	1	.937	-2	93	82	O38(2/23/13)		-0.9
Total	5	548	1811	303	454	82	32	23	220	265	8	201	.251	.349	.369	100	6	69	.974	-3	102	86	O510(22/173/328)		-2.3

BARRETT, MARTY   Martin F. B11.1860 Port Henry NY   D1.29.1910 Holyoke MA   BR/TR/5-9/170   d6.24

YEAR	TM LG	G	AB	R	H	2B	3B	HR	RBI	BB-IB	HP	SO	AVG	OBP	SLG	AOPS	ABR	SB-CS	FA	FR	RNG	THR	GAMES AT POSITION	DL	BFW
1884	Bos N	3	6	0	0	0	0	0	0	0		4	.000	.000	.000	-99	-1		.900	-1			C3		-0.2
	Ind AA	5	13	1	1	1	0	0		1		0	.077	.143	.154	-3	-1		.808	-2			C4/OR		-0.3
Total	8	19	1	1	1	0	0	0	1		4	.053	.100	.105	-34	-2		.833	-3			C7/OR		-0.5

BARRETT, MARTY   Martin Glenn B6.23.1958 Arcadia CA   BR/TR/5-10/176*   [BosA79 S1/1]   d9.6 b-Tom Col Arizona St.

YEAR	TM LG	G	AB	R	H	2B	3B	HR	RBI	BB-IB	HP	SO	AVG	OBP	SLG	AOPS	ABR	SB-CS	FA	FR	RNG	THR	GAMES AT POSITION	DL	BFW
1982	Bos A	8	18	0	1	0	0	0	0	0-0	0	1	.056	.056	.056	-65	-3	0-0	1.000	4	157	124	2b7		0.0
1983	Bos A	33	44	7	10	1	1	0	2	3-0	0	5	.227	.271	.295	53	-3	0-0	.984	-4	75	83	2b23,D5		-0.6
1984	Bos A	139	475	56	144	23	3	3	45	42-2	1	25	.303	.358	.383	101	2	5-3	.987	0	103	72	2b136		1.0
1985	Bos A	156	534	59	142	26	0	5	56	56-3	2	50	.266	.336	.343	83	-11	7-5	.987	16	103	101	2b155		1.4
1986	†Bos A	158	625	94	179	39	4	4	60	65-1	3	31	.286	.353	.381	100	2	15-7	.982	-3	95	102	2b158		0.8
1987	Bos A	137	559	72	164	23	0	3	43	51-0	1	38	.293	.351	.351	85	-10	15-2	.988	33	108	116	2b137	16	3.0
1988	†Bos A	150	612	83	173	28	1	1	65	40-1	7	35	.283	.330	.337	84	-12	7-3	.990	5	90	100	2b150		-0.2
1989	Bos A	86	336	31	86	18	0	1	27	32-0	2	12	.256	.320	.318	77	-9	4-1	.975	-0	97	99	2b80,D4	61	-0.7
1990	†Bos A	62	159	15	36	4	0	1	13	15-1	1	13	.226	.294	.252	52	-10	4-0	.992	-2	97	79	2b60/3D		-1.0
1991	SD N	12	16	1	3	1	0	1	3	1-0	0	2	.188	.235	.438	82	0	0-0	1.000	1	101	291	2b3,3b2	33	0.1
Total	10	941	3378	418	938	163	9	18	314	304-7	16	209	.278	.337	.347	86	-55	57-21	.986	51	99	98	2b908,D10,3b3	110	3.8

BARRETT, MICHAEL   Michael Patrick B10.22.1976 Atlanta GA   BR/TR/6-2/200(185-210)   [MonN95 1/28]   d9.19

YEAR	TM LG	G	AB	R	H	2B	3B	HR	RBI	BB-IB	HP	SO	AVG	OBP	SLG	AOPS	ABR	SB-CS	FA	FR	RNG	THR	GAMES AT POSITION	DL	BFW
1998	Mon N	8	23	3	7	2	0	2	3-0	1	6		.304	.407	.522	146	1	0-0	.963	1	41	268	C3,3b3		0.3
1999	Mon N	126	433	53	127	32	3	8	52	32-4	3	39	.293	.345	.436	100	0	0-2	.943	-5	102	40	3b66,C59,S2	18	-0.2
2000	Mon N	89	271	28	58	15	2	4	22	23-5	1	35	.214	.277	.288	43	-24	0-1	.891	-4	95	107	3b55,C28		-2.6
2001	Mon N	132	472	42	118	33	2	6	38	25-2	2	54	.250	.289	.367	69	-22	2-1	.993	-16	74	66	C131		-2.9
2002	Mon N	117	376	41	99	20	1	12	49	40-7	1	65	.263	.332	.418	95	-4	6-3	.989	11	101	88	C110,1b6		1.4
2003	Mon N	70	226	33	47	9	2	10	30	21-7	2	37	.208	.280	.398	73	-10	0-0	.998	0	195	70	C68	45	-0.5
2004	Chi N	134	456	55	131	32	6	16	65	33-4	5	64	.287	.337	.489	108	5	1-4	.994	3	93	93	C130		1.4
2005	Chi N	133	424	48	117	32	4	16	61	40-3	7	61	.276	.345	.479	110	7	0-3	.994	-9	87	87	C122/D		0.5
Total	8	809	2681	303	704	175	18	70	319	217-32	22	361	.263	.320	.420	89	-46	9-14	.992	-19	98	83	C651,3b124,1b6,S2/D	63	-2.6

BARRETT, BOB   Robert Schley "Jumbo" B1.27.1899 Atlanta GA   D1.18.1982 Atlanta GA   BR/TR/5-11/175   d4.30

YEAR	TM LG	G	AB	R	H	2B	3B	HR	RBI	BB-IB	HP	SO	AVG	OBP	SLG	AOPS	ABR	SB-CS	FA	FR	RNG	THR	GAMES AT POSITION	DL	BFW
1923	Chi N	3	3	0	1	0	0	0	0	0	0	0	.333	.333	.333	76	0	0	—	0			/H		0.0
1924	Chi N	54	133	12	32	2	3	5	21	7	0	29	.241	.279	.414	82	-4	1-0	.943	-2	98	93	2b25,1b10,3b8		-0.6
1925	Chi N	14	32	1	10	1	0	0	7	1	0	4	.313	.333	.344	72	-1	1-2	1.000	-1	35	356	3b6,2b4		-0.3
	Bro N	1	1	0	0	0	0	0	0	0	0	0	.000	.000	.000	-99	0	0-0	—	0			/H		0.0
	Year	15	33	1	10	1	0	0	8	1	0	4	.303	.324	.333	67	-1	1-2	1.000	-1	35	356	3b6,2b4		-0.3
1927	Bro N	99	355	29	92	14	5	3	38	14	1	22	.259	.289	.341	68	-17	1	.920	-7	94	87	3b96		-1.8
1929	Bos N	68	126	15	34	10	0	3	19	10	0	6	.270	.324	.349	75	-4	3-1	.938	5	133	62	3b34,1b4,2b2/OL		0.2
Total	5	239	650	57	169	23	5	10	86	32	1	61	.260	.296	.357	72	-26	6-3	.924	-5	100	85	3b144,2b31,1b14/OL		-2.5

BARRETT, TOM   Thomas Loren B4.2.1960 San Fernando CA   BB/TR/5-9/170(157-170)   [NYA82 26/667]   d7.2 b-Marty Col Arizona   [DL 1990 Phi N 178]

YEAR	TM LG	G	AB	R	H	2B	3B	HR	RBI	BB-IB	HP	SO	AVG	OBP	SLG	AOPS	ABR	SB-CS	FA	FR	RNG	THR	GAMES AT POSITION	DL	BFW
1988	Phi N	36	54	5	11	0	0	0	3	7-0	1	8	.204	.306	.222	53	-3	0-0	.959	2	123	104	2b10		-0.1
1989	Phi N	14	27	3	6	0	0	0	1	1-0	0	7	.222	.250	.222	36	-2	0-0	.978	2	86	197	2b9		0.0

YEAR	TM LG	G	AB	R	H	2B	3B	HR	RBI	BB-IB	HP	SO	AVG	OBP	SLG	AOPS	ABR	SB-CS	FA	FR	RNG	THR	GAMES AT POSITION	DL	BFW
1992	Bos A	4	3	1	0	0	0	0	0	2-0	0	0	.000	.400	.000	19	0	0-0	1.000	-1	76	0	2b2		-0.1
Total	3	54	84	9	17	1	0	0	4	10-0	1	15	.202	.295	.214	47	-5	0-0	.970	3	103	132	2b21	178	-0.2

BARRETT, BILL William B Washington DC d7.8

YEAR	TM LG	G	AB	R	H	2B	3B	HR	RBI	BB-IB	HP	SO	AVG	OBP	SLG	AOPS	ABR	SB-CS	FA	FR	RNG	THR	GAMES AT POSITION	DL	BFW
1871	Kek NA	1	5	1	1	1	0	0	1	0		0	.200	.200	.400	66	0	0-0	1.000	1			/C3		0.0
1872	Oly NA	1	4	0	0	0	0	0	0	0		0	.000	.000	.000	-99	-1	0-0	.400	-2			/C		-0.2
1873	Bal NA	1	4	0	1	0	0	0	0	0		0	.250	.250	.250	49	0	0-1	.667	-1	31	0	/SOR		-0.1
Total	3 NA	3	13	1	2	1	0	0	1	0		0	.154	.154	.231	12	-1	0-1	.769	-2			C2/ORS3		-0.3

BARRETT, BILL William Joseph "Whispering Bill" B5.28.1900 Cambridge MA D1.26.1951 Cambridge MA BR/TR/6-0/175 d5.13 OF(74/28/400)

YEAR	TM LG	G	AB	R	H	2B	3B	HR	RBI	BB-IB	HP	SO	AVG	OBP	SLG	AOPS	ABR	SB-CS	FA	FR	RNG	THR	GAMES AT POSITION	DL	BFW
1921	Phi A	14	30	3	7	2	1	0	3	0	0	5	.233	.233	.367	51	-2	0-0	.925	1	116	29	S8,P4,3b2/1		-0.1
1923	Chi A	44	162	17	44	7	2	2	23	9	-0	24	.272	.310	.377	81	-5	12-3	.940	-1	100	100	O40(40/1/0)/3		-0.7
1924	Chi A	119	406	52	110	18	5	2	56	30	3	38	.271	.326	.355	78	-15	15-10	.904	-14	87	91	S77,O28(25/3/0),3b8		-2.1
1925	Chi A	81	245	44	89	23	3	3	40	24	0	27	.363	.420	.518	145	17	5-6	.943	-5	100	110	2b41,O27(3/1/23),S4,3b4		1.1
1926	Chi A	111	368	46	113	31	4	6	61	25	1	26	.307	.353	.462	115	7	9-7	.969	-2	103	78	O102(1/0/102),1b2		-0.2
1927	Chi A	147	556	62	159	35	9	4	83	52	0	46	.286	.347	.403	96	-3	20-13	.963	7	103	140	O147(0/12/136)		-0.7
1928	Chi A	76	235	34	65	11	2	3	26	14	1	30	.277	.320	.379	84	-6	8-4	.988	-1	104	187	O37(4/1/32),2b25		-0.9
1929	Chi A	3	1	0	0	0	0	0	0	2	0	0	.000	.667	.000	87	0	0-0	—	0			/H		0.0
	Bos A	111	370	57	100	23	4	3	35	51	3	38	.270	.363	.378	93	-2	11-8	.974	7	104	164	O109(1/10/101)/3		-0.3
	Year	114	371	57	100	23	4	3	35	53	3	38	.270	.365	.377	94	-2	11-8	.974	7	104	164	O109(1/10/101)/3		-0.3
1930	Bos A	6	18	3	3	1	0	0	1	1	0	3	.167	.211	.222	10	-2	0-0	1.000	-1	71	0	O5R		-0.3
	Was A	6	4	0	0	0	0	0	0	1	0	2	.000	.200	.000	-44	-1	0-0	1.000	0	157	0	/OR		-0.1
	Year	12	22	3	3	1	0	0	1	2	0	5	.136	.208	.182	-0	-3	0-0	1.000	-1	78	0	O6R		-0.4
Total	9	718	2395	318	690	151	30	23	328	209	8	239	.288	.347	.405	97	-12	80-51	.964	-8	102	133	O496R,S89,2b66,3b16,P4,1b3		-4.3

BARRIOS, JOSE Jose Manuel B6.26.1957 New York NY BR/TR/6-4/195 [SFN75 3/56] d4.23

YEAR	TM LG	G	AB	R	H	2B	3B	HR	RBI	BB-IB	HP	SO	AVG	OBP	SLG	AOPS	ABR	SB-CS	FA	FR	RNG	THR	GAMES AT POSITION	DL	BFW
1982	SF N	10	19	2	3	0	0	0	1-0	0	4	.158	.200	.158	1	-3	0-0	1.000	-1	0	111	1b7		-0.4

BARRON, TONY Anthony Dirk B8.17.1966 Portland OR BR/TR/6-0/185* [LAN87 7/170] d6.2 Col Willamette

YEAR	TM LG	G	AB	R	H	2B	3B	HR	RBI	BB-IB	HP	SO	AVG	OBP	SLG	AOPS	ABR	SB-CS	FA	FR	RNG	THR	GAMES AT POSITION	DL	BFW
1996	Mon N	1	1	0	0	0	0	0	0	0-0	0	1	.000	.000	.000	-98	0	0-0	—	0			/H		0.0
1997	Phi N	57	189	22	54	12	1	4	24	12-0	2	38	.286	.330	.423	98	-1	0-1	.983	3	121	82	O53R		0.0
Total	2	58	190	22	54	12	1	4	24	12-0	2	39	.284	.329	.421	97	-1	0-1	.983	3	121	82	O53R		0.0

BARRON, RED David Irenus B6.21.1900 Clarksville GA D10.4.1982 Atlanta GA BR/TR/5-11.5/185 d6.10 Col Georgia Tech

YEAR	TM LG	G	AB	R	H	2B	3B	HR	RBI	BB-IB	HP	SO	AVG	OBP	SLG	AOPS	ABR	SB-CS	FA	FR	RNG	THR	GAMES AT POSITION	DL	BFW
1929	Bos N	10	21	3	4	1	0	0	1	1	0	4	.190	.227	.238	16	-3	2	.929	1	114	291	O6L		-0.2

BARROWS, FRANK Franklin Lee B10.22.1844 Hudson OH D2.6.1922 Fitchburg MA d5.20

YEAR	TM LG	G	AB	R	H	2B	3B	HR	RBI	BB-IB	HP	SO	AVG	OBP	SLG	AOPS	ABR	SB-CS	FA	FR	RNG	THR	GAMES AT POSITION	DL	BFW
1871	Bos NA	18	86	13	13	2	1	0	11	0		1	.151	.151	.198	-1	-11	1-0	.829	-2	52	0	O17(13/0/4)/2		-0.8

BARROWS, CUKE Roland B10.20.1883 Gray ME D2.10.1955 Gorham ME BL/TR/5-8/158 d9.18

YEAR	TM LG	G	AB	R	H	2B	3B	HR	RBI	BB-IB	HP	SO	AVG	OBP	SLG	AOPS	ABR	SB-CS	FA	FR	RNG	THR	GAMES AT POSITION	DL	BFW
1909	Chi A	5	20	1	3	0	0	0	0	0		0	.150	.190	.150	8	-2	0	.923	1	228	562	O5L		-0.2
1910	Chi A	6	20	0	4	0	0	0	1	3		0	.200	.304	.200	61	-1	0	.875	-1	77	0	O6L		-0.2
1911	Chi A	13	46	5	9	2	0	0	4	7	1		.196	.315	.239	57	-2	2	1.000	-1	113	0	O13R		-0.4
1912	Chi A	8	13	0	3	0	0	0	2	2	0		.231	.333	.231	64	0	1	1.000	0	31	320	O3R		-0.1
Total	4	32	99	6	19	2	0	0	9	12	1	2	.192	.292	.212	50	-5	3	.950	-1	129	176	O27(11/0/16)		-0.9

BARRY, JEFF Jeffrey Finas B9.22.1969 Medford OR BB/TR/6-1/200(190-204) d6.9 Col San Diego St.

YEAR	TM LG	G	AB	R	H	2B	3B	HR	RBI	BB-IB	HP	SO	AVG	OBP	SLG	AOPS	ABR	SB-CS	FA	FR	RNG	THR	GAMES AT POSITION	DL	BFW
1995	NY N	15	15	2	2	1	0	0	1-0	0	8	.133	.188	.200	2	-2	0-0	1.000	0	134	0	O2(1/0/1)		-0.2
1998	Col N	15	34	4	6	1	0	0	2	2-0	0	11	.176	.216	.206	11	-4	0-0	1.000	1	115	207	O10(1/8/5)		-0.3
1999	Col N	74	168	19	45	16	0	5	26	19-1	2	29	.268	.341	.452	80	-5	0-4	1.000	1	95	167	O56(14/32/15)		-0.5
Total	3	104	217	25	53	18	0	5	28	22-1	2	48	.244	.314	.396	66	-11	0-4	1.000	2	99	170	O68(16/40/21)		-1.0

BARRY, SHAD John C. B10.27.1878 Newburgh NY D11.27.1936 Los Angeles CA BR/TR d5.30 Col Niagara OF(214/39/371)

YEAR	TM LG	G	AB	R	H	2B	3B	HR	RBI	BB-IB	HP	SO	AVG	OBP	SLG	AOPS	ABR	SB-CS	FA	FR	RNG	THR	GAMES AT POSITION	DL	BFW
1899	Was N	78	247	31	71	7	5	1	33	12	3		.287	.328	.368	92	-4	11	.946	-9	80	0	O23(20/0/3),1b22,S13,3b13,2b7		-1.1
1900	Bos N	81	254	40	66	10	7	1	37	13	2		.260	.301	.366	74	-10	9	.956	-12	134	268	O24(22/1/1),S18,2b16,1b10/3		-2.1
1901	Bos N	11	40	3	7	2	0	0	6	2	1		.175	.233	.225	30	-4	1	.926	-1	68	0	O11L		-0.5
	Phi N	67	252	35	62	10	0	1	22	15	2		.246	.294	.298	70	-9	13	.903	-13	92	65	2b35,3b16,O13(3/9/1)/S		-2.2
	Year	78	292	38	69	12	0	1	28	17	3		.236	.285	.288	64	-13	14	.903	-13	92	65	2b35,O24(14/9/1),3b16/S		-2.7
1902	Phi N	**138**	543	65	156	20	6	3	58	44	2		.287	.343	.363	118	11	14	.939	-6	82	60	O137(7/0/130)/1		-0.1
1903	Phi N	138	550	75	152	24	5	1	60	30	6		.276	.331	.344	92	-6	26	.970	-2	94	52	O107(105/2/0),1b30/3		-1.4
1904	Phi N	35	122	15	25	2	0	0	3	11	2		.205	.281	.221	58	-6	2	.979	11	300	322	O32(11/6/15)/3		0.4
	Chi N	73	263	29	69	7	2	1	26	17	1		.262	.310	.316	93	-4	10	.917	-4	74	0	O30(0/13/17),1b8,3b16,S8,2b2		-0.8
	Year	108	385	44	94	9	2	1	29	28	3		.244	.300	.286	82	-8	14	.955	7	195	172	O62(11/19/32),1b18,3b17,S8,2b2		-0.4
1905	Chi N	27	104	10	22	2	0	0	10	5	1		.212	.255	.231	43	-7	5	.982	0	106	87	1b26		-0.8
	Cin N	125	494	90	160	11	12	1	56	33	5		.324	.364	.401	118	10	16	.982	-7	79	117	1b124,O2(1/1/0)		0.1
	Year	152	598	100	182	13	12	1	66	38	6		.304	.352	.371	105	3	21	.982	-6	84	**112**	1b150,O2(1/1/0)		-0.7
1906	Cin N	73	279	38	80	10	5	1	33	26	3		.287	.354	.369	120	7	11	.993	-0	90	113	1b43,O30(14/7/9)		0.4
	Stl N	62	237	26	59	9	1	0	12	15	2		.249	.294	.295	89	-3	6	.930	-3	82	109	O35R,1b21,3b6		-0.9
	Year	135	516	64	139	19	6	1	45	41	5		.269	.329	.335	107	4	17	.922	-3	130	0	O65(14/7/44),1b64,3b6		-0.5
1907	Stl N	81	294	30	73	5	2	0	19	28	3		.248	.320	.279	91	-2	4	.963	-5	103	0	O81R		-1.2
1908	Stl N	74	268	24	61	8	1	0	11	19	3		.228	.286	.265	80	-6	9	.967	1	104	0	O69R,S2		-0.9
	NY N	37	67	5	10	1	1	0	5	9	1		.149	.260	.194	43	-4	1	.971	-2	0	0	O31(20/0/10),S2		-0.8
	Year	111	335	29	71	9	2	0	16	28	4		.212	.281	.251	71	-10	10	.968	-1	92	0	O100(20/0/79),S2		-1.7
Total	10	1100	4014	516	1073	128	47	10	391	279	37		.267	.321	.330	94	-35	140	.955	-50	106	58	O625R,1b295,2b60,3b54,S42		-11.9

BARRY, JACK John Joseph B4.26.1887 Meriden CT D4.23.1961 Shrewsbury MA BR/TR/5-9/158 d7.13 Mil 1918 M1 Col Holy Cross

YEAR	TM LG	G	AB	R	H	2B	3B	HR	RBI	BB-IB	HP	SO	AVG	OBP	SLG	AOPS	ABR	SB-CS	FA	FR	RNG	THR	GAMES AT POSITION	DL	BFW
1908	Phi A	40	135	13	30	4	3	0	8	10	3		.222	.291	.296	85	-2	5	.966	-7	102	53	2b20,S14,3b3		-0.9
1909	Phi A	124	409	56	88	11	2	1	23	44	10		.215	.307	.259	77	-8	17	.927	-26	88	**106**	S124		-3.5
1910	†Phi A	145	487	64	126	19	5	3	60	52	5		.259	.336	.337	112	8	14	.916	-27	87	**114**	S145		-1.6
1911	†Phi A	127	442	73	117	18	7	1	63	38	7		.265	.333	.344	90	-6	30	**.944**	-11	92	**108**	S127		-0.7
1912	Phi A	140	483	75	126	19	9	0	55	47	7		.261	.335	.337	96	-2	22	.925	-6	103	**125**	S139		0.1
1913	†Phi A	134	455	62	125	20	6	3	85	44	8	32	.275	.349	.365	111	7	15	.953	-5	96	116	S134		1.1
1914	†Phi A	140	467	57	113	12	0	0	42	53	4	34	.242	.324	.268	81	-9	22-13	.947	7	107	120	S140		0.9
1915	Phi A	54	194	16	43	6	2	0	15	15	2		.222	.284	.273	69	-4	6-5	.952	-2	95	87	S54		-0.7
	†Bos A	78	248	30	65	13	2	0	26	24	6	11	.262	.342	.331	104	2	6-5	.962	-4	100	76	2b78		-0.1
	Year	132	442	46	108	19	4	0	41	39	8		.244	.317	.305	89	-6	6-5	.962	-6	100	76	2b78,S54		-0.8
1916	Bos A	94	330	28	67	6	1	0	20	17	**17**	24	.203	.277	.227	52	-19	8	.974	1	102	84	2b94		-1.9
1917	Bos A	116	388	65	83	9	0	2	30	47	4	27	.214	.305	.253	71	-12	12	**.974**	-5	104	93	2b116,M		-1.7
1919	Bos A	31	108	13	26	5	1	0	2	5	3	5	.241	.293	.306	72	-4	2	.922	-5	99	92	2b31		-0.9
Total	11	1223	4146	532	1009	142	38	10	429	396	76	142	.243	.321	.303	88	-53	153-18	.935	-90	95	112	S877,2b339,3b3		-9.9

BARRY, RICH Richard Donovan B9.12.1940 Berkeley CA BR/TR/6-4/205 d7.4

YEAR	TM LG	G	AB	R	H	2B	3B	HR	RBI	BB-IB	HP	SO	AVG	OBP	SLG	AOPS	ABR	SB-CS	FA	FR	RNG	THR	GAMES AT POSITION	DL	BFW
1969	Phi N	20	32	4	6	0	0	0	5-0	1	8	.188	.316	.219	53	-2	0-0	.938	0	134	0	O9L		-0.2

BARTEE, KIMERA Kimera Anotchi B7.21.1972 Omaha NE BR/TR (BB 1998)/6-0/185(175-200) [BalA93 14/399] d4.3 Col Creighton

YEAR	TM LG	G	AB	R	H	2B	3B	HR	RBI	BB-IB	HP	SO	AVG	OBP	SLG	AOPS	ABR	SB-CS	FA	FR	RNG	THR	GAMES AT POSITION	DL	BFW
1996	Det A	110	217	32	55	-6	1	1	14	17-0	0	77	.253	.308	.304	55	-15	20-10	.991	3	119	23	O99(4/95/2),D2		-1.0
1997	Det A	12	5	4	1	0	0	0	0	2-0	1	2	.200	.500	.200	93	0	3-1	1.000	-0	83	0	O6(3/3/0),D3		0.0
1998	Det A	57	98	20	19	5	1	3	15	6-0	0	35	.194	.238	.357	52	-7	9-5	.964	2	105	239	O29(11/18/1),D10		-0.6
1999	Det A	41	77	11	15	1	3	0	9	9-0	0	20	.195	.279	.286	44	-7	3-3	.985	0	113	0	O38C/D		-0.7
2000	Cin N	11	4	2	0	0	0	0	0	0-0	1	2	.000	.200	.000	-42	-1	1-0	1.000	-0	68	0	O3(2/1/0)		-0.1
2001	Col N	12	15	0	0	0	0	0	1	2-1	1	5	.000	.158	.000	-43	-3	0-0	.889	-1	92	0	O10(9/2/0)		-0.4
Total	6	243	416	69	90	12	5	4	33	36-1	3	141	.216	.282	.298	48	-33	36-19	.983	4	114	52	O185(29/157/3),D16		-2.8

BARTELL, DICK Richard William "Rowdy Richard" B11.22.1907 Chicago IL D8.4.1995 Alameda CA BR/TR/5-9/160 d10.2 Mil 1944-45 C7

YEAR	TM LG	G	AB	R	H	2B	3B	HR	RBI	BB-IB	HP	SO	AVG	OBP	SLG	AOPS	ABR	SB-CS	FA	FR	RNG	THR	GAMES AT POSITION	DL	BFW
1927	Pit N	1	2	0	0	0	0	0	0	0-0	0	0	.000	.500	.000	41	0	0	1.000	0	69	198	/S		0.0
1928	Pit N	72	233	27	71	8	4	1	36	21	6	18	.305	.377	.386	96	-1	4	.974	-2	96	110	2b39,S27/3		0.1
1929	Pit N	143	610	101	184	40	13	2	57	40	2	29	.302	.347	.420	87	-13	11	.953	-6	94	89	S74,2b70		-0.9
1930	Pit N	129	475	69	152	32	13	4	75	39	5	34	.320	.378	.467	102	2	8	.941	5	103	**115**	S126		1.8

YEAR	TM LG	G	AB	R	H	2B	3B	HR	RBI	BB-IB	HP	SO	AVG	OBP	SLG	AOPS	ABR	SB-CS	FA	FR	RNG	THR	GAMES AT POSITION	DL	BFW
1931	Phi N	135	554	88	160	43	7	0	34	27	3	38	.289	.325	.392	85	-11	6	.948	4	98	96	S133,2b3		0.3
1932	Phi N	154	614	118	189	48	7	1	53	64	6	47	.308	.379	.414	101	4	8	.963	9	102	82	S154		2.4
1933	Phi N★	152	587	78	159	25	5	1	37	56	5	46	.271	.340	.336	83	-11	6	.951	9	101	96	S152		0.9
1934	Phi N	146	604	102	187	30	4	0	37	64	9	59	.310	.384	.373	91	-4	13	.954	18	106	108	S146		2.4
1935	NY N	137	539	60	141	28	4	14	53	37	6	52	.262	.316	.406	94	-5	5	.954	7	101	102	S137		1.1
1936	†NY N	145	510	71	152	31	3	8	42	40	5	36	.298	.355	.418	109	7	6	.956	43	122	125	S144		5.7
1937	†NY N★	128	516	91	158	38	2	14	62	40	10	38	.306	.367	.469	124	18	5	.958	36	114	134	S128		6.1
1938	NY N	127	481	67	126	26	1	9	49	55	8	60	.262	.347	.376	98	1	4	.952	26	111	115	S127		3.6
1939	Chi N	105	336	37	80	24	2	3	34	42	7	25	.238	.335	.348	82	-7	6	.943	-4	94	93	S101/3		-0.3
1940	†Det A	139	528	76	123	24	3	7	53	76	5	53	.233	.335	.330	67	-25	12-2	.953	13	100	89	S139		0.1
1941	Det A	5	12	0	2	1	0	0	1	2	1	2	.167	.333	.250	51	-1	0-1	.920	-1	84	67	S5		-0.1
	NY N	104	373	44	113	20	0	5	35	52	4	29	.303	.394	.397	121	13	6	.959	-5	96	102	3b84,S21		1.3
1942	NY N	90	316	53	77	10	3	5	24	44	8	34	.244	.351	.342	102	3	4	.965	3	109	140	3b52,S31		1.0
1943	NY N	99	337	48	91	14	0	5	28	47	7	27	.270	.371	.356	110	7	5	.980	15	115	84	3b54,S33		2.7
1946	NY N	5	2	0	0	0	0	0	0	0	0	0	.000	.000	.000	-99	-1	0	1.000	0	226	0	3b4,2b2		0.0
Total	18	2016	7629	1130	2165	442	71	79	710	748	97	627	.284	.355	.391	90	-24	109-3	.953	171	104	102	S1679,3b196,2b114		28.2

BARTIROME, TONY Anthony Joseph B5.9.1932 Pittsburgh PA BL/TL/5-10/155 d4.19 Mil 1953-54 C3

YEAR	TM LG	G	AB	R	H	2B	3B	HR	RBI	BB-IB	HP	SO	AVG	OBP	SLG	AOPS	ABR	SB-CS	FA	FR	RNG	THR	GAMES AT POSITION	DL	BFW
1952	Pit N	124	355	32	78	10	3	0	16	26	1	37	.220	.273	.265	48	-25	3-3	.989	1	108	98	1b118		-2.9

BARTLETT, JASON Jason Alan B10.30.1979 Mountain View CA BR/TR/6-0/180* [SDN01 13/390] d8.3 Col Oklahoma

YEAR	TM LG	G	AB	R	H	2B	3B	HR	RBI	BB-IB	HP	SO	AVG	OBP	SLG	AOPS	ABR	SB-CS	FA	FR	RNG	THR	GAMES AT POSITION	DL	BFW
2004	Min A	8	12	2	1	0	0	0	1	1-0	1		.083	.154	.083	-35	-2	2-0	.889	2	152	199	S5/2D		0.0
2005	Min A	74	224	33	54	10	1	3	16	21-0	4	37	.241	.316	.335	72	-9	4-0	.979	10	118	117	S68,D5		0.7
Total	2	82	236	35	55	10	1	3	17	22-0	4	38	.233	.308	.322	67	-11	6-0	.974	12	119	120	S73,D6/2		0.7

BARTLEY, BOYD Boyd Owen B2.11.1920 Chicago IL BR/TR/5-8.5/165 d5.30 Mil 1943-46 Col Illinois

YEAR	TM LG	G	AB	R	H	2B	3B	HR	RBI	BB-IB	HP	SO	AVG	OBP	SLG	AOPS	ABR	SB-CS	FA	FR	RNG	THR	GAMES AT POSITION	DL	BFW
1943	Bro N	9	21	0	1	0	0	0	0	1	0	3	.048	.091	.048	-59	-4	0	.897	0	99	72	S9		-0.4

BARTLING, IRV Henry Irving B6.27.1914 Bay City MI D6.12.1973 Westland MI BR/TR/6-0/175 d9.8 Col Michigan St.

YEAR	TM LG	G	AB	R	H	2B	3B	HR	RBI	BB-IB	HP	SO	AVG	OBP	SLG	AOPS	ABR	SB-CS	FA	FR	RNG	THR	GAMES AT POSITION	DL	BFW
1938	Phi A	14	46	5	8	1	0	0	5	3	0	7	.174	.224	.239	17	-6	0-0	.914	-3	86	83	S13/3		-0.8

BARTON, HARRY Harry Lamb B1.20.1875 Chester PA D1.25.1955 Upland PA BB/TR/5-6.5/155 d4.15

YEAR	TM LG	G	AB	R	H	2B	3B	HR	RBI	BB-IB	HP	SO	AVG	OBP	SLG	AOPS	ABR	SB-CS	FA	FR	RNG	THR	GAMES AT POSITION	DL	BFW
1905	Phi A	29	60	5	10	2	1	0	3	3	0		.167	.206	.233	39	-4	2	.954	-4	101	124	C13,1b2,3b2/OR		-0.8

BARTON, BOB Robert Wilbur B7.30.1941 Norwood OH BR/TR/6-0/175(175-190) d9.17

YEAR	TM LG	G	AB	R	H	2B	3B	HR	RBI	BB-IB	HP	SO	AVG	OBP	SLG	AOPS	ABR	SB-CS	FA	FR	RNG	THR	GAMES AT POSITION	DL	BFW
1965	SF N	4	7	1	4	0	0	0	1	0-0	0	0	.571	.571	.571	217	1	0-0	1.000	1	0	0	C2		0.2
1966	SF N	43	91	4	16	2	1	0	3	5-2	0	5	.176	.216	.220	22	-10	0-0	.994	1	84	169	C39		-0.8
1967	SF N	7	19	0	4	0	0	0	1	0-0	1	2	.211	.250	.211	34	-2	0-0	1.000	1	230	66	C7		-0.1
1968	SF N	46	92	4	24	2	0	0	5	7-1	0	18	.261	.310	.283	80	-2	0-0	.995	6	109	131	C45		0.6
1969	SF N	49	106	5	18	2	0	0	4	9-1	1	19	.170	.241	.189	22	-11	0-0	.985	-8	76	60	C49		-1.9
1970	SD N	61	188	15	41	6	0	4	16	15-2	1	37	.218	.278	.314	61	-11	1-1	.995	4	71	148	C59		-0.5
1971	SD N	121	376	23	94	17	2	5	29	35-11	2	49	.250	.317	.346	94	-3	0-5	.981	10	89	147	C119		1.1
1972	SD N	29	88	1	17	1	0	0	9	2-0	0	19	.193	.209	.205	20	-10	2-0	.989	-4	125	110	C29		-1.3
1973	Cin N	3	1	0	0	0	0	0	0	1-0	0	0	.000	.500	.000	52	0	0-0	1.000	0	0	0	C2		0.0
1974	SD N	30	81	4	19	1	0	0	7	13-1	0	19	.235	.333	.247	69	-3	0-0	.981	6	87	245	C29	36	0.4
Total	10	393	1049	54	237	31	3	9	66	87-18	5	168	.226	.287	.287	64	-51	3-6	.987	17	91	141	C380	36	-2.3

BARTON, VINCE Vincent David B2.1.1908 Edmonton AL, Can. D9.13.1973 Toronto ON, Can. BL/TR/6-0/180 d7.17

YEAR	TM LG	G	AB	R	H	2B	3B	HR	RBI	BB-IB	HP	SO	AVG	OBP	SLG	AOPS	ABR	SB-CS	FA	FR	RNG	THR	GAMES AT POSITION	DL	BFW
1931	Chi N	66	239	45	57	10	1	13	50	21	9	40	.238	.323	.452	104	1	1	.964	-4	101	27	O61R		-0.7
1932	Chi N	36	134	19	30	2	3	3	15	8	1	22	.224	.273	.351	67	-7	0	1.000	-1	90	89	O34R		-1.0
Total	2	102	373	64	87	12	4	16	65	29	10	62	.233	.306	.416	91	-6	1	.976	-5	97	49	O95R		-1.7

BARTOSCH, DAVE David Robert B3.24.1917 St.Louis MO BR/TR/6-1/190 d4.28

YEAR	TM LG	G	AB	R	H	2B	3B	HR	RBI	BB-IB	HP	SO	AVG	OBP	SLG	AOPS	ABR	SB-CS	FA	FR	RNG	THR	GAMES AT POSITION	DL	BFW
1945	StL N	24	47	9	12	1	0	0	3	6	0		.255	.340	.277	71	-2	0	.964	1	120	112	O11(4/0/7)		-0.1

BASGALL, MONTY Romanus B2.8.1922 Pfeifer KS D9.22.2005 Sierra Vista AZ BR/TR/5-10.5/175* d4.19 C14 Col Sterling

YEAR	TM LG	G	AB	R	H	2B	3B	HR	RBI	BB-IB	HP	SO	AVG	OBP	SLG	AOPS	ABR	SB-CS	FA	FR	RNG	THR	GAMES AT POSITION	DL	BFW
1948	Pit N	38	51	12	11	1	0	2	6	3	0	13	.216	.259	.353	63	-3	0	1.000	3	110	60	2b22		0.0
1949	Pit N	107	308	25	67	9	1	2	26	31	1	32	.218	.291	.273	51	-21	1	.972	-3	96	98	2b98,3b3		-2.0
1951	Pit N	55	153	15	32	5	2	0	9	12	1	14	.209	.271	.268	44	-12	0-0	.969	6	106	100	2b55		-0.4
Total	3	200	512	52	110	15	3	4	41	46	2	51	.215	.282	.279	50	-36	1-0	.973	5	100	96	2b175,3b3		-2.4

BASHANG, AL Albert C. B8.22.1888 Cincinnati OH D6.23.1967 Cincinnati OH BB/TR/5-8/150 d7.30

YEAR	TM LG	G	AB	R	H	2B	3B	HR	RBI	BB-IB	HP	SO	AVG	OBP	SLG	AOPS	ABR	SB-CS	FA	FR	RNG	THR	GAMES AT POSITION	DL	BFW
1912	Det A	6	12	3	1	0	0	0	0	3	0		.083	.267	.083	2	-1	0	1.000	-0	92	0	O6(5/1/0)		-0.2
1918	Bro N	2	5	0	1	0	0	0	0	0	0		.200	.200	.200	22	-0	0	1.000	1	0	0	/O		0.0
Total	2	8	17	3	2	0	0	0	0	3	0	0	.118	.250	.118	8	-1	0	1.000	0	89	0	O7(5/1/0)		-0.2

BASHORE, WALT Walter Franklin (b Walter Franklin Beshore) B10.6.1909 Harrisburg PA D9.26.1984 Sebring FL BR/TR/6-0/170 d7.14

YEAR	TM LG	G	AB	R	H	2B	3B	HR	RBI	BB-IB	HP	SO	AVG	OBP	SLG	AOPS	ABR	SB-CS	FA	FR	RNG	THR	GAMES AT POSITION	DL	BFW
1936	Phi N	10	10	1	2	0	0	0	1	4	0	3	.200	.273	.200	26	-1	0	1.000	-1	58	0	O6C/3		-0.2

BASINSKI, EDDIE Edwin Frank "Bazooka","Fiddler" B11.4.1922 Buffalo NY BR/TR/6-1/172 d5.20

YEAR	TM LG	G	AB	R	H	2B	3B	HR	RBI	BB-IB	HP	SO	AVG	OBP	SLG	AOPS	ABR	SB-CS	FA	FR	RNG	THR	GAMES AT POSITION	DL	BFW
1944	Bro N	39	105	13	27	4	1	0	9	6	2	10	.257	.310	.314	77	-3	1	.960	-3	89	73	2b37,S3		-0.5
1945	Bro N	108	336	30	88	9	4	0	33	11	4	33	.262	.293	.313	69	-15	0	.926	-10	92	119	S101,2b6		-1.9
1947	Pit N	56	161	15	32	6	2	4	17	18	0	27	.199	.279	.335	61	-10	0	.972	-5	95	102	2b56		-1.2
Total	3	203	602	58	147	19	7	4	59	35	6	70	.244	.292	.319	68	-28	1	.925	-19	92	117	S104,2b99		-3.6

BASS, JOHN John Elias B1848 Charleston SC D9.25.1888 Denver CO 5-6/150 d5.4

YEAR	TM LG	G	AB	R	H	2B	3B	HR	RBI	BB-IB	HP	SO	AVG	OBP	SLG	AOPS	ABR	SB-CS	FA	FR	RNG	THR	GAMES AT POSITION	DL	BFW
1871	Cle NA	22	89	18	27	1	10	3	18	3		4	.303	.326	.640	179	8	0-1	.779	-7	74	59	S22/C		0.1
1872	Atl NA	2	7	0	1	0	0	0	1	0			.143	.143	.286	24	-1	0-0	.500	-1	0	0	O2R		-0.1
1877	Har N	1	4	1	1	0	0	0	0	0			.250	.250	.250	65	0		—	-0	0	0	/OL		0.0
Total	2 NA	24	96	18	28	2	10	3	19		1	0	.292	.313	.615	166	7	0-1	.779	-7	74	59	S22,O2R/C		0.0

BASS, KEVIN Kevin Charles B5.12.1959 Redwood City CA BB/TR/6-0/183* [MilA77 2/29] d4.9

YEAR	TM LG	G	AB	R	H	2B	3B	HR	RBI	BB-IB	HP	SO	AVG	OBP	SLG	AOPS	ABR	SB-CS	FA	FR	RNG	THR	GAMES AT POSITION	DL	BFW
1982	Mil A	18	9	4	0	0	0	0	0	1-0	0	1	.000	.100	.000	-73	-1	0-0	1.000	-1	72	0	O14(0/6/8),D2		-0.3
	Hou N	12	24	2	1	0	0	0	1	0-0	0	8	.042	.042	.042	-83	-6	0-0	.917	-1	72	0	O7(4/4/0)		-0.8
1983	Hou N	88	195	25	46	7	3	2	18	6-1	0	27	.236	.257	.333	67	-10	2-2	.945	-3	93	37	O52(0/5/47)		-1.6
1984	Hou N	121	331	33	86	17	5	2	29	6-1	1	57	.260	.279	.360	84	-9	5-5	.975	-0	101	93	O81(0/31/52)	11	-1.4
1985	Hou N	150	539	72	145	27	5	16	68	31-1	6	63	.269	.315	.427	108	4	19-8	.997	4	105	117	O141(10/105/39)		0.7
1986	†Hou N★	157	591	83	184	33	5	20	79	38-11	6	72	.311	.357	.486	134	26	22-13	.984	3	104	107	O155(2/41/133)		2.3
1987	Hou N	157	592	83	168	31	5	19	85	53-13	4	77	.284	.344	.449	113	10	21-8	.987	5	104	115	O155R		0.4
1988	Hou N	157	541	57	138	27	2	14	72	42-10	6	65	.255	.314	.390	106	3	31-6	.979	1	100	103	O147R		0.4
1989	Hou N	87	313	42	94	19	4	5	44	29-3	1	44	.300	.357	.435	131	13	11-4	.985	4	109	127	O84(31/0/53)	75	1.6
1990	SF N	61	214	25	54	9	1	7	32	14-3	2	26	.252	.303	.402	96	-2	2-2	.968	-7	79	51	O55R	99	-1.1
1991	SF N	124	361	36	84	10	4	10	40	36-8	4	56	.233	.307	.366	92	-5	7-4	.977	-0	90	142	O101(23/0/79)	34	-0.8
1992	SF N	89	265	25	71	11	3	0	30	16-1	1	53	.268	.310	.411	109	2	7-7	.983	-4	92	30	O72(56/0/21)	13	-0.5
	NY N	46	137	15	37	12	2	2	9	7-2	0	17	.270	.303	.431	107	1	7-2	.987	2	115	58	O39(28/0/13)		0.2
	Year	135	402	40	108	23	5	9	39	23-3	1	70	.269	.308	.418	108	3	14-9	.985	-2	100	40	O111(84/0/34)		-0.3
1993	Hou N	111	229	31	65	18	0	3	37	26-3	1	31	.284	.359	.402	107	3	7-1	.989	-2	89	85	O64(12/2/50)		0.0
1994	Hou N	82	203	37	63	15	1	6	35	28-6	1	24	.310	.393	.483	134	11	2-3	.977	-1	94	93	O57(11/0/47)		0.0
1995	Bal A	111	295	32	72	12	0	5	32	24-0	2	47	.244	.303	.336	65	-15	8-8	.984	-0	101	72	O77(32/0/53),D19		-2.0
Total	14	1571	4839	609	1308	248	40	118	611	357-63	37	668	.270	.323	.411	105	24	151-73	.982	-2	100	97	O1301(209/194/953),D21	232	-1.9

BASS, RANDY Randy William B3.13.1954 Lawton OK BL/TR/6-1/210(206-225) [MinA72 7/152] d9.3

YEAR	TM LG	G	AB	R	H	2B	3B	HR	RBI	BB-IB	HP	SO	AVG	OBP	SLG	AOPS	ABR	SB-CS	FA	FR	RNG	THR	GAMES AT POSITION	DL	BFW
1977	Min A	9	19	0	2	0	0	0	0	0-0	0	5	.105	.105	.105	-43	-4	0-0	—	0			D6		-0.4
1978	KC A	2	2	0	0	0	0	0	0	0-0	0	2	.000	.000	.000	-97	-1	0-0	—	0			/H		-0.1
1979	Mon N	2	1	0	0	0	0	0	0	0-0	0	1	.000	.000	.000	-99	0	0-0	1.000	0	0	0	/1		0.0
1980	SD N	19	49	5	14	0	1	3	8	7-1	1	7	.286	.386	.510	159	4	0-0	.985	-1	83	104	1b15		0.2
1981	SD N	69	176	13	37	4	1	4	20	20-1	1	28	.210	.293	.313	79	-5	0-1	.993	3	124	101	1b50		-0.6
1982	SD N	13	30	1	6	0	0	1	8	2-0	1	4	.200	.265	.300	64	-2	0-0	1.000	-0	84	159	1b9		-0.2

YEAR	TM LG	G	AB	R	H	2B	3B	HR	RBI	BB-IB	HP	SO	AVG	OBP	SLG	AOPS	ABR	SB-CS	FA	FR	RNG	THR	GAMES AT POSITION	DL	BFW
	Tex A	16	48	5	10	2	0	1	6	1-0	1	7	.208	.231	.313	53	-3	0-0	1.000	-0	83	156	1b6,D7		-0.4
Total 6		130	325	24	69	6	2	9	42	30-2	4	51	.212	.284	.326	77	-11	0-1	.993	1	109	112	1b81,D13		-1.5

BASS, DOC   William Capers (Also Played One Game in 1918 Under Name of Johnson)   B12.4.1898 Macon GA   D1.12.1970 Macon GA   BL/TL/5-10/165   d7.29 Col Mercer

YEAR	TM LG	G	AB	R	H	2B	3B	HR	RBI	BB-IB	HP	SO	AVG	OBP	SLG	AOPS	ABR	SB-CS	FA	FR	RNG	THR	GAMES AT POSITION	DL	BFW
1918	Bos N	2	1	1	1	0	0	0	0	0	0	1	1.000	1.000	1.000	533	0						/H		0.1

BASSETT, CHARLEY   Charles Edwin   B2.9.1863 Central Falls RI   D5.28.1942 Pawtucket RI   BR/TR/5-8/150   d7.22 Col Brown

YEAR	TM LG	G	AB	R	H	2B	3B	HR	RBI	BB-IB	HP	SO	AVG	OBP	SLG	AOPS	ABR	SB-CS	FA	FR	RNG	THR	GAMES AT POSITION	DL	BFW
1884	Pro N	27	79	10	11	2	1	0	6	4		15	.139	.181	.190	17	-7		.815	-2	100	75	3b13,S7,O2(1/1/0)/2		-0.8
1885	Pro N	82	285	21	41	8	2	0	16	19		60	.144	.197	.186	25	-23		.900	3	103	114	2b39,S23,3b20/C		-1.6
1886	KC N	90	342	41	89	19	8	2	32	36		43	.260	.331	.380	109	4	6	.886	9	111	95	S82,3b8		1.3
1887	Ind N	119	452	41	104	14	6	1	47	25	5	31	.230	.278	.294	61	-23	25	**.931**	18	**115**	111	2b119		-0.1
1888	Ind N	128	481	58	116	20	3	2	60	32	6	41	.241	.297	.308	91	-4	24	.922	-14	103	84	2b128		-1.3
1889	Ind N	127	477	64	117	12	5	4	68	37	3	38	.245	.304	.317	72	-20	15	.937	13	109	114	2b127		-0.2
1890	NY N	100	410	52	98	13	8	0	54	29	7	25	.239	.300	.310	78	-13	14	**.952**	19	109	107	2b100		0.9
1891	NY N	130	524	60	136	19	8	4	68	36	4	29	.260	.312	.349	96	-4	16	**.908**	6	96	101	3b121,2b9		0.4
1892	NY N	35	130	9	27	2	3	0	16	6	2	11	.208	.254	.269	59	-7	0	.938	8	115	94	2b30,3b5		0.2
	Lou N	79	313	36	67	5	5	2	35	15	0	19	.214	.250	.281	66	-14	16	.861	-1	109	118	3b73,2b6		-1.3
	Year	114	443	45	94	7	8	2	51	21	2	30	.212	.251	.278	64	-22	16	.858	7	109	119	3b78,2b36		-1.1
Total 9		917	3493	392	806	114	49	15	402	239	27	312	.231	.285	.304	76	-111	116	.932	59	109	108	2b559,3b240,S112,O2(1/1/0)/C		-2.5

BASSLER, JOHNNY   John Landis   B6.3.1895 Mechanics Grove PA   D6.29.1979 Santa Monica CA   BL/TR/5-9/170   d7.11 C4

YEAR	TM LG	G	AB	R	H	2B	3B	HR	RBI	BB-IB	HP	SO	AVG	OBP	SLG	AOPS	ABR	SB-CS	FA	FR	RNG	THR	GAMES AT POSITION	DL	BFW
1913	Cle A	1	2	0	0	0	0	0	0	0	0	0	.000	.000	.000	-97	-1		.500	-1	62	0	/C		-0.2
1914	Cle A	43	77	5	14	1	1	0	6	15	1	8	.182	.323	.221	61	-3	3-2	.946	-2	88	129	C25/3OR		-0.3
1921	Det A	119	388	37	119	18	5	0	56	58	*3	16	.307	.401	.379	101	4	2-1	.975	-4	88	115	C114		0.8
1922	Det A	121	372	41	120	14	0	0	41	62	2	12	.323	.422	.360	109	10	2-1	.980	-9	80	106	C118		0.9
1923	Det A	135	383	45	114	12	3	0	49	76	0	13	.298	.414	.345	103	7	2-2	.988	9	113	140	C128		2.2
1924	Det A	124	379	43	131	20	3	1	68	62	3	11	.346	.441	.422	125	19	2-1	.979	-6	94	104	C122		2.0
1925	Det A	121	344	40	96	19	3	0	52	74	1	6	.279	.408	.352	96	3	1-1	.983	-10	87	87	C118		0.0
1926	Det A	66	174	20	53	8	1	0	22	45	0	6	.305	.447	.362	111	7	0-0	1.000	1	85	124	C63		1.1
1927	Det A	81	200	19	57	7	0	0	24	45	0	9	.285	.416	.320	92	1	1-0	.974	-1	91	101	C67		0.4
Total 9		811	2319	250	704	99	16	1	318	437	10	81	.304	.416	.341	104	47	13-8	.980	-21	92	112	C756/OR3		6.9

BASTIAN, CHARLIE   Charles J.   B7.4.1860 Philadelphia PA   D1.18.1932 Pennsauken NJ   BR/TR/5-6.5/145   d8.18

YEAR	TM LG	G	AB	R	H	2B	3B	HR	RBI	BB-IB	HP	SO	AVG	OBP	SLG	AOPS	ABR	SB-CS	FA	FR	RNG	THR	GAMES AT POSITION	DL	BFW
1884	Wil U	**17**	60	6	12	1	3	2		3			.200	.238	.417	92	-3		.907	11	153	60	2b16/PS		0.8
	KC U	11	46	6	9	3	0	1		4			.196	.260	.326	88	-2		.950	1	108	83	2b11		-0.1
	Year	28	106	12	21	4	3	3		7			.198	.248	.377	90	-5		.923	12	135	69	2b27/PS		0.7
1885	Phi N	103	389	63	65	11	5	4	29	35		82	.167	.236	.252	59	-17		.890	8	102	117	S103		-0.6
1886	Phi N	105	373	46	81	9	11	2	38	33		73	.217	.281	.316	81	-9	29	**.945**	-5	108	59	2b87,S10,3b8		-1.0
1887	Phi N	60	221	33	47	11	1	1	21	19	3	29	.213	.284	.285	55	-13	11	.921	-11	92	95	2b39,S18,3b4		-1.9
1888	Phi N	80	275	30	53	4	1	1	17	27	7	41	.193	.282	.225	60	-11	12	.945	10	116	59	2b65,3b14/S		0.1
1889	Chi N	46	155	19	21	0	0	0	10	25		46	.135	.256	.135	10	-19	1	.919	-3	103	58	S45/2		-1.8
1890	Chi P	80	283	38	54	10	5	0	29	33	5	37	.191	.287	.261	45	-23	4	.880	-0	94	98	S64,2b12,3b4		-2.5
1891	Cin AA	1	4	0	0	0	0	0	0	0			.000	.000	.000	-92	-1	0	1.000	1	118	199	/2		0.0
	Phi N	1	0	0	0	0	0	0	0	0			—	—	—			0	1.000	0	133	0	/S		0.0
Total 8		504	1806	241	342	49	26	11	144	179	15	308	.189	.268	.264	57	-98	57	.892	1	99	106	S243,2b232,3b30/P		-7.0

BATCH, EMIL   Emil "Heinie","Ace"   B1.21.1880 Brooklyn NY   D8.23.1926 Brooklyn NY   BR/TR/5-7/170   d9.13

YEAR	TM LG	G	AB	R	H	2B	3B	HR	RBI	BB-IB	HP	SO	AVG	OBP	SLG	AOPS	ABR	SB-CS	FA	FR	RNG	THR	GAMES AT POSITION	DL	BFW
1904	Bro N	28	94	9	24	1	2	2	7	1	1		.255	.271	.372	100	-1	6	.880	-1	104	100	3b28		-0.2
1905	Bro N	145	568	64	143	20	11	5	49	26	0		.252	.285	.352	96	-6	21	.887	-5	91	116	3b145		-0.8
1906	Bro N	59	203	23	52	7	6	0	11	15	1		.256	.311	.350	115	2	3	.964	0	78	0	O50(47/0/3),3b2		0.0
1907	Bro N	116	388	38	96	10	3	0	31	23	1		.247	.291	.289	89	-6	7	.937	-4	95	109	O102(81/1/20),3b2/2S		-1.9
Total 4		348	1253	134	315	38	22	7	98	65	3		.251	.290	.334	98	-11	37	.886	-11	93	112	3b177,O152(128/1/23)/S2		-2.9

BATEMAN, JOHN   John Alvin   B7.21.1940 Killeen TX   D12.3.1996 Sand Springs OK   BR/TR/6-3/220(200-225)   d4.19

YEAR	TM LG	G	AB	R	H	2B	3B	HR	RBI	BB-IB	HP	SO	AVG	OBP	SLG	AOPS	ABR	SB-CS	FA	FR	RNG	THR	GAMES AT POSITION	DL	BFW
1963	Hou N	128	404	23	85	8	6	10	59	13-1	9	103	.210	.249	.334	71	-17	0-0	.971	-1	88	109	C115		-1.3
1964	Hou N	74	221	18	42	8	0	5	19	17-5	1	48	.190	.249	.294	56	-13	0-1	.987	5	70	67	C72		-0.5
1965	Hou N	45	142	15	28	3	1	7	14	12-3	0	37	.197	.256	.380	83	-4	0-1	.985	-0	144	97	C39		-0.3
1966	Hou N	131	433	39	121	24	3	17	70	20-9	5	74	.279	.315	.467	123	12	0-0	.981	2	103	75	C121		2.0
1967	Hou N	76	252	16	48	9	0	2	17	17-11	2	53	.190	.245	.250	44	-18	0-0	.989	0	90	85	C71		21	-1.6
1968	Hou N	111	350	28	87	19	0	4	33	23-16	3	46	.249	.297	.337	93	-3	1-1	.985	-2	80	63	C108		0.0
1969	Mon N	74	235	16	49	4	0	8	19	12-6	1	42	.209	.250	.328	60	-14	0-2	.985	-2	72	77	C66		21	-1.4
1970	Mon N	139	520	51	123	21	5	15	68	28-9	1	75	.237	.275	.383	75	-21	8-4	.983	6	143	115	C137		-0.9
1971	Mon N	139	492	34	119	17	3	10	56	19-3	4	87	.242	.273	.350	75	-18	1-0	.985	-2	83	110	C137		-2.0
1972	Mon N	18	29	2	7	1	0	0	3	3-0	0	4	.241	.313	.276	67	-1	0-0	1.000	-1	281	0	C7		-0.2
	Phi N	82	252	10	56	9	0	3	17	8-6	1	39	.222	.246	.294	52	-16	0-1	.972	-1	86	110	C80		-1.6
	Year	100	281	10	63	10	0	3	20	11-6	1	43	.224	.253	.292	54	-17	0-1	.973	-2	100	87	C87		-1.8
Total 10		1017	3330	250	765	123	18	81	375	172-69	27	610	.230	.271	.350	76	-113	10-10	.982	-1	98	92	C953	42	-7.8

BATES, CHARLIE   Charles William   B9.17.1907 Philadelphia PA   D1.29.1980 Topeka KS   BR/TR/5-10/165   d9.22

YEAR	TM LG	G	AB	R	H	2B	3B	HR	RBI	BB-IB	HP	SO	AVG	OBP	SLG	AOPS	ABR	SB-CS	FA	FR	RNG	THR	GAMES AT POSITION	DL	BFW
1927	Phi A	9	38	5	9	2	2	0	2	3	0	5	.237	.293	.395	73	-2	3-1	.857	-1	91	98	O9(0/1/8)		-0.3

BATES, DEL   Delbert Oakley   B6.12.1940 Seattle WA   BL/TR/6-2/195   d5.6 Col Everett (WA) CC

YEAR	TM LG	G	AB	R	H	2B	3B	HR	RBI	BB-IB	HP	SO	AVG	OBP	SLG	AOPS	ABR	SB-CS	FA	FR	RNG	THR	GAMES AT POSITION	DL	BFW
1970	Phi N	22	60	1	8	2	0	0	1	6-1	1	15	.133	.257	.167	16	-7	0-1	.992	-0	62	125	C20		-0.7

BATES, BUD   Hubert Edgar   B3.16.1912 Los Angeles CA   D4.29.1987 Long Beach CA   BR/TR/6-0/165   d9.16

YEAR	TM LG	G	AB	R	H	2B	3B	HR	RBI	BB-IB	HP	SO	AVG	OBP	SLG	AOPS	ABR	SB-CS	FA	FR	RNG	THR	GAMES AT POSITION	DL	BFW
1939	Phi N	15	58	6	15	2	0	1	2	2	0	8	.259	.283	.345	70	-3	1	.978	1	116	82	O14(1/13/0)		-0.2

BATES, JASON   Jason Charles   B1.5.1971 Downey CA   BB/TR/5-11/170(170-192)   [ColN92 7/207]   d4.26 Col Arizona

YEAR	TM LG	G	AB	R	H	2B	3B	HR	RBI	BB-IB	HP	SO	AVG	OBP	SLG	AOPS	ABR	SB-CS	FA	FR	RNG	THR	GAMES AT POSITION	DL	BFW
1995	†Col N	116	322	42	86	17	4	8	46	42-3	2	70	.267	.355	.419	80	-8	3-6	.991	-3	98	114	2b82,S20,3b15		-0.3
1996	Col N	88	160	19	33	8	1	1	9	23-1	2	34	.206	.312	.287	48	-11	2-1	.978	-3	111	93	2b37,S18,3b12		-1.2
1997	Col N	62	121	17	29	10	0	3	11	15-1	3	27	.240	.338	.397	75	-4	0-1	1.000	-4	71	148	2b22,S16,3b6		-0.7
1998	Col N	53	74	10	14	3	0	0	3	8-6	0	21	.189	.268	.230	27	-8	0-0	.974	-5	89	62	2b17,3b3,S3	24	-1.2
Total 4		319	677	88	162	38	5	12	69	88-6	7	152	.239	.332	.363	66	-31	5-8	.987	-9	97	108	2b158,S57,3b36	24	-3.4

BATES, JOHNNY   John William   B1.10.1884 Steubenville OH   D2.10.1949 Steubenville OH   BL/TR/5-7/168   d4.12

YEAR	TM LG	G	AB	R	H	2B	3B	HR	RBI	BB-IB	HP	SO	AVG	OBP	SLG	AOPS	ABR	SB-CS	FA	FR	RNG	THR	GAMES AT POSITION	DL	BFW
1906	Bos N	140	504	52	127	21	5	6	54	36	10		.252	.315	.349	110	5	9	.958	-11	70	91	O140(7/133/0)		-1.4
1907	Bos N	126	447	52	116	18	12	2	49	39	7		.260	.329	.367	118	9	11	.979	-3	107	111	O120(1/1/118)		0.0
1908	Bos N	127	445	48	115	14	6	1	29	35			.258	.315	.324	106	3	25	.948	-4	100	54	O117(101/8/8)		-0.9
1909	Bos N	63	236	27	68	15	3	1	23	20	4		.288	.354	.390	125	7	15	.945	5	178	0	O60L		0.9
	Phi N	77	266	43	78	11	1	1	15	28	2		.293	.364	.353	122	8	22	.959	-1	123	141	O73(11/62/0)		0.4
	Year	140	502	70	146	26	4	2	38	48	6		.291	.360	.371	123	15	37	.952	4	149		O133(71/62/0)		1.3
1910	Phi N	135	498	91	152	26	11	3	61	61	4	49	.305	.385	.420	130	20	31	.954	5	101	131	O131(25/103/3)		2.0
1911	Cin N	148	518	89	151	24	13	1	61	103	6	59	.292	.415	.394	131	29	33	.966	1	103	96	O147(0/145/2)		1.3
1912	Cin N	81	239	45	69	12	7	1	29	47	0	16	.289	.406	.410	127	11	10	.950	5	103	151	O65(1/64/0)		1.1
1913	Cin N	131	407	63	113	13	7	6	51	67	6	30	.278	.387	.388	122	15	21-9	.946	2	96	131	O111(0/24/88)		1.3
1914	Cin N	58	155	29	39	7	5	2	15	28	4	17	.252	.380	.400	158	7	4	.913	-6	95	71	O54C		-0.3
	Chi N	9	8	2	1	0	0	0	1	1	1		.125	.300	.125	28	-1	0	1.000	0	196		O3(0/2/1)		0.0
	Year	67	163	31	40	7	5	2	16	29	5		.245	.376	.387	124	6	4	.917	-5	99	92	O57(0/56/1)		-0.3
	Bal F	59	190	24	58	6	3	1	29	38	3	18	.305	.429	.384	119	5	6	.950	-1	99	99	O59(12/48/0)		0.0
Total 9		1154	3913	565	1087	169	73	25	417	503	49	190	.278	.367	.377	121	118	187-9	.955	-7	103	100	O1080(218/644/220)		5.1

BATES, RAY   Raymond   B2.8.1890 Paterson NJ   D8.15.1970 Tucson AZ   BR/TR/6-0/165   d5.31 Mil 1918

YEAR	TM LG	G	AB	R	H	2B	3B	HR	RBI	BB-IB	HP	SO	AVG	OBP	SLG	AOPS	ABR	SB-CS	FA	FR	RNG	THR	GAMES AT POSITION	DL	BFW
1913	Cle A	27	30	4	5	0	0	0	4	3	1	9	.167	.265	.300	63	-2	3	.905	0	114	244	3b12,O2C		-0.1
1917	Phi A	127	485	47	115	20	7	2	66	21	6	39	.237	.277	.320	83	-12	12	.933	9	104	86	3b124		0.0
Total 2		154	515	51	120	20	9	2	70	24	7	48	.233	.277	.318	82	-14	15	.932	9	104	93	3b136,O2C		-0.1

YEAR	TM LG	G	AB	R	H	2B	3B	HR	RBI	BB-IB	HP	SO	AVG	OBP	SLG	AOPS	ABR	SB-CS	FA	FR	RNG	THR	GAMES AT POSITION	DL	BFW

BATES, BILLY   William Derrick   B12.7.1963 Houston TX   BL/TR/5-7/155*   [MilA85 4/81]   d8.17   Col Texas

1989	Mil A	7	14	3	3	0	0	0	0	0-0	0	1	.214	.214	.214	21	-2	2-0	.938	3	125	251	2b7	20	0.2
1990	Mil A	14	29	6	3	1	0	0	0	4-0	0	7	.103	.206	.138	-0	-4	4-0	.962	-0	113	84	2b14		-0.3
	†Cin N	8	5	2	0	0	0	0	0	0-0	0	2	.000	.000	.000	-96	-1	2-1	1.000	-1	35	0	/2		-0.3
Total	2	29	48	11	6	1	0	0	0	4-0	0	10	.125	.189	.146	-4	-7	8-1	.953	1	111	125	2b22	20	-0.4

BATHE, BILL   William David   B10.14.1960 Downey CA   BR/TR/6-2/200*   [OakA81 8/196]   d4.12   Col Pepperdine

1986	Oak A	39	103	9	19	3	0	5	11	2-0	1	20	.184	.208	.359	54	-7	0-0	.991	-3	64	92	C39		-0.9
1989	†SF N	30	32	3	9	1	0	0	6	0-0	0	7	.281	.273	.313	71	-1	0-0	1.000	1	54	203	C7		-0.1
1990	SF N	52	48	3	11	0	0	3	12	7-2	0	12	.229	.321	.458	118	1	0-0	1.000	-0	111	113	C8	59	0.1
Total	3	121	183	15	39	4	1	8	29	9-2	1	39	.213	.251	.377	75	-7	0-0	.992	-3	67	97	C54	59	-0.9

BATISTA, TONY   Leocadio Francisco   B12.9.1973 Puerto Plata, D.R.   BR/TR/6-0/190(165-210)   d6.3

1996	Oak A	74	238	38	71	10	2	6	25	19-0	1	49	.298	.350	.433	98	-1	7-3	.988	9	120	106	2b52,3b18,S4,D4		1.0
1997	Oak A	68	188	22	38	10	1	4	18	14-0	2	31	.202	.265	.330	54	-13	2-2	.970	7	112	96	S61,3b4/2D	16	-0.3
1998	Ari N	106	293	46	80	16	1	18	41	18-0	3	52	.273	.318	.519	116	5	1-1	.994	-1	93	116	2b41,S34,3b15		0.8
1999	Ari N	44	144	16	37	5	0	5	21	16-3	2	17	.257	.335	.396	85	-3	2-0	.979	9	114	123	S43		0.9
	Tor A	98	375	61	107	25	1	26	79	22-1	0	79	.285	.328	.565	121	10	2-0	.975	8	106	104	S98		2.4
2000	Tor A★	154	620	96	163	32	2	41	114	35-1	6	121	.263	.307	.519	101	-3	5-4	.963	12	107	**120**	3b154		0.9
2001	Tor A	72	271	29	56	11	1	13	45	13-1	4	66	.207	.251	.399	67	-14	0-1	.953	7	111	173	3b72		-0.7
	Bal A	84	308	41	82	16	5	12	42	19-0	1	47	.266	.305	.468	106	1	5-1	.934	2	103	102	D33,3b29,S20		0.4
	Year	156	579	70	138	27	6	25	87	32-1	5	113	.238	.280	.435	87	-14	5-2	.948	9	109	153	3b101,D33,S20		-0.3
2002	Bal A★	161	615	90	150	36	1	31	87	50-9	11	107	.244	.309	.457	106	4	5-4	.962	6	107	134	3b154,D7		1.0
2003	Bal A	161	631	76	148	20	1	26	99	28-4	5	102	.235	.270	.393	73	-28	4-3	.950	0	104	119	3b154,D7		-2.6
2004	Mon N	157	606	76	146	30	2	32	110	26-4	4	78	.241	.272	.455	81	-20	14-6	.954	3	109	**123**	3b155		-1.4
Total	9	1179	4289	591	1078	211	17	214	681	260-23	42	749	.251	.298	.458	93	-62	47-25	.956	62	107	127	3b755,S260,2b94,D52	16	2.4

BATISTA, RAFAEL   Rafael (Sanchez)   B10.20.1947 San Pedro de Macoris, D.R.   BL/TL/6-1/195*   d6.17

1973	Hou N	12	15	2	4	0	0	0	2	1-1	0	6	.267	.313	.267	62	-1	0-0	1.000	-0	56	40	1b8		-0.1
1975	Hou N	10	10	0	3	1	0	0	0	0-0	0	4	.300	.300	.400	100	0	0-0			0		/H		0.0
Total	2	22	25	2	7	1	0	0	2	1-1	0	10	.280	.308	.320	77	-1	0-0	1.000	-0	56	40	1b8		-0.1

BATISTE, KEVIN   Kevin Wade   B10.21.1966 Galveston TX   BR/TR/6-2/187   [TorA85 2/53]   d6.13

1989	Tor A	6	8	1	2	0	0	0	0	0-0	0	5	.250	.250	.250	42	-1	1-0	1.000	0	135	0	O5(2/0/3)		0.0

BATISTE, KIM   Kimothy Emil   B3.15.1968 New Orleans LA   BR/TR/6-0/193(175-200)   [PhiN87 3/78]   d9.8

1991	Phi N	10	27	2	6	0	0	1	1	1-1	0	8	.222	.250	.222	34	-2	0-1	.970	1	111	113	S7		-0.2
1992	Phi N	44	136	9	28	4	0	1	10	4-1	0	18	.206	.224	.257	37	-12	0-0	.922	-11	76	79	S41		-2.2
1993	†Phi N	79	156	14	44	7	1	5	29	3-2	1	29	.282	.298	.436	96	-2	0-1	.956	5	86	51	3b58,S24		0.4
1994	Phi N	64	209	17	49	6	0	1	13	1-0	1	32	.234	.239	.278	34	-21	1-1	.919	-3	94	64	3b42,S17		-2.2
1996	SF N	54	130	17	27	6	0	3	11	5-1	0	33	.208	.235	.323	47	-11	3-3	.847	-5	85	188	3b25,S7	15	-1.6
Total	5	251	658	59	154	23	1	10	64	14-5	2	120	.234	.250	.318	52	-48	4-6	.908	-15	89	92	3b125,S96	15	-5.8

BATSCH, BILL   William McKinley   B5.18.1892 Mingo Junction OH   D12.31.1963 Canton OH   BR/TR/5-10.5/168   d9.9   Col Bethany

1916	Pit N	1	1	0	1	0	0	0	1	0-0	0	0	—	1.000	—	218	0	0-0			0		/H		0.0

BATTAM, LARRY   Lawrence J.   B5.1.1878 Brooklyn NY   D1.27.1938 Brooklyn NY   5-11/166   d9.28

1895	NY N	2	4	0	1	0	0	0	2	0-0	0	1	.250	.500	.250	99	0	0-0	.667	-1	83	0	3b2		0.0

BATTEN, GEORGE   George Burnett   B10.7.1891 Haddonfield NJ   D8.4.1972 New Port Richey FL   BR/TR/5-11/165   d9.28

1912	NY A	1	3	0	0	0	0	0	0	0-0	0	0	.000	.000	.000	-94	-1	0-0	1.000	-0	55	0	/2		-0.1

BATTEY, EARL   Earl Jesse   B1.5.1935 Los Angeles CA   D11.15.2003 Ocala FL   BR/TR/6-1/205(205-225)   d9.10

1955	Chi A	5	7	1	2	0	0	0	1	1-0	1	0	.286	.444	.286	97	0	0-0	1.000	1	*0*	*181*	C5		0.1
1956	Chi A	4	4	1	1	0	0	0	0	1-0	0	1	.250	.400	.250	74	0	0-0	.800	1	*0*	*0*	C3		-0.1
1957	Chi A	48	115	12	20	2	3	3	6	11-1	0	38	.174	.246	.322	54	-8	0-2	.989	3	*110*	*107*	C43		-0.4
1958	Chi A	68	168	24	38	8	0	8	26	24-1	2	34	.226	.325	.417	106	2	1-0	.988	2	*98*	*105*	C49		0.6
1959	Chi A	26	64	9	14	1	2	2	7	8-0	0	13	.219	.306	.391	91	-1	0-0	.990	2	*90*	*147*	C20		0.2
1960	Was A	137	466	49	126	24	1	15	60	48-5	8	68	.270	.346	.427	110	7	4-5	.982	10	**154**	**141**	C136		2.3
1961	Min A	133	460	70	139	24	1	17	55	53-3	3	66	.302	.377	.470	118	13	3-3	.993	11	139	78	C131		2.9
1962	Min A★	148	522	58	146	20	3	11	57	57-3	0	48	.280	.348	.393	96	-2	0-0	.991	14	148	95	C147		1.9
1963	Min A	147	508	64	145	17	1	26	84	61-8	8	75	.285	.369	.476	133	24	0-0	.994	0	133	79	C146		4.0
1964	Min A	131	405	33	110	17	1	12	52	51-6	1	49	.272	.348	.407	111	7	1-1	.990	-1	113	78	C125		1.2
1965	†Min A★	131	394	36	117	22	2	6	60	50-7	2	23	.297	.375	.409	119	12	0-0	.986	7	**158**	110	C128		2.6
1966	Min A★	115	364	30	93	12	1	4	34	43-7	3	30	.255	.337	.327	87	-5	4-1	.995	12	109	92	C113		1.4
1967	Min A	48	109	6	18	3	1	0	8	13-1	0	24	.165	.254	.211	36	-8	0-0	.987	-1	68	89	C41	23	-0.9
Total	13	1141	3586	393	969	150	17	104	449	421-42	28	470	.270	.349	.409	106	41	13-12	.990	66	*131*	*98*	C1087	23	15.8

BATTIN, JOE   Joseph V.   B11.11.1851 Philadelphia PA   D12.10.1937 Akron OH   BR/TR   d8.11   M2/U2

1871	Cle NA	1	3	0	0	0	0	0	1			0	.000	.250	.000	-21	0	0-0	1.000	0	*0*	*0*	/OR		0.0
1873	Ath NA	1	5	4	3	0	0	0	2	1		0	.600	.667	.600	260	1	0-0	.667	0	*491*	*0*	/OC		0.1
1874	Ath NA	51	226	40	52	11	1	0	27	1		7	.230	.233	.288	61	-11	3-2	.813	3	*108*	*174*	2b41,O7(0/2/5),S5		-0.8
1875	StL NA	67	284	31	71	6	3	0	33	0		6	.250	.250	.292	97	0	15-3	.861	14	**115**	*130*	2b62,3b6,C2/OC		1.0
1876	StL N	64	283	34	85	11	4	0	46	6		6	.300	.315	.367	134	11		**.867**	15	**115**	**203**	3b63/2		2.3
1877	StL N	57	226	28	45	3	7	1	22	6		17	.199	.220	.288	62	-10		.823	-3	114	161	3b32,2b21,O5C/P		-0.9
1882	Pit AA	34	133	13	28	5	1	1		3			.211	.228	.286	76	-3		.876	17	137	135	3b34		1.3
1883	Pit AA	98	388	42	83	9	6	1		11			.214	.236	.276	67	-14		**.891**	29	**127**	97	3b98,P2,M		1.5
1884	Pit AA	43	158	10	28	1	2	0		3	1		.177	.198	.209	33	-12		.919	8	122	73	3b43,M		-0.3
	CP U	18	69	8	13	2	0	0		0			.188	.188	.217	23	-9		.908	3	125	151	3b18,M		0.0
	Bal U	17	59	3	6	1	0	0		0			.102	.102	.119	-30	-11		.813	2	122	60	3b17		-0.8
	Year	35	128	11	19	3	0	0		0			.148	.148	.172	-3	-20		.868	10	124	112	3b35		-0.8
1890	Syr AA	29	119	15	25	2	1	0	13	8	0		.210	.260	.244	54	-7	8	.794	-6	89	39	3b29		-1.1
Total	4 NA	120	518	75	126	17	4	0	62	3		13	.243	.248	.292	80	-10	18-5	.842	17	112	148	2b103,O10(0/4/6),3b6,S5,C2		0.3
Total	6	360	1435	163	309	34	21	3		37	1	23	.218	.238	.277	67	-55	8	.876	69	120	121	3b334,2b22,O5C,P3		2.0

BATTLE, ALLEN   Allen Zelmo   B11.29.1968 Grantham NC   BR/TR/6-0/170*   [StLN91 10/259]   d4.26   Col South Alabama

1995	StL N	61	118	13	32	5	0	0	2	15-0	1	26	.271	.358	.314	78	-3	3-3	.984	1	121	0	O32(15/7/14)		-0.4
1996	Oak A	47	130	20	25	3	0	1	5	17-1	2	26	.192	.293	.238	38	-12	10-2	.988	-1	96	84	O47(24/27/0)		-1.1
Total	2	108	248	33	57	8	0	1	7	32-1	3	52	.230	.324	.274	56	-15	13-5	.986	-0	107	48	O79(39/34/14)		-1.5

BATTLE, HOWARD   Howard Dion   B3.25.1972 Biloxi MS   BR/TR/6-0/208(197-210)   [TorA90 4/123]   d9.5

1995	Tor A	9	15	3	3	0	0	0	4	4-0	0	8	.200	.368	.200	53	-1	1-0	1.000	-1	75	0	3b6/D		-0.2
1996	Phi N	5	5	0	0	0	0	0	0	0-0	0	2	.000	.000	.000	-99	-1	0-0	—	-0	0	0	/3		-0.2
1999	†Atl N	15	17	2	6	0	0	1	5	2-0	0	3	.353	.421	.529	140	1	0-0	1.000	-0	76	0	3b6		0.1
Total	3	29	37	5	9	0	0	1	9	6-0	0	13	.243	.349	.324	75	-1	1-0	1.000	-2	73	0	3b13/D		-0.3

BATTLE, JIM   James Milton   B3.26.1901 Bailey TX   D9.30.1965 Chico CA   BR/TR/6-1/170   d9.9

1927	Chi A	5	8	1	3	0	0	0	1	0-0	0	0	.375	.375	.625	160	0	0-0	1.000	-1	68	0	3b4,S2		0.0

BATTS, MATT   Matthew Daniel   B10.16.1921 San Antonio TX   BR/TR/5-11/200(200-214)   d9.10   Col Baylor

1947	Bos A	7	16	3	8	1	0	1	5	1	0	1	.500	.529	.750	236	3	0-0	1.000	-0	*121*	*98*	C6		0.3
1948	Bos A	46	118	13	37	12	0	1	24	15	0	9	.314	.391	.441	115	3	0-0	.986	-1	*120*	*88*	C41		0.4
1949	Bos A	60	157	23	38	9	1	3	31	25	1	22	.242	.350	.369	84	-3	1-0	.977	1	*145*	*82*	C50		-0.3
1950	Bos A	75	238	27	65	15	3	4	34	18	1	19	.273	.327	.412	80	-8	0-0	.994	1	*121*	*64*	C73		-0.3
1951	Bos A	11	29	1	4	1	0	0	2	1	0	6	.138	.167	.172	-8	-4	0-0	.975	-0	*138*	*148*	C11		-0.4
	StL A	79	248	26	75	17	1	5	31	21	0	21	.302	.357	.440	111	4	2-0	.960	-8	*91*	*113*	C64		-0.1
	Year	90	277	27	79	18	1	5	33	22	0	23	.285	.338	.412	98	-1	2-0	.962	-8	*96*	*117*	C75		-0.5
1952	Det A	56	173	11	41	4	1	3	13	14	1	22	.237	.298	.324	72	-7	1-0	.983	2	*104*	*134*	C55	33	-0.2

YEAR	TM LG	G	AB	R	H	2B	3B	HR	RBI	BB-IB	HP	SO	AVG	OBP	SLG	AOPS	ABR	SB-CS	FA	FR	RNG	THR	GAMES AT POSITION	DL	BFW
1953	Det A	116	374	38	104	24	3	6	42	24	0	36	.278	.322	.406	97	-3	2-3	.986	-15	77	114	C103		-1.4
1954	Det A	12	21	1	6	1	0	0	5	2	0	4	.286	.333	.333	89	0	0-0	.967	1	153	167	C8		0.1
	Chi A	55	158	16	36	7	1	3	19	17	0	15	.228	.299	.342	74	-6	0-1	.992	5	124	104	C42		0.1
	Year	67	179	17	42	8	1	3	24	19	0	19	.235	.303	.341	76	-6	0-1	.989	6	127	111	C50		0.2
1955	Cin N	26	71	4	18	4	1	0	13	4-0	0	11	.254	.286	.338	63	-4	0-0	.986	0	119	81	C21		-0.3
1956	Cin N	3	2	0	0	0	0	0	0	1-0	0	1	.000	.333	.000	0	0	0-0	—	0			/H		0.0
Total	10	546	1605	163	432	95	11	26	219	143-0	3	163	.269	.329	.391	89	-25	6-4	.983	-15	108	102	C474	33	-1.8

BAUER, HANK   Henry Albert B7.31.1922 E.St.Louis IL   BR/TR/6-0/192* d9.6   M8/C1

YEAR	TM LG	G	AB	R	H	2B	3B	HR	RBI	BB-IB	HP	SO	AVG	OBP	SLG	AOPS	ABR	SB-CS	FA	FR	RNG	THR	GAMES AT POSITION	DL	BFW
1948	NY A	19	50	6	9	1	1	1	9	4	0	13	.180	.268	.300	51	-4	1-0	.964	0	103	115	O14(8/0/7)		-0.4
1949	†NY A	103	301	56	82	6	6	10	45	37	1	42	.272	.354	.432	107	1	2-2	.977	1	92	169	O95(21/25/60)		-0.1
1950	†NY A	113	415	72	133	16	2	13	70	35	5	41	.320	.380	.463	118	10	2-3	.987	2	105	93	O110(36/0/82)		0.7
1951	†NY A	118	348	53	103	19	3	10	54	42	1	39	.296	.373	.454	128	13	5-2	.990	2	103	108	O107(51/1/62)		1.1
1952	†NY A★	141	553	86	162	31	6	17	74	50	3	61	.293	.355	.463	134	23	6-7	.984	-3	89	141	O139(18/0/122)		1.5
1953	†NY A★	133	437	77	133	20	6	10	57	59	6	45	.304	.394	.446	131	21	2-3	.992	3	102	123	O126(3/1/124)		1.8
1954	NY A★	114	377	73	111	16	5	12	54	40	4	42	.294	.360	.459	128	13	4-4	.989	-2	97	85	O108(8/0/104)		0.7
1955	†NY A	139	492	97	137	20	5	20	53	56-1	8	65	.278	.360	.461	122	14	8-4	.981	5	106	136	O133(5/0/131)/C		1.5
1956	†NY A	147	539	96	130	18	7	26	84	59-3	2	72	.241	.316	.445	103	-1	4-2	.969	-6	90	98	O146(7/0/143)		-1.1
1957	†NY A	137	479	70	124	22	9	18	65	42-4	1	64	.259	.321	.455	112	6	7-2	.986	-5	93	93	O135(3/0/134)		-0.3
1958	†NY A	128	452	62	121	22	6	12	50	32-1	1	56	.268	.316	.423	106	2	3-2	.980	-5	93	79	O123(2/0/121)		-0.7
1959	NY A	114	341	44	81	20	0	9	39	33-1	2	54	.238	.307	.375	90	-5	4-2	.972	-8	88	41	O111(4/0/108)		-1.6
1960	KC A	95	255	30	70	15	0	3	31	21-1	1	36	.275	.326	.369	89	-4	1-0	.978	-5	79	107	O67R		-1.1
1961	KC A	43	106	11	28	-3	1	3	18	9-0	0	6	.264	.319	.396	89	-2	1-0	.958	-2	85	103	O35(11/2/27),M		-0.5
Total	14	1544	5145	833	1424	229	57	164	703	521-11	34	638	.277	.346	.439	114	87	50-33	.982	-21	95	106	O1449(177/29/1292)/C		1.5

BAUGHMAN, JUSTIN   Justin Reis B8.1.1974 Mountain View CA   BR/TR/5-11/180* [CalA95 5/116] d5.17   Col Lewis & Clark   [DL 1999 Ana A 182]

YEAR	TM LG	G	AB	R	H	2B	3B	HR	RBI	BB-IB	HP	SO	AVG	OBP	SLG	AOPS	ABR	SB-CS	FA	FR	RNG	THR	GAMES AT POSITION	DL	BFW
1998	Ana A	63	196	24	50	11	1	1	20	9-0	1	36	.255	.277	.327	56	-13	10-4	.977	-1	101	64	2b59,S3/D		-1.0
2000	Ana A	16	22	4	5	2	0	0	1-0	1	5	.227	.261	.318	44	-2	3-0	.958	-0	132	147	2b5,S5,D4		-0.1
Total	2	79	218	28	55	11	1	1	20	7-0	1	38	.252	.275	.326	55	-15	13-4	.976	-2	103	70	2b64,S8,D5	182	-1.1

BAUMANN, PADDY   Charles John B12.20.1885 Indianapolis IN   D11.20.1969 Indianapolis IN   BR/TR/5-9/160   d8.10

YEAR	TM LG	G	AB	R	H	2B	3B	HR	RBI	BB-IB	HP	SO	AVG	OBP	SLG	AOPS	ABR	SB-CS	FA	FR	RNG	THR	GAMES AT POSITION	DL	BFW
1911	Det A	26	94	8	24	2	4	0	11	6	1		.255	.307	.362	82	-3	1-0	.956	4	116	77	2b23,O3R		0.1
1912	Det A	16	42	3	11	1	0	0	7	6	0		.262	.354	.286	86	0	4	.786	-2	95	0	3b6,2b5,O2(1/1/0)		-0.3
1913	Det A	50	191	31	57	7	4	1	22	16	0	18	.298	.353	.393	120	4	4	.943	-6	98	83	2b49		-0.1
1914	Det A	3	11	1	0	0	0	0	2	0	1		1.000	.154	.000	-52	-2	0	1.000	-1	93	101	2b3		-0.3
1915	NY A	76	219	30	64	13	1	2	28	28	3	32	.292	.380	.388	130	3	9-10	.978	1	96	113	2b43,3b19/OC		1.0
1916	NY A	79	237	35	68	5	3	1	25	19	5	16	.287	.352	.346	108	2	10	.958	-6	94	30	O28(12/1/15),3b26,2b9		-0.4
1917	NY A	49	110	10	24	2	1	0	8	4	0	9	.218	.246	.255	52	-7	2	.941	-6	70	126	2b18,O7(4/1/2)/3		-1.5
Total	7	299	904	118	248	30	13	4	101	81	9	76	.274	.340	.350	103	3	30-10	.953	-16	97	95	2b150,3b52,O41(17/4/20)		-1.5

BAUMER, JIM   James Sloan B1.29.1931 Tulsa OK   D7.8.1996 Paoli PA   BR/TR/6-2/185* d9.14

YEAR	TM LG	G	AB	R	H	2B	3B	HR	RBI	BB-IB	HP	SO	AVG	OBP	SLG	AOPS	ABR	SB-CS	FA	FR	RNG	THR	GAMES AT POSITION	DL	BFW
1949	Chi A	8	10	2	4	1	1	0	2	2	1	.400	.571	.700	243	2	0-0	.938	1	126	170	S7		0.3
1961	Cin N	10	24	0	3	0	0	0	0-0	1	9	.125	.125	.125	-33	-5	0-0	1.000	-3	64	39	2b9		-0.8
Total	2	18	34	2	7	1	1	0	2	2-0	2	10	.206	.289	.294	55	-3	0-0	1.000	-3	64	39	2b9,S7		-0.5

BAUMGARTNER, JOHN   John Edward B5.29.1931 Birmingham AL   BR/TR/6-1/190 d4.14   Col Alabama

YEAR	TM LG	G	AB	R	H	2B	3B	HR	RBI	BB-IB	HP	SO	AVG	OBP	SLG	AOPS	ABR	SB-CS	FA	FR	RNG	THR	GAMES AT POSITION	DL	BFW
1953	Det A	7	27	3	5	0	0	0	2	0	0	5	.185	.185	.185	0	-4	0-0	.913	-1	79	119	3b7		-0.5

BAUMHOLTZ, FRANK   Frank Conrad B10.7.1918 Midvale OH   D12.14.1997 Winter Springs FL   BL/TL/5-10.5/175* d4.15   Col Ohio U.

YEAR	TM LG	G	AB	R	H	2B	3B	HR	RBI	BB-IB	HP	SO	AVG	OBP	SLG	AOPS	ABR	SB-CS	FA	FR	RNG	THR	GAMES AT POSITION	DL	BFW
1947	Cin N	151	643	96	182	32	9	5	56	56	1	53	.283	.341	.384	93	-7	6	.977	-7	84	136	O150(0/29/136)		-1.9
1948	Cin N	128	415	57	123	19	5	4	30	27	3	32	.296	.344	.395	103	1	8	.987	3	100	145	O110(20/23/67)		0.0
1949	Cin N	27	81	12	19	5	3	1	8	6	1	8	.235	.295	.407	86	-2	0	.964	1	115	53	O20(13/0/7)		-0.3
	Chi N	58	164	15	37	4	2	1	15	9	1	21	.226	.270	.293	52	-12	2	.986	-2	86	90	O43(0/7/38)		-1.5
	Year	85	245	27	56	9	5	2	23	15	2	29	.229	.279	.331	64	-14	2	.976	-1	97	77	O63(13/7/45)		-1.8
1951	Chi N	146	560	62	159	28	10	2	50	49	4	36	.284	.346	.380	94	-5	5-4	.975	-10	94	47	O140(17/64/60)		-2.1
1952	Chi N	103	409	59	133	17	4	4	35	27	3	27	.325	.371	.416	116	3	5-7	.974	3	107	99	O101(0/47/65)	38	0.7
1953	Chi N	133	520	75	159	36	7	3	25	42	1	36	.306	.359	.419	100	1	3-3	.980	-6	96	56	O130(0/69/64)		-1.0
1954	Chi N	90	303	38	90	12	6	4	22	20	1	15	.297	.340	.416	95	-3	1-3	.988	-4	95	37	O71(10/61/13)		-1.1
1955	Chi N	105	280	23	81	12	5	1	27	16-2	1	24	.289	.325	.379	88	-5	0-1	.993	0	105	63	O63(40/0/23)		-0.9
1956	Phi N	76	100	13	27	0	0	0	9	6-0	1	6	.270	.309	.270	61	-5	0-2	.962	1	98	185	O15(0/1/14)		-0.6
1957	Phi N	2	2	0	0	0	0	0	0-0	1		.000	.000	.000	-99	-1	0-0	—	0			/H		-0.1
Total	10	1019	3477	450	1010	165	51	25	272	258-2	17	258	.290	.342	.389	95	-29	30-20	.980	-22	96	88	O843(100/301/487)	38	-8.8

BAUTISTA, DANNY   Daniel (Alcantara) B5.24.1972 Santo Domingo, D.R.   BR/TR/5-11/170(170-225) d9.15

YEAR	TM LG	G	AB	R	H	2B	3B	HR	RBI	BB-IB	HP	SO	AVG	OBP	SLG	AOPS	ABR	SB-CS	FA	FR	RNG	THR	GAMES AT POSITION	DL	BFW
1993	Det A	17	61	6	19	3	0	1	9	1-0	0	10	.311	.317	.410	95	-1	3-1	1.000	1	103	207	O16(0/9/8)/D		0.1
1994	Det A	31	99	12	23	4	1	4	15	3-0	0	18	.232	.255	.414	68	-5	1-2	1.000	0	109	0	O30(0/14/16)/D	53	-0.6
1995	Det A	89	271	28	55	9	0	7	27	12-0	0	68	.203	.237	.314	42	-25	4-1	.988	-0	105	56	O86(2/0/84)/D		-2.7
1996	Det A	25	64	12	16	2	0	2	8	9-0	0	15	.250	.342	.375	81	-2	1-2	.974	-1	102	0	O22(12/0/12)/D		-0.4
	Atl N	17	20	1	3	0	0	0	1	2-0	1	5	.150	.261	.150	11	-3	0-0	1.000	-0	96		O14(2/2/10)	94	-0.3
1997	†Atl N	64	103	14	25	3	2	3	9	5-1	1	24	.243	.282	.398	75	-4	2-2	.984	1	110	51	O57(48/1/10)	22	-0.4
1998	†Atl N	82	144	17	36	11	0	3	17	7-0	0	21	.250	.281	.389	76	-5	1-0	.959	-4	79	0	O58(53/1/4)/D	43	-1.0
1999	Fla N	70	205	32	59	10	1	5	24	4-0	1	30	.288	.303	.420	86	-6	3-0	.979	7	137	98	O60(22/18/31)		0.1
2000	Fla N	44	89	9	17	4	0	4	12	5-0	0	20	.191	.234	.371	52	-7	1-0	.980	1	103	143	O38(25/5/17)		-0.6
	Ari N	87	262	45	83	16	7	7	47	20-4	3	30	.317	.366	.511	116	6	5-2	.987	3	103	108	O82(2/21/67)		0.6
	Year	131	351	54	100	20	7	11	59	25-4	3	50	.285	.333	.476	102	-1	6-2	.985	4	103	147	O120(27/26/84)		0.0
2001	†Ari N	100	222	26	67	11	2	5	26	14-1	1	31	.302	.346	.437	94	-2	3-2	1.000	2	101	146	O61(3/28/33)		-0.1
2002	Ari N	40	154	22	50	5	2	6	23	11-2	0	21	.325	.367	.500	118	3	3-2	.985	-3	92		O39(0/5/37)	130	-0.1
2003	Ari N	88	284	29	78	16	3	4	36	21-2	4	50	.275	.330	.394	82	-7	3-2	.961	·7	88	23	O79(3/18/59)	34	-1.7
2004	Ari N	141	539	64	154	27	1	11	65	35-2	4	66	.286	.332	.401	83	-13	6-2	.986	3	104	76	O137(0/2/135)/D		-1.6
Total	12	895	2517	317	685	121	19	62	319	149-12	15	409	.272	.315	.409	83	-71	37-16	.984	3	103	76	O779(172/124/523),D6	376	-8.7

BAUTISTA, JOSE   Jose Antonio B10.19.1980 Santo Domingo, D.R.   BR/TR/6-0/190* [PitN00 20/599] d4.4

YEAR	TM LG	G	AB	R	H	2B	3B	HR	RBI	BB-IB	HP	SO	AVG	OBP	SLG	AOPS	ABR	SB-CS	FA	FR	RNG	THR	GAMES AT POSITION	DL	BFW
2004	Bal A	16	11	3	3	0	0	0	1-0	0	3	.273	.333	.273	61	-1	0-0	1.000	-0	71	542	O6R,3b4,D2		-0.1
	TB A	12	12	1	2	0	0	0	3-0	0	7	.167	.333	.167	37	-1	0-1	1.000	-0	63	0	O8(5/0/3),3b2/D		-0.2
	KC A	13	25	1	5	1	0	0	1	1-0	0	12	.200	.231	.240	23	-3	0-0	.957	2	130	172	3b11/OR		-0.1
	Year	41	48	·5	10	1	0	0	2	5-0	0	22	.208	.283	.229	36	-5	0-1	.960	1	127	149	3b17,O15(5/0/10),D3		-0.4
	Pit N	23	40	1	8	2	0	0	2-0	0	18	.200	.238	.250	26	-4	0-0	.864	-1	110	0	O12(0/3/9)		-0.5
2005	Pit N	11	28	3	4	1	0	0	1	3-0	0	7	.143	.226	.179	4	-1	1-0	.952	1	99	150	3b8		-0.3
Total	2	75	116	9	22	4	0	0	3	10-0	0	47	.190	.254	.224	26	-13	1-1	.903	1	92	102	O27(5/3/19),3b25,D3		-1.2

BAXES, JIM   Dimitrios Speros B7.5.1928 San Francisco CA   D11.14.1996 Garden Grove CA   BR/TR/6-1/200 d4.11   b-Mike

YEAR	TM LG	G	AB	R	H	2B	3B	HR	RBI	BB-IB	HP	SO	AVG	OBP	SLG	AOPS	ABR	SB-CS	FA	FR	RNG	THR	GAMES AT POSITION	DL	BFW
1959	LA N	11	33	4	10	1	0	2	5	4-0	1	7	.303	.395	.515	130	-2	1-0	.952	3	129	113	3b10		0.5
	Cle A	77	247	35	59	11	0	15	34	21-0	0	47	.239	.299	.466	111	2	0-1	.956	-13	84	93	2b48,3b22		-0.8
Total	2	88	280	39	69	12	0	17	39	25-0	1	54	.246	.310	.471	113	4	1-1	.956	-10	84	93	2b48,3b32		-0.3

BAXES, MIKE   Michael B12.18.1930 San Francisco CA   BR/TR/5-10/175* d4.17   b-Jim

YEAR	TM LG	G	AB	R	H	2B	3B	HR	RBI	BB-IB	HP	SO	AVG	OBP	SLG	AOPS	ABR	SB-CS	FA	FR	RNG	THR	GAMES AT POSITION	DL	BFW
1956	KC A	73	106	9	24	3	1	1	5	18-1	0	15	.226	.339	.302	70	-4	0-1	.944	2	114	75	S62/2		0.0
1958	KC A	73	231	31	49	10	1	8	21-0	3	24	.212	.286	.346	52	-15	1-6	.969	-2	102	96	2b61,S4		-1.5
Total	2	146	337	40	73	13	2	1	13	39-1	3	39	.217	.303	.276	58	-19	1-7	.946	-0	114	71	S66,2b62		-1.5

BAXTER, MOOSE   John Morris B7.27.1876 Chippewa Falls WI   D8.7.1926 Portland OR   BL/TR/6-2/200 d4.19

YEAR	TM LG	G	AB	R	H	2B	3B	HR	RBI	BB-IB	HP	SO	AVG	OBP	SLG	AOPS	ABR	SB-CS	FA	FR	RNG	THR	GAMES AT POSITION	DL	BFW
1907	StL N	6	21	1	4	0	0	0	0	0			.190	.190	.190	20	-2	0	.921	-1	118	34	1b6		-0.3

BAY, HARRY   Harry Elbert "Deerfoot" B1.17.1878 Pontiac IL   D3.20.1952 Peoria IL   BL/TL/5-8/138 d7.23

YEAR	TM LG	G	AB	R	H	2B	3B	HR	RBI	BB-IB	HP	SO	AVG	OBP	SLG	AOPS	ABR	SB-CS	FA	FR	RNG	THR	GAMES AT POSITION	DL	BFW
1901	Cin N	41	157	25	33	1	2	1	3	13	1		.210	.275	.280	60	-8	4	.953	-1	60	217	O40(0/25/15)		-1.1
1902	Cin N	6	16	3	6	0	0	0	1	2	1		.375	.474	.375	148	1	0	.778	0	211	0	O3L		0.1
	Cle A	108	455	71	132	10	5	0	23	36	1		.290	.343	.334	92	-4	22	**.973**	1	92	105	O107(24/79/4)		-0.8

YEAR	TM LG	G	AB	R	H	2B	3B	HR	RBI	BB-IB	HP	SO	AVG	OBP	SLG	AOPS	ABR	SB-CS	FA	FR	RNG	THR	GAMES AT POSITION	DL	BFW
1903	Cle A	140	579	94	169	15	12	1	35	29		3		.292	.329	.364	110	6	45	.950	-5	83	79	O140(26/114/0)		-0.7
1904	Cle A	132	506	69	122	12	9	3	36	43		5		.241	.307	.318	99	0	38	.987	6	105	166	O132(5/127/0)		0.0
1905	Cle A	144	552	90	166	18	10	0	22	36		5		.301	.349	.370	126	16	36	.970	-2	89	115	O144C		0.8
1906	Cle A	68	280	47	77	8	3	0	14	26		0		.275	.337	.325	109	3	17	.979	-5	91	117	O68C		-0.6
1907	Cle A	34	95	14	17	1	1	0	7	10		2		.179	.271	.211	53	-5	7	.968	2	143	127	O31(7/23/1)		-0.5
1908	Cle A	2	0	0	0	0	0	0	0	0		0		—	—	—	—	0	0		0			/R		0.0
Total	8	675	2640	413	722	65	42	5	141	195		18		.273	.328	.336	103	9	169	.968	-4	93	122	O665(65/580/20)		-2.8

BAY, JASON   Jason Raymond B9.20.1978 Trail BC, Can.   BR/TR/6-2/200*   [MonN00 22/645]   d5.23   Col Gonzaga

YEAR	TM LG	G	AB	R	H	2B	3B	HR	RBI	BB-IB	HP	SO	AVG	OBP	SLG	AOPS	ABR	SB-CS	FA	FR	RNG	THR	GAMES AT POSITION	DL	BFW
2003	SD N	3	8	2	2	1	0	1	2	1-0		1		.250	.400	.750	210	1	0-0	1.000	1	159	0	O3C	43	0.2
	Pit N	27	79	13	23	6	1	3	12	18-0		0	28	.291	.423	.506	139	6	3-1	.976	-2	85	67	O26(24/2/1)		0.3
	Year	30	87	15	25	7	1	4	14	19-0		1	29	.287	.421	.529	145	7	3-1	.980	-1	91	61	O29(24/5/1)		0.5
2004	Pit N	120	411	61	116	24	4	26	82	41-2		10	129	.282	.358	.550	131	18	4-6	.991	-0	106	49	O119(117/5/0)	33	1.2
2005	Pit N☆	162	599	110	183	44	6	32	101	95-9		4	142	.306	.402	.559	151	47	21-1	.988	-4	102	43	O162(146/30/0)		4.2
Total	3	312	1097	186	324	75	11	62	197	155-11		17	300	.295	.387	.553	143	72	28-8	.988	-5	103	47	O310(287/40/1)	76	5.9

BAYLESS, DICK   Harry Owen B9.6.1883 Joplin MO D12.16.1920 Santa Rita NM   BL/TR/5-9/178   d9.9

YEAR	TM LG	G	AB	R	H	2B	3B	HR	RBI	BB-IB	HP	SO	AVG	OBP	SLG	AOPS	ABR	SB-CS	FA	FR	RNG	THR	GAMES AT POSITION	DL	BFW
1908	Cin N	19	71	7	16	1	0	1	3	6		2		.225	.304	.282	90	-1	0	.946	3	251	345	O19(0/2/17)		0.1

BAYLOR, DON   Don Edward B6.28.1949 Austin TX   BR/TR/6-1/195(190-210)   [BalA67 2/39]   d9.18   M9/C7

YEAR	TM LG	G	AB	R	H	2B	3B	HR	RBI	BB-IB	HP	SO	AVG	OBP	SLG	AOPS	ABR	SB-CS	FA	FR	RNG	THR	GAMES AT POSITION	DL	BFW
1970	Bal A	8	17	4	4	0	0	0	4	2-0		0	3	.235	.300	.235	53	-1	1-1	1.000	0	125	0	O6(3/4/0)		-0.1
1971	Bal A	1	2	0	0	0	0	0	1	2-0		1		.000	.600	.000	82	0	0-0	1.000	0	195	0	/OR		0.1
1972	Bal A	102	320	33	81	13	3	11	38	29-0		9	50	.253	.300	.416	117	7	24-2	.975	-4	100	35	O84(35/13/48),1b9		0.3
1973	†Bal A	118	405	64	116	20	4	11	51	35-3		13	48	.286	.357	.437	123	13	32-9	.981	-1	100	67	O110L,1b6/D		1.0
1974	†Bal A	137	489	66	133	22	4	10	59	43-6		10	56	.272	.341	.382	111	8	29-12	.978	-16	85	11	O129(112/2/26),1b8/D		-1.4
1975	Bal A	145	524	79	148	21	6	25	76	53-8		13	64	.282	.360	.489	147	32	32-17	.982	-6	91	77	O135(127/5/6),1b2,D7		1.9
1976	Oak A	157	595	85	147	25	4	15	68	58-4		20	72	.247	.329	.368	110	9	52-12	.981	-6	97	18	O76(27/2/50),1b69,D23		0.0
1977	Cal A	154	561	87	141	27	0	25	75	62-7		12	76	.251	.334	.433	113	11	26-12	.966	-2	97	59	O77(48/11/19),D61,1b18		0.4
1978	Cal A	158	591	103	151	26	0	34	99	56-9		18	71	.255	.342	.472	130	23	22-9	.974	-3	100	47	O102,O39L,1b17		1.6
1979	†Cal A★	162	628	120	186	33	3	36	139	71-6		11	51	.296	.371	.530	146	41	22-12	.976	-3	101	43	O97(78/0/19),D65/1		3.2
1980	Cal A	90	340	39	85	12	2	5	51	24-4		11	32	.250	.316	.341	82	-8	6-6	.969	1	106	99	O54(37/0/18),D36	46	-1.1
1981	Cal A	103	377	52	90	18	1	17	66	42-1		7	53	.239	.322	.427	115	7	3-3	1.000	1	116	60	D97,1b4/OL		0.5
1982	†Cal A	157	608	80	160	24	1	24	93	57-7		7	69	.263	.329	.424	105	4	10-4	—	0	0	0	D155		0.0
1983	NY A	144	534	82	162	33	3	21	85	40-11		13	85	.303	.361	.494	138	28	17-7	1.000	0	101	0	D136,O5(2/0/4)/1		2.5
1984	NY A	134	493	84	129	29	1	27	89	38-6		23	68	.262	.341	.489	131	21	1-1	.889	-1	0	98	D127,O5(1/0/4)		1.7
1985	NY A	142	477	70	110	24	1	23	91	52-6		24	90	.231	.330	.430	110	8	0-4	—	0	0	0	D140		0.2
1986	†Bos A	160	585	93	139	23	1	31	94	62-8		35	111	.238	.344	.439	111	11	3-5	.986	-2	43	74	D143,1b13,O3L		0.2
1987	Bos A	108	339	64	81	8	0	16	57	40-3		24	47	.239	.355	.404	99	1	5-2	—	0	0	0	D97		-0.1
	†Min A	20	49	3	14	1	0	0	6	5-0		4	12	.286	.397	.306	87	0	0-1	—	0	0	0	D14		-0.1
	Year	128	388	67	95	9	0	16	63	45-3		28	59	.245	.360	.392	98	1	5-3	—	0	0	0	D111		-0.2
1988	†Oak A	92	264	28	58	7	0	7	34	34-2		12	44	.220	.332	.326	89	-3	0-1	—	0	0	0	D80		-0.6
Total	19	2292	8198	1236	2135	366	28	338	1276	805-91		267	1069	.260	.342	.436	118	212	285-120	.977	-41	97	46	D1285,O822(623/37/195),1b148	46	10.2

BEACH, JACK   Stonewall Jackson B1862 Alexandria VA D7.23.1896 Alexandria VA   d5.1

YEAR	TM LG	G	AB	R	H	2B	3B	HR	RBI	BB-IB	HP	SO	AVG	OBP	SLG	AOPS	ABR	SB-CS	FA	FR	RNG	THR	GAMES AT POSITION	DL	BFW
1884	Was AA	8	31	3	3	0	0	0						.097	.097	.161	-20	-4		.667	-1	128	335	O8(1/0/7)		-0.4

BEADLE, DAVE   David A. B1.1864 New York NY D9.22.1925 New York NY   BL/6-2/200   d6.17

YEAR	TM LG	G	AB	R	H	2B	3B	HR	RBI	BB-IB	HP	SO	AVG	OBP	SLG	AOPS	ABR	SB-CS	FA	FR	RNG	THR	GAMES AT POSITION	DL	BFW
1884	Det N	1	3	0	0	0	0	0	0	0		0	2	.000	.000	.000	-99	-1		.500	-1	0	0	/O(1/0/1)C		-0.1

BEALL, JOHNNY   John Woolf B3.12.1882 Beltsville MD D6.13.1926 Beltsville MD   BL/TR/6-0/180   d4.17

YEAR	TM LG	G	AB	R	H	2B	3B	HR	RBI	BB-IB	HP	SO	AVG	OBP	SLG	AOPS	ABR	SB-CS	FA	FR	RNG	THR	GAMES AT POSITION	DL	BFW
1913	Cle A	6	6	0	1	0	0	0	1	0		0	2	.167	.167	.167	-2	-1	0	—	0			/H		-0.1
	Chi A	17	60	10	16	0	1	2	3	0		1		.267	.279	.400	99	-1	1	.953	0	100	110	O17C		-0.2
	Year	23	66	10	17	0	1	2	4	0		1	2	.258	.269	.379	89	-2	1	.953	0	100	110	O17C		-0.3
1915	Cin N	10	34	3	8	1	0	0	3	5		1	10	.235	.350	.265	86	0	0-1	.960	1	99	153	O10(9/1/0)		0.0
1916	Cin N	6	21	3	7	2	0	1	4	3		0	1	.333	.417	.571	207	3	1	1.000	1	82	334	O6L		0.4
1918	StL N	19	49	2	11	1	0	0	6	3		0	6	.224	.269	.245	59	-2	0	1.000	-0	97	81	O18R		-0.4
Total	4	58	170	18	43	4	1	3	17	11		2	25	.253	.306	.341	95	-1	2-1	.972	1	97	136	O51(14/18/18)		-0.3

BEALL, BOB   Robert Brooks B4.24.1948 Portland OR   BB/TL/5-11/180*   [PhiN70 28/653]   d5.12   Col Oregon St.

YEAR	TM LG	G	AB	R	H	2B	3B	HR	RBI	BB-IB	HP	SO	AVG	OBP	SLG	AOPS	ABR	SB-CS	FA	FR	RNG	THR	GAMES AT POSITION	DL	BFW
1975	Atl N	20	31	2	7	2	0	0	1	6-0		0	9	.226	.351	.290	77	-1	0-0	.984	-0	91	104	1b8		-0.2
1978	Atl N	108	185	29	45	8	0	1	16	36-0		1	27	.243	.368	.303	81	-3	4-5	.987	-1	119	87	1b40,O8(6/2/0)		-0.5
1979	Atl N	17	15	1	2	2	0	0	1	3-0		0	4	.133	.263	.267	46	-1	0-0	1.000	0	111	0	1b3	98	-0.1
1980	Pit N	3	3	0	0	0	0	0	0	0-0		0	1	.000	.000	.000	-97	-1	0-0	—	0			/H		-0.1
Total	4	148	234	32	54	12	0	1	18	45-0		1	41	.231	.355	.295	76	-6	4-5	.987	0	114	87	1b51,O8(6/2/0)	98	-0.9

BEALS, TOMMY   Thomas L. (aka W.Thomas in 1871-1873) B8.1850 NY D10.2.1915 San Francisco CA   BR/5-5/144   d7.27

YEAR	TM LG	G	AB	R	H	2B	3B	HR	RBI	BB-IB	HP	SO	AVG	OBP	SLG	AOPS	ABR	SB-CS	FA	FR	RNG	THR	GAMES AT POSITION	DL	BFW
1871	Oly NA	10	36	6	7	1	0	0	1	2				.194	.237	.194	27	-3	2-0	.778	2	92	0	O8(4/0/4),2b2		0.0
1872	Oly NA	9	36	6	11	1	1	0	5	1			1	.306	.324	.389	125	1	0-0	.853	1	146	95	2b5,S2,O2C		0.1
1873	Was NA	37	169	35	46	9	5	0	22	1			1	.272	.276	.385	97	0	3-0	.870	9	112	109	2b26,C13/OL		0.5
1874	Bos NA	19	97	20	19	3	4	0	17	0				.196	.196	.309	56	-5	0-1	.849	1	108	61	2b12,O9(1/2/6)		-0.4
1875	Bos NA	35	155	38	41	2	6	0	16	3			6	.265	.278	.355	114	1	1-0	.867	-0	43	126	O30(3/19/8),2b8		0.1
1880	Chi N	13	46	4	7	0	0	0	3	1			6	.152	.170	.152	10	-4		.889	-5	55	0	O10R,2b3		-0.9
Total	5 NA	110	493	105	124	15	16	0	61	7			5	.252	.262	.347	90	-6	6-1	.864	13	112	115	2b53,O50(9/23/18),C13,S2		0.3

BEAMON, CHARLIE   Charles Alfonzo Jr. B12.4.1953 Oakland CA   BL/TL/6-1/183(170-183)   d9.11   f-Charlie   Col Laney (CA) JC

YEAR	TM LG	G	AB	R	H	2B	3B	HR	RBI	BB-IB	HP	SO	AVG	OBP	SLG	AOPS	ABR	SB-CS	FA	FR	RNG	THR	GAMES AT POSITION	DL	BFW
1978	Sea A	10	11	2	2	0	0	0	0	1-0		0	1	.182	.250	.182	23	-1	0-0	1.000	1	279	109	1b2,D6		0.0
1979	Sea A	27	25	5	5	1	0	0	0	2-0		1	5	.200	.200	.240	18	-3	1-0	1.000	0	125	0	1b7,O2L,D5		-0.3
1981	Tor A	8	15	1	3	1	0	0	0	2-0		1	2	.200	.294	.267	59	-1	0-0	1.000	-0	0	0	D4/1		-0.1
Total	3	45	51	8	10	2	0	0	0	5-0		2	8	.196	.241	.235	32	-5	1-0	1.000	1	175	46	D15,1b10,O2L		-0.4

BEAMON, TREY   Clifford B2.11.1974 Dallas TX   BL/TR/6-3/195*   [PitN92 2/61]   d8.4

YEAR	TM LG	G	AB	R	H	2B	3B	HR	RBI	BB-IB	HP	SO	AVG	OBP	SLG	AOPS	ABR	SB-CS	FA	FR	RNG	THR	GAMES AT POSITION	DL	BFW
1996	Pit N	24	51	7	11	2	0	0	6	4-0		0	6	.216	.273	.255	39	-5	1-1	.960	-0	107	0	O14(5/0/10)		-0.6
1997	SD N	43	65	5	18	3	0	0	7	2-0		1	17	.277	.309	.323	70	-3	1-2	.909	0	76	368	O20(15/0/5)		-0.3
1998	Det A	28	42	4	11	4	0	0	2	5-0		0	13	.262	.340	.357	81	-1	1-0	1.000	0	200	0	D11,O4(2/0/2)	83	-0.1
Total	3	95	158	16	40	9	0	0	15	11-0		1	36	.253	.306	.310	63	-9	3-3	.944	-1	99	172	O38(22/0/17),D11	83	-1.0

BEAN, JOE   Joseph William B3.18.1874 Boston MA D2.15.1961 Atlanta GA   BR/TR/5-8/138   d4.28

YEAR	TM LG	G	AB	R	H	2B	3B	HR	RBI	BB-IB	HP	SO	AVG	OBP	SLG	AOPS	ABR	SB-CS	FA	FR	RNG	THR	GAMES AT POSITION	DL	BFW
1902	NY N	50	182	13	40	2	1	0	5	5		2		.220	.249	.242	52	-11	9	.880	-8	96	109	S50		-1.8

BEAN, BILLY   William Daro B5.11.1964 Santa Ana CA   BL/TL/6-1/185*   [DetA86 4/99]   d4.25   Col Loyola Marymount

YEAR	TM LG	G	AB	R	H	2B	3B	HR	RBI	BB-IB	HP	SO	AVG	OBP	SLG	AOPS	ABR	SB-CS	FA	FR	RNG	THR	GAMES AT POSITION	DL	BFW
1987	Det A	26	66	6	17	2	0	0	4	5-0		0	11	.258	.310	.288	62	-4	1-1	1.000	3	129	111	O24(5/17/3)		-0.1
1988	Det A	10	11	2	2	0	1	0	2	0-0		0	4	.182	.182	.364	50	-1	0-0	1.000	0	83	0	O4(0/2/3),1b2/D		-0.1
1989	Det A	9	11	0	0	0	0	0	0	2-0		1	3	.000	.214	.000	-35	-2	0-0	.833	-1	88	0	O6(4/1/2),1b2		-0.3
	LA N	51	71	7	14	6	0	0	3	4-0		1	10	.197	.250	.254	45	-5	0-2	1.000	-0	103	0	O44(28/11/7)		-0.7
1993	SD N	88	177	19	46	9	0	5	32	6-1		2	29	.260	.284	.395	81	-5	2-4	.987	1	94	250	O54(11/17/32),1b12		-0.6
1994	SD N	84	135	7	29	5	1	0	14	7-1		0	25	.215	.248	.267	37	-13	0-0	1.000	0	110	0	O39(17/7/15),1b16		-1.5
1995	SD N	4	7	1	0	0	0	0	0	1-0		0	6	.000	.125	.000	-65	-2	0-0	.750	-1	72	0	O4L		-0.2
Total	6	272	478	42	108	20	2	5	53	25-2		4	84	.226	.266	.308	55	-32	3-6	.988	2	104	105	O175(69/55/62),1b32/D		-3.5

BEANE, BILLY   William Lamar B3.29.1962 Orlando FL   BR/TR/6-4/195(195-210)   [NYN80 1/23]   d9.13

YEAR	TM LG	G	AB	R	H	2B	3B	HR	RBI	BB-IB	HP	SO	AVG	OBP	SLG	AOPS	ABR	SB-CS	FA	FR	RNG	THR	GAMES AT POSITION	DL	BFW
1984	NY N	5	10	1	1	0	0	0	0	0-0		0	3	.100	.100	.100	-44	-2	0-1	1.000	-0	55	0	O5(2/1/2)		-0.3
1985	NY N	8	8	0	2	1	0	0	0	0-0		1	2	.250	.250	.375	74	-0	0-0	1.000	-0	39	0	O2(1/0/1)		-0.1
1986	Min A	80	183	20	39	6	0	3	15	11-0		0	54	.213	.258	.295	49	-13	2-3	.989	-1	120		O67(64/5/1),D5	14	-1.4
1987	Min A	12	15	1	4	2	0	0	1	0-0		0	6	.267	.267	.400	71	-1	0-0	1.000	0	152	0	O7R		0.0
1988	Det A	6	6	1	1	0	0	0	0	0-0		0	2	.167	.167	.167	-7	-1	0-0	1.000	0	93	0	O6(4/1/1)		-0.1
1989	Oak A	37	79	8	19	5	0	0	11	0-0		0	13	.241	.237	.304	54	-5	3-1	1.000	1	114	0	O25(4/0/21),1b4/C3D	21	-0.5
Total	6	148	301	30	66	14	0	3	29	11-0		0	80	.219	.256	.296	48	-22	5-5	1.000	2	116	0	O112(75/7/33),D9,1b4/3C	35	-2.4

YEAR	TM LG	G	AB	R	H	2B	3B	HR	RBI	BB-IB	HP	SO	AVG	OBP	SLG	AOPS	ABR	SB-CS	FA	FR	RNG	THR	GAMES AT POSITION	DL	BFW

BEARD, TED   Cramer Theodore   B1.7.1921 Woodsboro MD   BL/TL/5-8/165*   d9.5

1948	Pit N	25	81	15	16	1	3	0	7	12	2	18	.198	.316	.284		62	-4	5	1.000	-1	105	0	O22C		-0.6
1949	Pit N	14	24	1	2	0	0	0	1	2	0	2	.083	.154	.083		-34	-5	0	.900	-1	91	0	O10R		-0.6
1950	Pit N	61	177	32	41	6	2	4	12	27	0	45	.232	.333	.356		79	-5	3	.983	2	109	108	O49(1/21/27)	38	-0.5
1951	Pit N	22	48	7	9	1	0	1	3	6	1	14	.188	.291	.271		51	-3	0-0	1.000	0	87	195	O15(12/4/0)		-0.4
1952	Pit N	15	44	5	8	2	1	0	3	7	0	9	.182	.294	.273		57	-3	2-0	1.000	0	103	83	O13(0/3/10)		-0.3
1957	Chi A	38	78	15	16	1	0	0	7	18-2	0	14	.205	.354	.218		59	-3	3-2	.974	2	89	342	O28(0/3/25)		-0.3
1958	Chi A	19	22	5	2	0	0	1	2	6-0	0	5	.091	.286	.227		44	-2	3-0	1.000	-0	105	0	O15(10/6/1)		-0.2
Total	7	194	474	80	94	11	6	6	35	78-2	3	107	.198	.315	.285		61	-25	16-2	.987	2	102	120	O152(23/59/73)	38	-2.9

BEARD, OLLIE   Oliver Perry   B5.2.1862 Lexington KY   D5.28.1929 Cincinnati OH   BR/TR/5-11/180   d4.17

1889	Cin AA	141	558	96	159	13	14	1	77	35	1	39	.285	.328	.364		94	-8	36	.896	18	109	126	S141		1.2
1890	Cin N	122	492	64	132	17	15	3	72	44	2	13	.268	.331	.382		108	3	30	.897	-1	108	117	S113,3b9		0.5
1891	Lou AA	68	257	35	62	4	5	0	24	33	1	9	.241	.330	.296		80	-6	7	.879	3	105	150	3b61,S7		-0.2
Total	3	331	1307	195	353	34	34	4	173	112	4	61	.270	.330	.357		97	-11	73	.896	20	109	121	S261,3b70		1.5

BEASLEY, LEW   Lewis Paige   B8.27.1948 Sparta VA   BL/TR/5-10/172   [BalA67*2/38]   d5.21

| 1977 | Tex A | 25 | 32 | 5 | 7 | 1 | 0 | 0 | 2 | 2 | 0 | 2 | .219 | .257 | .250 | | 41 | -3 | 1-1 | .833 | -3 | 53 | 0 | O18(14/0/4)/SD | | -0.6 |

BEATTY, DESMOND   Desmond Aloysius "Desperate"   B4.7.1893 Baltimore MD   D10.6.1969 Norway ME   BR/TR/5-8.5/158   d9.28

| 1914 | NY N | 2 | 3 | 0 | 0 | 0 | 0 | 0 | 0 | 0 | 0 | 0 | .000 | .000 | .000 | | -99 | -1 | 0 | .400 | -1 | 47 | 0 | /S3 | | -0.2 |

BEAUCHAMP, JIM   James Edward   B8.21.1939 Vinita OK   BR/TR/6-2/205(190-205)   d9.22   C8

1963	StL N	4	3	0	0	0	0	0	0	0-0	0	2	.000	.000	.000		-91	-1	0-0		—	0		/H		-0.1
1964	Hou N	23	55	6	9	2	0	2	4	5-0	1	16	.164	.246	.309		58	-3	0-0	.913	-1	86	0	O15(11/4/0),1b2		-0.5
1965	Hou N	24	53	5	10	1	0	2	4	5-0	0	11	.189	.259	.208		36	-5	0-2	1.000	1	70	199	O9L,1b3		-0.5
	Mil N	4	3	0	0	0	0	0	0	1-0	0	1	.000	.250	.000		-23	0	0-1	1.000	-0	0	123	1b2		-0.1
	Year	28	56	5	10	1	0	2	4	6-0	0	12	.179	.258	.196		32	-5	0-3	1.000	1	70	199	O9L,1b5		-0.6
1967	Atl N	4	3	0	0	0	0	0	0	1	0	0	.000	.000	.000		-99	-1	0-0		—	0		/H		-0.1
1968	Cin N	31	57	10	15	2	0	2	14	4-1	0	19	.263	.306	.404		107	0	0-0	1.000	1	118	0	O13(1/11/1)/1		0.1
1969	Cin N	43	60	8	15	1	0	1	8	5-2	0	13	.250	.308	.317		71	-2	0-0	1.000	0	113	0	O9(5/4/0),1b3		-0.3
1970	Hou N	31	26	3	5	0	0	1	4	3-0	1	7	.192	.276	.308		58	-2	0-1	1.000	-1	83	0	O16(13/3/0)		-0.3
	StL N	44	58	8	15	2	0	1	6	8-0	0	11	.259	.338	.345		84	-1	2-0	1.000	1	113	245	O10(2/6/2),1b5		0.0
	Year	75	84	11	20	2	0	2	10	11-0	1	18	.238	.320	.333		77	-3	2-1	1.000	1	101	145	O26(15/9/2),1b5		-0.3
1971	StL N	77	162	24	38	8	3	2	16	9-1	1	26	.235	.274	.358		76	-6	3-1	.982	-2	85	87	1b44/OL		-1.1
1972	NY N	58	120	11	29	1	0	5	19	7-1	1	33	.242	.282	.375		89	-2	0-0	.979	-2	67	88	1b35,O5L		-0.7
1973	†NY N	50	61	5	17	1	1	0	14	7-1	0	11	.279	.343	.328		90	-1	1-0	.969	-1	73	123	1b11	22	-0.2
Total	10	393	661	79	153	18	4	14	90	54-6	3	150	.231	.288	.334		75	-24	6-5	.980	-2	91	90	1b106,O78(47/28/3)	22	-3.8

BEAUMONT, GINGER   Clarence Howeth   B7.23.1876 Rochester WI   D4.10.1956 Burlington WI   BL/TR/5-8/190   d4.21   Col Beloit

1899	Pit N	111	437	90	154	15	8	3	38	41	7		.352	.416	.444		136	23	31	.924	-0	123	140	O100(3/96/1),1b2		1.5
1900	†Pit N	138	567	105	158	14	9	5	50	40	4		.279	.331	.362		90	-9	27	.944	-15	52	67	O138C		-3.0
1901	Pit N	133	558	120	185	14	5	8	72	44	2		.332	.382	.418		128	20	36	.943	-7	47	52	O133C		0.6
1902	Pit N	130	541	100	**193**	21	6	0	67	39	4		**.357**	.404	.418		148	31	33	.975	-2	85	204	O130C		2.4
1903	†Pit N	141	613	**137**	**209**	30	6	7	68	44	5		.341	.390	.444		133	26	23	.948	-11	76	45	O141C		0.8
1904	Pit N	153	615	97	**185**	12	12	3	54	34	1		.301	.338	.374		117	10	28	.968	-7	74	110	O153C		-0.4
1905	Pit N	103	384	60	126	12	8	3	40	22	0		.328	.365	.424		131	13	21	.972	0	99	178	O97C		0.9
1906	Pit N	80	310	48	82	9	3	2	32	19	2		.265	.311	.332		96	-2	1	.945	-5	63	96	O78C		-1.2
1907	Bos N	150	580	67	**187**	19	14	4	62	37	3		.322	.366	.424		148	29	25	.962	4	150	**224**	O149C		3.0
1908	Bos N	125	476	66	127	20	6	2	52	42	1		.267	.328	.347		117	9	13	.965	-3	112	80	O121C		0.0
1909	Bos N	123	407	35	107	11	4	0	60	35	0		.263	.321	.310		92	-4	12	.969	1	101	80	O111C		-0.9
1910	†Chi N	76	172	30	46	5	1	2	22	28	1	14	.267	.373	.343		110	3	4	.957	-2	98	73	O56(15/34/7)		-0.1
Total	12	1463	5660	955	1759	182	82	39	617	425	30	14	.311	.362	.393		122	149	254	.956	-48	89	114	O1407(18/1380/8),1b2		3.6

BEAVENS, ED   Edward P. (aka Edward P. Bevens)   B1848 Troy NY   TR/5-8/138   d5.9

1871	Tro NA	3	15	7	6	0	0	0	5	0		0	.400	.400	.400		129	0	2-0	.818	1	120	166	2b3		0.1
1872	Atl NA	10	43	6	9	2	0	0	2	1		0	.209	.227	.256		41	-3	0-0	.683	-6	92	50	2b10/SOL		-0.7
Total	2 NA	13	58	13	15	2	0	0	7	1		0	.259	.271	.293		62	-3	2-0	.720	-5	99	78	2b13/OLS		-0.6

BECHTEL, GEORGE   George A.   B1848 Philadelphia PA   5-11/165   d5.20   ▲

1871	Ath NA	20	94	24	33	9	1	1	21	2		2	.351	.365	.500		147	6	4-0	.821	1	124	354	O15(1/3/11),P3,3b3		0.4
1872	Mut NA	51	247	61	74	11	3	0	42	7		3	.300	.319	.368		118	7	9-1	.823	-0	79	111	O50(13/0/37)/1		0.8
1873	Phi NA	**53**	258	53	63	12	1	1	39	9		1	.244	.270	.310		69	-10	2-1	.853	6	121	152	O52(0/2/50),P3		0.0
1874	Phi NA	32	151	29	42	4	5	1	34	2		1	.278	.288	.391		111	1	0-0	.731	-4	87	0	O28(1/0/28),P6		-0.1
1875	Cen NA	**14**	61	12	17	5	0	0	7	1		1	.279	.290	.361		136	4	0-0	.791	-1	91	138	P14		0.0
	Ath NA	35	164	33	46	6	2	0	20	1		3	.280	.285	.341		105	0	2-0	.810	0	73	101	O31(0/3/29),P4		0.2
	Year	49	225	45	63	11	2	0	27	2		4	.280	.286	.347		113	2	2-0	.810	-1	73	101	O31(0/3/29),P18		0.2
1876	Lou N	14	55	2	10	1	0	0	2	0		1	.182	.182	.200		23	-5		.882	-1	49	0	O14R		-0.5
	NY N	2	10	2	3	0	0	0	0	0		1	.300	.300	.300		115	0		.429	-2	0	0	O2C		-0.1
	Year	16	65	4	13	1	0	0	2	0		1	.200	.200	.215		34	-5		.750	-3	41	0	O16(0/2/14)		-0.6
Total	5 NA	205	975	212	275	47	12	3	163	22		11	.282	.298	.364		105	8	17-2	.816	1	81	122	O176(15/8/155),P30,3b3/1		1.3

BECK, CLYDE   Clyde Eugene "Jersey"   B1.6.1900 Bassett CA   D7.15.1988 Temple City CA   BR/TR/5-10/176   d5.19

1926	Chi N	30	81	10	16	0	0	1	4	7	0	15	.198	.261	.235		34	-8	0	.993	8	107	150	2b30		0.1
1927	Chi N	117	391	44	101	20	5	2	44	43	0	37	.258	.332	.350		83	-9	0	.969	11	106	107	2b99,3b17/S		0.6
1928	Chi N	131	483	72	124	18	4	3	52	58	4	58	.257	.341	.329		77	-15	3	.958	3	92	161	3b87,S47/2		-0.2
1929	Chi N	54	190	28	40	7	0	0	19	9	0	24	.211	.282	.247		32	-20	3	.978	7	124	116	3b33,S14		-0.9
1930	Chi N	83	244	32	52	7	0	6	34	36	0	32	.213	.314	.316		53	-19	2	.953	-3	96	99	S57,2b24,3b2		-1.4
1931	Cin N	53	136	17	21	4	2	0	19	21	1	14	.154	.272	.213		34	-12	1	.960	0	103	204	3b38,S6		-1.1
Total	6	468	1525	203	354	56	11	12	162	184	5	180	.232	.317	.307		63	-83	9	.959	27	103	163	3b177,2b154,S125		-2.9

BECK, ERVE   Ervin Thomas "Dutch"   B7.19.1878 Toledo OH   D12.23.1916 Toledo OH   BR/TR/5-10/168   d9.19

1899	Bro N	8	24	2	4	2	0	0	2	0		0	.167	.167	.250		13	-3	0	.931	-1	126	52	2b6,S2		-0.3
1901	Cle A	135	539	78	156	26	8	6	79	23	1		.289	.320	.401		103	1	7	.927	-8	99	71	2b132		-0.6
1902	Cin N	48	187	19	57	10	3	1	20	3	1		.305	.319	.406		113	2	2	.936	-2	99	83	2b32,1b6,O6(3/0/3)		0.0
	Det A	41	162	23	48	4	0	2	22	4	0		.296	.313	.358		84	-4	3	.971	2	134	113	1b36,O5R		-0.3
Total	3	232	912	122	265	42	11	9	123	30	2		.291	.313	.390		99	-4	12	.929	-9	100	75	2b170,1b42,O11(3/0/8),S2		-1.2

BECK, FRED   Frederick Thomas   B11.17.1886 Havana IL   D3.12.1962 Havana IL   BL/TL/6-1/180   d4.14

1909	Bos N	96	334	20	66	5	6	2	27	17	4		.198	.245	.266		56	-19	5	.966	2	99	244	O57(12/42/2),1b33		-2.2
1910	Bos N	154	571	52	157	32	6	**10**	64	19	7	55	.275	.307	.415		105	0	8	.963	0	100	108	O134(2/125/7),1b19		-0.7
1911	Cin N	41	87	7	16	1	2	2	20	1	0	13	.184	.193	.310		41	-8	2	1.000	-0	99	109	O16(4/5/7),1b6		-0.5
	Phi N	66	210	26	59	8	3	3	25	17	4	21	.281	.346	.390		105	1	3	.957	-3	87	94	O61(11/1/50)		-0.5
	Year	107	297	33	75	9	5	5	45	18	4	34	.253	.304	.367		88	-7	5	.966	-3	89	97	O77(15/6/57),1b6		-1.4
1914	Chi F	**157**	555	51	155	23	4	11	77	44	8	66	.279	.341	.395		106	-5	9	.982	-13	66	119	1b157		-2.4
1915	Chi F	121	373	35	83	9	3	5	38	24	4	38	.223	.277	.303		67	-24	4	.992	-6	70	105	1b117		-3.6
Total	5	635	2130	191	536	78	27	33	251	122	27	193	.252	.301	.360		89	-55	31	.984	-20	72	110	1b332,O268(29/173/66)		-10.3

BECK, ZINN   Zinn Bertram   B9.30.1885 Steubenville OH   D3.19.1981 W.Palm Beach FL   BR/TR/5-10.5/160   d9.14

1913	StL N	10	30	4	5	1	0	0	4	0	1	4	.167	.265	.200		34	-2	1	.833	0	107	94	S5,3b5		-0.2
1914	StL N	137	457	42	106	15	11	3	45	28	4	32	.232	.282	.333		84	-12	14	.935	3	108	**150**	3b122,S16		-0.4
1915	StL N	70	223	21	52	9	4	0	15	12	3	31	.233	.282	.309		79	-6	3-10	.935	1	110	126	3b62,S4,2b2		-0.7
1916	StL N	62	184	8	41	7	1	0	10	14	1	21	.223	.281	.272		71	-6	3	.910	-2	98	100	3b52/12		-0.8
1918	NY A	11	8	0	0	0	0	0	1	0	0	1	.000	.000	.000		-98	-2	0	1.000	0	197	205	1b5/3		-0.2
Total	5	290	902	75	204	32	16	3	73	58	8	95	.226	.279	.307		76	-28	21-10	.932	2	107	132	3b242,S25,1b6,2b3		-2.3

YEAR	TM LG	G	AB	R	H	2B	3B	HR	RBI	BB-IB	HP	SO	AVG	OBP	SLG	AOPS	ABR	SB-CS	FA	FR	RNG	THR	GAMES AT POSITION	DL	BFW

BECKENDORF, HEINIE Henry Ward B6.15.1884 New York NY D9.15.1949 Jackson Heights NY BR/TR/5-9/174 d4.16

1909	Det A	15	27	1	7	1	0	0	1	2	0		.259	.310	.296	88	0	0	.957	-0	96	88	C15		0.0
1910	Det A	3	7	0	3	0	0	0	2	1	0		.429	.500	.429	179	1	0	.909	-0	115	54	C2		0.1
	Was A	37	103	8	15	1	0	0	10	5	3		.146	.207	.155	14	-10	0	.991	2	103	64	C36		-0.6
	Year	40	110	8	18	1	0	0	12	6	3		.164	.227	.173	26	-9	0	.988	1	104	63	C38		-0.5
Total	2	55	137	9	25	2	0	0	13	8	3		.182	.243	.197	39	-9	0	.983	1	102	68	C53		-0.5

BECKER, BEALS David Beals B7.5.1886 El Dorado KS D8.16.1943 Huntington Park CA BL/TL/5-9/170 d4.19

1908	Pit N	20	65	4	10	0	1	0	0	2	1		.154	.191	.185	20	-6	2	1.000	1	226	0	O17R		-0.7
	Bos N	43	171	13	47	3	1	0	7	7	0		.275	.303	.304	96	-1	7	.941	-1	182	93	O43(0/1/42)		-0.4
	Year	63	236	17	57	3	2	0	7	9	1		.242	.272	.271	74	-8	9	.958	-0	195	66	O60(0/1/59)		-1.1
1909	Bos N	152	562	60	138	15	6	6	24	47	1		.246	.305	.326	91	-7	21	.932	-2	123	150	O152R		-1.7
1910	NY N	80	126	18	36	4	6	3	24	14	0	25	.286	.357	.437	131	4	11	.972	3	107	178	O45(6/23/14)/1		0.6
1911	†NY N	88	172	28	45	11	1	1	20	26	0	22	.262	.359	.355	97	0	19	.975	1	101	129	O55(17/6/33)		-0.1
1912	†NY N	125	402	66	106	18	8	6	58	54	2	35	.264	.354	.393	101	1	30	.958	3	99	125	O117(1/93/26)		-0.3
1913	Cin N	30	108	11	32	5	3	0	14	6	0	12	.296	.333	.398	109	1	0-4	.971	1	110	77	O28(9/8/11)		-0.1
	Phi N	88	306	53	99	19	10	9	44	22	0	30	.324	.369	.539	151	19	11-12	.983	-1	103	58	O77(42/36/2)/1		1.2
	Year	118	414	64	131	24	13	9	58	28	0	42	.316	.360	.502	140	20	11-16	.980	-0	105	63	O105(51/44/13)/1		1.1
1914	Phi N	138	514	76	167	25	5	9	66	37	0	59	.325	.370	.446	133	20	16	.947	4	108	108	O126(87/32/8)		1.9
1915	†Phi N	112	338	38	83	16	4	11	35	26	1	48	.246	.301	.414	114	5	12-15	.943	-6	99	46	O98(90/0/8)		-0.9
Total	8	876	2764	367	763	114	43	45	292	241	5	231	.276	.335	.397	112	36	129-31	.955	4	114	106	O758(252/199/313),1b2		-0.5

BECKER, HEINZ Heinz Reinhard "Dutch" B8.26.1915 Berlin, Germany D11.11.1991 Dallas TX BB/TR (BL 1946)/6-2/200 d4.21

1943	Chi N	24	69	5	10	0	0	0	2	9	0	6	.145	.244	.145	14	-8	0	.983	1	132	66	1b18		-0.8
1945	†Chi N	67	133	25	38	8	2	2	27	17	2	16	.286	.375	.421	124	5	0	1.000	-1	72	132	1b28		0.2
1946	Chi N	9	7	0	2	0	0	0	1	1	0	1	.286	.375	.286	91	0	0	—	0			/H		0.0
	Cle A	50	147	15	44	10	1	0	17	23	0	18	.299	.401	.381	127	7	1-0	.995	-0	91	95	1b44		0.6
1947	Cle A	2	2	0	0	0	0	0	0	0	0	1	.000	.000	.000	-99	-1	0	—	0			/H		-0.1
Total	4	152	358	45	94	18	3	2	47	50	4	42	.263	.359	.346	102	3	1-0	.994	-0	94	100	1b90		-0.1

BECKER, JOE Joseph Edward B6.25.1908 St.Louis MO D1.11.1998 Sunset Hills MO BR/TR/6-1/180 d5.10 C16

1936	Cle A	22	50	5	9	3	1	1	11	5	0	4	.180	.255	.340	45	-5	0-0	.977	-2	89	42	C15		-0.6
1937	Cle A	18	33	3	11	2	1	0	2	3	1	4	.333	.405	.455	116	1	0-0	.949	-1	82	205	C12		0.1
Total	2	40	83	8	20	5	2	1	13	8	1	8	.241	.315	.386	73	-4	0-0	.964	-3	86	112	C27		-0.5

BECKER, MARTY Martin Henry B12.25.1893 Tiffin OH D9.25.1957 Cincinnati OH BB/TL/5-8.5/155 d9.8

1915	NY N	17	52	5	13	2	0	0	3	2	0	9	.250	.278	.288	76	-2	3	.917	1	86	230	O16(0/16/1)		-0.1

BECKER, RICH Richard Godhard B2.1.1972 Aurora IL BL/TL (BB 1993-94, 95p)/5-10/199(180-199) [MinA90 3/85] d9.10

1993	Min A	3	7	3	2	0	0	0	5-0		0	4	.286	.583	.571	210	2	1-1	.875	-0	109	0	O3C	21	0.2
1994	Min A	28	98	12	26	3	0	1	8	13-0	0	25	.265	.351	.327	76	-3	6-1	.989	4	124	135	O26(1/23/2)/D	18	0.2
1995	Min A	106	392	45	93	15	1	2	33	34-0	4	95	.237	.303	.296	57	-25	8-9	.986	7	104	227	O105(2/99/5)		-1.7
1996	Min A	148	525	92	153	31	4	12	71	68-1	2	118	.291	.372	.434	102	3	19-5	.993	17	114	209	O146(15/121/10)		2.1
1997	Min A	132	443	61	117	22	3	10	45	62-1	1	130	.264	.354	.395	94	-3	17-5	.985	1	105	78	O128(3/114/14)		0.1
1998	NY N	49	100	15	19	4	2	3	10	21-2	0	42	.190	.331	.360	84	-2	3-1	.984	3	106	238	O41(17/14/13)		0.0
	Bal A	79	113	22	23	1	0	3	11	22-0	2	34	.204	.343	.292	69	-5	2-0	.984	-3	87	46	O60(5/13/43)/D		-0.8
1999	Mil N	89	139	15	35	5	2	5	16	33-0	0	38	.252	.395	.424	107	3	5-0	.970	0	93	140	O50(16/19/17),D2		0.3
	Oak A	40	125	21	33	3	0	1	10	25-0	2	43	.264	.395	.312	86	-1	3-2	.986	0	85	197	O39(17/32/8)		-0.1
2000	Oak A	23	47	11	9	2	0	1	5	11-0	1	17	.234	.390	.340	88	0	1-0	.949	2	111	306	O19(8/14/1),D2		0.2
	Det A	92	238	48	58	12	0	7	34	56-0	0	70	.244	.383	.382	97	1	1-2	.956	-3	94	78	O80(14/24/47),D3		-0.3
	Year	115	285	59	69	14	0	8	39	67-0	1	87	.242	.384	.375	96	1	2-2	.954	-1	97	116	O99(22/38/48),D5		-0.1
Total	8	789	2227	345	570	100	12	45	243	350-4	12	616	.256	.358	.372	88	-30	66-26	.983	29	104	158	O697(104/476/160),D9	39	0.2

BECKERT, GLENN Glenn Alfred B10.12.1940 Pittsburgh PA BR/TR/6-1/190* d4.12 Mil 1966 Col Allegheny

1965	Chi N	154	614	73	147	21	3	3	30	28-0	3	52	.239	.275	.298	60	-33	6-8	.973	5	108	102	2b153		-1.7
1966	Chi N	153	656	73	188	23	7	1	59	26-0	4	36	.287	.317	.348	84	-15	10-4	.970	-14	96	86	2b152/S		-1.6
1967	Chi N	146	597	91	167	32	3	5	40	30-1	0	25	.280	.314	.369	91	-7	10-3	.968	-2	103	100	2b144		0.4
1968	Chi N	155	643	98	189	28	4	4	37	31-0	2	20	.294	.326	.369	102	2	8-4	.977	10	104	117	2b155		2.9
1969	Chi N★	131	543	69	158	22	1	1	37	24-0	6	24	.291	.325	.341	78	-15	6-0	.965	11	112	91	2b129	21	0.6
1970	Chi N★	143	591	99	170	15	6	3	36	32-0	0	22	.288	.323	.349	71	-24	4-1	.970	13	107	105	2b138/OC		-0.1
1971	Chi N★	131	530	80	181	18	5	2	42	24-0	0	24	.342	.367	.406	104	3	3-2	.986	-1	100	89	2b129		1.2
1972	Chi N★	120	474	51	128	22	2	3	43	23-1	2	17	.270	.304	.344	76	-14	2-1	.976	15	112	101	2b118		0.9
1973	Chi N	114	372	38	95	13	0	0	29	30-1	-2	15	.255	.313	.290	64	-17	0-2	.984	-7	98	88	2b88	22	-2.1
1974	SD N	64	172	11	44	1	0	0	7	11-0	1	19	.256	.301	.262	61	-9	0-0	.938	-10	84	67	2b36/3	69	-1.8
1975	SD N	9	16	2	6	1	0	0	1	0-0	0	1	.375	.412	.438	145	1	0-0	1.000	-0	106	0	3b4		0.1
Total	11	1320	5208	685	1473	196	31	22	360	260-3	19	243	.283	.318	.345	81	-128	49-25	.973	19	104	98	2b1242,3b5/OCS	112	-1.2

BECKLEY, JAKE Jacob Peter "Eagle Eye" B8.4.1867 Hannibal MO D6.25.1918 Kansas City MO BL/TL/5-10/200 d6.20 HF1971

1888	Pit N	71	283	35	97	15	3	0	27	7		22	.343	.363	.417	162	20	20	.979	-3	73	110	1b71		1.0
1889	Pit N	123	522	91	157	24	10	9	97	29	6	29	.301	.345	.437	130	19	11	.982	2	98	111	1b122/OR		0.8
1890	Pit P	121	516	109	167	38	22	9	120	42	6	32	.324	.381	.535	156	40	18	.976	-0	97	91	1b121		2.3
1891	Pit N	133	554	94	162	20	19	4	73	44	8	46	.292	.353	.419	128	18	13	.982	13	147	90	1b133		1.6
1892	Pit N	151	614	102	145	21	19	10	96	31	14	44	.236	.288	.381	102	-3	30	.978	20	163	101	1b151		1.5
1893	Pit N	131	542	108	164	32	15	5	106	54	20	26	.303	.386	.459	127	21	15	.986	11	130	106	1b131		2.5
1894	Pit N	132	537	123	185	36	19	7	122	43	19	21	.345	.412	.521	125	22	21	.978	5	115	94	1b132		2.0
1895	Pit N	130	534	104	175	31	19	5	111	24	21	20	.328	.380	.485	129	22	20	.978	-7	75	98	1b130		1.2
1896	Pit N	59	217	44	55	7	5	3	32	22	10	28	.253	.349	.373	94	-1	8	.982	-0	99	120	1b56,O3C/2		-0.2
	NY N	46	182	37	55	8	4	6	38	9	5	7	.302	.352	.489	124	5	11	.982	-1	96	69	1b45,O2L		0.4
	Year	105	399	81	110	15	9	9	70	31	15	35	.276	.351	.426	108	4	19	.982	-1	98	98	1b101,O5(2/3/0)/2		0.2
1897	NY N	17	68	8	17	2	3	1	11	2	3		.250	.301	.412	90	-2	2	.973	2	152	130	1b17		0.0
	Cin N	97	365	76	126	17	9	7	76	18	12		.345	.393	.499	127	12	23	.979	-3	85	114	1b97		0.8
	Year	114	433	84	143	19	12	8	87	20	15		.330	.380	.485	121	11	25	.978	-1	96	117	1b114		0.8
1898	Cin N	118	459	86	135	20	12	4	72	28	10		.294	.348	.416	111	5	6	.983	-1	92	107	1b118		0.8
1899	Cin N	135	517	87	172	27	16	3	99	40	10		.333	.392	.464	132	22	20	.986	5	107	97	1b135		2.4
1900	Cin N	141	558	98	190	26	10	2	94	40	8		.341	.389	.434	130	23	23	.980	5	115	115	1b140		1.6
1901	Cin N	140	580	78	178	36	13	3	79	28	7		.307	.346	.429	133	23	4	.977	-4	89	104	1b140		1.6
1902	Cin N	129	531	82	175	23	7	5	69	34	6		.330	.377	.427	135	21	15	.983	2	87	119	1b129/P		1.7
1903	Cin N	120	459	85	150	29	10	2	81	42	1		.327	.384	.447	123	13	23	.976	4	114	96	1b119		1.4
1904	StL N	142	551	72	179	22	9	1	67	35	9		.325	.375	.403	147	30	17	.988	-12	67	113	1b142		1.7
1905	StL N	134	514	48	147	20	10	1	57	30	6		.286	.333	.370	113	7	12	.982	-8	80	79	1b134		-0.3
1906	StL N	87	320	29	79	16	6	0	44	13	1		.247	.283	.334	96	-3	5	.987	-4	78	90	1b85		-1.0
1907	StL N	32	115	6	23	1	0	0	7	3	1		.200	.222	.235	45	-8	0	.988	-2	71	107	1b32		-1.2
Total	20	2389	9538	1602	2934	473	244	87	1578	616	183	270	.308	.361	.436	126	306	315	.981	19	102	102	1b2380,Q6(2/3/1)/P2		23.0

BECQUER, JULIO Julio (Villegas) B12.20.1931 Havana, Cuba BL/TL/5-11.5/178(162-178) d9.13

1955	Was A	10	14	3	3	0	0	0	1	0-0	0	1	.214	.214	.214	16	-2	0-0	1.000	0	205	124	1b2		-0.1
1957	Was A	105	186	14	42	6	2	2	22	10-2	1	29	.226	.269	.312	59	-11	3-3	1.000	-0	90	86	1b43		-1.4
1958	Was A	86	164	10	39	6	1	0	12	8-3	0	21	.238	.270	.256	47	-12	1-2	.994	5	149	74	1b42/OL		-1.0
1959	Was A	108	220	20	59	12	5	1	26	8-2	1	17	.268	.296	.382	85	-5	3-2	.990	1	113	102	1b53		-0.7
1960	Was A	110	298	41	75	15	7	4	35	12-3	1	35	.252	.282	.389	81	-10	1-3	.989	-3	87	93	1b77/P		-0.9
1961	LA A	11	8	0	0	0	0	0	0	1-0	0	5	.000	.111	.000	-61	-2	0-0	1.000	0	92	0	1b5		-0.2
	Min A	57	84	13	20	1	2	5	18	2-1	0	12	.238	.253	.476	86	-3	0-1	1.000	-0	60	126	1b18,O5L/P		-0.4
	Year	68	92	13	20	1	2	5	18	3-1	0	17	.217	.240	.435	72	-5	0-1	1.000	-0	65	105	1b23,O5L/P		-0.6
1963	Min A	1	0	0	0	0	0	0	0	0-0	0		—	—	—			0-0	—	0			/H		0.0
Total	7	488	974	100	238	37	16	12	114	41-11	3	120	.244	.276	.352	70	-45	8-11	.993	3	100	91	1b240,O6L,P2		-5.6

YEAR	TM LG	G	AB	R	H	2B	3B	HR	RBI	BB-IB	HP	SO	AVG	OBP	SLG	AOPS	ABR	SB-CS	FA	FR	RNG	THR	GAMES AT POSITION	DL	BFW

BEDELL, HOWIE Howard William B9.29.1935 Clearfield PA BL/TR/6-1/185* d4.10 C2 Col West Chester

1962	Mil N	58	138	15	27	1	2	0	2	11-0	0	22	.196	.255	.232	33	-14	1-0	.955	-1	108	0	O45(44/2/0)		-1.6
1968	Phi N	9	7	0	1	0	0	0	1	1-0	0	0	.143	.250	.143	20	-1	0-0	—	0			/H		-0.1
Total	2	67	145	15	28	1	2	0	3	12-0	0	22	.193	.253	.228	32	-15	1-0	.955	-1	108	0	O45(44/2/0)		-1.7

BEDFORD, GENE William Eugene B12.2.1896 Dallas TX D10.6.1977 San Antonio TX BB/TR/5-8/170 d6.25 Col SMU

| 1925 | Cle A | 2 | 3 | 1 | 0 | 0 | 0 | 0 | 0 | 0-0 | 0 | 1 | .000 | .000 | .000 | -99 | -1 | 0-0 | 1.000 | -1 | 57 | 0 | 2b2 | | -0.2 |

BEECHER, ED Edward Harry B7.2.1860 Guilford CT D9.12.1935 Hartford CT BL/TL/5-10/185 d6.28

1887	Pit N	41	169	15	41	8	0	2	22	7	2	8	.243	.281	.325	73	-6	8	.915	5	167	79	O41(18/22/1)		-0.2
1889	Was N	42	179	20	53	9	0	0	30	5	1	4	.296	.319	.346	91	-2	3	.861	-2	93	64	O39(1/0/38),1b3		-0.4
1890	Buf P	126	536	69	159	22	10	3	90	29	7	23	.297	.341	.392	104	3	14	.810	-5	102	72	O126(119/0/7)/P		-0.4
1891	Was AA	58	235	35	57	11	3	2	28	27	5	9	.243	.333	.340	97	0	17	.824	0	116	142	O58(52/6/0)		-0.1
	Phi AA	16	71	9	15	2	4	0	7	3	0	4	.211	.243	.352	70	-4	7	1.000	-0	81	0	O16R		-0.4
	Year	74	306	44	72	13	7	2	35	30	5	13	.235	.314	.343	91	-4	24	.845	0	110	116	O74(52/6/16)		-0.5
Total	4	283	1190	148	325	52	17	7	177	71	15	48	.273	.322	.363	94	-9	49	.843	-2	112	84	O280(190/28/62),1b3/P		-1.5

BEELER, JODIE Joseph Sam B11.26.1921 Dallas TX D10.8.2002 Mesquite TX BR/TR/6-0/170 d9.21

| 1944 | Cin N | 3 | 3 | 0 | 0 | 0 | 0 | 0 | 0 | 0-0 | 0 | 2 | .000 | .000 | .000 | -99 | -1 | 0 | .000 | -1 | 0 | 0 | /23 | | -0.2 |

BEGLEY, GENE Eugene T. B6.7.1861 Brooklyn NY d9.11

| 1886 | NY N | 5 | 16 | 1 | 2 | 0 | 0 | 0 | 1 | 1 | | 3 | .125 | .176 | .125 | -7 | -2 | 1 | .864 | -0 | | | C3,O2R | | -0.2 |

BEGLEY, JIM James Lawrence "Imp" B9.19.1902 San Francisco CA D2.22.1957 San Francisco CA BR/TR/5-6/145 d5.28 Col San Francisco

| 1924 | Cin N | 2 | 5 | 1 | 1 | 0 | 0 | 0 | 2 | 0-0 | 0 | 0 | .200 | .429 | .200 | 75 | 0 | 0-0 | .933 | 0 | 118 | 0 | 2b2 | | 0.0 |

BEHEL, STEVE Stephen Arnold Douglas B11.6.1860 Earlville IL D2.15.1945 Los Angeles CA d9.27

1884	Mil U	9	33	5	8	1	0	0		3			.242	.306	.273	140	1		1.000	-0	64	0	O9L		0.1
1886	NY AA	59	224	32	46	5	2	0	17	22	1		.205	.279	.246	71	-6	16	.858	-4	76	0	O59(26/33/0)		-1.0
Total	2	68	257	37	54	6	2	0	17	25	1		.210	.283	.249	76	-5	16	.865	-4	75	0	O68(35/33/0)		-0.9

BEJMA, OLLIE Alojzy Frank B9.12.1907 South Bend IN D1.3.1995 South Bend IN BR/TR/5-10/165 d4.24

1934	StL A	95	262	39	71	16	3	2	29	40	4	36	.271	.376	.378	87	-4	3-2	.952	-6	93	107	S32,2b14,3b13,O9R		-0.6
1935	StL A	64	198	18	38	8	2	2	26	27	0	21	.192	.289	.283	46	-16	1-0	.952	-4	101	95	2b47,S8,3b2		-1.6
1936	StL A	67	139	19	36	2	3	2	18	27	0	21	.259	.380	.360	81	-4	0-0	.963	-9	88	43	2b32,3b7/S		-0.9
1939	Chi A	90	307	52	77	9	3	8	44	36	1	27	.251	.331	.378	79	-11	1-3	.981	-8	95	84	2b81/S3		-1.3
Total	4	316	906	128	222	35	11	14	117	130	5	105	.245	.343	.354	75	-35	5-5	.967	-26	94	78	2b174,S42,3b23,O9R		-4.4

BELANGER, MARK Mark Henry B6.8.1944 Pittsfield MA D10.6.1998 New York NY BR/TR/6-1/170* d8.7

1965	Bal A	11	3	1	1	0	0	0	0	0-0	0	1	.333	.333	.333	88	0	0-1	1.000	0	61	662	S4		0.0
1966	Bal A	8	19	2	3	1	0	0	0	0-0	0	3	.158	.158	.211	5	-2	0-0	1.000	3	136	106	S6		0.1
1967	Bal A	69	184	19	32	5	0	1	10	12-1	0	46	.174	.224	.217	31	-16	6-1	.952	2	93	90	S38,2b26,3b2		-1.0
1968	Bal A	145	472	40	98	13	0	2	21	40-2	4	114	.208	.272	.248	59	-23	10-1	.969	19	106	105	S145		1.2
1969	†Bal A	150	530	76	152	17	4	2	50	53-5	2	54	.287	.351	.345	95	-2	14-6	.968	-8	97	108	S148		0.8
1970	†Bal A	145	459	53	100	6	5	1	36	52-3	5	65	.218	.303	.259	56	-27	13-2	.970	-2	101	110	S143		-1.2
1971	†Bal A	150	500	67	133	19	4	0	35	73-6	2	48	.266	.365	.320	91	1	10-8	.978	-1	97	103	S149		1.8
1972	Bal A	113	285	36	53	9	1	2	16	18-1	2	53	.186	.236	.246	43	-20	6-3	.975	9	101	114	S105		-0.1
1973	†Bal A	154	470	60	106	15	1	0	27	49-1	5	54	.226	.302	.262	61	-23	13-6	.971	5	106	118	S154		0.0
1974	†Bal A	155	493	54	111	14	4	5	36	51-0	2	69	.225	.298	.300	75	-16	17-7	.984	3	106	110	S155		0.8
1975	Bal A	152	442	44	100	11	1	3	27	36-0	1	53	.226	.286	.276	63	-22	16-4	.978	30	116	139	S152		2.7
1976	Bal A★	153	522	66	141	22	2	1	40	51-0	2	64	.270	.336	.326	100	1	27-17	.982	16	112	111	S153		3.7
1977	Bal A	144	402	39	83	13	4	2	30	43-1	3	68	.206	.287	.274	57	-24	15-8	.985	19	108	117	S142		0.9
1978	Bal A	135	348	39	74	13	0	0	16	40-1	6	55	.213	.299	.250	61	-17	6-6	.985	30	118	119	S134		2.5
1979	†Bal A	101	198	28	33	6	2	0	9	29-0	1	33	.167	.273	.217	36	-17	5-1	.990	-4	93	99	S98	32	-1.3
1980	Bal A	113	268	37	61	7	3	0	22	12-0	0	25	.228	.261	.276	48	-20	6-3	.975	-3	97	92	S109		-1.4
1981	Bal A	64	139	9	23	3	2	1	10	12-0	2	25	.165	.242	.237	39	-11	2-1	.973	-0	102	64	S63		-0.6
1982	LA N	54	50	6	12	1	0	0	4	5-1	0	10	.240	.309	.260	62	-2	1-0	.953	-4	99	40	S44/2		-0.4
Total	18	2016	5784	676	1316	175	33	20	389	576-22	42	839	.228	.300	.280	67	-240	167-75	.977	114	105	109	S1942,2b27,3b2	32	8.5

BELARDI, WAYNE Carroll Wayne B9.5.1930 St.Helena CA D10.21.1993 Santa Cruz CA BL/TL/6-1/185* d4.18 Col Santa Clara

1950	Bro N	10	10	0	0	0	0	0	0	0-0	0	4	.000	.000	.000	-98	-3	0	1.000	-0	0	0	/1		-0.3
1951	Bro N	3	3	1	1	0	1	0	0	0	0	0	.333	.333	1.000	240	0	0-0	—	0			/H		0.0
1953	†Bro N	69	163	19	39	3	2	11	34	16	1	40	.239	.311	.485	101	-1	0-0	.984	-1	95	124	1b38	30	-0.3
1954	Bro N	11	9	0	2	0	0	0	1	2	0	3	.222	.364	.222	55	-1	0-0	—	0			/H		-0.2
	Det A	88	250	27	58	7	1	11	24	33	5	34	.232	.330	.400	102	0	1-0	.988	2	111	89	1b79		-0.2
1955	Det A	3	3	0	0	0	0	0	0	0-0	0	1	.000	.000	.000	-99	-1	0-0	—	0			/H		-0.1
1956	Det A	79	154	24	43	3	1	6	15	15-1	2	13	.279	.371	.429	111	3	0-0	.988	-1	94	78	1b31,O2(2/0/1)		0.0
Total	6	263	592	71	143	13	5	28	74	66-1	14	97	.242	.330	.422	100	-3	1-0	.987	-0	103	95	1b149,O2(2/0/1)	30	-0.9

BELCHER, KEVIN Kevin Donnell B8.8.1967 Waco TX BR/TR/6-0/170 [TexA87 6/155] d9.3 Col Navarro (TX) JC

| 1990 | Tex A | 16 | 15 | 4 | 1 | 0 | 0 | 0 | 0 | 2-0 | 0 | 6 | .133 | .235 | .200 | 23 | -2 | 0-0 | 1.000 | 0 | 115 | 0 | O9(2/5/2) | | -0.1 |

BELDEN, IRA Ira Allison B4.16.1874 Cleveland OH D7.15.1916 Lakewood OH BL/TR/5-11/175 d9.17

| 1897 | Cle N | 8 | 30 | 5 | 8 | 0 | 2 | 0 | 4 | 2 | 1 | | .267 | .333 | .400 | 88 | -1 | 0 | 1.000 | 1 | 159 | 0 | O8R | | 0.0 |

BELK, TIM Timothy William B4.6.1970 Cincinnati OH BR/TR/6-3/200 [CinN92 15/409] d6.25 Col Lubbock Christian

| 1996 | Cin N | 7 | 15 | 2 | 3 | 0 | 0 | 0 | 2 | 2-0 | 0 | 2 | .200 | .250 | .200 | 22 | -0 | 0-0 | 1.000 | -1 | 0 | 57 | 1b6 | | -0.3 |

BELL, BUDDY David Gus B8.27.1951 Pittsburgh PA BR/TR/6-2/185(180-200) [CleA69 16/373] d4.15 M7/C5 f-Gus s-David s-Mike OF(11/64/66)

1972	Cle A	132	466	49	119	21	1	9	36	34-8	3	29	.255	.310	.363	96	-2	5-6	.990	5	104	121	O123(0/63/65),3b6		-0.3
1973	Cle A★	156	631	86	169	23	7	14	59	49-2	6	47	.268	.325	.393	100	-1	7-15	.958	27	117	141	3b154,O2(0/1/1)		2.1
1974	Cle A	116	423	51	111	15	1	7	46	35-1	3	29	.262	.322	.352	95	-3	1-3	.963	15	115	127	3b115/D	45	1.1
1975	Cle A	153	553	66	150	20	4	10	59	51-6	1	72	.271	.332	.376	100	-0	6-5	.950	-0	95	95	3b153		-0.2
1976	Cle A	159	604	75	170	26	2	7	60	44-3	2	49	.281	.329	.366	105	3	3-8	.956	8	104	86	3b158,1b2		0.8
1977	Cle A	129	479	64	140	23	4	11	64	45-5	1	63	.292	.351	.426	115	10	1-8	.960	13	110	106	3b118,O11L		1.7
1978	Cle A	142	556	71	157	27	8	6	62	39-1	0	43	.282	.328	.392	103	1	1-3	.970	27	116	108	3b139/D		2.5
1979	Tex A	162	670	89	200	42	3	18	101	30-4	3	45	.299	.327	.451	110	7	5-4	.969	28	123	84	3b147,S33		3.4
1980	Tex A★	129	490	76	161	24	4	17	83	40-11	0	39	.329	.379	.498	142	28	3-1	.981	27	115	100	3b120,S3	15	5.1
1981	Tex A★	97	360	44	106	16	1	10	64	42-10	3	30	.294	.364	.428	137	18	3-3	.961	34	144	110	3b96/S		5.1
1982	Tex A★	148	537	62	159	27	2	13	67	70-8	2	50	.296	.376	.426	126	22	5-4	.976	38	127	113	3b145,S4		5.6
1983	Tex A	156	618	75	171	35	3	14	66	50-5	4	48	.277	.332	.411	105	5	3-5	.967	18	113	88	3b154		1.8
1984	Tex A★	148	553	88	174	36	5	11	83	63-8	3	54	.315	.382	.458	128	23	2-1	.958	24	117	104	3b147		4.5
1985	Tex A	84	313	33	74	13	3	4	32	33-1	1	21	.236	.308	.335	76	-10	3-2	.942	17	122	139	3b83		0.6
	Cin N	67	247	28	54	15	2	6	36	34-2	0	27	.219	.311	.368	86	-4	0-1	.946	-11	77	117	3b67		-1.7
1986	Cin N	155	568	89	158	29	3	20	75	73-4	5	49	.278	.362	.445	118	15	2-8	.975	-9	97	111	3b151/2		0.6
1987	Cin N	143	522	74	148	29	2	17	70	71-3	1	39	.284	.369	.425	106	6	4-1	.979	-24	82	73	3b142		-1.9
1988	Cin N	21	54	3	10	0	0	3	7-1	0	3	.185	.270	.185	34	-4	0-0	.968	-1	89	105	3b13,1b2	33	-0.6
	Hou N	74	269	24	68	10	1	7	38	19-1	0	29	.253	.301	.375	97	-2	1-1	.924	-10	88	79	3b66,1b7	15	-1.4
	Year	95	323	27	78	10	1	7	40	26-2	0	32	.241	.295	.344	86	-7	1-1	.931	-11	88	83	3b79,1b9		-2.0
1989	Tex A	34	82	4	15	4	0	0	3	7-0	0	16	.183	.247	.232	35	-7	0-0	1.000	0	96	0	D22,3b9/1	15	-0.8
Total	18	2405	8995	1151	2514	425	56	201	1106	836-84	38	776	.279	.341	.406	108	105	55-79	.964	229	110	104	3b2183,O136R,S41,D24,1b12/2	123	28.0

BELL, DAVID David Michael B9.14.1972 Cincinnati OH BR/TR/5-10/175(170-195) [CleA90 7/190] d5.3 f-Buddy gf-Gus b-Mike

1995	Cle A	2	2	0	0	0	0	0	0	0-0	0	1	.000	.000	.000	-98	-1	0-0	1.000	0	252	0	3b2		0.0
	StL N	39	144	13	36	7	2	2	19	4-0	2	25	.250	.278	.368	68	-7	1-2	.967	-2	100	116	2b37,3b3		-0.8
1996	StL N	62	145	12	31	6	0	1	9	10-2	1	22	.214	.268	.276	44	-12	1-1	.953	-4	110	24	3b45,2b20/S		-0.7
1997	StL N	66	142	9	30	7	2	1	12	10-2	1	28	.211	.261	.310	49	-11	1-0	.913	-4	99	34	3b35,2b23,S13	62	-1.4
1998	StL N	4	9	2	2	1	0	0	0	0-0	0	1	.222	.222	.333		-1	0-0	1.000	-1	53	0	3b4/2		-0.2

YEAR	TM LG	G	AB	R	H	2B	3B	HR	RBI	BB-IB	HP	SO	AVG	OBP	SLG	AOPS	ABR	SB-CS	FA	FR	RNG	THR	GAMES AT POSITION	DL	BFW
	Cle A	107	340	37	89	21	2	10	41	22-4	2	54	.262	.306	.424	85	-8	0-4	.982	13	107	99	2b101,3b6/1S		0.7
	Sea A	21	80	11	26	8	0	0	8	5-0	0	8	.325	.365	.425	104	1	0-0	.984	3	111	132	2b14,1b5,3b5/OL		0.4
	Year	128	420	48	115	29	2	10	49	27-4	2	62	.274	.331	.432	89	-7	0-4	.982	16	108	103	2b115,3b11,1b6/SOL		1.1
1999	†Sea A	157	597	92	160	31	2	21	78	58-0	2	90	.268	.331	.432	95	-6	7-4	.978	2	101	105	2b154,1b4/S		0.3
2000	†Sea A	133	454	57	112	24	2	11	47	42-0	6	66	.247	.305	.381	78	-16	2-3	.944	-10	93	94	3b93,2b48,1b2/S		-2.2
2001	†Sea A	135	470	62	122	28	0	15	64	28-1	3	59	.260	.303	.415	92	-6	2-1	.961	2	102	112	3b134,1b2		-0.4
2002	†SF N	154	552	82	144	29	2	20	73	54-2	9	80	.261	.333	.429	107	2	1-2	.973	-7	98	86	3b139,2b12,S3,1b2		-0.4
2003	Phi N	85	297	32	58	14	0	4	37	41-1	4	40	.195	.296	.283	58	-18	0-0	.966	6	106	117	3b85,2b3	74	-1.1
2004	Phi N	143	533	67	155	33	1	18	77	57-4	6	75	.291	.363	.458	108	7	1-1	.943	3	109	89	3b142		1.1
2005	Phi N	150	557	53	138	31	1	10	61	47-6	5	69	.248	.310	.361	73	-21	0-1	.951	10	106	85	3b150		-1.1
Total 11		1258	4322	527	1103	240	14	113	526	378-22	40	619	.255	.318	.396	86	-97	16-19	.955	18	103	91	3b843,2b413,S20,1b16/OL	136	-5.8

BELL, GUS David Russell B11.15.1928 Louisville KY D5.7.1995 Montgomery OH BL/TR/6-2/196* d5.30 s-Buddy gs-David gs-Mike

YEAR	TM LG	G	AB	R	H	2B	3B	HR	RBI	BB-IB	HP	SO	AVG	OBP	SLG	AOPS	ABR	SB-CS	FA	FR	RNG	THR	GAMES AT POSITION	DL	BFW
1950	Pit N	111	422	62	119	22	11	8	53	28	4	46	.282	.333	.443	99	-2	4	.977	5	109	131	O104R		-0.1
1951	Pit N	149	600	80	167	27	12	16	89	42	4	41	.278	.330	.443	103	0	1-4	.986	1	95	136	O145R		-0.4
1952	Pit N	131	468	53	117	21	5	16	59	36	2	72	.250	.306	.419	97	-7	1-4	.972	-7	90	73	O123R		-1.7
1953	Cin N★	151	610	102	183	37	5	30	105	48	3	72	.300	.354	.525	124	21	0-2	.977	5	103	111	O151(0/145/6)		1.7
1954	Cin N	153	619	104	185	38	7	17	101	44	4	58	.299	.349	.465	108	7	5-3	.986	-2	97	102	O153C		-0.2
1955	Cin N	154	610	88	188	30	6	27	104	54-2	1	57	.308	.361	.510	122	19	4-4	.987	-13	91	34	O154C		-0.2
1956	Cin N★	150	603	82	176	31	4	29	84	50-4	3	66	.292	.347	.501	117	15	6-2	.986	-11	84	110	O149C		-0.3
1957	Cin N	121	510	65	149	20	3	13	61	30-5	3	54	.292	.332	.420	95	-4	0-1	.988	-5	96	79	O121C		-1.5
1958	Cin N	112	385	42	97	16	2	10	46	36-7	1	40	.252	.314	.382	80	-11	2-3	.996	-4	93	86	O107(20/87/0)		-2.1
1959	Cin N	148	580	59	170	27	2	19	115	29-1	2	44	.293	.325	.445	101	-1	2-3	.996	4	99	132	O145(6/0/141)		-0.3
1960	Cin N	143	515	65	135	19	5	12	62	29-3	1	40	.262	.300	.388	86	-11	4-3	.988	1	100	112	O131(41/0/97)		-1.6
1961	†Cin N	103	235	27	60	10	1	3	33	18-3	0	21	.255	.298	.345	72	-9	1-1	.991	-1	106	20	O75(43/1/33)		-1.4
1962	NY N	30	101	8	15	2	0	1	6	10-0	1	7	.149	.221	.198	14	-12	0-1	.979	3	90	327	O26R		-1.1
	Mil N	79	214	28	61	11	3	5	24	12-2	0	17	.285	.322	.435	104	0	0-0	.987	-1	93	90	O58(52/1/8)		-0.3
	Year	109	315	36	76	13	3	6	30	22-2	0	24	.241	.288	.359	74	-12	0-1	.984	3	92	173	O84(52/1/34)		-1.4
1963	Mil N	3	3	0	1	0	0	0	0	0-0	0	0	.333	.333	.333	94	0	0-0	—	0			/H	130	0.0
1964	Mil N	3	3	0	0	0	0	0	0	0-0	0	1	.000	.000	.000	-99	-1	0-0	—	0			/H		-0.1
Total 15		1741	6478	865	1823	311	66	206	942	470-27	27	636	.281	.330	.445	102	7	30-31	.985	-26	96	101	O1642(162/811/683)	130	-9.6

BELL, DEREK Derek Nathaniel B12.11.1968 Tampa FL BR/TR/6-2/215(200-215) [TorA87 2/49] d6.28

YEAR	TM LG	G	AB	R	H	2B	3B	HR	RBI	BB-IB	HP	SO	AVG	OBP	SLG	AOPS	ABR	SB-CS	FA	FR	RNG	THR	GAMES AT POSITION	DL	BFW
1991	Tor A	18	28	5	4	0	0	0	1	6-0	1	5	.143	.314	.143	30	-2	3-2	.889	-2	75	0	O13(7/6/0)		-0.5
1992	†Tor A	61	161	23	39	6	3	2	15	15-1	5	34	.242	.324	.354	86	-3	7-2	1.000	2	104	139	O56(24/18/15)/D	29	-0.1
1993	SD N	150	542	73	142	19	1	21	72	23-5	12	122	.262	.303	.417	91	-9	26-5	.976	1	104	125	O125(1/119/6),3b19		-0.3
1994	SD N	108	434	54	135	20	0	14	54	29-5	1	88	.311	.354	.454	113	7	24-8	.962	-5	99	55	O108C		0.6
1995	Hou N	112	452	63	151	21	2	8	86	33-2	8	71	.334	.385	.442	127	18	27-9	.963	4	87	132	O110(0/30/82)		1.3
1996	Hou N	158	627	84	165	40	3	17	113	40-8	8	123	.263	.311	.418	99	-3	29-3	.977	2	95	153	O157(0/0/157)		-0.3
1997	†Hou N	129	493	67	136	29	3	15	71	40-3	12	94	.276	.344	.438	107	4	15-7	.967	-8	92	61	O125(0/36/89)/D	30	-0.6
1998	†Hou N	156	630	111	198	41	2	22	108	51-0	4	126	.314	.364	.490	127	25	13-13	.973	-3	95	78	O154R		1.5
1999	†Hou N	128	509	61	120	22	0	12	66	50-1	4	129	.236	.306	.350	67	-26	18-6	.985	-14	79	49	O126R	15	-4.3
2000	†NY N	144	546	87	145	31	4	18	69	65-0	6	125	.266	.348	.425	100	0	8-4	.988	-7	90	58	O143(0/5/142)/P		-1.2
2001	Pit N	46	156	14	27	3	0	5	13	25-5	0	38	.173	.287	.288	48	-12	0-2	.988	-1	88	103	O46(5/1/43)	127	-1.6
Total 11		1210	4578	642	1262	232	15	134	668	377-30	61	955	.276	.336	.421	100	-1	170-51	.975	-39	92	92	O1163(37/325/814),3b19,D2/P	201	-5.5

BELL, FERN Fernando Jerome Lee (b Fern Oran Bell) "Danny" B1.21.1913 Ada OK D8.29.2000 Rancho Mirage CA BR/TR/6-0/180 d4.17

YEAR	TM LG	G	AB	R	H	2B	3B	HR	RBI	BB-IB	HP	SO	AVG	OBP	SLG	AOPS	ABR	SB-CS	FA	FR	RNG	THR	GAMES AT POSITION	DL	BFW
1939	Pit N	83	262	44	75	5	8	2	34	42	0	18	.286	.385	.389	110	5	2	.975	-1	100	120	O67(15/46/7)/3		0.2
1940	Pit N	6	3	0	0	0	0	0	1	1	0	1	.000	.250	.000	-26	0	0	—	0			/H		0.0
Total 2		89	265	44	75	5	8	2	35	43	0	19	.283	.383	.385	109	5	2	.975	-1	100	120	O67(15/46/7)/3		0.2

BELL, FRANK Frank Gustav B1863 Cincinnati OH D4.14.1891 Cincinnati OH 6-0/? d7.7 b-Charlie

YEAR	TM LG	G	AB	R	H	2B	3B	HR	RBI	BB-IB	HP	SO	AVG	OBP	SLG	AOPS	ABR	SB-CS	FA	FR	RNG	THR	GAMES AT POSITION	DL	BFW
1885	Bro AA	10	29	5	5	0	1	0	2	1			.172	.200	.241	39	-2		.739	-4			C5,O4(0/3/1),3b2		-0.5

BELL, GEORGE George Antonio (Mathey) B10.21.1959 San Pedro de Macoris, D.R. BR/TR/6-1/190(185-210) d4.9 b-Juan

YEAR	TM LG	G	AB	R	H	2B	3B	HR	RBI	BB-IB	HP	SO	AVG	OBP	SLG	AOPS	ABR	SB-CS	FA	FR	RNG	THR	GAMES AT POSITION	DL	BFW
1981	Tor A	60	163	19	38	2	1	5	12	5-1	0	27	.233	.256	.350	69	-7	3-2	.969	2	110	108	O44(26/0/18),D8		-0.7
1983	Tor A	39	112	5	30	5	4	2	17	4-1	2	17	.268	.305	.438	95	-1	1-1	.954	-1	98	45	O34(28/0/6),D2		-0.4
1984	Tor A	159	606	85	177	39	4	26	87	24-2	8	86	.292	.326	.498	120	15	11-2	.971	-3	93	114	O147(66/0/90),3b3,D7		0.7
1985	†Tor A	157	607	87	167	28	6	28	95	43-6	8	90	.275	.327	.479	115	11	21-6	.968	-2	93	124	O157L,3b2		0.5
1986	Tor A	159	641	101	198	38	6	31	108	41-3	2	62	.309	.349	.532	133	27	7-8	.966	-3	85	173	O147L,D11,3b2		1.5
1987	Tor A★	156	610	111	188	32	4	47	134	39-9	7	75	.308	.352	.605	145	37	5-1	.960	9		146	O148L/23D		2.5
1988	Tor A	156	614	78	165	27	5	24	97	34-5	1	66	.269	.304	.446	108	3	4-2	.946	-12	85	94	O149L,D7		-1.3
1989	†Tor A	153	613	88	182	41	2	18	104	33-3	4	80	.297	.330	.458	124	18	4-3	.963	-10	92	48	O134L,D19		0.3
1990	Tor A★	142	562	67	149	25	0	21	86	32-7	3	80	.265	.303	.422	100	-2	3-2	.979	-1	102	58	O106L,D36		-0.8
1991	Chi N★	149	558	63	159	27	0	25	86	32-6	2	62	.285	.323	.468	116	10	2-6	.962	-10	84	74	O146L		-0.5
1992	Chi A	155	627	74	160	27	0	25	112	31-8	6	97	.255	.294	.418	99	-4	5-2	.964	-2	87	0	D140,O15L		-1.1
1993	Chi A	102	410	36	89	17	2	13	64	13-2	1	49	.217	.243	.363	63	-24	1-1	—	0	0		D102	41	-2.9
Total 12		1587	6123	814	1702	308	34	265	1002	331-53	49	771	.278	.316	.469	113	83	67-36	.964	-45	91	104	O1227(1123/0/114),D339,3b8/2	41	-2.2

BELL, JAY Jay Stuart B12.11.1965 Eglin A.F.B. FL BR/TR/6-1/185* [MinA84 1/8] d9.29 C1

YEAR	TM LG	G	AB	R	H	2B	3B	HR	RBI	BB-IB	HP	SO	AVG	OBP	SLG	AOPS	ABR	SB-CS	FA	FR	RNG	THR	GAMES AT POSITION	DL	BFW
1986	Cle A	5	14	3	5	2	0	1	4	2-0	0	3	.357	.438	.714	210	2	0-0	.778	-0	148	101	2b2,D2		0.2
1987	Cle A	38	125	14	27	9	1	2	13	8-0	1	31	.216	.269	.352	62	-7	2-0	.947	-1	95	100	S38		-0.4
1988	Cle A	73	211	23	46	5	1	2	21	21-0	1	53	.218	.289	.280	59	-12	4-2	.965	-17	84	83	S72/D		-2.4
1989	Pit N	78	271	33	70	13	3	2	27	19-0	1	47	.258	.307	.351	91	-4	5-3	.968	-9	95	111	S78		-0.8
1990	†Pit N	159	583	93	148	28	7	7	52	65-0	3	109	.254	.329	.362	94	-4	10-6	.970	1	102	112	S159		0.9
1991	†Pit N	157	608	96	164	32	8	16	67	52-1	4	99	.270	.330	.428	113	9	10-6	.968	8	106	106	S156		3.0
1992	†Pit N	159	632	87	167	36	6	9	55	55-0	4	103	.264	.326	.383	101	1	7-5	.973	15	112	112	S159		3.0
1993	Pit N★	154	604	102	187	32	9	9	51	77-6	6	122	.310	.392	.437	122	22	16-10	.986	22	112	106	S154		5.4
1994	Pit N	110	424	68	117	35	4	9	45	49-1	3	82	.276	.353	.441	104	4	2-0	.973	18	115	99	S110		2.9
1995	Pit N	138	530	79	139	28	4	13	55	55-1	4	110	.262	.336	.404	92	-6	2-5	.978	11	105	105	S136,3b3		1.3
1996	Pit N	151	527	65	132	26	3	13	71	54-5	5	108	.250	.323	.391	85	-11	6-4	.986	6	106	82	S151		0.5
1997	KC A	153	573	89	167	28	3	21	92	71-2	4	101	.291	.368	.461	113	12	10-6	.985	8	106	111	S149,3b4		2.9
1998	Ari N	155	549	79	138	29	5	20	67	81-3	7	129	.251	.353	.432	105	6	3-5	.971	-11	101	99	S138,2b15		0.4
1999	†Ari N★	151	589	132	170	32	6	38	112	82-2	4	132	.289	.374	.557	132	28	7-4	.968	-19	87	99	2b148/SD		1.5
2000	Ari N	149	565	87	151	30	6	18	68	70-0	3	88	.267	.348	.437	94	-5	7-3	.988	-3	94	101	2b145/D		-0.9
2001	†Ari N	129	428	59	106	24	1	13	46	65-3	4	79	.248	.349	.400	88	-6	0-1	.994	-11	84	105	2b80,3b40,D3		-1.3
2002	Ari N	32	49	3	8	1	0	2	11	5-0	1	9	.163	.250	.306	45	-4	0-0	1.000	0	81	234	3b6,1b5,2b2,S2	110	-0.4
2003	NY N	72	116	11	21	1	0	0	3	22-1	0	38	.181	.319	.190	39	-10	0-0	.952	-4	93	101	2b14,3b14,1b13,S12/D	15	-1.3
Total 18		2063	7398	1123	1963	394	67	195	860	853-25	57	1443	.265	.343	.416	101	15	91-60	.975	14	105	104	S1515,2b406,3b67,1b18,D10	125	15.4

BELL, RUDY John (b Rudolph Fred Baerwald) B1.1.1881 Wausau WI D7.28.1955 Albuquerque NM BR/TR/5-8.5/158 d9.16

YEAR	TM LG	G	AB	R	H	2B	3B	HR	RBI	BB-IB	HP	SO	AVG	OBP	SLG	AOPS	ABR	SB-CS	FA	FR	RNG	THR	GAMES AT POSITION	DL	BFW
1907	NY A	17	52	4	11	2	1	0	3	1	1		.212	.268	.288	72	-2	4	.897	-1		0	O17(12/0/5)		-0.4

BELL, JUAN Juan (Mathey) B3.29.1968 San Pedro de Macoris, D.R. BR/TR (BB 1995)/5-11/176(157-176) d9.6 b-George

YEAR	TM LG	G	AB	R	H	2B	3B	HR	RBI	BB-IB	HP	SO	AVG	OBP	SLG	AOPS	ABR	SB-CS	FA	FR	RNG	THR	GAMES AT POSITION	DL	BFW
1989	Bal A	8	4	2	0	0	0	0	0	0-0	0	1	.000	.000	.000	-99	-1	1-0	1.000	1	172	263	2b2,S2,D4		0.0
1990	Bal A	5	2	1	0	0	0	0	0	0-0	0	1	.000	.000	.000	-99	-1	0-0	1.000	0	101	0	/SD		-0.1
1991	Bal A	100	209	26	36	9	2	1	15	8-0	0	51	.172	.201	.249	25	-22	0-0	.973	-2	106	197	2b77,S15/OLD		-2.3
1992	Phi N	46	147	12	30	3	1	1	8	18-5	1	29	.204	.292	.259	58	-8	5-0	.972	2	100	88	S46		-0.2
1993	Phi N	24	65	5	13	6	1	0	7	5-0	1	12	.200	.268	.323	58	-4	0-1	.909	-2	95	93	S22		-0.4
	Mil N	91	286	42	67	6	2	5	29	36-0	1	64	.234	.321	.322	74	-10	6-6	.983	-4	87	111	2b47,S40,O3(0/1/2),D2		-1.0
1994	Mon N	38	97	12	27	4	0	2	9	15-0	0	21	.278	.372	.381	97	-3	4-0	.991	4	116	128	2b25,3b3/S		0.6
1995	Bos A	17	26	7	4	2	0	1	2	2-0	0	10	.154	.207	.346	42	-2	0-0	.857	-1	79	30	S6,2b5/3		-0.3
Total 7		329	836	107	177	30	6	10	71	84-5	3	189	.212	.284	.298	70	-48	16-7	.981	-2	102	110	2b156,S133,D11,3b4,O4(1/1/2)		-3.7

YEAR	TM LG	G	AB	R	H	2B	3B	HR	RBI	BB-IB	HP	SO	AVG	OBP	SLG	AOPS	ABR	SB-CS	FA	FR	RNG	THR	GAMES AT POSITION	DL	BFW

BELL, KEVIN   Kevin Robert B7.13.1955 Los Angeles CA BR/TR/6-0/195* [ChiA74*1/7] d6.16 Col Mt. San Antonio (CA) JC

YEAR	TM LG	G	AB	R	H	2B	3B	HR	RBI	BB-IB	HP	SO	AVG	OBP	SLG	AOPS	ABR	SB-CS	FA	FR	RNG	THR	GAMES AT POSITION	DL	BFW
1976	Chi A	68	230	24	57	7	6	5	20	18-0	1	56	.248	.302	.396	104	0	2-1	.970	-1	91	84	3b67/D		-0.1
1977	Chi A	9	28	4	5	1	0	1	6	3-0	0	8	.179	.250	.321	57	-2	0-0	.909	1	87	159	S5,3b4/OL	100	-0.1
1978	Chi A	54	68	9	13	0	0	2	5	5-0	1	19	.191	.257	.279	50	-5	1-0	.946	6	121	124	3b52/D		0.1
1979	Chi A	70	200	20	49	8	1	4	22	15-0	0	43	.245	.296	.355	75	-7	2-4	.923	2	106	90	3b68,S2		-0.8
1980	Chi A	92	191	16	34	5	2	1	11	29-1	0	37	.178	.284	.241	46	-14	0-0	.925	2	109	91	3b83,S3,D3		-1.3
1982	Oak A	4	9	1	3	1	0	0	0	0-0	0	4	.333	.333	.444	115	0	0-0	.857	-0	71	216	3b3/D		0.0
Total	6	297	726	74	161	22	9	13	64	70-1	2	165	.222	.289	.331	73	-28	5-5	.940	9	104	97	3b277,S10,D6/OL	100	-2.2

BELL, LES   Lester Rowland B12.14.1901 Harrisburg PA D12.26.1985 Hershey PA BR/TR/5-11/165 d9.18

YEAR	TM LG	G	AB	R	H	2B	3B	HR	RBI	BB-IB	HP	SO	AVG	OBP	SLG	AOPS	ABR	SB-CS	FA	FR	RNG	THR	GAMES AT POSITION	DL	BFW
1923	StL N	15	51	5	19	2	1	0	9	9	0	7	.373	.467	.451	146	4	1-0	.917	-2	97	94	S15		0.4
1924	StL N	17	57	5	14	3	2	1	5	3	1	7	.246	.295	.421	91	-1	0-0	.905	-4	78	75	S17		-0.3
1925	StL N	153	586	80	167	29	9	11	88	43	0	47	.285	.334	.422	89	-10	4-5	.924	1	99	143	3b153/S		-0.1
1926	†StL N	155	581	85	189	33	14	17	100	54	0	62	.325	.383	.518	135	28	9	.950	-24	83	100	3b155		1.3
1927	StL N	115	390	48	101	26	6	9	65	34	1	63	.259	.320	.426	95	-3	5	.904	-16	83	98	3b100,S10		-1.2
1928	Bos N	153	591	58	164	36	7	10	91	40	0	45	.277	.323	.413	96	-5	1	.948	7	102	122	3b153		1.1
1929	Bos N	139	483	58	144	23	5	9	72	50	0	42	.298	.364	.422	98	-1	4	.953	-21	83	79	3b127/2S		-1.3
1930	Chi N	74	248	35	69	15	4	5	47	24	0	27	.278	.342	.431	85	-6	1	.948	-2	90	126	3b70,1b2		-0.4
1931	Chi N	75	252	30	71	17	1	4	32	19	0	22	.282	.332	.405	95	-2	0	.944	4	103	162	3b70		0.5
Total	9	896	3239	404	938	184	49	66	509	276	2	322	.290	.346	.438	102	4	25-5	.939	-57	92	116	3b828,S44,1b2/2		0.0

BELL, MIKE   Michael Allen B4.22.1968 Lewiston NY BL/TL/6-1/175* [AtlN86 4/86] d5.2

YEAR	TM LG	G	AB	R	H	2B	3B	HR	RBI	BB-IB	HP	SO	AVG	OBP	SLG	AOPS	ABR	SB-CS	FA	FR	RNG	THR	GAMES AT POSITION	DL	BFW
1990	Atl N	36	45	8	11	5	1	1	5	2-0	1	9	.244	.292	.467	100	0	0-1	.981	1	130	79	1b24		-0.1
1991	Atl N	17	30	4	4	0	0	1	1	2-0	0	7	.133	.188	.233	17	-3	1-0	.975	-0	97	142	1b14		-0.4
Total	2	53	75	12	15	5	1	2	6	4-0	1	16	.200	.250	.373	67	-3	1-1	.979	0	116	107	1b38		-0.5

BELL, MIKE   Michael John B12.7.1974 Cincinnati OH BR/TR/6-2/210 [TexA93 S1/30] d7.20 f-Buddy gf-Gus b-David

YEAR	TM LG	G	AB	R	H	2B	3B	HR	RBI	BB-IB	HP	SO	AVG	OBP	SLG	AOPS	ABR	SB-CS	FA	FR	RNG	THR	GAMES AT POSITION	DL	BFW
2000	Cin N	19	27	5	6	0	0	2	4	4-0	0	7	.222	.323	.444	88	-1	0-0	.900	2	150	193	3b13		0.1

BELL, BEAU   Roy Chester B8.20.1907 Bellville TX D9.14.1977 College Station TX BR/TR/6-2/185 d4.16 Col Texas A&M-Commerce

YEAR	TM LG	G	AB	R	H	2B	3B	HR	RBI	BB-IB	HP	SO	AVG	OBP	SLG	AOPS	ABR	SB-CS	FA	FR	RNG	THR	GAMES AT POSITION	DL	BFW
1935	StL A	76	220	20	55	8	3	2	17	16	1	16	.250	.304	.345	65	-12	1-1	.918	-4	92	68	O37(10/0/27),1b15,3b3		-1.9
1936	StL A	155	616	100	212	40	12	11	123	60	1	55	.344	.403	.502	119	18	4-1	.974	0	103	85	O142(12/0/133),1b17		0.8
1937	StL A☆	156	642	82	218	51	8	14	117	53	1	54	.340	.391	.509	124	24	2-2	.984	3	87	178	O131R,1b26,3b2		1.5
1938	StL A	147	526	91	138	35	3	13	84	71	0	46	.262	.350	.414	91	-7	1-3	.979	3	106	104	O132R,1b4		-1.2
1939	StL A	11	32	4	7	1	0	1	5	4	1	3	.219	.324	.344	69	-1	0-0	1.000	-0	105	0	O9L		-0.2
	Det A	54	134	14	32	4	2	0	24	24	1	16	.239	.358	.299	65	-7	0-1	1.000	2	100	179	O37L		-0.6
	Year	65	166	18	39	5	2	1	29	28	2	19	.235	.352	.307	66	-8	0-1	1.000	2	100	143	O46L		-0.8
1940	Cle A	120	444	55	124	22	2	4	58	34	1	41	.279	.332	.365	83	-11	2-2	.971	2	107	69	O97R,1b14		-1.7
1941	Cle A	48	104	12	20	4	1	1	9	10	1	8	.192	.270	.288	50	-8	1-2	1.000	-2	94	0	O14R,1b10		-1.2
Total	7	767	2718	378	806	165	32	46	437	272	7	239	.297	.362	.432	99	-4	11-12	.976	2	100	109	O599(68/0/534),1b86,3b5		-4.5

BELL, TERRY   Terence William B10.27.1962 Dayton OH BR/TR/6-0/195* [SeaA83 1/17] d9.3 Col Old Dominion

YEAR	TM LG	G	AB	R	H	2B	3B	HR	RBI	BB-IB	HP	SO	AVG	OBP	SLG	AOPS	ABR	SB-CS	FA	FR	RNG	THR	GAMES AT POSITION	DL	BFW
1986	KC A	8	3	0	0	0	0	0	0	2-0	0	1	.000	.400	.000	20	0	0-0	1.000	-1	117	0	C8		-0.1
1987	Atl N	1	1	0	0	0	0	0	0	0-0	0	1	.000	.000	.000	-96	0	0-0	—	0			/H		0.0
Total	2	9	4	0	0	0	0	0	0	2-0	0	2	.000	.333	.000	-0	0	0-0	1.000	-1	117	0	C8		-0.1

BELLA, ZEKE   John B8.23.1930 Greenwich CT BR/TL/5-11/185* d9.11

YEAR	TM LG	G	AB	R	H	2B	3B	HR	RBI	BB-IB	HP	SO	AVG	OBP	SLG	AOPS	ABR	SB-CS	FA	FR	RNG	THR	GAMES AT POSITION	DL	BFW
1957	NY A	5	10	0	1	0	0	0	0	1-0	0	2	.100	.182	.100	-21	-2	0-0	1.000	1	106	402	O4(1/0/3)		-0.1
1959	KC A	47	82	10	17	2	1	1	9	9-0	1	14	.207	.293	.293	60	-4	0-0	1.000	0	83	240	O25(11/0/14)/1		-0.5
Total	2	52	92	10	18	2	1	1	9	10-0	1	16	.196	.282	.272	52	-6	0-0	1.000	1	88	273	O29(12/0/17)/1		-0.6

BELLAN, STEVE   Esteban Enrique B1850 , Cuba D8.8.1932 Havana, Cuba 5-6/154 d5.9

YEAR	TM LG	G	AB	R	H	2B	3B	HR	RBI	BB-IB	HP	SO	AVG	OBP	SLG	AOPS	ABR	SB-CS	FA	FR	RNG	THR	GAMES AT POSITION	DL	BFW
1871	Tro NA	29	128	26	32	3	3	0	23	9		2	.250	.299	.320	77	-4	4-4	.713	-2	83	100	3b28/S		-0.4
1872	Tro NA	23	115	22	30	4	0	0	17	0		2	.261	.261	.296	70	-4	1-0	.673	-7	69	0	S9,3b8,O6C		-0.8
1873	Mut NA	8	32	4	7	2	0	0	3	2		0	.219	.265	.281	63	-1	0-0	.488	-6	46	327	3b7,2b3		-0.5
Total	3 NA	60	275	52	69	9	3	0	43	11		2	.251	.280	.305	73	-9	5-4	.674	-14	76	141	3b43,S10,O6C,2b3		-1.7

BELLE, ALBERT   Albert Jojuan "Joey" B8.25.1966 Shreveport LA BR/TR/6-2/210(200-225) [CleA87 2/47] d7.15 Col Louisiana St. [DL 2001 Bal A 190, 2002 Bal A 183, 2003 Bal A 183]

YEAR	TM LG	G	AB	R	H	2B	3B	HR	RBI	BB-IB	HP	SO	AVG	OBP	SLG	AOPS	ABR	SB-CS	FA	FR	RNG	THR	GAMES AT POSITION	DL	BFW
1989	Cle A	62	218	22	49	8	4	7	37	12-0	2	55	.225	.269	.394	84	-6	2-2	.979	1	102	97	O144(15/0/31),D17		-0.8
1990	Cle A	9	23	1	4	0	0	1	3	1-0	0	6	.174	.208	.304	42	-2	0-0	—	0	0	0	/OLD		-0.2
1991	Cle A	123	461	60	130	31	2	28	95	25-2	5	99	.282	.323	.540	134	19	3-1	.952	1	98	168	O89(88/0/2),D32		1.7
1992	Cle A	153	585	81	152	23	1	34	112	52-5	4	128	.260	.320	.477	123	15	8-2	.969	-4	92	30	D100,O52L		0.8
1993	Cle A★	159	594	93	172	36	3	38	129	76-13	8	96	.290	.370	.552	146	39	23-12	.986	11	106	170	O150L,D9		4.2
1994	Cle A	106	412	90	147	35	2	36	101	58-9	5	71	.357	.438	.714	190	57	9-6	.973	-3	89	103	O104L,D2		4.5
1995	†Cle A★	143	546	121	173	52	1	50	126	73-5	6	80	.317	.401	.690	174	60	5-2	.981	-1	99	70	O142L/D		5.0
1996	†Cle A☆	158	602	124	187	38	3	48	148	99-15	7	87	.311	.410	.623	157	55	11-0	.970	-2	94	101	O152L,D6		4.5
1997	Chi A☆	161	634	90	174	45	1	30	116	53-6	6	105	.274	.332	.491	116	14	4-4	.972	2	116	10	O154L,D7		0.9
1998	Chi A☆	163	609	113	200	48	2	49	152	81-10	7	84	.328	.399	.655	173	67	6-4	.976	2	102	115	O159L,D4		5.8
1999	Bal A	161	610	108	181	36	1	37	117	101-15	7	82	.297	.400	.541	143	43	17-3	.985	-5	83	159	O154R,D7		3.0
2000	Bal A	141	559	71	157	37	1	23	103	52-11	2	68	.281	.342	.474	110	8	0-5	.986	-0	98	107	O110R,D31		0.8
Total	12	1539	5853	974	1726	389	21	381	1239	683-91	55	961	.295	.369	.564	144	369	88-41	.976	1	99	106	O1311(1017/0/297),D222	556	29.3

BELLHORN, MARK   Mark Christian B8.23.1974 Boston MA BB/TR/6-1/205(190-209) [OakA95 2/35] d6.10 Col Auburn-Montgomery OF(1/3/3)

YEAR	TM LG	G	AB	R	H	2B	3B	HR	RBI	BB-IB	HP	SO	AVG	OBP	SLG	AOPS	ABR	SB-CS	FA	FR	RNG	THR	GAMES AT POSITION	DL	BFW
1997	Oak A	68	224	33	51	9	1	6	19	32-0	1	70	.228	.324	.357	78	-7	7-1	.951	7	103	114	3b40,2b17/SD		0.2
1998	Oak A	11	12	1	1	1	0	0	0	3-0	1	4	.083	.313	.167	30	-1	2-0	1.000	-0	144	0	3b5,S2/2D		-0.1
2000	Oak A	9	13	2	2	0	0	0	0	2-0	0	6	.154	.267	.154	10	-2	0-0	.953	-1	37	0	2b2,3b2/S		-0.2
2001	Oak A	38	74	11	10	1	2	1	4	7-0	0	37	.135	.210	.243	19	-9	0-0	.953	-2	99	74	2b12,3b9,S5/ORD		-1.0
2002	Chi N	146	445	86	115	24	4	27	56	76-3	6	144	.258	.374	.512	134	21	7-5	.980	-8	93	98	3b77,2b36,1b22,S12/OL		1.6
2003	Chi N	51	139	15	29	7	1	2	22	29-1	1	46	.209	.341	.317	74	-4	3-3	.938	-1	96	58	3b42		-0.5
	Col N	48	110	12	26	3	0		4	21-0	2	32	.236	.368	.264	60	-5	2-3	.973	-1	105	59	2b20,3b15,S6,O5(0/3/2)/1	22	-0.6
	Year	99	249	27	55	10	1	2	26	50-1	1	78	.221	.353	.293	67	-10	5-6	.944	-1	98	56	3b57,2b20,S6,O5(0/3/2)/1		-1.1
2004	†Bos A	138	523	93	138	37	3	17	82	88-1	5	177	.264	.373	.444	106	8	6-1	.980	-4	97	84	2b124,3b16/S	18	0.9
2005	Bos A	85	283	41	61	20	0	7	28	49-1	0	109	.216	.328	.360	80	-7	3-0	.985	4	106	55	2b83/S	32	0.2
	†NY A	9	17	2	2	0	0	1	3	3-0	0	3	.118	.250	.294	44	-1	0-0	1.000	2	75	0	3b4,2b2,S2		0.1
	Year	94	300	43	63	20	0	8	30	52-1	0	112	.210	.324	.357	78	-8	3-0	.983	6	108	56	2b85,3b4,S3		0.3
Total	8	603	1840	296	435	102	11	61	218	310-6	15	628	.236	.349	.403	95	-7	30-13	.979	-3	101	92	3b338,2b169,S31,1b23,D9,O7C	72	0.6

BELLIARD, RAFAEL   Rafael Leonidas (Matias) B10.24.1961 Pueblo Nuevo, D.R. BR/TR (BB 1982)/5-6/150(139-160) d9.6

YEAR	TM LG	G	AB	R	H	2B	3B	HR	RBI	BB-IB	HP	SO	AVG	OBP	SLG	AOPS	ABR	SB-CS	FA	FR	RNG	THR	GAMES AT POSITION	DL	BFW
1982	Pit N	9	2	3	1	0	0	0	0	0-0	0	0	.500	.500	.500	173	0	1-0	1.000	0	91	0	S4		0.1
1983	Pit N	4	1	1	0	0	0	0	0	0-0	0	1	.000	.000	.000	-97	0	0-0	1.000	1	170	300	S3		0.1
1984	Pit N	20	22	3	5	0	0	0	0	0-0	0	1	.227	.227	.227	28	-2	4-1	.889	-3	64	113	S12/2	61	-0.5
1985	Pit N	17	20	1	4	0	0	0	0	0-0	0	5	.200	.200	.200	12	-2	0-0	.947	1	112	72	S12		0.0
1986	Pit N	117	309	33	72	5	2	0	31	26-6	3	54	.233	.298	.262	55	-19	12-2	.970	10	114	90	S96,2b23	15	-0.9
1987	Pit N	81	203	26	42	4	3	1	15	20-6	3	25	.207	.286	.271	48	-15	5-1	.979	2	99	85	S71,2b7	39	-0.6
1988	Pit N	122	286	28	61	0	4	0	11	26-3	4	47	.213	.288	.241	54	-17	7-1	.977	-11	96	101	S117,2b3	15	-2.2
1989	Pit N	67	154	10	33	4	0	0	8	8-2	0	22	.214	.253	.240	43	-12	5-2	.978	-4	101	82	S40,2b20,3b6		-1.4
1990	Pit N	47	54	10	11	3	0	0	6	5-0	1	13	.204	.283	.259	52	-3	1-2	1.000	-1	76	135	2b21,S10,3b5		-0.5
1991	†Atl N	149	353	36	88	9	0	0	27	22-2	2	63	.249	.296	.286	61	-18	3-1	.967	7	106	100	S145		-0.3
1992	†Atl N	144	285	20	60	6	1	0	14	14-4	3	43	.211	.255	.239	38	-23	0-1	.969	-1	100	93	S139/2		-1.9
1993	†Atl N	91	79	6	18	5	1	0	6	3-0	3	12	.228	.291	.291	55	-5	0-0	1.000	6	113	144	S58,2b24		0.2
1994	†Atl N	46	120	9	29	7	1	0	9	2-1	0	29	.242	.264	.317	49	-7	0-2	.984	-7	72	78	S26,2b18		-1.3
1995	†Atl N	75	180	12	40	2	1	0	7	6-2	1	28	.222	.255	.244	31	-18	2-2	.992	3	92	64	S40,2b32		-0.9
1996	†Atl N	87	142	9	24	7	0	3	9	3-1	2	28	.169	.179	.218	4	-20	3-1	.983	7	105	115	S63,2b15		-0.9
1997	Atl N	72	71	8	15	3	0	1	3	1-0	0	17	.211	.219	.296	34	-7	0-1	.990	-4	85	106	S53,2b7		-0.9
1998	Atl N	7	20	1	5	0	0	0	0	0-0	1	1	.250	.250	.250	32	-2	0-0	.952	-1	75	128	S7	171	-0.3
Total	17	1155	2301	217	508	55	14	2	142	136-26	23	384	.221	.270	.259	45	-172	43-17	.974	2	100	95	S896,2b172,3b11	301	-11.6

YEAR	TM LG	G	AB	R	H	2B	3B	HR	RBI	BB-IB	HP	SO	AVG	OBP	SLG	AOPS	ABR	SB-CS	FA	FR	RNG	THR	GAMES AT POSITION	DL	BFW

BELLIARD, RON   Ronald B4.7.1975 Bronx NY   BR/TR/5-8/180(180-200)   [MilA94 8/207]   d9.12

YEAR	TM LG	G	AB	R	H	2B	3B	HR	RBI	BB-IB	HP	SO	AVG	OBP	SLG	AOPS	ABR	SB-CS	FA	FR	RNG	THR	GAMES AT POSITION	DL	BFW
1998	Mil N	8	5	1	1	0	0	0	0	0-0	0	1	.200	.200	.200	6	-1	0-0	—	-0	0	0	/2		-0.1
1999	Mil N	124	457	60	135	29	4	8	58	64-0	0	59	.295	.379	.429	104	5	4-5	.978	-1	105	95	2b119/3S		0.8
2000	Mil N	152	571	83	150	30	9	8	54	82-4	3	84	.263	.354	.389	89	-8	7-5	.976	1	102	125	2b151		0.0
2001	Mil N	101	364	69	96	30	3	11	36	35-2	0	65	.264	.335	.453	104	2	5-2	.990	13	107	107	2b96	52	2.0
2002	Mil N	104	289	30	61	13	0	3	26	18-0	1	46	.211	.257	.287	47	-24	2-3	.975	-9	89	88	2b49,3b42		-3.2
2003	Col N	116	447	73	124	31	2	8	50	49-0	2	71	.277	.351	.409	86	-8	7-2	.973	-2	103	100	2b113	21	-0.4
2004	Cle A★	152	599	78	169	48	1	12	70	60-5	2	98	.282	.348	.426	104	6	3-2	.981	-6	99	90	2b151/D		0.6
2005	Cle A	145	536	71	152	36	1	17	78	35-0	1	72	.284	.325	.450	108	6	2-2	.981	3	102	112	2b141		1.5
Total	8	902	3268	465	888	217	20	67	372	343-11	14	495	.272	.341	.412	94	-22	30-21	.979	-2	102	104	2b821,3b43/DS	73	1.2

BELLINGER, CLAY   Clayton Daniel B11.18.1968 Oneonta NY   BR/TR/6-3/195(195-215)   [SFN89 2/44]   d4.9   Col Rollins   OF(32/36/7)

YEAR	TM LG	G	AB	R	H	2B	3B	HR	RBI	BB-IB	HP	SO	AVG	OBP	SLG	AOPS	ABR	SB-CS	FA	FR	RNG	THR	GAMES AT POSITION	DL	BFW
1999	†NY A	32	45	12	9	2	0	1	2	1-0	0	10	.200	.217	.311	33	-5	0-0	1.000	1	89	65	3b16,1b8,O2L/2SD		-0.4
2000	†NY A	98	184	33	38	8	2	6	21	17-1	5	48	.207	.288	.370	67	-10	5-0	.968	0	91	71	O46(17/26/5),2b21,3b18,1b10,S6		-0.8
2001	†NY A	51	81	12	13	1	1	5	12	4-0	1	23	.160	.207	.383	51	-7	1-2	1.000	3	81	0	O25(13/10/2),3b17,1b6,S2		-0.4
2002	Ana A	2	1	0	0	0	0	0	0	0-0	0	1	.000	.000	.000	-99	-0	0-0	1.000	-0	0	0	1b2		0.0
Total	4	183	311	57	60	11	3	12	35	22-1	6	82	.193	.257	.363	58	-22	6-2	.977	4	88	48	O73C,3b51,1b26,2b22,S9,D4		-1.6

BELLMAN, JACK   John Hutchins "Happy Jack" B3.4.1864 Taylorsville KY   D12.8.1931 Louisville KY   d4.23

YEAR	TM LG	G	AB	R	H	2B	3B	HR	RBI	BB-IB	HP	SO	AVG	OBP	SLG	AOPS	ABR	SB-CS	FA	FR	RNG	THR	GAMES AT POSITION	DL	BFW
1889	StL AA	1	2	1	1	0	0	0	0	0	0	0	.500	.667	.500	207	0	0-0	1.000	-0			/C		0.0

BELLOIR, ROB   Robert Edward B7.13.1948 Heidelberg, Germany   BR/TR/5-10/155(155-170)   [CleA69 8/181]   d8.2   Col Mercer

YEAR	TM LG	G	AB	R	H	2B	3B	HR	RBI	BB-IB	HP	SO	AVG	OBP	SLG	AOPS	ABR	SB-CS	FA	FR	RNG	THR	GAMES AT POSITION	DL	BFW
1975	Atl N	43	105	11	23	2	1	0	9	7-0	0	8	.219	.268	.257	45	-8	0-0	.922	-6	100	81	S38/2		-1.1
1976	Atl N	30	60	5	12	2	0	0	4	5-1	0	7	.200	.262	.233	39	-5	0-0	.929	-5	80	114	S12,3b10,2b5		-0.9
1977	Atl N	6	1	2	0	0	0	0	0	0-0	0	0	.000	.000	.000	-90	-0	0-0	1.000	0	141	0	S3		-0.0
1978	Atl N	2	1	0	1	1	0	0	0	0-0	0	0	1.000	1.000	2.000	651	1	0-0	1.000	-0	141	0	/S3		0.1
Total	4	81	167	18	36	5	1	0	13	12-1	0	15	.216	.268	.257	46	-12	0-0	.924	-11	97	95	S54,3b11,2b6		-1.9

BELTRAN, CARLOS   Carlos Ivan B4.24.1977 Manati, PR   BB/TR/6-1/190(175-190)   [KCA95 2/49]   d9.14

YEAR	TM LG	G	AB	R	H	2B	3B	HR	RBI	BB-IB	HP	SO	AVG	OBP	SLG	AOPS	ABR	SB-CS	FA	FR	RNG	THR	GAMES AT POSITION	DL	BFW
1998	KC A	14	58	12	16	5	3	0	7	3-0	1	12	.276	.317	.466	98	0	3-0	.978	1	127	0	O14C		0.1
1999	KC A	156	663	112	194	27	7	22	108	46-2	4	123	.293	.337	.454	97	-5	27-8	.972	-1	96	158	O154C,D2		-0.1
2000	KC A	98	372	49	92	15	4	7	44	35-2	0	69	.247	.309	.366	67	-20	13-9	.975	-1	101	108	O88(2/83/3),D7	61	-1.5
2001	KC A	155	617	106	189	32	12	24	101	52-2	5	120	.306	.362	.514	116	14	31-1	.988	5	102	158	O152C,D3		2.5
2002	KC A	162	637	114	174	44	7	29	105	71-1	4	135	.273	.346	.501	109	8	35-7	.983	1	99	148	O149C,D12		1.5
2003	KC A	141	521	102	160	14	10	26	100	72-4	2	81	.307	.389	.522	130	23	41-4	.987	7	106	195	O130C,D8	19	3.6
2004	KC A	69	266	51	74	19	2	15	51	37-7	2	44	.278	.367	.534	132	13	14-3	.985	4	112	116	O69C		1.9
	†Hou N★	90	333	70	86	17	7	23	53	55-3	5	57	.258	.368	.559	132	16	28-0	.977	3	102	194	O89C		2.5
2005	NY N★	151	582	83	155	34	2	16	78	56-5	25	96	.266	.330	.414	97	-3	17-6	.990	1	107	65	O150C		0.1
Total	8	1036	4049	600	1140	207	54	162	647	427-26	25	737	.282	.350	.470	108	46	209-29	.982	20	103	137	O995(2/990/3),D32	80	10.6

BELTRE, ADRIAN   Adrian (Perez) B4.7.1979 Santo Domingo, D.R.   BR/TR/5-11/220(165-220)   d6.24

YEAR	TM LG	G	AB	R	H	2B	3B	HR	RBI	BB-IB	HP	SO	AVG	OBP	SLG	AOPS	ABR	SB-CS	FA	FR	RNG	THR	GAMES AT POSITION	DL	BFW
1998	LA N	77	195	18	42	9	0	7	22	14-0	3	37	.215	.278	.369	72	-9	3-1	.925	6	114	127	3b74,S2		-0.2
1999	LA N	152	538	84	148	27	5	15	67	61-12	6	105	.275	.352	.428	102	2	18-7	.932	-1	99	98	3b152		0.3
2000	LA N	138	510	71	148	30	2	20	85	56-2	2	80	.290	.360	.475	115	11	12-5	.944	17	110	124	3b138/S	19	2.8
2001	LA N	126	475	59	126	22	4	13	60	28-1	5	82	.265	.310	.411	90	-9	13-4	.952	6	100	88	3b124,S2	41	-0.1
2002	LA N	159	587	70	151	26	5	21	75	37-4	4	96	.257	.303	.426	98	-7	7-5	.954	-10	92	63	3b157/S		-1.6
2003	LA N	158	559	50	134	30	2	23	80	37-4	5	103	.240	.290	.424	86	-14	2-2	.957	9	98	130	3b157/S		-0.4
2004	†LA N	156	598	104	200	32	0	48	121	53-9	2	87	.334	.388	.629	160	51	7-2	.978	8	103	123	3b155/S		5.9
2005	Sea A	156	603	69	154	36	1	19	87	38-6	5	108	.255	.303	.413	95	-6	3-1	.967	-5	92	100	3b155/D		-0.9
Total	8	1122	4065	525	1103	212	19	166	597	324-38	32	698	.271	.327	.455	106	19	65-27	.953	29	100	113	3b1112,S7/D	60	5.8

BELTRE, ESTEBAN   Esteban (Valera) B12.26.1967 Ingenio Quisquella, D.R.   BR/TR/5-10/172(155-172)   d9.3

YEAR	TM LG	G	AB	R	H	2B	3B	HR	RBI	BB-IB	HP	SO	AVG	OBP	SLG	AOPS	ABR	SB-CS	FA	FR	RNG	THR	GAMES AT POSITION	DL	BFW
1991	Chi A	8	6	0	1	0	0	0	0	1-0	0	1	.167	.286	.167	29	-1	1-0	1.000	-2	61	63	S8		-0.2
1992	Chi A	49	110	21	21	2	0	1	10	3-0	0	18	.191	.211	.236	26	-11	1-0	.924	-11	87	54	S43,D4		-2.0
1994	Tex A	48	131	12	37	5	0	0	12	16-0	0	25	.282	.358	.321	77	-4	2-5	.961	6	116	91	S41,3b5/2		0.3
1995	Tex A	54	92	7	20	8	0	0	7	4-0	0	15	.217	.250	.304	42	-8	0-0	.969	-4	85	93	S36,2b8,5/3		-0.9
1996	Bos A	27	62	6	16	2	0	0	6	4-0	0	14	.258	.299	.290	50	-5	1-0	1.000	-4	66	45	3b13,2b8,S6/D		-0.7
Total	5	186	401	46	95	17	0	1	35	28-0	0	73	.237	.285	.287	51	-29	5-5	.951	-15	95	75	S134,2b24,3b19,D5		-3.5

BEMIS, HARRY   Harry Parker B2.1.1874 Farmington NH   D5.23.1947 Cleveland OH   BR/TR/5-7.5/175   d4.23

YEAR	TM LG	G	AB	R	H	2B	3B	HR	RBI	BB-IB	HP	SO	AVG	OBP	SLG	AOPS	ABR	SB-CS	FA	FR	RNG	THR	GAMES AT POSITION	DL	BFW
1902	Cle A	93	317	42	99	12	7	1	29	19		8	.312	.366	.404	118	8	3	.964	1	93	111	C87,O2R/2		1.6
1903	Cle A	92	314	31	82	20	3	1	41	8		7	.261	.295	.354	96	-2	5	.988	-2	102	97	C74,1b10/2		0.3
1904	Cle A	97	336	35	76	11	6	0	25	8		7	.226	.259	.295	76	-10	6	.958	1	119	97	C79,1b13/2		-0.2
1905	Cle A	70	226	27	66	13	0	3	28	13		5	.292	.344	.376	127	7	3	.972	-4	102	81	C58,2b4,3b2/1		1.0
1906	Cle A	93	297	28	82	13	5	2	30	12		5	.276	.311	.374	116	4	8	.963	-3	116	75	C81		1.0
1907	Cle A	65	172	12	43	7	0	0	19	7		1	.250	.282	.291	82	-4	5	.957	-5	99	79	C51,1b2		-0.5
1908	Cle A	91	277	23	62	9	1	0	33	7		4	.224	.253	.264	68	-10	14	.964	-1	143	78	C76,1b2		-0.4
1909	Cle A	42	123	4	23	2	3	0	13	0		1	.187	.194	.252	39	-9	2	.971	1	109	77	C36		-0.7
1910	Cle A	61	167	12	36	5	1	1	16	5		0	.216	.238	.275	60	-8	3	.961	-7	84	101	C46		-1.2
Total	9	704	2229	214	569	92	29	5	234	79		36	.255	.292	.329	92	-24	49	.966	-18	109	90	C588,1b28,2b7,3b2,O2R		1.0

BENARD, MARVIN   Marvin Larry B1.20.1971 Bluefields, Nicaragua   BL/TL/5-9/185(180-191)   [SFN92 50/1391]   d9.5   Col Lewis-Clark St.

YEAR	TM LG	G	AB	R	H	2B	3B	HR	RBI	BB-IB	HP	SO	AVG	OBP	SLG	AOPS	ABR	SB-CS	FA	FR	RNG	THR	GAMES AT POSITION	DL	BFW
1995	SF N	13	34	5	13	2	0	1	4	1-0	1	9	.382	.400	.529	146	2	1-0	1.000	0	124	0	O7C		0.3
1996	SF N	135	488	89	121	17	4	5	27	59-2	4	84	.248	.333	.330	78	-15	25-11	.984	6	110	104	O132(5/102/38)		-0.8
1997	†SF N	84	114	13	26	4	0	1	13	13-0	1	29	.228	.315	.289	62	-6	3-1	.967	-1	72	164	O36(14/6/18)/D		-0.8
1998	SF N	121	286	41	92	21	1	3	36	34-1	2	39	.322	.396	.434	125	12	11-4	.982	-5	89	24	O79(12/9/64),D2		0.5
1999	SF N	149	562	100	163	36	5	16	64	55-2	6	97	.290	.359	.457	112	10	27-14	.988	-3	100	67	O142(4/123/20)		0.8
2000	†SF N	149	560	102	147	27	6	12	55	63-0	6	97	.262	.342	.396	92	-7	22-7	.997	6	104	137	O141(21/128/38)		0.8
2001	SF N	129	392	70	104	19	2	15	44	29-2	4	66	.265	.320	.439	100	-1	10-5	.965	-0	101	94	O109(15/75/37)		-0.2
2002	SF N	65	123	16	34	9	2	1	13	7-0	1	26	.276	.321	.407	96	-2	5-1	1.000	3	113	213	O38(14/6/20)	61	-0.8
2003	SF N	46	71	5	14	3	1	0	4	4-0	1	9	.197	.237	.268	32	-7	1-0	1.000	3	139	224	O21(17/0/4)	98	-0.5
Total	9	891	2630	441	714	138	21	54	260	265-7	25	454	.271	.343	.402	96	-14	105-43	.986	8	103	101	O705(102/456/239),D3	159	-0.6

BENAVIDES, FREDDIE   Alfredo B4.7.1966 Laredo TX   BR/TR/6-2/180*   [CinN87 2/50]   d5.14   C1   Col TCU

YEAR	TM LG	G	AB	R	H	2B	3B	HR	RBI	BB-IB	HP	SO	AVG	OBP	SLG	AOPS	ABR	SB-CS	FA	FR	RNG	THR	GAMES AT POSITION	DL	BFW
1991	Cin N	24	63	11	18	1	0	0	3	1-1	1	15	.286	.303	.302	69	-1	0-0	.974	0	102	61	S20,2b3		-0.1
1992	Cin N	74	173	14	40	10	1	1	17	10-4	1	34	.231	.277	.318	66	-8	0-1	1.000	-1	93	61	2b37,S34/3		-0.8
1993	Col N	74	213	20	61	10	3	3	26	6-1	0	27	.286	.305	.404	75	-8	3-2	.937	-5	92	67	S48,2b19,3b5/1	41	-0.6
1994	Mon N	47	85	8	16	5	1	0	6	3-1	1	15	.188	.222	.271	28	-9	0-0	.976	-6	71	92	2b36,3b5,1b3,S3		-1.5
Total	4	219	534	53	135	26	5	4	52	20-7	3	91	.253	.282	.343	65	-28	4-3	.948	-12	95	92	S105,2b95,3b11,1b4	41	-3.3

BENCH, JOHNNY   Johnny Lee B12.7.1947 Oklahoma City OK   BR/TR/6-1/208(187-215)   [CinN65 2/36]   d8.28   HF1989   OF(55/2/54)

YEAR	TM LG	G	AB	R	H	2B	3B	HR	RBI	BB-IB	HP	SO	AVG	OBP	SLG	AOPS	ABR	SB-CS	FA	FR	RNG	THR	GAMES AT POSITION	DL	BFW
1967	Cin N	26	86	7	14	3	1	1	6	0	0	19	.163	.207	.256	29	-8	0-1	.995	3	214	69	C26		-0.5
1968	Cin N★	154	564	67	155	40	2	15	82	31-8	2	96	.275	.311	.433	115	10	1-5	.991	9	130	111	C154		2.9
1969	Cin N★	148	532	83	156	23	1	26	90	49-7	4	86	.293	.353	.487	128	19	6-6	.992	6	193	104	C147		3.2
1970	†Cin N★	158	605	97	177	35	4	45	148	54-9	0	102	.293	.345	.587	145	36	5-2	.986	20	211	89	C139,O24(15/2/6),1b12/3		5.9
1971	Cin N★	149	562	80	134	19	2	27	61	49-7	0	83	.238	.299	.423	104	0	2-1	.988	11	162	83	C141,1b12,O12(10/0/3),3b3		1.7
1972	†Cin N★	147	538	87	145	22	2	40	125	100-23	2	84	.270	.379	.541	169	51	6-6	.992	7	250	86	C129,O17R,1b7,3b4		6.5
1973	†Cin N★	152	557	83	141	17	3	25	104	83-14	2	83	.253	.345	.429	120	15	4-1	.995	10	204	79	C134,O23R,1b4/3		3.2
1974	Cin N★	160	621	108	174	38	2	33	129	80-15	3	90	.280	.363	.507	144	36	5-4	.993	14	212	86	C137,3b36,1b5		5.7
1975	†Cin N★	142	530	83	150	39	1	28	110	65-12	2	108	.283	.359	.519	141	29	11-5	.993	5	198	82	C121,O19(16/0/3),1b9		5.5
1976	†Cin N★	135	465	62	109	24	1	16	74	81-6	1	95	.234	.348	.394	108	8	13-2	.997	7	136	101	C128,O5L/1		2.4
1977	Cin N★	142	494	67	136	34	2	31	109	58-8	1	95	.275	.348	.540	133	22	2-4	.987	3	143	91	C135,O8(7/0/1),1b4/3		2.9
1978	Cin N★	120	393	52	102	17	1	23	73	50-10	1	83	.260	.340	.483	120	14	4-2	.989	8	150	100	C107,1b11,O2(1/0/1)		2.9
1979	†Cin N★	130	464	73	128	19	0	22	80	67-8	0	73	.276	.364	.459	124	11	4-2	.986	5	134	92	C126,1b2		2.8
1980	Cin N★	114	360	52	90	12	0	24	68	41-2	0	64	.250	.327	.483	127	12	4-2	.991	-11	107	81	C105		0.5
1981	Cin N	52	178	14	55	8	0	8	25	17-3	0	21	.309	.366	.489	127	10	0-2	.983	-2	84	123	1b38,C7	85	0.5

YEAR	TM LG	G	AB	R	H	2B	3B	HR	RBI	BB-IB	HP	SO	AVG	OBP	SLG	AOPS	ABR	SB-CS	FA	FR	RNG	THR	GAMES AT POSITION	DL	BFW
1982	Cin N	119	399	44	103	16	0	13	38	37-2	0	58	.258	.320	.396	99	-1	1-2	.917	-17	80	62	3b107,1b8/C		-2.1
1983	Cin N★	110	310	32	79	15	2	12	54	24-1	0	38	.255	.308	.432	100	-1	0-1	.933	-7	87	85	3b42,1b32,C5/OL		-1.1
Total	17	2158	7658	1091	2048	381	24	389	1376	891-135	19	1278	.267	.342	.476	127	269	68-43	.990	83	173	91	C1742,3b195,1b145,O111L	85	42.7

BENEDICT, ART Arthur Melville B3.31.1862 Cornwall IL D1.14.1948 Denver CO BR/TR d5.14

YEAR	TM LG	G	AB	R	H	2B	3B	HR	RBI	BB-IB	HP	SO	AVG	OBP	SLG	AOPS	ABR	SB-CS	FA	FR	RNG	THR	GAMES AT POSITION	DL	BFW
1883	Phi N	3	15	3	4	1	0	0		4		.267	.267	.333	89	0		.571	-3	62	0	2b3		-0.3

BENEDICT, BRUCE Bruce Edwin B8.18.1955 Birmingham AL BR/TR/6-1/190(175-195) [AtlN76 5/99] d8.18 C3 Col Nebraska-Omaha

YEAR	TM LG	G	AB	R	H	2B	3B	HR	RBI	BB-IB	HP	SO	AVG	OBP	SLG	AOPS	ABR	SB-CS	FA	FR	RNG	THR	GAMES AT POSITION	DL	BFW
1978	Atl N	22	52	3	13	2	0	1	6-2	0	6	.250	.328	.288	66	-1	0-0	.990	-0	80	188	C22		-0.2
1979	Atl N	76	204	14	46	11	0	0	15	33-3	0	18	.225	.331	.279	65	-8	1-3	.984	-7	78	84	C76		-1.4
1980	Atl N	120	359	40	91	14	1	2	34	28-8	1	36	.253	.308	.315	74	-12	3-3	.988	6	140	93	C120		-0.2
1981	Atl N★	90	295	26	78	12	1	5	35	33-4	3	21	.264	.341	.363	100	1	1-1	.986	5	88	131	C90		1.0
1982	†Atl N★	118	386	34	95	11	1	3	44	37-9	3	40	.246	.315	.303	73	-13	4-4	.993	4	110	93	C118		-0.5
1983	Atl N★	134	423	43	126	13	1	2	43	61-16	1	24	.298	.385	.348	98	-2	1-3	.992	9	92	102	C134		1.6
1984	Atl N	95	300	26	67	8	1	4	25	34-3	1	25	.223	.301	.297	65	-14	1-2	.991	-7	96	71	C95		-1.8
1985	Atl N	70	208	12	42	6	0	0	20	22-1	1	12	.202	.279	.231	42	-16	0-1	.989	-7	85	102	C70		-2.2
1986	Atl N	64	160	11	36	10	1	0	13	15-1	2	10	.225	.298	.300	63	-8	1-0	.993	-4	173	86	C57		-1.0
1987	Atl N	37	95	4	14	1	0	1	5	17-0	0	15	.147	.277	.189	25	-10	0-1	.989	0	77	90	C35		-0.9
1988	Atl N	90	236	11	57	7	0	0	19	19-1	0	26	.242	.296	.271	62	-11	0-2	.989	3	109	120	C89		-0.5
1989	Atl N	66	160	12	31	3	0	1	6	23-4	1	18	.194	.299	.231	52	-9	0-0	.995	8	107	139	C65		0.2
Total	12	982	2878	214	696	98	6	18	260	328-52	13	251	.242	.320	.299	72	-100	12-20	.990	10	105	102	C971		-5.9

BENES, JOE Joseph Anthony "Bananas" B1.8.1901 Long Island City NY D3.7.1975 Elmhurst NY BR/TR/5-8.5/158 d5.9

YEAR	TM LG	G	AB	R	H	2B	3B	HR	RBI	BB-IB	HP	SO	AVG	OBP	SLG	AOPS	ABR	SB-CS	FA	FR	RNG	THR	GAMES AT POSITION	DL	BFW
1931	StL N	10	12	1	2	0	0	0	2	1		1	.167	.333	.167	37	-1	0	1.000	-0	109	78	S6,2b2/3		-0.1

BENGOUGH, BENNY Bernard Oliver B7.27.1898 Niagara Falls NY D12.22.1968 Philadelphia PA BR/TR/5-7.5/168 d5.18 C19 Col Niagara

YEAR	TM LG	G	AB	R	H	2B	3B	HR	RBI	BB-IB	HP	SO	AVG	OBP	SLG	AOPS	ABR	SB-CS	FA	FR	RNG	THR	GAMES AT POSITION	DL	BFW
1923	NY A	19	53	1	7	2	0	0	3	4	0	2	.132	.193	.170	-4	-8	0-0	.973	1	130	111	C19		-0.7
1924	NY A	11	16	4	5	1	1	0	3	2	0	0	.313	.389	.500	128	1	0-0	1.000	2	125	69	C11		0.3
1925	NY A	95	283	17	73	14	2	0	23	19	0	9	.258	.305	.322	60	-18	0-2	.993	6	96	114	C94		-0.7
1926	NY A	36	84	9	32	6	0	0	14	7	1	4	.381	.435	.452	134	5	1-0	.973	5	100	171	C35		1.1
1927	†NY A	31	85	6	21	3	3	0	10	4	0	4	.247	.281	.353	66	-5	0-3	.986	7	126	90	C30		0.3
1928	†NY A	58	161	12	43	3	1	0	9	7	1	8	.267	.302	.298	60	-10	0-0	.992	9	95	116	C58		-0.3
1929	NY A	23	62	5	12	2	1	0	7	0	0	2	.194	.194	.258	16	-8	0-0	.982	-3	90	71	C23		-1.0
1930	NY A	44	102	10	24	4	2	0	12	3	0	8	.235	.257	.314	46	-9	1-0	.990	4	103	97	C44		-0.2
1931	StL A	40	140	6	35	4	1	0	12	4	0	4	.250	.271	.293	46	-11	0-3	.986	1	104	98	C37		-0.8
1932	StL A	54	139	13	35	7	1	0	15	12	0	4	.252	.311	.317	60	-8	0-1	.989	5	118	135	C47		-0.5
Total	10	411	1125	83	287	46	12	0	108	62	2	45	.255	.295	.317	59	-71	2-9	.988	31	105	113	C398		-2.1

BENIQUEZ, JUAN Juan Jose (Torres) B5.13.1950 San Sebastian, PR BR/TR/5-11/165(148-175) d9.4 OF(295/735/184)

YEAR	TM LG	G	AB	R	H	2B	3B	HR	RBI	BB-IB	HP	SO	AVG	OBP	SLG	AOPS	ABR	SB-CS	FA	FR	RNG	THR	GAMES AT POSITION	DL	BFW
1971	Bos A	16	57	8	17	2	0	0	4	3-0	1	4	.298	.333	.333	83	-1	3-1	.895	-8	61	56	S15		-0.8
1972	Bos A	33	99	10	24	4	1	1	8	7-0	0	11	.242	.287	.333	81	-2	2-0	.900	1	108	114	S27		0.3
1974	Bos A	106	389	60	104	14	3	5	33	25-2	1	61	.267	.313	.357	86	-7	19-11	.978	-2	104	58	O97(7/91/0),D4	25	-1.2
1975	†Bos A	78	254	43	74	14	4	2	17	25-1	2	26	.291	.358	.402	106	2	7-10	.991	1	119	104	O44(31/13/2),D20,3b14	16	-0.1
1976	Tex A	145	478	49	122	14	4	0	33	39-1	3	56	.255	.315	.301	80	-12	17-6	.986	13	109	178	O141C/2		-0.1
1977	Tex A	123	424	56	114	19	6	10	50	43-0	1	43	.269	.336	.413	102	1	26-18	.988	-2	96	115	O123C	15	-0.3
1978	Tex A	127	473	61	123	17	3	11	50	20-1	3	59	.260	.292	.378	87	-10	10-12	.972	-10	89	98	O126C	30	-2.3
1979	NY A	62	142	19	36	6	1	4	17	9-0	0	17	.254	.299	.394	89	-3	3-3	.981	1	95	137	O60(18/38/4),3b3	60	-0.1
1980	Sea A	70	237	26	54	10	0	6	21	17-0	0	25	.228	.278	.346	69	-4	2-3	.957	-1	104	70	O65(2/63/0)/D	74	-1.3
1981	Cal A	58	166	18	30	5	0	3	13	15-0	1	16	.181	.251	.265	49	-11	2-1	.959	-4	95	0	O55(15/36/7)/D		-1.8
1982	†Cal A	112	196	25	52	11	2	3	24	15-1	1	21	.265	.321	.388	92	-2	3-0	.983	-6	77	92	O107(37/25/51)		-1.0
1983	Cal A	92	315	44	96	15	0	3	34	15-0	4	29	.305	.343	.381	100	0	4-2	.968	-0	94	141	O64(38/30/31),D6	50	-0.3
1984	Cal A	110	354	60	119	17	0	8	39	18-0	1	43	.336	.370	.452	127	13	0-3	.971	0	104	85	O98(64/8/50)		0.8
1985	Cal A	132	411	54	125	13	5	8	42	34-3	5	46	.304	.364	.418	114	8	4-3	1.000	-9	84	26	O71(18/36/22),1b46,D14/3S		-0.6
1986	Bal A	113	343	48	103	15	0	6	36	40-1	3	49	.300	.372	.397	112	8	2-3	.963	-1	108	34	O54(44/3/9),3b25,D16,1b14		0.2
1987	KC A	57	174	14	41	7	0	3	26	11-1	1	26	.236	.282	.328	60	-10	0-0	1.000	-7	81	0	O22(17/2/4),D15,1b6,3b6		-1.9
	Tor A	39	81	6	23	5	1	5	21	5-0	1	13	.284	.330	.556	127	3	0-0	.875	-2	62	0	D15,O7(3/0/4),1b2		0.1
	Year	96	255	20	64	12	1	8	47	16-1	2	39	.251	.297	.400	81	-7	0-0	.976	-9	77	0	D30,O29(20/2/8),1b8,3b6		-1.8
1988	Tor A	27	58	9	17	2	0	1	8	8-0	1	6	.293	.373	.379	112	1	0-0	—	0	0	0	D19/OL		0.1
Total	17	1500	4651	610	1274	190	30	79	476	349-11	31	551	.274	.327	.379	95	-32	104-76	.977	-35	98	95	O1155C,D111,1b68,3b48,S43/2	270	-10.5

BENITEZ, YAMIL Yamil Antonio B10.5.1972 San Juan, PR BR/TR/6-2/195(180-195) d9.15

YEAR	TM LG	G	AB	R	H	2B	3B	HR	RBI	BB-IB	HP	SO	AVG	OBP	SLG	AOPS	ABR	SB-CS	FA	FR	RNG	THR	GAMES AT POSITION	DL	BFW
1995	Mon N	14	39	8	15	2	1	2	7	1-0	0	7	.385	.400	.641	163	3	0-2	.950	0	101	160	O14(3/4/8)		0.2
1996	Mon N	11	12	0	2	0	0	0	2	0-0	0	4	.167	.167	.167	-11	-2	0-0	.500	-0	52	0	O4(3/0/1)		-0.2
1997	KC A	53	191	22	51	7	1	8	21	10-0	1	49	.267	.307	.440	89	-4	2-2	.965	-1	108	0	O52(31/0/22)		-0.8
1998	Ari N	91	206	17	41	7	1	9	30	14-1	4	46	.199	.262	.374	65	-12	2-2	.972	4	115	129	O62(49/0/13),D2		-1.0
Total	4	169	448	47	109	16	3	19	60	25-1	5	106	.243	.290	.420	82	-15	4-6	.963	2	110	69	O132(86/4/44),D2		-1.8

BENJAMIN, STAN Alfred Stanley B5.20.1914 Framingham MA BR/TR/6-2/194 d9.16 Col McDaniel

YEAR	TM LG	G	AB	R	H	2B	3B	HR	RBI	BB-IB	HP	SO	AVG	OBP	SLG	AOPS	ABR	SB-CS	FA	FR	RNG	THR	GAMES AT POSITION	DL	BFW
1939	Phi N	12	50	4	7	2	1	0	2	1	0	6	.140	.157	.220	0	-7	1	.867	0	98	240	O7(4/2/2),3b5		-0.7
1940	Phi N	8	9	1	2	0	0	0	1	1	0	1	.222	.300	.222	48	-1	0	1.000	1	108	871	O2R		0.0
1941	Phi N	129	480	47	113	20	7	3	27	20	0	81	.235	.266	.325	68	-23	17	.980	-1	92	132	O110(2/26/86),1b8,2b2/3		-3.1
1942	Phi N	78	210	24	47	8	3	2	8	10	1	27	.224	.262	.319	73	-8	5	.976	1	92	207	O45(0/25/21),1b15		-1.1
1945	Cle A	14	21	1	7	2	0	0	3	0	0	0	.333	.333	.429	126	1	0-1	1.000	2	108	547	O4(3/0/1)		0.2
Total	5	241	770	77	176	32	11	5	41	32	1	115	.229	.260	.318	66	-38	23-1	.975	2	93	173	O168(9/53/112),1b23,3b6,2b2		-4.7

BENJAMIN, MIKE Michael Paul B11.22.1965 Euclid OH BR/TR/6-0/169(169-195) [SFN87 3/74] d7.7 Col Arizona St. [DL 2001 Pit N 190]

YEAR	TM LG	G	AB	R	H	2B	3B	HR	RBI	BB-IB	HP	SO	AVG	OBP	SLG	AOPS	ABR	SB-CS	FA	FR	RNG	THR	GAMES AT POSITION	DL	BFW
1989	SF N	14	6	1	1	0	0	0	0-0	0	1	.167	.167	.167	-5	-7	0-0	1.000	-1	74	0	S8		-0.1
1990	SF N	22	56	7	12	3	1	2	3-1	0	10	.214	.254	.411	82	-2	1-0	.988	4	122	117	S21		0.4
1991	SF N	54	106	12	13	3	0	2	8	7-2	1	26	.123	.188	.208	12	-13	3-0	.984	11	120	131	S51/3		0.1
1992	SF N	40	75	4	13	3	1	1	3	4-1	0	15	.173	.215	.267	38	-7	1-0	.991	-1	101	102	S33,3b2		-0.5
1993	SF N	63	146	22	29	7	0	4	16	9-2	4	23	.199	.264	.329	59	-9	0-0	.991	12	103	230	S23,2b23,3b16	29	0.5
1994	SF N	38	62	9	16	5	1	1	9	5-1	0	16	.258	.343	.419	101	0	5-0	.968	7	156	172	S18,2b10,3b5		0.9
1995	SF N	68	186	19	41	6	0	3	8	8-3	1	51	.220	.256	.301	47	-15	11-1	.964	1	114	53	3b43,S16,2b8		-1.1
1996	SF N	35	103	13	23	5	1	4	13	12-5	2	21	.223	.316	.408	89	-2	3-1	.954	-2	99	78	S31/2	97	-0.1
1997	Bos A	49	116	12	27	9	1	0	7	4-0	1	27	.233	.262	.328	52	-8	2-3	.929	3	137	140	3b19,S16,2b5,1b4/PD		-0.4
1998	†Bos A	124	349	46	95	23	0	4	39	15-1	6	73	.272	.312	.372	76	-12	3-0	.994	4	89	95	2b87,S20,3b11,1b10,D2		-0.3
1999	Pit N	110	368	42	93	26	7	1	37	20-3	2	90	.247	.288	.364	64	-21	10-1	.982	35	128	148	S93,2b12,3b6	19	2.1
2000	Pit N	93	233	28	63	18	2	2	19	12-0	3	45	.270	.313	.391	77	-9	5-4	.974	25	150	116	3b34,S30,2b27/1		1.7
2002	Pit N	108	120	7	18	2	1	0	3	7-0	1	31	.150	.202	.183	5	-17	0-4	.979	4	104	91	3b62,S15,2b11/1OR		-1.4
Total	13	818	1926	227	442	109	15	24	169	106-19	25	429	.229	.277	.339	61	-116	44-14	.980	102	118	116	S375,3b199,2b184,1b16,D3/ORP	395	1.8

BENNERS, IKE Isaac B. B6.7.1856 Philadelphia PA D4.18.1932 Philadelphia PA BL/?/175 d5.1

YEAR	TM LG	G	AB	R	H	2B	3B	HR	RBI	BB-IB	HP	SO	AVG	OBP	SLG	AOPS	ABR	SB-CS	FA	FR	RNG	THR	GAMES AT POSITION	DL	BFW
1884	Bro AA	49	189	25	38	11	5	1		7	2		.201	.237	.328	82	-4		.821	-4	11	0	O49L		-0.8
	Wil U	6	22	0	1	0	0	0		1			.045	.087	.045	-57	-5		.750	-0	62	358	O6(0/3/3)		-0.5
Total	1	55	211	25	39	11	5	1		8			.185	.222	.299	66	-9		.813	-5	17	43	O55(49/3/3)		-1.3

BENNETT, CHARLIE Charles Wesley B11.21.1854 New Castle PA D2.24.1927 Detroit MI BR/TR/5-11/180 d5.1 OF(25/25/20)

YEAR	TM LG	G	AB	R	H	2B	3B	HR	RBI	BB-IB	HP	SO	AVG	OBP	SLG	AOPS	ABR	SB-CS	FA	FR	RNG	THR	GAMES AT POSITION	DL	BFW
1878	Mil N	49	184	16	45	9	0	1	12	10		26	.245	.284	.310	89	-2		.831	-12			C35,O20(0/16/4)		-1.3
1880	Wor N	51	193	20	44	9	3	0	18	10		30	.228	.266	.306	86	-3		.913	0			C46,O6(0/3/3)		-0.2
1881	Det N	76	299	44	90	18	7	7	64	18		37	.301	.341	.478	149	16		.962	17			C70,3b5,O3(1/2/0)		3.2
1882	Det N	84	342	43	103	16	10	5	51	20		33	.301	.340	.450	151	19		.945	6			C65,3b11,2b7/S1		2.8
1883	Det N	92	371	56	113	34	7	5	55	26		59	.305	.350	.474	155	26		.944	2			C72,2b15,O12(1/4/7)		3.0
1884	Det N	90	341	37	90	18	6	3	40	36		40	.264	.334	.378	132	15		.917	3			C80,O5(1/0/4),S4/321		2.2
1885	Det N	91	349	49	84	24	13	5	60	47		37	.249	.356	.456	161	25		.919	5			C62,O19(18/0/1),3b10		3.3
1886	Det N	72	235	37	57	13	7	4	34	48		29	.243	.371	.391	127	10	4	.955	13			C69,O4(3/0/1)/S		2.5
1887	†Det N	46	160	26	39	6	5	2	20	30		22	.244	.363	.400	108	2	7	.951	7			C45,OL1		1.0
1888	Det N	74	258	32	68	12	4	5	29	31		40	.264	.347	.399	136	12	4	.966	8			C73/1		2.5

YEAR	TM LG	G	AB	R	H	2B	3B	HR	RBI	BB-IB	HP	SO	AVG	OBP	SLG	AOPS	ABR	SB-CS	FA	FR	RNG	THR	GAMES AT POSITION	DL	BFW
1889	Bos N	82	247	42	57	8	2	4	28	21	2	43	.231	.296	.328	70	-11	7	**.955**	7			C82		0.2
1890	Bos N	85	281	59	60	17	2	4	40	72	2	56	.214	.377	.320	96	2	6	**.959**	19	*128*	86	C85		2.5
1891	Bos N	75	256	35	55	9	3	5	39	42	3	61	.215	.332	.332	84	-5	3	**.960**	18	*127*	89	C75		1.7
1892	†Bos N	35	114	19	23	4	0	1	16	27	0	23	.202	.355	.263	80	-1	6	.948	5	*132*	72	C35		0.6
1893	Bos N	60	191	34	40	6	0	4	27	40	2	36	.209	.352	.304	69	-8	5	.953	2	*131*	58	C60		-0.1
Total	15	1062	3821	549	978	203	67	55	533	478	11	572	.256	.340	.387	118	97	42	.942	100	*129*	79	C954,O70L,3b27,2b23,S6,1b4		23.9

BENNETT, GARY Gary David B4.17.1972 Waukegan IL BR/TR/6-0/210(190-210) [PhiN90 11/293] d9.24

YEAR	TM LG	G	AB	R	H	2B	3B	HR	RBI	BB-IB	HP	SO	AVG	OBP	SLG	AOPS	ABR	SB-CS	FA	FR	RNG	THR	GAMES AT POSITION	DL	BFW
1995	Phi N	1	1	0	0	0	0	0	0	0-0	0	1	.000	.000	.000	-99	0	0-0	—	0			/H		0.0
1996	Phi N	6	16	0	4	0	0	0	1	2-1	0	6	.250	.333	.250	56	-1	0-0	1.000	3	177	212	C5		0.2
1998	Phi N	9	31	4	9	0	0	0	3	5-0	0	5	.290	.378	.290	82	-1	0-0	1.000	-4	559	0	C9		-0.4
1999	Phi N	36	88	7	24	4	0	1	21	4-0	0	11	.273	.298	.352	65	-5	0-0	.971	-6	78	46	C32		-0.9
2000	Phi N	31	74	8	18	5	0	2	5	13-0	2	15	.243	.371	.392	93	0	0-0	.995	1	111	87	C31		0.3
2001	NY N	1	1	0	1	0	0	0	0	0-0	0	0	1.000	1.000	1.000	451	1	0-0	—	0			/H		0.0
	Phi N	26	75	8	16	3	1	1	6	9-1	0	19	.213	.294	.320	63	-4	0-0	.987	-2	129	99	C24		-0.4
	Col N	19	55	7	15	3	0	1	4	3-3	1	5	.273	.317	.382	67	-3	0-0	1.000	-3	63	48	C19		-0.5
	Year	46	131	15	32	6	1	2	10	12-4	1	24	.244	.308	.351	67	-6	0-0	.992	-5	102	78	C43		-0.9
2002	Col N	90	291	26	77	10	2	4	26	15-2	6	45	.265	.314	.354	69	-14	1-3	.992	-13	115	55	C90		-2.3
2003	SD N	96	307	26	73	15	0	2	42	24-3	2	48	.238	.296	.306	63	-17	3-0	.996	-24	88	64	C91	36	-3.4
2004	Mil N	75	219	18	49	14	0	3	20	22-3	2	32	.224	.297	.329	62	-12	1-0	.993	-16	103	81	C75		-2.3
2005	Was N	68	199	11	44	7	0	1	21	21-3	2	37	.221	.298	.271	56	-13	0-1	.986	1	127	73	C64		-0.8
Total	10	458	1357	115	330	61	3	15	149	118-16	15	224	.243	.308	.326	66	-69	5-4	.991	-62	116	68	C440	36	-10.5

BENNETT, HERSCHEL Herschel Emmett B9.21.1896 Elwood MO D9.9.1964 Springfield MO BL/TR/5-9.5/160 d4.19

YEAR	TM LG	G	AB	R	H	2B	3B	HR	RBI	BB-IB	HP	SO	AVG	OBP	SLG	AOPS	ABR	SB-CS	FA	FR	RNG	THR	GAMES AT POSITION	DL	BFW
1923	StL A	5	4	0	0	0	0	0	0	1	0	1	.000	.200	.000	-42	-1	0-0	1.000	0	116	0	/OC		-0.1
1924	StL A	41	94	16	31	4	3	1	11	3	2	6	.330	.364	.468	107	-1	1-0	.966	-1	84	109	O21(12/0/9)		-0.1
1925	StL A	93	298	46	83	11	6	2	37	18	2	16	.279	.324	.376	73	-13	4-10	.916	-1	91	155	O73(41/12/21)		-2.1
1926	StL A	80	225	33	60	14	2	1	26	22	2	21	.267	.337	.360	78	-7	2-1	.950	3	98	114	O50(36/6/9)		-0.8
1927	StL A	93	256	40	68	12	2	3	30	14	3	21	.266	.311	.363	72	-11	6-2	.946	1	110	86	O55(12/2/42)		-1.3
Total	5	312	877	135	242	41	13	7	104	58	9	65	.276	.327	.376	77	-32	13-13	.937	2	98	136	O200(101/21/81)		-4.4

BENNETT, FRED James Fred "Red" B3.15.1902 Atkins AR D5.12.1957 Atkins AR BR/TR/5-9/185 d4.13

YEAR	TM LG	G	AB	R	H	2B	3B	HR	RBI	BB-IB	HP	SO	AVG	OBP	SLG	AOPS	ABR	SB-CS	FA	FR	RNG	THR	GAMES AT POSITION	DL	BFW
1928	StL A	7	8	0	2	1	0	0	0	0	0	2	.250	.250	.375	60	0	0-0	1.000	0	158	0	/OR		0.0
1931	Pit N	32	89	6	25	5	0	1	7	7	0	4	.281	.333	.371	90	-1	0-0	.951	-0	90	143	O21(3/0/18)		-0.3
Total	2	39	97	6	27	6	0	1	7	7	0	6	.278	.327	.371	87	-1	0-0	.953	-0	93	138	O22(3/0/19)		-0.3

BENNETT, JOE Joseph Rosenblum B7.2.1900 New York NY D7.11.1987 Morro Bay CA BR/TR/5-9/168 d7.5 Col NYU

YEAR	TM LG	G	AB	R	H	2B	3B	HR	RBI	BB-IB	HP	SO	AVG	OBP	SLG	AOPS	ABR	SB-CS	FA	FR	RNG	THR	GAMES AT POSITION	DL	BFW
1923	Phi N	1	0	0	0	0	0	0	0	0	0	0	—	—	—		0	0-0	1.000	0	154	0	/3		0.0

BENNETT, PUG Justin Titus B2.20.1874 Ponca NE D9.12.1935 Kirkland WA BR/TR/5-11/165 d4.12 Col Blackburn

YEAR	TM LG	G	AB	R	H	2B	3B	HR	RBI	BB-IB	HP	SO	AVG	OBP	SLG	AOPS	ABR	SB-CS	FA	FR	RNG	THR	GAMES AT POSITION	DL	BFW
1906	StL N	153	595	66	156	16	7	1	34	56	8		.262	.334	.318	108	6	20	.948	-8	99	83	2b153		0.0
1907	StL N	87	324	20	72	8	2	0	21	21	1		.222	.272	.259	69	-12	7	.939	-10	89	88	2b83,3b3		-2.5
Total	2	240	919	86	228	24	9	1	55	77	9		.248	.312	.297	94	-6	27	.945	-18	96	85	2b236,3b3		-2.5

BENSON, VERN Vernon Adair B9.19.1924 Granite Quarry NC BL/TR/5-11/180* d7.31 Mil 1943-45 M1/C18 Col Catawba

YEAR	TM LG	G	AB	R	H	2B	3B	HR	RBI	BB-IB	HP	SO	AVG	OBP	SLG	AOPS	ABR	SB-CS	FA	FR	RNG	THR	GAMES AT POSITION	DL	BFW
1943	Phi A	2	2	0	0	0	0	0	0	0	0	0	.000	.000	.000	-99	-1	0-0	—	0			/H		-0.1
1946	Phi A	7	5	1	0	0	0	0	0	1	0	3	.000	.167	.000	-51	-1	0-0	1.000	0	203	0	O2L		-0.1
1951	StL N	13	46	8	12	3	1	1	7	6	0	8	.261	.346	.435	108	1	0-0	.950	1	125	190	3b9,O4L		0.1
1952	StL N	20	47	6	9	2	0	2	5	5	0	9	.191	.269	.362	73	-2	0-0	.889	-0	114	159	3b15		-0.2
1953	StL N	13	4	2	0	0	0	0	0	1	0	0	.000	.200	.000	-42	-1	0-0	—	0			/H		-0.1
Total	5	55	104	17	21	5	1	3	12	13	0	23	.202	.291	.356	75	-4	0-0	.911	1	118	170	3b24,O6L		-0.4

BENTLEY, JACK John Needles B3.8.1895 Sandy Spring MD D10.24.1969 Olney MD BL/TL/5-11.5/200 d9.6 ▲

YEAR	TM LG	G	AB	R	H	2B	3B	HR	RBI	BB-IB	HP	SO	AVG	OBP	SLG	AOPS	ABR	SB-CS	FA	FR	RNG	THR	GAMES AT POSITION	DL	BFW
1913	Was A	3	3	0	0	0	0	0	0	0	0	0	.000	.000	.000	-98	-1	0	1.000	0	154	0	P3		0.0
1914	Was A	30	40	7	11	2	0	0	4	0	0	5	.275	.275	.325	77	2	0	.930	-1	86	85	P30		0.0
1915	Was A	4	2	0	0	0	0	0	0	0	0	1	.000	.000	.000	-98	0	0	.750	-0	61	0	P4		0.0
1916	Was A	2	0	0	0	0	0	0	0	0	0	0	—	—	—		0	0	1.000	0	352	0	P2		0.0
1923	†NY N	52	89	9	38	6	2	1	14	3	0	4	.427	.446	.573	169	15	0-0	.977	-1	89	47	P31		0.0
1924	†NY N	46	98	12	26	5	1	0	6	3	0	13	.265	.287	.337	68	4	0-0	.979	-1	94	139	P28		0.0
1925	NY N	64	99	10	30	5	2	3	18	9	0	11	.303	.361	.485	119	3	0-0	.930	-1	89	91	P28,O3R/1		-0.1
1926	Phi N	75	240	19	62	12	3	2	27	5	0	0	.258	.273	.358	66	-12	0-0	.993	-1	90	81	1b56,P7		-1.6
	NY N	3	4	0	1	0	0	0	0	0	0	0	.250	.250	.250	35	0	0-0	—	-0	0	0	/P		0.0
	Year	78	244	19	63	12	3	2	27	5	0	4	.258	.273	.357	65	-13	0-0	.993	-1	90	81	1b56,P8		-1.6
1927	NY N	8	9	1	2	0	0	1	2	1	0	1	.222	.300	.556	125	0	0-0	.750	-0	91	0	P4,1b2		0.0
Total	9	287	584	58	170	30	8	7	71	21	0	39	.291	.316	.406	91	12	0-0	.949	-5	90	84	P138,1b59,O3R		-1.7

BENTON, BUTCH Alfred Lee B8.24.1957 Tampa FL BR/TR/6-1/193* [NYN75 1/6] d9.14

YEAR	TM LG	G	AB	R	H	2B	3B	HR	RBI	BB-IB	HP	SO	AVG	OBP	SLG	AOPS	ABR	SB-CS	FA	FR	RNG	THR	GAMES AT POSITION	DL	BFW
1978	NY N	4	4	1	2	0	0	0	2	0-0	1	0	.500	.600	.500	216	1	0-0	1.000	-0	0	0	/C		0.1
1980	NY N	12	21	0	1	0	0	0	0	2-0	1	4	.048	.167	.048	-38	-4	0-0	.935	-2	96	47	C4		-0.6
1982	Chi N	4	7	0	1	0	0	0	1	0-0	0	1	.143	.143	.143	-19	-1	0-0	1.000	2	87	0	C4		0.1
1985	Cle A	31	67	5	12	4	0	0	7	3-2	0	9	.179	.208	.239	24	-7	0-0	.957	-5	118	95	C26		-1.1
Total	4	51	99	6	16	4	0	0	10	5-2	2	14	.162	.213	.202	16	-11	0-0	.959	-5	109	77	C39		-1.5

BENTON, STAN Stanley W. "Rabbit" B9.29.1901 Cannel City KY D6.7.1984 Mesquite TX BR/TR/5-7/150 d9.13

YEAR	TM LG	G	AB	R	H	2B	3B	HR	RBI	BB-IB	HP	SO	AVG	OBP	SLG	AOPS	ABR	SB-CS	FA	FR	RNG	THR	GAMES AT POSITION	DL	BFW
1922	Phi N	6	19	1	4	1	0	0	3	2	0	1	.211	.286	.263	39	-1	0-0	.889	-1	103	0	2b5		-0.2

BENZINGER, TODD Todd Eric B2.11.1963 Dayton KY BB/TR/6-1/190* [BosA81 4/96] d6.21

YEAR	TM LG	G	AB	R	H	2B	3B	HR	RBI	BB-IB	HP	SO	AVG	OBP	SLG	AOPS	ABR	SB-CS	FA	FR	RNG	THR	GAMES AT POSITION	DL	BFW
1987	Bos A	73	223	36	62	11	1	8	43	22-3	2	41	.278	.344	.444	105	2	5-4	.987	9	131	157	O61(14/5/47),1b2		0.7
1988	†Bos A	120	405	47	103	28	1	13	70	22-4	1	80	.254	.293	.425	95	-4	2-3	.991	-3	78	89	1b85,O48(5/0/43)/D	19	-1.4
1989	Cin N	161	628	79	154	28	3	17	76	44-13	2	120	.245	.293	.381	89	-10	3-7	.995	-12	69	84	1b158		-3.8
1990	†Cin N	118	376	35	95	14	2	5	46	19-4	4	69	.253	.291	.340	72	-15	3-4	.992	-1	86	102	1b95,O10L		-2.5
1991	Cin N	51	123	7	23	3	2	1	11	10-2	0	20	.187	.244	.268	43	-10	2-0	.986	1	113	62	1b21,O15L		-1.1
	KC A	78	293	29	86	15	3	2	40	17-2	3	46	.294	.338	.386	99	-1	2-6	.996	-7	68	89	1b75/D		-1.4
1992	LA N	121	293	24	70	16	2	4	31	15-1	0	54	.239	.272	.348	76	-10	2-4	.989	-1	97	37	O51(18/0/33),1b42		-1.6
1993	SF N	86	177	25	51	7	2	6	26	13-1	0	35	.288	.332	.452	112	2	0-0	1.000	-3	66	120	1b40,O7L/3		-0.4
1994	SF N	107	328	32	87	13	2	9	31	17-4	2	84	.265	.304	.399	85	-9	2-1	.994	-5	83	102	1b99		-2.1
1995	SF N	9	10	2	2	0	0	1	2	2-1	0	3	.200	.308	.500	119	0	0-0	1.000	-1	0	0	1b5		0.0
Total	9	924	2856	316	733	135	18	66	376	181-35	14	552	.257	.301	.386	88	-55	21-29	.994	-22	77	94	1b622,O192(69/5/123),D2/3	19	-13.6

BERARDINO, JOHNNY John "Bernie" B5.1.1917 Los Angeles CA D5.19.1996 Los Angeles CA BR/TR/6-0/180* d4.22 Mil 1942-45 C1 Col USC

YEAR	TM LG	G	AB	R	H	2B	3B	HR	RBI	BB-IB	HP	SO	AVG	OBP	SLG	AOPS	ABR	SB-CS	FA	FR	RNG	THR	GAMES AT POSITION	DL	BFW
1939	StL A	126	468	42	120	24	5	5	58	37		36	.256	.314	.361	71	-22	0-0	.958	-1	99	76	2b114,3b8,S2		-1.4
1940	StL A	142	523	71	135	31	4	16	85	32	0	46	.258	.301	.424	84	-15	6-8	.939	-10	*105*	112	S112,2b13,3b9		0.3
1941	StL A	128	469	48	127	30	4	5	89	41	2	27	.271	.332	.384	86	-10	3-5	.954	-10	91	104	S123/3		-1.2
1942	StL A	29	74	11	21	6	0	1	10	4	1	2	.284	.329	.405	104	0	3-1	.950	-0	73	76	S6,3b6,1b5,2b4		0.1
1946	StL A	144	582	70	154	29	5	5	68	34	1	58	.265	.306	.357	81	-16	2-4	.972	-2	101	91	2b143		0.1
1947	StL A	90	306	29	80	22	1	1	20	44	2	26	.261	.358	.350	95	-1	6-5	.977	-4	90	99	2b86		0.1
1948	Cle A	66	147	19	28	5	1	2	10	27	3	16	.190	.328	.279	64	-7	0-1	.988	2	99	110	2b20,1b18,S12,3b3		-0.5
1949	Cle A	50	116	11	23	6	1	0	13	14	2	11	.198	.295	.267	50	-8	0-1	.935	-3	97	68	3b25,2b8,S3		-1.1
1950	Cle A	4	5	1	2	0	0	0	3	1	0	0	.400	.500	.400	137	0	0-0	1.000	-0	66	86	/23		0.0
	Pit N	40	131	12	27	3	1	1	12	19	0	11	.206	.307	.267	51	-9	0	.964	2	112	102	2b36,3b3		-0.5
1951	Pit N	39	119	13	27	7	1	0	13	17	0	18	.227	.324	.303	68	-5	1-1	.917	-5	77	84	3b31,2b2/1OL		-1.0
1952	Cle A	35	32	5	3	0	0	0	2	10	0	8	.094	.310	.094	17	-3	0-1	.960	1	138	66	2b8,S8,3b4,1b2		-0.2
	Pit N	19	56	2	8	4	0	0	4	4	0	6	.143	.200	.214	14	-6	0-0	.960	4	125	109	2b18		-0.2
Total	11	912	3028	334	755	167	23	36	387	284	13	268	.249	.316	.355	77	-101	27-29	.968	-6	101	91	2b453,S266,3b91,1b26/OL		-6.8

YEAR	TM LG	G	AB	R	H	2B	3B	HR	RBI	BB-IB	HP	SO	AVG	OBP	SLG	AOPS	ABR	SB-CS	FA	FR	RNG	THR	GAMES AT POSITION	DL	BFW

BERBERET, LOU Louis Joseph B11.20.1929 Long Beach CA D4.6.2004 Las Vegas NV BL/TR/5-11/212(200-212) d9.17 Col Santa Clara

1954	NY A	5	5	1	2	0	0	0	3	1	0	1	.400	.500	.400	154	0	0-0	1.000	1	0	0	C3		0.1
1955	NY A	2	5	1	2	0	0	0	1	1-0	0	0	.400	.500	.400	147	0	0-0	1.000	0	0	0	/C		0.1
1956	Was A	95	207	25	54	6	3	4	27	46-9	3	33	.261	.402	.377	107	4	0-0	.997	-2	82	134	C59		0.5
1957	Was A	99	264	24	69	11	2	7	36	41-5	2	38	.261	.359	.398	110	5	0-1	1.000	-5	75	144	C77		0.4
1958	Was A	5	6	0	1	0	0	0	0	4-0	0	1	.167	.500	.167	94	0	0-0	.917	0	55	252	C2		0.1
	Bos A	57	167	11	35	5	3	2	18	31-1	1	32	.210	.337	.311	74	-5	0-2	.984	-4	131	88	C49		-0.7
	Year	62	173	11	36	5	3	2	18	35-1	1	33	.208	.344	.306	76	-5	0-2	.981	-3	128	94	C51		-0.6
1959	Det A	100	338	38	73	8	2	13	44	35-1	0	59	.216	.284	.367	75	-13	0-0	.989	-6	115	107	C95		-1.5
1960	Det A	85	232	18	45	4	0	5	23	41-4	1	31	.194	.313	.276	60	-12	2-0	.993	1	116	116	C81		-0.7
Total	7	448	1224	118	281	34	10	31	153	200-20	7	195	.230	.337	.350	86	-21	2-3	.992	-15	102	118	C367		-1.7

BERBLINGER, JEFF Jeffrey James B11.19.1970 Wichita KS BR/TR/6-0/190 [StLN93 7/200] d9.7 Col Kansas

| 1997 | StL N | 7 | 5 | 1 | 0 | 0 | 0 | 0 | 0 | 0-0 | 0 | 1 | .000 | .000 | .000 | -99 | -1 | 0-0 | 1.000 | 1 | 108 | 258 | 2b4 | | -0.1 |

BERG, DAVE David Scott B9.3.1970 Roseville CA BR/TR/5-11/185(185-196) [FlaN93 38/1079] d4.2 Col Miami OF(38/0/16)

1998	Fla N	81	182	18	57	11	0	2	21	26-1	0	46	.313	.393	.407	120	7	3-0	1.000	0	84	86	2b27,3b25,S17		0.9
1999	Fla N	109	304	42	87	18	1	3	25	27-0	5	59	.286	.348	.382	90	-5	2-2	.969	1	108	62	S37,2b29,3b19,O3L		0.0
2000	Fla N	82	210	23	53	14	1	1	21	25-0	5	46	.252	.340	.343	79	-6	3-0	.957	-5	98	110	S49,3b13,2b11	21	-0.6
2001	Fla N	82	215	26	52	12	1	4	16	14-0	2	39	.242	.292	.363	71	-10	0-1	.965	-7	101	111	2b34,S19,3b16		-1.4
2002	Tor A	109	374	42	101	26	2	4	39	26-1	5	57	.270	.322	.382	84	-8	0-2	.966	-3	99	115	2b52,3b20,S13,O13(3/0/10),1b10,D8		-1.0
2003	Tor A	61	161	26	41	6	1	4	18	11-0	0	34	.255	.301	.379	75	-6	0-1	.978	-6	92	61	2b24,3b17,O6(1/0/5),1b2/SD	30	-1.1
2004	Tor A	58	154	13	39	4	0	3	23	4-0	1	27	.253	.278	.338	57	-10	0-1	.974	-5	70	68	O31(31/0/1),1b7,2b4,3b3,D7		-1.6
Total	7	582	1600	190	430	91	6	21	163	133-2	16	308	.269	.328	.373	83	-38	8-7	.981	-24	98	94	2b181,S136,3b113,O53L,D22,1b19	51	-4.8

BERG, MOE Morris B3.2.1902 New York NY D5.29.1972 Belleville NJ BR/TR/6-1/185 d6.27 C2 Col Princeton

1923	Bro N	49	129	9	24	3	2	0	6	2	0	5	.186	.198	.240	16	-16	1-0	.906	-5	93	83	S47/2		-1.6
1926	Chi A	41	113	4	25	6	0	0	7	6	0	9	.221	.261	.274	41	-10	0-2	.948	4	106	147	S31,2b2/3		-0.4
1927	Chi A	35	69	4	17	4	0	0	4	4	0	10	.246	.288	.304	55	-5	0-0	.952	-4	117	87	2b11,C10,S6,3b3		-0.7
1928	Chi A	76	224	25	55	16	0	0	29	14	4	25	.246	.302	.317	64	-12	3-1	.990	7	139	96	C73		0.0
1929	Chi A	107	352	32	101	7	0	0	47	17	2	16	.287	.323	.307	64	-19	5-1	.982	-1	99	101	C106		-1.2
1930	Chi A	20	61	4	7	3	0	0	7	1	0	5	.115	.129	.164	-27	-12	0-0	.986	-0	95	126	C20		-1.1
1931	Cle A	10	13	1	1	0	0	0	0	1	0	1	.077	.143	.154	-21	-2	0-0	.889	12	174	247	C8		-0.2
1932	Was A	75	195	16	46	8	1	1	26	8	0	13	.236	.266	.303	48	-16	1-1	1.000	6	168	105	C75		-0.6
1933	Was A	40	65	8	12	3	0	2	9	4	0	5	.185	.232	.323	46	-5	0-0	1.000	2	221	72	C35		-0.2
1934	Was A	33	86	5	21	4	0	0	6	6	1	4	.244	.301	.291	55	-6	2-0	.988	-3	149	87	C31		-0.6
	Cle A	29	97	4	25	3	1	0	9	1	0	7	.258	.265	.309	47	-8	0-0	.980	1	127	68	C28		-0.4
	Year	62	183	9	46	7	1	0	15	7	1	11	.251	.283	.301	51	-14	2-0	.983	-1	137	76	C59		-1.0
1935	Bos A	38	98	13	28	5	0	2	12	5	0	3	.286	.320	.398	79	-3	0-0	.991	3	111	145	C37		0.1
1936	Bos A	39	125	9	30	4	1	0	19	2	2	6	.240	.264	.288	34	-14	0-0	.986	9	96	158	C39		-0.2
1937	Bos A	47	141	13	36	3	1	0	20	5	0	4	.255	.281	.291	43	-13	0-0	.979	2	115	91	C47		-0.8
1938	Bos A	10	12	0	4	0	0	0	0	0	0	1	.333	.333	.333	64	-1	0-0	1.000	0	113	155	C7/1		0.0
1939	Bos A	14	33	3	9	1	0	1	5	2	0	3	.273	.314	.394	77	-1	0-0	.965	2	101	178	C13		0.1
Total	15	663	1813	150	441	71	6	6	206	78	9	117	.243	.278	.299	49	-143	12-5	.986	24	127	107	C529,S84,2b14,3b4/1		-7.8

BERGAMO, AUGIE August Samuel B2.14.1917 Detroit MI D8.19.1974 Grosse Pointe MI BL/TL/5-9/165 d4.25

1944	†StL N	80	192	35	55	6	3	2	19	35	1	23	.286	.399	.380	118	6	0	.988	-4	94	0	O50(31/1/19),1b2		0.0
1945	StL N	94	304	51	96	17	2	3	44	43	0	21	.316	.401	.414	124	12	0	.969	2	101	140	O77(7/0/70),1b2		0.9
Total	2	174	496	86	151	23	5	5	63	78	1	44	.304	.400	.401	122	18	0	.975	-2	98	87	O127(38/1/89),1b4		0.9

BERGEN, MARTY Martin B10.25.1871 N.Brookfield MA D1.19.1900 N.Brookfield MA TR/5-10/170 d4.17 b-Bill

1896	Bos N	65	245	39	66	6	4	4	37	11	3	22	.269	.309	.376	75	-10	4	.920	8	113	115	C63/1		0.3
1897	†Bos N	87	327	47	81	11	3	2	45	18	4		.248	.295	.318	58	-21	5	.963	14	154	71	C85/OC		0.1
1898	Bos N	120	446	62	125	16	5	3	60	13	1		.280	.302	.359	85	-11	9	.962	5	117	92	C117,1b2		0.2
1899	Bos N	72	260	32	67	11	3	1	34	10	2		.258	.290	.335	65	-13	4	.955	6	119	96	C72		-0.1
Total	4	344	1278	180	339	44	15	10	176	52	10	22	.265	.299	.347	72	-55	24	.954	33	126	92	C337,1b3/OC		0.7

BERGEN, BILL William Aloysius B6.13.1878 N.Brookfield MA D12.19.1943 Worcester MA BR/TR/6-0/184 d5.6 b-Marty

1901	Cin N	87	308	15	55	6	4	1	17	8	0		.179	.199	.234	27	-30	2	.970	-3	110	105	C87		-2.5
1902	Cin N	89	322	19	58	8	3	0	36	14	0		.180	.214	.224	32	-26	2	.959	19	125	101	C89		0.2
1903	Cin N	58	207	21	47	4	2	0	19	7	0		.227	.252	.266	43	-16	2	.980	4	123	102	C58		-0.6
1904	Bro N	96	329	17	60	4	2	0	12	9	0		.182	.204	.207	28	-29	3	.959	13	100	111	C93/1		-0.7
1905	Bro N	79	247	12	47	3	2	0	22	7	0		.190	.213	.219	31	-22	4	.954	0	82	128	C76		-1.5
1906	Bro N	103	353	9	56	3	0	0	19	7	0		.159	.175	.184	13	-38	2	.977	-5	97	104	C103		-2.9
1907	Bro N	51	138	2	22	3	0	0	14	1	0		.159	.165	.181	9	-15	1	.968	-2	87	123	C51		-1.5
1908	Bro N	99	302	8	53	8	2	0	15	5	0		.175	.189	.215	30	-25	1	.989	10	87	105	C99		-0.6
1909	Bro N	112	346	16	48	1	1	1	15	10	0		.139	.163	.156	-1	-42	4	.976	11	93	125	C112		-2.3
1910	Bro N	89	249	11	40	2	1	0	14	6	0	39	.161	.180	.177	4	-31	0	.981	13	99	114	C89		-1.1
1911	Bro N	84	227	8	30	3	1	0	14	11	0	42	.132	.183	.154	-6	-33	2	.981	5	87	118	C84		-2.2
Total	11	947	3028	138	516	45	21	2	193	88	0	81	.170	.194	.201	20	-307	23	.972	73	99	112	C941/1		-15.7

BERGER, BRANDON Brandon Charles B2.21.1975 Covington KY BR/TR/5-11/205* [KCA96 14/409] d9.9 Col Eastern Kentucky

2001	KC A	6	16	4	5	1	1	2	2	2-0	0	2	.313	.389	.875	199	2	0-0	1.000	-1	69	0	O5L/D		0.1
2002	KC A	51	134	16	27	5	1	6	17	8-2	2	32	.201	.255	.388	61	-8	1-0	1.000	2	101	221	O36(14/4/21),D10/1		-0.7
2003	KC A	13	32	3	7	0	0	3	5-0	0	4	.219	.324	.219	44	-2	0-0	1.000	1	96	211	O11R/D		-0.3
2004	KC A	11	35	5	7	2	0	0	0-0	0	7	.200	.200	.257	18	-4	1-1	1.000	1	132	178	O11(10/0/1)		-0.3
Total	4	81	217	28	46	8	2	8	24	15-2	2	45	.212	.268	.378	63	-12	2-1	1.000	3	103	191	O63(29/4/33),D12/1		-1.1

BERGER, CLARENCE Clarence Edward B11.1.1894 E.Cleveland OH D6.30.1959 Washington DC BL/TR/6-0/185 d9.23

| 1914 | Pit N | 6 | 13 | 2 | 1 | 0 | 0 | 0 | 4 | .077 | .143 | .077 | -36 | -2 | 0 | 1.000 | -1 | 53 | 0 | O5R | | -0.3 |

BERGER, JOHNNY John Henne B8.27.1901 Philadelphia PA D5.7.1979 Lake Charles LA BR/TR/5-9/165 d4.20

1922	Phi A	2	1	0	1	0	0	0	0	0	0	0	1.000	1.000	1.000	412	0	1-0	1.000	0	0	0	C2		0.1
1927	Was A	9	15	1	4	0	0	0	1	2	0	3	.267	.353	.267	63	-1	0-0	.926	-0	144	0	C9		-0.1
Total	2	11	16	1	5	0	0	0	1	2	0	3	.313	.389	.313	85	-1	1-0	.935	0	129	0	C11		0.0

BERGER, TUN John Henry B12.6.1867 Pittsburgh PA D6.10.1907 Pittsburgh PA TR/?/204 d5.9

1890	Pit N	104	391	64	104	18	4	0	40	35	7	23	.266	.337	.332	108	6	11	.912	-13	160	54	O41(4/3/36),S33,C21,2b6/3		-0.3
1891	Pit N	43	134	15	32	2	1	1	14	12	3	10	.239	.315	.291	79	-3	4	.920	-10	106	112	C18,2b17,S6,O2(0/1/1)		-1.0
1892	Was N	26	97	9	14	2	1	0	3	7	1	9	.144	.210	.186	20	-9	3	.872	-7	84	54	S18,C9		-1.4
Total	3	173	622	88	150	22	6	1	57	54	11	42	.241	.313	.301	87	-6	18	.837	-30	84	53	S57,C48,O43(4/4/37),2b23/3		-2.7

BERGER, JOE Joseph August "Fats" B12.20.1886 St.Louis MO D3.5.1956 Rock Island IL BR/TR/5-10.5/170 d4.11

1913	Chi A	79	223	27	48	6	2	2	20	36	2	28	.215	.330	.287	82	-4	5	.959	3	111	82	2b71,S4/3		0.0
1914	Chi A	48	148	11	23	3	1	0	3	13	0	9	.155	.224	.189	25	-14	2-8	.922	0	104	86	S28,2b12,3b7		-1.6
Total	2	127	371	38	71	9	3	2	23	49	2	37	.191	.289	.248	60	-18	7-8	.956	3	110	89	2b83,S32,3b8		-1.6

BERGER, BOZE Louis William B5.13.1910 Baltimore MD D11.3.1992 Bethesda MD BR/TR/6-2/180 d8.17 Col Maryland-Baltimore Co.

1932	Cle A	1	1	0	0	0	0	0	0	0	1	.000	.000	.000	-94	0	0-0	1.000	0	98	0	/S		0.0
1935	Cle A	124	461	62	119	27	5	5	43	34	1	97	.258	.310	.371	74	-19	7-5	.964	12	106	119	3b120,S3,1b2/3		0.1
1936	Cle A	28	52	1	9	2	0	0	5	1	0	14	.173	.189	.212	-1	-9	0-0	.959	1	93	56	1b8,2b8,3b7,S2		-0.6
1937	Chi A	52	130	19	31	5	0	5	13	15	1	24	.238	.322	.392	79	-5	1-1	.931	-1	101	118	3b40/2S		-0.4
1938	Chi A	118	470	60	102	15	3	3	36	43	1	80	.217	.284	.281	41	-44	4-1	.946	-8	108	119	S67,2b42,3b9		-4.0
1939	Bos A	20	30	4	9	2	0	0	2	1	0	10	.300	.323	.367	73	-1	0-0	.947	1	97	48	S10,3b5,2b2		0.0
Total	6	343	1144	146	270	51	8	13	97	94	3	226	.236	.296	.329	50	-78	12-7	.954	5	104	111	2b173,S84,3b62,1b10		-4.9

YEAR	TM LG	G	AB	R	H	2B	3B	HR	RBI	BB-IB	HP	SO	AVG	OBP	SLG	AOPS	ABR	SB-CS	FA	FR	RNG	THR	GAMES AT POSITION	DL	BFW

BERGER, WALLY Walter Anton B10.10.1905 Chicago IL D11.30.1988 Redondo Beach CA BR/TR/6-2/198 d4.15

1930	Bos N	151	555	98	172	27	14	38	119	54	4	69	.310	.375	.614	139	31	3	.966	3	106	98	O145L		2.0
1931	Bos N	156	617	94	199	44	8	19	84	55	2	70	.323	.386	.512	143	37	13	.977	4	102	118	O156C/1		3.6
1932	Bos N	145	602	90	185	34	6	17	73	33	3	66	.307	.346	.468	121	17	5	**.993**	-2	100	79	O134C,1b11		1.0
1933	Bos N★	137	528	84	165	37	8	27	106	41	3	77	.313	.365	.566	**177**	50	2	.977	-2	103	61	O136C		4.7
1934	Bos N★	150	615	92	183	35	4	34	121	49	3	65	.298	.352	.546	148	38	2	.978	-6	94	80	O150C		2.7
1935	Bos N★	150	589	91	174	39	4	**34**	**130**	50	4	80	.295	.355	.548	151	40	3	.965	9	**119**	67	O149C		4.4
1936	Bos N☆	138	534	88	154	23	3	25	91	53	8	84	.288	.361	.483	134	25	1	.966	-3	99	95	O133C		1.8
1937	Bos N	30	113	14	31	9	1	5	22	11	1	33	.274	.344	.504	140	6	0	1.000	-1	94	52	O28L		0.3
	†NY N	59	199	40	58	11	2	12	43	18	3	30	.291	.359	.548	141	11	3	.965	-3	88	97	O52(3/46/3)		0.6
	Year	89	312	54	89	20	3	17	65	29	4	63	.285	.354	.532	141	17	3	.976	-5	90	82	O80(31/46/3)		0.9
1938	NY N	16	32	5	6	0	0	0	4	2	0	4	.188	.235	.188	17	-4	0	1.000	0	120	0	O9(0/8/1)		-0.4
	Cin N	99	407	74	125	23	4	16	56	29	2	44	.307	.356	.501	137	19	2	.966	-2	95	94	O98L		1.2
	Year	115	439	79	131	23	4	16	60	31	2	48	.298	.347	.478	128	15	2	.970	-2	97	85	O107(98/8/1)		0.8
1939	†Cin N	97	329	36	85	15	1	14	44	36	5	63	.258	.341	.438	107	3	1	.970	-8	80	99	O95(66/29/0)		-0.9
1940	Cin N	2	2	0	0	0	0	0	0	0	0	1	.000	.000	.000	-99	-1	0	—	0			/H		-0.1
	Phi N	20	41	3	13	2	0	1	5	4	0	7	.317	.378	.439	130	2	1	.947	-1	103	0	O11(4/2/5)/1		0.1
	Year	22	43	3	13	2	0	1	5	4	0	8	.302	.362	.419	119	1	1	.947	-1	103	0	O11(4/2/5)/1		0.0
Total	11	1350	5163	809	1550	299	59	242	898	435	38	693	.300	.359	.522	140	274	36	.974	-11	100	86	O1296(344/943/9),1b13		21.0

BERGERON, PETER Peter Francis B11.9.1977 Greenfield MA BL/TR/6-2/185* [LAN96 4/118] d9.7

1999	Mon N	16	45	12	11	4	0	1	9-0		1	9	.244	.370	.289	73	-1	0-0	.967	2	118	287	O13(13/3/0)		0.0
2000	Mon N	148	518	80	127	25	7	5	31	58-0	0	100	.245	.320	.349	69	-25	11-13	.985	5	99	**201**	O146(32/117/0)		-2.1
2001	Mon N	102	375	53	79	11	4	3	16	28-2	1	87	.211	.275	.285	45	-32	10-7	.996	-4	95	113	O101C		-3.4
2002	Mon N	31	123	24	23	3	2	0	7	22-0	0	44	.187	.310	.244	49	-9	10-3	.974	-2	100	0	O31C		-1.0
2004	Mon N	11	42	2	9	0	0	0	1	6	0	16	.214	.250	.214	21	-5	0-1	.913	-2	78	0	O11C	35	-0.7
Total	5	308	1103	171	249	41	13	8	56	119-2	5	252	.226	.303	.308	57	-72	31-24	.984	-1	98	143	O302(45/263/0)	35	-7.2

BERGH, JOHN John Baptist B10.8.1857 Boston MA D4.17.1883 Boston MA d8.5

1876	Phi N	1	4	0	0	0	0	0	0			2	.000	.000	.000	-99	-1		1.000	-0	0	0	/OCC		-0.1
1880	Bos N	11	40	2	8	3	0	0	2			5	.200	.238	.275	76	-1		.844	-3			C11		-0.3
Total	2	12	44	2	8	3	0	0	2			7	.182	.217	.250	59	-2		.841	-3			C12/OC		-0.4

BERGHAMMER, MARTY Martin Andrew "Pepper" B6.18.1888 Elliott PA D12.21.1957 Pittsburgh PA BL/TR/5-9/172 d9.8

1911	Chi A	2	5	0	0	0	0	0	0	0	1		.000	.167	.000	-54	-1	0	1.000	-0	51	0	2b2		-0.1
1913	Cin N	74	188	25	41	4	1	1	13	10	3	29	.218	.269	.266	53	-12	16-10	.909	4	107	97	S54,2b13		-0.5
1914	Cin N	77	112	15	25	2	0	0	6	10	0	18	.223	.287	.241	56	-6	4	.906	6	124	68	S33,2b13		0.1
1915	Pit F	132	469	96	114	10	6	0	33	83	12	44	.243	.371	.290	88	-9	26	**.943**	-15	90	113	S132		-1.6
Total	4	285	774	136	180	16	7	1	52	103	16	91	.233	.335	.275	75	-28	46-10	.931	-5	97	106	S219,2b28		-2.1

BERGMAN, AL Alfred Henry "Dutch" B9.27.1890 Peru IN D6.20.1961 Fort Wayne IN BR/TR/5-7/155 d8.29 Col Notre Dame

| 1916 | Cle A | 8 | 14 | 2 | 3 | 0 | 0 | 0 | | | 0 | 4 | .214 | .313 | .357 | 95 | -0 | | .889 | -1 | 92 | 0 | 2b3 | | -0.1 |

BERGMAN, DAVE David Bruce B6.6.1953 Evanston IL BL/TL/6-1.5/185(180-195) [NYA74 2/36] d8.26 Col Illinois St.

1975	NY A	7	17	0	0	0	0	0	0	2-0	0	4	.000	.105	.000	-69	-4	0-0	.917	1	109	258	O6R		-0.4
1977	NY A	5	4	1	1	0	0	0	1	0-0	0	1	.250	.200	.250	37	0	0-0	1.000	1	157	0	O3(1/1/1),1b2		0.0
1978	Hou N	104	186	15	43	5	1	0	12	39-9	0	32	.231	.361	.269	85	-2	2-0	.993	-3	80	109	1b66,O29L		-0.7
1979	Hou N	13	15	4	6	0	0	1	2	0-0	0	3	.400	.400	.600	179	1	0-0	1.000	-0	0	93	1b4		0.1
1980	†Hou N	90	78	12	20	6	1	0	3	10-2	0	10	.256	.341	.359	104	1	1-0	.995	1	116	158	1b59,O5(3/0/2)		0.1
1981	Hou N	6	6	1	1	0	0	1	1	0-0	0	0	.167	.167	.667	135	0	0-0	1.000	0	626	0	/1		0.0
	SF N	63	145	16	37	9	0	3	13	19-3	0	18	.255	.339	.379	108	2	2-0	.992	2	136	99	1b33,O15L		0.2
	Year	69	151	17	38	9	0	4	14	19-3	0	18	.252	.333	.391	109	2	2-0	.992	2	140	92	1b34,O15L		0.2
1982	SF N	100	121	22	33	3	1	4	14	18-3	0	11	.273	.364	.413	119	3	3-0	.991	-0	92	76	1b69,O6(4/0/3)		0.2
1983	SF N	90	140	16	40	4	1	6	24	24-2	1	21	.286	.394	.457	139	3	2-1	.994	3	129	87	1b50,O6L		0.9
1984	†Det A	120	271	42	74	8	5	7	44	33-2	3	40	.273	.351	.417	114	5	3-4	.989	5	122	103	1b114,O2(1/0/1)		0.5
1985	Det A	69	140	8	25	2	0	3	7	14-0	0	15	.179	.250	.257	40	-12	0-0	.991	-1	93	88	1b44/OLD	37	-1.5
1986	Det A	65	130	14	30	6	1	1	9	21-0	0	16	.231	.338	.315	79	-3	0-0	.986	1	118	119	1b41,O2(1/0/1),D8		-0.4
1987	†Det A	91	172	25	47	7	3	6	22	30-4	1	23	.273	.379	.453	126	7	0-1	.992	-2	91	98	1b65,O7(3/0/4),D7	15	0.2
1988	Det A	116	289	37	85	14	0	5	35	38-2	0	34	.294	.372	.394	120	9	0-2	.990	1	110	86	1b64,D30,O13L		0.5
1989	Det A	137	385	38	103	13	1	7	37	44-3	2	44	.268	.345	.361	101	3	1-3	.993	5	**119**	88	1b123/OLD		-0.1
1990	Det A	100	205	21	57	10	1	2	26	33-3	0	17	.278	.375	.366	108	4	3-2	.995	-1	83	93	D51,1b27,O5L		-0.1
1991	Det A	86	194	23	46	10	1	7	29	35-2	0	40	.237	.351	.407	108	3	1-1	.997	-0	100	106	1b49,D13,O4L		-0.1
1992	Det A	87	181	17	42	3	0	1	10	20-1	0	19	.232	.305	.265	61	-9	1-0	.986	-3	80	84	1b55,D12/OL		-1.6
Total	17	1349	2679	312	690	100	16	54	289	380-36	7	347	.258	.348	.367	102	15	19-14	.992	8	107	97	1b866,D133,O106(88/1/18)	52	-2.2

BERGOLLA, WILLIAM William Jose B2.4.1983 Valencia, Venez BR/TR/6-0/175 d5.9

| 2005 | Cin N | 17 | 38 | 3 | 5 | 0 | 0 | 0 | 1 | 0-0 | 0 | 0 | .132 | .132 | .132 | -32 | -7 | 0-0 | 1.000 | 3 | 147 | 120 | 2b9/S | | -0.4 |

BERKENSTOCK, NATE Nathan B1831 PA D2.23.1900 Philadelphia PA d10.30

| 1871 | Ath NA | 1 | 4 | 0 | 0 | 0 | 0 | 0 | 0 | | | 3 | .000 | .000 | .000 | -99 | -1 | 0-0 | 1.000 | 0 | 0 | 0 | /OR | | 0.0 |

BERKLEBACH, FRANK Frank Pierce B7.27.1853 Philadelphia PA D6.10.1932 Merchantville NJ 6-0/182 d7.4

| 1884 | Cin AA | 6 | 25 | 3 | 6 | 0 | 0 | 0 | | | | 2 | .240 | .296 | .320 | 96 | 0 | | .667 | -1 | 0 | 0 | O6L | | -0.2 |

BERKMAN, LANCE William Lance B2.10.1976 Waco TX BB/TL/6-1/205(205-220) [HouN97 1/16] d7.16 Col Rice

1999	Hou N	34	93	10	22	2	0	4	15	12-0	0	21	.237	.321	.387	80	-3	5-1	.955	-2	94	0	O27(22/0/8)/1		-0.5
2000	Hou N	114	353	76	105	28	1	21	67	56-1	1	73	.297	.388	.561	128	16	6-2	.968	0	99	107	O96(40/0/63),1b2		1.2
2001	†Hou N★	156	577	110	191	55	5	34	126	92-5	13	121	.331	.430	.620	157	54	7-9	.981	-2	100	61	O155(128/40/7)		4.4
2002	Hou N★	158	578	106	169	35	2	42	**128**	107-20	4	118	.292	.405	.578	148	40	8-4	.977	-10	88	70	O156(76/122/12)		2.9
2003	Hou N	153	538	110	155	35	6	25	93	107-13	9	108	.288	.412	.515	133	31	5-3	.989	-3	92	108	O153(153/1/0)		2.2
2004	Hou N★	160	544	104	172	40	3	30	106	127-14	10	101	.316	.450	.566	156	55	9-7	.992	-5	86	124	O160(70/2/90),1b4		4.1
2005	†Hou N	132	468	76	137	34	1	24	82	91-12	4	72	.293	.411	.524	143	34	4-1	.994	-3	93	120	1b96,O49(39/0/11),D3	33	2.2
Total	7	907	3151	592	951	229	18	180	617	592-65	41	614	.302	.416	.557	144	227	44-27	.980	-23	92	90	O796(528/165/191),1b103,D3	33	16.5

BERMAN, BOB Robert Leon B1.24.1899 New York NY D8.2.1988 Bridgeport CT BR/TR/5-7.5/158 d6.4 Col Fordham

| 1918 | Was A | 2 | 0 | 0 | 0 | 0 | 0 | 0 | 0 | | | | | | | | | | 1.000 | 0 | 0 | 0 | /C | | 0.0 |

BERNARD, CURT Curtis Henry B2.18.1878 Parkersburg WV D4.10.1955 Culver City CA BL/TR/5-10/150 d9.17

1900	NY N	20	71	9	18	2	0	0	8	6			.254	.329	.282	73	-2	1	.929	-2	39	0	O19R/S		-0.4
1901	NY N	23	76	11	17	0	2	0	6	7			.224	.289	.276	67	-3	2	.800	-2	189	0	O15(0/8/7),2b4,S2/3		-0.6
Total	2	43	147	20	35	2	2	0	14	13			.238	.309	.279	70	-5	3	.857	-4	110	0	O34(0/8/26),2b4,S3/3		-1.0

BERNAZARD, TONY Antonio (Garcia) B8.24.1956 Caguas, PR BB/TR/5-9/160* d7.13

1979	Mon N	22	40	11	12	2	1	0	8	15-0	1	12	.300	.500	.425	154	5	1-2	.982	-3	97	54	2b14		0.2
1980	Mon N	82	183	26	41	7	5	2	18	17-4	0	41	.224	.289	.355	78	-6	9-2	.976	-3	104	90	2b39,S22		-0.3
1981	Chi A	106	384	53	106	14	4	6	34	54-6	2	66	.276	.367	.380	118	11	4-4	.987	6	103	91	2b104/S		2.3
1982	Chi A	137	540	90	138	25	9	11	56	67-0	2	88	.256	.337	.396	101	1	11-0	.985	31	**112**	119	2b137	21	4.2
1983	Chi A	59	233	30	61	16	2	2	26	17-0	0	45	.262	.306	.373	84	-5	2-1	.976	2	111	99	2b59		0.0
	Sea A	80	300	35	80	18	1	6	30	38-3	2	52	.267	.351	.393	101	2	21-8	.971	5	100	89	2b79		1.3
	Year	139	533	65	141	34	3	8	56	55-3	2	97	.265	.332	.385	94	-3	23-9	.973	7	105	93	2b138		1.3
1984	Cle A	140	439	44	97	15	4	2	38	43-0	2	76	.221	.290	.290	76	-23	20-13	.978	2	103	101	2b136/D		-1.5
1985	Cle A	153	500	73	137	26	3	11	59	69-2	1	72	.274	.361	.404	110	-10	17-9	.978	-10	97	83	2b147/S		0.8
1986	Cle A	146	562	88	169	28	4	17	73	53-5	6	77	.301	.365	.456	124	19	17-8	.979	3	104	91	2b146		3.0
1987	Cle A	79	293	39	70	12	1	11	30	25-2	1	49	.239	.300	.399	83	-8	7-4	.983	-14	90	71	2b78		-1.7
	Oak A	61	214	34	57	14	1	3	19	30-0	0	30	.266	.354	.383	103	2	4-4	.953	-15	85	64	2b59,D3		-1.0
	Year	140	507	73	127	26	2	14	49	55-2	1	79	.250	.323	.393	91	-6	11-8	.971	-30	88	68	2b137,D3		-2.7

YEAR	TM LG	G	AB	R	H	2B	3B	HR	RBI	BB-IB	HP	SO	AVG	OBP	SLG	AOPS	ABR	SB-CS	FA	FR	RNG	THR	GAMES AT POSITION	DL	BFW
1991	Det A	6	12	0	2	0	0	0	0	0-0	0	4	.167	.167	.167	-7	-2	0-0	.900	1	165	328	2b2,D2		-0.1
Total	10	1071	3700	523	970	177	30	75	391	428-22	17	606	.262	.339	.387	99	5	113-55	.978	7	102	92	2b1000,S24,D6	21	7.2

BERNHARDT, JUAN Juan Ramon (Coradin) B8.31.1953 San Pedro de Macoris, D.R. BR/TR/5-11/175(160-175) d7.10

YEAR	TM LG	G	AB	R	H	2B	3B	HR	RBI	BB-IB	HP	SO	AVG	OBP	SLG	AOPS	ABR	SB-CS	FA	FR	RNG	THR	GAMES AT POSITION	DL	BFW
1976	NY A	10	21	1	4	1	0	0	1	0-0	0	4	.190	.190	.238	25	-2	0-0	.800	-1	77	0	O4(1/0/3)/3D		-0.3
1977	Sea A	89	305	32	74	9	2	7	30	5-0	2	26	.243	.259	.354	66	-16	2-3	.982	1	102	28	D54,3b21,1b8	15	-1.8
1978	Sea A	54	165	13	38	9	0	2	12	9-1	1	10	.230	.270	.321	67	-7	1-1	.989	0	151	87	1b25,3b22,D2		-1.0
1979	Sea A	1	1	0	1	0	0	0	0	0-0	0	0	1.000	1.000	1.000	432	0	0-0	—	0			/H		0.0
Total	4	154	492	46	117	19	2	9	43	14-1	3	40	.238	.261	.339	65	-25	3-4	.965	0	94	26	D58,3b44,1b33,O4(1/0/3)	15	-3.1

BERNIER, CARLOS Carlos (Rodriguez) B1.28.1927 Juana Diaz, PR D4.6.1989 Juana Diaz, PR BR/TR/5-9/180 d4.22

YEAR	TM LG	G	AB	R	H	2B	3B	HR	RBI	BB-IB	HP	SO	AVG	OBP	SLG	AOPS	ABR	SB-CS	FA	FR	RNG	THR	GAMES AT POSITION	DL	BFW
1953	Pit N	105	310	48	66	7	8	3	31	51	4	53	.213	.332	.316	70	-13	15-14	.970	3	107	111	O86(11/57/18)		-1.5

BERO, JOHNNY John George B12.22.1922 Gary WV D5.11.1985 Gardena CA BL/TR/6-0/170* d9.26 Col Western Michigan

YEAR	TM LG	G	AB	R	H	2B	3B	HR	RBI	BB-IB	HP	SO	AVG	OBP	SLG	AOPS	ABR	SB-CS	FA	FR	RNG	THR	GAMES AT POSITION	DL	BFW
1948	Det A	4	9	2	0	0	0	0	0	1	0	1	.000	.100	.000	-70	-2	0-0	1.000	-1	59	0	2b2		-0.3
1951	StL A	61	160	24	34	5	0	5	17	26	0	30	.213	.323	.338	76	-5	1-1	.954	-7	97	73	S55/2		-0.9
Total	2	65	169	26	34	5	0	5	17	27	0	31	.201	.311	.320	69	-7	1-1	.954	-8	97	73	S55,2b3		-1.2

BERRA, DALE Dale Anthony B12.13.1956 Ridgewood NJ BR/TR/6-0/190* [PitN75 1/20] d8.22 f-Yogi

YEAR	TM LG	G	AB	R	H	2B	3B	HR	RBI	BB-IB	HP	SO	AVG	OBP	SLG	AOPS	ABR	SB-CS	FA	FR	RNG	THR	GAMES AT POSITION	DL	BFW
1977	Pit N	17	40	0	7	1	0	0	3	1-0	0	8	.175	.195	.200	6	-5	0-0	.973	-0	88	62	3b14		-0.6
1978	Pit N	56	135	16	28	2	0	6	14	13-3	2	20	.207	.285	.356	75	-5	3-1	.908	-5	91	161	3b55,S2		-1.1
1979	Pit N	44	123	11	26	5	0	3	15	11-2	0	17	.211	.272	.325	60	-7	0-0	.940	-7	86	101	S22,3b22		-1.3
1980	Pit N	93	245	21	54	8	2	6	31	16-6	1	52	.220	.269	.343	68	-11	2-0	.968	-11	98	138	3b48,S45,2b4		-2.0
1981	Pit N	81	232	21	56	12	0	2	27	17-4	3	34	.241	.302	.319	72	-8	11-1	.976	-6	100	114	3b42,S30,2b18		-1.0
1982	Pit N	156	529	64	139	25	5	10	61	33-12	4	83	.263	.306	.386	90	-8	6-6	.961	5	103	90	S153,3b6		1.3
1983	Pit N	161	537	51	135	25	1	10	52	61-**19**	0	84	.251	.327	.358	87	-8	8-5	.963	14	100	138	S161		2.4
1984	Pit N	136	450	31	100	16	0	9	52	34-8	1	78	.222	.273	.318	67	-21	1-3	.955	-2	103	86	S135/3	15	-1.0
1985	NY A	48	109	8	25	5	1	1	8	7-0	0	20	.229	.276	.321	64	-6	1-1	.917	2	107	160	3b41,S6		-0.4
1986	NY A	42	108	10	25	7	0	2	13	9-0	1	14	.231	.294	.352	76	-4	0-0	.972	-0	93	88	S19,3b18,D4		-0.2
1987	Hou N	19	45	3	8	3	0	0	2	8-3	0	12	.178	.296	.244	49	-3	0-0	.963	-2	96	53	S18,2b3		-0.4
Total	11	853	2553	236	603	109	9	49	278	210-57	12	422	.236	.294	.344	76	-86	32-17	.959	-12	99	92	S591,3b247,2b25,D4	15	-4.3

BERRA, YOGI Lawrence Peter B5.12.1925 St.Louis MO BL/TR/5-8/194(183-194) d9.22 M7/C20 HF1972 s-Dale

YEAR	TM LG	G	AB	R	H	2B	3B	HR	RBI	BB-IB	HP	SO	AVG	OBP	SLG	AOPS	ABR	SB-CS	FA	FR	RNG	THR	GAMES AT POSITION	DL	BFW
1946	NY A	7	22	3	8	1	0	2	4	1	0	1	.364	.391	.682	193	2	0-0	1.000	3	94	187	C6		0.4
1947	†NY A	83	293	41	82	15	3	11	54	13	0	12	.280	.310	.464	115	3	0-1	.972	-5	86	55	C51,O24(12/0/12)		0.0
1948	NY A☆	125	469	70	143	24	10	14	98	25	1	24	.305	.341	.488	120	9	3-3	.979	-2	92	115	C71,O50R		0.8
1949	†NY A★	116	415	59	115	20	2	20	91	22	6	25	.277	.323	.480	111	2	2-1	.989	10	81	108	C109		1.7
1950	†NY A★	151	597	116	192	30	6	28	124	55	4	12	.322	.383	.533	136	29	4-2	.985	4	128	103	C148		3.8
1951	†NY A★	141	547	92	161	19	4	27	88	44	3	20	.294	.350	.492	131	19	5-4	.984	9	115	124	C141		3.5
1952	†NY A★	142	534	97	146	17	1	30	98	66	4	24	.273	.358	.478	139	26	2-3	.992	1	93	102	C140		3.5
1953	†NY A★	137	503	80	149	23	5	27	108	50	3	32	.296	.363	.523	142	27	0-3	.986	7	122	85	C133		3.8
1954	†NY A★	151	584	88	179	28	6	22	125	56	4	29	.307	.367	.488	139	29	0-1	.990	7	132	97	C149/3		4.4
1955	†NY A★	147	541	84	147	20	3	27	108	60-6	1	20	.272	.349	.470	121	14	1-0	.984	4	134	76	C145		2.5
1956	†NY A★	140	521	93	155	29	2	30	105	65-7	5	29	.298	.378	.534	144	32	3-2	.986	6	125	95	C135/OL		4.3
1957	†NY A★	134	482	74	121	14	2	24	82	57-10	1	24	.251	.329	.438	110	6	1-2	.995	12	116	140	C121,O6(5/0/1)		2.4
1958	†NY A★	122	433	60	115	17	3	22	90	35-5	2	35	.266	.319	.471	120	10	3-0	1.000	4	100	128	C88,O21R,1b2		1.8
1959	†NY A	131	472	64	134	25	1	19	69	43-5	4	38	.284	.347	.462	125	16	1-2	.997	6	127	101	C116,O7(1/0/6)		2.7
1960	†NY A★	120	359	46	99	14	1	15	62	38-6	3	23	.276	.347	.446	120	10	2-1	.989	-2	120	99	C63,O36(20/0/17)		0.8
1961	†NY A★	119	395	62	107	11	0	22	61	35-4	2	28	.271	.330	.466	117	8	2-0	.988	4	103	114	O87(81/0/8),C15		0.8
1962	†NY A	86	232	25	52	8	0	10	35	24-4	2	18	.224	.297	.388	87	-5	0-1	.990	5	154	83	C31,O28L		0.0
1963	†NY A	64	147	20	43	6	0	8	28	15-2	1	17	.293	.360	.497	139	2	1-0	.988	8	81	56	C35		1.8
1965	NY N	4	9	1	2	0	0	0	0	0-0	0	3	.222	.222	.222	27	-1	0-0	.941	9	49	0	C2		0.0
Total	19	2120	7555	1175	2150	321	49	358	1430	704-49	52	414	.285	.348	.482	126	244	30-26	.989	78	115	103	C1699,O260(148/0/115),1b2/3		39.0

BERRAN, DENNIS Dennis Martin B10.8.1887 Merrimac MA D4.28.1943 Boston MA BL/TL d8.11

YEAR	TM LG	G	AB	R	H	2B	3B	HR	RBI	BB-IB	HP	SO	AVG	OBP	SLG	AOPS	ABR	SB-CS	FA	FR	RNG	THR	GAMES AT POSITION	DL	BFW
1912	Chi A	2	4	1	1	0	0	0	0	0	0		.250	.250	.250	44	0	0	1.000	-0	66	0	O2L		-0.1

BERRES, RAY Raymond Frederick B8.31.1907 Kenosha WI BR/TR/5-9/170 d4.24 C20

YEAR	TM LG	G	AB	R	H	2B	3B	HR	RBI	BB-IB	HP	SO	AVG	OBP	SLG	AOPS	ABR	SB-CS	FA	FR	RNG	THR	GAMES AT POSITION	DL	BFW
1934	Bro N	39	79	7	17	4	0	0	3	1	0	16	.215	.225	.266	32	-8	0	.969	-2	93	148	C37		-0.8
1936	Bro N	105	267	16	64	10	1	1	13	14	1	35	.240	.280	.296	55	-17	1	.988	10	65	125	C105		-0.3
1937	Pit N	2	6	0	1	0	0	0	0	0	0	0	.167	.167	.167	-9	-1	0	1.000	0	67	173	C2		0.0
1938	Pit N	40	100	7	23	2	0	0	6	8	0	10	.230	.287	.250	48	-7	0	.993	3	98	139	C40		-0.2
1939	Pit N	81	231	22	53	6	1	0	16	11	1	25	.229	.267	.264	44	-19	1	.993	0	112	88	C80		-1.5
1940	Pit N	21	32	2	6	0	0	0	2	1	0	1	.188	.212	.188	11	-4	0	.980	1	69	178	C21		-0.3
	Bos N	85	229	12	44	1	0	1	14	18	0	19	.192	.251	.218	32	-22	0	.981	1	102	121	C85		-1.7
	Year	106	261	14	50	1	0	1	16	19	0	20	.192	.246	.215	29	-26	0	.981	2	98	128	C106		-2.0
1941	Bos N	120	279	21	56	10	0	1	19	17	0	20	.201	.247	.247	41	-22	2	.995	4	93	117	C120		-1.3
1942	NY N	12	32	0	6	0	0	0	1	2	0	3	.188	.235	.188	24	-3	0	.973	-1	147	40	C12		-0.4
1943	NY N	20	28	1	4	1	0	0	0	1	0	4	.143	.172	.179	1	-4	0	.981	2	90	187	C17		-0.2
1944	NY N	16	17	4	4	0	0	1	2	1	1	0	.471	.526	.647	230	3	0	1.000	0	112	241	C12		0.4
1945	NY N	20	30	4	5	0	0	0	2	2	0	2	.167	.219	.167	8	-4	0	1.000	1	187	41	C20		-0.2
Total	11	561	1330	96	287	37	3	3	78	76	3	134	.216	.260	.255	43	-108	4	.989	19	95	118	C551		-6.5

BERROA, ANGEL Angel Maria (Selmo) B1.27.1978 Santo Domingo, D.R. BR/TR/6-0/175* d9.18

YEAR	TM LG	G	AB	R	H	2B	3B	HR	RBI	BB-IB	HP	SO	AVG	OBP	SLG	AOPS	ABR	SB-CS	FA	FR	RNG	THR	GAMES AT POSITION	DL	BFW
2001	KC A	15	53	8	16	2	0	4	3-0	1	0	10	.302	.339	.340	72	-2	2-0	.953	1	114	108	S14		0.1
2002	KC A	20	75	8	17	7	1	0	5	7-1	1	10	.227	.301	.347	64	-4	3-0	.964	4	116	92	S20		0.2
2003	KC A	158	567	92	163	28	7	17	73	29-3	18	100	.287	.338	.451	100	-1	21-5	.968	3	105	98	S158		1.6
2004	KC A	134	512	72	134	27	6	8	43	23-0	12	87	.262	.308	.385	79	-17	14-8	.955	-4	100	105	S133	15	-0.9
2005	KC A	159	608	68	164	21	5	11	55	18-3	14	108	.270	.305	.375	85	-15	7-5	.965	-1	100	93	S159	15	-0.4
Total	5	486	1815	248	494	85	19	36	180	80-7	45	315	.272	.317	.399	87	-39	47-18	.963	4	103	98	S484		0.6

BERROA, GERONIMO Geronimo Emiliano Letta (b Geronimo Emiliano Letta (Berroa)) B3.18.1965 Santo Domingo, D.R. BR/TR/6-0/195(195-210) d4.5

YEAR	TM LG	G	AB	R	H	2B	3B	HR	RBI	BB-IB	HP	SO	AVG	OBP	SLG	AOPS	ABR	SB-CS	FA	FR	RNG	THR	GAMES AT POSITION	DL	BFW
1989	Atl N	81	136	7	36	4	0	2	9	7-1	0	32	.265	.301	.338	81	-4	0-1	.971	3	135	72	O34(1/0/33)		-0.2
1990	Atl N	7	4	0	0	0	0	0	0	1-1	0	1	.000	.200	.000	-38	-1	0-0	1.000	-0	86	0	O3L		-0.1
1992	Cin N	13	15	2	4	1	0	0	0	2-0	1	1	.267	.389	.333	103	0	0-1	1.000	5	50	1067	O3L		0.0
1993	Fla N	14	34	3	4	1	0	0	0	2-0	0	7	.118	.167	.147	-14	-6	0-0	.833	-1	63	181	O9(1/0/8)		-0.7
1994	Oak A	96	340	55	104	18	2	13	65	41-0	3	62	.306	.379	.485	133	18	7-2	1.000	3	116	169	D44,O42(36/0/7),1b9	10	1.6
1995	Oak A	141	546	87	152	22	3	22	88	63-2	1	98	.278	.351	.451	113	10	7-4	.971	2	105	118	D72,O71(17/0/54)		0.4
1996	Oak A	153	586	101	170	32	1	36	106	47-0	4	122	.290	.344	.532	119	15	0-3	.980	-3	80	151	D91,O61(17/0/54)		0.4
1997	Oak A	73	261	40	81	12	0	16	42	36-2	1	58	.310	.395	.540	141	16	3-2	.986	-3	87	38	O43R,D32		0.9
	†Bal A	83	300	48	78	13	0	10	48	40-2	0	62	.260	.347	.403	100	1	1-2	.959	-2	95	43	D42,O40R		-0.6
	Year	156	561	88	159	25	0	26	90	76-4	1	120	.283	.369	.467	119	17	4-4	.955	-5	91	40	O83R,D74		0.3
1998	Cle A	20	65	6	13	3	1	0	3	7-0	0	17	.200	.278	.277	43	-6	1-0	1.000	1	104	130	O14L,D5	31	-0.5
	Det A	52	126	17	30	4	1	0	10	17-1	2	27	.238	.338	.310	69	-5	0-1	1.000	-0	101	0	D37,O4(2/0/2)		-0.7
	Year	72	191	23	43	7	2	1	13	24-1	2	44	.225	.318	.298	61	-11	1-1	1.000	1	104	113	D42,O18(16/0/2)		-1.2
1999	Tor A	22	62	11	12	3	0	1	6	9-0	2	15	.194	.315	.290	55	-4	0-0	1.000	0	111	0	D17,O2L	106	-0.5
2000	LA N	24	31	2	9	0	0	0	5	4-1	0	8	.258	.343	.323	73	-1	0-0	1.000	1	135	0	O6(4/0/2),1b2	123	-0.1
Total	10	779	2506	379	692	113	9	101	382	276-10	17	510	.276	.349	.449	109	33	19-16	.977	0	99	112	D340,O332(100/0/243),1b11	270	-0.1

BERRY, KEN Allen Kent B5.10.1941 Kansas City MO BR/TR/5-11/180* d9.9 Col Wichita St.

YEAR	TM LG	G	AB	R	H	2B	3B	HR	RBI	BB-IB	HP	SO	AVG	OBP	SLG	AOPS	ABR	SB-CS	FA	FR	RNG	THR	GAMES AT POSITION	DL	BFW
1962	Chi A	3	6	2	2	0	0	0	0	0-0	0	0	.333	.333	.333	80	0	0-0	1.000	1	120	1134	O2(1/1/1)		0.1
1963	Chi A	4	5	2	1	0	0	0	0	0-0	0	1	.200	.333	.200	55	0	0-0	.857	0	199	0	O2L/2		0.0
1964	Chi A	12	32	4	12	1	0	1	4	5-0	0	3	.375	.459	.500	171	3	0-1	1.000	-2	62	0	O12C		0.0
1965	Chi A	157	472	51	103	17	4	12	42	28-5	5	96	.218	.268	.347	79	-15	4-2	.980	-2	101	96	O156C		-2.3
1966	Chi A	147	443	56	120	20	2	8	34	28-4	2	63	.271	.316	.379	106	3	7-10	.991	-3	88	127	O141(101/13/41)		-1.0
1967	Chi A★	147	485	49	117	14	4	7	41	46-4	2	68	.241	.310	.330	93	-5	9-8	.992	-6	88	97	O143(50/38/86)		-2.2
1968	Chi A	153	504	49	127	21	2	7	32	25-1	1	64	.252	.288	.343	90	-7	6-6	.981	-2	98	108	O151(0/149/2)		-1.7

YEAR	TM LG	G	AB	R	H	2B	3B	HR	RBI	BB-IB	HP	SO	AVG	OBP	SLG	AOPS	ABR	SB-CS	FA	FR	RNG	THR	GAMES AT POSITION	DL	BFW
1969	Chi A	130	297	25	69	12	2	4	18	24-5	3	50	.232	.296	.327	71	-12	1-2	**1.000**	1	101	121	O120(2/116/2)		-1.5
1970	Chi A	141	463	45	128	12	2	7	50	43-10	6	61	.276	.344	.356	91	-5	6-4	.988	-1	102	103	O138C		-1.0
1971	Cal A	111	298	29	66	17	0	3	22	18-0	3	33	.221	.269	.309	69	-13	3-2	.988	4	111	91	O101(8/94/0)	15	-1.3
1972	Cal A	119	409	41	118	15	3	5	39	35-2	2	47	.289	.347	.377	122	11	5-3	**1.000**	8	106	**191**	O116C		1.8
1973	Cal A	136	415	48	118	11	2	3	36	26-0	1	50	.284	.327	.342	96	-3	1-6	**.997**	4	113	63	O129(15/111/4)		-0.5
1974	Mil A	98	267	21	64	9	2	1	24	18-0	3	26	.240	.295	.300	72	-10	3-1	.995	5	107	169	O82(5/74/5),D13		-0.7
1975	Cle A	25	40	6	8	1	0	0	1	1-0	1	7	.200	.238	.225	31	-4	0-1	.926	1	111	130	O18L,D5		-0.4
Total	14	1383	4136	422	1053	150	23	58	343	298-31	30	569	.255	.308	.344	90	-57	45-46	.989	8	100	114	O1311(202/1018/141),D18/2	15	-10.7

BERRY, CHARLIE Charles Francis B10.18.1902 Phillipsburg NJ D9.6.1972 Evanston IL BR/TR/6-0/185 d6.15 C5/U21 f-Charlie Col Lafayette

YEAR	TM LG	G	AB	R	H	2B	3B	HR	RBI	BB-IB	HP	SO	AVG	OBP	SLG	AOPS	ABR	SB-CS	FA	FR	RNG	THR	GAMES AT POSITION	DL	BFW
1925	Phi A	10	14	1	3	1	0	0	3	0	0	2	.214	.214	.286	24	-2	0-0	.900	-1	122	0	C4		-0.2
1928	Bos A	80	177	18	46	7	3	1	19	21	0	19	.260	.342	.350	84	-4	0-1	.959	-8	73	132	C63		-0.9
1929	Bos A	77	207	19	50	11	4	1	21	15	3	29	.242	.302	.348	69	-10	2-6	.983	3	106	130	C72		-0.5
1930	Bos A	88	256	31	74	9	6	6	35	16	0	22	.289	.331	.441	98	-2	2-0	.988	8	**165**	104	C85		1.0
1931	Bos A	111	357	41	101	16	2	6	49	29	0	38	.283	.337	.389	96	-3	4-0	.985	-0	116	98	C102		0.4
1932	Bos A	10	32	0	6	3	0	0	6	3	0	2	.188	.257	.281	40	-3	0-0	.944	-1	66	105	C10		-0.3
	Chi A	72	226	33	69	15	6	4	31	21	0	23	.305	.364	.478	124	8	3-0	.981	-2	81	156	C70		1.0
	Year	82	258	33	75	18	6	4	37	24	0	25	.291	.351	.453	114	5	3-0	.977	-3	79	**150**	C80		0.7
1933	Chi A	86	271	25	69	8	3	2	28	17	1	16	.255	.301	.328	70	-13	0-0	.987	-10	84	76	C83		-1.7
1934	Phi A	99	269	14	72	10	2	0	34	22	0	23	.268	.323	.320	69	-13	0-0	.987	-2	86	110	C99		-0.9
1935	Phi A	62	190	14	48	7	3	3	29	10	0	20	.253	.290	.368	70	-10	0-0	.987	-1	72	145	C56		-0.8
1936	Phi A	13	17	0	1	1	0	0	1	6	0	2	.059	.304	.118	8	-2	0-0	.971	-0	77	117	C12		-0.2
1938	Phi A	1	2	0	0	0	0	0	0	0	0	0	.000	.000	.000	-99	-1	0-0	1.000	0	0	857	/C		0.0
Total	11	709	2018	196	539	88	29	23	256	160	5	196	.267	.322	.374	83	-55	13-7	.982	-14	101	115	C657		-3.1

BERRY, CHARLIE Charles Joseph B9.6.1860 Elizabeth NJ D1.22.1940 Phillipsburg NJ BR/TR/5-11/175 d4.30 s-Charlie

YEAR	TM LG	G	AB	R	H	2B	3B	HR	RBI	BB-IB	HP	SO	AVG	OBP	SLG	AOPS	ABR	SB-CS	FA	FR	RNG	THR	GAMES AT POSITION	DL	BFW
1884	Alt U	7	25	2	6	0	0	0		0			.240	.240	.240	45	-2		.862	-5	54	0	2b7		-0.6
	KC U	29	118	15	29	6	1	1		1			.246	.252	.339	89	-5		.887	1	102	83	2b22,O8(1/7/0)/3		-0.3
	CP U	7	27	4	3	2	0	0		0			.111	.111	.185	-12	-4		.833	-0	95	46	2b7		-0.4
	Year	43	170	21	38	8	1	1		1			.224	.228	.300	64	-13		.871	-4	92	59	2b36,O8(1/7/0)/3		-1.3

BERRY, CLAUDE Claude Elzy "Admiral" B2.14.1880 Losantville IN D2.1.1974 Richmond IN BR/TR/5-7/165 d4.22

YEAR	TM LG	G	AB	R	H	2B	3B	HR	RBI	BB-IB	HP	SO	AVG	OBP	SLG	AOPS	ABR	SB-CS	FA	FR	RNG	THR	GAMES AT POSITION	DL	BFW
1904	Chi A	3	1	1	0	0	0	0	0	1	0		.000	.500	.000	68	0	0	1.000	0	0	175	C3		0.1
1906	Phi A	10	30	2	7	0	0	0	2	2	0		.233	.281	.233	60	-1	1	.938	3	107	180	C10		0.3
1907	Phi A	8	19	2	4	2	0	0	1	2	0		.211	.286	.316	90	0		.944	-2	84	64	C8		-0.1
1914	Pit F	124	411	35	98	18	9	2	36	26	0	50	.238	.284	.341	70	-26	6	.970	1	103	101	C122		-1.5
1915	Pit F	100	292	32	56	11	1	1	26	29	2	42	.192	.269	.247	46	-25	7	.980	6	116	101	C99		-1.2
Total	5	245	753	72	165	31	10	3	65	60	2	92	.219	.279	.299	61	-52	14	.971	8	108	104	C242		-2.4

BERRY, NEIL Cornelius John B1.11.1922 Kalamazoo MI BR/TR/5-10/170* d4.20 Col Western Michigan

YEAR	TM LG	G	AB	R	H	2B	3B	HR	RBI	BB-IB	HP	SO	AVG	OBP	SLG	AOPS	ABR	SB-CS	FA	FR	RNG	THR	GAMES AT POSITION	DL	BFW
1948	Det A	87	256	46	68	8	1	0	16	37	0	23	.266	.358	.305	75	-8	1-3	.930	-1	98	113	S41,2b26		-0.6
1949	Det A	109	329	38	78	9	1	0	18	27	2	24	.237	.299	.271	51	-24	4-2	.970	-8	93	86	2b95,S4		-2.6
1950	Det A	39	40	9	10	1	0	0	7	6	0	11	.250	.348	.275	59	-2	0-0	.944	2	100	181	S12,2b2/3		0.0
1951	Det A	67	157	17	36	5	2	0	9	10	0	15	.229	.275	.287	52	-11	4-2	.944	3	112	81	S38,2b10,3b7		-0.6
1952	Det A	73	189	22	43	4	3	0	13	22	1	19	.228	.311	.280	65	-9	1-3	.965	3	105	78	S66,3b2		-0.4
1953	StL A	57	99	14	28	1	2	0	11	9	0	10	.283	.343	.333	82	-3	1-2	.825	-3	77	35	3b18,2b15,S6		-0.5
	Chi A	5	8	1	1	0	0	0	0	1	0	0	.125	.222	.125	-4	-1	0-0	1.000	1	162	63	2b3		-0.0
	Year	62	107	15	29	1	2	0	11	10	0	11	.271	.333	.318	75	-4	1-2	.825	-2	77	35	3b18,2b18,S6		-0.5
1954	Bal A	5	9	1	1	0	0	0	0	1	0	2	.111	.200	.111	-14	-1	0-0	1.000	1	0	90 113	S5		-0.1
Total	7	442	1087	148	265	28	9	0	74	113	3	105	.244	.317	.286	62	-59	11-12	.949	-4	105	99	S172,2b151,3b28		-4.8

BERRY, JOE Joseph Howard Jr. "Nig" B12.31.1894 Philadelphia PA D4.29.1976 Philadelphia PA BB/TR/5-10.5/159 d7.18 f-Joe Col Penn

YEAR	TM LG	G	AB	R	H	2B	3B	HR	RBI	BB-IB	HP	SO	AVG	OBP	SLG	AOPS	ABR	SB-CS	FA	FR	RNG	THR	GAMES AT POSITION	DL	BFW
1921	NY N	9	6	0	2	0	1	0	2	1	0	1	.333	.429	.667	185	1		.875	0	155	0	2b7		0.1
1922	NY N	6	0	0	0	0	0	0	0	0	0	0	—	—	—		0			0			/R		0.0
Total	2	15	6	0	2	0	1	0	2	1	0	1	.333	.429	.667	185	1		.875	0	155	0	2b7		0.1

BERRY, JOE Joseph Howard Sr. "Hodge" B9.10.1872 Wheeling WV D3.13.1961 Allenwood NJ BB/TR/5-9/172 d9.4 s-Joe

YEAR	TM LG	G	AB	R	H	2B	3B	HR	RBI	BB-IB	HP	SO	AVG	OBP	SLG	AOPS	ABR	SB-CS	FA	FR	RNG	THR	GAMES AT POSITION	DL	BFW
1902	Phi N	1	4	0	1	0	0	0	1	1	0	1	.250	.400	.250	101	0	1	1.000	-1	57	0	/C		-0.1

BERRY, SEAN Sean Robert B3.22.1966 Santa Monica CA BR/TR/5-11/210* [KCA86*S1/9] d9.17 Col UCLA

YEAR	TM LG	G	AB	R	H	2B	3B	HR	RBI	BB-IB	HP	SO	AVG	OBP	SLG	AOPS	ABR	SB-CS	FA	FR	RNG	THR	GAMES AT POSITION	DL	BFW
1990	KC A	8	23	2	5	1	0	0	4	2-0	0	5	.217	.280	.348	76	-1	0-0	.944	-0	78	148	3b8		-0.1
1991	KC A	31	60	5	8	3	0	0	1	5-0	1	23	.133	.212	.183	10	-7	0-0	.970	5	134	73	3b30		-0.2
1992	Mon N	24	57	5	19	1	0	1	4	1-0	0	11	.333	.345	.404	112	1	2-1	.879	-3	73	45	3b20		-0.3
1993	Mon N	122	299	50	78	15	2	14	49	41-6	2	70	.261	.348	.465	112	6	12-2	.936	1	101	105	3b96		0.9
1994	Mon N	103	320	43	89	19	2	11	41	32-7	3	50	.278	.347	.453	106	3	0-0	.938	-10	84	78	3b100		-0.3
1995	Mon N	103	314	38	100	22	1	14	55	25-1	2	53	.318	.367	.529	129	13	3-8	.947	2	97	153	3b83,1b3		1.3
1996	Hou N	132	431	55	121	38	1	17	95	23-1	9	58	.281	.328	.492	122	13	12-6	.922	-1	99	76	3b110		1.3
1997	†Hou N	96	301	37	77	24	1	8	43	25-1	5	53	.256	.318	.422	96	-2	1-5	.921	-1	102	94	3b85,D3	30	-0.4
1998	†Hou N	102	299	48	94	17	1	13	52	31-3	7	50	.314	.387	.508	138	17	3-1	.953	-0	97	105	3b87/D		1.7
1999	Mil N	106	259	26	59	11	1	2	23	17-0	3	50	.228	.281	.301	48	-21	0-0	.989	-3	80	109	1b64		-2.8
2000	Mil N	32	46	1	7	2	0	1	4	4-0	0	13	.152	.220	.261	21	-6	0-1	1.000	-3	36	82	3b9		-0.9
	Bos A	1	4	0	0	0	0	0	0	0-0	0	2	.000	.000	.000	-97	-1	0-0	—	-1	0	0	/3		-0.2
Total	11	860	2413	310	657	153	10	81	369	206-19	32	438	.272	.334	.445	104	15	47-24	.937	-15	96	98	3b629,1b67,D4	30	-0.0

BERRY, TOM Thomas Haney B12.31.1842 Chester PA D6.6.1915 Chester PA 5-6/140 d9.2

YEAR	TM LG	G	AB	R	H	2B	3B	HR	RBI	BB-IB	HP	SO	AVG	OBP	SLG	AOPS	ABR	SB-CS	FA	FR	RNG	THR	GAMES AT POSITION	DL	BFW
1871	Ath NA	1	4	0	1	0	0	0	0	0		0	.250	.250	.250	45	0	0-0	.000	-0	0	0	/OR		0.0

BERRYHILL, DAMON Damon Scott B12.3.1963 South Laguna CA BB/TR/6-0/205* [ChiN84*1/4] d9.5 Col Orange Coast (CA) JC

YEAR	TM LG	G	AB	R	H	2B	3B	HR	RBI	BB-IB	HP	SO	AVG	OBP	SLG	AOPS	ABR	SB-CS	FA	FR	RNG	THR	GAMES AT POSITION	DL	BFW
1987	Chi N	12	28	2	5	1	0	0	1	3-0	0	5	.179	.258	.214	26	-3	0-1	.909	-5	80	34	C11		-0.8
1988	Chi N	95	309	19	80	19	1	7	38	17-5	0	56	.259	.295	.395	93	-3	1-0	.982	-0	113	**149**	C90	15	0.2
1989	Chi N	91	334	37	86	13	0	5	41	16-4	2	54	.257	.291	.341	76	-11	1-0	.992	-0	179	90	C89	69	-0.6
1990	Chi N	17	53	6	10	4	0	1	9	5-1	0	14	.189	.254	.321	55	-3	0-0	.978	-2	109	37	C15	128	-1.6
1991	Chi N	62	159	13	30	7	0	5	14	11-1	1	41	.189	.244	.327	57	-9	1-2	.967	-7	101	61	C48		-1.6
	Atl N	1	1	0	0	0	0	0	0	0-0	0	1	.000	.000	.000	-95	-0	0-0	1.000	0	0	0	/C		
	Year	63	160	13	30	7	0	5	14	11-1	1	42	.188	.243	.325	56	-10	1-2	.967	-7	100	60	C49		-1.6
1992	†Atl N	101	307	21	70	16	1	10	43	17-4	1	67	.228	.268	.384	79	-9	0-2	.998	-9	83	71	C84		-1.5
1993	†Atl N	115	335	24	82	18	2	8	43	21-1	2	64	.245	.291	.382	77	-11	0-0	.990	-7	105	92	C105		0.2
1994	Bos A	82	255	30	67	17	2	6	34	19-0	0	59	.263	.312	.416	82	-7	0-1	.995	-1	70	111	C67,D6		-0.4
1995	Cin N	34	82	6	15	3	0	2	11	10-2	0	19	.183	.260	.293	48	-6	0-0	.988	1	109	80	C29/1	39	0.0
1997	†SF N	73	167	17	43	8	0	3	23	20-5	0	29	.257	.335	.359	84	-4	0-0	.990	1	101	112	C51/1	38	0.0
Total	10	683	2030	175	488	106	6	47	257	106-19	6	409	.240	.288	.368	77	-66	3-6	.988	-15	111	96	C590,D6,1b2	289	-5.4

BERTE, HARRY Harry Thomas B5.10.1872 Covington KY D5.6.1952 Los Angeles CA TR/5-10/160 d9.17

YEAR	TM LG	G	AB	R	H	2B	3B	HR	RBI	BB-IB	HP	SO	AVG	OBP	SLG	AOPS	ABR	SB-CS	FA	FR	RNG	THR	GAMES AT POSITION	DL	BFW
1903	StL N	4	15	1	5	0	0	0	1	1	0		.333	.375	.333	106	0	0	.778	-3	67	137	2b3/S		-0.3

BERTELL, DICK Richard George B11.21.1935 Oak Park IL D12.20.1999 Mission Viejo CA BR/TR/6-0.5/200* d9.22 Col Iowa St. [DL 1966 SF N 67]

YEAR	TM LG	G	AB	R	H	2B	3B	HR	RBI	BB-IB	HP	SO	AVG	OBP	SLG	AOPS	ABR	SB-CS	FA	FR	RNG	THR	GAMES AT POSITION	DL	BFW
1960	Chi N	5	15	0	2	0	0	0	2	3-0	0	1	.133	.263	.133	17	-2	0-0	1.000	-1	68	146	C5		-0.3
1961	Chi N	92	267	20	73	7	1	2	33	15-3	1	33	.273	.308	.330	70	-12	0-0	.982	3	113	111	C90		-0.5
1962	Chi N	77	215	19	65	6	2	2	18	13-5	1	30	.302	.343	.377	90	-3	0-1	.986	-10	71	115	C76		-1.0
1963	Chi N	100	322	15	75	7	2	2	33	24-6	4	41	.233	.284	.286	62	-16	0-2	.988	17	**137**	**162**	C99		0.6
1964	Chi N	112	353	29	84	11	3	4	35	33-8	2	67	.238	.305	.320	74	-12	2-1	.981	-3	137	132	C110		-1.0
1965	Chi N	34	84	6	18	2	0	0	7	11-2	0	14	.214	.302	.238	54	-5	0-0	.981	1	113	217	C34		-0.3
	SF N	22	48	1	9	1	0	0	3	7-3	0	5	.188	.291	.208	42	-3	0-0	.992	0	66	95	C22		-0.3
	Year	56	132	7	27	3	0	0	10	18-5	0	19	.205	.298	.227	50	-8	0-0	.986	1	96	172	C56		-0.6
1967	Chi N	2	6	1	1	0	0	1	1	0-0	0	2	.167	.167	.500	80	0	0-0	1.000	0	0	137	C2		0.0
Total	7	444	1310	91	327	34	9	10	112	106-27	3	188	.250	.306	.312	70	-53	2-4	.985	7	116	137	C438	67	-2.8

YEAR	TM LG	G	AB	R	H	2B	3B	HR	RBI	BB-IB	HP	SO	AVG	OBP	SLG	AOPS	ABR	SB-CS	FA	FR	RNG	THR	GAMES AT POSITION	DL	BFW

BERTHRONG, HARRY   Henry W.   B1.1.1844 Mumford NY   D4.28.1928 Chelsea MA   TR/5-6.5/140   d5.5

| 1871 | Oly NA | 17 | 73 | 17 | 17 | 1 | 1 | 0 | 8 | 4 | | 2 | .233 | .273 | .274 | 61 | -3 | 3-1 | .806 | -4 | 0 | 0 | O12(11/1/0),2b5/C | | -0.4 |

BERTOIA, RENO   Reno Peter   B1.8.1935 St.Vito Udine, Italy   BR/TR/5-11.5/185*   d9.22

1953	Det A	1	1	0	0	0	0	0	0	0	0	1	.000	.000	.000	-99	0	0-0	.500	-1	0	0	/2		-0.1
1954	Det A	54	37	13	6	2	0	1	2	5	0	9	.162	.262	.297	54	-2	1-0	.969	8	175	109	2b15,3b8,S3		0.6
1955	Det A	38	68	13	14	2	1	1	10	5-1	0	11	.206	.253	.309	54	-5	0-0	.923	3	113	196	3b14,2b6,S5		-0.1
1956	Det A	22	66	7	12	2	0	1	5	6-0	1	12	.182	.260	.258	37	-6	0-0	.982	5	111	122	2b18,3b2		0.0
1957	Det A	97	295	28	81	16	2	4	28	19-2	4	43	.275	.326	.383	91	-4	2-3	.953	-14	82	60	3b83,S7,2b2		-1.9
1958	Det A	86	240	28	56	6	0	6	27	20-2	2	35	.233	.290	.333	68	-10	5-2	.950	4	104	100	3b68,S5/OL		-0.7
1959	Was A	90	308	33	73	10	0	8	29	29-3	1	48	.237	.302	.347	79	-9	2-5	.971	-5	102	84	2b71,3b5/S		-1.1
1960	Was A	121	460	44	122	17	4	4	45	26-2	6	58	.265	.313	.359	83	-12	3-5	.961	-5	100	80	3b112,2b21		-1.9
1961	Min A	35	104	17	22	2	0	1	8	20-1	0	12	.212	.333	.260	59	-5	0-0	.900	-6	86	46	3b32		-1.2
	KC A	39	120	12	29	2	0	0	13	9-0	0	15	.242	.286	.258	48	-9	1-0	.942	4	118	93	3b29,2b6		-0.5
	Det A	24	46	6	10	1	0	1	4	3-0	0	8	.217	.265	.304	50	-3	0-0	.931	-2	77	100	3b13,2b7/S		-0.5
	Year	98	270	35	61	5	0	2	25	32-1	0	35	.226	.302	.267	53	-18	3-0	.923	-4	97	73	3b74,2b13/S		-2.2
1962	Det A	5	0	3	0	0	0	0	0	0-0	0	0	—	—	—	—	0	0-0	1.000	0	162	0	/2S3		0.0
Total	10	612	1745	204	425	60	10	27	171	142-11	16	252	.244	.303	.336	73	-65	16-15	.949	-9	97	83	3b367,2b148,S23/OL		-7.4

BESCHER, BOB   Robert Henry   B2.25.1884 London OH   D11.29.1942 London OH   BB/TL/6-1/200   d9.5   Col Wittenberg

1908	Cin N	32	114	16	31	5	5	0	17	9	2		.272	.336	.404	140	5	10	1.000	3	46	190	O32L		0.6
1909	Cin N	124	446	73	107	17	6	1	34	56			.240	.335	.312	102	3	54	.953	0	85	105	O117(115/0/2)		-0.4
1910	Cin N	150	589	95	147	20	10	4	48	81	4	75	.250	.344	.338	104	4	70	.947	2	108	81	O150L		-0.3
1911	Cin N	153	599	106	165	32	10	1	45	102	5	78	.275	.385	.367	115	18	81	.954	-8	87	95	O153L		0.3
1912	Cin N	145	548	120	154	29	11	4	38	83	6	61	.281	.381	.396	116	16	67	.963	2	110	68	O143L		1.1
1913	Cin N	141	511	86	132	22	11	1	37	94	3	68	.258	.377	.350	109	11	38-23	.968	4	100	119	O138L		1.0
1914	NY N	135	512	82	138	23	4	6	35	45	6	48	.270	.336	.365	112	8	36	.960	1	103	90	O126(15/111/0)		0.0
1915	StL N	130	486	71	128	15	7	4	34	52	6	53	.263	.342	.348	109	6	27-19	.971	-2	100	78	O129(128/0/1)		-0.2
1916	StL N	151	561	78	132	24	8	6	43	60	6	50	.235	.316	.339	102	2	39-12	.965	-0	98	114	O151(151/2/1)		0.0
1917	StL N	42	110	10	17	1	1	1	8	20	1	13	.155	.290	.227	56	-5	3	.984	-5	88	0	O32(27/4/0)		-1.3
1918	Cle A	25	60	12	20	2	1	0	6	17	1	5	.333	.487	.400	153	6	3	.969	0	92	135	O17(0/3/14)		0.5
Total	11	1228	4536	749	1171	190	74	28	345	619	48	451	.258	.353	.351	109	74	428-54	.960	-3	97	94	O1188(1052/120/18)		1.3

BESTICK, WILLIAM   William   B New York NY   d6.10

| 1872 | Eck NA | 4 | 14 | 0 | 4 | 0 | 0 | 0 | 0 | 0 | | 0 | .286 | .286 | .286 | 90 | 0 | 0-0 | .760 | -2 | | | C4/S | | -0.1 |

BESWICK, JIM   James William   B2.12.1958 Wilkinsburg PA   BB/TR/6-1/180   [SDN76 5/101]   d8.9

| 1978 | SD N | 17 | 20 | 2 | 1 | 0 | 0 | 0 | 0 | 1-0 | 0 | 7 | .050 | .095 | .050 | -63 | -4 | 0-0 | 1.000 | -0 | 99 | 0 | O6(0/2/4) | | -0.5 |

BETANCOURT, YUNIESKY   Yuniesky (Perez)   B1.31.1982 Santa Clara, Cuba   BR/TR/5-10/190   d7.28

| 2005 | Sea A | 60 | 211 | 24 | 54 | 11 | 5 | 1 | 15 | 11-0 | 2 | 24 | .256 | .296 | .370 | 82 | -6 | 1-3 | .978 | -3 | 93 | 102 | S53,2b9 | | -0.6 |

BETCHER, FRANK   Franklin Lyle (b Franklin Lyle Bettger)   B2.15.1888 Philadelphia PA   D11.27.1981 Wynnewood PA   BB/TR/5-11/173   d5.21

| 1910 | StL N | 35 | 89 | 7 | 18 | 2 | 0 | 0 | 6 | 7 | 2 | 14 | .202 | .276 | .225 | 48 | -6 | 1 | .928 | 0 | 105 | 72 | S12,3b7,2b6,O2(1/1/0) | | -0.6 |

BETEMIT, WILSON   Wilson   B11.2.1981 Santo Domingo, D.R.   BB/TR/6-2/155(155-190)   d9.18

2001	Atl N	8	3	1	0	0	0	0	0	2-0	0	3	.000	.400	.000	17	0	1-0	—	-0	0	0	/S		0.0
2004	†Atl N	22	47	2	8	0	0	0	3	4-0	0	16	.170	.231	.170	7	-7	0-1	.933	0	122	95	S11,3b7		-0.6
2005	†Atl N	115	246	36	75	12	4	4	20	22-4	0	55	.305	.359	.435	105	2	1-3	.952	-8	98	65	3b63,S25/2		-0.6
Total	3	145	296	39	83	12	4	4	23	28-4	0	74	.280	.339	.389	89	-5	2-4	.955	-8	96	80	3b70,S37/2		-1.2

BETHEA, BILL   William Lamar "Spot"   B1.1.1942 Houston TX   BR/TR/6-0/175   d9.13   Col Texas

| 1964 | Min A | 10 | 30 | 4 | 5 | 1 | 0 | 0 | 2 | 4-0 | 0 | 4 | .167 | .265 | .200 | 31 | -3 | 0-0 | 1.000 | -2 | 83 | 129 | 2b7,S3 | | -0.4 |

BETTENCOURT, LARRY   Lawrence Joseph   B9.22.1905 Newark CA   D9.15.1978 New Orleans LA   BR/TR/5-11/195   d6.2   Col St. Marys (CA)

1928	StL A	67	159	30	45	9	4	4	24	22	2	19	.283	.377	.465	117	4	2-1	.946	-6	88	59	3b41,O2R/C		0.0
1931	StL A	74	206	27	53	9	2	3	26	31	1	35	.257	.337	.364	87	-3	4-3	.963	-1	94	118	O58(2/0/56)		-0.7
1932	StL A	27	30	4	4	1	0	1	3	7	0	6	.133	.297	.267	45	-2	1-0	1.000	3	122		O4(2/0/3),3b2		-0.2
Total	3	168	395	61	102	19	6	8	53	60	3	60	.258	.360	.397	95	-1	7-4	.966	-6	95	111	O64(4/0/61),3b43/C		-0.9

BETZEL, BRUNO   Christian Frederick Albert John Henry David   B12.6.1894 Chattanooga OH   D2.7.1965 W.Hollywood FL   BR/TR/5-9/158   d9.3

1914	StL N	7	9	2	0	0	0	0	1	0	1	0	.000	.100	.000	-70	-2	0	1.000	1	157	0	2b4/3		-0.1
1915	StL N	117	367	42	92	12	4	0	27	18	3	48	.251	.291	.305	80	-9	10-13	.937	4	112	74	3b105,2b3,S2		-0.6
1916	StL N	142	510	49	119	15	11	1	37	39	0	77	.233	.288	.312	85	-10	22-16	.960	29	112	132	2b113,3b33,O7(1/2/4)		2.3
1917	StL N	106	328	24	71	4	3	1	17	20	2	47	.216	.266	.256	62	-15	9	.962	12	113	138	2b75,O23(12/1/9),3b4		-0.6
1918	StL N	76	230	18	51	6	7	0	13	12	0	16	.222	.260	.309	76	-8	8	.914	-2	103	60	3b34,O21(1/7/15),2b10		-1.2
Total	5	448	1444	135	333	37	25	2	94	90	5	189	.231	.274	.298	76	-44	49-29	.956	44	113	132	2b205,3b177,O51(14/10/28),S2		-0.2

BEVACQUA, KURT   Kurt Anthony   B1.23.1947 Miami Beach FL   BR/TR/6-1/185(180-195)   [CinN67 S2/26]   d6.22   Col Miami-Dade North (FL) CC   OF(47/0/25)

1971	Cle A	55	137	9	28	3	1	3	13	4-1	0	28	.204	.222	.307	46	-10	0-0	.971	-3	91	53	2b36,O5(2/0/3),3b3,S2		-1.3
1972	Cle A	19	35	2	4	0	0	1	1	3-1	0	10	.114	.184	.200	14	-4	0-0	.900	0	65	0	O11(8/0/3)/3		-0.5
1973	KC A	99	276	39	71	8	3	2	40	25-1	1	42	.257	.317	.330	78	-8	2-3	.935	-10	81	92	3b40,2b16,D16,O10(5/0/5),1b9		-2.0
1974	KC A	39	90	10	19	0	0	0	3	9-0	1	20	.211	.290	.211	44	-6	1-1	.987	-3	54	154	1b14,3b13,2b7,S2,D3		-1.1
1975	Mil A	104	258	30	59	14	0	2	24	26-1	1	45	.229	.300	.306	72	-9	3-4	.948	-6	90	108	3b60,2b32,S5,1b3/D		-1.4
1976	Mil A	12	7	3	1	0	0	0	0	0-0	0	0	.143	.143	.143	-16	-1	0-0	1.000	1	257	0	2b2,D3		0.0
1977	Tex A	39	96	13	32	7	2	5	28	6-1	0	13	.333	.365	.604	159	7	0-1	1.000	-1	61	0	1b4(6/0/8),3b11,1b5,2b5,D3		0.6
1978	Tex A	90	248	21	55	12	0	6	30	18-0	0	31	.222	.271	.343	72	-10	1-2	.877	-5	95	88	3b49,D16,2b13/1		-1.6
1979	SD N	114	297	23	75	12	4	1	34	38-2	0	25	.253	.331	.330	88	-4	2-5	.954	2	105	135	3b64,2b16,1b8,O8L		-0.5
1980	SD N	62	71	4	19	6	1	0	12	6-0	1	7	.268	.321	.380	103	0	1-1	.929	-0	109	127	3b13,O4L,2b2/1		0.0
	Pit N	22	43	1	7	1	0	0	4	6-0	1	7	.163	.280	.186	31	-4	0-0	.958	1	117	90	3b9,1b2		-0.4
	Year	84	114	5	26	7	1	0	16	12-0	1	8	.228	.305	.307	75	-4	1-1	.947	0	114	105	3b22,O4L,1b3,2b2		-0.4
1981	Pit N	29	27	2	7	1	0	1	4	4-0	0	6	.259	.333	.407	110	0	0-0	.941	1	128	214	2b4,3b2		0.2
1982	SD N	64	123	15	31	9	0	2	24	17-4	0	22	.252	.333	.325	93	2	2-0	.989	-1	94	72	1b30,O3(2/0/1)/3		-0.3
1983	SD N	74	156	17	38	7	0	2	24	14-1	0	33	.244	.320	.327	83	-3	0-3	.995	1	89	93	1b27,3b12,O12(9/0/3)		-0.5
1984	†SD N	59	80	7	16	3	0	1	9	14-1	1	19	.200	.326	.275	70	-3	0-0	1.000	-2	87	114	1b20,3b10,O3(1/0/2)		-0.6
1985	SD N	71	138	17	33	6	0	3	25	25-5	0	17	.239	.349	.348	98	1	0-0	.946	0	93	145	3b33,1b9/OL		0.0
Total	15	970	2117	214	499	90	11	27	275	221-19	5	329	.236	.305	.327	78	-59	12-20	.938	-28	94	121	3b329,2b133,1b129,O72L,D42,S9		-10.2

BEVAN, HAL   Harold Joseph   B11.15.1930 New Orleans LA   D10.5.1968 New Orleans LA   BR/TR/6-2/198*   d4.24

1952	Bos A	1	1	0	0	0	0	0	0	0-0	0	0	.000	.000	.000	-93	-0	0	—	-0	0	0	/3		0.0
	Phi A	8	17	1	6	0	0	0	4	0-0	0	1	.353	.353	.353	91	0	2-0	1.000	0	105	0	3b6	106	0.0
	Year	9	18	1	6	0	0	0	4	0-0	0	1	.333	.333	.333	81	-1	2-0	1.000	0	102	0	3b7		0.0
1955	KC A	3	3	0	0	0	0	0	0	0-0	0	0	.000	.000	.000	-99	-1	0-0	1.000	-0	0	0	/3		-0.1
1961	Cin N	3	3	1	1	0	0	1	1	0-0	0	2	.333	.333	1.333	311	1	0-0	—	0			/H		0.1
Total	3	15	24	2	7	0	0	1	5	0-0	0	3	.292	.292	.417	89	-2	2-0	1.000	0	97	0	3b8	106	0.0

BEVILLE, MONTE   Henry Monte   B2.24.1875 Dublin IN   D1.24.1955 Grand Rapids MI   BL/TR/5-11/180   d4.24

1903	NY A	82	258	23	50	14	1	0	29	16	4		.194	.252	.256	49	-15	4	.960	-7	105	81	C75,1b3		-1.6
1904	NY A	9	22	2	6	2	0	0	2	2	0		.273	.333	.364	115	1	0	.906	-2	56	0	1b4,C3		-0.1
	Det A	54	174	14	36	5	1	0	13	8	2		.207	.250	.247	59	-8	2	.957	-4	86	82	C30,1b24		-1.1
	Year	63	196	16	42	7	1	0	15	10	2		.214	.260	.260	66	-7	2	.950	-5	86	83	C33,1b28		-1.2
Total	2	145	454	39	92	21	2	0	44	26	6		.203	.255	.258	56	-22	6	.957	-12	99	82	C108,1b31		-2.8

BIANCALANA, BUDDY   Roland Americo   B2.2.1960 Larkspur CA   BB/TR/5-11/160*   [KCA78 1/25]   d9.12   [DL 1989 KC A 182]

1982	KC A	3	2	1	0	1	0	0	0	1-0	0	1	.500	.667	1.500	471	1	0-0	1.000	2	199	137	S3		0.3
1983	KC A	6	15	2	3	0	0	0	0	0-0	0	7	.200	.200	.200	10	-2	1-0	.914	2	138	97	S6		0.1
1984	†KC A	66	134	18	26	6	4	1	9	6-0	0	44	.194	.229	.299	44	-11	1-2	.946	-2	116	85	S33,2b29/D		-0.9

YEAR	TM LG	G	AB	R	H	2B	3B	HR	RBI	BB-IB	HP	SO	AVG	OBP	SLG	AOPS	ABR	SB-CS	FA	FR	RNG	THR	GAMES AT POSITION	DL	BFW
1985	†KC A	81	138	21	26	5	1	1	6	17-0	0	34	.188	.277	.261	48	-10	1-4	.961	4	110	98	S74,2b4,D2	18	-0.1
1986	KC A	100	190	24	46	4	4	2	8	15-0	0	50	.242	.298	.337	71	-8	5-1	.946	-5	97	102	S89,2b12		-0.6
1987	KC A	37	47	4	10	1	0	1	7	1-0	0	10	.213	.229	.298	37	-4	0-0	.886	-3	102	73	S22,2b12/D	15	-0.6
	Hou N	18	24	1	1	0	0	0	0	1-0	0	12	.042	.080	.042	-69	-6	0-0	.889	-2	78	53	S16,2b3		-0.8
Total 6		311	550	70	113	16	7	6	30	41-0	0	157	.205	.261	.293	50	-40	8-7	.945	-4	106	95	S243,2b60,D4	215	-2.6

BIANCO, TOMMY　Thomas Anthony　B12.16.1952 Rockville Centre NY　BB/TR/5-11/190　[MilA71 1/3]　d5.28

YEAR	TM LG	G	AB	R	H	2B	3B	HR	RBI	BB-IB	HP	SO	AVG	OBP	SLG	AOPS	ABR	SB-CS	FA	FR	RNG	THR	GAMES AT POSITION	DL	BFW
1975	Mil N	18	34	6	6	1	0	0	0	3-0	1	7	.176	.263	.206	34	-3	0-0	.941	-0	108	0	3b7,1b5,D2		-0.4

BIASATTI, HANK　Henry Arcado　B1.14.1922 Beano, Italy　D4.20.1996 Dearborn MI　BL/TL/5-11/175　d4.23

| 1949 | Phi A | 21 | 24 | 6 | 2 | 2 | 0 | 0 | 2 | 8 | 0 | 5 | .083 | .313 | .167 | 30 | -2 | 0-0 | .979 | -1 | 59 | 78 | 1b8 | | -0.3 |

BICHETTE, DANTE　Alphonse Dante　B11.18.1963 W.Palm Beach FL　BR/TR/6-3/225(212-238)　[CalA84 17/424]　d9.5 Col Palm Beach (FL) CC

YEAR	TM LG	G	AB	R	H	2B	3B	HR	RBI	BB-IB	HP	SO	AVG	OBP	SLG	AOPS	ABR	SB-CS	FA	FR	RNG	THR	GAMES AT POSITION	DL	BFW
1988	Cal A	21	46	1	12	2	0	0	8	0-0	0	7	.261	.240	.304	59	-3	0-0	.979	2	107	261	O21(3/17/5)		-0.1
1989	Cal A	48	138	13	29	7	0	3	15	6-0	0	24	.210	.240	.326	60	-8	3-0	.990	6	116	232	O40(12/6/23)/D		-0.2
1990	Cal A	109	349	40	89	15	1	15	53	16-1	3	79	.255	.292	.433	102	-1	5-2	.965	2	93	195	O105(51/16/53)		-0.1
1991	Mil A	134	445	53	106	18	3	15	59	22-4	1	107	.238	.272	.393	84	-12	14-8	.976	9	109	160	O127(1/7/120)/3		-0.6
1992	Mil A	112	387	37	111	27	2	5	41	16-3	3	74	.287	.318	.406	103	1	18-7	.990	-5	90	87	O101(0/1/101),D4		-0.6
1993	Col N	141	538	93	167	43	5	21	89	28-2	7	99	.310	.348	.526	113	10	14-8	.973	9	112	137	O137(0/9/134)		1.3
1994	Col N★	116	484	74	147	33	2	27	95	19-3	4	70	.304	.334	.548	107	5	21-8	.991	-1	94	116	O116R		-0.1
1995	†Col N★	139	579	102	197	38	2	40	128	22-5	4	96	.340	.364	.620	121	-8	13-9	.986	-8	82	103	O136(120/0/35)		0.3
1996	Col N★	159	633	114	198	39	3	31	141	45-4	6	105	.313	.359	.531	107	7	31-12	.967	-12	87	49	O156(19/0/138)		-1.0
1997	Col N	151	561	81	173	31	2	26	118	30-1	5	90	.308	.343	.510	98	-1	6-5	.987	-6	89	46	O139(128/0/16),D5		-1.3
1998	Col N★	161	662	97	219	48	2	22	122	28-2	1	76	.331	.357	.509	103	4	14-4	.965	6	99	138	O156(134/0/29)/D		0.5
1999	Col N	151	593	104	177	38	2	34	133	54-3	2	84	.298	.354	.541	98	-1	6-6	.951	6	87	193	O144L,D2		-0.7
2000	Cin N	125	461	67	136	27	2	16	76	41-3	4	69	.295	.353	.466	103	2	5-2	.969	3	101	148	O121R		-0.1
	Bos A	30	114	13	33	5	0	7	14	8-0	0	22	.289	.336	.518	109	1	0-0	—	0	0	0	D30		-0.1
2001	Bos A	107	391	45	112	30	1	12	49	20-1	3	76	.286	.325	.460	104	2	2-2	.955	-2	85	137	O53(37/0/16),D46		-0.5
Total 14		1704	6381	934	1906	401	27	274	1141	355-32	41	1078	.299	.336	.499	104	23	152-73	.974	2	95	128	O1552(649/56/907),D89/3		-3.3

BIECHER, ED　Edward "Scrap Iron"　B5.1876 IN　D7.15.1939 St.Louis MO　d9.26

1897	StL N	3	-12	1	4	0	0	0	1	0	0		.333	.333	.333	78	0	1	1.000	-0	0	0	O3L		-0.1
1898	Cle N	8	25	1	5	2	0	0	0	0	0		.200	.200	.280	38	-2	0	.846	-1	121	0	O8C		-0.3
Total 2		11	37	2	9	2	0	0	1	0	0		.243	.243	.297	51	-2	1	.895	-1	83	0	O11(3/8/0)		-0.4

BIELASKI, OSCAR　Oscar　B3.21.1847 Washington DC　D11.8.1911 Washington DC　BR/TR/5-10.5/170　d4.24

1872	Nat NA	10	46	13	8	0	0	0	3	0			.174	.174	.174	6	-6	0-0	.737	-1	0	0	O10R		-0.4
1873	Was NA	38	173	35	49	3	2	0	20	4			.283	.299	.324	88	-2	1-3	.755	2	128	0	O38(2/0/36)		0.1
1874	Bal NA	43	187	24	45	0	0	0	8	2			.241	.249	.241	58	-9	3-1	.806	5	156	72	O43(0/1/43)/1		-0.1
1875	Chi NA	51	201	21	48	1	0	0	11	2			.239	.246	.244	70	-6	5-5	.748	-1	140	130	O51(4/0/48)		-0.4
1876	Chi N	32	139	24	29	3	0	0	10	2			.209	.220	.230	45	-9		.763	-3	76	106	O32R		-1.0
Total 4 NA		142	607	93	150	4	2	0	42	8			15	.247	.257	.260	66	-23	9-9	.767	5	132	68	O142(6/1/137)/1		-0.8

BIERBAUER, LOU　Louis W.　B9.28.1865 Erie PA　D1.31.1926 Erie PA　BL/TR/5-8/140　d4.17　▲

1886	Phi AA	137	522	56	118	17	5	2	47	21	0		.226	.256	.289	70	-20	19	.910	-5	104	85	2b133,C4,S2,P2		-1.7
1887	Phi AA	126	530	74	144	19	7	1	82	13	0		.272	.289	.340	75	-20	40	.921	-7	99	87	2b126/P		-1.8
1888	Phi AA	134	535	83	143	20	9	0	80	25	1		.267	.301	.338	105	2	34	.916	22	110	95	2b121,3b13/P		2.6
1889	Phi AA	130	549	80	167	27	7	7	105	29	4	30	.304	.344	.417	118	11	17	.941	36	107	127	2b130/C		4.3
1890	Bro P	133	589	128	180	31	11	7	99	40	0	15	.306	.350	.431	102	-2	16	.931	21	112	113	2b133		1.9
1891	Pit N	121	500	60	103	13	6	1	47	28	3	19	.206	.252	.262	51	-33	12	.929	-0	98	82	2b121		-2.6
1892	Pit N	152	649	81	153	20	9	4	65	25	0	29	.236	.264	.331	79	-20	11	.950	29	117	102	2b152		1.4
1893	Pit N	128	528	84	150	19	11	4	94	36	4	12	.284	.335	.384	93	-8	11	.939	14	105	123	2b128		1.0
1894	Pit N	131	528	87	160	20	13	3	109	26	2	10	.303	.338	.407	80	-20	19	.939	6	109	93	2b131		-0.6
1895	Pit N	118	470	54	122	13	11	1	71	19	2	8	.260	.291	.340	66	-26	18	.947	9	108	102	2b118		-0.9
1896	Pit N	59	258	33	74	10	6	0	39	5	0	7	.287	.300	.372	80	-9	7	.966	8	108	127	2b59		0.1
1897	StL N	12	46	1	10	0	0	0	1	0	0		.217	.217	.217	15	-6	2	.921	-1	97	91	2b12		-0.6
1898	StL N	4	9	0	0	0	0	0	0	1	0		.000	.100	.000	-69	-2		.429	-1	83	0	2b2/S3		-0.3
Total 13		1385	5713	821	1524	209	95	34	839	268	16	130	.267	.301	.354	84	-153	206	.935	130	107	102	2b1366,3b14,C5,P4,S3		2.8

BIERMAN, CHARLIE　Charles S.　B1845 Hoboken NJ　D8.4.1879 Hoboken NJ　6-0/180　d6.21

| 1871 | Kek NA | 1 | 2 | 0 | 0 | 0 | 0 | 0 | 0 | 1 | | | .000 | .333 | .000 | 6 | 0 | 0-0 | .818 | -0 | 0 | 0 | /1 | | 0.0 |

BIESER, STEVE　Steven Ray　B8.4.1967 Perryville MO　BL/TR/5-10/170*　[PhiN89 32/820]　d4.1 Col Southeast Missouri

1997	NY N	47	69	16	17	3	0	0	4	7-1	4	20	.246	.346	.290	73	-2	2-3	1.000	2	112	287	O21(9/13/1),C2		-0.1
1998	Pit N	13	11	2	3	1	0	0	1	2-0	0	2	.273	.385	.364	97	-0	0-0	—	-0	0	0	/OL		0.0
Total 2		60	80	18	20	4	0	0	5	9-1	4	22	.250	.351	.300	77	-2	2-3	1.000	2	109	279	O22(10/13/1),C2		-0.1

BIGBEE, CARSON　Carson Lee "Skeeter"　B3.31.1895 Waterloo OR　D10.17.1964 Portland OR　BL/TR/5-9/157　d8.25 b-Lyle Col Oregon

1916	Pit N	43	164	17	41	3	6	0	3	7	1	14	.250	.285	.341	91	-3	8	.946	-5	107	64	2b23,O19L/3		-0.9
1917	Pit N	133	469	46	112	11	6	0	21	37	5	16	.239	.301	.288	79	-11	19	.961	-4	107	64	O107(85/5/17),2b16,S2		-2.3
1918	Pit N	92	310	47	79	11	3	1	19	42	0	10	.255	.344	.319	99	2	19	.958	0	93	129	O92(87/0/5)		-0.3
1919	Pit N	125	478	61	132	11	4	2	27	37	3	26	.276	.332	.328	95	-2	31	.971	15	119	128	O124(50/75/0)		0.3
1920	Pit N	137	550	78	154	19	15	4	32	45	6	28	.280	.341	.391	106	4	31-15	.971	3	103	104	O133(128/6/0)		0.3
1921	Pit N	147	632	100	204	23	17	3	42	41	0	19	.323	.364	.427	106	5	21-20	.977	12	105	142	O146(133/13/0)		0.3
1922	Pit N	150	614	113	215	29	15	5	99	56	1	13	.350	.405	.471	124	23	24-15	.956	14	111	146	O150(146/4/0)		2.3
1923	Pit N	123	499	79	149	18	7	0	54	43	1	15	.299	.355	.363	88	-8	10-9	.990	8	111	105	O122L		-1.1
1924	Pit N	89	282	42	74	4	1	0	15	26	3	12	.262	.331	.284	65	-13	15-7	.943	1	101	118	O75L		-1.7
1925	†Pit N	66	126	31	30	7	0	0	8	7	0	8	.238	.278	.294	43	-11	2-2	.942	1	106	105	O42(30/2/10)		-1.2
1926	Pit N	42	68	15	15	3	1	2	4	3	1	0	.221	.264	.382	69	-3	2	.966	1	101	175	O21(17/4/0)		-0.4
Total 11		1147	4192	629	1205	139	75	17	324	344	21	161	.287	.345	.369	96	-17	182-68	.966	44	107	119	O1031(892/109/32),2b39,S2/3		-4.4

BIGBEE, LYLE　Lyle Randolph "Al"　B8.22.1893 Sweet Home OR　D8.5.1942 Portland OR　BL/TR/6-0/180　d4.15 b-Carson Col Oregon　▲

1920	Phi A	38	75	14	14	2	0	1	8	9	1	12	.187	.282	.253	42	-6	1-0	.857	-3	85	0	O13(11/0/1),P12		-0.8
1921	Pit N	5	2	0	0	0	0	0	0	0	0	1	.000	.000	.000	-97	-0	0-0	1.000	-0	96	0	P5		0.0
Total 2		43	77	5	14	2	0	1	8	9	1	13	.182	.276	.247	39	-6	1-0	1.000	-3	103	0	P17,O13(11/0/1)		-0.8

BIGBIE, LARRY　Larry Robert　B11.4.1977 Hobart IN　BL/TR/6-4/190(190-210)　[BalA99 1/21]　d6.23 Col Ball St.

2001	Bal A	47	131	15	30	6	0	2	11	17-1	0	42	.229	.318	.321	73	-5	4-1	1.000	-2	91	91	O40(5/18/17)		-0.6
2002	Bal A	16	34	1	6	1	0	0	3	1-0	0	11	.176	.194	.206	9	-5	1-0	1.000	0	107	0	O12(6/1/6)		-0.4
2003	Bal A	83	287	43	87	15	1	9	31	29-3	1	60	.303	.365	.456	116	7	7-1	.994	2	102	105	O80(76/2/5)	66	0.7
2004	Bal A	139	478	76	134	23	1	15	68	45-0	1	113	.280	.341	.427	100	0	8-3	.993	1	107	42	O134(114/30/0),D2	16	-0.2
2005	Bal A	67	206	22	51	9	1	5	21	21-1	0	49	.248	.314	.374	83	-5	3-3	1.000	2	96	92	O62(57/6/0)	17	-0.9
	Col N	23	66	5	14	1	1	0	2	3-0	0	18	.212	.257	.258	31	-7	2-0	1.000	1	108	127	O15(0/11/5)	16	-0.1
Total 5		375	1202	162	322	55	4	31	136	116-5	2	293	.268	.331	.398	91	-15	25-8	.996	0	102	75	O343(258/68/33),D2	115	-2.0

BIGELOW, ELLIOT　Elliot Allardice "Babe","Gilly"　B10.13.1897 Tarpon Springs FL　D8.13.1933 Tampa FL　BL/TL/5-11/185　d4.18

| 1929 | Bos A | 100 | 211 | 23 | 60 | 16 | 0 | 1 | 26 | 23 | 1 | 18 | .284 | .357 | .374 | 91 | 2 | 1-4 | .944 | -3 | 85 | 125 | O59(2/2/55) | | -0.8 |

BIGGIO, CRAIG　Craig Alan　B12.14.1965 Smithtown NY　BR/TR/5-11/180*　[HouN87 1/22]　d6.26 Col Seton Hall OF(109/255/2)

1988	Hou N	50	123	14	26	6	1	3	5	7-2	0	29	.211	.254	.350	74	-5	6-1	.991	6	67	121	C50		0.5
1989	Hou N	134	443	64	114	21	2	13	60	49-8	6	64	.257	.336	.402	115	-9	21-3	.990	-20	66	67	C125,O5(1/4/0)		0.0
1990	Hou N	150	555	53	153	24	2	4	42	53-1	2	79	.276	.342	.348	93	-4	25-11	.985	-5	78	104	C113,O50(17/34/2)		-0.2
1991	Hou N★	149	546	79	161	23	4	4	46	53-3	2	71	.295	.358	.374	112	10	19-6	.990	-10	89	84	C139,2b3,O2(1/1/0)		1.1
1992	Hou N★	162	613	96	170	32	3	6	39	94-9	7	95	.277	.378	.369	117	19	38-11	.984	-27	84	84	2b161		-0.1
1993	Hou N★	155	610	98	175	41	5	21	64	77-7	10	93	.287	.373	.474	130	28	15-17	.982	0	95	101	2b155		3.2
1994	Hou N★	114	437	88	139	44	5	6	56	62-1	8	58	.318	.411	.483	139	30	39-4	.988	-4	98	89	2b113		3.7
1995	Hou N★	141	553	123	167	30	2	22	77	80-1	22	85	.302	.406	.483	140	40	33-8	.986	6	100	83	2b141		4.4

YEAR	TM LG	G	AB	R	H	2B	3B	HR	RBI	BB-IB	HP	SO	AVG	OBP	SLG	AOPS	ABR	SB-CS	FA	FR	RNG	THR	GAMES AT POSITION	DL	BFW
1996	Hou N★	**162**	605	113	174	24	4	15	75	75-0	**27**	72	.288	.386	.415	122	23	25-7	.988	-2	96	70	2b162		3.1
1997	†Hou N★	**162**	619	**146**	191	37	8	22	81	84-6	**34**	107	.309	.415	.501	144	46	47-10	.979	25	**111**	116	2b160/D		8.2
1998	†Hou N★	160	646	123	210	**51**	2	20	88	64-6	23	113	.325	.403	.503	141	42	50-8	.980	-0	102	98	2b159/D		5.5
1999	Hou N	160	639	123	188	**56**	0	16	73	88-9	11	107	.294	.386	.457	114	19	28-14	.985	19	100	**124**	2b155,O6L,D2		4.3
2000	Hou N	101	377	67	101	13	5	8	35	61-3	16	73	.268	.388	.393	92	-2	12-2	.987	-5	99	87	2b100	60	0.0
2001	†Hou N	155	617	118	180	35	3	20	70	66-4	**28**	100	.292	.382	.455	108	11	7-4	.984	-16	90	96	2b154/D		0.2
2002	Hou N	145	577	96	146	36	3	15	58	50-2	17	111	.253	.330	.404	88	-11	16-2	.988	-4	88	96	2b142/OL		-0.6
2003	Hou N	153	628	102	166	44	2	15	62	57-3	**27**	112	.264	.350	.412	93	-4	8-4	.997	-5	94	111	O150C		-0.7
2004	†Hou N	156	633	100	178	47	0	24	63	40-0	15	94	.281	.337	.469	102	2	7-2	.966	-8	92	58	O149(83/66/0)/D		-0.6
2005	†Hou N	155	590	94	156	40	1	26	69	37-2	17	90	.264	.325	.468	105	3	11-1	.976	11	104	104	2b141,D5		2.2
Total	18	2564	9811	1697	2795	604	52	260	1063	1097-67	273	1557	.285	.370	.437	115	256	407-119	.984	-51	97	96	2b1746,C427,O363C,D11	60	34.2

BIGLER, PETE Ivan Edward B12.13.1892 Bradford OH D4.1.1975 Coldwater MI BR/TR/5-9/150 d5.6 Col Springfield

YEAR	TM LG	G	AB	R	H	2B	3B	HR	RBI	BB-IB	HP	SO	AVG	OBP	SLG	AOPS	ABR	SB-CS	FA	FR	RNG	THR	GAMES AT POSITION	DL	BFW
1917	StL A	1	0	0	0	0	0	0	0	0-0	0	0	—	—	—	—	0	0	—	0			/R		0.0

BIGNELL, GEORGE George William B7.18.1858 Taunton MA D1.16.1925 Providence RI 5-9/160 d9.27

| 1884 | Mil U | 4 | 9 | 4 | 2 | 0 | 0 | 0 | | | | | .222 | .300 | .222 | 111 | 0 | | .951 | 1 | | | C4 | | 0.1 |

BIITTNER, LARRY Lawrence David B7.27.1945 Pocahontas IA BL/TL/6-2/205* [TexA68 10/212] d7.17 Col Buena Vista

1970	Was A	2	0	0	0	0	0	0	0	0-0	0	0	.000	.000	.000	-99	-1	0-0	—	0			/H		-0.1
1971	Was A	66	171	12	44	4	1	0	16	16-3	1	20	.257	.323	.292	79	-5	0-0	.940	1	95	227	O41(7/0/38),1b3		-0.6
1972	Tex A	137	382	34	99	18	1	3	31	29-5	2	37	.259	.313	.335	97	-2	1-3	.991	1	126	82	1b65,O65(28/8/32)		-1.0
1973	Tex A	83	258	19	65	8	2	1	12	20-0	1	21	.252	.307	.310	77	-8	1-0	.980	3	93	177	O57(19/2/38),1b20,D3		-0.9
1974	Mon N	18	26	2	7	1	0	0	3	2-0	0	2	.269	.269	.308	58	-2	0-0	1.000	1	107	444	O4L		-0.1
1975	Mon N	121	346	34	109	13	5	3	28	34-8	0	33	.315	.376	.408	112	6	2-1	.972	0	95	127	O93(35/4/55)		0.1
1976	Mon N	11	32	2	6	1	0	0	1	0-0	0	3	.188	.188	.219	14	-4	0-0	.947	1	125	189	O7(3/0/4)		-0.3
	Chi N	78	192	21	47	13	1	0	17	10-3	1	6	.245	.286	.323	66	-8	0-2	.985	5	174	92	1b33,O24(22/0/3)	15	-0.8
	Year	89	224	23	53	14	1	0	18	10-3	1	9	.237	.272	.308	59	-12	0-2	.985	6	174		1b33,O31(25/0/7)		-1.1
1977	Chi N	138	493	74	147	28	1	12	62	35-2	1	36	.298	.345	.432	97	-2	2-1	.987	4	139	93	1b80,O52L/P		-0.4
1978	Chi N	120	343	32	88	15	1	4	50	23-4	1	37	.257	.300	.341	72	-13	0-1	.987	5	149	120	1b62,O29L		-1.4
1979	Chi N	111	272	35	79	13	1	6	50	21-1	0	23	.290	.339	.393	91	-3	1-1	.925	-3	70	113	O44(23/1/21),1b32		-0.9
1980	Chi N	127	273	21	68	12	2	1	34	18-2	2	33	.249	.294	.319	67	-12	1-3	.996	2	105	62	1b41,O38(20/0/17)		-1.5
1981	Cin N	42	61	1	13	4	0	0	8	4-1	0	4	.213	.258	.279	54	-4	0-0	1.000	1	75	48	1b8,O3R		-0.3
1982	Cin N	97	184	18	57	9	2	2	24	17-2	2	16	.310	.369	.413	120	5	1-0	.978	1	96	113	O31(26/0/6),1b15		0.5
1983	Tex A	66	116	5	32	5	1	0	18	9-5	0	16	.276	.323	.336	84	-2	0-0	.987	1	139	99	1b22,O2R,D9		-0.2
Total	14	1217	3151	310	861	144	20	29	354	236-36	11	287	.273	.324	.359	87	-55	10-12	.970	23	91	133	O490(268/15/219),1b381,D12/P	15	-7.9

BILARDELLO, DANN Dann James B5.26.1959 Santa Cruz CA BR/TR/6-0/190* [LAN78 S1/7] d4.11 Col Cabrillo (CA) JC

1983	Cin N	109	298	27	71	18	0	9	38	15-3	1	49	.238	.274	.389	80	-9	2-1	.991	-2	104	121	C105		-0.7
1984	Cin N	68	182	16	38	7	0	2	10	19-3	1	33	.209	.287	.280	57	-10	0-1	.992	3	121	129	C68		-0.5
1985	Cin N	42	102	6	17	0	0	1	9	4-1	1	15	.167	.206	.196	12	-12	0-0	.986	7	122	179	C42		-0.4
1986	Mon N	79	191	12	37	5	0	4	17	14-3	0	32	.194	.249	.283	46	-15	1-0	.982	-1	104	80	C77		-1.3
1989	Pit N	33	80	11	18	6	0	2	8	2-0	0	18	.225	.244	.375	77	-3	1-2	.970	1	76	134	C33		0.0
1990	Pit N	19	37	1	2	0	0	0	3	4-1	0	10	.054	.146	.054	-44	-7	0-0	1.000	3	192	128	C19		-0.4
1991	SD N	15	26	4	7	2	1	0	5	3-0	0	4	.269	.345	.423	111	0	0-0	1.000	4	109	128	C13		0.5
1992	SD N	17	33	2	4	1	0	0	1	0-0	0	8	.121	.216	.152	6	-4	0-0	1.000	1	51	173	C14		-0.2
Total	8	382	949	79	194	39	1	18	91	65-12	3	170	.204	.259	.324	55	-60	4-4	.988	17	109	124	C371	57	-3.0

BILKO, STEVE Stephen Thomas B11.13.1928 Nanticoke PA D3.7.1978 Wilkes-Barre PA BR/TR/6-1/230* d9.22

1949	StL N	6	17	3	5	2	0	0	2	5	0	6	.294	.455	.412	128	0	0	1.000	0	109	26	1b5		0.1
1950	StL N	10	33	1	6	1	0	0	2	4	0	10	.182	.270	.212	27	-3	0	.989	1	123	98	1b9		-0.3
1951	StL N	21	72	5	16	4	0	2	12	9	0	15	.222	.309	.361	79	-2	0-0	.984	0	106	104	1b19		-0.3
1952	StL N	20	72	7	19	6	1	1	6	4	0	15	.264	.303	.417*	97	0	0-0	.995	5	184	63	1b20		0.4
1953	StL N	154	570	72	143	23	3	21	84	70	1	125	.251	.334	.412	93	-6	0-1	.991	9	**121**	106	1b154		0.0
1954	StL N	8	14	1	2	0	0	0	1	3	0	5	.143	.294	.143	18	-2	0-0	1.000	2	299	102	1b6		0.0
	Chi N	47	92	11	22	8	1	4	12	11	0	24	.239	.320	.478	104	-1	0-0	1.000	6	200	97	1b22		0.5
	Year	55	106	12	24	8	1	4	13	14	0	25	.226	.317	.434	92	-1	0-0	1.000	8	214	95	1b28		0.5
1958	Cin N	31	87	12	23	4	2	4	17	10-0	0	23	.264	.330	.494	111	1	0-0	.995	-1	81	106	1b21		-0.1
	LA N	47	101	13	21	1	2	7	18	8-0	0	37	.208	.264	.465	86	-3	0-0	.995	2	127	100	1b25		-0.2
	Year	78	188	25	44	5	4	11	35	18-0	0	57	.234	.295	.479	98	-2	0-0	.995	1	104	103	1b46		-0.3
1960	Det A	78	222	20	46	11	2	9	25	27-0	0	31	.207	.292	.396	82	-6	0-1	.991	-0	97	95	1b62		-1.0
1961	LA A	114	294	49	82	16	1	20	59	58-2	0	81	.279	.395	.544	134	16	1-1	.989	3	112	82	1b86,O3R		1.3
1962	LA A	64	164	26	47	9	1	8	38	25-0	2	35	.287	.374	.500	141	10	1-1	.995	-1	90	97	1b50	31	0.7
Total	10	600	1738	220	432	85	13	76	276	234-2	3	395	.249	.336	.444	103	6	2-4	.992	25	119	97	1b479,O3R	31	0.6

BILLINGS, JOSH John Augustus B11.30.1892 Grantville KS D12.30.1981 Santa Monica CA BR/TR/5-11/165 d9.9 Mil 1918 Col Oklahoma St.

1913	Cle A	1	3	0	0	0	0	0	0	0	0	3	.000	.000	.000	-97	-1	0	.857	1	125	99	/C		-0.1
1914	Cle A	11	8	3	2	1	0	0	0	1	0	1	.250	.333	.375	109	0	1	.813	1	0	147	C3		-0.2
1915	Cle A	8	21	2	4	1	0	0	0	0	0	6	.190	.190	.238	28	-2	1	1.000	-0	94	63	C7/OC		-0.2
1916	Cle A	22	31	2	5	0	0	0	1	2	0	11	.161	.212	.161	12	-3	0	.981	2	126	76	C12		-0.1
1917	Cle A	66	129	8	23	3	2	0	9	8	3	21	.178	.243	.233	42	-9	2	.974	2	108	118	C48		-0.4
1918	Cle A	2	3	0	1	0	0	0	1	0	0	0	.333	.333	.333	92	0	0	1.000	0	0		/C		0.0
1919	StL A	38	76	9	15	1	0	0	3	1	1	12	.197	.218	.237	27	-4	0	.982	3	102	128	C26/1		-0.3
1920	StL A	66	155	19	43	5	2	0	11	11	7	10	.277	.353	.400	80	-4	1-0	.967	-4	92	104	C40		-0.5
1921	StL A	20	46	2	10	0	0	0	4	0	1	7	.217	.217	.217	11	-6	0-0	.982	1	110	88	C12		-0.3
1922	StL A	5	7	0	3	1	0	0	1	0	0	0	.429	.429	.571	153	1	0-0	1.000	-0	64	191	C3		0.0
1923	StL A	4	9	0	0	0	0	0	0	0	0	1	.000	.000	.000	-95	-3	0-0	.917	0	141	173	C4		-0.2
Total	11	243	488	45	106	12	5	0	29	23	11	73	.217	.268	.262	47	-35	5-0	.970	4	102	109	C157/1OC		-2.2

BILLINGS, DICK Richard Arlin B12.4.1942 Detroit MI BR/TR/6-1/195* [TexA65 16/622] d9.11 Col Michigan St.

1968	Was A	12	33	3	6	1	0	0	3	5-0	0	13	.182	.282	.303	82	-1	0-0	.929	1	93	219	O8L,3b4		-0.1
1969	Was A	27	37	3	5	0	0	0	0	6-0	0	8	.135	.256	.135	13	-4	0-1	1.000	0	78	0	O6(5/1/0)/3		-0.5
1970	Was A	11	24	3	6	2	0	1	1	2-0	0	1	.250	.308	.458	113	0	0-0	1.000	-2	86	178	C8		-0.1
1971	Was A	116	349	32	86	14	0	6	48	21-1	5	54	.246	.296	.338	84	-8	2-5	.992	-4	62	121	C62,O32(22/0/12),3b2		-1.3
1972	Tex A	133	469	41	119	15	1	5	58	29-5	2	77	.254	.296	.322	88	-6	1-5	.981	-1	77	136	C92,O41(39/0/2),3b5/1		-1.0
1973	Tex A	81	280	17	50	11	0	3	32	20-2	1	43	.179	.237	.250	39	-23	1-1	.975	-16	66	110	C72,O4(3/0/1),1b3,D2	16	-3.8
1974	Tex A	16	31	2	7	1	0	0	4	4-0	0	6	.226	.314	.258	68	-1	2-0	1.000	0	136	91	C13/OLD	50	0.0
	StL N	1	5	0	1	0	0	0	1	0-0	0	1	.200	.200	.200	12	-1	0-0	1.000	0	0	0	O/C		-0.1
1975	StL N	3	3	0	0	0	0	0	0	0-0	0	2	.000	.000	.000	-96	-1	0-0	—	0			/H		-0.1
Total	8	400	1231	101	280	44	1	16	142	87-8	9	207	.227	.281	.304	72	-47	6-12	.984	-22	72	122	C248,O92(78/1/15),3b12,1b4,D3	66	-7.0

BINKS, GEORGE George Alvin "Bingo" (b George Alvin Binkowski) B7.11.1916 Chicago IL BL/TL/6-0/175 d9.23

1944	Was A	5	12	0	3	0	0	0	1	1-0	0	1	.250	.250	.250	45	-1	0-0	1.000	-0	97	0	O3R		-0.1
1945	Was A	145	550	62	153	32	6	6	81	34	3	52	.278	.324	.391	117	9	11-7	.977	5	106	117	O128(27/79/26),1b20		0.8
1946	Phi A	65	134	13	26	3	0	0	12	6	0	16	.194	.229	.216	26	-14	1-0	1.000	1	112	53	O28(15/9/5)		-1.5
1947	Phi A	104	333	33	86	19	4	2	34	23	1	36	.258	.308	.357	83	-8	8-2	.965	2	101	149	O75(25/0/51),1b13		-1.0
1948	Phi A	17	41	2	4	1	0	0	2	2	0	8	.098	.140	.122	-10	-4	1-0	1.000	1	92	146	O14(2/0/12)		-0.8
	StL A	15	23	2	5	0	1	0	1	2	0	1	.217	.280	.304	32	-2	0-0	1.000	1	96	0	O5(2/0/3),1b4		-0.3
	Year	32	64	4	9	1	1	0	3	4	0	9	.141	.191	.156	-7	-10	1-0	1.000	-1	93	106	O19(4/0/15),1b4		-1.1
Total	5	351	1093	114	277	55	10	8	150	67	4	108	.253	.299	.344	86	-24	21-9	.977	7	104	118	O253(71/88/100),1b37		-2.9

BIRAS, STEVE Stephen Alexander B2.26.1922 E.St.Louis IL D4.21.1965 St.Louis MO BR/TR/5-11/185 d9.15

| 1944 | Cle A | 2 | 2 | 0 | 2 | 0 | 0 | 0 | 2 | 0 | 0 | 0 | 1.000 | 1.000 | 1.000 | 491 | 1 | 0-0 | .667 | -0 | 77 | 0 | /2 | | 0.1 |

BIRCHALL, JUD Adoniram Judson B9.12.1855 Philadelphia PA D12.22.1887 Philadelphia PA d5.2

| 1882 | Phi AA | **75** | 338 | 65 | 89 | 12 | 1 | 0 | 27 | 8 | | | .263 | .280 | .305 | 91 | -4 | | .860 | 0 | 80 | 0 | O74L/2 | | -0.5 |
| 1883 | Phi AA | 96 | 448 | 95 | 108 | 10 | 1 | 1 | 24 | 20 | | | .241 | .274 | .275 | 70 | -16 | | .809 | 5 | 116 | 0 | O96L | | -1.2 |

YEAR	TM LG	G	AB	R	H	2B	3B	HR	RBI	BB-IB	HP	SO	AVG	OBP	SLG	AOPS	ABR	SB-CS	FA	FR	RNG	THR	GAMES AT POSITION	DL	BFW
1884	Phi AA	54	221	36	57	2	2	0		4		5	.258	.287	.285	82	-5		.838	2	65	62	O52(51/0/1),3b2		-0.4
Total	3	225	1007	196	254	24	4	1	51	32		5	.252	.279	.287	80	-25		.832	7	92	15	O222(221/0/1),3b2/2		-2.1

BIRD, FRANK Frank Zepherin "Dodo" B3.10.1869 Spencer MA D5.20.1958 Worcester MA BR/TR/5-10/195 d4.16

YEAR	TM LG	G	AB	R	H	2B	3B	HR	RBI	BB-IB	HP	SO	AVG	OBP	SLG	AOPS	ABR	SB-CS	FA	FR	RNG	THR	GAMES AT POSITION	DL	BFW
1892	StL N	17	50	3	10	3	1	1	6	0		11	.200	.286	.360	100	0	2	.920	-3	96	96	C17		-0.2

BIRD, GEORGE George Raymond B6.23.1850 Stillman Valley IL D11.9.1940 Rockford IL BR/TR/5-9/150 d5.6

YEAR	TM LG	G	AB	R	H	2B	3B	HR	RBI	BB-IB	HP	SO	AVG	OBP	SLG	AOPS	ABR	SB-CS	FA	FR	RNG	THR	GAMES AT POSITION	DL	BFW
1871	Rok NA	25	106	19	28	2	5	0	13	3		2	.264	.284	.377	92	-1	1-0	.756	-5	66	0	O25(1/25/0)		-0.4

BIRDSALL, DAVE David Solomon B7.16.1838 New York NY D12.30.1896 Boston MA BR/TR/5-9/126 d5.5

YEAR	TM LG	G	AB	R	H	2B	3B	HR	RBI	BB-IB	HP	SO	AVG	OBP	SLG	AOPS	ABR	SB-CS	FA	FR	RNG	THR	GAMES AT POSITION	DL	BFW
1871	Bos NA	29	152	51	46	3	3	0	24	4		4	.303	.321	.362	93	-2	6-0	.769	0	110	208	O27R,C7		0.0
1872	Bos NA	16	76	11	16	3	0	0	15	1		0	.211	.221	.250	42	-5	0-2	.826	2			C12,O7(4/0/3)		-0.3
1873	Bos NA	3	11	4	1	0	0	0	0	2		0	.091	.231	.091	-1	-1	1-0	.200	-2	-0	0	O3(1/0/3)		-0.2
Total	3 NA	48	239	66	63	6	3	0	39	7		4	.264	.285	.314	73	-8	7-2	.720	0			O37(5/0/33),C19		-0.5

BIRMINGHAM, JOE Joseph Leo "Dode" B8.6.1884 Elmira NY D4.24.1946 Tampico, Tamaulipas, Mexico BR/TR/5-10/185 d9.12 M4 Col Cornell

YEAR	TM LG	G	AB	R	H	2B	3B	HR	RBI	BB-IB	HP	SO	AVG	OBP	SLG	AOPS	ABR	SB-CS	FA	FR	RNG	THR	GAMES AT POSITION	DL	BFW
1906	Cle A	10	40	5	11	2	1	0	6	1		0	.275	.293	.375	110	0	2	1.000	1	155	0	O9L/3		0.0
1907	Cle A	137	476	55	112	10	9	1	33	16	3		.235	.265	.300	79	-13	23	.949	12	**168**	213	O133(17/101/16),S3		-0.8
1908	Cle A	122	413	32	88	10	1	2	38	19	3		.213	.252	.257	65	-16	15	.957	4	**148**	179	O121(1/119/1)/S		-2.0
1909	Cle A	100	343	29	99	10	5	1	38	19	4		.289	.333	.356	113	4	12	.948	2	124	75	O98C		0.2
1910	Cle A	104	367	41	84	11	2	0	35	23	5		.229	.284	.270	72	-12	18	.961	11	107	**159**	O103(1/102/0)/3		-0.6
1911	Cle A	125	447	55	136	18	5	2	51	15	5		.304	.334	.380	98	-3	16	.973	3	101	110	O102(3/96/3),3b16		-0.6
1912	Cle A	107	369	49	94	19	3	1	45	26	4		.255	.311	.331	81	-9	15	.952	2	93	129	O96(3/93/0),1b9,M		-1.4
1913	Cle A	47	131	16	37	9	1	0	15	8		22	.282	.324	.366	99	0	7	.974	-2	102	39	O36(4/32/0),M		-0.5
1914	Cle A	19	47	2	6	0	0	0	4	2		5	.128	.163	.128	-12	-7	0-1	1.000	-0	92	90	O14(0/6/8),M		-0.9
Total	9	771	2633	284	667	89	27	7	265	129	24	27	.253	.294	.316	84	-56	108-1	.958	33	125	141	O712(38/647/28),3b18,1b9,S4		-6.6

BISCHOFF, JOHN John George "Smiley" B10.28.1894 Granite City IL D12.28.1981 Granite City IL BR/TR/5-7/165 d4.18

YEAR	TM LG	G	AB	R	H	2B	3B	HR	RBI	BB-IB	HP	SO	AVG	OBP	SLG	AOPS	ABR	SB-CS	FA	FR	RNG	THR	GAMES AT POSITION	DL	BFW
1925	Chi A	7	11	1	1	0	0	0	1	0		0	.091	.167	.091	-35	-2	0-0	1.000	-0	110	212	C4		-0.2
	Bos A	41	133	13	37	9	1	0	16	6		11	.278	.309	.383	75	-6	1-2	.952	-4	70	100	C40		-0.7
	Year	48	144	14	38	9	1	0	16	7		16	.264	.298	.361	67	-8	1-2	.955	-4	72	106	C44		-0.9
1926	Bos A	59	127	6	33	11	2	0	19	15		16	.260	.343	.378	91	-2	1-3	.974	-4	66	87	C46		-0.4
Total	2	107	271	20	71	20	3	1	35	22	1	32	.262	.320	.369	78	-10	2-5	.964	-8	69	97	C90		-1.3

BISHOP, FRANK Frank H. B9.21.1860 Belvidere IL D6.18.1929 Chicago IL d5.27

YEAR	TM LG	G	AB	R	H	2B	3B	HR	RBI	BB-IB	HP	SO	AVG	OBP	SLG	AOPS	ABR	SB-CS	FA	FR	RNG	THR	GAMES AT POSITION	DL	BFW
1884	CP U	4	16	1	3	1	0	0		0			.188	.188	.250	32	-2		.667	-2	49	0	3b3/S		-0.3

BISHOP, MAX Max Frederick "Tilly","Camera Eye" B9.5.1899 Waynesboro PA D2.24.1962 Waynesboro PA BL/TR/5-8.5/165 d4.15 Col CC of Baltimore (MD)

YEAR	TM LG	G	AB	R	H	2B	3B	HR	RBI	BB-IB	HP	SO	AVG	OBP	SLG	AOPS	ABR	SB-CS	FA	FR	RNG	THR	GAMES AT POSITION	DL	BFW
1924	Phi A	91	294	52	75	13	2	2	21	54	5	30	.255	.380	.333	84	-4	4-3	.969	10	114	108	2b80		0.7
1925	Phi A	105	368	66	103	18	4	4	27	87	2	37	.280	.420	.383	98	4	5-9	.957	5	**109**	90	2b104		0.9
1926	Phi A	122	400	77	106	20	2	0	33	116	1	41	.265	.431	.325	94	5	4-5	.987	6	102	95	2b119		1.3
1927	Phi A	117	372	80	103	15	1	0	22	105	5	28	.277	.442	.323	95	6	8-6	.967	2	103	85	2b106		1.0
1928	Phi A	126	472	104	149	27	5	6	50	100	3	36	.316	.438	.432	126	25	6-10	.978	-6	92	92	2b125		1.9
1929	†Phi A	129	475	102	110	19	6	3	36	**128**	3	44	.232	.398	.316	83	-5	1-4	.970	-20	88	77	2b129		-2.1
1930	†Phi A	130	441	117	111	27	6	10	38	128	6	60	.252	.426	.408	108	13	3-2	.976	-1	101	81	2b127		1.4
1931	†Phi A	130	497	115	146	30	4	5	37	112	2	51	.294	.426	.400	111	15	3-1	.984	2	98	116	2b130		2.4
1932	Phi A	114	409	89	104	24	2	5	37	110	1	43	.254	.412	.359	98	6	2-2	.988	-1	100	106	2b106		1.1
1933	Phi A	117	391	80	115	27	1	4	42	106	1	46	.294	.446	.399	124	23	1-5	.975	-7	101	70	2b113		2.0
1934	Bos A	97	253	66	65	13	1	1	22	82	2	22	.261	.445	.332	96	5	3-2	.990	3	98	105	2b57,1b15		0.9
1935	Bos A	60	122	19	28	3	1	1	14	28	1	14	.230	.377	.295	71	-4	0-2	.978	-3	93	55	2b34,1b11,S2		-0.6
Total	12	1338	4494	966	1216	236	35	41	379	1156	31	452	.271	.423	.366	102	89	40-51	.976	-10	100	91	2b1230,1b26,S2		10.9

BISHOP, MIKE Michael David B11.5.1958 Santa Maria CA D2.8.2005 Bakersfield CA BR/TR/6-2/225 [AnaA76 12/270] d4.16

YEAR	TM LG	G	AB	R	H	2B	3B	HR	RBI	BB-IB	HP	SO	AVG	OBP	SLG	AOPS	ABR	SB-CS	FA	FR	RNG	THR	GAMES AT POSITION	DL	BFW
1983	NY N	3	8	2	1	0	0	0	3-0	0	1	.125	.364	.250	73	0	0-0	.944	-0	86	79	C3		0.0

BISLAND, RIVINGTON Rivington Martin B2.17.1890 New York NY D1.11.1973 Salzburg, Austria BR/TR/5-9/155 d9.13

YEAR	TM LG	G	AB	R	H	2B	3B	HR	RBI	BB-IB	HP	SO	AVG	OBP	SLG	AOPS	ABR	SB-CS	FA	FR	RNG	THR	GAMES AT POSITION	DL	BFW
1912	Pit N	1	1	0	0	0	0	0	0	0		0	.000	.000	.000	-99	0	0		-0		0	/H		0.0
1913	StL A	12	44	3	6	0	0	0	3	2	1	5	.136	.191	.136	-4	-6	0	.963	-3	89	66	S12		-0.4
1914	Cle A	18	57	9	6	1	0	0	2	6	0	2	.105	.190	.123	-5	-7	2-5	.962	0	100	92	S15/3		-0.8
Total	3	31	102	12	12	1	0	0	5	8	1	7	.118	.189	.127	-6	-13	2-5	.962	-2	95	81	S27/3		-1.7

BISSONETTE, DEL Delphia Louis B9.6.1899 Winthrop ME D6.9.1972 Augusta ME BL/TL/5-11/180 d4.11 M1/C2 Col Georgetown

YEAR	TM LG	G	AB	R	H	2B	3B	HR	RBI	BB-IB	HP	SO	AVG	OBP	SLG	AOPS	ABR	SB-CS	FA	FR	RNG	THR	GAMES AT POSITION	DL	BFW
1928	Bro N	**155**	587	90	188	30	13	25	106	70	4	75	.320	.396	.543	145	38	5	.987	-3	90	74	1b155		2.4
1929	Bro N	116	431	68	121	28	10	12	75	46	1	58	.281	.351	.476	105	-2	3	.987	-9	67	74	1b113		-1.3
1930	Bro N	146	572	102	192	33	13	16	113	56	1	66	.336	.396	.523	121	19	4	.987	-9	78	**118**	1b146		0.1
1931	Bro N	152	587	90	170	19	14	12	87	59	0	53	.290	.354	.431	111	8	4	.990	-6	79	104	1b152		-1.3
1933	Bro N	35	114	9	28	7	0	1	10	2	0	17	.246	.259	.333	71	-5	2	.988	-0	97	100	1b32		-0.8
Total	5	604	2291	359	699	117	50	66	391	233	6	269	.305	.371	.486	119	62	17	.988	-28	80	94	1b598		-0.9

BITTMAN, RED Henry Peter B7.22.1862 Cincinnati OH D11.8.1929 Cincinnati OH d10.10

YEAR	TM LG	G	AB	R	H	2B	3B	HR	RBI	BB-IB	HP	SO	AVG	OBP	SLG	AOPS	ABR	SB-CS	FA	FR	RNG	THR	GAMES AT POSITION	DL	BFW
1889	KC AA	4	14	2	4	0	0	0		1		0	.286	.333	.286	72	-1	1	1.000	1	112	104	2b4		0.0

BJORKMAN, GEORGE George Anton B8.26.1956 Ontario CA BR/TR/6-2/190 [StLN78 4/93] d7.10 Col Oral Roberts

YEAR	TM LG	G	AB	R	H	2B	3B	HR	RBI	BB-IB	HP	SO	AVG	OBP	SLG	AOPS	ABR	SB-CS	FA	FR	RNG	THR	GAMES AT POSITION	DL	BFW
1983	Hou N	29	75	8	17	4	0	2	14	16-4	1	29	.227	.370	.360	109	2	0	.993	-3	95	73	C29		0.0

BLACK, JOHN John Falcnor "Jack" (b John Falcnor Haddow) B2.23.1890 Covington KY D3.20.1962 Rutherford NJ BR/TR/6-1/185 d6.20

YEAR	TM LG	G	AB	R	H	2B	3B	HR	RBI	BB-IB	HP	SO	AVG	OBP	SLG	AOPS	ABR	SB-CS	FA	FR	RNG	THR	GAMES AT POSITION	DL	BFW
1911	StL A	54	186	13	28	4	0	0	7	10	2		.151	.202	.172	5	-24	4	.972	0	111	121	1b54		-2.6

BLACK, BILL John William "Jigger" B8.12.1899 Philadelphia PA D1.14.1968 Philadelphia PA BL/TR/5-11/168 d5.4

YEAR	TM LG	G	AB	R	H	2B	3B	HR	RBI	BB-IB	HP	SO	AVG	OBP	SLG	AOPS	ABR	SB-CS	FA	FR	RNG	THR	GAMES AT POSITION	DL	BFW
1924	Chi A	6	5	0	1	0	0	0	0	0		0	.200	.200	.200	3	-1	0-0	—	-0	0	0	/2		-0.1

BLACK, BOB Robert Benjamin B12.10.1862 Cincinnati OH D3.21.1933 Sioux City IA 5-5.5/155 d8.19 ▲

YEAR	TM LG	G	AB	R	H	2B	3B	HR	RBI	BB-IB	HP	SO	AVG	OBP	SLG	AOPS	ABR	SB-CS	FA	FR	RNG	THR	GAMES AT POSITION	DL	BFW
1884	KC U	38	146	25	36	14	2	1		10			.247	.295	.390	122	0		.784	-0	94	0	O19(5/7/7),P16,2b6/S		-0.1

BLACKABY, ETHAN Ethan Allen B7.24.1940 Cincinnati OH BL/TL/5-11/190* d9.6 Col Illinois

YEAR	TM LG	G	AB	R	H	2B	3B	HR	RBI	BB-IB	HP	SO	AVG	OBP	SLG	AOPS	ABR	SB-CS	FA	FR	RNG	THR	GAMES AT POSITION	DL	BFW
1962	Mil N	6	13	0	2	1	0	0	1-0		0	8	.154	.214	.231	20	-1	0-0	1.000	-1	50	0	O3(2/1/0)		-0.2
1964	Mil N	9	12	0	1	0	0	0	1-0		0	2	.083	.154	.083	-31	-2	0-0	.500	-1	21	0	O5(2/0/3)		-0.4
Total	2	15	25	0	3	1	0	0	2-0		0	10	.120	.185	.160	-4	-3	0-0	.800	-2	36	0	O8(4/1/3)		-0.6

BLACKBURN, EARL Earl Stuart B11.1.1892 Leesville OH D8.3.1966 Mansfield OH BR/TR/5-11/180 d9.17

YEAR	TM LG	G	AB	R	H	2B	3B	HR	RBI	BB-IB	HP	SO	AVG	OBP	SLG	AOPS	ABR	SB-CS	FA	FR	RNG	THR	GAMES AT POSITION	DL	BFW
1912	Pit N	1	0	0	0	0	0	0	0	0		0	—	—	—		0	0	1.000	0	0	0	/C		0.0
	Cin N	1	0	0	0	0	0	0	0	1		0	—	1.000	—	191	0	0	1.000	0	0	0	/C		0.1
	Year	2	0	0	0	0	0	0	0	1		0	—	1.000	—	190	0	0	1.000	0	0	0	C2		0.1
1913	Cin N	17	27	1	7	3	0	0	3	2		5	.259	.310	.259	64	-1	2-1	.848	-2	108	86	C12		-0.2
1915	Bos N	3	6	0	1	0	0	0	0	1		1	.167	.375	.167	70	0	0-0	1.000	-0	94	126	C3		0.0
1916	Bos N	47	110	12	30	4	4	0	7	9		21	.273	.328	.382	123	3	2	.972	3	173	67	C44		1.0
1917	Cin N	2	2	0	0	0	0	0	0	0		0	.000	.000	.000	-93	0		—	0			/H		-0.1
Total	5	71	145	13	38	4	4	0	10	14		27	.262	.327	.345	107	2	4-1	.954	2	156	71	C61		0.8

BLACKBURNE, LENA Russell Aubrey "Slats" B10.23.1886 Clifton Heights PA D2.29.1968 Riverside NJ BR/TR/5-11/160 d4.14 M2/C13

YEAR	TM LG	G	AB	R	H	2B	3B	HR	RBI	BB-IB	HP	SO	AVG	OBP	SLG	AOPS	ABR	SB-CS	FA	FR	RNG	THR	GAMES AT POSITION	DL	BFW
1910	Chi A	75	242	16	42	3	1	0	10	19	4		.174	.245	.194	39	-17	4	.911	11	107	117	S74		-0.4
1912	Chi A	5	1	0	0	0	0	0	0	1			.000	.500	.000	48	0	1	.800	-0	57	570	S4/3		0.0
1914	Chi A	144	474	52	105	10	5	1	35	66	6	58	.222	.324	.270	80	-9	25-15	.963	4	**109**	67	2b143		-0.3
1915	Chi A	96	283	33	61	5	1	0	25	35	1	34	.216	.304	.240	61	-13	13-11	.949	-9	88	108	3b83,S9		-2.2
1918	Cin N	125	435	34	99	8	10	1	45	25	1	30	.228	.271	.299	75	-15	6	.938	11	99	**126**	S125		0.5
1919	Bos N	31	80	5	21	3	1	0	4	6	1	7	.262	.322	.325	99	0	3	.948	1	96	100	3b24/12S		0.2
	Phi N	72	291	32	58	10	5	2	19	10	1	22	.199	.228	.289	51	-18	2	.933	7	114	94	3b72/1		-1.0
	Year	103	371	37	79	13	6	2	23	16	2	29	.213	.249	.296	61	-18	5	.937	8	**110**	96	3b96,1b2/2S		-0.8
1927	Chi A	1	1	1	1	0	0	0	1	0		0	1.000	1.000	1.000	431	0	0-0	—	0		0	/H		0.0

YEAR	TM LG	G	AB	R	H	2B	3B	HR	RBI	BB-IB	HP	SO	AVG	OBP	SLG	AOPS	ABR	SB-CS	FA	FR	RNG	THR	GAMES AT POSITION	DL	BFW
1929	Chi A	1	0	0	0	0	0	0	0	0-0	0	0	—	—	—	—	0	0-0	—	0	0	0	/PM		0.0
Total	8	550	1807	173	387	39	23	4	139	162	14	151	.214	.284	.268	67	-72	54-26	.927	25	102	124	S213,3b180,2b144,1b2/P		-3.2

BLACKERBY, GEORGE   George Franklin B11.10.1903 Luther OK D5.30.1987 Wichita Falls TX BR/TR/6-1/176 d8.10

| 1928 | Chi A | 30 | 83 | 8 | 21 | 0 | 0 | 0 | 12 | 4 | 0 | 10 | .253 | .287 | .253 | 44 | -7 | 2-1 | .953 | -1 | 95 | 54 | O20L | | -0.9 |

BLACKWELL, FRED   Fredrick William "Blacky" B9.7.1891 Bowling Green KY D12.8.1975 Morgantown KY BL/TR/5-11.5/160 d9.25 Mil 1918

1917	Pit N	3	10	1	2	0	0	0	2	0	0	3	.200	.200	.200	22	-1	0	1.000	0	84	102	C3		-0.1
1918	Pit N	8	13	1	2	0	0	0	4	3	0	4	.154	.313	.154	42	-1	0	.926	0	148	87	C8		0.0
1919	Pit N	24	65	3	14	3	0	0	4	3	1	9	.215	.261	.262	55	-3	0	.964	1	135	75	C22		-0.1
Total	3	35	88	5	18	3	0	0	10	6	1	16	.205	.263	.239	50	-5	0	.961	1	132	80	C33		-0.2

BLACKWELL, TIM   Timothy P B8.19.1952 San Diego CA BB/TR/5-11/180(170-185) [BosA70 13/311] d7.3

1974	Bos A	44	122	9	30	1	1	0	8	21	1	21	.246	.308	.270	63	-6	1-1	.971	-4	82	105	C44		-0.8
1975	Bos A	59	132	15	26	3	2	0	6	19-0	1	13	.197	.303	.250	53	-8	0-0	.984	1	82	104	C57,D2		-0.5
1976	Phi N	4	8	0	2	0	0	0	1	0-0	0	1	.250	.250	.250	41	-1	0-0	1.000	1	0	0	C4		0.1
1977	Phi N	1	0	1	0	0	0	0	0	0-0	0	0	—	—	—	—	0	0-0	1.000	0	0	0	/C		0.0
	Mon N	16	22	3	2	1	0	0	0	2-1	0	7	.091	.167	.136	-18	-4	0-0	.925	-3	48	0	C14		-0.7
	Year	17	22	4	2	1	0	0	0	2-1	0	7	.091	.167	.136	-18	-4	0-0	.929	-3	46	0	C15		-0.7
1978	Chi N	49	103	8	23	3	0	0	7	23-1	1	17	.223	.367	.252	69	-3	0-0	.987	4	101	44	C49		0.3
1979	Chi N	63	122	8	20	3	1	0	12	32-1	1	25	.164	.338	.205	48	-7	0-0	.975	-4	85	105	C63		-1.0
1980	Chi N	103	320	24	87	16	4	5	30	41-6	0	62	.272	.352	.394	100	1	0-1	.982	13	99	158	C103		1.9
1981	Chi N	58	158	21	37	10	2	1	11	23-4	0	23	.234	.331	.342	86	-2	2-1	.993	-6	61	115	C56		-0.6
1982	Mon N	23	42	2	8	1	0	0	3	3-0	0	11	.190	.244	.286	46	-3	0-0	.985	-2	71	86	C18		-0.4
1983	Mon N	6	15	0	3	1	0	0	2	1-0	0	5	.200	.250	.267	43	-1	0-0	.935	-2	39	0	C5		-0.3
Total	10	426	1044	91	238	40	11	6	80	154-14	4	183	.228	.328	.305	73	-34	3-3	.981	-9	84	110	C414,D2		-2.0

BLADES, RAY   Francis Raymond B8.6.1896 Mt.Vernon IL D5.18.1979 Lincoln IL BR/TR/5-7.5/163 d8.19 M3/C11

1922	StL N	37	130	27	39	2	4	3	21	25	4	21	.300	.428	.446	132	8	3-3	.931	-1	103	169	O29(28/0/1),S4/3		0.4
1923	StL N	98	317	48	78	21	5	5	44	37	3	46	.246	.342	.391	95	-1	4-2	.967	6	110	138	O83(81/1/3),3b4		-0.1
1924	StL N	131	456	86	142	21	13	11	68	35	10	38	.311	.373	.487	131	19	7-9	.956	-1	114	55	O109(106/3/1),2b7,3b7		0.9
1925	StL N	122	462	112	158	37	8	12	57	59	6	47	.342	.423	.535	140	30	6-8	.979	9	114	127	O114L/3		2.7
1926	StL N	107	416	81	127	17	12	8	43	62	11	45	.305	.409	.462	129	19	6	.980	0	101	94	O105L		1.1
1927	StL N	61	180	33	57	8	5	2	29	28	2	22	.317	.414	.450	127	8	3	.914	-9	74	0	O50(29/0/21)		-0.4
1928	†StL N	51	85	9	20	7	1	1	19	20	2	26	.235	.393	.376	100	1	0	.972	-1	87	56	O19(4/0/15)		-0.1
1930	†StL N	45	101	26	40	6	2	4	25	21	1	15	.396	.504	.614	163	12	1	.957	-1	107	33	O32(13/0/21)		0.7
1931	†StL N	35	67	10	19	4	0	1	5	10	2	7	.284	.392	.388	106	1	1	.871	-2	83	70	O20(7/0/13)		-0.2
1932	StL N	80	201	35	46	10	1	3	29	34	6	31	.229	.340	.333	80	-5	2	.975	-1	106	42	O62(13/0/49)/3		-0.9
Total	10	767	2415	467	726	133	51	50	340	331	47	310	.301	.395	.460	123	92	33-22	.963	-1	105	87	O623(500/4/124),3b14,2b7,S4		4.1

BLADT, RICK   Richard Alan B12.9.1946 Santa Cruz CA BR/TR/6-1/160* d6.15 Col Foothill (CA) JC

1969	Chi N	10	13	1	2	0	0	0	1	0-0	0	5	.154	.154	.154	-12	-2	0-0	1.000	1	141	401	O7(2/5/1)		-0.1
1975	NY A	52	117	13	26	3	1	1	11	11-0	1	8	.222	.292	.291	66	-5	6-2	.973	2	106	154	O51C		-0.4
Total	2	62	130	14	28	3	1	1	12	11-0	1	13	.215	.280	.277	58	-7	6-2	.976	3	109	178	O58(2/56/1)		-0.5

BLAEMIRE, RAE   Rae Bertrum B2.8.1911 Gary IN D12.23.1975 Champaign IL BR/TR/6-0/178 d9.13

| 1941 | NY N | 2 | 5 | 0 | 2 | 0 | 0 | 0 | 0 | 0-0 | 0 | 0 | .400 | .400 | .400 | 123 | 1 | 0-0 | 1.000 | -0 | 0 | 0 | C2 | | 0.0 |

BLAIR, FOOTSIE   Clarence Vick B7.13.1900 Enterprise OK D7.1.1982 Texarkana TX BL/TR/6-1/180 d4.28

1929	†Chi N	26	72	10	23	5	0	0	8	3	0	4	.319	.347	.431	91	-1	1	.897	-0	88	0	3b8,1b7,2b2		-0.1
1930	Chi N	134	578	97	158	24	12	6	59	20	7	58	.273	.306	.388	66	-35	9	.958	4	105	101	2b115,3b13		-2.4
1931	Chi N	86	240	31	62	19	4	3	29	14	1	26	.258	.302	.408	88	-5	1	.956	-7	89	67	2b44,1b23/3		-1.1
Total	3	246	890	138	243	48	16	10	96	37	8	88	.273	.308	.397	73	-41	11	.958	-4	101	94	2b161,1b30,3b22		-3.6

BLAIR, BUDDY   Louis Nathan B9.10.1910 Columbia MS D6.7.1996 Monroe LA BL/TR/6-0/186 d4.14 Mil 1943-45 Col Louisiana St.

| 1942 | Phi A | 137 | 484 | 48 | 135 | 26 | 8 | 5 | 66 | 30 | 3 | 30 | .279 | .325 | .397 | 103 | 0 | 1-6 | .931 | -5 | 95 | 84 | 3b126 | | -0.3 |

BLAIR, PAUL   Paul L D B2.1.1944 Cushing OK BR/TR (BB 1971p)/6-0/171* d9.9 OF(31/1801/58)

1964	Bal A	8	1	0	0	0	0	0	0	0-0	0	0	1.000	1.000	.000	-99	0	0-1	1.000	-0	83	0	O6C		-0.1
1965	Bal A	119	364	49	85	19	2	5	25	32-3	4	52	.234	.302	.338	80	-9	8-5	.992	-1	101	110	O116C		-1.4
1966	†Bal A	133	303	35	84	20	2	6	33	15-0	0	36	.277	.306	.416	109	3	5-6	.990	-3	98	73	O127(2/125/0)		-0.4
1967	Bal A	151	552	72	162	27	12	11	64	50-3	5	68	.293	.353	.446	137	25	8-6	.985	9	113	151	O146C		3.2
1968	Bal A	141	421	48	89	22	1	7	38	37-4	2	60	.211	.277	.318	80	-10	4-2	.993	4	104	135	O132C/3		-1.0
1969	†Bal A★	150	625	102	178	32	5	26	76	40-0	2	72	.285	.327	.477	122	15	20-6	.988	12	114	144	O150C		2.6
1970	Bal A	133	480	79	128	24	2	18	65	56-1	3	93	.267	.344	.438	113	9	24-11	.990	11	121	122	O128C/3		1.9
1971	†Bal A	141	516	75	135	24	8	10	44	32-2	1	94	.262	.306	.397	97	-4	14-11	.991	-4	101	48	O138C		-1.3
1972	Bal A	142	477	47	111	20	8	8	49	25-0	0	78	.233	.267	.358	83	-12	7-8	.991	5	109	122	O139C		-1.3
1973	†Bal A★	146	500	73	140	25	3	10	64	43-4	2	72	.280	.334	.402	107	4	18-8	.990	6	105	139	O144C/D		0.8
1974	†Bal A	151	552	77	144	27	4	17	62	43-0	2	59	.261	.313	.417	112	7	27-9	.985	-1	106	62	O151C		0.5
1975	Bal A	140	440	51	96	13	4	5	31	25-0	0	82	.218	.257	.300	61	-24	17-11	.991	-1	101	93	O138C/1D		-3.0
1976	Bal A	145	375	59	74	16	0	3	16	22-2	2	49	.197	.245	.264	52	-23	15-6	.979	-1	104	71	O139C/D		-2.7
1977	†NY A	83	164	20	43	4	3	4	25	9-1	1	16	.262	.303	.396	91	-3	3-2	.969	-1	101	28	O79(6/42/33)/D		-0.5
1978	†NY A	75	125	10	22	5	0	2	13	9-0	0	17	.176	.231	.264	40	-10	1-1	.989	-2	98	0	O64(1/49/16),2b5,S4,3b3		-1.4
1979	NY A	2	5	0	1	0	0	0	0	0-0	0	1	.200	.200	.200	8	-1	0-0	1.000	0	173	0	O2(0/1/1)		0.0
	Cin N	75	140	7	21	4	1	2	15	11-3	0	27	.150	.209	.236	22	-16	0-0	.992	2	109	96	O67(16/56/2)		-1.5
1980	NY A	12	2	2	0	0	0	0	0	0-0	0	0	.000	.000	.000	-99	-1	0-0	1.000	0	155	0	O12(6/1/6)		0.0
Total	17	1947	6042	776	1513	282	55	134	620	449-23	23	877	.250	.302	.382	96	-50	171-93	.988	37	107	104	O1878C,2b5,3b5,S4,D4/1	21	-5.6

BLAIR, WALTER   Walter Allen "Heavy" B10.13.1883 Landrus PA D8.20.1948 Lewisburg PA BR/TR/6-0/185 d9.17 M1 Col Bucknell

1907	NY A	7	22	1	4	0	0	0	1	2	0		.182	.250	.182	35	2	1	.922	1	99	112	C7		0.0
1908	NY A	76	211	9	40	1	1	1	13	11	2		.190	.237	.237	53	-11	4	.956	-12	74	99	C60,O9(2/0/7),1b3		-2.1
1909	NY A	42	110	5	23	2	0	1	11	7	2		.209	.269	.264	68	-4	2	.964	-5	86	87	C42		-0.7
1910	NY A	6	22	2	5	0	1	0	2	0	0		.227	.227	.318	67	-1	0	.970	-1	87	125	C6		-0.2
1911	NY A	85	222	18	43	9	2	0	26	16	3		.194	.257	.252	40	-18	2	.970	2	96	105	C84/1		-1.0
1914	Buf F	128	378	22	92	11	2	0	33	32	1	64	.243	.304	.283	59	-27	6	.984	11	114	100	C128		-0.6
1915	Buf F	98	290	23	65	15	3	2	20	18	2	32	.224	.274	.317	65	-19	4	.981	-2	75	119	C97,M		-1.4
Total	7	442	1255	80	272	42	11	3	106	86	10	96	.217	.272	.275	56	-82	18	.974	-6	93	105	C424,O9(2/0/7),1b4		-6.0

BLAKE, HARRY   Harry Cooper B6.16.1874 Portsmouth OH D10.14.1919 Chicago IL BR/TR/5-7/165 d7.7

1894	Cle N	73	296	51	78	15	4	1	51	30	2	2	.264	.335	.351	63	-18	1	.932	2	133	148	O73(0/4/69)		-1.5
1895	†Cle N	85	318	50	88	10	1	3	45	31	1	33	.277	.343	.343	73	-13	11	.898	-5	99	113	O84R		-1.8
1896	†Cle N	104	383	66	92	12	5	1	43	46	0	30	.240	.322	.305	62	-21	10	.944	-2	111	145	O103(0/12/92)/S		-2.5
1897	Cle N	32	117	17	30	3	1	1	15	12	1		.256	.331	.325	70	-5	5	.989	3	63	238	O32(2/25/5)		-0.4
1898	Cle N	136	474	65	116	18	7	0	58	69	1		.245	.342	.312	89	-4	12	.952	6	133	74	O136(1/22/114),1b2		-0.4
1899	StL N	97	292	50	70	9	4	2	41	43	2		.240	.341	.318	80	-7	16	.979	1	85	100	O87(9/69/9),2b4/S1C		-1.0
Total	6	527	1880	299	474	67	22	8	253	231	7	85	.252	.336	.324	73	-68	55	.944	6	111	121	O515(12/132/373),2b4,1b3,S2/C		-7.6

BLAKE, CASEY   William Casey B8.23.1973 Des Moines IA BR/TR/6-2/205(195-210) [TorA96 7/189] d8.14 Col Wichita St.

1999	Tor A	14	39	6	10	2	0	1	1	2-0	0	7	.256	.293	.385	70	2	0-0	1.000	3	119	230	3b14		0.1
2000	Min A	7	16	1	3	2	0	0	1	3-0	1	7	.188	.333	.313	65	-1	0-0	1.000	-1	70	0	3b5/1D		-0.2
2001	Min A	13	22	1	7	1	0	0	2	1-0	0	4	.318	.400	.364	98	-0	1-0	.800	-3	80	0	3b5,1b3,D4		0.0
	Bal A	6	15	2	2	0	0	1	2	1-0	0	4	.133	.188	.333	35	-2	2-0	.967	-1	0	80	1b5/D		-0.3
	Year	19	37	3	9	1	0	1	4	4-1	0	12	.243	.317	.351	74	-1	3-0	.979	-2	49	77	1b8,3b5,D5		-0.3
2002	Min A	9	20	2	4	1	0	0	1	2-0	0	7	.200	.273	.250	39	-2	0-0	.846	-2	64	104	3b5,1b3		-0.3
2003	Cle A	152	557	80	143	35	0	17	67	38-1	10	109	.257	.312	.411	90	-8	7-9	.952	6	108	128	3b140,1b31		-0.4
2004	Cle A	152	587	90	159	36	4	28	88	68-2	9	139	.271	.354	.486	121	18	5-8	.939	-2	99	92	3b152,1b8		1.5

YEAR	TM LG	G	AB	R	H	2B	3B	HR	RBI	BB-IB	HP	SO	AVG	OBP	SLG	AOPS	ABR	SB-CS	FA	FR	RNG	THR	GAMES AT POSITION	DL	BFW
2005	Cle A	147	523	72	126	32	1	1	23	58	43-3	10	116	.241	.308	.438	100	-1	4-5	.973	-0	105	38	O138R,3b6,1b4		-0.9
Total	7	500	1779	257	454	109	4	70	220	160-7	30	397	.255	.324	.439	101	2	19-22	.945	3	103	112	3b327,O138R,1b55,D6		-0.5

BLAKELY, LINC Lincoln Howard B2.12.1912 Oakland CA D9.28.1976 Oakland CA BR/TR/6-0/180 d4.29

YEAR	TM LG	G	AB	R	H	2B	3B	HR	RBI	BB-IB	HP	SO	AVG	OBP	SLG	AOPS	ABR	SB-CS	FA	FR	RNG	THR	GAMES AT POSITION	DL	BFW
1934	Cin N	34	102	11	23	1	1	0	10	5		1	14	.225	.269	.255	42	-9	1	.987	3	109	211	O28(6/22/0)		-0.6

BLAKISTON, BOB Robert J. (b Robert J. Blackstone) B10.2.1855 San Francisco CA D12.25.1918 San Francisco CA 5-8.5/180 d5.2

YEAR	TM LG	G	AB	R	H	2B	3B	HR	RBI	BB-IB	HP	SO	AVG	OBP	SLG	AOPS	ABR	SB-CS	FA	FR	RNG	THR	GAMES AT POSITION	DL	BFW
1882	Phi AA	72	281	40	64	4	1	0	20	9				.228	.252	.249	65	-11		.855	-1	154	0	O38(0/4/34),3b34/2		-1.1
1883	Phi AA	44	167	26	41	3	3	0	26	9				.246	.284	.299	81	-4		.857	-1	93	7	O37(2/35/0),1b6,3b5		-0.5
1884	Phi AA	32	128	21	33	6	0	0	11	4				.258	.336	.305	104	1		.911	-3	119		O28(0/27/1),3b2/12S		-0.2
	Ind AA	6	18	0	4	1	0	0	1	0				.222	.263	.278	79	0		.884	-4	155	0	1b5/OR		-0.1
	Year	38	146	21	37	7	0	0	12	4				.253	.327	.301	101	1		.914	-3	51	115	O29(0/27/3),1b6,3b2/2S		-0.3
Total	3	154	594	87	142	14	4	0	46	22				.239	.280	.276	79	-14		.874	-5	103	37	O104(2/66/37),3b41,1b12,2b2/S		-1.9

BLALOCK, HANK Hank Joe B11.21.1980 San Diego CA BL/TR/6-1/192* [TexA99 3/105] d4.1

YEAR	TM LG	G	AB	R	H	2B	3B	HR	RBI	BB-IB	HP	SO	AVG	OBP	SLG	AOPS	ABR	SB-CS	FA	FR	RNG	THR	GAMES AT POSITION	DL	BFW
2002	Tex A	49	147	16	31	8	0	3	17	20-1	1	43	.211	.306	.327	68	-7	0-0	.943	-5	88	86	3b46		-1.1
2003	Tex A★	143	567	89	170	33	3	29	90	44-1	1	97	.300	.350	.522	118	-2	2-3	.959	6	99	128	3b141,2b4		1.9
2004	Tex A★	159	624	107	172	38	3	32	110	75-7	6	149	.276	.355	.500	116	15	2-2	.957	-5	98	123	3b159		1.1
2005	Tex A	161	647	80	170	34	0	25	92	51-1	3	132	.263	.318	.431	94	-6	1-0	.973	-6	99	95	3b158,D2		-1.1
Total	4	512	1985	292	543	113	6	89	309	190-10	11	421	.274	.338	.471	106	16	5-5	.962	-10	98	106	3b504,2b4,D2		0.8

BLANCHARD, JOHNNY John Edwin B2.26.1933 Minneapolis MN BL/TR/6-1/198* d9.25

YEAR	TM LG	G	AB	R	H	2B	3B	HR	RBI	BB-IB	HP	SO	AVG	OBP	SLG	AOPS	ABR	SB-CS	FA	FR	RNG	THR	GAMES AT POSITION	DL	BFW
1955	NY A	1	3	0	0	0	0	0	0	1-0	0	1	.000	.000	.000	-29	-1	0-0	1.000	0	0	0	/C		0.0
1959	NY A	49	59	6	10	1	0	2	4	7-0	0	12	.169	.258	.288	51	-4	0-0	.963	-1	137	0	C12,O8(1/0/7)/1		-0.6
1960	†NY A	53	99	8	24	3	1	4	14	6-1	1	17	.242	.292	.414	94	-2	0-0	.988	5	100	37	C28	32	0.5
1961	†NY A	93	243	38	74	10	1	21	54	27-9	4	28	.305	.382	.613	170	23	1-0	.990	-1	96	72	C48,O15(8/0/7)		2.4
1962	†NY A	93	246	33	57	7	0	13	39	28-0	1	32	.232	.309	.419	98	-1	0-0	.987	-9	90	78	O47(15/0/32),C15,1b2		-1.1
1963	†NY A	76	218	22	49	4	0	16	45	26-3	0	30	.225	.305	.463	114	3	0-0	.987	-6	74	54	O64(22/0/42)		-0.7
1964	†NY A	77	161	18	41	8	0	7	28	24-4	1	24	.255	.344	.435	115	4	0-0	.984	-5	120	68	C25,O14(6/0/8),1b3		-0.1
1965	NY A	12	34	1	5	1	0	1	3	7-2	0	3	.147	.286	.265	60	-2	0-0	.961	-1	100	79	C12		-0.2
	KC A	52	120	10	24	2	0	2	11	8-1	1	16	.200	.267	.267	49	-8	0-0	1.000	-5	84	0	O20(1/0/19),C14		-1.4
	Year	64	154	11	29	3	0	3	14	15-3	1	19	.188	.259	.266	52	-10	0-0	.971	-6	72	64	C26,O20(1/0/19)		-1.6
	Mil N	10	10	1	1	0	0	1	2	2-0	0	1	.100	.250	.400	79	0	0-0	—	0			OL		-0.1
Total	8	516	1193	137	285	36	2	67	200	136-20	7	163	.239	.317	.441	109	12	2-0	.987	-21	82	55	O169(54/0/115),C155,1b6	32	-1.3

BLANCO, ANDRES Andres Eloy (Perez) B4.11.1984 Urama, Venez BB/TR/5-10/150(150-180) d4.17

YEAR	TM LG	G	AB	R	H	2B	3B	HR	RBI	BB-IB	HP	SO	AVG	OBP	SLG	AOPS	ABR	SB-CS	FA	FR	RNG	THR	GAMES AT POSITION	DL	BFW
2004	KC A	19	60	9	19	2	2	0	5	5-0	1	6	.317	.379	.417	107	1	1-2	.959	4	116	135	S19		0.5
2005	KC A	26	79	6	17	0	1	0	5	0-0	1	5	.215	.220	.241	26	-9	0-1	.977	7	110	140	2b24,S7		-0.1
Total	2	45	139	15	36	2	3	0	10	5-0	2	11	.259	.291	.317	63	-8	1-3	.964	11	113	130	S26,2b24		0.4

BLANCO, DAMASO Damaso (Caripe) B11.12.1941 Curiepe, Venez BR/TR/5-10/165* d5.26

YEAR	TM LG	G	AB	R	H	2B	3B	HR	RBI	BB-IB	HP	SO	AVG	OBP	SLG	AOPS	ABR	SB-CS	FA	FR	RNG	THR	GAMES AT POSITION	DL	BFW
1972	SF N	39	20	5	7	1	0	0	2	4-0	0	3	.350	.440	.400	143	2	2-1	.889	-1	91	182	3b19,S8,2b3		0.1
1973	SF N	28	12	4	0	0	0	0	0	1-0	0	2	.000	.077	.000	-74	-3	0-0	1.000	-1	50	0	3b7,S5,2b3		-0.4
1974	SF N	5	1	0	0	0	0	0	0	0-0	0	1	.000	.000	.000	-96	0	1-0	—	0			/H		0.0
Total	3	72	33	9	7	1	0	0	2	5-0	0	6	.212	.308	.242	58	-1	3-1	.929	-2	81	139	3b26,S13,2b6		-0.3

BLANCO, HENRY Henry Ramon B8.29.1971 Caracas, Venez BR/TR/5-11/190(168-225) d7.25 [DL 1998 LA N 120]

YEAR	TM LG	G	AB	R	H	2B	3B	HR	RBI	BB-IB	HP	SO	AVG	OBP	SLG	AOPS	ABR	SB-CS	FA	FR	RNG	THR	GAMES AT POSITION	DL	BFW
1997	LA N	3	5	1	2	0	0	1	1	0-0	0	1	.400	.400	1.000	269	-0	0-0	1.000	-0	0	0	/13		0.1
1999	Col N	88	263	30	61	12	3	6	28	34-1	1	38	.232	.320	.369	59	-16	1-1	.992	19	102	161	C86/OL		0.7
2000	Mil N	93	284	29	67	24	0	7	31	36-6	0	60	.236	.318	.394	80	-8	0-3	.991	14	184	165	C88	16	0.9
2001	Mil N	104	314	33	66	18	0	6	31	34-6	2	72	.210	.290	.344	65	-17	0-1	.992	10	131	113	C102		0.0
2002	†Atl N	81	221	17	45	9	1	6	22	20-5	1	51	.204	.267	.335	62	-14	0-2	.993	-0	106	115	C79	15	-1.0
2003	Atl N	55	151	11	30	8	0	1	13	10-2	1	21	.199	.252	.272	37	-14	0-0	.996	-4	67	109	C52		-1.5
2004	†Min A	114	315	36	65	19	1	10	37	21-0	3	56	.206	.260	.368	60	-19	0-3	.991	12	160	127	C114		-0.2
2005	Chi N	54	161	16	39	6	0	6	25	11-1	0	24	.242	.287	.391	74	-7	0-0	.998	13	126	189	C54		1.0
Total	8	592	1714	173	375	96	8	43	188	166-21	8	323	.219	.288	.359	64	-94	4-10	.993	63	131	138	C575/OL31	151	0.9

BLANCO, OSSIE Oswaldo Carlos (Diaz) B9.8.1945 Caracas, Venez BR/TR/6-0/185* d5.26

YEAR	TM LG	G	AB	R	H	2B	3B	HR	RBI	BB-IB	HP	SO	AVG	OBP	SLG	AOPS	ABR	SB-CS	FA	FR	RNG	THR	GAMES AT POSITION	DL	BFW
1970	Chi A	34	66	4	13	0	0	0	8	3-0	0	14	.197	.225	.197	19	-7	0-1	.993	-0	103	83	1b22/OL		-0.9
1974	Cle A	18	36	1	7	0	0	0	2	7-0	0	4	.194	.326	.194	53	-2	0-3	.992	-2	50	104	1b16/D		-0.6
Total	2	52	102	5	20	0	0	0	10	10-0	0	18	.196	.263	.196	31	-9	0-4	.993	-2	76	94	1b38/DOL		-1.5

BLANCO, TONY Tony Hemiphere (Cabrera) B11.10.1981 San Juan de Maguana, D.R. BR/TR/6-1/175 d4.4

YEAR	TM LG	G	AB	R	H	2B	3B	HR	RBI	BB-IB	HP	SO	AVG	OBP	SLG	AOPS	ABR	SB-CS	FA	FR	RNG	THR	GAMES AT POSITION	DL	BFW
2005	Was N	56	62	7	11	3	0	1	7	2-0	1	19	.177	.215	.274	29	-7	1-0	1.000	-0	86	288	O11(9/0/2),3b5,1b3	25	-0.7

BLANK, COONIE Frank Ignatz B10.18.1892 St.Louis MO D12.8.1961 St.Louis MO BR/TR/5-11/165 d8.15

YEAR	TM LG	G	AB	R	H	2B	3B	HR	RBI	BB-IB	HP	SO	AVG	OBP	SLG	AOPS	ABR	SB-CS	FA	FR	RNG	THR	GAMES AT POSITION	DL	BFW
1909	StL N	1	2	0	0	0	0	0	0	0-0	0	0	.000	.000	.000	-99	0	0-0	1.000	-0	55	0	/C		-0.1

BLANKENSHIP, CLIFF Clifford Douglas B4.10.1880 Columbus GA D4.26.1956 Oakland CA BR/TR/5-10.5/165 d4.17

YEAR	TM LG	G	AB	R	H	2B	3B	HR	RBI	BB-IB	HP	SO	AVG	OBP	SLG	AOPS	ABR	SB-CS	FA	FR	RNG	THR	GAMES AT POSITION	DL	BFW
1905	Cin N	19	56	8	11	1	1	0	7	4	0		.196	.250	.250	44	-4	1	.960	-3	47	97	1b15		-0.7
1907	Was A	37	102	4	23	2	0	0	6	3	0		.225	.248	.245	62	-5	3	.991	-1	85	123	C22,1b9		-0.8
1909	Was A	39	60	4	15	1	0	0	9	0	0		.250	.250	.267	66	-3	2	.907	-6	69	83	C17,O4(1/1/2)		-0.4
Total	3	95	218	16	49	4	1	0	22	7	0		.225	.249	.252	58	-12	6	.964	-9	80	110	C39,1b24,O4(1/1/2)		-1.9

BLANKENSHIP, LANCE Lance Robert B12.6.1963 Portland OR BR/TR/6-0/185* [OakA86 10/249] d9.4 Col California-Davis OF(71/66/71) [DL 1994 Oak A 131]

YEAR	TM LG	G	AB	R	H	2B	3B	HR	RBI	BB-IB	HP	SO	AVG	OBP	SLG	AOPS	ABR	SB-CS	FA	FR	RNG	THR	GAMES AT POSITION	DL	BFW
1988	Oak A	10	3	1	0	0	0	0	0	0-0	0	1	.000	.000	.000	-99	-4	0-1	1.000	-1	42	0	2b4,D4		-0.2
1989	†Oak A	58	125	22	29	5	1	1	4	8-0	0	31	.232	.276	.312	68	-6	5-1	1.000	-1	120	0	O25(4/0/21),2b4,D10		-0.5
1990	†Oak A	86	136	18	26	3	0	0	10	20-0	0	23	.191	.295	.213	46	-9	3-1	.947	-2	99	62	3b28,O28(10/1/17),2b20/1D		-1.1
1991	Oak A	90	185	33	46	8	0	3	21	23-0	3	42	.249	.336	.341	94	-1	12-3	.983	10	107	107	2b45,O28(18/0/11),3b14,D6		1.1
1992	†Oak A	123	349	59	84	24	1	3	34	82-2	6	57	.241	.393	.341	113	13	21-7	.992	7	104	104	2b78,O51(22/16/20),1b7,D3	33	2.3
1993	Oak A	94	252	43	48	8	1	2	23	67-0	2	64	.190	.363	.254	73	-6	13-5	.994	-0	109	29	O66(17/49/2),2b19,1b6,S2,D5	49	-0.4
Total	6	461	1050	176	233	48	3	9	92	200-2	11	218	.222	.350	.299	86	-10	54-18	.987	15	112	33	O198L,2b190,3b42,D34,1b14,S2	213	1.2

BLANKS, LARVELL Larvell B1.28.1950 Del Rio TX BR/TR/5-8/167* [AtlN69 3/60] d7.19

YEAR	TM LG	G	AB	R	H	2B	3B	HR	RBI	BB-IB	HP	SO	AVG	OBP	SLG	AOPS	ABR	SB-CS	FA	FR	RNG	THR	GAMES AT POSITION	DL	BFW
1972	Atl N	33	85	10	28	5	1	1	7	7-0	0	12	.329	.376	.424	118	2	0-0	1.000	5	116	113	2b18,S4,3b2		0.9
1973	Atl N	17	18	1	4	0	0	0	1	1-0	0	3	.222	.263	.222	33	-2	0-0	—	-1	0	0	3b3,2b2,S2		-0.3
1974	Atl N	3	8	0	2	0	0	0	1	0-0	0	0	.250	.250	.250	39	-1	0-0	.889	-1	111	0	S2		-0.1
1975	Atl N	141	471	49	110	13	3	3	38	38-1	2	43	.234	.292	.293	61	-25	4-3	.960	-8	106	85	S129,2b12		-1.9
1976	Cle A	104	328	45	92	8	7	5	44	30-0	0	31	.280	.337	.393	115	5	1-2	.977	-7	86	116	S56,2b46,3b2,D3		-0.6
1977	Cle A	105	322	43	92	10	4	6	38	19-1	0	37	.286	.324	.398	99	-1	3-0	.960	-11	83	75	S66,3b18,2b12,D6		-0.6
1978	Cle A	70	193	19	49	10	0	2	20	10-0	0	16	.254	.285	.337	77	-6	0-0	.926	-4	98	100	S43,2b17,3b3/D		-0.6
1979	Tex A	68	120	13	24	5	0	1	15	11-0	0	9	.200	.259	.267	45	-9	0-0	.972	-7	90	108	S49,2b16/D		-1.3
1980	Atl N	88	221	23	45	6	0	2	12	16-1	0	27	.204	.255	.258	44	-17	1-2	.947	13	117	138	S56,3b43/2		-0.3
Total	9	629	1766	203	446	57	14	20	172	132-3	3	178	.253	.300	.335	78	-54	9-7	.957	-21	99	94	S407,2b124,3b71,D11		-3.6

BLASINGAME, DON Don Lee B3.16.1932 Corinth MS D4.13.2005 Fountain Hills AZ BR/TR/5-10/165* d9.20

YEAR	TM LG	G	AB	R	H	2B	3B	HR	RBI	BB-IB	HP	SO	AVG	OBP	SLG	AOPS	ABR	SB-CS	FA	FR	RNG	THR	GAMES AT POSITION	DL	BFW
1955	StL N	5	16	4	6	1	0	0	1	6-1	0	1	.375	.545	.438	165	2	1-1	.955	0	124	37	2b3,S2		0.3
1956	StL N	150	587	94	153	22	7	0	27	72-0	3	52	.261	.344	.322	81	-14	8-8	.986	17	106	132	2b98,S49,3b2		1.3
1957	StL N	154	650	108	176	25	7	8	58	71-4	1	49	.271	.343	.368	89	-8	21-9	.984	20	110	125	2b154		2.5
1958	StL N★	143	547	71	150	19	10	2	36	57-2	1	47	.274	.343	.356	83	-13	20-5	.964	-2	100	95	2b137		-0.3
1959	StL N	150	615	90	178	26	7	1	24	67-2	2	42	.289	.361	.359	87	-9	15-15	.979	20	107	103	2b150		2.0
1960	SF N	136	523	72	123	12	8	2	31	49-1	2	53	.235	.302	.300	70	-22	14-2	.979	-4	95	84	2b133		-1.5
1961	SF N	3	1	1	0	0	0	0	0	2-0	0	1	.000	.667	.000	100	0	0-0	—	0			/H		0.0
	†Cin N	123	450	59	100	18	4	1	21	39-0	2	38	.222	.286	.287	52	-31	4-3	.972	-15	90	68	2b116		-3.7
	Year	126	451	60	100	18	4	1	21	41-0	2	39	.222	.288	.286	53	-30	4-3	.972	-15	90	68	2b116		-3.7
1962	Cin N	141	494	77	139	9	7	2	35	63-2	2	44	.281	.364	.340	88	-7	4-3	.976	-4	96	79	2b137		0.1
1963	Cin N	18	31	4	9	0	0	0	0	7-0	0	5	.161	.316	.226	57	-1	0-1	.974	-1	72	0	2b11,3b2		-0.3
	Was A	69	254	29	65	10	2	2	12	24-1	0	18	.256	.320	.335	84	-5	3-2	.991	10	110	130	2b64		1.1

YEAR	TM LG	G	AB	R	H	2B	3B	HR	RBI	BB-IB	HP	SO	AVG	OBP	SLG	AOPS	ABR	SB-CS	FA	FR	RNG	THR	GAMES AT POSITION	DL	BFW
1964	Was A	143	506	56	135	17	2	1	34	40-1	0	44	.267	.320	.314	78	-15	8-5	.977	-12	102	88	2b135		-1.7
1965	Was A	129	403	47	90	8	8	1	18	35-1	2	45	.223	.287	.290	66	-19	5-4	.984	2	100	105	2b110		-1.0
1966	Was A	68	200	18	43	9	0	1	11	18-0	0	21	.215	.280	.275	61	-10	2-1	.984	-1	100	105	2b58/S		-0.6
	KC A	12	19	1	3	0	0	0	1	2-0	0	3	.158	.238	.158	17	-2	0-1	1.000	1	122	112	2b4		-0.2
	Year	80	219	19	46	9	0	1	12	20-0	0	24	.210	.276	.265	57	-12	2-2	.985	0	101	105	2b62/S		-0.8
Total	12	1444	5296	731	1366	178	62	21	308	552-15	15	462	.258	.329	.327	78	-154	105-60	.979	30	101	100	2b1310,S52,3b4		-2.0

BLATNIK, JOHNNY John Louis B3.10.1921 Bridgeport OH D1.21.2004 Lansing OH BR/TR/6-0/195* d4.21

YEAR	TM LG	G	AB	R	H	2B	3B	HR	RBI	BB-IB	HP	SO	AVG	OBP	SLG	AOPS	ABR	SB-CS	FA	FR	RNG	THR	GAMES AT POSITION	DL	BFW
1948	Phi N	121	415	56	108	27	8	6	45	31	2	77	.260	.315	.407	96	-4	3	.946	-0	100	110	O105L		-1.2
1949	Phi N	6	8	3	1	0	0	0	0	4		1	.125	.417	.125	53	0	0	1.000	-0	84	0	O2R		0.0
1950	Phi N	4	4	0	1	0	0	0	0	2	0	3	.250	.500	.250	106	0	0	1.000	0	114	0	/OL		0.0
	StL N	7	20	0	3	0	0	0	1	3		1	.150	.261	.150	11	-3	0	.875	-2	66	279	O7(2/0/7)		-0.3
	Year	11	24	0	4	0	0	0	1	5	0	5	.167	.310	.167	29	-2	0	.900	-0	73	239	O8(3/0/7)		-0.3
Total	3	138	447	59	113	27	8	6	46	40	2	82	.253	.317	.389	91	-7	3	.945	-1	98	115	O115(108/0/9)		-1.5

BLATTNER, BUDDY Robert Garnett B2.8.1920 St.Louis MO BR/TR/6-0.5/180 d4.18 Mil 1943-45

YEAR	TM LG	G	AB	R	H	2B	3B	HR	RBI	BB-IB	HP	SO	AVG	OBP	SLG	AOPS	ABR	SB-CS	FA	FR	RNG	THR	GAMES AT POSITION	DL	BFW
1942	StL N	19	23	3	1	0	0	0	1	3	1	4	.043	.185	.043	-29	-4	0	.900	-1	92	68	S13,2b3		-0.4
1946	NY N	126	420	63	107	18	6	11	49	56	6	52	.255	.351	.405	113	8	12	.976	4	101	93	2b114/1		1.9
1947	NY N	55	153	28	40	9	2	0	13	21	0	19	.261	.351	.346	85	-3	4	.947	-1	110	64	2b34,3b11		-0.2
1948	NY N	8	20	3	4	1	0	0	0	3	0	2	.200	.304	.250	51	-1	2	1.000	2	152	129	2b7		0.1
1949	Phi N	64	97	15	24	6	0	5	21	19	0	17	.247	.371	.464	126	4	0	.981	-6	87	69	2b15,3b12/S		-0.1
Total	5	272	713	112	176	34	8	16	84	102	7	96	.247	.347	.384	102	4	18	.971	-1	103	87	2b173,3b23,S14/1		1.3

BLAUSER, JEFF Jeffrey Michael B11.8.1965 Los Gatos CA BR/TR/6-0/170(190-190) [AtlN84 S1/5] d7.5 Col Sacramento (CA) City

YEAR	TM LG	G	AB	R	H	2B	3B	HR	RBI	BB-IB	HP	SO	AVG	OBP	SLG	AOPS	ABR	SB-CS	FA	FR	RNG	THR	GAMES AT POSITION	DL	BFW
1987	Atl N	51	165	11	40	6	3	2	15	18-1	3	34	.242	.328	.352	77	-5	7-3	.962	4	116	93	S50		0.4
1988	Atl N	18	67	7	16	3	1	2	7	2-0	1	11	.239	.268	.403	88	-1	0-1	.967	1	143	69	2b9,S8		0.0
1989	Atl N	142	456	63	123	24	2	12	46	38-2	1	101	.270	.325	.410	107	4	5-2	.929	-16	97	85	3b78,2b39,S30,O2C		-1.0
1990	Atl N	115	386	46	104	24	3	8	39	35-1	5	70	.269	.338	.409	99	0	3-5	.961	-3	100	90	S93,2b14,3b9/OC	16	0.4
1991	†Atl N	129	352	49	91	14	3	11	54	54-4	2	59	.259	.358	.409	109	6	5-6	.948	-14	83	91	S85,2b32,3b18		-0.5
1992	†Atl N	123	343	61	90	19	3	14	46	46-2	4	82	.262	.354	.458	121	11	5-5	.968	-14	91	75	S106,2b21/3		0.1
1993	†Atl N★	161	597	110	182	29	2	15	73	85-0	16	109	.305	.401	.436	122	24	16-6	.970	-16	93	106	S161		2.1
1994	†Atl N	96	380	56	98	21	4	6	45	38-0	5	64	.258	.329	.382	83	-9	1-3	.970	4	100	85	S96	18	0.2
1995	†Atl N	115	431	60	91	16	2	12	31	57-2	12	107	.211	.319	.341	71	-17	8-5	.970	3	97	102	S115		-0.6
1996	Atl N	83	265	48	65	14	1	10	35	40-3	6	54	.245	.356	.419	98	0	6-0	.926	-14	89	95	S79	67	-0.7
1997	†Atl N★	151	519	90	160	31	4	17	70	70-6	20	101	.308	.405	.482	131	27	5-1	.973	-18	88	107	S149/D		2.0
1998	†Chi N	119	361	49	79	11	3	4	26	60-1	8	93	.219	.340	.299	68	-15	2-2	.965	-22	88	58	S106	15	-2.9
1999	Chi N	104	200	41	48	5	1	9	26	26-0	8	52	.240	.347	.420	94	-2	2-2	.961	-5	78	92	2b25,S22,3b18/OL		-0.5
Total	13	1407	4522	691	1187	217	33	122	513	569-22	91	937	.262	.354	.406	101	23	65-41	.964	-110	93	91	S1100,3b140,3b124,O4(1/3/0)/D	116	-1.0

BLAYLOCK, MARV Marvin Edward B9.30.1929 Ft.Smith AR D10.23.1993 Conway AR BL/TL/6-1.5/175* d9.26 Col Arkansas-Fort Smith [JC]

YEAR	TM LG	G	AB	R	H	2B	3B	HR	RBI	BB-IB	HP	SO	AVG	OBP	SLG	AOPS	ABR	SB-CS	FA	FR	RNG	THR	GAMES AT POSITION	DL	BFW
1950	NY N	1	1	0	0	0	0	0	0	0	0	0	.000	.000	.000	-99	0	0			0		/H		0.0
1955	Phi N	113	259	30	54	7	7	3	24	31-2	1	43	.208	.293	.324	66	-13	6-1	.991	2	98	69	1b77,O6(4/0/2)		-1.4
1956	Phi N	136	460	61	117	14	8	10	50	50-2	2	86	.254	.327	.385	93	-5	5-1	.992	-4	85	91	1b124/OR		-1.5
1957	Phi N	37	26	5	4	0	0	2	4	3-0	3	8	.154	.313	.385	89	-1	0-0	1.000	1	76	0	1b12/OR		-0.1
Total	4	287	746	96	175	21	15	15	78	84-4	6	137	.235	.314	.363	83	-18	11-2	.992	-2	89	82	1b213,O8(4/0/5)		-3.0

BLEFARY, CURT Curtis Le Roy B7.5.1943 Brooklyn NY D1.28.2001 Pompano Beach FL BL/TR/6-2/195(195-210) d4.14 Col Wagner OF(323/0/232)

YEAR	TM LG	G	AB	R	H	2B	3B	HR	RBI	BB-IB	HP	SO	AVG	OBP	SLG	AOPS	ABR	SB-CS	FA	FR	RNG	THR	GAMES AT POSITION	DL	BFW
1965	Bal A	144	462	72	120	23	4	22	70	88-4	3	73	.260	.381	.470	138	26	4-2	.979	1	96	121	O136(63/0/73)		2.0
1966	†Bal A	131	419	73	107	14	2	23	64	73-3	6	56	.255	.371	.468	142	26	1-4	.976	-2	92	82	O109,1b20		1.7
1967	Bal A	155	554	69	134	19	5	22	81	73-11	8	94	.242	.337	.413	122	16	4-4	.968	11	94	188	O103(86/0/19),1b52		1.9
1968	Bal A	137	451	50	90	8	1	15	39	65-11	4	66	.200	.301	.322	90	-4	6-3	.962	-6	102	183	O92(55/0/46),C40,1b12		-1.6
1969	Hou N	155	542	66	137	26	7	12	67	77-10	4	79	.253	.347	.393	109	8	8-7	.987	6	109	96	1b152/OL		0.1
1970	NY A	99	269	34	57	6	0	9	37	43-3	3	37	.212	.324	.335	87	-4	1-3	.972	-9	80	21	O79R,1b6		-1.9
1971	NY A	21	36	4	7	1	0	1	2	3-0	1	5	.194	.256	.306	61	1	0-0	.875	-2	70	335	O6R,1b4		-0.3
	†Oak A	50	101	15	22	2	0	5	12	15-2	1	15	.218	.325	.386	103	0	0-1	.975	-2	63	112	C14,O14(8/0/6),3b5,2b2		-0.2
	Year	71	137	19	29	3	0	6	14	18-2	1	20	.212	.308	.365	92	-2	0-1	.958	-2	85	233	O20(8/0/12),C14,3b5,1b4,2b2		-0.5
1972	Oak A	8	11	2	5	2	0	0	1	0-0	1	0	.455	.417	.636	233	2	0-0	—	0	0	0	/120L		0.2
	SD N	74	102	10	20	3	0	3	9	19-3	0	18	.196	.320	.314	88	-1	0-0	.982	-3	50	125	O12,1b6,3b3,O3R		-0.5
Total	9	974	2947	394	699	104	20	112	382	456-47	29	444	.237	.342	.400	115	67	24-24	.972	-5	93	126	O544L,1b253,C66,3b8,2b3		1.4

BLESSITT, IKE Isaiah B9.30.1949 Detroit MI BR/TR/5-11/185 [DetA67 15/295] d9.7

YEAR	TM LG	G	AB	R	H	2B	3B	HR	RBI	BB-IB	HP	SO	AVG	OBP	SLG	AOPS	ABR	SB-CS	FA	FR	RNG	THR	GAMES AT POSITION	DL	BFW
1972	Det A	4	5	0	0	0	0	0	0	0-0	1	2	.000	.000	.000	-97	-1	0-0	1.000	0	168	0	/O(1/0/1)		-0.1

BLIGH, NED Edwin Forrest B6.30.1864 Brooklyn NY D4.18.1892 Brooklyn NY BR/TR/5-11/172 d6.26

YEAR	TM LG	G	AB	R	H	2B	3B	HR	RBI	BB-IB	HP	SO	AVG	OBP	SLG	AOPS	ABR	SB-CS	FA	FR	RNG	THR	GAMES AT POSITION	DL	BFW
1886	Bal AA	3	9	0	0	0	0	0	1	0			.000	.100	.000	-69	-2	0	.833	-1			C3		-0.3
1888	Cin AA	3	5	0	0	0	0	0	0	0			.000	.000	.000	-95	-1	0	1.000	-0			C2/OR		-0.1
1889	Col AA	28	93	6	13	1	1	0	5	4	3	14	.140	.200	.172	7	-12	2	.927	-3			C28		-1.1
1890	Col AA	8	29	2	6	2	0	0	5	2	0		.207	.258	.276	62	-1	0	.933	1	105	141	C8		0.0
	†Lou AA	24	73	9	15	0	1	1	9	9	0		.205	.293	.247	60	-4	1	.921	2	135	92	C24		0.0
	Year	32	102	11	21	2	1	1	14	11	0		.206	.283	.255	61	-5	1	.925	3	127	98	C32		0.0
Total	4	66	209	17	34	3	1	1	19	16	3	14	.163	.232	.201	28	-20	3	.923	-2	127	98	C65/OR		-1.5

BLISS, FRANK Frank Eugene B12.10.1852 Chicago IL D1.8.1929 Nashville TN d6.20 Col Michigan

YEAR	TM LG	G	AB	R	H	2B	3B	HR	RBI	BB-IB	HP	SO	AVG	OBP	SLG	AOPS	ABR	SB-CS	FA	FR	RNG	THR	GAMES AT POSITION	DL	BFW
1878	Mil N	2	8	0	1	0	0	0		0			.125	.125	.125	-17	-1		1.000	-1	93	0	/3C		-0.1

BLISS, JACK John Joseph Albert B1.9.1882 Vancouver WA D10.23.1968 Temple City CA BR/TR/5-9/185 d5.10 Col California-Davis

YEAR	TM LG	G	AB	R	H	2B	3B	HR	RBI	BB-IB	HP	SO	AVG	OBP	SLG	AOPS	ABR	SB-CS	FA	FR	RNG	THR	GAMES AT POSITION	DL	BFW
1908	StL N	44	136	9	29	4	0	1	5	8	2		.213	.267	.265	73	-9	3	.992	-2	67	117	C43		-0.2
1909	StL N	35	113	12	25	2	1	1	8	12	2		.221	.307	.283	89	-1	2	.951	-2	79	96	C32		-0.1
1910	StL N	16	33	2	2	0	0	0	3	4	0	8	.061	.162	.061	-36	-6	0	.980	-2	80	C13		-0.7
1911	StL N	97	258	36	59	6	4	1	27	42	2	25	.229	.341	.295	81	-5	5	.952	-15	75	105	C84/S		-1.4
1912	StL N	49	114	11	28	3	1	0	18	19	4	14	.246	.372	.289	84	-1	3	.973	-6	69	96	C41		-0.4
Total	5	241	654	70	143	15	6	3	61	85	10	47	.219	.318	.274	76	-17	13	.966	-27	73	103	C213/S		-2.8

BLOCK, BRUNO James John (b James John Blochowicz) B3.13.1885 Wisconsin Rapids WI D8.6.1937 S.Milwaukee WI BR/TR/5-9/185 d8.5

YEAR	TM LG	G	AB	R	H	2B	3B	HR	RBI	BB-IB	HP	SO	AVG	OBP	SLG	AOPS	ABR	SB-CS	FA	FR	RNG	THR	GAMES AT POSITION	DL	BFW
1907	Was A	24	57	3	8	2	1	0	4		0		.140	.169	.211	23	-5	0	.949	-4	78	102	C21		-0.9
1910	Chi A	55	152	12	32	1	1	0	9	13	0		.211	.273	.230	60	-7	3	.964	2	120	102	C47		0.0
1911	Chi A	39	115	11	35	6	1	1	18	6	0		.304	.339	.400	109	1	1	.972	0	145	74	C38		0.4
1912	Chi A	46	136	8	35	5	6	0	26	7			.257	.294	.382	96	-2	1	.980	2	99	93	C46		0.3
1914	Chi F	45	106	8	21	4	1	0	14	11	0	17	.198	.274	.255	47	-10	1	.966	3	140	88	C34		-0.5
Total	5	209	566	42	131	18	10	1	69	39	0	17	.231	.281	.304	74	-23	5	.969	3	120	91	C186		-0.7

BLOCK, CY Seymour B5.4.1919 Brooklyn NY D9.22.2004 Manhasset NY BR/TR/6-0/180 d9.7 Mil 1943-45

YEAR	TM LG	G	AB	R	H	2B	3B	HR	RBI	BB-IB	HP	SO	AVG	OBP	SLG	AOPS	ABR	SB-CS	FA	FR	RNG	THR	GAMES AT POSITION	DL	BFW
1942	Chi N	9	33	6	12	1	1	0	4	3	0	3	.364	.417	.455	161	2	2	.917	-2	70	59	3b8/2		0.1
1945	†Chi N	2	7	1	1	0	0	0	1	0	0	1	.143	.143	.143	-21	-1	0	1.000	1	147	0	/23		-0.1
1946	Chi N	6	13	2	3	0	0	0	4	4	0		.231	.412	.231	86	0	0	1.000	1	105	582	3b4		0.1
Total	3	17	53	9	16	1	1	0	5	7	0	3	.302	.383	.358	118	1	2	.947	-1	82	195	3b13,2b2		0.1

BLOCKER, TERRY Terry Fennell B8.18.1959 Columbia SC BL/TL/6-2/195* [NYN81 1/4] d4.11 Col Tennessee St.

YEAR	TM LG	G	AB	R	H	2B	3B	HR	RBI	BB-IB	HP	SO	AVG	OBP	SLG	AOPS	ABR	SB-CS	FA	FR	RNG	THR	GAMES AT POSITION	DL	BFW
1985	NY N	18	15	1	1	0	0	0	0	1-0	0	5	.067	.125	.067	-46	-3	0-0	1.000	-0	75	0	O5(3/1/1)	15	-0.4
1988	Atl N	66	198	13	42	4	2	2	10	10-3	1	20	.212	.250	.283	51	-13	1-1	.994	1	108	37	O61C		-1.4
1989	Atl N	26	31	1	7	1	0	1	1	1-0	0	5	.226	.250	.258	45	-2	1-0	1.000	-0	93	0	O8(2/2/4)/P		-0.2
Total	3	110	244	15	50	5	2	3	11	12-3	1	30	.205	.242	.266	44	-18	2-1	.994	0	106	33	O74(5/6/4/5)/P	15	-2.0

BLOGG, WES Wesley Collins B1855 Norfolk VA D3.10.1897 Baltimore MD 5-8/155 d6.20

YEAR	TM LG	G	AB	R	H	2B	3B	HR	RBI	BB-IB	HP	SO	AVG	OBP	SLG	AOPS	ABR	SB-CS	FA	FR	RNG	THR	GAMES AT POSITION	DL	BFW
1883	Pit AA	9	34	0	5	0	0	0					.147	.147	.147	-5	-4		.881	-2			C6,O3R		-0.5

BLOMBERG, RON Ronald Mark "Boomer" B8.23.1948 Atlanta GA BL/TR/6-1/205(185-205) [NYA67 1/1] d9.10 [DL 1977 NY A 180]

YEAR	TM LG	G	AB	R	H	2B	3B	HR	RBI	BB-IB	HP	SO	AVG	OBP	SLG	AOPS	ABR	SB-CS	FA	FR	RNG	THR	GAMES AT POSITION	DL	BFW
1969	NY A	4	6	0	3	0	0	0		1-0	0	0	.500	.571	.500	209	1	0-0	1.000	-0	70	0	O2L		0.1
1971	NY A	64	199	30	64	6	2	7	31	14-3	0	23	.322	.363	.477	144	10	2-4	.970	-4	91	27	O57R		0.3
1972	NY A	107	299	36	80	22	1	14	49	38-4	3	26	.268	.355	.488	153	20	0-2	.985	-7	72	127	1b95		0.6
1973	NY A	100	301	45	99	13	1	12	57	34-4	0	25	.329	.395	.498	154	22	2-0	.980	1	122	128	D55,1b41		1.9
1974	NY A	90	264	39	82	11	2	10	48	29-2	2	33	.311	.375	.481	149	17	2-1	1.000	1	108	175	D58,O19(2/0/17)		1.6
1975	NY A	34	106	18	27	8	2	4	17	13-1	0	10	.255	.336	.481	130	4	0-0	1.000	0	112	0	D27/OR	106	0.3
1976	NY A	1	2	0	0	0	0	0	0	0-0	0	0	.000	.000	.000	-99	-1	0-0	—		0		/D	148	-0.1
1978	Chi A	61	156	16	36	7	0	5	22	11-2	0	17	.231	.280	.372	81	-4	0-0	.986	-1	69	35	D36,1b7		-0.7
Total	8	461	1333	184	391	67	8	52	224	140-16	5	134	.293	.360	.473	140	69	6-7	.983	-10	86	122	D177,1b143,O79(4/0/75)	434	4.0

BLONG, JOE Joseph Myles B9.17.1853 St.Louis MO D9.17.1892 St.Louis MO BR/TR d5.4 ▲

YEAR	TM LG	G	AB	R	H	2B	3B	HR	RBI	BB-IB	HP	SO	AVG	OBP	SLG	AOPS	ABR	SB-CS	FA	FR	RNG	THR	GAMES AT POSITION	DL	BFW
1875	RS NA	16	68	3	10	1	0	0	5	0		7	.147	.147	.176	13	-5	1-0	.927	3	134	82	P15,O4(2/2/0)		0.1
1876	StL N	62	264	30	62	7	4	0	30	2		9	.235	.241	.292	81	-5		.895	-1	124	123	O62R/P		-0.5
1877	StL N	58	218	17	47	8	3	0	13	4		22	.216	.230	.280	63	-8		.835	-2	86	0	O40(13/4/23),P25		-0.7
Total	2	120	482	47	109	15	7	0	43	6		31	.226	.236	.286	72	-13		.867	-3	110	77	O102(13/4/85),P26		-1.2

BLOODWORTH, JIMMY James Henry B7.26.1917 Tallahassee FL D8.17.2002 Apalachicola FL BR/TR/5-11/180* d9.14 Mil 1944-46

YEAR	TM LG	G	AB	R	H	2B	3B	HR	RBI	BB-IB	HP	SO	AVG	OBP	SLG	AOPS	ABR	SB-CS	FA	FR	RNG	THR	GAMES AT POSITION	DL	BFW
1937	Was A	15	50	3	11	2	1	0	8	5	0	8	.220	.291	.300	51	-4	0-1	.946	-1	102	98	2b14		-0.4
1939	Was A	83	318	34	92	24	1	4	40	10	1	26	.289	.313	.409	90	-6	3-1	.972	12	101	135	2b73,O5R		0.9
1940	Was A	119	469	47	115	17	8	11	70	16	1	71	.245	.272	.386	73	-23	3-1	.978	14	97	106	2b96,1b17,3b6		-0.4
1941	Was A	142	506	59	124	24	3	7	66	41	1	58	.245	.303	.346	75	-20	1-1	.971	27	109	114	2b132,3b6/S		1.5
1942	Det A	137	533	62	129	23	1	13	57	35	5	63	.242	.295	.362	78	-17	2-8	.972	10	104	75	2b134,S2		-0.1
1943	Det A	129	474	41	114	23	4	9	52	29	3	59	.241	.289	.344	79	-14	4-7	.972	15	104	86	2b129		0.8
1946	Det A	76	249	25	61	8	1	5	36	12	2	26	.245	.285	.345	71	-10	3-3	.974	-1	94	107	2b71		-0.8
1947	Pit N	88	316	27	79	9	0	7	48	16	2	39	.250	.290	.345	66	-16	1	.979	-16	84	95	2b87		-2.8
1949	Cin N	134	452	40	118	20	1	9	59	27	1	36	.261	.304	.385	83	-12	1	.981	-4	100	93	2b92,1b23,3b8		-1.2
1950	Cin N	4	14	1	3	1	0	0	1	2	0	0	.214	.313	.286	58	-1	0	1.000	-2	58	0	2b4		-0.2
†Phi N		54	96	6	22	2	0	0	13	6	0	12	.229	.275	.250	40	-9	0	1.000	-1	96	100	2b27,1b7,3b2		-0.8
Year		58	110	7	25	3	0	0	14	8	0	12	.227	.280	.255	42	-9	0	1.000	-3	91	86	2b31,1b7,3b2		-1.0
1951	Phi N	21	42	2	6	0	0	0	1	3	0	9	.143	.200	.143	-6	-6	1-0	.975	-1	99	64	2b8,1b6		-0.7
Total	11	1002	3519	347	874	160	20	62	451	202	16	407	.248	.292	.358	74	-138	19-22	.975	52	100	98	2b867,1b53,3b22,O5R,S3		-4.2

BLOOMFIELD, BUD Clyde Stalcup B1.5.1936 Oklahoma City OK BR/TR/5-11.5/175* d9.25 Col Tulsa

YEAR	TM LG	G	AB	R	H	2B	3B	HR	RBI	BB-IB	HP	SO	AVG	OBP	SLG	AOPS	ABR	SB-CS	FA	FR	RNG	THR	GAMES AT POSITION	DL	BFW
1963	StL N	1	0	0	0	0	0	0		0-0	0	0					0-0		—	-0	0	0	/3		0.0
1964	Min A	7	7	1	1	0	0	0	0	0-0	0	0	.143	.143	.143	-20	-1	0-0	1.000	-0	119	197	2b3,S2		-0.1
Total	2	8	7	1	1	0	0	0	0	0-0	0	0	.143	.143	.143	-20	-1	0-0	1.000	-0	119	197	2b3,S2/3		-0.1

BLOOMQUIST, WILLIE William Paul B11.27.1977 Bremerton WA BR/TR/5-11/185* [SeaA99 3/95] d9.1 Col Arizona St. OF(26/16/1)

YEAR	TM LG	G	AB	R	H	2B	3B	HR	RBI	BB-IB	HP	SO	AVG	OBP	SLG	AOPS	ABR	SB-CS	FA	FR	RNG	THR	GAMES AT POSITION	DL	BFW
2002	Sea A	12	33	11	15	4	0	0	7	5-0	0	2	.455	.526	.576	200	5	3-1	1.000	1	121	0	O7L,2b4		0.6
2003	Sea A	89	196	30	49	7	2	1	14	19-1	1	39	.250	.317	.321	74	-7	4-1	.970	-6	80	65	3b37,S18,D12,O11(10/0/1),2b7,1b3		-1.2
2004	Sea A	93	188	27	46	10	0	2	18	10-0	0	48	.245	.283	.330	62	-11	13-2	.923	-7	76	145	3b31,S20,1b19,O9(8/1/0)/2D	19	-1.4
2005	Sea A	82	249	27	64	15	2	0	22	11-0	1	38	.257	.289	.333	70	-11	14-1	.986	-9	96	113	2b32,S24,O15(1/15/0),3b6/1D	34	-1.4
Total	4	276	666	95	174	36	4	3	61	45-1	2	127	.261	.308	.341	76	-24	34-5	.949	-22	78	96	3b74,S62,2b44,O42L,1b23,D19	53	-3.4

BLOSSER, GREG Gregory Brent B6.26.1971 Manatee FL BL/TL/6-3/205* [BosA89 1/16] d9.5

YEAR	TM LG	G	AB	R	H	2B	3B	HR	RBI	BB-IB	HP	SO	AVG	OBP	SLG	AOPS	ABR	SB-CS	FA	FR	RNG	THR	GAMES AT POSITION	DL	BFW
1993	Bos A	17	28	1	2	1	0	0	1	2-0	0	7	.071	.133	.107	-32	-5	1-0	1.000	1	105	328	O9L/D		-0.5
1994	Bos A	5	11	2	1	0	0	0	1	4-0	0	4	.091	.333	.091	16	-1	0-0	.727	0	184	0	O3(1/0/2)/D		-0.1
Total	2	22	39	3	3	1	0	0	2	6-0	0	11	.077	.200	.103	-16	-6	1-0	.870	1	129	229	O12(10/0/2),D2		-0.5

BLOTT, JACK John Leonard B8.24.1902 Girard OH D6.11.1964 Ann Arbor MI BR/TR/6-0/210 d7.30 Col Michigan

YEAR	TM LG	G	AB	R	H	2B	3B	HR	RBI	BB-IB	HP	SO	AVG	OBP	SLG	AOPS	ABR	SB-CS	FA	FR	RNG	THR	GAMES AT POSITION	DL	BFW
1924	Cin N	2	1	0	0	0	0	0	0	0-0	0	0	.000	.000	.000	-99	-1	0-0	1.000	-0	0	0	/C		0.0

BLOWERS, MIKE Michael Roy B4.24.1965 Wurzburg, W.Germany BR/TR/6-2/210(190-210) [MonN86 10/252] d9.1 Col Washington

YEAR	TM LG	G	AB	R	H	2B	3B	HR	RBI	BB-IB	HP	SO	AVG	OBP	SLG	AOPS	ABR	SB-CS	FA	FR	RNG	THR	GAMES AT POSITION	DL	BFW
1989	NY A	13	38	2	10	0	0	0	3	3-0	0	13	.263	.317	.263	66	-2	0-0	.852	-4	62	148	3b13		-0.5
1990	NY A	48	144	16	27	4	0	5	21	12-1	1	50	.188	.255	.319	59	-8	1-0	.899	-11	74	51	3b45,D2		-2.0
1991	NY A	15	35	3	7	0	0	1	1	4-0	0	3	.200	.282	.286	57	-2	0-0	.870	-3	77	49	3b14		-0.5
1992	Sea A	31	73	7	14	3	0	1	2	6-0	0	20	.192	.253	.274	47	-5	0-0	.984	1	90	193	3b29,1b3		-0.5
1993	Sea A	127	379	55	106	23	3	15	57	44-3	2	98	.280	.357	.475	119	10	1-5	.951	7	107	75	3b117,O2(1/0/1)/C1D		1.6
1994	Sea A	85	270	37	78	13	0	9	49	25-2	1	60	.289	.348	.437	99	0	2-2	.939	5	108	64	3b48,1b20,O9(8/0/1),D9		0.3
1995	†Sea A	134	439	59	113	24	1	23	96	53-0	1	128	.257	.335	.474	107	4	2-1	.947	-14	79	43	3b126,1b7,O5(2/0/3)		-1.7
1996	LA N	92	317	31	84	19	2	6	38	37-2	1	77	.265	.341	.394	100	1	0-0	.951	-18	72	66	3b90,1b6/S	74	-1.7
1997	†Sea A	68	150	22	44	5	0	5	20	21-1	0	33	.293	.376	.427	110	3	0-0	.990	1	125	93	1b49,3b10,O6(5/0/1)/D		0.1
1998	Oak A	129	409	56	97	24	2	11	71	39-1	1	116	.237	.302	.386	79	-13	1-0	.927	-9	96	95	3b120,1b8,D2		-2.0
1999	Sea A	19	46	2	11	1	0	2	7	4-0	0	12	.239	.300	.391	75	-2	0-0	1.000	1	125	163	1b14,3b4/D		-0.2
Total	11	761	2300	290	591	116	8	78	365	248-10	6	610	.257	.329	.416	96	-14	7-8	.938	-44	89	74	3b616,1b108,O22(16/0/6),D18/SC	74	-6.3

BLUE, BERT Bird Wayne B12.9.1877 Bettsville OH D9.2.1929 Detroit MI BR/TR/6-3/200 d6.15

YEAR	TM LG	G	AB	R	H	2B	3B	HR	RBI	BB-IB	HP	SO	AVG	OBP	SLG	AOPS	ABR	SB-CS	FA	FR	RNG	THR	GAMES AT POSITION	DL	BFW
1908	StL A	11	24	2	9	1	2	0	1	3	0		.375	.444	.583	232	3	0	.942	1	141	57	C8		0.5
	Phi A	6	18	2	3	0	0	0	1	0	0		.167	.167	.167	8	-2	0	1.000	0	73	123	C6		-0.1
	Year	17	42	4	12	1	2	0	2	3	0		.286	.333	.405	136	1	0	.967	1	113	84	C14		0.4

BLUE, LU Luzerne Atwell B3.5.1897 Washington DC D7.28.1958 Alexandria VA BB/TL/5-10/165 d4.14

YEAR	TM LG	G	AB	R	H	2B	3B	HR	RBI	BB-IB	HP	SO	AVG	OBP	SLG	AOPS	ABR	SB-CS	FA	FR	RNG	THR	GAMES AT POSITION	DL	BFW
1921	Det A	153	585	103	180	33	11	5	75	103	5	47	.308	.416	.427	116	20	13-17	.990	-6	85	68	1b152		0.1
1922	Det A	145	584	131	175	31	9	6	45	82	7	48	.300	.392	.414	114	15	8-5	.991	0	101	101	1b144		0.6
1923	Det A	129	504	100	143	27	7	4	46	96	4	40	.284	.402	.371	106	11	10-11	.992	5	113	79	1b129		0.5
1924	Det A	108	395	81	123	26	7	2	53	64	4	26	.311	.413	.428	119	14	9-4	.986	3	114	93	1b108		1.0
1925	Det A	150	532	91	163	18	9	3	94	83	3	29	.306	.403	.391	104	6	19-5	.985	1	102	94	1b148		0.0
1926	Det A	128	429	92	123	24	14	1	52	90	2	18	.287	.413	.415	115	13	13-7	.985	-6	82	108	1b109/OC		0.0
1927	Det A	112	365	71	95	17	9	1	42	71	2	28	.260	.384	.364	94	-1	13-7	.984	-2	98	120	1b104		-0.8
1928	StL A	**154**	549	116	154	32	11	14	80	105	4	43	.281	.400	.455	120	20	12-7	.989	2	106	103	1b154		1.2
1929	StL A	151	573	111	168	40	10	6	61	126	2	32	.293	.422	.429	115	21	12-6	.994	-3	92	107	1b151		0.7
1930	StL A	117	425	85	100	27	5	4	42	81	4	44	.235	.363	.351	79	-11	12-7	.987	-0	104	100	1b111		-1.6
1931	Chi A	155	589	119	179	23	15	1	62	127	3	60	.304	.430	.399	126	32	13-3	.990	-3	95	81	1b155		1.5
1932	Chi A	112	373	51	93	21	2	0	43	64	3	21	.249	.364	.316	83	-6	17-6	.986	8	**138**	116	1b105		-0.5
1933	Bro N	1	1	0	0	0	0	0	0	0	0	0	.000	.000	.000	-99	-0	0-0	1.000	-0	0	0	/1		0.0
Total	13	1615	5904	1151	1696	319	109	44	695	1092	43	436	.287	.402	.401	109	134	151-85	.989	-2	101	96	1b1571/OC		2.7

BLUEGE, OSSIE Oswald Louis B10.24.1900 Chicago IL D10.14.1985 Edina MN BR/TR/5-11/162 d4.24 M5/C3 b-Otto

YEAR	TM LG	G	AB	R	H	2B	3B	HR	RBI	BB-IB	HP	SO	AVG	OBP	SLG	AOPS	ABR	SB-CS	FA	FR	RNG	THR	GAMES AT POSITION	DL	BFW
1922	Was A	19	61	5	12	1	0	0	2	7	2	7	.197	.300	.213	37	-5	0	.925	-2	95	101	3b17,S2		-0.6
1923	Was A	109	379	48	93	15	7	2	42	48	3	53	.245	.334	.338	84	-8	5-3	.936	4	103	144	3b106,2b4		0.3
1924	†Was A	117	402	59	113	15	4	7	49	39	9	36	.281	.358	.353	86	-7	7-5	.943	-13	92	65	3b102,2b10,S4		-1.4
1925	†Was A	145	522	77	150	27	4	4	79	59	2	56	.287	.362	.377	89	-7	16-15	.953	1	100	108	3b144,S4		0.1
1926	Was A	139	487	69	132	19	8	3	65	70	5	46	.271	.368	.361	93	-3	12-9	.952	-16	91	64	3b134,S8		-1.0
1927	Was A	146	503	71	138	21	10	6	66	57	5	47	.274	.354	.362	87	-9	15-15	.961	15	112	71	3b146		1.5
1928	Was A	146	518	78	154	33	7	2	75	46	**8**	27	.297	.364	.400	101	2	18-6	.960	10	110	133	3b144/2		2.2
1929	Was A	64	220	35	65	6	0	5	31	19	1	15	.295	.354	.391	91	-3	6-4	.967	4	117	132	3b35,2b14,S10		0.4
1930	Was A	134	476	64	138	27	7	3	69	51	2	40	.290	.368	.395	93	-3	15-8	.964	-1	101	91	3b134		0.4
1931	Was A	152	570	82	155	25	7	8	98	50	5	39	.272	.336	.402	88	-11	16-10	**.960**	-7	94	97	3b152/S		-1.1
1932	Was A	149	507	64	131	22	4	5	64	83	4	41	.258	.367	.347	87	-6	9-7	.970	5	105	119	3b149		0.3
1933	†Was A	140	501	63	131	14	0	6	71	55	3	34	.261	.338	.325	77	-15	6-7	.965	-10	97	116	3b138		-2.1
1934	Was A	99	285	39	70	9	2	2	33	30	2	15	.246	.306	.291	57	-19	2-1	.950	7	120	136	3b41,S30,2b5,O5L		-0.7
1935	Was A★	100	320	44	84	14	3	0	34	37	1	21	.262	.341	.325	75	-11	2-2	.967	-2	99	85	S58,3b25,2b4		-0.4
1936	Was A	90	319	43	92	12	1	1	55	38	6	16	.288	.375	.342	83	-7	5-3	.993	4	97	108	2b52,S23,3b15		0.2
1937	Was A	42	127	12	36	12	1	0	13	13	1	11	.283	.355	.370	87	-7	3-1	.952	-2	96	100	S28,1b2,3b2		-0.5
1938	Was A	58	184	25	48	11	1	0	21	21	1	11	.261	.340	.337	75	-7	3-1	.990	0	104	101	2b38,S10/13		-0.3

YEAR	TM LG	G	AB	R	H	2B	3B	HR	RBI	BB-IB	HP	SO	AVG	OBP	SLG	AOPS	ABR	SB-CS	FA	FR	RNG	THR	GAMES AT POSITION	DL	BFW
1939	Was A	18	59	5	9	0	0	0	3	7	0		.153	.242	.153	3	-9	1-0	.989	0	127	114	1b11,2b2,S2,3b2		-0.8
Total	18	1867	6440	883	1751	276	67	43	848	723	71	515	.272	.352	.356	85	-132	140-87	.957	3	102	104	3b1487,S180,2b130,1b14,O5L		-3.2

BLUEGE, OTTO Otto Adam "Squeaky" B7.20.1909 Chicago IL D6.28.1977 Chicago IL BR/TR/5-10/154 d4.12 b-Ossie

YEAR	TM LG	G	AB	R	H	2B	3B	HR	RBI	BB-IB	HP	SO	AVG	OBP	SLG	AOPS	ABR	SB-CS	FA	FR	RNG	THR	GAMES AT POSITION	DL	BFW
1932	Cin N	1	0	1	0	0	0	0	0	0	0	0	—	—	—	0	0			0			/R		0.0
1933	Cin N	108	291	17	62	6	2	0	18	26	0	29	.213	.278	.247	52	-18	0	.937	-8	99	98	S95,2b10/3		-2.1
Total	2	109	291	18	62	6	2	0	18	26	0	29	.213	.278	.247	52	-18	0	.937	-8	99	98	S95,2b10/3		-2.1

BLUHM, RED Harvey Fred B6.27.1894 Cleveland OH D5.7.1952 Flint MI BR/TR/5-11/165 d7.3

YEAR	TM LG	G	AB	R	H	2B	3B	HR	RBI	BB-IB	HP	SO	AVG	OBP	SLG	AOPS	ABR	SB-CS	FA	FR	RNG	THR	GAMES AT POSITION	DL	BFW
1918	Bos A	1	1	0	0	0	0	0	0	0	0	0	.000	.000	.000	-99	0	0		0			/H		0.0

BLUM, GEOFF Geoffrey Edward B4.26.1973 Redwood City CA BB/TR/6-3/200* [MonN94 7/196] d8.9 Col California-Davis OF(52/0/4)

YEAR	TM LG	G	AB	R	H	2B	3B	HR	RBI	BB-IB	HP	SO	AVG	OBP	SLG	AOPS	ABR	SB-CS	FA	FR	RNG	THR	GAMES AT POSITION	DL	BFW
1999	Mon N	45	133	21	32	7	2	8	18	17-3	0	25	.241	.327	.504	110	1	1-0	.928	-13	82	48	S42,2b2		-0.8
2000	Mon N	124	343	40	97	20	2	11	45	26-2	3	60	.283	.335	.449	96	-3	1-4	.952	12	117	70	3b55,S44,2b13,1b11		1.0
2001	Mon N	148	453	57	107	25	0	9	50	43-8	10	94	.236	.313	.351	73	-18	9-5	.966	2	103	105	3b72,O35L,2b25,1b14,S4		-1.6
2002	Hou N	130	368	45	104	20	4	10	52	49-5	1	70	.283	.367	.440	107	3	2-0	.971	15	113	147	3b104,O10(9/0/3),S2/12		1.8
2003	Hou N	123	420	51	110	19	0	10	52	20-1	2	50	.262	.295	.379	71	-18	0-0	.971	-7	96	144	3b83,2b25,S11,1b6,O2(1/0/1)		-2.4
2004	TB A	112	339	38	73	21	0	8	35	24-1	0	58	.215	.266	.348	60	-21	2-3	.934	-10	98	108	3b59,2b52,O7L,1b2/SD		-2.8
2005	SD N	78	224	26	54	13	1	5	22	24-0	3	28	.241	.321	.375	86	-4	3-2	.965	1	125	144	3b34,2b19,S14,1b2	18	-0.2
†Chi A		31	95	6	19	2	1	1	3	4-0	0	15	.200	.232	.274	33	-9	0-1	1.000	0	91	88	1b12,3b12,S6,2b2		-1.0
Total	7	791	2375	284	596	127	10	62	277	207-20	19	400	.251	.314	.391	81	-69	18-15	.961	-0	108	123	3b419,2b139,S124,O54L,1b48,D2	18	-6.0

BOAK, CHET Chester Robert B6.19.1935 New Castle PA D11.28.1983 Emporium PA BR/TR/6-0/180* d9.18

YEAR	TM LG	G	AB	R	H	2B	3B	HR	RBI	BB-IB	HP	SO	AVG	OBP	SLG	AOPS	ABR	SB-CS	FA	FR	RNG	THR	GAMES AT POSITION	DL	BFW
1960	KC A	5	13	1	2	0	0	0	1	0-0	1	2	.154	.200	.154	1	-2	0-0	.957	-0	95	125	2b5		-0.2
1961	Was A	5	7	0	0	0	0	0	0	1-0	0	1	.000	.125	.000	-64	-2	1-0	1.000	-1	71	0	/2		-0.2
Total	2	10	20	1	2	0	0	0	1	1-0	1	3	.100	.174	.100	-22	-4	1-0	.962	-1	90	100	2b6		-0.4

BOARDMAN, FREDERICK Frederick d8.29

YEAR	TM LG	G	AB	R	H	2B	3B	HR	RBI	BB-IB	HP	SO	AVG	OBP	SLG	AOPS	ABR	SB-CS	FA	FR	RNG	THR	GAMES AT POSITION	DL	BFW
1874	Bal NA	1	4	0	1	0	0	0	0	0-0	0	0	.250	.250	.250	61	0	0-0	—	0	0	0	/OR		0.0

BOBB, RANDY Mark Randall B1.1.1948 Los Angeles CA D6.13.1982 Carnelian Bay CA BR/TR/6-1/190(185-200) [ChiN67 S1/2] d8.15 Col Arizona St.

YEAR	TM LG	G	AB	R	H	2B	3B	HR	RBI	BB-IB	HP	SO	AVG	OBP	SLG	AOPS	ABR	SB-CS	FA	FR	RNG	THR	GAMES AT POSITION	DL	BFW
1968	Chi N	7	8	0	1	0	0	0	0	1-0	0	2	.125	.222	.125	6	-1	0-0	1.000	-0	0	258	C7		-0.1
1969	Chi N	3	2	0	0	0	0	0	0	0-0	0	1	.000	.000	.000	-89	-1	0-0	1.000	-1	35	0	C2		-0.1
Total	2	10	10	0	1	0	0	0	0	1-0	0	3	.100	.182	.100	-14	-1	0-0	1.000	-1	8	200	C9		-0.2

BOCACHICA, HIRAM Hiram (Colon) B3.4.1976 Ponce, PR BR/TR/5-11/165(165-180) [MonN94 1/21] d9.13

YEAR	TM LG	G	AB	R	H	2B	3B	HR	RBI	BB-IB	HP	SO	AVG	OBP	SLG	AOPS	ABR	SB-CS	FA	FR	RNG	THR	GAMES AT POSITION	DL	BFW
2000	LA N	8	10	2	3	0	0	0	0	0-0	0	1	.300	.300	.300	55	-1		1.000	3	252	255	2b2		0.2
2001	LA N	75	133	15	31	11	1	2	9	9-0	1	33	.233	.287	.376	74	-5	4-1	.941	-4	100	95	2b19,O13(10/0/3),3b8	17	-0.8
2002	LA N	49	65	12	14	3	0	4	9	5-0	0	19	.215	.271	.446	93	-1	1-1	.960	-1	99	0	O22(19/3/2)		-0.3
	Det A	34	103	14	23	4	0	4	8	5-0	0	22	.223	.259	.379	69	-5	2-2	.966	-1	91	235	O32(1/27/4),2b2/D		-0.5
2003	Det A	6	22	1	1	1	0	0	0	0-0	0	7	.045	.045	.091	-68	-5	0-0	1.000	-1	80	377	O6(1/5/0)		-0.5
2004	Sea A	50	90	9	22	5	0	3	6	12-0	1	27	.244	.337	.400	96	0	5-4	1.000	-2	93	0	O44(1/32/12),D3		-0.3
2005	Oak A	9	19	2	2	0	0	0	0	0-0	0	7	.105	.105	.105	-43	-4	0-0	1.000	-0	92	0	O6(0/1/5),3b2/D		-0.4
Total	7	231	442	55	96	24	1	13	32	31-0	2	117	.217	.271	.364	68	-21	12-8	.978	-4	93	93	O123(32/68/26),2b23,3b10,D5	17	-2.6

BOCCABELLA, JOHN John Dominic B6.29.1941 San Francisco CA BR/TR/6-1/200(195-210) d9.2 Col Santa Clara

YEAR	TM LG	G	AB	R	H	2B	3B	HR	RBI	BB-IB	HP	SO	AVG	OBP	SLG	AOPS	ABR	SB-CS	FA	FR	RNG	THR	GAMES AT POSITION	DL	BFW
1963	Chi N	24	74	7	14	4	1	1	5	6-0	0	21	.189	.247	.311	57	-4	0-1	.996	-1	82	183	1b24		-0.7
1964	Chi N	9	23	4	9	2	1	0	6	0-0	0	3	.391	.391	.565	159	2	0-0	1.000	-0	121	104	1b5,O2L		0.1
1965	Chi N	6	12	2	4	0	0	2	4	1-0	0	2	.333	.385	.833	227	2	0-0	1.000	-0	107	0	1b2/OL		0.2
1966	Chi N	75	206	22	47	9	0	6	25	14-1	0	39	.228	.274	.359	74	-7	0-1	.981	3	101	155	O33L,1b30,C5	39	-0.8
1967	Chi N	25	35	0	6	1	1	0	8	3-1	1	7	.171	.237	.257	45	-3	0-0	1.000	-1	131	0	O9(4/0/5),1b3/C		-0.4
1968	Chi N	7	14	0	1	0	0	1	2	2-0	0	2	.071	.176	.071	-19	-2	0-0	1.000	-0	47	0	C4/OL		-0.2
1969	Mon N	40	86	4	9	2	0	1	6	6-1	1	30	.105	.170	.163	-6	-12	1-0	1.000	-1	79	181	C32		-1.3
1970	Mon N	61	145	18	39	3	1	5	17	11-2	0	24	.269	.321	.407	93	-2	0-1	.993	6	178	111	1b33,C24/3		0.3
1971	Mon N	74	177	15	39	11	0	3	15	14-2	1	26	.220	.278	.333	72	-6	0-1	.979	-3	118	97	C37,1b37,3b2		-1.1
1972	Mon N	83	207	14	47	8	1	1	10	9-3	1	29	.227	.259	.290	56	-12	1-2	.983	6	99	164	C73,1b7/3		-0.6
1973	Mon N	118	403	25	94	13	0	7	46	26-8	1	57	.233	.279	.318	63	-21	1-1	.980	5	100	119	C117/1	22	-1.1
1974	SF N	29	80	6	11	3	0	0	5	4-2	0	6	.138	.176	.175	-1	-11	0-0	.991	-1	110	46	C26		-1.1
Total	12	551	1462	117	320	56	5	26	148	96-20	5	246	.219	.267	.317	62	-76	3-7	.984	14	101	125	C319,1b142,O46(41/0/5),3b4	61	-6.7

BOCEK, MILT Milton Francis B7.16.1912 Chicago IL BR/TR/6-1/185 d9.3

YEAR	TM LG	G	AB	R	H	2B	3B	HR	RBI	BB-IB	HP	SO	AVG	OBP	SLG	AOPS	ABR	SB-CS	FA	FR	RNG	THR	GAMES AT POSITION	DL	BFW
1933	Chi A	11	22	3	8	1	0	1	3	4	0	6	.364	.462	.545	173	3	0-0	1.000	1	76	0	O6(3/1/2)		0.2
1934	Chi A	19	38	3	8	1	0	0	3	5	0	5	.211	.302	.237	39	-3	0-0	1.000	2	117	238	O10(9/1/0)		-0.2
Total	2	30	60	6	16	2	0	1	6	9	0	11	.267	.360	.300	86	0	0-0	1.000	1	106	175	O16(12/2/2)		0.0

BOCHTE, BRUCE Bruce Anton B11.12.1950 Pasadena CA BL/TL/6-3/200* [AnaA72 2/34] d7.19 Col Santa Clara

YEAR	TM LG	G	AB	R	H	2B	3B	HR	RBI	BB-IB	HP	SO	AVG	OBP	SLG	AOPS	ABR	SB-CS	FA	FR	RNG	THR	GAMES AT POSITION	DL	BFW
1974	Cal A	57	196	24	53	4	1	5	26	18-0	1	23	.270	.332	.378	110	2	6-3	.985	-3	96	87	O39(32/5/3),1b24		-0.4
1975	Cal A	107	375	41	107	19	3	3	48	45-5	2	43	.285	.362	.376	118	10	3-4	.987	-6	75	103	1b105/D	50	-0.5
1976	Cal A	146	466	53	120	17	1	2	49	64-11	2	53	.258	.346	.311	101	3	4-5	.988	1	104	55	O86(71/0/18),1b59/D		-0.6
1977	Cal A	25	100	12	29	4	0	2	8	7-0	0	4	.290	.336	.390	101	3	3-2	1.000	0	79	304	O24C/D		-0.2
	Cle A	112	392	52	119	19	1	5	43	40-3	0	38	.304	.364	.395	111	7	3-2	.966	3	109	130	O76(74/3/1),1b36/D		0.5
	Year	137	492	64	148	23	1	7	51	47-3	0	42	.301	.358	.394	109	7	6-4	.974	3	102	173	O100(74/27/1),1b36,D2		0.5
1978	Sea A	140	486	58	128	25	3	11	51	60-3	1	47	.263	.342	.395	108	6	3-4	.984	-5	84	114	O91(82/19/0),D43/1		-0.4
1979	Sea A★	150	554	81	175	38	6	16	100	67-8	2	64	.316	.385	.493	134	28	2-2	.991	5	114	103	1b147		2.4
1980	Sea A	148	520	62	156	34	4	13	78	72-13	0	81	.300	.381	.456	127	22	2-3	.996	7	119	116	1b133,D11		2.0
1981	Sea A	99	335	39	87	16	0	6	30	47-5	2	53	.260	.354	.361	102	3	1-3	.995	-4	94	97	1b82,O14L/D		-0.8
1982	Sea A	144	509	58	151	21	0	12	70	67-5	3	71	.297	.380	.409	113	12	8-5	.988	-5	83	91	O99(99/1/0),1b34,D12		0.0
1984	Oak A	148	469	58	124	23	0	5	52	52-3	0	59	.264	.333	.345	95	-1	2-5	.993	-13	68	98	1b144,D2		-2.4
1985	Oak A	137	424	48	125	17	1	14	60	49-6	0	58	.295	.367	.439	129	17	3-1	.990	-10	73	86	1b128		0.1
1986	Oak A	125	407	57	104	13	1	6	65	65-3	0	68	.256	.357	.337	97	1	3-2	.991	0	100	86	1b115/D		-0.5
Total	12	1538	5233	643	1478	250	21	100	658	653-65	13	662	.282	.360	.396	113	110	43-41	.992	-29	93	98	1b1008,O429(372/52/22),D74	50	-0.6

BOCHY, BRUCE Bruce Douglas B4.16.1955 Landes de Bussac, France BR/TR/6-4/210(205-234) [HouN75 S1/23] d7.19 M11/C2 Col Brevard (FL) CC

YEAR	TM LG	G	AB	R	H	2B	3B	HR	RBI	BB-IB	HP	SO	AVG	OBP	SLG	AOPS	ABR	SB-CS	FA	FR	RNG	THR	GAMES AT POSITION	DL	BFW
1978	Hou N	54	154	8	41	8	0	3	15	11-4	0	35	.266	.311	.377	99	-1	0-0	.974	-1	71	128	C55		0.1
1979	Hou N	56	129	11	28	4	0	1	6	13-4	1	25	.217	.294	.271	59	-7	0-0	.970	-3	80	121	C55		-0.9
1980	†Hou N	22	22	0	4	1	0	0	0	5-1	1	7	.182	.357	.227	72	0	0-0	1.000	-1	74	0	C10/1		-0.1
1982	NY N	17	49	4	15	4	0	2	8	4-0	1	6	.306	.358	.510	140	3	0-0	.961	0	82	139	C16/1		0.4
1983	SD N	23	42	2	9	1	1	0	3	0-0	0	9	.214	.205	.286	39	-4	0-0	1.000	1	151	186	C11		-0.3
1984	†SD N	37	92	10	21	5	1	4	15	3-0	0	21	.228	.250	.435	89	-2	0-1	.988	1	98	69	C36		0.0
1985	SD N	48	112	16	30	2	0	6	13	6-1	0	30	.268	.305	.446	109	0	0-0	.988	-4	76	88	C46		-0.2
1986	SD N	63	127	16	32	9	0	8	22	14-3	0	23	.252	.326	.512	130	5	1-0	.991	1	91	107	C48		0.8
1987	SD N	38	75	8	12	3	0	2	11	11-1	0	21	.160	.264	.280	47	-6	0-1	.962	-5	86	15	C23	23	-1.1
Total	9	358	802	75	192	37	2	26	93	67-14	2	177	.239	.298	.388	92	-12	1-2	.979	-10	85	103	C298,1b2	23	-1.3

BOCKMAN, EDDIE Joseph Edward B7.26.1920 Santa Ana CA BR/TR/5-9/175 d9.11

YEAR	TM LG	G	AB	R	H	2B	3B	HR	RBI	BB-IB	HP	SO	AVG	OBP	SLG	AOPS	ABR	SB-CS	FA	FR	RNG	THR	GAMES AT POSITION	DL	BFW
1946	NY A	4	12	2	1	1	0	0	0	1	0	4	.083	.154	.167	-10	-2	0-0	.933	1	77	375	3b4		-0.1
1947	Cle A	46	66	8	17	2	2	1	14	5	0	17	.258	.310	.394	97	-1	0-0	.946	5	135	241	3b12,2b4/SOL		0.4
1948	Pit N	70	176	23	42	7	1	4	23	17	0	35	.239	.309	.358	79	-6	2	.962	7	119	129	3b51/2		0.2
1949	Pit N	79	220	21	49	6	1	6	19	23	0	31	.223	.296	.341	69	-10	3	.959	5	108	120	3b68,2b5		-0.5
Total	4	199	474	54	109	16	4	11	56	46	0	87	.230	.299	.350	74	-19	5-0	.958	18	114	143	3b135,2b10/OLS		0.0

BODIE, PING Frank Stephan (b Francesco Stephano Pezzolo) B10.8.1887 San Francisco CA D12.17.1961 San Francisco CA BR/TR/5-8/195 d4.22

YEAR	TM LG	G	AB	R	H	2B	3B	HR	RBI	BB-IB	HP	SO	AVG	OBP	SLG	AOPS	ABR	SB-CS	FA	FR	RNG	THR	GAMES AT POSITION	DL	BFW
1911	Chi A	145	551	75	159	27	13	4	97	49	1		.289	.348	.407	114	9	14	.969	-2	94	111	O128(0/107/21),2b16		-0.2
1912	Chi A	138	472	58	139	24	7	5	72	43	4		.294	.358	.420	123	14	12	.969	-10	88	63	O130(8/72/50)		-0.4
1913	Chi A	127	406	39	107	14	8	8	48	35	2	57	.264	.325	.397	112	4	5	.968	-5	94	81	O119(43/76/0)		-0.8
1914	Chi A	107	327	21	75	9	5	3	29	21	1	35	.229	.278	.315	79	-10	12-11	.959	-3	89	120	O95(2/92/1)		-2.2
1917	Phi A	148	557	51	162	28	11	7	74	53	3	40	.291	.356	.418	138	24	13	.963	7	93	**168**	O145L/1		2.8
1918	NY A	91	324	32	83	12	6	3	46	27	3	24	.256	.318	.358	102	0	6	.971	4	97	139	O90L		-0.1

YEAR	TM LG	G	AB	R	H	2B	3B	HR	RBI	BB-IB	HP	SO	AVG	OBP	SLG	AOPS	ABR	SB-CS	FA	FR	RNG	THR	GAMES AT POSITION	DL	BFW
1919	NY A	134	475	45	132	27	8	6	59	36	4	46	.278	.334	.406	107	3	15	.959	-11	89	68	O134(0/129/5)		-1.8
1920	NY A	129	471	63	139	26	12	7	79	40	0	30	.295	.350	.446	106	3	6-14	.968	-12	88	77	O129C		-2.1
1921	NY A	31	87	5	15	2	2	0	12	8	0	8	.172	.241	.241	23	-11	0-1	.944	-3	75	90	O25(5/20/0)		-1.4
Total	9	1050	3670	393	1011	169	72	43	516	312	18	240	.275	.335	.396	110	36	83-26	.965	-35	91	102	O995(293/625/77),2b16/1		-6.2

BOECKEL, TONY Norman Doxie B8.25.1892 Los Angeles CA D2.16.1924 LaJolla CA BR/TR/5-10.5/175 d7.23 Mil 1918

YEAR	TM LG	G	AB	R	H	2B	3B	HR	RBI	BB-IB	HP	SO	AVG	OBP	SLG	AOPS	ABR	SB-CS	FA	FR	RNG	THR	GAMES AT POSITION	DL	BFW
1917	Pit N	64	219	16	58	11	1	0	23	8	2	31	.265	.297	.324	88	-3	6	.935	-3	95	89	3b62		-0.5
1919	Pit N	45	152	18	38	9	2	0	16	18	1	20	.250	.333	.336	98	0	11	.930	-7	88	38	3b45		-0.5
	Bos N	95	365	42	91	11	5	1	26	35	1	13	.249	.317	.315	94	-2	10	.960	1	104	85	3b93		0.1
	Year	140	517	60	129	20	7	1	42	53	2	33	.250	.322	.321	95	-2	21	.951	-6	99	70	3b138		-0.4
1920	Bos N	153	582	70	156	28	5	3	62	38	1	50	.268	.314	.349	94	-5	18-15	.936	-6	91	110	3b149,S3/2		-0.8
1921	Bos N	153	592	93	185	20	13	10	84	52	2	41	.313	.370	.441	120	17	20-15	.933	-13	91	67	3b153		1.3
1922	Bos N	119	402	61	116	19	6	6	47	35	2	32	.289	.349	.410	99	-1	14-8	.952	-9	86	75	3b106		-0.2
1923	Bos N	148	568	72	169	32	4	7	79	51	2	31	.298	.357	.405	105	5	11-8	.939	-9	94	100	3b147/S		0.4
Total	6	777	2880	362	813	130	36	27	337	237	11	218	.282	.339	.381	102	11	90-46	.941	-45	93	86	3b755,S4/2		-0.2

BOEHMER, LEN Leonard Joseph Stephen B6.28.1941 Flint Hill MO BR/TR/6-1/192* d6.18 Col St. Louis

YEAR	TM LG	G	AB	R	H	2B	3B	HR	RBI	BB-IB	HP	SO	AVG	OBP	SLG	AOPS	ABR	SB-CS	FA	FR	RNG	THR	GAMES AT POSITION	DL	BFW
1967	Cin N	2	3	0	0	0	0	0	0	0-0		0	.000	.000	.000	-90	-1	0-0	1.000	0	149	0	/2		-0.1
1969	NY A	45	108	5	19	4	0	0	7	8-2	1	10	.176	.233	.213	26	-11	0-1	.995	1	98	103	1b21,3b8/2S		-1.2
1971	NY A	3	5	0	0	0	0	0	0	0-0	0	0	.000	.000	.000	-99	-1	0-1	1.000	-0	51	0	/3		-0.2
Total	3	50	116	5	19	4	0	0	7	8-2	1	10	.164	.218	.198	18	-13	0-1	.995	1	98	103	1b21,3b9,2b2/S		-1.5

BOGAR, TIM Timothy Paul B10.28.1966 Indianapolis IN BR/TR/6-2/198* [NYN87 8/212] d4.21 Col Eastern Illinois

YEAR	TM LG	G	AB	R	H	2B	3B	HR	RBI	BB-IB	HP	SO	AVG	OBP	SLG	AOPS	ABR	SB-CS	FA	FR	RNG	THR	GAMES AT POSITION	DL	BFW
1993	NY N	78	205	19	50	13	0	3	25	14-2	3	29	.244	.300	.351	75	-7	0-1	.972	9	109	99	S66,3b7,2b6	16	0.6
1994	NY N	50	52	5	8	0	0	2	5	4-1	0	11	.154	.211	.269	25	-6	1-0	.909	5	81	0	3b22,2b14,S7/2OL	34	-0.1
1995	NY N	78	145	17	42	7	0	1	21	9-0	0	25	.290	.329	.359	85	-3	1-0	.971	3	97	55	S27,3b25,1b10,2b7/OL		0.1
1996	NY N	91	89	17	19	4	0	0	6	8-0	2	20	.213	.287	.258	49	-6	1-3	1.000	1	70	113	1b32,3b25,S19,2b8		-0.6
1997	Hou N	97	241	30	60	14	4	4	30	24-1	3	42	.249	.320	.390	89	-4	4-1	.985	11	109	140	S80,3b14/1	24	1.2
1998	Hou N	79	156	12	24	4	1	1	8	9-2	2	36	.154	.208	.212	11	-21	2-1	.989	5	116	77	S55,2b11,3b11/D		-1.3
1999	†Hou N	106	309	44	74	16	2	4	31	38-5	1	52	.239	.328	.343	72	-13	3-5	.977	26	117	144	S90,3b12/2		1.7
2000	Hou N	110	304	32	63	9	2	7	33	35-7	3	56	.207	.292	.319	51	-24	1-0	.971	3	106	102	S95,2b2,P2/3		-1.3
2001	LA N	12	15	4	5	2	0	0	2	2-0	0	1	.333	.412	.867	232	3	0-0	1.000	-2	0	128	1b3,S2/3	168	0.1
Total	9	701	1516	180	345	69	9	24	161	143-18	17	272	.228	.298	.332	64	-81	13-12	.978	61	111	116	S441,3b118,1b60,2b36,P2,O2L/D	242	0.4

BOGENER, TERRY Terry Wayne B9.28.1955 Hannibal MO BL/TL/6-0/193 [TexA78 6/150] d6.14 Col Oklahoma

YEAR	TM LG	G	AB	R	H	2B	3B	HR	RBI	BB-IB	HP	SO	AVG	OBP	SLG	AOPS	ABR	SB-CS	FA	FR	RNG	THR	GAMES AT POSITION	DL	BFW
1982	Tex A	24	60	6	13	2	1	1	4	4-0	2	8	.217	.288	.333	73	-2	2-0	1.000	-1	84	0	O16(4/10/2),D4		-0.4

BOGGS, WADE Wade Anthony B6.15.1958 Omaha NE BL/TR/6-2/197(185-197) d4.10 C1 HF2005

YEAR	TM LG	G	AB	R	H	2B	3B	HR	RBI	BB-IB	HP	SO	AVG	OBP	SLG	AOPS	ABR	SB-CS	FA	FR	RNG	THR	GAMES AT POSITION	DL	BFW
1982	Bos A	104	338	51	118	14	1	5	44	35-4	0	21	.349	.406	.441	126	14	1-0	.994	20	156	95	1b49,3b44/OLD		2.9
1983	Bos A	153	582	100	210	44	7	5	74	92-2	1	36	.361	.444	.486	146	43	3-3	.947	4	103	112	3b153		4.4
1984	Bos A	158	625	109	203	31	4	6	55	89-6	0	44	.325	.407	.416	123	24	3-2	.959	22	111	100	3b156,D2		4.4
1985	Bos A★	161	653	107	240	42	3	8	78	96-5	4	61	.368	.450	.478	148	51	2-1	.965	9	104	94	3b161		5.6
1986	†Bos A★	149	580	107	207	47	2	8	71	105-14	0	44	.357	.453	.486	155	54	0-1	.953	6	99	118	3b149		5.4
1987	Bos A★	147	551	108	200	40	6	24	89	105-19	2	48	.363	.461	.588	172	65	1-3	.965	8	102	129	3b145/1D		6.5
1988	†Bos A★	155	584	128	214	45	6	5	58	125-18	1	34	.366	.476	.490	165	62	2-3	.971	3	92	69	3b151,D3		6.4
1989	Bos A★	156	621	113	205	51	7	3	54	107-19	7	51	.330	.430	.449	140	41	2-6	.958	3	95	111	3b152,D3		4.3
1990	†Bos A★	155	619	89	187	44	5	6	63	87-19	1	68	.302	.386	.418	120	21	0-1	.946	-15	86	63	3b152,D3		0.6
1991	Bos A★	144	546	93	181	42	2	8	51	89-25	0	32	.332	.421	.460	137	33	1-2	.968	5	99	133	3b140		3.8
1992	Bos A★	143	514	62	133	22	4	7	50	74-19	4	31	.259	.353	.358	94	-2	1-3	.952	-0	98	118	3b117,D21		-0.4
1993	NY A★	143	560	83	169	26	1	2	59	74-4	0	49	.302	.378	.363	104	7	0-1	.970	21	121	131	3b134,D8		2.8
1994	NY A★	97	366	61	125	19	1	11	55	61-3	1	29	.342	.433	.489	143	27	2-1	.962	9	116	137	3b93,1b4		3.3
1995	†NY A★	126	460	76	149	22	4	5	63	74-5	0	50	.324	.412	.422	120	18	1-1	.981	-2	96	62	3b117,1b9		1.5
1996	†NY A★	132	501	80	156	29	2	2	41	67-7	0	32	.311	.389	.389	99	-4	1-2	.974	-4	91	116	3b123,D4		-0.1
1997	NY A	104	353	55	103	23	1	4	28	48-3	0	38	.292	.373	.397	103	4	0-1	.978	2	100	131	3b76,D19/P		0.4
1998	TB A	123	435	51	122	23	4	7	52	46-6	0	54	.280	.348	.400	92	-5	3-2	.973	1	101	108	3b78,D33	21	-0.4
1999	TB A	90	292	40	88	14	1	2	29	38-2	0	23	.301	.377	.377	93	-2	1-0	.942	-7	83	116	3b74,1b4/PD	46	-0.8
Total	18	2440	9180	1513	3010	578	61	118	1014	1412-180	23	745	.328	.415	.443	129	457	24-35	.962	84	101	107	3b2215,D107,1b67,P2/OL	67	50.6

BOHNE, SAM Samuel Arthur (b Samuel Arthur Cohen) B10.22.1896 San Francisco CA D5.23.1977 Palo Alto CA BR/TR/5-8.5/175 d9.9

YEAR	TM LG	G	AB	R	H	2B	3B	HR	RBI	BB-IB	HP	SO	AVG	OBP	SLG	AOPS	ABR	SB-CS	FA	FR	RNG	THR	GAMES AT POSITION	DL	BFW
1916	StL N	14	38	3	9	0	0	0	4			0	6	.237	.310	.237	69	-1	3	.870	-3	98	63	S14		-0.4
1921	Cin N	153	613	98	175	28	16	3	44	54	4	38	.285	.347	.398	101	1	26-22	.973	10	97	120	2b102,3b53		1.6
1922	Cin N	112	383	53	105	14	5	3	51	39	2	18	.274	.344	.360	83	-9	13-8	.958	13	114	128	2b85,S20		0.8
1923	Cin N	139	539	77	136	18	10	3	47	48	1	37	.252	.316	.340	74	-21	16-19	.975	9	104	86	2b96,3b35,S9/1		-0.8
1924	Cin N	100	349	42	89	15	9	4	46	18	1	24	.255	.293	.384	81	-11	9-6	.941	-5	95	74	2b48,S40,3b12		-1.0
1925	Cin N	73	214	24	55	9	1	2	24	14	0	14	.257	.303	.336	65	-12	6-4	.933	-5	98	102	S49,2b10,O4(1/0/4),1b2,3b2		-1.1
1926	Cin N	25	54	8	11	0	2	0	5	4	0	8	.204	.259	.278	46	-5	1	.931	-2	100	91	S20		-0.5
	Bro N	47	125	4	25	3	2	1	11	12	0	9	.200	.270	.280	49	-9	1	.965	5	109	60	2b31,3b15		-0.3
	Year	72	179	12	36	3	4	1	16	16	0	17	.201	.267	.279	48	-14	2	.965	3	109	60	2b31,S20,3b15		-0.8
Total	7	663	2315	309	605	87	45	16	228	193	9	154	.261	.321	.359	81	-67	75-59	.966	23	103	102	2b372,S152,3b117,O4(1/0/4),1b3		-1.7

BOISCLAIR, BRUCE Bruce Armand B12.9.1952 Putnam CT BL/TL/6-2/190(185-200) [NYN70 20/486] d9.11

YEAR	TM LG	G	AB	R	H	2B	3B	HR	RBI	BB-IB	HP	SO	AVG	OBP	SLG	AOPS	ABR	SB-CS	FA	FR	RNG	THR	GAMES AT POSITION	DL	BFW
1974	NY N	7	12	0	3	1	0	0	1	0-0		4	.250	.308	.333	80	0	0-0	.923	2	112	837	O5(2/3/0)		0.1
1976	NY N	110	286	42	82	13	3	2	13	28-5	0	55	.287	.350	.374	111	3	9-5	.981	0	104	66	O87(35/39/20)		0.2
1977	NY N	127	307	41	90	21	1	4	44	31-0	1	57	.293	.359	.407	109	5	6-4	.959	-4	101	20	O91(30/9/55),1b9		-0.3
1978	NY N	107	214	24	48	7	1	4	15	23-3	0	43	.224	.293	.322	76	-7	3-3	.983	2	115	71	O69(12/2/58)/1		-0.9
1979	NY N	59	98	7	18	5	1	0	4	3-0	1	24	.184	.210	.255	29	-10	0-2	1.000	0	97	137	O24(8/0/17)/1	60	-1.2
Total	5	410	917	114	241	47	6	10	77	86-8	2	183	.263	.324	.360	93	-8	18-14	.975	0	105	71	O276(87/53/150),1b11	60	-2.1

BOKEN, BOB Robert Anthony B2.23.1908 Maryville IL D10.6.1988 Las Vegas NV BR/TR/6-2/165 d4.25

YEAR	TM LG	G	AB	R	H	2B	3B	HR	RBI	BB-IB	HP	SO	AVG	OBP	SLG	AOPS	ABR	SB-CS	FA	FR	RNG	THR	GAMES AT POSITION	DL	BFW
1933	Was A	55	133	19	37	5	2	3	26	9	0	16	.278	.324	.414	95	-3	0-0	.969	-3	103	94	2b31,3b19,S10		-0.2
1934	Was A	11	27	5	6	1	1	0	6	3	0	1	.222	.300	.333	66	-2	1-0	.864	1	112	268	3b6/2		0.0
	Chi A	81	297	30	70	9	1	3	40	15	1	32	.236	.275	.303	47	-24	2-1	.929	-15	92	69	2b57,S22		-3.2
	Year	92	324	35	76	10	2	3	46	18	1	33	.235	.277	.306	49	-26	4-1	.929	-14	92	73	2b58,S22,3b6		-3.2
Total	2	147	457	54	113	15	4	6	72	27	1	49	.247	.291	.337	62	-28	4-1	.941	-17	95	79	2b89,S32,3b25		-3.4

BOLAND d9.4

YEAR	TM LG	G	AB	R	H	2B	3B	HR	RBI	BB-IB	HP	SO	AVG	OBP	SLG	AOPS	ABR	SB-CS	FA	FR	RNG	THR	GAMES AT POSITION	DL	BFW
1875	Atl NA	1	4	0	0	0	0	0	0	0		0	.000	.000	.000	-99	-1	0-0	.750	-0	55	0	/3		-0.1

BOLAND, ED Edward John B4.18.1908 Long Island City NY D2.5.1993 Clearwater FL BL/TL/5-10/165 d9.18

YEAR	TM LG	G	AB	R	H	2B	3B	HR	RBI	BB-IB	HP	SO	AVG	OBP	SLG	AOPS	ABR	SB-CS	FA	FR	RNG	THR	GAMES AT POSITION	DL	BFW
1934	Phi N	8	30	2	9	1	1	0	5	0	0	2	.300	.300	.400	76	-1	1	.778	-1	55	207	O7R		-0.2
1935	Phi N	30	47	5	10	0	0	0	4	4	0	6	.213	.275	.213	30	-5	1	.833	-2	88	0	O10(2/2/6)		-0.6
1944	Was A	19	59	4	16	4	0	0	14	0	0	6	.271	.271	.339	77	-2	0-0	.889	-2	92	245	O14R		-0.3
Total	3	57	136	11	35	5	1	0	23	4	0	14	.257	.279	.309	59	-8	2-0	.852	-2	83	161	O31(2/2/27)		-1.1

BOLD, CHARLIE Charles Dickens "Dutch" B10.27.1894 Karlskrona, Sweden D7.29.1978 Chelsea MA BR/TR/6-2/185 d8.24 Col Georgetown

YEAR	TM LG	G	AB	R	H	2B	3B	HR	RBI	BB-IB	HP	SO	AVG	OBP	SLG	AOPS	ABR	SB-CS	FA	FR	RNG	THR	GAMES AT POSITION	DL	BFW
1914	StL A	2	1	0	0	0	0	0	0	0		0	.000	.000	.000	-99	-0		.500	-0		0	/1		-0.1

BOLES, CARL Carl Theodore B10.31.1934 Center Point AR BR/TR/5-11/188 d8.2 Col Arkansas-Pine Bluff

YEAR	TM LG	G	AB	R	H	2B	3B	HR	RBI	BB-IB	HP	SO	AVG	OBP	SLG	AOPS	ABR	SB-CS	FA	FR	RNG	THR	GAMES AT POSITION	DL	BFW
1962	SF N	19	24	4	9	0	0	1	0	1-0	0	6	.375	.375	.375	104	0	0-0	.833	-1	75	0	O7L		-0.1

BOLEY, JOE John Peter (b John Peter Bolinsky) B7.19.1896 Mahanoy City PA D12.30.1962 Mahanoy City PA BR/TR/5-11/170 d4.12

YEAR	TM LG	G	AB	R	H	2B	3B	HR	RBI	BB-IB	HP	SO	AVG	OBP	SLG	AOPS	ABR	SB-CS	FA	FR	RNG	THR	GAMES AT POSITION	DL	BFW
1927	Phi A	118	370	49	115	18	8	1	52	26	3	14	.311	.361	.411	95	-4	8-5	.951	-7	97	88	S114		0.1
1928	Phi A	132	425	49	112	20	3	0	49	32	1	11	.264	.317	.325	67	-20	5-1	.949	-17	87	78	S132		-2.3
1929	†Phi A	91	303	36	76	17	6	2	47	24	2	16	.251	.310	.366	71	-14	1-0	.963	-11	87	104	S88/3		-1.4
1930	†Phi A	121	420	41	116	22	2	4	55	32	5	26	.276	.335	.367	74	-16	0-0	.970	-6	88	99	S120		-0.9
1931	†Phi A	67	224	26	51	9	3	0	20	15	2	13	.228	.282	.295	49	-17	1-1	.954	-8	87	111	S62/2		-2.0
1932	Phi A	10	34	2	7	2	0	0	4	1	0	4	.206	.229	.265	26	-4	0-1	.897	-4	76	44	S10		-0.7
	Cle A	1	4	0	1	0	0	0	0	0	0	0	.250	.250	.250	28	0	0-0	—	-0	0	0	/S		-0.1

YEAR	TM LG	G	AB	R	H	2B	3B	HR	RBI	BB-IB	HP	SO	AVG	OBP	SLG	AOPS	ABR	SB-CS	FA	FR	RNG	THR	GAMES AT POSITION	DL	BFW
	Year	11	38	2	8	2	0	0	4	1	0	4	.211	.231	.263	27	-4	0-1	.897	-4	75	43	S11		-0.8
Total	6	540	1780	203	478	88	22	7	227	130	13	84	.269	.323	.354	72	-75	15-8	.957	-53	89	93	S527/23		-7.3

BOLGER, JIM   James Cyril "Dutch" B2.23.1932 Cincinnati OH BR/TR/6-2/180* d6.24

YEAR	TM LG	G	AB	R	H	2B	3B	HR	RBI	BB-IB	HP	SO	AVG	OBP	SLG	AOPS	ABR	SB-CS	FA	FR	RNG	THR	GAMES AT POSITION	DL	BFW
1950	Cin N	2	1	0	0	0	0	0	0	0	0	0	.000	.000	.000	-99	0	0	—	-0	0	0	O2L		0.0
1951	Cin N	2	0	1	0	0	0	0	0	0	0	0	—	—	—	—	0	1-0	—	0			/R		0.0
1954	Cin N	5	3	1	1	0	0	0	0	0	0	1	.333	.333	.333	72	0	0-0	—	-0	0	0	O2C		0.0
1955	Chi N	64	160	19	33	5	4	0	7	9-1	2	17	.206	.257	.287	45	-13	2-2	.955	-2	105	28	O51(3/49/0)		-1.8
1957	Chi N	112	273	28	75	4	1	5	29	10-1	3	36	.275	.303	.352	78	-9	0-1	.987	2	111	91	O63(24/28/17),3b3		-1.1
1958	Chi N	84	120	15	27	4	1	1	11	9-0	1	20	.225	.285	.300	56	-8	0-1	.940	-0	106	61	O37(28/6/5)		-1.0
1959	Cle A	8	7	0	0	0	0	0	0	1-0	0	1	.000	.125	.000	-65	-2	0-0	—	0			/H		-0.2
	Phi N	35	48	1	4	1	0	0	1	3-1	0	8	.083	.135	.104	-34	-9	0-0	.938	-0	110	0	O9(7/1/1)		-1.0
Total	7	312	612	65	140	14	6	6	48	32-3	6	83	.229	.272	.301	54	-41	3-4	.966	-1	108	61	O164(64/86/23),3b3		-5.1

BOLICK, FRANK   Frank Charles B6.28.1966 Ashland PA BB/TR/5-10/180(180-200) [MilA87 9/227] d4.5 Col Georgia Tech

YEAR	TM LG	G	AB	R	H	2B	3B	HR	RBI	BB-IB	HP	SO	AVG	OBP	SLG	AOPS	ABR	SB-CS	FA	FR	RNG	THR	GAMES AT POSITION	DL	BFW
1993	Mon N	95	213	25	45	13	0	4	24	23-2	4	37	.211	.298	.329	65	-10	1-0	.992	4	135	106	1b51,3b24		-0.9
1998	Ana A	21	45	3	7	2	0	1	2	11-0	0	8	.156	.321	.267	54	-3	0-0	1.000	-1	72	0	3b7/1ORD		-0.3
Total	2	116	258	28	52	15	0	5	26	34-2	4	45	.202	.302	.318	63	-13	1-0	.992	3	134	109	1b52,3b31,D9/OR		-1.2

BOLLING, FRANK   Frank Elmore B11.16.1931 Mobile AL BR/TR/6-1/175* d4.13 Mil 1955 b-Milt Col Spring Hill

YEAR	TM LG	G	AB	R	H	2B	3B	HR	RBI	BB-IB	HP	SO	AVG	OBP	SLG	AOPS	ABR	SB-CS	FA	FR	RNG	THR	GAMES AT POSITION	DL	BFW
1954	Det A	117	368	46	87	15	2	6	38	36	0	51	.236	.302	.337	77	-12	3-5	.974	-20	88	77	2b113		-2.8
1956	Det A	102	366	53	103	21	7	7	45	42-1	2	51	.281	.354	.434	108	-4	6-2	.978	-9	95	92	2b102		0.3
1957	Det A	146	576	72	149	27	6	15	40	57-3	2	64	.259	.327	.405	96	-3	4-9	.980	-5	98	106	2b146		0.1
1958	Det A	154	610	91	164	25	4	14	75	54-1	4	54	.269	.328	.392	92	-6	6-4	.985	11	106	96	2b154		1.6
1959	Det A	127	459	56	122	18	3	13	55	45-2	7	37	.266	.339	.403	98	-1	2-2	.987	4	99	101	2b126		1.2
1960	Det A	139	536	64	136	20	4	9	59	40-2	2	48	.254	.308	.356	77	-18	7-4	.978	-2	97	93	2b138		-1.0
1961	Mil N★	148	585	86	153	16	4	15	56	57-1	3	62	.262	.329	.379	93	-6	7-3	.988	-1	110	107	2b148		0.6
1962	Mil N★	122	406	43	110	17	4	9	43	35-3	4	45	.271	.333	.399	99	-1	2-2	.989	-7	99	104	2b119		0.2
1963	Mil N	142	542	73	132	18	2	5	43	41-3	3	47	.244	.299	.312	77	-16	2-1	.981	2	101	133	2b141		-0.2
1964	Mil N	120	352	35	70	11	1	5	34	21-3	2	44	.199	.245	.278	48	-25	0-1	.985	-5	94	117	2b117		-2.4
1965	Mil N	148	535	55	141	26	3	7	50	24-6	3	41	.264	.295	.363	84	-12	0-4	.976	-11	94	97	2b147		-1.3
1966	Atl N	75	227	16	48	7	0	1	18	10-3	1	14	.211	.244	.256	40	-18	1-1	.983	-9	90	92	2b67		-2.5
Total	12	1540	5562	692	1415	221	40	106	556	462-28	30	558	.254	.313	.366	85	-114	40-38	.982	-52	99	102	2b1518		-6.2

BOLLING, JACK   John Edward B2.20.1917 Mobile AL D4.13.1998 Panama City FL BL/TL/5-11/168 d6.10 Mil 1944-46 Col Alabama

YEAR	TM LG	G	AB	R	H	2B	3B	HR	RBI	BB-IB	HP	SO	AVG	OBP	SLG	AOPS	ABR	SB-CS	FA	FR	RNG	THR	GAMES AT POSITION	DL	BFW
1939	Phi N	69	211	27	61	11	0	3	13	11	0	10	.289	.324	.384	92	-3	6	.982	2	123	77	1b48		-0.5
1944	Bro N	56	131	21	46	14	1	1	25	14	1	4	.351	.418	.496	159	11	0	.991	1	114	30	1b27		1.1
Total	2	125	342	48	107	25	1	4	38	25	1	14	.313	.361	.427	118	8	6	.985	3	120	60	1b75		0.6

BOLLING, MILT   Milton Joseph B8.9.1930 Mississippi City MS BR/TR/6-1/180* d9.10 b-Frank

YEAR	TM LG	G	AB	R	H	2B	3B	HR	RBI	BB-IB	HP	SO	AVG	OBP	SLG	AOPS	ABR	SB-CS	FA	FR	RNG	THR	GAMES AT POSITION	DL	BFW
1952	Bos A	11	36	4	8	1	0	1	3	3	0	5	.222	.282	.333	66	-2	0-1	.984	3	124	80	S11		0.2
1953	Bos A	109	323	30	85	12	1	5	28	23	3	41	.263	.318	.353	77	-11	1-4	.956	5	104	110	S109		0.1
1954	Bos A	113	370	42	92	20	1	6	36	47	4	55	.249	.337	.368	84	-7	2-4	.946	9	111	97	S107,3b5		1.1
1955	Bos A	6	5	0	1	0	0	0	0	0-0	1	1	.200	.200	.200	7	-1	0-0	.800	-0	109	0	S2	63	-0.1
1956	Bos A	45	118	19	25	3	2	3	8	18-1	1	20	.212	.319	.347	68	-6	0-1	.947	6	94	78	S26,3b11/2		-0.9
1957	Bos A	1	1	0	0	0	0	0	0	0-0	0	0	.000	.000	.000	-95	0	0-0	—	0			/H		0.0
	Was A	91	277	29	63	12	1	4	19	18-0	2	59	.227	.277	.321	64	-14	2-2	.982	7	110	94	2b53,S37/3		-0.2
	Year	92	278	29	63	12	1	4	19	18-0	2	59	.227	.276	.320	64	-14	2-2	.982	7	110	94	2b53,S37/3		-0.2
1958	Det A	24	31	3	6	2	0	0	3	5-0	0	7	.194	.306	.258	53	-2	0-0	.946	1	96	151	S13/23		-0.1
Total	7	400	1161	127	280	50	7	19	94	114-1	10	188	.241	.313	.345	74	-43	5-12	.952	20	107	100	S305,2b55,3b18	63	0.1

BOLLWEG, DON   Donald Raymond B2.12.1921 Wheaton IL D5.26.1996 Wheaton IL BL/TL/6-1/190* d9.28

YEAR	TM LG	G	AB	R	H	2B	3B	HR	RBI	BB-IB	HP	SO	AVG	OBP	SLG	AOPS	ABR	SB-CS	FA	FR	RNG	THR	GAMES AT POSITION	DL	BFW
1950	StL N	4	11	1	2	0	0	0	1	0	0	1	.182	.250	.182	15	-1	0-0	1.000	-1	0	115	1b4		-0.2
1951	StL N	6	9	1	1	0	0	0	2	0	0	1	.111	.111	.222	-13	-1	0-0	.941	-1	0	155	1b2		-0.2
1953	†NY A	70	155	24	46	6	4	6	24	21	1	31	.297	.384	.503	143	9	1-0	.983	-4	66	116	1b43		0.4
1954	Phi A	103	268	35	60	15	3	5	24	35	3	33	.224	.319	.358	85	-5	1-0	.978	2	119	83	1b71		-0.7
1955	KC A	12	9	1	1	0	0	0	2	3-2	0	2	.111	.333	.111	23	-1	0-0	1.000	-0	0	377	1b3		-0.1
Total	5	195	452	62	110	22	7	11	53	60-2	4	68	.243	.337	.396	100	1	2-0	.980	-3	95	98	1b123		-0.8

BOLTON, CECIL   Cecil Glenford "Glenn" B2.13.1904 Booneville MS D8.25.1993 Jackson MS BL/TR/6-4/195 d9.21 Col Mississippi St.

YEAR	TM LG	G	AB	R	H	2B	3B	HR	RBI	BB-IB	HP	SO	AVG	OBP	SLG	AOPS	ABR	SB-CS	FA	FR	RNG	THR	GAMES AT POSITION	DL	BFW
1928	Cle A	4	13	1	2	0	2	0	2	0	2	.154	.267	.462	87	-1	0-0	.955	-1	42	93	1b4		-0.2

BOLTON, CLIFF   William Clifton B4.10.1907 High Point NC D4.21.1979 Lexington NC BL/TR/5-9/160 d4.20

YEAR	TM LG	G	AB	R	H	2B	3B	HR	RBI	BB-IB	HP	SO	AVG	OBP	SLG	AOPS	ABR	SB-CS	FA	FR	RNG	THR	GAMES AT POSITION	DL	BFW
1931	Was A	23	43	3	11	1	1	0	6	1	0	5	.256	.273	.326	56	-3	0-0	.947	-3	103	92	C13		-0.5
1933	†Was A	33	39	4	16	1	1	0	6	6	1	3	.410	.500	.487	164	4	0-0	.889	-1	160	75	C9/OR		0.3
1934	Was A	42	148	12	40	9	1	1	17	11	0	9	.270	.321	.365	80	-5	2-0	.981	-3	152	120	C39		-0.4
1935	Was A	110	375	47	114	18	11	2	55	58	1	13	.304	.399	.427	117	11	0-1	.971	-23	75	87	C106		-0.5
1936	Was A	86	289	41	84	18	4	2	51	25	1	12	.291	.349	.401	90	-5	1-2	.979	-2	86	114	C83		-0.2
1937	Det A	27	57	6	15	2	0	1	7	8	0	6	.263	.354	.351	76	-2	0-0	.982	0	89	121	C13		-0.1
1941	Was A	14	11	0	0	0	0	0	0	1	0	2	.000	.083	.000	-80	-7	0-0	1.000	0	0	0	C3		-0.3
Total	7	335	962	113	280	49	18	6	143	110	3	50	.291	.366	.398	98	-3	3-3	.974	-32	94	102	C266/OR		-1.7

BOND, WALT   Walter Franklin B10.19.1937 Denmark TN D9.14.1967 Houston TX BL/TR/6-7/228(222-235) d4.19 Col Lane

YEAR	TM LG	G	AB	R	H	2B	3B	HR	RBI	BB-IB	HP	SO	AVG	OBP	SLG	AOPS	ABR	SB-CS	FA	FR	RNG	THR	GAMES AT POSITION	DL	BFW
1960	Cle A	40	131	19	29	2	1	5	18	13-2	3	14	.221	.302	.366	84	-3	4-1	1.000	1	110	93	O36(5/11/20)		-0.3
1961	Cle A	38	52	7	9	1	1	2	7	6-0	1	10	.173	.267	.346	65	-3	1-0	1.000	0	98	155	O12(0/1/11)		-0.3
1962	Cle A	12	50	10	19	3	0	6	17	4-1	0	9	.380	.426	.800	228	9	1-0	1.000	-0	107	0	O12(3/0/10)		0.8
1964	Hou N	148	543	63	138	16	7	20	85	38-8	8	90	.254	.304	.420	110	5	2-2	.989	-10	75	83	1b76,O71(28/1/42)		-1.4
1965	Hou N	117	407	46	107	17	2	7	47	42-8	5	51	.263	.337	.366	106	4	2-1	.983	-5	96	92	1b74,O38(18/0/21)		-0.8
1967	Min A	10	16	4	5	1	0	1	5	3-0	0	1	.313	.400	.563	174	2	0-0	.875	1	0	160	O3L		0.2
Total	6	365	1199	149	307	40	11	41	179	106-19	17	175	.256	.323	.410	110	14	10-4	.974	-13	99	37	O172(57/13/104),1b150		-1.8

BONDS, BARRY   Barry Lamar B7.24.1964 Riverside CA BL/TL/6-1/190(185-230) [PitN85 1/6] d5.30 f-Bobby Col Arizona St.

YEAR	TM LG	G	AB	R	H	2B	3B	HR	RBI	BB-IB	HP	SO	AVG	OBP	SLG	AOPS	ABR	SB-CS	FA	FR	RNG	THR	GAMES AT POSITION	DL	BFW
1986	Pit N	113	413	72	92	26	3	16	48	65-2	2	102	.223	.330	.416	102	2	36-7	.983	4	108	140	O110C		1.1
1987	Pit N	150	551	99	144	34	9	25	59	54-3	3	88	.261	.329	.492	113	9	32-10	.986	16	117	172	O145(101/46/1)		2.4
1988	Pit N	144	538	97	152	30	5	24	58	72-14	2	82	.283	.368	.491	146	33	17-11	.980	2	107	60	O136(135/3/0)		3.3
1989	Pit N	159	580	96	144	34	6	19	58	93-22	1	93	.248	.351	.426	126	22	32-10	.984	12	111	154	O156L		3.5
1990	†Pit N★	151	519	104	156	32	3	33	114	93-15	3	83	.301	.406	.565	171	54	52-13	.983	8	107	126	O150(149/2/0)		6.4
1991	†Pit N★	153	510	95	149	28	5	25	116	107-25	4	73	.292	.410	.514	162	48	43-13	.991	6	106	147	O150(150/4/0)		5.6
1992	†Pit N★	140	473	109	147	36	5	34	103	127-32	5	69	.311	.456	.624	205	75	39-8	.991	-0	104	57	O139L	19	7.9
1993	SF N★	159	539	129	181	38	4	46	123	126-43	2	79	.336	.458	.677	207	90	29-12	.984	-3	100	59	O157L		8.0
1994	SF N★	112	391	89	122	18	1	37	81	74-18	6	43	.312	.426	.647	182	50	29-9	.986	1	92	144	O112L		4.8
1995	SF N★	144	506	109	149	30	7	33	104	120-22	5	83	.294	.431	.577	168	56	31-10	.980	5	104	130	O143L		5.6
1996	SF N★	158	517	122	159	27	3	42	129	151-30	1	76	.308	.461	.615	186	75	40-7	.980	-4	104	114	O152(149/6/0)		7.6
1997	†SF N★	159	532	123	155	26	5	40	101	145-34	8	87	.291	.446	.585	172	65	37-8	.984	-0	100	95	O159L		6.2
1998	SF N★	156	552	120	167	44	7	37	122	130-29	8	92	.303	.438	.609	182	74	28-12	.984	-1	105	20	O155L		6.6
1999	SF N	102	355	91	93	20	2	34	83	73-9	3	62	.262	.389	.617	160	34	15-2	.984	-0	100	69	O96L,D4	52	3.0
2000	†SF N★	143	480	129	147	28	4	49	106	117-22	3	77	.306	.440	.688	193	73	11-3	.989	5	104	99	O141L		6.8
2001	SF N★	153	476	129	156	32	2	73	137	177-35	9	93	.328	.515	.863	263	133	13-3	.977	-4	94	82	O143L,D6		11.7
2002	†SF N★	143	403	117	149	31	2	46	110	198-68	9	47	.370	.582	.799	274	126	9-2	.968	-2	100	49	O135L,D5		11.5
2003	SF N★	130	390	111	133	22	1	45	90	148-61	10	58	.341	.529	.749	226	87	7-0	.992	2	106	67	O123L,D6		8.2
2004	SF N★	147	373	129	135	27	3	45	101	232-120	9	41	.362	.609	.812	255	119	6-1	.983	-2	91	150	O133L,D7		10.6
2005	SF N	14	42	8	12	1	0	5	10	9-3	0	6	.286	.404	.667	170	4	0-0	1.000	-1	87	0	O13L	162	0.3
Total	20	2730	9140	2078	2742	564	77	708	1853	2311-607	93	1434	.300	.442	.611	183	1229	506-141	.984	51	103	101	O2648(2489/171/1),D28	233	121.1

BONDS, BOBBY   Bobby Lee B3.15.1946 Riverside CA D8.23.2003 San Carlos CA BR/TR/6-1/190* d6.25 C8 s-Barry Col Riverside (CA) CC

YEAR	TM LG	G	AB	R	H	2B	3B	HR	RBI	BB-IB	HP	SO	AVG	OBP	SLG	AOPS	ABR	SB-CS	FA	FR	RNG	THR	GAMES AT POSITION	DL	BFW
1968	SF N	81	307	55	78	10	5	9	35	38-0	1	84	.254	.336	.407	123	9	16-7	.978	1	105	98	O80(0/35/62)		0.8
1969	SF N	158	622	120	161	25	6	32	90	81-3	10	187	.259	.351	.473	131	26	45-4	.978	-1	104	77	O155(0/77/99)		2.8

YEAR	TM LG	G	AB	R	H	2B	3B	HR	RBI	BB-IB	HP	SO	AVG	OBP	SLG	AOPS	ABR	SB-CS	FA	FR	RNG	THR	GAMES AT POSITION	DL	BFW
1970	SF N	157	663	134	200	36	10	26	78	77-7	2	189	.302	.375	.504	135	32	48-10	.969	6	105	131	O157(1/32/141)		3.7
1971	†SF N★	155	619	110	178	32	4	33	102	62-6	5	137	.288	.355	.512	145	36	26-8	.994	2	104	93	O154(0/33/133)		3.5
1972	SF N	153	626	118	162	29	5	26	80	60-4	5	137	.259	.326	.446	116	12	44-6	.978	5	115	70	O153(0/12/143)		1.8
1973	SF N★	160	643	131	182	34	4	39	96	87-9	4	148	.283	.370	.530	141	36	43-17	.970	6	115	84	O158(0/2/158)		3.9
1974	SF N	150	567	97	145	22	8	21	71	95-8	4	134	.256	.358	.434	118	16	41-11	.966	2	107	106	O148(0/8/141)		1.6
1975	NY A★	145	529	93	143	26	3	32	85	89-8	3	137	.270	.375	.512	151	38	30-17	.987	5	107	122	O129(1/44/90),D12		3.8
1976	Cal A	99	378	48	100	10	3	10	54	41-6	3	90	.265	.337	.386	120	9	30-15	.977	3	101	130	O98R/D	67	0.9
1977	Cal A	158	592	103	156	23	9	37	115	74-5	2	141	.264	.342	.520	138	29	41-18	.986	0	104	53	O140R,D18		2.3
1978	Chi A	26	90	8	25	4	0	2	8	10-1	0	10	.278	.347	.389	106	1	6-2	.956	0	89	188	O22R,D3		0.1
	Tex A	130	475	85	126	15	4	29	82	69-6	2	110	.265	.356	.497	138	24	37-20	.970	-1	90	154	O111R,D18		-1.8
	Year	156	565	93	151	19	4	31	90	79-7	2	120	.267	.355	.480	133	25	43-22	.968	-1	90	159	O133R,D21		1.9
1979	Cle A	146	538	93	148	24	1	25	85	74-4	8	135	.275	.367	.463	123	19	34-23	.979	7	116	107	O116R,D29		1.8
1980	StL N	86	231	37	47	5	3	5	24	33-3	2	74	.203	.305	.316	71	-9	15-5	.967	-0	97	107	O70(63/0/15)	22	-1.1
1981	Chi N	45	163	26	35	7	1	6	19	24-5	2	44	.215	.323	.380	93	-1	5-6	.982	-3	94	65	O45(0/42/3)	65	-0.5
Total	14	1849	7043	1258	1886	302	66	332	1024	914-75	53	1757	.268	.353	.471	129	277	461-169	.977	32	106	100	O1736(65/285/1472),D81	154	27.2

BONE, GEORGE George Drummond B8.28.1876 New Haven CT D5.26.1918 West Haven CT BB/TR/5-7/152 d9.18

YEAR	TM LG	G	AB	R	H	2B	3B	HR	RBI	BB-IB	HP	SO	AVG	OBP	SLG	AOPS	ABR	SB-CS	FA	FR	RNG	THR	GAMES AT POSITION	DL	BFW
1901	Mil A	12	43	6	13	2	0	0	6	4	0	0	.302	.362	.349	103	0	0	.869	-1	87	148	S12		0.0

BONGIOVANNI, NINO Anthony Thomas B12.21.1911 New Orleans LA BL/TL/5-10/175 d4.23

YEAR	TM LG	G	AB	R	H	2B	3B	HR	RBI	BB-IB	HP	SO	AVG	OBP	SLG	AOPS	ABR	SB-CS	FA	FR	RNG	THR	GAMES AT POSITION	DL	BFW
1938	Cin N	2	7	0	2	1	0	0	0	0	0	0	.286	.286	.429	97	0	0	1.000	0	123	0	O2L		0.0
1939	†Cin N	66	159	17	41	6	0	0	16	9	0	8	.258	.298	.296	60	-9	0	.989	1	119	31	O39(6/1/32)		-1.0
Total	2	68	166	17	43	7	0	0	16	9	0	8	.259	.297	.301	61	-9	0	.990	1	119	29	O41(8/1/32)		-1.0

BONILLA, JUAN Juan Guillermo B2.12.1955 Santurce, PR BR/TR/5-9/170* d4.9 Col Florida St.

YEAR	TM LG	G	AB	R	H	2B	3B	HR	RBI	BB-IB	HP	SO	AVG	OBP	SLG	AOPS	ABR	SB-CS	FA	FR	RNG	THR	GAMES AT POSITION	DL	BFW
1981	SD N	99	369	30	107	13	2	1	25	25-5	2	23	.290	.337	.344	102	1	4-9	.976	-8	98	108	2b97		-0.4
1982	SD N	45	182	21	51	6	2	0	8	11-0	1	15	.280	.325	.335	90	-3	0-1	.975	-4	100	100	2b45	124	-0.5
1983	SD N	152	556	55	132	17	4	4	45	50-11	3	40	.237	.301	.304	71	-22	3-0	.986	-9	97	104	2b149		-2.3
1985	NY A	8	16	0	2	1	0	0	2	0-0	0	3	.125	.125	.188	-16	-3	0-0	.955	0	109	105	2b7		-0.2
1986	Bal A	102	284	33	69	10	1	1	18	25-0	0	21	.243	.311	.296	67	-13	0-0	.981	-4	90	107	2b70,3b33,D2		-1.3
1987	NY A	23	55	6	14	3	0	1	3	5-0	0	6	.255	.317	.364	80	-2	0-0	.965	-2	91	89	2b22/3D		-0.3
Total	6	429	1462	145	375	50	9	7	101	116-16	9	108	.256	.314	.317	79	-42	7-10	.980	-27	96	104	2b390,3b34,D3	124	-5.0

BONILLA, BOBBY Roberto Martin Antonio B2.23.1963 Bronx NY BB/TR/6-3/240(210-240) d4.9 OF(206/10/698) [DL 1985 Pit N 102]

YEAR	TM LG	G	AB	R	H	2B	3B	HR	RBI	BB-IB	HP	SO	AVG	OBP	SLG	AOPS	ABR	SB-CS	FA	FR	RNG	THR	GAMES AT POSITION	DL	BFW
1986	Chi A	75	234	27	63	10	2	2	26	33-2	1	49	.269	.361	.355	93	-1	4-1	.989	1	110	79	O43(39/4/4),1b30		-0.3
	Pit N	63	192	28	46	6	2	1	17	29-1	1	39	.240	.342	.307	78	-5	4-4	.974	-0	85	94	O51(37/6/24),1b4,3b4		-0.8
1987	Pit N	141	466	58	140	33	3	15	77	39-4	2	64	.300	.351	.481	118	12	3-5	.932	-10	92	93	3b89,O46(17/0/34),1b6		-0.2
1988	Pit N★	159	584	87	160	32	7	24	100	85-19	4	82	.274	.366	.476	142	34	3-5	.935	3	108	66	3b159		3.8
1989	Pit N★	163	616	96	173	37	10	24	86	76-20	1	93	.281	.358	.490	146	36	8-8	.929	5	108	121	3b156,1b8/OR		4.2
1990	†Pit N★	160	625	112	175	39	7	32	120	45-9	1	103	.280	.322	.518	134	25	4-3	.961	-5	91	73	O149R,3b14,1b3		1.6
1991	†Pit N★	157	577	102	174	44	6	18	100	90-8	2	67	.302	.391	.492	150	43	2-4	.989	3	93	113	O104R,3b67,1b4		4.3
1992	NY N	128	438	62	109	23	0	19	70	66-10	1	73	.249	.348	.432	121	13	4-3	.992	4	108	93	O121R,1b6		1.4
1993	NY N★	139	502	81	133	21	3	34	87	72-11	0	96	.265	.352	.522	134	23	3-3	.969	-2	88	105	O85R,3b52,1b6	16	1.6
1994	NY N	108	403	60	117	24	1	20	67	55-9	0	101	.290	.374	.504	128	18	1-3	.942	6	111	153	3b107		2.3
1995	NY N★	80	317	49	103	25	4	18	53	31-10	1	48	.325	.385	.599	161	27	0-3	.882	-5	88	122	3b46,O31L,1b10		1.9
	Bal A	61	237	47	79	12	4	10	46	23-0	1	31	.333	.394	.544	139	13	0-2	.971	1	94	83	O39(1/0/38),3b24		1.0
1996	†Bal A	159	595	107	171	27	5	28	116	75-7	5	85	.287	.363	.491	116	15	1-3	.975	-8	86	107	O108R,D44,1b9,3b4		-0.1
1997	†Fla N	153	562	77	167	39	3	17	96	73-8	5	94	.297	.378	.468	127	24	6-6	.938	-17	81	115	3b149,1b2,D3		0.8
1998	Fla N	28	97	11	27	5	0	4	15	12-1	0	22	.278	.355	.454	119	3	0-1	.922	-4	84	117	3b26	12	-0.1
	LA N	72	236	28	56	6	1	7	30	29-3	0	37	.237	.315	.360	83	-6	1-1	.912	-9	80	85	3b59,O12L	36	-1.5
	Year	100	333	39	83	11	1	11	45	41-4	0	59	.249	.326	.387	93	-4	1-2	.915	-13	81	95	3b85,O12L		-1.6
1999	†NY N	60	119	12	19	5	0	4	18	19-1	1	16	.160	.277	.303	50	-10	0-1	.974	1	100	168	O25(2/0/23),1b4,D3	80	-1.4
2000	†Atl N	114	239	23	61	13	3	5	28	37-2	1	51	.255	.356	.397	91	-3	0-0	.927	-10	57	34	O64(63/0/1)/3D		-1.4
2001	StL N	93	174	17	37	7	0	5	21	23-3	1	51	.213	.308	.339	66	-9	1-1	.992	-2	61	139	1b33,O10(4/0/6)/PD	8	-1.3
Total	16	2113	7213	1084	2010	408	61	287	1173	912-128	28	1204	.279	.358	.472	124	252	45-57	.931	-49	100	108	3b957,O889R,1b125,D53/P	254	16.2

BONIN, LUTHER Ernest Luther "Bonnie" B1.13.1888 Greenhill IN D1.3.1966 Sycamore OH BL/TR/5-9.5/178 d4.13

YEAR	TM LG	G	AB	R	H	2B	3B	HR	RBI	BB-IB	HP	SO	AVG	OBP	SLG	AOPS	ABR	SB-CS	FA	FR	RNG	THR	GAMES AT POSITION	DL	BFW
1913	StL A	1	1	0	0	0	0	0	0	0	0	0	.000	.000	.000	-99	0	0	—	0			/H		0.0
1914	Buf F	20	76	6	14	4	1	0	4	7	0	11	.184	.253	.263	40	-8	3	.970	0	94	122	O20R		-0.9
Total	2	21	77	6	14	4	1	0	4	7	0	11	.182	.250	.260	38	-8	3	.970	0	94	122	O20R		-0.9

BONNELL, BARRY Robert Barry B10.27.1953 Mariemont OH BR/TR/6-3/200(190-208) [PhiN75*S1/1] d5.4 Col Ohio St. OF(395/344/214)

YEAR	TM LG	G	AB	R	H	2B	3B	HR	RBI	BB-IB	HP	SO	AVG	OBP	SLG	AOPS	ABR	SB-CS	FA	FR	RNG	THR	GAMES AT POSITION	DL	BFW
1977	Atl N	100	360	41	108	11	0	1	45	37-8	2	32	.300	.368	.339	82	-7	7-5	.989	6	124	76	O75(2/63/10),3b32	22	-0.3
1978	Atl N	117	304	36	73	11	3	1	16	20-1	0	30	.240	.287	.306	59	-16	12-6	.984	7	105	159	O105(53/55/11),3b15		-1.2
1979	Atl N	127	375	47	97	20	4	12	45	26-2	3	55	.259	.311	.424	93	-4	8-7	.983	-1	92	106	O124(77/74/0)/3		-0.9
1980	Tor A	130	463	55	124	22	4	13	56	37-2	2	59	.268	.322	.417	98	-2	3-4	.973	-1	92	164	O122(5/57/61),D3	19	-0.7
1981	Tor A	66	227	21	50	7	4	4	28	12-0	1	25	.220	.242	.339	68	-10	4-3	.975	1	103	112	O66(9/18/41)		-1.3
1982	Tor A	140	437	59	128	26	3	6	49	32-4	1	51	.293	.342	.407	97	-1	14-2	.979	-6	93	45	O125(99/3/7),3b9,D6		-0.8
1983	Tor A	121	377	49	120	21	3	10	54	33-5	1	52	.318	.369	.469	122	12	10-7	.986	-1	94	95	O117(62/22/51),3b4/D		0.6
1984	Sea A	110	363	42	96	15	4	8	48	25-3	2	51	.264	.315	.394	95	-3	5-2	.994	-0	89	153	O94(70/16/20),3b10,1b5,D8		-1.0
1985	Sea A	48	111	9	27	8	0	1	10	6-1	0	19	.243	.282	.342	69	-5	1-2	.976	-0	101	164	O22(9/0/13),1b5,D2	30	-0.6
1986	Sea A	17	51	4	10	2	0	0	4	1-0	0	13	.196	.208	.235	21	-5	0-1	.941	1	99	0	O9L,1b8,D2		-0.6
Total	10	976	3068	363	833	143	24	56	355	229-26	13	387	.272	.323	.389	90	-42	64-39	.982	2	97	114	O859L,3b71,D22,1b18	71	-6.8

BONNER, FRANK Frank J B8.20.1869 Lowell MA D12.31.1905 Kansas City MO BR/TR/5-7.5/169 d4.26

YEAR	TM LG	G	AB	R	H	2B	3B	HR	RBI	BB-IB	HP	SO	AVG	OBP	SLG	AOPS	ABR	SB-CS	FA	FR	RNG	THR	GAMES AT POSITION	DL	BFW
1894	†Bal N	33	118	27	38	10	2	0	24	17	1	5	.322	.412	.441	101	7	12	.904	-9	82	74	2b27,O4(2/1/1),3b2/S		-0.5
1895	Bal N	11	42	9	14	1	1	0	7	5	0	4	.333	.404	.405	106	0	4	.742	-4	76	159	3b11		-0.2
	StL N	15	59	3	8	0	1	1	8	1	1	8	.136	.164	.254	-1	-10	2	.656	-5	72	0	3b10,O5R/C		-1.2
	Year	26	101	12	22	1	2	1	15	6	1	9	.218	.269	.297	46	-9	6	.698	-8	74	83	3b21,O5R/C		-1.4
1896	Bro N	9	34	8	6	2	0	0	5	2	2	5	.176	.263	.235	34	-3	1	.915	0	129	84	2b9		-0.2
1899	Was N	85	347	41	95	20	4	2	44	18	2		.274	.313	.372	88	-6	6	.940	3	102	94	2b85		0.1
1902	Cle A	34	132	14	37	6	0	0	14	5	1		.280	.312	.326	80	-4	1	.907	-6	95	39	2b34		-0.9
	Phi A	11	44	2	8	0	0	0	3	0	1		.182	.200	.182	6	-6	0	.937	-1	95	80	2b11		-0.7
	Year	45	176	16	45	6	0	0	17	5	2		.256	.284	.290	61	-10	1	.915	-7	95	50	2b45		-1.6
1903	Bos N	48	173	11	38	5	0	1	10	7	3		.220	.262	.266	53	-11	2	.957	-1	99	145	2b26,S22		-1.0
Total	6	246	949	115	244	44	8	4	115	55	11	22	.257	.305	.333	73	-39	28	.931	-21	99	87	2b190,S23,3b23,O9(2/1/6)/C		-4.6

BONNER, BOBBY Robert Averill B8.12.1956 Uvalde TX BR/TR/6-0/185* [BalA78 3/74] d9.12 Col Texas A&M-Commerce

YEAR	TM LG	G	AB	R	H	2B	3B	HR	RBI	BB-IB	HP	SO	AVG	OBP	SLG	AOPS	ABR	SB-CS	FA	FR	RNG	THR	GAMES AT POSITION	DL	BFW
1980	Bal A	4	4	0	0	0	0	0	0	0-0	0	0	.000	.000	.000	-99	0	0-0	.889	-0	110	91	S3		-0.1
1981	Bal A	10	27	6	8	2	0	0	1	0-0	0	0	.296	.310	.370	99	0	1-0	.976	2	109	163	S9		0.3
1982	Bal A	41	77	8	13	0	0	0	5	3-0	0	12	.169	.198	.234	19	-9	0-0	.959	-12	76	62	S38,2b3		-1.8
1983	Bal A	6	0	0	0	0	0	0	0	0-0	0	0	—	—	—	—	0	0-0	1.000	-1	0	0	2b5/D		-0.1
Total	4	61	108	15	21	5	1	0	8	4-0	0	16	.194	.219	.259	34	-10	1-0	.980	-10	85	85	S50,2b8/D		-1.7

BONURA, ZEKE Henry John B9.20.1908 New Orleans LA D3.9.1987 New Orleans LA BR/TR/6-0/210 d4.17 Mil 1941-45

YEAR	TM LG	G	AB	R	H	2B	3B	HR	RBI	BB-IB	HP	SO	AVG	OBP	SLG	AOPS	ABR	SB-CS	FA	FR	RNG	THR	GAMES AT POSITION	DL	BFW
1934	Chi A	127	510	86	154	35	4	27	110	64	0	31	.302	.380	.545	132	23	0-2	.996	4	109	81	1b127		1.3
1935	Chi A	138	550	107	162	34	4	21	92	57	3	28	.295	.364	.485	115	11	4-0	.994	2	105	93	1b138		0.1
1936	Chi A	148	587	120	194	39	7	12	138	94	4	29	.330	.426	.482	119	22	4-2	.996	11	134	118	1b146		1.7
1937	Chi A	116	447	79	154	41	2	19	100	49	2	24	.345	.412	.573	146	32	5-1	.989	-2	97	132	1b115		1.9
1938	Was A	137	540	72	156	27	3	22	114	44	1	29	.289	.346	.472	111	6	2-2	.993	3	109	107	1b129		-0.4
1939	NY N	123	455	75	146	26	3	11	85	56	2	22	.321	.388	.477	130	20	1	.992	6	118	104	1b122		1.5
1940	Was A	79	311	41	85	16	3	3	45	40	1	13	.273	.358	.373	96	-1	2-0	.982	-4	85	97	1b79		-1.1
	Chi N	49	182	20	48	14	0	4	20	10	2	4	.264	.302	.407	96	-1	1	.991	6	151	99	1b44		0.0
Total	7	917	3582	600	1099	232	29	119	704	404	17	180	.307	.384	.487	121	112	19-7	.992	26	112	104	1b900		5.0

YEAR	TM LG	G	AB	R	H	2B	3B	HR	RBI	BB-IB	HP	SO	AVG	OBP	SLG	AOPS	ABR	SB-CS	FA	FR	RNG	THR	GAMES AT POSITION	DL	BFW

BOOE, EVERETT Everett Little B9.28.1891 Mocksville NC D5.21.1969 Kenedy TX BL/TR/5-8.5/165 d4.13 Col Davidson

YEAR	TM LG	G	AB	R	H	2B	3B	HR	RBI	BB-IB	HP	SO	AVG	OBP	SLG	AOPS	ABR	SB-CS	FA	FR	RNG	THR	GAMES AT POSITION	DL	BFW
1913	Pit N	29	80	9	16	0	2	0	2	6	0	9	.200	.256	.250	47	-6	2-4	1.000	1	89	162	O22(1/21/0)		-0.8
1914	Ind F	20	31	5	7	1	0	0	6	7	0	6	.226	.368	.258	65	-2	4	.778	-1	96	0	O5(4/1/0),S3		-0.3
	Buf F	76	241	29	54	9	2	0	14	21	1	50	.224	.289	.278	54	-19	8	.959	-3	97	90	O58(23/0/35),S8,3b2/2		-2.6
	Year	96	272	34	61	10	2	0	20	28	1	56	.224	.299	.276	55	-21	12	.944	-5	97	84	O63(27/1/35),S11,3b2/2		-2.9
Total	2	125	352	43	77	10	4	0	22	34	1	65	.219	.289	.270	54	-27	14-4	.959	-4	95	102	O85(28/22/35),S11,3b2/2		-3.7

BOOKER, BUDDY Richard Lee B5.28.1942 Lynchburg VA BL/TR/5-10/170(170-185) d6.4

YEAR	TM LG	G	AB	R	H	2B	3B	HR	RBI	BB-IB	HP	SO	AVG	OBP	SLG	AOPS	ABR	SB-CS	FA	FR	RNG	THR	GAMES AT POSITION	DL	BFW
1966	Cle A	18	28	6	6	1	0	2	5	2-0	0	6	.214	.267	.464	105	0	0-0	.964	-4	85	66	C12		-0.4
1968	Chi A	5	5	0	0	0	0	0	0	1-0	0	2	.000	.167	.000	-46	-1	0-0	1.000	-1	28	56	C3		-0.2
Total	2	23	33	6	6	1	0	2	5	3-0	0	8	.182	.250	.394	83	-1	0-0	.967	-4	80	60	C15		-0.6

BOOKER, ROD Roderick Stewart B9.4.1958 Los Angeles CA BL/TR/6-0/175* [MinA80 4/90] d4.29 Col California-Davis

YEAR	TM LG	G	AB	R	H	2B	3B	HR	RBI	BB-IB	HP	SO	AVG	OBP	SLG	AOPS	ABR	SB-CS	FA	FR	RNG	THR	GAMES AT POSITION	DL	BFW
1987	StL N	44	47	9	13	1	1	0	8	7-1	0	7	.277	.370	.340	88	-1	2-0	.960	1	105	57	2b18,3b4/S		0.2
1988	StL N	18	35	6	12	3	0	0	3	4-0	0	3	.343	.410	.429	139	2	2-2	.889	-2	85	0	3b13/2		0.0
1989	StL N	10	8	1	2	0	0	0	0	0-0	0	1	.250	.250	.250	42	-1	0-0	.867	1	149	177	2b5/3		0.0
1990	Phi N	73	131	19	29	5	2	0	10	15-7	0	26	.221	.301	.290	64	-6	3-1	.976	-11	76	93	S27,2b23,3b10		-1.6
1991	Phi N	28	53	2	12	1	0	0	7	1-1	0	7	.226	.236	.245	37	-5	0-0	1.000	-5	75	29	S20,3b3		-0.9
Total	5	173	274	38	68	10	3	0	28	27-9	0	44	.248	.315	.307	72	-11	7-3	.985	-16	76	68	S48,2b47,3b31		-2.3

BOOL, AL Albert B8.24.1897 Lincoln NE D9.27.1981 Lincoln NE BR/TR/5-11/180 d9.29

YEAR	TM LG	G	AB	R	H	2B	3B	HR	RBI	BB-IB	HP	SO	AVG	OBP	SLG	AOPS	ABR	SB-CS	FA	FR	RNG	THR	GAMES AT POSITION	DL	BFW
1928	Was A	2	7	0	1	0	0	0	1	0	0	0	.143	.143	.143	-25	-1	0-0	1.000	0	111	121	C2		-0.1
1930	Pit N	78	216	30	56	12	4	7	46	25	0	29	.259	.336	.449	87	-5	0	.967	1	95	135	C65		0.0
1931	Bos N	49	85	5	16	1	0	0	6	9	0	13	.188	.266	.200	28	-9	0	.989	-0	103	101	C37		-0.8
Total	3	129	308	35	73	13	4	7	53	34	0	42	.237	.313	.373	71	-15	0-0	.973	1	98	125	C104		-0.9

BOONE, AARON Aaron John B3.9.1973 LaMesa CA BR/TR/6-2/200* [CinN94 3/72] d6.20 b-Bret f-Bob gf-Ray Col USC [DL 2004 Cle A 100]

YEAR	TM LG	G	AB	R	H	2B	3B	HR	RBI	BB-IB	HP	SO	AVG	OBP	SLG	AOPS	ABR	SB-CS	FA	FR	RNG	THR	GAMES AT POSITION	DL	BFW
1997	Cin N	16	49	5	12	1	0	0	5	2-0	0	5	.245	.275	.265	41	-4	1-0	.917	-1	100	0	3b13/2		-0.4
1998	Cin N	58	181	24	51	13	2	2	28	15-1	5	36	.282	.350	.409	99	0	6-1	.950	0	103	82	3b52/2S		0.2
1999	Cin N	139	472	56	132	26	5	14	72	30-2	6	79	.280	.330	.445	92	-7	17-6	.958	2	103	89	3b136,S6		-0.3
2000	Cin N	84	291	44	83	18	0	12	43	24-1	10	52	.285	.354	.471	104	2	6-1	.964	3	103	144	3b84,S2	83	0.6
2001	Cin N	103	381	54	112	26	2	14	62	29-1	8	71	.294	.351	.482	108	6	6-3	.936	5	114	94	3b103	62	1.0
2002	Cin N★	162	606	83	146	38	2	26	87	56-4	10	111	.241	.314	.439	96	-7	32-8	.954	16	122	142	3b154,S16		1.5
2003	†NY A	54	189	31	48	13	0	6	31	11-0	3	30	.254	.302	.418	89	-3	8-0	.961	5	109	83	3b54		2.0
2005	Cle A	143	511	61	124	19	1	16	60	35-3	9	92	.243	.299	.378	83	-14	9-3	.955	2	105	88	3b142/D		-1.0
Total	8	865	3083	419	818	173	15	108	453	237-14	58	550	.265	.327	.436	97	-22	100-25	.954	43	110	106	3b821,S30,2b21/D	245	4.0

BOONE, BRET Bret Robert B4.6.1969 El Cajon CA BR/TR/5-10/180* [SeaA90 5/134] d8.19 b-Aaron f-Bob gf-Ray Col USC

YEAR	TM LG	G	AB	R	H	2B	3B	HR	RBI	BB-IB	HP	SO	AVG	OBP	SLG	AOPS	ABR	SB-CS	FA	FR	RNG	THR	GAMES AT POSITION	DL	BFW
1992	Sea A	33	129	15	25	4	0	4	15	4-0	1	34	.194	.224	.318	50	-9	1-1	.965	1	104	94	2b32,3b6		-0.8
1993	Sea A	76	271	31	68	12	2	12	38	17-1	4	52	.251	.301	.443	96	-3	2-3	.991	-5	89	116	2b74/D		-0.5
1994	Cin N	108	381	59	122	25	2	12	68	24-1	6	74	.320	.368	.491	123	13	3-4	.974	-18	94	127	2b106,3b2		-0.1
1995	†Cin N	138	513	63	137	34	2	15	68	41-0	6	84	.267	.326	.429	97	-3	5-1	.994	-8	94	127	2b138		-0.4
1996	Cin N	142	520	56	121	21	3	12	69	31-0	3	100	.233	.275	.354	65	-28	3-2	.991	3	98	95	2b141	15	-1.9
1997	Cin N	139	443	40	99	25	1	7	46	45-4	4	101	.223	.298	.332	64	-23	5-5	.997	-4	94	95	2b136		-2.1
1998	Cin N☆	157	583	76	155	38	1	24	95	48-3	4	104	.266	.324	.458	102	1	6-4	.988	-7	94	101	2b156		0.1
1999	†Atl N	152	608	102	153	38	1	20	63	47-0	5	112	.252	.310	.416	82	-18	14-9	.982	2	107	90	2b151		-0.9
2000	SD N	127	463	61	116	18	2	19	74	50-7	5	97	.251	.326	.421	94	-6	8-4	.977	-5	94	102	2b126		-0.5
2001	†Sea A★	158	623	118	206	37	3	37	141	40-5	9	110	.331	.372	.578	156	49	5-5	.986	-16	93	106	2b156,D2		3.7
2002	Sea A	155	608	88	169	34	3	24	107	53-4	6	102	.278	.339	.462	115	12	12-5	.989	-18	91	94	2b153/D		0.2
2003	Sea A★	159	622	111	183	35	5	35	117	68-3	7	125	.294	.366	.535	142	38	16-3	.990	-15	91	117	2b158		3.1
2004	Sea A	148	593	74	149	30	0	24	83	56-2	3	52	.251	.317	.423	96	-5	10-5	.978	-35	84	94	2b148		-3.0
2005	Sea A	74	273	30	63	15	3	7	34	24-2	3	52	.231	.299	.385	86	-6	4-2	.979	-15	89	87	2b74		-1.7
	Min A	14	53	3	9	0	0	3	4	1-0	0	13	.170	.241	.170	12	-7	0-0	.974	1	91	132	2b14		-0.5
	Year	88	326	33	72	15	3	7	37	28-2	4	65	.221	.290	.350	73	-13	4-2	.978	-14	89	94	2b88		-2.2
Total	14	1780	6683	927	1775	366	28	252	1021	552-32	69	1295	.266	.325	.442	101	5	94-53	.986	-140	93	102	2b1763,3b8,D4	50	-5.3

BOONE, IKE Isaac Morgan B2.17.1897 Samantha AL D8.1.1958 Northport AL BL/TR/6-0/195 d4.22 b-Dan Col Alabama

YEAR	TM LG	G	AB	R	H	2B	3B	HR	RBI	BB-IB	HP	SO	AVG	OBP	SLG	AOPS	ABR	SB-CS	FA	FR	RNG	THR	GAMES AT POSITION	DL	BFW
1922	NY N	2	2	0	1	0	0	0	0	0	0	1	.500	.500	.500	157	0	0-0	—	0			/H		0.0
1923	Bos A	5	15	1	4	0	0	0	2	1	0	1	.267	.313	.400	86	0	0-1	.929	-0	114	0	O4C		-0.1
1924	Bos A	128	487	72	164	31	4	13	98	54	1	32	.337	.404	.497	131	23	2-2	.976	-9	82	96	O124R		0.3
1925	Bos A	133	476	79	157	34	5	9	68	60	1	19	.330	.406	.479	124	19	1-4	.941	-9	90	73	O118R		0.0
1927	Chi A	29	53	10	12	4	0	1	11	3	0	4	.226	.268	.358	63	-3	0-0	1.000	-1	100	0	O11(1/0/10)		-0.4
1930	Bro N	40	101	13	30	9	1	3	13	14	0	8	.297	.383	.495	111	0	0-0	.960	-0	105	63	O27L		0.0
1931	Bro N	6	6	0	1	0	0	0	0	1	0	0	.200	.333	.200	47	0	0	—	0			/H		0.0
1932	Bro N	13	21	2	3	1	0	0	2	5	0	2	.143	.308	.190	38	-2	0	1.000	0	83	245	O8(2/0/6)		-0.1
Total	8	356	1160	177	372	79	11	26	194	138	2	67	.321	.394	.475	121	39	3-7	.960	-19	88	82	O292(30/4/258)		-0.3

BOONE, LUTE Lute Joseph "Danny" B5.6.1890 Pittsburgh PA D7.29.1982 Pittsburgh PA BR/TR/5-9/160 d9.9

YEAR	TM LG	G	AB	R	H	2B	3B	HR	RBI	BB-IB	HP	SO	AVG	OBP	SLG	AOPS	ABR	SB-CS	FA	FR	RNG	THR	GAMES AT POSITION	DL	BFW
1913	NY A	6	12	1	4	0	0	0	1	3	0	1	.333	.467	.333	134	1	0	.857	-1	87	64	S4		0.0
1914	NY A	106	370	34	82	8	2	0	21	31	2	41	.222	.285	.254	63	-17	10-18	.960	18	111	115	2b90,3b9/OR		-0.2
1915	NY A	130	431	44	88	12	2	5	43	41	8	53	.204	.285	.276	68	-17	14-17	.965	21	117	140	2b115,S11,3b4		0.3
1916	NY A	46	124	16	23	4	0	1	8	8	3	10	.185	.252	.242	47	-8	7	.973	3	119	148	3b25,S12,2b8		-0.4
1918	Pit N	27	91	7	18	3	0	0	3	8	0	9	.198	.263	.231	49	-5	1	.921	-3	95	60	S26/2		-0.8
Total	5	315	1028	102	215	27	4	6	76	91	13	111	.209	.282	.261	63	-44	32-35	.960	14	114	128	2b214,S53,3b38/OR		-1.1

BOONE, RAY Raymond Otis "Ike" B7.27.1923 San Diego CA D10.17.2004 San Diego CA BR/TR/6-1/188* d9.3 s-Bob gs-Bret gs-Aaron

YEAR	TM LG	G	AB	R	H	2B	3B	HR	RBI	BB-IB	HP	SO	AVG	OBP	SLG	AOPS	ABR	SB-CS	FA	FR	RNG	THR	GAMES AT POSITION	DL	BFW
1948	†Cle A	6	5	0	2	0	0	0	1	0	0	1	.400	.400	.600	168	0	0-0	.889	0	129	0	S4		0.1
1949	Cle A	86	258	39	65	4	4	4	26	38	2	17	.252	.352	.345	87	-5	0-2	.947	0	97	117	S76		-0.1
1950	Cle A	109	365	53	110	14	6	7	58	56	2	27	.301	.397	.430	116	10	4-3	.945	-7	93	96	S102		0.8
1951	Cle A	151	544	73	127	14	1	12	51	48	5	36	.233	.302	.329	75	-21	5-3	.957	-1	98	106	S151		-1.3
1952	Cle A	103	316	57	83	8	2	7	45	53	2	33	.263	.372	.367	113	7	0-1	.941	-4	98	102	S96,3b2/2		-0.9
1953	Cle A	34	112	21	27	1	2	4	21	24	1	21	.241	.375	.393	110	2	1-2	.952	1	100	122	S31		0.6
	Det A	101	385	73	120	16	6	22	93	48	5	47	.312	.395	.556	156	30	2-1	.958	1	99	125	3b97,S3		3.0
	Year	135	497	94	147	17	8	26	114	72	6	68	.296	.390	.516	146	32	3-3	.958	3	99	125	3b97,S34		3.6
1954	Det A★	148	543	76	160	19	7	20	85	71	2	53	.295	.376	.466	133	24	4-2	.964	2	103	80	3b148/S		2.6
1955	Det A	135	500	61	142	22	7	20	116	50-2	1	49	.284	.346	.476	123	14	1-1	.953	-2	98	133	3b126		1.2
1956	Det A★	131	481	77	148	14	6	25	81	77-8	3	46	.308	.403	.518	142	30	0-0	.959	-4	91	83	3b130		2.5
1957	Det A	129	462	48	126	25	3	12	65	57-6	3	47	.273	.353	.418	108	6	1-1	.990	-12	61	101	1b117,3b4		-1.3
1958	Det A	39	114	16	27	4	1	6	20	14-1	1	13	.237	.323	.447	103	0	0-2	.988	-1	82	101	1b32		-0.3
	Chi A	77	246	25	60	12	1	7	41	18-1	1	33	.244	.295	.386	89	-4	1-1	.986	-2	91	85	1b63		-1.1
	Year	116	360	41	87	16	2	13	61	32-2	2	46	.242	.304	.406	93	-4	1-3	.986	-3	88	90	1b95		-1.4
1959	Chi A	9	21	3	5	0	0	1	5	7-0	0	5	.238	.400	.381	126	1	1-0	.955	0	141	46	1b6		0.1
	KC A	61	132	19	36	6	0	4	12	27-2	0	17	.273	.396	.364	108	3	1-0	.983	1	117	70	1b38,3b3		0.3
	Year	70	153	22	41	6	0	5	17	34-2	0	22	.268	.398	.366	111	4	2-0	.980	2	63	224	1b44,3b3		0.4
	Mil N	13	15	3	3	0	0	0	3	4-0	0	2	.200	.368	.400	114	0	0-0	1.000	-0	63	224	1b3		0.0
1960	Mil N	7	12	3	3	1	0	0	4	5-0	0	1	.250	.471	.333	135	1	0-0	1.000	1	121	108	1b4		0.1
	Bos A	34	78	6	16	1	0	1	11	11-0	0	5	.205	.300	.256	51	-5	0-0	.994	-0	90	103	1b6		-0.7
Total	13	1373	4589	645	1260	162	46	151	737	608-20	27	463	.275	.361	.429	115	93	21-19	.958	-27	98	103	3b510,S464,1b285/2		7.4

BOONE, BOB Robert Raymond B11.19.1947 San Diego CA BR/TR/6-2/202(195-210) [PhiN69 6/124] d9.10 M6/C1 f-Ray s-Bret s-Aaron Col Stanford

YEAR	TM LG	G	AB	R	H	2B	3B	HR	RBI	BB-IB	HP	SO	AVG	OBP	SLG	AOPS	ABR	SB-CS	FA	FR	RNG	THR	GAMES AT POSITION	DL	BFW
1972	Phi N	16	51	4	14	1	0	1	4	5-2	0	7	.275	.333	.353	94	0	1-0	.936	-4	140	101	C14		-0.4
1973	Phi N	145	521	42	136	20	2	10	61	41-8	0	36	.261	.311	.365	85	-11	3-4	.990	14	120	138	C145		0.9
1974	Phi N	146	488	41	118	24	3	3	52	35-9	4	29	.242	.295	.322	70	-20	3-1	.976	-3	89	112	C146		-1.6
1975	Phi N	97	289	28	71	14	2	2	20	32-6	1	14	.246	.322	.329	77	-8	1-3	.990	2	138	117	C92,3b3		-0.4
1976	†Phi N★	121	361	40	98	18	2	4	54	45-14	1	44	.271	.356	.366	100	2	2-5	.993	-8	125	62	C108,1b4		-0.4

YEAR	TM LG	G	AB	R	H	2B	3B	HR	RBI	BB-IB	HP	SO	AVG	OBP	SLG	AOPS	ABR	SB-CS	FA	FR	RNG	THR	GAMES AT POSITION	DL	BFW
1977	†Phi N	132	440	55	125	26	4	11	66	42-5	2	54	.284	.343	.436	104	3	5-5	.989	7	119	85	C131,3b2		1.5
1978	†Phi N★	132	435	48	123	18	4	12	62	46-10	1	37	.283	.347	.425	114	8	2-5	.991	-1	133	84	C129,1b3/OL		1.1
1979	Phi N★	119	398	38	114	21	3	9	58	49-9	2	33	.286	.367	.422	110	7	1-4	.988	-3	152	101	C117,3b2		0.8
1980	†Phi N	141	480	34	110	23	1	9	55	48-12	1	41	.229	.299	.338	73	-17	3-4	.979	3	102	108	C138		-0.9
1981	Phi N	76	227	19	48	17	0	4	24	22-2	0	16	.211	.279	.295	60	-12	2-2	.985	-12	72	78	C75		-2.3
1982	†Cal A	143	472	42	121	17	0	7	58	39-2	0	34	.256	.310	.337	78	-14	0-2	.989	15	193	130	C143		0.6
1983	Cal A★	142	468	46	120	18	0	9	52	24-1	0	42	.256	.289	.353	77	-16	4-3	.980	10	148	111	C142		0.0
1984	Cal A	139	450	33	91	16	1	3	32	25-1	0	45	.202	.242	.262	40	-37	3-3	.984	4	148	93	C137		-2.4
1985	Cal A	150	460	37	114	17	0	5	55	37-2	3	35	.248	.306	.317	72	-18	1-2	.987	10	154	104	C147		-0.2
1986	†Cal A	144	442	48	98	12	2	7	49	43-1	0	30	.222	.287	.305	63	-23	1-0	.988	19	210	94	C144		0.2
1987	Cal A	128	389	42	94	18	0	3	33	35-0	1	36	.242	.304	.311	66	-18	0-2	.983	5	207	92	C127/D		-0.9
1988	Cal A	122	352	38	104	17	0	5	39	29-2	2	26	.295	.352	.386	109	5	2-2	.986	-3	118	127	C121		0.8
1989	KC A	131	405	33	111	13	2	1	43	49-4	2	37	.274	.351	.323	93	-2	3-2	.991	11	138	110	C129		1.6
1990	KC A	40	117	11	28	3	0	0	9	17-0	0	12	.239	.336	.265	71	-4	1-1	.985	-3	78	78	C40	64	-0.4
Total	19	2264	7245	679	1838	303	26	105	826	663-90	20	608	.254	.315	.346	82	-175	38-50	.986	66	140	104	C2225,1b7,3b7/DOL	64	-2.4

BOOTH d5.1

YEAR	TM LG	G	AB	R	H	2B	3B	HR	RBI	BB-IB	HP	SO	AVG	OBP	SLG	AOPS	ABR	SB-CS	FA	FR	RNG	THR	GAMES AT POSITION	DL	BFW
1875	NH NA	1	2	0	0	0	0	0	0	0		1	.000	.000	.000	-99	0	0-0	.500	-0	66	0	/S		-0.1

BOOTH, AMOS Amos Smith "Darling" B9.14.1848 Lebanon OH D7.1.1921 Miamisburg OH BR/TR/5-9/159 d4.25 ▲

YEAR	TM LG	G	AB	R	H	2B	3B	HR	RBI	BB-IB	HP	SO	AVG	OBP	SLG	AOPS	ABR	SB-CS	FA	FR	RNG	THR	GAMES AT POSITION	DL	BFW
1876	Cin N	63	272	31	71	3	0	0	14	9		11	.261	.285	.272	101	3		.760	-16	77	0	3b24,C24,S22,O3R,P3		-1.0
1877	Cin N	44	157	16	27	2	1	0	13	12		10	.172	.231	.197	41	-9		.853	-5	107	28	S13,C12,P12,2b10,3b3/OL		-0.9
1880	Cin N	1	2	0	0	0	0	0	0	0		0	.000	.000	.000	-99	0		—	-0	0	0	0/3		-0.1
1882	Bal AA	1	3	0	0	0	0	0	0				.000	.000	.000	-99	-1		1.000	0	66	0	/3		-0.1
	Lou AA	1	4	0	0	0	0	0	0				.000	.000	.000	-99	-1		1.000	0	103	0	/2		-0.1
	Year	2	7	0	0	0	0	0	0				.000	.000	.000	-99	-1		1.000	0	66	0	/32		-0.2
Total	4	110	438	47	98	5	1	0	27	21		21	.224	.259	.240	73	-8		.746	-21			C36,S35,3b29,P15,2b11,O4(1/0/3)		-2.2

BOOTH, EDDIE Edward H. B Brooklyn NY d4.26

YEAR	TM LG	G	AB	R	H	2B	3B	HR	RBI	BB-IB	HP	SO	AVG	OBP	SLG	AOPS	ABR	SB-CS	FA	FR	RNG	THR	GAMES AT POSITION	DL	BFW
1872	Man NA	24	116	25	37	5	2	0	15	0		1	.319	.319	.397	126	4	0-2	.775	4	120	92	2b20,O4(0/3/1)		0.4
	Atl NA	15	62	10	19	4	0	0	7	0		0	.306	.306	.371	92	-1	0-2	.808	2	358	0	O14(6/0/8)/2		0.0
	Year	39	178	35	56	9	2	0	22	0		1	.315	.315	.388	111	2	0-4	.780	6	121	97	2b21,O18(6/3/9)		0.4
1873	Res NA	18	74	11	21	5	2	0	6	0		1	.284	.284	.405	111	1	0-0	.875	-3	41	0	O17(15/0/2)/2		-0.1
	Atl NA	16	70	8	14	3	1	0	7	2		0	.200	.222	.271	51	-3	0-1	.788	0	130	0	O16(0/4/12)		-0.2
	Year	34	144	19	35	8	3	0	13	2		1	.243	.253	.340	82	-2	0-1	.831	-3	84	0	O33(15/4/14)/2		-0.3
1874	Atl NA	44	185	24	47	4	3	1	16	3		3	.254	.266	.324	100	2	0-0	.809	-4	44	0	O44L/2		-0.4
1875	Mut NA	68	281	33	56	3	4	0	18	0		2	.199	.199	.238	49	-15	4-3	.827	1	158	103	O63(3/1/60),2b8		-0.9
1876	NY N	57	228	17	49	2	1	0	7	2		4	.215	.222	.232	59	-8		.764	-5	132	0	O53(0/2/51),2b5/P		-1.2
Total	4 NA	185	788	111	194	24	12	1	69	5		7	.246	.251	.311	81	-12	4-8	.824	-3	130	41	O158(68/8/83),2b31		-1.2

BOOTY, JOSH Joshua Gibson B4.29.1975 Starkville MS BR/TR/6-3/210* [FlaN94 1/5] d9.24

YEAR	TM LG	G	AB	R	H	2B	3B	HR	RBI	BB-IB	HP	SO	AVG	OBP	SLG	AOPS	ABR	SB-CS	FA	FR	RNG	THR	GAMES AT POSITION	DL	BFW
1996	Fla N	2	2	1	0	0	0	0	0	0-0	0	0	.500	.500	.500	169	0	0-0	—	-0	0	0	/3		0.0
1997	Fla N	4	5	1	3	0	0	0	1	1-0	0	1	.600	.667	.600	246	1	0-0	.857	1	174	387	3b4		0.2
1998	Fla N	7	19	0	3	1	0	0	3	3-0	0	8	.158	.273	.211	31	-2	0-0	.833	-1	95	83	3b7		-0.3
Total	3	13	26	3	7	1	0	0	4	4-0	0	9	.269	.367	.308	84	-1	0-0	.840	-0	109	143	3b12		-0.1

BORCHARD, JOE Joseph Edward B11.25.1978 Los Angeles CA BB/TR/6-5/220* [ChiA00 1/12] d9.2 Col Stanford

YEAR	TM LG	G	AB	R	H	2B	3B	HR	RBI	BB-IB	HP	SO	AVG	OBP	SLG	AOPS	ABR	SB-CS	FA	FR	RNG	THR	GAMES AT POSITION	DL	BFW
2002	Chi A	16	36	5	8	0	0	2	5	1-0	0	14	.222	.243	.389	62	-2	0-0	1.000	-1	90	0	O15(10/5/3)		-0.3
2003	Chi A	16	49	5	9	1	0	1	5	1-0	0	18	.184	.246	.265	37	-5	0-1	1.000	-2	83	0	O16C		-0.7
2004	Chi A	63	201	26	35	4	1	9	20	19-1	1	57	.174	.249	.338	49	-16	1-0	.972	-2	92	112	O56(0/2/54),D4		-2.0
2005	Chi A	7	12	0	5	2	0	0	0	0-0	0	4	.417	.417	.583	155	1	0-1	1.000	0	184	0	O2R,D3		0.1
Total	4	102	298	36	57	7	1	12	30	21-1	1	93	.191	.254	.342	53	-22	1-2	.982	-4	91	75	O89(10/23/59),D7		-2.9

BORDAGARAY, FRENCHY Stanley George B1.3.1910 Coalinga CA D4.13.2000 Ventura CA BR/TR/5-7.5/175 d4.17 Col Cal St.-Fresno

YEAR	TM LG	G	AB	R	H	2B	3B	HR	RBI	BB-IB	HP	SO	AVG	OBP	SLG	AOPS	ABR	SB-CS	FA	FR	RNG	THR	GAMES AT POSITION	DL	BFW
1934	Chi A	29	87	12	28	3	1	0	2	3	0	8	.322	.344	.379	84	-2	1-2	.938	-1	86	156	O17(2/1/14)		-0.4
1935	Bro N	120	422	69	119	19	6	1	39	17	6	29	.282	.319	.363	85	-10	18	.980	2	95	164	O105(17/61/27)		-1.1
1936	Bro N	125	372	63	117	21	3	4	31	17	1	42	.315	.346	.419	104	3	2 12	.991	2	111	117	O92(14/46/33),2b11,3b6		-1.1
1937	StL N	96	300	43	88	11	4	1	37	15	2	25	.293	.331	.367	88	-6	11	.942	-6	82	32	3b50,O28(3/7/15)		-1.1
1938	StL N	81	156	19	44	5	1	0	21	8	2	9	.282	.325	.327	76	-5	2	.959	0	112	133	O29(6/14/9),3b4		-0.6
1939	†Cin N	63	122	19	24	5	1	0	12	9	0	10	.197	.252	.254	36	-11	3	1.000	-0	104	0	O43(21/3/19),2b2		-1.3
1941	†NY A	36	73	10	19	1	0	0	4	6	1	8	.260	.325	.274	61	-4	1-0	.967	-1	94	75	O19(6/0/13)		-0.3
1942	Bro N	48	58	11	14	2	0	0	5	3	0	9	.241	.279	.276	62	-3	2	1.000	0	117	0	O17(0/10/7)		-0.3
1943	Bro N	89	268	47	81	18	2	0	19	30	3	15	.302	.379	.384	120	9	6	.989	-7	99	147	O53(28/6/20),3b25		0.0
1944	Bro N	130	501	85	141	26	4	6	51	36	1	22	.281	.331	.385	103	1	3	.945	-15	79	78	3b98,O25(5/15/8)		-1.4
1945	Bro N	113	273	32	70	9	6	2	49	29	0	15	.256	.332	.355	91	-4	7	.886	-9	86	72	3b57,O22(9/7/6)		-1.3
Total	11	930	2632	410	745	120	28	14	270	173	16	186	.283	.331	.366	91	-33	66-2	.982	-32	103	113	O450(111/170/171),3b240,2b13		-7.9

BORDERS, PAT Patrick Lance B5.14.1963 Columbus OH BR/TR/6-2/200(190-205) [TorA82 6/134] d4.6

YEAR	TM LG	G	AB	R	H	2B	3B	HR	RBI	BB-IB	HP	SO	AVG	OBP	SLG	AOPS	ABR	SB-CS	FA	FR	RNG	THR	GAMES AT POSITION	DL	BFW
1988	Tor A	56	154	15	42	6	3	5	21	3-0	0	24	.273	.285	.448	101	-1	0-0	.973	2	120	160	C43/23D	45	0.4
1989	†Tor A	94	241	22	62	11	1	3	29	11-2	1	45	.257	.290	.349	81	-7	2-1	.980	1	88	136	C68,D18		-0.4
1990	Tor A	125	346	36	99	24	2	15	49	18-2	0	57	.286	.319	.497	123	9	0-1	.993	4	110	128	C115/D		1.8
1991	†Tor A	105	291	22	71	17	0	5	36	11-1	1	45	.244	.271	.354	70	-13	0-0	.993	13	98	107	C102		-0.8
1992	†Tor A	138	480	47	116	26	2	13	53	33-3	2	75	.242	.290	.385	84	-11	1-1	.991	4	83	103	C137		0.1
1993	†Tor A	138	488	38	124	30	0	9	55	20-2	2	66	.254	.285	.371	74	-19	2-2	.986	1	80	102	C138		-0.9
1994	Tor A	85	295	24	73	13	1	3	26	15-0	0	50	.247	.284	.329	57	-20	1-1	.988	6	84	105	C85		-0.8
1995	KC A	52	143	14	33	8	1	4	13	7-1	0	22	.231	.267	.385	66	-8	0-0	1.000	1	196	97	C45,D3		-0.4
	Hou N	11	35	1	4	0	0	0	3	2-1	0	7	.114	.162	.114	-27	-7	0-0	.987	1	118	198	C11		-0.5
1996	StL N	26	69	3	22	3	0	0	4	1-0	0	14	.319	.329	.362	82	-2	0-1	.984	5	198	127	C17/1		0.3
	Cal A	19	57	6	13	3	0	2	8	3-0	0	11	.228	.267	.386	61	-4	0-1	.984	2	69	113	C19		-0.4
	Chi A	31	94	6	26	1	0	3	6	5-0	0	18	.277	.313	.383	78	-4	0-0	.982	-3	75	129	C30/D		-0.4
	Year	50	151	12	39	4	0	5	14	8-0	0	29	.258	.296	.384	72	-7	0-1	.983	-0	73	123	C49/D		-0.5
1997	Cle A	55	159	17	47	7	1	4	15	9-0	2	27	.296	.341	.428	95	-1	0-2	1.000	4	80	96	C53		0.1
1998	Cle A	54	160	12	38	6	0	6	10	6-0	2	40	.237	.289	.275	47	-13	0-1	.974	-4	97	98	C53/3		-1.4
1999	Cle A	6	20	2	6	0	1	0	3	1-0	0	3	.300	.300	.400	73	-1	0-1	.943	-2	36	0	C5		-0.3
	Tor A	6	14	1	3	0	0	1	3	0-0	0	2	.214	.267	.429	72	-1	0-0	1.000	-0	0	200	C3/3D		-0.1
	Year	12	34	3	9	0	1	1	6	1-0	0	5	.265	.286	.412	73	-2	0-1	.955	-3	27	51	C8,D3/3		-0.4
2001	Sea A	5	6	1	3	0	0	0	1	0-0	0	1	.500	.500	.500	174	1	0-0	.923	-0	150	153	C5		0.0
2002	Sea A	4	4	0	2	1	0	0	1	0-0	0	5	.500	.500	.750	234	1	0-0	1.000	-0	0	0	C2,D2		0.0
2003	Sea A	12	14	1	2	1	0	0	1	0-0	0	5	.143	.200	.214	10	-2	0-0	1.000	1	111	308	C7,3b2		-0.1
2004	Sea A	19	53	6	10	2	0	1	5	1-0	0	12	.189	.204	.283	26	-6	1-1	.992	5	131	187	C19		0.0
	†Min A	19	42	3	12	4	0	0	5	0-0	1	10	.286	.302	.381	74	-2	0-0	.968	-1	69	153	C19		-0.1
	Year	38	95	9	22	6	0	1	10	1-0	1	22	.232	.247	.326	48	-7	3-1	.982	4	102	171	C38		-0.1
2005	Sea A	39	117	12	23	5	0	1	7	4-1	0	22	.197	.228	.265	33	-11	0-0	.990	-7	74	128	C39		-1.6
Total	17	1099	3282	289	831	168	12	69	346	155-13	12	557	.253	.288	.375	76	-122	9-14	.988	27	96	117	C1015,D35,3b5/12	45	-3.8

BORDICK, MIKE Michael Todd B7.21.1965 Marquette MI BR/TR/5-11/175* d4.11 Col Maine

YEAR	TM LG	G	AB	R	H	2B	3B	HR	RBI	BB-IB	HP	SO	AVG	OBP	SLG	AOPS	ABR	SB-CS	FA	FR	RNG	THR	GAMES AT POSITION	DL	BFW
1990	†Oak A	25	14	0	1	0	0	0	0	4-0	0	4	.071	.133	.071	-43	-3	0-0	1.000	-3	79	0	3b10,S9,2b7		-0.6
1991	Oak A	90	235	21	56	5	1	0	21	14-0	0	37	.238	.289	.268	63	-14	3-4	.972	-6	96	89	S84,2b5/3		-1.5
1992	†Oak A	154	504	62	151	19	4	3	48	40-2	9	59	.300	.358	.371	111	8	12-6	.987	5	101	98	2b95,S70		2.1
1993	Oak A	159	546	60	136	21	2	3	48	60-2	11	58	.249	.332	.312	79	-14	10-10	.982	-15	92	99	S159/2		-1.8
1994	Oak A	114	391	38	99	18	4	2	37	38-1	3	44	.253	.320	.335	76	-14	0-4	.974	6	98	113	S112,2b4		0.1
1995	Oak A	126	428	46	113	13	0	8	44	35-2	5	44	.264	.325	.350	80	-11	11-3	.983	8	95	113	S126/D	19	0.6
1996	Oak A	155	525	46	126	18	4	5	54	39-0	5	59	.240	.307	.318	60	-33	5-6	.979	10	108	115	S155		-1.2
1997	†Bal A	153	509	55	120	19	1	7	46	33-1	2	66	.236	.283	.318	59	-32	0-1	.980	-3	97	105	S153		-2.3
1998	Bal A	151	465	59	121	29	1	13	51	39-0	10	65	.260	.328	.411	93	-5	6-7	.990	21	107	102	S150		2.4
1999	Bal A	160	631	93	175	35	7	10	77	54-1	5	102	.277	.334	.403	98	-9	14-4	.989	35	114	125	S159		3.6

YEAR	TM LG	G	AB	R	H	2B	3B	HR	RBI	BB-IB	HP	SO	AVG	OBP	SLG	AOPS	ABR	SB-CS	FA	FR	RNG	THR	GAMES AT POSITION	DL	BFW
2000	Bal A★	100	391	70	116	22	1	16	59	34-0	1	71	.297	.350	.481	114	8	6-5	.979	-13	89	81	S100		0.2
	†NY N	56	192	18	50	8		4	21	15-0	2	28	.260	.321	.365	77	-7	3-1	.968	-7	90	77	S56		-1.0
2001	Bal A	58	229	32	57	13	0	7	30	17-1	6	36	.249	.314	.397	92	-3	9-3	.977	-5	92	76	S58	116	-0.3
2002	Bal A	117	367	37	85	19	3	8	36	35-0	5	63	.232	.302	.365	81	-10	7-4	.998	26	117	125	S117	32	2.4
2003	Tor A	102	343	39	94	18	2	5	54	33-0	2	60	.274	.340	.382	87	-6	3-1	.987	12	100	124	S69,3b22,2b13/D		1.1
Total	14	1720	5770	676	1500	257	30	91	626	500-10	63	800	.260	.323	.362	83	-147	96-58	.982	71	101	105	S1577,2b125,3b33,D2	167	3.8

BORGMANN, GLENN Glenn Dennis B5.25.1950 Paterson NJ BR/TR/6-4/210* [MinA71 D1/9] d7.1 Col South Alabama

YEAR	TM LG	G	AB	R	H	2B	3B	HR	RBI	BB-IB	HP	SO	AVG	OBP	SLG	AOPS	ABR	SB-CS	FA	FR	RNG	THR	GAMES AT POSITION	DL	BFW
1972	Min A	56	175	11	41	4	0	3	14	25-8	0	25	.234	.325	.309	86	-2	0-0	.965	2	124	91	C56		0.2
1973	Min A	12	34	7	9	2	0	0	9	6-0	0	10	.265	.375	.324	94	0	0-0	1.000	-4	90	76	C12		-0.3
1974	Min A	128	345	33	87	8	1	3	45	39-0	1	44	.252	.323	.307	82	-7	2-1	.997	-2	89	108	C128		-0.4
1975	Min A	125	352	34	73	15	2	2	33	47-1	2	59	.207	.303	.278	65	-15	0-1	.989	2	102	120	C125		-0.9
1976	Min A	24	65	10	16	3	0	1	6	19-0	0	7	.246	.417	.338	121	3	1-1	.976	-2	68	117	C24		0.2
1977	Min A	17	43	12	11	1	0	2	7	11-0	0	9	.256	.407	.419	127	2	0-0	1.000	-3	53	98	C17	73	0.0
1978	Min A	49	123	16	26	4	1	3	15	18-0	0	17	.211	.306	.333	80	-3	0-0	.990	-1	129	120	C46/D		0.0
1979	Min A	31	70	4	14	3	0	0	8	12-0	0	11	.200	.317	.243	51	-4	1-0	.993	3	78	81	C31		0.0
1980	Chi N	32	87	10	19	2	0	2	14	14-0	0	9	.218	.320	.310	76	-3	0-0	1.000	5	106	169	C32		0.3
Total	9	474	1294	137	296	42	4	16	151	191-9	3	191	.229	.325	.304	79	-29	4-3	.989	1	99	112	C471/D	73	-0.9

BORKOWSKI, BOB Robert Vilarian B1.27.1926 Dayton OH BR/TR/6-0/182* d4.22

YEAR	TM LG	G	AB	R	H	2B	3B	HR	RBI	BB-IB	HP	SO	AVG	OBP	SLG	AOPS	ABR	SB-CS	FA	FR	RNG	THR	GAMES AT POSITION	DL	BFW
1950	Chi N	85	256	27	70	7	4	4	29	16	1	30	.273	.319	.379	84	-7	1	.975	-2	99	56	O65(7/29/30)/1		-1.2
1951	Chi N	58	89	9	14	1	0	0	10	3	0	16	.157	.185	.169	-4	-13	0-0	.933	-0	109	68	O25(7/9/9)		-1.4
1952	Cin N	126	377	42	95	11	4	4	24	26	0	53	.252	.300	.334	76	-13	1-3	.991	-2	103	58	O103(15/64/26),1b5		-2.0
1953	Cin N	94	249	32	67	11	1	7	29	21	1	41	.269	.328	.406	89	-4	0-1	.982	-3	94	71	O67(3/3/61),1b2		-0.9
1954	Cin N	73	162	13	43	12	1	1	19	8	1	18	.265	.299	.370	73	-6	0-1	1.000	1	107	114	O36(13/0/23),1b3		-0.8
1955	Cin N	25	18	1	3	1	0	0	1	1-0	0	2	.167	.211	.222	14	-2	0-0	1.000	0	151	0	O11L/1		-0.2
	Bro N	9	19	2	2	0	0	0	0	1-0	0	6	.105	.150	.105	-30	-4	0-0	1.000	-1	84	0	O9(3/2/4)		-0.4
	Year	34	37	3	5	1	0	0	1	2-0	0	8	.135	.179	.162	-8	-6	0-0	1.000	-0	103	0	O20(14/2/4)/1		-0.6
Total	6	470	1170	126	294	43	10	16	112	76-0	3	166	.251	.298	.346	71	-49	2-6	.982	-6	101	66	O316(59/107/153),1b12		-6.9

BOROM, RED Edward Jones B10.30.1916 Spartanburg SC BL/TR/5-10/175 d4.23

YEAR	TM LG	G	AB	R	H	2B	3B	HR	RBI	BB-IB	HP	SO	AVG	OBP	SLG	AOPS	ABR	SB-CS	FA	FR	RNG	THR	GAMES AT POSITION	DL	BFW
1944	Det A	7	14	1	1	0	0	0	1	2	0	2	.071	.188	.071	-23	-2	0-0	.950	0	154	44	2b4/S		-0.2
1945	†Det A	55	130	19	35	4	0	0	9	7	0	8	.269	.307	.300	72	-5	4-2	.966	4	119	96	2b28,3b4,S2		0.1
Total	2	62	144	20	36	4	0	0	10	9	0	10	.250	.294	.278	62	-7	4-2	.964	5	123	90	2b32,3b4,S3		-0.1

BOROS, STEVE Stephen B9.3.1936 Flint MI BR/TR/6-0/185* d6.19 M3/C10 Col Michigan

YEAR	TM LG	G	AB	R	H	2B	3B	HR	RBI	BB-IB	HP	SO	AVG	OBP	SLG	AOPS	ABR	SB-CS	FA	FR	RNG	THR	GAMES AT POSITION	DL	BFW
1957	Det A	24	41	4	6	1	0	0	2	1-0	0	8	.146	.167	.171	-7	-6	0-0	.906	1	122	63	3b9,S5		-0.6
1958	Det A	6	2	0	0	0	0	0	0	0-0	0	1	.000	.000	.000	-93	-1	0-0	1.000	0	0	0	/2		-0.1
1961	Det A	116	396	51	107	18	2	5	62	68-2	8	42	.270	.382	.364	99	3	4-2	.953	-21	80	69	3b116	39	-1.8
1962	Det A	116	356	46	81	14	1	16	47	53-3	3	62	.228	.331	.407	95	-1	3-1	.931	-17	77	87	3b105,2b6		-1.9
1963	Chi N	41	90	9	19	5	1	3	7	12-0	1	19	.211	.304	.389	93	-1	0-2	.975	-1	82	77	1b14,O11R		-0.4
1964	Cin N	117	370	31	95	12	3	2	31	47-14	2	43	.257	.342	.322	86	-5	4-1	.961	-3	90	107	3b114		-0.9
1965	Cin N	2	0	0	0	0	0	0	0	0-0	0	0	—	—	—	—	-0	0-0	1.000	0	114	0	3b2		0.0
Total	7	422	1255	141	308	50	7	26	149	181-19	13	174	.245	.344	.359	90	-12	11-6	.948	-41	84	87	3b346,1b14,O11R,2b7,S5	39	-5.7

BORTON, BABE William Baker B8.14.1888 Marion IL D7.29.1954 Berkeley CA BL/TL/6-0/178 d9.2

YEAR	TM LG	G	AB	R	H	2B	3B	HR	RBI	BB-IB	HP	SO	AVG	OBP	SLG	AOPS	ABR	SB-CS	FA	FR	RNG	THR	GAMES AT POSITION	DL	BFW
1912	Chi A	31	105	15	39	3	1	0	17	8	0		.371	.416	.419	143	6	1	.997	0	92	103	1b30		0.5
1913	Chi A	28	80	9	22	5	0	0	13	23	1	5	.275	.442	.338	130	6	1	.991	-2	71	136	1b26		0.3
	NY A	33	108	8	14	2	0	0	11	18	1	19	.130	.260	.148	20	-10	1	.978	4	157	87	1b33		-0.8
	Year	61	188	17	36	7	0	0	24	41	2	24	.191	.342	.229	68	-5	2	.984	2	118	109	1b59		-0.5
1915	StL F	159	549	97	157	20	14	3	83	92	7	64	.286	.395	.390	115	8	17	.993	-10	65	113	1b159		-0.6
1916	StL A	66	98	10	22	1	2	1	12	19	1	13	.224	.350	.306	102	1	1	.991	-1	73	69	1b22		-0.1
Total	4	317	940	139	254	31	17	4	136	160	9	101	.270	.381	.352	108	11	21	.991	-8	80	108	1b270		-0.7

BOSCH, DON Donald John B7.15.1942 San Francisco CA BB/TR/5-10/160* d9.19

YEAR	TM LG	G	AB	R	H	2B	3B	HR	RBI	BB-IB	HP	SO	AVG	OBP	SLG	AOPS	ABR	SB-CS	FA	FR	RNG	THR	GAMES AT POSITION	DL	BFW
1966	Pit N	3	2	0	0	0	0	0	0	0-0	0	0	.000	.000	.000	-99	-1	0-0	—	-0	0	0	/OC		-0.1
1967	NY N	44	93	7	13	0	1	0	2	5-0	0	24	.140	.184	.161	-0	-12	3-1	1.000	-1	89	131	O39C		-1.5
1968	NY N	50	111	14	19	1	0	3	7	9-1	0	33	.171	.231	.261	48	-7	0-2	.974	3	120	174	O33(4/30/0)		-0.6
1969	Mon N	49	112	13	20	5	0	1	4	8-0	0	20	.179	.233	.250	35	-10	1-0	.964	-1	98	67	O32(2/29/1)		-1.2
Total	4	146	318	34	52	6	1	4	13	22-1	0	77	.164	.217	.226	28	-30	4-3	.972	2	102	126	O105(6/99/1)		-3.4

BOSETTI, RICK Richard Alan B8.5.1953 Redding CA BR/TR/5-11/185* [PhiN73*7/114] d9.9 Col Shasta (CA) JC

YEAR	TM LG	G	AB	R	H	2B	3B	HR	RBI	BB-IB	HP	SO	AVG	OBP	SLG	AOPS	ABR	SB-CS	FA	FR	RNG	THR	GAMES AT POSITION	DL	BFW
1976	Phi N	13	18	6	5	0	0	0	1	0-0	0	1	.278	.316	.333	81	0	3-0	1.000	0	86	377	O6(1/4/1)		0.0
1977	StL N	41	69	12	16	0	0	0	3	6-0	1	11	.232	.303	.232	46	-5	4-4	1.000	2	100	227	O35(27/7/3)		-0.5
1978	Tor A	136	568	61	147	25	5	5	42	30-0	1	65	.259	.299	.347	80	-16	6-10	.986	14	112	194	O135C	15	-0.5
1979	Tor A	162	619	59	161	35	2	8	65	22-0	3	70	.260	.286	.362	73	-24	13-12	.974	9	105	167	O162C		-1.7
1980	Tor A	53	188	24	40	7	1	4	18	15-1	2	29	.213	.277	.324	62	-10	4-6	.985	-4	88	112	O51C	105	-1.5
1981	Tor A	25	47	5	11	2	0	0	4	2-0	0	6	.234	.265	.277	53	-2	0-2	1.000	0	107		O19(5/13/2)/D		-0.4
	†Oak A	9	19	4	2	0	0	1	0	3-0	0	3	.105	.227	.105	-2	-2	0-0	1.000	0	129		O5(0/4/1),D2		-0.2
	Year	34	66	9	13	2	0	1	4	5-0	0	9	.197	.254	.227	38	-5	0-2	1.000	0	111		O24(5/17/3),D3		-0.6
1982	Oak A	6	15	1	3	0	0	0	0	0-0	0	1	.200	.200	.200	11	-2	0-0	1.000	2	116	643	O6C		0.0
Total	7	445	1543	172	385	70	8	17	133	79-1	9	188	.250	.288	.338	71	-62	30-34	.982	25	105	173	O419(33/382/7),D3	120	-4.8

BOSLEY, THAD Thaddis B9.17.1956 Oceanside CA BL/TL/6-3/175* [CalA74 4/82] d6.29 C5

YEAR	TM LG	G	AB	R	H	2B	3B	HR	RBI	BB-IB	HP	SO	AVG	OBP	SLG	AOPS	ABR	SB-CS	FA	FR	RNG	THR	GAMES AT POSITION	DL	BFW
1977	Cal A	58	212	19	63	10	2	0	19	16-0	1	32	.297	.346	.363	98	0	5-4	.963	-1	110	28	O55(20/35/1)	27	-0.2
1978	Chi A	66	219	25	59	5	1	2	13	13-1	0	32	.269	.308	.329	79	-7	12-11	.975	3	114	82	O64(15/39/14)	18	-0.6
1979	Chi A	36	77	13	24	1	1	1	8	9-0	0	14	.312	.384	.390	109	1	4-1	.967	4	149	143	O22(2/1/5)/D		0.5
1980	Chi A	70	147	12	33	2	0	2	14	10-3	0	27	.224	.272	.279	52	-10	3-2	.958	-0	108	38	O52(32/18/4)	55	-1.2
1981	†Mil A	42	105	11	24	2	0	0	3	6-0	0	13	.229	.270	.248	52	-7	2-1	.966	-2	93	54	O37(7/8/22)/D		-1.0
1982	Sea A	22	46	3	8	1	0	0	4	4-0	0	6	.174	.240	.196	21	-5	3-1	1.000	-3	44	128	O19(15/3/2)		-0.8
1983	Chi N	43	72	12	21	4	1	2	12	10-1	0	12	.292	.373	.458	125	1	1-1	1.000	1	102	102	O20(16/1/3)		0.3
1984	†Chi N	55	98	17	29	2	2	1	14	13-2	0	22	.296	.375	.418	114	2	5-1	.976	0	99	139	O33(11/2/21)		0.2
1985	Chi N	108	180	25	59	6	3	7	27	20-1	0	29	.328	.391	.511	138	9	5-1	.988	2	133		O55(46/7/8)		1.1
1986	Chi N	87	120	15	33	4	1	1	9	18-3	0	24	.275	.370	.350	93	-1	3-0	.969	-2	86		O41(32/2/8)		-0.3
1987	KC A	80	140	13	39	6	1	1	16	9-2	0	26	.279	.318	.357	78	-5	0-0	.966	-1	96		O28(13/1/14),D13		-0.7
1988	KC A	15	21	1	4	0	0	0	2	2-1	0	6	.190	.250	.190	28	-2	0-0	1.000	0	83		O6(1/4/1),D4	16	0.0
	Cal A	35	75	9	21	5	0	0	7	6-0	0	12	.280	.321	.347	93	-1	1-1	.965	1	120		O26(24/0/2),D2		0.0
	Year	50	96	10	25	5	0	0	9	8-1	0	18	.260	.306	.313	78	-3	1-1	.967	1	117		O32(25/4/3),D6		-0.2
1989	Tex A	37	40	5	9	2	0	1	3	3-0	1	11	.225	.273	.350	75	-1	2-0	1.000	2	216	603	O8(6/0/2),D5		0.1
1990	Tex A	30	29	3	4	0	0	0	2	4-1	0	7	.138	.242	.241	36	-3	1-0	1.000	-1	51		O9(7/1/1),D4		-0.4
Total	14	784	1581	183	430	50	12	19	158	143-15	1	275	.272	.330	.357	89	-27	47-24	.972	4	109	57	O481(267/122/108),D30	116	-3.2

BOSS, HARLEY Elmer Harley "Lefty" B11.19.1908 Hodge LA D5.15.1964 Nashville TN BL/TL/5-11.5/185 d7.19 Col Louisiana Tech

YEAR	TM LG	G	AB	R	H	2B	3B	HR	RBI	BB-IB	HP	SO	AVG	OBP	SLG	AOPS	ABR	SB-CS	FA	FR	RNG	THR	GAMES AT POSITION	DL	BFW
1928	Was A	12	12	1	3	0	0	0	3	0	0	1	.250	.400	.250	75	-1	0-0	.970	-1	0	106	1b5		-0.1
1929	Was A	28	66	9	18	2	1	0	6	2	0	6	.273	.294	.333	61	-4	0-0	.977	0	117	126	1b18		-0.5
1930	Was A	3	3	0	0	0	0	0	0	0	0	0	.000	.000	.000	-99	-0	0-0	1.000	0	0	0	/1		-0.1
1933	Cle A	112	438	54	118	17	7	1	53	25	1	27	.269	.310	.347	71	-20	2-5	.994	5	119	112	1b110		-2.5
Total	4	155	519	64	139	19	8	1	61	30	1	34	.268	.309	.341	69	-25	2-5	.992	5	116	113	1b134		-3.2

BOSTICK, HENRY Henry Landers (b Henry Lipschitz) B1.12.1895 Boston MA D9.16.1968 Denver CO BR/TR d5.18 Col Denver

YEAR	TM LG	G	AB	R	H	2B	3B	HR	RBI	BB-IB	HP	SO	AVG	OBP	SLG	AOPS	ABR	SB-CS	FA	FR	RNG	THR	GAMES AT POSITION	DL	BFW
1915	Phi A	2	7	0	0	0	0	0	0	0	0		.000	.125	.000	-4	-1	0-0	1.000	1	78	0	3b2		-0.2

BOSTOCK, LYMAN Lyman Wesley B11.22.1950 Birmingham AL D9.23.1978 Gary IN BL/TR/6-1/180* [MinA72 26/596] d4.8 Col Cal St.-Northridge

YEAR	TM LG	G	AB	R	H	2B	3B	HR	RBI	BB-IB	HP	SO	AVG	OBP	SLG	AOPS	ABR	SB-CS	FA	FR	RNG	THR	GAMES AT POSITION	DL	BFW
1975	Min A	98	369	52	104	21	5	0	29	28-2	0	42	.282	.331	.366	96	-2	2-3	.985	-5	97	43	O92(12/28/55)/D	31	-1.2
1976	Min A	128	474	75	153	21	9	4	60	33-5	1	37	.323	.364	.430	131	17	12-6	.988	1	99	115	O124(0/121/3)		1.6
1977	Min A	153	593	104	199	36	12	14	90	51-5	6	59	.336	.389	.508	145	38	16-7	.989	-2	99	93	O149(60/90/3)		3.3

YEAR	TM LG	G	AB	R	H	2B	3B	HR	RBI	BB-IB	HP	SO	AVG	OBP	SLG	AOPS	ABR	SB-CS	FA	FR	RNG	THR	GAMES AT POSITION	DL	BFW
1978	Cal A	147	568	74	168	24	4	5	71	59-8	2	36	.296	.362	.379	113	11	15-12	.989	4	109	69	O146(0/58/90)/D		0.9
Total	4	526	2004	305	624	102	30	23	250	171-20	9	174	.311	.365	.427	124	64	45-28	.988	-2	102	82	O511(72/297/151),D2	31	4.6

BOSTON, DARYL Daryl Lamont B1.4.1963 Cincinnati OH BL/TL/6-3/203(185-210) [ChiA81 1/7] d5.13

YEAR	TM LG	G	AB	R	H	2B	3B	HR	RBI	BB-IB	HP	SO	AVG	OBP	SLG	AOPS	ABR	SB-CS	FA	FR	RNG	THR	GAMES AT POSITION	DL	BFW
1984	Chi A	35	83	8	14	3	1	0	3	4-0	0	20	.169	.207	.229	19	-9	6-0	.910	-2	95	130	O34(0/30/5)/D		-1.0
1985	Chi A	95	232	20	53	13	1	3	15	14-1	0	44	.228	.271	.332	62	-12	8-6	.989	3	101	168	O93(0/90/4),D2		-1.1
1986	Chi A	56	199	29	53	11	3	5	22	21-3	0	33	.266	.335	.427	102	1	9-5	.969	1	107	105	O53C/D		0.2
1987	Chi A	103	337	51	87	21	2	10	29	25-2	0	68	.258	.307	.421	89	-6	12-6	.991	-1	100	58	O92(51/45/0),D5		-0.8
1988	Chi A	105	281	37	61	12	2	15	31	21-5	0	44	.217	.271	.434	94	-4	9-3	.951	-1	101	97	O85(44/43/1),D5		-0.5
1989	Chi A	101	218	34	55	3	4	5	23	24-3	0	31	.252	.325	.372	98	-1	7-2	.971	1	110	54	O75(57/2/21),D9		-0.1
1990	Chi A	5	1	0	0	0	0	0	0	0-0	0	0	.000	.000	.000	-99	0	1-0	—	-0	0	0	/ORD		0.0
	NY N	115	366	65	100	21	2	12	45	28-2	2	50	.273	.328	.440	109	4	18-7	.986	-5	95	65	O109(1/108/0)		0.0
1991	NY N	137	255	40	70	16	4	4	21	30-0	0	42	.275	.350	.416	115	6	15-8	.981	-0	104	52	O115(9/74/37)		0.5
1992	NY N	130	289	37	72	14	2	11	35	38-6	3	60	.249	.338	.426	117	7	12-6	.993	-2	90	141	O95(66/16/14)		0.4
1993	Col N	124	291	46	76	15	1	14	40	26-1	2	57	.261	.325	.464	93	-3	1-6	.985	-4	85	110	O79(41/31/9)		-1.0
1994	NY A	52	77	11	14	2	0	4	14	6-0	1	20	.182	.250	.364	58	-5	0-1	1.000	-0	74	221	O16(7/7/2),D9		-0.6
Total	11	1058	2629	378	655	131	22	83	278	237-23	8	469	.249	.312	.410	94	-22	98-50	.977	-10	98	96	O847(276/499/94),D35		-4.0

BOSWELL, KEN Kenneth George B2.23.1946 Austin TX BL/TR/6-0/172* [NYN65 4/66] d9.18 Col Sam Houston St.

YEAR	TM LG	G	AB	R	H	2B	3B	HR	RBI	BB-IB	HP	SO	AVG	OBP	SLG	AOPS	ABR	SB-CS	FA	FR	RNG	THR	GAMES AT POSITION	DL	BFW
1967	NY N	11	40	2	9	3	0	1	4	1-0	0	5	.225	.233	.375	76	-1	0-0	.971	3	139	76	2b6,3b4		0.2
1968	NY N	75	284	37	74	7	2	4	11	16-0	1	27	.261	.300	.342	92	-3	7-2	.965	-1	101	93	2b69		0.3
1969	†NY N	102	362	48	101	14	7	3	32	36-3	2	47	.279	.347	.381	101	1	7-3	.959	-14	92	100	2b96	56	-0.7
1970	NY N	105	351	32	89	13	2	5	44	41-8	2	32	.254	.331	.345	81	-9	5-4	.996	-10	91	86	2b101		-1.3
1971	NY N	116	392	46	107	20	1	5	40	36-4	2	31	.273	.334	.367	100	1	5-2	.973	-26	78	86	2b109		-2.0
1972	NY N	100	355	35	75	9	1	9	33	32-1	0	35	.211	.274	.318	70	-15	2-2	.990	-23	72	97	2b94		-3.5
1973	†NY N	76	110	12	25	2	1	2	14	12-2	0	11	.227	.303	.318	73	-4	0-0	.973	0	90	116	3b17,2b3		-0.4
1974	NY N	96	222	19	48	6	1	2	15	18-1	1	19	.216	.277	.279	57	-13	0-1	1.000	5	92	69	2b28,3b20,O7(2/0/5)		-0.8
1975	Hou N	86	178	16	43	8	2	0	21	30-7	1	12	.242	.349	.309	92	-1	0-3	.991	-5	102	74	2b31,3b23		-0.6
1976	Hou N	91	126	12	33	8	1	0	18	8-2	0	8	.262	.301	.341	91	-2	1-0	.933	-4	81	152	3b16,2b3/OL		-0.5
1977	Hou N	72	97	7	21	1	1	0	12	10-1	1	12	.216	.287	.247	50	-7	0-0	1.000	-1	81	118	2b26,3b2		-0.8
Total	11	930	2517	266	625	91	19	31	244	240-29	9	239	.248	.313	.337	84	-53	27-17	.979	-76	87	90	2b566,3b82,O8(3/0/5)	56	-10.1

BOTTARINI, JOHN John Charles B9.14.1908 Crockett CA D10.8.1976 Jemez Springs NM BR/TR/6-0/190 d4.22

YEAR	TM LG	G	AB	R	H	2B	3B	HR	RBI	BB-IB	HP	SO	AVG	OBP	SLG	AOPS	ABR	SB-CS	FA	FR	RNG	THR	GAMES AT POSITION	DL	BFW
1937	Chi N	26	40	3	11	3	0	1	7	5	1	10	.275	.370	.425	111	1	0-1	1.000	0	115	134	C18/OL		0.2

BOTTOMLEY, JIM James Leroy "Sunny Jim" B4.23.1900 Oglesby IL D12.11.1959 St.Louis MO BL/TL/6-0/180 d8.18 M1/C1 HF1974

YEAR	TM LG	G	AB	R	H	2B	3B	HR	RBI	BB-IB	HP	SO	AVG	OBP	SLG	AOPS	ABR	SB-CS	FA	FR	RNG	THR	GAMES AT POSITION	DL	BFW
1922	Stl N	37	151	29	49	8	5	5	35	6	2	13	.325	.358	.543	136	7	3-1	.986	-3	65	81	1b34		0.2
1923	Stl N	134	523	79	194	34	14	8	94	45	4	44	.371	.425	.535	155	42	4-6	.986	-12	61	88	1b130		1.9
1924	Stl N	137	528	87	167	31	12	14	111	35	3	35	.316	.362	.500	131	22	5-4	.982	-11	67	94	1b133/2		0.1
1925	Stl N	153	619	92	227	44	12	21	128	47	2	36	.367	.413	.578	147	43	3-4	.987	-3	91	107	1b153		2.7
1926	†Stl N	154	603	98	180	40	14	19	120	58	4	52	.299	.364	.500	126	22	4	.989	-15	61	101	1b154		-0.3
1927	Stl N	152	574	95	174	31	15	19	124	74	5	49	.303	.387	.509	134	28	8	.989	-12	73	130	1b152		0.6
1928	†Stl N	149	576	123	187	42	20	31	136	71	3	54	.325	.402	.628	163	51	10	.987	-14	61	94	1b148		2.5
1929	Stl N	146	560	108	176	31	12	29	137	70	1	54	.314	.391	.568	133	28	3	.991	-5	83	102	1b145		1.2
1930	Stl N	131	487	92	148	33	7	15	97	44	5	36	.304	.368	.493	102	1	5	.990	-14	53	111	1b124		-1.8
1931	†Stl N	108	382	73	133	34	5	9	75	34	1	24	.348	.403	.534	144	25	3	.987	-4	81	118	1b93		1.2
1932	Stl N	91	311	45	92	16	3	11	48	25	1	32	.296	.350	.473	115	7	2	.986	-3	81	108	1b74		-0.4
1933	Cin N	145	549	57	137	23	9	13	83	42	7	28	.250	.311	.395	102	0	3	.991	-9	78	102	1b145		-2.4
1934	Cin N	142	556	72	158	31	11	11	78	33	0	40	.284	.324	.439	105	2	1	.989	-4	93	92	1b139		-1.5
1935	Cin N	107	399	44	103	21	1	1	49	18	2	24	.258	.294	.323	68	-18	3	.992	-2	88	101	1b97		-2.9
1936	Stl A	140	544	72	162	39	11	12	95	44	3	55	.298	.354	.476	100	-2	0-0	.992	-9	67	80	1b140		-2.1
1937	Stl A	65	109	11	26	7	0	1	12	18	0	15	.239	.346	.330	71	-4	1-0	.995	1	113	86	1b24,M		-0.5
Total	16	1991	7471	1177	2313	465	151	219	1422	664	43	591	.310	.369	.500	124	254	58-15	.988	-120	74	101	1b1885/2		-1.5

BOTTS, JASON Jason Carl B7.26.1980 Paso Robles CA BR/TR/6-6/250 d9.14 Col Glendale (CA) JC

YEAR	TM LG	G	AB	R	H	2B	3B	HR	RBI	BB-IB	HP	SO	AVG	OBP	SLG	AOPS	ABR	SB-CS	FA	FR	RNG	THR	GAMES AT POSITION	DL	BFW
2005	Tex A	10	27	4	8	0	0	3	3	3-0	0	13	.296	.367	.296	77	-1	0-0	.900	0	87	398	O7L,D3		-0.1

BOUCHEE, ED Edward Francis B3.7.1933 Livingston MT BL/TL/6-1/205* d9.19 Col Washington St.

YEAR	TM LG	G	AB	R	H	2B	3B	HR	RBI	BB-IB	HP	SO	AVG	OBP	SLG	AOPS	ABR	SB-CS	FA	FR	RNG	THR	GAMES AT POSITION	DL	BFW
1956	Phi N	9	22	0	6	2	0	1	5-0		0	6	.273	.407	.364	112	1	0-0	1.000	-0	69	123	1b6		0.0
1957	Phi N	154	574	78	168	35	8	17	76	84-6	14	91	.293	.394	.470	136	33	1-0	.988	6	110	77	1b154		3.1
1958	Phi N	89	334	55	86	19	5	9	39	51-4	0	74	.257	.355	.425	107	5	1-0	.993	-1	95	74	1b89		-0.1
1959	Phi N	136	499	75	142	29	4	15	74	70-4	5	74	.285	.375	.449	117	15	0-4	.986	-2	95	89	1b134		0.4
1960	Phi N	22	65	1	17	4	0	0	8	9-2	1	11	.262	.355	.323	89	0	0-0	.994	0	105	79	1b22		-0.1
	Chi N	98	299	33	71	11	1	5	44	45-4	2	51	.237	.335	.331	86	-4	2-0	.991	-0	100	88	1b80		-0.9
	Year	120	364	34	88	15	1	5	52	54-6	3	62	.242	.339	.330	86	-5	2-0	.992	0	101	86	1b102		-1.0
1961	Chi N	112	319	49	79	12	3	12	38	58-7	0	77	.248	.371	.417	108	6	1-4	.983	1	109	112	1b107		-0.1
1962	NY N	50	87	7	14	2	0	3	10	18-2	0	17	.161	.302	.287	59	-5	0-0	.976	4	208	106	1b19		-0.2
Total	7	670	2199	298	583	114	21	61	290	340-29	27	400	.265	.368	.419	112	51	3-12	.988	8	105	88	1b611		2.1

BOUCHER, AL Alexander Francis "Bo" B11.13.1881 Franklin MA D6.23.1974 Torrance CA BR/TR/5-8.5/156 d4.16

YEAR	TM LG	G	AB	R	H	2B	3B	HR	RBI	BB-IB	HP	SO	AVG	OBP	SLG	AOPS	ABR	SB-CS	FA	FR	RNG	THR	GAMES AT POSITION	DL	BFW
1914	Stl F	147	516	62	119	26	4	2	49	52	2	88	.231	.304	.308	64	-33	13	.916	-4	95	79	3b147		-3.6

BOUCHER, MEDRIC Medric Charles Francis B3.12.1886 St.Louis MO D3.12.1974 Martinez CA BR/TR/5-10/165 d5.20

YEAR	TM LG	G	AB	R	H	2B	3B	HR	RBI	BB-IB	HP	SO	AVG	OBP	SLG	AOPS	ABR	SB-CS	FA	FR	RNG	THR	GAMES AT POSITION	DL	BFW
1914	Bal F	16	16	2	5	1	1	0	2	1	0	1	.313	.353	.500	127	0	0	.950	0	151	41	C7/1OR		0.1
	Pit F	1	1	0	0	0	0	0	0	0	0	0	.000	.000	.000	-99	0	0	—	0			/H		0.0
	Year	17	17	2	5	1	1	0	2	1	0	1	.294	.333	.471	114	0	0	.950	0	151	41	C7/1OR		0.1

BOUDREAU, LOU Louis B7.17.1917 Harvey IL D8.20.2001 Olympia Fields IL BR/TR/5-11/185* d9.9 M16 HF1970 Col Illinois

YEAR	TM LG	G	AB	R	H	2B	3B	HR	RBI	BB-IB	HP	SO	AVG	OBP	SLG	AOPS	ABR	SB-CS	FA	FR	RNG	THR	GAMES AT POSITION	DL	BFW
1938	Cle A	1	1	0	0	0	0	0	0	1	0	0	.000	.000	.000	36	0	0-0	—	-0	0	0	/3		-0.0
1939	Cle A	53	225	42	58	15	4	0	19	28	0	24	.258	.340	.360	82	-6	2-1	.953	6	109	95	S53		0.4
1940	Cle A★	155	627	97	185	46	10	9	101	73	2	39	.295	.370	.443	113	14	6-3	.968	12	100	134	S155		3.5
1941	Cle A★	148	579	95	149	45	8	10	56	85	3	57	.257	.355	.415	108	9	9-4	.966	13	103	101	S147		3.2
1942	Cle A★	147	506	57	143	18	10	2	58	75	4	39	.283	.379	.370	118	15	7-16	.965	-2	101	124	S146,M		2.0
1943	Cle A☆	152	539	69	154	32	7	3	67	90	0	31	.286	.388	.388	135	29	4-7	.970	25	108	126	S152/CM		6.8
1944	Cle A☆	150	584	91	191	45	5	3	67	73	5	39	.327	.406	.437	146	39	11-3	.978	20	103	123	S149/CM		7.5
1945	Cle A★	97	345	50	106	24	1	3	48	35	2	20	.307	.374	.409	133	15	0-4	.983	4	94	120	S97,M		2.7
1946	Cle A	140	515	51	151	30	6	6	62	40	1	14	.293	.345	.410	118	11	6-7	.970	17	99	105	S139,M		3.7
1947	Cle A	150	538	79	165	45	3	4	67	67	4	10	.307	.388	.424	129	24	1-0	.982	19	106	123	S148,M		5.3
1948	†Cle A★	152	560	116	199	34	6	18	106	98	2	9	.355	.453	.534	166	58	3-2	.975	8	103	121	S151/CM		7.1
1949	Cle A	134	475	53	135	20	3	4	60	70	4	10	.284	.381	.364	100	2	0-1	.982	8	105	131	S88,3b38,1b6/2M		1.5
1950	Cle A	81	260	23	70	13	2	1	29	31	1	5	.269	.349	.346	81	-7	1-2	.986	2	95	106	S61,1b8,2b2,3b2,M		-0.2
1951	Bos A	82	273	37	73	18	1	5	47	30	6	12	.267	.353	.396	93	-2	1-0	.951	1	104	126	S52,3b15,1b2		0.2
1952	Bos A	4	2	1	0	0	0	0	2	0	0	0	.000	.000	.000	-93	-1	0-0	1.000	-0	151	0	/S3M		0.0
Total	15	1646	6029	861	1779	385	66	68	789	796	34	309	.295	.380	.415	121	200	51-50	.973	134	102	119	S1539,3b57,1b16,2b3,C3		43.6

BOURJOS, CHRIS Christopher B10.16.1955 Chicago IL BR/TR/6-0/187 d8.31 Col Northern Illinois

YEAR	TM LG	G	AB	R	H	2B	3B	HR	RBI	BB-IB	HP	SO	AVG	OBP	SLG	AOPS	ABR	SB-CS	FA	FR	RNG	THR	GAMES AT POSITION	DL	BFW
1980	SF N	13	22	4	5	1	0	1	2	2-0	0	7	.227	.292	.409	97	0	0-0	1.000	-1	67	0	O6(2/0/4)		-0.1

BOURNIGAL, RAFAEL Rafael Antonio (Pelletier) B5.12.1966 Azua, D.R. BR/TR/5-11/165(160-176) [LAN87 19/482] d9.1 Col Florida St.

YEAR	TM LG	G	AB	R	H	2B	3B	HR	RBI	BB-IB	HP	SO	AVG	OBP	SLG	AOPS	ABR	SB-CS	FA	FR	RNG	THR	GAMES AT POSITION	DL	BFW
1992	LA N	10	20	1	3	1	0	0	1	0-0	1	2	.150	.227	.200	22	-2	0-0	.967	0	91	157	S9		-0.1
1993	LA N	8	18	0	9	1	0	0	3	0-0	1	2	.500	.500	.556	192	2	0-0	1.000	1	47	0	2b4,S4		0.3
1994	LA N	40	116	12	26	3	1	0	11	9-1	2	5	.224	.291	.267	50	-9	0-0	.981	-4	87	109	S40		-1.0
1996	Oak A	88	252	33	61	14	2	0	18	16-0	1	19	.242	.290	.313	53	-18	4-3	.993	3	109	99	2b64,S23		-1.1
1997	Oak A	79	222	29	62	9	4	1	20	16-1	4	19	.279	.339	.333	76	-7	2-1	.980	5	114	91	S74,2b7	30	0.3
1998	Oak A	85	209	23	47	11	0	1	19	10-1	2	19	.225	.265	.292	46	-17	6-1	1.000	-3	93	102	2b48,S38/D		-1.5
1999	Sea A	55	95	16	26	5	0	2	14	7-0	0	6	.274	.317	.389	82	-3	0-0	.987	-8	105	116	S28,2b17,3b8/OLD		0.1
Total	7	365	932	104	234	44	3	4	85	59-3	10	64	.251	.301	.318	62	-54	12-5	.986	3	103	101	S216,2b140,3b8,D2/OL	30	-3.0

YEAR	TM LG	G	AB	R	H	2B	3B	HR	RBI	BB-IB	HP	SO	AVG	OBP	SLG	AOPS	ABR	SB-CS	FA	FR	RNG	THR	GAMES AT POSITION	DL	BFW

BOURQUE, PAT Patrick Daniel B3.23.1947 Worcester MA BL/TL/6-0/210* d9.6 Col Holy Cross

YEAR	TM LG	G	AB	R	H	2B	3B	HR	RBI	BB-IB	HP	SO	AVG	OBP	SLG	AOPS	ABR	SB-CS	FA	FR	RNG	THR	GAMES AT POSITION	DL	BFW
1971	Chi N	14	37	3	7	0	1	1	3	3-0	0	9	.189	.250	.324	54	-2	0-0	.957	2	187	73	1b11		-0.2
1972	Chi N	11	27	3	7	1	0	0	5	2-0	0	2	.259	.310	.296	66	-1	0-0	1.000	1	148	162	1b7		-0.1
1973	Chi N	57	139	11	29	6	0	7	20	16-1	2	21	.209	.297	.403	86	-3	1-1	.986	4	145	109	1b38		-0.2
	†Oak A	23	42	8	8	4	1	2	9	15-2	0	10	.190	.390	.476	154	4	0-0	1.000	-1	0	111	D15,1b5		0.3
1974	Oak A	73	96	6	22	4	0	1	16	15-1	0	20	.229	.327	.302	89	-1	0-2	.988	-1	83	127	1b39,D8		-0.4
	Min A	23	64	5	14	2	0	1	8	7-0	0	11	.219	.296	.297	69	-2	0-0	.987	3	168	99	1b21		-0.1
	Year	96	160	11	36	6	1	2	24	22-1	0	31	.225	.315	.300	82	-3	0-2	.988	2	125	113	1b60,D8		-0.5
Total	4	201	405	36	87	17	2	12	61	58-4	2	73	.215	.313	.356	87	-5	1-3	.985	9	138	110	1b121,D23		-0.7

BOWA, LARRY Lawrence Robert B12.6.1945 Sacramento CA BB/TR/5-10/155* d4.7 M6/C13 Col Sacramento (CA) City

YEAR	TM LG	G	AB	R	H	2B	3B	HR	RBI	BB-IB	HP	SO	AVG	OBP	SLG	AOPS	ABR	SB-CS	FA	FR	RNG	THR	GAMES AT POSITION	DL	BFW
1970	Phi N	145	547	50	137	17	6	0	34	21-1	0	48	.250	.277	.303	57	-35	24-13	.979	-23	91	79	S143/2		-4.1
1971	Phi N	159	650	74	162	18	5	0	25	36-2	5	61	.249	.293	.292	66	-30	28-11	.987	5	105	95	S157		-0.3
1972	Phi N	152	579	67	145	11	13	1	31	32-1	2	51	.250	.291	.320	72	-24	17-9	.987	2	101	97	S150		-0.4
1973	Phi N	122	446	42	94	11	3	0	23	24-8	1	31	.211	.252	.249	38	-38	10-6	.979	2	96	113	S122	37	-2.3
1974	Phi N★	162	669	97	184	19	10	1	36	23-0	1	52	.275	.294	.338	75	-25	39-11	.984	-13	90	103	S162		-1.4
1975	Phi N★	136	583	79	178	18	9	2	38	24-0	2	32	.305	.334	.377	93	-8	24-6	.962	-11	90	104	S135	27	0.1
1976	†Phi N★	156	624	71	155	15	9	0	49	32-3	0	31	.248	.283	.301	64	-31	30-8	.975	-14	95	105	S156		-2.4
1977	†Phi N	154	624	93	175	19	3	4	41	32-2	0	32	.280	.313	.340	72	-25	32-3	.983	3	103	111	S154		0.0
1978	†Phi N★	156	654	78	192	31	5	3	43	24-1	1	40	.294	.319	.370	90	-10	27-5	.986	6	102	112	S156		1.7
1979	Phi N★	147	539	74	130	17	11	0	31	61-5	1	32	.241	.316	.314	70	-22	20-9	.991	-6	96	96	S146	15	-1.2
1980	†Phi N	147	540	57	144	16	4	2	39	24-7	3	28	.267	.300	.322	70	-22	21-6	.975	-20	92	80	S147		-2.6
1981	†Phi N	103	360	34	102	14	3	0	31	26-2	0	17	.283	.331	.339	86	-6	16-7	.975	-7	99	83	S102		-0.2
1982	Chi N	142	499	50	123	15	7	0	29	39-5	1	38	.246	.302	.305	68	-22	8-3	.973	-22	93	81	S140		-3.0
1983	Chi N	147	499	73	133	20	5	2	43	35-1	1	30	.267	.312	.339	77	-16	7-3	.984	26	112	122	S145		2.6
1984	†Chi N	133	391	46	87	14	2	0	17	28-5	0	24	.223	.274	.269	49	-26	10-4	.974	12	106	93	S132		-0.1
1985	Chi N	72	195	13	48	6	4	0	13	11-2	1	20	.246	.285	.318	63	-10	5-1	.970	4	107	93	S66		0.0
	NY N	14	19	2	2	1	0	0	2	2-0	1	2	.105	.190	.158	-2	-3	0-0	.882	-2	50	140	S9,2b4		-0.4
	Year	86	214	15	50	7	4	0	15	13-2	2	22	.234	.276	.304	58	-12	5-1	.965	2	103	96	S75,2b4		-0.4
Total	16	2247	8418	987	2191	262	99	15	525	474-45	17	569	.260	.300	.320	70	-353	318-105	.980	-58	98	99	S2222,2b5	79	-14.0

BOWCOCK, BENNY Benjamin James B10.28.1879 Fall River MA D6.16.1961 Taunton MA BR/TR/5-7/150 d9.18

YEAR	TM LG	G	AB	R	H	2B	3B	HR	RBI	BB-IB	HP	SO	AVG	OBP	SLG	AOPS	ABR	SB-CS	FA	FR	RNG	THR	GAMES AT POSITION	DL	BFW
1903	StL A	14	50	7	16	3	1	1	10	3	0		.320	.358	.480	154	3	1	.885	-6	79	85	2b14		-0.2

BOWDEN, TIM David Timon B8.15.1891 McDonough GA D10.25.1949 Emory (now part of Atlanta) GA BL/TR/5-10/175 d9.17 Col Georgia

YEAR	TM LG	G	AB	R	H	2B	3B	HR	RBI	BB-IB	HP	SO	AVG	OBP	SLG	AOPS	ABR	SB-CS	FA	FR	RNG	THR	GAMES AT POSITION	DL	BFW
1914	StL A	7	9	0	2	0	0	0	1	0-0	0	6	.222	.300	.222	60	0	0	1.000	0	123	0	O4(0/1/3)		-0.1

BOWEN, CHICK Emmons Joseph B7.26.1897 New Haven CT D8.9.1948 New Haven CT BR/TR/5-7/165 d9.15 Col Holy Cross

YEAR	TM LG	G	AB	R	H	2B	3B	HR	RBI	BB-IB	HP	SO	AVG	OBP	SLG	AOPS	ABR	SB-CS	FA	FR	RNG	THR	GAMES AT POSITION	DL	BFW
1919	NY N	3	5	0	1	0	0	0	1	1	0	2	.200	.333	.200	63	0		1.000	-0	108	0	O2(0/1/1)		0.0

BOWEN, ROB Robert McClure B2.24.1981 Bedford TX BB/TR/6-2/210* [MinA99 2/56] d9.1

YEAR	TM LG	G	AB	R	H	2B	3B	HR	RBI	BB-IB	HP	SO	AVG	OBP	SLG	AOPS	ABR	SB-CS	FA	FR	RNG	THR	GAMES AT POSITION	DL	BFW
2003	Min A	7	10	0	1	0	0	0	1	0-0	0	4	.100	.091	.100	-45	-2	0-0	.944	-2	18	0	C7		-0.4
2004	Min A	17	27	1	3	0	0	1	2	4-0	0	10	.111	.226	.222	17	-3	0-0	.985	-1	78	45	C15		-0.4
Total	2	24	37	1	4	0	0	1	3	4-0	0	14	.108	.190	.189	1	-5	0-0	.976	-3	65	35	C22		-0.8

BOWEN, SAM Samuel Thomas B9.18.1952 Brunswick GA BR/TR/5-9/167* [BosA74 7/164] d8.25 Col Valdosta St.

YEAR	TM LG	G	AB	R	H	2B	3B	HR	RBI	BB-IB	HP	SO	AVG	OBP	SLG	AOPS	ABR	SB-CS	FA	FR	RNG	THR	GAMES AT POSITION	DL	BFW
1977	Bos A	3	2	0	0	0	0	0	0	0-0	0	2	.000	.000	.000	-90	-1	0-0	1.000	0	229		O3(2/1/0)		0.0
1978	Bos A	6	7	3	1	0	0	1	1	1-0	0	4	.143	.250	.571	113	0	0-0	1.000	-1	28	0	O4(1/3/0)		-0.1
1980	Bos A	7	13	0	2	0	0	0	0	2-0	0	3	.154	.267	.154	17	-1	1-0	1.000	2	142	290	O6(1/4/1)		0.0
Total	3	16	22	3	3	0	0	1	1	3-0	0	7	.136	.240	.273	38	-2	1-0	1.000	1	110	172	O13(4/8/1)		-0.1

BOWENS, SAM Samuel Edward B3.3.1939 Wilmington NC D3.28.2003 Wilmington NC BR/TR/6-1.5/195(190-209) d9.7 Negro Lg 1957-58 Col Tennessee St.

YEAR	TM LG	G	AB	R	H	2B	3B	HR	RBI	BB-IB	HP	SO	AVG	OBP	SLG	AOPS	ABR	SB-CS	FA	FR	RNG	THR	GAMES AT POSITION	DL	BFW
1963	Bal A	15	48	8	16	3	1	1	5	3-0	0	5	.333	.385	.500	151	3	1-1	.952	-2	86	0	O13R		0.1
1964	Bal A	139	501	58	132	25	2	22	71	42-1	4	99	.263	.323	.453	114	9	4-3	.981	3	107	103	O135(32/0/120)		0.3
1965	Bal A	84	203	16	33	4	1	7	20	10-0	0	41	.163	.199	.296	39	-17	7-1	.982	1	105	82	O68(11/0/58)		-2.1
1966	Bal A	89	243	26	51	9	1	6	20	17-2	5	52	.210	.275	.329	74	-8	9-3	.960	3	102	192	O68(32/4/41)		-0.9
1967	Bal A	62	120	13	22	2	1	5	12	11-0	1	43	.183	.258	.342	76	-4	3-4	.977	-1	86	111	O32(16/0/16)		-0.8
1968	Was A	57	115	14	22	4	0	4	7	11-0	0	39	.191	.262	.330	81	-3	0-0	.957	0	100	142	O27(11/3/14)		-0.5
1969	Was A	33	57	6	11	1	0	0	4	5-0	0	14	.193	.258	.211	34	-5	1-1	.971	-0	102	77	O30(6/3/22)		-0.7
Total	7	479	1287	141	287	48	6	45	143	100-4	10	293	.223	.283	.375	87	-25	25-13	.974	4	102	114	O373(108/10/284)		-4.6

BOWERMAN, FRANK Frank Eugene "Mike" B12.5.1868 Romeo MI D11.30.1948 Romeo MI BR/TR/6-2/190 d8.24 M1 Col Michigan

YEAR	TM LG	G	AB	R	H	2B	3B	HR	RBI	BB-IB	HP	SO	AVG	OBP	SLG	AOPS	ABR	SB-CS	FA	FR	RNG	THR	GAMES AT POSITION	DL	BFW
1895	Bal N	1	1	0	0	0	0	0	0	0	0	0	.000	.000	.000	-97	-0	0	1.000	0	0		/C		0.0
1896	Bal N	4	16	0	2	0	0	0	4	1	0	0	.125	.176	.125	-20	-3	0	.900	-0	118	167	C3/1		-0.2
1897	†Bal N	38	130	16	41	5	0	1	21	1	2		.315	.331	.377	87	-3	3	.948	-0	103	76	C36		0.0
1898	Bal N	5	16	5	7	1	0	0	1	2	1		.438	.526	.500	191	2	1	.950	-0	115	163	C4		0.2
	Pit N	69	241	17	66	6	3	0	29	7	1		.274	.297	.324	79	-8	4	.946	2	104	106	C59,1b9		0.0
	Year	74	257	22	73	7	3	0	30	9	2		.284	.313	.335	87	-5	5	.946	2	105	110	C63,1b9		0.2
1899	Pit N	110	427	51	111	16	10	3	53	12	5		.260	.288	.365	79	-15	10	.947	13	121	109	C80,1b28		0.5
1900	NY N	80	270	25	65	5	3	1	42	6	4		.241	.268	.293	57	-17	10	.929	11	110	125	C75,S2		0.1
1901	NY N	59	191	20	38	5	3	0	14	7	2		.199	.235	.257	44	-14	3	.950	4	96	113	C46,2b3,S3,3b3/1		-0.6
1902	NY N	109	373	38	93	14	6	0	27	13	1		.249	.276	.319	85	-8	12	.954	2	96	111	C100,1b3		0.3
1903	NY N	64	210	22	58	6	2	1	31	6	3		.276	.306	.338	81	-6	5	.977	3	118	85	C55,1b4/OC		0.2
1904	NY N	93	289	36	67	11	4	2	27	16	7		.232	.288	.318	84	-6	7	.977	8	143	98	C79,1b9,2b2/P		1.0
1905	NY N	98	297	37	80	8	1	3	41	12	11		.269	.322	.333	93	-2	6	.982	5	150	80	C72,1b17/2		0.9
1906	NY N	103	285	23	65	7	3	1	42	15	3		.228	.274	.284	72	-10	5	.984	7	113	109	C67,1b20		0.3
1907	NY N	96	311	31	81	8	2	2	32	17	5		.260	.309	.299	88	-5	11	.990	-2	127	91	C62,1b29		-0.1
1908	Bos N	86	254	16	58	8	1	1	25	13	4		.228	.274	.280	78	-7	4	.971	-3	88	94	C63,1b11		-0.5
1909	Bos N	33	99	6	21	2	0	0	4	2	0		.212	.228	.232	41	-7	0	.928	-1	91	90	C27,M		-0.6
Total	15	1048	3410	345	853	102	38	13	393	130	48		.250	.287	.314	77	-109	81	.963	48	114	102	C829,1b132,2b6,S5,3b3/POC		1.5

BOWERS, BRENT Brent Raymond B5.2.1971 Bridgeview IL BL/TR/6-3/200 [TorA89 2/60] d8.16

YEAR	TM LG	G	AB	R	H	2B	3B	HR	RBI	BB-IB	HP	SO	AVG	OBP	SLG	AOPS	ABR	SB-CS	FA	FR	RNG	THR	GAMES AT POSITION	DL	BFW
1996	Bal A	21	39	6	12	1	0	0	3	0-0	0	7	.308	.308	.359	68	-2	0-0	1.000	1	95	250	O21L		-0.1

BOWERS, BILLY Grover Bill B3.25.1922 Parkin AR D9.17.1996 Wynne AR BL/TR/5-9.5/176 d4.24

YEAR	TM LG	G	AB	R	H	2B	3B	HR	RBI	BB-IB	HP	SO	AVG	OBP	SLG	AOPS	ABR	SB-CS	FA	FR	RNG	THR	GAMES AT POSITION	DL	BFW
1949	Chi A	26	78	5	15	2	1	0	6	4	0	5	.192	.232	.244	27	-9	1-1	.980	0	102	132	O20(3/10/8)		-0.9

BOWES, FRANK Frank M. B1865 Bath NY D1.21.1895 New York NY TR/5-9/160 d4.17

YEAR	TM LG	G	AB	R	H	2B	3B	HR	RBI	BB-IB	HP	SO	AVG	OBP	SLG	AOPS	ABR	SB-CS	FA	FR	RNG	THR	GAMES AT POSITION	DL	BFW
1890	Bro AA	61	232	28	51	5	2	0		1			.220	.246	.259	50	-16	11	.813	-11	82	96	C25,O19(4/2/13),3b13,1b3,S2		-2.2

BOWIE, JIM James R. B2.17.1965 Tokyo, Japan BL/TL/6-0/205 [SeaA86 12/297] d8.3 Col Louisiana St.

YEAR	TM LG	G	AB	R	H	2B	3B	HR	RBI	BB-IB	HP	SO	AVG	OBP	SLG	AOPS	ABR	SB-CS	FA	FR	RNG	THR	GAMES AT POSITION	DL	BFW
1994	Oak A	6	14	0	3	0	0	0		0-0	0	2	.214	.214	.214	12	-2	0-0	1.000	-0	66	138	1b6		-0.2

BOWLIN, WELDON Lois Weldon "Hoss" B12.10.1940 Paragould AR BR/TR/5-9/155 d9.16 Col Arkansas St.

YEAR	TM LG	G	AB	R	H	2B	3B	HR	RBI	BB-IB	HP	SO	AVG	OBP	SLG	AOPS	ABR	SB-CS	FA	FR	RNG	THR	GAMES AT POSITION	DL	BFW
1967	KC A	2	5	0	1	0	0	0	0	0-0	0	0	.200	.200	.200	19	-1	0-0	1.000	0	133	0	3b2		0.0

BOWLING, STEVE Stephen Shaddon B6.26.1952 Tulsa OK BR/TR/6-0/185* [MilA74 7/150] d9.7 Col Tulsa

YEAR	TM LG	G	AB	R	H	2B	3B	HR	RBI	BB-IB	HP	SO	AVG	OBP	SLG	AOPS	ABR	SB-CS	FA	FR	RNG	THR	GAMES AT POSITION	DL	BFW
1976	Mil A	14	42	4	7	2	0	0	5		0	5	.167	.205	.214	23	-4	0-0	.975	1	118	116	O13C/D		-0.3
1977	Tor A	89	194	19	40	8	1	1	13	37-1	0	42	.206	.330	.273	67	-7	2-3	.987	8	98	304	O87(20/24/47)		-0.3
Total	2	103	236	23	47	10	1	1	15	39-1	0	47	.199	.310	.263	60	-11	2-3	.985	9	101	276	O100(20/37/47)/D		-0.6

BOWMAN, ELMER Elmari Wilhelm "Big Bow" B3.19.1897 Proctor VT D12.17.1985 Los Angeles CA BR/TR/6-0.5/193 d8.3 Col Vermont

YEAR	TM LG	G	AB	R	H	2B	3B	HR	RBI	BB-IB	HP	SO	AVG	OBP	SLG	AOPS	ABR	SB-CS	FA	FR	RNG	THR	GAMES AT POSITION	DL	BFW
1920	Was A	2	1	0	0	0	0	0	0	0-0	0	0	.000	.000	.000	42	0	0-0	—	0			/H		0.0

BOWMAN, ERNIE Ernest Ferrell B7.28.1935 Johnson City TN BR/TR/5-10/160* d4.12

YEAR	TM LG	G	AB	R	H	2B	3B	HR	RBI	BB-IB	HP	SO	AVG	OBP	SLG	AOPS	ABR	SB-CS	FA	FR	RNG	THR	GAMES AT POSITION	DL	BFW
1961	SF N	38	38	10	8	0	0	0	2	1-0	0	8	.211	.231	.316	45	-3	2-0	.885	-4	81	57	2b13,S12,3b7		-0.6
1962	†SF N	46	42	9	8	1	0	1	4	1-0	1	10	.190	.227	.286	37	-4	0-1	1.000	-5	76	19	2b17,3b11,S10		-0.9

YEAR	TM LG	G	AB	R	H	2B	3B	HR	RBI	BB-IB	HP	SO	AVG	OBP	SLG	AOPS	ABR	SB-CS	FA	FR	RNG	THR	GAMES AT POSITION	DL	BFW
1963	SF N	81	125	10	23	3	0	0	4	0-0	0	15	.184	.181	.208	13	-14	1-2	.952	-8	79	75	S40,2b26,3b12		-2.1
Total	3	165	205	29	39	4	2	1	10	2-0	1	33	.190	.200	.244	24	-21	3-3	.950	-17	83	68	S62,2b56,3b30		-3.6

BOWMAN, BOB Robert Leroy B5.10.1931 Laytonville CA BR/TR/6-1/195* d4.16 Col San Jose St.

YEAR	TM LG	G	AB	R	H	2B	3B	HR	RBI	BB-IB	HP	SO	AVG	OBP	SLG	AOPS	ABR	SB-CS	FA	FR	RNG	THR	GAMES AT POSITION	DL	BFW
1955	Phi N	3	3	0	0	0	0	0	0	0-0	0	1	.000	.000	.000	-99	-1	0-0	1.000	0	134	0	O2(1/0/1)		-0.1
1956	Phi N	6	16	2	3	0	1	1	2	0-0	0	6	.188	.188	.500	78	-1	0-0	.833	-1	75	0	O5(0/1/4)		-0.2
1957	Phi N	99	237	31	63	8	2	6	23	27-1	6	50	.266	.352	.392	104	2	0-0	.929	1	98	162	O81(3/0/79)		0.0
1958	Phi N	91	184	31	53	11	2	8	24	16-2	0	30	.288	.343	.500	122	5	0-1	.988	-1	105	30	O57(20/1/37)		0.2
1959	Phi N	57	79	7	10	0	0	2	5	5-0	0	23	.127	.176	.203	1	-12	0-0	1.000	1	114	101	O20(11/2/7),P5		-1.1
Total	5	256	519	71	129	19	5	17	54	48-3	6	109	.249	.317	.403	93	-7	0-1	.955	0	102	108	O165(35/4/128),P5		-1.2

BOWMAN, BILL William George B1869 Chicago IL 5-11/180 d6.18

YEAR	TM LG	G	AB	R	H	2B	3B	HR	RBI	BB-IB	HP	SO	AVG	OBP	SLG	AOPS	ABR	SB-CS	FA	FR	RNG	THR	GAMES AT POSITION	DL	BFW
1891	Chi N	15	45	2	4	1	0	0	5	5	1	9	.089	.196	.111	-10	-6	0	.915	-2	130	99	C15		-0.7

BOWSER, RED James Harvey B9.20.1881 Freeport PA D5.22.1943 Moundsville WV d9.13

YEAR	TM LG	G	AB	R	H	2B	3B	HR	RBI	BB-IB	HP	SO	AVG	OBP	SLG	AOPS	ABR	SB-CS	FA	FR	RNG	THR	GAMES AT POSITION	DL	BFW
1910	Chi A	1	2	0	0	0	0	0	0	0-0	0	0	.000	.000	.000	-99	0	0	—	0	0	0	/O		-0.1

BOYD, FRANK Frank Jay B4.2.1868 West Middletown PA D12.16.1937 Oil City PA BR/TR/?/168 d5.18

YEAR	TM LG	G	AB	R	H	2B	3B	HR	RBI	BB-IB	HP	SO	AVG	OBP	SLG	AOPS	ABR	SB-CS	FA	FR	RNG	THR	GAMES AT POSITION	DL	BFW
1893	Cle N	2	5	3	1	1	0	0	3	1	0		.200	.333	.400	89	0	0	1.000	0	98	174	C2		0.0

BOYD, JAKE Jacob Henry B1.19.1874 Martinsburg WV D8.12.1932 Gettysburg PA TL/?/160 d9.20 ▲

YEAR	TM LG	G	AB	R	H	2B	3B	HR	RBI	BB-IB	HP	SO	AVG	OBP	SLG	AOPS	ABR	SB-CS	FA	FR	RNG	THR	GAMES AT POSITION	DL	BFW
1894	Was N	6	21	1	3	0	0	0	1	1	0	4	.143	.182	.143	-22	-4	2	.833	1	410	0	O3(1/0/2),P3		-0.1
1895	Was N	52	159	29	43	5	1	1	16	20	7	28	.270	.376	.333	85	-2	2	.786	-7	82	160	O21(3/0/18),P15,2b10,S8/3		-0.8
1896	Was N	4	13	1	1	0	0	0	1	1	1	1	.077	.200	.077	-25	-1	0	.909	0	113	0	P4		0.0
Total	3	62	193	31	47	5	1	1	18	22	8	33	.244	.345	.295	66	-7	4	.794	-6	132	136	O24(4/0/20),P22,2b10,S8/3		-0.9

BOYD, BOB Robert Richard "The Rope" B10.1.1919 Potts Camp MS D9.7.2004 Wichita KS BL/TL/5-10/170* d9.8 Negro Lg 1946-50

YEAR	TM LG	G	AB	R	H	2B	3B	HR	RBI	BB-IB	HP	SO	AVG	OBP	SLG	AOPS	ABR	SB-CS	FA	FR	RNG	THR	GAMES AT POSITION	DL	BFW
1951	Chi A	12	18	3	3	0	0	0	4	3	0	5	.167	.286	.278	54	-1	0-0	1.000	-1	38	244	1b6		-0.2
1953	Chi A	55	165	20	49	6	2	3	23	13	1	11	.297	.352	.412	103	0	1-4	1.000	-1	84	97	1b29,O16(15/0/1)		-0.4
1954	Chi A	29	56	10	10	3	0	0	5	4	0	3	.179	.233	.232	27	-6	2-0	.955	-0	108	175	O13L,1b12		-0.6
1956	Bal A	70	225	28	70	8	3	2	11	30-2	1	14	.311	.395	.400	119	7	0-5	.990	-6	68	92	1b60,O8(3/0/5)	85	-0.2
1957	Bal A	141	485	73	154	16	8	4	34	55-3	2	31	.318	.388	.408	126	18	2-4	.991	-3	91	100	1b132/OL		0.7
1958	Bal A	125	401	38	124	21	5	7	36	25-1	2	24	.309	.350	.439	123	12	1-1	.994	0	98	106	1b99		0.6
1959	Bal A	128	415	42	110	20	2	3	41	29-1	1	14	.265	.312	.345	83	-10	3-1	.985	-9	71	108	1b109		-2.5
1960	Bal A	71	82	9	26	5	2	0	9	6-1	0	5	.317	.364	.427	114	2	0-0	1.000	-0	82	144	1b17		0.1
1961	KC A	26	48	7	11	2	0	0	9	1-0	0	2	.229	.240	.271	37	-4	0-2	1.000	-1	44	66	1b8		-0.6
	Mil N	36	41	3	10	0	0	0	3	1-0	0	7	.244	.256	.244	38	-4	0-0	1.000	1	280	149	1b3		-0.3
Total	9	693	1936	253	567	81	23	19	175	167-8	7	114	.293	.349	.388	105	14	9-17	.991	-17	84	103	1b475,O38(32/0/6)	85	-3.4

BOYD, BILL William J. B12.22.1852 New York NY D10.1.1912 Jamaica NY d4.22 M1/U1

YEAR	TM LG	G	AB	R	H	2B	3B	HR	RBI	BB-IB	HP	SO	AVG	OBP	SLG	AOPS	ABR	SB-CS	FA	FR	RNG	THR	GAMES AT POSITION	DL	BFW
1872	Mut NA	36	170	27	44	6	1	1	32	6		7	.259	.284	.324	92	0	4-2	.730	-12	75	54	3b34/2OR		-0.9
1873	Atl NA	48	228	31	63	5	4	1	30	2		4	.276	.283	.346	96	1	1-1	.716	3	172	84	O43R,3b8		0.4
1874	Har NA	26	117	22	41	8	4	0	19	1		5	.350	.356	.487	160	7	1-0	.664	-9	75	93	3b25/OR		-0.2
1875	Atl NA	36	151	14	44	11	0	1	10	1		0	.291	.296	.384	154	0	0-0	.774	-7	95	59	2b15,O12R,3b9,1b2/PSM		0.2
Total	4 NA	146	666	94	192	30	9	3	91	10		13	.288	.299	.374	119	18	6-3	.704	-24	79	88	3b76,O57R,2b16,1b2/SP		-0.5

BOYER, CLETE Cletis Leroy B2.9.1937 Cassville MO BR/TR/6-0/182(165-188) d6.5 C10 b-Cloyd b-Ken

YEAR	TM LG	G	AB	R	H	2B	3B	HR	RBI	BB-IB	HP	SO	AVG	OBP	SLG	AOPS	ABR	SB-CS	FA	FR	RNG	THR	GAMES AT POSITION	DL	BFW
1955	KC A	47	79	3	19	1	0	0	6	3-0	0	17	.241	.268	.253	40	-7	0-0	.963	2	89	120	S12,3b11,2b10		-0.4
1956	KC A	67	129	15	28	3	1	1	4	11-1	1	24	.217	.284	.279	49	-10	1-1	.971	11	120	117	2b51,3b7		0.3
1957	KC A	10	0	0	0	0	0	0	0	0-0	0	0	—	—	—	0	0	0-0	—	-0	0	0	/23		0.0
1959	NY A	47	114	4	20	2	0	0	3	6-2	1	23	.175	.215	.193	14	-14	1-0	.990	4	100	110	S26,3b16		-0.8
1960	†NY A	124	393	54	95	20	1	14	46	23-1	3	85	.242	.285	.405	90	-7	2-3	.967	24	120	132	3b99,S33		1.8
1961	†NY A	148	504	61	113	19	5	11	55	63-4	2	83	.224	.308	.347	80	-14	1-3	.967	28	118	140	3b141,S12/OR		1.3
1962	†NY A	158	566	85	154	24	1	18	68	51-8	3	106	.272	.331	.413	104	2	3-2	.964	34	122	151	3b157		3.6
1963	†NY A	152	557	59	140	20	3	12	54	33-11	2	91	.251	.295	.363	84	-13	4-2	.954	22	108	134	3b141,S9/2		1.0
1964	†NY A	147	510	43	111	10	6	8	52	36-11	1	93	.218	.269	.304	59	-30	6-1	.968	8	110	139	3b123,S21		-2.0
1965	NY A	148	514	69	129	23	6	18	58	39-10	2	79	.251	.304	.424	106	2	4-1	.968	21	114	160	3b147,S2		2.5
1966	NY A	144	500	59	120	22	4	14	57	46-4	2	48	.240	.303	.384	101	0	6-0	.966	20	127	80	3b85,S59		2.8
1967	Atl N	154	572	63	140	18	3	26	96	39-3	2	81	.245	.292	.423	105	1	6-3	.970	7	97	123	3b150,S6		0.8
1968	Atl N	71	273	19	62	7	2	4	17	16-3	2	32	.227	.275	.311	75	-9	2-0	.981	4	101	141	3b69	25	-0.6
1969	†Atl N	144	496	57	124	16	1	14	57	55-6	4	87	.250	.328	.371	95	-3	3-7	.965	7	104	83	3b141		0.1
1970	Atl N	134	475	44	117	14	1	16	62	41-8	1	71	.246	.305	.381	79	-15	2-5	.954	11	112	94	3b126,S5		-0.6
1971	Atl N	30	98	10	24	1	0	6	19	8-2	1	11	.245	.299	.439	101	0	0-0	.961	1	93	133	3b25/S		0.1
Total	16	1725	5780	.645	1396	200	33	162	654	470-74	25	931	.242	.299	.372	87	-117	41-28	.965	204	112	126	3b1439,S186,2b63/OR	25	9.9

BOYER, KEN Kenton Lloyd B5.20.1931 Liberty MO D9.7.1982 St.Louis MO BR/TR/6-2/200* d4.12 M3/C2 b-Clete b-Cloyd

YEAR	TM LG	G	AB	R	H	2B	3B	HR	RBI	BB-IB	HP	SO	AVG	OBP	SLG	AOPS	ABR	SB-CS	FA	FR	RNG	THR	GAMES AT POSITION	DL	BFW
1955	StL N	147	530	78	140	27	2	18	62	37-5	1	67	.264	.311	.425	94	-6	22-17	.952	2	103	104	3b139,S18		-0.4
1956	StL N★	150	595	91	182	30	2	26	98	38-7	1	65	.306	.347	.494	123	19	8-3	.961	9	109	149	3b149		2.8
1957	StL N	142	544	79	144	18	3	19	62	44-8	1	77	.265	.318	.414	94	-6	12-8	.996	-3	102	27	O105C,3b41		-1.4
1958	StL N	150	570	101	175	21	9	23	90	49-8	3	53	.307	.360	.496	121	16	11-6	.962	24	115	135	3b144,O6C/S		4.0
1959	StL N★	149	563	86	174	18	5	28	94	67-7	2	77	.309	.384	.508	127	22	12-6	.956	13	109	133	3b143,S12		3.5
1960	StL N★	151	552	95	168	26	10	32	97	56-10	4	77	.304	.370	.562	139	30	8-7	.959	16	107	149	3b146		4.5
1961	StL N★	153	589	109	194	26	11	24	95	68-9	1	91	.329	.397	.533	132	28	6-3	.951	14	116	76	3b153		4.1
1962	StL N★	160	611	92	178	27	5	24	98	75-7	1	104	.291	.369	.470	113	12	12-7	.956	4	102	120	3b160		1.6
1963	StL N★	159	617	86	176	28	2	24	111	70-10	2	90	.285	.358	.454	121	19	1-0	.925	-16	91	97	3b159		0.3
1964	†StL N★	162	628	100	185	30	10	24	119	70-12	2	85	.295	.365	.489	128	24	3-5	.951	0	102	118	3b162		2.3
1965	StL N	144	535	71	139	18	2	13	75	57-3	1	73	.260	.328	.374	90	-1	2-7	.968	-1	91	79	3b143		-2.2
1966	NY N	136	496	62	132	28	2	14	61	30-5	1	64	.266	.304	.415	101	0	4-3	.951	14	116	126	3b130,1b2		1.4
1967	NY N	56	166	17	39	7	2	3	13	26-3	0	22	.235	.335	.355	100	1	2-1	.949	-0	104	97	3b44,1b8		0.0
	Chi A	57	180	17	47	5	1	4	21	7-0	0	25	.261	.287	.367	96	-2	0-2	.957	-1	101	87	3b33,1b18		-0.5
1968	Chi A	10	24	0	3	0	0	0	1	1-0	0	6	.125	.160	.125	-13	-3	0-0	.900	-1	84	140	3b5/1		-0.5
	LA N	83	221	20	60	7	2	6	41	16-3	1	34	.271	.317	.403	126	6	2-2	.922	1	108	92	3b34,1b32		0.6
1969	LA N	25	34	0	7	2	0	0	4	2-0	0	7	.206	.250	.265	47	-2	0-0	.971	-0	91	236	1b4		-0.3
Total	15	2034	7455	1104	2143	318	68	282	1141	713-97	20	1017	.287	.349	.462	115	151	105-77	.952	64	105	115	3b1785,O111C,1b65,S31		19.8

BOYLAND, DOE Dorian Scott B1.6.1955 Chicago IL BL/TL/6-4/200* [PitN76 2/45] d9.4 Col Wisconsin-Oshkosh

YEAR	TM LG	G	AB	R	H	2B	3B	HR	RBI	BB-IB	HP	SO	AVG	OBP	SLG	AOPS	ABR	SB-CS	FA	FR	RNG	THR	GAMES AT POSITION	DL	BFW
1978	Pit N	6	8	1	2	0	0	0	1	0-0	0	1	.250	.250	.250	38	-1	0-0	1.000	-0	0	0	/1		-0.1
1979	Pit N	4	3	0	0	0	0	0	0	0-0	0	2	.000	.000	.000	-95	-1	0-0	—	-0	0	0	/H		-0.1
1981	Pit N	11	8	0	0	0	0	0	0	1-0	0	3	.000	.111	.000	-63	-2	0-0	—	0	0	0	/H		-0.2
Total	3	21	19	1	2	0	0	0	1	1-0	0	6	.105	.150	.105	-26	-4	0-0	1.000	0	0	0	/1		-0.4

BOYLE, EDDIE Edward J. B5.8.1874 Cincinnati OH D2.9.1941 Cincinnati OH BR/TR/6-3/200 d4.17 b-Jack

YEAR	TM LG	G	AB	R	H	2B	3B	HR	RBI	BB-IB	HP	SO	AVG	OBP	SLG	AOPS	ABR	SB-CS	FA	FR	RNG	THR	GAMES AT POSITION	DL	BFW
1896	Lou N	3	9	0	0	0	0	0	2	2	0		.000	.182	.000	-52	-2	0	.938	-0	78	93	C3		-0.2
	Pit N	2	5	0	0	0	0	0	0	0	0	1	.000	.000	.000	-99	-1	0	.833	-1	75	75	C2		-0.2
	Year	5	14	0	0	0	0	0	2	2	0		.000	.125	.000	-68	-3	0	.909	-1	77	88	C5		-0.4

BOYLE, HENRY Henry J. "Handsome Henry" B9.20.1860 Philadelphia PA D5.25.1932 Philadelphia PA BR/TR d7.9 OF(54/18/13) ▲

YEAR	TM LG	G	AB	R	H	2B	3B	HR	RBI	BB-IB	HP	SO	AVG	OBP	SLG	AOPS	ABR	SB-CS	FA	FR	RNG	THR	GAMES AT POSITION	DL	BFW
1884	StL U	65	262	41	68	10	3	4		9			.260	.284	.366	92	-11		.885	4	137	140	O43(40/2/2),P19,3b4/S21		-0.4
1885	StL N	72	258	24	52	9	1	1	21	13		38	.202	.240	.256	64	-9		.907	-4	86	172	P42,O31(12/10/9),2b2		-0.8
1886	StL N	30	108	9	27	2	2	1	13	5		19	.250	.283	.333	93	-1	0	.852	0	112	90	P25,O6(0/5/1)		-0.4
1887	Ind N	41	141	17	27	9	1	2	13	9	2	18	.191	.250	.312	57	-8	2	.912	-6	67	134	P38,O4(2/1/1)		-0.4
1888	Ind N	37	125	15	18	2	0	1	6	6	1	31	.144	.189	.184	19	-11	1	.933	-2	120	59	P37/1		0.1
1889	Ind N	46	155	17	38	10	0	1	17	9	1	23	.245	.291	.329	72	-6	4	.958	-5	69	0	P46/3		-0.2
Total	6	291	1049	120	230	42	7	10	70	51	4	129	.219	.258	.301	69	-46	7	.912	-8	87	103	P207,O84L,3b5,2b3,1b2/S		-1.7

BOYLE, JIM James John B1.19.1904 Cincinnati OH D12.24.1958 Cincinnati OH BR/TR/6-0/180 d6.20 b-Buzz Col Xavier

YEAR	TM LG	G	AB	R	H	2B	3B	HR	RBI	BB-IB	HP	SO	AVG	OBP	SLG	AOPS	ABR	SB-CS	FA	FR	RNG	THR	GAMES AT POSITION	DL	BFW
1926	NY N	1	0	0	0	0	0	0	0	0-0	0	0	—	—	—	0	0	0-0	—	0	0	0	/C		0.0

YEAR	TM LG	G	AB	R	H	2B	3B	HR	RBI	BB-IB	HP	SO	AVG	OBP	SLG	AOPS	ABR	SB-CS	FA	FR	RNG	THR	GAMES AT POSITION	DL	BFW

BOYLE, JACK John Anthony "Honest Jack" B3.22.1866 Cincinnati OH D1.7.1913 Cincinnati OH BR/TR/6-4/190 d10.8 b-Eddie OF(6/2/7)

1886	Cin.AA	1	5	0	1	0	0	0	0	0	0		.200	.200	.200	25	0	0	.769	-1			/C		-0.1
1887	†StL AA	88	350	48	66	3	1	2	41	20			.189	.237	.220	25	-38	7	.897	-9			C86,O2R,1b2/3		-3.3
1888	†StL AA	71	257	33	62	8	1	1	23	13			.241	.284	.292	77	-8	11	.932	13			C70/OC		1.1
1889	StL AA	99	347	54	85	11	5	3	42	21	7	42	.245	.301	.331	71	-16	5	.947	9			C80,3b12,O5(3/0/2),1b4/2		-0.1
1890	Chi P	100	369	56	96	9	5	1	49	44	5	29	.260	.347	.320	76	-13	11	.940	-2	116	98	C50,3b30,S16,1b7,O2R		-0.8
1891	StL AA	121	434	76	122	18	8	5	79	44	12	35	.281	.353	.394	102	-1	18	.936	-3	116	78	C91,S25,3b7,O3(1/1/1),2b3,1b3		0.3
1892	NY N	120	436	52	80	8	9	0	32	36	4	41	.183	.252	.239	49	-28	10	.922	-3	70	152	C79,1b40,O2L,S2		-2.3
1893	Phi N	116	504	105	144	29	9	4	81	41	10	30	.286	.351	.403	100	-1	22	.988	6	119	101	1b112,C6,2b2		0.4
1894	Phi N	117	510	103	152	23	10	4	89	46	3	27	.298	.360	.406	86	-12	23	.982	0	98	106	1b117/32		-0.9
1895	Phi N	**133**	565	90	143	17	4	0	67	35	5	23	.253	.302	.297	55	-39	13	.973	-6	84	82	1b133		-3.7
1896	Phi N	40	145	17	43	4	1	0	28	6	5	7	.297	.346	.359	87	-3	3	.920	-7	102	81	C28,1b12		-0.6
1897	Phi N	75	288	37	73	9	1	2	36	19	3		.253	.306	.313	65	-15	3	.962	-6	103	89	C50,1b24		-1.4
1898	Phi N	6	22	0	2	0	1	0	3	1	0		.091	.130	.182	-11	-3	0	.919	-1	120	94	1b4,C3		-0.4
Total	13	1087	4232	671	1069	139	54	23	570	326	59	234	.253	.315	.327	72	-177	126	.929	-9	*100*	*103*	C544,1b458,3b51,S43,O15R,2b7		-11.8

BOYLE, JACK John Bellew B7.9.1889 Morris IL D4.3.1971 Ft.Lauderdale FL BL/TR/5-11.5/165 d6.28 Col Chicago

| 1912 | Phi N | 15 | 25 | 4 | 7 | 1 | 0 | 0 | 2 | 5 | | | .280 | .308 | .320 | 67 | -1 | 0 | .905 | 3 | 164 | 292 | 3b6,S2 | | 0.2 |

BOYLE, BUZZ Ralph Francis B2.9.1908 Cincinnati OH D11.12.1978 Cincinnati OH BL/TL/5-11.5/170 d9.11 b-Jim Col Xavier

1929	Bos N	17	57	8	15	2	1	1	2	6		0	11	.263	.333	.386	81		1.000	1	106	101	O17L		-0.2
1930	Bos N	1	1	0	0	0	0	0	0	0		0	0	.000	.000	.000	-99	0	0	—	-0	0	0	/OC		0.0
1933	Bro N	93	338	38	101	13	4	0	31	16		0	24	.299	.331	.361	102	0	7	.975	-3	103	32	O90(45/34/10)		-0.7
1934	Bro N	128	472	88	144	26	10	7	48	51	3	44	.305	.376	.447	126	18	8	.970	9	103	189	O121(18/19/86)		1.9
1935	Bro N	127	475	51	129	17	9	4	45	42	0	45	.272	.332	.371	90	-7	7	.963	4	99	152	O124(0/17/107)		-0.9
Total	5	366	1343	185	389	58	24	12	125	116	3	125	.290	.347	.395	105	9	24	.970	11	102	135	O353(80/71/203)		0.1

BRACK, GIBBY Gilbert Herman B3.29.1908 Chicago IL D1.20.1960 Greenville TX BR/TR/5-9/170 d4.23

1937	Bro N	112	372	60	102	27	9	5	38	44	0	93	.274	.351	.435	111	6	9	.969	2	102	130	O101(37/44/21)		0.4
1938	Bro N	40	56	10	12	2	1	1	6	4	0	14	.214	.267	.339	64	-3	1	1.000	3	124	350	O13(7/0/6)		-0.1
	Phi N	72	282	40	81	20	4	4	28	18	1	30	.287	.332	.429	111	4	2	.964	-0	103	88	O68(12/38/24)		0.1
	Year	112	338	50	93	22	5	5	34	22	1	44	.275	.321	.414	102	0	3	.969	3	106	132	O81(19/38/30)		0.0
1939	Phi N	91	270	40	78	21	4	6	41	26	0	49	.289	.351	.463	121	8	1	.959	-3	98	102	O48(2/6/40),1b19		0.0
Total	3	315	980	150	273	70	18	16	113	92	1	186	.279	.341	.436	111	15	13	.967	2	103	122	O230(58/88/91),1b19		0.4

BRADFORD, BUDDY Charles William B7.25.1944 Mobile AL BR/TR/5-11/191(170-191) d9.9

1966	Chi A	14	28	3	4	0	0	0	0	2-0		6	.143	.200	.143	0	-4	0-0	.833	-2	37	0	O9(5/0/4)		-0.7
1967	Chi A	24	20	6	2	1	0	0	1	1-1		7	.100	.143	.150	-14	-3	1-0	.900	-1	75	0	O14(6/1/8)		-0.5
1968	Chi A	103	281	32	61	11	0	5	24	23-2	2	67	.217	.277	.310	78	-7	8-4	.965	-1	103	78	O99(35/25/58)		-1.5
1969	Chi A	93	273	36	70	8	2	11	27	34-4	4	75	.256	.347	.421	109	3	5-2	.961	-5	89	91	O88(0/48/59)		-0.5
1970	Chi A	32	91	8	17	3	0	2	8	10-0	1	30	.187	.265	.286	51	-6	1-2	.979	2	86	65	O27(2/20/9)		-1.0
	Cle A	75	163	25	32	6	1	7	23	21-1	1	43	.196	.290	.374	79	-5	0-1	.984	1	115	36	O64(1/58/5)/3		-0.6
	Year	107	254	33	49	9	1	9	31	31-1	1	73	.193	.281	.343	69	-11	1-3	.982	-1	105	46	O91(3/78/14)/3		-1.6
1971	Cle A	20	38	4	6	2	1	0	3	6-1	0	10	.158	.273	.263	48	-3	0-0	.930	1	122	123	O18C		-0.2
	Cin N	79	100	17	20	3	0	2	12	14-4	3	23	.200	.316	.290	73	-3	4-2	.986	-0	89	96	O66(36/26/5)		-0.5
1972	Chi A	35	48	13	13	2	0	2	8	4-0	1	13	.271	.340	.438	127	2	3-2	1.000	3	100	109	O28(3/22/3)		0.1
1973	Chi A	53	168	24	40	3	1	8	15	17-1	2	43	.238	.316	.411	100	-1	4-5	.992	3	94	257	O51(1/48/2)	32	0.0
1974	Chi A	39	96	16	32	2	0	5	10	13-0	1	11	.333	.414	.510	162	8	1-2	.980	1	103	118	O32(10/0/24)/D	82	0.7
1975	Chi A	25	58	4	9	3	1	2	15	8-0	2	22	.155	.274	.345	78	-2	3-2	.966	-0	98	90	O18(3/0/15),D4		-0.3
	StL N	50	81	22	22	1	0	4	15	12-0	0	24	.272	.366	.432	115	2	0-2	.935	1	123	85	O25(3/1/21)		0.1
1976	Chi A	55	160	20	35	5	2	4	14	19-2	2	47	.219	.309	.350	92	-2	6-0	.978	-2	104	91	O48(2/0/46),D3		-0.4
Total	11	697	1605	224	363	50	8	52	175	184-16	19	411	.226	.311	.364	91	-21	36-24	.971	-7	99	91	O587(107/267/259),D8/3	114	-5.3

BRADFORD, VIC Henry Victor B3.5.1915 Brownsville TN D6.10.1994 Paris KY BR/TR/6-2/190 d5.1 Mil 1944-46 Col Alabama

| 1943 | NY N | 6 | 5 | 1 | 1 | 0 | 0 | 0 | 1 | 1 | 0 | 1 | .200 | .333 | .200 | 55 | 0 | 0 | 1.000 | 0 | 185 | 0 | /OL | | 0.0 |

BRADLEY, AL Albert Joseph B5.23.1856 Bradys Bend PA D2.5.1937 Altoona PA 5-10/185 d5.21

| 1884 | Was U | 3 | 1 | 0 | 0 | 0 | 0 | 0 | 0 | 2 | | | .000 | .400 | .000 | 77 | 0 | | 1.000 | 0 | 0 | 0 | /OC | | 0.0 |

BRADLEY, GEORGE George Washington "Grin" B7.13.1852 Reading PA D10.2.1931 Philadelphia PA BR/TR/5-10.5/175 d5.4 OF(11/19/16) ▲

1875	StL NA	60	254	28	62	7	3	0	24	1			19	.244	.247	.295	96	0	3-3	.896	0	108	193	P60,S2/2OL		-0.1
1876	StL N	**64**	265	29	66	7	6	0	28	3		12	.249	.257	.321	97	3		.919	2	96	188	P64		0.0
1877	Chi N	55	214	31	52	7	3	0	12	6		19	.243	.264	.304	70	-8		.950	-2	101	100	P50,3b16,1b3/OR		-0.3
1879	Tro N	63	251	36	62	9	5	0	23	1		20	.247	.250	.323	93	-2		.867	6	130		P54,3b5,1b3/ORS		0.3
1880	Pro N	82	309	32	70	7	6	0	23	5		38	.227	.239	.288	80	-7		.858	17	147	166	3b57,P28,O7(1/0/6),1b2		1.2
1881	Det N	1	4	0	0	0	0	0	0	0			.000	.000	.000	-96	-1		.667	-1	38	396	/S		-0.1
	Cle N	60	241	21	60	10	1	2	18	4		25	.249	.261	.324	88	-3		.865	-12	76	83	3b48,P6,S6/OL		-1.2
	Year	61	245	21	60	10	1	2	18	4		25	.245	.257	.318	84	-4		.865	-12	76	87	3b48,S7,P6/OL		-1.3
1882	Cle N	30	115	16	21	5	0	0	6	4		16	.183	.210	.226	41	-7		.897	3	151	607	P18,O9(5/4/0),1b6		-0.2
1883	Cle N	4	16	0	5	0	1	0	1	0			.313	.313	.438	126	-0		.792	-1	79	178	S4		0.0
	Phi AA	76	312	47	73	8	5	1	36	8			.234	.253	.301	71	-11		.779	1	118	129	3b44,P26,O11C,1b2		-0.5
1884	Cin U	58	226	31	43	4	7	0		7			.190	.215	.270	43	-24		.912	-1	105	152	P41,O16(4/4/8),S5,1b2		-1.0
1886	Phi AA	13	48	1	4	0	1	0	1	1	0		.083	.102	.125	-29	-7	2	.849	1	115	49	S13		-0.6
1888	Bal AA	1	3	0	0	0	0	0	0	0			.000	.000	.000	-99	-1	0	.600	-1	34	0	/S		-0.2
Total	10	507	2004	244	456	57	35	3	148	39	0	131	.228	.242	.295	72	-68	2	.896	12	110	136	P287,3b170,O46C,S31,1b18		-2.6

BRADLEY, GEORGE George Washington B4.1.1914 Greenwood AR D10.19.1982 Lawrenceburg TN BR/TR/6-1.5/185 d4.28

| 1946 | StL A | 4 | 12 | 2 | 2 | 0 | 0 | 0 | 3 | 0 | | 1 | .167 | .167 | .250 | 15 | -1 | 0-0 | 1.000 | -0 | 86 | 0 | O3C | | -0.2 |

BRADLEY, HUGH Hugh Frederick "Corns" B5.23.1885 Grafton MA D1.26.1949 Worcester MA BR/TR/5-10/175 d4.25 Col Holy Cross

1910	Bos A	32	83	8	14	6	2	0	7	5	0		.169	.216	.289	57	-4	2	.995	-1	69	115	1b21,C3/OR		-0.7
1911	Bos A	12	41	9	13	2	0	1	4	2	1		.317	.364	.439	125	1	1	.993	1	101	126	1b12		0.1
1912	Bos A	40	137	16	26	11	1	1	19	15	1		.190	.275	.307	63	-7	3	.989	0	94	80	1b40		-0.7
1914	Pit F	118	427	41	131	20	6	0	61	27	8	27	.307	.359	.382	103	-5	7	.990	-0	98	118	1b118		-0.8
1915	Pit F	26	66	3	18	4	1	0	6	4	0	5	.273	.314	.364	91	-2	2	.952	-1	99	0	O15R		-0.4
	Bro F	37	126	7	31	3	2	0	18	4	0	9	.246	.269	.302	61	-9	6	.996	3	156	47	1b26,O7R/C		-0.8
	New F	12	33	0	5	0	0	0	2	2	2	3	.152	.243	.152	13	-4	2	.986	-1	23	58	1b8		-0.7
	Year	75	225	10	54	7	3	0	26	10	2	17	.240	.278	.298	63	-15	10	.994	0	125	58	1b34,O22R/C		-1.9
Total	5	277	913	84	238	46	12	2	117	59	12	44	.261	.314	.344	84	-30	23	.991	-1	99	84	1b225,O23R,C4		-4.0

BRADLEY, JACK John Thomas B9.20.1893 Denver CO D3.18.1969 Tulsa OK BR/TR/5-11/175 d6.18 Col Illinois

| 1916 | Cle A | 2 | 3 | 0 | 0 | 0 | 0 | 0 | 0 | 1 | | | .000 | .000 | .000 | -94 | -1 | 0 | 1.000 | -0 | 51 | 0 | /C | | -0.1 |

BRADLEY, MARK Mark Allen B12.3.1956 Elizabethtown KY BR/TR/6-1/180* [LAN75 1/24] d9.3

1981	LA N	9	6	2	1	1	0	0	0	0-0	0	1	.167	.167	.333	41	0	0-0	1.000	1	91	704	O6(1/0/5)		0.0
1982	LA N	8	3	1	1	0	0	0	0	0-0	0	0	.333	.333	.333	90	0	0-0	1.000	0	76	0	O3(1/0/2)		0.0
1983	NY N	73	104	10	21	4	0	3	5	11-1	0	35	.202	.278	.327	67	-5	4-2	1.000	-0	91	133	O35(14/7/16)		-0.6
Total	3	90	113	13	23	5	0	3	5	11-1	0	36	.204	.274	.327	67	-5	4-2	1.000	1	91	171	O44(16/7/23)		-0.6

BRADLEY, MILTON Milton Obelle B4.15.1978 Harbor City CA BB/TR/6-0/180(180-205) [MonN96 2/40] d7.19

2000	Mon N	42	154	20	34	8	1	2	15	14-0	1	32	.221	.288	.325	55	-11	2-3	.979	1	96	262	O40C		-0.9
2001	Mon N	67	220	19	49	16	3	1	19	19-0	1	62	.223	.287	.336	61	-13	7-4	.988	4	111	145	O65(13/52/2)		-0.9
	Cle A	10	18	3	4	1	0	0	3	2-0	0	5	.222	.300	.278	52	-1	1-0	.929	0	99	361	O9(0/8/1)/D		-0.1
2002	Cle A	98	325	48	81	18	3	9	38	32-2	0	58	.249	.317	.406	89	-6	6-3	.982	3	99	205	O94C/D	51	-0.2
2003	Cle A	101	377	61	121	34	2	10	56	64-8	5	73	.321	.421	.501	144	29	17-7	.992	-2	94	133	O93C,D8	65	2.7
2004	†LA N	141	516	72	138	24	0	19	67	71-3	6	123	.267	.362	.424	104	5	15-11	.977	5	109	109	O138(17/93/31)		0.7

YEAR	TM LG	G	AB	R	H	2B	3B	HR	RBI	BB-IB	HP	SO	AVG	OBP	SLG	AOPS	ABR	SB-CS	FA	FR	RNG	THR	GAMES AT POSITION	DL	BFW
2005	LA N	75	283	49	82	14	1	13	38	25-1	2	47	.290	.350	.484	116	6	6-1	.989	3	105	161	O72C	95	1.1
Total	6	534	1893	272	509	115	10	54	233	227-14	15	398	.269	.350	.426	102	9	54-28	.984	14	103	157	O511(30/452/34),D10	211	2.4

BRADLEY, PHIL Philip Poole B3.11.1959 Bloomington IN BR/TR/6-0/185(175-190) [SeaA81 3/53] d9.2 Col Missouri

YEAR	TM LG	G	AB	R	H	2B	3B	HR	RBI	BB-IB	HP	SO	AVG	OBP	SLG	AOPS	ABR	SB-CS	FA	FR	RNG	THR	GAMES AT POSITION	DL	BFW
1983	Sea A	23	67	8	18	2	0	0	5	8-0	0	5	.269	.342	.299	76	-2	3-1	.974	-3	76	94	O21C/D		-0.4
1984	Sea A	124	322	49	97	12	4	0	24	34-2	3	61	.301	.373	.363	105	4	21-8	.992	1	105	51	O117(48/68/14),D3		0.4
1985	Sea A★	159	641	100	192	33	8	26	88	55-4	12	129	.300	.365	.498	132	28	22-9	.986	-1	97	99	O159(126/28/10)		2.2
1986	Sea A	143	526	88	163	27	4	12	50	77-1	8	134	.310	.405	.445	130	26	21-12	.996	-6	85	120	O140(138/5/0)	17	1.4
1987	Sea A	158	603	101	179	38	10	14	84	84-2	8	119	.297	.387	.463	119	19	40-10	.983	-5	87	122	O158L		1.2
1988	Phi N	154	569	77	150	30	5	11	56	54-0	16	106	.264	.341	.392	108	8	11-9	.990	5	102	151	O153(153/3/1)		0.8
1989	Bal A	144	545	83	151	23	10	11	55	70-4	7	103	.277	.364	.417	123	18	20-6	.990	-6	93	46	O140L,D2		1.0
1990	Bal A	72	289	39	78	9	4	5	26	30-2	7	35	.270	.352	.349	100	1	10-4	.987	-1	98	65	O70L,D2	26	-0.1
	Chi A	45	133	20	30	5	1	0	5	20-3	4	26	.226	.344	.278	78	-3	7-3	.973	-1	100	54	O38(23/14/6),D7		-0.4
	Year	117	422	59	108	14	2	4	31	50-5	11	61	.256	.349	.327	93	-2	17-7	.982	-1	99	62	O108(93/14/6),D9		-0.5
Total	8	1022	3695	565	1058	179	43	78	376	432-18	65	718	.286	.369	.421	117	99	155-62	.988	-17	94	98	O996(856/139/31),D15	43	6.1

BRADLEY, SCOTT Scott William B3.22.1960 Glen Ridge NJ BL/TR/5-11/185* [NYA81 3/64] d9.9 Col North Carolina-Asheville

YEAR	TM LG	G	AB	R	H	2B	3B	HR	RBI	BB-IB	HP	SO	AVG	OBP	SLG	AOPS	ABR	SB-CS	FA	FR	RNG	THR	GAMES AT POSITION	DL	BFW
1984	NY A	9	21	3	6	1	0	0	2	1-0	0	1	.286	.318	.333	83	0	0-0	1.000	-0	103	0	O5L,C3		-0.1
1985	NY A	19	49	4	8	2	1	0	1	1-0	1	5	.163	.196	.245	20	-6	0-0	.923	-2	56	118	C3,D9	54	-0.7
1986	Chi A	9	21	3	6	0	0	0	2	1-0	0	2	.286	.375	.286	80	-1	0-2	—	-0	0	0	/OLD		-0.1
	Sea A	68	199	17	60	8	3	5	28	12-4	2	7	.302	.344	.447	113	3	1-0	.990	-6	103	75	C59,D3		-0.1
	Year	77	220	20	66	8	3	5	28	13-4	4	7	.300	.347	.432	110	3	1-2	.990	-6	103	75	C59,D9/OL		-0.2
1987	Sea A	102	342	34	95	15	1	5	43	15-1	3	18	.278	.310	.371	77	-12	0-1	.983	-3	84	86	C82,3b8,O2R,D6		-1.2
1988	Sea A	103	335	45	86	17	1	4	33	17-1	2	16	.257	.295	.340	77	-11	1-1	.991	5	84	102	C85,O4R,3b3,1b2,D4		-0.1
1989	Sea A	103	270	21	74	16	0	3	37	21-4	1	23	.274	.322	.367	93	-2	1-1	.993	-0	74	75	C70,1b2/OLD		0.1
1990	Sea A	101	233	11	52	9	0	1	28	15-2	0	20	.223	.264	.275	52	-15	0-1	.995	1	78	97	C63,3b5/1D		-1.1
1991	Sea A	83	172	10	35	7	0	0	11	19-2	1	19	.203	.280	.244	47	-12	0-0	.993	-5	80	46	C65,3b4/1D		-1.5
1992	Sea A	2	1	0	0	0	0	0	0	1-0	0	1	.000	.500	.000	50	0	0-0	1.000	1	0	0	/C		0.1
	Cin N	5	5	1	2	0	0	0	1	1-0	0	1	.400	.500	.400	154	0	0-0	1.000	-1	36	0	C2		0.0
Total	9	604	1648	149	424	75	6	18	184	104-14	11	110	.257	.302	.343	76	-55	3-6	.990	-10	83	83	C433,D42,3b20,O13(7/0/6),1b6	54	-4.7

BRADLEY, BILL William Joseph B2.13.1878 Cleveland OH D3.11.1954 Cleveland OH BR/TR/6-0/185 d8.26 M2

YEAR	TM LG	G	AB	R	H	2B	3B	HR	RBI	BB-IB	HP	SO	AVG	OBP	SLG	AOPS	ABR	SB-CS	FA	FR	RNG	THR	GAMES AT POSITION	DL	BFW
1899	Chi N	35	129	26	40	6	1	2	18	12	2		.310	.378	.419	121	4	4	.884	-4	97	157	3b30,S5		0.1
1900	Chi N	122	444	63	125	21	8	5	49	27	5		.282	.330	.399	104	1	14	.882	14	111	75	3b106,1b15		1.6
1901	Cle A	133	516	95	151	28	13	1	55	26	8		.293	.336	.403	109	5	15	.930	12	102	125	3b133/P		1.9
1902	Cle A	137	550	104	187	39	12	11	77	27	4		.340	.375	.515	151	36	11	.923	12	107	107	3b137		4.8
1903	Cle A	136	536	101	168	36	22	6	68	25	3		.313	.348	.496	154	33	21	.924	11	114	130	3b136		4.8
1904	Cle A	154	609	94	183	32	8	6	83	26	5		.300	.334	.409	136	23	23	.955	9	104	132	3b154		4.0
1905	Cle A	146	541	63	145	34	6	0	51	27	15		.268	.321	.353	112	8	22	.945	13	108	141	3b146,M		2.7
1906	Cle A	82	302	32	83	16	2	2	25	18	4		.275	.324	.361	116	6	13	.966	1	103	80	3b82		1.0
1907	Cle A	139	498	48	111	20	1	0	34	35	9		.223	.286	.267	76	-12	20	.938	6	101	130	3b139		-0.3
1908	Cle A	148	548	70	133	24	7	1	46	29	13		.243	.297	.318	99	-1	18	.939	-25	88	110	3b118,S30		-2.5
1909	Cle A	95	334	30	62	6	3	0	22	19	3		.186	.236	.222	43	-22	9	.957	-5	94	164	3b87,1b3,2b3		-2.9
1910	Cle A	61	214	12	42	3	0	0	12	10	1		.196	.236	.210	39	-15	6	.956	-2	95	86	3b61		-1.8
1914	Bro F	7	6	0	3	1	0	0	3	0	0		.500	.500	.667	218	-1	0	—		0		/HM		0.1
1915	KC F	66	203	15	38	9	1	0	19	9	1	18	.187	.225	.241	33	-22	5	.949	-3	98	60	3b61		-2.6
Total	14	1461	5430	754	1471	275	84	34	552	290	73	18	.271	.317	.371	108	40	181	.933	40	103	118	3b1390,S35,1b18,2b3/P		10.9

BRADSHAW, DALLAS Dallas Carl "Windy" B11.23.1895 Wolf Creek IL D12.11.1939 Herrin IL BL/TR/5-7/145 d6.5

YEAR	TM LG	G	AB	R	H	2B	3B	HR	RBI	BB-IB	HP	SO	AVG	OBP	SLG	AOPS	ABR	SB-CS	FA	FR	RNG	THR	GAMES AT POSITION	DL	BFW
1917	Phi A	2	4	0	0	0	0	0	0	1-0	0	1	.000	.000	.000	-99	-1	0-0	1.000	0	61	196	/2		-0.1

BRADSHAW, GEORGE George Thomas B9.12.1924 Salisbury NC D11.4.1994 Hendersonville NC BR/TR/6-2/185 d8.10

YEAR	TM LG	G	AB	R	H	2B	3B	HR	RBI	BB-IB	HP	SO	AVG	OBP	SLG	AOPS	ABR	SB-CS	FA	FR	RNG	THR	GAMES AT POSITION	DL	BFW
1952	Was A	10	23	3	5	2	0	0	6	1	1	2	.217	.280	.304	65	-1	0-0	.917	-2	83	0	C9		-0.3

BRADSHAW, TERRY Terry Leon B2.3.1969 Franklin VA BL/TR/6-0/180(180-195) [StLN90 9/249] d5.4 Col Norfolk St.

YEAR	TM LG	G	AB	R	H	2B	3B	HR	RBI	BB-IB	HP	SO	AVG	OBP	SLG	AOPS	ABR	SB-CS	FA	FR	RNG	THR	GAMES AT POSITION	DL	BFW
1995	StL N	19	44	6	10	1	1	0	2	2-0	0	10	.227	.261	.295	45	-4	1-2	.952	1	121	202	O10(6/3/1)		-0.3
1996	StL N	15	21	4	7	1	0	0	3	3-0	0	2	.333	.417	.381	112	1	0-1	1.000	-1	50	0	O7(4/3/1)		-0.1
Total	2	34	65	10	17	2	1	0	5	5-0	0	12	.262	.314	.323	68	-3	1-3	.960	-0	97	135	O17(10/6/2)		-0.4

BRADY, BRIAN Brian Phelan B7.11.1962 Elmhurst NY BL/TL/5-11/185 [CalA84 6/138] d4.16 Col New York Tech

YEAR	TM LG	G	AB	R	H	2B	3B	HR	RBI	BB-IB	HP	SO	AVG	OBP	SLG	AOPS	ABR	SB-CS	FA	FR	RNG	THR	GAMES AT POSITION	DL	BFW
1989	Cal A	2	2	1	1	0	0	0	1	.500	.500	1.000	318	-1	0	2		—	-0	0	0	/OR		0.1

BRADY, CLIFF Clifford Francis B3.6.1897 St.Louis MO D9.25.1974 Belleville IL BR/TR/5-5.5/140 d8.8

YEAR	TM LG	G	AB	R	H	2B	3B	HR	RBI	BB-IB	HP	SO	AVG	OBP	SLG	AOPS	ABR	SB-CS	FA	FR	RNG	THR	GAMES AT POSITION	DL	BFW
1920	Bos A	53	180	16	41	5	1	0	12	13	1	12	.228	.284	.267	48	-14	0-1	.974	11	124	95	2b53		-0.2

BRADY, SPIKE Michael T. B12.1854 Chicago IL d9.25

YEAR	TM LG	G	AB	R	H	2B	3B	HR	RBI	BB-IB	HP	SO	AVG	OBP	SLG	AOPS	ABR	SB-CS	FA	FR	RNG	THR	GAMES AT POSITION	DL	BFW
1875	Chi NA	1	4	1	1	0	0	0		0			.250	.250	.750	231	0	0-0	.625	-0	247	0	/OC		0.0

BRADY, BOB Robert Jay B11.8.1922 Lewistown PA D4.22.1996 Manchester CT BL/TR/6-1/175 d8.24

YEAR	TM LG	G	AB	R	H	2B	3B	HR	RBI	BB-IB	HP	SO	AVG	OBP	SLG	AOPS	ABR	SB-CS	FA	FR	RNG	THR	GAMES AT POSITION	DL	BFW
1946	Bos N	3	5	0	1	0	0	0	1		0	1	.200	.333	.200	52	-0	0	.857	-0	47	275	/C		0.0
1947	Bos N	1	1	0	0	0	0	0	0		0	0	.000	.000	.000	-99	-0	0	—	0			/H		0.0
Total	2	4	6	0	1	0	0	0	1		0	1	.167	.286	.167	29	-0	0	.857	-0	47	275	/C		0.0

BRADY, STEVE Stephen A. B7.14.1851 Worcester MA D11.1.1917 Hartford CT 5-9.5/165 d7.23

YEAR	TM LG	G	AB	R	H	2B	3B	HR	RBI	BB-IB	HP	SO	AVG	OBP	SLG	AOPS	ABR	SB-CS	FA	FR	RNG	THR	GAMES AT POSITION	DL	BFW
1874	Har NA	27	118	19	37	5	1	0	14	2		10	.314	.325	.373	117	2	1-2	.662	-9	58	0	3b16,O11(0/5/6)/S		-0.6
1875	Was NA	21	91	7	13	0	0	0	3	0		4	.143	.143	.143	-0	-9	5-0	.815	-5	107	26	2b18,O2(1/0/1)/C1		-1.2
	Har NA	1	4	0	0	0	0	0	0	0			1.000	.000	.000	-95	-1	0-0	1.000	1	454	0	/OC		0.0
	Year	22	95	7	13	0	0	0	3	0		5	.137	.137	.137	-5	-10	5-0	.815	-4	107	26	2b18,O3(1/1/1)/C1		-1.2
1883	NY AA	97	432	69	117	12	6	0		11			.271	.289	.326	94	-4		.961	3	121	101	1b81,O16R		-0.8
1884	†NY AA	112	485	102	122	11	3	0		21	0		.252	.283	.293	90	-5		.918	-2	124	38	O110R,1b5/2		-0.4
1885	NY AA	108	434	60	128	14	5	3	58	25	6		.295	.342	.371	131	16		.879	-5	58	88	O105R,1b4,2b2/3		0.9
1886	NY AA	124	466	56	112	8	5	0	39	35	3		.240	.298	.279	88	-4	16	.836	-4	123	27	O123R/1		-0.8
Total	2 NA	49	213	26	50	5	1	0	17	2		15	.235	.242	.268	68	-8	6-2	.815	-13	107	26	2b18,3b16,O14(1/6/7)/1CS		-1.8
Total	4	441	1817	287	479	45	19	4	97	92	9	0	.264	.302	.316	100	3	16	.877	-4	102	63	O354R,1b91,2b3/3		-1.1

BRADY, DOUG Stephen Douglas B11.23.1969 Jacksonville IL BB/TR/5-11/165 [ChiA91 12/332] d9.5 Col Liberty

YEAR	TM LG	G	AB	R	H	2B	3B	HR	RBI	BB-IB	HP	SO	AVG	OBP	SLG	AOPS	ABR	SB-CS	FA	FR	RNG	THR	GAMES AT POSITION	DL	BFW
1995	Chi A	12	21	4	4	1	0	0	1	2-0	0	6	.190	.261	.238	32	-2	0-0	1.000	3	141	108	2b6,D3		0.1

BRAGAN, BOBBY Robert Randall "Nig" B10.30.1917 Birmingham AL BR/TR/5-10.5/175 d4.16 Mil 1945-46 M7/C2

YEAR	TM LG	G	AB	R	H	2B	3B	HR	RBI	BB-IB	HP	SO	AVG	OBP	SLG	AOPS	ABR	SB-CS	FA	FR	RNG	THR	GAMES AT POSITION	DL	BFW
1940	Phi N	132	474	36	105	14	1	4	44	28	0	34	.222	.265	.300	58	-29	2	.936	4	105	100	S132,3b2		-1.5
1941	Phi N	154	557	37	140	19	3	4	69	26	0	29	.251	.285	.318	72	-23	7	.944	-7	95	88	S154,2b2/3		-2.0
1942	Phi N	109	335	17	73	12	2	2	15	20	1	21	.218	.264	.284	63	-17	0	.939	8	108	106	S78,C22,2b4,3b3		-0.2
1943	Bro N	74	220	17	58	7	2	2	24	15		16	.264	.311	.341	88	-4	0	.973	0	97	114	C57,3b12		-0.1
1944	Bro N	94	266	26	71	8	4	0	17	13	1	14	.267	.304	.327	79	-8	2	.954	-3	91	64	S51,C35,3b6/2		0.1
1947	†Bro N	25	36	3	7	2	0	0	3	7		0	.194	.326	.250	53	-2	1	1.000	2	88	94	C21		0.1
1948	Bro N	9	12	0	2	0	0	0	0	1		1	.167	.231	.167	9	-2	0	1.000	-0	70	214	C5		-0.2
Total	7	597	1900	136	456	62	12	15	172	110	2	117	.240	.282	.309	69	-85	12	.941	4	100	93	S415,C140,3b24,2b7		-4.6

BRAGG, DARREN Darren William B9.7.1969 Waterbury CT BL/TR/5-9/180* [SeaA91 22/578] d4.12 Col Georgia Tech

YEAR	TM LG	G	AB	R	H	2B	3B	HR	RBI	BB-IB	HP	SO	AVG	OBP	SLG	AOPS	ABR	SB-CS	FA	FR	RNG	THR	GAMES AT POSITION	DL	BFW
1994	Sea A	8	19	4	3	1	0	0	2	2-1	0	5	.158	.238	.211	17	-2	0-0	1.000	-0	47	0	O3L,D3		-0.3
1995	Sea A	52	145	20	34	5	1	3	12	18-1	4	37	.234	.331	.345	77	-5	9-0	.989	6	112	280	O47(32/0/17),D2		0.1
1996	Sea A	69	195	36	53	12	1	7	25	33-4	2	35	.272	.376	.451	109	4	8-5	.992	4	106	186	O63(48/5/16)		0.6
	Bos A	58	222	38	56	14	1	3	22	36-2	2	39	.252	.357	.365	83	-5	6-4	.986	2	100	140	O58(7/47/29)		-0.3
	Year	127	417	74	109	26	2	10	47	69-6	4	74	.261	.366	.405	97	-8	14-9	.989	6	103	162	O121(55/52/45)		0.3
1997	Bos A	153	513	65	132	35	2	9	57	61-5	3	102	.257	.337	.386	87	-8	10-6	.987	6	105	142	O150(1/118/41)/3		-0.3
1998	†Bos A	129	409	51	114	29	3	8	57	42-0	6	99	.279	.351	.423	99	0	5-3	.996	-3	97	75	O124(7/12/112),D4		-0.7
1999	StL N	93	273	38	71	12	1	6	26	44-1	3	67	.260	.369	.377	88	-4	3-0	.982	0	95	157	O88(22/43/33)	62	-0.7
2000	Col N	71	149	16	33	7	1	3	21	17-1	0	41	.221	.296	.342	50	-11	4-1	1.000	-3	84	0	O43(34/0/9)		-1.5

YEAR	TM LG	G	AB	R	H	2B	3B	HR	RBI	BB-IB	HP	SO	AVG	OBP	SLG	AOPS	ABR	SB-CS	FA	FR	RNG	THR	GAMES AT POSITION	DL	BFW
2001	NY N	18	57	4	15	6	0	0	5	4-0	1	23	.263	.323	.368	84	-1	3-2	1.000	-1	78	114	O16(8/2/10)		-0.3
	NY A	5	4	1	1	0	0	0	0	1-0	0	0	.250	.250	.500	90	0	0-0	1.000	0	118	0	O3R		0.0
2002	†Atl N	109	212	34	57	15	2	3	15	24-0	2	52	.269	.347	.401	100	0	5-2	.971	-1	100	67	O63(12/18/36),D3		-0.3
2003	†Atl N	104	162	21	39	5	1	0	9	13-1	2	38	.241	.305	.284	55	-11	2-1	.988	4	86	36	O78(29/21/35)		-1.6
2004	SD N	9	7	2	1	0	0	0	0	2-0	0	2	.143	.333	.143	31	-1	0-0	—	0			/H		-0.1
	Cin N	38	94	11	18	3	1	4	9	8-1	0	29	.191	.255	.372	61	-6	1-0	.984	3	126	164	O26(2/14/11)		-0.3
	Year	47	101	13	19	3	1	4	9	10-1	0	31	.188	.261	.356	59	-7	1-0	.984	3	126	164	O26(2/14/11)		-0.4
Total	11	916	2461	341	627	145	14	46	260	304-17	25	570	.255	.340	.381	85	-50	56-24	.988	9	100	124	O762(205/280/352),D12/3	62	-5.4

BRAGGS, GLENN Glenn Erick B10.17.1962 San Bernardino CA BR/TR/6-3/210* [MilA83 2/54] d7.18 Col Hawaii-Manoa

YEAR	TM LG	G	AB	R	H	2B	3B	HR	RBI	BB-IB	HP	SO	AVG	OBP	SLG	AOPS	ABR	SB-CS	FA	FR	RNG	THR	GAMES AT POSITION	DL	BFW
1986	Mil A	58	215	19	51	8	2	4	18	11-0	1	47	.237	.274	.349	67	-11	1-1	.910	-0	103	141	O56(51/3/5),D2		-1.3
1987	Mil A	132	505	67	136	28	7	13	77	47-7	4	96	.269	.332	.430	98	-1	12-5	.972	10	128	71	O123R,D8		0.3
1988	Mil A	72	272	30	71	14	0	10	42	14-0	5	60	.261	.307	.423	102	0	6-4	.978	1	114	29	O54R,D18	93	-0.1
1989	Mil A	144	514	77	127	12	3	15	66	42-4	4	111	.247	.305	.370	91	-8	17-5	.972	-1	100	77	O132(127/0/9),D13		-1.2
1990	Mil A	37	113	17	28	5	0	3	13	12-2	3	21	.248	.328	.372	98	0	5-3	.965	3	131	48	O32(13/0/20),D2		0.2
	†Cin N	72	201	22	60	9	1	6	28	26-1	3	43	.299	.383	.443	123	7	3-4	.968	6	102	266	O60(26/0/35)		1.1
1991	Cin N	85	250	36	65	10	0	11	39	23-3	2	46	.260	.323	.432	107	2	11-3	.966	1	112	52	O74(55/0/27)	42	0.3
1992	Cin N	92	266	40	63	16	3	8	38	36-5	2	48	.237	.330	.410	106	3	3-1	.946	-7	78	85	O79(56/0/29)	15	-0.6
Total	7	692	2336	308	601	102	16	70	321	211-22	24	472	.257	.322	.405	98	-8	58-26	.963	13	108	92	O610(328/3/302),D43	150	-1.3

BRAIN, DAVE David Leonard B1.24.1879 Hereford, England D5.25.1959 Los Angeles CA BR/TR/5-10/170 d4.24 OF(26/15/5)

YEAR	TM LG	G	AB	R	H	2B	3B	HR	RBI	BB-IB	HP	SO	AVG	OBP	SLG	AOPS	ABR	SB-CS	FA	FR	RNG	THR	GAMES AT POSITION	DL	BFW
1901	Chi A	5	20	2	7	1	0	0	5	1	0		.350	.381	.400	120	1	0	.909	0	96	189	2b5		0.1
1903	StL N	119	464	44	107	8	15	1	60	25	0		.231	.270	.319	70	-22	21	.908	7	104	121	S72,3b46		-1.1
1904	StL N	127	488	57	130	24	12	7	72	17	0		.266	.291	.408	120	8	18	.927	-3	100	108	S59,3b30,O19(7/11/1),2b13,1b4		0.8
1905	StL N	44	158	11	36	4	5	1	17	8	1		.228	.269	.335	82	-4	4	.910	-1	83	36	S29,3b6,O6(0/4/2)		-1.1
	Pit N	85	307	31	79	17	6	3	46	15	2		.257	.296	.381	99	-2	8	.923	6	116	152	3b78,S4		0.7
	Year	129	465	42	115	21	11	4	63	23	3		.247	.287	.366	93	-6	12	.929	-1	117	141	3b84,S33,O6(0/4/2)		-0.4
1906	Bos N	139	525	43	131	19	5	5	45	29	3		.250	.293	.333	98	-4	11	.917	25	116	152	3b139		2.8
1907	Bos N	133	509	60	142	24	9	**10**	56	29	5		.279	.324	.420	134	17	10	.916	24	121	148	3b130,O3L		4.8
1908	Cin N	16	55	4	6	0	0	0	1	8	0		.109	.222	.109	7	-6	0	.947	-1	0	0	O16L		-0.8
	NY N	11	17	2	3	0	0	0	1	2	0		.176	.263	.176	39	-1	1	.867	-2	92	1	2b3,O3R,3b2/S		-0.4
	Year	27	72	6	9	0	0	0	2	10	0		.125	.232	.125	14	-7	1	.947	-3	0	0	O19(16/0/2),2b3,3b2/S		-1.2
Total	7	679	2543	254	641	97	52	27	303	134	11		.252	.292	.363	101	-13	73	.913	50	116	142	3b431,S165,O47L,2b21,1b4		5.8

BRAINERD, FRED Frederick F. B2.17.1892 Champaign IL D4.17.1959 Galveston TX BR/TR/6-0/176 d10.6 Col Illinois

YEAR	TM LG	G	AB	R	H	2B	3B	HR	RBI	BB-IB	HP	SO	AVG	OBP	SLG	AOPS	ABR	SB-CS	FA	FR	RNG	THR	GAMES AT POSITION	DL	BFW
1914	NY N	2	5	1	1	0	0	0	0	1	0	0	.200	.333	.200	62	0	0	.923	0	94	130	2b2		0.0
1915	NY N	91	249	31	50	7	2	1	21	21	1	44	.201	.266	.257	62	-12	6-7	.988	4	149	141	1b43,3b15,S9/2OC		-1.0
1916	NY N	2	7	0	0	0	0	0	0	0	0	0	.000	.000	.000	-99	-2	0	.625	-1	46	0	3b2		-0.4
Total	3	95	261	32	51	7	2	1	21	22	1	44	.195	.261	.249	58	-14	6-7	.988	3	149	141	1b43,3b17,S9,2b3/OC		-1.4

BRAMHALL, ART Arthur Washington B2.22.1909 Oak Park IL D9.4.1985 Madison WI BR/TR/5-11/170 d4.18 Col DePaul

YEAR	TM LG	G	AB	R	H	2B	3B	HR	RBI	BB-IB	HP	SO	AVG	OBP	SLG	AOPS	ABR	SB-CS	FA	FR	RNG	THR	GAMES AT POSITION	DL	BFW
1935	Phi N	2	1	0	0	0	0	0	0	0	0	0	.000	.000	.000	-91	0	0	1.000	0	146	0	/S3		0.0

BRANCATO, AL Albert "Bronk" B5.29.1919 Philadelphia PA BR/TR/5-9.5/188 d9.7 Mil 1942-45

YEAR	TM LG	G	AB	R	H	2B	3B	HR	RBI	BB-IB	HP	SO	AVG	OBP	SLG	AOPS	ABR	SB-CS	FA	FR	RNG	THR	GAMES AT POSITION	DL	BFW
1939	Phi A	21	68	12	14	5	0	1	8	8	1	9	.206	.299	.324	60	-4	1-0	.939	-1	106	48	3b20/S		-0.4
1940	Phi A	107	298	42	57	11	2	1	23	28	2	36	.191	.265	.252	36	-29	3-1	.949	-3	96	85	S80,3b25		-2.5
1941	Phi A	144	530	60	124	20	9	2	49	59	0	49	.234	.311	.317	68	-25	1-5	.915	-17	101	88	S139,3b7		-3.3
1945	Phi A	10	34	3	4	1	0	0	0	3	0	6	.118	.143	.147	-16	-5	0-0	.959	-1	88	86	S10		-0.6
Total	4	282	930	117	199	37	11	4	80	96	3	92	.214	.290	.290	54	-63	5-6	.927	-21	99	87	S230,3b52		-6.8

BRAND, RON Ronald George B1.13.1940 Los Angeles CA BR/TR/5-8/170* d5.26 Col Los Angeles Valley (CA) JC

YEAR	TM LG	G	AB	R	H	2B	3B	HR	RBI	BB-IB	HP	SO	AVG	OBP	SLG	AOPS	ABR	SB-CS	FA	FR	RNG	THR	GAMES AT POSITION	DL	BFW
1963	Pit N	46	66	8	19	2	0	1	7	10-0	1	11	.288	.390	.364	118	2	0-0	.968	5	115	121	C33,2b2,3b2		0.8
1965	Hou N	117	391	27	92	6	3	2	37	19-2	6	34	.235	.281	.281	63	-20	10-5	.988	-6	96	87	C102,3b6,O5L		-2.3
1966	Hou N	56	123	12	30	2	0	0	10	9-3	2	13	.244	.301	.260	64	-6	0-2	.986	1	100	72	C25,2b9,O3L/3		-0.4
1967	Hou N	84	215	22	52	8	1	0	18	23-7	2	17	.242	.321	.288	78	-5	4-0	.998	-3	94	119	C67/2OL	21	-0.4
1968	Hou N	43	81	7	13	2	0	0	4	9-0	2	11	.160	.261	.185	36	-6	1-1	1.000	3	95	51	C29/3OR		-0.2
1969	Mon N	103	287	19	74	12	0	0	20	30-4	1	19	.258	.327	.300	77	-8	2-3	.985	-7	75	118	C84,O2(1/1/0)		-1.3
1970	Mon N	72	126	10	30	2	3	0	9	9-0	0	16	.238	.287	.302	58	-8	2-1	.952	1	117	120	S19,3b12,C9,O5(1/3/1),2b3		-0.5
1971	Mon N	47	56	3	12	0	0	0	5	4-0	0	10	.214	.254	.214	33	-5	1-1	.957	5	126	135	S22,3b4,O4(3/1/0)/C2		0.1
Total	8	568	1345	108	322	34	7	3	106	112-16	14	126	.239	.303	.282	68	-56	20-13	.988	-1	91	100	C350,S41,3b26,O21(14/5/2),2b16	21	-4.2

BRANDT, JACKIE John George B4.28.1934 Omaha NE BR/TR/5-11/170(165-185) d4.21 Mil 1957-58

YEAR	TM LG	G	AB	R	H	2B	3B	HR	RBI	BB-IB	HP	SO	AVG	OBP	SLG	AOPS	ABR	SB-CS	FA	FR	RNG	THR	GAMES AT POSITION	DL	BFW
1956	StL N	27	42	9	12	3	0	1	3	4-0	1	5	.286	.362	.429	111	1	0-1	1.000	1	115	81	O26(3/3/20)		0.1
	NY N	98	351	45	105	16	8	11	47	17-2	0	31	.299	.330	.484	116	6	3-4	.989	1	98	130	O96(86/3/26)		0.2
	Year	125	393	54	117	19	8	12	50	21-2	1	36	.298	.333	.478	116	7	3-5	**.990**	2	100	123	O122(89/6/46)		0.3
1958	SF N	18	52	7	13	1	0	0	3	6-0	0	5	.250	.328	.269	62	-3	1-0	1.000	-1	103	0	O14(11/1/3)		-0.4
1959	SF N	137	429	63	116	16	5	12	57	35-2	0	69	.270	.324	.415	98	-3	11-4	.984	-0	99	137	O116(111/4/6),3b18,1b3/2		-0.8
1960	Bal A	145	511	73	130	24	6	15	65	47-3	0	59	.254	.317	.413	98	-3	5-3	.983	0	101	127	O142(17/102/51),3b2/1		-0.9
1961	Bal A★	139	516	93	153	18	5	16	72	62-0	1	51	.297	.371	.444	122	16	10-2	.974	-7	95	74	O136(21/120/34)/3		0.5
1962	Bal A	143	505	76	129	29	5	19	75	55-2	4	64	.255	.330	.446	116	10	9-3	.976	1	104	135	O138(0/109/30),3b2		0.7
1963	Bal A	142	451	49	112	15	5	15	61	34-3	2	75	.248	.298	.404	99	-2	4-5	.986	2	105	114	O134(30/92/39)/3		-0.7
1964	Bal A	137	523	66	127	25	1	13	47	45-5	3	104	.243	.305	.369	87	-9	1-4	.981	13	116	156	O134(10/131/0)		-0.2
1965	Bal A	96	243	35	59	17	0	8	24	21-0	0	40	.243	.303	.412	99	0	1-2	.961	4	111	167	O84(39/37/22)		0.0
1966	Phi N	82	164	16	41	6	1	1	15	17-2	0	36	.250	.317	.317	78	-4	0-2	.988	-4	82	95	O71(17/49/6)		-1.1
1967	Phi N	16	19	1	2	1	0	0	1	0-0	0	6	.105	.105	.158	-25	-3	0-0	1.000	-0	53	0	O3L		-0.4
	Hou N	41	89	7	21	4	1	1	15	8-1	0	9	.236	.296	.337	85	-2	0-0	.991	-2	76	46	1b14,O6L/3		-0.5
	Year	57	108	8	23	5	1	1	16	8-1	0	15	.213	.265	.306	65	-5	0-0	.991	-2	76	46	1b14,O9L/3		-0.9
Total	11	1221	3895	540	1020	175	37	112	485	351-20	12	574	.262	.323	.412	102	4	45-30	.980	9	102	122	O1100(354/651/237),3b25,1b18/2		-3.5

BRANNAN, OTIS Otis Owen B3.13.1899 Greenbrier AR D6.6.1967 Little Rock AR BL/TR/5-9/160 d4.11 Col Arkansas St.

YEAR	TM LG	G	AB	R	H	2B	3B	HR	RBI	BB-IB	HP	SO	AVG	OBP	SLG	AOPS	ABR	SB-CS	FA	FR	RNG	THR	GAMES AT POSITION	DL	BFW
1928	StL A	135	483	68	118	18	3	6	66	60	4	19	.244	.333	.356	79	-15	3-9	.964	-6	101	98	2b135		-1.9
1929	StL A	23	51	4	15	1	0	1	8	4	0	4	.294	.345	.373	82	-1	0-0	.975	0	105	76	2b19		-0.1
Total	2	158	534	72	133	19	3	11	74	64	4	23	.249	.334	.358	79	-16	3-9	.966	-6	101	96	2b154		-2.0

BRANNOCK, MIKE Michael J. B10.25.1851 Douglas MA D10.7.1881 Chicago IL 5-8/162 d10.21

YEAR	TM LG	G	AB	R	H	2B	3B	HR	RBI	BB-IB	HP	SO	AVG	OBP	SLG	AOPS	ABR	SB-CS	FA	FR	RNG	THR	GAMES AT POSITION	DL	BFW
1871	Chi NA	3	14	2	1	0	0	0	0	0		0	.071	.071	.071	-53	-3	0-0	.500	-2	40	0	3b3		-0.3
1875	Chi NA	2	9	2	1	0	0	0	0	0		0	.111	.111	.111	-22	-1	2-0	.500	-1	83	0	3b2		-0.2
Total	2 NA	5	23	4	2	0	0	0	0	0		0	.087	.087	.087	-43	-4	2-0	.500	-3	59	0	3b5		-0.5

BRANOM, DUD Edgar Dudley B11.30.1897 Sulphur Springs TX D2.4.1980 Sun City AZ BL/TL/6-1/190 d4.12

YEAR	TM LG	G	AB	R	H	2B	3B	HR	RBI	BB-IB	HP	SO	AVG	OBP	SLG	AOPS	ABR	SB-CS	FA	FR	RNG	THR	GAMES AT POSITION	DL	BFW
1927	Phi A	30	94	8	22	1	0	0	13	2		5	.234	.250	.245	27	-10	2-1	.973	-0	108	105	1b26		-1.2

BRANSFIELD, KITTY William Edward B1.7.1875 Worcester MA D5.1.1947 Worcester MA BR/TR/5-11/207 d8.22 U1

YEAR	TM LG	G	AB	R	H	2B	3B	HR	RBI	BB-IB	HP	SO	AVG	OBP	SLG	AOPS	ABR	SB-CS	FA	FR	RNG	THR	GAMES AT POSITION	DL	BFW
1898	Bos N	5	9	2	2	0	1	0	1	0			.222	.222	.444	85	0	0	.889	-1	97	0	C4/1		-0.1
1901	Pit N	139	566	92	167	26	16	0	91	29	5		.295	.335	.398	109	5	23	.981	-10	66	117	1b139		-0.8
1902	Pit N	102	413	49	126	21	8	0	69	17	2		.305	.336	.395	121	9	23	.984	-7	69	82	1b101		0.0
1903	†Pit N	127	505	69	134	23	7	2	57	33	3		.265	.314	.350	87	-10	13	.981	5	117	**136**	1b127		-0.7
1904	Pit N	139	520	47	116	17	9	0	60	22	3		.223	.259	.290	68	-21	11	.981	-2	97	**121**	1b139		-2.8
1905	Phi N	151	580	55	150	23	9	3	76	27	1		.259	.294	.345	93	-7	27	.985	-2	94	99	1b151		-1.2
1906	Phi N	140	524	47	144	28	5	1	60	16	4		.275	.300	.353	104	0	12	.980	-1	100	86	1b139		-0.5
1907	Phi N	94	348	25	81	15	2	0	38	14	0		.233	.262	.287	73	-12	8	.978	-3	93	101	1b92		-1.8
1908	Phi N	144	507	40	152	20	5	0	71	23	2		.304	.335	.395	128	15	30	.986	-1	98	111	1b143		1.3
1909	Phi N	140	527	47	154	27	6	1	59	18	3		.292	.319	.372	114	6	17	**.989**	7	117	138	1b138		1.1
1910	Phi N	123	427	39	102	17	4	3	52	20	1	34	.239	.275	.319	71	-18	10	.982	-4	83	**130**	1b110		-2.6
1911	Phi N	23	43	4	11	1	0	0	2	2		5	.256	.326	.326	61	-3	1	.987	-0	95	47	1b8		-0.3
	Chi N	3	10	0	4	0	0	0	2	0		2	.400	.400	.600	207	2	0	1.000	-0	62	398	1b3		0.1

YEAR TM LG	G	AB	R	H	2B	3B	HR	RBI	BB-IB	HP	SO	AVG	OBP	SLG	AOPS	ABR	SB-CS	FA	FR	RNG	THR	GAMES AT POSITION	DL	BFW
Year	26	53	4	15	3	1	0	3	2		0	7	.283	.309	.377	91	-1	1	.991	-0	86	143	1b11		-0.2
Total 12	1330	4999	529	1351	225	75	13	637	221		24	41	.270	.304	.353	97	-34	175	.983	-18	94	110	1b1291,C4		-8.3

BRANSON, JEFF   Jeffery Glenn B1.26.1967 Waynesboro MS   BL/TR/6-0/180*   [CinN88 2/45]   d4.12   Col West Alabama

YEAR TM LG	G	AB	R	H	2B	3B	HR	RBI	BB-IB	HP	SO	AVG	OBP	SLG	AOPS	ABR	SB-CS	FA	FR	RNG	THR	GAMES AT POSITION	DL	BFW
1992 Cin N	72	115	12	34	7	1	0	15	5-2	0	16	.296	.322	.374	95	2	0-1	.946	2	103	161	2b33,3b8/S		0.1
1993 Cin N	125	381	40	92	15	1	3	22	19-2	0	73	.241	.275	.310	57	-24	4-1	.978	0	96	94	S59,2b45,3b14/1		-1.8
1994 Cin N	58	109	18	31	4	1	6	16	5-2	0	16	.284	.316	.505	110	1	0-0	.980	-5	69	57	2b19,3b18,S8,1b2		-0.4
1995 †Cin N	122	331	43	86	18	2	12	45	44-14	2	69	.260	.345	.435	104	3	2-1	.971	13	107	191	3b98,S32,2b6/1		1.7
1996 Cin N	129	311	34	76	16	4	9	37	31-4	1	67	.244	.312	.408	87	-6	2-0	.932	-4	102	157	3b64,S38,2b31		-0.7
1997 Cin N	65	98	9	15	3	1	1	5	7-1	0	23	.153	.210	.235	16	-13	1-0	.971	-0	95	202	3b27,2b14,S11		-1.2
†Cle A	29	72	5	19	4	0	2	7	7-0	1	17	.264	.329	.403	89	-1	0-2	.986	-1	104	91	2b19,3b6,S2/D		-0.1
1998 Cle A	63	100	6	20	4	1	1	9	3-0	0	21	.200	.221	.290	31	-11	0-0	.960	0	88	155	2b31,3b20,1b3,S2	30	-0.9
2000 LA N	18	17	3	4	1	0	0	0	1-0	0	6	.235	.278	.294	47	-1	0-0	1.000	-1	68	0	S7,2b3,3b3		-0.2
2001 LA N	13	21	3	6	0	0	0	0	0-0	0	4	.286	.286	.286	52	-2	0-0	1.000	-1	96	93	2b6,S2/3		-0.2
Total 9	694	1555	173	383	72	11	34	156	122-25	4	312	.246	.300	.372	77	-55	9-5	.957	2	103	161	3b259,2b207,S162,1b7/D	30	-3.7

BRANT, MARSHALL   Marshall Lee B9.17.1955 Garberville CA   BR/TR/6-5/185*   [NYN75*4/73]   d10.1   Col Sonoma St.

YEAR TM LG	G	AB	R	H	2B	3B	HR	RBI	BB-IB	HP	SO	AVG	OBP	SLG	AOPS	ABR	SB-CS	FA	FR	RNG	THR	GAMES AT POSITION	DL	BFW
1980 NY A	3	6	0	0	0	0	0	0	0-0	0	3	.000	.000	.000	-99	-2	0-0	1.000	0	135	181	1b2/D		-0.2
1983 Oak A	5	14	2	2	0	0	0	2	0-0	0	3	.143	.143	.143	-22	-2	0-0	.905	-1	0	161	1b3/D		-0.4
Total 2	8	20	2	2	0	0	0	2	0-0	0	6	.100	.100	.100	-47	-4	0-0	.935	-1	44	167	1b5,D2		-0.6

BRANTLEY, MICKEY   Michael Charles B6.17.1961 Catskill NY   BR/TR/5-10/180*   [SeaA83 2/35]   d8.9   C2   Col Coastal Carolina   [DL 1990 Sea A 6]

YEAR TM LG	G	AB	R	H	2B	3B	HR	RBI	BB-IB	HP	SO	AVG	OBP	SLG	AOPS	ABR	SB-CS	FA	FR	RNG	THR	GAMES AT POSITION	DL	BFW
1986 Sea A	27	102	12	20	3	2	3	7	10-0	0	21	.196	.268	.353	66	-5	1-1	.983	-1	81	222	O25(1/25/0)		-0.7
1987 Sea A	92	351	52	106	23	2	14	54	24-0	0	44	.302	.344	.499	114	7	13-4	.982	-5	89	68	O82(6/51/35),D8	46	0.1
1988 Sea A	149	577	76	152	25	4	15	56	26-0	1	64	.263	.296	.399	89	-10	18-7	.982	-0	103	65	O147(118/49/4),D2		-1.3
1989 Sea A	34	108	14	17	5	0	0	8	7-0	0	7	.157	.207	.204	16	-12	2-2	1.000	1	109	68	O23(12/0/11),D7		-1.3
Total 4	302	1138	154	295	56	8	32	125	67-0	2	136	.259	.300	.407	89	-20	34-14	.984	-6	97	81	O277(137/125/50),D17	52	-3.2

BRANYAN, RUSSELL   Russell Oles B12.19.1975 Warner Robins GA   BL/TR/6-3/195*   [CleA94 7/185]   d9.26

YEAR TM LG	G	AB	R	H	2B	3B	HR	RBI	BB-IB	HP	SO	AVG	OBP	SLG	AOPS	ABR	SB-CS	FA	FR	RNG	THR	GAMES AT POSITION	DL	BFW
1998 Cle A	1	4	0	0	0	0	0	0	0-0	0	2	.000	.000	.000	-96	-0		1.000	-0	75	0	/3		-0.1
1999 Cle A	11	38	4	8	2	0	1	6	3-0	1	19	.211	.286	.342	56	-3	0-0	.960	3	159	0	3b8,D3		0.0
2000 Cle A	67	193	32	46	7	2	16	38	22-1	2	76	.238	.327	.544	112	2	0-0	.968	1	114	123	O33(18/0/15),D23/3		0.1
2001 †Cle A	113	315	48	73	16	2	20	54	38-1	3	132	.232	.316	.486	104	1	1-1	.930	-2	95	77	3b72,O33(31/0/2),D7		-0.1
2002 Cle A	50	161	16	33	4	0	8	17	17-0	0	65	.205	.278	.379	72	-7	1-2	.986	-2	87	180	O42L,3b8/D		-1.0
Cin N	84	217	34	53	9	4	16	39	34-3	2	86	.244	.349	.516	124	6	3-1	.951	-0	93	235	O25L,1b18,3b16,D4		0.4
2003 Cin N	74	176	22	38	12	0	9	26	27-0	1	69	.216	.322	.438	101	0	0-0	.968	6	153	153	3b20,O17L,1b14/D	75	0.5
2004 Mil N	51	158	21	37	11	1	11	27	20-0	1	68	.234	.324	.525	114	2	1-0	.962	5	114	96	3b44,1b2		0.8
2005 Mil N	85	202	23	52	11	0	12	31	39-10	0	80	.257	.378	.490	125	8	1-0	.946	-7	77	104	3b59,1b5,O3L/D	32	0.1
Total 8	536	1464	200	340	72	6	93	238	200-15	13	597	.232	.327	.480	107	9	7-4	.944	5	100	92	3b229,O153(136/0/17),D40,1b39	107	0.7

BRASHEAR, ROY   Roy Parks B1.3.1874 Ashtabula OH   D4.20.1951 Los Angeles CA   BR/TR/5-11/190   d4.25   b-Kitty

YEAR TM LG	G	AB	R	H	2B	3B	HR	RBI	BB-IB	HP	SO	AVG	OBP	SLG	AOPS	ABR	SB-CS	FA	FR	RNG	THR	GAMES AT POSITION	DL	BFW
1902 StL N	110	388	36	107	8	2	1	40	32	1		.276	.333	.314	104	2		.980	-5	92	120	1b67,2b21,O16(1/7/8),S3		-0.4
1903 Phi N	20	75	9	17	3	0	0	4	6	0		.227	.284	.267	59	-4	2	.918	-3	84	124	2b18,1b2		-0.7
Total 2	130	463	45	124	11	2	1	44	38	1		.268	.327	.307	96	-2	11	.978	-8	92	119	1b69,2b39,O16(1/7/8),S3		-1.1

BRATCHER, JOE   Joseph Warlick "Goobers" B7.22.1898 Grand Saline TX   D10.13.1977 Fort Worth TX   BL/TR/5-8.5/140   d8.26

YEAR TM LG	G	AB	R	H	2B	3B	HR	RBI	BB-IB	HP	SO	AVG	OBP	SLG	AOPS	ABR	SB-CS	FA	FR	RNG	THR	GAMES AT POSITION	DL	BFW
1924 StL N	4	1	1	0	0	0	0	0	0-0	0	0	.000	.000	.000	-99	-0	0-0		0	0	0	/OC		0.0

BRATSCHI, FRED   Frederick Oscar "Fritz" B1.16.1892 Alliance OH   D1.10.1962 Massillon OH   BR/TR/5-10/170   d7.24

YEAR TM LG	G	AB	R	H	2B	3B	HR	RBI	BB-IB	HP	SO	AVG	OBP	SLG	AOPS	ABR	SB-CS	FA	FR	RNG	THR	GAMES AT POSITION	DL	BFW
1921 Chi A	16	28	0	8	1	0	0	3	0-0	0	2	.286	.286	.321	55	-2	0-0	1.000	1	88	350	O5(1/0/4)		-0.1
1926 Bos A	72	167	12	46	10	1	0	19	14	1	15	.275	.335	.347	81	-5	0-1	.949	-5	80	30	O37(29/0/8)		-1.2
1927 Bos A	1	1	0	0	0	0	0	0	0-0	0	0	.000	.000	.000	-99	-0	0-0	—	0			/H		0.0
Total 3	89	196	12	54	11	1	0	22	14	1	17	.276	.327	.342	76	-7	0-1	.956	-4	81	66	O42(30/0/12)		-1.3

BRAUN, STEVE   Stephen Russell B5.8.1948 Trenton NJ   BL/TR/5-10/180*   [MinA66 10/200]   d4.6   C1   OF(465/0/35)

YEAR TM LG	G	AB	R	H	2B	3B	HR	RBI	BB-IB	HP	SO	AVG	OBP	SLG	AOPS	ABR	SB-CS	FA	FR	RNG	THR	GAMES AT POSITION	DL	BFW
1971 Min A	128	343	51	87	12	2	5	35	48-4	1	50	.254	.350	.344	95	-10	8-3	.933	-10	81	54	3b73,2b28,S10,O2L		-0.8
1972 Min A	121	402	40	116	21	0	2	50	45-1	2	38	.289	.360	.356	109	7	4-5	.970	-10	100	103	3b74,2b20,S11,O9(8/0/1)		-0.3
1973 Min A	115	361	46	102	28	5	6	42	74-8	3	48	.283	.408	.438	133	20	4-3	.941	-7	91	114	3b102,O6L		1.2
1974 Min A	129	453	53	127	12	1	8	40	56-4	2	51	.280	.361	.364	106	2	4-4	.964	2	89	143	O108L,3b17		0.1
1975 Min A	136	453	70	137	18	3	11	45	66-5	1	55	.302	.389	.428	130	21	0-2	.971	-2	96	84	O106L,1b9,3b2/2D		1.2
1976 Min A	122	417	73	120	12	3	3	61	67-2	1	43	.288	.384	.353	116	12	12-4	.971	2	111	203	D71,O32(30/0/3),3b16		1.3
1977 Sea A	139	451	51	106	19	1	5	31	80-2	2	59	.235	.351	.315	84	-6	8-3	.975	4	98	159	O100L,D32/3		-0.7
1978 Sea A	32	74	11	17	4	0	3	15	9-1	0	5	.230	.310	.405	101	0	1-0	1.000	-0	81	0	D14,O4(2/0/2)		-0.1
†KC A	64	137	16	36	10	1	0	14	28-1	0	16	.263	.386	.350	106	3	3-2	.964	-2	108	63	O33L,3b11		0.0
Year	96	211	27	53	14	1	3	29	37-2	0	21	.251	.360	.370	104	3	4-2	.967	-2	105	56	O37(35/0/2),D14,3b11		-0.1
1979 KC A	58	116	15	31	2	0	4	10	22-2	0	11	.267	.384	.388	106	2	0-0	1.000	1	85	353	O18L,D11,3b2	34	0.2
1980 KC A	14	23	0	1	0	0	0	1	2-0	0	2	.043	.120	.043	-52	-5	0-0	1.000	0	27	0	O5(3/0/2)/D		-0.6
Tor A	37	55	4	15	2	0	1	9	8-1	0	5	.273	.365	.364	96	0	0-0	1.000	0	437	0	D13/3		0.0
Year	51	78	4	16	2	0	1	10	10-1	0	7	.205	.295	.269	54	-5	0-0	1.000	-1	27	0	D14,O5(3/0/2)/3		-0.6
1981 StL N	44	46	9	9	2	1	0	2	15-0	1	7	.196	.393	.283	90	1	1-0	1.000	1	114	346	O12(6/0/6)/3		0.2
1982 †StL N	58	62	6	17	4	0	0	4	11-0	0	10	.274	.384	.339	101	1	0-0	1.000	0	62	0	O8(6/0/2),3b5	15	-0.1
1983 StL N	78	92	8	25	2	1	3	7	21-0	0	7	.272	.404	.413	127	4	0-1	1.000	0	84	0	O22(18/0/5),3b4		0.4
1984 StL N	86	98	6	27	3	1	0	16	17-0	0	17	.276	.383	.327	103	1	0-0	1.000	-2	48	123	O19(12/0/7)/3		-0.1
1985 StL N	64	67	7	16	4	0	1	6	10-1	1	9	.239	.342	.343	94	0	0-0	1.000	1	107	205	O14(7/0/7)		0.0
Total 15	1425	3650	466	989	155	19	52	388	579-32	17	433	.271	.371	.367	108	65	45-27	.973	-23	94	136	O498L,3b310,D151,2b49,S21,1b9	49	1.9

BRAVO, ANGEL   Angel Alfonso (Urdaneta) B8.4.1942 Maracaibo, Venez   BL/TL/5-8/150*   d6.6

YEAR TM LG	G	AB	R	H	2B	3B	HR	RBI	BB-IB	HP	SO	AVG	OBP	SLG	AOPS	ABR	SB-CS	FA	FR	RNG	THR	GAMES AT POSITION	DL	BFW
1969 Chi A	27	90	10	26	4	2	1	3	3-0	1	5	.289	.319	.411	98	-1	2-2	.978	-2	90	0	O25(2/24/3)		-0.3
1970 †Cin N	65	65	10	18	1	1	0	3	0-0	0	13	.277	.365	.323	85	-1	0-1	.947	0	100	204	O22(5/12/5)		-0.1
1971 Cin N	5	5	0	1	0	0	0	0	0-0	0	1	.200	.200	.200	14	-1	0-0	—	0			/H		-0.1
SD N	52	58	6	9	2	0	0	6	8-1	0	12	.155	.265	.190	34	-5	0-1	.833	-2	41	0	O9(5/3/1)		-0.8
Year	57	63	6	10	2	0	0	6	8-1	0	13	.159	.260	.190	32	-5	0-1	.833	-2	41	0	O9(5/3/1)		-0.9
Total 3	149	218	26	54	7	3	1	12	20-1	2	31	.248	.315	.321	77	-8	2-2	.957	-4	84	46	O56(12/39/9)		-1.3

BRAY, BUSTER   Clarence Wilbur B4.1.1913 Birmingham AL   D9.4.1982 Evansville IN   BL/TL/6-0/170   d4.18

YEAR TM LG	G	AB	R	H	2B	3B	HR	RBI	BB-IB	HP	SO	AVG	OBP	SLG	AOPS	ABR	SB-CS	FA	FR	RNG	THR	GAMES AT POSITION	DL	BFW
1941 Bos A	4	11	2	2	1	0	0	2	0-0	0	2	.091	.167	.182	-2	-2	0	1.000	0	98		O3C		-0.2

BRAZELL, CRAIG   Craig Walter B5.10.1980 Montgomery AL   BL/TR/6-3/210   [NYN98 5/154]   d8.17

YEAR TM LG	G	AB	R	H	2B	3B	HR	RBI	BB-IB	HP	SO	AVG	OBP	SLG	AOPS	ABR	SB-CS	FA	FR	RNG	THR	GAMES AT POSITION	DL	BFW
2004 NY N	24	34	3	9	2	0	1	3	1-0	0	7	.265	.286	.412	79	-1	0-0	.974	0	158	30	1b7		-0.1

BRAZILL, FRANK   Frank Leo B8.11.1899 Spangler PA   D11.3.1976 Oakland CA   BL/TR/5-11.5/175   d4.13

YEAR TM LG	G	AB	R	H	2B	3B	HR	RBI	BB-IB	HP	SO	AVG	OBP	SLG	AOPS	ABR	SB-CS	FA	FR	RNG	THR	GAMES AT POSITION	DL	BFW
1921 Phi A	66	177	17	48	3	1	0	19	23	2	21	.271	.361	.299	70	-7	2-4	.984	-2	98	114	1b36,3b9		-1.1
1922 Phi A	6	13	0	1	0	0	0	1	0	0	1	.077	.077	.077	-58	-3	0-0	.750	-1	50	0	3b2		-0.4
Total 2	72	190	17	49	3	1	0	20	23	2	22	.258	.344	.284	62	-10	2-4	.984	-4	98	114	1b36,3b11		-1.5

BREAM, SID   Sidney Eugene B8.3.1960 Carlisle PA   BL/TL/6-4/220*   [LAN81 2/48]   d9.1   Col Liberty

YEAR TM LG	G	AB	R	H	2B	3B	HR	RBI	BB-IB	HP	SO	AVG	OBP	SLG	AOPS	ABR	SB-CS	FA	FR	RNG	THR	GAMES AT POSITION	DL	BFW
1983 LA N	15	11	0	2	0	0	0	2	2-0	0	2	.182	.308	.182	39	-1	0-0	1.000	-0	0	116	1b4		-0.1
1984 LA N	27	49	2	9	3	0	0	6	6-2	0	7	.184	.263	.245	46	-3	1-0	1.000	2	153	102	1b14		-0.2
1985 LA N	24	53	4	7	0	0	0	6	7-3	0	10	.132	.230	.302	50	-4	0-0	.994	2	151	72	1b16		-0.3
Pit N	26	95	14	27	7	0	3	15	11-2	0	14	.284	.355	.453	126	4	0-2	.992	2	124	102	1b25		0.3
Year	50	148	18	34	7	0	6	21	18-5	0	24	.230	.310	.399	99	0	0-2	.993	4	134	91	1b41		0.0
1986 Pit N	154	522	73	140	37	5	16	77	60-5	1	73	.268	.341	.450	114	11	13-7	.989	21	152	95	1b153,O2L		2.4
1987 Pit N	149	516	64	142	25	3	13	65	49-11	0	69	.275	.336	.411	96	-3	9-8	.988	2	153	144	1b144		-1.5
1988 Pit N	148	462	50	122	37	0	10	65	47-6	1	64	.264	.328	.409	113	4	9-9	.995	19	152	98	1b138		1.9
1989 Pit N	19	36	3	8	0	0	0	2	10-0	0	10	.222	.417	.305	113	2	0-0	.992	-0	94	66	1b13	149	-0.1
1990 †Pit N	147	389	39	105	23	2	15	67	48-5	2	65	.270	.349	.455	125	14	8-4	.993	10	133	113	1b142		1.6
1991 †Atl N	91	265	32	67	12	0	11	45	25-5	0	31	.253	.313	.423	100	0	0-3	.996	1	103	114	1b85	61	-0.6
1992 †Atl N	125	372	30	97	25	1	10	61	46-2	1	51	.261	.340	.414	107	3	6-0	.989	0	103	97	1b120		-0.1

YEAR TM LG	G	AB	R	H	2B	3B	HR	RBI	BB-IB	HP	SO	AVG	OBP	SLG	AOPS	ABR	SB-CS	FA	FR	RNG	THR	GAMES AT POSITION	DL	BFW
1993 †Atl N	117	277	33	72	14	1	9	35	31-3	0	43	.260	.332	.415	97	-1	4-2	.996	6	123	122	1b90		-0.2
1994 Hou N	46	61	7	21	5	0	0	7	9-1	0	9	.344	.429	.426	130	3	0-1	.986	2	207	141	1b10	31	0.5
Total 12	1088	3108	351	819	191	12	90	455	353-45	5	450	.264	.336	.420	107	36	50-40	.992	72	130	104	1b954,O2L	241	4.6

BREAZEALE, JIM James Leo B10.3.1949 Houston TX BL/TR/6-2/210(195-215) [AtlN68*1/8] d9.13 [DL 1973 Atl N 53]

YEAR TM LG	G	AB	R	H	2B	3B	HR	RBI	BB-IB	HP	SO	AVG	OBP	SLG	AOPS	ABR	SB-CS	FA	FR	RNG	THR	GAMES AT POSITION	DL	BFW
1969 Atl N	2	1	1	0	0	0	0	0	2-0	0	0	.000	.667	.000	100	0	0-0	.833	-0	0	0	/1		0.0
1971 Atl N	10	21	1	4	0	0	1	3	0-0	0	3	.190	.182	.333	43	-2	0-0	1.000	-0	68	82	1b4		-0.3
1972 Atl N	52	85	10	21	2	0	5	17	6-1	0	12	.247	.297	.447	100	0	0-1	1.000	-2	36	95	1b16/3		-0.4
1978 Chi A	25	72	8	15	3	0	3	13	8-0	0	10	.208	.284	.375	84	-2	0-0	.992	-3	29	75	1b19,D4		-0.6
Total 4	89	179	20	40	5	0	9	33	16-1	0	25	.223	.284	.402	88	-4	0-1	.993	-6	36	82	1b40,D4/3	53	-1.3

BREDE, BRENT Brent David B9.13.1971 Belleville IL BL/TL/6-4/190(190-208) [MinA90 5/140] d9.8

YEAR TM LG	G	AB	R	H	2B	3B	HR	RBI	BB-IB	HP	SO	AVG	OBP	SLG	AOPS	ABR	SB-CS	FA	FR	RNG	THR	GAMES AT POSITION	DL	BFW
1996 Min A	10	20	2	6	0	1	0	2	1-0	0	5	.300	.333	.400	83	-1	0-0	1.000	1	127	304	O7R		0.0
1997 Min A	61	190	25	52	11	1	3	21	21-0	1	38	.274	.347	.389	91	-2	7-2	.957	-3	90	0	O42(30/0/40),1b15/D		-0.7
1998 Ari N	98	212	23	48	9	3	2	17	24-2	2	43	.226	.311	.325	67	-10	1-0	.964	-2	92	67	O58(26/0/39),1b12/D		-1.4
Total 3	169	422	50	106	20	5	5	40	46-2	3	86	.251	.328	.358	79	-13	8-2	.964	-4	93	52	O107(29/0/86),1b27,D2		-2.1

BREEDEN, DANNY Danny Richard B6.27.1942 Albany GA BR/TR/5-11.5/185* d7.24 b-Hal Col Troy St.

YEAR TM LG	G	AB	R	H	2B	3B	HR	RBI	BB-IB	HP	SO	AVG	OBP	SLG	AOPS	ABR	SB-CS	FA	FR	RNG	THR	GAMES AT POSITION	DL	BFW
1969 Cin N	3	8	0	1	0	0	0	0	1-0	0	3	.125	.125	.125	-28	-7	1-0	.941	-1	65	0	C3		-0.2
1971 Chi N	25	65	3	10	1	0	0	4	9-0	1	18	.154	.263	.169	22	-6	0-0	.975	3	101	56	C25		-0.2
Total 2	28	73	3	11	1	0	0	5	9-0	1	21	.151	.250	.164	18	-7	0-0	.972	3	96	49	C28		-0.4

BREEDEN, HAL Harold Noel B6.28.1944 Albany GA BR/TL/6-2/200* d4.7 b-Danny

YEAR TM LG	G	AB	R	H	2B	3B	HR	RBI	BB-IB	HP	SO	AVG	OBP	SLG	AOPS	ABR	SB-CS	FA	FR	RNG	THR	GAMES AT POSITION	DL	BFW
1971 Chi N	23	36	1	5	1	0	1	2	2-0	0	7	.139	.184	.250	19	-4	0-0	.982	1	164	39	1b8		-0.4
1972 Mon N	42	87	6	20	2	0	3	10	7-1	0	15	.230	.281	.356	80	-2	0-0	.994	-0	91	84	1b26/OL		-0.5
1973 Mon N	105	258	36	71	10	6	15	43	29-3	2	45	.275	.353	.535	138	12	0-1	.991	3	118	99	1b66		1.0
1974 Mon N	79	190	14	47	13	0	2	20	24-0	1	35	.247	.330	.347	85	-3	0-1	.987	0	104	127	1b56		-0.7
1975 Mon N	24	37	4	5	2	0	0	1	7-3	0	5	.135	.273	.189	28	-3	0-0	.989	-1	77	72	1b12		-0.5
Total 5	273	608	61	148	28	6	21	76	69-7	2	107	.243	.321	.413	99	0	0-2	.990	3	110	102	1b168/OL		-1.1

BREEDING, MARV Marvin Eugene B3.8.1934 Decatur AL BR/TR/6-0/175* d4.19 Col Samford

YEAR TM LG	G	AB	R	H	2B	3B	HR	RBI	BB-IB	HP	SO	AVG	OBP	SLG	AOPS	ABR	SB-CS	FA	FR	RNG	THR	GAMES AT POSITION	DL	BFW
1960 Bal A	152	551	69	147	25	2	3	43	35-2	3	80	.267	.313	.336	77	-18	10-4	.977	9	102	112	2b152		0.2
1961 Bal A	90	244	32	51	8	0	1	16	14-1	0	33	.209	.250	.254	37	-22	5-2	.970	4	99	123	2b80		-1.2
1962 Bal A	95	240	27	59	10	1	2	18	8-0	1	41	.246	.273	.321	63	-13	2-2	.977	10	113	120	2b73/S3		0.2
1963 Was A	58	197	20	54	7	2	1	14	7-0	0	21	.274	.299	.345	60	-6	1-1	.914	-1	100	91	2b29,2b22,S2		-0.5
LA N	20	36	6	6	0	0	0	1	2-0	0	5	.167	.211	.167	11	-4	1-0	.972	-5	74	0	2b17/S3		-1.0
Total 4	415	1268	154	317	50	5	7	92	66-3	4	180	.250	.288	.314	65	-63	19-9	.975	18	103	112	2b344,3b31,S4		-2.3

BREMER, HERB Herbert Frederick B10.26.1913 Chicago IL D11.28.1979 Columbus GA BR/TR/6-0/195 d9.16

YEAR TM LG	G	AB	R	H	2B	3B	HR	RBI	BB-IB	HP	SO	AVG	OBP	SLG	AOPS	ABR	SB-CS	FA	FR	RNG	THR	GAMES AT POSITION	DL	BFW
1937 StL N	11	33	2	7	1	0	0	2	4	0	4	.212	.257	.242	36	-0	0	.979	-0	81	107	C10		-0.3
1938 StL N	50	151	14	33	5	1	2	14	9	0	36	.219	.262	.305	53	-10	1	.977	2	91	123	C50		-0.6
1939 StL N	9	9	0	1	0	0	0	1	0	0	2	.111	.111	.111	-38	-2	0	1.000	-0	67	0	C8		-0.2
Total 3	70	193	16	41	6	1	2	18	11	0	42	.212	.255	.285	45	-15	1	.979	2	88	115	C68		-1.1

BRENEGAN, SAM Olaf Selmar B9.1.1890 Galesville WI D4.20.1956 Galesville WI BL/TR/6-2/185 d4.24

YEAR TM LG	G	AB	R	H	2B	3B	HR	RBI	BB-IB	HP	SO	AVG	OBP	SLG	AOPS	ABR	SB-CS	FA	FR	RNG	THR	GAMES AT POSITION	DL	BFW
1914 Pit N	1	0	0	0	0	0	0	0	0	0	0	—				-0	0	0			/C		0.0

BRENLY, BOB Robert Earl B2.25.1954 Coshocton OH BR/TR/6-2/210* d8.14 M4/C4 Col Ohio U.

YEAR TM LG	G	AB	R	H	2B	3B	HR	RBI	BB-IB	HP	SO	AVG	OBP	SLG	AOPS	ABR	SB-CS	FA	FR	RNG	THR	GAMES AT POSITION	DL	BFW
1981 SF N	19	45	5	15	2	1	1	4	6-0	1	4	.333	.423	.489	163	-4	0-1	.964	-4	104	50	C14,3b3/OL		0.0
1982 SF N	65	180	26	51	4	1	4	15	18-4	1	26	.283	.348	.383	107	2	6-2	.961	-3	85	143	C61/3	38	0.1
1983 SF N	104	281	36	63	12	2	7	34	37-6	2	48	.224	.317	.356	89	-4	10-7	.983	6	110	**132**	C90,1b10,O2(1/0/1)		0.5
1984 SF N★	145	506	74	147	28	0	20	80	48-3	3	52	.291	.352	.464	132	22	6-9	.986	-13	100	125	C127,1b22,O3(1/0/2)		1.1
1985 SF N	133	440	41	97	16	1	19	56	57-5	2	62	.220	.311	.391	100	-1	1-4	.984	-9	103	103	C110,3b17,1b10		-0.2
1986 SF N	149	472	60	116	26	0	16	62	74-10	3	97	.246	.350	.403	113	10	10-6	**.995**	2	126	121	C101,3b45,1b19		1.5
1987 †SF N	123	375	55	100	19	1	18	51	47-3	3	85	.267	.348	.467	121	11	10-7	.988	13	115	140	C108,1b6,3b2		2.7
1988 SF N	73	206	13	39	7	0	5	22	20-3	2	40	.189	.265	.296	64	-10	1-2	.984	-1	118	73	C69		-0.8
1989 Tor A	48	88	9	15	3	1	1	6	10-0	1	17	.170	.255	.261	46	-6	1-0	.975	-3	53	81	D28,C13,1b5		-1.0
SF N	12	22	1	4	0	0	0	2	0-0	0	9	.182	.208	.273	40	-2	0-0	1.000	0	278	39	C12		-0.1
Total 9	871	2615	321	647	119	7	91	333	318-35	17	438	.247	.330	.403	107	26	45-38	.984	-7	109	118	C705,1b72,3b68,D28,O6(3/0/3)	38	3.8

BRENNAN, JIM Jack (b John Gottlieb Dorn) B1862 St.Louis MO ?/155 d4.20

YEAR TM LG	G	AB	R	H	2B	3B	HR	RBI	BB-IB	HP	SO	AVG	OBP	SLG	AOPS	ABR	SB-CS	FA	FR	RNG	THR	GAMES AT POSITION	DL	BFW
1884 StL U	56	231	38	50	6	1	0	12				.216	.255	.251	52	-20		.891	2			C33,O16(7/4/6),3b7/S		-1.4
1885 StL U	3	10	0	1	0	0	0	1	1			.100	.182	.100	-7	-1		.750	-1	0	0	O2L/3		-0.2
1888 KC AA	34	118	5	20	2	0	0	6	3	2		.169	.203	.186	24	-10	3	.884	-2			C25,O5(2/1/2),3b5		-0.9
1889 Phi AA	31	113	12	25	4	0	0	15	10	0	15	.221	.285	.257	55	-6	1	.818	-2			C13,O7(0/4/3),2b7,3b4		-0.6
1890 Cle P	59	233	32	59	3	7	0	26	13	4	29	.253	.304	.326	74	-9	8	.845	-2	70	104	C42,3b14,O6(2/0/4)		-1.5
Total 5	183	705	87	155	15	8	0	48	39	6	45	.220	.267	.264	54	-46	12	.869	-15	70	104	C113,O36(13/9/15),3b31,2b7/S		-4.6

BRENZEL, BILL William Richard B3.3.1910 Oakland CA D6.12.1979 Oakland CA BR/TR/5-10/173 d4.13

YEAR TM LG	G	AB	R	H	2B	3B	HR	RBI	BB-IB	HP	SO	AVG	OBP	SLG	AOPS	ABR	SB-CS	FA	FR	RNG	THR	GAMES AT POSITION	DL	BFW
1932 Pit N	9	24	0	1	0	0	0	2	0	0	4	.042	.042	.083	-69	-6	0	1.000	1	89	46	C9		-0.5
1934 Cle A	15	51	4	11	3	0	0	3	2	0	1	.216	.245	.275	33	-5	0-0	1.000	2	112	103	C15		-0.3
1935 Cle A	52	142	12	31	5	1	0	14	6	0	10	.218	.250	.268	33	-15	2-2	.975	-4	105	113	C51		-1.6
Total 3	76	217	16	43	9	1	0	19	8	0	15	.198	.227	.249	23	-26	2-2	.985	-2	105	102	C75		-2.4

BRESNAHAN, ROGER Roger Philip "The Duke of Tralee" B6.11.1879 Toledo OH D12.4.1944 Toledo OH BR/TR/5-9/200 d8.27 M5/C6 HF1945 OF(19/221/41) ▲

YEAR TM LG	G	AB	R	H	2B	3B	HR	RBI	BB-IB	HP	SO	AVG	OBP	SLG	AOPS	ABR	SB-CS	FA	FR	RNG	THR	GAMES AT POSITION	DL	BFW
1897 Was N	6	16	1	6	0	0	0	3	1	0		.375	.412	.375	109	0	0	1.000	-1	75	0	P6/OC		0.0
1900 Chi N	2	2	0	0	0	0	0	0	0	0		.000	.000	.000	-99	-1	0	—	-0	0	0	/OF		-0.1
1901 Bal A	86	295	40	79	9	9	1	32	23	1		.268	.323	.369	88	-6	10	.919	-12	98	85	C69,O8(7/0/1),3b4,P2,2b2		-1.1
1902 Bal A	65	235	30	64	8	6	4	34	21	2		.272	.337	.409	102	0	12	.880	-7	92	89	3b30,C22,O15C		-0.5
NY N	51	178	16	51	9	3	1	22	16	2		.287	.352	.388	130	6	6	.946	0	191	126	O27R,C16,1b4,S4/3		0.8
1903 NY N	113	406	87	142	30	8	4	55	61	7		.350	.443	.493	161	36	34	.965	-0	122	235	O84(4/79/1),1b13,C11,3b4		3.1
1904 NY N	109	402	81	114	22	7	5	33	58	5		.284	.381	.410	138	21	13	.954	-1	123	314	O93(7/81/5),1b10,S4/23		1.6
1905 †NY N	104	331	58	100	18	3	0	46	50	11		.302	.411	.375	132	18	11	.970	8	**152**	100	C87,O8(0/2/4)		3.4
1906 NY N	124	405	69	114	22	4	0	43	81	**15**		.281	**.419**	.356	139	26	25	.974	6	118	**120**	C82,O40(0/39/3)		4.2
1907 NY N	110	328	57	83	9	7	4	38	61	6		.253	.380	.360	128	14	15	.986	-2	125	81	C95,1b6,O2C/3		2.3
1908 NY N	140	449	70	127	25	3	1	54	**83**	6		.283	.401	.356	136	25	14	.985	-5	125	85	C139		3.8
1909 StL N	72	234	27	57	4	1	0	23	46	1		.244	.370	.269	105	5	11	.960	-9	74	118	C59,2b9/3M		0.1
1910 StL N	88	234	35	65	15	3	0	27	55	2	17	.278	.419	.368	135	15	13	.961	-15	74	99	C77,O2(1/1/0)/PM		0.8
1911 StL N	81	227	22	63	17	8	3	41	45	3	19	.278	.404	.463	146	16	4	.968	-10	76	110	C77,2b2,M		1.2
1912 StL N	48	108	8	36	7	2	1	15	14	2	9	.333	.419	.463	145	7	4	.974	2	79	125	C28,M		1.1
1913 Chi N	69	162	20	37	5	2	1	21	21	2	11	.228	.324	.302	79	-4	7-1	.963	-2	109	98	C58		0.0
1914 Chi N	101	248	42	69	10	4	0	24	49	2	20	.278	.401	.351	125	11	14	.978	-4	88	101	C85,2b14/OC		1.5
1915 Chi N	77	221	19	45	8	1	1	19	29	1	23	.204	.296	.262	70	-7	19-3	.982	1	99	101	C68,M		0.3
Total 17	1446	4481	682	1252	218	71	26	530	714	67	99	.279	.386	.377	126	182	212-4	.971	-52	106	99	C974,O281C,3b42,1b33,2b28,P9,S8		22.5

BRESSLER, RUBE Raymond Bloom B10.23.1894 Coder PA D11.7.1966 Cincinnati OH BR/TL/6-0/187 d4.24 Mil 1918 ▲

YEAR TM LG	G	AB	R	H	2B	3B	HR	RBI	BB-IB	HP	SO	AVG	OBP	SLG	AOPS	ABR	SB-CS	FA	FR	RNG	THR	GAMES AT POSITION	DL	BFW
1914 Phi A	29	51	6	11	1	0	1	4	6	1	7	.216	.310	.275	79	4	0	.941	-3	61	138	P29		0.0
1915 Phi A	33	55	9	8	1	1	1	4	9	1	13	.145	.277	.236	56	-1	0	.900	1	106	0	P32		0.0
1916 Phi A	4	5	1	1	0	0	0	1	0	0	2	.200	.200	.600	147	1	0	1.000	-0	47	0	P4		0.0
1917 Cin N	3	5	0	1	0	0	0	0	0	0	2	.200	.200	.200	24	0	0	1.000	-0	39	0	P2		0.0
1918 Cin N	23	62	10	17	5	0	0	6	5	0	4	.274	.328	.355	110	3	0	.982	3	137	152	P17,O3(3/0/1)		0.1
1919 Cin N	61	165	22	34	3	4	2	15	26	3	11	.206	.311	.309	89	-2	2	.965	-1	111	63	O48(41/0/7),P13		-0.4
1920 Cin N	21	30	4	8	1	0	0	3	3	0	4	.267	.290	.300	71	-1	1-0	1.000	-1	90	502	P10,O3(3/0/1/2),1b2		-0.2
1921 Cin N	109	323	41	99	18	6	1	54	39	2	20	.307	.385	.409	115	9	5-5	.953	-5	100	56	O50(9/0/76),1b6		-0.3
1922 Cin N	52	53	7	14	0	2	0	8	4	0	4	.264	.316	.340	70	-3	1-0	1.000	-1	0	0	1b3,O2(1/0/1)		-0.3
1923 Cin N	54	119	25	33	3	1	0	18	20	4	4	.277	.399	.319	93	0	3-1	.983	-2	79	73	1b22,O6(3/0/3)		-0.2
1924 Cin N	115	383	41	133	14	13	4	49	22	4	20	.347	.389	.483	134	17	9-10	.990	2	122	104	1b50,O49(45/0/4)		1.0

YEAR	TM LG	G	AB	R	H	2B	3B	HR	RBI	BB-IB	HP	SO	AVG	OBP	SLG	AOPS	ABR	SB-CS	FA	FR	RNG	THR	GAMES AT POSITION	DL	BFW
1925	Cin N	97	319	43	111	17	6	4	61	40	2	16	.348	.424	.476	133	18	9-5	.982	-5	79	126	1b52,O38(36/0/2)		0.7
1926	Cin N	86	297	58	106	15	9	1	51	37	3	20	.357	.433	.478	149	22	3	.970	-5	95	52	O80L,1b4		1.1
1927	Cin N	124	467	43	136	14	8	3	77	32	1	22	.291	.338	.375	94	-5	4	.972	5	104	132	O120L		-0.9
1928	Bro N	145	501	78	148	29	13	4	70	80	5	33	.295	.398	.429	118	16	2	**.985**	-6	93	68	O137L		-0.1
1929	Bro N	136	456	72	145	22	8	9	77	67	1	27	.318	.406	.461	117	14	4	.954	1	107	87	O122L		0.5
1930	Bro N	109	335	53	100	12	8	3	52	51	2	19	.299	.394	.409	96	-1	4	.995	7	118	83	O90L,1b7		-0.1
1931	Bro N	67	153	22	43	4	5	0	26	11	0	10	.281	.329	.373	89	-3	0	.982	-2	91	58	O35(23/7/3)/1		-0.6
1932	Phi N	27	83	9	19	6	1	0	6	2	0	5	.229	.247	.325	47	-6	0	1.000	3	110	360	O18L		-0.4
	StL N	10	19	0	3	0	0	0	2	0	0	1	.158	.158	.158	-14	-3	0	1.000	-0	104	0	O4L		-0.3
	Year	37	102	9	22	6	1	0	8	2	0	6	.216	.231	.294	37	-9	0	1.000	3	109	298	O22L		-0.7
Total	19	1305	3881	544	1170	164	87	32	586	449	28	246	.301	.378	.413	110	79	47-21	.971	-8	102	85	O840(732/8/99),1b147,P107		-0.4

BRESSOUD, EDDIE   Edward Francis B5.2.1932 Los Angeles CA BR/TR/6-1/175* d6.14

YEAR	TM LG	G	AB	R	H	2B	3B	HR	RBI	BB-IB	HP	SO	AVG	OBP	SLG	AOPS	ABR	SB-CS	FA	FR	RNG	THR	GAMES AT POSITION	DL	BFW
1956	NY N	49	163	15	37	4	2	0	9	12-1	1	20	.227	.284	.276	52	-11	1-0	.950	-8	92	90	S48		-1.6
1957	NY N	49	127	11	34	2	1	5	10	4-1	2	19	.268	.299	.433	94	-2	0-1	.940	-1	105	88	S33,3b12		-0.1
1958	SF N	66	137	19	36	5	3	0	8	14-1	0	22	.263	.331	.343	81	-4	0-1	.966	-4	93	87	2b57,3b6,S4		-0.5
1959	SF N	104	315	36	79	17	2	9	26	28-6	0	55	.251	.311	.403	91	-5	0-0	.974	-7	96	72	S92/123		-0.5
1960	SF N	116	386	37	87	19	6	9	43	35-12	2	72	.225	.290	.376	87	-8	1-2	.960	2	102	83	S115		0.3
1961	SF N	59	114	14	24	6	0	3	11	11-4	0	23	.211	.276	.342	66	-6	1-1	.964	-10	72	71	S34,3b3/2		-1.3
1962	Bos A	153	599	79	166	40	9	14	68	46-4	1	118	.277	.329	.444	103	2	2-3	.965	23	**109**	106	S153		3.7
1963	Bos A	140	497	61	129	23	6	20	60	52-2	2	93	.260	.329	.451	113	9	1-1	.962	-13	88	94	S137		0.8
1964	Bos A☆	158	566	86	166	41	3	15	55	72-4	1	99	.293	.372	.456	123	21	1-1	.972	-8	92	78	S158		2.7
1965	Bos A	107	296	29	67	11	1	8	25	29-4	1	77	.226	.297	.351	79	-8	0-1	.963	-9	94	101	S86,3b2/OL		-0.2
1966	NY N	133	405	48	91	15	5	10	49	47-4	1	107	.225	.304	.360	87	-7	2-2	.960	10	110	109	S94,3b32,1b9,2b7		1.0
1967	†StL N	52	67	8	9	1	1	1	1	5-0	0	18	.134	.237	.224	33	-6	0-0	.929	-9	77	92	S48/3		-1.5
Total	12	1186	3672	443	925	184	40	94	365	359-44	12	723	.252	.319	.401	96	-25	9-13	.963	-26	97	90	S1002,2b66,3b57,1b10/OL		2.8

BRETON, JIM   John Frederick B7.15.1891 Chicago IL D5.30.1973 Beloit WI BR/TR/5-10.5/178 d8.25 Col Illinois

YEAR	TM LG	G	AB	R	H	2B	3B	HR	RBI	BB-IB	HP	SO	AVG	OBP	SLG	AOPS	ABR	SB-CS	FA	FR	RNG	THR	GAMES AT POSITION	DL	BFW
1913	Chi A	12	30	1	5	1	1	0	2	1	0	5	.167	.194	.267	35	-3	0	.938	2	152	112	S7,3b3		0.0
1914	Chi A	81	231	21	49	7	2	0	24	24	1	42	.212	.292	.260	67	-9	9-6	.910	1	107	63	3b79		-0.7
1915	Chi A	16	36	3	5	1	0	0	1	5	1	9	.139	.262	.167	27	-3	2-1	.882	-2	74	126	3b14/2S		-0.5
Total	3	109	297	25	59	9	3	0	27	30	2	56	.199	.279	.249	59	-15	11-7	.906	1	103	69	3b96,S8/2		-1.2

BRETT, GEORGE   George Howard B5.15.1953 Glen Dale WV BL/TR/6-0/200(180-205) [KCA71 2/29] d8.2 HF1999 b-Ken OF(22/0/14)

YEAR	TM LG	G	AB	R	H	2B	3B	HR	RBI	BB-IB	HP	SO	AVG	OBP	SLG	AOPS	ABR	SB-CS	FA	FR	RNG	THR	GAMES AT POSITION	DL	BFW
1973	KC A	13	40	2	5	2	0	0	0	0-0	0	5	.125	.125	.175	-10	-6	0-0	.974	2	126	88	3b13		-0.4
1974	KC A	133	457	49	129	21	5	2	47	21-3	0	38	.282	.313	.363	89	-7	8-5	.948	-7	102	56	3b132/S		-1.6
1975	KC A	159	634	84	**195**	35	**13**	11	89	46-6	2	49	.308	.353	.456	125	19	13-10	.949	2	104	86	3b159/S		2.0
1976	†KC A★	159	645	94	**215**	34	**14**	7	67	49-4	1	36	**.333**	.377	.462	145	35	21-11	.948	3	103	86	3b157,S4		4.1
1977	†KC A★	139	564	105	176	32	13	22	88	55-9	2	24	.312	.373	.532	142	32	14-12	.957	18	114	**137**	3b135/SD		4.6
1978	†KC A★	128	510	79	150	**45**	8	9	62	39-6	1	35	.294	.342	.467	123	15	23-7	.961	4	104	108	3b128/S		2.0
1979	†KC A★	154	645	119	**212**	42	**20**	23	107	51-14	0	36	.329	.376	.563	146	40	17-10	.944	14	114	99	3b149,1b8/D	33	4.9
1980	†KC A★	117	449	87	175	33	9	24	118	58-16	1	22	**.390**	**.454**	**.664**	201	64	15-6	.955	4	106	123	3b112/1	29	**6.5**
1981	†KC A★	89	347	42	109	27	7	6	43	27-7	1	23	.314	.361	.484	143	19	14-6	.946	-10	91	46	3b88		0.9
1982	KC A★	144	552	101	166	32	9	21	82	71-14	1	51	.301	.378	.505	140	31	6-1	.959	-7	96	83	3b134,O12L		2.2
1983	†KC A★	123	464	90	144	38	2	25	93	57-13	1	39	.310	.385	**.563**	156	37	0-1	.919	-16	87	117	3b102,1b14,O13(6/0/7)/D	21	1.7
1984	†KC A★	104	377	42	107	21	3	13	69	38-6	0	37	.284	.344	.459	120	10	0-2	.949	4	110	114	3b101	46	0.2
1985	†KC A★	155	550	108	184	38	5	30	112	103-**31**	3	49	.335	.436	**.585**	177	64	9-1	.967	5	105	116	3b152/D		6.6
1986	KC A★	124	441	70	128	28	4	16	73	80-**18**	4	45	.290	.401	.481	136	26	1-2	.952	-1	99	88	3b115,S2,D7		2.3
1987	KC A	115	427	71	124	18	2	22	78	72-14	1	47	.290	.388	.496	130	21	6-3	.993	-3	88	101	1b83,D21,3b11	50	1.1
1988	KC A★	157	589	90	180	42	3	24	103	82-15	3	51	.306	.389	.509	149	41	14-3	.992	-7	81	102	1b124,D33/S		2.7
1989	KC A	124	457	67	129	26	3	12	80	59-14	3	47	.282	.362	.431	125	17	14-4	.998	4	106	82	1b104,D17,O2L	41	1.4
1990	KC A	142	544	82	179	**45**	7	14	87	56-14	0	63	**.329**	.387	.515	153	40	9-2	.993	-3	86	98	1b102,D32,O9(2/0/7)/3		3.0
1991	KC A	131	505	77	129	40	2	10	61	58-10	0	75	.255	.327	.402	101	2	2-0	.989	-1	69	72	D118,1b10	31	-0.3
1992	KC A	152	592	55	169	35	5	7	61	35-6	4	69	.285	.330	.397	100	-1	8-6	.987	-0	109	70	D132,1b15,3b3		3.0
1993	KC A	145	560	69	149	31	3	19	75	39-9	3	67	.266	.312	.434	93	-7	7-5	—	0	0	0	D140		-1.4
Total	21	2707	10349	1583	3154	665	137	317	1595	1096-229	33	908	.305	.369	.487	134	492	201-97	.951	4	103	98	3b1692,D506,1b461,O36L,S11	251	42.8

BREWER, TONY   Anthony Bruce B11.25.1957 Coushatta LA BR/TR/5-11/190 d8.1 b-Mike Col Miami

YEAR	TM LG	G	AB	R	H	2B	3B	HR	RBI	BB-IB	HP	SO	AVG	OBP	SLG	AOPS	ABR	SB-CS	FA	FR	RNG	THR	GAMES AT POSITION	DL	BFW
1984	LA N	24	37	3	4	1	0	1	4	4-1	0	9	.108	.195	.216	15	-4	1-0	1.000	-1	72	0	O10(8/0/2)		-0.6

BREWER, MIKE   Michael Quinn B10.24.1959 Shreveport LA BR/TR/6-5/190 [KCA79*1/22] d6.11 b-Tony Col Foothill (CA) JC

YEAR	TM LG	G	AB	R	H	2B	3B	HR	RBI	BB-IB	HP	SO	AVG	OBP	SLG	AOPS	ABR	SB-CS	FA	FR	RNG	THR	GAMES AT POSITION	DL	BFW
1986	KC A	12	18	0	3	0	0	0	6	0-0	0	6	.167	.250	.222	29	-2	0-1	1.000	-1	85	0	O9R/D		-0.3

BREWER, ROD   Rodney Lee B2.24.1966 Eustis FL BL/TL/6-3/210* [StLN87 5/124] d9.5 Col Florida

YEAR	TM LG	G	AB	R	H	2B	3B	HR	RBI	BB-IB	HP	SO	AVG	OBP	SLG	AOPS	ABR	SB-CS	FA	FR	RNG	THR	GAMES AT POSITION	DL	BFW
1990	StL N	14	25	2	6	2	0	0	2	0-0	0	4	.240	.240	.280	42	-2	0-0	.981	1	167	143	1b9		-0.2
1991	StL N	19	13	0	1	0	0	0	0	0-0	0	5	.077	.077	.077	-56	-3	0-0	1.000	0	107	86	1b15,O3R		-0.3
1992	StL N	29	103	11	31	6	0	0	10	8-0	1	12	.301	.354	.359	106	1	0-1	1.000	1	102	102	1b27,O4L		0.0
1993	StL N	110	147	15	42	8	0	2	20	17-5	1	26	.286	.359	.381	100	1	1-0	.960	-2	103	57	O33(15/0/19),1b32/P		-0.3
Total	4	172	288	30	80	15	0	2	33	25-5	2	47	.278	.336	.351	91	-3	1-1	.995	-0	100	117	1b83,O40(19/0/22)/P		-0.8

BREWSTER, CHARLIE   Charles Lawrence B12.27.1916 Marthaville LA D10.1.2000 Alma GA BR/TR/5-8.5/175 d5.2

YEAR	TM LG	G	AB	R	H	2B	3B	HR	RBI	BB-IB	HP	SO	AVG	OBP	SLG	AOPS	ABR	SB-CS	FA	FR	RNG	THR	GAMES AT POSITION	DL	BFW
1943	Cin N	7	8	0	1	0	0	0	0	0	0	1	.125	.125	.125	-28	-1	0	1.000	-0	72	177	2b2		-0.1
	Phi N	49	159	13	35	2	0	0	12	10	2	19	.220	.275	.233	49	-11	1	.901	-18	79	70	S46		-2.7
	Year	56	167	13	36	2	0	0	12	10	2	20	.216	.268	.228	45	-12	1	.901	-18	79	70	S46,2b2		-2.8
1944	Chi N	10	44	4	11	2	0	0	2	5	0	7	.250	.327	.295	76	-1	0	.903	-1	86	148	S10		-0.1
1946	Cle A	3	2	0	0	0	0	0	0	1	0	1	.000	.333	.000	-1	0	0-0	1.000	1	151	0	/S		0.0
Total	3	69	213	17	47	4	0	0	14	16	2	28	.221	.281	.239	52	-13	1-0	.902	-18	81	85	S57,2b2		-2.9

BRICKELL, FRITZ   Fritz Darrell B3.19.1935 Wichita KS D10.15.1965 Wichita KS BR/TR/5-5.5/157* d4.30 f-Fred

YEAR	TM LG	G	AB	R	H	2B	3B	HR	RBI	BB-IB	HP	SO	AVG	OBP	SLG	AOPS	ABR	SB-CS	FA	FR	RNG	THR	GAMES AT POSITION	DL	BFW
1958	NY A	2	0	0	0	0	0	0	0	0-0	0	—	—	—	—	—	-1	0-0	1.000	0	165	0	2b2		0.0
1959	NY A	18	39	4	10	1	0	1	4	1-0	0	10	.256	.275	.359	75	-2	0-0	.925	-1	108	46	S15,2b3		-0.1
1961	LA A	21	49	3	6	0	0	0	3	6-0	0	9	.122	.218	.122	-6	-7	0-0	.901	-1	86	123	S17		-0.7
Total	3	41	88	7	16	1	0	1	7	7-0	0	19	.182	.242	.227	26	-9	0-0	.911	-1	96	85	S32,2b5		-0.8

BRICKELL, FRED   George Frederick B11.9.1906 Saffordville KS D4.8.1961 Wichita KS BL/TR/5-7/160 d8.19 s-Fritz

YEAR	TM LG	G	AB	R	H	2B	3B	HR	RBI	BB-IB	HP	SO	AVG	OBP	SLG	AOPS	ABR	SB-CS	FA	FR	RNG	THR	GAMES AT POSITION	DL	BFW
1926	Pit N	24	55	11	19	3	1	0	4	3	2	6	.345	.400	.436	119	2	0	.920	1	88	279	O14L		0.2
1927	†Pit N	32	21	6	6	1	0	1	4	1	0	0	.286	.318	.476	103	0	0	1.000	0	128	0	O3(0/1/2)		0.0
1928	Pit N	81	202	34	65	4	4	3	41	20	0	18	.322	.383	.426	107	2	5	.958	3	108	157	O50(44/0/8)		0.1
1929	Pit N	60	118	13	37	4	2	0	17	7	0	12	.314	.352	.381	80	-4	3	1.000	2	110	151	O27(14/0/13)		-0.3
1930	Pit N	68	219	36	65	9	3	1	14	15	0	20	.297	.342	.379	74	-9	3	.951	-1	102	73	O61(11/50/0)		-1.1
	Phi N	53	240	33	59	12	6	0	17	13	2	21	.246	.290	.346	49	-20	1	.963	2	104	135	O53C		-1.9
	Year	121	459	69	124	21	9	1	31	28	2	41	.270	.315	.362	61	-30	4	.958	1	103	105	O114(11/103/0)		-3.0
1931	Phi N	130	514	77	130	14	5	1	31	42	5	39	.253	.316	.305	63	-26	5	.978	0	103	79	O122C		-3.0
1932	Phi N	45	66	9	22	6	1	0	2	4	2	5	.333	.389	.455	112	2	2	.935	1	99	230	O12(1/11/0)		0.2
1933	Phi N	8	13	2	4	1	0	0	1	1	0	1	.308	.357	.538	136	1	0	1.000	1	130	354	O4L		0.1
Total	8	501	1448	221	407	54	23	6	131	106	11	121	.281	.335	.363	75	-52	19	.967	9	104	119	O346(88/237/23)		-5.7

BRICKLEY, GEORGE   George Vincent B7.19.1894 Everett MA D2.23.1947 Everett MA BR/TR/5-9/180 d9.26

YEAR	TM LG	G	AB	R	H	2B	3B	HR	RBI	BB-IB	HP	SO	AVG	OBP	SLG	AOPS	ABR	SB-CS	FA	FR	RNG	THR	GAMES AT POSITION	DL	BFW
1913	Phi A	5	12	0	2	1	0	0	1	0	0		.167	.231	.333	66	-0		1.000	-0	66	0	O4R		-0.1

BRIDEWESER, JIM   James Ehrenfeld B2.13.1927 Lancaster OH D8.25.1989 El Toro CA BR/TR/6-0/165* d9.29 Col USC

YEAR	TM LG	G	AB	R	H	2B	3B	HR	RBI	BB-IB	HP	SO	AVG	OBP	SLG	AOPS	ABR	SB-CS	FA	FR	RNG	THR	GAMES AT POSITION	DL	BFW
1951	NY A	2	8	1	3	0	0	0	0	0	0	1	.375	.375	.375	107	-0		.818	-0	87	225	S2		0.0
1952	NY A	42	38	12	10	1	0	0	2	3	0	5	.263	.317	.263	67	-2	0-0	.935	1	132	94	S22,2b4/3		-0.1
1953	NY A	7	3	3	3	0	1	0	3	1	0	0	1.000	1.000	1.667	631	2	0-0	.833	-0	0	0	S3		0.2
1954	Bal A	73	204	18	54	7	2	0	12	15	1	27	.265	.314	.319	81	-6	1-1	.944	-8	95	89	S48,2b19		-1.0
1955	Chi A	34	58	6	12	3	2	0	4	3-0	0	7	.207	.246	.328	52	-4	0-0	.949	3	108	142	S26,3b3,2b2		0.0
1956	Chi A	10	11	0	2	1	0	0	1	0-0	1	3	.182	.250	.273	47	-1	0-0	.938	-0	110	58	S10		-0.1

YEAR	TM LG	G	AB	R	H	2B	3B	HR	RBI	BB-IB	HP	SO	AVG	OBP	SLG	AOPS	ABR	SB-CS	FA	FR	RNG	THR	GAMES AT POSITION	DL	BFW
	Det A	70	156	23	34	4	0	0	10	20-2	0	19	.218	.307	.244	47	-12	3-1	.987	6	113	117	S32,2b31,3b4		-0.2
	Year	80	167	23	36	5	0	0	11	20-2	1	22	.216	.303	.246	46	-13	3-1	.979	5	112	105	S42,2b31,3b4		-0.3
1957	Bal A	91	142	16	38	7	1	1	18	21-2	0	16	.268	.362	.352	102	1	2-0	.943	-0	98	112	S74,3b3/2		0.5
Total	7	329	620	79	156	22	6	1	50	63-4	2	78	.252	.322	.311	75	-22	6-2	.946	-0	101	108	S217,2b57,3b11		-0.7

BRIDGES, ROCKY Everett Lamar B8.7.1927 Refugio TX BR/TR/5-8/175* d4.17 C7

YEAR	TM LG	G	AB	R	H	2B	3B	HR	RBI	BB-IB	HP	SO	AVG	OBP	SLG	AOPS	ABR	SB-CS	FA	FR	RNG	THR	GAMES AT POSITION	DL	BFW
1951	Bro N	63	134	13	34	7	0	1	15	10	0	10	.254	.306	.328	69	-6	0-0	.871	-1	98	148	3b40,2b10,S9		-0.6
1952	Bro N	51	56	9	11	3	0	0	2	7	0	9	.196	.286	.250	49	-4	0-1	.986	6	112	162	2b24,S13,3b6		0.3
1953	Cin N	122	432	52	98	13	2	1	21	37	0	42	.227	.288	.273	47	-34	6-3	.976	14	106	122	2b115,S6,3b3		-1.1
1954	Cin N	53	52	4	12	1	0	0	2	7	0	7	.231	.322	.250	50	-4	0-1	1.000	6	122	73	S20,2b19,3b13		0.3
1955	Cin N	95	168	20	48	4	0	1	18	15-2	0	19	.286	.341	.327	75	-6	1-1	.965	4	106	95	3b59,S26,2b9		-0.1
1956	Cin N	71	19	9	4	0	0	1	4	4-0	0	3	.211	.348	.211	52	-1	1-2	.966	3	97	85	3b51,2b8,S7/OL		0.2
1957	Cin N	5	1	1	0	0	0	0	0	1-0	0	1	.000	.500	.000	46	0	0-0	1.000	-1	0	0	2b2/S3		-0.1
	Was A	120	391	40	89	17	2	3	47	40-4	2	32	.228	.298	.304	67	-17	0-2	.971	23	111	93	S108,2b14/3		1.5
1958	Was A☆	116	377	38	99	14	3	5	28	27-1	3	32	.263	.315	.355	86	-8	0-3	.976	9	105	97	S112,2b3,3b3		1.0
1959	Det A	116	381	38	102	16	3	3	35	30-2	1	35	.268	.320	.349	80	-10	1-2	.952	-1	93	110	S110,2b5		-0.3
1960	Det A	10	5	0	1	0	0	0	0	0	0	0	.200	.200	.200	8	-1	0-0	1.000	1	126	0	3b7,S3		0.0
	Cle A	10	27	1	9	0	0	0	3	1-1	0	2	.333	.357	.333	91	0	0-0	1.000	2	127	81	S7,3b3		0.2
	Year	20	32	1	10	0	0	0	3	1-1	0	2	.313	.333	.313	76	-1	0-0	1.000	3	120	114	3b10,S10		0.2
	StL N	3	0	0	0	0	0	0	0	0	0	0	—	—	—	—	0	0-0	1.000	1	80	360	2b3		0.1
1961	LA A	84	229	20	55	5	1	2	15	26-0	1	37	.240	.320	.297	59	-13	1-0	.988	5	105	64	2b58,S25,3b4		-0.1
Total	11	919	2272	245	562	81	16	16	187	205-10	7	229	.247	.310	.313		-104	10-15	.968	71	104	99	S447,2b270,3b191/OL		1.3

BRIDWELL, AL Albert Henry B1.4.1884 Friendship OH D1.23.1969 Portsmouth OH BL/TR/5-9/170 d4.16 OF(3/2/14)

YEAR	TM LG	G	AB	R	H	2B	3B	HR	RBI	BB-IB	HP	SO	AVG	OBP	SLG	AOPS	ABR	SB-CS	FA	FR	RNG	THR	GAMES AT POSITION	DL	BFW
1905	Cin N	82	254	17	64	3	1	0	17	19		2	.252	.309	.272	66	-10	8	.944	4	105	122	3b43,O18(3/2/13),2b7,S5/1		-0.6
1906	Bos N	120	459	41	104	9	1	0	22	44	2		.227	.297	.251	73	-14	9	.930	18	104	101	S119/OR		0.9
1907	Bos N	140	509	49	111	8	2	0	26	61	6		.218	.309	.242	73	-13	17	.942	5	102	111	S140		-0.5
1908	NY N	147	467	53	133	14	4	0	46	52	6		.285	.364	.319	113	10	20	.933	9	103	98	S147		2.7
1909	NY N	145	476	59	140	11	5	0	55	67	4		.294	.386	.338	123	16	32	.940	2	99	115	S145		2.5
1910	NY N	142	492	74	136	15	7	0	48	73	4	23	.276	.374	.335	107	8	14	.946	4	95	96	S141		1.7
1911	NY N	76	263	28	71	10	1	0	31	33	3	10	.270	.358	.316	86	-3	8	.917	5	104	96	S76		0.6
	Bos N	51	182	29	53	5	0	0	10	33	1	8	.291	.403	.319	95	1	2	.950	-4	100	83	S51		0.0
	Year	127	445	57	124	15	1	0	41	66	4	18	.279	.377	.317	90	-2	10	.929	0	102	91	S127		0.6
1912	Bos N	31	106	6	25	5	1	0	14	5		5	.236	.270	.302	55	-7	2	.936	-5	89	112	S31		-1.0
1913	Chi N	136	405	35	97	6	5	0	37	74	1	28	.240	.358	.291	87	-4	12-16	.948	3	100	96	S136		0.5
1914	StL F	117	381	46	90	6	5	1	33	71	2	18	.236	.359	.286	73	-17	9	.944	-4	96	96	S103,2b11		-1.4
1915	StL F	65	175	20	41	3	2	0	9	25	1	6	.229	.328	.269	65	-10	6	.952	1	104	94	2b42,3b15/1		-0.9
Total	11	1252	4169	457	1064	95	32	2	348	557	32	98	.255	.347	.295	89	-43	136-16	.939	36	100	102	S1094,2b60,3b58,O19R,1b2		4.5

BRIEF, BUNNY Anthony Vincent (b Anthony John Grzeszkowski) B7.3.1892 Remus MI D2.11.1963 Milwaukee WI BR/TR/6-0/185 d9.22

YEAR	TM LG	G	AB	R	H	2B	3B	HR	RBI	BB-IB	HP	SO	AVG	OBP	SLG	AOPS	ABR	SB-CS	FA	FR	RNG	THR	GAMES AT POSITION	DL	BFW
1912	StL A	15	42	9	13	3	0	0	5	6	1		.310	.408	.381	131	2	2	.826	-1	109	0	O9L,1b4		0.1
1913	StL A	85	258	24	56	11	6	1	26	21	3	46	.217	.284	.318	78	-8	3	.986	-1	93	122	1b62,O8L		-1.2
1915	Chi A	48	154	13	33	6	2	2	17	16	4	28	.214	.305	.318	84	-3	8-6	.986	-2	86	104	1b46		-0.7
1917	Pit N	36	115	15	25	5	1	2	11	15	2	21	.217	.318	.330	96	0	4	.988	2	121	107	1b34		0.1
Total	4	184	569	61	127	25	9	5	59	58	10	95	.223	.306	.325	87	-9	17-6	.987	-3	98	114	1b146,O17L		-1.7

BRIGGS, CHARLIE Charles R. B9.1860 Batavia IL D3.10.1920 Seattle WA 5-7/170 d5.2

YEAR	TM LG	G	AB	R	H	2B	3B	HR	RBI	BB-IB	HP	SO	AVG	OBP	SLG	AOPS	ABR	SB-CS	FA	FR	RNG	THR	GAMES AT POSITION	DL	BFW
1884	CP U	49	182	29	31	8	2	1		11			.170	.218	.253	42	-18		.814	-6	69	79	O37(3/28/6),2b12,S2		-2.2

BRIGGS, DAN Dan Lee B11.18.1952 Scotia CA BL/TL/6-0/180* [AnaA70 2/34] d9.10

YEAR	TM LG	G	AB	R	H	2B	3B	HR	RBI	BB-IB	HP	SO	AVG	OBP	SLG	AOPS	ABR	SB-CS	FA	FR	RNG	THR	GAMES AT POSITION	DL	BFW
1975	Cal A	13	31	-3	7	1	0	1	3	2-0	0	6	.226	.273	.355	82	-1	0-2	.953	-1	36	111	1b6,O5L,D2		-0.3
1976	Cal A	77	248	19	53	13	2	1	14	13-3	1	47	.214	.254	.294	65	-12	0-3	.993	1	101	122	1b44,O40(2/32/9)/D		-1.7
1977	Cal A	59	74	6	12	2	0	1	4	8-1	0	14	.162	.241	.230	31	-7	0-0	.993	0	110	75	1b45,O13(0/12/1)		-0.8
1978	Cle A	15	49	4	8	0	1	1	4	4-0	0	9	.163	.226	.265	38	-4	0-0	1.000	2	120	90	O15R		-0.4
1979	SD N	104	227	34	47	4	3	8	30	18-5	5	45	.207	.277	.357	77	-9	2-1	.986	5	137	72	1b50,O44(25/16/3)		-0.7
1981	Mon N	9	11	0	1	0	0	0	0	0-0	0	3	.091	.091	.091	-47	-2	0-1	1.000	0	161	81	1b3,O3(1/2/1)		-0.3
1982	Chi N	48	48	1	6	0	0	1	0	0-0	1	9	.125	.143	.125	-24	-8	0-0	.875	1	77	800	O10(8/1/1),1b4		-0.8
Total	7	325	688	67	134	20	6	12	53	45-9	7	133	.195	.249	.294	55	-43	2-7	.989	8	114	94	1b152,O130(41/63/30),D3		-5.0

BRIGGS, GRANT Grant B3.16.1865 Pittsburgh PA D5.31.1928 Pittsburgh PA 5-11/170 d4.17

YEAR	TM LG	G	AB	R	H	2B	3B	HR	RBI	BB-IB	HP	SO	AVG	OBP	SLG	AOPS	ABR	SB-CS	FA	FR	RNG	THR	GAMES AT POSITION	DL	BFW
1890	Syr AA	86	316	44	57	6	5	0	21	16	1		.180	.222	.231	37	-26	7	.928	-10	78	101	C46,O33(4/25/4),3b5,S4		-2.9
1891	Lou AA	1	4	0	1	0	0	0	0	0	0	0	.250	.250	.250	44	0	0	1.000	-0	79	103	/C		0.0
1892	StL N	22	55	2	4	1	0	0	1	5	1	14	.073	.164	.091	-24	-8	2	.902	-8	96	81	C15,O8(2/1/5)		-1.5
1895	Lou N	1	3	0	0	0	0	0	0	0	0	1	.000	.000	.000	-99	-1	0	1.000	-0	108	0	/C		-0.1
Total	4	110	378	46	62	7	5	0	22	21	2	15	.164	.212	.209	27	-35	9	.925	-19	82	96	C63,O41(6/26/9),3b5,S4		-4.5

BRIGGS, JOHNNY John Edward B3.10.1944 Paterson NJ BL/TL/6-1/195* d4.17 Col Seton Hall

YEAR	TM LG	G	AB	R	H	2B	3B	HR	RBI	BB-IB	HP	SO	AVG	OBP	SLG	AOPS	ABR	SB-CS	FA	FR	RNG	THR	GAMES AT POSITION	DL	BFW
1964	Phi N	61	66	16	17	2	0	1	6	9-0	0	12	.258	.347	.333	94	0	1-1	.957	1	114	164	O19(9/9/1)/1		0.0
1965	Phi N	93	229	47	54	9	4	4	23	42-1	0	44	.236	.349	.362	104	3	3-2	.982	-3	95	66	O66(4/62/0)		-0.2
1966	Phi N	81	255	43	72	13	5	10	23	41-3	0	55	.282	.380	.490	140	15	3-2	.977	-5	90	70	O69(2/68/0)		0.9
1967	Phi N	106	332	47	77	12	4	9	30	41-1	0	72	.232	.315	.373	96	-2	3-5	.979	-1	104	41	O94(31/65/1)		-0.8
1968	Phi N	110	338	36	86	13	1	9	31	58-4	1	72	.254	.364	.361	119	11	8-5	.968	-3	100	24	O65(10/34/21),1b36		0.4
1969	Phi N	124	361	51	86	20	3	12	46	64-3	0	78	.238	.351	.410	116	10	9-6	.971	4	112	107	O108(76/32/12),1b2		0.9
1970	Phi N	110	341	43	92	15	7	9	47	39-5	0	65	.270	.342	.434	110	4	5-4	.980	7	120	113	O95(79/11/15)	32	0.6
1971	Phi N	10	22	3	4	1	0	0	3	6-1	0	2	.182	.357	.227	68	-1	0-0	.846	4	89	246	O8L		-0.1
	Mil A	125	375	51	99	11	1	21	59	71-7	1	79	.264	.378	.467	141	22	1-2	.958	5	113	127	O65(55/0/11),1b60		2.0
1972	Mil A	135	418	58	111	14	1	21	65	54-4	1	77	.266	.347	.455	141	21	1-2	.980	0	104	82	O106(98/12/0),1b28		1.5
1973	Mil A	142	488	78	120	20	7	18	57	87-6	2	83	.246	.361	.426	123	17	15-9	.968	3	101	90	O137L/D		1.2
1974	Mil A	154	554	72	140	30	8	17	73	71-2	0	102	.253	.337	.428	119	14	9-7	.973	0	98	91	O149(148/1/0),D2		0.6
1975	Mil A	28	74	12	22	1	0	3	5	20-0	0	13	.297	.447	.432	148	6	0-2	.962	3	110	204	O21L/D		0.7
	Min A	87	264	44	61	9	2	7	39	60-10	0	41	.231	.371	.360	107	6	6-2	.983	9	165	97	1b49,O35(20/0/17),D2		0.9
	Year	115	338	56	83	10	2	10	44	80-10	0	54	.246	.388	.376	116	11	6-4	.983	11	168	134	O56(41/0/17),1b49,D3		1.6
Total	12	1366	4117	601	1041	170	43	139	507	663-47	5	785	.253	.355	.416	120	125	64-49	.973	19	104	88	O1037(698/294/78),1b176,D6	80	8.6

BRIGHT, HARRY Harry James B9.22.1929 Kansas City MO D3.13.2000 Sacramento CA BR/TR/6-0/190* d8.7

YEAR	TM LG	G	AB	R	H	2B	3B	HR	RBI	BB-IB	HP	SO	AVG	OBP	SLG	AOPS	ABR	SB-CS	FA	FR	RNG	THR	GAMES AT POSITION	DL	BFW
1958	Pit N	15	24	4	6	1	0	1	3	1-0	0	6	.250	.269	.417	84	-1	0-0	1.000	0	112	0	3b7		-0.1
1959	Pit N	40	48	4	12	1	0	3	8	5-0	0	10	.250	.321	.458	105	0	0-0	1.000	-1	81	0	O4(3/0/1),3b3/2		-0.1
1960	Pit N	4	4	0	0	0	0	0	0	0-0	0	2	.000	.000	.000	-99	-1	0-0	—	0			/H		-0.1
1961	Was A	72	183	20	44	6	0	4	21	19-1	0	25	.240	.310	.339	75	-7	0-0	.928	7	123	174	3b40,C8/2		0.0
1962	Was A	113	392	55	107	15	4	17	67	26-0	7	51	.273	.319	.462	109	3	2-1	.989	0	108	106	1b99,C3/3		-0.3
1963	Cin N	1	1	0	0	0	0	0	0	0-0	0	1	.000	.000	.000	-97	0	0-0	1.000	0	0	0	0/1		0.0
†NY A		60	157	15	37	7	0	7	23	13-1	1	31	.236	.297	.414	98	-1	0-0	.985	-4	42	159	1b35,3b12		-0.7
1964	NY A	4	5	0	1	0	0	0	0	1-0	0	1	.200	.333	.200	52	0	0-0	1.000	-0	0	0	1b2		-0.1
1965	Chi N	27	25	1	7	1	0	0	4	0-0	0	8	.280	.269	.320	67	-1	0-0	—	0			/H		-0.1
Total	8	336	839	99	214	31	4	32	126	65-2	3	133	.255	.309	.416	96	-8	2-3	.988	2	92	117	1b137,3b63,C11,O4(3/0/1),2b2		-1.5

BRILEY, GREG Gregory "Peewee" B5.24.1965 Greenville NC BL/TR/5-8/165(165-180) [SeaA86 S1/12] d6.27 Col North Carolina St.

YEAR	TM LG	G	AB	R	H	2B	3B	HR	RBI	BB-IB	HP	SO	AVG	OBP	SLG	AOPS	ABR	SB-CS	FA	FR	RNG	THR	GAMES AT POSITION	DL	BFW
1988	Sea A	13	36	6	9	2	0	1	4	5-1	0	6	.250	.333	.389	99	0	0-1	.929	-2	64	0	O11L		-0.3
1989	Sea A	115	394	52	105	22	4	13	52	39-1	5	82	.266	.336	.442	115	8	11-5	.958	1	96	92	O105(96/0/10),2b10,D2		0.7
1990	Sea A	125	337	40	83	18	2	5	29	37-0	1	48	.246	.319	.356	88	-5	16-4	.989	-1	100	67	O107(43/0/67),D4		-0.7
1991	Sea A	139	381	39	99	17	3	2	26	27-0	1	51	.260	.307	.336	78	-12	23-11	.980	-4	93	82	O125(94/4/46)/23D		-1.8
1992	Sea A	86	200	18	55	10	0	5	12	13-0	1	34	.275	.290	.400	91	-3	3-3	.967	-5	98	74	O42(27/13/4),D12,2b4,3b4	48	-0.8
1993	Fla N	120	170	17	33	6	0	3	12	12-0	1	42	.194	.250	.282	40	-15	6-2	.986	1	107	80	O67(32/1/36)		-1.5
Total	6	598	1518	172	384	75	9	29	135	124-2	8	260	.253	.310	.372	88	-27	65-25	.975	-10	96	76	O457(303/18/163),D20,2b15,3b5	48	-4.4

BRINKER, BILL William Hutchinson "Dode" B8.30.1883 Warrensburg MO D2.5.1965 Arcadia CA BB/TR/6-1/190 d4.24 Col Washington

YEAR	TM LG	G	AB	R	H	2B	3B	HR	RBI	BB-IB	HP	SO	AVG	OBP	SLG	AOPS	ABR	SB-CS	FA	FR	RNG	THR	GAMES AT POSITION	DL	BFW
1912	Phi N	9	18	1	4	1	0	0	2	2		3	.222	.300	.278	55	-1	0	.778	-1	84	0	3b2,O2(1/1/0)		-0.2

BRINKMAN, CHUCK
Charles Ernest B9.16.1944 Cincinnati OH BR/TR/6-1/185* [ChiA66 16/318] d7.10 b-Ed Col Ohio St.

YEAR	TM LG	G	AB	R	H	2B	3B	HR	RBI	BB-IB	HP	SO	AVG	OBP	SLG	AOPS	ABR	SB-CS	FA	FR	RNG	THR	GAMES AT POSITION	DL	BFW
1969	Chi A	14	15	2	1	0	0	0		1-0	0	5	.067	.125	.067	-43	-3	0-0	1.000	-1	103	57	C14		-0.4
1970	Chi A	9	20	4	5	1	0	0		3-0	0	3	.250	.348	.300	77	0	0-0	.974	0	303	101	C9		0.0
1971	Chi A	15	20	0	4	0	0	0	1	3-1	0	5	.200	.304	.200	44	-1	0-0	1.000	-2	33	196	C14		-0.3
1972	Chi A	35	52	1	7	0	0	0	0	4-0	0	7	.135	.196	.135	-0	-6	0-0	.985	3	80	150	C33		-0.3
1973	Chi A	63	139	13	26	6	0	1	10	11-0	1	37	.187	.252	.252	41	-11	0-0	.987	4	105	114	C63		-0.5
1974	Chi A	8	14	1	2	0	0	0		1-0	0	3	.143	.200	.143	-0	-2	0-0	1.000	-2	73	57	C8	15	-0.4
	Pit N	4	7	1	1	0	0	0		1-0	0	3	.143	.125	.143	-20	-1	0-0	1.000	-1	157	0	C4		-0.2
Total	6	148	267	22	46	7	0	1	12	23-1	1	60	.172	.240	.210	28	-24	0-0	.988	1	109	117	C145	15	-2.1

BRINKMAN, ED
Edwin Albert B12.8.1941 Cincinnati OH BR/TR/6-0/170* d9.6 C8 b-Chuck Col Cincinnati

YEAR	TM LG	G	AB	R	H	2B	3B	HR	RBI	BB-IB	HP	SO	AVG	OBP	SLG	AOPS	ABR	SB-CS	FA	FR	RNG	THR	GAMES AT POSITION	DL	BFW
1961	Was A	4	11	0	1	0	0	0	0	0-1	0	1	.091	.167	.091	-30	-2	0-0	.889	-0	104	166	3b3		-0.2
1962	Was A	54	133	8	22	7	1	0	4	11-0	0	28	.165	.228	.233	25	-14	1-0	.942	-8	86	101	S38,3b10		-1.9
1963	Was A	145	514	44	117	20	3	7	45	31-4	0	86	.228	.276	.319	67	-24	5-3	.950	4	111	109	S143		-0.7
1964	Was A	132	447	54	100	20	4	8	34	26-1	4	99	.224	.271	.336	68	-20	2-2	.969	2	104	104	S125		-0.8
1965	Was A	154	444	35	82	13	2	5	35	38-7	2	82	.185	.251	.257	46	-32	1-2	.964	0	95	93	S150		-2.2
1966	Was A	158	582	42	133	18	9	7	48	29-4	0	105	.229	.263	.326	70	-25	7-9	.965	7	106	94	S158		-0.6
1967	Was A	109	320	21	60	9	2	1	18	24-1	4	58	.188	.252	.237	47	-21	1-3	.979	2	108	100	S109		-1.2
1968	Was A	77	193	12	36	3	0	0	6	19-5	0	31	.187	.259	.202	43	-13	0-0	.967	-4	105	74	S74,2b2/OL		-1.4
1969	Was A	151	576	71	153	18	5	2	43	50-3	5	42	.266	.328	.325	88	-9	2-2	.976	20	113	104	S150		2.9
1970	Was A	158	625	63	164	17	2	1	40	60-0	5	41	.262	.330	.301	79	-17	8-9	.974	31	117	105	S157		3.3
1971	Det A	159	527	40	120	18	2	1	37	44-7	1	54	.228	.293	.275	60	-27	1-4	.980	4	102	94	S159		-0.5
1972	†Det A	156	516	42	105	19	1	6	49	38-9	3	51	.203	.259	.279	59	-26	0-0	.990	2	98	89	S156		-0.6
1973	Det A★	162	515	55	122	16	4	7	40	34-1	1	79	.237	.284	.324	67	-24	0-1	.968	-17	90	89	S162		-2.2
1974	Det A	153	502	55	111	15	3	14	54	29-0	1	71	.221	.266	.347	73	-19	2-0	.972	6	101	89	S151,3b2		0.6
1975	StL N	28	75	6	18	4	0	1	6	7-2	1	10	.240	.306	.333	76	-2	0-0	.948	0	97	108	S24		0.0
	Tex N	1	2	0	0	0	0	0	0	0-0	0	1	.000	.000	.000	-99	-1	0-0	1.000	-0	82	0	/3		-0.1
	NY A	44	63	2	11	4	1	0	2	3-0	1	6	.175	.224	.270	39	-5	0-0	.933	-6	84	112	S39,2b3,3b3		-0.9
	Year	45	65	2	11	4	1	0	2	3-0	1	7	.169	.217	.262	35	-6	0-0	.933	-6	84	112	S39,3b4,2b3		-1.0
Total	15	1845	6045	550	1355	201	38	60	461	444-44	40	845	.224	.280	.300	65	-281	30-35	.970	46	103	97	S1795,3b19,2b5/OL		-6.5

BRINKOPF, LEON
Leon Clarence B10.20.1926 Cape Girardeau MO D7.2.1998 Cape Girardeau MO BR/TR/5-11.5/185 d4.18

YEAR	TM LG	G	AB	R	H	2B	3B	HR	RBI	BB-IB	HP	SO	AVG	OBP	SLG	AOPS	ABR	SB-CS	FA	FR	RNG	THR	GAMES AT POSITION	DL	BFW
1952	Chi N	9	22	1	4	0	0	0	2	4	0	5	.182	.308	.182	38	-2	0-0	.955	-1	110	30	S6		-0.3

BRIODY, FATTY
Charles F. "Alderman" B8.13.1858 Lansingburg NY D6.22.1903 Chicago IL TR/5-8.5/190 d6.16

YEAR	TM LG	G	AB	R	H	2B	3B	HR	RBI	BB	HP	SO	AVG	OBP	SLG	AOPS	ABR	SB-CS	FA	FR	RNG	THR	GAMES AT POSITION	DL	BFW
1880	Tro N	1	4	0	0	0	0	0	0	0			.000	.000	.000	-95	-1		.700	-1			/C		-0.2
1882	Cle N	53	194	30	50	13	0	0	13	9		13	.258	.291	.325	101	1		.902	1			C53		0.6
1883	Cle N	40	145	23	34	5	1	0	10	3		13	.234	.250	.283	62	-7		.900	5			C33,2b4,1b2/3		0.1
1884	Cle N	43	148	17	25	6	0	1	12	6		19	.169	.201	.230	34	-11		.922	10			C42/OR		0.3
	Cin U	22	89	11	30	2	2	0		1			.337	.344	.404	117	-1		.943	12			C22		1.1
1885	StL N	62	215	14	42	9	0	1	17	12		23	.195	.238	.251	62	-8		.893	-7			C60/OC32		-1.0
1886	KC N	56	215	14	51	10	3	0	29	3		35	.237	.248	.312	65	-10	0	.919	-1			C54,O2(0/1/1)/1		-0.6
1887	Det N	33	128	24	29	6	1	1	26	9	1	10	.227	.283	.313	63	-7	6	.907	6			C33		0.2
1888	KC AA	13	48	1	10	1	0	0	8	1	0		.208	.224	.229	43	-3	0	.896	-3			C13		-0.5
Total	8	323	1186	134	271	52	7	3	115	44	1	113	.228	.257	.292	68	-47	6	.910	22			C311,2b5,O4(0/2/2),1b3,3b2		-0.5

BRISTOW, GEORGE
George T. B5.1870 Paw Paw IL TR d4.15

YEAR	TM LG	G	AB	R	H	2B	3B	HR	RBI	BB	HP	SO	AVG	OBP	SLG	AOPS	ABR	SB-CS	FA	FR	RNG	THR	GAMES AT POSITION	DL	BFW
1899	Cle N	3	8	0	1	1	0	0	0	0	1		.125	.222	.250	32	-1	0	1.000	1	279	0	O3(1/0/2)		0.0

BRITO, BERNARDO
Bernardo B12.4.1963 San Cristobal, D.R. BR/TR/6-1/190(190-210) d9.15

YEAR	TM LG	G	AB	R	H	2B	3B	HR	RBI	BB-IB	HP	SO	AVG	OBP	SLG	AOPS	ABR	SB-CS	FA	FR	RNG	THR	GAMES AT POSITION	DL	BFW
1992	Min A	8	14	1	2	1	0	0	2	0-0	0	4	.143	.133	.214	-1	-2	0-1	.750	-0	86	0	O3L/D		-0.3
1993	Min A	27	54	8	13	0	0	4	9	1-0	1	20	.241	.255	.500	97	-1	0-0	1.000	1	97	272	O10L,D7		-0.3
1995	Min A	5	5	1	1	0	0	1	1	0-0	1	3	.200	.333	.800	182	1	0-0	—	0			D3		0.0
Total	3	40	73	10	16	3	0	5	12	1-0	1	27	.219	.237	.466	85	-2	0-1	.941	0	95	211	O13L,D11		-0.4

BRITO, JORGE
Jorge Manuel (Uceta) B6.22.1966 Moncion, D.R. BR/TR/6-1/190* d4.30

YEAR	TM LG	G	AB	R	H	2B	3B	HR	RBI	BB-IB	HP	SO	AVG	OBP	SLG	AOPS	ABR	SB-CS	FA	FR	RNG	THR	GAMES AT POSITION	DL	BFW
1995	Col N	18	51	5	11	3	0	0	7	2-0	1	17	.216	.259	.275	32	-5	1-0	.991	4	160	108	C18		0.0
1996	Col N	8	14	1	1	0	0	0	0	1-0	2	8	.071	.235	.071	-12	-2	0-0	1.000	3	97	64	C8	27	0.1
Total	2	26	65	6	12	3	0	0	7	3-0	3	25	.185	.254	.231	23	-7	1-0	.994	6	143	96	C26	27	0.1

BRITO, JUAN
Juan Ramon B11.7.1979 Santiago Rodriguez, D.R. BR/TR/5-11/205* d5.3

YEAR	TM LG	G	AB	R	H	2B	3B	HR	RBI	BB-IB	HP	SO	AVG	OBP	SLG	AOPS	ABR	SB-CS	FA	FR	RNG	THR	GAMES AT POSITION	DL	BFW
2002	KC A	9	23	1	7	2	0	0	1	0-0	0	3	.304	.304	.391	74	-1	0-0	.978	-1	53	230	C9		-0.1
2004	Ari N	54	171	17	35	7	0	3	12	9-1	1	41	.205	.246	.298	38	-16	1-0	.990	-0	82	146	C54		-1.2
Total	2	63	194	18	42	9	0	3	13	9-1	1	44	.216	.252	.309	42	-17	1-0	.989	-1	79	156	C63		-1.3

BRITO, TILSON
Tilson Manuel (Jimenez) B5.28.1972 Santo Domingo, D.R. BR/TR/6-0/175* d4.1

YEAR	TM LG	G	AB	R	H	2B	3B	HR	RBI	BB-IB	HP	SO	AVG	OBP	SLG	AOPS	ABR	SB-CS	FA	FR	RNG	THR	GAMES AT POSITION	DL	BFW
1996	Tor A	26	80	10	19	7	0	1	7	10-0	3	18	.237	.344	.363	79	-2	1-1	.956	-1	99	124	2b18,S5,D2		-0.1
1997	Tor A	49	126	9	28	3	0	0	8	9-0	2	28	.222	.281	.246	40	-11	1-0	.989	-2	96	103	2b25,3b17,S8		-1.1
	Oak A	17	46	8	13	2	1	2	6	1-0	0	10	.283	.298	.500	103			.920	2	124	151	3b10,S6,2b2	22	0.3
	Year	66	172	17	41	5	1	2	14	10-0	2	38	.238	.285	.314	57	-11	1-0	.961	-1	100	124	2b27,3b27,S14		-0.9
Total	2	92	252	27	60	12	1	3	21	20-0	5	56	.238	.305	.329	64	-13	2-1	.989	-1	100	124	2b45,3b27,S19,D2	22	-1.0

BRITTAIN, GUS
August Schuster B11.29.1909 Wilmington NC D2.16.1974 Wilmington NC BR/TR/5-10/192 d7.22

YEAR	TM LG	G	AB	R	H	2B	3B	HR	RBI	BB	HP	SO	AVG	OBP	SLG	AOPS	ABR	SB-CS	FA	FR	RNG	THR	GAMES AT POSITION	DL	BFW
1937	Cin N	3	6	1	0	0	0	0	0	0		3	.167	.167	.167	-10	-1	0	1.000	0	0	0	/C		-0.1

BRITTON, GIL
Stephen Gilbert B9.21.1891 Parsons KS D6.20.1983 Parsons KS BR/TR/5-10/160 d9.20

YEAR	TM LG	G	AB	R	H	2B	3B	HR	RBI	BB	HP	SO	AVG	OBP	SLG	AOPS	ABR	SB-CS	FA	FR	RNG	THR	GAMES AT POSITION	DL	BFW
1913	Pit N	3	12	0	0	0	0	0	0	0		2	.000	.000	.000	-99	-3	0	.824	-1	95	183	S3		-0.4

BROCK, GREG
Gregory Allen B6.14.1957 McMinnville OR BL/TR/6-3/205* [LAN79 13/336] d9.1 Col Wyoming

YEAR	TM LG	G	AB	R	H	2B	3B	HR	RBI	BB-IB	HP	SO	AVG	OBP	SLG	AOPS	ABR	SB-CS	FA	FR	RNG	THR	GAMES AT POSITION	DL	BFW
1982	LA N	18	17	1	2	1	0	0	1	1-1	0	5	.118	.167	.176	-4	-2	0-0	1.000	-0	0	0	1b3		-0.3
1983	†LA N	146	455	64	102	14	2	20	66	83-12	1	81	.224	.343	.396	105	5	5-1	.991	6	114	94	1b140		0.3
1984	LA N	88	271	33	61	6	0	14	34	39-3	0	37	.225	.319	.402	103	1	8-0	.995	7	129	99	1b83	26	0.5
1985	†LA N	129	438	64	110	19	0	21	66	54-4	0	72	.251	.332	.438	117	9	4-2	.994	5	113	97	1b122		0.7
1986	LA N	115	325	33	76	13	0	16	52	37-5	0	60	.234	.309	.422	108	2	2-5	.996	13	148	70	1b99	21	0.8
1987	Mil A	141	532	81	159	29	3	13	85	57-4	6	63	.299	.371	.438	110	10	5-4	.993	5	112	95	1b141	15	0.6
1988	Mil A	115	364	53	77	16	1	6	50	63-16	3	49	.212	.329	.310	80	-7	2-4	.993	10	135	110	1b114/D	46	-0.3
1989	Mil A	107	373	40	99	16	0	12	52	43-8	3	49	.265	.345	.405	112	6	6-1	.995	-4	87	106	1b100,D7	58	-0.3
1990	Mil A	123	367	42	91	23	0	7	50	43-9	2	45	.248	.324	.368	95	-1	4-2	.993	-4	89	96	1b115		-1.3
1991	Mil A	31	60	9	17	4	0	1	6	14-1	0	9	.283	.419	.400	130	4	1-1	1.000	-1	76	116	1b25		0.1
Total	10	1013	3202	420	794	141	6	110	462	434-63	15	469	.248	.338	.399	104	27	41-18	.994	37	114	96	1b942,D8	166	0.7

BROCK, JOHN
John Roy B10.16.1896 Hamilton IL D10.27.1951 Clayton MO BR/TR/5-6.5/165 d8.10

YEAR	TM LG	G	AB	R	H	2B	3B	HR	RBI	BB	HP	SO	AVG	OBP	SLG	AOPS	ABR	SB-CS	FA	FR	RNG	THR	GAMES AT POSITION	DL	BFW
1917	StL N	7	15	4	6	1	0	0	2	0		3	.400	.400	.467	170	1	2	.944	-0	140	92	C4		0.1
1918	StL N	27	52	9	11	2	0	0	4	3	0	10	.212	.255	.250	56	-3	5	.951	-2	81	137	C18/OR		-0.4
Total	2	34	67	13	17	3	0	0	6	3	0	13	.254	.286	.299	81	-2	7	.949	-2	93	128	C22/OR		-0.3

BROCK, LOU
Louis Clark B6.18.1939 El Dorado AR BL/TL/5-11.5/170* d9.10 HF1985 Col Southern A&M

YEAR	TM LG	G	AB	R	H	2B	3B	HR	RBI	BB-IB	HP	SO	AVG	OBP	SLG	AOPS	ABR	SB-CS	FA	FR	RNG	THR	GAMES AT POSITION	DL	BFW
1961	Chi N	4	11	1	1	0	0	0	0	1-0	0	3	.091	.167	.091	-29	-1	0-0	.750	-1	101	0	O3C		-0.3
1962	Chi N	123	434	73	114	24	7	9	35	35-4	3	96	.263	.319	.412	92	-5	16-7	.965	-3	98	101	O106C		-1.0
1963	Chi N	148	547	79	141	19	11	9	37	31-2	4	122	.258	.300	.382	91	-8	24-12	.973	10	112	160	O140R		-0.6
1964	Chi N	52	215	30	54	9	2	2	14	13-0	2	40	.251	.300	.340	77	-7	10-3	.959	-0	88	197	O52(0/2/51)		-0.9
	†StL N	103	419	81	146	21	9	12	44	27-0	2	87	.348	.387	.527	143	24	33-15	.949	2	103	102	O102(99/2/4)		2.3
	Year	155	634	111	200	30	11	14	58	40-0	4	127	.315	.358	.464	121	18	43-18	.953	3	98	136	O154(99/4/55)		1.4
1965	StL N	155	631	107	182	35	8	16	69	45-6	10	116	.288	.345	.445	110	9	63-27	.959	4	103	126	O153(150/2/7)		0.9
1966	StL N	156	643	94	183	24	12	15	46	31-6	3	134	.285	.320	.429	106	3	74-18	.936	-2	99	83	O154(122/0/34)		0.1
1967	†StL N★	159	689	113	206	32	12	21	76	24-6	6	109	.299	.327	.472	128	21	52-18	.956	2	102	121	O157L		2.1
1968	†StL N	159	660	92	184	46	14	6	51	46-7	3	124	.279	.328	.414	125	19	62-12	.952	1	105	88	O156L		2.3

YEAR	TM LG	G	AB	R	H	2B	3B	HR	RBI	BB-IB	HP	SO	AVG	OBP	SLG	AOPS	ABR	SB-CS	FA	FR	RNG	THR	GAMES AT POSITION	DL	BFW
1969	StL N	157	655	97	195	33	10	12	47	50-15	2	115	.298	.349	.434	117	14	**53**-14	.949	-3	94	81	O157L		0.9
1970	StL N	155	664	114	202	29	5	13	57	60-12	1	99	.304	.361	.422	106	6	51-15	.962	-7	91	78	O152(149/0/3)		-0.4
1971	StL N	157	640	**126**	200	37	7	7	61	76-5	1	107	.313	.385	.425	124	23	**64**-19	.951	-7	92	68	O157(156/0/1)		1.5
1972	StL N☆	153	621	81	193	26	8	3	42	47-12	1	93	.311	.359	.393	115	12	**63**-18	.952	-7	88	60	O149L		0.4
1973	StL N	160	650	110	193	29	8	7	63	71-15	0	112	.297	.364	.398	111	11	**70**-20	.963	-6	93	27	O159L		0.4
1974	StL N★	153	635	105	194	25	7	3	48	61-16	2	88	.306	.368	.381	110	9	**118**-33	.967	-4	93	73	O152L		1.1
1975	StL N★	136	528	78	163	27	6	3	47	38-6	1	64	.309	.359	.400	105	4	56-16	.966	-2	101	53	O128L		0.1
1976	StL N	133	498	73	150	24	5	4	67	35-7	1	75	.301	.344	.394	108	5	56-19	.983	-3	94	72	O123L		0.1
1977	StL N	141	489	69	133	22	6	2	46	30-2	2	74	.272	.317	.354	80	-14	35-24	.954	-6	91	29	O130L		-2.7
1978	StL N	92	298	31	66	9	0	0	12	17-2	0	29	.221	.263	.252	45	-22	17-5	.975	-5	86	36	O79L		-3.1
1979	StL N★	120	405	56	123	15	4	5	38	23-1	3	43	.304	.342	.398	100	0	21-12	.958	-4	84	100	O98L		-0.8
Total	19	2616	10332	1610	3023	486	141	149	900	761-124	49	1730	.293	.343	.410	108	102	938-307	.959	-40	96	85	O2507(2164/115/240)		2.4

BROCK, TARRIK Tarrik Jumaan B12.25.1973 Goleta CA BL/TL/6-3/185 [DetA91 2/59] d3.29

2000	Chi N	13	12	1	2	0	0	0	0	4-0	0	4	.167	.375	.167	44	-1	1-1	.889	-0	97	0	O10(9/2/0)		-0.1

BRODERICK, MATT Matthew Thomas B12.1.1877 Lattimer PA D2.26.1940 Freeland PA BR/TR/5-6.5/135 d5.1 Col Villanova

1903	Bro N	2	2	0	0	0	0	0	0	0-0	0		.000	.000	.000	-99	-1	0	1.000	0	0	1331	/2		0.0

BRODIE, STEVE Walter Scott B9.11.1868 Warrenton VA D10.30.1935 Baltimore MD BL/TR/5-11/180 d4.21

1890	Bos N	132	514	77	152	19	9	0	67	66	11	20	.296	.387	.368	111	9	29	**.953**	2	82	140	O132(2/19/114)		0.8
1891	Bos N	133	523	84	136	13	6	2	78	63	10	39	.260	.351	.319	85	-10	25	.951	8	122	**294**	O133(1/102/31)		-0.5
1892	StL N	154	602	85	153	10	9	4	60	52	4	31	.254	.318	.321	98	-2	28	.943	3	92	77	O137(1/121/17),2b16,3b2		-0.7
1893	StL N	107	469	71	149	16	8	2	79	33	11	16	.318	.376	.399	106	3	41	.951	5	112	181	O107(0/102/5)		0.1
	Bal N	25	97	18	35	7	2	0	19	12	3	2	.361	.446	.474	142	7	8	.963	-1	55	0	O25(2/24/0)		0.3
	Year	**132**	566	89	184	23	10	2	98	45	14	18	.325	.389	.412	112	10	49	.953	4	103	152	O132(2/126/5)		0.4
1894	†Bal N	129	573	134	210	25	11	3	113	18	13	8	.366	.399	.464	103	1	42	.950	-7	65	81	O129C		-1.1
1895	†Bal N	131	528	85	184	27	10	2	134	26	14	15	.348	.394	.449	114	10	35	.965	3	119	51	O131C		0.4
1896	†Bal N	132	516	98	153	19	11	2	87	36	18	17	.297	.363	.388	96	-3	25	.972	7	117	139	O132C		-0.4
1897	Pit N	100	370	47	108	7	12	2	53	25	7		.292	.348	.392	99	-2	11	**.983**	2	83	39	O100C		-0.5
1898	Pit N	42	156	15	41	5	0	0	21	6	3		.263	.303	.295	73	-6	3	.958	2	67	76	O42C		-0.6
	Bal N	23	98	12	30	3	2	0	19	5	1		.306	.346	.378	105	0	3	.923	1	144	0	O23C		0.0
	Year	65	254	27	71	8	2	0	40	11	4		.280	.320	.327	86	-5	6	.946	3	95	48	O65C		-0.6
1899	Bal N	137	531	82	164	26	1	3	87	31	23		.309	.373	.379	101	2	19	**.979**	-1	73	95	O137(0/136/1)		-0.7
1901	Bal A	83	306	41	95	6	6	2	41	25	8		.310	.378	.389	108	4	9	.963	-2	40	0	O83(11/72/0)		-0.2
1902	NY N	110	420	37	118	8	2	3	42	22	6		.281	.326	.331	104	1	11	.953	7	157	**215**	O110C		0.4
Total	12	1438	5703	886	1728	191	89	25	900	420	132	148	.303	.365	.381	102	14	289	.959	28	97	119	O1421(17/1243/168),2b16,3b2		-2.7

BROGNA, RICO Rico Joseph B4.18.1970 Turners Falls MA BL/TL/6-2/205* [DetA88 1/26] d8.8

1992	Det A	9	26	3	5	1	0	1	3	3-0	1	5	.192	.276	.346	72	-1	0-0	.982	0	126	151	1b8,D2		-0.1
1994	NY N	39	131	16	46	11	2	7	20	6-0	0	29	.351	.380	.626	158	11	1-0	.997	1	110	112	1b35		0.8
1995	NY N	134	495	72	143	27	2	22	76	39-7	2	111	.289	.342	.485	119	12	0-0	**.998**	0	100	101	1b131		0.1
1996	NY N	55	188	18	48	10	1	7	30	19-1	0	50	.255	.318	.431	102	0	0-0	.996	-2	84	114	1b52	102	-0.7
1997	Phi N	148	543	68	137	36	1	20	81	33-4	0	116	.252	.293	.433	99	-11	12-3	.994	9	114	89	1b145		-1.3
1998	Phi N	153	565	77	150	36	4	20	104	49-8	0	125	.265	.319	.446	100	-1	7-7	.996	13	126	89	1b151		-0.2
1999	Phi N	157	619	90	172	29	4	24	102	54-7	2	132	.278	.336	.454	97	-5	8-5	.995	8	120	96	1b157		-1.0
2000	Phi N	38	129	12	32	14	0	1	13	7-1	2	28	.248	.295	.380	70	-6	1-0	.996	-1	83	86	1b34	70	-0.9
	Bos A	43	56	8	11	3	0	1	8	3-0	0	13	-.196	.237	.304	35	-6	0-0	.983	-2	74	87	1b37,D2		-0.8
2001	Atl N	72	206	15	51	9	0	3	21	14-1	1	42	.248	.297	.335	63	-12	3-1	.994	3	122	73	1b67		-1.3
Total	9	848	2958	379	795	176	13	106	458	227-29	7	655	.269	.320	.445	97	-19	32-16	.995	30	112	94	1b817,D4	172	-5.4

BROHAMER, JACK John Anthony B2.26.1950 Maywood CA BL/TR (BB 1972p)/5-10/165* [CleA67 34/638] d4.18

1972	Cle A	136	527	49	123	13	2	5	35	27-0	1	46	.233	.271	.294	66	-23	3-2	.977	4	106	103	2b132/3		-1.2
1973	Cle A	102	300	29	66	12	1	4	29	32-3	0	23	.220	.291	.307	68	-12	0-2	.971	10	108	103	2b97		0.3
1974	Cle A	101	315	33	85	11	1	2	30	26-0	1	22	.270	.329	.330	91	-3	2-1	.987	4	107	107	2b99	31	0.7
1975	Cle A	69	217	15	53	5	0	6	16	14-0	0	14	.244	.289	.350	80	-7	2-2	.976	-1	91	123	2b66	30	-0.4
1976	Chi A	119	354	33	89	12	2	7	40	44-9	3	28	.251	.333	.356	103	2	1-3	.984	14	106	98	2b117/3		2.3
1977	Chi A	59	152	26	39	10	3	2	20	21-4	1	8	.257	.347	.401	104	2	0-0	.923	-3	112	146	3b38,2b18/D		-0.1
1978	Bos A	81	244	34	57	14	1	1	25	25-1	0	13	.234	.300	.311	67	-10	1-3	.974	-6	91	97	3b30,D25,2b23		-1.8
1979	Bos A	64	192	25	51	7	1	1	11	15-1	0	15	.266	.316	.328	71	-8	0-3	.982	-1	95	92	2b36,3b22	17	-0.8
1980	Bos A	21	57	5	18	2	0	1	6	4-0	0	3	.316	.361	.404	103	0	0-0	.900	-1	92	150	3b13,2b4,D3		-0.1
	Cle A	53	142	13	32	5	1	1	15	14-4	0	6	.225	.291	.296	62	-7	0-1	.979	-4	93	90	2b47/D		-1.0
	Year	74	199	18	50	7	1	2	21	18-4	0	9	.251	.311	.327	74	-7	0-1	.981	-5	93	83	2b51,3b13,D4		-1.1
Total	9	805	2500	262	613	91	12	30	227	222-22	8	178	.245	.306	.327	-66		9-17	.979	14	102	102	2b639,3b105,D30	78	-2.1

BRONKIE, HERMAN Herman Charles "Dutch" B3.31.1885 S.Manchester CT D5.27.1968 Somers CT BR/TR/5-9/165 d9.20

1910	Cle A	5	10	1	2	0	0	0	1	1	0		.200	.273	.200	48	-1	1	.625	-2	46	0	3b3/S		-0.3
1911	Cle A	2	6	0	1	0	0	0	0	1	0		.167	.167	.167	-7	-1	0	1.000	-0	37	0	3b2		-0.1
1912	Cle A	6	16	1	0	0	0	0	0	1	0		.000	.059	.000	-80	-4	0	.917	1	128	120	3b6		-0.2
1914	Chi N	1	1	1	1	1	0	0	1	0	0		0	1.000	1.000	1.000	786	1	0	.000	-1	0	0	/3		0.0
1918	StL N	18	68	7	15	3	0	1	7	2	0		4	.221	.243	.309	70	-3	0	.984	-1	107	63	3b18		-0.2
1919	StL A	67	196	23	50	6	4	0	14	23	1		23	.255	.336	.327	84	-4	2	.939	4	115	133	3b34,2b16,1b2		0.1
1922	StL A	23	64	7	18	4	1	0	2	6	0		7	.281	.343	.375	84	-1	0-2	.917	-0	88	245	3b18		-0.1
Total	7	122	361	40	87	14	5	1	24	33		34	.241	.306	.316	74	-13	3-2	.931	2	105	132	3b82,2b16,1b2/S		-0.8

BROOKENS, TOM Thomas Dale B8.10.1953 Chambersburg PA BR/TR/5-10/170* {DetA75*1/4} d7.10 Col Mansfield OF(0/2/6)

1979	Det A	60	190	23	50	5	2	4	21	11-0	2	40	.263	.309	.374	81	-6	10-3	.945	8	123	148	3b42,2b19/D		0.4
1980	Det A	151	509	64	140	25	9	10	66	32-3	1	71	.275	.315	.418	98	-3	13-11	.931	6	105	100	3b138,2b9/SD		0.1
1981	Det A	71	239	19	58	10	1	4	25	14-0	2	43	.243	.284	.343	79	-7	5-3	.952	3	104	114	3b71		-0.5
1982	Det A	140	398	40	92	15	3	9	58	27-0	0	63	.231	.277	.352	72	-16	5-9	.939	5	113	112	3b113,2b26,S9/OC		-1.4
1983	Det A	138	332	50	71	13	3	6	32	29-2	2	46	.214	.276	.325	68	-15	10-4	.928	3	111	129	3b103,S30,2b10/D		-0.8
1984	†Det A	113	224	32	55	11	4	5	26	19-0	1	33	.246	.306	.397	93	-2	6-6	.969	6	104	172	3b68,S28,2b26/D	16	0.6
1985	Det A	156	485	54	115	34	6	7	47	27-0	0	78	.237	.277	.375	77	-16	14-5	.943	3	99	106	3b151,S8,2b3/CD		-1.4
1986	Det A	98	281	42	76	11	2	3	25	20-0	1	42	.270	.319	.356	84	-6	11-8	.955	-8	99	76	3b35,2b31,S14,D14,O3(0/1/3)		-1.3
1987	†Det A	143	444	59	107	15	3	13	59	33-3	2	63	.241	.295	.376	80	-14	7-4	.954	-4	101	73	3b122,S16,2b11		-1.7
1988	Det A	136	441	62	107	23	5	5	38	44-2	3	74	.243	.313	.351	90	-6	4-4	.952	4	96	78	3b136,S3/2		-1.0
1989	NY A	66	168	14	38	6	0	4	14	11-1	0	27	.226	.272	.333	71	-7	1-3	.926	-5	95	60	3b51,S7,2b5,O3R,D3	39	-1.3
1990	Cle A	72	138	14	41	7	2	1	20	14-1	0	26	.297	.360	.399	102	3	3-2	.923	3	122	103	3b26,S21,S3,1b2/D	15	0.1
Total	12	1336	3865	477	950	175	40	71	431	281-12	14	605	.246	.296	.367	82	-100	86-60	.943	19	103	102	3b1065,2b162,S119,D23,O7R,1b2/C	70	-8.2

BROOKS, HUBIE Hubert B9.24.1956 Los Angeles CA BR/TR/6-0/200(178-205) [NYN78 1/3] d9.4 Col Arizona St. OF(7/0/576)

1980	NY N	24	81	8	25	2	1	1	10	5-0	0	9	.309	.364	.395	113	1	1-1	.966	-1	91	58	3b23		0.0
1981	NY N	98	358	40	110	21	2	4	38	23-2	1	65	.307	.345	.411	116	7	9-5	.924	1	104	93	3b93,O3(1/0/2)/S		0.8
1982	NY N	126	457	40	114	21	2	2	40	28-5	5	76	.249	.297	.317	72	-17	6-3	.931	-9	95	78	3b126	24	-2.9
1983	NY N	150	586	53	147	18	4	5	58	24-2	4	96	.251	.284	.357	72	-27	6-4	.950	6	**112**	104	3b145,2b7		-2.5
1984	NY N	153	561	61	159	23	2	16	73	48-15	2	79	.283	.341	.417	114	9	6-5	.929	-12	87	102	3b129,S26		-0.3
1985	Mon N	156	605	67	163	34	7	13	100	34-6	5	79	.269	.310	.413	107	3	6-9	.958	-35	90	89	S155		-1.7
1986	Mon N★	80	306	50	104	18	5	14	58	25-3	2	60	.340	.388	.569	163	25	4-2	.958	-7	96	82	S80	65	2.7
1987	Mon N★	112	430	57	113	22	3	14	72	24-2	1	72	.263	.301	.426	97	-9	4-3	.953	-23	87	91	S109	44	-2.2
1988	Mon N	151	588	61	164	35	2	20	90	35-3	1	108	.279	.318	.447	112	8	7-3	.968	-5	93	111	O149R		0.0
1989	Mon N	148	542	56	145	30	1	14	70	39-2	4	108	.268	.317	.404	104	1	6-11	.964	-6	92	84	O150R		-1.1
1990	LA N	153	568	74	151	28	1	20	91	33-10	6	108	.266	.307	.424	103	1	2-5	.964	-7	90	90	O150R		-1.3
1991	NY N	103	357	48	85	11	1	16	50	14-8	1	62	.238	.324	.409	106	3	3-1	.972	-0	96	90	O100R	49	-0.2
1992	Cal A	82	306	28	66	13	0	8	36	12-3	1	46	.216	.247	.337	61	-17	3-3	.986	-0	97	71	D70,1b6	76	-2.1
1993	KC A	75	168	14	48	12	0	1	24	11-1	1	27	.286	.331	.375	84	-3	0-1	.966	1	98	157	O40(6/0/34),1b3,D9		-0.4

YEAR	TM LG	G	AB	R	H	2B	3B	HR	RBI	BB-IB	HP	SO	AVG	OBP	SLG	AOPS	ABR	SB-CS	FA	FR	RNG	THR	GAMES AT POSITION	DL	BFW
1994	KC A	34	61	5	14	2	0	1	14	2-0	0	10	.230	.239	.311	43	-5	1-0	1.000	-0	45	117	D19,1b4		-0.6
Total	15	1645	5974	656	1608	290	31	149	824	387-62	38	1005	.269	.315	.403	99	-18	64-56	.966	-99	93	97	O582R,3b516,S371,D98,1b13,2b7	258	-11.8

BROOKS, JERRY Jerome Edward B3.23.1967 Syracuse NY BR/TR/6-0/195* [LAN88 12/296] d9.6 Col Clemson

YEAR	TM LG	G	AB	R	H	2B	3B	HR	RBI	BB-IB	HP	SO	AVG	OBP	SLG	AOPS	ABR	SB-CS	FA	FR	RNG	THR	GAMES AT POSITION	DL	BFW
1993	LA N	9	9	2	2	1	0	1	1	0-0	-1	1	.222	.222	.667	134	1	0-0	—	-0	0	0	O2R		0.0
1996	Fla N	8	5	2	2	0	1	0	3	1-0	-1	1	.400	.571	.400	264	1	0-0	1.000	0	129	0	O2R/1		0.1
Total	2	17	14	4	4	1	1	1	4	1-0	-1	3	.286	.375	.714	190	1	0-0	1.000	-1	75	0	O4R/1		0.1

BROOKS, MANDY Jonathan Joseph (b Jonathan Joseph Brozek) B8.18.1897 Milwaukee WI D6.17.1962 Kirkwood MO BR/TR/5-9/165 d5.30

YEAR	TM LG	G	AB	R	H	2B	3B	HR	RBI	BB-IB	HP	SO	AVG	OBP	SLG	AOPS	ABR	SB-CS	FA	FR	RNG	THR	GAMES AT POSITION	DL	BFW
1925	Chi N	90	349	55	98	25	7	14	72	19	2	28	.281	.322	.513	108	2	10-3	.977	3	105	111	O89C		0.3
1926	Chi N	26	48	7	9	1	0	1	6	5	1	5	.188	.278	.271	48	-4	0	1.000	1	97	161	O18(4/5/9)		-0.3
Total	2	116	397	62	107	26	7	15	78	24	3	33	.270	.316	.484	101	-2	10-3	.979	4	104	117	O107(4/94/9)		0.0

BROOKS, BOBBY Robert B11.1.1945 Los Angeles CA D10.11.1994 Harbor City CA BR/TR/5-8.5/165* [OakA65 9/256] d9.1 Col Los Angeles Harbor (CA) JC

YEAR	TM LG	G	AB	R	H	2B	3B	HR	RBI	BB-IB	HP	SO	AVG	OBP	SLG	AOPS	ABR	SB-CS	FA	FR	RNG	THR	GAMES AT POSITION	DL	BFW
1969	Oak A	29	79	13	19	5	0	3	10	20-1	0	24	.241	.396	.418	134	5	0-2	1.000	-1	84	116	O21(16/0/5)		0.3
1970	Oak A	7	18	2	6	1	0	2	5	1-0	0	7	.333	.368	.722	200	2	0-1	1.000	-1	53	0	O5(4/0/2)		0.1
1972	Oak A	15	39	4	7	0	0	0	5	8-1	0	8	.179	.319	.179	54	-2	0-1	.930	1	137	0	O11C		-0.2
1973	Cal A	4	7	0	1	0	0	0	0	3	0	3	.143	.143	.143	-21	-1	0-0	—	-0	0	0	/OL		-0.2
Total	4	55	143	19	33	6	0	5	20	29-2	0	42	.231	.362	.378	115	4	0-4	.964	-1	95	65	O38(21/11/7)		0.0

BROSIUS, SCOTT Scott David B8.15.1966 Hillsboro OR BR/TR/6-1/185(185-202) [OakA87 20/511] d8.7 Col Linfield OF(37/68/74)

YEAR	TM LG	G	AB	R	H	2B	3B	HR	RBI	BB-IB	HP	SO	AVG	OBP	SLG	AOPS	ABR	SB-CS	FA	FR	RNG	THR	GAMES AT POSITION	DL	BFW
1991	Oak A	36	68	9	16	2	0	2	4	3-0	0	11	.235	.268	.397	86	-2	3-1	1.000	-1	67	59	2b18,O13(5/0/10),3b7/D		-0.2
1992	Oak A	38	87	13	19	2	0	4	13	3-1	2	13	.218	.258	.379	81	-3	3-0	1.000	-3	75	112	O20(4/0/19),3b12,1b3/SD	45	-0.6
1993	Oak A	70	213	26	53	10	1	6	25	14-0	1	37	.249	.296	.390	88	-5	6-0	.991	-2	97	81	O46(8/34/6),1b11,3b10,S6,D2		-0.5
1994	Oak A	96	324	31	77	14	1	14	49	24-0	2	57	.238	.289	.417	87	-8	2-6	.946	5	102	125	3b85,O7(2/2/4)/1	18	-0.4
1995	Oak A	123	389	69	102	19	2	17	46	41-0	8	67	.262	.342	.452	111	6	4-2	.918	-2	107	89	3b60,O49(8/22/22),1b18,2b3,S3,D2		0.2
1996	Oak A	114	428	73	130	25	0	22	71	59-4	7	85	.304	.393	.516	130	21	7-2	.969	15	121	124	3b109,1b10,O4(3/2/0)	51	3.4
1997	Oak A	129	479	59	97	20	1	11	41	34-1	4	102	.203	.259	.317	50	-37	9-4	.977	17	112	124	3b107,S30,O22(6/6/11)	22	-1.8
1998	†NY A★	152	530	86	159	34	0	19	98	52-1	10	97	.300	.371	.472	123	19	11-8	.948	9	106	105	3b150,1b3/OR		2.7
1999	†NY A	133	473	64	117	26	1	17	71	39-2	6	74	.247	.307	.414	85	-12	9-3	.962	4	100	97	3b132/D	15	-0.6
2000	†NY A	135	470	57	108	20	0	16	64	45-1	2	73	.230	.299	.374	70	-23	0-3	.968	-3	92	99	3b134,1b2,O2(1/0/1)/D	20	-2.4
2001	†NY A	120	428	57	123	25	2	13	49	34-2	5	83	.287	.343	.446	106	4	3-1	.935	2	92	110	3b120,O2C	36	0.6
Total	11	1146	3889	544	1001	200	8	141	531	348-12	47	699	.257	.323	.422	94	-40	57-30	.956	41	105	114	3b934,O166R,1b48,S40,2b21,D8	207	0.4

BROSKIE, SIG Sigmund Theodore "Chops" B3.23.1911 Iselin PA D5.17.1975 Canton OH BR/TR/5-11.5/200 d9.11

YEAR	TM LG	G	AB	R	H	2B	3B	HR	RBI	BB-IB	HP	SO	AVG	OBP	SLG	AOPS	ABR	SB-CS	FA	FR	RNG	THR	GAMES AT POSITION	DL	BFW
1940	Bos N	11	22	1	6	1	0	0	2	2	0	2	.273	.304	.318	76	-1	0	.935	5	125	148	C11		0.0

BROTTEM, TONY Anton Christian B4.30.1891 Halstad MN D8.5.1929 Chicago IL BR/TR/6-0.5/176 d4.17 Mil 1918

YEAR	TM LG	G	AB	R	H	2B	3B	HR	RBI	BB-IB	HP	SO	AVG	OBP	SLG	AOPS	ABR	SB-CS	FA	FR	RNG	THR	GAMES AT POSITION	DL	BFW
1916	Stl N	26	33	3	6	1	0	0	4	1	0	10	.182	.250	.212	43	-2	1	.950	-1	75	172	C15,O2(0/1/1)		-0.3
1918	Stl N	2	4	0	0	0	0	0	0	1	0	0	.000	.200	.000	-39	-1	0	1.000	1	384	0	1b2		0.0
1921	Was A	4	7	1	1	0	0	0	2	0	0	1	.143	.333	.143	26	-1	0-0	1.000	1	143	81	C4		0.0
	Pit N	30	91	6	22	2	0	0	9	3	0	11	.242	.266	.264	40	-8	0-1	.983	-0	135	86	C29		-0.7
Total	3	62	135	10	29	3	0	0	15	5	0	22	.215	.264	.237	38	-12	1-1	.977	1	124	103	C48,1b2,O2(0/1/1)		-1.0

BROUGHTON, CAL Cecil Calvert B12.28.1860 Magnolia WI D3.15.1939 Evansville WI BR/TR/5-10/180 d5.2

YEAR	TM LG	G	AB	R	H	2B	3B	HR	RBI	BB-IB	HP	SO	AVG	OBP	SLG	AOPS	ABR	SB-CS	FA	FR	RNG	THR	GAMES AT POSITION	DL	BFW
1883	Cle N	4	10	2	2	0	0	0	2				.200	.333	.200	68	-0		.950	0			C4		0.0
	Bal AA	9	32	1	6	0	0	0	1				.188	.212	.188	29	-3		.825	-2			C8/OR		-0.4
1884	Mil U	11	39	5	12	5	0	0	0				.308	.308	.436	226	-9		.937	-1			C7,O5(1/4/0)		0.4
1885	Stl AA	4	17	1	1	0	0	0	1	0			.059	.059	.059	-60	-3		.889	-1			C4		-0.3
	NY AA	11	41	1	6	0	0	0	1	0			.146	.167	.171	7	-4		.860	-1			C11		-0.4
	Year	15	58	2	7	1	0	0	2	1			.121	.136	.138	-14	-7		.867	-2			C15		-0.7
1888	Det N	1	4	0	0	0	0	0	0	0			.000	.000	.000	-99	-1	0	1.000	1			/C		0.0
Total	4	40	143	10	27	6	0	0	6	1			.189	.211	.231	43	-6		.887	-4			C35,O6(1/4/1)		-0.7

BROUHARD, MARK Mark Steven B5.22.1956 Burbank CA BR/TR/6-1/210* [AnaA76*/74] d4.12 Col Los Angeles Pierce (CA) JC

YEAR	TM LG	G	AB	R	H	2B	3B	HR	RBI	BB-IB	HP	SO	AVG	OBP	SLG	AOPS	ABR	SB-CS	FA	FR	RNG	THR	GAMES AT POSITION	DL	BFW
1980	Mil A	45	125	17	29	5	0	5	16	7-0	1	24	.232	.278	.400	86	-3	1-0	.964	0	121	0	D21,O12(4/0/8),1b10		-0.4
1981	Mil A	60	186	19	51	6	3	2	20	7-1	2	41	.274	.305	.371	99	-1	1-1	.990	3	95	206	O51(7/0/46),D7		-0.1
1982	†Mil A	40	108	16	29	4	1	4	10	9-0	2	17	.269	.336	.435	116	2	0-3	.986	2	119	103	O30(7/0/23),D7		0.2
1983	Mil A	56	185	25	51	10	1	7	23	9-0	2	39	.276	.315	.454	117	4	0-4	.991	3	122	30	O42(38/0/8),D11	20	0.3
1984	Mil A	66	197	20	47	7	0	6	22	16-3	2	36	.239	.298	.365	87	-4	0-3	.983	5	107	186	O52(48/0/4),D8		-0.2
1985	Mil A	37	108	11	28	7	2	1	13	5-1	1	26	.259	.298	.389	86	-2	0-0	.964	-2	98	0	O29(10/0/21)/D		-0.5
Total	6	304	909	108	235	40	7	25	104	53-5	10	183	.259	.305	.400	98	-4	2-11	.983	11	109	112	O216(114/0/110),D55,1b10	20	-0.7

BROUSSARD, BEN Benjamin Isaac B9.24.1976 Beaumont TX BL/TL/6-2/220* [CinN99 2/65] d6.22 Col McNeese St.

YEAR	TM LG	G	AB	R	H	2B	3B	HR	RBI	BB-IB	HP	SO	AVG	OBP	SLG	AOPS	ABR	SB-CS	FA	FR	RNG	THR	GAMES AT POSITION	DL	BFW
2002	Cle A	39	112	10	27	4	0	4	9	7-1	1	25	.241	.292	.384	76	-4	0-0	.960	-2	91	66	O32L,1b4,D3		-0.7
2003	Cle A	116	386	53	96	21	3	16	55	32-2	5	75	.249	.312	.443	97	-2	5-2	.991	2	96	98	1b114	7	-1.3
2004	Cle A	139	418	57	115	28	5	17	82	52-3	12	95	.275	.370	.488	126	17	4-2	.994	1	103	109	1b133		0.8
2005	Cle A	142	466	59	119	30	5	19	68	52-5	4	98	.255	.307	.464	105	2	2-2	.992	-6	80	122	1b138,D2		-1.5
Total	4	436	1382	179	357	83	13	56	214	123-11	22	293	.258	.327	.459	107	13	11-6	.993	-9	92	110	1b389,O32L,D5	7	-2.7

BROUTHERS, ART Arthur H. B11.25.1882 Montgomery AL D9.28.1959 Charleston SC BR/TR/6-1/? d4.14

YEAR	TM LG	G	AB	R	H	2B	3B	HR	RBI	BB-IB	HP	SO	AVG	OBP	SLG	AOPS	ABR	SB-CS	FA	FR	RNG	THR	GAMES AT POSITION	DL	BFW
1906	Phi A	37	144	18	30	5	1	0	14	5	1		.208	.240	.257	54	-8	4	.900	-3	86	0	3b35/2		-1.1

BROUTHERS, DAN Dennis Joseph "Big Dan" B5.8.1858 Sylvan Lake NY D8.2.1932 E.Orange NJ BL/TL/6-2/207 d6.23 HF1945 ▲

YEAR	TM LG	G	AB	R	H	2B	3B	HR	RBI	BB-IB	HP	SO	AVG	OBP	SLG	AOPS	ABR	SB-CS	FA	FR	RNG	THR	GAMES AT POSITION	DL	BFW
1879	Tro N	39	168	17	46	12	1	4	17	1		18	.274	.278	.429	138	7		.926	-5	63	59	1b37,P3		0.1
1880	Tro N	3	12	0	2	0	0	0	0	0			.167	.231	.167	35	-1		.893	-1	70		1b3		-0.2
1881	Buf N	65	270	60	86	18	9	8	45	18		22	.319	.361	.541	182	25		.797	-6	72	62	O35(33/0/2),1b30		1.5
1882	Buf N	84	351	71	129	23	11	6	63	21		7	.368	.403	.547	198	38		.974	1	84	84	1b84		2.8
1883	Buf N	98	425	85	159	41	17	3	97	16		17	.374	.397	.572	186	43		.961	1	108	92	1b97/3P		3.0
1884	Buf N	94	398	82	130	22	15	14	79	33		20	.327	.378	.563	186	38		.964	0	112	93	1b93/3		2.7
1885	Buf N	98	407	87	146	32	11	7	59	34		10	.359	.408	.543	199	44		.975	-2	78	92	1b98		3.1
1886	Det N	121	489	139	181	40	15	11	72	66		16	.370	.445	.581	203	63	21	.968	-8	58	123	1b121		3.9
1887	†Det N	123	500	153	169	36	20	12	101	71		6	.338	.426	.504	166	46	34	.969	-4	80	103	1b123		2.6
1888	Det N	129	522	118	160	33	11	9	66	66	12	13	.307	.399	.464	172	47	34	.971	-2	101	94	1b129		3.3
1889	Bos N	126	485	105	181	26	9	7	118	66	14	6	.373	.462	.507	161	42	22	.974	1	104	119	1b126		2.8
1890	Bos P	123	460	117	152	36	9	1	97	99	18	17	.330	.466	.454	137	32	28	.963	2	119	109	1b123		1.8
1891	Bos AA	130	486	117	170	26	19	5	109	87	24	20	.350	.471	.512	184	60	31	.978	-7	63	105	1b130		3.5
1892	Bro N	152	588	121	197	30	26	5	124	84	16	30	.335	.432	.480	182	64	31	.982	12	129	82	1b152		6.8
1893	Bro N	77	282	57	95	21	11	2	59	52	6		.337	.450	.511	163	29	9	.986	4	113	110	1b77		2.6
1894	†Bal N	123	525	137	182	39	23	9	128	67	5	9	.347	.425	.560	130	25	38	.976	-2	95	110	1b123		1.7
1895	Bal N	5	23	2	6	2	0	0	5	1	0		.261	.292	.348	63	-1	0	1.000	0	119	322	1b5		-0.1
	Lou N	24	97	13	30	10	1	2	15	11	0		.309	.380	.495	133	5	1	.953	-2	79	87	1b24		0.2
	Year	29	120	15	36	12	1	2	20	12	0		.300	.364	.467	119	4	1	.960	-2	86	126	1b29		0.1
1896	Phi N	57	218	42	75	13	3	1	41	44	4	11	.344	.462	.445	141	17	7	.983	-3	74	116	1b57		1.0
1904	NY N	2	5	0	0	0	0	0	0	0			.000	.000	.000	-96	-1	0	1.000	1			/1		-0.1
Total	19	1673	6711	1523	2296	460	205	106	1296	840	105	238	.342	.423	.519	169	622	256	.971	-20	94	102	1b1633,O35(33/0/2),P4,3b2		43.2

BROVIA, JOE Joseph John "Ox" B2.18.1922 Davenport CA D8.15.1994 Santa Cruz CA BR/TR/6-3/195 d7.3

YEAR	TM LG	G	AB	R	H	2B	3B	HR	RBI	BB-IB	HP	SO	AVG	OBP	SLG	AOPS	ABR	SB-CS	FA	FR	RNG	THR	GAMES AT POSITION	DL	BFW
1955	Cin N	21	18	0	2	1	0	0	2	0		4	.111	.150	.111	-25	-3		—	0			/H		-0.3

BROWER, FRANK Frank Willard "Turkeyfoot" B3.26.1893 Gainesville VA D11.20.1960 Baltimore MD BL/TR/6-2/180 d8.14 Col Washington and Lee ▲

YEAR	TM LG	G	AB	R	H	2B	3B	HR	RBI	BB-IB	HP	SO	AVG	OBP	SLG	AOPS	ABR	SB-CS	FA	FR	RNG	THR	GAMES AT POSITION	DL	BFW
1920	Was A	36	119	21	37	7	2	1	13	9	3		.311	.374	.429	115	-1	3	1-1	.900	-1	85	141	O20(1/0/19),1b9/3	0.1
1921	Was A	83	203	31	53	12	3	5	35	18	3	7	.261	.330	.365	81	-6	1-1	.917	4	112	148	O46R,1b4		-0.6
1922	Was A	139	471	61	138	20	6	9	71	52	10	25	.293	.375	.418	112	9	8-6	.978	-3	100	70	O121R,1b7		-0.3
1923	Cle A	126	397	77	113	25	8	16	66	62	8	32	.285	.392	.509	136	21	6-5	.988	-1	100	110	1b112,O4(1/0/3)		1.3
1924	Cle A	66	107	16	30	10	1	3	20	27	2	9	.280	.434	.477	133	7	1-1	.990	1	117	67	1b26,P4,O3(2/0/1)		0.5
Total	5	450	1297	206	371	74	20	30	205	168	26	84	.286	.379	.443	117	34	17-14	.952	-0	101	96	O194(4/0/190),1b158,P4/3		1.0

YEAR	TM LG	G	AB	R	H	2B	3B	HR	RBI	BB-IB	HP	SO	AVG	OBP	SLG	AOPS	ABR	SB-CS	FA	FR	RNG	THR	GAMES AT POSITION	DL	BFW

BROWER, LOUIS Louis Lester B7.1.1900 Cleveland OH D3.4.1994 Tyler TX BR/TR/5-10/155 d6.13

1931	Det A	21	62	3	10	1	0	0	6	8	2	5	.161	.278	.177	21	-7	1-0	.886	-6	71	95	S20,2b2		-1.1

BROWN, BOB Robert Richard B1.10.1960 Jamaica NY BR/TR/5-11/190* d9.3 Col Duke

1986	Tex A	21	9	3	1	1	0	0	0	0-0	0	3	.111	.111	.222	-12	-1	1-2	1.000	-1	79	0	O17(16/1/1)/D		-0.3
1987	Tex A	127	303	63	79	10	3	14	46	36-0	0	66	.261	.338	.452	107	2	15-9	.964	-4	95	47	O106(45/67/6),D7		-0.3
1988	Tex A	82	201	29	45	7	0	1	11	27-0	0	38	.224	.316	.274	65	-9	10-5	.972	-3	89	81	O59(26/33/4),D13	23	-1.3
1989	NY A	26	69	9	16	3	0	2	3	6-0	0	11	.232	.293	.362	84	-2	3-1	.970	3	131	142	O25(1/9/15)/D	13	0.2
Total	4	256	582	104	141	21	3	17	60	69-0	0	118	.242	.322	.376	88	-10	29-17	.968	-4	97	68	O207(88/110/26),D22	36	-1.7

BROWN, ADRIAN Adrian Demond B2.7.1974 McComb MS BB/TR/6-0/185(175-200) [PitN92 48/1351] d5.16

1997	Pit N	48	147	17	28	6	0	1	10	13-0	4	18	.190	.273	.252	38	-13	8-4	.987	-1	90	169	O38(0/35/3)		-1.4
1998	Pit N	41	152	20	43	4	1	0	5	9-0	0	18	.283	.323	.322	70	-7	4-0	.977	1	103	137	O38(3/34/1)		-0.5
1999	Pit N	116	226	34	61	5	2	4	17	33-2	1	39	.270	.364	.363	85	-5	5-3	.966	-4	90	82	O96(4/29/66)		-1.0
2000	Pit N	104	308	64	97	18	3	4	28	29-1	0	34	.315	.373	.432	103	2	13-1	.976	-1	93	164	O92(7/71/15)	51	0.3
2001	Pit N	8	31	3	6	0	0	1	2	3-0	0	9	.194	.265	.290	42	-1	2-1	1.000	-0	104	0	O7C	179	-0.3
2002	Pit N	91	208	20	45	10	2	1	21	19-0	1	34	.216	.284	.298	55	-14	10-6	.974	-1	92	34	O71(0/64/9)		-1.9
2003	†Bos A	9	15	2	3	0	0	0	1	1-0	0	4	.200	.250	.200	20	-2	2-0	1.000	-0	85	0	O9(3/6/0)		-0.2
2004	KC A	5	11	0	3	0	0	0	0	0-0	0	2	.273	.273	.273	43	-1	0-0	1.000	0	141	0	O5(4/0/1)		-0.1
Total	8	422	1098	160	286	43	8	11	84	107-3	6	152	.260	.328	.344	74	-43	44-15	.977	-9	94	109	O356(21/246/95)	230	-5.1

BROWN, BRANT Brant Michael B6.22.1971 Porterville CA BL/TL/6-3/205(205-220) [ChiN92 3/79] d6.15 Col Cal St.-Fresno

1996	Chi N	29	69	11	21	1	0	5	9	2-1	1	17	.304	.329	.536	120	2	3-3	1.000	2	151	35	1b18		0.2
1997	Chi N	46	137	15	32	7	1	5	15	7-0	1	28	.234	.286	.409	77	-3	2-1	1.000	0	102	204	O27L,1b12		-0.7
1998	†Chi N	124	347	56	101	17	7	14	48	30-2	1	95	.291	.348	.501	116	7	4-5	.963	-3	101	20	O102(48/69/0),1b7	29	0.2
1999	Pit N	130	341	49	79	20	3	16	58	22-3	4	114	.232	.283	.449	82	-12	3-4	.981	1	108	96	O82(0/23/59),1b7,D6		-1.3
2000	Fla N	41	73	4	14	6	0	2	6	3-0	0	33	.192	.224	.356	46	-7	0-1	.923	1	85	0	O13(8/0/5),1b5		-0.7
	Chi N	54	89	7	14	1	0	3	10	10-0	1	29	.157	.248	.270	32	-10	2-1	1.000	1	110	0	O28(18/9/3),1b7		-1.0
	Year	95	162	11	28	7	0	5	16	13-0	1	62	.173	.237	.309	38	-16	3-1	.980	-2	102	0	O41(26/9/8),1b12		-1.7
Total	5	424	1056	142	261	52	11	45	146	74-6	10	316	.247	.301	.445	88	-25	15-14	.975	-9	104	65	O252(101/101/67),1b56,D6	29	-3.3

BROWN, CURTIS Curtis B9.14.1945 Sacramento CA BR/TR/5-11/180 d5.27 b-Leon

| 1973 | Mon N | 1 | 4 | 0 | 0 | 0 | 0 | 0 | 0 | 0-0 | 0 | 0 | .000 | .000 | .000 | -96 | -1 | 0-0 | 1.000 | 0 | 159 | 0 | /OL | | -0.1 |

BROWN, DARRELL Darrell Wayne B10.29.1955 Oklahoma City OK BB/TR/6-0/184* [DetA77 3/57] d4.11 Col Cal St.-Los Angeles

1981	Det A	16	4	4	1	0	0	0	0	0-0	0	1	.250	.250	.250	43	0	1-0	1.000	-0	70	0	O6(1/2/3),D4		0.0
1982	Oak A	8	18	2	6	0	1	0	3	1-0	0	2	.333	.368	.444	126	0	1-0	1.000	-1	90	0	O7(1/0/6)/D		0.0
1983	Min A	91	309	40	84	6	2	0	22	10-0	1	28	.272	.297	.304	-63	-16	3-3	.995	-4	95	44	O81(5/76/0),D3		-2.1
1984	Min A	95	260	36	71	9	3	1	19	14-1	0	16	.273	.309	.342	76	-9	4-1	.993	3	109	115	O55(19/35/0),D13		-0.7
Total	4	210	591	82	162	15	6	1	44	25-1	1	47	.274	.304	.325	-71	-25	9-4	.994	-2	100	70	O149(26/113/9),D21		-2.8

BROWN, DELOS Delos Hight B10.4.1892 Anna IL D12.21.1964 Carbondale IL BR/TR/5-9/160 d6.12 Col Millikin

| 1914 | Chi A | 1 | 1 | 0 | 0 | 0 | 0 | 0 | 0 | 0-0 | 0 | 1 | .000 | .000 | .000 | -99 | 0 | 0 | — | 0 | | | /H | | 0.0 |

BROWN, DEE Dermal Bram B3.27.1978 Bronx NY BL/TR/6-0/215(210-225) [KCA96 1/14] d9.14

1998	KC A	5	3	2	0	0	0	0	0	0-0	0	1	.000	.000	.000	-96	-1	0-0	1.000	0	144	0	O2R,D3		-0.1
1999	KC A	12	25	1	2	0	0	0	0	2-0	0	7	.080	.148	.080	-38	-5	0-0	.929	2	195	501	O3L,D2		-0.4
2000	KC A	15	25	4	4	1	0	0	4	3-0	0	9	.160	.250	.200	15	-3	0-0	1.000	1	145	0	O5L		-0.3
2001	KC A	106	380	39	93	19	0	7	40	22-4	1	81	.245	.286	.350	61	-22	5-3	.988	-3	91	58	O83(77/4/3),D20	40	-2.8
2002	KC A	16	51	5	12	3	1	1	7	4-0	0	20	.235	.291	.392	70	-2	0-0	.923	-1	71	0	O8L,D5		-0.4
2003	KC A	50	132	16	30	7	0	2	14	8-1	2	37	.227	.280	.326	56	-8	1-1	.985	3	120	132	O33(17/0/17),D11	52	-0.7
2004	KC A	59	195	19	49	7	0	4	24	11-0	1	50	.251	.293	.349	67	-10	2-2	.970	-0	98	143	O53L/D	24	-1.2
Total	7	263	811	86	190	37	1	14	89	50-5	4	205	.234	.281	.334	57	-51	8-6	.978	-0	100	97	O187(163/4/22),D42	116	-5.9

BROWN, DRUMMOND Drummond Nicol B1.31.1885 Los Angeles CA D1.27.1927 Parkville MO BR/TR/6-0/180 d4.25

1913	Bos N	15	34	3	11	1	0	1	2	2	0	9	.324	.361	.441	126	1	0	.960	-3	92	58	C12		-0.1
1914	KC F	31	58	4	11	3	0	0	5	7	0	6	.190	.277	.241	44	-5	1	.954	2	106	116	C23,1b2		-0.2
1915	KC F	77	227	13	55	10	1	1	26	12	3	23	.242	.289	.308	71	-13	3	.961	-2	94	103	C65/1		-1.0
Total	3	123	319	20	77	14	1	2	33	21	3	38	.241	.294	.310	72	-17	4	.960	-3	96	101	C100,1b3		-1.3

BROWN, ED Edward P. B Chicago IL TR/?/178 d8.19 ▲

1882	StL AA	17	60	4	11	0	0	0		4			.183	.234	.183	41	-4		.808	-2	92	0	O15(2/0/13),2b2/P		-0.5
1884	Tol AA	42	153	13	27	3	0	0		2	0		.176	.187	.196	24	-13		.815	-8	77	24	3b40,O2L/CP		-1.8
Total	2	59	213	17	38	3	0	0		6			.178	.201	.192	29	-17		.815	-10	77	24	3b40,O17(4/0/13),P2,2b2/C		-2.3

BROWN, EDDIE Edward William "Glass Arm Eddie" B7.17.1891 Milligan NE D9.10.1956 Vallejo CA BR/TR/6-3/190 d9.26 Col Syracuse

1920	NY N	3	8	1	1	0	0	0	0	0	0	3	.125	.125	.250	6	-1	0	1.000	-0	97	0	O2C		-0.2
1921	NY N	70	128	16	36	6	2	0	12	4	4	11	.281	.324	.359	80	-4	1-0	.956	-1	101	56	O30(2/26/2)		-0.6
1924	Bro N	114	455	56	140	30	4	5	78	26	0	15	.308	.345	.424	108	5	3-5	.975	-4	106	24	O114C		-0.4
1925	Bro N	153	618	88	189	39	11	5	99	22	2	18	.306	.332	.429	95	-6	3-4	.972	1	108	49	O153C		-1.2
1926	Bos N	153	612	71	201	31	8	2	84	23	2	20	.328	.355	.415	117	12	5	.965	3	110	69	O153(73/80/0)		0.6
1927	Bos N	155	558	64	171	35	6	2	75	28	4	11	.306	.340	.401	106	4	11	.980	3	111	74	O150L/1		-0.4
1928	Bos N	142	523	45	140	28	2	2	59	24	0	22	.268	.305	.340	72	-22	6	.960	-3	103	56	O129(80/50/1)/1		-3.3
Total	7	790	2902	341	878	170	33	16	407	127	12	109	.303	.334	.400	99	-12	29-9	.970	-1	108	56	O731(305/425/3),1b2		-5.5

BROWN, RANDY Edwin Randolph B8.29.1944 Leesburg FL BL/TR/5-7/170* [AnaA66 18/348] d9.11 Col Florida St.

1969	Cal A	13	25	3	4	1	0	0		6-0	0	1	.160	.323	.200	51	-1	0-0	1.000	0	77	143	C10/OC		-0.1
1970	Cal A	5	4	0	0	0	0	0		0-0	0	0	.000	.000	.000	-99	-1	0-0	1.000	-2	42	0	C5		-0.3
Total	2	18	29	3	4	1	0	0		6-0	0	1	.138	.286	.172	32	-2	0-0	1.000	-2	70	113	C15/OC		-0.4

BROWN, EMIL Emil Quincy B12.29.1974 Chicago IL BR/TR/6-2/192* [OakA94 6/149] d4.3 Col Indian River (FL) CC

1997	Pit N	66	95	16	17	2	1	2	6	10-1	7	32	.179	.304	.284	54	-6	5-1	.948	2	117	134	O42(30/8/4)		-0.5
1998	Pit N	13	39	2	10	1	0	3	1	1-0	1	11	.256	.293	.282	52	-3	0-0	1.000	2	119	333	O10(9/1/1)		-0.1
1999	Pit N	6	14	0	2	0	0	0	0	0-0	1	3	.143	.143	.214	-11	-2	0-0	1.000	0	113	0	O6L		-0.2
2000	Pit N	50	119	13	26	5	0	3	16	11-0	3	34	.218	.299	.336	60	-7	3-1	1.000	0	90	165	O38(14/12/18)	14	-0.8
2001	Pit N	61	123	18	25	4	1	3	13	15-1	2	42	.203	.300	.325	60	-7	10-4	.988	1	99	216	O54(2/51/2)		-0.5
	SD N	13	14	3	1	0	0	0		1-0	0	7	.071	.133	.071	-49	-3	2-0	1.000	-1	83	0	O11(4/6/2)		-0.3
	Year	74	137	21	26	4	1	3	13	16-1	2	49	.190	.284	.299	51	-10	12-4	.989	1	97	188	O65(6/57/4)		-0.8
2005	KC A	150	545	75	156	31	5	17	86	48-1	8	108	.286	.349	.455	120	16	10-1	.958	-2	98	115	O139(11/0/129),D10.		0.8
Total	6	359	949	127	237	44	7	25	124	86-3	21	237	.250	.323	.390	89	-12	30-7	.969	3	100	141	O300(76/78/156),D10	14	-1.6

BROWN, FRED Fred Herbert B4.12.1879 Ossipee NH D2.3.1955 Somersworth NH BR/TR/5-10.5/190 d5.4 Col Dartmouth

1901	Bos N	7	14	1	2	0	0	0	2	0	0		.143	.143	.143	-16	-2	0	1.000	1	205	0	O5(3/0/2)		-0.2
1902	Bos N	2	6	1	2	1	0	0	0	0	0		.333	.333	.500	155	0	0	1.000	1	726	0	O2R		0.1
Total	2	9	20	2	4	1	0	0	2	0	0		.200	.200	.250	30	-2	0	1.000	1	314	0	O7(3/0/4)		-0.1

BROWN, IKE Isaac B4.13.1942 Memphis TN D5.17.2001 Memphis TN BR/TR/6-1/205* d6.17 Negro Lg 1960-61 OF(44/0/7)

1969	Det A	70	170	24	39	4	3	5	12	26-4	2	43	.229	.338	.376	96	-1	2-3	.962	-8	96	77	2b45,3b12,O3(1/0/2)/S		-0.7
1970	Det A	56	94	17	27	5	0	4	15	13-0	1	26	.287	.376	.468	131	4	0-0	.935	-7	65	65	2b23,O4(3/0/1)/3		-0.2
1971	Det A	59	110	20	28	1	0	8	19	19-1	0	25	.255	.359	.482	132	5	0-1	1.000	-0	92	45	1b17,O9(8/0/1),2b8,3b4/S		0.3
1972	†Det A	51	84	12	21	3	2	1	9	15-2	0	23	.250	.376	.357	115	2	1-2	1.000	5	188	103	O22(20/0/3),1b13,2b3/S		0.6
1973	Det A	42	76	12	22	2	1	1	9	15-1	0	13	.289	.407	.382	116	2	0-1	.983	-0	123	87	1b21,O12L,3b2/2		0.0
1974	Det A	2	2	0	0	0	0	0	0	0-0	0	0	.000	.000	.000	-97	-1	0-0	1.000	0	64	0	3b2		0.0
Total	6	280	536	85	137	15	6	20	65	90-7	3	130	.256	.364	.410	115	11	3-7	.956	-11	89	75	2b79,1b51,O50L,3b22,S3,D2		0.0

YEAR	TM LG	G	AB	R	H	2B	3B	HR	RBI	BB-IB	HP	SO	AVG	OBP	SLG	AOPS	ABR	SB-CS	FA	FR	RNG	THR	GAMES AT POSITION	DL	BFW
BROWN, JIM	James Donaldson "Don","Moose" B3.31.1897 Laurel MD BR/TR/6-0/178 d9.13																								
1915	StL N	1	2	0	1	0	0	0	2		0	1	.500	.750	.500	281	1	0	1.000	-0	61	0	/OC		0.1
1916	Phi A	14	42	6	10	2	1	1	5	4	0	9	.238	.340	.405	119	1	0	.895	-1	79	155	O12(0/6/6)		-0.1
Total	2	15	44	6	11	2	1	1	5	6	0	10	.250	.340	.409	131	2	0	.900	-1	78	145	O13(0/7/6)		0.0
BROWN, JIMMY	James Roberson B4.25.1910 Jamesville NC D12.29.1977 Bath NC BB/TR/5-8.5/165 d4.23 Mil 1944-45 C3 Col North Carolina St.																								
1937	StL N	138	525	86	145	20	9	2	53	27	1	29	.276	.313	.360	81	-15	10	.964	-14	101	85	2b112,S25/3		-2.1
1938	StL N	108	382	50	115	12	6	0	38	27	5	26	.301	.350	.364	91	-4	7	.968	-0	100	120	2b49,S30,3b24		0.1
1939	StL N	147	645	88	192	31	8	3	51	32	4	18	.298	.335	.384	87	-12	4	.957	-4	101	98	S104,2b50		-0.6
1940	StL N	107	454	56	127	17	4	0	30	24	1	15	.280	.317	.335	76	-15	9	.977	-17	93	107	2b48,3b41,S28		-2.7
1941	StL N	132	549	81	168	28	9	3	56	45	4	22	.306	.363	.406	109	7	2	.965	2	101	102	3b123,2b11		1.4
1942	†StL N★	145	606	75	155	28	4	1	71	52	0	11	.256	.315	.320	80	-15	4	.970	-7	89	125	2b82,3b66,S12		-1.5
1943	StL N	34	110	6	20	4	2	0	8	6	1	5	.182	.224	.255	37	-9	0	.978	2	98	102	2b19,3b9,S6		-0.7
1946	Pit N	79	241	23	58	6	0	0	12	18	0	5	.241	.293	.266	58	-13	3	.960	-2	99	82	S30,2b21,3b9		-1.3
Total	8	890	3512	465	980	146	42	9	319	231	12	110	.279	.326	.352	84	-76	39	.968	-42	97	103	2b392,3b273,S235		-7.4
BROWN, JIM	James W. H. B12.12.1860 Clinton Co. PA D4.6.1908 Williamsport PA d4.17 ▲																								
1884	Alt U	21	88	12	22	2	1			1			.250	.258	.352	82	-5		.615	-3	60	0	O14(2/4/8),P11		-0.6
	NY N	1	3	0	0	0	0	0	0	0		1	.000	.000	.000	-98	-1		.333	-0	54	0	/P		0.0
	StP U	6	16	5	5	4	0	0		1			.313	.353	.563	318	4		.706	-3	148	0	P6/1OR		0.1
1886	Phi AA	1	3	0	0	0	0	0	0	0		0	.000	.000	.000	-99	-1	0	1.000	-0	73	0	/P		0.0
Total	2	29	110	17	27	6	1	0	2	0	1	.245	.259	.364	93	-3	0	.741	-4	117	0	P19,O15(2/4/9)/1		-0.5
BROWN, JARVIS	Jarvis Ardel B3.26.1967 Waukegan IL BR/TR/5-7/170* [MinA86*1/9] d7.2 Col Triton (IL) JC																								
1991	†Min A	38	37	10	8	0	0	0	2-0		1	8	.216	.256	.216	31	-1	4	7-1	.955	-2	74	0	O32(3/11/19),D4		-0.5
1992	Min A	35	15	8	1	0	0	0	2-0	1	4	.067	.222	.067	-15	-2	2-2	.952	-0	108	0	O31(4/9/18),D2		-0.3
1993	SD N	47	133	21	31	9	2	0	8	15-0	6	26	.233	.335	.331	79	-3	3-3	.982	4	121	104	O43(5/40/0)		0.0
1994	Atl N	17	15	3	2	1	0	1	1	0-0	1	4	.133	.133	.400	31	-2	0-0	1.000	0	108	0	O9(3/4/2)		-0.2
1995	Bal A	18	27	2	4	1	0	1	1	7-0	0	9	.148	.324	.185	36	-2	1-1	1.000	-2	73	0	O17(0/13/5)	24	-0.4
Total	5	155	227	44	46	11	2	1	10	26-0	7	49	.203	.303	.282	57	-13	13-7	.978	-0	104	53	O132(15/77/44),D6	24	-1.4
BROWN, JAKE	Jerald Ray B3.22.1948 Sumrall MS D12.18.1981 Houston TX BR/TR/6-2/200 [SFN69 S1/2] d5.17 Col Southern A&M																								
1975	SF N	41	43	6	9	3	0	0	4	5-0	0	13	.209	.292	.279	57	-2	0-0	.857	-0	87	211	O14(9/1/4)		-0.3
BROWN, CHRIS	John Christopher B8.15.1961 Jackson MS BR/TR/6-2/210(185-210) [SFN79 2/44] d9.3																								
1984	SF N	23	84	6	24	7	0	1	11	9-0	1	19	.286	.358	.405	118	3	2-1	.900	-2	88	72	3b23		0.0
1985	SF N	131	432	50	117	20	3	16	61	38-4	11	78	.271	.345	.442	124	13	2-3	.971	4	97	74	3b120		1.5
1986	SF N★	116	416	57	132	16	3	7	49	33-4	9	43	.317	.376	.421	127	15	13-9	.933	-10	88	100	3b111,S2		0.3
1987	SF N	38	132	17	32	6	0	6	17	9-1	3	16	.242	.306	.424	95	-1	1-3	.905	-3	88	87	3b37/S	44	-0.6
	SD N	44	155	17	36	3	0	6	23	11-0	3	30	.232	.294	.368	77	-6	3-1	.942	-4	88	170	3b43		-1.0
	Year	82	287	34	68	9	0	12	40	20-1	6	46	.237	.299	.394	86	-7	4-4	.923	-7	88	132	3b80/S		-1.6
1988	SD N	80	247	14	58	6	0	2	19	19-3	3	49	.235	.295	.283	69	-10	0-0	.949	2	101	143	3b72		-0.8
1989	Det A	17	57	3	11	3	0	0	4	1-0	0	17	.193	.203	.246	28	-6	0-0	.909	-1	84	138	3b17		-0.7
Total	6	449	1523	164	410	61	6	38	184	120-12	30	252	.269	.333	.392	105	8	21-17	.943	-15	93	105	3b423,S3	44	-1.3
BROWN, LINDSAY	John Lindsay "Red" B7.22.1911 Mason TX D1.1.1967 San Antonio TX BR/TR/5-10/160 d7.13																								
1937	Bro N	48	115	16	13	0	1	0	4	5-0	1	17	.270	.288	.313	62	-6	1	.937	2	100	123	S45		-0.2
BROWN, JOE	Joseph E. B4.4.1859 Warren PA D6.28.1888 Warren PA 5-10/162 d8.16 ▲																								
1884	Chi N	15	61	6	13	1	0	0	3	0		15	.213	.213	.230	36	-5		.750	-1	98	0	O9(0/1/9),P7/1C		-0.3
1885	Bal AA	5	19	2	3	0	0	0	0	0		0	.158	.158	.158*	-0	-2		1.000	0	80	0	P4/2		0.0
Total	2	20	80	8	16	1	0	0	3	0	0	15	.200	.200	.213	28	-7		.895	-1	96	0	P11,O9(0/1/9)/2C1		-0.3
BROWN, KEVIN	Kevin Lee B4.21.1973 Valparaiso IN BR/TR/6-2/215(200-224) [TexA94 2/56] d9.12 Col Southern Indiana																								
1996	Tex A	3	4	1	0	0	0	1	1	2-0		2	.000	.375	.000	20	0	0-0	1.000	1	0	221	C2/D		0.1
1997	Tex A	4	5	1	2	0	0	1	1	0-0	0	0	.400	.400	1.000	234	1	0-0	.900	-0	101	0	C4		0.1
1998	Tor A	52	110	17	29	7	1	2	15	9-0	2	31	.264	.320	.400	89	-2	0-0	.993	3	84	107	C52	17	0.3
1999	Tor A	2	9	1	4	2	0	1	1	0-0	0	3	.444	.444	.667	175	1	0-0	1.000	-1	130	155	C2		0.1
2000	Mil N	5	17	3	4	3	0	1	1	1-0	0	5	.235	.278	.412	72	-1	0-0	.957	-2	70	0	C5		-0.3
2001	Mil N	17	43	7	9	0	1	4	12	2-0	1	18	.209	.261	.535	100	-1	0-0	1.000	-2	77	131	C16		-0.1
2002	Bos A	2	1	0	0	0	0	0		0-0	0	0	.000	.000	.000	-98	-0	0-0	1.000	-0	0	0	C2		0.0
Total	7	85	189	30	48	12	2	7	31	14-0	4	59	.254	.311	.450	96	-2	0-0	.990	-2	81	105	C83/D	17	0.2
BROWN, LARRY	Larry Leslie B3.1.1940 Shinnston WV BR/TR/5-11/165(157-168) d7.6 b-Dick																								
1963	Cle A	74	247	28	63	6	0	5	18	22-0	1	27	.255	.316	.340	85	-5	4-3	.938	-9	97	68	S46,2b27		-0.9
1964	Cle A	115	335	33	77	12	1	12	40	24-3	2	55	.230	.283	.379	84	-4	5-7	.981	7	108	92	2b103,S4		0.6
1965	Cle A	124	438	52	111	22	2	8	40	38-0	5	62	.253	.315	.368	93	-4	5-7	.977	1	96	110	S95,2b26		0.6
1966	Cle A	105	340	29	78	12	0	3	17	36-3	3	58	.229	.309	.291	73	-11	0-1	.961	-6	91	90	S90,2b10	42	-1.0
1967	Cle A	152	485	38	110	16	2	7	37	53-6	6	62	.227	.308	.311	84	-9	4-4	.967	-3	93	109	S150		0.1
1968	Cle A	154	495	43	116	18	3	6	35	43-10	5	46	.234	.300	.319	90	-6	1-1	.966	-16	84	95	S154		-1.0
1969	Cle A	132	469	48	112	10	2	4	24	44-2	1	43	.239	.304	.294	66	-21	5-3	.959	-8	92	99	S101,3b29,2b5		-1.8
1970	Cle A	72	155	17	40	5	2	0	15	20-1	0	14	.258	.339	.316	79	-4	1-0	.950	0	91	108	S27,3b17,2b16		0.0
1971	Cle A	13	50	4	11	1	0	0	5	3-0	1	3	.220	.278	.240	44	-4	0-0	.980	-6	61	45	S13		-0.9
	Oak A	70	189	14	37	2	1	1	9	7-0	1	19	.196	.228	.233	31	-18	1-2	.959	-1	93	101	S31,2b23,3b10		-1.6
	Year	83	239	18	48	3	1	1	14	10-0	2	22	.201	.239	.234	35	-21	1-2	.965	-7	82	104	S44,2b23,3b10		-2.5
1972	Oak A	47	142	11	26	2	0	0	4	13-1	0	8	.183	.250	.197	36	-11	0-0	.974	-2	96	117	2b46/3	108	-1.2
1973	†Bal A	17	28	4	7	0	1	5	5-0	0	6	.250	.353	.357	103	0	0-0	.880	-2	77	155	3b15/2		-0.2
1974	Tex A	54	76	10	15	2	0	0	5	9-0	1	13	.197	.279	.224	48	-5	0-0	.931	3	119	171	3b47,2b8/S		-0.2
Total	12	1129	3449	331	803	108	13	47	254	317-26	22	414	.233	.300	.313	76	-106	22-23	.964	-41	91	99	S712,2b265,3b119	150	-7.5
BROWN, LEON	Leon B11.16.1949 Sacramento CA BR/TR/6-0/185 [BalA66 9/176] d5.19 b-Curtis Col Cal St.-Sacramento																								
1976	NY N	64	70	11	15	3	0	2	4	4-0	0	17	.257	.257	.257	48	-0	3-3	1.000	3	102	254	O43(39/28/6)		-0.4
BROWN, LEW	Lewis J. "Blower" B2.1.1858 Leominster MA D1.15.1889 Boston MA BR/TR/5-10.5/185 d6.17																								
1876	Bos N	45	195	23	41	6	6	2	21	3		22	.210	.222	.333	82	-4		.856	1			C45/O(0/1/1)		-0.2
1877	Bos N	58	221	27	56	12	8	1	31	6		33	.253	.273	.394	104	0		.897	15			C55,1b4		1.5
1878	Pro N	58	243	44	74	21	6	1	43	7		37	.305	.324	.453	153	14		.880	3			C45,1b15/ORP		1.6
1879	Pro N	53	229	23	59	13	4	2	38	4		24	.258	.270	.376	112	3		.847	-6			C48,O6R		-0.1
	Chi N	6	21	2	6	1	0	0	3	1		4	.286	.318	.333	109	0		.974	0	138	206	1b6		0.0
	Year	59	250	25	65	14	4	2	41	5		28	.260	.275	.372	112	3		.847	-5			C48,O6R,1b6		-0.1
1881	Det N	27	108	16	26	3	1	3	14	3		16	.241	.261	.370	93	-1		.959	-4	84	134	1b27		-0.3
	Pro N	18	75	9	18	3	1	0	10	4		13	.240	.278	.307	85	-1		.833	-2	42	0	O13R,1b5		-0.3
	Year	45	183	25	44	6	2	3	24	7		29	.240	.268	.344	90	-2		.960	-3	80	136	1b32,O13R		-0.6
1883	Bos N	14	54	5	13	4	1	0	9	3		6	.241	.281	.352	89	-1		.943	-2	43	111	1b14		-0.3
	Lou AA	14	60	6	11	2	1	0		1			.183	.197	.250	46	-3		.891	-2	121	91	1b14/C		-0.6
1884	Bos U	85	325	50	75	18	3	1	13				.231	.260	.314	74	-20		.914	10			C54,1b33,O2R/P		-0.7
Total	7	378	1531	205	379	83	31	10	169	45		155	.248	.269	.362	99	-13		.884	17			C248,1b118,O23(0/1/23),P2		0.6
BROWN, MARTY	Marty Leo B1.23.1963 Lawton OK BR/TR/6-1/190* [CinN85 12/292] d9.4 Col Georgia																								
1988	Cin N	10	16	0	3	0	0	0	2	1-0	0	2	.188	.235	.250	38	-1	0-1	1.000	-0	100	0	3b8		-0.2
1989	Cin N	16	30	2	5	2	0	0	4	4-0	0	8	.167	.257	.200	34	-3	0-0	.913	0	116	147	3b11		-0.2
1990	Bal A	9	15	1	3	0	0	0		1-0	0	7	.200	.250	.200	20	-1	0-0	1.000	-1	47	0	2b3,3b2,D4		-0.3
Total	3	35	61	3	11	2	0	0	6	6-0	0	18	.180	.250	.213	34	-5	0-1	.943	-1	108	88	3b21,D4,2b3		-0.7
BROWN, MIKE	Michael Charles B12.29.1959 San Francisco CA BR/TR/6-2/195* [CalA80 7/176] d7.21 Col San Jose St.																								
1983	Cal A	31	104	12	24	5	1	3	9	7-0	0	20	.231	.279	.385	81	-3	1-0	.949	-2	76	167	O31(18/3/11)		-0.6
1984	Cal A	62	148	19	42	8	3	7	22	13-1	0	23	.284	.342	.520	135	6	0-2	.968	-2	78	181	O44(2/0/43),D3		0.2

YEAR	TM LG	G	AB	R	H	2B	3B	HR	RBI	BB-IB	HP	SO	AVG	OBP	SLG	AOPS	ABR	SB-CS	FA	FR	RNG	THR	GAMES AT POSITION	DL	BFW
1985	Cal A	60	153	23	41	9	1	4	20	7-0	1	21	.268	.304	.418	96	-1	0-1	1.000	1	100	115	O48(1/1/46),D7		-0.3
	Pit N	57	205	29	68	18	2	5	33	22-4	0	27	.332	.391	.512	153	15	2-2	.938	-4	85	81	O56R		0.8
1986	Pit N	87	243	18	53	7	0	4	26	27-3	0	32	.218	.293	.296	62	-12	2-3	.973	-3	92	59	O71R		-2.1
1988	Cal A	18	50	4	11	2	0	0	3	1-0	0	12	.220	.235	.260	39	-4	0-0	.946	1	103	226	O18(18/0/2)		-0.4
Total	5	315	903	105	239	49	7	23	113	77-8	1	135	.265	.321	.411	101	1	5-8	.964	-10	88	115	O268(39/4/229),D10		-2.4

BROWN, OLIVER Oliver S. B1849 Brooklyn NY D9.23.1932 Brooklyn NY d8.1

YEAR	TM LG	G	AB	R	H	2B	3B	HR	RBI	BB-IB	HP	SO	AVG	OBP	SLG	AOPS	ABR	SB-CS	FA	FR	RNG	THR	GAMES AT POSITION	DL	BFW
1872	Atl NA	4	15	0	2	0	0	0	0			1	.133	.133	.133	-15	-2	0-0	.889	0	0	0	O4R		-0.1
1875	Atl NA	3	10	0	0	0	0	0	0			0	.000	.000	.000	-99	-2	0-0	.833	-1	0	0	1b2,O2(0/1/1)		-0.2
Total	2 NA	7	25	0	2	0	0	0	0			1	.080	.080	.080	-46	-4	0-0	.846	-0	0	0	O6(0/1/5),1b2		-0.3

BROWN, OLLIE Ollie Lee "Downtown" B2.11.1944 Tuscaloosa AL BR/TR/6-3/200(175-200) d9.10 b-Oscar

YEAR	TM LG	G	AB	R	H	2B	3B	HR	RBI	BB-IB	HP	SO	AVG	OBP	SLG	AOPS	ABR	SB-CS	FA	FR	RNG	THR	GAMES AT POSITION	DL	BFW
1965	SF N	6	10	0	2	1	0	0	0	0-0	0	2	.200	.200	.300	38	-1	0-0	1.000	-0	88	0	O4R		-0.1
1966	SF N	115	348	32	81	7	1	7	33	33-7	2	66	.233	.303	.319	71	-13	2-5	.978	-2	88	167	O114(1/16/107)		-2.4
1967	SF N	120	412	44	110	12	1	13	53	25-7	4	65	.267	.312	.396	104	-1	0-2	.985	-6	91	93	O115(0/10/111)		-1.4
1968	SF N	40	95	7	22	4	0	0	11	3-0	2	23	.232	.270	.274	64	-4	1-0	1.000	-3	71	51	O35(3/3/30)		-1.0
1969	SD N	151	568	76	150	18	3	20	61	44-3	3	97	.264	.319	.412	107	3	10-6	.976	2	100	122	O148R		-0.2
1970	SD N	139	534	79	156	34	1	23	89	34-8	0	78	.292	.331	.489	122	14	5-3	.964	1	99	106	O137R		0.9
1971	SD N	145	484	36	132	16	0	9	55	52-5	3	74	.273	.346	.362	108	6	3-3	.982	2	96	88	O134(0/1/134)		0.0
1972	SD N	23	70	5	12	2	0	0	3	5-2	0	9	.171	.224	.200	24	-7	0-0	1.000	0	108	80	O17R		-0.9
	Oak A	20	54	5	13	1	0	1	4	6-1	0	14	.241	.317	.315	93	0	1-1	1.000	-1	97	0	O16(0/9/9)		-0.2
	Mil A	66	179	21	50	8	0	3	25	17-3	1	24	.279	.342	.374	116	4	0-2	.992	9	124	227	O56R/3		1.0
	Year	86	233	26	63	9	0	4	29	23-4	1	38	.270	.336	.361	111	3	1-3	.994	8	118	176	O72(0/9/65)/3		0.8
1973	Mil A	97	296	28	83	10	1	7	32	33-1	2	53	.280	.355	.392	112	-1	4-1	.994	-1	21	0	D82,O4R		0.3
1974	Hou N	27	69	8	15	1	0	3	6	4-0	0	15	.217	.260	.362	76	-3	0-0	1.000	1	132	0	O20R		-0.3
	Phl N	43	99	11	24	5	2	4	13	6-1	0	20	.242	.286	.455	100	-1	0-1	.921	-2	83	67	O33(24/0/9)		-0.5
	Year	70	168	19	39	6	2	7	19	10-1	0	35	.232	.275	.417	91	-4	0-1	.961	-1	103	39	O53(24/0/29)		-0.8
1975	Phl N	84	145	19	44	12	0	6	26	15-1	0	29	.303	.369	.510	135	7	1-1	1.000	-1	103	0	O63(23/0/48)		0.4
1976	†Phl N	92	209	30	53	10	1	5	30	33-5	0	33	.254	.350	.383	105	3	2-1	.949	2	100	162	O75(9/0/69)		0.2
1977	†Phl N	53	70	5	17	3	1	1	13	4-1	0	14	.243	.280	.357	87	-3	1-1	1.000	-1	79	135	O21(15/0/7)		-0.5
Total	13	1221	3642	404	964	144	11	102	454	314-45	17	616	.265	.324	.394	103	11	30-27	.977	1	97	110	O992(75/39/910),D82/3		-4.7

BROWN, OSCAR Oscar Lee B2.8.1946 Long Beach CA BR/TR/6-0/175* [AtlN66 S1/7] d9.3 b-Ollie Col USC

YEAR	TM LG	G	AB	R	H	2B	3B	HR	RBI	BB-IB	HP	SO	AVG	OBP	SLG	AOPS	ABR	SB-CS	FA	FR	RNG	THR	GAMES AT POSITION	DL	BFW
1969	Atl N	7	4	2	1	0	0	0	0	0-0	0	1	.250	.250	.250	40	0	0-0	1.000	-0	90	0	O3(0/2/1)		0.0
1970	Atl N	28	47	6	18	2	1	1	7	7-0	1	7	.383	.464	.532	159	4	0-2	.960	-1	93	0	O25(8/12/5)		0.2
1971	Atl N	27	43	4	9	4	0	0	5	3-0	0	8	.209	.261	.302	55	-2	0-0	1.000	0	66	118	O15(6/7/3)		-0.3
1972	Atl N	76	164	19	37	5	1	3	16	4-0	0	29	.226	.244	.323	55	-10	0-2	.899	4	111	254	O59(28/3/28)		-1.0
1973	Atl N	22	58	3	12	3	0	0	0	3-0	0	10	.207	.246	.259	37	-5	0-0	1.000	1	119	102	O13(5/3/5)	65	-0.5
Total	5	160	316	34	77	14	2	4	28	17-0	1	55	.244	.284	.339	69	-13	0-4	.939	4	104	164	O115(47/27/42)	65	-1.6

BROWN, DICK Richard Ernest B1.17.1935 Shinnston WV D4.17.1970 Baltimore MD BR/TR/6-3/190(175-190) d6.20 b-Larry

YEAR	TM LG	G	AB	R	H	2B	3B	HR	RBI	BB-IB	HP	SO	AVG	OBP	SLG	AOPS	ABR	SB-CS	FA	FR	RNG	THR	GAMES AT POSITION	DL	BFW
1957	Cle A	34	114	10	30	4	0	4	22	4-1	0	23	.263	.281	.404	88	-3	1-1	.986	-0	79	108	C33		-0.2
1958	Cle A	68	173	20	41	5	0	7	20	14-1	3	27	.237	.304	.387	91	-2	1-0	.987	1	90	127	C62		0.1
1959	Cle A	48	141	15	31	7	0	5	16	11-1	1	39	.220	.288	.376	85	-3	0-0	.996	1	92	114	C48		0.0
1960	Chi A	16	43	4	7	0	0	3	5	3-0	0	11	.163	.217	.372	57	-3	0-0	.986	2	54	39	C14		-0.1
1961	Det A	93	308	32	82	12	2	16	45	22-2	0	57	.266	.312	.474	105	0	0-2	.990	6	142	148	C91	47	1.0
1962	Det A	134	431	40	104	12	0	12	40	21-7	2	66	.241	.279	.353	67	-22	0-1	.994	8	131	57	C132		-0.8
1963	Bal A	59	171	13	42	7	0	2	13	15-6	1	35	.246	.310	.322	80	-4	1-0	.986	2	123	85	C58		0.1
1964	Bal A	88	230	24	59	6	0	8	32	12-4	1	45	.257	.294	.387	89	-4	2-0	.988	-1	106	107	C84		-0.2
1965	Bal A	96	255	17	59	9	1	5	30	17-8	1	53	.231	.278	.333	73	-10	2-2	.983	2	107	147	C92	47	-0.4
Total	9	636	1866	175	455	62	3	62	223	119-30	11	356	.244	.291	.380	83	-51	7-6	.989	21	114	106	C614	47	-0.5

BROWN, ROBERT Robert d7.29

YEAR	TM LG	G	AB	R	H	2B	3B	HR	RBI	BB-IB	HP	SO	AVG	OBP	SLG	AOPS	ABR	SB-CS	FA	FR	RNG	THR	GAMES AT POSITION	DL	BFW
1874	Bal NA	2	9	0	0	0	0	0	0	0		0	.000	.000	.000	-99	-2	0-0	.727	-1	78	0	S2		-0.2

BROWN, BOBBY Robert William "Doc" B10.25.1924 Seattle WA BL/TR/6-1/180* d9.22 Mil 1952-54 Col Tulane

YEAR	TM LG	G	AB	R	H	2B	3B	HR	RBI	BB-IB	HP	SO	AVG	OBP	SLG	AOPS	ABR	SB-CS	FA	FR	RNG	THR	GAMES AT POSITION	DL	BFW
1946	NY A	7	24	1	8	1	0	0	4		0	0	.333	.429	.375	124	1	0-0	1.000	-2	73	39	S5,3b2		0.0
1947	†NY A	69	150	21	45	6	1	1	18	21	1	9	.300	.384	.373	114	4	0-2	.932	-7	73	73	3b27,S11,O3(0/2/1)		-0.4
1948	NY A	113	363	62	109	19	5	3	48	48	1	16	.300	.383	.405	111	7	0-1	.946	-13	84	104	3b41,S26,2b17,O4(3/0/1)		-0.4
1949	†NY A	104	343	61	97	14	4	6	61	38	3	18	.283	.359	.399	101	0	4-3	.949	-3	94	88	3b86,O3(1/0/2)		-0.4
1950	†NY A	95	277	33	74	4	2	4	37	39	1	18	.267	.360	.339	82	-7	3-1	.958	-4	94	89	3b82		-1.0
1951	†NY A	103	313	44	84	15	2	6	51	47	3	18	.268	.369	.387	108	5	1-1	.955	-6	91	96	3b90		-0.1
1952	NY A	29	89	6	22	2	0	1	14	9	1	6	.247	.323	.303	80	-2	1-1	.894	2	118	73	3b24		-0.1
1954	NY A	28	60	5	13	1	0	1	7	8	0	11	.217	.304	.283	65	-3	0-1	1.000	1	102	78	3b17		-0.3
Total	8	548	1619	233	452	62	14	22	237	214	10	88	.279	.367	.376	100	5	9-10	.948	-32	93	87	3b369,S42,2b17,O10(4/2/4)		-2.7

BROWN, BOBBY Rogers Lee B5.24.1954 Norfolk VA BB/TR (BL 1979)/6-1/205(198-231) [BalA72 11/264] d4.5

YEAR	TM LG	G	AB	R	H	2B	3B	HR	RBI	BB-IB	HP	SO	AVG	OBP	SLG	AOPS	ABR	SB-CS	FA	FR	RNG	THR	GAMES AT POSITION	DL	BFW
1979	Tor A	4	10	1	0	0	0	0	0	2-0	0	1	.000	.167	.000	-50	-2	0-0	1.000	0	110	0	O4(2/0/2)		-0.2
	NY A	30	68	7	17	3	1	0	3	2-0	0	17	.250	.271	.324	61	-4	2-1	.949	-0	113	0	O27(7/20/0)/D		-0.5
	Year	34	78	8	17	3	1	0	3	4-0	0	18	.218	.256	.282	46	-6	2-1	.955	-0	113	0	O31(9/20/2)/D		-0.7
1980	NY A	137	412	65	107	12	5	14	47	29-4	0	82	.260	.306	.415	98	-3	27-8	.972	3	105	89	O131(28/81/25)/D		0.0
1981	†NY A	31	62	5	14	1	0	0	6	5-0	0	15	.226	.279	.242	53	-4	4-2	.949	3	126	166	O29(6/11/14),D2		-0.2
1982	Sea A	79	245	29	59	7	1	4	17	17-2	0	32	.241	.288	.327	67	-12	28-6	.968	2	105	128	O68(51/14/4),D3	21	-0.8
1983	SD N	57	225	40	60	5	3	5	22	23-0	0	38	.267	.333	.382	101	0	27-9	.963	-4	97	24	O54(52/4/0)		-0.4
1984	†SD N	85	171	28	43	7	2	3	29	11-0	0	33	.251	.292	.368	85	-4	16-4	.971	2	115	69	O53(27/13/16)		-0.2
1985	SD N	79	84	8	13	0	0	0	6	5-0	0	20	.155	.200	.190	10	-10	6-4	1.000	0	79	246	O28(9/9/12)		-1.1
Total	7	502	1277	183	313	38	12	26	130	94-6	0	238	.245	.295	.355	80	-39	110-34	.968	6	106	87	O394(182/152/73),D7	21	-3.4

BROWN, ROOSEVELT Roosevelt Lawayne B8.3.1975 Vicksburg MS BL/TR/5-11/195* [AtlN93 20/572] d5.18

YEAR	TM LG	G	AB	R	H	2B	3B	HR	RBI	BB-IB	HP	SO	AVG	OBP	SLG	AOPS	ABR	SB-CS	FA	FR	RNG	THR	GAMES AT POSITION	DL	BFW
1999	Chi N	33	64	6	14	6	1	1	10	2-0	0	14	.219	.239	.391	57	-5	1-0	.955	-2	70	122	O18(13/5/1)		-0.6
2000	Chi N	45	91	11	32	8	0	3	14	4-0	1	22	.352	.378	.538	132	4	0-1	1.000	2	110	104	O28(24/1/5)		0.5
2001	Chi N	39	83	13	22	6	1	4	22	7-0	0	22	.265	.326	.506	115	2	0-0	.952	-2	77	0	O22(21/1/3),D3		-0.1
2002	Chi N	111	204	14	43	12	0	3	23	23-0	3	50	.211	.299	.314	65	-11	2-2	.975	-1	99	42	O64(48/13/4)/D		-1.4
Total	4	228	442	44	111	32	2	11	69	36-0	4	108	.251	.311	.407	80	-12	3-5	.972	-2	93	58	O132(106/20/13),D4		-1.6

BROWN, SAM Samuel Wakefield B5.21.1878 Webster PA D11.8.1931 Mount Pleasant PA BR/TR d4.21 Col Grove City

YEAR	TM LG	G	AB	R	H	2B	3B	HR	RBI	BB-IB	HP	SO	AVG	OBP	SLG	AOPS	ABR	SB-CS	FA	FR	RNG	THR	GAMES AT POSITION	DL	BFW
1906	Bos N	71	231	12	48	6	0	0	20	13		4	.208	.262	.242	59	-11	4	.970	-2	85	124	C35,O13(6/4/1),3b12,1b3,2b2		-1.1
1907	Bos N	70	208	17	40	6	0	0	14	12		4	.192	.250	.221	48	-12	0	.970	-4	80	111	C63,1b2		-1.1
Total	2	141	439	29	88	12	1	0	34	25		8	.200	.256	.232	54	-23	4	.970	-6	82	116	C98,O13(6/4/1),3b12,1b5,2b2		-2.2

BROWN, TOMMY Thomas Michael "Buckshot" B12.6.1927 Brooklyn NY BR/TR/6-1/170* d8.3 Mil 1946-47 OF(87/0/6)

YEAR	TM LG	G	AB	R	H	2B	3B	HR	RBI	BB-IB	HP	SO	AVG	OBP	SLG	AOPS	ABR	SB-CS	FA	FR	RNG	THR	GAMES AT POSITION	DL	BFW
1944	Bro N	46	146	17	24	4	0	0	8		0	17	.164	.208	.192	13	-17	0	.925	-10	82	87	S46		-2.5
1945	Bro N	57	196	13	48	3	4	2	19	6	0	16	.245	.267	.332	66	-11	3	.918	-6	97	92	S55/OR		-1.2
1947	Bro N	15	34	3	8	1	0	0	2	1	0	6	.235	.257	.265	37	-3	0	1.000	1	102	0	3b6,O3L/S		-0.2
1948	Bro N	54	145	18	35	4	0	2	20	7	1	17	.241	.281	.310	58	-9	1	.936	3	84	120	3b43/1		-1.2
1949	†Bro N	41	89	14	27	2	0	3	18	6	0	8	.303	.347	.427	102	0	0	.931	-0	110	55	O27L		0.5
1950	Bro N	48	86	15	25	2	1	8	20	11	1	9	.291	.378	.616	153	6	0	.917	1	101	191	O16L		-0.3
1951	Bro N	11	25	2	4	2	0	0	4	1	0	4	.160	.222	.240	24	-1	0-0	.909	-0	83	224	O5L		-0.3
	Phl N	78	196	24	43	2	1	10	32	16	1	21	.219	.278	.393	80	-7	1-2	.966	-6	100	39	O32L,2b14,1b12/3		-1.6
	Year	89	221	26	47	4	1	10	33	17	1	25	.213	.272	.376	73	-10	1-2	.957	-7	102	39	O37L,2b14,1b12/3		-1.9
1952	Phl N	18	25	2	4	1	0	0	1	2	0	3	.160	.276	.320	65	-1	0-0	1.000	0	142	0	1b3,O3L		-0.1
	Chi N	61	200	24	64	11	0	3	24	12		24	.320	.358	.420	114	4	1-2	.911	-16	82	75	S39,2b10,1b5		-1.1
	Year	79	225	26	68	12	0	4	26	16		27	.302	.349	.409	109	3	1-2	.911	-16	82	75	S39,2b10,1b8,O3L		-1.2
1953	Chi N	65	138	19	27	7	1	2	13	13		17	.196	.279	.304	51	-10	1-0	.903	-5	92	77	S25,O6(1/0/5)		-1.2
Total	9	494	1280	151	309	39	7	31	159	85		6	142	.241	.292	.355	74	-51	7-4	.916	-45	89	86	S166,O93L,3b50,2b24,1b21		-9.1

YEAR	TM LG	G	AB	R	H	2B	3B	HR	RBI	BB-IB	HP	SO	AVG	OBP	SLG	AOPS	ABR	SB-CS	FA	FR	RNG	THR	GAMES AT POSITION	DL	BFW

BROWN, TOM   Thomas Tarlton   B9.21.1860 Liverpool, England   D10.25.1927 Washington DC   BL/TR/5-10/168   d7.6   M2/U4 ▲

YEAR	TM LG	G	AB	R	H	2B	3B	HR	RBI	BB-IB	HP	SO	AVG	OBP	SLG	AOPS	ABR	SB-CS	FA	FR	RNG	THR	GAMES AT POSITION	DL	BFW
1882	Bal AA	45	181	30	55	5	2	1	23	6			.304	.326	.370	146	9		.728	-1	155	82	O45R,P2		0.7
1883	Col AA	97	420	69	115	12	7	5	32	20			.274	.307	.371	127	14		.808	-1	121	123	O96R,P3		1.1
1884	Col AA	107	451	93	123	9	11	5	32	24	4		.273	.343	.375	135	18		.847	-6	88	180	O107R,P4		1.0
1885	Pit AA	108	437	81	134	16	12	4	68	34	7		.307	.366	.426	152	27		.828	-5	111	61	O108R,P2		1.8
1886	Pit AA	115	460	106	131	11	11	1	51	56	2		.285	.365	.363	129	17	30	.837	6	156	381	O115(1/1/115)/P		1.9
1887	Pit N	47	192	30	47	3	4	0	6	11	1	40	.245	.289	.302	69	-8	12	.870	2	112	0	O47C		-0.7
	Ind N	36	140	20	25	3	0	2	9	8	1	25	.179	.228	.243	32	-13	13	.813	-3	110	156	O36(0/17/19)		-1.4
	Year	83	332	50	72	6	4	2	15	19	2	65	.217	.263	.277	53	-21	25	.851	-1	111	65	O83(0/64/19)		-2.1
1888	Bos N	107	420	62	104	10	7	9	49	30	1	68	.248	.299	.369	109	4	46	.896	-6	94	80	O107(6/2/99)		-0.4
1889	Bos N	90	362	93	84	10	5	2	24	59	1	56	.232	.341	.304	76	-11	63	.901	2	73	33	O90(88/0/2)		-0.3
1890	Bos P	128	543	146	149	23	14	4	61	86	3	84	.274	.377	.390	98	-1	79	.911	2	136	172	O128C		-0.3
1891	Bos AA	137	589	177	189	30	21	5	72	70	4	96	.321	.397	.469	150	37	106	.878	-12	95	150	O137C		1.8
1892	Lou N	153	660	105	150	16	8	2	45	47	5	94	.227	.284	.285	78	-18	78	.919	16	151	156	O153C		-1.1
1893	Lou N	122	529	104	127	15	5	0	54	56	5	63	.240	.319	.323	77	-17	66	.929	26	192	273	O122C		0.1
1894	Lou N	130	541	123	137	22	14	0	57	60	3	74	.253	.331	.396	80	-19	66	.912	2	97	147	O130C		-2.0
1895	StL N	84	355	73	78	11	4	1	31	48	2	44	.220	.316	.282	56	-23	34	.951	7	120	166	O84(1/83/0)		-1.7
	Was N	34	134	25	32	8	3	2	16	18	0	16	.239	.329	.388	85	-3	8	.909	-5	23	0	O34C		-0.8
	Year	118	489	98	110	19	7	3	47	66	2	60	.225	.320	.311	64	-26	42	.942	2	95	123	O118(1/117/0)		-2.5
1896	Was N	116	435	87	128	17	6	2	59	58	6	49	.294	.385	.375	101	3	28	.928	-4	46	47	O116(0/114/2)		-0.6
1897	Was N	116	469	91	137	17	2	5	45	52	1		.292	.364	.369	94	-3	25	.928	-2	102	149	O115C,M		-1.0
1898	Was N	16	55	8	9	1	0	0	2	5	0		.164	.233	.182	19	-6	3	.925	0	49	0	O15C,M		-0.6
Total	17	1788	7373	1523	1954	239	138	64	736	748	46	709	.265	.336	.361	101	7	657	.890	18	114	144	O1785(96/1098/593),P12		-3.2

BROWN, TOM   Thomas William   B12.12.1940 Laureldale PA   BB/TL/6-1/190   d4.8   Col Maryland-Baltimore Co.

YEAR	TM LG	G	AB	R	H	2B	3B	HR	RBI	BB-IB	HP	SO	AVG	OBP	SLG	AOPS	ABR	SB-CS	FA	FR	RNG	THR	GAMES AT POSITION	DL	BFW
1963	Was A	61	116	8	17	4	0	1	4	11-0	1	45	.147	.227	.207	23	-12	2-1	1.000	-2	82	0	O16(10/5/1),1b14		-1.6

BROWN, WILLARD   Willard Jessie   B6.26.1915 Shreveport LA   D8.4.1996 Houston TX   BR/TR/5-11.5/200   d7.19   Negro Lg 1934-51   Mil 1944-45

YEAR	TM LG	G	AB	R	H	2B	3B	HR	RBI	BB-IB	HP	SO	AVG	OBP	SLG	AOPS	ABR	SB-CS	FA	FR	RNG	THR	GAMES AT POSITION	DL	BFW
1947	StL A	21	67	4	12	3	1	1	6	0	0	7	.179	.179	.269	23	-7	2-2	1.000	1	124	0	O18(0/1/17)		-0.8

BROWN, GATES   William James "Gator"   B5.2.1939 Crestline OH   BL/TR/5-11/220(200-225)   d6.19   C7

YEAR	TM LG	G	AB	R	H	2B	3B	HR	RBI	BB-IB	HP	SO	AVG	OBP	SLG	AOPS	ABR	SB-CS	FA	FR	RNG	THR	GAMES AT POSITION	DL	BFW
1963	Det A	55	82	16	22	3	1	2	14	8-0	1	13	.268	.333	.402	104	3	2-1	1.000	4	138	320	O16L		0.4
1964	Det A	123	426	65	116	22	6	15	54	31-0	4	53	.272	.326	.458	114	7	11-4	.981	6	116	78	O106L		0.9
1965	Det A	96	227	33	58	14	2	10	43	17-1	0	33	.256	.305	.467	115	4	6-0	.973	3	121	33	O56(49/0/7)		0.5
1966	Det A	88	169	27	45	5	1	7	27	18-2	2	19	.266	.337	.432	119	4	3-0	.980	-2	71	177	O43L		0.1
1967	Det A	51	91	17	17	1	1	2	9	13-0	0	15	.187	.286	.286	68	-4	0-0	1.000	0	85	102	O20L	63	-0.5
1968	†Det A	67	92	15	34	7	2	6	15	12-1	1	4	.370	.442	.685	231	15	0-0	1.000	-1	78	120	O17L/1		1.5
1969	Det A	60	93	13	19	1	2	1	6	5-0	1	17	.204	.250	.290	49	-7	0-0	.906	1	127	108	O14L		-0.7
1970	Det A	81	124	18	28	3	2	3	24	20-0	1	14	.226	.331	.323	82	-2	0-0	.950	0	102	76	O26L		-0.4
1971	Det A	82	195	37	66	2	3	11	29	21-2	2	17	.338	.408	.549	162	15	4-2	.986	-2	90	78	O56L	24	1.2
1972	†Det A	103	252	33	58	5	0	10	31	26-3	2	28	.230	.304	.369	97	-1	3-0	.977	5	123	118	O72L		0.1
1973	Det A	125	377	48	89	11	1	12	50	52-6	1	41	.236	.328	.366	90	-4	1-1	1.000	0	43	0	D119,O2L		-0.8
1974	Det A	73	99	7	24	2	0	4	17	10-2	0	15	.242	.312	.384	96	-1	0-0	—	0	0	0	D13		-0.1
1975	Det A	47	35	1	6	2	0	1	3	9-1	1	6	.171	.356	.314	87	0	0-0	—	0	0	0	/H		-0.1
Total	13	1051	2262	330	582	78	19	84	322	242-18	15	275	.257	.330	.420	109	26	30-8	.977	13	108	100	O428(421/0/7),D132/1	87	2.1

BROWN, WILLARD   William M. "Big Bill","California"   B1866 San Francisco CA   D12.20.1897 San Francisco CA   BR/TR/6-2/190   d5.10

YEAR	TM LG	G	AB	R	H	2B	3B	HR	RBI	BB-IB	HP	SO	AVG	OBP	SLG	AOPS	ABR	SB-CS	FA	FR	RNG	THR	GAMES AT POSITION	DL	BFW
1887	NY N	49	170	17	37	3	2	0	25	10	3	15	.218	.273	.259	51	-11	10	.914	-2			C46,3b3,O2R		-0.8
1888	†NY N	20	59	4	16	1	0	0	6	1	0	8	.271	.283	.288	84	-1	1	.893	-1			C20		-0.1
1889	†NY N	40	139	16	36	10	0	1	29	9	3	9	.259	.318	.353	87	-2	6	.846	-5			C37,O3C		-0.5
1890	NY P	60	230	47	64	8	4	4	43	13	1	13	.278	.320	.400	84	-7	5	.900	-4	100	107	C34,O13(2/0/11),1b9,3b3,2b2		-0.8
1891	Phi N	115	441	62	107	20	4	0	50	34	4	35	.243	.303	.306	75	-14	7	.989	4	111	113	1b97,C19,O2C		-1.6
1893	Bal N	7	32	5	4	3	0	0	5	1	0	3	.125	.152	.219	-2	-9	0	.985	-0	80	67	1b7		-0.4
	Lou N	111	461	80	140	23	7	1	85	50	1	32	.304	.373	.390	112	10	9	.989	-1	86	103	1b111/C		0.7
	Year	118	493	85	144	26	7	1	90	51	1	35	.292	.360	.379	104	5	9	.988	-1	86	101	1b118/C		0.3
1894	Lou N	13	48	5	10	2	0	0	9	5	0	7	.208	.283	.250	31	-5	1	.977	4	231	67	1b13		-0.1
	StL N	3	9	0	1	0	0	0	0	0	0	2	.111	.111	.111	-46	-2	0	1.000	1	120	107	1b3		-0.2
	Year	16	57	5	11	2	0	0	9	5	0	9	.193	.258	.228	19	-8	1	.982	4	211	74	1b16		-0.3
Total	7	418	1589	236	415	70	17	6	252	123	12	124	.261	.319	.338	82	-37	39	.987	-5	105	103	1b240,C157,O20(2/5/13),3b6,2b2		-3.8

BROWN, BILL   William Verna "Verna"   B7.8.1893 Coleman TX   D5.13.1965 Lubbock TX   BL/TL/5-8/185   d8.15

YEAR	TM LG	G	AB	R	H	2B	3B	HR	RBI	BB-IB	HP	SO	AVG	OBP	SLG	AOPS	ABR	SB-CS	FA	FR	RNG	THR	GAMES AT POSITION	DL	BFW
1912	StL A	9	20	0	4	0	0	0	1	2	0		.200	.200	.200	15	-2	0	.909	-0	111	0	O7(6/1/0)		-0.3

BROWNE, BYRON   Byron Ellis   B12.27.1942 St.Joseph MO   BR/TR/6-2/200(185-200)   d9.9   Col Missouri Western

YEAR	TM LG	G	AB	R	H	2B	3B	HR	RBI	BB-IB	HP	SO	AVG	OBP	SLG	AOPS	ABR	SB-CS	FA	FR	RNG	THR	GAMES AT POSITION	DL	BFW
1965	Chi N	4	6	0	0	0	0	0	0	0-0	0	2	.000	.000	.000	-98	-2	0-0	.667	-0	67	0	O4L		-0.2
1966	Chi N	120	419	46	102	15	7	16	51	40-1	5	143	.243	.316	.427	103	1	3-3	.967	-8	91	38	O114(67/42/10)		-1.3
1967	Chi N	10	19	3	3	2	0	0	2	4-1	0	5	.158	.304	.263	61	-1	1-1	1.000	-0	103	0	O8(0/2/6)		-0.2
1968	Hou N	10	13	0	3	0	0	0	1	4-0	0	6	.231	.412	.231	99	0	0-0	1.000	2	192	604	O2R		0.2
1969	StL N	22	53	9	12	0	1	1	9	11-1	0	14	.226	.359	.321	91	0	0-0	1.000	4	130	320	O16(5/5/8)		0.3
1970	Phi N	104	270	29	67	17	2	10	36	33-5	0	72	.248	.327	.437	106	2	1-2	.975	1	105	86	O88(6/23/61)		0.0
1971	Phi N	58	68	5	14	3	0	3	5	8-0	0	23	.206	.289	.382	89	-1	0-0	1.000	-2	79	0	O30(17/4/10)		-0.4
1972	Phi N	21	21	2	4	0	0	0	1	1-0	0	8	.190	.227	.190	19	-2	0-0	1.000	-1	37	0	O9(0/3/6)		-0.1
Total	8	349	869	94	205	37	10	30	102	101-8	5	273	.236	.318	.405	98	-3	5-6	.973	-5	98	72	O271(99/79/103)		-1.9

BROWNE, EARL   Earl James "Snitz"   B3.5.1911 Louisville KY   D1.12.1993 Whittier CA   BL/TL/6-0/175   d9.12

YEAR	TM LG	G	AB	R	H	2B	3B	HR	RBI	BB-IB	HP	SO	AVG	OBP	SLG	AOPS	ABR	SB-CS	FA	FR	RNG	THR	GAMES AT POSITION	DL	BFW
1935	Pit N	9	32	6	8	2	0	0	6	2	0	8	.250	.294	.313	61	-2	0	1.000	0	93	70	1b9		-0.2
1936	Pit N	8	23	7	7	1	2	0	3	1	0	4	.304	.333	.522	124	0	0	1.000	1	95	385	O4L/1		0.1
1937	Phi N	105	332	42	97	19	3	6	52	21	4	41	.292	.342	.422	98	-1	4	.980	3	94	146	O54(8/5/43),1b23		-0.3
1938	Phi N	21	74	4	19	4	0	0	8	5	0	11	.257	.304	.311	71	-3	0	.978	-0	101	78	1b16,O2L		-0.5
Total	4	143	461	59	131	26	5	6	69	29	4	64	.284	.332	.401	93	-6	4	.983	4	96	156	O60(14/5/43),1b49		-0.9

BROWNE, GEORGE   George Edward   B1.12.1876 Richmond VA   D12.9.1920 Hyde Park NY   BL/TR/5-10.5/160   d9.27

YEAR	TM LG	G	AB	R	H	2B	3B	HR	RBI	BB-IB	HP	SO	AVG	OBP	SLG	AOPS	ABR	SB-CS	FA	FR	RNG	THR	GAMES AT POSITION	DL	BFW
1901	Phi N	8	26	2	5	1	0	0	4	1			.192	.250	.231	39	-2	2	1.000	-0	0	0	O8(6/1/1)		-0.3
1902	Phi N	70	281	41	73	7	1	0	26	16	2		.260	.304	.292	84	-5	11	.910	6	137	36	O70L		0.4
	NY N	53	216	30	69	9	5	0	14	9	3		.319	.355	.407	137	8	13	.895	-1	92	52	O53(51/0/2)		0.4
	Year	123	497	71	142	16	6	0	40	25	5		.286	.326	.342	107	3	24	.904	4	118	43	O123(121/0/2)		0.0
1903	NY N	141	591	105	185	20	3	3	45	43	4		.313	.364	.372	106	5	27	.918	-6	66	91	O141(1/0/140)		-0.7
1904	NY N	150	596	99	169	16	5	4	39	39	4		.284	.332	.347	105	3	24	.925	-6	106	148	O149R		-1.0
1905	†NY N	127	536	95	157	16	14	4	43	20	2		.293	.321	.397	111	4	26	.915	-9	54	29	O127R		-1.1
1906	NY N	122	477	61	126	10	4	0	38	27	0		.264	.304	.302	87	-9	32	.934	-3	113	87	O121R		-2.1
1907	NY N	127	458	54	119	11	10	5	37	31	1		.260	.308	.360	105	1	15	.941	-7	88	137	O121R		-1.2
1908	Bos N	138	536	61	122	10	6	1	34	36	0		.228	.276	.274	77	-15	17	.950	2	111	181	O138(12/17/109)		-2.3
1909	Chi N	12	39	7	8	0	1	0	1	5	0		.205	.295	.256	70	-1	3	.944	0	73	0	O12(0/11/1)		-0.3
	Was A	103	393	40	107	15	5	1	16	17	3		.272	.308	.344	111	3	13	.935	-3	92	96	O101(63/4/34)		-0.5
1910	Was A	22	71	4	4	0	0	0	0	4	0		.182	.217	.182	26	-2	0	.667	-1	64	0	O5L		-0.4
	Chi A	30	112	17	27	4	1	0	4	12	0		.241	.315	.295	95	0	5	.952	-3	79	53	O29(0/20/9)		-0.6
	Year	37	134	18	31	4	1	0	4	13	0		.231	.299	.276	84	-2	5	.917	-5	77	46	O34(5/20/9)		-1.0
1911	Bro N	8	12	1	4	0	0	0	3	2	1		.333	.385	.333	106	0	0	1.000	-0	121	0	O2R		0.0
1912	Phi N	6	5	0	1	0	0	0	0	0	0		.200	.333	.200	45	0	0	—	0			/H		0.0
Total	12	1102	4300	614	1176	119	55	18	303	265	20		.273	.317	.339	100	-10	190	.927	-36	93	100	O1077(208/53/816)		-10.5

BROWNE, JERRY   Jerome Austin   B2.13.1966 Christiansted, V.I.   BB/TR/5-10/170*   d9.6   OF(98/67/25)

YEAR	TM LG	G	AB	R	H	2B	3B	HR	RBI	BB-IB	HP	SO	AVG	OBP	SLG	AOPS	ABR	SB-CS	FA	FR	RNG	THR	GAMES AT POSITION	DL	BFW
1986	Tex A	12	24	6	10	2	0	0	3	1-0	0	4	.417	.440	.500	151	2	0-2	.923	-2	86	97	2b8		0.0
1987	Tex A	132	454	63	123	16	6	1	38	61-0	2	50	.271	.358	.339	86	-7	27-17	.980	-4	92	77	2b130/D	15	-0.4
1988	Tex A	73	214	26	49	9	1	1	17	25-0	1	21	.229	.308	.304	71	-8	7-6	.958	-25	75	62	2b70/D		-3.3
1989	Cle A	153	598	83	179	31	4	5	45	68-10	1	64	.299	.370	.390	113	12	14-6	.979	-38	87	70	2b151,D2		-2.2

YEAR	TM LG	G	AB	R	H	2B	3B	HR	RBI	BB-IB	HP	SO	AVG	OBP	SLG	AOPS	ABR	SB-CS	FA	FR	RNG	THR	GAMES AT POSITION	DL	BFW
1990	Cle A	140	513	92	137	26	5	6	50	72-1	2	46	.267	.353	.372	105	6	12-7	.985	-11	96	73	2b139		-0.2
1991	Cle A	107	290	28	66	5	2	1	29	27-0	1	29	.228	.292	.269	57	-17	2-4	.964	-3	98	65	2b47,O17L,3b15,D7		-2.1
1992	†Oak A	111	324	43	93	12	2	3	40	40-0	4	40	.287	.366	.364	112	7	3-3	.965	-7	89	108	3b58,O43(17/23/6),2b19/SD		-0.1
1993	Oak A	76	260	27	65	13	0	2	19	22-0	0	17	.250	.306	.323	74	-10	4-0	.985	-0	109	33	O56(30/26/4),3b13,2b1b2	90	-1.0
1994	Fla N	101	329	42	97	17	4	3	30	52-3	2	23	.295	.392	.398	103	4	3-0	.931	-1	90	118	3b62,O30(23/7/4),2b15		0.4
1995	Fla N	77	184	21	47	4	0	1	17	25-0	1	20	.255	.346	.293	70	-7	1-5	.959	6	109	158	O29(11/11/11),2b27,3b7	43	-0.1
Total	10	982	3190	431	866	135	25	23	288	393-14	13	325	.271	.351	.351	95	-18	73-45	.977	-85	90	71	2b609,O175L,3b155,D12,1b2/S	148	-9.0

BROWNE, PIDGE Prentice Almont B3.21.1929 Peekskill NY D6.3.1997 Houston TX BL/TL/6-1/190 d4.13

YEAR	TM LG	G	AB	R	H	2B	3B	HR	RBI	BB-IB	HP	SO	AVG	OBP	SLG	AOPS	ABR	SB-CS	FA	FR	RNG	THR	GAMES AT POSITION	DL	BFW
1962	Hou N	65	100	8	21	4	2	1	10	13-0	1	9	.210	.298	.320	72	-4	0-0	.983	1	117	74	1b26		-0.4

BROWNING, PETE Louis Rogers "The Gladiator" B6.17.1861 Louisville KY D9.10.1905 Louisville KY BR/TR/6-0/180 d5.2 OF(477/490/35)

YEAR	TM LG	G	AB	R	H	2B	3B	HR	RBI	BB-IB	HP	SO	AVG	OBP	SLG	AOPS	ABR	SB-CS	FA	FR	RNG	THR	GAMES AT POSITION	DL	BFW
1882	Lou AA	69	288	67	109	17	3	5		26			.378	.430	.510	229	41		.890	9	104	117	2b42,S18,3b13		4.6
1883	Lou AA	84	358	95	121	15	9	4		23			.338	.378	.464	183	34		.861	-9	48	81	O48(34/11/3),S26,3b10,2b3/1		2.2
1884	Lou AA	103	447	101	150	33	8	4	47	13	2		.336	.357	.472	176	37		.806	-12	67	81	3b52,O24(1/23/0),1b23,2b4/P		2.1
1885	Lou AA	112	481	98	174	34	10	9	73	25	0		.362	.393	.530	190	48		.900	3	104	115	O112C		4.2
1886	Lou AA	112	467	86	159	29	6	2	68	30	7		.340	.389	.441	151	27	26	.791	-13	74	74	O112(31/82/0)		0.9
1887	Lou AA	134	547	137	220	35	16	4	118	55	8		.402	.464	.547	178	59	103	.868	-6	93	152	O134C		3.8
1888	Lou AA	99	383	58	120	22	8	3	72	37	4		.313	.380	.436	164	29	36	.888	-1	104	226	O99(20/79/0)		2.3
1889	Lou AA	83	324	39	83	19	5	2	32	34	0	30	.256	.327	.364	98	0	21	.882	-4	74	96	O83L		-0.6
1890	Cle P	118	493	112	184	40	8	5	93	75	3	36	.373	.459	.517	175	60	35	.893	5	82	82	O118L		4.9
1891	Pit N	50	203	35	59	14	1	4	28	27	1	31	.291	.377	.429	138	11	4	.904	3	92		O50(48/0/2)		1.1
	Cin N	55	216	29	74	10	3	0	33	24	2	23	.343	.413	.417	141	12	12	.924	-2	65	128	O55(54/1/0)		0.8
	Year	105	419	64	133	24	4	4	61	51	3	54	.317	.395	.422	139	23	16	.913	1	79		O105(102/1/2)		1.9
1892	Lou N	21	77	10	19	4	0	0	4	12	0	7	.247	.348	.299	104	1	5	.911	-1	28	273	O21L		-0.2
	Cin N	83	307	47	93	12	5	3	52	40	2	26	.303	.383	.404	140	16	8	.917	-2	99		O82(23/46/16),1b2		0.8
	Year	104	384	57	112	16	5	3	56	52	2	33	.292	.376	.383	133	18	13	.916	-3	84	58	O103(44/46/16),1b2		0.6
1893	Lou N	57	220	38	78	11	3	1	37	44	2	15	.355	.466	.445	155	22	8	.881	-4	51	44	O57(44/0/13)		1.2
1894	StL N	2	7	1	1	0	0	0	0	0	0		.143	.143	.143	-31	-2	0	1.000	-0	0	0	O2C		-0.2
	Bro N	1	2	1	2	0	0	0	2	1	0	0	1.000	1.000	1.000	412	1	0	1.000	-0	0	0	/OR		0.1
	Year	3	9	2	3	0	0	0	2	1	0	0	.333	.400	.333	80	0	0	1.000	-1	0	0	O3(0/2/1)		-0.1
Total	13	1183	4820	954	1646	295	85	46	659	466	29	168	.341	.403	.467	164	396	258	.883	-35	82	103	O998C,3b75,2b49,S44,1b26/P		28.0

BRUBAKER, BILL Wilbur Lee B11.7.1910 Cleveland OH D4.2.1978 Laguna Hills CA BR/TR/6-2/185 d9.8 gs-Dennis Rasmussen Col UCLA

YEAR	TM LG	G	AB	R	H	2B	3B	HR	RBI	BB-IB	HP	SO	AVG	OBP	SLG	AOPS	ABR	SB-CS	FA	FR	RNG	THR	GAMES AT POSITION	DL	BFW
1932	Pit N	7	24	3	10	3	0	0	3	0	0	4	.417	.481	.542	178	3	1	.909	0	103	176	3b7		0.3
1933	Pit N	2	2	0	0	0	0	0	0	0	0	0	.000	.000	.000	-99	-1	0	1.000	0	148	0	/3		0.0
1934	Pit N	3	6	0	2	1	0	0	1	1	0	0	.333	.429	.500	144	0	0	1.000	1	139	395	3b3		0.1
1935	Pit N	6	11	1	0	0	0	0	0	0	0	5	.000	.154	.000	-53	-2	0	.889	-0	96	0	3b5		-0.3
1936	Pit N	145	554	77	160	27	4	6	102	50	4	96	.289	.352	.384	96	-2	5	.940	-12	90	49	3b145		-0.9
1937	Pit N	120	413	57	105	20	4	6	48	47	3	51	.254	.335	.366	90	-5	2	.952	5	108	116	3b115,S3/1		0.4
1938	Pit N	45	112	18	33	5	0	3	19	9	0	14	.295	.347	.420	109	1	2	.875	-3	85	137	3b18,1b9,S3/OL		-0.1
1939	Pit N	100	345	41	80	23	1	7	43	29	3	51	.232	.297	.365	78	-11	3	.950	5	102	100	2b65,3b32/S		-0.1
1940	Pit N	38	78	8	15	3	1	0	7	8	0	16	.192	.267	.256	45	-6	0	.955	4	117	133	3b19,S8,1b4		-0.2
1943	Bos N	13	19	3	8	3	0	0	1	2	0	2	.421	.476	.579	207	3	0	.778	-1	95	0	3b5,1b3		0.2
Total	10	479	1564	208	413	85	10	22	225	151	10	239	.264	.333	.373	90	-20	13	.938	-2	102	85	3b350,2b65,1b17,S15/OL		-0.6

BRUCE, LOU Louis R. B1.16.1877 St.Regis NY D2.9.1968 Ilion NY BL/TR/5-5/145 d6.2 Col Syracuse ▲

YEAR	TM LG	G	AB	R	H	2B	3B	HR	RBI	BB-IB	HP	SO	AVG	OBP	SLG	AOPS	ABR	SB-CS	FA	FR	RNG	THR	GAMES AT POSITION	DL	BFW
1904	Phi A	30	101	9	27	3	0	0	9				.267	.302	.297	85	-2	2	.969	-0	131	350	O25(11/10/5),P2/23		-0.3

BRUCKER, EARLE Earle Francis Jr. B8.29.1925 Los Angeles CA BL/TR/6-2/210 d10.2 f-Earle Col San Diego St.

YEAR	TM LG	G	AB	R	H	2B	3B	HR	RBI	BB-IB	HP	SO	AVG	OBP	SLG	AOPS	ABR	SB-CS	FA	FR	RNG	THR	GAMES AT POSITION	DL	BFW
1948	Phi A	2	6	0	1	0	0	0	1		0	1	.167	.286	.333	64	0	0-0	1.000	0	0	0	C2		0.0

BRUCKER, EARLE Earle Francis Sr. B5.6.1901 Albany NY D5.8.1981 San Diego CA BR/TR/5-11/175 d4.19 M1/C11 s-Earle

YEAR	TM LG	G	AB	R	H	2B	3B	HR	RBI	BB-IB	HP	SO	AVG	OBP	SLG	AOPS	ABR	SB-CS	FA	FR	RNG	THR	GAMES AT POSITION	DL	BFW
1937	Phi A	102	317	40	82	16	5	6	37	48	0	30	.259	.356	.397	91	-5	1-2	.971	-5	87	106	C92		-0.4
1938	Phi A	53	171	26	64	21	1	3	35	19	0	16	.374	.437	.561	152	15	1-1	.986	-4	79	87	C44/1		1.2
1939	Phi A	62	172	18	50	15	1	3	31	24	1	16	.291	.381	.442	112	4	0-1	1.000	-6	72	84	C47		0.1
1940	Phi A	23	46	3	9	1	1	0	2	6	0	3	.196	.288	.261	44	-4	0-0	.966	-0	71	134	C13		-0.3
1943	Phi A	1	1	0	0	0	0	0	0	0	0	0	.000	.000	.000	-99	-0	0-0	—	0			/H		0.0
Total	5	241	707	87	205	53	8	12	105	97	1	65	.290	.376	.438	108	11	2-4	.980	-15	81	98	C196/1		0.6

BRUETT, J. T. Joseph Timothy B10.8.1967 Milwaukee WI BL/TL/5-11/175* [MinA88 11/285] d6.3 Col Minnesota

YEAR	TM LG	G	AB	R	H	2B	3B	HR	RBI	BB-IB	HP	SO	AVG	OBP	SLG	AOPS	ABR	SB-CS	FA	FR	RNG	THR	GAMES AT POSITION	DL	BFW
1992	Min A	56	76	7	19	4	0	0	2	6-1	1	12	.250	.313	.303	71	-3	6-3	.979	-1	94	81	O45(5/20/22),D3		-0.4
1993	Min A	17	20	2	5	2	0	0	1	1-0	1	4	.250	.318	.350	79	-1	0-0	.857	-1	105	0	O13(2/4/8)		-0.1
Total	2	73	96	9	24	6	0	0	3	7-1	2	16	.250	.314	.313	72	-4	6-3	.952	-1	96	64	O58(7/24/30),D3		-0.5

BRUGGY, FRANK Frank Leo B5.4.1891 Elizabeth NJ D4.5.1959 Elizabeth NJ BR/TR/5-11/195 d4.13 Col Seton Hall

YEAR	TM LG	G	AB	R	H	2B	3B	HR	RBI	BB-IB	HP	SO	AVG	OBP	SLG	AOPS	ABR	SB-CS	FA	FR	RNG	THR	GAMES AT POSITION	DL	BFW
1921	Phi N	96	277	28	86	11	2	5	28	23	3	37	.310	.370	.419	100	1	6-2	.953	-11	69	104	C86,1b2		-0.4
1922	Phi A	53	111	10	31	7	0	0	9	6	1	11	.279	.322	.342	71	-5	0-0	.925	-2	113	121	C31		-0.5
1923	Phi A	54	105	4	22	3	0	1	6	4	1	9	.210	.245	.267	34	-10	1-1	.950	-1	110	131	C34,1b5		-1.0
1924	Phi A	50	113	9	30	6	0	0	8	8	0	15	.265	.314	.319	63	-6	4-4	.928	-6	98	83	C44		-0.9
1925	Cin N	6	14	2	3	0	0	0	1	2	0	2	.214	.313	.214	38	-1	0-0	.870	-1	85	107	C6		-0.2
Total	5	259	620	53	172	27	2	6	52	43	5	72	.277	.329	.356	71	-21	12-5	.941	-19	88	106	C201,1b7		-3.0

BRUMBAUGH, CLIFF Clifford Michael B4.21.1974 Wilmington DE BR/TR/6-2/205 d5.30 Col Delaware

YEAR	TM LG	G	AB	R	H	2B	3B	HR	RBI	BB-IB	HP	SO	AVG	OBP	SLG	AOPS	ABR	SB-CS	FA	FR	RNG	THR	GAMES AT POSITION	DL	BFW
2001	Tex A	7	10	1	0	0	0	0	0	1-0	0	5	.000	.091	.000	-71	-3	0-0	1.000	-0	84	0	O6(2/0/4)		-0.3
	Col N	14	36	5	10	2	0	1	4	2-0	0	9	.278	.316	.417	72	-1	0-1	1.000	-1	94	0	O11(4/0/8)		-0.3
Total	1	21	46	6	10	2	0	1	4	3-0	0	14	.217	.265	.326	45	-4	0-1	1.000	-1	91	0	O17(6/0/12)		-0.6

BRUMFIELD, JACOB Jacob Donnell B5.27.1965 Bogalusa LA BR/TR/6-0/185(170-190) [ChiN83 7/164] d4.6

YEAR	TM LG	G	AB	R	H	2B	3B	HR	RBI	BB-IB	HP	SO	AVG	OBP	SLG	AOPS	ABR	SB-CS	FA	FR	RNG	THR	GAMES AT POSITION	DL	BFW
1992	Cin N	24	30	6	4	0	0	0	2	2-1	1	4	.133	.212	.133	-0	-4	6-0	1.000	2	132	279	O16(7/8/1)		-0.1
1993	Cin N	103	272	40	73	17	3	6	23	21-4	1	47	.268	.321	.419	96	-2	20-8	.978	3	101	156	O96(24/68/5),2b4		0.3
1994	Cin N	68	122	36	38	10	2	4	11	15-0	0	18	.311	.381	.525	135	7	6-3	.987	2	111	65	O43(14/24/6)		0.8
1995	Pit N	116	402	64	109	23	2	4	26	37-0	5	71	.271	.339	.368	85	-8	22-12	.969	5	109	159	O104C	15	-0.1
1996	Pit N	29	80	11	20	9	0	2	8	5-0	0	17	.250	.294	.438	87	-2	3-1	.946	-2	82	110	O22C		-0.3
	Tor A	90	308	52	79	19	2	12	52	24-1	1	58	.256	.316	.448	92	-5	12-3	.982	1	96	155	O83(18/39/37),D5		-0.4
1997	Tor A	58	174	22	36	1	2	3	20	14-0	1	31	.207	.268	.282	44	-15	4-4	1.000	3	98	266	O47(14/24/10),D4	15	-1.3
1999	LA N	18	17	4	5	0	1	0	1	1-0	0	5	.294	.294	.412	80	-1	0-0	1.000	0	122	0	O11(7/4/0)		-0.1
	Tor A	62	170	25	40	8	3	2	19	19-0	1	39	.235	.307	.353	68	-9	1-2	.978	3	110	161	O53(10/36/8),D6		-0.6
Total	7	568	1575	260	404	91	14	32	162	137-7	12	290	.257	.318	.393	84	-39	74-33	.979	17	104	163	O475(94/329/67),D15,2b4	30	-1.8

BRUMLEY, MIKE Anthony Michael B4.9.1963 Oklahoma City OK BB/TR/5-10/165* [BosA83 2/33] d6.16 f-Mike Col Texas

YEAR	TM LG	G	AB	R	H	2B	3B	HR	RBI	BB-IB	HP	SO	AVG	OBP	SLG	AOPS	ABR	SB-CS	FA	FR	RNG	THR	GAMES AT POSITION	DL	BFW
1987	Chi N	39	104	18	21	2	2	1	9	10-1	1	30	.202	.276	.288	48	-8	7-1	.965	1	101	123	S34/2		-0.2
1989	Det A	92	212	33	42	5	2	1	11	14-0	1	45	.198	.251	.255	44	-16	8-4	.980	-14	86	49	S42,2b24,3b11,O4(1/1/2),D8		-2.8
1990	Sea A	62	147	19	33	5	4	0	7	10-0	0	22	.224	.272	.313	63	-8	2-0	.983	-2	92	88	S47,2b6,3b3,O2(1/1/0)/D		-0.6
1991	Bos A	63	118	16	25	5	0	0	5	10-0	1	22	.212	.273	.254	44	-9	2-0	.950	7	119	69	S31,3b17,2b7,O4C,D2		0.1
1992	Bos A	2	1	0	0	0	0	0	0	0-0	0	0	.000	.000	.000	-93	-0	0-0	—	0			/H		0.0
1993	Hou N	8	10	1	3	0	0	0	2	1-0	0	3	.300	.364	.300	83	0	0-1	—	0			/3SO(1/0/1)		-0.1
1994	Oak A	11	25	0	6	0	0	0	2	1-0	1	4	.240	.269	.240	36	-3	0-0	.929	-2	86	102	2b4,3b4,O3L/S		-0.2
1995	Hou N	18	18	1	1	0	0	0	0	0-0	0	5	.056	.056	.222	-33	-4	1-0	1.000	-1	42	0	S3,O3L/13		-0.4
Total	8	295	635	78	131	17	8	3	38	46-1	2	136	.206	.261	.272	47	-48	20-6	.972	-10	97	82	S159,2b42,3b37,O17(9/6/3),D11/1	35	-4.4

BRUMLEY, MIKE Tony Mike B7.10.1938 Granite OK BL/TR/5-10/195* d4.18 s-Mike Col Oklahoma

YEAR	TM LG	G	AB	R	H	2B	3B	HR	RBI	BB-IB	HP	SO	AVG	OBP	SLG	AOPS	ABR	SB-CS	FA	FR	RNG	THR	GAMES AT POSITION	DL	BFW
1964	Was A	136	426	36	104	19	2	2	35	40-6	1	54	.244	.309	.312	74	-14	1-1	.991	-4	114	102	C132		-1.3
1965	Was A	79	216	15	45	4	0	3	15	20-6	2	33	.208	.280	.269	58	-12	1-1	.990	1	74	112	C66		-0.9
1966	Was A	9	18	1	2	1	0	0	0	0-0	0	2	.111	.111	.167	-22	-3	0-0	1.000	-0	0	89	C7		-0.3
Total	3	224	660	52	151	24	2	5	50	60-12	3	89	.229	.296	.294	67	-29	2-2	.991	-4	98	105	C205		-2.5

BRUMMER, GLENN Glenn Edward B11.23.1954 Olney IL BR/TR/6-0/200(185-200) d5.25 Col Lake Land (IL) JC

YEAR	TM LG	G	AB	R	H	2B	3B	HR	RBI	BB-IB	HP	SO	AVG	OBP	SLG	AOPS	ABR	SB-CS	FA	FR	RNG	THR	GAMES AT POSITION	DL	BFW
1981	StL N	21	30	2	6	1	0	0	2	1-0	0	10	.200	.219	.233	0	-3	0-0	1.000	-1	84	98	C19		-0.4
1982	†StL N	35	64	4	15	4	0	0	8	0-0	0	12	.234	.234	.297	46	-5	2-0	.970	-1	161	49	C32		-0.5
1983	StL N	45	87	7	24	7	0	0	9	10-1	0	11	.276	.351	.356	96	0	1-3	.978	5	68	64	C41		-0.4
1984	StL N	28	58	3	12	0	0	1	3	3-0	0	7	.207	.246	.259	43	-5	0-0	.973	2	164	117	C26	46	-0.2
1985	Tex A	49	108	7	30	4	0	0	5	11-1	2	22	.278	.355	.315	84	-2	1-5	.989	-8	84	40	C47/ORD		-1.0
Total	5	178	347	23	87	16	0	1	27	25-2	2	54	.251	.304	.305	69	-15	4-8	.981	-12	115	66	C165/DOR	46	-2.5

BRUNANSKY, TOM Thomas Andrew B8.20.1960 Covina CA BR/TR/6-4/211(205-220) [CalA78 1/14] d4.9

YEAR	TM LG	G	AB	R	H	2B	3B	HR	RBI	BB-IB	HP	SO	AVG	OBP	SLG	AOPS	ABR	SB-CS	FA	FR	RNG	THR	GAMES AT POSITION	DL	BFW
1981	Cal A	11	33	7	5	0	0	0	8	6-0	0	10	.152	.317	.424	111	1	0-1	.938	2	107	363	O11L		0.2
1982	Min A	127	463	77	126	30	1	20	46	71-0	8	101	.272	.377	.471	127	20	1-2	.986	11	123	91	O127(3/38/97)		2.6
1983	Min A	151	542	70	123	24	5	28	82	61-4	4	95	.227	.308	.445	101	-1	2-5	.985	13	114	146	O146(0/38/119),D4		0.5
1984	Min A	155	567	75	144	21	0	32	85	57-2	0	94	.254	.320	.460	108	5	4-5	.984	0	95	135	O153R/D		-0.4
1985	Min A★	157	567	71	137	28	4	27	90	71-7	0	86	.242	.320	.448	103	2	5-3	.984	1	96	135	O155(0/1/155)		-0.5
1986	Min A	157	593	69	152	28	1	23	75	53-4	1	98	.256	.315	.423	97	-3	6-2	.982	3	105	97	O152(0/1/152),D2		-0.7
1987	†Min A	155	532	83	138	22	2	32	85	74-5	4	104	.259	.352	.489	116	13	11-11	.990	3	104	108	O138(58/0/107),D17		0.7
1988	Min A	14	49	5	9	1	0	1	6	7-0	0	11	.184	.286	.265	54	-3	1-2	.864	-3	70	0	O13(1/0/12)/D		-0.7
	StL N	143	523	69	128	22	4	22	79	79-6	4	82	.245	.345	.428	120	15	16-6	**.996**	-1	92	136	O143(1/0/143)		1.1
1989	StL N	158	556	67	133	29	3	20	85	59-3	2	107	.239	.312	.410	102	1	5-9	.977	-2	96	107	O155(0/1/155)/1		-0.8
1990	StL N	19	57	5	9	3	0	1	2	12-0	1	10	.158	.310	.263	60	-3	0-0	.950	0	106	93	O17R		-0.3
	†Bos A	129	461	61	123	24	5	15	71	54-7	3	105	.267	.342	.438	113	8	5-10	.982	0	105	56	O121(0/1/121),D7		0.6
1991	Bos A	142	459	54	105	24	1	16	70	49-2	3	72	.229	.303	.390	87	-9	1-2	.989	0	105	56	O137(0/1/136)/D		-1.3
1992	Bos A	138	458	47	122	31	3	15	74	66-2	0	96	.266	.354	.441	115	11	2-5	.989	0	101	99	O92R,1b28,D17		0.5
1993	Mil A	80	224	20	41	7	3	6	29	25-0	0	59	.183	.265	.321	57	-15	3-4	.987	3	113	86	O71R,D6	60	-1.5
1994	Mil A	16	28	2	6	2	0	0	0	1-0	0	9	.214	.241	.286	34	-3	0-0	1.000	-1	46	0	O6R,1b2,D2		-0.4
	Bos A	48	177	22	42	10	1	10	34	23-1	0	48	.237	.319	.475	98	-1	0-2	.989	-1	101	33	O42(14/0/33),1b5,D3		-0.6
	Year	64	205	24	48	12	1	10	34	24-1	0	57	.234	.309	.449	89	-4	0-2	.989	-3	98	31	O48(14/0/39),1b7,D5		-1.0
Total	14	1800	6289	804	1543	306	33	271	919	770-43	30	1187	.245	.337	.434	105	38	69-70	.984	33	104	108	O1679(88/81/1569),D61,1b36	60	-1.0

BRUNSBERG, ARLO Arlo Adolph B8.15.1940 Fertile MN BL/TR/6-0/195 d9.23 Col Concordia College (MN)

YEAR	TM LG	G	AB	R	H	2B	3B	HR	RBI	BB-IB	HP	SO	AVG	OBP	SLG	AOPS	ABR	SB-CS	FA	FR	RNG	THR	GAMES AT POSITION	DL	BFW
1966	Det A	2	3	1	1	0	0	0	0	1-0	0	1	.333	.500	.667	227	1	0-0	1.000	-0	0	0	C2		0.1

BRUNTLETT, ERIC Eric Kevin B3.29.1978 Lafayette IN BR/TR/6-0/200* [HouN00 9/277] d6.27 Col Stanford

YEAR	TM LG	G	AB	R	H	2B	3B	HR	RBI	BB-IB	HP	SO	AVG	OBP	SLG	AOPS	ABR	SB-CS	FA	FR	RNG	THR	GAMES AT POSITION	DL	BFW
2003	Hou N	31	54	3	14	3	0	1	4	0-0	0	10	.259	.255	.370	58	-3	0-0	.963	-2	66	68	S10,2b9,O2(1/1/0)/3		-0.4
2004	Hou N	45	52	14	13	2	0	4	8	7-0	0	13	.250	.328	.519	114	1	4-0	.938	-5	68	103	S33,2b5,O2(1/1/0)		-0.2
2005	†Hou N	91	109	19	24	5	2	4	14	10-0	1	25	.220	.292	.413	82	-3	7-2	.929	2	62	56	2b28,O26(11/14/1),S10,3b8/1		0.0
Total	3	167	215	36	51	10	2	9	26	17-0	1	48	.237	.292	.428	84	-5	11-2	.962	-5	80	98	S53,2b42,O30(13/16/1),3b9/1		-0.6

BRUSH, BOB Robert B3.8.1875 Osage IA D4.2.1944 San Bernardino CA d4.20

YEAR	TM LG	G	AB	R	H	2B	3B	HR	RBI	BB-IB	HP	SO	AVG	OBP	SLG	AOPS	ABR	SB-CS	FA	FR	RNG	THR	GAMES AT POSITION	DL	BFW
1907	Bos N	2	2	0	0	0	0	0	0	0-0	0	0	.000	.000	.000	-99	0	0	1.000	-0	0	0	/1		-0.1

BRUTON, BILL William Haron B11.9.1925 Panola AL D12.5.1995 Marshallton DE BL/TR/6-0.5/169* d4.13 Negro Lg 1949

YEAR	TM LG	G	AB	R	H	2B	3B	HR	RBI	BB-IB	HP	SO	AVG	OBP	SLG	AOPS	ABR	SB-CS	FA	FR	RNG	THR	GAMES AT POSITION	DL	BFW
1953	Mil N	151	613	82	153	18	14	1	41	44	6	100	.250	.306	.330	70	-29	**26**-11	.979	0	98	111	O150C		-3.3
1954	Mil N	142	567	89	161	20	7	4	30	40	4	78	.284	.336	.365	88	-11	**34**-13	.981	4	94	**134**	O141C		-1.6
1955	Mil N	149	636	106	175	30	12	9	47	43-6	4	72	.275	.325	.403	97	-5	**25**-11	.968	9	106	148	O149C		-0.2
1956	Mil N	147	525	73	143	23	**15**	8	56	26-11	1	63	.272	.304	.419	99	-4	8-6	.969	-3	100	92	O145C		-1.4
1957	Mil N	79	306	41	85	16	9	5	30	19-4	1	35	.278	.317	.438	110	3	11-4	.981	-4	94	83	O79C	73	-0.4
1958	†Mil N	100	325	47	91	11	3	3	28	27-4	2	37	.280	.336	.360	93	-4	4-1	.977	-7	90	86	O96C	40	-1.4
1959	Mil N	133	478	72	138	22	6	6	41	35-2	1	54	.289	.338	.397	104	2	13-5	.991	-2	101	83	O133C		-0.5
1960	Mil N	151	629	**112**	180	27	**13**	12	54	41-1	2	97	.286	.330	.428	115	10	22-13	.986	-6	94	89	O149C		-0.3
1961	Det A	160	596	99	153	15	5	17	63	61-0	3	66	.257	.327	.384	87	-12	22-6	.988	4	114	51	O155C		-0.9
1962	Det A	147	561	90	156	27	5	16	74	55-0	5	67	.278	.346	.430	104	4	14-7	.983	8	**119**	74	O145C		0.8
1963	Det A	145	524	84	134	21	8	8	48	59-3	0	70	.256	.330	.372	93	-4	14-7	.991	1	110	72	O138C		0.2
1964	Det A	106	296	42	82	11	5	5	33	32-1	0	54	.277	.347	.399	105	2	14-5	.987	1	95	155	O81(10/70/1)		-0.2
Total	12	1610	6056	937	1651	241	102	94	545	482-32	29	793	.273	.328	.393	96	-48	207-89	.981	1	102	97	O1561(10/1550/1)	113	-9.6

BRUYETTE, ED Edward T. B8.31.1874 Manawa WI D8.5.1940 Peshastin WA BL/TR/5-10/170 d8.6

YEAR	TM LG	G	AB	R	H	2B	3B	HR	RBI	BB-IB	HP	SO	AVG	OBP	SLG	AOPS	ABR	SB-CS	FA	FR	RNG	THR	GAMES AT POSITION	DL	BFW
1901	Mil A	26	82	7	15	3	0	0	4	12	0	12	.183	.295	.220	46	-5	1-0	.778	-4	45	0	O21C,2b3/S3		-1.0

BRYAN, BILLY William Ronald B12.4.1938 Morgan GA BL/TR/6-4/200(200-215) d9.12

YEAR	TM LG	G	AB	R	H	2B	3B	HR	RBI	BB-IB	HP	SO	AVG	OBP	SLG	AOPS	ABR	SB-CS	FA	FR	RNG	THR	GAMES AT POSITION	DL	BFW
1961	KC A	9	19	2	3	0	0	1	2	2-0	0	7	.158	.238	.316	46	-2	0-0	1.000	-1	0	0	C4		-0.2
1962	KC A	25	74	5	11	2	1	2	7	5-0	0	32	.149	.203	.284	28	-8	0-0	.976	-3	59	25	C22		-1.1
1963	KC A	24	65	11	11	1	1	3	7	9-5	0	22	.169	.270	.354	69	-3	0-0	.981	2	101	30	C24		0.1
1964	KC A	93	220	19	53	9	2	13	36	16-1	0	69	.241	.290	.477	107	1	0-0	.991	-9	74	86	C65		-0.6
1965	KC A	108	305	36	82	11	5	14	51	29-5	2	87	.252	.315	.446	116	6	0-0	.984	-4	84	89	C95		0.6
1966	KC A	32	76	0	10	4	0	0	7	6-0	0	17	.132	.193	.184	10	-9	0-0	.965	1	36	107	C21,1b3		-0.8
	NY A	27	69	5	15	2	0	4	5	5-0	0	19	.217	.270	.420	99	0	0-0	.988	-0	80	181	C14,1b3		-0.8
	Year	59	145	5	25	6	0	4	12	11-0	0	36	.172	.229	.297	52	-9	0-0	.975	1	58	144	C35,1b6		-0.8
1967	NY A	16	12	1	2	0	0	1	2	5-0	0	3	.167	.412	.417	151	1	0-0	1.000	0	0	0	/C		0.1
1968	Was A	40	108	7	22	3	0	3	8	14-2	1	27	.204	.301	.315	90	-1	0-1	.983	-3	85	107	C28		-0.3
Total	8	374	968	86	209	32	9	41	125	91-13	3	283	.216	.284	.395	91	-15	0-1	.984	-17	77	85	C274,1b6		-2.2

BRYANT, DEREK Derek Roszell B10.9.1951 Lexington KY BR/TR/5-11/185 [OakA73 8/191] d4.24 Col Kentucky

YEAR	TM LG	G	AB	R	H	2B	3B	HR	RBI	BB-IB	HP	SO	AVG	OBP	SLG	AOPS	ABR	SB-CS	FA	FR	RNG	THR	GAMES AT POSITION	DL	BFW
1979	Oak A	39	106	8	19	2	1	0	13	10-1	0	10	.179	.246	.217	29	-11	0-0	1.000	-1	93	94	O33(25/0/10),D2		-1.3

BRYANT, DON Donald Ray B7.13.1941 Jasper FL BR/TR/6-5/200* d7.17 C7

YEAR	TM LG	G	AB	R	H	2B	3B	HR	RBI	BB-IB	HP	SO	AVG	OBP	SLG	AOPS	ABR	SB-CS	FA	FR	RNG	THR	GAMES AT POSITION	DL	BFW
1966	Chi N	13	26	2	8	2	0	0	4	1-0	1	4	.308	.357	.385	105	0	1-0	.978	-0	58	51	C10		0.1
1969	Hou N	31	59	2	11	1	0	1	6	4-1	0	13	.186	.250	.254	42	-5	0-0	.993	-1	59	21	C28		-0.6
1970	Hou N	15	24	2	5	0	0	0	3	1-0	0	8	.208	.231	.208	22	-3	0-0	.957	-2	26	125	C13		-0.5
Total	3	59	109	6	24	3	0	1	13	6-1	1	25	.220	.271	.275	34	-8	1-0	.983	-4	52	48	C51		-1.0

BRYANT, GEORGE George F. B2.10.1857 Bridgeport CT D6.12.1907 Boston MA d8.6

YEAR	TM LG	G	AB	R	H	2B	3B	HR	RBI	BB-IB	HP	SO	AVG	OBP	SLG	AOPS	ABR	SB-CS	FA	FR	RNG	THR	GAMES AT POSITION	DL	BFW
1885	Det N	1	4	0	0	0	0	0	0	1	0	2	.000	.000	.000	-99	-1		1.000	-0	46	339	/2		-0.1

BRYANT, RALPH Ralph Wendell B5.20.1961 Fort Gaines GA BL/TR/6-2/200* [LAN81 S1/22] d9.8 Col Abraham Baldwin (GA) JC

YEAR	TM LG	G	AB	R	H	2B	3B	HR	RBI	BB-IB	HP	SO	AVG	OBP	SLG	AOPS	ABR	SB-CS	FA	FR	RNG	THR	GAMES AT POSITION	DL	BFW
1985	LA N	6	6	0	2	0	0	0	0	0-0	0	2	.333	.333	.333	89	0	0-0	—	-0	0	0	O3(2/0/1)		0.0
1986	LA N	27	75	15	19	4	2	6	15	3-0	1	25	.253	.305	.600	155	5	0-1	.953	1	100	131	O26R		0.4
1987	LA N	46	69	7	17	2	1	2	10	10-2	1	24	.246	.346	.391	98	0	2-1	.917	-1	97	0	O19(8/0/12)		-0.2
Total	3	79	150	22	38	6	3	8	24	15-2	2	51	.253	.325	.493	125	5	2-2	.940	-0	103	79	O48(10/0/39)		0.2

BRYE, STEVE Stephen Robert B2.4.1949 Alameda CA BR/TR/6-0/190* [MinA67 1/17] d9.3

YEAR	TM LG	G	AB	R	H	2B	3B	HR	RBI	BB-IB	HP	SO	AVG	OBP	SLG	AOPS	ABR	SB-CS	FA	FR	RNG	THR	GAMES AT POSITION	DL	BFW
1970	Min A	9	11	1	2	1	0	0	2	2-0	0	4	.182	.308	.273	60	-1	0-0	1.000	-1	66	0	O6(6/0/1)		-0.1
1971	Min A	28	107	10	24	1	0	3	11	7-0	0	15	.224	.270	.318	65	-5	3-1	.966	1	93	231	O28(25/7/0)		-0.6
1972	Min A	100	253	18	61	9	3	0	12	17-1	1	38	.241	.292	.300	73	-9	3-1	.994	9	114	165	O93(74/20/2)		-0.4
1973	Min A	92	278	39	73	9	5	6	33	35-1	0	43	.263	.343	.396	104	3	3-5	.986	2	108	71	O87(12/74/4)/D		0.0
1974	Min A	135	488	52	138	32	1	2	41	22-1	5	59	.283	.319	.365	94	-4	1-3	**.997**	-2	97	120	O129(0/128/1)		-1.0
1975	Min A	86	246	41	62	13	1	9	34	21-2	2	37	.252	.315	.423	106	1	2-1	.983	-0	93	146	O72(19/5/48),D6	21	-0.3
1976	Min A	87	258	33	68	11	0	2	23	13-0	0	31	.264	.295	.329	82	-6	1-2	.987	-6	88	21	O78(11/57/17),D3		-1.6
1977	Mil A	94	241	27	60	14	3	7	28	16-0	1	39	.249	.297	.419	93	-3	1-0	1.000	7	111	173	O48(27/4/17),D6		0.2
1978	Pit N	66	115	16	29	7	1	3	11	4-1	1	10	.252	.305	.322	72	-4	2-1	.983	-1	96	85	O47(28/7/12)		-0.6
Total	9	697	1997	237	515	97	13	30	193	144-6	10	276	.258	.309	.365	90	-30	16-14	.991	9	101	119	O623(204/339/102),D16	21	-4.3

BUBELA, JAIME Jaime Lee B6.6.1978 Houston TX BL/TR/6-1/200 d9.15 Col Baylor

YEAR	TM LG	G	AB	R	H	2B	3B	HR	RBI	BB-IB	HP	SO	AVG	OBP	SLG	AOPS	ABR	SB-CS	FA	FR	RNG	THR	GAMES AT POSITION	DL	BFW
2005	Sea A	11	19	3	2	0	0	0	0	1-0	0	4	.105	.150	.105	-32	-4	1-0	1.000	1	125	0	O7(1/6/0)/D		-0.1

BUBSER, HAL Harold Fred B9.28.1895 Chicago IL D6.22.1959 Melrose Park IL BR/TR/5-11/170 d4.15

YEAR	TM LG	G	AB	R	H	2B	3B	HR	RBI	BB-IB	HP	SO	AVG	OBP	SLG	AOPS	ABR	SB-CS	FA	FR	RNG	THR	GAMES AT POSITION	DL	BFW
1922	Chi A	3	3	0	0	0	0	0	0	0-0	0	2	.000	.000	.000	-99	-1	0-0	—		0		/H		-0.1

YEAR	TM	LG	G	AB	R	H	2B	3B	HR	RBI	BB-IB	HP	SO	AVG	OBP	SLG	AOPS	ABR	SB-CS	FA	FR	RNG	THR	GAMES AT POSITION	DL	BFW

BUCHA, JOHNNY   John George   B1.22.1925 Allentown PA   D4.28.1996 Bethlehem PA   BR/TR/5-11/190*   d5.2

1948	StL	N	2	1	0	0	0	0	0	1		0	0	.000	.500	.000	43	0	0	1.000	-0		0	/C		0.0
1950	StL	N	22	36	5	5	1	0	0	1	4	0	7	.139	.225	.167	5	-5	0	.959	-0	146	86	C17		-0.5
1953	Det	A	60	158	17	35	9	0	1	14	20	0	14	.222	.309	.297	65	-7	1-1	.984	-6	81	118	C56		-1.1
Total	3		84	195	18	40	10	0	1	15	25	0	21	.205	.295	.272	53	-12	1-1	.980	-6	92	112	C74		-1.6

BUCHANAN, BRIAN   Brian James   B7.21.1973 Miami FL   BR/TR/6-4/230*   [NYA94 1/24]   d5.19   Col Virginia

2000	Min	A	30	82	10	19	3	0	1	8	8-0		2	.232	.301	.305	52	-6	0-2	1.000	-2	77	67	O25(2/0/24),D2		-0.9
2001	Min	A	69	197	28	54	12	0	10	32	19-0	2	58	.274	.342	.487	110	3	1-1	.973	-0	105	45	O46(7/0/39),D19	15	0.0
2002	Min	A	44	135	19	34	5	1	5	15	6-0	2	33	.252	.294	.415	83	-4	2-1	1.000	1	127	0	O24R,D17	15	-0.4
	SD	N	48	92	12	27	5	0	6	13	9-0	1	26	.293	.363	.543	151	6	0-1	1.000	-0	108	79	1b15,O14R		0.4
2003	SD	N	115	198	29	52	10	2	8	29	24-1	3	51	.263	.346	.455	119	5	6-2	1.000	1	114	144	O43(15/0/29),1b24,D5		0.4
2004	SD	N	38	60	7	12	2	0	2	6	6-2	1	19	.200	.279	.333	62	-4	0-0	1.000	-2	58	0	O18(15/0/3),1b3	25	-0.6
	NY	N	2	3	0	0	0	0	0	0	1-0	0	1	.000	.250	.000	-28	-1	0-0	1.000	0	154	115	/1		-0.1
	Year		40	63	7	12	2	0	2	6	7-2	1	20	.190	.278	.317	57	-4	0-0	1.000	-2	58	0	O18(15/0/3),1b4		-0.7
Total	5		346	767	105	198	37	3	32	103	73-3	10	210	.258	.328	.439	101	-1	9-7	.987	-3	99	65	O170(39/0/133),1b43,D43	55	-1.2

BUCHEK, JERRY   Gerald Peter   B5.9.1942 St.Louis MO   BR/TR/5-11/185*   d6.30

1961	StL	N	31	90	6	12	1	1	0	9	0-0		2	28	.133	.151	.156	-16	-15	0-0	.912	-8	78	115	S31		-2.1
1963	StL	N	3	4	1	1	0	0	0	0-0		0	2	.250	.250	.250	41	0	0-0	1.000	-0	59	309	/S		0.0
1964	†StL	N	35	30	7	6	0	2	0	1	3-0		0	11	.200	.273	.333	64	-2	0-0	.929	2	116	70	S20,2b9/3		0.2
1965	StL	N	55	166	17	41	8	3	3	21	13-2	0	46	.247	.300	.386	84	-4	1-0	.994	8	105	120	2b33,S18/3	30	0.9
1966	StL	N	100	284	23	67	10	4	4	25	23-4	0	71	.236	.288	.342	75	-10	0-5	.974	-6	105	132	2b49,S48,3b4		-1.1
1967	NY	N	124	411	35	97	11	2	14	41	26-5	2	101	.236	.283	.375	89	-8	3-5	.977	-3	96	90	2b95,3b17,S9		-0.4
1968	NY	N	73	192	8	35	4	0	1	11	10-5	3	53	.182	.234	.219	36	-15	1-1	.935	-1	101	117	3b37,2b12,O9L		-1.9
Total	7		421	1177	96	259	35	11	22	108	75-16	7	312	.220	.269	.325	67	-54	5-11	.978	-8	100	105	2b198,S127,3b60,O9L	30	-4.4

BUCHER, JIM   James Quinter   B3.24.1911 Manassas VA   D10.21.2004 Elizabethtown PA   BL/TR/5-11/170   d4.18

1934	Bro	N	47	84	12	19	5	2	0	8	4		0	7	.226	.261	.333	61	-5	1	.920	-2	93	117	2b20,3b6		-0.6
1935	Bro	N	123	473	72	143	22	1	7	58	10	0	33	.302	.317	.397	93	-6	4	.950	-2	100	113	2b41,3b39,O37(21/0/16)		-0.7
1936	Bro	N	110	370	49	93	12	8	2	41	29	0	27	.251	.306	.343	74	-15	5	.910	-6	108	86	3b39,2b32,O30(7/0/23)		-2.0
1937	Bro	N	125	380	44	96	11	2	4	37	20	3	18	.253	.295	.324	67	-18	5	.951	-10	79	97	2b49,3b43,O6(4/1/1)		-2.4
1938	StL	N	17	57	7	13	3	1	0	7	2		0	2	.228	.254	.316	53	-4	0	.955	-1	83	115	2b14/3		-0.6
1944	Bos	A	80	277	39	76	4	2	4	31	19	2	13	.274	.326	.365	98	-1	3-3	.958	-4	96	119	3b44,2b21		-0.4
1945	Bos	A	52	151	19	34	4	3	0	11	7	1	13	.225	.264	.291	60	-8	1-3	.940	1	111	125	3b32,2b2		-0.9
Total	7		554	1792	242	474	66	19	17	193	91	6	113	.265	.302	.351	78	-57	19-6	.939	-25	102	102	3b204,2b179,O73(32/1/40)		-7.6

BUCK, JOHN   Johnathan R.   B7.7.1980 Kemmerer WY   BR/TR/6-3/210*   [HouN98 7/212]   d6.25

2004	KC	A	71	238	36	56	9	0	12	30	15-0		0	79	.235	.280	.424	80	-8	1-1	.992	-5	114	91	C68,D3		-0.9
2005	KC	A	118	401	40	97	21	1	12	47	23-2	3	94	.242	.287	.389	83	-11	2-2	.996	-11	100	123	C117		-1.4
Total	2		189	639	76	153	30	1	24	77	38-2	3	173	.239	.284	.402	82	-19	3-3	.995	-16	105	111	C185,D3		-2.3

BUCKLEY, KEVIN   Kevin John   B1.16.1959 Quincy MA   BR/TR/6-1/200   [TexA81 17/424]   d9.4   Col Maine

| 1984 | Tex | A | 5 | 7 | 1 | 2 | 1 | 0 | 0 | 2-0 | | 1 | .286 | .444 | .429 | 138 | 1 | 0-0 | — | 0 | | | D3 | | 0.0 |

BUCKLEY, DICK   Richard D.   B9.21.1858 Troy NY   D12.12.1929 Pittsburg PA   BR/TR/5-10/195   d4.20

1888	Ind	N	71	260	28	71	9	3	5	22	6		0	24	.273	.289	.388	112	3	4	.898	-14			C51,3b22/OR1		-0.7
1889	Ind	N	68	260	35	67	11	0	8	41	15	1	32	.258	.301	.392	91	-5	5	.877	-13			C55,3b12/OL1		-1.2
1890	NY	N	70	266	39	68	11	0	2	26	23	4	35	.256	.324	.320	88	-4	3	.931	7	98	127	C62,3b8		0.7
1891	NY	N	75	253	23	55	9	1	4	31	11	3	30	.217	.258	.308	67	-11	3	.958	4	82	106	C74/3		-0.1
1892	StL	N	121	410	43	93	17	4	5	52	22	5	34	.227	.275	.324	85	-9	7	.937	-9	95	85	C119,1b2		-0.7
1893	StL	N	9	23	2	4	1	0	0	1	0		0	0	.174	.174	.217	4	-3	0	.914	-2		86	100	C9		-0.2
1894	StL	N	29	89	5	16	1	2	1	6	3	1	3	.180	.240	.270	23	-12	1	.936	2	106	118	C27/1		-0.6
	Phi	N	43	160	18	47	7	3	1	26	6	2	13	.294	.327	.394	75	-7	0	.966	-1	92	90	C42/1		-0.4
	Year		72	249	23	63	8	5	2	29	12	3	16	.253	.295	.349	56	-20	1	.954	1	97	100	C69,1b2		-1.0
1895	Phi	N	38	112	20	28	6	1	0	14	9		5	22	.250	.333	.321	69	-5	2	.919	-1	93	84	C38		-0.2
Total	8		524	1833	213	449	72	14	26	216	98		21	188	.245	.291	.342	81	-53	25	.931	-25	93	100	C477,3b43,1b6,O2(1/0/1)		-3.4

BUCKNER, BILL   William Joseph   B12.14.1949 Vallejo CA   BL/TL/6-0/185(182-195)   [LAN68 2/25]   d9.21   C2

1969	LA	N	1	1	0	0	0	0	0	0-0		0	.000	.000	.000	-99	0	0-0	—	0			/H		0.0
1970	LA	N	28	68	6	13	3	1	0	4	3-1	0	7	.191	.225	.265	32	-7	0-1	1.000	-1	121	81	O20(19/0/1)/1		-0.7
1971	LA	N	108	358	37	99	*15	1	5	41	11-4	5	18	.277	.306	.366	95	-4	4-1	.994	4	110	91	O86(6/0/81),1b11		-0.5
1972	LA	N	105	383	47	122	14	3	5	37	17-2	1	13	.319	.348	.410	117	7	10-3	.992	2	112	24	O61(19/0/52),1b35		0.5
1973	LA	N	140	575	68	158	20	6	8	46	17-5	3	34	.275	.297	.351	82	-16	12-2	.998	-2	94	137	1b93,O48(35/0/13)		-2.7
1974	†LA	N	145	580	83	182	30	3	7	58	30-10	4	24	.314	.351	.412	117	12	31-13	.976	-6	94	44	O137(134/0/4),1b6		-0.1
1975	LA	N	92	288	30	70	11	2	6	31	17-7	2	15	.243	.286	.358	82	-8	8-3	.986	2	108	80	O72L	21	-1.0
1976	LA	N	154	642	76	193	28	4	7	60	26-6	1	26	.301	.326	.389	104	1	28-9	.985	-2	99	62	O153(149/0/5)/1		-0.8
1977	Chi	N	122	426	40	121	27	0	11	60	21-2	1	23	.284	.314	.425	88	-7	7-5	.990	-2	92	102	1b99	13	-1.6
1978	Chi	N	117	446	47	144	26	1	5	74	18-5	0	17	.323	.345	.419	102	1	7-5	.995	7	128	103	1b105	15	0.2
1979	Chi	N	149	591	72	168	34	7	14	66	30-6	2	28	.284	.319	.437	95	-5	9-4	.993	15	136	103	1b140		0.2
1980	Chi	N	145	578	69	187	41	3	10	68	30-11	0	18	**.324**	.353	.457	116	13	1-2	.993	5	123	91	1b94,O50(42/0/12)		1.0
1981	Chi N★		**106**	421	45	131	**35**	3	10	75	26-9	1	16	.311	.349	.480	127	15	5-2	.984	0	105	95	1b105		0.9
1982	Chi	N	161	657	93	201	34	5	15	105	36-7	5	26	.306	.342	.441	115	12	15-5	.993	12	125	72	1b161		1.6
1983	Chi	N	153	626	79	175	**38**	6	16	66	25-5	5	30	.280	.310	.436	101	-1	12-4	.992	22	**153**	116	1b144,O15L		1.3
1984	Chi	N	21	43	3	9	0	0	2	1-1		1	2	.209	.239	.209	26	-4	0-0	1.000	1	126	114	1b7,O2L		-0.3
	Bos	A	114	439	51	122	21	2	11	67	24-5	5	38	.278	.321	.410	96	-3	2-2	.986	6	117	75	1b113		-0.4
1985	Bos	A	162	673	89	201	46	3	16	110	30-5	2	36	.299	.325	.447	106	5	18-4	.992	25	**150**	96	1b162		2.2
1986	†Bos	A	153	629	73	.168	39	2	18	102	40-9	4	25	.267	.311	.421	98	-3	6-4	.989	20	**142**	73	1b138,D15		0.7
1987	Bos	A	75	286	29	78	6	1	2	42	13-1	0	19	.273	.299	.322	64	-15	1-3	.991	2	109	88	1b74	16	-1.7
	Cal	A	57	183	16	56	12	1	3	32	9-1	0	7	.306	.337	.432	106	1	1-0	1.000	-0	62	93	D39,1b5		0.0
	Year		132	469	39	134	18	2	5	74	22-2	0	26	.286	.314	.365	80	-14	2-3	.992	2	106	85	1b79,D39		-1.7
1988	Cal	A	19	43	1	9	0	0	0	4-0		0	2	.209	.271	.209	39	-4	2-0	1.000	0	1146	972	D11/1		-0.3
	KC	A	89	242	18	62	14	0	3	34	13-5	0	19	.256	.290	.351	79	-7	3-1	.994	-0	91	75	D42,1b21		-1.0
	Year		108	285	19	71	14	0	3	43	17-5	0	19	.249	.287	.330	73	-10	5-1	.973	-0	97	75	D53,1b22		-1.3
1989	KC	A	79	176	7	38	4	1	1	16	6-2	0	11	.216	.240	.267	43	-14	1-0	.985	-1	89	113	1b24,D19		-1.7
1990	Bos	A	22	43	4	8	0	1	3	3-2		1	5	.186	.234	.256	37	-4	0-0	1.000	-1	-0	86	73	1b15		-0.3
Total	22		2517	9397	1077	2715	498	49	174	1208	450-111	42	453	.289	.321	.408	99	-35	183-73	.992	112	125	97	1b1555,O644(493/0/168),D126	65	-4.7

BUDASKA, MARK   Mark David   B12.27.1952 Sharon PA   BB/TL/6-0/180*   d6.6   Col Los Angeles Pierce (CA) JC

1978	Oak	A	4	4	1	1	0	0	0	1-0		0	2	.250	.400	.500	159	0	0-0	.500	-1	42	0	O2(1/0/1)		0.0
1981	Oak	A	9	32	3	5	1	0	0	2	4-0		0	10	.156	.250	.188	29	-3	0-1	—	0			D9		-0.4
Total	2		13	36	3	6	2	0	0	2	5-0		0	12	.167	.268	.222	44	-3	0-1	.500	-1	42	0	D9,O2(1/0/1)		-0.4

BUDD   B Cleveland OH   d9.10

| 1890 | Cle | P | 1 | 4 | 0 | 0 | 0 | 0 | 0 | 0 | | | 0 | 3 | .000 | .000 | .000 | -99 | 0 | 0 | 1.000 | 0 | 0 | 0 | /OL | | -0.1 |

BUDDIN, DON   Donald Thomas   B5.5.1934 Turbeville SC   BR/TR/5-11/178*   d4.17

1956	Bos	A	114	377	49	90	24	0	5	37	65-1	4	62	.239	.352	.342	76	-11	2-0	.953	7	105	**123**	S113		0.6
1958	Bos	A	136	497	74	118	25	2	12	43	82-1	4	106	.237	.349	.368	92	-3	0-4	.958	14	108	107	S136		2.2
1959	Bos	A	151	485	75	117	24	1	10	53	92-0	5	91	.241	.366	.357	95	1	6-1	.949	-10	96	95	S150		0.4
1960	Bos	A	124	428	62	105	21	5	6	36	62-5	1	59	.245	.338	.360	87	-6	4-2	.951	-2	96	91	S124		0.2
1961	Bos	A	115	339	58	89	22	3	6	42	72-7	2	45	.263	.394	.398	110	9	2-1	.956	-2	96	99	S109		1.6
1962	Hou	N	40	80	10	13	4	1	2	10	17-2	1	17	.162	.316	.313	75	-2	0-0	.952	-1	92	94	S27,3b9		-0.1
	Det	A	31	83	14	19	3	0	4	20-0		1	16	.229	.385	.265	76	-2	1-0	.978	-2	94	118	S19,2b5,3b2		-0.2
Total	6		711	2289	342	551	123	12	41	225	410-16	18	404	.241	.358	.359	90	-14	15-8	.954	4	100	103	S678,3b11,2b5		4.7

YEAR	TM LG	G	AB	R	H	2B	3B	HR	RBI	BB-IB	HP	SO	AVG	OBP	SLG	AOPS	ABR	SB-CS	FA	FR	RNG	THR	GAMES AT POSITION	DL	BFW

BUDZINSKI, MARK   Mark Joseph B8.26.1973 Baltimore MD BL/TL/6-2/180 [CleA95 21/586] d8.3 Col Richmond

| 2003 | Cin N | 4 | 7 | 0 | 0 | 0 | 0 | 0 | 0 | 0-0 | 0 | 4 | .000 | .000 | .000 | -99 | -2 | 0-0 | 1.000 | 0 | 133 | 0 | /OC | | -0.2 |

BUECHELE, STEVE   Steven Bernard B9.26.1961 Lancaster CA BR/TR/6-2/190* [TexA82 5/122] d7.19 Col Stanford

1985	Tex A	69	219	22	48	6	3	6	21	14-2	2	38	.219	.271	.356	69	-10	3-2	.969	7	107	132	3b69/2		-0.5
1986	Tex A	153	461	54	112	19	2	18	54	35-1	5	98	.243	.302	.410	89	-8	5-8	.968	15	108	81	3b137,2b33,O2L		0.5
1987	Tex A	136	363	45	86	20	0	13	50	28-3	1	66	.237	.290	.399	81	-11	2-2	.964	-5	97	65	3b123,2b18,O2L		-1.6
1988	Tex A	155	503	68	126	21	4	16	58	65-6	5	79	.250	.342	.404	105	4	2-4	.962	7	106	97	3b153,2b2		1.0
1989	Tex A	155	486	60	114	22	2	16	59	36-0	5	107	.235	.294	.387	89	-8	1-3	.969	19	106	98	3b145,2b18/SD		1.0
1990	Tex A	91	251	30	54	10	0	7	30	27-1	2	63	.215	.294	.339	77	-8	1-0	.966	5	104	48	3b88,2b4	65	-0.2
1991	Tex A	121	416	58	111	17	2	18	66	39-4	5	69	.267	.335	.447	117	9	0-4	**.991**	15	115	92	3b111,2b13,S4		2.3
	†Pit N	31	114	16	28	5	1	4	19	10-0	1	28	.246	.315	.412	105		0-1	.956	-0	100	106	3b31		0.0
1992	Pit N	80	285	27	71	14	1	8	43	34-4	2	61	.249	.331	.389	104	2	0-2	.957	1	109	80	3b80		0.0
	Chi N	65	239	25	66	9	3	1	21	18-2	5	44	.276	.338	.351	93	-2	1-1	.960	1	105	59	3b63,2b2		-0.1
	Year	145	524	52	137	23	4	9	64	52-6	7	105	.261	.334	.372	99	-0	1-3	.958	3	**107**	71	3b143,2b2		0.2
1993	Chi N	133	460	53	125	27	2	15	65	48-5	5	87	.272	.345	.437	109	6	1-1	**.975**	-2	99	121	3b129,1b6	15	0.5
1994	Chi N	104	339	33	82	11	1	14	52	39-2	4	80	.242	.325	.404	89	-6	1-0	.974	-11	84	90	3b99,1b6/2		-1.6
1995	Chi N	32	106	10	20	2	0	1	9	11-0	1	19	.189	.265	.236	33	-10	0-0	.942	-2	93	59	3b32	24	-1.2
	Tex A	9	24	0	3	0	0	0	0	4-1	0	5	.125	.250	.125	1	-4	0-0	1.000	-0	84	161	3b9		-0.3
Total	11	1334	4266	501	1046	183	21	137	547	408-31	43	842	.245	.316	.394	93	-46	17-28	.968	50	103	90	3b1269,2b92,1b12,S5,O4L/D	104	0.1

BUELOW, CHARLIE   Charles John B1.12.1877 Dubuque IA D5.4.1951 Dubuque IA BR/TR d6.1

| 1901 | NY N | 22 | 72 | 3 | 8 | 4 | 0 | 0 | 4 | 2 | 1 | | .111 | .147 | .167 | -10 | -10 | 0 | .853 | 3 | 131 | 109 | 3b17,2b2 | | -0.7 |

BUELOW, FRITZ   Frederick William Alexander B2.13.1876 Berlin, Germany D12.27.1933 Detroit MI BR/TR/5-10.5/170 d9.28

1899	StL N	7	15	4	7	0	2	0	2	2	1		.467	.556	.733	246	3	0	1.000	-0	141	30	C4,O2L		0.3
1900	StL N	6	17	2	4	0	0	0	3	0	0		.235	.235	.235	30	-2	0	.864	-1	100	104	C4/OL		-0.2
1901	Det A	70	231	28	52	5	5	2	29	11	3		.225	.269	.316	59	-14	2	.967	6	118	108	C69		-0.1
1902	Det A	66	224	23	50	5	2	2	29	9	1		.223	.256	.290	50	-16	3	.927	-5	84	119	C63,1b2		-1.4
1903	Det A	63	192	24	41	3	6	1	13	6	3		.214	.249	.307	68	-8	4	.961	-3	79	112	C60,1b2		-0.7
1904	Det A	42	136	6	15	1	1	0	5	8	0		.110	.160	.132	-7	-17	2	.975	-1	87	110	C42		-1.6
	Cle A	42	119	11	21	4	1	0	5	11	1		.176	.252	.227	52	-6	2	.979	2	118	85	C42		-0.0
	Year	84	255	17	36	5	2	0	10	19	1		.141	.204	.176	21	-23	4	.977	1	102	98	C84		-1.6
1905	Cle A	75	239	11	41	4	1	1	18	6	1		.172	.198	.209	29	-20	7	.960	-4	102	105	C60,O8R,1b3,3b2		-2.0
1906	Cle A	34	86	7	14	2	0	0	7	9	1		.163	.250	.186	38	-6	0	.938	1	128	115	C33/1		-0.2
1907	StL A	26	75	9	11	1	0	0	1	7	0		.147	.220	.160	21	-6	0	.983	-0	89	126	C25		-0.5
Total	9	431	1334	125	256	25	18	6	112	69	12		.192	.238	.251	46	-92	20	.960	-5	100	109	C402,O11(3/0/8),1b8,3b2		-6.4

BUES, ART   Arthur Frederick B3.3.1888 Milwaukee WI D11.7.1954 Whitefish Bay WI BR/TR/5-11/184 d4.17

1913	Bos N	2	1	0	0	0	0	0	0	0	0	1	.000	.000	.000	-98	-0	0	—	-0	0	0	/23		-0.1
1914	Chi N	14	45	3	10	1	1	0	4	5	0	6	.222	.300	.289	76	-1	1	.968	-2	76	0	3b12		-0.3
Total	2	16	46	3	10	1	1	0	4	5	0	7	.217	.294	.283	72	-1	1	.968	-2	75	0	3b13/2		-0.4

BUFFINTON, CHARLIE   Charles G. B6.14.1861 Fall River MA D9.23.1907 Fall River MA BR/TR/6-1/180 d5.17 M1 ▲

1882	Bos N	15	50	5	13	1	0	0		3			.260	.288	.280	83	-1		.615	-2	108	0	O7R,P5,1b4		-0.3
1883	Bos N	86	341	28	81	8	3	1	26	6			.238	.251	.287	62	-16		.756	-6	93	197	O51(0/13/40),P43,1b2		-1.4
1884	Bos N	87	352	48	94	18	3	1	39	16			.267	.299	.344	102	1		.946	-3	98	64	P67,O13(0/13/1),1b11		-0.6
1885	Bos N	82	338	26	81	12	3	1	33	3			.240	.246	.302	79	-8		.912	1	121	178	P51,O18(1/11/6),1b15		-0.6
1886	Bos N	44	176	27	51	4	1	1	30	4			.290	.313	.341	102	0	3	.968	-5	54	73	1b19,P18,O9(0/1/8)		-0.6
1887	Phi N	66	269	34	72	12	1	1	46	11	1	3	.268	.299	.331	70	-11	8	.931	3	144	236	P40,O22(7/7/8),1b10		-0.5
1888	Phi N	46	160	14	29	4	1	0	12	7	0	5	.181	.216	.219	37	-11	1	.939	9	**141**	168	P46/OL		0.4
1889	Phi N	47	154	16	32	2	0	0	21	9	1	5	.208	.256	.221	31	-15	0	.916	1	107	131	P47/OL		0.0
1890	Phi P	42	150	24	41	3	2	1	24	9	1	3	.273	.319	.340	74	-6	1	.864	1	105	210	P36,O5(1/2/2),1b3,M		0.0
1891	Bos AA	58	181	16	34	2	1	1	16	19	1	15	.188	.269	.227	43	-14	1	.934	5	134	119	P48,O10(5/0/6),1b4		0.0
1892	Bal N	13	43	7	15	1	1	0	4	3	0	6	.349	.391	.419	141	4	1	.892	1	138	115	P13		0.0
Total	11	586	2214	245	543	67	16	7	255	91	4	114	.245	.276	.299	71	-77	14	.916	6	116	147	P414,O137(16/47/78),1b68		-3.4

BUFORD, DAMON   Damon Jackson B6.12.1970 Baltimore MD BR/TR/5-10/170* [BalA90 10/283] d5.4 f-Don Col USC

1993	Bal A	53	79	18	18	5	0	2	9	9-0	1	19	.228	.315	.367	79	-2	2-2	.984	1	98	146	O30(5/24/1),D17		-0.3
1994	Bal A	4	2	2	1	0	0	0	0	0-0	0	1	.500	.500	.500	151	0	0-0	—	-0	0	0	/OLD		0.0
1995	Bal A	24	32	6	2	0	0	0	2	6-0	0	7	.063	.205	.063	-24	-6	3-1	1.000	1	126	0	O24(0/15/9)		-0.4
	NY N	44	136	24	32	5	0	4	12	19-0	5	28	.235	.346	.360	91	-1	7-7	.972	-2	92	93	O39(25/16/0)		-0.2
1996	†Tex A	90	145	30	41	9	0	6	20	15-0	0	34	.283	.348	.469	98	0	8-5	1.000	-1	95	101	O80(14/25/44)		-1.6
1997	Tex A	122	366	49	82	18	4	8	39	30-0	2	83	.224	.287	.339	59	-22	18-7	.990	3	105	129	O117C,D3		-1.6
1998	†Bos A	86	216	37	61	14	4	10	42	22-1	1	43	.282	.349	.523	121	6	6-5	1.000	-1	94	116	O67C,D15/23	31	0.4
1999	†Bos A	91	297	39	72	15	2	6	38	21-0	2	74	.242	.294	.367	66	-16	9-2	.985	1	100	127	O84(5/82/0),D5	17	-1.3
2000	Chi N	150	495	64	124	18	3	15	48	47-3	8	118	.251	.324	.390	81	-16	4-6	.986	-4	103	49	O148(2/140/7)		-1.9
2001	Chi N	35	85	11	15	2	0	3	8	4-0	0	23	.176	.213	.306	33	-9	0-0	1.000	-1	101	0	O34(0/33/1)		-0.7
Total	9	699	1853	280	448	86	9	54	218	173-4	20	430	.242	.311	.385	77	-66	56-35	.989	-3	101	93	O624(52/519/62),D41/32	48	-6.7

BUFORD, DON   Donald Alvin B2.2.1937 Linden TX BB/TR/5-8/165(160-175) d9.14 C6 s-Damon Col USC

1963	Chi A	12	42	9	12	1	2	0	5	5-0	0	7	.286	.354	.405	116	1	1-0	.955	-4	62	65	3b9,2b2		-0.3
1964	Chi A	135	442	62	116	14	6	4	30	46-2	5	62	.262	.337	.348	94	-3	12-7	.968	-2	92	133	2b92,3b37		0.2
1965	Chi A	155	586	93	166	22	5	10	47	67-4	4	76	.283	.358	.389	120	17	17-7	.981	22	108	**129**	2b139,3b41		**5.3**
1966	Chi A	**163**	607	85	148	26	7	8	52	69-3	3	71	.244	.323	.399	100	1	51-22	.939	11	**117**	119	3b133,2b37,O11(8/0/3)		1.9
1967	Chi A	156	535	61	129	10	9	4	32	65-3	1	51	.241	.322	.316	93	-4	34-21	.948	6	108	100	3b121,2b51/OL		0.5
1968	Bal A	130	426	65	120	13	4	15	46	57-5	4	46	.282	.367	.437	144	24	27-12	1.000	2	107	106	O65(27/41/2),2b58,3b2		3.3
1969	†Bal A	144	554	99	161	31	11	64	96-7	5	62		.291	.397	.447	127	26	19-18	.983	-4	93	67	O128L,2b10,3b6		1.3
1970	†Bal A	144	504	99	137	15	2	17	66	109-8	8	55	.272	.406	.411	125	23	16-8	.987	2	98	160	O130L,2b3,3b3		1.9
1971	†Bal A★	122	449	**99**	130	19	4	19	54	89-15	7	62	.290	.413	.477	151	35	15-7	.987	-0	103	84	O115(114/0/1)		3.1
1972	†Bal A	125	408	46	84	6	2	5	22	69-10	4	43	.206	.326	.267	75	-10	8-3	.989	-2	91	91	O105(104/0/1)		-2.3
Total	10	1286	4553	718	1203	157	44	93	418	672-57	41	575	.264	.362	.379	115	110	200-105	.988	28	98	100	O555(512/41/7),2b392,3b352		14.9

BUHNER, JAY   Jay Campbell B8.13.1964 Louisville KY BR/TR/6-3/205(205-222) [PitN84*S2/36] d9.11 Col McLennan (TX) CC

1987	NY A	7	22	0	5	2	0	0	1	1-0	0	6	.227	.261	.318	53	-1	0-0	1.000	0	78	259	O7(2/3/2)		-0.2
1988	NY A	25	69	8	13	0	0	3	13	3-0	3	25	.188	.250	.319	59	-4	0-0	.964	1	107	218	O22(3/16/3)		-0.3
	Sea A	60	192	28	43	13	1	10	25	25-1	3	68	.224	.320	.458	111	3	1-1	.993	7	112	206	O59(1/2/55)		0.8
	Year	85	261	36	56	13	1	13	38	28-1	6	93	.215	.302	.421	98	-1	1-1	.985	8	111	209	O81(4/18/58)		0.5
1989	Sea A	58	204	27	56	15	1	9	33	19-0	2	55	.275	.341	.490	128	7	1-4	.966	-1	90	140	O57(0/2/56)	51	0.3
1990	Sea A	51	163	16	45	12	0	7	33	17-1	4	50	.276	.357	.479	130	6	2-2	.966	-5	77	41	O40(0/1/39),D10	120	0.1
1991	Sea A	137	406	64	99	14	4	27	77	53-5	6	117	.244	.337	.498	128	14	0-1	.981	7	102	177	O131(1/3/131)		1.8
1992	Sea A	152	543	69	132	16	3	25	79	71-2	6	146	.243	.333	.422	110	7	0-6	.994	4	97	135	O150(0/2/150)		0.4
1993	Sea A	158	563	91	153	28	3	27	98	100-11	2	144	.272	.379	.476	127	24	2-5	.978	-9	88	75	O148R,D10		0.6
1994	Sea A	101	358	74	100	23	4	21	68	66-5	3	63	.279	.394	.542	136	21	0-1	.990	-3	96	166	O96(0/1/95),D4	16	1.7
1995	†Sea A	126	470	86	123	23	0	40	121	60-7	1	120	.262	.343	.566	131	19	0-1	.989	-9	82	67	O120R,D4		1.1
1996	Sea A★	150	564	107	153	29	0	44	138	84-5	9	159	.271	.369	.557	131	27	0-1	.989	-6	87	90	O142R,D8		1.6
1997	†Sea A	157	540	104	131	18	2	40	109	119-3	5	175	.243	.383	.506	130	27	0-0	**.997**	-2	97	53	O154R,D2		1.6
1998	Sea A	72	244	33	59	7	1	15	45	38-0	1	71	.242	.344	.463	107	2	0-0	.985	1	100	110	O70R/D	85	0.0
1999	Sea A	87	266	37	59	11	0	14	38	60-0	6	100	.222	.388	.421	108	6	0-0	.993	-4	79	126	O85R/1	57	-0.2
2000	†Sea A	112	364	50	92	20	0	26	82	59-3	4	98	.253	.361	.522	123	13	0-2	1.000	-3	94	63	O104R/D	14	0.4
2001	†Sea A	19	45	4	10	2	0	2	8	5-0	0	20	.222	.340	.400	99	0	0-0	1.000	1	88	0	O12(10/0/2),D4	153	-0.1
Total	15	1472	5013	798	1273	233	19	310	965	702-56	56	1404	.254	.359	.494	123	172	6-24	.988	-17	93	109	O1397(17/30/1356),D44/1	496	8.3

BUKER, HARRY   Henry L. "Happy" B1859 Chicago IL D8.10.1899 Chicago IL ?/140 d6.11

| 1884 | Det N | 30 | 111 | 5 | 15 | 1 | 0 | 0 | | 3 | 4 | | .135 | .144 | .144 | 15 | -13 | | .867 | 1 | 109 | 106 | S19,O11R | | -1.0 |

YEAR	TM	LG	G	AB	R	H	2B	3B	HR	RBI	BB-IB	HP	SO	AVG	OBP	SLG	AOPS	ABR	SB-CS	FA	FR	RNG	THR	GAMES AT POSITION	DL	BFW

BULLARD, GEORGE George Donald "Curly" B10.24.1928 Lynn MA D12.23.2002 Lynn MA BR/TR/5-9.5/165 d9.17

| 1954 | Det | A | 4 | 1 | 0 | 0 | 0 | 0 | 0 | 0 | 0-0 | 0 | 0 | .000 | .000 | .000 | -99 | 0 | 0-0 | .800 | 0 | 116 | 0 | /S | | 0.0 |

BULLAS, SIM Simeon Edward B4.10.1861 Cleveland OH D1.14.1908 Cleveland OH 5-7.5/150 d5.2

| 1884 | Tol | AA | 13 | 45 | 4 | 4 | 0 | 1 | 0 | | 1 | 0 | | .089 | .109 | .133 | -21 | -6 | | .909 | -3 | | | C12,O2L | | -0.8 |

BULLETT, SCOTT Scott Douglas B12.25.1968 Martinsburg WV BL/TL (BB 1993)/6-2/200(190-220) d9.3

1991	Pit	N	11	4	2	0	0	0	0	0	0-0	1	3	.000	.000	.000	-39	-1	1-1	1.000	-0	82	0	O3(1/1/1)		-0.1
1993	Pit	N	23	55	2	11	0	2	0	4	3-0	0	15	.200	.237	.273	37	-5	3-2	1.000	-1	92	124	O19(0/18/1)		-0.6
1995	Chi	N	104	150	19	41	5	7	3	22	12-2	1	30	.273	.331	.460	106	-3	8-3	.968	-2	94	51	O64(54/12/0)		-0.1
1996	Chi	N	109	165	26	35	5	0	3	16	10-0	0	54	.212	.256	.297	44	-14	7-3	.986	3	119	111	O58(28/11/22)		-1.1
Total	4		247	374	49	87	10	9	6	42	25-2	2	102	.233	.283	.356	67	-20	19-9	.983	1	103	87	O144(83/42/24)	21	-1.9

BULLING, BUD Terry Charles "Terry" B12.15.1952 Lynwood CA BR/TR/6-1/200(195-210) [MinA74 14/326] d7.3 Col Cal St.-Los Angeles

1977	Min	A	15	32	2	5	0	0	0	5	5-1	0	5	.156	.270	.188	28	-3	0-0	.952	-1	57	34	C10,D3		-0.4
1981	Sea	A	62	154	15	38	3	0	2	15	21-0	1	20	.247	.341	.305	83	-3	0-0	.977	-6	80	103	C62		-0.7
1982	Sea	A	56	154	17	34	7	0	1	8	19-2	0	16	.221	.306	.286	62	-8	2-1	.991	2	103	123	C56		-0.3
1983	Sea	A	5	5	0	0	0	0	0	0	0-0	0	0	.000	.000	.000	-96	-1	0-0	1.000	0	155	0	C5	15	-0.1
Total	4		138	345	34	77	11	0	3	28	45-3	1	41	.223	.315	.281	66	-15	2-1	.983	-5	90	105	C133,D3	15	-1.5

BULLOCK, ERIC Eric Gerald B2.16.1960 Los Angeles CA BL/TL/5-11/185* [HouN81 S1/20] d8.26 Col Los Angeles Harbor (CA) JC

1985	Hou	N	18	25	3	7	2	0	0	2	1-0	0	3	.280	.308	.360	88	0	0-1	.750	-1	83	0	O7(4/0/3)		-0.2
1986	Hou	N	6	21	0	1	0	0	0	1	0-0	0	3	.048	.048	.048	-76	-5	2-0	.875	-1	71	0	O6L		-0.6
1988	Min	A	16	17	3	5	0	0	0	3	3-0	0	1	.294	.400	.294	95	0	1-0	.875	0	175	0	O4(3/0/2),D2		0.1
1989	Phi	N	6	4	1	0	0	0	0	0	0-0	0	2	.000	.000	.000	-99	-1	0-0	1.000	0	194	0	O3(0/1/2)		-0.1
1990	Mon	N	4	2	0	1	0	0	0	0	0-0	0	0	.500	.500	.500	182	0	0-0	—	0			/H		0.0
1991	Mon	N	73	72	6	16	4	0	1	6	9-0	0	13	.222	.305	.319	78	-2	6-1	1.000	0	100		O9(6/0/3),1b3		-0.2
1992	Mon	N	8	0	0	0	0	0	0	0	0-0	0	1	.000	.000	.000	-99	-1	0-0	—	0			/H		-0.2
Total	7		131	146	13	30	6	0	1	12	13-0	0	23	.205	.269	.267	52	-9	9-2	.892	-1	98		O29(19/1/10),1b3,D2		-1.1

BUMBRY, AL Alonza Benjamin (b Alonza Benjamin Bumbrey) B4.21.1947 Fredericksburg VA BL/TR/5-8/175* [BalA68 11/238] d9.5 C9 Col Virginia St.

1972	†Bal	A	9	11	5	4	0	1	0	0	0-0	0	1	.364	.364	.545	161	0	1-1	1.000	0	119	0	O2L		0.1
1973	†Bal	A	110	356	73	120	15	11	7	34	34-0	3	49	.337	.398	.500	151	24	23-10	.978	-7	86	36	O86(62/1/29),D7		1.4
1974	†Bal	A	94	270	35	63	10	3	1	19	21-2	1	46	.233	.288	.304	73	-10	12-4	.953	0	96	159	O67L,D7		-1.3
1975	Bal	A	114	349	47	94	19	4	2	32	32-3	4	81	.269	.336	.364	104	-2	16-3	1.000	-2	87	70	O48,O39(35/3/1)/3		-0.1
1976	Bal	A	133	450	71	113	15	7	9	36	43-2	1	76	.251	.316	.376	108	4	42-10	.989	0	99	113	O116(82/57/0),D10		0.5
1977	Bal	A	133	518	74	164	31	3	4	41	45-4	2	88	.317	.371	.411	120	16	19-8	.991	-1	102	76	O130(52/112/0)	15	1.6
1978	Bal	A	33	114	21	27	5	2	2	6	17-0	2	15	.237	.346	.368	107	2	5-3	.985	-1	93	111	O28(16/17/0)	112	0.0
1979	†Bal	A	148	569	80	162	29	1	7	49	43-3	3	74	.285	.336	.376	96	-3	37-12	.982	-4	97	76	O146(5/146/0)		-0.4
1980	Bal	A★	160	645	118	205	29	9	9	53	78-8	3	75	.318	.392	.433	128	28	44-11	.990	5	110	62	O160(1/160/0)		3.6
1981	Bal	A	101	392	61	107	18	2	1	27	51-2	2	51	.273	.358	.337	102	3	22-15	.992	-2	96	100	O100C		0.0
1982	Bal	A	150	562	77	147	20	4	5	44	44-4	0	77	.262	.314	.338	80	-16	10-5	.986	6	108	98	O147(3/146/0)/D		-1.1
1983	†Bal	A	124	378	63	104	14	4	3	31	31-2	0	33	.275	.328	.357	90	-5	12-5	.988	-2	99	54	O104(17/99/0),D11		-0.8
1984	Bal	A	119	344	47	93	12	1	3	24	25-0	0	35	.270	.317	.337	83	-8	9-5	.988	3	101	125	O99(28/82/0),D9		-0.6
1985	SD	N	68	95	6	19	3	0	1	10	7-0	0	9	.200	.255	.263	46	-7	2-0	.939	0	126	0	O17(12/5/1)		-0.7
Total	14		1496	5053	778	1422	220	52	54	402	471-30	21	709	.281	.343	.378	104	31	254-92	.986	-4	100	85	O1241(382/928/31),D93/3	127	2.2

BUNCE, JOSH Joshua B5.10.1847 Brooklyn NY D4.28.1912 Brooklyn NY d8.27

| 1877 | Har | N | 1 | 4 | 0 | 0 | 0 | 0 | 0 | | 0 | | | .000 | .000 | .000 | -99 | -1 | | 1.000 | -0 | 0 | 0 | /OL | | -0.1 |

BURBRINK, NELSON Nelson Edward B12.28.1921 Cincinnati OH D4.12.2001 Largo FL BR/TR/5-10/195 d6.5

| 1955 | StL | N | 58 | 170 | 11 | 47 | 8 | 1 | 0 | 15 | 14-1 | 1 | 13 | .276 | .333 | .335 | 79 | -5 | 1-1 | .979 | -2 | 106 | 118 | C55 | | -0.5 |

BURCH, AL Albert William B10.7.1883 Albany NY D10.5.1926 Brooklyn NY BL/TL/5-8.5/160 d6.19

1906	StL	N	91	335	40	89	5	1	0	11	37	0		.266	.339	.287	99	1	15	.934	-1	131	210	O91(0/58/33)		-0.5
1907	StL	N	48	154	18	35	3	1	0	5	17	0		.227	.304	.260	79	-3	7	.922	-1	152	235	O48C		-0.7
	Bro	N	40	120	12	35	2	2	0	12	11	0		.292	.351	.342	127	4	5	.890	2	180	0	O36(27/5/2)/2		0.4
	Year		88	274	30	70	5	3	0	17	28	0		.255	.325	.296	100	0	12	.908	1	164	134	O84(27/53/5)/2		-0.3
1908	Bro	N	123	456	45	111	8	4	2	18	33	0		.243	.294	.292	91	-6	15	.971	9	151	156	O116(47/44/28)		-0.4
1909	Bro	N	152	601	80	163	20	6	1	30	51	0		.271	.329	.329	108	5	38	.955	-0	126	77	O151(41/102/9)/1		0.0
1910	Bro	N	103	352	41	83	8	3	1	20	22	0	30	.236	.281	.284	67	-16	13	.957	-2	91	110	O70(0/26/45),1b13		-2.3
1911	Bro	N	54	167	18	38	2	3	0	7	15	0	22	.228	.291	.275	61	-9	3	.972	1	102	97	O43(0/41/3),2b3		-1.1
Total	6		611	2185	254	554	48	20	4	103	186	1	52	.254	.312	.299	91	-24	96	.950	11	126	130	O555(115/324/123),1b14,2b4		-4.6

BURCH, ERNIE Ernest A. B9.9.1856 DeKalb Co. IL D10.12.1892 Guthrie OK BL/5-10/190 d8.15

1884	Cle	N	32	124	9	26	4	0	0	7	5		24	.210	.240	.242	50	-7		.899	5	162	94	O32(23/0/9)		-0.3
1886	Bro	AA	113	456	78	119	22	6	2	72	39	1		.261	.321	.349	109	5	16	.884	-10	56	89	O113L		-0.7
1887	Bro	AA	49	188	47	55	4	4	2	26	29	3		.293	.395	.388	118	6	15	.899	1	101	56	O49L		0.4
Total	3		194	768	134	200	30	10	4	24	73	4	24	.260	.328	.341	102	4	31	.891	-4	85	81	O194(185/0/9)		-0.6

BURDA, BOB Edward Robert B7.16.1938 St.Louis MO BL/TL/5-11/180* d8.25 Col Illinois

1962	StL	N	7	14	0	1	0	0	0	0	3-0	0	1	.071	.235	.071	-12	-2	1-0	.917	0	145	0	O6(1/0/5)		-0.2
1965	SF	N	31	27	0	3	0	0	0	5	5-0	0	6	.111	.235	.111	6	-3	0-0	.969	-1	0	37	1b11/OL		-0.5
1966	SF	N	37	43	3	7	3	0	0	2	2-0	0	5	.163	.196	.233	19	-5	0-0	1.000	-0	132	0	1b7,O4(3/0/1)		-0.6
1969	SF	N	97	161	20	37	8	0	6	27	21-3	0	12	.230	.317	.391	99	0	0-1	.995	-0	92	93	1b45,O19(5/0/15)		-0.3
1970	SF	N	28	23	1	6	0	0	0	5	5-2	1	2	.261	.414	.261	86	0	0-0	.933	-1	0	63	1b8/OL		-0.1
	Mil	A	78	222	19	55	9	0	4	20	16-1	3	17	.248	.303	.342	79	-7	1-0	.987	-5	76	87	O64R,1b7		-1.5
1971	StL	N	65	71	6	21	0	0	1	12	10-2	1	11	.296	.386	.338	103	1	0-0	1.000	1	127	0	1b13/OR		0.1
1972	Bos	A	45	73	4	12	1	0	2	9	8-3	0	11	.164	.241	.260	48	-5	0-0	.992	0	81	103	1b15/OL		-0.7
Total	7		388	634	53	142	21	0	13	78	70-11	5	65	.224	.302	.319	74	-21	2-1	.992	-7	83	81	1b106,O97(12/0/86)		-3.8

BURDOCK, JACK John Joseph "Black Jack" B4.1852 Brooklyn NY D11.27.1931 Brooklyn NY BR/TR/5-9.5/158 d5.2 M1/U3

1872	Atl	NA	37	174	27	47	3	0	0	14	1		1	.270	.274	.287	62	-10	0-1	.743	-7	94	22	S36,C4,2b2		-1.3
1873	Atl	NA	55	245	56	62	7	1	2	36	7		4	.253	.274	.314	83	-2	3-2	.818	-6	105	94	2b55,C2		-0.5
1874	Mut	NA	61	273	45	75	11	4	1	26	1		5	.275	.277	.355	98	-1	4-1	.820	10	93	97	3b60,O3(2/1/0)		0.6
1875	Har	NA	74	350	72	103	12	5	0	35	3		13	.294	.300	.357	121	6	20-11	.895	-3	84	134	2b73,3b2/C		-0.1
1876	Har	N	69	309	66	80	9	1	0	23	13		16	.259	.289	.294	87	-5		.895	2	89	98	2b69/3		0.0
1877	Har	N	58	277	35	72	6	0	0	9	2		16	.260	.265	.282	81	-5		.903	7	99	128	2b55,3b3		0.4
1878	Bos	N	60	246	37	64	12	6	5	25	3		17	.260	.269	.358	97	-2		.918	21	103	151	2b60		2.0
1879	Bos	N	84	359	64	86	10	3	0	36	9		28	.240	.258	.284	77	-9		.911	12	100	147	2b84		0.6
1880	Bos	N	86	356	58	90	17	4	2	35	8		26	.253	.269	.340	108	3		.923	15	100	101	2b86		2.1
1881	Bos	N	73	282	36	67	12	4	1	24	7		18	.238	.256	.319	84	-5		.911	-8	91	98	2b72/S		-1.0
1882	Bos	N	83	319	36	76	6	7	0	27	9		24	.238	.259	.301	79	-8		.932	6	99	82	2b83		2.0
1883	Bos	N	96	400	80	132	27	8	5	88	14		35	.330	.353	.475	145	21		.921	1	93	103	2b96,M		2.2
1884	Bos	N	87	361	65	97	14	4	6	49	15		52	.269	.298	.380	112	5		.922	2	100	82	2b87/3		0.9
1885	Bos	N	45	169	18	24	6	0	0	7	8		18	.142	.181	.172	15	-15		.917	-3	96	83	2b45		-1.6
1886	Bos	N	59	221	26	48	6	1	0	25	11		27	.217	.254	.253	56	-11	3	.904	-10	92	87	2b59		-1.8
1887	Bos	N	65	237	36	61	6	0	0	29	18	4	22	.257	.320	.283	68	-9	19	.882	-16	94	124	2b65		-2.0
1888	Bos	N	22	59	7	12	5	0	0	3	6	1	5	.203	.232	.203	38	-6	1	.903	-1	100	116	2b22		-0.6
	Bro	AA	70	246	15	30	1	2	1	8	17	5		.122	.166	.154	3	-27	9	.904	-3	104	101	2b70		-2.5
1891	Bro	N	3	12	1	1	0	0	0	1	1			.083	.154	.083	-31	-2	0	1.000	-0	88	83	2b3		-0.2
Total	4 NA		227	1042	200	287	33	10	3	111	12		23	.275	.284	.335	95	-7	27-15	.859	-1	93	116	2b130,3b62,S36,C7,O3(2/1/0)		-1.3
Total	14		960	3873	578	944	131	40	15	390	128		305	.244	.270	.310	83	-75	32	.912	26	97	106	2b956,3b5/S		-1.5

BURG, JOE Joseph Peter B6.4.1882 Chicago IL D4.28.1969 Joliet IL BR/TR/5-10/150 d9.26

| 1910 | Bos | N | 13 | 46 | 5 | 15 | 0 | 1 | 0 | 10 | 7 | 0 | 12 | .326 | .415 | .348 | 124 | 2 | 5 | .867 | 1 | 123 | 58 | 3b12/S | | 0.3 |

YEAR	TM LG	G	AB	R	H	2B	3B	HR	RBI	BB-IB	HP	SO	AVG	OBP	SLG	AOPS	ABR	SB-CS	FA	FR	RNG	THR	GAMES AT POSITION	DL	BFW

BURGESS, SMOKY Forrest Harrill B2.6.1927 Caroleen NC D9.15.1991 Asheville NC BL/TR/5-8/187(171-198) d4.19

1949	Chi N	46	56	4	15	0	0	1	12	4	0	4	.268	.317	.321	73	-2	0	1.000	1	78	250	C8		-0.1
1951	Chi N	94	219	21	55	4	2	2	20	21	0	12	.251	.317	.315	69	-10	2-0	.980	-4	58	129	C64		-1.1
1952	Phi N	110	371	49	110	27	2	6	56	49	1	21	.296	.380	.429	125	15	3-1	.978	-4	94	97	C104		1.8
1953	Phi N	102	312	31	91	17	5	4	36	37	2	17	.292	.370	.417	105	4	3-2	.993	-4	102	46	C95		0.4
1954	Phi N★	108	345	41	127	27	5	4	46	42	0	11	.368	.432	.510	146	26	1-5	.975	-3	111	69	C91		2.5
1955	Phi N	7	21	4	4	2	0	1	1	3-1	0	1	.190	.292	.429	90	0	0-0	1.000	1	90	0	C6		0.1
	Cin N★	116	421	67	129	15	3	20	77	47-4	1	35	.306	.373	.499	123	14	1-1	.986	-3	120	62	C107		1.6
	Year	123	442	71	133	17	3	21	78	50-5	1	36	.301	.369	.495	122	14	1-1	.987	-3	118	59	C113		1.7
1956	Cin N	90	229	28	63	10	0	12	39	26-4	0	18	.275	.346	.476	112	4	0-1	1.000	-2	91	77	C55		0.5
1957	Cin N	90	205	29	58	14	1	14	39	24-5	0	16	.283	.353	.566	134	10	0-0	.988	-5	117	80	C45		0.7
1958	Cin N	99	251	28	71	12	1	6	31	22-3	0	20	.283	.343	.410	93	-2	0-0	.988	3	131	86	C58		0.4
1959	Pit N★	114	377	41	112	28	5	11	59	31-9	2	16	.297	.349	.485	122	12	0-0	.984	-12	99	91	C101		0.5
1960	†Pit N★	110	337	33	99	15	2	7	39	35-12	0	13	.294	.356	.412	110	5	0-1	.994	5	163	91	C89		1.5
1961	Pit N★	100	323	37	98	17	3	12	52	30-8	2	16	.303	.365	.486	123	11	1-0	.991	-5	167	61	C92		1.0
1962	Pit N	103	360	38	118	19	2	13	61	31-9	0	19	.328	.375	.500	134	17	0-1	.988	-3	106	76	C101		1.8
1963	Pit N	91	264	20	74	10	1	6	37	24-8	1	14	.280	.338	.394	111	4	0-1	.990	-6	76	102	C72		0.1
1964	Pit N☆	68	171	9	42	3	1	2	17	13-3	1	14	.246	.303	.310	73	-6	2-1	.992	-5	82	67	C44		-1.0
	Chi A	7	5	1	1	0	0	1	1	2-2	0	2	.200	.429	.800	239	4	0-0	—	0			/H		0.1
1965	Chi A	80	77	2	22	4	0	2	24	11-4	0	7	.286	.371	.416	132	4	0-0	1.000	1	130	155	C5		0.5
1966	Chi A	79	67	0	21	5	0	0	15	11-2	1	8	.313	.412	.388	143	5	0-0	1.000	0	0	0	C2		0.5
1967	Chi A	77	60	2	8	1	0	2	11	14-6	1	8	.133	.303	.250	69	-2	0-0	—	0			/H		-0.2
Total	18	1691	4471	485	1318	230	33	126	673	477-80	13	270	.295	.362	.446	116	110	13-14	.988	-45	111	80	C1139		11.6

BURGESS, TOM Thomas Roland "Tim" B9.1.1927 London ON, Can. BL/TL/6-0/180* d4.17 C2

1954	StL N	17	21	2	1	1	0	0	1	3	0	9	.048	.167	.095	-29	-4	0-0	.750	-1	65	0	O4R		-0.5
1962	LA A	87	143	17	28	7	1	2	13	36-8	0	20	.196	.354	.301	82	-2	2-0	.997	-3	68	101	1b35,O2L		-0.6
Total	2	104	164	19	29	8	1	2	14	39-8	0	29	.177	.332	.274	67	-6	2-0	.997	-3	68	101	1b35,O6(2/0/4)		-1.1

BURGO, BILL William Ross B11.15.1919 Johnstown PA D10.19.1988 Morgan City LA BR/TR/5-8/185 d9.22

1943	Phi A	17	70	12	26	4	2	1	9	4	2	1	.371	.421	.529	178	7	0-2	.979	1	108	137	O17L		0.7
1944	Phi A	27	88	6	21	2	0	1	3	7	3	3	.239	.316	.295	76	-3	1-3	.955	1	119	52	O22(14/0/8)		-0.4
Total	2	44	158	18	47	6	2	2	12	11	5	4	.297	.362	.399	121	4	1-5	.965	2	114	88	O39(31/0/8)		0.3

BURICH, BILL William Max B5.29.1918 Calumet MI BR/TR/6-0/180 d4.15 Mil 1943-46

1942	Phi N	25	80	3	23	1	0	0	7	6	0	13	.287	.337	.300	92	-1	2	.917	-4	83	54	S19,3b3		-0.3
1946	Phi N	2	1	1	0	0	0	0	0	0	0	0	.000	.000	.000	-99	0	0	—	-0	0	0	S/3		0.0
Total	2	27	81	4	23	1	0	0	7	6	0	13	.284	.333	.296	89	-1	2	.917	-4	83	54	S19,3b4		-0.3

BURK, MACK Mack Edwin B4.21.1935 Nacogdoches TX BR/TR/6-4/180* d5.25 Mil 1957-58 Col Texas

1956	Phi N	15	1	3	1	0	0	0	0	0-0	0	1	1.000	1.000	1.000	449	0	0-0	1.000	0	0	0	/C		0.0
1958	Phi N	1	1	0	0	0	0	0	0	0-0	0	1	.000	.000	.000	-99	0	0-0	—	0			/H		0.0
Total	2	16	2	3	1	0	0	0	0	0-0	0	1	.500	.500	.500	171	0	0-0	1.000	0	0	0	/C		0.0

BURKAM, CHRIS Chauncey De Pew B10.13.1892 Benton Harbor MI D5.9.1964 Kalamazoo MI BL/TR/5-11/175 d6.24

| 1915 | StL A | 1 | 1 | 0 | 0 | 0 | 0 | 0 | 0 | 0 | 0 | 0 | .000 | .000 | .000 | -99 | 0 | | — | 0 | | | /H | | 0.0 |

BURKE, CHRIS Christopher Allen B3.11.1980 Louisville KY BR/TR/5-11/180* [HouN01 1/10] d7.4 Col Tennessee

2004	Hou N	17	17	2	1	0	0	0	0	3-0	0	3	.059	.200	.059	-27	-3	0-0	1.000	3	174	164	2b7		0.0
2005	†Hou N	108	318	49	79	19	2	5	26	23-0	6	62	.248	.309	.368	77	-11	11-6	.992	-4	90	73	O84(83/6/0),2b18		-1.7
Total	2	125	335	51	80	19	2	5	26	26-0	6	65	.239	.303	.352	71	-14	11-6	.992	-1	90	73	O84(83/6/0),2b25		-1.7

BURKE, DAN Daniel L. B10.25.1868 Abington MA D3.20.1933 Taunton MA BR/TR/5-10/190 d4.18

1890	Roc AA	32	102	14	22	1	0	0	9	17	1		.216	.333	.225	70	-2	2	.944	-1	189	122	O29(0/19/10),C4,1b2		-0.3
	Syr AA	9	20	1	0	0	0	0	0	5	1		.000	.231	.000	-35	-3	0	.900	-1	79	65	C9		-0.3
	Year	41	122	15	22	1	0	0	9	22	2		.180	.315	.189	53	-5	2	.944	-2	189	122	O29(0/19/10),C13,1b2		-0.6
1892	Bos N	1	4	0	0	0	0	0	0	0	0	2	.000	.000	.000	-92	-1	0	.900	0	107	80	/C		0.0
Total	2	42	126	15	22	1	0	0	9	22	2	2	.175	.307	.183	48	-6	2	.944	-2	189	122	O29(0/19/10),C14,1b2		-0.6

BURKE, EDDIE Edward D. B10.6.1866 Northumberland PA D11.26.1907 Utica NY BL/TR/5-6/161 d4.19

1890	Phi N	100	430	85	113	16	11	4	50	49	8	40	.263	.349	.379	109	5	38	.904	1	138	113	O96C,2b4		0.2
	Pit N	31	124	17	26	5	2	1	7	14	1	9	.210	.295	.306	85	-2	6	.911	0	38	71	O31C		-0.2
	Year	131	554	102	139	21	13	5	57	63	9	49	.251	.337	.363	105	3	44	.906	1	114	103	O127C,2b4		0.0
1891	Mil AA	35	144	31	34	9	0	5	21	12	10	19	.236	.337	.340	78	-5	7	.918	2	131	254	O35C		-0.3
1892	Cin N	15	41	6	6	1	0	0	4	9	0	4	.146	.300	.171	44	-2	2	1.000	-1	138	334	O14(3/5/6)/3		-0.3
	NY N	89	363	81	94	10	5	6	41	46	5	37	.259	.350	.364	118	9	42	.857	-5	98	74	2b59,O30L		0.4
	Year	104	404	87	100	11	5	6	45	55	5	41	.248	.345	.344	110	7	44	.857	-6	98	74	2b59,O44(33/5/6)/3		0.1
1893	NY N	135	537	122	150	23	10	9	80	51	25	32	.279	.384	.410	106	5	54	.911	0	82	41	O135L		-0.6
1894	†NY N	138	574	124	176	23	11	4	77	39	10	35	.307	.361	.406	85	-15	36	.934	-6	71	58	O138L		-2.6
1895	NY N	39	167	38	43	6	2	1	12	7	3	9	.257	.299	.335	65	-9	14	.914	1	128	144	O39L		-1.0
	Cin N	56	228	52	61	8	6	1	28	22	4	14	.268	.343	.368	80	-7	19	.899	1	89	99	O56(56/0/1)		-0.9
	Year	95	395	90	104	14	8	2	40	29	7	23	.263	.325	.354	74	-16	33	.905	2	105	117	O95(95/0/1)		-1.9
1896	Cin N	122	521	120	177	24	9	1	52	41	4	29	.340	.392	.426	108	6	53	.935	2	74	74	O122(116/5/1)		-0.3
1897	Cin N	95	387	71	103	17	1	1	41	29	6		.266	.327	.323	67	-18	22	.940	5	78	152	O95(94/0/1)		-1.9
Total	8	855	3516	747	983	142	57	30	413	319	76	228	.280	.352	.378	94	-33	293	.921	0	90	93	O791(611/172/9),2b63/3		-7.5

BURKE, FRANK Frank Aloysius B2.16.1880 Carbon Co. PA D9.17.1946 Los Angeles CA TR d9.14

1906	NY N	8	9	2	3	1	1	0	1	1	0		.333	.400	.667	227	1	1	.667	-1	0	0	O4(0/3/1)		0.1
1907	Bos N	43	129	6	23	0	1	0	8	11	0		.178	.243	.194	37	-9	3	.955	-3	60	0	O36(32/4/1)		-1.7
Total	2	51	138	8	26	1	2	0	9	12	0		.188	.253	.225	50	-8	4	.942	-4	57	0	O40(32/7/2)		-1.6

BURKE, GLENN Glenn Lawrence B11.16.1952 Oakland CA D5.30.1995 San Leandro CA BR/TR/6-0/205* [LAN72 17/401] d4.9 Col Merritt (CA) JC [DL 1980 Oak A 33]

1976	LA N	25	46	9	11	2	0	0	5	3-0	1	8	.239	.300	.283	67	-2	3-2	.971	-2	89	0	O20(5/15/0)		-0.5
1977	†LA N	83	169	16	43	8	0	1	13	5-1	1	22	.254	.280	.320	60	-10	13-5	.971	-7	81	31	O74(5/64/6)		-1.7
1978	LA N	16	19	2	4	0	0	0	0	2-0	0	4	.211	.211	.211	18	-2	1-0	1.000	-1	69	0	O15(4/11/0)		-0.3
	Oak A	78	200	19	47	6	1	1	14	10-1	0	26	.235	.270	.290	61	-11	15-8	.987	0	109	27	O67(13/45/14)/1D	23	-1.2
1979	Oak A	23	89	2	19	2	1	0	4	4-1	0	10	.213	.247	.258	38	-8	3-1	1.000	0	93	115	O23(22/0/2)		-0.9
Total	4	225	523	50	124	18	2	2	38	22-3	2	70	.237	.270	.291	56	-33	35-16	.983	-10	94	38	O199(49/135/22),D2/1	56	-4.6

BURKE, JAMIE James Eugene B9.24.1971 Roseburg OR BR/TR/6-0/195(195-220) [AnaA93 9/243] d5.9 Col Oregon St.

2001	Ana A	9	5	1	1	0	0	0	0	0-0	0	2	.200	.200	.200	6	-1	0-0	1.000	1	82	0	C8/1D		0.0
2003	Chi A	6	8	1	3	0	0	0	2	0-0	0	0	.375	.375	.375	95	1	0-0	1.000	-1	57	0	C4/1D		-0.1
2004	Chi A	57	120	22	40	9	0	0	15	10-0	1	13	.333	.386	.408	105	2	0-0	.987	0	156	103	C45,1b2,3b2,O2R,D3		0.4
2005	Chi A	1	1	0	0	0	0	0	0	0-0	0	0	.000	.000	.000	-96	0	0-0	—	0	0	0	/1		0.0
Total	4	73	134	23	44	9	0	0	17	10-0	1	15	.328	.377	.396	99	1	0-0	.988	-0	148	94	C57,D5,1b5,O2R,3b2		0.3

BURKE, JIMMY James Timothy "Sunset Jimmy" B10.12.1874 St.Louis MO D3.26.1942 St.Louis MO BR/TR/5-7/160 d10.6 M4/C15

1898	Cle N	13	38	1	4	1	0	0	1	2	0		.105	.150	.132	-19	-6	1	.853	-2	93	0	3b13		-0.8
1899	StL N	2	6	1	2	0	0	0	0	1	0		.333	.429	.333	108	0	0	.923	1	131	277	2b2		0.1
1901	Mil A	64	233	24	48	8	0	0	26	17			.206	.266	.240	43	-17	6	.860	-8	92	53	3b64		-2.1
	Chi A	42	148	20	39	5	0	0	21	12	2		.264	.327	.297	76	-4	11	.867	-4	98	97	S31,3b11		-0.6
	Year	106	381	44	87	13	0	0	47	29	4		.228	.290	.262	56	-21	17	.859	-12	124	224	3b75,S31		-2.7
	Pit N	14	51	4	10	0	0	0	4	4	1		.196	.268	.196	35	-4	0	.877	2	124	244	3b14		-0.1
1902	Pit N	60	203	24	60	12	2	0	26	17	3		.296	.359	.374	122	6	9	.895	-3	102	88	2b27,O18(7/0/11),3b9,S4		0.3
1903	StL N	115	431	55	123	13	2	0	42	23	3		.285	.326	.329	90	-6	28	.911	9	107	138	3b93,2b15,O5(4/0/1)		0.5
1904	StL N	118	406	37	92	10	3	0	37	15	10		.227	.271	.266	69	-15	17	.897	-7	94	84	3b118		-2.0

YEAR	TM LG	G	AB	R	H	2B	3B	HR	RBI	BB-IB	HP	SO	AVG	OBP	SLG	AOPS	ABR	SB-CS	FA	FR	RNG	THR	GAMES AT POSITION	DL	BFW
1905	StL N	122	431	34	97	9	5	1	30	21	9		.225	.275	.276	67	-18	15	.924	4	104	90	3b122,M		-1.2
Total	7	550	1947	200	475	58	13	6	187	112	30		.244	.295	.289	73	-64	87	.899	-8	101	91	3b444,2b44,S35,O23(11/0/12)		-5.9

BURKE, JOE   Joseph Aloysius   B12.7.1867 Nashville TN   D11.3.1940 Cincinnati OH   5-7/160   d9.26

YEAR	TM LG	G	AB	R	H	2B	3B	HR	RBI	BB-IB	HP	SO	AVG	OBP	SLG	AOPS	ABR	SB-CS	FA	FR	RNG	THR	GAMES AT POSITION	DL	BFW
1890	StL AA	2	6	3	4	0	0	0	2	1			.667	.750	.667	278	2	0	.750	-0	131	0	3b2		0.1
1891	Cin AA	1	4	0	1	0	0	0	1	0		2	.250	.250	.250	40	0	0	1.000	1	134	0	/2		0.0
Total	2	3	10	3	5	0	0	0	3	1		2	.500	.583	.500	193	2	0	.750	1	131	0	3b2/2		0.1

BURKE, LEO   Leo Patrick   B5.6.1934 Hagerstown MD   BR/TR/5-10/190(175-190)   d9.7   Col VPI

YEAR	TM LG	G	AB	R	H	2B	3B	HR	RBI	BB-IB	HP	SO	AVG	OBP	SLG	AOPS	ABR	SB-CS	FA	FR	RNG	THR	GAMES AT POSITION	DL	BFW
1958	Bal A	7	11	4	5	1	0	1	4	1-0		2	.455	.500	.818	271	3	0-0	1.000	-1	63	0	O3(1/1/1)/3		0.2
1959	Bal A	5	10	0	2	0	0	0	1	0-0	1	5	.200	.273	.200	33	-1	0-0	1.000	-1	64	0	2b3,3b2		-0.2
1961	LA A	6	5	0	0	0	0	0	0	0-0		1	.000	.000	.000	-90	-1	0-0	—	0		/H		-0.1
1962	LA A	19	64	8	17	1	0	4	14	5-1		11	.266	.329	.469	115	1	0-0	.958	-1	108	0	O12(4/0/8),3b4/S		-0.1
1963	StL N	30	49	6	10	2	1	1	5	4-0	0	12	.204	.264	.347	68	-2	0-0	1.000	0	136	0	O11(2/0/9),3b5		-0.3
	Chi N	27	49	4	9	0	0	2	7	4-1	0	13	.184	.241	.306	55	-3	0-1	.925	3	128	140	2b10,1b4		0.0
	Year	57	98	10	19	2	1	3	12	8-1	0	25	.194	.252	.327	61	-5	0-1	1.000	3	136	0	O11(2/0/9),2b10,3b5,1b4		-0.3
1964	Chi N	59	103	11	27	3	1	1	14	7-1	1	31	.262	.315	.340	81	-3	0-0	1.000	-1	113	107	O18R,2b5,3b4,1b2/C		-0.5
1965	Chi N	12	10	0	2	0	0	0	0	0-0		1	.200	.200	.200	13	-1	0-0	1.000	-0	0		C2/OR		-0.1
Total	7	165	301	33	72	7	2	9	45	21-3	3	79	.239	.294	.365	81	-7	0-1	.985	-2	112	42	O45(7/1/37),2b17,3b16,1b6,C3/S		-1.1

BURKE, LES   Leslie Kingston "Buck"   B12.18.1902 Lynn MA   D5.6.1975 Danvers MA   BL/TR/5-9/168   d5.2

YEAR	TM LG	G	AB	R	H	2B	3B	HR	RBI	BB-IB	HP	SO	AVG	OBP	SLG	AOPS	ABR	SB-CS	FA	FR	RNG	THR	GAMES AT POSITION	DL	BFW
1923	Det A	7	10	2	1	0	0	0	2	0		1	.100	.100	.100	-48	-2	0-0	.500	-1	44	0	3b2/2		-0.3
1924	Det A	72	241	30	61	10	4	0	17	22	2	20	.253	.321	.328	69	-12	2-4	.957	-2	102	102	2b58,S6		-1.3
1925	Det A	77	180	32	52	6	3	0	24	17	2	8	.289	.357	.356	82	-5	4-1	.962	4	105	115	2b52		0.0
1926	Det A	38	75	9	17	1	0	0	4	7	1	3	.227	.301	.240	42	-6	1-2	.942	1	106	123	2b15,3b7/S		-0.5
Total	4	194	506	73	131	17	7	0	47	46	5	32	.259	.327	.320	67	-25	7-7	.958	1	104	109	2b126,3b9,S7		-2.1

BURKE, MIKE   Michael E.   B1854 NY   D6.9.1889 Albany NY   BR/TR/6-0/190   d5.1

YEAR	TM LG	G	AB	R	H	2B	3B	HR	RBI	BB-IB	HP	SO	AVG	OBP	SLG	AOPS	ABR	SB-CS	FA	FR	RNG	THR	GAMES AT POSITION	DL	BFW
1879	Cin N	28	117	13	26	3	0	0	8	2		5	.222	.235	.248	63	-4		.786	-6	87	70	S19,O5(0/1/4),3b5		-0.9

BURKE, PAT   Patrick Edward   B5.13.1901 St.Louis MO   D7.7.1965 St.Louis MO   BR/TR/5-10.5/170   d9.23

YEAR	TM LG	G	AB	R	H	2B	3B	HR	RBI	BB-IB	HP	SO	AVG	OBP	SLG	AOPS	ABR	SB-CS	FA	FR	RNG	THR	GAMES AT POSITION	DL	BFW
1924	StL A	1	3	0	0	0	0	0	1	0		0	.000	.000	.000	-94	-1	0-0	—	-0	0	0	/3		-0.1

BURKETT, JESSE   Jesse Cail "Crab"   B12.4.1868 Wheeling WV   D5.27.1953 Worcester MA   BL/TL/5-8/155   d4.22   C1   HF1946 ▲

YEAR	TM LG	G	AB	R	H	2B	3B	HR	RBI	BB-IB	HP	SO	AVG	OBP	SLG	AOPS	ABR	SB-CS	FA	FR	RNG	THR	GAMES AT POSITION	DL	BFW
1890	NY N	101	401	67	124	23	13	4	60	33	3	52	.309	.366	.461	140	19	14	.824	1	142	115	O90(11/2/77),P21		1.3
1891	Cle N	40	167	29	45	7	4	0	13	23	0	19	.269	.358	.359	105	1	1	.892	-2	82	90	O40(6/2/35)		-0.1
1892	†Cle N	145	608	119	167	15	14	6	66	67	1	59	.275	.348	.375	114	9	36	.904	2	86	161	O145L		-0.2
1893	Cle N	125	511	145	178	25	15	6	82	98	7	23	.348	.459	.491	144	36	39	.849	-7	89	115	O125L		1.4
1894	Cle N	125	523	138	187	27	14	8	94	84	1	27	.358	.447	.509	125	24	28	.915	-4	81	106	O125L/P		0.7
1895	†Cle N	**132**	555	153	**225**	22	13	5	83	74	8	32	**.405**	.482	.519	149	44	41	.884	-4	84	98	O132(131/0/1)		2.3
1896	†Cle N	133	586	**160**	**240**	27	16	6	72	49	7	19	**.410**	.461	.541	155	46	34	.926	-4	92	92	O133L		2.5
1897	Cle N	127	517	129	198	28	7	2	60	76	7		.383	.468	.476	142	37	28	.949	-1	100	84	O127(127/1/0)		2.1
1898	Cle N	150	624	114	213	18	9	0	42	69	9		.341	.415	.399	135	32	19	.938	-7	81	67	O150(148/1/1)		1.2
1899	StL N	141	558	116	221	21	8	7	71	67	2		.396	.463	.500	160	49	25	.938	-3	92	100	O140(139/0/1)/2		3.1
1900	StL N	**141**	559	88	203	11	15	7	68	62	3		.363	.429	.474	150	39	32	.934	6	89	123	O141(140/1/0)		3.0
1901	StL N	**142**	601	**142**	**226**	20	15	10	75	59	10		**.376**	**.440**	.509	**184**	66	27	.923	-1	93	88	O142L		**5.5**
1902	StL A	138	553	97	169	29	9	5	52	71	5		.306	.390	.418	126	22	23	.924	5	94	144	O137L/PS3		1.9
1903	StL A	132	515	73	151	20	7	3	40	52	3		.293	.361	.377	125	18	17	.941	-3	69	112	O132L		0.7
1904	StL A	147	575	72	156	15	10	2	27	78	5		.271	.363	.343	132	25	12	.942	5	145	92	O147L		2.4
1905	Bos A	148	573	78	147	12	13	4	47	67	4		.257	.339	.344	115	11	13	.929	-2	67	0	O148L		0.1
Total	16	2067	8426	1720	2850	320	182	75	952	1029	75	231	.338	.415	.446	140	478	389	.917	-19	93	96	O2054(1936/7/115),P23/3S2		27.9

BURKHART, MORGAN   Morgan   B1.29.1972 St.Louis MO   BB/TL/5-11/225*   d6.27   Col Central Missouri

YEAR	TM LG	G	AB	R	H	2B	3B	HR	RBI	BB-IB	HP	SO	AVG	OBP	SLG	AOPS	ABR	SB-CS	FA	FR	RNG	THR	GAMES AT POSITION	DL	BFW
2000	Bos A	25	73	16	21	3	0	4	18	17-1	4	25	.288	.442	.493	134	5	0-0	.964	-1	52	42	D19,1b5/OL		0.3
2001	Bos A	11	33	3	6	1	0	1	4	1-0	1	15	.182	.206	.303	32	-3	0-0	1.000	-0	68	117	1b5,D6		-0.4
2003	KC A	6	15	1	3	0	0	0	1	1-0	0	2	.200	.250	.200	20	-2	0-0	1.000	-0	0	140	1b2,D2		-0.2
Total	3	42	121	20	30	4	0	5	23	19-1	4	42	.248	.366	.405	96	0	0-0	.986	-1	50	96	D27,1b12/OL		-0.3

BURKS, ELLIS   Ellis Rena   B9.11.1964 Vicksburg MS   BR/TR/6-2/205(175-209)   [BosA83*1/20]   d4.30   Col Ranger (TX) JC

YEAR	TM LG	G	AB	R	H	2B	3B	HR	RBI	BB-IB	HP	SO	AVG	OBP	SLG	AOPS	ABR	SB-CS	FA	FR	RNG	THR	GAMES AT POSITION	DL	BFW
1987	Bos A	133	558	94	152	30	2	20	59	41-0	2	98	.272	.324	.441	97	7	27-6	.988	7	99	**269**	O132C/D		0.7
1988	†Bos A	144	540	93	159	37	5	18	92	62-1	3	89	.294	.367	.481	130	23	25-9	.977	3	103	147	O142C,D2	8	2.7
1989	Bos A	97	399	73	121	19	6	12	61	36-2	5	52	.303	.365	.471	127	14	21-5	.977	-0	98	137	O95C/D	47	1.6
1990	†Bos A*	152	588	89	174	33	8	21	89	48-4	1	82	.296	.349	.486	125	18	9-11	.994	-10	88	97	O143C,D6		0.6
1991	Bos A	130	474	56	119	33	3	14	56	39-2	6	81	.251	.314	.422	97	-2	6-11	.993	-10	91	33	O126C,D2		-1.5
1992	Bos A	66	235	35	60	8	3	8	30	25-2	1	48	.255	.327	.417	100	0	5-2	.984	-10	72	88	O63C/D	102	-1.1
1993	†Chi A	146	499	75	137	24	4	17	74	60-2	4	97	.275	.352	.441	115	11	6-9	.982	-0	106	60	O146(0/21/132)		0.2
1994	Col N	42	149	33	48	8	3	13	24	16-3	0	39	.322	.388	.678	146	10	3-1	.964	-4	85	98	O39C	74	0.7
1995	Col N★	103	278	41	74	10	6	14	49	39-0	2	72	.266	.359	.496	96	-2	7-3	.970	1	109	83	O80(23/65/1)	10	0.0
1996	Col N★	156	613	**142**	211	45	8	40	128	61-2	6	114	.344	.408	**.639**	139	35	32-6	.983	-2	97	71	O152(129/32/0)		3.3
1997	Col N	119	424	91	123	19	2	32	82	47-0	3	75	.290	.363	.571	114	9	7-2	.982	-5	87	104	O112(66/89/0)	31	0.3
1998	Col N	100	357	54	102	22	5	16	54	39-0	2	80	.286	.355	.510	103	2	3-7	.975	-5	89	84	O98(45/78/0)		-0.5
	SF N	42	147	22	45	6	1	5	22	19-1	3	31	.306	.387	.463	132	7	8-1	.989	-3	96	39	O41(0/36/10)		0.6
	Year	142	504	76	147	28	6	21	76	58-1	5	111	.292	.365	.496	110	8	11-8	.979	-8	91	70	O139(45/114/10)		0.1
1999	SF N	120	390	73	110	19	0	31	96	89-2	6	86	.282	.394	.569	151	32	7-5	.991	-0	105	45	O107R,D3	17	2.4
2000	†SF N	122	393	74	135	21	5	24	96	56-5	1	49	.344	.419	.606	168	42	5-1	.982	2	109	64	O108R,D2	14	3.7
2001	†Cle A	124	439	83	123	29	1	28	74	62-2	5	85	.280	.369	.542	133	22	5-1	1.000	-0	79	202	D102,O20(18/0/2)	16	1.5
2002	Cle A	138	518	92	156	28	0	32	91	44-3	6	108	.301	.362	.541	133	24	2-3	1.000	-1	66	0	D127,O6L		1.5
2003	Cle A	55	198	27	52	11	1	6	28	27-2	2	46	.263	.360	.419	105	2	1-1	1.000	0	154	0	D51,O2L	113	0.0
2004	Bos A	11	33	6	6	0	1	1	3	0	1	8	.182	.270	.273	40	-1	2-0	—	0			D9	150	-0.3
Total	18	2000	7232	1253	2107	402	63	352	1206	793-33	60	1340	.291	.363	.510	123	241	181-84	.983	-35	96	100	O1612(289/1062/360),D307	582	16.4

BURLESON, RICK   Richard Paul "Rooster"   B4.29.1951 Lynwood CA   BR/TR/5-10/160*   [BosA70*S1/5]   d5.4   C5   [DL 1985 Cal A 182]

YEAR	TM LG	G	AB	R	H	2B	3B	HR	RBI	BB-IB	HP	SO	AVG	OBP	SLG	AOPS	ABR	SB-CS	FA	FR	RNG	THR	GAMES AT POSITION	DL	BFW
1974	Bos A	114	384	36	109	22	0	4	44	21-0	2	34	.284	.320	.372	93	-3	3-3	.957	-3	99	86	S88,2b31,3b2		0.6
1975	†Bos A	158	580	66	146	25	1	6	62	45-1	3	44	.252	.305	.329	74	-20	8-5	.963	2	103	110	S158		0.1
1976	Bos A	152	540	75	157	27	1	7	42	60-2	5	37	.291	.365	.383	107	7	14-9	.957	3	103	101	S152		2.9
1977	Bos A★	154	663	80	194	36	7	3	52	47-1	2	69	.293	.338	.382	87	-11	13-12	.970	20	107	**125**	S154		2.4
1978	Bos A★	145	626	75	155	32	5	5	49	40-2	4	71	.248	.296	.339	71	-24	8-8	.981	20	109	113	S144	14	1.0
1979	Bos A★	153	627	93	174	32	5	5	60	35-0	3	54	.278	.315	.366	80	-18	9-5	**.980**	30	113	108	S153		2.8
1980	Bos A	155	644	89	179	29	2	8	51	62-0	2	51	.278	.341	.366	90	-8	12-13	.974	**31**	110	**136**	S155		3.7
1981	Cal A★	109	430	53	126	17	1	5	33	42-2	3	38	.293	.357	.372	110	7	4-6	.979	27	115	123	S109		4.5
1982	Cal A	11	45	4	7	1	0	0	2	6-2	0	1	.156	.255	.178	21	-1	0-0	.986	4	126	157	S11	169	0.1
1983	Cal A	33	119	22	34	7	0	0	11	12-0	0	12	.286	.348	.345	93	-1	0-2	.969	2	110	82	S31	102	0.3
1984	Cal A	7	4	2	0	0	0	0	0	0		0	.000	.000	.000	-99	-1	0-0	—	0			/H	152	-0.1
1986	†Cal A	93	271	35	77	14	0	5	29	33-1	1	32	.284	.363	.391	107	4	1-3	.984	-5	96	72	D38,S37,2b6,3b4		0.0
1987	Bal A	62	206	26	43	9	1	2	14	17-0	3	18	.209	.279	.316	59	-12	0-2	.976	-6	93	109	2b55,D7		-1.5
Total	13	1346	5139	656	1401	256	23	50	449	420-11	28	477	.273	.328	.361	87	-85	72-68	.971	126	108	113	S1192,2b92,D45,3b6	619	16.8

BURNETT, HERCULES   Hercules H.   B8.13.1865 Louisville KY   D10.4.1936 Louisville KY   BR/5-11/177   d6.26

YEAR	TM LG	G	AB	R	H	2B	3B	HR	RBI	BB-IB	HP	SO	AVG	OBP	SLG	AOPS	ABR	SB-CS	FA	FR	RNG	THR	GAMES AT POSITION	DL	BFW
1888	Lou AA	1	4	1	0	0	0	0	0			0	.000	.200	.000	-34	-1	1	.667	-0	0	0	/OR		-0.1
1895	Lou N	5	17	6	7	1	1	2	3	3		2	.412	.474	.882	212	4	2	.769	-1	147	0	O4C/1		0.2
Total	2	6	21	7	7	1	1	2	3	3		2	.333	.417	.714	152	3	3	.750	-1	110	0	O5(0/4/1)/1		0.1

BURNETT, JOHNNY   John Henderson   B11.1.1904 Bartow FL   D8.12.1959 Tampa FL   BL/TR/5-11/175   d5.7   Col Florida

YEAR	TM LG	G	AB	R	H	2B	3B	HR	RBI	BB-IB	HP	SO	AVG	OBP	SLG	AOPS	ABR	SB-CS	FA	FR	RNG	THR	GAMES AT POSITION	DL	BFW
1927	Cle A	17	8	5	0	0	0	0	0	3		3	.000	.000	.000	-99	-2	1-0	.833	1	163	284	2b2		-0.2
1928	Cle A	3	10	3	5	0	0	0	1	0		0	.500	.500	.500	162	1	0	.867	0	95	†89	S2		0.1
1929	Cle A	19	33	2	5	1	0	0	2	1		2	.152	.200	.182	-1	-5	0-0	.923	2	135	64	S10,2b8		-0.2
1930	Cle A	54	170	28	53	13	0	0	20	17	1	8	.312	.378	.388	91	-1	2-2	.973	-1	107	42	3b27,S19		0.1

YEAR	TM LG	G	AB	R	H	2B	3B	HR	RBI	BB-IB	HP	SO	AVG	OBP	SLG	AOPS	ABR	SB-CS	FA	FR	RNG	THR	GAMES AT POSITION	DL	BFW
1931	Cle A	111	427	85	128	25	5	1	52	39	1	25	.300	.360	.389	92	-5	5-2	.938	-1	99	108	S63,2b35,3b21/OR		0.1
1932	Cle A	129	512	81	152	23	5	4	53	46	4	27	.297	.359	.385	87	-9	2-5	.946	-19	97	83	S103,2b26		-1.9
1933	Cle A	83	261	39	71	11	2	1	29	23	1	14	.272	.333	.341	76	-9	3-2	.938	-2	101	98	S41,2b17,3b12		-0.7
1934	Cle A	72	208	28	61	11	2	3	30	18	1	11	.293	.352	.409	94	-2	1-1	.981	-5	88	123	3b42,S9,2b3,O2(1/0/1)		-0.6
1935	StL A	70	206	17	46	10	1	0	26	19	0	16	.223	.289	.282	46	-17	1-0	.939	-3	104	123	3b31,S18,2b12		-1.6
Total	9	558	1835	288	521	94	15	9	213	163	9	107	.284	.345	.366	81	-49	15-12	.935	-29	100	95	S265,3b133,2b103,O3(1/0/2)		-4.9

BURNETT, JACK John Jeirus (b John Jeirus Barnett) B12.16.1879 Ventura CA D9.3.1923 Modoc Co. CA BB d7.2

YEAR	TM LG	G	AB	R	H	2B	3B	HR	RBI	BB-IB	HP	SO	AVG	OBP	SLG	AOPS	ABR	SB-CS	FA	FR	RNG	THR	GAMES AT POSITION	DL	BFW
1907	StL N	59	206	18	49	8	4	0	12	15	2		.238	.296	.316	95	-2	5	.955	-5	102	49	O59C		-1.0

BURNITZ, JEROMY Jeromy Neal B4.15.1969 Westminster CA BL/TR/6-0/205(180-216) [NYN90 1/17] d6.21 Col Oklahoma St.

YEAR	TM LG	G	AB	R	H	2B	3B	HR	RBI	BB-IB	HP	SO	AVG	OBP	SLG	AOPS	ABR	SB-CS	FA	FR	RNG	THR	GAMES AT POSITION	DL	BFW
1993	NY N	86	263	49	64	10	6	13	38	38-4	1	66	.243	.339	.475	117	6	3-6	.977	1	101	113	O79(0/20/61)		0.3
1994	NY N	45	143	26	34	4	0	3	15	23-0	1	45	.238	.347	.329	78	-4	1-1	.970	-6	77	32	O42R		-1.2
1995	Cle A	9	7	4	4	1	0	0	0	0-0	0	5	.571	.571	.714	227	1	0-0	1.000	1	191	0	O6(5/1/0),D2		0.2
1996	Cle A	71	128	30	36	10	0	7	26	25-1	2	31	.281	.406	.523	133	8	2-1	1.000	-1	105	0	O30(10/6/14),D15		0.5
	Mil A	23	72	8	17	4	0	2	14	8-1	2	16	.236	.321	.375	74	-3	2-0	.975	-2	81	71	O22(0/8/14)		-0.5
	Year	94	200	38	53	14	0	9	40	33-2	4	47	.265	.377	.470	112	5	4-1	.988	-3	93	36	O52(10/14/28),D15		0.0
1997	Mil A	153	494	85	139	37	8	27	85	75-8	5	111	.281	.382	.553	138	29	20-13	.975	-3	89	153	O149(5/26/124)		1.9
1998	Mil N	161	609	92	160	28	1	38	125	70-7	4	118	.263	.339	.499	116	13	7-4	.972	-2	98	92	O161(0/1/161)		0.3
1999	Mil N★	130	467	87	126	33	2	33	103	91-7	16	124	.270	.402	.561	141	33	7-3	.982	0	100	92	O127R,D3	33	2.5
2000	Mil N	161	564	91	131	29	2	31	98	99-10	14	121	.232	.356	.456	105	6	6-4	.979	-2	96	113	O158R/D		-0.5
2001	Mil N	154	562	104	141	32	4	34	100	80-9	5	150	.251	.347	.504	119	16	0-4	.981	1	97	127	O153R		0.7
2002	NY N	154	479	65	103	15	0	19	54	58-5	10	135	.215	.311	.365	85	-13	10-7	.966	-4	96	80	O140R/D		-2.4
2003	NY N	65	234	38	64	18	0	18	45	21-6	4	55	.274	.344	.581	141	13	1-4	.986	-1	104	50	O65(10/21/48)	30	0.9
	LA N	61	230	25	47	4	0	13	32	14-3	1	57	.204	.252	.391	66	-13	4-0	.946	-5	79	90	O60(54/12/2)		-1.1
	Year	126	464	63	111	22	0	31	77	35-9	5	112	.239	.299	.487	104	0	5-4	.970	-6	92	69	O125(64/33/50)		-1.1
2004	Col N	150	540	94	153	30	4	37	110	58-7	5	124	.283	.356	.559	117	14	5-6	.974	-7	85	126	O143(21/69/79),D3		0.2
2005	Chi N	160	605	84	156	31	2	24	87	57-3	3	109	.258	.322	.435	94	-6	5-4	.984	2	109	71	O160(0/3/158)		-1.2
Total	13	1583	5397	882	1375	286	29	299	932	717-71	73	1302	.255	.348	.485	113	100	73-57	.977	-27	96	99	O1495(105/167/1281),D25	63	-0.3

BURNS, C.B. Charles Birmingham B5.15.1879 Bay View MD D6.6.1968 Havre de Grace MD BR/TR/6-0/175 d8.19

YEAR	TM LG	G	AB	R	H	2B	3B	HR	RBI	BB-IB	HP	SO	AVG	OBP	SLG	AOPS	ABR	SB-CS	FA	FR	RNG	THR	GAMES AT POSITION	DL	BFW
1902	Bal A	1	1	0	1	0	0	0	0	0	0	0	1.000	1.000	1.000	436	0	0	—	0			/H		0.0

BURNS, ED Edward James B10.31.1888 San Francisco CA D5.30.1942 Monterey CA BR/TR/5-6/165 d6.25 Col St. Marys (CA)

YEAR	TM LG	G	AB	R	H	2B	3B	HR	RBI	BB-IB	HP	SO	AVG	OBP	SLG	AOPS	ABR	SB-CS	FA	FR	RNG	THR	GAMES AT POSITION	DL	BFW
1912	StL N	1	1	0	0	0	0	0	1	0	0	0	.000	.000	.000	-99	0	0	—	0	0	0	/C		0.0
1913	Phi N	17	30	3	6	3	0	0	3	6	1	3	.200	.351	.300	83	0	2	.980	-2	94	90	C15		-0.1
1914	Phi N	70	139	8	36	3	4	0	16	20	0	12	.259	.352	.338	99	0	5	.947	-5	73	122	C55		-0.2
1915	†Phi N	67	174	11	42	5	0	0	16	20	2	12	.241	.327	.270	81	-3	1	.981	-1	106	93	C62		0.1
1916	Phi N	78	219	14	51	8	1	0	14	16	3	18	.233	.294	.279	74	-6	3	.981	-6	105	90	C75/SOC		-0.7
1917	Phi N	20	49	2	10	1	0	0	6	1	0	5	.204	.220	.224	35	-4	2	.971	-0	108	131	C15		-1.0
1918	Phi N	68	184	10	38	1	1	0	9	20	1	9	.207	.288	.223	53	-10	1	.981	-4	96	111	C68		-0.4
Total	7	321	796	48	183	21	6	0	65	83	7	59	.230	.308	.271	73	-23	14	.974	-19	97	103	C291/OCS		-2.3

BURNS, GEORGE George Henry "Tioga George" B1.31.1893 Niles OH D1.7.1978 Kirkland WA BR/TR/6-1.5/180 d4.14

YEAR	TM LG	G	AB	R	H	2B	3B	HR	RBI	BB-IB	HP	SO	AVG	OBP	SLG	AOPS	ABR	SB-CS	FA	FR	RNG	THR	GAMES AT POSITION	DL	BFW
1914	Det A	137	478	55	139	22	5	5	57	32	12	56	.291	.348	.389	119	10	23-13	.982	-6	91	106	1b137		0.2
1915	Det A	105	392	49	99	18	3	5	50	22	5	51	.253	.301	.352	91	-6	9-3	.986	-4	90	123	1b104		-1.2
1916	Det A	135	479	60	137	22	6	4	73	22	7	30	.286	.327	.382	109	3	12	.985	-10	72	97	1b124		-1.1
1917	Det A	119	407	42	92	14	10	1	40	15	6	33	.226	.264	.317	77	-14	3	.990	-4	84	72	1b104		-2.3
1918	Det A	130	505	61	178	22	9	6	70	23	8	25	.352	.390	.467	157	32	8	.983	6	124	132	1b128,O2(1/0/1)		3.8
1919	Phi A	126	470	63	139	29	9	8	57	19	12	18	.296	.339	.447	118	9	15	.980	2	120	83	1b86,O34R		0.7
1920	Phi A	22	60	1	14	3	0	1	7	6	1	7	.233	.313	.333	71	-2	4-0	.958	0	84	164	O13R		-0.2
	†Cle A	44	56	7	15	4	1	0	13	4	2	3	.268	.339	.375	86	-1	1-0	.979	1	159	21	1b12/OR		0.0
	Year	66	116	8	29	7	1	1	20	10	3	10	.250	.326	.353	78	-4	5-0	.958	1	83	161	O14R,1b12		-0.2
1921	Cle A	84	244	52	88	21	4	0	49	13	2	19	.361	.398	.480	121	8	3-1	.990	2	111	108	1b73		0.6
1922	Bos A	147	558	71	171	32	5	12	73	20	9	28	.306	.341	.446	104	1	8-2	.987	-1	103	101	1b140		-0.7
1923	Bos A	146	551	91	181	47	5	7	82	45	3	33	.328	.386	.470	124	20	9-7	.990	-1	97	90	1b127		0.8
1924	Cle A	129	462	64	143	37	5	4	68	29	15	27	.310	.370	.437	106	4	14-5	.987	9	130	90	1b127		0.6
1925	Cle A	127	488	69	164	41	4	6	79	24	3	24	.336	.371	.473	112	6	16-11	.989	1	102	92	1b126		0.0
1926	Cle A	151	603	97	216	64	3	4	114	24	8	33	.358	.394	.494	130	27	13-7	.990	1	107	115	1b151		1.8
1927	Cle A	140	549	84	175	51	2	3	78	42	7	27	.319	.375	.435	109	9	13-11	.990	4	112	99	1b139		0.3
1928	Cle A	82	209	29	52	12	1	5	30	17	6	11	.249	.323	.388	85	-5	2-3	.984	2	126	108	1b53		-0.6
	NY A	4	4	1	2	0	0	0	0	0	0	1	.500	.500	.500	169	0	0-0	1.000	-0	0		1b2		0.0
	Year	86	213	30	54	12	1	5	30	17	6	12	.254	.326	.390	87	-4	2-3	.985	2	125	107	1b55		-0.6
1929	NY A	9	9	0	0	0	0	0	0	0	0	4	.000	.000	.000	-99	-3	0-0	—	0			/H		-0.3
	†Phi A	29	49	5	13	5	0	1	11	2	0	3	.265	.294	.429	81	-1	1-0	1.000	-0	77	110	1b19		-0.2
	Year	38	58	5	13	5	0	1	11	2	0	7	.224	.250	.362	55	-4	1-0	1.000	-0	77	110	1b19		-0.5
Total	16	1866	6573	901	2018	444	72	72	951	363	110	433	.307	.354	.429	112	99	154-63	.987	2	104	101	1b1671,O50(1/0/49)		2.2

BURNS, GEORGE George Joseph B11.24.1889 Utica NY D8.15.1966 Gloversville NY BR/TR/5-7/160 d10.3 C1

YEAR	TM LG	G	AB	R	H	2B	3B	HR	RBI	BB-IB	HP	SO	AVG	OBP	SLG	AOPS	ABR	SB-CS	FA	FR	RNG	THR	GAMES AT POSITION	DL	BFW
1911	NY N	6	17	2	1	0	0	0	1	0	0	0	.059	.111	.059	-50	-3	0	1.000	-1	89	0	O6(1/4/1)		-0.4
1912	NY N	29	51	11	15	4	0	0	3	8	1	8	.294	.400	.373	109	1	7	1.000	1	94	163	O23(13/5/5)		0.2
1913	†NY N	150	605	81	173	37	4	2	54	58	4	74	.286	.352	.370	106	7	40-35	.963	1	101	102	O150(119/0/32)		-0.3
1914	NY N	154	561	100	170	35	10	3	60	89	5	53	.303	.403	.417	149	39	62	.950	0	106	82	O154(102/0/54)		3.4
1915	NY N	155	622	83	169	27	14	3	51	56	1	57	.272	.333	.375	121	15	27-20	.960	-7	93	72	O155(140/0/15)		-0.1
1916	NY N	155	623	105	174	24	8	5	41	63	1	47	.279	.346	.368	126	20	37-26	.962	-0	97	117	O155L		1.4
1917	†NY N	152	597	103	180	25	13	5	45	75	1	55	.302	.380	.412	148	30	40	.974	2	105	83	O152L		3.5
1918	NY N	119	465	80	135	22	6	4	51	43	1	37	.290	.354	.389	129	17	40	.965	9	125	80	O119L		2.3
1919	NY N	139	534	86	162	30	9	2	46	82	0	37	.303	.396	.404	142	33	40	.990	2	105	85	O139L		3.1
1920	NY N	154	631	115	181	35	9	6	46	76	2	48	.287	.365	.399	121	20	22-22	.983	11	123	74	O154(154/1/0)		2.3
1921	†NY N	149	605	111	181	28	9	4	61	80	6	24	.299	.386	.395	107	10	19-20	.972	-7	96	75	O149(90/59/0)/3		-0.9
1922	Cin N	156	631	104	180	20	10	1	53	78	2	38	.285	.366	.353	88	-9	30-23	.976	-4	95	97	O156(0/109/47)		-2.2
1923	Cin N	154	614	99	168	27	13	3	45	101	0	46	.274	.376	.375	101	5	12-14	.960	-6	101	60	O154(0/3/151)		-1.5
1924	Cin N	93	336	43	86	19	2	2	33	29	0	21	.256	.315	.342	77	-10	3-6	.963	2	99	129	O90(12/1/79)		-1.7
1925	Phi N	88	349	65	102	29	1	5	32	78	0	20	.292	.353	.390	82	-8	4-8	.990	2	102	99	O88(66/4/22)		-1.4
Total	15	1853	7241	1188	2077	362	108	41	611	872	26	565	.287	.366	.384	115	173	383-174	.970	6	103	88	O1844(1262/186/406)/3		7.7

BURNS, JIM James M. B St.Louis MO D2.17.1909 Chicago IL 5-7/168 d9.25

YEAR	TM LG	G	AB	R	H	2B	3B	HR	RBI	BB-IB	HP	SO	AVG	OBP	SLG	AOPS	ABR	SB-CS	FA	FR	RNG	THR	GAMES AT POSITION	DL	BFW
1888	KC AA	15	66	13	20	1	0	0	4	1			.303	.343	.303	101	0	6	.853	1	155	300	O15L		0.1
1889	KC AA	134	579	103	176	23	11	5	97	20	7	68	.304	.335	.408	105	-1	56	.913	-8	44	65	O134C/3		-1.1
1891	Was AA	20	82	15	26	6	0	0	10	6	2	10	.317	.378	.390	126	3	2	.771	-4	31		O20(0/5/16)/S		-0.1
Total	3	169	727	131	222	29	11	5	111	27	12	78	.305	.341	.396	107	2	64	.897	-10	53	81	O169(15/139/16)/S3		-1.1

BURNS, JACK John Irving "Slug" B8.31.1907 Cambridge MA D4.18.1975 Brighton MA BL/TL/5-10.5/175 d9.17 C5

YEAR	TM LG	G	AB	R	H	2B	3B	HR	RBI	BB-IB	HP	SO	AVG	OBP	SLG	AOPS	ABR	SB-CS	FA	FR	RNG	THR	GAMES AT POSITION	DL	BFW
1930	StL A	8	30	5	9	3	0	0	2	5	0		.300	.400	.400	100	0	0-0	1.000	1	138	165	1b8		0.1
1931	StL A	144	570	75	148	27	7	4	70	42	1	58	.260	.312	.353	72	-25	19-12	.993	19	159	114	1b143		-1.8
1932	StL A	150	617	111	188	33	8	11	70	61	2	43	.305	.368	.438	102	2	17-11	.992	5	111	99	1b150		-0.7
1933	StL A	144	556	89	160	43	4	7	71	56	1	51	.288	.353	.417	97	-1	11-11	.992	3	108	114	1b143		-1.3
1934	StL A	154	612	86	157	28	4	13	73	62	2	47	.257	.327	.392	78	-22	9-3	.992	-0	97	98	1b154		-3.3
1935	StL A	143	549	77	157	28	1	6	67	68	1	49	.286	.366	.368	86	-9	3-2	.992	9	74	92	1b141		-2.9
1936	StL A	9	14	2	3	1	0	0	0	3	0	6	.214	.353	.286	58	-1	0-0	1.000	-0	73	120	1b2		-0.1
	Det A	138	558	96	158	36	3	4	63	79	3	45	.283	.375	.380	87	-9	4-8	.994	1	99	109	1b138		-2.1
	Year	147	572	98	161	37	3	4	64	82	3	46	.281	.374	.378	86	-10	4-8	.994	1	99	109	1b140		-2.2
Total	7	890	3506	541	980	199	31	44	417	376	8	299	.280	.351	.392	87	-65	63-47	.992	19	108	105	1b879		-12.1

YEAR	TM	LG	G	AB	R	H	2B	3B	HR	RBI	BB-IB	HP	SO	AVG	OBP	SLG	AOPS	ABR	SB-CS	FA	FR	RNG	THR	GAMES AT POSITION	DL	BFW

BURNS, JACK John Joseph B5.13.1880 Avoca PA D6.24.1957 Waterford CT BR/TR/5-10/160 d9.11

YEAR	TM	LG	G	AB	R	H	2B	3B	HR	RBI	BB-IB	HP	SO	AVG	OBP	SLG	AOPS	ABR	SB-CS	FA	FR	RNG	THR	GAMES AT POSITION	DL	BFW
1903	Det	A	11	37	2	10	0	0	0	3	1	2		.270	.325	.270	82	-1	0	.981	2	109	135	2b11		0.1
1904	Det	A	4	16	3	2	0	0	0	1	1	0		.125	.176	.125	-4	-2	1	.952	-1	72	77	2b4		-0.4
Total	2		15	53	5	12	0	0	0	4	2	2		.226	.281	.226	57	-3	1	.973	0	98	118	2b15		-0.3

BURNS, JOE Joseph Francis B3.26.1889 Ipswich MA D7.12.1987 Beverly MA BL/TL/5-11/170 d6.19

YEAR	TM	LG	G	AB	R	H	2B	3B	HR	RBI	BB-IB	HP	SO	AVG	OBP	SLG	AOPS	ABR	SB-CS	FA	FR	RNG	THR	GAMES AT POSITION	DL	BFW
1910	Cin	N	1	1	0	1	0	0	0	0	0		0	1.000	1.000	1.000	506	0	1	—	0			/H		0.1
1913	Det	A	4	13	0	5	0	0	0	1	2	1	4	.385	.500	.385	162	1	0	1.000	-0	99	0	O4L		0.1
Total	2		5	14	0	6	0	0	0	1	2	1	4	.429	.529	.429	184	1	1	1.000	-0	99	0	O4L		0.2

BURNS, JOE Joseph Francis B2.25.1900 Trenton NJ D1.7.1986 Trenton NJ BR/TR/6-0/175 d4.18

YEAR	TM	LG	G	AB	R	H	2B	3B	HR	RBI	BB-IB	HP	SO	AVG	OBP	SLG	AOPS	ABR	SB-CS	FA	FR	RNG	THR	GAMES AT POSITION	DL	BFW
1924	Chi	A	8	19	1	2	0	0	0	0	0		2	.105	.105	.105	-47	-4	0-0	.933	-1	72	56	C6		-0.5

BURNS, JOE Joseph James B6.17.1916 Bryn Mawr PA D6.24.1974 Bryn Mawr PA BR/TR/5-10.5/175 d4.24

YEAR	TM	LG	G	AB	R	H	2B	3B	HR	RBI	BB-IB	HP	SO	AVG	OBP	SLG	AOPS	ABR	SB-CS	FA	FR	RNG	THR	GAMES AT POSITION	DL	BFW
1943	Bos	N	52	135	12	28	3	0	1	5	8	2	25	.207	.262	.252	49	-9	2	.933	2	116	125	3b34,O4(1/1/2)		-0.7
1944	Phi	A	28	75	5	18	2	0	1	8	4	0	8	.240	.278	.307	68	-3	0-1	.919	-5	79	98	3b17,2b9		-0.9
1945	Phi	A	31	90	7	23	1	1	0	3	4	0	17	.256	.287	.289	68	-4	0-1	1.000	-2	83	63	O19R,3b5/1		-0.8
Total	3		111	300	24	69	6	1	2	16	16	2	50	.230	.274	.277	60	-16	2-2	.920	-5	104	110	3b56,O23(1/1/21),2b9/1		-2.4

BURNS, PAT Patrick d8.11

YEAR	TM	LG	G	AB	R	H	2B	3B	HR	RBI	BB-IB	HP	SO	AVG	OBP	SLG	AOPS	ABR	SB-CS	FA	FR	RNG	THR	GAMES AT POSITION	DL	BFW
1884	Bal	AA	6	25	3	5	2	1	0		3	0		.200	.286	.360	105	-1		.953	-1	46	70	1b6		-0.1
	Bal	U	1	4	0	2	0	0	0		0			.500	.500	.500	185	0		.917	-0	0	238	/1		0.0
Total	1		7	29	3	7	2	1	0		3	0		.241	.313	.379	117	0		.947	-1	39	96	1b7		-0.1

BURNS, DICK Richard Simon B12.26.1863 Holyoke MA D11.16.1937 Holyoke MA BL/TL/5-7/140 d5.3 ▲

YEAR	TM	LG	G	AB	R	H	2B	3B	HR	RBI	BB-IB	HP	SO	AVG	OBP	SLG	AOPS	ABR	SB-CS	FA	FR	RNG	THR	GAMES AT POSITION	DL	BFW
1883	Det	N	37	140	11	26	7	1	0		5	2	22	.186	.197	.250	36	-10		.758	-4	89	132	O24(1/1/23),P17		-0.9
1884	Cin	U	79	350	84	107	17	12	4		5			.306	.315	.457	122	-3		.827	-2	95	78	O44(6/33/7),P40,S2		-0.4
1885	StL	N	14	54	2	12	2	1	0		4	3	8	.222	.263	.296	86	-1		.682	-2	93	334	O14C/P		-0.3
Total	3		130	544	97	145	26	14	4		9	10	30	.267	.280	.388	98	-14		.785	-8	93	135	O82(7/48/30),P58,S2		-1.6

BURNS, TOM Thomas Everett B3.30.1857 Honesdale PA D3.19.1902 Jersey City NJ BR/TR/5-7/152 d5.1 M3/U1 OF(10/2/2)

YEAR	TM	LG	G	AB	R	H	2B	3B	HR	RBI	BB-IB	HP	SO	AVG	OBP	SLG	AOPS	ABR	SB-CS	FA	FR	RNG	THR	GAMES AT POSITION	DL	BFW
1880	Chi	N	85	333	47	103	17	3	0	43	12		23	.309	.333	.378	133	11		.864	-25	76	54	S79,3b9,C2/P		-1.1
1881	Chi	N	84	342	41	95	20	3	4	42	14		22	.278	.306	.389	112	4		.870	-4	96	88	S80,3b3,2b3		0.4
1882	Chi	N	84	355	55	88	23	6	0	48	15		28	.248	.278	.346	95	-2		.911	-2	93	119	2b43,S41		-0.1
1883	Chi	N	97	405	69	119	37	7	2	67	13		31	.294	.316	.435	116	7		.872	3	106	113	S79,2b19/OL		1.1
1884	Chi	N	83	343	54	84	14	2	7	44	13		50	.245	.272	.359	89	-5		.838	-4	103	113	S80,3b3		-0.6
1885	†Chi	N	111	445	82	121	23	9	7	71	16		48	.272	.297	.411	112	3		.844	-4	101	114	S111/2		0.2
1886	†Chi	N	112	445	64	123	18	10	3	65	14		40	.276	.298	.382	92	-7	15	.890	11	106	101	3b112		0.5
1887	Chi	N	115	424	57	112	20	10	3	60	34	1	32	.264	.320	.380	83	-12	32	.872	17	110	134	3b107,O8(6/2/0)		0.6
1888	Chi	N	134	483	60	115	12	6	3	70	26	3	49	.238	.281	.306	81	-11	34	.905	17	105	89	3b134		0.8
1889	Chi	N	136	525	64	135	27	6	4	66	32	2	57	.257	.302	.354	79	-18	18	.880	-3	100	124	3b136		-1.6
1890	Chi	N	139	538	86	149	17	6	5	86	57	2	45	.277	.348	.359	102	1	44	.898	2	101	122	3b139		0.4
1891	Chi	N	59	243	36	55	8	1	1	17	21	0	21	.226	.288	.280	66	-11	18	.892	-1	90	150	3b53,S4,O2L		-1.0
1892	Pit	N	12	39	7	8	0	0	0	4	3	0	8	.205	.262	.205	41	-3	1	.690	-4	0	3	3b8,O3(1/0/2),M		-0.7
Total	13		1251	4920	722	1307	236	69	39	683	270	8	454	.266	.305	.365	96	-43	162	.886	2	102	115	3b704,S474,2b66,O14L,C2/P		-1.1

BURNS, TOMMY Thomas P. "Oyster" B9.6.1864 Philadelphia PA D11.11.1928 Brooklyn NY BL/TR/5-8/183 d8.18 OF(100/15/781) ▲

YEAR	TM	LG	G	AB	R	H	2B	3B	HR	RBI	BB-IB	HP	SO	AVG	OBP	SLG	AOPS	ABR	SB-CS	FA	FR	RNG	THR	GAMES AT POSITION	DL	BFW
1884	Wil	U	2	7	0	1	0	1	0		1			.143	.250	.429	99	0		.778	-0	101	0	S2		0.0
	Bal	AA	35	131	34	39	2	6	0	23	7	3		.298	.348	.542	179	10		.826	-4	64	210	O24R,2b10,P2/3		0.6
1885	Bal	AA	78	321	47	74	11	6	5	37	16	6		.231	.280	.349	99	0		.908	-1	193	254	O45(1/0/44),P15,S10,3b6,2b6/1		0.1
1887	Bal	AA	140	551	122	188	33	19	9	99	63	5		.341	.414	.519	169	53	58	.841	-17	84	85	S98,3b42,P3/2		3.2
1888	Bal	AA	79	325	54	97	18	9	4	42	24	1		.298	.349	.446	158	21	23	.855	-7	29	42	O56(46/0/10),S23,P5,3b2/2		1.1
	Bro	AA	52	204	40	58	9	6	2	25	14	3		.284	.339	.417	142	9	21	.851	-9	90	84	S36,O14C,2b3		0.1
	Year		131	529	94	155	27	15	6	67	38	4		.293	.345	.435	152	30	44	.847	-16	24	35	O70(46/14/10),S59,P5,2b4,3b2		1.2
1889	†Bro	AA	131	504	105	153	19	13	5	100	68	4	26	.304	.391	.423	131	22	32	.920	-7	97	113	O113R,S19		1.2
1890	†Bro	N	119	472	102	134	22	12	12	128	51	4	42	.284	.359	.464	139	21	21	.941	-2	120	108	O116R,3b3		1.6
1891	Bro	N	123	470	75	134	24	13	4	83	53	0	30	.285	.358	.417	126	15	21	.922	-1	91	164	O113R,S6,3b5		1.2
1892	Bro	N	141	542	88	171	27	18	4	96	65	6	42	.315	.395	.454	162	42	33	.937	-12	79	96	O129(2/0/127),3b7,S5		2.2
1893	Bro	N	109	415	68	112	22	8	7	60	36	4	16	.270	.334	.412	103	0	14	.932	-0	109	136	O108(0/1/108)/S		-0.4
1894	Bro	N	126	513	107	182	32	14	5	109	44	3	18	.355	.409	.501	127	24	30	.949	-5	72	78	O126R		1.0
1895	Bro	N	20	76	7	14	0	1	0	7	8	1	2	.184	.271	.211	27	-8	0	.918	1	132	156	O19L		-0.8
	NY	N	33	114	21	35	5	3	1	25	14	1	6	.307	.388	.430	113	3	10	.870	-2	123	0	O32L/1		-0.1
	Year		53	190	28	49	5	4	1	32	22	2	8	.258	.341	.342	80	-5	10	.893	-1	127	67	O51L/1		-0.9
Total	11		1188	4645	870	1392	224	129	65	834	464	41	182	.300	.368	.445	135	212	263	.920	-64	94	114	O895R,S200,3b66,P25,2b21,1b2		11.0

BURR, ALEX Alexander Thomson B11.1.1893 Chicago IL D10.12.1918 Cazaux, France BR/TR/6-3.5/190 d4.21 Col Williams

YEAR	TM	LG	G	AB	R	H	2B	3B	HR	RBI	BB-IB	HP	SO	AVG	OBP	SLG	AOPS	ABR	SB-CS	FA	FR	RNG	THR	GAMES AT POSITION	DL	BFW
1914	NY	A	1	0	0	0	0	0	0	0	0		0	—	—	—		0	0	—	-0	0	0	/OC		0.0

BURRELL, BUSTER Frank Andrew B12.22.1866 Weymouth MA D5.8.1962 Weymouth MA BR/TR/5-10/165 d8.1

YEAR	TM	LG	G	AB	R	H	2B	3B	HR	RBI	BB-IB	HP	SO	AVG	OBP	SLG	AOPS	ABR	SB-CS	FA	FR	RNG	THR	GAMES AT POSITION	DL	BFW
1891	NY	N	15	53	1	5	0	0	0	1	3	1	12	.094	.158	.094	-27	-9	2	.856	-6	82	104	C15/OC		-1.3
1895	Bro	N	12	28	7	4	0	1	0	5	4	0	3	.143	.250	.250	32	-3	0	.838	-1	129	77	C12		-0.3
1896	Bro	N	62	206	19	62	11	3	0	23	15	0	13	.301	.348	.383	98	0	1	.928	-6	104	74	C60		-0.1
1897	Bro	N	33	103	15	25	2	0	2	18	10	0		.243	.310	.320	70	-4	1	.884	-5	89	93	C27,1b4		-0.6
Total	4		122	390	42	96	13	3	3	47	32	1	28	.246	.305	.318	70	-16	4	.896	-18	100	83	C114,1b4/OC		-2.3

BURRELL, PAT Patrick Brian B10.10.1976 Eureka Springs AR BR/TR/6-4/225* [PhiN98 1/1] d5.24 Col Miami

YEAR	TM	LG	G	AB	R	H	2B	3B	HR	RBI	BB-IB	HP	SO	AVG	OBP	SLG	AOPS	ABR	SB-CS	FA	FR	RNG	THR	GAMES AT POSITION	DL	BFW
2000	Phi	N	111	408	52	106	27	1	18	79	63-2	1	139	.260	.359	.463	107	5	0-0	.988	-6	60	80	1b58,O48L,D4		-0.7
2001	Phi	N	155	539	70	139	29	2	27	89	70-7	5	162	.258	.346	.469	114	11	2-1	.972	0	87	186	O146L,D5		0.6
2002	Phi	N	157	586	96	165	39	2	37	116	89-9	3	153	.282	.376	.544	153	43	1-0	.979	-5	92	80	O157L		3.2
2003	Phi	N	146	522	57	109	31	4	21	64	72-2	4	142	.209	.309	.404	91	-8	0-0	.976	-4	94	84	O140L,D2		-1.7
2004	Phi	N	127	448	66	115	17	0	24	84	78-7	2	130	.257	.365	.455	108	7	0-0	.983	-1	100	132	O122L		-0.5
2005	Phi	N	154	562	78	158	27	1	32	117	99-6	3	160	.281	.389	.504	128	26	0-0	.972	-4	87	121	O153L	30	1.6
Total	6		850	3065	424	792	170	10	159	549	471-33	18	886	.258	.358	.476	118	84	5-1	.976	-17	91	126	O766L,1b58,D11	30	3.4

BURRIGHT, LARRY Larry Allen "Possum" B7.10.1937 Roseville IL BR/TR/5-11/170* d4.12 Col Fullerton (CA) JC

YEAR	TM	LG	G	AB	R	H	2B	3B	HR	RBI	BB-IB	HP	SO	AVG	OBP	SLG	AOPS	ABR	SB-CS	FA	FR	RNG	THR	GAMES AT POSITION	DL	BFW
1962	LA	N	115	249	35	51	6	4	3	30	21-5	0	67	.205	.264	.317	60	-15	4-3	.962	-1	99	71	2b109/S		-1.0
1963	NY	N	41	100	9	22	2	1	0	3	8-1	2	25	.220	.291	.260	59	-5	1-0	.946	10	131	90	S19,2b15/3		0.8
1964	NY	N	3	7	0	0	0	0	0	0	0-0	0	0	.000	.000	.000	-99	-2	0-0	1.000	4	191	215	2b3		0.2
Total	3		159	356	44	73	8	6	4	33	29-6	2	92	.205	.267	.295	56	-22	5-3	.964	13	105	83	2b127,S20/3		0.0

BURRIS, PAUL Paul Robert B7.21.1923 Hickory NC D10.3.1999 Charlotte NC BR/TR/6-0/190* d10.2

YEAR	TM	LG	G	AB	R	H	2B	3B	HR	RBI	BB-IB	HP	SO	AVG	OBP	SLG	AOPS	ABR	SB-CS	FA	FR	RNG	THR	GAMES AT POSITION	DL	BFW
1948	Bos	N	2	4	0	2	0	0	0	0	0	0	0	.500	.500	.500	174	0	0	1.000	1	0	0	C2		0.1
1950	Bos	N	10	23	1	4	1	0	0	3	1	0	2	.174	.208	.217	13	-3	0	1.000	1	87	0	C8		-0.2
1952	Bos	N	55	168	14	37	4	0	2	21	7	1	19	.220	.256	.280	50	-12	0-0	1.000	-3	91	68	C50		-1.3
1953	Mil	N	2	1	0	0	0	0	0	0	0	0	0	.000	.000	.000	-99	-0	0-0	1.000	0	0	0	C2	77	0.0
Total	4		69	196	15	43	5	0	2	24	8	1	21	.219	.254	.276	47	-15	0-0	1.000	-2	88	57	C62	77	-1.4

BURROUGHS, HENRY Henry S. B1845 NJ D3.31.1878 Newark NJ 5-8/147 d5.5

YEAR	TM	LG	G	AB	R	H	2B	3B	HR	RBI	BB-IB	HP	SO	AVG	OBP	SLG	AOPS	ABR	SB-CS	FA	FR	RNG	THR	GAMES AT POSITION	DL	BFW
1871	Oly	NA	12	63	11	15	2	3	1	14	1			.238	.250	.413	91	-1	0-0	.706	-2	107	0	O8(4/0/4),3b5/2		-0.1
1872	Oly	NA	2	7	1	1	0	0	0	1	0			.143	.143	.143	25	-1	0-0	.625	-0	305	0	O2C		-0.1
Total	2 NA		14	70	12	16	2	3	1	14	1			.229	.250	.386	85	-2	0-0	.680	-2	162	0	O10(4/2/4),3b5/2		-0.2

BURROUGHS, JEFF Jeffrey Alan B3.7.1951 Long Beach CA BR/TR/6-1/200* [TexA69 1/1] d7.20 s-Sean

YEAR	TM	LG	G	AB	R	H	2B	3B	HR	RBI	BB-IB	HP	SO	AVG	OBP	SLG	AOPS	ABR	SB-CS	FA	FR	RNG	THR	GAMES AT POSITION	DL	BFW
1970	Was	A	6	12	1	2	0	0	0		2-0	0	5	.167	.286	.167	29	-1	0-0	1.000	-0	89	0	O3R		-0.2
1971	Was	A	59	181	20	42	9	0	5	25	22-0	1	55	.232	.319	.365	98	0	1-0	.966	-2	90	98	O50(34/0/23)		-0.5
1972	Tex	A	22	65	4	12	1	0	1	3	5-0	0	22	.185	.243	.246	47	-4	0-2	.935	-1	85	154	O19(17/0/2)/1	19	-0.8
1973	Tex	A	151	526	71	147	17	1	30	85	67-3	1	88	.279	.355	.487	142	29	0-0	.975	10	112	139	O148(43/0/106),1b3/D		3.1
1974	Tex	A★	152	554	84	167	33	2	25	118	91-12	5	104	.301	.397	.504	164	50	2-3	.972	-13	81	89	O150R,1b2/D		3.0

YEAR	TM LG	G	AB	R	H	2B	3B	HR	RBI	BB-IB	HP	SO	AVG	OBP	SLG	AOPS	ABR	SB-CS	FA	FR	RNG	THR	GAMES AT POSITION	DL	BFW
1975	Tex A	152	585	81	132	20	0	29	94	79-11	1	155	.226	.315	.409	105	4	4-4	.966	-15	83	77	O148R,D3		-2.0
1976	Tex A	158	604	71	143	22	2	18	86	69-4	2	93	.237	.315	.369	98	-1	0-0	.987	-6	89	104	O155R,D3		-1.6
1977	Atl N	154	579	91	157	19	1	41	114	86-2	0	126	.271	.362	.520	121	17	4-1	.974	-12	86	77	O154R		-0.2
1978	Atl N☆	153	488	72	147	30	6	23	77	117-12	0	92	.301	.432	.529	152	41	1-2	.975	-4	85	115	O146L		3.2
1979	Atl N	116	397	49	89	14	1	11	47	73-7	3	75	.224	.347	.348	85	-5	2-2	.963	-3	86	102	O110L		-1.4
1980	Atl N	99	278	35	73	14	0	13	51	35-6	2	57	.263	.347	.453	121	8	1-1	.977	-7	89	0	O73L		-0.2
1981	Sea A	89	319	32	81	13	1	10	41	41-3	0	64	.254	.339	.395	106	3	0-1	.985	-11	72	65	O87(1/0/86)/D		-1.3
1982	Oak A	113	285	42	79	13	2	16	48	45-0	0	61	.277	.372	.505	144	18	1-3	.981	-2	97	0	D114		1.3
1983	Oak A	121	401	43	108	15	1	10	56	47-4	0	79	.269	.341	.387	107	5	0-2	—	0	0	0	D114		0.0
1984	Oak A	58	71	5	15	1	0	2	8	18-0	0	23	.211	.367	.310	96	1	0-0	1.000	0	55	0	D75		0.0
1985	†Tor A	86	191	19	49	9	3	6	28	34-1	0	36	.257	.366	.429	114	5	0-1	—	0	0	0	D78		-0.2
Total	16	1689	5536	720	1443	230	20	240	882	831-65	15	1135	.261	.355	.439	121	170	16-22	.974	-65	88	90	O1281(445/0/845),D269,1b6	19	2.6

BURROUGHS, SEAN Sean Patrick B9.12.1980 Atlanta GA BL/TR/6-2/200* [SDN98 1/9] d4.2 f-Jeff

YEAR	TM LG	G	AB	R	H	2B	3B	HR	RBI	BB-IB	HP	SO	AVG	OBP	SLG	AOPS	ABR	SB-CS	FA	FR	RNG	THR	GAMES AT POSITION	DL	BFW
2002	SD N	63	192	18	52	6	1	1	11	12-1	1	30	.271	.317	.323	79	-8	2-0	.935	0	93	61	3b48,2b13	47	-0.6
2003	SD N	146	517	62	148	27	6	7	58	44-4	11	75	.286	.352	.402	106	5	7-2	.966	1	95	105	3b137		0.7
2004	SD N	130	523	76	156	23	3	2	47	31-4	9	52	.298	.348	.365	89	-5	5-4	.957	-5	91	121	3b125		-1.2
2005	†SD N	93	284	20	71	7	2	1	17	24-4	5	41	.250	.318	.299	67	-14	4-0	.962	3	103	116	3b78/SP		-0.9
Total	4	432	1516	176	427	62	12	11	133	111-13	26	198	.282	.340	.360	89	-26	18-6	.959	-1	95	108	3b388,2b13/PS	47	-2.0

BURRUS, DICK Maurice Lennon B1.29.1898 Hatteras NC D2.2.1972 Elizabeth City NC BL/TL/5-11/175 d6.23 Col North Carolina St.

YEAR	TM LG	G	AB	R	H	2B	3B	HR	RBI	BB-IB	HP	SO	AVG	OBP	SLG	AOPS	ABR	SB-CS	FA	FR	RNG	THR	GAMES AT POSITION	DL	BFW
1919	Phi A	70	194	17	50	7	8	0	8	9	1	25	.258	.294	.314	70	-9	2	.986	-3	91	72	1b38,O10(0/2/8)		-1.4
1920	Phi A	71	135	11	25	8	0	0	10	5	2	7	.185	.225	.244	24	-15	0-3	.989	-1	97	142	1b31,O2R		-1.7
1925	Bos N	152	588	82	200	41	4	5	87	51	3	29	.340	.396	.449	126	26	8-9	.990	1	102	87	1b151		1.4
1926	Bos N	131	486	59	131	21	4	3	61	37	2	16	.270	.324	.335	85	-10	4	.991	12	140	88	1b128		-0.6
1927	Bos N	72	220	22	70	8	3	0	32	17	1	10	.318	.370	.382	110	3	3	.972	1	120	103	1b61		0.0
1928	Bos N	64	137	15	37	6	0	3	13	19	2	8	.270	.367	.380	101	1	1	.977	-2	87	101	1b32		-0.3
Total	6	560	1760	206	513	87	12	11	211	138	11	95	.291	.347	.373	97	-4	18-12	.986	8	114	92	1b441,O12(0/2/10)		-2.6

BURT, FRANK Frank J. B Camden NJ d5.2

YEAR	TM LG	G	AB	R	H	2B	3B	HR	RBI	BB-IB	HP	SO	AVG	OBP	SLG	AOPS	ABR	SB-CS	FA	FR	RNG	THR	GAMES AT POSITION	DL	BFW
1882	Bal AA	10	36	2	4	2	1	0		1			.111	.135	.222	20	-3		.815	-1	40	335	O10L		-0.4

BURTON, ELLIS Ellis Narrington B8.12.1936 Los Angeles CA BB/TR/5-11/165(150-165) d9.18

YEAR	TM LG	G	AB	R	H	2B	3B	HR	RBI	BB-IB	HP	SO	AVG	OBP	SLG	AOPS	ABR	SB-CS	FA	FR	RNG	THR	GAMES AT POSITION	DL	BFW
1958	StL N	8	30	5	7	0	1	2	4	3-0	1	8	.233	.324	.500	110	0	0-1	1.000	-1	88	0	O7(5/0/2)		-0.1
1960	StL N	29	28	5	6	1	0	0	2	4-0	0	14	.214	.313	.250	52	-2	0-2	1.000	-4	54	0	O23(14/5/4)		-0.5
1963	Cle A	26	31	6	6	3	0	1	1	4-0	0	4	.194	.286	.387	87	0	0-0	1.000	-1	53	182	O16(9/0/7)		-0.2
	Chi N	93	322	45	74	16	1	12	41	36-1	4	59	.230	.311	.398	98	0	6-3	.975	-9	79	101	O90(1/76/21)		-1.3
1964	Chi N	42	105	12	20	3	2	2	17	17-0	0	22	.190	.303	.314	71	-4	4-0	.981	-2	95	0	O29(1/21/11)		-0.7
1965	Chi N	17	40	6	7	1	0	0	4	1-0	0	10	.175	.186	.200	11	-5	1-0	1.000	1	109	214	O12(2/10/0)		-0.4
Total	5	215	556	79	120	24	4	17	59	65-1	5	117	.216	.300	.365	85	-11	11-6	.981	-14	81	84	O177(32/112/45)		-3.2

BUSBY, JIM James Franklin B1.8.1927 Kenedy TX D7.8.1996 Augusta GA BR/TR/6-1/175* d4.23 C18 Col TCU

YEAR	TM LG	G	AB	R	H	2B	3B	HR	RBI	BB-IB	HP	SO	AVG	OBP	SLG	AOPS	ABR	SB-CS	FA	FR	RNG	THR	GAMES AT POSITION	DL	BFW
1950	Chi A	18	48	5	10	0	0	0	4	1	0	5	.208	.224	.208	12	-7	0-2	.964	1	92	233	O12(0/12/1)		-0.7
1951	Chi A★	143	477	59	135	15	2	5	68	40	4	46	.283	.344	.354	91	-7	26-11	.982	7	106	127	O139C		-0.1
1952	Chi A	16	39	5	5	0	0	0	2		0	7	.128	.171	.128	-16	-6	0-2	1.000	1	118	0	O16C		-0.7
	Was A	129	512	58	125	24	4	2	47	22	4	48	.244	.281	.318	69	-24	5-6	.993	6	114	38	O128C		-2.3
	Year	145	551	63	130	24	4	2	47	24	4	55	.236	.273	.305	62	-30	5-8	.994	7	114	35	O144C		-3.0
1953	Was A	150	586	68	183	28	7	6	82	38	4	45	.312	.358	.415	111	8	13-6	.988	13	113	112	O150C		1.4
1954	Was A	155	628	83	187	22	7	7	80	43	3	56	.298	.342	.389	107	3	17-2	.988	5	114	40	O155C		0.4
1955	Was A	47	191	23	44	6	2	6	14	13-1	0	22	.230	.279	.377	79	-7	5-0	.993	-1	104	35	O47C		-0.9
	Chi A	99	337	38	82	13	4	1	27	25-0	0	37	.243	.294	.315	62	-19	7-3	.984	1	100	111	O99C		-2.2
	Year	146	528	61	126	19	6	7	41	38-1	0	59	.239	.289	.337	68	-26	12-3	.987	0	101	85	O146C		-3.1
1956	Cle A	135	494	72	116	17	3	12	50	43-2	4	47	.235	.301	.354	71	-22	8-3	.989	0	109	37	O133C		-2.7
1957	Cle A	30	74	9	14	2	1	2	4	1-0	0	8	.189	.200	.324	41	-7	0-1	.978	0	103	163	O26(2/25/0)		-0.8
	Bal A	86	288	31	72	10	1	3	19	23-0	0	36	.250	.304	.323	77	-10	6-3	.984	2	103	128	O85C		-1.3
	Year	116	362	40	86	12	2	5	23	24-0	0	44	.238	.284	.323	69	-17	6-4	.983	2	103	121	O111(2/110/0)		-2.1
1958	Bal A	113	215	32	51	7	2	3	19	24-0	3	37	.237	.320	.330	84	-4	6-4	.995	2	114	-25	O103C/3		-0.6
1959	Bos A	61	102	16	23	8	0	1	5	5-0	1	18	.225	.266	.333	61	-4	0-1	.980	0	104	75	O34(8/25/1)		-0.7
1960	Bos A	1	0	0	0	0	0	0	0	0-0	0	0	—	—	—	—	0	0-0	—	-0	0	0	/OL		0.0
	Bal A	79	159	25	41	7	1	0	12	20-1	0	14	.258	.341	.314	79	-4	2-3	.985	2	115	70	O71C		-0.5
	Year	80	159	25	41	7	1	0	12	20-1	0	14	.258	.341	.314	79	-4	2-3	.985	2	115	70	O72(1/71/0)		-0.5
1961	Bal A	75	89	15	23	3	1	0	6	8-0	0	10	.258	.316	.315	73	-3	2-0	.987	0	105	127	O71C		-0.4
1962	Hou N	15	11	2	2	0	0	0	1	2-0	0	3	.182	.308	.182	38	-1	0-1	1.000	-1	60	0	O10(1/8/1)/C		-0.2
Total	13	1352	4250	541	1113	162	35	48	438	310-4	23	439	.262	.314	.350	82	-115	97-48	.988	37	109	76	O1280(12/1267/3)/C3		-12.3

BUSBY, PAUL Paul Miller "Red" B8.25.1918 Waynesboro MS BL/TR/6-1/175 d9.14

YEAR	TM LG	G	AB	R	H	2B	3B	HR	RBI	BB-IB	HP	SO	AVG	OBP	SLG	AOPS	ABR	SB-CS	FA	FR	RNG	THR	GAMES AT POSITION	DL	BFW
1941	Phi N	10	16	3	5	0	0	0	2	2	0	1	.313	.313	.313	79	-1	0	1.000	-0	78	0	O3(0/2/1)		-0.1
1943	Phi N	26	40	13	10	1	0	0	5	2	0	5	.250	.286	.275	65	-2	2	1.000	0	121	0	O10(2/0/8)		-0.3
Total	2	36	56	16	15	1	0	0	7	4	0	6	.268	.293	.286	69	-3	2	1.000	-0	115	0	O13(2/2/9)		-0.4

BUSCH, ED Edgar John B11.16.1917 Lebanon IL D1.17.1987 St.Clair Co. IL BR/TR/5-10/175 d9.30

YEAR	TM LG	G	AB	R	H	2B	3B	HR	RBI	BB-IB	HP	SO	AVG	OBP	SLG	AOPS	ABR	SB-CS	FA	FR	RNG	THR	GAMES AT POSITION	DL	BFW
1943	Phi A	4	17	2	5	0	0	0		1	1	2	.294	.368	.294	95	0	0-1	.941	-2	55	39	S4		-0.2
1944	Phi A	140	484	41	131	11	3	0	40	29	1	17	.271	.313	.306	78	-15	5-3	.940	-21	93	74	S111,2b27,3b4		-2.7
1945	Phi A	126	416	37	104	10	3	0	35	32	1	9	.250	.305	.288	73	-15	2-3	.952	1	105	93	S116,2b2,3b2/1		-0.6
Total	3	270	917	80	240	21	6	0	75	62	3	28	.262	.311	.298	76	-30	7-7	.946	-22	98	83	S231,2b29,3b6/1		-3.5

BUSCH, MIKE Michael Anthony B7.7.1968 Davenport IA BR/TR/6-5/220(175-249) [LAN90 4/110] d8.30 Col Iowa St.

YEAR	TM LG	G	AB	R	H	2B	3B	HR	RBI	BB-IB	HP	SO	AVG	OBP	SLG	AOPS	ABR	SB-CS	FA	FR	RNG	THR	GAMES AT POSITION	DL	BFW
1995	LA N	13	17	3	4	0	0	3	6	0-0	0	7	.235	.235	.765	162	1	0-0	.875	1	76	0	3b10,1b2		0.0
1996	LA N	38	83	8	18	4	0	4	17	5-0	0	33	.217	.261	.410	78	-3	0-0	.932	-3	73	36	3b23/1	34	-0.6
Total	2	51	100	11	22	4	0	7	23	5-0	0	40	.220	.257	.470	92	-2	0-0	.923	-4	73	30	3b33,1b3	34	-0.6

BUSH, HOMER Homer Giles B11.12.1972 East St.Louis IL BR/TR/5-11/180* [SDN91 7/185] d8.16 [DL 1996 SD N 133]

YEAR	TM LG	G	AB	R	H	2B	3B	HR	RBI	BB-IB	HP	SO	AVG	OBP	SLG	AOPS	ABR	SB-CS	FA	FR	RNG	THR	GAMES AT POSITION	DL	BFW
1997	NY A	10	11	2	4	0	0	3	0-0	0	4	.364	.364	.364	91	0	0-0	.913	1	137	92	2b8/D		0.1
1998	†NY A	45	71	17	27	3	0	1	5	5-0	0	19	.380	.421	.465	136	4	6-3	.971	-3	73	50	2b24,D12,3b3,S2	33	1.6
1999	Tor A	128	485	69	155	26	4	5	55	21-0	6	82	.320	.353	.421	95	-4	32-8	.984	10	109	107	2b109,S18		1.9
2000	Tor A	76	297	38	64	8	0	1	18	18-0	5	60	.215	.271	.253	33	-31	9-4	.986	18	113	128	2b75	76	-0.3
2001	Tor A	78	271	32	83	11	1	3	27	8-1	6	50	.306	.336	.387	89	-4	13-4	.990	19	115	141	2b78		
2002	Tor A	23	78	9	18	2	0	1	2	2-0	1	12	.231	.268	.295	48	-6	2-0	.990	-2	95	84	2b22/D		-1.3
	Fla N	40	54	7	12	0	0	0	5	3-0	0	13	.222	.263	.222	33	-6	2-1	.962	-7	64	37	2b12,S4		-0.2
2004	NY A	9	7	2	0	0	0	0	0-0	1	2	.000	.125	.000	-63	-2	0-0	1.000	-1	50	184	2b4,D2		
Total	7	409	1274	176	363	50	5	11	115	57-1	20	238	.285	.324	.358	75	-49	65-20	.985	35	107	115	2b332,S24,D16,3b3	321	0.8

BUSH, DONIE Owen Joseph B10.8.1887 Indianapolis IN D3.28.1972 Indianapolis IN BB/TR/5-6/140 d9.18 M7

YEAR	TM LG	G	AB	R	H	2B	3B	HR	RBI	BB-IB	HP	SO	AVG	OBP	SLG	AOPS	ABR	SB-CS	FA	FR	RNG	THR	GAMES AT POSITION	DL	BFW
1908	Det A	20	68	13	20	1	1	0		4			.294	.360	.338	122	2	2	.938	-2	93	140	S20		0.1
1909	†Det A	157	532	114	145	18	2	0	33	88	4		.273	.380	.314	114	15	53	.925	10	110	73	S157		2.3
1910	Det A	142	496	90	130	13	4	3	34	78	2		.262	.365	.323	108	8	49	.940	10	110	61	S141/3		2.6
1911	Det A	150	561	126	130	18	5	1	36	98	3		.232	.349	.287	74	-15	40	.925	13	112	72	S150		0.8
1912	Det A	144	511	107	118	14	8	2	38	117	3		.231	.377	.301	98	6	37	.929	27	121	88	S144		1.2
1913	Det A	152	597	98	150	19	10	1	40	80	4	32	.251	.344	.322	96	-1	44	.938	2	106	94	S152		1.2
1914	Det A	157	596	97	150	18	4	0	32	112	3	54	.252	.373	.295	98	6	35-26	.944	32	114	106	S157		5.1
1915	Det A	155	561	99	128	12	8	1	44	118	2	44	.228	.342	.305	89	-1	35-27	.937	6	105	109	S155		1.4
1916	Det A	145	550	73	124	5	9	0	34	75	1	42	.225	.319	.267	74	-16	19	.954	-16	96	73	S144		-2.5
1917	Det A	147	581	112	163	18	5	0	24	80	2	36	.281	.370	.328	111	12	34	.932	-17	95	64	S147		0.6
1918	Det A	128	500	74	117	10	3	0	22	79	1	31	.234	.340	.266	86	-5	9	.931	-20	91	54	S128		-1.7
1919	Det A	129	509	82	124	11	6	0	26	75	2	36	.244	.343	.289	80	-11	22	.943	-10	95	80	S129		-1.2
1920	Det A	141	506	85	133	18	5	0	33	73	1	32	.263	.357	.324	83	-9	15-7	.938	-15	95	95	S140		-1.2
1921	Det A	104	402	72	113	6	5	0	27	45	2	23	.281	.360	.321	74	-15	8-11	.949	-6	101	87	S81,2b23		-1.2

YEAR	TM LG	G	AB	R	H	2B	3B	HR	RBI	BB-IB	HP	SO	AVG	OBP	SLG	AOPS	ABR	SB-CS	FA	FR	RNG	THR	GAMES AT POSITION	DL	BFW
	Was A	23	84	15	18	1	0	0	2	12		0	4	.214	.313	.226	41	-7	2-2	.932	-2	99	119	S21		-0.7
	Year	127	486	87	131	7	5	0	29	57		1	27	.270	.347	.305	69	-22	10-13	.946	-8	101	93	S102,2b23		-1.9
1922	Was A	41	134	17	32	4	1	0	7	21		0	7	.239	.342	.284	68	-6	1-1	.957	2	106	183	3b37/2		-0.2
1923	Was A	10	22	6	9	0	0	0	0	0		0	1	.409	.409	.409	122	1	1-1	.813	-1	90	0	3b5,2b2,M		0.0
Total	16	1945	7210	1280	1804	186	74	9	436	1158		29	346	.250	.356	.300	91	-36	406-75	.936	3	104	81	S1866,3b43,2b26		9.4

BUSH, RANDY Robert Randall B10.5.1958 Dover DE BL/TL/6-1/186* [MinA79 2/37] d5.1 Col New Orleans

YEAR	TM LG	G	AB	R	H	2B	3B	HR	RBI	BB-IB	HP	SO	AVG	OBP	SLG	AOPS	ABR	SB-CS	FA	FR	RNG	THR	GAMES AT POSITION	DL	BFW
1982	Min A	55	119	13	29	6	1	4	13	8-0	3	28	.244	.305	.412	92	-1	0-0	1.000	-0	88	0	D26,O6L		-0.3
1983	Min A	124	373	43	93	24	3	11	56	34-8	7	51	.249	.323	.418	98	-1	0-1	1.000	1	165	38	D103,1b3		-0.4
1984	Min A	113	311	46	69	17	1	11	43	31-6	4	60	.222	.292	.389	85	-6	1-2	1.000	-0	0	154	D89,1b2		-1.0
1985	Min A	97	234	26	56	13	3	10	35	24-1	5	30	.239	.321	.449	102	1	3-0	.969	-3	92	0	O41(39/0/4),D28/1		-0.4
1986	Min A	130	357	50	96	19	7	7	45	39-2	4	63	.269	.347	.420	105	3	5-3	.977	-3	100	37	O102(90/0/13),1b3,D6		-0.4
1987	†Min A	122	293	46	74	10	2	11	46	43-5	3	49	.253	.349	.413	99	0	10-3	.982	-4	99	25	O75(2/0/72),1b9,D9		-0.5
1988	Min A	136	394	51	103	20	3	14	51	58-14	9	49	.261	.365	.434	120	13	8-6	.979	-1	101	56	O109(1/0/108),1b6,D7		0.8
1989	Min A	141	391	60	103	17	4	14	54	48-6	3	73	.263	.347	.435	112	7	5-8	.986	3	109	111	O109(34/1/88),1b25,D5		0.4
1990	Min A	73	181	17	44	8	0	6	18	21-2	6	27	.243	.338	.387	97	0	0-3	1.000	0	103	57	O32(2/0/32),D29,1b6	76	-0.3
1991	†Min A	93	165	21	50	10	1	6	23	24-3	3	25	.303	.401	.485	137	9	0-2	1.000	-1	95	54	O38(7/0/32),1b12,D10		0.6
1992	Min A	100	182	14	39	8	1	2	22	11-3	2	37	.214	.263	.302	57	-11	1-1	1.000	-0	110	0	O24(3/0/21),D24,1b8		-1.3
1993	Min A	35	45	1	7	2	0	0	3	7-1	0	13	.156	.269	.200	28	-4	0-0	1.000	-1	0	132	1b4/ORD		-0.5
Total	12	1219	3045	388	763	154	26	96	409	348-51	49	505	.251	.334	.413	101	10	33-29	.983	-9	101	53	O537(184/1/371),D341,1b79	76	-3.3

BUSHONG, DOC Albert John B9.15.1856 Philadelphia PA D8.19.1908 Brooklyn NY BR/TR/5-11/165 d7.19 Col Penn

YEAR	TM LG	G	AB	R	H	2B	3B	HR	RBI	BB-IB	HP	SO	AVG	OBP	SLG	AOPS	ABR	SB-CS	FA	FR	RNG	THR	GAMES AT POSITION	DL	BFW
1875	Atl NA	1	5	0	3	0	1	0	0	0		0	.600	.600	1.000	511	2	0-0	.800	-0			/C		0.1
1876	Phi N	5	21	4	1	0	0	0	1	0		0	.048	.048	.048	-69	-4	0-0	.769	-2			C5		-0.5
1880	Wor N	41	146	13	25	3	0	0	19	1		16	.171	.177	.192	23	-12	0-0	.918	13			C40/OR3		0.2
1881	Wor N	76	275	35	64	7	4	0	21	21		23	.233	.287	.287	77	-7	0-0	.918	9			C76		0.4
1882	Wor N	69	253	20	40	4	1	1	15	5		17	.158	.174	.194	18	-23	0-0	.897	-3			C69		-1.8
1883	Cle N	63	215	15	37	5	0	0	9	7		19	.172	.198	.195	21	-20	0-0	.909	13			C63		-0.1
1884	Cle N	62	203	24	48	6	1	0	10	17		11	.236	.295	.276	78	-5	0-0	.886	0			C62/OC		0.1
1885	†StL AA	85	300	42	80	13	5	0	21	11	2		.267	.297	.343	97	-2	0-0	.932	12			C85/3		1.6
1886	†StL AA	107	386	56	86	8	0	1	31	31	0		.223	.281	.251	64	-16	12	.942	15			C106/1		0.7
1887	†StL AA	53	201	35	51	4	0	0	26	11	2		.254	.299	.274	55	-13	14	.927	-4			C52,O2R,3b2		-0.4
1888	Bro AA	69	253	23	53	5	1	0	16	5	2		.209	.231	.237	50	-15	0-0	.915	-4			C69		-1.2
1889	†Bro AA	25	84	15	13	1	0	0	8	9	0	7	.155	.237	.167	16	-9	2	.894	-0			C25		-0.7
1890	†Bro N	16	55	5	13	2	0	0	7	6	0	4	.236	.311	.273	70	-2	2	.913	-2	86	62	C15,O2C		-0.2
Total	12	671	2392	287	511	58	12	2	184	124	6	97	.214	.254	.250	55	-128	39	.916	57	86	62	C667,O6(0/3/3),3b4/1		-1.9

BUSKEY, JOE Joseph Henry "Jazzbow" B12.18.1902 Cumberland MD D4.11.1949 Cumberland MD BR/TR/5-10/175 d4.19

YEAR	TM LG	G	AB	R	H	2B	3B	HR	RBI	BB-IB	HP	SO	AVG	OBP	SLG	AOPS	ABR	SB-CS	FA	FR	RNG	THR	GAMES AT POSITION	DL	BFW
1926	Phi N	1	8	1	0	0	0	0	0	1		0	1	1.000	.111	.000	-65	-2	0	.810	-1	93	48	S5		-0.3

BUSKEY, MIKE Michael Thomas B1.13.1949 San Francisco CA BR/TR/5-11/165 d9.5 Col San Francisco

YEAR	TM LG	G	AB	R	H	2B	3B	HR	RBI	BB-IB	HP	SO	AVG	OBP	SLG	AOPS	ABR	SB-CS	FA	FR	RNG	THR	GAMES AT POSITION	DL	BFW
1977	Phi N	6	7	1	2	0	1	0	1	0-0	1		.286	.375	.571	142	0	0-0	.882	1	102	227	S6		0.1

BUSSE, RAY Raymond Edward B9.25.1948 Daytona Beach FL BR/TR/6-4/175* d7.24 Col Daytona Beach (FL) JC

YEAR	TM LG	G	AB	R	H	2B	3B	HR	RBI	BB-IB	HP	SO	AVG	OBP	SLG	AOPS	ABR	SB-CS	FA	FR	RNG	THR	GAMES AT POSITION	DL	BFW
1971	Hou N	10	34	2	5	3	0	0	4	2-0		9	.147	.194	.235	22	-3	0-0	.929	-6	56	0	S5,3b3		-1.0
1973	StL N	24	70	6	10	4	2	2	5	5-2		21	.143	.200	.343	47	-6	0-1	.898	1	107	136	S23		-0.3
	Hou N	15	17	1	1	0	0	0	1	0-1		12	.059	.111	.059	-52	-4	0-0	1.000	1	120	93	S5,3b3		-0.3
	Year	39	87	7	11	4	2	2	6	5-2		33	.126	.183	.287	28	-9	0-1	.906	1	108	132	S28,3b3	15	-0.6
1974	Hou N	19	34	3	7	1	0	0	3	0-0		12	.206	.270	.235	44	-3	0-0	.864	-0	120	77	3b8		-0.3
Total	3	68	155	12	23	8	2	2	9	11-2		54	.148	.205	.265	30	-16	0-1	.908	-5	98	107	S33,3b14	15	-1.9

BUTCHER, HANK Henry Joseph B7.12.1886 Chicago IL D12.28.1979 Hazel Crest IL BR/TR/5-10/180 d7.8

YEAR	TM LG	G	AB	R	H	2B	3B	HR	RBI	BB-IB	HP	SO	AVG	OBP	SLG	AOPS	ABR	SB-CS	FA	FR	RNG	THR	GAMES AT POSITION	DL	BFW
1911	Cle A	38	133	22	32	7	3	1	11	11	1		.241	.303	.361	84	-3	9	.984	1	104	102	O34(24/4/6)		-0.3
1912	Cle A	26	82	9	16	4	1	1	10	6	0		.195	.250	.305	57	-5	1	.920	1	106	103	O21L		-0.5
Total	2	64	215	31	48	11	4	2	21	17	1		.223	.283	.340	74	-8	10	.956	2	105	106	O55(45/4/6)		-0.8

BUTERA, SAL Salvatore Philip B9.25.1952 Richmond Hill NY BR/TR/6-0/190* d4.10 C2 Col Suffolk (NY) CC

YEAR	TM LG	G	AB	R	H	2B	3B	HR	RBI	BB-IB	HP	SO	AVG	OBP	SLG	AOPS	ABR	SB-CS	FA	FR	RNG	THR	GAMES AT POSITION	DL	BFW
1980	Min A	34	85	4	23	1	0	2	3-0	1	6	.271	.300	.282	57	-5	0-0	.950	-6	115	111	C32,D2		-1.0
1981	Min A	62	167	13	40	7	1	0	18	22-0	1	14	.240	.325	.293	75	-4	0-0	.970	5	131	147	C59/1D		0.3
1982	Min A	54	126	9	32	2	0	0	8	17-0	1	12	.254	.347	.270	70	-5	0-0	.988	3	91	101	C53		0.0
1983	Det A	4	5	1	1	0	0	0	0	1-0	0	0	.200	.200	.200	11	-1	0-0	.929	1	107	0	C4		0.0
1984	Mon N	3	3	0	0	0	0	0	0	1-0	0	1	.000	.250	.000	-26	-0	0-0	1.000	1	90	0	C2		0.0
1985	Mon N	67	120	11	24	1	0	3	12	13-1	1	12	.200	.281	.283	62	-6	0-0	.984	-6	64	76	C66/P		-1.1
1986	Cin N	56	113	14	27	4	1	2	16	21-3	0	10	.239	.356	.363	90	0	0-0	.979	-2	105	86	C53/P		-0.1
1987	Cin N	5	11	1	2	0	1	0	2	1-0	0	6	.182	.250	.455	79	0	0-0	.920	0	49	240	C5		0.0
	†Min A	51	111	7	19	5	0	1	12	7-0	0	16	.171	.217	.243	22	-13	0-0	.983	-5	65	123	C51		-1.6
1988	Tor A	23	60	3	14	2	1	1	6	1-0	0	9	.233	.246	.350	64	-3	0-0	.991	-1	110	71	C23		-0.3
Total	9	359	801	63	182	24	3	8	76	86-4	3	85	.227	.302	.295	65	-37	0-0	.978	-12	97	107	C348,D3,P2/1		-3.8

BUTKA, ED Edward Luke "Babe" B1.7.1916 Canonsburg PA D4.21.2005 Pittsburgh PA BR/TR/6-3/193 d9.26

YEAR	TM LG	G	AB	R	H	2B	3B	HR	RBI	BB-IB	HP	SO	AVG	OBP	SLG	AOPS	ABR	SB-CS	FA	FR	RNG	THR	GAMES AT POSITION	DL	BFW
1943	Was A	3	9	0	3	1	0	0	1	0		0	.333	.333	.444	132	0	0-0	1.000	1	217	57	1b3		0.1
1944	Was A	15	41	1	8	1	0	0	1	2		11	.195	.233	.220	31	-4	0-0	.972	-0	109	84	1b14		-0.5
Total	2	18	50	1	11	2	0	0	2	2		14	.220	.250	.260	48	-4	0-0	.977	1	127	80	1b17		-0.4

BUTLER, ART Arthur Edward (b Arthur Edward Bouthillier) B12.19.1887 Fall River MA D10.7.1984 Fall River MA BR/TR/5-9/160 d4.14

YEAR	TM LG	G	AB	R	H	2B	3B	HR	RBI	BB-IB	HP	SO	AVG	OBP	SLG	AOPS	ABR	SB-CS	FA	FR	RNG	THR	GAMES AT POSITION	DL	BFW
1911	Bos N	27	68	11	12	2	0	2	6		2	6	.176	.263	.206	30	-6	0	.930	-2	107	45	3b14,2b4/S		-0.9
1912	Pit N	43	154	19	42	4	2	1	17	15	0	13	.273	.337	.344	88	-3	2	.960	-15	80	75	2b43		-1.7
1913	Pit N	82	214	40	60	9	3	0	20	32	2	14	.280	.379	.350	114	6	9-5	.919	-15	82	75	2b28,S26,3b2,O2R		-0.7
1914	StL N	86	274	29	55	12	3	1	24	39	5	23	.201	.311	.277	76	-6	14	.927	-16	93	90	S83/OC		-1.8
1915	StL N	130	469	73	119	12	5	1	31	47	1	34	.254	.323	.307	91	-4	26-14	.916	-32	88	84	S125,2b2		-3.1
1916	StL N	86	110	9	23	5	0	0	7	7	0	12	.209	.256	.255	57	-5	3	.882	-3	77	0	O15(2/9/4),2b8/S3		-1.0
Total	6	454	1289	181	311	44	13	5	101	146	10	102	.241	.323	.303	85	-18	54-19	.919	-83	89	82	S236,2b85,O18(2/10/6),3b17		-9.2

BUTLER, BRETT Brett Morgan B6.15.1957 Los Angeles CA BL/TL/5-10/160* [AtlN79 23/573] d8.20 C1 Col Southeastern Oklahoma

YEAR	TM LG	G	AB	R	H	2B	3B	HR	RBI	BB-IB	HP	SO	AVG	OBP	SLG	AOPS	ABR	SB-CS	FA	FR	RNG	THR	GAMES AT POSITION	DL	BFW
1981	Atl N	40	126	17	32	2	3	0	4	19-0	0	17	.254	.352	.317	91	-1	9-1	.987	-0	103	70	O37(25/11/5)		-0.1
1982	†Atl N	89	240	35	52	2	0	0	7	25-0	0	35	.217	.291	.225	45	-17	21-8	1.000	-6	87	56	O77C		-2.3
1983	Atl N	151	549	84	154	21	13	5	37	54-3	2	56	.281	.344	.393	98	-2	39-23	.987	6	101	140	O143(109/38/4)		0.0
1984	Cle A	159	602	108	162	25	9	3	49	86-1	4	62	.269	.361	.355	98	2	52-22	.991	2	101	123	O156(0/155/1)		0.6
1985	Cle A	152	591	106	184	28	14	5	50	63-2	1	42	.311	.377	.431	122	19	47-20	.998	14	108	199	O150C/D		3.4
1986	Cle A	161	587	92	163	17	14	4	51	70-1	4	65	.278	.356	.375	101	2	32-15	.993	1	101	104	O159C		0.3
1987	Cle A	137	522	91	154	25	8	9	41	91-0	1	55	.295	.399	.425	118	18	33-16	.990	7	112	66	O136C	19	2.4
1988	SF N	157	568	109	163	27	9	6	43	97-4	0	64	.287	.393	.398	134	30	43-20	.988	3	101	104	O155C		3.0
1989	†SF N	154	594	100	168	22	4	4	36	59-2	3	69	.283	.349	.354	105	5	31-16	.986	-3	101	43	O152C		0.9
1990	SF N	160	622	108	192	20	9	3	44	90-1	6	62	.309	.397	.384	121	22	51-19	.986	-8	99	44	O159C		1.8
1991	LA N★	161	615	112	182	13	5	2	38	108-4	1	79	.296	.401	.343	113	17	38-28	1.000	-5	97	91	O161C		1.0
1992	LA N	157	553	86	171	14	11	3	39	95-3	5	67	.309	.413	.391	130	27	41-21	.995	-7	92	108	O155C		2.2
1993	LA N	156	607	80	181	21	10	1	42	86-1	5	69	.298	.387	.371	111	13	39-19	1.000	-11	90	72	O155C		0.6
1994	LA N	111	417	79	131	13	9	8	33	68-0	2	52	.314	.411	.446	131	22	27-8	.993	1	99	138	O111C		2.6
1995	NY N	90	367	54	114	13	7	1	25	43-2	0	42	.311	.381	.392	109	5	21-7	.995	-0	98	124	O90C		0.8
	†LA N	39	146	24	40	5	2	0	13	24-0	0	9	.274	.368	.336	96	5	11-1	.987	-4	87	0	O38C		-0.1
	Year	129	513	78	154	18	9	1	38	67-2	0	51	.300	.377	.376	105	6	32-8	.993	-5	95	87	O128C		0.7
1996	LA N	34	131	22	35	1	1	0	13	22-0	1	22	.267	.313	.290	66	-1	8-3	.957	7	101	62	O34C	127	-0.6
1997	LA N	105	343	52	97	9	0	0	18	42-0	1	40	.283	.363	.324	87	-5	15-10	1.000	-1	95	88	O91(47/49/0)/D	27	-0.8
Total	17	2213	8180	1359	2375	277	131	54	578	1129-23	38	907	.290	.377	.376	110	150	558-257	.992	-13	99	100	O2159(181/1986/10),D2	173	15.7

BUTLER, FRANK Frank Dean "Stuffy","Goldbrick" B7.18.1860 Savannah GA D7.10.1945 Jacksonville FL BL/TL/5-7/155 d7.30

YEAR	TM LG	G	AB	R	H	2B	3B	HR	RBI	BB-IB	HP	SO	AVG	OBP	SLG	AOPS	ABR	SB-CS	FA	FR	RNG	THR	GAMES AT POSITION	DL	BFW
1895	NY N	5	22	5	6	1	0	0	2	1		0	1	.273	.304	.318	62	-1	0	1.000	-0	0	0	O5(4/0/1)		-0.2

YEAR	TM LG	G	AB	R	H	2B	3B	HR	RBI	BB-IB	HP	SO	AVG	OBP	SLG	AOPS	ABR	SB-CS	FA	FR	RNG	THR	GAMES AT POSITION	DL	BFW

BUTLER, KID Frank Edward B5.1861 Boston MA D4.9.1921 S.Boston MA 5-6/140 d5.20

| 1884 | Bos U | 71 | 255 | 36 | 43 | 15 | 0 | 0 | 12 | | | | .169 | .206 | .227 | 32 | -29 | | .810 | -4 | 67 | 58 | O53(37/7/9),2b12,S6,3b2 | | -3.0 |

BUTLER, JOHN John Albert (aka Frederick King in 1901) B7.26.1879 Boston MA D2.2.1950 Boston MA BR/TR/5-7/170 d9.28 Col Fordham

1901	Mil A	1	3	0	0	0	0	0	0	1	0		.000	.250	.000	-28	0	0	1.000	-1	46	0	/C		-0.1
1904	StL N	12	37	0	6	1	0	0	1	4	1		.162	.262	.189	42	-2	0	.968	-2	82	67	C12		-0.4
1906	Bro N	1	0	0	0	0	0	0	0	0	0		—	—	—	—	0	0	1.000	0	297	0	/C		0.0
1907	Bro N	30	79	6	10	1	0	0	2	9	0		.127	.216	.139	12	-8	0	.946	-5	85	99	C28/OL		-1.2
Total	4	44	119	6	16	2	0	0	3	14	1		.134	.231	.151	21	-10	0	.953	-8	83	90	C42/OL		-1.7

BUTLER, JOHNNY John Stephen "Trolley Line" B3.20.1893 Fall River KS D4.29.1967 Seal Beach CA BR/TR/6-0/175 d4.18 C1

1926	Bro N	147	501	54	135	27	5	1	68	54	5	44	.269	.346	.349	89	-6	6	.949	-2	95	68	S102,3b42,2b8		0.5
1927	Bro N	149	521	39	124	13	6	2	57	34	6	33	.238	.292	.298	58	-32	9	.959	-5	87	98	S90,3b60		-2.3
1928	Chi N	62	174	17	47	7	0	0	16	19	3	7	.270	.352	.310	75	-5	2	.950	5	109	93	3b59,S2		0.3
1929	StL N	17	55	5	9	1	1	0	5	4	0	5	.164	.220	.218	9	-8	0	.964	-1	78		3b9,S8		-0.7
Total	4	375	1251	115	315	48	12	3	146	111	14	89	.252	.320	.317	70	-51	17	.954	-3	91	82	S202,3b170,2b8		-2.2

BUTLER, BRENT Justin Brent B2.11.1978 Laurinburg NC BR/TR/6-0/180* [StLN96 3/68] d7.4

2001	Col N	53	119	17	29	7	1	1	14	7-0	1	7	.244	.287	.345	53	-8	1-1	.959	-2	103	118	2b23,S10,3b9		-0.9
2002	Col N	113	344	55	89	18	4	9	42	10-3	5	40	.259	.287	.413	75	-14	2-6	.974	-9	101	101	2b72,3b33,S13		-2.1
2003	Col N	37	90	13	19	3	1	1	4	7-2	1	13	.211	.276	.300	44	-7	1-0	.988	-4	99	74	2b20,3b8,S4		-1.0
Total	3	203	553	85	137	28	6	11	60	24-5	7	60	.248	.285	.380	65	-29	4-7	.973	-14	101	99	2b115,3b50,S27		-4.0

BUTLER, RICH Richard Dwight B5.1.1973 Toronto ON, Can. BL/TR/6-1/190(180-205) d9.6 b-Rob

1997	Tor A	7	14	3	4	1	0	2	2	2-0	1	5	.286	.375	.357	92	0	0-1	1.000	-0	83	0	O3L/D		-0.1
1998	TB A	72	217	25	49	3	3	7	20	15-0	2	37	.226	.278	.364	65	-13	4-2	1.000	1	100	109	O61(39/0/22)	36	-1.3
1999	TB A	7	20	2	3	1	0	0	0	2-0	1	4	.150	.227	.200	10	-3	0-0	1.000	-1	80	0	O6(2/0/4)	11	-0.3
Total	3	86	251	30	56	5	3	7	22	19-0	4	44	.223	.280	.351	62	-16	4-3	1.000	-0	98	95	O70(44/0/26)/D	47	-1.7

BUTLER, DICK Richard H. B12.1869 Brooklyn NY D7.16.1917 New York NY d6.16

1897	Lou N	10	38	3	7	0	0	0		2	0		.184	.184	.184	-3	-6	1	.818	-3	93	119	C10		-0.7
1899	Was N	12	36	4	10	0	1	0	1	2	0		.278	.316	.333	79	-1	1	.892	-4	77	133	C11		-0.4
Total	2	22	74	7	17	0	1	0	-3	2	0		.230	.250	.257	37	-7	2	.852	-6	85	126	C21		-1.1

BUTLER, ROB Robert Frank John B4.10.1970 E.York ON, Can. BL/TL/5-11/185* d6.12 b-Rich

1993	†Tor A	17	48	8	13	4	0	0	2	7-0	1	12	.271	.375	.354	95	0	2-2	.970	0	118	0	O16(15/1/0)	70	0.0
1994	Tor A	41	74	13	13	0	1	0	5	7-0	1	8	.176	.250	.203	20	-9	0-1	.977	-1	96	0	O31(17/13/2)/D		-1.0
1997	Phi N	43	89	10	26	9	1	0	13	5-0	1	8	.292	.326	.416	95	-1	1-0	1.000	2	92	334	O25(4/14/8)	22	0.1
1999	Tor A	8	7	1	1	0	0	0	1	0-0	0	4	.143	.250	.143	4	-1	0-0	1.000	-0	49	0	O2L,D3	76	-0.1
Total	4	109	218	32	53	13	2	0	21	19-0	3	32	.243	.309	.321	66	-11	3-3	.982	1	99	113	O74(38/28/10),D4	168	-1.0

BUTLER, BILL William J. B1861 New Orleans LA d6.29

| 1884 | Ind AA | 9 | 31 | 7 | 7 | 3 | 2 | 0 | | 1 | 0 | | .226 | .250 | .452 | 128 | 1 | | .700 | -1 | 157 | 0 | O9(1/1/7) | | 0.0 |

BUTLER, KID Willis Everett B8.9.1887 Franklin PA D2.22.1964 Richmond CA BR/TR/5-11/155 d4.30

| 1907 | StL A | 20 | 59 | 4 | 13 | 2 | 0 | 0 | 6 | 2 | 0 | | .220 | .246 | .254 | 60 | -3 | 1 | .940 | 0 | 118 | 70 | 2b11,3b5/S | | -0.2 |

BUTTERY, FRANK Frank B5.13.1851 Silvermine CT D12.16.1902 Norwalk CT d4.26 ▲

| 1872 | Man NA | 18 | 93 | 16 | 20 | 0 | 0 | 0 | 2 | | | | .215 | .215 | .215 | 35 | -7 | 0-0 | .842 | -0 | 131 | 0 | P8,O8R,3b5 | | -0.3 |

BUZAS, JOE Joseph John B10.2.1919 Alpha NJ D3.19.2003 Salt Lake City UT BR/TR/6-1/180 d4.17 Col Bucknell

| 1945 | NY A | 30 | 65 | 8 | 17 | 2 | 1 | 0 | 6 | 2 | 0 | 5 | .262 | .284 | .323 | 73 | -3 | 2-0 | .898 | -2 | 100 | 89 | S12 | | -0.4 |

BYERS, BURLEY Burley (b Christopher A. Bayer) B12.19.1875 Louisville KY D5.30.1933 Louisville KY ?/175 d6.17

| 1899 | Lou N | 1 | 3 | 0 | 0 | 0 | 0 | 0 | 0 | 0 | 0 | | .000 | .000 | .000 | -99 | -1 | 0 | .600 | -1 | 36 | 0 | /S | | -0.2 |

BYERS, BILL James William B10.3.1877 Bridgeton IN D9.8.1948 Baltimore MD BL/TR/5-7/210 d4.15

| 1904 | StL N | 19 | 60 | 3 | 13 | 0 | 0 | 0 | 4 | 1 | 0 | | .217 | .230 | .217 | 40 | -4 | 0 | .971 | -2 | 89 | 55 | C16/1 | | -0.5 |

BYERS, RANDY Randell Parker B10.2.1964 Bridgeton NJ BL/TR/6-2/180* [SDN84*S1/8] d9.7 Col CC of Baltimore (MD)

1987	SD N	10	16	1	5	1	0	0	1	1-0	0	5	.313	.353	.375	97	0	1-0	1.000	0	83	391	O5L		0.0
1988	SD N	11	10	0	2	1	0	0	0	0-0	0	5	.200	.200	.300	43	-1	0-0	—	-0	0	0	O2(1/0/1)		-0.1
Total	2	21	26	1	7	2	0	0	1	1-0	0	10	.269	.296	.346	77	-1	1-0	1.000	0	80	379	O7(6/0/1)		-0.1

BYNUM, FREDDIE Freddie Lee B3.15.1980 Wilson NC BL/TR/6-1/180 d8.30 Col Pitt Co. (NC) CC

| 2005 | Oak A | 7 | 7 | 0 | 2 | 1 | 0 | 0 | 1 | 0-0 | 1 | 3 | .286 | .286 | .429 | 85 | 0 | 0-0 | — | -1 | 0 | 0 | 2b3,O2(1/1/0) | | -0.1 |

BYRD, JIM James Edward B10.3.1968 Wewahitchka FL BR/TR/6-1/185 [BosA87 8/214] d5.31 Col Seminole St. (OK) JC

| 1993 | Bos A | 2 | 0 | 0 | 0 | 0 | 0 | 0 | 0 | 0-0 | 0 | 0 | — | — | — | — | — | 0-0 | — | — | | | /R | | 0.0 |

BYRD, MARLON Marlon Jerrard B8.30.1977 Boynton Beach FL BR/TR/6-0/225* [PhiN99 10/306] d9.8 Col Georgia Perimeter JC

2002	Phi N	10	35	2	8	2	0	1	1	1-0	0	9	.229	.250	.371	68	-2	0-2	1.000	-1	82	0	O10(0/8/2)	15	-0.4
2003	Phi N	135	495	86	150	28	4	7	45	44-3	7	94	.303	.366	.418	113	10	11-1	.984	-4	99	72	O131C		1.0
2004	Phi N	106	346	48	79	13	2	5	33	22-1	7	68	.228	.287	.321	55	-23	2-2	.990	-4	93	92	O92C		-2.6
2005	Was N	74	216	20	57	15	2	2	26	18-1	1	47	.264	.318	.380	89	-3	5-1	.985	-4	109	155	O65(54/11/4),D2	30	0.0
	Phi N	5	13	0	4	0	0	0	0	1-0	1	3	.308	.400	.308	86	0	0-0	1.000	-1	67	0	O5C		-0.1
	Year	79	229	20	61	15	2	2	26	19-1	2	50	.266	.323	.376	89	-4	5-1	.985	-4	106	145	O70(54/16/4),D2		-0.1
Total	4	330	1105	156	298	58	8	15	105	86-5	16	220	.270	.329	.377	88	-18	18-6	.986	-5	98	91	O303(54/247/6),D2	45	-2.1

BYRD, SAMMY Samuel Dewey "Babe Ruth's Legs" B10.15.1907 Bremen GA D5.11.1981 Mesa AZ BR/TR/5-10.5/175 d5.11

1929	NY A	62	170	32	53	12	0	5	28	28	0	18	.312	.409	.471	135	10	1-4	.950	3	110	128	O54(6/16/32)		0.8
1930	NY A	92	218	46	62	12	2	6	31	30	0	18	.284	.371	.440	110	4	5-1	.992	1	110	48	O85(47/12/26)		0.1
1931	NY A	115	248	51	67	18	2	3	32	29	1	26	.270	.349	.395	101	1	5-0	.974	0	106	58	O88(26/34/34)		-0.1
1932	†NY A	105	209	49	62	12	1	8	30	30	0	20	.297	.385	.478	129	10	1-2	.964	-1	98	96	O91(11/70/11)		0.6
1933	NY A	85	107	26	30	6	1	2	11	15	0	12	.280	.369	.411	113	2	0-1	.987	3	131	42	O71(23/15/35)		0.3
1934	NY A	106	191	32	47	8	0	3	23	18	2	22	.246	.318	.335	73	-8	1-2	**.988**	6	132	44	O104(34/13/59)		-0.5
1935	Cin N	121	416	51	109	25	4	9	52	37	0	51	.262	.322	.406	97	-2	4	.970	-1	98	109	O115(39/76/0)		-0.7
1936	Cin N	59	141	17	35	8	0	2	13	11	0	11	.248	.303	.348	80	-4	0	.989	1	112	43	O37(15/22/0)		-0.4
Total	8	745	1700	304	465	101	10	38	220	198	3	178	.274	.350	.412	104	13	17-10	.975	11	109	78	O645(201/258/197)		0.1

BYRNE, BOBBY Robert Matthew B12.31.1884 St.Louis MO D12.31.1964 Wayne PA BR/TR/5-7.5/145 d4.11

1907	StL N	149	559	55	143	11	5	0	29	35	6		.256	.307	.293	91	-7	21	.920	21	112	117	3b148/S		2.0
1908	StL N	127	439	27	84	7	1	0	14	23	4		.191	.238	.212	46	-27	16	.925	10	105	91	3b122,S4		-1.6
1909	StL N	105	421	61	90	13	6	1	33	46	7		.214	.302	.280	86	-6	21	.922	13	116	74	3b105		1.1
	†Pit N	46	168	31	43	6	2	0	7	32	4		.256	.387	.315	109	4	8	.987	3	115	60	3b46		1.0
	Year	151	589	92	133	19	8	1	40	78	11		.226	.327	.290	93	-1	29	.939	16	**116**	70	3b151		2.1
1910	Pit N	148	602	101	**178**	**43**	12	2	52	66	7	27	.296	.366	.417	121	17	36	.929	-7	101	56	3b148		1.4
1911	Pit N	153	598	96	155	24	17	2	52	67	8	41	.259	.342	.366	94	-5	23	.930	-2	100	112	3b152		-0.3
1912	Pit N	130	528	99	152	31	11	3	35	54	7	40	.288	.358	.405	110	8	20	**.948**	-24	76	90	3b110		-1.2
1913	Pit N	113	448	54	121	22	0	1	47	29	5	28	.270	.322	.326	89	-6	10-16	.940	-10	83	96	3b110		-1.7
	Phi N	19	58	9	13	1	0	0	4	5	2	3	.224	.308	.293	69	-2	2-3	.963	0	104	0	3b15		-0.2
	Year	132	506	63	134	23	0	1	51	34	7	31	.265	.320	.322	86	-7	12-19	.943	-10	86	84	3b125		-1.9
1914	Phi N	126	467	61	127	12	1	3	46	50	7	44	.272	.339	.302	85	-7	9	.934	-1	109	47	2b101,3b22		-0.6
1915	†Phi N	105	387	50	81	6	4	0	21	39	5	28	.209	.290	.245	62	-17	4-12	**.969**	-5	94	75	3b105		-2.5
1916	Phi N	48	141	22	33	10	1	0	9	14	1	2	.234	.308	.319	89	-1	6	.933	1	99	149	3b40		0.1
1917	Phi N	13	14	1	5	0	1	0	2	2	1	2	.357	.400	.357	128	0	1	1.000	0	33	0	3b4		0.0
	Chi A	1	1	0	0	0	0	0	0	0	0	0	.000	.000	.000	-98	0	0	1.000	0	154	0	/2		0.0
Total	11	1283	4831	667	1225	186	60	10	329	456	49	220	.254	.324	.323	91	-49	176-31	.934	1	99	90	3b1147,2b102,S5		-2.5

YEAR	TM LG	G	AB	R	H	2B	3B	HR	RBI	BB-IB	HP	SO	AVG	OBP	SLG	AOPS	ABR	SB-CS	FA	FR	RNG	THR	GAMES AT POSITION	DL	BFW

BYRNES, ERIC Eric James B2.16.1976 Redwood City CA BR/TR/6-2/205* [OakA98 8/225] d8.22 Col UCLA

2000	Oak A	10	10	5	3	0	0	0	0	0-0	1	1	.300	.364	.300	72	0	2-1	1.000	0	131	0	O4(1/0/3),D2		0.0
2001	†Oak A	19	38	9	9	0	0	3	5	4-0	1	6	.237	.326	.500	113	1	1-0	.933	-2	74	0	O12(8/2/5),D5		-0.1
2002	†Oak A	90	94	24	23	4	2	3	11	4-0	3	17	.245	.291	.426	90	-2	3-0	.982	-3	84	56	O79(52/10/22),D6		-0.5
2003	†Oak A	121	414	64	109	27	9	12	51	42-4	2	71	.263	.333	.459	106	3	10-2	.991	-11	80	92	O117(44/82/2),D2		-0.7
2004	Oak A	143	569	91	161	39	3	20	73	46-0	12	111	.283	.347	.467	111	10	17-1	.989	-5	90	136	O141(109/33/20)/D		0.4
2005	Oak A	59	192	30	51	15	2	7	24	14-0	7	27	.266	.336	.474	111	3	2-2	.984	5	120	153	O54(51/2/4),D4		0.6
	Col N	15	53	2	10	2	0	0	5	7-0	0	11	.189	.283	.226	37	-5	2-0	.976	3	144	133	O14(4/4/8)		-0.3
	Bal A	52	167	17	32	7	1	3	11	11-0	1	33	.192	.246	.299	44	-14	3-0	.969	1	108	87	O51(51/1/1)		-1.4
Total	6	509	1537	242	398	95	17	48	180	128-4	27	277	.259	.325	.437	98	-4	40-6	.984	-11	94	111	O472(320/134/65),D20		-2.0

BYRNES, JIM James Joseph B1.5.1880 San Francisco CA D7.31.1941 San Francisco CA BR/TR/5-9/150 d4.19

1906	Phi A	10	23	2	4	0	0	0	0	0	0		.174	.174	.261	34	-2	0	.889	-0	103	122	C9		-0.2

BYRNES, MILT Milton John "Skippy" B11.15.1916 St.Louis MO D2.1.1979 St.Louis MO BL/TL/5-10.5/170 d4.21

1943	StL A	129	429	58	120	28	7	4	50	53	2	49	.280	.362	.406	122	13	1-4	**.997**	7	104	150	O114(23/66/26)		1.4
1944	†StL A	128	407	63	120	20	4	4	45	68	0	50	.295	.396	.393	119	13	1-7	.976	0	105	73	O122(41/52/36)		0.6
1945	StL A	133	442	53	110	29	4	8	59	78	1	84	.249	.363	.387	112	10	1-3	.988	7	111	105	O125(31/56/47),1b2		1.0
Total	3	390	1278	174	350	77	15	16	154	199	3	183	.274	.373	.395	117	36	3-14	.987	14	107	109	O361(95/174/109),1b2		3.0

CABALLERO, PUTSY Ralph Joseph B11.5.1927 New Orleans LA BR/TR/5-11/175* d9.14

1944	Phi N	4	4	0	0	0	0	0	0	0	0	1	.000	.000	.000	-99	-1	0	.889	1	119	0	3b2		-0.1
1945	Phi N	9	1	1	0	0	0	0	1	0	0	0	.000	.000	.000	-99	0	0	.857	0	87	417	3b5		-0.1
1947	Phi N	2	7	2	1	0	0	0	1	0	0	0	.143	.143	.143	7	-1	0	1.000	0	117	102	2b2/3		-0.1
1948	Phi N	113	351	33	86	12	1	0	19	24	0	18	.245	.293	.285	58	-21	7	.962	5	103	114	3b79,2b23		-1.5
1949	Phi N	29	68	8	19	3	0	0	3	0	0	9	.279	.279	.324	63	-4	0	.981	0	92	106	2b21/S		-0.2
1950	†Phi N	46	24	12	4	0	0	0	2	0	0	2	.167	.231	.167	-3	-1	7	.950	2	127	146	2b5,3b4,S2		-0.1
1951	Phi N	84	161	15	30	3	2	1	11	12	0	7	.186	.243	.248	33	-16	1-2	.985	-1	95	109	2b54,3b3/S		-1.5
1952	Phi N	35	42	10	10	3	0	0	2	2	0	0	.238	.273	.310	62	-1	1-0	.857	-0	110	148	S8,2b7,3b7		-0.2
Total	8	322	658	81	150	21	3	1	40	41	0	34	.228	.273	.274	49	-48	10-4	.968	7	96	104	2b112,3b101,S12		-3.7

CABELL, ENOS Enos Milton B10.8.1949 Fort Riley KS BR/TR/6-5/185(172-190) d9.17 Col Los Angeles Harbor (CA) JC OF(42/1/72)

1972	Bal A	3	5	0	0	0	0	0	0	0-0	0	0	.000	.000	.000	-96	-1	0-0	1.000	0	0	134	/1		-0.2
1973	Bal A	32	47	12	10	2	0	1	3	0-0	0	7	.213	.250	.319	62	-2	1-3	.991	-2	54	149	1b23/3		-0.6
1974	†Bal A	80	174	24	42	4	2	3	17	7-1	0	20	.241	.269	.339	76	-6	5-3	.995	-0	109	118	1b28,O22(1/0/22),3b19/2D		-0.9
1975	Hou N	117	348	43	92	17	6	2	43	18-1	3	53	.264	.303	.365	92	-6	12-3	.973	3	85	231	O67(37/0/32),1b25,3b22		-0.5
1976	Hou N	144	586	85	160	13	7	2	43	29-1	2	79	.273	.309	.329	89	-12	35-8	.958	-2	97	88	3b143,1b3		-1.0
1977	Hou N	150	625	101	176	36	7	16	68	27-2	3	55	.282	.313	.438	108	3	42-22	.948	-1	97	76	3b144,1b8/S		0.2
1978	Hou N	162	660	92	195	31	8	7	71	22-1	5	80	.295	.321	.398	108	4	33-15	.958	-7	91	58	3b153,1b14/S		-0.5
1979	Hou N	155	603	60	164	30	5	6	67	21-7	3	68	.272	.299	.368	86	-14	37-18	.957	-20	76	54	3b132,1b51		-3.8
1980	†Hou N	152	604	69	167	23	8	2	55	26-6	1	84	.276	.305	.351	91	-11	21-13	.927	-12	89	71	3b150/1		-2.6
1981	SF N	96	396	41	101	20	1	2	36	10-0	1	47	.255	.274	.326	72	-16	6-7	.987	-2	134	99	1b69,3b22		-2.6
1982	Det A	125	464	45	121	20	1	2	37	15-2	1	48	.261	.284	.323	66	-22	15-6	.992	-1	123	127	1b83,3b59,O3(1/0/2)		-2.7
1983	Det A	121	392	62	122	23	5	5	46	16-2	1	41	.311	.335	.434	114	6	4-8	.997	5	121	108	1b106,3b4/SD		0.4
1984	Hou N	127	436	52	135	17	3	8	44	21-5	1	47	.310	.341	.417	120	10	8-11	.993	-1	95	123	1b112		0.0
1985	Hou N	60	143	20	35	4	1	2	14	16-0	0	15	.245	.321	.357	91	-2	3-1	.994	-1	92	106	1b49		-0.5
	†LA N	57	192	20	56	11	0	0	22	14-1	0	21	.292	.340	.349	95	-1	6-2	.920	3	117	137	3b32,1b21,O4(1/0/3)		0.1
	Year	117	335	40	91	19	1	2	36	30-1	0	36	.272	.332	.352	93	-2	9-3	.993	2	79	90	1b70,3b32,O4(1/0/3)		-0.3
1986	LA N	107	277	27	71	11	0	2	29	14-2	2	26	.256	.294	.318	75	-10	10-4	.987	3	105	85	1b61,O16(2/1/13),3b7		-1.1
Total	15	1688	5952	753	1647	263	66	60	596	259-31	23	691	.277	.308	.370	93	-81	238-124	.944	-33	92	74	3b888,1b655,O112R,D9,S3/2		-16.2

CABRERA, ALEX Alexander Alberto B12.24.1971 Caripito, Venez BR/TR/6-2/220 d6.26

2000	Ari N	31	80	10	21	2	1	5	14	4-0	2	21	.262	.299	.500	95	-1	0-0	1.000	1	84	104	1b15,O12(1/0/11)	14	-0.1

CABRERA, AL Alfredo A. B5.11.1881 Canary Islands, Spain D1964 Batabano, Cuba TR d5.16

1913	StL N	1	2	0	0	0	0	0	0	0	0	0	.000	.000	.000	-99	-1	0	—	-0	0	0	/S		-0.1

CABRERA, FRANCISCO Francisco (Paulino) B10.10.1966 Santo Domingo, D.R. BR/TR/6-4/193* d7.24

1989	Tor A	3	12	1	2	1	0	0	1	1-0	0	3	.167	.231	.250	36	-1	0-0	—	0			D3		-0.1
	Atl N	4	14	0	3	2	0	0	0	1-0	0	3	.214	.214	.357	59	-1	0-0	1.000	-1	69	68	1b2/C		-0.2
1990	Atl N	63	137	14	38	5	1	7	25	5-0	0	21	.277	.301	.482	106	0	1-0	.990	-1	90	64	1b48,C3		-0.2
1991	†Atl N	44	95	7	23	6	0	4	23	6-0	0	20	.242	.284	.432	94	-1	1-1	.987	-1	104	78	C17,1b14		-0.2
1992	†Atl N	12	10	2	3	0	0	2	3	1-0	1	5	.300	.364	.900	232	2	0-0	—	-0	0	0	/C		0.1
1993	†Atl N	70	83	8	20	3	0	4	11	8-1	0	21	.241	.308	.422	91	-1	0-0	1.000	2	174	69	1b12,C2.		0.0
Total	5	196	351	32	89	17	1	17	62	21-1	1	69	.254	.294	.453	99	-2	2-1	.989	-1	113	66	1b76,C24,D3		-0.6

CABRERA, JOLBERT Jolbert Alexis B12.8.1972 Cartagena, Colombia BR/TR/6-0/177(177-195) d4.12 b-Orlando OF(124/128/66)

1998	Cle A	1	2	0	0	0	0	0	0	0-0	0	1	.000	.000	.000	-96	-1	0-0	1.000	0	122	0	/S		0.0
1999	Cle A	30	37	6	7	1	0	0	1	1-0	1	8	.189	.231	.216	14	-5	3-0	.957	1	109	0	O16(4/12/0),2b6		-0.3
2000	Cle A	100	175	27	44	3	1	2	15	8-0	2	15	.251	.290	.314	52	-13	6-4	.989	4	105	145	O74(24/26/29),2b19,S8,D2		-0.9
2001	†Cle A	141	287	50	75	16	3	1	38	16-0	6	41	.261	.312	.348	72	-12	10-4	.978	-0	93	40	O83(36/35/18),2b28,3b27,S14/D		-1.0
2002	Cle A	38	72	5	8	1	0	0	7	5-0	1	13	.111	.177	.125	-17	-12	1-1	1.000	-1	89	0	O34(5/16/13),2b3/D	32	-1.3
	LA N	10	12	3	4	1	0	0	1	2-0	0	2	.333	.429	.417	135	1	0-0	1.000	1	158	0	O4(3/0/1),3b3/2		0.1
2003	LA N	128	347	43	98	32	2	6	37	17-3	10	62	.282	.332	.438	102	1	6-4	.967	-2	67	143	O63(31/38/4),2b59,S9,1b8,3b5		-0.2
2004	Sea A	113	359	38	97	19	2	6	47	16-1	8	70	.270	.312	.384	85	-8	10-3	.970	-4	106	135	3b36,1b23,O23(21/1/1),2b18,S14,D5		-1.1
Total	7	561	1291	172	333	73	8	15	145	65-4	28	212	.258	.305	.362	74	-49	36-16	.981	-4	94	97	O297C,2b134,3b71,S46,1b31,D9	32	-4.7

CABRERA, MIGUEL Jose Miguel (Torres) B4.18.1983 Maracay, Venez BR/TR/6-2/180(180-210) d6.20

2003	†Fla N	87	314	39	84	21	3	12	62	25-3	3	84	.268	.325	.468	108	3	0-2	.972	-4	102	151	O55L,3b34		-0.3
2004	Fla N★	160	603	101	177	31	1	33	112	68-5	6	148	.294	.366	.512	132	28	5-2	.968	-3	91	142	O158(59/0/100)/D		1.8
2005	Fla N★	158	613	106	198	43	2	33	116	64-12	2	125	.323	.385	.561	154	48	1-0	.976	-6	81	168	O134L,3b29		3.6
Total	3	405	1530	246	459	95	6	78	290	157-20	11	357	.300	.366	.523	136	79	6-4	.971	-12	89	153	O347(248/0/100),3b63/D		5.1

CABRERA, MELKY Melky B8.11.1984 Santo Domingo, D.R. BB/TL/5-11/170 d7.7

2005	NY A	6	19	1	4	0	0	0	0	0-0	0	2	.211	.211	.211	13	-2	0-0	1.000	-1	64	0	O6C		-0.4

CABRERA, ORLANDO Orlando Luis B11.2.1974 Cartagena, Colombia BR/TR/5-10/175(150-190) d9.3 b-Jolbert

1997	Mon N	16	18	4	4	0	0	0	2	1-0	0	3	.222	.263	.222	29	-2	1-2	.875	1	150	126	S6,2b4		-0.1
1998	Mon N	79	261	44	73	16	5	3	22	18-1	0	27	.280	.325	.414	96	-2	6-2	.984	-5	91	69	S52,2b28		-0.1
1999	Mon N	104	382	48	97	23	5	4	39	18-4	3	38	.254	.293	.403	77	-16	2-2	.979	15	107	98	S102	56	0.6
2000	Mon N	125	422	47	100	25	1	13	55	25-3	1	28	.237	.279	.393	60	-23	4-4	.981	8	108	104	S124/2	30	-0.6
2001	Mon N	162	626	64	173	41	6	14	96	43-5	4	54	.276	.324	.428	94	-7	19-7	**.986**	29	113	105	S162		3.5
2002	Mon N	153	563	64	148	43	1	7	56	48-4	2	53	.263	.321	.380	83	-15	25-7	.962	21	113	103	S153		2.1
2003	Mon N	162	626	95	186	47	2	17	80	52-3	1	64	.297	.347	.460	107	7	24-7	.975	6	101	104	S162		2.9
2004	Mon N	103	390	41	96	19	2	4	31	28-0	2	31	.246	.298	.336	62	-22	12-3	.984	4	103	109	S101		-0.2
	†Bos A	58	228	33	67	19	1	6	31	11-0	1	23	.294	.320	.465	98	-1	4-1	.966	-6	94	68	S57		-0.2
2005	†LA A	141	540	70	139	28	3	8	57	38-4	3	50	.257	.309	.365	80	-16	21-2	**.988**	-15	87	96	S140	105	-1.6
Total	9	1103	4056	510	1083	261	26	80	469	282-24	17	371	.267	.315	.403	85	-97	118-32	.978	58	104	99	S1059,2b33	105	5.5

CACEK, CRAIG Craig Thomas B9.10.1954 Hollywood CA BR/TR/6-1/200 [NYN72 9/205] d6.18

1977	Hou N	7	20	0	1	0	0	0	0	0-0	0	4	.050	.095	.050	-65	-5	0-0	.981	-1	31	161	1b6		-0.7

CACERES, EDGAR Edgar F. B6.6.1964 Barquisimeto, Venez BB/TR/6-1/170 d6.8

1995	KC A	55	117	13	28	6	2	1	17	8-0	1	15	.239	.291	.350	65	-6	2-2	.992	0	102	66	2b36,S8,1b6,3b3,D3	15	-0.5

CADY, CHARLIE Charles B. B12.1865 Chicago IL D6.7.1909 Kankakee IL 5-11/180 d9.5 ▲

1883	Cle N	3	11	0	0	0	0	0	0		0	5	.000	.083	.000	-73	-2		1.000	-0	0	0	O2R/P		-0.1
1884	CP U	6	20	4	2	1	1	0	1		0		.100	.143	.250	17	-3		.909	-0	76	0	P4,O2C		-0.1

YEAR	TM LG	G	AB	R	H	2B	3B	HR	RBI	BB-IB	HP	SO	AVG	OBP	SLG	AOPS	ABR	SB-CS	FA	FR	RNG	THR	GAMES AT POSITION	DL	BFW
	KC U	2	3	0	0	0	0	0	0				.000	.000	.000	-99	-1		.600	-2			/C2		-0.3
	Year	8	23	4	2	1	1	0	1				.087	.125	.217	2	-4		.909	-2	76	0	P4,O2C/C2		-0.4
Total	2	11	34	4	2	1	1	0	0	2			5	.059	.111	.147	-23	-6		.917	-3			P5,O4(0/2/2)/2C		-0.5

CADY, HICK Forrest Leroy (b Forrest Leroy Bergland) B1.26.1886 Bishop Hill IL D3.3.1946 Cedar Rapids IA BR/TR/6-2/179 d4.26

YEAR	TM LG	G	AB	R	H	2B	3B	HR	RBI	BB-IB	HP	SO	AVG	OBP	SLG	AOPS	ABR	SB-CS	FA	FR	RNG	THR	GAMES AT POSITION	DL	BFW
1912	†Bos A	47	135	19	35	13	2	0	9	10	3			.259	.324	.385	98	0		.990	9	126	93	C43,1b4		1.2
1913	Bos A	40	96	10	24	5	2	0	6	5	1	14		.250	.294	.344	84	-2	1	.992	4	98	91	C39		0.4
1914	Bos A	61	159	14	41	6	1	0	8	12	0	22		.258	.310	.308	86	-3	2-1	.971	2	121	109	C58		0.4
1915	†Bos A	78	205	25	57	10	2	0	17	19	1	25		.278	.342	.346	109	2	0-2	.980	4	117	87	C77		1.2
1916	†Bos A	78	162	5	31	6	3	0	13	15	1	16		.191	.264	.265	59	-9		.967	-5	126	72	C63,1b3		-1.1
1917	Bos A	17	46	4	7	1	1	0	2	1	0	6		.152	.170	.217	18	-5	0	.959	1	125	99	C14		-0.4
1919	Phi N	34	98	6	21	6	0	1	19	4	1	8		.214	.252	.306	63	-4	1	.984	-6	74	111	C29		-0.9
Total	7	355	901	83	216	47	11	1	74	66	7	91		.240	.297	.320	82	-21	4-3	.979	8	115	93	C323,1b7		0.8

CAFEGO, TOM Thomas B8.21.1911 Whipple WV D10.29.1961 Detroit MI BL/TR/5-10/160 d9.3

YEAR	TM LG	G	AB	R	H	2B	3B	HR	RBI	BB-IB	HP	SO	AVG	OBP	SLG	AOPS	ABR	SB-CS	FA	FR	RNG	THR	GAMES AT POSITION	DL	BFW
1937	StL A	4	4	1	0	0	0	0	0	0				.000	.000	.000	-99	-1	0-0	.500	-0	83	0	/OL		-0.1

CAFFIE, JOE Joseph Clifford "Rabbit" B2.14.1931 Ramer AL BL/TR/5-10.5/180* d9.13 Negro Lg 1950

YEAR	TM LG	G	AB	R	H	2B	3B	HR	RBI	BB-IB	HP	SO	AVG	OBP	SLG	AOPS	ABR	SB-CS	FA	FR	RNG	THR	GAMES AT POSITION	DL	BFW
1956	Cle A	12	38	7	13	0	1	1	4	4-0	-	2	8	.342	.432	.342	104	1	3-2	1.000	1	106	134	O10L		0.1
1957	Cle A	32	89	14	24	2	1	3	10	4-2	0	11	.270	.301	.416	95	0	0-1	.976	0	118	0	O19(3/0/18)		-0.3
Total	2	44	127	21	37	2	1	3	11	8-2		2	13	.291	.343	.394	99	0	3-3	.984	1	114	46	O29(13/0/18)		-0.2

CAFFYN, BEN Benjamin Thomas B2.10.1880 Peoria IL D11.22.1942 Peoria IL BL/TL/5-10/175 d8.21

YEAR	TM LG	G	AB	R	H	2B	3B	HR	RBI	BB-IB	HP	SO	AVG	OBP	SLG	AOPS	ABR	SB-CS	FA	FR	RNG	THR	GAMES AT POSITION	DL	BFW
1906	Cle A	30	103	16	20	4	0	0	3	12		2		.194	.291	.233	65	-3	2	.909	-3	60	308	O29(28/1/0)		-0.9

CAGE, WAYNE Wayne Levell B11.23.1951 Monroe LA BL/TL/6-4/175(175-205) [CleA71 3/55] d4.22

YEAR	TM LG	G	AB	R	H	2B	3B	HR	RBI	BB-IB	HP	SO	AVG	OBP	SLG	AOPS	ABR	SB-CS	FA	FR	RNG	THR	GAMES AT POSITION	DL	BFW
1978	Cle A	36	98	11	24	6	1	4	13	9-0	1	28	.245	.308	.449	111	1	1-2	.988	1	140	131	D20,1b11		0.0
1979	Cle A	29	56	6	13	2	0	1	6	5-0	0	16	.232	.295	.321	66	-3	0-2	1.000	0	126	72	1b7,D9		-0.3
Total	2	65	154	17	37	8	1	5	19	14-0	1		44	.240	.304	.403	94	-2	1-4	.992	1	135	111	D29,1b18		-0.3

CAHILL, JOHN John Patrick Parnell "Patsy" B4.30.1865 San Francisco CA D10.31.1901 Pleasanton CA BR/TR/5-7.5/168 d5.31 ▲

YEAR	TM LG	G	AB	R	H	2B	3B	HR	RBI	BB-IB	HP	SO	AVG	OBP	SLG	AOPS	ABR	SB-CS	FA	FR	RNG	THR	GAMES AT POSITION	DL	BFW
1884	Col AA	59	210	28	46	3	3	0		6	2			.219	.248	.262	72	-6		.843	-0	79	0	O56L,S5,P2		-0.7
1886	StL A	125	463	43	92	17	6	1	32	9		79		.199	.214	.268	49	-28	16	.866	2	141	131	O124(0/1/123),P2/S3		-2.5
1887	Ind N	68	263	22	54	4	3	0	26	9	1	5		.205	.234	.243	34	-24	34	.826	-5	108	49	O56(0/3/53),3b9,P6/S		-2.4
Total	3	252	936	93	192	24	12	1	58	24	3	84		.205	.227	.260	49	-58	50	.851	-4	119	81	O236(56/4/176),3b10,P10,S7		-5.6

CAHILL, TOM Thomas H. B10.1868 Fall River MA D12.25.1894 Scranton PA 5-7/150 d4.9 Col Penn

YEAR	TM LG	G	AB	R	H	2B	3B	HR	RBI	BB-IB	HP	SO	AVG	OBP	SLG	AOPS	ABR	SB-CS	FA	FR	RNG	THR	GAMES AT POSITION	DL	BFW
1891	Lou AA	119	430	68	109	17	7	3	44	41	4	6	51	.253	.327	.347	94	-4	38	.930	-8	83	122	C55,S49,O12(9/2/1),2b6,3b2		-0.5

CAIRO, MIGUEL Miguel Jesus B5.4.1974 Anaco, Venez BR/TR/6-1/160(160-210) d4.17 OF(49/0/12)

YEAR	TM LG	G	AB	R	H	2B	3B	HR	RBI	BB-IB	HP	SO	AVG	OBP	SLG	AOPS	ABR	SB-CS	FA	FR	RNG	THR	GAMES AT POSITION	DL	BFW
1996	Tor A	9	27	5	6	2	0	0	1	2-0	1	9	.222	.300	.296	52	-2	0-0	1.000	-1	77	95	2b9		-0.2
1997	Chi N	16	29	7	7	1	0	0	1	2-0	1	4	.241	.313	.276	54	-2	0-0	1.000	0	83	129	2b9,S2		-0.1
1998	TB A	150	515	49	138	26	5	5	46	24-0	6	44	.268	.307	.367	73	-21	19-8	.978	17	107	122	2b148,D2		0.3
1999	TB A	120	465	61	137	15	5	3	36	24-0	7	46	.295	.335	.368	79	-15	22-7	.986	27	111	117	2b108,D2	39	1.8
2000	TB A	119	375	49	98	18	2	1	34	29-0	2	34	.261	.314	.328	65	-20	28-7	.983	5	99	111	2b108,D2		-0.4
2001	Chi N	66	123	20	35	3	1	2	9	16-1	0	21	.285	.364	.374	95	-1	2-1	.900	-2	73	145	3b40,2b11/S		-0.1
	†StL N	27	33	5	11	5	0	1	7	2-0	0	23	.333	.371	.576	137	2	0-0	1.000	-0	174	0	O6L,2b5,3b3/1S		0.1
	Year	93	156	25	46	8	1	3	16	18-1	0	23	.295	.366	.417	104	1	2-1	.882	-5	71	142	3b43,2b16,O6L,S2/1		-0.3
2002	†StL N	108	184	28	46	9	2	2	23	13-2	3	36	.250	.307	.353	77	-7	1-1	.905	-2	94	0	O24(19/0/5),2b18,3b7,S6,1b4,D3		-0.9
2003	StL N	92	261	41	64	15	2	5	32	13-1	6	30	.245	.289	.375	75	-10	4-1	.986	-14	87	75	2b40,O27(22/0/6),3b12,S7,1b3	40	-2.3
2004	†NY A	122	360	48	105	17	5	6	42	18-1	14	49	.292	.346	.417	99	-1	11-3	.987	-5	93	97	2b113,3b8,S3/1	17	0.1
2005	NY N	100	327	31	82	18	0	2	19	19-2	4	31	.251	.296	.324	65	-17	13-3	.984	-1	99	122	2b82,1b8,3b3,O3(2/0/1)	17	-1.3
Total	10	929	2699	344	729	129	22	27	250	162-7	44	305	.270	.318	.364	77	-94	100-31	.983	23	101	112	2b660,3b73,O60L,S20,1b17,D9	96	-3.5

CAITHAMER, GEORGE George Theodore "Sidee" B7.22.1910 Chicago IL D6.1.1954 Chicago IL BR/TR/5-10/168 d9.17

YEAR	TM LG	G	AB	R	H	2B	3B	HR	RBI	BB-IB	HP	SO	AVG	OBP	SLG	AOPS	ABR	SB-CS	FA	FR	RNG	THR	GAMES AT POSITION	DL	BFW
1934	Chi A	5	19	1	6	0	0	0	3	1	0	5	.316	.350	.368	83	0	0-0	.958	-1	59	75	C5		-0.1

CALDERON, IVAN Ivan (Perez) B3.19.1962 Fajardo, PR D12.27.2003 Loiza, PR BR/TR/6-1/220(160-221) d8.10

YEAR	TM LG	G	AB	R	H	2B	3B	HR	RBI	BB-IB	HP	SO	AVG	OBP	SLG	AOPS	ABR	SB-CS	FA	FR	RNG	THR	GAMES AT POSITION	DL	BFW
1984	Sea A	11	24	2	5	1	0	1	1	2-0	1	5	.208	.269	.375	77	-1	1-0	1.000	0	110	0	O11(4/6/1)	17	-0.1
1985	Sea A	67	210	37	60	16	4	8	28	19-1	2	45	.286	.349	.514	132	9	4-2	.981	-1	95	151	O53(33/11/22),1b2,D3		0.7
1986	Sea A	37	131	13	31	5	0	2	13	6-0	1	33	.237	.275	.321	61	-7	3-1	.937	-1	86	187	O32(2/2/31)		-0.9
	Chi A	13	33	3	10	2	1	0	2	3-1	0	6	.303	.361	.424	109	0	0-0	.900	0	135	0	O5L,D6		-0.1
	Year	50	164	16	41	7	1	2	15	9-1	1	39	.250	.293	.341	71	-7	3-1	.932	-1	90	170	O37(7/2/31),D6		-0.9
1987	Chi A	144	542	93	159	38	2	28	83	60-6	1	109	.293	.362	.526	129	23	10-5	.984	-1	101	76	O139(6/0/135),D3	15	1.4
1988	Chi A	73	264	40	56	14	0	14	35	34-2	0	66	.212	.299	.424	101	0	4-4	.954	-1	96	119	O67(4/0/63),D3	79	-0.3
1989	Chi A	157	622	83	178	34	9	14	87	43-7	3	94	.286	.332	.437	118	13	7-1	.978	-2	99	84	O103(17/0/89),D36,1b26		0.5
1990	Chi A	158	607	85	166	44	2	14	74	51-7	1	79	.273	.327	.422	111	9	32-16	.975	-1	100	43	O122L,1b4		0.7
1991	Mon N★	134	470	69	141	22	3	19	75	53-4	3	64	.300	.368	.481	140	26	31-16	.974	-1	104	85	O130(130/0/3),D27,1b2		2.1
1992	Mon N	48	170	19	45	14	2	3	24	14-1	1	22	.265	.323	.424	111	2	1-2	.988	-1	92	100	O46L	119	-0.1
1993	Bos A	73	213	25	47	8	2	1	19	21-1	1	28	.221	.291	.291	54	-14	4-2	1.000	1	111	69	O47(9/2/39),D19	19	-1.5
	Chi A	9	26	1	3	2	0	0	3	0-0	0	5	.115	.115	.192	-19	-4	0-0	—				D6		-2.0
	Year	82	239	26	50	10	2	1	22	21-1	1	33	.209	.274	.280	47	-18	4-2	1.000	1	111	69	O47(9/2/39),D25		-2.0
Total	10	924	3312	470	901	200	25	104	444	306-30	13	556	.272	.333	.442	113	56	97-49	.976	-5	100	90	O755(378/11/383),D103,1b34	249	-0.3

CALDERONE, SAM Samuel Francis B2.6.1926 Beverly NJ BR/TR/5-10.5/185* d4.19 Mil 1951-52

YEAR	TM LG	G	AB	R	H	2B	3B	HR	RBI	BB-IB	HP	SO	AVG	OBP	SLG	AOPS	ABR	SB-CS	FA	FR	RNG	THR	GAMES AT POSITION	DL	BFW
1950	NY N	34	67	9	20	1	0	1	12	2	0	5	.299	.319	.358	77	-2	0	.972	-2	156	81	C33		-0.3
1953	NY N	35	45	4	10	2	0	0	8	1	0	4	.222	.239	.267	31	-5	0-0	.966	0	157	101	C31		-0.4
1954	Mil N	22	29	3	11	2	0	1	5	4	0	4	.379	.441	.448	146	2	0-0	1.000	2	102	67	C16		0.4
Total	3	91	141	16	41	5	0	1	25	7	0	13	.291	.322	.348	76	-5	0-0	.978	-0	144	84	C80		-0.3

CALDWELL, BRUCE Bruce B2.8.1906 Ashton RI D2.15.1959 West Haven CT BR/TR/6-0/195 d6.30 Col Yale

YEAR	TM LG	G	AB	R	H	2B	3B	HR	RBI	BB-IB	HP	SO	AVG	OBP	SLG	AOPS	ABR	SB-CS	FA	FR	RNG	THR	GAMES AT POSITION	DL	BFW
1928	Cle A	18	27	2	6	1	0	0	3	2	1	2	.222	.300	.333	66	-1	1-0	1.000	0	97	159	O10R/1		-0.2
1932	Bro N	7	11	2	1	0	0	0	2	2	0	2	.091	.231	.091	-10	-2	0	.875	-1	0	0	1b6		-0.3
Total	2	25	38	4	7	1	0	0	5	4	1	4	.184	.279	.263	44	-3	1-0	1.000	-1	97	159	O10R,1b7		-0.5

CALDWELL, RAY Raymond Benjamin "Rube","Sum" B4.26.1888 Corydon PA D8.17.1967 Salamanca NY BL/TR/6-2/190 d9.9 ▲

YEAR	TM LG	G	AB	R	H	2B	3B	HR	RBI	BB-IB	HP	SO	AVG	OBP	SLG	AOPS	ABR	SB-CS	FA	FR	RNG	THR	GAMES AT POSITION	DL	BFW
1910	NY A	6	6	0	0	0	0	0	0	0			.000	.000	.000	-95	-1	0	1.000	-0	66	0	P6		0.0
1911	NY A	59	147	16	40	4	1	0	17	11	0		.272	.323	.313	73	-5	5	.953	-2	76	103	P41,O11(5/0/5)		0.6
1912	NY A	44	76	18	18	1	2	0	6	5	0		.237	.284	.303	64	-4	0	.938	1	111	125	P30/OL		0.6
1913	NY A	59	97	10	28	3	2	0	11	3	0	15	.289	.310	.361	96	-1	3	1.000	-4	87	63	P27,O3(0/1/2)		-0.5
1914	NY A	59	113	9	22	4	0	0	10	7	1	24	.195	.248	.230	44	-8	2-1	.967	-4	74	101	P31,1b6		-0.5
1915	NY A	72	144	27	35	4	1	4	20	9	1	32	.243	.288	.368	96	8	4-3	.988	-3	80	161	P36		0.0
1916	NY A	45	93	6	19	2	0	0	4	17	2	17	.204	.221	.226	34	-8	1	.960	-0	93	111	P21,O2		-0.7
1917	NY A	63	124	12	32	6	1	2	12	16	0	16	.258	.343	.371	117	3	2	.973	-2	88	43	P32,O8(0/5/3)		-0.1
1918	NY A	65	151	14	44	10	1	1	18	13	1	23	.291	.352	.377	117	3	2	.977	-3	73	49	P24,O19(2/12/5)		-0.1
1919	Bos A	33	48	5	13	1	0	1	8	9	0	9	.271	.393	.375	73	-2	0	.950	-2	78	0	P18,O2L		0.0
	Cle A	6	23	4	8	0	0	2	6	0	0	4	.348	.348	.522	134	3	0	.900	-1	56	0	P6		-0.1
	Year	39	71	9	21	1	0	3	14	9	0	13	.296	.296	.394	97	-1	0	.933	-3	70	0	P24,O2L		-0.1
1920	†Cle A	41	89	17	19	3	0	0	7	2	0	13	.213	.300	.247	45	1	0-2	.917	-3	80	0	P34		0.6
1921	Cle A	38	53	2	11	4	0	1	2	1	0	5	.208	.236	.340	45	0	0	.930	-3	93	83	P37		0.6
Total	12	590	1164	138	289	46	8	8	114	78	3	158	.248	.297	.322	78	-11	23-6	.960	-21	80	80	P343,O46(11/18/15),1b6		-1.2

CALHOUN, JACK John Charles "Red" B12.14.1879 Pittsburgh PA D2.27.1947 Cincinnati OH BR/TR/6-0/185 d6.27

YEAR	TM LG	G	AB	R	H	2B	3B	HR	RBI	BB-IB	HP	SO	AVG	OBP	SLG	AOPS	ABR	SB-CS	FA	FR	RNG	THR	GAMES AT POSITION	DL	BFW
1902	StL N	20	64	3	10	2	1	0	8	8	1		.156	.260	.219	50	-4	1	.972	-1	89	66	3b12,1b5/OR		-0.8

CALHOUN, BILL William Davitte "Mary" B6.23.1890 Rockmart GA D1.28.1955 Sandersville GA BL/TL/6-0/180 d4.24 Col Georgia Tech

YEAR	TM LG	G	AB	R	H	2B	3B	HR	RBI	BB-IB	HP	SO	AVG	OBP	SLG	AOPS	ABR	SB-CS	FA	FR	RNG	THR	GAMES AT POSITION	DL	BFW
1913	Bos N	6	13	0	1	0	0	0		0		3	.077	.077	.077	-55	-3	0	.970	-0	67	70	1b3		-0.

YEAR	TM LG	G	AB	R	H	2B	3B	HR	RBI	BB-IB	HP	SO	AVG	OBP	SLG	AOPS	ABR	SB-CS	FA	FR	RNG	THR	GAMES AT POSITION	DL	BFW
CALLAGHAN, MARTY			Martin Francis	B6.9.1900	Norwood MA			D6.23.1975	Norfolk MA		BL/TL/5-10/157	d4.13													
1922	Chi N	74	175	31	45	7	4	0	20	17	1	17	.257	.326	.343	71	-7	2-3	.946	-4	96	38	O53(12/10/31)		-1.4
1923	Chi N	61	129	18	29	1	3	0	14	8	1	18	.225	.275	.279	47	-10	2-5	.969	-0	100	98	O38(19/0/19)		-1.4
1928	Cin N	81	238	29	69	11	4	0	24	27	0	10	.290	.362	.370	93	-2	5	.980	-1	97	97	O69(48/22/1)		-0.6
1930	Cin N	79	225	28	62	9	2	0	16	19	1	25	.276	.335	.333	66	-12	1	.986	1	106	71	O54(16/38/0)		-1.3
Total	4	295	767	106	205	28	13	0	74	71	3	70	.267	.332	.338	72	-31	10-8	.973	-4	100	77	O214(95/70/51)		-4.7
CALLAGHAN, PAT			Patrick J.	B New York NY			d5.1																		
1884	Ind AA	61	258	38	67	8	5	2		8		0	.260	.282	.353	109	2		.812	-9	83	67	3b61		-0.5
CALLAHAN, DAVE			David Joseph	B7.20.1888	Seneca IL		D10.28.1969	Ottawa IL	BL/TR/5-10/165	d9.14															
1910	Cle A	13	44	6	8	1	0	0	2	4	1		.182	.265	.205	47	-3	5	1.000	-0	123	0	O12L		-0.4
1911	Cle A	6	16	1	4	0	1	0	0	1	0		.250	.294	.375	85	-1	0	.875	1	64	342	O4C		0.0
Total	2	19	60	7	12	1	1	0	2	5	1		.200	.273	.250	58	-4	5	.972	1	111	71	O16(12/4/0)		-0.4
CALLAHAN, ED			Edward Joseph	B12.11.1857	Boston MA		D2.5.1947	New York NY	d7.19																
1884	StL U	1	3	0	0	0	0	0		0			.000	.000	.000	-96	-1		1.000	1	708	0	/OL		0.0
	KC U	3	11	0	4	0	0	0		0			.364	.364	.364	139	0		.800	1	139	192	S3		0.1
	Bos U	4	13	2	5	0	0	0		1			.385	.429	.385	150	1		.750	-1	0	0	O4(1/0/3)		0.0
	Year	8	27	2	9	0	0	0		1			.333	.357	.333	116	0		.778	1	86	0	O5(2/0/3),S3		0.1
CALLAHAN, NIXEY			James Joseph	B3.18.1874	Fitchburg MA	D10.4.1934	Boston MA	BR/TR/5-10.5/180	d5.12	M7	OF(401/30/59) ▲														
1894	Phi N	9	21	4	5	0	0	0	0	0		7	.238	.238	.238	15	-1	0	.923	1	125	0	P9		0.0
1897	Chi N	94	360	60	105	18	6	3	47	10	5		.292	.320	.400	86	-9	12	.918	3	102	95	2b30,P23,O21(12/9/0),S18,3b2		-0.3
1898	Chi N	43	164	27	43	7	5	0	22	4	0		.262	.280	.366	85	-5	3	.947	-2	93	145	P31,O9(1/0/8),S21		-0.3
1899	Chi N	47	150	21	39	4	3	0	18	8	2		.260	.306	.327	76	-5	9	.904	4	128	95	P35,O9(0/7/2),S2/2		0.0
1900	Chi N	32	115	16	27	3	2	0	9	6	0		.235	.273	.296	59	2	5	.975	6	131	104	P32		0.2
1901	Chi A	45	118	15	39	7	3	1	19	10	0		.331	.383	.466	138	6	10	.944	4	135	159	P27,3b6,2b2		0.2
1902	Chi A	70	218	27	51	7	2	0	13	6	2		.234	.261	.284	53	-14	4	.941	4	129	250	P35,O23(6/3/15)/S		-0.4
1903	Chi A	118	439	47	128	26	5	2	56	20	1		.292	.324	.387	118	9	24	.895	-5	106	47	3b102,O8(6/0/2),P3,M		0.6
1904	Chi A	132	482	66	126	23	2	0	54	39	1		.261	.318	.317	105	5	29	.977	-13	81	0	O104L,2b28,M		-1.6
1905	Chi A	96	345	50	94	18	6	1	43	29	4		.272	.336	.368	128	11	26	.956	-5	104	0	O93(71/1/21)		0.2
1911	Chi A	120	466	64	131	13	5	3	60	15	2		.281	.306	.350	86	-12	45	.963	-11	85	56	O114(93/10/11)		-2.8
1912	Chi A	111	408	45	111	9	7	1	52	12	3		.272	.298	.336	84	-11	19	.939	-16	81	22	O107L,M		-3.2
1913	Chi A	6	9	0	2	0	0	0	1	0	0	2	.222	.222	.222	30	-1	0	1.000	-0	108	0	/OLM		-0.1
Total	13	923	3295	442	901	135	46	11	394	159	20	9	.273	.311	.352	94	-25	186	.953	-30	94	26	O489L,P195,3b110,2b62,S22/1		-7.7
CALLAHAN, JIM			James Timothy "Red" (b James Timothy Callaghan)	B1.12.1879	Allegheny Co. PA	D3.9.1968	Carnegie PA	BR/TR/5-9/145	d5.25																
1902	NY N	1	4	0	0	0	0	0		0			.000	.200	.000	-38	-1	0	—	0	0	0	/OR		-0.1
CALLAHAN, LEO			Leo David	B8.9.1890	Jamaica Plain MA	D5.2.1982	Erie PA	BL/TL/5-8/142	d4.9																
1913	Bro N	33	41	6	7	1	0	0	3	4		5	.171	.244	.293	52	-3	0	.857	-1	105	0	O8(2/4/2)		-0.4
1919	Phi N	81	235	26	54	14	4	1	9	29	1	19	.230	.317	.336	90	-2	5	.950	2	91	162	O58(12/9/38)		-0.4
Total	2	114	276	32	61	17	5	1	12	33	1	24	.221	.306	.330	84	-5	5	.941	1	92	148	O66(14/13/40)		-0.8
CALLAHAN, WESLEY			Wesley Leroy	B7.3.1888	Lyons IN	D9.13.1953	Dayton OH	BR/TR/5-7.5/155	d9.7																
1913	StL N	7	14	0	4	0	0	0	1	2		2	.286	.375	.286	91	0	1	.920	0	112	119	S6		0.1
CALLAWAY, FRANK			Frank Burnett	B2.26.1898	Knoxville TN	D8.21.1987	Knoxville TN	BR/TR/6-0/170	d9.17	Col Tennessee															
1921	Phi A	14	50	7	12	1	1	0	4	2	1	11	.240	.283	.300	49	-4	1-0	.878	-5	96	28	S14		-0.7
1922	Phi A	29	48	5	13	0	2	0	4	0	0	13	.271	.271	.354	60	-3	0-0	.880	0	126	112	2b11,3b5,S4		-0.2
Total	2	43	98	12	25	1	3	0	8	2	1	24	.255	.277	.327	54	-7	1-0	.889	-5	96	26	S18,2b11,3b5		-0.9
CALLISON, JOHNNY			John Wesley	B3.12.1939	Qualls OK	BL/TR/5-10/175*	d9.9																		
1958	Chi A	18	64	10	19	4	2	1	12	6	0	14	.297	.352	.469	128	2	1-0	.976	1	98	164	O18L		0.2
1959	Chi A	49	104	12	18	3	0	3	12	13-0	1	20	.173	.271	.288	54	-7	0-1	.983	1	92	161	O41L		-0.8
1960	Phi N	99	288	36	75	11	5	9	30	45-2	0	70	.260	.360	.427	114	7	0-4	.989	6	115	104	O86(32/16/47)		-0.7
1961	Phi N	138	455	74	121	20	11	9	47	69-5	5	87	.266	.363	.418	109	7	10-4	.967	1	101	98	O124(90/1/35)		0.2
1962	Phi N★	157	603	107	181	26	10	23	83	54-1	6	96	.300	.363	.491	131	25	10-3	.980	22	125	194	O152(3/5/151)		3.7
1963	Phi N	157	626	96	178	36	11	26	78	50-4	2	111	.284	.339	.502	140	31	8-3	.994	19	114	225	O157(2/1/156)		4.2
1964	Phi N★	162	654	101	179	30	10	31	104	36-3	6	95	.274	.316	.492	126	19	6-3	.988	14	114	161	O162(2/0/162)		2.3
1965	Phi N☆	160	619	93	162	25	16	32	101	57-2	6	117	.262	.328	.509	135	26	6-5	.982	15	112	199	O159R		3.1
1966	Phi N	155	612	93	169	40	7	11	55	56-4	3	83	.276	.338	.418	109	9	8-8	.990	2	102	111	O154R		-0.1
1967	Phi N	149	556	62	145	30	5	14	64	55-17	3	63	.261	.329	.408	109	7	6-12	.977	5	107	113	O147R		-0.1
1968	Phi N	121	398	46	97	18	4	14	40	42-4	3	70	.244	.319	.415	120	10	4-3	1.000	2	100	117	O109R		0.4
1969	Phi N	134	495	66	131	29	5	16	64	49-11	3	73	.265	.332	.440	118	11	2-1	.990	12	119	124	O129R	20	1.7
1970	Chi N	147	477	65	126	23	2	19	68	60-11	2	63	.264	.348	.440	98	0	7-2	.973	-0	104	143	O144(0/3/143)		-0.7
1971	Chi N	103	290	27	61	12	1	8	38	36-8	2	55	.210	.298	.341	71	-10	2-1	.982	-2	102	51	O89(1/0/88)		-1.8
1972	NY A	92	275	28	71	10	0	9	34	18-1	1	34	.258	.299	.393	108	2	3-0	.992	-2	92	79	O74R		-0.4
1973	NY A	45	136	10	24	4	0	1	10	4-0	2	24	.176	.197	.228	21	-15	1-1	.960	-2	82	103	O32R,D10		-1.8
Total	16	1886	6652	926	1757	321	89	226	840	650-73	41	1064	.264	.331	.441	114	124	74-51	.984	90	108	137	O1777(189/26/1586),D10	52	10.6
CALLOWAY, RON			Ronald Isiah	B9.4.1976	San Jose CA	BL/TL/6-1/210*	[AriN97 8/263]	d3.31	Col Canada (CA)	JC															
2003	Mon N	126	340	36	81	17	1	9	52	20-1	2	80	.238	.282	.374	68	-17	9-2	.983	1	105	76	O97(50/2/47)		-1.8
2004	Mon N	46	84	4	14	2	0	1	10	5-0	0	22	.167	.211	.226	13	-11	2-0	1.000	-1	90	0	O20(6/0/15)		-1.3
Total	2	172	424	40	95	19	1	10	62	25-1	2	102	.224	.268	.344	57	-28	11-2	.985	-1	103	-64	O117(56/2/62)		-3.1
CALVO, JACK			Jacinto (Gonzalez) (Born Jacinto Del Calvo)	B6.11.1894	Havana, Cuba	D6.15.1965	Miami FL	BL/TL/5-10/156	d5.9																
1913	Was A	17	33	5	8	0	0	1	2	1	0	4	.242	.265	.333	73	-1	0	.900	-0	64	212	O13(6/0/7)		-0.2
1920	Was A	17	23	5	1	0	1	0	2	2	0	2	.043	.120	.130	-35	-5	0-0	1.000	-1	79	0	O10(6/1/3)		-0.6
Total	2	34	56	10	9	0	1	1	4	3	0	6	.161	.203	.250	27	-6	0-0	.938	-1	69	137	O23(12/1/10)		-0.8
CALZADO, NAPOLEON			Napolean	B2.9.1977	Santo Domingo, D.R.	BR/TR/6-3/200	d5.29																		
2005	Bal A	4	5	0	1	0	0	0	0	0	0	2	.200	.200	.200	7	-1	0-0	1.000	-0	99	0	O2(1/1/0)		-0.1
CAMELLI, HANK			Henry Richard	B12.12.1914	Gloucester MA	D7.14.1996	Wellesley MA	BR/TR/5-11/190	d10.3																
1943	Pit N	1	3	0	0	0	0	0	0	0	0	0	.000	.250	.000	-24	0	0	1.000	0	0	0	/C		0.0
1944	Pit N	63	125	14	37	5	1	1	10	18	0	12	.296	.385	.376	110	2	0	.959	2	100	85	C61		0.7
1945	Pit N	1	2	0	0	0	0	0	0	0	0	0	.000	.333	.000	-3	0	0	1.000	0	0	0	/C		0.0
1946	Pit N	42	96	8	20	2	2	0	5	8	0	9	.208	.269	.271	52	-6	0	.971	1	69	117	C39		-0.4
1947	Bos N	52	150	10	29	8	1	1	11	18	0	18	.193	.280	.280	50	-11	0	.977	2	83	90	C51		-0.6
Total	5	159	376	33	86	15	4	2	26	46	0	39	.229	.313	.306	70	-15	0	.970	5	84	93	C153		-0.3
CAMERON, JACK			John Stanley "Happy Jack"	B9.22.1884	Sydney NS, Can.	D7.12.1963	Charlotte NC	BR/TR/5-10/170	d9.13																
1906	Bos N	18	61	3	11	0	0	0	4	2	0		.180	.206	.180	21	-6	0	.852	-1	150	193	O16(15/0/1),P2		-0.8
CAMERON, MIKE			Michael Terrance	B1.8.1973	LaGrange GA	BR/TR/6-2/190*	[ChiA91 18/488]	d8.27																
1995	Chi A	28	38	4	7	2	0	1	2	3-0	0	15	.184	.244	.316	46	-3	0-0	1.000	1	111	108	O28(0/3/26)		-0.3
1996	Chi A	11	11	1	1	0	0	0	0	1-0	0	3	.091	.167	.091	-34	-2	0-1	1.000	-0	79	0	O8(2/4/5),D2		-0.3
1997	Chi A	116	379	63	98	18	3	14	55	55-1	5	105	.259	.356	.433	109	6	23-2	.985	13	124	88	O112(0/102/37),D4		2.2
1998	Chi A	141	396	53	83	16	5	8	43	37-0	6	101	.210	.285	.336	62	-23	27-11	.988	2	106	83	O138(0/136/2)		-1.7
1999	Cin N	146	542	93	139	34	9	21	66	80-5	6	145	.256	.357	.469	104	3	38-12	.979	-1	104	88	O146C		0.8
2000	†Sea A	155	543	96	145	28	4	19	78	78-0	3	143	.267	.365	.438	105	6	24-7	.985	1	106	68	O155(0/155/1)		1.0
2001	†Sea A★	150	540	99	144	30	4	25	110	69-3	10	155	.267	.353	.480	125	21	34-5	.986	5	106	96	O149C/D		3.2
2002	Sea A	158	545	84	130	26	5	25	80	79-3	7	176	.239	.340	.442	110	9	31-8	.988	3	107	76	O155C		1.6
2003	Sea A	147	534	74	135	31	5	18	76	70-1	5	137	.253	.344	.431	109	8	17-7	.992	16	126	45	O147C		2.5
2004	NY N	140	493	76	114	30	1	30	76	57-2	8	143	.231	.319	.479	106	3	22-6	.978	2	106	86	O135C		0.8

YEAR	TM LG	G	AB	R	H	2B	3B	HR	RBI	BB-IB	HP	SO	AVG	OBP	SLG	AOPS	ABR	SB-CS	FA	FR	RNG	THR	GAMES AT POSITION	DL	BFW
2005	NY N	76	308	47	84	23	2	12	39	29-0	4	85	.273	.342	.477	115	6	13-1	.962	-3	98	68	O76(0/10/68)	84	0.3
Total	11	1268	4329	690	1080	238	39	173	625	558-12	60	1198	.249	.340	.442	105	34	229-60	.985	38	110	78	O1249(2/1142/139),D7	84	10.1

CAMILLI, DOLPH Adolph Louis B4.23.1907 San Francisco CA D10.21.1997 San Mateo CA BL/TL/5-10/185 d9.9 s-Doug

YEAR	TM LG	G	AB	R	H	2B	3B	HR	RBI	BB-IB	HP	SO	AVG	OBP	SLG	AOPS	ABR	SB-CS	FA	FR	RNG	THR	GAMES AT POSITION	DL	BFW
1933	Chi N	16	58	8	13	2	1	2	7	4	0	11	.224	.274	.397	90	-1	3	.994	2	130	166	1b16		-0.1
1934	Chi N	32	120	17	33	8	0	4	19	.5	2	25	.275	.315	.442	102	0	1	.988	2	123	108	1b32		-0.1
	Phi N	102	378	52	100	20	3	12	68	48	2	69	.265	.350	.429	95	-2	3	.985	-3	92	97	1b102		-1.4
	Year	134	498	69	133	28	3	16	87	53	4	94	.267	.342	.432	96	-2	4	.986	-1	99	100	1b134		-1.5
1935	Phi N	156	602	88	157	23	5	25	83	65	3	113	.261	.336	.440	97	-3	9	.987	-2	98	92	1b156		-1.9
1936	Phi N	151	530	106	167	29	13	28	102	116	3	84	.315	.441	.577	156	47	5	.988	-11	77	93	1b150		2.2
1937	Phi N	131	475	101	161	23	7	27	80	90	2	82	.339	.446	.587	165	47	6	.994	4	108	92	1b131		3.8
1938	Bro N	146	509	106	128	25	11	24	100	119	0	101	.251	.393	.485	137	30	6	.995	-1	95	104	1b145		1.5
1939	Bro N★	157	565	105	164	30	12	26	104	110	4	107	.290	.409	.524	144	38	1	.990	9	122	106	1b157		3.2
1940	Bro N	142	512	92	147	29	13	23	96	89	4	83	.287	.397	.529	145	33	9	.992	-5	84	79	1b140		1.4
1941	†Bro N✱	149	529	92	151	29	6	34	120	104	4	115	.285	.407	.556	162	46	3	.989	1	101	99	1b148		3.3
1942	Bro N	150	524	89	132	23	7	26	109	97	3	85	.252	.372	.471	144	31	10	.992	-1	94	121	1b150		1.7
1943	Bro N	95	353	56	87	15	6	6	43	65	1	48	.246	.365	.374	113	0	2	.992	-1	94	91	1b95		0.3
1945	Bos A	63	198	24	42	5	2	2	19	35	0	38	.212	.330	.288	78	-4	2-0	.991	2	110	132	1b54		-0.5
Total	12	1490	5353	936	1482	261	86	239	950	947	28	961	.277	.388	.492	134	270	60-0	.990	-5	98	100	1b1476		13.4

CAMILLI, DOUG Douglas Joseph B9.22.1936 Philadelphia PA BR/TR/5-11/195(180-195) d9.25 C6 f-Dolph Col Stanford

YEAR	TM LG	G	AB	R	H	2B	3B	HR	RBI	BB-IB	HP	SO	AVG	OBP	SLG	AOPS	ABR	SB-CS	FA	FR	RNG	THR	GAMES AT POSITION	DL	BFW
1960	LA N	6	24	4	8	2	0	1	3	1-0	1	4	.333	.385	.542	141	1	0-0	.980	-0	121	0	C6		0.1
1961	LA N	13	30	3	4	0	0	3	4	1-0	0	9	.133	.161	.433	47	-3	0-0	.986	2	91	57	C12		0.0
1962	LA N	45	88	16	25	5	2	4	22	12-1	0	21	.284	.366	.523	145	6	0-0	.983	-5	82	66	C39		0.1
1963	LA N	49	117	9	19	1	1	3	10	11-6	0	22	.162	.234	.265	47	-9	0-0	.977	3	99	29	C47		-0.4
1964	LA N	50	123	1	22	3	0	0	8-1		0	19	.179	.226	.203	25	-12	0-0	.990	2	128	109	C46		-0.9
1965	Was A	75	193	13	37	6	1	3	18	16-2	1	34	.192	.257	.280	53	-12	0-0	.980	1	123	127	C59		-0.9
1966	Was A	44	107	5	22	4	0	2	8	3-0	1	19	.206	.234	.299	53	-7	0-0	.990	2	127	167	C39	66	-0.4
1967	Was A	30	82	5	15	1	0	2	5	4-0	0	16	.183	.221	.268	46	-6	0-0	.992	-5	76	117	C24		-1.0
1969	Was A	1	3	0	1	0	0	0	0	0-0	0	2	.333	.333	.333	92	0	0-0	1.000	0	0	0	/C		0.0
Total	9	313	767	56	153	22	4	18	80	56-10	3	146	.199	.256	.309	61	-42	0-0	.984	-2	109	99	C273	66	-3.4

CAMILLI, LOU Louis Steven B9.24.1946 El Paso TX BB/TR/5-10/170* [CleA67 S3/55] d8.9 Col Texas A&M-Commerce

YEAR	TM LG	G	AB	R	H	2B	3B	HR	RBI	BB-IB	HP	SO	AVG	OBP	SLG	AOPS	ABR	SB-CS	FA	FR	RNG	THR	GAMES AT POSITION	DL	BFW
1969	Cle A	13	14	0	0	0	0	0	0	0-0	0	3	.000	.000	.000	-97	-4	0-0	1.000	2	91	83	3b13		-0.2
1970	Cle A	16	15	0	0	0	0	0	0	2-0	0	2	.000	.118	.000	-62	-3	0-0	1.000	1	143	0	S3,2b2/3		-0.3
1971	Cle A	39	81	5	16	2	0	0	0	8-1	0	10	.198	.270	.222	37	-7	0-0	.938	-3	95	50	S23,2b16		-0.8
1972	Cle A	39	41	2	6	2	0	0	3	3-0	0	8	.146	.205	.195	19	-4	0-0	1.000	-1	79	91	S8,2b2		-0.5
Total	4	107	151	7	22	4	0	0	3	13-1	0	23	.146	.213	.172	11	-18	0-0	.951	-2	94	56	S34,2b20,3b14		-1.8

CAMINITI, KEN Kenneth Gene B4.21.1963 Hanford CA D10.10.2004 Bronx NY BB/TR/6-0/200* [HouN84 3/71] d7.16 Col San Jose St.

YEAR	TM LG	G	AB	R	H	2B	3B	HR	RBI	BB-IB	HP	SO	AVG	OBP	SLG	AOPS	ABR	SB-CS	FA	FR	RNG	THR	GAMES AT POSITION	DL	BFW
1987	Hou N	63	203	10	50	7	1	3	23	12-1	0	44	.246	.287	.335	67	-10	0-0	.949	2	92	127	3b61		-0.9
1988	Hou N	30	83	5	15	2	0	1	7	5-0	0	18	.181	.225	.241	36	-7	0-0	.948	1	96	57	3b28		-0.9
1989	Hou N	161	585	71	149	31	3	10	72	51-9	3	93	.255	.316	.369	99	-1	4-1	.954	11	108	103	3b160		1.2
1990	Hou N	153	541	52	131	20	2	4	51	48-7	0	97	.242	.302	.309	71	-22	9-4	.945	-9	93	108	3b149		-3.1
1991	Hou N	152	574	65	145	30	3	13	80	46-7	5	85	.253	.312	.383	100	-1	4-5	.948	14	107	114	3b152		1.3
1992	Hou N	135	506	68	149	31	2	13	62	44-13	1	68	.294	.350	.441	128	18	10-4	.966	-7	88	88	3b129	22	1.3
1993	Hou N	143	543	75	142	31	0	13	75	49-10	0	88	.262	.321	.390	93	-6	8-5	.942	11	103	106	3b143		0.6
1994	Hou N★	111	406	63	115	28	2	18	75	43-13	2	71	.283	.352	.495	125	14	4-3	.969	-5	103	102	3b108		1.9
1995	SD N	143	526	74	159	33	0	26	94	69-8	1	94	.302	.380	.513	138	30	12-5	.936	14	106	122	3b143		4.5
1996	†SD N★	146	546	109	178	37	2	40	130	78-16	4	99	.326	.408	.621	176	62	11-5	.954	15	112	128	3b145	15	7.4
1997	SD N★	137	486	92	141	28	0	26	90	80-9	3	118	.290	.389	.508	143	33	11-2	.941	16	121	84	3b133	21	5.0
1998	†SD N	131	452	87	114	29	0	29	82	71-4	4	108	.252	.353	.509	134	23	6-2	.931	-9	90	80	3b126	86	1.4
1999	†Hou N	78	273	45	78	11	3	13	56	46-4	1	58	.286	.386	.476	120	10	6-2	.932	4	103	150	3b58	107	0.7
2000	Hou N	59	208	42	63	13	0	15	45	42-8	1	37	.303	.419	.596	139	14	3-0	.915	-7	85	77	3b53	15	-0.3
2001	Tex A	54	185	24	43	8	1	9	25	22-2	2	41	.232	.318	.432	93	-2	0-0	.940	-1	97	105	3b53		-1.2
	†Atl N	64	171	12	38	9	0	6	16	21-1	0	44	.222	.306	.380	76	-6	0-1	.977	-3	80	91	1b33,3b13/D		-1.2
Total	15	1760	6288	894	1710	348	17	239	983	727-112	29	1163	.272	.347	.447	116	149	88-39	.946	53	102	106	3b1676,1b33/D	266	20.4

CAMP, HOWIE Howard Lee "Red" B7.1.1893 Hopeful AL D5.8.1960 Eastaboga AL BL/TR/5-9/169 d9.19 Mil 1918

YEAR	TM LG	G	AB	R	H	2B	3B	HR	RBI	BB-IB	HP	SO	AVG	OBP	SLG	AOPS	ABR	SB-CS	FA	FR	RNG	THR	GAMES AT POSITION	DL	BFW
1917	NY A	5	21	3	6	1	0	0	4		0		.286	.318	.333	98	-0		.857	0	82	263	O5(0/4/1)		0.0

CAMP, LEW Robert Plantagenet Llewellan B2.23.1868 Columbus OH D10.1.1948 Omaha NE BL/TR/6-0/175 d8.26 b-Kid

YEAR	TM LG	G	AB	R	H	2B	3B	HR	RBI	BB-IB	HP	SO	AVG	OBP	SLG	AOPS	ABR	SB-CS	FA	FR	RNG	THR	GAMES AT POSITION	DL	BFW
1892	StL N	42	145	19	30	3	1	2	13	17	1	27	.207	.294	.283	79	-3	12	.780	-13	78	68	3b39,O3(0/2/1)		-1.5
1893	Chi N	38	156	37	41	7	7	2	17	19	1	19	.263	.347	.436	109	1	30	.847	-5	79	71	3b16,O11C,2b9,S3		-0.3
1894	Chi N	8	33	1	6	2	0	0	1	1	0	6	.182	.206	.242	7	-5	0	.830	-4	68	92	2b8		-0.7
Total	3	88	334	57	77	12	8	4	31	37	2	52	.231	.311	.350	85	-7	42	.801	-22	78	69	3b55,2b17,O14(0/13/1),S3		-2.5

CAMPANELLA, ROY Roy B11.19.1921 Philadelphia PA D6.26.1993 Woodland Hills CA BR/TR/5-8/200(200-215) d4.20 HF1969 Negro Lg 1937-45 [DL 1958 LA N 168]

YEAR	TM LG	G	AB	R	H	2B	3B	HR	RBI	BB-IB	HP	SO	AVG	OBP	SLG	AOPS	ABR	SB-CS	FA	FR	RNG	THR	GAMES AT POSITION	DL	BFW
1948	Bro N	83	279	32	72	11	3	9	45	36	1	45	.258	.345	.416	102	1	3	.981	8	130	146	C78		1.2
1949	†Bro N★	130	436	65	125	22	2	22	82	67	3	36	.287	.385	.498	130	20	3	.985	1	140	110	C127		3.1
1950	Bro N★	126	437	70	123	19	3	31	89	55	2	51	.281	.364	.551	134	21	1	.985	-3	126	92	C123		2.4
1951	Bro N★	143	505	90	164	33	1	33	108	53	4	51	.325	.393	.590	158	41	1-2	.986	12	254	107	C140		5.9
1952	†Bro N★	128	468	73	126	18	1	22	97	57	3	59	.269	.352	.453	120	13	8-4	.994	-3	147	101	C122		1.8
1953	†Bro N★	144	519	103	162	26	3	41	142	67	6	58	.312	.395	.611	154	41	4-2	.989	5	166	98	C140		5.0
1954	Bro N★	111	397	43	82	14	3	19	51	42	2	49	.207	.285	.401	74	-17	1-4	.989	-1	148	109	C111		-1.3
1955	†Bro N★	123	446	81	142	20	1	32	107	56-9	6	41	.318	.395	.583	153	35	2-3	.992	4	118	73	C121		4.3
1956	†Bro N★	124	388	39	85	6	1	20	73	66-15	1	61	.219	.333	.394	88	-6	1-0	.989	4	134	88	C121		0.5
1957	Bro N	103	330	31	80	9	0	13	62	34-6	4	50	.242	.316	.388	81	-8	1-0	.993	15	136	108	C100		1.2
Total	10	1215	4205	627	1161	178	18	242	856	533-30	30	501	.276	.360	.500	123	141	25-15	.988	46	153	102	C1183	168	24.1

CAMPANERIS, BERT Dagoberto (Blanco) "Campy" (b Dagoberto Campaneria (Blanco)) B3.9.1942 Pueblo Nuevo, Cuba BR/TR/5-10/160* d7.23 OF(68/2/1)

YEAR	TM LG	G	AB	R	H	2B	3B	HR	RBI	BB-IB	HP	SO	AVG	OBP	SLG	AOPS	ABR	SB-CS	FA	FR	RNG	THR	GAMES AT POSITION	DL	BFW
1964	KC A	67	269	27	69	14	3	4	22	15-0	4	41	.257	.306	.375	86	-5	10-2	.981	-7	89	59	S38,O27L,3b6		-0.9
1965	KC A	144	578	67	156	23	12	6	42	41-0	9	71	.270	.326	.382	103	1	51-19	.938	-9	93	82	S109,O39(38/2/1)/PC123		0.3
1966	KC A	142	573	82	153	29	10	5	42	25-1	5	72	.267	.302	.379	98	-3	52-10	.951	-15	89	92	S138		0.2
1967	KC A	147	601	85	149	29	6	3	32	36-2	7	82	.248	.297	.331	89	-9	55-16	.954	-13	89	92	S145		-0.3
1968	Oak A★	159	642	87	177	25	9	4	38	50-2	4	69	.276	.330	.361	115	10	62-22	.956	8	102	106	S155,O3L		4.2
1969	Oak A	135	547	71	142	15	2	2	25	30-4	4	62	.260	.302	.305	73	-21	62-8	.967	-3	103	100	S125		0.2
1970	Oak A	147	603	97	168	28	4	22	64	36-1	4	73	.279	.321	.448	114	9	42-10	.973	-2	99	115	S143		3.4
1971	†Oak A★	134	569	80	143	18	4	5	47	29-1	2	64	.251	.287	.323	75	-21	34-7	.960	3	98	120	S133	20	0.4
1972	†Oak A☆	149	625	85	150	25	2	8	32	32-0	2	88	.240	.278	.325	80	-18	52-14	.977	-5	101	113	S148		1.6
1973	†Oak A★	151	601	89	150	17	6	4	46	50-1	4	79	.250	.308	.318	81	-16	34-10	.969	-3	101	103	S149		0.3
1974	†Oak A★	134	527	77	153	18	8	2	41	47-2	0	81	.290	.347	.366	112	8	34-15	.966	-2	98	104	S133/D	15	2.4
1975	†Oak A	137	509	69	135	15	3	4	46	50-2	1	71	.265	.337	.330	92	-5	24-12	.962	-16	93	82	S137		-0.4
1976	Oak A	149	536	67	137	14	1	1	52	63-0	2	80	.256	.331	.291	88	-5	54-12	.969	-1	106	79	S149		1.9
1977	Tex A★	150	552	77	140	19	7	5	46	47-1	4	66	.254	.314	.341	78	-17	27-20	.968	26	113	113	S149	18	2.3
1978	Tex A	98	269	30	50	5	3	1	17	20-0	1	36	.186	.245	.238	37	-23	22-4	.954	4	104	93	S89,D4		-0.7
1979	Tex A	8	9	2	1	0	0	0	0	1-0	0	1	.111	.200	.111	-14	-1	1-0	.962	3	117	219	S8		0.2
	†Cal A	85	239	27	56	4	4	0	15	19-0	2	34	.234	.294	.285	59	-14	12-4	.957	11	102	142	S82/D		0.6
	Year	93	248	29	57	4	4	0	15	20-0	2	35	.230	.290	.278	56	-16	13-4	.957	14	103	146	S90/D		0.8
1980	Cal A	77	210	32	53	8	1	2	18	14-0	1	33	.252	.300	.329	74	-6	10-5	.957	-9	86	99	S64/2D		-1.1
1981	Cal A	55	82	11	21	2	1	1	10	5-0	0	10	.256	.295	.341	83	-2	5-2	.900	-8	83	106	3b45,S3,2b2		-0.2
1983	NY A	60	143	19	46	5	0	1	11	8-0	0	9	.322	.355	.357	100	0	6-7	.964	-1	99	101	S2097,3b76,O69L,2b36,D8/1CP	15	-0.3
Total	19	2328	8684	1181	2249	313	86	79	646	618-15	52	972	.259	.311	.342	89	-137	649-199	.964	-24	99	101	S2097,3b76,O69L,2b36,D8/1CP	68	13.4

CAMPANIS, AL Alexander Sebastian (b Alessandro Campani) B11.2.1916 Kos, Dodecanese Islands D6.21.1998 Fullerton CA BB/TR/6-0/185 d9.23 Mil 1944-45 s-Jim Col NYU

YEAR	TM LG	G	AB	R	H	2B	3B	HR	RBI	BB-IB	HP	SO	AVG	OBP	SLG	AOPS	ABR	SB-CS	FA	FR	RNG	THR	GAMES AT POSITION	DL	BFW
																									-0.1
1943	Bro N	7	20	3	2	0	0	0	0	4	0	5	.100	.250	.100	3	-2	0	1.000	1	90	67	2b7		

CAMPANIS, JIM James Alexander B2.9.1944 New York NY BR/TR/6-0/195* d9.20 f-Al

YEAR	TM LG	G	AB	R	H	2B	3B	HR	RBI	BB-IB	HP	SO	AVG	OBP	SLG	AOPS	ABR	SB-CS	FA	FR	RNG	THR	GAMES AT POSITION	DL	BFW
1966	LA N	1	1	0	0	0	0	0	0	0-0	0	0	.000	.000	.000	-99	0	0-0	1.000	0	0	0	/C		0.0
1967	LA N	41	62	3	10	1	0	2	2	9-1	0	14	.161	.268	.274	60	-3	0-0	.990	1	69	54	C23		-0.2
1968	LA N	4	11	0	1	0	0	0	0	1-0	0	2	.091	.167	.091	-23	-2	0-0	.960	0	51	206	C4		-0.2
1969	KC A	30	83	4	13	5	0	0	5	5-1	0	19	.157	.202	.217	18	-9	0-0	.982	1	67	78	C26		-0.8
1970	KC A	31	54	6	7	0	0	2	2	4-1	0	14	.130	.203	.241	22	-6	0-0	.986	-3	36	162	C13/OR		-0.9
1973	Pit N	6	6	0	1	0	0	0	0	0-0	0	0	.167	.167	.167	-8	-1	0-0	—	0			/H		-0.1
Total	6	113	217	13	32	6	0	4	9	19-3	1	49	.147	.218	.230	27	-21	0-0	.983	-1	59	99	C67/OR		-2.2

CAMPAU, COUNT Charles Columbus B10.17.1863 Detroit MI D4.3.1938 New Orleans LA BL/TR/5-11/160 d7.7 M1

YEAR	TM LG	G	AB	R	H	2B	3B	HR	RBI	BB-IB	HP	SO	AVG	OBP	SLG	AOPS	ABR	SB-CS	FA	FR	RNG	THR	GAMES AT POSITION	DL	BFW
1888	Det N	70	251	28	51	5	3	1	18	19	0	36	.203	.259	.259	65	-10	27	.933	-4	85	138	O70R		-1.4
1890	StL AA	75	314	68	101	9	12	9	75	26	0		.322	.374	.513	141	12	36	.934	2	106	36	O74(39/2/33)/31M		1.1
1894	Was N	2	7	1	1	0	0	0	0	1	0	4	.143	.250	.143	-3	-1	0	1.000	-0	0	0	O2L		-0.1
Total	3	147	572	97	153	14	15	10	93	46	0	40	.267	.322	.397	109	1	63	.934	-2	95	84	O146(41/2/103)/13		-0.4

CAMPBELL, VIN Arthur Vincent B1.30.1888 St.Louis MO D11.16.1969 Towson MD BL/TR/6-0/185 d6.6 Col Vanderbilt

YEAR	TM LG	G	AB	R	H	2B	3B	HR	RBI	BB-IB	HP	SO	AVG	OBP	SLG	AOPS	ABR	SB-CS	FA	FR	RNG	THR	GAMES AT POSITION	DL	BFW
1908	Chi N	1	1	0	0	0	0	0	0	0	0		.000	.000	.000	-96	0						/H		0.0
1910	Pit N	97	282	42	92	9	5	4	21	26	4	23	.326	.391	.436	133	12	17	.895	-4	100	83	O74(38/17/18)		0.5
1911	Pit N	42	93	12	29	3	1	0	10	8	0	7	.312	.366	.366	101	-0	6	.923	-2	101	38	O21(9/1/11)		-0.2
1912	Bos N	145	624	102	185	32	9	3	48	32	1	44	.296	.334	.391	96	-5	19	.938	-5	99	89	O144C		-2.0
1914	Ind F	134	544	92	173	23	11	7	44	37	6	47	.318	.368	.439	108	-2	26	.925	-8	88	95	O132(1/94/37)		-1.8
1915	New F	127	525	78	163	18	10	1	44	29	5	35	.310	.352	.389	115	1	24	.947	-9	87	84	O126(0/12/115)		-1.7
Total	6	546	2069	326	642	85	36	15	167	132	18	156	.310	.357	.408	109	6	92	.929	-27	93	86	O497(48/268/181)		-5.2

CAMPBELL, BRUCE Bruce Douglas B10.20.1909 Chicago IL D6.17.1995 Ft.Myers Beach FL BL/TR/6-1/185 d9.12 Mil 1942-45

YEAR	TM LG	G	AB	R	H	2B	3B	HR	RBI	BB-IB	HP	SO	AVG	OBP	SLG	AOPS	ABR	SB-CS	FA	FR	RNG	THR	GAMES AT POSITION	DL	BFW
1930	Chi A	5	10	4	5	1	1	0	5	1	0	2	.500	.545	.800	245	2	0-0	1.000	0	128	0	O4L		0.2
1931	Chi A	4	17	4	7	2	0	2	5	0	1	4	.412	.444	.882	256	4	0-0	.900	-0	101	0	O4L		0.3
1932	Chi A	7	18	3	4	1	0	0	2	0	0	2	.222	.222	.278	31	-2	0-1	1.000	-0	81	0	O4(3/0/1)		-0.3
	StL A	139	593	83	169	35	11	14	85	40	6	102	.285	.336	.452	97	-5	7-5	.935	4	107	119	O139R		-0.9
	Year	146	611	86	173	36	11	14	87	40	6	104	.283	.333	.447	95	-6	7-6	.935	6	116	117	O143(3/0/140)		-1.2
1933	StL A	148	567	87	157	38	8	16	106	69	2	77	.277	.357	.457	108	6	10-4	.950	-5	87	134	O144R		-0.6
1934	StL A	138	481	62	134	25	6	9	74	51	2	64	.279	.350	.412	88	-9	5-4	.935	1	97	147	O123R		-1.5
1935	Cle A	80	308	56	100	26	3	7	54	31	2	33	.325	.390	.497	126	12	2-1	.992	-7	88	32	O75R		0.1
1936	Cle A	76	172	35	64	15	2	6	30	19	2	17	.372	.440	.587	150	14	2-1	.960	0	95	121	O47R		1.1
1937	Cle A	134	448	82	135	42	11	4	61	67	0	49	.301	.392	.471	116	13	4-5	.978	-0	91	129	O123R		0.4
1938	Cle A	133	511	90	148	27	12	12	72	53	3	57	.290	.360	.460	106	3	11-7	.967	-1	97	124	O122R		-0.4
1939	Cle A	130	450	84	129	23	13	8	72	67	3	48	.287	.383	.449	116	12	7-6	.942	-4	87	134	O115R		0.0
1940	†Det A	103	297	56	84	15	5	8	44	45	2	28	.283	.381	.448	104	3	2-7	.959	-1	97	108	O74R		-0.4
1941	Det A	141	512	72	141	28	10	15	93	68	3	67	.275	.364	.457	105	4	3-3	.976	-8	95	41	O133R		-1.2
1942	Was A	122	378	41	105	17	5	5	63	37	1	34	.278	.344	.389	107	3	0-6	.955	0	109	63	O87(20/0/68)		-0.4
Total	13	1360	4762	759	1382	295	87	106	766	548	27	584	.290	.367	.455	108	60	53-50	.956	-20	95	107	O1194(31/0/1164)		-3.6

CAMPBELL, SOUP Clarence B3.7.1915 Sparta VA D2.16.2000 Sparta VA BL/TR/6-1/188 d4.21 Mil 1942-46 Col Hampden-Sydney

YEAR	TM LG	G	AB	R	H	2B	3B	HR	RBI	BB-IB	HP	SO	AVG	OBP	SLG	AOPS	ABR	SB-CS	FA	FR	RNG	THR	GAMES AT POSITION	DL	BFW
1940	Cle A	35	62	8	14	1	0	0	2	7	0	12	.226	.304	.242	45	-5	0-0	1.000	1	121	0	O16(8/5/4)		-0.5
1941	Cle A	104	328	36	82	10	4	3	35	31	1	21	.250	.317	.332	75	-12	1-9	.981	0	101	92	O78(20/59/0)		-1.7
Total	2	139	390	44	96	11	4	3	37	38	1	33	.246	.315	.318	70	-17	1-9	.984	1	104	80	O94(28/64/4)		-2.2

CAMPBELL, DAVE David Wilson B1.14.1942 Manistee MI BR/TR/6-0/185* d9.17 Col Michigan

YEAR	TM LG	G	AB	R	H	2B	3B	HR	RBI	BB-IB	HP	SO	AVG	OBP	SLG	AOPS	ABR	SB-CS	FA	FR	RNG	THR	GAMES AT POSITION	DL	BFW
1967	Det A	2	2	0	0	0	0	0	0	0-0	0	1	1.000	.000	.000	-97	0	0-0	.500	-0	0	0	/1		-0.1
1968	Det A	9	8	1	1	0	0	1	2	1-0	0	3	.125	.222	.500	111	0	0-0	1.000	-1	64	113	2b5		0.0
1969	Det N	32	39	4	4	1	0	0	2	4-0	1	15	.103	.205	.128	-5	-5	0-1	.967	-2	41	137	1b13,2b5/3		-0.9
1970	SD N	154	581	71	127	28	2	12	40	40-2	1	115	.219	.268	.336	64	-32	18-6	.974	18	111	96	2b153		-0.2
1971	SD N	108	365	38	83	14	2	7	29	37-0	0	75	.227	.299	.334	84	-8	9-6	.968	2	111	95	2b69,3b40,S4,1b2,O2L		-0.3
1972	SD N	33	100	6	24	5	0	0	3	11-2	0	12	.240	.315	.290	79	-3	0-4	.988	1	101	53	3b31/2	97	-0.4
1973	SD N	33	98	2	22	3	0	0	8	7-1	0	15	.224	.271	.255	52	-6	1-1	.979	4	103	107	2b27,1b3,3b2		-0.2
	StL N	13	21	1	0	0	0	0	1	1-0	0	6	.000	.043	.000	-86	-5	0-0	.933	-3	68	41	2b6		-0.8
	Hou N	9	15	1	4	2	0	0	2	0-0	1	4	.267	.267	.400	83	0	0-0	1.000	2	161	146	3b5,1b2/OL		0.1
	Year	55	134	4	26	5	0	0	11	8-1	0	25	.194	.234	.231	33	-12	1-1	.975	3	98	98	2b33,3b7,1b5/OL		-0.9
1974	Hou N	35	23	4	2	1	0	0	2	1-0	0	8	.087	.125	.130	-30	-4	1-0	.895	3	102	198	2b9,1b6,3b2/OL	44	-0.2
Total	8	428	1252	128	267	54	4	20	89	102-5	2	254	.213	.272	.311	63	-63	29-18	.971	22	109	96	2b275,3b81,1b27,O4L,S4	141	-3.0

CAMPBELL, JIM James Robert B6.24.1937 Palo Alto CA BR/TR/6-0/190* d7.17

YEAR	TM LG	G	AB	R	H	2B	3B	HR	RBI	BB-IB	HP	SO	AVG	OBP	SLG	AOPS	ABR	SB-CS	FA	FR	RNG	THR	GAMES AT POSITION	DL	BFW
1962	Hou N	27	86	6	19	3	0	0	6	6-0	1	23	.221	.272	.372	77	-3	0-0	.970	3	70	133	C25		0.1
1963	Hou N	55	158	9	35	3	0	4	19	10-3	0	40	.222	.268	.316	72	-6	0-0	.979	-3	77	86	C42		-0.8
Total	2	82	244	15	54	7	0	7	25	16-3	1	63	.221	.269	.336	74	-9	0-0	.975	-0	74	103	C67		-0.7

CAMPBELL, JIM James Robert B1.10.1943 Hartsville SC BL/TR/6-0/205 d4.11

YEAR	TM LG	G	AB	R	H	2B	3B	HR	RBI	BB-IB	HP	SO	AVG	OBP	SLG	AOPS	ABR	SB-CS	FA	FR	RNG	THR	GAMES AT POSITION	DL	BFW
1970	StL N	13	13	0	3	0	0	0	1	0-0	0	3	.231	.231	.231	23	-1	0-0	—	0			/H		-0.1

CAMPBELL, JOE Joseph Earl B3.10.1944 Louisville KY BR/TR/6-1/175 [NYN65 26/808] d5.3 Col Morehead St.

YEAR	TM LG	G	AB	R	H	2B	3B	HR	RBI	BB-IB	HP	SO	AVG	OBP	SLG	AOPS	ABR	SB-CS	FA	FR	RNG	THR	GAMES AT POSITION	DL	BFW
1967	Chi N	1	3	0	0	0	0	0	0	0-0	0	3	.000	.000	.000	-96	-1	0-0	—	-0	0	0	/OR		-0.1

CAMPBELL, HUTCH Marc Thaddeus B11.29.1884 Punxsutawney PA D2.13.1946 New Bethlehem PA BB/TR/5-9/155 d9.30 Col Lock Haven

YEAR	TM LG	G	AB	R	H	2B	3B	HR	RBI	BB-IB	HP	SO	AVG	OBP	SLG	AOPS	ABR	SB-CS	FA	FR	RNG	THR	GAMES AT POSITION	DL	BFW
1907	Pit N	2	4	0	1	0	0	0	1	0	0	1	.250	.400	.250	102	0	0	.889	0	132	0	S2		0.0

CAMPBELL, MAT Mathew B8.1.1850 , Ireland D1.12.1926 Scotch Plains NJ d4.28 b-Hugh

YEAR	TM LG	G	AB	R	H	2B	3B	HR	RBI	BB-IB	HP	SO	AVG	OBP	SLG	AOPS	ABR	SB-CS	FA	FR	RNG	THR	GAMES AT POSITION	DL	BFW
1873	Res NA	21	84	9	12	2	0	0	2	2		6	.143	.163	.167	-2	-10	1-0	.938	-2	75	89	1b18,S3/OR		-0.8

CAMPBELL, PAUL Paul McLaughlin B9.1.1917 Paw Creek NC BL/TL/5-10/185* d4.15 Mil 1943-45

YEAR	TM LG	G	AB	R	H	2B	3B	HR	RBI	BB-IB	HP	SO	AVG	OBP	SLG	AOPS	ABR	SB-CS	FA	FR	RNG	THR	GAMES AT POSITION	DL	BFW
1941	Bos A	1	0	0	0	0	0	0	0	0	0		—	—	—		0	0-0	—	0			/R		0.0
1942	Bos A	26	15	4	1	0	0	0	1	0	0	5	.067	.125	.067	-44	-3	1-0	1.000	0	162	0	O4C		-0.3
1946	†Bos A	28	26	3	3	1	0	0	2	0	0	7	.115	.179	.154	-6	-4	0-0	1.000	-0	50	81	1b5		-0.4
1948	Det A	59	83	15	22	1	1	1	11	1	0	10	.265	.274	.337	60	-5	0-0	.969	2	164	71	1b27		-0.4
1949	Det A	87	255	38	71	15	4	3	30	24	1	32	.278	.343	.404	97	-2	3-3	.988	-3	83	108	1b74		-0.7
1950	Det A	3	1	0	0	0	0	0	0	0	0	0	.000	.000	.000	-97	0	0-0	—	0			/H		0.0
Total	6	204	380	61	97	17	5	4	41	28	1	54	.255	.308	.358	76	-14	4-3	.984	-1	98	99	1b106,O4C		-1.8

CAMPBELL, RON Ronald Thomas B4.5.1940 Chattanooga TN BR/TR/6-1/180* d9.1 Col Tennessee Wesleyan

YEAR	TM LG	G	AB	R	H	2B	3B	HR	RBI	BB-IB	HP	SO	AVG	OBP	SLG	AOPS	ABR	SB-CS	FA	FR	RNG	THR	GAMES AT POSITION	DL	BFW
1964	Chi N	26	92	7	25	6	1	1	10	1-0	0	21	.272	.277	.391	83	-2	0-1	.941	8	134	100	2b26		0.8
1965	Chi N	2	2	0	0	0	0	0	0	0-0	0	0	.000	.000	.000	-98	-1	0-0	—	0			/H		-0.1
1966	Chi N	24	60	4	13	1	0	0	4	6-2	0	5	.217	.284	.233	46	-4	1-1	.980	4	133	104	S11,3b7		0.0
Total	3	52	154	11	38	7	1	1	14	7-2	0	26	.247	.276	.325	67	-7	1-2	.941	12	134	100	2b26,S11,3b7		0.7

CAMPBELL, SAM Samuel B Philadelphia PA d10.11

YEAR	TM LG	G	AB	R	H	2B	3B	HR	RBI	BB-IB	HP	SO	AVG	OBP	SLG	AOPS	ABR	SB-CS	FA	FR	RNG	THR	GAMES AT POSITION	DL	BFW
1890	Phi AA	2	5	0	0	0	0	0	0	1	0		.000	.167	.000	-51	-1	0	.833	-1	25	0	2b2		-0.2

CAMPBELL, GILLY William Gilthorpe B2.13.1908 Kansas City KS D2.21.1973 Los Angeles CA BL/TR/5-7.5/182 d4.25

YEAR	TM LG	G	AB	R	H	2B	3B	HR	RBI	BB-IB	HP	SO	AVG	OBP	SLG	AOPS	ABR	SB-CS	FA	FR	RNG	THR	GAMES AT POSITION	DL	BFW
1933	Chi N	46	89	11	25	3	1	1	10	7	2	4	.281	.347	.371	105	1	3	.949	-1	142	83	C20		0.1
1935	Cin N	88	218	26	56	7	0	3	30	42	1	7	.257	.379	.330	95	1	3	.986	-1	90	117	C66,1b5/OL		0.3
1936	Cin N	89	235	28	63	13	1	1	40	43	1	14	.268	.384	.345	104	4	2	.984	3	97	119	C71/1		1.1
1937	Cin N	18	40	3	11	2	0	0	2	5	0	1	.275	.356	.325	90	0	0	.967	-0	86	117	C17		0.0
1938	Bro N	54	126	10	31	5	0	0	11	19	2	9	.246	.354	.286	76	-3	0	.958	-1	82	121	C44		-0.1
Total	5	295	708	78	186	30	2	5	93	116	6	35	.263	.371	.332	96	3	5	.975	0	95	113	C218,1b6/OL		1.4

CAMPOS, FRANK Francisco Jose (Lopez) B5.11.1924 Havana, Cuba BL/TL/5-11/180* d9.11 [DL 1954 Was A 64]

YEAR	TM LG	G	AB	R	H	2B	3B	HR	RBI	BB-IB	HP	SO	AVG	OBP	SLG	AOPS	ABR	SB-CS	FA	FR	RNG	THR	GAMES AT POSITION	DL	BFW
1951	Was A	8	26	4	11	3	0	0	1	1	0	1	.423	.423	.615	182	3	0-0	1.000	-1	74	0	O7R		0.2
1952	Was A	53	112	9	29	6	1	0	8	1	2	13	.259	.280	.330	71	-5	0-0	.978	-1	104	0	O23(13/1/10)		-0.7

YEAR	TM LG	G	AB	R	H	2B	3B	HR	RBI	BB-IB	HP	SO	AVG	OBP	SLG	AOPS	ABR	SB-CS	FA	FR	RNG	THR	GAMES AT POSITION	DL	BFW
1953	Was A	10	9	0	1	0	0	0	2	1	0	0	.111	.200	.111	-14	-1	0-0	—	0			/H		-0.1
Total	3	71	147	13	41	9	2	0	13	2	2	14	.279	.298	.367	86	-3	0-0	.981	-2	99	0	O30(13/1/17)	64	-0.6

CAMPUSANO, SIL Silvestre (Diaz) B12.31.1965 Santo Domingo, D.R. BR/TR/6-0/175(160-190) d4.4

YEAR	TM LG	G	AB	R	H	2B	3B	HR	RBI	BB-IB	HP	SO	AVG	OBP	SLG	AOPS	ABR	SB-CS	FA	FR	RNG	THR	GAMES AT POSITION	DL	BFW
1988	Tor A	73	142	14	31	10	2	2	12	9-0	4	33	.218	.282	.359	78	-4	0-0	.934	-2	96	82	O69(15/35/19),D2	29	-0.7
1990	Phi N	66	85	10	18	1	1	2	9	6-0	1	16	.212	.269	.318	62	-5	1-0	.976	-3	78	78	O47(16/25/7)		-0.8
1991	Phi N	15	35	2	4	0	0	1	2	1-0	0	10	.114	.139	.200	-6	-5	0-0	1.000	1	111	177	O15(1/15/0)	18	-0.5
Total	3	154	262	26	53	11	3	5	23	16-0	5	59	.202	.260	.324	62	-14	1-0	.953	-4	93	94	O131(32/75/26),D2	47	-2.0

CANALE, GEORGE George Anthony B8.11.1965 Memphis TN BL/TR/6-1/190* [MilA86 6/139] d9.3 Col VPI

YEAR	TM LG	G	AB	R	H	2B	3B	HR	RBI	BB-IB	HP	SO	AVG	OBP	SLG	AOPS	ABR	SB-CS	FA	FR	RNG	THR	GAMES AT POSITION	DL	BFW
1989	Mil A	13	26	5	5	1	0	1	3	2-0	0	3	.192	.250	.346	67	-1	0-1	.989	-1	70	58	1b11		-0.3
1990	Mil A	10	13	4	1	1	0	0	0	2-0	0	6	.077	.200	.154	0	-2	0-1	1.000	0	124	24	1b6,D3		-0.2
1991	Mil A	21	34	6	6	2	0	3	10	8-0	0	6	.176	.318	.500	130	1	0-0	.983	2	166	85	1b19		0.3
Total	3	44	73	15	12	4	0	4	13	12-0	0	15	.164	.276	.384	85	-2	0-2	.988	2	127	65	1b36,D3		-0.2

CANATE, WILLIE Emisael William (Librada) B12.11.1971 Maracaibo, Venez BR/TR/6-0/170 d4.16

YEAR	TM LG	G	AB	R	H	2B	3B	HR	RBI	BB-IB	HP	SO	AVG	OBP	SLG	AOPS	ABR	SB-CS	FA	FR	RNG	THR	GAMES AT POSITION	DL	BFW
1993	†Tor A	38	47	12	10	0	0	1	5	3-0	2	15	.213	.309	.277	59	-3	1-1	1.000	2	111	205	O31(17/6/9),D	32	-0.1

CANAVAN, JIM James Edward B11.26.1866 New Bedford MA D5.27.1949 New Bedford MA BR/TR/5-8/160 d4.8 OF(105/10/106)

YEAR	TM LG	G	AB	R	H	2B	3B	HR	RBI	BB-IB	HP	SO	AVG	OBP	SLG	AOPS	ABR	SB-CS	FA	FR	RNG	THR	GAMES AT POSITION	DL	BFW
1891	Cin AA	101	426	74	97	13	14	7	66	27	5	44	.228	.282	.373	80	-16	21	.860	-14	95	85	S101		-2.3
	Mil AA	35	142	33	38	2	4	3	21	16	0	10	.268	.342	.401	94	-3	7	.864	-2	107	44	2b24,S11		-0.3
	Year	136	568	107	135	15	18	10	87	43	5	54	.238	.297	.380	84	-18	28	.860	-15	96	80	S112,2b24		-2.6
1892	Chi N	118	439	48	73	10	11	0	32	48	0	48	.166	.248	.239	47	-29	33	.923	-11	96	86	2b112,O4(1/3/0),S2		-3.3
1893	Cin N	121	461	65	104	13	7	5	64	51	2	20	.226	.305	.317	64	-26	31	.931	-0	76	0	O117(96/6/16),2b5/3		-2.9
1894	Cin N	103	364	81	100	16	10	13	74	64	0	25	.275	.383	.481	104	1	13	.897	-1	64	153	O97(8/1/90),S3,3b2/21		-0.4
1897	Bro N	63	240	25	52	9	3	2	34	26	2		.217	.299	.304	63	-13	9	.909	-17	84	84	2b63		-2.4
Total	5	541	2072	326	464	63	49	30	291	232	9	147	.224	.305	.345	74	-86	114	.917	-45	73	66	O218R,2b205,S117,3b3/1		-11.6

CANCEL, ROBINSON Robinson Castro B5.4.1976 Lajas, PR BR/TR/6-0/195 [MilA94 16/431] d9.3 [DL 2000 Mil N 149]

YEAR	TM LG	G	AB	R	H	2B	3B	HR	RBI	BB-IB	HP	SO	AVG	OBP	SLG	AOPS	ABR	SB-CS	FA	FR	RNG	THR	GAMES AT POSITION	DL	BFW
1999	Mil N	15	44	5	8	2	0	0	5	2-0	1	12	.182	.234	.227	17	-6	0-0	.980	3	83	107	C15		-0.2

CANDAELE, CASEY Casey Todd B1.12.1961 Lompoc CA BB/TR/5-9/165* d6.5 Col Arizona OF(86/78/38)

YEAR	TM LG	G	AB	R	H	2B	3B	HR	RBI	BB-IB	HP	SO	AVG	OBP	SLG	AOPS	ABR	SB-CS	FA	FR	RNG	THR	GAMES AT POSITION	DL	BFW
1986	Mon N	30	104	9	24	4	1	0	6	5-0	0	15	.231	.264	.288	53	-7	3-5	.983	1	103	96	2b24,3b4		-0.6
1987	Mon N	138	449	62	122	23	4	1	23	38-3	2	28	.272	.330	.347	77	-14	7-10	.985	3	106	77	2b68,O67(8/45/16),S25/1		-1.0
1988	Mon N	36	116	9	20	5	1	0	4	10-1	0	11	.172	.238	.233	34	-10	1-0	.988	-1	100	94	2b35		-1.1
	Hou N	21	31	2	5	3	0	0	1	1-0	0	6	.161	.188	.258	28	-3	0-1	1.000	2	121	105	2b10,O5(0/3/2)/3		-0.1
	Year	57	147	11	25	8	1	0	5	11-1	0	17	.170	.228	.238	33	-13	1-1	.990	1	104	96	2b45,O5(0/3/2)/3		-1.2
1990	Hou N	130	262	30	75	8	6	3	22	31-5	1	42	.286	.364	.397	112	5	7-5	1.000	1	111	55	O58(36/12/13),2b49,S13/3		0.6
1991	Hou N	151	461	44	121	20	7	4	50	40-7	0	49	.262	.319	.362	97	-3	9-3	.982	5	100	94	2b109,O26(18/5/4),3b9		0.5
1992	Hou N	135	320	19	68	12	1	1	18	24-3	1	36	.213	.269	.266	56	-19	7-1	.968	3	107	124	S65,3b29,O21(20/1/1),2b9		-0.7
1993	Hou N	75	121	18	29	8	0	1	7	10-0	0	14	.240	.298	.331	70	-5	2-3	1.000	-2	69	57	2b19,O17(4/12/2),S14,3b4	23	-0.7
1996	†Cle A	24	44	8	11	2	0	1	4	1-0	0	9	.250	.267	.364	57	-3	0-0	1.000	4	130	219	2b11,3b3/S		0.3
1997	Cle A	14	26	5	8	1	0	0	4	1-0	1	1	.308	.333	.346	75	-1	1-0	1.000	6	174	124	2b9/3D		0.4
Total	9	754	1934	206	483	86	20	11	139	161-19	6	211	.250	.308	.332	77	-60	37-28	.987	26	102	94	2b343,O194L,S118,3b54/D1	23	-2.4

CANGELOSI, JOHN John Anthony B3.10.1963 Brooklyn NY BB/TL/5-8/160* d6.30 Col Miami-Dade North (FL) CC

YEAR	TM LG	G	AB	R	H	2B	3B	HR	RBI	BB-IB	HP	SO	AVG	OBP	SLG	AOPS	ABR	SB-CS	FA	FR	RNG	THR	GAMES AT POSITION	DL	BFW
1985	Chi A	5	2	2	0	0	0	0	0	0-0	0	1	1.000	.333	.000		-1	31		0			O3C,D2		-0.1
1986	Chi A	137	438	65	103	16	3	2	32	71-0	7	61	.235	.349	.299	76	-12	50-17	.969	-7	90	102	O129(29/98/5),D3		-1.6
1987	Pit N	104	182	44	50	8	3	4	18	46-1	3	33	.275	.427	.418	124	9	21-6	.962	0	99	129	O47(27/16/8)		1.1
1988	Pit N	75	118	18	30	4	1	0	8	17-0	1	16	.254	.353	.305	91	-1	9-4	.963	0	117		O24(11/12/3)/P	21	0.0
1989	Pit N	112	160	18	35	4	2	0	9	35-2	3	20	.219	.365	.269	88	0	11-8	.973	1	114	67	O46(12/24/10)		0.0
1990	Pit N	58	76	13	15	2	0	0	1	11-0	1	12	.197	.307	.224	50	-5	7-2	1.000	1	86	0	O12(3/9/0)		-0.6
1992	Tex A	73	85	12	16	2	0	1	6	18-0	0	16	.188	.330	.247	66	-3	6-5	.964	3	106	212	O65(36/24/10),D6		-0.2
1994	NY N	62	111	14	28	4	0	0	4	19-1	2	20	.252	.371	.288	76	-3	5-1	1.000	4	104	264	O50(24/13/19)		0.1
1995	Hou N	90	201	46	64	5	2	2	18	48-2	4	42	.318	.457	.393	136	15	21-5	.950	-1	95	116	O59(26/32/1)/P		1.6
1996	Hou N	108	262	49	69	11	4	1	16	44-0	5	41	.263	.378	.347	101	3	17-9	.975	1	97	156	O78(53/29/0)		0.3
1997	†Fla N	103	192	28	47	8	0	1	12	19-1	3	33	.245	.321	.302	68	-9	5-1	1.000	1	112	46	O58(34/23/6)/P		-0.8
1998	Fla N	104	171	19	43	8	0	1	10	30-0	1	23	.251	.365	.316	87	-2	2-3	.969	-1	96	56	O45(9/33/8)/D		-0.4
1999	Col N	7	6	0	1	1	0	0	0	0-0	0	1	.167	.167	.333	18	-1	0-0	1.000	0	226	0	/OL		-0.1
Total	13	1038	2004	328	501	73	15	12	134	358-7	31	322	.250	.370	.319	90	-9	154-61	.972	-1	99	114	O617(265/317/70),D12,P3	21	-0.7

CANIZARO, JAY Jason Kyle B7.4.1973 Beaumont TX BR/TR/5-9/170* [SFN93 4/106] d4.28 Col Oklahoma St. [DL 2001 Min A 190]

YEAR	TM LG	G	AB	R	H	2B	3B	HR	RBI	BB-IB	HP	SO	AVG	OBP	SLG	AOPS	ABR	SB-CS	FA	FR	RNG	THR	GAMES AT POSITION	DL	BFW
1996	SF N	43	120	11	24	4	1	2	8	9-0	1	38	.200	.260	.300	49	-9	0-2	.972	-1	103	89	2b35,S7		-0.9
1999	SF N	12	18	5	8	2	0	1	9	1-0	0	2	.444	.474	.722	211	3	1-0	1.000	-1	89	74	2b4		0.2
2000	Min A	102	346	43	93	21	1	7	40	24-0	1	57	.269	.318	.396	74	-14	4-2	.982	-24	86	71	2b90,D2		-3.1
2002	Min A	38	112	14	24	8	1	0	11	10-0	1	22	.214	.280	.304	55	-7	0-1	.990	-4	91	90	2b30,3b8		-1.0
Total	4	195	596	73	149	35	3	10	68	44-0	3	119	.250	.303	.369	70	-27	5-5	.981	-29	90	78	2b159,3b8,S7,D2	190	-4.8

CANNELL, RIP Virgin Wirt B1.23.1880 S.Bridgton ME D8.26.1948 Bridgton ME BR/TR/5-10.5/180 d4.14 Col Tufts

YEAR	TM LG	G	AB	R	H	2B	3B	HR	RBI	BB-IB	HP	SO	AVG	OBP	SLG	AOPS	ABR	SB-CS	FA	FR	RNG	THR	GAMES AT POSITION	DL	BFW
1904	Bos N	100	346	32	81	5	1	0	18	23	2		.234	.286	.254	70	-12	10	.897	-10	44	26	O93(15/10/69)		-2.9
1905	Bos N	154	567	52	140	14	4	0	36	51	2		.247	.311	.286	80	-13	17	.935	-11	69	117	O154(3/149/3)		-3.3
Total	2	254	913	84	221	19	5	0	54	74	4		.242	.302	.274	76	-25	27	.923	-21	60	83	O247(18/159/72)		-6.2

CANNIZZARO, CHRIS Christopher John B5.3.1938 Oakland CA BR/TR/6-0/190* d4.17 C3

YEAR	TM LG	G	AB	R	H	2B	3B	HR	RBI	BB-IB	HP	SO	AVG	OBP	SLG	AOPS	ABR	SB-CS	FA	FR	RNG	THR	GAMES AT POSITION	DL	BFW
1960	StL N	7	9	0	2	0	0	0	1	1-0	0	3	.222	.273	.222	42	-1	0-0	1.000	1	134	0	C6		0.0
1961	StL N	6	2	0	1	0	0	0	0	0-0	0	0	.500	.500	.500	151	0	0-0	1.000	-0	0	0	C5		0.0
1962	NY N	59	133	9	32	2	1	0	9	19-1	1	26	.241	.335	.271	65	-6	1-1	.973	-1	131	193	C56/OR		-0.5
1963	NY N	16	33	4	8	1	0	0	1	1-0	0	8	.242	.257	.273	54	-2	0-1	1.000	-1	421	139	C15		-0.2
1964	NY N	60	164	11	51	10	0	0	10	14-2	1	28	.311	.367	.372	112	3	0-0	.988	1	168	135	C53		0.5
1965	NY N	114	251	17	46	8	2	0	7	28-4	2	60	.183	.270	.231	44	-18	0-2	.977	3	152	136	C112		-1.2
1968	Pit N	25	58	5	14	2	1	0	7	9-4	0	13	.241	.343	.397	123	2	0-0	.976	0	145	119	C25		0.3
1969	SD N☆	134	418	23	92	14	3	4	33	42-8	0	81	.220	.290	.297	67	-19	0-1	.988	-10	92	118	C132		-2.4
1970	SD N	111	341	27	95	13	3	5	42	48-8	1	49	.279	.366	.378	104	4	2-7	.980	-9	116	89	C110		-0.2
1971	SD N	21	63	2	12	1	0	1	8	11-0	1	10	.190	.320	.254	69	-2	0-0	.992	-0	118	68	C19		-0.2
	Chi N	71	197	18	42	8	1	5	23	28-2	1	24	.213	.311	.340	74	-6	0-0	.983	-12	81	99	C70		-1.6
	Year	92	260	20	54	9	1	6	31	39-2	2	34	.208	.314	.319	73	-8	0-0	.985	-12	90	92	C89		-1.8
1972	LA N	73	200	14	48	6	0	2	18	31-5	0	38	.240	.341	.300	85	-3	0-1	.983	-6	99	56	C72		-0.6
1973	LA N	17	21	0	4	0	0	0	3	1-0	0	3	.190	.280	.190	37	-2	0-0	1.000	-2	100	0	C13		-0.4
1974	SD N	26	60	2	11	1	0	0	4	6-0	0	11	.183	.258	.200	31	-6	0-0	.979	-2	93	87	C26		-0.7
Total	13	740	1950	132	458	66	12	18	169	241-35	7	354	.235	.319	.309	77	-56	3-17	.982	-37	121	110	C714/OR		-7.2

CANNON, JOE Joseph Jerome B7.13.1953 Camp Lejeune NC BL/TR/6-3/185* [HouN74*1/16] d9.22 Col Pensacola (FL) JC

YEAR	TM LG	G	AB	R	H	2B	3B	HR	RBI	BB-IB	HP	SO	AVG	OBP	SLG	AOPS	ABR	SB-CS	FA	FR	RNG	THR	GAMES AT POSITION	DL	BFW
1977	Hou N	9	17	3	2	0	0	0	0	1-0	0	5	.118	.118	.235	-9	-3	1-1	1.000	0	125	0	O3L		-0.3
1978	Hou N	8	18	1	4	0	0	0	0	0-0	0	1	.222	.222	.222	26	-2	0-1	.778	-1	87	0	O5(3/2/0)		-0.3
1979	Tor A	61	142	14	30	1	1	1	5	1-0	0	31	.211	.217	.254	26	-15	7-0	1.000	3	104	176	O57(17/0/40)		-1.2
1980	Tor A	70	50	16	4	0	0	0	0	0-0	1	14	.080	.098	.080	-49	-10	2-2	.968	1	80	96	O33(18/16/0)/D		-1.2
Total	4	148	227	34	40	3	1	1	10	1-0	1	54	.176	.183	.211	7	-30	15-6	.977	1	98	136	O91(41/18/40)/D		-3.0

CANO, ROBINSON Robinson Jose (Mercedes) B10.22.1982 San Pedro de Macoris, D.R. BL/TR/6-0/175 d5.3 f-Jose

YEAR	TM LG	G	AB	R	H	2B	3B	HR	RBI	BB-IB	HP	SO	AVG	OBP	SLG	AOPS	ABR	SB-CS	FA	FR	RNG	THR	GAMES AT POSITION	DL	BFW
2005	†NY A	132	522	78	155	34	4	14	62	16-1	3	68	.297	.320	.458	103	1	1-3	.978	4	103	87	2b131		1.1

CANSECO, JOSE Jose (Capas) B7.2.1964 Havana, Cuba BR/TR/6-4/240(195-240) [OakA82 15/392] d9.2 twb-Ozzie

YEAR	TM LG	G	AB	R	H	2B	3B	HR	RBI	BB-IB	HP	SO	AVG	OBP	SLG	AOPS	ABR	SB-CS	FA	FR	RNG	THR	GAMES AT POSITION	DL	BFW
1985	Oak A	29	96	16	29	3	0	5	13	4-0	0	31	.302	.330	.490	130	3	1-1	.951	1	104	117	O26(13/1/16)		0.2
1986	Oak A☆	157	600	85	144	29	1	33	117	65-1	8	175	.240	.318	.457	117	14	15-7	.958	-7	98	39	O155(124/0/46)/D		0.1
1987	Oak A	159	630	81	162	35	3	31	113	50-2	2	157	.257	.310	.470	111	8	15-3	.975	6	104	141	O130L,D30		0.9
1988	†Oak A★	158	610	120	187	34	0	**42**	**124**	78-10	10	128	.307	.391	**.569**	171	60	40-16	.978	2	99	123	O144R,D13		5.9
1989	†Oak A✻	65	227	40	61	9	1	17	57	23-4	2	69	.269	.333	.542	150	14	6-3	.976	2	105	120	O56R,D5	101	1.4

YEAR	TM LG	G	AB	R	H	2B	3B	HR	RBI	BB-IB	HP	SO	AVG	OBP	SLG	AOPS	ABR	SB-CS	FA	FR	RNG	THR	GAMES AT POSITION	DL	BFW
1990	†Oak A★	131	481	83	132	14	2	37	101	72-8	5	158	.274	.371	.543	159	38	19-10	.995	1	102	109	O88R,D43	15	3.6
1991	Oak A	154	572	115	152	32	1	**44**	122	78-7	9	152	.266	.359	.556	159	46	26-6	.965	-7	96	54	O131R,D24		3.7
1992	Oak A*	97	366	66	90	11	0	22	72	48-1	3	104	.246	.325	.456	127	12	5-7	.988	1	103	95	O77R,D20	15	0.9
	Tex A	22	73	8	17	4	0	4	15	15-1	3	24	.233	.385	.452	138	5	1-0	.970	1	126	0	O13R,D8		0.5
	Year	119	439	74	107	15	0	26	87	63-2	6	128	.244	.344	.456	129	17	6-7	.985	2	106	81	O90R,D28		1.4
1993	Tex A	60	231	30	59	14	1	10	46	16-2	3	62	.255	.308	.455	107	1	6-6	.970	-1	92	110	O49R/P	102	-0.3
1994	Tex A	111	429	88	121	19	2	31	90	69-8	5	114	.282	.386	.552	137	24	15-8	—	0	0	0	D111		1.7
1995	†Bos A	102	396	64	121	25	1	24	81	42-4	7	93	.306	.378	.556	136	21	4-0	1.000	-0	64	0	D101/OR	36	1.5
1996	Bos A	96	360	68	104	22	1	28	82	63-3	6	82	.289	.400	.589	144	26	3-1	1.000	-1	80	140	D84,O11(10/0/2)	68	1.9
1997	Oak A	108	388	56	91	19	0	23	74	51-1	3	122	.235	.325	.461	103	1	8-2	.938	-4	86	73	D56,O44(19/0/27)	52	-0.6
1998	Tor A	151	583	98	138	26.	0	46	107	65-5	6	159	.237	.318	.518	112	8	29-17	.960	-1	95	101	D78,O73(50/0/26)		1.4
1999	TB A*	113	430	75	120	18	1	34	95	58-3	7	135	.279	.369	.563	132	20	3-0	1.000	0	77	338	D106,O6L	41	1.4
2000	TB A	61	218	31	56	15	0	9	30	41-1	4	65	.257	.383	.450	112	6	2-0	—	0	0	0	D60	53	0.2
	†NY A	37	111	16	27	3	0	6	19	23-1	0	37	.243	.365	.432	105	1	0-0	.818	-0	118	0	D26,O5(4/0/1)		-0.1
	Year	98	329	47	83	18	0	15	49	64-2	4	102	.252	.377	.444	109	7	2-0	.730	-0	118	0	D86,O5(4/0/1)		0.2
2001	Chi A	76	256	46	66	8	0	16	49	45-1	5	75	.258	.366	.477	114	6	2-1	1.000	-1	34	0	D62,O2R		0.2
Total	17	1887	7057	1186	1877	340	14	462	1407	906-63	84	1942	.266	.353	.515	132	314	200-88	.971	-8	99	94	O1011(356/1/679),D834/P	483	23.2

CANSECO, OZZIE Osvaldo (Capas) B7.2.1964 Havana, Cuba BR/TR/6-2/220* [NYA83*2/40] d7.18 twb-Jose Col Miami-Dade Kendall (FL) CC [DL 1989 Oak A 24]

YEAR	TM LG	G	AB	R	H	2B	3B	HR	RBI	BB-IB	HP	SO	AVG	OBP	SLG	AOPS	ABR	SB-CS	FA	FR	RNG	THR	GAMES AT POSITION	DL	BFW
1990	Oak A	9	19	1	2	1	0	0	1	1-0	0	10	.105	.150	.158	-14	-3	0-0	1.000	-0	86	0	O2(1/0/1),D4		-0.3
1992	StL N	9	29	7	8	5	0	0	3	7-0	0	4	.276	.417	.448	148	3	0-0	.889	-2	48	0	O8(7/0/1)		0.0
1993	StL N	6	17	0	3	0	0	0	0	1-0	0	3	.176	.222	.176	8	-2	0-0	.500	-2	13	0	O5L		-0.4
Total	3	24	65	8	13	6	0	0	4	9-0	0	17	.200	.297	.292	66	-2	0-0	.857	-4	42	0	O15(13/0/2),D4	24	-0.7

CANTU, JORGE Jorge Luis (Guzman) B1.30.1982 McAllen TX BR/TR/6-1/184* d7.17

YEAR	TM LG	G	AB	R	H	2B	3B	HR	RBI	BB-IB	HP	SO	AVG	OBP	SLG	AOPS	ABR	SB-CS	FA	FR	RNG	THR	GAMES AT POSITION	DL	BFW
2004	TB A	50	173	25	52	20	1	2	17	9-0	2	44	.301	.341	.462	110	3	0-0	.964	-4	95	91	2b33,3b11/SD		0.0
2005	TB A	150	598	73	171	40	1	28	117	19-1	6	83	.286	.311	.497	114	10	1-0	.971	-35	85	70	2b80,3b62,D13		-2.1
Total	2	200	771	98	223	60	2	30	134	28-1	8	127	.289	.318	.489	113	13	1-0	.969	-39	88	76	2b113,3b73,D17/S		-2.1

CANTZ, BART Bartholomew L. B1.29.1860 Philadelphia PA D2.12.1943 Philadelphia PA d7.25

YEAR	TM LG	G	AB	R	H	2B	3B	HR	RBI	BB-IB	HP	SO	AVG	OBP	SLG	AOPS	ABR	SB-CS	FA	FR	RNG	THR	GAMES AT POSITION	DL	BFW
1888	Bal AA	37	126	7	21	2	1	0	9	2	0		.167	.180	.198	22	-11	0	.904	-7			C33,O4(1/0/3)		-1.5
1889	Bal AA	20	69	6	12	2	0	0	8	4	0	14	.174	.219	.203	20	-7	2	.860	-5			C18,O2R		-0.9
1890	Phi AA	5	22	1	1	0	0	0	1	0	0		.045	.045	.045	-74	-5	0	.893	-2	84	127	C5		-0.6
Total	3	62	217	14	34	4	1	0	18	6	0	14	.157	.179	.184	11	-23	2	.890	-14	84	127	C56,O6(1/0/5)		-3.0

CAPRA, NICK Nick Lee B3.8.1958 Denver CO BR/TR/5-8/165* [TexA79 3/69] d9.6 Col Oklahoma

YEAR	TM LG	G	AB	R	H	2B	3B	HR	RBI	BB-IB	HP	SO	AVG	OBP	SLG	AOPS	ABR	SB-CS	FA	FR	RNG	THR	GAMES AT POSITION	DL	BFW
1982	Tex A	13	15	2	4	0	0	1	1	3-0	1	4	.267	.421	.467	150	1	2-1	1.000	2	131	586	O9(4/1/4)		0.3
1983	Tex A	8	2	2	0	0	0	0	0	0-0	0	0	.000	.000	.000	-99	-1	0-0	—	-0	0	0	O4(1/1/2)		-0.1
1985	Tex A	8	8	1	1	0	0	0	0	0-0	0	1	.125	.125	.125	-31	-1	0-0	1.000	-1	158	0	O8(1/3/4)		-0.1
1988	KC A	14	29	3	4	1	0	0	2	2-0	0	3	.138	.194	.172	3	-4	1-0	1.000	-1	77	0	O11(2/7/2)/D		-0.5
1991	Tex A	2	0	1	0	0	0	0	0	1-0	0	0	—	1.000	.000	-205	0	0-0	1.000	0	242	0	O2(1/1/0)		0.1
Total	5	45	54	9	9	1	0	1	1	6-0	1	7	.167	.262	.241	41	-5	3-1	1.000	2	111	175	O34(9/13/12)/D		-0.3

CAPRI, PAT Patrick Nicholas B11.27.1918 New York NY D6.14.1989 New York NY BR/TR/6-0.5/170 d7.16 Col Brooklyn

YEAR	TM LG	G	AB	R	H	2B	3B	HR	RBI	BB-IB	HP	SO	AVG	OBP	SLG	AOPS	ABR	SB-CS	FA	FR	RNG	THR	GAMES AT POSITION	DL	BFW
1944	Bos N	7	1	1	0	0	0	0	0	0-0	0	0	1.000	.000	.000	-96	0		1.000	1	287	732	/2		0.0

CAPRON, RALPH Ralph Earl B6.16.1889 Minneapolis MN D9.19.1980 Los Angeles CA BL/TR/5-11.5/165 d4.25 Col Minnesota

YEAR	TM LG	G	AB	R	H	2B	3B	HR	RBI	BB-IB	HP	SO	AVG	OBP	SLG	AOPS	ABR	SB-CS	FA	FR	RNG	THR	GAMES AT POSITION	DL	BFW
1912	Pit N	1	0	0	0	0	0	0	0	0	0	0	—	—	—				—				/R		0.0
1913	Phi N	2	1	1	0	0	0	0	0	0	0	0	.000	.000	.000	-96	0	0-0	—	-0	0	0	/OL		0.0
Total	2	3	1	1	0	0	0	0	0	0	0	0	.000	.000	.000	-96	0	0	.000	-0	0	0	/OL		0.0

CARABALLO, RAMON Ramon (Sanchez) B5.23.1969 Rio San Juan, D.R. BB/TR/5-7/150* d9.9

YEAR	TM LG	G	AB	R	H	2B	3B	HR	RBI	BB-IB	HP	SO	AVG	OBP	SLG	AOPS	ABR	SB-CS	FA	FR	RNG	THR	GAMES AT POSITION	DL	BFW
1993	Atl N	6	0	0	0	0	0	0	0	0-0	0	0						0-0	1.000	1	116	0	2b5		0.1
1995	StL N	34	99	10	20	4	1	2	3	6-0	3	33	.202	.269	.323	54	-7	3-2	.956	4	115	139	2b24		-0.1
Total	2	40	99	10	20	4	1	2	3	6-0	3	33	.202	.269	.323	54	-7	3-2	.958	5	115	134	2b29		0.0

CARBINE, JOHN John C. B10.12.1855 Syracuse NY D9.11.1915 Chicago IL 6-0/187 d5.8

YEAR	TM LG	G	AB	R	H	2B	3B	HR	RBI	BB-IB	HP	SO	AVG	OBP	SLG	AOPS	ABR	SB-CS	FA	FR	RNG	THR	GAMES AT POSITION	DL	BFW
1875	Wes NA	10	36	0	3	0	0	0	2	0		1	.083	.083	.083	-40	-5	0-0	.950	1	154	111	1b10		-0.4
1876	Lou N	7	25	3	4	0	0	0	1	0		0	.160	.160	.160	6	-3		.878	-0	88	219	1b6/OR		-0.3

CARBO, BERNIE Bernardo B8.5.1947 Detroit MI BL/TR/6-0/175* [CinN65 1/16] d9.2

YEAR	TM LG	G	AB	R	H	2B	3B	HR	RBI	BB-IB	HP	SO	AVG	OBP	SLG	AOPS	ABR	SB-CS	FA	FR	RNG	THR	GAMES AT POSITION	DL	BFW
1969	Cin N	4	3	0	0	0	0	0	0	0		2	.000	.000	.000	-95	-1	0-0	—	0			/H		-0.1
1970	†Cin N	125	365	54	113	19	3	21	63	94-9	4	77	.310	.454	.551	167	41	10-4	.979	-1	93	101	O119(118/0/1)		3.4
1971	Cin N	106	310	33	68	20	1	5	20	54-4	2	56	.219	.338	.339	93	0	2-1	.982	1	94	118	O90L		-0.5
1972	Cin N	19	21	2	3	0	0	0	0	6-1	1	3	.143	.357	.143	49	-1	0-0	1.000	0	146	0	O4R		-0.1
	StL N	99	302	42	78	13	1	7	34	57-9	5	56	.258	.381	.377	118	11	0-1	.967	7	103	236	O92R/3		1.3
	Year	118	323	44	81	13	1	7	34	63-10	6	59	.251	.380	.362	114	10	0-1	.969	7	105	228	O96R/3		1.2
1973	StL N	111	308	42	88	18	0	8	40	58-7	1	52	.286	.397	.422	127	15	2-0	.978	3	104	139	O94(2/0/93)		1.4
1974	Bos A	117	338	40	84	20	0	12	61	58-7	4	90	.249	.364	.414	116	9	4-3	.994	-0	100	82	O87(33/0/56),D15		0.5
1975	†Bos A	107	319	64	82	21	3	15	50	83-5	1	69	.257	.409	.483	140	21	2-4	.976	1	100	114	O85(38/0/47),D13		1.7
1976	Bos A	17	55	5	13	4	0	2	6	8-1	0	17	.236	.333	.418	107	1	1-0	1.000	0	100	0	D15/OL		0.0
	Mil A	69	183	20	43	7	0	3	15	33-3	0	55	.235	.352	.322	100	2	1-2	1.000	5	122	243	O33(4/0/29),D24		0.5
	Year	86	238	25	56	11	0	5	21	41-4	0	72	.235	.348	.345	102	2	2-2	1.000	5	122	239	D39,O34(5/0/29)		0.5
1977	Bos A	86	228	36	66	6	1	15	34	47-3	0	72	.289	.409	.522	137	13	1-2	.951	2	111	115	O67(8/0/59),D7		1.2
1978	Bos A	17	46	7	12	3	0	1	6	8-0	0	8	.261	.370	.391	104	1	1-1	1.000	1	155	0	O9(1/0/8),D8		0.1
	Cle A	60	174	21	50	8	0	4	16	20-1	1	31	.287	.362	.402	116	4	1-0	1.000	-1	23	0	D49,O4R		0.2
	Year	77	220	28	62	11	0	5	22	28-1	1	39	.282	.364	.400	113	5	2-1	.976	1	127	0	D57,O13(1/0/12)		0.3
1979	StL N	52	64	6	18	1	0	3	12	10-0	1	22	.281	.368	.438	120	2	1-0	1.000	-2	57	0	O17(4/0/13)		0.0
1980	StL N	14	11	0	2	0	0	0	0	1-0	0	1	.182	.250	.182	21	-1	0-0	—				/H		-0.2
	Pit N	7	6	0	2	0	0	0	1	1-0	0	1	.333	.429	.333	111	0	0-0	—	0			/H		0.0
	Year	21	17	0	4	0	0	0	1	2-0	0	1	.235	.316	.235	54	-1	0-0	—	0					-0.2
Total	12	1010	2733	372	722	140	9	96	358	538-50	19	611	.264	.387	.427	125	117	26-18	.978	17	101	131	O702(299/0/406),D131/3		9.4

CARDENAL, JOSE Jose Rosario Domec (b Jose Rosario Domec (Cardenal)) B10.7.1943 Matanzas, Cuba BR/TR/5-10/150* d4.14 C11 OF(427/847/549)

YEAR	TM LG	G	AB	R	H	2B	3B	HR	RBI	BB-IB	HP	SO	AVG	OBP	SLG	AOPS	ABR	SB-CS	FA	FR	RNG	THR	GAMES AT POSITION	DL	BFW
1963	SF N	9	5	1	1	0	0	0	0	1-0	0	1	.200	.333	.200	58	0	0-1	—	-0	0	0	O2(0/1/1)		-0.1
1964	SF N	20	15	3	0	0	0	0	0	2-0	0	3	.000	.118	.000	-62	-3	2-0	.909	1	83	549	O16(8/2/6)		-0.2
1965	Cal A	134	512	58	128	23	2	11	57	27-1	2	72	.250	.287	.367	87	-10	37-15	.964	3	100	**221**	O129C,3b2/2		-0.8
1966	Cal A	154	561	67	155	15	3	16	48	34-5	4	69	.276	.320	.399	109	5	24-11	.992	3	105	113	O146(7/140/0)		0.6
1967	Cal A	108	381	40	90	13	5	6	27	15-0	2	63	.236	.268	.344	83	-10	10-5	.986	3	102	173	O101(27/70/1)		-1.1
1968	Cle A	157	583	78	150	21	6	7	44	39-3	2	74	.257	.305	.353	101	-1	40-18	.974	7	108	124	O153C		0.4
1969	Cle A	146	557	75	143	26	3	11	45	49-3	6	58	.257	.314	.373	90	-8	36-6	.982	2	108	109	O142(1/141/0),3b5		-0.4
1970	StL N	148	552	73	162	32	6	10	74	45-0	1	70	.293	.348	.428	104	3	26-9	.969	-9	91	78	O134(0/133/1)		-0.7
1971	StL N	89	301	37	73	12	4	7	48	29-1	0	35	.243	.303	.379	90	-4	12-3	.969	7	118	162	O83(0/8/78)		0.0
	Mil A	53	198	20	51	10	0	3	32	13-0	1	20	.258	.297	.354	87	-4	9-5	.979	3	107	183	O52(0/45/7)		-0.2
1972	Chi N	143	533	96	155	24	6	17	70	55-3	1	58	.291	.356	.454	117	12	25-14	.971	9	85	112	O137(8/16/125)		-0.3
1973	Chi N	145	522	80	158	33	2	11	68	58-9	5	62	.303	.375	.437	116	14	19-7	.980	-5	92	106	O142(1/2/142)		0.4
1974	Chi N	143	542	75	159	35	3	13	72	56-3	1	67	.293	.359	.441	118	14	23-9	.965	4	101	157	O137(32/1/108)		1.3
1975	Chi N	154	574	85	182	30	2	9	68	77-5	4	50	.317	.397	.423	123	22	34-12	.976	9	107	126	O151(137/0/108)		2.7
1976	Chi N	136	521	64	156	25	2	8	47	32-0	1	39	.299	.339	.401	101	1	23-14	.981	3	97	116	O128(127/0/2)		-0.3
1977	Chi N	100	226	33	54	12	1	3	18	28-2	1	30	.239	.324	.341	71	-8	5-4	.989	-4	84	30	O62(54/6/2)/2S	18	-1.6
1978	†Phi N	87	201	27	50	12	0	4	33	23-2	0	16	.249	.323	.368	92	-2	2-3	.990	-5	71	136	1b50,O13(10/0/4)		-1.0
1979	Phi N	29	48	4	10	3	0	0	4	6-0	0	8	.208	.321	.271	61	-2	1-0	1.000	-1	65	0	O12(9/0/6)/1		-0.1
	NY N	11	37	8	11	4	0	2	4	6-0	1	3	.297	.409	.568	168	4	1-0	1.000	-1	102	0	O9R,1b2	40	0.3
	Year	40	85	12	21	7	0	2	13	14-1	1	11	.247	.360	.400	104	1	2-0	1.000	-2	93	0	O21(9/0/15),1b3		-0.1
1980	NY N	26	42	4	7	1	0	0	4	5-0	0	5	.167	.265	.190	31	-4	0-1	1.000	1	141	268	O6(2/0/4),1b5		-0.4
	†KC A	25	53	8	18	2	0	0	5	5-0	0	5	.340	.377	.377	112	1	0-0	.970	-1	84	150	O23(4/0/19)		0.0
Total	18	2017	6964	936	1913	333	46	138	775	608-38	26	807	.275	.333	.395	92	20	329-137	.976	13	100	129	O1778C,1b58,3b7,2b2/S	58	-1.8

YEAR	TM	LG	G	AB	R	H	2B	3B	HR	RBI	BB-IB	HP	SO	AVG	OBP	SLG	AOPS	ABR	SB-CS	FA	FR	RNG	THR	GAMES AT POSITION	DL	BFW

CARDENAS, LEO   Leonardo Lazaro (Alfonso) "Chico"   B12.17.1938 Matanzas, Cuba   BR/TR/5-10/163(150-163)   d7.25

1960	Cin	N	48	142	13	33	2	4	1	12	6-0	0	32	.232	.264	.324	59	-9	0-0	.958	0	103	130	S47		-0.5
1961	†Cin	N	74	198	23	61	18	1	5	24	15-1	0	39	.308	.353	.485	119	6	1-0	.973	-11	87	66	S63		0.0
1962	Cin	N	153	589	57	173	31	4	10	60	39-4	5	99	.294	.341	.411	98	-1	2-5	.972	-11	94	89	S149		0.0
1963	Cin	N	158	565	42	133	22	4	7	48	23-6	4	101	.235	.270	.326	69	-23	3-5	**.972**	-3	92	99	S157		-1.5
1964	Cin	N★	**163**	597	61	150	32	2	9	69	41-10	2	110	.251	.299	.357	82	-14	4-4	.960	-11	85	97	S163		-1.2
1965	Cin	N★	156	557	65	160	25	11	11	57	60-25	1	100	.287	.355	.431	113	11	1-4	.975	-2	90	93*	S155		2.2
1966	Cin	N★	**160**	568	59	145	25	4	20	81	45-18	1	87	.255	.309	.419	93	-6	9-4	**.980**	-14	87	88	S160		-0.5
1967	Cin	N	108	379	30	97	14	3	2	21	34-16	2	77	.256	.320	.325	76	-10	4-5	.971	-10	90	87	S108	60	-1.3
1968	Cin	N★	137	452	45	106	13	4	7	41	36-18	2	83	.235	.292	.319	79	-11	2-1	.955	-22	91	82	S136		-2.6
1969	†Min	A	160	578	67	162	24	4	10	70	66-12	4	96	.280	.353	.388	106	6	5-6	.965	23	112	**134**	S160		4.9
1970	†Min	A	160	588	67	145	34	4	11	65	42-2	4	101	.247	.300	.374	84	-14	2-5	.978	5	100	100	S160		0.9
1971	Min	A☆	153	554	59	146	25	4	18	75	51-5	1	69	.264	.321	.421	107	4	3-3	**.985**	0	95	96	S153		2.4
1972	Cal	A	150	551	25	123	11	2	6	42	35-4	2	73	.223	.272	.283	69	-23	1-2	.970	8	98	90	S150		0.2
1973	Cle	A	72	195	9	42	4	0	0	12	13-0	1	42	.215	.264	.236	41	-15	1-4	.964	-12	84	86	S67,3b5		-2.2
1974	Tex	A	34	92	5	25	3	0	0	7	2-1	0	14	.272	.287	.304	72	-4	1-0	1.000	2	106	29	3b21,S10,D4		-0.1
1975	Tex	A	55	102	15	24	2	0	1	5	14-0	0	12	.235	.328	.284	75	-3	0-0	.956	8	122	153	3b43,S5,2b3		0.5
Total	16		1941	6707	662	1725	285	49	118	689	522-122	28	1135	.257	.311	.367	88	-106	39-48	.971	-49	94	96	S1843,3b69,D4,2b3	60	1.2

CARDONA, JAVIER   Javier Peterson   B9.15.1975 Santurce, PR   BR/TR/6-1/185*   [DetA94 23/641]   d5.31 Col Lake Land (IL) JC

2000	Det	A	26	40	1	7	1	0	0	2	0-0	1	9	.175	.190	.275	17	-5	0-0	.973	-4	99	58	C26		-0.7
2001	Det	A	46	96	10	25	8	0	1	10	2-0	1	12	.260	.280	.375	73	-4	0-1	.980	-8	199	111	C44/D		-0.9
2002	SD	N	15	39	2	4	1	0	0	2	2-0	0	10	.103	.143	.128	-28	-8	0-0	.976	-2	134	131	C14		-0.9
Total	3		87	175	13	36	10	0	2	14	4-0	2	31	.206	.228	.297	39	-17	0-1	.977	-13	161	102	C84/D		-2.5

CAREW, ROD   Rodney Cline   B10.1.1945 Gatun, Canal Zone   BL/TR/6-0/182(170-182)   d4.11 C10 HF1991

1967	Min	A★	137	514	66	150	22	7	8	51	37-4	2	91	.292	.341	.409	112	7	5-9	.976	-2	97	86	2b134		1.6
1968	Min	A★	127	461	46	126	27	4	1	42	26-1	1	71	.273	.312	.347	95	-3	12-4	.968	-5	96	77	2b117,S4		0.5
1969	†Min	A★	123	458	79	152	30	4	8	56	37-0	3	72	**.332**	.386	.467	134	21	19-8	.970	-6	102	116	2b118		2.5
1970	†Min	A★	51	191	27	70	12	3	4	28	11-0	2	28	.366	.407	.524	152	13	4-6	.961	-5	101	99	2b45/1	69	1.0
1971	Min	A★	147	577	88	177	16	10	2	48	45-1	1	81	.307	.356	.380	106	4	6-7	.976	-21	87	80	2b142,3b2		-1.0
1972	Min	A★	142	535	61	170	21	6	0	51	43-9	2	60	.318	.369	.379	118	12	12-6	.978	2	100	103	2b139		2.6
1973	Min	A★	149	580	98	**203**	30	**11**	6	62	62-9	2	55	**.350**	.411	.471	143	34	41-16	.984	10	98	96	2b147		5.8
1974	Min	A★	153	599	86	**218**	30	5	3	55	74-9	1	49	**.364**	**.433**	.446	149	42	38-16	.960	13	100	104	2b148		6.9
1975	Min	A★	143	535	89	192	24	4	14	80	64-18	1	40	**.359**	**.421**	.497	159	44	35-9	.973	-12	106	95	2b123,1b14,D2		6.7
1976	Min	A★	156	605	97	200	29	12	9	90	67-14	1	52	.331	.395	.463	149	38	49-22	.989	-3	97	**113**	1b152,2b7		2.7
1977	Min	A★	155	616	**128**	**239**	38	**16**	14	100	69-15	3	55	**.388**	**.449**	.570	178	69	23-13	.994	7	114	**124**	1b151,2b4/D		6.5
1978	Min	A★	152	564	85	188	26	10	5	70	78-19	1	62	**.333**	**.411**	.441	138	32	27-7	.989	-0	105	111	1b148,2b4/OL		2.6
1979	†Cal	A★	110	409	78	130	15	3	3	44	73-7	0	46	.318	.419	.391	124	19	18-8	.988	-8	72	108	1b103,D6	46	0.5
1980	Cal	A★	144	540	74	179	34	7	3	59	59-7	1	38	.331	.396	.437	131	25	23-15	.994	-4	82	81	1b103,D32		1.3
1981	Cal	A★	93	364	57	111	17	1	2	21	45-7	0	45	.305	.380	.374	117	10	16-9	.995	-1	98	114	1b90,D2		0.4
1982	†Cal	A★	138	523	88	167	25	5	3	44	67-5	2	49	.319	.396	.433	120	17	10-17	.992	1	106	105	1b134		0.6
1983	Cal	A★	129	472	66	160	24	2	2	44	57-9	1	48	.339	.409	.411	128	21	6-7	.994	-9	72	112	1b89,D24,2b2		0.5
1984	Cal	A★	93	329	42	97	8	1	3	31	40-1	0	39	.295	.367	.353	102	2	4-3	.981	-3	99	108	1b83/D	23	-0.6
1985	Cal	A	127	443	69	124	17	3	2	39	64-9	1	47	.280	.371	.345	98	5	5-5	.990	-10	73	**128**	1b116	21	-1.6
Total	19		2469	9315	1424	3053	445	112	92	1015	1018-144	25	1028	.328	.393	.429	130	409	353-187	.991	-32	94	111	1b1184,2b1130,D68,S4,3b2/OL	159	39.5

CAREY, ANDY   Andrew Arthur (b Andrew Arthur Hexem)   B10.18.1931 Oakland CA   BR/TR/6-1/195(185-198)   d5.2 Col St. Marys (CA)

1952	NY	A	16	40	6	6	0	0	0	1	3	0	10	.150	.209	.150	1	-5	0-0	.889	-1	102	185	3b14/S		-0.7
1953	NY	A	51	81	14	26	5	0	4	8	9	0	12	.321	.389	.531	152	6	2-1	.988	5	121	172	3b40,S2/2		1.1
1954	NY	A	122	411	60	124	14	6	8	65	43	7	38	.302	.373	.423	123	13	5-5	.967	13	105	**141**	3b120		2.5
1955	†NY	A	135	510	73	131	19	**11**	7	47	44-6	1	51	.257	.313	.378	88	-11	3-3	.954	10	102	**138**	3b135		-0.2
1956	†NY	A	132	422	54	100	18	2	7	50	45-4	2	53	.237	.310	.339	75	-16	9-6	.947	-3	101	102	3b131		-1.9
1957	†NY	A	85	247	30	63	6	3	6	35	15-3	5	42	.255	.309	.393	92	-4	2-2	.977	1	101	72	3b81		-0.3
1958	†NY	A	102	315	39	90	19	4	12	45	34-4	6	43	.286	.364	.486	137	16	1-2	.961	10	107	125	3b99		2.6
1959	NY	A	41	101	11	26	1	0	3	9	7-0	0	17	.257	.306	.356	84	-3	1-1	.916	-1	85	203	3b34	70	-0.4
1960	NY	A	4	3	1	1	0	0	0	1	0-0	0	1	.333	.333	.333	86	0	0-0	1.000	0	143	0	3b2/OL		0.0
	KC	A	102	343	30	80	14	4	12	53	26-0	1	52	.233	.287	.402	84	-9	0-0	.975	3	100	135	3b91		-0.7
	Year		106	346	31	81	14	4	12	54	26-0	1	53	.234	.287	.402	85	-9	0-0	.975	3	100	134	3b93/OL		-0.7
1961	KC	A	39	123	20	30	6	2	3	11	15-0	2	23	.244	.336	.398	94	-1	0-0	.944	-3	93	147	3b39		-0.4
	Chi	A	56	143	21	38	12	3	0	14	11-0	2	24	.266	.323	.392	93	-1	0-1	.961	-10	81	49	3b54		-1.2
	Year		95	266	41	68	18	5	3	25	26-0	4	47	.256	.329	.395	93	-2	0-1	.953	-13	87	94	3b93		-1.6
1962	LA	N	53	111	12	26	5	1	2	13	16-1	1	24	.234	.333	.351	90	-1	0-0	.942	-3	88	71	3b42		-0.4
Total	11		938	2850	371	741	119	38	64	350	268-18	27	389	.260	.327	.396	97	-16	23-21	.958	22	100	122	3b882,S3/OL2	70	-0.0

CAREY, SCOOPS   George C.   B12.4.1870 Pittsburgh PA   D12.17.1916 E.Liverpool OH   BR/TR/5-11/175   d4.26 Col West Virginia

1895	†Bal	N	123	490	59	128	21	6	1	75	27	4	32	.261	.305	.335	63	-29	2	**.987**	-7	65	**112**	1b123/OCS3		-2.9
1898	Lou	N	8	32	1	6	1	1	0	1	1	0		.188	.212	.281	42	-3	0	.961	-0	118	92	1b8		1.1
1902	Was	A	120	452	46	142	35	11	0	60	20	5		.314	.350	.440	117	10	3	**.989**	4	107	76	1b120		1.1
1903	Was	A	48	183	8	37	3	2	0	23	4	1		.202	.223	.240	38	-14	0	.977	-3	81	75	1b47		-1.9
Total	4		299	1157	114	313	60	20	1	159	52	10	32	.271	.308	.360	80	-36	5	.986	-5	86	91	1b298/3SOC		-4.0

CAREY, MAX   Max George "Scoops" (b Maximilian Carnarius)   B1.11.1890 Terre Haute IN   D5.30.1976 Miami FL   BB/TR/5-11.5/170   d10.3 M2/C1 HF1961

1910	Pit	N	2	6	2	3	0	1	0	2	2	0	1	.500	.625	.833	307	2	0	1.000	1	149	239	O2L		0.3
1911	Pit	N	129	427	77	110	15	10	5	43	44	4	75	.258	.337	.375	95	-4	27	.975	7	**121**	66	O122(46/76/0)		-0.3
1912	Pit	N	150	587	114	177	23	8	5	66	61	5	79	.302	.372	.394	111	10	45	.968	3	106	77	O150(145/6/0)		0.6
1913	Pit	N	154	620	**99**	172	23	10	5	49	55	3	67	.277	.339	.371	107	6	**61**-17	.961	11	107	127	O154(144/11/0)		1.7
1914	Pit	N	156	593	76	144	25	**17**	1	31	59	2	56	.243	.313	.347	101	-1	38	.965	7	105	117	O154L		-0.1
1915	Pit	N	140	564	76	143	26	5	3	27	57	4	58	.254	.326	.333	101	1	**36**-17	.982	11	109	126	O139L		1.0
1916	Pit	N	154	599	90	158	23	11	7	42	59	7	58	.264	.337	.374	117	13	**63**-19	.983	22	113	**166**	O154(21/134/0)		3.6
1917	Pit	N	155	588	82	174	21	12	1	51	58	10	38	.296	.369	.378	125	20	46	.979	21	**121**	136	O153C		3.4
1918	Pit	N	**126**	468	70	128	14	6	3	48	**62**	4	25	.274	.363	.348	113	10	**58**	.958	13	110	**146**	O126C		1.6
1919	Pit	N	66	244	41	75	10	2	0	9	25	2	24	.307	.376	.365	119	7	18	.947	1	114	63	O63C		0.4
1920	Pit	N	130	485	74	140	18	4	1	35	59	3	31	.289	.369	.348	104	5	**52**-10	.967	-5	103	52	O129C		-0.1
1921	Pit	N	140	521	85	161	34	4	7	56	70	4	30	.309	.395	.430	115	16	**37**-12	.957	5	**115**	71	O139C		1.8
1922	Pit	N	**155**	629	140	207	28	12	10	70	**80**	2	23	.329	.408	.459	122	23	**51**-2	.969	10	109	116	O155(3/152/0)		3.5
1923	Pit	N	153	610	120	188	32	**19**	6	63	73	7	28	.308	.388	.452	119	18	**51**-8	.962	12	108	137	O153C		3.0
1924	Pit	N	149	599	113	178	30	9	8	55	58	7	17	.297	.366	.417	108	8	**49**-13	.965	2	103	97	O149C		1.0
1925	†Pit	N	133	542	109	186	39	13	5	44	66	4	19	.343	.418	.491	123	26	**46**-11	.950	2	99	**160**	O130C		2.4
1926	Pit	N	86	324	46	72	14	5	0	28	30	0	14	.222	.288	.296	55	-21	10	.943	1	104	104	O82C		-2.3
	Bro	N	27	100	18	26	3	1	0	7	8	0	5	.260	.315	.310	70	-4	0	.933	-3	100	0	O27C		-0.8
	Year		113	424	64	98	17	6	0	35	38	0	19	.231	.294	.300	58	-25	10	.941	-2	103	78	O109C		-3.1
1927	Bro	N	144	538	70	143	30	10	1	54	64	1	18	.266	.345	.364	90	-6	32	.970	3	101	112	O141(1/38/108)		-1.4
1928	Bro	N	108	296	41	73	11	0	2	19	47	2	24	.247	.354	.304	74	-9	18	.986	1	102	109	O95(1/75/35)		-0.2
1929	Bro	N	19	23	2	7	0	0	0	1	3	1	2	.304	.407	.304	81	0	1	1.000	0	101	0	O4(0/2/2)		-0.1
Total	20		2476	9363	1545	2665	419	159	70	800	1040	77	695	.285	.361	.386	107	117	738-109	.966	127	108	111	O2421(656/1645/145)		18.0

CAREY, PAUL   Paul Stephan   B1.8.1968 Boston MA   BL/TR/6-4/215   [MiaI90 3/100]   d5.25 Col Stanford   [DL 1994 Bal A 99]

| 1993 | Bal | A | 18 | 47 | 1 | 10 | 4 | 0 | 1 | 6 | 5-0 | 0 | 14 | .213 | .288 | .234 | 40 | -4 | 0-0 | .970 | -2 | 21 | 122 | 1b9,D5 | | -0.6 |

CAREY, ROGER   Roger J.   B1865 NY   D2.8.1895 New York NY   d7.9

| 1887 | NY | N | 1 | 4 | 0 | 0 | 0 | 0 | 0 | 1 | 0 | 0 | 1 | .000 | .000 | .000 | -99 | -1 | 0 | .800 | 0 | 143 | 193 | /2 | | -0.1 |

CAREY, TOM   Thomas Francis Aloysius "Scoops"   B10.11.1906 Hoboken NJ   D2.21.1970 Rochester NY   BR/TR/5-8.5/170   d7.19 Mil 1943-45 C2

| 1935 | StL | A | 76 | 296 | 29 | 86 | 18 | 4 | 0 | 42 | 13 | 0 | 11 | .291 | .320 | .378 | 77 | -11 | 0-2 | .961 | -3 | 100 | 93 | 2b76 | | -1.0 |
| 1936 | StL | A | 134 | 488 | 58 | 133 | 27 | 6 | 1 | 57 | 27 | 3 | 25 | .273 | .315 | .359 | 64 | -29 | 2-1 | .967 | -1 | **105** | 86 | 2b128/S | | -2.0 |

YEAR	TM LG	G	AB	R	H	2B	3B	HR	RBI	BB-IB	HP	SO	AVG	OBP	SLG	AOPS	ABR	SB-CS	FA	FR	RNG	THR	GAMES AT POSITION	DL	BFW
1937	StL A	130	487	54	134	24	1	1	40	21	1	26	.275	.306	.335	61	-30	1-2	.983	-2	99	89	2b87,S44/3		-2.2
1939	Bos A	54	161	17	39	6	2	0	20	3	2	9	.242	.265	.304	44	-14	0-0	1.000	6	111	106	2b35,S10		-0.6
1940	Bos A	43	62	4	20	4	0	0	7	2	0	1	.323	.344	.387	86	-1	0-0	.953	3	121	162	S20,2b4,3b4		0.3
1941	Bos A	25	21	7	4	0	0	0	2	0	0	2	.190	.190	.190	1	-3	0-0	1.000	2	105	169	2b9,S8/3		-0.1
1942	Bos A	1	1	0	1	0	0	0	1	0	0	0	1.000	1.000	1.000	448	-0	0-0	1.000	-0	-0	0	/2		0.0
1946	Bos A	3	5	0	1	0	0	0	0	0	0	1	.200	.200	.200	11	-1	0-0	.900	1	139	202	2b3		0.0
Total	8	466	1521	169	418	79	13	2	169	66	6	75	.275	.308	.348	63	-89	3-5	.973	5	103	91	2b343,S83,3b6		-5.6

CAREY, TOM Thomas John B1849 Brooklyn NY BR/TR/5-8/145 d5.4 M2/U2

YEAR	TM LG	G	AB	R	H	2B	3B	HR	RBI	BB-IB	HP	SO	AVG	OBP	SLG	AOPS	ABR	SB-CS	FA	FR	RNG	THR	GAMES AT POSITION	DL	BFW
1871	Kek NA	19	87	16	20	2	0	0	10	2		1	.230	.247	.253	43	-6	5-0	.857	0	96	74	2b19		-0.4
1872	Bal NA	42	196	42	57	7	0	2	27	2		2	.291	.298	.357	96	-2	4-1	.815	-13	63	39	2b29,S9,3b3,O3R/1		-1.1
1873	Bal NA	56	291	76	98	18	3	1	55	1		4	.337	.339	.430	127	10	2-3	.847	-3	94	106	2b54,3b4,S3,M		0.2
1874	Mut NA	64	287	56	82	10	3	1	38	2		4	.286	.291	.352	102	-6	3-0	.776	-19	80	61	S51,2b13,M		-1.6
1875	Har NA	86	382	63	101	6	2	0	38	1		3	.264	.266	.291	89	-6	13-3	.844	-13	83	136	S86/2		-1.7
1876	Har N	68	289	51	78	7	0	0	26	3		4	.270	.277	.294	84	-6		.882	0	99	84	S68		-0.8
1877	Har N	60	274	38	70	3	2	1	20	0		9	.255	.255	.292	81	-5		.826	-7	107	84	S60		-0.8
1878	Pro N	61	253	30	60	10	3	0	24	0		14	.237	.237	.300	76	-7		.874	2	107	55	S61		-0.2
1879	Cle N	80	335	30	80	14	1	0	32	5		20	.239	.250	.287	77	-8		.864	-3	99	67	S80		-0.7
Total	5 NA	267	1243	253	358	43	8	4	168	8		14	.288	.293	.345	99	-4	27-7	.813	-47	82	105	S149,2b116,3b7,O3R/1		-4.6
Total	4	269	1151	152	288	34	6	1	102	8		47	.250	.255	.293	79	-26		.862	-8	103	72	S269		-1.9

CARFREY, ED Edwin d4.19

| 1890 | Phi AA | 1 | 4 | 0 | 1 | 0 | 0 | 0 | 0 | 0 | | 0 | .250 | .250 | .250 | 48 | 0 | 0 | .750 | -0 | 86 | 74 | /S | | -0.1 |

CARGO, BOBBY Robert J. B10.1868 Pittsburgh PA D4.27.1904 Atlanta GA BR/TR d10.6

| 1892 | Pit N | 2 | 4 | 0 | 1 | 0 | 0 | 0 | 0 | 0 | | 0 | .250 | .250 | .250 | 51 | 0 | 0 | .636 | -0 | 109 | 404 | S2 | | -0.1 |

CARISCH, FRED Frederick Behlmer B11.14.1881 Fountain City WI D4.19.1977 San Gabriel CA BR/TR/5-10.5/174 d8.31 C2

1903	Pit N	5	18	4	6	4	0	1	5	0	0		.333	.333	.722	192	2	0	.969	1	143	102	C4		0.3
1904	Pit N	37	125	9	31	3	1	0	8	9	0		.248	.299	.288	79	-3	3	.984	2	108	109	C22,1b14		0.1
1905	Pit N	32	107	7	22	0	3	0	8	2	1		.206	.227	.262	44	-8	1	.973	3	126	97	C30		-0.3
1906	Pit N	4	12	0	1	0	0	0	1	0	0		.083	.154	.083	-25	-2	1	.909	-1	114	107	C4		-0.2
1912	Cle A	24	69	4	19	3	1	0	5	1	0		.275	.286	.348	78	-2	3	.952	4	103	125	C23		0.4
1913	Cle A	82	222	11	48	4	2	0	26	21	1	19	.216	.287	.252	56	-12	6	.971	14	126	94	C79		0.8
1914	Cle A	40	102	8	22	3	2	0	5	12	0	18	.216	.298	.284	72	-3	2-2	.962	-1	89	90	C38		-0.2
1923	Det A	2	0	0	0	0	0	0	0	0	0						0	0-0	1.000	-0	-0	0	C2		0.0
Total	8	226	655	43	149	17	9	1	57	46	2	37	.227	.280	.285	66	-28	16-2	.968	22	115	99	C202,1b14		0.9

CARL, FRED Frederick E. B9.8.1858 Baltimore MD D1.13.1899 Baltimore MD BL/TL/5-6/158 d7.25

| 1889 | Lou AA | 25 | 99 | 13 | 20 | 2 | 2 | 0 | 13 | 16 | | 22 | .202 | .313 | .263 | 66 | -4 | 0 | .735 | 0 | 128 | 125 | O18(2/4/12),2b6/3 | | -0.3 |

CARL, LEW Lewis Adolph B1836 Baltimore MD D5.19.1885 Newark NJ d9.9

| 1874 | Bal NA | 1 | 3 | 0 | 0 | 0 | 0 | 0 | 0 | 0 | | | .000 | .000 | .000 | -99 | -1 | 0-0 | .250 | -1 | | | /C | | -0.1 |

CARLETON, JIM James Leslie B8.20.1848 NY D4.25.1910 Detroit MI 5-8/155 d5.4

1871	Cle NA	29	127	31	32	8	1	0	18	8		3	.252	.296	.331	85	-1	2-1	.898	-3	87	78	1b29		-0.2
1872	Cle NA	7	38	8	12	1	0	0	4	1		0	.316	.333	.342	114	1	1-0	.956	2	483	135	1b7		0.2
Total	2 NA	36	165	39	44	9	1	0	22	9		3	.267	.305	.333	91	0	3-1	.908	-1	165	89	1b36		0.0

CARLIN, JIM James Arthur B2.23.1918 Wylam AL BR/TR/5-11/165 d7.26 Mil 1942-45 Col Southeastern Louisiana

| 1941 | Phi N | 16 | 21 | 2 | 3 | 1 | 0 | 1 | 2 | 3 | | 4 | .143 | .250 | .333 | 66 | -1 | 0 | 1.000 | -1 | 55 | 0 | O9(0/4/5),3b2 | | -0.2 |

CARLISLE, WALTER Walter G. "Rosy" B7.6.1883 Yorkshire, England D5.27.1945 Los Angeles CA BB/TR/5-9/154 d5.8

| 1908 | Bos A | 3 | 10 | 1 | 1 | 0 | 0 | 0 | 0 | 1 | | 0 | .100 | .182 | .100 | -8 | -1 | 1 | 1.000 | 1 | 298 | 0 | O3L | | -0.1 |

CARLSTROM, SWEDE Albin Oscar B10.26.1886 Elizabeth NJ D4.28.1935 Elizabeth NJ BR/TR/6-0/167 d9.12

| 1911 | Bos A | 2 | 6 | 0 | 1 | 0 | 0 | 0 | 0 | 0 | | 0 | .167 | .167 | .167 | -7 | -1 | 0 | 1.000 | 0 | 108 | 165 | S2 | | 0.0 |

CARLYLE, CLEO Hiram Cleo B9.7.1902 Fairburn GA D11.12.1967 Los Angeles CA BL/TR/6-0/170 d5.16 b-Roy

| 1927 | Bos A | 95 | 278 | 31 | 65 | 12 | 8 | 1 | 28 | 36 | 1 | 40 | .234 | .324 | .345 | 75 | -11 | 4-4 | .965 | -2 | 88 | 132 | O83(30/3/50) | | -1.8 |

CARLYLE, ROY Roy Edward "Dizzy" B12.10.1900 Buford GA D11.22.1956 Norcross GA BL/TR/6-2.5/195 d4.16 b-Cleo Col Oglethorpe

1925	Was N	1	1	0	0	0	0	0	0	0		0	1.000	.000	.000	-99	-0	0-0	—	0			/H		0.0
	Bos A	93	276	36	90	20	3	7	49	16	1	28	.326	.365	.496	117	6	1-1	.909	-5	93	70	O67(43/0/24)		-0.4
	Year	94	277	36	90	20	3	7	49	16	1	29	.325	.364	.495	116	6	1-1	.909	-5	93	70	O67(43/0/24)		-0.4
1926	Bos A	45	165	22	47	6	2	2	16	4	2	18	.285	.313	.382	82	-5	0-0	.904	-5	81	88	O38R		-1.3
	NY A	35	62	3	20	5	1	0	11	4	1	9	.323	.373	.435	112	1	0-0	.941	-1	85	96	O15R		0.0
	Year	80	227	25	67	11	3	2	27	8	3	27	.295	.328	.396	91	-4	0-0	.911	-5	82	90	O53R		-1.3
Total	2	174	504	61	157	31	6	9	76	24	4	56	.312	.348	.450	105	2	1-1	.910	-11	88	78	O120(43/0/77)		-1.7

CARMAN, GEORGE George Wartman B3.29.1866 Philadelphia PA D6.16.1929 Lancaster PA d9.4

| 1890 | Phi AA | 27 | 93 | 9 | 16 | 2 | 0 | 0 | 7 | 8 | 1 | | .172 | .245 | .194 | 30 | -8 | 5 | .768 | -8 | 86 | 74 | S14,O10R,2b2/3 | | -1.5 |

CARMEL, DUKE Leon James B4.23.1937 New York NY BL/TL/6-3/202* d9.10

1959	StL N	10	23	2	3	1	0	0	3	1-0		6	.130	.167	.174	-9	-4	0-1	1.000	-0	97	0	O10(2/8/3)		-0.5
1960	StL N	4	3	0	0	0	0	0	0	1-0		1	.000	.250	.000	-23	-0	1-1	1.000	0	225	102	1b2/OR		0.0
1963	StL N	57	44	9	10	1	0	1	2	9-0		11	.227	.358	.318	88	0	0-0	.974	2	159	0	O38(26/6/8)/1		0.1
	NY N	47	149	11	35	5	3	3	18	16-2		37	.235	.307	.369	93	-1	2-2	.980	-2	99	74	O21C,1b18		-0.6
	Year	104	193	20	45	6	3	4	20	25-2		48	.233	.320	.358	90	-2	2-2	.977	0	123	45	O59(26/27/8),1b19		-0.5
1965	NY A	6	8	0	0	0	0	0	0	0		5	.000	.000	.000	-99	-0	0-0	1.000	0	127	0	1b2		-0.2
Total	4	124	227	22	48	7	3	4	23	27-2		60	.211	.294	.322	73	-7	3-4	.981	0	118	37	O70(28/35/12),1b23		-1.2

CARNETT, EDDIE Edwin Elliott "Lefty" B10.21.1916 Springfield MO BL/TL/6-0/185 d4.19 Mil 1945-46 Col Santa Ana (CA) JC

1941	Bos N	2	0	0	0	0	0	0	0	0		0					0	0-0	—	-0	-0	0	P2		0.0
1944	Chi A	126	457	51	126	18	8	1	60	26		35	.276	.322	.357	95	-4	5-2	.949	-5	97	92	O88(62/25/6),1b25,P2		-1.5
1945	Cle A	30	73	5	16	7	0	0	7	2	1	9	.219	.250	.315	66	-3	0-1	.971	-0	100	68	O16(8/1/7),P2		-0.5
Total	3	158	530	56	142	25	8	1	67	28	6	44	.268	.312	.351	91	-7	5-3	.952	-5	97	88	O104(70/26/13),1b25,P6		-2.0

CARNEY, JOHN John Joseph "Handsome Jack" B11.10.1866 Salem MA D10.19.1925 Litchfield NH BR/TR/5-10.5/175 d4.24

1889	Was N	69	273	25	63	7	0	1	29	14		14	.231	.271	.267	54	-17	12	.957	-6	67	85	1b53,O16(1/0/15)		-2.5
1890	Buf P	28	107	11	29	3	0	0	13	7		3	.271	.333	.299	76	-3	2	.972	1	79	107	1b24,O4(1/0/3)		-0.5
	Cle P	25	89	15	31	5	3	0	21	14		5	.348	.442	.472	157	8	6	.857	-2	97	0	O19R,1b6		0.4
	Year	53	196	26	60	8	3	0	34	21		4	.306	.385	.378	113	5	8	.969	-4	72	115	1b30,O23(1/0/22)		-0.1
1891	Cin AA	99	367	47	102	10	8	3	43	35		18	.278	.346	.373	98	-3	15	.974	1	111	71	1b99		-1.0
	Mil AA	31	110	22	33	5	2	3	23	13		8	.300	.389	.464	120	2	5	.986	4	160	101	1b31		0.3
	Year	130	477	69	135	15	10	6	66	48		26	.283	.356	.394	103	-1	20	.977	5	123	78	1b130		-0.7
Total	3	252	946	120	258	30	13	7	129	83	11	59	.273	.338	.354	92	-13	40	.971	-5	102	85	1b213,O39(2/0/37)		-3.3

CARNEY, PAT Patrick Joseph "Doc" B8.7.1876 Holyoke MA D1.9.1953 Worcester MA BL/TL/6-0/200 d9.20 Col Holy Cross ▲

1901	Bos N	13	55	6	16	2	1	0	6	3		1	.291	.339	.364	95	-0	0	.933	-2	97	0	O13R		-0.3
1902	Bos N	137	522	75	141	17	4	2	65	42	12		.270	.339	.330	105	5	27	.930	-8	106	158	O137(3/0/135),P2		-1.0
1903	Bos N	110	392	37	94	12	4	1	49	28	4		.240	.297	.298	73	-14	10	.953	-3	86	135	O92(3/0/90),P10/1		-1.9
1904	Bos N	78	279	24	57	5	2	0	11	12	1		.204	.240	.237	49	-17	6	.953	-1	145	181	O71(2/9/60),P4/1		-2.1
Total	4	338	1248	142	308	36	11	3	131	85	18		.247	.304	.300	82	-26	43	.942	-14	105	151	O313(8/9/298),P16,1b2		-5.3

CARNEY, BILL William John B3.25.1874 St.Paul MN D7.31.1938 Hopkins MN BB/TR/5-10/? d8.22

| 1904 | Chi N | 2 | 7 | 0 | 0 | 0 | 0 | 0 | 0 | 1 | | 0 | .000 | .125 | .000 | -60 | -1 | 0 | 1.000 | 0 | 580 | 0 | O2R | | -0.1 |

CARPENTER, BUBBA Charles Sydney B7.23.1968 Dallas TX BL/TL/6-1/195 d5.13 Col Arkansas-Monticello

| 2000 | Col N | 15 | 27 | 4 | 6 | 0 | 0 | 3 | 5 | 4-0 | | 13 | .222 | .323 | .556 | 94 | 0 | 0-0 | 1.000 | -1 | 39 | 0 | O6(5/0/1),D2 | | -0.2 |

YEAR	TM LG	G	AB	R	H	2B	3B	HR	RBI	BB-IB	HP	SO	AVG	OBP	SLG	AOPS	ABR	SB-CS	FA	FR	RNG	THR	GAMES AT POSITION	DL	BFW

CARPENTER, HICK Warren William B8.16.1855 Grafton MA D4.18.1937 San Diego CA BR/TL/5-11/186 d5.1

1879	Syr N	65	261	30	53	6	0	0	20	2		15	.203	.209	.226		49	-13	.948	-5	117	72	1b34,3b18,O11R,2b3		-1.7
1880	Cin N	77	300	32	72	6	4	0	23	2		15	.240	.245	.287		80	-7	.853	-0	89	109	3b67,1b9/S		-0.5
1881	Wor N	83	347	40	75	12	2	1	31	3		19	.216	.223	.240		54	-19	.848	3	104	100	3b83		-1.3
1882	Cin AA	80	351	78	120	15	5	1	67	10			.342	.360	.422		154	18	.835	-3	92	93	3b80		1.5
1883	Cin AA	95	435	99	130	18	4	3	40	19			.299	.328	.379		120	9	.870	-5	92	68	3b95		0.5
1884	Cin AA	108	474	80	121	16	2	4	60	6	4		.255	.271	.323		89	-7	.881	-9	86	135	3b108/OR		-1.3
1885	Cin AA	112	473	89	131	12	8	1	61	9	3		.277	.295	.349		101	-1	.860	-7	90	104	3b112		-0.6
1886	Cin AA	111	458	67	101	8	5	2	61	18	6	20	.221	.282	.273		66	-20	8	.841	-7	99	136	3b111		-2.2
1887	Cin AA	127	498	70	124	12	6	1	50	19	4		.249	.282	.303		62	-28	44	.846	-14	95	95	3b127		-3.2
1888	Cin AA	136	551	68	147	14	5	3	67	5	5		.267	.280	.327		89	-10	59	.866	-14	97	81	3b136		-2.0
1889	Cin AA	123	486	67	127	23	6	0	63	18	4	41	.261	.293	.333		76	-17	47	.835	-25	82	87	3b121,1b2		-3.5
1892	StL N	1	3	0	1	0	0	0	0	1	0	1	.333	.500	.333		161	0	0	.714	-0	90	0	/3		0.0
Total	12	1118	4637	720	1202	142	47	18	543	112	28	91	.259	.281	.322		86	-95	158	.853	-86	92	98	3b1059,1b45,O12R,2b3/S		-14.3

CARR, CHARLIE Charles Carbitt B12.27.1876 Coatesville PA D11.25.1932 Memphis TN BR/TR/6-2/195 d9.15 Col Lehigh

1898	Was N	20	73	6	14	2	0	0	4	2	0		.192	.213	.219		24	-7	2	.950	-2	84	114	1b20		-0.9
1901	Phi A	2	8	0	1	0	0	0	0	0	0		.125	.125	.125		-29	-1	0	.926	0	174	0	1b2		-0.1
1903	Det A	135	548	59	154	23	11	2	79	10	2		.281	.296	.374		103	0	10	.982	13	134	114	1b135		1.0
1904	Det A	92	360	29	77	13	3	0	40	14	1		.214	.245	.267		64	-15	6	.983	16	169	109	1b92		-0.1
	Cle A	32	120	9	27	5	1	0	7	4	0		.225	.250	.283		69	-4	0	.973	-0	105	94	1b32		-0.6
	Year	124	480	38	104	18	4	0	47	18	1		.217	.246	.271		65	-20	6	.980	16	152	105	1b124		-0.7
1905	Cle A	89	306	29	72	12	4	1	31	13	1		.235	.266	.310		82	-7	12	.991	-1	89	96	1b87		-1.1
1906	Cin N	22	94	9	18	2	3	0	10	2	1		.191	.216	.277		51	-6	0	.983	1	112	147	1b22		-0.6
1914	Ind F	115	441	44	129	11	10	3	69	26	1	47	.293	.333	.383		86	-16	19	.991	1	98	110	1b115		-1.9
Total	7	507	1950	185	492	68	32	6	240	71	5	47	.252	.280	.329		81	-56	49	.984	27	120	102	1b505		-4.3

CARR, CHUCK Charles Lee Glenn B8.10.1967 San Bernardino CA BB/TR (BR 1995p)/5-10/165* [CinN86 9/228] d4.28

1990	NY N	4	2	0	0	0	0	0	0	0-0	0	2	.000	.000	.000		-99	-1	1-0	—	-0	0	0	/OL		0.0
1991	NY N	12	11	1	2	0	0	0	1	0-0	0	3	.182	.182	.182		3	-1	1-0	1.000	5	153	0	O9C	15	-0.1
1992	StL N	22	64	8	14	3	0	0	3	9-0	0	6	.219	.315	.266		68	-2	10-2	1.000	-0	100	98	O19(5/9/6)		-0.2
1993	Fla N	142	551	75	147	19	2	4	41	49-0	2	74	.267	.327	.330		73	-20	58-22	.985	7	112	99	O139C	17	-0.7
1994	Fla N	106	433	61	114	19	2	2	30	22-1	5	61	.263	.305	.330		64	-23	32-8	.980	6	118	72	O104C		-1.2
1995	Fla N	105	308	54	70	20	0	2	20	46-1	1	49	.227	.330	.312		70	-12	25-11	.987	6	111	179	O103C	27	-0.3
1996	Mil A	27	106	18	29	6	1	1	11	6-0	0	21	.274	.310	.377		70	-5	5-4	1.000	5	123	271	O27C	141	0.0
1997	Mil A	26	46	3	6	3	0	0	0	2-0	1	11	.130	.184	.196		-1	-7	1-0	1.000	-1	77	152	O23C/D		-0.8
†Hou N	63	192	34	53	11	2	4	17	15-2	2	37	.276	.333	.417		98	-1	11-5	.966	-1	98	126	O59(1/58/0)		-0.1
Total	10	507	1713	254	435	81	7	13	123	149-4	12	273	.254	.316	.332		70	-72	144-52	.984	22	111	122	O484(7/472/6)/D	200	-3.4

CARR, LEW Lewis Smith B8.15.1872 Union Springs NY D6.15.1954 Moravia NY BR/TR/6-2/200 d7.4 Col Hobart and William Smith

| 1901 | Pit N | 9 | 28 | 2 | 7 | 1 | 1 | 0 | 4 | 2 | | | .250 | .344 | .357 | | 100 | -1 | | .886 | -3 | 82 | 130 | S9/3 | | -0.3 |

CARRASQUEL, CHICO Alfonso (Colon) B1.23.1928 Caracas, Venez D5.26.2005 Caracas, Venez BR/TR/6-0/170* d4.18

1950	Chi A	141	524	72	148	21	5	4	46	66	5	46	.282	.368	.365		91	-6	0-2	.961	11	107	106	S141		1.2
1951	Chi A★	147	538	41	142	22	4	2	58	46	3	39	.264	.325	.331		79	-16	14-4	.975	12	110	108	S147		0.6
1952	Chi A	100	359	36	89	7	4	1	42	33	2	27	.248	.315	.298		71	-15	2-2	.964	-11	89	88	S99		-2.1
1953	Chi A★	149	552	72	154	30	4	2	47	38	4	47	.279	.330	.359		83	-13	5-3	.976	5	100	94	S149		0.5
1954	Chi A★	155	620	106	158	28	3	12	62	85	5	67	.255	.348	.368		93	-4	7-6	.975	13	103	110	S155		2.3
1955	Chi A★	145	523	83	134	11	2	11	52	61-0	4	59	.256	.335	.368		83	-13	1-1	.973	4	101	102	S144		0.3
1956	Cle A	141	474	60	115	15	1	7	48	52-0	6	61	.243	.323	.323		70	-20	0-4	.967	-20	84	85	S141/3		-3.0
1957	Cle A	125	392	37	108	14	1	8	57	41-2	8	53	.276	.351	.378		102	2	0-2	.960	-8	93	84	S122		0.3
1958	Cle A	49	156	14	40	6	0	2	21	14-1	0	12	.256	.318	.333		81	-4	0-0	.931	-13	76	80	3b32,S22		-1.5
	KC A	59	160	19	34	5	1	2	13	21-0	0	15	.213	.304	.294		64	-8	0-1	.976	-4	92	175	3b32,S22		-1.1
	Year	108	316	33	74	11	1	4	34	35-1	0	27	.234	.311	.313		72	-12	0-1	.947	-17	83	72	S54,3b46		-2.6
1959	Bal A	114	346	28	77	13	4	0	28	34-1	1	41	.223	.292	.295		64	-17	2-3	.970	-7	96	133	S89,2b22,3b2/1		-1.7
Total	10	1325	4644	568	1199	172	25	55	474	491-4	38	467	.258	.333	.342		82	-114	31-28	.969	-6	99	99	S1241,3b49,2b22/1		-4.2

CARREON, CAM Camilo B8.6.1937 Colton CA D9.2.1987 Tucson AZ BR/TR/6-0/198(185-198) d9.27 s-Mark

1959	Chi A	1	1	0	0	0	0	0	0	0-0	0	0	.000	.000	.000		-99	-1	0-0	1.000	0	0	0	/C		0.0
1960	Chi A	8	17	2	4	0	0	0	2	1-0	0	3	.235	.278	.235		41	-1	0-0	1.000	0	197	0	C7		-0.1
1961	Chi A	78	229	32	62	5	1	4	27	21-2	1	24	.271	.331	.354		85	-5	0-1	.995	9	97	74	C71		0.7
1962	Chi A	106	313	31	80	19	1	4	37	33-2	1	37	.256	.328	.361		86	-6	1-1	.995	6	86	61	C93		0.5
1963	Chi A	101	270	28	74	10	1	2	35	23-2	1	32	.274	.332	.341		91	-3	1-0	.987	-1	91	100	C92		0.0
1964	Chi A	37	95	12	26	5	0	0	4	7-3	1	13	.274	.330	.326		86	-2	0-0	.987	-1	264	63	C34	32	-0.2
1965	Cle A	19	52	6	12	2	1	1	7	9-3	0	6	.231	.344	.365		101	0	1-0	1.000	-1	115	82	C19		0.0
1966	Bal A	4	9	2	2	2	0	0	2	3-0	0	2	.222	.417	.444		150	1	0-0	1.000	0	61	278	C3		0.1
Total	8	354	986	113	260	43	4	11	114	97-12	3	117	.264	.331	.349		87	-16	3-4	.993	13	106	81	C320	32	1.0

CARREON, MARK Mark Steven B7.19.1963 Chicago IL BR/TL/6-0/195(170-195) [NYN81 8/185] d9.8 f-Cam

1987	NY N	9	12	0	3	0	0	1	1	1-0	0	1	.250	.308	.250		52	-1	0-1	.800	-0	87	0	O5L		-0.2
1988	NY N	7	9	5	5	2	0	1	1	2-0	0	1	.556	.636	1.111		409	4	0-0	1.000	-1	26	0	O4L		0.3
1989	NY N	68	133	20	41	6	0	6	16	12-0	1	17	.308	.370	.489		150	8	2-3	.983	-1	103	0	O39(18/0/21)	21	0.6
1990	NY N	82	188	30	47	12	0	10	26	15-0	2	29	.250	.312	.473		113	3	1-0	1.000	-3	92	40	O60(16/36/13)	44	-0.1
1991	NY N	106	254	18	66	6	0	4	21	12-2	2	26	.260	.297	.331		77	-8	2-1	.971	-4	82	122	O77(43/22/22)		-1.4
1992	Det A	101	336	34	78	11	1	10	41	22-2	1	57	.232	.278	.360		77	-12	3-1	.979	1	105	91	O83(64/1/19),D13	18	-1.3
1993	SF N	78	150	22	49	9	1	7	33	13-2	1	16	.327	.373	.540		149	10	0-0	.943	-3	76	90	O41(9/5/30),1b3		0.5
1994	SF N	51	100	8	27	4	0	3	20	7-0	2	20	.270	.324	.400		93	-1	0-0	.978	-2	98	0	O33(10/0/24)	16	-0.4
1995	SF N	117	396	53	119	24	0	17	65	23-1	4	37	.301	.343	.490		120	10	0-1	.993	-7	79	103	1b81,O22(3/0/19)		-0.4
1996	SF N	81	292	40	76	22	3	9	51	22-2	2	25	.260	.317	.449		102	0	2-3	.986	-5	77	114	1b73,O5(3/0/2)		-1.2
	Cle A	38	142	16	46	12	0	2	14	11-0	3	6	.324	.385	.451		110	3	1-1	.994	-25	92	88	1b34,O5(0/4/1),D2	37	-0.2
Total	10	738	2012	246	557	108	5	69	289	140-9	19	246	.277	.327	.438		107	16	12-11	.974	-25	92	114	O374(175/68/151),1b191,D15	136	-3.7

CARRIGAN, BILL William Francis "Rough" B10.22.1883 Lewiston ME D7.8.1969 Lewiston ME BR/TR/5-9/175 d7.7 M7 Col Holy Cross

1906	Bos A	37	109	5	23	0	0	0	10	5	1		.211	.252	.211		45	-7	3	.940	-4	84	104	C35		-0.8
1908	Bos A	57	149	13	35	5	2	0	14	3	1		.235	.255	.295		77	-4	1	.955	5	102	118	C47,1b3		1.1
1909	Bos A	94	280	25	83	13	2	1	36	17	2		.296	.341	.368		121	7	2	.972	2	112	105	C77,1b8		1.9
1910	Bos A	114	342	36	85	11	5	0	53	23	6		.249	.307	.313		92	-3	10	.962	-16	100	84	C110		-1.0
1911	Bos A	72	232	29	67	6	1	1	30	26	5		.289	.373	.336		99	1	5	.972	-0	96	106	C62,1b6		0.6
1912	†Bos A	87	266	34	70	7	1	0	24	38	2		.263	.359	.297		84	-4	7	.970	-4	110	86	C87		-0.1
1913	Bos A	87	256	17	62	15	5	0	28	27	2	26	.242	.319	.340		91	-3	6	.979	-7	87	109	C82,M		-0.3
1914	Bos A	82	178	18	45	5	1	1	22	40	2	18	.253	.395	.309		112	6	1-2	.984	8	126	83	C78,M		2.1
1915	†Bos A	46	95	10	19	3	0	0	7	16	1	12	.200	.321	.232		68	-3	0	.975	7	128	106	C44,M		0.8
1916	†Bos A	33	63	7	17	2	1	0	11	11	0	9	.270	.378	.333		113	2	2	1.000	5	151	58	C27,M		0.9
Total	10	709	1970	194	506	67	14	6	235	206	22	59	.257	.334	.314		94	-8	37-2	.971	-3	107	96	C649,1b17		4.6

CARRILLO, MATIAS Matias (Garcia) B2.24.1963 Los Mochis, Sinaloa, Mexico BL/TL/5-11/190* d5.23

1991	Mil A	3	0	0	0	0	0	0	0	0-0	0	—	—	—	—		-99	-0	0-0	—	-0	0	0	O3L		0.0
1993	Fla N	24	55	4	14	6	0	0	3	1-0	1	7	.255	.281	.364		67	-2	0-0	1.000	-1	85	0	O16(4/5/9)		-0.4
1994	Fla N	80	136	13	34	7	0	0	9	9-0	0	31	.250	.295	.301		54	-9	3-3	.982	0	81	246	O49(20/8/25)		-1.0
Total	3	107	191	17	48	13	0	0	12	10-0	1	38	.251	.291	.319		58	-11	3-3	.987	-1	81	174	O68(27/13/34)		-1.4

CARROLL d4.17

| 1884 | Was U | 4 | 16 | 1 | 4 | 0 | 0 | 0 | | 0 | | | .250 | .250 | .250 | | 54 | -1 | | .500 | -1 | 98 | 0 | O4L | | -0.2 |

CARROLL, DIXIE Dorsey Lee B5.9.1891 Paducah KY D10.13.1984 Jacksonville FL BL/TR/5-11/165 d9.12

| 1919 | Bos N | 15 | 49 | 10 | 13 | 3 | 1 | 0 | 7 | 7 | 2 | 1 | .265 | .379 | .367 | | 130 | 2 | 5 | .921 | 1 | 89 | 255 | O13(6/8/1) | | 0.3 |

YEAR	TM LG	G	AB	R	H	2B	3B	HR	RBI	BB-IB	HP	SO	AVG	OBP	SLG	AOPS	ABR	SB-CS	FA	FR	RNG	THR	GAMES AT POSITION	DL	BFW

CARROLL, FRED Frederick Herbert B7.2.1864 Sacramento CA D11.7.1904 San Rafael CA BR/TR/5-11/185 d5.1 Col St. Marys (CA) OF(144/67/108)

1884	Col AA	69	252	46	70	13	5	6		13		5	.278	.326	.440	161	18		.944	7			C54,O15(12/2/1)		2.6
1885	Pit AA	71	280	45	75	13	8	0	30	7		5	.268	.298	.371	112	3		.926	1			C60,O12(10/2/0)		0.8
1886	Pit AA	122	486	92	140	28	11	5	64	52		4	.288	.342	.422	146	27	20	.921	0			C70,O27(15/10/2),1b25/S		2.7
1887	Pit N	102	421	71	138	24	15	6	54	36		2	21	.328	.384	.499	154	32	23	.833	-16	114	0	O46(8/33/5),C40,1b17/S	1.4
1888	Pit N	97	366	62	91	14	5	2	48	32	10	31	.249	.326	.331	120	11	18	.897	-11			C54,O38(31/2/5),1b5/3		0.4
1889	Pit N	91	318	80	105	21	11	2	51	85	11	26	.330	.486	.484	190	50	19	.930	-8			C43,O41(24/12/5),1b7/3		3.7
1890	Pit P	111	416	95	124	20	7	2	71	75	11		.298	.418	.394	128	25	35	.856	-13	103	69	C56,O49(42/6/1),1b7		1.2
1891	Pit N	91	353	55	77	13	4	4	48	48	2	36	.218	.315	.312	85	-6	22	.915	4	81	80	O91(2/0/89)		-0.2
Total	8	754	2892	546	820	146	66	27	366	348	50	136	.284	.370	.408	137	160	137	.903	-35	103	69	C377,O319L,1b61,3b2,S2		12.6

CARROLL, JAMEY Jamey Blake B2.18.1974 Evansville IN BR/TR/5-10/175* [MonN96 14/400] d9.11 Col Evansville

2002	Mon N	16	71	16	22	5	3	1	6	4-0	0	12	.310	.347	.507	118	-1	1-0	.917	-1	98	71	3b13,S3/2		0.1
2003	Mon N	105	227	31	59	10	1	1	10	19-0	3	39	.260	.323	.326	69	-10	5-2	.969	10	128	93	3b67,S14,2b11/D		0.2
2004	Mon N	102	218	36	63	14	2	0	16	32-1	1	21	.289	.378	.372	92	-1	3-3	.995	-3	84	125	2b51,3b13,S10,O2L		0.0
2005	Was N	113	303	44	76	8	1	0	22	34-1	5	55	.251	.333	.284	69	-13	3-4	.980	-9	99	102	2b63,S41,3b12		-1.8
Total	4	336	819	127	220	37	7	2	54	89-2	9	127	.269	.344	.338	80	-23	14-7	.987	-2	92	113	2b126,3b105,S68,O2L/D		-1.5

CARROLL, SCRAPPY John E. B8.27.1860 Buffalo NY D11.14.1942 Buffalo NY BR/5-7.5/? d9.27

1884	StP U	9	31	3	3	1	0	0		2			.097	.152	.129	-26	-6		.824	3	305	334	O8R,3b2		-0.2
1885	Buf N	13	40	1	3	0	0	0	1	2		8	.075	.119	.075	-35	-6		.917	2	202	0	O13(7/6/0)		-0.4
1887	Cle AA	57	216	30	43	5	1	0	19	15	4		.199	.264	.231	40	-17	19	.843	-3	86	47	O54(14/0/40),3b3/2		-1.7
Total	3	79	287	34	49	6	1	0	20	19	4	8	.171	.232	.199	26	-29	19	.853	1	126	68	O75(21/6/48),3b5/2		-2.3

CARROLL, PAT Patrick B3.1853 Philadelphia PA D2.14.1916 Philadelphia PA d5.10

1884	Alt U	11	49	4	13	1	0	0		1			.265	.280	.286	71	-3		.920	-2			C8,O3R		-0.4
	Phi U	5	19	1	3	1	0	0					.158	.158	.211	12	-3		.804	-2			C5		-0.4
	Year	16	68	5	16	2	0	0		1			.235	.246	.265	56	-6		.865	-4			C13,O3R		-0.8

CARROLL, DOC Ralph Arthur "Red" B12.28.1891 Worcester MA D6.27.1983 Worcester MA BR/TR/6-0/170 d6.27 Col Tufts

| 1916 | Phi A | 10 | 22 | 1 | 2 | 0 | 0 | 0 | 1 | | | 8 | .091 | .167 | .091 | -24 | -3 | 0 | .942 | -2 | 63 | 214 | C10 | | -0.5 |

CARROLL, CLIFF Samuel Clifford B10.18.1859 Clay Grove IA D6.12.1923 Portland OR BB/TR/5-8/163 d8.3

1882	Pro N	10	41	4	5	0	0	0	2	0		4	.122	.122	.122	-21	-5		1.000	1	94	508	O10(2/0/8)		-0.4
1883	Pro N	58	238	37	63	12	3	1	20	4		28	.265	.277	.353	87	-4		.902	3	80	209	O58(56/1/1)		-0.2
1884	†Pro N	113	452	90	118	16	4	3	54	29		39	.261	.306	.334	103	2		.904	0	46	34	O113L		0.0
1885	Pro N	104	426	62	99	12	3	1	40	29		29	.232	.281	.282	85	-6		.886	4	51	75	O104L		-0.5
1886	Was N	111	433	73	99	11	6	2	22	44		26	.229	.300	.296	88	-4	31	.862	-0	101	106	O111(109/1/1)		-0.6
1887	Was N	103	420	79	104	17	4	4	37	17	9	30	.248	.291	.336	79	-11	40	.902	1	105	183	O103(102/1/0)		-1.1
1888	Pit N	5	20	1	0	0	0	0	0	0	0	8	.000	.000	.000	-99	-5	2	.667	-1	128	0	O5(1/0/4)		-0.6
1890	Chi N	136	582	134	166	16	6	7	65	53	7	34	.285	.352	.366	106	3	34	.936	11	114	151	O136(112/0/24)		1.0
1891	Chi N	130	515	87	132	20	8	7	80	50	15	42	.256	.340	.367	106	4	31	.915	-5	75	153	O130(0/1/130)		-0.1
1892	StL N	101	407	82	111	14	8	4	49	47	11	22	.273	.363	.376	130	17	30	.901	5	121	28	O101(99/0/3)		1.2
1893	Bos N	120	438	80	98	7	5	2	54	88	5	28	.224	.360	.342	65	-20	29	.917	2	89	127	O120(33/0/89)		-2.1
Total	11	991	3972	729	995	125	47	31	423	361	47	290	.251	.320	.329	93	-29	197	.905	21	88	119	O991(731/4/260)		-3.4

CARROLL, TOM Thomas Edward B9.17.1936 Jamaica NY BR/TR/6-3/186* d5.7 Mil 1958 Col Notre Dame

1955	†NY A	14	6	3	2	0	0	0		0-0	0	2	.333	.333	.333	81	0	0-0	.875	1	177	0	S4		0.1
1956	NY A	36	17	11	6	0	0	0		1-0	0	3	.353	.389	.353	100	1	0-0	.857	3	262	452	3b11/S		0.3
1959	KC A	14	7	1	1	0	0	0	1	0-0	0	1	.143	.143	.143	-21	-1	0-0	1.000	2	144	66	S9,3b3		0.1
Total	3	64	30	15	9	0	0	1	1	1-0	0	6	.300	.323	.300	69	-1	1-0	.813	5	234	373	3b14,S14		0.5

CARSON, KIT Walter Lloyd B11.15.1912 Colton CA D6.21.1983 Long Beach CA BL/TL/6-0/180 d7.21

1934	Cle A	5	18	4	5	2	1	0	2	1		3	.278	.350	.500	115	0	0-0	1.000	-1	41	0	O4R		0.0
1935	Cle A	16	22	1	5	2	0	0	2	1		6	.227	.292	.318	57	-1	0-1	1.000	-0	105	0	O4R		-0.2
Total	2	21	40	5	10	4	1	0	4	2		9	.250	.318	.400	83	-1	0-1	1.000	-1	78	0	O8R		-0.2

CARSWELL, FRANK Frank Willis "Tex", "Wheels" B11.6.1919 Palestine TX D10.16.1998 Houston TX BR/TR/6-0/195 d4.17 Col Rice

| 1953 | Det A | 16 | 15 | 2 | 4 | 0 | 0 | 2 | 3 | 0 | | 1 | .267 | .389 | .267 | 81 | 0 | 0-0 | 1.000 | -0 | 60 | 0 | O3L | | 0.0 |

CARTER, GARY Gary Edmund B4.8.1954 Culver City CA BR/TR/6-2/215* [MonN72 3/53] d9.16 HF2003

1974	Mon N	9	27	5	11	0	1	1	6	1-0	0	2	.407	.414	.593	174	2	2-0	1.000	0	338	58	C6,O2R		0.3
1975	Mon N★	144	503	58	136	20	1	17	68	72-8	1	83	.270	.360	.416	110	8	5-2	.974	-9	92	17	O92R,C66/3		-0.2
1976	Mon N	91	311	31	68	8	1	6	38	30-2	1	43	.219	.287	.336	67	-14	0-0	.994	11	146	138	C60,O36(2/0/34)	46	-0.3
1977	Mon N	154	522	86	148	29	2	31	84	58-5	5	103	.284	.356	.525	137	27	5-5	.990	4	103	87	C146/OL		3.6
1978	Mon N	157	533	76	136	27	1	20	72	62-11	5	70	.255	.336	.422	112	9	10-6	.989	22	149	104	C152/1		3.9
1979	Mon N★	141	505	74	143	26	5	22	75	40-3	5	62	.283	.338	.485	123	14	3-2	.989	22	138	122	C138		4.3
1980	Mon N★	154	549	76	145	25	5	29	101	58-11	1	78	.264	.331	.486	124	16	3-2	.993	25	138	103	C149		5.0
1981	†Mon N★	100	374	48	94	20	2	16	68	35-4	1	35	.251	.313	.444	110	4	1-5	.993	13	157	108	C100/1		2.1
1982	Mon N★	154	557	91	163	32	1	29	97	78-11	6	64	.293	.381	.510	143	34	2-5	.991	25	133	109	C153		6.7
1983	Mon N★	145	541	63	146	37	3	17	79	51-7	7	57	.270	.336	.444	116	12	1-1	.995	25	151	115	C144/1		4.3
1984	Mon N★	159	596	75	175	32	1	27	106	64-9	6	57	.294	.366	.487	144	35	2-2	.993	4	112	91	C143,1b25		4.5
1985	NY N*	149	555	83	156	17	1	32	100	69-16	6	46	.281	.365	.488	140	29	1-1	.992	9	120	98	C143,1b6/OR		4.5
1986	†NY N★	132	490	81	125	14	2	24	105	62-9	6	63	.255	.337	.439	117	11	1-0	.991	8	102	82	C122,1b9,O4(2/0/2)/3	15	2.5
1987	NY N★	139	523	55	123	18	2	20	83	42-1	1	73	.235	.290	.392	83	-15	0-0	.991	1	99	91	C135,1b4/OR		-0.9
1988	†NY N★	130	455	39	110	16	2	11	46	34-1	1	52	.242	.301	.358	93	-5	0-2	.990	-10	75	74	C119,1b10/3		-0.9
1989	NY N	50	153	14	28	8	0	2	15	12-0	0	15	.183	.241	.275	50	-10	0-0	.980	-5	68	132	C47/1	74	-1.4
1990	SF N	92	244	24	62	10	0	9	27	25-3	1	31	.254	.324	.406	103	5	1-1	.992	-5	85	93	C80,1b3	16	-0.1
1991	LA N	101	248	22	61	14	0	6	26	22-1	7	26	.246	.323	.375	98	0	2-2	.988	4	81	121	C68,1b10		0.6
1992	Mon N	95	285	24	62	18	1	5	29	33-4	2	29	.218	.299	.340	82	-6	0-0	.989	-3	58	135	C85,1b5		-0.6
Total	19	2296	7971	1025	2092	371	31	324	1225	848-106	68	997	.262	.335	.439	115	152	39-42	.991	140	120	104	C2056,O137(5/0/132),1b76,3b3	151	37.9

CARTER, HOWIE John Howard B10.13.1904 New York NY D7.24.1991 New York NY BR/TR/5-10/154 d6.21 Col Fordham

| 1926 | Cin N | 5 | 1 | 0 | 0 | 0 | 0 | 0 | 0 | 0 | 0 | 0 | .000 | .000 | .000 | -99 | 0 | 0 | 1.000 | 0 | 172 | 0 | 2b3/S | | 0.0 |

CARTER, JOE Joseph Chris B3.7.1960 Oklahoma City OK BR/TR/6-3/215(215-230) [ChiN81 1/2] d7.30 Col Wichita St. OF(775/432/624)

1983	Chi N	23	51	6	9	1	1	0	1	0-0	1	21	.176	.176	.235	13	-6	1-0	1.000	-0	100	0	O16(14/2/1)		0.2
1984	Cle A	66	244	32	67	6	1	13	41	11-0	1	48	.275	.307	.467	109	2	2-4	.956	4	103	253	O59(48/14/0),1b7	15	0.4
1985	Cle A	143	489	64	128	27	0	15	59	25-2	2	74	.262	.298	.409	92	-6	24-6	.983	7	108	137	O135(122/4/30),1b11/23D		-0.1
1986	Cle A	162	663	108	200	36	9	29	121	32-3	5	95	.302	.335	.514	130	24	29-7	.976	4	113	114	O104(45/9/78),1b70		2.3
1987	Cle A	149	588	83	155	27	2	32	106	27-6	5	105	.264	.304	.480	103	3	31-6	.983	-0	77	86	1b84,O62(42/13/14),D5		-0.9
1988	Cle A	157	621	85	168	36	6	27	98	35-6	7	82	.271	.314	.478	116	11	27-5	.985	0	101	106	O156C		1.4
1989	Cle A	162	651	84	158	32	4	35	105	39-8	8	112	.243	.292	.465	109	4	13-5	.978	-2	96	72	O146(56/103/1),1b11,D8		-0.1
1990	SD N	162	634	79	147	27	1	24	115	48-18	7	93	.232	.290	.391	86	-14	22-6	.988	2	104	143	O150(51/112/0),1b14		-1.3
1991	†Tor A★	162	638	89	174	42	3	33	108	49-12	10	112	.273	.330	.503	123	19	20-9	.974	-3	91	127	O151(57/0/100),D11		1.1
1992	†Tor A★	158	622	97	164	30	7	34	119	36-4	11	109	.264	.309	.498	119	12	12-5	.971	3	100	119	O129(6/0/123),D24,1b4		0.9
1993	†Tor A★	155	603	92	153	33	5	33	121	47-5	9	113	.254	.312	.489	111	7	8-3	.974	-5	97	70	O151(55/0/96),D3		-0.5
1994	Tor A	111	435	70	118	25	2	27	103	33-6	6	64	.271	.317	.524	113	6	11-0	.991	-3	100	153	O110R/D		0.0
1995	Tor A	139	558	70	141	23	0	25	76	37-5	3	87	.253	.300	.428	87	-13	12-1	.975	-0	99	108	O128(116/20/0),1b7,D5		-1.4
1996	Tor A★	157	625	84	158	35	7	30	107	44-2	7	106	.253	.306	.475	95	-8	7-6	.961	-13	74	94	O115L,1b41,D15		-2.8
1997	Tor A	157	612	76	143	30	4	21	102	40-5	7	105	.234	.284	.399	77	-23	8-2	.972	-2	108	103	O55(41/0/10),1b42		-3.3
1998	Bal A	85	283	36	70	15	1	11	34	18-4	2	48	.247	.297	.424	86	-7	3-1	.962	-3	115	132	O50(3/0/47),D32/1		-0.7
	SF N	41	105	15	31	7	0	7	29	6-0	1	26	.295	.322	.562	137	5	1-0	1.000	-3	62	0	O17(4/0/14),1b16		0.1
Total	16	2189	8422	1170	2184	432	53	396	1445	527-86	90	1387	.259	.306	.464	104	13	231-66	.977	-18	99	103	O1730L,1b308,D176/32	15	-5.8

YEAR	TM LG	G	AB	R	H	2B	3B	HR	RBI	BB-IB	HP	SO	AVG	OBP	SLG	AOPS	ABR	SB-CS	FA	FR	RNG	THR	GAMES AT POSITION	DL	BFW

CARTER, BLACKIE Otis Leonard B9.30.1902 Langley SC D9.10.1976 Greenville SC BR/TR/5-10/175 d10.3 Col Furman

1925	NY N	1	4	0	0	0	0	0	0	0	0	1	.000	.000	.000	-99	-1	0-0	1.000	1	46	1047	/OL		-0.1
1926	NY N	5	17	4	4	1	0	1	1	1	0	0	.235	.278	.471	100	0	0-0	.917	-0	112	0	O4(3/0/1)		-0.1
Total	2	6	21	4	4	1	0	1	1	1	0	1	.190	.227	.381	61	-1	0-0	.929	0	100	185	O5(4/0/1)		-0.2

CARTER, STEVE Steven Jerome B12.3.1964 Charlottesville VA BL/TR/6-4/200* [PitN87 17/424] d4.16 Col Georgia

1989	Pit N	9	16	2	2	1	0	1	3	2-1	0	5	.125	.222	.375	70	-1	0-0	1.000	-1	51	0	O5R		-0.2
1990	Pit N	5	5	0	1	0	0	0	0	0-0	0	1	.200	.200	.200	11	-1	0-0	1.000	0	155	0	O3(1/2/1)		0.0
Total	2	14	21	2	3	1	0	1	3	2-1	0	6	.143	.217	.333	56	-2	0-0	1.000	-1	73	0	O8(1/2/6)		-0.2

CARTWRIGHT, ED Edward Charles "Jumbo" B10.6.1859 Johnstown PA D9.3.1933 St.Petersburg FL BR/TR/5-10/220 d7.10

1890	StL AA	75	300	70	90	12	4	8	60	29	3		.300	.367	.447	123	6	26	.976	-1	85	101	1b75		-0.1
1894	Was N	132	507	88	149	35	13	12	106	57	8	43	.294	.374	.485	109	7	31	.973	-1	100	71	1b132		0.4
1895	Was N	122	472	95	156	34	17	3	90	54	1	41	.331	.400	.494	131	22	50	.984	15	149	86	1b122		2.9
1896	Was N	133	499	76	138	15	10	1	62	54	2	44	.277	.350	.353	85	-10	28	.978	0	100	86	1b133		-0.9
1897	Was N	33	124	19	29	4	0	0	15	8	1		.234	.286	.266	46	-10	9	.963	2	143	92	1b33		-0.7
Total	5	495	1902	348	562	100	44	24	333	202	15	128	.295	.368	.432	106	15	144	.977	16	113	85	1b495		1.6

CARTY, RICO Ricardo Adolfo Jacobo (b Ricardo Adolfo Jacobo (Carty)) B9.1.1939 San Pedro de Macoris, D.R. BR/TR/6-3/200(190-210) d9.15 [DL 1968 Atl N 175, 1971 Atl N 122]

1963	Mil N	2	2	0	0	0	0	0	0	0-0	0	2	.000	.000	.000	-99	-1	0-0	—	0			/H		-0.1
1964	Mil N	133	455	72	150	28	4	22	88	43-4	3	78	.330	.388	.554	162	38	1-2	.978	-0	97	72	O121(118/1/2)		3.2
1965	Mil N	83	271	37	84	18	1	10	35	17-0	3	44	.310	.355	.494	136	13	1-4	.958	1	106	86	O73L		1.0
1966	Atl N	151	521	73	170	25	2	15	76	60-7	0	74	.326	.391	.468	137	28	4-6	.971	4	106	95	O126(126/0/1),C17,1b2/3		2.6
1967	Atl N	134	444	41	113	16	2	15	64	49-10	2	70	.255	.329	.401	110	6	4-3	.959	1	105	98	O112(97/0/15),1b9		-0.1
1969	†Atl N	104	304	47	104	15	0	16	58	32-3	0	28	.342	.401	.549	164	26	0-2	.952	-3	96	0	O79L	22	1.8
1970	Atl N★	136	478	84	175	23	2	25	101	77-6	2	46	.366	.454	.584	167	49	1-2	.974	-0	105	57	O133L		4.0
1972	Atl N	86	271	31	75	12	2	6	29	44-4	1	33	.277	.378	.402	112	6	0-0	.979	2	104	63	O78L	33	0.5
1973	Tex A	86	306	24	71	12	0	3	33	36-2	1	39	.232	.311	.301	77	-9	2-0	1.000	-1	96	62	O53L,D31	22	-1.3
	Chi N	22	70	4	15	0	0	1	8	6-0	0	10	.214	.276	.257	45	-5	0-0	.947	-0	104	0	O19L		-0.7
	Oak A	7	8	1	2	1	0	1	1	2-0	0	1	.250	.400	.750	228	1	0-0	—	0			D2		0.1
1974	Cle A	33	91	6	33	5	0	1	16	5-0	0	9	.363	.396	.451	144	5	0-0	.985	-2	22	147	D14,1b8		2.0
1975	Cle A	118	383	57	118	19	1	18	64	45-3	2	31	.308	.378	.504	149	25	2-2	.990	-1	100	113	D72,1b26,O12L		2.7
1976	Cle A	152	552	67	171	34	0	13	83	67-9	0	45	.310	.379	.442	142	32	1-1	1.000	-1	41	97	D137,1b12/OL		2.7
1977	Cle A	127	461	50	129	23	1	15	80	56-6	0	51	.280	.355	.432	117	12	1-2	1.000	1	226	263	D123,1b2	19	0.9
1978	Tor A	104	387	51	110	16	0	20	68	36-5	0	41	.284	.340	.481	127	13	1-1	—	0	0	0	D101		1.0
	Oak A	41	141	19	39	5	1	11	31	21-2	0	16	.277	.368	.560	166	12	0-0	—	0	0	0	D41		1.1
	Year	145	528	70	149	21	1	31	99	57-7	0	57	.282	.348	.502	137	25	1-1	.640	-1	0	0	D142		2.1
1979	Tor A	132	461	48	118	26	0	12	55	46-4	1	45	.256	.322	.390	91	-6	3-1	—	0	0	0	D129		-0.9
Total	15	1651	5606	712	1677	278	17	204	890	642-65	13	663	.299	.369	.464	131	245	21-26	.970	-0	102	68	O807(789/1/18),D650,1b59,C17/3	393	18.1

CARUSO, MIKE Michael John B5.27.1977 Queens NY BL/TR/6-1/172* [SFN96 2/42] d3.31 [DL 2000 Chi A 52]

1998	Chi A	133	523	81	160	17	6	3	55	14-0	7	38	.306	.331	.390	89	-10	22-6	.944	-8	98	107	S131		-0.6
1999	Chi A	136	529	60	132	11	4	2	35	20-0	3	36	.250	.280	.297	47	-44	12-14	.957	-23	92	94	S132,D2		-5.6
2002	KC A	12	20	3	2	0	0	0	0	1-0	0	2	.100	.143	.100	-30	-4	0-0	1.000	-1	135	0	S2,b4,3b2		-0.4
Total	3	281	1072	144	294	28	10	7	90	35-0	10	76	.274	.302	.339	65	-58	34-20	.951	-32	95	99	S268,2b4,3b2,D2	52	-6.6

CARUTHERS, BOB Robert Lee "Parisian Bob" B1.5.1864 Memphis TN D8.5.1911 Peoria IL BL/TR/5-7/138 d9.7 M1/U2 ▲

1884	StL AA	23	82	15	22	2	0	2		4	0		.268	.302	.366	113	1		.750	-4	47	0	O16R,P13		-0.3
1885	†StL AA	60	222	37	50	10	2	1	12	20	0		.225	.289	.302	83	-4		.902	-1	97	233	P53,O7(6/0/1)		0.2
1886	†StL AA	87	317	91	106	21	14	4	61	64	1		.334	.448	.527	196	38	26	.897	4	80	112	P44,O43(1/0/42),2b2		1.3
1887	†StL AA	98	364	102	130	23	11	8	73	66	6		.357	.463	.547	164	33	49	.903	8	121	56	O54(3/2/50),P39,1b7		1.8
1888	Bro AA	94	335	58	77	10	5	5	53	45	4		.230	.328	.334	113	7	23	.899	-1	58	183	O51(4/16/31),P44		0.1
1889	†Bro AA	59	172	45	43	8	3	2	31	44	2	17	.250	.408	.366	121	8	9	.968	1	103	166	P56,O3(0/1/2),1b2		0.0
1890	†Bro N	71	238	46	63	7	4	1	29	47	5	18	.265	.397	.340	115	8	13	.860	-1	74	0	O39(37/1/1),P37		0.0
1891	Bro N	56	171	24	48	5	3	2	23	25	0	13	.281	.372	.380	120	5	4	.940	-1	108	91	P38,O17(1/2/14)/2		0.0
1892	StL N	143	513	76	142	16	8	3	69	86	5	29	.277	.386	.357	131	25	24	.892	-9	75	47	O122(6/7/110),P16,2b6,1b4,M		0.8
1893	Chi N	1	3	0	0	0	0	0	0	1	0	0	.000	.250	.000	-32	-1	0	1.000	-0	0	0	/OC		-0.1
	Cin N	13	48	14	14	2	0	1	8	15	1	2	.292	.469	.396	128	3	4	.857	-1	45	0	O13R		0.1
	Year	14	51	14	14	2	0	1	8	16	1	2	.275	.456	.373	119	3	4	.862	-1	43	0	O14(0/1/13)		0.0
Total	10	705	2465	508	695	104	50	29	359	417	24	79	.282	.391	.400	135	123	152	.875	-14	90	87	O366(58/30/280),P340,1b13,2b9		3.6

CASANOVA, PAUL Paulino (Ortiz) B12.21.1941 Colon, Cuba BR/TR/6-4/200* d9.18

1965	Was A	5	13	2	4	0	0	1	1-0	0	3	.308	.357	.385	112	0	0-0	.938	-2	53	0	C4		-0.2
1966	Was A	122	429	45	109	16	5	13	44	14-2	1	78	.254	.278	.406	95	-5	1-2	.981	-2	142	102	C119		-0.2
1967	Was A☆	141	528	47	131	19	1	9	53	17-5	2	65	.248	.273	.339	84	-13	1-1	.984	1	153	92	C137		-0.6
1968	Was A	96	322	19	63	6	0	4	25	7-1	0	52	.196	.210	.252	42	-24	0-1	.989	-8	119	87	C92		-3.3
1969	Was A	124	379	26	82	9	2	4	37	18-7	3	52	.216	.254	.282	54	-25	0-0	.992	-3	110	85	C122		-2.4
1970	Was A	104	328	25	75	17	3	6	30	10-2	1	47	.229	.251	.354	69	-16	0-0	.988	0	166	96	C100		-1.2
1971	Was A	94	311	19	63	9	1	5	26	14-1	1	52	.203	.238	.286	51	-22	0-3	.985	-3	112	75	C83		-2.5
1972	Atl N	49	136	8	28	3	0	2	10	4-2	0	28	.206	.229	.272	38	-11	0-1	.975	-8	176	78	C43		-1.9
1973	Atl N	82	236	18	51	7	0	7	18	11-3	1	36	.216	.254	.335	58	-14	0-2	.977	-7	54	153	C78		-2.0
1974	Atl N	42	104	5	21	1	0	0	8	5-2	0	17	.202	.232	.202	23	-11	0-0	.986	-2	101	134	C33		-1.2
Total	10	859	2786	214	627	87	12	50	252	101-25	9	430	.225	.252	.319	64	-141	2-10	.985	-33	128	96	C811		-15.5

CASANOVA, RAUL Raul B8.23.1972 Humacao, PR BB/TR/6-0/195(192-230) [NYN90 8/226] d5.24 [DL 1999 Det A 98]

1996	Det A	25	85	6	16	1	0	4	9	6-0	0	18	.188	.242	.341	45	-4	0-0	.978	-4	45	150	C22,D3	55	-1.0
1997	Det A	101	304	27	74	10	1	5	24	26-1	3	48	.243	.308	.332	68	-15	1-1	.985	1	74	108	C92/D		-0.8
1998	Det A	16	42	4	6	2	0	1	3	5-0	1	10	.143	.250	.262	33	-4	0-0	.967	1	78	182	C14	101	-0.2
2000	Mil N	86	231	20	57	13	0	6	36	26-1	4	48	.247	.331	.407	86	-5	1-2	.990	-3	95	65	C72,D3		-0.4
2001	Mil N	71	192	21	50	10	0	11	33	12-2	1	29	.260	.303	.484	102	0	0-0	.991	-6	71	90	C56,D2	58	-0.3
2002	Mil N	31	87	3	16	1	0	1	8	10-4	1	18	.184	.273	.230	38	-8	0-0	.994	-2	68	137	C28	98	-0.9
	Bal A	2	1	0	0	0	0	0	0	0-0	0	1	.000	.000	.000	-99	0	0-0	1.000	0	0	0	C2		0.0
2005	Chi A	6	5	0	1	0	0	0	0	0-0	0	1	.200	.200	.200	7	-1	0-0	1.000	-0	0	0	C6		-0.1
Total	7	338	947	81	220	37	4	28	113	85-8	10	173	.232	.300	.369	73	-41	2-3	.987	-13	75	103	C292,D9	410	-3.7

CASE, GEORGE George Washington B11.11.1915 Trenton NJ D1.23.1989 Trenton NJ BR/TR/6-0/183 d9.8 C4

1937	Was A	22	90	14	26	6	2	0	11	3	0	5	.289	.312	.400	82	-3	2-1	.945	-0	112	50	O22(8/1/14)		-0.4
1938	Was A	141	433	69	132	27	3	2	40	39	0	28	.305	.362	.395	96	-2	11-6	.956	-6	93	73	O101(0/19/82)		-1.2
1939	Was A☆	128	530	103	160	20	7	2	35	56	0	36	.302	.369	.377	98	-1	51-17	.955	-2	103	66	O123(7/79/38)		-0.2
1940	Was A	154	656	109	192	29	5	5	56	52	5	39	.293	.349	.375	94	-6	35-10	.970	-3	99	86	O154(0/118/36)		-0.9
1941	Was A	153	649	95	176	32	8	2	53	51	1	37	.271	.325	.354	84	-17	33-9	.975	12	108	153	O151(115/0/36)		-0.9
1942	Was A	125	513	101	164	26	2	5	43	44	3	30	.320	.377	.407	122	15	44-6	.951	-3	105	43	O120(86/0/34)		1.3
1943	Was A★	141	613	102	180	36	5	1	52	41	3	27	.294	.341	.374	113	9	61-14	.985	2	106	76	O140(18/0/122)		1.1
1944	Was A*	119	464	63	116	14	2	2	32	49	3	22	.250	.326	.302	83	-9	49-18	.979	9	108	70	O114(83/7/28)		-1.1
1945	Was A*	123	504	72	148	19	5	1	31	49	3	27	.294	.360	.357	118	12	30-16	.979	9	108	137	O123(87/15/27)		1.5
1946	Cle A	118	484	46	109	23	4	1	22	34	3	38	.225	.280	.295	65	-18	28-11	.968	-6	90	65	O118L		-3.9
1947	Was A	36	80	11	12	1	0	0	2	8	0	8	.150	.227	.162	10	-10	5-1	.963	1	113	73	O21(12/4/5)		-1.0
Total	11	1226	5016	785	1415	233	43	21	377	426	21	297	.282	.341	.358	95	-36	349-109	.970	5	103	87	O1187(534/243/422)		-5.7

CASEY, DENNIS Dennis Patrick B3.30.1858 Binghamton NY D1.19.1909 Binghamton NY BL/TR/5-9/164 d8.18 b-Dan

1884	Wil U	2	8	1	2	1	0	0		0	0		.250	.250	.375	85	0		1.000	0	0	0	O2C		0.0
	Bal AA	37	149	20	37	7	4	3		5	0		.248	.273	.409	115	2		.898	0	79	208	O37C		0.1
1885	Bal AA	63	264	50	76	10	5	3	29	21	3		.288	.347	.398	137	12		.821	-5	96	0	O63C		0.4
Total	2	102	421	71	115	18	9	6	29	26	3		.273	.320	.401	128	14		.847	-5	89	71	O102C		0.5

YEAR	TM LG	G	AB	R	H	2B	3B	HR	RBI	BB-IB	HP	SO	AVG	OBP	SLG	AOPS	ABR	SB-CS	FA	FR	RNG	THR	GAMES AT POSITION	DL	BFW
CASEY, DOC	James Patrick B3.15.1870 Lawrence MA D12.31.1936 Detroit MI BB/TR/5-6/157 d9.14 Col Maryland-Baltimore Co.																								
1898	Was N	28	112	13	31	2	0	0	15	3	1		.277	.302	.295	71	-4	15	.893	-2	101	120	3b22,S4,C3		-0.5
1899	Was N	9	34	3	4	2	0	0	2	2	0		.118	.167	.176	-6	-5	1	.853	-1	87	209	3b9		-0.5
	Bro N	134	525	75	141	14	8	1	43	25	9		.269	.331	.331	75	-19	27	.892	-16	88	107	3b134		-3.0
	Year	143	559	78	145	16	8	1	45	27	9		.259	.304	.322	70	-24	28	.889	-16	88	113	3b143		-3.5
1900	Bro N	1	3	0	1	0	0	0	1	0	1		.333	.500	.333	125	0	0	1.000	0	103	0	/3		0.0
1901	Det A	128	540	105	153	16	9	2	46	32	10		.283	.335	.357	88	-9	34	.887	3	112	137	3b127		-0.3
1902	Det A	132	520	69	142	18	7	3	55	44	7		.273	.338	.352	90	-7	22	.904	3	106	87	3b132		0.0
1903	Chi N	112	435	56	126	8	3	1	40	19	3		.290	.324	.329	88	-8	11	.915	-19	84	47	3b112		-2.3
1904	Chi N	136	548	71	147	20	4	1	43	18	7		.268	.300	.325	90	-6	21	.911	-10	91	84	3b134,C2		-1.3
1905	Chi N	144	526	66	122	21	10	1	56	41	6		.232	.295	.316	79	-14	22	**.949**	-10	94	50	3b142/S		-2.2
1906	Bro N	149	571	71	133	17	8	0	34	52	8		.233	.306	.291	93	-4	22	.919	-16	93	64	3b149		-1.8
1907	Bro N	141	527	55	122	19	5	0	19	34	3		.231	.282	.279	82	-11	16	.955	-7	95	87	3b138		-1.7
Total	10	1114	4341	584	1122	137	52	9	354	270	55		.258	.310	.320	85	-87	191	.915	-74	96	84	3b1100,C5,S5		-13.6
CASEY, JOE	Joseph Felix B8.15.1887 Boston MA D6.2.1966 Melrose MA BR/TR/5-9/180 d10.1 Col Boston College																								
1909	Det A	3	5	1	0	0	0	0	0	1	0		.000	.167	.000	-45	-1	0	1.000	1	125	193	C3		0.0
1910	Det A	23	62	3	12	3	0	0	2	2	1		.194	.231	.242	45	-4	1	.964	3	114	104	C22		0.2
1911	Det A	15	33	2	5	0	0	0	3	3	0		.152	.222	.152	5	-4	0	.956	-2	103	84	C12,O3C		-0.5
1918	Was A	9	17	3	4	0	0	0	2	2	0	2	.235	.316	.235	67	-1	0	1.000	1	105	72	C8		0.1
Total	4	50	117	9	21	3	0	0	7	8	1	2	.179	.238	.205	32	-10	1	.970	4	111	100	C45,O3C		-0.2
CASEY, BOB	Orrin Robinson B1.26.1859 Adolphustown ON, Can. D11.28.1936 Syracuse NY BR/5-11/190 d7.17																								
1882	Det N	9	39	5	9	2	1	1	7	0		15	.231	.231	.410	101	0		.667	-5	58	0	3b8/2		-0.5
CASEY, SEAN	Sean Thomas B7.2.1974 Willingboro NJ BL/TR/6-4/225(215-235) [CleA95 2/53] d9.12 Col Richmond																								
1997	Cle A	6	10	1	2	0	0	0	1	1-0	1	1	.200	.333	.200	42	-1	0-0	1.000	-0	0	0	/1D		-0.1
1998	Cin N	96	302	44	82	21	1	7	52	43-3	3	45	.272	.365	.417	105	4	1-1	.994	-8	62	104	1b86	32	-1.2
1999	Cin N★	151	594	103	197	42	3	25	99	61-13	9	88	.332	.399	.539	131	30	0-2	.995	-15	59	101	1b148/D		0.1
2000	Cin N	133	480	69	151	33	2	20	85	52-4	7	80	.315	.385	.517	123	18	1-0	.995	-10	72	107	1b129	15	-0.3
2001	Cin N★	145	533	69	165	40	0	13	89	43-8	9	63	.310	.369	.458	107	7	3-1	.994	-10	74	84	1b136,D3		-1.4
2002	Cin N	120	425	56	111	25	0	6	42	43-6	5	47	.261	.334	.362	84	-11	2-1	.993	-2	96	101	1b108/D	37	-2.3
2003	Cin N	147	573	71	167	19	3	14	80	51-4	2	58	.291	.350	.408	102	1	4-0	.996	-10	78	87	1b144		-2.0
2004	Cin N★	146	571	101	185	44	2	24	99	46-5	10	36	.324	.381	.534	137	32	2-0	.994	-18	57	70	1b145/D	16	-0.9
2005	Cin N	137	529	75	165	32	0	9	58	48-3	5	44	.312	.371	.423	112	11	2-0	**.998**	-9	70	76	1b134/D		-0.9
Total	9	1081	4017	589	1225	256	11	118	605	388-46	51	467	.305	.371	.462	114	91	15-5	.995	-81	71	90	1b1031,D10	100	-7.9
CASH, DAVE	David B6.11.1948 Utica NY BR/TR/5-11/172* [PitN66 5/95] d9.13 C2																								
1969	Pit N	18	61	8	17	3	1	0	4	9-0	0	6	.279	.371	.361	108	1	2-0	.990	6	129	82	2b17		0.9
1970	†Pit N	64	210	30	66	7	6	1	28	17-3	1	25	.314	.365	.419	111	3	5-2	.974	8	103	127	2b55		1.5
1971	†Pit N	123	478	79	138	17	4	2	34	46-0	0	33	.289	.349	.354	99	0	13-5	.987	-1	102	120	2b105,3b24,S3		0.8
1972	†Pit N	99	425	58	120	22	4	3	30	22-1	0	31	.282	.316	.374	97	-3	9-9	.992	25	114	136	2b97		2.9
1973	Pit N	116	436	59	118	21	2	2	31	38-0	0	36	.271	.328	.342	88	-7	2-5	.979	5	103	75	2b92,3b17		0.3
1974	Phi N★	**162**	687	89	206	26	11	2	58	46-4	9	33	.300	.351	.378	100	-1	20-8	.977	31	109	127	2b162		4.4
1975	Phi N★	**162**	699	111	**213**	40	3	4	57	56-5	4	34	.305	.356	.388	102	4	13-6	.981	18	104	123	2b162		3.4
1976	†Phi N★	160	666	92	189	14	**12**	1	56	54-3	2	13	.284	.337	.345	91	-8	10-12	**.988**	10	96	**126**	2b158		1.0
1977	Mon N	153	650	91	188	42	7	0	43	52-5	2	33	.289	.343	.375	95	-4	21-12	.986	-15	96	79	2b153		-1.0
1978	Mon N	159	658	66	166	26	3	3	43	37-2	0	29	.252	.291	.315	70	-28	12-6	**.986**	-7	98	103	2b159		-2.8
1979	Mon N	76	187	24	60	11	1	2	19	12-0	0	12	.321	.358	.422	113	3	7-4	.971	-5	99	75	2b47		0.1
1980	SD N	130	397	25	90	14	2	1	23	35-5	0	21	.227	.287	.280	64	-20	6-5	.987	6	104	102	2b123		-0.8
Total	12	1422	5554	732	1571	243	56	21	426	424-28	18	309	.283	.334	.358	92	-60	120-74	.984	81	103	110	2b1330,3b41,S3		10.7
CASH, KEVIN	Kevin Forrest B12.6.1977 Tampa FL BR/TR/6-0/185* d9.6 Col Florida St.																								
2002	Tor A	7	14	1	2	0	0	0	1	1-0	1	4	.143	.200	.143	-6	-2	0-0	.968	0	79	88	C7		-0.2
2003	Tor A	34	106	10	15	3	0	1	8	4-0	1	22	.142	.179	.198	-0	-16	0-0	.995	-4	130	78	C34		-1.7
2004	Tor A	60	181	18	35	9	0	4	21	10-0	4	59	.193	.249	.309	43	-16	0-0	.994	8	145	118	C60	17	-0.9
2005	TB A	13	31	4	5	1	0	2	5	1-0	1	13	.161	.212	.387	56	-2	0-0	1.000	0	167	135	C13	34	-0.1
Total	4	114	332	33	57	13	0	7	31	16-0	6	98	.172	.221	.274	28	-36	0-0	.994	5	140	106	C114	51	-2.4
CASH, NORM	Norman Dalton B11.10.1934 Justiceburg TX D10.12.1986 Beaver Island MI BL/TL/6-0/190(165-190) d6.18 Col Sul Ross St.																								
1958	Chi A	13	8	2	2	0	0	0	0	0-0	0	1	.250	.250	.250	39	-1	0-0	1.000	0	126	0	O4(1/0/3)		-0.1
1959	†Chi A	58	104	16	25	0	1	4	16	18-3	5	9	.240	.372	.375	109	2	1-1	.984	-1	86	93	1b31		-0.1
1960	Det A	121	353	64	101	16	3	18	63	65-1	6	58	.286	.402	.501	140	22	4-2	.991	-1	98	85	1b99,O4(3/0/1)		1.6
1961	Det A★	159	535	119	**193**	22	8	41	132	124-**19**	9	85	**.361**	**.487**	.662	198	83	11-5	.992	5	109	97	1b157		**7.6**
1962	Det A	148	507	94	123	16	2	39	89	104-12	**13**	82	.243	.382	.513	134	28	6-3	.992	8	114	80	1b146,O3R		2.7
1963	Det A	147	493	67	133	19	1	26	79	89-8	6	76	.270	.386	.471	135	27	2-3	.994	3	105	88	1b142		2.2
1964	Det A	144	479	63	123	15	5	23	83	70-4	3	66	.257	.351	.453	121	15	2-1	**.997**	4	107	93	1b137		1.1
1965	Det A	142	467	79	124	23	1	30	82	77-5	4	62	.266	.371	.512	147	31	6-6	.992	6	**115**	96	1b139		3.0
1966	Det A★	160	603	98	168	18	3	32	93	66-4	4	91	.279	.351	.478	133	26	2-1	.988	4	108	96	1b158		2.1
1967	Det A	152	488	64	118	16	5	22	72	81-9	4	100	.242	.352	.430	127	19	3-2	**.995**	10	121	99	1b146		2.2
1968	†Det A	127	411	50	108	15	1	25	63	39-7	3	70	.263	.329	.487	141	20	1-1	.992	9	**127**	91	1b117		2.4
1969	Det A	142	483	81	135	15	4	22	74	63-5	6	80	.280	.368	.464	127	18	2-1	.994	7	**114**	98	1b134		1.4
1970	Det A	130	370	58	96	18	2	15	53	72-6	5	58	.259	.383	.441	127	17	0-1	.989	3	110	83	1b114		1.1
1971	Det A★	135	452	72	128	10	3	32	91	59-7	7	86	.283	.372	.531	148	28	1-0	.992	1	101	96	1b131		2.0
1972	†Det A★	137	440	51	114	16	0	22	61	50-13	4	64	.259	.342	.445	128	15	0-2	.993	2	102	103	1b134		0.7
1973	Det A	121	363	51	95	19	0	19	40	47-7	8	73	.262	.357	.471	124	12	1-0	.991	2	107	85	1b114,D3		0.7
1974	Det A	53	149	14	34	3	2	7	12	19-2	3	30	.228	.327	.416	109	-4	1-1	.985	-0	101	83	1b44		-0.2
Total	17	2089	6705	1046	1820	241	41	377	1103	1043-112	90	1091	.271	.374	.488	138	364	43-30	.992	62	109	92	1b1943,O11(4/0/7),D3		30.4
CASH, RON	Ronald Forrest B11.20.1949 Atlanta GA BR/TR/6-0/180* d9.4 Col Florida St.																								
1973	Det A	14	39	8	16	1	1	0	6	5-0	1	5	.410	.467	.487	162	3	0-0	.900	0	104	357	O7L,3b6		0.4
1974	Det A	20	62	6	14	2	0	1	5	0-0	0	11	.226	.222	.258	38	-5	0-1	.979	-1	87	93	1b15,3b4	23	-0.9
Total	2	34	101	14	30	3	1	1	11	5-0	1	16	.297	.324	.347	89	-2	0-1	.979	-1	87	93	1b15,3b10,O7L	23	-0.5
CASIMIRO, CARLOS	Carlos Rafael B11.8.1976 San Pedro de Macoris, D.R. BR/TR/5-11/179 d7.31																								
2000	Bal A	2	8	0	1	1	0	0	3	0-0	0	1	.125	.125	.250	-9	-1	0-0	—	0			D2		-0.1
CASKIN, ED	Edward James B12.30.1851 Danvers MA D10.9.1924 Danvers MA BR/TR/5-9.5/165 d5.1																								
1879	Tro N	70	304	32	78	13	2	0	21	2		14	.257	.261	.313	95	-1		.902	6	121	94	S42,C22,2b6		0.7
1880	Tro N	82	333	36	75	5	4	0	28	7		24	.225	.241	.264	68	-12		.885	6	112	73	S82,C2		-0.2
1881	Tro N	63	234	33	53	7	1	0	21	13		29	.226	.267	.265	65	-9		.906	3	102	94	S63		-0.4
1883	NY N	95	383	47	91	11	2	1	40	14		25	.238	.264	.285	68	-15		.855	-5	98	62	S81,2b13/C		-1.5
1884	NY N	100	351	49	81	11	1	1	40	34		55	.231	.299	.276	80	-7		.883	5	98	125	S96,C6		0.1
1885	StL N	71	262	31	47	3	0	0	12	12		22	.179	.215	.191	34	-18		.884	-3	101	56	3b69,C2/S		-1.9
1886	NY N	1	4	1	2	0	0	0	1	0		1	.500	.500	.500	203	0		1.000	1	0	0	/S		0.0
Total	7	482	1871	229	427	50	10	2	163	82		170	.228	.261	.269	70	-62		.883	11	104	90	S366,3b69,C33,2b19		-3.2
CASSADY, HARRY	Harry Delbert (b Harry Delbert Cassaday) B7.20.1880 Bellflower IL D4.19.1969 Fresno CA BL/TL/5-8/145 d8.8 Col Illinois Wesleyan																								
1904	Pit N	12	44	8	9	0	0	0	2	2			.205	.239	.205	-36	-3	2-0	.867	-0	243	0	O12R		-0.4
1905	Was A	10	30	1	4	0	0	0	1	0			.133	.133	.133	-16	-4	0	1.000	1	113	0	O9R		-0.4
Total	2	22	74	9	13	0	0	0	4	2			.176	.197	.176	17	-7	2	.933	1	184	0	O21R		-0.8
CASSIDY, JOHN	John P. B1857 Brooklyn NY D7.2.1891 Brooklyn NY BR/TL/5-8/168 d4.24 OF(1/147/411) ▲																								
1875	Atl NA	41	166	14	29	3	2	1	6	0		4	.175	.175	.235	47	-7	0-0	.782	-4	110	43	P30,O12(1/0/11),1b10,2b2		-0.5
	NH NA	6	22	3	3	1	0	0	1	0		1	.136	.136	.182	11	-2	0-1	.988	1	84	14	1b6		-0.1
	Year	**47**	188	17	32	4	2	1	7	0		5	.170	.170	.229	43	-9	0-1	.782	-3	110	43	P30,1b16,O12(1/0/11),2b2		-0.6
1876	Har N	12	47	6	13	2	0	0	8	1		0	.277	.292	.319	95	0		1.000	1	189	0	O8R,1b4		0.1

YEAR	TM	LG	G	AB	R	H	2B	3B	HR	RBI	BB-IB	HP	SO	AVG	OBP	SLG	AOPS	ABR	SB-CS	FA	FR	RNG	THR	GAMES AT POSITION	DL	BFW
1877	Har	N	**60**	251	43	95	10	5	0	27	3		3	.378	.386	.458	147	24		.722	-5	147	117	O58(0/1/57),P2		1.6
1878	Chi	N	60	256	33	68	7	1	0	29	9		11	.266	.291	.301	89	-3		.810	7	190	**265**	O60R/C		0.3
1879	Tro	N	9	37	4	7	1	0	0	1	2		4	.189	.231	.216	52	-2		.889	-1	76	0	O8(0/3/5),1b2		-0.3
1880	Tro	N	**83**	352	40	89	14	8	0	29	12		34	.253	.277	.338	102	-0		.880	-4	95	28	O82(0/47/35)/2		-0.5
1881	Tro	N	**85**	370	57	82	13	3	1	11	18		21	.222	.258	.281	66	-15		.872	-12	87	0	O84C/S		-2.8
1882	Tro	N	29	121	14	21	3	1	0	9	3		16	.174	.194	.215	32	-9		.778	-8	66	140	O16(0/12/4),3b13		-1.6
1883	Pro	N	89	366	46	87	16	5	0	42	9		38	.238	.256	.309	69	-14		.864	-0	133	73	O88(1/0/87)/21		-1.3
1884	Bro	AA	106	433	57	109	11	6	2		19	2			.252	.286	.319	96	-2		.847	-8	132	162	O101R,3b4/S		-1.0
1885	Bro	AA	54	221	36	47	6	2	1	28	8	3		.213	.250	.271	64	-9		.852	-6	83	197	O54R		-1.4
Total	10		587	2454	336	618	83	31	4	_184_	84	5	_127_	.252	.278	.316	89	-30		.845	-35	122	108	O559R,3b17,1b7,S2,2b2,P2/C		-6.9

CASSIDY, JOE   Joseph Phillip   B2.8.1883 Chester PA   D3.25.1906 Chester PA   BR/TR   d4.18   Col Villanova

YEAR	TM	LG	G	AB	R	H	2B	3B	HR	RBI	BB-IB	HP	SO	AVG	OBP	SLG	AOPS	ABR	SB-CS	FA	FR	RNG	THR	GAMES AT POSITION	DL	BFW
1904	Was	A	152	581	63	140	12	**19**	1	33	15	4		.241	.265	.332	90	-10	17	.937	7	96	111	S99,O32(1/20/11),3b23		-0.1
1905	Was	A	151	576	67	124	16	4	1	43	25	2		.215	.250	.262	65	-24	23	.934	**35**	**115**	104	S151		1.7
Total	2		303	1157	130	264	28	23	2	76	40	6		.228	.258	.297	78	-34	40	.935	42	108	107	S250,O32(1/20/11),3b23		1.6

CASSIDY, PETE   Peter Francis   B4.8.1873 Wilmington DE   D7.9.1929 Wilmington DE   BR/TR/5-10/165   d4.18

YEAR	TM	LG	G	AB	R	H	2B	3B	HR	RBI	BB-IB	HP	SO	AVG	OBP	SLG	AOPS	ABR	SB-CS	FA	FR	RNG	THR	GAMES AT POSITION	DL	BFW
1896	Lou	N	49	184	16	39	1	1	0	12	7	4	7	.212	.256	.228	29	-19	5	.973	-7	89	56	1b38,S11		-2.2
1899	Bro	N	6	20	2	3	1	0	0	4	1	2		.150	.261	.200	27	-2	1	1.000	-2	77	0	3b3,S2		-0.4
	Was	N	46	178	21	56	13	0	3	32	9	5		.315	.365	.438	121	5	5	.970	-2	92	111	1b37,3b6,S3		0.3
	Year		52	198	23	59	14	0	3	36	10	7		.298	.353	.414	101	3	6	.970	-5	92	111	1b37,3b9,S5		-0.1
Total	2		101	382	39	98	15	1	3	48	17	11	_7_	.257	.307	.325	72	-16	11	.972	-11	91	84	1b75,S16,3b9		-2.3

CASSINI, JACK   Jack Dempsey "Gabby","Scat"   B10.26.1919 Dearborn MI   BR/TR/5-10/175   d4.19

YEAR	TM	LG	G	AB	R	H	2B	3B	HR	RBI	BB-IB	HP	SO	AVG	OBP	SLG	AOPS	ABR	SB-CS	FA	FR	RNG	THR	GAMES AT POSITION	DL	BFW
1949	Pit	N	8	0	3	0	0	0	0	0	0	0	0	—	—	—		0	0	—	0			/R		0.0

CASTELLANO, PEDRO   Pedro Orlando (Arrieta)   B3.11.1970 Lara, Venez   BR/TR/6-1/175*   d5.30

YEAR	TM	LG	G	AB	R	H	2B	3B	HR	RBI	BB-IB	HP	SO	AVG	OBP	SLG	AOPS	ABR	SB-CS	FA	FR	RNG	THR	GAMES AT POSITION	DL	BFW
1993	Col	N	34	71	12	13	2	0	3	7	8-0	0	16	.183	.266	.338	52	-5	1-1	.909	-2	97	61	3b13,1b10,S5,2b4		-0.7
1995	Col	N	4	5	0	0	0	0	0	0	2-0	0	3	.000	.286	.000	-13	-1	0-0	1.000	-1	0	0	3b3		-0.1
1996	Col	N	13	17	1	2	0	0	0	2	3-1	1	6	.118	.286	.118	9	-2	0-0	1.000	1	167	136	2b3/3OL		-0.1
Total	3		51	93	13	15	2	0	3	9	13-1	1	25	.161	.271	.280	40	-8	1-1	.917	-2	89	53	3b17,1b10,2b7,S5/OL		-0.9

CASTIGLIA, JIM   James Vincent   B9.30.1918 Passaic NJ   BL/TR/5-11/200   d4.14   Mil 1942-45   Col Georgetown

YEAR	TM	LG	G	AB	R	H	2B	3B	HR	RBI	BB-IB	HP	SO	AVG	OBP	SLG	AOPS	ABR	SB-CS	FA	FR	RNG	THR	GAMES AT POSITION	DL	BFW
1942	Phi	A	16	18	2	_7_	0	0	0	2	1	0	3	.389	.421	.389	129	1	0-0	.875	-1	72	198	C3		0.0

CASTIGLIONE, PETE   Peter Paul   B2.13.1921 Greenwich CT   BR/TR/5-11/175*   d9.10

YEAR	TM	LG	G	AB	R	H	2B	3B	HR	RBI	BB-IB	HP	SO	AVG	OBP	SLG	AOPS	ABR	SB-CS	FA	FR	RNG	THR	GAMES AT POSITION	DL	BFW
1947	Pit	N	13	50	6	14	0	0	0	1	2	0	5	.280	.308	.280	55	-3	0	.970	-0	100	74	S13		-0.3
1948	Pit	N	4	2	0	0	0	0	0	0	0	0	0	.000	.000	.000	-98	-1	1	1.000	0	145	0	/S		-0.1
1949	Pit	N	118	448	57	120	20	2	6	43	20	0	43	.268	.299	.362	74	-17	2	.957	4	103	128	3b98,S17,O2R		-1.3
1950	Pit	N	94	263	29	67	10	3	3	22	23	1	23	.255	.317	.350	73	-11	1	.970	-11	86	115	3b35,S29,2b9,1b3		-2.0
1951	Pit	N	132	482	62	126	19	4	7	42	34	1	28	.261	.311	.361	78	-16	2-2	.957	8	115	103	3b99,S28		-0.7
1952	Pit	N	67	214	27	57	9	1	4	18	17	1	8	.266	.323	.374	90	-3	3-3	.951	4	111	64	3b57/1OL		0.0
1953	Pit	N	45	159	14	33	2	1	4	21	5	1	14	.208	.236	.308	41	-15	1-1	.978	1	113	64	3b43		-1.1
	StL	N	67	52	9	9	2	0	0	3	2	0	5	.173	.204	.212	9	-7	0-0	.967	4	121	211	3b51,2b9,S3		-0.3
	Year		112	211	23	42	4	1	4	24	7	1	19	.199	.228	.284	33	-22	1-1	.976	8	114	90	3b94,2b9,S3		-1.4
1954	StL	N	5	0	1	0	0	0	0	0	0	0	0	—	—	—		0	0-0	1.000	0	142	0	3b5		0.0
Total	8		545	1670	205	426	62	11	24	150	103	4	126	.255	.300	.349	71	-73	10-6	.960	12	108	102	3b388,S91,2b18,1b4,O3(1/0/2)		-5.8

CASTILLA, VINNY   Vinicio (Soria)   B7.4.1967 Oaxaca, Oaxaca, Mexico   BR/TR/6-1/200(175-205)   d9.1

YEAR	TM	LG	G	AB	R	H	2B	3B	HR	RBI	BB-IB	HP	SO	AVG	OBP	SLG	AOPS	ABR	SB-CS	FA	FR	RNG	THR	GAMES AT POSITION	DL	BFW
1991	Atl	N	12	5	1	1	0	0	0	0	0-0	0	2	.200	.200	.200	12	-1	0-0	1.000	-1	65	0	S12		-0.2
1992	Atl	N	9	16	1	4	1	0	0	1	1-1	1	4	.250	.333	.313	79	0	0-0	.875	-0	72	0	3b4,S4		0.0
1993	Col	N	105	337	36	86	9	7	9	30	13-4	2	45	.255	.283	.404	71	-15	2-5	.975	4	103	105	S104	15	-0.6
1994	Col	N	52	130	16	43	11	1	3	18	7-1	0	23	.331	.357	.500	105	1	2-1	.984	-0	98	119	S18,2b14,3b9,1b2		0.3
1995	†Col	N★	139	527	82	163	34	2	32	90	30-2	4	87	.309	.347	.564	106	5	2-8	.958	-7	99	87	3b137,S5		-0.3
1996	Col	N	160	629	97	191	34	0	40	113	35-7	5	88	.304	.343	.548	106	5	7-2	.960	**34**	**130**	**150**	3b160		3.9
1997	Col	N	159	612	94	186	25	2	40	113	44-9	8	108	.304	.356	.547	108	7	2-4	.954	12	116	135	3b157		1.8
1998	Col	N★	**162**	645	108	206	28	4	46	144	40-7	6	89	.319	.362	.589	120	18	5-9	.970	0	102	125	3b162/S		1.7
1999	Col	N	158	615	83	169	24	1	33	102	53-7	1	75	.275	.331	.478	81	-18	2-3	.954	-1	101	107	3b157		-1.7
2000	TB	A	85	331	22	73	9	1	6	42	14-3	3	41	.221	.254	.308	43	-30	1-2	.967	14	126	135	3b83	60	-1.5
2001	TB	A	24	93	7	20	6	0	2	9	3-0	1	22	.215	.247	.344	55	-6	0-0	.934	2	101	119	3b24		-0.4
	†Hou	N	122	445	62	120	28	1	23	82	32-3	3	86	.270	.320	.492	99	-1	1-4	.963	9	107	91	3b121,S3		0.7
2002	†Atl	N	143	543	56	126	23	2	12	61	22-4	7	69	.232	.268	.348	64	-32	4-1	**.982**	-18	91	90	3b139		-4.9
2003	†Atl	N	147	542	65	150	28	3	22	76	26-3	3	86	.277	.310	.461	99	-3	1-2	.955	0	104	100	3b147		-0.2
2004	Col	N	148	583	93	158	43	3	35	**131**	51-6	6	113	.271	.332	.535	107	6	0-0	**.987**	7	104	96	3b148		1.3
2005	Was	N	142	494	53	125	36	1	12	66	43-7	5	82	.253	.319	.403	95	-4	4-2	.970	-10	85	91	3b138		-1.3
Total	15		1767	6640	881	1821	339	28	315	1078	428-64	57	1020	.274	.324	.483	95	-68	33-43	.965	45	105	110	3b1586,S147,2b14,1b2	75	-1.4

CASTILLO, ALBERTO   Alberto Terrero   B2.10.1970 San Juan de la Maguana, D.R.   BR/TR/6-0/185(184-215)   d5.28

YEAR	TM	LG	G	AB	R	H	2B	3B	HR	RBI	BB-IB	HP	SO	AVG	OBP	SLG	AOPS	ABR	SB-CS	FA	FR	RNG	THR	GAMES AT POSITION	DL	BFW
1995	NY	N	13	29	2	3	0	0	0	0	3-0	1	9	.103	.212	.103	-14	-5	1-0	.974	3	198	154	C12		-0.1
1996	NY	N	6	11	1	4	0	0	0	0	0-0	0	4	.364	.364	.364	97	0	0-0	1.000	-1	76	0	C6		-0.1
1997	NY	N	35	59	3	12	1	0	0	7	5-0	0	16	.203	.304	.220	44	-5	0-1	.987	2	159	42	C34		-0.1
1998	NY	N	38	83	13	17	4	0	2	7	9-0	1	17	.205	.290	.325	64	-4	0-2	.990	2	137	188	C35/D		-0.1
1999	StL	N	93	255	21	67	8	0	4	31	24-1	2	48	.263	.326	.341	69	-12	0-0	.991	11	159	157	C91		0.3
2000	Tor	A	66	185	14	39	7	0	1	16	21-0	0	36	.211	.287	.265	41	-17	0-0	.993	9	133	116	C66		-0.4
2001	Tor	A	66	131	9	26	4	0	1	4	7-0	1	30	.198	.255	.252	34	-13	1-1	.989	7	98	103	C66		-0.3
2002	NY	A	15	37	3	5	1	0	4	4	1-0	0	12	.135	.158	.216	-2	-6	0-0	.990	3	79	166	C14		-0.2
2003	SF	A	11	15	2	3	1	0	1	4	0-0	0	5	.200	.200	.467	66	-1	0-0	.975	2	219	61	C10	30	0.1
2004	KC	A	29	89	12	24	6	0	1	11	14-0	0	10	.270	.365	.371	94	0	0-2	.995	8	103	123	C29		0.8
2005	KC	A	34	100	13	21	5	1	1	14	12-0	0	21	.210	.292	.310	65	-5	0-0	.992	8	285	84	C34		0.5
	Oak	A	1	1	0	0	0	0	0	0	0-0	0	1	.000	.000	.000	-99	-0	0-0	1.000	0	0	0	/C		0.0
	Year		35	101	13	21	5	1	1	14	12-0	0	22	.208	.289	.307	63	-5	0-0	.992	8	282	83	C35		0.5
Total	11		407	995	93	221	37	2	11	98	100-1	7	209	.222	.295	.296	54	-68	3-6	.990	53	149	123	C398/D	30	0.4

CASTILLO, TONY   Anthony   B6.14.1957 San Jose CA   BR/TR/6-4/190   [SDN75 3/50]   d9.22

YEAR	TM	LG	G	AB	R	H	2B	3B	HR	RBI	BB-IB	HP	SO	AVG	OBP	SLG	AOPS	ABR	SB-CS	FA	FR	RNG	THR	GAMES AT POSITION	DL	BFW
1978	SD	N	5	8	0	1	0	0	0	1	0-0	0	2	.125	.125	.125	-32	-1	0-0	.950	1	226	187	C5		0.0

CASTILLO, BRAULIO   Braulio Robinson Medrano (b Braulio Robinson Medrano (Castillo))   B5.13.1968 Elias Pina, D.R.   BR/TR/6-0/160*   d8.18

YEAR	TM	LG	G	AB	R	H	2B	3B	HR	RBI	BB-IB	HP	SO	AVG	OBP	SLG	AOPS	ABR	SB-CS	FA	FR	RNG	THR	GAMES AT POSITION	DL	BFW
1991	Phi	N	28	52	3	9	3	0	2	2	1-0	0	15	.173	.189	.231	17	-6	1-1	.977	0	98	208	O26(0/24/2)		-0.6
1992	Phi	N	28	76	12	15	3	1	2	7	4-0	0	15	.197	.237	.342	62	-4	1-0	.956	-1	102	9	O24(2/6/16)		-0.6
Total	2		56	128	15	24	6	1	4	9	5-0	0	30	.188	.218	.297	44	-10	2-1	.966	-1	100	98	O50(2/30/18)		-1.2

CASTILLO, MANNY   Esteban Manuel Antonio (Cabrera)   B4.1.1957 Santo Domingo, D.R.   BB/TR/5-9/160(160-180)   d9.1

YEAR	TM	LG	G	AB	R	H	2B	3B	HR	RBI	BB-IB	HP	SO	AVG	OBP	SLG	AOPS	ABR	SB-CS	FA	FR	RNG	THR	GAMES AT POSITION	DL	BFW
1980	KC	A	7	10	1	2	0	0	0	0	0-0	0	1	.200	.200	.200	10	-1	0-0	1.000	0	103	0	3b3/2D		0.0
1982	Sea	A	138	506	49	130	29	1	3	49	22-2	2	35	.257	.286	.336	69	-21	2-8	.938	-16	81	74	3b130,2b9		-4.2
1983	Sea	A	91	203	13	42	6	3	0	24	7-2	1	20	.207	.233	.266	37	-18	1-1	.971	8	112	94	3b55,1b11,2b5/PD		-1.1
Total	3		236	719	63	174	35	4	3	73	29-4	3	56	.242	.270	.314	59	-40	3-9	.949	-8	89	78	3b188,2b15,1b11,D8/P		-5.4

CASTILLO, JOSE   Jose (Rondon)   B3.19.1981 Las Mercedes, Venez   BR/TR/6-1/200*   d4.7

YEAR	TM	LG	G	AB	R	H	2B	3B	HR	RBI	BB-IB	HP	SO	AVG	OBP	SLG	AOPS	ABR	SB-CS	FA	FR	RNG	THR	GAMES AT POSITION	DL	BFW
2004	Pit	N	129	383	44	98	15	2	8	39	23-5	1	92	.256	.298	.368	71	-17	3-2	.980	4	100	113	2b123,S2		-0.8
2005	Pit	N	101	370	49	99	16	3	11	53	23-3	0	59	.268	.307	.416	89	-8	2-3	.977	16	108	139	2b100	69	1.2
Total	2		230	753	93	197	31	5	19	92	46-8	1	151	.262	.303	.392	80	-25	5-5	.979	20	104	125	2b223,S2	69	0.4

CASTILLO, JUAN   Juan (Bryas)   B1.25.1962 San Pedro de Macoris, D.R.   BB/TR (BR 1988-89)/5-11/162*   d4.12

YEAR	TM	LG	G	AB	R	H	2B	3B	HR	RBI	BB-IB	HP	SO	AVG	OBP	SLG	AOPS	ABR	SB-CS	FA	FR	RNG	THR	GAMES AT POSITION	DL	BFW
1986	Mil	A	26	54	6	9	0	1	0	5	5-0	1	12	.167	.250	.204	24	-6	1-1	1.000	-2	83	77	2b17,S4,3b2/ORD		-0.7
1987	Mil	A	116	321	44	72	11	4	3	28	33-0	3	76	.224	.302	.312	61	-18	15-7	.973	-11	90	93	2b97,S13,3b7	15	-2.2
1988	Mil	A	54	90	10	20	0	0	0	2	3-0	0	14	.222	.247	.222	32	-8	2-0	.932	0	129	105	2b18,3b17,S13/OLD	38	-0.7
1989	Mil	A	3	4	0	0	0	0	0	0	0-0	0	2	.000	.000	.000	-99	-1	0-0	1.000	0	90	83	2b3		-0.1
Total	4		199	469	60	101	11	5	3	38	41-0	4	104	.215	.282	.279	54	-33	18-8	.972	-13	93	92	2b135,S30,3b26,D5,O2(1/0/1)	53	-3.7

YEAR	TM	LG	G	AB	R	H	2B	3B	HR	RBI	BB-IB	HP	SO	AVG	OBP	SLG	AOPS	ABR	SB-CS	FA	FR	RNG	THR	GAMES AT POSITION	DL	BFW

CASTILLO, LUIS Luis Antonio (Donato) B9.12.1975 San Pedro de Macoris, D.R. BB/TR (BR 1998p)/5-11/175(155-196) d8.8

1996	Fla	N	41	164	26	43	2	1	1	8	14-0	0	46	.262	.320	.305	68	-8	17-4	.986	7	104	143	2b41		0.3
1997	Fla	N	75	263	27	63	8	0	0	8	27-0	0	53	.240	.310	.270	56	-17	16-10	.971	-3	94	106	2b70	15	-1.6
1998	Fla	N	44	153	21	31	3	2	1	10	22-0	1	33	.203	.307	.268	56	-10	3-0	.970	-1	93	105	2b44		-0.8
1999	Fla	N	128	487	76	147	23	4	0	28	67-0	0	85	.302	.384	.366	97	1	50-17	.976	-12	97	88	2b126		-0.1
2000	Fla	N	136	539	101	180	17	3	2	17	78-0	0	86	.334	.418	.388	111	13	**62**-22	.983	-4	98	92	2b136	19	2.1
2001	Fla	N	134	537	76	141	16	10	2	45	67-0	1	90	.263	.344	.341	81	-15	33-16	.980	10	104	**118**	2b133		0.3
2002	Fla	N★	146	606	86	185	18	5	2	39	55-4	2	76	.305	.364	.361	99	-3	**48**-15	.981	-12	97	94	2b144		-0.3
2003	†Fla	N★	152	595	99	187	19	6	6	39	63-0	2	60	.314	.381	.397	108	8	21-19	.986	4	103	99	2b152		1.6
2004	Fla	N	150	564	91	164	12	7	2	47	75-2	1	68	.291	.373	.348	93	-4	21-4	.991	1	99	111	2b148		0.7
2005	Fla	N★	122	439	72	132	12	4	4	30	65-1	1	32	.301	.391	.374	108	8	10-7	.988	20	109	109	2b120		3.2
Total	10		1128	4347	675	1273	130	42	20	271	533-7	8	629	.293	.370	.356	94	-27	281-114	.983	10	100	103	2b1114	34	5.4

CASTILLO, MARTY Martin Horace B1.16.1957 Long Beach CA BR/TR/6-1/190(190-205) [DetA78 5/116] d8.19 Col Chapman

1981	Det	A	6	8	1	1	0	0	0	0	0-0	0	2	.125	.125	.125	-27	-1	0-0	1.000	2	147	642	3b4/COL		0.1
1982	Det	A	1	0	0	0	0	0	0	0	0-0	0	0	—	—	—		0	0-0	1.000	-0	7	0	/C		0.0
1983	Det	A	67	119	10	23	4	0	2	10	7-0	0	22	.193	.238	.277	42	-10	2-0	.990	0	94	82	3b58,C10		-1.0
1984	†Det	A	70	141	16	33	5	2	4	17	10-0	0	33	.234	.285	.383	83	-4	1-0	.970	-6	101	111	C36,3b33/D		-0.8
1985	Det	A	57	84	4	10	2	0	2	5	2-0	0	19	.119	.138	.214	-5	-12	0-2	.977	0	109	157	C32,3b25		-1.2
Total	5		201	352	31	67	11	2	8	32	19-0	0	76	.190	.231	.301	46	-27	3-2	.978	-4	97	91	3b120,C80/DOL		-2.9

CASTILLO, CARMEN Monte Carmelo B6.8.1958 San Pedro de Macoris, D.R. BR/TR/6-1/190(185-201) d7.17

1982	Cle	A	47	120	11	25	4	0	2	11	6-2	2	17	.208	.258	.292	50	-8	0-0	.978	1	123	0	O43(19/8/20),D2		-0.9
1983	Cle	A	23	36	9	10	2	1	1	3	4-0	1	6	.278	.366	.472	124	1	1-1	.929	1	99	343	O19R/D		0.2
1984	Cle	A	87	211	36	55	9	2	10	36	21-0	2	32	.261	.329	.464	116	4	1-3	.933	-2	106	57	O70R,D2		-0.1
1985	Cle	A	67	184	27	45	5	1	11	25	11-0	3	40	.245	.298	.462	105	0	3-0	.953	-0	116	0	O51R,D9		-0.2
1986	Cle	A	85	205	34	57	9	0	8	32	9-0	1	48	.278	.310	.439	103	0	2-1	.939	2	106	209	O37R,D35		0.0
1987	Cle	A	89	220	27	55	17	0	11	31	16-0	0	52	.250	.296	.477	101	0	1-1	1.000	1	92	264	D43,O23(1/0/22)		-0.1
1988	Cle	A	66	176	12	48	8	0	4	14	5-1	1	31	.273	.297	.386	87	-4	6-2	.933	-2	96	49	O45(30/0/16),D9		-0.6
1989	Min	A	94	218	23	56	13	3	8	33	15-1	1	40	.257	.305	.454	105	1	1-2	.976	2	113	81	O67(7/0/61),D16		0.1
1990	Min	A	64	137	11	30	4	0	0	12	3-1	1	23	.219	.239	.248	35	-12	0-1	.923	-1	104	0	D35,O21(2/0/21)		-1.5
1991	Min	A	9	12	0	2	1	0	0	0	0-0	1	1	.167	.231	.333	52	-1	0-0	1.000	1	126	0	O4(1/0/3),D2		-0.1
Total	10		631	1519	190	383	71	8	55	197	90-5	13	291	.252	.298	.418	93	-19	15-11	.953	3	109	80	O380(60/8/320),D154		-3.2

CASTINO, JOHN John Anthony B10.23.1954 Evanston IL BR/TR/5-11/175* [MinA76 3/58] d4.6 Col Rollins [DL 1985 Min A 181]

1979	Min	A	148	393	49	112	13	6	5	52	27-0	1	72	.285	.331	.397	92	-6	5-2	.963	9	109	**136**	3b143,S5		0.2
1980	Min	A	150	546	67	165	17	7	13	64	29-1	0	67	.302	.336	.430	101	-1	7-5	.961	21	114	122	3b138,S18		2.0
1981	Min	A	101	381	41	102	13	**9**	6	36	18-3	1	52	.268	.301	.396	94	-5	4-5	**.975**	17	113	125	3b98,2b4		1.1
1982	Min	A	117	410	48	99	12	6	6	37	36-1	2	51	.241	.304	.344	76	-14	2-5	.995	-0	90	100	2b96,3b21,O6(5/1/0)/D	14	-1.2
1983	Min	A	142	563	83	156	30	4	11	57	62-1	1	54	.277	.348	.403	102	3	4-2	.990	10	104	92	2b132,3b8/D		2.0
1984	Min	A	8	27	5	12	1	0	0	3	5-2	0	2	.444	.531	.481	173	3	0-0	1.000	-1	81	74	3b8	140	0.2
Total	6		666	2320	293	646	86	34	41	249	177-8	5	298	.278	.329	.398	95	-20	22-19	.967	56	112	126	3b416,2b232,S23,O6(5/1/0),D2	335	4.3

CASTINO, VINCE Vincent Charles B10.11.1917 Willisville IL D3.6.1967 Sacramento CA BR/TR/5-9/175 d6.24

1943	Chi	A	33	101	14	23	1	0	2	16	12	0	14	.228	.310	.297	78	-3	0-0	.971	-5	88	47	C30		-0.6
1944	Chi	A	29	78	8	18	5	0	0	3	10	1	13	.231	.326	.295	79	-2	0-1	.990	1	120	137	C26		0.1
1945	Chi	A	26	36	2	8	1	0	0	4	3	0	7	.222	.282	.250	56	-2	0-0	.951	-1	160	111	C25		-0.3
Total	3		88	215	24	49	7	0	2	23	25	1	31	.228	.311	.288	75	-7	0-1	.976	-5	112	92	C81		-0.8

CASTLE, DON Donald Hardy B2.1.1950 Kokomo IN BL/TL/6-1/205 [TexA68 1/8] d9.11

| 1973 | Tex | A | 4 | 13 | 0 | 4 | 1 | 0 | 0 | 2 | 1-0 | 0 | 3 | .308 | .357 | .385 | 113 | 0 | 0-0 | — | 0 | | | D3 | | 0.0 |

CASTLE, JOHN John Francis B6.1.1883 Honey Brook PA D4.13.1929 Philadelphia PA 5-10.5/? d4.25

| 1910 | Phi | N | 3 | 4 | 1 | 1 | 0 | 0 | 0 | 0 | 0 | 0 | | .250 | .250 | .250 | 44 | 0 | 1 | — | -0 | 0 | 0 | O2(1/1/0) | | 0.0 |

CASTLEMAN, FOSTER Foster Ephraim B1.1.1931 Nashville TN BR/TR/6-0/175* d8.4

1954	NY	N	13	12	0	3	0	0	0	1	0	1	3	.250	.308	.250	47	-1	0-0	—	-0	0	0	3b2		-0.1
1955	NY	N	15	28	3	6	1	0	2	4	2-0	0	4	.214	.267	.464	89	-1	0-0	1.000	-2	73	57	2b6/3		-0.2
1956	NY	N	124	385	33	87	16	3	14	45	15-2	2	50	.226	.256	.392	72	-17	2-1	.947	3	108	61	3b107,S2/2		-1.4
1957	NY	N	18	37	7	6	2	0	1	1	2-0	0	4	.162	.205	.297	33	-4	0-0	.867	-1	101	106	3b7/2S		-0.5
1958	Bal	A	98	200	15	34	5	0	3	14	16-2	3	34	.170	.242	.240	35	-18	2-0	.964	-15	85	95	S91,2b4,3b4/OL		-2.8
Total	5		268	662	58	136	24	3	20	65	35-4	6	99	.205	.250	.341	60	-41	4-1	.944	-14	107	63	3b121,S94,2b12/OL		-5.0

CASTRO, BERNIE Bernabel B7.14.1979 Santo Domingo, D.R. BB/TR/5-10/165 d9.1

| 2005 | Bal | A | 24 | 80 | 14 | 23 | 3 | 1 | 0 | 7 | 9-0 | 0 | 10 | .287 | .360 | .350 | 90 | -1 | 6-2 | .941 | -1 | 99 | 92 | 2b11/OLD | | -0.1 |

CASTRO, JUAN Juan Gabriel B6.20.1972 Los Mochis, Sinaloa, Mexico BR/TR/5-10/187(163-195) d9.2

1995	LA	N	11	4	0	1	0	0	0	0	1-0	0	1	.250	.400	.250	82	0	0-0	1.000	1	153	0	3b7,S4		0.1
1996	†LA	N	70	132	16	26	5	3	0	5	10-0	0	27	.197	.254	.280	43	-11	1-0	.982	-5	90	137	S30,3b23,2b9/OL		-1.4
1997	LA	N	40	75	3	11	3	1	0	4	7-1	0	20	.147	.220	.213	15	-10	0-0	1.000	-2	82	77	S22,2b14,3b3	58	-1.1
1998	LA	N	89	220	25	43	7	0	2	14	15-0	0	37	.195	.245	.255	34	-22	0-0	.954	3	102	143	S47,2b38,3b12		-1.5
1999	LA	N	2	1	0	0	0	0	0	0	0-0	0	1	.000	.000	.000	-99	0	0-0	1.000	1	408	463	/2S		0.1
2000	Cin	N	82	224	20	54	12	2	4	23	14-1	0	33	.241	.283	.366	61	-14	0-2	.994	-7	95	101	S57,2b21,3b7		-1.6
2001	Cin	N	96	242	27	54	10	3	13	13-2	0	50	.223	.261	.302	43	-21	0-0	.944	-14	89	68	S46,2b37,3b19/1		-3.1
2002	Cin	N	54	82	5	18	3	0	2	11	7-0	0	18	.220	.278	.329	60	-5	0-0	.964	-0	96	125	S25,2b17/13	62	-0.4
2003	Cin	N	113	320	28	81	14	1	9	33	18-1	0	58	.253	.290	.387	79	-11	2-3	.984	-1	108	94	2b56,3b30,S24/1	15	-0.9
2004	Cin	N	111	299	36	73	21	2	5	26	14-1	0	51	.244	.277	.378	69	-15	1-0	.958	3	91	84	3b78,S31,2b12,1b4	21	-0.9
2005	Min	A	97	272	27	70	18	1	5	33	9-1	0	39	.257	.279	.353	73	-11	0-1	.985	15	124	134	S73,3b22,2b5	22	0.9
Total	11		765	1871	187	471	93	10	30	162	108-7	0	335	.230	.271	.339	55	-120	4-6	.978	-6	102	117	S360,2b210,3b202,1b7/OL	178	-9.8

CASTRO, LOUIS Louis Manuel "Jud" B1877 , Colombia D9.24.1941 New York NY BR/TR/5-7/? d4.23 Col Manhattan

| 1902 | Phi | A | 42 | 143 | 18 | 35 | 8 | 1 | 1 | 15 | 4 | 0 | | .245 | .265 | .336 | 63 | -8 | 2 | .918 | -11 | 82 | 70 | 2b36,O3(0/2/1)/S | | -1.8 |

CASTRO, RAMON Ramon Abraham B3.1.1976 Vega Baja, PR BR/TR/6-3/225* [HouN94 1/17] d8.27

1999	Fla	N	24	67	4	12	4	0	2	10	4-3	0	14	.179	.282	.328	58	-4	0-0	.992	-1	141	143	C24		-0.4
2000	Fla	N	50	138	10	33	4	0	2	14	16-7	1	36	.239	.318	.312	65	-8	0-0	.980	-1	93	128	C50		-0.6
2001	Fla	N	7	11	0	2	0	0	0	1	1-0	0	1	.182	.250	.182	15	-1	0-0	1.000	-1	94	0	C3		-0.2
2002	Fla	N	54	101	11	24	4	0	6	18	14-3	0	24	.238	.322	.455	112	1	0-0	1.000	-4	78	119	C37/D	22	-0.1
2003	Fla	N	40	53	6	15	2	0	5	8	4-0	0	11	.283	.333	.604	143	3	0-0	.982	-1	176	0	C18/D		0.3
2004	Fla	N	32	96	9	13	3	0	3	8	11-2	1	30	.135	.231	.260	28	-11	0-0	.990	-1	163	89	C31	124	-0.8
2005	NY	N	99	209	26	51	16	0	8	41	25-2	0	58	.244	.321	.435	99	0	1-0	.993	-3	133	80	C99	18	0.2
Total	7		306	675	66	150	33	0	26	94	81-17	2	174	.222	.304	.387	82	-20	1-0	.990	-9	124	100	C262,D2	164	-1.6

CASTRO, RAMON Ramon Alfredo B10.23.1979 Valencia, Venez BR/TR/6-0/195 d6.21

| 2004 | Oak | A | 9 | 15 | 2 | 2 | 1 | 0 | 0 | 3 | 1-1 | 0 | 3 | .133 | .188 | .200 | 1 | -2 | 0-0 | 1.000 | -1 | 60 | 0 | 3b6/SD | | -0.3 |

CATALANOTTO, FRANK Frank John B4.27.1974 Smithtown NY BL/TR/6-0/195(170-195) [DetA92 10/280] d9.3 OF(317/0/59)

1997	Det	A	13	26	2	8	2	0	0	3	3-0	0	7	.308	.379	.385	101	0	0-0	1.000	-2	81	0	2b6,D3		-0.1
1998	Det	A	89	213	23	60	13	2	6	25	12-1	4	39	.282	.325	.446	99	-1	3-2	.974	-0	86	108	2b31,D23,1b18,3b3		-0.6
1999	Det	A	100	286	41	79	19	0	11	35	15-1	9	49	.276	.327	.458	97	-2	3-4	1.000	-10	72	130	1b32,2b32,3b21,D9		-1.2
2000	Tex	A	103	282	55	82	13	3	10	42	33-0	6	36	.291	.375	.457	108	4	6-2	.966	-5	101	73	2b49,D20,1b17/OR	22	0.0
2001	Tex	A	133	463	77	153	31	5	11	54	39-3	8	55	.330	.391	.490	127	19	15-5	.995	-1	106	36	O92(78/0/15),2b13,3b11,1b5,D5		1.6
2002	Tex	A	68	212	42	57	16	4	3	23	25-0	8	27	.269	.364	.443	111	4	9-5	.971	-3	84	0	O26L,2b23,1b15,D8	92	0.0
2003	Tor	A	133	489	83	146	34	6	13	59	35-1	6	62	.299	.351	.472	111	4	2-2	.993	-8	79	74	O100(61/0/43),D21,1b5		-0.6
2004	Tor	A	75	249	27	73	19	1	1	26	17-1	4	33	.293	.344	.390	87	-4	1-0	.971	-1	95	51	O41L,D29	95	-0.8
2005	Tor	A	130	419	56	126	29	5	8	59	37-0	10	53	.301	.367	.451	111	8	0-2	**1.000**	-3	94	84	O111L,D15		0.0
Total	9		844	2639	406	784	176	27	63	326	216-7	55	361	.297	.357	.456	109	36	39-22	.992	-32	92	59	O371L,2b154,D133,1b92,3b35	209	-1.4

YEAR	TM LG	G	AB	R	H	2B	3B	HR	RBI	BB-IB	HP	SO	AVG	OBP	SLG	AOPS	ABR	SB-CS	FA	FR	RNG	THR	GAMES AT POSITION	DL	BFW
CATER, DANNY	Danny Anderson B2.25.1940 Austin TX BR/TR/5-11.5/180(170-198) d4.14 OF(293/2/16)																								
1964	Phi N	60	152	13	45	9	1	1	13	7-1	0	15	.296	.325	.388	102	0	1-0	.981	-9	98	218	O39(36/1/2),1b7/3	40	0.0
1965	Chi A	142	514	74	139	18	4	14	55	33-0	3	65	.270	.316	.403	110	5	3-3	.978	-10	80	82	O127(127/1/0),3b11,1b3		-1.3
1966	Chi A	21	60	3	11	1	1	0	4	0-0	1	10	.183	.194	.233	25	-6	3-1	.909	-3	70	0	O18(16/0/3)		-1.0
	KC A	116	425	47	124	16	3	7	52	28-2	1	37	.292	.334	.393	113	6	1-4	.994	-2	100	111	1b53,3b42,O22(21/0/1)		-0.2
	Year	137	485	50	135	17	4	7	56	28-2	2	47	.278	.317	.373	102	0	4-5	.994	-5	100	111	1b53,3b42,O40(37/0/4)		-1.2
1967	KC A	142	529	55	143	17	4	4	46	34-9	4	56	.270	.317	.340	98	-2	4-5	.916	-10	76	36	3b56,O55L,1b44		-2.0
1968	Oak A	147	504	53	146	28	3	6	62	35-3	2	43	.290	.336	.393	126	15	8-7	.995	-3	87	108	1b121,O20(19/0/2)/2		0.4
1969	Oak A	152	584	64	153	24	2	10	76	28-3	2	40	.262	.296	.361	87	-13	1-4	.992	2	112	114	1b132,O20(19/0/1),2b4		-2.5
1970	NY A	155	582	64	175	26	5	6	76	34-6	2	44	.301	.340	.393	107	4	4-2	.992	-4	98	96	1b131,3b42,O7R		-1.0
1971	NY A	121	428	39	118	16	5	4	50	19-4	2	25	.276	.308	.364	95	-5	0-3	.995	10	159	110	1b78,3b52		-0.1
1972	Bos A	92	317	32	75	17	1	8	39	15-2	2	33	.237	.270	.372	86	-6	0-1	.993	5	121	88	1b90		-0.9
1973	Bos A	63	195	30	61	12	0	1	24	10-1	1	22	.313	.348	.390	102	1	0-0	.997	2	88	134	1b37,3b21,D3		-0.1
1974	Bos A	56	126	14	31	5	0	5	20	10-1	2	13	.246	.309	.405	98	0	1-0	1.000	4	100	63	1b23,D14		-0.2
1975	StL N	22	35	3	8	2	0	0	2	1-1	0	3	.229	.250	.286	46	-3	0-0	.981	-9	99	80	1b12		-0.3
Total	12	1289	4451	491	1229	191	29	66	519	254-33	22	406	.276	.316	.377	101	-4	26-30	.994	-12	108	105	1b731,O308L,3b225,D17,2b5	40	-9.2
CATES, ELI	Eli Eldo B1.26.1877 Greens Fork IN D5.29.1964 Anderson IN BR/TR/5-9.5/175 d4.20 ▲																								
1908	Was A	40	59	5	11	1	1	0	3	6	1		.186	.273	.237	72	-2	0	.907	-0	118	107	P19,2b3		-0.1
CATHER, TED	Theodore Physick B5.20.1889 Chester PA D4.9.1945 Elkton MD BR/TR/5-10.5/178 d9.23																								
1912	StL N	5	19	4	8	1	1	0	2	0	0	4	.421	.421	.579	176	2	1	.944	1	110	213	O5(0/4/1)		0.2
1913	StL N	67	183	16	39	8	4	0	12	9	0	24	.213	.250	.301	58	-11	7-6	.915	-2	86	139	O57(11/44/2)/P1		-1.6
1914	StL N	39	99	11	27	7	0	0	13	3	0	15	.273	.294	.343	90	-1	4	.981	1	99	129	O28(23/5/0)		-0.2
	†Bos N	50	145	19	43	11	2	0	27	7	2	28	.297	.338	.400	120	3	7	.953	-3	85	81	O48(23/7/20)		-0.1
	Year	89	244	30	70	18	2	0	40	10	2	43	.287	.320	.377	108	2	11	.966	-2	91	101	O76(46/12/20)		-0.3
1915	Bos N	40	102	10	21	3	1	2	18	15	2	19	.206	.319	.314	96	0	2-4	.902	-3	75	72	O32(31/0/2)		-0.6
Total	4	201	548	60	138	30	8	2	72	34	4	90	.252	.300	.347	91	-7	21-10	.938	-6	87	113	O170(91/17/65)/1P		-2.3
CATON, HOWDY	James Howard "Buster" B7.16.1896 Zanesville OH D1.8.1948 Zanesville OH BR/TR/5-6/165 d9.17 Mil 1918																								
1917	Pit N	14	57	6	12	1	0	0	4	6	0	7	.211	.286	.298	77	-2	0	.895	-3	99	75	S14		-0.4
1918	Pit N	80	303	37	71	5	7	0	17	32	2	16	.234	.312	.297	83	-6	12	.928	-7	101	112	S79		-0.9
1919	Pit N	39	102	13	18	1	2	0	5	12	0	10	.176	.263	.225	46	-7	2	.927	-9	65	65	S17,3b14/OC		-1.6
1920	Pit N	98	352	29	83	11	5	0	27	33	2	19	.236	.305	.295	71	-13	4-9	.929	-22	89	97	S96		-3.3
Total	4	231	814	85	184	18	16	0	53	83	4	52	.226	.301	.287	72	-28	18-9	.926	-41	93	99	S206,3b14/OC		-6.2
CATTERSON, TOM	Thomas Henry B8.25.1884 Warwick RI D2.5.1920 Portland ME BL/TL/5-10/170 d9.19 Col Villanova																								
1908	Bro N	19	68	5	13	1	1	1	2	5	1		.191	.257	.279	74	-2	0	.976	0	42	0	O18L		-0.4
1909	Bro N	9	18	0	4	0	0	0	1	3	0		.222	.333	.222	75	0	0	.833	-1	0	0	O6C		-0.2
Total	2	28	86	5	17	1	1	1	3	8	1		.198	.274	.267	75	-2	0	.957	-1	35	0	O24(18/6/0)		-0.6
CAULFIELD, JAKE	John Joseph B11.23.1917 Los Angeles CA D12.16.1986 San Francisco CA BR/TR/5-11/170 d4.24 Col San Francisco																								
1946	Phi A	44	94	13	26	8	0	0	10	4	0	11	.277	.306	.362	87	-4	0-0	.929	-4	85	.87	S31/3		-0.4
CAUSEY, WAYNE	James Wayne B12.26.1936 Ruston LA BL/TR/5-10.5/175* d6.5																								
1955	Bal A	68	175	14	34	2	1	1	9	17-1	1	25	.194	.269	.234	39	-16	0-1	.912	-6	101	122	3b55,2b7/S		-2.2
1956	Bal A	53	88	7	15	0	1	1	4	8-0	1	23	.170	.237	.227	26	-10	0-0	.980	1	117	130	3b30,2b7		-0.9
1957	Bal A	14	10	2	2	0	0	0	1	5-2	1	2	.200	.471	.200	105	1	0-0	.960	1	125	90	2b6,3b5		0.2
1961	KC A	104	312	37	86	14	1	8	49	37-0	0	28	.276	.348	.404	100	0	0-0	.955	17	121	116	3b88,S11,2b9		1.8
1962	KC A	117	305	40	77	14	1	4	38	41-5	2	30	.252	.340	.344	82	-6	2-0	.953	3	102	71	S51,3b26,2b9		0.1
1963	KC A	139	554	72	155	32	4	8	44	56-3	0	54	.280	.345	.395	101	3	4-2	.978	12	106	101	S135,3b2		2.7
1964	KC A	157	604	82	170	31	4	8	49	88-3	7	65	.281	.377	.386	110	13	0-1	.967	2	95	89	S131,2b17,3b9		2.9
1965	KC A	144	513	48	134	17	8	3	34	61-4	2	48	.261	.341	.343	97	-1	1-3	.972	-16	94	93	S62,2b45,3b35		-1.0
1966	KC A	28	79	1	18	0	0	0	5	7-1	0	6	.228	.284	.228	53	-5	1-0	.871	-6	46	114	3b15,S10		-1.1
	Chi A	78	164	23	40	8	2	0	13	24-0	1	13	.244	.333	.317	97	0	2-0	.980	-4	102	65	2b60/S3		0.1
	Year	106	243	24	58	8	2	0	18	31-1	1	19	.239	.318	.288	83	-5	3-0	.980	-10	102	65	2b60,3b16,S11		-1.0
1967	Chi A	124	292	21	66	10	3	1	28	32-4	1	35	.226	.302	.291	80	-7	2-5	.978	-4	109	94	2b96,S2		-0.7
1968	Chi A	59	100	8	18	2	0	0	7	14-2	1	7	.180	.284	.200	49	-6	0-0	.971	-5	93	87	2b41		-1.0
	Cal A	4	11	0	0	0	0	0	0	0-0	0	1	.000	.000	.000	-99	-3	0-0	1.000	1	132	184	2b4		-0.2
	Year	63	111	8	18	2	0	0	7	14-2	1	8	.162	.260	.180	36	-8	0-0	.975	-4	62	59	2b45		-1.2
	Atl N	16	37	2	4	0	1	1	4	0-0	1	4	.108	.103	.243	3	-5	0-0	1.000	-4	62	59	2b6,S2,3b2		-1.0
Total	11	1105	3244	357	819	130	26	35	285	390-25	15	341	.252	.333	.341	89	-42	12-12	.969	-6	100	91	S406,2b307,3b268		-0.3
CAVANAUGH, JOHN	John J. B6.5.1900 Scranton PA D1.14.1961 New Brunswick NJ BR/TR/5-9/158 d7.7																								
1919	Phi N	1	1	0	0	0	0	0	0	0-0	0	0	.000	.000	.000	-93	0	0	—	-0	0	0	/3		0.0
CAVARRETTA, PHIL	Philip Joseph B7.19.1916 Chicago IL BL/TL/5-11.5/175* d9.16 M3/C4																								
1934	Chi N	7	21	5	8	1	1	1	6	2	0	3	.381	.435	.619	182	2	1	1.000	1	148	151	1b5		0.2
1935	†Chi N	146	589	85	162	28	12	8	82	39	2	61	.275	.322	.404	93	-7	4	.986	2	108	**128**	1b145		-1.8
1936	Chi N	124	458	55	125	18	1	9	56	17	5	36	.273	.306	.376	81	-14	8	.987	-2	95	113	1b115		-2.5
1937	Chi N	106	329	43	94	18	7	5	56	32	0	35	.286	.349	.429	106	3	7	.972	9	191	159	O55(7/47/1),1b43		0.0
1938	†Chi N	92	268	29	64	11	4	1	28	14	4	27	.239	.287	.321	65	-13	4	.962	-2	84	138	O52(7/8/37),1b28		-2.0
1939	Chi N	22	59	4	15	3	1	0	0	4	0	3	.254	.322	.364	82	-1	2	.991	-1	76	94	1b13/OR		-0.3
1940	Chi N	65	193	34	54	11	4	2	22	31	3	18	.280	.388	.409	122	7	3	.991	-1	94	138	1b52		0.2
1941	Chi N	107	346	46	99	18	4	6	40	53	2	28	.286	.384	.413	129	-15	2	.992	-5	97	69	O66(8/53/6),1b33		0.6
1942	Chi N	136	482	59	130	28	4	3	54	71	1	42	.270	.365	.363	118	14	7	.989	0	97	72	O70(4/67/0),1b61		0.7
1943	Chi N	143	530	93	154	27	9	8	73	75	3	42	.291	.382	.421	134	25	3	.987	-11	74	95	1b134,O7C		0.7
1944	Chi N★	152	614	106	**197**	35	15	5	82	67	3	42	.321	.390	.451	137	31	4	.992	-7	80	107	1b139,O13C		1.8
1945	†Chi N★	132	498	94	177	34	10	6	97	81	4	34	**.355**	**.449**	.500	167	50	5	.993	-1	92	104	1b120,O11L		4.1
1946	Chi N★	139	510	89	150	28	10	8	78	88	3	54	.294	.401	.435	140	30	2	.967	3	108	80	O86(7/13/78),1b51		3.0
1947	Chi N★	127	459	56	144	22	5	2	63	58	0	35	.314	.391	.397	114	11	2	.977	-2	90	149	O100(69/26/8),1b24		0.3
1948	Chi N	111	334	41	93	16	5	3	40	35	1	29	.278	.349	.383	102	1	4	.998	1	110	147	1b41,O40(30/0/10)		-0.2
1949	Chi N	105	360	46	106	22	4	8	49	45	1	31	.294	.374	.444	122	12	2	.993	9	142	89	1b70,O25(3/0/21)		1.7
1950	Chi N	82	256	49	70	11	1	10	31	40	2	31	.273	.376	.441	115	7	1	.986	0	107	88	1b67,O3R		0.5
1951	Chi N	89	206	24	64	7	1	6	28	27	1	28	.311	.393	.442	122	7	0-0	.994	3	122	110	1b53,M		0.9
1952	Chi N	41	63	7	15	1	1	1	8	9	0	3	.238	.333	.333	84	-1	0-0	.991	1	129	136	1b13,M		0.1
1953	Chi N	27	21	3	6	3	0	0	3	6	0	3	.286	.444	.429	126	1	0-0	—	0			/HM		0.1
1954	Chi A	71	158	21	50	6	1	3	24	26	2	12	.316	.417	.411	124	7	4-0	.993	-2	83	114	1b44,O9(2/0/7)		0.4
1955	Chi A	6	4	1	0	0	0	0	0	0-0	0	0	.000	.000	.000	-97	-1	0-0	1.000	-0	0	63	1b3		-0.1
Total	22	2030	6754	990	1977	347	99	95	920	820-0	37	598	.293	.372	.416	118	186	65-0	.990	-10	99	105	1b1254,O538(148/234/172)		8.1
CAVENEY, IKE	James Christopher B12.10.1894 San Francisco CA D7.6.1949 San Francisco CA BR/TR/5-9/168 d4.12																								
1922	Cin N	118	394	41	94	12	9	3	54	29	6	33	.239	.301	.338	66	-21	6-6	.934	-5	100	**121**	S118		-1.3
1923	Cin N	138	488	58	135	21	9	4	63	26	1	41	.277	.315	.381	84	-13	5-4	.942	-1	98	109	S138		0.1
1924	Cin N	95	337	36	92	19	1	4	32	14	4	21	.273	.310	.371	83	-8	2-3	.924	-3	99	112	S90,2b5		-0.2
1925	Cin N	115	358	38	89	9	5	2	47	28	0	31	.249	.303	.318	60	-22	2-0	.941	5	105	**129**	S111		-0.6
Total	4	466	1577	173	410	61	24	13	196	97	11	126	.260	.307	.354	74	-64	15-13	.936	-4	100	117	S457,2b5		-2.0
CEDENO, ANDUJAR	Andujar (Donastorg) B8.21.1969 LaRomana, D.R. D10.28.2000 Santo Domingo, D.R. BR/TR/6-1/168* d9.2 b-Domingo																								
1990	Hou N	7	8	0	0	0	0	0	0	0-0	0	5	.000	.000	.000	-99	-2	0-0	.833	-2	39	0	S3		-0.4
1991	Hou N	67	251	27	61	13	2	9	36	9-1	1	74	.243	.270	.418	96	-3	4-3	.930	-18	80	104	S66		-1.7
1992	Hou N	71	220	15	38	13	2	2	13	14-2	3	71	.173	.232	.277	45	-16	2-0	.959	-8	96	77	S70		-2.1
1993	Hou N	149	505	69	143	24	4	11	56	48-9	3	97	.283	.346	.412	106	5	9-7	.955	-21	91	99	S149/3		-0.6
1994	Hou N	98	342	38	90	26	0	9	49	29-15	4	79	.263	.334	.418	100	0	1-1	.947	1	101	**122**	S95		0.8
1995	SD N	120	390	42	82	16	2	6	31	28-7	5	92	.210	.271	.308	54	-27	5-3	.965	-3	96	93	S116/3		-2.2
1996	SD N	49	154	10	36	2	1	3	18	9-2	1	32	.234	.279	.318	46	-10	3-2	.946	-1	106	115	S47,3b2		-0.8

YEAR	TM LG	G	AB	R	H	2B	3B	HR	RBI	BB-IB	HP	SO	AVG	OBP	SLG	AOPS	ABR	SB-CS	FA	FR	RNG	THR	GAMES AT POSITION	DL	BFW
	Det A	52	179	19	35	4	2	7	20	4-0	0	37	.196	.213	.358	41	-18	2-1	.948	-2	106	70	S51/3		-1.5
	Hou N	3	2	1	0	0	0	0	0	2-0	0	1	.000	.500	.000	50	0	0-0	1.000	2	194	440	S2/3		0.2
Total	7	616	2051	221	485	98	13	47	223	143-36	21	488	.236	.292	.366	77	-71	26-17	.952	-52	95	99	S599,3b6		-8.3

CEDENO, CESAR Cesar (Encarnacion) B2.25.1951 Santo Domingo, D.R. BR/TR/6-2/195(175-200) d6.20

YEAR	TM LG	G	AB	R	H	2B	3B	HR	RBI	BB-IB	HP	SO	AVG	OBP	SLG	AOPS	ABR	SB-CS	FA	FR	RNG	THR	GAMES AT POSITION	DL	BFW
1970	Hou N	90	355	46	110	21	4	7	42	15-2	2	57	.310	.340	.451	115	6	17-4	.968	-2	108	19	O90(0/75/17)		0.4
1971	Hou N	161	611	85	161	40	6	10	81	25-5	3	102	.264	.293	.398	98	-4	20-9	.989	-6	85	59	O157(11/125/30),1b2		-1.5
1972	Hou N★	139	559	103	179	39	8	22	82	56-5	5	62	.320	.385	.537	165	47	55-21	.981	2	103	108	O137C		5.3
1973	Hou N★	139	525	86	168	35	2	25	70	41-7	7	79	.320	.376	.537	152	36	56-15	.981	6	109	117	O136C		4.6
1974	Hou N★	160	610	95	164	29	5	26	102	64-6	4	103	.269	.338	.461	129	21	57-17	.993	6	109	110	O157C		3.1
1975	Hou N	131	500	93	144	31	3	13	63	62-9	7	52	.288	.371	.440	135	25	50-17	.982	-4	96	96	O131C	19	2.3
1976	Hou N★	150	575	89	171	26	5	18	83	55-9	1	51	.297	.357	.454	141	29	58-15	.980	-2	99	119	O146C		3.3
1977	Hou N	141	530	92	148	36	8	14	71	47-7	11	50	.279	.346	.457	124	18	61-14	.997	1	98	156	O137C	7	2.7
1978	Hou N	50	192	31	54	8	2	7	23	15-1	0	24	.281	.333	.453	126	6	23-2	.987	4	118	73	O50C	104	1.4
1979	Hou N	132	470	57	123	27	4	6	54	64-8	3	52	.262	.348	.374	105	-5	30-13	.981	-10	55	122	1b91,O40C		-0.9
1980	†Hou N	137	499	71	154	32	8	10	73	66-11	0	72	.309	.389	.465	150	35	48-15	.977	-5	95	98	O136C		3.6
1981	†Hou N	82	306	42	83	19	0	5	34	24-2	1	31	.271	.321	.382	106	2	12-7	.991	-3	88	88	1b46,O34C		-0.4
1982	Cin N	138	492	52	142	35	1	8	57	41-2	4	41	.289	.346	.413	112	9	16-11	.990	-6	97	53	O131C/1		0.1
1983	Cin N	98	332	40	77	16	0	9	39	33-2	3	53	.232	.302	.361	82	-8	13-9	.993	0	110	106	O73(0/1/73),1b17		-1.4
1984	Cin N	110	380	59	105	24	2	10	47	25-4	1	54	.276	.321	.429	105	2	19-3	.980	2	108	143	O77(52/14/19),1b44	15	0.2
1985	Cin N	83	220	24	53	12	0	3	30	19-1	3	35	.241	.307	.336	77	-6	9-5	.990	1	116	32	O53(46/4/4),1b34		-0.8
	†StL N	28	76	14	33	4	1	6	19	5-2	0	7	.434	.463	.750	237	13	5-1	.993	-3	46	132	1b23,O2(1/0/1)		1.0
	Year	111	296	38	86	16	1	9	49	24-3	3	42	.291	.347	.443	116	6	14-6	.993	-2	69	126	1b57,O55(47/4/5)		0.2
1986	LA N	37	78	5	18	2	1	0	6	7-0	0	13	.231	.294	.282	64	-4	1-1	.944	-2	85	76	O31(28/3/0)		-0.7
Total	17	2006	7310	1084	2087	436	60	199	976	664-83	56	938	.285	.347	.443	124	232	550-179	.985	-21	101	94	O1718(138/1457/144),1b258	145	22.3

CEDENO, DOMINGO Domingo Antonio (Donastorg) B11.4.1968 LaRomana, D.R. BB/TR/6-1/170* d5.19 b-Andujar

YEAR	TM LG	G	AB	R	H	2B	3B	HR	RBI	BB-IB	HP	SO	AVG	OBP	SLG	AOPS	ABR	SB-CS	FA	FR	RNG	THR	GAMES AT POSITION	DL	BFW
1993	Tor A	15	46	5	8	0	0	0	7	1-0	0	10	.174	.188	.174	-1	-7	1-0	.973	-2	107	69	S10,2b5		-0.7
1994	Tor A	47	97	14	19	2	3	0	10	10-0	1	31	.196	.261	.278	42	-9	1-2	.935	-7	87	78	2b28,S8,3b6/OL		-1.4
1995	Tor A	51	161	18	38	6	1	4	14	10-0	2	35	.236	.289	.360	68	-8	0-1	.980	3	106	88	S30,2b20/3		-0.3
1996	Tor A	77	282	44	79	10	2	2	17	15-0	2	60	.280	.320	.351	70	-13	5-3	.969	3	95	118	2b62,3b6,S5		-0.6
	Chi A	12	19	2	3	2	0	0	3	0-0	0	4	.158	.143	.263	4	-3	1-0	—	-2	0	0	2b2,S2/D		-0.4
	Year	89	301	46	82	12	2	2	20	15-0	2	64	.272	.308	.346	67	-16	6-3	.969	1	93	116	2b64,S7,3b6/D		-1.0
1997	Tex A	113	365	49	103	19	6	4	36	27-0	2	77	.282	.334	.400	85	-6	3-3	.960	-6	102	76	2b65,S43,3b3,D2	37	-0.9
1998	Tex A	61	141	19	37	9	1	2	21	10-0	0	32	.262	.309	.383	75	-5	2-1	.963	-7	87	79	S35,D14,2b7		-1.0
1999	Sea A	21	42	4	9	2	0	2	8	5-0	1	9	.214	.313	.405	82	-1	1-1	.941	-2	120	112	S20/23		0.1
	Phi N	32	66	5	10	4	0	1	5	5-0	0	22	.152	.211	.258	18	-9	0-1	.982	-2	88	68	S19/2		-1.0
Total	7	429	1219	160	306	54	13	15	121	83-0	7	264	.251	.300	.354	67	-63	14-12	.964	-19	97	90	2b191,S172,D17,3b17/OL	37	-6.2

CEDENO, ROGER Roger Leandro B8.16.1974 Valencia, Venez BB/TR/6-1/205(165-205) d6.20

YEAR	TM LG	G	AB	R	H	2B	3B	HR	RBI	BB-IB	HP	SO	AVG	OBP	SLG	AOPS	ABR	SB-CS	FA	FR	RNG	THR	GAMES AT POSITION	DL	BFW
1995	LA N	40	42	4	10	2	0	0	3	3-0	0	10	.238	.283	.286	56	-3	1-0	.977	2	135	0	O36(19/13/5)		-0.1
1996	LA N	86	211	26	52	11	1	2	18	24-0	1	47	.246	.326	.336	80	-6	5-1	.983	1	105	73	O71(20/50/4)		-0.5
1997	LA N	80	194	31	53	10	2	3	17	25-2	3	44	.273	.362	.392	105	2	9-1	.987	5	131	38	O71(13/55/4)	54	0.9
1998	LA N	105	240	33	58	11	1	2	17	27-2	0	57	.242	.317	.321	72	-10	8-2	.978	-4	77	117	O77(45/29/10)	24	-1.3
1999	†NY N	155	453	90	142	23	4	4	36	60-3	3	100	.313	.396	.408	109	9	66-17	.989	4	105	118	O149(13/21/127)/2		1.6
2000	Hou N	74	259	54	73	2	5	6	26	43-0	0	47	.282	.383	.398	91	-3	25-11	.978	-3	100	26	O67(23/29/17)	83	-0.5
2001	Det A	131	523	79	153	14	11	6	48	36-1	2	83	.293	.337	.396	96	-5	55-15	.953	-12	87	68	O120(0/67/55),D7		-1.2
2002	NY N	149	511	65	133	19	2	7	41	42-1	2	92	.260	.318	.346	83	-16	25-4	.966	-5	100	26	O132L		-2.2
2003	NY N	148	484	70	129	25	4	7	37	38-3	1	86	.267	.320	.378	85	-12	14-9	.987	1	104	71	O128(0/17/111)		-1.6
2004	†StL N	95	200	22	53	9	2	3	23	19-2	0	41	.265	.327	.375	80	-6	5-1	1.000	-5	64	85	O54(23/0/35)/D	32	-1.2
2005	StL N	37	57	4	9	1	0	0	8	2-0	1	6	.158	.197	.175	-0	-9	0-2	.818	-2	53	0	O16(6/0/10)	18	-1.2
Total	11	1100	3174	478	865	127	32	40	274	319-14	13	613	.273	.340	.371	88	-59	213-63	.976	-19	99	67	O921(294/281/378),D8/2	211	-7.3

CEDENO, RONNY Ronny Alexander (Salazar) B2.2.1983 Carabobo, Venez BR/TR/6-0/180 d4.23

YEAR	TM LG	G	AB	R	H	2B	3B	HR	RBI	BB-IB	HP	SO	AVG	OBP	SLG	AOPS	ABR	SB-CS	FA	FR	RNG	THR	GAMES AT POSITION	DL	BFW
2005	Chi N	41	80	13	24	3	0	1	6	5-1	2	11	.300	.356	.375	89	-1	0-0	.986	-3	75	72	S29/2		-0.3

CEPEDA, ORLANDO Orlando Manuel (Penne) "Baby Bull","Cha Cha" B9.17.1937 Ponce, PR BR/TR/6-2/210* d4.15 C1 HF1999

YEAR	TM LG	G	AB	R	H	2B	3B	HR	RBI	BB-IB	HP	SO	AVG	OBP	SLG	AOPS	ABR	SB-CS	FA	FR	RNG	THR	GAMES AT POSITION	DL	BFW
1958	SF N	148	603	88	188	38	4	25	96	29-7	3	84	.312	.342	.512	126	21	15-11	.989	-2	96	95	1b147		0.9
1959	SF N★	151	605	92	192	35	4	27	105	33-10	5	100	.317	.355	.522	134	27	23-9	.984	-5	97	89	1b122,O44L,3b4		1.6
1960	SF N★	151	569	81	169	36	3	24	96	34-9	8	91	.297	.343	.497	135	26	15-6	.983	-2	104	143	O91L,1b63		1.7
1961	SF N★	152	585	105	182	28	4	46	142	39-11	9	91	.311	.362	.609	158	45	12-8	.997	-3	85	79	1b81,O80(64/0/17)		3.2
1962	†SF N★	162	625	105	191	26	1	35	114	37-8	6	97	.306	.347	.518	132	26	10-4	.991	-7	83	99	1b160,O2(1/0/1)		1.0
1963	SF N☆	156	579	100	183	33	4	34	97	37-11	10	70	.316	.366	.563	166	48	8-3	.985	-10	82	80	1b150,O3L		3.2
1964	SF N★	142	529	75	161	27	2	31	97	43-7	8	83	.304	.361	.539	148	33	9-4	.986	-7	84	85	1b139/OL		1.9
1965	SF N	33	34	1	6	1	0	1	5	3-1	0	9	.176	.225	.294	49	-2	0-0	1.000	0	131	64	1b4,O2L	103	-0.2
1966	SF N	19	49	5	14	2	0	3	15	4-2	1	11	.286	.352	.510	132	2	0-1	.778	-2	64	0	O8L,1b6		-0.1
	StL N	123	452	65	137	24	0	17	58	34-10	13	68	.303	.362	.469	130	20	9-8	.989	-5	85	119	1b120		0.7
	Year	142	501	70	151	26	0	20	73	38-12	14	79	.301	.361	.473	130	22	9-9	.990	-7	83	120	1b126,O8L		0.6
1967	†StL N★	151	563	91	183	37	0	25	111	62-23	12	75	.325	.399	.524	166	51	11-2	.993	0	99	91	1b151		4.6
1968	†StL N	157	600	71	149	26	2	16	73	43-13	9	96	.248	.306	.378	107	4	8-6	.988	-5	91	99	1b154		-1.2
1969	†Atl N	154	573	74	147	28	2	22	88	55-10	5	76	.257	.325	.428	109	6	12-5	.994	1	103	84	1b153		-0.4
1970	Atl N	148	567	87	173	33	0	34	111	47-11	9	75	.305	.365	.543	133	26	6-5	.992	4	107	87	1b148		1.7
1971	Atl N	71	250	31	69	10	1	14	44	22-7	0	29	.276	.330	.492	123	7	3-6	.992	1	108	107	1b63	36	0.1
1972	Atl N	28	84	6	25	3	0	4	9	7-1	0	17	.298	.352	.476	122	2	0-0	1.000	1	106	88	1b22		0.1
	Oak A	3	3	0	0	0	0	0	0	0-0	0	0	.000	.000	.000	-99	-1	0-0	—	0			/H	85	-0.1
1973	Bos A	142	550	51	159	25	0	20	86	50-13	3	81	.289	.350	.444	116	11	0-2	—	0	0	0	D142		0.7
1974	KC A	33	107	3	23	5	0	1	18	9-0	1	16	.215	.282	.290	61	-5	1-0	—	0	0	0	D26		-0.6
Total	17	2124	7927	1131	2351	417	27	379	1365	588-154	102	1169	.297	.350	.499	133	347	142-80	.990	-40	92	92	1b1683,O231(214/0/18),D168,3b4	224	18.8

CEPICKY, MATT Matthew William B11.10.1977 St.Louis MO BL/TR/6-2/215* [MonN99 4/120] d7.31 Col Missouri St.

YEAR	TM LG	G	AB	R	H	2B	3B	HR	RBI	BB-IB	HP	SO	AVG	OBP	SLG	AOPS	ABR	SB-CS	FA	FR	RNG	THR	GAMES AT POSITION	DL	BFW
2002	Mon N	32	74	7	16	3	0	3	15	4-1	0	21	.216	.256	.378	63	-4	0-0	1.000	-2	76	0	O17(16/0/1)		-0.7
2003	Mon N	5	8	0	2	1	0	0	0	0-0	0	2	.250	.250	.375	59	0	0-0	1.000	-1	27	0	O4(3/0/1)		-0.1
2004	Mon N	32	60	4	13	4	0	1	3	1-0	0	18	.217	.230	.333	41	-5	1-0	1.000	0	111	0	O11(9/0/2),D2		-0.4
2005	Was N	11	25	1	6	3	0	0	3	1-0	0	8	.240	.269	.360	68	-1	0-1	1.000	1	175	0	O6(5/0/1)		0.0
Total	4	80	167	12	37	11	0	4	21	6-1	0	49	.222	.249	.359	56	-10	1-1	1.000	0	110		O38(33/0/5),D2		-1.2

CERMAK, ED Edward Hugo B3.10.1882 Cleveland OH D11.22.1911 Cleveland OH BR/TR/5-11/170 d9.9

YEAR	TM LG	G	AB	R	H	2B	3B	HR	RBI	BB-IB	HP	SO	AVG	OBP	SLG	AOPS	ABR	SB-CS	FA	FR	RNG	THR	GAMES AT POSITION	DL	BFW
1901	Cle A	4	4	0	0	0	0	0	0	0-0	0		.000	.000	.000	-99	-1	0	1.000	1	450	1792	/OR		0.0

CERONE, RICK Richard Aldo B5.19.1954 Newark NJ BR/TR/5-11/192(184-195) [CleA75 1/7] d8.17 Col Seton Hall

YEAR	TM LG	G	AB	R	H	2B	3B	HR	RBI	BB-IB	HP	SO	AVG	OBP	SLG	AOPS	ABR	SB-CS	FA	FR	RNG	THR	GAMES AT POSITION	DL	BFW
1975	Cle A	7	12	1	3	1	0	0	0	0-0	0	2	.250	.308	.333	81	0	0-0	1.000	-1	125	68	C7		-0.1
1976	Cle A	7	16	1	2	0	0	0	0	0-0	0	2	.125	.125	.125	-27	-3	0-0	.963	-1	86	59	C6/D		-0.3
1977	Tor A	31	100	7	20	4	0	1	10	6-0	0	12	.200	.245	.270	40	-8	0-0	.994	2	183	86	C31		-0.6
1978	Tor A	88	282	25	63	8	2	3	20	23-0	1	32	.223	.284	.298	63	-14	0-3	.992	1	112	103	C84,D2		-1.1
1979	Tor A	136	469	47	112	27	4	7	61	37-1	1	40	.239	.294	.358	75	-17	1-4	.980	3	129	97	C136		-1.0
1980	†NY A	147	519	70	144	30	4	14	85	32-2	6	56	.277	.321	.432	108	4	1-3	.990	18	172	116	C147		2.7
1981	†NY A	71	234	23	57	13	2	2	21	12-0	1	24	.244	.276	.342	79	-7	0-0	.992	-3	116	80	C69	35	-0.8
1982	NY A	89	300	29	68	10	0	5	28	19-1	1	27	.227	.271	.310	61	-16	0-2	.989	-11	100	69	C89	64	-2.5
1983	NY A	80	246	18	54	7	0	2	15	15-1	1	29	.220	.267	.272	50	-17	0-1	.991	-6	103	60	C78/3		-2.0
1984	NY A	38	120	8	25	3	0	2	13	9-0	1	15	.208	.269	.283	55	-8	1-0	.996	-1	120	104	C38	59	-0.7
1985	Atl N	96	282	15	61	9	0	3	25	16-1	1	28	.216	.288	.280	57	-16	0-3	.986	-5	99	100	C91	15	-2.0
1986	Mil A	68	216	22	56	14	0	4	18	15-0	1	28	.259	.304	.380	84	-5	1-1	.991	4	109	168	C68		0.2
1987	NY A	113	284	28	69	12	1	4	23	30-0	4	46	.243	.320	.335	76	-9	0-1	.998	8	123	111	C111,P2,1b2		0.2
1988	Bos A	84	264	31	71	13	1	3	27	20-0	3	32	.269	.326	.360	88	-4	0-0	1.000	-1	91	71	C83/D		-0.2
1989	Bos A	102	296	28	72	16	1	4	48	34-1	2	40	.243	.320	.345	84	-6	0-0	.984	-3	73	116	C97/ORD		-0.4
1990	NY A	49	139	12	42	6	0	2	11	5-0	0	13	.302	.324	.388	98	-1	0-0	.995	2	146	158	C35/2D	64	0.3

YEAR	TM LG	G	AB	R	H	2B	3B	HR	RBI	BB-IB	HP	SO	AVG	OBP	SLG	AOPS	ABR	SB-CS	FA	FR	RNG	THR	GAMES AT POSITION	DL	BFW
1991	NY N	90	227	18	62	13	0	2	16	30-2	1	24	.273	.360	.357	103	2	1-1	.987	2	**138**	121	C81		0.8
1992	Mon N	33	63	10	17	4	0	1	7	3-0	1	5	.270	.313	.381	96	0	1-2	1.000	-1	82	66	C28		-0.1
Total	18	1329	4069	393	998	190	15	59	436	320-9	24	450	.245	.301	.343	78	-125	6-22	.990	5	120	102	C1279,D11,1b2,P2/2OR3	237	-7.6

CERV, BOB   Robert Henry   B5.5.1926 Weston NE   BR/TR/6-0/202(202-226)   d8.1 Col Nebraska

YEAR	TM LG	G	AB	R	H	2B	3B	HR	RBI	BB-IB	HP	SO	AVG	OBP	SLG	AOPS	ABR	SB-CS	FA	FR	RNG	THR	GAMES AT POSITION	DL	BFW
1951	NY A	12	28	4	6	1	0	0	2	4	0	6	.214	.313	.250	55	-2	0-0	.875	-1	101	0	O9R		-0.3
1952	NY A	36	87	11	21	3	2	1	8	9	0	22	.241	.313	.356	91	-1	0-1	1.000	0	102	68	O27(15/12/0)		-0.3
1953	NY A	8	6	0	0	0	0	0	1	0	0	1	.000	.143	.000	-61	-1	0-0	—	0			/H		-0.1
1954	NY A	56	100	14	26	6	0	5	13	11	0	17	.260	.330	.470	122	3	0-2	.897	-2	73	94	O24L		-0.1
1955	†NY A	55	85	17	29	4	2	3	22	7-0	3	16	.341	.411	.541	157	7	4-0	1.000	-1	88	105	O20(13/7/1)		0.6
1956	†NY A	54	115	16	35	5	6	3	25	18-0	0	13	.304	.396	.530	148	8	0-1	.984	1	93	190	O44(29/15/1)		0.7
1957	KC A	124	345	35	94	14	2	11	44	20-1	1	57	.272	.312	.420	97	-3	1-1	.964	-2	92	118	O89(40/35/22)		-0.9
1958	KC A★	141	515	93	157	20	7	38	104	50-10	5	82	.305	.371	.592	158	39	3-3	.985	15	118	161	O136L		4.6
1959	KC A	125	463	61	132	22	4	20	87	35-5	3	87	.285	.332	.479	120	11	3-2	.980	2	100	107	O119L		0.7
1960	KC A	23	78	14	20	1	1	6	12	10-1	0	17	.256	.337	.526	130	3	0-0	.977	2	92	279	O21L		0.4
	†NY A	87	216	32	54	11	1	8	28	30-2	3	36	.250	.349	.421	114	5	0-0	.982	4	103	182	O51(50/1/1),1b3		0.6
	Year	110	294	46	74	12	2	14	40	40-3	3	53	.252	.346	.449	119	8	0-0	.980	5	100	211	O72(71/1/1),1b3		1.0
1961	LA A	18	57	3	9	3	0	2	6	1-0	0	8	.158	.169	.316	25	-6	0-0	.944	-2	68	0	O15L		-1.0
	NY A	57	118	17	32	5	1	6	20	12-0	1	17	.271	.344	.483	125	4	1-0	.983	3	117	112	O30(28/2/0),1b3		0.5
	Year	75	175	20	41	8	1	8	26	13-0	1	25	.234	.289	.429	91	-3	1-0	.974	-2	100	72	O45(43/2/0),1b3		-0.5
1962	NY A	14	17	1	2	1	0	0	0	2-0	1	3	.118	.250	.176	18	-2	0-0	1.000	-0	82	0	O3(1/0/2)		-0.2
	Hou N	19	31	2	7	0	0	2	3	2-0	1	10	.226	.273	.419	89	-1	0-0	.833	-1	47	297	O6L		-0.2
Total	12	829	2261	320	624	96	26	105	374	212-19	17	392	.276	.340	.481	122	64	12-10	.976	18	101	135	O594(497/72/36),1b6		5.0

CEY, RON   Ronald Charles "The Penguin"   B2.15.1948 Tacoma WA   BR/TR/5-10/185*   [LAN68 S3/53]   d9.3 Col Washington St.

YEAR	TM LG	G	AB	R	H	2B	3B	HR	RBI	BB-IB	HP	SO	AVG	OBP	SLG	AOPS	ABR	SB-CS	FA	FR	RNG	THR	GAMES AT POSITION	DL	BFW
1971	LA N	2	2	0	0	0	0	0	0	0-0	0	2	.000	.000	.000	-99	-1	0-0	—	0			/H		-0.1
1972	LA N	11	37	3	10	1	0	1	3	7-0	1	10	.270	.400	.378	124	2	0-0	.900	-2	84	60	3b11		-0.1
1973	LA N	152	507	60	124	18	4	15	80	74-7	2	77	.245	.338	.385	105	4	1-1	.961	5	101	159	3b146		0.9
1974	†LA N★	159	577	88	151	20	2	18	97	76-13	7	68	.262	.349	.397	114	12	1-1	.959	14	103	91	3b158		2.5
1975	LA N★	158	566	72	160	29	2	25	101	78-15	7	74	.283	.372	.473	140	32	5-2	.960	-3	94	100	3b158		3.0
1976	LA N	145	502	69	139	18	3	23	80	89-13	3	74	.277	.386	.462	142	31	0-4	.965	9	111	91	3b144		3.9
1977	†LA N★	153	564	77	136	22	3	30	110	93-6	2	106	.241	.347	.450	112	11	3-4	.964	12	105	129	3b153		2.0
1978	†LA N★	159	555	84	150	32	0	23	84	96-9	7	96	.270	.380	.452	133	29	2-5	.966	3	102	107	3b158		2.9
1979	LA N★	150	487	77	137	20	1	28	81	86-8	2	85	.281	.389	.499	144	32	3-3	**.977**	6	101	102	3b150		3.6
1980	LA N	157	551	81	140	25	0	28	77	69-5	5	92	.254	.342	.452	123	17	2-2	.972	6	101	109	3b157		2.2
1981	†LA N	85	312	42	90	15	2	13	50	40-3	3	55	.288	.372	.474	146	19	0-2	.941	4	100	119	3b84		2.2
1982	LA N	150	556	62	141	23	1	24	79	57-6	4	99	.254	.323	.428	113	9	3-2	.963	-1	100	103	3b149		0.6
1983	Chi N	159	581	73	160	33	1	24	90	62-11	5	85	.275	.346	.460	117	14	0-0	.955	-13	95	47	3b157		-0.2
1984	†Chi N	146	505	71	121	27	0	25	97	61-10	6	108	.240	.324	.442	106	4	3-2	**.967**	-12	88	76	3b144		-1.1
1985	Chi N	145	500	64	116	18	2	22	63	58-9	4	106	.232	.316	.408	92	-5	1-1	.943	-8	99	87	3b140		-1.7
1986	Chi N	97	256	42	70	21	0	13	36	44-1	5	66	.273	.384	.508	134	14	0-0	.952	-6	92	59	3b77		0.7
1987	Oak A	45	104	12	23	6	0	4	11	22-1	1	32	.221	.359	.394	107	2	0-0	.961	-2	25	71	D30,1b7,3b3		-0.1
Total	17	2073	7162	977	1868	328	21	316	1139	1012-117	62	1235	.261	.354	.445	121	226	24-29	.961	11	100	101	3b1989,D30,1b7		21.2

CHACON, ELIO   Elio (Rodriguez)   B10.26.1936 Caracas, Venez   D4.24.1992 Caracas, Venez   BR/TR/5-9/170*   d4.20

YEAR	TM LG	G	AB	R	H	2B	3B	HR	RBI	BB-IB	HP	SO	AVG	OBP	SLG	AOPS	ABR	SB-CS	FA	FR	RNG	THR	GAMES AT POSITION	DL	BFW
1960	Cin N	49	116	14	21	1	0	0	7	14-1	1	23	.181	.271	.190	29	-11	7-1	.980	1	99	114	2b43,O2R		-0.6
1961	†Cin N	61	132	26	35	4	2	1	5	21-0	2	22	.265	.374	.371	97	0	1-4	.989	-0	100	90	2b42,O7(3/0/5)		0.2
1962	NY N	118	368	49	87	10	3	2	27	76-3	1	64	.236	.368	.296	80	-7	12-7	.961	-2	103	88	S110,2b2/3		0.0
Total	3	228	616	89	143	15	5	4	39	111-4	4	109	.232	.351	.292	74	-18	20-12	.961	-1	103	92	S110,2b87,O9(3/0/7)/3		-0.4

CHADBOURNE, CHET   Chester James "Pop"   B10.28.1884 Parkman ME   D6.21.1943 Los Angeles CA   BL/TR/5-9/170   d9.17

YEAR	TM LG	G	AB	R	H	2B	3B	HR	RBI	BB-IB	HP	SO	AVG	OBP	SLG	AOPS	ABR	SB-CS	FA	FR	RNG	THR	GAMES AT POSITION	DL	BFW
1906	Bos A	11	43	7	13	1	0	0	3	3	0		.302	.348	.326	111	1	1	.926	2	131	78	2b11/S		0.3
1907	Bos A	10	38	0	11	0	0	0	1	7	0		.289	.400	.289	121	1	1	1.000	-0	78	0	O10L		0.1
1914	KC F	147	581	92	161	22	8	1	37	69	5	49	.277	.359	.348	97	-10	42	.979	9	95	**157**	O146L		-0.7
1915	KC F	152	587	75	133	16	9	1	35	62	6	29	.227	.307	.290	71	-32	29	.979	-4	91	109	O152(5/147/0)		-5.1
1918	Bos N	27	104	9	27	2	1	0	6	5	1		.260	.300	.298	86	-2	5	.925	-3	90	57	O27C		-0.8
Total	5	347	1353	183	345	41	18	2	82	146	12	83	.255	.333	.316	86	-42	78	.969	4	92	123	O335(161/174/0),2b11/S		-6.2

CHALK, DAVE   David Lee   B8.30.1950 Del Rio TX   BR/TR/5-10/175*   [AnaA72 1/10]   d9.4 Col Texas   [DL 1979 Cal A 30]

YEAR	TM LG	G	AB	R	H	2B	3B	HR	RBI	BB-IB	HP	SO	AVG	OBP	SLG	AOPS	ABR	SB-CS	FA	FR	RNG	THR	GAMES AT POSITION	DL	BFW
1973	Cal A	24	69	14	16	2	0	0	6	9-0	1	13	.232	.329	.261	73	-2	0-0	.962	2	96	148	S22		0.3
1974	Cal A★	133	465	44	117	9	3	5	31	30-1	7	57	.252	.304	.316	84	-11	10-10	.938	6	91	93	S99,3b38		0.5
1975	Cal A☆	149	513	59	140	24	2	3	56	66-4	2	49	.273	.353	.345	107	7	6-9	.976	5	99	100	3b149		1.0
1976	Cal A	142	438	39	95	14	1	0	33	49-3	10	62	.217	.308	.253	70	-14	0-0	.971	3	98	83	S102,3b49		0.0
1977	Cal A	149	519	58	144	27	2	3	45	52-2	5	69	.277	.345	.355	96	-1	12-8	.948	-2	93	81	3b141,2b7,S4		-0.5
1978	Cal A	135	470	42	119	12	0	1	34	38-0	1	34	.253	.318	.285	73	-16	5-8	.955	-11	88	86	S97,2b29,3b22/D		-2.0
1979	Tex A	9	8	0	2	0	0	0	0	0-0	0		.250	.250	.250	36	-1	0-0	1.000	0	210	0	S3/2D		0.0
	Oak A	66	212	15	47	6	0	2	13	29-0	1	14	.222	.317	.278	66	-9	2-1	.988	-10	89	78	2b37,S16,3b16		-1.6
	Year	75	220	15	49	6	0	2	13	29-0	1	14	.223	.315	.277	64	-10	2-1	.988	-10	88	77	2b38,S19,3b16,D2		-1.6
1980	†KC A	69	167	19	42	10	1	1	20	18-0	2	27	.251	.326	.341	83	-3	1-1	.964	-7	95	54	3b33,2b17/SD		-1.0
1981	KC A	27	49	2	11	3	0	0	5	4-0	0	2	.224	.283	.286	64	-2	0-1	.955	-4	66	203	3b14,2b10/S		-0.7
Total	9	903	2910	292	733	107	9	15	243	295-10	35	327	.252	.325	.310	84	-52	36-38	.962	-19	95	101	3b462,S345,2b101,D9	30	-4.0

CHAMBERLAIN, JOE   Joseph Jeremiah   B5.10.1910 San Francisco CA   D1.28.1983 San Francisco CA   BR/TR/6-1/175   d4.17

YEAR	TM LG	G	AB	R	H	2B	3B	HR	RBI	BB-IB	HP	SO	AVG	OBP	SLG	AOPS	ABR	SB-CS	FA	FR	RNG	THR	GAMES AT POSITION	DL	BFW
1934	Chi A	43	141	13	34	5	1	2	16	7	0	38	.241	.272	.333	54	-10	1	.896	-5	112	66	S26,3b14/2		-1.3

CHAMBERLAIN, WES   Wesley Polk   B4.13.1966 Chicago IL   BR/TR/6-2/210(210-230)   [PitN87 4/86]   d8.31 Col Jackson St.

YEAR	TM LG	G	AB	R	H	2B	3B	HR	RBI	BB-IB	HP	SO	AVG	OBP	SLG	AOPS	ABR	SB-CS	FA	FR	RNG	THR	GAMES AT POSITION	DL	BFW
1990	Phi N	18	46	9	13	3	0	2	4	1-0	0	9	.283	.298	.478	110	-0	4-0	.958	-0	111	0	O10(10/0/2)		0.1
1991	Phi N	101	383	51	92	16	3	13	50	31-0	2	73	.240	.300	.399	96	-3	9-4	.985	-1	99	70	O98(95/0/3)		-0.7
1992	Phi N	76	275	26	71	18	0	9	41	10-2	1	55	.258	.285	.422	98	-2	4-0	.971	-2	97	72	O73(28/0/48)	47	-0.5
1993	†Phi N	96	284	34	80	20	2	12	45	17-3	1	51	.282	.320	.493	117	6	2-1	.993	6	103	207	O76R	18	0.8
1994	Phi N	24	69	7	19	5	0	2	6	3-0	0	12	.275	.306	.435	89	-1	0-0	1.000	1	93	217	O18R	16	-0.1
	Bos A	51	164	13	42	9	1	4	20	12-2	0	38	.256	.307	.396	76	-6	0-2	1.000	3	105	207	O34R,D12		-0.6
1995	Bos A	19	45	4	5	1	0	1	2	1-0	0	11	.119	.178	.214	5	-6	1-0	.955	1	109	158	O12R,D5		-0.6
Total	6	385	1263	144	322	72	6	43	167	77-7	4	249	.255	.299	.424	95	-12	20-7	.984	8	100	126	O321(133/0/193),D17	81	-1.6

CHAMBERS, AL   Albert Eugene   B3.24.1961 Harrisburg PA   BL/TL/6-4/217*   [SeaA79 1/1]   d7.23

YEAR	TM LG	G	AB	R	H	2B	3B	HR	RBI	BB-IB	HP	SO	AVG	OBP	SLG	AOPS	ABR	SB-CS	FA	FR	RNG	THR	GAMES AT POSITION	DL	BFW
1983	Sea A	31	67	11	14	3	0	1	7	18-1	0	20	.209	.376	.299	85	-1	0-1	1.000	-1	52	0	D22,O3L		-0.2
1984	Sea A	22	49	4	11	1	0	1	4	3-0	0	12	.224	.269	.306	59	-3	2-1	.947	-1	89	0	O13L/D		-0.4
1985	Sea A	4	4	0	0	0	0	0	0	0-0	0	2	.000	.000	.000	-99	-1	0-0	—	0			/H		-0.1
Total	3	57	120	15	25	4	0	2	11	21-1	0	34	.208	.326	.292	70	-4	2-2	.955	-2	81	0	D23,O16L		-0.7

CHAMBLEE, JIM   James Nathaniel   B5.6.1975 Denton TX   BR/TR/6-4/170   [BosA95 12/326]   d8.24 Col Odessa (TX) JC

YEAR	TM LG	G	AB	R	H	2B	3B	HR	RBI	BB-IB	HP	SO	AVG	OBP	SLG	AOPS	ABR	SB-CS	FA	FR	RNG	THR	GAMES AT POSITION	DL	BFW
2003	Cin N	2	0	0	0	0	0	0	0	0-0	0	0	.000	.000	.000	-99	-1	0-0	—	0			/3		-0.1

CHAMBLISS, CHRIS   Carroll Christopher   B12.26.1948 Dayton OH   BL/TR/6-1/215(195-225)   [CleA70*1/1]   d5.28 C11 Col UCLA

YEAR	TM LG	G	AB	R	H	2B	3B	HR	RBI	BB-IB	HP	SO	AVG	OBP	SLG	AOPS	ABR	SB-CS	FA	FR	RNG	THR	GAMES AT POSITION	DL	BFW
1971	Cle A	111	415	49	114	20	4	9	48	40-1	0	83	.275	.341	.407	102	5	2-0	.992	-6	77	83	1b108		-1.4
1972	Cle A	121	466	51	136	27	2	6	44	26-2	0	63	.292	.327	.397	111	6	3-4	.993	-8	74	109	1b119		-1.4
1973	Cle A	155	572	70	156	30	2	11	53	58-8	3	76	.273	.342	.390	104	4	4-8	.991	4	110	107	1b154		0.3
1974	Cle A	17	67	8	22	4	0	0	7	5-1	0	5	.328	.375	.388	121	2	0-1	.982	-3	53	93	1b17		-0.3
	NY A	110	400	38	97	16	3	6	43	23-1	0	43	.243	.282	.343	80	-11	0-0	.992	6	120	101	1b106		-1.5
	Year	127	467	46	119	20	3	6	50	28-2	0	48	.255	.296	.349	86	-9	0-1	.990	3	110	100	1b123		-1.8
1975	NY A	150	562	66	171	38	4	9	72	29-9	1	50	.304	.336	.434	119	12	0-1	.991	4	106	97	1b147		0.4
1976	†NY A★	156	641	79	188	32	6	17	96	27-1	3	80	.293	.323	.441	124	16	1-0	.994	-2	98	106	1b155/D		0.1
1977	†NY A	157	600	90	172	32	6	17	90	45-5	2	73	.287	.336	.445	112	9	4-0	.989	-3	94	106	1b157		-0.3
1978	†NY A	162	625	81	171	26	3	12	90	41-3	5	60	.274	.321	.382	99	-1	2-1	**.997**	4	105	102	1b155,D7		-0.7
1979	NY A	149	554	61	155	27	3	18	63	34-4	5	73	.280	.324	.437	106	3	3-2	.995	3	107	118	1b134,D16		0.3
1980	Atl N	158	602	83	170	37	2	18	72	49-6	4	73	.282	.338	.440	115	12	7-3	.993	-2	97	**120**	1b158		0.1

YEAR	TM LG	G	AB	R	H	2B	3B	HR	RBI	BB-IB	HP	SO	AVG	OBP	SLG	AOPS	ABR	SB-CS	FA	FR	RNG	THR	GAMES AT POSITION	DL	BFW
1981	Atl N	107	404	44	110	25	2	8	51	44-10	1	41	.272	.343	.403	112	7	4-1	.997	6	117	97	1b107		0.7
1982	†Atl N	157	534	57	144	25	2	20	86	57-13	0	57	.270	.337	.436	113	9	7-3	.993	11	126	132	1b151		1.2
1983	Atl N	131	447	59	125	24	3	20	78	63-15	0	68	.280	.366	.481	125	16	2-7	.996	0	98	123	1b126	15	0.7
1984	Atl N	135	389	47	100	14	0	9	44	58-12	1	54	.257	.350	.362	95	0	1-2	.993	-1	97	106	1b109		-0.9
1985	Atl N	101	170	16	40	7	0	3	21	18-4	0	22	.235	.307	.329	74	-6	0-0	.997	1	110	109	1b39		-0.7
1986	Atl N	97	122	13	38	8	0	2	14	15-4	0	24	.311	.384	.426	119	4	0-2	.993	-2	53	124	1b20		0.0
1988	NY A	1	1	0	0	0	0	0	0	0-0	0	1	.000	.000	.000	-99	0	0-0	—	0			/H		0.0
Total	17	2175	7571	912	2109	392	42	185	972	632-99	27	926	.279	.334	.415	108	83	40-35	.993	12	101	108	1b1962,D24	15	-5.0

CHAMPION, MIKE Robert Michael B2.10.1955 Montgomery AL BR/TR/6-0/180* [SDN73 2/28] d9.14

YEAR	TM LG	G	AB	R	H	2B	3B	HR	RBI	BB-IB	HP	SO	AVG	OBP	SLG	AOPS	ABR	SB-CS	FA	FR	RNG	THR	GAMES AT POSITION	DL	BFW
1976	SD N	11	38	4	9	2	0	1	2	1-0	0	3	.237	.256	.368	82	-1	0-0	.940	-3	87	31	2b11		-0.4
1977	SD N	150	507	35	116	14	6	1	43	27-3	2	85	.229	.271	.286	55	-35	3-3	.974	-29	90	86	2b149		-5.8
1978	SD N	32	53	3	12	0	2	0	4	5-0	0	13	.226	.293	.302	72	-2	0-0	.932	1	120	151	2b20,3b4		-0.1
Total	3	193	598	42	137	16	8	2	49	33-3	2	101	.229	.274	.293	58	-38	3-3	.968	-31	97	88	2b180,3b4		-6.3

CHANCE, FRANK Frank Leroy "Husk","The Peerless Leader" B9.9.1877 Fresno CA D9.15.1924 Los Angeles CA BR/TR/6-0/190 d4.29 M11 HF1946

YEAR	TM LG	G	AB	R	H	2B	3B	HR	RBI	BB	HP	SO	AVG	OBP	SLG	AOPS	ABR	SB-CS	FA	FR	RNG	THR	GAMES AT POSITION	DL	BFW
1898	Chi N	53	147	32	41	4	3	1	14	7			.279	.338	.367	102	0	7	.950	-1	155	74	C33,O17(1/1/15),1b3		-0.1
1899	Chi N	64	192	37	55	6	2	1	22	15	4		.286	.351	.354	96	-1	10	.950	0	108	105	C57/OL1		0.4
1900	Chi N	56	149	26	44	9	3	0	13	15	15		.295	.413	.396	129	8	8	.932	-3	94	109	C51/1		0.8
1901	Chi N	69	241	38	67	12	4	0	36	29	9		.278	.376	.361	119	8	27	.932	-2	125	0	O51(4/1/46),C13,1b6		0.5
1902	Chi N	76	242	40	70	9	4	1	31	37	8		.289	.407	.372	143	15	29	.969	-2	89	105	1b38,C30,O4R		1.6
1903	Chi N	125	441	83	144	24	10	2	81	78	10		.327	.439	.440	155	38	67	.972	-3	97	89	1b121,C2		3.1
1904	Chi N	124	451	89	140	16	10	6	49	36	16		.310	.382	.430	150	27	42	.990	11	128	101	1b123/C		3.8
1905	Chi N	118	392	92	124	16	12	2	70	78	17		.316	.450	.434	157	35	38	.990	2	99	105	1b115,M		3.5
1906	†Chi N	136	474	103	151	24	10	3	71	70	12		.319	.419	.430	156	35	57	.989	-1	92	125	1b136,M		3.4
1907	†Chi N	111	382	58	112	19	2	1	49	51	13		.293	.395	.361	129	17	35	.992	7	119	135	1b109,M		2.5
1908	†Chi N	129	452	65	123	27	4	2	55	37	8		.272	.338	.363	119	11	27	.989	5	110	111	1b126,M		1.5
1909	Chi N	93	324	53	88	16	4	0	46	30	4		.272	.341	.346	110	4	29	.994	-2	82	115	1b92,M		0.1
1910	†Chi N	88	295	54	88	12	8	0	36	37	10	15	.298	.395	.393	131	13	16	.996	-1	83	111	1b87,M		1.1
1911	Chi N	31	88	23	21	6	3	1	17	25	5	13	.239	.432	.409	136	6	9	.990	-2	66	77	1b29,M		0.4
1912	Chi N	2	5	2	1	0	0	0	0	3	0	0	.200	.500	.200	96	0	1	1.000	-0	0	88	1b2,M		0.0
1913	NY A	12	24	3	5	0	0	0	6	8	0	1	.208	.406	.208	81	0	1	1.000	-0	106	47	1b7,M		0.0
1914	NY A	1	0	0	0	0	0	0	0	0	0	0	—	—	—	—	0	0	1.000	-0	0	0	/1M		0.0
Total	17	1288	4299	798	1274	200	79	20	596	556	137	29	.296	.394	.394	135	216	403	.987	8	101	109	1b997,C187,O73(6/2/65)		22.6

CHANCE, BOB Robert B9.10.1940 Statesboro GA BL/TR/6-2/219(196-219) d9.4

YEAR	TM LG	G	AB	R	H	2B	3B	HR	RBI	BB-IB	HP	SO	AVG	OBP	SLG	AOPS	ABR	SB-CS	FA	FR	RNG	THR	GAMES AT POSITION	DL	BFW
1963	Cle A	16	52	5	15	4	0	2	7	1-0	0	16	.288	.302	.481	116	1	0-1	.909	-1	95	0	O14R		-0.1
1964	Cle A	120	390	45	109	16	1	14	75	40-8	3	101	.279	.346	.433	118	10	3-3	.988	-11	51	78	1b81,O31(1/0/30)		-0.8
1965	Was A	72	199	20	51	9	0	4	14	18-2	0	44	.256	.317	.362	94	-1	0-1	.988	-2	86	100	1b48,O3R		-0.7
1966	Was A	37	57	1	10	3	0	1	8	2-0	0	23	.175	.200	.281	38	-5	0-0	.974	-1	53	89	1b13		-0.7
1967	Was A	27	42	5	9	2	0	3	7	7-0	1	13	.214	.340	.476	144	3	0-0	1.000	-0	87	97	1b10		0.2
1969	Cal A	5	7	0	1	0	0	0	1	0-0	0	4	.143	.143	.143	-21	-1	0-0	.909	-0	0	0	/1		-0.2
Total	6	277	747	76	195	34	1	24	112	68-10	4	195	.261	.323	.406	106	7	3-5	.987	-16	65	87	1b153,O48(1/0/47)		-2.3

CHANEY, DARREL Darrel Lee B3.9.1948 Hammond IN BB/TR (BL 1973p, 74-75)/6-1/190* [CinN66 2/33] d4.11

YEAR	TM LG	G	AB	R	H	2B	3B	HR	RBI	BB-IB	HP	SO	AVG	OBP	SLG	AOPS	ABR	SB-CS	FA	FR	RNG	THR	GAMES AT POSITION	DL	BFW
1969	Cin N	93	209	21	40	5	2	0	15	24-4	1	75	.191	.278	.234	43	-16	1-0	.947	-14	91	102	S91		-2.3
1970	†Cin N	57	95	7	22	3	0	1	4	3-1	1	26	.232	.263	.295	49	-7	1-1	.941	1	92	46	S30,2b18,3b3		-0.4
1971	Cin N	10	24	2	3	0	0	1	1	1-0	0	6	.125	.160	.125	-19	-4	0-1	1.000	-1	86	26	S7/23		-0.5
1972	†Cin N	83	196	29	49	7	2	2	19	29-7	0	28	.250	.345	.337	100	1	1-3	.963	-12	90	84	S64,2b12,3b10		-0.6
1973	†Cin N	105	227	27	41	7	1	0	14	26-5	1	50	.181	.267	.220	38	-19	4-3	.964	2	105	119	S75,2b14,3b12		-0.9
1974	Cin N	117	135	27	27	6	1	2	16	26-6	0	33	.200	.327	.304	79	-3	1-2	.952	-1	86	49	3b81,2b38,S12		-0.2
1975	†Cin N	71	160	18	35	6	0	2	26	14-2	0	38	.219	.280	.294	59	-9	3-0	.961	9	122	116	S34,2b23,3b13		0.5
1976	Atl N	153	496	42	125	20	8	1	50	54-7	0	92	.252	.324	.331	82	-11	5-7	.950	5	102	93	S151/23		1.0
1977	Atl N	74	209	22	42	7	2	3	15	17-2	0	44	.201	.260	.297	44	-17	0-0	.979	9	104	72	S41,2b24		-0.3
1978	Atl N	89	245	27	55	9	1	3	20	25-7	0	48	.224	.295	.306	62	-12	1-0	.976	-2	98	77	S77,3b8/2		-0.8
1979	Atl N	63	117	15	19	5	0	0	10	19-2	0	34	.162	.277	.205	32	-10	2-1	.945	-5	92	86	S39,2b5,3b4/C		-1.3
Total	11	915	2113	237	458	75	17	14	190	238-43	4	471	.217	.296	.288	61	-107	19-18	.959	-10	100	93	S621,2b137,3b133/C	54	-5.8

CHANNELL, LES Lester Clark "Goat","Gint" B3.3.1886 Crestline OH D5.8.1954 Denver CO BL/TL/6-0/180 d5.11

YEAR	TM LG	G	AB	R	H	2B	3B	HR	RBI	BB	HP	SO	AVG	OBP	SLG	AOPS	ABR	SB-CS	FA	FR	RNG	THR	GAMES AT POSITION	DL	BFW
1910	NY A	6	19	3	6	0	0		3	2	0	0	.316	.381	.316	112	0	2	1.000	-0	111	0	O6L		0.0
1914	NY A	1	1	0	0	0	0	0	0	0	0	0	1.000	1.000	2.000	803	1	0	1.000	-0		0	/H		0.1
Total	2	7	20	3	6	0	0		3	2	0	0	.350	.409	.400	145	1	2	1.000	-0	111	0	O6L		0.1

CHANT, CHARLIE Charles Joseph B8.7.1951 Bell CA BR/TR/6-0/185* [OakA69 19/439] d9.12

YEAR	TM LG	G	AB	R	H	2B	3B	HR	RBI	BB-IB	HP	SO	AVG	OBP	SLG	AOPS	ABR	SB-CS	FA	FR	RNG	THR	GAMES AT POSITION	DL	BFW
1975	Oak A	5	5	1	0	0	0	0	0	0-0	0	0	.000	.000	.000	-99	-1	0-0	1.000	-0	36	0	O5(3/0/2)/D		-0.2
1976	StL N	15	14	0	2	0	0	0	0	0-0	0	4	.143	.143	.143	-18	-2	0-0	1.000	2	149	270	O14(7/2/5)		-0.1
Total	2	20	19	1	2	0	0	0	0	0-0	0	4	.105	.105	.105	-40	-3	0-0	1.000	1	124	210	O19(10/2/7)/D		-0.3

CHAPLIN, ED Bert Edgar (b Bert Edgar Chapman) B9.25.1893 Pelzer SC D8.15.1978 Sanford FL BL/TR/5-7/158 d9.4 Col South Carolina-Aiken

YEAR	TM LG	G	AB	R	H	2B	3B	HR	RBI	BB-IB	HP	SO	AVG	OBP	SLG	AOPS	ABR	SB-CS	FA	FR	RNG	THR	GAMES AT POSITION	DL	BFW
1920	Bos A	4	5	2	1	0	0	0	1	0-0	0	1	.200	.556	.400	163	1	0-0	.900	-0	108	0	C2		0.1
1921	Bos A	3	2	0	0	0	0	0	0	0-0	0	0	.000	.000	.000	-99	-1	0-0	1.000	0	0	968	/C		-0.1
1922	Bos A	28	69	8	13	1	0	0	6	9	0	9	.188	.282	.232	35	-7	2-1	.960	-2	80	78	C21		-0.7
Total	3	35	76	10	14	2	1	0	7	13	0	11	.184	.303	.237	43	-7	2-1	.953	-2	82	81	C24		-0.7

CHAPMAN, CALVIN Calvin Louis B12.20.1910 Courtland MS D4.1.1983 Batesville MS BL/TR/5-9/160 d9.10 b-Ed

YEAR	TM LG	G	AB	R	H	2B	3B	HR	RBI	BB	HP	SO	AVG	OBP	SLG	AOPS	ABR	SB-CS	FA	FR	RNG	THR	GAMES AT POSITION	DL	BFW
1935	Cin N	15	53	6	18	1	0	0	3	4	0	5	.340	.386	.358	105	0	2	.949	-1	96	141	S12,2b4		0.0
1936	Cin N	96	219	35	54	7	3	1	22	16	1	19	.247	.301	.320	72	-9	5	.961	-5	81	129	O31(21/1/9),2b23/3		-1.5
Total	2	111	272	41	72	8	3	1	25	20	1	24	.265	.317	.327	78	-9	7	.961	-7	81	129	O31(21/1/9),2b27,S12/3		-1.5

CHAPMAN, GLENN Glenn Justice "Pete" B1.21.1906 Cambridge City IN D11.5.1988 Richmond IN BR/TR/5-11.5/170 d4.18

YEAR	TM LG	G	AB	R	H	2B	3B	HR	RBI	BB	HP	SO	AVG	OBP	SLG	AOPS	ABR	SB-CS	FA	FR	RNG	THR	GAMES AT POSITION	DL	BFW
1934	Bro N	67	93	19	26	5	1	1	10	7	0	19	.280	.330	.387	96	1	1	1.000	2	123	0	O40(27/0/14),2b14		0.1

CHAPMAN, HARRY Harry E. B10.26.1887 Severance KS D10.21.1918 Nevada MO BR/TR/5-11/160 d10.6

YEAR	TM LG	G	AB	R	H	2B	3B	HR	RBI	BB	HP	SO	AVG	OBP	SLG	AOPS	ABR	SB-CS	FA	FR	RNG	THR	GAMES AT POSITION	DL	BFW
1912	Chi N	1	4	1	1	0	1	0	1	0	0	0	.250	.250	.750	169	0	1	1.000	1	177	142	/C		0.1
1913	Cin N	2	2	1	1	0	0	0	0	0	0	1	.500	.500	.500	187	0	0	—	0			/H		0.0
1914	StL F	64	181	16	38	2	1	0	14	13	2	27	.210	.270	.232	36	-19	2	.973	-5	83	98	C51/12OC		-2.1
1915	StL F	62	186	19	37	6	3	1	29	22	1	24	.199	.284	.280	56	-14	4	.989	6	107	98	C53		-0.4
1916	StL A	18	31	2	3	0	0	0	2	0	0	5	.097	.152	.097	-7	-5	0	.981	1	96	155	C14		-0.4
Total	5	147	404	38	80	8	5	1	44	37	2	57	.198	.269	.250	43	-38	7	.982	-2	97	103	C119/OC21		-2.8

CHAPMAN, JACK John Curtis "Death To Flying Things" B5.8.1843 Brooklyn NY D6.10.1916 Brooklyn NY TR/5-11/170 d5.5 M11

YEAR	TM LG	G	AB	R	H	2B	3B	HR	RBI	BB	HP	SO	AVG	OBP	SLG	AOPS	ABR	SB-CS	FA	FR	RNG	THR	GAMES AT POSITION	DL	BFW
1874	Atl NA	53	242	32	64	10	2	0	24	4		11	.264	.276	.322	103	4	2-1	.741	1	167	0	O53(0/1/52)/1		0.6
1875	StL NA	43	195	28	44	5	3	0	30	1		7	.226	.230	.282	84	-2	4-1	.733	-5	81	159	O43R/1		-0.3
1876	Lou N	17	67	4	16	1	0	0	5	1		3	.239	.250	.254	58	-3		.750	-3	78		O17(5/1/11)/3M		-0.6
Total	2 NA	96	437	60	108	15	5	0	54	5		18	.247	.256	.304	95	2	6-2	.738	-4	126	75	O96(0/1/95),1b2		0.3

CHAPMAN, JOHN John Joseph B10.15.1899 Centralia PA D11.3.1953 Philadelphia PA BR/TR/5-10.5/175 d6.28 Col Mount St. Marys

YEAR	TM LG	G	AB	R	H	2B	3B	HR	RBI	BB	HP	SO	AVG	OBP	SLG	AOPS	ABR	SB-CS	FA	FR	RNG	THR	GAMES AT POSITION	DL	BFW
1924	Phi A	19	71	7	20	4	1	0	7	3	0	10	.282	.329	.366	78	-2	0-0	.958	-5	73	116	S19		-0.6

CHAPMAN, KELVIN Kelvin Keith B6.2.1956 Willits CA BR/TR/5-11/173* d4.5 Col Santa Rosa (CA) JC

YEAR	TM LG	G	AB	R	H	2B	3B	HR	RBI	BB-IB	HP	SO	AVG	OBP	SLG	AOPS	ABR	SB-CS	FA	FR	RNG	THR	GAMES AT POSITION	DL	BFW
1979	NY N	35	80	7	12	1	2	0	4	5-0	0	15	.150	.198	.213	13	-10	0-0	.980	-2	86	121	2b22/3		-1.1
1984	NY N	75	197	27	57	13	0	3	23	19-0	2	30	.289	.356	.401	114	4	8-7	.979	-4	87	103	2b57,3b3		0.3
1985	NY N	62	144	16	25	3	0	0	7	9-0	2	15	.174	.231	.194	21	-15	5-4	.970	-10	82	79	2b48/3		-2.6
Total	3	172	421	50	94	17	2	3	34	33-0	4	60	.223	.284	.295	63	-21	13-11	.976	-16	85	98	2b127,3b5		-3.4

CHAPMAN, RAY Raymond Johnson B1.15.1891 Beaver Dam KY D8.17.1920 New York NY BR/TR/5-10/170 d8.30

YEAR	TM LG	G	AB	R	H	2B	3B	HR	RBI	BB	HP	SO	AVG	OBP	SLG	AOPS	ABR	SB-CS	FA	FR	RNG	THR	GAMES AT POSITION	DL	BFW
1912	Cle A	31	109	29	34	6	3	0	19	10	1		.312	.375	.422	124	3	10	.904	-7	77	98	S31		-0.2
1913	Cle A	141	508	83	131	19	7	3	39	46	2	51	.258	.322	.341	91	-6	29	.936	-9	92	106	S138/OR		-0.6

YEAR	TM LG	G	AB	R	H	2B	3B	HR	RBI	BB-IB	HP	SO	AVG	OBP	SLG	AOPS	ABR	SB-CS	FA	FR	RNG	THR	GAMES AT POSITION	DL BFW
1914	Cle A	106	375	59	103	16	10	2	42	48	1	48	.275	.358	.387	119	9	24-9	.913	-13	86	77	S72,2b33	0.5
1915	Cle A	**154**	570	101	154	14	17	3	64	70	3	82	.270	.353	.370	114	9	36-15	.944	10	100	66	S154	3.4
1916	Cle A	109	346	50	80	10	5	0	27	50	1	46	.231	.330	.289	81	-7	21-14	.935	7	102	92	S52,3b36,2b16	0.6
1917	Cle A	156	563	59	170	28	13	2	36	61	0	52	.302	.370	.409	128	19	52	.938	24	111	107	S156	5.8
1918	Cle A	128	446	84	119	19	8	1	32	84	6	46	.267	.390	.352	113	12	35	.936	7	101	85	S128/OC	3.0
1919	Cle A	115	433	75	130	23	10	3	53	31	3	38	.300	.351	.420	109	4	18	.944	2	100	107	S115	1.4
1920	Cle A	111	435	97	132	27	8	3	49	52	2	38	.303	.380	.423	109	7	13-9	.959	14	106	106	S111	2.7
Total 9		1051	3785	671	1053	162	81	17	364	452	19	414	.278	.358	.377	110	50	238-47	.939	34	100	94	S957,2b49,3b36,O2(0/1/1)	16.6

CHAPMAN, SAM Samuel Blake B4.11.1916 Tiburon CA BR/TR/6-1/190* d5.16 Mil 1942-45 Col California-Davis

YEAR	TM LG	G	AB	R	H	2B	3B	HR	RBI	BB-IB	HP	SO	AVG	OBP	SLG	AOPS	ABR	SB-CS	FA	FR	RNG	THR	GAMES AT POSITION	DL BFW
1938	Phl A	114	406	60	105	17	7	17	63	55	4	94	.259	.353	.461	105	1	3-4	.952	0	102	103	O110(103/8/0)	-0.4
1939	Phl A	140	498	74	134	24	6	15	64	51	1	62	.269	.338	.432	98	-4	11-4	.955	1	106	107	O117C,1b19	-0.6
1940	Phl A	134	508	88	140	26	3	23	75	46	1	96	.276	.337	.474	110	6	2-6	.963	5	104	142	O129C	0.5
1941	Phl A	143	552	97	178	29	9	25	106	47	2	49	.322	.378	.543	145	32	6-9	.967	12	106	**174**	O141(0/140/1)	3.7
1945	Phl A	9	30	3	6	2	0	0	1	2	0	4	.200	.250	.267	50	-2	0-0	1.000	-1	90	0	O8C	-0.3
1946	Phl A★	146	545	77	142	22	5	20	67	54	0	66	.261	.327	.429	111	6	1-3	.970	8	108	134	O145(89/59/0)	0.5
1947	Phl A	149	551	84	139	18	5	14	83	65	0	70	.252	.331	.379	95	-4	3-4	.987	8	103	161	O146(12/134/0)	-0.1
1948	Phl A	123	445	58	115	18	4	13	70	55	1	50	.258	.341	.413	100	-2	6-1	.982	1	104	79	O118C	-0.3
1949	Phl A	**154**	589	89	164	24	4	24	108	80	2	68	.278	.367	.455	121	16	3-4	.979	3	104	101	O154C	1.4
1950	Phl A	144	553	93	139	20	6	23	95	68	4	79	.251	.338	.434	98	-4	3-3	.978	5	104	90	O140C	-0.3
1951	Phl A	18	65	7	11	1	0	0	5	12	0	12	.169	.299	.185	32	-6	0-0	.957	-2	91	57	O17C	-0.8
	Cle A	94	246	24	56	9	1	6	36	27	0	32	.228	.304	.346	80	-8	3-0	.985	-4	93	40	O84(38/44/7)/1	-1.4
	Year	112	311	31	67	10	1	6	41	39	0	44	.215	.303	.312	69	-14	3-0	.978	-6	93	44	O101(38/61/7)/1	-2.2
Total 11		1368	4988	754	1329	210	52	180	773	562	15	682	.266	.342	.438	107	31	41-38	.972	36	104	117	O1309(242/1068/8),1b20	1.9

CHAPMAN, TRAVIS Travis Adrian B6.5.1978 Jacksonville FL BR/TR/6-2/180 [PhiN00 17/505] d9.9 Col Mississippi St.

YEAR	TM LG	G	AB	R	H	2B	3B	HR	RBI	BB-IB	HP	SO	AVG	OBP	SLG	AOPS	ABR	SB-CS	FA	FR	RNG	THR	GAMES AT POSITION	DL BFW
2003	Phi N	1	1	0	0	0	0	0	0	0	0	0	.000	.000	.000	-99	0	0-0	—	0	0	0	/3	-0.1

CHAPMAN, BEN William Benjamin B12.25.1908 Nashville TN D7.7.1993 Hoover AL BR/TR/6-0/190 d4.15 M4/C1 OF(404/583/541) ▲

YEAR	TM LG	G	AB	R	H	2B	3B	HR	RBI	BB-IB	HP	SO	AVG	OBP	SLG	AOPS	ABR	SB-CS	FA	FR	RNG	THR	GAMES AT POSITION	DL BFW
1930	NY A	138	513	74	162	31	10	10	81	43	2	58	.316	.371	.474	118	13	14-6	.912	-9	92	71	3b91,2b45	1.1
1931	NY A	149	600	120	189	28	11	17	122	75	5	77	.315	.396	.483	138	34	**61-23**	.963	6	106	125	O137(90/0/50),2b11	3.4
1932	†NY A	151	581	101	174	41	15	10	107	71	3	55	.299	.381	.473	126	24	**38-18**	.949	5	104	122	O150(81/0/86)	1.9
1933	NY A★	147	565	112	176	36	4	9	98	72	4	45	.312	.393	.437	127	25	**27-18**	.975	14	107	**190**	O147(76/0/77)	2.9
1934	NY A★	149	588	82	181	21	**13**	5	86	67	3	68	.308	.381	.413	113	11	26-16	.967	4	106	100	O149(41/87/23)	0.9
1935	NY A★	140	553	118	160	38	8	8	74	61	1	39	.289	.361	.430	110	8	17-10	.964	13	103	**243**	O138C	1.7
1936	NY A	36	139	19	37	14	3	1	21	15	0	20	.266	.338	.432	92	-2	1-2	.965	1	106	93	O36C	-0.2
	Was A★	97	401	91	133	36	7	4	60	69	1	18	.332	.431	.486	133	25	19-7	.959	-1	97	112	O97C	2.1
	Year	133	540	110	170	50	10	5	81	84	1	38	.315	.408	.472	123	23	20-9	.961	-0	99	107	O133C	1.9
1937	Was A	35	130	23	34	7	1	0	12	26	0	7	.262	.385	.331	86	-1	8-0	.957	-1	104	34	O32C	-0.2
	Bos A	113	423	76	130	23	11	7	57	57	1	35	.307	.391	.463	110	7	27-12	.985	5	114	85	O112(2/10/100)/S	0.6
	Year	148	553	99	164	30	12	7	69	83	1	42	.297	.389	.432	105	6	**35-12**	.978	4	**112**	74	O144(2/42/100)/S	0.4
1938	Bos A	127	480	92	163	40	8	6	80	65	0	33	.340	.418	.494	122	19	13-6	.966	5	106	.130	O146(1/0/125)/3	1.6
1939	Cle A	149	545	101	158	31	9	6	82	87	2	30	.290	.390	.413	109	11	18-6	.971	-6	93	100	O146(2/137/9)	0.3
1940	Cle A	143	548	82	157	40	8	4	50	78	2	45	.286	.377	.403	105	8	13-7	.964	1	103	94	O140(62/18/62)	0.2
1941	Was A	28	110	9	28	6	0	1	10	10	0	6	.255	.317	.336	76	-4	2-2	.983	0	100	142	O26L	-0.4
	Chi A	57	190	26	43	9	1	2	19	19	0	14	.226	.297	.316	63	-10	2-2	.992	0	100	91	O49(21/22/7)	-1.2
	Year	85	300	35	71	15	1	3	29	29	0	20	.237	.304	.323	68	-14	4-4	.989	1	100	108	O75(47/22/7)	-1.6
1944	Bro N	20	38	11	14	4	0	0	11	5	0	4	.368	.442	.474	161	7	0	.900	-2	40	0	P11	0.0
1945	Bro N	13	22	2	3	0	0	0	3	2	0	1	.136	.208	.136	-3	-1	0	.938	1	123	172	P10	0.0
	Phi N	24	51	4	16	2	0	0	4	2	0	2	.314	.340	.353	95	0	0	.933	-1	80	183	O10(2/6/2),3b4,P3,M	-0.2
	Year	37	73	6	19	2	0	0	7	4	0	2	.260	.299	.288	65	-4	0	.941	-1	117	152	P13,O10(2/6/2),3b4	-0.2
1946	Phi N	1	1	0	0	0	0	0	0	0	0	0	.000	.000	.000	-99	0	0	—	0	0	0	/PM	0.0
Total 15		1717	6478	1144	1958	407	107	90	977	824	26	556	.302	.383	.440	115	174	287-135	.967	36	104	127	O1495C,3b96,2b56,P25/S	14.5

CHAPMAN, FRED William Fred "Chapple" B7.17.1916 Liberty NC D3.27.1997 Kannapolis NC BR/TR/6-1/185 d9.15 Mil 1943-45

YEAR	TM LG	G	AB	R	H	2B	3B	HR	RBI	BB-IB	HP	SO	AVG	OBP	SLG	AOPS	ABR	SB-CS	FA	FR	RNG	THR	GAMES AT POSITION	DL BFW
1939	Phl A	15	49	5	14	1	1	0	1	1	0	10	.286	.300	.347	66	-3	1-0	.899	-3	98	59	S15	-0.4
1940	Phl A	26	69	6	11	1	0	0	4	6	0	10	.159	.227	.174	6	-10	1-1	.862	-6	88	88	S25	-1.4
1941	Phl A	35	69	1	11	1	0	0	4	4	0	15	.159	.205	.174	1	-10	1-2	.917	-1	121	66	S28,3b2/2	-1.1
Total 3		76	187	12	36	3	1	0	9	11	0	28	.193	.237	.219	20	-23	3-3	.889	-10	101	74	S68,3b2/2	-2.9

CHAPPAS, HARRY Harry Perry B10.26.1957 Mt.Rainier MD BB/TR/5-3/150* [ChiA76*S6/94] d9.7 Col Miami-Dade North (FL) CC

YEAR	TM LG	G	AB	R	H	2B	3B	HR	RBI	BB-IB	HP	SO	AVG	OBP	SLG	AOPS	ABR	SB-CS	FA	FR	RNG	THR	GAMES AT POSITION	DL BFW
1978	Chi A	20	75	11	20	1	0	0	6	6-0	1	11	.267	.318	.280	72	-3	1-2	1.000	1	107	66	S20	0.0
1979	Chi A	26	59	9	17	0	0	1	4	5-0	1	5	.288	.354	.356	92	-1	1-1	.929	1	107	104	S23	0.2
1980	Chi A	26	50	6	8	2	0	0	2	4-0	1	10	.160	.236	.200	21	-5	0-2	.981	3	113	139	S19/2D	-0.2
Total 3		72	184	26	45	4	0	1	12	15-0	3	26	.245	.307	.283	65	-9	2-5	.967	5	108	95	S62,D2/2	0.0

CHAPPELL, LARRY La Verne Ashford B2.19.1890 McClusky IL D11.8.1918 San Francisco CA BL/TR/6-0/186 d7.18

YEAR	TM LG	G	AB	R	H	2B	3B	HR	RBI	BB-IB	HP	SO	AVG	OBP	SLG	AOPS	ABR	SB-CS	FA	FR	RNG	THR	GAMES AT POSITION	DL BFW
1913	Chi A	60	208	20	48	8	1	0	15	18	1	22	.231	.295	.279	69	-8	7	.952	-3	98	59	O59(52/7/0)	-1.6
1914	Chi A	21	39	3	9	0	0	0	1	4	0	11	.231	.302	.231	61	-2	0	.929	-1	93	0	O9(7/0/2)	-0.4
1915	Chi A	1	1	0	0	0	0	0	0	0	0	0	.000	.000	.000	-97	0	1	—	0			/H	0.0
1916	Cle A	3	2	0	0	0	0	0	0	1	0	0	.000	.333	.000	1	0	1	—	0			/H	0.0
	Bos N	20	53	4	12	1	1	0	9	2	1	8	.226	.288	.283	72	-2	1	.957	-2	93	0	O14(12/0/2)	-0.5
1917	Bos N	4	2	0	0	0	0	0	0	1	0	1	.000	.000	.000	-99	-1	0	—	-0	0	0	/OC	-0.1
Total 5		109	305	27	69	9	2	0	26	25	2	42	.226	.289	.269	66	-12	9	.951	-6	97	44	O83(71/8/4)	-2.6

CHARBONEAU, JOE Joseph B6.17.1955 Belvidere IL BR/TR/6-2/200* [PhiN76 S2/35] d4.11 Col West Valley (CA) CC

YEAR	TM LG	G	AB	R	H	2B	3B	HR	RBI	BB-IB	HP	SO	AVG	OBP	SLG	AOPS	ABR	SB-CS	FA	FR	RNG	THR	GAMES AT POSITION	DL BFW
1980	Cle A	131	453	76	131	17	2	23	87	49-0	3	70	.289	.358	.488	129	18	2-4	.963	-1	95	128	O67(67/0/1),D57	1.2
1981	Cle A	48	138	14	29	7	1	4	18	7-0	0	22	.210	.247	.362	74	-5	1-0	.963	-1	97	58	O27(24/0/5),D14	-0.8
1982	Cle A	22	56	7	12	2	1	2	9	5-0	1	7	.214	.286	.393	85	-1	0-0	.955	-3	72	0	O18(9/0/8)/D	-0.5
Total 3		201	647	97	172	26	4	29	114	61-0	4	99	.266	.329	.453	115	12	3-4	.962	-4	92	94	O112(100/0/14),D72	-0.1

CHARLES, ED Edwin Douglas B4.29.1933 Daytona Beach FL BR/TR/5-10/170* d4.11

YEAR	TM LG	G	AB	R	H	2B	3B	HR	RBI	BB-IB	HP	SO	AVG	OBP	SLG	AOPS	ABR	SB-CS	FA	FR	RNG	THR	GAMES AT POSITION	DL BFW
1962	KC A	147	535	81	154	24	7	17	74	54-0	4	70	.288	.356	.454	111	9	20-4	.964	14	110	102	3b140,2b2	2.5
1963	KC A	158	603	82	161	28	2	15	79	58-7	5	79	.267	.332	.395	99	0	15-8	.949	-1	104	62	3b158	0.8
1964	KC A	150	557	69	134	25	4	16	49	64-2	4	92	.241	.321	.379	92	-5	12-7	.954	-14	89	86	3b147	-2.1
1965	KC A	134	480	55	129	19	7	8	56	44-0	4	72	.269	.332	.387	106	-4	13-4	.971	5	98	104	3b128/2S	1.0
1966	KC A	118	385	52	110	18	4	9	42	30-2	4	53	.286	.337	.444	127	12	12-5	.963	-1	104	108	3b104/1OL	1.2
1967	KC A	19	61	6	15	1	0	0	5	12-1	1	13	.246	.378	.262	95	1	1-0	.966	3	117	35	3b18	0.4
	NY N	101	323	50	77	13	2	3	31	24-1	7	58	.238	.300	.319	80	-8	4-1	.944	14	119	106	3b89	0.7
1968	NY N	117	369	41	102	11	1	15	53	28-4	2	57	.276	.328	.434	127	11	5-4	.954	1	103	114	3b106,1b2	1.3
1969	†NY N	61	169	21	35	8	1	3	18	18-3	1	31	.207	.286	.320	68	-7	4-2	.946	-1	96	131	3b52	-0.9
Total 8		1005	3482	438	917	147	30	86	421	332-20	28	525	.263	.330	.397	103	-1	86-35	.957	19	103	95	3b942,1b3,2b3/OLS	4.0

CHARLES, FRANK Franklin Scott B2.23.1969 Fontana CA BR/TR/6-4/210 [SFN91 17/453] d9.5 Col Cal St.-Fullerton

YEAR	TM LG	G	AB	R	H	2B	3B	HR	RBI	BB-IB	HP	SO	AVG	OBP	SLG	AOPS	ABR	SB-CS	FA	FR	RNG	THR	GAMES AT POSITION	DL BFW
2000	Hou N	4	7	1	3	1	0	0	2	0-0	0	2	.429	.429	.571	139	0	0-0	1.000	1	61	0	/C	0.1

CHARLES, CHAPPY Raymond (b Charles Shuh Achenbach) B3.25.1881 Phillipsburg NJ D8.4.1959 Bethlehem PA BR/TR/5-11/175 d4.15

YEAR	TM LG	G	AB	R	H	2B	3B	HR	RBI	BB-IB	HP	SO	AVG	OBP	SLG	AOPS	ABR	SB-CS	FA	FR	RNG	THR	GAMES AT POSITION	DL BFW
1908	StL N	121	454	39	93	14	3	1	17	19	1		.205	.238	.256	61	-22	15	.921	-6	98	26	2b65,S31,3b23	-3.0
1909	StL N	99	339	33	80	7	3	0	29	31	5		.236	.309	.274	87	-5	7	.918	-8	96	108	2b71,S26,3b2	-1.2
	Cin N	13	43	3	11	2	0	0	5	4	0		.256	.319	.302	94	-1	2	.932	-1	107	34	2b10,S3	-0.1
	Year	112	382	36	91	9	3	0	34	35	5		.238	.310	.277	87	-5	9	.920	-9	97	100	2b81,S29,3b2	-1.3
1910	Cin N	4	15	1	2	0	0	0	1	0	0	1	.133	.133	.267	17	-2	0	.818	-1	82	119	S4	-0.3
Total 3		237	851	76	186	23	7	1	51	54	6	1	.219	.270	.266	72	-29	24	.920	-15	98	68	2b146,S64,3b25	-4.6

CHARTAK, MIKE Michael George "Shotgun" B4.28.1916 Brooklyn NY D7.25.1967 Cedar Rapids IA BL/TL/6-2/180 d9.13

YEAR	TM LG	G	AB	R	H	2B	3B	HR	RBI	BB-IB	HP	SO	AVG	OBP	SLG	AOPS	ABR	SB-CS	FA	FR	RNG	THR	GAMES AT POSITION	DL BFW
1940	NY A	11	15	2	2	1	0	0	3	5	0	5	.133	.350	.200	49	-1	0-0	1.000	-0	87	0	O3R	-0.1
1942	NY A	5	5	0	0	0	0	0	0	0	0	2	.000	.000	.000	-99	-1	0-0	—	0			/H	-0.1

YEAR	TM LG	G	AB	R	H	2B	3B	HR	RBI	BB-IB	HP	SO	AVG	OBP	SLG	AOPS	ABR	SB-CS	FA	FR	RNG	THR	GAMES AT POSITION	DL	BFW
	Was A	24	92	11	20	4	2	1	8	14	0	16	.217	.321	.337	86	-2	0-1	.926	0	103	116	O24R		-0.4
	StL A	73	237	37	59	11	2	3	43	40	2	27	.249	.362	.426	119	7	3-3	.974	5	104	199	O64R		0.8
	Year	102	334	48	79	15	4	10	51	54	2	43	.237	.346	.395	107	4	3-4	.962	5	104	177	O88R		0.3
1943	StL A	108	344	38	88	16	2	10	37	39	1	55	.256	.333	.401	112	5	1-3	.970	-0	109	78	O77R,1b18		-0.2
1944	†StL A	35	72	8	17	2	1	1	7	6	1	9	.236	.304	.333	77	-2	0-0	1.000	0	88	63	1b12,O7(4/0/3)		-0.3
Total 4		256	765	96	186	34	7	21	98	104	4	112	.243	.337	.388	105	6	4-7	.967	5	106	127	O175(4/0/171),1b30		-0.3

CHASE, HAL Harold Homer "Prince Hal" B2.13.1883 Los Gatos CA D5.18.1947 Colusa CA BR/TL/6-0/175 d4.14 M2 Col Santa Clara

YEAR	TM LG	G	AB	R	H	2B	3B	HR	RBI	BB-IB	HP	SO	AVG	OBP	SLG	AOPS	ABR	SB-CS	FA	FR	RNG	THR	GAMES AT POSITION	DL	BFW
1905	NY A	128	465	60	116	16	6	3	49	15	3		.249	.277	.329	83	-11	22	.976	-9	78	125	1b124,S2/2		-2.4
1906	NY A	151	597	84	193	23	10	0	76	13	3		.323	.341	.395	118	10	28	.980	-2	95	89	1b150/2		0.6
1907	NY A	125	498	72	143	23	3	2	68	19	1		.287	.315	.357	106	2	32	.973	0	103	84	1b121,O4L		0.0
1908	NY A	106	405	50	104	11	3	1	36	15	1		.257	.285	.306	91	-5	27	.980	-3	91	73	1b98,2b3,O3L/3P		-1.2
1909	NY A	118	474	60	134	17	3	4	63	20	4		.283	.317	.357	112	5	25	.978	-2	100	89	1b118/S		0.1
1910	NY A	130	524	67	152	20	5	3	73	16	1		.290	.312	.365	106	1	40	.981	-4	88	120	1b130,M		-0.6
1911	NY A	133	527	82	166	32	7	3	62	21	1		.315	.342	.419	105	2	36	.974	-2	101	108	1b124,O7C,2b2,M		-0.3
1912	NY A	131	522	61	143	21	9	4	58	17	2		.274	.299	.372	86	-12	33	.979	-1	111	80	1b122,2b7		-1.7
1913	NY A	39	146	15	31	2	4	0	9	11	0	13	.212	.268	.281	60	-8	5	.982	-4	88	97	1b29,2b5,O5C		-1.4
	Chi A	102	384	49	110	11	10	2	39	16	3	41	.286	.320	.383	107	0	9	.976	1	114	104	1b102		-0.1
	Year	141	530	64	141	13	14	2	48	27	3	54	.266	.305	.355	94	-8	14	.977	-3	108	102	1b131,2b5,O5C		-1.5
1914	Chi A	58	206	27	55	10	5	0	20	23	1	19	.267	.343	.364	114	4	9	.981	2	116	103	1b58		0.5
	Buf F	75	291	43	101	19	9	3	48	6	2	31	.347	.365	.471	133	7	10	.980	-1	99	89	1b73		0.5
1915	Buf F	145	567	85	165	31	10	**17**	89	20	1	50	.291	.316	.471	118	1	23	.983	0	103	101	1b143/OR		-0.3
1916	Cin N	142	542	66	**184**	29	12	4	82	19	1	48	**.339**	.363	.459	155	32	22-11	.980	-5	79	116	1b98,O25(14/14/0),2b16		2.8
1917	Cin N	152	602	71	167	28	15	4	86	15	1	49	.277	.296	.394	115	7	21	.983	-3	98	103	1b151		0.0
1918	Cin N	74	259	30	78	12	6	2	38	13	2	15	.301	.339	.417	133	9	5	.980	-2	93	146	1b67,O2L		0.6
1919	Cin N	110	408	58	116	17	7	5	45	17	3	40	.284	.318	.390	115	6	16	.984	-1	101	**111**	1b107		0.2
Total 15		1919	7417	980	2158	322	124	57	941	276	30	306	.291	.319	.391	110	50	363-15	.980	-35	98	102	1b1815,O47(23/26/1),2b35,S3/P3		-2.7

CHATHAM, BUSTER Charles L B12.25.1901 West TX D12.15.1975 Waco TX BR/TR/5-5/150 d6.1

YEAR	TM LG	G	AB	R	H	2B	3B	HR	RBI	BB-IB	HP	SO	AVG	OBP	SLG	AOPS	ABR	SB-CS	FA	FR	RNG	THR	GAMES AT POSITION	DL	BFW
1930	Bos N	112	404	48	108	20	11	5	56	37	2	41	.267	.332	.408	80	-14	8	.920	-11	88	158	3b92,S17		-1.6
1931	Bos N	17	44	4	10	1	0	1	3	6	0	6	.227	.320	.318	75	-2	0	.762	-4	51	99	S6,3b6		-0.5
Total 2		129	448	52	118	21	11	6	59	43	2	47	.263	.331	.400	80	-16	8	.924	-15	90	155	3b98,S23		-2.1

CHATTERTON, JIM James M. B10.14.1864 Brooklyn NY D12.15.1944 Tewksbury MA d6.7

YEAR	TM LG	G	AB	R	H	2B	3B	HR	RBI	BB-IB	HP	SO	AVG	OBP	SLG	AOPS	ABR	SB-CS	FA	FR	RNG	THR	GAMES AT POSITION	DL	BFW
1884	KC U	4	15	4	2	1	0	0		2			.133	.235	.200	38	-1		1.000	1	590	0	O2R,1b2/P		-0.1

CHAVARRIA, OSSIE Osvaldo (Quijano) B8.5.1940 Colon, Pan BR/TR/5-11/155* d4.14

YEAR	TM LG	G	AB	R	H	2B	3B	HR	RBI	BB-IB	HP	SO	AVG	OBP	SLG	AOPS	ABR	SB-CS	FA	FR	RNG	THR	GAMES AT POSITION	DL	BFW
1966	KC A	86	191	26	46	10	0	2	10	18-1	0	43	.241	.306	.325	84	-4	3-2	.939	-3	83	82	O26(19/0/7),S23,2b14,1b8,3b5		-0.6
1967	KC A	38	59	2	6	2	0	0	4	7-0	1	16	.102	.209	.136	4	-7	1-0	1.000	1	105	144	2b17,3b7,O3(2/0/1),S2		-0.5
Total 2		124	250	28	52	12	0	2	14	25-1	1	59	.208	.283	.280	65	-11	4-2	.990	-2	100	108	2b31,O29(21/0/8),S25,3b12,1b8		-1.1

CHAVEZ, ANGEL Angel Aristides (Castro) B7.22.1981 David, Pan BR/TR/6-1/195 d8.30

YEAR	TM LG	G	AB	R	H	2B	3B	HR	RBI	BB-IB	HP	SO	AVG	OBP	SLG	AOPS	ABR	SB-CS	FA	FR	RNG	THR	GAMES AT POSITION	DL	BFW
2005	SF N	10	19	1	5	1	0	0	1	0-0	0		.263	.263	.316	49	-1	0-0	1.000	-4	63	0	2b5,S4/3		-0.5

CHAVEZ, ENDY Endy De Jesus B2.7.1978 Valencia, Venez BL/TL/6-0/165* d5.29

YEAR	TM LG	G	AB	R	H	2B	3B	HR	RBI	BB-IB	HP	SO	AVG	OBP	SLG	AOPS	ABR	SB-CS	FA	FR	RNG	THR	GAMES AT POSITION	DL	BFW
2001	KC A	29	77	4	16	2	0	0	5	3-0	0	8	.208	.237	.234	23	-9	0-2	1.000	0	91	162	O28(22/5/2)		-0.9
2002	Mon N	36	125	20	37	8	5	1	9	5-0	0	16	.296	.321	.464	102	-1	3-5	.989	5	109	402	O35C		0.4
2003	Mon N	141	483	66	121	25	5	5	47	31-3	1	59	.251	.294	.354	67	-24	18-7	.990	1	100	138	O135C		-2.1
2004	Mon N	132	502	65	139	20	6	5	34	30-0	1	40	.277	.318	.371	74	-20	32-7	.984	2	100	144	O127C		-1.2
2005	Was N	7	9	2	2	1	0	0	1	3-0	0	1	.222	.417	.333	107	0	0-1	1.000	-1	68	0	O6C		0.0
	Phi N	91	107	17	23	3	0	0	10	4-0	0	13	.215	.243	.299	40	-10	2-1	.980	3	100	365	O51(20/28/5)		-0.8
	Year	98	116	19	25	4	3	0	11	7-0	0	14	.216	.260	.302	46	-10	2-2	.981	2	100	365	O57(20/34/5)		-0.8
Total 5		436	1303	174	338	59	19	11	106	76-3	1	137	.259	.299	.359	69	-64	55-23	.987	11	100	182	O382(42/336/7)		-4.6

CHAVEZ, ERIC Eric Cesar B12.7.1977 Los Angeles CA BL/TR/6-0/204(195-206) [OakA96 1/10] d9.8

YEAR	TM LG	G	AB	R	H	2B	3B	HR	RBI	BB-IB	HP	SO	AVG	OBP	SLG	AOPS	ABR	SB-CS	FA	FR	RNG	THR	GAMES AT POSITION	DL	BFW
1998	Oak A	16	45	6	14	4	1	0	6	3-1	0	5	.311	.354	.444	107	2	1-1	1.000	2	109	119	3b13		0.2
1999	Oak A	115	356	47	88	21	2	13	50	46-4	0	56	.247	.333	.427	95	-3	1-1	.961	-8	90	81	3b105,S2,D3	29	-0.9
2000	†Oak A	153	501	89	139	23	4	26	86	62-8	1	94	.277	.355	.495	115	10	2-2	.951	-6	99	66	3b146,S2		0.5
2001	†Oak A	151	552	91	159	43	0	32	114	41-9	4	99	.288	.338	.540	127	21	8-2	**.972**	12	**108**	119	3b149/1SD		3.3
2002	Oak A	153	585	87	161	31	3	34	109	65-13	1	119	.275	.348	.513	126	21	8-3	.961	12	**108**	105	3b143/OLD		3.3
2003	†Oak A	156	588	94	166	39	5	29	101	62-10	1	89	.282	.350	.514	124	20	8-3	.971	23	**112**	137	3b154		4.2
2004	Oak A	125	475	87	131	20	0	29	77	**95**-10	2	99	.276	.397	.501	134	27	6-3	.968	14	**109**	150	3b125/OL	37	3.9
2005	Oak A	160	625	92	168	40	1	27	101	58-4	2	129	.269	.329	.466	108	7	6-0	.966	8	102	111	3b153,D6		1.6
Total 8		1029	3727	593	1026	221	16	190	644	432-59	12	690	.275	.350	.496	119	103	40-15	.965	57	105	111	3b988,D19,S5,O2L/1	66	16.1

CHAVEZ, RAUL Raul Alexander B3.18.1973 Valencia, Venez BR/TR/5-11/210(175-215) d8.30

YEAR	TM LG	G	AB	R	H	2B	3B	HR	RBI	BB-IB	HP	SO	AVG	OBP	SLG	AOPS	ABR	SB-CS	FA	FR	RNG	THR	GAMES AT POSITION	DL	BFW
1996	Mon N	4	5	1	1	0	0	0	0	1-0	0	1	.200	.333	.200	44	0	1-0	1.000	1	0	0	C3		0.0
1997	Mon N	13	26	0	7	0	0	0	2	0-0	0	5	.269	.259	.269	42	-2	1-0	1.000	1	121	108	C13		-0.1
1998	Sea A	1	1	0	0	0	0	0	0	0-0	0	0	.000	.000	.000	-99	0	0-0	1.000	-0	0	0	/C		0.0
2000	Hou N	14	43	3	11	2	0	1	5	3-2	0	6	.256	.298	.372	65	-2	0-0	.986	-4	83	57	C14		-0.6
2002	Hou N	2	4	1	1	1	0	0	0	1-0	1	0	.250	.500	.500	157	1	0-0	1.000	-1	0	0	C2		0.0
2003	Hou N	19	37	5	10	1	1	1	4	1-0	0	6	.270	.289	.432	81	-1	0-0	1.000	-1	223	150	C16		-0.2
2004	†Hou N	64	162	9	34	8	0	0	23	10-3	0	38	.210	.256	.259	33	-16	0-1	.991	7	112	109	C61		-0.7
2005	†Hou N	37	99	6	17	3	0	2	6	4-0	1	18	.172	.210	.263	23	-12	0-0	.991	8	207	185	C36		-0.2
Total 8		154	377	25	81	15	1	4	40	20-5	2	74	.215	.256	.292	41	-32	3-1	.992	9	140	123	C146		-1.8

CHEEK, HARRY Harry G. B1879 Sedalia MO D6.25.1956 Paramus NJ TR d4.30

YEAR	TM LG	G	AB	R	H	2B	3B	HR	RBI	BB-IB	HP	SO	AVG	OBP	SLG	AOPS	ABR	SB-CS	FA	FR	RNG	THR	GAMES AT POSITION	DL	BFW
1910	Phi N	2	4	1	2	1	0	0	0	0	0		.500	.500	.750	255	1	0	1.000	1	87	0	C2		0.0

CHEN, CHIN-FENG Chin-Feng B10.28.1977 Tainan City, Taiwan BR/TR/6-1/189* d9.14

YEAR	TM LG	G	AB	R	H	2B	3B	HR	RBI	BB-IB	HP	SO	AVG	OBP	SLG	AOPS	ABR	SB-CS	FA	FR	RNG	THR	GAMES AT POSITION	DL	BFW
2002	LA N	3	5	1	0	0	0	0	0	1-0	0	3	.000	.167	.000	-53	-1	0-0	1.000	0	163	0	/OL		-0.1
2003	LA N	1	1	0	0	0	0	0	0	0-0	0	0	.000	.000	.000	-99	0	0-0	—	0			/H		0.0
2004	LA N	8	8	1	0	0	0	0	0	2-0	0	3	.000	.200	.000	-42	-2	0-0	1.000	1	247	0	O3L		-0.1
2005	LA N	7	8	1	2	0	0	0	0	0-0	0	4	.250	.250	.250	32	-1	0-0	1.000	0	82	0	O3L		-0.1
Total 4		19	22	3	2	0	0	0	0	3-0	0	10	.091	.200	.091	-20	-4	0-0	1.000	1	176	0	O7L		-0.3

CHERVINKO, PAUL Paul B7.23.1910 Trauger PA D6.3.1976 Danville IL BR/TR/5-8/185 d5.30 Col Illinois

YEAR	TM LG	G	AB	R	H	2B	3B	HR	RBI	BB-IB	HP	SO	AVG	OBP	SLG	AOPS	ABR	SB-CS	FA	FR	RNG	THR	GAMES AT POSITION	DL	BFW
1937	Bro N	30	48	1	7	0	1	0	2	3	0	16	.146	.196	.188	5	-7	0	1.000	0	81	85	C26		-0.5
1938	Bro N	12	27	0	4	0	0	0	3	2	0	16	.148	.207	.148	-1	-4	0	.974	0	102	120	C12		-0.3
Total 2		42	75	1	11	0	1	0	5	5	0	16	.147	.200	.173	3	-11	0	.990	0	90	99	C38		-0.8

CHILDS, CUPID Clarence Algernon B8.14.1867 Calvert Co. MD D11.8.1912 Baltimore MD BL/TR/5-8/185 d4.23

YEAR	TM LG	G	AB	R	H	2B	3B	HR	RBI	BB-IB	HP	SO	AVG	OBP	SLG	AOPS	ABR	SB-CS	FA	FR	RNG	THR	GAMES AT POSITION	DL	BFW
1888	Phi N	2	4	0	0	0	0	0	0	0	0		.000	.000	.000	-95	-1	0	.857	0	108	248	2b2		-0.1
1890	Syr AA	126	493	109	170	**33**	14	2	89	72	6		.345	.434	.481	189	**61**	56	.928	14	105	103	2b125/S		**6.8**
1891	Cle N	141	551	120	155	21	12	2	83	97	7	32	.281	.395	.374	119	18	39	.910	-12	99	84	2b141		0.9
1892	†Cle N	145	558	**136**	177	14	11	3	53	117	9	20	.317	**.443**	.398	149	41	26	.938	-5	99	97	2b145		3.9
1893	Cle N	124	485	145	159	19	10	3	65	120	4	12	.326	.463	.425	129	28	27	.926	9	107	101	2b123		3.4
1894	Cle N	118	479	143	169	21	12	2	52	101	5	11	.353	.475	.459	121	24	17	.916	-1	101	99	2b118		2.2
1895	†Cle N	120	466	96	134	15	4	4	90	74	6	24	.288	.392	.363	90	-5	20	.921	10	106	91	2b120		0.9
1896	†Cle N	132	498	106	177	24	9	1	106	100	4	18	.355	.467	.446	133	31	25	.942	**39**	**117**	**147**	2b132		6.3
1897	Cle N	114	444	105	150	15	9	1	61	74	2		.338	.435	.419	119	16	25	.944	18	106	116	2b114		3.3
1898	Cle N	110	413	90	119	9	4	1	31	69	4		.288	.395	.337	112	11	9	.931	12	**110**	95	2b110		2.5
1899	StL N	125	464	73	123	11	11	1	48	74	5		.265	.369	.333	93	-2	11	.934	-14	91	97	2b125		-0.9
1900	Chi N	137	531	67	128	14	5	0	44	57	7		.241	.323	.286	71	-19	15	.935	15	110	105	2b137		0.2
1901	Chi N	63	236	24	61	9	0	0	21	30	7		.258	.359	.297	95	1	3	.939	9	106	154	2b63		1.0
Total 13		1457	5622	1214	1721	205	101	20	743	991	63	117	.306	.416	.389	119	204	269	.930	94	105	106	2b1455/S		30.4

YEAR	TM LG	G	AB	R	H	2B	3B	HR	RBI	BB-IB	HP	SO	AVG	OBP	SLG	AOPS	ABR	SB-CS	FA	FR	RNG	THR	GAMES AT POSITION	DL	BFW

CHILDS, PETE   Peter Pierre B11.15.1871 Philadelphia PA D2.15.1922 Philadelphia PA TR d4.24

1901	StL N	29	79	12	21	1	0	0	8	14	2		.266	.389	.278	100	1	0	.907	-5	94	66	2b19,O2(1/1/0)/S		-0.3
	Chi N	60	210	23	48	5	1	0	14	26			.229	.319	.262	72	-6	4	.958	12	116	92	2b60		0.6
	Year	89	289	35	69	6	1	0	22	40	4		.239	.339	.266	80	-5	4	.947	7	111	86	2b79,O2(1/1/0)/S		0.3
1902	Phi N	123	403	25	78	5	0	0	25	34	0		.194	.256	.206	43	-26	6	.945	-8	97	53	2b123		-3.6
Total	2	212	692	60	147	11	1	0	47	74	4		.212	.292	.231	59	-31	10	.946	-1	102	66	2b202,O2(1/1/0)/S		-3.3

CHILDS, SAM   Samuel Beresford B11.6.1861 East Hartford CT D5.21.1938 Denver CO d5.31 Col Yale

1883	Col AA	1	4	0	0	0	0	0					.000	.000	.000	-99	-1		1.000	0	0	0	/1		-0.1

CHILES, PEARCE   Pearce Nuget "What's the Use" B5.28.1867 Deepwater MO BR/TR/5-11/185 d4.18

1899	Phi N	97	338	57	108	28	7	2	76	16	1		.320	.352	.462	127	11	6	.944	-10	96	247	O46(13/2/31),1b25,2b16		0.0
1900	Phi N	33	111	13	24	6	2	1	23	6	0		.216	.256	.333	63	-6	4	.987	-1	102	132	1b16,2b12,O3R		-0.6
Total	2	130	449	70	132	34	9	3	99	22	1		.294	.328	.430	111	5	10	.947	-11	90	232	O49(13/2/34),1b41,2b28		-0.6

CHILES, RICH   Richard Francis B11.22.1949 Sacramento CA BL/TL/5-11/170* [HouN68 2/23] d4.20

1971	Hou N	67	119	12	27	5	1	2	15	16-0	1	20	.227	.268	.336	73	-4	0-1	1.000	-1	67	0	O27(25/0/2)		-0.8
1972	Hou N	9	11	0	3	1	0	0	2	1-0	1	0	.273	.333	.364	101	0	0-0	1.000	0	149	0	O2L		0.0
1973	NY N	8	25	2	3	2	0	0	1	0-0	0	2	.120	.120	.200	-13	-4	0-0	1.000	2	143	249	O8C		-0.2
1976	Hou N	5	4	1	2	1	0	0	0	0-0	0	1	.500	.500	.750	273	1	0-0	1.000	0	427	0	/OL	19	0.1
1977	Min A	108	261	31	69	16	1	3	36	23-2	2	17	.264	.323	.368	90	-3	0-1	.946	-2	97	0	D61,O22(1/0/21)		-0.7
1978	Min A	87	198	22	53	12	0	1	22	20-2	2	25	.268	.333	.343	91	-2	1-2	.965	0	101	88	O61(58/0/3),D8		-0.4
Total	6	284	618	68	157	37	2	6	76	50-4	6	65	.254	.310	.350	85	-13	1-4	.972	-1	97	62	O121(87/8/26),D69	19	-2.0

CHIOZZA, DINO   Dino Joseph "Dynamo" B6.30.1912 Memphis TN D4.23.1972 Memphis TN BL/TR/6-0/170 d7.14 b-Lou

1935	Phi N	2	0	1	0	0	0	0	0	0-0	0	0	—	—	—	—	0	0	1.000	-0	0	0	S2		0.0

CHIOZZA, LOU   Louis Peo B5.17.1910 Tallulah LA D2.28.1971 Memphis TN BL/TR/6-0/172 d4.17 b-Dino

1934	Phi N	134	484	66	147	28	5	0	44	34	6	35	.304	.357	.382	86	-8	9	.938	-18	93	73	2b85,3b26,O17(13/0/4)		-2.1
1935	Phi N	124	472	71	134	26	6	3	47	33		39	.284	.333	.383	84	-10	7	.947	4	106	74	2b120,3b2		0.1
1936	Phi N	144	572	83	170	32	6	1	48	37	6	39	.297	.346	.379	87	-10	17	.972	-6	100	108	O90(4/85/1),2b33,3b26		-1.5
1937	†NY N	117	439	49	102	11	2	4	29	20		30	.232	.266	.294	51	-31	6	.939	-4	96	93	3b93,O12C,2b2		-3.2
1938	NY N	57	179	15	42	7	2	3	17	12		7	.235	.283	.346	72	-8	5	.944	-3	109	49	2b34,O16(5/10/0)/3		-0.9
1939	NY N	40	142	19	38	3	1	3	12	9	0	10	.268	.311	.366	81	-4	3	.915	-2	97	137	3b30,S8		-0.5
Total	6	616	2288	303	633	107	22	14	197	145	14	165	.277	.324	.361	78	-71	45	.943	-28	102	70	2b274,3b178,O135(22/107/5),S8		-8.1

CHIPPLE, WALT   Walter John (b Walter John Chlipala) B9.26.1918 Utica NY D6.8.1988 Tonawanda NY BR/TR/6-0.5/168 d4.17

1945	Was A	18	44	4	6	0	0	0	5	5	0	6	.136	.224	.136	6	-5	0-1	.978	2	121	172	O13(1/11/1)		-0.4

CHISM, TOM   Thomas Raymond B5.9.1955 Chester PA BL/TL/6-1/195 [BalA74 S4/36] d9.13 Col Widener

1979	Bal A	6	3	0	0	0	0	0	0	0-0	0	1	.000	.000	.000	-99	-1	0-0	1.000	0	0	0	1b4		-0.1

CHITI, HARRY   Harry B11.16.1932 Kincaid IL D1.31.2002 Haines City FL BR/TR/6-3/225* d9.27 Mil 1953-54

1950	Chi N	3	6	0	2	0	0	0	0	0	0	3	.333	.333	.333	77	-0	0	1.000	-0	0	534	/C		-0.1
1951	Chi N	9	31	1	11	2	0	0	5	2	0	4	.355	.394	.419	117	1	0-0	.913	-1	63	188	C8		0.0
1952	Chi N	32	113	14	31	5	0	5	13	5	0	8	.274	.305	.451	106	0	0-1	.984	2	66	65	C32		0.4
1955	Chi N	113	338	24	78	6	1	11	41	25-8	1	68	.231	.282	.352	68	-17	0-0	.984	-4	66	131	C113		-1.5
1956	Chi N	72	203	17	43	6	4	4	18	19-3	1	35	.212	.281	.340	68	-10	0-0	.981	0	78	136	C67		-0.7
1958	KC A	103	295	32	79	11	3	9	44	18-4	3	48	.268	.311	.417	98	-2	3-2	.987	1	130	94	C83		0.3
1959	KC A	55	162	20	44	11	1	5	25	17-1	1	26	.272	.344	.444	113	3	0-1	.988	2	115	72	C47		0.7
1960	KC A	58	190	16	42	7	0	5	28	17-0	1	33	.221	.288	.337	68	-9	1-0	.983	-1	76	70	C52		-0.7
	Det A	37	104	9	17	0	0	2	5	10-1	0	12	.163	.235	.221	24	-11	0-3	.984	-2	69	95	C36		-1.3
	Year	95	294	25	59	7	0	7	33	27-1	1	45	.201	.269	.296	52	-20	1-3	.984	-3	73	80	C88		-2.0
1961	Det A	5	12	0	1	0	0	0	0	1-0	0	2	.083	.154	.083	-34	-2	0-0	1.000	-0	69	364	C5		-0.3
1962	NY N	15	41	2	8	1	0	0	1	1-0	0	8	.195	.233	.220	22	-5	0-0	.971	-1	64	79	C14		-0.5
Total	10	502	1495	135	356	49	9	41	179	115-17	8	242	.238	.294	.365	77	-52	4-7	.983	-4	86	107	C458		-3.7

CHOI, HEE-SEOP   Hee-Seop B3.16.1979 Chun-Nam, South Korea BL/TL/6-5/235* d9.3

2002	Chi N	24	50	6	9	1	0	2	4	7-0	0	15	.180	.281	.320	60	-3	0-0	.983	-1	81	133	1b22		-0.5
2003	Chi N	80	202	31	44	17	0	8	28	37-1	4	71	.218	.350	.421	98	1	1-1	.991	2	102	97	1b69	22	-0.3
2004	Fla N	95	281	48	76	16	1	15	40	52-4	3	78	.270	.388	.495	133	16	1-0	.990	-6	75	93	1b89		0.3
	†LA N	31	62	5	10	5	0	0	6	11-2	1	18	.161	.289	.242	42	-5	0-0	.994	-1	89	141	1b23		-0.7
	Year	126	343	53	86	21	1	15	46	63-6	4	96	.251	.370	.449	116	10	1-0	.990	-6	78	102	1b112		-0.4
2005	LA N	133	320	40	81	15	2	15	42	34-1	8	80	.253	.336	.453	106	2	1-3	.997	5	124	94	1b83	22	0.0
Total	4	363	915	130	220	54	3	40	120	141-8	16	262	.240	.349	.437	105	11	3-4	.992	0	98	100	1b286	22	-1.2

CHOO, SHIN-SOO   Shin-Soo B7.30.1982 Pusan, South Korea BL/TL/5-11/180 d4.21

2005	Sea A	10	18	1	1	0	0	0	1	3-0	0	4	.056	.190	.056	-32	-3	0-0	1.000	1	139	0	O5L		-0.2

CHOUINARD, FELIX   Felix George B10.5.1887 Chicago IL D4.28.1955 Hines IL BR/TR/5-7/150 d9.11

1910	Chi A	24	82	6	16	3	2	0	9	8			.195	.275	.280	77	-2	4	.962	2	90	197	O23C/2		-0.1
1911	Chi A	14	17	3	3	0	0	0	0	0			.176	.176	.176	-2	-2	0	.857	1	103	313	2b4,O4(0/3/1)		-0.2
1914	Pit F	9	30	2	9	1	0	1	3	0		4	.300	.300	.433	99	-1	1	.917	0	101	189	2b4,O3(2/1/0)/S		-0.1
	Bro F	32	79	7	20	1	2	0	8	4	0	13	.253	.289	.316	65	-6	3	.929	1	106	119	O20(5/14/2)		-0.6
	Bal F	5	9	3	4	0	0	0	1	0			1.000	.444	.444	138	-0	0	1.000	-0	96	0	O2(1/1/0)		0.0
	Year	46	118	12	33	2	2	1	12	4			.280	.303	.356	79	-6	4	.941	0	102	123	O25(8/16/2),2b4/S		-0.7
1915	Bro F	4	4	1	2	0	0	0	2	0			.500	.500	.500	183	0	0	1.000	-0	61	0	O2(1/1/0)		0.0
Total	4	88	221	22	54	5	4	1	23	12	1	18	.244	.286	.317	75	-11	8	.948	3	96	161	O54(9/43/3),2b9/S		-1.0

CHOZEN, HARRY   Harry B9.27.1915 Winnebago MN D9.16.1994 Houston TX BR/TR/5-9.5/190 d9.21

1937	Cin N	1	4	0	1	0	0	0	0	0	0	0	.250	.250	.250	38	0	0	.833	-0	42	0	/C		-0.1

CHRISLEY, NEIL   Barbra O'Neil B12.16.1931 Calhoun Falls SC BL/TR/6-3/187* d4.15

1957	Was A	26	51	6	8	2	1	0	3	7-0	0	7	.157	.259	.235	36	-5	0-0	.810	-1	80	139	O11(4/0/7)		-0.7
1958	Was A	105	233	19	50	7	4	5	26	16-2	0	46	.215	.265	.343	67	-12	1-3	.992	2	99	147	O69(38/7/25)/3		-1.4
1959	Det A	65	106	7	14	3	0	6	11	12-0	1	10	.132	.215	.330	48	-8	0-0	1.000	-1	98	0	O21(3/1/17)		-1.0
1960	Det A	96	220	27	56	10	3	5	24	19-0	1	26	.255	.311	.395	89	-4	2-0	.981	-1	110	66	O47(31/4/12),1b2		-0.5
1961	Mil N	10	9	1	2	0	0	0	0	1-0	0	0	.222	.300	.222	44	-1	0-0	—	0			/H		-0.1
Total	5	302	619	60	130	22	8	16	64	55-2	2	62	.210	.275	.349	69	-30	3-3	.975	1	101	100	O148(76/12/61),1b2/3		-3.7

CHRISTENBURY, LLOYD   Lloyd Reid "Low" B10.19.1893 Mecklenburg Co. NC D12.13.1944 Birmingham AL BL/TR/5-7/165 d9.20 Col Davidson

1919	Bos N	7	31	5	9	1	0	0	4	2	0	2	.290	.333	.323	102	0	0	.941	1	93	208	O7L		0.1
1920	Bos N	65	106	17	22	2	2	0	14	13	1	12	.208	.300	.264	66	-4	0-1	.895	-3	84	86	O14(0/7/7),S7,2b6,3b2		-0.8
1921	Bos N	62	125	34	44	6	2	3	16	21	1	7	.352	.449	.504	161	12	3-4	.914	-10	81	69	2b32,S2,3b2		0.3
1922	Bos N	71	152	22	38	5	2	1	13	18	2	11	.250	.337	.329	76	-5	2-4	.946	2	109	139	O32(30/0/2),2b5,3b2		-0.6
Total	4	205	414	78	113	14	6	4	47	54	4	32	.273	.362	.365	101	3	5-9	.936	-10	102	141	O53(37/7/9),2b43,S9,3b6		-1.0

CHRISTENSEN, BRUCE   Bruce Ray B2.22.1948 Madison WI BL/TR/5-11/165 [AnaA66 17/328] d7.17

1971	Cal A	29	63	4	17	4	0	0	3	6-1	0	5	.270	.333	.286	82	-1	0-1	.988	-2	97	123	S24		-0.1

CHRISTENSEN, JOHN   John Lawrence B9.5.1960 Downey CA BR/TR/6-0/180* [NYN81 2/38] d9.13 Col Cal St.-Fullerton

1984	NY N	5	11	2	3	0	0	0	3	1-0	0	2	.273	.308	.455	121	0	0-1	.500	1	20	0	O5(3/0/2)		-0.1
1985	NY N	51	113	10	21	4	1	3	13	19-1	0	23	.186	.303	.319	75	-4	1-2	.956	-4	69	93	O38(6/2/31)		-1.0
1987	Sea A	53	132	19	32	6	1	2	12	12-0	1	28	.242	.306	.348	69	-6	2-0	1.000	1	98	136	O43(2/0/41),D8	39	-0.6
1988	Min A	23	38	5	10	4	0	0	5	3-1	1	5	.263	.349	.368	98	0	0-0	1.000	-0	99	0	O17R/D	39	-0.1
Total	4	132	294	36	66	16	2	5	33	35-2	2	58	.224	.308	.344	77	-10	3-3	.977	-5	83	95	O103(11/2/91),D9	39	-1.7

YEAR	TM LG	G	AB	R	H	2B	3B	HR	RBI	BB-IB	HP	SO	AVG	OBP	SLG	AOPS	ABR	SB-CS	FA	FR	RNG	THR	GAMES AT POSITION	DL	BFW

CHRISTENSEN, MC KAY McKay Andrew B8.14.1975 Upland CA BL/TL/5-11/180* [AnaA94 1/6] d4.6

1999	Chi A	28	53	10	12	1	0	1	6	4-0	0	7	.226	.271	.302	48	-4	2-1	.943	-0	116	0	O27C		-0.4
2000	†Chi A	32	19	4	2	0	0	0	1	2-0	1	6	.105	.227	.105	-11	-3	1-1	1.000	0	91	235	O29C		-0.3
2001	Chi A	7	4	0	1	0	0	0	0	0-0	1	2	.250	.400	.250	73	0	0-0	1.000	-1	37	0	O6C		-0.1
	LA N	28	49	7	16	2	0	1	7	3-0	1	10	.327	.400	.429	122	2	3-2	.917	-1	88	0	O14(3/11/0)		0.0
2002	NY N	4	3	1	1	0	0	0	0	1-0	0	1	.333	.500	.333	137	0	0-0	1.000	0	190	0	O3(2/1/0)		0.0
Total	4	99	128	22	32	3	0	2	14	10-0	5	26	.250	.324	.320	68	-5	6-4	.951	-2	100	51	O79(5/74/0)		-0.8

CHRISTENSEN, CUCKOO Walter Niels "Seacap" B10.24.1899 San Francisco CA D12.20.1984 Menlo Park CA BL/TL/5-6.5/156 d4.13

1926	Cin N	114	329	41	115	15	7	0	41	40	4	18	.350	.426	.438	136	19	8	.978	-5	92	71	O93(72/19/9)		0.9
1927	Cin N	57	185	25	47	6	0	0	16	20	1	16	.254	.330	.286	68	-8	4	.957	-2	87	119	O50(11/35/4)		-1.2
Total	2	171	514	66	162	21	7	0	57	60	5	34	.315	.392	.383	112	11	12	.970	-7	90	88	O143(83/54/13)		-0.3

CHRISTENSON, RYAN Ryan Alan B3.28.1974 Redlands CA BR/TR/6-0/191(175-191) [OakA95 10/260] d4.20 Col Pepperdine

1998	Oak A	117	370	56	95	22	2	5	40	36-0	1	106	.257	.321	.368	80	-10	5-6	.983	2	104	105	O116(1/113/4)		-0.8
1999	Oak A	106	268	41	56	12	1	4	24	38-0	1	58	.209	.306	.306	59	-16	7-5	.969	-1	105	60	O104C/D		-1.6
2000	†Oak A	121	129	31	32	2	0	4	18	19-0	1	33	.248	.349	.388	87	-3	1-2	.951	-2	92	78	O114(76/27/14)		-0.5
2001	Ari N	19	4	3	1	1	0	0	1	1-0	0	1	.250	.400	.500	122	0	1-0	1.000	-2	69	0	O5(4/1/0)		0.0
	Oak A	7	4	1	0	0	0	0	0	0-0	0	1	.000	.000	.000	-99	-1	0-0	1.000	-0	61	0	O4(1/1/3)/D		-0.1
2002	Mil N	22	58	5	9	4	0	1	3	5-0	0	13	.155	.222	.276	32	-6	0-0	1.000	-1	103	0	O21(6/16/0)		-0.7
2003	Tex A	60	165	22	29	7	2	6	16	15-0	3	44	.176	.255	.255	33	-16	2-2	1.000	-0	107	0	O59C		-1.6
Total	6	452	998	159	222	48	5	16	102	114-0	6	256	.222	.303	.329	65	-52	16-15	.973	-3	100	88	O423(88/321/21),D2		-5.3

CHRISTIAN, BOB Robert Charles B10.17.1945 Chicago IL D2.20.1974 San Diego CA BR/TR/5-10/180* d9.2 Col Grossmont (CA) JC

1968	Det A	3	3	0	1	1	0	0	0	0-0	0	0	.333	.333	.667	192	0	0-0	1.000	0		0	/1OR		0.0
1969	Chi A	39	129	11	28	4	0	3	16	10-1	1	19	.217	.273	.318	63	-7	3-0	.958	-0	99	105	O38(37/0/1)		-0.9
1970	Chi A	12	15	3	4	0	0	1	3	1-0	0	4	.267	.313	.467	108	0	0-0	1.000	-1	51	0	O4L		-0.1
Total	3	54	147	14	33	5	0	4	19	11-1	1	23	.224	.278	.340	70	-7	3-0	.959	-1	96	98	O43(41/0/2)/1		-1.0

CHRISTMAN, MARK Marquette Joseph B10.21.1913 Maplewood MO D10.9.1976 St.Louis MO BR/TR/5-11/180 d4.20

1938	Det A	95	318	35	79	6	4	1	44	27	0	21	.248	.307	.302	50	-25	5-2	.983	10	109	118	3b69,S21		-1.1
1939	Det A	6	16	0	4	2	0	0	0	0	0	2	.250	.250	.375	54	-1	0-0	.900	1	72	155	3b5		-0.1
	StL A	79	222	27	48	6	3	0	20	20	1	10	.216	.281	.270	41	-20	2-1	.960	14	112	103	S64/2		-0.2
	Year	85	238	27	52	8	3	0	20	20	1	12	.218	.279	.277	42	-22	2-1	.960	13	112	103	S64,3b5/2		-0.3
1943	StL A	98	336	31	91	11	5	2	35	19	4	29	.271	.318	.351	94	-4	0-3	.991	2	111	78	3b37,S24,1b20,2b14		-0.2
1944	†StL A	148	547	56	148	25	1	6	83	47	3	37	.271	.332	.353	90	-6	5-2	.972	4	98	125	3b145,1b3		-0.1
1945	StL A	78	289	32	80	7	4	4	34	19	3	19	.277	.328	.370	98	-2	1-0	.973	-1	94	94	3b77		-0.2
1946	StL A	128	458	40	118	22	2	1	41	22	2	29	.258	.295	.321	68	-20	0-0	.975	9	116	125	3b77,S47		-0.9
1947	Was A	110	374	27	83	15	2	1	33	32	2	16	.222	.287	.281	60	-21	4-4	.978	-8	94	100	S106/2		-2.2
1948	Was A	120	409	38	106	17	4	1	40	25	1	19	.259	.303	.318	67	-21	0-0	.969	-25	85	75	S102,3b9,2b3		-4.0
1949	Was A	49	112	8	24	2	0	3	18	8	1	7	.214	.273	.313	56	-8	0-0	.967	3	122	157	3b23,1b6,S4/2		-0.5
Total	9	911	3081	294	781	113	29	19	348	219	16	179	.253	.306	.324	71	-128	17-14	.975	8	104	115	3b442,S368,1b29,2b20		-9.5

CHRISTMAS, STEVE Stephen Randall B12.9.1957 Orlando FL BL/TR/6-0/190* d9.1 Col Southwestern Oklahoma

1983	Cin N	9	17	0	1	0	0	0	1	0-0	0	3	.059	.105	.059	-50	-4	0-0	1.000	1	122	168	C7		-0.2
1984	Chi A	12	11	1	4	1	0	1	4	0-0	0	2	.364	.364	.727	184	1	0-0	1.000	0	6	0	/C		0.1
1986	Chi N	3	9	0	1	1	0	0	2	0-0	0	1	.111	.111	.222	-10	-1	0-0	1.000	0	32	224	/C1	69	-0.1
Total	3	24	37	1	6	2	0	1	7	1-0	0	6	.162	.179	.297	30	-4	0-0	1.000	1	102	175	C9/1	69	-0.2

CHRISTOPHER, JOE Joseph O'Neal B12.13.1935 Frederiksted, V.I. BR/TR/5-10/176* d5.26

1959	Pit N	15	12	6	0	0	0	0	0	1-0	0	4	.000	.077	.000	-78	-3	0-0	1.000	0	119	0	O9R		-0.3
1960	†Pit N	50	56	21	13	2	0	1	3	5-0	0	8	.232	.295	.321	68	-2	1-0	1.000	-1	92	0	O17(11/5/1)		-0.4
1961	Pit N	76	186	25	49	7	3	0	14	18-0	0	24	.263	.327	.333	76	-6	6-4	.978	-1	98	53	O55(45/5/5)		-1.0
1962	NY N	119	271	36	66	10	2	6	32	35-0	4	42	.244	.338	.362	87	-4	11-3	.972	-3	90	89	O94(19/34/42)		-1.0
1963	NY N	64	149	19	33	5	1	1	8	13-0	3	21	.221	.295	.289	68	-6	1-3	.983	-2	97	39	O45(6/0/40)		-1.1
1964	NY N	154	543	78	163	26	8	16	76	48-5	6	92	.300	.360	.466	135	25	6-5	.974	-3	96	93	O145(7/10/129)		1.3
1965	NY N	148	437	38	109	18	3	5	40	35-0	6	82	.249	.311	.339	87	-7	4-4	.989	-5	94	44	O112(62/0/51)		-2.0
1966	Bos A	12	13	1	1	0	0	0	0	1-0	0	4	.077	.200	.077	-15	-2	0-0	1.000	-0	47	0	O2L		-0.2
Total	8	638	1667	224	434	68	17	29	173	157-8	19	277	.260	.329	.374	96	-5	29-19	.979	-15	95	67	O479(152/54/277)		-4.7

CHRISTOPHER, LOYD Loyd Eugene B12.31.1919 Richmond CA D9.5.1991 Richmond CA BR/TR/6-2/190 d4.20 b-Russ

1945	Bos A	8	14	4	4	0	0	0	4	3	0	2	.286	.412	.286	101	0	0-0	1.000	-0	78	0	O3C		0.0
	Chi N	1	0	0	0	0	0	0	0	0	0	0	—	—	—	—	0	0-0	—	-0	0	0	/OL		0.0
1947	Chi A	7	23	1	5	0	1	0	2	0	0	4	.217	.280	.304	65	-1	0-1	1.000	1	114	192	O7L		-0.1
Total	2	16	37	5	9	0	1	0	4	5	0	6	.243	.333	.297	80	-1	0-1	1.000	1	104	143	O11(8/3/0)		-0.1

CHURCH, HI Hiram Lincoln B11.23.1863 Central Square NY D2.23.1926 Jacksonville FL d8.23 Col Syracuse

| 1890 | Bro AA | 3 | 9 | 1 | 1 | 0 | 0 | 0 | 0 | 0-0 | | 0 | .111 | .111 | .111 | -36 | -2 | 0 | 1.000 | -1 | 0 | 0 | O3L | | -0.2 |

CHURCH, RYAN Ryan Matthew B10.14.1978 Santa Barbara CA BL/TL/6-1/190* [CleA00 14/426] d8.21 Col Nevada-Reno

2004	Mon N	30	63	6	11	1	0	1	6	7-1	0	16	.175	.257	.238	28	-7	0-0	1.000	3	124	360	O18(12/2/6)		-0.4
2005	Was N	102	268	41	77	15	3	9	42	24-0	5	70	.287	.353	.466	122	8	3-2	1.000	4	118	50	O85(51/20/21)	35	1.0
Total	2	132	331	47	88	16	3	10	48	31-1	5	86	.266	.335	.423	102	1	3-2	1.000	8	119	104	O103(63/22/27)	35	0.6

CHURRY, JOHN John B11.26.1900 Johnstown PA D2.8.1970 Zanesville OH BR/TR/5-9/172 d5.24

1924	Chi N	6	7	0	1	1	0	0	0	0-0	0	0	.143	.333	.286	67	-0	0-0	1.000	0	90	135	C3		0.0
1925	Chi N	3	6	1	3	0	0	0	1	0-0	0	0	.500	.500	.500	154	0	0-0	1.000	0	61	422	C3		0.0
1926	Chi N	2	4	0	0	0	0	0	0	1-0	0	2	.000	.200	.000	-42	-1	0	1.000	0	0	0	/C		-0.1
1927	Chi N	1	1	0	1	0	0	0	0	0-0	0	0	1.000	1.000	1.000	436	0	0	1.000	0	0	0	/C		0.1
Total	4	12	18	1	5	1	0	0	1	3	0	2	.278	.381	.333	89	-1	0-0	1.000	0	52	170	C8		0.0

CIAFFONE, LARRY Lawrence Thomas "Symphony Larry" B8.17.1924 Brooklyn NY D12.14.1991 Brooklyn NY BR/TR/5-9.5/185 d4.17

| 1951 | StL N | 5 | 5 | 0 | 0 | 0 | 0 | 0 | 0 | 1 | 0 | 2 | .000 | .167 | .000 | -51 | -1 | 0-0 | 1.000 | 0 | 103 | 0 | /OL | | -0.1 |

CIANFROCCO, ARCHI Angelo Dominic B10.6.1966 Rome NY BR/TR/6-5/215(200-215) [MonN87 5/122] d4.8 Col Purdue OF(8/0/17)

1992	Mon N	86	232	25	56	5	2	6	30	11-0	1	66	.241	.276	.358	79	-8	3-0	.993	1	117	164	1b56,3b19,O5L		-1.0
1993	Mon N	12	17	3	4	1	0	0	0	1-0	0	5	.235	.235	.471	80	-1	0-0		-0	62	173	1b11		-0.1
	SD N	84	279	27	68	10	2	11	47	17-1	3	64	.244	.289	.412	86	-7	2-0	.932	-7	76	85	3b64,1b31		-1.4
	Year	96	296	30	72	11	2	12	48	17-1	3	69	.243	.287	.416	85	-7	2-0	.932	-7	76	85	3b64,1b42		-1.5
1994	SD N	59	146	9	32	6	0	4	13	4-0	4	39	.219	.252	.356	59	-9	2-0	.920	3	106	42	3b37,1b16/S		-0.7
1995	SD N	51	118	22	31	7	0	5	31	11-1	2	28	.263	.333	.449	108	1	0-2	1.000	0	88	84	1b30,S15,O7(2/0/5),2b3,3b3		0.1
1996	†SD N	79	192	21	54	13	3	2	32	8-0	2	56	.281	.315	.411	94	-2	1-0	1.000	-5	96	83	1b33,3b11,S10,O8(1/0/7),2b6/C	31	-0.8
1997	SD N	89	220	25	54	12	0	4	26	25-1	3	80	.245	.328	.355	85	-5	7-1	.983	7	110	80	1b39,3b38,2b12,S5,O2R		0.2
1998	SD N	40	72	4	9	3	0	1	5	3-0	1	24	.125	.192	.208	6	-10	1-0	1.000	1	138	136	1b19,3b13,O3R	29	-1.0
Total	7	500	1276	136	308	59	7	34	185	80-3	16	360	.241	.292	.379	80	-41	16-3	.994	0	113	91	1b235,3b185,S31,O25R,2b24/C	60	-4.7

CIAS, DARRYL Darryl Richard B4.23.1957 New York NY BR/TR/5-11/190 [BalA75 6/143] d4.27

| 1983 | Oak A | 19 | 18 | 1 | 6 | 1 | 0 | 0 | 1 | 2-0 | 0 | 4 | .333 | .400 | .389 | 125 | 1 | 1-0 | .967 | -3 | 55 | 45 | C19 | | -0.2 |

CICERO, JOE Joseph Francis "Dode" B11.18.1910 Atlantic City NJ D3.30.1983 Clearwater FL BR/TR/5-8/167 d9.20

1929	Bos A	10	32	6	10	2	2	0	4	0-0	0	2	.313	.313	.500	108	0	0-0	1.000	-0	101	0	O7(1/6/0)		-0.1
1930	Bos A	18	30	5	5	1	2	0	4	1	0	5	.167	.194	.333	32	-4	0-0	—	-0	0	0	O5(1/0/4),3b2		-0.3
1945	Phi A	12	19	3	3	0	0	0	0	1	0	6	.158	.238	.158	16	-2	0-0	1.000	-0	91	0	O7(1/0/6)		-0.3
Total	3	40	81	14	18	3	4	0	8	2	0	13	.222	.250	.358	60	-6	0-0	1.000	0	94	0	O19(3/6/10),3b2		-0.7

CIESLAK, TED Thaddeus Walter B11.22.1912 Milwaukee WI D5.9.1993 Milwaukee WI BR/TR/5-10/175 d4.18

| 1944 | Phi N | 85 | 220 | 18 | 54 | 10 | 0 | 2 | 11 | 21 | 1 | 17 | .245 | .314 | .318 | 81 | -5 | 1 | .877 | -12 | 81 | 14 | 3b48,O5L | | -1.8 |

YEAR	TM LG	G	AB	R	H	2B	3B	HR	RBI	BB-IB	HP	SO	AVG	OBP	SLG	AOPS	ABR	SB-CS	FA	FR	RNG	THR	GAMES AT POSITION	DL	BFW
CIHOCKI, AL	Albert Joseph B5.7.1924 Nanticoke PA BR/TR/5-11/185 d4.17																								
1945	Cle A	92	283	21	60	9	3	0	24	11	0	48	.212	.241	.265	49	-20	2-1	.946	-2	100	117	S41,3b29,2b23		-1.9
CIHOCKI, ED	Edward Joseph "Cy" B5.9.1907 Wilmington DE D11.9.1987 Newark DE BR/TR/5-8/163 d5.29																								
1932	Phi A	1	1	0	0	0	0	0	0	0	0	0	.000	.000	.000	-97	0	0-0	—	0			/H		0.0
1933	Phi A	33	97	6	14	2	3	0	9	7	0	16	.144	.202	.227	13	-13	0-0	.904	-2	95	120	S28/23		-1.3
Total	2	34	98	6	14	2	3	0	9	7	0	16	.143	.200	.224	12	-13	0-0	.904	-2	95	120	S28/32		-1.3
CIMOLI, GINO	Gino Nicholas (b Gino Anichletto Cimoli) B12.18.1929 San Francisco CA BR/TR/6-2/200(180-205) d4.19																								
1956	†Bro N	73	36	3	4	1	0	0	4	1-1	0	8	.111	.135	.139	-24	-6	1-0	.946	1	132	0	O62(52/8/3)		-0.6
1957	Bro N★	142	532	88	156	22	5	10	57	39-1	4	86	.293	.343	.410	93	-2	3-1	.979	-2	94	112	O138(81/24/51)		-1.4
1958	LA N	109	325	35	80	6	3	9	27	18-0	3	49	.246	.292	.366	71	-15	3-0	.974	-0	93	152	O104(34/68/12)		-2.0
1959	StL N	143	519	61	145	40	7	8	72	37-2	2	83	.279	.327	.430	94	-4	7-0	.979	-1	94	121	O141(43/45/55)		-1.0
1960	†Pit N	101	307	36	82	14	4	0	28	32-3	1	43	.267	.336	.339	85	-5	0-0	.964	-3	99	76	O91(27/58/17)		-1.2
1961	Pit N	21	67	4	20	3	1	0	6	2-0	0	13	.299	.319	.373	83	-2	0-0	.971	-0	100	76	O19(14/5/0)		-0.3
	Mil N	37	117	12	23	5	0	3	4	11-0	0	15	.197	.266	.316	57	-7	1-0	.985	-4	88	0	O31(0/30/1)		-1.2
	Year	58	184	16	43	8	1	3	10	13-0	0	28	.234	.284	.337	67	-9	1-0	.980	-4	92	28	O50(14/35/1)		-1.5
1962	KC A	152	550	67	151	20	**15**	10	71	40-2	2	89	.275	.323	.420	95	-6	2-1	.968	-7	89	101	O147(5/10/138)		-2.3
1963	KC A	145	529	56	139	19	11	4	48	39-3	2	72	.263	.313	.363	85	-11	3-1	.985	4	100	156	O136(2/13/130)		-1.7
1964	KC A	4	9	1	0	0	0	0	0	0-0	0	1	.000	.000	.000	-97	-2	0-0	1.000	0	152	0	O4(1/0/3)		-0.2
	Bal N	38	58	6	8	3	2	0	3	2-1	0	13	.138	.164	.259	16	-7	0-0	.893	-2	84	0	O35(11/2/23)		-1.1
	Year	42	67	7	8	3	2	0	3	2-1	0	14	.119	.143	.224	1	-9	0-0	.912	-2	92	0	O39(12/2/26)		-1.3
1965	Cal A	4	5	1	0	0	0	0	1	0-0	0	2	.000	.000	.000	-99	-1	0-0	1.000	0	162	0	/OR		-0.2
Total	10	969	3054	370	808	133	48	44	321	221-13	14	474	.265	.315	.383	84	-70	21-6	.974	-14	95	110	O909(270/263/434)		-13.1
CINTRON, ALEX	Alexander B12.17.1978 Humacao, PR BB/TR/6-1/170(170-200) [AriN97 36/1103] d7.24																								
2001	Ari N	8	7	0	2	0	1	0	0	0-0	0	0	.286	.286	.571	106	0	0-0	1.000	0	112	0	S7		0.0
2002	†Ari N	38	75	11	16	6	0	4	12-2	0		13	.213	.322	.293	60	-4	0-0	1.000	-0	76	103	2b18,3b9,S8		-0.3
2003	Ari N	117	448	70	142	26	6	13	51	29-0	2	33	.317	.359	.489	110	6	2-3	.979	-2	89	101	S93,3b16,2b9		1.1
2004	Ari N	154	564	56	148	31	7	4	49	31-2	2	59	.262	.301	.363	67	-28	3-3	.972	-1	103	72	S133,2b19/3		-1.9
2005	Ari N	122	330	36	90	19	2	8	48	12-3	1	33	.273	.298	.415	81	-10	1-2	.966	-3	111	92	S39,3b32,2b23		-1.0
Total	5	439	1424	173	398	82	16	25	152	84-7	5	138	.279	.320	.412	84	-36	6-8	.974	-6	99	86	S280,2b69,3b58		-2.1
CIPRIANI, FRANK	Frank Dominick B4.14.1941 Buffalo NY BR/TR/6-0/185 d9.8 Col Fordham																								
1961	KC A	13	36	4	9	0	0	0	2	2-0	0	4	.250	.289	.250	45	-3	0-0	1.000	-0	109	0	O11R		-0.4
CIRILLO, JEFF	Jeffrey Howard B9.23.1969 Pasadena CA BR/TR/6-2/193(180-200) [MilA91 11/286] d5.11 Col USC																								
1994	Mil A	39	126	17	30	9	0	3	12	11-0	2	16	.238	.309	.381	73	-5	0-1	.965	-3	92	144	3b37/2		-0.8
1995	Mil A	125	328	57	91	19	4	9	39	47-0	4	42	.277	.371	.442	105	4	7-2	.938	10	117	**168**	3b108,2b25,1b3,S2		1.5
1996	Mil A	158	566	101	184	46	5	15	83	58-0	7	69	.325	.391	.504	120	19	7-4	.950	-14	92	69	3b154,1b2/2D		0.3
1997	Mil A★	154	580	74	167	46	2	10	82	60-0	14	74	.288	.367	.426	105	7	4-3	.963	**24**	117	119	3b149,1b6		3.0
1998	Mil N	156	604	97	194	31	1	14	68	79-3	4	88	.321	.402	.445	121	22	10-4	.976	22	113	164	3b149,1b6		4.4
1999	Mil N	157	607	96	198	35	1	15	88	75-4	5	83	.326	.401	.461	118	20	7-4	.967	7	105	130	3b155		2.7
2000	Col N★	157	598	111	195	53	2	11	115	67-4	9	72	.326	.392	.477	97	1	3-4	.964	7	106	**144**	3b155		0.8
2001	Col N	138	528	72	165	26	4	17	83	43-6	5	63	.313	.364	.473	96	-2	12-2	**.982**	18	**117**	105	3b137	16	1.8
2002	Sea A	146	485	51	121	20	0	6	54	31-0	9	67	.249	.301	.328	71	-20	8-4	**.973**	1	92	118	3b141,1b11		-1.7
2003	Sea A	87	258	24	53	11	0	2	23	24-1	5	32	.205	.284	.271	51	-18	1-1	.977	-10	78	60	3b85/1	26	-2.7
2004	SD N	33	75	12	16	3	0	1	7	5-0	4	6	.213	.259	.293	46	-6	0-0	1.000	-3	59	60	3b11,1b10,2b4/OL	37	-1.0
2005	Mil N	77	185	29	52	15	0	4	23	23-0	4	22	.281	.373	.427	109	3	4-2	.951	-5	82	104	3b53,2b3/1	68	-0.1
Total	12	1427	4940	743	1466	314	19	107	677	523-18	65	642	.297	.368	.433	101	25	60-36	.966	54	104	120	3b1335,1b34,2b34,D5,S2/OL	147	8.2
CISAR, GEORGE	George Joseph B8.25.1912 Chicago IL BR/TR/6-0/175 d9.9																								
1937	Bro N	20	29	8	6	0	0	0	2	4	2	0	6	.207	.258	.207	27	-3	3	1.000	0	119	0	O13(9/0/4)	-0.3
CISSELL, BILL	Chalmer William B1.3.1904 Perryville MO D3.15.1949 Chicago IL BR/TR/5-11/170 d4.11																								
1928	Chi A	125	443	66	115	22	3	1	60	29	1	41	.260	.307	.330	68	-21	18-6	.938	1	102	107	S123		-0.5
1929	Chi A	**152**	618	83	173	27	12	5	62	28	1	53	.280	.312	.387	80	-22	25-17	.933	-3	100	97	S152		-0.8
1930	Chi A	141	562	82	152	28	9	2	48	28	2	32	.270	.307	.363	72	-26	16-9	.948	-9	97	88	2b107,3b24,S10		-2.7
1931	Chi A	109	409	42	90	13	5	1	46	16	1	26	.220	.256	.284	44	-35	18-6	.944	-7	97	96	S83,2b23/3		-3.2
1932	Chi A	12	43	7	11	1	1	1	5	1	0	4	.256	.273	.395	76	-2	0-0	.928	-1	72	120	S12		-0.2
	Cle A	131	541	78	173	35	6	6	93	28	1	25	.320	.354	.440	98	-2	18-15	.964	5	**106**	99	2b129,S6		0.9
	Year	143	584	85	184	36	7	7	98	29	1	25	.315	.349	.437	97	-4	18-15	.964	4	**106**	99	2b129,S18		0.7
1933	Cle A	112	409	53	94	21	3	6	33	31	0	29	.230	.284	.340	62	-24	6-6	.947	-3	98	88	2b62,S46/3		-1.9
1934	Bos A	102	416	71	111	13	4	4	44	28	1	23	.267	.315	.344	66	-22	11-4	.959	-3	96	94	2b96,S7,3b2		-1.7
1937	Phi A	34	117	15	31	7	0	1	14	17	0	10	.265	.358	.350	81	-3	0-0	.962	1	107	69	2b33		0.0
1938	NY N	38	149	19	40	6	0	2	18	6	1	11	.268	.297	.349	76	-5	1	.977	2	115	99	2b33,3b6		0.5
Total	9	956	3707	516	990	173	43	29	423	212	10	250	.267	.308	.360	73	-162	113-63	.958	-12	101	88	2b483,S439,3b34		-9.6
CLABAUGH, MOOSE	John William B11.13.1901 Albany MO D7.11.1984 Tucson AZ BL/TR/6-0/185 d8.30																								
1926	Bro N	11	14	2	1	1	0	0	1	0	1	1	.071	.133	.143	-26	-3	0	.600	-1	84	0	O2L		-0.3
CLACK, BOBBY	Robert Suter "Gentlemanly Bob" B6.13.1850 , England D10.22.1933 Danvers MA BR/TR/5-9/153 d5.13																								
1874	Atl NA	33	135	22	23	1	0	0	13	4		2	.170	.194	.178	23	-10	0-0	.779	-3	110	0	O31(1/30/0),1b2		-1.0
1875	Atl NA	17	59	1	6	0	0	0	1	0		3	.102	.102	.102	-33	-7	0-0	.867	2	154	325	O17(0/16/1)/1		-0.4
1876	Cin N	32	118	10	19	0	1	0	5	5		12	.161	.195	.178	29	-8		.736	-2	90	0	O17(0/3/14),2b8,1b5,3b3/P		-0.8
Total	2 NA	50	194	23	29	1	0	0	14	4		5	.149	.167	.155	7	-17	0-0	.811	-0	125	108	O48(1/46/1),1b3		-1.4
CLAIRE, DAVEY	David Matthew B11.17.1897 Ludington MI D1.7.1956 Las Vegas NV BR/TR/5-8/164 d9.17																								
1920	Det A	3	7	1	1	0	0	0	0	0	0	0	.143	.143	.143	-25	-1	0-0	.800	-1	105	0	S3		-0.2
CLANCY, AL	Albert Harrison B8.14.1888 Santa Fe NM D10.17.1951 Las Cruces NM BR/TR/5-10.5/175 d6.20																								
1911	StL A	3	5	0	0	0	0	0	0	0	0	0	.000	.167	.000	-54	-1	0	.800	-1	120	532	3b2		-0.1
CLANCY, BUD	John William B9.15.1900 Odell IL D9.26.1968 Ottumwa IA BL/TL/6-0/170 d8.29																								
1924	Chi A	13	35	5	9	1	0	0	6	3	0	2	.257	.316	.286	58	-2	3-2	.947	-2	54	67	1b8		-0.4
1925	Chi A	4	3	0	0	0	0	0	0	1	0	0	.000	.250	.000	-34	-1	0-0	—	0			/H		-0.1
1926	Chi A	12	38	3	13	2	2	0	7	1	1	1	.342	.375	.500	132	1	0-0	.991	-0	94	153	1b10		0.1
1927	Chi A	130	464	46	139	21	2	2	53	24	2	24	.300	.337	.373	86	-10	4-3	.991	-1	97	85	1b123		-1.9
1928	Chi A	130	487	64	132	19	11	2	37	42	2	25	.271	.331	.368	85	-12	6-9	.991	4	**112**	104	1b128		-1.8
1929	Chi A	92	290	36	82	14	6	3	45	16	0	19	.283	.320	.403	86	-7	3-1	.991	2	113	83	1b74		-0.9
1930	Chi A	68	234	28	57	8	3	3	27	12	2	18	.244	.286	.342	61	-15	3-1	.995	-3	72	79	1b60		-2.0
1932	Bro N	53	196	14	60	4	2	0	16	6	0	13	.306	.327	.347	83	-5	0	.996	3	116	153	1b53		-0.7
1934	Phi N	20	49	8	12	0	0	1	7	6	1	4	.245	.339	.306	65	-2	0	1.000	-1	65	134	1b10		-0.4
Total	9	522	1796	204	504	69	26	12	198	111	8	106	.281	.325	.368	82	-53	19-16	.992	2	101	96	1b466		-8.1
CLANCY, BILL	William Edward B4.12.1879 Redfield NY D2.10.1948 Oriskany NY BR/TR/6-2/180 d4.14																								
1905	Pit N	56	227	23	52	11	3	2	34	4	0		.229	.246	.330	69	-10	3	.983	-3	81	118	1b52,O4R		-1.4
CLANTON, UKE	Eucal "Cat" B2.19.1898 Powell MO D2.24.1960 Antlers OK BL/TL/5-8/165 d9.21 Col Oklahoma																								
1922	Cle A	1	1	0	0	0	0	0	0	1	0	0	.000	.000	.000	-99	-0	0-0	.500	-0	0	0	/1		-0.1
CLAPINSKI, CHRIS	Christopher Alan B8.20.1971 Buffalo NY BB/TR/6-0/175* d7.17 Col California-Davis																								
1999	Fla N	36	56	6	13	1	2	0	2	9-0	1	12	.232	.348	.321	75	-2	1-0	.882	-1	65	72	3b9,S6,O3L,2b2/D		-0.2
2000	Fla N	34	49	12	15	4	1	1	7	5-0	0	7	.306	.370	.490	121	2	0-0	.933	-2	97	65	2b14,3b3,O3L/S		0.1
Total	2	70	105	18	28	5	3	1	9	14-0	1	19	.267	.358	.400	97	0	1-0	.935	-2	101	64	2b16,3b12,S7,O6L/D		-0.1
CLAPP, AARON	Aaron Bronson B7.1856 Ithaca NY D1.13.1914 Sayre PA TR/5-8/175 d5.1 b-John																								
1879	Tro N	36	146	24	39	9	3	0	18	6		10	.267	.296	.370	126	5		.935	-3	63	80	1b25,O11(7/1/3)		0.0

YEAR	TM LG	G	AB	R	H	2B	3B	HR	RBI	BB-IB	HP	SO	AVG	OBP	SLG	AOPS	ABR	SB-CS	FA	FR	RNG	THR	GAMES AT POSITION	DL	BFW

CLAPP, JOHN   John Edgar   B7.17.1851 Ithaca NY   D12.18.1904 Ithaca NY   BR/TR/5-7/194   d4.26   M6   b-Aaron   OF(62/19/21)

YEAR	TM LG	G	AB	R	H	2B	3B	HR	RBI	BB-IB	HP	SO	AVG	OBP	SLG	AOPS	ABR	SB-CS	FA	FR	RNG	THR	GAMES AT POSITION	DL	BFW
1872	Man NA	19	97	30	27	7	1	1	16	1		0	.278	.286	.402	116	2	2-1	.845	-1			C19,S2/1OCM		0.1
1873	Ath NA	45	204	36	62	10	2	1	27	2		2	.304	.311	.387	99	-2	4-5	.893	2			C43,S6/2OC		0.0
1874	Ath NA	39	165	46	48	7	4	3	19	1		1	.291	.295	.436	121	3	2-0	.861	7			C27,O15(0/1/14)/S		0.8
1875	Ath NA	60	292	65	77	8	7	0	39	7		1	.264	.281	.339	103	-1	9-5	.874	18			C60		1.5
1876	StL N	64	298	60	91	4	2	0	29	8		2	.305	.324	.332	125	9		.874	10			C61,O4(0/1/3)/2		1.8
1877	StL N	60	255	47	81	6	6	0	34	8		6	.318	.338	.388	135	10		.887	-5			C53,O10(2/0/9)/1		0.6
1878	Ind N	63	263	42	80	10	2	0	29	.13		8	.304	.337	.357	148	16		.890	-3	48	0	O44L,1b12,C9,S3/2M		0.9
1879	Buf N	70	292	47	77	12	5	1	36	11		11	.264	.290	.349	107	2		.906	-8			C63,O7R,M		-0.4
1880	Cin N	80	323	33	91	16	4	1	20	21		10	.282	.326	.365	135	13		.897	19			C73,O10(1/9/0),M		3.2
1881	Cle N	68	261	47	66	12	2	0	25	35		6	.253	.341	.314	113	7		.890	-3			C48,O21(15/6/0),M		0.4
1883	NY N	20	73	6	13	0	0	0	5	5		4	.178	.231	.178	27	-6		.895	3			C16,O5(0/3/2),M		-0.2
Total	4 NA	163	758	177	214	32	14	5	101	11		4	.282	.293	.381	107	2	17-11	.873	26			C149,O17(0/3/14),S9/21		2.4
Total	7	425	1765	282	499	60	21	2	178	101		47	.283	.322	.344	122	51		.892	14			C323,O101L,1b13,S3,2b2		6.3

CLAPP, STUBBY   Richard Keith   B2.24.1973 Windsor ON, Can.   BL/TR/5-8/175   [StLN96 36/1058]   d6.18   Col Texas Tech

YEAR	TM LG	G	AB	R	H	2B	3B	HR	RBI	BB-IB	HP	SO	AVG	OBP	SLG	AOPS	ABR	SB-CS	FA	FR	RNG	THR	GAMES AT POSITION	DL	BFW
2001	StL N	23	25	0	5	2	0	0	1	1-0		7	.200	.231	.280	30	-3	0-0	1.000	0	174	0	2b4,O4L		-0.2

CLARE, DENNY   Dennis J.   B1.1853 Brooklyn NY   D11.26.1928 Brooklyn NY   d9.14

YEAR	TM LG	G	AB	R	H	2B	3B	HR	RBI	BB-IB	HP	SO	AVG	OBP	SLG	AOPS	ABR	SB-CS	FA	FR	RNG	THR	GAMES AT POSITION	DL	BFW
1872	Atl NA	2	7	1	1	0	0	0	0	0		0	.143	.143	.143	-10	-1	0-0	.857	-1	195	0	2b2/S		-0.2

CLAREY, DOUG   Douglas William   B4.20.1954 Los Angeles CA   BR/TR/6-0/180   [MinA72 6/128]   d4.20

YEAR	TM LG	G	AB	R	H	2B	3B	HR	RBI	BB-IB	HP	SO	AVG	OBP	SLG	AOPS	ABR	SB-CS	FA	FR	RNG	THR	GAMES AT POSITION	DL	BFW
1976	StL N	9	4	2	1	0	0	0	1	0-0		1	.250	.250	1.000	238	1	0-0	1.000	-1	27	0	2b7		-0.1

CLARK, ALLIE   Alfred Aloysius   B6.16.1923 S.Amboy NJ   BR/TR/5-11/185*   d8.5

YEAR	TM LG	G	AB	R	H	2B	3B	HR	RBI	BB-IB	HP	SO	AVG	OBP	SLG	AOPS	ABR	SB-CS	FA	FR	RNG	THR	GAMES AT POSITION	DL	BFW
1947	†NY A	24	67	9	25	5	0	1	14	5	0	2	.373	.417	.493	154	5	0-0	1.000	0	115	0	O16(6/0/10)		0.4
1948	†Cle A	81	271	43	84	5	2	9	38	23	0	13	.310	.364	.443	117	5	0-2	.982	-3	89	95	O65(21/0/44),3b5/1		-0.2
1949	Cle A	35	74	8	13	4	0	1	9	4	0	7	.176	.218	.270	29	-8	0-0	1.000	-2	65	98	O17(1/0/16)/1		-1.0
1950	Cle A	59	163	19	35	6	1	6	21	11	0	10	.215	.264	.374	64	-10	0-1	.987	-1	97	70	O41(25/0/17)		-1.3
1951	Cle A	3	10	3	3	2	0	1	3	1	0	2	.300	.364	.800	221	2	0-0	1.000	-0	73	0	O3R		0.1
	Phi A	56	161	20	40	10	1	4	22	15	2	7	.248	.320	.398	91	-2	2-0	.984	0	102	95	O32(1/1/30),3b10		-0.2
	Year	59	171	23	43	12	1	5	25	16	2	9	.251	.323	.421	98	-1	2-0	.985	0	100	88	O35(1/1/33),3b10		-0.1
1952	Phi A	71	186	23	51	12	0	7	29	10	1	19	.274	.315	.452	105	0	0-2	.988	-1	100	61	O48(7/2/39),1b2		-0.3
1953	Phi A	20	74	6	15	4	0	3	13	3	0	5	.203	.234	.378	61	-5	0-0	1.000	-0	92	117	O19R		-0.6
	Chi A	9	15	0	1	0	0	0	0	0	0	5	.067	.067	.067	-62	-3	0-0	1.000	-0	0	279	/1OL		-0.4
	Year	29	89	6	16	4	0	3	13	3	0	10	.180	.207	.326	40	-8	0-0	1.000	-1	91	117	O20(1/0/19)/1		-1.0
Total	7	358	1021	131	267	48	4	32	149	72	3	70	.262	.312	.410	92	-16	2-5	.988	-8	95	78	O242(62/3/178),3b15,1b5		-3.5

CLARK, DAD   Alfred Robert "Fred"   B7.16.1873 San Francisco CA   D7.26.1956 Ogden UT   BL/TL/5-11/170   d7.3

YEAR	TM LG	G	AB	R	H	2B	3B	HR	RBI	BB-IB	HP	SO	AVG	OBP	SLG	AOPS	ABR	SB-CS	FA	FR	RNG	THR	GAMES AT POSITION	DL	BFW
1902	Chi N	12	43	1	8	1	0	0	2	4		0	.186	.255	.209	45	-3	1	.938	-2	88	147	1b12		-0.5

CLARK, TONY   Anthony Christopher   B6.15.1972 Newton KS   BB/TR/6-7/245(205-250)   [DetA90 1/2]   d9.3

YEAR	TM LG	G	AB	R	H	2B	3B	HR	RBI	BB-IB	HP	SO	AVG	OBP	SLG	AOPS	ABR	SB-CS	FA	FR	RNG	THR	GAMES AT POSITION	DL	BFW
1995	Det A	27	101	10	24	5	1	3	11	8-0	0	30	.238	.294	.396	77	-4	0-0	.985	-1	94	99	1b27		-0.7
1996	Det A	100	376	56	94	14	0	27	72	29-1	0	127	.250	.299	.503	99	-3	0-1	.993	-2	90	92	1b86,D12		-1.3
1997	Det A	159	580	105	160	28	3	32	117	93-13	3	144	.276	.376	.500	127	25	1-3	.993	-3	94	101	1b158/D		0.7
1998	Det A	157	602	84	175	37	0	34	103	63-5	3	128	.291	.358	.522	124	21	3-3	.991	-0	104	111	1b142,D15		0.7
1999	Det A	143	536	74	150	29	0	31	99	64-7	6	133	.280	.361	.507	117	14	2-1	.992	2	106	95	1b132,D11		0.3
2000	Det A	60	208	32	57	14	0	13	37	24-2	0	51	.274	.349	.529	119	6	0-0	.993	3	121	104	1b58/D	90	0.3
2001	Det A★	126	428	67	123	29	3	16	75	62-10	1	108	.287	.374	.481	128	19	0-1	.996	-1	99	108	1b78,D42		0.9
2002	Bos A	90	275	24	57	12	1	3	29	21-0	1	57	.207	.265	.291	47	-21	0-0	.992	4	118	99	1b85,D2		-2.3
2003	NY N	125	254	29	59	13	0	16	43	24-2	1	73	.232	.300	.472	102	-1	0-0	.992	-4	71	83	1b80/OL		-1.0
2004	†NY A	106	253	37	56	12	0	16	49	26-3	2	92	.221	.297	.458	93	-3	0-0	.994	0	99	112	1b99/D		-0.9
2005	Ari N	130	349	47	106	22	2	30	87	37-6	1	88	.304	.366	.636	155	25	0-0	.997	-1	95	90	1b83,D7	105	1.7
Total	11	1223	3962	566	1061	215	10	221	722	451-49	18	1031	.268	.343	.494	114	78	6-9	.993	-3	100	100	1b1028,D92/OL	105	-1.6

CLARK, EARL   Bailey Earl   B11.6.1907 Washington DC   D1.16.1938 Washington DC   BR/TR/5-10/160   d8.17

YEAR	TM LG	G	AB	R	H	2B	3B	HR	RBI	BB-IB	HP	SO	AVG	OBP	SLG	AOPS	ABR	SB-CS	FA	FR	RNG	THR	GAMES AT POSITION	DL	BFW
1927	Bos N	13	44	6	12	1	0	0	3	2		4	.273	.304	.295	66	-2	0	1.000	-0	114	0	O13(10/3/0)		-0.3
1928	Bos N	28	112	18	34	9	1	0	10	4		2	.304	.339	.402	98	0	0	.987	-2	103	0	O27C		-0.3
1929	Bos N	84	279	43	88	13	3	1	30	12		1	.315	.346	.394	86	-6	6	.978	4	109	100	O74(4/70/1)		-0.8
1930	Bos N	82	233	29	69	11	3	3	28	7		1	.296	.320	.408	77	-10	3	.977	3	118	55	O63(1/40/22)		-0.8
1931	Bos N	16	50	8	11	2	0	0	4	7		0	.220	.316	.260	58	-3	1	.970	1	98	257	O14L		-0.3
1932	Bos N	50	44	11	11	2	0	0	4	2		7	.250	.283	.295	58	-3	1	1.000	3	136	394	O16(6/3/6)		0.0
1933	Bos N	7	23	3	8	0	0	0	1	2		1	.348	.400	.391	138	1	0	1.000	-1	81	0	O6(3/3/0)		0.0
1934	StL A	13	41	4	7	2	0	0	1	1		3	.171	.190	.220	5	-6	0-0	1.000	0	115	0	O9(2/0/7)		-0.6
Total	8	293	826	122	240	41	7	4	81	37		4	.291	.324	.372	78	-29	11-0	.981	8	111	81	O222(40/146/36)		-2.9

CLARK, BRADY   Brady William   B4.18.1973 Portland OR   BR/TR/6-2/195*   d9.3   Col San Diego

YEAR	TM LG	G	AB	R	H	2B	3B	HR	RBI	BB-IB	HP	SO	AVG	OBP	SLG	AOPS	ABR	SB-CS	FA	FR	RNG	THR	GAMES AT POSITION	DL	BFW
2000	Cin N	11	11	1	3	1	0	0	2	0-0	0	2	.273	.273	.364	57	-1	0-0	1.000	1	237	0	O5(2/0/3)		0.0
2001	Cin N	89	129	22	34	3	0	6	18	22-1	1	16	.264	.373	.426	101	1	4-1	.981	-1	103	0	O43(26/7/14)/D		-0.1
2002	Cin N	51	66	6	10	3	0	0	9	6-2	1	9	.152	.233	.197	16	-8	1-2	.938	-1	78	0	O22(15/3/6)		-1.1
	NY N	10	12	3	5	1	0	0	1	1-0	0	2	.417	.462	.500	167	1	0-0	1.000	-0	93	0	O6(1/2/3)		0.1
	Year	61	78	9	15	4	0	0	10	7-2	1	11	.192	.267	.244	38	-7	1-2	.950	-2	81	0	O28(16/5/9)		-1.0
2003	Mil N	128	315	33	86	21	1	6	40	21-0	9	40	.273	.330	.403	92	-3	13-2	.973	5	114	100	O105(25/6/82)	16	0.0
2004	Mil N	138	353	41	99	18	1	7	46	53-2	3	48	.280	.385	.397	103	4	15-8	.984	10	127	82	O133(3/9/123)		1.0
2005	Mil N	145	599	94	183	31	1	13	53	47-1	18	55	.306	.372	.426	109	9	10-13	.995	11	119	69	O145C	15	1.9
Total	6	572	1485	200	420	78	3	32	169	150-6	38	172	.283	.361	.404	99	3	43-26	.986	24	118	72	O459(72/172/231)/D	31	1.8

CLARK, DANNY   Daniel Curran   B1.18.1894 Meridian MS   D5.23.1937 Meridian MS   BL/TR/5-9/167   d4.12

YEAR	TM LG	G	AB	R	H	2B	3B	HR	RBI	BB-IB	HP	SO	AVG	OBP	SLG	AOPS	ABR	SB-CS	FA	FR	RNG	THR	GAMES AT POSITION	DL	BFW
1922	Det A	83	185	31	54	11	3	3	26	15		11	.292	.345	.432	105	1	1-0	.945	-3	101	88	2b38,O5R/3		-0.1
1924	Bos A	104	325	36	90	23	3	2	54	51		2	.277	.378	.385	97	-1	4-7	.943	-0	105	56	3b94		0.4
1927	StL N	58	72	8	17	2	2	0	13	8		7	.236	.313	.319	67	-3	0	.929	1	118	81	O9R		-0.4
Total	3	245	582	75	161	36	8	5	93	74		2	.277	.360	.392	96	-1	5-7	.943	-2	105	56	3b95,2b38,O14R		-0.1

CLARK, DAVE   David Earl   B9.3.1962 Tupelo MS   BL/TR/6-2/210(198-213)   [CleA83 1/11]   d9.3   C2   Col Jackson St.

YEAR	TM LG	G	AB	R	H	2B	3B	HR	RBI	BB-IB	HP	SO	AVG	OBP	SLG	AOPS	ABR	SB-CS	FA	FR	RNG	THR	GAMES AT POSITION	DL	BFW
1986	Cle A	18	58	10	16	1	0	3	9	7-0	0	11	.276	.348	.448	118	1	1-0	1.000	1	127	0	O10R,D7		0.2
1987	Cle A	29	87	11	18	5	0	3	12	2-0	0	24	.207	.225	.368	53	-6	1-0	1.000	1	118	136	O13(1/0/12),D12		-0.6
1988	Cle A	63	156	11	41	4	1	3	18	17-2	0	28	.263	.333	.359	92	-2	0-2	.947	-2	89	0	D27,O23(10/1/15)		-0.6
1989	Cle A	102	253	21	60	12	0	8	29	30-5	0	63	.237	.317	.379	94	-2	0-2	.964	-3	70	0	D55,O21(12/0/11)		-0.8
1990	Chi N	84	171	22	47	4	2	5	20	8-1	0	40	.275	.304	.409	89	-3	7-1	1.000	-1	87	85	O39L		-0.4
1991	KC A	11	10	1	2	0	0	0	1	1-0	0	1	.200	.273	.200	33	-1	0-0	—	-0	0	0	/ORD		-0.1
1992	Pit N	23	33	3	7	0	0	2	7	6-0	0	8	.212	.325	.394	106	0	0-0	1.000	-1	71	0	O8(1/0/7)		-0.1
1993	Pit N	110	277	43	75	11	2	11	46	38-5	1	58	.271	.358	.444	114	6	1-0	.957	-6	90	53	O91(40/0/53)		-0.2
1994	Pit N	86	223	37	66	11	1	10	46	22-0	1	48	.296	.355	.489	116	5	2-2	.974	2	102	130	O57(10/0/48)		0.4
1995	Pit N	77	196	30	55	6	0	4	24	24-1	1	38	.281	.359	.372	92	-2	3-3	.961	0	113	32	O61(34/0/29)	47	-0.4
1996	Pit N	92	211	28	58	12	2	8	35	31-3	0	51	.275	.366	.464	114	5	2-1	.969	-1	93	102	O61(34/0/28)		0.2
	†LA N	15	15	0	3	0	0	0	1	3-0	0	2	.200	.333	.200	48	-1	0-0	—	-0	0	0	/OL		-0.1
	Year	107	226	28	61	12	2	8	36	34-3	0	53	.270	.364	.447	110	4	2-1	.988	-1	91	100	O62(35/0/28)		0.1
1997	Chi N	102	143	19	43	8	0	5	32	19-3	5	34	.301	.386	.462	118	4	1-0	.953	-2	113	165	O25(24/0/1),D4		0.5
1998	†Hou N	93	131	12	27	7	0	0	14	14-1	1	45	.206	.288	.260	47	-10	1-1	.885	-2	79	102	O22(9/0/13),D4		-1.2
Total	13	905	1964	248	518	81	8	62	284	222-21	5	451	.264	.338	.422	102	-6	19-12	.969	-11	96	73	O433(215/1/228),D110	47	-3.2

CLARK, DOUG   Douglas Dwyer   B3.5.1976 Springfield MA   BL/TR/6-2/205   d9.14   Col Massachusetts

YEAR	TM LG	G	AB	R	H	2B	3B	HR	RBI	BB-IB	HP	SO	AVG	OBP	SLG	AOPS	ABR	SB-CS	FA	FR	RNG	THR	GAMES AT POSITION	DL	BFW
2005	SF N	8	5	2	0	0	0	0	0	1-0	0	2	.000	.167	.000	-49	-1	0-0	—	0			/H		-0.2

CLARK, GLEN   Glen Ester   B3.7.1941 Austin TX   BB/TR/6-1/190   d6.3

YEAR	TM LG	G	AB	R	H	2B	3B	HR	RBI	BB-IB	HP	SO	AVG	OBP	SLG	AOPS	ABR	SB-CS	FA	FR	RNG	THR	GAMES AT POSITION	DL	BFW
1967	Atl N	4	4	0	0	0	0	0	0	0-0	0	1	.000	.000	.000	-99	-1	0-0	—	0			/H		-0.1

YEAR	TM LG	G	AB	R	H	2B	3B	HR	RBI	BB-IB	HP	SO	AVG	OBP	SLG	AOPS	ABR	SB-CS	FA	FR	RNG	THR	GAMES AT POSITION	DL	BFW

CLARK, PEP Harry B3.20.1883 Union City OH D6.8.1965 Milwaukee WI BR/TR/5-7.5/175 d9.11

| 1903 | Chi A | 15 | 65 | 7 | 20 | 4 | 2 | 0 | 9 | 2- | 1 | | .308 | .338 | .431 | 135 | 3 | 5 | .877 | -1 | 118 | 58 | 3b15 | | 0.3 |

CLARK, HOWIE Howard Roddy B2.13.1974 San Diego CA BL/TR/5-10/195(180-195) [BalA92 27/744] d7.16 OF(17/0/12)

2002	Bal A	14	53	3	16	5	0	0	4	3-0	2	6	.302	.362	.396	107	1	0-0	1.000	0	119	0	O4L/1D		0.1
2003	Tor A	38	70	9	25	3	1	0	7	3-0	2	6	.357	.400	.429	114	2	0-1	.957	1	114	239	3b13,O5(4/0/1),2b3,1b2/SD		0.2
2004	Tor A	40	115	17	25	6	0	3	12	13-0	0	15	.217	.292	.348	64	-6	0-1	.972	-1	108	214	O19(9/0/11),1b11,23D		-0.8
Total 3		92	238	29	66	14	1	3	23	19-0	4	27	.277	.338	.382	87	-3	0-1	.980	1	105	148	O28L,D19,3b14,1b14,2b4/S		-0.5

CLARK, JACK Jack Anthony B11.10.1955 New Brighton PA BR/TR/6-2/205(170-210) [SFN73 13/294] d9.12 C3 OF(11/23/1014)

1975	SF N	8	17	3	4	0	0	0	2	1-0	0	2	.235	.263	.235	42	-1	1-0	1.000	0	110	0	O3(1/2/1),3b2		-0.1
1976	SF N	26	102	14	23	6	2	2	10	8-0	0	18	.225	.277	.382	85	-2	6-2	.987	3	113	168	O26(5/20/8)		0.0
1977	SF N	136	413	64	104	17	4	13	51	49-2	2	73	.252	.332	.407	97	-2	12-4	.975	6	110	135	O114(0/1/113)		0.0
1978	SF N★	156	592	90	181	46	8	25	98	50-8	1	72	.306	.358	.537	154	41	15-11	.982	8	107	127	O152R		4.1
1979	SF N★	143	527	84	144	25	2	26	86	63-6	1	95	.273	.348	.476	133	23	11-8	.982	2	97	118	O140R,3b2		1.8
1980	SF N	127	437	77	124	20	8	22	82	74-13	2	55	.284	.382	.517	156	35	2-5	.967	-4	98	66	O120R	16	2.4
1981	SF N	99	385	60	103	19	2	17	53	45-6	1	45	.268	.341	.460	131	15	1-1	.981	5	99	168	O98R		1.6
1982	SF N	157	563	90	154	30	2	27	103	90-7	1	91	.274	.372	.481	139	32	6-9	.980	-4	96	89	O155R		1.9
1983	SF N	135	492	82	132	25	0	20	66	74-6	1	79	.268	.361	.441	126	19	5-3	.967	6	101	183	O133R,1b2		1.9
1984	SF N	57	203	33	65	9	1	11	44	43-7	0	29	.320	.434	.537	178	23	1-1	.990	-1	90	82	O54R,1b4	72	2.0
1985	†StL N★	126	442	71	124	26	3	22	87	83-14	2	88	.281	.393	.502	151	33	1-4	.988	-9	81	112	1b121,O12R	15	1.7
1986	StL N	65	232	34	55	12	2	9	23	45-4	1	61	.237	.362	.422	116	7	1-1	.995	-6	75	137	1b64	103	-0.3
1987	†StL N★	131	419	93	120	23	1	35	106	136-13	0	139	.286	.459	.597	173	53	1-2	.989	-5	92	116	1b126/OR		3.9
1988	NY A	150	496	81	120	14	0	27	93	113-6	2	141	.242	.381	.433	129	24	3-2	.951	-1	99	91	D112,O19(5/0/14),1b10	11	1.9
1989	SD N	142	455	76	110	19	1	26	94	132-18	2	145	.242	.410	.459	149	37	6-2	.988	-1	107	119	1b131,O12R		3.2
1990	SD N	115	334	59	89	12	1	25	62	104-11	2	91	.266	.441	.533	166	37	4-3	.994	-1	95	104	1b109	29	2.9
1991	Bos A	140	481	75	120	18	1	28	87	96-3	3	133	.249	.374	.466	125	19	0-2	—	0	0	0	D135		1.4
1992	Bos A	81	257	32	54	11	0	5	33	56-3	1	87	.210	.350	.311	82	-4	1-1	.992	0	106	74	D64,1b13		-0.7
Total 18		1994	6847	1118	1826	332	39	340	1180	1262-127	24	1441	.267	.379	.476	137	389	77-61	.978	1	101	122	O1039R,1b580,D311,3b4	246	29.6

CLARK, JIM James (b James Petrosky) B9.21.1927 Baggaley PA D10.24.1990 Santa Monica CA BR/TR/5-9/150 d8.17

| 1948 | Was A | 9 | 12 | 1 | 3 | 0 | 0 | 0 | 2 | 2-0 | 0 | 4 | .250 | .250 | .250 | 34 | -1 | 0-0 | 1.000 | 0 | 95 | 0 | /S3 | | -0.1 |

CLARK, JIM James Edward B4.30.1947 Kansas City KS BR/TR/6-1/190 d7.16

| 1971 | Cle A | 13 | 18 | 2 | 3 | 0 | 1 | 0 | 0 | 2-0 | 0 | 7 | .167 | .250 | .278 | 45 | -1 | 0-0 | 1.000 | 0 | 150 | 0 | O3(2/0/1)/1 | | -0.1 |

CLARK, JIM James Francis B12.26.1887 Brooklyn NY D3.20.1969 Beaumont TX BR/TR/5-11/175 d9.2 Col Bucknell

1911	StL N	14	18	2	3	0	1	0	3	3-	0	4	.167	.286	.278	60	-1	2	1.000	-1	83	0	O8(1/6/1)		-0.2
1912	StL N	2	1	0	0	0	0	0	0	0-	0	1	.000	.000	.000	-99	0		—	0			/H		0.0
Total 2		16	19	2	3	0	1	0	3	3-	0	5	.158	.273	.263	51	-1	2	1.000	-1	83	0	O8(1/6/1)		-0.2

CLARK, JERALD Jerald Dwayne B8.10.1963 Crockett TX BR/TR/6-4/202(189-205) [SDN85 12/310] d9.19 b-Phil Col Lamar

1988	SD N	6	15	0	3	1	0	0	3	0-0	0	4	.200	.200	.267	33	-1	0-0	1.000	1	152	496	O4L		0.0
1989	SD N	17	41	5	8	2	0	1	7	3-0	0	9	.195	.250	.317	61	-2	0-1	.947	0	80	356	O14(10/0/4)		-0.3
1990	SD N	53	101	12	27	4	1	5	11	5-0	0	24	.267	.299	.475	109	1	0-0	1.000	0	93	49	1b15,O13(5/0/9)		0.0
1991	SD N	118	369	26	84	16	0	10	47	31-2	6	90	.228	.295	.352	80	-10	2-1	.994	-5	86	91	O96(85/0/13),1b16	19	-2.0
1992	SD N	146	496	45	120	22	6	12	58	22-3	4	97	.242	.278	.383	84	-12	3-0	.990	7	110	153	O134(115/1/22),1b11		-1.0
1993	Col N	140	478	65	135	26	6	13	67	20-2	10	60	.282	.324	.444	89	-8	3-0	.966	-15	100	90	O96(80/0/17),1b37		-1.6
1995	Min A	36	109	17	37	8	3	3	15	2-0	1	11	.339	.354	.550	131	4	3-0	1.000	-1	99	77	O23(12/10/5),1b11,D3	106	0.3
Total 7		516	1609	170	414	79	16	44	208	83-7	21	295	.257	.301	.408	89	-28	17-8	.983	2	102	124	O380(311/11/70),1b90,D3	125	-4.6

CLARK, JERMAINE Jermaine Marcel B9.29.1976 Berkeley CA BL/TR/5-10/175* [SeaA97 5/163] d4.3 Col San Francisco

2001	Det A	3	0	1	0	0	0	0	0	0-0	0		—	—	—	—	0	0-0	—	0			R2		0.0
2003	Tex A	10	9	0	0	0	0	0	0	3-0	0	3	.000	.250	.000	-24	-2	0-0	1.000	-8	16	0	O6(5/1/0),2b2/D		-1.0
	SD N	1	2	0	0	0	0	0	0	1-0	0	1	.000	.000	.000	-99	-1	0-1	1.000	0	107	0	/OL		-0.1
	Tex A	14	37	2	8	2	0	0	6	3-0	0	4	.216	.268	.270	42	-3	2-1	1.000	-1	16	0	O11L,2b5/D		-0.4
2004	Cin N	14	30	4	4	1	0	0	2	1-0	2	8	.133	.212	.167	-0	-5	1-0	1.000	0	106	333	O8(1/1/6),2b2		-0.4
2005	Oak A	4	0	2	0	0	0	0	0	1-0	0	0	—	1.000	—	197	0	0-0	—	0	0	0	2b2/OL		0.0
Total 4		46	78	9	12	3	0	0	9	6-0	2	13	.154	.244	.192	18	-11	3-2	1.000	-9	68	164	O27(19/2/6),2b11,D2		-1.9

CLARK, CAP John Carrol B9.19.1906 Snow Camp NC D2.16.1957 Fayetteville NC BL/TR/5-11/180 d4.23 Col Elon

| 1938 | Phi N | 52 | 74 | 11 | 19 | 1 | 0 | 4 | 9 | 0- | 0 | 10 | .257 | .337 | .297 | 78 | -2 | 0 | .936 | -4 | 57 | 107 | C29 | | -0.5 |

CLARK, MEL Melvin Earl B7.7.1926 Letart WV BR/TR/6-0/180* d9.11 Col Ohio U.

1951	Phi N	10	31	2	10	1	0	1	3	0-	0	3	.323	.323	.452	108	0	0-1	1.000	-0	102	0	O7(1/0/6)		-0.1
1952	Phi N	47	155	20	52	6	4	1	15	6-	1	13	.335	.364	.445	125	4	2-1	1.000	3	108	146	O38(12/0/27)/3		0.6
1953	Phi N	60	198	31	59	10	4	0	19	11-	0	17	.298	.338	.389	89	-3	1-0	.991	1	109	53	O51(1/0/51)		-0.4
1954	Phi N	83	233	26	56	9	7	1	24	17-	0	21	.240	.291	.352	67	-12	0-1	.961	4	101	192	O63(21/0/42)		-1.2
1955	Phi N	10	32	3	5	0	0	0	1	3-0	0	4	.156	.229	.250	27	-3	0-0	1.000	3	114	401	O8R		-0.2
1957	Det A	5	7	0	0	0	0	0	0	0-	0	0	.000	.000	.000	-97	-2	0-0	1.000	0	143	0	O2L		-0.2
Total 6		215	656	82	182	29	15	3	63	37-0	2	61	.277	.318	.381	85	-16	3-3	.983	3	106	140	O169(37/0/134)/3		-1.4

CLARK, SPIDER Owen F. B9.16.1867 Brooklyn NY D2.8.1892 Brooklyn NY TR/5-10/150 d5.2 OF(5/4/34)

1889	Was N	38	145	19	37	7	2	3	22	6-	0	18	.255	.285	.393	94	-2	8	.887	4			C14,S13,O9R,3b2,2b2		0.3
1890	Buf P	69	260	45	69	11	1	2	25	20-	3	16	.265	.325	.338	84	-5	8	.938	-3	106	149	O34(5/4/25),C14,2b13,1b6,3b3/SP		-0.5
Total 2		107	405	64	106	18	3	5	47	26-	3	34	.262	.311	.358	88	-7	16	.952	2			O43R,C28,2b15,S14,1b6,3b5/P		-0.2

CLARK, PHIL Phillip Benjamin B5.6.1968 Crockett TX BR/TR/6-0/200(180-205) [DetA86 1/18] d5.27 b-Jerald

1992	Det A	23	54	3	22	4	0	1	5	6-1	0	9	.407	.467	.537	178	6	1-0	.931	1	138	0	O13(4/0/9),D7		0.7
1993	SD N	102	240	33	75	17	0	9	33	8-2	5	31	.313	.345	.496	122	7	2-0	.963	10	142	254	O36(22/0/15),1b24,C11,3b5		1.5
1994	SD N	61	149	14	32	6	0	5	20	5-1	1	18	.215	.250	.356	59	-10	1-2	.992	-2	100	104	1b24,O17(12/0/5),C5/3		-1.4
1995	SD N	75	97	12	21	3	0	2	7	8-1	1	18	.216	.278	.309	58	-6	0-2	1.000	-2	86	0	O34(14/0/21),1b2		-0.9
1996	Bos A	3	3	0	0	0	0	0	0	0-0	0	1	.000	.000	.000	-98	-1	0-0	1.000	0	0	0	/13D		-0.1
Total 5		264	543	62	150	30	0	17	65	27-5	9	76	.276	.317	.425	97	-4	4-4	.951	7	121	103	O100(52/0/50),1b51,C16,D8,3b7		-0.2

CLARK, BOBBY Robert Cale B6.13.1955 Sacramento CA BR/TR/6-0/190* [AnaA75*S5/87] d8.21 Col California-Riverside

1979	†Cal A	19	54	8	16	2	1	5	5	5-0	0	11	.296	.356	.463	122	1	1-1	.978	4	132	372	O19(16/3/2)		0.5
1980	Cal A	78	261	26	60	10	1	5	23	11-0	2	45	.230	.266	.333	64	-14	0-0	.982	8	122	119	O77(33/46/0)		-0.7
1981	Cal A	34	88	12	22	2	1	4	19	7-0	1	18	.250	.305	.432	109	1	0-0	1.000	4	112	290	O34(27/8/1)		0.4
1982	†Cal A	102	90	11	19	1	0	2	8	0-0	0	29	.211	.209	.289	35	-8	1-0	1.000	1	101	80	O102(24/24/57)		-0.9
1983	Cal A	76	212	17	49	9	1	5	21	9-0	0	45	.231	.261	.354	68	-10	0-0	1.000	-5	93	7	O72(43/4/28)/3D	45	-1.8
1984	Mil A	58	169	14	44	7	2	2	16	16-0	1	35	.260	.324	.361	94	-1	1-5	.981	-8	80	0	O56(3/42/16)	30	-1.2
1985	Mil A	29	93	6	21	3	0	0	8	7-0	0	19	.226	.277	.258	49	-7	1-1	1.000	2	116	61	O27(1/17/12)		-0.6
Total 7		396	967	97	231	34	7	19	100	55-0	3	199	.239	.281	.347	73	-38	4-8	.990	6	105	91	O387(147/144/116),D2/3	75	-4.3

CLARK, BOB Robert H. B3.18.1863 Covington KY D8.21.1919 Covington KY BR/TR/5-10/175 d4.17

1886	Bro AA	71	269	37	58	8	2	0	26	17-	0		.216	.262	.260	63	-12	14	.864	-7			C44,O17(6/1/11),S12		-1.3
1887	Bro AA	48	177	24	47	3	1	0	18	7-	1		.266	.297	.294	64	-9	15	.871	-2			C45,O3R		-0.6
1888	Bro AA	45	150	23	36	3	1	0	20	9-	2		.240	.292	.333	100	0	11	.884	-2			C36,O8(1/6/1)/1		0.1
1889	†Bro AA	53	182	32	50	5	2	0	22	26-	1	7	.275	.368	.324	98	1	18	.870	-0			C53		0.4
1890	†Bro N	43	151	24	33	3	0	1	15	15-	4	9	.219	.306	.278	70	-6	10	.836	-15	86	76	C42/OR		-1.5
1891	Cin N	16	54	2	9	1	0	0	3	5-	0	9	.167	.213	.111	-5	-7	3	.868	-4	91	91	C16		-0.9
1893	Lou N	12	28	3	3	1	0	0	3	5-	0	5	.107	.242	.143	4	-4	0	.947	-1	102	149	C10/ORS		-0.3
Total 7		288	1011	145	233	25	11	1	107	85-	9	29	.230	.296	.280	71	-37	71	.867	-31	89	86	C246,O30(7/2/22),S13/1		-4.1

CLARK, RON Ronald Bruce B1.14.1943 Ft.Worth TX BR/TR/5-10/175* d9.11 C6

| 1966 | Min A | 5 | 1 | 1 | 1 | 0 | 0 | 0 | 1 | 0-0 | 0 | 0 | .000 | .500 | 1.000 | 448 | 0 | 0-0 | — | -0 | 0 | 0 | /3 | | -0.0 |
| 1967 | Min A | 20 | 60 | 7 | 10 | 3 | 1 | 2 | 11 | 4-0 | 0 | 15 | .167 | .215 | .350 | 61 | -3 | 0-0 | .891 | -2 | 101 | 0 | 3b16 | 81 | -0.5 |

YEAR	TM LG	G	AB	R	H	2B	3B	HR	RBI	BB-IB	HP	SO	AVG	OBP	SLG	AOPS	ABR	SB-CS	FA	FR	RNG	THR	GAMES AT POSITION	DL	BFW
1968	Min A	104	227	14	42	5	1	1	13	16-2	2	44	.185	.245	.229	42	-16	3-2	.932	-4	113	109	3b52,S43,2b10		-1.9
1969	Min A	5	8	0	1	0	0	0	0	0-0	0	1	.125	.125	.125	-29	-1	0-0	1.000	-1	31	0	3b2		-0.3
	Sea A	57	163	9	32	5	0	0	12	13-2	1	29	.196	.258	.227	37	-14	1-0	.966	-9	83	69	S38,3b15,2b5/1		-2.0
	Year	62	171	9	33	5	0	0	12	13-2	1	29	.193	.253	.222	34	-15	1-0	.966	-10	83	69	S38,3b17,2b5/1		-2.3
1971	Oak A	2	1	0	0	0	0	0	0	1-0	0	1	.000	.500	.000	53	0	0-0	—	0			/H		0.0
1972	Oak A	14	15	1	4	2	0	0	1	2-0	0	4	.267	.353	.400	130	1	0-0	1.000	1	93	211	2b11,3b3		0.2
	Mil A	22	54	8	10	1	1	2	5	5-0	0	11	.185	.250	.352	80	-2	0-0	.963	4	142	108	2b11,3b10		0.3
	Year	36	69	9	14	3	1	2	6	7-0	0	15	.203	.273	.362	92	-1	0-0	.974	5	126	142	2b22,3b13		0.5
1975	Phi N	1	1	0	0	0	0	0	0	0-0	0	1	.000	.000	.000	-95	0	0-0	—	0			/H		0.0
Total	7	230	530	40	100	16	3	5	43	41-4	3	98	.189	.249	.258	48	-35	4-2	.904	-12	105	89	3b99,S81,2b37/1	81	-4.2

CLARK, ROY Roy Elliott "Pepper" B5.11.1874 New Haven CT D11.1.1925 Bridgeport CT BL/TR/5-8/170 d4.19 Col Brown

YEAR	TM LG	G	AB	R	H	2B	3B	HR	RBI	BB-IB	HP	SO	AVG	OBP	SLG	AOPS	ABR	SB-CS	FA	FR	RNG	THR	GAMES AT POSITION	DL	BFW
1902	NY N	22	80	4	12	1	0	0	3	1	0		.150	.160	.162	-0	-10	5	.964	-1	88	174	O21(3/9/9)		-1.2

CLARK, WILL William Nuschler B3.13.1964 New Orleans LA BL/TL/6-1/190(185-200) [SFN85 1/2] d4.8 Col Mississippi St.

YEAR	TM LG	G	AB	R	H	2B	3B	HR	RBI	BB-IB	HP	SO	AVG	OBP	SLG	AOPS	ABR	SB-CS	FA	FR	RNG	THR	GAMES AT POSITION	DL	BFW
1986	SF N	111	408	66	117	27	2	11	41	34-10	3	76	.287	.343	.444	122	12	4-7	.989	-3	93	102	1b102	50	0.1
1987	†SF N	150	529	89	163	29	5	35	91	49-11	5	98	.308	.371	.580	155	40	5-17	.991	1	104	125	1b139		2.7
1988	SF N★	**162**	575	102	162	31	6	29	**109**	**100-27**	4	129	.282	.386	.508	163	**51**	9-1	.993	-3	94	120	1b158		4.0
1989	†SF N★	159	588	**104**	196	38	9	23	111	74-14	5	103	.333	.407	.546	176	60	8-3	.994	-1	100	115	1b158		5.1
1990	SF N★	154	600	91	177	25	5	19	95	62-9	3	97	.295	.357	.448	126	21	8-2	.992	-1	101	108	1b153		1.0
1991	SF N★	148	565	84	170	32	7	29	116	51-12	2	91	.301	.359	**.536**	153	38	4-2	**.997**	5	109	119	1b144		3.4
1992	SF N★	144	513	69	154	40	1	16	73	73-23	4	82	.300	.384	.476	152	39	12-7	.993	1	103	132	1b141		3.1
1993	SF N	132	491	82	139	27	2	14	73	63-6	6	68	.283	.367	.432	118	15	12-2	.988	-2	98	127	1b129	15	0.1
1994	Tex A★	110	389	73	128	24	2	13	80	71-11	3	59	.329	.431	.501	139	27	5-1	.990	2	108	95	1b107/D		1.8
1995	Tex A	123	454	85	137	27	3	16	92	68-6	4	50	.302	.389	.480	123	18	0-1	.994	1	102	117	1b122/D		0.6
1996	†Tex A	117	436	69	124	25	1	13	72	64-5	1	67	.284	.377	.436	100	2	2-1	.996	-2	93	90	1b117	48	-0.9
1997	Tex A	110	393	56	128	29	1	12	51	49-11	3	62	.326	.403	.496	125	16	0-0	.996	-1	95	101	1b100,D7	52	0.6
1998	†Tex A	149	554	98	169	41	1	23	102	72-5	3	97	.305	.384	.507	124	21	1-0	.989	-9	79	98	1b134,D15		0.0
1999	Bal A	77	251	40	76	15	0	10	29	38-2	2	42	.303	.395	.482	128	12	2-2	.995	2	111	101	1b63,D3	87	0.8
2000	Bal A	79	256	40	77	15	1	9	28	47-3	4	45	.301	.413	.473	131	15	4-2	.991	-1	93	90	1b72,D6	14	0.7
	†StL N	51	171	29	59	15	1	12	42	22-0	3	24	.345	.426	.655	165	18	1-0	.992	-2	94	175	1b50		1.1
Total	15	1976	7173	1186	2176	440	47	284	1205	937-155	59	1190	.303	.384	.497	137	405	67-48	.992	-14	98	111	1b1889,D33	266	24.2

CLARK, WILLIE William Otis "Wee Willie" B8.16.1872 Pittsburgh PA D11.13.1932 Pittsburgh PA BL/TL/6-0/195 d6.20

YEAR	TM LG	G	AB	R	H	2B	3B	HR	RBI	BB-IB	HP	SO	AVG	OBP	SLG	AOPS	ABR	SB-CS	FA	FR	RNG	THR	GAMES AT POSITION	DL	BFW
1895	NY N	23	88	9	23	3	2	0	16	5	0	6	.261	.301	.341	67	-5	1	.974	1	119	124	1b23		-0.3
1896	NY N	72	247	38	72	12	4	0	33	15	0	12	.291	.352	.372	94	-2	8	.975	-4	75	105	1b65		-0.5
1897	NY N	116	431	63	122	17	12	1	75	37	9		.283	.352	.385	97	-2	18	.984	3	106	122	1b107,O7L/3		0.0
1898	Pit N	57	209	29	64	9	7	1	31	22	2		.306	.378	.431	134	9	0	.984	1	98	90	1b57		0.9
1899	Pit N	81	300	49	85	13	10	0	44	35	10		.283	.377	.393	112	6	11	.989	0	89	78	1b79		0.5
Total	5	349	1275	188	366	54	35	2	199	114	29	18	.287	.359	.389	104	6	38	.983	0	95	102	1b331,O7L/3		0.6

CLARK, WIN William Winfield B4.11.1875 Circleville OH D4.15.1959 Los Angeles CA BR/TR/5-10/175 d7.12

YEAR	TM LG	G	AB	R	H	2B	3B	HR	RBI	BB-IB	HP	SO	AVG	OBP	SLG	AOPS	ABR	SB-CS	FA	FR	RNG	THR	GAMES AT POSITION	DL	BFW
1897	Lou N	4	16	2	3	0	0	0	1	2	0		.188	.235	.188	13	-2	1	.810	-2	75	80	2b3/3		-0.3

CLARKE, ARTIE Arthur Franklin B5.6.1865 Providence RI D11.14.1949 Brookline MA BR/TR/5-8/155 d4.19 Col Williams

YEAR	TM LG	G	AB	R	H	2B	3B	HR	RBI	BB-IB	HP	SO	AVG	OBP	SLG	AOPS	ABR	SB-CS	FA	FR	RNG	THR	GAMES AT POSITION	DL	BFW
1890	NY N	101	395	55	89	12	8	0	49	32	4	38	.225	.290	.296	71	-16	44	.908	-2	98	146	C36,O33(3/1/30),3b16,2b15/S		-1.3
1891	NY N	48	174	17	33	2	2	0	21	15	0	16	.190	.254	.224	41	-13	5	.916	-11	82	120	C42,3b5,O2(0/1/1)		-1.9
Total	2	149	569	72	122	14	10	0	70	47	4	54	.214	.279	.274	62	-29	49	.912	-13	90	132	C78,O35(3/2/31),3b21,2b15/S		-3.2

CLARKE, FRED Fred Clifford "Cap" B10.3.1872 Winterset IA D8.14.1960 Winfield KS BL/TR/5-10.5/165 d6.30 M19/C1 HF1945 b-Josh

YEAR	TM LG	G	AB	R	H	2B	3B	HR	RBI	BB-IB	HP	SO	AVG	OBP	SLG	AOPS	ABR	SB-CS	FA	FR	RNG	THR	GAMES AT POSITION	DL	BFW
1894	Lou N	76	314	55	86	11	7	7	48	26	4	27	.274	.337	.420	88	-8	26	.886	4	118	62	O76L		-0.8
1895	Lou N	132	550	96	191	21	5	4	82	34	10	24	.347	.396	.425	119	18	40	.881	13	103	80	O132L		1.6
1896	Lou N	131	517	96	168	15	18	9	79	43	14	34	.325	.392	.476	133	24	34	.908	2	101	38	O131L		1.2
1897	Lou N	130	526	122	205	30	13	6	67	45	25		.390	.461	.530	167	55	59	.927	5	96		O129(128/3/0),M		4.1
1898	Lou N	149	599	116	184	23	12	3	47	48	15		.307	.373	.401	123	19	40	.940	7	90	58	O149(148/0/2),M		1.1
1899	Lou N	149	606	122	206	23	9	5	70	49	16		.340	.404	.432	130	26	49	.964	-1	89	34	O145L,S3,M		1.2
1900	Pit N	106	399	84	110	15	12	3	32	51	7		.276	.368	.396	110	6	21	.944	2	55	58	O104L,M		-0.1
1901	Pit N	129	527	118	171	24	15	6	60	51	10		.324	.395	.461	143	30	23	.970	2	80	0	O127L/S3M		2.4
1902	Pit N	113	459	103	145	27	14	2	53	51	14		.316	.401	.449	157	33	29	.958	-1	83	57	O113(110/0/4),M		2.6
1903	†Pit N	104	427	88	150	**32**	15	5	70	41	5		.351	.414	**.532**	164	35	21	.962	-8	71	95	O101L,S2,M		2.0
1904	Pit N	72	278	51	85	7	11	0	25	22	5		.306	.367	.410	136	11	11	.979	-1	44	76	O70L,M		0.7
1905	Pit N	141	525	95	157	18	15	2	51	55	2		.299	.368	.402	126	17	24	.976	5	9		O137L,M		1.5
1906	Pit N	118	417	69	129	14	**13**	1	39	40	1		.309	.371	.412	138	18	18	.974	5	107	98	O110L,M		1.8
1907	Pit N	148	501	97	145	18	13	2	59	68	8		.289	.383	.389	140	26	37	**.987**	8	77	44	O144L,M		2.9
1908	Pit N	151	551	83	146	18	15	2	53	65	6		.265	.349	.363	127	18	24	.973	10	79	47	O151(150/1/0),M		2.3
1909	†Pit N	152	550	97	158	16	11	3	68	**80**	6		.287	.384	.373	124	19	31	**.987**	7	79	47	O152L,M		1.9
1910	Pit N	123	429	57	113	23	9	2	63	53	4	23	.263	.350	.373	105	3	12	.967	3	113		O118L,M		0.0
1911	Pit N	110	392	73	127	25	13	5	49	53	2	27	.324	.407	.492	146	24	10	.970	-1	108	56	O101L,M		1.9
1913	Pit N	9	13	0	1	1	0	0	0	0	0	0	.077	.077	.154	-37	-2	0	1.000	-0	77		O2L,M		-0.3
1914	Pit N	2	2	0	0	0	0	0	0	0	0		.000	.000	.000	-99	-1	0	—	0			/HM		-0.1
1915	Pit N	1	2	1	1	0	0	0	0	0	0	0	.500	.500	.500	206	0	0	—	-0	0	0	/OLM		0.0
Total	21	2246	8584	1622	2678	361	220	67	1015	875	154	135	.312	.386	.429	137	371	509	.952	62	83	49	O2193(2187/4/6),S6/3		27.9

CLARKE, HARRY Harry Corson B1.13.1861 New York NY D3.3.1923 Los Angeles CA d8.28

YEAR	TM LG	G	AB	R	H	2B	3B	HR	RBI	BB-IB	HP	SO	AVG	OBP	SLG	AOPS	ABR	SB-CS	FA	FR	RNG	THR	GAMES AT POSITION	DL	BFW
1889	Was N	1	3	0	0	0	0	0	0	0	0		1.000	.000	.000	-99	-1	0	1.000	1	915	0	/OR		0.0

CLARKE, HORACE Horace Meredith B6.2.1940 Frederiksted, V.I. BB/TR/5-9/178(170-182) d5.13

YEAR	TM LG	G	AB	R	H	2B	3B	HR	RBI	BB-IB	HP	SO	AVG	OBP	SLG	AOPS	ABR	SB-CS	FA	FR	RNG	THR	GAMES AT POSITION	DL	BFW
1965	NY A	51	108	13	28	1	0	1	9	6-0	1	6	.259	.296	.296	70	-4	2-1	.923	2	134	129	3b17,2b7/S		-0.3
1966	NY A	96	312	37	83	10	4	6	28	27-4	1	24	.266	.324	.381	107	2	5-3	.970	-11	86	106	S63,2b16,3b4		-0.2
1967	NY A	143	588	74	160	17	0	3	29	42-2	0	64	.272	.321	.316	92	-6	21-4	**.990**	16	116	97	2b140		2.8
1968	NY A	148	579	52	133	6	1	2	26	23-0	0	46	.230	.258	.254	58	-32	20-7	.984	29	119	103	2b139		1.3
1969	NY A	156	641	82	183	26	7	4	48	53-1	0	41	.285	.339	.367	101	0	33-13	.982	2	101	119	2b156		1.6
1970	NY A	158	686	81	172	24	2	4	46	35-5	2	35	.251	.286	.309	68	-8	23-7	.979	-8	104	96	2b157		-2.7
1971	NY A	159	625	76	156	23	7	2	41	64-2	2	43	.250	.321	.318	86	-12	17-7	.981	-3	106	98	2b156		-0.3
1972	NY A	147	547	65	132	20	2	3	37	56-4	4	44	.241	.315	.302	86	-8	18-6	.985	15	**115**	114	2b143		2.0
1973	NY A	148	590	60	155	21	0	2	35	47-0	2	48	.263	.317	.308	79	-16	11-10	.979	16	107	111	2b147		0.9
1974	NY A	24	47	3	11	1	0	0	4	4-0	0	5	.234	.294	.255	60	-2	1-0	1.000	1	88	62	2b20/D		-0.3
	SD N	42	90	5	17	1	0	0	4	8-0	0	6	.189	.255	.200	30	-9	0-0	.978	-0	100	51	2b21		-0.3
Total	10	1272	4813	548	1230	150	23	27	304	365-18	11	362	.256	.308	.313	82	-119	151-58	.983	58	109	104	2b1102,S64,3b21/D		4.0

CLARKE, NIG Jay Justin B12.15.1882 Amherstburg ON, Can. D6.15.1949 River Rouge MI BL/TR (BB 1907)/5-8/165 d4.26

YEAR	TM LG	G	AB	R	H	2B	3B	HR	RBI	BB-IB	HP	SO	AVG	OBP	SLG	AOPS	ABR	SB-CS	FA	FR	RNG	THR	GAMES AT POSITION	DL	BFW
1905	Cle A	5	9	2	1	1	0	0	1	1	0		.111	.200	.222	-1	0	1.000	-1	76	55	C5		-0.2
	Det A	3	7	1	3	0	0	1	1	0	1		.429	.500	.857	326	2	0	1.000	0	71	116	C2		0.2
	Cle A	37	114	9	23	5	1	0	8	10	1		.202	.266	.263	67	-4	0	.961	-2	76	55	C37		-0.3
	Year	45	130	12	27	6	1	1	10	11	1		.208	.275	.292	79	-3	0	.965	-3	103	92	C44		-0.3
1906	Cle A	57	179	22	64	12	4	1	21	13	1		.358	.404	.486	181	17	3	.982	2	117	93	C54		2.5
1907	Cle A	120	390	44	105	19	6	3	33	35	2		.269	.333	.372	123	11	3	.961	-8	100	87	C115		1.5
1908	Cle A	97	290	34	70	8	4	2	27	30	1		.241	.315	.321	106	2	6	.969	-4	**137**	101	C90		1.1
1909	Cle A	55	164	15	45	4	2	0	14	9	1		.274	.316	.323	98	-1	1	.952	-1	106	111	C44		0.3
1910	Cle A	21	58	4	9	2	0	0	2	6	0		.155	.258	.190	40	-4	0	.974	-0	90	121	C17		-0.2
1911	StL A	82	256	22	55	10	1	0	18	26	1		.215	.287	.262	56	-15	2	.926	-12	76	104	C73,1b4		-2.1
1919	Phi N	26	62	4	15	3	0	0	2	4	1	5	.242	.299	.290	72	-2	1	.969	-2	83	138	C22		-0.2
1920	Pit N	3	9	0	0	0	0	0	0	2	0	4	.000	.222	.000	-32	-0	0-0	1.000	1	101	105	C3		0.0
Total	9	506	1536	157	390	64	20	6	127	138	7	9	.254	.333	.333	102	4	16-0	.960	-23	105	99	C462,1b4		2.6

YEAR	TM LG	G	AB	R	H	2B	3B	HR	RBI	BB-IB	HP	SO	AVG	OBP	SLG	AOPS	ABR	SB-CS	FA	FR	RNG	THR	GAMES AT POSITION	DL	BFW

CLARKE, JOSH   Joshua Baldwin "Pepper" B3.8.1879 Winfield KS   D7.2.1962 Ventura CA   BL/TR/5-10/180   d6.15   b-Fred

YEAR	TM LG	G	AB	R	H	2B	3B	HR	RBI	BB-IB	HP	SO	AVG	OBP	SLG	AOPS	ABR	SB-CS	FA	FR	RNG	THR	GAMES AT POSITION	DL	BFW
1898	Lou N	6	18	0	3	0	0	0			0		.167	.211	.167	9	-2	0	.917	-0	0	0	O5(2/0/4)		-0.3
1905	StL N	50	167	31	43	3	2	3	18	27	0		.257	.361	.353	117	4	8	.942	-8	29	0	O26(2/5/19),2b16,S4		-0.4
1908	Cle A	131	492	70	119	8	4	1	21	76	4		.242	.348	.280	104	7	37	.963	-3	84	26	O131(130/1/0)		-0.5
1909	Cle A	4	12	1	0	0	0	0	0	2	0		.000	.143	.000	-52	-2	0	.600	-1	0	0	O4L		-0.4
1911	Bos N	32	120	16	28	7	3	1	4	29	1	22	.233	.387	.367	103	2	6	.938	3	107	153	O30L		0.3
Total	5	223	809	118	193	18	9	5	43	135	5	22	.239	.351	.302	102	9	51	.949	-10	77	42	O196(168/6/23),2b16,S4		-1.3

CLARKE, GREY   Richard Grey "Noisy" B9.26.1912 Fulton AL   D11.25.1993 Kannapolis NC   BR/TR/5-9/183   d4.19

YEAR	TM LG	G	AB	R	H	2B	3B	HR	RBI	BB-IB	HP	SO	AVG	OBP	SLG	AOPS	ABR	SB-CS	FA	FR	RNG	THR	GAMES AT POSITION	DL	BFW
1944	Chi A	63	169	14	44	10	1	0	27	22	2	6	.260	.352	.331	97	1	0-4	.941	1	110	77	3b45		0.0

CLARKE, SUMPTER   Sumpter Mills B10.18.1897 Savannah GA   D3.16.1962 Knoxville TN   BR/TR/5-11/170   d9.27   b-Rufe   Col South Carolina-Aiken

YEAR	TM LG	G	AB	R	H	2B	3B	HR	RBI	BB-IB	HP	SO	AVG	OBP	SLG	AOPS	ABR	SB-CS	FA	FR	RNG	THR	GAMES AT POSITION	DL	BFW
1920	Chi N	1	3	0	1	0	0	0	0	0	0	1	.333	.333	.333	90	0	0-0	1.000	-0	91	0	/3		0.0
1923	Cle A	1	3	0	0	0	0	0	0	0	0	0	.000	.000	.000	-99	-1	0-0	1.000	0	0	0	/O		-0.1
1924	Cle A	35	104	17	24	6	1	0	11	6	0	12	.231	.273	.308	49	-8	0-0	1.000	-1	97	67	O33(2/9/22)		-1.0
Total	3	37	110	17	25	6	1	0	11	6	0	13	.227	.267	.300	46	-9	0-0	1.000	-1	97	67	O34(2/9/22)/3		-1.1

CLARKE, TOMMY   Thomas Aloysius B5.9.1888 New York NY   D8.14.1945 Corona NY   BR/TR/5-11/175   d8.26   C5

YEAR	TM LG	G	AB	R	H	2B	3B	HR	RBI	BB-IB	HP	SO	AVG	OBP	SLG	AOPS	ABR	SB-CS	FA	FR	RNG	THR	GAMES AT POSITION	DL	BFW
1909	Cin N	18	52	8	13	3	2	0	10	6	0		.250	.328	.385	122	1	3	.965	2	102	119	C17		0.5
1910	Cin N	64	151	19	42	6	5	1	20	19	3	17	.278	.370	.404	131	6	1	.971	2	123	85	C56		1.3
1911	Cin N	86	203	20	49	6	7	1	25	25	1	22	.241	.328	.355	94	-2	4	.970	8	133	86	C81/1		1.1
1912	Cin N	72	146	19	41	7	2	0	22	28	1	14	.281	.400	.356	111	4	9	.983	3	98	95	C63		1.1
1913	Cin N	114	330	29	87	11	8	1	38	39	2	40	.264	.345	.355	100	1	2-1	.979	-5	99	89	C100		0.4
1914	Cin N	113	313	30	82	13	7	2	25	31	2	30	.262	.332	.367	105	2	6	.973	2	92	98	C106		1.2
1915	Cin N	96	226	23	65	7	2	0	21	33	1	22	.288	.381	.336	116	6	7-3	.981	-3	93	91	C72		1.0
1916	Cin N	78	177	10	42	10	1	0	17	24	0	20	.237	.328	.305	97	1	8	.965	-9	75	96	C51		-0.6
1917	Cin N	58	110	11	32	3	3	1	13	11	1	12	.291	.361	.400	139	5	2	.991	-3	81	82	C29		0.4
1918	Chi N	1	0	0	0	0	0	0	0	0	0		—	—	—	—	—	0	.000	0	0	0	/C		0.0
Total	10	700	1708	169	453	66	37	6	191	216	11	177	.265	.351	.358	109	24	42-4	.975	-4	100	93	C576/1		6.4

CLARKE, BOILERYARD   William Jones B10.18.1868 New York NY   D7.29.1959 Princeton NJ   BR/TR/5-11.5/170   d5.1

YEAR	TM LG	G	AB	R	H	2B	3B	HR	RBI	BB-IB	HP	SO	AVG	OBP	SLG	AOPS	ABR	SB-CS	FA	FR	RNG	THR	GAMES AT POSITION	DL	BFW
1893	Bal N	49	183	23	32	1	3	1	24	19	6	14	.175	.274	.230	34	-18	2	.909	-5	90	100	C38,1b11		-1.6
1894	Bal N	28	100	18	24	8	0	1	19	16	3	14	.240	.361	.350	69	-5	2	.903	-1	121	89	C23,1b5		-0.2
1895	†Bal N	67	241	38	70	15	3	0	35	13	9	18	.290	.350	.378	85	-5	8	.938	15	149	115	C60,1b6		1.2
1896	Bal N	80	300	48	89	14	7	2	71	14	8	12	.297	.345	.410	97	-2	7	.948	-3	111	86	C67,1b14		0.0
1897	†Bal N	64	241	32	65	7	1	1	38	9	9		.270	.320	.320	69	-11	5	.939	-9	102	64	C59,1b4		-1.2
1898	Bal N	82	285	26	69	5	2	0	27	4	15		.242	.289	.274	60	-15	2	.962	3	113	96	C70,1b10		-0.5
1899	Bos N	60	223	25	50	3	2	2	32	10	4		.224	.270	.283	47	-17	2	.940	3	119	88	C60		-0.8
1900	Bos N	81	270	35	85	5	2	1	30	9	3		.315	.344	.359	84	-7	0	.928	4	107	107	C67,1b8		0.3
1901	Was A	110	422	58	118	15	5	3	54	23	12		.280	.335	.360	94	-3	7	.952	-5	108	96	C107,1b3		0.2
1902	Was A	87	291	31	78	15	0	6	40	23	4		.268	.330	.381	96	-1	1	**.972**	-4	99	102	C87		0.3
1903	Was A	126	465	35	111	14	6	2	38	15	7		.239	.273	.308	72	-16	12	.981	-14	80	94	1b88,C37		-2.9
1904	Was A	85	275	23	58	8	1	0	17	17	5		.211	.269	.247	65	-10	5	.977	-4	73	125	C52,1b29		-1.1
1905	NY N	31	50	2	9	0	0	1	4	4	0		.180	.241	.240	42	-4	1	.973	-1	66	96	1b15,C12		-0.4
Total	13	950	3346	394	858	110	32	20	429	176	85	58	.256	.310	.326	75	-114	54	.947	-18	106	98	C739,1b193		-6.7

CLARKE, STU   William Stuart B1.24.1906 San Francisco CA   D8.26.1985 Hayward CA   BR/TR/5-8.5/160   d7.17

YEAR	TM LG	G	AB	R	H	2B	3B	HR	RBI	BB-IB	HP	SO	AVG	OBP	SLG	AOPS	ABR	SB-CS	FA	FR	RNG	THR	GAMES AT POSITION	DL	BFW
1929	Pit N	57	178	20	47	5	7	2	21	19	1	21	.264	.338	.404	81	-6	3	.919	-9	97	78	S41,3b15/2		-0.9
1930	Pit N	4	9	2	4	0	1	0	2	1	0		.444	.500	.667	178	1	0	1.000	-1	64	0	2b2		0.0
Total	2	61	187	22	51	5	8	2	23	20	1	21	.273	.346	.417	86	-5	3	.919	-9	97	78	S41,3b15,2b3		-0.9

CLARKSON, BUS   James Buster B3.13.1915 Hopkins SC   D1.18.1989 Jeannette PA   BR/TR/5-11/210   d4.30   Negro Lg 1937-50 Mil 1943-45 Col Wilberforce

YEAR	TM LG	G	AB	R	H	2B	3B	HR	RBI	BB-IB	HP	SO	AVG	OBP	SLG	AOPS	ABR	SB-CS	FA	FR	RNG	THR	GAMES AT POSITION	DL	BFW
1952	Bos N	14	25	3	5	0	0	1	3		0	3	.200	.286	.200	38	-2	0-0	.938	-2	60	0	S6,3b2		-0.4

CLARY, ELLIS   Ellis "Cat" B9.11.1916 Valdosta GA   D6.2.2000 Valdosta GA   BR/TR/5-8/160   d6.7   C7

YEAR	TM LG	G	AB	R	H	2B	3B	HR	RBI	BB-IB	HP	SO	AVG	OBP	SLG	AOPS	ABR	SB-CS	FA	FR	RNG	THR	GAMES AT POSITION	DL	BFW
1942	Was A	76	240	34	66	9	0	0	16	45	2	25	.275	.394	.313	101	4	2-0	.969	-15	86	75	2b69,3b2		-0.7
1943	Was A	73	254	36	65	19	1	0	19	44	2	31	.256	.370	.339	112	4	8-4	.945	-6	90	49	3b68/S		0.3
	StL A	23	69	15	19	2	0	0	5	11	0	6	.275	.375	.304	98	0	1-2	.972	0	107	135	3b14,2b3		0.1
	Year	96	323	51	84	21	1	0	24	55	2	37	.260	.371	.331	109	7	9-6	.949	-5	93	62	3b82,2b3/S		0.4
1944	†StL A	25	49	6	13	1	1	0	4	12	0	9	.265	.410	.327	106	1	1-0	1.000	-0	94	118	3b11,2b6		0.1
1945	StL A	26	38	6	8	1	0	1	2	2	0	3	.211	.250	.316	61	-2	0-2	.947	0	106	171	3b16,2b3		-0.3
Total	4	223	650	97	171	32	2	1	46	114	4	74	.263	.376	.323	103	10	12-8	.953	-20	94	78	3b111,2b81/S		-0.5

CLAY, DAIN   Dain Elmer "Sniffy","Ding-A-Ling" B7.10.1919 Hicksville OH   D8.28.1994 Chula Vista CA   BR/TR/5-10.5/160   d6.12   Col Kent St.

YEAR	TM LG	G	AB	R	H	2B	3B	HR	RBI	BB-IB	HP	SO	AVG	OBP	SLG	AOPS	ABR	SB-CS	FA	FR	RNG	THR	GAMES AT POSITION	DL	BFW
1943	Cin N	49	93	19	25	2	4	0	9	8	1	14	.269	.333	.376	106	0	1	.936	-2	81	103	O33(1/29/3)		-0.3
1944	Cin N	110	356	51	89	15	0	0	17	17	3	18	.250	.290	.292	67	-16	8	.993	-2	103	45	O98(5/93/0)		-2.2
1945	Cin N	153	656	81	184	29	2	1	50	37	2	58	.280	.321	.335	84	-15	19	.989	1	104	77	O152C		-1.9
1946	Cin N	121	435	52	99	17	0	2	22	53	5	40	.228	.318	.280	73	-14	11	**.988**	-5	94	85	O120(11/107/2)		-2.5
Total	4	433	1540	203	397	63	6	3	98	115	11	130	.258	.314	.312	79	-45	39	.987	-9	99	73	O403(17/381/5)		-6.9

CLAY, BILL   Frederick C. B11.23.1874 Baltimore MD   D10.12.1917 York PA   TL/?/175   d8.8

YEAR	TM LG	G	AB	R	H	2B	3B	HR	RBI	BB-IB	HP	SO	AVG	OBP	SLG	AOPS	ABR	SB-CS	FA	FR	RNG	THR	GAMES AT POSITION	DL	BFW
1902	Phi N	3	8	1	2	0	0	0		1	0		.250	.250	.250	54	0	0	.750	-1	0	0	O3L		-0.1

CLAYTON, ROYCE   Royce Spencer B1.2.1970 Burbank CA   BR/TR/6-0/183* [SFN88 1/15]   d9.20

YEAR	TM LG	G	AB	R	H	2B	3B	HR	RBI	BB-IB	HP	SO	AVG	OBP	SLG	AOPS	ABR	SB-CS	FA	FR	RNG	THR	GAMES AT POSITION	DL	BFW
1991	SF N	9	26	0	3	1	0	0	2	1-0	0	6	.115	.148	.154	-15	-4	0-0	.880	-6	30	29	S8		-1.0
1992	SF N	98	321	31	72	7	4	4	24	26-3	5	63	.224	.281	.308	71	-14	8-4	.973	-2	99	107	S94/3		-0.9
1993	SF N	153	549	54	155	21	5	6	70	38-2	5	91	.282	.331	.372	92	-7	11-10	.963	4	98	126	S153		0.7
1994	SF N	108	385	38	91	14	6	3	30	30-2	5	74	.236	.295	.327	65	-21	23-3	.973	8	106	105	S108		-0.1
1995	SF N	138	509	56	124	29	3	5	58	38-1	3	109	.244	.298	.342	70	-22	24-9	.969	3	104	115	S136		-0.7
1996	†StL N	129	491	64	136	20	4	6	35	33-4	1	89	.277	.321	.371	82	-13	33-15	.972	0	101	101	S113		-0.2
1997	StL N★	154	576	75	153	39	5	9	61	33-4	3	109	.266	.306	.398	83	-15	30-10	.973	11	106	107	S153		1.0
1998	StL N	90	355	59	83	19	1	4	29	40-1	2	51	.234	.313	.327	69	-15	19-6	.970	5	111	96	S89		15	-0.1
	†Tex A	52	186	30	53	12	1	5	24	13-0	1	32	.285	.330	.441	94	-2	5-5	.972	0	102	76	S52		0.2
1999	†Tex A	133	465	69	134	21	5	14	52	39-1	4	100	.288	.346	.445	95	-4	8-6	.961	5	107	100	S133		20	-0.9
2000	Tex A	148	513	70	124	21	5	14	54	42-1	3	92	.242	.301	.384	71	-24	11-7	.977	-6	95	87	S148		-1.8
2001	Chi A	135	433	62	114	21	4	9	60	33-2	3	72	.263	.315	.393	81	-12	10-7	.988	-1	103	94	S133		-0.4
2002	Chi A	112	342	51	86	14	2	7	35	20-0	3	67	.251	.295	.365	73	-14	5-1	.989	6	101	113	S109		0.0
2003	Mil N	146	483	49	110	16	1	11	39	49-10	3	92	.228	.301	.333	66	-25	5-2	.977	-15	96	82	S141		-2.8
2004	Col N	146	574	95	160	36	4	8	54	48-0	4	125	.279	.338	.397	79	-16	10-5	**.986**	-7	100	86	S144		-1.1
2005	Ari N	143	522	59	141	28	4	2	44	48-0	1	105	.270	.320	.351	73	-20	13-3	.982	-1	104	101	S141		-1.0
Total	15	1894	6730	862	1739	319	54	107	671	521-31	39	1277	.258	.313	.370	78	-228	215-93	.974	6	102	100	S1855/3		35	-7.3

CLEMENS, CHET   Chester Spurgeon B5.10.1917 San Fernando CA   D2.10.2002 San Clemente CA   BR/TR/6-0/175   d9.13   Mil 1944-46

YEAR	TM LG	G	AB	R	H	2B	3B	HR	RBI	BB-IB	HP	SO	AVG	OBP	SLG	AOPS	ABR	SB-CS	FA	FR	RNG	THR	GAMES AT POSITION	DL	BFW
1939	Bos N	9	23	2	5	0	0	0	1	1	0	3	.217	.250	.217	29	-2	1	.867	-1	102	0	O7L		-0.3
1944	Bos N	19	17	7	3	1	1	0	2	2	0	2	.176	.263	.353	69	-1	0	1.000	-0	123	0	O7L		-0.1
Total	2	28	40	9	8	1	1	0	3	3	0	5	.200	.256	.275	46	-3	1	.905	-1	108	0	O14L		-0.4

CLEMENS, CLEM   Clement Lambert "Count" (b Clement Lambert Ulatowski) B11.21.1886 Chicago IL   D11.2.1967 St.Petersburg FL   BR/TR/5-11/176   d5.15   Col Notre Dame

YEAR	TM LG	G	AB	R	H	2B	3B	HR	RBI	BB-IB	HP	SO	AVG	OBP	SLG	AOPS	ABR	SB-CS	FA	FR	RNG	THR	GAMES AT POSITION	DL	BFW
1914	Chi F	13	27	4	4	0	0	2	3	0	0		.148	.233	.148	6	-4	0	.950	-0	144	69	C8		-0.4
1915	Chi F	11	22	3	3	1	0	0	3	1	0		.136	.174	.182	0	-3	0	1.000	-0	122	61	C9,2b2		-0.3
1916	Chi N	10	15	0	0	0	0	0	0	5	0	6	.000	.063	.000	-72	-3	0	.941	0	128	101	C9		-0.3
Total	3	34	64	7	7	1	0	2	5	6	0	6	.109	.174	.125	-15	-10	0	.962	0	132	76	C26,2b2		-1.0

CLEMENS, DOUG   Douglas Horace B6.9.1939 Leesport PA   BL/TR/6-0/180*   d10.2   Col Syracuse

YEAR	TM LG	G	AB	R	H	2B	3B	HR	RBI	BB-IB	HP	SO	AVG	OBP	SLG	AOPS	ABR	SB-CS	FA	FR	RNG	THR	GAMES AT POSITION	DL	BFW
1960	StL N	1	0	0	0	0	0	0	0	0-0	0		—	—	—		0	0-0	1.000	0	330	0	/OR		0.0
1961	StL N	6	12	1	2	1	0	0	0	0-0	0		.167	.333	.250	53	-1	0-0	.667	-1	41	0	O3(2/0/2)		-0.2
1962	StL N	48	93	12	22	1	1	1	12	17-1	1	19	.237	.355	.301	71	-3	0-0	.974	-3	90	0	O34(7/1/27)		-0.7

YEAR	TM LG	G	AB	R	H	2B	3B	HR	RBI	BB-IB	HP	SO	AVG	OBP	SLG	AOPS	ABR	SB-CS	FA	FR	RNG	THR	GAMES AT POSITION	DL	BFW
1963	StL N	5	6	1	1	0	0	1	2	1-0	0	2	.167	.286	.667	151	0	0-0	1.000	1	96	809	O3(2/0/1)		0.1
1964	StL N	33	78	8	16	4	3	1	9	6-0	1	16	.205	.271	.372	73	-3	0-0	.970	0	93	158	O22(17/0/5)		-0.4
	Chi N	54	140	23	39	10	2	2	12	18-2	1	22	.279	.363	.421	116	4	0-0	.923	2	106	191	O40(1/2/38)	30	0.3
	Year	87	218	31	55	14	5	3	21	24-2	2	38	.252	.331	.404	100	1	0-0	.937	2	101	179	O62(18/2/43)		-0.1
1965	Chi N	128	340	36	75	11	0	4	26	38-4	2	53	.221	.300	.288	66	-14	5-8	.981	-4	86	122	O105(44/13/49)		-2.7
1966	Phi N	79	121	10	31	1	0	1	15	16-0	2	25	.256	.353	.289	81	-2	1-0	1.000	2	112	71	O28(24/2/3)/1		-0.2
1967	Phi N	69	73	2	13	5	0	4	8	8-0	1	15	.178	.262	.247	48	-5	0-0	1.000	1	52	0	O10(9/0/1)		-0.7
1968	Phi N	29	57	6	12	1	1	2	8	7-1	0	13	.211	.292	.368	99	0	0-0	1.000	-1	93	83	O17(3/0/15)		-0.2
Total	9	452	920	99	211	34	7	12	88	114-8	7	166	.229	.317	.321	78	-24	6-8	.969	-4	92	116	O263(109/18/142)/1	30	-4.7

CLEMENS, BOB   Robert Baxter B8.9.1886 Odessa MO D4.5.1964 Marshall MO BR/TR/5-9/163 d9.17 Col Missouri Valley

YEAR	TM LG	G	AB	R	H	2B	3B	HR	RBI	BB-IB	HP	SO	AVG	OBP	SLG	AOPS	ABR	SB-CS	FA	FR	RNG	THR	GAMES AT POSITION	DL	BFW
1914	StL A	7	13	1	3	0	2	0	1	2-1	0	1	.231	.375	.385	134	1		.750	-0	76	201	O5(2/1/2)		-0.1

CLEMENT, WALLY   Wallace Oakes B7.21.1881 Auburn ME D11.1.1953 Coral Gables FL BL/TR/5-11/175 d8.17 Col Tufts

1908	Phi N	16	36	0	8	3	0	0	1	0	0		.222	.222	.306	66	-1	2	1.000	2	71	312	O8L		0.0
1909	Phi N	3	3	0	0	0	0	0	0	0	0		.000	.000	.000	-99	-1	0	—	0			/H		-0.1
	Bro N	92	340	35	88	8	4	0	17	18	0		.259	.296	.306	90	-5	11	.965	2	108	129	O88(84/0/4)		-0.9
	Year	95	343	35	88	8	4	0	17	18	0		.257	.294	.303	88	-6	11	.965	2	108	129	O88(84/0/4)		-1.0
Total	2	111	379	35	96	11	4	0	18	18	0		.253	.287	.303	86	-7	13	.970	4	104	149	O96(92/0/4)		-1.0

CLEMENTE, EDGARD   Edgard Alexis (Velazquez) (b Edgard Alexis Velazquez) B12.15.1975 Santurce, PR BR/TR/5-11/188* [ColN93 10/296] d9.10

1998	Col N	11	17	2	6	0	1	0	2	2-0	0	8	.353	.421	.471	111	0	0-0	.857	-1	56	0	O7(0/1/6)		-0.1
1999	Col N	57	162	24	41	10	2	8	25	7-0	0	46	.253	.282	.488	72	-7	0-0	.972	0	104	91	O49(2/45/4)		-0.7
2000	Ana A	46	78	4	17	2	0	0	5	0-0	1	27	.218	.228	.244	19	-10	0-1	1.000	0	95	180	O32(15/5/12),D11		-1.0
Total	3	114	257	30	64	12	3	8	32	9-0	1	81	.249	.276	.412	61	-17	0-1	.974	-1	97	108	O88(17/51/22),D11		-1.8

CLEMENTE, ROBERTO   Roberto (Walker) "Bob" B8.18.1934 Carolina, PR D12.31.1972 San Juan, PR BR/TR/5-11/175* d4.17 HF1973

1955	Pit N	124	474	48	121	23	11	5	47	18-3	2	60	.255	.284	.382	76	-18	2-5	.978	11	109	181	O118(1/10/111)		-1.3
1956	Pit N	147	543	66	169	30	7	7	60	13-2	4	58	.311	.330	.431	105	3	6-6	.957	3	102	152	O139(26/22/101),2b2/3		-0.1
1957	Pit N	111	451	42	114	17	7	4	30	23-1	0	45	.253	.288	.348	72	-19	0-4	.979	7	117	101	O109(0/14/97)		-1.8
1958	Pit N	140	519	69	150	24	10	6	50	31-1	0	41	.289	.327	.408	96	-4	8-2	.982	19	122	190	O135R		1.1
1959	Pit N	105	432	60	128	17	7	4	50	15-2	3	51	.296	.322	.396	91	-7	2-3	.948	3	108	112	O104R	40	-0.9
1960	†Pit N★	144	570	89	179	22	6	16	94	39-4	2	72	.314	.357	.458	121	16	4-5	.971	-1	91	141	O142R		0.9
1961	Pit N★	146	572	100	201	30	10	23	89	35-10	3	59	.351	.390	.559	148	38	4-1	.969	9	97	205	O144(0/1/144)		3.7
1962	Pit N★	144	538	95	168	28	9	10	74	35-9	1	73	.312	.352	.454	115	11	6-4	.973	10	111	163	O142R		1.0
1963	Pit N★	152	600	77	192	23	8	17	76	31-6	4	64	.320	.356	.470	135	26	12-2	.958	-7	92	97	O151(0/8/143)		1.2
1964	Pit N★	155	622	95	211	40	7	12	87	51-16	2	87	.339	.388	.484	145	38	5-2	.968	4	107	115	O154R		3.3
1965	Pit N★	152	589	91	194	21	14	10	65	43-14	5	78	.329	.378	.463	136	27	8-0	.968	1	106	157	O145(0/5/143)		2.7
1966	Pit N★	154	638	105	202	31	11	29	119	46-13	0	109	.317	.360	.536	146	38	7-5	.965	10	113	152	O154(0/1/154)		3.7
1967	Pit N★	147	585	103	209	26	10	23	110	41-17	2	103	.357	.400	.554	170	51	9-1	.970	5	100	158	O145(0/2/144)		5.1
1968	Pit N	132	502	74	146	18	12	18	57	51-27	1	77	.291	.355	.482	152	31	2-3	.984	5	120	79	O131R		3.2
1969	Pit N★	138	507	87	175	20	12	19	91	56-16	3	73	.345	.411	.544	170	47	4-1	.980	6	104	152	O135R		4.8
1970	†Pit N★	108	412	65	145	22	10	14	60	38-14	2	66	.352	.407	.556	156	32	3-0	.966	3	98	171	O104R		3.0
1971	†Pit N★	132	522	82	178	29	8	13	86	26-5	0	65	.341	.370	.502	144	28	1-2	.993	7	112	122	O124R		3.0
1972	Pit N★	102	378	68	118	19	7	10	60	29-7	0	49	.312	.356	.479	139	18	0-0	1.000	3	115	72	O94R		1.7
Total	18	2433	9454	1416	3000	440	166	240	1305	621-167	35	1230	.317	.359	.475	130	356	83-46	.973	107	107	141	O2370(27/63/2302),2b2/3	40	34.3

CLEMENTS, ED   Edward B Philadelphia PA d6.24

| 1890 | Pit N | 1 | 1 | 0 | 0 | 0 | 0 | 0 | 0 | 0 | 0 | 0 | .000 | .000 | .000 | -99 | -1 | 0 | .400 | -1 | 52 | 0 | /S | | -0.1 |

CLEMENTS, JACK   John J. B7.24.1864 Philadelphia PA D5.23.1941 Norristown PA BL/TL/5-8.5/204 d4.22 M1

1884	Phi U	41	177	37	50	13	2	3		9			.282	.317	.429	135	3		.764	-2	210	156	O22(5/0/17),C20/S		0.1
	Phi N	9	30	3	7	0	0	0		4		8	.233	.324	.233	82	0		.827	-2			C9		-0.1
1885	Phi N	52	188	14	36	11	3	1	14	2		30	.191	.200	.298	61	-8		.891	-4			C41,O11(2/7/2)		-0.9
1886	Phi N	54	185	15	38	5	1	0	11	7		34	.205	.234	.243	45	-12	4	.930	7			C47,O7(1/0/6)		-0.2
1887	Phi N	66	246	48	69	13	7	1	47	9	4	24	.280	.317	.402	93	-3	7	.940	8			C59,3b4,S3		0.8
1888	Phi N	86	326	26	80	8	4	1	32	10	4	36	.245	.276	.304	80	-8	3	.927	0			C85/OR		0.0
1889	Phi N	78	310	51	88	17	1	4	35	29	1	21	.284	.347	.384	96	-3	3	.916	-6			C78		-0.2
1890	Phi N	97	381	64	120	23	8	7	74	45	3	30	.315	.392	.472	148	23	10	.944	4	105	80	C91,1b5,M		3.0
1891	Phi N	107	423	58	131	29	4	4	75	43	5	19	.310	.380	.445	131	18	3	.927	-6	93	86	C107,1b2		1.8
1892	Phi N	109	402	50	106	25	6	8	76	43	3	40	.264	.339	.415	128	14	7	.950	13	135	66	C109		3.3
1893	Phi N	94	376	64	107	20	3	17	80	39	5	29	.285	.360	.489	125	12	3	.942	-3	128	69	C92/1		1.4
1894	Phi N	48	171	26	60	6	5	3	36	26	9		.351	.461	.497	134	12	6	.940	-5	91	70	C48		0.8
1895	Phi N	88	322	64	127	27	2	13	75	22	9	7	.394	.446	.612	170	34	3	.969	-8	94	89	C88		2.6
1896	Phi N	57	184	35	66	5	7	5	45	17	5	14	.359	.427	.543	157	15	2	.966	-3	104	103	C53		1.4
1897	Phi N	55	185	18	44	4	2	6	36	12	6		.238	.305	.378	82	-6	3	.962	-2	103	80	C49		-0.3
1898	StL N	99	335	39	86	19	5	3	41	21	7		.257	.314	.370	94	-4	1	.971	-12	74	90	C86		-0.7
1899	Cle N	4	12	1	3	0	0	0	0	0			.250	.308	.250	58	-1	0	.938	-1	61	150	C4		-0.1
1900	Bos N	16	42	6	13	0	0	1	10	3	1		.310	.370	.405	101	0	0	.948	1	99	63	C10		0.2
Total	17	1160	4295	619	1231	226	60	77	687	341	62	301	.287	.348	.421	116	86	55	.937	-21	105	80	C1076,O41(8/7/26),1b8,3b4,S4		12.9

CLEMONS, VERNE   Verne James "Stinger","Tubby" B9.8.1891 Clemons IA D5.5.1959 Bay Pines FL BR/TR/5-9.5/190 d4.22

1916	StL A	4	7	0	1	1	0	0	0	0	0	1	.143	.143	.286	30	-1	0	.889	-0	85	160	C2		-0.1
1919	StL N	88	239	14	63	13	2	2	22	26	0	13	.264	.336	.360	116	6	4	.982	3	104	97	C75		1.6
1920	StL N	112	338	17	95	10	6	1	36	30	0	12	.281	.340	.355	103	2	1-1	.977	-7	85	90	C103		0.3
1921	StL N	117	341	29	109	16	2	2	48	33	0	17	.320	.380	.396	108	5	0-0	.985	-1	95	95	C107		1.0
1922	StL N	71	160	9	41	4	0	0	15	18	0	5	.256	.331	.281	62	-8	1-0	.996	2	106	121	C63		-0.3
1923	StL N	57	130	6	37	9	1	0	13	10	2	11	.285	.345	.369	90	-1	0-0	.981	1	105	102	C41		0.2
1924	StL N	25	56	3	18	3	0	0	6	2	0	3	.321	.345	.375	94	0	0-0	.983	-1	98	90	C17		-0.1
Total	7	474	1271	78	364	56	11	5	140	119	2	62	.286	.348	.360	99	3	6-1	.983	-4	96	98	C408		2.6

CLENDENON, DONN   Donn Alvin B7.15.1935 Neosho MO D9.17.2005 Sioux Falls SD BR/TR/6-3.5/210(201-220) d9.22 Col Morehouse

1961	Pit N	9	35	7	11	1	1	0	2	5-0	0	14	.314	.400	.400	113	1	0-0	1.000	-0	91	123	O8(1/0/7)		0.0
1962	Pit N	80	222	39	67	8	5	7	28	26-3	1	58	.302	.376	.477	128	9	16-4	.990	-2	79	122	1b52,O19(16/1/2)		0.5
1963	Pit N	154	563	65	155	28	7	15	57	39-3	5	136	.275	.326	.430	116	11	22-13	.991	5	112	130	1b151		0.7
1964	Pit N	133	457	53	129	23	8	12	64	26-2	2	96	.282	.321	.446	115	8	12-8	.990	-1	99	124	1b119		0.0
1965	Pit N	162	612	89	184	32	14	14	96	48-7	3	128	.301	.351	.467	129	23	9-9	.984	2	112	132	1b158/3		1.5
1966	Pit N	155	571	80	171	22	10	28	98	52-7	2	142	.299	.358	.520	141	30	8-7	.985	-1	103	147	1b152		2.0
1967	Pit N	131	478	46	119	15	2	13	56	34-4	1	107	.249	.298	.370	90	-7	4-4	.988	5	121	118	1b123		-1.1
1968	Pit N	158	584	63	150	20	6	17	87	47-4	1	163	.257	.309	.399	114	9	10-3	.990	8	123	112	1b155		0.9
1969	Mon N	38	129	14	31	6	1	4	14	6-1	0	32	.240	.272	.395	85	-3	0-2	.987	3	144	112	1b24,O11(9/1/1)		-0.3
	†NY N	72	202	31	51	5	0	12	37	19-4	2	62	.252	.321	.455	113	3	3-2	.984	-3	81	131	1b58/OL		-0.5
	Year	110	331	45	82	11	1	16	51	25-5	2	94	.248	.303	.432	102	0	3-4	.985	0	100	125	1b82,O12(10/1/1)		-0.8
1970	NY N	121	396	65	114	18	3	22	97	39-4	1	91	.288	.348	.515	128	14	4-1	.991	-0	96	102	1b100		0.7
1971	NY N	88	263	29	65	10	0	11	37	21-3	1	78	.247	.302	.411	101	0	1-2	.985	-2	88	101	1b72		-0.8
1972	StL N	61	136	13	26	4	0	4	9	17-4	0	37	.191	.279	.309	68	-6	1-2	.986	2	127	132	1b36		-0.7
Total	12	1362	4648	594	1273	192	57	159	682	379-46	21	1140	.274	.328	.442	118	76	90-57	.988	16	108	124	1b1200,O39(27/2/10)/3		2.9

CLEVELAND, ELMER   Elmer Ellsworth B9.15.1862 Washington DC D10.8.1913 Zimmerman PA BR/TR/5-11/190 d8.29

1884	Cin U	29	115	24	37	9	2	0		4			.322	.345	.435	125	0		.843	1	99	0	3b29		0.1
1888	NY N	9	34	6	8	0	2	2	3	1		5	.235	.297	.529	161	2	1	.667	-4	42	0	3b9		-0.2
	Pit N	30	108	10	24	2	1	2	9	5		23	.222	.270	.315	94	-1	3	.831	-5	90	86	3b30		-0.6
	Year	39	142	16	32	2	3	4	16	8		24	.225	.276	.366	111	2	4	.806	-10	80	67	3b39		-0.8
1891	Col AA	12	41	12	7	0	0	0	4	12	1	9	.171	.370	.171	59	-1	4	.843	1	111	43	3b12		0.0
Total	3	80	298	52	76	11	5	4	20	24		33	.255	.317	.366	110	0	8	.830	-8	93	37	3b80		-0.7

YEAR	TM LG	G	AB	R	H	2B	3B	HR	RBI	BB-IB	HP	SO	AVG	OBP	SLG	AOPS	ABR	SB-CS	FA	FR	RNG	THR	GAMES AT POSITION	DL	BFW

CLIBURN, STAN Stanley Gene B12.19.1956 Jackson MS BR/TR/6-0/195 [AnaA74 5/106] d5.6 twb-Stew
| 1980 | Cal A | 54 | 56 | 7 | 10 | 2 | 0 | 2 | 6 | 3-0 | 0 | 9 | .179 | .217 | .321 | 47 | -4 | 0-0 | .971 | -1 | 60 | 93 | C54 | | -0.5 |

CLIFT, HARLOND Harlond Benton "Darkie" B8.12.1912 El Reno OK D4.27.1992 Yakima WA BR/TR/5-11/180 d4.17
1934	StL A	147	572	104	149	30	10	14	56	84	2	100	.260	.357	.421	92	-7	7-2	.929	-14	89	98	3b141		-1.4
1935	StL A	137	475	101	140	26	4	11	69	83	6	39	.295	.406	.436	113	12	0-3	.934	-6	102	63	3b127,2b6		0.9
1936	StL A	152	576	145	174	40	11	20	73	115	7	68	.302	.424	.514	127	28	12-4	.951	5	105	99	3b152		3.4
1937	StL A☆	155	571	103	175	36	7	29	118	98	6	80	.306	.413	.546	139	36	8-5	.947	41	129	141	3b155		7.4
1938	StL A	149	534	119	155	25	7	34	118	118	5	67	.290	.423	.554	143	39	10-5	.962	15	102	105	3b149		5.3
1939	StL A	151	526	90	142	25	2	15	84	111	5	55	.270	.402	.411	106	10	4-3	.953	13	107	99	3b149		2.6
1940	StL A	150	523	92	143	29	5	20	87	104	2	62	.273	.396	.463	119	19	9-8	.959	9	110	104	3b147		3.0
1941	StL A	154	584	108	149	33	9	17	84	113	0	93	.255	.376	.430	109	10	6-4	.959	5	104	94	3b154		2.0
1942	StL A	143	541	108	148	39	4	7	55	106	2	48	.274	.394	.399	122	22	6-4	.941	-1	101	106	3b141/S		2.6
1943	StL A	105	379	43	88	11	3	3	25	54	1	37	.232	.329	.301	83	-7	5-4	.950	16	118	98	3b104		1.1
	Was A	8	30	4	9	0	0	0	4	5	1	3	.300	.417	.300	115	1	0-0	.968	-1	69	0	3b8 ▲		0.0
	Year	113	409	47	97	11	3	3	29	59	2	40	.237	.336	.301	85	-6	5-4	.951	15	114	91	3b112		1.1
1944	Was A	12	44	4	7	3	0	0	3	3	0	3	.159	.213	.227	27	-4	0-0	.842	-2	90	95	3b12		-0.7
1945	Was A	119	375	49	79	12	0	8	53	76	4	58	.211	.349	.307	99	4	2-1	.934	-4	98	95	3b111		0.1
Total	12	1582	5730	1070	1558	309	62	178	829	1070	41	713	.272	.390	.441	115	163	69-43	.948	75	106	100	3b1550,2b6/S		26.3

CLIFTON, FLEA Herman Earl B12.12.1909 Cincinnati OH D12.22.1997 Cincinnati OH BR/TR/5-10/160 d4.29
1934	Det A	16	16	3	1	0	0	0	1	1	0	2	.063	.118	.063	-52	-4	0-0	1.000	1	141	0	3b4/2		-0.3
1935	†Det A	43	110	15	28	5	0	0	9	5	1	13	.255	.293	.300	56	-7	2-1	.934	-1	89	74	3b21,2b5,S4		-0.7
1936	Det A	13	26	5	5	1	0	0	1	4	0	3	.192	.300	.231	33	-3	0-1	.926	-1	84	95	S6,3b2/2		-0.3
1937	Det A	15	43	4	5	1	0	0	2	7	0	10	.116	.240	.140	-2	-7	3-0	.958	-2	94	66	3b7,S4,2b3		-0.7
Total	4	87	195	27	39	7	0	0	13	17	1	28	.200	.268	.236	30	-21	5-2	.937	-3	94	85	3b34,S14,2b10		-2.0

CLINE, MONK John P. B3.3.1858 Louisville KY D9.23.1916 Louisville KY BL/TL/5-4/150 d7.4
1882	Bal AA	44	172	18	38	6	2	0		3			.221	.234	.279	79	-3		.825	4	165	87	O39(1/38/0),S8,2b2/3		-0.1
1884	Lou AA	94	396	91	115	16	7	2	39	27	4		.290	.342	.381	142	20		.875	4	142	44	O90(8/81/3),S6		1.9
1885	Lou AA	2	9	0	2	0	0	0	2	0	0		.222	.222	.333	74	0		1.000	-0	0	0	/OL3		0.0
1888	KC AA	73	293	45	69	13	2	0	19	20	2		.235	.289	.294	82	-6	29	.883	5	192	135	O70(32/0/38),2b3/3		-0.2
1891	Lou AA	19	70	11	21	3	1	0	11	16	0	2	.300	.430	.371	131	4	2	.929	-1	72	0	O19L		0.2
Total	5	232	940	165	245	39	12	2	71	66	6	2	.261	.313	.334	110	15	31	.868	12	157	78	O219(61/119/41),S14,2b5,3b3		1.8

CLINE, TY Tyrone Alexander B6.15.1939 Hampton SC BL/TL/6-0.5/170* d9.14 Col Clemson
1960	Cle A	7	26	2	8	1	1	0	2	0	0	4	.308	.308	.423	99	0	0-0	1.000	1	161	0	O6C		0.1
1961	Cle A	12	43	9	9	2	1	0	1	6-0	0	1	.209	.333	.302	73	-1	1-0	1.000	-2	70	0	O12C		-0.4
1962	Cle A	118	375	53	93	15	5	2	28	28-0	5	50	.248	.308	.331	74	-14	5-4	.992	1	109	67	O107C		-1.6
1963	Mil N	72	174	17	41	2	1	0	10	10-0	2	31	.236	.283	.259	58	-9	2-1	.992	5	114	173	O62C		-0.6
1964	Mil N	101	116	22	35	4	2	1	13	8-0	3	22	.302	.359	.397	113	2	0-1	.982	2	106	286	O54(3/49/2),1b6		0.3
1965	Mil N	123	220	27	42	5	3	0	10	16-2	1	50	.191	.246	.241	37	-19	2-2	.969	5	120	178	O86(17/58/12),1b5		-1.7
1966	Chi N	7	17	3	6	0	0	0	2	0-0	0	2	.353	.353	.353	96	0	1-0	1.000	-0	97	0	O5C		0.0
	Atl N	42	71	12	18	0	0	0	6	3-0	2	11	.254	.303	.254	56	-4	2-1	1.000	-1	111	142	O19(7/5/10),1b6		-0.6
	Year	49	88	15	24	0	0	0	8	3-0	2	13	.273	.312	.273	63	-4	3-1	1.000	-1	108	108	O24(7/10/10),1b6		-0.6
1967	Atl N	10	8	0	0	0	0	0	0	1	3	.000	.111	.000	-66	-2	0-0	1.000	0	514	0	/OL		-0.2
	SF N	64	122	18	33	5	1	0	4	9-0	1*	13	.270	.326	.393	106	1	2-1	1.000	-2	90	0	O37(17/21/3)	21	-0.3
	Year	74	130	18	33	5	1	0	4	9-0	2	16	.254	.312	.369	96	-1	2-1	1.000	-2	92	0	O38(18/21/3)		-0.5
1968	SF N	116	291	37	65	6	3	1	28	11-1	1	26	.223	.253	.275	59	-15	0-2	.971	1	99	170	O70(48/13/10),1b24		-2.2
1969	Mon N	101	209	26	50	5	3	2	12	32-1	2	22	.239	.346	.321	87	-3	4-3	.988	1	110	103	O41(7/35/0),1b17		-0.4
1970	Mon N	2	2	0	1	0	0	0	0	0-0	0	0	.500	.500	.500	168	0	0-0	—	0			/H	65	0.2
	†Cin N	48	63	13	17	7	1	0	8	12-1	0	11	.270	.387	.413	114	2	1-2	.966	1	124	138	O20(6/8/6),1b2		0.2
	Year	50	65	13	18	7	1	0	8	12-1	0	11	.277	.390	.415	115	2	1-2	.966	1	124	138*	O20(6/8/6),1b2		0.2
1971	Cin N	69	97	12	19	1	0	0	1	18-0	2	16	.196	.333	.206	56	-5	2-2	1.000	-1	95	0	O28(6/21/1),1b2		-0.7
Total	12	892	1834	251	437	53	25	6	125	153-5	21	262	.238	.304	.304	72	-67	22-19	.986	12	108	116	O548(112/402/44),1b62	86	-8.1

CLINES, GENE Eugene Anthony B10.6.1946 San Pablo CA BR/TR/5-9/170* [PitN66 6/115] d6.28 C19
1970	Pit N	31	37	4	15	2	0	0	3	2-0	0	5	.405	.436	.459	141	2	2-1	1.000	-1	45	0	O7(2/2/3)		0.1
1971	†Pit N	97	273	52	84	12	4	1	24	22-0	1	36	.308	.366	.392	114	5	15-6	.981	4	100	202	O74(20/43/13)		0.8
1972	†Pit N	107	311	52	104	15	6	0	17	16-1	2	47	.334	.369	.421	126	10	12-6	.958	-2	91	138	O83(38/17/39)		0.6
1973	Pit N	110	304	42	80	11	3	1	23	26-0	3	46	.263	.327	.329	84	-6	8-7	.968	-2	96	121	O77(7/45/25)	21	-1.2
1974	†Pit N	107	276	29	62	5	1	0	14	30-2	1	40	.225	.307	.250	59	-14	14-2	.989	5	111	137	O78(19/51/11)		-1.0
1975	NY N	82	203	25	46	6	3	0	10	11-1	1	21	.227	.269	.286	56	-13	4-4	.982	5	95	297	O60(35/34/2)		-1.2
1976	Tex A	116	446	52	123	14	3	0	38	16-0	4	52	.276	.304	.316	81	-12	11-9	.987	3	103	144	O103(96/5/4),D10		-1.6
1977	Chi N	101	239	27	70	12	2	3	41	25-2	1	25	.293	.358	.397	93	-1	1-2	.986	-6	68	88	O63(50/3/11)	16	-1.0
1978	Chi N	109	229	31	59	10	2	0	17	21-1	1	28	.258	.321	.319	71	-8	4-3	.978	-1	85	155	O66(35/10/24)		-1.2
1979	Chi N	10	10	0	2	0	0	0	0	0-0	0	1	.200	.200	.200	9	-1	0-0	—	0			/H		-0.2
Total	10	870	2328	314	645	85	24	5	187	169-7	19	291	.277	.329	.341	87	-38	71-40	.979	6	95	151	O611(302/210/132),D10	37	-5.9

CLINGMAN, BILLY William Frederick B11.21.1869 Cincinnati OH D5.14.1958 Cincinnati OH BB/TR/5-11/150 d9.9
1890	Cin N	7	27	7	7	1	0	0	5	1	0	0	.259	.286	.296	70	-1	0	.892	-1	107	181	S6/2		-0.1
1891	Cin AA	1	5	0	1	1	0	0	0	0	0	0	.200	.200	.400	66	-0	0	.667	-1	84	0	/2		-0.1
1895	Pit N	107	386	69	99	16	4	0	45	41	2	43	.256	.331	.319	72	-15	19	.888	12	114	102	3b107		0.0
1896	Lou N	121	423	57	99	10	2	2	37	57	3	51	.234	.329	.281	64	-20	19	.925	24	114	104	3b121		0.5
1897	Lou N	115	403	61	92	14	7	2	47	37	5		.228	.301	.313	64	-21	14	.947	30	124	106	3b115		0.9
1898	Lou N	154	538	65	138	12	6	0	50	51	5		.257	.327	.301	81	-12	15	.914	7	112	101	3b79,S74/OC2		0.0
1899	Lou N	110	369	68	97	15	5	0	45	46	3		.263	.349	.347	91	-3	13	.913	-3	106	112	S110		-0.1
1900	Chi N	47	159	15	33	6	0	0	11	17	2		.208	.292	.245	51	-10	6	.872	-11	91	107	S47		-1.8
1901	Was A	137	480	66	116	10	7	2	55	42	4		.242	.308	.304	71	-18	10	.932	22	107	112	S137		0.7
1903	Cle A	21	64	10	18	1	0	0	7	11	0		.281	.387	.328	118	2	2	.932	1	114	64	2b11,S7,3b3		0.4
Total	10	820	2854	413	700	86	32	8	302	303	24	94	.245	.323	.306	74	-98	98	.919	81	113	106	3b425,S381,2b14/OC		0.4

CLINTON, JIM James Lawrence "Big Jim" B8.10.1850 New York NY D9.3.1921 Brooklyn NY BR/TR/5-8.5/174 d5.18 U1 OF NA(0/8/9) ▲
1872	Eck NA	25	98	11	24	4	1	0	6			3	.245	.245	.306	81	-4	0-1	.712	-4	105	0	3b11,O9(0/7/2),2b3,C2,S2/P		-0.4
1873	Res NA	9	39	5	9	2	0	0	4	0			.231	.231	.282	56	-2	0-1	.687	-2	84	58	3b9		-0.3
1874	Atl NA	2	11	3	2	1	0	0	0	0			.182	.182	.273	49	-0	0-0	.444	-1	72	0	/2OC		0.0
1875	Atl NA	22	81	3	10	0	0	0	0	0			.123	.123	.123	-16	-8	0-0	.830	3	125	75	P17,O7R,1b5/2		0.0
1876	Lou N	16	65	8	22	0	0	0		0			.338	.338	.369	115	0		.783	0	168	231	O14R/1P		0.0
1882	Wor N	26	98	9	16	2	0	0	3	7		13	.163	.219	.184	30	-7		.734	-4	67	63	O26(21/1/4)		-1.1
1883	Bal AA	94	399	69	125	16	8	0		27			.313	.357	.393	137	17		.842	4	102	85	O92L,2b2		1.6
1884	Bal AA	104	437	82	118	12	6	4		29	13		.270	.344	.352	119	10		.807	-4	83	161	O104(37/67/0)/2		0.3
1885	Cin AA	105	408	48	97	5	5	0	34	15	7		.238	.277	.275	73	-13		.877	-2	78	114	O105C		-1.7
1886	Bal AA	23	83	8	15	1	0	0	6	4	1		.181	.227	.193	33	-6	3	.894	-1	26	142	O23C		-0.7
Total	4 NA	58	229	22	45	7	1	0	12	0		7	.197	.197	.236	43	-11	0-1	.698	-4	94	29	3b20,P18,O17R,1b5,2b5,S2,C2		-0.8
Total	6	368	1490	224	393	38	19	4	43	82	21	13	.264	.311	.323	101	1	3	.838	-6	85	123	O364(150/196/18),2b3/P1		-1.6

CLINTON, LOU Lucian Louis B10.13.1937 Ponca City OK D12.6.1997 Wichita KS BR/TR/6-1/185* d4.22
1960	Bos A	96	298	37	68	17	5	6	37	20-1	3	66	.228	.278	.419	75	-11	4-3	.966	2	113	178	O89R		-1.3
1961	Bos A	17	51	4	13	2	1	0	3	2-0	0	10	.255	.283	.333	63	-3	0-0	1.000	3	121	308	O13R		-0.1
1962	Bos A	114	398	63	117	24	10	18	75	34-3	1	79	.294	.349	.540	132	16	2-1	.979	1	103	106	O103R		1.0
1963	Bos A	148	560	71	130	23	7	22	77	49-6	1	118	.232	.294	.416	94	-6	0-0	.982	7	118	73	O146R		-1.0
1964	Bos A	37	120	15	31	4	3	6	9	11-0	0	33	.258	.310	.417	95	-1	1-0	1.000	5	115	333	O35R		0.2
	LA A	91	306	30	76	18	0	9	38	31-0	1	40	.248	.317	.395	108	3	3-0	.985	1	84	235	O86R		-0.1
	Year	128	426	45	107	22	3	12	44	40-1	1	73	.251	.315	.401	104	2	4-0	.990	6	92	262	O121R		0.1
1965	Cal A	89	222	29	54	12	3	1	44	23-1	1	37	.243	.316	.338	88	-3	2-3	.983	1	96	151	O73(1/0/72)		-0.8
	KC A	1	1	0	0	0	0	0	0	0-0	0	0	.000	.000	.000	-99	0	0-0	—	-0	0	0	/OR		0.0

YEAR	TM LG	G	AB	R	H	2B	3B	HR	RBI	BB-IB	HP	SO	AVG	OBP	SLG	AOPS	ABR	SB-CS	FA	FR	RNG	THR	GAMES AT POSITION	DL	BFW
	Cle A	12	34	2	6	1	0	1	2	3-0	0	7	.176	.243	.294	51	-2	0-0	.941	0	91	189	O9(9/1/1)		-0.3
	Year	102	257	31	60	13	3	2	10	26-1	1	44	.233	.305	.331	83	-6	2-3	.977	1	95	155	O83(10/1/74)		-1.1
1966	NY A	80	159	18	35	10	2	5	21	16-1	0	27	.220	.288	.403	101	0	0-0	.976	-1	97	77	O63(5/1/57)		-0.4
1967	NY A	6	4	1	2	0	0	0	2	1-1	0	1	.500	.600	.750	308	1	0-0	—	-0	0	0	/OL		0.1
Total	8	691	2153	270	532	112	31	65	269	188-14	7	418	.247	.308	.418	99	-6	12-7	.980	18	105	133	O619(16/2/603)		-2.7

CLOSSER, J.D. Jeffrey Darrin B1.15.1980 Beech Grove IN BB/TR/5-10/175(175-195) [AriN98 5/163] d6.30

YEAR	TM LG	G	AB	R	H	2B	3B	HR	RBI	BB-IB	HP	SO	AVG	OBP	SLG	AOPS	ABR	SB-CS	FA	FR	RNG	THR	GAMES AT POSITION	DL	BFW
2004	Col N	36	113	5	36	6	0	1	10	6-0	2	22	.319	.364	.398	86	-2	0-0	.986	3	85	147	C32		0.3
2005	Col N	92	237	31	52	12	2	7	27	32-1	1	48	.219	.314	.376	70	-10	1-0	.982	-9	64	81	C80		-1.4
Total	2	350	36	88	18	2	8	37	38-1	3	70	.251	.329	.383	75	-12	1-0	.983	-6	71	102	C112		-1.1

CLOUGH, ED Edgar George "Big Ed","Spec" B10.28.1906 Wiconisco PA D1.30.1944 Harrisburg PA BL/TL/6-0/188 d8.28 ▲

YEAR	TM LG	G	AB	R	H	2B	3B	HR	RBI	BB-IB	HP	SO	AVG	OBP	SLG	AOPS	ABR	SB-CS	FA	FR	RNG	THR	GAMES AT POSITION	DL	BFW
1924	StL N	7	14	0	1	0	0	0	1	0-0	0	3	.071	.071	.071	-63	-3	0-0	1.000	1	139	227	O6(5/0/1)		-0.2
1925	StL N	3	4	0	1	0	0	0	0	0-0	0	0	.250	.250	.250	28	0	0-0	1.000	-0	42	0	P3		0.0
1926	StL N	1	1	0	0	0	0	0	0	0-0	0	0	.000	.000	.000	-96	0	0-0	—	-0	-0	0	/P		0.0
Total	3	11	19	0	2	0	0	0	1	0-0	0	3	.105	.105	.105	-44	-3	0-0	1.000	1	139	227	O6(5/0/1),P4		-0.2

CLYBURN, DANNY Danny B4.6.1974 Lancaster SC BR/TR/6-3/220* [PitN92 2/47] d9.15

YEAR	TM LG	G	AB	R	H	2B	3B	HR	RBI	BB-IB	HP	SO	AVG	OBP	SLG	AOPS	ABR	SB-CS	FA	FR	RNG	THR	GAMES AT POSITION	DL	BFW
1997	Bal A	2	3	0	0	0	0	0	0	0-0	0	2	.000	.000	.000	-99	-1	0-0	—	-0	0	0	/OL		-0.1
1998	Bal A	11	25	6	7	0	0	1	3	1-0	0	10	.280	.308	.400	84	-1	0-0	1.000	-0	108	0	O8(5/0/5)/D		-0.1
1999	TB A	28	81	8	16	4	0	3	5	7-0	1	21	.198	.270	.358	57	-6	0-0	1.000	2	106	244	O24(14/0/10),D4	77	-0.4
Total	3	41	109	14	23	4	0	4	8	8-0	1	33	.211	.271	.358	59	-8	0-0	1.000	2	105	188	O33(20/0/15),D5	77	-0.6

CLYMER, OTIS Otis Edgar B1.27.1876 Pine Grove PA D2.27.1926 St.Paul MN BB/TR/5-11/180 d4.14

YEAR	TM LG	G	AB	R	H	2B	3B	HR	RBI	BB-IB	HP	SO	AVG	OBP	SLG	AOPS	ABR	SB-CS	FA	FR	RNG	THR	GAMES AT POSITION	DL	BFW
1905	Pit N	96	365	74	108	11	5	0	23	19	1		.296	.332	.353	102	-2	0	23	.986	-2	61	188	O89(4/0/85)/1	-0.6
1906	Pit N	11	45	7	11	0	1	0	1	3	0		.244	.292	.289	78	-1	1	.900	-1	69	0	O11R	-0.3
1907	Pit N	22	66	8	15	2	0	0	4	5	3		.227	.311	.258	77	-1	4	.923	-2	0	0	O15R/1	-0.5
	Was A	57	206	30	65	5	5	1	16	18	4		.316	.382	.403	163	15	18	.912	-2	64	0	O51(27/1/24)/1	1.1
1908	Was A	110	368	32	93	11	4	1	35	20	0		.253	.291	.313	105	1	19	.933	-1	185	299	O82(1/0/81),2b13,3b2	-0.4
1909	Was A	45	138	11	27	5	2	0	6	17	0		.196	.284	.261	76	-3	7	.922	-2	65	91	O41(0/1/40)	-0.8
1913	Chi N	30	105	16	24	5	1	0	7	14	0	18	.229	.319	.295	76	-3	9-5	.933	-3	92	57	O26(0/24/2)	-0.7
	Bos N	14	37	4	12	3	1	0	6	3	0	3	.324	.375	.459	135	2	2-1	.880	-1	104	0	O11(1/7/4)	0.0
	Year	44	142	20	36	8	2	0	13	17	0	21	.254	.333	.338	91	-1	11-6	.918	-4	95	41	O37(1/31/6)	-0.7
Total	6	385	1330	182	355	42	19	2	98	99	8	21	.267	.322	.332	106	10	83-6	.939	-15	94	142	O326(33/33/262),2b13,1b3,3b2	-2.2

CLYMER, BILL William Johnston "Derby Day Bill" B12.18.1873 Philadelphia PA D12.26.1936 Philadelphia PA d6.25 C1

YEAR	TM LG	G	AB	R	H	2B	3B	HR	RBI	BB-IB	HP	SO	AVG	OBP	SLG	AOPS	ABR	SB-CS	FA	FR	RNG	THR	GAMES AT POSITION	DL	BFW
1891	Phi N	3	11	0	0	0	0	0	0	0			.000	.154	.000	-55	-2	1	.867	1	55	0	S3		-0.3

COACHMAN, PETE Bobby Dean B11.11.1961 Cottonwood AL BR/TR/5-9/175 [CalA84 11/268] d8.18 Col South Alabama

YEAR	TM LG	G	AB	R	H	2B	3B	HR	RBI	BB-IB	HP	SO	AVG	OBP	SLG	AOPS	ABR	SB-CS	FA	FR	RNG	THR	GAMES AT POSITION	DL	BFW
1990	Cal A	16	45	3	14	3	0	0	5	1-0	2	7	.311	.354	.378	107	0	0-1	.958	0	100	183	3b9,2b2,D2		0.0

COAN, GIL Gilbert Fitzgerald B5.18.1922 Monroe NC BL/TR/6-0/180* d4.27

YEAR	TM LG	G	AB	R	H	2B	3B	HR	RBI	BB-IB	HP	SO	AVG	OBP	SLG	AOPS	ABR	SB-CS	FA	FR	RNG	THR	GAMES AT POSITION	DL	BFW
1946	Was A	59	134	17	28	3	2	3	9	7	4	37	.209	.269	.328	70	-6	2-2	.969	-1	102	0	O29(27/0/2)		-1.0
1947	Was A	11	42	5	21	3	2	0	3	5	1	6	.500	.553	.667	245	8	2-1	1.000	1	103	128	O11R		0.9
1948	Was A	138	513	56	119	13	9	7	60	41	7	78	.232	.298	.333	70	-26	23-9	.970	12	119	116	O131L		-2.1
1949	Was A	111	358	36	78	7	8	3	25	29	1	48	.218	.278	.307	56	-26	9-6	.975	-9	115	109	O97(68/29/0)		-3.1
1950	Was A	104	366	58	111	17	4	5	50	28	4	46	.303	.359	.429	106	2	10-5	.970	-0	105	54	O98(95/3/1)	35	-0.4
1951	Was A	135	538	85	163	25	7	9	62	39	6	62	.303	.357	.426	113	8	8-5	.965	18	121	162	O132L		1.6
1952	Was A	107	332	50	68	11	6	5	20	32	1	35	.205	.277	.319	68	-16	9-4	.984	0	101	77	O86L		-2.2
1953	Was A	68	168	28	33	1	4	2	17	22	3	23	.196	.301	.286	60	-10	7-0	1.000	3	114	62	O46(45/1/0)		-0.8
1954	Bal A	94	265	29	74	11	1	2	20	16	1	17	.279	.320	.351	90	-4	9-4	.968	-3	100	21	O67(36/32/0)		-1.1
1955	Bal A	61	130	18	31	7	1	1	11	13-0	1	15	.238	.313	.331	79	-4	4-2	.983	5	85	201	O43(42/0/1)		-0.5
	Chi A	17	17	0	3	0	0	0	1	0-0	0	5	.176	.176	.176	-5	-3	0-0	1.000	0	127	0	O3(1/0/2)		-0.3
	Year	78	147	18	34	7	1	1	12	13-0	1	20	.231	.298	.313	68	-7	4-2	.984	0	88	0	O46(43/0/3)		-0.8
	NY N	9	13	0	2	0	0	0	0	0-0	0	4	.154	.154	.154	-18	-2	0-0	1.000	-0	88	0	O6(1/2/4)		-0.3
1956	NY N	4	1	0	0	0	0	0	0	0-0	0	1	.000	.000	.000	-99	0	0-0	—	-0	0	0	/H		0.0
Total	11	918	2877	384	731	98	44	39	278	232-0	28	384	.254	.316	.359	84	-79	83-38	.973	29	108	99	O749(664/67/21)	35	-9.3

COBB, JOE Joseph Stanley (b Joseph Stanley Serafin) B1.24.1895 Hudson PA D12.24.1947 Allentown PA BR/TR/5-9/170 d4.25 Mil 1918

YEAR	TM LG	G	AB	R	H	2B	3B	HR	RBI	BB-IB	HP	SO	AVG	OBP	SLG	AOPS	ABR	SB-CS	FA	FR	RNG	THR	GAMES AT POSITION	DL	BFW
1918	Det A	1	0	0	0	0	0	0	1	0	0		—	1.000	—	210	0			—	-0	0	0	/H		0.0

COBB, TY Tyrus Raymond "The Georgia Peach" B12.18.1886 Narrows (Banks Co.) GA D7.17.1961 Atlanta GA BL/TR/6-1/175 d8.30 M6 HF1936 OF(35/2194/706)

YEAR	TM LG	G	AB	R	H	2B	3B	HR	RBI	BB-IB	HP	SO	AVG	OBP	SLG	AOPS	ABR	SB-CS	FA	FR	RNG	THR	GAMES AT POSITION	DL	BFW
1905	Det A	41	150	19	36	6	0	1	15	10	0		.240	.287	.300	86	-2	2	.958	2	141	96	O41(2/39/0)		-0.2
1906	Det A	98	358	45	113	15	5	1	34	19	5		.316	.355	.394	131	12	23	.961	4	112	134	O96(18/55/24)		1.2
1907	†Det A	150	605	97	**212**	28	14	5	**119**	24	5		**.350**	.380	**.468**	164	40	53	.961	12	156	**267**	O150R		4.9
1908	†Det A	150	581	88	**188**	**36**	20	4	**108**	34	6		**.324**	.367	**.475**	166	40	39	.944	3	132	101	O150R		4.1
1909	†Det A	156	573	**116**	216	33	10	**9**	**107**	48	6		**.377**	**.431**	**.517**	190	59	76	.946	2	120	162	O156R		**6.0**
1910	Det A	140	506	**106**	194	35	13	8	91	64	4		**.383**	**.456**	**.551**	202	61	65	.958	3	112	87	O137(0/111/26)		6.3
1911	Det A	146	591	**147**	**248**	**47**	**24**	8	**127**	44	8		**.420**	**.467**	**.621**	193	**72**	**83**	.957	7	111	95	O146C		**6.6**
1912	Det A	140	553	120	**226**	30	23	7	83	43	5		**.409**	**.456**	**.584**	203	72	61	.940	-4	98	96	O140C		5.6
1913	Det A	122	428	70	167	18	16	4	67	58	4	31	**.390**	**.467**	.535	196	54	51	.947	-1	97	112	O118(0/116/2)/2		4.6
1914	Det A	98	345	69	127	22	11	2	57	57	6	22	**.368**	**.466**	**.513**	188	41	35-17	.949	-14	79	61	O96C		2.3
1915	Det A	**156**	563	**144**	**208**	31	13	3	99	118	10	43	**.369**	**.486**	.487	182	67	**96-38**	.951	-9	88	95	O156C		5.7
1916	Det A	145	542	**113**	201	31	10	5	68	78	2	39	**.371**	**.452**	**.493**	177	55	**68-24**	.953	-8	93	85	O143C/1		4.6
1917	Det A	152	588	107	**225**	**44**	**24**	6	102	61	4	34	**.383**	**.444**	**.570**	210	76	55	.973	4	100	116	O152(0/123/29)		**7.4**
1918	Det A	111	421	83	161	19	**14**	3	64	41	2	21	**.382**	**.440**	.515	**196**	48	34	.975	-1	99	88	O95(0/92/3),1b13,P2/23		**4.3**
1919	Det A	124	497	92	**191**	36	13	1	70	38	1	22	**.384**	.429	.515	168	45	28	.973	-6	88	107	O123C		3.1
1920	Det A	112	428	86	143	28	8	2	63	58	2	28	.334	.416	.451	133	23	15-10	.966	-11	90	57	O112C		0.4
1921	Det A	128	507	124	197	37	16	12	101	56	5	19	.389	.452	.596	167	52	22-15	.970	6	96	**169**	O121C,M		4.8
1922	Det A	137	526	99	211	42	16	4	99	55	4	24	.401	.462	.565	172	58	9-13	.980	-5	93	96	O134(0/133/1),M		4.2
1923	Det A	145	556	103	189	40	7	6	88	66	3	14	.340	.413	.469	135	30	9-10	.969	3	107	92	O141C,M		2.5
1924	Det A	155	625	115	211	38	10	4	79	85	5	18	.338	.418	.450	126	27	23-14	**.986**	0	101	82	O155C,M		2.0
1925	Det A	121	415	97	157	31	12	12	102	65	5	12	.378	.468	.598	**171**	43	13-9	.948	0	96	82	O105(0/101/4)/PM		3.5
1926	Det A	79	233	48	79	18	5	4	62	26	1	2	.339	.408	.511	137	13	9-4	.950	-4	89	80	O55(15/39/1),M		0.7
1927	Phi A	133	490	104	175	32	7	5	93	67	1	12	.357	.440	.482	131	26	22-16	.969	-5	96	73	O127(0/52/75)		1.2
1928	Phi A	95	353	54	114	27	4	1	40	34	4	16	.323	.389	.431	112	9	6-8	.964	-1	104	35	O85R		-0.1
Total	24	3034	11434	2246	4189	724	295	117	1938	1249	94	357	.366	.433	.512	167	1025	897-178	.961	-28	104	108	O2934C,1b14,P3,2b2/3		85.7

COBLE, DAVE David Lamar B12.24.1912 Monroe NC D10.15.1971 Orlando FL BR/TR/6-1/183 d5.1 Col South Carolina-Aiken

YEAR	TM LG	G	AB	R	H	2B	3B	HR	RBI	BB-IB	HP	SO	AVG	OBP	SLG	AOPS	ABR	SB-CS	FA	FR	RNG	THR	GAMES AT POSITION	DL	BFW
1939	Phi N	15	25	2	7	1	0	0	3	8	0	3	.280	.280	.320	63	-1	0	.938	-2	49	121	C13		-0.3

COCHRAN, GEORGE George Leslie B2.12.1889 Rusk TX D5.21.1960 Harbor City CA TR d7.29

YEAR	TM LG	G	AB	R	H	2B	3B	HR	RBI	BB-IB	HP	SO	AVG	OBP	SLG	AOPS	ABR	SB-CS	FA	FR	RNG	THR	GAMES AT POSITION	DL	BFW
1918	Bos A	24	60	7	7	0	0	0	3	10	2	6	.117	.264	.117	15	-6	3	.960	-1	102	133	3b22/S		-0.7

COCHRANE, DAVE David Carter B1.31.1963 Riverside CA BB/TR/6-2/180* [NYN81 4/81] d9.2 OF(42/0/12)

YEAR	TM LG	G	AB	R	H	2B	3B	HR	RBI	BB-IB	HP	SO	AVG	OBP	SLG	AOPS	ABR	SB-CS	FA	FR	RNG	THR	GAMES AT POSITION	DL	BFW
1986	Chi A	19	62	4	12	2	0	1	2	5-1	0	22	.194	.254	.274	42	-5	0-0	.872	-4	95	33	3b18/S		-0.9
1989	Sea A	54	102	13	24	4	1	3	7	14-0	1	27	.235	.333	.382	98	0	0-2	.905	-5	89	151	S30,1b9,3b9,2b4,O3L,C2		-0.6
1990	Sea A	15	20	3	3	0	0	0	0	0-0	1	8	.150	.150	.150	-16	-3	0-0	1.000	1	58	0	S5,1b3,3b3/C		-0.2
1991	Sea A	65	178	16	44	13	0	2	22	9-0	1	36	.247	.286	.354	76	-6	0-1	.969	-6	84	0	O26(2/0/3),C19,3b13,1b4/D		-1.3
1992	Sea A	65	152	10	38	5	0	2	12	12-0	0	34	.250	.309	.322	76	-5	1-0	.879	-1	83	293	O25(16/0/9),C21,3b10,1b3,S3,D2/2	66	-0.3
Total	5	218	514	43	121	24	1	8	43	40-1	3	129	.235	.294	.333	73	-19	1-3	.925	-15	82	125	O54L,3b53,C43,S39,1b19,2b5,D3	66	-3.6

COCHRANE, MICKEY Gordon Stanley B4.6.1903 Bridgewater MA D6.28.1962 Lake Forest IL BL/TR/5-10.5/180 d4.14 M5/C1 HF1947 Col Boston U.

YEAR	TM LG	G	AB	R	H	2B	3B	HR	RBI	BB-IB	HP	SO	AVG	OBP	SLG	AOPS	ABR	SB-CS	FA	FR	RNG	THR	GAMES AT POSITION	DL	BFW
1925	Phi A	134	420	69	139	21	5	6	55	44	2	19	.331	.397	.448	107	5	7-4	.984	-6	96	80	C133		0.7
1926	Phi A	120	370	50	101	8	9	8	47	56	2	15	.273	.369	.408	97	-2	5-2	.975	12	109	96	C115		1.7
1927	Phi A	126	432	80	146	20	6	12	80	50	2	7	.338	.409	.495	127	17	9-6	.986	5	**117**	72	C123		2.8
1928	Phi A	131	468	92	137	26	12	10	57	76	3	25	.293	.395	.464	122	17	7-5	.966	5	109	63	C130		2.8
1929	†Phi A	135	514	113	170	37	8	7	95	69	2	8	.331	.412	.475	123	21	7-7	.983	6	93	62	C135		3.3

YEAR	TM LG	G	AB	R	H	2B	3B	HR	RBI	BB-IB	HP	SO	AVG	OBP	SLG	AOPS	ABR	SB-CS	FA	FR	RNG	THR	GAMES AT POSITION	DL	BFW
1930	†Phi A	130	487	110	174	42	5	10	85	55	1	18	.357	.424	.526	133	27	5-0	.993	6	99	77	C130		3.8
1931	†Phi A	122	459	87	160	31	6	17	89	56	3	21	.349	.423	.553	146	31	2-3	.986	11	128	89	C117		4.5
1932	Phi A	139	518	118	152	35	4	23	112	100	4	22	.293	.412	.510	132	29	0-1	.993	9	107	92	C137/OL		4.2
1933	Phi A	130	429	104	138	30	4	15	60	106	3	22	.322	**.459**	.515	156	43	8-6	.989	-6	88	82	C128		4.1
1934	†Det A★	129	437	74	.140	32	1	2	76	78	4	26	.320	.428	.412	117	17	8-4	.988	1	135	119	C124,M		2.4
1935	†Det A☆	115	411	93	131	33	3	5	47	96	4	15	.319	.452	.450	139	32	5-5	.989	-0	129	83	C110,M		3.6
1936	Det A	44	126	24	34	8	0	2	17	46	0	15	.270	.465	.381	111	6	1-1	.983	-6	118	61	C42,M		0.2
1937	Det A	27	98	27	30	10	1	2	12	25	1	4	.306	.452	.490	134	7	0-1	1.000	-2	89	69	C27,M		0.6
Total	13	1482	5169	1041	1652	333	64	119	832	857	29	217	.320	.419	.478	127	250	64-45	.985	37	109	82	C1451/OL		34.7

COCKMAN, JIM James B4.26.1873 Guelph ON, Can. D9.28.1947 Guelph ON, Can. BR/TR/5-6/145 d9.28

YEAR	TM LG	G	AB	R	H	2B	3B	HR	RBI	BB-IB	HP	SO	AVG	OBP	SLG	AOPS	ABR	SB-CS	FA	FR	RNG	THR	GAMES AT POSITION	DL	BFW
1905	NY A	13	38	5	4	0	0	0	2	4	0		.105	.190	.105	-5	-4	2	.875	-2	90	0	3b13		-0.6

COCKRELL, ALAN Atlee Alan B12.5.1962 Kansas City KS BR/TR/6-2/212 [SFN84 1/9] d9.7 C1 Col Tennessee

| 1996 | Col N | 9 | 8 | 0 | 2 | 1 | 0 | 0 | 2 | 0-0 | 0 | 4 | .250 | .222 | .375 | 50 | -1 | 0-0 | — | -0 | 0 | 0 | /OR | | -0.1 |

COFFEY, JACK John Francis B1.28.1887 New York NY D2.14.1966 Bronx NY BR/TR/5-11/178 d6.23 Col Fordham

1909	Bos N	73	257	21	48	4	4	0	20	11	3		.187	.229	.233	41	-19	2	.896	-7	102	67	S73		-2.6
1918	Det A	22	67	7	14	0	2	0	4	8	1	6	.209	.303	.269	75	-2	2	.957	-2	89	64	2b22		-0.4
	Bos A	15	44	5	7	1	0	1	2	3	0	2	.159	.213	.250	40	-3	2	.955	1	115	0	3b14/2		-0.2
	Year	37	111	12	21	1	2	1	6	11	1	8	.189	.268	.261	62	-6	4	.959	-0	93	61	2b23,3b14		-0.6
Total	2	110	368	33	69	5	6	1	26	22	4	8	.188	.241	.242	48	-24	6	.896	-7	102	67	S73,2b23,3b14		-3.2

COFFIE, IVANON Ivanon Angelino B5.16.1977 Willemstad, Curacao, Netherlands Antilles BL/TR/6-1/192 d7.15

| 2000 | Bal A | 23 | 60 | 6 | 13 | 4 | 0 | 1 | 6 | 5-0 | 1 | 11 | .217 | .284 | .317 | 56 | -4 | 1-0 | .971 | 0 | 113 | 40 | 3b15,S4/D | | -0.3 |

COGGINS, FRANK Franklin B5.22.1944 Griffin GA BB/TR/6-2/187* d9.10

1967	Was A	19	75	9	23	3	0	1	8	2-0	0	17	.307	.321	.387	114	1	1-0	.964	3	121	101	2b19		0.6
1968	Was A	62	171	15	30	6	1	0	7	9-2	0	33	.175	.215	.222	34	-14	1-1	.953	-5	92	109	2b52		-1.7
1972	Chi N	6	1	1	0	0	0	0	0	1-0	0	0	.000	.500	.000	48	0	0-0	—				/H		0.0
Total	3	87	247	25	53	9	1	1	15	12-2	0	50	.215	.249	.271	59	-13	2-1	.957	-2	100	107	2b71		-1.1

COGGINS, RICH Richard Allen B12.7.1950 Indianapolis IN BL/TL/5-8/170* [BalA68 21/475] d8.29

1972	Bal A	16	39	5	13	4	0	1	1-0		0	6	.333	.350	.436	128	1	0-2	1.000	4	172	148	O13(0/9/6)		0.4
1973	†Bal A	110	389	54	124	19	9	7	41	28-2	0	24	.319	.363	.468	132	15	17-9	.987	1	102	88	O101(0/39/76)/D		1.3
1974	†Bal A	113	411	53	100	13	3	4	32	29-3	5	31	.243	.299	.319	80	-11	26-6	.984	-3	102	37	O105(2/30/87)		-1.6
1975	Mon N	13	37	1	10	3	1	0	4	1-0	0	7	.270	.289	.405	87	-1	0-0	1.000	-1	89	0	O10(9/0/2)	45	-0.2
	NY A	51	107	7	24	1	0	1	6	7-0	0	16	.224	.272	.262	52	-7	3-3	.970	1	105	118	O36(3/25/8),D9		-0.7
1976	NY A	7	4	1	1	0	0	0	1	0-0	0	1	.250	.250	.250	47	0	1-0	1.000	0	201	0	O2(0/1/1)/D		0.0
	Chi A	32	96	4	15	2	0	0	6	6-0	0	15	.156	.206	.177	13	-11	3-1	1.000	-3	81	52	O26(6/2/23)		-1.6
	Year	39	100	5	16	2	0	0	6	6-0	0	16	.160	.208	.180	14	-11	4-1	1.000	-2	84	51	O28(6/3/24)/D		-1.6
Total	5	342	1083	125	287	42	13	12	90	72-5	5	100	.265	.312	.361	93	-14	50-21	.986	-1	103	67	O293(20/106/203),D11	45	-2.4

COGSWELL, ED Edward B2.25.1854 , England D7.27.1888 Fitchburg MA BR/TR/5-8/150 d7.11

1879	Bos N	49	236	51	76	8	1	1	18	8			.322	.344	.377	135	9		.967	1	78	120	1b49		0.6
1880	Tro N	47	209	41	63	7	3	0	13	11		10	.301	.336	.364	130	6		.961	1	117	76	1b47		0.5
1882	Wor N	13	51	10	7	1	0	0	1	6		6	.137	.228	.157	26	-4		.937	-1	82	128	1b13		-0.6
Total	3	109	496	102	146	16	4	1	32	25		21	.294	.328	.349	121	11		.960	1	95	102	1b109		0.5

COHEN, ALTA Alta Albert "Schoolboy" B12.25.1908 New York NY D3.11.2003 Maplewood NJ BL/TL/5-10.5/170 d4.15

1931	Bro N	1	3	1	2	0	0	0	0	0	0	0	.667	.667	.667	261	1	0	1.000	1	46	1623	/OR		0.2
1932	Bro N	9	32	1	5	1	0	0	1	3	0	7	.156	.229	.188	14	-4	0	.850	1	73	517	O8(5/3/0)		-0.4
1933	Phi N	19	32	6	6	1	0	0	1	6	0	4	.188	.316	.219	49	-2	0	1.000	0	116	0	O7L		-0.2
Total	3	29	67	8	13	2	0	0	2	9	0	11	.194	.289	.224	42	-5	0	.925	2	90	369	O16(12/3/1)		-0.4

COHEN, ANDY Andrew Howard B10.25.1904 Baltimore MD D10.29.1988 El Paso TX BR/TR/5-8/155 d6.6 M1/C1 b-Syd Col Alabama

1926	NY N	32	35	4	9	0	1	0	4	1	2	2	.257	.278	.314	60	-2	0	.792	0	123	0	2b10,S10,3b2		-0.2
1928	NY N	129	504	64	138	24	7	9	59	31	2	17	.274	.314	.403	87	-11	3	.969	2	103	115	2b126,S3/3		-0.6
1929	NY N	101	347	40	102	12	2	5	47	11	2	15	.294	.319	.383	73	-16	3	.964	10	108	106	2b94/S3		-0.3
Total	3	262	886	108	249	36	10	14	114	43	4	34	.281	.317	.392	81	-29	6	.964	11	105	110	2b230,S14,3b4		-1.1

COKER, JIMMIE Jimmie Goodwin B3.28.1936 Holly Hill SC D10.29.1991 Throckmorton TX BR/TR/5-11/195* d9.11

1958	Phi N	2	6	0	1	0	0	0	0	0-0	0	1	.167	.167	.167	-12	-1	0-0	1.000	-0	52	0	C2		-0.1
1960	Phi N	81	252	18	54	5	3	6	34	23-2	4	45	.214	.289	.329	69	-11	0-3	.982	-1	54	116	C76		-1.0
1961	Phi N	11	25	3	10	1	0	1	4	7-1	0	4	.400	.531	.560	193	4	0-0	.984	-0	34	52	C11		0.4
1962	Phi N	5	3	0	0	0	0	0	1	1-0	0	1	.000	.200	.000	-27	-1	0-0	—				/H		-0.1
1963	SF N	4	5	0	1	0	0	0	0	1-0	0	1	.200	.333	.200	58	0	0-0	1.000	-1	12	0	C2		-0.1
1964	Cin N	11	32	3	10	2	0	1	4	3-1	0	5	.313	.371	.469	130	1	0-0	1.000	1	86	293	C11		0.3
1965	Cin N	24	61	3	15	2	0	2	9	8-1	0	16	.246	.329	.377	93	0	0-0	.993	3	53	115	C19		0.3
1966	Cin N	50	111	9	28	3	0	4	14	8-1	0	5	.252	.300	.387	83	-3	0-1	.979	5	165	156	C39,O2L		-0.1
1967	Cin N	45	97	8	18	2	1	2	4	4-1	0	20	.186	.218	.289	39	-8	0-1	.976	-2	80	92	C34		-1.0
Total	9	233	592	44	137	15	4	16	70	55-7	4	99	.231	.299	.351	77	-19	1-5	.983	0	64	127	C194,O2L		-1.4

COLANGELO, MIKE Michael Gus B10.22.1976 Teaneck NJ BR/TR/6-1/185* [AnaA97 21/627] d6.13 Col George Mason [DL 2000 Ana A 181]

1999	Ana A	1	2	0	1	0	0	0	1-0		0	0	.500	.667	.500	204	1	0-0	1.000	1	72	2192	/OL	112	0.1
2001	SD N	50	91	10	22	3	3	2	8	8-0	1	30	.242	.310	.407	90	-2	0-0	.979	-0	95	74	O40(25/14/4)		-0.3
2002	Oak A	20	23	2	4	1	0	0	0	1-0	1	2	.174	.240	.217	23	-3	0-0	1.000	-1	95	0	O19(14/1/5)		-0.3
Total	3	71	116	12	27	4	3	2	8	10-0	2	32	.233	.305	.371	79	-5	0-0	.985	-0	94	100	O60(40/15/9)	293	-0.5

COLAVITO, ROCKY Rocco Domenico B8.10.1933 New York NY BR/TR/6-3/190(183-199) d9.10 C6

1955	Cle A	5	9	3	4	2	0	0	0	0-0	0	2	.444	.444	.667	189	1	0-0	1.000	1	133	463	O2R		0.2
1956	Cle A	101	322	55	89	11	4	21	65	49-0	2	46	.276	.372	.531	134	15	0-1	.968	-1	99	89	O98R		1.0
1957	Cle A	134	461	66	116	26	0	25	84	71-0	1	80	.252	.348	.471	124	16	1-6	.962	8	118	127	O130R		1.8
1958	Cle A	143	489	80	148	26	3	41	113	84-6	2	89	.303	.405	**.620**	183	57	0-2	.981	-0	97	127	O129(1/0/129),1b11/P		5.1
1959	Cle A★	154	588	90	151	24	0	**42**	111	71-8	2	86	.257	.337	.512	135	27	3-3	.985	5	114	81	O154R		2.5
1960	Det A	145	555	67	138	18	1	35	87	53-4	4	80	.249	.317	.474	108	4	3-6	.976	1	100	118	O144R		-0.2
1961	Det A★	163	583	129	169	30	2	45	140	113-2	2	75	.290	.402	.580	156	49	1-2	.975	7	103	129	O161(150/0/20)		4.6
1962	Det A★	161	601	90	164	30	2	37	112	96-7	2	68	.273	.371	.514	132	29	2-0	.992	12	111	105	O161L		3.2
1963	Det A	160	597	91	162	29	2	22	91	84-9	1	78	.271	.358	.437	119	18	0-0	.988	6	105	89	O159(142/0/23)		1.4
1964	KC A★	160	588	89	161	31	2	34	102	83-4	5	56	.274	.366	.507	136	31	3-1	.973	-3	102	0	O159(3/0/157)		1.3
1965	Cle A★	**162**	592	92	170	25	2	26	**108**	93-11	3	63	.287	.383	.468	140	35	1-1	**1.000**	-1	98	92	O162(1/0/162)		2.3
1966	Cle A★	151	533	68	127	13	0	30	72	76-4	3	81	.238	.336	.432	119	14	2-1	.982	3	104	127	O146R		0.8
1967	Cle A	63	191	10	46	9	0	5	21	24-0	1	31	.241	.329	.366	104	2	2-2	.962	-2	93	107	O50(28/0/31)		-0.4
	Chi A	60	190	20	42	4	1	3	29	25-2	0	10	.221	.306	.300	85	-3	1-1	.977	-4	87	56	O58(11/0/54)		-1.2
	Year	123	381	30	88	13	1	8	50	49-2	1	41	.231	.317	.333	95	-2	3-3	.970	-5	90	60	O108(39/0/85)		-1.6
1968	LA N	40	113	8	23	0	3	11	15-1		0	18	.204	.295	.310	89	-1	0-1	1.000	-1	91	95	O33(21/0/13)		-0.5
	NY A	39	91	13	20	7	0	5	22	14-0	1	12	.220	.330	.451	139	4	0-0	.933	4	63	69	O28(6/0/22)/P		-0.2
Total	14	1841	6503	971	1730	283	21	374	1159	951-58	29	880	.266	.359	.489	132	298	19-27	.980	28	103	105	O1774(524/0/1285),1b11,P2		22.3

COLBERN, MIKE Michael Malloy B4.19.1955 Santa Monica CA BR/TR/6-3/205* [ChiA76 2/32] d7.18 Col Arizona St.

1978	Chi A	48	141	11	38	5	1	2	20	1-0	2	36	.270	.281	.362	80	-4	0-1	.969	-1	96	104	C47/D		-0.4
1979	Chi A	32	83	5	20	5	1	0	8	4-0	0	25	.241	.276	.325	61	-5	0-0	.971	-0	77	161	C32	30	-0.4
Total	2	80	224	16	58	10	2	2	28	5-0	2	61	.259	.279	.348	73	-9	0-1	.970	-2	89	126	C79/D	30	-0.8

COLBERT, CRAIG Craig Charles B2.13.1965 Iowa City IA BR/TR/6-0/190(190-214) [SFN86 20/500] d4.6 Col Oral Roberts

1992	SF N	49	126	10	29	5	2	1	16	9-0	0	22	.230	.277	.325	75	-5	1-0	.994	-3	122	98	C35,3b9,2b2	15	-0.6
1993	SF N	23	37	2	6	2	0	1	5	3-1	0	13	.162	.225	.297	40	-3	0-0	.982	2	271	81	C10,2b2/3	79	-0.1
Total	2	72	163	12	35	7	2	2	21	12-1	0	35	.215	.266	.319	67	-8	1-0	.990	-1	156	94	C45,3b10,2b4	94	-0.7

YEAR	TM LG	G	AB	R	H	2B	3B	HR	RBI	BB-IB	HP	SO	AVG	OBP	SLG	AOPS	ABR	SB-CS	FA	FR	RNG	THR	GAMES AT POSITION	DL	BFW

COLBERT, NATE Nathan B4.9.1946 St.Louis MO BR/TR/6-2/209(190-209) d4.14

1966	Hou N	19	7	3	0	0	0	0	0	0-0	0	4	.000	.000	.000	-99	-2	0-0	—	0			/H	16	-0.2
1968	Hou N	20	53	5	8	1	0	0	4	1-0	0	23	.151	.164	.170	1	-6	1-1	.952	-1	107	163	O11(3/5/3),1b5		-1.0
1969	SD N	139	483	64	123	20	9	24	66	45-7	3	123	.255	.322	.482	127	14	6-4	.990	.0	107	85	1b134		0.4
1970	SD N	156	572	84	148	17	6	38	86	56-8	4	150	.259	.328	.509	125	17	3-5	.991	-8	84	95	1b153/3		-0.4
1971	SD N★	156	565	81	149	25	3	27	84	63-6	4	119	.264	.339	.462	134	24	5-2	.993	3	104	92	1b153		1.6
1972	SD N★	151	563	87	141	27	2	38	111	70-14	2	127	.250	.333	.508	147	33	15-6	.996	6	112	88	1b150		2.9
1973	SD N★	145	529	73	143	25	2	22	80	54-9	8	146	.270	.343	.450	130	21	9-8	.992	5	111	100	1b144		1.3
1974	SD N	119	368	53	76	16	0	14	54	62-6	1	108	.207	.319	.364	96	-1	10-2	.988	9	133	80	1b79,O48L		0.2
1975	Det A	45	156	16	23	4	2	4	18	17-0	0	52	.147	.231	.276	41	-13	0-2	.982	-4	72	80	1b44/D		-2.2
	Mon N	38	81	10	14	4	1	4	11	5-3	1	31	.173	.230	.395	67	-4	0-0	.988	-1	83	123	1b22		-0.7
1976	Mon N	14	40	5	8	2	0	2	6	9-1	0	16	.200	.347	.400	106	1	3-1	1.000	1	90	644	O7L,1b6		0.2
	Oak A	2	5	0	0	0	0	0	0	1-1	0	3	.000	.167	.000	-50	-1	0-0	—	0			D2		-0.1
Total	10	1004	3422	481	833	141	25	173	520	383-55	23	902	.243	.322	.451	120	83	52-31	.991	10	103	91	1b890,O66(58/5/3),D3/3	16	2.0

COLBRUNN, GREG Gregory Joseph B7.26.1969 Fontana CA BR/TR/6-0/205(190-215) [MonB87 6/148] d7.9 [DL 2005 Tex A 183]

1992	Mon N	52	168	12	45	8	0	2	18	6-1	2	34	.268	.294	.351	85	-4	3-2	.992	-1	90	81	1b47	16	-0.9
1993	Mon N	70	153	15	39	9	0	4	23	6-1	1	33	.255	.282	.392	76	-5	4-2	.995	-1	94	101	1b61	100	-0.9
1994	Fla N	47	155	17	47	10	0	6	31	9-0	2	27	.303	.345	.484	110	2	1-1	.988	-2	91	92	1b41	63	-0.3
1995	Fla N	138	528	70	146	22	1	23	89	22-4	6	69	.277	.311	.453	97	-4	11-3	.996	-3	90	97	1b134		-1.8
1996	Fla N	141	511	60	146	26	2	16	69	25-1	14	76	.286	.333	.438	105	3	4-5	.995	4	111	124	1b134	15	-0.5
1997	Min A	70	217	24	61	14	0	5	26	8-1	1	38	.281	.307	.415	85	-5	1-2	.988	-0	103	135	1b64,D2		-1.0
	†Atl N	28	54	3	15	3	0	2	9	2-0	1	11	.278	.316	.444	95	-1	0-0	.984	1	120	60	1b14,D3		-0.1
1998	Col N	62	122	12	38	8	2	2	13	8-0	1	23	.311	.359	.459	93	-1	3-3	.992	1	125	93	1b27,O5R/C		-0.2
	†Atl N	28	44	6	13	3	0	1	10	2-0	3	11	.295	.367	.432	110	1	1-0	1.000	0	84	41	1b9/ORD		0.0
	Year	90	166	18	51	11	2	3	23	10-0	4	34	.307	.361	.452	98	0	4-3	.993	1	115	81	1b36,O6R,D3/C		-0.2
1999	†Ari N	67	135	20	44	5	3	5	24	12-0	4	23	.326	.392	.519	128	6	1-1	.996	1	116	105	1b39,3b2,D2		0.4
2000	Ari N	116	329	48	103	22	1	15	57	43-2	10	45	.313	.405	.523	128	16	0-1	.989	1	102	96	1b99/3D		0.8
2001	Ari N	59	97	12	28	8	0	4	18	9-0	2	14	.289	.373	.495	114	2	0-0	.987	-1	160	107	1b14,3b10	70	0.1
2002	Ari N	72	171	30	57	16	2	10	27	13-1	0	19	.333	.378	.626	148	11	0-0	.993	-4	64	71	1b40,3b5,D3	25	0.5
2003	Sea A	22	58	7	16	1	1	3	7	4-0	0	16	.276	.323	.483	114	1	0-1	.989	-1	68	64	1b14,D4	107	-0.1
2004	Ari N	20	27	1	3	0	0	0	1	0-0	5	6	.111	.143	.111	-31	-5	0-0	1.000	0	155	0	1b2,D2	114	-0.5
Total	13	992	2769	337	801	155	12	98	422	170-11	49	444	.289	.338	.460	105	17	29-21	.993	-4	99	102	1b739,D21,3b18,O6R/C	693	-4.5

COLE, ALEX Alexander B8.17.1965 Fayetteville NC BL/TL/6-0/170(170-184) [StLN85*2/43] d7.27 Col Manatee (FL) CC

1990	Cle A	63	227	43	68	5	4	0	13	28-0	1	38	.300	.379	.357	107	3	40-9	.961	-1	99	104	O59C/D		0.7
1991	Cle A	122	387	58	114	17	3	0	21	58-2	1	47	.295	.386	.354	106	6	27-17	.970	0	102	118	O107(8/101/0),D6	22	0.5
1992	Cle A	41	97	11	20	1	0	0	5	10-0	1	21	.206	.284	.216	43	-7	9-2	.971	-2	80	81	O24(18/5/2),D4		-0.9
	†Pit N	64	205	33	57	3	7	0	10	18-1	0	46	.278	.335	.361	98	-1	7-4	.989	-2	87	151	O53(0/1/52)		-0.3
1993	Col N	126	348	50	89	9	4	0	24	43-3	2	58	.256	.339	.305	64	-17	30-13	.982	-1	98	111	O93C		-1.5
1994	Min A	105	345	68	102	15	5	4	23	44-2	1	60	.296	.375	.403	100	1	29-8	.969	-1	107	79	O100(16/84/0)/D		0.5
1995	Min A	28	79	10	27	3	2	1	14	8-0	1	15	.342	.409	.468	127	3	1-3	.938	-1	93	109	O23C,D2	111	-0.3
1996	Bos A	24	72	13	16	5	1	0	7	8-0	0	11	.222	.296	.319	56	-5	5-3	.974	-2	79	90	O24C		-0.6
Total	7	573	1760	286	493	58	26	5	117	217-8	7	296	.280	.360	.351	90	-17	148-59	.971	-8	98	107	O483(42/390/54),D14	133	-1.5

COLE, DICK Richard Roy B5.6.1926 Long Beach CA BR/TR/6-2/175* d4.27 C1

1951	StL N	15	36	4	7	1	0	0	3	6	0	5	.194	.310	.222	45	-3	0-0	.969	3	142	125	2b14		0.1
	Pit N	42	106	9	25	4	0	1	11	15	0	9	.236	.331	.302	69	-4	0-1	.981	-1	92	77	2b34,S8		-0.4
	Year	57	142	13	32	5	0	1	14	21	0	14	.225	.325	.282	63	-7	0-1	.978	2	105	90	2b48,S8		-0.3
1953	Pit N	97	235	29	64	13	1	0	23	38	0	26	.272	.374	.336	87	-2	2-2	.965	-5	95	85	S77,2b7/1		-0.2
1954	Pit N	138	486	40	131	22	5	1	40	41	0	48	.270	.323	.342	75	-17	0-0	.949	-8	100	68	S66,3b55,2b17		-1.9
1955	Pit N	77	239	16	54	8	3	0	21	18-1	2	22	.226	.285	.285	53	-16	0-0	.935	1	103	112	3b33,2b24,S12		-1.3
1956	Pit N	72	99	7	21	2	1	0	9	11-0	0	9	.212	.291	.253	49	-7	0-0	.947	-3	106	163	3b18,2b12,S6		-1.0
1957	Mil N	15	14	1	1	0	0	0	0	3-1	0	5	.071	.235	.071	-13	-2	0-0	.952	0	89	212	2b10/13		-0.2
Total	6	456	1215	106	303	50	10	2	107	132-2	2	124	.249	.322	.312	69	-51	2-3	.961	-13	98	78	S169,2b118,3b107,1b2		-4.9

COLE, STU Stewart Bryan B2.7.1966 Charlotte NC BR/TR/6-1/175 [KCA87 3/67] d9.5 Col North Carolina-Charlotte

| 1991 | KC A | 9 | 7 | 1 | 1 | 0 | 0 | 0 | 0 | 2-0 | 0 | 2 | .143 | .333 | .143 | 36 | -1 | 0-0 | 1.000 | -1 | 111 | 0 | 2b5/SD | | -0.2 |

COLE, WILLIS Willis Russell B1.6.1882 Milton Junction WI D10.11.1965 Madison WI BR/TR/5-8/170 d8.22

1909	Chi A	46	165	17	39	7	3	0	16	16	1		.236	.308	.315	101	0	3	.889	-5	85	84	O46C		-0.8
1910	Chi A	22	80	6	14	2	1	0	2	4	1		.175	.224	.225	42	-6	0	.974	1	77	205	O22C		-0.7
Total	2	68	245	23	53	9	4	0	18	20	2		.216	.281	.286	82	-6	3	.912	-5	82	122	O68C		-1.5

COLEMAN, CHOO CHOO Clarence B8.25.1937 Orlando FL BL/TR/5-9/165* d4.16

1961	Phi N	34	47	3	6	1	0	0	4	2-0	1	8	.128	.180	.149	-12	-8	0-0	.977	-2	49	55	C14		-0.9
1962	NY N	55	152	24	38	7	2	6	17	11-2	1	24	.250	.303	.441	96	-1	2-4	.995	-4	90	102	C44		-0.4
1963	NY N	106	247	22	44	0	0	3	9	24-3	5	49	.178	.264	.215	39	-19	5-5	.969	7	103	141	C91/OL		-1.1
1966	NY N	6	16	2	3	0	0	0	0	0-0	0	4	.188	.188	.188	5	-2	0-0	.963	-2	36	143	C5		-0.4
Total	4	201	462	51	91	8	2	9	30	37-5	7	85	.197	.266	.281	52	-30	7-9	.977	-1	93	123	C154/OL		-2.9

COLEMAN, CURT Curtis Hancock B2.18.1887 Salem OR D7.1.1980 Newport OR BL/TR/5-11/180 d4.13 Col Oregon

| 1912 | NY A | 12 | 37 | 8 | 9 | 4 | 0 | 0 | 4 | 7 | 0 | | .243 | .364 | .351 | 99 | 0 | 0 | .865 | -0 | 113 | 67 | 3b10 | | 0.1 |

COLEMAN, DAVE David Lee B10.26.1950 Dayton OH BR/TR/6-3/195 [BosA69 18/419] d4.13

| 1977 | Bos A | 12 | 12 | 1 | 0 | 0 | 0 | 0 | 0 | 0-0 | 0 | 3 | .000 | .077 | .000 | -69 | -3 | 0-0 | 1.000 | -1 | 59 | 0 | O9(3/5/1) | | -0.4 |

COLEMAN, JERRY Gerald Francis B9.14.1924 San Jose CA BR/TR/6-0/170* d4.20 Mil 1952-53 M1

1949	†NY A	128	447	54	123	21	5	2	42	63	2	44	.275	.367	.358	92	-4	8-6	.981	5	95	111	2b122,S4		0.7
1950	NY A★	153	522	69	150	19	6	6	69	67	3	38	.287	.372	.381	96	-2	3-2	.977	-12	89	111	2b152,S6		-0.6
1951	†NY A	121	362	48	90	11	2	3	43	31	4	36	.249	.315	.315	73	-14	6-1	.968	6	96	123	2b102,S18		-0.2
1952	NY A	11	42	6	17	2	1	0	4	5	0	4	.405	.468	.500	180	1	0-1	.971	2	98	200	2b11		0.7
1953	NY A	8	10	1	2	0	0	0	0	2	0	2	.200	.200	.200	9	-1	0-0	1.000	1	102	191	2b7/S		0.1
1954	NY A	107	300	39	65	7	1	3	21	26	0	29	.217	.278	.277	54	-20	3-0	.977	15	114	132	2b79,S30/3		0.2
1955	†NY A	43	96	12	22	5	0	0	8	11-0	2	11	.229	.321	.281	64	-4	0-2	.966	-1	84	142	S29,2b13/3	88	-0.4
1956	†NY A	80	183	15	47	5	1	0	18	12-2	1	18	.257	.305	.295	61	-11	1-2	.979	8	111	136	2b41,S24,3b18		0.1
1957	†NY A	72	157	23	42	7	2	2	12	20-0	1	21	.268	.354	.376	101	1	1-1	.969	3	105	152	2b45,3b21,S4		0.6
Total	9	723	2119	267	558	77	18	16	217	235-2	13	218	.263	.340	.339	83	-50	22-15	.976	26	98	122	2b572,S116,3b41	88	1.1

COLEMAN, GORDY Gordon Calvin B7.5.1934 Rockville MD D3.12.1994 Cincinnati OH BL/TR/6-2/218(208-220) d9.19

1959	Cle A	6	15	5	8	0	1	0	2	1-0	0	2	.533	.563	.667	245	3	0-0	.955	0	184	46	1b3		0.3
1960	Cin N	66	251	26	68	10	1	6	32	12-1	2	32	.271	.308	.390	89	-4	1-1	.998	7	135	132	1b66		0.3
1961	†Cin N	150	520	63	149	27	4	26	87	45-11	2	67	.287	.341	.504	120	14	1-3	.991	6	113	78	1b150		1.1
1962	Cin N	136	476	73	132	13	1	28	86	36-4	3	68	.277	.331	.485	113	7	2-3	.989	-1	95	95	1b128		-0.3
1963	Cin N	123	365	38	90	20	2	14	59	29-1	2	51	.247	.303	.427	105	2	1-0	.987	2	105	96	1b107		-0.1
1964	Cin N	89	198	18	48	6	2	5	27	13-1	1	30	.242	.291	.369	82	-5	2-0	.990	3	126	92	1b49		-0.4
1965	Cin N	108	325	39	98	19	0	14	57	24-4	1	38	.302	.348	.489	125	11	0-0	.991	0	94	82	1b89		0.7
1966	Cin N	91	227	20	57	7	0	5	37	16-2	0	45	.251	.299	.348	73	-8	2-1	.986	-1	88	76	1b65		-1.3
1967	Cin N	4	7	0	0	0	0	0	1	1-1	0	0	.000	.125	.000	-55	-1	0-0	1.000	0	122	0	1b2		-0.2
Total	9	773	2384	282	650	102	11	98	387	177-25	11	333	.273	.324	.448	106	19	9-8	.990	16	107	91	1b659		-0.4

COLEMAN, JOHN John Francis B3.6.1863 Saratoga Springs NY D5.31.1922 Detroit MI BL/TR (BB 1887)/5-9.5/170 d5.1 Col Syracuse ▲

1883	Phi N	90	354	33	83	12	8	0	32	15		39	.234	.266	.314	83	-7		.886	6	111	53	P65,O31(19/12/0)/2		0.2
1884	Phi N	43	171	16	42	7	2	0	22	8		20	.246	.279	.310	89	-2		.844	3	120	224	O27(3/19/5),P21,1b2		0.0
	Phi AA	28	107	16	22	3	2	0		5	0		.206	.241	.336	81	-3		.743	-1	147	165	O24(11/13/0),P3,1b2		-0.4
1885	Phi AA	96	398	71	119	15	11	3	70	25	3		.299	.345	.415	131	13		.844	1	153	170	O93(1/17/76),P8		1.0
1886	Phi AA	121	492	67	121	18	16	0	65	33	2		.246	.348	.348	100	-2	28	.862	2	122	160	O115(0/5/110),1b6,P3/2		-0.1

YEAR	TM LG	G	AB	R	H	2B	3B	HR	RBI	BB-IB	HP	SO	AVG	OBP	SLG	AOPS	ABR	SB-CS	FA	FR	RNG	THR	GAMES AT POSITION	DL	BFW
	Pit AA	11	43	3	15	2	1	0	9	2	0		.349	.378	.442	157	3	1	.786	-1	69		O11L		0.1
	Year	132	535	70	136	20	17	0	74	35	2		.254	.302	.355	105	1	29	.858	0	118	148	O126(11/5/110),1b6,P3/2		0.0
1887	Pit N	115	475	75	139	21	11	2	54	31	1	40	.293	.337	.396	111	8	25	.899	-1	83	83	O115(0/2/113),1b2		0.5
1888	Pit N	116	438	49	101	11	4	0	26	29	4	52	.231	.285	.274	86	-5	15	.928	2	130	66	O91(0/3/88),1b25		-0.6
1889	Phi AA	6	19	1	1	0	0	0	1	1	0		.053	.100	.053	-57	-4	1	.929	0	148	0	P5/OL		0.0
1890	Pit N	3	11	1	2	0	0	0	0	3	0		.182	.357	.182	66	0	1	1.000	-1	0	0	O2(1/0/1),P2		0.0
Total	8	629	2508	332	645	88	56	7	279	152	10	154	.257	.302	.345	101	1	71	.873	10	123	132	O510(47/71/393),P107,1b37,2b2		0.7

COLEMAN, MICHAEL   Michael Donnell B8.16.1975 Nashville TN BR/TR/5-11/180(180-225) [BosA94 18/495] d9.1 [DL 2000 Bos A 96, 2002 Bos A 25]

YEAR	TM LG	G	AB	R	H	2B	3B	HR	RBI	BB-IB	HP	SO	AVG	OBP	SLG	AOPS	ABR	SB-CS	FA	FR	RNG	THR	GAMES AT POSITION	DL	BFW
1997	Bos A	8	24	2	4	1	0	0	2	0-0	0	11	.167	.167	.208	-3	-4	1-0	.941	-1	90	0	O7C		-0.4
1999	Bos A	2	5	1	1	0	0	0	0	1-0	0	2	.200	.333	.200	39	0	0-0	—	-1	0	0	O2(1/1/0)		-0.1
2001	NY A	12	38	5	8	0	0	1	7	0-0	0	15	.211	.205	.289	30	-4	0-1	1.000	-2	51	0	O9(1/7/3),D3		-0.6
Total	3	22	67	8	13	1	0	1	9	1-0	0	26	.194	.203	.254	19	-8	1-1	.960	-4	63	0	O18(2/15/3),D3	121	-1.1

COLEMAN, ED   Parke Edward B12.1.1901 Canby OR D8.5.1964 Oregon City OR BL/TR/6-2/200 d4.15 Col Oregon St.

YEAR	TM LG	G	AB	R	H	2B	3B	HR	RBI	BB-IB	HP	SO	AVG	OBP	SLG	AOPS	ABR	SB-CS	FA	FR	RNG	THR	GAMES AT POSITION	DL	BFW
1932	Phi A	26	73	13	25	7	1	1	13	1	0	6	.342	.351	.507	115	1	1-0	1.000	2	92	299	O16R		0.2
1933	Phi A	102	388	48	109	26	3	6	68	19	2	51	.281	.318	.410	91	-6	0-0	.948	-2	105	63	O89(1/0/88)		-1.3
1934	Phi A	101	329	53	92	14	6	14	60	29	2	34	.280	.342	.486	116	5	0-1	.980	1	94	134	O86R		0.1
1935	Phi A	10	13	0	1	0	0	0	0	0	0	3	.077	.077	.077	-61	-3	0-0	—	-0	0	0	/OR		-0.3
	StL A	108	397	66	114	15	9	17	71	53	1	41	.287	.373	.499	118	9	0-2	.974	-2	90	131	O102R		0.1
	Year	118	410	66	115	15	9	17	71	53	1	44	.280	.364	.485	113	7	0-2	.974	-2	90	131	O103R		-0.2
1936	StL A	92	137	13	40	5	4	2	34	15	1	17	.292	.366	.431	93	-2	0-0	.939	-2	93	0	O18R		-0.4
Total	5	439	1337	193	381	67	23	40	246	117	6	152	.285	.345	.459	105	4	1-3	.966	-4	96	112	O312(1/0/311)		-1.6

COLEMAN, RAY   Raymond Leroy B6.4.1922 Dunsmuir CA BL/TR/5-11/170* d4.22

YEAR	TM LG	G	AB	R	H	2B	3B	HR	RBI	BB-IB	HP	SO	AVG	OBP	SLG	AOPS	ABR	SB-CS	FA	FR	RNG	THR	GAMES AT POSITION	DL	BFW
1947	StL A	110	343	34	89	9	7	2	30	26	1	32	.259	.314	.344	81	-10	2-5	.984	1	100	115	O93(21/0/73)		-1.4
1948	StL A	17	29	2	5	0	1	0	2	2	0	5	.172	.226	.241	24	-3	1-0	.889	-1	88	0	O5R		-0.4
	Phi A	68	210	32	51	6	6	0	21	31	0	17	.243	.340	.329	78	-7	4-3	.978	1	92	166	O53(0/32/21)		-0.8
	Year	85	239	34	56	6	7	0	23	33	0	22	.234	.327	.318	72	-10	5-3	.972	0	92	153	O58(0/32/26)		-1.2
1950	StL A	117	384	54	104	25	6	8	55	32	2	37	.271	.330	.430	90	-7	7-5	.985	3	107	86	O98(27/43/28)		-0.8
1951	StL A	91	341	41	96	16	5	5	55	24	0	32	.282	.329	.402	94	-4	3-4	.975	2	100	138	O87(47/5/42)		-0.7
	Chi A	51	181	21	50	8	7	3	21	15	0	14	.276	.332	.448	112	1	2-3	.980	3	117	69	O51(23/29/12)		0.2
	Year	142	522	62	146	24	12	8	76	39	0	46	.280	.330	.418	100	-3	5-7	.977	5	106	113	O138(70/34/54)		-0.5
1952	Chi A	85	195	19	42	7	1	2	14	13	0	17	.215	.264	.292	54	-13	0-0	.978	2	104	129	O73(28/33/15)		-1.4
	StL A	20	46	5	9	3	0	0	1	5	1	4	.196	.288	.261	52	-3	0-0	1.000	-0	107	0	O16(5/5/6)		-0.4
	Year	105	241	24	51	10	1	2	15	18	1	21	.212	.269	.286	54	-15	0-0	.982	2	105	107	O89(33/38/21)		-1.8
Total	5	559	1729	208	446	74	33	20	199	148	4	158	.258	.318	.374	84	-46	19-20	.980	11	103	112	O476(151/147/202)		-5.7

COLEMAN, BOB   Robert Hunter B9.26.1890 Huntingburg IN D7.16.1959 Boston MA BR/TR/6-2/190 d6.13 M3/C3

YEAR	TM LG	G	AB	R	H	2B	3B	HR	RBI	BB-IB	HP	SO	AVG	OBP	SLG	AOPS	ABR	SB-CS	FA	FR	RNG	THR	GAMES AT POSITION	DL	BFW
1913	Pit N	24	50	5	9	2	0	0	9	7	0	8	.180	.281	.220	46	-3	0	.978	-3	83	89	C24		-0.5
1914	Pit N	73	150	11	40	4	1	1	14	15	0	32	.267	.333	.327	101	0	3	.977	2	113	89	C72		0.7
1916	Cle A	19	28	3	6	2	0	0	4	7	0	6	.214	.371	.286	92	0	0	.972	-1	99	136	C12		0.0
Total	3	116	228	19	55	8	1	1	27	29	0	46	.241	.327	.298	87	-3	3	.976	-2	105	94	C108		0.2

COLEMAN, VINCE   Vincent Maurice B9.22.1961 Jacksonville FL BB/TR/6-0/185(170-195) [StLN82 10/257] d4.18 Col Florida A&M

YEAR	TM LG	G	AB	R	H	2B	3B	HR	RBI	BB-IB	HP	SO	AVG	OBP	SLG	AOPS	ABR	SB-CS	FA	FR	RNG	THR	GAMES AT POSITION	DL	BFW
1985	†StL N	151	636	107	170	20	10	1	40	50-1	0	115	.267	.320	.335	84	-15	110-25	.979	5	101	143	O150(138/17/10)		0.0
1986	StL N	154	600	94	139	13	8	0	29	60-0	2	98	.232	.301	.280	62	-31	107-14	.972	-1	96	111	O149(131/20/0)		-2.1
1987	†StL N	151	623	121	180	14	10	3	43	70-0	1	126	.289	.363	.358	90	-8	109-22	.970	-0	93	146	O150L		0.1
1988	StL N★	153	616	77	160	20	10	3	38	49-4	1	111	.260	.313	.339	86	-12	81-27	.971	-3	92	152	O150(127/24/0)		-1.1
1989	StL N★	145	563	94	143	21	9	2	28	50-0	2	90	.254	.316	.334	83	-12	65-10	.962	-10	86	63	O142L		-1.7
1990	StL N	124	497	73	145	18	9	6	39	35-1	2	88	.292	.340	.400	102	3	77-17	.981	2	96	135	O120(118/0/2)		1.0
1991	NY N	72	278	45	71	7	5	1	17	39-0	0	47	.255	.347	.327	91	-3	37-14	.979	-7	82	135	O70C	84	-0.7
1992	NY N	71	229	37	63	11	1	2	21	27-9	2	41	.275	.355	.358	104	2	24-9	.991	-2	93	73	O61(41/21/0)	77	0.1
1993	NY N	92	373	64	104	14	8	2	25	21-1	0	58	.279	.316	.375	86	-3	38-13	.982	-3	96	76	O90L		-1.1
1994	KC A	104	438	61	105	14	12	2	33	29-0	1	72	.240	.285	.340	58	-29	50-8	.962	-4	79	155	O99L,D5		-2.7
1995	KC A	75	293	39	84	13	4	2	20	27-1	1	40	.287	.348	.399	92	-4	26-9	.975	-5	74	143	O69(57/2/13),D4		-0.8
	†Sea A	40	162	27	47	10	2	1	9	10-1	1	32	.290	.335	.395	88	-3	16-7	.988	2	116	84	O38L		-0.1
	Year	115	455	66	131	23	6	5	29	37-2	2	80	.288	.343	.398	91	-7	42-16	.980	-3	89	122	O107(95/2/13),D4		-0.9
1996	Cin N	33	84	10	13	1	1	1	4	9-0	0	31	.155	.237	.226	22	-10	12-2	.968	0	92	203	O20L		-0.8
1997	Det A	6	14	0	1	0	0	0	0	0-0	0	3	.071	.133	.071	-45	-3	0-0	1.000	-0	84	0	O3(2/1/0),D		-0.3
Total	13	1371	5406	849	1425	176	89	28	346	477-12	15	960	.264	.324	.345	83	-136	752-177	.974	-26	92	123	O1311(1153/155/25),D10	161	-10.2

COLES, CAD   Cadwallader B1.17.1886 Rock Hill SC D6.30.1942 Miami FL BL/TR/6-0.5/174 d4.16 Col Clemson

YEAR	TM LG	G	AB	R	H	2B	3B	HR	RBI	BB-IB	HP	SO	AVG	OBP	SLG	AOPS	ABR	SB-CS	FA	FR	RNG	THR	GAMES AT POSITION	DL	BFW
1914	KC F	78	194	17	49	7	3	1	25	5	0	30	.253	.271	.335	67	-13	6	.889	-5	77	82	O39(3/31/6),1b3		-2.2

COLES, CHUCK   Charles Edward B6.27.1931 Fredericktown PA D1.25.1996 Myrtle Beach SC BL/TL/5-9/180 d9.19 Col Waynesburg

YEAR	TM LG	G	AB	R	H	2B	3B	HR	RBI	BB-IB	HP	SO	AVG	OBP	SLG	AOPS	ABR	SB-CS	FA	FR	RNG	THR	GAMES AT POSITION	DL	BFW
1958	Cin N	5	11	0	2	1	0	0	2	2-0	0	6	.182	.308	.273	52	-1	0-0	1.000	0	132	0	O4(3/1/0)		-0.1

COLES, DARNELL   Darnell B6.2.1962 San Bernardino CA BR/TR/6-1/185(170-190) [SeaA80 1/6] d9.4 OF(123/0/228)

YEAR	TM LG	G	AB	R	H	2B	3B	HR	RBI	BB-IB	HP	SO	AVG	OBP	SLG	AOPS	ABR	SB-CS	FA	FR	RNG	THR	GAMES AT POSITION	DL	BFW
1983	Sea A	27	92	9	26	7	0	1	6	7-0	0	12	.283	.333	.391	95	0	3-3	.941	-2	84	136	3b26		-0.4
1984	Sea A	48	143	15	23	3	1	0	6	17-0	2	26	.161	.259	.196	28	-14	2-1	.918	-4	82	130	3b42,O3L,D3	22	-1.9
1985	Sea A	27	59	8	14	4	0	1	5	9-0	1	17	.237	.338	.356	92	0	0-1	.918	1	113	130	S15,3b7,O2L,D2		0.2
1986	Det A	142	521	67	142	30	2	20	86	45-3	6	84	.273	.333	.453	112	9	6-2	.938	-4	97	105	3b133,S2,O2R,D7	15	0.3
1987	Det A	53	149	14	27	5	1	4	15	15-1	2	23	.181	.263	.309	54	-10	1-0	.847	-1	109	87	3b36,1b9,O8(2/0/6)/SD	33	-1.2
	Pit N	40	119	20	27	8	0	6	24	19-2	1	20	.227	.333	.445	104	1	1-3	1.000	-4	63	60	O26(1/0/26),3b10/1		-0.5
1988	Pit N	68	211	20	49	13	1	5	36	20-1	3	41	.232	.299	.374	96	-1	1-1	.990	-5	92	0	O55R/13		-0.8
	Sea A	55	195	32	57	10	1	10	34	17-0	4	26	.292	.356	.508	134	9	3-2	.986	-4	75	122	O47(43/0/4)/1D		0.4
1989	Sea A	146	535	54	135	21	3	10	59	27-1	6	61	.252	.294	.359	81	-15	5-4	.975	7	101	136	O89(7/0/83),3b26,1b18,D12		-1.2
1990	Sea A	37	107	9	23	5	1	2	16	4-1	1	17	.215	.248	.336	62	-6	0-0	.970	1	91	0	O20R,3b6,1b4/D		-0.6
	Det A	52	108	13	22	2	0	1	4	12-1	0	21	.204	.281	.250	50	-7	0-4	1.000	2	96	0	D30,O11(4/0/9),3b8		-0.8
	Year	89	215	22	45	7	1	3	20	16-2	1	38	.209	.265	.293	56	-13	0-4	.977	3	92	0	O31(4/0/29),D31,3b14,1b4		-1.4
1991	SF N	11	14	1	3	0	0	0	0	0-0	0	2	.214	.214	.214	21	-2	0-0	—	-1	0	0	O3R/1		-0.2
1992	Cin N	55	141	16	44	11	2	3	18	3-0	0	15	.312	.322	.482	123	4	1-0	1.000	0	103	38	3b23,1b20,O5(3/0/2)	40	0.3
1993	Tor A	64	194	26	49	9	1	4	26	16-1	4	29	.253	.319	.371	84	-1	1-1	.957	-6	91	45	O44(31/0/13),3b16/1D		-1.2
1994	Tor A	48	143	15	30	6	1	4	15	10-0	1	25	.210	.263	.350	56	-10	0-0	.980	-2	108	63	O29(24/0/5),3b10,b7/D		-1.3
1995	StL N	63	138	13	31	7	0	3	16	16-1	3	20	.225	.316	.341	73	-5	0-0	.951	-8	64	32	3b22,1b18/OL		-1.4
1997	Col N	21	22	1	7	1	0	1	2	0-0	1	6	.318	.348	.500	97	0	0-0	1.000	-0	123	0	3b3,O2L		0.0
Total	14	957	2891	333	709	142	14	75	368	237-12	35	445	.245	.307	.382	88	-51	20-23	.923	-30	97	93	3b366,O347R,1b84,D67,S18	110	-10.3

COLETTA, CHRIS   Christopher Michael B8.2.1944 Brooklyn NY BL/TL/5-11/190 d8.15

YEAR	TM LG	G	AB	R	H	2B	3B	HR	RBI	BB-IB	HP	SO	AVG	OBP	SLG	AOPS	ABR	SB-CS	FA	FR	RNG	THR	GAMES AT POSITION	DL	BFW
1972	Cal A	14	30	5	9	1	0	1	7	1-0	0	4	.300	.323	.433	130	1	0-0	1.000	1	35	0	O7(5/0/2)		-0.1

COLGAN, ED   William H. B E.St.Louis IL D8.8.1895 Great Falls MT ?/180 d5.3

YEAR	TM LG	G	AB	R	H	2B	3B	HR	RBI	BB-IB	HP	SO	AVG	OBP	SLG	AOPS	ABR	SB-CS	FA	FR	RNG	THR	GAMES AT POSITION	DL	BFW
1884	Pit AA	48	161	10	25	4	0	0		3	0		.155	.171	.193	18	-14		.906	1			C44,O4(2/0/2)		-0.9

COLLIER, LOU   Louis Keith B8.21.1973 Chicago IL BR/TR/5-10/182(180-191) [PitN92 31/875] d6.28 Col Triton (IL) JC

YEAR	TM LG	G	AB	R	H	2B	3B	HR	RBI	BB-IB	HP	SO	AVG	OBP	SLG	AOPS	ABR	SB-CS	FA	FR	RNG	THR	GAMES AT POSITION	DL	BFW
1997	Pit N	18	37	3	5	0	0	0	3	1-0	0	11	.135	.158	.135	-22	-7	1-0	1.000	1	116	106	S18		-0.5
1998	Pit N	110	334	30	82	13	6	2	34	31-6	6	70	.246	.316	.338	73	-13	2-2	.960	1	100	96	S107	16	-0.5
1999	Mil N	74	135	18	35	9	0	2	21	14-0	0	31	.259	.325	.370	76	-5	3-2	.948	-0	88	52	S31,O10(9/0/1),3b7,2b4		-1.1
2000	Mil N	14	32	9	7	1	0	1	2	6-0	0	4	.219	.333	.344	75	-1	0-0	1.000	1	86	401	O10(5/7/0)/3		-0.1
2001	Mil N	50	127	19	32	9	1	2	14	17-0	1	30	.252	.340	.378	89	-2	5-1	.976	1	108	99	O23(12/11/0),3b16/D		0.0
2002	Mon N	13	11	3	1	0	0	0	0	1-1	0	3	.091	.231	.182	12	-1	0-0	1.000	-1	90	0	O7(3/3/1),2b2/3		-0.2
2003	Bos A	4	1	0	0	0	0	0	0	0-0	0	1	.000	.000	.000	-96	0	0-1	1.000	0	167	0	3b2,O2(1/1/0)		-0.1
2004	Phi N	32	36	7	10	1	0	1	4	5-0	0	10	.278	.381	.389	97	0	1-0	1.000	-1	41	0	O8L/3		-0.1
Total	8	315	713	89	172	33	7	8	78	75-7	9	160	.241	.317	.341	72	-29	12-6	.962	-6	99	90	S156,O60(38/22/2),3b28,2b6/D	16	-2.6

YEAR	TM LG	G	AB	R	H	2B	3B	HR	RBI	BB-IB	HP	SO	AVG	OBP	SLG	AOPS	ABR	SB-CS	FA	FR	RNG	THR	GAMES AT POSITION	DL	BFW

COLLINS d9.12

| 1892 | StL N | 1 | 2 | 0 | 0 | 0 | 0 | 0 | 0 | 0 | 0 | 2 | .000 | .000 | .000 | -99 | 0 | 0 | 1.000 | 0 | 0 | 0 | /OR | | -0.1 |

COLLINS, CHUB Charles Augustine B10.12.1857 Dundas ON, Can. D5.20.1914 Dundas ON, Can. BB/TR/5-11.5/165 d5.1

1884	Buf N	45	169	24	30	6	0	0	20	14		36	.178	.240	.213	42	-11		.914	2	105	94	2b42,S3		-0.6
	Ind AA	38	138	18	31	3	1	0		9	0		.225	.272	.261	77	-3		.886	-6	90	58	2b38		-0.7
1885	Det N	14	55	8	10	0	2	0	6	0		11	.182	.182	.255	40	-4		.792	-5	83	73	S14		-0.9
Total	2	97	362	50	71	9	3	0	26	23		47	.196	.244	.238	55	-18		.901	-9	98	77	2b80,S17		-2.2

COLLINS, WILSON Cyril Wilson B5.7.1889 Pulaski TN D2.28.1941 Knoxville TN BR/TR/5-9.5/165 d5.12 Col Vanderbilt

1913	Bos N	16	3	3	1	0	0	0	0	0	0	1	.333	.333	.333	89	0	0	1.000	0	180	0	O9(5/3/1)		0.0
1914	Bos N	27	35	5	9	0	0	0	1	2	0	8	.257	.297	.257	66	-2	0	.917	-0	120	0	O19(9/3/7)		-0.3
Total	2	43	38	8	10	0	0	0	1	2	0	9	.263	.300	.263	68	-2	0	.926	-0	125	0	O28(14/6/8)		-0.3

COLLINS, DAN Daniel Thomas B7.12.1854 St.Louis MO D9.21.1883 New Orleans LA d6.8 ▲

| 1874 | Chi NA | 3 | 12 | 1 | 1 | 1 | 0 | 0 | 0 | | | 2 | .083 | .083 | .167 | -22 | -2 | 1-0 | 1.000 | 0 | 243 | 0 | P2,O2R/S | | -0.1 |
| 1876 | Lou N | 7 | 28 | 3 | 4 | 1 | 0 | 0 | 9 | 0 | | 5 | .143 | .143 | .179 | 5 | -3 | | .909 | 1 | 179 | 492 | O7(0/2/5) | | -0.2 |

COLLINS, DAVE David S B10.20.1952 Rapid City SD BB/TL/5-11/175* [CalA72 S1/6] d6.7 C8 Col Mesa (AZ) CC

1975	Cal A	93	319	41	85	13	4	3	29	36-1	1	55	.266	.340	.361	106	3	24-10	.988	3	112	59	O75(74/1/0),D12		0.3
1976	Cal A	99	365	45	96	12	1	4	28	40-2		55	.263	.335	.334	103	2	32-19	.994	2	110	64	O71(52/19/0),D22		0.0
1977	Sea A	120	402	46	96	9	3	5	28	33-0	3	66	.239	.299	.313	68	-18	25-10	.985	1	95	127	O73(67/3/3),D40		-2.0
1978	Cin N	102	102	13	22	1	0	0	7	15-0	0	18	.216	.311	.225	53	-6	7-7	.969	1	103	140	O24(3/17/4)		-0.6
1979	†Cin N	122	396	59	126	16	4	3	35	27-2	2	68	.318	.364	.402	109	5	16-9	.976	-4	101	31	O91(45/3/50),1b10		-0.3
1980	Cin N	144	551	94	167	20	4	3	35	53-2	3	68	.303	.366	.370	108	8	79-21	.986	4	112	60	O141(18/119/6)		2.1
1981	Cin N	95	360	63	98	18	6	3	23	41-1	6	41	.272	.355	.381	110	6	26-10	.977	0	108	60	O94(1/0/93)		0.4
1982	NY A	111	348	41	88	12	3	3	25	28-3	5	49	.253	.315	.330	79	-10	13-8	.992	-1	98	145	O60(20/20/25),1b52/D		-1.5
1983	Tor A	118	402	55	109	12	4	1	34	43-1	2	67	.271	.343	.328	81	-9	31-7	.989	10	115	73	O112(112/2/1),1b5/D	18	0.0
1984	Tor A	128	441	59	136	24	**15**	2	44	33-0	5	41	.308	.366	.444	119	11	60-14	.991	-2	87	110	O108(106/2/0),1b6,D4		1.3
1985	Oak A	112	379	52	95	16	4	4	29	29-2	1	37	.251	.303	.346	84	-9	29-8	.978	2	113	17	O91L		-0.8
1986	Det A	124	419	44	113	18	2	1	27	44-0	2	49	.270	.340	.329	84	-8	27-12	.995	1	109	34	O94(76/10/11),D24		-1.0
1987	Cin N	57	85	19	25	5	0	0	5	11-0	2	12	.294	.388	.353	94	0	9-0	1.000	1	135	0	O21(18/2/1)		0.3
1988	Cin N	99	174	12	41	6	2	0	14	11-0	2	27	.236	.286	.293	65	-8	7-2	.965	-1	96	139	O35(13/5/18),1b3		-1.0
1989	Cin N	78	106	12	25	4	0	0	7	10-0	0	17	.236	.302	.274	64	-5	3-1	1.000	5	165	0	O16L		-0.2
1990	StL N	99	58	12	13	1	0	0	3	13-2	0	10	.224	.366	.241	70	-2	7-1	1.000	-4	0	72	1b49,O12(4/1/8)		-0.5
Total	16	1701	4907	667	1335	187	52	32	373	467-16	38	660	.272	.338	.351	93	-40	395-139	.986	15	107	71	O1118(716/204/220),1b125,D104	18	-3.5

COLLINS, EDDIE Edward Trowbridge Jr. B11.23.1916 Lansdowne PA D11.2.2000 Jennersville PA BL/TR/5-10/175 d7.4 Mil 1942-45 f-Eddie Col Yale

1939	Phi A	32	21	6	5	1	0	0		3			.238	.238	.286	34	-2	1-0	1.000	0	202	0	O6R/2		-0.2
1941	Phi A	80	219	29	53	6	3	0	12	20	0	24	.242	.305	.297	61	-13	2-1	.968	1	113	65	O50(4/9/38)		-1.4
1942	Phi A	20	34	6	8	2	0	0	4	4	0	2	.235	.316	.294	72	-1	1-0	.800	-1	70	0	O9(1/3/6)		-0.3
Total	3	132	274	41	66	9	3	0	16	24	0	29	.241	.302	.296	61	-16	4-1	.959	0	113	56	O65(5/12/50)/2		-1.9

COLLINS, EDDIE Edward Trowbridge Sr. "Cocky" (aka Sullivan in 1906) B5.2.1887 Millerton NY D3.25.1951 Boston MA BL/TR/5-9/175 d9.17 Mil 1918 M3/C2 HF1939 s-Eddie Col Columbia

1906	Phi A	6	15	2	3	0	0	0		0			.200	.200	.200	25	-1	1	.900	-1	91	0	S3/23		-0.2
1907	Phi A	14	23	0	8	0	1	0		2	0		.348	.385	.435	146	1	0	.833	-1	78	99	S6		0.0
1908	Phi A	102	330	39	90	18	7	1	40	16	3		.273	.312	.379	116	5	8	.944	-10	89	34	2b47,S28,O10(2/3/5)		-0.5
1909	Phi A	**153**	571	104	198	30	10	3	56	62	6		.347	.416	.450	170	48	63	**.967**	4	93	114	2b152/S		5.9
1910	†Phi A	153	581	81	188	16	15	3	81	49	6		.324	.382	.418	152	34	**81**	**.972**	30	104	136	2b153		7.0
1911	†Phi A	132	493	92	180	22	13	3	73	62	15		.365	.451	.481	163	46	38	.967	-0	90	107	2b132		4.6
1912	Phi A	**153**	543	**137**	189	25	11	0	64	101	0		.348	.450	.435	159	50	63	.955	14	103	**125**	2b153		6.4
1913	†Phi A	148	534	**125**	184	23	13	3	73	85	7	37	.345	.441	.453	165	49	55	.965	16	**106**	107	2b148		**7.0**
1914	†Phi A	152	526	**122**	181	23	14	2	85	97	6	31	.344	**.452**	.452	**179**	**58**	58-30	.970	2	91	116	2b152		6.9
1915	Chi A	**155**	521	118	173	22	10	4	77	**119**	5	27	.332	.460	.436	163	50	46-30	**.974**	11	104	103	2b155		**6.6**
1916	Chi A	**155**	545	87	168	14	17	0	52	86	3	36	.308	.405	.396	139	29	40-21	**.976**	-7	91	**131**	2b155		2.9
1917	†Chi A	**156**	564	91	163	18	12	0	67	89	5	16	.289	.363	.363	127	22	53	.969	-26	85	110	2b156		-0.1
1918	Chi A	97	330	51	91	8	2	2	30	73	0	13	.276	.407	.330	121	14	22	.974	-1	95	131	2b96		1.6
1919	†Chi A	**140**	518	87	165	19	7	4	80	68	2	27	.319	.400	.405	126	20	**33**	.974	3	97	**125**	2b140		2.7
1920	Chi A	153	602	117	224	38	13	3	76	69	2	19	.372	.438	.493	146	43	20-8	**.976**	10	99	115	2b153		5.4
1921	Chi A	139	526	79	177	20	10	2	58	66	5	15	.337	.412	.424	115	15	12-10	.968	31	**112**	110	2b136		4.4
1922	Chi A	154	598	92	194	20	12	1	69	73	4	16	.324	.401	.403	110	12	20-12	**.976**	-13	93	87	2b154		0.4
1923	Chi A	145	505	89	182	22	5	5	67	84	4	8	.360	.455	.453	141	37	48-29	.975	-6	93	93	2b142		3.4
1924	Chi A	152	556	108	194	27	7	6	86	89	3	16	.349	.441	.455	136	35	42-17	**.977**	-10	95	94	2b150,M		3.0
1925	Chi A	118	425	80	147	26	3	3	80	87	4	8	.346	.461	.442	137	32	19-6	.970	-3	93	110	2b116,M		2.3
1926	Chi A	106	375	66	129	32	4	1	62	62	5	8	.344	.441	.459	140	27	13-8	.973	-8	93	99	2b101,M		2.1
1927	Phi A	95	226	50	76	12	1	1	15	56	0	9	.336	.468	.412	123	12	6-2	.965	-5	88	107	2b56/S		0.9
1928	Phi A	36	33	3	10	3	0	0	7	4		4	.303	.378	.394	100	0	0-0	—	-1	0	0	2b2/S		-0.1
1929	Phi A	9	7	0	0	0	0	0	0	2	0	0	.000	.222	.000	-37	-1	0-0	—	0			/H		-0.1
1930	Phi A	3	2	1	1	0	0	0	0	0	0	0	.500	.500	.500	148	0	0-0	—	0			/H		0.0
Total	25	2826	9949	1821	3315	438	187	47	1300	1499	77	286	.333	.424	.429	142	637	741-173	.970	21	97	111	2b2650,S40,O10(2/3/5)/3		72.5

COLLINS, HUB Hubert B. B4.15.1864 Louisville KY D5.21.1892 Brooklyn NY BR/TR/5-8/160 d9.4 OF(241/31/0)

1886	Lou AA	27	101	12	29	3	2	0	10	5			.287	.321	.356	106	0	7	.885	-2	46	0	O24(22/2/0),3b2/S21		-0.2
1887	Lou AA	130	559	122	162	22	8	1	66	39		2	.290	.338	.363	94	-6	71	.887	-7	103	27	O109L,1b10,1b8,S4/3		-1.2
1888	Lou AA	116	485	117	149	26	11	2	50	41		4	.307	.366	.419	154	30	62	.890	3	124	162	O82(57/26/0),2b19,S15		2.8
	Bro AA	12	42	16	13	5	1	0	3	9		1	.310	.442	.476	195	-2	9	.897	-2	88	106	2b12		0.3
	Year	128	527	133	162	31	12	2	53	50		5	.307	.373	.423	158	36	71	.890	0	124	162	O82(57/26/0),2b31,S15		3.1
1889	†Bro AA	138	560	139	149	18	3	2	73	80		7	41	.266	.365	.320	95	0	65	.929	-3	101	99	2b138		0.2
1890	†Bro N	129	510	**148**	142	32	7	3	69	85		3	47	.278	.385	.386	124	20	85	.945	-3	104	118	2b129		2.4
1891	Bro N	107	435	82	120	16	5	3	31	59		2	63	.276	.365	.356	111	8	32	.910	-21	91	58	2b72,O35(32/3/0)		-1.0
1892	Bro N	21	87	17	26	5	1	0	17	14		0	13	.299	.396	.379	140	5	4	.925	-2	0	0	O21L		0.1
Total	7	2779	653	790	127	38	11	319	332		19	164	.284	.365	.373	115	62	335	.928	-32	99	92	2b381,O271L,S20,1b9,3b3		3.4

COLLINS, RIPPER James Anthony B3.30.1904 Altoona PA D4.15.1970 New Haven CT BB/TL/5-9/165 d4.18 C3

1931	†StL N	89	279	34	84	20	10	4	59	18		3	24	.301	.350	.487	118	0	1	.995	4	123	104	1b68,O3(1/0/2)		0.4
1932	StL N	149	549	82	153	28	8	21	91	38		3	67	.279	.329	.474	110	6	4	.999	-1	83	107	1b81,O60(15/0/45)		-0.6
1933	StL N	132	493	66	153	26	7	10	68	38		3	49	.310	.363	.452	125	16	7	.994	3	102	83	1b123		0.8
1934	†StL N	154	600	116	200	40	12	**35**	128	57		2	50	.333	.393	**.615**	155	46	2	.991	8	**118**	74	1b154		3.7
1935	StL N★	150	578	109	181	36	10	23	122	65		3	45	.313	.385	.529	138	31	0	.987	1	102	102	1b150		1.7
1936	StL N★	103	277	48	79	13	3	13	48	48		1	30	.285	.399	.509	143	6	1	.990	-1	61	0	1b61,O9(1/0/8)		1.1
1937	Chi N★	115	456	77	125	16	5	16	71	32		5	46	.274	.329	.436	102	0	2	.991	1	101	106	1b111		-1.0
1938	†Chi N	143	490	78	131	22	8	13	61	54		3	48	.267	.344	.424	107	5	1	**.996**	8	118	108	1b135		0.8
1941	Pit N	49	62	5	13	2	2	0	11	6		0	14	.210	.279	.306	65	-3	0	.947	1	180	65	1b11,O3R		-0.3
Total	9	1084	3784	615	1121	205	65	135	659	356		23	373	.296	.360	.492	125	125	18	.992	23	107	101	1b894,O75(17/0/58)		5.8

COLLINS, JIMMY James Joseph B1.16.1870 Buffalo NY D3.6.1943 Buffalo NY BR/TR/5-9/178 d4.19 M6 HF1945

1895	Bos N	11	38	10	8	3	0	1	8	4		2	.211	.302	.368	67	-2	0	.714	-2	81	0	O10R		-0.3
	Lou N	96	373	65	104	17	5	6	49	33		9	16	.279	.352	.399	100	1	12	.926	20	116	95	3b77,O18(0/7/11),2b2/S		1.7
	Year	107	411	75	112	20	5	7	57	37		10	20	.273	.347	.397	96	-2	12	.926	19	116	95	3b77,O28(0/7/21),2b2/S		1.4
1896	Bos N	84	304	48	90	10	9	1	46	30		8	12	.296	.374	.398	98	-1	10	.909	16	118	137	3b80,S4		1.4
1897	†Bos N	134	529	103	183	28	13	6	132	41		7		.346	.400	.482	125	18	14	.917	19	113	129	3b134		3.3
1898	Bos N	**152**	597	107	196	35	5	**15**	111	40		7		.328	.377	.479	138	27	12	.932	12	103	108	3b152		3.9
1899	Bos N	151	599	98	166	28	11	5	92	40		12		.277	.335	.386	89	-11	12	.943	18	109	115	3b151		0.8
1900	Bos N	**142**	586	104	178	25	6	6	95	34		10		.304	.352	.394	94	-6	23	.935	10	96	113	3b141/S		0.6
1901	Bos A	**138**	564	108	187	42	16	6	94	34		5		.332	.375	.495	142	31	19	.914	13	106	**142**	3b138,M		4.2
1902	Bos A	108	429	71	138	21	10	6	61	24		2		.322	.360	.459	130	12	18	**.954**	8	105	96	3b107,M		2.1

YEAR	TM LG	G	AB	R	H	2B	3B	HR	RBI	BB-IB	HP	SO	AVG	OBP	SLG	AOPS	ABR	SB-CS	FA	FR	RNG	THR	GAMES AT POSITION	DL	BFW
1903	†Bos A	130	540	88	160	33	17	5	72	24	2		.296	.329	.448	125	14	23	.952	10	103	149	3b130,M		2.9
1904	Bos A	156	631	85	171	33	13	3	67	27	5		.271	.306	.379	110	6	19	.945	5	104	121	3b156,M		1.7
1905	Bos A	131	508	66	140	26	5	4	65	37	4		.276	.330	.370	120	12	18	.923	5	103	115	3b131,M		2.2
1906	Bos A	37	142	17	39	8	4	1	16	4	0		.275	.295	.408	120	2	1	.911	2	107	64	3b32,M		0.5
1907	Bos A	41	158	13	46	8	0	0	10	10	0		.291	.333	.342	116	3	4	.874	-6	89	53	3b41		-0.2
	Phi A	99	364	38	99	21	0	0	35	24	8		.272	.331	.330	108	5	4	.904	-2	94	116	3b98		0.5
	Year	140	522	51	145	29	0	0	45	34	8		.278	.332	.333	110	8	8	.895	-9	93	98	3b139		0.3
1908	Phi A	115	433	34	94	14	3	0	30	20	4		.217	.258	.263	65	-17	5	.928	-7	92	109	3b115		-2.3
Total	14	1725	6795	1055	1999	352	116	65	983	426	84	32	.294	.343	.409	112	94	194	.929	122	104	117	3b1683,O28(0/7/21),S6,2b2		23.0

COLLINS, ZIP   John Edgar   B5.4.1892 Brooklyn NY   D12.19.1983 Manassas VA   BL/TL/5-11/152   d7.31

YEAR	TM LG	G	AB	R	H	2B	3B	HR	RBI	BB-IB	HP	SO	AVG	OBP	SLG	AOPS	ABR	SB-CS	FA	FR	RNG	THR	GAMES AT POSITION	DL	BFW
1914	Pit N	49	182	14	44	2	0	0	15	8	1	10	.242	.277	.253	61	-9	3	.962	1	103	107	O49(0/11/40)		-1.2
1915	Pit N	101	354	51	104	8	5	1	23	24	1	38	.294	.340	.353	112	4	6-7	.942	1	104	103	O89C		-0.2
	Bos N	5	14	3	4	1	1	0	0	2	0	1	.286	.375	.500	171	1	1	1.000	0	88	245	O4L		0.2
	Year	106	368	54	108	9	6	1	23	26	1	39	.293	.342	.359	114	5	7-7	.944	2	103	108	O93(4/89/0)		0.0
1916	Bos N	93	268	39	56	1	6	1	18	18	1	42	.209	.261	.269	66	-12	4	.947	-1	89	131	O78(26/27/27)		-2.0
1917	Bos N	9	27	3	4	0	1	0	2	0	0	4	.148	.148	.222	14	-3	0	1.000	-0	86	116	O5(1/0/4)		-0.4
1921	Phi A	24	71	14	20	5	1	0	5	6	2	5	.282	.354	.380	87	-1	1-2	.915	-1	99	112	O20C		-0.3
Total	5	281	916	124	232	17	14	2	63	58	5	100	.253	.301	.309	85	-20	15-9	.946	1	99	112	O245(31/147/71)		-3.9

COLLINS, SHANO   John Francis   B12.4.1885 Charlestown MA   D9.10.1955 Newton MA   BR/TR/6-0/185   d4.21   M2   gs-Bob Gallagher

YEAR	TM LG	G	AB	R	H	2B	3B	HR	RBI	BB-IB	HP	SO	AVG	OBP	SLG	AOPS	ABR	SB-CS	FA	FR	RNG	THR	GAMES AT POSITION	DL	BFW
1910	Chi A	97	315	29	62	10	8	1	24	25	1		.197	.258	.289	74	-11	10	.949	2	96	118	O66(19/7/40),1b28		-1.4
1911	Chi A	106	370	48	97	16	12	4	48	20	5		.262	.309	.403	101	-2	14	.978	4	118	117	1b98,2b3,O3L		-0.1
1912	Chi A	153	579	75	168	34	10	2	81	29	5		.290	.332	.394	110	5	27	.969	0	100	70	O105(1/17/85),1b46		-0.2
1913	Chi A	148	535	53	128	26	9	1	47	32	3	60	.239	.286	.327	80	-16	22	.949	2	111	87	O147(2/0/145)		-2.3
1914	Chi A	154	598	61	164	34	9	3	65	27	6	49	.274	.312	.376	108	3	30-24	.970	1	100	103	O154(7/45/103)		-0.7
1915	Chi A	153	576	73	148	24	17	2	85	28	6	50	.257	.298	.368	96	-7	38-19	.963	-0	106	96	O104(20/21/64),1b47		-1.3
1916	Chi A	143	527	74	128	28	12	0	42	59	3	51	.243	.323	.342	98	-1	16	.959	5	104	119	O137(23/2/112),1b4		-0.4
1917	†Chi A	82	252	38	59	13	3	1	14	10	2	27	.234	.269	.321	78	-8	14	.992	3	119	72	O73(9/0/64)		-0.9
1918	Chi A	103	365	30	100	18	11	1	56	17	1	29	.274	.310	.392	111	2	7	.973	12	117	151	O93(16/34/42),1b5		0.9
1919	†Chi A	63	179	21	50	6	3	1	16	7	1	11	.279	.317	.363	90	-3	3	.957	4	115	135	O46(2/7/37),1b8		-0.1
1920	Chi A	133	495	70	150	21	10	1	63	23	4	24	.303	.339	.392	93	-7	12-9	.988	-7	82	106	1b116,O13(2/1/10)		-1.7
1921	Bos A	141	542	63	155	29	12	4	69	18	4	26	.286	.314	.406	85	-16	15-8	.966	4	99	124	O139(1/44/94),1b3		-1.9
1922	Bos A	135	472	33	128	24	7	1	52	7	5	30	.271	.289	.358	68	-24	7-9	.951	-4	104	49	O117(11/45/63),/1		-3.7
1923	Bos A	97	342	41	79	10	5	0	18	11	5	29	.231	.265	.289	46	-29	7-8	.953	-0	86	112	O89(0/57/32)		-3.4
1924	Bos A	89	240	37	70	17	5	0	28	18	3	17	.292	.349	.404	94	-3	4-6	.957	-8	79	66	O56(18/11/27),1b12		-1.5
1925	Bos A	2	3	1	1	0	0	0	1	0	0	0	.333	.333	.333	70	0	0-0	—	-0	0	0	/OC		0.0
Total	16	1799	6390	747	1687	310	133	22	709	331	57	405	.264	.306	.364	90	-117	226-83	.962	17	103	103	O1343(133/292/918),1b368,2b3		-18.7

COLLINS, JOE   Joseph Edward (b Joseph Edward Kollonige)   B12.3.1922 Scranton PA   D8.30.1989 Union NJ   BL/TL/6-0/185*   d9.25

YEAR	TM LG	G	AB	R	H	2B	3B	HR	RBI	BB-IB	HP	SO	AVG	OBP	SLG	AOPS	ABR	SB-CS	FA	FR	RNG	THR	GAMES AT POSITION	DL	BFW
1948	NY A	5	5	0	1	1	0	0	2	0	0	1	.200	.200	.400	58	0	0-0					/H		0.0
1949	NY A	7	10	2	1	0	0	0	4	6	0	1	.100	.438	.100	46	0	0-0	.920	-1	0	60	1b5		-0.1
1950	†NY A	108	205	47	48	8	3	8	28	31	0	34	.234	.335	.420	95	-2	5-0	.987	0	101	111	1b99,O2R		-0.3
1951	†NY A	125	262	52	75	8	5	9	48	34	0	23	.286	.368	.458	127	9	9-7	.987	5	126	110	1b114,O15R		1.1
1952	†NY A	122	428	69	120	16	8	18	59	55	1	47	.280	.364	.481	142	23	4-2	.990	-3	90	124	1b119		1.7
1953	†NY A	127	387	72	104	11	2	17	44	59	0	36	.269	.365	.439	121	11	2-6	.989	1	106	116	1b113,O4R		0.5
1954	†NY A	130	343	67	93	20	2	12	46	51	0	37	.271	.365	.446	126	13	2-2	.992	2	108	142	1b117		1.0
1955	†NY A	105	278	40	65	9	1	13	45	44-2	2	32	.234	.339	.414	104	2	0-2	.998	7	135	146	1b73,O27R		0.4
1956	†NY A	100	262	38	59	5	3	7	43	34-2	1	33	.225	.313	.347	78	-9	3-1	.990	5	103	60	O51(25/7/24),1b43		-0.7
1957	†NY A	79	149	17	30	1	0	2	10	24-2	0	18	.201	.310	.248	56	-9	2-1	.987	-1	93	107	1b32,O15(2/2/11)		-1.1
Total	10	908	2329	404	596	79	24	86	329	338-6	4	263	.256	.350	.421	112	38	27-21	.990	16	110	124	1b715,O114(27/9/83)		2.5

COLLINS, KEVIN   Kevin Michael "Casey"   B8.4.1946 Springfield MA   BL/TR/6-2/190*   d9.1

YEAR	TM LG	G	AB	R	H	2B	3B	HR	RBI	BB-IB	HP	SO	AVG	OBP	SLG	AOPS	ABR	SB-CS	FA	FR	RNG	THR	GAMES AT POSITION	DL	BFW
1965	NY N	11	23	4	4	1	0	0	1-0	0	0	9	.174	.208	.217	21	-2	0-1	1.000	-2	101	128	3b7,S3		-0.5
1967	NY N	4	10	1	1	0	0	0	0-0	0	0	3	.100	.100	.100	-43	-2	1-0	1.000	-0	117	0	2b2		-0.2
1968	NY N	58	154	12	31	5	2	1	13	7-2	0	37	.201	.233	.279	54	-9	0-1	.955	-5	77	110	3b40,2b6/S		-1.7
1969	NY N	16	40	1	6	3	0	1	2	3-1	0	9	.150	.209	.300	40	-3	0-0	.925	1	113	114	3b14		-0.2
	Mon N	52	96	5	23	5	1	2	12	8-0	0	16	.240	.292	.375	87	-2	0-0	1.000	-5	76	40	2b20,3b16		-0.7
	Year	68	136	6	29	8	1	3	14	11-1	0	26	.213	.268	.353	73	-5	0-0	.917	-4	93	95	3b30,2b20		-0.9
1970	Det A	25	24	2	5	1	0	1	3	1-0	0	10	.208	.240	.375	66	-1	0-0	1.000	0	158	0	/1		-0.1
1971	Det A	35	41	6	11	2	1	1	4	0-0	0	12	.268	.268	.439	93	-1	0-0	1.000	1	114	0	3b4,O2(1/0/1)/2	23	0.0
Total	6	201	388	30	81	17	4	6	34	20-3	0	97	.209	.245	.320	62	-20	1-2	.944	-11	85	103	3b81,2b29,S4,O2(1/0/1)/1	155	-3.4

COLLINS, ORTH   Orth Stein "Buck"   B4.27.1880 Lafayette IN   D12.13.1949 Ft.Lauderdale FL   BL/TR/6-0/150   d6.1

YEAR	TM LG	G	AB	R	H	2B	3B	HR	RBI	BB-IB	HP	SO	AVG	OBP	SLG	AOPS	ABR	SB-CS	FA	FR	RNG	THR	GAMES AT POSITION	DL	BFW
1904	NY A	5	17	3	6	1	1	0	1	0	0		.353	.389	.529	180	1	0	1.000	3	1145	0	O5(0/5/1)		0.4
1909	Was A	8	7	0	0	0	0	0	0	0	0		.000	.000	.000	-99	-2	0	1.000	-0	0	0	O2(0/1/1)/P		-0.2
Total	2	13	24	3	6	1	1	0	1	0	0		.250	.280	.375	104	-1	0	1.000	3	954	0	O7(0/6/2)/P		0.2

COLLINS, RIP   Robert Joseph   B9.18.1909 Pittsburgh PA   D4.19.1969 Pittsburgh PA   BR/TR/5-11/176   d4.28

YEAR	TM LG	G	AB	R	H	2B	3B	HR	RBI	BB-IB	HP	SO	AVG	OBP	SLG	AOPS	ABR	SB-CS	FA	FR	RNG	THR	GAMES AT POSITION	DL	BFW
1940	Chi N	47	120	11	25	3	0	1	14	14	0	18	.208	.296	.258	55	-7	4	.951	-3	104	109	C42		-0.8
1944	NY A	3	3	0	1	0	0	0	0	1	0	0	.333	.500	.333	136	0	0-0	1.000	0	0	0	C3		0.1
Total	2	50	123	11	26	3	0	1	14	15	0	18	.211	.302	.260	58	-7	4-0	.953	-3	101	105	C45		-0.7

COLLINS, PAT   Tharon Leslie   B9.13.1896 Sweet Sprgs. MO   D5.20.1960 Kansas City KS   BR/TR/5-9/178   d9.5

YEAR	TM LG	G	AB	R	H	2B	3B	HR	RBI	BB-IB	HP	SO	AVG	OBP	SLG	AOPS	ABR	SB-CS	FA	FR	RNG	THR	GAMES AT POSITION	DL	BFW
1919	StL A	11	21	2	3	1	0	0	1	4	0		.143	.280	.190	32	-2	0	.929	-0	107	87	C5		-0.2
1920	StL A	23	28	5	6	1	0	0	6	3	0	5	.214	.290	.250	43	-2	0-0	1.000	-1	82	61	C7		-0.3
1921	StL A	58	111	9	27	3	0	1	10	16	0	17	.243	.339	.297	60	-6	1-0	.961	-1	113	80	C31		-0.5
1922	StL A	63	127	14	39	6	0	8	23	21	0	21	.307	.405	.543	140	8	0-1	.980	4	133	92	C28,1b5		1.2
1923	StL A	85	181	9	32	8	0	3	30	15	0	45	.177	.264	.271	32	-18	0-0	.980	-0	96	102	C47		-1.6
1924	StL A	32	54	9	17	2	0	1	11	11	0	14	.315	.431	.407	110	1	0-1	.969	-1	95	97	C20		0.1
1926	†NY A	102	290	41	83	11	3	7	35	73	2	57	.286	.433	.417	124	15	3-2	.971	1	89	95	C100		2.2
1927	†NY A	92	251	38	69	9	3	7	36	54	2	24	.275	.407	.418	118	9	0-1	.976	-3	103	59	C89		1.1
1928	†NY A	70	136	18	30	5	0	6	14	35	0	16	.221	.380	.390	106	3	0-0	.977	-4	88	100	C70		0.2
1929	Bos N	7	5	1	0	0	0	0	2	3	0		.000	.375	.000	2	-1	0	1.000	0	91	75	C6		0.0
Total	10	543	1204	146	306	46	6	33	168	235	4	202	.254	.378	.385	98	7	4-5	.974	-5	99	87	C403,1b5		2.2

COLLINS, BILLY   William J.   B1863 Dublin, Ireland   D6.8.1893 Brooklyn NY   BR/?/150   d8.1

YEAR	TM LG	G	AB	R	H	2B	3B	HR	RBI	BB-IB	HP	SO	AVG	OBP	SLG	AOPS	ABR	SB-CS	FA	FR	RNG	THR	GAMES AT POSITION	DL	BFW
1887	NY AA	1	4	1	1	0	0	0	0	0	0		.250	.250	.250	42	0	0	.250	-2			/C		-0.2
1889	Phi AA	1	4	0	1	0	0	0	1	1	0		.250	.400	.250	88	0	1	.800	-1			/C		0.0
1890	Phi AA	1	1	0	0	0	0	0	0	0	0		.000	.000	.000	-99	0	0	.500	-1	86	74	/S		-0.1
1891	Cle N	2	3	0	0	0	0	0	0	0	0		.000	.000	.000	-96	-1	0	—	1	0	0	/ORC		0.0
Total	4	5	12	1	2	0	0	0	1	1	0	0	.167	.231	.167	14	-1	1	.737	-2			C3/ORS		-0.3

COLLINS, BILL   William Shirley   B3.27.1882 Chesterton IN   D6.26.1961 San Bernardino CA   BB/TR/6-0/170   d4.14

YEAR	TM LG	G	AB	R	H	2B	3B	HR	RBI	BB-IB	HP	SO	AVG	OBP	SLG	AOPS	ABR	SB-CS	FA	FR	RNG	THR	GAMES AT POSITION	DL	BFW
1910	Bos N	151	584	67	141	6	7	3	40	43	13	48	.241	.305	.291	72	-22	36	.977	8	108	109	O151(129/10/13)		-2.4
1911	Bos N	17	44	8	6	1	0	0	1	3	0	8	.136	.156	.205	-6	-6	4	1.000	1	127	61	O13(3/8/2)/3		-0.6
	Chi N	7	3	2	1	1	0	0	0	1	0		.333	.500	.667	225	0	0	1.000	0	101	0	O4(2/2/0)		0.1
	Year	24	47	10	7	2	0	0	1	4	0		.149	.184	.234	16	-6	4	1.000	1	126	59	O17(5/10/2)/3		-0.5
1913	Bro N	32	95	8	18	1	0	0	4	8	2	11	.189	.267	.200	33	-8	2-4	.921	-2	102	29	O27(13/15/0)		-1.4
1914	Buf F	21	47	6	8	1	1	0	4	4	2	8	.149	.167	.277	-2	-7	0	.864	1	75	260	O15(3/2/1/13)		-0.6
Total	4	228	773	91	173	11	10	3	54	54	15	75	.224	.287	.276	60	-42	42-4	.966	8	106	105	O210(149/36/28)/3		-4.9

COLLVER, BILL   William J.   B3.21.1867 Clyde OH   D3.24.1888 Detroit MI   d7.4

YEAR	TM LG	G	AB	R	H	2B	3B	HR	RBI	BB-IB	HP	SO	AVG	OBP	SLG	AOPS	ABR	SB-CS	FA	FR	RNG	THR	GAMES AT POSITION	DL	BFW
1885	Bos N	1	4	0	0	0	0	0		0	0		.000	.000	.000	-99	-1		—	-0	0	0	/OR		-0.1

YEAR	TM LG	G	AB	R	H	2B	3B	HR	RBI	BB-IB	HP	SO	AVG	OBP	SLG	AOPS	ABR	SB-CS	FA	FR	RNG	THR	GAMES AT POSITION	DL	BFW

COLMAN, FRANK Frank Lloyd B3.2.1918 London ON, Can. D2.19.1983 London ON, Can. BL/TL/5-11/188 d9.12

1942	Pit N	10	37	2	5	0	0	1	2	2	0	2	.135	.179	.216	15	-4	0	1.000	1	93	285	O8R		-0.4
1943	Pit N	32	59	9	16	2	2	0	4	8	0	7	.271	.358	.373	108	1	0	1.000	-0	111	0	O11R		-0.1
1944	Pit N	99	226	30	61	9	5	6	53	25	1	27	.270	.345	.434	113	4	0	.964	-1	103	77	O53(3/0/50),1b6		0.0
1945	Pit N	77	153	18	32	11	1	4	30	9	0	16	.209	.253	.373	70	-7	0	.993	1	131	83	1b22,O12(6/0/5)		-0.8
1946	Pit N	26	53	3	9	3	0	1	6	2	1	7	.170	.214	.283	39	-4	0	1.000	0	100	142	O8(4/0/4),1b2		-0.5
	NY A	5	15	2	4	0	0	1	5	1	0	1	.267	.313	.467	114	0	0-0	1.000	-0	110	0	O4R		0.0
1947	NY A	22	28	2	3	0	0	2	6	2	0	6	.107	.167	.321	34	-3	0-0	1.000	1	96	450	O6L		-0.3
Total	6	271	571	66	130	25	8	15	106	49	2	66	.228	.291	.378	85	-13	0-0	.980	1	102	93	O103(19/0/83),1b30		-2.1

COLON, CRIS Cristobal B1.3.1969 LaGuaira, Venez BB/TR/6-2/180 d9.18

| 1992 | Tex A | 14 | 36 | 5 | 6 | 0 | 0 | 0 | 1 | 1-0 | 0 | 9 | .167 | .189 | .167 | 0 | -5 | 0-0 | .946 | 0 | 104 | 63 | S14 | | -0.4 |

COLUCCIO, BOB Robert Pasquali B10.2.1951 Centralia WA BR/TR/5-11/183* [MilA69 17/403] d4.15

1973	Mil A	124	438	65	98	21	8	15	58	54-2	3	92	.224	.311	.411	104	1	13-6	.992	8	110	165	O108(18/14/79),D11		0.5
1974	Mil A	138	394	42	88	13	4	6	31	43-2	1	61	.223	.305	.322	81	-10	15-9	.989	6	108	109	O131(4/103/34),D2		-0.8
1975	Mil A	22	62	8	12	0	1	1	5	11-0	1	11	.194	.320	.274	70	-2	1-4	1.000	-0	102	67	O22C		-0.4
	Chi A	61	161	22	33	4	2	4	13	13-1	1	34	.205	.269	.329	67	-8	4-0	.980	1	104	113	O59(14/3/44)/D	36	-0.8
	Year	83	223	30	45	4	3	5	18	24-1	2	45	.202	.284	.314	68	-10	5-4	.987	1	103	98	O81(14/25/44)/D		-1.2
1977	Chi A	20	37	4	10	0	0	0	7	6-0	0	2	.270	.356	.270	78	-1	0-2	1.000	1	101	113	O19(9/8/3)		-0.1
1978	StL N	5	3	0	0	0	0	0	0	1-0	0	2	.000	.250	.000	-25	0	0-0	—	-0	91	0	O2(1/0/1)		-0.1
Total	5	370	1095	141	241	38	15	26	114	128-5	8	202	.220	.305	.353	87	-20	33-21	.990	15	107	126	O341(46/150/161),D14	36	-1.7

COMBS, EARLE Earle Bryan "The Kentucky Colonel" B5.14.1899 Pebworth KY D7.21.1976 Richmond KY BL/TR/6-0/185 d4.16 C16 HF1970 Col Eastern Kentucky

1924	NY A	24	35	10	14	5	0	0	2	4	0	2	.400	.462	.543	159	3	0-1	1.000	-1	98	0	O11(5/3/3)		0.2
1925	NY A	150	593	117	203	36	13	3	61	65	4	43	.342	.411	.462	123	23	12-13	.979	-5	98	73	O150(12/138/0)		0.8
1926	†NY A	145	606	113	181	31	12	8	55	47	3	23	.299	.352	.429	105	2	8-6	.970	-3	103	57	O145C		-0.7
1927	†NY A	152	648	137	231	36	23	6	64	62	2	31	.356	.414	.511	143	40	15-6	.968	-6	104	39	O152C		2.8
1928	†NY A	149	626	118	194	33	21	7	56	77	2	33	.310	.387	.463	127	24	11-8	.980	0	106	66	O149C		1.7
1929	NY A	142	586	119	202	33	15	3	65	69	0	32	.345	.414	.468	135	33	12-7	.966	-7	94	69	O141C		1.9
1930	NY A	137	532	129	183	30	22	7	82	74	0	26	.344	.424	.523	145	38	16-10	.969	-4	99	51	O135(60/45/30)		2.3
1931	NY A	138	563	120	179	31	13	5	58	68	3	34	.318	.394	.446	128	24	11-3	.974	-8	95	49	O129C		1.3
1932	†NY A	144	591	143	190	32	10	9	65	81	2	16	.321	.405	.455	129	28	3-9	.967	-9	94	52	O139(42/115/1)		1.1
1933	NY A	122	417	86	125	22	16	5	64	47	1	19	.300	.372	.465	128	16	6-4	.975	-5	98	41	O104(23/80/2)		0.7
1934	NY A	63	251	47	80	13	5	2	25	40	0	11	.319	.412	.434	127	12	3-1	.993	-3	99	21	O62(12/51/0)		0.7
1935	NY A	89	298	47	84	7	4	3	35	36	0	10	.282	.359	.362	92	-3	1-3	.993	-1	102	39	O70(57/13/1)		-0.8
Total	12	1455	5746	1186	1866	309	154	58	632	670	17	278	.325	.397	.462	127	240	98-71	.974	-51	99	53	O1387(211/1161/37)		12.0

COMBS, MERL Merrill Russell B12.11.1919 Los Angeles CA D7.7.1981 Riverside CA BL/TR/6-0/172* d9.12 C2 Col USC

1947	Bos A	17	68	8	15	1	0	1	6	9	0	9	.221	.329	.279	65	-3	0-0	1.000	3	117	181	3b17		0.0
1949	Bos A	14	24	5	5	1	0	0	1	9	0	3	.208	.424	.250	75	0	0-0	.923	-1	81	120	3b9/S		-0.1
1950	Bos A	1	0	0	0	0	0	0	0	1	0	0	—	1.000	—	158	0	0-0	—	0			/H		0.0
	Was A	37	102	19	25	1	0	0	6	22	0	16	.245	.379	.255	68	-4	0-0	.966	0	107	89	S30		-0.2
	Year	38	102	19	25	1	0	0	6	23	0	16	.245	.384	.255	69	-3	0-0	.966	0	107	89	S30		-0.2
1951	Cle A	19	28	3	5	2	0	0	2	2	0	3	.179	.233	.250	32	-3	0-0	.960	3	131	87	S16		0.0
1952	Cle A	52	139	11	23	1	1	1	10	14	0	15	.165	.242	.209	28	-14	0-1	.972	8	115	113	S49,2b3		-0.4
Total	5	140	361	45	73	6	1	2	25	57	0	43	.202	.314	.241	52	-24	0-1	.968	13	113	101	S96,3b26,2b3		-0.7

COMER, WAYNE Harry Wayne B2.3.1944 Shenandoah VA BR/TR/5-10/175* d9.17

1967	Det A	4	3	0	1	0	0	0	0-0	0	0	.333	.333	.333	95	0	0-0	—	-0	0	0	/OC		0.0
1968	†Det A	48	48	8	6	0	1	1	3	2-0	0	7	.125	.160	.229	16	-5	0-0	1.000	0	113	0	O27(26/0/1)/C		-0.6
1969	Sea A	147	481	88	118	18	1	15	54	82-2	1	79	.245	.354	.380	107	7	18-7	.980	7	105	161	O139(20/92/46)/C3		1.1
1970	Mil A	13	17	1	1	0	0	0	1	0-0	0	3	.059	.059	.059	-67	-4	0-0	1.000	0	109	0	O5(1/2/2)		-0.4
	Was A	77	129	21	30	4	0	0	8	22-0	1	16	.233	.346	.264	75	-3	4-1	.960	-2	91	84	O58(18/21/20)/3	21	-0.7
	Year	90	146	22	31	4	0	0	9	22-0	1	19	.212	.318	.240	59	-7	4-1	.962	-2	92	79	O63(19/23/22)/3		-1.1
1972	Det A	27	9	1	1	0	0	0	1	0-0	0	2	.111	.100	.111	-33	-1	0-1	1.000	-1	69	0	O17(15/1/1)		-0.3
Total	5	316	687	119	157	22	2	16	67	106-2	2	106	.229	.331	.336	89	-6	22-9	.978	4	102	131	O247(80/117/70),3b2,C2	21	-0.9

COMISKEY, CHARLIE Charles Albert "Commy","The Old Roman" B8.15.1859 Chicago IL D10.26.1931 Eagle River WI BR/TR/6-0/180 d5.2 M12 HF1939 ▲

1882	StL AA	78	329	58	80	9	5	1	45	4			.243	.252	.310	85	-6		.967	-1	73	73	1b77,P2		-1.3
1883	StL AA	96	401	87	118	17	9	2	64	11			.294	.313	.397	120	7		.963	-1	70	135	1b96/OLM		-0.2
1884	StL AA	108	460	76	109	17	6	2	84	5	5		.237	.253	.313	81	-11		.969	2	101	116	1b108/2PM		-1.7
1885	†StL AA	83	340	68	87	15	7	2	44	14	4		.256	.293	.359	101	-1		.969	1	110	92	1b83,M		-0.6
1886	†StL AA	131	578	95	147	15	9	3	76	10	0		.254	.267	.327	82	-16	41	.975	5	125	125	1b122,2b9,O2R,M		-2.0
1887	†StL AA	125	538	139	180	22	5	4	103	27	7		.335	.374	.416	109	3	117	.976	4	135	115	1b116,2b9,O3R,M		-0.2
1888	†StL AA	137	576	102	157	22	5	6	83	12	4		.273	.292	.359	98	-5	72	.970	-4	95	109	1b133,O5(0/2/3),2b3,M		-2.0
1889	StL AA	137	587	105	168	28	10	3	102	19	3	19	.286	.312	.383	86	-16	65	.970	-1	95	106	1b134,O3(0/1/2),2b3/PM		-2.4
1890	Chi P	88	377	53	92	11	3	0	59	14	3	17	.244	.277	.289	49	-29	34	.965	-3	92	106	1b88,M		-3.2
1891	StL AA	139	572	84	148	16	2	2	88	33	7	25	.259	.307	.304	65	-29	38	.979	4	110	106	1b139,O2L,M		-3.3
1892	Cin N	141	551	61	125	14	6	3	71	32	4	16	.227	.274	.290	72	-20	30	.984	1	96	132	1b141,M		-1.9
1893	Cin N	64	259	38	57	12	1	0	26	11	2	2	.220	.257	.274	40	-23	9	.979	-6	59	143	1b64,M		-2.5
1894	Cin N	63	228	26	61	9	1	0	38	5	4	5	.268	.295	.307	44	-22	10	.973	-3	82	101	1b62/ORM		-1.9
Total	13	1390	5796	992	1529	207	68	28	883	197	43	84	.264	.293	.337	81	-168	416	.973	-3	99	113	1b1363,2b25,O17(3/3/11),P4		-23.2

COMMAND, JIM James Dalton "Igor" B10.15.1928 Grand Rapids MI BL/TR/6-2/200* d6.20

1954	Phi N	9	18	4	4	1	0	1	6	2	0	4	.222	.300	.444	91	0	0-0	.929	-0	96	0	3b6		-0.1
1955	Phi N	5	5	0	0	0	0	0	0	0	0	0	.000	.000	.000	-99	-1	0-0	—	0			/H		-0.1
Total	2	14	23	4	4	1	0	1	6	2-0	0	4	.174	.240	.348	52	-1	0-0	.929	-0	96	0	3b6		-0.2

COMOROSKY, ADAM Adam Anthony B12.9.1905 Swoyersville PA D3.2.1951 Swoyersville PA BR/TR/5-10/167 d9.13

1926	Pit N	8	15	2	4	1	1	0	0	1	0	2	.267	.313	.467	102	0	1	1.000	-0	108	0	O6L		0.0
1927	Pit N	18	61	5	14	1	0	0	4	3	0	1	.230	.266	.246	35	-6	0	.978	1	123	65	O16(15/1/0)		-0.6
1928	Pit N	51	176	22	52	6	3	2	34	15	1	6	.295	.354	.398	92	0	1	.968	1	113	52	O49(38/9/5)		-0.4
1929	Pit N	127	473	86	152	26	11	6	97	40	2	22	.321	.377	.461	104	2	19	.963	-1	102	73	O121L		-0.7
1930	Pit N	152	597	112	187	47	23	12	119	51	4	33	.313	.371	.539	114	12	14	.969	2	102	107	O152(130/30/0)		0.3
1931	Pit N	99	350	37	85	12	1	1	48	34	0	28	.243	.310	.291	63	-18	11	.978	3	110	81	O90(89/0/1)		-2.0
1932	Pit N	108	370	54	106	18	4	4	46	25	3	20	.286	.337	.389	96	-2	7	.981	5	116	62	O92(74/18/0)		-0.1
1933	Pit N	64	162	18	46	8	1	1	15	4	0	9	.284	.301	.364	89	-3	2	1.000	1	101	42	O30L		-0.5
1934	Cin N	127	446	46	115	12	6	0	40	34	3	23	.258	.315	.312	70	-19	1	.970	-1	107	48	O122(47/9/66)		-2.7
1935	Cin N	59	137	22	34	3	1	2	14	7	1	14	.248	.290	.328	68	-7	1	.953	1	105	116	O40(25/10/5)		-0.7
Total	10	813	2787	404	795	134	51	28	417	214	14	158	.285	.339	.400	91	-43	57	.972	10	107	74	O718(575/77/77)		-7.4

COMPTON, PETE Anna Sebastian "Bash" B9.28.1889 San Marcos TX D2.3.1978 Kansas City MO BL/TL/5-11/170 d9.6

1911	StL A	28	107	9	29	4	0	0	5	8	0		.271	.322	.308	79	-3	2	.917	1	94	149	O28R		-0.3
1912	StL A	103	268	26	75	6	4	2	30	22	2		.280	.339	.354	102	0	11	.925	2	112	99	O72(50/0/22)		-0.1
1913	StL A	63	100	14	18	5	2	2	17	13	0	13	.180	.274	.330	79	-3	2	.862	-2	79	85	O21(8/5/8)		-0.6
1915	StL F	2	8	0	2	0	0	0	3	0	0	0	.250	.250	.250	39	-1	0	1.000	-0	62	0	O2C		-0.1
	Bos N	35	116	10	28	7	1	1	12	8	0	11	.241	.290	.345	96	-4	4-1	.971	1	108	58	O31(0/20/11)		-0.2
1916	Bos N	34	98	13	20	2	0	0	8	7	1	7	.204	.264	.224	53	-5	0-0	.939	-1	101	64	O30(3/26/1)		-0.9
	Pit N	5	16	1	1	0	0	0	0	1	0	5	.063	.211	.063	-14	-2	0	.917	-0	120	0	O5R		-0.3
	Year	39	114	14	21	2	0	0	8	8	1	12	.184	.256	.202	43	-7	0	.936	-1	104	53	O35(3/26/6)		-1.2
1918	NY N	21	60	5	13	0	1	0	5	5	0	2	.217	.277	.250	64	-3	2	.971	1	106	169	O19(12/2/5)		-0.2
Total	6	291	773	78	186	24	8	5	80	65	4	40	.241	.303	.312	83	-18	26-1	.933	1	104	95	O208(73/55/80)		-2.7

COMPTON, MIKE Michael Lynn B8.15.1944 Stamford TX BR/TR/5-10/180 d4.17 Col Sul Ross St.

| 1970 | Phi N | 47 | 110 | 8 | 18 | 0 | 1 | 1 | 9 | 9-3 | 2 | 22 | .164 | .240 | .209 | 22 | -13 | 0-0 | .986 | -1 | 87 | 119 | C40 | | -1.2 |

YEAR	TM	LG	G	AB	R	H	2B	3B	HR	RBI	BB-IB	HP	SO	AVG	OBP	SLG	AOPS	ABR	SB-CS	FA	FR	RNG	THR	GAMES AT POSITION	DL	BFW

CONATSER, CLINT   Clinton Astor "Connie" (b Astor Clinton Conatser)   B7.24.1921 Los Angeles CA   BR/TR/5-11/182   d4.21 Col Los Angeles (CA) City

1948	†Bos	N	90	224	30	69	6	3	3	23	32	1	27	.277	.370	.384	106	3	0	.974	-2	99	68	O76(24/52/0)		-0.1
1949	Bos	N	53	152	10	40	6	0	3	16	14	0	19	.263	.325	.362	89	-3	0	.951	1	103	151	O44(15/13/16)		-0.3
Total	2		143	376	40	102	15	3	6	39	46	1	46	.271	.352	.375	99	0	0	.965	-1	101	102	O120(39/65/16)		-0.4

CONCEPCION, DAVE   David Ismael (Benitez)   B6.17.1948 Aragua, Venez   BR/TR/6-1/180(155-200)   d4.6

1970	†Cin	N	101	265	38	69	6	3	1	19	23-5	3	45	.260	.324	.317	73	-10	10-2	.945	-3	101	110	S93,2b3		-0.2
1971	Cin	N	130	327	24	67	4	4	1	20	18-2	0	51	.205	.246	.251	42	-26	9-3	.974	-2	99	115	S112,2b10,3b7,O5C	15	-1.8
1972	†Cin	N	119	378	40	79	13	2	2	29	32-8	2	65	.209	.272	.270	58	-21	13-6	.969	1	103	114	S114,3b9/2		-0.7
1973	Cin	N*	89	328	39	94	18	3	8	46	21-3	1	55	.287	.327	.433	115	6	22-5	.974	6	104	110	S88,O2C	72	2.5
1974	Cin	N	160	594	70	167	25	1	14	82	44-10	6	79	.281	.335	.397	106	4	41-6	.963	11	105	113	S160/OC		4.1
1975	†Cin	N★	140	507	62	139	23	1	5	49	39-4	2	51	.274	.326	.353	88	-8	33-6	.977	17	109	141	S130,3b6		3.0
1976	†Cin	N★	152	576	74	162	28	7	9	69	49-11	1	68	.281	.335	.401	106	4	21-10	.968	17	105	105	S150		4.2
1977	Cin	N★	156	572	59	155	26	3	8	64	46-6	0	77	.271	.322	.369	84	-13	29-7	.986	16	100	115	S156		2.3
1978	Cin	N★	153	565	75	170	33	4	6	67	51-4	1	83	.301	.351	.405	113	11	23-10	.969	4	100	83	S152		3.3
1979	†Cin	N*	149	590	91	166	25	3	16	84	64-5	0	73	.281	.348	.415	109	7	19-7	.967	20	107	120	S148		4.5
1980	Cin	N★	156	622	72	162	31	8	5	77	37-2	1	107	.260	.300	.360	86	-13	12-2	.978	-9	91	112	S155/2		-0.4
1981	Cin	N★	106	421	57	129	28	0	5	67	37-1	1	61	.306	.358	.409	119	12	4-5	.960	8	98	113	S106		3.2
1982	Cin	N★	147	572	48	164	25	4	5	53	45-4	0	61	.287	.337	.371	98	-1	13-6	.977	19	101	112	S145/13		3.4
1983	Cin	N	143	528	54	123	22	0	1	47	56-9	0	81	.233	.303	.280	61	-26	14-9	.979	-6	93	83	S139,3b6/1		-1.9
1984	Cin	N	154	531	46	130	26	1	4	58	52-5	0	72	.245	.307	.320	74	-17	22-6	.978	-27	83	71	S104,3b54,1b6		-3.5
1985	Cin	N	155	560	59	141	19	2	7	48	50-3	3	67	.252	.314	.330	77	-17	16-12	.962	-31	87	75	S151,3b5		-3.5
1986	Cin	N	90	311	42	81	13	2	3	30	26-1	0	43	.260	.314	.344	79	-9	13-2	.965	-1	101	97	S60,1b12,3b2b10,3b10	52	-0.2
1987	Cin	N	104	279	32	89	15	0	1	33	28-5	0	24	.319	.377	.384	100	1	4-3	.992	5	102	126	2b59,1b26,3b13,S2		0.7
1988	Cin	N	84	197	11	39	9	0	0	8	18-5	0	23	.198	.265	.244	45	-14	3-2	.994	3	99	127	2b46,1b16,S13,3b9/P	15	-1.0
Total	19		2488	8723	993	2326	389	48	101	950	736-93	21	1186	.267	.322	.357	89	-130	321-109	.971	47	99	106	S2178,2b130,3b120,1b62,O8C/P	154	18.0

CONCEPCION, ONIX   Onix Cardona (Cardona)   B10.5.1957 Dorado, PR   BR/TR/5-6/180(160-180)   d8.30 [DL 1986 KC A 45]

1980	†KC	A	12	15	1	2	0	0	0	2	0-0	0	1	.133	.133	.133	-26	-3	0-0	.833	-2	81	39	S6		-0.5
1981	KC	A	2	0	0	0	0	0	0	0	0-0	0	0	—	—	—	—	0	0-0	—	-0	0	0	/S		0.0
1982	KC	A	74	205	17	48	9	1	0	15	5-0	1	18	.234	.256	.288	49	-15	2-1	.948	-8	100	100	S46,2b24/D	18	-1.8
1983	KC	A	80	219	22	53	11	3	0	20	12-0	1	12	.242	.282	.320	65	-11	10-3	.913	-7	89	132	3b31,2b28,S21/D		-1.4
1984	†KC	A	90	287	36	81	9	2	1	23	14-0	3	33	.282	.319	.338	82	-7	9-6	.972	9	114	114	S85,2b6/3	41	1.1
1985	†KC	A	131	314	32	64	5	1	2	20	16-0	6	29	.204	.255	.245	38	-27	4-4	.959	6	114	94	S128,2b2		-1.1
1987	Pit	N	1	1	0	1	0	0	0	0	0-0	0	0	1.000	1.000	1.000	427	0	0-0	—	0	0	0	/H	68	0.0
Total	7		390	1041	108	249	34	7	3	80	47-0	11	93	.239	.278	.294	57	-63	25-14	.960	-3	109	100	S287,2b60,3b32,D2	172	-3.7

CONDE, RAMON   Ramon Luis (Roman) "Wito"   B12.29.1934 Juana Diaz, PR   BR/TR/5-8/172   d7.17

| 1962 | Chi | A | 14 | 16 | 0 | 0 | 0 | 0 | 0 | 1 | 3-0 | 0 | 3 | .000 | .158 | .000 | -54 | -4 | 0-0 | .889 | -1 | 57 | 0 | 3b7 | | -0.5 |

CONE, FRED   Joseph Frederick   B5.1848 Rockford IL   D4.13.1909 Chicago IL   5-9.5/171   d5.5

| 1871 | Bos | NA | 19 | 77 | 17 | 27 | 3 | 0 | 0 | 14 | 3-0 | 2 | 2 | .260 | .329 | .325 | 86 | -1 | 12-1 | .854 | -1 | 90 | 0 | O18(18/0/1) | | 0.1 |

CONGALTON, BUNK   William Millar   B1.24.1875 Guelph ON, Can.   D8.19.1937 Cleveland OH   BL/TL/5-11/190   d4.17

1902	Chi	N	47	188	16	45	3	0	1	27	7	0		.239	.267	.271	68	-8	4	.988	0	96	67	O47(0/5/43)		-1.0
1905	Cle	A	12	47	4	17	0	0	0	5	2	0		.362	.388	.362	136	2	3	.923	-1	152	0	O12R		0.0
1906	Cle	A	117	419	51	134	13	5	3	50	24	3		.320	.361	.396	139	18	12	.957	-9	41	0	O114(21/1/93)		0.4
1907	Cle	A	9	22	3	4	0	0	0	2	4	0		.182	.308	.182	56	-1	0	1.000	0	125	0	O6R		-0.1
	Bos	A	124	496	44	142	11	8	2	47	20	3		.286	.318	.353	115	6	13	.969	-3	113	119	O123R		-0.3
	Year		133	518	46	146	11	8	2	49	24	3		.282	.317	.346	112	5	13	.971	-2	114	113	O129R		-0.4
Total	4		309	1172	117	342	27	13	4	131	57	6		.292	.328	.352	116	17	32	.967	-12	85	59	O302(21/6/277)		-1.0

CONIGLIARO, TONY   Anthony Richard   B1.7.1945 Revere MA   D2.24.1990 Salem MA   BR/TR/6-3/185(185-205)   d4.16   b-Billy [DL 1968 Bos A 175]

1964	Bos	A	111	404	69	117	21	2	24	52	35-1	5	78	.290	.354	.530	135	19	2-4	.973	1	97	134	O106(81/25/2)	37	1.4
1965	Bos	A	138	521	82	140	21	5	32	81	51-6	5	116	.269	.338	.512	131	20	4-2	.976	9	117	117	O137(0/2/135)		2.1
1966	Bos	A	150	558	77	148	26	7	28	93	52-8	5	112	.265	.330	.487	120	14	0-2	.973	-5	93	95	O146R		-0.1
1967	Bos	A★	95	349	59	100	11	5	20	67	27-2	5	58	.287	.341	.519	141	17	4-6	.983	3	114	86	O95R	40	1.3
1969	Bos	A	141	506	57	129	21	3	20	82	48-6	4	111	.255	.321	.427	104	2	2-4	.981	-11	88	39	O137R		-1.9
1970	Bos	A	146	560	89	149	20	1	36	116	43-4	8	93	.266	.324	.498	117	11	4-2	.977	-3	98	75	O146R		0.0
1971	Cal	A	74	266	23	59	18	0	4	15	23-1	1	52	.222	.285	.335	81	-7	3-3	.994	4	109	122	O72R	80	-0.7
1975	Bos	A	21	57	8	7	1	0	2	9	8-0	0	9	.123	.221	.246	32	-5	1-0	—	0	0	0	D15		-0.6
Total	8		876	3221	464	849	139	23	166	516	287-28	33	629	.264	.327	.476	118	71	20-23	.979	-2	101	94	O839(81/27/733),D15	332	1.5

CONIGLIARO, BILLY   William Michael   B8.15.1947 Revere MA   BR/TR/6-0/190* [BosA65 1/5]   d4.11   b-Tony

1969	Bos	A	32	80	14	23	6	2	4	7	9-0	1	23	.287	.367	.563	150	5	1-0	.926	-5	57	0	O24(3/18/6)		-0.1
1970	Bos	A	114	398	59	108	16	3	18	58	35-0	7	73	.271	.339	.462	112	6	3-7	.968	2	102	122	O108(77/25/20)		0.0
1971	Bos	A	101	351	42	92	26	1	11	33	25-4	1	68	.262	.310	.436	102	1	3-2	.983	-1	101	81	O100(1/79/20)		-0.4
1972	Mil	A	52	191	22	44	6	2	7	16	8-0	0	54	.230	.261	.393	94	-3	1-0	.992	5	121	138	O52(2/6/45)		-0.5
1973	†Oak	A	48	110	5	22	2	2	0	14	9-1	0	26	.200	.252	.255	48	-8	1-0	1.000	3	104	227	O40(21/18/3)/2	59	-0.2
Total	5		347	1130	142	289	56	10	40	128	86-5	8	244	.256	.311	.429	103	1	9-10	.980	3	102	114	O322(104/146/94)/2	59	-1.2

CONINE, JEFF   Jeffrey Guy   B6.26.1966 Tacoma WA   BR/TR/6-1/220(200-220)   [KCA87 58/1226]   d9.16 Col UCLA

1990	KC	A	9	20	3	5	2	0	0	2	2-0	0	5	.250	.318	.350	88	0	0-0	.977	-0	99	146	1b9		-0.1
1992	KC	A	28	91	10	23	5	2	0	9	8-1	0	23	.253	.313	.352	83	-2	0-0	1.000	-1	88	71	O23(22/0/1),1b4		-0.5
1993	Fla	N	162	595	75	174	24	3	12	79	52-2	5	135	.292	.351	.403	97	-2	2-2	.992	-2	90	104	O147L,1b43		-1.1
1994	Fla	N☆	115	451	60	144	27	6	18	82	40-4	1	92	.319	.373	.525	127	17	1-2	.974	1	103	71	O97L,1b46		1.2
1995	Fla	N★	133	483	72	146	26	2	25	105	66-5	1	94	.302	.379	.520	134	25	2-0	.976	0	96	101	O118L,1b14		2.0
1996	Fla	N	157	597	84	175	32	2	26	95	62-1	4	121	.293	.360	.484	124	21	1-4	.975	2	86	114	O128L,1b48		0.5
1997	†Fla	N	151	405	46	98	13	1	17	61	57-3	2	89	.242	.337	.405	98	-1	2-0	.992	9	127	112	1b145/OL		-0.2
1998	KC	A	93	309	30	79	26	0	8	43	26-1	2	68	.256	.312	.417	86	-6	3-0	.993	-3	88	130	1b99,D20,O13(7/0/6),3b4	58	-1.3
1999	Bal	A	139	444	54	129	31	1	13	75	30-0	3	40	.291	.335	.453	103	2	0-3	.993	-3	88	130	1b99,D20,O13(7/0/6),3b4		-1.1
2000	Bal	A	119	409	53	116	20	2	13	46	36-0	2	53	.284	.341	.438	101	0	4-3	.932	4	107	153	1b80,O36(22/0/16),3b17,D12		1.0
2001	Bal	A	139	524	75	163	23	2	14	97	64-6	5	75	.311	.386	.443	126	22	12-8	.994	-2	83	94	1b80,O36(22/0/16),3b17,D12		1.3
2002	Bal	A	116	451	44	123	26	4	15	63	25-6	2	66	.273	.307	.448	105	-3	8-0	.990	-8	79	115	1b103,O6L,D7	53	-1.4
2003	Bal	A	124	493	75	143	33	3	15	80	37-5	5	60	.290	.338	.460	111	8	5-0	.992	-2	97	100	1b118,O8(6/0/2)/3		0.6
	†Fla	N	25	84	13	20	3	0	1	15	13-0	0	10	.238	.337	.452	109	1	0-0	1.000	2	105	210	O25L		0.2
2004	Fla	N	140	521	55	146	35	1	14	83	48-3	2	78	.280	.340	.432	104	3	5-5	.994	13	122	114	O83L,1b57		0.7
2005	Fla	N	131	335	42	102	20	2	3	33	38-2	3	58	.304	.374	.403	112	7	2-0	.973	-3	111	70	O61(37/0/28),1b45,D3		0.4
Total	15		1781	6212	791	1786	346	31	198	968	604-40	37	1067	.288	.350	.449	110	96	47-27	.992	11	104	109	1b862,O845(756/0/96),3b66,D65	111	0.6

CONLAN, JOCKO   John Bertrand   B12.6.1899 Chicago IL   D4.16.1989 Scottsdale AZ   BL/TL/5-7.5/165   d7.6 U24 HF1974

1934	Chi	A	63	225	35	56	11	3	0	16	19	1	7	.249	.310	.324	62	-13	2-2	.955	-3	89	116	O54(0/54/4)		-1.7
1935	Chi	A	65	140	20	40	7	1	0	15	14	1	6	.286	.355	.350	81	-4	3-3	.961	-0	96	120	O37(0/21/16)		-0.5
Total	2		128	365	55	96	18	4	0	31	33	2	13	.263	.327	.334	69	-17	5-5	.957	-3	92	117	O91(0/75/20)		-2.2

CONLON, JOCKO   Arthur Joseph   B12.10.1897 Woburn MA   D8.5.1987 Falmouth MA   BR/TR/5-7/145   d4.17 Col Harvard

| 1923 | Bos | N | 59 | 147 | 23 | 32 | 3 | 0 | 0 | 17 | 11 | 6 | 11 | .218 | .299 | .238 | 45 | -11 | 0-3 | .955 | -2 | 102 | 77 | 2b36,S6,3b4 | | -1.2 |

CONN, BERT   Albert Thomas   B9.22.1879 Philadelphia PA   D11.2.1944 Philadelphia PA   TR/6-0/178   d9.16 ▲

1898	Phi	N	1	3	1	1	0	1	0	1	0	0		.333	.333	1.000	291	1	0	1.000	-0	58	0	/P		0.0
1900	Phi	N	6	9	4	3	1	0	0	1	0	0		.333	.333	.444	115	1	0	.667	-1	23	0	P4		0.0
1901	Phi	N	5	18	2	4	1	0	0	0	1	0		.222	.263	.278	56	-1	0	.880	-2	93	0	2b5		-0.2
Total	3		12	30	7	8	2	1	0	2	1	0		.267	.290	.400	74	1	0	.880	-2	93	0	2b5,P5		-0.2

YEAR	TM LG	G	AB	R	H	2B	3B	HR	RBI	BB-IB	HP	SO	AVG	OBP	SLG	AOPS	ABR	SB-CS	FA	FR	RNG	THR	GAMES AT POSITION	DL	BFW

CONNALLY, FRITZIE Fritzie Lee B5.19.1958 Bryan TX BR/TR/6-3/210* [ChiN80 7/167] d9.9 Col Baylor

1983	Chi N	8	10	0	1	0	0	0	0	0-0	0	5	.100	.100	.100	-42	-2	0-0	1.000	0	109	0	3b3		-0.2
1985	Bal A	50	112	16	26	4	0	3	15	19-0	1	21	.232	.329	.348	94	-2	0-0	.976	-2	96	50	3b46,1b2/D		-0.2
Total	2	58	122	16	27	4	0	3	15	19-0	1	26	.221	.329	.328	83	-2	0-0	.977	-2	97	48	3b49,1b2/D		-0.4

CONNATSER, BRUCE Broadus Milburn B9.19.1902 Sevierville TN D1.27.1971 Terre Haute IN BR/TR/5-11.5/170 d9.15 Col Alabama

1931	Cle A	12	49	5	14	3	0	0	4	2	1	3	.286	.327	.347	73	-2	0-0	1.000	1	138	41	1b12		-0.2
1932	Cle A	23	60	8	14	3	1	0	4	4	0	8	.233	.281	.317	51	-4	1-0	1.000	0	108	75	1b14		-0.5
Total	2	35	109	13	28	6	1	0	11	4	1	11	.257	.302	.330	61	-6	1-0	1.000	2	123	58	1b26		-0.7

CONNAUGHTON, FRANK Frank Henry B1.1.1869 Clinton MA D12.1.1942 Boston MA BR/TR/5-9/165 d5.28

1894	Bos N	46	171	42	59	9	2	2	33	16	2	8	.345	.407	.456	100	0	3	.892	0	106	87	S33,C7,O4(2/2/0)		0.2
1896	NY N	88	315	53	82	3	2	2	43	25	2	7	.260	.319	.302	66	-16	22	.892	5	116	88	S54,O30L		-0.9
1906	Bos N	12	44	3	9	0	0	0	1	3	1		.205	.271	.205	50	-3	1	.918	-1	88	54	S11/2		-0.4
Total	3	146	530	98	150	12	4	4	77	44	5	15	.283	.344	.343	78	-19	26	.894	5	110	84	S98,O34(32/2/0),C7/2		-1.1

CONNELL, GENE Eugene Joseph B5.10.1906 Hazleton PA D8.31.1937 Waverly NY BR/TR/6-0.5/180 d7.4 b-Joe Col Penn

| 1931 | Phi N | 6 | 12 | 1 | 3 | 0 | 0 | 0 | 0 | 0 | 0 | 3 | .250 | .250 | .250 | 32 | -1 | 0 | 1.000 | -1 | 57 | 104 | C6 | | -0.2 |

CONNELL, JOE Joseph Bernard B1.16.1902 Bethlehem PA D9.21.1977 Trexlertown PA BL/TL/5-8/165 d6.15 b-Gene Col Villanova

| 1926 | NY N | 2 | 1 | 1 | 0 | 0 | 0 | 0 | 0 | 0 | 0 | 0 | -99 | -99 | -99 | 0 | | | — | 0 | | | /H | | 0.0 |

CONNELL, PETE Peter J. (b Patrick J. O'Connell) B1862 Brooklyn NY D5.5.1892 Brooklyn NY 6-1/180 d9.3

1886	NY AA	1	5	0	0	0	0	0	0	0	0		.000	.000	.000	-99	-1	0	.667	-1	55	0	/3		-0.2
1890	Bro AA	11	40	7	9	2	1	0	3	7	0		.225	.340	.325	100	0	3	.830	-1	100	106	3b10/1		-0.1
Total	2	12	45	7	9	2	1	0	3	7	0		.200	.308	.289	80	-1	3	.820	-2	96	97	3b11/1		-0.3

CONNELL, TERRY Terence G. B6.17.1855 Philadelphia PA D3.25.1924 Narberth PA d6.20

| 1874 | Chi NA | 1 | 4 | 0 | 0 | 0 | 0 | 0 | 0 | 0 | 0 | | .000 | .000 | .000 | -99 | -1 | 0-0 | .429 | -1 | | | /C | | -0.1 |

CONNELLY, TOM Thomas Martin B10.20.1897 Chicago IL D2.18.1941 Hines IL BL/TR/5-11.5/165 d9.24

1920	NY A	1	1	0	0	0	0	0	0	0	0	0	.000	.000	.000	-97	0	0-0	—	0			/H		0.0
1921	NY A	4	5	0	1	0	0	0	0	1	0	0	.200	.333	.200	38	0	0-0	1.000	0	146	0	O3(0/1/2)		0.0
Total	2	5	6	0	1	0	0	0	0	1	0	0	.167	.286	.167	18	0	0-0	1.000	0	146	0	O3(0/1/2)		0.0

CONNOLLY, ED Edward Joseph Sr. B7.17.1908 Brooklyn NY D11.12.1963 Pittsfield MA BR/TR/5-8.5/180 d9.20 s-Ed

1929	Bos A	5	8	0	0	0	0	0	0	0	0	2	.000	.000	.000	-99	-2	0-0	.889	-0	104	124	C5		-0.3
1930	Bos A	27	48	1	9	2	0	0	7	4	0	3	.188	.250	.229	23	-6	0-0	1.000	0	141	122	C26		-0.4
1931	Bos A	42	93	3	7	1	0	0	3	5	1	18	.075	.131	.086	-44	-20	0-0	.981	-1	116	82	C41		-1.8
1932	Bos A	75	222	9	50	8	4	0	21	20	0	27	.225	.289	.297	54	-16	0-1	.957	-2	69	130	C75		-1.3
Total	4	149	371	13	66	11	4	0	31	29	1	50	.178	.239	.229	23	-44	0-1	.966	-3	90	117	C147		-3.8

CONNOLLY, RED John M. B1863 New York NY D3.2.1896 New York NY BB d7.1

| 1886 | StL N | 2 | 7 | 0 | 0 | 0 | 0 | 0 | 0 | 0 | 0 | 3 | .000 | .000 | .000 | -99 | -2 | 0 | — | -0 | 0 | 0 | O2C | | -0.2 |

CONNOLLY, JOEY Joseph Francis B2.1.1884 N.Smithfield RI D9.1.1943 N.Smithfield RI BL/TR/5-7.5/165 d4.10

1913	Bos N	126	427	79	120	18	11	5	57	66	1	47	.281	.379	.410	123	15	18-21	.954	-5	88	100	O124L		0.0
1914	†Bos N	120	399	64	122	28	10	9	65	49	8	36	.306	.393	.494	164	33	12	.974	-1	84	144	O118(115/0/5)		2.9
1915	Bos N	104	305	48	91	14	8	0	23	39	5	35	.298	.387	.397	144	18	13-12	.971	1	98	103	O93(81/3/9)		1.4
1916	Bos N	62	110	11	25	5	2	0	12	14	1	13	.227	.320	.309	98	0	5	.980	1	98	138	O31(14/4/12)		0.0
Total	4	412	1241	202	358	65	31	14	157	168	15	131	.288	.380	.425	139	66	48-33	.967	-5	90	117	O366(334/7/26)		4.3

CONNOLLY, JOE Joseph H. "Coaster Joe" B6.27.1894 San Francisco CA D3.30.1960 San Francisco CA BR/TR/6-0/170 d10.1

1921	NY N	2	4	0	0	0	0	0	0	1	0	1	.000	.000	.000	-42	-1	0-0	1.000	0	-101	0	/OL		-0.1
1922	Cle A	12	45	6	11	2	1	0	6	5	0	3	.244	.320	.333	70	-1	1-0	.972	1	103	153	O12C		-0.2
1923	Cle A	52	109	25	33	10	1	3	25	13	0	7	.303	.377	.495	129	5	1-2	.957	-3	82	60	O39(2/3/34)		-0.1
1924	Bos A	14	10	1	1	0	0	0	1	2	0	7	.100	.250	.100	-7	-2	0-0	1.000	0	130	0	O3R		-0.2
Total	4	80	168	32	45	12	2	3	32	21	0	18	.268	.349	.417	100	1	2-2	.966	-2	91	86	O55(3/15/37)		-0.6

CONNOLLY, BUD Mervin Thomas "Mike" B5.25.1901 San Francisco CA D6.12.1964 Berkeley CA BR/TR/5-8/154 d5.3

| 1925 | Bos A | 43 | 107 | 12 | 28 | 7 | 1 | 0 | 21 | 23 | 0 | 9 | .262 | .392 | .346 | 88 | -1 | 0-3 | .950 | -4 | 88 | 75 | S34,3b2 | | -0.2 |

CONNOLLY, TOM Thomas Francis "Blackie","Ham" B12.30.1892 Boston MA D5.14.1966 Boston MA BL/TR/5-11/175 d5.12 Col Georgetown

| 1915 | Was A | 50 | 141 | 14 | 26 | 3 | 2 | 0 | 14 | 23 | 2 | 19 | .184 | .268 | .234 | 49 | -9 | 5-4 | .970 | -2 | 88 | 102 | 3b24,O19(11/0/8),S4 | | -1.2 |

CONNOR, NED Edward B1850 NY D1.28.1898 Philadelphia PA 5-9/156 d5.18

| 1871 | Tro NA | 7 | 33 | 6 | 7 | 0 | 0 | 0 | 2 | 0 | | | .212 | .212 | .212 | 22 | -3 | 0-0 | .878 | -1 | 167 | 50 | 1b4,O3R | | -0.2 |

CONNOR, JIM James Matthew (b James Matthew O'Connor) B5.11.1863 Port Jervis NY D9.3.1950 Providence RI BR/TR/5-10.5/179 d7.11

1892	Chi N	9	34	2	2	0	0	0	1	1	1	7	.059	.111	.059	-48	-6	0	.917	-4	76	0	2b9		-1.0
1897	Chi N	77	285	40	83	10	5	3	38	24	4		.291	.355	.393	94	-3	10	.936	19	118	138	2b76		1.6
1898	Chi N	138	505	51	114	9	9	0	67	42	3		.226	.289	.279	63	-25	11	.946	-7	100	143	2b138		-2.4
1899	Chi N	69	234	26	48	7	1	0	24	18	1		.205	.265	.244	41	-19	6	.942	2	111	126	2b44,3b25		-1.3
Total	4	293	1058	117	247	26	15	3	129	85	9	7	.233	.296	.295	64	-53	27	.942	10	106	135	2b267,3b25		-3.1

CONNOR, JOE Joseph Francis B12.8.1874 Waterbury CT D11.8.1957 Waterbury CT BR/TR/6-2/185 d9.9 b-Roger

1895	StL N	2	7	0	0	0	0	0	0	0	0	2	.000	.000	.000	-99	-2	0	1.000	1	138	0	3b2		-0.1
1900	Bos N	7	19	2	4	0	0	0	4	2	0		.211	.286	.211	34	-2	1	.971	2	98	127	C7		0.0
1901	Mil A	38	102	10	28	3	1	1	9	6	1		.275	.321	.353	91	-1	4	.949	-3	74	120	C30/23OC		-0.2
	Cle A	37	121	13	17	3	1	0	6	7	2		.140	.200	.182	7	-15	2	.942	-1	94	93	C32,O4R/S		-1.3
	Year	75	223	23	45	6	2	1	15	13	3		.202	.255	.260	45	-17	6	.946	-4	85	105	C62,O5(0/1/4)/23S		-1.5
1905	NY A	8	22	4	5	0	0	0	2	3	0		.227	.320	.273	79	0	1	.978	1	117	142	C6,1b2		0.2
Total	4	92	271	29	54	7	2	1	23	18	3		.199	.257	.251	43	-20	8	.952	-1	89	111	C75,O5(0/1/4),3b3,1b2/S2		-1.4

CONNOR, ROGER Roger B7.1.1857 Waterbury CT D1.4.1931 Waterbury CT BL/TL/6-3/220 d5.1 M1 HF1976 b-Joe

1880	Tro N	**83**	340	53	113	18	8	3	47	13		21	.332	.357	.459	166	22		.821	-11	93	108	3b83		1.3
1881	Tro N	**85**	367	55	107	17	6	2	31	15		20	.292	.319	.387	115	6		.950	2	128	105	1b85		0.3
1882	Tro N	81	349	65	115	22	**18**	4	42	13		20	.330	.354	.530	188	33		.951	0	183	123	1b43,O24(5/19/0),3b14		2.6
1883	NY N	**98**	409	80	146	28	15	1	50	25		16	.357	.394	.506	173	36		.958	3	125	75	1b98		2.6
1884	NY N	**116**	477	98	151	28	4	4	82	38		32	.317	.367	.417	143	24		.860	-1	94	103	2b67,O37C,3b12		2.2
1885	NY N	110	455	102	169	23	15	1	65	51		8	**.371**	**.435**	.495	**203**	54		.975	3	109	138	1b110		**4.3**
1886	NY N	118	485	105	172	29	**20**	7	71	41		15	.355	.405	.540	183	48	17	.973	10	**147**	104	1b118		4.2
1887	NY N	127	471	113	134	26	22	17	104	75		8	.285	.392	.541	164	44	43	**.993**	5	96	100	1b127		3.1
1888	†NY N	134	481	98	140	15	17	14	71	**73**	4	44	.291	.389	.480	**178**	45	27	.982	1	88	100	1b133/2		3.3
1889	†NY N	**131**	496	117	157	32	17	13	**130**	93	2	46	.317	.426	**.528**	166	46	21	.977	-8	56	96	1b131/3		2.3
1890	NY P	123	484	133	169	24	15	**14**	103	88	1	32	.349	.450	**.548**	154	37	22	**.985**	10	**129**	111	1b123		2.8
1891	NY N	129	479	112	139	29	13	7	94	83	4	39	.290	.399	.449	153	37	27	.983	1	96	112	1b129		2.3
1892	Phi N	**155**	564	123	166	**37**	11	12	73	116	6	39	.294	.420	.463	167	53	22	**.985**	-6	71	118	1b155		4.2
1893	NY N	135	511	111	156	25	8	11	105	91	3	26	.305	.413	.450	129	24	24	.974	2	110	83	1b135/3		2.1
1894	NY N	22	82	10	24	7	1	1	14	8	0		.293	.356	.415	86	-2	2	.976	2	131	108	1b21/OR		0.0
	StL N	99	380	83	122	28	25	7	79	51	6	17	.321	.410	.582	137	21	17	.974	5	122	114	1b99		1.9
	Year	121	462	93	146	35	25	8	93	59	6	17	.316	.400	.552	128	19	19	.974	6	**123**	113	1b120/OR		1.9
1895	StL N	104	401	78	131	29	4	8	78	63	3	10	.327	.422	.504	140	27	9	.986	5	111	90	1b104		2.5
1896	StL N	126	483	71	137	21	9	11	72	52	2	14	.284	.356	.433	112	8	10	**.988**	13	**139**	57	1b126,M		1.7
1897	StL N	22	83	13	19	3	1	1	12	13	0		.229	.333	.325	76	-3	3	.984	-0	95	41	1b22		-0.2
Total	18	1998	7797	1620	2467	441	233	138	1323	1002	39	449	.316	.397	.486	154	560	244	.978	33	109	100	1b1759,3b111,2b68,O62(5/56/1)		43.4

CONNORS, JERRY Jeremiah B Cleveland OH d7.11

| 1892 | Phi N | 1 | 3 | 0 | 0 | 0 | 0 | 0 | 0 | 0 | 0 | 1 | .000 | .000 | .000 | -99 | -1 | 0 | — | -0 | 0 | 0 | /OR | | -0.1 |

YEAR	TM LG	G	AB	R	H	2B	3B	HR	RBI	BB-IB	HP	SO	AVG	OBP	SLG	AOPS	ABR	SB-CS	FA	FR	RNG	THR	GAMES AT POSITION	DL	BFW

CONNORS, CHUCK Kevin Joseph Aloysius B4.10.1921 Brooklyn NY D11.10.1992 Los Angeles CA BL/TL/6-5/190* d5.1 Col Seton Hall

YEAR	TM LG	G	AB	R	H	2B	3B	HR	RBI	BB-IB	HP	SO	AVG	OBP	SLG	AOPS	ABR	SB-CS	FA	FR	RNG	THR	GAMES AT POSITION	DL	BFW
1949	Bro N	1	1	0	0	0	0	0	0	0	0	0	.000	.000	.000	-96	0	0	—	0			/H		0.0
1951	Chi N	66	201	16	48	5	1	2	18	12	0	25	.239	.280	.303	56	-13	4-0	.984	-2	95	84	1b57		-1.5
Total	2	67	202	16	48	5	1	2	18	12	0	25	.238	.280	.302	56	-13	4-0	.984	-2	95	84	1b57		-1.5

CONNORS, MERV Mervin James B1.23.1914 Berkeley CA BR/TR/6-2/192 d9.4

YEAR	TM LG	G	AB	R	H	2B	3B	HR	RBI	BB-IB	HP	SO	AVG	OBP	SLG	AOPS	ABR	SB-CS	FA	FR	RNG	THR	GAMES AT POSITION	DL	BFW
1937	Chi A	28	103	12	24	4	1	2	12	14	0	19	.233	.325	.350	70	-5	2-1	.926	-2	98	158	3b28		-0.5
1938	Chi A	24	62	14	22	4	0	6	13	9	0	17	.355	.437	.710	178	7	0-0	.979	0	117	131	1b16		0.6
Total	2	52	165	26	46	8	1	8	25	23	0	36	.279	.367	.485	111	2	2-1	.926	-1	98	158	3b28,1b16		0.1

CONROY, BEN Bernard Patrick B3.14.1871 Philadelphia PA D11.25.1937 Philadelphia PA ?/160 d4.21

YEAR	TM LG	G	AB	R	H	2B	3B	HR	RBI	BB-IB	HP	SO	AVG	OBP	SLG	AOPS	ABR	SB-CS	FA	FR	RNG	THR	GAMES AT POSITION	DL	BFW
1890	Phi AA	117	404	45	69	13	1	0	21	45	5		.171	.262	.208	39	-30	17	.893	-1	107	98	S74,2b42,OC		-2.5

CONROY, WID William Edward B4.5.1877 Philadelphia PA D12.6.1959 Mt.Holly NJ BR/TR/5-9/158 d4.25 C1 OF(224/76/10)

YEAR	TM LG	G	AB	R	H	2B	3B	HR	RBI	BB-IB	HP	SO	AVG	OBP	SLG	AOPS	ABR	SB-CS	FA	FR	RNG	THR	GAMES AT POSITION	DL	BFW
1901	Mil A	131	503	74	129	20	6	5	64	36	8		.256	.316	.350	89	-7	21	.922	17	106	97	S118,3b12		1.3
1902	Pit N	99	365	55	89	10	6	1	47	24	5		.244	.299	.372	86	-7	10	.925	8	104	132	S95,O3(2/0/1)		0.4
1903	NY A	126	503	54	137	23	12	1	45	32	5		.272	.322	.372	101	1	33	.919	3	104	88	3b123,S4		0.7
1904	NY A	140	489	58	119	18	12	1	52	43	7		.243	.314	.335	100	1	30	.944	7	108	86	3b110,S27,O3C		1.2
1905	NY A	101	385	55	105	19	11	2	35	32	0		.273	.329	.395	116	6	25	.928	0	87	23	3b48,O25(20/3/2),S17,1b10,2b3		0.7
1906	NY A	148	567	67	139	17	10	4	54	47	0		.245	.303	.332	89	-7	32	.968	-2	95	38	O97(37/66/0),S49,3b2		-1.4
1907	NY A	140	530	58	124	12	11	3	51	30	3		.234	.279	.315	83	-12	41	.955	8	76	60	O100L,S38		-1.0
1908	NY A	141	531	44	126	22	3	1	39	14	1		.237	.258	.296	79	-14	23	.939	14	107·	83	3b119,2b12,O10(5/1/4)		0.3
1909	Was A	139	488	44	119	13	4	1	20	37	1		.244	.298	.293	91	-5	24	.938	3	103	95	3b120,2b13,O5(2/3/0)/S		0.1
1910	Was A	103	351	36	89	11	3	1	27	30	1		.254	.314	.311	100	0	11	.961	9	94	102	3b46,O46(44/0/2),2b5		-0.9
1911	Was A	106	349	40	81	11	4	2	28	20	4		.232	.282	.304	64	-18	12	.930	8	116	102	3b85,O15(14/0/1)/2		-0.9
Total	11	1374	5061	605	1257	176	82	22	452	345	35		.248	.301	.329	91	-62	262	.934	67	104	86	3b665,S349,O304L,2b34,1b10		1.4

CONROY, BILL William Frederick "Pep" B1.9.1899 Chicago IL D1.23.1970 Chicago IL BR/TR/5-8.5/160 d4.18

YEAR	TM LG	G	AB	R	H	2B	3B	HR	RBI	BB-IB	HP	SO	AVG	OBP	SLG	AOPS	ABR	SB-CS	FA	FR	RNG	THR	GAMES AT POSITION	DL	BFW
1923	Was A	18	60	6	8	2	2	0	2	4	0	9	.133	.188	.233	11	-8	0-0	.926	-1	67	0	3b10,1b6/OC		-0.9

CONROY, BILL William Gordon B2.26.1915 Bloomington IL D11.13.1997 Citrus Heights CA BR/TR/6-0/185 d9.21 Mil 1945 Col Illinois Wesleyan

YEAR	TM LG	G	AB	R	H	2B	3B	HR	RBI	BB-IB	HP	SO	AVG	OBP	SLG	AOPS	ABR	SB-CS	FA	FR	RNG	THR	GAMES AT POSITION	DL	BFW
1935	Phi A	1	4	0	1	1	0	0	0	1	0	0	.250	.400	.500	133	0	0-0	1.000	0	73	0	/C		0.0
1936	Phi A	1	2	0	1	0	0	0	0	0	0	1	.500	.500	.500	151	0	0-0	1.000	-0	0	0	/C		0.0
1937	Phi A	26	60	4	12	1	1	0	3	7	0	9	.200	.284	.250	36	-6	1-0	1.000	-1	87	79	C18/1		-0.5
1942	Bos A	83	250	22	50	4	2	4	20	40	2	47	.200	.315	.280	66	-11	2-0	.971	-4	113	93	C83		-0.6
1943	Bos A	39	89	13	16	5	0	1	6	18	3	19	.180	.336	.270	77	-1	0-0	.969	0	108	92	C38		0.1
1944	Bos A	19	47	6	10	2	0	0	4	11	0	9	.213	.362	.255	79	-1	0-0	.972	-0	103	105	C19		0.0
Total	6	169	452	45	90	13	3	5	33	77	5	85	.199	.322	.274	66	-19	3-0	.974	-2	107	91	C160/1		-1.0

CONSOLO, BILLY William Angelo B8.18.1934 Cleveland OH BR/TR/5-11/180* d4.20 C15

YEAR	TM LG	G	AB	R	H	2B	3B	HR	RBI	BB-IB	HP	SO	AVG	OBP	SLG	AOPS	ABR	SB-CS	FA	FR	RNG	THR	GAMES AT POSITION	DL	BFW
1953	Bos A	47	65	9	14	2	1	1	6	2	0	23	.215	.239	.323	48	-5	1-2	.808	5	121	185	3b16,2b11		0.0
1954	Bos A	91	242	23	55	7	1	1	11	33	2	69	.227	.324	.277	59	-12	2-1	.953	-2	97	84	S50,3b18,2b12		-1.0
1955	Bos A	8	18	4	4	0	0	0	1	5-0	0	5	.222	.391	.222	63	-1	0-0	.889	-3	49	35	2b4		-0.3
1956	Bos A	48	11	13	2	0	0	0	1	3-0	1	5	.182	.357	.182	41	-1	0-0	.920	4	207	215	2b25		0.3
1957	Bos A	68	196	26	53	6	1	4	19	23-0	0	48	.270	.345	.372	91	-2	1-3	.933	9	124	110	S42,2b16,3b2		1.1
1958	Bos A	46	72	13	9	2	1	0	6	5-0	0	14	.125	.192	.181	3	-10	0-0	.925	-1	91	124	2b13,S11/3		-0.5
1959	Bos A	10	14	3	3	1	0	0	0	2	0	5	.214	.313	.286	63	-1	0-0	.818	-1	46	70	S2		-0.2
	Was A	79	202	25	43	5	3	0	10	36-0	0	54	.213	.332	.267	67	-8	1-0	.952	10	114	105	S75,2b4		0.8
	Year	89	216	28	46	6	3	0	10	38-0	0	59	.213	.331	.269	66	-9	1-0	.948	9	112	104	S77,2b4		0.6
1960	Was A	100	174	23	36	4	2	·3	15	25-1	0	29	.207	.310	.305	68	-8	1-1	.938	-10	94	100	S82,2b12,3b2		-1.3
1961	Min A	11	5	1	0	0	0	0	0	0-0	0	1	.000	.000	.000	-95	-1	0-0	1.000	-1	34	0	2b3,S3/3		0.0
1962	Phi N	13	5	3	2	0	0	0	0	0-0	0	1	.400	.400	.400	119	0	0-0		-0	0	0	/3		0.0
	LA A	28	20	4	2	0	0	0	0	3-0	0	11	.100	.217	.100	-12	-3	2-0	.917	0	69	207	3b20,S4/2		-0.2
	KC A	54	154	11	37	4	2	0	16	23-2	0	33	.240	.337	.292	68	-6	1-3	.950	-3	98	88	S48		-0.7
	Year	82	174	15	39	4	2	0	16	26-2	0	42	.224	.323	.270	61	-9	3-3	.944	-3	102	84	S52,3b20/2		-0.9
Total	10	603	1178	158	260	31	11	9	83	161-3	3	297	.221	.315	.289	63	-58	9-10	.945	12	107	105	S317,2b101,3b61		-2.3

CONTI, JASON Stanley Jason B1.27.1975 Pittsburgh PA BL/TR/5-11/180* [AriN96 32/965] d6.29 Col Pittsburgh

YEAR	TM LG	G	AB	R	H	2B	3B	HR	RBI	BB-IB	HP	SO	AVG	OBP	SLG	AOPS	ABR	SB-CS	FA	FR	RNG	THR	GAMES AT POSITION	DL	BFW
2000	Ari N	47	91	11	21	4	3	1	15	7-2	1	30	.231	.293	.374	64	-5	3-0	.983	4	117	290	O35(2/4/33)		-0.2
2001	Ari N	5	4	1	1	0	0	0	0	1-0	0	2	.250	.400	.250	69	0	0-0	—	-0	0	0	/OR		0.0
2002	TB A	78	222	26	57	15	2	3	21	18-1	1	55	.257	.315	.383	86	-4	4-2	.966	7	114	214	O74(21/28/28)		0.1
2003	Mil N	30	48	3	11	2	0	2	7	2-0	0	18	.229	.255	.396	68	-3	0-1	.909	1	133	139	O20(1/1/19)		-0.2
2004	Tex A	22	55	6	10	3	0	4	5	5-0	0	19	.182	.250	.236	27	-6	0-2	1.000	1	116	0	O21(1/20/0)		-0.6
Total	5	182	420	47	100	24	5	6	47	33-3	2	124	.238	.296	.362	71	-18	7-5	.968	12	117	192	O151(25/53/81)		-0.9

CONWAY, CHARLIE Charles Connell B4.28.1886 Youngstown OH D9.12.1968 Youngstown OH BR/TR d4.15

YEAR	TM LG	G	AB	R	H	2B	3B	HR	RBI	BB-IB	HP	SO	AVG	OBP	SLG	AOPS	ABR	SB-CS	FA	FR	RNG	THR	GAMES AT POSITION	DL	BFW
1911	Was A	2	3	0	1	0	1	0	0	0	0	0	.333	.333	1.000	272	0	0	.000	-0	0	0	O2		0.0

CONWAY, JACK Jack Clements B7.30.1919 Bryan TX D6.11.1993 Waco TX BR/TR/5-11.5/175 d9.9 Mil 1942-45 Col Texas

YEAR	TM LG	G	AB	R	H	2B	3B	HR	RBI	BB-IB	HP	SO	AVG	OBP	SLG	AOPS	ABR	SB-CS	FA	FR	RNG	THR	GAMES AT POSITION	DL	BFW
1941	Cle A	2	2	0	1	0	0	0	1	0	0	0	.500	.500	.500	174	0	0-0	1.000	1	151	0	S2		0.1
1946	Cle A	68	258	24	58	6	2	0	18	20	0	36	.225	.281	.264	56	-16	2-2	.955	-9	85	74	2b50,S14,3b3		-2.4
1947	Cle A	34	50	3	9	2	0	0	5	3	0	8	.180	.226	.220	25	-5	0-0	.877	-1	106	131	S24,2b5/3		-0.5
1948	NY N	24	49	8	12	2	1	1	3	5	0	10	.245	.315	.388	89	-1	0	.985	4	120	143	2b13,S6,3b3		0.3
Total	4	128	359	35	80	10	3	1	27	28	0	54	.223	.279	.276	57	-22	2-2	.962	-6	91	84	2b68,S46,3b7		-2.5

CONWAY, OWEN Owen Sylvester B10.23.1890 New York NY D3.12.1942 Philadelphia PA TR d6.21

YEAR	TM LG	G	AB	R	H	2B	3B	HR	RBI	BB-IB	HP	SO	AVG	OBP	SLG	AOPS	ABR	SB-CS	FA	FR	RNG	THR	GAMES AT POSITION	DL	BFW
1915	Phi A	4	15	2	1	0	0	0	0	0	0	3	.067	.067	.067	-62	-3	0	.750	0	115	197	3b4		-0.3

CONWAY, PETE Peter J. B10.30.1866 Burmont PA D1.13.1903 Clifton Heights PA BR/TR/5-10.5/162 d8.10 b-Jim ▲

YEAR	TM LG	G	AB	R	H	2B	3B	HR	RBI	BB-IB	HP	SO	AVG	OBP	SLG	AOPS	ABR	SB-CS	FA	FR	RNG	THR	GAMES AT POSITION	DL	BFW
1885	Buf N	29	90	7	10	5	0	1	7	5		28	.111	.158	.200	15	-8		.889	-1	112	0	P27,O2R/S1		-0.1
1886	KC N	51	194	22	47	8	2	1	18	5		34	.242	.261	.320	71	-7	3	.857	-3	122	172	O31(3/20/8),P23		-0.6
	Det N	12	43	10	8	1	0	2	3	1		8	.186	.205	.349	63	-2	0	.846	-1	101	0	P11/OL		0.0
	Year	63	237	32	55	9	2	3	21	·6		42	.232	.251	.325	70	-9	3	.826	-3	89	49	P34,O32(4/20/8)		-0.6
1887	†Det N	24	95	16	22	5	1	1	7	·2	0	9	.232	.247	.337	58	-6	0	.979	1	131	0	P17,O8L		-0.2
1888	Det N	45	167	28	46	4	2	3	23	8	3	25	.275	.320	.377	120	4	1	.938	2	114	230	P45/OL		0.1
1889	Pit N	3	10	2	1	0	0	0		1		3	.100	.182	.400	67	-1	1	.875	0	139	·0	P3/OL		0.0
Total	5	164	599	85	134	23	5	9	60	22	3	107	.224	.255	.324	73	-20	·5	.907	-0	110	99	P126,O44(14/20/10)/1S		-0.8

CONWAY, RIP Richard Daniel B4.18.1896 White Bear Lake MN D12.2.1972 St.Paul MN BL/TR/5-6/160 d4.16 Mil 1918 Col St. Thomas (MN)

YEAR	TM LG	G	AB	R	H	2B	3B	HR	RBI	BB-IB	HP	SO	AVG	OBP	SLG	AOPS	ABR	SB-CS	FA	FR	RNG	THR	GAMES AT POSITION	DL	BFW
1918	Bos N	14	24	4	4	0	0	0	2	2	0	4	.167	.231	.167	23	-2	1	.810	-3	61	0	2b5/3		-0.6

CONWAY, BILL William F. B11.28.1861 Lowell MA D12.18.1943 Somerville MA BR/TR/5-8/170 d7.28 b-Dick

YEAR	TM LG	G	AB	R	H	2B	3B	HR	RBI	BB-IB	HP	SO	AVG	OBP	SLG	AOPS	ABR	SB-CS	FA	FR	RNG	THR	GAMES AT POSITION	DL	BFW
1884	Phi N	1	4	0	0	0	0	0	0	0		1	.000	.000	.000	-99	-1		1.000	0			/C		-0.1
1886	Bal AA	7	14	4	2	0	0	0	3	7	0		.143	.429	.143	84	1	0	.925	-3			C7		-0.2
Total	2	8	18	4	2	0	0	0	3	7	0	1	.111	.360	.111	52	0	0	.936	-3			C8		-0.2

CONWELL, ED Edward James "Irish" B1.29.1890 Chicago IL D5.1.1926 Chicago IL BR/TR/5-11/155 d9.22

YEAR	TM LG	G	AB	R	H	2B	3B	HR	RBI	BB-IB	HP	SO	AVG	OBP	SLG	AOPS	ABR	SB-CS	FA	FR	RNG	THR	GAMES AT POSITION	DL	BFW
1911	StL N	1	1	0	0	0	0	0	0	0	0		.000	.000	.000	-99	-0		.000	-1	0	0	/3		-0.1

CONYERS, HERB Herbert Leroy B1.8.1921 Cowgill MO D9.16.1964 Cleveland OH BL/TR/6-4/205 d4.18

YEAR	TM LG	G	AB	R	H	2B	3B	HR	RBI	BB-IB	HP	SO	AVG	OBP	SLG	AOPS	ABR	SB-CS	FA	FR	RNG	THR	GAMES AT POSITION	DL	BFW
1950	Cle A	7	9	2	3	0	0	1	4	1	0	2	.333	.400	.667	175	1	1-0	1.000	-0	0	0	/1		0.1

COOGAN, DALE Dale Roger B8.14.1930 Los Angeles CA D3.8.1989 Mission Viejo CA BL/TL/6-1/190 d4.22

YEAR	TM LG	G	AB	R	H	2B	3B	HR	RBI	BB-IB	HP	SO	AVG	OBP	SLG	AOPS	ABR	SB-CS	FA	FR	RNG	THR	GAMES AT POSITION	DL	BFW
1950	Pit N	53	129	19	31	6	1	1	13	17	2	24	.240	.338	.326	73	-5	0	.980	2	135	96	1b32		-0.3

COOGAN, DAN Daniel George B2.16.1875 Philadelphia PA D10.28.1942 Philadelphia PA 5-8/128 d4.25 Col Penn

YEAR	TM LG	G	AB	R	H	2B	3B	HR	RBI	BB-IB	HP	SO	AVG	OBP	SLG	AOPS	ABR	SB-CS	FA	FR	RNG	THR	GAMES AT POSITION	DL	BFW
1895	Was N	26	77	9	17	2	1	0	7	13	0	6	.221	.333	.273	58	-4	1	.746	-9	81	71	S18,C5,O2R/3		-1.0

YEAR	TM LG	G	AB	R	H	2B	3B	HR	RBI	BB-IB	HP	SO	AVG	OBP	SLG	AOPS	ABR	SB-CS	FA	FR	RNG	THR	GAMES AT POSITION	DL	BFW

COOK, JIM   James Fitchie   B11.10.1879 Dundee IL   D6.17.1949 St.Louis MO   BR/TR/5-9/163   d7.2   Col Illinois

| 1903 | Chi N | 8 | 26 | 3 | 4 | 1 | 0 | 0 | 2 | 2 | | 1 | .154 | .241 | .192 | 25 | -2 | 1 | 1.000 | -1 | 0 | 0 | O5C,2b2/1 | | -0.4 |

COOK, DOC   Luther Almus   B6.24.1886 Whitt TX   D6.30.1973 Lawrenceburg TN   BL/TR/6-0/170   d8.7   Col Vanderbilt

1913	NY A	20	72	9	19	2	1	0	1	10	2	4	.264	.369	.319	101	1	1	.939	-0	101	88	O20(0/13/7)		-0.1
1914	NY A	132	470	59	133	11	3	1	40	44	9	60	.283	.356	.326	105	4	26-32	.949	-3	94	97	O127(1/10/116)		-1.2
1915	NY A	132	476	70	129	16	5	1	33	62	8	43	.271	.364	.338	111	8	29-18	.959	-1	93	123	O131R		0.1
1916	NY A	4	10	0	1	0	0	0	1	0	0	2	.100	.100	.100	-39	-2	0	1.000	-0	98	0	O3R		-0.2
Total	4	288	1028	138	282	29	9	3	75	116	19	109	.274	.359	.329	106	11	56-50	.953	-5	94	108	O281(1/23/257)		-1.4

COOK, PAUL   Paul   B5.5.1863 Caledonia NY   D5.25.1905 Rochester NY   BR/TR/5-10/185   d9.13

1884	Phi N	3	12	0	1	0	0	0		2			.083	.083	.083	-50	-2		.818	-2			C3		-0.4
1886	Lou AA	66	262	28	54	5	2	0	14	10	0		.206	.235	.240	46	-17	6	.945	-7	98	104	1b43,C21,O2(1/0/1)		-2.3
1887	Lou AA	61	223	34	55	4	2	0	17	11	4		.247	.294	.283	60	-12	15	.916	-4			C55,1b6		-1.0
1888	Lou AA	57	185	20	34	2	0	0	13	5	4		.184	.222	.195	35	-13	9	.901	-8			C53,O4(1/0/3)/S		-1.6
1889	Lou AA	81	286	34	65	10	1	0	15	15	9	48	.227	.287	.269	60	-15	11	.925	3			C74,O7(0/2/5)/S1		-0.5
1890	Bro P	58	218	32	55	3	3	0	31	14	2	18	.252	.303	.294	56	-15	7	.890	3	129	120	C36,1b21/OR		-0.8
1891	Lou AA	45	153	21	35	3	1	0	23	11	1	17	.229	.285	.261	57	-9	4	.909	-10	83	105	C35,1b10		-1.5
	StL AA	7	25	3	5	0	0	0	1	1	1	2	.200	.259	.200	28	-2	0	.921	1	116	88	C7		0.0
	Year	52	178	24	40	3	1	0	24	12	2	19	.225	.281	.253	52	-11	4	.912	-8	90	101	C42,1b10		-1.5
Total	7	378	1364	172	304	27	9	0	114	67	21	87	.223	.270	.256	52	-85	52	.906	-22	109	110	C284,1b81,O14(2/2/10),S2		-8.1

COOK, CLIFF   Raymond Clifford   B8.20.1936 Dallas TX   BR/TR/6-0/188*   d9.9

1959	Cin N	9	21	3	8	2	1	0	5	2-1	0	8	.381	.435	.571	161	2	1-0	.909	0	104	190	3b9		0.2
1960	Cin N	54	149	9	31	7	0	3	13	8-1	0	51	.208	.247	.315	52	-10	0-0	.954	-2	91	108	3b47,O4(3/1/0)		-1.3
1961	Cin N	4	5	0	0	0	0	0	0	0-0	0	4	.000	.000	.000	-99	-1	0-0	1.000	0	186	0	/3		-0.1
1962	Cin N	6	5	0	0	0	0	0	0	0-0	0	2	.000	.000	.000	-97	-1	0-0	1.000	-1	0	0	3b4		-0.2
	NY N	40	112	12	26	6	1	2	9	4-0	0	34	.232	.275	.357	68	-5	1-0	.875	-6	73	66	3b16,O10R	33	-1.1
	Year	46	117	12	26	6	1	2	9	4-0	0	36	.222	.264	.342	61	-7	1-0	.878	-6	68	61	3b20,O10R		-1.3
1963	NY N	50	106	9	15	2	1	2	8	12-4	0	37	.142	.229	.236	34	-9	0-1	1.000	3	92	174	O21(8/1/12),3b9,1b5		-0.8
Total	5	163	398	33	80	17	3	7	35	26-6	0	136	.201	.254	.312	54	-24	2-1	.937	-5	95	95	3b86,O35(11/2/22),1b5	33	-3.3

COOKE, DUSTY   Allen Lindsey   B6.23.1907 Swepsonville NC   D11.21.1987 Raleigh NC   BL/TR/6-1/205   d4.15   M1/C5

1930	NY A	92	216	43	55	12	3	6	29	32	1	61	.255	.353	.421	100	0	4-6	.978	1	111	47	O73(21/28/24)		-0.3
1931	NY A	27	39	10	13	1	0	1	6	8	0	11	.333	.447	.436	141	3	4-1	1.000	1	136	0	O11(7/0/6)		0.3
1932	NY A	3	0	1	0	0	0	0	0	1	0	0	–.000	–.000		191	0	0-0		0			/H		0.0
1933	Bos A	119	454	86	133	35	10	5	54	67	2	71	.293	.386	.447	121	16	7-5	.956	-5	98	62	O118(47/70/30)		0.6
1934	Bos A	74	168	34	41	8	5	1	26	36	0	25	.244	.377	.369	87	-2	7-2	.976	-2	95	33	O44(9/14/21)		-0.5
1935	Bos A	100	294	51	90	18	6	3	34	46	0	24	.306	.400	.439	109	5	6-8	.972	-2	100	66	O82(7/35/44)		-0.1
1936	Bos A	111	341	58	93	20	3	6	47	72	1	48	.273	.401	.402	93	-1	4-3	.972	-1	108	55	O91(24/1/67)		-0.7
1938	Cin N	82	233	41	64	15	1	2	33	28	1	36	.275	.355	.373	103	2	0	.963	1	106	89	O51(46/0/7)		0.0
Total	8	608	1745	324	489	109	28	24	229	290	5	276	.280	.384	.416	106	23	32-25	.969	-7	104	55	O470(161/148/199)		-0.7

COOKE, FRED   Frederick B.   B Paulding OH   D1.22.1923 Gallipolis OH   5-10/164   d7.30

| 1897 | Cle N | 5 | 17 | 2 | 5 | 2 | 0 | 0 | 3 | 3 | 0 | | .294 | .400 | .412 | 109 | 0 | 0 | .857 | 1 | 490 | 0 | O5R | | 0.1 |

COOKSON, BRENT   Brent Adam   B9.7.1969 Van Nuys CA   BR/TR/5-11/200*   [OakA91 15/411]   d8.12   Col Cal St.-Long Beach

1995	KC A	22	35	2	5	1	0	0	5	2-0	0	7	.143	.189	.171	-5	-6	1-0	1.000	-0	98	0	O12(10/0/2),D2		-0.6
1999	LA N	3	5	0	1	0	0	0	0	0-0	0	1	.200	.200	.200	2	-1	0-0	1.000	0	146	0	O3(2/0/1)		-0.1
Total	2	25	40	2	6	1	0	0	5	2-0	0	8	.150	.190	.175	-4	-7	1-0	1.000	-0	106	0	O15(12/0/3),D2		-0.7

COOLBAUGH, MIKE   Michael Robert   B6.5.1972 Binghamton NY   BR/TR/6-1/185*   [TorA90 16/447]   d7.16   b-Scott

2001	Mil N	39	70	10	14	6	0	2	7	5-0	2	16	.200	.273	.371	66	-4	0-0	.971	-1	92	189	3b27,S3		-0.4
2002	StL N	5	12	0	1	0	0	0	0	1-0	0	3	.083	.154	.083	-34	-2	0-0	1.000	1	143	530	3b4		-0.1
Total	2	44	82	10	15	6	0	2	7	6-0	2	19	.183	.256	.329	51	-6	0-0	.977	0	101	247	3b31,S3		-0.5

COOLBAUGH, SCOTT   Scott Robert   B6.13.1966 Binghamton NY   BR/TR/5-11/185*   [TexA87 3/77]   d9.2   b-Mike   Col Texas

1989	Tex A	25	51	7	14	1	0	2	7	4-0	0	12	.275	.321	.412	105	0	0-0	.958	4	133	113	3b23,D2		0.4
1990	Tex A	67	180	21	36	6	0	2	13	15-0	1	47	.200	.264	.267	49	-12	1-0	.941	6	111	118	3b66		-0.6
1991	SD N	60	180	12	39	8	1	2	15	19-2	1	45	.217	.294	.306	67	-8	0-3	.952	0	105	101	3b54		-0.9
1994	StL N	15	21	4	4	0	0	2	6	1-0	0	4	.190	.217	.476	77	-1	0-0	1.000	-1	0	146	1b4,3b4		-0.2
Total	4	167	432	44	93	15	1	8	41	39-2	2	108	.215	.281	.310	65	-21	1-3	.949	11	112	108	3b147,1b4,D2		-1.3

COOLEY, DUFF   Duff Gordon "Dick"   B3.29.1873 Leavenworth KS   D8.9.1937 Dallas TX   BL/TR/5-11/158   d7.27   OF(549/479/69)

1893	StL N	29	107	20	37	2	3	0	21	8	0	9	.346	.391	.421	115	2	8	.947	-5	50	1	O15R,C10,S5		-0.2
1894	StL N	54	206	35	61	3	1	1	21	12	6	16	.296	.335	.335	62	-13	7	.833	-11	15	63	O39(8/4/28),3b13/S1		-2.0
1895	StL N	133	567	108	194	9	20	7	75	37	3	29	.342	.386	.466	121	14	27	.934	5	86	21	O125(116/8/1),3b5,S3/C		0.9
1896	StL N	40	166	29	51	5	3	0	13	7	0	13	.307	.335	.373	90	-3	12	.959	-2	33	0	O40L		-0.7
	Phi N	64	287	63	88	6	4	2	22	18	0	16	.307	.348	.376	92	-4	18	.901	-4	71	86	O64(22/40/2)		-1.0
	Year	104	453	92	139	11	7	2	35	25	0	19	.307	.343	.375	91	-7	30	.923	-6	55	50	O104(62/40/2)		-1.7
1897	Phi N	133	566	124	186	14	13	4	40	51	2		.329	.386	.420	116	13	31	.960	3	84	162	O131(0/108/23),1b2		0.7
1898	Phi N	149	629	123	196	24	12	4	55	48	4		.312	.364	.407	126	21	17	.943	1	73	40	O149C		1.1
1899	Phi N	94	406	75	112	15	8	1	31	29	4		.276	.330	.360	92	-5	15	.971	-6	88	126	1b79,O14C/2		-1.0
1900	Pit N	66	249	30	50	8	1	0	22	14	0		.201	.243	.241	34	-23	9	.989	-5	53	118	1b66		-2.7
1901	Bos N	63	240	27	62	13	3	0	27	14	1		.258	.302	.338	78	-7	5	.943	-1	68	59	O53(29/24/0),1b10		-1.1
1902	Bos N	135	548	71	162	26	8	0	58	34	2		.296	.339	.372	118	11	17	.952	-7	40	46	O127(94/33/0),1b7		-0.3
1903	Bos N	138	553	76	160	26	10	1	70	44	5		.289	.342	.378	109	6	27	.952	-5	62	88	O126(124/3/0),1b13		-0.6
1904	Bos N	122	467	41	127	18	7	5	70	24	3		.272	.312	.373	115	7	14	.976	-7	20	82	O116L,1b6		-0.7
1905	Det A	97	377	25	93	11	9	1	32	26	1		.247	.297	.332	99	-2	7	.959	5	113	192	O96C		-0.1
Total	13	1317	5368	849	1579	180	102	26	557	366	20	73	.294	.342	.380	104	17	224	.945	-34	63	78	O1095L,1b184,3b18,C11,S9/2		-7.7

COOMBS, CECIL   Cecil Lysander   B3.18.1888 Moweaqua IL   D11.25.1975 Fort Worth TX   BR/TR/5-9/160   d8.7

| 1914 | Chi A | 7 | 23 | 1 | 4 | 1 | 0 | 0 | 1 | 1 | 0 | 7 | .174 | .208 | .217 | 28 | -2 | 0-1 | 1.000 | 1 | 93 | 245 | O7C | | -0.2 |

COOMBS, JACK   John Wesley "Colby Jack"   B11.18.1882 LeGrand IA   D4.15.1957 Palestine TX   BB/TR/6-0/185   d7.5   M1/C1   Col Colby ▲

1906	Phi A	24	67	9	16	2	0	0	3	1	1		.239	.261	.269	64	1	2	.967	-1	80	288	P23		0.0
1907	Phi A	24	48	4	8	0	1	0	4	0	0		.167	.167	.229	25	-1	1	.979	-0	89	185	P23		0.0
1908	Phi A	78	220	24	56	9	5	1	23	9	1		.255	.287	.355	101	-1	6	.990	5	106	194	O47(1/11/35),P26/1		0.3
1909	Phi A	37	83	4	14	4	0	0	10	4	1		.169	.216	.217	36	1	1	.973	-9	95	127	P30		0.0
1910	†Phi A	46	132	20	29	3	0	0	9	7	2		.220	.270	.242	61	1	3	.990	-5	68	74	P45		0.0
1911	†Phi A	52	141	31	45	6	1	2	23	8	0		.319	.356	.418	118	13	5	.913	-3	77	118	P47		0.0
1912	Phi A	56	110	10	28	2	0	0	13	14	1		.255	.344	.273	80	6	1	1.000	-1	87	40	P40		0.0
1913	Phi A	2	3	1	1	1	0	0		0	0	2	.333	.333	.667	195	1	0	.500	-0	0	0	P2		0.0
1914	Phi A	5	11	0	3	1	0	0	2	1	0		.273	.333	.364	114	0	0-1	1.000	-0	44	0	P2,O2C		0.0
1915	Bro N	29	75	8	21	1	0	0	5	2	0	17	.280	.299	.320	86	4	0-1	.980	-4	58	110	P29		0.0
1916	†Bro N	27	61	2	11	0	0	1	5	0	0	10	.180	.206	.213	28	0	1	1.000	-6	36	82	P27		0.0
1917	Bro N	32	44	4	10	0	1	0	2	4	0	9	.227	.292	.273	72	2	1	.971	-5	65	76	P31		0.0
1918	Bro N	46	113	6	19	3	2	0	9	4	1	5	.168	.223	.230	38	1		.962	-4	75	0	P27,O13(0/3/11)		-0.5
1920	Det A	2	2	0	0	0	0	0	0	0	0		.000	.000	.000	-99	-0	0	1.000	-0	65	0	P2		0.0
Total	14	460	1110	123	261	34	10	4	100	59	7	44	.235	.278	.295	74	20	21-2	.966	-23	75	118	P354,O62(1/16/46)/1		-0.2

COOMER, RON   Ronald Bryan   B11.18.1966 Crest Hill IL   BR/TR/5-11/206(195-225)   [OakA87 14/355]   d8.1   Col Taft (CA) JC

1995	Min A	37	101	15	26	3	1	5	19	9-0	1	11	.257	.324	.455	100	-1	0-0	.993	1	111	92	1b22,3b13/ORD		-0.1
1996	Min A	95	233	34	69	12	1	12	41	17-1	2	24	.296	.340	.511	110	3	0-0	.993	2	161	83	1b57,O23R,3b9,D3		0.1
1997	Min A	140	523	63	156	30	2	13	85	22-5	0	91	.298	.324	.438	95	-5	4-3	.966	-3	99	102	3b119,1b9,O7R,D7		-0.8
1998	Min A	137	529	54	146	22	1	15	72	18-1	0	72	.276	.295	.406	79	-18	2-2	.972	-4	90	83	3b75,1b54,D13,O3R		-2.5
1999	Min A★	127	467	54	123	25	1	16	65	30-1	1	69	.263	.307	.424	90	-15	2-1	.996	9	130	108	1b71,3b57/ORD		-1.1

YEAR	TM LG	G	AB	R	H	2B	3B	HR	RBI	BB-IB	HP	SO	AVG	OBP	SLG	AOPS	ABR	SB-CS	FA	FR	RNG	THR	GAMES AT POSITION	DL	BFW
2000	Min A	140	544	64	147	29	1	16	82	36-2	4	50	.270	.317	.415	79	-18	2-0	.995	2	92	94	1b124,3b5,D9		-2.5
2001	Chi N	111	349	25	91	19	1	8	53	29-1	2	70	.261	.316	.390	85	-8	0-0	.954	1	91	105	3b76,1b36/D	22	-0.8
2002	†NY A	55	148	14	39	7	0	3	17	6-1	0	23	.264	.299	.372	75	-6	0-0	.882	-4	78	58	3b26,D15,1b11		-1.1
2003	LA N	69	125	11	30	4	0	4	15	10-2	1	19	.240	.299	.368	75	-5	0-0	1.000	-0	115	96	1b24,3b11,D4	26	-0.6
Total	9	911	3019	333	827	151	8	92	449	177-14	9	429	.274	.313	.421	86	-73	13-7	.996	3	115	97	1b408,3b391,D63,O35R	48	-9.4

COON, WILLIAM   William K. B3.21.1855 PA D8.30.1915 Burlington NJ d9.4

YEAR	TM LG	G	AB	R	H	2B	3B	HR	RBI	BB-IB	HP	SO	AVG	OBP	SLG	AOPS	ABR	SB-CS	FA	FR	RNG	THR	GAMES AT POSITION	DL	BFW
1875	Ath NA	4	12	1	2	0	0	0		0		0	.167	.167	.167	15	-1	1-0	.810	-0			C4/OR		-0.1
1876	Phi N	54	220	30	50	5	1	0	22	2		4	.227	.234	.259	65	-8		.761	-13	160	76	O29(0/2/29),C18,3b4,2b4,P2		-1.8

COONEY, JIMMY   James Edward "Scoops" B8.24.1894 Cranston RI D8.7.1991 Warwick RI BR/TR/5-11/160 d9.22 Mil 1918 f-Jimmy b-Johnny

YEAR	TM LG	G	AB	R	H	2B	3B	HR	RBI	BB-IB	HP	SO	AVG	OBP	SLG	AOPS	ABR	SB-CS	FA	FR	RNG	THR	GAMES AT POSITION	DL	BFW
1917	Bos A	11	36	4	8	1	0	0	3	6	0	2	.222	.333	.250	79	-1	0	1.000	3	107	167	2b10/S		0.3
1919	NY N	5	14	3	3	0	0	0	1	0	0	0	.214	.214	.214	29	-1	0	1.000	1	100	170	S4/2		-0.1
1924	StL N	110	383	44	113	20	8	1	57	20	0	20	.295	.330	.397	96	-3	12-10	.969	4	97	102	S99,3b7/2		1.1
1925	StL N	54	187	27	51	11	2	0	18	4	1	5	.273	.292	.353	62	-11	1-3	.976	-4	87	110	S37,2b15/OL		-1.2
1926	Chi N	141	513	52	129	18	5	1	47	23	3	10	.251	.288	.312	61	-29	11	.972	18	102	120	S141		0.4
1927	Chi N	33	132	16	32	2	0	0	6	8	0	7	.242	.286	.258	46	-10	1	.973	-1	97	66	S33		-0.8
	Phi N	76	259	33	70	12	1	0	15	13	0	9	.270	.305	.324	68	-12	4	.980	15	110	114	S74		1.0
	Year	109	391	49	102	14	1	0	21	21	0	16	.261	.299	.302	61	-22	5	.978	13	106	98	S107		0.2
1928	Bos N	18	51	2	7	0	0	0	3	2	0	5	.137	.170	.137	-20	-9	-1	.982	1	99	150	S11,2b4		-0.7
Total	7	448	1575	181	413	64	16	2	150	76	4	58	.262	.298	.327	67	-76	30-13	.974	34	100	110	S400,2b31,3b7/OL		0.0

COONEY, JIMMY   James Joseph B7.9.1865 Cranston RI D7.1.1903 Cranston RI BB/TR/5-9/155 d4.19 s-Jimmy s-Johnny

YEAR	TM LG	G	AB	R	H	2B	3B	HR	RBI	BB-IB	HP	SO	AVG	OBP	SLG	AOPS	ABR	SB-CS	FA	FR	RNG	THR	GAMES AT POSITION	DL	BFW
1890	Chi N	135	574	114	156	19	10	4	52	73	6	23	.272	.360	.361	106	5	45	.936	-1	98	114	S135/C		0.8
1891	Chi N	118	465	84	114	15	3	0	42	48	2	17	.245	.318	.290	78	-12	21	.917	9	113	102	S118		0.0
1892	Chi N	65	238	18	41	1	0	0	20	23	1	5	.172	.248	.176	29	-20	10	.912	-3	101	72	S65		-1.9
	Was N	6	25	5	4	0	1	0	4	4	0	3	.160	.276	.240	58	-1	1	.862	-2	72	49	S6		-0.3
	Year	71	263	23	45	1	1	0	24	27	1	8	.171	.251	.183	31	-22	11	.908	-5	99	71	S71		-2.2
Total	3	324	1302	221	315	35	14	4	118	148	9	48	.242	.324	.300	82	-28	77	.923	3	104	100	S324/C		-1.4

COONEY, JOHNNY   John Walter B3.18.1901 Cranston RI D7.8.1986 Sarasota FL BR/TL/5-10/165 d4.19 M1/C21 f-Jimmy b-Jimmy ▲

YEAR	TM LG	G	AB	R	H	2B	3B	HR	RBI	BB-IB	HP	SO	AVG	OBP	SLG	AOPS	ABR	SB-CS	FA	FR	RNG	THR	GAMES AT POSITION	DL	BFW
1921	Bos N	8	5	0	1	0	0	0	0	0	0	1	.200	.200	.200	7	0	0-0	1.000	0	91	0	P8		0.0
1922	Bos N	4	8	0	0	0	0	0	0	0	0	1	.000	.000	.000	-99	-1	0-0	1.000	0	103	392	P4		0.0
1923	Bos N	42	66	7	25	1	0	0	3	4	0	2	.379	.394	.394	119	2	0-1	1.000	0	61	79	P23,O11(2/8/1)/1		0.1
1924	Bos N	55	130	10	33	2	1	0	4	9	0	5	.254	.302	.285	61	-7	0-4	.962	-1	72	132	P34,O16(0/15/1)/1		-0.5
1925	Bos N	54	103	17	33	7	0	0	13	3	1	6	.320	.346	.388	96	-1	1-0	.949	1	104	167	P31,1b3/OL		0.0
1926	Bos N	64	126	17	38	3	2	0	18	13	0	7	.302	.367	.357	105	1	6	.996	4	160	121	1b31,P19/OR		0.3
1927	Bos N	10	1	0	0	0	0	0	0	0	0	0	.000	.000	.000	-99	0		—	0			/H		0.0
1928	Bos N	33	41	2	7	0	0	0	2	4	0	3	.171	.244	.171	11	-5	0	1.000	3	153	231	P24,1b3,O2(0/1/1)		0.0
1929	Bos N	41	72	10	23	4	1	0	6	3	1	0	.319	.355	.403	91	-1	1	1.000	3	121	0	O16(4/10/2),P14		0.0
1930	Bos N	4	3	0	0	0	0	0	0	0	0	0	.000	.000	.000	-99	-0	0-0	1.000	0	283	0	P2		0.0
1935	Bro N	10	29	3	9	1	0	1	3	0	0	2	.310	.375	.379	106	0	0	1.000	-0	109	0	O10C		0.0
1936	Bro N	130	507	71	143	17	5	0	30	24	0	15	.282	.315	.335	74	-19	3	.994	9	108	131	O130C		-1.3
1937	Bro N	120	430	61	126	18	5	0	37	22	0	10	.293	.327	.358	85	-10	5	.976	5	108	105	O111(5/104/3),1b2		-0.7
1938	Bos N	120	432	45	117	25	5	0	17	22	1	12	.271	.308	.352	90	-7	2	.982	-2	101	68	O110(17/15/84),1b13		-1.6
1939	Bos N	118	368	39	101	8	1	2	27	21	2	8	.274	.317	.318	77	-13	2	.992	2	99	128	O116(0/112/5),1b2		-1.4
1940	Bos N	108	365	40	116	14	3	0	21	25	1	9	.318	.363	.373	109	5	4	.992	1	106	-67	O99(0/98/1),1b7		0.2
1941	Bos N	123	442	52	141	25	2	0	29	27	0	15	.319	.358	.385	114	4	3	.996	3	104	106	O111C,1b4		0.8
1942	Bos N	74	198	23	41	6	0	0	7	23	0	5	.207	.290	.237	56	-10	2	.984	-2	96	77	O54(5/16/34),1b23		-1.7
1943	Bro N	37	34	7	7	0	0	0	2	4	0	3	.206	.289	.206	44	-2	1	1.000	0	89	0	1b3,O2C		-0.3
1944	Bro N	7	4	0	3	0	0	0	1	0	0	0	.750	.750	.750	329	1	0	1.000	0	120	0	O2(1/1/0)		0.1
	NY A	10	8	1	1	0	0	0	1	1	0	0	.125	.222	.125	1	-1	0-0	.988	25	105	98	O2L		-0.1
Total	20	1172	3372	408	965	130	26	2	219	208	6	107	.286	.329	.342	87	-61	30-5	.988	25	105	98	O794(37/633/133),P159,1b93		-6.1

COONEY, PHIL   Philip Clarence (b Philip Clarence Cohen) B9.14.1882 New York NY D10.6.1957 New York NY BL/TR/5-8/155 d9.27

YEAR	TM LG	G	AB	R	H	2B	3B	HR	RBI	BB-IB	HP	SO	AVG	OBP	SLG	AOPS	ABR	SB-CS	FA	FR	RNG	THR	GAMES AT POSITION	DL	BFW
1905	NY A	1	3	0	0	0	0	0	0	0	0	0	.000	.000	.000	-90	-1	0	1.000	-0	74	0	/3		-0.1

COONEY, BILL   William Ambrose "Cush" B4.7.1883 Boston MA D11.6.1928 Roxbury MA TR d9.22 Col Princeton

YEAR	TM LG	G	AB	R	H	2B	3B	HR	RBI	BB-IB	HP	SO	AVG	OBP	SLG	AOPS	ABR	SB-CS	FA	FR	RNG	THR	GAMES AT POSITION	DL	BFW
1909	Bos N	5	10	3	3	0	0	0	0	0	0		.300	.300	.300	82	0	0	.500	-0	60	0	P3/2S		0.0
1910	Bos N	8	12	2	3	0	0	0	1	2	0	0	.250	.357	.250	74	0	0	—	-0	60	0	O2R		0.0
Total	2	13	22	2	6	0	0	0	1	2	0	0	.273	.333	.273	78	0	0	.500	-0	60	0	P3,O2R/S2		0.0

COOPER, CECIL   Cecil Celester B12.20.1949 Brenham TX BL/TL/6-2/190(165-190) [BosA68 6/128] d9.8 C2

YEAR	TM LG	G	AB	R	H	2B	3B	HR	RBI	BB-IB	HP	SO	AVG	OBP	SLG	AOPS	ABR	SB-CS	FA	FR	RNG	THR	GAMES AT POSITION	DL	BFW
1971	Bos A	14	42	9	13	4	1	0	3	5-1	1	4	.310	.388	.452	130	2	1-0	.988	-2	43	62	1b11		0.0
1972	Bos A	12	17	4	4	1	0	0	2	2-1	0	6	.235	.316	.294	78	0	0-0	1.000	-1	0	94	1b3		-0.1
1973	Bos A	30	101	12	24	2	0	3	11	7-1	0	12	.238	.284	.347	73	-4	1-2	.984	-1	99	103	1b29		-0.7
1974	Bos A	121	414	55	114	24	1	8	43	32-3	1	74	.275	.327	.396	101	1	2-5	.983	-2	96	112	1b74,D41		-1.0
1975	†Bos A	106	305	49	95	17	6	14	44	19-6	1	33	.311	.355	.544	140	15	1-4	.995	2	126	105	1b66,D53		1.2
1976	Bos A	123	451	66	127	22	6	15	78	16-6	1	62	.282	.304	.457	109	3	7-1	.994	-2	91	96	1b66,D53		-0.5
1977	Mil A	160	643	86	193	31	7	20	78	28-4	0	110	.300	.326	.463	113	9	13-8	.988	7	116	104	1b148,D10		0.6
1978	Mil A	107	407	60	127	23	2	13	54	32-3	0	72	.312	.359	.474	133	17	3-4	.988	4	125	108	1b84,D19	42	1.5
1979	Mil A★	150	590	83	182	44	1	24	106	16-0	0	77	.308	.364	.508	133	28	15-3	.993	-8	84	103	1b135,D15		1.4
1980	Mil A★	153	622	96	219	33	4	25	122	39-15	2	42	.352	.387	.539	156	46	17-6	.997	5	115	125	1b142,D11		4.3
1981	†Mil A★	106	416	70	133	35	1	12	60	28-2	3	30	.320	.363	.495	153	28	5-4	.992	1	109	123	1b101,D5		2.3
1982	†Mil A★	155	654	104	205	38	3	32	121	32-7	3	51	.313	.342	.528	143	35	2-3	.997	1	100	117	1b154/D		2.5
1983	Mil A	160	661	106	203	37	3	30	126	37-7	1	63	.307	.341	.508	141	34	2-1	.993	-10	79	100	1b158,D2		1.4
1984	Mil A	148	603	63	166	28	3	11	67	27-6	2	59	.275	.307	.386	94	-6	8-2	.991	3	108	100	1b122,D26		-1.1
1985	Mil A★	154	631	82	185	39	8	16	99	30-3	2	77	.293	.322	.456	112	9	10-3	.986	-2	100	93	1b123,D30	11	-2.3
1986	Mil A	134	542	46	140	24	1	12	75	41-2	1	87	.258	.310	.373	83	-13	1-2	.988	-3	90	102	1b90,D44		-1.1
1987	Mil A	63	250	25	62	13	0	6	36	17-2	0	51	.248	.293	.372	73	-10	-1	—	0	0	0	D62	3	-1.1
Total	17	1896	7349	1012	2192	415	47	241	1125	448-79	17	911	.298	.337	.466	121	194	89-49	.992	-8	101	107	1b1475,D373	56	8.3

COOPER, CLAUDE   Claude William B4.1.1892 Troup TX D1.21.1974 Plainview TX BL/TL/5-9/158 d4.14 Mil 1918 Col TCU

YEAR	TM LG	G	AB	R	H	2B	3B	HR	RBI	BB-IB	HP	SO	AVG	OBP	SLG	AOPS	ABR	SB-CS	FA	FR	RNG	THR	GAMES AT POSITION	DL	BFW
1913	†NY N	27	30	11	9	4	0	0	4		0	6	.300	.382	.433	132	2	3-3	.895	-0	106	108	O15(6/10/0)		0.1
1914	Bro F	113	399	56	96	14	11	2	25	26	4	60	.241	.294	.346	74	-23	25	.926	-2	106	74	O101(45/21/38)		-3.2
1915	Bro F	153	527	75	155	26	12	2	63	77	4	78	.294	.388	.400	123	12	31	.958	13	111	150	O121(112/7/2),1b32		2.0
1916	Phi N	56	104	9	20	2	0	0	11	7	1	15	.192	.250	.212	41	-7	1	.945	-1	107	39	O29(15/13/1)/1		-1.0
1917	Phi N	24	29	5	3	1	0	0	1	5	0	4	.103	.235	.138	15	-3	0	.923	-1	108	108	O12(9/3/2)		-0.4
Total	5	373	1089	156	283	47	23	4	104	119	9	163	.260	.338	.356	95	-19	60-3	.943	10	108	108	O278(187/54/43),1b33		-2.5

COOPER, GARY   Gary Clifton B8.13.1964 Lynwood CA BR/TR/6-1/200 [HouN86 7/172] d9.15 Col Brigham Young

YEAR	TM LG	G	AB	R	H	2B	3B	HR	RBI	BB-IB	HP	SO	AVG	OBP	SLG	AOPS	ABR	SB-CS	FA	FR	RNG	THR	GAMES AT POSITION	DL	BFW
1991	Hou N	9	16	1	4	1	0	0	2	3-0	0	6	.250	.368	.313	99	0	0-0	.833	-2	32	0	3b4		-0.2

COOPER, GARY   Gary Nathaniel B12.22.1956 Savannah GA BB/TR/6-3/175 [AtlN75 3/66] d8.25

YEAR	TM LG	G	AB	R	H	2B	3B	HR	RBI	BB-IB	HP	SO	AVG	OBP	SLG	AOPS	ABR	SB-CS	FA	FR	RNG	THR	GAMES AT POSITION	DL	BFW
1980	Atl N	21	23	0	0	0	0	0	0	0	0	0	.000	.000	.000	-99	-1	2-1	1.000	1	89	511	O13(11/2/0)		0.0

COOPER, PAT   Orge Patterson B11.26.1917 Albemarle NC D3.15.1993 Charlotte NC BR/TR/6-3/180 d5.11

YEAR	TM LG	G	AB	R	H	2B	3B	HR	RBI	BB-IB	HP	SO	AVG	OBP	SLG	AOPS	ABR	SB-CS	FA	FR	RNG	THR	GAMES AT POSITION	DL	BFW
1946	Phi A	1	0	0	0	0	0	0	0	0	0	0					0	0-0	—	-0	0	0	/P		0.0
1947	Phi A	13	16	0	4	0	0	0	3	0	0	5	.250	.250	.375	71	-1	0-0	1.000	-0	125	0	/1		-0.1
Total	2	14	16	0	4	0	0	0	3	0	0	5	.250	.250	.375	71	-1	0-0	1.000	-0	125	0	1/1P		-0.1

COOPER, SCOTT   Scott Kendrick B10.13.1967 St.Louis MO BL/TR/6-3/205(200-215) [BosA86 3/69] d9.5

YEAR	TM LG	G	AB	R	H	2B	3B	HR	RBI	BB-IB	HP	SO	AVG	OBP	SLG	AOPS	ABR	SB-CS	FA	FR	RNG	THR	GAMES AT POSITION	DL	BFW
1990	Bos A	2	1	0	0	0	0	0	0	0	0	0	.000	.000	.000	-95	-0		—	0			/H		0.0
1991	Bos A	14	35	6	6	2	0	0	7	4-0	0	9	.171	.256	.229	50	-2	0-0	.933	1	112	56	3b13		0.6
1992	Bos A	123	337	34	93	21	0	5	33	37-0	0	51	.276	.346	.383	97	0	1-1	.990	6	101	107	1b62,3b7/2SD		0.2
1993	Bos A★	156	526	67	147	29	3	9	63	58-15	5	81	.279	.355	.397	96	-2	5-2	.937	-11	89	87	3b154,1b2/S		-1.1
1994	Bos A★	104	369	49	104	16	4	13	53	30-2	1	68	.282	.333	.453	97	-3	0-3	.944	10	116	125	3b104	8	0.6

YEAR	TM LG	G	AB	R	H	2B	3B	HR	RBI	BB-IB	HP	SO	AVG	OBP	SLG	AOPS	ABR	SB-CS	FA	FR	RNG	THR	GAMES AT POSITION	DL	BFW
1995	StL N	118	374	29	86	18	2	3	40	49-3	3	85	.230	.321	.313	68	-16	0-3	.945	9	111	141	3b110		-0.8
1997	KC A	75	159	12	32	6	1	3	15	17-0	2	32	.201	.283	.308	54	-11	1-1	1.000	-2	94	80	3b39,1b8,D5		-1.3
Total	7	592	1801	197	478	94	12	33	211	193-20	11	299	.265	.337	.386	89	-27	7-10	.948	12	104	106	3b467,1b72,D7,S2/2	48	-1.8

COOPER, WALKER William Walker "Walk" B1.8.1915 Atherton MO D4.11.1991 Scottsdale AZ BR/TR/6-3/210(195-215) d9.25 Mil 1945 C2 b-Mort

YEAR	TM LG	G	AB	R	H	2B	3B	HR	RBI	BB-IB	HP	SO	AVG	OBP	SLG	AOPS	ABR	SB-CS	FA	FR	RNG	THR	GAMES AT POSITION	DL	BFW
1940	StL N	6	19	3	6	1	0	0	2	2-0	0	2	.316	.381	.368	102	0	0	1.000	-0	86	144	C6		0.0
1941	StL N	68	200	19	49	9	1	1	20	13	0	14	.245	.291	.315	66	-9	1	.966	3	123	122	C63		-0.3
1942	†StL N★	125	438	58	123	32	7	7	65	29	1	29	.281	.327	.434	113	6	4	.972	7	158	103	C115		2.1
1943	†StL N★	122	449	52	143	30	4	9	81	19	2	19	.318	.349	.463	128	14	4	.975	1	169	75	C112		2.3
1944	†StL N★	112	397	56	126	25	5	13	72	20	1	19	.317	.352	.504	136	17	4	.980	5	146	74	C97		2.8
1945	StL N	4	18	3	7	0	0	0	1	0	0	1	.389	.389	.389	114	0	0	.966	0	115	66	C4		0.1
1946	NY N★	87	280	29	75	10	1	8	46	17	0	12	.268	.310	.396	99	-2	0	.972	-7	87	103	C73		-0.6
1947	NY N★	140	515	79	157	24	8	35	122	24	3	43	.305	.339	.586	141	24	2	.979	-6	163	67	C132		2.5
1948	NY N★	91	290	40	77	12	0	16	54	28	1	29	.266	.332	.472	115	5	1	.979	-7	118	44	C79		0.2
1949	NY N	42	147	14	31	4	2	4	21	7	3	8	.211	.261	.347	62	-9	0	.982	-1	91	83	C40		-0.7
	Cin N☆	82	307	34	86	9	2	16	62	21	2	24	.280	.330	.479	113	4	0	.978	-3	118	105	C77		0.6
	Year	124	454	48	117	13	4	20	83	28	5	32	.258	.308	.436	97	-5	0	.979	-3	109	98	C117		-0.1
1950	Cin N	15	47	3	9	3	0	0	4	0	0	5	.191	.191	.255	16	-6	0	.972	-0	73	104	C13		-0.6
	Bos N☆	102	337	52	111	19	3	14	60	30	3	26	.329	.389	.528	148	23	1	.973	-3	82	114	C88		2.4
	Year	117	384	55	120	22	3	14	64	30	3	31	.313	.367	.495	132	17	1	.973	-4	81	113	C101		1.8
1951	Bos N	109	342	42	107	14	1	18	59	28	1	18	.313	.367	.518	145	20	1-1	.981	-2	78	138	C90		2.3
1952	Bos N	102	349	33	82	12	1	10	55	22	1	32	.235	.282	.361	80	-11	1-0	.983	-5	93	114	C89		-1.1
1953	Mil N	53	137	12	30	6	0	3	16	12	1	15	.219	.287	.328	64	-7	1-0	.983	-3	86	54	C35		-0.8
1954	Pit N	14	15	0	3	2	0	1	2	0	1	1	.200	.294	.333	64	-1	0-0	1.000	-0	36	0	C2		-0.1
	Chi N	57	158	21	49	10	2	7	32	21	2	23	.310	.398	.532	138	9	0-0	.978	-3	59	132	C48		0.8
	Year	71	173	21	52	12	2	7	33	23	2	24	.301	.389	.514	132	9	0-0	.978	-3	58	128	C50		0.7
1955	Chi N	54	111	11	31	8	1	7	15	6-1	1	19	.279	.322	.559	128	4	0-0	.961	-7	58	96	C31		-0.2
1956	StL N	40	68	5	18	5	1	2	14	3-1	1	8	.265	.296	.456	98	0	0-0	.984	-2	87	46	C16		-0.2
1957	StL N	48	78	7	21	5	1	2	15	12-1	1	10	.269	.310	.474	106	0	0-0	.957	-2	93	87	C13		-0.1
Total	18	1473	4702	573	1341	240	40	173	812	309-3	22	357	.285	.332	.464	116	81	18-1	.977	-32	118	97	C1223		11.4

COQUILLETTE, TRACE Trace Robert B6.4.1974 Carmichael CA BR/TR/6-0/185* [MonN93 10/286] d9.7 Col Sacramento (CA) City

YEAR	TM LG	G	AB	R	H	2B	3B	HR	RBI	BB-IB	HP	SO	AVG	OBP	SLG	AOPS	ABR	SB-CS	FA	FR	RNG	THR	GAMES AT POSITION	DL	BFW
1999	Mon N	17	49	2	13	3	0	1	4	4-0	1	7	.265	.333	.327	71	-2	1-0	.944	-1	81	59	3b11,2b6		-0.2
2000	Mon N	34	59	6	12	4	0	1	8	7-0	0	19	.203	.284	.322	53	-4	0-0	.958	-1	105	93	3b19,2b8,O2(2/0/1)		-0.5
Total	2	51	108	8	25	7	0	1	12	11-0	1	26	.231	.306	.324	61	-6	1-0	.952	-2	94	77	3b30,2b14,O2(2/0/1)		-0.7

CORA, ALEX Jose Alexander B10.18.1975 Caguas, PR BL/TR/6-0/180(180-200) [LAN96 3/88] d6.7 b-Joey Col Miami

YEAR	TM LG	G	AB	R	H	2B	3B	HR	RBI	BB-IB	HP	SO	AVG	OBP	SLG	AOPS	ABR	SB-CS	FA	FR	RNG	THR	GAMES AT POSITION	DL	BFW
1998	LA N	29	33	1	4	0	1	0	4	2-0	1	8	.121	.194	.182	-0	-5	0-0	.956	3	83	117	S21,2b4		-0.2
1999	LA N	11	30	2	5	1	0	0	3	0-0	1	4	.167	.194	.200	-0	-5	0-0	1.000	0	94	80	S8,2b3	83	-0.4
2000	LA N	109	353	39	84	18	6	4	32	26-4	1	53	.238	.302	.357	69	-18	4-1	.972	3	99	123	S101,2b8		-0.7
2001	LA N	134	405	38	88	18	3	4	29	31-6	8	58	.217	.285	.306	57	-27	0-2	.962	-5	97	88	S132/2		-2.3
2002	LA N	115	258	37	75	14	4	5	28	26-4	7	38	.291	.371	.434	121	7	7-2	.977	-3	94	105	S61,2b40		0.9
2003	LA N	148	477	39	119	24	3	4	34	16-3	10	59	.249	.287	.338	64	-26	4-2	.978	31	106	146	2b141,S15		1.1
2004	†LA N	138	405	47	107	9	4	10	47	47-10	18	41	.264	.364	.380	95	-2	3-4	.987	3	101	124	2b138		0.6
2005	Cle A	49	146	11	30	5	2	1	8	5-0	4	18	.205	.250	.288	45	-12	6-0	.974	9	127	85	S24,2b15/OL		0.1
	†Bos A	47	104	14	28	3	2	2	16	6-0	1	12	.269	.310	.394	83	-3	1-2	.983	3	90	108	2b35,S11,3b5		0.1
	Year	96	250	25	58	8	4	3	24	11-0	5	30	.232	.275	.332	61	-15	7-2	.989	12	101	118	2b50,S35,3b5/OL		0.2
Total	8	780	2211	228	540	92	25	30	197	159-27	57	291	.244	.310	.349	74	-91	25-13	.982	43	103	131	2b385,S373,3b5/OL	83	-0.8

CORA, JOEY Jose Manuel (Amaro) B5.14.1965 Caguas, PR BB/TR/5-8/152(150-162) [SDN85 1/23] d4.6 C2 b-Alex Col Vanderbilt

YEAR	TM LG	G	AB	R	H	2B	3B	HR	RBI	BB-IB	HP	SO	AVG	OBP	SLG	AOPS	ABR	SB-CS	FA	FR	RNG	THR	GAMES AT POSITION	DL	BFW
1987	SD N	77	241	23	57	7	2	0	13	28-1	1	26	.237	.317	.282	63	-12	15-11	.975	1	109	82	2b66,S6		-0.9
1989	SD N	12	19	5	6	1	0	0	1	1-0	0	0	.316	.350	.368	105	0	1-0	.960	1	110	93	S7,3b2/2		0.2
1990	SD N	51	100	12	27	3	0	0	2	6-1	0	9	.270	.311	.300	68	-4	8-3	.833	-7	50	49	S21,2b15/C		-1.0
1991	Chi A	100	228	37	55	2	3	0	18	20-0	5	21	.241	.313	.276	67	-10	11-6	.970	-13	95	82	2b80,S5,D2	19	-2.2
1992	Chi A	68	122	27	30	7	1	0	9	22-1	4	13	.246	.371	.320	98	1	10-3	.984	-2	99	118	2b28,D18,S6,3b5		0.1
1993	†Chi A	153	579	95	155	15	13	2	51	67-0	1	63	.268	.351	.349	91	-7	20-8	.974	-17	93	89	2b151,3b3		-1.4
1994	Chi A	90	312	55	86	13	4	2	30	38-0	2	32	.276	.353	.362	87	-5	8-4	.978	-9	84	106	2b84/D	15	-0.9
1995	†Sea A	120	427	64	127	19	2	3	39	37-0	6	31	.297	.359	.372	90	-5	18-7	.955	-16	84	72	2b112/SD		-1.3
1996	Sea A	144	530	90	154	37	6	6	45	35-1	5	32	.291	.340	.417	90	-8	5-5	.979	-2	90	102	2b140/3		-0.5
1997	†Sea A★	149	574	105	172	40	4	11	54	53-2	5	49	.300	.359	.441	109	9	6-7	.973	-7	86	91	2b142		0.7
1998	Chi A	131	519	95	147	23	6	6	26	62-0	4	50	.283	.362	.385	94	-3	13-5	.962	-24	82	87	2b130		-1.9
	†Cle A	24	83	16	19	4	0	0	6	11-0	1	9	.229	.326	.277	57	-5	2-1	.986	-11	65	60	2b21		-1.5
	Year	155	602	111	166	27	6	6	32	73-0	5	59	.276	.357	.370	89	-8	15-6	.965	-35	80	83	2b151		-3.4
Total	11	1119	3734	624	1035	174	41	30	294	380-6	44	358	.277	.348	.369	90	-49	117-60	.971	-105	89	91	2b970,S46,D22,3b11/C	34	-10.6

CORBETT, GENE Eugene Louis B10.25.1913 Winona MN BL/TR/6-1.5/190 d9.19

YEAR	TM LG	G	AB	R	H	2B	3B	HR	RBI	BB-IB	HP	SO	AVG	OBP	SLG	AOPS	ABR	SB-CS	FA	FR	RNG	THR	GAMES AT POSITION	DL	BFW
1936	Phi N	6	21	1	3	0	0	0	2	2	0	3	.143	.217	.143	-1	-3	0	1.000	-1	54	149	1b6		-0.4
1937	Phi N	7	12	4	4	2	0	0	1	0	0	0	.333	.333	.500	114	0	0	.800	-1	92	0	3b3/2		0.0
1938	Phi N	24	75	7	6	1	0	2	7	6	0	11	.080	.148	.173	-12	-12	0	.995	-1	86	88	1b22		-1.5
Total	3	37	108	12	13	3	0	2	10	8	0	14	.120	.181	.204	5	-15	0	.996	-2	79	101	1b28,3b3/2		-1.9

CORBITT, CLAUDE Claude Elliott B7.21.1915 Sunbury NC D5.1.1978 Cincinnati OH BR/TR/5-10/170 d9.23 Col Duke

YEAR	TM LG	G	AB	R	H	2B	3B	HR	RBI	BB-IB	HP	SO	AVG	OBP	SLG	AOPS	ABR	SB-CS	FA	FR	RNG	THR	GAMES AT POSITION	DL	BFW
1945	Bro N	2	4	1	2	0	0	0	0	0	0	0	.500	.600	.500	209	1	0	1.000	0	118	433	3b2		0.1
1946	Cin N	82	274	25	68	10	1	1	16	23	1	13	.248	.309	.303	77	-9	3	.947	-6	101	109	S77		-1.1
1948	Cin N	87	258	24	66	11	0	0	18	14	1	16	.256	.297	.298	64	-13	4	.973	-4	96	68	2b52,3b16,S11		-1.4
1949	Cin N	44	94	10	17	1	0	0	3	9	0	1	.181	.252	.191	20	-11	1	.984	-5	77	127	S18,2b17/3		-1.5
Total	4	215	630	60	153	22	1	1	37	47	2	30	.243	.297	.286	63	-32	8	.956	-15	96	106	S106,2b69,3b19		-3.9

CORCORAN, ART Arthur Andrew "Bunny" B11.23.1894 Roxbury MA D7.27.1958 Chelsea MA TR/5-11/185 d9.9 Col Georgetown

YEAR	TM LG	G	AB	R	H	2B	3B	HR	RBI	BB-IB	HP	SO	AVG	OBP	SLG	AOPS	ABR	SB-CS	FA	FR	RNG	THR	GAMES AT POSITION	DL	BFW
1915	Phi A	1	4	0	0	0	0	0	0	0	0	2	.000	.000	.000	-99	-1	0	1.000	-0	59	0	/3		-0.1

CORCORAN, JOHN John A. B1873 Cincinnati OH D11.2.1901 Cincinnati OH TL d9.17

YEAR	TM LG	G	AB	R	H	2B	3B	HR	RBI	BB-IB	HP	SO	AVG	OBP	SLG	AOPS	ABR	SB-CS	FA	FR	RNG	THR	GAMES AT POSITION	DL	BFW
1895	Pit N	6	20	0	3	0	0	0	1	0	0	2	.150	.150	.150	-24	-4	0	.895	-1	100	0	S4,3b2		-0.4

CORCORAN, JACK John H. B5.15.1858 Lowell MA D12.28.1935 Jersey City NJ d5.1

YEAR	TM LG	G	AB	R	H	2B	3B	HR	RBI	BB-IB	HP	SO	AVG	OBP	SLG	AOPS	ABR	SB-CS	FA	FR	RNG	THR	GAMES AT POSITION	DL	BFW
1884	Bro AA	52	185	17	39	4	3	0		2		11	.211	.251	.265	68	-6		.873	-7			C38,O9(4/2/3),2b4,S2/P		-1.0

CORCORAN, LARRY Lawrence J. B8.10.1859 Brooklyn NY D10.14.1891 Newark NJ BL/TR (TB 1884p)/?/120 d5.1 b-Mike ▲

YEAR	TM LG	G	AB	R	H	2B	3B	HR	RBI	BB-IB	HP	SO	AVG	OBP	SLG	AOPS	ABR	SB-CS	FA	FR	RNG	THR	GAMES AT POSITION	DL	BFW
1880	Chi N	72	286	41	66	11	1	0	25	10		33	.231	.257	.276	76	-7		.957	5	114	117	P63,O8(0/5/3),S8		0.1
1881	Chi N	47	189	25	42	8	0	0	9	5		22	.222	.242	.265	57	-9		.893	-1	83	0	P45,S2/OL		-0.1
1882	Chi N	40	169	23	35	10	2	1	24	6		18	.207	.234	.308	69	-6		.915	-0	95	55	P39/3		0.0
1883	Chi N	68	263	40	55	12	7	0	25	6		62	.209	.227	.308	56	-15		.906	-2	94	113	P56,O13(8/4/1),S3/2		-0.4
1884	Chi N	64	251	43	61	3	4	1	19	10		33	.243	.272	.299	73	-9		.882	7	125	145	P60,O4R,S2		0.3
1885	Chi N	7	22	6	6	1	0	0	2	0		1	.273	.429	.318	127	1		.905	-0	98	0	P7/S		0.0
	NY N	3	14	3	5	0	0	0	4	0		1	.357	.357	.357	133	1		1.000	1	177	1558	P3		0.0
	Year	10	36	9	11	1	0	0	6	0		2	.306	.405	.333	129	1		.935	1	122	464	P10/S		0.0
1886	NY N	1	4	0	0	0	0	0	0	0		2	.000	.000	.000	-99	-1	0	.000	-1	0	0	/OR		-0.1
	Was N	21	81	9	15	2	1	0		14		14	.185	.250	.235	52	-4	3	.619	-3	178	256	O11R,S9,P2		-0.6
	Year	22	85	9	15	2	1	0		7		16	.176	.231	.235	44	-5	3	.591	-4	166	239	O12R,S9,P2		-0.7
1887	Ind N	3	10	2	2	0	0	0		0		0	.200	.333	.200	53	-1	2	1.000	0	0	0	O2(0/1/1),P2		0.0
Total	8	326	1289	192	287	47	15	2	111	52		187	.223	.253	.287	67	-50	5	.910	6	105	104	P277,O40(9/10/21),S25/23		-0.8

CORCORAN, MICKEY Michael Joseph B8.26.1882 Buffalo NY D12.9.1950 Buffalo NY BR/TR/5-8/165 d9.15

YEAR	TM LG	G	AB	R	H	2B	3B	HR	RBI	BB-IB	HP	SO	AVG	OBP	SLG	AOPS	ABR	SB-CS	FA	FR	RNG	THR	GAMES AT POSITION	DL	BFW
1910	Cin N	14	46	3	10	3	0	0	7	5	1	9	.217	.308	.283	76	-1	0	.911	-2	108	86	2b14		-0.3

CORCORAN, TOMMY Thomas William "Corky" B1.4.1869 New Haven CT D6.25.1960 Plainfield CT BR/TR/5-9/164 d4.19 U1

YEAR	TM LG	G	AB	R	H	2B	3B	HR	RBI	BB-IB	HP	SO	AVG	OBP	SLG	AOPS	ABR	SB-CS	FA	FR	RNG	THR	GAMES AT POSITION	DL	BFW
1890	Pit P	123	503	80	117	14	13	1	61	38		2	45	.233	.289	.318	68	-24	43	.884	6	106	76	S123		-1.2
1891	Phi AA	133	511	84	130	11	15	7	71	29	10	56	.254	.307	.376	95	-8	30	.911	12	104	11	S133		0.7
1892	Bro N	151	613	77	145	11	6	1	74	34	4	51	.237	.281	.279	72	-22	39	.925	-6	96	93	S151		-1.9
1893	Bro N	115	459	61	126	11	10	2	58	27		2	12	.275	.318	.355	82	-14	14	.907	13	111	93	S115		0.5
1894	Bro N	129	576	123	173	21	20	5	92	25	0	17	.300	.329	.432	88	-15	33	.904	-4	99	79	S129		-1.0
1895	Bro N	128	540	83	145	17	10	2	69	23	3	11	.269	.302	.348	73	-23	17	.925	-17	111	100	S128		0.0
1896	Bro N	132	532	63	154	15	7	3	73	15	1	13	.289	.310	.361	81	-17	16	.926	26	108	126	S132		1.3
1897	Cin N	109	445	76	128	30	5	3	57	13		2		.288	.311	.398	81	-14	15	.913	4	97	142	S63,2b47		-0.5
1898	Cin N	153	619	80	155	28	15	2	87	26		2		.250	.283	.354	77	-23	19	.932	10	108	119	S153		-0.5
1899	Cin N	138	540	93	150	11	8	0	81	29		2		.278	.317	.328	76	-20	32	.930	0	98	115	S124,2b14		-1.1
1900	Cin N	127	523	64	128	21	9	1	54	22		2		.245	.278	.325	68	-5	27	.921	-7	97	114	S124,2b5		-2.3
1901	Cin N	31	115	14	24	3	3	0	15	11	0			.209	.278	.287	68	-5	6	.919	1	102	150	S30		-0.2
1902	Cin N	138	538	54	136	18	4	0	54	11	1			.253	.268	.301	69	-21	20	.926	-11	92	101	S137/2		-1.2
1903	Cin N	115	459	61	113	18	7	2	73	12	1			.246	.267	.329	63	-25	12	.943	9	100	105	S115		-2.1
1904	Cin N	150	578	55	133	17	9	2	74	19	1			.230	.257	.301	66	-25	19	.936	0	100	109	S150		0.2
1905	Cin N	151	605	70	150	21	11	2	85	23	1			.248	.277	.329	72	-23	28	.952	20	107	105	S151		-2.2
1906	Cin N	117	430	29	89	13	1	1	33	19		1		.207	.242	.249	51	-25	8	.941	2	99	124	S117		-1.3
1907	NY N	62	226	21	60	9	2	0	24	7		0		.265	.288	.323	88	-4	9	.939	-8	98	71	2b62		-1.3
Total	18	2202	8812	1188	2256	289	155	34	1135	383	35	205	.256	.290	.336	74	-333	387	.924	84	102	100	S2075,2b129		-15.8

CORCORAN, TIM Timothy Michael B3.19.1953 Glendale CA BL/TL/5-11/175* d5.18 Col Cal St.-Los Angeles

YEAR	TM LG	G	AB	R	H	2B	3B	HR	RBI	BB-IB	HP	SO	AVG	OBP	SLG	AOPS	ABR	SB-CS	FA	FR	RNG	THR	GAMES AT POSITION	DL	BFW
1977	Det A	55	103	13	29	3	0	3	15	6-1		0	9	.282	.315	.398	90	-2	0-1	1.000	-1	101	0	O18(4/6/8),D3		-0.3
1978	Det A	116	324	37	86	13	1	1	27	24-2	5	27	.265	.322	.321	80	-8	3-2	.985	-4	93	84	O9(3/0/6),1b5,D2		-1.7
1979	Det A	18	22	4	5	1	0	0	6	4-1	0	2	.227	.333	.273	67	-1	1-1	1.000	1	142	391	O9(3/0/6),1b5,D2		0.0
1980	Det A	84	153	20	44	7	1	3	18	22-2	1	10	.288	.379	.405	113	4	0-2	.985	-1	90	116	1b48,O18(7/0/11),D5		-0.1
1981	Min A	22	51	4	9	3	0	0	4	6-0	1	7	.176	.259	.235	42	-1	0-0	1.000	0	103	84	1b16,D3		-0.4
1983	Phi N	3	0	0	0	0	0	0	0	0-0	0	0	—	—	—	—		0-0	1.000	-0	0	0	1b3		0.0
1984	Phi N	102	208	30	71	13	1	5	36	37-5	1	27	.341	.440	.486	158	19	0-1	.997	-2	91	70	1b51,O17(4/0/13)	15	1.4
1985	Phi N	103	182	11	39	6	1	0	22	29-4	0	20	.214	.312	.258	63	-8	0-0	.993	-1	88	73	1b59,O3(2/0/2)		-1.3
1986	NY N	6	7	1	0	0	0	0	0	2-1	0	0	.000	.222	.000	-34	-1	0-0	1.000	0	134	136	/1		-0.1
Total	9	509	1050	120	283	46	4	12	128	130-16	7	102	.270	.349	.355	96	-1	4-7	.993	-7	90	84	1b183,O174(20/8/147),D14	15	-2.5

CORDERO, WIL Wilfredo (Nieva) B10.3.1971 Mayaguez, PR BR/TR/6-2/195(185-230) d7.24 OF(400/0/17)

YEAR	TM LG	G	AB	R	H	2B	3B	HR	RBI	BB-IB	HP	SO	AVG	OBP	SLG	AOPS	ABR	SB-CS	FA	FR	RNG	THR	GAMES AT POSITION	DL	BFW
1992	Mon N	45	126	17	38	4	1	2	8	9-0	1	31	.302	.353	.397	113	2	0-0	.949	-8	85	72	S35,2b9		-0.4
1993	Mon N	138	475	56	118	32	2	10	58	34-8	1	60	.248	.308	.387	81	-13	12-3	.941	-20	96	83	S134,3b2		-2.1
1994	Mon N★	110	415	65	122	30	3	15	63	41-3	6	62	.294	.363	.489	119	12	16-3	.952	-13	95	93	S109		1.0
1995	Mon N	131	514	64	147	35	2	10	49	36-4	9	88	.286	.341	.420	99	1	9-5	.960	-25	87	78	S105,O26L		-2.0
1996	Bos A	59	198	29	57	14	0	3	37	11-4	2	31	.288	.330	.404	83	-5	2-1	.949	-2	97	66	2b37,D13/1		-0.5
1997	Bos A	140	570	82	160	26	3	18	72	31-7	4	122	.281	.320	.432	92	-8	1-3	.992	-5	89	90	O137L/2D		-1.8
1998	Chi A	96	341	58	91	18	2	13	49	22-0	3	66	.267	.314	.446	97	-3	2-1	.992	4	131	115	1b83,O11(4/0/8)		-0.5
1999	†Cle A	54	194	35	58	15	0	8	32	15-0	6	37	.299	.364	.500	113	4	0-1	.981	-2	90	0	O29L,D23	91	0.0
2000	Pit N	89	348	46	98	24	3	16	51	25-1	4	58	.282	.336	.506	109	3	1-2	.983	-10	69	57	O85L/D		-0.6
	Cle A	38	148	18	39	11	2	0	17	7-0	3	18	.264	.310	.365	68	-7	0-0	1.000	2	110	96	O38L		-1.0
2001	Cle A	89	268	30	67	11	1	4	21	22-2	4	50	.250	.313	.343	71	-11	0-0	.985	-5	81	41	O51(49/0/4),1b22,D12	15	-1.9
2002	Cle A	6	18	1	4	0	0	1	1	0-0	0	3	.222	.222	.222	18	-2	0-0	1.000	1	107	916	O4L/1		-0.1
	Mon N	66	143	21	39	9	0	6	29	17-0	2	26	.273	.349	.462	111	2	2-0	.958	1	109	73	O28(24/0/5),1b10,D2	15	0.1
2003	Mon N	130	436	57	121	27	0	16	71	49-5	4	90	.278	.354	.450	106	5	1-1	.996	-6	82	96	1b123/OLD		-1.1
2004	Fla N	27	66	6	13	3	0	1	6	3-0	2	19	.197	.250	.288	42	-6	1-0	.991	-1	54	116	1b13,O3L	113	-0.8
2005	Was N	29	51	2	6	2	0	0	2	3-1	0	14	.118	.161	.157	-15	-9	0-0	1.000	-9	38	74	1b12,D3	52	-1.1
Total	14	1247	4311	587	1178	261	19	152	566	325-35	57	775	.273	.330	.428	95	-38	49-19	.980	-90	88	74	O413L,S383,1b265,D58,2b47,3b2	369	-12.8

CORDOVA, MARTY Martin Keevin B7.10.1969 Las Vegas NV BR/TR/6-0/206(193-206) [MinA89 10/269] d4.26 Col Orange Coast (CA) JC [DL 2004 Bal A 183]

YEAR	TM LG	G	AB	R	H	2B	3B	HR	RBI	BB-IB	HP	SO	AVG	OBP	SLG	AOPS	ABR	SB-CS	FA	FR	RNG	THR	GAMES AT POSITION	DL	BFW
1995	Min A	137	512	81	142	27	4	24	84	52-1	10	111	.277	.352	.486	116	11	20-7	.986	14	117	127	O137(132/11/0)		2.1
1996	Min A	145	569	97	176	46	1	16	111	53-4	8	96	.309	.371	.478	112	12	11-5	.991	5	107	87	O145L		1.1
1997	Min A	103	378	44	93	18	4	15	51	30-2	3	92	.246	.305	.434	89	-8	5-3	.991	9	109	186	O101L,D2	46	-0.3
1998	Min A	119	438	52	111	20	2	10	69	50-3	5	103	.253	.333	.377	83	-10	3-6	.978	4	114	73	O115L,D4	15	-1.1
1999	Min A	124	425	62	121	28	3	14	70	48-2	9	96	.285	.365	.464	105	4	13-4	.927	-4	80	0	D85,O29(6/0/25)		-0.3
2000	Tor A	62	200	23	49	7	0	4	18	18-0	1	35	.245	.317	.340	64	-11	3-2	.982	-6	67	39	O41(23/0/18),D15		-1.9
2001	†Cle A	122	409	61	123	20	2	20	69	23-0	8	81	.301	.348	.506	117	9	0-3	.990	6	109	138	O106(83/2/30),D7		1.0
2002	Bal A	131	458	55	116	25	2	18	64	47-3	3	111	.253	.325	.434	106	3	1-6	.971	-5	86	44	O72L,D56	12	-0.9
2003	Bal A	9	30	5	7	1	0	1	4	8-1	1	5	.233	.410	.367	108	1	1-0	1.000	1	85	815	O4L,D5	159	0.2
Total	9	952	3419	480	938	192	18	122	540	329-16	50	730	.274	.344	.448	102	11	57-36	.984	24	105	107	O750(681/13/73),D174	415	-0.1

COREY, FRED Frederick Harrison B1855 Coventry RI D11.27.1912 Providence RI BR/TR/5-7/160 d5.1 OF(8/29/46) ▲

YEAR	TM LG	G	AB	R	H	2B	3B	HR	RBI	BB-IB	HP	SO	AVG	OBP	SLG	AOPS	ABR	SB-CS	FA	FR	RNG	THR	GAMES AT POSITION	DL	BFW
1878	Pro N	7	21	3	3	0	0	0	1	0			2	.143	.143	.143	-6	-2		1.000	0	42	0	P5,2b2/1		-0.1
1880	Wor N	41	138	11	24	8	1	0	6	4			27	.174	.197	.246	45	-8		.759	-7	68	135	O29(2/6/21),P25,S3/31		-1.0
1881	Wor N	51	203	22	45	8	4	0	10	5			10	.222	.240	.300	65	-9		.827	1	96	96	O25(1/0/24),P23,S7		-0.4
1882	Wor N	64	255	33	63	7	12	0	29	5			31	.247	.262	.369	97	-2		.847	-5	100	58	S26,P21,O15(5/10/0),3b6,1b5		-0.6
1883	Phi AA	71	298	45	77	16	2	1	40	12				.258	.287	.336	91	-3		.799	-1	116	109	3b34,P18,O14(0/13/1),2b9/SC		-0.3
1884	Phi AA	104	439	64	121	17	16	5		17		2		.276	.306	.421	127	10		.887	12	110	91	3b104		2.2
1885	Phi AA	94	384	61	94	14	8	1	38	17		3		.245	.282	.331	88	-7		.872	7	106	103	3b92/SP		0.2
Total	7	432	1738	239	427	70	43	7	124	60	5	70	.246	.273	.348	93	-21		.863	7	108	96	3b237,P93,O83R,S38,2b11,1b7/C		0.0

COREY, MARK Mark Mundell B11.3.1955 Tucumcari NM BR/TR/6-2/200* [BalA76*/43] d9.1 Col Central Arizona JC

YEAR	TM LG	G	AB	R	H	2B	3B	HR	RBI	BB-IB	HP	SO	AVG	OBP	SLG	AOPS	ABR	SB-CS	FA	FR	RNG	THR	GAMES AT POSITION	DL	BFW
1979	Bal A	13	13	1	2	0	0	0	1	0-0	0	4	.154	.154	.154	-17	-2	1-0	1.000	0	116	0	O11R/D		-0.2
1980	Bal A	36	36	7	10	2	0	1	2	5-0	0	7	.278	.366	.417	116	-1	0-1	1.000	-2	72	0	O34(15/0/19)		-0.2
1981	Bal A	10	8	0	0	0	0	0	0	2-0	0	2	.000	.200	.000	-38	-1	0-0	1.000	0	78	388	O9(7/0/2)		-0.1
Total	3	59	57	10	12	2	0	1	3	7-0	0	13	.211	.297	.298	65	-2	1-1	1.000	-2	82	65	O54(22/0/32)/D		-0.5

CORGAN, CHUCK Charles Howard B12.4.1902 Wagoner OK D6.13.1928 Wagoner OK BB/TR/5-11/180 d9.19 Col Arkansas-Monticello

YEAR	TM LG	G	AB	R	H	2B	3B	HR	RBI	BB-IB	HP	SO	AVG	OBP	SLG	AOPS	ABR	SB-CS	FA	FR	RNG	THR	GAMES AT POSITION	DL	BFW
1925	Bro N	14	47	4	8	1	0	0	3			0	9	.170	.220	.234	16	-6		.908	1	115	56	S14		-0.3
1927	Bro N	19	57	3	15	1	0	1	4	4		0	4	.263	.311	.281	59	-3	0	.969	6	116	65	2b13,S3		-0.3
Total	2	33	104	7	23	2	0	1	7			0	13	.221	.270	.260	40	-9	0-0	.900	7	108	58	S17,2b13		-0.6

CORHAN, ROY Roy George "Irish" B10.21.1887 Indianapolis IN D11.24.1958 San Francisco CA BR/TR/5-9.5/165 d4.20

YEAR	TM LG	G	AB	R	H	2B	3B	HR	RBI	BB-IB	HP	SO	AVG	OBP	SLG	AOPS	ABR	SB-CS	FA	FR	RNG	THR	GAMES AT POSITION	DL	BFW
1911	Chi A	43	131	14	28	6	2	0	8	15			2	.214	.304	.290	68	-5	2	.924	10	112	137	S43		0.7
1916	StL N	92	295	30	62	6	3	0	18	20		2	31	.210	.265	.251	59	-14	15	.917	1	106	92	S84		-0.9
Total	2	135	426	44	90	12	5	0	26	35		4	31	.211	.277	.263	62	-19	17	.920	10	108	107	S127		-0.2

CORIDAN, PHIL Philip F. B8.19.1858 Walpole (now Fortville) IN D7.1.1915 Indianapolis IN BL d7.16

YEAR	TM LG	G	AB	R	H	2B	3B	HR	RBI	BB-IB	HP	SO	AVG	OBP	SLG	AOPS	ABR	SB-CS	FA	FR	RNG	THR	GAMES AT POSITION	DL	BFW
1884	CP U	2	7	1	1	0	0	0	0					.143	.143	.143	-13	-1		.800	-1	81	0	2b2/OL		-0.2

CORKHILL, POP John Stewart B4.11.1858 Parkesburg PA D4.3.1921 Pennsauken NJ BL/TR/5-10/180 d5.1 OF(6/615/420) ▲

YEAR	TM LG	G	AB	R	H	2B	3B	HR	RBI	BB-IB	HP	SO	AVG	OBP	SLG	AOPS	ABR	SB-CS	FA	FR	RNG	THR	GAMES AT POSITION	DL	BFW
1883	Cin AA	88	375	53	81	10	8	2	46	3				.216	.222	.301	63	-17		.930	0	60		O85(0/15/70),S2,2b2,1b2		-1.5
1884	Cin AA	110	452	85	124	13	11	4	70	6		4		.274	.290	.378	111	3		.934	8	162	181	O92R,S11,1b6,3b3/P		0.9
1885	Cin AA	112	440	64	111	10	8	1	53	7		7		.252	.275	.318	85	-9		.938	17	189	139	O110R,P8,1b3		0.6
1886	Cin AA	129	540	81	143	9	7	5	97	23		6		.265	.302	.335	96	-5	24	.918	-0	136	166	O112R,3b12,1b7,S3/P		-0.5
1887	Cin AA	128	541	99	168	19	11	5	97	14				.311	.333	.414	105	0	30	.952	12	136	164	O128(0/121/7),P5		0.6
1888	Cin AA	118	490	68	133	11	9	1	74	15		4		.271	.299	.337	98	-4	27	.958	1	86	123	O116(4/112/0),P2/12		-0.7
	Bro AA	19	71	17	27	4	3	1	19	4		2		.380	.429	.563	217	9	3	.980	0	60		O19C		0.8
	Year	137	561	85	160	15	12	2	93	19		6		.285	.316	.365	113	5	30	.961	1	82	105	O135(4/131/0),P2/12		0.1
1889	†Bro AA	138	537	91	134	21	9	8	78	42		3	24	.250	.308	.367	91	-8	22	.949	9	131	146	O138C/S1		-0.4
1890	Bro N	51	204	23	46	4	2	1	21	15		0	11	.225	.279	.279	62	-10	6	.977	2	71	62	O48C,1b6		-0.9
1891	Phi AA	83	349	50	73	7	7	3	31	26		2	15	.209	.268	.269	54	-23	12	.956	4	94	97	O83(0/73/10)		-1.8
	Cin N	1	4	0	0	0	0	0	0	0		0		1.000	.000	.000	-99	-1		1.000	0	0	0	/OC		-0.1

YEAR	TM LG	G	AB	R	H	2B	3B	HR	RBI	BB-IB	HP	SO	AVG	OBP	SLG	AOPS	ABR	SB-CS	FA	FR	RNG	THR	GAMES AT POSITION	DL	BFW
	Pit N	41	145	16	33	1	1	3	20	7	1	10	.228	.268	.310	70	-6	7	.935	3	160	316	O41(1/40/0)		-0.4
	Year	42	149	16	33	1	1	3	20	7	1	11	.221	.261	.302	65	-7	7	.939	3	160	296	O42(1/41/0)		-0.5
1892	Pit N	68	256	23	47	1	4	0	25	12	3	19	.184	.229	.219	35	-21	6	.953	5	114	163	O68(1/48/19)		-2.0
Total	10	1086	4404	650	1120	110	80	31	631	174	36	80	.254	.288	.337	87	-92	137	.947	59	122	134	O1041C,1b26,P17,S17,3b15,2b3		-5.4

CORRALES, PAT   Patrick   B3.20.1941 Los Angeles CA   BR/TR/6-0/195*   d8.2   M9/C21   Col Fresno (CA) City

YEAR	TM LG	G	AB	R	H	2B	3B	HR	RBI	BB-IB	HP	SO	AVG	OBP	SLG	AOPS	ABR	SB-CS	FA	FR	RNG	THR	GAMES AT POSITION	DL	BFW
1964	Phi N	2	1	1	0	0	0	0		1-0	0	0	.000	.500	.000	55	0	0-0	—	0			/H		0.0
1965	Phi N	63	174	16	39	8	1	2	15	25-5	1	42	.224	.323	.316	83	-3	0-0	.982	-8	99	76	C62		-0.8
1966	StL N	28	72	5	13	2	0	0	3	2-0	2	17	.181	.221	.208	21	-8	1-0	.975	6	223	199	C27		-0.1
1968	Cin N	20	56	3	15	4	0	0	6	6-0	1	16	.268	.349	.339	101	1	0-0	.991	-2	64	68	C20		-0.1
1969	Cin N	29	72	10	19	5	0	0	5	8-0	1	17	.264	.346	.375	97	0	0-1	.986	1	87	52	C29		0.2
1970	†Cin N	43	106	9	25	5	1	1	10	8-1	0	22	.236	.289	.330	65	-5	0-0	.983	1	196	103	C42		-0.3
1971	Cin N	40	94	6	17	2	0	0	6	6-1	0	17	.181	.230	.202	24	-10	0-0	.980	-3	107	14	C39		-1.2
1972	Cin N	2	1	0	0	0	0	0		2-1	0	0	.000	.667	.000	109	0	0-0	1.000	1	0	341	C2		0.1
	SD N	44	119	6	23	0	0	0	6	11-1	1	26	.193	.267	.193	35	-10	0-0	.993	-1	93	81	C43		-1.0
	Year	46	120	6	23	0	0	0	6	13-2	1	26	.192	.276	.192	38	-10	0-0	.993	-0	91	88	C45		-0.9
1973	SD N	29	72	7	15	2	1	0	3	6-1	1	10	.208	.275	.264	55	-5	0-0	.986	-5	71	76	C28		-0.9
Total	9	300	767	63	166	28	3	4	54	75-10	7	167	.216	.291	.276	61	-40	1-1	.984	-10	117	83	C292		-4.1

CORREIA, ROD   Ronald Douglas   B9.13.1967 Providence RI   BR/TR/5-11/185*   [OakA88 15/385]   d6.20   Col Massachusetts-Dartmouth

YEAR	TM LG	G	AB	R	H	2B	3B	HR	RBI	BB-IB	HP	SO	AVG	OBP	SLG	AOPS	ABR	SB-CS	FA	FR	RNG	THR	GAMES AT POSITION	DL	BFW
1993	Cal A	64	128	12	34	5	0	0	9	6-0	4	20	.266	.319	.305	66	-6	2-4	.981	-1	105	79	S40,2b11,3b3,D6		-0.3
1994	Cal A	6	17	4	4	1	0	0	0	0-0	2	0	.235	.316	.294	58	-1	0-0	1.000	-2	52	69	2b5/S		-0.3
1995	Cal A	14	21	3	5	1	1	0	3	0-0	0	5	.238	.238	.381	58	-1	0-0	.850	-0	81	143	S7,2b3,3b2/D		-0.1
Total	3	84	166	19	43	7	1	0	12	6-0	6	25	.259	.309	.313	65	-8	2-4	.968	-1	102	89	S48,2b19,D7,3b5		-0.7

CORRELL, VIC   Victor Crosby   B2.5.1946 Washington DC   BR/TR/5-10/185*   [CleA67 9/171]   d10.4   Col Georgia Southern

YEAR	TM LG	G	AB	R	H	2B	3B	HR	RBI	BB-IB	HP	SO	AVG	OBP	SLG	AOPS	ABR	SB-CS	FA	FR	RNG	THR	GAMES AT POSITION	DL	BFW
1972	Bos A	1	4	1	2	0	0	0	1	0-0	0	1	.500	.500	.500	187	0	0-0	1.000	1	0	0	/C		0.1
1974	Atl N	73	202	20	48	15	1	4	29	21-3	4	38	.238	.317	.381	93	-2	0-0	.988	5	94	61	C59		0.6
1975	Atl N	103	325	37	70	12	1	11	39	42-5	1	66	.215	.305	.360	82	-8	0-2	.973	-5	84	99	C97		-1.0
1976	Atl N	69	200	26	45	6	2	5	16	21-5	1	37	.225	.302	.350	80	-6	0-1	.981	-3	76	110	C65		-0.7
1977	Atl N	54	144	16	30	7	0	7	16	22-1	1	33	.208	.314	.403	82	-3	2-3	.973	-6	60	120	C49		-0.8
1978	Cin N	52	105	9	25	7	0	1	6	8-3	0	17	.238	.292	.333	74	-4	0-2	.980	-3	118	110	C52		-0.6
1979	Cin N	48	133	14	31	12	0	1	15	14-2	1	26	.233	.309	.346	79	-3	0-0	.992	-1	77	62	C47		-0.2
1980	Cin N	10	19	1	8	1	0	0	3	0-0	0	2	.421	.421	.474	152	1	0-0	.919	-3	48	41	C10	145	-0.1
Total	8	410	1132	124	259	60	4	29	125	128-19	8	220	.229	.310	.366	84	-25	2-8	.979	-15	83	92	C380	145	-2.7

CORRIDEN, JOHN   John Michael Jr.   B1.6.1918 Logansport IN   D6.4.2001 Indianapolis IN   BB/TR/5-6/160   d4.20   f-Red   Col Indiana

YEAR	TM LG	G	AB	R	H	2B	3B	HR	RBI	BB-IB	HP	SO	AVG	OBP	SLG	AOPS	ABR	SB-CS	FA	FR	RNG	THR	GAMES AT POSITION	DL	BFW
1946	Bro N	1	0	1	0	0	0	0	0	0-0	0	0	-	-	-	0	0	0-0	—	0			/R		0.0

CORRIDEN, RED   John Michael Sr.   B9.4.1887 Logansport IN   D9.28.1959 Indianapolis IN   BR/TR/5-9/165   d9.8   M1/C18   s-John

YEAR	TM LG	G	AB	R	H	2B	3B	HR	RBI	BB-IB	HP	SO	AVG	OBP	SLG	AOPS	ABR	SB-CS	FA	FR	RNG	THR	GAMES AT POSITION	DL	BFW
1910	StL A	26	84	19	13	3	0	1	4	13	4		.155	.297	.226	68	-2	5	.902	2	115	49	S14,3b12		0.1
1912	Det A	38	138	22	28	6	0	0	5	15	1		.203	.286	.246	54	-8	4	.929	-2	102	138	3b25,2b7,S3		-0.9
1913	Chi N	46	97	13	17	3	0	2	9	10	0	14	.175	.252	.268	49	-7	4-3	.907	-2	102	127	S37,2b2/3		-0.7
1914	Chi N	107	318	42	73	9	5	3	29	35	9	33	.230	.323	.318	91	-3	13	.894	-27	78	95	S91,3b8,2b3		-2.6
1915	Chi N	6	3	1	0	0	0	0	0	2	1		.000	.571	.000	79	1	0	.667	-1	56	0	/3OC		0.0
Total	5	223	640	97	131	21	5	6	47	75	16	48	.205	.304	.281	74	-19	26-3	.896	-29	88	94	S145,3b47,2b12/OC		-4.1

CORTAZZO, JESS   John Francis   B9.26.1904 Wilmerding PA   D3.4.1963 Pittsburgh PA   BR/TR/5-3.5/142   d9.1

YEAR	TM LG	G	AB	R	H	2B	3B	HR	RBI	BB-IB	HP	SO	AVG	OBP	SLG	AOPS	ABR	SB-CS	FA	FR	RNG	THR	GAMES AT POSITION	DL	BFW
1923	Chi A	1	1	0	0	0	0	0	0	0-0	0	0	.000	.000	.000	-99	0	0-0	—	0			/H		0.0

CORTEZ, FERNANDO   Fernando   B8.10.1981 Stockton CA   BL/TR/6-1/175   d7.5   Col Grossmont (CA) CC

YEAR	TM LG	G	AB	R	H	2B	3B	HR	RBI	BB-IB	HP	SO	AVG	OBP	SLG	AOPS	ABR	SB-CS	FA	FR	RNG	THR	GAMES AT POSITION	DL	BFW
2005	TB A	8	13	0	1	0	0	0	1	1-0	0	3	.077	.143	.077	-40	-3	0-0	1.000	-3	41	0	2b3,S2/3		-0.5

COSCARART, JOE   Joseph Marvin   B11.18.1909 Escondido CA   D4.5.1993 Sequim WA   BR/TR/6-0/185   d4.26   b-Pete

YEAR	TM LG	G	AB	R	H	2B	3B	HR	RBI	BB-IB	HP	SO	AVG	OBP	SLG	AOPS	ABR	SB-CS	FA	FR	RNG	THR	GAMES AT POSITION	DL	BFW
1935	Bos N	86	284	30	67	11	2	1	29	16	0	28	.236	.277	.299	59	-17	2	.962	-3	120	87	3b41,S27,2b15		-1.6
1936	Bos N	104	367	28	90	11	2	2	44	19	5	37	.245	.292	.302	64	-19	0	.935	1	109	136	3b97,S6/2		-1.5
Total	2	190	651	58	157	22	4	3	73	35	5	65	.241	.285	.301	62	-36	2	.943	-2	112	123	3b138,S33,2b16		-3.1

COSCARART, PETE   Peter Joseph   B6.16.1913 Escondido CA   D7.24.2002 Escondido CA   BR/TR/5-11.5/175   d4.26   b-Joe   Col San Diego St.

YEAR	TM LG	G	AB	R	H	2B	3B	HR	RBI	BB-IB	HP	SO	AVG	OBP	SLG	AOPS	ABR	SB-CS	FA	FR	RNG	THR	GAMES AT POSITION	DL	BFW
1938	Bro N	32	79	10	12	3	0	0	6	9	2	18	.152	.256	.190	24	-8	0	.955	1	97	115	2b27		-0.6
1939	Bro N	115	419	59	116	22	2	4	43	46	4	56	.277	.354	.368	91	-4	10	.960	-10	98	102	2b107,3b4,S2		-0.7
1940	Bro N★	143	506	55	120	24	4	9	58	53	1	59	.237	.311	.354	78	-15	5	.958	-34	85	73	2b140		-4.1
1941	†Bro N	43	62	13	8	1	0	0	5	7	0	12	.129	.217	.145	3	-8	1	.948	1	111	74	2b19/S		-0.7
1942	Pit N	133	487	57	111	12	4	3	29	38	3	56	.228	.288	.287	67	-21	2	.952	-19	97	80	S108,2b25		-3.3
1943	Pit N	133	491	57	119	19	6	0	48	46	0	48	.242	.304	.305	75	-16	10	.961	-3	103	105	2b85,S47/3		-1.2
1944	Pit N	139	554	89	146	30	4	4	42	41	1	57	.264	.315	.354	85	-11	10	.967	-3	99	91	2b136,S4/OR		-0.7
1945	Pit N	123	392	59	95	17	2	8	38	55	4	55	.242	.341	.357	91	-4	2	.978	21	**116**	**124**	2b122/S		2.3
1946	Pit N	3	2	0	1	1	0	0	0	0	0	0	.500	.500	1.000	312	1	0	—	-0	0	0	/S		0.0
Total	9	864	2992	399	728	129	22	28	269	295	15	361	.243	.314	.329	78	-86	34	.963	-47	99	97	2b661,S164,3b5/OR		-9.0

COSEY, RAY   Donald Ray   B2.15.1956 San Rafael CA   BL/TL/5-10/185   d4.14

YEAR	TM LG	G	AB	R	H	2B	3B	HR	RBI	BB-IB	HP	SO	AVG	OBP	SLG	AOPS	ABR	SB-CS	FA	FR	RNG	THR	GAMES AT POSITION	DL	BFW
1980	Oak A	9	9	0	1	0	0	0	0	0-0	0	0	.111	.111	.111	-41	-2	0-0	—	0			/H		-0.2

COSTA, SHANE   Shane Jeremy   B12.12.1981 Visalia CA   BL/TR/6-0/220   d6.2   Col Cal St.-Fullerton

YEAR	TM LG	G	AB	R	H	2B	3B	HR	RBI	BB-IB	HP	SO	AVG	OBP	SLG	AOPS	ABR	SB-CS	FA	FR	RNG	THR	GAMES AT POSITION	DL	BFW
2005	KC A	27	81	13	19	2	0	2	7	5-0	1	11	.235	.287	.333	69	-4	0-0	1.000	-1	81	100	O20L,D4		-0.6

COSTELLO, DAN   Daniel Francis "Dashing Dan"   B9.9.1891 Jessup PA   D3.26.1936 Pittsburgh PA   BL/TR/6-0.5/185   d7.2   Col Mount St. Marys

YEAR	TM LG	G	AB	R	H	2B	3B	HR	RBI	BB-IB	HP	SO	AVG	OBP	SLG	AOPS	ABR	SB-CS	FA	FR	RNG	THR	GAMES AT POSITION	DL	BFW
1913	NY A	2	2	1	1	0	0	0	0	0-0	0	0	.500	.500	.500	192	0	0	—	0			/H		0.0
1914	Pit N	21	64	7	19	1	0	0	5	8	0	16	.297	.375	.313	110	1	2	.970	0	100	107	O20R		0.1
1915	Pit N	71	125	16	27	4	1	0	11	7	0	23	.216	.258	.264	59	-6	7-1	.893	-3	70	52	O22(5/12/5)/1		-1.1
1916	Pit N	60	159	11	38	1	3	0	8	6	0	23	.239	.267	.283	68	-7	3	.976	-1	114	0	O41(33/1/7)		-1.1
Total	4	154	350	35	85	6	4	0	24	21	0	62	.243	.286	.283	73	-12	12-1	.959	-4	101	37	O83(38/13/32)/1		-2.1

COSTO, TIM   Timothy Roger   B2.16.1969 Melrose Park IL   BR/TR/6-5/220*   [CleA90 1/8]   d9.18   Col Iowa

YEAR	TM LG	G	AB	R	H	2B	3B	HR	RBI	BB-IB	HP	SO	AVG	OBP	SLG	AOPS	ABR	SB-CS	FA	FR	RNG	THR	GAMES AT POSITION	DL	BFW
1992	Cin N	12	36	3	8	2	0	0	5	0-0	0	6	.222	.310	.278	68	-1	0-0	1.000	0	104	203	1b12		-0.2
1993	Cin N	31	98	13	22	5	0	3	12	4-0	1	17	.224	.250	.367	64	-5	0-0	.980	0	104	56	O26(11/0/16),1b2,3b2		-0.7
Total	2	43	134	16	30	7	0	3	14	9-0	0	23	.224	.267	.343	65	-6	0-0	.980	1	104	56	O26(11/0/16),1b14,3b2		-0.9

COTA, HUMBERTO   Humberto Figueroa   B2.7.1979 San Luis Rio Colorado, Sonora, Mexico   BR/TR/6-0/180(175-210)   d9.9

YEAR	TM LG	G	AB	R	H	2B	3B	HR	RBI	BB-IB	HP	SO	AVG	OBP	SLG	AOPS	ABR	SB-CS	FA	FR	RNG	THR	GAMES AT POSITION	DL	BFW
2001	Pit N	7	9	0	2	0	0	0	1	0-0	0	5	.222	.222	.222	15	-1	0-0	1.000	1	0	0	C3		0.0
2002	Pit N	7	17	2	5	1	0	0	1	1-1	0	4	.294	.333	.353	82	0	0-0	1.000	1	262	83	C7		-0.1
2003	Pit N	10	16	1	4	1	0	0	1	1-0	0	5	.250	.294	.313	58	-1	0-0	1.000	0	129	171	C4		-0.1
2004	Pit N	36	66	10	15	1	1	5	8	3-1	1	20	.227	.271	.500	93	-1	0-0	.991	-1	205	32	C24	66	-0.2
2005	Pit N	93	297	29	72	20	2	7	43	17-2	2	80	.242	.285	.387	75	-11	0-0	.992	0	119	79	C87	16	-0.6
Total	5	153	405	42	98	23	2	12	53	22-4	3	114	.242	.284	.398	77	-14	0-0	.993	1	137	74	C125	82	-0.8

COTE, HENRY   Henry Joseph   B2.19.1864 Troy NY   D4.28.1940 Troy NY   5-9.5/165   d9.16

YEAR	TM LG	G	AB	R	H	2B	3B	HR	RBI	BB-IB	HP	SO	AVG	OBP	SLG	AOPS	ABR	SB-CS	FA	FR	RNG	THR	GAMES AT POSITION	DL	BFW
1894	Lou N	10	31	7	9	2	0	0	3	5	0	6	.290	.389	.484	117	-1	2	.918	3	100	145	C10		0.4
1895	Lou N	10	33	10	10	0	0	0	5	3	0	3	.303	.361	.303	77	-1	2	.872	-3	90	53	C10		-0.3
Total	2	20	64	17	19	2	0	0	8	8	0	9	.297	.375	.391	98	0	4	.900	-0	95	102	C20		0.1

COTE, PETE   Warren Peter   B8.30.1902 Cambridge MA   D10.17.1987 Middleton MA   BR/TR/5-6/148   d6.18   Col Holy Cross

YEAR	TM LG	G	AB	R	H	2B	3B	HR	RBI	BB-IB	HP	SO	AVG	OBP	SLG	AOPS	ABR	SB-CS	FA	FR	RNG	THR	GAMES AT POSITION	DL	BFW
1926	NY N	2	1	0	0	0	0	0	0	0-0	0	0	.000	.000	.000	-99	0	0	—	0			/H		0.0

COTTER, ED   Edward Christopher   B7.4.1904 Hartford CT   D6.14.1959 Hartford CT   BR/TR/6-0/185   d6.12   Col Villanova

YEAR	TM LG	G	AB	R	H	2B	3B	HR	RBI	BB-IB	HP	SO	AVG	OBP	SLG	AOPS	ABR	SB-CS	FA	FR	RNG	THR	GAMES AT POSITION	DL	BFW
1926	Phi N	17	26	3	8	0	1	0	1	1	0	4	.308	.333	.385	-1	-1	1	.833	-1	111	0	3b8,S5		-0.1

YEAR	TM LG	G	AB	R	H	2B	3B	HR	RBI	BB-IB	HP	SO	AVG	OBP	SLG	AOPS	ABR	SB-CS	FA	FR	RNG	THR	GAMES AT POSITION	DL	BFW

COTTER, HOOKS Harvey Louis B5.22.1900 Holden MO D8.6.1955 Los Angeles CA BL/TL/5-10/160 d4.15

1922	Chi N	1	1	0	1	1	0	0	0	0	0	0	1.000	1.000	2.000	644	1	0-0	—	0			/H		0.1
1924	Chi N	98	310	39	81	16	4	4	33	36	0	31	.261	.338	.377	91	-3	3-5	.989	4	119	99	1b90		-0.7
Total 2		99	311	39	82	17	4	4	33	36	0	31	.264	.340	.383	92	-2	3-5	.989	4	119	99	1b90		-0.6

COTTER, DICK Richard Raphael B10.12.1889 Manchester NH D4.4.1945 Brooklyn NY BR/TR/5-11/172 d8.17 Col Manhattan

1911	Phi N	20	46	2	13	0	0	0	5	5	0	7	.283	.353	.283	78	-1	1	.975	-2	81	133	C17		-0.2
1912	Chi N	26	54	6	15	0	2	0	10	6	1	13	.278	.361	.352	96	0	1	.954	-1	128	85	C24		0.0
Total 2		46	100	8	28	0	2	0	15	11	1	20	.280	.357	.320	87	-1	2	.964	-3	107	107	C41		-0.2

COTTER, TOM Thomas Benedict B9.30.1866 Waltham MA D11.22.1906 Brookline MA BR/TR/5-10.5/149 d9.3

1891	Bos AA	6	12	1	3	0	0	0	4	1	0		.250	.308	.250	61	-1	0	.938	-0	154	106	C5/OR		0.0

COTTIER, CHUCK Charles Keith B1.8.1936 Delta CO BR/TR/5-10.5/175* d4.17 M3/C18

1959	Mil N	10	24	1	3	1	0	0	1	3-0	0	7	.125	.222	.167	6	-3	0-0	.976	-0	106	43	2b10		-0.3
1960	Mil N	95	229	29	52	8	0	3	19	14-3	2	21	.227	.273	.301	63	-12	1-0	.968	5	108	90	2b92		-0.2
1961	Det A	10	7	2	2	0	0	0	1	1-0	0	1	.286	.375	.286	77	0	0-0	.889	-0	19	96	S8,2b2		0.0
	Was A	101	337	37	79	14	4	2	34	30-1	1	51	.234	.296	.318	66	-17	9-1	.982	11	116	104	2b100		0.4
	Year	111	344	39	81	14	4	2	35	31-1	1	52	.235	.297	.317	66	-17	9-1	.982	11	117	106	2b102,S8		0.4
1962	Was A	136	443	50	107	14	6	6	40	44-0	2	57	.242	.310	.341	76	-15	14-8	.981	24	108	123	2b134		1.9
1963	Was A	113	337	30	69	16	4	5	21	24-6	0	63	.205	.257	.320	61	-18	2-1	.963	2	105	94	2b85,S24/3		-0.8
1964	Was A	73	137	16	23	6	2	3	10	19-1	0	33	.168	.268	.307	60	-7	2-0	.982	-2	96	113	2b53,3b3,S2		-0.5
1965	Was A	7	1	1	0	0	0	0	0	0-0	0	0	.000	.000	.000	-99	0	0-0	—	0			/H		0.0
1968	Cal A	33	67	2	13	4	1	0	1	0-0	0	15	.194	.217	.284	52	-4	0-0	.963	-1	98	59	3b27,2b4		-0.6
1969	Cal A	2	2	0	0	0	0	0	0	0-0	0	0	.000	.000	.000	-99	-1	0-0	1.000	-0	79	0	2b2	22	-0.1
Total 9		580	1584	168	348	63	17	19	127	137-11	5	248	.220	.282	.317	65	-77	28-10	.976	39	108	105	2b482,S34,3b31	22	-0.2

COTTO, HENRY Henry B1.5.1961 New York NY BR/TR/6-2/178* d4.5

1984	†Chi N	105	146	24	40	5	0	0	8	10-2	1	23	.274	.325	.308	73	-5	9-3	.984	7	131	123	O88(47/34/10)	41	0.2
1985	NY A	34	56	4	17	1	0	1	6	3-0	0	12	.304	.339	.375	97	0	1-1	.977	1	100	185	O30(14/20/1)		-0.6
1986	NY A	35	80	11	17	3	0	1	6	2-0	0	17	.213	.229	.287	41	-7	3-0	1.000	1	108	77	O29(11/19/0)/D		-0.7
1987	NY A	68	149	21	35	10	0	5	20	6-0	1	35	.235	.269	.403	75	-6	4-2	.989	-1	96	102	O57(15/41/2)		-0.7
1988	Sea A	133	386	50	100	18	1	8	33	23-0	2	53	.259	.302	.373	85	-8	27-3	.992	-3	93	130	O120C,D2		-0.7
1989	Sea A	100	295	44	78	11	2	9	33	12-3	1	44	.264	.300	.407	94	-3	10-4	.988	3	95	212	O118(41/18/67),D3		-0.1
1990	Sea A	127	355	40	92	14	4	4	33	22-2	4	52	.259	.307	.349	83	-9	21-3	.990	2	108	70	O56(38/19/8),D6		-0.6
1991	Sea A	66	177	35	54	6	2	6	23	10-0	2	27	.305	.347	.463	122	5	16-3	.981	3	116	88	O58(38/17/8),D5	65	0.9
1992	Sea A	108	294	42	76	11	5	5	27	14-3	1	49	.259	.294	.354	80	-9	23-2	1.000	1	112	45	O92(63/30/6),D3		-0.5
1993	Sea A	54	105	10	20	1	0	2	7	2-0	1	22	.190	.213	.257	25	-12	6-3	.983	1	117	0	O34(23/9/4),D15		-1.2
	Fla N	54	135	15	40	9	3	4	14	3-0	1	18	.296	.312	.415	89	-2	11-1	.977	2	120	46	O46(13/15/21)		0.1
Total 10		884	2178	296	569	87	9	44	210	107-10	16	352	.261	.299	.370	83	-56	130-26	.989	16	106	104	O760(322/355/133),D32	106	-3.2

COUGHLIN, DENNIS Dennis H. B1844 NY D5.14.1913 Washington DC d4.27

1872	Nat NA	8	37	5	11	1	0	0	7	0		0	.297	.297	.324	78	-1	0-0	.941	1	187	646	O5C/12S		-0.1

COUGHLIN, ED Edward E. B8.5.1861 Hartford CT D12.25.1952 Hartford CT d5.15

1884	Buf N	1	4	0	1	0	0	0		0	0		.250	.250	.250	56	0		.750	-0	0	0	/ORP		0.0

COUGHLIN, BILL William Paul "Scranton Bill" B7.12.1878 Scranton PA D5.7.1943 Scranton PA BR/TR/5-9/140 d8.9

1899	Was N	6	24	2	3	0	1	0	3	1	0		.125	.160	.208	1	-4	1	.818	-1	85	0	3b6		-0.4
1901	Was A	137	506	75	139	17	13	6	68	25	6		.275	.317	.395	98	-3	16	.922	3	92	85	3b137		0.3
1902	Was A	123	469	84	141	27	4	6	71	26	6		.301	.348	.414	110	6	29	.926	7	106	60	3b66,S31,2b26		1.5
1903	Was A	125	473	56	116	18	3	1	31	9	5		.245	.267	.302	69	-18	30	.952	3	98	96	3b119,S4,2b2		-1.2
1904	Was A	65	265	28	73	15	4	0	17	9	3		.275	.307	.362	113	3	10	.939	4	99	105	3b64		1.0
	Det A	56	206	22	47	6	0	0	17	5	3		.228	.257	.257	65	-8	1	.929	-5	99	84	3b56		-1.3
	Year	121	471	50	120	21	4	0	34	14	6		.255	.285	.316	92	-5	11	.935	-1	99	74	3b120		-0.3
1905	Det A	137	489	48	123	20	6	0	44	34	7		.252	.309	.317	98	-1	16	.914	-7	96	96	3b136		-0.5
1906	Det A	147	498	54	117	15	5	2	60	36	5		.235	.293	.297	83	-10	31	.940	-12	90	103	3b147		-1.9
1907	†Det A	134	519	80	126	10	2	0	46	35	8		.243	.301	.270	79	-11	15	.930	-9	89	66	3b133		-1.9
1908	†Det A	119	405	32	87	5	1	0	23	29	7		.215	.269	.232	61	-17	10	.941	-13	92	91	3b119		-3.2
Total 9		1049	3854	481	972	133	39	15	380	203	52		.252	.299	.319	86	-63	159	.931	-30	94	86	3b983,S35,2b28		-7.6

COUGHTRY, MARLAN James Marlan B9.11.1934 Hollywood CA BL/TR/6-1/170* d9.2 Col Long Beach (CA) City

1960	Bos A	15	19	3	3	0	0	0		5-0	0	8	.158	.333	.158	36	-1	0-0	.909	-1	95	22	2b13/3		-0.2
1962	LA A	11	22	0	4	0	0	0	2	0-0	0	6	.182	.182	.182	-2	-3	0-0	.867	3	136	142	3b5,2b2		-0.1
	KC A	6	11	1	2	0	0	0	1	4-0	0	3	.182	.400	.182	60	0	0-0	.917	1	179	174	3b3		0.1
	Cle A	3	2	1	1	0	0	0	1	1-0	0	1	.500	.667	.500	226	1	0-0	—	0			/H		0.1
	Year	20	35	2	7	0	0	0	4	5-0	0	10	.200	.300	.200	38	-3	0-0	.889	4	155	156	3b8,2b2		0.1
Total 2		35	54	5	10	0	0	0	4	10-0	0	18	.185	.313	.185	37	-3	0-0	.915	3	108	81	2b15,3b9		-0.1

COULSON, BOB Robert Jackson B6.17.1887 Courtney PA D9.11.1953 Washington PA BR/TR/5-10.5/175 d8.4 Col Penn St.

1908	Cin N	8	18	3	6	1	1	0	1	3	0		.333	.429	.500	202	0	1	1.000	1	126	0	O6(4/1/1)		0.1
1910	Bro N	25	89	14	22	3	4	1	13	6	1	14	.247	.302	.404	109	0	9	.922	0	101	111	O25R		-0.1
1911	Bro N	146	521	52	122	23	7	0	50	42	8	78	.234	.301	.305	73	-20	32	.968	0	145	0	O145(0/2/144)		-2.7
1914	Pit F	18	64	7	13	1	0	0	3	7	0	10	.203	.282	.219	38	-7	2	.931	-1	97	39	O18(11/0/7)		-0.5
Total 4		197	692	76	163	28	12	1	67	58	9	102	.236	.303	.315	77	-25	43	.960	-0	101	95	O194(15/3/177)		-3.4

COULTER, CHIP Thomas Lee B6.5.1945 Steubenville OH BB/TR/5-10/172 d9.18

1969	StL N	6	19	3	6	1	1	0	2	0	6		.316	.381	.474	137	1	0-1	.960	-1	100	146	2b6		0.0

COUNSELL, CRAIG Craig John B8.21.1970 South Bend IN BL/TR/6-0/175(170-185) [ColN92 11/319] d9.17 Col Notre Dame

1995	Col N	3	1	0	0	0	0	0	0	0-0	0	0	.000	.500	.000	36	0	0-0	1.000	-0	60	275	S3		0.0
1997	Col N	1	0	0	0	0	0	0	0	0-0	0	0	—	—	—	0	0	0-0	—	0			/R		0.0
	†Fla N	51	164	20	49	9	2	1	16	18-2	3	17	.299	.376	.396	108	3	1-1	.989	13	107	121	2b51		1.
	Year	52	164	20	49	9	2	1	16	18-2	3	17	.299	.376	.396	107	2	1-1	.989	13	107	121	2b51	55	1.
1998	Fla N	107	335	43	84	19	5	4	40	51-7	4	47	.251	.355	.373	98	1	3-0	.991	5	104	94	2b104		-1.
1999	Fla N	37	66	4	10	1	0	0	2	5-0	0	10	.152	.211	.167	-3	-11	0-0	.980	-2	98	56	2b12		-1.
	LA N	50	108	20	28	6	0	0	9	9-0	0	14	.259	.311	.315	63	-6	1-0	.993	3	114	79	2b38,S2		-1.
	Year	87	174	24	38	7	0	0	11	14-0	0	24	.218	.274	.259	38	-17	1-0	.989	2	110	73	2b50,S2		-1.
2000	Ari N	67	152	23	48	8	1	2	11	20-0	2	18	.316	.400	.421	105	2	3-3	.974	2	100	122	2b25,3b23,S6		0.
2001	†Ari N	141	458	76	126	22	3	4	38	61-3	2	76	.275	.359	.362	83	-10	6-8	.975	14	90	121	S58,2b55,3b38,1b2	52	0.
2002	Ari N	112	436	63	123	22	1	1	35	45-3	1	52	.282	.348	.351	81	-12	7-5	.974	11	110	104	3b57,S26,2b10,1b2	61	-0.
2003	Ari N	89	303	40	71	6	3	3	21	41-0	2	32	.234	.328	.304	68	-22	11-4	.986	11	110	104	S129/3		-1.
2004	Mil N	140	473	59	114	19	5	2	23	59-9	5	88	.241	.330	.315	68	-22	17-4	.983	-10	99	90	S129/3		2.
2005	Ari N	150	578	85	148	34	4	9	42	78-4	8	69	.256	.350	.375	87	-8	26-7	.990	22	113	100	2b143/S		3.
Total 10		948	3074	433	801	146	24	27	253	388-28	27	423	.261	.346	.350	80	-80	75-32	.990	74	108	103	2b451,S247,3b213,1b4	168	3.

COURTNEY, CLINT Clinton Dawson "Scrap Iron" B3.16.1927 Hall Summit LA D6.16.1975 Rochester NY BL/TR/5-8/180* d9.29 C1

1951	NY A	1	2	0	0	0	0	0	0	0	1		1.000	.333	.000	-5	0	0-0	.800	0	511	0	/C		0.
1952	StL A	119	413	38	118	24	3	5	50	39	1	26	.286	.349	.395	104	2	0-2	.996	1	97	113	C113		0.
1953	StL A	106	355	28	89	12	2	4	19	25	1	20	.251	.302	.330	69	-16	0-1	.980	-7	91	126	C103		-1.
1954	Bal A	122	397	25	107	18	4	3	37	30	4	7	.270	.323	.360	95	-4	2-1	.990	-5	82	125	C111		-0.
1955	Chi A	19	37	7	14	3	0	1	10	7-2	1	0	.378	.467	.541	168	4	0-0	1.000	0	113	54	C17		0.
	Was A	75	238	26	71	8	4	7	30	19-4	1	9	.298	.349	.391	105	1	0-0	.983	-9	78	128	C67		0.
	Year	94	275	33	85	11	4	8	40	26-6	2	9	.309	.366	.411	114	5	0-0	.985	-9	83	117	C84		0.
1956	Was A	101	283	31	85	20	3	5	44	20-4	9	10	.300	.362	.445	113	5	0-5	.979	-11	75	134	C76		0.
1957	Was A	91	232	23	62	14	1	6	27	16-5	12	11	.267	.346	.414	108	3	1-5	.994	-5	75	127	C59		-0.
1958	Was A	134	450	46	113	18	0	8	62	48-3	9	14	.251	.332	.344	89	-5	1-5	.991	-8	60	115	C128		-0.

YEAR	TM LG	G	AB	R	H	2B	3B	HR	RBI	BB-IB	HP	SO	AVG	OBP	SLG	AOPS	ABR	SB-CS	FA	FR	RNG	THR	GAMES AT POSITION	DL	BFW
1959	Was A	72	189	10	44	4	1	2	18	20-1	1	19	.233	.308	.296	68	-8	0-1	.987	-11	55	49	C53	30	-1.7
1960	Bal A	83	154	14	35	3	0	1	12	30-3	8	14	.227	.374	.266	79	-2	0-1	.975	2	66	138	C58		0.1
1961	KC A	1	1	0	0	0	0	0	0	0-0	0	0	.000	.000	.000	-98	0	0-0	—	0			/H		0.0
	Bal A	22	45	3	12	2	0	0	4	10-0	0	3	.267	.400	.311	96	0	0-0	1.000	1	116	79	C16		0.2
	Year	23	46	3	12	2	0	0	4	10-0	0	3	.261	.393	.304	92	0	0-0	1.000	1	116	79	C16		0.2
Total	11	946	2796	260	750	126	17	38	313	264-22	46	143	.268	.339	.366	94	-20	3-16	.987	-51	79	118	C802	30	-3.7

COURTNEY, ERNIE Edward Ernest B1.20.1875 Des Moines IA D2.29.1920 Buffalo NY BL/TR/5-8/168 d4.17 OF(40/1/6)

YEAR	TM LG	G	AB	R	H	2B	3B	HR	RBI	BB-IB	HP	SO	AVG	OBP	SLG	AOPS	ABR	SB-CS	FA	FR	RNG	THR	GAMES AT POSITION	DL	BFW
1902	Bos A	48	165	23	36	3	0	0	17	13	4		.218	.291	.236	62	-7	3	.974	-0	92	0	O39(36/1/3),S3		-1.0
	Bal A	1	4	3	2	0	1	0	1	1	0		.500	.600	1.000	324	1	0	1.000	0	66	0	/3		0.1
1903	NY A	25	79	7	21	3	3	1	8	7	2		.266	.341	.418	119	2	1	.916	1	116	122	S19,2b4/1		0.3
	Det A	23	74	7	17	0	0	0	6	5	3		.230	.305	.230	64	-3	1	.938	-2	59	80	3b13,S9		-0.5
	Year	48	153	14	38	3	3	1	14	12	5		.248	.324	.327	94	-1	2	.921	-1	116	94	S28,3b13,2b4/1		-0.2
1905	Phi A	155	601	77	165	14	7	2	77	47	7		.275	.344	.331	102	2	17	.923	-20	83	73	3b155		-1.4
1906	Phi A	116	398	53	94	12	2	0	42	45	1		.236	.315	.276	84	-6	6	.923	-9	90	86	3b96,1b13,O3R/S		-1.5
1907	Phi A	130	440	42	107	17	4	2	43	55	6		.243	.335	.314	105	5	6	.907	-5	93	118	3b75,1b48,O4L,2b2,S2		0.1
1908	Phi A	60	160	14	29	3	0	0	6	15	2		.181	.260	.200	46	-9	1	.915	-3	92	46	3b22,1b13,2b5,S2		-1.4
Total	6	558	1921	226	471	52	17	5	200	188	25		.245	.321	.298	91	-15	35	.920	-40	87	84	3b362,1b75,O46L,S36,2b11		-5.3

COUSINEAU, DEE Edward Thomas B12.16.1898 Watertown MA D7.14.1951 Watertown MA BR/TR/6-0/170 d10.6 Col Fordham

YEAR	TM LG	G	AB	R	H	2B	3B	HR	RBI	BB-IB	HP	SO	AVG	OBP	SLG	AOPS	ABR	SB-CS	FA	FR	RNG	THR	GAMES AT POSITION	DL	BFW
1923	Bos N	1	2	1	2	0	0	0	2	0	0	0	1.000	1.000	1.000	447	1	0-0		0	0	0	/C		0.1
1924	Bos N	3	2	0	0	0	0	0	0	0	0	0	.000	.000	.000	-99	-1	0-0	.500	-0	0	0	C3		-0.1
1925	Bos N	1	0	0	0	0	0	0	0	0	0	0	—	—	—		0	0-0		0	0	0	/C		0.0
Total	3	5	4	1	2	0	0	0	2	0	0	0	.500	.500	.500	174	0	0-0	.500	-0	0	0	C5		0.0

COVENEY, JACK John Patrick B6.10.1880 S.Natick MA D3.28.1961 Wayland MA BR/TR/5-9/175 d9.19 Col St. Anselm

YEAR	TM LG	G	AB	R	H	2B	3B	HR	RBI	BB-IB	HP	SO	AVG	OBP	SLG	AOPS	ABR	SB-CS	FA	FR	RNG	THR	GAMES AT POSITION	DL	BFW
1903	StL N	4	14	0	2	0	0	0	0	0			.143	.143	.143	-19	-2	0	.923	0	94	172	C4		-0.2

COVINGTON, SAM Clarence Calvert B11.18.1894 Denison TX D1.4.1963 Denison TX BL/TR/6-1/190 d8.25 Mil 1918 b-Tex

YEAR	TM LG	G	AB	R	H	2B	3B	HR	RBI	BB-IB	HP	SO	AVG	OBP	SLG	AOPS	ABR	SB-CS	FA	FR	RNG	THR	GAMES AT POSITION	DL	BFW
1913	StL A	20	60	0	9	1	0	0	4	4	0	6	.150	.203	.183	14	-7	3	.994	3	184	83	1b16		-0.4
1917	Bos N	17	66	8	13	2	0	1	10	5	1	5	.197	.264	.273	69	-2	1	.994	0	99	166	1b17		-0.3
1918	Bos N	3	3	0	1	0	0	0	0	0	0	0	.333	.333	.333	108	0	0		0			/H		0.0
Total	3	40	129	11	23	2	1	1	14	9	1	11	.178	.237	.233	43	-9	4	.994	4	139	127	1b33		-0.7

COVINGTON, WES John Wesley B3.27.1932 Laurinburg NC BL/TR/6-1/205* d4.19

YEAR	TM LG	G	AB	R	H	2B	3B	HR	RBI	BB-IB	HP	SO	AVG	OBP	SLG	AOPS	ABR	SB-CS	FA	FR	RNG	THR	GAMES AT POSITION	DL	BFW
1956	Mil N	75	138	17	39	4	0	2	16	16-3	1	20	.283	.361	.355	100	0	1-0	.979	-1	85	115	O35(34/0/1)		-0.2
1957	†Mil N	96	328	51	93	8	4	21	65	29-7	5	35	.284	.339	.537	143	17	4-1	.981	0	90	155	O89L		1.3
1958	†Mil N	90	294	43	97	12	1	24	74	20-7	5	35	.330	.380	.622	175	30	0-0	.953	-4	90	60	O82L		2.2
1959	Mil N	103	373	38	104	17	3	7	45	26-8	3	41	.279	.329	.397	101	0	1-0	.962	-4	88	86	O94L		-1.0
1960	Mil N	95	281	25	70	16	1	10	35	15-1	1	37	.249	.288	.420	99	-2	1-2	.964	-6	86	37	O72L		-1.2
1961	Mil N	9	21	3	4	1	0	0	0	2-0	0	4	.190	.261	.238	36	-2	0-0	1.000	-1	38	0	O5L		-0.3
	Chi A	22	59	5	17	1	0	4	15	4-1	0	5	.288	.333	.508	123	2	0-0	.900	-1	64	204	O14(11/0/3)		0.0
	KC A	17	44	3	7	0	0	1	6	4-0	2	7	.159	.260	.227	31	-4	0-0	1.000	-2	69	0	O12(11/0/1)		-0.7
	Year	39	103	8	24	1	0	5	21	8-1	2	12	.233	.301	.388	83	-3	0-0	.941	-3	75	115	O26(22/0/4)		-0.7
	Phi N	57	165	23	50	9	0	7	26	15-1	0	17	.303	.355	.485	124	6	0-0	.950	-3	75	115	O45(10/0/36)		0.0
1962	Phi N	116	304	36	86	12	1	9	44	19-1	2	44	.283	.324	.418	102	0	0-0	.944	-4	84	65	O88L		-0.8
1963	Phi N	119	353	46	107	24	1	17	64	26-7	2	56	.303	.354	.521	150	23	1-0	.937	-5	84	81	O101L		1.4
1964	Phi N	129	339	37	95	18	0	13	58	38-6	3	50	.280	.355	.448	127	13	0-0	.972	-5	78	84	O99(97/1/2)		0.5
1965	Phi N	101	235	27	58	10	1	15	45	26-8	1	47	.247	.322	.489	128	6	0-0	.968	0	102	71	O64L		0.6
1966	Chi N	9	11	0	1	0	0	0	0	1-1	0	2	.091	.167	.091	-26	-2	0-0	1.000	0	115	0	/OL		-0.2
	†LA N	37	33	1	4	0	1	1	6	10-0	2	5	.121	.293	.273	63	-2	0-0	1.000	0	36	0	O2L		-0.2
	Year	46	44	1	5	0	1	1	6	11-1	2	7	.114	.264	.227	41	-4	0-0	1.000	0	66	0	O3L		-0.4
Total	11	1075	2978	355	832	128	17	131	499	247-51	24	414	.279	.337	.466	123	87	7-4	.961	-36	85	86	O803(761/1/43)		1.4

COWAN, BILLY Billy Rolland B8.28.1938 Calhoun City MS BR/TR/6-0/170* d9.9 Col Utah

YEAR	TM LG	G	AB	R	H	2B	3B	HR	RBI	BB-IB	HP	SO	AVG	OBP	SLG	AOPS	ABR	SB-CS	FA	FR	RNG	THR	GAMES AT POSITION	DL	BFW
1963	Chi N	14	36	4	9	1	1	2	0-0	1	11		.250	.250	.417	84	-1	0-1	.917	-1	58	183	O10(1/7/2)		-0.3
1964	Chi N	139	497	52	120	16	4	19	50	18-5	1	128	.241	.268	.404	83	-13	12-3	.968	-10	99	23	O134C		-2.7
1965	NY N	82	156	16	28	8	2	3	9	4-1	1	45	.179	.205	.314	45	-12	3-2	1.000	-2	90	87	O61(2/59/0),2b2/S		-1.6
	Mil N	19	27	4	5	1	0	0	6	0-0	0	9	.185	.185	.222	14	-3	0-0	1.000	-1	81	0	O10(7/3/0)		-0.4
	Year	101	183	20	33	9	2	3	9	4-1	1	54	.180	.202	.301	41	-15	3-2	1.000	-2	89	76	O71(9/62/0),2b2/S		-2.0
1967	Phi N	34	59	11	9	0	0	3	6	4-0	0	14	.153	.203	.305	44	-5	1-0	1.000	-2	80	0	O20(16/0/4)/23		-0.8
1969	NY A	32	48	5	8	0	0	1	3	3-0	0	9	.167	.216	.229	25	-5	0-0	1.000	-0	82	140	O14(8/4/2)		-0.6
	Cal A	28	56	10	17	1	0	4	10	3-1	1	9	.304	.350	.536	151	3	0-0	1.000	↑	95	482	O13(3/2/8),1b6		0.4
	Year	60	104	15	25	1	0	5	13	6-1	1	18	.240	.288	.394	93	-2	0-0	1.000	↑	88	301	O27(11/6/10),1b6		-0.2
1970	Cal A	68	134	20	37	9	1	5	25	11-2	1	29	.276	.336	.470	124	4	0-1	.929	-3	79	0	O27(3/1/23),1b14,3b2		-0.1
1971	Cal A	74	174	12	48	8	0	4	20	7-1	0	41	.276	.304	.391	103	0	1-1	1.000	-0	108	47	O40(38/0/2),1b5		-0.3
1972	Cal A	3	2	0	0	0	0	0	0	0-0	0	2	.000	.000	.000	-99	-1	0-0	—	0			/H		-0.1
Total	8	493	1190	131	281	44	8	40	125	50-10	4	297	.236	.269	.387	83	-33	17-8	.977	-16	94	56	O329(78/210/41),1b25,3b3,2b3/S		-6.5

COWENS, AL Alfred Edward B10.25.1951 Los Angeles CA D3.11.2002 Downey CA BR/TR/6-2/200* [KCA69 75/1026] d4.6

YEAR	TM LG	G	AB	R	H	2B	3B	HR	RBI	BB-IB	HP	SO	AVG	OBP	SLG	AOPS	ABR	SB-CS	FA	FR	RNG	THR	GAMES AT POSITION	DL	BFW
1974	KC A	110	269	28	65	7	1	1	25	23-0	1	38	.242	.303	.286	69	-11	5-0	.988	2	89	219	O102(6/24/75),3b2,D4		-1.2
1975	KC A	120	328	44	91	13	8	4	42	28-1	4	36	.277	.340	.402	107	2	12-7	.978	-0	107	55	O113(22/35/65),D2		-0.2
1976	†KC A	152	581	71	154	23	6	3	59	26-0	3	50	.265	.298	.341	89	-2	23-16	.986	3	101	115	O148(0/12/142)/D		-1.8
1977	†KC A	162	606	98	189	32	14	23	112	41-4	8	64	.312	.361	.525	137	29	16-12	.982	0	96	127	O159(0/26/141)/D		2.1
1978	†KC A	132	485	63	133	24	8	5	63	31-3	6	54	.274	.319	.388	97	-3	14-6	.990	-1	99	106	O127(0/16/119),3b5,D2	25	-0.5
1979	KC A	136	516	69	152	18	7	9	73	40-4	3	44	.295	.345	.409	101	0	10-8	.986	-7	99	29	O134(0/1/134)/D	21	-1.4
1980	Cal A	34	119	11	27	5	0	1	17	12-1	1	21	.227	.303	.294	65	-5	1-2	1.000	-0	95	133	O30(3/10/19)/D		-0.7
	Det A	108	403	58	113	15	3	5	42	37-4	1	40	.280	.339	.370	93	-4	5-6	.986	-3	92	97	O107R/D		-1.4
	Year	142	522	69	140	20	3	6	59	49-5	2	61	.268	.331	.352	87	-9	6-8	.989	-3	93	105	O137(3/10/126),D2		-2.1
1981	Det A	85	253	27	66	11	4	1	18	22-3	1	36	.261	.319	.348	90	-3	3-3	.994	-4	93	68	O83(0/65/18)		-0.9
1982	Sea A	146	560	72	151	39	2	20	78	46-3	1	71	.270	.325	.475	113	9	1-1	.987	-2	94	133	O145R/D		-0.1
1983	Sea A	110	356	39	73	19	2	7	35	23-0	2	38	.205	.255	.329	58	-21	10-2	.985	2	101	157	O70(2/4/65),D34	29	-2.2
1984	Sea A	139	524	60	145	34	2	15	78	27-2	2	83	.277	.312	.435	106	3	9-5	.987	-4	92	108	O130(0/2/130),D7		-0.7
1985	Sea A	122	452	59	120	32	5	14	69	30-3	1	56	.265	.310	.451	105	2	0-0	.967	-1	92	140	O110R,D5		-0.5
1986	Sea A	28	82	5	15	4	0	0	6	3-0	0	18	.183	.209	.232	20	-9	1-0	.971	-6	87	161	O19(1/0/18)/D		-1.0
Total	13	1584	5534	704	1494	276	68	108	717	389-28	34	659	.270	.319	.403	98	-22	120-74	.985	-12	96	111	O1477(34/195/1288),D61,3b7	75	-10.5

COX, STEVE Charles Steven B10.31.1974 Delano CA BL/TL/6-4/222* [OakA92 5/144] d9.19

YEAR	TM LG	G	AB	R	H	2B	3B	HR	RBI	BB-IB	HP	SO	AVG	OBP	SLG	AOPS	ABR	SB-CS	FA	FR	RNG	THR	GAMES AT POSITION	DL	BFW
1999	TB A	6	19	4	4	0	0	0	2	2-0	0	2	.211	.211	.263	20	-2	0-0	1.000	-1	52	157	1b4,O2L		-0.3
2000	TB A	116	318	44	90	19	1	11	35	45-2	5	47	.283	.379	.453	111	7	1-2	.948	6	107	94	O56(26/0/30),1b24,D17		0.1
2001	TB A	108	342	37	88	22	0	12	51	24-0	10	75	.257	.323	.427	97	-1	2-2	.998	0	96	101	1b78,O8(6/0/2),D4	17	-0.8
2002	TB A	148	560	65	142	30	1	16	72	60-5	7	116	.254	.330	.396	95	-3	5-0	.993	5	119	101	1b110,D35		-0.9
Total	4	378	1239	146	324	72	2	39	158	129-7	22	240	.262	.340	.417	99	1	8-4	.994	3	106	99	1b216,O66(34/0/32),D56	17	-1.9

COX, DICK Elmer Joseph B9.30.1895 Pasadena CA D6.1.1966 Morro Bay CA BR/TR/5-7.5/158 d4.16

YEAR	TM LG	G	AB	R	H	2B	3B	HR	RBI	BB-IB	HP	SO	AVG	OBP	SLG	AOPS	ABR	SB-CS	FA	FR	RNG	THR	GAMES AT POSITION	DL	BFW
1925	Bro N	122	434	68	143	23	10	7	64	37	0	29	.329	.382	.477	121	14	4-3	.968	-3	93	96	O111(3/0/108)		0.2
1926	Bro N	124	398	53	118	17	4	1	45	46	4	20	.296	.375	.367	102	3	6	.964	-3	95	86	O117(0/1/116)		-0.8
Total	2	246	832	121	261	40	14	8	109	83	4	49	.314	.379	.424	112	17	10-3	.966	-6	94	91	O228(3/1/224)		-0.6

COX, FRANK Francis Bernard "Runt" B8.29.1857 Waltham MA D6.24.1928 Hartford CT 5-6/? d8.13

YEAR	TM LG	G	AB	R	H	2B	3B	HR	RBI	BB-IB	HP	SO	AVG	OBP	SLG	AOPS	ABR	SB-CS	FA	FR	RNG	THR	GAMES AT POSITION	DL	BFW
1884	Det N	27	102	6	13	3	1	0		36			.127	.144	.176	0	-1		.812	-3	99	106	S27		-1.2

COX, JIM James Charles B5.28.1950 Bloomington IL BR/TR/5-11/175* [MonN72*S1/2] d7.19 Col Iowa

YEAR	TM LG	G	AB	R	H	2B	3B	HR	RBI	BB-IB	HP	SO	AVG	OBP	SLG	AOPS	ABR	SB-CS	FA	FR	RNG	THR	GAMES AT POSITION	DL	BFW
1973	Mon N	9	15	1	2	1	0	0	0	1-0	0	4	.133	.188	.200	7	-2	0-0	.950	-2	75	33	2b7		-0.4
1974	Mon N	77	236	29	52	9	1	2	26	23-2	1	36	.220	.288	.292	60	-12	2-3	.968	5	104	106	2b72	27	-0.4
1975	Mon N	11	27	1	7	1	0	1	5	1-1	0	2	.259	.276	.407	86	-1	1-0	1.000	-1	103	145	2b8		-0.1

YEAR	TM LG	G	AB	R	H	2B	3B	HR	RBI	BB-IB	HP	SO	AVG	OBP	SLG	AOPS	ABR	SB-CS	FA	FR	RNG	THR	GAMES AT POSITION	DL	BFW
1976	Mon N	13	29	2	5	0	1	0	2	2-0	0	2	.172	.226	.241	31	-3	0-0	.958	-1	86	96	2b11		-0.3
Total	4	110	307	33	66	11	2	3	33	27-3	1	44	.215	.276	.293	58	-18	3-3	.969	1	101	104	2b98	27	-1.2

COX, DARRON James Darron B11.21.1967 Oklahoma City OK BR/TR/6-1/205 [CinN89 5/134] d4.6 Col Oklahoma

YEAR	TM LG	G	AB	R	H	2B	3B	HR	RBI	BB-IB	HP	SO	AVG	OBP	SLG	AOPS	ABR	SB-CS	FA	FR	RNG	THR	GAMES AT POSITION	DL	BFW
1999	Mon N	15	25	2	6	1	0	0	5	.240			.296	.400	77	-1	0-0	.963	3	227	55	C14		99	0.2

COX, JEFF Jeffrey Lindon B11.9.1955 Los Angeles CA BR/TR/5-11/170* d7.1 C7

YEAR	TM LG	G	AB	R	H	2B	3B	HR	RBI	BB-IB	HP	SO	AVG	OBP	SLG	AOPS	ABR	SB-CS	FA	FR	RNG	THR	GAMES AT POSITION	DL	BFW
1980	Oak A	59	169	20	36	3	0	0	9	14-0	0	23	.213	.273	.231	42	-13	8-5	.979	-18	86	72	2b58		-2.8
1981	Oak A	2	0	0	0	0	0	0	0	0-0	0	0	—	—	—		0	0-0	1.000	0	264	0	/2		0.0
Total	2	61	169	20	36	3	0	0	9	14-0	0	23	.213	.273	.231	42	-13	8-5	.979	-17	86	72	2b59		-2.8

COX, LARRY Larry Eugene B9.11.1947 Bluffton OH D2.17.1990 Bellefontaine OH BR/TR/5-11/190(178-190) d4.18 C2

YEAR	TM LG	G	AB	R	H	2B	3B	HR	RBI	BB-IB	HP	SO	AVG	OBP	SLG	AOPS	ABR	SB-CS	FA	FR	RNG	THR	GAMES AT POSITION	DL	BFW
1973	Phi N	1	0	0	0	0	0	0	0	0-0	0	0	—	—	—		0	0-0	1.000	0	0	0	/C		0.0
1974	Phi N	30	53	5	9	2	0	0	4	4-0	1	9	.170	.241	.208	25	-5	0-0	.990	-3	76	19	C29	28	-0.8
1975	Phi N	11	5	0	1	0	0	0	1	1-0	0	1	.200	.286	.200	48	0	1-0	1.000	-1	138	0	C10		-0.1
1977	Sea A	35	93	6	23	6	0	2	6	10-0	0	12	.247	.320	.376	90	-1	1-1	.970	-4	72	158	C35	13	-0.1
1978	Chi N	59	121	10	34	5	0	2	18	12-0	0	16	.281	.346	.372	90	-1	1-0	.967	-1	110	108	C58	39	-0.1
1979	Sea A	100	293	32	63	11	3	4	36	22-0	0	39	.215	.266	.314	56	-19	2-1	.981	-7	68	119	C99		-2.2
1980	Sea A	105	243	18	49	6	2	4	20	19-0	0	36	.202	.260	.292	50	-17	1-2	**.993**	7	102	108	C104		-0.7
1981	Tex A	5	13	0	3	1	0	0	0	0-0	0	4	.231	.231	.308	57	-1	0-0	1.000	1	43	0	C5		0.0
1982	Chi N	2	4	1	0	0	0	0	0	2-1	0	0	.000	.333	.000	1	0	0-0	1.000	1	48	306	C2		0.0
Total	9	348	825	72	182	31	5	12	85	70-1	1	117	.221	.280	.314	61	-44	5-4	.983	-8	86	110	C343	80	-4.3

COX, BOBBY Robert Joseph B5.21.1941 Tulsa OK BR/TR/5-11/180* d4.14 M24/C1

YEAR	TM LG	G	AB	R	H	2B	3B	HR	RBI	BB-IB	HP	SO	AVG	OBP	SLG	AOPS	ABR	SB-CS	FA	FR	RNG	THR	GAMES AT POSITION	DL	BFW
1968	NY A	135	437	33	100	15	1	7	41	41-7	5	85	.229	.300	.316	90	-5	3-2	.957	-5	105	97	3b132		-1.2
1969	NY A	85	191	17	41	7	1	2	17	34-7	1	41	.215	.332	.293	80	-4	0-1	.935	6	114	149	3b56,2b6		0.2
Total	2	220	628	50	141	22	2	9	58	75-14	6	126	.225	.310	.309	87	-9	3-3	.950	1	107	111	3b188,2b6		-1.0

COX, BILLY William Richard B8.29.1919 Newport PA D3.30.1978 Harrisburg PA BR/TR/5-10/150* d9.20 Mil 1942-45

YEAR	TM LG	G	AB	R	H	2B	3B	HR	RBI	BB-IB	HP	SO	AVG	OBP	SLG	AOPS	ABR	SB-CS	FA	FR	RNG	THR	GAMES AT POSITION	DL	BFW
1941	Pit N	10	37	4	10	3	1	0	2	3	0	2	.270	.325	.405	105	-1	1	.943	1	118	142	S10		0.2
1946	Pit N	121	411	32	119	22	6	2	36	26	1	15	.290	.333	.387	101	0	4	.935	-13	94	83	S114		-0.7
1947	Pit N	132	529	75	145	30	7	15	54	29	1	28	.274	.313	.442	96	-6	5	.968	-11	99	78	S129		-0.8
1948	Bro N	88	237	36	59	13	2	3	15	38	0	19	.249	.353	.359	90	-2	3	.958	-5	93	75	3b70,S6/2		-0.7
1949	†Bro N	100	390	48	91	18	2	8	40	30	1	18	.233	.290	.351	68	-18	5	.964	7	100	145	3b100		-1.2
1950	Bro N	119	451	62	116	17	2	8	44	35	0	24	.257	.311	.357	74	-18	6	**.957**	12	108	165	3b107,2b13,S9		-0.5
1951	Bro N	142	455	62	127	25	4	9	51	37	2	32	.279	.336	.411	98	-2	5-5	.970	-5	95	87	3b139/S		-0.8
1952	†Bro N	116	455	56	118	12	3	6	34	25	2	32	.259	.301	.338	76	-16	10-12	.970	-7	88	175	3b100,S10,2b9		-2.5
1953	†Bro N	100	327	44	95	18	1	10	44	37	0	21	.291	.363	.443	106	4	2-2	.974	-2	90	123	3b89/S6/2		0.1
1954	Bro N	77	226	26	53	9	2	2	17	21	0	13	.235	.297	.319	59	-14	0-0	.961	1	98	85	3b58,2b11,S8		-1.2
1955	Bal A	53	194	25	41	7	2	3	14	17-0	0	16	.211	.275	.330	63	-11	1-2	.969	-5	100	71	3b37,2b18,S6		-1.7
Total	11	1058	3712	470	974	174	32	66	351	298-0	7	218	.262	.318	.380	85	-83	42-21	.965	-27	96	124	3b700,S299,2b53		-9.8

COX, TED William Ted B1.24.1955 Oklahoma City OK BR/TR/6-3/195(190-205) [BosA73 1/17] d9.18

YEAR	TM LG	G	AB	R	H	2B	3B	HR	RBI	BB-IB	HP	SO	AVG	OBP	SLG	AOPS	ABR	SB-CS	FA	FR	RNG	THR	GAMES AT POSITION	DL	BFW
1977	Bos A	13	58	11	21	3	1	1	6	3-0	0	6	.362	.393	.500	127	2	0-0	—	0	0	0	D13		0.2
1978	Cle A	82	227	14	53	7	4	1	19	16-1	1	30	.233	.286	.278	60	-12	0-1	.980	-4	78	156	O38(33/0/5),3b20,D12,1b7/S		-2.0
1979	Cle A	78	189	17	40	6	0	4	22	14-1	2	27	.212	.272	.307	56	-12	3-4	.964	-1	95	142	3b52,O16L,2b4/D		-1.5
1980	Sea A	83	247	17	60	9	0	2	23	19-3	0	25	.243	.295	.304	64	-12	0-0	.945	-4	95	135	3b80		-1.8
1981	Tor A	16	50	6	15	4	0	2	9	5-0	0	10	.300	.364	.500	138	-1	0-1	.897	-4	75	40	3b14/1D		-0.2
Total	5	272	771	65	189	29	1	10	79	57-5	3	98	.245	.298	.324	71	-31	3-6	.947	-14	91	120	3b166,O54(49/0/5),D27,1b8,2b4/S		-5.3

COYNE, TOOTS Martin Albert B10.20.1894 St.Louis MO D9.18.1939 St.Louis MO TR d9.28

YEAR	TM LG	G	AB	R	H	2B	3B	HR	RBI	BB-IB	HP	SO	AVG	OBP	SLG	AOPS	ABR	SB-CS	FA	FR	RNG	THR	GAMES AT POSITION	DL	BFW
1914	Phi A	1	2	0	0	0	0	0	0	0	0	2	.000	.000	.000	-99	-1	0	1.000	-0	112	0	/3		-0.1

CRABTREE, ESTEL Estel Crayton "Crabby" B8.19.1903 Crabtree OH D1.4.1967 Logan OH BL/TR/6-0/168 d4.18 C2

YEAR	TM LG	G	AB	R	H	2B	3B	HR	RBI	BB-IB	HP	SO	AVG	OBP	SLG	AOPS	ABR	SB-CS	FA	FR	RNG	THR	GAMES AT POSITION	DL	BFW
1929	Cin N	1	1	0	0	0	0	0	0	0	0	0	.000	.000	.000	-99	-0	0	—	0			/H		0.0
1931	Cin N	117	443	70	119	12	12	4	37	23	3	26	.269	.309	.377	89	-10	3	.974	10	107	172	O101(9/16/76),3b4,1b2		-0.5
1932	Cin N	108	402	38	110	14	9	2	35	23	2	26	.274	.316	.368	86	-9	2	.990	5	108	103	O95(14/73/9)		-0.7
1933	StL N	23	34	6	9	3	0	0	3	2	0	3	.265	.306	.353	83	-1	1	.947	0	128	0	O7(0/4/3)		-0.1
1941	StL N	77	167	27	57	6	3	5	28	26	0	3	.341	.439	.503	154	13	1	1.000	-2	91	71	O50(17/16/19)/3		1.0
1942	StL N	10	9	1	3	0	0	0	2	1	0	3	.333	.400	.556	166	1	0	—	0			/H		0.1
1943	Cin N	95	254	25	70	12	0	2	26	25	2	17	.276	.345	.346	101	1	1	.939	-6	89	66	O65(2/44/17)		-0.8
1944	Cin N	58	98	7	28	6	1	0	11	13	0	6	.286	.369	.347	106	1	0	1.000	-1	80	86	O19(15/3/1),1b2		-0.1
Total	8	489	1408	174	396	53	25	13	142	113	10	109	.281	.339	.382	100	-4	8	.976	6	101	111	O337(57/156/125),3b5,1b4		-1.1

CRADLE, RICKEY Rickey Nelson B6.20.1973 Norfolk VA BR/TR/6-2/180 [TorA91 5/146] d7.1

YEAR	TM LG	G	AB	R	H	2B	3B	HR	RBI	BB-IB	HP	SO	AVG	OBP	SLG	AOPS	ABR	SB-CS	FA	FR	RNG	THR	GAMES AT POSITION	DL	BFW
1998	Sea A	5	7	0	1	0	0	0	0	1	0	5	.143	.250	.143	9	-1	1-0	1.000	-0	57	0	O4(1/2/1)	27	-0.1

CRAFT, HARRY Harry Francis "Wildfire" B4.19.1915 Ellisville MS D8.3.1995 Conroe TX BR/TR/6-1/185 d9.19 M7/C5 Col Mississippi College

YEAR	TM LG	G	AB	R	H	2B	3B	HR	RBI	BB-IB	HP	SO	AVG	OBP	SLG	AOPS	ABR	SB-CS	FA	FR	RNG	THR	GAMES AT POSITION	DL	BFW
1937	Cin N	10	42	7	13	2	1	0	4	1	0	3	.310	.326	.405	102	0	1	1.000	0	94	131	O10C		0.0
1938	Cin N	**151**	612	70	165	28	9	15	83	29	2	46	.270	.305	.418	100	-4	3	.983	7	110	112	O151C		0.0
1939	†Cin N	134	502	58	129	20	7	13	67	27	3	54	.257	.299	.402	86	-12	5	.981	-3	91	122	O134C		-1.9
1940	†Cin N	115	422	47	103	18	5	6	48	17	2	46	.244	.277	.353	72	-18	2	**.997**	0	103	76	O109(0/106/3),1b2		-2.1
1941	Cin N	119	413	48	103	15	2	10	59	33	4	43	.249	.308	.368	90	-7	4	.983	-2	102	68	O115C		-1.2
1942	Cin N	37	113	7	20	2	1	0	6	3	1	11	.177	.205	.212	22	-12	0	.987	2	101	147	O33C		-1.2
Total	6	566	2104	237	533	85	25	44	267	110	10	203	.253	.294	.380	85	-53	14	.986	4	102	100	O552(0/549/3),1b2		-6.4

CRAIG, ROD Rodney Paul B1.12.1958 Los Angeles CA BB/TR/6-1/195* d9.11 Col San Jacinto North (TX) JC

YEAR	TM LG	G	AB	R	H	2B	3B	HR	RBI	BB-IB	HP	SO	AVG	OBP	SLG	AOPS	ABR	SB-CS	FA	FR	RNG	THR	GAMES AT POSITION	DL	BFW
1979	Sea A	16	52	9	20	8	1	0	6	5	0	5	.385	.396	.577	155	4	1-1	.923	-2	87	0	O15R		0.1
1980	Sea A	70	240	30	57	15	4	3	20	17-3	0	35	.237	.293	.346	73	-9	3-6	.987	-5	90	45	O63(3/58/2)	15	-1.6
1982	Cle A	49	65	7	15	2	0	0	1	4-0	0	6	.231	.275	.262	48	-5	3-1	.966	-1	105	0	O22(11/4/7),D4		-0.5
1986	Chi A	10	10	3	2	0	0	0	0	2-0	0	2	.200	.333	.200	4	-1	0-0	—	-0	0	0	O2(1/0/1)		-0.1
Total	4	145	367	49	94	25	2	3	27	24-3	2	48	.256	.305	.360	80	-11	7-8	.977	-8	91	32	O102(15/62/26),D4	15	-2.1

CRAMER, DOC Roger Maxwell "Flit" B7.22.1905 Beach Haven NJ D9.9.1990 Manahawkin NJ BL/TR/6-2/185 d9.18 C4

YEAR	TM LG	G	AB	R	H	2B	3B	HR	RBI	BB-IB	HP	SO	AVG	OBP	SLG	AOPS	ABR	SB-CS	FA	FR	RNG	THR	GAMES AT POSITION	DL	BFW
1929	Phi A	2	6	0	0	0	0	0	0	0	0	0	.000	.000	.000	-97	-2	0-0	1.000	0	167	0	/OL		-0.2
1930	Phi A	30	82	12	19	1	1	0	6	2	0	8	.232	.250	.268	30	-9	0-0	.927	-1	97	85	O21(6/13/2)/S		-1.0
1931	†Phi A	65	223	37	58	8	2	2	20	11	2	15	.260	.301	.341	64	-12	2-1	.979	-9	97	118	O55(2/47/6)		-1.0
1932	Phi A	92	384	73	129	27	7	3	46	17	2	27	.336	.367	.461	109	5	3-1	.976	4	110	98	O86(0/45/42)		0.5
1933	Phi A	152	661	109	195	27	8	8	75	36	0	24	.295	.331	.396	91	-11	5-4	.971	-0	100	121	O152C		-1.4
1934	Phi A	153	649	99	202	29	4	8	46	40	2	35	.311	.353	.411	100	-2	1-5	.985	2	101	102	O152C		-0.8
1935	Phi A★	149	644	96	214	37	4	3	70	37	5	34	.332	.373	.416	105	4	6-7	.975	-1	104	51	O149C		-0.2
1936	Bos A	154	643	99	188	31	7	0	41	49	5	20	.292	.347	.362	71	-29	4-6	.975	11	106	149	O154C		-1.2
1937	Bos A☆	133	560	90	171	22	11	0	51	35	4	14	.305	.351	.384	82	-17	8-6	.969	2	103	100	O133C		-1.9
1938	Bos A★	148	658	116	198	36	6	0	71	51	3	19	.301	.354	.380	80	-20	4-9	.986	6	104	106	O148C/P		-2.1
1939	Bos A★	137	589	110	183	30	6	0	56	36	2	17	.311	.352	.382	85	-14	3-3	.984	-5	92	100	O135C		-2.1
1940	Bos A☆	150	661	94	200	27	12	1	51	36	1	29	.303	.340	.384	84	-17	3-5	.969	-7	91	98	O149(16/96/37)		-2.9
1941	Was A	154	660	93	180	25	4	2	66	37	6	15	.273	.317	.338	77	-24	4-1	.984	-11	90	71	O152C		-3.3
1942	Det A	151	630	75	166	24	4	0	43	43	3	18	.263	.314	.317	72	-24	4-4	.981	-4	90	139	O150C		-3.1
1943	Det A	140	606	79	182	18	4	1	43	31	1	13	.300	.335	.348	93	-7	4-3	.989	-5	95	86	O138C		-1.1
1944	Det A	143	578	69	169	20	9	2	42	37	2	21	.292	.337	.369	96	-4	2-9	.980	-12	86	59	O140C		-2.2
1945	†Det A	141	541	74	144	22	8	6	58	37	3	21	.266	.315	.370	97	-3	2-9	**.991**	-15	84	69	O50C		-0.7
1946	Det A	68	204	26	60	8	1	1	26	15	0	8	.294	.342	.368	93	-2	3-0	1.000	-4	83	73	O35C		0.1
1947	Det A	73	157	21	42	7	2	2	30	20	1	9	.268	.350	.344	91	-2	0-4	.965	-1	93	149	O36C		0.0
1948	Det A	4	4	1	0	0	0	0	0	1	0	3	.000	.429	.000	19	-0	0-0	1.000	-0	69	0	/OC		-0.0
Total	20	2239	9140	1357	2705	396	109	37	842	572	41	345	.296	.340	.375	87	-190	62-73	.979	-40	96	99	O2142(25/2031/87)/PS		-29.4

CRAMER, DICK William B. B Brooklyn NY D8.11.1885 Camden NJ d5.12

YEAR	TM LG	G	AB	R	H	2B	3B	HR	RBI	BB-IB	HP	SO	AVG	OBP	SLG	AOPS	ABR	SB-CS	FA	FR	RNG	THR	GAMES AT POSITION	DL	BFW
1883	NY N	2	6	0	0	0	0	0	0	0	1		5	.000	.143	.000	-52	-1		—	-0	0	0	O2(0/1/1)		-0.

YEAR	TM LG	G	AB	R	H	2B	3B	HR	RBI	BB-IB	HP	SO	AVG	OBP	SLG	AOPS	ABR	SB-CS	FA	FR	RNG	THR	GAMES AT POSITION	DL	BFW

CRANDALL, DEL   Delmar Wesley B3.5.1930 Ontario CA   BR/TR/6-1/195(185-205) d6.17 Mil 1951-52 M6/C1

YEAR	TM LG	G	AB	R	H	2B	3B	HR	RBI	BB-IB	HP	SO	AVG	OBP	SLG	AOPS	ABR	SB-CS	FA	FR	RNG	THR	GAMES AT POSITION	DL	BFW
1949	Bos N	67	228	21	60	10	1	4	34	9	0	18	.263	.291	.368	80	-8	2	.982	4	99	117	C63		0.0
1950	Bos N	79	255	21	56	11	0	4	37	13	0	24	.220	.291	.310	52	-19	0	.967	0	82	132	C75/1		-1.5
1953	Mil N	116	382	55	104	13	1	15	51	33	0	47	.272	.330	.429	102	0	2-1	.986	11	90	140	C108		1.6
1954	Mil N☆	138	463	60	112	18	2	21	64	40	3	56	.242	.305	.425	94	-6	0-3	.989	11	97	117	C136		1.0
1955	Mil N★	133	440	61	104	15	2	26	62	40-11	2	56	.236	.299	.457	103	0	2-1	.985	-2	126	117	C131		0.4
1956	Mil N★	112	311	37	74	14	2	16	48	35-15	1	30	.238	.313	.450	110	4	1-2	.996	5	147	100	C109		1.3
1957	†Mil N	118	383	45	97	11	2	15	46	30-9	1	38	.253	.308	.410	98	-3	1-2	.987	-3	87	116	C102,O9(1/0/9)/1		-0.2
1958	†Mil N★	131	427	50	116	23	1	18	63	48-18	1	38	.272	.348	.457	122	14	4-1	.990	7	126	105	C124		2.7
1959	Mil N★	150	518	65	133	19	2	21	72	46-8	3	48	.257	.318	.423	105	2	5-1	.994	9	163	89	C146		1.9
1960	Mil N★	142	537	81	158	14	1	19	77	34-6	4	36	.294	.334	.430	118	12	4-6	.988	-8	167	68	C141		1.0
1961	Mil N	15	30	3	6	3	0	0	1	1-0	0	0	.200	.226	.300	40	-3	0-0	1.000	-1	89	91	C5		1.0
1962	Mil N★	107	350	35	104	12	3	8	45	27-2	2	24	.297	.348	.417	108	4	3-4	.994	4	174	92	C90,1b5	56	-0.3
1963	Mil N	86	259	18	52	4	7	3	28	18-5	0	22	.201	.251	.251	46	-18	1-4	.991	-4	89	103	C75,1b7		1.1
1964	SF N	69	195	12	45	8	1	3	11	22-9	0	21	.231	.309	.328	78	-5	0-3	.993	6	107	80	C65		-2.2
1965	Pit N	60	140	11	30	2	0	2	10	14-7	1	10	.214	.288	.271	59	-8	1-0	.996	3	207	112	C60		0.3
1966	Cle A	50	108	10	25	2	0	4	14	14-5	0	9	.231	.320	.361	95	-1	0-0	.991	7	105	81	C49	20	0.9
Total	16	1573	5026	585	1276	179	18	179	657	424-95	21	477	.254	.312	.404	97	-35	26-28	.989	51	126	104	C1479,1b14,O9(1/0/9)	76	7.8

CRANDALL, DOC   James Otis B10.8.1887 Wadena IN D8.17.1951 Bell CA   BR/TR/5-10.5/180 d4.24 C4 ▲

YEAR	TM LG	G	AB	R	H	2B	3B	HR	RBI	BB-IB	HP	SO	AVG	OBP	SLG	AOPS	ABR	SB-CS	FA	FR	RNG	THR	GAMES AT POSITION	DL	BFW
1908	NY N	34	72	8	16	4	0	2	6	4	1		.222	.273	.361	97	0	0	.985	-2	85	131	P32/2		-0.1
1909	NY N	30	41	4	10	0	1	1	1	1	0		.244	.262	.366	93	2	0	.941	2	116	432	P30		-0.1
1910	NY N	45	73	10	25	2	4	1	13	5	0	7	.342	.385	.521	163	5	0	.984	-2	84	164	P42/S		-0.1
1911	†NY N	61	113	12	27	1	4	2	21	8	1	16	.239	.295	.372	83	-4	2	.958	-0	110	114	P41,S6,2b3		0.0
1912	†NY N	50	80	9	25	6	2	0	19	6	0	7	.313	.360	.438	114	1	0	.957	-0	101		P37,2b2/1		-0.1
1913	†NY N	31	25	4	7	2	1	0	2	1	0	5	.280	.308	.440	111	0	0	1.000	1	120		P24,2b2		0.0
	StL N	2	5	0	0	0	0	0	0	0	0	2	.000	.000	.000	-99	-1	0	—	0			/H		-0.1
	†NY N	15	22	3	8	2	0	0	2	2	0	3	.364	.417	.455	148	3	0	1.000	1	120		P11		0.0
	Year	48	49	7	15	4	1	0	4	3	0	10	.306	.346	.429	120	1	0	1.000	1	124		P35,2b2		0.0
1914	StL F	118	278	40	86	16	5	2	41	58	0	32	.309	.429	.424	126	10	3	.926	-13	96	48	2b63,P27/SOC		-0.4
1915	StL F	84	141	18	40	2	2	1	19	27	2	15	.284	.406	.348	107	13	4	.958	-1	103	105	P51		0.0
1916	StL A	16	12	0	1	0	0	0	0	2	0	4	.083	.214	.083	-11	-7	0	.000	-0	-0		P2		0.0
1918	Bos N	14	28	1	8	0	0	0	2	4	0	3	.286	.375	.286	107	0	0	1.000	-0	101	302	P5,O3R		0.0
Total	10	500	887	109	253	35	19	9	126	118	4	94	.285	.372	.398	114	29	9	.962	-13	99	129	P302,2b71,S8,O4(0/1/2)/1		-0.7

CRANE, ED   Edward Nicholas "Cannon-Ball" B5.27.1862 Boston MA D9.20.1896 Rochester NY   BR/TR/5-10.5/204 d4.17 ▲

YEAR	TM LG	G	AB	R	H	2B	3B	HR	RBI	BB-IB	HP	SO	AVG	OBP	SLG	AOPS	ABR	SB-CS	FA	FR	RNG	THR	GAMES AT POSITION	DL	BFW
1884	Bos U	101	428	83	122	23	6	12		14			.285	.308	.451	129	2		.826	-6	127	125	O57(18/0/39),C42,1b5,P4		-0.3
1885	Pro N	1	2	0	0	0	0	0	0	1			1.000	.333	1.000	15	0		.500	0	663	0	/OL		0.0
	Buf N	13	51	5	14	0	1	2	9	3		8	.275	.315	.431	135	2		.769	-3	-0		O13(10/3/0)		-0.1
	Year	14	53	5	14	0	1	2	9	4		9	.264	.316	.415	135	2		.750	-2	38	0	O14(11/3/0)		-0.1
1886	Was N	80	292	20	50	11	3	0	20	13		54	.171	.207	.229	35	-22	8	.866	1	113	162	O68(8/9/51),P10,C4		-1.8
1888	†NY N	12	37	3	6	2	0	1	2	1	0	11	.162	.225	.297	66	1	1	.867	1	115	0	P12		0.0
1889	†NY N	29	103	16	21	1	0	2	11	13	0	21	.204	.293	.272	58	-6	6	.762	-4	51	57	P29/1		-0.2
1890	NY P	43	146	27	46	5	4	0	16	10	1	26	.315	.363	.404	96	7	5	.846	-4	83	0	P43		0.0
1891	Cin AA	34	110	13	17	0	0	1	7	8	0	28	.155	.212	.182	12	-13	4	.822	-3	92	0	P32,O3(0/1/2)		-0.3
	Cin N	15	46	3	5	0	0	0	2	3	0	12	.109	.163	.109	-20	-3	3	.906	0	108	239	P15		-0.3
1892	NY N	48	163	20	40	1	0	0	14	11	1	30	.245	.297	.264	71	-6	2	.814	-2	85	140	P47/OR		-0.2
1893	NY N	12	26	8	12	1	0	0	3	7	0	0	.462	.576	.500	186	4	0	.889	-1	93	0	P10/1OR		0.0
	Bro N	3	5	1	2	1	0	0	0	0	0	0	.400	.400	.600	172	1	0	.500	-1		0	P2/OR		0.0
	Year	15	31	9	14	2	0	0	3	7	0	0	.452	.553	.516	186	5	0	.850	-1	81	0	P12,O2R/1		0.0
Total	9	391	1409	199	335	45	15	18	84	86	2	191	.238	.283	.329	81	-33	29	.840	-21	86	59	P204,O145(37/13/95),C46,1b7		-2.9

CRANE, FRED   Frederic William Hotchkiss B11.4.1840 Old Saybrook CT D4.27.1925 Brooklyn NY   5-9/135 d5.26

YEAR	TM LG	G	AB	R	H	2B	3B	HR	RBI	BB-IB	HP	SO	AVG	OBP	SLG	AOPS	ABR	SB-CS	FA	FR	RNG	THR	GAMES AT POSITION	DL	BFW
1873	Res NA	1	4	0	1	0	0	0		0			.250	.250	.250	53	0	0-0	.667	-1	79	0	/2		-0.1
1875	Atl NA	21	81	7	17	1	0	0		4	0	4	.210	.210	.222	58	-3	0-0	.953	2	255	136	1b20/SOR		0.0
Total	2 NA	22	85	7	18	1	0	0		5	0	4	.212	.212	.224	57	-3	0-0	.953	1	255	136	1b20/ORS2		-0.1

CRANE, SAM   Samuel Byren "Lucky","Red" B9.13.1894 Harrisburg PA D11.12.1955 Philadelphia PA   BR/TR/5-11.5/154 d10.2

YEAR	TM LG	G	AB	R	H	2B	3B	HR	RBI	BB-IB	HP	SO	AVG	OBP	SLG	AOPS	ABR	SB-CS	FA	FR	RNG	THR	GAMES AT POSITION	DL	BFW
1914	Phi A	2	6	0	0	0	0	0	0	2	0	3	.000	.250	.000	-25	-1	-1 0	.929	0	111	0	S2		-0.1
1915	Phi A	8	23	3	2	2	0	0	1	0	0	4	.087	.087	.174	-23	-4	0	.900	0	106	66	S6/2		-0.3
1916	Phi A	2	4	1	1	0	0	0	0	2	0	1	.250	.500	.250	132	0	0	1.000	0	120	0	S2		0.1
1917	Was A	32	95	6	17	2	0	0	4	4	0	14	.179	.212	.200	26	-9	0	.889	-4	90	108	S32		-1.2
1920	Cin N	54	144	20	31	4	0	0	9	7	2	9	.215	.261	.243	46	-10	5-4	.945	-7	81	112	S25,3b10,2b4,O3R		-1.7
1921	Cin N	73	215	20	50	10	2	0	16	14	4	14	.233	.292	.298	59	-12	2-5	.953	-14	85	106	S63,3b2/OR		-2.1
1922	Bro N	3	8	1	2	1	0	0	0	1	1	2	.250	.333	.375	83	0	0	.875	1	115	103	S3		0.1
Total	7	174	495	51	103	19	2	0	30	29	7	46	.208	.262	.255	46	-36	7-9	.931	-23	88	102	S133,3b12,2b5,O4R		-5.2

CRANE, SAM   Samuel Newhall B1.2.1854 Springfield MA D6.26.1925 New York NY   BR/TR/6-0/190 d5.1 M2

YEAR	TM LG	G	AB	R	H	2B	3B	HR	RBI	BB-IB	HP	SO	AVG	OBP	SLG	AOPS	ABR	SB-CS	FA	FR	RNG	THR	GAMES AT POSITION	DL	BFW
1880	Buf N	10	31	4	4	0	0	0	2	1		8	.129	.156	.129	-2	-3		.866	-1	90	114	2b10/OCM		-0.4
1883	NY AA	96	349	57	82	8	5	0		13			.235	.262	.287	73	-11		.859	-12	86	84	2b96/OC		-1.7
1884	Cin N	80	309	56	72	9	3	1		11			.233	.259	.291	62	-24		.858	-12	97	124	2b80,M		-3.0
1885	Det N	68	245	23	47	4	6	1	20	13		45	.192	.233	.269	62	-11		.908	-4	93	72	2b68		-1.2
1886	Det N	47	185	24	26	2	2	1	12	8		34	.141	.176	.189	11	-20	8	.903	-1	96	134	2b38,S8,O4(1/0/3)		-1.8
	StL N	39	116	10	20	3	1	0	7	13		27	.172	.256	.216	48	-7	6	.897	-4	93	91	2b39		-0.8
	Year	86	301	34	46	5	3	1	19	21		61	.153	.208	.199	25	-27	14	.900	-5	95	113	2b77,S8,O4(1/0/3)		-2.6
1887	Was N	7	30	6	9	1	0	1	1	1	0	6	.300	.323	.400	106	0	5	.865	-0	98	139	S7		0.0
1890	NY N	2	6	0	0	0	0	0	0	0	0	0	.000	.000	.000	-99	-2	1	.778	-1		0	/1OR		-0.2
	Pit N	22	82	3	16	0	0	0	3	0	1		.195	.205	.232	31	-7	5	.880	2	117	53	2b15,S7/OR		-0.4
	NY N	2	6	0	0	0	0	0	0	0	0		.000	.000	.000	-99	-2	0	1.000	0	114	433	2b2		-0.1
	Year	26	94	3	16	0	0	0	3	0		7	.170	.179	.202	12	-11	5	.883	1	117	67	2b17,S7,O2R/1		-0.7
Total	7	373	1359	183	276	30	18	3	45	60	1	127	.203	.237	.258	53	-87	25	.878	-33	93	97	2b348,S22,O8(1/2/5)/1		-9.6

CRAVATH, GAVY   Clifford Carlton "Cactus" B3.23.1881 Poway CA D5.23.1963 Laguna Beach CA   BR/TR/5-10.5/186 d4.18 M2/C1

YEAR	TM LG	G	AB	R	H	2B	3B	HR	RBI	BB-IB	HP	SO	AVG	OBP	SLG	AOPS	ABR	SB-CS	FA	FR	RNG	THR	GAMES AT POSITION	DL	BFW
1908	Bos A	94	277	43	71	10	11	1	34	38	4		.256	.354	.383	136	12	6	.925	-1	80	127	O77(62/0/15),1b5		0.8
1909	Chi A	19	50	7	9	0	0	1	8	19	0		.180	.406	.240	109	2	3	.944	-2	0		O18C		-0.1
	Was A	4	6	0	0	0	0	0	1	1	0		.000	.143	.000	-57	-1	0	1.000	1	685	0	/OR		-0.1
	Year	23	56	7	9	0	0	1	9	20	0		.161	.382	.214	93	1	3	.947	-2	43	0	O19(0/18/1)		-0.2
1912	Phi N	130	436	63	124	30	9	11	70	47	3	77	.284	.358	.470	118	10	15	.966	6	94	154	O113(30/14/73),1b5		0.9
1913	Phi N	147	525	78	179	34	14	19	128	55	3	63	.341	.407	.568	169	47	10-11	.958	-8	84	106	O141(3/7/133)		3.0
1914	Phi N	149	499	76	149	27	8	19	100	83	3	72	.299	.402	.499	157	38	14	.958	1	85	148	O143(1/0/142)		3.3
1915	†Phi N	150	522	89	149	31	7	24	115	86	6	77	.285	.393	.510	170	47	11-9	.946	9	101	173	O149R		5.2
1916	Phi N	137	448	70	127	21	8	11	70	64	5	89	.283	.379	.440	146	27	9	.966	-5	86	106	O130R		1.7
1917	Phi N	140	503	70	141	29	16	12	83	70	5		.280	.369	.473	151	32	6	.946	-7	89	94	O139R		2.0
1918	Phi N	121	426	41	99	27	5	8	54	54	1	46	.232	.320	.376	105	4	7	.931	-8	85	98	O118(7/0/110)		-1.2
1919	Phi N	83	214	34	73	18	5	12	45	35	2		.341	.438	.640	207	29	8	.914	-2	94	94	O56(2/1/53),M		2.7
1920	Phi N	46	45	2	13	5	0	1	11	9	0	12	.289	.407	.467	144	3	0-0	.667	-1	43	0	O5(3/0/2),M		-0.7
Total	11	1220	3951	575	1134	232	83	119	719	561	28	514	.287	.380	.478	149	250	89-20	.944	-18	88	122	O1090(108/40/947),1b5		18.4

CRAVER, BILL   William H. B6.1844 Troy NY D6.17.1901 Troy NY   BR/TR/5-9/160 d5.9 M4 OF NA(0/7/5)

YEAR	TM LG	G	AB	R	H	2B	3B	HR	RBI	BB-IB	HP	SO	AVG	OBP	SLG	AOPS	ABR	SB-CS	FA	FR	RNG	THR	GAMES AT POSITION	DL	BFW
1871	Tro NA	27	118	26	38	8	1	0	26	3			.322	.339	.407	112	2	6-3	.870	7	110	167	2b18,S4,C3,1b2/ORM		0.5
1872	Bal NA	35	178	55	50	3	3	0	24	5		2	.281	.301	.331	90	-3	9-1	.876	7			C27,2b5,O4R,3b2,M		0.5
1873	Bal NA	41	197	45	57	9	3	2	30	1		5	.289	.296	.365	96	-1	5-4	.933	6			C22,S15,O7C,1b3		0.3
1874	Phi NA	55	265	68	91	19	11	0	56	4		2	.343	.353	.498	164	18	11-3	.807	-4	95	156	2b54,C5/1		1.5
1875	Cen NA	14	65	8	18	4	0	0	5	2		4	.277	.299	.400	153	4	1-0	.773	2	135	95	S9,3b4/1M		0.5
	Ath NA	54	240	71	64	8	2	0	40	4		5	.319	.330	.469	157	12	8-4	.856	-4	93	174	2b54,C2/3		0.4

YEAR	TM LG	G	AB	R	H	2B	3B	HR	RBI	BB-IB	HP	SO	AVG	OBP	SLG	AOPS	ABR	SB-CS	FA	FR	RNG	THR	GAMES AT POSITION	DL	BFW
	Year	68	325	79	101	15	**13**	2	45	6		9	.311	.323	.455	156	16	9-4	.856	-2	93	**174**	2b54,S9,3b5,C2/1		0.9
1876	NY N	56	246	24	55	4	0	0	22	2		7	.224	.230	.240	65	-7		.814	-24	69	41	2b42,C11,S6,M		-2.6
1877	Lou N	57	238	33	63	5	2	0	29	5		11	.265	.280	.303	71	-9		.904	-1	98	124	S57		-0.7
Total	5 NA	226	1083	273	337	54	31	2	177	20		16	.311	.324	.424	130	32	40-15	.834	22			2b131,C59,S28,O12C,3b7,1b7		3.5
Total	2	113	484	57	118	9	2	0	51	7		18	.244	.255	.271	69	-16		.897	-26			S63,2b42,C11		-3.3

CRAWFORD, CARL Carl Demonte B8.5.1981 Houston TX BL/TL/6-2/203(203-220) [TBA99 2/52] d7.20

YEAR	TM LG	G	AB	R	H	2B	3B	HR	RBI	BB-IB	HP	SO	AVG	OBP	SLG	AOPS	ABR	SB-CS	FA	FR	RNG	THR	GAMES AT POSITION	DL	BFW
2002	TB A	63	259	23	67	11	6	2	30	9-0	3	41	.259	.290	.371	76	-10	9-5	.994	6	118	127	O63L		-0.6
2003	TB A	151	630	80*	177	18	9	5	54	26-4	1	102	.281	.309	.362	78	-22	**55**-10	.992	11	112	112	O146(137/13/0)/D		-0.8
2004	TB A★	152	626	104	185	26	**19**	11	55	35-2	1	81	.296	.331	.450	104	1	**59**-15	.994	9	**119**	64	O145(122/30/0),D5		1.3
2005	TB A	156	644	101	194	33	**15**	15	81	27-1	5	84	.301	.331	.469	114	10	46-8	.995	9	**123**	37	O154(147/8/0)/D		1.9
Total	4	522	2159	308	623	88	49	33	220	97-7	10	308	.289	.320	.421	96	-21	169-38	.994	35	118	78	O508(469/51/0),D7		1.8

CRAWFORD, PAT Clifford Rankin B1.28.1902 Society Hill SC D1.25.1994 Morehead City NC BL/TR/5-11/170 d4.18 Col Davidson

YEAR	TM LG	G	AB	R	H	2B	3B	HR	RBI	BB-IB	HP	SO	AVG	OBP	SLG	AOPS	ABR	SB-CS	FA	FR	RNG	THR	GAMES AT POSITION	DL	BFW
1929	NY N	65	57	13	17	3	0	3	24	11		0	5	.298	.412	.509	127	3	1	1.000	-0	79	33	1b7/3	0.2
1930	NY N	25	76	11	21	3	2	3	17	7	1	2	.276	.345	.487	100	0	0	.966	-1	93	108	2b18/1	-0.1
	Cin N	76	224	24	65	7	1	3	26	23	1	10	.290	.359	.371	81	-7	2	.969	-4	99	73	2b54,1b13	-0.9
	Year	101	300	35	86	10	3	6	43	30	2	12	.287	.355	.400	86	-7	2	.968	-8	97	82	2b72,1b14	-1.0
1933	StL N	91	224	24	60	8	2	0	21	14	2	9	.268	.317	.321	78	-6	1	.986	1	117	87	1b29,2b15,3b7	-0.7
1934	†StL N	61	70	3	19	2	0	0	16	5		4	.271	.320	.300	63	-4	0	.900	1	100	0	3b9,2b4	-0.3
Total	4	318	651	75	182	23	5	9	104	60	4	29	.280	.344	.372	85	-14	4	.969	-4	99	87	2b91,1b50,3b17	-1.8

CRAWFORD, FORREST Forrest A. B5.10.1881 Rockdale TX D3.29.1908 Austin TX BL/TR d7.30

YEAR	TM LG	G	AB	R	H	2B	3B	HR	RBI	BB-IB	HP	SO	AVG	OBP	SLG	AOPS	ABR	SB-CS	FA	FR	RNG	THR	GAMES AT POSITION	DL	BFW
1906	StL N	45	145	8	30	3	1	0	11	7	1		.207	.248	.241	55	-8	1	.927	-6	97	57	S39,3b6	-1.5
1907	StL N	7	22	0	5	0	0	0	3	2		0	.227	.292	.227	65	-1	0	.912	-1	94	90	S7	-0.1
Total	2	52	167	8	35	3	1	0	14	9	1		.210	.254	.240	56	-9	1	.924	-7	97	62	S46,3b6	-1.6

CRAWFORD, GEORGE George d10.8

YEAR	TM LG	G	AB	R	H	2B	3B	HR	RBI	BB-IB	HP	SO	AVG	OBP	SLG	AOPS	ABR	SB-CS	FA	FR	RNG	THR	GAMES AT POSITION	DL	BFW
1890	Phi AA	5	17	1	2	0	0	0	3	0		0	.118	.118	.118	-31	-3	1	1.000	1	0	0	O4R/S	-0.2

CRAWFORD, GLENN Glenn Martin "Shorty" B12.2.1913 North Branch MI D1.2.1972 Saginaw MI BL/TR/5-9/165 d4.22

YEAR	TM LG	G	AB	R	H	2B	3B	HR	RBI	BB-IB	HP	SO	AVG	OBP	SLG	AOPS	ABR	SB-CS	FA	FR	RNG	THR	GAMES AT POSITION	DL	BFW
1945	StL N	4	3	0	0	0	0	0	0	1		0	.000	.250	.000	-26	0	0	—	-0	0	0	/OL	-0.1
	Phi N	82	302	41	89	13	2	2	24	36	1	15	.295	.372	.371	110	5	5	.976	3	98	87	O38(6/0/32),S34,2b14	0.8
	Year	86	305	41	89	13	2	2	24	37	1	15	.292	.370	.367	108	5	5	.976	3	98	87	O39(7/0/32),S34,2b14	0.7
1946	Phi N	1	1	0	0	0	0	0	0	0		0	.000	.000	.000	-99	0	0	—	-0	0	0	/H	0.0
Total	2	87	306	41	89	13	2	2	24	37	1	15	.291	.369	.366	108	5	5	.000	3	98	87	O39(7/0/32),S34,2b14	0.7

CRAWFORD, KEN Kenneth Daniel B10.31.1894 South Bend IN D11.11.1976 Pittsburgh PA BL/TR/5-9/145 d9.6 Col Pittsburgh

YEAR	TM LG	G	AB	R	H	2B	3B	HR	RBI	BB-IB	HP	SO	AVG	OBP	SLG	AOPS	ABR	SB-CS	FA	FR	RNG	THR	GAMES AT POSITION	DL	BFW
1915	Bal F	23	82	4	20	2	1	0	7	1		0	18	.244	.253	.293	52	-7	0	.978	-2	81	37	1b14,O4(1/0/3)	-1.0

CRAWFORD, JAKE Rufus B3.20.1928 Campbell MO BR/TR/6-1.5/185 d9.7 Col Missouri

YEAR	TM LG	G	AB	R	H	2B	3B	HR	RBI	BB-IB	HP	SO	AVG	OBP	SLG	AOPS	ABR	SB-CS	FA	FR	RNG	THR	GAMES AT POSITION	DL	BFW
1952	StL A	7	11	1	2	1	0	0	0	5		.182	.250	.273	44	-1	1-0	1.000	0	116	0	O3(0/2/1)		-0.1

CRAWFORD, SAM Samuel Earl "Wahoo Sam" B4.18.1880 Wahoo NE D6.15.1968 Hollywood CA BL/TL/6-0/190 d9.10 HF1957

YEAR	TM LG	G	AB	R	H	2B	3B	HR	RBI	BB-IB	HP	SO	AVG	OBP	SLG	AOPS	ABR	SB-CS	FA	FR	RNG	THR	GAMES AT POSITION	DL	BFW
1899	Cin N	31	127	25	39	7	1	20	2			.307	.318	.465	111	0	6	.970	3	212	183	O31(9/22/0)		0.2
1900	Cin N	101	389	68	101	15	15	7	59	28	3		.260	.314	.429	107	1	14	.948	4	119	51	O95(70/12/12)		-0.4
1901	Cin N	131	515	91	170	20	16	**16**	104	37	3		.330	.378	.524	112	44	13	.923	2	124	134	O127(1/0/126)		3.9
1902	Cin N	140	555	92	185	18	**22**	3	78	47	1		.333	.386	.461	147	29	16	.932	3	130	105	O140(7/0/133)		2.7
1903	Det A	**137**	550	88	184	23	**25**	4	89	25	2		.335	.366	.489	159	36	18	.960	5	109	79	O137(45/0/92)		3.6
1904	Det A	150	562	49	143	22	16	2	73	44	0		.254	.309	.361	115	9	20	.973	5	110	177	O150(1/0/149)		0.7
1905	Det A	**154**	575	73	171	38	10	6	75	50	3		.297	.357	.430	148	31	22	**.988**	13	166	113	O103R,1b51		4.2
1906	Det A	145	563	65	166	25	16	2	72	38	1		.295	.341	.407	130	18	24	.984	5	136	60	O116(0/2/116),1b32		1.9
1907	†Det A	144	582	**102**	188	34	17	4	81	37	2		.323	.366	.460	157	35	18	.965	7	122	48	O144C,1b2		3.9
1908	†Det A	152	591	102	184	33	16	**7**	80	37	3		.311	.355	.457	157	35	15	.970	-10	61	47	O134C,1b17		2.1
1909	†Det A	156	589	83	185	**35**	14	6	97	47	1		.314	.366	.452	151	33	30	.965	-15	38	50	O139C,1b18		1.2
1910	Det A	154	588	83	170	26	**19**	5	**120**	37	1		.289	.332	.423	128	16	20	.963	-8	102	49	O153(0/26/127)/1		0.1
1911	Det A	146	574	109	217	36	14	7	115	61	0		.378	.438	.526	160	47	37	.975	-13	86	63	O146R		2.6
1912	Det A	149	581	81	189	30	21	4	109	42	2		.325	.373	.470	145	31	42	.984	-16	72	72	O149R		0.6
1913	Det A	**153**	609	78	193	32	**23**	9	83	52	0	28	.317	.371	.489	154	37	13	.964	-11	91	63	O140R,1b13		1.9
1914	Det A	**157**	582	74	183	22	**26**	8	**104**	69	1	31	.314	.388	.483	157	38	25-16	.977	-10	82	86	O157R		2.1
1915	Det A	**156**	612	81	183	31	**19**	4	**112**	66	0	29	.299	.367	.431	132	23	24-14	.974	-17	87	40	O156R		-0.3
1916	Det A	100	322	41	92	11	13	0	42	37	0	10	.286	.359	.401	124	9	10	.988	-3	22	62	1b15,O3R		-1.3
1917	Det A	61	104	6	18	4	0	2	12	4	0	6	.173	.204	.269	44	-8	0							-0.4
Total	19	2517	9570	1391	2961	458	309	97	1525	760	23	104	.309	.362	.452	143	464	367-30	.965	-65	100	78	O2299(134/479/1687),1b151		29.3

CRAWFORD, WILLIE Willie Murphy B9.7.1946 Los Angeles CA D8.27.2004 Los Angeles CA BL/TL/6-1/205* d9.16

YEAR	TM LG	G	AB	R	H	2B	3B	HR	RBI	BB-IB	HP	SO	AVG	OBP	SLG	AOPS	ABR	SB-CS	FA	FR	RNG	THR	GAMES AT POSITION	DL	BFW
1964	LA N	10	16	3	5	0	0	0	1-0	0	7	.313	.353	.375	113	0	1-1	1.000	1	129	0	O4(1/0/3)		0.0
1965	†LA N	52	27	10	4	0	0	0	2-0	0	8	.148	.207	.148	2	-4	2-0	1.000	-0	86	0	O8(2/1/5)		-0.4
1966	LA N	6	0	1	0				0-0	0					—	0	0-0	—	0			/R		0.0
1967	LA N	4	4	0	1	0	0	0	1-0	0	3	.250	.400	.250	98	0	0-0	.000	-0	0	0	/OR		0.0
1968	LA N	61	175	25	44	12	1	4	14	20-0	2	64	.251	.335	.400	129	7	1-3	.966	5	116	223	O48(45/1/4)		1.0
1969	LA N	129	389	64	96	17	5	11	41	49-3	2	85	.247	.331	.401	111	5	4-5	.973	-2	96	79	O113(56/22/38)		-0.3
1970	LA N	109	299	48	70	8	6	8	40	33-4	2	88	.234	.313	.381	89	-6	4-4	.960	4	105	157	O94(34/4/64)		0.2
1971	LA N	114	342	64	96	16	6	9	40	28-2	1	49	.281	.334	.442	125	10	5-2	.981	-1	86	79	O97(63/5/35)		-0.3
1972	LA N	96	243	29	61	7	3	8	27	35-3	2	55	.251	.349	.403	115	5	4-2	.983	-4	91	43	O74(51/0/28)		-0.3
1973	LA N	145	457	75	135	26	2	14	66	78-12	1	91	.295	.396	.453	140	29	12-5	.978	-1	94	109	O138(11/5/125)		2.2
1974	†LA N	139	468	73	138	23	4	11	61	64-9	0	88	.295	.376	.432	131	-21	7-8	.966	-9	94	34	O133(0/2/132)		0.4
1975	LA N	124	373	46	98	15	2	9	44	49-11	0	43	.263	.345	.386	108	4	5-5	.990	-2	105	29	O113(25/0/93)		0.7
1976	StL N	120	392	49	119	17	5	9	50	37-6	1	53	.304	.360	.441	126	13	2-1	.982	-1	103	70	O107(3/0/105)		-0.4
1977	Hou N	42	114	14	29	3	0	2	18	16-1	0	10	.254	.341	.333	90	-1	0-0	.959	-2	91	0	O30L		-0.4
	Oak A	59	136	7	25	7	1	1	16	20	4	20	.184	.277	.272	52	-9	0-0	.978	2	108	219	O22(2/0/20),D18		-0.8
Total	14	1210	3435	507	921	152	35	86	419	431-55	9	664	.268	.349	.408	116	74	47-36	.975	-13	98	82	O982(323/40/653),D18		1.2

CREAMER, GEORGE George W. (b George W. Triebel) B1855 Philadelphia PA D6.27.1886 Philadelphia PA BR/TR/6-2/? d5.1 M1

YEAR	TM LG	G	AB	R	H	2B	3B	HR	RBI	BB-IB	HP	SO	AVG	OBP	SLG	AOPS	ABR	SB-CS	FA	FR	RNG	THR	GAMES AT POSITION	DL	BFW
1878	Mil N	50	193	30	41	7	3	0	15	5		15	.212	.232	.280	63	-8		.839	-2	120	47	2b28,O17(0/16/4),3b6		-0.9
1879	Syr N	15	60	3	13	2	0	0	3	1		2	.217	.230	.250	65	-2		.825	-8	87	23	2b10,S3,O2(0/1/1)		-0.9
1880	Wor N	**85**	306	40	61	6	3	0	27	4		21	.199	.210	.239	47	-17		.883	-8	97	101	2b85		-2.1
1881	Wor N	80	309	42	64	9	2	0	25	11		27	.207	.234	.249	49	-18		.904	-9	96	87	2b80		-2.2
1882	Wor N	81	286	27	65	16	6	1	29	14		24	.227	.263	.336	88	-4		.907	11	**112**	107	2b81		0.9
1883	Pit AA	91	369	54	94	7	9	0		20			.255	.293	.322	102	1		.897	8	102	101	2b91		1.1
1884	Pit AA	98	339	38	62	8	5	0		16	2		.183	.224	.236	51	-18		**.937**	16	110	97	2b98,M		0.2
Total	7	500	1862	234	400	55	28	1	**99**	71	2	89	.215	.244	.276	67	-66		.901	8	104	94	2b473,O19(0/17/5),3b6,S3		-3.9

CREDE, JOE Joseph B4.26.1978 Jefferson City MO BR/TR/6-3/195* [ChiA96 5/137] d9.12

YEAR	TM LG	G	AB	R	H	2B	3B	HR	RBI	BB-IB	HP	SO	AVG	OBP	SLG	AOPS	ABR	SB-CS	FA	FR	RNG	THR	GAMES AT POSITION	DL	BFW
2000	Chi A	7	14	2	5	1	0	0	3	0-0		3	.357	.333	.429	94	0	0-0	.933	1	129	156	3b6/D		0.1
2001	Chi A	17	50	1	11	1	1	0	7	3-0	1	11	.220	.273	.280	45	-4	1-0	1.000	-1	71	136	3b15		-0.5
2002	Chi A	53	200	28	57	10	0	12	35	8-0	2	40	.285	.311	.515	110	2	0-2	.938	-5	89	138	3b53		-0.3
2003	Chi A	151	536	68	140	31	2	19	75	32-1	6	75	.261	.308	.433	89	-9	1-1	.964	-0	95	121	3b151		-0.8
2004	Chi A	144	490	67	117	26	0	21	69	34-0	10	81	.239	.299	.418	82	-14	1-2	.965	-8	93	102	3b144		-2.0
2005	†Chi A	132	432	54	109	21	0	22	62	25-3	8	66	.252	.303	.454	90	-30	1-1	.971	-14	94	122	3b499,D2/S	15	-0.4
Total	6	504	1722	220	439	89	2	74	251	102-4	25	276	.255	.303	.439	90	-30	4-6	.965	-14	94	122	3b499,D2/S	15	-3.9

CREE, BIRDIE William Franklin B10.23.1882 Khedive PA D11.8.1942 Sunbury PA BR/TR/5-6/150 d9.17 Col Penn St.

YEAR	TM LG	G	AB	R	H	2B	3B	HR	RBI	BB-IB	HP	SO	AVG	OBP	SLG	AOPS	ABR	SB-CS	FA	FR	RNG	THR	GAMES AT POSITION	DL	BFW
1908	NY A	21	78	5	21	0	2	0	4	7	2		.269	.345	.321	115	1	1.000	1	186	302	O21C		0.2
1909	NY A	104	343	48	90	6	3	2	27	30	9		.262	.338	.315	105	3	10	.949	-1	100	93	O79(24/32/25),S6,2b4/3		-0.1
1910	NY A	134	467	58	134	19	16	4	73	40	8		.287	.353	.422	135	18	28	.955	-8	92	67	O134(49/85/0)		-0.2
1911	NY A	137	520	90	181	30	22	4	88	56	5		.348	.415	.513	149	33	48	.964	-9	90	90	O132(122/7/3),S4,2b2		2.4

YEAR	TM LG	G	AB	R	H	2B	3B	HR	RBI	BB-IB	HP	SO	AVG	OBP	SLG	AOPS	ABR	SB-CS	FA	FR	RNG	THR	GAMES AT POSITION	DL	BFW
1912	NY A	50	190	25	63	11	6	0	22	20	5		.332	.409	.453	138	10	12	.948	4	124	77	O50L		1.1
1913	NY A	145	534	51	145	25	6	1	63	50	4	51	.272	.338	.346	100	1	22	.988	-4	91	89	O144L		-1.0
1914	NY A	77	275	45	85	18	5	0	40	30	6	24	.309	.389	.411	141	15	4-9	.976	4	109	98	O76C		1.2
1915	NY A	74	196	23	42	8	2	0	15	36	6	22	.214	.333	.276	88	0	1	.945	-4	89	84	O53(0/37/16)		-0.9
Total	8	742	2603	345	761	117	62	11	332	269	43	97	.292	.368	.398	124	81	132-17	.965	-10	101	91	O689(389/258/44),S10,2b6/3		3.3

CREEDEN, CONNIE Cornelius Stephen B7.21.1915 Danvers MA D11.30.1969 Santa Ana CA BL/TL/6-1/200 d4.28

1943	Bos N	5	4	0	1	0	0	0	1	1	0	0	.250	.400	.250	91	0	0			0		/H		0.0

CREEDEN, PAT Patrick Francis "Whoops" B5.23.1906 Newburyport MA D4.20.1992 Brockton MA BL/TR/5-8/175 d4.14   Col Boston College

1931	Bos A	5	8	0	0	0	0	0	1	0	0	3	.000	.111	.000	-73	-2	0-0	.846	-1	83	87	2b2		-0.2

CREEGAN, MARTY Mark (b Marcus Kragen) B7.31.1864 San Francisco CA D9.29.1920 San Francisco CA ?/161 d4.17

1884	Was U	9	33	4	5	0	0	0		1			.152	.176	.152	0	-5		.667	-2	77	950	O6(0/5/1),C3,3b2/1		-0.6

CREELY, GUS August L. B6.6.1870 Florissant MO D4.22.1934 St.Louis MO 5-6/150 d10.9

1890	StL AA	4	15	0	0	0	0	0	0	0	0		.000	.000	.000	-88	-4	1	.769	-2	76	0	S4		-0.5

CREGAN, PETE Peter James "Peekskill Pete" B4.13.1875 Kingston NY D5.18.1945 New York NY BR/TR/5-7.5/150 d9.8

1899	NY N	1	2	0	0	0	0	0	0	0	0		.000	.000	.000	-99	-1	0	1.000	-0	0	0	/OR		-0.1
1903	Cin N	6	19	0	2	0	0	0	0	1	1		.105	.190	.105	-13	-3	0	.769	-1	0	0	O6(5/0/1)		-0.4
Total	2	7	21	0	2	0	0	0	0	1	1		.095	.174	.095	-21	-4	0	.786	-1	0	0	O7(5/0/2)		-0.5

CREGER, BERNIE Bernard Odell B3.21.1927 Wytheville VA D11.30.1997 Lynchburg VA BR/TR/6-0/175 d4.29

1947	StL N	15	16	3	3	1	0	0	3	1	0	3	.188	.235	.250	28	-2	1	.828	-2	96	58	S13		-0.4

CRESPI, CREEPY Frank Angelo Joseph B2.16.1918 St.Louis MO D3.1.1990 Florissant MO BR/TR/5-8.5/175 d9.14   Mil 1943-46

1938	StL N	7	19	2	5	2	0	0	1	2	0		.263	.333	.368	88	0		.813	-3	66	111	S7		-0.3
1939	StL N	15	29	3	5	1	0	0	6	3	0	6	.172	.250	.207	23	-3	0	.962	-0	114	34	2b6,S4		-0.3
1940	StL N	3	11	2	3	1	0	0	0	1	0		.273	.333	.364	87	0	1	1.000	-1	27	0	3b2/S		-0.1
1941	StL N	146	560	85	156	24	2	4	46	57	9	58	.279	.355	.350	93	-3	3	.962	-2	98	115	2b145		0.4
1942	†StL N	93	292	33	71	4	2	0	35	27	1	29	.243	.309	.271	65	-13	4	.967	-6	85	101	2b83,S5		-1.5
Total	5	264	911	125	240	32	4	4	88	90	10	102	.263	.336	.321	82	-19	8	.963	-13	94	109	2b234,S17,3b2		-1.8

CRESPO, CESAR Cesar Antonio (Claudio) B5.23.1979 Rio Piedras, PR BB/TR/5-11/170* [NYN97 3/90] d5.29 b-Felipe

2001	SD N	55	153	27	32	6	0	4	12	25-0	0	50	.209	.320	.327	73	-6	6-2	.970	-5	85	71	2b34,O18(6/11/2),3b2/S		-0.9
2002	SD N	25	29	5	5	2	0	0	3	3-0	0	6	.172	.250	.241	36	-3	3-2	1.000	-1	57	903	O7(6/1/1),2b4,3b4/S		-0.4
2004	Bos A	52	79	6	13	2	1	0	2	0-0	0	20	.165	.165	.215	-2	-12	2-0	.943	-0	98	121	S27,O19(10/7/2),2b11		-1.0
Total	3	132	261	38	50	10	1	4	17	28	0	76	.192	.270	.284	46	-21	11-4	.976	-6	86	69	2b49,O44(22/19/5),S29,3b6		-2.3

CRESPO, FELIPE Felipe Javier (Clausio) B3.5.1973 Rio Piedras, PR BB/TR/5-11/200* [TorA90 3/95] d4.28 b-Cesar

1996	Tor A	22	49	6	9	4	0	0	4	12-0	3	13	.184	.375	.265	66	-2	1-0	.982	3	95	117	2b10,3b6,1b2	22	0.2
1997	Tor A	12	28	3	8	0	1	1	5	2-0	1	4	.286	.333	.464	105	-2	0-0	.933	-2	54	100	3b7/2D		-0.1
1998	Tor A	66	130	11	34	8	1	1	15	15-1	2	27	.262	.342	.362	84	-3	4-3	1.000	-1	102	54	O42(19/1/24),2b8,3b2/1D		-0.4
2000	†SF N	89	131	17	38	6	1	4	29	10-2	2	23	.290	.351	.443	108	-3	3-2	.962	-2	83	0	O26(18/0/9),1b11,2b7/D		-0.2
2001	SF N	40	66	8	13	1	0	4	10	7-1	2	26	.197	.286	.394	80	-2	1-1	.972	-2	44	111	1b16,2b2/ORD		-0.3
	Phi N	33	41	1	7	3	1	0	5	4-0	0	8	.171	.234	.293	40	-4	0-0	1.000	1	160	124	O4L,1b2/2		-0.3
	Year	73	107	9	20	4	1	4	15	11-1	2	34	.187	.266	.355	65	-6	1-1	.977	-3	38	124	1b18,O5(4/0/1),2b3/D		-0.9
Total	5	262	445	46	109	22	4	10	68	50-4	11	101	.245	.330	.380	86	-10	9-6	.989	-3	99	65	O73(41/1/34),1b32,2b29,3b15,D6	53	-1.4

CRIGER, LOU Louis B2.3.1872 Elkhart IN D5.14.1934 Tucson AZ BR/TR/5-10/165 d9.21

1896	Cle N	2	5	0	0	0	0	0	0	0	0		.000	.167	.000	-51	-1	1	1.000	1	138	123	/C		0.0
1897	Cle N	39	138	15	31	4	1	0	22	23	1		.225	.340	.268	58	-8	5	.937	0	113	86	C37,1b2		-0.3
1898	Cle N	84	287	43	80	13	4	1	32	40	5		.279	.377	.362	113	7	2	.957	16	114	101	C82		2.9
1899	StL N	77	258	39	66	4	5	2	44	28	2		.256	.333	.333	81	-7	14	.949	7	125	97	C75		0.6
1900	StL N	80	288	31	78	8	6	2	38	4	2		.271	.286	.361	78	-10	5	.953	4	94	104	C75/3		0.0
1901	Bos A	76	268	26	62	6	8	0	24	11	3		.231	.270	.276	52	-18	7	.967	19	113	109	C68,1b8		0.7
1902	Bos A	83	266	32	68	16	6	0	28	27	0		.256	.324	.361	87	-4	7	.965	14	133	104	C80/OL		1.7
1903	†Bos A	96	317	41	61	7	10	3	31	26	1		.192	.256	.306	65	-15	5	.979	23	125	114	C96		1.8
1904	Bos A	98	299	34	63	10	5	2	34	27	3		.211	.283	.298	79	-7	1	.981	18	142	91	C95		2.3
1905	Bos A	109	313	33	62	6	7	1	36	54	3		.198	.322	.272	88	-2	5	.972	5	127	104	C109		1.7
1906	Bos A	7	17	0	3	1	0	0	1	1	0		.176	.222	.235	43	-1	1	.981	2	112	70	C6		0.2
1907	Bos A	75	226	12	41	4	0	0	14	19	2		.181	.251	.199	44	-14	2	.978	4	112	100	C75		-0.3
1908	Bos A	84	237	12	45	4	2	0	25	13	0		.190	.232	.224	47	-14	1	.980	13	102	108	C84		0.7
1909	StL A	74	212	15	36	1	1	0	9	25	1		.170	.261	.184	44	-13	2	.986	6	98	96	C73		0.0
1910	NY A	27	69	3	13	2	0	0	4	10	0		.188	.291	.217	56	-3	0	.993	-1	101	87	C27		-0.1
1912	StL A	1	2	1	0	0	0	0	0	0	0		.000	.000	.000	-99	-1	0	1.000	0	120	104	/C		0.0
Total	16	1012	3202	337	709	86	50	11	342	309	23	0	.221	.295	.290	72	-111	58	.971	133	118	118	C984,1b10/OL3		11.9

CRIPE, DAVE David Gordon B4.7.1951 Ramona CA BR/TR/6-0/180 d9.10   Col William and Mary

1978	KC A	7	13	1	2	0	0	0	1	0-0	0	2	.154	.154	.154	-13	-2	0-0	1.000	-3	15	0	3b5		-0.5

CRISCIONE, DAVE David Gerald B9.2.1951 Dunkirk NY BR/TR/5-8/185 [TexA69 5/95] d7.17

1977	Bal A	9	9	1	3	0	0	0	1	0-0	1		.333	.333	.667	174	1	0-0	1.000	-1	88	0	C7		0.0

CRISCOLA, TONY Anthony Paul B7.9.1915 Walla Walla WA D7.10.2001 LaJolla CA BL/TR/5-11.5/180 d4.15   Col Whitman

1942	StL A	91	158	17	47	9	2	1	13	8		13	.297	.331	.399	103	-3	2-2	.955	-3	93	0	O52(37/13/2)		-0.5
1943	StL A	29	52	4	8	0	0	0	1	8	0	7	.154	.267	.154	24	-5	0-0	.960	-1	103	0	O13(10/2/1)		-0.7
1944	Cin N	64	157	14	36	3	2	0	14	14	1	12	.229	.297	.274	64	-8	0	.977	1	106	101	O35(3/0/32)		-1.0
Total	3	184	367	35	91	12	4	1	28	30	1	32	.248	.307	.311	75	-13	2-2	.966	-3	100	47	O100(50/15/35)		-2.2

CRISHAM, PAT Patrick J. B6.4.1877 Amesbury MA D6.12.1915 Syracuse NY 6-0/168 d5.5

1899	Bal N	53	172	23	50	5	3	0	20	4	1		.291	.311	.355	78	-6	4	.979	-1	94	37	1b26,C22		-0.5

CRISP, COCO Covelli Loyce B11.1.1979 Los Angeles CA BB/TR/6-0/185* [StLN99 7/222] d8.15   Col Los Angeles Pierce (CA) JC

2002	Cle A	32	127	16	33	9	2	1	9	11-0	0	19	.260	.314	.386	85	-3	4-1	.988	0	103	63	O32(2/31/0)		-0.2
2003	Cle A	99	414	55	110	15	6	3	27	23-1	0	51	.266	.302	.353	73	-17	15-9	.995	-2	95	100	O90(39/53/0),D7		-2.0
2004	Cle A	139	491	78	146	24	2	15	71	36-4	0	69	.297	.344	.446	108	5	20-13	.986	-3	97	78	O128(37/94/0),D6		0.1
2005	Cle A	145	594	86	178	42	4	16	69	44-1	0	81	.300	.345	.465	118	15	15-6	.985	0	108	38	O145(138/10/0)	15	1.1
Total	4	415	1626	235	467	90	14	35	176	114-6	0	220	.287	.332	.424	101	0	54-29	.988	-6	101	67	O395(216/188/0),D13	15	-1.0

CRISP, JOE Joseph Shelby B7.8.1889 Higginsville MO D2.5.1939 Kansas City MO BR/TR/6-4/200 d9.2

1910	StL A	1	1	0	0	0	0	0	0	0	0		.000	.000	.000	-99	-0	0	1.000	-0	45	0	/C		0.0
1911	StL A	1	1	0	1	0	0	0	0	0	0		1.000	1.000	1.000	477	0	0		0			/H		0.0
Total	2	2	2	0	1	0	0	0	0	0	0		.500	.500	.500	206	0	0	1.000	-0	45	0	/C		0.0

CRISS, DODE Dode B3.12.1885 Sherman MS D9.8.1955 Sherman MS BL/TR/6-2/200 d4.20 ▲

1908	StL A	64	82	15	28	6	0	14	9				.341	.407	.415	166	7	1	.933	-1	189	0	O11R,P9/1		0.6
1909	StL A	35	48	2	14	6	1	0	7	0	1		.292	.306	.458	152	6	0	1.000	-1	59	0	P11		0.1
1910	StL A	70	91	11	21	4	2	1	11	11	1		.231	.320	.352	118	2	2	.983	-1	66	90	1b11,P6		0.1
1911	StL A	58	83	10	21	3	1	2	15	11	1		.253	.347	.386	109	1	0	.956	-2	70	76	1b14,P4		-0.1
Total	4	227	304	38	84	19	4	3	47	31			.276	.349	.395	133	16	3	.964	-4	72	0	P30,1b26,O11R		0.6

CRIST, CHES Chester Arthur "Squak" B2.10.1882 Cozaddale OH D1.7.1957 Cincinnati OH BR/TR/5-11/165 d5.18

1906	Phi N	6	11	1	0	0	0	0	0	0	0		.000	.083	.000	-74	-2	0	.800	-2	71	43	C6		-0.5

CRITZ, HUGHIE Hugh Melville B9.17.1900 Starkville MS D1.10.1980 Greenwood MS BR/TR/5-8/147 d5.31   Col Mississippi St.

1924	Cin N	102	413	67	133	15	14	3	35	19	0	18	.322	.352	.448	115	6	19-11	.956	2	102	101	2b96/S		1.1
1925	Cin N	144	541	74	150	14	8	2	51	34	1	17	.277	.321	.344	72	-24	13-13	.970	20	110	126	2b144		-0.2
1926	Cin N	155	607	96	164	24	14	3	79	39	2	25	.270	.316	.371	87	-14	7	.981	23	110	128	2b155		1.4

YEAR	TM LG	G	AB	R	H	2B	3B	HR	RBI	BB-IB	HP	SO	AVG	OBP	SLG	AOPS	ABR	SB-CS	FA	FR	RNG	THR	GAMES AT POSITION	DL	BFW
1927	Cin N	113	396	50	110	10	8	4	49	16	0	18	.278	.306	.374	84	-11	7	.969	-1	103	114	2b113		-0.9
1928	Cin N	153	641	95	190	21	11	5	52	37	0	24	.296	.335	.387	90	-12	18	.971	-15	98	124	2b153		-2.2
1929	Cin N	107	425	55	105	17	9	1	50	27	0	21	.247	.292	.336	58	-30	9	.974	7	112	115	2b106/S		-1.8
1930	Cin N	28	104	15	24	3	2	0	11	6	0	6	.231	.273	.298	40	-11	1	.987	-1	105	91	2b28		-0.9
	NY N	124	558	93	148	17	11	4	50	24	0	26	.265	.296	.357	58	-41	7	.972	8	98	106	2b124		-2.7
	Year	152	662	108	172	20	13	4	61	30	0	32	.260	.292	.347	55	-51	8	.974	7	99	103	2b152		-3.6
1931	NY N	66	238	33	69	7	2	4	17	8	0	17	.290	.313	.387	89	-5	4	.984	2	98	83	2b54		0.1
1932	NY N	151	659	90	182	32	7	2	50	34	1	27	.276	.313	.355	81	-18	3	.974	6	100	103	2b151		0.3
1933	†NY N	133	558	68	137	18	5	2	33	23	3	24	.246	.279	.306	68	-24	4	.982	45	126	118	2b133		3.1
1934	NY N	137	571	77	138	17	1	6	40	19	2	24	.242	.269	.306	55	-38	5	.978	27	114	125	2b137		-0.2
1935	NY N	65	219	19	41	13	3	2	14	3	0	10	.187	.198	.242	18	-27	2	.966	-0	100	112	2b59		-2.2
Total	12	1478	5930	832	1591	195	95	38	531	289	9	257	.268	.303	.352	74	-249	97-24	.974	124	107	115	2b1453,S2		-5.7

CROCKETT, DAVEY Daniel Solomon B10.5.1875 Roanoke VA D2.23.1961 Charlottesville VA BL/TR/6-1/175 d7.11

1901	Det A	28	102	10	29	2	2	0	14	6	2		.284	.336	.343	85	-2	1	.968	-1	100	121	1b27		-0.3

CROFT, ART Arthur F. B1.23.1855 St.Louis MO D3.16.1884 St.Louis MO d5.4

1875	RS NA	19	75	5	15	3	0	0	2	0		2	.200	.200	.240	58	-2	5-1	.800	-3	0	0	O19(10/7/2)		-0.4
1877	StL N	54	220	23	51	5	2	0	27	1		15	.232	.235	.273	63	-9		.971	-3	79	81	1b28,O25(25/1/1)/2		-1.3
1878	Ind N	60	222	22	35	6	0	0	16	5		23	.158	.176	.185	22	-17		.963	-2	55	79	1b51,O9L		-2.1
Total	2	114	442	45	86	11	2	0	43	6		38	.195	.205	.229	43	-26		.965	-5	63	80	1b79,O34(34/1/1)/2		-3.4

CROFT, HARRY Henry T. B8.1.1875 Chicago IL D12.11.1933 Oak Park IL d5.19 Col Niagara

1899	Lou N	2	2	0	0	0	0	0	0	0	0	0	.000	.000	.000	-99	-1	0	—	0			/H		-0.1
	Phi N	2	7	0	1	0	0	0	0	1	0		.143	.250	.143	9	-1	0	1.000	-0	111	0	2b2		-0.2
	Year	4	9	0	1	0	0	0	0	1	0		.111	.200	.111	-14	-1	0	1.000	-0	111	0	2b2		0.2
1901	Chi N	3	12	1	4	0	0	0	4	0	0		.333	.333	.333	97	0	0	1.000	2	652	0	O3R		0.0
Total	2	7	21	1	5	0	0	0	4	1	0		.238	.273	.238	47	-2	0	1.000	2	652	0	O3R,2b2		

CROLIUS, FRED Fred Joseph B12.16.1876 Jersey City NJ D8.25.1960 Ormond Beach FL d4.19 Col Dartmouth

1901	Bos N	49	200	22	48	4	1	1	13	9	10		.240	.306	.285	66	-9	6	.850	-8	48	69	O49(0/3/46)		-1.8
1902	Pit N	9	38	4	10	2	1	0	7	0	0		.263	.263	.368	91	-1	0	1.000	-0	97	0	O9R		-0.1
Total	2	58	238	26	58	6	2	1	20	9	10		.244	.300	.298	69	-10	6	.868	-8	55	60	O58(0/3/55)		-1.9

CROMARTIE, WARREN Warren Livingston B9.29.1953 Miami Beach FL BL/TL/6-0/192(180-200) [MonN73 S1/5] d9.6 Col Miami-Dade North (FL) CC

1974	Mon N	8	17	2	3	0	0	0	3-0		0	3	.176	.300	.176	34	-1	1-0	1.000	-1	76	0	O6L		-0.2
1976	Mon N	33	81	8	17	1	0	0	2	1-0	0	5	.210	.220	.222	34	-8	1-2	.943	-1	98	74	O20(5/0/16)		-1.1
1977	Mon N	155	620	64	175	41	7	5	50	33-3	4	40	.282	.321	.395	93	7	10-3	.976	5	102	95	O155(153/0/4)		-0.8
1978	Mon N	159	607	77	180	32	6	10	56	33-5	7	60	.297	.337	.418	111	8	8-8	.978	17	114	180	O158(157/0/1),1b4		1.8
1979	Mon N	158	659	84	181	46	5	8	46	38-19	1	78	.275	.313	.396	92	-7	8-7	.976	10	109	126	O158L		-0.6
1980	Mon N	162	597	74	172	33	5	14	70	51-24	2	64	.288	.345	.430	113	11	8-8	.991	-5	90	87	1b158,O2L		-0.6
1981	†Mon N	99	358	41	109	19	2	6	42	39-12	0	27	.304	.370	.419	120	11	2-3	.992	-4	75	90	1b62,O38R		0.1
1982	Mon N	144	497	59	126	24	3	14	62	69-15	3	60	.254	.346	.398	105	5	3-0	.979	6	114	107	O136(2/0/135),1b9		0.5
1983	Mon N	120	360	37	100	26	2	3	43	43-7	1	48	.278	.352	.386	106	4	8-3	.973	11	124	187	O101R/1		1.2
1991	KC A	69	131	13	40	7	2	1	20	15-0	0	33	.305	.376	.420	121	4	1-3	.996	-4	46	90	1b29,O6(4/1/1)/D		-0.2
Total	10	1107	3927	459	1104	229	32	61	391	325-85	18	403	.281	.335	.402	103	20	50-37	.977	36	111	127	O780(487/1/296),1b263/D		0.1

CROMER, D.T. David Thomas B3.19.1971 Lake City SC BL/TR/6-2/220(190-220) [OakA92 11/312] d4.5 b-Tripp Col South Carolina-Aiken

2000	Cin N	35	47	7	16	4	0	2	8	1-1		14	.340	.360	.553	124	2	0-0	.964	-1	65	145	1b13		0.0
2001	Cin N	50	57	7	16	3	0	5	12	3-0	1	19	.281	.302	.596	122	1	0-0	.973	0	128	76	1b8/D		0.1
Total	2	85	104	14	32	7	0	7	20	4-1	1	33	.308	.327	.577	123	3	0-0	.967	-1	91	117	1b21/D		0.1

CROMER, TRIPP Roy Bunyan B11.21.1967 Lake City SC BR/TR/6-2/170* [StLN89 3/66] d9.7 b-D.T. Col South Carolina-Aiken

1993	StL N	10	23	1	2	0	0	0	1-0		0	6	.087	.125	.087	-42	-5	0-0	.912	-0	101	88	S9		-0.5
1994	StL N	2	0	1	0	0	0	0	0-0		0	0	—	—	—		-1	0-0	.000	-1	0	0	S2		-0.1
1995	StL N	105	345	36	78	19	4	5	18	14-2	4	66	.226	.261	.325	53	-24	0-0	.960	-1	106	113	S95,2b11		-1.8
1997	LA N	28	86	8	25	3	0	4	20	6-3	0	16	.291	.333	.465	115	1	0-1	.968	-3	84	85	2b17,S10/3	62	0.0
1998	LA N	6	6	1	1	0	0	1	1	0-0	0	2	.167	.167	.667	111	0	0-0		0			/H	140	0.0
1999	LA N	33	52	5	10	0	0	2	8	5-0	0	10	.192	.263	.308	46	-5	0-0	1.000	4	134	169	2b9,S9,3b2,O2(1/0/1)/1	58	0.0
2000	Hou N	9	8	2	1	0	0	0	1-0		0	1	.125	.222	.125	-9	-1	0-0	.500	-1	124	0	3b2/2S	37	-0.2
2003	Hou N	3	4	0	1	0	1	0	1-0		0	0	.250	.250	.750	140	0	0-0	1.000	2	202	445	/2		0.1
Total	8	196	524	54	118	22	1	12	48	27-5	4	101	.225	.266	.340	58	-34	0-1	.959	-0	106	110	S126,2b39,3b5,O2(1/0/1)/1	297	-2.5

CROMPTON, NED Edward B2.12.1889 Liverpool, England D9.28.1950 Aspinwall PA BL/TL/5-10.5/175 d9.13

1909	StL A	17	63	7	10	2	1	0	2	7	1		.159	.254	.222	54	-3	1	.909	1	178	191	O17L		-0.4
1910	Cin N	1	2	0	0	0	0	0	0	0	0		.000	.000	.000	-99	-1	0	—	-0	0	0	/OC		-0.1
Total	2	18	65	7	10	2	1	0	2	7	1	2	.154	.247	.215	49	-4	1	.909	1	177	190	O18(17/1/0)		-0.5

CROMPTON, HERB Herbert Bryan "Workhorse" B11.7.1911 Taylor Ridge IL D8.5.1963 Moline IL BR/TR/6-0/185 d4.26

1937	Was A	2	3	0	1	0	0	0	0	0	0	0	.333	.333	.333	72	0	0-0	1.000	1	0	449	C2		0.0
1945	NY A	36	99	6	19	3	0	0	12	2	0	7	.192	.208	.222	24	-10	0-0	.984	-1	80	136	C33		-1.0
Total	2	38	102	6	20	3	0	0	12	2	0	7	.196	.212	.225	25	-10	0-0	.984	-1	78	145	C35		-1.0

CRON, CHRIS Christopher John B3.31.1964 Albuquerque NM BR/TR/6-2/200* [AtlN84*S2/38] d8.15 Col Santa Ana (CA) JC

1991	Cal A	6	15	2	2	0	0	0	2-0		0	5	.133	.235	.133	5	-2	0-0	1.000	1	202	26	1b5/D		-0.1
1992	Chi A	6	10	0	0	0	0	0	0-0		0	4	.000	.000	.000	-99	-3	0-0	.923	0	162	69	1b5/OL		-0.3
Total	2	12	25	0	2	0	0	0	2-0	0	9	.080	.148	.080	-35	-5	0-0	.980	1	191	37	1b10/OLD		-0.4

CRONIN, DAN Daniel T. B4.1.1857 S.Boston MA D11.30.1885 Boston MA 5-8/170 d7.9

1884	CP U	1	4	1	1	0	0	0	0				.250	.250	.250	52	0		.200	-2	0	345	/2		-0.2
	StL U	1	5	0	0	0	0	0	0				.000	.000	.000	-96	-1		.000	-1	0	0	/OL		-0.2
	Year	2	9	1	1	0	0	0	0				.111	.111	.111	-32	-2		.000	-3	0	345	/2OL		-0.4

CRONIN, JIM James John B8.7.1905 Richmond CA D6.10.1983 Concord CA BB/TR/5-10.5/150 d7.4

1929	Phi A	25	56	7	13	2	1	0	4	5	0	7	.232	.295	.304	52	-4	0-0	.966	2	126	130	2b10,S9,3b4		-0.1

CRONIN, JOE Joseph Edward B10.12.1906 San Francisco CA D9.7.1984 Barnstable MA BR/TR/5-11.5/180 d4.29 M15 HF1956

1926	Pit N	38	83	9	22	2	2	0	11	6	0	15	.265	.315	.337	72	-3	0	.977	5	105	150	2b27,S7		0.2
1927	Pit N	12	22	2	5	1	0	0	3	2	0	7	.227	.292	.273	48	-2	0	1.000	-3	56	0	2b7,S4/1		-0.4
1928	Was A	63	227	23	55	10	4	0	25	22	0	27	.242	.309	.322	66	-11	4-0	.953	8	107	125	S63		0.4
1929	Was A	145	494	72	139	29	8	8	61	85	1	37	.281	.388	.421	107	9	5-9	.923	5	104	106	S143/2		2.6
1930	Was A	154	587	127	203	41	9	13	126	72	5	36	.346	.422	.513	135	34	17-10	.960	27	110	111	S154		6.9
1931	Was A	156	611	103	187	44	13	12	126	81	4	52	.306	.391	.480	127	26	10-9	.950	13	101	114	S155		4.5
1932	Was A	143	557	95	177	43	18	6	116	66	4	49	.318	.393	.492	129	25	7-5	.959	7	103	111	S141		3.8
1933	†Was A★	152	602	89	186	45	11	5	118	87	2	49	.309	.398	.445	124	25	5-4	.960	6	106	118	S152,M		3.9
1934	Was A★	127	504	68	143	30	9	7	101	53	1	28	.284	.353	.421	103	1	8-0	.951	13	114	127	S127,M		-0.1
1935	Bos A★	144	556	70	164	37	14	9	95	63	4	40	.295	.370	.460	106	5	3-3	.949	-15	95	98	S139,1b2,M		-0.8
1936	Bos A	81	295	36	83	22	4	2	43	32	1	21	.281	.354	.403	82	-8	1-0	.958	-16	87	95	S148,M		1.2
1937	Bos A★	148	570	102	175	40	4	18	110	84	1	73	.307	.402	.486	118	18	5-3	.954	7	103	115	S142,M		4.4
1938	Bos A★	143	530	98	172	51	5	17	94	91	5	60	.325	.428	.536	134	32	7-5	.954	4	99	105	S142,M		3.2
1939	Bos A★	143	520	97	160	33	3	19	107	87	0	48	.308	.407	.492	124	22	6-6	.948	-0	105	94	S146,3b2,M		2.7
1940	Bos A	149	548	104	156	35	6	24	111	83	0	55	.285	.380	.502	122	19	7-5	.958	-1	99	85	S119,3b22/OLM		3.5
1941	Bos A★	143	518	98	161	38	8	16	95	82	1	55	.311	.406	.508	137	30	1-4	.865	-1	103	200	3b11,1b5/SM		0.5
1942	Bos A	45	79	7	24	3	0	4	24	15	0	21	.304	.415	.494	150	6	0-1	.968	-0	98	95	3b10,M		0.8
1943	Bos A	59	77	9	24	5	0	5	29	11	0	19	.312	.398	.558	176	7	0-0	.981	-2	93	90	1b49,M		-0.3
1944	Bos A	76	191	24	46	7	0	5	28	34	1	19	.241	.358	.356	106	3	1-4	1.000	1	148	355	3b3,M	67	0.2
1945	Bos A	3	8	1	3	0	0	0	1	4	0	3	.375	.545	.375	165	1	0-0					S1843,3b69,1b57,2b35/OL	67	39.6
Total	20	2124	7579	1233	2285	515	118	170	1424	1059	34	700	.301	.390	.468	119	239	87-71	.951	53	102	105	S1843,3b69,1b57,2b35/OL		

YEAR	TM LG	G	AB	R	H	2B	3B	HR	RBI	BB-IB	HP	SO	AVG	OBP	SLG	AOPS	ABR	SB-CS	FA	FR	RNG	THR	GAMES AT POSITION	DL	BFW

CRONIN, BILL William Patrick "Crungy" B12.26.1902 W.Newton MA D10.26.1966 Newton MA BR/TR/5-9/167 d7.4

1928	Bos N	3	2	1	0	0	0	0	1		0	0	.000	.333	.000	-6	0	0	1.000	0	0	0	C3		0.0
1929	Bos N	6	9	0	1	0	0	0	0	1	0	0	.111	.111	.111	-47	-2	0	1.000	1	157	88	C6		-0.1
1930	Bos N	66	178	19	45	9	1	0	17	4	2	8	.253	.277	.305	44	-16	0	.983	4	117	90	C64		-0.7
1931	Bos N	51	107	8	22	6	1	0	10	7	2	5	.206	.267	.280	49	-8	0	.941	0	105	94	C50		-0.6
Total	4	126	296	28	68	15	2	0	27	12	4	13	.230	.269	.294	43	-26	0	.968	5	113	91	C123		-1.4

CROOKE, TOM Thomas Aloysius B7.26.1884 Washington DC D4.5.1929 Quantico VA BR/TR/6-0/180 d9.29

1909	Was A	3	7	2	2	1	0	0	2	2	0		.286	.444	.429	184	1	1	.969	-1	0	207	1b3		0.0
1910	Was A	8	21	1	4	1	0	0	1	1	0		.190	.227	.238	48	-1	0	1.000	-0	75	97	1b5		-0.2
Total	2	11	28	3	6	2	0	0	3	3	0		.214	.290	.286	85	0	1	.988	-1	47	138	1b8		-0.2

CROOKS, JACK John Charles B11.9.1865 St.Paul MN D2.2.1918 St.Louis MO BR/TR/5-10/170 d9.26 M1

1889	Col AA	12	43	13	14	2	3	0	7	10	1	4	.326	.463	.512	187	6	10	.987	4	123	64	2b12		0.8
1890	Col AA	135	485	86	107	5	4	1	62	96	7		.221	.357	.254	86	-1	57	.937	-1	93	121	2b134/3OL		0.3
1891	Col AA	138	519	110	127	19	13	0	46	103	9	47	.245	.379	.331	110	14	50	.957	18	98	129	2b138		3.2
1892	StL N	128	445	82	95	7	4	7	38	136	2	52	.213	.400	.294	116	22	23	.928	-5	94	96	2b100,3b26,O2R,M		2.0
1893	StL N	128	448	93	106	10	9	1	48	121	9	37	.237	.408	.306	91	2	31	.908	2	99	87	3b123,S4/C		0.6
1895	Was N	118	412	81	117	19	8	6	58	70	8	39	.284	.398	.413	111	10	36	.956	18	104	79	2b118		2.6
1896	Was N	25	84	20	24	3	0	3	20	16	1	8	.286	.406	.429	120	-3	2	.916	-2	86	60	2b20,3b4		0.1
	Lou N	39	122	19	29	5	1	2	15	20	2	8	.238	.354	.344	88	-1	8	.925	1	92	130	2b39		0.1
	Year	64	206	39	53	8	1	5	35	36	3	16	.257	.376	.379	101	2	10	.922	-2	90	107	2b59,3b4		0.2
1898	StL N	72	225	33	52	4	2	1	20	40	5		.231	.359	.280	82	-3	3	.959	-5	99	81	2b66,3b3,S2/O(1/1/0)		0.2
Total	8	795	2783	537	671	74	44	21	314	612	44	195	.241	.386	.322	102	52	220	.946	37	97	104	2b627,3b157,S6,O4(2/1/2)/C		9.9

CROSBY, ED Edward Carlton B5.26.1949 Long Beach CA BL/TR/6-2/180* [StLN69*2/43] d7.12 s-Bobby Col Long Beach (CA) City

1970	StL N	38	95	9	24	4	1	0	6	7-0	1	5	.253	.308	.316	66	-5	0-0	.954	2	109	94	S35,3b3,2b2		0.0
1972	StL N	101	276	27	60	9	1	0	19	18-1	2	27	.217	.269	.257	51	-18	1-1	.979	-4	94	112	S43,2b38,3b14		-1.7
1973	StL N	22	39	4	5	2	1	0	1	4-1	0	4	.128	.209	.231	22	-4	0-0	.938	-3	86	99	S7,2b5,3b4		-0.7
	†Cin N	36	51	4	11	1	1	0	5	7-1	0	12	.216	.333	.275	73	-2	0-1	.953	1	116	86	S29,2b5		-0.6
	Year	58	90	8	16	3	2	0	6	11-2	0	16	.178	.282	.256	51	-6	0-1	.950	-2	111	88	S36,2b10,3b4		0.1
1974	Cle A	37	86	11	18	3	0	0	6	6-0	0	12	.209	.258	.244	46	-6	0-1	.926	-3	71	99	3b18,S13,2b3		-0.9
1975	Cle A	61	128	12	30	5	0	0	7	13-0	0	14	.234	.305	.258	60	-6	0-4	.974	-1	100	84	S30,2b19,3b13		-0.5
1976	Cle A	2	2	0	1	0	0	0	0	0-0	0	0	.500	.500	.500	195	0	0-0	1.000	1	293	0	/3D		0.1
Total	6	297	677	67	149	22	4	0	44	55-3	5	74	.220	.282	.264	55	-41	1-7	.964	-7	104	92	S157,2b72,3b53/D		-3.6

CROSBY, BUBBA Richard Stephen B8.11.1976 Houston TX BL/TL/5-11/180* [LAN98 1/23] d5.29 Col Rice

2003	LA N	9	12	1	1	0	0	0	1	0-0	0	3	.083	.083	.083	-58	-3	0-0	.667	-0	114	0	/OL		-0.3
2004	†NY A	55	53	8	8	2	0	2	7	2-0	1	13	.151	.196	.302	27	-6	2-0	.973	-1	98	0	O45(11/12/25),D2		-0.7
2005	†NY A	76	98	15	27	0	1	1	6	4-0	0	14	.276	.304	.327	67	-5	4-1	1.000	3	120	125	O67(4/41/23),D4		-0.2
Total	3	140	163	23	36	2	1	3	14	6-0	1	30	.221	.253	.301	45	-14	6-1	.984	2	112	79	O113(16/53/48),D6		-1.2

CROSBY, BOBBY Robert Edward B1.12.1980 Lakewood CA BR/TR/6-3/200* [OakA01 1/25] d9.2 f-Ed Col Cal St.-Long Beach

2003	Oak A	11	12	1	0	0	0	0	0	1-0	1	5	.000	.143	.000	-57	-3	0-0	.889	2	165	144	S9,D2		-0.1
2004	Oak A	151	545	70	130	34	1	22	64	58-0	9	141	.239	.319	.426	93	-5	7-3	.975	16	110	111	S151		2.1
2005	Oak A	84	333	66	92	25	4	9	38	35-0	1	54	.276	.346	.456	110	5	0-0	.981	5	103	120	S84		1.6
Total	3	246	890	137	222	59	5	31	102	94-0	11	200	.249	.326	.431	97	-3	7-3	.976	23	108	114	S244,D2	77	3.6

CROSETTI, FRANKIE Frank Peter Joseph "Crow" B10.4.1910 San Francisco CA D2.11.2002 Stockton CA BR/TR/5-10/165 d4.12 Def 1944 C25

1932	†NY A	116	398	47	96	20	9	5	57	51	5	51	.241	.335	.374	88	-7	3-2	.937	-5	89	104	S84,3b33/2		-0.5
1933	NY A	136	451	71	114	20	5	9	60	55	2	40	.253	.337	.379	95	-3	4-1	.936	-8	91	75	S133		-0.1
1934	NY A	138	554	85	147	22	10	11	67	61	5	58	.265	.344	.401	98	-3	5-6	.945	-11	91	111	S119,3b23/2		-0.5
1935	NY A	87	349	49	78	17	6	8	50	41	4	27	.256	.351	.430	107	3	3-1	.963	-7	94	88	S87		0.2
1936	†NY A★	151	632	137	182	35	7	15	78	90	12	83	.288	.387	.437	107	9	18-7	.948	-13	94	96	S151		0.8
1937	†NY A	149	611	127	143	29	5	11	49	86	12	105	.234	.340	.352	74	-23	13-7	.948	0	98	101	S147		-1.1
1938	†NY A	157	631	113	166	35	3	9	55	106	15	97	.263	.382	.371	90	-5	27-12	.948	18	106	119	S157		2.4
1939	†NY A☆	152	656	109	153	25	5	10	56	65	13	81	.233	.315	.332	67	-34	11-7	.968	10	97	148	S152		-1.2
1940	NY A	145	546	84	106	23	4	4	31	72	10	77	.194	.299	.273	52	-39	14-8	.954	-13	97	91	S145		-3.9
1941	NY A	50	148	13	33	2	2	1	22	18	3	14	.223	.320	.284	62	-8	0-2	.944	5	100	107	S32,3b13		-0.1
1942	†NY A	74	285	50	69	5	5	4	23	31	9	33	.242	.335	.337	91	-3	1-1	.951	0	88	140	3b62,S8,2b2		-0.1
1943	†NY A	95	348	36	81	8	1	2	20	36	7	47	.233	.317	.279	74	-11	4-4	.946	-0	96	107	S90		-0.4
1944	NY A	55	197	20	47	4	2	5	30	11	6	21	.239	.299	.355	84	-5	3-0	.960	-5	88	94	S55		-0.5
1945	NY A	130	441	57	105	12	0	4	48	59	10	65	.238	.341	.293	84	-8	7-1	.946	-5	96	115	S126		-0.3
1946	NY A	28	59	4	17	3	0	0	3	8	1	2	.288	.382	.339	101	1	0-3	.940	5	124	146	S24		0.6
1947	NY A	3	1	0	0	0	0	0	0	0	0	0	.000	.000	.000	-99	0	0-0	—	-0	0	0	/2S		-0.1
1948	NY A	17	14	4	4	0	1	0	2	2	0	2	.286	.375	.429	115	0	0-0	1.000	0	117	251	2b6,S5		0.0
Total	17	1683	6277	1006	1541	260	65	98	649	792	114	799	.245	.341	.354	84	-136	113-62	.949	-30	96	107	S1516,3b131,2b11		-4.8

CROSS, AMOS Amos C. B1861 , Czechoslovakia D7.16.1888 Cleveland OH d4.22 b-Frank b-Lave

1885	Lou AA	35	130	11	37	2	1	0	14	0	1		.285	.290	.315	91	-2		.936	-0			C35		0.1
1886	Lou AA	74	283	51	78	14	6	1	42	44	1		.276	.375	.378	129	11	13	.910	-7			C51,1b20,S2/OL		0.5
1887	Lou AA	8	28	0	3	0	0	0	0	1	0		.107	.138	.107	-31	-5	0	.808	-2			C5,1b2/OR		-0.6
Total	3	117	441	62	118	16	7	1	56	45	2		.268	.338	.342	108	4	13	.916	-10			C91,1b22,O2(1/0/1),S2		0.0

CROSS, CLARENCE Clarence (b Clarence Crause) B3.4.1856 St.Louis MO D6.23.1931 Seattle WA d5.5

1884	Alt U	2	7	1	4	1	0	0		2			.571	.667	.714	315	2		.500	-2	22	0	3b2		0.0
	Phi U	2	9	0	2	0	0	0		0			.222	.222	.222	38	-1		.545	-2	84	0	S2		-0.2
	KC U	25	93	13	20	1	0	0		6			.215	.263	.226	57	-7		.836	4	137	68	S24/3		-0.2
	Year	29	109	14	26	2	0	0		8			.239	.291	.257	76	-6		.813	1	133	62	S26,3b3		-0.4
1887	NY AA	16	55	9	11	2	1	0	5	2	3		.200	.267	.273	53	-3	0	.833	-1	105	34	S13,3b4		-0.4
Total	2	45	164	23	37	4	1	0	5	10	3		.226	.282	.262	67	-9	0	.818	-1	125	54	S39,3b7		-0.8

CROSS, FRANK Frank Atwell "Mickey" B1.20.1873 Cleveland OH D11.2.1932 Geauga Lake OH TR/5-9/161 d5.20 b-Amos b-Lave

| 1901 | Cle A | 1 | 5 | 0 | 3 | 0 | 0 | 0 | 3 | 0 | | | .600 | .600 | .600 | 243 | 1 | 0 | — | -0 | 0 | 0 | /OR | | 0.1 |

CROSS, JEFF Joffre James B8.28.1918 Tulsa OK D7.23.1997 Huntsville TX BR/TR/5-11/160 d9.27 Mil 1943-45 Col Oklahoma

1942	StL N	1	4	0	1	0	0	0	0	0	0		.250	.250	.250	43	0	0	1.000	-0	123	0	/S		0.0
1946	StL N	49	69	17	15	3	0	0	6	10	0	8	.217	.316	.261	62	-3	4	.970	3	113	154	S17,2b8/3		0.0
1947	StL N	51	49	4	5	1	0	0	3	10	0	6	.102	.254	.122	3	-7	0	.947	2	129	118	3b15,S14,2b2		-0.4
1948	StL N	2	0	0	0	0	0	0	0	0	0		—	—	—		-4	0	—	-0		0	/R		0.0
	Chi N	16	20	1	2	0	0	0	0	0	0	4	.100	.100	.100	-48	-4	0	.786	-3	79	0	S9/2		-0.7
	Year	18	20	1	2	0	0	0	0	0	0	4	.100	.100	.100	-47	-4	0	.786	-3	79	0	S9/2		-0.7
Total	4	119	142	22	23	4	0	0	10	20	0	18	.162	.265	.190	26	-14	4	.932	2	107	135	S41,3b16,2b11		-1.1

CROSS, LAVE Lafayette Napoleon B5.12.1866 Milwaukee WI D9.6.1927 Toledo OH BR/TR/5-8.5/155 d4.23 M1 b-Amos b-Frank OF(13/34/72)

1887	Lou AA	54	203	32	54	8	3	0	26	15	1		.266	.320	.335	81	-5	15	.916	-2			C44,O10(3/1/6)		-0.3
1888	Lou AA	47	181	20	41	3	0	0	15	12	1		.227	.239	.243	56	-9	10	.929	-7			C37,O12(2/0/10),S2		-0.4
1889	Phi AA	55	199	22	44	8	2	0	23	14	0	9	.221	.272	.281	58	-11	11	.934	14			C55		0.6
1890	Phi P	63	245	42	73	7	8	3	47	12	0		.298	.331	.429	100	-2	5	.885	3	98	120	C49,O15(0/5/10)		0.3
1891	Phi AA	110	402	66	121	20	14	5	52	38	3	23	.301	.366	.458	135	16	14	.971	1	145	279	O43R,C43,3b24/S2		1.8
1892	Phi N	140	541	84	149	15	10	4	69	39	3	16	.275	.328	.362	109	4	18	.921	6	107	103	3b65,C39,O25(8/17/0),2b14,S5		1.2
1893	Phi N	96	415	81	124	17	6	4	78	26	1	7	.299	.342	.398	96	-4	18	.974	15	128	97	C40,3b30,O10(0/9/1),S10,1b6		1.2
1894	Phi N	122	542	128	210	35	10	7	132	31	3	7	.387	.424	.528	131	27	23	.916	23	120	148	3b103,C16,S7/2		4.0
1895	Phi N	125	535	95	145	26	9	2	101	35	3		.271	.319	.364	76	-21	21	.940	32	121	121	3b125		1.1
1896	Phi N	106	406	63	104	23	5	1	73	32	1	14	.256	.312	.345	74	-16	21	.937	13	110	95	3b61,S37,2b6,O2C/C		0.0
1897	Phi N	38	344	37	89	17	5	3	51	10	1		.259	.282	.363	71	-16	10	.912	-1	98	81	3b47,2b38,O2R/S		-1.2
1898	StL N	151	602	71	191	28	8	3	79	28	0		.317	.350	.401	111	8	14	.945	20	112	90	3b149,S2		2.8

YEAR	TM LG	G	AB	R	H	2B	3B	HR	RBI	BB-IB	HP	SO	AVG	OBP	SLG	AOPS	ABR	SB-CS	FA	FR	RNG	THR	GAMES AT POSITION	BFW
1899	Cle N*	38	154	15	44	5	0	0	20	8	1		.286	.325	.338	88	-2	2	.955	5	98	99	3b38,M	0.3
	StL N	103	403	61	122	14	5	4	64	17	1		.303	.330	.392	94	-4	11	.960	31	122	178	3b103	2.5
	Year	141	557	76	166	19	5	5	84	25	2		.298	.330	.377	94	-6	13	.959	36	116	157	3b141	2.8
1900	StL N	16	61	6	18	1	0	0	6	1	0		.295	.306	.311	71	-3	1	.962	2	120	56	3b16	-0.1
	†Bro N	117	461	73	135	14	6	4	67	25	2		.293	.332	.375	90	-8	20	.943	3	101	61	3b117	-0.3
	Year	133	522	79	153	15	6	4	73	26	2		.293	.329	.368	88	-11	21	.945	5	103	60	3b133	-0.4
1901	Phi A	100	424	82	139	28	12	2	73	19	1		.328	.358	.465	121	11	23	.919	7	107	49	3b100	1.8
1902	Phi A	137	559	90	191	39	8	0	108	27	2		.342	.374	.440	120	15	25	.942	6	99	69	3b137	2.3
1903	Phi A	137	559	60	163	22	4	2	90	10	0		.292	.304	.356	93	-6	14	.950	-3	88	100	3b136/1	-0.5
1904	Phi A	155	607	73	176	31	10	1	71	13	5		.290	.310	.379	112	6	10	.936	-9	83	111	3b155	0.2
1905	†Phi A	147	587	69	156	29	5	0	77	26	1		.266	.299	.332	98	-2	8	.952	-4	93	65	3b130	-1.1
1906	Was A	130	494	55	130	14	6	1	46	28	0		.263	.303	.322	100	-1	19	.978	8	124	46	3b41	-0.1
1907	Was A	41	161	13	32	8	0	0	10	10	0		.199	.246	.248	62	-7	3	.928	-12	85	49	3b147	0.3
Total	21	2278	9085	1338	2651	412	136	47	1378	466	31	90	.292	.329	.383	100	-30	303	.938	160	103	92	3b1724,C324,O119R,S65,2b60,1b7	16.4

CROSS, MONTE Montford Montgomery B8.31.1869 Philadelphia PA D6.21.1934 Philadelphia PA BR/TR/5-8.5/148 d9.27 U1 -0.6

YEAR	TM LG	G	AB	R	H	2B	3B	HR	RBI	BB-IB	HP	SO	AVG	OBP	SLG	AOPS	ABR	SB-CS	FA	FR	RNG	THR	GAMES AT POSITION	BFW
1892	Bal N	15	50	5	8	0	0	0	2	4	0	10	.160	.222	.160	16	-5	2	.864	-2	100	41	S15	0.7
1894	Pit N	13	43	14	19	1	5	2	13	5	2		.442	.520	.837	225	8	6	.924	-0	89	127	S13	-1.7
1895	Pit N	109	397	67	101	14	13	3	54	38	3	38	.254	.324	.378	85	-10	39	.884	-17	87	95	S108/2	-1.3
1896	StL N	125	427	66	104	10	6	6	52	58	6	48	.244	.342	.337	83	-9	40	.892	-13	94	54	S125	3.6
1897	StL N	132	465	60	133	17	11	4	55	62	7		.286	.378	.396	107	6	38	.918	30	117	81	S132	2.1
1898	Phi N	149	525	68	135	25	5	1	50	55	8		.257	.337	.330	95	-1	20	.907	16	103	103	S149	0.2
1899	Phi N	154	557	85	143	25	6	3	65	56	10		.257	.335	.339	88	-7	26	.909	2	94	119	S154	-2.8
1900	Phi N	131	466	59	94	11	3	0	62	51	6		.202	.289	.258	52	-30	19	.928	-7	94	94	S131	-4.0
1901	Phi N	139	483	49	95	14	1	1	44	52	5		.197	.289	.236	50	-29	24	.924	-16	93	139	S139	-1.2
1902	Phi A	137	497	72	115	22	2	3	59	32	8		.231	.289	.302	61	-26	17	.927	9	99	62	S137/2	0.9
1903	Phi A	137	470	44	116	21	2	0	45	49	6		.247	.326	.319	90	-3	31	.940	8	92	78	S153	-3.3
1904	Phi A	153	503	33	95	23	4	1	38	46	7		.189	.266	.256	62	-20	19	.937	-15	86	58	S77,2b2	-0.3
1905	†Phi A	79	252	28	67	17	2	0	24	19	6		.266	.332	.349	114	5	8	.929	-10	84	97	S134	-0.4
1906	Phi A	134	445	32	89	23	3	1	40	50	7		.200	.291	.272	74	-11	22	.938	3	91	111	S74	0.9
1907	Phi A	77	248	37	51	9	5	0	18	39	1		.206	.316	.282	89	-1	17	.954	8	97	84	S1678,2b4	-7.2
Total	15	1684	5828	719	1365	232	68	31	621	616	82	100	.234	.316	.313	80	-133	328	.920	-4	96	84		

CROSSIN, FRANK Frank Patrick B6.15.1891 Avondale PA D12.6.1965 Kingston PA BR/TR/5-10/160 d9.24 -0.5

YEAR	TM LG	G	AB	R	H	2B	3B	HR	RBI	BB-IB	HP	SO	AVG	OBP	SLG	AOPS	ABR	SB-CS	FA	FR	RNG	THR	GAMES AT POSITION	BFW
1912	StL A	8	22	5	5	0	0	0	2	1	1		.227	.261	.227	41	-2	1	.920	-3	70	81	C8	0.0
1913	StL A	4	4	1	1	0	0	0	0	1	1	1	.250	.500	.250	124	0	0	.857	-1	85	73	C2	-0.8
1914	StL A	43	90	5	11	1	1	0	5	10	2	10	.122	.225	.156	15	-9	3	.934	-2	101	90	C41	-0.8
Total	3	55	116	8	17	1	1	0	7	12	3	11	.147	.244	.172	25	-11	4	.930	-5	96	88	C51	-1.3

CROTTY, JOE Joseph P. B12.24.1860 Cincinnati OH D6.22.1926 Minneapolis MN BR/TR d5.4

YEAR	TM LG	G	AB	R	H	2B	3B	HR	RBI	BB-IB	HP	SO	AVG	OBP	SLG	AOPS	ABR	SB-CS	FA	FR	RNG	THR	GAMES AT POSITION	BFW
1882	Lou AA	5	20	1	2	0	0	0	0				.100	.100	.100	-34	-3		.882	0			C5	-0.2
	StL AA	8	28	2	4	1	0	0	3				.143	.226	.179	37	-2		.882	-1			C7/OC	-0.2
	Year	13	48	3	6	1	0	0	3				.125	.176	.146	10	-4		.882	-0			C12/OC	-0.4
1884	Cin U	21	84	11	22	4	2	1	1				.262	.271	.393	91	-4		.896	-3			C21	-0.5
1885	Lou AA	39	129	14	20	2	0	0	7	3	3		.155	.193	.171	15	-12		.931	0			C38/1	-0.8
1886	NY AA	14	47	6	8	0	1	0	2	4	1		.170	.250	.213	50	-3	3	.933	-0			C14	-0.2
Total	4	87	308	34	56	7	3	1	9	11	4		.182	.220	.234	43	-24	3	.915	-4			C85/1OC	-1.9

CROUCH, JACK Jack Albert "Roxy" B10.12.1903 Salisbury NC D8.25.1972 Leesburg FL BR/TR/5-9/165 d9.18 -0.1

YEAR	TM LG	G	AB	R	H	2B	3B	HR	RBI	BB-IB	HP	SO	AVG	OBP	SLG	AOPS	ABR	SB-CS	FA	FR	RNG	THR	GAMES AT POSITION	BFW
1930	StL A	6	14	1	2	1	0	0	1	1	0	3	.143	.200	.214	5	-2	0-0	1.000	1	197	146	C5	-0.3
1931	StL A	8	12	0	0	0	0	0	0	1	0	4	.000	.000	.000	-97	-3	0-0	.895	0	171	87	C7	-0.3
1933	StL A	19	30	1	5	0	0	0	5	2	0	6	.167	.219	.267	26	-3	0-0	1.000	-0	88	206	C9	-0.1
	Cin N	10	16	5	2	0	0	0	1	0	0	2	.125	.222	.125	1	-2	1-0	.976	1	84	70	C6	-0.8
Total	3	43	72	7	9	1	0	0	8	3	2	13	.125	.182	.181	-3	-10	1-0	.976	1	129	130	C27	

CROUCHER, FRANK Frank Donald "Dingle" B7.23.1914 San Antonio TX D5.21.1980 Houston TX BR/TR/5-11/165 d4.18 Mil 1943-45 -1.7

YEAR	TM LG	G	AB	R	H	2B	3B	HR	RBI	BB-IB	HP	SO	AVG	OBP	SLG	AOPS	ABR	SB-CS	FA	FR	RNG	THR	GAMES AT POSITION	BFW
1939	Det A	97	324	38	87	15	0	5	40	16	0	42	.269	.303	.361	64	-18	2-2	.934	-6	98	93	S93,2b3	-1.1
1940	†Det A	37	57	3	6	0	0	0	2	4	0	5	.105	.164	.105	-26	-11	0-0	.936	-2	100	45	S26,2b7/3	-2.1
1941	Det A	136	489	51	124	21	4	2	39	33	3	72	.254	.305	.325	61	-28	2-0	.935	-4	94	96	S136	0.0
1942	Was A	26	65	2	18	1	1	0	5	3	0	9	.277	.309	.323	79	-2	0-0	.950	1	116	75	2b18	-4.9
Total	4	296	935	94	235	37	5	7	86	56	3	128	.251	.296	.324	58	-59	4-2	.934	-10	96	92	S255,2b28/3	

CROUSE, BUCK Clyde Ellsworth B1.6.1897 Anderson IN D10.23.1983 Muncie IN BL/TR/5-8/158 d8.1 -0.4

YEAR	TM LG	G	AB	R	H	2B	3B	HR	RBI	BB-IB	HP	SO	AVG	OBP	SLG	AOPS	ABR	SB-CS	FA	FR	RNG	THR	GAMES AT POSITION	BFW
1923	Chi A	23	70	6	18	1	1	0	7	3	1		.257	.297	.357	73	-3	0-0	.955	-2	73	107	C22	-1.2
1924	Chi A	94	305	30	79	10	1	1	44	23	4	12	.259	.319	.308	64	-17	3-2	.945	-2	80	127	C90	0.6
1925	Chi A	54	131	18	46	7	0	2	25	12	1	4	.351	.410	.450	125	5	1-2	.952	-0	185	138	C48	-0.4
1926	Chi A	49	135	10	32	4	1	0	17	14	0	7	.237	.309	.281	57	-9	0-0	.985	2	137	106	C45	-0.2
1927	Chi A	85	222	22	53	11	0	0	20	21	1	14	.239	.307	.288	57	-14	4-1	.972	7	117	142	C76	-0.5
1928	Chi A	78	218	17	55	5	2	2	20	19	1		.252	.315	.321	68	-10	3-4	.959	2	131	128	C81	0.3
1929	Chi A	45	107	11	29	7	0	2	12	5	2		.271	.316	.393	82	-3	2-0	.979	3	115	104	C40	0.2
1930	Chi A	42	118	14	30	8	1	0	15	17	0	10	.254	.348	.339	78	-3	1-1	.979	4	107	120	C38	-1.6
Total	8	470	1306	128	342	54	6	8	160	114	10	68	.262	.326	.331	72	-54	14-10	.964	13	116	125	C440	

CROW, DON Donald Le Roy B8.18.1958 Yakima WA BR/TR/6-4/200 [LAN79 3/76] d7.25 Col Washington St. -0.2

YEAR	TM LG	G	AB	R	H	2B	3B	HR	RBI	BB-IB	HP	SO	AVG	OBP	SLG	AOPS	ABR	SB-CS	FA	FR	RNG	THR	GAMES AT POSITION	BFW
1982	LA N	4	4	0	0	0	0	0	0	0	0		.000	.000	.000	-99	-1		1.000	-1	43	123	C4	

CROWE, GEORGE George Daniel "Big George" B3.22.1921 Whiteland IN BL/TL/6-2/212* d4.16 Col Indianapolis -0.1

YEAR	TM LG	G	AB	R	H	2B	3B	HR	RBI	BB-IB	HP	SO	AVG	OBP	SLG	AOPS	ABR	SB-CS	FA	FR	RNG	THR	GAMES AT POSITION	BFW
1952	Bos N	73	217	25	56	13	1	4	20	18	5	25	.258	.329	.382	100	0	0-1	.985	1	112	82	1b55	0.1
1953	Mil N	47	42	6	12	2	0	2	6	2	1	7	.286	.333	.476	115	1	0-0	1.000	0	161	65	1b9	1.3
1955	Mil N	104	303	41	85	12	4	15	55	45-8	1	44	.281	.374	.495	135	16	0-1	.989	2	111	88	1b79	0.1
1956	Cin N	77	144	22	36	2	1	10	23	11-1	2	28	.250	.312	.486	104	0	0-0	.988	2	128	69	1b32	-0.9
1957	Cin N	133	494	71	134	20	1	31	92	32-3	1	62	.271	.314	.504	108	5	1-1	.989	1	99	88	1b120	0.6
1958	Cin N☆	111	345	31	95	12	5	7	61	41-3	0	51	.275	.348	.400	94	-3	0-0	1.000	2	172	104	1b93/2	-0.1
1959	StL N	77	103	14	31	6	0	4	29	5-2	0	12	.301	.330	.592	132	4	0-0	1.000	0	112	51	1b5	-0.1
1960	StL N	73	72	5	17	3	0	4	13	5-1	0	16	.236	.278	.444	89	-1	0-0	.990	0	106	86	1b5	
1961	StL N	7	7	1	0	0	0	0	0	0-0	0	1	.143	.143	.143	-22	-1	0-0	—	0			/H	
Total	9	702	1727	215	467	70	12	81	299	159-18	10	246	.270	.333	.466	109	21	3-2	.990	5	106	86	1b407/2	

CROWLEY, ED Edgar Jewel B8.20.1906 Watkinsville GA D4.14.1970 Birmingham AL BR/TR/6-1/180 d6.21 Col Georgia Tech -0.1

YEAR	TM LG	G	AB	R	H	2B	3B	HR	RBI	BB-IB	HP	SO	AVG	OBP	SLG	AOPS	ABR	SB-CS	FA	FR	RNG	THR	GAMES AT POSITION	BFW
1928	Was A	2	1	0	0	0	0	0	0	0	0		.000	.000	.000	-99	-0	0-0	.000	-1	0		3b2	

CROWLEY, JOHN John A. B1.12.1862 Lawrence MA D9.23.1896 Lawrence MA 5-10/164 d5.1 -1.3

YEAR	TM LG	G	AB	R	H	2B	3B	HR	RBI	BB-IB	HP	SO	AVG	OBP	SLG	AOPS	ABR	SB-CS	FA	FR	RNG	THR	GAMES AT POSITION	BFW
1884	Phi N	48	168	26	41	7	3	0	19	15		21	.244	.306	.321	102	1		.832	-20			C48	

CROWLEY, TERRY Terrence Michael B2.16.1947 Staten Island NY BL/TL/6-0/180(170-182) [BalA66 11/216] d9.4 C19 Col Long Island-Brooklyn 0.0

YEAR	TM LG	G	AB	R	H	2B	3B	HR	RBI	BB-IB	HP	SO	AVG	OBP	SLG	AOPS	ABR	SB-CS	FA	FR	RNG	THR	GAMES AT POSITION	BFW
1969	Bal A	7	18	2	6	0	0	0	3	1-0	0	4	.333	.350	.333	96	0	0-0	1.000	0	135	179	1b3,O2L	-0.1
1970	†Bal A	83	152	25	39	5	0	5	20	35-3	0	26	.257	.394	.388	115	5	2-0	.973	-4	85	0	O27(6/0/22),1b23	-0.3
1971	Bal A	18	23	2	4	0	0	0	4	5	0	4	.174	.269	.174	27	-2	0-0	1.000	-1	73	0	O6(1/0/5),1b2	-0.4
1972	Bal A	97	247	30	57	10	0	11	29	32-5	1	26	.231	.319	.405	111	4	0-0	.990	-3	87	49	O68(3/0/65),1b15	-0.7
1973	†Bal A	54	131	16	27	4	0	3	15	16-1	1	14	.206	.297	.305	70	-5	0-0	1.000	0	94	88	O12(1/0/21),1b7	-0.3
1974	Cin N	84	125	11	30	12	0	1	20	10-0	1	16	.240	.293	.360	86	-2	1-0	1.000	2	161	180	1b4,O4(3/0/1)	0.2
1975	†Cin N	66	71	8	19	6	0	1	11	7-1	0	6	.268	.333	.394	100	0	0-0	1.000	0			/H	-0.2
1976	Atl N	7	6	0	0	0	0	0	0	0-0	0	0	.000	.000	.000	-94	-2	0-0	—	0			/H	-0.2
	Bal A	33	61	5	15	1	0	3	7	7-1	0	11	.246	.333	.426	108	-1	0-0	1.000	0	178	74	D17/1	0.2
1977	Bal A	18	22	3	8	0	0	1	9	1-0	0	3	.364	.391	.545	161	1	0-0	1.000	0	0		/1D	-0.3
1978	Bal A	62	95	9	24	2	0	0	12	8-0	1	12	.253	.314	.274	72	-3	0-0	1.000	1	143	97	D17,O2L/1	0.5
1979	†Bal A	61	63	8	20	5	1	1	8	14-2	1	13	.317	.449	.476	155	6	0-0	1.000	-0	0	188	D15,1b2	0.5

YEAR	TM LG	G	AB	R	H	2B	3B	HR	RBI	BB-IB	HP	SO	AVG	OBP	SLG	AOPS	ABR	SB-CS	FA	FR	RNG	THR	GAMES AT POSITION	DL	BFW
1980	Bal A	92	233	33	67	8	0	12	50	29-2	0	21	.288	.364	.476	131	10	0-0	1.000	2	357	52	D65,1b3		0.9
1981	Bal A	68	134	12	33	6	0	4	25	29-5	0	12	.246	.376	.381	120	5	0-0	1.000	0	105	79	D42,1b4		0.4
1982	Bal A	65	93	8	22	2	0	3	17	21-1	0	9	.237	.377	.355	103	1	0-0	.988	0	107	167	D14,1b10		0.0
1983	Mon N	50	44	2	8	0	0	0	3	9-0	1	4	.182	.327	.182	46	-3	0-0	1.000	-1	0	116	1b4		-0.4
Total	15	865	1518	174	379	62	1	42	229	222-21	7	181	.250	.345	.375	104	15	3-0	.980	-4	88	76	D195,O141(20/0/122),1b87		-0.7

CROWLEY, BILL William Michael B4.8.1857 Philadelphia PA D7.14.1891 Gloucester NJ BR/TR/5-7.5/159 d4.26 OF(82/150/254)

YEAR	TM LG	G	AB	R	H	2B	3B	HR	RBI	BB-IB	HP	SO	AVG	OBP	SLG	AOPS	ABR	SB-CS	FA	FR	RNG	THR	GAMES AT POSITION	DL	BFW
1875	Phi NA	9	37	4	3	0	0	0	3	1		0	.081	.105	.081	-33	-5	0-0	.800	-1	80	0	3b4,O4C/1		-0.5
1877	Lou N	61	238	30	67	9	3	1	23	4		13	.282	.293	.357	88	-5		.849	7	185	121	O58(0/57/2),S2,C2/32		0.0
1879	Buf N	60	261	41	75	9	5	0	30	6		14	.287	.303	.360	115	4		.809	-1	143	403	O43(3/1/39),C10,1b7,2b3		0.2
1880	Buf N	85	354	57	95	16	4	0	20	19		23	.268	.306	.336	115	6		.824	-2	126	80	O74(8/21/48),C22		0.3
1881	Bos N	72	279	33	71	12	0	0	31	14		15	.254	.290	.297	89	-2		.880	-3	88	170	O72(0/47/26)		-0.6
1883	Phi AA	23	96	16	24	4	3	0	16	3			.250	.273	.354	92	-1		.810	-2	78	0	O22(0/21/1)/1		-0.4
	Cle N	11	41	3	12	5	0	0	5	1		7	.293	.310	.415	119	1		.923	-2	0		O11R		-0.1
1884	Bos N	108	407	50	110	14	6	6	61	33		74	.270	.325	.378	121	10		.870	-7	96	168	O108(0/2/107)		0.2
1885	Buf N	92	344	29	83	14	1	1	36	21		32	.241	.285	.297	85	-5		.874	-4	47	37	O92(71/1/20)		0.4
Total	7	512	2020	259	537	83	22	8	222	101		178	.266	.301	.341	103	8		.853	-13	103	136	O480R,C34,1b8,2b4,S2/3		-1.5

CROZIER, ERIC Eric Le Roi B8.11.1978 Columbus OH BL/TL/6-4/200 [CleA00 41/1234] d9.4 Col Norfolk St.

| 2004 | Tor A | 14 | 33 | 5 | 5 | 2 | 0 | 2 | 4 | 6-0 | 0 | 19 | .152 | .282 | .394 | 70 | -2 | 0-0 | .972 | -0 | 74 | 57 | 1b5,D8 | | -0.2 |

CRUISE, WALTON Walton Edwin B5.6.1890 Childersburg AL D1.9.1975 Sylacauga AL BL/TR/6-0/175 d4.14 Mil 1918

YEAR	TM LG	G	AB	R	H	2B	3B	HR	RBI	BB-IB	HP	SO	AVG	OBP	SLG	AOPS	ABR	SB-CS	FA	FR	RNG	THR	GAMES AT POSITION	DL	BFW
1914	StL N	95	256	20	58	9	3	4	28	25	3	42	.227	.303	.332	90	-3	3	.976	-1	102	66	O81(43/38/0)		-1.0
1916	StL N	3	3	0	2	0	0	0	1	0	0	1	.667	.750	.667	339	1	0	1.000	0	118	0	O2(1/1/0)		0.1
1917	StL N	153	529	70	156	20	10	5	59	38	1	73	.295	.343	.399	131	18	16	.965	-11	88	77	O152(49/85/26)		-0.1
1918	StL N	70	240	34	65	5	4	6	39	30	3	26	.271	.359	.400	136	11	2	.964	-8	83	51	O65(48/0/17)		0.0
1919	StL N	9	21	0	2	1	0	0	1	0	0	6	.095	.136	.143	-17	-3	0	.833	-1	70	0	O5(0/4/1),1b2		-0.4
	Bos N	73	241	23	52	7	0	1	21	17	0	29	.216	.267	.257	61	-11	8	.978	-2	96	87	O66(31/23/14)		-1.9
	Year	82	262	23	54	8	0	1	21	18	0	35	.206	.257	.248	55	-14	8	.971	-3	95	83	O71(31/27/15),1b2		-2.3
1920	Bos N	91	288	40	80	7	5	1	21	31	2	26	.278	.352	.347	106	3	5-3	.950	-6	81	99	O82R		-0.8
1921	Bos N	108	344	47	119	16	7	8	55	48	2	24	.346	.429	.503	154	29	10-8	.963	-1	115	18	O102(100/2/0),1b2		2.0
1922	Bos N	104	352	51	98	15	10	4	46	44	1	20	.278	.360	.412	103	2	4-4	.948	2	113	76	O100(37/0/64),1b2		-0.4
1923	Bos N	21	38	4	8	2	0	0	3	3	2	2	.211	.268	.263	42	-3	1-0	.952	-0	119	0	O9(8/0/1)		-0.3
1924	Bos N	9	9	4	4	1	0	1	3	0	0	2	.444	.444	.889	260	2	0-0	—	0			/H		0.2
Total	10	736	2321	293	644	83	39	30	272	238	12	250	.277	.348	.386	114	46	49-15	.962	-27	97	66	O664(317/153/205),1b6		-2.6

CRUMLING, GENE Eugene Leon B4.5.1922 Wrightsville PA BR/TR/6-0/180 d9.11

| 1945 | StL N | 6 | 12 | 0 | 1 | 0 | 0 | 0 | 1 | 0 | | 1 | .083 | .083 | .083 | -52 | -3 | 0 | 1.000 | 1 | 83 | 183 | C6 | | -0.1 |

CRUMP, BUDDY Arthur Elliott B11.29.1901 Norfolk VA D9.26.1976 Raleigh NC BL/TL/5-10/156 d9.28

| 1924 | NY N | 4 | 1 | 0 | 0 | 0 | 0 | 0 | 0 | 0 | 0 | 1 | .000 | .000 | .000 | -99 | -1 | 0-0 | .500 | -1 | 47 | 0 | /OC | | -0.2 |

CRUTHERS, PRESS Charles Preston B9.8.1890 Marshallton DE D12.27.1976 Kenosha WI BR/TR/5-9/152 d9.29

YEAR	TM LG	G	AB	R	H	2B	3B	HR	RBI	BB-IB	HP	SO	AVG	OBP	SLG	AOPS	ABR	SB-CS	FA	FR	RNG	THR	GAMES AT POSITION	DL	BFW
1913	Phi A	3	12	3	3	1	0	0	0	0	0	2	.250	.250	.333	72	-0	3	.923	-2	55	93	2b3		-0.2
1914	Phi A	4	15	1	3	0	1	0	0	0	0	0	.200	.200	.333	63	-1	0-1	1.000	1	91	74	2b4		-0.1
Total	2	7	27	1	6	1	1	0	0	0	0	2	.222	.222	.333	67	-1	0-1	.973	-1	76	82	2b7		-0.3

CRUZ, TOMMY Cirilo (Dilan) B2.15.1951 Arroyo, PR BL/TL/5-9/165* d9.4 b-Hector b-Jose

1973	StL N	3	0	1	0	0	0	0	0	0		0					0	0-0	—	-0	0	0	/OL		0.0
1977	Chi A	4	2	1	0	0	0	0	0	0-0		0	.000	.000	.000	-99	-1	0-0	1.000	0	112	0	O2L		-0.1
Total	2	7	2	2	0	0	0	0	0	0-0		0	.000	.000	.000	-99	-1	0-0	1.000	-0	75	0	O3L		-0.1

CRUZ, DEIVI Deivi (Garcia) B11.16.1972 Bani, D.R. BR/TR/6-0/184(175-205) d4.1

YEAR	TM LG	G	AB	R	H	2B	3B	HR	RBI	BB-IB	HP	SO	AVG	OBP	SLG	AOPS	ABR	SB-CS	FA	FR	RNG	THR	GAMES AT POSITION	DL	BFW
1997	Det A	147	436	35	105	26	0	2	40	14-0	0	55	.241	.263	.314	50	-32	3-6	.979	9	109	112	S147		-1.4
1998	Det A	135	454	52	118	22	3	5	45	13-0	3	55	.260	.284	.355	64	-25	3-4	.983	16	115	115	S135		0.1
1999	Det A	155	518	64	147	35	0	13	58	12-0	4	57	.284	.302	.427	83	-15	1-4	.983	7	104	103	S155		0.2
2000	Det A	156	583	68	176	46	5	10	82	13-2	4	43	.302	.318	.449	93	-8	1-4	.982	7	106	112	S156		0.9
2001	Det A	110	414	39	106	28	1	7	52	17-0	4	46	.256	.291	.379	77	-14	4-1	.964	-10	101	96	S109,3b7		-1.5
2002	SD N	151	514	49	135	28	2	7	47	22-2	3	58	.263	.294	.366	83	-17	2-3	.973	-8	98	91	S147/1		-1.6
2003	Bal A	152	548	61	137	24	2	14	65	13-1	2	49	.250	.269	.378	69	-27	1-2	.975	1	102	98	S147,D5		-1.4
2004	SF N	127	397	46	116	30	2	7	55	17-6	3	32	.292	.322	.431	90	-6	1-3	.980	-4	100	104	S104,2b2/3		-0.4
2005	SF N	81	209	26	56	10	1	5	19	10-1	0	31	.268	.301	.397	78	-7	0-1	.985	-1	93	110	2b33,S16,3b5		-1.0
	Was N	20	51	2	13	1	0	0	1	1	3	.255	.283	.275	50	-4	0-0	1.000	-1	91	165	2b16,S8		-0.6
	Year	101	260	28	69	11	1	5	20	11-1	3	34	.265	.298	.373	73	-11	0-1	.989	-2	93	123	2b49,S24,3b5		-1.0
Total	9	1234	4124	442	1109	250	16	70	464	132-12	24	429	.269	.293	.388	77	-155	16-28	.978	18	105	104	S1124,2b51,3b13,D5/1	67	-6.1

CRUZ, ENRIQUE Enrique Michael B11.21.1981 Santo Domingo, D.R. BR/TR/6-1/180 d4.2

| 2003 | Mil N | 60 | 71 | 6 | 6 | 1 | 0 | 2 | 4-0 | 1 | 30 | .085 | .145 | .099 | -35 | -14 | 0-0 | 1.000 | -4 | 82 | 54 | S13,2b6,3b2 | | -1.8 |

CRUZ, FAUSTO Fausto (Santiago) B5.1.1972 Monte Cristi, D.R. BR/TR/5-10/165* d4.10

YEAR	TM LG	G	AB	R	H	2B	3B	HR	RBI	BB-IB	HP	SO	AVG	OBP	SLG	AOPS	ABR	SB-CS	FA	FR	RNG	THR	GAMES AT POSITION	DL	BFW
1994	Oak A	17	28	2	3	0	0	0	4-0	0	6	.107	.219	.107	-13	-5	0-0	.960	3	109	105	S10,3b4/2		-0.1
1995	Oak A	8	23	0	5	0	0	0	5	3-0	0	5	.217	.286	.217	42	-2	1-1	.971	-1	104	37	S8		-0.2
1996	Det A	14	38	5	9	2	0	0	1-0	0	11	.237	.256	.289	38	-4	0-0	.906	-2	104	56	2b8,S4/D		-0.5
Total	3	39	89	7	17	2	0	0	5	8-0	0	22	.191	.253	.213	23	-11	1-1	.934	1	107	66	S22,2b9,3b4/D		-0.8

CRUZ, HECTOR Hector Louis (Dilan) "Heity" B4.2.1953 Arroyo, PR BR/TR/5-11/173* d8.11 b-Tommy b-Jose

YEAR	TM LG	G	AB	R	H	2B	3B	HR	RBI	BB-IB	HP	SO	AVG	OBP	SLG	AOPS	ABR	SB-CS	FA	FR	RNG	THR	GAMES AT POSITION	DL	BFW
1973	StL N	11	11	1	0	0	0	0	0	1-0	0	3	.000	.083	.000	-75	-3	0-0	1.000	0	111	0	O5(1/4/0)		-0.3
1975	StL N	23	48	7	7	2	2	0	6	2-0	0	6	.146	.176	.271	23	-5	0-0	.800	-2	42	0	3b12,O6(4/0/2)		-0.9
1976	StL N	151	526	54	120	17	1	13	71	42-7	2	119	.228	.286	.338	76	-18	1-0	.934	-23	89	68	3b148		-4.5
1977	StL N	118	339	50	80	19	2	6	42	46-1	1	56	.236	.326	.357	85	-6	4-3	.964	-3	87	130	O106(27/0/85),3b2		-1.5
1978	Chi N	30	76	8	18	5	0	2	9	3-1	0	6	.237	.266	.382	70	-3	0-0	1.000	-2	93	0	O46(1/14/0),3b7		-0.5
	SF N	79	197	19	44	8	1	6	24	21-2	1	39	.223	.301	.365	88	-3	0-2	.978	-2	97	159	O53(31/17/14),3b14		-0.8
	Year	109	273	27	62	13	1	8	33	24-3	1	45	.227	.292	.370	83	-7	0-2	.983	-4	96	123	O67(32/31/14),3b21		-1.3
1979	SF N	16	25	2	3	0	0	1	3-0	0	7	.120	.214	.120	-7	-4	0-0	1.000	-1	94	0	O6(5/0/1),3b2		-0.5
	†Cin N	74	182	24	44	10	2	4	27	31-3	0	39	.242	.350	.385	101	1	0-1	.984	4	100	185	O69(13/23/49)		0.2
	Year	90	207	26	47	10	2	4	28	34-3	0	46	.227	.335	.353	89	-2	0-1	.985	3	100	176	O75(18/23/50),3b2		-0.3
1980	Cin N	52	75	5	16	4	1	1	5	8-1	0	16	.213	.289	.333	75	-3	0-0	.955	-0	122	0	O29(15/1/15)		-0.4
1981	Chi A	53	109	15	25	5	0	7	15	17-0	0	24	.229	.331	.468	118	3	2-2	.925	-1	97	0	3b18,O16(8/0/10)		0.1
1982	Chi N	17	19	1	4	1	0	0	0	1-0	0	4	.211	.286	.263	52	-1	0-0	1.000	-1	30	0	O4(4/0/1)		-0.2
Total	9	624	1607	186	361	71	9	39	200	176-15	4	317	.225	.301	.353	81	-42	7-8	.975	-31	96	122	O308(109/59/177),3b203		-9.3

CRUZ, HENRY Henry (Acosta) B2.27.1952 Christiansted, V.I. BL/TL/6-0/175* d4.18

YEAR	TM LG	G	AB	R	H	2B	3B	HR	RBI	BB-IB	HP	SO	AVG	OBP	SLG	AOPS	ABR	SB-CS	FA	FR	RNG	THR	GAMES AT POSITION	DL	BFW
1975	LA N	53	94	8	25	1	0	5	7-0	0	6	.266	.317	.319	80	-3	1-1	.960	-2	89	0	O41(17/23/4)		-0.7
1976	LA N	49	88	8	16	2	1	4	14	9-3	0	11	.182	.258	.364	76	-3	0-2	.976	-0	96	68	O23(5/5/17)		-0.6
1977	Chi A	16	21	3	6	0	0	2	5	1-1	0	5	.286	.318	.571	137	1	0-0	.833	-1	57	0	O9(1/2/6)		-0.1
1978	Chi A	53	77	13	17	2	1	2	10	8-0	1	11	.221	.292	.351	82	-2	0-1	1.000	3	96	270	O40(10/24/6)/D		0.0
Total	4	171	280	32	64	3	2	8	34	25-4	1	31	.229	.291	.361	84	-7	1-4	.974	-1	91	107	O113(33/54/33)/D		-1.4

CRUZ, JACOB Jacob B1.28.1973 Oxnard CA BL/TL/6-0/179(175-210) [SFN94 1/32] d7.18 Col Arizona St.

YEAR	TM LG	G	AB	R	H	2B	3B	HR	RBI	BB-IB	HP	SO	AVG	OBP	SLG	AOPS	ABR	SB-CS	FA	FR	RNG	THR	GAMES AT POSITION	DL	BFW
1996	SF N	33	77	10	18	3	0	3	10	12-0	2	24	.234	.352	.390	97	0	0-1	.977	0	106	75	O23(6/0/17)		-0.1
1997	SF N	16	25	3	4	1	0	0	3	3-0	0	8	.160	.241	.200	20	-3	0-0	.933	2	124	535	O12(2/0/10)		-0.1
1998	SF N	3	3	0	0	0	0	0	0-0	0	2	.000	.000	.000	-99	-1	0-0	—	0			/H		-0.1
	Cle A	1	1	0	0	0	0	0	0	0-0	0	0	.000	.000	.000	-96	0	0-0	—	0			/H		0.0
1999	Cle A	32	88	14	29	5	0	3	17	5-0	1	13	.330	.368	.511	116	2	0-2	1.000	0	115	0	O24(11/15/2),D2	82	0.1
2000	Cle A	11	29	3	7	0	0	0	4	4-0	0	8	.241	.361	.345	80	-1	1-0	1.000	0	91	277	O9(1/8/0),D2	154	0.0
2001	Cle A	28	68	12	15	3	0	3	11	5-0	3	23	.221	.303	.412	83	-2	0-2	.976	0	116	0	O22(3/15/5)		0.0
	Col N	44	76	7	16	1	0	1	7	10-0	1	27	.211	.303	.263	42	-6	0-2	.931	-2	80	85	O24(18/1/6)	31	-1.0
2002	Det A	35	88	12	24	1	2	1	6	13-0	3	20	.273	.377	.398	92	2	3-1	.929	-2	63	0	D14,O12(3/0/9),1b4	116	-0.1

YEAR	TM LG	G	AB	R	H	2B	3B	HR	RBI	BB-IB	HP	SO	AVG	OBP	SLG	AOPS	ABR	SB-CS	FA	FR	RNG	THR	GAMES AT POSITION	DL	BFW
2004	Cin N	96	147	22	33	8	0	3	28	16-2	4	43	.224	.317	.340	72	-6	0-0	1.000	-1	92	79	O29(4/0/26),1b6,D2		-0.8
2005	Cin N	110	127	12	30	10	0	4	18	16-1	1	46	.236	.324	.409	95	-1	0-0	1.000	-1	56	156	O20(8/0/12),1b5/D		-0.3
Total	9	409	729	95	176	38	2	19	105	85-3	16	207	.241	.331	.377	84	-16	4-8	.977	-3	95	88	O174(56/39/87),D21,1b15	383	-2.6

CRUZ, JOSE Jose (Dilan) B8.8.1947 Arroyo, PR BL/TL/6-0/175(170-185) d9.19 C9 b-Tommy b-Hector s-Jose [DL 1969 StL N 34]

YEAR	TM LG	G	AB	R	H	2B	3B	HR	RBI	BB-IB	HP	SO	AVG	OBP	SLG	AOPS	ABR	SB-CS	FA	FR	RNG	THR	GAMES AT POSITION	DL	BFW
1970	StL N	6	17	2	6	1	0	0	1	4-0	1	0	.353	.500	.412	143	2	0-0	1.000	1	195	0	O4(1/0/3)		0.3
1971	StL N	83	292	46	80	13	2	9	27	49-6	1	35	.274	.377	.425	122	10	6-3	.975	-4	97	43	O83(1/82/0)		0.4
1972	StL N	117	332	33	78	14	4	2	23	36-3	1	54	.235	.309	.319	80	-8	9-3	.979	-4	104	162	O102(10/87/7)		-0.6
1973	StL N	132	406	51	92	22	5	10	57	51-4	1	66	.227	.310	.379	91	-5	10-4	.979	-2	112	24	O118(1/85/37)		-1.1
1974	StL N	107	161	24	42	4	3	5	20	20-5	0	27	.261	.341	.416	.111	2	4-2	.975	1	110	84	O53(21/8/24)/1		0.1
1975	Hou N	120	315	44	81	15	2	9	49	52-6	1	44	.257	.358	.403	121	10	6-3	.980	5	116	102	O94(27/2/65)		1.2
1976	Hou N	133	439	49	133	21	5	4	61	53-5	0	46	.303	.377	.401	132	20	28-11	.972	7	108	118	O125(85/13/27)		2.4
1977	Hou N	157	579	87	173	31	10	17	87	69-13	0	67	.299	.368	.475	136	30	44-23	.973	-2	102	91	O155(0/6/155)		2.2
1978	Hou N	153	565	79	178	34	9	10	83	57-9	0	57	.315	.376	.460	142	32	37-9	.975	-2	112	33	O152R,1b2		2.8
1979	Hou N	157	558	73	161	33	9	9	72	72-16	0	66	.289	.367	.421	122	19	36-14	.959	1	104	59	O156L		1.7
1980	†Hou N☆	160	612	79	185	29	7	11	91	60-13	0	66	.302	.360	.426	131	25	36-11	.969	7	101	136	O156L		3.0
1981	†Hou N	107	409	53	109	16	5	13	55	35-4	0	49	.267	.319	.425	118	8	5-7	.984	4	116	54	O105L		0.6
1982	Hou N	155	570	62	157	27	2	9	68	60-12	1	67	.275	.342	.377	111	9	21-11	.964	6	111	72	O155L		0.9
1983	Hou N	160	594	85	189	28	8	14	92	65-10	1	86	.318	.385	.463	142	34	30-16	.979	-1	100	71	O160L		2.8
1984	Hou N	160	600	96	187	28	13	12	95	73-10	0	68	.312	.381	.462	147	38	22-8	.976	2	101	87	O160L		3.6
1985	Hou N★	141	544	69	163	34	4	9	79	43-10	0	74	.300	.349	.426	119	14	16-5	.971	4	100	62	O134L	12	0.2
1986	†Hou N	141	479	48	133	22	4	10	72	55-12	0	86	.278	.351	.403	111	7	3-4	.984	1	104	62	O97L		-0.6
1987	Hou N	126	365	47	88	17	4	11	38	36-3	0	65	.241	.307	.400	89	-7	4-1	.984	4	108	85	O97L		-0.7
1988	NY A	38	80	9	16	2	0	1	8	8-0	0	18	.200	.273	.262	51	-5	0-1	.889	-1	74	0	D12,O8(4/0/4)	21	-0.7
Total	19	2353	7917	1036	2251	391	94	165	1077	898-142	7	1031	.284	.354	.420	121	235	317-136	.971	35	106	82	O2156(1411/284/474),D12,1b3	67	20.5

CRUZ, JOSE Jose Javier B4.19.1974 Arroyo, PR BB/TR/6-0/200(190-210) [SeaA95 1/3] d5.31 f-Jose Col Rice

YEAR	TM LG	G	AB	R	H	2B	3B	HR	RBI	BB-IB	HP	SO	AVG	OBP	SLG	AOPS	ABR	SB-CS	FA	FR	RNG	THR	GAMES AT POSITION	DL	BFW
1997	Sea A	49	183	28	49	12	1	12	34	13-0	0	45	.268	.315	.541	119	4	1-0	.966	-3	99	35	O49L		0.0
	Tor A	55	212	31	49	7	0	14	34	28-2	0	72	.231	.316	.462	101	0	6-2	.981	-2	89	89	O55(51/4/0)		-0.4
	Year	104	395	59	98	19	1	26	68	41-2	0	117	.248	.315	.499	109	3	7-2	.974	-5	94	64	O104(100/4/0)		-0.4
1998	Tor A	105	352	55	89	14	3	11	42	57-3	0	99	.253	.354	.403	97	-1	11-4	.984	-1	97	113	O105(6/103/0)	15	0.9
1999	Tor A	106	349	63	84	19	3	14	45	64-5	0	91	.241	.358	.433	99	0	14-4	.990	7	112	129	O106(9/97/0)		-0.8
2000	Tor A	162	603	91	146	32	5	31	76	71-3	2	129	.242	.323	.466	94	-8	15-5	.993	-4	96	109	O162C	15	-0.4
2001	Tor A	146	577	92	158	38	4	34	88	45-4	1	138	.274	.326	.530	118	13	32-5	.990	-19	79	60	O143(14/133/0)	36	-0.4
2002	Tor A	124	466	64	114	26	5	18	70	51-1	0	106	.245	.317	.438	95	-4	7-1	.992	3	101	127	O119(56/21/47),D2		1.0
2003	†SF N	158	539	90	135	26	2	20	68	102-6	0	121	.250	.366	.414	103	5	5-8	.994	15	111	176	O158(0/3/157)		-0.8
2004	TB A	153	545	76	132	25	8	21	78	76-8	2	117	.242	.333	.433	101	1	11-6	.970	-1	100	97	O152(0/1/151)		-0.2
2005	Bos A	4	12	0	3	1	0	0	1	0-0	0	4	.250	.308	.333	67	-1	0-0	1.000	-1	28	0	O4R	29	-0.7
	Ari N	64	202	23	43	9	0	12	28	42-2	0	54	.213	.347	.436	100	1	0-1	.980	-7	77	70	O58(3/53/6)		0.3
	LA N	47	156	23	47	14	2	6	22	23-1	0	43	.301	.391	.532	139	10	0-1	.954	3	124	124	O45(1/0/45)		1.0
	Year	111	358	46	90	23	2	18	50	65-3	0	97	.251	.366	.478	116	10	0-2	.967	-4	98	94	O103(4/53/51)		0.3
Total	9	1173	4196	636	1049	223	32	193	585	573-35	5	1019	.250	.338	.456	103	20	102-37	.985	-11	98	109	O1156(189/577/410),D2	95	-0.4

CRUZ, JULIO Julio Luis B12.2.1954 Brooklyn NY BB/TR/5-9/165(159-180) d7.4 Col San Bernardino Valley (CA) JC

YEAR	TM LG	G	AB	R	H	2B	3B	HR	RBI	BB-IB	HP	SO	AVG	OBP	SLG	AOPS	ABR	SB-CS	FA	FR	RNG	THR	GAMES AT POSITION	DL	BFW
1977	Sea A	60	199	25	51	3	1	1	7	24-1	0	29	.256	.336	.296	75	-6	15-6	.983	1	103	79	2b54/D		-0.1
1978	Sea A	147	550	77	129	14	1	1	25	69-0	1	66	.235	.319	.269	68	-22	59-10	.987	13	111	104	2b141,S5/D	59	2.7
1979	Sea A	107	414	70	112	16	2	1	29	62-0	0	61	.271	.363	.326	86	-5	49-9	.979	20	112	107	2b107	15	-0.1
1980	Sea A	119	422	66	88	9	3	2	16	59-0	1	49	.209	.306	.258	56	-25	45-7	.983	10	106	102	2b115,D3		1.9
1981	Sea A	94	352	57	90	12	3	2	24	39-0	3	40	.256	.332	.324	86	-5	43-8	.982	12	107	108	2b92/S		0.2
1982	Sea A	154	549	83	133	22	5	8	49	57-1	3	71	.242	.316	.344	79	-16	46-13	.984	3	98	97	2b151,S2/3D		1.1
1983	Sea A	61	181	24	46	10	1	2	12	20-1	2	22	.254	.332	.354	86	-3	33-6	.984	6	99	96	2b97		0.7
	†Chi A	99	334	47	84	9	4	1	40	29-0	2	44	.251	.311	.311	70	-14	24-6	.983	12	107	113	2b97/D		1.8
	Year	160	515	71	130	19	5	3	52	49-1	4	66	.252	.318	.326	76	-16	57-12	.983	19	104	107	2b157/D		1.2
1984	Chi A	143	415	42	92	14	4	5	43	45-0	0	58	.222	.295	.311	65	-19	14-6	.976	24	114	113	2b141		-0.4
1985	Chi A	91	234	28	46	2	3	0	15	32-0	2	40	.197	.297	.231	45	-17	8-5	.982	9	101	116	2b87,D2	45	-1.3
1986	Chi A	81	209	38	45	2	0	0	19	42-0	1	28	.215	.343	.225	57	-11	7-2	.985	-8	96	97	2b78,D3	136	-1.3
Total	10	1156	3859	557	916	113	27	23	279	478-3	14	508	.237	.321	.299	71	-143	343-78	.983	103	106	104	2b1123,D13,S8/3	136	6.8

CRUZ, IVAN Luis Ivan B5.3.1968 Fajardo, PR BL/TL/6-3/210(210-225) [DetA89 28/733] d7.18 Col Jacksonville

YEAR	TM LG	G	AB	R	H	2B	3B	HR	RBI	BB-IB	HP	SO	AVG	OBP	SLG	AOPS	ABR	SB-CS	FA	FR	RNG	THR	GAMES AT POSITION	DL	BFW
1997	NY A	11	20	5	5	1	0	0	3	2-0	0	4	.250	.318	.300	63	-1	0-0	1.000	-0	0	0	1b3/OLD	92	-0.1
1999	Pit N	5	10	3	4	0	1	0	2	0-0	0	2	.400	.400	.700	170	1	0-0	1.000	0	149	356	/1OR		0.1
2000	Pit N	8	11	0	1	0	0	0	0	0-0	0	8	.091	.091	.091	-54	-3	0-0	1.000	-0	0	0	/1		-0.3
2002	StL N	17	14	2	5	0	0	1	3	1-0	0	3	.357	.400	.571	155	1	0-0	1.000	0	95	0	1b7		0.1
Total	4	41	55	5	15	1	0	2	8	3-0	0	17	.273	.310	.400	83	-2	0-0	1.000	-0	67	80	1b12,D4,O2(1/0/1)	92	-0.2

CRUZ, NELSON Nelson Ramon B7.1.1980 Monte Cristi, D.R. BR/TR/6-3/175 d9.17

YEAR	TM LG	G	AB	R	H	2B	3B	HR	RBI	BB-IB	HP	SO	AVG	OBP	SLG	AOPS	ABR	SB-CS	FA	FR	RNG	THR	GAMES AT POSITION	DL	BFW
2005	Mil N	8	5	1	1	1	0	0	0	2-0	0	2	.200	.429	.400	119	0	0-0	1.000	0	104	0	O8(2/0/6)		0.0

CRUZ, TODD Todd Ruben B11.23.1955 Highland Park MI BR/TR/6-0/175(170-180) [PhiN73 2/26] d9.4 [DL 1981 Chi A 56]

YEAR	TM LG	G	AB	R	H	2B	3B	HR	RBI	BB-IB	HP	SO	AVG	OBP	SLG	AOPS	ABR	SB-CS	FA	FR	RNG	THR	GAMES AT POSITION	DL	BFW
1978	Phi N	3	4	0	2	0	0	0	2	0-0	0	1	.500	.500	.500	177	0	0-1	1.000	1	183	0	S2		0.1
1979	KC A	55	118	9	24	7	0	2	15	3-0	1	19	.203	.224	.314	44	-10	0-1	.974	-6	95	58	S48,3b9		-1.2
1980	Cal A	18	40	5	11	3	0	1	5	5-1	0	8	.275	.356	.425	115	1	0-0	.860	-5	90	109	S12,3b4/2OL		-0.3
	Chi A	90	293	23	68	11	1	2	18	9-0	2	54	.232	.259	.297	52	-20	2-1	.956	4	105	86	S90		-0.7
	Year	108	333	28	79	14	1	3	23	14-1	2	62	.237	.271	.312	60	-19	2-1	.948	-1	104	88	S102,3b4/2OL		-1.0
1982	Sea A	136	492	44	113	20	2	16	57	12-1	0	95	.230	.246	.376	66	-25	2-10	.964	16	103	122	S136	15	0.9
1983	Sea A	65	216	21	41	4	1	7	21	7-2	2	56	.190	.221	.324	46	-17	1-3	.964	5	108	134	3b79,2b2		-1.3
	†Bal A	81	221	16	46	9	1	3	27	15-0	1	52	.208	.259	.299	54	-14	3-4	.942	3	108	134	3b79,S63,2b2		-0.4
	Year	146	437	37	87	13	3	10	48	22-2	3	108	.199	.241	.311	51	-31	4-7	.955	-8	108	134	3b89/PD		-0.7
1984	Bal A	96	142	15	31	4	0	3	9	8-0	1	33	.218	.263	.310	59	-8	1-4	.960	37	106	103	3b351,3b181,2b3/DPOL	71	-3.0
Total	6	544	1526	133	336	58	6	34	154	59-4	7	317	.220	.251	.333	58	-93	9-24	.960	37	106	103	S351,3b181,2b3/DPOL	71	-3.0

CUBBAGE, MIKE Michael Lee B7.21.1950 Charlottesville VA BL/TR/6-0/180* [TexA71 D2/25] d4.7 M1/C14 Col Virginia

YEAR	TM LG	G	AB	R	H	2B	3B	HR	RBI	BB-IB	HP	SO	AVG	OBP	SLG	AOPS	ABR	SB-CS	FA	FR	RNG	THR	GAMES AT POSITION	DL	BFW
1974	Tex A	9	15	0	0	0	0	0	0	0-0	0	4	.000	.000	.000	-99	-4	0-0	1.000	2	129	0	3b3,2b2		-0.2
1975	Tex A	58	143	12	32	6	0	4	21	18-2	0	14	.224	.305	.350	87	-2	0-0	.962	1	112	105	2b37,3b3,D2		0.1
1976	Tex A	14	32	2	7	0	0	0	0	7-0	0	7	.219	.359	.219	70	-1	0-0	1.000	-1	75	118	2b5/3D		-0.2
	Min A	104	342	40	89	19	5	3	49	42-3	3	37	.260	.344	.371	108	5	1-1	.940	7	112	129	3b99,2b2,D2		1.2
	Year	118	374	42	96	19	5	3	49	49-3	3	44	.257	.346	.358	105	4	1-1	.940	6	112	129	3b100,D8,2b7		1.0
1977	Min A	129	417	60	110	16	5	9	55	37-6	0	49	.264	.321	.391	95	-4	1-4	.952	-0	118	133	3b126/D		0.7
1978	Min A	125	394	40	111	12	7	7	57	40-3	1	44	.282	.348	.401	108	4	3-1	.971	7	113	122	3b115,2b5		1.0
1979	Min A	94	243	26	67	10	1	2	23	39-2	0	26	.276	.371	.350	93	-1	1-1	.928	-7	89	95	3b63,D21/12	18	-1.1
1980	Min A	103	285	29	70	9	0	8	42	23-4	1	37	.246	.301	.361	76	-10	0-1	.996	8	124	108	1b72,3b32/2D	15	-0.6
1981	NY N	67	80	9	17	2	1	4	9	9-1	0	15	.213	.289	.325	75	-3	0-0	.963	0	112	0	3b12		-0.3
Total	8	703	1951	218	503	74	20	34	251	215-21	5	233	.258	.330	.369	94	-16	6-15	.952	31	111	121	3b454,1b73,2b53,D33	33	0.7

CUCCINELLO, AL Alfred Edward B8.26.1914 Long Island City NY D3.29.2004 Malverne NY BR/TR/5-10/165 d5.17 b-Tony

YEAR	TM LG	G	AB	R	H	2B	3B	HR	RBI	BB-IB	HP	SO	AVG	OBP	SLG	AOPS	ABR	SB-CS	FA	FR	RNG	THR	GAMES AT POSITION	DL	BFW
1935	NY N	54	165	27	41	7	1	4	20	1	2	20	.248	.262	.376	70	-1	0	.951	1	102	119	2b48,3b2		-0.4

CUCCINELLO, TONY Anthony Francis "Cooch","Chick" B11.8.1907 Long Island City NY D9.21.1995 Tampa FL BR/TR/5-7/160 d4.15 C21 b-Al

YEAR	TM LG	G	AB	R	H	2B	3B	HR	RBI	BB-IB	HP	SO	AVG	OBP	SLG	AOPS	ABR	SB-CS	FA	FR	RNG	THR	GAMES AT POSITION	DL	BFW
1930	Cin N	125	443	64	138	22	5	10	78	47	2	44	.312	.380	.451	105	5	5	.920	-2	96	82	3b109,2b15,S4		0.0
1931	Cin N	154	575	67	181	39	11	2	93	54	0	23	.315	.374	.431	123	19	1	.969	7	103	126	2b154		3.5
1932	Bro N	154	597	76	168	32	6	12	77	46	4	47	.281	.337	.415	103	3	5	.973	21	109	118	2b154		3.2
1933	Bro N★	134	485	58	122	31	4	9	65	44	2	40	.252	.316	.388	105	3	4	.977	-17	88	87	2b120,3b14		-0.7
1934	Bro N	140	528	59	138	32	2	14	94	49	1	45	.261	.325	.409	100	4	0	.974	9	107	90	2b101,3b43		1.6
1935	Bro N	102	360	49	105	20	3	8	53	40	2	35	.292	.366	.431	116	9	3	.977	8	100	147	2b64,3b36		2.1
1936	Bos N	150	565	68	174	26	3	7	86	58	2	49	.308	.374	.402	116	15	1	.971	18	110	141	2b150		4.0
1937	Bos N	152	575	77	156	36	4	11	80	61	2	49	.271	.341	.405	112	10	2	.967	-13	104	110	2b154		0.7

YEAR	TM LG	G	AB	R	H	2B	3B	HR	RBI	BB-IB	HP	SO	AVG	OBP	SLG	AOPS	ABR	SB-CS	FA	FR	RNG	THR	GAMES AT POSITION	DL	BFW
1938	Bos N☆	147	555	62	147	25	2	9	76	52	3	32	.265	.331	.366	102	1	4	.974	-30	94	92	2b147		-1.9
1939	Bos N	81	310	42	95	17	1	2	40	26	0	26	.306	.360	.387	109	4	5	.970	-5	97	121	2b80		0.5
1940	Bos N	34	126	14	34	9	0	0	19	8	1	9	.270	.319	.341	87	-2	1	.978	2	110	164	3b33		0.1
	NY N	88	307	26	64	9	2	5	36	16	0	42	.208	.248	.300	50	-22	1	.987	7	105	69	2b47,3b37		0.1
	Year	122	433	40	98	18	2	5	55	24	1	51	.226	.269	.312	60	-25	2	.971	9	108	144	3b70,2b47		-1.2
1942	Bos N	40	104	8	21	3	0	1	8	9	0	11	.202	.265	.260	55	-6	0	.907	-0	90	188	3b20,2b14		-1.1
1943	Bos N	13	19	0	0	0	0	0	2	3	0	1	.000	.136	.000	-60	-4	0	.929	0	118	346	3b4,2b2/S		-0.6
	Chi A	34	103	5	28	5	0	2	11	13	0	13	.272	.353	.379	114	2	3-1	.965	-1	92	100	3b30,2b6		-0.4
1944	Chi A	38	130	5	34	3	0	0	17	8	0	16	.262	.304	.285	70	-5	0-0	.959	-1	98	97	3b30,2b6		0.2
1945	Chi A★	118	402	50	124	25	3	2	49	45	1	19	.308	.379	.400	130	17	6-2	.936	-6	101	109	3b112		-0.7
Total	15	1704	6184	730	1729	334	46	94	884	579	18	497	.280	.343	.394	105	49	42-3	.973	-14	102	112	2b1205,3b468,S5		11.7

CUDDYER, MICHAEL   Michael Brent B3.27.1979 Norfolk VA   BR/TR/6-2/202(202-220)   [MinA97 1/9]   d9.23   OF(8/0/70)

YEAR	TM LG	G	AB	R	H	2B	3B	HR	RBI	BB-IB	HP	SO	AVG	OBP	SLG	AOPS	ABR	SB-CS	FA	FR	RNG	THR	GAMES AT POSITION	DL	BFW
2001	Min A	8	18	1	4	2	0	0	1	2-0	0	6	.222	.300	.333	63	-1	1-0	.975	-1	68	111	1b5,3b2/D		-0.2
2002	†Min A	41	112	12	29	7	0	4	13	8-0	1	30	.259	.311	.429	92	-1	2-0	.980	2	125	85	O25R,3b10,1b6,D3		0.0
2003	†Min A	35	102	14	25	1	3	4	8	12-0	0	19	.245	.325	.431	94	-1	1-1	1.000	-5	73	107	O18(1/0/17),3b7,1b5/2D		-0.7
2004	Min A	115	339	49	89	22	1	12	45	37-2	3	74	.263	.339	.440	98	0	5-5	.982	-11	107	75	2b48,3b43,O15(7/0/8),1b10,D5		-1.0
2005	Min A	126	422	55	111	25	3	12	42	41-5	3	93	.263	.330	.422	96	-2	4-0	.942	-4	104	95	3b95,O20R,2b11,1b8	17	-0.7
Total	5	325	993	131	258	57	7	32	109	100-7	7	222	.260	.330	.428	96	-5	12-10	.941	-18	92	97	3b157,O78R,2b60,1b34,D11	17	-2.6

CUDWORTH, JIM   James Alaric "Cuddy" B8.22.1858 Fairhaven MA   D12.21.1943 Middleboro MA   BR/TR/6-0/165   d7.27 ▲

YEAR	TM LG	G	AB	R	H	2B	3B	HR	RBI	BB-IB	HP	SO	AVG	OBP	SLG	AOPS	ABR	SB-CS	FA	FR	RNG	THR	GAMES AT POSITION	DL	BFW
1884	KC U	32	116	7	17	3	1	0			7		.147	.161	.190		-17		.963	2	123	132	1b19,O12C,P2		-1.4

CUETO, MANUEL   Manuel "Patato" B2.8.1892 Guanajay, Cuba   D6.29.1942 Regla, Cuba   BR/TR/5-5/157   d6.25

YEAR	TM LG	G	AB	R	H	2B	3B	HR	RBI	BB-IB	HP	SO	AVG	OBP	SLG	AOPS	ABR	SB-CS	FA	FR	RNG	THR	GAMES AT POSITION	DL	BFW
1914	StL F	19	43	2	4	0	0	0	2	5	0	7	.093	.188	.093	-21	-8	0	.941	-2	89	0	3b10,S5,2b2		-1.0
1917	Cin N	56	140	10	28	3	0	1	11	16	1	17	.200	.287	.243	66	-5	4	.963	1	109	70	O38(32/4/3),2b6,C5		-0.6
1918	Cin N	47	108	14	32	5	1	0	14	19	1	6	.296	.406	.361	137	6	4	.929	-7	92	60	O19(12/1/4),2b10,S9,C6		0.0
1919	Cin N	29	88	10	22	2	0	0	4	10	2	4	.250	.340	.273	88	-1	5	.982	3	101	192	O25(7/0/18)/3		0.1
Total	4	151	379	36	86	10	1	1	31	50	4	33	.227	.323	.266	80	-8	13	.964	-4	103	111	O82(51/5/25),2b18,S14,C11,3b11		-1.5

CUFF, JOHN   John Patrick B6.1864 Jersey City NJ   D12.5.1916 Hoboken NJ   d9.11

YEAR	TM LG	G	AB	R	H	2B	3B	HR	RBI	BB-IB	HP	SO	AVG	OBP	SLG	AOPS	ABR	SB-CS	FA	FR	RNG	THR	GAMES AT POSITION	DL	BFW
1884	Bal U	3	11	1	1	0	0	0					.091	.167	.182	5	-2		.920	1			C3		-0.1

CULBERSON, LEON   Delbert Leon "Lee" B8.6.1919 Halls GA   D9.17.1989 Rome GA   BR/TR/5-11/180   d5.16

YEAR	TM LG	G	AB	R	H	2B	3B	HR	RBI	BB-IB	HP	SO	AVG	OBP	SLG	AOPS	ABR	SB-CS	FA	FR	RNG	THR	GAMES AT POSITION	DL	BFW
1943	Bos A	81	312	36	85	16	6	3	34	31	0	35	.272	.338	.391	111	4	14-0	.978	2	98	150	O79(28/51/0)		0.6
1944	Bos A	75	282	41	67	11	5	2	21	20	1	20	.238	.288	.333	78	-9	6-4	.979	-1	99	94	O72C		-1.2
1945	Bos A	97	331	26	91	21	6	6	45	20	0	37	.275	.316	.429	113	4	4-3	.967	3	96	190	O91(1/89/1)		0.4
1946	†Bos A	59	179	34	56	10	1	3	18	16	0	19	.313	.369	.430	116	4	3-2	.967	-3	95	31	O49(6/18/26),3b4		-0.1
1947	Bos A	47	84	10	20	1	0	0	11	12	3	10	.238	.354	.250	65	-3	1-1	.974	-1	92	162	O25(5/4/16),3b4		-0.5
1948	Was A	12	29	1	5	0	0	0	2	8	0	5	.172	.351	.172	43	-2	0-0	1.000	-1	74	162	O11C		-0.3
Total	6	371	1217	148	324	59	18	14	131	107	3	126	.266	.327	.379	100	-2	28-10	.974	0	96	134	O327(40/245/43),3b8		-1.1

CULLEN, JOHN   John Joseph B7.9.1854 New Orleans LA   D2.11.1921 Ukiah CA   5-10.5/171   d8.18

YEAR	TM LG	G	AB	R	H	2B	3B	HR	RBI	BB-IB	HP	SO	AVG	OBP	SLG	AOPS	ABR	SB-CS	FA	FR	RNG	THR	GAMES AT POSITION	DL	BFW
1884	Wil U	9	31	2	6	0	0	0					.194	.219	.194	25	-4		.750	-2	63	0	O6(4/0/2),S3		-0.5

CULLEN, TIM   Timothy Leo B2.16.1942 San Francisco CA   BR/TR/6-1/185*   d8.8   Col Santa Clara

YEAR	TM LG	G	AB	R	H	2B	3B	HR	RBI	BB-IB	HP	SO	AVG	OBP	SLG	AOPS	ABR	SB-CS	FA	FR	RNG	THR	GAMES AT POSITION	DL	BFW
1966	Was A	18	34	4	9	0	0	0	2-0	0	8	.235	.278	.265	57	-2	0-0	.889	-1	71	99	3b8,2b5		-0.3
1967	Was A	124	402	35	95	7	0	2	31	40-2	1	47	.236	.306	.269	74	-12	4-5	.951	15	121	114	S69,2b46,3b15/OR		1.1
1968	Chi A	72	155	16	31	7	0	2	13	15-5	1	23	.200	.275	.284	69	-6	0-0	.966	-2	109	113	2b71		-0.4
	Was A	47	114	8	31	4	2	1	16	7-1	2	12	.272	.323	.368	114	2	0-0	.968	-4	93	83	S33,2b16,3b3		0.0
	Year	119	269	24	62	11	2	3	29	22-6	3	35	.230	.295	.320	87	-4	0-0	.965	-7	109	107	2b87,S33,3b3		-0.4
1969	Was A	119	249	22	52	7	0	1	15	14-1	2	27	.209	.253	.249	44	-19	1-1	.981	4	103	102	2b105,S9/3		-1.1
1970	Was A	123	262	22	56	10	2	1	18	31-6	3	38	.214	.301	.279	65	-12	3-2	.994	12	111	119	2b112,S6		0.6
1971	Was A	125	403	34	77	13	4	2	26	33-4	0	47	.191	.252	.258	47	-29	2-0	.997	15	113	99	2b78,S62		-0.4
1972	†Oak A	72	142	10	37	8	1	0	16	5-0	0	17	.261	.284	.331	87	-3	0-1	.952	-4	100	93	2b65,3b4/S		-0.4
Total	7	700	1761	155	387	57	9	9	134	147-19	9	219	.220	.282	.278	65	-81	10-9	.979	35	108	106	2b498,S180,3b31/OR		-0.9

CULLENBINE, ROY   Roy Joseph B10.18.1913 Nashville TN   D5.28.1991 Mt.Clemens MI   BB/TR/6-1/190   d4.19

YEAR	TM LG	G	AB	R	H	2B	3B	HR	RBI	BB-IB	HP	SO	AVG	OBP	SLG	AOPS	ABR	SB-CS	FA	FR	RNG	THR	GAMES AT POSITION	DL	BFW
1938	Det A	25	67	12	19	1	3	0	9	12	0	9	.284	.392	.388	91	-1	2-0	1.000	0	104	88	O17L		-0.1
1939	Det A	75	179	31	43	9	2	4	23	34	0	29	.240	.362	.413	91	-2	0-1	.902	-2	96	70	O46(24/4/19),1b2		-0.7
1940	Bro N	22	61	8	11	1	0	1	9	23	0	11	.180	.405	.246	78	0	2	1.000	1	93	206	O19R		-0.1
	StL A	86	257	42	59	11	2	7	31	50	2	34	.230	.359	.370	87	-3	0-1	.975	-1	94	105	O57(11/0/49),1b6		-0.8
1941	StL A★	149	501	82	159	29	9	9	98	121	2	43	.317	.452	.465	138	36	6-4	.964	-1	94	113	O120(108/7/5),3b28,1b22		2.6
1942	StL A	38	109	15	21	7	1	2	14	30	1	20	.193	.367	.330	95	1	0-1	.930	1	81	228	O27L,1b5		-0.1
	Was A	64	241	30	69	19	0	2	35	44	0	18	.286	.396	.390	123	10	1-2	.966	6	108	222	O35L,3b28		1.5
	†NY A	21	77	16	28	7	0	2	17	18	0	2	.364	.484	.532	190	11	0-1	.980	1	111	128	O19R/1		1.0
	Year	123	427	61	118	33	1	6	66	92	0	40	.276	.405	.400	127	22	1-4	.959	8	100	199	O81(62/0/19),3b28,1b6		2.4
1943	Cle A	138	488	66	141	24	4	8	56	96	1	58	.289	.407	.404	146	34	3-4	.981	3	96	157	O121R,1b13		2.9
1944	Cle A☆	154	571	98	162	34	5	16	80	87	2	46	.284	.380	.445	141	33	4-4	.967	-3	89	142	O151(0/1/150)		0.0
1945	Cle A	8	13	1	1	1	0	0	0	11	0	0	.077	.500	.154	97	2	0-0	1.000	-1	105	0	O4R,3b3		0.0
	†Det A	146	523	80	145	27	5	18	93	102	3	36	.277	.398	.451	137	29	2-0	.980	9	105	152	O146(2/0/145)		3.1
	Year	154	536	83	146	28	5	18	93	113	3	36	.272	.402	.444	137	31	2-0	.980	8	105	150	O150(2/0/149),3b3		3.1
1946	Det A	113	328	63	110	21	0	15	56	88	1	39	.335	.477	.537	172	39	3-0	.965	2	86	191	O81(12/0/69),1b21		3.9
1947	Det A	142	464	82	104	18	1	24	78	137	1	51	.224	.401	.422	125	23	3-2	.989	18	144	72	1b138		3.6
Total	10	1181	3879	627	1072	209	32	110	599	853	11	399	.276	.408	.432	132	212	26-20	.969	32	96	146	O843(236/12/600),1b208,3b31		18.8

CULLER, DICK   Richard Broadus B1.15.1915 High Point NC   D6.16.1964 Chapel Hill NC   BR/TR/5-9.5/155   d9.19   Col High Point

YEAR	TM LG	G	AB	R	H	2B	3B	HR	RBI	BB-IB	HP	SO	AVG	OBP	SLG	AOPS	ABR	SB-CS	FA	FR	RNG	THR	GAMES AT POSITION	DL	BFW
1936	Phi A	9	38	3	9	0	0	0	1	1	0	3	.237	.256	.237	23	-5	0-0	.946	-2	71	86	2b7,S2		-0.6
1943	Chi A	53	148	9	32	5	1	0	11	16	1	11	.216	.297	.264	65	-6	4-5	.950	7	98	188	3b26,2b19,S3		0.1
1944	Bos N	8	28	2	2	0	0	0	0	4	0	2	.071	.188	.071	-24	-5	0	.904	1	120	117	S8		-0.3
1945	Bos N	136	527	87	138	12	1	2	30	50	2	35	.262	.328	.300	75	-17	7	.954	-9	99	103	S126,3b6		-1.7
1946	Bos N	134	482	70	123	15	3	0	33	62	2	18	.255	.342	.299	82	-10	7	.948	-4	95	92	S132		-0.6
1947	Bos N	77	214	20	53	5	1	0	19	19	0	15	.248	.309	.280	59	-13	1	.967	2	109	84	S77		-0.7
1948	Chi N	48	89	4	15	2	0	0	5	13	0	3	.169	.275	.191	29	-9	0	.968	10	120	99	S43,2b2		0.3
1949	NY N	7	1	0	0	0	0	0	0	0	0	0	.000	.500	.000	45	0	0	.889	1	141	90	S7		0.1
Total	8	472	1527	195	372	39	6	2	99	166	5	87	.244	.320	.281	68	-65	19-5	.954	4	102	96	S398,3b32,2b28		-3.4

CULLOP, NICK   Henry Nicholas "Tomato Face" (b Heinrich Nicholas Kolop) B10.16.1900 St.Louis MO   D12.8.1978 Westerville OH   BR/TR/6-0/200   d4.14

YEAR	TM LG	G	AB	R	H	2B	3B	HR	RBI	BB-IB	HP	SO	AVG	OBP	SLG	AOPS	ABR	SB-CS	FA	FR	RNG	THR	GAMES AT POSITION	DL	BFW
1926	NY A	2	2	0	1	0	0	0	0	0	0	1	.500	.500	.500	164	0	0-0					/H		0.0
1927	Was A	15	23	2	5	2	0	0	1	1	0	6	.217	.250	.304	44	-2	0-0	1.000	-0	102	0	O5(2/0/3)/1		-0.2
	Cle A	32	68	9	16	2	3	1	8	9	1	19	.235	.333	.397	88	-2	0-4	.982	2	110	199	O20(0/13/7)/P		-0.2
	Year	47	91	11	21	4	3	1	9	10	1	25	.231	.314	.374	78	-3	0-4	.984	2	109	172	O25(2/13/10)/1P		-0.3
1929	Bro N	13	41	7	8	2	2	1	5	8	0	9	.195	.327	.415	84	-1	0	1.000	1	92	222	O11(5/6/2)/1		-0.1
1930	Cin N	7	22	2	4	0	0	1	5	1	0	9	.182	.217	.318	29	-1	0	1.000	1	70	651	O5C		-0.1
1931	Cin N	104	334	29	88	23	7	8	48	21	1	86	.263	.309	.446	107	1	1	.968	1	93	O83L		-0.2
Total	5	173	490	49	122	29	12	11	67	40	2	128	.249	.308	.424	96	-7	1-4	.975	4	101	153	O124(90/24/12),1b2/P		-0.8

CULMER, WIL   Wilfred Hillard B11.11.1957 Nassau, Bahamas   D10.14.2003 Nassau, Bahamas   BR/TR/6-4/210   d4.12   Col Chipola (FL) JC

YEAR	TM LG	G	AB	R	H	2B	3B	HR	RBI	BB-IB	HP	SO	AVG	OBP	SLG	AOPS	ABR	SB-CS	FA	FR	RNG	THR	GAMES AT POSITION	DL	BFW
1983	Cle A	19	2	0	0	0	0	0	0	4	0	0	.105	.100	.105	-40	-4	0-1	1.000	-1	32	0	O4R,D2		-0.5

CULP, BENNY   Benjamin Baldy B1.19.1914 Philadelphia PA   D10.23.2000 Philadelphia PA   BR/TR/5-9/175   d9.17   Mil 1944-45 C2

YEAR	TM LG	G	AB	R	H	2B	3B	HR	RBI	BB-IB	HP	SO	AVG	OBP	SLG	AOPS	ABR	SB-CS	FA	FR	RNG	THR	GAMES AT POSITION	DL	BFW
1942	Phi N	1	0	0	0	0	0	0	0	0	0						-0		.500	-0	0	0	/C		0.0
1943	Phi N	10	24	4	5	1	0	0	2	3	0	3	.208	.296	.250	61	-1	0	.958	-1	103	62	C10		-0.2
1944	Phi N	4	2	1	0	0	0	0	0	0	0	0	.000	.000	.000	-99	-0	0	1.000	-0	0	0	/C		-0.1
Total	3	15	26	5	5	1	0	0	2	3	0	6	.192	.276	.231	49	-2	0	.926	-2	95	57	C12		-0.3

YEAR	TM LG	G	AB	R	H	2B	3B	HR	RBI	BB-IB	HP	SO	AVG	OBP	SLG	AOPS	ABR	SB-CS	FA	FR	RNG	THR	GAMES AT POSITION	DL	BFW

CUMMINGS, JACK John William B4.1.1904 Pittsburgh PA D10.5.1962 W.Mifflin PA BR/TR/6-0/195 d9.11
1926	NY N	7	16	3	5	3	0	0	4	4	0	2	.313	.450	.500	157	2	0	.958	0	87	149	C6		0.2
1927	NY N	43	80	8	29	6	1	2	14	5	0	10	.363	.407	.538	151	6	0	.974	-3	113	77	C34		0.4
1928	NY N	33	27	4	9	2	0	2	9	3	0	4	.333	.400	.630	165	2	0	.833	-0	0	0	C4		0.2
1929	NY N	3	3	0	1	0	0	0	0	0	0	0	.333	.333	.333	66	0	0	1.000	-0	0	0	/C		0.0
	Bos N	3	6	0	1	0	0	0	1	0	0	2	.167	.167	.167	-18	-1	0	.667	-1	85	0	C3		-0.2
	Year	6	9	0	2	0	0	0	1	0	0	2	.222	.222	.222	11	-1	0	.714	-1	74	0	C4		-0.2
Total	4	89	132	15	45	11	1	4	28	12	1	18	.341	.400	.530	145	9	0	.947	-4	101	84	C48		0.6

CUMMINGS, MIDRE Midre Almeric B10.14.1971 St.Croix, V.I. BL/TR/6-0/195(190-225) [MinA90 1/29] d9.10
1993	Pit N	13	36	5	4	1	0	0	3	4-0	0	9	.111	.195	.139	-7	-6	0-0	1.000	-1	97	0	O11(5/5/1)		-0.6
1994	Pit N	24	86	11	21	4	0	1	12	4-0	1	18	.244	.283	.326	58	-5	0-0	.962	-0	104	67	O24(18/5/4)		-0.6
1995	Pit N	59	152	13	37	7	1	2	15	13-3	0	30	.243	.303	.342	68	-7	1-0	.988	2	110	98	O41(8/20/14)		-0.7
1996	Pit N	24	85	11	19	3	1	3	7	7-0	0	16	.224	.221	.388	55	-6	0-0	.980	-0	111	0	O21(0/11/10)		-0.7
1997	Pit N	52	106	11	20	6	2	3	8	8-0	1	26	.189	.252	.368	59	-7	0-0	1.000	-0	98	71	O25(14/0/11)		0.3
	Phi N	63	208	24	63	16	4	1	23	23-0	0	30	.303	.369	.433	112	4	2-3	.991	-0	106	44	O54(0/53/2)		-0.5
	Year	115	314	35	83	22	6	4	31	31-0	1	56	.264	.330	.411	93	-3	2-3	.993	-1	104	52	O79(14/53/13)		-0.2
1998	†Bos A	67	120	20	34	8	0	5	15	17-0	2	19	.283	.381	.475	118	4	3-3	.941	-1	85	0	D29,O17R	40	0.0
1999	Min A	16	38	1	10	0	0	1	9	3-0	0	7	.263	.310	.342	65	-2	2-0	1.000	-1	75	0	O5(1/0/5),D5		-0.2
2000	Min A	77	181	28	50	10	0	4	22	11-1	3	25	.276	.328	.398	77	-6	0-0	1.000	4	110	226	O40(7/0/33),D15		-0.4
	Bos A	21	25	1	7	0	0	0	2	6-0	0	3	.280	.419	.280	80	0	0-0	1.000	-0	106	0	O4(0/1/3)/D		-0.1
	Year	98	206	29	57	10	0	4	24	17-1	3	28	.277	.341	.383	78	-7	0-0	1.000	3	110	201	O44(7/1/36),D16		-0.1
2001	†Ari N	20	20	1	6	1	0	0	1	0-0	0	4	.300	.286	.350	63	-1	0-0	1.000	0	216	0	O4(3/0/1)		0.1
2004	TB A	22	54	10	15	4	0	2	7	5-0	2	12	.278	.361	.463	115	1	1-0	1.000	-0	78	0	D12,O2L		0.1
2005	Bal A	2	2	0	0	0	0	0	0	0-0	0	1	.000	.000	.000	-99	-1	0-0	—	-0	0	0	/OL		-3.8
Total	11	460	1113	136	286	60	8	22	124	94-4	9	200	.257	.318	.385	80	-32	9-6	.987	-1	105	71	O249(59/95/101),D62	40	-3.8

CUNNINGHAM, JOE Joseph Robert B8.27.1931 Paterson NJ BL/TL/6-1/190* d6.30 C1
1954	StL N	85	310	40	88	11	3	11	50	43	2	40	.284	.375	.445	112	6	1-1	.989	1	107	119	1b85		0.2
1956	StL N	4	3	1	0	0	0	0	0	1	0	1	.000	.250	.000	-25	-1	0-0	1.000	-0	0	0	/1		1.0
1957	StL N	122	261	50	83	15	0	9	52	56-6	5	29	.318	.439	.479	146	22	3-3	1.000	-5	78	73	1b67,O46R		1.0
1958	StL N	131	337	61	105	20	3	12	57	82-3	3	23	.312	.449	.496	144	28	4-4	.997	-4	87	52	1b67,O66(24/0/42)		1.5
1959	StL N★	144	458	65	158	28	6	7	60	88-9	5	47	.345	.453	.478	140	33	2-6	.972	-1	108	64	O121(20/0/109),1b35		2.5
1960	StL N	139	492	68	138	28	3	6	39	59-4	6	59	.280	.363	.386	97	1	1-7	.950	-5	97	63	O86(1/1/85),1b15		-1.2
1961	StL N	113	322	60	92	11	2	7	40	53-3	11	32	.286	.403	.398	104	5	1-0	.964	-8	30	104	O8(1/1/85),1b10		1.3
1962	Chi A	149	526	91	155	32	7	8	70	101-3	7	59	.295	.410	.428	128	27	3-3	.994	-5	87	104	1b143,O5R		1.3
1963	Chi A	67	210	32	60	12	1	1	31	33-2	4	23	.286	.388	.367	116	7	1-0	.996	-6	63	95	1b58	90	-0.2
1964	Chi A	40	108	13	27	7	0	0	10	14-1	3	15	.250	.352	.315	90	-1	0-1	.996	-1	86	123	1b33		-1.2
	Was A	49	126	15	27	4	0	0	7	23-0	2	13	.214	.344	.246	68	-4	0-1	.997	-4	56	97	1b41		-1.1
	Year	89	234	28	54	11	0	0	17	37-1	5	28	.231	.348	.278	78	-5	0-2	.997	-5	70	109	1b74		-1.3
1965	Was A	95	201	29	46	9	1	3	20	46-0	1	27	.229	.375	.328	103	4	0-1	.986	-3	81	110	1b59		0.5
1966	Was A	3	8	0	1	0	0	0	0	0-0	0	1	.125	.125	.125	-28	-1	0-0	1.000	1	264	56	1b3		0.4
Total	12	1141	3362	525	980	177	26	64	436	599-31	49	369	.291	.403	.417	119	126	16-27	.993	-37	84	101	1b607,O440(46/1/403)	90	3.

CUNNINGHAM, RAY Raymond Lee B1.17.1905 Mesquite TX D7.30.2005 Pearland TX BR/TR/5-7.5/150 d9.16
1931	StL N	3	4	0	0	0	0	0	1	0	0	0	.000	.000	.000	-96	-1	0-0	1.000	1	184	0	3b3		0.4
1932	StL N	11	22	4	4	1	0	0	3	0	0	4	.182	.261	.227	37	-2	0-0	1.000	2	92	0	3b8,2b2		0.4
Total	2	14	26	4	4	1	0	0	4	0	0	4	.154	.241	.192	18	-3	0-0	1.000	2	109	0	3b11,2b2		0.8

CUNNINGHAM, BILL William Aloysius B7.30.1895 San Francisco CA D9.26.1953 Colusa CA BR/TR/5-8/155 d7.14 C1 Col St.Marys (CA)
1921	NY N	40	76	10	21	2	1	1	12	3	1	3	.276	.313	.368	79	-2	0-1	1.000	-1	97	49	O20(1/18/1)		-0.
1922	†NY N	85	229	37	75	15	2	2	33	7	1	9	.328	.350	.437	101	0	4-5	.988	-1	96	93	O71(2/68/0)/3		-0.
1923	†NY N	79	203	22	55	7	1	5	27	10	0	9	.271	.305	.389	83	-6	5-2	.992	-1	89	120	O68(10/58/0),2b4		-1.
1924	Bos N	114	437	44	119	15	8	1	40	32	3	27	.272	.326	.350	85	-10	8-5	.970	5	102	141	O109(95/15/0)		-2.
Total	4	318	945	113	270	39	12	9	112	52	5	48	.286	.326	.381	88	-18	17-13	.982	3	97	119	O268(108/159/1),2b4/3		-2.

CUNNINGHAM, BILL William John B6.9.1888 Schenectady NY D2.21.1946 Schenectady NY BR/TR/5-9/170 d9.12
1910	Was A	21	74	3	22	5	1	0	14	12	1		.297	.402	.392	156	6	4	.957	-2	94	105	2b21		0.
1911	Was A	94	331	34	63	10	5	3	37	19	2		.190	.239	.278	45	-26	10	.932	-9	98	59	2b93		-3.
1912	Was A	8	27	5	5	1	0	1	8	3	0		.185	.267	.333	71	-1	2	.962	-2	95	47	2b7/S		-3.
Total	3	123	432	42	90	16	6	4	59	34	3		.208	.271	.301	64	-21	16	.938	-12	97	66	2b121/S		-3.

CURLEY, DOC Walter James B3.12.1874 Upton MA D9.23.1920 Worcester MA BR/TR d9.12 Col Virginia
| 1899 | Chi N | 10 | 37 | 7 | 4 | 0 | 1 | 0 | 2 | 3 | | 3 | .108 | .233 | .162 | 9 | -5 | 0 | .907 | -3 | 95 | 58 | 2b10 | | -0. |

CURREN, PETE Peter B Baltimore MD ?/175 d9.12
| 1876 | Phi N | 3 | 12 | 5 | 4 | 1 | 0 | 0 | 2 | 0 | | | .333 | .333 | .417 | 150 | 1 | | .588 | -2 | | | C2/OR | | -0. |

CURRIN, PERRY Perry Gilmore B9.27.1928 Washington DC BL/TR/6-0/175 d6.29
| 1947 | StL A | 3 | 2 | 0 | 0 | 0 | 0 | 0 | 0 | 1 | 0 | | .000 | .333 | .000 | -3 | 0 | 0-0 | 1.000 | 1 | 115 | 477 | /S | | 0. |

CURRY, TONY George Anthony B12.22.1938 Nassau, Bahamas BL/TL/5-11/185* d4.12
1960	Phi N	95	245	26	64	14	2	6	34	16-2	1	53	.261	.308	.408	94	-2	0-2	.925	-5	90	43	O64(51/3/14)		-1.
1961	Phi N	15	36	3	7	2	0	0	3	1-0	0	8	.194	.216	.250	24	-4	0-0	.833	0	64	367	O8L		-0.
1966	Cle A	19	16	4	2	0	0	0	3	3-0	0	8	.125	.263	.125	16	-2	0-0	—	0			/H		-0.
Total	3	129	297	33	73	16	2	6	40	20-2	1	69	.246	.295	.374	82	-8	0-2	.915	-5	87	79	O72(59/3/14)		-1.

CURRY, JIM James L. B3.10.1893 Camden NJ D8.2.1938 Grenloch NJ BR/TR/5-11/160 d10.2
1909	Phi A	1	4	1	1	0	0	0	0	0		0	.250	.250	.250	57	0	0	1.000	-0	105	0	/2		-0.
1911	NY A	4	11	3	2	0	0	0	0	1		0	.182	.250	.182	20	-1	0	.773	-2	56	78	2b4		-0.
1918	Det A	5	20	1	5	1	0	0	1	1		1	.250	.286	.300	80	-1	0	.952	-2	92	56	2b5		-0.
Total	3	10	35	5	8	1	0	0	1	1		1	.229	.270	.257	56	-2	0	.867	-4	78	32	2b10		-0.

CURTIS, CHAD Chad David B11.6.1968 Marion IN BR/TR/5-10/175* [CalA89 45/1157] d4.8 Col Grand Canyon
1992	Cal A	139	441	59	114	16	2	10	46	51-2	6	71	.259	.341	.372	99	0	43-18	.978	1	90	199	O135(48/35/62)/D		0
1993	Cal A	152	583	94	166	25	3	6	59	70-2	4	89	.285	.361	.369	95	-2	48-24	.980	7	105	155	O151C,2b3		0
1994	Cal A	114	453	67	116	23	4	11	50	37-0	5	69	.256	.317	.397	82	-13	25-11	.988	7	109	116	O114C		-0
1995	Det A	144	586	96	157	29	3	21	67	70-3	1	93	.268	.349	.435	104	3	27-15	.992	-8	93	66	O144C		-0
1996	Det A	104	400	65	105	20	1	10	37	53-0	1	73	.262	.346	.393	87	-7	16-10	.985	1	102	150	O40C		-0
	†LA N	43	104	20	22	5	0	2	9	17-0	0	15	.212	.322	.317	74	-4	2-1	1.000	-0	104	0	O19(3/12/4)		0
1997	Cle A	22	29	8	6	1	0	3	5	7-0	0	10	.207	.361	.552	129	1	0-0	1.000	-0	104	0	O92(53/43/5)	26	0
	†NY A	93	320	51	93	21	1	12	50	36-1	5	49	.291	.362	.475	120	10	12-6	.978	-5	87	117	O111(56/55/9)		0
	Year	115	349	59	99	22	1	15	55	43-1	5	59	.284	.362	.481	120	11	12-6	.980	-5	88	107	O111(56/55/9)		0
1998	†NY A	151	456	79	111	21	1	10	56	75-3	7	80	.243	.355	.360	92	-3	21-5	.984	4	108	99	O148(100/45/9),D2		0
1999	†NY A	96	195	37	51	6	0	5	24	43-0	3	35	.262	.398	.369	100	2	8-4	.990	-4	86	55	O81(72/6/3),D14		0
2000	Tex A	108	335	48	91	25	1	8	48	37-0	1	71	.272	.343	.424	92	-3	3-3	.965	-2	96	91	O80(51/0/30),D16		-0
2001	Tex A	38	115	24	29	3	0	3	10	14-0	1	21	.252	.338	.357	81	-3	7-1	.988	3	120	112	O33(10/16/9),D2	98	0
Total	10	1204	4017	648	1061	195	16	101	461	510-11	40	676	.264	.349	.396	95	-19	212-98	.982	1	99	118	O1141(385/686/122),D35,2b3	124	-1

CURTIS, ERVIN Ervin Duane B12.27.1861 Coldwater MI D2.14.1945 N.Adams MA BL/TL/5-8.5/157 d7.15
1891	Cin N	27	108	11	29	3	1	1	9	11		1	.269	.331	.380	106	0	3	.862	-2	136	134	O27(0/24/3)		-0
	Was AA	29	103	17	26	3	2	0	12	13		2	.252	.347	.320	96	0	2	.797	-1	141	0	O29(0/20/9)		-0
Total	2	56	211	28	55	6	5	1	21	24		3	.261	.339	.351	101	0	5	.829	-3	138	68	O56(0/44/12)		-0

CURTIS, GENE Eugene Holmes "Eude" B5.5.1883 Bethany WV D1.1.1919 Steubenville OH BR/TR/6-3/220 d9.21 Col West Virginia
| 1903 | Pit N | 5 | 19 | 2 | 8 | 1 | 0 | 0 | 3 | 1 | 0 | | .421 | .450 | .474 | 158 | 1 | 0 | .833 | -1 | 129 | 0 | O5L | | 0 |

YEAR	TM LG	G	AB	R	H	2B	3B	HR	RBI	BB-IB	HP	SO	AVG	OBP	SLG	AOPS	ABR	SB-CS	FA	FR	RNG	THR	GAMES AT POSITION	DL	BFW

CURTIS, FRED Frederick Marion B10.30.1880 Beaver Lake MI D4.5.1939 Minneapolis MN BR/TR/6-1/? d7.24

| 1905 | NY A | 2 | 9 | 0 | 2 | 1 | 0 | 0 | 2 | 1 | 0 | | .222 | .300 | .333 | 90 | 0 | 1 | 1.000 | -0 | 72 | 0 | 1b2 | | 0.0 |

CURTIS, HARRY Harry Albert B2.19.1883 Portland ME D8.1.1951 Evanston IL TR/5-10.5/170 d8.28 Col Notre Dame

| 1907 | NY N | 6 | 9 | 2 | 2 | 0 | 0 | 0 | 1 | 2 | 0 | | .222 | .364 | .222 | 81 | 0 | 2 | .909 | -0 | 112 | 107 | C6 | | 0.0 |

CURTRIGHT, GUY Guy Paxton B10.18.1912 Holliday MO D8.23.1997 Sun City Center FL BR/TR/5-11/200 d4.21 Col Truman St.

1943	Chi A	138	488	67	142	20	7	3	48	69	3	60	.291	.382	.379	123	17	13-12	.972	-2	102	66	O128L		0.6
1944	Chi A	72	198	22	50	8	2	2	23	23	0	29	.253	.330	.343	94	-1	4-3	.948	3	98	207	O51(35/0/17)		-0.2
1945	Chi A	98	324	51	91	15	7	4	32	39	0	29	.281	.358	.407	125	10	3-4	.986	1	100	110	O84(26/46/13)		0.7
1946	Chi A	23	55	7	11	2	0	0	5	11	0	14	.200	.333	.236	63	-2	0-1	1.000	1	99	164	O15(2/2/11)		-0.2
Total	4	331	1065	147	294	45	16	9	108	142	3	124	.276	.363	.374	115	24	20-20	.973	2	101	109	O278(191/48/41)		0.9

CUSICK, TONY Andrew Daniel "Andy" B12.1857 Fall River MA D8.6.1929 Chicago IL BR/TR/5-9.5/190 d8.21

1884	Wil U	11	34	0	5	0	0	0		1			.147	.171	.147	-3	-5		.871	0			C6,S3,O3(1/1/1)/23		-0.4
	Phi N	9	29	2	4	0	0	0	1	0		3	.138	.138	.138	-14	-4		.930	2			C9		-0.1
1885	Phi N	39	141	12	25	1	0	0	5	1		24	.177	.183	.184	19	-13		.808	-5			C38/OC		-1.4
1886	Phi N	29	104	10	23	5	1	0	4	3		14	.221	.243	.288	61	-5	1	.891	-3			C25,O3(1/0/2)/1		-0.6
1887	Phi N	7	24	3	7	1	0	0	5	3	1		.292	.393	.333	98	0	0	.643	-4			C4,1b3/2		-0.3
Total	4	95	332	27	64	7	1	0	15	8	1	42	.193	.214	.220	35	-27	1	.844	-10			C82,O7(2/2/3),1b4,S3,2b2/3		-2.8

CUSICK, JACK John Peter B6.12.1928 Weehawken NJ D11.17.1989 Englewood NJ BR/TR/6-0/170* d4.24

1951	Chi N	65	164	16	29	3	2	2	16	17		29	.177	.254	.256	37	-15	2-1	.953	-2	104	78	S56		-1.4
1952	Bos N	49	78	5	13	1	0	0	6	6	0	9	.167	.226	.179	14	-9	0-1	.969	-3	89	31	S28,3b3		-1.1
Total	2	114	242	21	42	4	2	2	22	23	0	38	.174	.245	.231	30	-24	2-2	.958	-4	100	65	S84,3b3		-2.5

CUST, JACK John Joseph B1.16.1979 Flemington NJ BL/TR/6-2/205(200-230) [AriN97 1/30] d9.26

2001	Ari N	3	2	0	1	0	0	0		1-0	0	0	.500	.667	.500	195	0	0-0	—	-0	0	0	/OL		0.0
2002	Col N	35	65	8	11	2	0	1	8	12-0	0	32	.169	.295	.246	43	-5	0-1	.960	-1	92	0	O18L		-0.8
2003	Bal A	27	73	7	19	2	0	4	11	10-0	1	25	.260	.357	.521	128	3	0-0	1.000	0	254	0	D23/OL		0.2
2004	Bal A	1	1	0	0	0	0	0	0	0-0	0	1	.000	.000	.000	-99	0	0-0	—	0			/H		0.0
Total	4	66	141	15	31	9	0	5	19	23-0	1	58	.220	.331	.390	86	-2	0-1	.964	-1	97	0	D23,O20L		-0.6

CUTHBERT, NED Edgar Edward B6.20.1845 Philadelphia PA D2.6.1905 St.Louis MO BR/TR/5-6/140 d5.20 M1/U1

1871	Ath NA	**28**	150	47	37	7	5	3	30	10		2	.247	.294	.420	103	1	16-2	.890	4	93	0	O27L/C		0.5
1872	Ath NA	**47**	260	83	88	10	0	1	47	6		10	.338	.353	.388	127	8	14-4	.858	-3	39	0	O47L		0.6
1873	Phi NA	51	279	78	77	5	3	2	34	2		4	.276	.281	.337	80	-8	14-2	.842	-6	27	76	O51L		-0.7
1874	Chi NA	58	295	65	79	6	1	2	24	5		5	.268	.280	.315	90	-3	8-0	.806	-1	121	66	O55(55/2/0),C4		-0.5
1875	StL NA	68	319	68	78	9	2	0	17	3		9	.245	.252	.285	95	0	18-1	.860	-12	18	0	O67(65/2/0),C3/2		-0.5
1876	StL N	63	283	46	70	10	1	0	25	7		4	.247	.266	.290	90	-4		.843	-7	68	125	O63L		-1.1
1877	Cin N	12	56	6	10	5	0	0	2	1		2	.179	.193	.268	49	-3		.830	4	219	413	O12L		0.1
1882	StL AA	60	233	28	52	16	5	0		17			.223	.276	.335	101	1		.896	-3	90	0	O60L,M		-0.3
1883	StL AA	21	71	3	12	1	0	0	3	4			.169	.213	.183	27	-6		.794	-1	127	0	O20(18/1/1)/1		-0.7
1884	Bal U	44	168	29	34	5	0	0		10			.202	.247	.232	42	-17		.750	-5	104	0	O44C		-2.0
Total 5 NA		252	1303	341	359	37	11	8	152	26		29	.276	.290	.339	98	-2	70-9	.845	-18	56	31	O247(245/4/0),C8/2		-0.1
Total	5	200	811	112	178	37	6	0	30	39		6	.219	.255	.280	73	-27		.833	-11	98	68	O199(153/45/1)/1		-4.0

CUTSHAW, GEORGE George William "Clancy" B7.29.1886 Wilmington IL D8.22.1973 San Diego CA BR/TR/5-9/160 d4.25 Col Notre Dame

1912	Bro N	102	357	41	100	14	9	0	28	31	2	16	.280	.344	.342	91	-4	16	.958	4	108	80	2b91,3b5/S		0.1
1913	Bro N	147	592	72	158	23	13	7	80	39	3	22	.267	.315	.385	97	-5	39-17	.957	17	101	134	2b147		1.8
1914	Bro N	153	583	69	150	22	12	2	78	30	3	32	.257	.297	.346	89	-10	34	.959	28	99	127	2b153		2.1
1915	Bro N	**154**	566	68	139	18	9	0	62	34	4	35	.246	.293	.309	81	-14	28-23	**.971**	14	106	82	2b154		0.1
1916	†Bro N	154	581	58	151	21	4	2	63	25	1	32	.260	.292	.320	85	-11	27-20	.958	6	101	88	2b154		-0.4
1917	Bro N	135	487	42	126	17	7	4	49	21	2	26	.259	.292	.347	93	-5	22	.963	-1	94	71	2b134		-1.6
1918	Pit N	**126**	463	56	132	16	10	3	68	27	1	18	.285	.326	.395	116	7	25	.964	-3	93	119	2b126		0.7
1919	Pit N	**139**	512	49	124	15	8	3	51	30	2	22	.242	.287	.320	79	-14	36	**.980**	-9	89	107	2b139		-2.2
1920	Pit N	131	488	56	123	16	8	0	47	23	1	10	.252	.287	.318	71	-19	17-14	.968	1	97	105	2b129		-1.8
1921	Pit N	98	350	46	119	18	4	0	53	11	1	11	.340	.362	.414	102	5	14-5	.951	-23	85	92	2b84		-1.8
1922	Det A	132	499	57	133	14	8	2	61	20	4	13	.267	.300	.339	68	-25	11-5	.972	5	101	97	2b132		-1.6
1923	Det A	45	143	15	32	1	2	0	13	9	2	5	.224	.279	.259	43	-12	2-1	.988	8	116	86	2b43,3b2		-0.4
Total	12	1516	5621	629	1487	195	89	25	653	300	26	242	.265	.305	.344	86	-111	271-85	.965	37	98	101	2b1486,3b7/S		-5.0

CUYLER, KIKI Hazen Shirley B8.30.1898 Harrisville MI D2.11.1950 Ann Arbor MI BR/TR/5-10.5/180 d9.29 C4 HF1968

1921	Pit N	1	3	0	0	0	0	0	0	0	0	1	.000	.000	.000	-97	-1	0-0	1.000	-0	90	0	/OR		-0.1
1922	Pit N	1	1	0	0	0	0	0	0	0	0	0	—	—	—	0	0	0-0	—	0			/R		0.0
1923	Pit N	11	40	4	10	1	1	0	2	5	1	3	.250	.348	.325	77	-1	2-3	.931	-0	105	88	O11(10/3/0)		-0.3
1924	Pit N	117	466	94	165	27	16	9	85	30	7	62	.354	.402	.539	147	30	32-11	.943	3	98	145	O114(78/4/35)		2.7
1925	†Pit N	**153**	617	**144**	220	43	**26**	18	102	58	**13**	56	.357	.423	.598	148	44	41-13	.967	2	104	97	O153(0/25/129)		3.6
1926	Pit N	**157**	614	**113**	197	31	15	8	92	50	9	66	.321	.380	.459	119	16	**35**	.968	7	106	117	O157(62/79/18)		1.3
1927	Pit N	85	285	60	88	13	7	3	31	37	3	36	.309	.394	.435	114	7	20	.980	0	105	76	O73(12/49/13)		0.3
1928	Chi N	133	499	92	142	25	9	17	79	51	7	61	.285	.359	.473	117	12	37	.982	1	91	140	O127(13/7/108)		0.2
1929	†Chi N	139	509	111	183	29	7	15	102	66	5	56	.360	.438	.532	139	34	**43**	.974	1	98	110	O129(16/8/114)		2.2
1930	Chi N	**156**	642	155	228	50	17	13	134	72	**10**	49	.355	.428	.547	133	37	**37**	.980	6	104	108	O156(29/0/131)		2.6
1931	Chi N	154	613	110	202	37	12	9	88	72	5	54	.330	.404	.473	133	31	13	.970	-9	93	68	O153(0/66/84)		1.5
1932	†Chi N	110	446	58	130	19	9	10	77	29	4	43	.291	.340	.442	109	5	9	.969	-11	87	65	O109(0/49/60)		-1.1
1933	Chi N	70	262	37	83	13	3	5	35	21	4	29	.317	.376	.447	135	12	4	.978	-5	91	39	O69(35/15/19)		0.4
1934	Chi N★	142	559	80	189	**42**	8	6	69	31	4	62	.338	.377	.474	129	23	15	.971	-3	90	151	O142(0/136/6)		1.5
1935	Chi N	45	157	22	42	5	1	4	18	10	5	16	.268	.331	.389	92	-2	3	.981	-1	91	147	O42(0/41/2)		-0.3
	Cin N	62	223	36	56	8	3	2	22	27	2	18	.251	.337	.341	85	-4	5	.985	-4	85	109	O57(5/49/3)		-0.9
	Year	107	380	58	98	13	4	6	40	37	7	34	.258	.335	.361	88	-6	8	.983	-4	88	125	O99(5/90/5)		-1.2
1936	Cin N	144	567	96	185	29	11	7	74	47	2	50	.326	.380	.453	132	25	16	.974	-5	94	87	O140(22/105/14)		1.5
1937	Cin N	117	406	48	110	12	4	0	32	36	2	50	.271	.333	.320	82	-10	10	.973	-5	86	107	O106(41/47/16)		-1.9
1938	Bro N	82	253	45	69	14	3	2	23	23	2	23	.273	.348	.399	107	3	6	.993	3	98	171	O68(8/17/43)		0.3
Total	18	1879	7161	1305	2299	394	157	128	1065	676	85	752	.321	.386	.474	125	261	328-27	.972	-20	96	108	O1807(331/700/796)		13.5

CUYLER, MILT Milton B10.7.1968 Macon GA BB/TR/5-10/185* [DetA86 2/46] d9.6

1990	Det A	19	51	8	13	3	1	0	8	5-0	0	10	.255	.316	.353	87	-1	1-2	.976	0	91	245	O17(0/17/1)		-0.1
1991	Det A	154	475	77	122	15	7	3	33	52-0	5	92	.257	.335	.337	85	-9	41-10	.986	3	107	91	O151(1/150/0)		-0.1
1992	Det A	89	291	39	70	11	1	3	28	10-0	4	62	.241	.275	.316	64	-15	8-5	.983	-4	95	80	O89(0/88/1)		-2.0
1993	Det A	82	249	46	53	11	7	0	19	19-0	3	53	.213	.276	.313	58	-16	13-2	.968	1	110	50	O80C	71	-1.1
1994	Det A	48	116	20	28	3	1	1	11	13-0	1	21	.241	.318	.310	63	-6	5-3	.975	-3	85	47	O45(13/29/8)	56	-0.9
1995	Det A	41	88	15	18	1	4	0	5	8-0	1	16	.205	.271	.307	50	-7	2-1	.929	-1	92	111	O36(34/1/1),D2	60	-0.9
1996	Bos N	50	110	19	22	1	2	2	12	13-0	3	19	.200	.299	.300	54	-9	7-3	.972	2	128	0	O45(0/30/22),D2	109	-0.6
1998	Tex A	7	6	3	3	2	0	1	3	1-0	0	6	.500	.571	1.333	355	2	0-0	1.000	0	106	0	O3C,D3		0.2
Total	8	490	1386	227	329	47	23	10	119	121-0	16	273	.237	.305	.326	71	-61	77-26	.977	-1	103	77	O466(48/398/33),D7	296	-5.5

CYPERT, AL Alfred Boyd "Cy" B8.8.1889 Little Rock AR D1.9.1973 Washington DC BR/TR/5-10.5/150 d6.27 Col Harvard

| 1914 | Cle A | 1 | 1 | 1 | 1 | 0 | 0 | 0 | | 0 | 0 | | 1.000 | .000 | .000 | -96 | 0 | 0 | — | -0 | 0 | 0 | /3 | | 0.0 |

DADE, PAUL Lonnie Paul B12.7.1951 Seattle WA BR/TR/6-0/195* [AnaA70 1/10] d9.12

1975	Cal A	11	30	5	6	4	0	0	1	3-0	0	7	.200	.333	.333	95	0	0-0	1.000	1	145	0	O3(1/0/2)/3D		0.1
1976	Cal A	13	9	2	1	0	0	0	1	3-0	0	3	.111	.333	.111	36	-1	0-0	.750	1	88	1254	O4(3/0/1),2b2/3D		0.1
1977	Cle A	134	461	65	134	15	3	3	45	32-4	2	58	.291	.333	.366	92	-5	16-8	.989	-2	87	156	O99(32/28/46),3b26/2D		-1.0
1978	Cle A	93	307	37	78	12	1	3	29	34-1	2	45	.254	.331	.329	87	-3	12-9	.962	3	109	111	O81(1/7/75),D9		-0.6
1979	Cle A	44	170	22	48	4	1	3	18	12-1	0	22	.282	.326	.371	88	-3	12-6	.962	1	109	151	O37(20/0/17),3b2,D4		-0.3
	SD N	76	283	34	78	19	2	1	19	14-0	2	48	.276	.311	.367	91	-4	13-5	.949	5	115	101	3b70,O4(1/3/0)		0.1

YEAR	TM LG	G	AB	R	H	2B	3B	HR	RBI	BB-IB	HP	SO	AVG	OBP	SLG	AOPS	ABR	SB-CS	FA	FR	RNG	THR	GAMES AT POSITION	DL	BFW
1980	SD N	68	53	17	10	0	0	0	3	12-0	0	10	.189	.338	.189	54	-3	4-5	.846	-1	97	80	3b21,O8(4/3/1)/2	22	-0.5
Total	6	439	1313	186	355	54	7	10	107	113-6	6	193	.270	.328	.345	89	-20	57-33	.970	6	97	150	O236(62/41/142),3b121,D28,2b4	22	-2.1

DAGRES, ANGELO Angelo George "Junior" B8.22.1934 Newburyport MA BL/TL/5-11/175 d9.11 Col Rhode Island

YEAR	TM LG	G	AB	R	H	2B	3B	HR	RBI	BB-IB	HP	SO	AVG	OBP	SLG	AOPS	ABR	SB-CS	FA	FR	RNG	THR	GAMES AT POSITION	DL	BFW
1955	Bal A	8	15	5	4	0	0	0	3	1-0	0	2	.267	.278	.267	61	-1	0-0	.818	-1	100	0	O5(1/0/4)		-0.2

DAHLEN, BILL William Frederick "Bad Bill" B1.5.1870 Nelliston NY D12.5.1950 Brooklyn NY BR/TR/5-9/180 d4.22 M4

YEAR	TM LG	G	AB	R	H	2B	3B	HR	RBI	BB-IB	HP	SO	AVG	OBP	SLG	AOPS	ABR	SB-CS	FA	FR	RNG	THR	GAMES AT POSITION	DL	BFW
1891	Chi N	135	549	114	143	18	13	9	76	67	7	60	.260	.348	.390	115	10	21	.887	4	108	108	3b84,O37(30/0/7),S15		1.4
1892	Chi N	143	581	114	170	23	19	5	58	45	5	56	.293	.349	.423	132	19	60	.909	15	91	113	S72,3b68,O2C/2		3.6
1893	Chi N	116	485	113	146	28	15	5	64	58	5	30	.301	.381	.452	123	16	31	.892	6	101	86	S67,3b55		2.1
1894	Chi N	122	507	150	182	32	14	15	108	76	3	33	.359	.445	.566	135	29	43	.900	26	107	129	S67,3b55		4.5
1895	Chi N	129	516	106	131	19	10	7	62	61	10	51	.254	.344	.370	79	-17	38	.904	35	119	119	S129/OC		1.9
1896	Chi N	125	474	137	167	30	19	9	74	64	8	36	.352	.438	.553	154	38	51	.915	22	107	120	S125		5.5
1897	Chi N	75	276	67	80	18	8	6	40	43	7		.290	.399	.478	126	11	15	.930	24	110	152	S75		3.3
1898	Chi N	142	521	96	151	35	8	1	79	58	23		.290	.385	.393	123	20	27	.921	20	108	138	S142		4.3
1899	Bro N	121	428	87	121	22	7	4	76	67	15		.283	.398	.395	115	13	29	.941	14	100	116	S110,3b11		2.9
1900	†Bro N	133	483	87	125	16	11	1	69	73	7		.259	.364	.344	90	-4	31	.938	21	107	110	S133		2.1
1901	Bro N	131	511	69	136	17	9	4	82	30	5		.266	.313	.358	92	-6	23	.929	14	103	97	S129,2b2		1.1
1902	Bro N	138	527	67	139	25	8	2	74	43	8		.264	.329	.353	110	6	20	.916	-6	98	76	S138		0.6
1903	Bro N	138	474	71	124	17	9	1	64	82	2		.262	.373	.342	107	9	34	.948	19	109	99	S138		3.1
1904	NY N	145	523	70	140	26	2	2	**80**	44	1		.268	.326	.337	100	1	47	.930	25	108	139	S145		3.2
1905	†NY N	148	520	67	126	20	4	7	81	62	12		.242	.337	.337	99	2	37	.948	20	102	114	S147/OL		2.7
1906	NY N	143	471	63	113	18	3	1	49	76	10		.240	.357	.297	102	6	16	.938	2	101	79	S143		1.4
1907	NY N	143	464	40	96	20	1	0	34	51			.207	.291	.254	69	-15	11	.941	6	100	88	S143		-0.4
1908	Bos N	144	524	50	125	23	2	3	48	35	8		.239	.296	.307	94	-3	10	.952	38	120	131	S49,2b6,3b2		4.5
1909	Bos N.	69	197	22	46	6	1	2	16	29			.234	.332	.305	93	-1	4	.908	6	117	99	S49,2b6,3b2		-0.1
1910	Bro N	3	2	0	0	0	0	0	0	0	0	0	.000	.000	.000	-99	-1	0	—	0			/HM		-0.1
1911	Bro N	1	3	0	0	0	0	0	0	0	0	0	.000	.000	.000	-99	-1	0	1.000	1	159	246	/SM		0.0
Total	21	2444	9036	1590	2461	413	163	84	1234	1064	140	269	.272	.358	.382	109	132	548	.927	310	106	111	S2133,3b223,O58(36/11/11),2b19		48.5

DAHLGREN, BABE Ellsworth Tenney B6.15.1912 San Francisco CA D9.4.1996 Arcadia CA BR/TR/6-0/190 d4.16 C1

YEAR	TM LG	G	AB	R	H	2B	3B	HR	RBI	BB-IB	HP	SO	AVG	OBP	SLG	AOPS	ABR	SB-CS	FA	FR	RNG	THR	GAMES AT POSITION	DL	BFW
1935	Bos A	149	525	77	138	27	7	9	63	56	3	67	.263	.337	.392	83	-14	6-5	.988	-6	86	89	1b149		-3.3
1936	Bos A	16	57	6	16	3	1	1	7	7	0	1	.281	.359	.421	87	-1	2-1	.980	-0	99	78	1b16		-0.3
1937	NY A	1	1	0	0	0	0	0	0	0	0	0	.000	.000	.000	-99	0	0	—	0			/H		0.0
1938	NY A	27	43	8	8	1	0	0	1	1	0	7	.186	.205	.209	4	-7	0-0	.826	2	58	0	3b8,1b6		-0.8
1939	†NY A	144	531	71	125	18	6	15	89	57	2	54	.235	.312	.377	76	-21	2-3	.991	-7	78	**133**	1b144		-4.0
1940	NY A	**155**	568	51	150	24	4	12	73	60	2	54	.264	.325	.384	86	-13	1-1	.990	-11	74	116	1b155		-3.7
1941	Bos N	44	166	20	39	8	1	7	30	16	1	13	.235	.306	.422	108	1	0	.993	2	116	136	1b39,3b5		-0.1
	Chi N	99	359	50	101	20	1	16	59	43	1	39	.281	.360	.476	139	18	2	.991	-8	64	105	1b98		0.1
	Year	143	525	70	140	28	2	23	89	59	2	52	.267	.343	.459	129	19	2	.992	-6	79	**114**	1b137,3b5		0.0
1942	Chi N	17	56	4	12	1	0	0	6	4	0	2	.214	.267	.232	48	-4	0	.986	0	116	63	1b14		-0.5
	StL A	2	2	0	0	0	0	0	0	0	0	0	.000	.000	.000	-99	-1	0-0	—	0			/H		-0.1
	Bro N	17	19	2	1	0	0	0	0	4	0	5	.053	.217	.053	-19	-3	0	1.000	3	143	192	1b10		-1.2
1943	Phi N★	136	508	55	146	19	2	5	54	50	2	39	.287	.354	.362	111	8	2	.988	-17	97	104	1b73,3b35,S25/C		0.8
1944	Pit N	**158**	599	67	173	28	7	12	101	47	6	56	.289	.347	.419	110	7	2	.987	9	126	85	1b158		-1.8
1945	Pit N	144	531	57	133	24	8	5	75	51	2	51	.250	.318	.354	84	-12	1	.981	1	126	81	1b24		-0.9
1946	StL A	28	80	2	14	1	0	0	9	8	0	13	.175	.250	.188	22	-8	0-1	.981	1	126	81	1b24		-0.8
Total	12	1137	4045	470	1056	174	37	82	569	390	22	401	.261	.329	.383	92	-50	18-11	.990	-37	93	106	1b1030,3b48,S25/C		-16.1

DAILEY, JOHN John J. B1854 Brooklyn NY d4.29

YEAR	TM LG	G	AB	R	H	2B	3B	HR	RBI	BB-IB	HP	SO	AVG	OBP	SLG	AOPS	ABR	SB-CS	FA	FR	RNG	THR	GAMES AT POSITION	DL	BFW
1875	Was NA	27	110	16	20	5	4	0	13	0		1	.182	.182	.300	67	-3	3-2	.810	-2	114	39	S20,3b5,2b2		-0.5
	Atl NA	2	8	3	1	0	0	0	0	0		1	.125	.125	.125	-15	-1	0-0	1.000	-2	0	0	O2R/1S		-0.3
	Year	29	118	19	21	5	4	0	13	0		2	.178	.178	.288	62	-4	3-2	.797	-4	108	37	S21,3b5,2b2,O2R/1		-0.8

DAILEY, VINCE Vincent Perry B12.25.1864 Osceola PA D11.14.1919 Hornell NY 6-0/200 d4.21

YEAR	TM LG	G	AB	R	H	2B	3B	HR	RBI	BB-IB	HP	SO	AVG	OBP	SLG	AOPS	ABR	SB-CS	FA	FR	RNG	THR	GAMES AT POSITION	DL	BFW
1890	Cle N	64	246	41	71	5	7	0	32	33	0	23	.289	.373	.366	118	6	17	.859	0	116	80	O64R,P2		0.5

DAILY, CON Cornelius F. B9.11.1864 Blackstone MA D6.14.1928 Brooklyn NY BL/6-0/192 d6.9 b-Ed

YEAR	TM LG	G	AB	R	H	2B	3B	HR	RBI	BB-IB	HP	SO	AVG	OBP	SLG	AOPS	ABR	SB-CS	FA	FR	RNG	THR	GAMES AT POSITION	DL	BFW
1884	Phi U	2	8	0	0	0	0	0	0	0			.000	.000	.000	-99	-1		.857	-1			C2		-0.1
1885	Pro N	60	223	20	58	6	1	0	19	12		20	.260	.298	.296	95	-1		.876	1			C48,1b7,O6(1/3/2)		0.3
1886	Bos N	50	180	25	43	4	2	0	21	19		29	.239	.312	.283	84	-3	2	.911	-9			C49/OL		-0.7
1887	Bos N	36	120	12	19	5	0	0	13	9	2	8	.158	.229	.200	20	-13	7	.889	-2			C36		-1.1
1888	Ind N	57	202	14	44	6	1	0	14	10		28	.218	.255	.257	63	-8	15	.893	-4			C42,O5R,3b5,1b5/2		-0.9
1889	Ind N	62	219	35	55	6	2	0	26	28	4	21	.251	.347	.297	79	-5	14	.887	-11			C51,O6(1/3/2),1b6/3		-1.2
1890	Bro P	46	168	20	42	6	0	0	35	15		14	.250	.315	.321	66	-9	6	.879	-0	129	80	C40,1b6/OR		-0.8
1891	Bro N	60	206	25	66	10	4	0	30	15	4	13	.320	.378	.379	121	6	7	.925	1	97	107	C55,O3R,S2/1		0.4
1892	Bro N	80	278	38	65	10	1	0	28	38	1	21	.234	.328	.277	87	-2	18	.943	1	104	108	C68,O13(2/3/8)		-0.2
1893	Bro N	61	215	33	57	4	2	1	32	20	5	12	.265	.342	.316	79	-6	13	.935	-1	99	80	C51,O9(2/0/7)		-0.0
1894	Bro N	67	234	40	60	14	7	0	32	31	3	22	.256	.351	.376	81	-7	8	.930	-5	90	101	C60,1b7		-0.6
1895	Bro N	40	142	17	30	3	2	1	11	10	1	18	.211	.268	.282	45	-12	3	.956	1	132	64	C39/OL		-0.6
1896	Chi N	9	27	1	2	0	0	0	1	1	0	2	.074	.107	.074	-50	-6	1	.969	-1	93	104	C9		-0.2
Total	13	630	2222	280	541	74	22	2	262	208	21	208	.243	.314	.299	75	-68	94	.912	-33	105	93	C550,O45(8/9/28),1b32,3b6,S2/2		-4.5

DAILY, ED Edward M. B9.7.1862 Providence RI D10.21.1891 Washington DC BR/TR/5-10.5/174 d5.4 b-Con ▲

YEAR	TM LG	G	AB	R	H	2B	3B	HR	RBI	BB-IB	HP	SO	AVG	OBP	SLG	AOPS	ABR	SB-CS	FA	FR	RNG	THR	GAMES AT POSITION	DL	BFW
1885	Phi N	50	184	22	38	8	2	1	13	0		25	.207	.207	.288	60	-0		.891	-4	88	78	P50		0.0
1886	Phi N	79	309	40	70	17	1	4	50	7		34	.227	.244	.327	72	-11	23	.827	3	148	129	O56(13/11/32),P27		-0.5
1887	Phi N	26	106	18	30	11	1	1	17	3	0	9	.283	.303	.434	96	-1	8	.659	-4	61	0	O22(1/20/1),P6		-0.2
	Was N	78	311	39	78	6	10	2	36	14	1	27	.251	.285	.354	82	-9	26	.855	-5	61	42	O77R/P		-1.2
	Year	104	417	57	108	17	11	3	53	17	1	36	.259	.285	.374	86	-9	34	.812	-9	62	34	O99(1/20/78),P7		-0.7
1888	Was N	110	453	56	102	8	4	7	39	7	1	42	.225	.239	.307	78	-12	44	.912	4	114	113	O100R,P9/1		-1.0
1889	Col AA	136	578	105	148	22	8	3	70	38		65	.256	.303	.337	87	-11	60	.854	-3	105	65	O136L,P2		-1.5
1890	Bro AA	91	394	68	94	15	7	1	39	24			.239	.284	.320	81	-11	49	.892	3	147	100	O64R,P27		-0.0
	NY N	4	15	1	2	1	0	0	1	0		4	.133	.133	.200	-3	-2	0	.500	1	432	0	O3(1/0/2),P2		-0.0
	†Lou AA	23	80	24	20	0	2	0	9	13			.250	.355	.300	95	-1	13	.925	2	166	203	P12,O11(0/2/9)		-0.2
1891	Lou AA	22	64	10	16	2	0	0	8	8	1	6	.250	.342	.281	80	-1	4	.884	-0	105	-0	P15,O7(2/0/5)		-0.5
	Was AA	21	79	13	18	2	0	0	6	11		10	.228	.322	.253	68	-3	8	.719	-3	59	117	O21R		-0.5
	Year	43	143	23	34	4	0	0	14	19	1	16	.238	.331	.266	73	-4	12	.750	-4	63	182	O28(2/0/26),P15		-0.5
Total	7	640	2573	396	616	92	35	19	288	125	5	222	.239	.276	.325	80	-61	235	.857	-6	108	87	O497(153/33/311),P151/1		-5.5

DAISY, GEORGE George R. B1857 Gloucester NJ D4.27.1931 Cumberland MD 5-11/190 d5.31

YEAR	TM LG	G	AB	R	H	2B	3B	HR	RBI	BB-IB	HP	SO	AVG	OBP	SLG	AOPS	ABR	SB-CS	FA	FR	RNG	THR	GAMES AT POSITION	DL	BFW
1884	Alt U	1	4	0	0	0	0	0	0	0			.000	.000	.000	-99	-1		.000	-1	0	0	/OL		-0.0

DALENA, PETE Peter Martin B6.26.1960 Fresno CA BL/TR/5-11/200 [NYA82 27/691] d7.7 Col Cal St.-Fresno

YEAR	TM LG	G	AB	R	H	2B	3B	HR	RBI	BB-IB	HP	SO	AVG	OBP	SLG	AOPS	ABR	SB-CS	FA	FR	RNG	THR	GAMES AT POSITION	DL	BFW
1989	Cle A	5	7	0	1	1	0	0	0	0		3	.143	.143	.286	18	-1	0-0	—	0			/D		-0.0

DALESANDRO, MARK Mark Anthony B5.14.1968 Chicago IL BR/TR/6-0/185* [CalA90 18/503] d6.6 Col Illinois

YEAR	TM LG	G	AB	R	H	2B	3B	HR	RBI	BB-IB	HP	SO	AVG	OBP	SLG	AOPS	ABR	SB-CS	FA	FR	RNG	THR	GAMES AT POSITION	DL	BFW
1994	Cal A	19	25	5	5	1	0	1	2	2-0		4	.200	.259	.360	57	-2	0-0	1.000	-2	223	0	C11,3b5,O2L		-0.0
1995	Cal A	11	10	1	1	1	0	0	0	0-0		2	.100	.100	.200	-25	-2	0-0	1.000	-1	48	161	C8/OLD		-0.0
1998	Tor A	32	67	8	20	5	0	2	14	1-0		9	.299	.304	.463	97	-1	0-0	.986	-6	97	75	C18,1b8,1b2/OR		-0.0
1999	Tor A	16	27	3	5	0	0	0	1	0-0		4	.185	.207	.185	3	-4	1-0	1.000	-0	49	207	C8,3b2,D5		-0.0
2001	Chi A	1	0	0	0	0	0	0	0	0-0		0	.000	.000	.000	—	-0	0-0	—	-0	-0	0	/C		-0.0
Total	5	79	129	17	31	7	0	3	17	3-0	1	14	.240	.259	.364	60	-9	1-0	.992	-9	103	91	C46,3b15,D6,O4(3/0/1),1b2		-0.0

DALEY, JOHN John Francis B5.25.1887 Pittsburgh PA D8.31.1988 Mansfield OH BR/TR/5-7.5/155 d7.19 Col Fordham

YEAR	TM LG	G	AB	R	H	2B	3B	HR	RBI	BB-IB	HP	SO	AVG	OBP	SLG	AOPS	ABR	SB-CS	FA	FR	RNG	THR	GAMES AT POSITION	DL	BFW
1912	StL A	18	52	7	9	0	0	1	3	9	2		.173	.317	.231	60	-2	4	.833	-4	96	129	S17		-0.0

YEAR	TM LG	G	AB	R	H	2B	3B	HR	RBI	BB-IB	HP	SO	AVG	OBP	SLG	AOPS	ABR	SB-CS	FA	FR	RNG	THR	GAMES AT POSITION	DL	BFW

DALEY, JUD Judson Lawrence B3.14.1884 S.Coventry CT D1.26.1967 Gadsden AL BL/TR/5-8/172 d9.19

1911	Bro N	19	65	8	15	2	1	0	7	2		3	8	.231	.286	.292	65	-3	2	.952	1	108	122	O16L		-0.3
1912	Bro N	61	199	22	51	9	1	1	13	24		2	17	.256	.342	.327	87	-3	2	.947	1	97	119	O55(24/24/7)		-0.5
Total	2	80	264	30	66	11	2	1	20	26		5	25	.250	.329	.318	82	-6	4	.949	2	100	120	O71(40/24/7)		-0.8

DALEY, PETE Peter Harvey B1.14.1930 Grass Valley CA BR/TR/6-0/195* d5.3

1955	Bos A	17	50	4	11	2	1	0	5	3-0	0	6	.220	.264	.300	47	-4	0-0	1.000	2	83	71	C14		-0.2
1956	Bos A	59	187	22	50	11	3	5	29	18-5	2	30	.267	.338	.439	92	-2	1-0	.992	-6	108	49	C57		-0.5
1957	Bos A	78	191	17	43	10	0	3	25	16-4	1	31	.225	.288	.325	64	-9	0-0	1.000	0	144	63	C77		-0.7
1958	Bos A	27	56	10	18	2	1	2	8	7-1	0	11	.321	.397	.500	136	3	0-0	.990	1	130	146	C27		0.5
1959	Bos A	65	169	9	38	7	0	1	11	13-1	0	31	.225	.279	.284	53	-11	1-1	.996	4	132	102	C58		0.5
1960	KC A	73	228	19	60	10	2	5	25	16-1	0	41	.263	.311	.390	88	-4	0-0	.990	-6	61	90	C61/OL		-0.5
1961	Was A	72	203	12	39	7	1	2	17	14-3	0	37	.192	.244	.266	37	-19	0-1	.988	1	64	132	C72		-0.7
Total	7	391	1084	93	259	49	8	18	120	87-15	3	187	.239	.297	.349	71	-46	2-2	.993	-5	101	91	C366/OL		-3.7

DALEY, TOM Thomas Francis "Pete" B11.13.1884 DuBois PA D12.2.1934 Los Angeles CA BL/TR/5-5/168 d8.29

1908	Cin N	14	46	5	5	0	0	0	1	3		2		.109	.196	.109	-2	-5	1	1.000	1	143	295	O13R		-0.6
1913	Phi A	62	141	13	36	2	1	0	11	13		2	28	.255	.327	.284	81	-3	4	.963	0	99	95	O39C		-0.6
1914	Phi A	28	86	17	22	1	3	0	7	12		1	14	.256	.347	.337	110	1	4-7	1.000	2	106	130	O24(15/10/0)		0.0
	NY A	69	191	36	48	6	4	0	9	38.		1	13	.251	.378	.325	112	5	8-8	.958	4	103	150	O58(28/29/0)		0.5
	Year	97	277	53	70	7	7	0	16	50		1	27	.253	.369	.329	111	6	12-15	.969	6	104	144	O82(43/39/0)		0.5
1915	NY A	10	8	2	2	0	0	0	1	2		0	2	.250	.400	.250	95	0	1	1.000	0	147	0	O2(1/0/1)		0.1
Total	4	183	472	73	113	9	8	0	29	68		5	57	.239	.341	.292	92	-2	18-15	.970	7	106	143	O136(44/77/14)		-0.6

DALLESSANDRO, DOM Nicholas Dominic "Dim Dom" B10.3.1913 Reading PA D4.29.1988 Indianapolis IN BL/TL/5-6/168 d4.24 Mil 1945

1937	Bos A	68	147	18	34	7	1	0	11	27		0	16	.231	.351	.293	61	-8	2-1	.965	-2	91	44	O35(30/1/4)		-1.1
1940	Chi N	107	287	33	77	19	6	1	36	34		1	13	.268	.348	.387	104	2	4	.969	-0	108	20	O74L		-0.2
1941	Chi N	140	486	73	132	36	2	6	85	68		1	37	.272	.362	.391	116	13	3	.987	-5	98	42	O131(69/62/0)		0.3
1942	Chi N	96	264	30	69	12	4	4	43	36		0	29	.261	.350	.383	119	7	4	.986	-1	92	115	O66(31/32/4)		0.3
1943	Chi N	87	176	13	39	8	3	1	31	40		1	14	.222	.369	.318	101	2	1	.967	-3	92	51	O45(31/14/0)		-0.3
1944	Chi N	117	381	53	116	19	4	8	74	61		0	29	.304	.400	.438	137	21	1	.982	-3	91	112	O106(91/16/0)		1.3
1946	Chi N	65	89	4	20	2	1	0	9	23		0	12	.225	.384	.326	104	2	1	.971	-1	103	0	O20(16/0/4)		0.0
1947	Chi N	66	115	18	33	7	1	1	14	21		0	11	.287	.397	.391	115	4	0	1.000	-1	95	55	O28L		0.1
Total	8	746	1945	242	520	110	23	22	303	310		3	150	.267	.369	.381	112	43	16-1	.980	-16	96	64	O505(370/125/12)		0.4

DALLIMORE, BRIAN Brian Scott B11.15.1973 Las Vegas NV BR/TR/6-1/180* [HouN96 9/264] d4.29 Col Stanford

2004	SF N	20	43	8	12	2	0	1	7	4-0	1	7	.279	.347	.395	90		0-1	.963	0	113	83	2b9,3b6		0.0
2005	SF N	7	7	1	1	1	0	0	0	0-0	0	0	.143	.143	.286	8	-1	0-0	1.000	1	173	354	2b2/S		0.0
Total	2	27	50	9	13	3	0	1	7	4-0	1	7	.260	.321	.380	80	-2	0-1	.970	1	124	132	2b11,3b6/S		0.0

DALRYMPLE, ABNER Abner Frank B9.9.1857 Gratiot WI D1.25.1939 Warren IL BL/TR/5-10.5/175 d5.1

1878	Mil N	61	271	52	96	10	4	0	15	6			29	.354	.368	.421	149	13		.832	7	69	120	O61L		1.5
1879	Chi N	71	333	47	97	25	1	0	23	4			29	.291	.300	.372	113	5		.728	-15	24	55	O71(66/1/4)		-1.4
1880	Chi N	86	382	91	126	25	12	0	36	3			18	.330	.335	.458	156	20		.859	4	92	125	O86L		1.8
1881	Chi N	82	362	72	117	22	4	1	37	15			22	.323	.350	.414	133	13		.835	-7	64	33	O82L		0.1
1882	Chi N	84	397	96	117	25	11	1	36	14			18	.295	.319	.421	129	12		.877	0	114	0	O84L		0.9
1883	Chi N	80	363	78	108	24	4	2	37	11			29	.298	.318	.402	108	3		.826	-2	65	99	O80L		-0.1
1884	Chi N	111	521	111	161	18	9	22	69	14			39	.309	.327	.505	146	23		.882	0	78	133	O111L		1.8
1885	†Chi N	113	492	109	135	27	12	11	61	46			42	.274	.336	.445	133	16		.879	-1	74	75	O113(112/1/0)		1.1
1886	†Chi N	82	331	62	77	7	12	3	26	33			44	.233	.302	.353	86	-7	16	.953	3	91	44	O82L		-0.6
1887	Pit N	92	358	45	76	18	5	2	31	45	6		43	.212	.311	.307	78	-8	29	.900	2	83	34	O92L		-0.6
1888	Pit N	57	227	19	50	9	2	0	14	6	2		28	.220	.247	.278	73	-7	7	.909	-2	98	0	O57(56/0/1)		-0.9
1891	Mil AA	32	135	31	42	7	5	1	22	7	0		18	.311	.345	.459	108	0	6	.909	-1	107	92	O32L		-0.2
Total	12	951	4172	813	1202	217	81	43	407	204	8		359	.288	.323	.410	120	83	58	.863	-10	79	79	O951(944/2/5)		3.4

DALRYMPLE, CLAY Clayton Errol B12.3.1936 Chico CA BL/TR/6-0/199* d4.24 Col Cal St.-Chico

1960	Phi N	82	158	11	43	6	2	4	21	15-4	3	21	.272	.343	.411	106	1	0-0	.966	-3	73	129	C48		0.1
1961	Phi N	129	378	23	83	11	1	5	42	30-9	4	30	.220	.281	.294	54	-25	0-2	.978	2	112	178	C122		-1.9
1962	Phi N	123	370	40	102	13	3	11	54	70-7	2	30	.276	.393	.416	122	15	1-3	.987	-1	137	104	C119		1.8
1963	Phi N	142	452	40	114	15	3	10	40	45-15	5	55	.252	.327	.365	100	1	0-2	.981	-1	100	124	C142		0.6
1964	Phi N	127	382	36	91	16	3	6	46	39-6	0	44	.238	.303	.343	84	-7	0-1	.991	4	144	107	C124		0.1
1965	Phi N	103	301	14	64	5	5	4	23	34-7	0	37	.213	.292	.302	69	-13	0-1	.993	20	122	154	C102		1.2
1966	Phi N	114	331	30	81	13	3	4	39	60-10	3	57	.245	.365	.338	97	2	0-0	.993	2	139	95	C110		0.9
1967	Phi N	101	268	12	46	7	1	3	21	36-6	1	49	.172	.271	.239	47	-18	1-2	.994	19	155	132	C97		0.5
1968	Phi N	85	241	19	50	9	1	3	26	22-9	1	57	.207	.272	.290	70	-8	1-2	.990	-2	100	102	C80		-0.8
1969	†Bal A	37	80	8	19	1	1	3	6	13-1	0	8	.237	.340	.387	103	0	0-0	1.000	0	123	175	C30		0.1
1970	Bal A	13	32	4	7	1	0	1	3	7-2	0	4	.219	.350	.344	93	0	0-0	1.000	4	87	241	C11	75	0.5
1971	Bal A	23	49	6	10	1	0	1	6	16-1	1	13	.204	.409	.286	99	1	0-0	.971	3	173	135	C18	75	0.5
Total	12	1079	3042	243	710	98	23	55	327	387-77	22	403	.233	.322	.335	85	-51	3-13	.987	45	124	128	C1003	75	3.6

DALRYMPLE, BILL William Dunn B2.7.1891 Baltimore MD D7.14.1967 San Diego CA TR d7.6

| 1915 | StL A | 3 | 2 | 0 | 0 | 0 | 0 | 0 | 0 | 0 | | 0 | 0 | .000 | .000 | .000 | -99 | -1 | 0 | 1.000 | 0 | 233 | 0 | /3 | | 0.0 |

DALTON, JACK Talbot Percy B7.3.1885 Henderson TN BR/TR/5-10.5/187 d6.20 Col Virginia

1910	Bro N	77	273	33	62	9	4	1	21	26		4	30	.227	.304	.300	79	-8	5	.966	1	101	110	O72R		-1.0
1914	Bro N	128	442	65	141	13	4	1	45	53		3	38	.319	.396	.391	131	19	19	.965	-9	93	50	O116(5/109/2)		0.2
1915	Buf F	132	437	68	128	17	3	2	46	50		3	28	.293	.368	.359	103	3	28	.966	-4	99	71	O119(10/60/52)		-1.5
1916	Det A	8	11	1	2	0	0	0	0	0		0	6	.182	.182	.182	9	-1	0	1.000	0	103	0	O4(1/0/3)		-0.2
Total	4	345	1163	167	333	39	15	4	112	129		9	112	.286	.362	.356	107	7	52	.966	-12	97	72	O311(16/169/129)		-2.5

DALY, BERT Albert Joseph B4.8.1881 Bayonne NJ D9.3.1952 Bayonne NJ BR/TR/5-9/170 d8.7 Col Maryland-Baltimore Co.

| 1903 | Phi A | 10 | 21 | 2 | 4 | 0 | 2 | 0 | 4 | 1 | | 0 | | .190 | .227 | .381 | 76 | 1 | 0 | .700 | -3 | 69 | 0 | 2b4,3b3/S | | -0.4 |

DALY, SUN James J. B1.6.1865 Port Henry NY D4.30.1938 Albany NY BL/?/184 d9.30

| 1892 | Bal N | 13 | 48 | 5 | 12 | 0 | 2 | 0 | 7 | 4 | | | | .250 | .265 | .333 | 79 | -2 | 0 | .923 | 1 | 106 | 211 | O13(10/3/0) | | -0.2 |

DALY, JOE Joseph John B9.21.1868 Conshohocken PA D3.21.1943 Philadelphia PA TR/5-8/157 d9.19 b-Tom

1890	Phi AA	21	75	8	21	4	1	0	7	3		0		.280	.308	.360	97	-1	1	.900	-5	168	0	O14(3/8/3),C9		-0.4
1891	Cle N	1	3	0	0	0	0	0	0	0		0	2	.000	.000	.000	-96	-1	0	1.000	0	0	0	/OR		-0.1
1892	Bos N	1	0	0	0	0	0	0	0	0		0		—	—	—		0	0	1.000	0	0	0	/C		0.0
Total	3	23	78	8	21	4	1	0	7	3		0	2	.269	.296	.346	90	-2	1	.909	-4	153	0	O15(3/8/4),C10		-0.5

DALY, TOM Thomas Daniel B12.12.1891 St.John NB, Can. D11.7.1946 Medford MA BR/TR/5-11.5/171 d9.23 C14

1913	Chi A	1	3	0	0	0	0	0	0	0		0		.000	.000	.000	-99	-1	0	1.000	0	127	97	/C		0.0
1914	Chi A	62	133	13	31	2	0	0	8	7		0	13	.233	.271	.248	57	-7	3-4	.909	-5	72	47	O23(14/0/10),3b5,C4,1b2		-1.5
1915	Chi A	29	47	5	9	1	0	0	3	5		0	9	.191	.269	.213	43	-3	0	.958	-1	178	55	C19/1		-0.5
1916	Cle A	31	73	3	16	1	1	0	8	4		0	2	.219	.230	.260	45	-5	0	.982	-1	108	107	C25/OR		-0.5
1918	Chi N	1	1	0	0	0	0	0	0	0		0		.000	.000	.000	-98	0	0	.667	-0	0	0	/C		-0.1
1919	Chi N	25	50	4	11	0	1	0	2	2		0	5	.220	.250	.260	53	-3	0	.956	1	95	61	C18		-0.4
1920	Chi N	44	90	12	28	6	0	0	13	2		1	6	.311	.333	.378	102	2	1-1	.981	-1	100	85	C29		0.1
1921	Chi N	51	143	12	34	7	1	0	22	8		0	8	.238	.278	.301	53	-10	1-2	.973	2	100	105	C47		-0.3
Total	8	244	540	49	129	17	3	0	55	25		1	43	.239	.274	.281	59	-29	5-7	.972	-6	109	89	C144,O24(14/0/11),3b5,1b3		-3.2

DALY, TOM Thomas Peter "Tido" B2.7.1866 Philadelphia PA D10.29.1938 Brooklyn NY BB/TR/5-7/170 d4.30 C1 b-Joe OF(9/17/29)

1887	Chi N	74	256	45	53	10	4	2	17	22		25	.207	.290	.301	52	-18	29	**.935**	29			C64,O8(2/3/3),S2,2b2,1b2		1.4
1888	Chi N	65	219	34	42	2	6	0	29	10		1	26	.192	.230	.256	51	-13	10	.939	14			C62,O4(0/1/3)		0.6
1889	Was N	71	250	39	75	13	5	1	40	38		1	28	.300	.394	.404	131	12	18	.917	4			C57,1b8,2b4,O3(1/0/2)/S		-1.8

YEAR	TM LG	G	AB	R	H	2B	3B	HR	RBI	BB-IB	HP	SO	AVG	OBP	SLG	AOPS	ABR	SB-CS	FA	FR	RNG	THR	GAMES AT POSITION	DL	BFW
1890	†Bro N	82	292	55	71	9	4	5	43	32	4	43	.243	.326	.353	97	-1	20	.953	2	87	82	C69,1b12/OR		0.5
1891	Bro N	58	200	29	50	11	5	2	27	21	2	34	.250	.327	.385	108	2	7	.881	-6	97	48	C26,1b15,S11,O7R		-0.3
1892	Bro N	124	446	76	114	15	6	4	51	64	5	62	.256	.355	.343	116	11	34	.897	-10	84	96	3b57,O30(5/13/12),C27,2b10		0.3
1893	Bro N	126	470	94	136	21	14	8	70	76	0	65	.289	.388	.445	127	20	32	.915	-26	96	55	2b82,3b45		-0.2
1894	Bro N	124	496	135	168	22	10	8	82	77	5	42	.339	.433	.472	127	27	51	.909	-21	91	87	2b124		0.9
1895	Bro N	121	460	90	129	17	8	2	68	52	3	52	.280	.357	.365	94	-2	28	.931	-22	92	85	2b121		-1.5
1896	Bro N	67	224	43	63	13	6	3	29	33	5	25	.281	.385	.433	122	9	19	.909	-7	93	115	2b66/C		0.4
1898	Bro N	23	73	11	24	3	1	0	11	14	1		.329	.443	.397	142	5	6	.993	3	107	127	2b23		0.8
1899	Bro N	141	498	95	156	24	9	5	88	69	12		.313	.409	.428	127	22	43	.929	16	104	131	2b141		3.9
1900	†Bro N	97	343	72	107	17	3	4	55	46	6		.312	.403	.414	118	11	27	.921	-7	91	105	2b93,1b3,O2(1/0/1)		0.7
1901	Bro N	133	520	88	164	**38**	10	3	90	42	4		.315	.371	.444	132	22	31	.944	10	94	98	2b133		3.2
1902	Chi A	137	489	57	110	22	3	1	54	55	0		.225	.303	.288	68	-20	19	.957	-15	90	129	2b137		-3.2
1903	Chi A	43	150	20	31	11	0	0	19	20	1		.207	.304	.280	80	-2	6	.948	-13	81	77	2b43		-1.6
	Cin N	80	307	42	90	14	9	1	38	16	2		.293	.332	.407	99	-2	5	.937	-7	97	86	2b79		-0.8
Total	16	1566	5693	1025	1583	262	103	49	811	687	52	402	.278	.361	.386	107	83	385	.931	-56	94	100	2b1058,C306,3b102,O55R,1b40,S14		6.9

DAM, BILL Elbridge Rust B4.4.1885 Cambridge MA D6.22.1930 Quincy MA BL/TL d8.23

1909	Bos N	2	1	2	1	1	0	0	1	0			.500	.667	1.000	398	1	0	1.000	-0	0	0	/OL		0.1

DAMASKA, JACK Jack Lloyd B8.21.1937 Beaver Falls PA BR/TR/5-11/168 d7.3

1963	StL N	5	5	1	1	0	0	0	1	0-0		4	.200	.200	.200	14	-1	0-0	—	-0	0	0	/2OL		-0.1

DAMON, JOHNNY Johnny David B11.5.1973 Fort Riley KS BL/TL/6-2/190(175-190) [KCA92 1/35] d8.12

1995	KC A	47	188	32	53	11	5	3	23	12-0	1	22	.282	.324	.441	96	-2	7-0	.991	-4	92	0	O47(0/44/4)		-0.4
1996	KC A	145	517	61	140	22	5	6	50	31-3	3	64	.271	.313	.368	72	-24	25-5	.983	-0	106	54	O144(0/89/63)/D		-2.0
1997	KC A	146	472	70	130	12	8	8	48	42-2	3	70	.275	.338	.386	86	-11	16-10	.988	5	112	67	O136(48/65/47),D5		-0.8
1998	KC A	161	642	104	178	30	10	18	66	58-4	4	84	.277	.339	.439	97	-4	26-12	.990	-2	96	101	O158(14/130/24)		-0.5
1999	KC A	145	583	101	179	39	9	14	77	67-5	3	50	.307	.379	.477	113	12	36-6	.987	-0	102	85	O140(132/8/3),D4		1.2
2000	KC A	159	655	**136**	214	42	10	16	88	65-4	1	60	.327	.382	.495	115	15	**46-9**	.986	2	105	59	O133(67/69/0),D25		2.0
2001	†Oak A	155	644	108	165	34	4	9	49	61-1	5	70	.256	.324	.363	81	-17	27-12	.991	-6	98	44	O154(67/86/5)		-2.2
2002	Bos A★	154	623	118	178	34	**11**	14	63	65-5	6	70	.286	.356	.443	110	9	31-6	.997	-5	93	92	O151C/D		0.0
2003	†Bos A	145	608	103	166	32	6	12	67	68-4	2	74	.273	.345	.405	94	-4	30-6	.997	-2	98	109	O144C/D		1.4
2004	†Bos A	150	621	123	189	35	6	20	94	76-1	2	71	.304	.380	.477	115	15	19-8	.986	-4	99	58	O148C/D		1.7
2005	†Bos A★	148	624	117	197	35	6	10	75	53-3	2	69	.316	.366	.439	108	8	18-1	.985	-12	101	74	O1502(328/1081/146),D39		1.4
Total	11	1555	6177	1073	1789	326	80	130	700	598-32	32	704	.290	.353	.431	100	-3	281-75	.989	-12	101	74			1.4

DAMRAU, HARRY Harry Robert (Also Known As Arthur Lee Whitehorn) B9.11.1890 Newburgh NY D8.21.1957 Staten Island NY BR/TR/5-10/178 d9.17

1915	Phi A	16	56	4	11	1	0	0	4	1	0	17	.196	.262	.214	44	-4	1-1	.870	-2	90	36	3b16		-0.6

DANIEL, JAKE Handley Jacob B4.22.1911 Roanoke AL D4.23.1996 LaGrange GA BL/TL/5-11/175 d7.24

1937	Bro N	12	27	3	5	1	0	0	3	3	0	4	.185	.267	.222	34	-2	0	1.000	-0	77	66	1b7		-0.3

DANIELS, BERT Bertram Elmer B10.31.1882 Danville IL D6.6.1958 Cedar Grove NJ BR/TR/5-10/170 d6.25 Col Bucknell

1910	NY A	95	356	68	90	13	8	1	17	41	**16**		.253	.356	.343	112	7	41	.957	-1	107	73	O85(79/6/0),3b6,1b4		0.1
1911	NY A	131	462	74	132	16	9	2	31	48	18		.286	.375	.372	102	3	40	.941	-5	101	73	O120(8/86/26)		-1.0
1912	NY A	135	496	72	136	25	11	2	41	51	**18**		.274	.363	.381	106	5	37	.945	3	115	74	O131(92/0/39)		0.2
1913	NY A	94	320	52	69	13	5	0	22	44	**18**	36	.216	.343	.287	85	-3	27	.966	1	97	114	O87R		-0.7
1914	Cin N	71	269	29	59	9	7	0	19	19	2	40	.219	.276	.305	70	-11	14	.974	-2	100	66	O71(11/26/38)		-1.9
Total	5	526	1903	295	486	76	40	5	130	203	72	76	.255	.349	.345	98	1	159	.953	-4	105	79	O494(190/118/190),3b6,1b4		-3.3

DANIELS, TONY Frederick Clinton B12.28.1924 Gastonia NC BR/TR/5-9.5/185 d6.12

1945	Phi N	76	230	15	46	9	2	0	10	12	3	22	.200	.249	.230	35	-21	1	.955	4	107	94	2b75/3		-1.4

DANIELS, JACK Harold Jack "Sour Mash Jack" B12.21.1927 Chester PA BL/TL/5-10/165 d4.18

1952	Bos N	106	219	31	41	5	1	2	14	28	3	30	.187	.288	.247	51	-14	3-3	.977	-1	96	102	O87(13/0/75)		-1.9

DANIELS, KAL Kalvoski B8.20.1963 Vienna GA BL/TR/5-11/195(185-205) [CinN82 S1/7] d4.9 Col Middle Georgia JC

1986	Cin N	74	181	34	58	10	4	6	23	22-1	2	30	.320	.398	.519	146	12	15-2	.967	-0	113	0	O47L	31	1.3
1987	Cin N	108	368	73	123	24	1	26	64	60-11	1	62	.334	.429	.617	167	37	26-8	.968	-1	101	78	O94L		3.5
1988	Cin N	140	495	95	144	29	1	18	64	87-10	3	94	.291	**.397**	.463	142	32	27-6	.982	-1	100	119	O137L	37	3.3
1989	Cin N	44	133	26	29	11	0	2	9	36-1	2	28	.218	.390	.346	109	4	6-4	1.000	-0	88	188	O38L	56	0.3
	LA N	11	38	7	13	2	0	2	8	7-0	0	5	.342	.435	.553	186	5	3-0	1.000	-0	102	0	O11L		0.8
	Year	55	171	33	42	13	0	4	17	43-1	2	33	.246	.399	.392	125	9	9-4	1.000	0	91	149	O49L		0.8
1990	LA N	130	450	81	133	23	1	27	94	68-1	3	104	.296	.389	.531	155	35	4-3	.987	1	87	161	O127L		3.3
1991	LA N	137	461	54	115	15	1	17	73	63-4	1	116	.249	.337	.397	109	6	6-1	.979	-2	88	132	O132L		0.1
1992	LA N	35	104	9	24	5	0	2	8	10-0	1	30	.231	.302	.337	82	-2	0-0	.964	-2	69	116	O21L,1b8	20	-0.6
	Chi N	48	108	12	27	6	0	4	17	12-0	1	24	.250	.328	.417	107	1	0-2	1.000	-1	70	277	O28L		-0.1
	Year	83	212	21	51	11	0	6	25	22-0	2	54	.241	.315	.377	95	-1	0-2	.984	-3	70	204	O49L,1b8		-0.7
Total	7	727	2338	391	666	125	8	104	360	365-28	14	493	.285	.382	.479	137	130	87-26	.980	-6	93	124	O635L,1b8	144	11.6

DANIELS, LAW Lawrence Long B7.14.1862 Newton MA D1.7.1929 Waltham MA BR/TR/5-10/170 d4.25

1887	Bal AA	48	165	23	41	5	1	0	32	8	1		.248	.287	.291	65	-7	7	.845	-8			C26,O15(10/5/0),1b4,2b2/S3		-1.2
1888	KC AA	61	218	32	45	2	0	2	28	14	3		.206	.264	.243	59	-10	20	.855	-3	174	253	O30(14/9/7),C29,3b2/S		-1.1
Total	2	109	383	55	86	7	1	2	60	22	4		.225	.274	.264	62	-17	27	.859	-12			C55,O45(24/14/7),1b4,3b3,S2,2b2		-2.3

DANNER, BUCK Henry Frederick B6.8.1891 Dedham MA D9.19.1949 Dedham MA BR/TR/5-11/140 d9.17

1915	Phi A	3	12	1	3	0	0	0	0	0	1	.250	.250	.250	51	-1	1	.750	-2	51	0	S3		-0.3

DANNING, HARRY Harry "Harry the Horse" B9.6.1911 Los Angeles CA D11.29.2004 Valparaiso IN BR/TR/6-1/190 d7.30 Mil 1943-45 b-Ike

1933	NY N	3	2	0	0	0	0	0	1	0	0	.000	.333	.000	2	-0	1	1.000	-0	0	0	/C		0.0
1934	NY N	53	97	8	32	9	0	1	7	1	0	9	.330	.337	.433	107	1	1	.989	0	112	124	C37		0.2
1935	NY N	65	152	16	37	11	1	2	20	9	0	16	.243	.286	.368	76	-5	0	.978	2	124	102	C44		-0.1
1936	†NY N	32	69	3	11	2	0	0	4	1	1	5	.159	.183	.246	15	-9	0	.988	2	138	83	C24		-0.6
1937	†NY N	93	292	30	84	12	4	8	53	18	1	20	.288	.331	.438	106	1	0	.982	1	161	101	C86		0.7
1938	NY N☆	120	448	59	137	26	9	9	60	23	4	40	.306	.345	.438	113	7	1	.984	-2	121	60	C114		1.2
1939	NY N☆	135	520	79	163	28	5	16	74	35	2	42	.313	.359	.479	122	15	4	.991	6	82	105	C132		2.9
1940	NY N★	140	525	67	157	34	4	13	91	35	5	31	.300	.349	.454	119	13	3	.980	9	**135**	89	C131		3.1
1941	NY N★	130	459	58	112	22	4	7	56	30	1	25	.244	.292	.355	80	-14	1	.993	7	117	100	C116/1		0.1
1942	NY N	119	408	45	114	20	3	1	34	34	0	29	.279	.335	.350	100	9	13	.985	-0	126	73	C116		0.7
Total	10	890	2971	363	847	162	26	57	397	187	14	217	.285	.330	.415	104	9	13		25	121	89	C801/1		8.2

DANNING, IKE Isaac B1.20.1905 Los Angeles CA D3.30.1983 Santa Monica CA BR/TR/5-10/160 d9.21 b-Harry

1928	StL A	2	6	0	3	0	0	0	2	1	0	2	.500	.571	.500	178	0	1	0-0	.917	0	123	220	C2		0.1

DANTONIO, FATS John James B12.31.1918 New Orleans LA D5.28.1993 New Orleans LA BR/TR/5-8/165 d9.18

1944	Bro N	3	7	0	1	0	0	0	0	0	0	1	.143	.143	.143	-20	-1	0	.846	-1	65	0	C3		-0.2
1945	Bro N	47	128	12	32	6	1	0	12	11	0	6	.250	.309	.313	74	-5	3	.929	-5	108	76	C45		-0.7
Total	2	50	135	12	33	6	1	0	12	11	0	7	.244	.301	.304	69	-6	3	.923	-5	105	72	C48		-0.9

DANZIG, BABE Harold Paul B4.30.1887 Binghamton NY D7.14.1931 San Francisco CA BR/TR/6-2/205 d4.12

1909	Bos A	6	13	0	2	0	0	0	2	1			.154	.313	.154	47	-1	0	.960	-1	0	212	1b3		-0.2

DAPPER, CLIFF Clifford Roland B1.2.1920 Los Angeles CA d4.19 Mil 1943-45

1942	Bro N	8	17	2	8	1	0	1	9	2	0	.471	.526	.706	255	3	0	1.000	0	145	82	C8		0.4

DARINGER, CLIFF Clifford Clarence "Shanty" B4.10.1885 Hayden IN D12.26.1971 Sacramento CA BL/TR/5-7.5/155 d4.20 b-Rolla

1914	KC F	64	160	12	42	2	1	0	16	11	3	7	.262	.322	.287	70	-9	9	.944	5	122	94	S24,3b19,2b14		-0.2

YEAR	TM LG	G	AB	R	H	2B	3B	HR	RBI	BB-IB	HP	SO	AVG	OBP	SLG	AOPS	ABR	SB-CS	FA	FR	RNG	THR	GAMES AT POSITION	DL	BFW

DARINGER, ROLLA Rolla Harrison B11.15.1888 N.Vernon IN D5.23.1974 Seymour IN BL/TR/5-10/155 d9.19 b-Cliff

1914	StL N	2	4	1	2	1	0	0	0	1	0	2	.500	.600	.750	304	1	0	.667	-1	81	373	/S		0.1
1915	StL N	10	23	3	2	0	0	0	9	0	0	5	.087	.344	.087	33	-1	0-1	.947	-2	91	151	S10		-0.3
Total	2	12	27	4	4	1	0	0	10	0	0	7	.148	.378	.185	72	0	0-1	.927	-2	90	171	S11		-0.2

DARK, ALVIN Alvin Ralph "Blackie" B1.7.1922 Comanche OK BR/TR/5-11/185* d7.14 M13/C2 Col Louisiana St. OF(39/0/4)

1946	Bos N	15	13	0	3	0	0	0	1	0	0	3	.231	.231	.462	93	0	0	.905	1	143	110	S12/OL		0.1
1948	†Bos N	137	543	85	175	39	6	3	48	24	2	36	.322	.353	.433	114	9	4	.963	-14	95	95	S133		0.4
1949	Bos N	130	529	74	146	23	5	3	53	31	1	43	.276	.317	.355	85	-13	5	.961	-3	98	100	S125,3b4		-0.8
1950	NY N	**154**	587	79	164	36	5	16	67	39	6	60	.279	.331	.440	100	-1	9	.962	-11	97	**106**	S154		-0.3
1951	†NY N★	156	646	114	196	**41**	7	14	69	42	6	39	.303	.352	.454	114	12	12-7	.944	4	100	**123**	S156		2.6
1952	NY N	151	589	92	177	29	3	14	73	47	5	49	.301	.357	.431	117	13	6-6	.965	5	96	**120**	S150		2.7
1953	NY N	**155**	647	126	194	41	6	23	88	28	6	34	.300	.335	.488	109	7	7-2	.967	8	105	107	S110,2b26,O17(13/0/4),3b8/P		2.5
1954	†NY N★	**154**	644	98	189	26	6	20	70	27	5	40	.293	.325	.446	98	-4	5-3	.956	2	102	105	S154		1.1
1955	NY N	115	475	77	134	20	3	9	45	22-2	5	32	.282	.319	.394	88	-9	2-1	.962	-12	93	94	S115		-1.1
1956	NY N	48	206	19	52	12	6	2	17	8-0	1	13	.252	.279	.340	67	-10	0-0	.961	-7	89	86	S48		-1.3
	StL N	100	413	54	118	14	7	4	37	21-0	2	33	.286	.320	.383	89	-7	3-1	.959	-1	100	104	S99		0.0
	Year	148	619	73	170	26	13	6	54	29-0	3	46	.275	.307	.372	82	-17	3-1	.960	-8	96	98	S147		-1.3
1957	StL N	140	583	80	169	25	8	4	64	29-4	4	56	.290	.326	.381	88	-10	3-4	.965	8	102	117	S139/3		0.9
1958	StL N	18	64	7	19	0	0	1	5	2-0	0	6	.297	.318	.344	72	-3	0-0	.943	-2	95	105	S8,3b8		-0.4
	Chi N	114	464	54	137	16	4	3	43	29-1	5	23	.295	.339	.366	89	-7	1-1	.949	1	99	105	3b111		-0.6
	Year	132	528	61	156	16	4	4	48	31-1	5	29	.295	.337	.364	87	-10	1-1	.948	-0	99	100	3b119,S8		-1.0
1959	Chi N	136	477	60	126	22	9	6	45	55-9	3	50	.264	.342	.386	95	-3	1-1	.948	1	106	103	3b131,1b4/S		-0.2
1960	Phi N	55	198	29	48	5	1	3	14	19-2	2	14	.242	.315	.323	75	-7	1-1	.953	-2	93	81	3b53/1		-1.0
	Mil N	50	141	16	42	6	2	1	18	7-2	1	13	.298	.329	.390	106	1	0-0	.960	-2	103	102	O25L,1b10,3b4,2b3		-0.3
	Year	105	339	45	90	11	3	4	32	26-4	3	27	.265	.321	.351	88	-6	1-1	.954	-4	91	78	3b57,O25L,1b11,2b3		-1.3
Total	14	1828	7219	1064	2089	358	72	126	757	430-20	54	534	.289	.333	.411	98	-32	59-27	.960	-24	99	107	S1404,3b320,O43L,2b29,1b15/P		4.3

DARLING, DELL Conrad B12.21.1861 Erie PA D11.20.1904 Erie PA BR/TR/5-8/170 d7.3

1883	Buf N	6	18	1	3	0	0	0	1	2		5	.167	.250	.167	29	-1		.875	-2			C6		-0.3
1887	Chi N	38	141	28	45	7	4	3	20	22	1	18	.319	.411	.489	132	6	19	.786	2	132	189	O20R,C20		0.8
1888	Chi N	20	75	12	16	3	1	2	7	3	1	12	.213	.253	.360	87	-1	0	.932	1			C20		0.2
1889	Chi N	36	120	14	23	1	1	0	7	25		22	.192	.331	.217	52	-7	5	.960	2			C36		-0.2
1890	Chi P	58	221	45	57	12	4	2	39	29	3	28	.258	.352	.376	91	-3	5	.957	-8	88	99	1b29,S15,C9,O7R,2b3,3b2		-1.0
1891	StL AA	17	53	9	7	1	3	0	9	10		11	.132	.270	.264	46	-4	0	.894	-0	117	117	C17,2b2/S		-0.3
Total	6	175	628	109	151	24	13	7	83	91	4	96	.240	.340	.354	87	-10	29	.923	-5	**115**	116	C108,1b29,O27R,S16,2b5,3b2		-0.8

DARR, MIKE Michael Curtis B3.21.1976 Corona CA D2.15.2002 Phoenix AZ BL/TR/6-3/205* [DetA94 2/52] d5.23

1999	SD N	25	48	6	13	1	0	2	3	5-0	1	18	.271	.340	.417	97	0	2-1	1.000	-0	110	0	O22(0/3/21)		-0.1
2000	SD N	58	205	21	55	14	4	1	30	23-1	0	45	.268	.342	.390	90	-3	9-1	1.000	5	107	203	O57(8/19/47)		0.1
2001	SD N	105	289	36	80	13	1	2	34	39-3	1	72	.277	.363	.349	93	-2	6-2	.990	5	112	123	O93(5/29/69)	21	0.1
Total	3	188	542	63	148	28	5	5	67	67-4	1	135	.273	.353	.371	92	-5	17-4	.994	10	110	142	O172(13/51/137)	21	0.1

DARRAGH, JIMMY James S. B7.17.1866 Ebensburg PA D8.12.1939 Rochester PA 6-2.5/180 d5.13 Col Penn

| 1891 | Lou AA | 1 | 2 | 0 | 1 | 0 | 0 | 0 | 0 | 0 | 0 | 0 | .500 | .500 | .500 | 188 | 0 | 0 | 1.000 | 0 | 353 | 0 | /1 | | 0.0 |

DARWIN, BOBBY Arthur Bobby Lee B2.16.1943 Los Angeles CA BR/TR/6-2/200* d9.30

1962	LA A	1	1	0	0	0	0	0	0	0-0	0	1	.000	.000	.000	-99	0	0-0	.000	-0	0	0	/P		0.0
1969	LA N	6	1	0	0	0	0	0	0	0-0	0	0	—	—	—	—	0	0-0	—	-0	-0	0	P3		0.0
1971	LA N	11	20	2	5	1	0	1	4	2-0	0	9	.250	.318	.450	121	1	0-0	1.000	0	131	0	O4R		0.1
1972	Min A	145	513	48	137	20	2	22	80	38-4	8	145	.267	.326	.442	121	13	2-3	.980	-8	92	84	O142(9/86/47)		-0.1
1973	Min A	145	560	69	141	20	2	18	90	46-5	3	137	.252	.309	.391	93	-6	5-2	.980	-4	88	142	O140R/D		-1.8
1974	Min A	152	575	67	152	13	4	25	94	37-2	14	127	.264	.322	.442	115	-7	1-3	.970	-7	93	75	O142R		-0.7
1975	Min A	48	169	26	37	6	0	5	18	18-1	4	44	.219	.307	.343	83	-4	2-0	.969	-4	56	140	O27R,D19		-0.9
	Mil A	55	186	19	46	6	2	8	23	11-0	3	54	.247	.300	.419	104	0	4-1	.978	3	103	165	O43(25/0/20),D9	34	0.1
	Year	103	355	45	83	12	2	13	41	29-1	7	98	.234	.304	.389	94	-4	6-1	.975	-1	84	155	O70(25/0/47),D28		-0.8
1976	Mil A	25	73	6	18	3	1	1	5	6-1	2	16	.247	.321	.356	100	-0	0-0	.977	1	117	79	O21(0/1/21)/D		0.0
	Bos A	43	106	9	19	5	2	3	13	2-0	3	35	.179	.216	.349	57	-6	1-0	.964	0	103	111	O17(3/0/14),D16		-0.7
	Year	68	179	15	37	8	3	4	18	8-1	5	51	.207	.260	.352	73	-7	1-0	.972	1	111	92	O38(3/1/35),D17		-0.7
1977	Bos A	4	9	1	2	1	0	0	1	0-0	0	4	.222	.222	.333	44	-1	0-0	.500	-0	225	0	/ORD		-0.1
	Chi N	11	12	2	2	1	0	0	0	0-0	0	5	.167	.167	.250	9	-2	0-0	—	0	0	0	/OR		-0.2
Total	9	646	2224	250	559	76	16	83	328	160-13	37	577	.251	.311	.412	103	4	15-9	.976	-19	91	106	O538(37/87/417),D48,P4	34	-4.3

DASCENZO, DOUG Douglas Craig B6.30.1964 Cleveland OH BB/TL/5-8/160* [ChiN85 12/312] d9.2 Col Oklahoma St.

1988	Chi N	26	75	9	16	3	0	0	4	9-1	0	4	.213	.298	.253	57	-4	6-1	1.000	2	118	121	O20C		-0.1
1989	Chi N	47	139	20	23	1	0	1	12	13-0	0	13	.165	.234	.194	23	-14	6-3	1.000	-1	103	0	O45(8/37/1)		-1.6
1990	Chi N	113	241	27	61	9	5	1	26	21-2	1	18	.253	.312	.344	76	-8	15-6	1.000	2	108	44	O107(65/38/22)/P		-0.7
1991	Chi N	118	239	40	61	11	0	1	18	24-2	1	26	.255	.327	.314	78	-6	14-7	.985	-4	95	0	O86(32/59/16),P3		-1.1
1992	Chi N	139	376	37	96	13	4	0	20	27-2	0	32	.255	.304	.311	73	-14	6-8	.978	-6	93	36	O122(25/80/28)		-2.4
1993	Tex A	76	146	20	29	5	1	2	10	8-0	0	22	.199	.239	.288	43	-13	2-0	.990	3	100	216	O68(16/35/25),D2		-1.0
1996	SD N	21	9	3	1	0	0	0	0	1-0	0	2	.111	.200	.111	-16	-2	0-1	1.000	-1	58	0	O10(0/1/9)		-0.2
Total	7	540	1225	156	287	42	10	5	90	103-7	3	117	.234	.293	.297	64	-61	49-26	.990	-4	100	53	O458(146/270/101),P4,D2		-7.1

DASHIELL, WALLY John Wallace B5.9.1902 Jewett TX D5.20.1972 Pensacola FL BR/TR/5-9.5/170 d4.20 Col Lon Morris (TX) JC

| 1924 | Chi A | 1 | 2 | 0 | 0 | 0 | 0 | 0 | 0 | 0-0 | 0 | 0 | .000 | .000 | .000 | -1 | 0 | 0-0 | .667 | -1 | 48 | 0 | /S | | -0.1 |

DATZ, JEFF Jeffrey William B11.28.1959 Camden NJ BR/TR/6-4/220 [HouN82 19/485] d9.5 C4 Col Rowan

| 1989 | Det A | 7 | 10 | 0 | 2 | 0 | 0 | 0 | 0 | 1-0 | 1 | 1 | .200 | .333 | .200 | 55 | -1 | 0-0 | 1.000 | 1 | 0 | 146 | C6/D | | 0.1 |

DAUBACH, BRIAN Brian Michael B2.11.1972 Belleville IL BL/TR/6-1/201(201-230) [NYN90 17/469] d9.10

1998	Fla N	10	15	0	3	1	0	0	3	1-0	1	5	.200	.294	.267	52	-1	0-0	1.000	-0	50	155	1b4		-0.2
1999	†Bos A	110	381	61	112	33	3	21	73	36-0	3	92	.294	.360	.562	126	15	0-1	.983	-0	101	80	1b61,D43,O2L/3		0.6
2000	Bos A	142	495	55	123	32	2	21	76	44-2	6	130	.248	.315	.448	89	-10	1-1	.996	2	102	79	1b83,D41,O8(7/0/1)/3		-1.6
2001	Bos A	122	407	54	107	28	3	22	71	53-7	5	108	.263	.350	.455	109	15	1-0	.988	0	101	83	1b106,O14(6/0/8)	17	0.5
2002	Bos A	137	444	62	118	24	2	20	78	51-4	7	126	.266	.348	.464	112	4	2-1	.990	-4	85	95	1b60,O48(35/0/13),D28		-0.3
2003	Chi A	95	183	26	42	11	0	6	21	34-1	1	54	.230	.352	.388	92	-1	1-0	.996	-1	99	84	1b45,D14,O12(3/0/9)		-0.6
2004	Bos A	30	75	9	17	8	0	2	8	10-1	1	21	.227	.326	.413	86	-1	0-0	.982	1	126	101	1b14,O7(6/0/1)		-0.2
2005	NY N	15	25	4	3	2	0	1	3	7-1	0	5	.120	.324	.320	74	-1	0-0	.977	-0	97	74	1b6,D2		-0.1
Total	8	661	2025	271	525	139	10	93	333	236-15	25	541	.259	.341	.476	107	24	5-3	.990	-2	99	85	1b379,D128,O91(59/0/32),3b2	17	-1.9

DAUBERT, HARRY Harry "Jake" B6.19.1892 Columbus OH D1.8.1944 Detroit MI BR/TR/6-0/160 d9.4

| 1915 | Pit N | 1 | 1 | 0 | 0 | 0 | 0 | 0 | 0 | 0 | 0 | 0 | .000 | .000 | .000 | -99 | 0 | | — | | 0 | 0 | /H | | 0.0 |

DAUBERT, JAKE Jacob Ellsworth B4.7.1884 Shamokin PA D10.9.1924 Cincinnati OH BL/TL/5-10.5/160 d4.14

1910	Bro N	144	552	67	146	15	15	8	50	47	5	53	.264	.328	.389	112	9	23	.989	-3	87	94	1b144		-0.1
1911	Bro N	149	573	89	176	17	8	5	45	51	2	56	.307	.366	.391	117	12	32	.989	2	104	**107**	1b149		1.0
1912	Bro N	145	559	81	172	19	16	3	66	48	6	45	.308	.369	.415	119	13	29	**.993**	1	97	87	1b143		1.0
1913	Bro N	139	508	76	178	17	7	2	52	44	3	40	**.350**	.405	.423	133	23	25-21	.991	3	105	**128**	1b139		2.1
1914	Bro N	126	474	89	156	17	7	6	45	30	5	34	**.329**	.375	.432	137	20	25	.993	-6	71	107	1b126		1.2
1915	Bro N	150	544	62	164	21	8	2	47	57	1	48	.301	.369	.381	125	17	11-13	.993	8	126	84	1b150		2.2
1916	Bro N	127	478	75	151	16	7	3	33	38	4	39	.316	.371	.397	132	19	21-7	**.993**	3	106	85	1b126		2.4
1917	Bro N	125	468	50	122	4	23	0	30	51	5	30	.261	.341	.299	94	-1	11	.991	6	**121**	76	1b125		0.2
1918	Bro N	108	396	50	122	12	**15**	2	47	27	5	18	.308	.360	.429	141	18	10	.991	-1	90	71	1b105		1.7
1919	†Cin N	**140**	537	79	148	10	12	2	44	35	2	23	.276	.332	.353	105	2	11	.989	-1	95	109	1b140		-0.4
1920	Cin N	142	553	97	168	28	13	4	48	47	3	29	.304	.362	.423	127	19	11-13	.990	8	75	101	1b140		-0.7
1921	Cin N	136	516	69	158	18	12	1	64	24	3	16	.306	.341	.399	100	-2	12-6	.993	3	106	109	1b136		-0.2
1922	Cin N	**156**	610	114	205	15	**22**	12	66	56	3	25	.336	.395	.492	130	25	14-17	**.994**	-0	97	**124**	1b156		1.1

YEAR	TM LG	G	AB	R	H	2B	3B	HR	RBI	BB-IB	HP	SO	AVG	OBP	SLG	AOPS	ABR	SB-CS	FA	FR	RNG	THR	GAMES AT POSITION	DL	BFW
1923	Cin N	125	500	63	146	27	10	2	54	40	4	20	.292	.349	.398	99	-1	11-12	.993	6	122	104	1b121		-0.4
1924	Cin N	102	405	47	114	14	9	1	31	28	2	17	.281	.331	.368	88	-7	5-10	.990	7	130	104	1b102		-1.0
Total	15	2014	7673	1117	2326	250	165	56	722	623	54	489	.303	.360	.401	117	162	251-99	.991	20	102	100	1b2002		10.9

DAUER, RICH Richard Fremont B7.27.1952 San Bernardino CA BR/TR/6-0/180(177-190) [BalA74 1/24] d9.11 C11 Col USC

1976	Bal A	11	39	4	4	0	0	0	3	1-0	1	3	.103	.143	.103	-28	-6	0-0	1.000	-2	82	118	2b10		-0.9
1977	Bal A	96	304	38	74	15	1	5	25	20-0	1	28	.243	.294	.349	79	-9	1-0	.982	11	109	126	2b83,3b9,D2		0.6
1978	Bal A	133	459	57	121	23	0	6	46	26-0	0	22	.264	.301	.353	89	-8	0-4	.998	5	95	115	2b87,3b52/D		-0.1
1979	†Bal A	142	479	63	123	20	0	9	61	36-2	1	36	.257	.305	.355	82	-13	0-1	.979	-11	91	115	2b103,3b44		-1.9
1980	Bal A	152	557	71	158	32	0	2	63	46-1	3	19	.284	.338	.352	92	-5	3-2	.991	3	94	124	2b137,3b35		0.4
1981	Bal A	96	369	41	97	27	0	4	38	27-0	3	18	.263	.317	.369	98	0	0-0	.989	-10	90	110	2b94,3b4		-0.1
1982	Bal A	158	558	75	156	24	2	8	57	50-1	1	34	.280	.337	.373	96	-2	0-1	.987	-29	84	91	2b123,3b61		-2.6
1983	†Bal A	140	459	49	108	19	0	5	41	47-2	2	29	.235	.306	.309	72	-17	1-1	.988	-22	89	94	2b131,3b17		-3.2
1984	Bal A	127	397	29	101	26	0	2	24	24-1	0	23	.254	.296	.335	76	-13	1-3	.980	-9	98	106	2b123,3b3		-1.6
1985	Bal A	85	208	25	42	7	0	2	14	20-0	1	7	.202	.275	.264	50	-14	0-1	.990	2	103	106	2b73,3b17/1		-0.9
Total	10	1140	3829	448	984	193	3	43	372	297-7	14	219	.257	.310	.343	83	-87	6-13	.987	-61	94	109	2b964,3b242,D3/1		-10.8

DAUGHERTY, DOC Harold Ray B10.12.1927 Paris PA BR/TR/6-0/180 d4.22

1951	Det A	1	1	0	0	0	0	0	0	0-0	0	0	1.000	.000	.000	-99	0	0-0	—	0			/H		0.0

DAUGHERTY, JACK John Michael B7.3.1960 Hialeah FL BB/TL/6-0/195* d9.1 Col Arizona

1987	Mon N	11	10	1	1	1	0	0	1	0-0	0	3	.100	.100	.200	-22	-2	0-0	1.000	0	383	0	/1		-0.1
1989	Tex A	52	106	15	32	4	2	1	10	11-0	1	21	.302	.364	.406	117	3	2-1	1.000	1	116	81	1b23,O5(4/0/1),D8		0.3
1990	Tex A	125	310	36	93	20	2	6	47	22-0	2	49	.300	.347	.435	118	7	0-0	.982	-0	71	183	O42(39/0/4),1b30,D21		0.4
1991	Tex A	58	144	8	28	3	2	1	11	16-1	0	23	.194	.270	.264	51	-10	1-0	.981	-2	91	64	O37(34/0/3),1b11/D	86	-1.3
1992	Tex A	59	127	13	26	9	0	0	9	16-1	1	21	.205	.295	.276	64	-6	2-1	.939	0	94	98	O26(16/1/11),D13,1b8	91	-0.7
1993	Hou N	4	3	0	1	0	0	0	0	0-0	0	0	.333	.333	.333	82	0	0-0	—	0	0	0	/1OR		0.0
	Cin N	46	59	7	13	2	0	2	9	11-0	0	15	.220	.338	.356	87	-1	0-0	.917	-2	67	0	O16(11/0/5),1b2		-0.3
	Year	50	62	7	14	2	0	2	9	11-0	0	15	.226	.338	.355	87	-1	0-0	.923	-1	72	0	O17(11/0/6),1b3		-0.3
Total	6	355	759	80	194	39	6	10	87	76-2	4	132	.256	.322	.362	92	-9	5-2	.969	-2	80	127	O127(104/1/25),1b76,D43	177	-1.7

DAUGHTERS, BOB Robert Francis "Red" B8.5.1914 Cincinnati OH D8.22.1988 Southbury CT BR/TR/6-2/185 d4.24 Col Holy Cross

1937	Bos A	1	1	0	0	0	0	0	0	0-0	0	0	—	—	—		0	0-0	—	0			/R		0.0

DAULTON, DARREN Darren Arthur B1.3.1962 Arkansas City KS BL/TR/6-2/190(180-207) [PhiN80 25/629] d9.25 C1

1983	Phi N	2	3	1	1	0	0	0	1	0-0	0	1	.333	.500	.333	136	0	0-0	1.000	0	51	0	C2		0.0
1985	Phi N	36	103	14	21	3	1	4	11	16-0	1	37	.204	.311	.369	87	-2	3-0	.994	1	90	101	C28	84	0.1
1986	Phi N	49	138	18	31	4	0	8	21	38-3	1	41	.225	.391	.428	122	6	2-3	.985	-4	78	104	C48	106	0.3
1987	Phi N	53	129	10	25	6	0	3	13	16-1	0	37	.194	.281	.310	55	-8	0-0	.991	-1	99	68	C40/1	10	-0.8
1988	Phi N	58	144	13	30	6	0	1	12	17-1	0	26	.208	.288	.271	61	-7	2-1	.977	-1	93	65	C44/1	36	-1.4
1989	Phi N	131	368	29	74	12	2	8	44	52-8	2	58	.201	.303	.310	76	-11	2-1	.984	-3	109	98	C126		-0.8
1990	Phi N	143	459	62	123	30	1	12	57	72-9	2	72	.268	.367	.416	116	13	7-1	.989	6	151	87	C139		2.9
1991	Phi N	89	285	36	56	12	0	12	42	41-4	2	66	.196	.297	.365	87	-5	5-0	.985	-14	84	51	C88	66	-1.3
1992	Phi N★	145	485	80	131	32	5	27	109	88-11	6	103	.270	.385	.524	156	39	11-2	.987	-3	122	92	C141		4.8
1993	†Phi N	147	510	90	131	35	4	24	105	117-12	2	111	.257	.392	.482	136	32	5-0	.991	-6	124	88	C146		3.7
1994	Phi N	69	257	43	77	17	1	15	56	33-2	1	43	.300	.380	.549	136	14	4-1	.994	7	78	99	C68	44	2.6
1995	Phi N★	98	342	44	85	19	3	9	55	55-2	5	52	.249	.359	.401	100	2	3-0	.994	-3	100	86	C95	37	0.5
1996	Phi N	5	12	3	2	0	0	0	0	7-0	1	5	.167	.500	.167	85	1	0-0	1.000	0	80	0	O5L	176	0.0
1997	Phi N	84	269	46	71	13	6	11	42	54-4	1	57	.264	.381	.480	128	12	4-0	.979	5	121	137	O70R,1b3,D6		1.4
	†Fla N	52	126	22	33	8	2	3	21	22-1	1	17	.262	.371	.429	115	4	2-1	.984	-2	83	98	O73(1/0/73),1b42,D7		-0.1
	Year	136	395	68	104	21	8	14	63	76-5	2	74	.263	.378	.463	124	16	6-1	.979	3	118	134	O73(1/0/73),1b42,D7		1.3
Total	14	1161	3630	511	891	197	25	137	588	629-58	24	726	.245	.357	.427	114	90	50-10	.989	-27	111	86	C965,O78(6/0/73),1b44,D7	559	11.9

DAVALILLO, YO-YO Pompeyo Antonio (Romero) B6.30.1931 Caracas, Venez BR/TR/5-3/154 d8.1 b-Vic

1953	Was A	19	58	10	17	1	0	0	2	1	0	7	.293	.305	.310	68	-3	1-0	.935	-2	90	96	S17		-0.3

DAVALILLO, VIC Victor Jose (Romero) B7.31.1936 Cabimas, Venez BL/TL/5-7/155* d4.9 b-Yo-Yo

1963	Cle A	90	370	44	108	18	5	7	36	16-0	1	41	.292	.321	.424	108	3	3-3	.988	9	121	180	O89C	59	0.9
1964	Cle A	150	577	64	156	26	2	6	51	34-2	1	77	.270	.309	.354	85	-12	21-11	.986	4	105	110	O143C		-1.3
1965	Cle A★	142	505	67	152	19	1	5	40	35-9	0	50	.301	.344	.372	103	2	26-7	.988	8	117	96	O134C		1.0
1966	Cle A	121	344	42	86	6	4	3	19	24-6	0	37	.250	.297	.317	77	-11	8-6	.986	2	107	118	O125(1/125/0)		-1.2
1967	Cle A	139	359	47	103	17	5	2	22	10-0	1	30	.287	.307	.379	101	-1	6-7	.986	-0	104	97	O125(1/125/0)		-0.6
1968	Cle A	51	180	15	43	7	3	2	13	3-0	1	19	.239	.254	.317	74	-7	8-6	.967	2	108	156	O49(3/2/48)		0.8
	Cal A	93	339	34	101	15	4	1	18	15-1	0	34	.298	.326	.355	116	5	17-10	.995	5	116	75	O86(0/70/17)		-0.2
	Year	144	519	49	144	17	7	3	31	18-1	1	53	.277	.301	.355	101	-2	25-16	.987	7	113	105	O135(3/72/65)		-0.9
1969	Cal A	33	71	10	11	1	1	0	1	6-1	1	5	.155	.231	.197	22	-8	3-0	1.000	-0	108	0	O22(0/2/20),1b3		-0.3
	StL N	63	98	15	26	3	0	2	10	7-0	0	8	.265	.314	.357	87	-2	1-1	1.000	0	113	0	O23(2/10/11),P2		0.2
1970	StL N	111	183	29	57	14	3	1	33	13-1	0	19	.311	.355	.437	108	2	4-1	.972	-5	97	157	O54(12/33/13)		-0.4
1971	†Pit N	99	295	48	84	14	6	1	33	11-1	2	31	.285	.312	.383	96	-3	10-2	.983	1	105	143	O61(11/20/31),1b16		1.1
1972	†Pit N	117	368	59	117	19	2	4	28	26-6	3	44	.318	.362	.413	123	11	14-1	.979	1	105	65	O97(64/7/26),1b8		-1.0
1973	Pit N	59	83	9	15	1	0	1	3	2-0	1	7	.181	.200	.229	19	-10	0-2	.977	2	165	108	1b10,O10(7/0/3)		-1.0
	†Oak A	38	64	5	12	1	0	0	4	3-1	0	4	.188	.224	.203	22	-7	0-0	.967	0	100	103	O19(8/1/10),1b8,D2		-0.8
1974	Oak A	17	23	0	4	0	0	0	1	0-0	0	2	.174	.174	.174	22	-2	0-0	1.000	-1	49	0	O6(2/2/2),D4		-0.4
1977	†LA N	24	48	3	15	2	0	0	4	0-0	0	6	.313	.313	.354	78	-1	0-0	1.000	-1	75	0	O12(1/4/8)		-0.3
1978	†LA N	75	77	15	24	1	1	1	11	3-0	0	7	.312	.333	.390	102	0	2-1	1.000	-0	91	0	O25(16/2/7)/1		-0.1
1979	LA N	29	27	2	7	1	0	0	2	2-0	0	5	.259	.310	.296	68	-1	0-0	1.000	-0	80	0	O3L		-0.1
1980	LA N	7	6	1	1	0	0	0	0	0-0	0	1	.167	.167	.167	-7	-1	0-0	1.000	0	1230	/1		-0.1
Total	16	1458	4017	509	1122	160	37	36	329	212-29	10	422	.279	.315	.364	94	-44	125-58	.986	30	109	106	O1066(131/752/196),1b47,D6,P2	59	-4.5

DaVANON, JERRY Frank Gerald B8.21.1945 Oceanside CA BR/TR/5-11/175* [StLN66 S1/17] d4.11 s-Jeff Col San Diego Mesa (CA) JC/San Diego (CA) City

1969	SD N	24	59	4	8	1	0	0	3	3-0	0	12	.136	.177	.153	-7	-9	0-3	.932	1	93	53	2b15,S7		-0.9
	StL N	16	40	7	12	3	0	1	7	6-1	0	8	.300	.391	.450	134	2	0-0	.958	2	105	90	S16		0.6
	Year	40	99	11	20	4	0	1	10	9-1	0	20	.202	.269	.273	53	-6	0-3	.959	3	118	97	S23,2b15		-0.3
1970	StL N	11	18	2	2	1	0	0	0	2-0	0	5	.111	.200	.167	-1	-3	0-0	1.000	2	88	442	3b5,2b3		0.0
1971	Bal A	38	81	14	19	5	0	0	4	12-0	1	20	.235	.340	.296	81	-0	0-0	.970	-5	86	74	2b20,S11,3b3/1		-0.5
1973	Cal A	41	49	6	12	3	0	0	3	3-0	0	9	.245	.288	.306	73	-2	1-2	.927	-2	100	101	S14,2b12,3b7		-0.3
1974	StL N	30	40	4	6	1	0	0	4	4-0	2	5	.150	.255	.175	24	-7	0-1	.840	-4	70	87	S14,3b8,2b7/OR		-0.7
1975	Hou N	32	97	15	27	4	2	1	10	16-1	1	7	.278	.384	.392	125	4	2-0	.944	3	102	102	S21,2b9,3b3		1.0
1976	Hou N	61	107	19	31	3	3	1	20	21-1	1	12	.290	.408	.402	143	7	0-2	.980	2	134	63	2b17,S17,3b9		1.1
1977	StL N	9	8	2	0	0	0	0	0	0-0	0	2	.000	.111	.000	-68	-2	0-0	.923	0	129	0	2b5		-0.2
Total	8	262	499	73	117	21	5	3	50	68-3	5	80	.234	.331	.315	85	-8	3-8	.936	-1	99	107	S100,2b88,3b35/OR1		0.1

DaVANON, JEFF Jeffrey Graham B12.8.1973 San Diego CA BB/TR/6-0/185(180-200) [OakA95 26/708] d9.7 f-Jerry Col San Diego St. [DL 2000 Ana A 181]

1999	Ana A	7	20	4	4	0	1	1	4	2-0	1	7	.200	.273	.450	80	-1	0-1	1.000	-1	60	0	O5(3/0/2),D2		-0.2
2001	Ana A	40	88	7	17	2	1	5	9	11-0	0	29	.193	.280	.409	78	-3	1-3	.980	-0	86	205	O29(0/13/17),D6		-0.5
2002	Ana A	16	30	3	5	3	0	1	4	2-0	0	6	.167	.219	.367	53	-2	1-0	1.000	-2	101	0	O10(3/4/4),D4		-0.2
2003	Ana A	123	330	56	93	16	1	12	43	42-0	1	59	.282	.360	.445	117	9	17-5	.983	4	118	41	O115(8/31/91)/D		1.1
2004	†Ana A	108	285	41	79	11	4	7	34	46-2	2	54	.277	.372	.418	112	6	18-3	.993	2	107	61	O81(24/39/29),D19	17	0.8
2005	†LA A	108	225	42	52	10	2	6	15	39-1	2	44	.231	.347	.311	79	-5	11-6	.991	0	120	47	O63(17/24/26),D30	198	-0.5
Total	6	402	978	153	250	42	8	28	109	142-3	3	199	.256	.348	.401	100	4	48-18	.987	7	111	63	O303(54/111/169),D62	198	0.5

DAVENPORT, JIM James Houston B8.17.1933 Siluria AL BR/TR/5-11/175* d4.15 M1/C15 Col Southern Mississippi

1958	SF N	134	434	70	111	22	3	12	41	30-0	7	72	.256	.317	.403	92	-6	1-3	.960	-7	97	89	3b130,S5		-1.4
1959	SF N	123	469	65	121	16	3	6	38	28-0	2	65	.258	.301	.343	73	-19	0-1	.978	-1	98	88	3b121/S		-2.1
1960	SF N	112	363	43	91	15	3	6	38	26-1	4	58	.251	.306	.358	87	-7	0-2	.961	-3	96	79	3b103,S7		-1.1
1961	SF N	137	436	64	121	28	4	12	65	45-1	2	65	.278	.342	.443	112	8	4-3	.965	7	101	114	3b132		1.4

YEAR	TM LG	G	AB	R	H	2B	3B	HR	RBI	BB-IB	HP	SO	AVG	OBP	SLG	AOPS	ABR	SB-CS	FA	FR	RNG	THR	GAMES AT POSITION	DL	BFW
1962	†SF N★	144	485	83	144	25	5	14	58	45-3	2	76	.297	.357	.456	119	13	2-5	.952	-2	97	120	3b141		0.9
1963	SF N	147	460	40	116	19	3	4	36	32-4	0	87	.252	.297	.333	83	-10	5-2	.962	-11	89	57	3b127,2b22/S		-2.2
1964	SF N	116	297	24	70	10	6	2	26	29-2	0	46	.236	.299	.330	77	-9	2-0	.979	-6	89	60	S64,3b41,2b30		-1.0
1965	SF N	106	271	29	68	14	3	4	31	21-2	1	47	.251	.304	.369	87	-5	0-0	.949	-16	101	76	3b39,S37,2b26		-1.8
1966	SF N	111	305	42	76	6	2	9	30	22-2	1	40	.249	.300	.370	83	-7	1-1	.961	-7	103	82	S58,3b36,2b21,1b2		-1.1
1967	SF N	124	295	42	81	10	3	5	30	39-6	4	50	.275	.366	.380	116	7	1-4	1.000	6	98	106	3b64,S28,2b12		1.5
1968	SF N	113	272	27	61	1	1	1	17	26-0	0	32	.224	.292	.246	63	-12	0-3	.960	-8	90	108	3b82,S17/2		-2.4
1969	SF N	112	303	20	73	10	1	2	42	29-1	0	37	.241	.304	.300	72	-11	0-1	.967	-2	96	111	3b104/1SOR		-1.5
1970	SF N	22	37	3	9	1	0	0	4	7-1	0	6	.243	.356	.270	73	-1	0-0	1.000	-4	46	0	3b10		-0.5
Total	13	1501	4427	552	1142	177	37	77	456	382-23	23	673	.258	.318	.367	90	-59	16-25	.964	-55	96	96	3b1130,S219,2b112,1b3/OR		-11.3

DAVID, ANDRE
Andre Anter B5.18.1958 Hollywood CA   BL/TL/6-0/170 (170-186)   [MinA80 8/194]   d6.29   C1   Col Cal St.-Fullerton

1984	Min A	33	48	5	12	2	0	1	5	7-2	1	11	.250	.351	.354	93	0	0-0	1.000	-1	74	0	O14(10/0/4),D2		-0.2
1986	Min A	5	5	0	1	0	0	0	0	0-0	1	2	.200	.333	.200	48	0	0-0	—	0			/D		0.0
Total	2	38	53	5	13	2	0	1	5	7-2	2	13	.245	.349	.340	88	0	0-0	1.000	-1	74	0	O14(10/0/4),D3		-0.2

DAVIDSON, CLAUDE
Claude Boucher "Davey" B10.13.1896 Boston MA   D4.18.1956 Weymouth MA   BL/TR/5-11/155   d4.25   Col Brown

1918	Phi A	31	81	4	15	1	0	0	4	5	0	9	.185	.233	.198	29	-7	0	.943	-1	91	99	2b15,O8(1/0/7)/3		-1.0
1919	Was A	2	7	1	3	0	0	0	0	1	0	1	.429	.500	.429	163	1	0	1.000	-0	90	0	3b2		0.1
Total	2	33	88	5	18	1	0	0	4	6	0	10	.205	.255	.216	41	-6	0	.943	-1	91	99	2b15,O8(1/0/7),3b3		-0.9

DAVIDSON, CLEATUS
Cleatus La Von B11.1.1976 Bartow FL   BB/TR/5-10/170   [MinA94 2/42]   d5.30

| 1999 | Min A | 12 | 22 | 3 | 3 | 0 | 0 | 0 | 3 | 0-0 | 0 | 4 | .136 | .136 | .136 | -29 | -4 | 2-0 | .973 | 4 | 162 | 221 | 2b6,S4 | 5 | 0.1 |

DAVIDSON, HOMER
Homer Hurd "Divvy" B10.14.1884 Cleveland OH   D7.26.1948 Detroit MI   BR/TR/5-10.5/155   d4.25   Col Penn

| 1908 | Cle A | 9 | 4 | 2 | 0 | 0 | 0 | 0 | 0 | 0 | 0 | | .000 | .000 | .000 | -99 | -1 | 0 | 1.000 | 1 | 0 | 124 | C5/OR | | 0.0 |

DAVIDSON, MARK
John Mark B2.15.1961 Knoxville TN   BR/TR/6-2/190*   [MinA82 11/266]   d6.20   Col Clemson

1986	Min A	36	68	5	8	3	0	2	6	0-0	0	22	.118	.189	.162	-3	-10	2-3	.980	-0	111	0	O31(20/5/7),D3		-1.1
1987	†Min A	102	150	32	40	4	1	1	14	13-1	0	26	.267	.321	.327	71	-6	9-2	1.000	1	103	102	O86(36/20/33),D9		-0.6
1988	Min A	100	106	22	23	7	0	1	10	10-0	1	20	.217	.288	.311	67	-5	3-3	.955	5	132	137	O91(4/4/84)/3D		-0.1
1989	Hou N	33	65	7	13	2	1	1	5	7-0	1	14	.200	.278	.308	70	-3	1-0	1.000	-0	104	0	O23(7/3/15)		-0.4
1990	Hou N	57	130	12	38	5	1	1	11	10-1	0	18	.292	.340	.369	99	0	0-3	.981	4	131	37	O51(26/1/27)	28	0.1
1991	Hou N	85	142	10	27	6	0	2	15	12-0	0	30	.190	.263	.275	54	-9	0-0	1.000	1	108	47	O63(32/4/32)		-1.0
Total	6	413	661	88	149	27	3	6	57	58-2	3	128	.225	.289	.303	64	-33	15-11	.983	10	116	67	O345(125/37/198),D15/3	28	-3.1

DAVIDSON, BILL
William Simpson B5.10.1884 Lafayette IN   D5.23.1954 Lincoln NE   BR/TR/5-10/170   d9.29

1909	Chi N	2	7	2	1	0	0	0	1	0	0		.143	.250	.143	22	-1	0	1.000	-0	0	0	O2(1/1/0)		-0.1
1910	Bro N	136	509	48	121	13	7	0	34	24	4	54	.238	.277	.291	68	-23	27	.961	-11	92	60	O131(0/127/4)		-4.3
1911	Bro N	87	292	33	68	3	4	1	26	16	1	21	.233	.275	.281	58	-18	19	.956	-6	99	37	O74C		-3.0
Total	3	225	808	83	190	16	11	1	60	41	5	75	.235	.276	.286	64	-42	46	.959	-17	94	51	O207(1/202/4)		-7.4

DAVIES, CHICK
Lloyd Garrison B3.6.1892 Peabody MA   D9.5.1973 Middletown CT   BL/TL/5-8/145   d7.11   Col Massachusetts ▲

1914	Phi A	19	46	6	11	3	1	0	5	5	0	13	.239	.314	.348	103	0	1	.926	-1	111	0	O10(9/0/1)/P		-0.1
1915	Phi A	56	132	13	24	5	3	0	11	14	2	31	.182	.270	.265	62	-6	2-4	.973	4	99	193	O32(7/21/4),P4		-0.6
1925	NY N	4	6	1	0	0	0	0	0	0	0	1	.000	.000	.000	-99	-2	0-0	1.000	0	182	0	P2/OR		-0.1
1926	NY N	38	18	4	4	0	0	0	1	3	0	5	.222	.333	.222	53	1	0	.938	1	118	174	P38		0.0
Total	4	117	202	24	39	8	4	0	17	22	2	50	.193	.279	.272	65	-7	3-4	.938	4	124	214	P45,O43(16/21/6)		-0.8

DAVIS, LEFTY
Alphonzo De Ford B2.4.1875 Nashville TN   D2.4.1919 Collins NY   BL/TL/5-10/170   d4.18

1901	Bro N	25	91	11	19	2	0	0	7	10	0		.209	.287	.231	50	-6	4	.822	-5	0	0	O24(12/2/10)/2		-1.1
	Pit N	87	335	87	105	8	11	2	33	56	2		.313	.415	.421	138	19	22	.975	5	158	273	O86R		2.0
	Year	112	426	98	124	10	11	2	40	66	2		.291	.389	.380	120	13	26	.942	1	126	217	O110(12/2/96)/2		0.9
1902	Pit N	59	232	52	65	7	3	0	20	35	1		.280	.377	.336	116	6	19	.945	-2	78	58	O59R		0.1
1903	NY A	104	372	54	88	10	0	0	25	43	2		.237	.319	.263	72	-11	11	.906	-8	60	35	O102(95/1/6)/S		-2.6
1907	Cin N	73	266	28	61	5	5	1	25	23	1		.229	.293	.297	82	-6	9	.972	3	113	124	O70(0/69/1)		-0.7
Total	4	348	1296	232	338	32	19	3	110	167	6		.261	.348	.322	98	2	65	.939	-6	95	116	O341(107/72/162)/S2		-2.3

DAVIS, ALVIN
Alvin Glenn B9.9.1960 Riverside CA   BL/TR/6-1/190*   [SeaA82 6/138]   d4.11   Col Arizona St.

1984	Sea A★	152	567	80	161	34	3	27	116	97-16	7	78	.284	.391	.497	146	40	5-4	.992	-2	90	80	1b147,D7		2.8
1985	Sea A	155	578	78	166	33	1	18	78	90-7	2	71	.287	.381	.441	124	23	1-2	.992	-3	91	93	1b154		1.0
1986	Sea A	135	479	66	130	18	1	18	72	76-10	3	68	.271	.373	.426	116	13	0-3	.986	1	106	122	1b101,D32	22	0.6
1987	Sea A	157	580	86	171	37	2	29	100	72-6	2	84	.295	.370	.516	126	23	0-0	.994	-5	87	107	1b157		0.8
1988	Sea A	140	478	67	141	24	1	18	69	95-13	4	53	.295	.412	.462	139	30	1-1	.994	-5	80	116	1b115,D25	19	1.6
1989	Sea A	142	498	84	152	30	1	21	95	101-15	6	49	.305	.424	.496	155	43	0-1	.992	-4	90	107	1b125,D14	16	3.0
1990	Sea A	140	494	63	140	21	0	17	68	85-10	4	68	.283	.387	.429	128	23	0-2	.994	-1	89	94	D87,1b52	15	1.5
1991	Sea A	145	462	39	102	15	1	12	69	56-9	0	78	.221	.299	.335	77	-15	0-3	1.000	-0	85	134	D126,1b14		-2.1
1992	Cal A	40	104	5	26	8	0	1	16	13-2	0	9	.250	.331	.327	85	-2	0-0	.995	-0	105	119	1b22,D9		-0.3
Total	9	1206	4240	568	1189	220	10	160	683	685-88	28	558	.280	.380	.450	126	178	7-16	.992	-19	90	103	1b887,D300	72	8.9

DAVIS, BILL
Arthur Willard B6.6.1942 Graceville MN   BL/TL/6-7/215 (215-226)   d9.16   Col Minnesota

1965	Cle A	10	10	0	3	1	0	0	0	0-0	0	1	.300	.300	.400	96	0	0-0	—	0			/H		0.0
1966	Cle A	23	38	2	6	1	0	1	4	6-0	0	9	.158	.267	.263	55	-2	0-0	.981	0	100	109	1b9		-0.3
1969	SD N	31	57	1	10	1	0	1	1	8-0	1	18	.175	.288	.193	38	-4	0-0	.992	-1	68	108	1b14		-0.7
Total	3	64	105	3	19	3	0	1	5	14-0	1	28	.181	.281	.238	50	-6	0-0	.988	-1	80	108	1b23		-1.0

DAVIS, BROCK
Bryshear Barnett B10.19.1943 Oakland CA   BL/TL/5-10/168*   d4.9   Col Cal St.-Los Angeles

1963	Hou N	34	55	7	11	2	0	1	4	2-1	0	10	.200	.254	.291	60	-3	0-0	.864	-0	95	155	O14(5/6/3)		-0.4
1964	Hou N	1	3	0	0	0	0	0	0	1-0	0	1	.000	.250	.000	-24	0	0-0	1.000	0	126	0	/OL		0.0
1966	Hou N	10	27	2	4	0	1	0	1	5-0	0	4	.148	.281	.185	35	-2	1-0	1.000	-0	101	0	O7C		-0.3
1970	Chi N	6	3	0	0	0	0	0	0	0-0	0	1	.000	.000	.000	-89	-1	0-0	—	-0	0	0	/OC		-0.1
1971	Chi N	106	301	36	77	7	5	0	28	35-0	2	34	.256	.335	.312	74	-9	0-6	.982	2	104	104	O93(3/85/5)		-1.3
1972	Mil A	85	154	17	49	2	0	0	12	12-0	0	23	.318	.365	.331	111	2	6-4	.970	-1	88	88	O43(19/19/5)		0.3
Total	6	242	543	48	141	12	5	1	43	57-1	2	73	.260	.331	.306	79	-13	7-10	.973	-1	101	98	O159(28/118/13)		-2.2

DAVIS, CHILI
Charles Theodore B1.17.1960 Kingston, Jamaica   BB/TR/6-3/210 (195-240)   d4.10

1981	SF N	8	15	1	2	0	0	0	0	1-0	0	2	.133	.188	.133	-8	-2	0-0	1.000	-0	92	0	O6(1/2/3)		-0.2
1982	SF N	154	641	86	167	27	6	19	76	45-2	2	115	.261	.308	.410	101	-1	24-13	.972	5	104	163	O153(13/142/1)		0.3
1983	SF N	137	486	54	113	21	2	11	59	55-6	0	108	.233	.305	.352	86	-10	10-12	.976	4	108	105	O133(0/121/12)		-1.0
1984	SF N★	137	499	87	157	21	6	21	81	42-6	1	74	.315	.368	.507	148	30	12-8	.971	3	106	121	O123(1/67/57)		3.1
1985	SF N	136	481	53	130	25	2	13	56	62-12	0	74	.270	.349	.412	119	13	15-7	.980	7	110	123	O126(0/36/91)		1.6
1986	SF N★	153	526	71	146	28	3	13	70	84-23	1	96	.278	.375	.416	125	21	16-13	.972	-1	104	83	O148(0/53/117)		1.3
1987	†SF N	149	500	80	125	22	1	24	76	72-15	2	109	.250	.344	.442	112	9	16-9	.975	-7	91	78	O135(18/114/36)		0.0
1988	Cal A	158	600	81	161	29	3	21	93	56-14	0	118	.268	.326	.432	114	11	9-10	.942	-10	89	103	O153(0/3/154),D3		-0.6
1989	Cal A	154	560	81	152	24	1	22	90	61-12	0	109	.271	.340	.436	120	15	3-0	.979	-11	87	56	O147L,D6		0.0
1990	Cal A	113	412	58	109	17	1	12	58	61-4	0	89	.265	.357	.398	114	9	1-2	.965	-3	79	159	D60,O52(46/0/7)	23	0.2
1991	†Min A	153	534	84	148	34	1	29	93	95-13	1	117	.277	.385	.507	139	31	5-6	1.000	-3	280		D150,O2L		2.5
1992	Min A	138	444	63	128	27	2	12	66	73-11	3	76	.288	.386	.439	128	20	4-5	1.000	0	130		D125,O4(1/0/3)/1		1.5
1993	Cal A	153	573	74	139	32	0	27	112	71-12	1	135	.243	.327	.440	101	-2	4-1	—	-0	0	0	D150/P		-0.7
1994	Cal A★	108	392	72	122	18	1	26	84	69-11	1	84	.311	.410	.561	146	29	3-2	1.000	6	124		D106,O2L		2.1
1995	Cal A	119	424	81	135	23	0	20	86	89-12	0	79	.318	.429	.514	148	35	3-3	—	0	0		D119	28	2.6
1996	Cal A	145	530	73	155	24	0	28	95	86-11	0	99	.292	.387	.496	125	19	5-2	—	0	0		D143		1.0
1997	KC A	140	477	71	133	20	0	30	90	85-16	1	96	.279	.386	.509	120	21	6-3	—	0	0		D133	13	1.4
1998	†NY A	35	103	11	30	7	0	3	9	14-1	0	18	.291	.373	.447	118	3	0-1	—	0	0		D34	136	0.1
1999	†NY A	146	476	59	128	25	1	19	78	73-7	2	100	.269	.366	.445	108	7	4-1	—	0	0		D132		0.1
Total	19	2436	8673	1240	2380	424	30	350	1372	1194-188	15	1698	.274	.360	.451	120	260	142-98	.971	-13	99	106	O1184(231/538/481),D1161/P1	200	15.3

YEAR	TM LG	G	AB	R	H	2B	3B	HR	RBI	BB-IB	HP	SO	AVG	OBP	SLG	AOPS	ABR	SB-CS	FA	FR	RNG	THR	GAMES AT POSITION	DL	BFW

DAVIS, DOUG   Douglas Raymond B9.24.1962 Bloomsburg PA BR/TR/6-0/180* [CalA84 9/216] d7.8 C2 Col North Carolina St.

1988	Cal A	6	12	1	0	0	0	0	0	0-0	1	3	.000	.077	.000	-78	-3	0-0	1.000	-2	99	226	C3,3b3		-0.8
1992	Tex A	1	1	0	1	0	0	0	0	0-0	0	0	1.000	1.000	1.000	476	0	0-0	—	-0	0	0	/C		0.0
Total	2	7	13	1	1	0	0	0	0	0-0	1	3	.077	.143	.077	-38	-3	0-0	1.000	-3	92	210	C4,3b3		-0.6

DAVIS, ERIC   Eric Keith B5.29.1962 Los Angeles CA BR/TR/6-3/185(165-200) [CinN80 8/201] d5.19

1984	Cin N	57	174	33	39	10	1	10	30	24-0	1	48	.224	.320	.466	113	3	10-2	.992	5	114	158	O51(2/46/10)	16	0.9
1985	Cin N	56	122	26	30	3	3	8	18	7-0	0	39	.246	.287	.516	114	1	16-3	.987	3	112	158	O47(24/28/5)		0.6
1986	Cin N	132	415	97	115	15	3	27	71	68-5	1	100	.277	.378	.523	141	24	80-11	.975	0	111	27	O121(72/71/16)		3.5
1987	Cin N★	129	474	120	139	23	4	37	100	84-8	1	134	.293	.399	.593	153	38	50-6	.990	16	124	136	O128(4/124/0)		5.9
1988	Cin N	135	472	81	129	18	3	26	93	65-10	3	124	.273	.363	.489	138	24	35-3	.981	-9	92	34	O130(0/125/5)		2.8
1989	Cin N★	131	462	74	130	14	2	34	101	68-12	1	116	.281	.367	.541	154	32	21-7	.984	-7	97	31	O125(4/118/3)	15	2.8
1990	†Cin N	127	453	84	118	26	2	24	86	60-6	2	100	.260	.347	.486	122	14	21-3	.993	-1	94	148	O122(56/66/0)	24	1.5
1991	Cin N	89	285	39	67	10	0	11	33	48-5	5	92	.235	.353	.386	104	3	14-2	.985	2	106	120	O81(7/77/0)	41	0.8
1992	LA N	76	267	21	61	8	1	5	32	36-2	3	71	.228	.325	.322	85	-4	19-1	.961	-7	84	0	O74(69/5/4)	50	-1.0
1993	LA N	108	376	57	88	17	0	14	53	41-6	1	88	.234	.308	.391	91	-5	33-5	.991	5	107	93	O103(101/3/0)		0.6
	Det A	23	75	14	19	1	1	6	15	14-1	0	18	.253	.371	.533	140	4	2-2	.981	0	111	0	O18C,D5		0.4
1994	Det A	37	120	19	22	4	0	3	13	18-0	0	45	.183	.290	.292	50	-9	5-0	.989	-2	96	56	O35C	73	-0.9
1996	Cin N	129	415	81	119	20	0	26	83	70-3	6	121	.287	.394	.523	138	25	23-9	.989	-1	105	51	O126(14/115/0)/1	15	0.2
1997	†Bal A	42	158	29	48	11	0	8	25	14-0	1	47	.304	.358	.525	132	7	6-0	.975	-5	68	0	O30R,D12	112	0.2
1998	Bal A	131	452	81	148	29	1	28	89	44-0	5	108	.327	.388	.582	152	35	7-6	.992	-3	90	88	O72(0/11/64),D53		2.4
1999	StL N	58	191	27	49	9	2	5	30	30-1	1	49	.257	.370	.503	91	-2	5-4	1.000	0	96	126	O51(0/3/50),D2	98	0.0
2000	†StL N	92	254	38	77	14	0	6	40	36-0	1	60	.303	.389	.429	105	3	1-1	.968	-1	108	28	O69R,D4		0.0
2001	SF N	74	156	17	32	7	3	4	22	13-0	1	38	.205	.269	.365	66	-9	1-1	.962	-0	106	44	O48R/D	19	-0.7
Total	17	1626	5321	938	1430	239	26	282	934	740-59	33	1398	.269	.359	.482	124	184	349-66	.984	-5	102	74	O1431(353/845/304),D77/1	463	20.4

DAVIS, GEORGE   George Stacey B8.23.1870 Cohoes NY D10.17.1940 Philadelphia PA BB/TR/5-9/180 d4.19 M3 HF1998 OF(12/243/48)

1890	Cle N	**136**	526	98	139	22	9	6	73	53		4	34	.264	.336	.375	109	6	22	.946	12	158	182	O133(0/129/4),2b2/S		1.2
1891	Cle N	136	570	115	165	35	12	3	89	53		4	29	.289	.354	.409	117	11	42	.931	8	154	32	O116(4/111/1),3b22,P3		1.8
1892	†Cle N	144	597	95	144	27	12	5	82	58		3	51	.241	.312	.352	97	-4	36	.914	-8	95	76	3b79,O44(0/3/41),S20,2b3		-1.1
1893	NY N	133	549	112	195	22	27	11	119	42		9	20	.355	.410	.554	154	38	37	.884	-1	99	114	3b133/S		3.1
1894	†NY N	124	486	125	171	27	19	9	93	67		4	10	.352	.434	.541	135	28	42	.908	-1	99	104	3b124		2.2
1895	NY N	110	430	108	146	36	9	5	101	55		2	12	.340	.417	.500	139	27	48	.881	11	103	150	3b80,1b14,2b10,O7(5/0/2),M		3.2
1896	NY N	124	494	98	158	25	12	5	99	50		4	24	.320	.387	.449	124	17	48	.917	15	109	99	3b74,S45,O3L,1b3		3.3
1897	NY N	131	521	112	184	31	10	10	135	43		7		.353	.410	.509	146	34	65	.926	20	99	139	S130		5.7
1898	NY N	121	486	80	149	20	5	2	86	32		1		.307	.351	.381	113	8	26	.933	30	101	112	S121		4.8
1899	NY N	109	419	69	141	22	5	1	59	38		2		.337	.394	.420	128	17	35	.946	46	112	119	S109		6.1
1900	NY N	114	426	69	136	20	4	3	61	35		2		.319	.376	.406	121	14	29	.944	29	111	105	S114,M		4.3
1901	NY N	130	491	69	148	26	7	7	65	40		2		.301	.356	.426	131	20	27	.939	24	102	89	S113,3b17,M		4.6
1902	Chi A	132	485	76	145	27	7	3	93	65		4		.299	.386	.402	124	20	31	.951	-3	96	134	S129,1b3		2.0
1903	NY N	4	15	2	4	0	0	0	1	1		0		.267	.313	.267	63	-1	0	.870	-2	68	0	S4		-0.2
1904	Chi A	152	563	75	142	27	15	1	69	43		5		.252	.311	.359	116	10	32	.937	18	107	149	S152		3.1
1905	Chi A	151	550	74	153	29	1	1	55	60		4		.278	.353	.340	125	19	31	.948	16	110	137	S151		4.4
1906	†Chi A	133	484	63	134	26	6	0	80	41		4		.277	.338	.355	120	13	27	.946	13	110	121	S129/2		3.1
1907	Chi A	132	466	59	111	16	2	1	52	47		4		.238	.313	.288	95	-1	15	.949	7	108	97	S132		1.3
1908	Chi A	128	419	41	91	14	1	0	26	41		7		.217	.298	.255	81	-6	22	.960	2	109	97	2b95,S23,1b4		-0.4
1909	Chi A	28	68	5	9	1	0	0	2	10		1		.132	.253	.147	28	-5	4	.986	1	143	93	1b17,2b2		-0.5
Total	20	2372	9045	1545	2665	453	163	73	1440	874		75	180	.295	.362	.405	121	265	619	.940	236	104	122	S1374,3b529,O303C,2b113,1b41,P3		50.7

DAVIS, KIDDO   George Willis B2.12.1902 Bridgeport CT D3.4.1983 Bridgeport CT BR/TR/5-11/178 d6.15 Col NYU

1926	NY A	1	0	0	0	0	0	0	0	0		0	0-0	—	—	—	—	-0	0	0	/OR		0.6
1932	Phi N	137	576	100	178	39	6	5	57	44		1	56	.309	.359	.424	98	0	16	.975	8	108	122	O133(1/132/0)		0.4
1933	†NY N	126	434	61	112	20	4	7	37	25		0	30	.258	.298	.371	92	-6	10	.988	-9	85	92	O120C		-1.9
1934	StL N	16	33	6	10	3	0	1	4	3		0	1	.303	.361	.485	117	1	1	.960	1	104	174	O9C		0.3
	Phi N	100	393	50	115	25	5	3	48	27		0	28	.293	.338	.405	86	-7	1	.991	15	115	178	O100C		0.3
	Year	116	426	56	125	28	5	4	52	30		0	29	.293	.340	.411	89	-6	2	.988	14	115	178	O109C		0.5
1935	NY N	47	91	16	24	7	1	2	6	10		1	4	.264	.343	.429	108	1	2	.977	-1	97	49	O21(2/2/17)		-0.1
1936	†NY N	47	67	6	16	1	0	0	5	6		0	5	.239	.301	.254	51	-5	0	1.000	2	107	229	O22(6/11/6)		-0.3
1937	NY N	56	76	20	20	10	0	0	9	10		1	7	.263	.356	.395	103	1	1	.932	-2	93	0	O37(11/25/0)		-0.1
	Cin N	40	136	19	35	6	0	1	5	16		1	6	.257	.340	.324	85	-2	1	.959	-1	104	33	O35(9/26/0)		-0.1
	Year	96	212	39	55	16	0	1	14	26		2	13	.259	.346	.349	90	-1	2	.951	-3	100	22	O72(20/51/0)		-0.1
1938	Cin N	5	18	3	5	1	0	0	1			0	4	.278	.316	.333	92	-17	32-0	1.000	0	92	265	O5(0/2/0/5)		0.0
Total	8	575	1824	281	515	112	16	19	171	142		4	141	.282	.336	.393	92	-17	32-0	.980	11	102	117	O483(31/425/29)		-2.2

DAVIS, GERRY   Gerald Edward B12.25.1958 Trenton NJ BR/TR/6-0/185* [SDN80 6/135] d9.20 Col Howard

1983	SD N	5	15	3	5	2	0	0	1	3-0	0	4	.333	.444	.467	157	1	1-0	1.000	0	91	306	O5R		0.1
1985	SD N	44	58	10	17	3	1	0	2	5-0	0	7	.293	.349	.379	105	0	0-0	.952	0	87	263	O23(7/1/14)		0.1
Total	2	49	73	13	22	5	1	0	3	8-0	0	11	.301	.370	.397	116	1	1-0	.967	1	88	276	O28(7/1/19)		0.2

DAVIS, GLENN   Glenn Earle B3.28.1961 Jacksonville FL BR/TR/6-3/210(200-212) [HouN81*S1/5] d9.2 Col Georgia

1984	Hou N	18	61	6	13	5	0	2	8	4-0	0	12	.213	.258	.393	87	-1	0-0	.988	2	144	109	1b16		-0.1
1985	Hou N	100	350	51	95	11	0	20	64	27-6	7	68	.271	.332	.474	127	11	0-0	.985	-2	97	109	1b89,O9R		1.1
1986	†Hou N★	158	574	91	152	32	3	31	101	64-6	9	72	.265	.344	.493	133	25	3-1	.992	2	98	85	1b156		2.7
1987	Hou N	151	578	70	145	35	2	27	93	47-10	5	84	.251	.310	.458	105	2	4-1	.991	3	101	79	1b151		-0.4
1988	Hou N	152	561	78	152	26	0	30	99	53-20	11	77	.271	.341	.478	140	28	4-3	**.996**	1	96	99	1b151		2.7
1989	Hou N★	158	581	87	156	26	1	34	89	69-17	7	123	.269	.350	.492	144	33	4-2	.992	2	106	92	1b156		2.2
1990	Hou N	93	327	44	82	15	4	22	64	46-17	8	54	.251	.357	.523	143	19	8-3	.995	-5	82	93	1b91	65	0.4
1991	Bal A	49	176	29	40	9	1	10	28	16-0	5	29	.227	.307	.460	114	3	4-0	.976	4	152	116	1b36,D12	116	0.2
1992	Bal A	106	398	46	110	15	2	13	48	37-2	2	65	.276	.338	.422	109	4	1-0	1.000	-0	65	59	D103,1b2	28	0.8
1993	Bal A	30	113	8	20	3	0	1	9	7-0	2	29	.177	.230	.230	23	-13	0-1	.990	-1	86	112	1b22,D7	91	-1.8
Total	10	1015	3719	510	965	177	13	190	603	370-78	55	613	.259	.332	.467	124	111	28-11	.991	6	101	93	1b870,D122,O9R	300	5.9

DAVIS, HARRY   Harry Albert "Stinky" B5.7.1908 Shreveport LA D3.3.1997 Shreveport LA BL/TL/5-10.5/160 d4.13 Col Centenary Louisiana

1932	Det A	141	590	92	159	32	13	4	74	60		2	53	.269	.339	.388	84	-14	12-7	.989	-4	87	105	1b141		-3.1
1933	Det A	66	173	24	37	8	2	0	14	22		0	8	.214	.303	.283	55	-11	2-3	.978	-5	57	104	1b44		-2.2
1937	StL A	120	450	89	124	25	3	3	35	71		0	26	.276	.374	.364	86	-7	7-6	.991	-4	86	98	1b112/OR		-2.1
Total	3	327	1213	205	320	65	18	7	123	153		2	87	.264	.347	.364	81	-32	21-16	.988	-13	82	102	1b297/OR		-7.4

DAVIS, HARRY   Harry H (b Harry Davis) "Jasper" B7.19.1873 Philadelphia PA D8.11.1947 Philadelphia PA BR/TR/5-10/180 d9.21 M1/C6 OF(50/19/11)

1895	NY N	7	24	1	7	0	1	0	6	2		0		.292	.346	.375	88	-1	1	.957	0	118	108	1b7		-0.1
1896	NY N	64	233	43	64	11	10	2	50	31		5	20	.275	.372	.433	115	5	16	.883	-5	34	0	O40(39/1/0),1b23		-0.1
	Pit N	44	168	24	32	5	6	0	23	13		2	21	.190	.257	.292	46	-14	9	.966	0	98	82	1b35,O10(9/0/1)/S		-1.1
	Year	108	401	67	96	16	16	2	73	44		7	41	.239	.325	.374	87	-9	25	.973	-5	96	91	1b58,O50(48/1/1)/S		-1.1
1897	Pit N	111	429	70	131	10	28	2	63	26		10		.305	.359	.473	123	11	21	.965	-12	84	78	1b64,3b32,O14(0/7/9)/S		-0.7
1898	Pit N	58	222	31	65	9	13	1	24	12		1		.293	.332	.464	130	6	7	.980	-5	85	99	1b53,O6C		-0.5
	Lou N	37	138	18	30	5	2	1	16	7		0		.217	.255	.304	61	-8	6	.967	-0	124	111	1b34,2b2/OR		-0.5
	Was N	1	3	0	0	0	0	0	0	0		0		.000	.000	.000	-99	-1	0	.875	-0	0	0	/1		-0.0
	Year	96	363	49	95	14	15	2	40	19		1		.262	.300	.399	102	-2	13	.974	-2	99	103	1b88,O7(0/6/1),2b2		-0.5
1899	Was N	18	64	9	12	2	3	0	8	8		1		.188	.288	.313	65	-3	2	.988	-1	48	53	1b18		-0.3
1901	Phi A	117	496	92	152	28	10	8	76	23		7	21	.306	.340	.452	113	7	21	.976	8	133	97	1b117		1.1
1902	Phi A	133	561	89	172	**43**	8	9	92	30		1	23	.307	.343	.444	112	8	28	.984	8	122	76	1b128,O5C		1.6
1903	Phi A	106	420	77	125	28	7	6	55	24		5		.298	.343	.440	128	14	24	.972	-1	98	77	1b104,O2L		1.2
1904	Phi A	102	404	64	125	23	11	**10**	62	23		2		.309	.350	.490	156	24	12	.983	-1	88	79	1b102		2.2
1905	†Phi A	150	607	**93**	173	**47**	6	8	**83**	43		2		.285	.334	.422	137	25	36	.985	0	92	71	1b150		2.8
1906	Phi A	145	551	94	161	42	7	**12**	**96**	49		8		.292	.355	.459	150	32	23	.975	0	100	109	1b145		3.3

YEAR	TM LG	G	AB	R	H	2B	3B	HR	RBI	BB-IB	HP	SO	AVG	OBP	SLG	AOPS	ABR	SB-CS	FA	FR	RNG	THR	GAMES AT POSITION	DL	BFW
1907	Phi A	149	582	84	155	35	8	8	87	42	2		.266	.318	.395	124	15	20	.977	4	109	79	1b149		1.7
1908	Phi A	147	513	65	127	23	9	5	62	61	4		.248	.332	.357	116	11	20	.986	1	96	68	1b147		1.0
1909	Phi A	149	530	73	142	22	11	4	75	51	5		.268	.338	.374	122	14	20	.988	-6	80	98	1b149		0.6
1910	†Phi A	139	492	61	122	19	4	1	41	53	9		.248	.332	.309	102	3	17	.986	-5	79	126	1b139		-0.5
1911	†Phi A	57	183	27	36	9	1	1	22	24	2		.197	.297	.273	60	-9	2	.977	2	113	94	1b53		-0.8
1912	Cle A	2	5	0	0	0	0	0	0	0	0		.000	.000	.000	-97	-1	0	.941	0	233	137	1b2,M		-0.1
1913	Phi A	7	17	2	6	2	0	0	4	1	0	4	.353	.389	.471	155	1	0	1.000	1	173	101	1b6		0.2
1914	Phi A	5	7	0	3	0	0	0	2	1	1	0	.429	.556	.429	204	1	0-2	1.000	-0	0	0	/1		0.0
1915	Phi A	5	3	0	1	0	0	0	4	0	0	0	.333	.333	.333	103	0	0	—	0	0	0	/1		0.0
1916	Phi A	1	0	0	0	0	0	0	0	1	0	0	—	1.000	—	213	0	0	—	0	0		/H		0.0
1917	Phi A	1	1	0	0	0	0	0	0	0	0	0	.000	.000	.000	-99	0	0	—	0			/H		0.0
Total	22	1755	6653	1001	1841	361	145	75	951	525	59	45	.277	.335	.408	119	140	285-2	.980	-7	99	89	1b1628,O78L,3b32,2b2,S2		10.9

DAVIS, TOMMY Herman Thomas B3.21.1939 Brooklyn NY BR/TR/6-2/205* d9.22 C1 OF(1101/122/56)

YEAR	TM LG	G	AB	R	H	2B	3B	HR	RBI	BB-IB	HP	SO	AVG	OBP	SLG	AOPS	ABR	SB-CS	FA	FR	RNG	THR	GAMES AT POSITION	DL	BFW
1959	LA N	1	1	0	0	0	0	0	0	0-0	1		1	.000	.000	.000	-93	-0	0-0	—	0			/H		0.0
1960	LA N	110	352	43	97	18	1	11	44	13-2	2	35	.276	.302	.426	92	-5	6-2	.975	-1	90	119	O87(24/55/10),3b5		-0.9
1961	LA N	132	460	60	128	13	2	15	58	32-4	2	53	.278	.325	.413	87	-9	10-4	.973	-3	113	59	O86(44/39/30),3b59		-1.4
1962	LA N★	163	665	120	230	27	9	27	153	33-6	2	65	.346	.374	.535	151	44	18-6	.961	0	105	100	O146(134/13/5),3b39		3.8
1963	†LA N★	146	556	69	181	19	3	16	88	29-5	4	59	.326	.359	.457	144	30	15-10	.969	-3	98	102	O129(120/14/3),3b40		2.1
1964	LA N	152	592	70	163	20	5	14	86	29-6	4	68	.275	.311	.397	106	2	11-8	.982	7	108	97	O148L		0.1
1965	LA N	17	60	3	15	1	1	0	9	2-1	0	4	.250	.270	.300	66	-3	2-1	1.000	0	93	129	O16L	143	-0.4
1966	†LA N	100	313	27	98	11	1	3	27	16-4	0	36	.313	.345	.383	111	4	3-3	.972	-0	86	109	O79L,3b2		0.0
1967	NY N	154	577	72	174	32	0	16	73	31-10	7	71	.302	.342	.440	125	18	9-3	.975	-3	99	59	O149L/1		0.9
1968	Chi N	132	456	30	122	5	3	8	50	16-3	0	48	.268	.289	.344	91	-7	4-2	.962	-4	87	112	O116(115/0/4),1b6		-2.1
1969	Sea A	123	454	52	123	29	1	6	80	30-5	4	46	.271	.318	.379	96	-3	19-4	.967	-9	85	36	O112L/1		-1.6
	Hou N	24	79	2	19	3	0	1	9	8-0	1	9	.241	.318	.316	79	-2	1-1	1.000	-0	88	102	O21(20/1/0)		-0.4
1970	Hou N	57	213	24	60	12	2	3	30	7-1	0	25	.282	.305	.399	90	-4	8-3	.949	-2	86	116	O53L		-0.8
	Oak A	66	200	17	58	9	1	1	27	8-1	1	18	.290	.318	.360	90	-3	2-4	.963	-5	74	43	O45(43/0/2),1b8		-1.2
	Chi N	11	42	4	11	2	0	2	8	1-0	0	1	.262	.279	.452	82	-1	0-0	.938	-1	98		O10L		-0.2
1971	†Oak A	79	219	26	71	8	1	3	42	15-1	0	19	.324	.363	.411	122	6	7-1	.989	4	150	102	1b35,O16L,2b3,3b2	15	0.8
1972	Chi N	15	26	3	7	1	0	0	6	2-0	0	3	.269	.321	.308	72	-1	0-1	1.000	-0	77	0	1b3,O2(1/0/1)		-0.2
	Bal A	26	82	9	21	3	0	0	6	6-0	0	18	.256	.307	.293	76	-2	0-1	1.000	1	104	0	O18(17/0/1),1b3		-0.3
1973	†Bal A	137	552	53	169	20	3	7	89	30-3	1	56	.306	.341	.391	106	3	11-3	.971	-3	0	107	D127,1b4		0.1
1974	†Bal A	158	626	67	181	20	1	11	84	34-9	3	49	.289	.325	.377	105	3	6-2	—	0	0	0	D155		-0.1
1975	Bal A	116	460	43	130	14	1	6	57	23-2	0	52	.283	.315	.357	95	-5	2-0	—	0	0	0	D111		-0.7
1976	Cal A	72	219	16	58	5	0	3	26	15-3	1	18	.265	.312	.329	94	-2	0-1	1.000	-0	0	0	D54/1		-0.4
	KC A	8	19	1	5	0	0	0	1-0	0	0	.263	.300	.263	65	-1	0-0	—	0			D3		-0.1
	Year	80	238	17	63	5	0	3	26	16-3	1	18	.265	.311	.324	92	-3	0-1	1.000	-0	0	0	D57/1		-0.5
Total	18	1999	7223	811	2121	272	35	153	1052	381-66	32	754	.294	.329	.405	108	62	136-59	.970	-19	96	85	O1233L,D450,3b147,1b62,2b3	158	-3.0

DAVIS, IKE Isaac Marion B6.14.1895 Pueblo CO D4.2.1984 Tucson AZ BR/TR/5-7/140 d4.23

YEAR	TM LG	G	AB	R	H	2B	3B	HR	RBI	BB-IB	HP	SO	AVG	OBP	SLG	AOPS	ABR	SB-CS	FA	FR	RNG	THR	GAMES AT POSITION	DL	BFW
1919	Was A	8	14	0	0	0	0	0	0	0	0	6	.000	.000	.000	-99	-4	0	.857	-2	24	101	S4		-0.6
1924	Chi A	10	33	4	8	1	1	0	4	2	0	5	.242	.286	.333	61	-2	0-0	.940	1	120	63	S10		-0.1
1925	Chi A	146	562	105	135	31	9	0	61	71	7	58	.240	.333	.327	72	-23	19-14	.937	7	106	113	S144		-0.1
Total	3	164	609	110	143	32	10	0	65	73	7	69	.235	.324	.320	68	-29	19-14	.936	6	105	110	S158		-0.8

DAVIS, IRA J. Ira "Slats" B7.8.1870 Philadelphia PA D12.21.1942 Brooklyn NY ?/162 d4.22 Col Penn

YEAR	TM LG	G	AB	R	H	2B	3B	HR	RBI	BB-IB	HP	SO	AVG	OBP	SLG	AOPS	ABR	SB-CS	FA	FR	RNG	THR	GAMES AT POSITION	DL	BFW
1899	NY N	6	17	3	4	1	1	0	2	0	0		.235	.235	.412	79	-1	1	.750	-0	114	289	S3,1b2		-0.1

DAVIS, JACKE Jacke Sylvesta B3.5.1936 Carthage TX BR/TR/5-11/185 d4.19 Col Baylor

YEAR	TM LG	G	AB	R	H	2B	3B	HR	RBI	BB-IB	HP	SO	AVG	OBP	SLG	AOPS	ABR	SB-CS	FA	FR	RNG	THR	GAMES AT POSITION	DL	BFW
1962	Phi N	48	75	9	16	0	1	1	6	4-0	0	20	.213	.253	.280	44	-6	1-0	.926	-2	86	0	O26(16/5/7)		-0.9

DAVIS, JUMBO James J. B9.5.1861 New York NY D2.14.1921 St.Louis MO BL/TR/5-11/195 d7.27 U1

YEAR	TM LG	G	AB	R	H	2B	3B	HR	RBI	BB-IB	HP	SO	AVG	OBP	SLG	AOPS	ABR	SB-CS	FA	FR	RNG	THR	GAMES AT POSITION	DL	BFW
1884	KC U	7	29	3	6	0	0	0		0			.207	.207	.207	30	-3		.633	-1	119	0	3b7		-0.4
1886	Bal AA	60	216	23	42	5	2	1	20	11	2		.194	.240	.250	55	-11	12	.848	4	96	71	3b60		-0.6
1887	Bal AA	130	485	81	150	23	19	8	109	28	5		.309	.353	.485	141	24	49	.826	1	116	56	3b87,S43		2.3
1888	KC AA	121	491	70	131	22	8	3	61	20	6		.267	.304	.363	106	1	42	.843	29	139	141	3b113,S8		2.9
1889	KC AA	62	241	40	64	4	3	0	30	17	2	35	.266	.319	.307	74	-9	25	.803	-3	103	111	3b62		-1.0
	StL AA	2	4	1	0	0	0	0	0	1	0	1	.000	.200	.000	-36	-1	0	1.000	0	0		/SOL		-0.1
	Year	64	245	41	64	4	3	0	30	18	2	36	.261	.317	.302	72	-10	25	.803	-4	103	111	3b62/SOL		-1.1
1890	StL AA	21	71	8	18	3	1	0	13	9	4		.254	.338	.324	83	-2	5	.731	-3	105	60	3b21		-0.4
	Bro AA	38	142	33	43	9	2	2	28	15	4		.303	.385	.437	147	9	10	.845	-4	105	132	3b38		0.5
	Year	59	213	41	61	12	3	2	41	24	4		.286	.369	.399	123	6	15	.800	-6	105	105	3b59		0.1
1891	Was AA	12	44	7	14	2	0	0	9	7	0	5	.318	.412	.477	162	4	8	.820	-1	91	94	3b12		0.3
Total	7	453	1723	266	468	69	37	14	270	108	19	41	.272	.322	.379	107	12	151	.824	22	115	99	3b400,S52/OL		3.5

DAVIS, J.J. Jerry C. B10.25.1978 Glendora CA BR/TR/6-4/250* [PitN97 1/8] d9.4

YEAR	TM LG	G	AB	R	H	2B	3B	HR	RBI	BB-IB	HP	SO	AVG	OBP	SLG	AOPS	ABR	SB-CS	FA	FR	RNG	THR	GAMES AT POSITION	DL	BFW
2002	Pit N	9	10	1	1	0	0	0		0-0	1	6	.100	.182	.100	-21	-2	0-0	1.000	-0	68	0	O4R		-0.2
2003	Pit N	19	35	1	7	0	0	1	4	3-0	0	13	.200	.263	.286	43	-3	0-1	1.000	-0	85	191	O10R		-0.4
2004	Pit N	25	35	4	5	1	0	0	3	4-0	0	10	.143	.225	.171	6	-5	2-0	.895	-0	91	178	O17(5/0/12)		-0.5
2005	Was N	14	26	0	6	0	0	0	2	2-0	0	7	.231	.286	.231	40	-2	1-1	1.000	1	122	258	O10(9/0/1)	118	-0.2
Total	4	67	106	6	19	1	0	1	9	9-0	1	34	.179	.248	.217	24	-12	3-2	.962	0	95	187	O41(14/0/27)	118	-1.3

DAVIS, JODY Jody Richard B11.12.1956 Gainesville GA BR/TR/6-3/210(192-210) [NYN76*3/62] d4.21 Col Middle Georgia JC

YEAR	TM LG	G	AB	R	H	2B	3B	HR	RBI	BB-IB	HP	SO	AVG	OBP	SLG	AOPS	ABR	SB-CS	FA	FR	RNG	THR	GAMES AT POSITION	DL	BFW
1981	Chi N	56	180	14	46	5	1	4	21	21-3	1	28	.256	.333	.361	93	-1	0-1	.972	1	118	130	C56		0.2
1982	Chi N	130	418	41	109	20	2	12	52	36-4	1	92	.261	.316	.404	98	-2	0-1	.984	5	115	114	C129		0.9
1983	Chi N	151	510	56	138	31	2	24	84	33-5	2	93	.271	.315	.480	113	7	0-2	.984	-12	101	78	C150		0.1
1984	†Chi N★	150	523	55	134	25	2	19	94	.47-15	1	99	.256	.315	.421	98	-2	5-6	.984	8	101	105	C146		1.1
1985	Chi N	142	482	47	112	30	0	17	58	48-5	0	83	.232	.300	.400	86	-9	1-0	.990	3	86	133	C138		0.0
1986	Chi N★	148	528	61	132	27	2	21	74	41-4	0	110	.250	.300	.428	93	-7	0-1	.992	10	137	142	C145/1		1.0
1987	Chi N	125	428	57	106	12	2	19	51	52-2	2	91	.248	.331	.418	93	-5	1-2	.989	-1	95	113	C123		-0.1
1988	Chi N	88	249	19	57	9	0	6	33	29-3	1	51	.229	.309	.337	82	-5	0-3	.995	-2	109	92	C74	16	-0.5
	Atl N	2	8	2	2	0	0	1	3	0-0	1	5	.250	.250	.625	138	0	0-0	1.000	1	95	135	C2		0.1
	Year	90	257	21	59	9	0	7	36	29-3	1	52	.230	.307	.346	84	-5	0-3	.995	-1	109	93	C76		-0.4
1989	Atl N	78	231	12	39	5	0	4	19	23-3	1	61	.169	.246	.242	40	-18	0-0	.985	1	131	117	C72,1b2		-1.5
1990	Atl N	12	28	0	2	0	0	1		3-0	0	3	.071	.161	.071	-32	-5	0-0	1.000	1	166	120	1b6,C4		-0.4
Total	10	1082	3585	364	877	164	11	127	490	333-44	9	712	.245	.307	.403	94	-7	7-16	.987	15	109	113	C1039,1b9	16	0.9

DAVIS, JOHN John Humphrey "Red" B7.15.1915 Wilkes-Barre PA D4.26.2002 Laurel MS BR/TR/5-11/172 d9.9 Mil 1942-45

YEAR	TM LG	G	AB	R	H	2B	3B	HR	RBI	BB-IB	HP	SO	AVG	OBP	SLG	AOPS	ABR	SB-CS	FA	FR	RNG	THR	GAMES AT POSITION	DL	BFW
1941	NY N	21	70	8	15	3	0	0	5	8	0	12	.214	.295	.257	55	-4	0	.970	1	108	108	3b21		-0.2

DAVIS, CRASH Lawrence Columbus B7.14.1919 Canon GA D8.31.2001 Greensboro NC BR/TR/6-0/173 d6.15 Mil 1943-45 Col Duke

YEAR	TM LG	G	AB	R	H	2B	3B	HR	RBI	BB-IB	HP	SO	AVG	OBP	SLG	AOPS	ABR	SB-CS	FA	FR	RNG	THR	GAMES AT POSITION	DL	BFW
1940	Phi A	23	67	4	18	1	1	0	9	3	1	10	.269	.310	.313	63	-4	1-0	.963	0	96	85	2b19/S		-0.2
1941	Phi A	39	105	8	23	3	0	0	8	11	0	16	.219	.293	.248	45	-8	0-0	.952	-2	108	94	2b20,1b12		-0.9
1942	Phi A	86	272	31	61	8	1	2	26	21	1	30	.224	.282	.283	60	-15	1-0	.965	-9	91	55	2b57,S26,1b3		-1.9
Total	3	148	444	43	102	12	2	2	43	35	2	56	.230	.289	.279	57	-27	2-0	.961	-10	96	70	2b96,S27,1b15		-3.0

DAVIS, MARK Mark Anthony B11.25.1964 San Diego CA BR/TR/6-0/180 [ChiA86 12/309] d7.2 b-Mike Col Stanford

YEAR	TM LG	G	AB	R	H	2B	3B	HR	RBI	BB-IB	HP	SO	AVG	OBP	SLG	AOPS	ABR	SB-CS	FA	FR	RNG	THR	GAMES AT POSITION	DL	BFW
1991	Cal A	3	2	0	0	0	0	0	0	0-0	0	0	.000	.000	.000	-99	-0	0-0	.500	-0	71	0	O3R		0.0

DAVIS, BEN Mark Christopher B3.10.1977 Chester PA BB/TR/6-4/215(205-225) [SDN95 1/2] d9.25

YEAR	TM LG	G	AB	R	H	2B	3B	HR	RBI	BB-IB	HP	SO	AVG	OBP	SLG	AOPS	ABR	SB-CS	FA	FR	RNG	THR	GAMES AT POSITION	DL	BFW
1998	SD N	1	1	0	0	0	0	0	0	0-0	0	0	.000	.000	.000	-99	0	0-0	1.000	0	0	0	/C		0.0
1999	SD N	76	266	29	65	14	1	5	30	25-3	0	70	.244	.307	.343	74	-11	2-1	.986	-6	115	94	C74		-1.1
2000	SD N	43	130	12	29	6	0	3	14	14-1	0	35	.223	.297	.338	64	-7	1-1	.996	-0	103	72	C38/D	19	-0.5
2001	SD N	138	448	56	107	20	0	11	57	66-5	4	112	.239	.337	.357	88	-7	4-4	.990	-6	94	115	C135,1b2		-0.5
2002	Sea A	80	228	24	59	10	1	7	43	18-1	2	58	.259	.313	.404	93	-3	1-1	.998	3	138	120	C77,1b2		0.4
2003	Sea A	80	246	25	58	18	0	6	42	18-2	0	61	.236	.284	.382	79	-8	0-0	.991	3	114	107	C73/D		-0.1

YEAR	TM LG	G	AB	R	H	2B	3B	HR	RBI	BB-IB	HP	SO	AVG	OBP	SLG	AOPS	ABR	SB-CS	FA	FR	RNG	THR	GAMES AT POSITION	DL	BFW
2004	Sea A	14	33	1	3	0	0	0	2	3-0		9	.091	.162	.091	-32	-7	0-0	1.000	1	277	76	C14		-0.5
	Chi A	54	160	21	37	9	0	6	16	9-0	1	40	.231	.276	.400	71	-7	1-1	.991	4	73	113	C53		0.0
	Year	68	193	22	40	9	0	6	18	12-0	1	49	.207	.256	.347	55	-14	1-1	.993	5	113	106	C67		-0.5
Total 7		486	1512	168	358	77	2	38	204	153-12	7	385	.237	.306	.366	78	-50	9-8	.992	-2	111	106	C465,1b4,D2	19	-2.3

DAVIS, MIKE   Michael Dwayne   B6.11.1959 San Diego CA   BL/TL/6-3/185(165-190)   [OakA77 3/69]   d4.10   b-Mark

YEAR	TM LG	G	AB	R	H	2B	3B	HR	RBI	BB-IB	HP	SO	AVG	OBP	SLG	AOPS	ABR	SB-CS	FA	FR	RNG	THR	GAMES AT POSITION	DL	BFW
1980	Oak A	51	95	11	20	2	1	1	8	7-0	0	14	.211	.262	.284	54	-6	2-1	1.000	2	116	201	O18(5/0/13),1b7,D6		-0.5
1981	†Oak A	17	20	0	1	1	0	0	0	2-0	0	4	.050	.136	.100	-32	-3	0-0	1.000	0	160	0	O2L/1D		-0.4
1982	Oak A	23	75	12	30	4	0	1	10	2-0	0	8	.400	.416	.493	153	5	3-2	.946	1	141	0	O13(8/3/5),1b7		0.5
1983	Oak A	128	443	61	122	24	4	8	62	27-1	5	74	.275	.322	.402	104	2	32-15	.974	11	111	186	O121(0/21/110),D3	16	0.9
1984	Oak A	134	382	47	88	18	3	9	46	31-2	1	66	.230	.285	.364	85	-9	14-9	.961	7	121	85	O127(1/16/121),D4		-0.8
1985	Oak A	154	547	92	157	34	1	24	82	50-8	2	99	.287	.348	.484	134	26	24-10	.979	5	116	59	O151(0/31/138)		2.5
1986	Oak A	142	489	77	131	28	3	19	55	34-2	1	91	.268	.314	.454	115	8	27-4	.973	6	113	106	O139(0/34/120)		1.3
1987	Oak A	139	494	69	131	32	1	22	72	42-5	1	94	.265	.320	.468	114	9	19-7	.942	-8	97	38	O124R,D14		-0.3
1988	†LA N	108	281	29	55	11	2	2	17	25-0	0	59	.196	.260	.270	54	-17	7-3	.961	-4	89	94	O76(1/23/63)		-2.4
1989	LA N	67	173	21	43	7	1	5	19	16-1	0	24	.249	.309	.387	100	0	6-5	.987	-2	90	43	O48(16/0/34)	62	-0.5
Total 10		963	2999	419	778	161	16	91	371	236-19	10	537	.259	.313	.415	104	15	134-56	.968	18	109	91	O819(33/128/728),D30,1b15	78	0.3

DAVIS, ODIE   Odie Ernest   B8.13.1955 San Antonio TX   BR/TR/6-1/178   [TexA77 7/165]   d9.3   Col Prairie View A&M

YEAR	TM LG	G	AB	R	H	2B	3B	HR	RBI	BB-IB	HP	SO	AVG	OBP	SLG	AOPS	ABR	SB-CS	FA	FR	RNG	THR	GAMES AT POSITION	DL	BFW
1980	Tex A	17	8	0	1	0	0	0	0	0-0	0	2	.125	.125	.125	-32	-1	0-0	.880	1	124	109	S13/3		0.0

DAVIS, OTIS   Otis Allen "Scat"   B9.24.1920 Charleston AR   BL/TR/6-0/160   d4.22

YEAR	TM LG	G	AB	R	H	2B	3B	HR	RBI	BB-IB	HP	SO	AVG	OBP	SLG	AOPS	ABR	SB-CS	FA	FR	RNG	THR	GAMES AT POSITION	DL	BFW
1946	Bro N	1	0	1	0	0	0	0	0	0-0	0	0	—	—	—	0	0		—	0			/R		0.0

DAVIS, DICK   Richard Earl   B9.25.1953 Long Beach CA   BR/TR/6-3/195*   d7.12   Col Snow (UT) JC

YEAR	TM LG	G	AB	R	H	2B	3B	HR	RBI	BB-IB	HP	SO	AVG	OBP	SLG	AOPS	ABR	SB-CS	FA	FR	RNG	THR	GAMES AT POSITION	DL	BFW
1977	Mil A	22	51	5	14	2	0	0	6	1-0	0	8	.275	.278	.314	64	-3	0-0	1.000	-2	67	0	O12L,D6		-0.5
1978	Mil A	69	218	28	54	10	1	5	26	7-0	2	23	.248	.273	.372	80	-6	2-5	1.000	1	108	123	D34,O28(18/4/8)		-0.9
1979	Mil A	91	335	51	89	13	1	12	41	16-0	0	46	.266	.298	.418	91	-6	3-3	.973	-1	103	39	D53,O35(32/0/3)		-1.0
1980	Mil A	106	365	50	99	26	2	4	30	11-0	1	43	.271	.297	.386	88	-7	5-3	.971	-1	87	112	D63,O38(13/0/27)		-1.1
1981	†Phi N	45	96	12	32	6	1	2	19	8-0	1	13	.333	.387	.479	138	5	1-2	1.000	-2	86	55	O32(1/0/31)		0.2
1982	Phi N	28	68	5	19	3	1	2	7	2-0	0	9	.279	.296	.441	102	0	1-0	1.000	0	114	0	O16R		-0.1
	Tor A	3	7	0	2	0	0	0	2	0-0	0	1	.286	.286	.286	53	0	0-0	1.000	0	97	0	/OLD		-0.1
	Pit N	39	77	7	14	2	1	2	10	5-0	0	9	.182	.224	.312	48	-6	1-0	.971	-2	93	0	O28(1/0/27)		-0.9
Total 6		403	1217	160	323	62	7	27	141	50-0	6	152	.265	.294	.394	89	-23	13-13	.981	-6	95	58	O190(78/4/112),D157		-4.4

DAVIS, BRANDY   Robert Brandon   B9.10.1927 Newark DE   D6.12.2005 Newark DE   BR/TR/6-0/170*   d4.15   C1   Col Duke

YEAR	TM LG	G	AB	R	H	2B	3B	HR	RBI	BB-IB	HP	SO	AVG	OBP	SLG	AOPS	ABR	SB-CS	FA	FR	RNG	THR	GAMES AT POSITION	DL	BFW
1952	Pit N	55	95	14	17	1	1	0	1	11	0	28	.179	.264	.211	32	-9	9-2	.932	-0	105	95	O29(9/9/12)		-0.9
1953	Pit N	12	39	5	8	2	0	0	2	0	0	3	.205	.205	.256	20	-5	0-2	.955	0	114	0	O9L		-0.6
Total 2		67	134	19	25	3	1	0	3	11	0	31	.187	.248	.224	29	-14	9-4	.938	-1	107	69	O38(18/9/12)		-1.5

DAVIS, BOB   Robert John Eugene   B3.1.1952 Pryor OK   BR/TR/6-0/180*   [SDN70 6/124]   d4.6

YEAR	TM LG	G	AB	R	H	2B	3B	HR	RBI	BB-IB	HP	SO	AVG	OBP	SLG	AOPS	ABR	SB-CS	FA	FR	RNG	THR	GAMES AT POSITION	DL	BFW
1973	SD N	5	11	1	1	0	0	0	0	0-0	0	5	.091	.091	.091	-54	-2	0-0	.941	0	66	87	C5		-0.2
1975	SD N	43	128	6	30	3	2	0	7	11-3	3	31	.234	.310	.289	72	-5	0-0	.986	0	100	99	C43		-0.3
1976	SD N	51	83	7	17	0	1	0	5	5-1	0	13	.205	.244	.229	40	-7	0-0	.965	0	105	117	C47		-0.6
1977	SD N	48	94	9	17	2	0	1	10	5-2	1	24	.181	.235	.234	30	-10	0-1	.975	-6	124	124	C46		-1.5
1978	SD N	19	40	3	8	1	0	0	2	1-1	0	5	.200	.220	.225	26	-4	0-0	.960	-4	78	123	C16		-0.9
1979	Tor A	32	89	6	11	2	0	1	8	6-0	1	15	.124	.180	.180	-0	-13	0-0	.984	-2	118	87	C32		-1.4
1980	Tor A	91	218	18	47	11	0	4	19	12-0	1	25	.216	.260	.321	56	-14	0-1	.983	-2	101	87	C89		-1.3
1981	Cal A	1	2	0	0	0	0	0	0	0-0	0	0	.000	.000	.000	-99	-1	0-0	1.000	1	21	0	/C		-0.1
Total 8		290	665	50	131	19	3	6	51	40-7	7	118	.197	.249	.262	42	-56	0-1	.978	-15	115	100	C279		-6.3

DAVIS, RON   Ronald Everette   B10.21.1941 Roanoke Rapids NC   D9.5.1992 Houston TX   BR/TR/6-0/180*   d8.1   Col Duke

YEAR	TM LG	G	AB	R	H	2B	3B	HR	RBI	BB-IB	HP	SO	AVG	OBP	SLG	AOPS	ABR	SB-CS	FA	FR	RNG	THR	GAMES AT POSITION	DL	BFW
1962	Hou N	6	14	1	3	0	0	0	1	1-0	0	7	.214	.267	.214	33	-1	1-0	1.000	-0	102	0	O5C		-0.1
1966	Hou N	48	194	21	48	10	1	2	19	13-2	4	26	.247	.308	.340	86	-4	2-2	.982	3	94	284	O48C		-0.2
1967	Hou N	94	285	31	73	19	1	7	38	17-2		48	.256	.303	.404	104	1	5-3	.976	2	96	166	O80(63/11/8)		-0.1
1968	Hou N	52	217	22	46	10	1	1	12	13-0	4	48	.212	.268	.281	67	-9	0-4	.971	3	111	124	O25(2/10/14)		-1.1
	†StL N	33	79	11	14	4	2	0	5	5-0	1	17	.177	.221	.278	51	-5	1-0	.979	1	97	178	O52C		-0.6
	Year	85	296	33	60	14	3	1	17	18-0	4	65	.203	.255	.280	63	-14	1-4	.973	4	107	140	O77(2/62/14)		-1.7
1969	Pit N	62	64	10	15	1	1	0	4	7-0	0	14	.234	.310	.287	68	-3	0-0	.933	-2	76	171	O51(22/12/20)		-0.6
Total 5		295	853	96	199	44	6	10	79	56-4	10	160	.233	.287	.334	82	-21	9-9	.974	6	98	171	O261(87/138/42)		-2.7

DAVIS, RUSS   Russell Stuart   B9.13.1969 Birmingham AL   BR/TR/6-0/195(170-200)   [NYA88 29/755]   d7.6   Col Shelton St. (AL) CC

YEAR	TM LG	G	AB	R	H	2B	3B	HR	RBI	BB-IB	HP	SO	AVG	OBP	SLG	AOPS	ABR	SB-CS	FA	FR	RNG	THR	GAMES AT POSITION	DL	BFW
1994	NY A	4	14	1	2	0	0	0	1	0-0	0	4	.143	.143	.143	-27	-3	0-0	1.000	-1	82	0	3b4		-0.3
1995	†NY A	40	98	14	27	5	2	2	12	10-0	1	26	.276	.349	.429	102	0	0-0	.968	-2	92	23	3b34,1b2,D4		-0.2
1996	Sea A	51	167	24	39	9	0	5	18	17-1	2	50	.234	.312	.377	73	-7	2-0	.933	-10	75	57	3b51	114	-1.5
1997	Sea A	119	420	57	114	29	1	20	63	27-2	2	100	.271	.317	.488	107	3	6-2	.939	-3	95	122	3b117/D	32	0.1
1998	Sea A	141	502	68	130	30	1	20	82	34-1	3	134	.259	.305	.442	92	-7	4-3	.906	-3	101	131	3b137,O3L		-0.9
1999	Sea A	124	432	55	106	17	1	21	59	32-1	5	111	.245	.304	.435	87	-11	3-3	.959	-15	87	78	3b124,S2		-2.3
2000	†SF N	80	180	27	47	5	0	9	24	9-0	2	29	.261	.302	.439	90	-4	0-3	.933	-11	68	52	3b43,1b6,D3		-1.5
2001	SF N	53	167	16	43	13	1	7	17	17-2	1	49	.257	.326	.473	111	2	1-0	.890	-12	74	122	3b46/D		-0.9
Total 8		612	1980	261	508	108	6	84	276	146-7	16	503	.257	.310	.444	93	-27	16-11	.932	-56	89	98	3b556,D9,1b8,O3L,S2	146	-7.5

DAVIS, STEVE   Steven Michael   B12.30.1953 Oakland CA   BR/TR/6-1/200   [ChiN76 14/319]   d9.23   Col Stanford

YEAR	TM LG	G	AB	R	H	2B	3B	HR	RBI	BB-IB	HP	SO	AVG	OBP	SLG	AOPS	ABR	SB-CS	FA	FR	RNG	THR	GAMES AT POSITION	DL	BFW
1979	Chi N	3	4	0	0	0	0	0	0	0-0	0	0	.000	.000	.000	-91	-1	0-0	1.000	-0	143	0	2b2/3		-0.1

DAVIS, TOMMY   Thomas James   B5.21.1973 Mobile AL   BR/TR/6-1/210   [BalA94 2/54]   d5.14   Col Southern Mississippi

YEAR	TM LG	G	AB	R	H	2B	3B	HR	RBI	BB-IB	HP	SO	AVG	OBP	SLG	AOPS	ABR	SB-CS	FA	FR	RNG	THR	GAMES AT POSITION	DL	BFW
1999	Bal A	5	6	0	1	0	0	0	0	0-0	0	2	.167	.167	.167	-15	-1	0-0	.909	-0	40	253	C4/1		-0.1

DAVIS, TOD   Thomas Oscar   B7.24.1924 Los Angeles CA   D12.31.1978 W.Covina CA   BR/TR/6-2/190*   d4.27

YEAR	TM LG	G	AB	R	H	2B	3B	HR	RBI	BB-IB	HP	SO	AVG	OBP	SLG	AOPS	ABR	SB-CS	FA	FR	RNG	THR	GAMES AT POSITION	DL	BFW
1949	Phi A	31	75	7	20	0	1	1	6	9	0	16	.267	.345	.333	83	-2	0-0	.912	-1	84	114	S14,3b12/2		-0.2
1951	Phi A	11	15	0	1	0	0	0	0	1	0	3	.067	.125	.067	-46	-3	0-0	1.000	-0	0	0	2b2/3		-0.3
Total 2		42	90	7	21	0	1	1	6	10	0	19	.233	.310	.289	61	-5	0-0	.912	-1	84	114	S14,3b13,2b3		-0.5

DAVIS, TRENCH   Trench Neal   B9.12.1960 Baltimore MD   BL/TL/6-3/171*   d6.4

YEAR	TM LG	G	AB	R	H	2B	3B	HR	RBI	BB-IB	HP	SO	AVG	OBP	SLG	AOPS	ABR	SB-CS	FA	FR	RNG	THR	GAMES AT POSITION	DL	BFW
1985	Pit N	2	7	1	1	0	0	0	0	0-0	0	0	.143	.143	.143	-20	-1	1-0	.667	-1	52	0	O2C		-0.2
1986	Pit N	15	23	2	3	0	0	0	1	0-0	0	4	.130	.125	.130	-27	-4	0-0	.917	0	87	350	O7C		-0.4
1987	Atl N	6	3	0	0	0	0	0	0	0-0	0	1	.000	.000	.000	-96	-1	0-0	—	0			/H		-0.1
Total 3		23	33	3	4	0	0	0	1	0-0	0	5	.121	.118	.121	-32	-6	1-0	.867	-1	78	263	O9C		-0.7

DAVIS, SPUD   Virgil Lawrence   B12.20.1904 Birmingham AL   D8.14.1984 Birmingham AL   BR/TR/6-1/197   d4.30   M1/C9

YEAR	TM LG	G	AB	R	H	2B	3B	HR	RBI	BB-IB	HP	SO	AVG	OBP	SLG	AOPS	ABR	SB-CS	FA	FR	RNG	THR	GAMES AT POSITION	DL	BFW
1928	StL N	2	5	1	1	0	0	1	0	0	0	1	.200	.333	.200	42	0	0-0	.750	-1	86	0	C2		-0.1
	Phi N	67	163	16	46	2	0	3	18	15	0	11	.282	.343	.350	79	-5	0-0	.980	-1	75	152	C49		-0.3
	Year	69	168	17	47	2	0	3	19	16	0	11	.280	.342	.345	78	-5	0-0	.971	-2	75	145	C51		-0.4
1929	Phi N	98	263	31	90	18	0	7	48	19	2	17	.342	.391	.490	110	4	1	.961	-10	92	103	C89		-0.1
1930	Phi N	106	329	41	103	16	1	14	65	17	1	20	.313	.349	.495	94	-4	1	.986	-9	73	110	C96		1.4
1931	Phi N	120	393	30	128	32	1	4	51	36	0	28	.326	.382	.443	112	9	0	.994	-1	75	118	C114		2.2
1932	Phi N	125	402	44	135	23	5	14	70	40	2	39	.336	.399	.522	130	18	1	.987	-3	88	82	C120		1.9
1933	Phi N	141	495	51	173	28	3	9	65	32	5	24	.349	.395	.473	130	21	2	.983	-10	74	106	C132		1.9
1934	†StL N	107	347	45	104	22	4	9	65	34	2	27	.300	.366	.464	113	7	0	.988	2	106	97	C94		1.4
1935	StL N	102	315	28	100	24	2	1	60	33	7	30	.317	.386	.416	111	7	0	**.992**	-2	114	33	C81,1b5		0.9
1936	StL N	112	363	30	99	26	2	4	59	35	3	34	.273	.342	.388	97	-1	0	.985	-7	116	99	C103,3b2		-0.2
1937	Cin N	76	209	19	56	10	1	3	33	23	0	15	.268	.341	.368	97	0	0	.980	4	74	102	C59		0.7
1938	Cin N	12	36	3	6	1	0	0	1	6	0	3	.167	.286	.194	35	-3	0	.962	0	154	119	C11		-0.2
	Phi N	70	215	11	53	7	0	2	23	14	1	14	.247	.293	.307	67	-10	1	.980	-10	60	94	C63		-1.7
	Year	82	251	14	59	8	0	2	24	19	1	20	.235	.292	.291	62	-13	1	.977	-10	58	98	C74		-1.9
1939	Phi N	87	202	10	62	8	1	0	23	24	1	20	.307	.383	.356	103	2	0	**1.000**	-6	54	124	C85		1.4
1940	Pit N	99	285	23	93	14	1	5	39	35	2	20	.326	.404	.435	132	14	0	.967	-5	73	139	C87		1.4
1941	Pit N	57	107	3	27	4	1	0	6	11	0	11	.252	.322	.308	78	-3	0	1.000	-0	101	90	C49		

YEAR	TM LG	G	AB	R	H	2B	3B	HR	RBI	BB-IB	HP	SO	AVG	OBP	SLG	AOPS	ABR	SB-CS	FA	FR	RNG	THR	GAMES AT POSITION	DL	BFW
1944	Pit N	54	93	6	28	7	0	2	14	10	0	8	.301	.369	.441	122	3	0	.966	0	95	94	C35		0.5
1945	Pit N	23	33	2	8	2	0	0	6	2	1	2	.242	.306	.303	67	-1	0	.968	-0	91	111	C13		-0.1
Total	16	1458	4255	388	1312	244	22	77	647	386	22	326	.308	.369	.430	108	58	6	.984	-59	85	102	C1282,1b5,3b2		7.0

DAVIS, BUTCH Wallace McArthur B6.19.1958 Martin Co. NC BR/TR/6-0/190* [KCA80 12/302] d8.23 Col East Carolina

YEAR	TM LG	G	AB	R	H	2B	3B	HR	RBI	BB-IB	HP	SO	AVG	OBP	SLG	AOPS	ABR	SB-CS	FA	FR	RNG	THR	GAMES AT POSITION	DL	BFW
1983	KC A	33	122	13	42	2	6	2	18	4-0	0	19	.344	.359	.508	136	5	4-3	.977	0	112	36	O33L		0.4
1984	KC A	41	116	11	17	3	0	2	12	10-0	0	19	.147	.211	.224	21	-13	4-3	.959	-0	104	90	O35(34/1/1),D2		-1.5
1987	Pit N	7	7	3	1	1	0	0	0	1-0	0	3	.143	.250	.286	41	-1	0-0	1.000	0	218	0	/OL		0.0
1988	Bal A	13	25	2	6	1	0	0	0	0-0	0	8	.240	.240	.280	46	-1	1-0	1.000	1	119	256	O10(2/0/8)/D		-0.1
1989	Bal A	5	6	1	1	1	0	0	0	0-0	0	3	.167	.167	.333	39	0	0-0	1.000	0	91	0	O3(2/0/1)/D		-0.1
1991	LA N	1	1	0	0	0	0	0	0	0-0	0	0	.000	.000	.000	-99	0	0-0	—	0			/H		0.0
1993	Tex A	62	159	24	39	10	4	3	20	5-1	1	28	.245	.273	.415	85	-5	3-1	.960	2	118	85	O44(23/10/17),D11	15	-0.4
1994	Tex A	4	17	2	4	3	0	0	0	0-0	0	3	.235	.235	.412	62	-1	1-0	1.000	0	75	343	O4R		0.0
Total	8	166	453	56	110	21	10	7	50	10-1	1	83	.243	.274	.380	77	-17	13-7	.969	4	111	89	O130(95/11/31),D15	15	-1.7

DAVIS, WILLIE William Henry B4.15.1940 Mineral Springs AR BL/TL/6-2.5/181* d9.8

YEAR	TM LG	G	AB	R	H	2B	3B	HR	RBI	BB-IB	HP	SO	AVG	OBP	SLG	AOPS	ABR	SB-CS	FA	FR	RNG	THR	GAMES AT POSITION	DL	BFW
1960	LA N	22	88	12	28	6	1	2	10	4-2	0	12	.318	.348	.477	116	2	3-5	.981	-0	103	67	O22C		-0.1
1961	LA N	128	339	56	86	19	6	12	45	27-4	0	46	.254	.316	.451	93	-4	12-5	.983	1	111	65	O114C		-0.4
1962	LA N	157	600	103	171	18	10	21	85	42-10	6	72	.285	.334	.453	117	12	32-7	.963	5	108	132	O156(1/155/0)		1.7
1963	†LA N	156	515	60	126	19	8	9	60	25-6	3	61	.245	.281	.365	92	-8	25-11	.978	10	109	182	O155C		-0.1
1964	LA N	157	613	91	180	23	7	12	77	22-1	1	59	.294	.316	.413	112	7	42-13	.983	15	119	164	O155C		2.3
1965	†LA N	142	558	52	133	24	3	10	57	14-3	7	81	.238	.263	.346	76	-20	25-9	.967	-1	105	77	O141C		-2.5
1966	†LA N	153	624	74	177	31	6	11	61	15-2	4	68	.284	.302	.405	104	0	21-10	.970	1	107	91	O152C		-0.3
1967	LA N	143	569	65	146	27	9	6	41	29-5	3	65	.257	.295	.367	97	-5	20-6	.971	-4	96	78	O138C		-1.2
1968	LA N	160	643	86	161	24	10	7	31	31-4	1	88	.250	.284	.351	98	-5	36-10	.973	-2	99	95	O158C		-0.9
1969	LA N	129	498	66	155	23	8	11	59	33-5	4	39	.311	.356	.456	135	21	24-10	.979	-2	99	106	O125C	21	1.9
1970	LA N	146	593	92	181	23	16	8	93	29-2	1	54	.305	.335	.438	111	5	38-14	.992	6	105	144	O143(0/139/4)		1.1
1971	LA N★	158	641	84	198	33	10	10	74	23-3	0	47	.309	.330	.438	123	15	20-8	.981	1	106	80	O157C		1.5
1972	LA N	149	615	81	178	22	7	19	79	27-4	3	61	.289	.317	.441	116	9	20-3	.987	0	101	110	O146C		0.9
1973	LA N★	152	599	82	171	29	9	16	77	29-12	5	62	.285	.320	.444	115	8	17-5	.980	-9	97	64	O146C		-0.2
1974	Mon N	153	611	86	180	27	9	12	89	27-9	3	69	.295	.322	.427	104	1	25-7	.969	-4	102	90	O151C		-0.4
1975	Tex A	42	169	16	42	8	2	5	17	4-0	1	25	.249	.270	.408	90	-3	13-5	.990	-3	94	35	O42C		-0.7
	StL N	98	350	41	102	19	6	6	50	14-1	4	27	.291	.319	.431	104	0	10-1	.970	3	112	88	O89(8/15/71)		0.1
1976	SD N	141	493	61	132	18	10	5	46	19-2	2	34	.268	.295	.375	92	-5	14-2	.992	3	110	77	O128C		-0.4
1979	†Cal N	43	56	9	14	2	1	0	2	4-0	0	7	.250	.300	.321	70	-3	1-0	1.000	-0	100	0	O7(1/0/6),D6		-0.3
Total	18	2429	9174	1217	2561	395	138	182	1053	418-75	51	977	.279	.311	.412	106	27	398-131	.978	20	105	103	O2323(10/2237/81),D6	21	2.0

DAWKINS, GOOKIE Travis Sentell B5.12.1979 Newberry SC BR/TR/6-1/180* [CinN97 2/66] d9.3

YEAR	TM LG	G	AB	R	H	2B	3B	HR	RBI	BB-IB	HP	SO	AVG	OBP	SLG	AOPS	ABR	SB-CS	FA	FR	RNG	THR	GAMES AT POSITION	DL	BFW
1999	Cin N	7	7	1	1	0	0	0		0-0	1	4	.143	.250	.143	3	-1	0-0	1.000	-1	69	88	S7		-0.2
2000	Cin N	14	41	5	9	2	0	0	3	2-1	0	7	.220	.256	.268	32	-4	0-0	.965	-2	102	179	S14		-0.2
2002	Cin N	31	48	2	6	0	0	0	6	6-0	0	21	.125	.222	.167	6	-7	2-1	.944	-8	82	64	S21,2b3		-1.3
2003	KC A	3	2	0	0	0	0	0		1-0	0	2	.000	.333	.000	-1	0	0-0	1.000	0	113	0	2b3		0.0
Total	4	55	98	8	16	4	0	0	9	11-2	1	34	.163	.241	.204	17	-12	2-1	.957	-6	89	114	S42,2b6		-1.7

DAWSON, ANDRE Andre Nolan B7.10.1954 Miami FL BR/TR/6-3/195(180-197) [MonN75 11/250] d9.11 Col Florida A&M

YEAR	TM LG	G	AB	R	H	2B	3B	HR	RBI	BB-IB	HP	SO	AVG	OBP	SLG	AOPS	ABR	SB-CS	FA	FR	RNG	THR	GAMES AT POSITION	DL	BFW
1976	Mon N	24	85	9	20	4	1	0	7	5-1	0	13	.235	.278	.306	62	-4	1-2	.969	1	112	64	O24(8/14/2)		-0.5
1977	Mon N	139	525	64	148	26	9	19	65	34-4	2	93	.282	.326	.474	115	8	21-7	.989	1	102	98	O136(13/129/3)		0.9
1978	Mon N	157	609	84	154	24	8	25	72	30-3	12	128	.253	.299	.442	105	1	28-11	.988	4	99	189	O153C		0.6
1979	Mon N	155	639	90	176	24	12	25	92	27-5	6	115	.275	.309	.468	109	-4	35-10	.988	-9	96	60	O153C		-0.3
1980	Mon N	151	577	96	178	41	7	17	87	44-7	6	69	.308	.358	.492	134	6	34-9	.986	7	106	140	O147C		3.8
1981	†Mon N★	103	394	71	119	21	3	24	64	35-14	7	50	.302	.365	.553	154	27	26-4	.980	12	121	140	O103C		4.4
1982	Mon N★	148	608	107	183	37	7	23	83	34-4	8	96	.301	.343	.498	129	22	39-10	.982	8	116	91	O147C		3.5
1983	Mon N★	159	633	104	189	36	10	32	113	38-12	9	81	.299	.338	.539	142	32	25-11	.980	-0	104	76	O157C		3.4
1984	Mon N	138	533	73	132	23	6	17	86	41-2	2	80	.248	.301	.409	103	0	13-5	.975	8	116	121	O134R		0.2
1985	Mon N	139	529	65	135	27	2	23	91	29-8	4	92	.255	.295	.444	111	5	13-4	.973	-2	97	103	O131(0/24/123)		-0.2
1986	Mon N	130	496	65	141	32	2	20	78	37-11	6	79	.284	.338	.478	124	15	18-12	.986	-4	89	110	O127R	25	0.4
1987	Chi N★	153	621	90	178	24	2	**49**	**137**	32-7	7	103	.287	.328	.568	127	20	11-3	.986	1	98	119	O152R		1.4
1988	Chi N★	157	591	78	179	31	8	24	79	37-12	4	73	.303	.344	.504	136	25	12-4	.989	-2	95	98	O147R		2.1
1989	†Chi N★	118	416	62	105	18	6	21	77	35-13	1	62	.252	.307	.476	114	6	8-5	.987	1	107	67	O112R	36	0.4
1990	Chi N	147	529	72	164	28	5	27	100	42-21	2	65	.310	.358	.535	134	24	16-2	.981	-4	90	103	O139R		1.8
1991	Chi N	149	563	69	153	21	4	31	104	22-3	5	80	.272	.302	.488	114	7	4-5	.988	-7	90	64	O137R		-0.6
1992	Chi N	143	542	60	150	27	2	22	90	30-8	4	70	.277	.316	.456	114	8	6-2	.992	-8	81	115	O139R		-0.4
1993	Bos A	121	461	44	126	29	1	13	67	17-4	13	49	.273	.313	.425	92	-6	2-1	1.000	-0	112	0	D97,O20R	19	-1.2
1994	Bos A	75	292	34	70	18	0	16	48	9-3	4	53	.240	.271	.466	82	-10	2-2	—	0			D74	31	-1.3
1995	Fla N	79	226	30	58	10	3	8	37	9-1	4	45	.257	.305	.434	92	-4	0-0	.908	-4	84	89	O59(12/0/47)	29	-1.0
1996	Fla N	42	58	6	16	2	0	2	14	2-0	1	13	.276	.311	.414	92	-1	0-0	.833	-1	52	0	O6L	79	-0.2
Total	21	2627	9927	1373	2774	503	98	438	1591	589-143	111	1509	.279	.323	.482	118	205	314-109	.983	1	100	104	O2323(39/1027/1284),D171	219	17.2

DAY, BOOTS Charles Frederick B8.31.1947 Ilion NY BL/TL/5-9/160* d6.15 Col Mohawk Valley (NY) CC

YEAR	TM LG	G	AB	R	H	2B	3B	HR	RBI	BB-IB	HP	SO	AVG	OBP	SLG	AOPS	ABR	SB-CS	FA	FR	RNG	THR	GAMES AT POSITION	DL	BFW
1969	StL N	11	6	1	0	0	0	0	0	1-0	0	1	.000	.143	.000	-56	-1	0-0	—	-0	0	0	/OC		-0.1
1970	Chi N	11	8	2	2	0	0	0	0	0-0	0	3	.250	.250	.250	31	-1	0-0	.875	1	116	763	O7C		0.0
	Mon N	41	108	14	29	4	0	0	5	6-2	0	18	.269	.307	.306	65	-5	3-2	.987	3	125	65	O35(5/30/0)		-0.4
	Year	52	116	16	31	4	0	0	5	6-2	0	21	.267	.303	.302	61	-6	3-2	.976	3	124	121	O42(5/37/0)		-0.4
1971	Mon N	127	371	53	105	10	2	4	33	33-5	1	39	.283	.342	.353	96	-2	9-4	.982	7	107	176	O120(3/118/0)		0.4
1972	Mon N	128	386	32	90	7	4	0	30	29-3	1	44	.233	.288	.272	59	-21	3-6	.979	-4	93	109	O117(0/103/15)		-3.2
1973	Mon N	101	207	36	57	7	0	4	28	21-1	0	28	.275	.342	.367	93	-2	0-3	1.000	-2	78	68	O51(12/45/6)		-0.7
1974	Mon N	52	65	8	12	0	0	2	5	5-0	0	8	.185	.239	.185	20	-7	0-0	1.000	-1	91	0	O16(14/0/2)		-0.9
Total	6	471	1151	146	295	28	6	8	98	95-11	2	141	.256	.314	.312	75	-39	15-15	.983	4	99	124	O347(34/304/23)		-4.9

DAYETT, BRIAN Brian Kelly B1.22.1957 New London CT BR/TR/5-10/180* [NYA78 16/416] d9.11 Col St. Leo

YEAR	TM LG	G	AB	R	H	2B	3B	HR	RBI	BB-IB	HP	SO	AVG	OBP	SLG	AOPS	ABR	SB-CS	FA	FR	RNG	THR	GAMES AT POSITION	DL	BFW
1983	NY A	11	29	3	6	1	0	1	5	2-0	1	4	.207	.258	.276	48	-1	0-0	1.000	2	142	167	O9L		-0.1
1984	NY A	64	127	14	31	8	0	4	23	9-0	1	14	.244	.295	.402	95	-1	0-0	.988	1	102	115	O62(55/0/10)/D		-0.2
1985	Chi N	22	26	1	6	0	0	1	4	0-0	1	6	.231	.259	.346	62	-1	0-0	1.000	-0	106	0	O10L		-0.2
1986	Chi N	24	67	7	18	4	0	4	11	6-0	0	10	.269	.316	.507	118	1	0-1	1.000	-1	88	72	O24(15/1/12)		-0.1
1987	Chi N	97	177	20	49	14	1	5	25	20-0	0	37	.277	.348	.452	106	2	0-0	1.000	-2	88	68	O78(68/0/12)		-0.2
Total	5	218	426	45	110	26	2	14	68	37-0	2	71	.258	.316	.427	99	-1	0-1	.995	-1	97	89	O183(158/1/34)/D	109	-0.8

DEAL, CHARLIE Charles Albert B10.30.1891 Wilkinsburg PA D9.16.1979 Covina CA BR/TR/6-0/160 d7.19

YEAR	TM LG	G	AB	R	H	2B	3B	HR	RBI	BB-IB	HP	SO	AVG	OBP	SLG	AOPS	ABR	SB-CS	FA	FR	RNG	THR	GAMES AT POSITION	DL	BFW
1912	Det A	42	142	13	32	4	2	0	11	9	0		.225	.272	.282	60	-8	4	.942	6	129	46	3b41		0.0
1913	Det A	16	50	3	11	0	2	0	3	1	0	7	.220	.235	.300	57	-3	2	.862	1	124	135	3b15		-0.2
	Bos N	10	36	6	11	1	0	0	3	2	1		.306	.359	.333	96	0	1-2	.935	-3	83	34	2b10		-0.3
1914	†Bos N	79	257	17	54	13	2	0	23	20	1	23	.210	.270	.276	63	-12	4	.948	-2	95	85	3b74/S		-1.3
1915	StL F	65	223	21	72	12	4	1	27	12	0	16	.323	.357	.426	114	1	10	.951	7	111	110	3b65		1.0
1916	StL A	23	74	7	10	1	0	0	10	6	0	8	.135	.200	.149	5	-9	4	.970	-2	91	136	3b22/2		-1.1
	Chi N	2	8	2	2	1	0	0	0	0	0	0	.250	.250	.375	82	0	0	1.000	1	167	296	3b2		0.1
1917	Chi N	135	449	46	114	11	3	0	47	19	0	18	.254	.289	.292	71	-16	10	.957	8	99	102	3b130		-0.5
1918	†Chi N	119	414	43	99	9	3	2	34	21	2	13	.239	.279	.290	72	-15	11	.942	-6	92	112	3b118		-1.9
1919	†Chi N	116	405	37	117	23	5	2	52	12	4	11	.289	.316	.385	110	4	11	**.973**	6	93	116	3b116		1.4
1920	Chi N	129	450	48	108	19	5	3	39	20	4	14	.240	.285	.304	85	-19	5-8	**.973**	11	109	101	3b128		-0.7
1921	Chi N	115	422	52	122	19	8	0	37	25	4	9	.289	.310	.393	85	-10	3-5	**.973**	13	109	89	3b112		0.8
Total	10	851	2930	295	752	104	34	11	318	135	16	121	.257	.302	.342	79		65-15	.958	40	103	99	3b823,2b11/S		-2.7

DEAL, LINDSAY Fred Lindsay B9.3.1911 Lenoir NC D4.18.1979 Little Rock AR BL/TR/6-0/175 d9.13

YEAR	TM LG	G	AB	R	H	2B	3B	HR	RBI	BB-IB	HP	SO	AVG	OBP	SLG	AOPS	ABR	SB-CS	FA	FR	RNG	THR	GAMES AT POSITION	DL	BFW
1939	Bro N	4	7	0	0	0	0	0	0	2-0	0	2	.000	.000	.000	-97	-2	0	1.000	-0	91	0	/OC		-0.2

YEAR	TM LG	G	AB	R	H	2B	3B	HR	RBI	BB-IB	HP	SO	AVG	OBP	SLG	AOPS	ABR	SB-CS	FA	FR	RNG	THR	GAMES AT POSITION	DL	BFW

DEAL, SNAKE John Wesley B1.21.1879 Lancaster PA D5.9.1944 Harrisburg PA BR/TR/6-0/164 d7.9 Col Villanova

| 1906 | Cin N | 65 | 231 | 13 | 48 | 4 | 3 | 0 | 21 | 6 | 0 | | .208 | .228 | .251 | 47 | -15 | 15 | .985 | 2 | 113 | 80 | 1b65 | | -1.6 |

DEALY, PAT Patrick E. B11.12.1861 Underhill VT D12.16.1924 Buffalo NY BR/TR/5-8/145 d9.30

1884	StP U	5	15	2	2	0	0	0		0			.133	.133	.133	-35	-3		.871	2			C4/OR		-0.1
1885	Bos N	35	130	18	29	4	1	1	9	2		14	.223	.235	.292	72	-4		.903	0			C29,3b3,O2(1/1/0),S2/1		-0.1
1886	Bos N	15	46	9	15	1	1	0	3	4		4	.326	.380	.391	139	2	5	.929	-2			C14/OL		0.1
1887	Was N	58	212	33	55	8	2	1	18	8	2	8	.259	.293	.330	78	-6	36	.931	-4			C28,S23,O5(4/1/0),3b5		-0.7
1890	Syr AA	18	66	9	12	1	0	0	4	5	1		.182	.250	.197	36	-5	4	.900	-5	77	94	C10,3b6,O2(0/1/1)		-0.9
Total	5	131	469	71	113	14	4	2	34	19	3	26	.241	.275	.301	75	-16	45	.914	-10	77	94	C85,S25,3b14,O11(6/3/2)/1		-1.7

DEAN, CHUBBY Alfred Lovell B8.24.1915 Mt.Airy NC D12.21.1970 Riverside NJ BL/TL/5-11/181 d4.14 Mil 1943-46 ▲

1936	Phi A	111	342	41	98	21	3	1	48	24	2	24	.287	.337	.374	77	-13	3-2	.989	-1	97	93	1b77		-1.8
1937	Phi A	104	309	36	81	14	4	2	31	42	0	10	.262	.350	.353	79	-9	2-1	.991	-2	89	81	1b78,P2		-1.7
1938	Phi A	16	20	3	6	2	0	0	1	1	0	4	.300	.333	.400	85	2	0-0	1.000	1	184	0	P6		0.0
1939	Phi A	80	77	12	27	4	0	0	19	8	0	9	.351	.412	.403	111	9	0-0	.935	1	131	258	P54		0.0
1940	Phi A	67	90	6	26	2	0	0	6	16	0	9	.289	.396	.311	88	-1	0-0	.976	1	125	54	P30/1		0.0
1941	Phi A	27	37	0	9	2	0	0	9	4	0	3	.243	.317	.297	65	-2	0-0	1.000	1	93	96	P18/1		0.0
	Cle A	17	25	2	4	1	0	0	2	3	0	2	.160	.250	.200	21	1	0-0	1.000	1	155	0	P8		0.0
	Year	44	62	2	13	3	0	0	11	7	0	5	.210	.290	.258	48	-5	0-0	1.000	1	118	57	P26/1		0.0
1942	Cle A	70	101	4	27	1	0	0	7	11	0	7	.267	.339	.277	79	8	0-0	.939	-3	69	0	P27		0.0
1943	Cle A	41	46	2	9	0	0	0	5	6	0	2	.196	.288	.196	45	1	0-0	.929	-1	71	106	P17		0.0
Total	8	533	1047	106	287	47	7	3	128	115	2	65	.274	.347	.341	79	-4	5-3	.964	-4	107	79	P162,1b157		-3.5

DEAN, TOMMY Tommy Douglas B8.30.1945 Iuka MS BR/TR/6-0/165* d9.17

1967	LA N	12	28	1	4	1	0	0	2	0	0	9	.143	.143	.179	-9	-4	0-0	.981	2	101	169	S12		-0.2
1969	SD N	101	273	14	48	9	2	2	9	27-4	1	54	.176	.251	.245	41	-22	0-3	.978	-6	100	77	S97,2b2		-2.0
1970	SD N	61	158	18	35	5	1	2	13	11-3	0	29	.222	.271	.304	56	-10	2-0	.974	-4	93	97	S55		-0.8
1971	SD N	41	70	2	8	0	0	1	1	4-0	0	13	.114	.162	.114	-22	-11	1-0	.969	-1	94	95	S28,3b11/2		-1.1
Total	4	215	529	35	95	15	3	4	25	42-7	1	105	.180	.240	.242	36	-47	3-3	.976	-10	97	91	S192,3b11,2b3		-4.1

DEANE, HARRY John Henry B5.6.1846 Trenton NJ D5.31.1925 Indianapolis IN 5-7/150 d7.12 M1

1871	Kek NA	6	22	3	4	0	0	0	2			0	.182	.250	.273	49	-2	0-0	1.000	2			O6L,M		0.0
1874	Bal NA	47	203	29	50	8	1	0	13	4		3	.246	.261	.296	79	-4	2-1	.818	-3	94	143	O46C,2b2/S		-0.7
Total	2 NA	53	225	32	54	8	1	0	15	6		3	.240	.260	.293	75	-6	2-1	.850	-3	83	126	O52(6/46/0),2b2/S		-0.7

DEAR, BUDDY Paul Stanford B12.1.1905 Norfolk VA D8.29.1989 Radford VA BR/TR/5-8/143 d9.9 Col VPI

| 1927 | Was A | 2 | 1 | 1 | 0 | 0 | 0 | 0 | 0 | 0 | 0 | 0 | .000 | .000 | .000 | -99 | 0 | 0-0 | — | -0 | 0 | 0 | /2 | | 0.0 |

DeARMOND, CHARLIE Charles Hommer "Hummer" B2.13.1877 Okeana OH D12.17.1933 Morning Sun OH BR/TR/5-10/165 d9.19

| 1903 | Cin N | 11 | 39 | 10 | 11 | 2 | 1 | 0 | 7 | 3 | 1 | | .282 | .349 | .385 | 98 | 0 | 1 | .878 | -1 | 74 | 92 | 3b11 | | -0.1 |

DEASLEY, JOHN John B1.1861 Philadelphia PA D12.25.1910 Philadelphia PA d6.17 b-Pat

1884	Was U	31	134	20	29	1	1	0		3			.216	.234	.239	45	-13		.836	1	99	141	S31		-1.0
	KC U	13	40	3	7	2	0	0		2			.175	.214	.239	38	-4		.833	1	109	207	S13		-0.2
	Year	44	174	23	36	3	1	0		5			.207	.229	.236	44	-17		.835	3	102	158	S44		-1.2

DEASLEY, PAT Thomas H. B11.17.1857 , Ireland D4.1.1943 Philadelphia PA BR/TR/5-8.5/154 d5.18 b-John

1881	Bos N	43	147	13	35	1	2	0	8	5		10	.238	.263	.299	80	-3		.914	-1			C28,O7(0/2/6),S7,1b2		-0.3
1882	Bos N	67	264	36	70	8	0	0	29	7		22	.265	.284	.295	86	-4		.958	2			C56,O14(1/0/13)/S		0.2
1883	StL AA	58	206	27	53	2	1	0	15	6			.257	.278	.277	75	-6		.930	8			C56,O2C		0.6
1884	StL AA	75	254	27	52	5	4	0		7	3		.205	.235	.256	58	-12		.919	9			C75,O2(1/0/1)/1		0.3
1885	NY N	54	207	22	53	5	1	0	24	9		20	.256	.287	.290	88	-3		.935	7			C54,O2C/S		0.8
1886	NY N	41	143	18	38	6	1	0	17	4		12	.266	.286	.322	84	-3	2	.925	4			C30,O15(1/6/8)		0.2
1887	NY N	30	118	12	37	5	1	0	23	9	1	7	.314	.367	.356	107	2	3	.867	-10			C24,3b7/S		-0.5
1888	Was N	34	127	6	20	1	0	0	4	2	0	18	.157	.171	.165	8	-13	2	.922	6			C31/ORS2		-0.4
Total	8	402	1466	161	358	37	9	0	120	49	4	89	.244	.271	.282	75	-42	7	.927	25			C354,O43(3/12/29),S11,3b7,1b3/2		0.9

DeBERRY, HANK John Herman B12.29.1894 Savannah TN D9.10.1951 Savannah TN BR/TR/5-11/195 d9.12 Mil 1918 Col Tennessee

1916	Cle A	15	33	7	9	4	0	0	4	6	0	9	.273	.385	.394	126	0	1	1.000	-1	94	91	C14		0.1
1917	Cle A	25	33	3	9	2	0	0	1	2	1	7	.273	.333	.333	96	0	0	.968	1	110	113	C9		0.1
1922	Bro N	85	259	29	78	10	1	3	35	20	1	9	.301	.354	.382	91	-3	4-1	.971	-5	75	94	C81		-0.3
1923	Bro N	78	235	21	67	11	6	1	48	20	2	12	.285	.346	.396	98	-1	2-1	.971	4	84	106	C60		0.7
1924	Bro N	77	218	20	53	10	3	3	26	20	1	21	.243	.307	.358	80	-6	0-1	.993	12	108	92	C63		1.0
1925	Bro N	67	193	26	50	8	1	2	24	16	2	9	.259	.322	.342	72	-8	2-2	.981	8	86	118	C55		0.3
1926	Bro N	48	115	6	33	11	0	0	13	8	0	5	.287	.333	.383	94	-1	0	.976	3	79	82	C37		0.5
1927	Bro N	68	201	15	47	3	2	1	21	17		0	.234	.294	.284	55	-13	1	.988	15	79	133	C67		0.6
1928	Bro N	82	258	19	65	8	2	0	23	18		15	.252	.301	.298	58	-16	3	.977	9	75	114	C80		-0.2
1929	Bro N	68	210	13	55	11	1	1	25	17		15	.262	.317	.338	64	-12	1	.991	-3	59	94	C68		-0.9
1930	Bro N	35	95	11	28	3	0	0	14	4		10	.295	.323	.326	58	-6	0	.978	7	101	74	C35		0.2
Total	11	648	1850	170	494	81	16	11	234	148	6	119	.267	.323	.346	76	-65	13-5	.982	51	82	103	C569		2.1

DEBUS, ADAM Adam Joseph B10.7.1892 Chicago IL D5.13.1977 Chicago IL BR/TR/5-10.5/150 d7.14 Mil 1918

| 1917 | Pit N | 38 | 131 | 9 | 30 | 5 | 4 | 0 | 7 | 2 | 1 | 4 | .229 | .279 | .328 | 83 | -3 | 2 | .898 | -7 | 91 | 60 | S21,3b18 | | -1.0 |

DeCINCES, DOUG Douglas Vernon B8.29.1950 Burbank CA BR/TR/6-2/194* [BalA70*S3/65] d9.9 Col Los Angeles Pierce (CA) JC

1973	Bal A	10	18	2	2	0	0	0	3	1-0	0	5	.111	.158	.111	-23	-3	0-0	.895	1	121	224	3b8,2b2/S		-0.2
1974	Bal A	1	1	0	0	0	0	0	0	1-0	0	0	.000	.500	.000	55	0	0-0	1.000	0	121	0	/3		0.0
1975	Bal A	61	167	20	42	6	3	4	23	13-2	1	32	.251	.306	.395	104	0	0-1	.947	6	122	153	3b34,S13,2b11,1b2		0.7
1976	Bal A	129	440	36	103	17	2	11	42	29-1	2	68	.234	.284	.357	92	-6	8-4	.941	-5	93	153	3b109,2b17,1b11,S2/D		-1.1
1977	Bal A	150	522	63	135	28	6	19	69	64-6	2	86	.259	.339	.433	116	12	8-8	.958	-3	99	128	3b148/12D		0.6
1978	Bal A	142	511	72	146	37	1	28	80	46-2	2	71	.286	.346	.526	151	33	7-7	.975	11	103	117	3b130,2b12		4.2
1979	†Bal A	120	422	67	97	27	1	16	61	54-5	3	68	.230	.318	.412	100	0	5-3	.964	-3	95	105	3b120	39	-0.5
1980	Bal A	145	489	64	122	23	2	16	64	49-5	3	83	.249	.319	.403	99	-1	11-6	.960	26	117	154	3b142/1		2.3
1981	Bal A	100	346	49	91	23	2	13	55	41-2	1	32	.263	.341	.454	128	13	0-3	.942	-2	92	173	3b100/1OL		5.7
1982	†Cal A	153	575	94	173	42	5	30	97	66-7	1	80	.301	.369	.548	148	38	7-5	.961	23	122	132	3b153,S2		5.7
1983	Cal A★	95	370	49	104	19	3	18	65	32-2	0	56	.281	.332	.495	126	12	2-0	.955	8	113	129	3b84,D10	36	1.9
1984	Cal A	146	547	77	147	23	3	20	82	53-4	0	79	.269	.327	.431	110	7	4-1	.964	0	103	87	3b140,D5		-0.9
1985	Cal A	120	427	50	104	22	1	20	78	47-11	2	71	.244	.317	.440	106	3	1-4	.958	-2	98	132	3b111,D3	19	-0.1
1986	†Cal A	140	512	69	131	20	3	26	96	52-4	2	74	.256	.325	.459	112	7	2-2	.965	-3	93	93	3b132/SD		0.2
1987	Cal A	133	453	65	106	23	0	16	63	70-6	2	87	.234	.337	.391	96	-1	3-4	.948	-6	99	109	3b128,1b4/SD		-0.9
	StL N	4	9	1	2	2	0	0	1	0-0	0	2	.222	.222	.444	69	0	0-0	.833	1	158	0	3b3		0.0
Total	15	1649	5809	778	1505	312	29	237	879	618-57	21	904	.259	.329	.445	115	114	58-48	.958	54	103	118	3b1543,2b43,D24,1b20,S20/OL	94	14.2

DECKER, HARRY Earle Harry B9.3.1864 Lockport IL BR/TR/5-11/180 d8.23 OF(12/4/8)

1884	Ind AA	4	15	1	4	0	0	0		1	0		.267	.313	.333	114	0		.870	-2			C4		-0.2
	KC U	23	75	8	10	2	0	0		5			.133	.188	.160	7	-11		.813	2	182	162	O16(6/4/6),C11		-0.7
1886	Det N	14	54	2	12	1	0	0	6	2		9	.222	.250	.241	48	-3	0	.871	2			C14/OL		0.0
	Was N	7	23	0	5	1	0	1	1	1		5	.217	.250	.348	87	0	0	.946	0			C4,3b2/S		0.0
	Year	21	77	2	17	2	0	1	7	3		14	.221	.250	.273	59	-4	0	.886	2			C18,3b2/OLS		0.0
1889	Phi N	11	30	4	3	0	0	0	5	0		6	.100	.156	.100	-25	-5	1	.857	-1	98	119	2b7,C3/OL		-0.5
1890	Phi N	5	19	5	7	0	0	2	4	1		1	.368	.478	.421	159	2	4	.938	-2	158	205	1b2,O2L/C		0.0
	Pit N	92	354	52	97	14	3	5	38	26		36	.274	.324	.373	116	7	8	.909	-37	65	93	C70,1b18,O4(2/0/2)/2S		-2.3
	Year	97	373	57	104	15	3	5	40	30		37	.279	.333	.375	119	9	12	.909	-39	65		C71,1b18,O6(4/0/2)/2S		-2.3
Total	4	156	570	72	138	20	4	5	49	41	0	56	.242	.293	.318	87	-10	13	.903	-38	65	92	C107,O24L,1b18,2b8,S2,3b2		-3.7

YEAR	TM LG	G	AB	R	H	2B	3B	HR	RBI	BB-IB	HP	SO	AVG	OBP	SLG	AOPS	ABR	SB-CS	FA	FR	RNG	THR	GAMES AT POSITION	DL	BFW

DECKER, FRANK Frank B2.26.1856 St.Louis MO D2.5.1940 St.Louis MO BR/TR d6.25

YEAR	TM LG	G	AB	R	H	2B	3B	HR	RBI	BB-IB	HP	SO	AVG	OBP	SLG	AOPS	ABR	SB-CS	FA	FR	RNG	THR	GAMES AT POSITION	DL	BFW
1879	Syr N	3	10	1	1	0	0	0	0	0	0	3	.100	.100	.100	-38	-1		.714	-2			C2/OR1		-0.3
1882	StL AA	2	8	0	2	0	0	0	1	0	0		.250	.250	.250	66	0		.813	-1	98	94	2b2		-0.1
Total	2	5	18	0	2	0	0	0	1	0	0	3	.167	.167	.167	12	-1		.813	-2			2b2,C2/1OR		-0.4

DECKER, GEORGE George A "Gentleman George" B6.1.1869 York PA D6.7.1909 Patton CA BL/TL/6-1/180 d7.11 OF(189/34/111)

YEAR	TM LG	G	AB	R	H	2B	3B	HR	RBI	BB-IB	HP	SO	AVG	OBP	SLG	AOPS	ABR	SB-CS	FA	FR	RNG	THR	GAMES AT POSITION	DL	BFW
1892	Chi N	78	291	32	66	6	7	1	28	20	0	49	.227	.277	.306	75	-10	9	.876	-7	126	156	O62R,2b16		-1.8
1893	Chi N	81	328	57	89	9	8	2	48	24	2	22	.271	.325	.366	85	-9	22	.878	-6	182	161	O33(23/0/10),1b27,2b20,S2		-1.4
1894	Chi N	93	393	76	122	17	7	8	93	24	5	20	.310	.358	.450	89	-10	23	.974	-7	56	86	1b49,O29(0/23/6),3b8,2b2/S		-1.4
1895	Chi N	73	297	51	82	9	7	2	41	17	4	22	.276	.324	.374	75	-13	11	.910	-7	36	0	O57(25/8/24),1b11,3b3/S2		-1.9
1896	Chi N	107	421	68	118	23	11	5	61	23	0	14	.280	.318	.423	91	-9	20	.928	-1	106	0	O71(67/3/1),1b36		-1.4
1897	Chi N	111	428	72	124	12	7	5	63	24	4	20	.290	.333	.386	86	-11	11	.925	-2	120	48	O75(74/0/1),1b38/2		-1.6
1898	StL N	76	286	26	74	10	0	1	45	20	3		.259	.314	.304	76	-9	4	.980	-7	48	67	1b75		-1.5
	Lou N	42	148	27	44	4	3	0	19	9	1		.297	.342	.365	104	0	9	.993	-0	82	96	1b32,O6R		0.0
	Year	118	434	53	118	14	3	1	64	29	4		.272	.323	.325	85	-9	13	.984	-7	58	75	1b107,O6R		-1.5
1899	Lou N	39	138	14	37	8	1	1	18	12			.268	.336	.362	92	-1	3	.968	-3	77	102	1b39		-0.4
	Was N	4	9	0	0	0	0	0	0	0	0		.000	.000	.000	-99	-3	0	.955	-0	97	72	1b2/OR		-0.3
	Year	43	147	14	37	8	1	1	18	12	0		.252	.317	.340	80	-4	3	.968	-3	78	100	1b41/OR		-0.4
Total	8	704	2739	423	756	98	51	25	416	173	21	127	.276	.324	.376	84	-75	112	.900	-40	117	57	O334L,1b309,2b40,3b11,S4		-11.7

DECKER, STEVE Steven Michael B10.25.1965 Rock Island IL BR/TR/6-3/205(205-220) [SFN88 21/542] d9.18 Col Lewis-Clark St.

YEAR	TM LG	G	AB	R	H	2B	3B	HR	RBI	BB-IB	HP	SO	AVG	OBP	SLG	AOPS	ABR	SB-CS	FA	FR	RNG	THR	GAMES AT POSITION	DL	BFW
1990	SF N	15	54	5	16	2	0	3	8	1-0	0	10	.296	.309	.500	123	1	0-0	.989	2	109	134	C15		0.4
1991	SF N	79	233	11	48	7	1	5	24	16-1	3	44	.206	.262	.309	63	-12	0-1	.984	1	115	103	C78		-0.8
1992	SF N	15	43	3	7	1	0	0	1	6-0	1	7	.163	.280	.186	36	-3	0-0	1.000	3	537	40	C15		0.0
1993	Fla N	8	15	0	0	0	0	0	1	3-0	0	3	.000	.158	.000	-48	-3	0-0	.968	1	70	78	C5	139	-0.2
1995	Fla N	51	133	12	30	2	1	3	13	19-1	0	22	.226	.318	.323	70	-6	1-0	.985	5	117	94	C46,1b2		0.2
1996	SF N	57	122	16	28	1	0	1	12	15-4	0	26	.230	.309	.262	55	-8	1-0	1.000	2	90	110	C30,1b3,3b2		-0.4
	Col N	10	25	8	8	2	0	1	8	3-0	0	3	.320	.393	.520	112	1	1-0	1.000	2	188	96	C10		0.4
	Year	67	147	24	36	3	0	2	20	18-4	0	29	.245	.323	.306	67	-7	1-0	1.000	4	112	105	C40,1b3,3b2		0.0
1999	Ana A	28	63	5	15	6	0	0	5	13-0	1	24	.238	.372	.333	83	-1	0-0	.987	-2	101	91	C17,1b6,D3		-0.2
Total		263	688	60	152	21	2	13	72	76-6	5	124	.221	.299	.314	68	-31	2-1	.988	13	143	98	C216,1b11,D3,3b2	139	-0.6

DEDE, ARTIE Arthur Richard B7.12.1895 Brooklyn NY D9.6.1971 Keene NH BR/TR/5-9/155 d10.4

YEAR	TM LG	G	AB	R	H	2B	3B	HR	RBI	BB-IB	HP	SO	AVG	OBP	SLG	AOPS	ABR	SB-CS	FA	FR	RNG	THR	GAMES AT POSITION	DL	BFW
1916	Bro N	1	1	0	0	0	0	0	0	0	0	0	.000	.000	.000	-97	0	0	1.000	-0	0	0	/C		-0.1

DEDEAUX, ROD Raoul Martial B2.17.1915 New Orleans LA BR/TR/5-11/160 d9.28 Col USC

YEAR	TM LG	G	AB	R	H	2B	3B	HR	RBI	BB-IB	HP	SO	AVG	OBP	SLG	AOPS	ABR	SB-CS	FA	FR	RNG	THR	GAMES AT POSITION	DL	BFW
1935	Bro N	2	4	0	1	0	0	0	1	0	0	0	.250	.250	.250	36	0	0	.857	0	116	159	S2		0.0

DEE, JIM James D. B Buffalo NY d7.30

YEAR	TM LG	G	AB	R	H	2B	3B	HR	RBI	BB-IB	HP	SO	AVG	OBP	SLG	AOPS	ABR	SB-CS	FA	FR	RNG	THR	GAMES AT POSITION	DL	BFW
1884	Pit AA	12	40	0	5	0	0	0		1	0		.125	.146	.125	-11	-5		.860	1	106	193	S12		-0.3

DEE, SHORTY Maurice Leo B10.4.1889 Halifax NS, Can. D8.12.1971 Jamaica Plain MA BR/TR/5-6/155 d9.14

YEAR	TM LG	G	AB	R	H	2B	3B	HR	RBI	BB-IB	HP	SO	AVG	OBP	SLG	AOPS	ABR	SB-CS	FA	FR	RNG	THR	GAMES AT POSITION	DL	BFW
1915	StL A	1	3	1	0	0	0	0	0	0-0	0		.000	.250	.000	-26	0	0-1	.500	-1	36	0	/S		-0.2

DEER, ROB Robert George B9.29.1960 Orange CA BR/TR/6-3/210(210-230) [SFN78 4/85] d9.4

YEAR	TM LG	G	AB	R	H	2B	3B	HR	RBI	BB-IB	HP	SO	AVG	OBP	SLG	AOPS	ABR	SB-CS	FA	FR	RNG	THR	GAMES AT POSITION	DL	BFW
1984	SF N	13	24	5	4	0	0	3	3	7-0	1	10	.167	.375	.542	159	2	1-1	.905	-0	111	0	O9L		0.1
1985	SF N	78	162	22	30	5	1	8	20	23-0	1	71	.185	.283	.377	88	-3	0-1	.982	-3	94	46	O37(21/0/17),1b10		-0.9
1986	Mil A	134	466	75	108	17	3	33	86	72-3	3	179	.232	.336	.494	119	12	5-2	.974	4	110	90	O131(1/0/131),1b4		0.8
1987	Mil A	134	474	71	113	15	2	28	80	86-6	5	186	.238	.360	.456	111	9	12-4	.974	6	110	124	O123(98/0/29),1b12,D4		1.0
1988	Mil A	135	492	71	124	24	0	23	85	51-4	7	153	.252	.338	.441	113	8	9-5	.990	3	100	124	O133(54/2/79)/D	23	0.7
1989	Mil A	130	466	72	98	18	2	26	65	60-5	4	158	.210	.305	.425	104	2	4-8	.972	1	102	105	O125(2/1/123),D5	16	-0.3
1990	Mil A	134	440	57	92	15	1	27	69	64-6	4	147	.209	.313	.432	107	4	2-3	.970	8	107	176	O117R,1b21/D		0.7
1991	Det A	134	448	64	80	14	2	25	64	89-1	0	175	.179	.314	.386	91	-5	1-3	.978	4	108	78	O132R,D2		-0.6
1992	Det A	110	393	66	97	20	1	32	64	51-1	3	131	.247	.337	.547	142	21	4-2	.983	0	100	106	O106R,D2	45	1.8
1993	Det A	90	323	48	70	11	0	14	39	38-1	3	120	.217	.302	.381	83	-8	3-2	.975	2	108	79	O86(0/2/84),D4	15	-1.0
	Bos A	38	143	18	28	6	1	7	16	20-0	2	49	.196	.303	.399	82	-4	2-0	.970	3	127	75	O36R,D2		-0.2
	Year	128	466	66	98	17	1	21	55	58-1	5	169	.210	.303	.386	83	-12	5-2	.973	5	114	78	O122(0/2/120),D6		-1.2
1996	SD N	25	50	6	9	3	0	4	9	14-0	5	30	.180	.359	.480	124	2	0-0	1.000	-0	106	0	O18(1/0/17)		0.1
Total	11	1155	3881	578	853	148	13	230	600	575-27	32	1409	.220	.324	.442	108	40	43-31	.977	27	106	104	O1053(186/5/871),1b47,D21	99	2.2

DEES, CHARLIE Charles Henry B6.24.1935 Birmingham AL BL/TL/6-1/173* d5.26

YEAR	TM LG	G	AB	R	H	2B	3B	HR	RBI	BB-IB	HP	SO	AVG	OBP	SLG	AOPS	ABR	SB-CS	FA	FR	RNG	THR	GAMES AT POSITION	DL	BFW
1963	LA A	60	202	23	62	11	1	3	27	11-1	8	31	.307	.362	.416	126	7	3-3	.986	-4	80	92	1b56		0.0
1964	LA A	26	26	3	2	1	0	0	1	1-0	1	7	.077	.143	.115	-30	-5	1-2	.981	-1	71	142	1b12		-0.7
1965	Cal A	12	32	1	5	0	0	0	1	1-0	0	5	.156	.182	.156	-3	-4	1-2	.986	-1	43	86	1b8		-0.7
Total	3	98	260	27	69	12	1	3	29	13-2	9	43	.265	.319	.354	95	-2	5-7	.986	-6	75	96	1b76		-1.4

DeFATE, TONY Clyde Herbert B2.22.1895 Kansas City MO D9.3.1963 New Orleans LA BR/TR/5-8.5/158 d4.18

YEAR	TM LG	G	AB	R	H	2B	3B	HR	RBI	BB-IB	HP	SO	AVG	OBP	SLG	AOPS	ABR	SB-CS	FA	FR	RNG	THR	GAMES AT POSITION	DL	BFW
1917	StL N	14	14	0	2	0	0	0	1	4	0	5	.143	.333	.143	50	-1	0	1.000	0	101	0	3b5/2		-0.1
	Det A	3	2	1	0	0	0	0	0	0	0	0	.000	.000	.000	-99	-0	0	1.000	-0	102	0	/2		-0.1
Total	1	17	16	1	2	0	0	0	1	4	0	6	.125	.300	.125	33	-1	0	1.000	-0	101	0	3b5,2b2		-0.2

DeFREITES, ARTURO Arturo Marcelino (Simon) B4.26.1953 San Pedro de Macoris, D.R. BR/TR/6-2/195* d9.7

YEAR	TM LG	G	AB	R	H	2B	3B	HR	RBI	BB-IB	HP	SO	AVG	OBP	SLG	AOPS	ABR	SB-CS	FA	FR	RNG	THR	GAMES AT POSITION	DL	BFW
1978	Cin N	9	19	1	4	1	0	2		1-0	0	4	.211	.238	.421	84	-1	0-0	1.000	0	97	131	1b6		-0.1
1979	Cin N	23	34	2	7	2	0	0	4	0-0	0	16	.206	.200	.265	27	-3	0-0	.974	-1	0	154	1b6/OR		-0.5
Total	2	32	53	3	11	3	0	1	6	1-0	0	20	.208	.214	.321	48	-4	0-0	.988	-1	52	142	1b12/OR		-0.6

DeGROFF, RUBE Edward Arthur B9.2.1879 Hyde Park NY D12.17.1955 Poughkeepsie NY BL/TL/5-11/? d9.22

YEAR	TM LG	G	AB	R	H	2B	3B	HR	RBI	BB-IB	HP	SO	AVG	OBP	SLG	AOPS	ABR	SB-CS	FA	FR	RNG	THR	GAMES AT POSITION	DL	BFW
1905	StL N	15	56	3	14	2	1	0	5	5	0		.250	.311	.321	91	-1	1	.909	0	149	197	O15(0/8/7)		-0.1
1906	StL N	1	4	1	0	0	0	0	0	0	0		.000	.000	.000	-99	-1	0	—	-0	0	0	/OR		-0.1
Total	2	16	60	4	14	2	1	0	5	5	0		.233	.292	.300	80	-2	1	.909	-0	148	196	O16(0/8/8)		-0.2

DeHAAN, KORY Korwin Jay B7.16.1976 Pella IA BL/TR/6-2/187* [PitN97 7/212] d4.25 Col Morningside

YEAR	TM LG	G	AB	R	H	2B	3B	HR	RBI	BB-IB	HP	SO	AVG	OBP	SLG	AOPS	ABR	SB-CS	FA	FR	RNG	THR	GAMES AT POSITION	DL	BFW
2000	SD N	90	103	19	21	7	0	2	13	5-0	0	39	.204	.239	.330	45	-9	4-2	1.000	1	99	188	O60(10/4/49)/D	20	-0.8
2002	SD N	12	11	1	1	0	0	0	0	0-0	0	6	.091	.091	.091	-56	-3	0-0	1.000	-0	108	0	O9(6/2/1)		-0.3
Total	2	102	114	20	22	7	0	2	13	5-0	0	45	.193	.225	.307	36	-12	4-2	1.000	1	100	168	O69(16/6/50)/D	20	-1.1

DEHLMAN, HERMAN Herman J. "Dutch" B1852 Brooklyn NY D3.13.1885 Wilkes-Barre PA d5.2 U1

YEAR	TM LG	G	AB	R	H	2B	3B	HR	RBI	BB-IB	HP	SO	AVG	OBP	SLG	AOPS	ABR	SB-CS	FA	FR	RNG	THR	GAMES AT POSITION	DL	BFW
1872	Atl NA	37	164	30	37	4	1	0	15	3		1	.226	.240	.262	46	-13	4-2	.928	-1	89	49	1b37		-0.9
1873	Atl NA	54	219	.50	52	5	1	0	18	11		9	.237	.274	.269	69	-5	5-0	.926	-3	72	87	1b54/S		-0.4
1874	Atl NA	53	218	40	49	3	1	0	18	7		5	.225	.249	.248	68	-5	2-0	.944	-3	46	87	1b53		-0.4
1875	StL NA	67	254	42	57	12	2	0	14	11		21	.224	.257	.287	98	2	23-9	.955	1	92	113	1b67,O2R		0.6
1876	StL N	64	245	40	45	6	0	0	9	9		10	.184	.213	.208	43	-13		.958	0	71	138	1b64		-1.4
1877	StL N	32	119	24	22	4	0	0	11	7		21	.185	.230	.218	44	-7		.931	-4	41	102	1b31/OL		-1.0
Total	4 NA	211	855	162	195	24	5	0	65	32		36	.228	.256	.268	71	-21	34-11	.940	-4	86	78	1b211,O2R/S		-1.1
Total	2	96	364	64	67	10	0	0	20	16		31	.184	.218	.212	43	-20		.950	-3	61	126	1b95/OL		-2.4

DEIDEL, JIM James Lawrence B6.6.1949 Denver CO BR/TR/6-2/195 d5.31

YEAR	TM LG	G	AB	R	H	2B	3B	HR	RBI	BB-IB	HP	SO	AVG	OBP	SLG	AOPS	ABR	SB-CS	FA	FR	RNG	THR	GAMES AT POSITION	DL	BFW
1974	NY A	2	2	0	0	0	0	0	0	0-0	0	0	.000	.000	.000	-99	-1	0-0	1.000	1	0	316	C2		0.0

DEININGER, PEP Otto Charles B10.10.1877 Wasseralfingen, Germany D9.25.1950 Boston MA BL/TL/5-8.5/180 d4.26 ▲

YEAR	TM LG	G	AB	R	H	2B	3B	HR	RBI	BB-IB	HP	SO	AVG	OBP	SLG	AOPS	ABR	SB-CS	FA	FR	RNG	THR	GAMES AT POSITION	DL	BFW
1902	Bos A	2	6	0	2	1	0	0		0	0		.333	.333	.833	210	1	0	1.000	-1	29	882	P2		0.0
1908	Phi N	1	0	0	0	0	0	0		0	0	0		.000	.000		0	-0	0	/OC					0.0
1909	Phi N	55	169	22	44	9	0	0	16	11	1		.260	.309	.314	93	-1	5	.989	-1	87	0	O45(1/38/6)/2		-0.5
Total	3	58	175	22	46	10	1	0	16	11	1		.263	.310	.331	97	0	5	.989	-2	87	0	O46(1/39/6),P2/2		-0.5

YEAR	TM LG	G	AB	R	H	2B	3B	HR	RBI	BB-IB	HP	SO	AVG	OBP	SLG	AOPS	ABR	SB-CS	FA	FR	RNG	THR	GAMES AT POSITION	DL	BFW

DEISEL, PAT Edward B4.29.1876 Ripley OH D4.17.1948 Cincinnati OH BR/TR/5-5 /145 d8.21

1902	Bro N	1	3	0	2	0	0	0	1	1	1		.667	.800	.667	351	1	0	1.000	0	70	0	/C		0.1
1903	Cin N	2	0	0	0	0	0	0	1	0			—	1.000	—	174	0		—	0	64	0	/C		
Total	2	3	3	0	2	0	0	0	1	2	1		.667	.833	.667	352	1	0	1.000	0	64	0	C2		0.1

DEITRICK, BILL William Alexander B4.30.1902 Hanover Co. VA D5.6.1946 Bethesda MD BR/TR/5-10/160 d9.19 Col Virginia

1927	Phi N	5	6	1	1	0	0	0	0	0		0	.167	.167	.167	-10	-1	0	.750	-1	46	220	S5		-0.2
1928	Phi N	52	100	13	20	6	0	0	7	17		1	10	.200	.322	.260	52	-6	1	1.000	0	101	208	O21(17/1/3),S8		-0.7
Total	2	57	106	14	21	6	0	0	7	17		1	10	.198	.315	.255	49	-7	1	1.000	-1	101	208	O21(17/1/3),S13		-0.9

DEJAN, MIKE Michael Dan B1.13.1915 Cleveland OH D2.2.1953 W.Los Angeles CA BL/TL/6-1/185 d7.13

| 1940 | Cin N | 12 | 16 | 1 | 3 | 0 | 1 | 0 | 2 | 3 | | | .188 | .316 | .313 | 73 | -1 | 0 | 1.000 | -0 | 90 | 0 | O2L | | -0.1 |

DeJESUS, DAVID David Christopher B12.20.1979 Brooklyn NY BL/TL/6-0/170(170-185) [KCA00 4/104] d9.2 Col Rutgers

2003	KC A	12	7	0	2	0	1	0	1	1-0		1	.286	.444	.571	155	-1	0-0	1.000	-1	30	0	O9(0/8/1)		0.0
2004	KC A	96	363	58	104	15	3	7	39	33-0		9	53	.287	.360	.402	99	0	8-11	.984	1	107	64	O94(4/85/6)		-0.1
2005	KC A	122	461	69	135	31	6	9	56	42-1		9	76	.293	.359	.445	121	15	5-5	.987	4	105	124	O119C		1.8
Total	3	230	831	127	241	46	10	16	95	76-1		19	131	.290	.361	.427	111	16	13-16	.986	4	105	96	O222(4/212/7)		1.7

DeJESUS, IVAN Ivan (Alvarez) B1.9.1953 Santurce, PR BR/TR/5-11/175(160-185) d9.13

1974	LA N	3	3	1	1	0	0	0	0	0-0			2	.333	.333	.333	90	0	0-0	1.000	-1	0	0	S2		-0.1
1975	LA N	63	87	10	16	2	1	0	2	11-0		0	15	.184	.276	.230	43	-7	1-2	.974	1	104	112	S63		-0.2
1976	LA N	22	41	4	7	2	1	0	2	4-0		0	9	.171	.244	.268	46	-3	0-1	.950	3	119	124	S13,3b7		0.1
1977	Chi N	155	624	91	166	31	7	3	40	56-4		4	90	.266	.328	.353	75	-21	24-12	.962	46	125	108	S154		4.2
1978	Chi N	160	619	104	172	24	7	3	35	74-5		2	78	.278	.356	.354	88	-7	41-12	.967	15	113	103	S160		3.1
1979	Chi N	160	636	92	180	26	10	5	52	59-1		2	82	.283	.345	.379	89	-9	24-20	.959	8	103	100	S160		1.4
1980	Chi N	157	618	78	160	26	3	3	33	60-2		4	81	.259	.327	.325	77	-17	44-16	.969	10	106	99	S156		1.3
1981	Chi N	106	403	49	78	8	4	0	13	46-2		0	61	.194	.280	.233	43	-30	21-9	.959	9	101	112	S106		-0.8
1982	Phi N	161	536	53	128	21	5	3	59	54-9		2	70	.239	.309	.313	73	-19	14-4	.973	-3	95	94	S154,3b7		-0.5
1983	†Phi N	158	497	60	126	15	7	4	45	53-18		0	77	.254	.333	.336	84	-11	11-4	.966	-17	91	71	S158		-1.6
1984	Phi N	144	435	40	112	15	3	0	35	43-7		2	76	.257	.325	.306	77	-12	12-5	.951	-18	98	78	S141		-0.6
1985	†StL N	59	72	11	16	5	0	0	7	4-0		0	16	.222	.260	.292	55	-4	2-2	1.000	-2	121	128	3b20,S13		-0.2
1986	NY A	7	4	1	0	0	0	0	0	1-0		0	1	.000	.200	.000	-40	-1	0-0	.900	-2	53	0	S7		0.0
1987	SF N	9	10	0	2	0	0	0	1	0-0		0	2	.200	.200	.200	7	-1	0-1	.840	1	132	100	S9		-0.4
1988	Det A	7	17	1	3	0	0	0	0	1-0		0	4	.176	.222	.176	14	-2	0-0	.893	-2	88	100	S7		4.6
Total	15	1371	4602	595	1167	175	48	21	324	466-48		16	664	.254	.323	.326	76	-144	194-88	.963	48	104	95	S1303,3b34		

DeJOHN, MARK Mark Stephen B9.18.1953 Middletown CT BB/TR/5-11/175 [NYN71 23/540] d4.28 C6

| 1982 | Det A | 24 | 21 | 1 | 4 | 2 | 0 | 0 | 1 | 4-0 | | 0 | 4 | .190 | .320 | .286 | 67 | -1 | 1-0 | .978 | 3 | 98 | 140 | S20,3b4/2 | | 0.3 |

DeKONING, BILL William Callahan B12.19.1918 Brooklyn NY D7.26.1979 Palm Harbor FL BR/TR/5-11/185 d5.27 Col Boston College

| 1945 | NY N | 3 | 1 | 0 | 0 | 0 | 0 | 0 | 0 | 0-0 | | 0 | .000 | .000 | .000 | -99 | 0 | 0-0 | 1.000 | -0 | 0 | 0 | C2 | | 0.0 |

DELAHANTY, ED Edward James "Big Ed" B10.30.1867 Cleveland OH D7.2.1903 Niagara Falls ON, Can. BR/TR/6-1/170 d5.22 HF1945 b-Frank b-Jim b-Joe b-Tom OF(1056/250/40)

1888	Phi N	74	290	40	66	12	2	1	31	12		1	26	.228	.261	.293	72	-9	38	.872	-9	94	101	2b56,O17(10/1/6)		-1.7
1889	Phi N	56	246	37	72	13	3	0	27	14		1	17	.293	.333	.370	89	-5	19	.956	-8	80	0	O31(30/0/1),2b24/S		-1.1
1890	Cle P	115	517	107	153	26	13	3	64	24		8	30	.296	.337	.414	109	5	25	.830	-6	99	98	S76,2b20,O18(4/11/3),3b3/1		0.1
1891	Phi N	128	543	92	132	19	9	5	86	33		8	50	.243	.296	.339	83	-14	25	.909	-4	139	108	O99(2/95/2),1b27,2b3		-2.2
1892	Phi N	123	477	79	146	30	21	6	91	31		9	32	.306	.360	.495	158	30	29	.944	7	126	150	O121(1/120/0),3b4		2.7
1893	Phi N	132	595	145	219	35	18	19	146	47		10	20	.368	.423	.583	167	53	37	.948	24	149	181	O117(100/17/0),2b15,1b6		5.4
1894	Phi N	116	495	148	200	39	19	4	133	60		7	16	.404	.475	.584	158	50	21	.927	12	147	106	O90(84/0/6),1b12,3b9,S8,2b6		4.2
1895	Phi N	116	480	149	194	49	10	11	106	86		6	31	.404	.500	.617	186	69	46	.944	-2	100	105	O103(98/5/0),S9,2b6/3		4.6
1896	Phi N	123	499	131	198	44	17	13	126	62		9	22	.397	.472	.631	192	68	37	.952	13	127	103	O99L,1b22/2		6.0
1897	Phi N	129	530	109	200	40	15	5	96	60		3		.377	.444	.538	163	50	26	.970	9	125	56	O129(128/0/1)/1		4.0
1898	Phi N	144	548	115	183	36	9	4	92	77		11		.334	.426	.454	159	48	58	.964	7	100	103	O144L		3.9
1899	Phi N	146	581	135	238	55	9	9	137	55		4		.410	.464	.582	193	76	30	.968	2	120	72	O143L		5.9
1900	Phi N	131	539	82	174	32	10	2	109	41		7		.323	.378	.430	124	18	16	.981	-4	88	109	1b130		1.3
1901	Phi N	139	542	106	192	38	16	8	108	65		4		.354	.427	.528	173	52	29	.949	-3	85	83	O84(82/1/1),1b58		4.1
1902	Was A	123	473	103	178	43	14	10	93	62		4		.376	.453	.590	186	58	16	.961	2	76	0	O111L,1b13		5.0
1903	Was A	42	156	22	52	11	1	1	21	12		2		.333	.388	.436	144	9	3	.962	2	139	86	O40(0/20/0)/1		0.9
Total	16	1837	7511	1600	2597	522	186	101	1466	741		94	244	.346	.411	.505	152	558	455	.951	41	118	96	O1346L,1b271,2b131,S94,3b17		43.1

DELAHANTY, FRANK Frank George "Pudgie" B12.29.1882 Cleveland OH D7.22.1966 Cleveland OH BR/TR/5-9/160 d8.23 b-Ed b-Jim b-Joe b-Tom

1905	NY A	9	27	0	6	1	0	0	3	1		0	.222	.250	.259	55	-1	0	.932	-1	68	0	1b5,O3L		-0.3
1906	NY A	92	307	37	73	11	8	2	41	16		3	.238	.282	.345	87	-6	11	.954	3	62	42	O86L		-0.9
1907	Cle A	15	52	5	9	0	1	0	4	4		0	.173	.232	.212	41	-4	2	.917	0	166	0	O15(9/0/6)		-0.5
1908	NY A	37	125	12	32	1	2	0	10	10		1	.256	.316	.296	98	-0	9	.957	-0	49	0	O36L		-0.3
1914	Buf F	79	274	29	55	4	7	2	27	23		1	19	.201	.265	.288	50	-25	21	.976	-4	91	73	O36(13/1/23),2b4		-3.4
	Pit F	41	159	25	38	4	4	1	7	11		2	11	.239	.297	.333	72	-9	7	.984	-2	102	90	O36(13/1/23),2b4		-1.3
	Year	120	433	54	93	8	11	3	34	34		3	30	.215	.277	.305	58	-35	28	.979	-5	94	78	O114(91/1/23),2b4		-4.7
1915	Pit F	14	42	3	10	1	0	0	3	1		0	.238	.256	.262	46	-4	0	1.000	1	108	154	O11L		-0.3
Total	6	287	986	109	223	22	22	5	94	66		7	30	.226	.280	.308	70	-49	50	.964	-3	81	53	O265(236/1/29),1b5,2b4		-7.0

DELAHANTY, JIM James Christopher B6.20.1879 Cleveland OH D10.17.1953 Cleveland OH BR/TR/5-10.5/170 d4.19 b-Ed b-Frank b-Joe b-Tom OF(176/1/12)

1901	Chi N	17	63	4	12	2	0	0	4	3		1	.190	.239	.222	35	-5	5	.877	-2	88	108	3b17/2		-0.6
1902	NY N	7	26	3	6	1	0	0	3	1		0	.231	.259	.269	64	-1	0	.917	-1	0	0	O7R		-0.2
1904	Bos N	142	499	56	142	27	8	3	60	27		9	.285	.333	.389	127	15	16	.888	2	102	88	3b113,2b18,O9(8/1/0)/P		2.0
1905	Bos N	125	461	50	119	18	5	8	55	28		10	.258	.315	.349	100	-1	12	.962	-7	98	24	O124(123/0/1)/P		-1.6
1906	Cin N	115	379	63	106	21	4	1	39	45		10	.280	.371	.364	124	13	21	.903	-15	85	34	3b105,S5,O2L		0.1
1907	StL A	33	95	8	21	3	0	0	6	5		2	.221	.275	.253	68	-3	6	.889	-2	86	50	3b21,O4R,2b2		-0.5
	Was A	108	404	44	118	18	7	2	54	36		12	.292	.367	.386	152	25	18	.941	-10	88	75	2b68,3b27,O9L,1b4		1.8
	Year	141	499	52	139	21	7	2	60	41		14	.279	.350	.361	121	21	24	.942	-11	89	74	2b70,3b48,O13(10/0/4),1b4		1.3
1908	Was A	83	287	33	91	11	4	1	30	24		3	.317	.376	.394	164	20	16	.963	-0	96	103	2b80		2.4
1909	Was A	90	302	18	67	13	5	1	21	23		6	.222	.290	.308	93	-2	4	.956	-1	94	89	2b85		-0.3
	†Det A	46	150	29	38	10	1	0	20	17		6	.253	.364	.333	115	4	9	.943	-5	101	88	2b46		0.0
	Year	136	452	47	105	23	6	1	41	40		15	.232	.316	.316	101	2	13	.951	-6	97	89	2b131		-0.3
1910	Det A	106	378	67	111	16	2	3	45	43		9	.294	.379	.370	126	14	15	.940	-15	91	95	2b106		1.5
1911	Det A	144	542	83	184	30	14	3	94	56		10	.339	.411	.463	137	28	15	.978	-13	45	48	1b71,2b59,3b13		1.5
1912	Det A	79	266	34	76	14	1	0	41	42		7	.286	.397	.346	117	9	9	.930	-3	107	130	2b44,O33L		-0.3
1914	Bro F	74	214	28	62	13	5	0	15	25		3	21	.290	.372	.397	106	1	4	.957	-12	93	76	2b55,1b5		-1.1
1915	Bro F	17	25	0	6	1	0	0	2	3		1	.240	.345	.280	77	-1	1	.857	-1	102	0	2b4		-0.3
Total	13	1186	4091	520	1159	191	59	19	489	378		92	24	.283	.357	.373	122	116	151	.946	-83	95	89	2b568,3b296,O188L,1b80,S5,P2		3.9

DELAHANTY, JOE Joseph Nicholas B10.18.1875 Cleveland OH D1.29.1936 Cleveland OH BR/TR/5-9/168 d9.30 b-Ed b-Frank b-Jim b-Tom

1907	StL N	7	22	3	7	0	1	0	2	0			.318	.318	.455	147	0	3	.933	-0	0	0	O7L		0.0
1908	StL N	140	499	37	127	14	11	1	44	32		7	.255	.309	.333	110	4	11	.977	-3	64	23	O138L		-0.8
1909	StL N	123	411	28	88	16	4	2	54	42		3	.214	.292	.287	85	-7	10	.985	-11	90	90	O63(14/45/7),2b48		-2.4
Total	3	270	932	68	222	30	15	4	100	74		10	.238	.301	.315	100	-2	24	.978	-15	70	43	O208(159/45/7),2b48		-3.2

DELAHANTY, TOM Thomas James B3.9.1872 Cleveland OH D1.10.1951 Sanford FL BL/TR/5-8/175 d9.29 b-Ed b-Frank b-Jim b-Joe

1894	Phi N	1	4	0	1	0	0	0	0	0		0	.250	.250	.250	21	-1	0	.875	-1	55	0	/2		-0.1
1896	Cle N	16	56	11	13	4	0	0	4	8		1	4	.232	.338	.304	66	-2	4	.823	-3	96	44	3b16		-0.4
	Pit N	1	3	1	1	0	0	0	0	0		0	.333	.333	.333	79	0	0	.750	-0	73	295	/S		0.0
	Year	17	59	12	14	4	0	0	4	8		4	.237	.338	.305	67	-3	4	.823	-3	96	44	3b16/S		-0.4
1897	Lou N	1	4	1	1	1	0	0	2	0			.250	.250	.500	99	0	0	.333	-1	0	0	/2		-0.1
Total	3	19	67	13	16	5	0	0	6	8		5	.239	.329	.313	66	-3	4	.823	-5	96	44	3b16,2b2/S		-0.6

YEAR	TM LG	G	AB	R	H	2B	3B	HR	RBI	BB-IB	HP	SO	AVG	OBP	SLG	AOPS	ABR	SB-CS	FA	FR	RNG	THR	GAMES AT POSITION	DL	BFW
DE LA HOZ, MIKE Miguel Angel (Piloto) B10.2.1938 Havana, Cuba BR/TR/5-11/175* d7.22																							
1960	Cle A	49	160	20	41	6	2	6	23	9-0	1	12	.256	.290	.431	98	-1	0-0	.950	-12	85	55	S38,3b8		-1.1
1961	Cle A	61	173	20	45	10	4	3	23	7-0	2	16	.260	.295	.370	79	-6	0-0	.969	0	105	22	2b17,S17,3b16		-0.3
1962	Cle A	12	12	0	1	0	0	0	0	0-0	0	3	.083	.083	.083	-57	-3	0-0	1.000	-0	123	0	2b2		-0.3
1963	Cle A	67	150	15	40	10	0	5	25	9-0	1	29	.267	.313	.433	107	1	0-0	.962	7	116	121	2b34,3b6,S2,O2L		1.1
1964	Mil N	78	189	25	55	7	1	4	12	14-4	2	22	.291	.346	.402	109	-8	1-1	.968	2	113	80	2b25,3b25,S8		0.6
1965	Mil N	81	176	15	45	3	2	2	11	8-1	2	21	.256	.293	.330	75	-6	0-1	.963	-0	91	111	S41,3b22,2b10/1		-0.5
1966	Atl N	71	110	11	24	3	0	2	7	5-1	0	18	.218	.250	.300	52	-7	0-1	.950	-5	88	78	3b30,2b8/S		-1.3
1967	Atl N	74	143	10	29	3	0	3	14	4-3	0	14	.203	.224	.287	46	-11	1-0	1.000	-4	72	112	2b23,3b22/S		-1.4
1969	Cin N	1	1	0	0	0	0	0	0	0-0	0	1	.000	.000	.000	-95	0	0-0	—	0			/H		0.0
Total	9	494	1114	116	280	42	5	25	115	56-9	8	130	.251	.290	.365	82	-31	2-3	.936	-12	97	98	3b129,2b119,S108,O2L/1		-3.2
DeLANCEY, BILL William Pinkney B11.28.1911 Greensboro NC D11.28.1946 Phoenix AZ BL/TR/5-11.5/185 d9.11																							
1932	StL N	8	26	1	5	0	2	0	2	2-0	0	1	.192	.250	.346	57	-2	0-0	.930	0	76	217	C8		-0.1
1934	†StL N	93	253	41	80	18	3	13	40	41	1	37	.316	.414	.565	150	19	1	.980	3	105	103	C77		2.5
1935	StL N	103	301	37	84	14	5	6	41	42	1	34	.279	.369	.419	107	4	0	.971	-2	110	31	C83		0.7
1940	StL N	15	18	0	4	0	0	0	2	0	0	2	.222	.222	.222	22	-2	0	.929	0	82	75	C12		-0.2
Total	4	219	598	79	173	32	10	19	85	85	2	74	.289	.380	.472	121	19	1	.972	1	106	71	C180		2.9
DELANEY, BILL William L. B3.4.1863 Cincinnati OH D3.1.1942 Canton OH BR/TR/5-10/170 d8.21																							
1890	Cle N	36	116	16	22	1	1	1	7	21	0	19	.190	.314	.241	64	-5	5	.926	-6	88	125	2b36		-0.8
DE LA ROSA, JESUS Jesus (b Jesus De Los Santos (De La Rosa)) B8.5.1953 Santo Domingo, D.R. BR/TR/6-1/153 d8.2																							
1975	Hou N	3	3	1	1	1	0	0	0	0-0	0	0	.333	.333	.667	186	0	0-0	—	0			/H		0.0
DE LA ROSA, TOMAS Tomas Agramonte B1.28.1978 LaVictoria, D.R. BR/TR/5-10/165* d7.17																							
2000	Mon N	32	66	7	19	3	1	2	9	7-0	1	11	.288	.365	.455	105	0	2-1	.980	2	107	55	S29		0.4
2001	Mon N	1	1	0	0	0	0	0	0	0-0	0	0	.000	.000	.000	-99	0	0-0	—	0			/H		0.0
Total	2	33	67	7	19	3	1	2	9	7-0	1	11	.284	.360	.448	102	0	2-1	.980	2	107	55	S29		0.4
DELGADO, ALEX Alexander B1.11.1971 Palmerejo, Venez BR/TR/6-0/160 d4.4																							
1996	Bos N	26	20	5	5	0	0	0	3	2-0	0	3	.250	.348	.250	54	-1	0-0	.889	-0	51		C14,O6(5/0/2),3b4/12		-0.2
DELGADO, CARLOS Carlos Juan (Hernandez) B6.25.1972 Mayaguez, PR BL/TR/6-3/225(215-230) d10.1																							
1993	Tor A	2	1	0	0	0	0	0	1	0-0	0	0	.000	.500	.000	46	0	0-0	1.000	0	0	0	/CD		0.0
1994	Tor A	43	130	17	28	2	0	9	24	25-4	3	46	.215	.352	.438	102	0	1-1	.966	-4	75	79	O41L/C		-0.5
1995	Tor A	37	91	7	15	3	0	3	11	6-0	0	26	.165	.212	.297	32	-10	0-0	1.000	1	113	101	O17L,1b4,D7		-0.9
1996	Tor A	138	488	68	132	28	2	25	92	58-2	9	139	.270	.353	.490	112	9	0-0	.983	-3	71	95	D108,1b27		-0.1
1997	Tor A	153	519	79	136	42	3	30	91	64-9	8	133	.262	.350	.528	125	19	0-3	.988	-6	80	105	1b119,D32		0.0
1998	Tor A	142	530	94	155	43	1	38	115	73-13	11	139	.292	.385	.592	150	41	0-0	.992	-6	83	95	1b141/D	24	2.1
1999	Tor A	152	573	113	156	39	0	44	134	86-7	15	141	.272	.377	.571	136	33	1-1	.990	-2	96	100	1b147,D5		1.6
2000	Tor A★	162	569	115	196	57	1	41	137	123-18	15	104	.344	.470	.664	178	77	0-1	.991	-10	78	105	1b162		4.7
2001	Tor A	162	574	102	160	31	1	39	102	111-22	16	136	.279	.408	.540	144	42	0-0	.994	-5	90	121	1b161		2.2
2002	Tor A	143	505	103	140	34	2	33	108	102-18	15	126	.277	.406	.549	147	39	1-0	.991	-1	99	99	1b140,D3	16	2.4
2003	Tor A★	161	570	117	172	38	1	42	145	109-23	19	137	.302	.426	.593	160	56	0-0	.993	1	102	109	1b147,D14		4.0
2004	Tor A	128	458	74	123	26	0	32	99	69-12	13	115	.269	.372	.535	127	20	0-1	.996	4	110	95	1b120,D8	37	1.2
2005	Fla N	144	521	81	157	41	3	33	115	72-20	17	121	.301	.399	.582	163	51	0-0	.989	-1	99	108	1b141/D	16	3.7
Total	13	1567	5529	970	1570	384	14	369	1173	899-148	139	1363	.284	.393	.559	142	377	9-7	.992	-32	92	104	1b1309,D180,O58L,C2	93	20.4
DELGADO, PUCHY Luis Felipe (Robles) B2.2.1954 Hatillo, PR BB/TL/5-11/170 d9.6																							
1977	Sea A	13	22	4	4	0	0	0	2	1-0	0	8	.182	.217	.182	10	-3	0-0	1.000	1	105	219	O13(1/2/10)		-0.2
DELGADO, WILSON Wilson (Duran) B7.15.1972 San Cristobal, D.R. BB/TR/5-11/160* d9.24																							
1996	SF N	6	22	3	8	0	0	0	2	1-0	2	5	.364	.440	.364	118	1	1-0	.960	-2	68	79	S6		-0.1
1997	SF N	8	7	1	1	1	0	0	0	0-0	0	2	.143	.143	.286	9	-1	0-0	1.000	-1	96	137	2b3/S		-0.1
1998	SF N	10	12	1	2	1	0	0	1	1-0	0	3	.167	.231	.250	28	-1	0-0	1.000	0	105	174	S6		-0.1
1999	SF N	35	71	7	18	2	1	0	3	5-0	1	9	.254	.312	.310	62	-4	1-0	.932	-4	102	142	S20,2b15		-0.7
2000	NY A	31	45	6	11	1	0	1	4	5-0	0	9	.244	.314	.333	67	-2	1-0	.950	-3	91	53	2b14,S11,3b5		-0.4
	KC A	33	83	15	22	1	0	0	7	6-0	0	17	.265	.311	.277	49	-7	1-1	1.000	12	151	138	2b19,S12,3b3		0.6
	Year	64	128	21	33	2	0	1	11	11-0	0	26	.258	.312	.297	55	-9	2-1	.986	9	130	108	2b33,S23,3b8		0.2
2001	KC A	14	25	1	3	0	0	0	1	3-0	0	10	.120	.214	.120	-8	-9	0-0	1.000	1	134	113	S6,3b3,2b2		-0.3
2002	StL N	12	20	2	4	0	0	2	5	0-0	0	6	.200	.200	.500	101	0	0-0	1.000	-3	63	32	S8		-0.2
2003	StL N	43	77	8	13	3	0	0	3	3-0	1	10	.169	.207	.208	10	-10	0-0	1.000	-3	117	78	2b12,3b11,S11		-1.3
	Ana N	19	50	4	16	0	0	0	4	8-0	0	8	.320	.414	.320	101	1	0-0	.867	0	98	212	3b9,S9/2		0.1
2004	NY N	42	130	11	38	4	1	2	13	15-3	0	29	.292	.366	.385	97	0	1-0	.957	2	112	113	S39		0.5
Total	9	253	542	59	136	15	2	5	43	47-3	4	108	.251	.314	.314	64	-27	5-1	.962	0	102	108	S129,2b66,3b31		-2.0
DelGRECO, BOBBY Robert George B4.7.1933 Pittsburgh PA BR/TR/5-11/190(175-190) d4.16																							
1952	Pit N	99	341	34	74	14	2	1	20	38	3	70	.217	.301	.279	60	-18	6-5	.977	2	102	119	O93(1/88/4)		-2.0
1956	Pit N	14	20	4	4	0	0	2	3	3-0	0	3	.200	.304	.500	114	0	0-0	1.000	0	112	0	O7C,3b3		0.0
	StL N	102	270	29	58	16	2	5	18	32-3	6	50	.215	.308	.344	76	-8	1-1	.987	-6	94	46	O99C		-1.9
	Year	116	290	33	62	16	2	7	21	35-3	6	53	.214	.307	.355	79	-8	1-1	.987	-6	95	44	O106C,3b3		-1.9
1957	Chi N	20	40	2	8	2	0	0	3	10-0	0	17	.200	.360	.250	69	-1	1-0	.967	0	88	238	O16C		-0.2
	NY A	8	7	3	3	0	0	0	0	2-0	0	2	.429	.556	.429	175	1	0-0	1.000	0	110	0	O6C		0.1
1958	NY A	12	5	1	1	0	0	0	0	1-0	0	1	.200	.333	.200	52	0	0-1	1.000	0	113	0	O12(11/1/0)		-0.1
1960	Phi N	100	300	48	71	16	4	10	26	54-0	1	64	.237	.355	.417	110	6	1-5	.970	10	119	160	O89(0/87/2)		1.1
1961	Phi N	41	112	14	29	5	0	2	11	12-3	1	17	.259	.344	.357	88	-1	0-0	1.000	0	112	46	O32(1/31/0)/23		-0.2
	KC A	74	239	34	55	14	1	5	21	30-2	1	31	.230	.317	.360	79	-7	0-0	.983	3	102	222	O73C		-0.5
1962	KC A	132	338	61	86	21	1	9	38	49-0	13	62	.254	.370	.402	103	4	4-1	.984	9	116	190	O124(33/95/4)		1.0
1963	KC A	121	306	40	65	7	1	8	29	40-1	5	52	.212	.311	.320	74	-10	1-2	.981	-1	105	87	O110(24/85/6),3b2		-1.5
1965	Phi N	8	4	1	0	0	0	0	0	0-0	0	3	.000	.000	.000	-99	-1	0-0	—	-0	0	0	O4L		-0.2
Total	9	731	1982	271	454	95	11	42	169	271-7	32	372	.229	.330	.352	84	-35	16-15	.981	17	106	130	O665(74/588/16),3b6/2		-4.4
DELIS, JUAN Juan Francisco B2.27.1928 Santiago de Cuba, Cuba D7.23.2003 Havana, Cuba BR/TR/5-11/170 d4.16																							
1955	Was A	54	132	12	25	3	1	0	11	4-1	0	15	.189	.218	.219	27	1	-15	.918	-1	112	144	3b24,O8(2/0/6)/2		-1.7
DELKER, EDDIE Edward Alberts B4.17.1906 Palo Alto PA D5.14.1997 Pottsville PA BR/TR/5-10.5/170 d4.28																							
1929	StL N	22	40	5	6	0	1	0	3	2	2	12	.150	.227	.200	7	-6	0	.750	-3	68	0	S9,2b7,3b3		-0.8
1931	StL N	1	2	0	1	0	0	0	2	0	0	0	.500	.500	1.000	283	1	0	1.000	-0	0	0	/3		0.0
1932	StL N	20	42	1	5	4	0	0	2	8	0	7	.119	.260	.214	28	-4	0	1.000	3	111	155	2b10,3b5,S4		-0.1
	Phi N	30	62	7	10	1	1	1	7	6	0	14	.161	.235	.258	29	-6	0	.925	-4	89	52	2b27		-1.0
	Year	50	104	8	15	5	1	1	9	14	0	21	.144	.246	.240	29	-10	0	.946	-2	95	78	2b37,3b5,S4		-1.1
1933	Phi N	25	41	6	7	3	1	0	1	0	0	12	.171	.171	.293	27	-1	0	.968	3	121	64	2b17,3b4		0.0
Total	4	98	187	19	29	3	1	1	15	16	2	45	.155	.229	.251	26	-19	0	.952	-2	100	76	2b61,3b13,S13		-1.9
DELLAERO, JASON Jason Christopher B12.17.1976 Mount Kisco NY BB/TR/6-2/195 [ChiA97 1/15] d9.7 Col South Florida																							
1999	Chi A	11	33	1	3	0	0	0	2	1-0	0	17	.091	.114	.091	-45	-7	0-0	.917	-2	96	71	S11		-0.8
DELLUCCI, DAVID David Michael B10.31.1973 Baton Rouge LA BL/TL/5-10/194(180-198) [BalA95 10/276] d6.3 Col U. of Mississippi																							
1997	Bal A	17	27	3	6	1	0	1	3	4-1	1	7	.222	.344	.370	89	0	0-0	1.000	2	168	281	O9(3/0/6),D5		0.1
1998	Ari N	124	416	43	108	19	**12**	5	51	33-2	3	103	.260	.318	.399	87	-9	3-5	.987	2	109	42	O117(95/19/15)		-1.2
1999	Ari N	63	109	27	43	7	1	1	15	11-0	3	24	.394	.463	.505	144	8	2-0	1.000	-1	93	81	O31(13/4/19)/D	71	0.7
2000	Ari N	34	50	2	15	3	0	0	2	4-0	0	9	.300	.352	.360	78	-2	0-2	1.000	0	107	0	O12(1/0/11)		-0.3
2001	†Ari N	115	217	28	60	10	2	10	40	22-4	2	52	.276	.349	.479	104	1	2-1	.989	-2	100	0	O58(8/18/35)		-0.2
2002	†Ari N	97	229	38	56	11	2	7	29	28-5	1	55	.245	.326	.402	86	-6	2-4	.967	-4	86	60	O64(20/2/45),D3	22	-1.3
2003	Ari N	70	165	18	40	11	3	2	19	19-1	5	45	.242	.328	.382	79	-5	9-0	.976	-1	103	40	O53(4/9/43)	15	-0.6
	†NY A	21	17	3	3	1	0	0	1	4	4-0	2	13	.176	.263	.255	38	-5	3-0	1.000	1	103	117	O18(2/1/16),D2	30	-0.4

YEAR	TM LG	G	AB	R	H	2B	3B	HR	RBI	BB-IB	HP	SO	AVG	OBP	SLG	AOPS	ABR	SB-CS	FA	FR	RNG	THR	GAMES AT POSITION	DL	BFW
2004	Tex A	107	331	59	80	13	1	17	61	47-3	5	88	.242	.342	.441	99	0	9-4	.989	-2	104		O94(84/7/6),D9		-0.5
2005	Tex A	128	435	97	109	17	5	29	65	76-0	5	121	.251	.367	.513	126	17	5-3	.970	-0	94	150	D67,O52(47/3/3)		1.1
Total	9	776	2030	319	526	93	26	73	289	248-16	25	517	.259	.345	.438	100	-1	35-19	.984	-5	102	51	O508(277/63/199),D87	138	-2.6

DELMAS, BERT Albert Charles B5.20.1911 San Francisco CA D12.4.1979 Huntington Beach CA BL/TR/5-11/165 d9.10 Col Stanford

YEAR	TM LG	G	AB	R	H	2B	3B	HR	RBI	BB-IB	HP	SO	AVG	OBP	SLG	AOPS	ABR	SB-CS	FA	FR	RNG	THR	GAMES AT POSITION	DL	BFW
1933	Bro N	12	28	4	7	0	0	0	0	1	0	7	.250	.276	.250	53	-2	0	.912	-3	82	75	2b10		-0.4

DE LOS SANTOS, LUIS Luis Manuel (Martinez) B12.29.1966 San Cristobal, D.R. BR/TR/6-5/205(190-225) [KCA84 2/44] d9.7

YEAR	TM LG	G	AB	R	H	2B	3B	HR	RBI	BB-IB	HP	SO	AVG	OBP	SLG	AOPS	ABR	SB-CS	FA	FR	RNG	THR	GAMES AT POSITION	DL	BFW
1988	KC A	11	22	1	2	1	1	0	1	4-0	0	4	.091	.231	.227	28	-2	0-0	1.000	-	50	125	1b5,D3		-0.3
1989	KC A	28	87	6	22	3	1	0	6	5-0	0	14	.253	.293	.310	70	-4	0-0	.986	-0	97	121	1b27		-0.6
1991	Det A	16	30	1	5	2	0	0	0	2-0	0	4	.167	.219	.233	25	-3	0-0	1.000	-1	155	0	O3L,1b2,3b2,D9		-0.4
Total	3	55	139	8	29	6	2	0	7	11-0	0	22	.209	.267	.281	53	-9	0-0	.988	-1	91	121	1b34,D12,O3L,3b2		-1.3

DelSAVIO, GARTON Garton Orville B11.26.1913 New York NY BR/TR/5-9.5/165 d4.24

YEAR	TM LG	G	AB	R	H	2B	3B	HR	RBI	BB-IB	HP	SO	AVG	OBP	SLG	AOPS	ABR	SB-CS	FA	FR	RNG	THR	GAMES AT POSITION	DL	BFW
1943	Phi N	4	11	0	1	0	0	0	0	1	0	0	.091	.167	.091	-26	-2	0	.857	-1	98	44	S4		-0.3

DELSING, JIM James Henry B11.13.1925 Rudolph WI BL/TR/5-10/175* d4.21

YEAR	TM LG	G	AB	R	H	2B	3B	HR	RBI	BB-IB	HP	SO	AVG	OBP	SLG	AOPS	ABR	SB-CS	FA	FR	RNG	THR	GAMES AT POSITION	DL	BFW
1948	Chi A	20	63	5	12	0	0	0	5	5	1	12	.190	.261	.190	22	-7	0-0	1.000	-1	93	90	O15C		-0.8
1949	NY A	9	20	5	7	1	0	1	3	1	0	2	.350	.381	.550	145	1	0-0	1.000	-1	71	0	O5C		0.0
1950	NY A	12	10	2	4	0	0	0	2	2	0	0	.400	.500	.400	137	1	0-0	—	0			/H		0.1
	StL A	69	209	25	55	5	2	0	15	20	0	23	.263	.328	.306	61	-12	1-4	.994	2	106	93	O53C		-1.2
	Year	81	219	27	59	5	2	0	17	22	0	23	.269	.336	.311	65	-12	1-4	.994	2	106	91	O53C		-1.1
1951	StL A	131	449	59	112	20	2	8	45	56	1	39	.249	.338	.356	85	-9	2-9	.983	8	108	128	O124(4/118/4)		-0.7
1952	StL A	93	298	34	76	13	6	1	34	25	5	29	.255	.323	.349	85	-7	3-3	.986	3	109	71	O85(34/44/10)		-0.8
	Det A	33	113	14	31	2	1	3	15	11	1	8	.274	.344	.389	103	-0	1-0	.958	-0	104	52	O32L		-0.2
	Year	126	411	48	107	15	7	4	49	36	6	37	.260	.329	.360	90	-6	4-3	.979	2	108	65	O117(66/44/10)		-1.0
1953	Det A	138	479	77	138	26	6	11	62	66	5	39	.288	.380	.436	121	16	1-3	.992	-6	96	60	O133C		0.3
1954	Det A	122	371	39	92	24	2	6	38	49	1	38	.248	.336	.372	96	-1	4-4	**.996**	3	107	75	O108(90/5/16)		-0.5
1955	Det A	114	356	49	85	15	2	10	60	48-2	1	40	.239	.328	.376	92	-4	2-0	.995	-6	91	39	O101(98/3/0)		-1.5
1956	Det A	10	12	0	0	0	0	0	0	3-0	1	3	.000	.250	.000	-29	-2	0-0	1.000	-0	88	0	O3L		-0.2
	Chi A	55	41	11	5	3	0	0	2	10-0	0	13	.122	.294	.195	31	-4	1-0	.957	1	119	164	O29(13/7/9)		-0.3
	Year	65	53	11	5	3	0	0	2	13-0	1	16	.094	.284	.151	17	-6	1-0	.962	1	114	135	O32(16/7/9)		-0.5
1960	KC A	16	40	2	10	3	0	0	5	3-0	0	5	.250	.302	.325	69	-2	0-0	1.000	1	120	0	O10L		-0.2
Total	10	822	2461	322	627	112	21	40	286	299-2	19	251	.255	.339	.366	91	-30	15-23	.989	3	102	76	O698(284/383/39)		-6.0

DeMAESTRI, JOE Joseph Paul "Oats" B12.9.1928 San Francisco CA BR/TR/6-0/174* d4.19

YEAR	TM LG	G	AB	R	H	2B	3B	HR	RBI	BB-IB	HP	SO	AVG	OBP	SLG	AOPS	ABR	SB-CS	FA	FR	RNG	THR	GAMES AT POSITION	DL	BFW
1951	Chi A	56	74	8	15	0	2	1	3	5	0	11	.203	.253	.297	49	-6	0-4	.959	2	121	141	S27,2b11,3b8		-0.4
1952	StL A	81	186	13	42	9	1	1	18	8	0	25	.226	.258	.301	54	-12	0-1	.939	-5	98	81	S77/23		-1.5
1953	Phi A	111	420	53	107	17	3	6	35	24	1	39	.255	.297	.352	72	-18	0-1	.964	-17	92	74	S108		-2.7
1954	Phi A	146	539	49	124	16	3	8	40	20	3	65	.230	.258	.315	57	-34	1-4	.965	-6	96	85	S142/23		-3.1
1955	KC A	123	457	42	114	14	1	6	37	20-1	3	47	.249	.284	.324	63	-26	3-5	.964	-12	97	93	S122		-2.9
1956	KC A	133	434	41	101	16	1	6	39	25-2	3	73	.233	.277	.316	57	-29	3-3	.964	9	109	110	S132,2b2		-1.0
1957	KC A☆	135	461	44	113	14	6	9	33	22-1	2	82	.245	.280	.360	73	-19	6-1	**.980**	-3	96	98	S134		-1.1
1958	KC A	139	442	32	97	11	1	6	38	16-1	1	84	.219	.247	.290	47	-33	1-0	**.980**	6	106	110	S137		-1.7
1959	KC A	118	352	31	86	16	5	6	34	28-8	4	65	.244	.305	.369	83	-9	1-0	.957	2	104	94	S115		0.2
1960	†NY A	49	35	8	8	1	0	0	2	0-0	0	9	.229	.229	.257	33	-3	0-0	.952	-1	74	107	2b19,S17		-0.3
1961	NY A	30	41	1	6	0	0	2	2	0-0	0	6	.146	.146	.146	-23	-7	0-0	.981	2	109	135	S18,2b5,3b4		-0.4
Total	11	1121	3441	322	813	114	23	49	281	168-13	17	511	.236	.274	.325	62	-196	15-19	.967	-21	100	95	S1029,2b39,3b14		-14.9

DEMAREE, FRANK Joseph Franklin (b Joseph Franklin Dimaria) B6.10.1910 Winters CA D8.30.1958 Los Angeles CA BR/TR/5-11.5/185 d7.22 Col St Marys (CA)

YEAR	TM LG	G	AB	R	H	2B	3B	HR	RBI	BB-IB	HP	SO	AVG	OBP	SLG	AOPS	ABR	SB-CS	FA	FR	RNG	THR	GAMES AT POSITION	DL	BFW
1932	†Chi N	23	56	4	14	3	0	0	6	2	1	7	.250	.288	.304	60	-3	0	1.000	1	92	173	O17(4/9/4)		-0.3
1933	Chi N	134	515	68	140	24	6	6	51	22	2	42	.272	.304	.377	94	-6	4	.965	-4	94	130	O133(10/123/0)		-1.4
1935	†Chi N	107	385	60	125	19	4	2	66	26	1	23	.325	.369	.410	108	5	6	.973	-2	88	157	O98(0/69/29)		0.0
1936	Chi N★	**154**	605	93	212	34	3	16	96	49	1	30	.350	.400	.496	137	32	4	.968	-2	97	107	O154(36/0/118)		2.0
1937	Chi N★	**154**	615	104	199	36	6	17	115	57	1	31	.324	.382	.485	129	25	6	.980	-0	97	107	O154R		1.5
1938	†Chi N	129	476	63	130	15	7	8	62	45	4	34	.273	.341	.384	96	-2	1	.972	-6	85	112	O125(9/0/119)		-1.6
1939	NY N	150	560	68	170	27	2	11	79	66	4	40	.304	.381	.418	114	13	2	.986	-8	90	86	O150(1/116/36)		0.0
1940	NY N	121	460	68	139	18	6	7	61	45	0	39	.302	.364	.413	113	8	5	.980	-8	89	65	O119(9/74/37)		-0.4
1941	NY N	16	35	3	6	0	0	0	1	4	0	1	.171	.256	.171	22	-4	0	1.000	0	98	156	O10(1/8/1)		-0.4
	Bos N	48	113	20	26	5	2	2	15	12	0	5	.230	.304	.363	91	-2	2	1.000	-2	88	58	O28(9/7/12)		-0.8
	Year	64	148	23	32	5	2	2	16	16	0	6	.216	.293	.318	74	-5	2	1.000	-1	91	80	O38(10/15/13)		-0.8
1942	Bos N	64	187	18	42	5	0	3	24	17	0	10	.225	.289	.299	74	-6	2	1.000	3	109	101	O49(27/0/22)		-0.8
1943	†StL N	39	86	5	25	2	0	0	8	8	0	4	.291	.351	.314	89	-1	1	1.000	-1	99	58	O23(12/0/12)		-0.3
1944	StL N	16	51	4	13	2	0	0	6	6	0	3	.255	.333	.294	76	-1	0	.969	-0	101	96	O16(15/0/1)		-0.2
Total	12	1155	4144	578	1241	190	36	72	591	359	14	269	.299	.357	.415	110	58	33-0	.978	-29	93	106	O1076(133/406/545)		-2.3

DeMARS, BILLY William Lester "Kid" B8.26.1925 Brooklyn NY BR/TR/5-10/160* d5.18 C19

YEAR	TM LG	G	AB	R	H	2B	3B	HR	RBI	BB-IB	HP	SO	AVG	OBP	SLG	AOPS	ABR	SB-CS	FA	FR	RNG	THR	GAMES AT POSITION	DL	BFW
1948	Phi A	18	29	3	5	0	0	0	1	5	0	3	.172	.294	.172	26	-3	0-0	.927	2	110	144	S9/23		-0.1
1950	StL A	61	178	25	44	5	1	0	13	22	0	13	.247	.330	.287	57	-11	0-1	.933	-9	88	81	S54,3b5		-1.7
1951	StL A	1	4	1	1	0	0	0	0	1	0	0	.250	.400	.250	76	0	0-0	1.000	-0	109	93	/S		0.0
Total	3	80	211	29	50	5	1	0	14	28	0	16	.237	.326	.270	53	-14	0-1	.933	-8	91	89	S64,3b6/2		-1.8

DeMERIT, JOHN John Stephen "Thumper" B1.8.1936 West Bend WI BR/TR/6-1.5/195(180-198) d6.18 Col Wisconsin-Madison

YEAR	TM LG	G	AB	R	H	2B	3B	HR	RBI	BB-IB	HP	SO	AVG	OBP	SLG	AOPS	ABR	SB-CS	FA	FR	RNG	THR	GAMES AT POSITION	DL	BFW
1957	†Mil N	33	34	4	5	0	0	0	1	0-0	0	8	.147	.147	.147	-6	-6	1-0	1.000	1	133		O13(2/11/0)		-0.6
1958	Mil N	3	3	1	2	0	0	0	0	0-0	0	0	.667	.667	.667	278	1	0-0	1.000	0	132	0	O2(0/1/1)		0.1
1959	Mil N	11	5	4	1	0	0	0	0	1-0	0	2	.200	.333	.200	51	0	0-0	1.000	0	195	0	O4(3/1/0)		0.0
1961	Mil N	32	74	5	12	3	0	2	5	5-0	1	19	.162	.225	.284	36	-7	0-0	1.000	0	102	114	O21(2/5/15)		-0.8
1962	NY N	14	16	3	3	0	0	1	1	2-0	0	4	.188	.278	.375	72	-1	0-0	1.000	-2	38	0	O9(3/2/4)		-0.3
Total	5	93	132	21	23	3	0	3	7	11	1	33	.174	.227	.265	32	-13	1-0	1.000	-1	103	66	O49(10/20/20)		-1.6

DEMETER, DON Donald Lee B6.25.1935 Oklahoma City OK BR/TR/6-4/190* d9.18

YEAR	TM LG	G	AB	R	H	2B	3B	HR	RBI	BB-IB	HP	SO	AVG	OBP	SLG	AOPS	ABR	SB-CS	FA	FR	RNG	THR	GAMES AT POSITION	DL	BFW
1956	Bro N	3	3	1	1	0	0	0	1	0	0	1	.333	.333	1.333	297	1	0-0	1.000	0	114	0	/OC		0.1
1958	LA N	43	106	11	20	2	0	5	8	5-0	0	32	.189	.225	.349	48	-9	2-3	1.000	-1	108	0	O39(11/25/4)		-1.1
1959	†LA N	139	371	55	95	11	1	18	70	16-1	6	87	.256	.294	.437	86	-9	5-6	.983	-3	97		O124C		-1.8
1960	LA N	64	168	23	46	7	1	9	29	8-1	1	34	.274	.306	.488	108	1	0-0	.989	-3	89	65	O62(0/61/1)		-0.4
1961	LA N	15	29	3	5	0	0	1	2	3-0	0	6	.172	.250	.276	36	-3	0-0	.950	1	126	154	O14(0/3/12)		0.1
	Phi N	106	382	54	98	18	4	20	68	19-2	5	74	.257	.300	.482	105	-0	2-1	.995	5	106	148	O79(23/44/17),1b22		0.1
	Year	121	411	57	103	18	4	21	70	22-2	5	80	.251	.297	.467	99	-3	2-1	.990	6	108	149	O93(23/47/29),1b22		-0.1
1962	Phi N	153	550	85	169	24	3	29	107	41-6	10	93	.307	.359	.520	139	29	2-7	.997	-5	99	100	3b105,O63(23/42/4)/1		1.9
1963	Phi N	154	515	63	133	20	2	22	83	31-10	6	93	.258	.306	.433	112	7	1-4	1.000	-1	98	116	O119(41/80/0),3b43,1b26		0.2
1964	Det A	134	441	57	113	22	1	22	80	17-6	5	85	.256	.290	.460	104	-4	4-1	1.000	-4	96	58	O88(24/52/13),1b23		-0.8
1965	Det A	122	389	50	98	16	4	16	58	23-3	6	65	.252	.305	.463	121	9	4-2	.988	-3	108	29	O82(1/56/25),1b34		0.2
1966	Det A	32	99	12	21	5	0	5	12	3-0	1	19	.212	.235	.414	81	-3	1-0	.985	5	136	152	O27(4/20/3),1b4		0.2
	Bos A	73	226	31	66	13	1	9	29	5-1	1	42	.292	.305	.478	111	3	1-0	.982	-17	89	93	O57(0/55/3),1b2		-0.2
	Year	105	325	43	87	18	1	14	41	8-1	1	61	.268	.284	.458	102	0	2-0	.984	-2	103	110	O84(4/75/6),1b6		0.2
1967	Bos A	20	43	7	12	5	0	1	4	3-0	0	11	.279	.326	.465	122	1	0-0	1.000	-1	97	175	O12(3/1/9)/3		0.2
	Cle A	51	121	15	25	4	0	5	12	6-1	2	16	.207	.256	.364	80	-3	1-0	.985	2	109	116	O35(13/28/1)/3		-0.3
	Year	71	164	22	37	9	0	6	16	9-1	2	27	.226	.274	.390	92	-2	0-0	.988	2	106	130	O47(16/29/10),3b2		-0.1
Total	11	1109	3443	467	912	147	17	163	563	180-31	42	658	.265	.307	.459	108	24	22-25	.990	-7	101	82	O802(143/592/92),3b150,1b112		-1.9

DEMETER, STEVE Stephen B1.27.1935 Homer City PA BR/TR/5-9.5/185* d7.29 C1

YEAR	TM LG	G	AB	R	H	2B	3B	HR	RBI	BB-IB	HP	SO	AVG	OBP	SLG	AOPS	ABR	SB-CS	FA	FR	RNG	THR	GAMES AT POSITION	DL	BFW
1959	Det A	11	18	1	2	1	0	0	1	0-0	0	1	.111	.111	.167	-24	-3	0-0	.909	0	95	196	3b4		-0.3
1960	Cle A	4	5	0	0	0	0	0	0	0-0	0	1	.000	.000	.000	-99	-1	0-0	1.000	0	55	513	3b3		-0.1
Total	2	15	23	1	2	1	0	0	1	0-0	0	2	.087	.087	.130	-40	-4	0-0	.933	1	86	271	3b7		-0.4

YEAR	TM LG	G	AB	R	H	2B	3B	HR	RBI	BB-IB	HP	SO	AVG	OBP	SLG	AOPS	ABR	SB-CS	FA	FR	RNG	THR	GAMES AT POSITION	DL	BFW

DEMMITT, RAY Charles Raymond B2.2.1884 Illiopolis IL D2.19.1956 Glen Ellyn IL BL/TR/5-8/170 d4.12 Col Illinois

YEAR	TM LG	G	AB	R	H	2B	3B	HR	RBI	BB-IB	HP	SO	AVG	OBP	SLG	AOPS	ABR	SB-CS	FA	FR	RNG	THR	GAMES AT POSITION	DL	BFW
1909	NY A	123	427	68	105	12	12	4	.30	55	6		.246	.340	.358	120	11	16	.908	-2	145	193	O109(0/70/39)		0.3
1910	StL A	10	23	4	4	1	0	0	2	3	1		.174	.296	.217	65	-1	0	1.000	1	108	198	O8R		0.0
1914	Det A	1	0	0	0	0	0	0	0	0	0		—	—	—	—	0	0	—				/R		0.0
	Chi A	146	515	63	133	13	12	2	46	61	6	48	.258	.344	.342	108	5	12-20	.953	-6	81	119	O142(127/4/12)		-1.3
	Year	147	515	63	133	13	12	2	46	61	6	48	.258	.344	.342	108	5	12-20	.953	-6	81	119	O142(127/4/12)		-1.3
1915	Chi A	9	6	0	0	0	0	0	0	1	0	2	.000	.143	.000	-55	-1	0	1.000	1	107	0	O3(1/0/2)		-0.1
1917	StL A	14	53	6	15	1	2	0	7	0	1	8	.283	.296	.377	109	0	1	1.000	-2	86	0	O14R		-0.2
1918	StL A	116	405	45	114	23	5	1	61	38	2	35	.281	.346	.370	120	10	10	.951	9	104	**164**	O114R		1.4
1919	StL A	79	202	19	48	11	2	1	19	14	1	27	.238	.290	.327	71	-8	3	.868	-4	80	103	O49R		-1.5
Total	7	498	1631	205	419	61	33	8	165	172	17	120	.257	.334	.349	108	16	42-20	.934	-4	105	147	O439(128/74/238)		-1.4

DeMONTREVILLE, GENE Eugene Napoleon B3.26.1874 St.Paul MN D2.18.1935 Memphis TN BR/TR/5-8/165 d8.20 b-Lee

YEAR	TM LG	G	AB	R	H	2B	3B	HR	RBI	BB-IB	HP	SO	AVG	OBP	SLG	AOPS	ABR	SB-CS	FA	FR	RNG	THR	GAMES AT POSITION	DL	BFW
1894	Pit N	2	8	0	2	0	0	0		1	0	4	.250	.333	.250	43	-1	0	.889	-0	116	0	S2		-0.1
1895	Was N	12	46	7	10	1	3	0	.9	3	0		.217	.265	.370	63	-3	5	.929	4	105	138	S12		0.1
1896	Was N	**133**	533	94	183	24	5	8	77	29	3	27	.343	.381	.452	119	13	28	.890	19	**110**	88	S133		3.3
1897	Was N	**133**	566	92	193	27	8	3	93	21	1		.341	.366	.433	111	7	30	.886	10	104	118	S99,2b33		1.9
1898	Bal N	151	567	93	186	19	2	0	86	52	10		.328	.394	.369	117	15	49	.944	3	101	81	2b123,S28		2.3
1899	Chi N	82	310	43	87	6	3	0	40	17	5		.281	.328	.319	80	-9	26	.902	7	108	123	S82		0.2
	Bal N	60	240	40	67	13	4	1	36	10	2		.279	.313	.379	85	-6	21	.961	4	102	70	2b60		0.1
	Year	142	550	83	154	19	7	1	76	27	7		.280	.322	.345	82	-14	47	.902	11	108	123	S82,2b60		0.3
1900	Bro N	69	234	34	57	8	1	0	28	10	3		.244	.283	.286	54	-15	21	.952	-1	97	83	2b48,S12,3b7/OC1		-1.3
1901	Bos N	**140**	577	83	173	14	4	5	72	17	1		.300	.321	.364	90	-9	25	**.954**	1	99	95	2b120,3b20		-0.7
1902	Bos N	124	481	51	125	16	5	0	53	12	0		.260	.284	.314	82	-12	23	.940	-17	88	59	2b112,S10		-3.0
1903	Was A	12	44	0	12	2	0	0	3	0	0		.273	.273	.318	75	-1	0	.931	-3	79	24	2b11/S		-0.5
1904	StL A	4	9	0	1	0	0	0	0	2	0		.111	.273	.111	25	-1	0	1.000	-0	95	0	2b3		-0.1
Total	11	922	3615	537	1096	130	35	17	497	174	25	35	.303	.340	.373	97	-22	228	.948	24	97	74	2b510,S379,3b27/1OC		2.2

DeMONTREVILLE, LEE Leon B9.23.1875 Washington Co. MN D3.22.1962 Pelham Manor NY BR/TR/5-7/140 d7.10 b-Gene

YEAR	TM LG	G	AB	R	H	2B	3B	HR	RBI	BB-IB	HP	SO	AVG	OBP	SLG	AOPS	ABR	SB-CS	FA	FR	RNG	THR	GAMES AT POSITION	DL	BFW
1903	StL N	26	70	8	17	3	1	0	7	8	2		.243	.318	.314	89	-1	3	.901	-2	104	152	S15,2b4/OR		-0.2

DEMPSEY, RICK John Rikard B9.13.1949 Fayetteville TN BR/TR (BB 1982p)/6-0/190(178-195) [MinA67 12/237] d9.23 C6

YEAR	TM LG	G	AB	R	H	2B	3B	HR	RBI	BB-IB	HP	SO	AVG	OBP	SLG	AOPS	ABR	SB-CS	FA	FR	RNG	THR	GAMES AT POSITION	DL	BFW
1969	Min A	5	6	1	3	1	0	0	0	1-0	0	0	.500	.571	.667	239	1	0-0	.833	-1	63	0	C3		0.0
1970	Min A	5	7	1	0	0	0	0	0	1-0	0	1	.000	.125	.000	-62	-2	0-0	.923	-1	40	0	C3		-0.2
1971	Min A	6	13	2	4	1	0	0	0	1-0	0	1	.308	.357	.385	107	0	0-0	.944	1	46	170	C6		0.1
1972	Min A	25	40	0	8	1	0	0	6	6-0	0	8	.200	.304	.225	56	-2	0-0	.986	-2	118	109	C23		-0.4
1973	NY A	6	11	0	2	0	0	0	0	1-0	0	3	.182	.250	.182	24	-1	0-0	.818	-3	65	0	C5		-0.4
1974	NY A	43	109	12	26	3	0	2	12	8-0	0	7	.239	.288	.321	77	-3	1-0	.978	6	291	150	C31,O2(1/0/1)/D		0.4
1975	NY A	71	145	18	38	8	0	1	11	21-1	0	15	.262	.353	.338	98	1	0-0	.977	2	83	72	C19,D18,O8(1/0/7)/3		0.2
1976	NY A	21	42	1	5	0	0	0	2	5-0	0	9	.119	.213	.119	-1	-5	0-0	1.000	3	160	119	C9,O4R		-0.2
	Bal A	59	174	11	37	2	0	0	10	13-0	2	17	.213	.275	.224	50	-11	1-1	.987	11	197	114	C58,O3(1/0/2)		0.2
	Year	80	216	12	42	2	0	0	12	18-0	2	21	.194	.263	.204	39	-16	1-1	.988	13	192	115	C67,O7(1/0/6)		0.0
1977	Bal A	91	270	27	61	7	4	3	34	34-1	2	50	.226	.314	.315	77	-8	2-3	.977	7	181	117	C91		0.2
1978	Bal A	136	441	41	114	26	0	6	32	48-2	1	54	.259	.327	.356	99	1	7-3	.985	4	138	108	C135		1.1
1979	†Bal A	124	368	48	88	23	0	6	41	38-1	0	37	.239	.307	.351	81	-9	0-1	.990	27	159	105	C124		2.1
1980	Bal A	119	362	51	95	26	3	9	40	36-1	3	45	.262	.333	.425	108	5	3-1	.987	11	118	**131**	C112,O6(3/0/3),1b2/D		2.0
1981	Bal A	92	251	24	54	10	1	6	15	32-1	1	36	.215	.306	.335	85	-4	0-1	**.998**	5	**154**	87	C90/D		0.4
1982	Bal A	125	344	35	88	15	1	5	36	46-1	0	37	.256	.339	.349	91	-3	0-3	.991	1	143	71	C124/D		0.2
1983	†Bal A	128	347	30	80	16	2	4	32	40-1	3	54	.231	.311	.323	77	-10	1-1	**.997**	19	129	93	C128		1.3
1984	Bal A	109	330	37	76	11	0	11	34	40-0	1	58	.230	.312	.364	89	-5	1-2	.992	-6	102	68	C108		-0.7
1985	Bal A	132	362	54	92	19	0	12	52	50-0	1	87	.254	.345	.406	107	5	0-1	.987	-11	95	83	C131		-0.1
1986	Bal A	122	327	42	68	15	1	13	29	45-0	3	78	.208	.309	.379	87	-4	1-0	.990	4	102	95	C121		0.3
1987	Cle A	60	141	16	25	10	0	1	9	23-0	1	29	.177	.295	.270	51	-9	0-0	.984	1	102	112	C59	51	-0.6
1988	†LA N	77	167	25	42	13	0	7	30	25-0	0	44	.251	.338	.455	133	8	1-0	.989	2	99	99	C74		1.4
1989	LA N	79	151	16	27	7	0	4	16	30-3	1	37	.179	.319	.305	80	-3	1-0	.984	4	131	160	C62		0.4
1990	LA N	62	128	13	25	5	0	2	15	23-0	0	29	.195	.318	.281	68	-5	1-0	.992	-1	96	130	C53	17	-0.4
1991	Mil A	61	147	15	34	6	0	4	21	23-1	0	20	.231	.329	.347	91	-2	0-2	.993	-2	101	81	C56,P2/1		-0.1
1992	Bal A	8	9	2	1	0	0	0	0	2-0	0	4	.111	.273	.111	11	-1	0-0	1.000	-2	64	0	C8		-0.3
Total	24	1766	4692	525	1093	223	12	96	471	592-13	18	736	.233	.319	.347	87	-67	20-19	.988	78	131	100	C1633,O23(6/0/17),D22,1b3,P2/3	111	6.9

DENNEHEY, TOD Thomas Francis B5.12.1899 Philadelphia PA D8.8.1977 Philadelphia PA BL/TL/5-10/180 d4.21

YEAR	TM LG	G	AB	R	H	2B	3B	HR	RBI	BB-IB	HP	SO	AVG	OBP	SLG	AOPS	ABR	SB-CS	FA	FR	RNG	THR	GAMES AT POSITION	DL	BFW
1923	Phi N	9	24	4	7	2	0	0	2	1	0	3	.292	.320	.375	74	-1	0-1	1.000	0	121	0	O9(7/0/2)		-0.1

DENNING, OTTO Otto George "Dutch" B12.28.1912 Hays KS D5.25.1992 Chicago IL BR/TR/6-0/180 d4.15

YEAR	TM LG	G	AB	R	H	2B	3B	HR	RBI	BB-IB	HP	SO	AVG	OBP	SLG	AOPS	ABR	SB-CS	FA	FR	RNG	THR	GAMES AT POSITION	DL	BFW
1942	Cle A	92	214	15	45	14	0	1	19	18	1	14	.210	.275	.290	62	-11	0-0	**.992**	1	*108*	89	C78,O2L		-0.7
1943	Cle A	37	129	8	31	6	0	0	13	5	0	1	.240	.269	.287	67	-6	3-1	.966	-4	78	135	1b34		-1.2
Total	2	129	343	23	76	20	0	1	32	23	1	15	.222	.272	.289	64	-17	3-1	.992	-3	*108*	89	C78,1b34,O2L		-1.9

DENNY, JERRY Jeremiah Dennis (b Jeremiah Dennis Eldridge) B3.16.1859 New York NY D8.16.1927 Houston TX BR/TR/5-11.5/180 d5.2 Col St. Marys (CA) OF(1/2/7)

YEAR	TM LG	G	AB	R	H	2B	3B	HR	RBI	BB-IB	HP	SO	AVG	OBP	SLG	AOPS	ABR	SB-CS	FA	FR	RNG	THR	GAMES AT POSITION	DL	BFW
1881	Pro N	**85**	320	38	77	16	2	1	24	5		44	.241	.252	.313	78	-8		.840	6	106	92	3b85		0.0
1882	Pro N	**84**	329	54	81	10	9	2	42	4		46	.246	.255	.350	92	-4		.861	11	114	72	3b84		0.8
1883	Pro N	**98**	393	73	108	26	8	8	55	9		48	.275	.291	.443	116	7		**.876**	10	96	115	3b98		1.6
1884	†Pro N	110	439	57	109	22	9	6	59	14		58	.248	.272	.380	105	2		.874	-5	86	52	3b99,1b9,2b3/C		-0.2
1885	Pro N	83	318	40	71	14	4	3	24	12		53	.223	.252	.321	87	-5		.869	1	96	96	3b83		-0.3
1886	StL N	119	475	58	122	24	6	9	62	14		68	.257	.278	.389	108	4	16	.895	25	**116**	161	3b117,S3		2.8
1887	Ind N	122	510	86	165	34	12	11	97	13	3		.324	.344	.502	137	23	29	.889	21	113	102	3b116,S4/OR2		3.9
1888	Ind N	126	524	92	137	27	7	12	63	9	2	79	.261	.277	.408	114	6	32	.894	16	109	95	3b96,S25,2b5/OCP		2.4
1889	Ind N	133	578	96	163	24	0	18	112	27	0		.282	.314	.417	101	-3	22	**.913**	13	107	53	3b123,2b7,S5		1.0
1890	NY N	114	437	50	93	18	7	3	42	28	6	62	.213	.270	.307	68	-20	11	.889	7	95	89	3b106,S7/2		-1.0
1891	NY N	4	16	0	4	1	0	0	1	0	0	3	.250	.250	.313	66	-1	2	.700	-2	24	190	3b4		-0.3
	Cle N	36	138	17	31	5	0	0	21	12	1	23	.225	.291	.261	59	-7	3	.884	-0	105	24	3b29,O7(1/1/6)		-0.6
	Phi N	19	73	5	21	1	1	0	11	4	0	6	.288	.325	.329	88	-1	1	.977	-1	36	75	1b12,3b7		-0.3
	Year	59	227	22	56	7	1	0	33	16	1	32	.247	.299	.286	69	-9	6	.876	-4	98	59	3b40,1b12,O7(1/1/6)		-1.2
1893	Lou N	44	175	22	43	5	4	1	22	9	0	15	.246	.283	.337	70	-4	4	.920	-4	99	99	S42,3b2		-0.4
1894	Lou N	60	221	26	61	11	7	0	32	13	1	12	.276	.325	.389	77	-10	8	.874	3	104	121	3b60		-0.4
Total	13	1237	4946	714	1286	238	76	74	667	173	15	602	.260	.287	.384	98	-25	130	.882	106	104	93	3b1109,S86,1b21,2b17,O9R/PC		9.0

DENORFIA, CHRIS Christopher Anthony B7.15.1980 Bristol CT BR/TR/6-1/195 d9.7 Col Wheaton (MA)

YEAR	TM LG	G	AB	R	H	2B	3B	HR	RBI	BB-IB	HP	SO	AVG	OBP	SLG	AOPS	ABR	SB-CS	FA	FR	RNG	THR	GAMES AT POSITION	DL	BFW
2005	Cin N	18	38	8	10	3	0	1	2	6-0	0	9	.263	.364	.421	109	1	1-0	.962	1	143	0	O12(2/10/2)		0.2

DENSON, DREW Andrew B11.16.1965 Cincinnati OH BB/TR/6-5/210* [AtlN84 1/19] d9.13

YEAR	TM LG	G	AB	R	H	2B	3B	HR	RBI	BB-IB	HP	SO	AVG	OBP	SLG	AOPS	ABR	SB-CS	FA	FR	RNG	THR	GAMES AT POSITION	DL	BFW
1989	Atl N	12	36	1	9	1	0	0	5	3-0	0	9	.250	.308	.278	67	-1	1-0	.988	2	170	46	1b12		0.0
1993	Chi A	4	5	0	1	0	0	0	0	0-0	0	2	.200	.200	.200	8	-1	0-0	.800	-0	176	1b3		-0.1
Total	2	16	41	1	10	1	0	0	5	3-0	0	11	.244	.295	.268	60	-2	1-0	.977	1	159	55	1b15		-0.1

DENT, BUCKY Russell Earl (b Russell Earl O'Dey) B11.25.1951 Savannah GA BR/TR/5-11/181(170-190) [ChiA70 S1/6] d6.1 M2/C11 Col Miami-Dade North (FL) CC

YEAR	TM LG	G	AB	R	H	2B	3B	HR	RBI	BB-IB	HP	SO	AVG	OBP	SLG	AOPS	ABR	SB-CS	FA	FR	RNG	THR	GAMES AT POSITION	DL	BFW
1973	Chi A	40	117	17	29	2	0	0	10	10-0	2	18	.248	.308	.265	62	-6	2-3	.963	7	118	96	S36,2b3/3		0.4
1974	Chi A	154	496	55	136	15	3	5	45	28-0	3	44	.274	.316	.347	88	-8	3-4	.972	6	100	112	S154		1.6
1975	Chi A★	157	602	52	159	29	4	3	58	36-3	0	48	.264	.301	.341	81	-16	2-4	**.981**	18	106	101	S157		2.1
1976	Chi A	158	562	44	138	18	4	2	52	43-3	2	45	.246	.300	.302	77	-17	3-5	.976	-4	94	96	S158		-0.4
1977	†NY A	158	477	54	118	18	4	8	49	39-0	1	28	.247	.300	.352	79	-14	1-1	.974	-10	95	108	S158		-0.8
1978	†NY A	123	379	40	92	11	1	5	40	23-1	2	24	.243	.286	.317	72	-15	3-1	.981	-9	97	91	S123	22	-0.7
1979	NY A	141	431	47	99	14	2	3	32	37-1	1	30	.230	.287	.285	57	-26	0-0	.977	32	**116**	122	S141		-2.0
1980	†NY A★	141	489	57	128	26	2	5	52	48-1	0	37	.262	.327	.354	89	-6	0-3	**.982**	12	105	99	S141	15	1.9
1981	NY A★	73	227	20	54	11	0	7	27	19-0	2	21	.238	.300	.379	96	-1	0-1	.970	-2	91	117	S73	35	0.4
1982	NY A	59	160	11	27	4	1	0	9	8-0	0	11	.169	.207	.188	20	-20	0-0	.962	6	108	89	S58		-0.9

YEAR	TM LG	G	AB	R	H	2B	3B	HR	RBI	BB-IB	HP	SO	AVG	OBP	SLG	AOPS	ABR	SB-CS	FA	FR	RNG	THR	GAMES AT POSITION	DL	BFW
	Tex A	46	146	16	32	9	0	1	14	13-0	0	10	.219	.280	.301	63	-7	0-0	.980	0	105	107	S45		-0.2
	Year	105	306	27	59	10	1	1	23	21-0	0	21	.193	.242	.242	35	-28	0-0	.970	7	107	97	S103		-1.1
1983	Tex A	131	417	36	99	15	2	2	34	23-0	1	31	.237	.278	.297	59	-24	3-7	**.979**	-12	97	98	S129/D		-2.4
1984	KC A	11	9	2	3	0	0	0	1	1-0	0	2	.333	.400	.333	104	0	0-0	1.000	-3	53	0	S9,3b2		-0.3
Total	12	1392	4512	451	1114	169	23	40	423	328-9	15	349	.247	.297	.321	74	-160	17-29	.976	46	101	102	S1382,3b3,2b3/D	72	2.7

DENTE, SAM   Samuel Joseph "Blackie"   B4.26.1922 Harrison NJ   D4.21.2002 Montclair NJ   BR/TR/5-11/175*   d7.10

YEAR	TM LG	G	AB	R	H	2B	3B	HR	RBI	BB-IB	HP	SO	AVG	OBP	SLG	AOPS	ABR	SB-CS	FA	FR	RNG	THR	GAMES AT POSITION	DL	BFW
1947	Bos A	46	168	14	39	4	2	0	11	19	0	15	.232	.310	.280	60	-9	0-1	.939	-3	96	138	3b46		-1.2
1948	StL A	98	267	26	72	11	2	0	22	22	1	8	.270	.328	.326	72	-11	1-3	.958	1	102	86	S76,3b6		-0.7
1949	Was A	153	590	48	161	24	4	1	53	31	0	24	.273	.309	.332	71	-27	4-4	.957	-7	101	82	S153		-2.5
1950	Was A	**155**	603	56	144	20	5	2	59	39	1	19	.239	.286	.299	52	-46	1-1	.952	-1	104	87	S128,2b29		-3.6
1951	Was A	88	273	21	65	8	1	0	29	25	0	10	.238	.302	.275	58	-16	3-0	.962	-1	102	97	S65,2b10,3b5		-1.2
1952	Chi A	62	145	12	32	0	1	0	11	5	2	8	.221	.257	.234	37	-13	0-0	.942	2	89	109	S27,3b18,2b6,O6(4/0/2),1b2		-1.0
1953	Chi A	2	0	0	0	0	0	0	0	0	0	0	—	—	—	-4	0	0-0	—	-0	0	0	/S		0.0
1954	†Cle A	68	169	18	45	7	1	1	19	14	0	4	.266	.319	.337	79	-5	0-0	.971	-2	100	131	S60,2b7		-0.3
1955	Cle A	73	105	10	27	4	0	0	10	12-1	0	6	.257	.331	.295	68	-4	0-0	.976	6	113	100	S53,3b13,2b4		-0.3
Total	9	745	2320	205	585	78	16	4	214	167-1	4	96	.252	.303	.305	62	-131	9-9	.958	-6	102	92	S563,3b88,2b56,O6(4/0/2),1b2		-10.2

DePANGHER, MIKE   Michael Anthony   B9.11.1858 Marysville CA   D7.7.1915 San Francisco CA   BL/5-8/190   d8.8

YEAR	TM LG	G	AB	R	H	2B	3B	HR	RBI	BB-IB	HP	SO	AVG	OBP	SLG	AOPS	ABR	SB-CS	FA	FR	RNG	THR	GAMES AT POSITION	DL	BFW
1884	Phi N	4	10	0	2	0	0	0		1		3	.200	.273	.200	54	0		.920	0			C4		0.0

DEPASTINO, JOE   Joseph Bernard   B9.4.1973 Philadelphia PA   BR/TR/6-2/210   [BosA92 7/198]   d8.5

YEAR	TM LG	G	AB	R	H	2B	3B	HR	RBI	BB-IB	HP	SO	AVG	OBP	SLG	AOPS	ABR	SB-CS	FA	FR	RNG	THR	GAMES AT POSITION	DL	BFW
2003	NY N	2	2	0	0	0	0	0	0	0-0	0	1	.000	.000	.000	-99	-1	0-0	1.000	0	0	0	/C		-0.1

DePHILLIPS, TONY   Anthony Andrew   B9.20.1912 New York NY   D5.5.1994 Port Jefferson NY   BR/TR/6-2/185   d4.25   Col Fordham

YEAR	TM LG	G	AB	R	H	2B	3B	HR	RBI	BB-IB	HP	SO	AVG	OBP	SLG	AOPS	ABR	SB-CS	FA	FR	RNG	THR	GAMES AT POSITION	DL	BFW
1943	Cin N	35	20	0	2	1	0	0	2	1	0	5	.100	.143	.150	-16	-3	0-0	.981	3	126	100	C35		0.1

DERBY, GENE   Eugene A.   B2.3.1860 Fitchburg MA   D9.13.1917 Waterbury CT   5-7/160   d9.3

YEAR	TM LG	G	AB	R	H	2B	3B	HR	RBI	BB-IB	HP	SO	AVG	OBP	SLG	AOPS	ABR	SB-CS	FA	FR	RNG	THR	GAMES AT POSITION	DL	BFW
1885	Bal AA	10	31	4	4	0	0	0		2	1		.129	.182	.129	-1	-3		.952	1			C9/OL		-0.2

DERNIER, BOB   Robert Eugene   B1.5.1957 Kansas City MO   BR/TR/6-0/165*   d9.7   Col Longview (MO) CC

YEAR	TM LG	G	AB	R	H	2B	3B	HR	RBI	BB-IB	HP	SO	AVG	OBP	SLG	AOPS	ABR	SB-CS	FA	FR	RNG	THR	GAMES AT POSITION	DL	BFW
1980	Phi N	10	7	5	4	0	0	0	1	1-0	0	0	.571	.625	.571	221	1	3-0	1.000	1	185	0	O3C		0.3
1981	Phi N	10	4	0	3	0	0	0	0	0-0	0	1	.750	.750	.750	309	1	2-1	1.000	-0	62	0	O5C		0.1
1982	Phi N	122	370	56	92	10	2	4	21	36-0	1	69	.249	.315	.319	76	-12	42-12	.981	8	**124**	83	O119(0/70/62)		-0.2
1983	†Phi N	122	221	41	51	10	0	1	15	18-0	0	21	.231	.287	.290	61	-12	35-7	.988	5	120	91	O107(12/68/31)		-0.3
1984	†Chi N	143	536	94	149	26	5	3	32	63-0	2	60	.278	.356	.362	94	-4	45-17	.986	-1	104	67	O140(1/139/0)		0.0
1985	Chi N	121	469	63	119	20	3	1	21	40-1	3	44	.254	.315	.316	70	-18	31-8	.972	1	112	58	O116C	22	-1.4
1986	Chi N	108	324	32	73	14	1	4	18	22-1	0	41	.225	.275	.312	57	-19	27-2	.987	-1	107	58	O105C	38	-1.6
1987	Chi N	93	199	38	63	4	4	8	21	19-0	1	19	.317	.379	.497	125	7	16-7	.989	-4	85	83	O71C		0.3
1988	Phi N	68	166	19	48	3	1	1	10	9-0	1	19	.289	.330	.337	90	-2	13-6	.980	0	101	116	O54(0/53/1)	39	-0.2
1989	Phi N	107	187	26	32	5	0	1	13	14-0	0	28	.171	.225	.214	27	-18	4-3	.970	1	108	0	O74(28/29/20)		-2.0
Total	10	904	2483	374	634	92	16	23	152	222-2	8	301	.255	.318	.333	78	-74	218-63	.982	10	110	72	O794(41/660/114)	99	-5.0

DeROSA, MARK   Mark Thomas   B2.26.1975 Passaic NJ   BR/TR/6-1/195(190-205)   [AtlN96 7/212]   d9.2   Col Penn   OF(8/0/30)

YEAR	TM LG	G	AB	R	H	2B	3B	HR	RBI	BB-IB	HP	SO	AVG	OBP	SLG	AOPS	ABR	SB-CS	FA	FR	RNG	THR	GAMES AT POSITION	DL	BFW
1998	Atl N	5	3	2	1	0	0	0	0	0-0	0	1	.333	.333	.333	77	0	0-0	1.000	-1	37	0	S4		-0.1
1999	Atl N	7	8	0	0	0	0	0	0	0-0	0	2	.000	.000	.000	-99	-2	0-0	1.000	0	87	0	S2		-0.2
2000	Atl N	22	13	9	4	1	0	0	3	2-0	0	1	.308	.400	.385	100	0	0-0	1.000	-2	59	85	S10		-0.1
2001	†Atl N	66	164	27	47	8	0	3	20	12-6	5	19	.287	.350	.390	91	-2	2-1	.960	-0	100	91	S48,2b5/3OLD		-0.1
2002	†Atl N	72	212	24	63	9	2	5	23	12-3	3	24	.297	.339	.429	105	-2	2-3	.974	6	116	131	2b32,S19,O7(2/0/5),3b4	60	0.8
2003	†Atl N	103	266	40	70	14	0	6	22	16-0	5	49	.263	.316	.383	82	-7	1-0	.984	4	105	119	2b29,3b25,S20,O2L/1D		-0.1
2004	Atl N	118	309	33	74	16	0	3	31	23-3	5	53	.239	.293	.320	60	-19	1-3	.939	-5	103	91	3b72,S11,2b5,O3L		-2.3
2005	Tex A	66	148	26	36	5	0	8	19	16-0	2	35	.243	.325	.439	97	-1	1-0	1.000	-1	106	79	O25R,2b17,S16,3b5/1D		-0.1
Total	8	459	1123	161	295	53	2	25	119	81-12	18	184	.263	.319	.380	82	-31	7-7	.972	2	107	114	S130,3b107,2b88,038R,D9,1b2	60	-2.0

DERRICK, CLAUD   Claud Lester "Deek"   B6.11.1886 Burton GA   D7.15.1974 Clayton GA   BR/TR/6-0/175   d9.8   Col Georgia

YEAR	TM LG	G	AB	R	H	2B	3B	HR	RBI	BB-IB	HP	SO	AVG	OBP	SLG	AOPS	ABR	SB-CS	FA	FR	RNG	THR	GAMES AT POSITION	DL	BFW
1910	Phi A	2	2	0	0	0	0	0		0	0		.000	.000	.000	-99	-1	0-0	.500	-1	0	0	/S		-0.1
1911	Phi A	36	100	14	23	1	2	0	5	7	2		.230	.284	.280	61	-5	7	.960	-0	99	113	2b21,S6,1b3,3b2		-0.5
1912	Phi A	21	58	7	14	0	1	0	7	5	1		.241	.313	.276	71	-2	1	.884	-1	109	93	S18		-0.2
1913	NY A	23	65	7	19	1	0	1	7	5	1	8	.292	.352	.354	106	0	2	.874	-2	102	108	S17,3b4/2		0.0
1914	Cin N	3	6	2	2	1	0	0	1	0	0	0	.333	.333	.500	142	0	1	.889	0	94	203	S2		0.1
	Chi N	28	96	5	21	3	1	0	13	5	0	13	.219	.257	.271	57	-5	2	.895	-3	94	85	S28		-0.6
	Year	31	102	7	23	4	1	0	14	5	0	13	.225	.262	.284	62	-5	3	.894	-3	94	90	S30		-0.6
Total	5	113	326	35	79	6	4	1	33	22	4	21	.242	.298	.294	72	-12	13	.892	-6	99	88	S72,2b22,3b6,1b3		-1.4

DERRICK, MIKE   James Michael   B9.19.1943 Columbia SC   BL/TR/6-0/190   d4.9

YEAR	TM LG	G	AB	R	H	2B	3B	HR	RBI	BB-IB	HP	SO	AVG	OBP	SLG	AOPS	ABR	SB-CS	FA	FR	RNG	THR	GAMES AT POSITION	DL	BFW
1970	Bos A	24	33	3	7	1	0	0	5	0-0	0	11	.212	.206	.242	23	-3	0-1	1.000	0	140	0	O2L/1		-0.4

DERRY, RUSS   Alva Russell   B10.7.1916 Princeton MO   D10.26.2004 Kansas City MO   BL/TR/6-1/180   d7.4

YEAR	TM LG	G	AB	R	H	2B	3B	HR	RBI	BB-IB	HP	SO	AVG	OBP	SLG	AOPS	ABR	SB-CS	FA	FR	RNG	THR	GAMES AT POSITION	DL	BFW
1944	NY A	38	114	14	29	3	0	4	14	20	0	19	.254	.366	.386	111	2	1-0	.949	-1	92	93	O28(16/0/12)		-0.1
1945	NY A	78	253	37	57	6	2	13	45	31	1	49	.225	.312	.419	107	1	1-0	.978	-0	105	68	O68(10/44/15)		-0.2
1946	Phi A	69	184	17	38	8	5	0	14	27	1	54	.207	.311	.304	73	-7	0-0	.985	4	116	87	O50(45/2/5)		-0.6
1949	StL N	2	2	0	0	0	0	0	0	0	0	2	.000	.000	.000	-96	-1	0	—	0			/H		-0.1
Total	4	187	553	68	124	17	7	17	73	78	2	124	.224	.322	.373	95	-5	2-0	.976	3	106	80	O146(71/46/32)		-1.0

DeSA, JOE   Joseph   B7.27.1959 Honolulu HI   D12.20.1986 San Juan, PR   BL/TL/5-11/170*   [StLN77 3/58]   d9.6

YEAR	TM LG	G	AB	R	H	2B	3B	HR	RBI	BB-IB	HP	SO	AVG	OBP	SLG	AOPS	ABR	SB-CS	FA	FR	RNG	THR	GAMES AT POSITION	DL	BFW
1980	StL N	7	11	0	3	0	0	0	0	0-0	0	2	.273	.273	.273	50	-1	0-0	1.000	-0	0	0	/1OR		-0.1
1985	Chi A	28	44	5	8	2	0	2	7	3-1	0	6	.182	.234	.364	58	-3	0-0	1.000	1	149	71	1b9/OLD		-0.2
Total	2	35	55	5	11	2	0	2	7	3-1	0	8	.200	.241	.345	57	-4	0-0	1.000	1	137	65	1b10,D4,O2(1/0/1)		-0.3

DESAUTELS, GENE   Eugene Abraham "Red"   B6.13.1907 Worcester MA   D11.5.1994 Flint MI   BR/TR/5-11/170   d6.22   Mil 1944-45   Col Holy Cross

YEAR	TM LG	G	AB	R	H	2B	3B	HR	RBI	BB-IB	HP	SO	AVG	OBP	SLG	AOPS	ABR	SB-CS	FA	FR	RNG	THR	GAMES AT POSITION	DL	BFW
1930	Det A	42	126	13	24	4	2	0	9	7	1	9	.190	.239	.254	25	-15	2-0	.996	3	74	115	C42		-0.8
1931	Det A	3	11	1	1	0	0	0	1	0	1	9	.091	.091	.091	-50	-2	0-0	1.000	-0	58	233	C3		-0.3
1932	Det A	28	72	8	17	2	0	0	2	13	1	11	.236	.360	.264	62	-3	0-0	.984	2	103	93	C24		0.0
1933	Det A	30	42	5	6	1	0	0	4	4	1	6	.143	.234	.167	8	-6	0-0	.973	0	73	69	C30		-0.4
1937	Bos A	96	305	33	74	10	3	0	27	36	1	26	.243	.325	.295	55	-21	1-2	**.993**	4	111	70	C94		-1.1
1938	Bos A	108	333	47	97	16	2	2	48	57	1	31	.291	.396	.369	89	-3	1-1	.985	4	110	106	C108		0.7
1939	Bos A	76	226	26	55	14	0	0	21	33	0	13	.243	.344	.305	64	-11	3-1	.994	-7	95	118	C73		-0.7
1940	Bos A	71	222	19	50	7	1	0	17	32	2	13	.225	.328	.266	54	-14	0-1	.992	-6	97	79	C70		-1.6
1941	Cle A	66	189	20	38	5	1	1	14	14	1	12	.201	.260	.254	38	-18	1-0	.997	5	112	94	C66		-0.8
1942	Cle A	62	162	14	40	5	0	0	9	12	1	13	.247	.303	.278	68	-7	1-0	.975	5	102	51	C61	71	-0.7
1943	Cle A	68	185	14	38	6	1	0	19	11	0	9	.205	.250	.249	49	-13	2-0	.982	3	147	78	C66		-0.7
1945	Cle A	10	9	1	1	0	0	0	0	1	0	1	.111	.200	.111	-9	-1	0-0	1.000	0	95	135	C10		-0.1
1946	Phi A	52	130	10	28	3	1	0	13	12	0	16	.215	.280	.254	51	-9	1-1	.989	3	118	160	C52		-0.4
Total	13	712	2012	211	469	73	11	3	187	232	9	168	.233	.315	.285	57	-123	12-6	.989	20	107	94	C699	71	-6.4

DeSHIELDS, DELINO   Delino Lamont   B1.15.1969 Seaford DE   BL/TR/6-1/175*   [MonN87 1/12]   d4.9   OF(118/3/1)

YEAR	TM LG	G	AB	R	H	2B	3B	HR	RBI	BB-IB	HP	SO	AVG	OBP	SLG	AOPS	ABR	SB-CS	FA	FR	RNG	THR	GAMES AT POSITION	DL	BFW
1990	Mon N	129	499	69	144	28	6	4	45	66-3	4	96	.289	.375	.393	116	13	42-12	.981	-5	99	101	2b128	26	1.4
1991	Mon N	151	563	83	134	15	4	10	51	95-2	3	151	.238	.347	.332	94	-1	56-23	.962	-21	95	91	2b148		-1.5
1992	Mon N	135	530	82	155	19	8	7	56	54-4	3	108	.292	.359	.398	115	11	46-15	.976	-22	89	91	2b134		-0.3
1993	Mon N	123	481	75	142	17	7	2	29	72-3	1	64	.295	.389	.372	101	4	43-10	.983	7	**108**	101	2b123	30	0.2
1994	LA N	89	320	51	80	11	3	2	33	54-0	1	53	.250	.357	.322	84	-6	27-7	.986	5	105	99	2b88,S10	25	0.7
1995	†LA N	127	425	66	109	18	3	8	37	63-4	1	85	.256	.353	.369	98	0	39-14	.980	-5	98	83	2b113		0.4
1996	†LA N	154	581	75	130	12	8	5	41	53-7	1	124	.224	.288	.298	59	-37	48-11	.975	-20	91	87	2b154		-4.2
1997	StL N	150	572	92	169	26	**14**	11	58	55-11	3	72	.295	.357	.500	110	7	55-14	.972	-8	96	108	2b147		1.3
1998	StL N	117	420	74	122	21	8	7	44	56-2	1	65	.290	.371	.429	111	8	26-10	.983	-10	93	93	2b111/1	36	-0.2
1999	Bal A	96	330	46	87	11	2	6	34	37-0	1	52	.264	.339	.364	82	-9	11-8	.977	-5	94	93	2b93	42	-1.0
2000	Bal A	151	561	84	166	43	5	10	86	69-2	1	82	.296	.369	.444	111	12	37-10	.975	-16	90	69	2b96,O41(39/2/0),D10		0.3
2001	Bal A	58	188	29	37	8	2	3	21	31-1	1	42	.197	.310	.309	69	-8	11-1	.967	-3	88	68	O47(46/1/0),D8		-1.0

YEAR	TM LG	G	AB	R	H	2B	3B	HR	RBI	BB-IB	HP	SO	AVG	OBP	SLG	AOPS	ABR	SB-CS	FA	FR	RNG	THR	GAMES AT POSITION	DL	BFW
	Chi N	68	163	26	45	9	3	2	16	28-0	0	35	.276	.380	.405	107	3	12-1	.976	-3	89	63	O33L,2b16,3b5/1		0.1
2002	Chi N	67	146	20	28	6	1	3	10	21-2	0	38	.192	.292	.308	61	-9	10-1	.970	2	99	67	2b41/OR	15	-0.3
Total 13		1615	5779	872	1548	244	74	80	561	754-31	20	1061	.268	.352	.377	97	-12	463-147	.977	-104	96	92	2b1392,O122L,D18,S10,3b5,1b2	174	-1.5

DESTRADE, ORESTES   Orestes (Cucuas) B5.8.1962 Santiago de Cuba, Cuba BB/TR/6-4/210(210-230) d9.11 Col Florida JC

YEAR	TM LG	G	AB	R	H	2B	3B	HR	RBI	BB-IB	HP	SO	AVG	OBP	SLG	AOPS	ABR	SB-CS	FA	FR	RNG	THR	GAMES AT POSITION	DL	BFW
1987	NY A	9	19	5	5	0	0	0	1	5-0	0	5	.263	.417	.263	86	0	0-0	1.000	0	62	103	1b3,D2		0.0
1988	Pit N	36	47	2	7	1	0	1	3	5-0	0	17	.149	.226	.234	34	-4	0-0	1.000	-1	47	73	1b8		-0.6
1993	Fla N	153	569	61	145	20	3	20	87	58-8	3	130	.255	.324	.406	89	-9	0-2	.987	-9	82	93	1b152		-3.2
1994	Fla N	39	130	12	27	4	0	5	15	19-1	2	32	.208	.316	.354	72	-5	1-0	.983	-3	75	100	1b37		-1.1
Total 4		237	765	80	184	25	3	26	106	87-9	5	184	.241	.319	.383	83	-18	1-2	.987	-13	79	94	1b200,D2		-4.9

DETHERAGE, BOB   Robert Wayne B9.20.1954 Springfield MO BR/TR/6-0/180 [LAN72 3/65] d4.11

YEAR	TM LG	G	AB	R	H	2B	3B	HR	RBI	BB-IB	HP	SO	AVG	OBP	SLG	AOPS	ABR	SB-CS	FA	FR	RNG	THR	GAMES AT POSITION	DL	BFW
1980	KC A	20	26	2	8	2	0	1	7	1-0	0	4	.308	.333	.500	123	1	1-1	1.000	-2	75	0	O20(12/0/11)		-0.2

DeTORE, GEORGE   George Francis B11.11.1906 Utica NY D2.7.1991 Utica NY BR/TR/5-8/170 d9.14 C1 Col Colgate

YEAR	TM LG	G	AB	R	H	2B	3B	HR	RBI	BB-IB	HP	SO	AVG	OBP	SLG	AOPS	ABR	SB-CS	FA	FR	RNG	THR	GAMES AT POSITION	DL	BFW
1930	Cle A	3	12	0	2	1	0	0	2	0	0	2	.167	.167	.250	4	-2	0-0	.750	-1	50	243	3b3		-0.3
1931	Cle A	30	56	3	15	6	0	0	7	8	0	2	.268	.359	.375	88	-1	0-2	.958	2	156	0	3b13,S10,2b3		0.2
Total 2		33	68	3	17	7	0	0	9	8	0	4	.250	.329	.353	74	-3	0-2	.929	1	131	58	3b16,S10,2b3		-0.1

DETWEILER, DUCKY   Robert Sterling B2.15.1919 Trumbauersville PA BR/TR/5-11/178 d9.12 Mil 1943-45

YEAR	TM LG	G	AB	R	H	2B	3B	HR	RBI	BB-IB	HP	SO	AVG	OBP	SLG	AOPS	ABR	SB-CS	FA	FR	RNG	THR	GAMES AT POSITION	DL	BFW
1942	Bos N	12	44	3	14	2	1	0	5	2	0	7	.318	.348	.409	123	1	0	.929	-2	80	104	3b12		-0.1
1946	Bos N	1	1	0	0	0	0	0	0	0	0	0	.000	.000	.000	-99	0	0	—	0			/H		0.0
Total 2		13	45	3	14	2	1	0	5	2	0	7	.311	.340	.400	118	1	0	.929	-2	80	104	3b12		-0.1

DEVAREZ, CESAR   Cesar Salvatore (Santana) B9.22.1969 San Francisco de Macoris, D.R. BR/TR/5-10/175* d6.3

YEAR	TM LG	G	AB	R	H	2B	3B	HR	RBI	BB-IB	HP	SO	AVG	OBP	SLG	AOPS	ABR	SB-CS	FA	FR	RNG	THR	GAMES AT POSITION	DL	BFW
1995	Bal A	6	4	0	0	0	0	0	0	0-0	0	0	.000	.000	.000	-98	0	0-0	1.000	0	32	0	C6		-0.1
1996	Bal A	10	18	3	2	0	1	0	3	1-0	0	3	.111	.158	.222	-5	-3	0-0	1.000	-0	67	69	C10		-0.3
Total 2		16	22	3	2	0	1	0	3	1-0	0	3	.091	.130	.182	-22	-4	0-0	1.000	0	59	54	C16		-0.4

DEVEREAUX, MIKE   Michael B4.10.1963 Casper WY BR/TR/6-0/195* [LAN85 5/116] d9.2 Col Arizona St.

YEAR	TM LG	G	AB	R	H	2B	3B	HR	RBI	BB-IB	HP	SO	AVG	OBP	SLG	AOPS	ABR	SB-CS	FA	FR	RNG	THR	GAMES AT POSITION	DL	BFW
1987	LA N	19	54	7	12	3	0	0	4	3-0	0	10	.222	.263	.278	45	-4	3-1	1.000	-1	81	111	O18(11/2/5)		-0.5
1988	LA N	30	43	4	5	1	0	0	2	2-0	0	10	.116	.156	.140	-15	-7	0-1	1.000	-0	102	0	O26(0/17/8)		-0.8
1989	Bal A	122	391	55	104	14	3	8	46	36-0	2	60	.266	.329	.379	102	1	22-11	.983	0	109	16	O112(4/80/35),D5		0.0
1990	Bal A	108	367	48	88	18	1	12	49	28-0	0	48	.240	.291	.392	93	-5	13-12	.983	2	108	78	O104C,D3	29	-0.5
1991	Bal A	149	608	82	158	27	10	19	59	47-2	2	115	.260	.313	.431	108	4	16-9	.993	4	104	131	O149(1/148/0)		0.7
1992	Bal A	156	653	76	180	29	11	24	107	44-1	4	94	.276	.321	.464	115	10	10-8	.989	-8	96	54	O155C		0.0
1993	Bal A	131	527	72	132	31	3	14	75	43-0	1	99	.250	.306	.400	85	-12	3-3	.988	-6	90	111	O130C	24	-1.7
1994	Bal A	85	301	35	61	8	2	9	33	22-0	1	72	.203	.256	.332	48	-25	1-2	.995	-2	97	71	O84C/D	15	-2.5
1995	Chi A	92	333	48	102	21	4	10	55	25-3	1	51	.306	.352	.465	116	7	6-6	.985	4	114	75	O90(0/9/87)		0.6
	†Atl N	29	55	7	14	3	0	1	8	2-0	0	11	.255	.281	.364	65	-3	2-0	1.000	2	138	0	O27(14/9/4)		-0.1
1996	†Bal A	127	323	49	74	11	2	8	34	34-0	2	53	.229	.305	.350	66	-18	8-2	.983	2	99	131	O112(35/30/62),D10		-1.7
1997	Tex A	29	72	8	15	3	0	0	7	7-0	0	10	.208	.275	.250	37	-7	1-0	1.000	-2	92	0	O28(5/3/24)		-0.9
1998	LA N	9	13	0	4	1	0	0	1	3-0	0	2	.308	.438	.385	125	1	0-1	1.000	1	128	489	O5(1/3/1)		0.1
Total 12		1086	3740	491	949	170	33	105	480	296-6	12	635	.254	.308	.401	91	-58	85-56	.988	-5	102	82	O1040(71/774/226),D19	68	-7.3

DEVINE, MICKEY   William Patrick B5.9.1892 Albany NY D10.1.1937 Albany NY BR/TR/5-10/165 d8.2

YEAR	TM LG	G	AB	R	H	2B	3B	HR	RBI	BB-IB	HP	SO	AVG	OBP	SLG	AOPS	ABR	SB-CS	FA	FR	RNG	THR	GAMES AT POSITION	DL	BFW
1918	Phi N	4	8	0	1	0	0	0	1	1	0	1	.125	.125	.250	13	-1	0	.909	-0	110	58	C3		-0.1
1920	Bos N	8	12	1	2	0	0	0	1	1	0	2	.167	.231	.167	7	-2	1-0	.955	0	102	53	C5		-0.1
1925	NY N	21	33	6	9	3	0	0	4	2	0	3	.273	.314	.364	76	-1	0-0	.933	1	113	116	C11/3		0.0
Total 3		33	53	7	12	4	0	0	4	3	0	6	.226	.268	.302	51	-4	1-0	.936	0	110	91	C19/3		-0.2

DeVIVEIROS, BERNIE   Bernard John B4.19.1901 Oakland CA D7.5.1994 Oakland CA BR/TR/5-7/160 d9.13

YEAR	TM LG	G	AB	R	H	2B	3B	HR	RBI	BB-IB	HP	SO	AVG	OBP	SLG	AOPS	ABR	SB-CS	FA	FR	RNG	THR	GAMES AT POSITION	DL	BFW
1924	Chi A	1	1	0	0	0	0	0	0	0	0	0	.000	.000	.000	-99	-1	0-0	.333	-1	0	0	/S		-0.1
1927	Det A	24	22	4	5	1	0	0	2	2	0	8	.227	.292	.273	46	-2	1-0	.913	-0	107	160	S14/3		-0.1
Total 2		25	23	4	5	1	0	0	2	2	0	8	.217	.280	.261	40	-2	1-0	.846	-1	97	144	S15/3		-0.2

DEVLIN, ART   Arthur McArthur B10.16.1879 Washington DC D9.18.1948 Jersey City NJ BR/TR/6-0/175 d4.14 C2 Col Georgetown

YEAR	TM LG	G	AB	R	H	2B	3B	HR	RBI	BB-IB	HP	SO	AVG	OBP	SLG	AOPS	ABR	SB-CS	FA	FR	RNG	THR	GAMES AT POSITION	DL	BFW
1904	NY N	130	474	81	133	16	8	1	66	62	6		.281	.371	.354	119	13	33	.907	5	108	81	3b130		2.3
1905	†NY N	153	525	74	129	14	7	2	61	66	13		.246	.344	.310	94	-1	59	.932	6	103	91	3b153		0.9
1906	NY N	148	498	76	149	23	8	2	65	74	6		.299	.396	.390	142	28	54	.944	29	122	136	3b148		6.6
1907	NY N	143	491	61	136	16	2	1	54	63	15		.277	.376	.324	116	14	38	.940	-2	96	69	3b140,S3		1.8
1908	NY N	157	534	59	135	18	4	2	45	62	14		.253	.346	.313	106	7	19	.947	12	105	110	3b157		2.6
1909	NY N	143	491	61	130	19	8	0	56	65	10		.265	.362	.336	115	12	26	.934	17	110	125	3b143		3.5
1910	NY N	147	493	71	128	17	5	2	67	62	9	32	.260	.353	.327	98	1	28	.933	6	101	102	3b147		1.1
1911	NY N	95	260	42	71	16	2	0	25	42	6	19	.273	.386	.350	103	4	9	.944	4	111	34	3b79,1b6,2b6,S6		1.0
1912	Bos N	124	436	59	126	18	8	0	54	51	3	37	.289	.367	.367	99	1	11	.992	-1	95	79	1b69,S26,3b26/OL		0.0
1913	Bos N	73	210	19	48	7	5	0	12	29	2	17	.229	.328	.310	81	-5	8-8	.973	5	106	45	3b69		0.2
Total 10		1313	4412	603	1185	164	57	10	505	576	84	105	.269	.364	.338	109	74	285-8	.938	81	107	97	3b1192,1b75,S35,2b6/OL		20.0

DEVLIN, JIM   James Alexander B6.6.1849 Philadelphia PA D10.10.1883 Philadelphia PA BR/TR/5-11/175 d4.21 ▲

YEAR	TM LG	G	AB	R	H	2B	3B	HR	RBI	BB-IB	HP	SO	AVG	OBP	SLG	AOPS	ABR	SB-CS	FA	FR	RNG	THR	GAMES AT POSITION	DL	BFW
1873	Phi NA	23	99	18	24	4	4	0	10	2			.242	.257	.364	79	-3	0-0	.938	-2	150	171	1b12,3b6,S4,O2R		-0.4
1874	Chi NA	45	203	26	58	5	0	0	26	2			.286	.293	.310	93	-2	2-1	.930	-2	63	57	1b24,O17R,3b5		-0.2
1875	Chi NA	69	318	60	92	17	6	0	40	4			.289	.298	.381	133	10	6-1	.934	1	134	71	1b42,P28,O4(0/3/1)		0.7
1876	Lou N	68	298	38	94	14	1	0	28	1			.315	.318	.369	109	1		.941	2	102	147	P68/1		0.1
1877	Lou N	61	268	38	72	6	3	1	27	7			.269	.287	.325	78	-1		.933	2	111	158	P61		0.0
Total 3 NA		137	620	104	174	26	10	0	76	8			.281	.290	.355	110	5	8-2	.933	-3	114	81	1b78,P28,O23(0/3/20),3b11,S4		0.1
Total 2		129	566	76	166	20	4	1	55	8			.293	.303	.348	94	0		.937	4	106	152	P129/1		0.1

DEVLIN, JIM   James Raymond B8.25.1922 Plains PA D1.15.2004 Danville PA BL/TR/5-11.5/165 d4.27

YEAR	TM LG	G	AB	R	H	2B	3B	HR	RBI	BB-IB	HP	SO	AVG	OBP	SLG	AOPS	ABR	SB-CS	FA	FR	RNG	THR	GAMES AT POSITION	DL	BFW
1944	Cle A	1	1	0	0	0	0	0	0	0	0	0	.000	.000	.000	-99		0-0	1.000	0	0	0	/C		0.0

DeVOGT, REX   Rex Eugene B1.4.1888 Clare MI D11.9.1935 Alma MI BR/TR/5-9/170 d4.17

YEAR	TM LG	G	AB	R	H	2B	3B	HR	RBI	BB-IB	HP	SO	AVG	OBP	SLG	AOPS	ABR	SB-CS	FA	FR	RNG	THR	GAMES AT POSITION	DL	BFW
1913	Bos N	3	6	0	0	0	0	0	0	0	0	3	.000	.000	.000	-98	-2	0	.941	1	137	142	C3		-0.1

DEVORE, DOUG   Douglas Rinehart B12.14.1977 Columbus OH BL/TL/6-4/215 [AriN99 12/358] d5.6 Col Indiana

YEAR	TM LG	G	AB	R	H	2B	3B	HR	RBI	BB-IB	HP	SO	AVG	OBP	SLG	AOPS	ABR	SB-CS	FA	FR	RNG	THR	GAMES AT POSITION	DL	BFW
2004	Ari N	50	107	8	24	3	2	3	13	7-0	0	31	.224	.272	.374	61	-7	1-1	1.000	3	123	146	O31(18/1/15)		-0.5

DEVORE, JOSH   Joshua M. B11.13.1887 Murray City OH D10.6.1954 Chillicothe OH BL/TL/5-6/160 d9.25

YEAR	TM LG	G	AB	R	H	2B	3B	HR	RBI	BB-IB	HP	SO	AVG	OBP	SLG	AOPS	ABR	SB-CS	FA	FR	RNG	THR	GAMES AT POSITION	DL	BFW
1908	NY N	5	6	1	1	0	0	0	2	1	0		.167	.286	.167	43	0	1	1.000	-0	0	0	O2R		-0.1
1909	NY N	22	28	6	4	1	0	0	1	2	2		.143	.250	.179	33	-2	3	.824	-1	103	0	O12(3/10/1)		-0.3
1910	NY N	133	490	92	149	11	10	2	27	46	6	67	.304	.371	.380	119	11	43	.929	-7	81	116	O130(106/2/22)		-0.1
1911	†NY N	149	565	96	158	19	10	3	50	81	6	69	.280	.376	.365	104	6	61	.934	0	89	143	O149(104/0/48)		-0.1
1912	†NY N	106	327	66	90	14	6	2	37	51	5	43	.275	.381	.373	104	4	27	.918	-5	86	106	O96(76/1/19)		-0.5
1913	NY N	16	21	4	4	0	1	0	1	3		4	.190	.320	.286	73	-1	6-2	1.000	0	68	214	O8(1/5/2)		0.0
	Cin N	66	217	30	58	6	4	3	14	12	1	21	.267	.309	.373	95	-3	17-7	.920	-2	88	126	O57(0/57/1)		-0.7
	Phi N	23	39	9	11	1	0	0	5	4	1	7	.282	.364	.308	89	0	0	.889	-1	81	185	O14(8/6/0)		-0.1
	Year	105	277	43	73	7	5	3	20	19	2	32	.264	.318	.357	92	-4	23-9	.919	-2	86	138	O79(9/68/3)		-0.8
1914	Phi N	30	53	5	16	2	0	0	7	4	0	5	.302	.351	.340	90	0	0	.947	3	86	399	O9(7/2/0)		0.2
	†Bos N	51	128	22	29	4	0	1	5	18	1	14	.227	.327	.281	82	-2	2	.915	-4	79	79	O42(23/20/0)		-0.8
	Year	81	181	27	45	6	0	1	12	22	1	19	.249	.333	.298	87	-2	2	.923	-1	80	147	O51(30/22/0)		-0.6
Total 7		601	1874	331	520	58	31	11	149	222	23	230	.277	.361	.359	103	13	160-9	.925	-16	85	126	O519(328/103/95)		-2.7

DeVORMER, AL   Albert E. B8.19.1891 Grand Rapids MI D8.29.1966 Grand Rapids MI BR/TR/6-0.5/175 d8.4

YEAR	TM LG	G	AB	R	H	2B	3B	HR	RBI	BB-IB	HP	SO	AVG	OBP	SLG	AOPS	ABR	SB-CS	FA	FR	RNG	THR	GAMES AT POSITION	DL	BFW
1918	Chi A	8	19	2	5	2	0	0	0	4		0	.263	.263	.368	90	0	1	1.000	-1	106	79	C6/OR		-0.1
1921	†NY A	22	49	6	17	4	0	0	7	2		4	.347	.373	.429	102	0	2-0	.950	-1	109	91	C17		0.1
1922	NY A	24	59	8	12	4	1	0	11	1		1	.203	.217	.305	34	-6	0-0	.968	-1	128	104	C17/1		-0.6
1923	Bos A	74	209	20	54	7	3	0	18	6		21	.258	.282	.321	58	-14	3-0	.979	-1	81	107	C55,1b2		-1.0

YEAR	TM LG	G	AB	R	H	2B	3B	HR	RBI	BB-IB	HP	SO	AVG	OBP	SLG	AOPS	ABR	SB-CS	FA	FR	RNG	THR	GAMES AT POSITION	DL	BFW
1927	NY N	68	141	14	35	3	1	2	21	11	2	11	.248	.312	.326	71	-6	1	.953	-3	122	103	C54,1b3		-0.7
Total	5	196	477	50	123	20	5	2	57	20	3	46	.258	.292	.333	65	-26	7-0	.967	-6	103	103	C149,1b6/OR		-2.3

DeVOY, WALT Walter Joseph B3.14.1886 St.Louis MO D12.17.1953 St.Louis MO BR/TR/5-11/165 d9.13

1909	StL A	19	69	7	17	3	1	0	8	3	0		.246	.278	.319	95	-1	4	.944	-0	127	0	O16R,1b3		-0.2

DeWILLIS, JEFF Jeffrey Allen B4.13.1965 Houston TX BR/TR/6-2/190 [TorA83 3/63] d4.19

1987	Tor A	13	25	2	3	1	0	0	1	0	0	12	.120	.185	.280	20	-3	0-0	.964	-1	174	160	C13		-0.3

DEXTER, CHARLIE Charles Dana B6.15.1876 Evansville IN D6.9.1934 Cedar Rapids IA BR/TR/5-7/155 d4.17 Col Univ. of the South OF(8/159/236)

1896	Lou N	107	402	65	112	18	7	3	37	17	6	34	.279	.318	.381	87	-9	21	.903	-9	79	120	C55,O47(0/46/1)		-1.4
1897	Lou N	76	257	43	72	12	5	2	46	21	3		.280	.342	.389	96	-2	12	.907	-1	252	404	O32(3/14/16),C23,3b14,S2		-0.2
1898	Lou N	112	421	76	132	13	5	1	66	26	7		.314	.363	.375	113	7	44	.958	-3	99	62	O95R,2b8,C7		0.1
1899	Lou N	81	298	47	76	7	1	1	34	21	5		.255	.315	.295	68	-13	21	.943	2	141	68	O72(1/0/71),S6		-1.3
1900	Chi N	40	125	7	25	5	0	2	20	1	1		.200	.243	.288	90	-11	2	.943	4	95	136	C22,O13R/2		-0.5
1901	Chi N	116	460	46	123	9	5	1	66	16	7		.267	.302	.315	82	-11	22	.982	2	131	106	1b54,3b25,O21(1/9/11),2b13,C3		-1.0
1902	Chi N	71	273	31	62	13	0	2	26	19	5		.227	.290	.297	83	-5	13	.846	-14	70	99	3b41,1b22,O10(1/4/5)		-2.0
	Bos N	48	183	33	47	3	0	1	18	16	2		.257	.323	.290	88	-2	16	.901	-3	100	78	S22,2b19,O7(0/4/3)/3		-0.5
	Year	119	456	64	109	16	0	3	44	35	7		.239	.303	.294	85	-7	29	.847	-17	70	98	3b42,1b22,S22,2b19,O17(1/8/8)		-2.5
1903	Bos N	123	457	82	102	15	1	3	34	61	6		.223	.328	.280	75	-12	32	.941	-9	91	165	O106(2/82/21),S9,C6		-2.4
Total	8	774	2876	430	751	95	24	16	347	198	42	34	.261	.318	.328	85	-58	183	.942	-30	114	108	O403R,C116,3b81,1b76,2b41,S39		-9.2

DIAZ, ALEX Alexis B10.5.1968 Brooklyn NY BB/TR/5-11/180* d7.25

1992	Mil A	22	9	5	1	0	0	0	1	0-0	0	0	.111	.111	.111	-38	-2	3-2	1.000	0	109	0	O11(2/10/0),D2		-0.2
1993	Mil A	32	69	9	22	2	0	0	1	0-0	0	12	.319	.319	.348	80	-2	5-3	.979	-0	99	77	O28(4/12/13)/D	119	-0.3
1994	Mil A	79	187	40	47	5	7	1	17	10-1	0	19	.251	.285	.369	65	-11	5-5	.993	1	96	150	O73(0/58/20),2b2/D	12	-1.0
1995	†Sea A	103	270	44	67	14	0	3	27	13-2	2	27	.248	.286	.333	60	-16	18-8	.987	-1	94	122	O88(17/69/4)		-1.5
1996	Sea A	38	79	11	19	2	0	1	5	2-0	2	8	.241	.274	.304	47	-7	6-3	.982	1	139	77	O28(19/5/5)/D	81	-0.4
1997	Tex A	28	90	8	20	4	0	2	12	5-0	1	13	.222	.268	.333	53	-6	1-1	.980	1	104	137	O23(3/0/20)/12		-0.6
1998	SF N	34	62	5	8	2	0	0	5	0-0	0	15	.129	.194	.161	-26	-12	1-1	1.000	1	105	268	O21(4/15/3)		-1.0
1999	Hou N	30	50	3	11	2	0	1	7	3-0	0	13	.220	.264	.320	47	-4	2-2	.900	1	64	258	O8(7/0/1)	71	-0.5
Total	8	366	816	102	195	31	7	8	75	33-3	5	107	.239	.271	.324	53	-60	41-25	.986	5	100	133	O280(56/169/66),D5,2b3/1	283	-5.5

DIAZ, BO Baudilio Jose (Seijas) B3.23.1953 Cua, Venez D11.23.1990 Caracas, Venez BR/TR/5-11/190(190-205) d9.6

1977	Bos A	2	1	0	0	0	0	0	0	0-0	0	0	1.000	1.000	1.000	-90	-0	0-0	1.000	1	0	0	C2		0.0
1978	Cle A	44	127	12	30	4	0	2	11	4-0	0	17	.236	.260	.315	61	-7	0-0	.971	-5	112	92	C44	61	-1.0
1979	Cle A	15	32	0	5	2	0	0	1	2-0	0	6	.156	.206	.219	15	-4	0-0	.958	-0	72	76	C15	55	-0.4
1980	Cle A	76	207	15	47	11	2	3	32	7-3	0	27	.227	.250	.343	61	-12	1-0	.989	2	78	83	C75		-0.8
1981	Cle A★	63	182	25	57	19	0	7	38	13-2	1	23	.313	.359	.533	156	13	2-2	.975	-3	122	84	C51,D3		1.2
1982	Phi N	144	525	69	151	29	1	18	85	36-5	3	87	.288	.333	.450	115	9	3-6	.989	-4	103	101	C144		1.0
1983	†Phi N	136	471	49	111	17	0	15	64	38-4	2	57	.236	.295	.367	83	-12	1-4	.986	18	106	114	C134		1.1
1984	Phi N	27	75	5	16	4	0	1	9	5-0	0	13	.213	.256	.307	58	-4	0-0	.992	-1	89	89	C23	97	-0.5
1985	Phi N	26	76	9	16	5	1	2	16	6-0	0	7	.211	.268	.382	78	-2	0-0	.972	2	86	125	C24	43	1.0
	Cin N	51	161	12	42	8	0	3	15	15-0	1	18	.261	.324	.366	89	-2	0-0	.988	13	116	98	C51		1.3
	Year	77	237	21	58	13	1	5	31	21-0	1	25	.245	.307	.371	86	-4	0-0	.983	15	107	106	C75		1.3
1986	Cin N	134	474	50	129	21	0	10	56	40-0	0	52	.272	.327	.380	91	-6	1-1	.984	3	115	98	C134		0.2
1987	Cin N★	140	496	49	134	28	1	15	82	19-1	5	73	.270	.300	.421	86	-11	1-0	.992	3	116	117	C137		-0.2
1988	Cin N	92	315	26	69	9	0	10	35	7-4	1	41	.219	.236	.343	63	-17	0-2	.990	5	126	127	C88	15	-1.0
1989	Cin N	43	132	6	27	5	0	1	8	6-3	0	17	.205	.239	.265	43	-10	0-2	.984	-1	96	55	C43	65	-1.0
Total	13	993	3274	327	834	162	5	87	452	198-22	13	429	.255	.297	.387	87	-65	9-17	.986	30	108	103	C965,D3	336	0.1

DIAZ, CARLOS Carlos Francisco B12.24.1964 Elizabeth NJ BR/TR/6-3/195 [TorA86 14/367] d5.8 Col Oklahoma St.

1990	Tor A	9	3	1	1	0	0	0	0	0-0	0	2	.333	.333	.333	85	0	0-0	1.000	2	97	197	C9		0.2

DIAZ, EDDY Eddy Javier B9.29.1971 Barquisimeto, Venez BR/TR/5-10/160 d4.17

1997	Mil A	16	50	4	11	2	1	0	7	1-0	0	5	.220	.235	.300	38	-5	0-0	1.000	1	100	132	2b14/3S		-0.3

DIAZ, EDGAR Edgar (Serrano) B2.8.1964 Santurce, PR BR/TR/6-0/160* d9.16 [DL 1987 Mil A 58]

1986	Mil A	5	13	0	3	0	0	0	1	0-0	0	3	.231	.286	.231	41	-1	0-0	.875	-3	62	70	S5		-0.3
1990	Mil A	86	218	27	59	2	2	0	14	21-0	1	32	.271	.338	.298	79	-6	3-2	.950	-5	96	93	S65,2b15,3b7/D		-0.7
Total	2	91	231	27	62	2	2	0	14	22-0	1	35	.268	.335	.294	77	-7	3-2	.946	-8	93	91	S70,2b15,3b7/D	58	-1.0

DIAZ, EDWIN Edwin (Rosario) B1.15.1975 Bayamon, PR BR/TR/5-11/170* [TexA93 2/52] d3.31

1998	Ari N	3	7	0	0	0	0	0	0	0-0	0	2	.000	.000	.000	-99	-2	0-0	.938	1	125	141	2b3		-0.1
1999	Ari N	4	5	2	2	2	0	0	1	3-1	0	1	.400	.625	.800	255	2	0-0	1.000	-0	250	0	2b2,S2	27	0.1
Total	2	7	12	2	2	2	0	0	1	3-1	0	3	.167	.333	.333	72	0	0-0	.947	1	146	118	2b5,S2	27	0.0

DIAZ, EINAR Einar Antonio B12.28.1972 Chiriqui, Pan BR/TR/5-10/165(165-200) d9.9

1996	Cle A	4	1	0	0	0	0	0	0	0-0	0	0	.000	.000	.000	-99	0	0-0	1.000	0	0	0	C4		0.0
1997	Cle A	5	7	1	1	1	0	0	1	0-0	0	2	.143	.143	.286	8	-1	0-0	.955	0	26	262	C5		-0.1
1998	†Cle A	17	48	8	11	1	0	2	9	3-0	2	2	.229	.286	.375	72	-2	0-0	.973	2	105	124	C17		0.0
1999	†Cle A	119	392	43	110	21	1	3	32	23-0	5	41	.281	.328	.362	72	-16	11-4	.988	3	96	112	C119		-0.4
2000	Cle A	75	250	29	68	14	2	4	25	11-0	8	29	.272	.323	.392	77	-9	4-2	.994	17	120	104	C74/3		1.2
2001	†Cle A	134	437	54	121	34	1	4	56	17-0	16	44	.277	.338	.387	84	-9	1-2	.992	14	111	133	C134/2		1.2
2002	Cle A	102	320	34	66	19	0	2	16	17-1	5	27	.206	.258	.284	44	-26	0-1	.989	3	65	149	C100	38	-1.6
2003	Tex A	101	334	30	86	14	1	4	35	9-0	10	32	.257	.294	.341	64	-18	3-1	.989	5	110	99	C101		-0.5
2004	Mon N	55	139	9	31	6	1	1	11	11-3	4	10	.223	.293	.302	54	-10	2-0	.990	5	90	64	C44/3		-0.2
2005	StL N	58	130	14	27	6	0	1	17	5-0	2	12	.208	.248	.277	37	-12	0-0	.995	1	160	112	C50,1b3		-0.9
Total	10	670	2058	222	521	116	6	21	202	96-4	53	199	.253	.302	.346	66	-103	21-10	.990	51	103	117	C648,1b3,3b2/2	38	-1.3

DIAZ, JUAN Juan Carlos B2.19.1974 San Jose de las Lajas, Cuba BR/TR/6-2/228 d6.12

2002	Bos A	4	7	2	2	2	0	1	3	0-0	0	3	.286	.375	.857	210	1	0-0	1.000	-0	0	0	/1D		0.1

DIAZ, MARIO Mario Rafael (Torres) B1.10.1962 Humacao, PR BR/TR/5-10/160* d9.12 [DL 1990 Sea A 25]

1987	Sea A	11	23	4	7	0	1	0	3	0-0	0	4	.304	.304	.391	78	-1	0-0	.972	3	130	155	S10		0.2
1988	Sea A	28	72	6	22	5	0	0	9	3-0	0	5	.306	.329	.375	94	-1	0-0	.985	-6	73	75	S21,2b4/13	17	-0.5
1989	Sea A	52	74	9	10	0	0	1	7	7-0	0	9	.135	.210	.176	9	-9	0-0	.930	-15	64	36	S37,2b14,3b3		-2.3
1990	NY N	16	22	0	3	1	0	0	1	0-0	0	3	.136	.130	.182	-13	-3	0-0	.958	1	131	42	S10/2		-0.2
1991	Tex A	96	182	24	48	7	0	1	22	15-0	0	18	.264	.318	.319	78	-5	0-1	.962	-3	91	95	S65,2b20,3b8/D	17	-0.5
1992	Tex A	19	31	2	7	1	0	0	1	1-1	0	2	.226	.250	.258	44	-2	0-1	.975	-2	83	30	S16,2b3/3		-0.5
1993	Tex A	71	205	24	56	10	1	2	24	8-0	1	13	.273	.297	.361	80	-6	1-0	.986	-3	93	88	S57,3b12/1		-0.5
1994	Fla N	32	77	10	25	4	2	0	11	6-0	1	6	.325	.376	.429	106	1	0-0	.964	1	105	211	3b11,2b7,S7		0.2
1995	Fla N	49	87	5	20	3	0	1	6	1-0	0	12	.230	.239	.299	40	-8	0-0	.944	-1	97	179	2b9,S5,3b3		-0.8
Total	9	374	773	84	198	31	4	5	84	41-1	2	70	.256	.292	.326	69	-34	1-2	.972	-24	88	81	S228,2b58,3b39,1b2/D	59	-4.9

DIAZ, MATT Matthew Edward B3.3.1978 Portland OR BR/TR/6-1/200* [TBA99 17/505] d7.19 Col Florida St.

2003	TB A	9	9	2	1	0	0	0	1	0-0	0	3	.111	.200	.111	-15	-2	0-0	.857	1	274	0	/OLD		-0.1
2004	TB A	10	21	3	4	1	1	1	3	1-0	2	6	.190	.292	.476	98	0	0-0	1.000	0	165	0	O4(3/0/1),D4		0.0
2005	KC A	34	89	7	25	4	2	1	9	1-0	2	15	.281	.323	.404	99	0	0-1	.950	-0	114	0	O21(19/0/2),D7	37	-0.1
Total	3	48	119	12	30	5	3	2	12	6-0	4	24	.252	.308	.395	90	-2	0-1	.948	1	130	0	O26(23/0/3),D13	37	-0.2

DIAZ, MIKE Michael Anthony B4.15.1960 San Francisco CA BR/TR/6-2/195(195-220) [ChiN78 30/685] d9.15

1983	Chi N	6	7	2	2	0	0	1	1	0-0	0	1	.286	.286	.429	91	0	0-0	1.000	-1	37	0	C3		-0.1
1986	Pit N	97	209	22	56	9	0	12	36	19-1	3	42	.268	.330	.483	120	5	0-1	.966	-3	96	50	O38(37/0/1),1b20,3b5/C		0.0
1987	Pit N	103	241	28	58	8	2	16	48	31-3	2	43	.241	.326	.490	114	4	1-0	.960	-1	86	105	O37(27/0/10),1b32,C8		0.0
1988	Pit N	47	74	6	17	3	0	0	5	16-1	0	13	.230	.367	.270	86	0	0-0	1.000	-2	66	0	O19(9/0/9),1b6/C	33	-0.3
	Chi A	40	152	12	36	6	0	3	12	5-0	1	30	.237	.266	.336	67	-7	0-1	.987	-1	95	92	1b39/D		-1.2
Total	4	293	683	70	169	27	2	31	102	71-4	6	128	.247	.319	.429	103	2	1-2	.988	-8	91	88	1b97,O94(73/0/20),C13,3b5/D	33	-1.6

YEAR	TM LG	G	AB	R	H	2B	3B	HR	RBI	BB-IB	HP	SO	AVG	OBP	SLG	AOPS	ABR	SB-CS	FA	FR	RNG	THR	GAMES AT POSITION	DL	BFW

DIAZ, VICTOR Victor Israel B12.10.1981 Santo Domingo, D.R. BR/TR/6-0/200* [LAN00 37/1107] d9.11 Col Grayson Co. (TX) JC

2004	NY N	15	51	8	15	3	0	3	8	1-0	1	15	.294	.321	.529	117	1	0-0	.935	-0	115	0	O14R		0.0
2005	NY N	89	280	41	72	17	3	12	38	30-7	1	82	.257	.329	.468	109	3	6-2	.981	-0	103	67	O81(3/0/78)		-0.1
Total	2	104	331	49	87	20	3	15	46	31-7	2	97	.263	.327	.477	110	4	6-2	.974	-0	105	58	O95(3/0/92)		-0.1

DICKEN, PAUL Paul Franklin B10.2.1943 DeLand FL BR/TR/6-5/195* d6.7 Col Manatee (FL) CC/Palm Beach (FL) CC

1964	Cle A	11	11	0	0	0	0	0	0	0-0	0	5	.000	.000	.000	-99	-3	0-0	—	0			/H		-0.3
1966	Cle A	2	2	0	0	0	0	0	0	0-0	0	1	.000	.000	.000	-99	-1	0-0	—	0			/H		-0.1
Total	2	13	13	0	0	0	0	0	0	0-0	0	6	.000	.000	.000	-99	-4	0-0	—	0			/H		-0.4

DICKERSON, BUTTERCUP Lewis Pessano B10.11.1858 Tyaskin MD D7.23.1920 Baltimore MD BL/TR/5-6/140 d7.15

1878	Cin N	29	123	17	38	5	1	0				7	.309	.309	.366	134	4		.877	-2	13	0	O29(10/19/0)		0.1
1879	Cin N	81	350	73	102	18	14	2	57	3		27	.291	.297	.440	147	17		.801	-4	50	48	O81L		0.7
1880	Tro N	30	119	15	23	2	2	0	10	2		3	.193	.207	.244	49	-6		.903	-4	91	207	O30(0/29/1)/S		-0.4
	Wor N	31	133	22	39	8	6	0	20	1		2	.293	.299	.444	136	4		.852	-4	53	155	O31C		-0.1
	Year	61	252	37	62	10	8	0	30	3		5	.246	.255	.369	96	-2		.883	0	72	181	O61(0/60/1)/S		-0.5
1881	Wor N	80	367	48	116	18	6	1	31	8		8	.316	.331	.406	123	9		.892	9	131	169	O80(79/0/1)		1.2
1883	Pit AA	85	354	62	88	15	1	0		18			.249	.285	.297	91	-2		.798	-1	184	97	O78(1/30/47),S8,2b2		-0.3
1884	StL U	46	211	49	77	15	1	0		8			.365	.388	.445	146	6		.895	4	113	145	O42L,3b4		0.8
	Bal AA	13	56	9	12	2	1	0		4	2		.214	.290	.286	85	-1		.941	-2	47	0	O12R/3		-0.2
	Lou AA	8	28	6	4	0	2	1		3	0		.143	.226	.393	103	0		.813	-1	149	0	O8(1/5/3)		0.0
	Year	21	84	15	16	2	3	1		7	2		.190	.269	.321	91	-1		.879	-2	86	0	O20(1/5/15)/3		-0.2
1885	Buf N	5	21	1	1	1	0	0	0	1		4	.048	.091	.095	-38	-3		1.000	1	226	0	O5(2/3/0)		-0.3
Total	7	408	1762	302	500	84	34	4	127	48		51	.284	.304	.377	118	28		.854	6	104	108	O396(216/117/64),S9,3b5,2b2		1.5

DICKEY, GEORGE George Willard "Skeets" B7.10.1915 Kensett AR D6.16.1976 DeWitt AR BB/TR/6-2/180 d9.21 Mil 1943-45 b-Bill

1935	Bos A	5	11	1	0	0	0	0	1	1	0	3	.000	.083	.000	-72	-1	0-0	1.000	-1	74	0	C4		-0.3
1936	Bos A	10	23	0	1	1	0	0	0	2	0	3	.043	.120	.087	-46	-5	0-0	.912	0	95	193	C10		-0.4
1941	Chi A	32	55	6	11	1	0	2	8	5	0	7	.200	.267	.327	57	-4	0-0	1.000	1	102	68	C17		-0.2
1942	Chi A	59	116	6	27	3	0	1	17	9	0	11	.233	.288	.284	63	-6	0-0	.918	-3	98	54	C29		-0.8
1946	Chi A	37	78	8	15	1	0	0	1	12	0	13	.192	.300	.205	45	-5	0-2	1.000	1	84	106	C30		-0.3
1947	Chi A	83	211	15	47	6	0	1	27	34	0	25	.223	.331	.265	69	-8	4-2	.985	-1	79	105	C80		-0.5
Total	6	226	494	36	101	12	0	4	54	63	0	62	.204	.294	.253	53	-31	4-4	.974	-2	86	95	C170		-2.5

DICKEY, BILL William Malcolm B6.6.1907 Bastrop LA D11.12.1993 Little Rock AR BL/TR/6-1.5/185 d8.15 Mil 1944-45 M1/C10 HF1954 b-George

1928	NY A	10	15	1	3	1	0	0	2	0	0	2	.200	.200	.400	56	-1	0-0	1.000	-1	71	102	C6		-0.2
1929	NY A	130	447	60	145	30	6	10	65	14	1	16	.324	.346	.485	120	10	4-6	.979	2	108	86	C127		1.8
1930	NY A	109	366	55	124	25	7	5	65	21	0	14	.339	.375	.486	122	11	7-1	.977	-10	85	92	C101		0.8
1931	NY A	130	477	65	156	17	10	6	78	39	0	20	.327	.378	.442	122	14	2-1	.996	-1	101	110	C125		2.0
1932	†NY A	108	423	66	131	20	4	15	84	34	0	13	.310	.361	.482	123	13	2-4	.987	-2	105	74	C108		1.6
1933	NY A☆	130	478	58	152	24	8	14	97	47	2	14	.318	.381	.490	134	25	3-4	.993	5	152	97	C127		3.5
1934	NY A★	104	395	56	127	24	4	12	72	38	2	18	.322	.384	.494	134	19	0-3	.986	-0	99	85	C104		2.3
1935	NY A	120	448	54	125	26	6	14	81	35	6	11	.279	.339	.458	111	5	1-1	.995	3	128	90	C118		1.4
1936	†NY A★	112	423	99	153	26	8	22	107	46	2	16	.362	.428	.617	161	39	0-2	.976	3	149	101	C107		4.2
1937	†NY A★	140	530	87	176	35	2	29	133	73	4	22	.332	.417	.570	145	38	3-2	.991	16	139	86	C137		5.6
1938	†NY A★	132	454	84	142	27	4	27	115	75	4	22	.313	.412	.568	144	32	3-0	.987	6	128	85	C126		4.1
1939	†NY A★	128	480	98	145	23	3	24	105	77	4	37	.302	.403	.512	135	27	5-0	.989	14	145	75	C126		4.5
1940	NY A	106	372	45	92	11	1	9	54	48	2	32	.247	.336	.355	83	-9	0-3	.994	2	139	104	C102		-0.2
1941	†NY A★	109	348	35	99	15	5	7	71	45	3	17	.284	.371	.417	110	5	2-1	.994	7	184	105	C104		1.3
1942	†NY A★	82	268	28	79	13	1	2	37	26	2	11	.295	.359	.373	108	3	2-2	.976	7	184	105	C80		1.4
1943	†NY A☆	85	242	29	85	18	2	4	33	41	0	12	.351	.445	.492	173	25	2-1	.994	4	170	83	C71		3.4
1946	NY A★	54	134	10	35	8	0	2	10	19	1	12	.261	.357	.366	101	1	0-1	.987	7	125	131	C39,M		1.0
Total	17	1789	6300	930	1969	343	72	202	1209	678	31	289	.313	.382	.486	128	257	36-32	.988	57	130	91	C1708		38.5

DICKSHOT, JOHNNY John Oscar "Ugly" (b John Oscar Dicksus) B1.24.1910 Waukegan IL D11.4.1997 Waukegan IL BR/TR/6-0/195 d4.16

1936	Pit N	9	9	2	2	0	0	0	1	1	0	2	.222	.300	.222	42	-1	0	—	-0	0	0	/OC		-0.1
1937	Pit N	82	264	42	67	8	4	3	33	26	1	36	.254	.323	.348	82	-7	0	.950	-1	94	115	O64(58/0/6)		-1.1
1938	Pit N	29	35	3	8	0	0	0	4	8	0	5	.229	.372	.229	68	-1	3	1.000	-0	103	0	O10(5/0/5)		-0.2
1939	Pit N	10	34	3	8	0	0	0	5	5	0	3	.235	.333	.235	55	-2	0	1.000	-0	78	130	O10R		-0.3
1944	Chi A	62	162	18	41	8	5	0	15	13	1	10	.253	.313	.364	94	-2	2-0	.974	-0	95	103	O40(35/0/5)		-0.4
1945	Chi A	130	486	74	147	19	4	4	58	48	1	41	.302	.366	.407	128	16	18-3	.971	0	97	115	O124L		1.3
Total	6	322	990	142	273	35	19	7	116	101	3	97	.276	.345	.371	100	3	23-3	.968	-2	95	110	O249(222/1/26)		-0.8

DIDIER, BOB Robert Daniel B2.16.1949 Hattiesburg MS BB/TR/6-0/190* d4.7 C5

1969	†Atl N	114	352	30	90	16	1	0	32	34-5	2	39	.256	.321	.307	76	-10	1-3	.994	-4	86	78	C114		-1.0
1970	Atl N	57	168	9	25	2	1	0	7	12-4	1	11	.149	.210	.173	3	-23	1-0	.988	-5	63	101	C57		-2.6
1971	Atl N	51	155	9	34	4	1	0	5	6-5	0	17	.219	.248	.258	41	-12	0-0	1.000	-0	126	47	C50		-1.1
1972	Atl N	13	40	5	12	2	1	0	5	2-0	1	4	.300	.341	.400	103	0	0-0	1.000	1	67	96	C11		0.1
1973	Det A	7	22	3	10	1	0	0	1	3-0	0	1	.455	.520	.500	177	3	0-0	1.000	2	85	96	C7		0.4
1974	Bos A	5	14	0	1	0	0	0	1	2-2	0	1	.071	.176	.071	-22	-2	0-0	.968	-1	44	104	C5		-0.3
Total	6	247	751	56	172	25	4	0	51	59-16	2	72	.229	.286	.273	54	-44	2-3	.994	-7	79	79	C244		-4.5

DIEHL, ERNIE Ernest Guy B10.2.1877 Cincinnati OH D11.6.1958 Miami FL BR/TR/6-1/190 d5.31

1903	Pit N	1	3	0	1	0	0	0		0	0		.333	.333	.333	87	0	0	—	-0	0	0	/OL		0.0
1904	Pit N	12	37	6	6	0	0	0	4	6	0		.162	.311	.162	46	-2	3	1.000	1	158	0	O7(2/0/5),S4		-0.1
1906	Bos N	3	11	1	5	1	0	0	0	0	0		.455	.455	.636	247	2	0	1.000	-0	0	0	O2L/S		0.1
1909	Bos N	1	4	1	2	1	0	0	0	0	0		.500	.500	.750	275	1	0	.800	1	485	0	/OL		0.1
Total	4	17	55	8	14	1	0	0	4	6	0		.255	.349	.309	101	1	3	.944	1	170	0	O11(6/0/5),S5		0.1

DIERING, CHUCK Charles Edward Allen B2.5.1923 St.Louis MO BR/TR/5-10/165* d4.15

1947	StL N	105	74	22	16	3	1	2	11	19	1	22	.216	.383	.365	95	0	3	1.000	3	118	190	O75(13/31/31)		0.3
1948	StL N	7	7	2	0	0	0	0	2	0	0	2	.000	.222	.000	-33	-1	1	1.000	1	102	672	O5L		-0.1
1949	StL N	131	369	60	97	21	8	3	38	35	1	49	.263	.328	.388	87	-7	1	.987	6	112	100	O124(0/123/1)		-0.3
1950	StL N	89	204	34	51	12	4	3	18	35	0	38	.250	.360	.353	84	-3	1	.989	7	111	157	O81(0/78/3)		0.2
1951	StL N	64	85	9	22	5	1	0	6	15	0	15	.259	.308	.341	74	-3	0-1	1.000	3	116	149	O44(6/33/5)		-0.2
1952	NY N	41	23	2	4	1	0	0	2	4	0	3	.174	.296	.304	66	-1	0-2	1.000	2	135	137	O36(27/4/5)		-0.1
1954	Bal A	128	418	35	108	14	1	2	29	56	4	57	.258	.349	.311	89	-4	3-7	.983	10	107	159	O119C		-0.2
1955	Bal A	137	371	38	95	16	2	3	31	57-1	0	45	.256	.355	.334	93	-2	5-8	.976	6	110	121	O107(2/105/0),3b34,S12		-0.1
1956	Bal A	50	97	15	18	4	0	1	4	23-0	0	19	.186	.342	.258	65	-4	2-5	1.000	2	107	210	O40(7/34/2),3b2		-0.5
Total	9	752	1648	217	411	76	14	14	141	237-1	6	250	.249	.345	.338	86	-25	16-23	.987	38	111	145	O631(60/527/47),3b36,S12		-1.0

DIETZ, DICK Richard Allen B9.18.1941 Crawfordsville IN D6.27.2005 Clayton GA BR/TR/6-1/185(175-195) d6.18

1966	SF N	13	24	1	1	0	0	0	0-0	1	9	.043	.083	.043	-62	-5	0-0	1.000	-1	65	235	C6		-0.6
1967	SF N	56	120	10	27	3	0	4	19	20-0	1	44	.225	.358	.350	106	2	0-1	.983	-3	85	109	C43		0.1
1968	SF N	98	301	21	82	14	2	6	38	34-3	1	68	.272	.347	.392	122	9	1-1	.976	-9	61	87	C90		0.5
1969	SF N	79	244	28	56	8	1	11	35	53-3	3	53	.230	.372	.406	120	9	0-0	.973	-1	107	96	C73		1.2
1970	SF N★	148	493	82	148	36	2	22	107	109-10	3	106	.300	.426	.515	153	44	0-1	.984	-21	80	56	C139		2.9
1971	†SF N	142	453	58	114	19	0	19	72	97-8	4	86	.252	.387	.419	130	23	1-3	.982	-9	102	45	C135		2.1
1972	LA N	27	56	4	9	1	0	1		14-2	0	11	.161	.329	.232	63	-2	0-0	1.000	4	142	136	C22		0.3
1973	Atl N	83	139	22	41	8	1	3	24	49-4	0	25	.295	.474	.432	143	13	0-0	.989	-2	121	76	1b36,C20	33	1.0
Total	8	646	1829	226	478	89	6	66	301	381-30	13	402	.261	.390	.425	129	93	4-6	.980	-41	88	72	C528,1b36	33	7.5

DIETZEL, ROY Leroy Louis B1.9.1931 Baltimore MD BR/TR/6-0/190 d9.2

| 1954 | Was A | 9 | 21 | 1 | 5 | 0 | 0 | 0 | 1 | 5 | 0 | 5 | .238 | .385 | .238 | 78 | 0 | 0-0 | .960 | -1 | 110 | 104 | 2b7,3b2 | | 0.0 |

YEAR	TM LG	G	AB	R	H	2B	3B	HR	RBI	BB-IB	HP	SO	AVG	OBP	SLG	AOPS	ABR	SB-CS	FA	FR	RNG	THR	GAMES AT POSITION	DL	BFW

DIFANI, JAY Clarence Joseph B12.21.1923 Crystal City MO BR/TR/6-0/170 d4.23 Col Missouri

1948	Was A	2	2	0	0	0	0	0	0	0-0	0	2	.000	.000	.000	-99	-1	0-0	—	0			/H		-0.1
1949	Was A	2	1	0	1	1	0	0	0	0-0	0	0	1.000	1.000	2.000	699	1	0-0	1.000	0	149	0	/2		0.1
Total	2	4	3	0	1	1	0	0	0	0-0	0	2	.333	.333	.667	166	0	0-0	1.000	0	149	0	/2		0.0

DIFELICE, MIKE Michael William B5.28.1969 Philadelphia PA BR/TR/6-2/205* [StLN91 11/26] d9.1 Col Tennessee

1996	StL N	4	7	0	2	1	0	0	2	0-0	0	1	.286	.286	.429	85	0	0-0	1.000	0	52	161	C4		0.0
1997	StL N	93	260	16	62	10	1	4	30	19-0	3	61	.238	.297	.331	64	-14	1-1	.991	15	95	122	C91/1		0.6
1998	TB A	84	248	17	57	12	3	3	23	15-0	1	56	.230	.274	.339	57	-16	0-0	.993	11	111	132	C84		0.7
1999	TB A	51	179	21	55	11	0	6	27	8-0	3	23	.307	.346	.469	104	1	0-0	.987	4	143	108	C51		-0.1
2000	TB A	60	204	23	49	13	1	6	19	12-0	0	40	.240	.280	.402	72	-10	0-0	.980	5	94	119	C59		-0.5
2001	TB A	48	149	13	31	5	1	2	9	8-0	1	39	.208	.259	.295	48	-12	1-1	.982	4	113	123	C48		-0.4
	Ari N	12	21	1	1	0	0	0	1	0-0	0	10	.048	.091	.048	-59	-5	0-0	.982	0	383	158	C12		0.1
2002	†StL N	70	174	17	40	11	0	4	19	17-3	1	42	.230	.297	.362	76	-7	0-0	.991	5	124	68	C61		0.3
2003	KC A	62	189	29	48	16	1	3	25	9-0	4	30	.254	.299	.397	77	-6	1-0	.994	5	78	127	C58,D2		-0.1
2004	Det A	13	22	3	3	0	1	0	2	3-0	0	1	.136	.240	.227	24	-3	0-0	1.000	1	344	63	C12/D		-0.1
	Chi N	4	3	0	0	0	0	0	0	0-0	0	1	.000	.000	.000	-97	-1	0-0	1.000	-0	-0	0	C4		-0.2
2005	NY N	11	17	0	2	0	0	0	0	2-0	0	5	.118	.211	.118	-11	-3	0-0	.976	1	278	84	C11		0.3
Total	10	512	1473	150	350	79	8	28	157	93-3	16	311	.238	.288	.359	67	-76	3-2	.989	51	117	115	C495,D3/1	

DIGNAN, STEVE Stephen E. B4.16.1859 Boston MA D7.11.1881 Boston, MA d6.1 Col Boston College

1880	Bos N	8	34	4	11	1	0	0	4	0-0		3	.324	.324	.353	133	1		.684	-0	148	501	O8(1/0/7)		0.1
	Wor N	3	10	1	3	0	1	0	2	0-0		1	.300	.300	.500	153	0		.750	-1	0	0	O3C		0.0
	Year	11	44	5	14	1	1	0	6	0-0		4	.318	.318	.386	137	1		.696	-1	116	393	O11(1/3/7)		0.1

DILLARD, DON David Donald B1.8.1937 Greenville SC BL/TR/6-1/200* d4.24

1959	Cle A	10	10	0	4	0	0	0	1	0-0	0	2	.400	.400	.400	125	0	0-0	—	0			/H		0.0
1960	Cle A	6	7	0	1	0	0	0	0	0-0	0	0	.143	.250	.143	9	-1	0-0	—	0	0	0	/OR		-0.1
1961	Cle A	74	147	27	40	5	0	7	17	15-1	0	28	.272	.340	.449	112	2	0-0	1.000	-1	101	0	O39(14/24/1)		0.0
1962	Cle A	95	174	22	40	5	1	5	14	11-1	0	25	.230	.276	.356	71	-8	0-1	.965	-4	74	54	O50(28/20/4)		-1.5
1963	Mil N	67	119	9	28	6	4	1	12	5-0	1	21	.235	.270	.378	86	-3	0-2	.951	1	83	337	O30(24/5/1)		-0.3
1965	Mil N	20	19	1	3	0	0	1	3	0-0	0	6	.158	.158	.316	30	-2	0-0	—	0	0	0	/OL		-0.2
Total	6	272	476	59	116	16	5	14	47	32-2	1	85	.244	.292	.387	86	-12	0-3	.976	-5	85	110	O121(67/49/7)		-2.1

DILLARD, PAT Robert Lee B6.12.1873 Chattanooga TN D7.22.1907 Denver CO BL/TR/6-0/180 d4.21

| 1900 | StL N | 57 | 183 | 24 | 42 | 5 | 2 | 0 | 12 | 13 | | 7 | .230 | .284 | .279 | 56 | -11 | 7 | .942 | -3 | 136 | 0 | O26(0/20/6),3b21,S3 | | -1.4 |

DILLARD, STEVE Stephen Bradley B2.8.1951 Memphis TN BR/TR/6-1/180* [BosA72 2/40] d9.28 Col U. of Mississippi

1975	Bos A	1	5	2	2	0	0	0	1	0-0	0	2	.400	.400	.400	117	0	1-0	1.000	1	136	147	/2		0.1
1976	Bos A	57	167	22	46	14	0	1	15	17-1	0	20	.275	.341	.377	99	1	6-4	.918	-7	102	168	3b18,2b17,S12,D7		-0.5
1977	Bos A	66	141	22	34	7	0	1	13	7-0	0	13	.241	.270	.312	54	-9	4-3	.967	-1	90	97	2b45,S9,D6		-0.7
1978	Det A	56	130	21	29	5	2	0	7	6-0	0	11	.223	.257	.292	53	-9	1-2	.958	-0	98	128	2b41,D4		-0.8
1979	Chi N	89	166	31	47	6	1	5	24	17-4	1	24	.283	.351	.422	101	0	1-0	.988	5	98	104	2b60,3b9		0.8
1980	Chi N	100	244	31	55	8	1	4	27	20-2	1	54	.225	.285	.316	63	-12	2-2	.908	-2	111	95	3b51,2b38,S2		-1.4
1981	Chi N	53	119	18	26	7	1	2	11	8-0	0	20	.218	.268	.345	69	-5	0-0	.974	4	118	122	2b32,3b7,S2		0.0
1982	Chi A	16	41	1	7	3	1	0	5	1-0	0	5	.171	.190	.293	30	-4	0-1	.959	2	118	57	2b16		-0.2
Total	8	438	1013	148	246	50	6	13	102	76-7	2	147	.243	.295	.343	72	-38	15-12	.973	2	101	100	2b250,3b85,S25,D17		-2.7

DILLHOEFER, PICKLES William Martin B10.13.1894 Cleveland OH D2.23.1922 St.Louis MO BR/TR/5-7/154 d4.16 Mil 1918

1917	Chi N	42	95	3	12	1	1	0	8	2	0	9	.126	.144	.158	-7	-12	1	.985	6	101	132	C37		-0.4
1918	Phi N	8	11	0	1	0	0	0	1	0	0	1	.091	.167	.091	-19	-2	2	.923	-1	93	92	C6		-0.2
1919	StL N	45	108	11	23	3	2	0	12	8	0	6	.213	.267	.278	68	-4	5	.967	-2	99	92	C39		-0.5
1920	StL N	76	224	26	59	8	3	0	13	13	0	7	.263	.304	.326	84	-5	2-1	.953	-5	90	86	C74		-0.4
1921	StL N	76	162	19	39	4	4	0	15	11	0	7	.241	.289	.315	61	-10	2-1	.953	-2	100	105	C69		-0.6
Total	5	247	600	59	134	16	10	0	48	35	0	30	.223	.266	.283	58	-33	12-2	.961	-2	96	100	C225		-2.1

DILLINGER, BOB Robert Bernard "Duke" B9.17.1918 Glendale CA BR/TR/5-11.5/170* d4.16 Col Idaho

1946	StL A	83	225	33	63	6	3	0	11	19	2	32	.280	.341	.333	85	-4	8-1	.922	-3	94	93	3b54/S		-0.7
1947	StL A	137	571	70	168	23	6	3	37	56	4	38	.294	.361	.371	102	2	34-13	.958	5	102	83	3b137		1.0
1948	StL A	153	644	110	207	34	10	2	44	65	1	34	.321	.385	.415	110	9	28-11	.955	-16	83	96	3b153		-0.5
1949	StL A★	137	544	68	176	22	13	1	51	51	3	40	.324	.385	.417	108	5	20-14	.938	-18	83	65	3b133		-1.3
1950	Phi A	84	356	55	110	21	9	3	41	31	0	20	.309	.366	.444	109	3	5-3	.957	1	100	95	3b84		-0.7
	Pit N	58	222	23	64	8	2	1	9	13	0	22	.288	.328	.356	77	-8	4	.957	1	101	110	3b51		-0.4
1951	Pit N	12	43	3	10	3	0	0	0	1	0	6	.233	.250	.302	47	-3	2-0	.963	-1	85	0	3b10		-1.4
	Chi A	89	299	39	90	6	4	0	20	15	1	17	.301	.337	.348	87	-7	5-5	.930	-6	94	82	3b70		
Total	6	753	2904	401	888	123	47	10	213	251	12	203	.306	.363	.391	100	-3	106-47	.948	-40	92	86	3b692/S		-3.8

DILLON, POP Frank Edward B10.17.1873 Normal IL D9.12.1931 Pasadena CA BL/TR/6-1/185 d9.8

1899	Pit N	30	121	21	31	5	0	0	20	5	0		.256	.286	.298	60	-7	5	.988	1	111	89	1b30		-0.5
1900	Pit N	5	18	3	2	1	0	0	1	0	0		.111	.111	.167	-24	-3	0	.981	0	189	86	1b5		-0.2
1901	Det A	74	281	40	81	14	6	1	42	15	0		.288	.324	.391	94	-3	14	.979	3	114	135	1b74		-0.2
1902	Det A	66	243	21	50	6	3	0	22	16	0		.206	.255	.255	41	-20	2	.976	5	140	111	1b66		-1.6
	Bal A	2	7	1	2	0	1	0	0	2	0		.286	.444	.571	173	1	0	.960	0	159	0	1b2		0.1
	Year	68	250	22	52	6	4	0	22	18	0		.208	.261	.264	45	-19	2	.975	5	141	107	1b68		-1.5
1904	Bro N	135	511	60	132	18	6	0	31	40	1		.258	.313	.317	97	-1	13	.982	4	112	96	1b134		-2.4
Total	5	312	1181	146	298	44	16	1	116	78	1		.252	.299	.319	79	-33	34	.980	14	120	107	1b311		

DILLON, JOHN John d5.8 b-Packy

| 1875 | RS NA | 1 | 1 | 0 | 0 | 0 | 0 | 0 | 0 | 0 | 0 | | .000 | .000 | .000 | -99 | 0 | 0-0 | — | -0 | 0 | 0 | /S | | 0.0 |

DILLON, JOE Joseph William B8.2.1975 Modesto CA BR/TR/6-2/200 d5.18 Col Texas Tech

| 2005 | Fla N | 27 | 36 | 6 | 6 | 1 | 0 | 1 | 1 | 1-0 | 1 | 8 | .167 | .211 | .278 | 28 | -4 | 0-0 | .923 | -1 | 84 | 98 | 2b4,O3L,3b2/1 | | -0.5 |

DILLON, PACKY Packard Andrew B St.Louis MO D1.8.1890 Guelph ON, Can. d5.4 b-John

| 1875 | RS NA | 3 | 13 | 1 | 3 | 1 | 0 | 0 | 1 | 0 | | | .231 | .231 | .308 | 94 | 0 | 0-0 | .923 | -2 | | | C3 | | -0.2 |

DILONE, MIGUEL Miguel Angel (Reyes) B11.1.1954 Santiago, D.R. BB/TR/6-0/160(150-175) d9.2

1974	Pit N	12	2	3	0	0	0	0	0	1-0	0	0	.000	.333	.000	-1	0	2-0	1.000	0	188	0	O2(0/1/1)		0.0
1975	Pit N	18	6	8	0	0	0	0	0	0-0	0	1	.000	.000	.000	-99	-2	2-2	1.000	-0	103	0	O2C		-0.2
1976	Pit N	16	17	7	4	0	0	0	0	0-0	0	0	.235	.235	.235	33	-2	5-1	1.000	1	146	0	O3(1/2/0)		0.0
1977	Pit N	29	44	5	6	0	0	0	0	2-0	0	3	.136	.174	.136	-15	-7	12-0	1.000	0	95	152	O17(9/7/2)		-0.5
1978	Oak A	135	258	34	59	8	1	0	14	23-0	1	30	.229	.294	.271	63	-12	50-23	.985	4	117	59	O99(47/25/36),D11,3b3		-0.9
1979	Oak A	30	91	15	17	1	2	0	6	6-0	0	11	.187	.237	.275	40	-8	25(5/0/20)	.959	-2	99	0	O25(5/0/20)		-1.2
	Chi N	43	36	14	11	0	0	0	1	2-0	0	5	.306	.342	.306	71	-1	15-5	1.000	-0	102	0	O22(4/18/0)		0.0
1980	Cle A	132	528	82	180	30	9	0	40	28-1	2	45	.341	.375	.432	119	14	61-18	.973	-1	102	85	O118(90/23/13),D11		1.6
1981	Cle A	72	269	33	78	5	9	0	18	18-1	0	28	.290	.334	.346	97	-2	29-10	.971	4	107	184	O56L,D11		0.7
1982	Cle A	104	379	50	89	12	3	3	25	25-0	2	36	.235	.286	.306	62	-20	33-5	.964	-3	95	55	O97(96/1/0)/D		-2.2
1983	Cle A	32	68	15	13	1	0	0	7	10-0	1	5	.191	.295	.265	53	-4	5-1	1.000	1	116	0	O19L		-0.4
	Chi A	4	3	1	0	0	0	0	0	0-0	0	0	.000	.000	.000	-96	-1	1-0	1.000	0	108	0	O2C,D2		-0.1
	Year	36	71	16	13	1	0	0	7	10-0	1	5	.183	.284	.254	47	-5	6-1	1.000	1	116	0	O21(19/2/0),D2		-0.5
	Pit N	7	0	1	0	0	0	0	0	0-0	0	0											/R		0.0
1984	Mon N	88	169	28	47	8	1	0	10	17-0	1	18	.278	.346	.367	105	1	27-2	.987	1	113	37	O41L		0.7
1985	Mon N	51	84	10	16	4	2	0	6	6-0	0	11	.190	.242	.238	37	-8	7-3	.974	-0	101	96	O22(8/13/2)		-0.8
	SD N	27	46	8	10	1	0	1	1	4-0	0	8	.217	.280	.261	53	-3	10-3	.917	-1	86	145	O14(4/9/1)		-0.3
	Year	78	130	18	26	5	2	1	7	10-0	0	19	.200	.255	.246	43	-11	17-6	.952	-1	95	115	O36(12/22/3)		-1.1
Total	12	800	2000	314	530	67	25	6	129	142-2	6	197	.265	.315	.333	81	-55	267-78	.975	4	105	76	O539(380/103/75),D36,3b3	40	-4.0

YEAR	TM LG	G	AB	R	H	2B	3B	HR	RBI	BB-IB	HP	SO	AVG	OBP	SLG	AOPS	ABR	SB-CS	FA	FR	RNG	THR	GAMES AT POSITION	DL	BFW

DiMAGGIO, DOM　Dominic Paul "The Little Professor"　B2.12.1917 San Francisco CA　BR/TR/5-9/168*　d4.16　Mil 1943-45　b-Joe b-Vince

1940	Bos A	108	418	81	126	32	6	8	46	41	2	46	.301	.367	.464	109	6	7-6	.977	6	96	208	O94(11/59/26)		0.7
1941	Bos A★	144	584	117	165	37	6	8	58	90	7	57	.283	.385	.408	107	10	13-6	.964	4	102	137	O151C		1.0
1942	Bos A☆	151	622	110	178	36	8	14	48	70	6	52	.286	.364	.437	121	17	16-10	.987	13	107	169	O151C		2.7
1946	†Bos A	142	534	85	169	24	7	7	73	66	1	58	.316	.393	.427	122	18	10-6	.985	2	104	94	O142C		1.7
1947	Bos A	136	513	75	145	21	5	8	71	74	3	62	.283	.376	.390	105	6	10-6	.977	15	109	213	O134C		1.8
1948	Bos A	155	648	127	185	40	4	9	87	101	2	58	.285	.383	.401	104	7	10-2	.981	9	109	98	O155C		1.2
1949	Bos A★	145	605	126	186	34	5	8	60	96	2	55	.307	.404	.420	110	12	9-7	.977	6	106	130	O144C		1.3
1950	Bos A★	141	588	131	193	30	11	7	70	82	4	68	.328	.414	.452	111	12	15-4	.983	3	101	126	O140C		1.3
1951	Bos A★	146	639	113	189	34	4	12	72	73	2	53	.296	.370	.418	103	3	4-7	.973	-8	92	99	O146C		-1.0
1952	Bos A★	128	486	81	143	20	1	6	33	57	2	61	.294	.371	.377	100	2	6-8	.975	-4	91	130	O123C		-0.6
1953	Bos A	3	3	1	1	0	0	0	0	0	0	1	.333	.333	.333	76	0	0	—	0			/H		0.0
Total	11	1399	5640	1046	1680	308	57	87	618	750	31	571	.298	.383	.419	109	93	100-62	.978	46	102	138	O1373(11/1338/26)		10.1

DiMAGGIO, JOE　Joseph Paul "Joltin' Joe","The Yankee Clipper"　B11.25.1914 Martinez CA　D3.8.1999 Hollywood FL　BR/TR/6-2/193*　d5.3　Mil 1943-45　C2 HF1955　b-Dom b-Vince

1936	†NY A★	138	637	132	206	44	15	29	125	24	4	39	.323	.352	.576	130	23	4-0	.978	8	100	171	O138(66/55/18)		2.2
1937	†NY A★	151	621	151	215	35	15	46	167	64	5	37	.346	.412	.673	168	60	3-0	.962	6	102	148	O150C		5.7
1938	†NY A★	145	599	129	194	32	13	32	140	59	2	21	.324	.386	.581	140	33	6-1	.963	-2	92	143	O145C		2.6
1939	†NY A★	120	462	108	176	32	6	30	126	52	4	20	.381	.448	.671	185	59	3-0	.986	5	102	129	O117C		5.5
1940	NY A★	132	508	93	179	28	9	31	133	61	3	30	.352	.425	.626	176	56	1-2	.978	-4	101	51	O130C		4.5
1941	†NY A★	139	541	122	193	43	11	30	125	76	4	13	.357	.440	.643	186	68	4-2	.978	-4	102	138	O139C		6.6
1942	†NY A★	154	610	123	186	29	13	21	114	68	2	36	.305	.376	.498	148	37	4-2	.981	-3	98	88	O154C		3.1
1946	NY A☆	132	503	81	146	20	8	25	95	59	2	24	.290	.367	.511	142	26	1-0	.982	2	95	179	O131(3/128/0)		2.6
1947	†NY A★	141	534	97	168	31	10	20	97	64	3	32	.315	.391	.522	154	38	3-0	.997	-14	87	23	O139C		2.2
1948	†NY A★	153	594	110	190	26	11	39	155	67	8	30	.320	.396	.598	164	50	1-1	.972	1	107	67	O152C		4.5
1949	†NY A★	76	272	58	94	14	6	14	67	55	2	18	.346	.459	.596	178	32	0-1	.985	-4	99	20	O76C		2.5
1950	†NY A★	139	525	114	158	33	10	32	122	80	1	33	.301	.394	.585	152	39	0-0	.976	-4	99	79	O137C/1		3.0
1951	†NY A☆	116	415	72	109	22	4	12	71	61	5	36	.263	.365	.422	117	11	0-0	.990	1	100	103	O113C		0.8
Total	13	1736	6821	1390	2214	389	131	361	1537	790	46	369	.325	.398	.579	156	532	30-9	.978	-1	99	106	O1721(69/1635/18)/1		45.8

DiMAGGIO, VINCE　Vincent Paul　B9.6.1912 Martinez CA　D10.3.1986 N.Hollywood CA　BR/TR/5-11/183　d4.19　b-Dom b-Joe

1937	Bos N	132	493	56	126	18	4	13	69	39	1	111	.256	.311	.387	98	-4	8	.982	8	99	180	O130(0/129/1)		0.1
1938	Bos N	150	540	71	123	28	3	14	61	65	2	134	.228	.313	.369	96	-3	11	.973	10	109	148	O149C/2		0.4
1939	Cin N	8	14	1	1	0	0	0	2	2	0	10	.071	.188	.143	-10	-2	0	1.000	1	100	275	O7(3/3/1)		-0.2
1940	Cin N	2	4	2	1	0	0	0	0	1	0	0	.250	.400	.250	82	0	0	1.000	-0	103		/OR		0.0
	Pit N	110	356	59	103	26	0	19	54	37	5	83	.289	.364	.522	143	21	11	.979	1	94	164	O108(1/103/4)		1.9
	Year	112	360	61	104	26	0	19	54	38	5	83	.289	.365	.519	142	21	11	.979	1	94	164	O109(1/103/5)		1.9
1941	Pit N	151	528	73	141	27	5	21	100	68	3	100	.267	.354	.456	128	19	10	.976	2	104	91	O151C		1.7
1942	Pit N	143	496	57	118	22	3	15	75	52	1	87	.238	.311	.385	101	-1	10	.978	12	111	151	O138C		0.9
1943	Pit N★	157	580	64	144	41	2	15	88	70	1	126	.248	.329	.403	107	6	11	.985	12	113	110	O156C/S		1.4
1944	Pit N★	109	342	46	82	20	4	9	50	33	0	83	.240	.307	.401	94	-3	6	.984	-1	97	100	O101C/3		-0.7
1945	Phi N	127	452	64	116	25	3	19	84	43	0	91	.257	.321	.451	117	8	12	.994	9	105	165	O121C		1.3
1946	Phi N	6	19	1	4	1	0	0	1	0	0	7	.211	.211	.263	35	-2	0	1.000	-9	96		O6C		-0.2
	NY N	15	25	2	0	0	0	0	0	2	0	5	.000	.074	.000	-78	-6	0	.967	0	125		O13C		-0.6
	Year	21	44	3	4	1	0	0	1	2	0	12	.091	.130	.114	-31	-8	0	.975	-0	116		O19C		-0.8
Total	10	1110	3849	491	959	209	24	125	584	412	12	837	.249	.324	.413	108	33	79	.981	52	105	137	O1081(4/1070/7)/3S2		6.0

DIMMEL, MIKE　Michael Wayne　B10.16.1954 Albert Lea MN　BR/TR/6-0/180*　[LAN73 6/138]　d9.2

1977	Bal A	25	5	8	0	0	0	0	0	0-0	0	1	1.000	.000	.000	-99	-1	1-0	1.000	2	151	314	O23(0/1/22)		0.0
1978	Bal A	8	0	2	0	0	0	0	0	0-0	0	0	—	—	—		0	0-1	.667	-0	89		O7(1/1/5)		-0.1
1979	StL N	6	3	1	1	0	0	0	0	0-0	0	0	.333	.333	.333	81	0	0-1	1.000	-0	105	0	O5(5/1/0)		-0.1
Total	3	39	8	11	1	0	0	0	0	0-0	0	1	.125	.125	.125	-33	-1	1-2	.952	1	132	202	O35(6/3/27)		-0.2

DINEEN, KERRY　Kerry Michael　B7.1.1952 Englewood NJ　BL/TL/5-11/165*　[NYA73 4/85]　d6.14　Col San Diego

1975	NY A	7	22	3	8	1	0	0	1	2-0	0	1	.364	.417	.409	135	1	5-0	1.000	1	128	0	O7C		0.1
1976	NY A	4	7	0	2	0	0	0	0	1-0	0	2	.286	.375	.286	96	0	1-1	.900	0	128	0	O4(0/2/2)		0.0
1978	Phi N	5	8	0	2	1	0	0	1	1-0	0	0	.250	.333	.375	96	0	0-0	1.000	-0	58	0	/OL		0.0
Total	3	16	37	3	12	2	0	0	2	4-0	0	3	.324	.390	.378	119	1	6-1	.967	1	121		O12(1/9/2)		0.1

DINGES, VANCE　Vance George　B5.29.1915 Elizabeth NJ　D10.4.1990 Harrisonburg VA　BL/TL/6-2/175　d4.17

1945	Phi N	109	397	46	114	15	4	1	36	35	1	17	.287	.346	.353	97	-1	5	.986	2	98	195	O65(16/18/33),1b42		-0.5
1946	Phi N	50	104	7	32	5	1	1	10	9	0	12	.308	.363	.404	127	3	2	.985	1	115	89	1b26/OL		0.3
Total	2	159	501	53	146	20	5	2	46	44	1	29	.291	.350	.363	102	2	7	.986	3	94	96	1b68,O66(17/18/33)		-0.2

DiPIETRO, BOB　Robert Louis Paul　B9.1.1927 San Francisco CA　BR/TR/5-11/185　d9.23　Col San Jose St.

1951	Bos A	4	11	0	1	0	0	0	0	1	0	1	.091	.167	.091	-26	-2	0-0	.833	0	71	501	O3R		-0.2

DiSARCINA, GARY　Gary Thomas　B11.19.1967 Malden MA　BR/TR/6-1/178(170-205)　[CalA88 6/143]　d9.23　Col Massachusetts　[DL 2001 Ana A 190]

1989	Cal A	2	0	0	0	0	0	0	0	0-0	0	0	—	—	—		0	0-0	—	-0	0	0	/S		0.0
1990	Cal A	18	57	8	8	1	1	0	0	3-0	0	10	.140	.183	.193	5	-8	1-0	.940	0	113	82	S14,2b3		-0.6
1991	Cal A	18	57	5	12	2	0	0	3	3-0	2	4	.211	.274	.246	45	-4	0-0	.915	-4	89	33	S10,2b7,3b2		-0.8
1992	Cal A	157	518	48	128	19	0	3	42	20-0	7	50	.247	.283	.301	63	-26	9-7	.967	3	99	108	S157		-1.2
1993	Cal A	126	416	44	99	20	1	3	45	15-0	2	36	.238	.273	.313	56	-27	5-7	.975	-8	96	96	S126	38	-2.6
1994	Cal A	112	389	53	101	14	2	3	33	18-0	2	28	.260	.294	.329	60	-24	3-7	.983	3	104	96	S110		-1.4
1995	Cal A★	99	362	61	111	28	6	5	41	20-0	2	25	.307	.344	.459	108	1	7-4	.986	-11	92	79	S98	44	0.0
1996	Cal A	150	536	62	137	26	4	5	48	21-0	2	36	.256	.286	.347	58	-36	2-1	.971	7	106	91	S150		-1.6
1997	Ana A	154	549	52	135	28	2	4	47	17-0	4	29	.246	.271	.326	55	-37	7-8	.977	-13	95	87	S153		-3.8
1998	Ana A	157	551	73	158	39	3	3	56	21-0	8	51	.287	.321	.385	81	-15	11-7	.980	-6	94	101	S157		-0.8
1999	Ana A	81	271	32	62	7	1	1	29	15-0	2	32	.229	.273	.273	40	-25	2-2	.963	2	104	111	S81	78	-1.7
2000	Ana A	12	38	6	15	2	0	1	1	1-0	1	3	.395	.425	.526	135	2	0-0	.934	6	139	154	S12	159	0.7
Total	12	1086	3744	444	966	186	20	28	355	154-0	36	306	.258	.292	.341	65	-196	47-44	.973	-21	99	96	S1069,2b10,3b2	509	-13.8

DISTEFANO, BENNY　Benito James　B1.23.1962 Brooklyn NY　BL/TL/6-1/195(195-210)　[PitN82*S2/29]　d5.18　Col Alvin (TX) CC

1984	Pit N	45	78	10	13	1	2	3	9	5-1	1	13	.167	.226	.346	59	-5	0-1	.946	4	135	224	O20(7/0/15),1b17		-0.3
1986	Pit N	31	39	3	7	1	0	1	5	1-0	0	5	.179	.190	.282	31	-4	0-0	1.000	0	136	0	O9R/1		-0.4
1988	Pit N	16	29	6	10	3	1	1	6	3-1	0	4	.345	.394	.621	193	3	0-0	1.000	0	100	34	1b5,O2R		0.3
1989	Pit N	96	154	12	38	8	0	2	15	17-3	3	30	.247	.333	.338	95	-4	1-0	.981	-4	73	93	1b48,C3/OR	15	-0.7
1992	Hou N	52	60	4	14	0	2	0	7	5-1	1	14	.233	.303	.300	74	-2	0-0	1.000	2	141	318	O12(7/0/5),1b6		-0.1
Total	5	240	360	35	82	13	5	7	42	31-6	5	66	.228	.296	.350	85	-8	1-1	.985	1	91	95	1b77,O44(14/0/32),C3	15	-1.2

DISTEL, DUTCH　George Adam　B4.15.1896 Madison IN　D2.12.1967 Madison IN　BR/TR/5-9/165　d6.21

1918	StL N	8	17	3	3	1	1	0	1	2	0	3	.176	.263	.353	90	-1	0	.900	-1	118	63	2b5,S2/OR		-0.2

DITTMER, JACK　John Douglas　B1.10.1928 Elkader IA　BL/TR/6-1/175*　d6.17　Col Iowa

1952	Bos N	93	326	26	63	7	2	4	41	26	1	26	.193	.255	.291	53	-22	1-0	.982	-1	100	94	2b90		-1.8
1953	Mil N	138	504	54	134	22	1	9	63	18	1	35	.266	.293	.367	75	-20	1-0	.965	-23	88	105	2b138		-3.2
1954	Mil N	66	192	22	47	8	0	6	20	19	3	17	.245	.319	.380	88	-4	0-1	.977	-2	100	89	2b55		-0.3
1955	Mil N	38	72	4	9	1	1	1	4	4-1	0	15	.125	.171	.208	0	-11	0-0	.977	-1	98	61	2b28		-1.0
1956	Mil N	44	102	8	25	4	0	1	6	8-0	0	8	.245	.300	.314	69	-4	0-0	.979	0	106	91	2b42		-0.2
1957	Det A	16	22	3	5	1	0	1	2	2	1	6	.227	.292	.273	54	-1	0-0	1.000	-1	63	0	3b3/2		-0.2
Total	6	395	1218	117	283	43	4	24	136	77-2	5	102	.232	.280	.333	66	-62	2-1	.974	-27	95	97	2b354,3b3		-6.7

DIVIS, MOXIE　Edward George　B1.16.1894 Cleveland OH　D12.19.1955 Lakewood OH　5-6/?　d8.4

1916	Phi A	3	6	0	1	0	0	0	1	0	0	2	.167	.167	.167	0	-1	0	1.000	1	46	720	/OL		0.0

YEAR	TM LG	G	AB	R	H	2B	3B	HR	RBI	BB-IB	HP	SO	AVG	OBP	SLG	AOPS	ABR	SB-CS	FA	FR	RNG	THR	GAMES AT POSITION	DL BFW

DIXON, LEO Leo Moses B9.4.1894 Chicago IL D4.11.1984 Chicago IL BR/TR/5-11/170 d4.14

1925	StL A	76	205	27	46	11	1	0	19	24	4	42	.224	.318	.302	55	-14	3-2	.981	4	91	153	C75	-0.6
1926	StL A	33	89	7	17	3	1	0	8	11	2	14	.191	.294	.247	40	-8	1-4	.977	3	135	137	C33	-0.4
1927	StL A	36	103	6	20	3	1	0	12	7	0	6	.194	.245	.243	26	-12	0-1	.937	1	118	142	C35	-0.9
1929	Cin N	14	30	0	5	2	0	0	2	3	0	7	.167	.242	.233	19	-4	0	1.000	2	113	121	C14	-0.1
Total 4		159	427	40	88	19	3	1	41	45	6	69	.206	.291	.272	43	-38	4-7	.971	9	109	144	C157	-2.0

DOBBEK, DAN Daniel John B12.6.1934 Ontonagon MI BL/TR/6-0/195* d9,9 Col Western Michigan

1959	Was A	16	60	8	15	1	2	1	5	5-1	0	13	.250	.308	.383	89	-1	0-0	1.000	-0	99	109	O16R	-0.2
1960	Was A	110	248	32	54	8	2	10	30	35-7	1	41	.218	.316	.387	90	-4	4-3	.973	0	101	130	O78(12/58/17)	-0.7
1961	Min A	72	125	12	21	3	1	4	14	13-1	2	18	.168	.255	.304	47	-10	1-2	.985	1	103	104	O48(32/10/13)	-1.2
Total 3		198	433	52	90	12	5	15	49	53-9	3	72	.208	.297	.363	77	-15	5-5	.980	1	103	104	O142(44/68/46)	-2.1

DOBBS, GREG Gregory Stuart B7.2.1978 Los Angeles CA BL/TR/6-1/205* d9.8 Col Oklahoma

2004	Sea A	18	53	4	12	1	0	1	9	1-0	1	14	.226	.250	.302	46	-4	0-0	.929	-2	90	147	3b14/D	-0.6
2005	Sea A	59	142	8	35	7	1	1	20	9-3	0	25	.246	.288	.331	70	-6	1-0	1.000	3	295	0	D24,1b5,O4L,3b2	-0.4
Total 2		77	195	12	47	8	1	2	29	10-3	1	39	.241	.278	.323	63	-10	1-0	.946	2	100	174	D25,3b16,1b5,O4L	-1.0

DOBBS, JOHN John Gordon B6.3.1875 Chattanooga TN D9.9.1934 Charlotte NC BL/TR/5-9.5/170 d4.20

1901	Cin N	109	435	71	119	17	4	2	27	36	6		.274	.338	.345	105	4	19	.948	-6	89	117	O100C,3b8	-0.6
1902	Cin N	63	256	39	76	7	3	1	16	19	1		.297	.348	.359	108	2	7	.963	6	121	86	O63L	0.5
	Chi N	59	235	31	71	8	2	0	35	18	0		.302	.352	.353	121	6	3	.977	2	106	332	O59C	0.5
	Year	122	491	70	147	15	5	1	51	37	1		.299	.350	.356	114	8	10	.970	8	114	198	O122(63/59/0)	1.0
1903	Chi N	16	61	8	14	1	0	0	4	7	2		.230	.329	.279	76	-2	0	1.000	0	46	0	O16C	-0.2
	Bro N	111	414	61	98	15	7	2	59	48	5		.237	.323	.320	86	-6	23	.966	2	72	109	O110C	-1.0
	Year	127	475	69	112	16	8	2	63	55	7		.236	.324	.316	85	-8	23	.970	2	69	95	O126C	-1.2
1904	Bro N	101	363	36	90	16	2	0	30	28	1		.248	.304	.303	90	-4	11	.936	-2	54	0	O92(2/86/3),2b2,S2	-1.0
1905	Bro N	123	460	59	117	21	4	2	36	31	2		.254	.304	.330	96	-2	15	.938	-5	72	24	O123C	-1.3
Total 5		582	2224	305	585	85	23	7	207	187	17		.263	.325	.331	98	-2	78	.954	-3	81	92	O563(65/494/3),3b8,S2,2b2	-3.1

DOBY, LARRY Lawrence Eugene B12.13.1923 Camden SC D6.18.2003 Montclair NJ BL/TR/6-1/182* d7.5 M1/C7 HF1998 Negro Lg 1942-47 Mil 1944-45 Col Long Island-Brooklyn

1947	Cle A	29	32	3	5	1	0	0	2	1	0	11	.156	.182	.188	3	-4	0-0	1.000	-1	111	0	2b4/1S	-0.5
1948	†Cle A	121	439	83	132	23	9	14	66	54	5	77	.301	.384	.490	135	21	9-9	.955	-3	94	128	O114(0/68/46)	1.3
1949	Cle A★	147	547	106	153	25	3	24	85	91	7	90	.280	.389	.468	129	23	10-9	.976	-11	92	61	O147(0/117/39)	0.7
1950	Cle A★	142	503	110	164	25	5	25	102	98	6	71	.326	.442	.545	156	47	8-6	.987	-9	99	17	O140C	3.2
1951	Cle A★	134	447	84	132	27	5	20	69	101	3	81	.295	.428	.512	163	45	4-1	.977	-2	98	99	O132C	3.8
1952	Cle A★	140	519	104	143	26	8	32	104	90	0	111	.276	.383	.541	166	46	5-2	.986	1	101	100	O136C	4.4
1953	Cle A★	149	513	92	135	18	5	29	102	96	6	121	.263	.385	.487	138	29	3-2	.984	-10	90	81	O146C	1.2
1954	†Cle A★	153	577	94	157	18	4	32	126	85	3	94	.272	.364	.484	130	23	3-1	.995	1	100	98	O153C	1.8
1955	Cle A☆	131	491	91	143	17	5	26	75	61-8	2	100	.291	.369	.505	124	19	2-0	.994	-6	93	80	O129C	0.8
1956	Chi A	140	504	89	135	22	3	24	102	102-6	4	105	.268	.392	.466	125	21	0-1	.987	-3	103	43	O137C	1.1
1957	Chi A	119	416	57	120	27	2	14	79	56-3	2	79	.288	.373	.464	127	17	2-3	.985	-9	93	39	O110C	0.8
1958	Cle A	89	247	41	70	10	1	13	45	26-2	0	49	.283	.348	.490	132	10	0-2	1.000	1	101	148	O68(8/59/1)	0.8
1959	Det A	18	55	5	12	3	1	0	4	8-0	0	9	.218	.313	.309	69	-2	0-0	.960	-0	92	125	O16(11/0/5)	-0.3
	Chi A	21	58	1	14	1	1	0	9	2-0	0	13	.241	.267	.293	54	-4	1-0	.955	-1	88	144	O12(1/2/10),1b2	-0.5
	Year	39	113	6	26	4	2	0	13	10-0	0	22	.230	.290	.301	62	-6	1-0	.957	-1	90	134	O28(12/2/15),1b2	-0.8
Total 13		1533	5348	960	1515	243	52	253	970	871-19	38	1011	.283	.386	.490	137	291	47-36	.983	-50	96	79	O1440(20/1329/101),2b4,1b3/S	18.1

DODD, ONA Ona Melvin. B10.14.1886 Springtown TX D12.17.1956 Carter OK BR/TR/5-8/150 d7.26 Col TCU

1912	Pit N	5	9	0	0	0	0	0	1	1	0	3	.000	.100	.000	-73	-2	0	1.000	0	109	0	3b4/2	-0.2

DODD, TOM Thomas Marion B8.15.1958 Portland OR BR/TR/6-0/190 [NYA80*S1/7] d7.25 Col Oregon

1986	Bal A	8	13	1	3	0	0	1	2	2-0	1	2	.231	.375	.462	128	1	0-0	—	-0	0	0	/3D	0.0

DODGE, JOHN John Lewis B4.27.1889 Bolivar TN D6.19.1916 Mobile AL BR/TR/5-11.5/165 d8.29

1912	Phi N	30	92	3	11	1	0	0	3	4	0	11	.120	.156	.130	-20	-15	2	1.000	4	119	177	3b23,2b5/S	-1.1
1913	Phi N	3	3	0	1	0	0	0	0	0	0		.333	.600	.333	164	1	0	1.000	-0	85	0	S3	0.0
	Cin N	94	323	35	78	8	8	4	45	10	2	34	.269	.353	.353	77	-12	11-7	.908	3	108	86	3b91	-0.7
	Year	97	326	35	79	8	8	4	45	12	2	34	.242	.274	.353	78	-11	11-7	.908	2	108	86	3b91,S3	-0.7
Total 2		127	418	38	90	9	8	4	48	16	2	45	.215	.248	.304	55	-26	13-7	.926	6	110	104	3b114,2b5,S4	-1.8

DODSON, PAT Patrick Neal B10.11.1959 Santa Monica CA BL/TL/6-4/210* d9.5 Col UCLA

1986	Bos A	9	12	3	5	2	0	1	3	3-0	0	3	.417	.533	.833	263	3	0-0	1.000	-1	38	230	1b7	0.2
1987	Bos A	26	42	4	7	3	0	2	6	8-1	0	13	.167	.288	.381	77	-1	0-0	1.000	-2	43	115	1b21/D	-0.4
1988	Bos A	17	45	5	8	3	1	1		6-0	0	17	.178	.275	.356	72	-2	0-0	1.000	1	119	64	1b17	-0.1
Total 3		52	99	12	20	8	1	4	10	17-1	0	33	.202	.314	.424	97	0	0-0	1.000	-1	77	104	1b45/D	-0.3

DOERR, BOBBY Robert Pershing B4.7.1918 Los Angeles CA BR/TR/5-11/175* d4.20 Mil 1944-45 C8 HF1986

1937	Bos A	55	147	22	33	5	1	2	14	18	1	25	.224	.313	.313	56	-10	2-4	.973	2	103	104	2b47	-0.6
1938	Bos A	145	509	70	147	26	7	5	80	59	0	39	.289	.363	.397	86	-11	5-10	.968	9	103	121	2b145	0.4
1939	Bos A	127	525	75	167	28	2	12	73	38	1	32	.318	.365	.448	103	2	1-10	.976	27	115	110	2b126	3.0
1940	Bos A	151	595	87	173	37	10	22	105	57	0	53	.291	.353	.497	113	10	10-5	.977	13	103	103	2b151	3.1
1941	Bos A★	132	500	74	141	28	4	16	93	43	0	43	.282	.339	.450	105	2	1-3	.971	-1	100	95	2b132	0.8
1942	Bos A☆	144	545	71	158	35	5	15	102	67	1	55	.290	.369	.455	127	20	4-4	.975	12	103	117	2b142	4.1
1943	Bos A★	155	604	78	163	32	3	16	75	62	1	59	.270	.339	.412	117	12	8-8	.990	9	104	115	2b155	3.2
1944	Bos A★	125	468	95	152	30	10	15	81	58	0	31	.325	.399	.528	166	40	5-2	.976	2	98	101	2b125	5.1
1946	†Bos A★	151	583	95	158	34	9	18	116	66	1	67	.271	.346	.453	115	11	5-6	.986	27	108	126	2b151	3.3
1947	Bos A★	146	561	79	145	23	10	17	95	59	0	47	.258	.329	.426	101	-1	3-3	.981	25	111	115	2b146	3.7
1948	Bos A★	140	527	94	150	23	6	27	111	83	4	49	.285	.386	.505	129	22	3-2	.993	9	102	116	2b138	3.8
1949	Bos A★	139	541	91	167	30	9	18	109	75	0	33	.309	.393	.497	126	19	2-2	.980	27	109	119	2b139	2.4
1950	Bos A★	149	586	103	172	29	11	27	120	67	1	42	.294	.367	.519	114	9	3-4	.988	6	99	99	2b149	1.9
1951	Bos A★	106	402	60	116	21	2	13	73	57	1	33	.289	.378	.448	112	8	2-1	.981	6	99	118	2b106	1.9
Total 14		1865	7093	1094	2042	381	89	223	1247	809	11	608	.288	.362	.461	114	133	54-64	.980	178	104	112	2b1852	40.3

DOHERTY, JOHN John Michael B8.22.1951 Woburn MA BL/TL/5-11/185* d6.1

1974	Cal A	74	223	20	57	14	1	3	15	8-1	0	13	.256	.280	.368	90	-4	2-1	.991	-2	83	100	1b70,D2	-1.0
1975	Cal A	30	94	7	19	3	0	1	12	8-1	0	12	.202	.262	.266	54	-6	1-1	.983	-1	83	93	1b26/D	-1.0
Total 2		104	317	27	76	17	1	4	27	16-2	0	25	.240	.275	.338	79	-10	3-2	.989	-3	83	98	1b96,D3	-2.0

DOLAN, COZY Albert J. (b James Alberts) B12.23.1889 Chicago IL D12.10.1958 Chicago IL BR/TR/5-10/160 d8.15 C3 OF(126/48/33)

1909	Cin N	3	6	2	1	0	0	0		0	0		.167	.375	.167	69	0	0	.750	-1	85	334	3b3	-0.1
1911	NY A	19	69	19	21	1	2	0	6	8	1		.304	.385	.377	106	1	12	.947	-1	90	159	3b19	0.0
1912	NY A	18	60	15	12	1	3	0	11	5	1		.200	.273	.317	64	-3	5	.768	-8	88	43	3b17	-0.7
	Phi N	11	50	8	14	2	2	0	7	1	0	10	.280	.294	.400	83	-2	3	.872	-1	94	64	3b11	-0.2
1913	Phi N	55	126	15	33	4	0	0	16	21	1	21	.262	.273	.294	59	-7	9-4	.905	-6	87	0	O12(8/0/4),S10,2b9,3b4/1	-1.3
	Pit N	35	133	22	27	5	2	0	9	15	0	14	.203	.289	.271	63	-6	14-7	.937	-1	97	171	3b35	-0.6
	Year	90	259	37	60	9	2	0	17	16	2	35	.232	.282	.282	61	-13	23-11	.932	-7	93	161	3b39,O12(8/0/4),S10,2b9/1	-1.9
1914	StL N	126	421	76	101	16	3	4	32	55	5	74	.240	.335	.321	96	0	42	.955	-11	93	77	O96(90/1/5),3b27	-0.2
1915	StL N	111	322	53	90	14	3	2	35	34	4	37	.280	.356	.398	127	11	17-11	.929	-8	98	38	O98(28/47/24)	-1.6
1922	NY N	1	0	0	0	0	0	0	0	0	0		—	—	—			0-0	—	0			/R	0.0
Total 7		379	1207	210	299	43	21	6	111	121	13	156	.252	.328	.339	95	-6	102-22	.940	-33	95	55	O206L,3b116,S10,2b9/1	-4.7

DOLAN, JOE Joseph B2.24.1873 Baltimore MD D3.24.1938 Omaha NE TR/5-10/155 d8.11

1896	Lou N	44	165	14	35	4	3		18	9		12	.212	.253	.291	45	-14	6	.940	7	108	118	S44	-0.4
1897	Lou N	36	133	10	28	2	2	0	7	8	3		.211	.271	.256	41	-12	6	.849	-5	83	72	S18,2b18	-1.3
1899	Lou N	61	222	27	57	6	3	1	30	11	6		.257	.298	.324	73	-9	3	.915	-6	107	47	2b61	-1.2
1900	Phi N	74	257	39	51	7	3	1	27	16	5		.198	.259	.261	44	-20	10	.931	0	111	81	3b31,2b29,S12	-1.7

YEAR	TM LG	G	AB	R	H	2B	3B	HR	RBI	BB-IB	HP	SO	AVG	OBP	SLG	AOPS	ABR	SB-CS	FA	FR	RNG	THR	GAMES AT POSITION	DL	BFW
1901	Phi N	10	37	0	3	0	0	0	2	2	0		.081	.128	.081	-38	-7	0	.973	-1	96	157	2b10		-0.8
	Phi A	98	338	50	73	21	2	1	38	26	5		.216	.282	.299	58	-19	3	.881	12	116	132	S61,3b35/2OR		-0.3
Total	5	323	1152	140	247	38	11	6	122	72	15	12	.214	.270	.282	51	-81	28	.902	8	107	118	S135,2b119,3b66/OR		-5.7

DOLAN, BIDDY Leon Mark B7.9.1881 Onalaska WI D7.15.1950 Indianapolis IN BR/TR/6-0/? d4.16

YEAR	TM LG	G	AB	R	H	2B	3B	HR	RBI	BB-IB	HP	SO	AVG	OBP	SLG	AOPS	ABR	SB-CS	FA	FR	RNG	THR	GAMES AT POSITION	DL	BFW
1914	Ind F	32	103	13	24	2	1	1	15	12	2	6	.233	.316	.330	69	-6	5	.979	1	113	82	1b31		-0.7

DOLAN, COZY Patrick Henry B12.3.1872 Cambridge MA D3.29.1907 Louisville KY BL/TL/5-10/160 d4.26 ▲

YEAR	TM LG	G	AB	R	H	2B	3B	HR	RBI	BB-IB	HP	SO	AVG	OBP	SLG	AOPS	ABR	SB-CS	FA	FR	RNG	THR	GAMES AT POSITION	DL	BFW
1895	Bos N	26	83	12	20	4	1	0	7	6		7	.241	.300	.313	54	-6	3	.949	3	138	145	P25/OC		0.1
1896	Bos N	6	14	4	2	0	0	0	0	0		1	.143	.143	.143	-23	-2	0	.765	-0	79	0	P6		0.0
1900	Chi N	13	48	5	13	1	0	0	2	2		0	.271	.300	.292	66	-2	2	.826	-1	63	0	O13R		-0.4
1901	Chi N	43	171	29	45	1	2	0	16	7	1		.263	.296	.292	74	-6	3	.878	1	163	209	O41R		-0.7
	Bro N	66	253	33	66	11	1	0	29	17	2		.261	.313	.312	79	-6	7	.967	0	123	104	O64(2/57/5)		-0.9
	Year	109	424	62	111	12	3	0	45	24	3		.262	.306	.304	77	-12	10	.931	0	140	149	O105(2/57/46)		-1.6
1902	Bro N	141	592	72	166	16	7	1	54	33	5		.280	.324	.336	103	1	24	.936	-11	53	45	O141(1/140/0)		-1.7
1903	Chi A	27	104	16	27	5	1	0	7	6	2		.260	.313	.327	96	0	5	.971	0	125	68	1b19,O4(2/2/0)		-0.1
	Cin N	93	385	64	111	20	3	0	58	28	2		.288	.340	.356	88	-6	11	.937	-3	97	73	O93R		-1.2
1904	Cin N	129	465	88	132	8	10	6	51	39	2		.284	.342	.383	113	6	19	.939	-2	105	0	O102(0/7/95),1b24		-0.1
1905	Cin N	22	77	7	18	2	1	0	4	7	1		.234	.306	.286	69	-3	2	.965	-3	86	87	1b13,O9(1/0/8)		-0.7
	Bos N	112	433	44	119	11	7	3	48	27	3		.275	.322	.353	103	1	21	.946	3	129	54	O111R,P2,1b2		-0.1
	Year	134	510	51	137	13	8	3	52	34	4		.269	.319	.343	97	-3	23	.931	-0	121	51	O120(1/0/119),1b15,P2		-0.8
1906	Bos N	152	549	54	136	20	4	0	39	55	2		.248	.318	.299	95	-2	17	.928	-1	146	87	O144(2/0/143),2b7,P2/1		-1.0
Total	9	830	3174	428	855	99	37	10	315	227	21	8	.269	.322	.333	94	-25	114	.931	-15	108	65	O723(8/207/509),1b59,P35,2b7		-6.8

DOLAN, TOM Thomas J. B9.1855 New York NY D1.16.1913 St.Louis MO BR/TR/5-11/185 d9.30

YEAR	TM LG	G	AB	R	H	2B	3B	HR	RBI	BB-IB	HP	SO	AVG	OBP	SLG	AOPS	ABR	SB-CS	FA	FR	RNG	THR	GAMES AT POSITION	DL	BFW
1879	Chi N	1	4	0	0	0	0	0	0	0		2	.000	.000	.000	-94	-1		1.000	1			/C		0.0
1882	Buf N	22	89	12	14	0	1	0	8	2		11	.157	.176	.180	14	-9		.941	-4			C18,O4(1/2/1),3b2		-1.0
1883	StL AA	81	295	32	63	9	2	1	18	9			.214	.237	.268	59	-14		.957	11			C42,O40(19/19/2)/P		-0.1
1884	StL AA	35	137	19	36	6	2	0		6	1		.263	.299	.336	103	0		.873	-6			C34,O2(1/1/0)		-0.3
	StL U	19	69	9	13	3	0	0		4			.188	.233	.232	40	-7		.897	7			C14,3b3,O2(0/1/1)		0.1
1885	StL N	3	9	1	2	0	0	0	0	2			.222	.364	.222	99	0		.810	-1			C3		-0.1
1886	StL N	15	44	8	11	3	0	0	1	7		9	.250	.353	.318	113	1	2	.928	5			C15		0.7
	Bal AA	38	125	13	19	3	2	0	6	3	0		.152	.203	.208	30	-10	8	.918	-4			C35,O3L		-1.0
1888	StL AA	11	36	1	7	1	0	0	1	1	0		.194	.216	.222	37	-3	1	.914	0			C11		-0.2
Total	7	225	808	95	165	25	7	1	40	39	1	23	.204	.242	.256	57	-43	11	.916	9			C173,O51(24/23/4),3b5/P		-1.9

DOLE, LESTER Lester Carrington B7.8.1855 Meriden CT D12.10.1918 Concord NH 5-11/? d5.27

YEAR	TM LG	G	AB	R	H	2B	3B	HR	RBI	BB-IB	HP	SO	AVG	OBP	SLG	AOPS	ABR	SB-CS	FA	FR	RNG	THR	GAMES AT POSITION	DL	BFW
1875	NH NA	1	4	1	2	0	0	0					.500	.500	.500	285	-1	0-0	.750	-0	0	0	/OC		0.0

DOLJACK, FRANK Frank Joseph "Dolie" B10.5.1907 Cleveland OH D1.23.1948 Cleveland OH BR/TR/5-11/175 d9.4

YEAR	TM LG	G	AB	R	H	2B	3B	HR	RBI	BB-IB	HP	SO	AVG	OBP	SLG	AOPS	ABR	SB-CS	FA	FR	RNG	THR	GAMES AT POSITION	DL	BFW
1930	Det A	20	74	10	19	5	1	3	17	2	1	11	.257	.286	.473	87	-2	0-1	.930	1	106	130	O20(0/4/16)		-0.3
1931	Det A	63	187	20	52	13	3	4	20	15	1	17	.278	.335	.444	100	-1	3-2	.925	2	101	183	O54(3/44/8)		-0.1
1932	Det A	8	26	5	10	1	0	1	7	2	0	4	.385	.429	.538	143	2	1-0	1.000	-1	67	0	O6L		0.1
1933	Det A	42	147	18	42	5	2	0	22	14	0	13	.286	.348	.347	83	-4	2-6	.941	1	92	160	O37(32/0/5)		-0.6
1934	†Det A	56	120	15	28	7	1	1	19	13	1	15	.233	.313	.333	67	-6	2-1	.943	0	98	174	O30(6/12/12),1b3		-0.6
1943	Cle A	3	7	1	0	0	0	0	0	1	0	0	.000	.125	.000	-66	-1	0-0	1.000	-0	75	0	O2(1/0/1)		-0.2
Total	6	192	561	68	151	31	7	9	85	47	3	60	.269	.329	.398	87	-12	8-10	.934	2	97	161	O149(48/60/42),1b3		-1.7

DOMINIQUE, ANDY Andrew John B10.30.1975 Tarzana CA BR/TR/6-0/220* [PhiN97 26/776] d5.25 Col Nevada-Reno

YEAR	TM LG	G	AB	R	H	2B	3B	HR	RBI	BB-IB	HP	SO	AVG	OBP	SLG	AOPS	ABR	SB-CS	FA	FR	RNG	THR	GAMES AT POSITION	DL	BFW
2004	Bos A	7	11	0	2	0	0	0	1	0-0	0	3	.182	.182	.182	-5	-2	0-0	.963	-1	67	118	1b5/C		-0.2
2005	Tor A	2	2	0	0	0	0	0	0	0-0	0	0	.000	.333	.000	0	0	0-0	1.000	-1	18	0	/C		-0.1
Total	2	9	13	0	2	0	0	0	1	0-0	1	3	.154	.214	.154	-1	-2	0-0	.963	-1	67	118	1b5,C2		-0.3

DONAHUE, SHE Charles Michael B6.29.1877 Oswego NY D8.28.1947 New York NY BR/TR/5-9/? d4.29

YEAR	TM LG	G	AB	R	H	2B	3B	HR	RBI	BB-IB	HP	SO	AVG	OBP	SLG	AOPS	ABR	SB-CS	FA	FR	RNG	THR	GAMES AT POSITION	DL	BFW
1904	StL N	4	15	1	4	0	0	0	2	0			.267	.267	.267	68	-1	3	.846	-2	70	125	2b3/S		-0.3
	Phi N	58	200	21	43	4	0	0	14	3	0		.215	.227	.235	44	-14	7	.857	-14	85	92	S29,3b24,1b3,2b2		-2.9
	Year	62	215	22	47	4	0	0	16	3	0		.219	.229	.237	46	-14	10	.852	-16	84	91	S30,3b24,2b5,1b3		-3.2

DONAHUE, JIM James Augustus B1.8.1862 Lockport IL D4.19.1935 Lockport IL BR/TR/6-0/175 d4.19

YEAR	TM LG	G	AB	R	H	2B	3B	HR	RBI	BB-IB	HP	SO	AVG	OBP	SLG	AOPS	ABR	SB-CS	FA	FR	RNG	THR	GAMES AT POSITION	DL	BFW
1886	NY AA	49	186	14	37	0	0	0	9	10			.199	.251	.199	45	-11	1	.803	-2	56	0	O32(12/21/1),C19		-1.1
1887	NY AA	60	220	33	62	4	1	1	29	21	2		.282	.350	.323	92	-1	6	.890	-6			C51,O5(0/2/3),1b4/32		-0.3
1888	KC AA	88	337	29	79	11	3	1	28	21	1		.234	.281	.294	79	-9	12	.902	-8			C67,O18(12/5/1),3b5/2		-1.0
1889	KC AA	67	252	30	59	5	4	0	32	21		20	.234	.293	.286	61	-14	12	.887	-6			C46,O14L,3b10		-1.4
1891	Col AA	77	280	27	61	4	3	0	35	31	1	18	.218	.298	.254	62	-13	2	.942	-9	74	115	C75/OR1		-1.5
Total	5	341	1275	133	298	24	11	2	133	104	7	38	.234	.295	.275	70	-48	33	.911	-31	74	115	C258,O70(38/28/6),3b16,1b5,2b2		-5.3

DONAHUE, JIGGS John Augustus B7.13.1879 Springfield OH D7.19.1913 Columbus OH BL/TL/6-1/178 d9.10 b-Pat

YEAR	TM LG	G	AB	R	H	2B	3B	HR	RBI	BB-IB	HP	SO	AVG	OBP	SLG	AOPS	ABR	SB-CS	FA	FR	RNG	THR	GAMES AT POSITION	DL	BFW
1900	Pit N	3	10	1	2	0	1	0	3	0			.200	.200	.400	63	-1	1	.889	-1	148	42	C2/OR		-0.1
1901	Pit N	2	0	0	0	0	0	0	0	0	0		—	—	—		0	0	—	-0	0	0	/COL		0.0
	Mil A	37	107	10	34	5	4	0	16	10	2		.318	.387	.439	135	5	4	.933	-4	77	105	C19,1b13		0.3
1902	StL A	30	89	11	21	1	1	1	7	12			.236	.327	.303	76	-3	2	.956	-1	116	104	C23,1b5		-0.2
1904	Chi A	102	367	46	91	9	7	1	48	25	1		.248	.298	.319	99	-1	18	.979	7	133	126	1b101		0.5
1905	Chi A	149	533	71	153	22	4	1	76	44	4		.287	.346	.349	126	17	32	.988	7	116	142	1b149		2.3
1906	†Chi A	154	556	70	143	17	7	1	57	48	3		.257	.320	.318	103	2	36	.988	9	119	107	1b154		0.9
1907	Chi A	157	609	75	158	16	4	0	68	28	3		.259	.295	.299	93	-6	27	.994	21	141	115	1b157		1.2
1908	Chi A	93	304	22	62	8	2	0	22	25	3		.204	.271	.243	69	-10	14	.994	4	114	95	1b83		-0.8
1909	Chi A	2	4	0	0	0	0	0	2	1	0		.000	.000	.000	-38	-1	0	1.000	-0	0	0	1b2		-0.1
	Was A	84	283	13	67	12	1	0	28	22	1		.237	.294	.286	87	-4	9	.984	-4	79	73	1b81		-1.0
	Year	86	287	13	67	12	1	0	30	23	1		.233	.293	.282	86	-4	9	.984	-4	78	72	1b83		-1.1
Total	9	813	2862	319	731	90	31	4	327	215	17		.255	.311	.313	99	-2	143	.987	38	119	115	1b745,C45,O2(1/0/1)		3.0

DONAHUE, JOHN John Frederick "Jiggs" B4.19.1894 Roxbury MA D10.3.1949 Boston MA BB/TR/5-8/170 d9.25

YEAR	TM LG	G	AB	R	H	2B	3B	HR	RBI	BB-IB	HP	SO	AVG	OBP	SLG	AOPS	ABR	SB-CS	FA	FR	RNG	THR	GAMES AT POSITION	DL	BFW
1923	Bos A	10	36	5	10	4	0	0	1	4	0		.278	.350	.389	94	0	0-1	1.000	3	105	294	O9R		0.1

DONAHUE, PAT Patrick William B11.8.1884 Springfield OH D1.31.1966 Springfield OH BR/TR/6-0/175 d5.29 b-Jiggs

YEAR	TM LG	G	AB	R	H	2B	3B	HR	RBI	BB-IB	HP	SO	AVG	OBP	SLG	AOPS	ABR	SB-CS	FA	FR	RNG	THR	GAMES AT POSITION	DL	BFW
1908	Bos A	35	86	8	17	2	0	1	6	9	2		.198	.289	.256	75	-2	0	.959	1	99	91	C32,1b3		0.2
1909	Bos A	65	177	14	42	4	1	2	25	17	1		.237	.308	.305	92	-2	2	.982	-1	113	78	C58		0.4
1910	Bos A	2	4	0	0	0	0	0	0	0			.000	.000	.000	-98	-1	0	1.000	0	120	0	/C		-0.1
	Phi A	14	34	2	5	0	0	0	4	3	1		.147	.237	.147	21	-3	1	1.000	3	114	118	C13		0.1
	Cle A	2	6	0	1	0	0	0	0	0			.167	.167	.167	4	-1	0	1.000	-0	83	75	C2/1		-0.1
	Phi A	1	1	0	0	0	0	0	0	0			.000	.000	.000	-99	-0	0	1.000	-0	114	118	/C		0.0
	Year	19	45	2	6	0	0	0	4	3	1		.133	.204	.133	6	-5	1	1.000	3	109	110	C17/1		-0.1
Total	3	119	308	24	65	6	1	3	35	29	4		.211	.287	.266	75	-9	3	.978	4	108	97	C107,1b4		0.5

DONAHUE, TIM Timothy Cornelius "Bridget" B6.8.1870 Raynham MA D6.12.1902 Taunton MA BL/TR/5-11/180 d7.28

YEAR	TM LG	G	AB	R	H	2B	3B	HR	RBI	BB-IB	HP	SO	AVG	OBP	SLG	AOPS	ABR	SB-CS	FA	FR	RNG	THR	GAMES AT POSITION	DL	BFW
1891	Bos AA	4	7	0	0	0	0	0	0	0		5	.000	.000	.000	-99	-2	0	.833	-1	111	74	C4		-0.2
1895	Chi N	63	219	29	59	9	1	2	36	20	3	15	.269	.339	.347	72	-9	5	.915	-5	94	70	C63		-0.7
1896	Chi N	57	188	27	41	10	4	0	20	11	4	15	.218	.276	.282	45	-15	11	.934	-1	93	104	C57		-0.9
1897	Chi N	38	188	28	45	7	3	0	21	9	2		.239	.281	.309	54	-13	3	.949	1	87	121	C55,S2/1		-0.6
1898	Chi N	122	396	52	87	12	3	0	39	49	8		.220	.318	.265	68	-15	17	.962	16	154	86	C122		1.2
1899	Chi N	92	278	39	69	9	3	0	29	34	7		.248	.345	.302	80	-6	10	.951	4	107	97	C91/1		0.6
1900	Chi N	67	216	21	51	10	1	0	17	19	5		.236	.308	.292	70	-8	8	.928	-7	95	79	C66/2		-0.8
1902	Was A	3	8	0	2	0	0	0	1	0			.250	.250	.250	39	-1	0	1.000	-0	89	142	C3		-0.1
Total	8	466	1500	196	354	57	12	2	163	142	29	45	.236	.314	.294	66	-69	54	.943	9	112	92	C461,1b2,S2/2		-1.5

DONALDSON, JOHN John David B5.5.1943 Charlotte NC BL/TR/5-11/165* d8.26

YEAR	TM LG	G	AB	R	H	2B	3B	HR	RBI	BB-IB	HP	SO	AVG	OBP	SLG	AOPS	ABR	SB-CS	FA	FR	RNG	THR	GAMES AT POSITION	DL	BFW
1966	KC A	15	30	4	4	0	0	1	4	3	2	-4	.133	.212	.133	2	-4	1-0	1.000	-2	64	44	2b9		-0.5
1967	KC A	105	377	27	104	16	5	0	28	37-3	2	39	.276	.343	.345	107	4	6-3	.982	-15	88	70	2b101/S		-0.2

YEAR	TM LG	G	AB	R	H	2B	3B	HR	RBI	BB-IB	HP	SO	AVG	OBP	SLG	AOPS	ABR	SB-CS	FA	FR	RNG	THR	GAMES AT POSITION	DL	BFW
1968	Oak A	127	363	37	80	9	2	2	27	45-0	0	44	.220	.307	.273	81	-7	5-5	.971	-2	102	95	2b98,3b5/S		-0.2
1969	Oak A	12	13	1	1	0	0	0	0	2-1	0	4	.077	.200	.077	-21	-2	0-0	.857	0	136	155	/2		-0.2
	Sea A	95	338	22	79	8	3	1	19	36-5	0	36	.234	.307	.284	67	-15	6-1	.974	-6	94	87	2b90,3b2/S		-1.4
	Year	107	351	23	80	8	3	1	19	38-6	0	40	.228	.303	.276	64	-17	6-1	.972	-5	94	88	2b91,3b2/S		-1.6
1970	Oak A	41	89	4	22	2	1	1	11	9-3	0	6	.247	.316	.326	80	-3	1-0	.986	-5	95	68	2b21,S6/3		-0.5
1974	Oak A	10	15	1	2	0	0	0	0	0-0	0	0	.133	.133	.133	-25	-2	0-0	.962	-2	152	207	2b7,3b3		-0.1
Total 6		405	1225	96	292	35	11	4	86	132-12	4	133	.238	.313	.295	80	-29	19-9	.976	-27	95	83	2b327,3b11,S9		-3.1

DONDERO, LEN Leonard Peter "Mike" B9.12.1903 Newark CA D1.1.1999 Fremont CA BR/TR/5-11/178 d4.21 Col St. Marys (CA)

1929	StL A	19	31	2	6	0	1	0	8	0-0	0	4	.194	.194	.290	22	-4	0-0	.857	-2	59	0	3b10,2b5		-0.5

DONLIN, MIKE Michael Joseph "Turkey Mike" B5.30.1878 Peoria IL D9.24.1933 Hollywood CA BL/TL/5-9/170 d7.19 ▲

1899	StL N	66	266	49	86	9	6	6	27	17	1		.323	.366	.470	126	8	20	.873	-8	91	102	O51(1/50/0),1b13,S3,P3		-0.4
1900	StL N	78	276	40	90	8	6	10	48	14	1		.326	.361	.507	139	12	14	.922	-4	110	311	O47(2/35/10),1b21		0.5
1901	Bal A	121	476	107	162	23	13	5	67	53	2		.340	.409	.475	138	25	33	.918	8	118	83	O74(73/1/0),1b47		2.5
1902	Cin N	34	143	30	41	5	4	0	9	9	1		.287	.333	.378	109	1	9	.877	-2	107	83	O32(30/0/2)/PS		-0.3
1903	Cin N	126	496	110	174	25	18	7	67	56	3		.351	.420	.516	150	31	26	.900	-5	86	96	O118(70/0/48),1b7		1.9
1904	Cin N	60	236	42	84	11	7	1	38	18	2		.356	.406	.475	158	16	21	.872	-4	126	58	O53(52/0/1),1b6		1.2
	NY N	42	132	17	37	7	3	2	14	10	2		.280	.340	.424	130	4	1	.918	-4	26	104	O37(23/11/3)		-0.1
	Year	102	368	59	121	18	10	3	52	28	4		.329	.382	.457	148	20	22	.886	-9	88	75	O90(75/11/4),1b6		1.1
1905	†NY N	150	606	**124**	216	31	16	7	80	56	2		.356	.413	.495	166	49	33	.934	-13	87	97	O150(4/147/0)		3.0
1906	NY N	37	121	15	38	5	1	1	14	11	0		.314	.371	.397	136	5	9	.929	-5	0	0	O29C/1		-0.1
1908	NY N	155	593	71	198	26	13	6	106	23	5		.334	.364	.452	153	32	30	.977	-0	106	23	O155(29/0/127)		2.8
1911	NY N	12	12	3	4	0	1	0	1	0	0	1	.333	.333	.583	150	1	5	1.000	-0	74	0	O3(0/2/1)		0.0
	Bos N	56	222	33	70	16	1	2	34	22	0	17	.315	.377	.423	115	5	7	.912	-3	93	100	O56C		-0.2
	Year	68	234	36	74	16	1	3	35	22	0	18	.316	.375	.432	117	6	9	.982	-0	100	94	O59(0/58/1)		0.3
1912	Pit N	77	244	27	77	9	8	2	35	20	1	16	.316	.370	.443	124	7	8	.982	-0	100	94	O62(2/10/51)		-0.1
1914	NY N	35	31	3	4	0	1	0	3	3	0	5	.161	.235	.355	77	-1	0	—	0			/H		-0.2
Total 12		1049	3854	669	1282	176	97	51	543	312	20	**39**	.333	.386	.468	142	195	213	.924	-37	94	88	O867(286/341/243),1b95,P4,S4		11.0

DONNELLY, JIM James B. B7.19.1865 New Haven CT D3.5.1915 New Haven CT BR/TR/5-10.5/155 d8.11

1884	Ind AA	40	134	22	34	2	2	0		5	4		.254	.301	.299	99	0		.850	-4	72	78	3b24,S8,O6(2/2/2),2b2		-0.3
1885	Det N	56	211	24	49	4	3	1	22	10		29	.232	.267	.294	81	-5		.850	-2	94	56	3b56		-0.6
1886	KC N	113	438	51	88	11	3	0	38	36		57	.201	.234	.256	50	-26	16	.845	1	107	87	3b113		-2.2
1887	Was N	117	425	51	85	9	6	1	46	16	3	26	.200	.234	.256	39	-35	42	.867	16	**120**	115	3b115,S2		-1.5
1888	Was N	122	428	43	86	9	4	0	23	20	3	16	.201	.242	.241	58	-20	44	.875	-1	103	92	3b117,S5		-1.9
1889	Was N	4	13	3	2	0	0	0	2	0	1	0	.154	.267	.154	20	-1	1	.667	-1	89	153	3b4		-0.2
1890	StL AA	11	42	11	14	0	0	0	3	8	1		.333	.451	.333	115	1	5	.795	-2	71	270	3b11		0.0
1891	Col AA	17	54	6	13	0	0	0	9	13	0		.241	.388	.241	85	0	7	.855	-4	99	106	3b106		0.2
1896	Bal N	106	396	70	130	14	10	0	71	34	4	11	.328	.387	.414	106	5	38	.920	2	106	19	3b44		0.3
1897	Pit N	44	161	22	31	4	0	0	14	16	1		.193	.270	.217	31	-16	14	.920	2	106	19	3b23		-1.2
	NY N	23	85	19	16	3	0	0	11	9	0		.188	.266	.224	31	-8	6	.869	-3	89	82	3b67		-1.0
	Year	67	246	41	47	7	0	0	25	25	1		.191	.268	.220	31	-24	20	.905	-1	100	39	3b67		-2.2
1898	StL N	1	1	0	1	0	0	0	0	0	0		1.000	1.000	1.000	463	0	0	.500	-1	135	0	/3		0.0
Total 11		654	2388	322	549	56	28	2	**237**	169	16	**144**	.230	.285	.279	66	-105	173	.865	3	104	94	3b631,S15,O6(2/2/2),2b2		-8.4

DONNELLY, JIM James J. 5-10.5/155 d7.11

1884	KC U	6	23	2	3	1	0	0		1			.130	.167	.174	4	-3		.536	-4	73	0	3b5/C		-0.6

DONNELLY, JOHN John B Elizabeth NJ d4.14 b-Pete

1873	Was NA	30	137	15	35	2	0	0	19	1		0	.255	.261	.270	60	-6	0-0	.750	0	83	119	S13,2b12,O6C/3		-0.5
1874	Phi NA	6	22	2	5	0	0	0	2	0		0	.227	.227	.227	45	-1	0-0	.667	-2	0	0	O3R,S2/2		-0.3
Total 2 NA		36	159	17	40	2	0	0	21	1		0	.252	.256	.264	58	-7	0-0	.734	-2	81	107	S15,2b13,O9(0/6/3)/3		-0.8

DONNELLY, PETE Peter J. B10.8.1849 Philadelphia PA D10.1.1890 Jersey City NJ d5.13 b-John

1871	Kek NA	9	34	7	7	1	1	0	3	1			.206	.229	.294	48	-2	0-0	.714	-4	0	0	O9(2/1/6),3b2		-0.4

DONNELS, CHRIS Chris Barton B4.21.1966 Los Angeles CA BL/TR/6-0/185* [NYN87 1/24] d5.7 Col Loyola Marymount

1991	NY N	37	89	7	20	0	0	0	5	14-1	0	19	.225	.330	.247	65	-4	1-1	1.000	4	114	106	1b15,3b11		-0.1
1992	NY N	45	121	8	21	4	0	0	6	17-0	0	25	.174	.275	.207	39	-9	1-0	.941	2	109	78	3b29,2b12		-0.8
1993	Hou N	88	179	18	46	14	2	2	19	19-0	0	33	.257	.327	.391	95	-1	2-0	.898	-1	108	152	3b31,1b23/2		-0.3
1994	Hou N	54	86	12	23	5	0	3	5	13-0	0	18	.267	.364	.430	111	2	1-0	1.000	-0	89	0	3b14,1b4,2b4		0.2
1995	Hou N	19	30	4	9	0	0	2	3	3-2	0	6	.300	.364	.300	83	-1	0-0	.818	-3	57	232	3b9/2		-0.3
	Bos A	40	91	13	23	2	2	2	11	9-0	0	18	.253	.317	.385	80	-3		1.000	-0	O6L,1b4,3b2/2		29	0.3
2000	LA N	27	34	8	10	3	0	4	9	6-1	1	7	.294	.390	.735	187	5	0-0	1.000	-4	143	0	1b6,3b3	16	-0.7
2001	LA N	66	88	8	15	2	0	3	8	12-2	0	25	.170	.277	.295	51	-7	0-0	.897	-3	110	115	3b14,1b7/P	32	-0.4
2002	†Ari N	74	80	5	19	4	1	3	16	10-1	0	14	.237	.312	.425	89	-2	0-0	1.000	-2	67	0	3b26/1	94	-2.4
Total 8		450	798	83	186	36	5	17	86	103-7	1	165	.233	.319	.355	82	-20	5-1	.932	-2	98	98	3b163,1b62,2b22,O6L/P		

DONOHUE, ALEX Alexander B1869 Altoona PA d8.24

1891	Phi N	6	22	3	7	0	0	0		3			.318	.375	.364	113	0	0	1.000	-1	0	0	O4C,S2		-0.1

DONOHUE, TOM Thomas James B11.15.1952 Mineola NY BR/TR/6-0/195* [AnaA72*1/9] d4.6 Col Nassau (NY) CC

																			.981	-8	86	122	.C38		-1.2
1979	Cal A	38	107	13	24	3	1	3	14	3-0	2	29	.224	.259	.355	66	-6	2-0	.981	-8	86	122	C38	15	-3.3
1980	Cal A	84	218	18	41	4	1	2	14	7-0	1	63	.188	.216	.243	26	-23	5-1	.986	-13	67	98	C84	15	-4.5
Total 2		122	325	31	65	7	2	5	28	10-0	3	92	.200	.230	.280	39	-29	7-1	.985	-21	73	105	C122		

DONOVAN, FRED Frederick Maurice B7.4.1864 Epping NH D3.7.1916 Bloomington IL BR/TR d6.23

1895	Cle N	3	12	1	1	0	0	0	1	1	0		.083	.154	.083	-36	-3	0	.938	-0	124	55	C3		-0.2

DONOVAN, JERRY Jeremiah Francis B9.3.1876 Lock Haven PA D6.27.1938 St.Petersburg FL BR/TR d4.12 b-Tom

1906	Phi N	61	166	11	33	4	0	0	15	6	2		.199	.236	.223	43	-11	2	.955	-4	90	80	C53/SOL		-1.2

DONOVAN, MIKE Michael Berchman B10.18.1881 Brooklyn NY D2.3.1938 New York NY BR/TR/5-8/155 d5.29

1904	Cle A	2	2	0	0	0	0	0	0	0	0		.000	.000	.000	-99	0	0	—	-0	0	0	/S		-0.1
1908	NY A	5	19	2	5	1	0	0	2	0	0		.263	.263	.316	87	0	0	1.000	1	86	0	3b5		0.1
Total 2		7	21	2	5	1	0	0	2	0	0		.238	.238	.286	69	0	0	1.000	1	86	0	3b5/S		0.0

DONOVAN, PATSY Patrick Joseph B3.16.1865 Co. Cork, Ireland D12.25.1953 Lawrence MA BL/TL/5-11.5/175 d4.19 M11

1890	Bos N	32	140	17	36	0	0	0		2	17		.257	.307	.257	60	-8	10	.891	-4	80	108	O32C		-1.1
	†Bro N	28	105	17	23	5	1	0	8	5	2		.219	.268	.286	61	-5	3	1.000	1	63	109	O28(1/24/3)		-0.5
	Year	60	245	34	59	5	1	0	17	13	4		.241	.290	.269	61	-13	13	.952	-3	72	108	O60(1/56/3)		-1.6
1891	Lou AA	105	439	73	141	10	3	2	53	30	1	18	.321	.375	.371	115	8	27	.912	3	79	0	O105L		0.7
	Was AA	17	70	9	14	1	0	0	3	4	0	5	.200	.243	.214	33	-6	1	.857	-2	78	154	O17(0/13/4)		-0.7
	Year	122	509	82	155	11	3	2	56	34	8	23	.305	.358	.350	104	2	28	.907	1	79	18	O122(105/13/4)		0.0
1892	Was N	40	163	29	39	3	0	0	12	11	2	13	.239	.295	.294	81	-4	16	.844	-4	144	213	O40(14/0/26)		-0.5
	Pit N	90	388	77	114	15	6	2	26	20	3	16	.294	.333	.363	110	4	40	.862	-1	135	159	O130(15/1/116)		-0.2
	Year	130	551	106	153	18	6	2	38	31	5	29	.278	.322	.343	100	0	56	.937	-2	86	133	O112R		-0.7
1893	Pit N	113	499	114	158	5	8	2	56	42	3		.317	.373	.371	100	4	46	.933	6	101	91	O133R		-0.6
1894	Pit N	**133**	577	147	175	21	10	4	76	36	5	12	.303	.350	.395	80	-20	41	.961	-6	59	49	O126(0/1/125)		-1.6
1895	Pit N	126	522	115	162	18	6	1	59	48	4	19	.310	.377	.374	99	4	36	.954	6	129	171	O131R		-0.8
1896	Pit N	131	573	113	183	20	5	1	59	35	11		.319	.370	.387	104	4	48	.949	1	101	154	O120R,M		0.3
1897	Pit N	120	479	92	154	16	7	0	57	25	4		.322	.360	.384	100	0	34	.928	-2	101	87	O147R		-0.5
1898	Pit N	147	610	112	184	16	9	0	37	34	7		.302	.346	.357	123	2	41	.942	-13	48	61	O122(0/1/121),M		-0.7
1899	Pit N	122	536	82	156	11	7	1	56	17	5		.291	.319	.343	82	-15	26	.951	-4	78	90	O124R		-3.1
1900	StL N	126	503	78	159	11	1	0	61	38	3		.316	.368	.342	97	-1	**45**	.951	-4	78	90	O124R		-1.0
1901	StL N	130	531	92	161	23	5	1	73	28	10		.303	.344	.371	113	9	28	.979	2	114	193	O129R,M		0.5
1902	StL N	126	502	70	158	12	4	0	35	28			.315	.363	.355	127	16	34	.959	9	**177**	126	O126R,M		2.0

YEAR	TM LG	G	AB	R	H	2B	3B	HR	RBI	BB-IB	HP	SO	AVG	OBP	SLG	AOPS	ABR	SB-CS	FA	FR	RNG	THR	GAMES AT POSITION	DL	BFW
1903	StL N	105	410	63	134	15	3	0	39	25	3		.327	.370	.378	117	9	25	.952	0	115	138	O105R,M		0.5
1904	Was A	125	436	30	100	6	0	0	19	24	1		.229	.271	.243	64	-18	17	.963	9	111	99	O122(0/2/120),M		-1.6
1906	Bro N	7	21	1	5	0	0	0	0	0			.238	.238	.238	53	-1	0	1.000	-0	0	0	O6R,M		-0.2
1907	Bro N	1	1	0	0	0	0	0	0	0			.000	.000	.000	-99	0	0	1.000	0	0	0	/ORM		0.0
Total	17	1824	7505	1321	2256	208	75	16	738	457	83	131	.301	.348	.355	98	-24	518	.941	5	102	112	O1816(121/74/1623)		-9.1

DONOVAN, TOM Thomas Joseph B1.1.1873 West Troy NY D3.25.1933 Watervliet NY BR/TR/6-2/168 d9.10 b-Jerry

YEAR	TM LG	G	AB	R	H	2B	3B	HR	RBI	BB-IB	HP	SO	AVG	OBP	SLG	AOPS	ABR	SB-CS	FA	FR	RNG	THR	GAMES AT POSITION	DL	BFW
1901	Cle A	18	71	9	18	4	1	0					.254	.254	.324	62	-4	1	.862	0	209	0	O18R/P		-0.4

DONOVAN, BILL William Edward "Wild Bill" B10.13.1876 Lawrence MA D12.9.1923 Forsyth NY BR/TR/5-11/190 d4.22 M4/C1 ▲

YEAR	TM LG	G	AB	R	H	2B	3B	HR	RBI	BB-IB	HP	SO	AVG	OBP	SLG	AOPS	ABR	SB-CS	FA	FR	RNG	THR	GAMES AT POSITION	DL	BFW
1898	Was N	39	103	11	17	2	2	2	8	4	2		.165	.211	.282	41	-9	2	.933	1	156	444	O20(6/6/8),P17/S2		-0.5
1899	Bro N	5	13	2	3	1	0	0	0	0	0		.231	.231	.308	46	0	0	.857	-0	79	444	P5		-0.5
1900	Bro N	5	13	0	0	0	0	0	2	0	0		.000	.000	.000	-94	-2	0	1.000	1	154	0	P5		0.0
1901	Bro N	46	135	16	23	3	0	2	13	8	0		.170	.217	.237	31	-1	1	.927	-1	84	176	P45		0.0
1902	Bro N	48	161	16	28	3	2	1	16	9	2		.174	.227	.236	43	-11	7	.948	1	94	97	P35,1b8,O4(2/0/2)/2		-0.3
1903	Det A	40	124	11	30	3	2	0	12	4	0		.242	.266	.298	71	-5	3	.938	-3	70	92	P35,S2/2OC		-0.1
1904	Det A	46	140	12	38	2	1	1	6	3	0		.271	.287	.321	95	-1	2	.967	-2	93	67	P34,1b8/OR		-0.3
1905	Det A	44	130	16	25	4	0	0	5	12	1		.192	.266	.223	55	-6	8	.933	-1	78	118	P34,O8(7/0/1),2b2		-0.1
1906	Det A	28	91	5	11	0	1	0	0	1	0		.121	.130	.143	-14	-12	6	.961	-2	97	53	P25,2b3/OC		-0.3
1907	†Det A	37	109	20	29	7	2	0	19	6	0		.266	.304	.367	110	7	4	.945	-6	66	0	P32		0.0
1908	†Det A	30	82	5	13	1	0	0	2	10	0		.159	.250	.171	36	0	2	.917	-6	53	0	P29		0.0
1909	†Det A	22	45	9	9	0	0	0	1	2	1		.200	.250	.200	41	0	0	.974	-2	67	88	P21		0.0
1910	Det A	26	69	6	10	1	0	0	2	5	0		.145	.203	.159	13	-2	0	.955	-6	50	112	P26		0.0
1911	Det A	24	60	11	12	3	1	0	6	11	0		.200	.324	.333	79	3	1	.935	-5	54	0	P26		0.0
1912	Det A	6	13	3	1	0	0	0	0	1	0		.077	.143	.077	-38	-2	0	1.000	-1	35	0	P3,1b2,O2R		-0.2
1915	NY A	10	12	1	1	0	0	0	0	1	0	6	.083	.154	.083	-29	-1	0	1.000	-1	70	0	P9,M		0.0
1916	NY A	1	0	0	0	0	0	0	0	0	0	0	—	—	—		0	0		-0	0	0	/PM		0.0
1918	Det A	2	2	1	1	0	0	0	1	0	0		.500	.500	.500	210	0	0	1.000	-0	62	0	P2		0.0
Total	18	459	1302	142	251	30	11	7	93	77	6	6	.193	.241	.249	49	-42	36	.944	-32	76	81	P378,O37(15/8/14),1b8,2b8,S3		-1.8

DOOIN, RED Charles Sebastian B6.12.1879 Cincinnati OH D5.14.1952 Rochester NY BR/TR/5-9.5/165 d4.18 M5 Col Xavier

YEAR	TM LG	G	AB	R	H	2B	3B	HR	RBI	BB-IB	HP	SO	AVG	OBP	SLG	AOPS	ABR	SB-CS	FA	FR	RNG	THR	GAMES AT POSITION	DL	BFW
1902	Phi N	94	333	20	77	7	3	0	35	10	4		.231	.262	.270	64	-15	8	.950	-6	83	110	C84,O6L		-1.4
1903	Phi N	62	188	18	41	5	1	0	14	8	1		.218	.254	.255	47	-14	9	.940	-7	85	114	C51/1OR		-1.5
1904	Phi N	108	355	41	86	11	4	6	36	8	1		.242	.261	.346	90	-6	15	.938	-3	85	113	C96,1b4,O3(1/2/0)/3		0.0
1905	Phi N	113	380	45	95	13	5	0	36	10	0		.250	.269	.311	75	-13	12	.965	11	120	96	C107/3		0.9
1906	Phi N	113	351	25	86	19	1	0	32	13	1		.245	.274	.305	80	-9	15	.948	-9	90	80	C107		-0.9
1907	Phi N	101	313	18	66	8	4	0	14	15	2		.211	.252	.262	62	-15	10	.959	8	124	92	C94/2OL		0.3
1908	Phi N	133	435	28	108	17	4	0	41	17	4		.248	.283	.306	85	-8	20	.966	19	130	110	C132		2.8
1909	Phi N	141	468	42	105	14	1	2	38	21	4		.224	.264	.271	66	-20	14	.958	6	102	97	C140		0.0
1910	Phi N	103	331	30	80	13	4	0	30	22	0	17	.242	.289	.305	71	-13	10	.956	-6	96	97	C91,O3(1/1/1),M		-1.0
1911	Phi N	74	247	18	81	15	1	1	16	14	1	12	.328	.366	.409	115	5	2	.967	-2	91	91	C74,M		1.0
1912	Phi N	69	184	20	43	9	0	0	22	5	2	12	.234	.262	.283	46	-14	8	.958	-1	90	98	C58,M		-1.1
1913	Phi N	55	129	6	33	4	1	0	13	3	1	9	.256	.273	.302	62	-7	1-4	.962	1	112	93	C50,M		-0.3
1914	Phi N	53	118	10	21	2	0	1	8	4	0	6	.178	.205	.220	25	-11	4	.967	-3	73	114	C40,O2L,M		-1.2
1915	Cin N	10	31	2	10	0	0	0	0	2	0	5	.323	.364	.323	106	0	1	.915	-3	87	62	C10		-0.2
	NY N	46	124	9	27	2	2	0	9	3	0	15	.218	.236	.266	55	-8	0-2	.964	-3	90	112	C46		-0.8
	Year	56	155	11	37	2	2	0	9	5	0	20	.239	.262	.277	66	-7	1-2	.956	-5	89	103	C56		-1.0
1916	NY N	15	17	1	2	0	0	0	0	0	0	3	.118	.118	.118	-29	-3	0	.972	0	131	25	C15		-0.2
Total	15	1290	4004	333	961	139	31	10	344	155	20	87	.240	.272	.298	72	-151	133-6	.957	5	102	99	C1195,O16(11/3/2),1b5,3b2/2		-3.6

DOOLAN, MICKEY Michael Joseph "Doc" (b Michael Joseph Doolittle) B5.7.1880 Ashland PA D11.1.1951 Orlando FL BR/TR/5-10.5/170 d4.14 C7 Col Villanova

YEAR	TM LG	G	AB	R	H	2B	3B	HR	RBI	BB-IB	HP	SO	AVG	OBP	SLG	AOPS	ABR	SB-CS	FA	FR	RNG	THR	GAMES AT POSITION	DL	BFW
1905	Phi N	136	492	53	125	27	11	4	48	24	2		.254	.292	.360	97	-4	17	.935	-16	96	86	S135		-1.5
1906	Phi N	154	535	41	123	19	7	1	55	27	2		.230	.270	.297	77	-17	16	.930	8	100	100	S154		-0.4
1907	Phi N	145	509	33	104	19	7	1	47	25	1		.204	.243	.275	63	-24	18	.929	15	105	125	S145		-0.5
1908	Phi N	129	445	29	104	25	4	2	49	17	3		.234	.267	.321	85	-9	5	.939	-2	100	86	S129		-0.7
1909	Phi N	147	493	39	108	12	10	1	35	37	2		.219	.276	.290	75	-16	10	.939	24	105	114	S147		1.4
1910	Phi N	148	536	58	141	31	6	2	57	35	6	56	.263	.315	.354	92	-6	16	.948	18	108	116	S148		1.7
1911	Phi N	146	512	51	122	23	6	1	49	44	2	65	.238	.301	.313	71	-21	14	.936	17	104	116	S145		0.6
1912	Phi N	146	532	47	137	26	6	1	62	34	2	59	.258	.305	.335	70	-23	6	.950	10	104	83	S146		-0.2
1913	Phi N	151	518	32	113	12	6	1	43	29	2	68	.218	.262	.270	50	-35	17-8	.941	9	103	113	S148,2b3		-1.5
1914	Bal F	145	486	58	119	23	6	1	53	40	7	47	.245	.311	.323	71	-27	30	.949	34	112	109	S145		1.7
1915	Bal F	119	404	41	75	13	7	2	21	24	4	39	.186	.238	.267	41	-40	10	.946	32	111	132	S119		0.1
	Chi F	24	86	9	23	1	1	0	9	2	1	7	.267	.292	.302	72	-5	5	.914	-1	107	56	S24		-0.5
	Year	143	490	50	98	14	8	2	30	26	5	46	.200	.248	.273	46	-45	15	.941	31	110	119	S143		-0.4
1916	Chi N	28	70	4	15	2	1	0	5	8	0	7	.214	.295	.271	67	-2	0	.918	0	105	86	S24		-0.1
	NY N	18	51	4	12	3	1	1	3	2	0	4	.235	.264	.392	106	0	1	.975	2	105	112	S16,2b2		0.3
	Year	46	121	8	27	5	2	1	8	10	0	11	.223	.282	.322	82	-3	1	.939	2	105	96	S40,2b2		0.2
1918	Bro N	92	308	14	55	8	2	0	18	22	0	24	.179	.233	.218	38	-23	8	.968	10	101	99	2b91		-1.3
Total	13	1728	5977	513	1376	244	81	15	554	370	34	376	.230	.279	.306	71	-252	173-8	.940	160	104	104	S1625,2b96		-0.9

DOOMS, HARRY Henry E. "Jack" B1.30.1867 St.Louis MO D12.14.1899 St.Louis MO d8.7

YEAR	TM LG	G	AB	R	H	2B	3B	HR	RBI	BB-IB	HP	SO	AVG	OBP	SLG	AOPS	ABR	SB-CS	FA	FR	RNG	THR	GAMES AT POSITION	DL	BFW
1892	Lou N	1	4	0	0	0	0	1	0	0		3	.000	.200	.000	-42	-1	0	.000	-1	0	0	/OR		-0.1

DORAN, TOM Thomas J. "Long Tom" B12.2.1880 Westchester Co. NY D6.22.1910 New York NY BL/TR/5-11/152 d4.19

YEAR	TM LG	G	AB	R	H	2B	3B	HR	RBI	BB-IB	HP	SO	AVG	OBP	SLG	AOPS	ABR	SB-CS	FA	FR	RNG	THR	GAMES AT POSITION	DL	BFW
1904	Bos A	12	32	1	4	0	1	0	4	4	1		.125	.243	.188	35	-2	1	.898	-3	131	41	C11		-0.5
1905	Bos A	3	3	0	0	0	0	0	0	0	0		.000	.000	.000	-99	-1	0	1.000	-0	0	330	/C		-0.1
	Det A	34	94	8	15	3	0	0	4	8	3		.160	.248	.191	40	-6	2	.963	-6	69	103	C32		-1.0
	Year	37	97	8	15	3	0	0	4	8	3		.155	.241	.186	35	-7	2	.964	-5	68	106	C33		-1.0
1906	Bos A	2	5	1	0	0	0	0	0	0	0		.000	.000	.000	-99	-1	0	1.000	0	91	137	C2		-0.1
Total	3	51	132	10	19	3	1	0	4	12	4		.144	.236	.182	33	-10	3	.950	-8	84	91	C46		-1.6

DORAN, BILL William Donald B5.28.1958 Cincinnati OH [HouN79 6/138] d9.6 C2 Col Miami-Ohio

YEAR	TM LG	G	AB	R	H	2B	3B	HR	RBI	BB-IB	HP	SO	AVG	OBP	SLG	AOPS	ABR	SB-CS	FA	FR	RNG	THR	GAMES AT POSITION	DL	BFW
1982	Hou N	26	97	11	27	3	0	0	6	4-0	0	11	.278	.304	.309	79	-3	5-0	.975	-4	94	111	2b26		-0.4
1983	Hou N	154	535	70	145	12	7	8	39	86-11	0	67	.271	.371	.364	111	10	12-12	.979	3	99	117	2b153		2.1
1984	Hou N	147	548	92	143	18	11	4	41	66-7	2	69	.261	.341	.356	103	2	21-12	.986	8	106	104	2b139,S13		2.0
1985	Hou N	148	578	84	166	31	6	14	59	71-6	0	69	.287	.362	.434	126	21	23-15	.980	6	100	112	2b147		3.6
1986	†Hou N	145	550	92	152	29	3	6	37	81-7	2	57	.276	.368	.373	109	10	42-19	.974	-34	78	81	2b144		-1.4
1987	Hou N	162	625	82	177	23	3	16	79	82-3	1	64	.283	.365	.406	109	10	31-11	.992	-13	91	72	2b162,S3		0.8
1988	Hou N	132	480	66	119	18	1	7	53	65-3	1	60	.248	.338	.333	97	0	17-4	.987	2	99	101	2b130		0.9
1989	Hou N	142	507	65	111	25	2	8	58	59-2	2	63	.219	.301	.323	82	-11	22-3	.980	-25	90	84	2b138		-3.1
1990	Hou N	109	344	49	99	21	2	6	32	71-1	0	53	.288	.405	.413	130	19	18-9	.989	-12	96	87	2b99		-0.9
	Cin N	17	59	10	22	8	0	1	5	8-1	0	5	.373	.448	.559	168	6	5-0	.985	1	111	97	2b12,3b4	15	1.0
	Year	126	403	59	121	29	2	7	37	79-2	0	58	.300	.411	.434	136	25	23-9	.988	-11	98	88	2b111,3b4		1.9
1991	Cin N	111	361	51	101	12	2	6	35	46-1	2	39	.280	.359	.374	103	3	5-4	.981	-9	91	108	2b88,O6L,1b4	22	-0.5
1992	Cin N	132	387	48	91	16	2	8	47	64-9	2	40	.235	.342	.349	94	-1	7-4	.988	-6	92	106	2b104,1b25		-0.6
1993	Mil A	28	60	7	13	4	0	0	8	6-1	0	3	.217	.284	.283	55	-4	1-0	.964	-3	79	91	2b17,1b4	45	-0.6
Total	12	1453	5131	727	1366	220	39	84	497	709-52	10	600	.266	.354	.373	106	62	209-93	.983	-85	94	97	2b1359,1b33,S16,O6L,3b4	82	4.7

DORAN, BILL William James B6.14.1898 San Francisco CA D3.9.1978 Santa Monica CA BL/TR/5-11.5/175 d6.23 Col St. Marys (CA)

YEAR	TM LG	G	AB	R	H	2B	3B	HR	RBI	BB-IB	HP	SO	AVG	OBP	SLG	AOPS	ABR	SB-CS	FA	FR	RNG	THR	GAMES AT POSITION	DL	BFW
1922	Cle A	3	2	0	1	0	0	0					.500	.667	.500	206	0	0-0	—	-0	0	0	3b2		0.0

DORGAN, JERRY Jeremiah F. B1856 Meriden CT D6.10.1891 New Haven CT BL/TR/?/165 d7.8 b-Mike

YEAR	TM LG	G	AB	R	H	2B	3B	HR	RBI	BB-IB	HP	SO	AVG	OBP	SLG	AOPS	ABR	SB-CS	FA	FR	RNG	THR	GAMES AT POSITION	DL	BFW
1880	Wor N	10	35	2	7	1	0	0				1	.200	.200	.229	41	-2		.750	-2	0	0	O9R/C		-0.4
1882	Phi AA	44	181	25	51	9	1	0	24	4			.282	.297	.343	108	1		.880	-2			C25,O22(1/1/20)/3		0.0
1884	Ind AA	34	141	22	42	6	1	0		2		2	.298	.324	.355	122	3		.793	-3	156	102	O29R,C5		0.1
	Bro AA	4	13	2	4	0	0	0		0		0	.308	.308	.308	101	0		.921	1			C4		0.1

YEAR TM LG	G	AB	R	H	2B	3B	HR	RBI	BB-IB	HP	SO	AVG	OBP	SLG	AOPS	ABR	SB-CS	FA	FR	RNG	THR	GAMES AT POSITION	DL	BFW
Year	38	154	24	46	6	1	0		2	2		.299	.316	.351	120	3		.793	-1	156	102	O29R,C9		0.2
1885 Det N	39	161	23	46	6	2	0	24	8		10	.286	.320	.348	115	3		.857	-3	71	200	O39(0/1/38)		0.0
Total 4	131	531	74	150	22	4	0	49	14		11	.282	.303	.339	109	5		.817	-9			O99(1/2/96),C35/3		-0.2

DORGAN, MIKE Michael Cornelius B10.2.1853 Middletown CT D4.26.1909 Hartford CT BR/TR/5-9/180 d5.8 M3 b-Jerry OF(29/17/556) ▲

YEAR TM LG	G	AB	R	H	2B	3B	HR	RBI	BB-IB	HP	SO	AVG	OBP	SLG	AOPS	ABR	SB-CS	FA	FR	RNG	THR	GAMES AT POSITION	DL	BFW
1877 StL N	60	266	45	82	9	7	0	23	9		13	.308	.331	.395	135	11		.824	-7	54	198	O50(20/1/29),C12,3b2/S2		0.2
1879 Syr N	59	270	38	72	11	5	1	17	4		13	.267	.277	.356	120	7		.954	-6	143	46	1b21,O16R,3b11,S6,C4,P2/2M		0.1
1880 Pro N	79	321	45	79	10	1	0	31	10		18	.246	.269	.283	90	-3		.858	-1	135	146	O77R,3b2/PM		-0.3
1881 Wor N	51	220	36	61	5	0	0	18	8		4	.277	.303	.300	85	-4		.953	-0	82	72	1b26,O23R,S2,M		-0.5
Det N	8	34	5	8	1	0	0	5	1		0	.235	.257	.265	62	-1		1.000	-1	70	0	O5(0/4/1),3b2/1		-0.2
Year	59	254	41	69	6	0	0	23	9		4	.272	.297	.295	82	-5		.897	-1	101	76	O28(0/4/24),1b27,S2,3b2		-0.7
1883 NY N	64	261	32	61	11	3	0	27	2		23	.234	.240	.299	63	-12		.847	-8	50	45	O59(0/9/51),C6/P		-1.7
1884 NY N	83	341	62	94	11	6	1	48	13		27	.276	.302	.352	103	0		.851	-2	93	124	O64(2/2/60),P14,C6,2b3		-0.2
1885 NY N	89	347	60	113	17	8	0	46	11		24	.326	.346	.421	149	18		.905	-4	66	212	O88R/1		1.3
1886 NY N	118	442	61	129	19	4	2	79	29		37	.292	.335	.367	112	7	9	.888	-10	57	122	O116(6/1/110),1b3		-0.4
1887 NY N	71	283	41	73	10	0	0	34	15	3	20	.258	.302	.293	69	-11	22	.870	-3	47	0	O69(1/0/68),1b2		-1.2
1890 Syr AA	33	139	19	30	8	0	0	18	16	1		.216	.301	.273	77	-3	8	.900	-2	92	77	O33R		-0.4
Total 10	715	2924	443	802	112	34	4	346	118	4	179	.274	.303	.340	102	9	39	.867	-43	77	126	O600R,1b54,C28,P18,3b17,S9,2b5		-3.3

DORMAN, RED Charles Dwight "Curlie" B10.3.1900 Jacksonville IL D12.7.1974 Anaheim CA BR/TR/5-10.5/180 d8.21

YEAR TM LG	G	AB	R	H	2B	3B	HR	RBI	BB-IB	HP	SO	AVG	OBP	SLG	AOPS	ABR	SB-CS	FA	FR	RNG	THR	GAMES AT POSITION	DL	BFW
1928 Cle A	25	77	12	28	6	0	0	11	9	0	6	.364	.430	.442	128	4	1-0	.915	-2	97	43	O24(5/19/0)		0.1

DORMAN, CHARLIE Charles William "Slats" B4.23.1898 San Francisco CA D11.15.1928 San Francisco CA BR/TR/6-2/185 d5.14

YEAR TM LG	G	AB	R	H	2B	3B	HR	RBI	BB-IB	HP	SO	AVG	OBP	SLG	AOPS	ABR	SB-CS	FA	FR	RNG	THR	GAMES AT POSITION	DL	BFW
1923 Chi A	1	2	0	1	0	0	0	0	0			.500	.500	.500	166	-0				0	391	/C		0.0

DORSETT, BRIAN Brian Richard B4.9.1961 Terre Haute IN BR/TR/6-3/220* [OakA83 10/241] d9.8 Col Indiana St. [DL 1988 Cle A 64]

YEAR TM LG	G	AB	R	H	2B	3B	HR	RBI	BB-IB	HP	SO	AVG	OBP	SLG	AOPS	ABR	SB-CS	FA	FR	RNG	THR	GAMES AT POSITION	DL	BFW
1987 Cle A	5	11	2	3	0	0	1	3	0-0	1	3	.273	.333	.545	126	0	0-0	1.000	-1	45	0	C4		-0.1
1988 Cal A	7	11	0	1	0	0	0	2	1-0	0	5	.091	.167	.091	-26	-2	0-0	1.000	-2	126	178	C7		-0.1
1989 NY A	8	22	3	8	1	0	0	4	1-0	0	4	.364	.391	.409	127	1	0-0	1.000	-0	209	104	C8		0.1
1990 NY A	14	35	2	5	2	0	0	4	2-0	0	3	.143	.189	.200	9	-4	0-0	1.000	-1	71	0	C9,D5		-0.6
1991 SD N	11	12	0	1	0	0	0	1	0-0	0	3	.083	.083	.083	-51	-2	0-0	1.000	0	244	0	1b2		-0.2
1993 Cin N	25	63	7	16	4	0	2	12	3-0	0	14	.254	.288	.413	84	-2	0-0	1.000	2	118	61	C18,1b3		-0.2
1994 Cin N	76	216	21	53	8	0	5	26	21-7	1	33	.245	.313	.352	74	-8	0-0	.991	3	133	104	C73/1		-0.2
1996 Chi N	17	41	3	5	0	0	1	3	4-0	0	8	.122	.196	.195	5	-6	0-0	1.000	4	405	94	C15		-0.1
Total 8	163	411	38	92	15	0	9	51	32-7	2	73	.224	.281	.326	61	-23	0-0	.995	6	157	92	C134,1b6,D5	64	-1.0

DORSEY, JERRY Jeremiah B1885 Oakland CA BL/TL/5-11/175 d9.23

YEAR TM LG	G	AB	R	H	2B	3B	HR	RBI	BB-IB	HP	SO	AVG	OBP	SLG	AOPS	ABR	SB-CS	FA	FR	RNG	THR	GAMES AT POSITION	DL	BFW
1911 Pit N	2	6	0	0	0	0	0	0	0		1	.000	.000	.000	-96	-2		1.000	0	118	0	/OC		-0.2

DOSCHER, HERM John Henry Sr. B12.20.1852 New York NY D3.20.1934 Buffalo NY BR/TR/5-10/182 d9.5 U4 s-Jack

YEAR TM LG	G	AB	R	H	2B	3B	HR	RBI	BB-IB	HP	SO	AVG	OBP	SLG	AOPS	ABR	SB-CS	FA	FR	RNG	THR	GAMES AT POSITION	DL	BFW
1872 Atl NA	6	24	4	9	0	0	0	5	0		1	.375	.375	.375	112	0	0-1	.714	-3	142	0	O6R		0.0
1873 Atl NA	1	6	1	1	0	0	0	1	0		0	.167	.167	.167	-1	-1	0-0	.500	-1	0	0	/OC		-0.1
1875 Was NA	22	81	5	15	4	0	0	5	0		6	.185	.185	.235	46	-4	1-0	.752	0	114	31	3b22		-0.4
1879 Tro N	47	191	16	42	8	0	0	18	2		10	.220	.228	.262	65	-6		.806	-3	100	111	3b47		-0.7
Chi N	3	11	1	2	0	0	0	1	0		3	.182	.182	.182	19	-1		.700	-1	90	0	3b3		-0.2
Year	50	202	17	44	8	0	0	19	2		13	.218	.225	.257	62	-7		.800	-4	99	105	3b50		-0.9
1881 Cle N	5	19	2	4	0	0	0	0	0		1	.211	.211	.211	35	-1		.895	-0	91	126	3b5		-0.2
1882 Cle N	25	104	7	25	2	0	0	10	0		11	.240	.240	.260	63	-4		.857	-1	96	73	3b22,O2L/S		-0.4
Total 3 NA	29	111	10	25	4	0	0	11	0		7	.225	.225	.261	62	-5	1-1	.752	-1	114	31	3b77,O7(0/1/6)		-0.5
Total 3	80	325	26	73	10	0	0	29	2		26	.225	.229	.255	61	-12		.823	-5	98	97	3b77,O2L/S		-1.5

DOSTER, DAVID David Eric B10.8.1970 Ft.Wayne IN BR/TR/5-10/185* [PhiN93 27/748] d6.16 Col Indiana St.

YEAR TM LG	G	AB	R	H	2B	3B	HR	RBI	BB-IB	HP	SO	AVG	OBP	SLG	AOPS	ABR	SB-CS	FA	FR	RNG	THR	GAMES AT POSITION	DL	BFW
1996 Phi N	39	105	14	28	8	0	1	8	7-0	0	21	.267	.313	.371	79	-3	0-0	.973	-2	90	85	2b24/3		-0.4
1999 Phi N	99	97	9	19	2	0	3	10	12-1	0	23	.196	.282	.309	49	-8	1-0	.993	7	104	132	2b77,3b6,S5		0.1
Total 2	138	202	23	47	10	0	4	18	19-1	0	44	.233	.297	.342	64	-11	1-0	.984	6	97	110	2b101,3b7,S5		-0.3

DOTTERER, DUTCH Henry John B11.11.1931.Syracuse NY D10.9.1999 Syracuse NY BR/TR/6-0/209(198-209) d9.25 Col Syracuse

YEAR TM LG	G	AB	R	H	2B	3B	HR	RBI	BB-IB	HP	SO	AVG	OBP	SLG	AOPS	ABR	SB-CS	FA	FR	RNG	THR	GAMES AT POSITION	DL	BFW
1957 Cin N	4	12	0	1	0	0	0	1	1-0	0	2	.083	.154	.083	-32	-0	0-0	1.000	-0	99	0	C4		-0.3
1958 Cin N	11	28	1	7	1	0	1	2	2-0	0	4	.250	.300	.393	77	-1	0-0	.981	2	120	136	C8		0.2
1959 Cin N	52	161	21	43	7	0	2	17	16-1	0	23	.267	.328	.348	79	-4	0-0	.992	1	126	91	C51		-0.1
1960 Cin N	33	79	4	18	5	0	2	11	13-0	0	10	.228	.337	.367	91	0	0-1	.979	-1	60	142	C31		-0.1
1961 Was A	7	19	1	5	2	0	0	1	3-0	0	5	.263	.364	.368	98	0	0-0	1.000	1	70	170	C7		0.2
Total 5	107	299	27	74	15	0	5	33	35-1	0	44	.247	.323	.348	79	-7	0-1	.988	3	102	112	C101		-0.1

DOUGHERTY, CHARLIE Charles William B2.7.1862 Darlington WI D2.18.1925 Milwaukee WI d4.17

YEAR TM LG	G	AB	R	H	2B	3B	HR	RBI	BB-IB	HP	SO	AVG	OBP	SLG	AOPS	ABR	SB-CS	FA	FR	RNG	THR	GAMES AT POSITION	DL	BFW
1884 Alt U	23	85	6	22	5	0	0	2				.259	.276	.318	79	-5		.854	-3	90	30	2b16,O8(2/2/4)/S		-0.6

DOUGHERTY, PATSY Patrick Henry B10.27.1876 Andover NY D4.30.1940 Bolivar NY BL/TR/6-2/190 d4.19

YEAR TM LG	G	AB	R	H	2B	3B	HR	RBI	BB-IB	HP	SO	AVG	OBP	SLG	AOPS	ABR	SB-CS	FA	FR	RNG	THR	GAMES AT POSITION	DL	BFW
1902 Bos A	108	438	77	150	12	6	0	34	42	6		.342	.407	.397	120	14	20	.899	-10	61	41	O102L/3		-0.1
1903 †Bos A	139	590	107	195	19	12	4	59	33	6		.331	.372	.424	131	22	35	.952	4	103	84	O139L		1.8
1904 Bos A	49	195	33	53	6	4	0	4	25	0		.272	.355	.338	113	4	10	.925	-0	72	240	O49L		0.1
NY A	106	452	80	128	13	10	6	22	19	3		.283	.316	.396	119	8	11	.925	-8	120	36	O106L		-0.6
Year	155	647	113	181	18	14	6	26	44	3		.280	.329	.379	117	12	21	.925	-8	104	102	O155L		-0.5
1905 NY A	116	418	56	110	16	6	3	29	28	6		.263	.319	.335	96	-2	17	.898	-3	97	75	O108L/3		-1.2
1906 NY A	12	52	3	10	2	0	0	4	0	0		.192	.192	.231	26	-4	0	1.000	2	197	315	O12L		-0.3
†Chi A	75	253	30	59	9	1	0	27	19	3		.233	.295	.312	92	-2	11	.985	-2	105	55	O74L		-0.9
Year	87	305	33	69	11	4	1	31	19	3		.226	.278	.298	81	-7	11	.987	1	118	91	O86L		-1.2
1907 Chi A	148	533	69	144	17	2	1	59	36	5		.270	.322	.315	107	5	33	.946	-7	98	98	O148L		-1.2
1908 Chi A	138	482	68	134	11	6	0	45	58	10		.278	.367	.326	128	18	47	.947	-15	47	28	O128L		-0.5
1909 Chi A	139	491	71	140	23	13	1	55	51	6		.285	.367	.391	146	25	36	.942	-14	57		O138L		0.4
1910 Chi A	127	443	45	110	8	6	1	43	41	4		.248	.318	.300	98	-1	22	.923	-12	81	59	O121L		-2.3
1911 Chi A	76	211	39	61	10	9	0	32	26	5		.289	.380	.422	128	8	19	.933	-6	80	72	O56L		0.0
Total 10	1233	4558	678	1294	138	78	17	413	378	54		.284	.346	.360	117	95	261	.935	-70	85	65	O1181L,3b2		-4.8

DOUGLAS, JOHN John Franklin B9.14.1917 Thayer WV D2.11.1984 Miami FL BL/TL/6-2.5/195 d4.21 Col Miami-Ohio

YEAR TM LG	G	AB	R	H	2B	3B	HR	RBI	BB-IB	HP	SO	AVG	OBP	SLG	AOPS	ABR	SB-CS	FA	FR	RNG	THR	GAMES AT POSITION	DL	BFW
1945 Bro N	5	9	0	0	0	0	0	2	2		4	.000	.182	.000	-47	-2	0	.971	-1	0	44	1b4		-0.3

DOUGLASS, ASTYANAX Astyanax Saunders B9.19.1897 Covington TX D1.26.1975 El Paso TX BL/TR/6-1/190 d7.30 Col TCU

YEAR TM LG	G	AB	R	H	2B	3B	HR	RBI	BB-IB	HP	SO	AVG	OBP	SLG	AOPS	ABR	SB-CS	FA	FR	RNG	THR	GAMES AT POSITION	DL	BFW
1921 Cin N	4	7	1	1	0	0	0	0	0		1	.143	.143	.143	-25	-1	0-0	1.000	0	114	185	C4		-0.1
1925 Cin N	7	17	1	3	0	0	0	1	1		3	.176	.222	.176	3	-3	0-0	.889	-1	79	172	C7		-0.3
Total 2	11	24	2	4	0	0	0	1	1		4	.167	.200	.167	-4	-4	0-0	.926	-1	89	176	C11		-0.4

DOUGLASS, KLONDIKE William Bingham B5.10.1872 Boston PA D12.13.1953 Bend OR BL/TR/6-0/200 d4.23 OF(68/9/55)

YEAR TM LG	G	AB	R	H	2B	3B	HR	RBI	BB-IB	HP	SO	AVG	OBP	SLG	AOPS	ABR	SB-CS	FA	FR	RNG	THR	GAMES AT POSITION	DL	BFW
1896 StL N	81	296	42	78	6	4	1	28	35	5	15	.264	.351	.321	81	-7	18	.894	-3	136	113	O74(29/5/41),C6,S2		-0.4
1897 StL N	126	519	77	170	15	3	6	50	52	13		.328	.402	.403	115	14	12	.948	-22	68	108	C61,O44(28/2/14),1b17,3b7/S		-0.1
1898 Phi N	146	582	105	150	26	4	2	48	55	11		.258	.333	.326	93	-3	18	.976	2	105	83	1b146		-0.1
1899 Phi N	77	275	26	70	6	6	0	27	10	6		.255	.296	.320	71	-12	7	.970	2	109	95	C66,3b4,1b4/OC		-0.2
1900 Phi N	50	160	23	48	9	4	0	25	13	2		.300	.360	.406	112	3	7	.934	-9	78	101	C47,3b2		-0.2
1901 Phi N	51	173	14	56	6	1	0	23	11	2		.324	.371	.370	113	3	10	.979	2	103	62	C41,1b6,O2(1/1/0)		0.8
1902 Phi N	109	408	37	95	12	3	0	37	23	0		.233	.274	.277	70	-15	6	.986	-6	84	68	1b69,C29,O10L		-2.2
1903 Phi N	105	377	43	96	5	4	1	36	28	1		.255	.308	.297	75	-13	6	.985	-1	91	80	1b97		-1.5
1904 Phi N	3	10	1	3	0	0	0	1	0	1		.300	.364	.300	109	0	0	.970	-1	52	72	1b3		0.0
Total 9	748	2800	368	766	85	29	10	275	227	41	15	.274	.337	.335	91	-30	84	.981	-35	94	78	1b342,C250,O131L,3b13,S3		-1.2

DOUMIT, RYAN Ryan Matthew B4.3.1981 Moses Lake WA BB/TR/6-0/200 d6.5

YEAR TM LG	G	AB	R	H	2B	3B	HR	RBI	BB-IB	HP	SO	AVG	OBP	SLG	AOPS	ABR	SB-CS	FA	FR	RNG	THR	GAMES AT POSITION	DL	BFW
2005 Pit N	75	231	25	59	13	1	6	35	11-1	13	48	.255	.324	.398	89	-4	2-1	.975	-1	119	137	C50,O3R,D6		-0.

YEAR	TM LG	G	AB	R	H	2B	3B	HR	RBI	BB-IB	HP	SO	AVG	OBP	SLG	AOPS	ABR	SB-CS	FA	FR	RNG	THR	GAMES AT POSITION	DL	BFW

DOUTHIT, TAYLOR Taylor Lee B4.22.1901 Little Rock AR D5.28.1986 Fremont CA BR/TR/5-11.5/175 d9.14 Col California-Davis

1923	StL N	9	27	3	5	0	2	0	0	0	0	4	.185	.185	.333	35	-3	1-0	1.000	1	104	168	O7(3/0/4)		-0.3
1924	StL N	53	173	24	48	13	1	0	13	16	3	19	.277	.349	.364	93	-1	4-3	.976	3	113	99	O50(9/22/19)		-0.1
1925	StL N	30	73	13	20	3	1	1	8	2	2	6	.274	.312	.384	75	-3	0-0	.981	1	113	61	O21(4/16/1)		-0.3
1926	†StL N	139	530	96	163	20	4	3	52	55	2	46	.308	.357	.377	99	1	23	.958	7	**111**	100	O138(1/137/0)		0.2
1927	StL N	130	488	81	128	29	6	5	50	52	2	45	.262	.336	.377	88	-8	6	.964	-1	107	55	O125(1/122/1)		-1.4
1928	†StL N	154	648	111	191	35	3	3	43	84	10	36	.295	.384	.372	97	2	11	.984	13	**120**	66	O154C		0.8
1929	StL N	150	613	128	206	42	7	9	62	79	5	49	.336	.416	.471	118	21	8	.974	-1	107	55	O150C		1.3
1930	†StL N	154	664	109	201	41	10	7	93	60	4	38	.303	.364	.426	87	-13	4	.964	0	106	65	O154C		-1.7
1931	StL N	36	133	21	44	11	2	1	21	11	1	9	.331	.386	.466	123	5	1	.972	-1	106	0	O36(0/35/1)		0.2
	Cin N	95	374	42	98	9	1	0	24	42	2	24	.262	.340	.291	76	-12	4	.983	1	104	72	O95C		-1.5
	Year	131	507	63	142	20	3	1	45	53	3	33	.280	.352	.337	89	-6	5	.980	-0	105	52	O131(0/130/1)		-1.3
1932	Cin N	96	333	28	81	12	1	0	25	31	2	29	.243	.311	.285	64	-16	3	.985	2	106	79	O82(2/86/0)		-1.6
1933	Cin N	1	0	1	0	0	0	0	0	0	0	0	—	—	—		0	0			0		/R		0.0
	Chi N	27	71	8	16	5	0	0	5	11	0	7	.225	.329	.296	80	-1	2	.930	-1	84	238	O18(5/13/0)		-0.2
	Year	28	71	9	16	5	0	0	5	11	0	7	.225	.329	.296	80	-1	2	.930	-1	84	238	O18(5/13/0)		-0.2
Total	11	1074	4127	665	1201	220	38	29	396	443	33	312	.291	.364	.384	93	-28	67-3	.972	24	109	72	O1036(25/984/26)		-4.4

DOW, CLARENCE Clarence G. B10.2.1854 Charlestown MA D3.11.1893 West Somerville MA d9.22

| 1884 | Bos U | 1 | 6 | 1 | 2 | 0 | 0 | 0 | | | | | .333 | .333 | .333 | 104 | 0 | 1 | 1.000 | 1 | 545 | 0 | /OC | | 0.1 |

DOWD, JOHN John Leo (b John Leo O'Dowd) B1.3.1891 Weymouth MA D1.31.1981 Ft.Lauderdale FL BR/TR/5-8/170 d7.3 Col Vermont

| 1912 | NY A | 10 | 31 | 1 | 6 | 1 | 0 | 0 | 6 | 1 | | | .194 | .342 | .226 | 60 | -1 | 0 | .840 | -3 | 96 | 31 | S10 | | -0.3 |

DOWD, SNOOKS Raymond Bernard B12.20.1897 Springfield MA D4.4.1962 Northampton MA BR/TR/5-8/163 d4.27 Col Lehigh

1919	Det A	1	0	0	0	0	0	0	0	0	0	0	—	—	—		0				0		/R		0.0
	Phi A	13	18	4	3	0	0	0	0	0	0	5	.167	.167	.167	-6	-3	2	.800	0	138	129	2b3,S2/3OC		-0.2
	Year	14	18	4	3	0	0	0	0	0	0	5	.167	.167	.167	-6	-3	2	.800	0	138	129	2b3,S2/3OC		-0.2
1926	Bro N	2	8	0	0	0	0	0	0	0	0	0	.000	.000	.000	-99	-2	0	1.000	-1	39	0	2b2		-0.4
Total	2	16	26	4	3	0	0	0	0	6	0	5	.115	.115	.115	-36	-5	2	.875	-1	92	0	2b5,S2/OC3		-0.6

DOWD, TOMMY Thomas Jefferson "Buttermilk Tommy" B4.20.1869 Holyoke MA D7.2.1933 Holyoke MA BR/TR/5-8/173 d4.8 M2 Col Brown OF(284/331/350)

1891	Bos AA	4	11	1	1	0	0	0	0	1			.091	.091	.091	-49	-2	0	—	-0	0	0	O4R		-0.2
	Was AA	112	464	66	120	9	10	1	44	19	2	44	.259	.294	.328	81	-15	39	.885	-13	94	75	2b107,O5L		-2.1
	Year	116	475	67	121	9	10	1	44	19	2	44	.255	.286	.322	78	-17	39	.885	-13	94	75	2b107,O9(5/0/4)		-2.3
1892	Was N	144	584	94	142	9	10	1	50	34	1	49	.243	.286	.298	79	-17	49	.891	-19	95	83	2b98,O23(7/0/16),3b18,S6		-3.1
1893	StL N	132	581	114	164	18	7	1	54	49	2	23	.282	.340	.343	81	-16	59	.944	3	121	196	O132(64/5/63)/2		-1.9
1894	StL N	123	524	92	142	16	8	4	62	54	2	33	.271	.341	.355	68	-28	31	.930	-7	73	89	O117(48/0/69),2b7/3		-3.2
1895	StL N	130	508	95	164	19	17	7	74	31	3	31	.323	.365	.469	116	9	32	.928	-4	67	76	O116(14/36/66),3b17,2b2		-0.1
1896	StL N	126	521	93	138	17	11	5	46	42	2	19	.265	.322	.369	85	-13	40	.920	-13	92	63	2b78,O48C,M		-2.2
1897	StL N	35	145	25	38	9	1	0	9	6	0		.262	.291	.338	67	-7	11	.915	-7	0	0	O30C,2b5,M		-1.3
	Phi N	91	391	68	114	14	4	0	43	19	0		.292	.324	.348	80	-12	30	.919	-5	98	169	O73(0/23/50),2b19		-1.7
	Year	126	536	93	152	23	5	0	52	25	0		.284	.316	.345	76	-19	41	.918	-12	68	117	O103(0/53/50),2b24		-3.0
1898	StL N	139	586	70	143	17	7	0	32	30	5		.244	.287	.297	66	-28	16	.920	-13	64	69	O129(9/42/82),2b11		-4.5
1899	Cle N	147	605	81	168	17	6	2	35	48	2		.278	.333	.336	90	-8	28	.954	-2	47	26	O147C		-1.7
1901	Bos A	**138**	594	104	159	18	7	3	52	38	3		.268	.315	.337	82	-15	33	.937	1	61	85	O137L,1b2/3		-1.9
Total	10	1321	5514	903	1493	163	88	24	501	370	22	**200**	.271	.319	.345	82	-152	368	.933	-78	71	98	O961R,2b328,3b37,S6,1b2		-23.9

DOWELL, KEN Kenneth Allen B1.19.1961 Sacramento CA BR/TR/5-9/160 [PhiN80 S3/61] d6.24 Col Sacramento (CA) City

| 1987 | Phi N | 15 | 39 | 4 | 5 | 0 | 0 | 1 | 2-0 | 0 | | 5 | .128 | .171 | .128 | -19 | -7 | 0-0 | 1.000 | -1 | 98 | 99 | S15 | | -0.6 |

DOWIE, JOE Joseph E. B7.15.1865 New Orleans LA D3.4.1917 New Orleans LA 5-8/150 d7.10

| 1889 | Bal AA | 20 | 75 | 12 | 17 | 5 | 0 | 0 | 8 | 2 | 2 | 10 | .227 | .266 | .293 | 58 | -4 | 5 | .947 | 0 | 54 | 0 | O20R | | -0.4 |

DOWNEY, RED Alexander Cummings B2.6.1889 Aurora IN D7.10.1949 Detroit MI BL/TL/5-11/174 d9.14 Col Georgetown

| 1909 | Bro N | 19 | 78 | 7 | 20 | 1 | 0 | 0 | 8 | 2 | | | .256 | .275 | .269 | 71 | -3 | 4 | 1.000 | -1 | 83 | 0 | O19(0/3/16) | | -0.5 |

DOWNEY, TOM Thomas Edward B1.1.1884 Lewiston ME D8.3.1961 Passaic NJ BR/TR/5-10/178 d5.7

1909	Cin N	119	416	39	96	9	6	1	32	32	1		.231	.287	.288	79	-11	16	.909	-6	98	124	S119/C		-1.4
1910	Cin N	111	378	43	102	9	7	0	32	34	3	28	.270	.335	.325	97	-2	12	.879	-8	95	64	S68,3b41		-0.6
1911	Cin N	111	360	50	94	16	7	0	36	44	2	38	.261	.345	.344	97	-1	10	.906	-11	94	72	S93,2b6,3b5,1b2/OR		-0.5
1912	Phi N	54	171	27	50	6	3	1	23	21	0	20	.292	.370	.380	99	0	3	.893	-5	87	49	3b46,S3		-0.4
	Chi N	13	22	4	4	0	2	0	4	1	0	5	.182	.217	.364	58	-2	0	.792	-0	108	0	S5,3b3/2		-0.2
	Year	67	193	31	54	6	5	1	27	22	0	25	.280	.353	.378	95	-2	3	.892	-6	88	47	3b49,S8/2		-0.6
1914	Buf F	151	541	69	118	20	3	2	42	40	1	55	.218	.273	.277	49	-47	35	**.962**	10	**109**	110	2b129,S16,3b5		-3.6
1915	Buf F	92	282	24	56	9	1	1	19	26	1	26	.199	.269	.248	45	-25	11	.930	-1	89	106	2b48,3b35,S2/1		-2.7
Total	6	651	2170	256	520	69	25	6	189	198	8	**172**	.240	.306	.304	74	-88	87	.901	-20	96	91	S306,2b184,3b135,1b3/ORC		-9.4

DOWNING, BRIAN Brian Jay B10.9.1950 Los Angeles CA BR/TR/5-10/194(170-205) d5.31 Col Cypress (CA) JC

1973	Chi A	34	73	5	13	1	0	2	4	10-1	0	17	.178	.277	.274	54	-5	0-0	1.000	5	95	144	O13(8/0/6),C11,3b8/D	38	0.0
1974	Chi A	108	293	41	66	12	1	10	39	51-3	2	72	.225	.344	.375	104	-5	0-1	.994	-2	79	105	C63,O39(5/0/34),D9		0.2
1975	Chi A	138	420	58	101	12	1	7	41	76-5	3	75	.240	.356	.324	93	0	13-4	.990	2	106	114	C137/D		1.0
1976	Chi A	104	317	38	81	14	0	3	30	40-0	1	55	.256	.338	.328	96	0	7-3	.988	-7	91	101	C93,D11		1.0
1977	Chi A	69	169	28	48	4	2	4	25	34-0	2	21	.284	.402	.402	122	7	1-2	.983	2	67	102	C61,O3(2/0/1),D2	16	-0.4
1978	Cal A	133	412	42	105	15	0	7	46	52-2	6	47	.255	.345	.342	97	1	3-2	.993	-7	71	138	C128,D2		1.0
1979	†Cal A★	148	509	87	166	27	3	12	75	77-4	5	57	.326	.418	.462	142	34	3-3	.985	-19	81	75	C129,D18		2.0
1980	Cal A	30	93	5	27	6	0	2	25	12-1	0	12	.290	.364	.419	118	4	0-2	1.000	-3	43	22	C16,D13	134	0.0
1981	Cal A	93	317	47	79	14	0	9	41	46-1	4	35	.249	.351	.379	109	6	1-1	.990	-4	87	28	O56L,C37,D5		0.0
1982	†Cal A	158	623	109	175	37	2	28	84	86-1	5	58	.281	.368	.482	131	29	2-1	**1.000**	-1	95	94	O158L		2.1
1983	Cal A	113	403	68	99	15	1	19	53	62-4	5	59	.246	.352	.429	114	9	1-2	.994	-2	88	133	O84L,D26	41	0.3
1984	Cal A	156	539	65	148	28	2	23	91	70-3	7	66	.275	.360	.462	127	22	0-4	**1.000**	-4	95	54	O131L,D21		1.0
1985	Cal A	150	520	80	137	23	1	20	85	78-3	13	61	.263	.371	.427	119	17	5-3	.992	-4	93	64	O121L,D25		0.7
1986	†Cal A	152	513	90	137	27	4	20	95	90-2	17	84	.267	.389	.462	131	27	4-4	.989	-4	94	57	O138L,D10		1.6
1987	Cal A	155	567	110	154	29	3	29	77	**106**-6	17	85	.272	.400	.487	138	37	5-5	1.000	-3	76	96	D118,O34L		2.8
1988	Cal A	135	484	80	117	18	2	25	64	81-5	14	63	.242	.360	.442	128	21	3-4	—	0	0	0	D132	16	1.6
1989	Cal A	142	544	59	154	25	2	14	59	56-3	6	87	.283	.354	.414	118	14	0-2	—	0	0	0	D141		0.9
1990	Cal A	96	330	47	90	18	2	14	51	50-2	6	45	.273	.374	.467	137	18	0-0	—	0	0	0	D87		1.6
1991	Tex A	123	407	76	113	17	2	17	49	58-7	8	70	.278	.377	.455	131	19	1-1	—	0	0	0	D109		1.5
1992	Tex A	107	320	53	89	18	0	10	39	62-2	8	58	.278	.407	.428	138	21	1-0	—	0	0	0	D93		1.8
Total	20	2344	7853	1188	2099	360	28	275	1073	1197-55	129	1127	.267	.370	.425	122	283	50-44	.995	-52	92	75	D824,O777(737/0/41),C675,3b8	245	19.6

DOWNS, RED Jerome Willis B8.22.1883 Neola IA D10.19.1939 Council Bluffs IA BR/TR/5-11/155 d5.2

1907	Det A	105	374	28	82	13	5	1	42	13	2		.219	.249	.289	69	-14	3	.930	-21	91	40	2b80,O20(12/8/0)/S3		-4.0
1908	†Det A	84	289	28	64	10	3	1	35	5	1		.221	.237	.287	67	-11	3	.925	-4	104	88	2b82/3		-1.7
1912	Bro N	9	32	2	8	3	0	0	3	1	0	5	.250	.273	.344	71	-1	3	.881	-2	100	61	2b9		-0.3
	Chi N	43	95	9	25	4	3	1	14	9	0	17	.263	.327	.400	99	-1	5	.907	2	101	147	2b16,S9,3b5		0.2
	Year	52	127	11	33	7	3	1	17	10	0	22	.260	.314	.386	92	-2	8	.896	0	101	110	2b25,S9,3b5		-0.1
Total	3	241	790	67	179	30	11	3	94	28	3	**22**	.227	.256	.304	72	-27	13	.924	-25	98	70	2b187,O20(12/8/0),S10,3b7		-5.8

DOWSE, TOM Thomas Joseph B8.12.1866 Mohill, Ireland D12.14.1946 Riverside CA BR/TR/5-11/175 d4.21

1890	Cle N	40	159	20	33	2	1	0	9	12	1	22	.208	.267	.233	47	-11	3	.870	0	177	226	O26(6/3/19),1b10,C3/P		-1.1
1891	Col AA	55	201	24	45	7	0	0	22	13	2	24	.224	.278	.259	57	-11	2	.919	-14	*74*	*81*	C51,O5(2/0/3)		-1.8
1892	Lou N	41	145	10	21	2	0	0	7	2	3	15	.145	.173	.159	1	-18	-1	.918	-1	*90*	*120*	C29,1b11,O3R/2		-1.6
	Cin N	1	4	0	0	0	0	0	0	0	0	0	.000	.000	.000	-99	-1	0	1.000	-0	*139*	0	/C		-0.1
	Phi N	16	54	3	10	0	0	0	6	2	1	4	.185	.228	.185	25	-5	1	.973	2	133	68	C15		-0.2
	Was N	7	27	5	7	1	0	0	4	0	0		.259	.259	.296	70	-1	0	.800	-1	0	0	O4L,C3		-0.1

YEAR	TM LG	G	AB	R	H	2B	3B	HR	RBI	BB-IB	HP	SO	AVG	OBP	SLG	AOPS	ABR	SB-CS	FA	FR	RNG	THR	GAMES AT POSITION	DL	BFW
	Year	65	230	18	38	3	0	0	15	4	4	22	.165	.193	.178	13	-25	2	.931	-0	102	104	C48,1b11,O7(4/0/3)/2		-2.0
Total	3	160	590	62	116	12	1	0	46	29	7	66	.197	.243	.220	38	-47	7	.921	-15	88	91	C102,O38(12/3/25),1b21/2P		-4.9

DOYLE, BRIAN Brian Reed B1.26.1955 Glasgow KY BL/TR/5-10/160* [TexA72 4/76] d4.30 b-Denny

YEAR	TM LG	G	AB	R	H	2B	3B	HR	RBI	BB-IB	HP	SO	AVG	OBP	SLG	AOPS	ABR	SB-CS	FA	FR	RNG	THR	GAMES AT POSITION	DL	BFW
1978	†NY A	39	52	6	10	0	0	0	0	0-0	0	3	.192	.192	.192	9	-7	0-3	.989	4	109	131	2b29,S7,3b5		-0.2
1979	NY A	20	32	2	4	2	0	0	5	3-0	0	1	.125	.200	.188	5	-4	0-0	.944	-2	116	107	2b13,3b6		-0.6
1980	NY A	34	75	8	13	1	0	1	5	6-0	0	7	.173	.235	.227	27	-8	1-1	.953	0	93	59	2b20,S12,3b2		-0.6
1981	Oak A	17	40	2	5	0	0	0	3	1-0	0	2	.125	.146	.125	-22	-6	0-1	1.000	-3	86	65	2b17	17	-1.0
Total	4	110	199	18	32	3	0	1	13	10-0	0	13	.161	.201	.191	10	-25	1-5	.977	-1	99	91	2b79,S19,3b13	17	-2.4

DOYLE, CONNY Cornelius J. B1862 , Ireland D7.29.1921 El Paso TX 5-10/185 d6.23

YEAR	TM LG	G	AB	R	H	2B	3B	HR	RBI	BB-IB	HP	SO	AVG	OBP	SLG	AOPS	ABR	SB-CS	FA	FR	RNG	THR	GAMES AT POSITION	DL	BFW
1883	Phi N	16	68	3	15	3	2	0	3	0		15	.221	.221	.324	69	-3		.788	-1	85	0	O16L		-0.4
1884	Pit AA	15	58	8	17	3	2	0		2	0		.293	.317	.414	138	2		.818	-1	41	0	O14L/S		0.1
Total	2	31	126	11	32	6	4	0	3	2	0	15	.254	.266	.365	101	-1		.800	-2	65	0	O30L/S		-0.3

DOYLE, DANNY Howard James B1.24.1917 McLoud OK D12.14.2004 Stillwater OK BB/TR/6-1/195 d9.14 Mil 1944-45 Col Oklahoma St.

YEAR	TM LG	G	AB	R	H	2B	3B	HR	RBI	BB-IB	HP	SO	AVG	OBP	SLG	AOPS	ABR	SB-CS	FA	FR	RNG	THR	GAMES AT POSITION	DL	BFW
1943	Bos A	13	43	2	9	1	0	0	6	7	0	9	.209	.320	.233	62	-2	0-1	.964	-2	87	91	C13		-0.4

DOYLE, JACOB Jacob Dixon B11.26.1855 Leesburg VA D8.15.1941 Waukegan IL d4.20

YEAR	TM LG	G	AB	R	H	2B	3B	HR	RBI	BB-IB	HP	SO	AVG	OBP	SLG	AOPS	ABR	SB-CS	FA	FR	RNG	THR	GAMES AT POSITION	DL	BFW
1872	Nat NA	9	41	6	11	1	0	0	9	0			.268	.268	.293	62	-2	0-0	.667	-4	86	0	S8/2		-0.5

DOYLE, JIM James Francis B12.25.1881 Detroit MI D2.1.1912 Syracuse NY BR/TR/5-10/168 d5.4 Col Niagara

YEAR	TM LG	G	AB	R	H	2B	3B	HR	RBI	BB-IB	HP	SO	AVG	OBP	SLG	AOPS	ABR	SB-CS	FA	FR	RNG	THR	GAMES AT POSITION	DL	BFW
1910	Cin N	7	13	1	2	2	0	0			0	2	.154	.154	.308	36	-1	0	.875	-1	44	0	3b3/OC		-0.2
1911	Chi N	130	472	69	133	23	12	5	62	40		54	.282	.340	.413	110	5	19	.922	8	116	145	3b127		1.6
Total	2	137	485	70	135	25	12	5	63	40	2	56	.278	.336	.410	109	4	19	.921	7	115	142	3b130/OC		1.4

DOYLE, JEFF Jeffrey Donald B10.2.1956 Havre MT BB/TR/5-9/160 [StLN77 6/136] d9.13 Col Oregon St.

YEAR	TM LG	G	AB	R	H	2B	3B	HR	RBI	BB-IB	HP	SO	AVG	OBP	SLG	AOPS	ABR	SB-CS	FA	FR	RNG	THR	GAMES AT POSITION	DL	BFW
1983	StL N	13	37	4	11	1	2	0	2	1-1	0	3	.297	.316	.432	105	0	0-0	.966	-0	91	164	2b12		0.0

DOYLE, JACK John Joseph "Dirty Jack" B10.25.1869 Killorglin, Ireland D12.31.1958 Holyoke MA BR/TR/5-9/155 d8.27 M2/U1 Col Fordham OF(13/45/76)

YEAR	TM LG	G	AB	R	H	2B	3B	HR	RBI	BB-IB	HP	SO	AVG	OBP	SLG	AOPS	ABR	SB-CS	FA	FR	RNG	THR	GAMES AT POSITION	DL	BFW
																							C7,O3R,2b2		0.0
1889	Col AA	11	36	6	10	1	1	0	3	6	0	6	.278	.381	.361	118	1	9	.897	-2			C38,S25,O9(2/6/1),2b6,3b3		0.1
1890	Col AA	77	298	47	80	17	7	2	44	13	0		.268	.299	.393	111	2	27	.887	-4	105	97	C29,O21(4/8/10),3b20/S		-0.1
1891	Cle N	69	250	43	69	14	4	0	43	26	3	44	.276	.351	.364	104	2	24	.875	-5	92	113	O12(1/0/11),C9/1S		0.2
1892	Cle N	24	88	17	26	4	1	1	14	6	0	10	.295	.340	.398	118	2	5	.875	0	145	261	O12(1/0/10,7),C9/1S		-0.6
	NY N	90	366	61	109	22	1	5	55	18	3	30	.298	.336	.404	126	10	42	.864	-20	91	62	2b31,C26,O17(0/10/7),3b13,S7		-0.4
	Year	114	454	78	135	26	2	6	69	24	3	40	.297	.337	.403	124	12	47	.890	-20	86	150	C35,2b31,O29(1/10/18),3b13,S8/1		0.6
1893	NY N	82	318	56	102	17	5	1	51	27	5	12	.321	.383	.415	111	5	40	.919	-1	98	130	C48,O29(0/21/8),S4,3b3/1		1.2
1894	†NY N	107	427	94	157	30	8	3	103	37	3	3	.368	.422	.496	121	16	44	.965	-1	106	90	1b101,C6		0.0
1895	NY N	82	319	52	100	21	3	1	66	24	2	13	.313	.365	.408	101	1	35	.968	-3	108	78	1b58,2b13,3b6,C4,M		0.0
1896	†Bal N	118	487	116	165	29	4	1	101	42	8	15	.339	.400	.421	115	13	73	.974	-12	64	126	1b118/2		1.6
1897	†Bal N	114	460	91	163	29	4	2	87	29	1		.354	.394	.448	122	15	62	.963	-1	96	93	1b114		-0.2
1898	Was N	43	177	26	54	2	2	2	26	7	1		.305	.335	.373	103	0	9	.860	-1	189	152	O38(6/0/32),1b24,S15,3b5/C2		-0.1
	NY N	82	297	42	84	15	3	1	43	12	3		.283	.317	.364	98	-2	14	.970	0	102	85	1b62,O38(6/0/32),S15,2b5,3b5,C2		-0.3
	Year	125	474	68	138	17	5	3	69	19	4		.291	.324	.367	100	-2	23	.970	0	102	105	1b62,O38(6/0/32),S15,2b5,3b5,C2		0.9
1899	NY N	119	452	56	135	16	7	3	77	33	4		.299	.352	.385	106	3	35	.976	6	129	102	1b114,C5		-0.5
1900	NY N	133	505	69	135	24	1	1	66	34	3		.267	.317	.325	81	-12	34	.971	7	130	112	1b133		-1.0
1901	Chi N	75	285	21	66	9	2	0	39	7	5		.232	.263	.277	59	-15	8	.973	7	145	87	1b75		0.9
1902	NY N	51	193	22	58	13	0	0	18	11	1		.301	.341	.368	120	5	12	.991	5	134	108	1b51		-1.7
	Was A	78	312	52	77	15	2	1	20	29	0		.247	.311	.317	74	-11	6	.929	-7	100	60	2b68,1b7,O4R,C2		1.7
1903	Bro N	139	524	84	164	27	6	0	91	54	5		.313	.383	.387	123	18	34	.981	2	103	107	1b139		0.2
1904	Bro N	8	22	2	5	1	0	0	2	6	1		.227	.414	.273	116	1	1	1.000	1	138	30	1b8		-0.3
	Phi N	66	236	20	52	10	3	1	22	19	1		.220	.281	.301	83	-5	4	.977	4	124	89	1b65/2		-0.1
	Year	74	258	22	57	11	3	1	24	25	2		.221	.295	.298	86	-4	5	.980	5	126	83	1b73/2		-0.2
1905	NY A	1	3	0	0	0	0	0	0	0	0		.000	.000	.000	-90	-1	0	.833	-1	0	0	/1		0.0
Total	17	1569	6055	977	1811	316	64	25	971	440	49	132	.299	.351	.385	106	48	518	.975	-18	113	104	1b1048,C176,O133R,2b127,S53,3b50		2.7

DOYLE, LARRY Lawrence Joseph "Laughing Larry" B7.31.1886 Caseyville IL D3.1.1974 Saranac Lake NY BL/TR/5-10/165 d7.22

YEAR	TM LG	G	AB	R	H	2B	3B	HR	RBI	BB-IB	HP	SO	AVG	OBP	SLG	AOPS	ABR	SB-CS	FA	FR	RNG	THR	GAMES AT POSITION	DL	BFW
1907	NY N	69	227	16	59	3	0	0	16	20		0	.260	.320	.273	83	-4	3	.917	-21	81	32	2b69		-2.9
1908	NY N	104	377	65	116	16	9	0	33	22		5	.308	.354	.398	134	13	17	.935	-8	96	108	2b102		0.7
1909	NY N	147	570	86	172	27	11	6	49	45		7	.302	.360	.419	140	25	31	.940	-17	84	116	2b144		1.0
1910	NY N	151	575	97	164	21	14	8	69	71		5	.285	.369	.412	128	20	39	.930	-18	91	100	2b151		0.3
1911	†NY N	143	526	102	163	25	25	13	77	71		5	.310	.397	.527	153	35	38	.944	-21	85	88	2b141		1.6
1912	NY N	143	558	98	184	33	8	10	90	56		2	.330	.393	.471	132	25	36	.948	-3	93	131	2b143		2.3
1913	†NY N	132	482	67	135	25	6	5	73	59		5	.280	.364	.388	114	11	38-14	.955	-14	87	118	2b130		0.2
1914	NY N	145	539	87	140	19	8	5	63	58	10	25	.260	.343	.353	111	8	17	.959	-17	89	119	2b145		-0.7
1915	NY N	150	591	86	189	40	10	4	70	32	3	28	.320	.358	.442	150	34	22-18	.947	-9	94	112	2b147		2.8
1916	NY N	113	441	55	118	24	10	2	47	27	4	23	.268	.316	.381	120	9	17	.960	14	103	123	2b113		2.8
	Chi N	9	38	6	15	5	1	1	7	1	0	1	.395	.410	.658	203	4	2	.982	4	122	265	2b9		0.9
	Year	122	479	61	133	29	11	3	54	28	4	24	.278	.323	.403	127	14	19	.962	18	104	134	2b122		3.7
1917	Chi N	135	476	48	121	19	5	6	61	48	0	28	.254	.323	.353	99	0	5	.952	2	94	96	2b128		0.5
1918	NY N	75	257	38	67	7	4	3	36	37	0	10	.261	.354	.354	118	7	10	.969	-7	101	90	2b73		0.1
1919	NY N	113	381	61	110	14	10	7	52	31	5	17	.289	.350	.433	136	16	12	.956	7	106	130	2b100		2.7
1920	NY N	137	441	34	124	21	2	4	50	47	2	28	.285	.352	.363	107	6	11-9	.949	-23	91	106	2b133		-1.7
Total	14	1766	6509	960	1887	299	123	74	793	625	53	274	.290	.357	.408	126	209	298-41	.945	-133	92	109	2b1728		10.6

DOYLE, DENNY Robert Dennis B1.17.1944 Glasgow KY BL/TR/5-9/174* d4.7 b-Brian Col Morehead St.

YEAR	TM LG	G	AB	R	H	2B	3B	HR	RBI	BB-IB	HP	SO	AVG	OBP	SLG	AOPS	ABR	SB-CS	FA	FR	RNG	THR	GAMES AT POSITION	DL	BFW
1970	Phi N	112	413	43	86	10	7	6	16	33-3	0	64	.208	.266	.281	48	-32	6-5	.978	-17	83	83	2b103		-4.4
1971	Phi N	95	342	34	79	12	1	3	24	19-0	5	31	.231	.280	.298	64	-16	4-2	.967	8	106	106	2b91	15	-0.2
1972	Phi N	123	442	33	110	14	2	1	26	31-2	0	33	.249	.295	.296	68	-19	6-7	.982	-11	92	90	2b119		-2.5
1973	Phi N	116	370	45	101	9	3	3	26	31-8	0	32	.273	.327	.338	83	-9	1-3	.974	3	103	100	2b114		0.0
1974	Cal A	147	511	47	133	19	2	1	34	25-2	1	49	.260	.295	.311	79	-15	6-7	.983	18	105	91	2b146,S2		1.1
1975	Cal A	8	15	0	1	0	0	0	0	0-0	0	1	.067	.125	.067	-48	-3	0-0	.926	1	112	70	2b6/3		-0.2
	†Bos A	89	310	50	96	21	2	4	36	14-0	1	11	.310	.339	.429	108	3	5-7	.974	-22	90	70	2b84,3b6,S2		-1.6
	Year	97	325	50	97	21	2	4	36	15-0	1	12	.298	.329	.412	102	0	5-7	.970	-21	91	70	2b90,3b7,S2		-1.8
1976	Bos A	117	432	51	108	15	5	0	26	22-0	0	39	.250	.285	.308	66	-19	8-5	.977	-13	97	100	2b112		-2.7
1977	Bos A	137	455	54	109	13	6	2	44	29-3	4	50	.240	.289	.308	57	-27	2-4	.979	-7	100	110	2b137	15	-2.8
Total	8	944	3290	357	823	113	28	16	237	205-18	11	310	.250	.295	.316	70	-137	38-40	.977	-40	97	95	2b912,3b7,S4	15	-13.3

DOZIER, D. J. William Henry B9.21.1965 Norfolk VA BR/TR/6-0/202 d5.6 Col Penn St.

YEAR	TM LG	G	AB	R	H	2B	3B	HR	RBI	BB-IB	HP	SO	AVG	OBP	SLG	AOPS	ABR	SB-CS	FA	FR	RNG	THR	GAMES AT POSITION	DL	BFW
1992	NY N	25	47	4	9	2	0	0	2	4-0	1	19	.191	.264	.234	44	-3	4-0	.971	1	122	0	O17L		-0.3

DRAKE, DELOS Delos Daniel B12.3.1886 Girard OH D10.3.1965 Findlay OH BR/TL/5-11.5/170 d4.30

YEAR	TM LG	G	AB	R	H	2B	3B	HR	RBI	BB-IB	HP	SO	AVG	OBP	SLG	AOPS	ABR	SB-CS	FA	FR	RNG	THR	GAMES AT POSITION	DL	BFW
1911	Det A	95	315	37	88	9	9	1	36	17	4		.279	.324	.375	90	-6	20	.942	-6	102	33	O83(74/5/5),1b2		-1.5
1914	StL F	138	514	51	129	18	8	3	42	31		57	.251	.295	.335	68	-32	17	.957	-0	103	98	O116(69/36/11),1b18		-4.1
1915	StL F	102	343	32	91	23	4	1	41	23		27	.265	.313	.364	86	-11	6	.974	-1	103	83	O97(7/62/33)/1		-1.9
Total	3	335	1172	120	308	50	21	5	119	71	6	84	.263	.308	.354	79	-49	43	.959	-7	103	76	O296(150/103/49),1b21		-7.5

DRAKE, LARRY Larry Francis B5.4.1921 McKinney TX D7.14.1985 Houston TX BL/TR/6-1.5/195 d7.20 Col Baylor

YEAR	TM LG	G	AB	R	H	2B	3B	HR	RBI	BB-IB	HP	SO	AVG	OBP	SLG	AOPS	ABR	SB-CS	FA	FR	RNG	THR	GAMES AT POSITION	DL	BFW
1945	Phi A	1	2	0	0	0	0	0	0	2		0	.000	.000	.000	-99	-1	0-0	1.000	0	116	0	/OL		-0.1
1948	Was A	4	7	0	2	0	0	0	1	1		5	.286	.375	.286	79	0	0-0	1.000	-0	95	0	O2R		0.0
Total	2	5	9	0	2	0	0	0	1	3		5	.222	.300	.222	44	-1	0-0	1.000	-0	102	0	O3(1/0/2)		-0.1

DRAKE, LYMAN Lyman Daniel B2.9.1852 Berea OH D2.6.1932 Muskegon MI 6-0/? d6.29

YEAR	TM LG	G	AB	R	H	2B	3B	HR	RBI	BB-IB	HP	SO	AVG	OBP	SLG	AOPS	ABR	SB-CS	FA	FR	RNG	THR	GAMES AT POSITION	DL	BFW
1884	Was AA	2	7	0	2	1	0	0	2	0			.286	.286	.429	147	-1	0	.000	-1	0	0	O2R		0.0

DRAKE, SAMMY Samuel Harrison B10.7.1934 Little Rock AR BB/TR/5-11/175* d4.17 b-Solly Col Philander Smith

YEAR	TM LG	G	AB	R	H	2B	3B	HR	RBI	BB-IB	HP	SO	AVG	OBP	SLG	AOPS	ABR	SB-CS	FA	FR	RNG	THR	GAMES AT POSITION	DL	BFW
1960	Chi N	15	15	5	1	0	0	0	0	1-0	0	4	.067	.125	.067	-46	-3	0-0	1.000	-2	58	0	3b6,2b2		-0.6
1961	Chi N	13	5	1	0	0	0	0	0	1-0	0	1	.000	.167	.000	-50	-1	0-0	1.000	-0	79	0	/OR		-0.1

YEAR	TM LG	G	AB	R	H	2B	3B	HR	RBI	BB-IB	HP	SO	AVG	OBP	SLG	AOPS	ABR	SB-CS	FA	FR	RNG	THR	GAMES AT POSITION	DL	BFW
1962	NY N	25	52	2	10	0	0	0	7	6-1	0	12	.192	.276	.192	28	-5	0-0	.977	-3	100	111	2b10,3b6		-0.7
Total	3	53	72	8	11	0	0	0	7	8-1	0	17	.153	.237	.153	8	-9	0-0	.978	-5	89	94	2b12,3b12/OR		-1.4

DRAKE, SOLLY Solomon Louis B10.23.1930 Little Rock AR BB/TR/6-0/170* d4.17 b-Sammy Col Philander Smith [DL 1955 Chi N 109]

YEAR	TM LG	G	AB	R	H	2B	3B	HR	RBI	BB-IB	HP	SO	AVG	OBP	SLG	AOPS	ABR	SB-CS	FA	FR	RNG	THR	GAMES AT POSITION	DL	BFW
1956	Chi N	65	215	29	55	9	1	2	15	23-0	1	35	.256	.331	.335	81	-5	9-5	.993	0	103	78	O53C		-0.7
1959	LA N	9	8	2	2	0	0	0	0	1-0	0	3	.250	.333	.250	54	0	1-0	.667	-0	82	0	O4R		-0.1
	Phi N	67	62	10	9	1	0	0	3	8-0	0	15	.145	.243	.161	10	-8	5-5	1.000	1	133	0	O37(22/11/9)		-0.8
	Year	76	70	12	11	1	0	0	3	9-0	0	18	.157	.253	.171	15	-8	6-5	.974	1	128	0	O41(22/11/13)		-0.9
Total	2	141	285	41	66	10	1	2	18	32-0	1	53	.232	.311	.295	64	-13	15-10	.989	1	108	62	O94(22/64/13)	109	-1.6

DRANSFELDT, KELLY Kelly Daniel B4.16.1975 Joliet IL BR/TR/6-2/195* [TexA96 4/113] d5.1 Col Michigan

YEAR	TM LG	G	AB	R	H	2B	3B	HR	RBI	BB-IB	HP	SO	AVG	OBP	SLG	AOPS	ABR	SB-CS	FA	FR	RNG	THR	GAMES AT POSITION	DL	BFW
1999	Tex A	16	53	3	10	1	0	1	5	3-0	0	12	.189	.232	.264	25	-6	0-0	.966	4	118	118	S16		-0.1
2000	Tex A	16	26	2	3	2	0	0	2	1-0	0	14	.115	.148	.192	-14	-5	0-0	1.000	3	125	143	S14,2b2		-0.1
2001	Tex A	4	3	0	0	0	0	0	0	0-0	0	0	.000	.000	.000	-97	-1	0-0	1.000	0	176	0	S3/3		-0.1
2004	Chi A	15	30	5	10	0	0	0	4	0-0	0	6	.333	.333	.333	72	-1	0-0	.947	6	106	35	S8,3b3/D		-0.1
Total	4	51	112	10	23	3	0	1	11	4-0	0	32	.205	.233	.259	25	-13	0-0	.974	6	120	108	S41,3b4,2b2/D		-0.5

DRAUBY, JAKE Jacob C. B1865 Harrisburg PA 5-10/163 d10.3

YEAR	TM LG	G	AB	R	H	2B	3B	HR	RBI	BB-IB	HP	SO	AVG	OBP	SLG	AOPS	ABR	SB-CS	FA	FR	RNG	THR	GAMES AT POSITION	DL	BFW
1892	Was N	10	34	3	7	0	1	0	3		0	12	.206	.250	.265	57	-2	0	.763	-2	88	135	3b10		-0.3

DREESEN, BILL William Richard B7.26.1904 New York NY D11.9.1971 Mt.Vernon NY BL/TR/5-7.5/160 d5.1

YEAR	TM LG	G	AB	R	H	2B	3B	HR	RBI	BB-IB	HP	SO	AVG	OBP	SLG	AOPS	ABR	SB-CS	FA	FR	RNG	THR	GAMES AT POSITION	DL	BFW
1931	Bos N	48	180	38	40	10	4	1	10	23	0	23	.222	.310	.339	77	-6	1	.910	-4	102	14	3b47		-0.9

DRESCHER, BILL William Clayton "Dutch" B5.23.1921 Congers NY D5.15.1968 Haverstraw NY BL/TR/6-2/190 d4.19

YEAR	TM LG	G	AB	R	H	2B	3B	HR	RBI	BB-IB	HP	SO	AVG	OBP	SLG	AOPS	ABR	SB-CS	FA	FR	RNG	THR	GAMES AT POSITION	DL	BFW
1944	NY A	4	7	0	1	0	0	0	0	0-0	0	0	.143	.143	.143	-18	-1	0-0	.875	-0	0	0	/C		-0.1
1945	NY A	48	126	10	34	3	1	0	15	8	0	5	.270	.313	.310	77	-4	0-2	.991	-6	68	93	C33		-0.9
1946	NY A	5	6	0	2	1	0	0	1	0	0	1	.333	.333	.500	129	0	0-0	1.000	1	0	0	C3		0.1
Total	3	57	139	10	37	4	1	0	16	8	0	5	.266	.306	.309	75	-5	0-2	.985	-5	63	86	C37		-0.9

DRESSEN, CHUCK Charles Walter B9.20.1898 Decatur IL D8.10.1966 Detroit MI BR/TR/5-5.5/146 d4.17 M16/C12

YEAR	TM LG	G	AB	R	H	2B	3B	HR	RBI	BB-IB	HP	SO	AVG	OBP	SLG	AOPS	ABR	SB-CS	FA	FR	RNG	THR	GAMES AT POSITION	DL	BFW
1925	Cin N	76	215	35	59	8	2	3	.19	12	2	4	.274	.319	.372	78	-8	5-3	.951	4	118	115	3b47,2b5,O4(3/0/1)		-0.1
1926	Cin N	127	474	76	126	27	11	4	48	49	3	31	.266	.338	.395	99	-1	0	.966	16	**122**	101	3b123/SOL		2.2
1927	Cin N	144	548	78	160	36	10	3	55	71	3	32	.292	.376	.405	113	13	7	**.967**	12	116	96	3b142,S2		3.3
1928	Cin N	135	498	72	145	26	3	1	59	43	6	22	.291	.355	.361	89	-7	10	.938	-2	103	110	3b135		0.0
1929	Cin N	110	401	49	98	22	3	1	36	41	4	21	.244	.321	.322	63	-23	8	.932	-13	89	70	3b98,2b8		-2.7
1930	Cin N	33	19	0	4	0	0	0	1	1	0	1	.211	.250	.211	14	-3	0	1.000	1	197	0	3b10,2b3		-0.1
1931	Cin N	5	15	0	1	0	0	0	0	1	0	1	.067	.125	.067	-50	-3	0	.846	-0	99	144	3b4		-0.4
1933	NY N	16	45	3	10	4	0	0	3	1	0	4	.222	.239	.311	57	-3	0	.972	-0	87	129	3b16		-0.3
Total	8	646	2215	313	603	123	29	11	221	219	18	118	.272	.343	.369	89	-35	30-3	.953	18	109	98	3b575,2b16,O5(4/0/1),S3		1.9

DRESSEN, LEE Leo August B7.23.1889 Ellinwood KS D6.30.1931 Diller NE BL/TL/6-0/165 d4.21

YEAR	TM LG	G	AB	R	H	2B	3B	HR	RBI	BB-IB	HP	SO	AVG	OBP	SLG	AOPS	ABR	SB-CS	FA	FR	RNG	THR	GAMES AT POSITION	DL	BFW
1914	StL N	46	103	16	24	2	1	0	7	11	0	20	.233	.307	.272	73	-3	2	.982	-1	89	116	1b38		-0.5
1918	Det A	31	107	10	19	1	2	0	3	21	2	10	.178	.323	.224	68	-3	2	.988	-4	55	62	1b30		-0.8
Total	2	77	210	26	43	3	3	0	10	32	2	30	.205	.316	.248	71	-6	4	.985	-5	71	87	1b68		-1.3

DREW, CAMERON Cameron Steward B2.12.1964 Boston MA BL/TR/6-5/230 [HouN85 1/12] d9.9 Col New Haven

YEAR	TM LG	G	AB	R	H	2B	3B	HR	RBI	BB-IB	HP	SO	AVG	OBP	SLG	AOPS	ABR	SB-CS	FA	FR	RNG	THR	GAMES AT POSITION	DL	BFW
1988	Hou N	7	16	1	3	0	1	0	1	0-0	0	1	.188	.188	.313	43	-1	0-0	1.000	0	123	0	O5(3/0/2)		-0.1

DREW, DAVE David d5.14

YEAR	TM LG	G	AB	R	H	2B	3B	HR	RBI	BB-IB	HP	SO	AVG	OBP	SLG	AOPS	ABR	SB-CS	FA	FR	RNG	THR	GAMES AT POSITION	DL	BFW
1884	Phi U	2	9	1	4	0	0	0		0			.444	.444	.444	184	1		—	0	0	0	/P2S		0.0
	Was U	13	53	8	16	1	2	0		1			.302	.315	.396	118	-1		.806	1	91	0	S8,1b5/OC		0.0
	Year	15	62	9	20	1	2	0		1			.323	.333	.403	127	0		.813	1	88	0	S9,1b5/P2OC		0.0

DREW, J.D. David Jonathan B11.20.1975 Tallahassee FL BL/TR/6-1/195* [StLN98 1/5] d9.8 b-Tim Col Florida St.

YEAR	TM LG	G	AB	R	H	2B	3B	HR	RBI	BB-IB	HP	SO	AVG	OBP	SLG	AOPS	ABR	SB-CS	FA	FR	RNG	THR	GAMES AT POSITION	DL	BFW
1998	StL N	14	36	9	15	3	1	5	13	4-0	0	10	.417	.463	.972	270	9	0-0	1.000	1	111	168	O11(6/2/5)		0.9
1999	StL N	104	368	72	89	16	6	13	39	50-0	6	77	.242	.340	.424	91	-6	19-3	.972	2	101	174	O98(1/97/0)	32	0.1
2000	†StL N	135	407	73	120	17	2	18	57	67-4	6	99	.295	.401	.479	119	14	17-9	.966	2	108	85	O127(24/26/98)	18	1.1
2001	†StL N	109	375	80	121	18	5	27	73	57-4	6	75	.323	.414	.613	158	34	13-3	.973	-1	99	104	O107(1/20/97)	43	2.9
2002	StL N	135	424	61	107	19	1	18	56	57-4	8	104	.252	.349	.429	107	3	8-2	.987	-2	103	54	O120(0/6/119)	15	-0.3
2003	StL N	100	287	60	83	13	3	15	42	36-0	3	48	.289	.374	.512	130	12	2-2	.994	4	106	161	O75(1/26/53)	44	1.4
2004	†Atl N	145	518	118	158	28	8	31	93	118-2	5	116	.305	.436	.569	150	57	12-3	.990	5	105	132	O142(0/8/138)/D	91	4.8
2005	LA N	72	252	48	72	12	1	15	36	51-3	5	52	.286	.412	.520	143	18	1-1	.987	-2	98	76	O72(0/30/44)		1.4
Total	8	814	2667	521	765	126	27	142	409	440-17	37	579	.287	.393	.514	132	134	72-23	.981	9	103	111	O752(33/215/554)/D	243	12.3

DREWS, FRANK Frank John B5.25.1916 Buffalo NY D4.22.1972 Buffalo NY BR/TR/5-10/175 d8.13

YEAR	TM LG	G	AB	R	H	2B	3B	HR	RBI	BB-IB	HP	SO	AVG	OBP	SLG	AOPS	ABR	SB-CS	FA	FR	RNG	THR	GAMES AT POSITION	DL	BFW
1944	Bos N	46	141	14	29	9	1	0	10	25	1	14	.206	.329	.284	71	-4	0	.959	1	98	102	2b46		-0.1
1945	Bos N	49	147	13	30	4	1	0	19	16	0	18	.204	.282	.245	47	-10	0	.976	2	111	111	2b48		-0.6
Total	2	95	288	27	59	13	2	0	29	41	1	32	.205	.306	.264	59	-14	0	.967	3	104	106	2b94		-0.7

DRIESSEN, DAN Daniel B7.29.1951 Hilton Head Island SC BL/TR/5-11/190(187-200) d6.9

YEAR	TM LG	G	AB	R	H	2B	3B	HR	RBI	BB-IB	HP	SO	AVG	OBP	SLG	AOPS	ABR	SB-CS	FA	FR	RNG	THR	GAMES AT POSITION	DL	BFW
1973	†Cin N	102	366	49	110	15	2	4	47	24-4	2	37	.301	.346	.385	107	3	8-3	.946	-4	93	139	3b87,1b35/OR		-0.2
1974	Cin N	150	470	63	132	23	6	7	56	48-5	1	62	.281	.347	.400	111	7	10-5	.915	-15	86	101	3b126,1b47,O3R		-1.0
1975	†Cin N	88	210	38	59	8	1	7	38	35-2	2	30	.281	.386	.429	125	8	10-3	.986	-3	101	144	1b41,O29(10/0/19)	8	0.3
1976	†Cin N	98	219	32	54	11	1	7	44	43-2	0	32	.247	.362	.402	116	6	14-1	.997	-2	93	124	1b40,O20L		0.4
1977	Cin N	151	536	75	161	31	4	17	91	64-8	3	85	.300	.375	.468	123	19	31-13	.994	-3	86	106	1b148		0.9
1978	Cin N	153	524	68	131	23	3	16	70	75-7	4	79	.250	.345	.397	107	7	28-9	.996	1	98	79	1b151		0.2
1979	†Cin N	150	515	72	129	24	3	18	75	60-11	3	77	.250	.330	.414	103	2	11-5	.993	-5	85	102	1b151		1.2
1980	Cin N	154	524	81	139	36	1	14	74	**93-17**	6	68	.265	.377	.418	125	23	19-6	.995	-5	85	102	1b151		-1.1
1981	Cin N	82	233	35	55	14	0	7	33	40-3	2	31	.236	.349	.386	110	5	2-4	.995	-7	60	104	1b74		-0.8
1982	Cin N	149	516	64	139	25	1	17	57	82-8	2	62	.269	.368	.421	121	17	11-6	**.998**	-8	73	109	1b144		0.0
1983	Cin N	122	386	57	107	17	1	12	57	75-10	0	51	.277	.390	.420	121	15	6-4	.996	-4	84	82	1b112	20	0.4
1984	Cin N	81	218	27	61	13	0	7	28	37-2	0	25	.280	.378	.436	124	9	2-1	.991	-4	72	64	1b70		0.1
	Mon N	51	169	20	43	11	0	9	32	17-6	0	15	.254	.321	.479	128	6	0-1	.995	-3	75	117	1b45		0.0
	Year	132	387	47	104	24	0	16	60	54-8	0	40	.269	.354	.455	128	14	2-2	.992	-7	73	86	1b115		0.0
1985	Mon N	91	312	31	78	18	0	6	35	33-9	2	29	.250	.324	.365	98	0	2-2	.997	2	109	118	1b88		-0.4
	SF N	54	181	22	42	8	0	3	22	17-3	1	22	.232	.297	.326	79	-5	0-0	.998	-1	89	83	1b49		-0.9
	Year	145	493	53	120	26	0	9	47	50-12	3	51	.243	.314	.351	91	-5	2-2	.997	2	102	106	1b137		-1.3
1986	SF N	15	16	2	3	2	0	0	0	4-1	0	4	.188	.350	.313	88	0	0-0	1.000	0	143	0	1b4		0.0
	Hou N	17	24	5	7	1	0	1	3	5-1	0	2	.292	.414	.458	144	2	0-0	1.000	-1	60	106	1b12		0.1
	Year	32	40	7	10	3	0	1	3	9-2	0	6	.250	.388	.400	122	2	0-0	1.000	-0	84	76	1b16		0.1
1987	†StL N	24	60	5	14	2	0	1	11	7-1	0	6	.233	.309	.317	66	-3	0-0	.993	-0	95	104	1b21		-0.4
Total	15	1732	5479	746	1464	282	23	153	763	761-100	28	719	.267	.356	.411	114	121	154-63	.995	-59	87	101	1b1375,3b213,O53(30/0/23)	28	-1.2

DRILL, LEW Lewis L B5.9.1877 Browerville MN D7.4.1969 St.Paul MN BR/TR/5-6/186 d4.23 Col Georgetown

YEAR	TM LG	G	AB	R	H	2B	3B	HR	RBI	BB-IB	HP	SO	AVG	OBP	SLG	AOPS	ABR	SB-CS	FA	FR	RNG	THR	GAMES AT POSITION	DL	BFW
1902	Was A	38	123	21	34	7	2	1	16	16	2		.276	.369	.390	110	2	0	.919	-10	94	78	C28,2b4,O4(1/0/3)/3		-0.5
	Bal A	2	8	2	2	0	0	0	0	0			.250	.250	.250	0	0	0	1.000	0	93	272	/C1		0.0
	Was A	33	98	12	24	3	2	0	13	10			.245	.327	.316	78	-3	5	.926	-4	94	78	C25,O4R/2		-0.4
	Year	73	229	35	60	10	4	1	29	26	4		.262	.347	.354	94	-1	5	.924	-13	97	86	C54,O8(1/0/7),2b5/31		-0.9
1903	Was A	51	154	11	39	9	3	0	23	15	3		.253	.331	.351	103	1	4	.966	-7	90	78	C47,1b3		-0.1
1904	Was A	46	142	17	38	7	1	1	11	21	6		.268	.385	.366	140	8	3	.934	-6	73	102	C29,O14(0/3/11)		0.6
	Det A	51	160	7	39	6	1	1	13	20	2		.244	.335	.294	103	2	2	.950	-6	83	96	C49,1b2		0.0
	Year	97	302	24	77	13	3	1	24	41	8		.255	.359	.328	121	10	5	.944	-12	79	98	C78,O14(0/3/11),1b2		0.0
1905	Det A	72	211	17	55	9	0	2	24	32	3		.261	.366	.303	112	5	7	.970	-6	72	92	C71		0.7
Total	4	293	896	87	231	41	10	2	100	114	18		.255	.359	.328	108	14	21	.953	-39	80	92	C250,O22(1/3/18),1b6,2b5/3		0.3

DRISCOLL, DENNIS Dennis F. B10.10.1862 Providence RI D2.21.1901 Providence RI d7.25

YEAR	TM LG	G	AB	R	H	2B	3B	HR	RBI	BB-IB	HP	SO	AVG	OBP	SLG	AOPS	ABR	SB-CS	FA	FR	RNG	THR	GAMES AT POSITION	DL	BFW
1885	Buf N	7	19	2	3	0	0	0	0	2		5	.158	.238	.158	20	-1		.719	-4	70	41	2b7		-0.5

YEAR	TM LG	G	AB	R	H	2B	3B	HR	RBI	BB-IB	HP	SO	AVG	OBP	SLG	AOPS	ABR	SB-CS	FA	FR	RNG	THR	GAMES AT POSITION	DL	BFW

DRISCOLL, JIM James Bernard B5.14.1944 Medford MA BL/TR/5-11/175* d6.17

1970	Oak A	21	52	2	10	0	0	1	2	2-0	1	15	.192	.236	.250	35	-5	0-0	.967	-3	94	143	2b7,S7		-0.7
1972	Tex A	15	18	0	0	0	0	0	0	2-1	0	3	.000	.100	.000	-71	-4	0-0	.900	1	107	203	2b4,3b2		-0.3
Total	2	36	70	2	10	0	0	1	2	4-1	1	18	.143	.200	.186	9	-9	0-0	.950	-2	97	155	2b11,S7,3b2		-1.0

DRISCOLL, DENNY John F. B11.19.1855 Lowell MA D7.11.1886 Lowell MA BL/TL/5-10.5/160 d7.1 ▲

1880	Buf N	18	65	1	10	1	0	0	4	1		7	.154	.167	.169	14	-6		.895	0	96	466	O14C,P6		-0.4
1882	Pit AA	23	80	12	11	2	0	1		3			.138	.169	.200	25	-2		.885	-4	75	111	P23		0.0
1883	Pit AA	41	148	19	27	2	1	0		4			.182	.204	.209	35	-10		.890	5	146	97	P41,O4(0/2/2)/3		0.2
1884	Lou AA	13	48	5	9	1	0	0	1	2	0		.188	.220	.208	42	-3		.816	2	181	561	P13,O2(1/1/0)		0.1
Total	4	95	341	37	57	6	1	1	5	10	0	7	.167	.191	.199	30	-21		.872	3	127	165	P83,O20(1/17/2)/3		-0.1

DRISCOLL, PADDY John Leo B1.11.1895 Evanston IL D6.28.1968 Chicago IL BR/TR/5-8.5/155 d6.12 Mil 1918 Col Northwestern

| 1917 | Chi N | 13 | 28 | 2 | 3 | 1 | 0 | 0 | 3 | 3 | | 6 | .107 | .167 | .143 | -4 | 3 | 2 | .882 | 0 | 114 | 166 | 2b8,3b2/S | | -0.4 |

DRISSEL, MIKE Michael F. B12.19.1864 St.Louis MO D2.26.1913 St.Louis MO BR/TR/5-11/? d9.5

| 1885 | StL AA | 6 | 20 | 1 | 1 | 0 | 0 | 0 | | 0 | | | .050 | .050 | .050 | -65 | -4 | | .971 | 0 | | | C6 | | -0.3 |

DROPO, WALT Walter "Moose" B1.30.1923 Moosup CT BR/TR/6-5/220* d4.19 Col Connecticut

1949	Bos A	11	41	3	6	2	0	0	1	3	0	7	.146	.205	.195	6	-6	0-0	1.000	-1	54	118	1b11		-0.7
1950	Bos A★	136	559	101	180	28	8	34	144	45	5	75	.322	.378	.583	130	22	0-0	.988	-3	90	104	1b134		1.3
1951	Bos A	99	360	37	86	14	0	11	57	38	0	52	.239	.312	.369	76	-13	0-0	.987	-0	100	98	1b93		-1.6
1952	Bos A	37	132	13	35	7	1	6	27	11	2	22	.265	.331	.470	112	2	0-0	.994	-1	85	95	1b35		0.0
	Det A	115	459	56	128	17	3	23	70	26	2	63	.279	.320	.479	120	8	2-2	.989	1	99	95	1b115		0.5
	Year	152	591	69	163	24	4	29	97	37	4	85	.276	.323	.477	118	10	2-2	.990	-0	96	95	1b150		0.5
1953	Det A	152	606	61	150	30	3	13	96	29	6	69	.248	.289	.371	78	-21	2-0	.990	13	131	77	1b150		-1.7
1954	Det A	107	320	27	90	14	2	4	44	24	1	41	.281	.328	.375	95	-3	0-1	.996	2	104	88	1b95		-0.7
1955	Chi A	141	453	55	127	15	2	19	79	42-8	2	71	.280	.343	.448	109	4	0-1	.995	-5	79	103	1b140		-0.9
1956	Chi A	125	361	42	96	13	1	8	52	37-2	3	51	.266	.334	.374	87	-7	1-0	.993	-4	83	111	1b117		-1.6
1957	Chi A	93	223	24	57	2	0	13	49	16-2	0	40	.256	.300	.439	101	-1	0-1	.987	2	122	108	1b69		-0.3
1958	Chi A	28	52	3	10	1	0	2	8	5-0	1	11	.192	.271	.327	67	-3	0-0	1.000	0	104		1b43		-0.3
	Cin N	63	162	18	47	7	2	7	31	12-0	1	31	.290	.335	.488	111	2	0-0	1.000	2	112	97	1b46		0.2
1959	Cin N	26	39	4	4	1	0	1	2	4-0	1	7	.103	.205	.205	9	-5	0-0	1.000	0	141	120	1b23		-0.4
	Bal A	62	151	21	42	9	0	6	21	12-0	0	20	.278	.329	.457	117	3	0-0	.990	-3	73	134	1b54,3b2		-0.2
1960	Bal A	79	179	16	48	8	0	4	21	20-0	1	19	.268	.343	.380	97	0	0-1	.993	-2	84	122	1b67/3		-0.5
1961	Bal A	14	27	1	7	0	0	1	2	4-0	0	9	.259	.355	.370	97	0	0-0	1.000	0	104	174	1b12		0.0
Total	13	1288	4124	478	1113	168	22	152	704	328-12	24	582	.270	.326	.432	100	-18	5-6	.992	2	99	100	1b1174,3b3		-6.9

DRUMRIGHT, KEITH Keith Alan B10.21.1954 Springfield MO BL/TR/5-10/170* [ChiN76 4/79] d9.1 Col Oklahoma

1978	Hou N	17	55	5	9	0	0	2	3-0	0	4	.164	.207	.164	5	-7	0-1	.944	-2	94	102	2b17		-0.9
1981	†Oak A	31	86	8	25	1	1	0	11	4-0	0	4	.291	.319	.326	90	-1	0-1	.989	-4	88	61	2b19,D5	15	-0.4
Total	2	48	141	13	34	1	1	0	13	7-0	0	8	.241	.275	.262	57	-8	0-1	.969	-5	91	80	2b36,D5	15	-1.3

DUBOIS, JASON Jason Bradford B3.26.1979 Virginia Beach VA BR/TR/6-5/220* [ChiN00 14/403] d5.19 Col Virginia Commonwealth

2004	Chi N	20	23	2	5	0	1	1	5	1-0	0	7	.217	.240	.435	70	-1	0-0	1.000	0	111		O5(1/0/4)/1		-0.1
2005	Chi N	52	142	15	34	12	0	7	22	7-1	3	49	.239	.289	.472	92	-2	0-1	.980	-2	81	114	O38L,D3		-0.5
	Cle A	14	45	6	10	0	0	2	2	5-0	0	25	.222	.300	.356	76	-2	0-0	1.000	0	110	0	O7(3/0/4),D7		-0.2
Total	2	86	210	23	49	12	1	10	29	13-1	3	81	.233	.286	.443	87	-5	0-1	.986	-2	87	90	O50(42/0/8),D10/1		-0.8

DUCEY, ROB Robert Thomas B5.24.1965 Toronto ON, Can. BL/TR/6-2/180* d5.1 Col Seminole (FL) CC

1987	Tor A	34	48	12	9	1	0	6	8-0	0	10	.188	.298	.271	53	-3	2-0	1.000	-1	97	0	O28(17/11/3)/D		-0.4
1988	Tor A	27	54	15	17	4	1	0	6	5-0	0	7	.315	.361	.426	122	2	1-0	1.000	-3	70	116	O26(1/25/0)/D		-0.1
1989	Tor A	41	76	5	16	4	0	0	7	9-1	0	25	.211	.294	.263	59	-4	2-1	1.000	2	102	170	O35(16/2/18)/D		0.1
1990	Tor A	19	53	7	16	5	0	0	7	7-0	1	15	.302	.387	.396	119	2	1-1	1.000	-1	104	0	O19L		-0.4
1991	†Tor A	39	68	8	16	2	2	1	4	6-0	0	26	.235	.297	.368	80	-2	2-0	.892	-2	89	95	O24(18/1/6),D2		-0.6
1992	Tor A	23	21	3	1	1	0	0	0-0	0	10	.048	.048	.095	-58	-4	0-1	1.000	-1	85	0	O13(3/2/8),D4		-0.4
	Cal A	31	59	4	14	3	0	0	2	5-0	1	12	.237	.292	.288	64	-3	2-3	.957	-1	92	129	O33(20/3/10),D5		-1.0
	Year	54	80	7	15	4	0	0	2	5-0	1	22	.188	.233	.237	32	-7	2-4	.971	-1	91	65	O26(1/14/13)		0.1
1993	Tex A	27	85	15	24	4	0	3	9	10-2	0	17	.282	.351	.494	131	3	2-3	1.000	-1	91	65	O26(1/14/13)		0.1
1994	Tex A	11	29	1	5	1	0	0	1	2-0	0	1	.172	.226	.207	12	-4	0-0	.882	-1	87	0	O10R		-0.5
1997	†Sea A	76	143	25	41	15	2	5	10	6-0	0	31	.287	.311	.524	114	3	3-3	.986	-2	88	130	O69(43/12/19)	18	-0.2
1998	Sea A	97	217	30	52	18	2	5	23	23-2	9	61	.240	.336	.410	92	-2	4-3	.970	2	111	102	O83(23/6/61)	20	0.4
1999	Phi N	104	188	29	49	10	2	8	33	38-1	0	57	.261	.383	.463	112	4	2-1	1.000	1	110	41	O58(39/9/11),D2		-0.6
2000	Phi N	70	106	16	20	3	1	6	20	20-0	1	36	.189	.317	.406	81	-3	1-0	.919	-2	82	76	O26(24/1/1),D5		-0.1
	Tor A	5	13	2	2	1	0	0	1	0-0	0	6	.154	.267	.231	27	-1	0-0	.889	-7	135	0	O7(4/1/2)		-1.1
	Phi N	42	46	8	10	1	0	5	9-1	0	11	.217	.333	.239	52	-3	0-0	1.000	-7	82	76	O3(1/1/1)	15	0.0
2001	Phi N	30	27	4	6	1	0	1	4	6-0	1	11	.222	.364	.370	95	0	0-0	1.000	1	117	160	O14(9/3/3),D3	77	0.1
	Mon N	27	46	6	11	2	0	2	8	10-0	1	14	.239	.379	.413	108	1	0-1	1.000	1	120	136	O17(10/4/4),D3		0.1
	Year	57	73	10	17	3	0	3	12	16-0	2	25	.233	.374	.397	104	1	0-1	1.000	1					0.1
Total	13	703	1279	190	309	78	13	31	146	166-7	11	346	.242	.331	.396	91	-14	22-17	.976	-13	93	83	O464(237/89/159),D20	215	-4.1

DUDRA, JOHN John Joseph B5.27.1916 Assumption IL D10.24.1965 Pana IL BR/TR/5-11.5/175 d9.7 Mil 1942-45

| 1941 | Bos N | 14 | 25 | 3 | 9 | 3 | 1 | 0 | 3 | 3 | | 4 | .360 | .429 | .560 | 185 | 3 | 0 | .933 | 0 | 116 | 182 | 2b5,3b5/1S | | 0.3 |

DUFF, PAT Patrick Henry B5.6.1875 Providence RI D9.11.1925 Providence RI TR/5-10/? d4.16 Col Manhattan

| 1906 | Was A | 1 | 1 | 0 | 0 | 0 | 0 | 0 | 0 | | 0 | .000 | .000 | .000 | -99 | 0 | | — | 0 | | | /H | | 0.0 |

DUFFEE, CHARLIE Charlie Edward "Home Run" B1.27.1866 Mobile AL D12.24.1894 Mobile AL BR/TR/5-5.5/151 d4.17 OF(152/257/48)

1889	StL AA	137	509	93	124	15	11	16	86	60	3	81	.244	.327	.411	97	-7	21	.936	14	167	136	O132(1/132/0),3b5,2b2		0.3
1890	StL AA	98	378	68	104	11	7	3	54	37	3		.275	.344	.365	96	-5	24	.951	8	144	324	O66(1/65/0),3b33/S		0.1
1891	Col AA	137	552	86	166	28	4	10	90	42	3	36	.301	.353	.420	129	19	41	.927	6	138	142	O128(73/55/0),3b7,S2		1.8
1892	Was N	132	492	64	122	12	11	6	51	36	2	33	.248	.302	.354	101	-2	28	.913	18	168	176	O125(73/55/48),3b6,1b4		0.7
1893	Cin N	4	12	3	2	1	0	0	0	5		0	.167	.412	.250	76	0	0	.400	-2	0	0	O4L		-0.2
Total	5	508	1943	314	518	67	33	35	281	180	11	150	.267	.332	.389	106	5	110	.927	44	154	175	O455C,3b51,1b4,S3,2b2		2.7

DUFFY, CHRIS Christopher Ellis B4.20.1980 Brattleboro VT BL/TL/5-10/185 d4.7 Col Arizona St.

| 2005 | Pit N | 39 | 126 | 22 | 43 | 4 | 2 | 1 | 9 | 7-0 | 2 | 22 | .341 | .385 | .429 | 114 | 2 | 2-2 | .988 | 1 | 115 | 66 | O34(0/33/1) | 38 | 0.4 |

DUFFY, ED Edward Charles B1844 , Ireland D6.21.1889 Brooklyn NY TR/5-7.5/152 d5.8

| 1871 | Chi NA | 26 | 121 | 30 | 28 | 5 | 0 | 0 | 15 | 3 | | 2 | .231 | .250 | .273 | 45 | -10 | 11-4 | .750 | -4 | 95 | 95 | S26/3 | | -0.8 |

DUFFY, FRANK Frank Thomas B10.14.1946 Oakland CA BR/TR/6-1/180* [CinN67 S1/6] d9.4 Col Stanford

1970	Cin N	6	11	1	2	2	0	0	1	1-0	0	2	.182	.250	.364	62	-1	1-0	1.000	1	127	221	S5		0.1
1971	Cin N	13	16	0	3	1	0	0	1	1-0	0	3	.188	.235	.250	38	-1	0-0	.944	3	144	165	S10		0.1
	†SF N	21	28	4	5	0	0	0	2	0-0	0	10	.179	.179	.179	1	-4	0-0	.968	2	104	164	S6/23		0.2
	Year	34	44	4	8	1	0	0	3	1-0	0	12	.182	.200	.205	15	-5	0-0	.955	5	124	165	S16/23		0.2
1972	Cle A	130	385	23	92	16	4	3	27	31-5	1	54	.239	.297	.325	82	-9	6-2	.977	-3	98	106	S126	25	2.2
1973	Cle A	116	361	34	95	16	4	8	50	25-0	2	41	.263	.312	.396	97	-2	6-6	.986	16	106	109	S115		-1.1
1974	Cle A	158	549	62	128	18	0	8	48	30-0	1	64	.233	.272	.310	68	-24	7-8	.980	-8	102	90	S158		-2.1
1975	Cle A	146	482	44	117	22	2	1	47	27-0	2	60	.243	.283	.303	66	-22	10-10	.977	15	109	101	S145		-0.1
1976	Cle A	133	392	38	83	11	2	3	30	29-2	2	50	.212	.268	.265	57	-21	10-0	.983	5	91	114	S132		-2.3
1977	Cle A	122	334	30	67	13	2	4	31	21-0	0	47	.201	.247	.287	47	-25	8-3	.967	-10	96	99	S121		-2.5
1978	Bos A	64	104	12	27	5	0	0	4	6-0	1	11	.260	.306	.308	66	-5	1-1	.960	-2	86	64	3b22,S21,2b12,D6		-0.2
1979	Bos A	6	3	0	0	0	0	0		0	0	3	.000	.000	.000	-95	-1	0-0	1.000	0			2b3/1		-0.1
Total	10	915	2665	248	619	104	14	26	240	171-7	8	342	.232	.279	.311	68	-115	49-30	.977	17	101	104	S839,3b23,2b16,D6/1	25	-0.6

YEAR	TM LG	G	AB	R	H	2B	3B	HR	RBI	BB-IB	HP	SO	AVG	OBP	SLG	AOPS	ABR	SB-CS	FA	FR	RNG	THR	GAMES AT POSITION	DL	BFW

DUFFY, HUGH Hugh B11.26.1866 Cranston RI D10.19.1954 Boston MA BR/TR/5-7/168 d6.23 M8/C1 HF1945 OF(574/677/437)

1888	Chi N	71	298	60	84	10	4	7	41	9		32	.282	.305	.413	118	5	13	.910	3	162	210	O67(3/0/64),S3/3		0.7
1889	Chi N	**136**	584	144	182	21	7	12	89	46	2	30	.312	.364	.433	116	10	52	.894	-16	76	46	O126R,S10		-0.6
1890	Chi P	**138**	596	**161**	**191**	36	16	7	82	59	2	20	.320	.384	.470	122	17	78	.917	9	130	103	O137(0/17/120)		1.9
1891	Bos AA	127	536	134	180	20	8	9	**110**	61	4		.336	.408	.453	149	34	85	.917	-2	104	70	O124(7/2/118),3b3/S		2.7
1892	†Bos N	147	612	125	184	28	12	5	81	60	1	37	.301	.364	.410	123	15	51	.942	-10	75	93	O146C,3b2		-0.4
1893	Bos N	**131**	560	147	203	23	7	6	118	50	1	13	**.363**	.416	.461	123	17	44	.953	-5	67	138	O131(0/128/3)		0.3
1894	Bos N	125	539	160	**237**	**51**	16	**18**	145	66	1	15	**.440**	.502	.694	172	64	48	.927	-3	131	105	O124(4/121/0),S2		4.5
1895	Bos N	131	533	112	188	30	6	9	100	65	5	17	.353	.428	.482	125	21	42	.946	3	106	194	O131C		1.2
1896	Bos N	131	527	97	158	16	8	5	113	52	2	19	.300	.365	.389	93	-6	39	.957	-2	86	48	O120(114/6/0),2b9,S2		-1.6
1897	†Bos N	134	550	130	187	25	10	11	129	52	6		.340	.403	.482	125	19	41	.975	-2	64	62	O129L,2b6,S2		0.5
1898	Bos N	**152**	568	97	169	13	8	8	108	59	1		.298	.365	.373	106	4	29	.956	1	83	45	O152(115/39/0)/31C		-0.6
1899	Bos N	147	588	103	164	29	7	5	102	39	3		.279	.327	.378	85	-14	26	.970	-7	38	18	O147(138/8/1)		-3.1
1900	Bos N	55	181	27	55	5	4	2	31	16	0		.304	.360	.403	100	-1	11	.957	-1	74	118	O49(44/5/0)/2		-0.5
1901	Mil A	79	285	40	86	15	9	2	45	16	1		.302	.341	.439	121	7	12	.967	-4	54	0	O77(12/65/0),M		-0.1
1904	Phi N	18	46	10	13	1	1	0	5	13	0		.283	.441	.348	150	4	3	.850	-2	73	0	O14(8/6/0),M		0.2
1905	Phi N	15	40	7	12	2	1	0	3	1	0		.300	.317	.400	117	1	0	.909	-0	76	0	O8(0/3/5),M		0.0
1906	Phi N	1	1	0	0	0	0	0	0	0	0			.000	.000	.000	-99	0	0	—	0			/HM		0.0
Total	17	1738	7044	1554	2293	325	119	106	1302	664		30	212	.326	.386	.451	121	197	574	.943	-31	88	85	O1682C,S20,2b16,3b7/C1		5.1

DUGAN, JOE Joseph Anthony "Jumping Joe" B5.12.1897 Mahanoy City PA D7.7.1982 Norwood MA BR/TR/5-11/160 d7.5 Col Holy Cross

1917	Phi A	43	134	9	26	8	0	0	16	3	3	16	.194	.229	.254	48	-9	0	.917	1	108	76	S39,2b2		-0.6
1918	Phi A	121	411	26	80	11	3	0	34	16	3	55	.195	.230	.258	47	-29	4	.930	17	106	126	S86,2b34		-0.6
1919	Phi A	104	387	25	105	17	2	1	30	11	5	30	.271	.300	.333	77	-13	9	.929	1	99	96	S98,2b4,3b2		-0.5
1920	Phi A	123	491	65	158	40	5	3	60	19	3	51	.322	.351	.442	108	5	5-8	.948	3	94	129	3b60,S32,2b31		1.0
1921	Phi A	119	461	54	136	22	6	10	58	28	5	45	.295	.342	.434	96	-4	5-1	.953	-22	84	85	3b119		-1.7
1922	Bos A	84	341	45	98	22	3	3	38	9	1	28	.287	.308	.396	83	-10	2-3	.943	-7	102	101	3b64,S21		-1.2
	†NY A	60	252	44	72	9	1	3	25	13	4	21	.286	.331	.365	79	-8	1-0	.967	-8	89	96	3b60		-1.2
	Year	144	593	89	170	31	4	6	63	22	5	49	.287	.318	.383	81	-18	3-3	.954	-16	96	**99**	3b124,S21		-2.4
1923	†NY A	146	644	111	182	30	7	7	67	25	2	41	.283	.311	.384	81	-21	4-2	**.974**	-13	91	113	3b146		-2.4
1924	NY A	148	610	105	184	31	7	3	56	31	5	33	.302	.341	.390	88	-13	1-2	.962	-12	86	94	3b148,2b2		-1.5
1925	NY A	102	404	50	118	19	4	0	31	19	4	20	.292	.330	.359	76	-16	2-4	.970	6	102	101	3b96		-0.5
1926	†NY A	123	434	39	125	19	5	1	64	25	1	16	.288	.328	.362	81	-13	2-4	.955	-13	89	53	3b122		-2.0
1927	†NY A	112	387	44	104	24	3	2	43	27	3	37	.269	.321	.362	79	-13	1-4	.938	-18	91	78	3b111		-2.4
1928	†NY A	94	312	33	86	15	0	6	34	16	3	15	.276	.317	.381	85	-7	1-0	.952	-16	79	91	3b91/2		-1.7
1929	Bos N	60	125	14	38	10	0	0	15	8	0	9	.304	.346	.384	84	-3	0	.918	-7	81	96	3b24,S5,2b2,O2L		-0.7
1931	Det A	8	17	1	4	0	0	0	0	0	0	3	.235	.235	.235	23	-2	0-0	.900	-1	81	0	3b5		-0.2
Total	14	1447	5410	665	1516	277	46	42	571	250		42	419	.280	.317	.372	82	-155	37-28	.957	-88	90	92	3b1048,S281,2b76,O2L		-16.2

DUGAN, BILL William H. B1864 New York NY D7.24.1921 New York NY d8.5 b-Ed

1884	Ric AA	9	28	4	3	1	0	0		0			.107	.138	.143	-8	-3		.889	-3			C9		-0.5
	KC U	3	6	0	0	0	0	0		0			.000	.000	.000	-99	-2		.400	-1	0	0	O3(1/2/0)		-0.2
Total	1	12	34	4	3	1	0	0		0			.088	.114	.118	-26	-5		.889	-3			C9,O3(1/2/0)		-0.7

DUGAS, GUS Augustin Joseph B3.24.1907 St.Jean de Matha QC, Can. D4.14.1997 Colchester CT BL/TL/5-9/165 d9.17

1930	Pit N	9	31	8	9	2	0	0	1	7	0	4	.290	.421	.355	90	0	0	.864	-1	93	90	O9R		-0.1
1932	Pit N	55	97	13	23	3	3	3	12	7	0	11	.237	.288	.423	90	-2	0	.952	-1	110	0	O20(6/1/13)		-0.4
1933	Phi N	37	71	4	12	3	0	0	9	1	0	9	.169	.181	.211	10	-8	0	.984	0	111	70	1b11/OC		-1.0
1934	Was A	24	19	2	1	1	0	0	1	3	0	3	.053	.182	.105	-25	-4	0-0	1.000	0	124	0	O2(0/1/1)		-0.3
Total	4	125	218	27	45	9	3	3	23	18	0	27	.206	.267	.317	54	-14	0-0	.926	-1	105	29	O32(6/3/23),1b11		-1.8

DUGDALE, DAN Daniel Edward B10.28.1864 Peoria IL D3.9.1934 Seattle WA BR/5-8/180 d5.20

1886	KC N	12	40	4	7	0	0	0				13	.175	.214	.175	18	-4	1	.884	-2			C7,O6(0/1/5)		-0.5
1894	Was N	38	134	19	32	4	2	0	16	13		14	.239	.306	.299	48	-12	7	.874	-8	71	112	C33,3b3,O2L		-1.3
Total	2	50	174	23	39	4	2	0	16	13		27	.224	.286	.270	42	-16	8	.877	-10	71	112	C40,O8(2/1/5),3b3		-1.8

DUGEY, OSCAR Oscar Joseph "Jake" B10.25.1887 Palestine TX D1.1.1966 Dallas TX BR/TR/5-8/160 d9.13 C5

1913	Bos N	5	8	1	2	0	0	0					.333	.333	.250	67	0	0	.500	-1	67	0	3b2/2S		-0.1
1914	Bos N	58	109	17	21	2	0	1	10	10	1	15	.193	.267	.239	51	-7	10	.933	-2	96	77	O16R,2b16/3		-1.0
1915	†Phi N	42	39	4	6	1	0	0	7	9	5	5	.154	.283	.179	41	-2	2-1	.941	2	134	49	2b14		-0.1
1916	Phi N	41	50	5	9	3	0	0	1	9	0	8	.220	.339	.280	88	0	2	.967	2	113	75	2b12		0.2
1917	Phi N	44	72	12	14	4	1	0	9	4	0	9	.194	.237	.278	55	-4	2	.871	-1	84	43	2b15,O4(1/2/0)		-0.6
1920	Bos N	5	0	2	0	0	0	0	0	0			—	—	—	—	0	0-0		0			/R		0.0
Total	6	195	278	45	54	10	1	1	20	31		38	.194	.277	.248	58	-13	17-1	.915	-2	100	64	2b58,O20(1/2/16),3b3/S		-1.6

DUGGAN, JIM James Elmer "Mer" B6.1.1885 Whiteland IN D12.5.1951 Indianapolis IN BL/TL/5-10/165 d6.29 Col Franklin

1911	StL A	1	4	1	0	0	0	0					.000	.200	.000	-44	-1	0	1.000	0	125	324	/1		-0.1

DUNBAR, TOM Thomas Jerome B11.24.1959 Graniteville SC BL/TL/6-2/192* [TexA80*S1/25] d9.7 Col Middle Georgia JC

1983	Tex A	12	24	3	6	0	0	0	5-0		0	5	.250	.379	.250	78	0	3-1	.875	-2	51	0	O9(2/0/7)/D		-0.2
1984	Tex A	34	97	9	25	2	0	2	10	6-1	0	16	.258	.301	.340	74	-4	1-0	.939	-2	85	0	O20(9/0/11),D6		-0.7
1985	Tex A	45	104	7	21	4	0	1	5	12-3	1	11	.202	.291	.269	53	-6	0-3	.933	-3	57	0	D18,O14(12/0/3)	16	-1.1
Total	3	91	225	19	52	6	0	3	18	23-4	1	32	.231	.305	.298	65	-10	4-4	.929	-7	70	0	O43(23/0/21),D25	16	-2.0

DUNCAN, CHRIS Christopher Edward B5.5.1981 Tucson AZ BL/TR/6-5/210 d9.10 f-Dave

2005	StL N	9	10	2	2	1	0	1	3	0-0	0	5	.200	.200	.600	97	0	0-0	1.000	-0	0	0	1b2/OR		0.0

DUNCAN, DAVE David Edwin B9.26.1945 Dallas TX BR/TR/6-2/200* d5.6 C28 s-Chris

1964	KC A	25	53	2	9	0	1	1	5	2-0	0	20	.170	.200	.264	27	-6	0-0	.981	-2	35	162	C22		-0.8
1967	KC A	34	101	9	19	4	0	5	19	4-0	0	50	.188	.219	.376	75	-4	0-1	.979	-4	55	53	C32		-0.7
1968	Oak A	82	246	15	47	4	0	7	28	25-3	1	68	.191	.266	.293	73	-8	1-2	.987	-1	88	104	C79		-0.7
1969	Oak A	58	127	11	16	3	0	3	22	19-4	0	41	.126	.236	.220	31	-12	0-0	.982	-12	81	100	C56		-2.4
1970	Oak A	86	232	21	60	7	0	10	29	22-2	1	38	.259	.320	.418	106	1	0-0	.978	2	100	97	C73		0.6
1971	†Oak A☆	103	363	39	92	13	1	15	40	28-2	1	77	.253	.307	.419	106	1	1-1	.984	-2	88	67	C102		0.5
1972	†Oak A	121	403	39	88	13	0	19	59	34-5	1	68	.218	.283	.392	106	-4	0-2	.993	-4	97	90	C113		0.1
1973	Cle A	95	344	43	80	11	1	17	43	35-1	0	86	.233	.309	.419	101	0	3-3	.988	-6	70	84	C86,D9		-0.3
1974	Cle A	136	425	46	85	10	1	16	46	42-3	2	91	.200	.274	.341	77	-14	0-4	.976	-7	124	73	C134,1b3/D	47	-1.7
1975	Bal A	96	307	30	63	7	0	12	41	16-0	1	82	.205	.245	.345	70	-14	0-0	.982	-3	**152**	78	C95		-1.4
1976	Bal A	93	246	20	58	7	0	4	25	25-0	1	56	.236	.304	.271	62	-14	0-0	.985	-11	103	77	C93		-2.2
Total	11	929	2885	274	617	79	4	109	341	252-20	14	677	.214	.279	.357	85	-69	5-13	.984	-52	100	82	C885,D10,1b3	47	-9.1

DUNCAN, JIM James William B7.1.1871 Saltsburg PA D10.16.1901 Foxburg PA BR/TR/5-8/140 d7.18

1899	Was N	15	47	5	11	2	0	0	5	4			.234	.294	.277	57	-3	1	.940	-2	77	117	C14		-0.4
	Cle N	31	105	9	24	2	3	2	9	4			.229	.257	.362	74	-5	0	.971	-6	76	104	1b17,C14		-0.9
	Year	46	152	14	35	4	3	2	14	8			.230	.269	.336	69	-7	1	.904	-9	70	117	C28,1b17		-1.3

DUNCAN, JEFF Jeffrey Matthew B12.9.1978 Harvey IL BL/TL/6-2/180* [NYN00 7/215] d5.20 Col Arizona St.

2003	NY N	56	139	13	27	0	2	1	10	17-3	2	41	.194	.291	.245	44	-12	4-2	1.000	5	134	0	O52(1/52/0)		-0.7
2004	NY N	13	15	2	1	0	0	0	1	1-0	0	5	.067	.125	.067	-50	-3	3-0	1.000	0	120	0	O4(2/2/0)		-0.3
Total	2	69	154	15	28	0	2	1	11	18-3	2	46	.182	.276	.227	35	-15	7-2	1.000	5	133	0	O56(3/54/0)		-1.0

DUNCAN, PAT Louis Baird B10.6.1893 Coalton OH D7.17.1960 Columbus OH BR/TR/5-9/170 d7.16 Mil 1918-19

1915	Pit N	3	5	0	1	0	0	0	0	0			.200	.200	.200	22	0	0	1.000	-0	74	0	/OC		-0.1
1919	†Cin N	31	90	9	22	3	3	2	17	8	0	7	.244	.306	.411	118	2	2	.982	0	103	94	O27L		0.1
1920	Cin N	**154**	576	75	170	16	11	2	83	42	7	42	.295	.350	.372	109	7	18-18	.964	5	105	87	O154L		-0.1
1921	Cin N	145	532	57	164	27	10	2	60	44	5	33	.308	.367	.408	110	8	7-18	.971	5	106	101	O145(129/16/1)		-0.3
1922	Cin N	151	607	94	199	44	12	8	94	40	1	31	.328	.370	.479	132	17	12-28	.971	1	100	100	O151L		-0.1

YEAR	TM LG	G	AB	R	H	2B	3B	HR	RBI	BB-IB	HP	SO	AVG	OBP	SLG	AOPS	ABR	SB-CS	FA	FR	RNG	THR	GAMES AT POSITION	DL	BFW
1923	Cin N	147	566	92	185	26	8	7	83	30	2	27	.327	.363	.438	113	9	15-13	.993	-5	93	78	O146(144/3/0)		-0.8
1924	Cin N	96	319	34	86	21	6	2	37	20	0	23	.270	.313	.392	89	-5	1-7	.927	-10	83	41	O83(82/0/1)		-2.3
Total	7	727	2695	361	827	137	50	23	374	184	15	164	.307	.355	.420	110	38	55-84	.970	-6	100	86	O707(687/20/2)		-3.6

DUNCAN, MARIANO   Mariano (Nalasco)   B3.13.1963 San Pedro de Macoris, D.R.   BR/TR (BB 1985-87)/6-0/185(160-200)   d4.9   OF(88/2/6)

YEAR	TM LG	G	AB	R	H	2B	3B	HR	RBI	BB-IB	HP	SO	AVG	OBP	SLG	AOPS	ABR	SB-CS	FA	FR	RNG	THR	GAMES AT POSITION	DL	BFW
1985	†LA N	142	562	74	137	24	6	6	39	38-4	3	113	.244	.293	.340	79	-17	38-8	.954	-7	99	86	S123,2b19		-0.5
1986	LA N	109	407	47	93	7	0	8	30	30-1	2	78	.229	.284	.305	67	-20	48-13	.951	-1	98	75	S106	29	-0.4
1987	LA N	76	261	31	56	8	1	6	18	17-1	2	62	.215	.267	.322	57	-17	11-1	.930	5	104	102	S67,2b7,O2(1/0/1)	64	-0.4
1989	LA N	49	84	9	21	5	1	0	8	0-0	2	15	.250	.267	.333	72	-3	3-3	.943	0	107	161	S16,2b8,O7(4/0/4)	30	-0.3
	Cin N	45	174	23	43	10	1	3	13	8-0	3	36	.247	.292	.368	85	-4	6-2	.955	-6	87	80	S44,2b5		-0.6
	Year	94	258	32	64	15	2	3	21	8-0	5	51	.248	.284	.357	81	-7	9-5	.952	-5	91	96	S60,2b13,O7(4/0/4)		-0.9
1990	†Cin N	125	435	67	133	22	11	10	55	24-4	3	67	.306	.345	.476	119	10	13-7	.973	5	98	93	2b115,S12/OL		1.8
1991	Cin N	100	333	46	86	7	4	12	40	12-0	3	57	.258	.288	.411	91	-6	5-4	.974	-4	90	95	2b62,S32,O7(6/2/0)	15	-0.7
1992	Phi N	142	574	71	153	40	3	8	50	17-0	5	108	.267	.292	.389	92	-8	23-3	.976	-10	103	36	O65L,2b52,S42,3b4		-1.3
1993	†Phi N	124	496	68	140	26	4	11	73	12-0	4	88	.282	.304	.417	92	-7	6-5	.969	-18	95	76	2b65,S59	15	-1.9
1994	Phi N★	88	347	49	93	22	1	8	48	17-1	4	72	.268	.306	.406	83	-9	10-2	.972	-8	100	107	2b37,3b28,S19,1b6	15	0.3
1995	Phi N	52	196	20	56	12	1	3	23	0-0	1	43	.286	.285	.403	80	-6	1-2	.957	9	102	131	2b24,S14,1b12/3		-0.2
	†Cin N	29	69	16	20	7	1	3	13	5-0	0	19	.290	.329	.478	111	1	0-1	.963	-3	76	81	2b7,1b6,S6,O3L		0.1
	Year	81	265	36	76	14	2	6	36	5-0	1	62	.287	.297	.423	88	-6	1-3	.958	6	96	119	2b31,S20,1b18,O3L/3	18	1.1
1996	†NY A	109	400	62	136	34	3	8	56	9-1	0	77	.340	.352	.500	113	7	4-3	.975	1	93	93	2b104,3b3,O3(2/0/1),D2		1.1
1997	NY A	50	172	16	42	8	0	1	13	6-0	0	39	.244	.270	.308	51	-13	2-1	.976	1	106	93	2b41,O6L,D2		-1.0
	Tor A	39	167	20	38	6	0	0	12	6-0	3	39	.228	.267	.263	39	-15	4-2	.984	3	98	106	2b39		-1.9
	Year	89	339	36	80	14	0	1	25	12-0	3	78	.236	.268	.286	45	-28	6-3	.972	-34	99	94	2b80,O6L,D2		-2.9
Total	12	1279	4677	619	1247	233	37	87	491	201-12	37	913	.267	.300	.388	86	-107	174-57	.972	-34	99	94	2b585,S540,O94L,3b36,1b24,D4	186	-6.2

DUNCAN, TAYLOR   Taylor McDowell   B5.12.1953 Memphis TN   D1.3.2004 Asheville NC   BR/TR/6-0/170(165-180)   [AtlN71 1/10]   d9.15

YEAR	TM LG	G	AB	R	H	2B	3B	HR	RBI	BB-IB	HP	SO	AVG	OBP	SLG	AOPS	ABR	SB-CS	FA	FR	RNG	THR	GAMES AT POSITION	DL	BFW
1977	StL N	8	12	2	4	0	0	1	2	2-0	0	1	.333	.400	.583	170	1	0-0	1.000	-2	35	0	3b5		-0.1
1978	Oak A	104	319	25	82	15	2	2	37	19-0	0	38	.257	.296	.335	82	-8	1-2	.953	-11	83	28	3b84,2b11/SD		-2.2
Total	2	112	331	27	86	15	2	3	39	21-0	0	39	.260	.301	.344	86	-7	1-2	.953	-13	81	27	3b89,2b11,D7/S		-2.3

DUNCAN, VERN   Vernon Van Duke   B1.6.1890 Clayton NC   D6.1.1954 Daytona Beach FL   BL/TR/5-9/155   d9.11   Col North Carolina-Asheville

YEAR	TM LG	G	AB	R	H	2B	3B	HR	RBI	BB-IB	HP	SO	AVG	OBP	SLG	AOPS	ABR	SB-CS	FA	FR	RNG	THR	GAMES AT POSITION	DL	BFW
1913	Phi N	8	12	3	5	1	0	0	1	0	0	3	.417	.417	.500	155	1	0	1.000	0	61	418	O3(1/0/2)		0.1
1914	Bal F	157	557	99	160	20	8	2	53	67	11	55	.287	.375	.363	98	-7	13	.914	-6	93	99	O148(36/101/11),3b8/2		-2.3
1915	Bal F	146	531	68	142	18	4	2	43	54	2	40	.267	.337	.328	85	-17	19	.965	-4	103	113	O124(60/64/0),3b21/2		-3.0
Total	3	311	1100	170	307	39	12	4	97	121	13	98	.279	.357	.347	93	-23	32	.939	-9	97	108	O275(97/165/13),3b29,2b2		-5.2

DUNDON, GUS   Augustus Joseph   B7.10.1874 Columbus OH   D9.1.1940 Pittsburgh PA   BR/TR/5-10/165   d4.14

YEAR	TM LG	G	AB	R	H	2B	3B	HR	RBI	BB-IB	HP	SO	AVG	OBP	SLG	AOPS	ABR	SB-CS	FA	FR	RNG	THR	GAMES AT POSITION	DL	BFW
1904	Chi A	108	373	40	85	9	3	0	36	30	4		.228	.292	.268	81	-7	19	.973	-13	95	95	2b103,3b3,S2		-2.2
1905	Chi A	106	364	30	70	7	3	0	22	23	4		.192	.248	.228	53	-19	14	.983	4	106	95	2b100,S6		-1.6
1906	Chi A	33	96	7	13	1	0	0	4	11	0		.135	.224	.146	17	-9	4	.921	1	96	90	2b18,S14		-0.8
Total	3	247	833	77	168	17	6	0	62	64	8		.202	.265	.236	61	-35	37	.972	-5	99	95	2b221,S22,3b3		-4.6

DUNDON, ED   Edward Joseph "Dummy"   B7.10.1859 Columbus OH   D8.18.1893 Columbus OH   TR/6-0/170   d6.2 ▲

YEAR	TM LG	G	AB	R	H	2B	3B	HR	RBI	BB-IB	HP	SO	AVG	OBP	SLG	AOPS	ABR	SB-CS	FA	FR	RNG	THR	GAMES AT POSITION	DL	BFW
1883	Col AA	26	93	8	15	1	0	0		3			.161	.188	.172	18	-8		.804	1	104	299	P20,O9(6/2/1)/2		-0.1
1884	Col AA	26	86	6	12	2	2	0		5	1		.140	.196	.209	35	-6		.966	3	125	460	O16(14/1/1),P11,1b3		-0.2
Total	2	52	179	14	27	3	2	0		8	1		.151	.191	.190	26	-14		.857	4	106	309	P31,O25(20/3/2),1b3/2		-0.2

DUNGAN, SAM   Samuel Morrison   B7.29.1866 Ferndale CA   D3.16.1939 Santa Ana CA   BR/5-11/180   d4.12

YEAR	TM LG	G	AB	R	H	2B	3B	HR	RBI	BB-IB	HP	SO	AVG	OBP	SLG	AOPS	ABR	SB-CS	FA	FR	RNG	THR	GAMES AT POSITION	DL	BFW
1892	Chi N	113	433	46	123	19	7	0	53	35	6	19	.284	.346	.360	112	6	15	.905	-9	43	53	O113(37/0/76)		-0.9
1893	Chi N	107	465	86	138	23	7	2	64	29	9	8	.297	.350	.389	98	-2	11	.920	3	112	74	O107(1/0/106)		-0.4
1894	Chi N	10	39	5	9	2	0	0	3	7	0	1	.231	.348	.282	50	-3	1	1.000	1	140	267	O10R		0.0
	Lou N	8	32	6	11	1	0	0	3	4	0	1	.344	.417	.375	99	0	2	.941	-0	69	274	O8R		-0.2
	Year	18	71	11	20	3	0	0	6	11	0	2	.282	.378	.324	70	-3	3	.971	1	104	271	O18R		-0.2
1900	Chi N	6	15	1	4	0	0	0	1	1	0		.267	.313	.267	63	-1	0	.800	-1	-0	0	O3C		-0.2
1901	Was A	138	559	70	179	26	12	1	73	40	2	29	.320	.356	.386	107	14	38	.924	-9	89	94	O345(39/3/303),1b35		-1.2
Total	5	382	1543	214	464	71	26	3	197	116	17	29	.301	.356	.386	107	14	38	.924	-9	89	94	O345(39/3/303),1b35		-1.2

DUNHAM, LEE   Leland Huffield   B6.9.1902 Atlanta IL   D5.11.1961 Atlanta IL   BL/TL/5-11/185   d4.17   Col Illinois Wesleyan

YEAR	TM LG	G	AB	R	H	2B	3B	HR	RBI	BB-IB	HP	SO	AVG	OBP	SLG	AOPS	ABR	SB-CS	FA	FR	RNG	THR	GAMES AT POSITION	DL	BFW
1926	Phi N	5	4	0	1	0	0	0	0	1	0	1	.250	.250	.250	33	0	0	1.000	-0	0	0	1b2		0.0

DUNLAP, FRED   Frederick C. "Sure Shot"   B5.21.1859 Philadelphia PA   D12.1.1902 Philadelphia PA   BR/TR/5-8/165   d5.1   M4

YEAR	TM LG	G	AB	R	H	2B	3B	HR	RBI	BB-IB	HP	SO	AVG	OBP	SLG	AOPS	ABR	SB-CS	FA	FR	RNG	THR	GAMES AT POSITION	DL	BFW
1880	Cle N	85	373	61	103	27	9	4	30	7		32	.276	.289	.429	143	17		.911	7	103	134	2b85		2.6
1881	Cle N	80	351	60	114	25	4	3	24	18		24	.325	.358	.444	159	25		.909	7	101	111	2b79/3		3.2
1882	Cle N	84	364	68	102	19	4	0	28	23		26	.280	.323	.354	121	17		.900	18	112	165	2b84,M		2.8
1883	Cle N	93	396	81	129	34	2	4	37	22		21	.326	.361	.452	147	24		.911	7	95	126	2b93/OR		2.9
1884	StL U	101	449	160	185	39	8	13		29			.412	.448	.621	213	50		.926	30	111	214	2b100/ORPM		7.1
1885	StL N	106	423	70	114	11	5	2	25	41		24	.270	.334	.333	124	14		.934	27	113	119	2b106,M		4.1
1886	StL N	71	285	53	76	15	2	3	32	28		30	.267	.332	.365	119	8	7	.931	-14	105	133	2b71/OC		2.2
	Det N	51	196	32	56	8	3	4	37	16		21	.286	.340	.418	125	6	13	.918	4	107	119	2b51		1.0
	Year	122	481	85	132	23	5	7	69	44		51	.274	.335	.387	122	14	20	.926	17	106	127	2b122/OC		3.2
1887	†Det N	65	272	60	72	13	10	5	45	25	0	12	.265	.327	.441	107	2	15	.940	11	104	143	2b82		1.8
1888	Pit N	82	321	41	84	12	4	1	36	16	3	30	.262	.303	.333	112	5	24	.950	-4	98	95	2b121,M		-1.2
1889	Pit N	121	451	59	106	19	0	6	65	46	2	33	.235	.309	.290	75	-13	21	.873	-2	105	48	2b17		-0.5
1890	Pit N	17	64	9	11	1	1	0	3	7	1	6	.172	.264	.219	46	-4	2	1.000	-1	47	0	/2		0.0
	NY P	1	4	1	2	0	0	0	0	0	0	0	.500	.500	.500	154	0	0					2b8		-0.1
1891	Was AA	8	25	4	5	1	0	0	1	4	1	2	.200	.355	.320	90	0	3	.818	-2	98	93	2b8		-0.1
Total	12	965	3974	759	1159	224	53	41	366	283	7	263	.292	.340	.406	132	144	85	.924	137	105	136	2b963,O3(0/1/2),P2/3		28.1

DUNLAP, GRANT   Grant Lester "Snap"   B12.20.1923 Stockton CA   BR/TR/6-2/180   d4.21   Col Pacific (CA)

YEAR	TM LG	G	AB	R	H	2B	3B	HR	RBI	BB-IB	HP	SO	AVG	OBP	SLG	AOPS	ABR	SB-CS	FA	FR	RNG	THR	GAMES AT POSITION	DL	BFW
1953	StL N	16	17	2	6	1	1	0	3	0	0	2	.353	.353	.647	154	1	0-0	—	-0	0	0	/OR		0.1

DUNLAP, BILL   William James   B5.1.1909 Palmer MA   D11.29.1980 Reading PA   d9.2

YEAR	TM LG	G	AB	R	H	2B	3B	HR	RBI	BB-IB	HP	SO	AVG	OBP	SLG	AOPS	ABR	SB-CS	FA	FR	RNG	THR	GAMES AT POSITION	DL	BFW
1929	Bos N	10	29	6	12	0	1	1	4	4	0	4	.414	.485	.586	171	3	0	.889	-1	103	0	O9(8/0/1)		0.2
1930	Bos N	16	29	3	2	1	0	0	0	0	0	6	.069	.069	.103	-61	-8	0	1.000	0	129	0	O7(0/2/5)		-0.7
Total	2	26	58	9	14	1	1	1	4	4	0	10	.241	.290	.345	57	-5	0	.939	-0	113	0	O16(8/2/6)		-0.5

DUNLEAVY, JACK   John Francis   B9.14.1879 Harrison NJ   D4.11.1944 S.Norwalk CT   BL/TL/5-6/167   d5.30   Col Amherst ▲

YEAR	TM LG	G	AB	R	H	2B	3B	HR	RBI	BB-IB	HP	SO	AVG	OBP	SLG	AOPS	ABR	SB-CS	FA	FR	RNG	THR	GAMES AT POSITION	DL	BFW
1903	StL N	61	193	23	48	3	3	0	10	13		9	.249	.306	.295	74	-7	10	.972	5	200	349	O38(6/0/32),P14		-0.2
1904	StL N	51	172	23	40	7	3	1	14	16	2		.233	.305	.326	99	0	8	.987	2	120	145	O44(5/3/36),P7		0.0
1905	StL N	119	435	52	105	8	1	1	25	55	1		.241	.328	.303	91	-3	15	.962	7	165	184	O118(13/0/115)/2		-0.1
Total	3	231	800	98	193	18	14	2	49	84	6		.241	.318	.306	89	-10	33	.969	15	163	210	O200(24/3/183),P21/2		-0.3

DUNLOP, GEORGE   George Henry   B7.19.1888 Meriden CT   D12.12.1971 Meriden CT   BR/TR/5-10/170   d9.9

YEAR	TM LG	G	AB	R	H	2B	3B	HR	RBI	BB-IB	HP	SO	AVG	OBP	SLG	AOPS	ABR	SB-CS	FA	FR	RNG	THR	GAMES AT POSITION	DL	BFW
1913	Cle A	7	17	3	4	1	0	0	0	1	0	5	.235	.235	.294	53	-1	0	.923	1	83	0	S4,3b3		0.0
1914	Cle A	1	3	0	0	0	0	0	0	0	0	1	1.000	.250	.000	-23	-0	0	1.000	-0	49	0	/S		-0.1
Total	2	8	20	3	4	1	0	0	0	1	0	6	.200	.238	.250	42	-1	0	.929	-0	75	0	S5,3b3		-0.1

DUNN, ADAM   Adam Troy   B11.9.1979 Houston TX   BL/TR/6-6/240(240-275)   [CinN98 2/50]   d7.20

YEAR	TM LG	G	AB	R	H	2B	3B	HR	RBI	BB-IB	HP	SO	AVG	OBP	SLG	AOPS	ABR	SB-CS	FA	FR	RNG	THR	GAMES AT POSITION	DL	BFW
2001	Cin N	66	244	54	64	18	1	19	43	38-2	12	74	.262	.371	.578	132	12	4-2	.986	2	108	69	O63(30/0/38)		1.1
2002	Cin N★	158	535	84	133	28	2	26	71	128-13	9	170	.249	.400	.454	124	22	19-9	.959	-4	90	136	O118(112/0/17),1b44/D	44	1.0
2003	Cin N	116	381	70	82	12	1	27	57	74-8	10	126	.215	.354	.465	118	11	8-2	.955	3	110	80	O102(99/0/4),1b19,D2		3.0
2004	Cin N	161	568	105	151	34	0	46	102	108-11	5	195	.266	.388	.569	146	41	6-1	.970	-5	89	117	O156L,1b10/D		3.0
2005	Cin N	160	543	107	134	35	2	40	101	114-14	12	168	.247	.387	.540	145	40	4-2	.981	-2	104	82	O133L,1b33	44	9.2
Total	5	661	2271	420	564	127	6	158	374	462-48	40	733	.248	.383	.518	134	126	41-16	.969	-6	98	101	O572(530/0/59),1b106,D4	44	9.2

DUNN, JACK   John Joseph   B10.6.1872 Meadville PA   D10.22.1928 Towson MD   BR/TR/5-9/?   d5.6   OF(8/10/41) ▲

YEAR	TM LG	G	AB	R	H	2B	3B	HR	RBI	BB-IB	HP	SO	AVG	OBP	SLG	AOPS	ABR	SB-CS	FA	FR	RNG	THR	GAMES AT POSITION	DL	BFW
1897	Bro N	36	131	20	29	4	0	0	17	4	0		.221	.244	.252	33	-13	2	.911	-2	111	119	P25,2b4,O3L,3b3/S		-0.4
1898	Bro N	51	167	21	41	0	1	0	19	7	1		.246	.280	.257	54	-10	3	.939	-1	88	75	P41,O4(1/2/1),S4,3b2		-0.3

YEAR	TM LG	G	AB	R	H	2B	3B	HR	RBI	BB-IB	HP	SO	AVG	OBP	SLG	AOPS	ABR	SB-CS	FA	FR	RNG	THR	GAMES AT POSITION	DL	BFW
1899	Bro N	43	122	21	30	2	1	0	16	3	1		.246	.270	.279	49	-9	3	.963	2	110	47	P41/S		0.1
1900	Bro N	10	26	2	6	0	0	0	1	1	0		.231	.259	.231	34	-1	0	.960	1	139	0	P10		0.0
	Phi N	10	33	3	10	1	0	0	5	0	0		.303	.303	.333	76	1	1	.920	-1	90	0	P10		0.0
	Year	20	59	5	16	1	0	0	6	1	0		.271	.283	.288	56	1	1	.940	0	112	0	P20		0.0
1901	Phi N	2	1	1	1	0	0	0	0	1	0		1.000	1.000	1.000	471	1	0	1.000	-0	79	7	P2		0.0
	Bal N	96	362	41	90	9	4	0	36	21	6		.249	.301	.296	63	-18	10	.872	-12	88	61	3b67,S19,P9/2OC		-2.5
1902	NY N	100	342	26	72	11	4	0	14	20	1		.211	.256	.249	56	-18	13	.962	-5	90	178	O43(0/3/40),S36,3b18,P3,2b2		-2.3
1903	NY N	78	257	35	62	15	1	0	37	15	3		.241	.291	.307	68	-11	12	.907	-3	94	207	S27,3b25,2b19/OL		-1.2
1904	NY N	64	181	27	56	12	2	1	19	11	2		.309	.356	.414	132	7	11	.914	-4	97	296	3b28,S10,2b9,O7(3/4/0)/P		0.4
Total 8		490	1622	197	397	54	10	1	164	83	14		.245	.287	.292	66	-71	55	.890	-25	91	114	3b143,P142,S98,O59R,2b35		-6.2

DUNN, JOE Joseph Edward B3.11.1885 Springfield OH D3.19.1944 Springfield OH BR/TR/5-9/160 d9.12

YEAR	TM LG	G	AB	R	H	2B	3B	HR	RBI	BB-IB	HP	SO	AVG	OBP	SLG	AOPS	ABR	SB-CS	FA	FR	RNG	THR	GAMES AT POSITION	DL	BFW
1908	Bro N	20	64	3	11	3	0	0	5	0	1		.172	.172	.219	26	-6	0	.957	4	92	149	C20		0.0
1909	Bro N	10	25	1	4	1	0	0	2	0	1		.160	.192	.200	23	-2	0	.952	-1	89	75	C7		-0.3
Total 2		30	89	4	15	4	0	0	7	0	1		.169	.178	.213	25	-8	0	.956	3	91	131	C27		-0.3

DUNN, RON Ronald Ray B1.24.1950 Oklahoma City OK BR/TR/5-11/180* [BalA68 5/94] d9.3

YEAR	TM LG	G	AB	R	H	2B	3B	HR	RBI	BB-IB	HP	SO	AVG	OBP	SLG	AOPS	ABR	SB-CS	FA	FR	RNG	THR	GAMES AT POSITION	DL	BFW
1974	Chi N	23	68	6	20	7	0	2	15	12-3	0	8	.294	.400	.485	141	4	0-0	.917	-6	86	57	2b21,3b6		-0.1
1975	Chi N	32	44	2	7	3	0	1	6	6-0	0	17	.159	.250	.295	51	-3	0-0	.957	-1	105	0	3b11,O2L/2		-0.4
Total 2		55	112	8	27	10	0	3	21	18-3	0	25	.241	.341	.411	106	1	0-0	.918	-7	86	56	2b22,3b17,O2L		-0.5

DUNN, STEVE Stephen B. B12.21.1858 London ON, Can. D5.5.1933 London ON, Can. BL/5-9.5/173 d9.27

YEAR	TM LG	G	AB	R	H	2B	3B	HR	RBI	BB-IB	HP	SO	AVG	OBP	SLG	AOPS	ABR	SB-CS	FA	FR	RNG	THR	GAMES AT POSITION	DL	BFW
1884	StP U	9	32	2	8	2	0	0					.250	.250	.313	127	0		.972	1	241	70	1b9/3		0.1

DUNN, STEVE Steven Robert B4.18.1970 Champaign IL BL/TL/6-4/225* [MinA88 4/103] d5.3

YEAR	TM LG	G	AB	R	H	2B	3B	HR	RBI	BB-IB	HP	SO	AVG	OBP	SLG	AOPS	ABR	SB-CS	FA	FR	RNG	THR	GAMES AT POSITION	DL	BFW
1994	Min A	14	35	4	8	5	0	0	4	1-0	0	12	.229	.250	.371	57	-2	0-0	.990	1	134	134	1b12		-0.2
1995	Min A	5	6	0	0	0	0	0	0	1-0	0	3	.000	.143	.000	-58	-1	0-0	1.000	-0	0	322	1b3		-0.2
Total 2		19	41	2	8	5	0	0	4	2-0	0	15	.195	.233	.317	40	-3	0-0	.990	1	125	147	1b15		-0.4

DUNN, TODD Todd Kent B7.29.1970 Tulsa OK BR/TR/6-5/220* [MilA93 1/35] d9.8 Col North Florida [DL 1998 Mil N 69]

YEAR	TM LG	G	AB	R	H	2B	3B	HR	RBI	BB-IB	HP	SO	AVG	OBP	SLG	AOPS	ABR	SB-CS	FA	FR	RNG	THR	GAMES AT POSITION	DL	BFW
1996	Mil A	6	10	2	3	1	0	0	1	0-0	0	3	.300	.300	.400	72	0	3-0	1.000	-0	105	0	O6(1/1/4)		-0.1
1997	Mil A	44	118	17	27	5	0	3	9	2-0	0	39	.229	.242	.347	51	-9	3-0	.909	-0	108	87	O27(19/2/7),D14		-1.0
Total 2		50	128	19	30	6	0	3	10	2-0	0	42	.234	.246	.352	52	-9	3-0	.920	-1	108	76	O33(20/3/11),D14	69	-1.1

DUNSTON, SHAWON Shawon Donnell B3.21.1963 Brooklyn NY BR/TR/6-1/175* [ChiN82 1/1] d4.9 OF(107/75/70)

YEAR	TM LG	G	AB	R	H	2B	3B	HR	RBI	BB-IB	HP	SO	AVG	OBP	SLG	AOPS	ABR	SB-CS	FA	FR	RNG	THR	GAMES AT POSITION	DL	BFW
1985	Chi N	74	250	40	65	12	4	4	18	19-3	1	42	.260	.310	.388	86	-4	11-3	.958	18	116	92	S73		2.2
1986	Chi N	150	581	66	145	37	3	17	68	21-5	3	114	.250	.278	.411	82	-16	13-11	.961	21	104	104	S149		2.1
1987	Chi N	95	346	40	85	18	3	5	22	10-1	1	68	.246	.267	.358	62	-20	12-3	.973	-6	99	93	S94	66	-0.5
1988	Chi N☆	155	575	69	143	23	6	9	56	16-8	2	108	.249	.271	.357	75	-20	30-9	.973	14	106	90	S151		0.8
1989	†Chi N	138	471	52	131	20	6	9	60	30-15	1	86	.278	.320	.403	99	-1	19-11	.972	5	102	114	S138		1.5
1990	Chi N★	146	545	73	143	22	8	17	66	15-1	1	87	.262	.283	.426	87	-12	25-5	.970	-1	99	95	S144		0.2
1991	Chi N	142	492	59	128	22	7	12	50	23-5	4	64	.260	.292	.407	92	-7	21-6	.968	-0	98	100	S142		0.6
1992	Chi N	18	73	8	23	3	1	0	2	3-0	0	13	.315	.342	.384	102	0	2-3	.986	-2	90	101	S18		-0.1
1993	Chi N	7	10	3	4	2	0	0	2	0-0	0	1	.400	.400	.600	165	0	0-0	1.000	-0	0	0	S2	153	0.1
1994	Chi N	88	331	38	92	19	0	11	35	16-3	2	48	.278	.313	.435	93	-4	3-8	.966	-7	94	98	S84	149	-0.7
1995	Chi N	127	477	58	141	30	6	14	69	10-5	6	75	.296	.317	.472	105	-1	10-5	.969	-8	97	73	S125		0.2
1996	SF N	82	287	27	86	12	2	5	25	13-0	1	40	.300	.331	.408	96	-3	8-0	.957	-1	99	108	S78	75	0.3
1997	Chi N	114	419	57	119	18	4	9	41	8-0	0	64	.284	.300	.411	82	-13	29-7	.970	-16	82	81	S108,O7L	15	-1.8
	Pit N	18	71	14	28	4	1	5	16	0-0	0	11	.394	.389	.690	174	7	3-1	.965	2	109	74	S18		1.0
	Year	132	490	71	147	22	5	14	57	8-0	0	75	.300	.312	.451	95	-6	32-8	.969	-15	86	80	S126,O7L		-0.8
1998	Cle A	62	156	26	37	11	3	3	12	6-0	1	18	.237	.265	.404	70	-6	9-2	.978	-3	100	76	2b24,S14,O12(11/1/0),D7		-0.7
	SF N	36	51	10	9	2	0	3	8	0-0	3	10	.176	.222	.392	60	-3	0-2	.938	-3	100	32	S9,O6C/2		-0.7
1999	StL N	62	150	23	46	5	2	5	25	2-0	2	23	.307	.327	.467	97	-2	6-3	1.000	-0	103	100	O27(9/16/5)/3	16	-0.2
	†NY N	42	93	12	32	6	1	0	16	0-0	2	16	.344	.354	.430	103	0	4-1	.978	1	102	97	O27(9/16/5)/3		0.1
	Year	104	243	35	78	11	3	5	41	2-0	5	39	.321	.341	.453	99	-1	10-4	.988	0	102	98	O50(18/27/9),1b8,S7,3b6,D2		-0.1
2000	†StL N	98	216	28	54	11	2	12	43	6-0	3	47	.250	.278	.486	87	-6	3-1	.989	1	115	44	O59(41/9/13),S8,1b6,3b5/D		-0.6
2001	SF N	88	186	26	52	10	3	9	25	2-0	2	32	.280	.293	.511	109	1	3-1	.966	2	102	178	O60(12/23/26)/1D	15	0.2
2002	†SF N	72	147	7	34	5	0	1	9	3-0	1	33	.231	.250	.286	45	-13	1-0	1.000	-4	79	0	O49(18/9/22)/1SD	38	-1.8
Total 18		1814	5927	736	1597	292	62	150	668	203-44	41	1000	.269	.296	.416	88	-123	212-82	.967	21	99	95	S1363,O242L,2b25,1b16,D14,3b11	527	2.2

DUNWOODY, TODD Todd Franklin B4.11.1975 Lafayette IN BL/TL/6-1/195(195-210) [FlaN93 7/211] d5.10

YEAR	TM LG	G	AB	R	H	2B	3B	HR	RBI	BB-IB	HP	SO	AVG	OBP	SLG	AOPS	ABR	SB-CS	FA	FR	RNG	THR	GAMES AT POSITION	DL	BFW
1997	Fla N	19	50	7	13	2	2	2	7	7-0	1	21	.260	.362	.500	129	2	2-0	.929	-1	101	0	O14(6/8/0)		0.1
1998	Fla N	116	434	53	109	27	7	5	28	21-0	4	113	.251	.292	.380	80	-15	5-1	.989	7	113	141	O111C		-0.5
1999	Fla N	64	186	20	41	6	3	2	20	12-0	1	41	.220	.270	.317	51	-15	3-4	.981	-3	89	110	O55(8/44/5)		-1.8
2000	KC A	61	178	12	37	9	0	1	23	8-0	1	42	.208	.238	.275	30	-19	3-0	.976	-2	101	0	O40(14/19/9),D11	60	-2.0
2001	Chi N	33	61	6	13	4	0	1	3	3-0	1	14	.213	.250	.328	49	-5	0-1	.973	1	120	112	O26(15/6/7)		-0.4
2002	Cle A	2	6	0	0	0	0	0	0	0-0	0	3	.000	.000	.000	-98	-2	0-0	1.000	-1	32	0	O2(1/0/1)	38	-0.2
Total 6		295	915	98	213	48	12	11	81	51-0	7	234	.233	.277	.348	63	-54	13-6	.982	3	105	100	O248(44/188/22),D11	98	-4.8

DURAN, DAN Daniel James B3.16.1954 Palo Alto CA BL/TL/5-11/190 [TexA73 30/646] d4.17 Col Foothill (CA) JC

YEAR	TM LG	G	AB	R	H	2B	3B	HR	RBI	BB-IB	HP	SO	AVG	OBP	SLG	AOPS	ABR	SB-CS	FA	FR	RNG	THR	GAMES AT POSITION	DL	BFW
1981	Tex A	13	16	1	4	0	0	0	0	1-0	0	1	.250	.294	.250	61	-1	0-0	1.000	0	65	335	O7L/1		-0.1

DURANT, MIKE Michael Joseph B9.14.1969 Columbus OH BR/TR/6-2/200 [MinA91 2/47] d4.3 Col Ohio St.

YEAR	TM LG	G	AB	R	H	2B	3B	HR	RBI	BB-IB	HP	SO	AVG	OBP	SLG	AOPS	ABR	SB-CS	FA	FR	RNG	THR	GAMES AT POSITION	DL	BFW
1996	Min A	40	81	15	17	3	0	0	5	10-0	0	15	.210	.293	.247	39	-8	3-0	.975	5	151	81	C37		0.0

DURAZO, ERUBIEL Erubiel (Cardenas) B1.23.1974 Hermosillo, Sonora, Mexico BL/TL/6-3/240(225-240) d7.26 Col Pima (AZ) CC

YEAR	TM LG	G	AB	R	H	2B	3B	HR	RBI	BB-IB	HP	SO	AVG	OBP	SLG	AOPS	ABR	SB-CS	FA	FR	RNG	THR	GAMES AT POSITION	DL	BFW
1999	†Ari N	52	155	31	51	4	2	11	30	26-1	1	43	.329	.422	.594	154	13	1-1	1.000	-1	83	84	1b44		0.8
2000	Ari N	67	196	35	52	11	0	8	33	34-2	1	43	.265	.373	.444	102	0	1-0	.989	-4	70	90	1b60	81	-0.6
2001	†Ari N	92	175	34	47	11	0	12	38	28-1	2	49	.269	.372	.537	124	7	0-0	.993	1	94	105	1b38,O2R,D7	17	0.5
2002	†Ari N	76	222	46	58	12	2	16	48	49-2	2	60	.261	.395	.550	137	12	0-1	.984	-3	79	73	1b56,O2R,D6	73	0.4
2003	†Oak A	154	537	92	139	29	0	21	77	100-12	2	105	.259	.374	.430	112	13	0-1	.981	-5	46	103	D121,1b33		-0.1
2004	Oak A	142	511	80	164	35	1	22	88	56-9	9	104	.321	.396	.523	138	31	3-2	.882	-1	79	114	D132,1b4		2.2
2005	Oak A	41	152	15	36	4	0	4	16	14-0	1	24	.237	.305	.368	77	-5	1-0	1.000	-0	277	0	D39/1	131	-0.7
Total 7		624	1948	333	547	108	6	94	330	307-27	18	428	.281	.381	.487	122	73	7-5	.988	-12	74	90	D305,1b236,O4R	302	2.5

DURBIN, KID Blaine Alphonsus B9.10.1886 Lamar MO D9.11.1943 Kirkwood MO BL/TL/5-8/155 d4.24 ▲

YEAR	TM LG	G	AB	R	H	2B	3B	HR	RBI	BB-IB	HP	SO	AVG	OBP	SLG	AOPS	ABR	SB-CS	FA	FR	RNG	THR	GAMES AT POSITION	DL	BFW
1907	Chi N	11	18	2	6	0	0	0	0	1			.333	.368	.333	113	0	0	1.000	1	106	0	P5,O5(1/0/4)		0.1
1908	Chi N	14	28	3	7	1	0	0	2	1			.250	.323	.286	91	0	0	1.000	1	0	0	O11C		-0.1
1909	Cin N	6	5	1	1	0	0	0	1	0			.200	.333	.200	66	0	0		0	0		/H		-0.1
	Pit N	1	0	0	0	0	0	0	0	0			—	—	—		0	0	—	0			/R		0.0
	Year	7	5	1	1	0	0	0	1	0			.200	.333	.200	65	0	0	—	0			/R		0.0
Total 3		32	51	6	14	1	0	0	4	1			.275	.339	.294	96	0	0	1.000	1	151	0	O16(1/11/4),P5		0.0

DURHAM, JOE Joseph Vann "Pop" B7.31.1931 Newport News VA BR/TR/6-1/186* d9.10 Mil 1955-56 †Negro Lg 1952 Col Shaw

YEAR	TM LG	G	AB	R	H	2B	3B	HR	RBI	BB-IB	HP	SO	AVG	OBP	SLG	AOPS	ABR	SB-CS	FA	FR	RNG	THR	GAMES AT POSITION	DL	BFW
1954	Bal A	10	40	4	9	0	1	3	4		0	7	.225	.295	.300	68	-2	0-0	.917	-1	90	0	O10(10/1/0)		-0.4
1957	Bal A	77	157	19	29	2	0	4	17	16-1	0	42	.185	.259	.274	49	-12	1-1	1.000	-1	101	45	O59(36/5/25)		-1.5
1959	StL N	6	5	2	0	0	0	0	0	0-0	0	1	.000	.000	.000	-94	-1	0-0	1.000	0	190	0	/OR		-0.1
Total 3		93	202	25	38	2	0	5	20	20-1	0	50	.188	.260	.272	49	-15	1-1	.979	-2	99	34	O70(46/6/26)		-2.0

DURHAM, LEON Leon B7.31.1957 Cincinnati OH BL/TL/6-2/210(185-215) [StLN76 1/15] d5.27

YEAR	TM LG	G	AB	R	H	2B	3B	HR	RBI	BB-IB	HP	SO	AVG	OBP	SLG	AOPS	ABR	SB-CS	FA	FR	RNG	THR	GAMES AT POSITION	DL	BFW
1980	StL N	96	303	42	82	15	4	8	42	18-1	1	55	.271	.309	.426	100	-1	8-5	.987	10	103	255	O78(35/2/43),1b8		0.5
1981	Chi N	87	328	42	95	14	6	10	35	27-6	1	53	.290	.344	.460	119	7	25-11	.970	-3	100	158	O83R,1b3	68	0.2
1982	Chi N	148	539	84	168	33	7	22	90	66-14	2	77	.312	.388	.521	147	35	28-14	.963	-3	98	116	O143(0/74/89)/1		2.9
1983	Chi N★	100	337	58	87	18	4	12	55	66-12	3	83	.258	.381	.466	128	15	12-6	.966	-11	98	34	O95(51/40/4),1b6	15	0.2
1984	†Chi N	137	473	86	132	30	4	23	96	69-11	2	86	.279	.369	.505	133	22	16-8	.994	9	100	96	1b130	18	1.9
1985	Chi N	153	542	58	155	21	1	21	75	64-24	0	99	.282	.357	.465	117	13	7-6	.995	3	100	98	1b151		0.7
1986	Chi N	141	484	66	127	18	7	20	65	67-16	1	98	.262	.350	.452	112	8	8-7	.995	-7	80	90	1b141		-0.9
1987	Chi N	131	439	70	120	22	1	27	63	51-9	2	92	.273	.348	.513	120	12	2-2	.990	-10	68	92	1b123		-0.6

YEAR	TM LG	G	AB	R	H	2B	3B	HR	RBI	BB-IB	HP	SO	AVG	OBP	SLG	AOPS	ABR	SB-CS	FA	FR	RNG	THR	GAMES AT POSITION	DL	BFW
1988	Chi N	24	73	10	16	6	1	3	6	9-2	0	20	.219	.305	.452	109	1	0-1	.995	1	110	114	1b20	21	0.0
	Cin N	21	51	4	11	3	0	1	2	5-1	0	12	.216	.286	.333	75	-2	0-0	.993	-1	69	86	1b17	67	-0.4
	Year	45	124	14	27	9	1	4	8	14-3	0	32	.218	.297	.403	95	-1	0-1	.994	0	93	102	1b37		-0.4
1989	StL N	29	18	2	1	1	0	0	1	2-0	1	4	.056	.182	.111	-11	-3	0-1	.961	0	145	209	1b18	23	-0.3
Total 10		1067	3587	522	992	192	40	147	530	444-96	9	679	.277	.356	.475	122	107	106-61	.994	-19	93	95	1b618,O399(86/116/219)	212	4.2

DURHAM, RAY   Ray B11.30.1971 Charlotte NC   BB/TR/5-8/180(170-195)   [ChiA90 5/132]   d4.26

YEAR	TM LG	G	AB	R	H	2B	3B	HR	RBI	BB-IB	HP	SO	AVG	OBP	SLG	AOPS	ABR	SB-CS	FA	FR	RNG	THR	GAMES AT POSITION	DL	BFW
1995	Chi A	125	471	68	121	27	6	7	51	31-2	6	83	.257	.309	.384	83	-13	18-5	.973	-22	86	78	2b122/D		-2.5
1996	Chi A	156	557	79	153	33	5	10	65	58-4	10	95	.275	.350	.406	95	-3	30-4	.984	-21	96	84	2b150,D3		-1.1
1997	Chi A	155	634	106	172	27	5	11	53	61-0	6	96	.271	.337	.382	91	-8	33-16	.974	-29	91	77	2b153/D		-2.7
1998	Chi A★	158	635	126	181	35	8	19	67	73-3	6	105	.285	.363	.455	113	13	36-9	.976	1	103	**128**	2b158		2.5
1999	Chi A	153	612	109	181	30	8	13	60	73-1	4	105	.296	.373	.435	104	5	34-11	.980	-6	98	97	2b151		0.9
2000	†Chi A★	151	614	121	172	35	9	17	75	75-0	7	105	.280	.361	.450	101	2	25-13	.980	4	99	**122**	2b150/D		1.2
2001	Chi A	152	611	104	163	42	10	20	65	64-3	4	110	.267	.337	.466	103	3	23-10	.986	6	107	94	2b150/D		1.6
2002	Chi A	96	345	71	103	20	2	9	48	49-0	5	59	.299	.390	.446	118	11	20-5	.968	6	103	107	2b92		2.2
	†Oak A	54	219	43	60	14	4	6	22	24-1	2	34	.274	.350	.457	113	4	6-2	.967	3	121	175	D43,2b11		0.6
	Year	150	564	114	163	34	6	15	70	73-1	7	93	.289	.374	.450	116	15	26-7	.968	9	105	115	2b103,D43	40	2.8
2003	†SF N	110	410	61	117	30	5	3	33	50-2	3	82	.285	.366	.441	108	6	7-7	.990	3	108	103	2b105	38	1.3
2004	SF N	120	471	95	133	28	8	17	65	57-3	6	60	.282	.364	.484	114	10	10-4	.972	-4	100	103	2b118		1.2
2005	SF N	142	497	67	144	33	4	12	62	48-2	5	59	.290	.356	.429	102	3	6-3	.982	-19	93	99	2b133/OC	78	-1.0
Total 11		1572	6076	1050	1700	354	70	149	666	663-21	66	993	.280	.354	.435	103	33	248-89	.978	-79	99	99	2b1491,D53/OC		4.2

DURNBAUGH, BOBBY   Robert Eugene "Scroggy" B1.15.1933 Dayton OH   BR/TR/5-8/170   d9.22

YEAR	TM LG	G	AB	R	H	2B	3B	HR	RBI	BB-IB	HP	SO	AVG	OBP	SLG	AOPS	ABR	SB-CS	FA	FR	RNG	THR	GAMES AT POSITION	DL	BFW
1957	Cin N	2	1	0	0	0	0	0	0	0-0	0	0	.000	.000	.000	-93	0	0-0	.500	-0	100	0	S2		-0.1

DURNING, GEORGE   George Dewey B5.9.1898 Philadelphia PA   D4.18.1986 Tampa FL   BR/TR/5-11/175   d9.12

YEAR	TM LG	G	AB	R	H	2B	3B	HR	RBI	BB-IB	HP	SO	AVG	OBP	SLG	AOPS	ABR	SB-CS	FA	FR	RNG	THR	GAMES AT POSITION	DL	BFW
1925	Phi N	5	14	3	5	0	0	0	1	2	0	1	.357	.438	.357	97	0	0-0	1.000	2	121	315	O4R		0.1

DUROCHER, LEO   Leo Ernest "The Lip" B7.27.1905 W.Springfield MA   D10.7.1991 Palm Springs CA   BR/TR (BB 1928-29)/5-10/160   d10.2   M24/C4   HF1994

YEAR	TM LG	G	AB	R	H	2B	3B	HR	RBI	BB-IB	HP	SO	AVG	OBP	SLG	AOPS	ABR	SB-CS	FA	FR	RNG	THR	GAMES AT POSITION	DL	BFW
																									0.0
1925	NY A	2	1	1	0	0	0	0	0	0	0	0	.000	.000	.000	-99	0	0-0	—	0			/H		-0.2
1928	†NY A	102	296	46	80	8	6	0	31	22	3	52	.270	.327	.338	77	-10	1-4	.948	5	108	106	2b66,S29		1.0
1929	NY A	106	341	53	84	4	5	0	32	34	3	33	.246	.320	.287	62	-20	3-1	.958	20	111	114	S93,2b12		-0.7
1930	Cin N	119	354	31	86	15	3	3	32	20	2	45	.243	.287	.328	51	-29	0	.959	11	107	111	S103,2b13		-1.8
1931	Cin N	121	361	26	82	11	5	1	29	18	0	32	.227	.264	.294	53	-26	0	.965	0	102	**121**	S120		-3.1
1932	Cin N	143	457	43	99	22	6	1	33	36	1	40	.217	.275	.293	55	-29	3	.960	-12	97	99	S142		0.1
1933	Cin N	16	51	6	11	1	0	1	3	4	0	5	.216	.273	.294	63	-3	0	.953	3	115	95	S16		-0.7
	StL N	123	395	45	102	18	4	2	41	26	1	32	.258	.306	.339	80	-10	3	.961	-5	93	86	S123		-0.6
	Year	139	446	51	113	19	4	3	44	30	1	37	.253	.302	.334	78	-13	3	.957	-3	90	111	S146		-1.3
1934	†StL N	146	500	62	130	26	5	3	70	33	2	40	.260	.308	.350	71	-20	2	.960	-3	96	87	S139		-1.4
1935	StL N	143	513	62	136	23	5	8	78	29	0	46	.265	.304	.376	79	-16	4	**.971**	-11	92	92	S136		-4.6
1936	StL N★	136	510	57	146	22	3	1	58	29	2	47	.286	.327	.347	82	-13	3	.959	-14	92	90	S134		-1.8
1937	StL N	135	477	46	97	11	3	1	47	38	1	36	.203	.262	.245	38	-42	6	**.966**	-3	95	105	S141		-2.1
1938	Bro N★	141	479	41	105	18	5	1	56	47	3	30	.219	.293	.284	58	-27	3	.957	-11	93	110	S113/3M		-1.3
1939	Bro N	116	390	42	108	21	6	1	34	27	1	24	.277	.325	.369	83	-9	2	.959	-3	92	91	S53,2b4,M		-0.8
1940	Bro N☆	62	160	10	37	9	1	1	14	12	1	13	.231	.285	.319	62	-8	1	.917	-0	110	70	S12/2M		-0.1
1941	Bro N	18	42	2	12	1	0	0	6	1	0	3	.286	.302	.310	70	-2	0	1.000	1	62	141	S6,M		-0.1
1943	Bro N	6	18	1	4	0	0	0	1	1	0	2	.222	.263	.222	41	-1	0	1.000	0	119	156	2b2,M		0.0
1945	Bro N	2	5	1	1	0	0	0	2	0	0	1	.200	.200	.200	11	-1	0	1.000	0	111	0	S1		-17.1
Total 17		1637	5350	575	1320	210	56	24	567	377	18	480	.247	.299	.320	66	-266	31-5	.961	-15	97	103	S1509,2b98/3		

DURRETT, RED   Elmer Cable B2.3.1921 Sherman TX   D1.17.1992 Waxahachie TX   BL/TL/5-10/170   d9.14

YEAR	TM LG	G	AB	R	H	2B	3B	HR	RBI	BB-IB	HP	SO	AVG	OBP	SLG	AOPS	ABR	SB-CS	FA	FR	RNG	THR	GAMES AT POSITION	DL	BFW
1944	Bro N	11	32	3	5	1	0	1	1	7	0	10	.156	.308	.281	68	-1	0	.933	1	124	111	O9(0/5/4)		-0.2
1945	Bro N	8	16	2	2	0	0	0	3	3	0	3	.125	.263	.125	10	-2	0	1.000	-0	93	0	O4C		-0.3
Total 2		19	48	5	7	1	0	1	1	10	0	13	.146	.293	.229	48	-3	0	.947	1	116	82	O13(0/9/4)		

DURRINGTON, TRENT   Trent John B8.27.1975 Sydney, New South Wales, Australia   BR/TR/5-10/172(172-198)   d8.6

YEAR	TM LG	G	AB	R	H	2B	3B	HR	RBI	BB-IB	HP	SO	AVG	OBP	SLG	AOPS	ABR	SB-CS	FA	FR	RNG	THR	GAMES AT POSITION	DL	BFW
																									-1.8
1999	Ana A	43	122	14	22	4	0	0	9	9-0	0	28	.180	.237	.197	12	-17	4-3	.966	-4	96	80	2b41		-0.2
2000	Ana A	4	3	0	0	0	0	0	0	0-0	0	0	.000	.000	.000	-97	-1	0-0	1.000	-1	67	0	/2		-0.3
2003	Ana A	12	14	5	2	0	0	0	1	3-0	0	0	.143	.294	.143	22	-2	1-1	1.000	-2	70	0	2b5,3b4/OLD		-0.6
2004	Mil N	53	82	13	19	2	3	2	4	4-0	0	23	.232	.267	.402	69	-4	4-0	.789	-2	82	0	3b11,2b6/PD		-0.2
2005	Mil N	28	14	3	3	1	0	0	2	1-0	0	3	.214	.267	.286	45	-1	5-2	.000	-1	0	0	/3		-3.1
Total 5		140	235	35	46	5	3	2	9	17-0	0	54	.196	.250	.268	33	-25	14-6	.971	-10	94	69	2b53,3b16,D3/POL		

DURST, CEDRIC   Cedric Montgomery B8.23.1896 Austin TX   D2.16.1971 San Diego CA   BL/TL/5-11/160   d5.30

YEAR	TM LG	G	AB	R	H	2B	3B	HR	RBI	BB-IB	HP	SO	AVG	OBP	SLG	AOPS	ABR	SB-CS	FA	FR	RNG	THR	GAMES AT POSITION	DL	BFW
																									0.0
1922	StL A	15	12	5	4	1	0	0	0	0	0	1	.333	.333	.417	91	0	0-0	.857	-0	133	0	O6(1/4/1)		-0.7
1923	StL A	45	85	11	18	2	0	5	11	8	0	14	.212	.280	.412	76	-4	0-0	1.000	-2	98	0	O10(4/5/1),1b8		-1.3
1926	StL A	80	219	32	52	7	5	3	16	22	1	19	.237	.310	.356	70	-11	0-3	.980	2	108	90	O57(5/42/10),1b4		-1.2
1927	†NY A	65	129	18	32	4	3	0	25	6	0	7	.248	.281	.326	59	-9	0-3	.980	-1	95	41	O36(13/6/17),1b2		-0.9
1928	†NY A	74	135	18	34	2	1	2	10	7	0	9	.252	.289	.326	63	-8	1-0	.983	1	105	79	O33(13/5/15),1b3		-0.6
1929	NY A	92	202	32	52	3	4	3	31	15	0	25	.257	.309	.361	77	-8	3-2	.987	6	128	89	O72(46/6/20)/1		-0.3
1930	NY A	8	19	0	3	1	0	0	5	0	0	1	.158	.158	.211	-8	-3	0-0	1.000	0	128	0	O6L		-2.3
	Bos A	102	302	29	74	19	5	1	24	17	2	24	.245	.290	.351	64	-17	3-1	.968	-2	98	65	O75(46/0/29)		-2.6
	Year	110	321	29	77	20	5	1	29	17	2	25	.240	.282	.343	60	-20	3-1	.970	-2	100	61	O81(52/0/29)		-2.8
Total 7		481	1103	145	269	39	17	15	122	75	3	100	.244	.294	.351	67	-60	7-11	.979	4	108	71	O295(134/68/93),1b18		-7.3

DUSAK, ERV   Ervin Frank "Four Sack" B7.29.1920 Chicago IL   D11.6.1994 Glendale Heights IL   BR/TR/6-2/185*   d9.18   Mil 1943-45 OF(105/106/67) ▲

YEAR	TM LG	G	AB	R	H	2B	3B	HR	RBI	BB-IB	HP	SO	AVG	OBP	SLG	AOPS	ABR	SB-CS	FA	FR	RNG	THR	GAMES AT POSITION	DL	BFW
1941	StL N	6	14	1	2	0	0	0	3	2	0	6	.143	.250	.143	12	-2	1	1.000	1	152	0	O4(1/2/1)		-0.1
1942	StL N	12	27	4	5	3	0	0	3	3	0	7	.185	.267	.296	60	-1	0	1.000	1	124	0	O8(5/0/3)/3		0.0
1946	†StL N	100	275	38	66	9	1	9	42	33	0	63	.240	.321	.378	94	-3	7	.993	7	100	203	O77(72/5/0),3b11,2b2		-0.1
1947	StL N	111	328	56	93	7	3	6	28	50	0	34	.284	.378	.378	97	0	1	.970	4	95	195	O89(22/28/47),3b7		-1.6
1948	StL N	114	311	60	65	9	2	6	19	49	0	55	.209	.317	.309	66	-14	3	.992	-2	94	76	O68(2/55/12),2b29,3b9/PS		0.0
1949	StL N	1	0	1	0	0	0	0	0	0	0	0					0	0	1.000	0		0	/R		0.0
1950	StL N	23	12	0	1	1	0	0	0	0	0	1	.083	.083	.167	-34	-2	0	1.000	1	108	211	P14,O2C		0.0
1951	StL N	5	2	1	1	0	0	1	1	0	0	1	.500	.500	2.000	537	1	0-0	1.000	-3	70	0	O12(1/10/1),P3,2b2,3b2		-0.2
	Pit N	21	39	6	12	3	1	1	7	3	0	11	.308	.357	.462	115	1	0-0	1.000	-3	70	0	O12(1/10/1),P8,2b2,3b2		-0.2
	Year	26	41	7	13	3	0	2	8	3	0	12	.317	.364	.537	136	2	0-0	.818	0	65	453	O11(2/4/3)		-0.1
1952	Pit N	20	27	1	6	0	1	0	3	2	0	8	.222	.276	.333	66	-1	0-0	.981	9	97	159	O271C,2b33,3b30,P23/S		-2.1
Total 9		413	1035	168	251	32	6	24	106	142	0	188	.243	.334	.355	84	-21	12-0	.981	9	97	159	O271C,2b33,3b30,P23/S		

DWIGHT, AL   Albert Ward B1.4.1856 New York NY   D2.20.1903 San Francisco CA   d6.19

YEAR	TM LG	G	AB	R	H	2B	3B	HR	RBI	BB-IB	HP	SO	AVG	OBP	SLG	AOPS	ABR	SB-CS	FA	FR	RNG	THR	GAMES AT POSITION	DL	BFW
1884	KC U	12	43	8	10	2	0	0		2			.233	.267	.279	75	-2		.953	0			C10/OC2		-0.2

DWYER, JIM   James Edward "Pig Pen" B1.3.1950 Evergreen Park IL   BL/TL/5-10/175(165-195)   [StLN71 11/253]   d6.10   Col Southern Illinois

YEAR	TM LG	G	AB	R	H	2B	3B	HR	RBI	BB-IB	HP	SO	AVG	OBP	SLG	AOPS	ABR	SB-CS	FA	FR	RNG	THR	GAMES AT POSITION	DL	BFW
																									-0.8
1973	StL N	28	57	7	11	1	9	0	1	1-0	0	5	.193	.207	.246	25	-6	0-0	1.000	-1	97	0	O20(9/10/1)		0.1
1974	StL N	74	86	13	24	1	0	2	11	11-2	1	16	.279	.360	.360	104	1	0-0	1.000	1	102	103	O25(8/1/16),1b3		-0.2
1975	StL N	21	31	4	6	1	0	0	1	4-0	0	6	.194	.286	.226	41	-2	0-0	1.000	1	126	0	O9(5/3/2)		0.1
	Mon N	60	175	22	50	7	1	3	20	23-0	0	30	.286	.365	.389	105	2	4-1	.959	1	90	214	O52(46/3/3)		-0.1
	Year	81	206	26	56	8	1	3	21	27-0	0	36	.272	.353	.364	95	-1	4-1	.966	2	94	188	O61(51/6/5)		-1.0
1976	Mon N	50	92	7	17	3	1	0	5	11-1	0	10	.185	.269	.239	44	-7	0-0	.970	-1	97	0	O19(15/0/5)		-0.2
	NY N	11	13	2	2	0	0	0	0	2-1	0	1	.154	.267	.154	23	-1	0-0	1.000	0	107	0	O2R		-1.2
	Year	61	105	9	19	3	1	0	5	13-2	0	11	.181	.269	.229	42	-8	0-0	1.000	-1	99	0	O21(15/0/7)		-0.3
1977	StL N	13	31	5	7	1	0	1	2	4-0	0	5	.226	.351	.258	67	-1	0-0	.952	-3	59	73	O22(18/0/5)		-0.5
1978	StL N	34	65	8	14	3	0	3	9	9-2	0	15	.215	.320	.308	76	-1	2-0	1.000	0	98	0	O13(6/6/1)		0.1
	SF N	73	173	22	39	9	2	6	22	28-3	1	29	.225	.327	.387	104	1	6-0	.987	3	98	330	O36(3/26/9),1b29		-0.1
	Year	107	238	30	53	12	2	9	26	37-4	1	32	.223	.325	.366	96	0	7-0	.979	0	84	235	O58(21/26/14),1b29		0.0
1979	Bos A	76	113	19	30	7	1	2	14	17-1	1	23	.265	.361	.381	96	3	3-1	.981	1	128	111	1b25,O19(6/1/12),D4		-0.2
1980	Bos A	93	260	34	74	11	1	9	38	28-5	2	23	.285	.357	.438	111	4	3-2	.975	-0	83	170	O65(11/29/27),D12,1b9		

(continued)

YEAR	TM	LG	G	AB	R	H	2B	3B	HR	RBI	BB-IB	HP	SO	AVG	OBP	SLG	AOPS	ABR	SB-CS	FA	FR	RNG	THR	GAMES AT POSITION	DL	BFW
1981	Bal	A	68	134	16	30	0	1	3	10	20-0	0	19	.224	.318	.306	83	-3	0-2	.977	-0	105	75	O59(43/2/19),1b3/D		-0.6
1982	Bal	A	71	148	28	45	4	3	6	15	27-4	0	24	.304	.407	.493	144	11	2-0	.976	-3	100	47	O49(16/0/37)/1D		0.7
1983	†Bal	A	100	196	37	56	17	1	8	38	31-3	0	29	.286	.382	.505	144	13	1-1	.966	-1	111	35	O56(7/0/49),D10,1b4		1.0
1984	Bal	A	76	161	22	41	9	1	2	21	23-0	0	24	.255	.337	.360	98	0	0-2	.966	0	99	119	O52(1/0/51),D3		0.7
1985	Bal	A	101	233	35	58	8	3	7	36	37-2	1	31	.249	.353	.399	108	3	0-2	.993	3	109	105	O78(46/0/33),D3	41	-0.2
1986	Bal	A	94	160	18	39	13	1	8	31	23-1	2	31	.244	.339	.488	125	6	0-2	1.000	3	110	300	O24(8/0/16),D24/1		0.2
1987	Bal	A	92	241	54	66	7	1	15	33	37-4	1	57	.274	.371	.498	131	11	4-1	1.000	-0	104	51	D41,O30(3/0/29)		0.7
1988	Bal	A	35	53	3	12	0	0	0	3	12-3	0	11	.226	.364	.226	73	-1	0-0	1.000	0	240	0	D17,O2(1/0/1)		0.8
	Min	A	20	41	6	12	1	0	2	15	13-1	1	8	.293	.464	.463	158	4	0-0	1.000	0	240	0	D13	50	-0.1
	Year		55	94	9	24	1	0	2	18	25-4	1	19	.255	.410	.330	112	3	0-0	1.000	0	240	0	D30,O2(1/0/1)		0.4
1989	Min	A	88	225	34	71	11	0	3	23	28-1	0	23	.316	.390	.404	117	6	2-0	.979	-0	0	0	D74/OR		0.3
	Mon	N	13	10	1	3	1	0	0	2	1-0	0	1	.300	.364	.400	116	0	0-0	—	0			/H		0.4
1990	Min	A	37	63	7	12	0	0	1	5	12-1	0	11	.190	.320	.238	55	-4	0-0	1.000	0	279	0	D23,O2(1/0/1)		0.0
Total	18		1328	2761	409	719	115	17	77	349	402-34	12	402	.260	.353	.398	107	35	26-15	.979	3	99	113	O634(250/75/329),D226,1b75	91	0.7

DWYER, JOHN John E. d5.16

YEAR	TM	LG	G	AB	R	H	2B	3B	HR	RBI	BB-IB	HP	SO	AVG	OBP	SLG	AOPS	ABR	SB-CS	FA	FR	RNG	THR	GAMES AT POSITION	DL	BFW
1882	Cle	N	1	3	0	0	0	0	0	1	0	0		.000	.000	.000	-99	-1		—	-1	0	0	/OLC		-0.1

DWYER, DOUBLE JOE Joseph Michael B3.27.1903 Orange NJ D10.21.1992 Glen Ridge NJ BL/TL/5-9/186 d4.20

YEAR	TM	LG	G	AB	R	H	2B	3B	HR	RBI	BB-IB	HP	SO	AVG	OBP	SLG	AOPS	ABR	SB-CS	FA	FR	RNG	THR	GAMES AT POSITION	DL	BFW
1937	Cin	N	12	11	2	3	0	0	0	1	1	0	0	.273	.333	.273	70	0			0			/H		0.0

DYBZINSKI, JERRY Jerome Matthew B7.7.1955 Cleveland OH BR/TR/6-2/180* [CleA77 15/375] d4.11 Col Cleveland St.

YEAR	TM	LG	G	AB	R	H	2B	3B	HR	RBI	BB-IB	HP	SO	AVG	OBP	SLG	AOPS	ABR	SB-CS	FA	FR	RNG	THR	GAMES AT POSITION	DL	BFW
1980	Cle	A	114	248	32	57	11	1	1	23	13-0	2	35	.230	.273	.294	55	-15	4-1	.971	14	110	93	S73,2b29,3b4,D2		0.6
1981	Cle	A	48	57	10	17	0	0	0	6	5-0	0	8	.298	.355	.298	90	-1	7-1	.970	2	104	73	S34,2b3,3b3/D		0.5
1982	Cle	A	80	212	19	49	6	2	0	22	21-0	3	25	.231	.305	.278	63	-11	3-5	.957	16	117	95	S77,3b3		1.1
1983	†Chi	A	127	256	30	59	10	1	1	32	18-0	2	29	.230	.283	.289	56	-15	11-4	.966	-2	93	96	S118,3b9		-0.7
1984	Chi	A	94	132	17	31	5	1	1	10	13-0	2	12	.235	.311	.311	70	-5	7-2	.974	6	114	121	S76,3b14/2D		0.7
1985	Pit	N	5	4	0	0	0	0	0	0	0-0	0	1	.000	.000	.000	-99	-1	0-0	.900	1	118	0	S5		-0.1
Total	6		468	909	108	213	32	5	3	93	70-0	9	109	.234	.293	.290	61	-48	32-13	.966	36	107	97	S383,3b33,2b33,D4		2.1

DYCK, JIM James Robert B2.3.1922 Omaha NE D1.11.1999 Cheney WA BR/TR/6-2/205(190-205) d9.27

YEAR	TM	LG	G	AB	R	H	2B	3B	HR	RBI	BB-IB	HP	SO	AVG	OBP	SLG	AOPS	ABR	SB-CS	FA	FR	RNG	THR	GAMES AT POSITION	DL	BFW
1951	StL	A	4	15	1	1	0	0	0	0	1	0	1	.067	.125	.067	-46	-3	0-0	1.000	0	80	107	3b4		-0.3
1952	StL	A	122	402	60	108	22	3	15	64	50	3	68	.269	.354	.450	119	0	0-4	.962	7	110	91	3b74,O48(39/8/2)		1.3
1953	StL	A	112	334	38	71	15	1	9	27	38	3	40	.213	.299	.344	72	-14	0-0	.981	-1	105	148	O55(32/19/8),3b51		-1.7
1954	Cle	A	2	1	0	1	0	0	0	1	1	0	0	1.000	1.000	1.000	441	1	0-0	—	0			/H		-1.7
1955	Bal	A	61	197	32	55	13	1	2	22	28-1	1	21	.279	.372	.386	112	4	1-0	.989	-0	100	116	O45L,3b17		0.1
1956	Cin	N	18	11	5	2	0	0	0	0	10-0	0	5	.217	.455	.304	112	2	0-0	.923	1	77	410	O9L		0.2
Total	6		330	983	139	242	52	5	26	114	131-1	9	135	.246	.339	.389	98	-1	4-6	.982	6	104	121	O157(125/27/10),3b147/1		-0.3

DYE, JERMAINE Jermaine Terrell B1.28.1974 Oakland CA BR/TR/6-4/220* [AtlN93 17/488] d5.17 Col Cosumnes River (CA) JC

YEAR	TM	LG	G	AB	R	H	2B	3B	HR	RBI	BB-IB	HP	SO	AVG	OBP	SLG	AOPS	ABR	SB-CS	FA	FR	RNG	THR	GAMES AT POSITION	DL	BFW
1996	†Atl	N	98	292	32	82	16	0	12	37	8-0	5	67	.281	.304	.459	93	-4	1-4	.950	-0	110	43	O92(25/4/71)		-0.8
1997	KC	A	75	263	26	62	14	0	7	22	17-0	1	51	.236	.284	.369	67	-13	2-1	.966	6	111	152	O75(1/0/75)	57	-1.1
1998	KC	A	60	214	24	50	5	1	5	23	11-2	1	46	.234	.270	.336	55	-15	2-2	.987	7	128	93	O59R	65	-1.1
1999	KC	A	158	608	96	179	44	8	27	119	58-4	1	119	.294	.354	.526	117	14	2-3	.984	14	113	151	O157R/D		1.8
2000	KC	A★	157	601	107	193	41	2	33	118	69-6	3	99	.321	.390	.561	130	29	0-1	.976	-3	95	108	O146R,D10		1.6
2001	KC	A	97	367	50	100	14	2	13	47	30-3	6	68	.272	.333	.417	88	-6	7-1	.984	-3	96	79	O93(0/2/92),D4		-1.3
	†Oak	A	61	232	41	69	17	1	13	59	27-3	1	44	.297	.366	.547	138	13	2-0	.972	-2	80	174	O61R		-1.3
	Year		158	599	91	169	31	1	26	106	57-6	7	112	.282	.346	.467	106	6	9-1	.979	-6	90	117	O154(0/2/153),D4		-0.5
2002	†Oak	A	131	488	74	123	27	4	24	86	52-2	10	108	.252	.333	.459	109	7	2-0	.972	-14	77	29	O111R,D19	26	-1.3
2003	†Oak	A	65	221	28	38	6	0	4	20	25-2	3	42	.172	.261	.253	38	-20	1-0	1.000	-4	88	30	O61(1/3/60),D3	91	-2.6
2004	Oak	A	137	532	87	141	29	4	23	80	49-4	4	128	.265	.329	.464	105	3	4-2	.992	-10	89	32	O134R,D2		-1.3
2005	†Chi	A	145	529	74	145	29	2	31	86	39-3	9	99	.274	.333	.512	115	11	11-4	.971	-6	90	107	O140R/1SD		-1.3
Total	11		1184	4347	639	1182	242	19	192	697	385-29	42	871	.272	.334	.469	104	19	34-18	.978	-14	97	91	O1129(27/9/1106),D40/S1	239	-5.4

DYER, BEN Benjamin Franklin B2.13.1893 Chicago IL D8.7.1959 Kenosha WI BR/TR/5-11/170 d5.23 Mil 1918

YEAR	TM	LG	G	AB	R	H	2B	3B	HR	RBI	BB-IB	HP	SO	AVG	OBP	SLG	AOPS	ABR	SB-CS	FA	FR	RNG	THR	GAMES AT POSITION	DL	BFW
1914	NY	N	7	4	1	1	0	0	0	0	0	0	1	.250	.250	.250	50	0	1	1.000	0	142	331	S6/2		0.0
1915	NY	N	7	19	4	4	0	1	0	0	4	1	3	.211	.375	.316	117	0	0	.889	-1	93	0	3b6/S		0.0
1916	Det	A	4	14	4	4	1	0	0	1	0	0	1	.286	.333	.357	104	0	0	1.000	-1	80	0	S4		-0.1
1917	Det	A	30	67	6	14	5	0	0	2	0	1	17	.209	.232	.284	57	-4	3	.846	-1	95	106	S14,3b8		-0.4
1918	Det	A	13	18	1	5	0	0	0	2	0	0	6	.278	.278	.278	71	-1	0	1.000	0	185	0	P2,1b2,O2(1/0/1)/2		0.0
1919	Det	A	44	85	11	21	4	0	0	15	8	0	19	.247	.312	.294	72	-3	0	.953	1	110	0	3b23,S11/OR		-0.1
Total	6		105	207	27	49	10	1	0	18	15	1	47	.237	.291	.295	74	-7	4	.937	-0	110	0	3b37,S36,O3(1/0/2),1b2,P2,2b2		-0.6

DYER, DUFFY Don Robert B8.15.1945 Dayton OH BR/TR/6-0/195* [NYN66 S1/9] d9.21 C11 Col Arizona St.

YEAR	TM	LG	G	AB	R	H	2B	3B	HR	RBI	BB-IB	HP	SO	AVG	OBP	SLG	AOPS	ABR	SB-CS	FA	FR	RNG	THR	GAMES AT POSITION	DL	BFW
1968	NY	N	1	3	0	1	0	0	0	0	1-0	0	1	.333	.500	.333	153	0	0-0	1.000	0	0	0	/C		0.1
1969	†NY	N	29	74	5	19	3	1	3	12	1-0	0	22	.257	.295	.446	102	0	0-0	.991	-2	97	58	C19		-0.2
1970	NY	N	59	148	8	31	1	0	2	12	21-4	0	32	.209	.308	.257	52	-10	1-1	.991	0	96	140	C57		-0.7
1971	NY	N	59	169	13	39	7	1	2	18	14-4	1	45	.231	.292	.320	74	-6	1-0	.992	-2	80	105	C53		-0.6
1972	NY	N	94	325	33	75	17	3	8	36	28-9	2	71	.231	.299	.375	93	-3	0-1	.993	17	123	**144**	C91/OR		1.9
1973	NY	N	70	189	9	35	6	1	1	9	13-1	2	40	.185	.245	.243	36	-17	0-1	.994	-2	109	117	C60		-1.7
1974	NY	N	63	142	14	30	1	1	0	10	18-2	1	15	.211	.302	.232	52	-9	0-0	.982	-7	87	96	C45		-1.5
1975	†Pit	N	48	132	8	30	5	2	3	16	6-0	1	22	.227	.266	.364	73	-6	0-0	.990	5	194	100	C36		0.1
1976	Pit	N	69	184	12	41	8	0	3	9	29-10	3	35	.223	.336	.315	85	-2	0-0	.994	6	120	125	C58		0.7
1977	Pit	N	94	270	27	65	11	1	3	19	54-11	3	49	.241	.370	.322	85	-3	6-0	**.996**	-0	100	98	C93		0.2
1978	Pit	N	58	175	7	37	8	1	0	13	18-3	2	32	.211	.294	.269	56	-10	2-1	.991	-1	72	96	C55		0.2
1979	Mon	N	28	74	4	18	6	0	1	8	9-4	0	17	.243	.325	.365	88	-1	0-0	.993	4	79	115	C27	17	-0.9
1980	Det	A	48	108	11	20	1	0	4	11	13-1	0	34	.185	.273	.306	57	-7	0-0	.986	-4	71	44	C37,D10		0.4
1981	Det	A	2	0	0	0	0	0	0	0	0-0	0	0	—	—	—	—	-0	0-0	—	-0	0	0	C2		-1.0
Total	14		722	1993	151	441	74	11	30	173	228-49	19	415	.221	.306	.315	72	-74	10-4	.992	14	104	110	C634,D10/OR	17	-3.2

DYER, EDDIE Edwin Hawley B10.11.1899 Morgan City LA D4.20.1964 Houston TX BL/TL/5-11.5/168 d7.8 M5 Col Rice ▲

YEAR	TM	LG	G	AB	R	H	2B	3B	HR	RBI	BB-IB	HP	SO	AVG	OBP	SLG	AOPS	ABR	SB-CS	FA	FR	RNG	THR	GAMES AT POSITION	DL	BFW
1922	StL	N	6	3	1	1	1	0	0	1	0		0	.333	.333	.667	159	0	0-0	1.000	0	0	0	P2		0.0
1923	StL	N	35	45	17	12	3	0	2	5	3	0	5	.267	.313	.467	105	0	1-0	1.000	-0	114	0	O8(7/2/0),P4		0.0
1924	StL	N	50	76	8	18	2	3	0	8	3	0	8	.237	.266	.342	63	-5	1-0	.909	1	119	57	P29/OC		0.0
1925	StL	N	31	31	4	3	1	0	0	3	0		1	.097	.176	.129	-20	-2	1-1	.917	0	114	85	P27		0.0
1926	StL	N	6	2	1	1	0	0	0	0	1	0		.500	.500	.500	164	0	0	1.000	0	134	0	P6		0.0
1927	StL	N	1	0	0	0	0	0	0	0	1	0		—	1.000	—	181	0		-0	0	0		P		0.0
Total	6		129	157	31	35	7	3	2	19	10	1	14	.223	.269	.344	61	-6	3-1	.921	1	112	58	P69,O9(7/3/0)		0.0

DYKES, JIMMY James Joseph B11.10.1896 Philadelphia PA D6.15.1976 Philadelphia PA BR/TR/5-9/185 d5.6 Mil 1918 M21/C10 OF(2/4/1)

YEAR	TM	LG	G	AB	R	H	2B	3B	HR	RBI	BB-IB	HP	SO	AVG	OBP	SLG	AOPS	ABR	SB-CS	FA	FR	RNG	THR	GAMES AT POSITION	DL	BFW
1918	Phi	A	59	186	13	35	3	3	0	13	19	1	32	.188	.267	.237	51	-11	3	.940	9	111	127	2b56/3		-0.2
1919	Phi	A	17	49	4	9	1	0	0	1	7	0	11	.184	.286	.204	38	-4	0	.945	3	129	73	2b16		0.0
1920	Phi	A	142	546	81	140	25	4	8	35	55	9	73	.256	.334	.361	83	-13	6-9	.957	16	110	71	2b108,3b34		0.4
1921	Phi	A	**155**	613	88	168	32	13	16	77	60	15	75	.274	.353	.447	102	1	6-5	.954	21	109	104	2b155		2.4
1922	Phi	A	145	501	66	138	23	7	12	68	55	11	98	.275	.359	.421	100	1	6-2	.945	-4	96	75	3b141,2b5		-0.8
1923	Phi	A	124	416	50	105	28	1	4	43	35	5	40	.252	.318	.353	76	-15	6-4	.964	2	106	95	2b102,S20,3b2		-0.4
1924	Phi	A	110	410	68	128	26	6	3	50	38	1	60	.312	.372	.427	105	0	3-3	.961	10	109	103	2b77,3b27,S4		1.5
1925	Phi	A	122	465	93	150	32	11	5	55	46	8	49	.323	.393	.471	111	8	1-3	.944	6	94	62	3b64,2b58,S2		1.8
1926	Phi	A	124	429	64	123	21	5	5	60	44	8	34	.287	.370	.392	94	-2	6-2	.950	16	107	128	3b82,2b44/S		2.0
1927	Phi	A	121	417	61	135	33	6	3	60	44	4	23	.324	.394	.453	113	9	2-3	.989	-5	91	125	3b82,2b4/S		0.2
1928	Phi	A	85	242	39	67	11	0	5	30	20	4	21	.277	.361	.384	93	-1	2-1	.982	-2	95	92	2b32,3b25,S5,O5(0/4/1),2b3,P2		0.0
1929	†Phi	A	119	401	76	131	34	6	13	79	51	**7**	29	.327	.400	.539	138	24	8-3	.928	-17	80	79	S60,3b48,2b12		0.0
1930	†Phi	A	125	435	69	131	28	4	6	73	74	**10**	53	.301	.414	.425	109	10	3-3	.960	-13	82	90	3b123/OL		1.7
1931	†Phi	A	101	355	48	97	28	5	7	46	49	6	47	.273	.361	.389	94	-1	1-2	.974	-2	93	93	3b87,S15		0.4
1932	Phi	A	153	558	71	148	29	5	7	90	77	4	65	.265	.358	.373	92	-9	8-2	**.980**	-9	89	89	3b141,S10/2		-1.1

YEAR	TM LG	G	AB	R	H	2B	3B	HR	RBI	BB-IB	HP	SO	AVG	OBP	SLG	AOPS	ABR	SB-CS	FA	FR	RNG	THR	GAMES AT POSITION	DL	BFW
1933	Chi A★	151	554	49	144	22	6	1	68	69	12	37	.260	.354	.327	85	-9	3-7	.953	-1	109	83	3b151		-0.6
1934	Chi A☆	127	456	52	122	17	4	7	82	64	4	28	.268	.363	.368	86	-8	1-1	.944	-5	113	59	3b74,1b27,2b27,M		-1.0
1935	Chi A	117	403	45	116	24	2	4	61	59	2	28	.288	.381	.387	97	0	4-3	.953	-6	96	96	3b98,1b16,2b3,M		-0.4
1936	Chi A	127	435	62	116	16	3	7	60	61	4	36	.267	.362	.366	77	-15	1-3	.951	-6	104	71	3b125,M		-1.6
1937	Chi A	30	85	10	26	5	0	1	23	9	0	7	.306	.372	.400	95	0	0-0	.993	0	65	108	1b15,3b11,M		-0.1
1938	Chi A	26	89	9	27	4	2	2	13	10	0	8	.303	.374	.461	105	1	0-0	.941	-3	92	76	2b23/S3M		-0.1
1939	Chi A	2	1	0	0	0	0	0	0	0	0	0	.000	.000	.000	-97	0	0-0	.667	-0	0	0	3b2,M		-0.1
Total	22	2282	8046	1108	2256	453	90	108	1071	958	115	850	.280	.365	.399	96	-32	70-55	.952	11	98	95	3b1257,2b722,1b148,S140,O7C,P2		4.9

DYKSTRA, LENNY Leonard Kyle "Nails" B2.10.1963 Santa Ana CA BL/TL/5-10/167(160-195) [NYN81 13/315] d5.3 [DL 1997 Phi N 181, 1998 Phi N 181]

YEAR	TM LG	G	AB	R	H	2B	3B	HR	RBI	BB-IB	HP	SO	AVG	OBP	SLG	AOPS	ABR	SB-CS	FA	FR	RNG	THR	GAMES AT POSITION	DL	BFW
																									0.6
1985	NY N	83	236	40	60	9	3	1	19	30-0	1	24	.254	.338	.331	90	-2	15-2	.994	6	114	167	O74C		2.7
1986	†NY N	147	431	77	127	27	7	8	45	58-1	5	55	.295	.377	.445	129	18	31-7	.990	4	110	125	O139(1/138/0)		1.2
1987	NY N	132	431	86	123	37	3	10	43	40-3	4	67	.285	.352	.455	116	11	27-7	.988	-1	103	73	O118C		1.2
1988	†NY N	126	429	57	116	19	3	8	33	30-2	3	43	.270	.321	.385	106	3	30-8	.996	5	114	71	O112C		1.2
1989	NY N	56	159	27	43	12	1	3	13	23-0	1	15	.270	.362	.415	129	7	13-1	.991	2	98	207	O88C		-0.9
	Phi N	90	352	39	78	20	3	4	19	37-1	1	38	.222	.297	.330	79	-9	17-11	.991	5	105	152	O139C		0.3
	Year	146	511	66	121	32	4	7	32	60-1	2	53	.237	.318	.356	95	-2	30-12	.988	7	113	84	O149C		4.8
1990	Phi N★	149	590	106	192	35	3	9	60	89-14	7	48	.325	.418	.441	137	36	33-5	.977	1	111	87	O63C	111	1.7
1991	Phi N	63	246	48	73	13	5	3	12	37-1	1	20	.297	.391	.427	131	12	24-4	.989	6	113	123	O85C	83	2.3
1992	Phi N	85	345	53	104	18	0	6	39	40-4	3	32	.301	.375	.406	122	12	30-5	.979	4	113	24	O160C		5.6
1993	†Phi N	161	637	143	194	44	6	19	66	129-9	2	64	.305	.420	.482	144	48	37-12	.984	4	114	88	O82C	35	1.8
1994	Phi N*	84	315	68	86	26	5	5	24	68-11	2	44	.273	.404	.435	117	12	15-4	.987	1	109	59	O61(9/52/0)	86	-0.2
1995	Phi N★	62	254	37	67	15	1	2	18	33-2	1	28	.264	.353	.354	88	-3	10-5	.987	1	110	59	O39C	134	0.9
1996	Phi N	40	134	21	35	6	3	3	13	26-2	2	25	.261	.387	.418	112	3	3-1	1.000	6	127	170	O39C	811	22.9
Total	12	1278	4559	802	1298	281	43	81	404	640-50	31	503	.285	.375	.419	119	148	285-72	.987	46	111	94	O1221(10/1213/0)		

DYLER, JOHN John F. B6.5.1852 Louisville KY D8.15.1916 Fort Myers FL d7.22 U1

																									-0.1
1882	Lou AA	1	4	0	0	0	0	0	0	0			.000	.000	.000	-99	-1		—	-0	0		/OL		

EADDY, DON Donald Johnson B2.16.1934 Grand Rapids MI BR/TR/5-11/170 d4.24 Col Michigan

																									-0.1
1959	Chi N	15	1	3	0	0	0	0	0	0-0	1	1	.000	.000	.000	-99	0	0-0	.500	-0	115	0	/3		

EAGAN, TRUCK Charles Eugene B8.10.1877 San Francisco CA D3.19.1949 San Francisco CA BR/TR/5-11/190 d5.1

																									-0.3
1901	Pit N	4	12	0	1	0	0	0	2	0		0	.083	.083	.083	-50	-2	1	.923	-1	105	0	S3		-0.1
	Cle A	5	18	2	3	0	1	0	2	1		0	.167	.211	.278	36	-2	0	1.000	1	139	0	2b5/3		-0.4
Total	2	9	30	2	4	0	1	0	4	1		0	.133	.161	.200	2	-4	1	1.000	0	139	0	2b5,S3/3		

EAGAN, BILL William "Bad Bill" B6.1.1869 Camden NJ D2.13.1905 Denver CO d4.8

																									0.8
1891	StL AA	82	297	49	65	11	4	4	43	44	3	53	.219	.326	.323	75	-11	21	.929	18	116	93	2b82		0.0
1893	Chi N	6	19	3	5	0	0	0	2	5	0		.263	.417	.263	83	0	4	.912	0	106	144	2b6		0.7
1898	Pit N	19	61	14	20	2	3	0	5	8	6		.328	.453	.459	165	6	1	.914	1	106	147	2b17		1.5
Total	3	107	377	66	90	13	7	4	50	57	9	58	.239	.352	.342	88	-5	26	.926	19	114	105	2b105		

EAGLE, BILL William Lycurgus B7.25.1877 Rockville MD D4.27.1951 Churchton MD d8.20

																									0.0
1898	Was N	4	13	0	4	1	0	0	2	0			.308	.308	.385	98	0	0	.750	-0	281	0	O4(1/0/1)		

EAKLE, CHARLIE Charles Emory B9.27.1887 MD D6.15.1959 Baltimore MD d8.20

																									-0.2
1915	Bal F	2	7	0	2	1	0	0	0	0			.286	.286	.429	97	0	1	.600	-2	47	0	2b2		

EARL, HOWARD Howard J. "Slim Jim" B2.27.1869 MA D12.22.1916 North Bay NY 6-2/180 d4.19

																									-1.5
1890	Chi N	92	384	57	95	10	3	7	51	18	2	47	.247	.285	.344	80	-13	17	.861	-6	107	71	O49R,2b39,S4,1b3		-0.8
1891	Mil AA	31	129	21	32	5	2	1	17	5	1	13	.248	.281	.341	65	-7	3	.978	-2	38	98	O30R,1b2		-2.3
Total	2	123	513	78	127	15	5	8	68	23	3	60	.248	.284	.343	76	-20	20	.904	-7	79	82	O79R,2b39,1b5,S4		

EARL, SCOTT William Scott B9.18.1960 Seymour IN BR/TR/5-11/165 [DetA81 14/354] d9.10 Col Eastern Kentucky

																									-0.5
1984	Det A	14	35	3	4	0	1	0	1	0-0		9	.114	.114	.171	-22	-6	1-0	.959	0	85	166	2b14		

EARLE, BILLY William Moffat "The Little Globetrotter" B11.10.1867 Philadelphia PA D5.30.1946 Omaha NE BR/TR/5-10.5/170 d4.27

																									0.3
1889	Cin N	53	169	37	45	4	7	4	31	30	3	24	.266	.386	.444	132	7	26	.776	-4	133	175	O26(2/1/23),C23,1b5		0.1
1890	StL AA	22	73	16	17	3	1	0	12	7	2		.233	.317	.301	72	-3	6	.955	3	100	105	C18,O3R/S32		0.4
1892	Pit N	5	13	5	7	2	0	0	3	4	0	1	.538	.647	.692	304	4	2	.909	-0	108	106	C5		0.1
1893	Pit N	27	95	21	24	4	4	2	15	7	0	6	.253	.304	.442	99	-1	1	.959	2	98	71	C27		0.4
1894	Lou N	21	65	10	23	1	0	0	7	9	1		.354	.432	.369	102	1	2	.954	3	98	169	C18/123OL		0.1
	Bro N	14	50	13	17	6	0	0	6	6	1	2	.340	.421	.460	121	2	4	.930	2	90	139	C12/2		0.5
	Year	35	115	23	40	7	0	0	13	15	1	5	.348	.427	.409	110	4	6	.944	1	97	113	C103,O30(3/1/26),1b6,2b3,3b2/S		1.4
Total	5	142	465	102	133	20	12	6	74	64	6	36	.286	.378	.419	114	10	41	.929	1	98	113	C103,O30(3/1/26),1b6,2b3,3b2/S		

EARLY, JAKE Jacob Willard B5.19.1915 Kings Mountain NC D5.31.1985 Melbourne FL BL/TR/5-11/168 d5.4 Mil 1944-45

																									-0.2
1939	Was A	32	84	8	22	7	2	0	14	5	0	14	.262	.303	.393	83	-3	0-0	.963	4	165	50	C24		0.3
1940	Was A	80	206	26	53	8	4	5	14	23	1	22	.257	.335	.408	98	-1	0-1	.969	2	88	135	C56		0.2
1941	Was A	104	355	42	102	20	7	10	54	24	3	38	.287	.338	.468	117	6	0-1	.965	-10	93	114	C100		-1.8
1942	Was A	104	353	31	72	14	2	3	46	37	1	37	.204	.281	.280	59	-20	0-0	.981	4	94	133	C98		1.1
1943	Was A★	126	423	37	109	23	3	5	60	53	4	43	.258	.346	.362	111	7	5-3	.980	-4	113	94	C122		-0.7
1946	Was A	64	189	13	38	6	0	4	18	23	0	27	.201	.288	.296	67	-9	0-0	.960	-2	96	146	C64		0.1
1947	StL A	87	214	25	48	9	3	3	19	54	1	34	.224	.381	.336	98	2	0-1	.991	-5	115	185	C92		-0.7
1948	Was A	97	246	22	54	7	2	1	28	36	1	33	.220	.322	.276	62	-13	2-1	.973	-5	82	101	C53		-0.6
1949	Was A	53	138	12	34	4	0	1	11	26	1	11	.246	.370	.297	79	-3	0-1	.976	-28	99	124	C694		-2.3
Total	9	747	2208	216	532	98	23	32	264	281	11	259	.241	.330	.350	89	-34	7-8	.976	-28	99	124	C694		

EASLER, MIKE Michael Anthony B11.29.1950 Cleveland OH BL/TR/6-1/196* [HouN69 14/312] d9.5 C6

																									-0.2
1973	Hou N	6	7	1	0	0	0	0	0	2-1		4	.000	.222	.000	-34	-1	0-0	.500	-1	27	0	O2(1/0/1)		-0.4
1974	Hou N	15	15	0	1	0	0	0	0	0-0		5	.067	.067	.067	-66	-3	0-0	—	0			/H		-0.4
1975	Hou N	5	5	0	0	0	0	0	0	0-0		1	.000	.000	.000	-99	-1	0-0	—	0			/H		-0.3
1976	Cal A	21	54	6	13	1	1	0	4	2-1		11	.241	.259	.296	69	-2	1-1	1.000	-0	103	0	O4(1/0/3)		0.2
1977	Pit N	10	18	3	8	2	0	1	5	0-0		1	.444	.421	.722	200	2	0-0	—	-1	0	0	O4(2/0/2)		0.0
1979	†Pit N	55	54	8	15	1	1	2	11	8-0		13	.278	.371	.444	115	1	0-1	—	-1	0	0	O119(91/0/42)		2.9
1980	Pit N	132	393	66	133	27	3	21	74	43-6		65	.338	.396	.583	166	35	5-9	.986	-1	100	74	O90(72/0/25)		0.5
1981	Pit N★	95	339	43	97	18	5	7	42	24-7		45	.286	.328	.431	110	4	4-7	.973	-1	98	78	O138(137/0/3)		0.0
1982	Pit N	142	475	52	131	27	2	15	58	40-12	6	85	.276	.337	.436	110	7	1-1	.965	-5	88	84	O105L	22	-0.2
1983	Pit N	115	381	44	117	17	2	10	54	22-1	3	64	.307	.349	.441	114	7	4-2	.976	3	138	82	D126,1b29		2.8
1984	Bos A	156	601	87	188	31	5	27	91	58-4	4	134	.313	.376	.516	137	31	1-1	.976	3	138	0	D130,O20(18/0/2)		-0.9
1985	Bos A	155	568	74	149	29	4	16	74	53-1	5	129	.262	.325	.412	97	-2	0-1	.958	0	122	0	D129,O11(8/0/3)		1.0
1986	NY A	146	490	64	148	26	4	14	78	49-13	0	87	.302	.362	.449	121	15	3-2	.981	2	101	222	O30L	15	-0.4
1987	Phi N	33	110	7	31	4	0	1	10	6-0	2	20	.282	.316	.345	73	-4	0-1	1.000	-1	89	106	D32,O15(14/0/1)		-0.3
	NY A	65	167	13	47	6	0	4	21	14-0	1	32	.281	.337	.389	94	-1	1-0	.974	0	97	97	D538(479/0/82),D433,1b29	37	4.5
Total	14	1151	3677	465	1078	189	25	118	522	321-46	17	696	.293	.349	.454	110	87	20-26	.974	1	97	97			

EASLEY, DAMION Jacinto Damion B11.11.1969 New York NY BR/TR/5-11/185(155-190) [CalA88 30/767] d8.13 Col Long Beach (CA) City OF(0/2/5)

																									0.0
1992	Cal A	47	151	14	39	5	0	1	12	8-0	3	26	.258	.307	.311	73	-5	9-5	.970	5	108	175	3b45,S3		0.0
1993	Cal A	73	230	33	72	13	2	2	22	28-2	3	35	.313	.392	.413	114	9	6-6	.978	-11	88	74	2b54,3b14/D	83	-0.3
1994	Cal A	88	316	41	68	16	1	6	30	29-0	4	48	.215	.288	.329	58	-20	4-5	.953	-4	92	54	3b47,2b40	18	-2.2
1995	Cal A	114	357	35	77	14	2	4	35	32-1	6	47	.216	.288	.300	55	-24	5-2	.981	-8	93	79	2b88,S25		-2.5
1996	Cal A	28	45	4	7	1	0	2	7	6-0	0	12	.156	.255	.311	42	-4	0-0	.943	-1	103	183	S13,2b9,3b3,O2C,D2	39	-0.4
	Det A	21	67	10	23	1	0	2	10	4-0	1	13	.343	.384	.448	111	1	3-1	.974	1	111	67	2b8,S8,3b2/D		0.2
	Year	49	112	14	30	2	0	4	17	10-0	1	25	.268	.331	.393	82	-3	3-1	.951	-0	103	154	S21,2b17,3b5,D3,O2C		-0.2
1997	Det A	151	527	97	139	37	3	22	72	68-3	16	102	.264	.362	.471	106	11	28-5	.985	26	113	118	2b140,S30,D2		3.6
1998	Det A★	153	594	84	161	38	2	27	100	39-2	19	124	.271	.332	.478	100	14	15-5	.989	7	99	115	2b147,S19		1.2
1999	Det A	151	549	83	146	30	1	20	65	51-2	15		.266	.346	.434	97	-2	11-3							

YEAR	TM LG	G	AB	R	H	2B	3B	HR	RBI	BB-IB	HP	SO	AVG	OBP	SLG	AOPS	ABR	SB-CS	FA	FR	RNG	THR	GAMES AT POSITION	DL	BFW
2000	Det A	126	464	76	120	27	2	14	58	55-1	11	79	.259	.350	.416	94	-3	13-4	**.990**	11	110	118	2b125	37	1.3
2001	Det A	154	585	77	146	27	7	11	65	52-3	13	90	.250	.323	.376	86	-12	10-5	.982	13	**112**	106	2b153		0.8
2002	Det A	85	304	29	68	14	1	8	30	27-3	11	43	.224	.307	.355	79	-9	1-3	.980	4	108	93	2b84	45	-0.1
2003	TB A	36	107	8	20	3	1	1	7	2-0	0	18	.187	.202	.262	21	-13	0-0	.922	-5	91	97	3b23,2b4,D8		-1.7
2004	Fla N	98	223	26	53	20	1	9	43	24-1	8	36	.238	.331	.457	107	3	4-1	.965	1	104	101	2b25,1b18,S15,3b6,O5R,D3		0.2
2005	Fla N	102	267	37	64	19	1	9	30	26-3	4	47	.240	.312	.419	96	-2	4-1	.978	4	95	102	2b46,S30,3b10		0.7
Total	14	1427	4786	654	1203	265	24	138	586	451-21	115	832	.251	.328	.403	90	-65	113-54	.984	31	104	104	2b1060,S164,3b150,D21,1b18,O7R	222	2.2

EAST, CARL   Carlton William   B8.27.1894 Marietta GA   D1.15.1953 Whitesburg GA   BL/TR/6-2/178   d8.24

YEAR	TM LG	G	AB	R	H	2B	3B	HR	RBI	BB-IB	HP	SO	AVG	OBP	SLG	AOPS	ABR	SB-CS	FA	FR	RNG	THR	GAMES AT POSITION	DL	BFW
1915	StL A	1	1	0	0	0	0	0	0	0	0	0	.000	.000	.000	-99	0		—	-0	0	0	/P		0.0
1924	Was A	2	6	1	2	1	0	0	2	2	0	1	.333	.500	.500	163	1	0-0	.800	-0	107	0	O2R		0.0
Total	2	3	7	1	2	1	0	0	2	2	0	1	.286	.444	.429	134	1	0-0	.800	-1	107	0	O2R/P		0.0

EAST, HARRY   Henry H.   B4.1863 St.Louis MO   D6.12.1905 St.Louis MO   d6.17

YEAR	TM LG	G	AB	R	H	2B	3B	HR	RBI	BB-IB	HP	SO	AVG	OBP	SLG	AOPS	ABR	SB-CS	FA	FR	RNG	THR	GAMES AT POSITION	DL	BFW
1882	Bal AA	1	4	0	0	0	0	0		0			.000	.000	.000	-99	-1		.600	-1	88	0	/3		-0.1

EASTER, LUKE   Luscious Luke   B8.4.1915 Jonestown MS   D3.29.1979 Euclid OH   BL/TR/6-4.5/240*   d8.11   C1   Negro Lg 1946-48

YEAR	TM LG	G	AB	R	H	2B	3B	HR	RBI	BB-IB	HP	SO	AVG	OBP	SLG	AOPS	ABR	SB-CS	FA	FR	RNG	THR	GAMES AT POSITION	DL	BFW
1949	Cle A	21	45	6	10	3	0	0	2	8	0	6	.222	.340	.289	68	-2	0-1	1.000	-2	61	0	O12R		-0.4
1950	Cle A	141	540	96	151	20	4	28	107	70	**10**	95	.280	.373	.487	123	17	0-3	.991	-3	91	94	1b128,O13R		0.8
1951	Cle A	128	486	65	131	12	5	27	103	37	9	71	.270	.333	.481	125	13	0-1	.988	-9	75	98	1b125		-0.1
1952	Cle A	127	437	63	115	10	3	31	97	44	5	84	.263	.337	.513	144	22	1-1	.983	1	107	91	1b118		2.0
1953	Cle A	68	211	26	64	9	0	7	31	15	4	35	.303	.361	.445	120	5	0-2	.981	-2	88	123	1b56	56	0.0
1954	Cle A	6	6	0	1	0	0	0	0	0	0	2	.167	.167	.167	-8	-1	0-0	—	0			/H		-0.1
Total	6	491	1725	256	472	54	12	93	340	174	28	293	.274	.350	.481	126	54	1-8	.986	-14	90	98	1b427,O25R	56	2.2

EASTERDAY, HENRY   Henry P.   B9.16.1864 Philadelphia PA   D3.30.1895 Philadelphia PA   BR/TR/5-6/145   d6.23

YEAR	TM LG	G	AB	R	H	2B	3B	HR	RBI	BB-IB	HP	SO	AVG	OBP	SLG	AOPS	ABR	SB-CS	FA	FR	RNG	THR	GAMES AT POSITION	DL	BFW
1884	Phi U	28	115	12	28	5	0	0		5			.243	.275	.287	76	-6		.875	7	123	111	S28		0.1
1888	KC A	115	401	42	76	7	6	3	37	31	5		.190	.256	.259	61	-18	23	.888	26	**125**	92	S115		1.0
1889	Col AA	95	324	43	56	5	8	4	34	41	2	57	.173	.270	.275	58	-18	10	.890	15	109	81	S89,2b5/3		-0.1
1890	Col AA	58	197	25	31	5	1	1	17	23	1		.157	.249	.208	37	-15	5	.879	5	107	133	S58		-0.7
	Phi AA	19	68	17	10	1	0	1	3	10	0		.147	.256	.206	37	-5	4	.876	-1	97	104	S19		-0.5
	Lou AA	7	24	2	2	0	0	0	1	2	1		.083	.185	.083	-21	-4	1	.886	0	123	66	S6/3		-0.3
	Year	84	289	44	43	6	1	2	21	35	2		.149	.245	.197	32	-24	10	.879	5	106	122	S83/3		-1.5
Total	4	322	1129	141	203	23	15	9	92	112	9	57	.180	.259	.251	54	-66	43	.885	52	115	98	S315,2b5,3b2		-0.5

EASTERLING, PAUL   Paul   B9.28.1905 Reidsville GA   D3.15.1993 Reidsville GA   BR/TR/5-11/180   d4.11

YEAR	TM LG	G	AB	R	H	2B	3B	HR	RBI	BB-IB	HP	SO	AVG	OBP	SLG	AOPS	ABR	SB-CS	FA	FR	RNG	THR	GAMES AT POSITION	DL	BFW
1928	Det A	43	114	17	37	7	1	3	12	8	1	24	.325	.374	.482	122	3	2-1	.921	-1	101	67	O34(32/0/2)		0.0
1930	Det A	29	79	7	16	6	0	1	14	6	0	18	.203	.259	.316	44	-7	0-1	1.000	1	91	216	O25(8/1/16)		-0.7
1938	Phi A	4	7	1	2	0	0	0	0	1	0	2	.286	.375	.286	70	0	0-0	.750	-0	81	0	/OC		-0.1
Total	3	76	200	25	55	13	1	4	26	15	1	44	.275	.329	.410	88	-4	2-2	.938	-0	97	116	O60(40/2/18)		-0.8

EASTERLY, TED   Theodore Harrison   B4.20.1885 Lincoln NE   D7.6.1951 Clearlake Highlands CA   BL/TR/5-8/165   d4.17

YEAR	TM LG	G	AB	R	H	2B	3B	HR	RBI	BB-IB	HP	SO	AVG	OBP	SLG	AOPS	ABR	SB-CS	FA	FR	RNG	THR	GAMES AT POSITION	DL	BFW
1909	Cle A	98	287	32	75	14	10	1	27	13			.261	.293	.390	111	2	8	.965	3	105	110	C76		1.3
1910	Cle A	110	363	34	111	16	6	0	55	21	0		.306	.344	.383	126	10	10	.964	-9	82	103	C65,O32R		0.7
1911	Cle A	99	287	34	93	19	5	1	37	8	4		.324	.345	.436	116	5	6	.910	-6	100	94	O54(0/2/52),C22		-0.2
1912	Cle A	65	186	17	55	4	0	2	21	7	2		.296	.328	.349	91	-3	3	.958	-1	91	92	C51		0.0
	Chi A	30	55	5	20	2	0	0	14	2	0		.364	.386	.400	129	2	2	.964	-2	87	86	C10/OL		0.1
	Year	95	241	22	75	6	0	2	35	9	2		.311	.341	.361	100	-1	5	.959	-3	90	91	C61/OL		0.1
1913	Chi A	60	97	3	23	1	0	0	8	4	0		.237	.267	.247	51	-6	2	.976	3	140	84	C19		-0.2
1914	KC F	134	436	58	146	20	12	1	67	31	4	25	.335	.384	.443	130	11	10	.969	-16	92	93	C128		0.5
1915	KC F	110	309	32	84	12	5	3	32	21	1	15	.272	.320	.372	99	-7	2	.969	3	98	96	C88		0.4
Total	7	706	2020	215	607	88	38	8	261	107	8	49	.300	.338	.394	112	14	43	.965	-27	95	97	C459,O87(1/2/84)		2.6

EASTERWOOD, ROY   Roy Charles "Shag"   B1.12.1915 Waxahachie TX   D8.24.1984 Graham TX   BR/TR/6-0.5/196   d4.21

YEAR	TM LG	G	AB	R	H	2B	3B	HR	RBI	BB-IB	HP	SO	AVG	OBP	SLG	AOPS	ABR	SB-CS	FA	FR	RNG	THR	GAMES AT POSITION	DL	BFW
1944	Chi N	17	33	1	7	2	0	1	2	2	0	11	.212	.235	.364	67	-2	0	1.000	-0	108	125	C12		-0.1

EASTON, JOHN   John David "Goose"   B3.4.1933 Trenton NJ   D7.28.2001 Princeton NJ   BR/TR/6-2/185*   d6.19   Col Princeton

YEAR	TM LG	G	AB	R	H	2B	3B	HR	RBI	BB-IB	HP	SO	AVG	OBP	SLG	AOPS	ABR	SB-CS	FA	FR	RNG	THR	GAMES AT POSITION	DL	BFW
1955	Phi N	1	0	0	0	0	0	0	0	0-0	0						0	0-0	—	0			/R		0.0
1959	Phi N	3	3	0	0	0	0	0	0	0-0	0	3	.000	.000	.000	-98	-1	0-0	—	0			/H		-0.1
Total	2	4	3	0	0	0	0	0	0	0-0	0	3	.000	.000	.000	-98	-1	0-0	—	0					-0.1

EAYRS, EDDIE   Edwin   B11.10.1890 Blackstone MA   D11.30.1969 Warwick RI   BL/TL/5-7/160   d6.30   Col Brown ▲

YEAR	TM LG	G	AB	R	H	2B	3B	HR	RBI	BB-IB	HP	SO	AVG	OBP	SLG	AOPS	ABR	SB-CS	FA	FR	RNG	THR	GAMES AT POSITION	DL	BFW
1913	Pit N	4	6	0	1	0	0	0		1	0	1	.167	.167	.167	-5	-0		.667	-0	97	0	P2		0.0
1920	Bos N	87	244	31	80	5	2	1	24	30	4	18	.328	.410	.377	133	12	4-3	.950	-3	87	85	O63(43/7/13),P7		0.5
1921	Bos N	15	15	0	1	0	0	0	1	2	0	4	.067	.067	.067	-68	-2	0-0	—	-0	0	0	P2		0.0
	Bro N	8	6	1	1	0	0	0	1	2	0	0	.167	.375	.167	47	0	0-0	—	-0	0	0	/OR		0.0
	Year	23	21	1	2	0	0	0	2	4	0	4	.095	.174	.095	-27	-4	0-0	—	-0	0	0	P2/OR		0.0
Total	3	114	271	32	83	5	2	1	26	32	4	23	.306	.388	.351	116	10	4-3	.950	-4	87	85	O64(43/7/14),P11		0.5

EBRIGHT, HI   Hiram C. "Buck"   B6.12.1859 Lancaster Co. PA   D10.24.1916 Milwaukee WI   BR/TR/5-9/180   d4.24

YEAR	TM LG	G	AB	R	H	2B	3B	HR	RBI	BB-IB	HP	SO	AVG	OBP	SLG	AOPS	ABR	SB-CS	FA	FR	RNG	THR	GAMES AT POSITION	DL	BFW
1889	Was N	16	59	7	15	2	2	1	6	3	1	8	.254	.302	.407	103	0	1	.875	3			C9,O4R,S3		0.3

ECHEVARRIA, ANGEL   Angel Santos   B5.25.1971 Bridgeport CT   BR/TR/6-3/226(214-230)   [ColN92 17/487]   d7.15   Col Rutgers

YEAR	TM LG	G	AB	R	H	2B	3B	HR	RBI	BB-IB	HP	SO	AVG	OBP	SLG	AOPS	ABR	SB-CS	FA	FR	RNG	THR	GAMES AT POSITION	DL	BFW
1996	Col N	26	21	2	6	0	0	0	6	2-0	1	5	.286	.346	.286	63	-1	0-0	1.000	-1	19	0	O11(4/0/7)		-0.2
1997	Col N	15	20	4	5	2	0	0	5	2-0	0	5	.250	.318	.350	61	-1	0-0	1.000	0	58	481	O7(2/2/3)		-0.1
1998	Col N	19	29	7	11	3	0	1	9	2-0	2	3	.379	.455	.586	141	2	0-0	1.000	-1	89	116	1b4,O4(3/0/1)		0.1
1999	Col N	102	191	28	56	7	0	11	35	17-0	3	34	.293	.360	.503	92	-2	1-3	.985	2	107	151	O49(20/0/31),1b10		-0.3
2000	Col N	10	9	0	1	0	0	0	2	0-0	0	2	.111	.111	.111	-36	-2	0-0	1.000	-0	262	0	1b2/OL		-0.2
	Mil N	31	42	3	9	2	0	1	4	7-0	0	9	.214	.327	.333	68	-2	0-0	1.000	-0	109	119	1b9,O5(2/0/3)		-0.2
	Year	41	51	3	10	2	0	1	6	7-0	0	11	.196	.293	.294	47	-4	0-0	1.000	-0	134	98	1b11,O6(3/0/3)		-0.4
2001	Mil N	75	133	12	34	11	0	5	13	8-0	3	29	.256	.310	.451	96	-1	0-1	.931	-3	75		O23(19/0/5),1b10/D		-0.6
2002	Chi N	50	98	14	30	7	0	3	21	8-0	1	17	.306	.351	.469	121	1	0-0	.971	1	138	123	O19(8/0/11),1b13		0.3
Total	7	328	543	70	152	32	0	21	90	46-0	10	104	.280	.343	.455	94	-4	1-4	.972	-2	94	125	O119(59/2/61),1b48/D		-1.2

ECHOLS, JOHNNY   John Gresham   B1.9.1917 Atlanta GA   D11.13.1972 Atlanta GA   BR/TR/5-10.5/175   d5.24

YEAR	TM LG	G	AB	R	H	2B	3B	HR	RBI	BB-IB	HP	SO	AVG	OBP	SLG	AOPS	ABR	SB-CS	FA	FR	RNG	THR	GAMES AT POSITION	DL	BFW
1939	StL N	2	0	0	0	0	0	0	0	0	0	0	—	—	—		0		—	0			/R		0.0

ECKHARDT, OX   Oscar George   B12.23.1901 Yorktown TX   D4.22.1951 Yorktown TX   BL/TR/6-1/185   d4.16   Col Texas

YEAR	TM LG	G	AB	R	H	2B	3B	HR	RBI	BB-IB	HP	SO	AVG	OBP	SLG	AOPS	ABR	SB-CS	FA	FR	RNG	THR	GAMES AT POSITION	DL	BFW
1932	Bos N	8	8	1	2	0	0	0	1	0	0	1	.250	.250	.250	36	-1	0	—	0			/H		-0.1
1936	Bro N	16	44	5	8	1	0	1	6	5	0	2	.182	.265	.273	45	-3	0	1.000	0	111	87	O10R		-0.4
Total	2	24	52	6	10	1	0	1	7	5	0	3	.192	.263	.269	43	-4	0	1.000	0	111	87	O10R		-0.5

ECKSTEIN, DAVID   David Mark   B1.20.1975 Sanford FL   BR/TR/5-6.5/170*   [BosA97 19/581]   d4.3   Col Florida

YEAR	TM LG	G	AB	R	H	2B	3B	HR	RBI	BB-IB	HP	SO	AVG	OBP	SLG	AOPS	ABR	SB-CS	FA	FR	RNG	THR	GAMES AT POSITION	DL	BFW
2001	Ana A	153	582	82	166	26	2	4	41	43-0	21	60	.285	.355	.357	87	-9	29-4	.971	-12	98	90	S126,2b14,D14		-0.7
2002	†Ana A	152	608	107	178	22	6	8	63	45-0	**27**	44	.293	.363	.388	103	4	21-13	.977	-13	96	106	S147,D3		0.2
2003	Ana A	120	452	59	114	22	1	3	31	36-0	15	45	.252	.325	.325	76	-14	16-5	.984	-3	94	94	S116,D3		-0.7
2004	†Ana A	142	566	92	156	24	1	2	35	42-1	13	49	.276	.339	.332	80	-16	16-5	**.988**	-25	81	90	S138/D	22	-2.7
2005	†StL N★	158	630	90	185	26	7	8	61	58-0	13	44	.294	.363	.395	97	-1	11-8	.981	**33**	**118**	**134**	S156		4.2
Total	5	725	2838	430	799	120	17	25	231	224-1	89	242	.282	.351	.362	90	-36	93-35	.980	-20	98	104	S683,D21,2b14	22	0.3

EDEN, CHARLIE   Charles M.   B1.18.1855 Lexington KY   D9.17.1920 Cincinnati OH   BL/TL/?/168   d8.17 ▲

YEAR	TM LG	G	AB	R	H	2B	3B	HR	RBI	BB-IB	HP	SO	AVG	OBP	SLG	AOPS	ABR	SB-CS	FA	FR	RNG	THR	GAMES AT POSITION	DL	BFW
1877	Chi N	15	55	9	12	0	1	0	5	3			.218	.259	.255	56	-3		.679	-2	78	229	O15R		-0.4
1879	Cle N	81	353	40	96	**31**	7	3	34	6		20	.272	.284	.425	131	13		.808	-4	118	138	O80(0/1/79),1b3/C		0.8
1884	Pit AA	32	122	12	33	7	4	1		7	6		.270	.341	.418	148	7		.759	-4	72	0	O31C,P2		0.2
1885	Pit AA	98	405	57	103	18	6	0	38	17	8		.254	.298	.328	99	0		.814	-6	43	71	O96L,P4,3b2		-1.6
Total	4	226	935	118	244	56	18	4	77	33	14	26	.261	.294	.372	115	17		.793	-26	77	97	O222(96/32/94),P6,1b3,3b2/C		-1.0

YEAR	TM LG	G	AB	R	H	2B	3B	HR	RBI	BB-IB	HP	SO	AVG	OBP	SLG	AOPS	ABR	SB-CS	FA	FR	RNG	THR	GAMES AT POSITION	DL	BFW

EDEN, MIKE   Edward Michael   B5.22.1949 Fort Clayton, Canal Zone   BB/TR/5-10/170*   d8.2   Col Southern Illinois

																									-0.2
1976	Atl N	5	8	0	0	0	0	0	1	0	0	0	.000	.000	.000	-94	-2	0-0	1.000	0	128	114	2b2		-0.2
1978	Chi A	10	17	1	2	0	0	0	0	4-0	0	0	.118	.286	.118	17	-2	0-0	.905	-0	91	136	S5,2b4		-0.2
Total	2	15	25	1	2	0	0	0	1	4-0	0	0	.080	.207	.080	-16	-4	0-0	1.000	0	85	141	2b6,S5		-0.4

EDINGTON, STUMP   Jacob Frank   B7.4.1891 Koleen IN   D11.11.1969 Bastrop LA   BL/TL/5-8/170   d6.20

1912	Pit N	15	53	4	16	0	2	0	12	3	0	1	.302	.339	.377	97	-1	0	1.000	1	101	155	O14R		0.0

EDLER, DAVE   David Delmar   B8.5.1956 Sioux City IA   BR/TR/6-0/185*   [SeaA78 21/520]   d9.4   Col Washington St.

1980	Sea A	28	89	11	20	1	0	3	9	8-1	0	16	.225	.289	.337	70	-4	2-3	.965	1	107	101	3b28		-0.4
1981	Sea A	29	78	7	11	3	0	0	5	11-0	1	13	.141	.250	.179	26	-7	3-3	.884	-4	89	90	3b26/S		-1.3
1982	Sea A	40	104	14	29	2	2	2	18	11-1	0	13	.279	.345	.394	100	0	4-2	.922	1	93	78	3b31,O2(1/0/1),D2		0.0
1983	Sea A	29	63	2	12	1	1	1	4	5-1	1	11	.190	.257	.286	48	-5	3-3	.875	-3	75	39	3b13,1b5/ORD		-0.9
Total	4	126	334	34	72	7	3	6	36	35-2	2	53	.216	.291	.308	65	-16	12-11	.922	-6	94	84	3b98,D8,1b5,O3(1/0/2)/S		-2.6

EDMONDS, JIM   James Patrick   B6.27.1970 Fullerton CA   BL/TL/6-1/218(190-218)   [CalA88 7/169]   d9.9

1993	Cal A	18	61	5	15	4	1	0	4	2-1	0	16	.246	.270	.344	62	-3	0-2	.981	5	140	354	O17(1/1/15)		0.0
1994	Cal A	94	289	35	79	13	1	5	37	30-3	1	72	.273	.343	.377	84	-7	4-2	.981	9	122	215	O77(59/5/19),1b22		-0.2
1995	Cal A★	141	558	120	162	30	4	33	107	51-4	5	130	.290	.352	.536	129	22	1-4	.998	12	116	119	O139C		3.1
1996	Cal A	114	431	73	131	28	3	27	66	46-2	4	101	.304	.375	.571	133	21	4-0	.997	1	104	94	O111C/D	51	2.1
1997	Ana A	133	502	82	146	27	0	26	80	60-5	4	80	.291	.368	.500	124	18	5-7	.985	8	111	159	O115C,1b11,D8	16	2.4
1998	Ana A	154	599	115	184	42	1	25	91	57-7	1	114	.307	.368	.506	122	20	7-5	.988	2	103	109	O153C		2.2
1999	Ana A	55	204	33	51	17	2	5	23	28-0	1	45	.250	.339	.426	94	-1	5-4	.992	3	105	120	O146C,1b6	119	4.2
2000	†StL N★	152	525	129	155	25	0	42	108	103-3	6	167	.295	.411	.583	146	40	10-3	.982	-5	93	156	O147C,1b2		3.4
2001	†StL N	150	500	95	152	38	1	30	110	93-12	4	136	.304	.410	.564	147	39	5-5	.986	6	107	147	O139C	15	4.9
2002	†StL N	144	476	96	148	31	2	28	83	86-14	8	134	.311	.420	.561	160	43	4-3	.986	13	116	178	O129(1/128/0),D2		5.0
2003	StL N★	137	447	89	123	32	2	39	89	77-6	4	127	.275	.385	.617	158	39	1-3	.988	-4	91	152	O146C/1D		5.1
2004	†StL N	153	498	102	150	38	3	42	111	101-12	5	150	.301	.418	.643	168	55	8-3	.994	-3	98	86	O139C		2.5
2005	StL N★	142	467	88	123	37	1	29	89	91-10	4	139	.263	.385	.533	136	27	5-5	.994	-3	98	86	O139C		2.5
Total	13	1587	5557	1063	1619	362	21	331	998	825-79	46	1411	.291	.384	.543	136	313	59-46	.989	48	105	138	O1500(61/1411/34),1b44,D21	201	34.7

EDMONDSON, BOB   Robert E.   B4.30.1879 Paris KY   D8.14.1931 Lawrence KS   BR/TR/5-11/185   d9.15 ▲

1906	Was A	3	3	1	1	0	0	0	0	0	0		.333	.333	.333	114	0	0	1.000	0	166	0	P2/OR		0.0
1908	Was A	26	80	5	15	4	1	0	2	7	1		.188	.261	.262	77	-2	0	.878	-2	75	140	O24(1/9/14)		-0.6
Total	2	29	83	6	16	4	1	0	2	7	1		.193	.264	.265	78	-2	0	.878	-2	74	139	O25(1/9/15),P2		-0.6

EDMONSON, EDDIE   Earl Edward   B11.20.1889 Hopewell PA   D5.10.1971 Leesburg FL   BL/TL/6-0/175   d10.4

1913	Cle A	2	5	0	0	0	0	0	0	0	0	0	.000	.000	.000	-97	-1	0	1.000	-0	0	0	/1O		-0.2

EDWARDS, BRUCE   Charles Bruce "Bull"   B7.15.1923 Quincy IL   D4.25.1975 Sacramento CA   BR/TR/5-7/194*   d6.23

1946	Bro N	92	292	24	78	13	5	1	25	34	2	20	.267	.348	.356	99	0	1	.982	8	152	108	C91		1.3
1947	†Bro N★	130	471	53	139	15	8	9	80	49	2	55	.295	.364	.418	103	2	2	.983	6	93	106	C128		1.4
1948	Bro N	96	286	36	79	17	2	8	54	26	2	28	.276	.341	.434	105	2	4	.984	-3	138	119	C48,O21L,3b14/1		0.0
1949	†Bro N	64	148	24	31	3	0	8	25	25	1	22	.209	.324	.392	87	-3	0	.990	-1	153	101	C41,O4L/3		-0.2
1950	Bro N	50	142	16	26	4	1	8	16	13	1	22	.183	.256	.394	67	-8	1	1.000	1	232	70	C9		-0.8
1951	Bro N	17	36	6	9	2	0	1	1	8	1	3	.250	.270	.389	74	-1	0-0	.962	-4	57	92	C28,1b9		-0.1
	Chi N☆	51	141	19	33	9	2	3	17	16	1	14	.234	.316	.390	87	-2	1-2	.971	-3	93	88	C37,1b9		-0.6
	Year	68	177	25	42	11	2	4	25	17	1	17	.237	.308	.390	85	-4	1-2	.989	-2	56	69	C22/2		-0.5
1952	Chi N	50	94	7	23	2	2	1	12	8	0	12	.245	.304	.340	77	-3	0-0	—	0			/H		0.0
1954	Chi N	4	3	1	0	0	0	0	1	2	0		.000	.400	.000	15	0	0-0	—	0			/H		0.1
1955	Was A	30	57	5	10	2	0	0	3	16-0	1	6	.175	.356	.211	58	-2	0-1	.980	3	112	179	C22,3b5		-0.1
1956	Cin N	7	5	0	1	0	0	0	0	0-0	1	2	.200	.200	.200	8	-1	0-0	.982	3	118	109	C429,O25L,3b21,1b12,2b2		0.6
Total	10	591	1675	191	429	67	20	39	241	190-0	8	179	.256	.335	.390	93	-16	9-3	.982	3	118	109			

EDWARDS, DAVE   David Leonard   B2.24.1954 Los Angeles CA   BR/TR/6-0/177(166-177)   [MinA71 7/167]   d9.11   b-Marshall b-Mike

1978	Min A	15	44	7	11	3	0	1	3	7-0	2	13	.250	.377	.386	112	1	1-1	.950	3	114	352	O15(10/8/0)		0.3
1979	Min A	96	229	42	57	8	0	8	35	24-1	1	45	.249	.323	.389	87	-4	6-3	.983	3	104	142	O86(37/31/23),D3		-0.3
1980	Min A	81	200	26	50	9	1	2	20	12-1	1	51	.250	.294	.335	68	-9	2-1	.932	-1	96	164	O72(27/47/2),D3	20	-1.1
1981	SD N	58	112	13	24	4	1	2	13	11-0	0	24	.214	.282	.321	78	-4	3-1	.970	3	99	236	O49(11/2/40)		-0.2
1982	SD N	71	55	7	10	2	0	1	2	1-0	1	14	.182	.196	.273	32	-5	0-0	.944	-1	108	0	O45(18/25/2)/1		-0.7
Total	5	321	640	95	152	26	2	14	73	55-2	4	147	.237	.301	.350	77	-21	12-6	.958	7	102	169	O267(103/113/67),D6/1	20	-2.0

EDWARDS, HANK   Henry Albert   B1.29.1919 Elmwood Place OH   D6.22.1988 Anaheim CA   BL/TL/6-0/190*   d9.10   Mil 1944-45

1941	Cle A	16	68	10	15	1	1	1	6	2	0	4	.221	.243	.309	47	-6	0-0	.929	-1	72	203	O16(2/0/14)		-0.8
1942	Cle A	13	48	6	12	2	1	0	7	5	0	8	.250	.321	.333	89	-1	2-1	.968	-1	99	0	O12C		0.2
1943	Cle A	92	297	38	82	18	6	3	28	30	0	34	.276	.343	.407	127	9	4-8	.983	-3	95	76	O74C		2.7
1946	Cle A	124	458	62	138	33	16	10	54	43	0	48	.301	.361	.509	151	28	1-3	.968	2	102	128	O123(0/1/122)		-0.9
1947	Cle A	108	393	54	102	12	3	15	59	31	1	55	.260	.315	.420	106	0	1-3	.990	-3	99	44	O100(39/0/67)	61	-0.3
1948	Cle A	55	160	27	43	9	2	3	18	18	1	18	.269	.346	.406	102	0	1-1	.987	-2	98	36	O41R		-0.1
1949	Cle A	5	15	3	4	0	0	1	1	1	0	2	.267	.313	.467	107	0	0-0	1.000	0	91	0	O5R		0.4
	Chi N	58	176	25	51	8	4	7	21	19	0	22	.290	.359	.500	131	7	0	.988	-1	89	103	O51(18/0/34)		0.6
1950	Chi N	41	110	13	40	11	1	2	21	10	0	13	.364	.417	.536	150	8	0	.976	-2	85	108	O29R		-0.1
1951	Bro N	35	31	1	7	1	0	0	3	4	0	9	.226	.314	.323	70	-1	0-0	—	0			/H		0.1
	Cin N	41	127	14	40	9	1	3	20	13	0	17	.315	.379	.472	126	5	0-2	.985	-2	102	0	O34(26/0/8)		0.0
	Year	76	158	15	47	12	1	3	23	17	0	26	.297	.366	.443	115	4	0-2	.988	0	105	63	O51(33/0/18)		0.3
1952	Cin N	74	184	24	52	7	6	6	28	19	2	22	.283	.350	.484	129	6	0-3	.988	0	115	0	O3L		-0.1
	Chi A	8	18	2	6	0	0	0	1	0	0	2	.333	.333	.333	85	0	0-0	1.000	0	97	142	O21(11/4/7)		-1.0
1953	StL A	65	106	6	21	3	0	0	9	13	0	10	.198	.286	.226	59	-9	0-1	1.000	0	142	71	O5R		0.8
Total	11	735	2191	285	613	116	41	51	276	208	2	264	.280	.343	.440	119	46	9-22	.981	-12	97	81	O560(132/91/345)	61	0.8

EDWARDS, DOC   Howard Rodney   B12.10.1936 Red Jacket WV   BR/TR/6-2/215(200-215)   d4.21   M3/C8   Col Mira Costa (CA) JC

1962	Cle A	53	143	13	39	6	0	3	9	9-0	2	14	.273	.325	.378	91	-2	0-1	.992	7	159	122	C39		0.7
1963	Cle A	10	31	6	8	2	0	0	0	2-2	0	6	.258	.303	.323	76	-1	0-0	.988	3	159	67	C10		-1.0
	KC A	71	240	16	60	12	0	6	35	11-6	2	23	.250	.287	.375	80	-7	0-1	.987	-6	63	100	C63		-0.7
	Year	81	271	22	68	14	0	6	35	13-8	2	29	.251	.289	.369	79	-7	0-1	.987	-3	76	96	C73		-1.5
1964	KC A	97	294	25	66	10	0	5	28	13-0	2	40	.224	.265	.310	57	-17	0-1	.986	0	62	111	C79,1b7		-0.3
1965	KC A	6	20	1	3	0	0	0	1	0-0	0	2	.150	.190	.150	-2	-3	0-0	1.000	0	225	86	C6		-0.6
	NY A	45	100	3	19	3	0	1	9	13-6	1	14	.190	.289	.250	55	-6	1-2	.986	-2	121	68	C43		-0.9
	Year	51	120	4	22	3	0	1	9	14-6	1	16	.183	.274	.233	46	-8	1-2	.988	-2	137	71	C49		-0.3
1970	Phi N	35	78	5	21	0	0	0	6	4-3	1	10	.269	.313	.269	59	-5	0-0	.970	1	47	191	C34		0.3
Total	5	317	906	69	216	33	0	15	87	53-17	9	109	.238	.287	.325	68	-41	1-4	.986	4	91	110	C274,1b7		-2.7

EDWARDS, JOHNNY   John Alban   B6.10.1938 Columbus OH   BL/TR/6-4/216(195-220)   d6.27   Col Ohio St.

1961	†Cin N	52	145	14	27	5	0	2	14	18-4	1	28	.186	.279	.262	45	-11	0-1	.982	-2	88	78	C52		-1.1
1962	Cin N	133	452	47	115	28	5	8	50	45-9	1	70	.254	.322	.392	88	-7	1-1	.987	13	121	98	C130		2.2
1963	Cin N★	148	495	46	128	19	4	11	67	45-5	4	93	.259	.322	.432	99	0	1-5	.995	15	110	107	C148		2.9
1964	Cin N★	126	423	47	119	23	1	7	55	34-9	1	65	.281	.331	.390	100	1	1-2	.992	8	98	129	C110		2.7
1965	Cin N☆	114	371	47	99	22	5	17	51	50-16	1	45	.267	.353	.474	123	13	0-0	.992	2	75	100	C98		-1.4
1966	Cin N	98	282	24	54	8	0	6	39	31-8	0	42	.191	.266	.284	50	-19	1-3	.990	13	95	111	C73		0.0
1967	Cin N	80	209	10	43	6	0	2	20	16-8	1	20	.206	.261	.263	46	-14	1-4	.992	3	199	92	C54		0.2
1968	†StL N	85	230	14	55	9	1	4	29	16-0	1	20	.239	.287	.326	86	-4	1-1	.994	8	105	129	C151		0.2
1969	Hou N	151	496	52	115	20	6	6	50	59-23	1	69	.232	.306	.333	81	-13	2-1	.995	11	117	140	C139		0.1
1970	Hou N	140	458	40	101	16	4	7	49	51-16	1	63	.221	.299	.319	72	-12	1-1	.995	9	120	104	C104		0.3
1971	Hou N	106	317	18	74	13	4	1	23	26-9	0	38	.233	.291	.309	72	-12	1-1	.988	-9	78	85	C105		0.3
1972	Hou N	108	332	33	89	9	2	5	40	50-12	1	39	.268	.358	.373	114	8	2-4	.989	-3	70	84	C76		0.3
1973	Hou N	79	250	24	61	10	2	5	27	19-7	2	23	.244	.301	.360	84	-6	1-0	.989	-3	70	84	C76	33	-0.6

YEAR	TM	LG	G	AB	R	H	2B	3B	HR	RBI	BB-IB	HP	SO	AVG	OBP	SLG	AOPS	ABR	SB-CS	FA	FR	RNG	THR	GAMES AT POSITION	DL	BFW
1974	Hou	N	50	117	8	26	7	1	1	10	11-3	1	12	.222	.292	.325	76	-4	1-1	.989	3	64	71	C32		0.1
Total	14		1470	4577	430	1106	202	32	81	524	465-118	16	635	.242	.311	.353	85	-89	15-23	.992	93	104	108	C1392	33	6.4

EDWARDS, MARSHALL Marshall Lynn B8.27.1952 Fort Lewis WA BL/TL/5-9/157* d4.11 b-David twb-Mike Col UCLA

1981	†Mil	A	40	58	10	14	1	1	0	4	0-0	0	2	.241	.241	.293	56	-4	6-2	.979	-1	92	79	O36(2/21/14)/D		-0.5
1982	†Mil	A	69	178	24	44	4	1	2	14	4-0	0	8	.247	.261	.315	61	-10	10-4	.984	1	109	57	O54(4/13/41),D6		-1.1
1983	Mil	A	51	74	14	22	1	1	0	5	1-0	0	9	.297	.303	.338	83	-2	5-5	1.000	2	102	225	O35(12/12/13),D4		-0.1
Total	3		160	310	48	80	6	3	2	23	5-0	0	19	.258	.267	.316	65	-16	21-11	.987	2	104	105			-1.7

EDWARDS, MIKE Michael Donald B11.24.1976 Goshen NY BR/TR/6-1/180* [CleA95 9/250] d9.20

2003	Oak	A	4	4	0	1	0	0	0	2-0	0	1	.250	.500	.250	106	0	0-0	—	-0	0	0	O2L,D2		0.0
2005	LA	N	88	239	23	59	9	2	3	15	16-0	2	34	.247	.300	.339	67	-12	1-1	.918	-5	89	82	3b39,O34(32/0/3)/SD		-1.8
Total	2		92	243	23	60	9	2	3	15	18-0	2	35	.247	.304	.337	68	-12	1-1	.918	-5	89	82	3b39,O36(34/0/3),D4/S		-1.8

EDWARDS, MIKE Michael Lewis B8.27.1952 Fort Lewis WA BR/TR/5-10/154* [PitN74 7/155] d9.10 b-Dave twb-Marshall Col UCLA

1977	Pit	N	7	6	1	0	0	0	0	0	0-0	1	3	.000	.143	.000	-56	-7	0-0	1.000	1	120	143	2b4		-0.1
1978	Oak	A	142	414	48	113	16	2	1	23	16-0	2	32	.273	.303	.329	81	-11	27-21	.964	-23	87	92	2b133,S9,D4		-3.0
1979	Oak	A	122	400	35	93	12	2	1	23	15-0	2	37	.233	.263	.280	49	-30	10-6	.962	-13	95	61	2b113,S3,D2		-3.6
1980	Oak	A	46	59	10	14	0	0	0	3	1-0	0	5	.237	.250	.237	36	-5	1-1	.971	-3	101	74	2b23/ORD		-0.8
Total	4		317	879	94	220	28	4	2	49	32-0	5	77	.250	.280	.298	62	-47	38-30	.964	-38	92	77	2b273,S12,D11/OR		-7.5

EDWARDS, RALPH Ralph Strunk B12.14.1882 Brewster NY D1.5.1949 White Plains NY BR/TR/5-9/165 d9.17

| 1915 | Phi | N | 2 | 5 | 0 | 0 | 0 | 0 | 0 | 0 | 0-0 | 0 | | .000 | .000 | .000 | -99 | -1 | 0 | 1.000 | -1 | 50 | 0 | /2 | | -0.2 |

EENHOORN, ROBERT Robert Franciscus B2.9.1968 Rotterdam, Netherlands BR/TR/6-3/185(170-185) [NYA90 2/45] d4.27 Col Davidson

1994	NY	A	3	4	1	2	1	0	0	0	0-0	0	0	.500	.500	.750	224	1	0-0	1.000	-1	41	206	S3		0.0
1995	NY	A	5	14	1	2	1	0	0	2	1-0	0	3	.143	.200	.214	8	-2	0-0	1.000	-1	82	123	2b3,S2		-0.2
1996	NY	A	12	14	2	1	0	0	0	2	0-0	0	3	.071	.167	.071	-31	-3	0-0	1.000	1	75	138	2b10,3b2		-0.2
	Cal	A	6	15	1	4	0	0	0	0	2-0	0	5	.267	.267	.267	35	-2	0-0	.875	1	74	52	S4,2b2		-0.2
	Year		18	29	3	5	0	0	0	2	2-0	0	8	.172	.212	.172	3	-4	0-0	.971	-1	85	137	2b12,S4,3b2		-0.4
1997	Ana	A	11	20	2	7	1	0	1	6	0-0	0	5	.350	.333	.550	130	3	0-0	.833	-3	59	0	3b5,S2,2b2		-0.2
Total	4		37	67	7	16	3	0	1	10	3-0	0	10	.239	.260	.328	53	-5	0-0	.963	-5	78	117	2b18,S11,3b7		-0.8

EGAN, BEN Arthur Augustus B11.20.1883 Augusta NY D2.18.1968 Sherrill NY BR/TR/6-0/195 d9.29 C2

1908	Phi	A	2	6	1	1	0	0	0	1		0		.167	.286	.333	95	0	0	.933	-0	76	105	C2		0.0
1912	Phi	A	49	138	9	24	3	4	0	13	6	0		.174	.208	.254	33	-13	3	.958	4	135	122	C46		-0.6
1914	Cle	A	29	88	7	20	2	1	0	11	3	3		.227	.277	.273	63	-4	0-1	.975	2	91	116	C27		0.0
1915	Cle	A	42	120	4	13	3	0	0	6	8	0	14	.108	.164	.133	-11	-17	0	.970	6	115	107	C40		-0.8
Total	4		122	352	21	58	9	5	0	30	18	3	34	.165	.212	.219	27	-34	3-1	.966	11	116	115	C115		-1.4

EGAN, JIM James K. "Troy Terrier" B1858 Derby CT D9.26.1884 New Haven CT TL d5.15 ▲

| 1882 | Tro | N | 30 | 115 | 15 | 23 | 2 | 0 | 1 | | 2 | 0 | | .200 | .207 | .261 | 51 | -6 | | .625 | -6 | 62 | 132 | O18(2/16/0),P12,C2 | | -0.8 |

EGAN, DICK Richard Joseph B6.23.1884 Portland OR D7.7.1947 Oakland CA BR/TR/5-11/162 d9.15 Col Fordham OF(11/2/14)

1908	Cin	N	18	68	8	14	3	1	0			0		.206	.229	.279	64	-3	7	.891	-2	92	202	2b18		-0.6
1909	Cin	N	127	480	59	132	14	3	2	53	37	2		.275	.329	.329	105	3	7	.950	24	117	112	2b116,S10		3.0
1910	Cin	N	135	474	70	116	11	5	0	46	53	1	38	.245	.322	.289	82	-10	41	.961	-10	101	80	2b131,S3		-2.0
1911	Cin	N	153	558	80	139	11	5	1	56	59	1	50	.249	.322	.292	75	-19	37	.949	-10	109	103	2b152		-0.6
1912	Cin	N	149	507	69	125	14	5	0	52	56	2	26	.247	.324	.294	72	-19	24	.973	1	101	85	2b149		-1.5
1913	Cin	N	60	195	15	55	7	3	0	22	15	0	13	.282	.333	.349	95	-1	6-10	.972	-1	96	113	2b37,S17,3b2		-0.2
1914	Bro	N	106	337	30	76	10	3	1	21	22	0	25	.226	.273	.294	64	-16	1	.914	-10	94	74	S83,3b10,O3(0/2/1),2b2/1		-2.2
1915	Bro	N	3	3	0	0	0	0	0	0	0	0		.000	.000	.000	-98	-1	0	—	0			/H		-0.1
	Bos	N	83	220	20	57	9	1	0	21	28	0	18	.259	.343	.309	102	0	3-4	.974	1	101	86	O24(11/0/13),2b22,S10,1b9,3b4		0.2
	Year		86	223	20	57	9	1	0	21	28	0	18	.256	.339	.305	100	1	3-4	.974	1	101	86	O24(11/0/13),2b22,S10,1b9,3b4		0.1
1916	Bos	N	83	238	23	53	8	3	0	16	19	0	21	.223	.280	.282	76	-7	2	.949	-18	83	60	2b59,S12,3b8		-2.7
Total	9		917	3080	374	767	87	29	4	292	291	6	191	.249	.315	.300	82	-70	167-14	.956	-5	104	98	2b686,S135,O27R,3b24,1b10		-6.7

EGAN, TOM Thomas Patrick B6.9.1946 Los Angeles CA BR/TR (BB 1974p, 75)/6-4/218* d5.27

1965	Cal	A	18	38	3	10	0	1	0	1	3-0	0	12	.263	.317	.316	82	-1	0-0	1.000	-2	115	0	C16	32	-0.3
1966	Cal	A	7	11	0	0	0	0	0		1-0	0	5	.000	.083	.000	-76	-3	0-0	1.000	2	0	0	C6		-0.1
1967	Cal	A	1	1	0	0	0	0	0	0	0-0	0	0	.000	.000	.000	-99	-1	0-0	1.000	0	0	0	/C		0.0
1968	Cal	A	16	43	2	5	1	0	1	4	2-0	0	15	.116	.156	.209	10	-5	0-0	1.000	0	53	91	C14		-0.5
1969	Cal	A	46	120	7	17	1	0	5	16	17-2	1	41	.142	.248	.275	50	-9	0-1	.985	4	96	147	C46	36	-0.3
1970	Cal	A	79	210	14	50	6	0	4	20	14-1	1	67	.238	.286	.324	71	-9	0-0	.988	-5	81	97	C79		-1.1
1971	Chi	A	85	251	29	60	11	1	10	34	26-1	4	94	.239	.320	.410	103	1	1-0	.986	5	59	82	C77/1		0.7
1972	Chi	A	50	141	8	27	3	0	2	9	4-0	2	48	.191	.224	.255	42	-11	0-0	.986	4	65	109	C46		-0.6
1974	Cal	A	43	94	4	11	0	0	4	8	1-0	0	40	.117	.194	.117	-9	-13	1-0	.996	5	59	125	C41		-0.7
1975	Cal	A	28	70	7	16	3	0	0	3	5-0	0	14	.229	.280	.300	69	-3	0-0	.965	-2	46	158	C28		-0.4
Total	10		373	979	74	196	25	3	22	91	80-4	9	336	.200	.266	.299	62	-53	2-1	.987	8	70	105	C354/1	68	-3.3

EGGERT, ELMER Elmer Albert "Mose" B1.29.1902 Rochester NY D4.9.1971 Rochester NY BR/TR/5-9/160 d4.27

| 1927 | Bos | A | 5 | 3 | 0 | 0 | 0 | 0 | 0 | 0 | 1-0 | 0 | 1 | .000 | .250 | .000 | -31 | -1 | 0-0 | — | -0 | 0 | 0 | /2 | | -0.1 |

EGGLER, DAVE David Daniel B4.30.1849 Brooklyn NY D4.5.1902 Buffalo NY BR/TR/5-9/165 d5.18

1871	Mut	NA	33	147	37	47	7	3	0	18	4		3	.320	.338	.408	124	6	14-3	.910	5	78	158	O33C		0.8
1872	Mut	NA	56	290	94	97	20	0	0	19	8		9	.334	.352	.403	141	17	18-6	.917	14	194	181	O56(1/55/0)		2.2
1873	Mut	NA	53	266	82	90	13	4	0	35	6		2	.338	.353	.417	129	9	3-2	.856	4	81	79	O53C/3		0.9
1874	Phi	NA	58	299	70	95	13	8	0	31	5		1	.318	.329	.415	132	9	5-6	.906	7	111	198	O57(7/50/0),2b2		1.2
1875	Ath	NA	66	295	66	89	13	7	0	33	1		10	.302	.304	.393	126	6	6-5	.921	4	68	162	O66(2/65/0)		0.7
1876	Phi	N	39	174	28	52	4	0	0	19	2		2	.299	.307	.322	111	2		.913	3	87	55	O39(1/37/1)		0.3
1877	Chi	N	33	136	20	36	3	0	0	20	1		5	.265	.270	.287	67	-5		.861	3	132	290	O33C		-0.4
1879	Buf	N	78	317	41	66	5	7	0	27	11		41	.208	.235	.268	64	-13		.919	-7	63	113	O78C		-2.2
1883	Bal	AA	53	202	15	38	2	0	0	7	1			.188	.192	.198	25	-17		.916	-0	76	53	O78C		-1.7
	Buf	N	38	153	13	38	2	1	0	13	2		29	.248	.258	.275	61	-8		.845	-4	43	70	O38(1/37/0)		-1.1
1884	Buf	N	63	241	25	47	3	1	0	20	6		54	.195	.215	.216	35	-18		.887	0	111	51	O63(2/61/0)		-1.9
1885	Buf	N	6	24	0	2	0	0	0	0	2		4	.083	.154	.083	-21	-3		.938	0	79	0	O6C		-0.3
Total	5 NA		266	1297	349	418	66	22	0	136	24		25	.322	.335	.407	131	47	46-22	.902	33	109	157	O265(10/256/0),2b2/3		5.8
Total	6		310	1247	142	279	19	9	0	106	25		137	.224	.239	.253	56	-62		.894	-5	80	98	O310(4/305/1)		-7.3

EHRET, RED Philip Sydney B8.31.1868 Louisville KY D7.28.1940 Cincinnati OH BR/TR/6-0/175 d7.7 ▲

1888	KC	AA	17	63	4	12	4	0	0	4	1			.190	.203	.254	43	-4	1	.750	-2	0	0	O10(5/2/3),P7/21		-0.4
1889	Lou	AA	67	258	27	65	6	6	1	31	4		0	23	.252	.263	.333	71	-12	4	.891	-2	123	121	P45,O22(6/1/15)/S32		-0.6
1890	†Lou	AA	43	146	11	31	2	1	0	10	1		0		.212	.218	.240	36	-3	1	.859	-3	89	105	P43		0.0
1891	Lou	AA	26	91	9	22	2	1	0	9	5		0	15	.242	.281	.286	63	1	0	.871	0	108	235	P26		0.0
1892	Pit	N	40	132	12	34	2	0	0	19	7		0	22	.258	.295	.273	72	3	1	.855	-4	81	41	P39		0.0
1893	Pit	N	40	136	16	24	3	0	1	17	10		0	18	.176	.233	.221	21	-6	1	.893	1	115	0	P39		0.0
1894	Pit	N	46	135	6	23	4	1	0	11	8		0	22	.170	.217	.215	4	-11	0	.859	-2	93	86	P46		0.0
1895	StL	N	37	96	13	21	2	1	1	9	6		0	12	.219	.265	.292	44	-2	0	.928	0	106	0	P37		0.0
1896	Cin	N	34	102	10	20	2	0	1	20	10		0	12	.196	.268	.245	33	-10	2	.923	-1	100	138	P34/1		0.0
1897	Cin	N	34	66	6	13	2	0	0	4	1		0		.197	.254	.227	26	-3	2	.957	-1	79	292	P34		0.0
1898	Lou	N	13	40	3	9	3	1	0	4	1		0		.225	.262	.350	76	1	0	.800	-2	77	0	P12		0.0
Total	11		397	1265	117	274	32	11	4	140	57		2	124	.217	.252	.269	44	-46	15	.882	-15	100	97	P362,O32(11/3/18),1b2,2b2/3S		-1.0

EIBEL, HACK Henry Hack B12.6.1893 Brooklyn NY D10.16.1945 Macon GA BL/TL/5-11/220 d6.13 ▲

1912	Cle	A	1	3	0	0	0	0	0	0	0-0	0		.000	.000	.000	-97	-1	0	—	-0	0	0	/OR		-0.1
1920	Bos	A	29	43	4	8	2	0	0	6	3		0	6	.186	.239	.233	26	-5	1-1	.800	-1	54	0	O5(3/0/2),P3/1		-0.5
Total	2		30	46	4	8	2	0	0	6	3		0	6	.174	.224	.217	19	-6	1-1	.800	-2	52	0	O6(3/0/3),P3/1		-0.6

YEAR	TM LG	G	AB	R	H	2B	3B	HR	RBI	BB-IB	HP	SO	AVG	OBP	SLG	AOPS	ABR	SB-CS	FA	FR	RNG	THR	GAMES AT POSITION	DL	BFW

EICHRODT, IKE Frederick George B1.6.1903 Chicago IL D7.14.1965 Indianapolis IN BR/TR/5-11.5/167 d9.7 — -0.6

1925	Cle A	15	52	4	12	3	1	0	4	2	0	7	.231	.259	.327	48	-4	0-0	.938	-2	96		O13C		-0.1
1926	Cle A	37	80	14	25	7	1	0	7	2	0	11	.313	.329	.425	95	-1	1-0	.976	1	100	173	O27(19/6/2)		-1.9
1927	Cle A	85	267	24	59	19	2	0	25	16	0	25	.221	.261	.307	48	-21	2-3	.979	5	98	183	O81(13/64/5)		-1.3
1931	Chi A	34	117	9	25	5	1	0	15	1	0	8	.214	.220	.274	31	-12	0-0	1.000	-1	104		O32(0/30/3)		-3.9
Total	4	171	516	51	121	34	5	0	51	21	0	51	.234	.264	.320	52	-38	2-3	.979	4	99	128	O153(32/113/10)		

EISENREICH, JIM James Michael B4.18.1959 St.Cloud MN BL/TL/5-11/195(175-200) [MinA80 16/402] d4.6 Col St. Cloud St.

1982	Min A	34	99	10	30	6	0	2	9	11-0	1	13	.303	.378	.424	116	3	0-0	.973	0	113		O30C	97	0.3
1983	Min A	2	7	1	2	1	0	0	0	1-0	0	1	.286	.375	.429	116	0	0-0	1.000	1	105	771	O2C	50	0.1
1984	Min A	12	32	1	7	1	0	0	3	2-1	0	4	.219	.250	.250	41	-3	2-0	1.000	-1	61		O3(0/2/1),D6	22	-0.3
1987	KC A	44	105	10	25	8	2	4	21	7-2	0	13	.238	.286	.467	92	-2	1-1	—	0	0		D26	15	-0.2
1988	KC A	82	202	26	44	8	1	1	19	6-1	0	31	.218	.236	.282	45	-15	9-3	.965	-1	117		O64(30/15/21),D13		-1.6
1989	KC A	134	475	64	139	33	7	9	59	37-9	0	44	.293	.341	.448	122	13	27-8	.989	-1	103	56	O123(26/67/58),D10	15	1.3
1990	KC A	142	496	61	139	29	7	5	51	42-2	1	51	.280	.335	.397	106	4	12-14	.996	-1	98	73	O138(70/19/78),D2		-0.3
1991	KC A	135	375	47	113	22	3	2	47	20-1	1	35	.301	.333	.392	101	0	5-3	.973	-6	87	21	O105(59/13/42),1b15/D		-0.9
1992	KC A	113	353	31	95	13	3	2	28	24-4	0	36	.269	.313	.340	81	-9	11-6	.995	-2	105	18	O88(24/1/66),D8	26	-1.4
1993	†Phi N	153	362	51	115	17	4	7	54	26-5.	1	36	.318	.363	.445	117	8	5-0	.989	3	115	69	O93(0/5/90)		0.3
1994	Phi N	104	290	42	87	15	4	4	43	33-3	1	31	.300	.371	.421	105	3	6-2	1.000	3	115	32	O111(39/6/68)		1.3
1995	Phi N	129	377	46	119	22	2	10	55	38-4	1	44	.316	.375	.464	134	12	10-0	.977	2	111	59	O91(43/3/50)		1.8
1996	Phi N	113	338	45	122	24	3	3	41	31-9	1	32	.361	.413	.476	134	18	11-1	.977	2	94	68	O55(43/0/13),1b29,D4		-0.8
1997	†Fla N	120	293	36	82	19	1	2	34	30-4	1	28	.280	.345	.372	93	-2	0-0	.987	-2	94	102	1b10,O8(5/0/3)		-0.6
1998	Fla N	30	64	9	16	1	0	1	7	4-1	0	14	.250	.294	.313	64	-4	2-0	.971	0	104	90	O24(22/0/2),1b9,D2		-1.2
	LA N	75	127	12	25	2	2	0	6	12-1	0	22	.197	.266	.244	37	-12	4-0	.977	-2	103	71	O32(27/0/5),1b19,D2		-1.8
	Year	105	191	21	41	3	2	1	13	16-2	0	36	.215	.275	.267	46	-16	6-0	.977	-2	103	71		225	-1.1
Total	15	1422	3995	492	1160	221	39	52	477	324-47	8	435	.290	.341	.404	103	14	105-38	.988	2	106	52	O1072(362/166/625),D72,1b64	225	-1.1

ELAND d4.14 — -0.1

| 1873 | Mar NA | 1 | 3 | 0 | 0 | 0 | 0 | 0 | 0 | 0 | | 0 | .000 | .000 | .000 | -99 | -1 | 0-0 | .667 | -0 | 0 | | /OR | | |

ELBERFELD, KID Norman Arthur "The Tabasco Kid" B4.13.1875 Pomeroy OH D1.13.1944 Chattanooga TN BR/TR/5-7/158 d5.30 M1 — -0.2

1898	Phi N	14	38	1	9	4	0	0	7	5	7		.237	.420	.342	124	3	0	.795	-3	70	57	3b14		-0.4
1899	Cin N	41	138	23	36	4	2	0	22	15	11		.261	.378	.319	90	0	5	.878	-8	90	75	S24,3b18		3.5
1901	Det A	121	432	76	133	21	11	3	76	57	7		.308	.397	.428	123	16	23	.907	19	104	134	S121		0.8
1902	Det A	130	488	70	127	17	6	1	64	51	11		.260	.348	.326	86	-7	19	.921	12	105	111	S130		1.6
1903	Det A	35	132	29	45	5.	3	0	19	11	5		.341	.412	.424	156	10	6	.932	5	107	89	S34/3		1.1
	NY A	90	349	49	100	18	5	0	45	22	10		.287	.346	.367	107	4	16	.914	4	100	130	S124/3		2.7
	Year	125	481	78	145	23	8	0	64	33	15		.301	.365	.383	120	13	22	.919	9	102	119	S124/3		2.2
1904	NY A	122	445	55	117	13	5	2	46	37	13		.263	.337	.328	106	5	18	.933	11	108	125	S122		-0.1
1905	NY A	111	390	48	102	18	2	0	53	23	16		.262	.329	.318	95	-1	18	.908	-4	98	104	S108		1.5
1906	NY A	99	346	59	106	11	5	2	31	30	15		.306	.378	.384	126	12	19	.925	-1	100	61	S98		2.4
1907	NY A	120	447	61	121	17	6	0	51	36	13		.271	.343	.336	108	5	22	.930	13	104	78	S118		-0.1
1908	NY A	19	56	11	11	3	0	0	5	6	5		.196	.328	.250	87	0	1	.916	-2	92	35	S17,M		0.4
1909	NY A	106	379	47	90	9	5	0	26	28	14		.237	.314	.288	89	-4	23	.943	4	93	112	S61,3b44		-0.3
1910	Was A	127	455	53	114	19	2	2	42	35	13		.251	.322	.292	97	-1	19	.957	7	98	99	2b68,3b52		2.2
1911	Was A	127	404	58	110	19	4	0	47	65	25		.272	.405	.339	110	13	24	.901	-3	77	122	S18/2		-0.6
1914	Bro N	30	62	7	14	1	0	0	1	2	5		.226	.304	.242	62	-3	0	.920	51	102	105	S18/2		14.0
Total	14	1292	4561	647	1235	169	56	10	535	427	165	4	.271	.355	.339	105	52	213	.920	51	102	105	S944,3b242,2b79		

ELDER, GEORGE George Rezin B3.10.1921 Lebanon KY BL/TR/5-11/180 d7.22 Col UCLA — -0.2

| 1949 | StL A | 41 | 44 | 9 | 11 | 3 | 0 | 0 | 2 | 4 | 0 | 11 | .250 | .313 | .318 | 64 | -2 | 0-0 | 1.000 | 1 | 129 | | O10L | | |

ELDRED, BRAD Bradley Ross B7.12.1980 Ft.Lauderdale FL BR/TR/6-6/270 d7.22 Col Florida International — -1.4

| 2005 | Pit N | 55 | 190 | 23 | 42 | 9 | 0 | 12 | 27 | 13-0 | 3 | 77 | .221 | .279 | .458 | 90 | -4 | 1-1 | .985 | -6 | 56 | 110 | 1b50 | | |

ELIA, LEE Lee Constantine B7.16.1937 Philadelphia PA BR/TR/5-11/175* d4.23 M4/C15 Col Delaware — -0.7

1966	Chi A	80	195	16	40	5	2	3	22	15-3	2	39	.205	.265	.297	67	-9	0-1	.954	-3	100	117	S75		-0.3
1968	Chi N	15	17	1	3	0	0	0	3	0-0	1	6	.176	.222	.176	20	-2	0-0	1.000	-1	45	0	S2/23		-1.0
Total	2	95	212	17	43	5	2	3	25	15-3	3	45	.203	.262	.288	63	-11	0-1	.954	-4	99	116	S77/32		

ELKO, PETE Peter "Piccolo Pete" B6.17.1918 Wilkes-Barre PA D9.17.1993 Wilkes-Barre PA BR/TR/5-11/185 d9.17 — -0.6

1943	Chi N	9	30	1	4	0	0	0	4	0			.133	.235	.133	8	-4	0	.852	-2	87	69	3b9		-0.2
1944	Chi N	7	22	2	5	1	0	0	0	4	0	6	.227	.227	.273	40	-2	0	1.000	0	94	140	3b6		-0.8
Total	2	16	52	3	9	1	0	0	4		0	6	.173	.232	.192	22	-6	0	.902	-2	89	92	3b15		

ELLAM, ROY Roy "Whitey","Slippery" B2.8.1886 W.Conshohocken PA D10.28.1948 Conshohocken PA BR/TR/5-10.5/203 d9.18 — 0.1

1909	Cin N	10	21	4	4	0	1	1	4	7	0		.190	.393	.429	156	2	1	.895	-1	93	158	S9		-1.0
1918	Pit N	26	77	9	10	1	1	0	2	17	2	17	.130	.302	.169	43	-4	2	.924	-6	87	69	S26		-0.9
Total	2	36	98	13	14	1	2	1	6	24	2	17	.143	.323	.224	67	-2	3	.917	-7	88	90	S35		

ELLERBE, FRANK Francis Rogers "Governor" B12.25.1895 Marion Co. SC D7.8.1988 Latta SC BR/TR/5-10.5/165 d8.28 Col Wofford — -0.5

1919	Was A	28	105	13	29	4	1	0	16	2	0	15	.276	.290	.333	75	-4	5	.945	-3	89	50	S28		-1.2
1920	Was A	101	336	38	98	14	2	0	36	19	1	23	.292	.331	.345	82	-9	5-4	.934	-6	100	65	3b75,S19/OR		-0.1
1921	Was A	10	10	1	2	0	0	0	1	0	0	2	.200	.200	.400	52	-1	0-0	—	0			/H		-0.8
	StL A	105	430	65	124	20	12	2	49	22	3	42	.288	.327	.405	81	-14	1-6	.953	1	97	44	3b105		-0.9
	Year	115	440	66	126	20	13	2	50	22	3	44	.286	.325	.405	81	-15	1-6	.953	1	97	44	3b105		-0.3
1922	StL A	91	342	42	84	16	3	1	33	25	3	36	.246	.303	.319	60	-20	1-1	.967	-2	81	113	3b14		-0.8
1923	StL A	18	49	6	9	0	0	1	1	1	0	5	.184	.200	.184	1	-7	0-1	.953	1	91	231	3b21		-0.6
1924	StL A	21	61	7	12	3	0	0	2	2	0	4	.197	.222	.246	19	-8	0-1	.975	5	120	38	3b39,2b2		-0.2
	Cle A	46	120	7	31	1	3	1	14	1	1	10	.258	.270	.342	56	-9	0-0	.967	-5	109	111	3b60,2b2		-0.8
	Year	67	181	14	43	4	3	1	16	3	1	14	.238	.254	.309	44	-17	0-1	.967	-5	109	111	3b60,2b2		
Total	6	420	1453	179	389	58	22	4	152	72	8	136	.268	.306	.346	68	-72	12-13	.952	8	102	81	3b345,S47,2b2/OR		-4.5

ELLICK, JOE Joseph J. B4.3.1854 Cincinnati OH D4.21.1923 Kansas City KS 5-10/162 d5.13 M1/U1 — -0.4

1875	RS NA	7	27	1	6	1	0	0				1	.222	.222	.259	74	0	1-0	.471	-4	60		3b5,O2C		-0.3
1878	Mil N	3	13	2	2	0	0	0	1	0			.154	.154	.154	1		-1	.769	-2			C2/3P		-0.3
1880	Wor N	5	18	1	1	0	0	0	0	1		2	.056	.105	.056	-40	-3		.882	0	116	0	3b5		-2.6
1884	CP U	92	394	71	93	11	0	6				16	.236	.266	.264	62	-30		.903	-0	98	52	O57(3/0/54),S33,2b4,M		-0.3
	KC U	2	8	0	0	0	0	0	0	0			.000	.000	.000	-99	-2		.714	-1	100	0	/2OR		-0.4
	Bal U	7	27	2	4	0	0	0		2			.148	.207	.148	8	-4		.714	-1	100	0	S6/OR		-3.3
	Year	101	429	73	97	11	0	6		19			.226	.257	.252	55	-36		.894	-2	101	94	O59(3/0/56),S39,2b5		-3.8
Total	6	109	460	76	100	11	0	6	1	19		3	.217	.248	.241	50	-40		.471	-3	101	94	O59(3/0/56),S39,3b6,2b5,C2/P		

ELLIOT, LARRY Lawrence Lee B3.5.1938 San Diego CA BL/TL/6-2/200* d4.19 Col San Diego (CA) City — 0.0

1962	Pit N	8	10	2	3	0	0	0	0	1	0	1	.300	.300	.600	135	0	0-0	1.000	0	127		O3R		-0.1
1963	Pit N	4	4	0	0	0	0	0	0	0	0	0	.000	.000	.000	-99	-1	0-0	—	0			/H		-0.4
1964	NY N	80	224	27	51	8	0	9	22	28-2	3	55	.228	.320	.384	100	1	1-2	.985	-2	100	52	O63(4/57/4)		-0.2
1966	NY N	65	199	24	49	14	2	5	32	17-1	0	46	.246	.306	.412	100	0	1-3	.912	1	83	288	O54(25/0/31)		-0.7
Total	4	157	437	53	103	22	2	15	56	45-3	3	105	.236	.311	.398	99	-1	1-3	.956	-1	93	158	O120(29/57/38)		

ELLIOTT, ALLEN Allen Clifford "Ace" B12.25.1897 St.Louis MO D5.6.1979 St.Louis MO BL/TR/6-0/170 d6.14 — -1.4

1923	Chi N	53	168	21	42	8	2	2	29	2	2	12	.250	.267	.357	63	-15	3-3	.992	-2	80	106	1b52		-0.3
1924	Chi N	10	14	0	2	0	0	0	0	0	0	1	.143	.143	.143	-23	2	0-0	1.000	0	43	88	1b10		-1.7
Total	2	63	182	21	44	8	2	2	29	2	2	13	.242	.258	.341	57	-12	3-3	.992	-2	77	104	1b62		

ELLIOTT, CARTER Carter Ward B11.29.1893 Atchison KS D5.21.1959 Palm Springs CA BL/TR/5-11/165 d9.10 — 0.1

| 1921 | Chi N | 12 | 28 | 5 | 7 | 2 | 0 | 0 | 5 | 0 | | | .250 | .364 | .321 | 83 | 0 | 0-0 | .964 | 2 | 104 | 85 | S10 | | |

YEAR	TM LG	G	AB	R	H	2B	3B	HR	RBI	BB-IB	HP	SO	AVG	OBP	SLG	AOPS	ABR	SB-CS	FA	FR	RNG	THR	GAMES AT POSITION	DL	BFW
ELLIOTT, GENE	Eugene Birminghouse B2.8.1889 Fayette Co. PA D1.5.1976 Huntingdon PA BL/TR/5-7/150 d4.13																						
1911	NY A	5	13	1	1	1	0	0	1	2			.077	.200	.154		-1	-2	0	—	-1	0	0	O2R/3		-0.2
ELLIOTT, ROWDY	Harold Bell B7.8.1890 Kokomo IN D2.12.1934 San Francisco CA BR/TR/5-9/160 d9.24 Mil 1918																						
1910	Bos N	3	2	0	0	0	0	0	0	0	0	0	.000	.000	.000		-96	0	0	1.000	-0	0	0	/C		-0.1
1916	Chi N	23	55	5	14	3	0	0	3	3	0	5	.255	.293	.309	77	-1	1	.969	-1	97	78	C18		-0.1
1917	Chi N	85	223	18	56	8	5	0	28	11	2	11	.251	.292	.332	84	-4	4	.969	4	97	115	C73		0.6
1918	Chi N	5	10	0	0	0	0	0	0	2	0	1	.000	.167	.000	-47	-2	0	.952	0	113	114	C5		-0.1
1920	Bro N	41	112	13	27	4	0	1	13	3	1	6	.241	.267	.304	62	-6	0-0	.964	1	102	117	C39		-0.1
Total	5	157	402	36	97	15	5	1	44	19	3	23	.241	.281	.311	73	-13	5-0	.967	5	99	110	C136		0.2
ELLIOTT, HARRY	Harry Lewis B12.30.1923 San Francisco CA BR/TR/5-9/175* d8.1 Col Minnesota																						
1953	StL N	24	59	6	15	4	1	1	6	3	1	8	.254	.302	.441	91	-1	0-0	1.000	0	111	75	O17(15/0/2)		-0.1
1955	StL N	68	117	9	30	4	0	1	12	11-3	1	9	.256	.321	.316	71	-5	0-2	.978	-1	103	56	O28(8/0/20)		-0.7
Total	2	92	176	15	45	10	1	2	18	14-3	2	17	.256	.314	.358	78	-6	0-2	.988	-0	106	64	O45(23/0/22)		-0.8
ELLIOTT, RANDY	Randy Lee B6.5.1951 Oxnard CA BR/TR/6-2/190* [SDN69 1/24] d9.10																						
1972	SD N	14	49	5	10	3	1	0	6	2-0	1	11	.204	.235	.306	57	-3	0-0	1.000	1	131	0	O13R		-0.3
1974	SD N	13	33	5	7	1	0	1	2	7-1	0	11	.212	.350	.333	96	0	0-1	1.000	-2	49	0	O11(7/0/4)/1		-0.3
1977	SF N	73	167	17	40	5	1	7	26	8-1	1	24	.240	.275	.407	81	-5	0-2	.973	2	93	200	O46L		-0.6
1980	Oak A	14	39	4	5	3	0	0	1	1-0	0	13	.128	.150	.205	-4	-6	0-0	—	0	0	0	D11		-0.6
Total	4	114	288	31	62	12	2	8	35	18-2	1	57	.215	.262	.354	69	-14	0-3	.982	0	94	127	O70(53/0/17),D11/1		-1.8
ELLIOTT, BOB	Robert Irving "Mr. Team" B11.26.1916 San Francisco CA D5.4.1966 San Diego CA BR/TR/6-0/185* d9.2 M1/C1 Col El Centro (CA) JC																						
1939	Pit N	32	129	18	43	10	3	1	19	9	0	4	.333	.377	.527	143	7	0	.978	0	110	39	O30C		0.7
1940	Pit N	148	551	88	161	34	11	5	64	45	0	28	.292	.348	.421	112	7	0	.978	4	107	104	O147(4/31/113)		0.3
1941	Pit N★	141	527	74	144	24	10	3	76	64	1	52	.273	.353	.374	105	4	6	.970	-0	106	76	O139(4/2/134)		-0.4
1942	Pit N	143	560	75	166	26	7	9	89	52	2	35	.296	.358	.416	123	16	2	.927	-1	102	82	3b142/OL		2.1
1943	Pit N	156	581	82	183	30	12	7	101	56	1	24	.315	.376	.444	132	23	4	.949	-4	101	137	3b151,2b2/S		2.2
1944	Pit N★	143	538	85	160	28	16	10	108	75	0	42	.297	.383	.465	132	24	9	.944	4	97	96	3b140/S		2.2
1946	Pit N	140	486	50	128	25	3	5	68	64	2	44	.263	.351	.358	99	1	6	.928	7	108	126	3b81,O61R		1.6
1947	Bos N★	150	555	93	176	35	5	22	113	87	0	60	.317	.410	.517	148	41	3	.995	6	108	89	O92R,3b43		0.4
1948	†Bos N★	151	540	99	153	24	5	23	100	131	0	57	.283	.423	.474	145	41	3	.956	-2	105	103	3b148		3.8
1949	Bos N	139	482	77	135	29	5	17	76	90	2	38	.280	.395	.467	138	29	0	.945	-12	97	78	3b150		2.9
1950	Bos N	142	531	94	162	28	5	24	107	68	2	67	.305	.386	.512	143	34	2	.963	11	108	99	3b130		4.0
1951	Bos N	136	480	73	137	29	2	15	70	65	1	56	.285	.371	.448	128	20	2-0	.952	-17	87	89	3b137		1.6
1952	NY N	98	272	33	62	6	2	10	35	36	2	20	.228	.323	.375	92	-1	1-0	.941	-8	93	103	3b127		1.3
1953	StL A	48	160	19	40	7	1	5	29	30	1	18	.250	.368	.400	105	2	0-1	.954	-1	85	151	O65(52/0/15),3b13		-0.8
	Chi A	67	208	24	54	11	1	4	32	31	1	21	.260	.358	.380	96	0	1-1	.963	-4	96	103	3b45		0.0
	Year	115	368	43	94	18	2	9	61	61	2	39	.255	.363	.389	100	2	1-2	.959	-5	91	74	3b58,O2L		-0.6
Total	15	1978	7141	1064	2061	382	94	170	1195	967	16	604	.289	.375	.440	124	260	60-2	.947	-28	99	99	3b1365,O537(63/63/415),S2,2b2		21.4
ELLIS, BEN	Alfred Benjamin B7.1870 New York NY D7.26.1931 Schenectady NY 5-10/165 d7.16																						
1896	Phi N	4	16	1	1	0	0	0	3	0		6	.063	.211	.063	-26	-3	0	.800	-1	69	126	S2,3b2		-0.3
ELLIS, RUBE	George William B11.17.1885 Downey CA D3.13.1938 Rivera CA BL/TL/6-0/170 d4.15																						
1909	StL N	149	575	76	154	10	9	3	46	54	3		.268	.334	.332	114	8	18	.955	13	135	175	O145(144/0/1)		1.4
1910	StL N	142	550	87	142	18	8	4	54	62	5	70	.258	.339	.342	102	2	25	.942	2	93	139	O141L		-0.5
1911	StL N	155	555	69	139	20	11	2	66	66	2	64	.250	.332	.337	90	-7	9	.938	0	101	100	O148L		-1.4
1912	StL N	109	305	47	82	18	2	4	33	34	0	36	.269	.342	.380	100	0	6	.929	-1	103	83	O76(65/4/7)		-1.4
Total	4	555	1985	279	517	66	30	13	199	216	10	170	.260	.336	.344	101	3	58	.943	14	109	130	O510(498/4/8)		-0.9
ELLIS, JOHN	John Charles B8.21.1948 New London CT BR/TR/6-2.5/220(210-225) d5.17 Col Mitchell (CT) JC																						
1969	NY A	22	62	3	18	4	0	1	8	1-0	1	11	.290	.308	.403	102	0	0-2	.978	-3	33	96	C15		-0.3
1970	NY A	78	226	24	56	12	1	7	29	18-0	1	47	.248	.305	.403	99	-1	0-1	.992	-2	123	100	1b53,3b5,C2		-0.7
1971	NY A	83	238	16	58	12	1	3	34	23-5	6	42	.244	.322	.340	93	-2	0-0	.990	-3	89	134	1b65,C2		-1.0
1972	NY A	52	136	13	40	5	1	5	25	8-0	0	22	.294	.333	.456	136	5	0-0	.965	2	109	72	C25,1b8		0.8
1973	Cle A	127	437	59	118	12	2	14	68	46-2	3	57	.270	.339	.403	107	4	0-0	.980	-17	105	96	C72,D38,1b12		-1.2
1974	Cle A	128	477	58	136	23	6	10	64	32-3	1	53	.285	.330	.421	116	9	1-2	.992	-4	86	100	1b69,C42,D21		0.9
1975	Cle A	92	296	22	68	11	1	7	32	14-2	1	33	.230	.266	.345	72	-12	0-1	.976	-6	97	104	C84,1b2,D3	29	-1.5
1976	Tex A	11	31	4	13	2	0	1	8	0-0	0	4	.419	.419	.581	187	3	0-0	1.000	-0	195	100	C14,1b2,D3	17	0.3
1977	Tex A	49	119	7	28	7	0	4	15	8-2	0	26	.235	.283	.395	82	-3	0-0	1.000	-2	59	32	C16,D15,1b8	148	-0.6
1978	Tex A	34	94	7	23	4	0	3	17	6-0	0	20	.245	.282	.383	77	-2	0-1	.958	-2	120	59	C22,D7		-0.3
1979	Tex A	111	316	33	90	12	0	12	61	15-1	2	55	.285	.318	.437	103	0	2-2	.978	-3	71	94	D62,1b30,C7		-0.6
1980	Tex A	73	182	12	43	9	1	1	23	14-1	1	23	.236	.290	.313	68	-8	3-0	.992	-2	65	83	1b39,D20,C3	21	-1.2
1981	Tex A	23	58	2	8	3	0	1	7	5	1	10	.138	.219	.241	34	-5	0-1	.993	-1	86	144	1b18/D		-0.7
Total	13	883	2672	259	699	116	13	69	391	190-17	17	403	.262	.312	.392	99	-12	6-10	.989	-42	86	103	1b304,C297,D170,3b5	215	-7.0
ELLIS, MARK	Mark William B6.6.1977 Rapid City SD BR/TR/5-11/180* [KCA99 9/271] d4.9 Col Florida [DL 2004 Oak A 183]																						
2002	†Oak A	98	345	58	94	16	4	6	35	44-1	4	54	.272	.359	.394	101	2	4-2	.978	6	101	93	2b85,S8,3b7/D		1.1
2003	†Oak A	154	553	78	137	31	5	9	52	48-4	7	94	.248	.313	.371	80	-16	6-2	.982	30	113	105	2b153		2.1
2005	Oak A	122	434	76	137	21	5	13	52	44-1	4	51	.316	.384	.477	125	17	1-3	.989	8	102	120	2b115,S7,1b2/D		2.8
Total	3	374	1332	212	368	68	14	28	139	136-6	15	199	.276	.348	.411	100	3	11-7	.983	44	107	107	2b353,S15,3b7,1b2,D2	183	6.0
ELLIS, ROB	Robert Walter B7.3.1950 Grand Rapids MI BR/TR/5-11/180* [MilA71 D1/3] d6.18 Col Michigan St.																						
1971	Mil A	36	111	9	22	2	0	0	6	12-0	1	24	.198	.278	.216	43	-8	0-2	.923	-6	70	144	3b19,O15(1/1/13)		-1.7
1974	Mil A	22	48	4	14	2	0	0	4	4-0	0	11	.292	.346	.333	97	0	0-0	1.000	1	78	493	O11(4/0/8)/3D		0.1
1975	Mil A	6	7	3	2	0	0	0	0	0-0	0	0	.286	.286	.286	61	0	0-0	1.000	-1	17	0	O5L/D		-0.2
Total	3	64	166	16	38	4	0	0	10	16-0	1	35	.229	.297	.253	59	-8	0-2	.976	-5	80	160	O31(10/1/21),3b20,D10		-1.8
ELLISON, BABE	Herbert Spencer "Bert" B11.15.1896 Ola AR D8.11.1955 San Francisco CA BR/TR/5-11/170 d9.18 Mil 1918 Col Arkansas-Monticello																						
1916	Det A	2	7	0	1	0	0	0	1	0	0	1	.143	.143	.143	-14	-1	0	1.000	-1	26	0	3b2		-0.2
1917	Det A	9	29	2	5	1	2	0	4	6	1	3	.172	.333	.448	139	1	0	.980	-2	17	96	1b9		-0.1
1918	Det A	7	23	1	6	1	0	0	2	3	0		.261	.346	.304	100	0	1	1.000	1	104	0	O4R,2b3		0.1
1919	Det A	56	134	18	29	4	0	0	11	13	0	24	.216	.291	.246	53	-8	4	.966	-2	99	80	2b25,O10(1/1/8)/S		-1.1
1920	Det A	61	155	11	34	7	2	0	21	8	0	26	.219	.258	.290	46	-13	4-1	.997	3	114	61	1b38,O4(0/2/2)/3		-1.1
Total	5	135	348	32	75	13	4	1	39	30	1	55	.216	.282	.284	58	-21	9-1	.982	-2	94	68	1b47,2b28,O18(1/3/14),3b3/S		-2.3
ELLISON, JASON	Jason Jerome B4.4.1978 Quincy CA BR/TR/5-10/180* [NYA95 47/1307] d5.9 Col Lewis-Clark St.																						
2003	SF N	7	10	1	1	0	0	0	0	0-0	0	2	.100	.100	.100	-47	-2	0-0	1.000	-0	77	0	O4(3/1/0)		-0.3
2004	SF N	13	4	4	2	0	1	3	3	0-0	0	1	.500	.500	1.250	320	1	2-0	1.000	4	178	0	O4C		0.2
2005	SF N	131	352	49	93	18	2	4	24	24-1	3	44	.264	.316	.361	74	-13	14-6	.968	5	112	103	O122(15/78/32)		-0.8
Total	3	150	366	54	96	18	2	5	27	24-1	3	46	.262	.312	.363	74	-14	16-6	.969	5	112	99	O130(18/83/32)		-0.9
ELMORE, VERDO	Verdo Wilson "Ellie" B12.10.1899 Gordo AL D8.5.1969 Birmingham AL BL/TR/5-11/185 d9.11 Col Alabama																						
1924	StL A	7	17	2	3	0	1	0	3	0		3	.176	.222	.353	44	-1	0-0	1.000	-1	0	0	O3R		-0.2
WELSH, ROY	Eugene Reybold B3.1.1892 Penns Grove NJ D11.12.1978 Philadelphia PA BR/TR/5-9/165 d4.19																						
1923	Chi A	81	209	28	52	7	0	0	24	16	1	23	.249	.305	.301	61	-12	16-8	.957	2	109	108	O57(50/6/1)		-1.3
1924	Chi A	60	147	21	45	9	1	0	11	10	0	14	.306	.358	.381	91	-2	6-1	.953	-1	104	79	O38(2/5/31),1b2		-0.4
1925	Chi A	32	48	6	9	1	0	0	4	5	0	7	.188	.264	.208	22	-6	2-0	.964	-2	112	183	O11(6/2/3),1b3		-0.4
Total	3	173	404	55	106	17	3	0	39	31	1	44	.262	.317	.319	67	-20	24-9	.957	2	108	107	O111(54/14/43),1b5		-2.1
ELSTER, KEVIN	Kevin Daniel B8.3.1964 San Pedro CA BR/TR/6-2/200(180-205) [NYN84*2/28] d9.2 Col Golden West (CA) JC																						
1986	†NY N	19	30	3	5	1	0	0	0	3-1	0	8	.167	.242	.200	24	-3	0-0	.962	2	112	108	S19		0.0
1987	NY N	5	10	1	4	2	0	0	1	0-0	0	1	.400	.400	.600	167	1	0-0	1.000	-0	98	0	S3		0.1
1988	†NY N	149	406	41	87	11	1	9	37	35-12	3	47	.214	.282	.313	73	-15	2-0	.977	2	93	98	S148		-0.3

YEAR	TM LG	G	AB	R	H	2B	3B	HR	RBI	BB-IB	HP	SO	AVG	OBP	SLG	AOPS	ABR	SB-CS	FA	FR	RNG	THR	GAMES AT POSITION	DL	BFW
																									1.0
1989	NY N	151	458	52	106	25	2	10	55	34-11	2	77	.231	.283	.360	88	-8	4-3	.976	7	95	96	S150	61	0.6
1990	NY N	92	314	36	65	20	1	9	45	30-2	1	54	.207	.274	.363	75	-11	2-0	.960	10	96	94	S92	15	0.8
1991	NY N	115	348	33	84	16	2	6	36	40-6	1	53	.241	.318	.351	89	-5	2-3	.970	5	104	82	S107	175	-0.2
1992	NY N	6	18	0	4	0	0	0	0	0-0	0	2	.222	.222	.222	26	-2	0-0	1.000	-1	76	121	S5	36	-0.3
1994	NY A	7	20	0	0	0	0	0	0	1-0	0	6	.000	.048	.000	-89	-6	0-0	1.000	2	130	171	S7		-0.3
1995	NY A	10	17	1	2	1	0	0	1	1-0	0	5	.118	.167	.176	-11	-3	0-0	1.000	-1	88	59	S10/2		-0.2
	Phi N	26	53	10	11	4	1	1	9	7-1	1	14	.208	.302	.377	80	-1	0-0	.982	-1	90	139	S19,1b4,3b2		0.7
1996	†Tex A	157	515	79	130	32	2	24	99	52-1	2	138	.252	.317	.462	90	-10	4-1	.981	5	99	91	S157		0.5
1997	Pit N	39	138	14	31	6	2	7	25	21-0	1	39	.225	.327	.449	100	0	0-2	.994	4	109	85	S39	135	-1.0
1998	Tex A	84	297	33	69	10	1	8	37	33-0	2	66	.232	.311	.354	69	-14	0-2	.976	-2	105	87	S84	15	-0.4
2000	LA N	80	220	29	50	8	0	14	32	36-5	1	59	.227	.341	.455	104	1	0-0	.946	-9	92	80	S55,3b8/1	30	-0.4
Total	13	940	2844	332	648	136	12	88	376	295-39	13	562	.228	.300	.377	82	-76	14-11	.974	23	98	94	S895,3b10,1b5/2	467	1.0

ELY, BONES   William Frederick   B6.7.1863 N.Girard PA   D1.10.1952 Berkeley CA   BR/TR/6-1/155   d6.19   OF(74/9/1) ▲

YEAR	TM LG	G	AB	R	H	2B	3B	HR	RBI	BB-IB	HP	SO	AVG	OBP	SLG	AOPS	ABR	SB-CS	FA	FR	RNG	THR	GAMES AT POSITION	DL	BFW
																			.000	-0	0	0	/ORP		-0.1
1884	Buf N	1	4	0	0	0	0	0		2	.000	.000	.000	-97	-1				1.000	-0	106	0	P6,O5(4/1/0)		-0.2
1886	Lou AA	10	32	5	5	0	0	0	6	2	0		.156	.206	.156	13	-3	1	1.000	-0	106	0	P6,O5(4/1/0)		-0.2
1890	Syr AA	119	496	72	130	16	6	0	64	31	2		.262	.308	.319	95	-4	44	.914	10	87	28	O78(70/8/0),S36,1b4,2b2/3P		0.4
1891	Bro N	31	111	9	17	0	1	0	11	7	0	9	.153	.203	.171	9	-13	4	.870	5	116	93	S28,3b2/2		-0.7
1893	StL N	44	178	25	45	1	6	0	16	17	0	13	.253	.318	.326	71	-8	2	.905	-5	91	90	S44		-0.9
1894	StL N	127	510	85	156	20	12	12	89	30	0	34	.306	.344	.463	93	-10	23	.901	1	101	95	S126/2P		-0.2
1895	StL N	118	471	68	122	16	2	1	47	19	0	18	.259	.288	.308	54	-33	29	.925	5	101	100	S118		-1.8
1896	Pit N	128	537	85	153	15	9	3	77	33	0	33	.285	.326	.363	85	-13	18	.918	-6	98	95	S128		-1.0
1897	Pit N	133	516	63	146	20	8	2	74	25	1		.283	.317	.364	83	-14	10	.927	8	106	100	S148		-0.3
1898	Pit N	148	519	49	110	14	5	2	44	24	0		.212	.247	.270	49	-36	6	.943	6	106	100	S133,2b6		-1.9
1899	Pit N	139	526	67	146	18	6	3	72	22	5		.278	.313	.352	82	-14	8	.928	-5	102	90	S133,2b6		-1.1
1900	†Pit N	130	475	60	116	6	6	0	51	17	1		.244	.272	.282	53	-33	6	.935	11	106	133	S130		-1.1
1901	Pit N	65	240	18	50	6	3	0	28	6	2		.208	.234	.258	41	-19	5	.916	-3	104	112	S64/3		-1.5
	Phi A	45	171	11	37	6	2	0	16	3	0		.216	.230	.275	38	-15	1	.913	2	106	108	S45		-1.9
1902	Was A	105	381	39	100	11	2	1	62	21	0	109	.262	.301	.310	69	-16	3	.923	-7	99	67	S105		-1.9
Total	14	1343	5167	656	1333	149	68	24	657	257	11	109	.258	.295	.327	70	-232	165	.923	21	102	97	S1238,O84L,2b10,P9,3b4,1b4		-14.0

EMERSON, CHESTER   Chester Arthur "Chuck"   B10.27.1889 Stow ME   D7.2.1971 Augusta ME   BL/TR/5-8/165   d9.27   Col Dartmouth

1911	Phi A	7	18	2	4	0	0	0		6	0		.222	.417	.222	82	0	1	1.000	-0	132	0	O7(0/1/6)		-0.1
1912	Phi A	1	1	0	0	0	0	0		0	0		.000	.000	.000	-99	0	0	—	0			/H		0.0
Total	2	8	19	2	4	0	0	0		6	0		.211	.400	.211	74	0	1	1.000	-0	132	0	O7(0/1/6)		-0.1

EMERY, CAL   Calvin Wayne   B6.28.1937 Centre Hall PA   BL/TL/6-2/205   d7.15   C1   Col Penn St.

| 1963 | Phi N | 16 | 19 | 0 | 3 | 1 | 0 | 0 | 0 | 0-0 | 0 | 2 | .158 | .158 | .211 | 5 | -2 | 0-0 | 1.000 | -0 | 0 | 0 | 1b2 | | -0.3 |

EMERY, SPOKE   Herrick Smith   B12.10.1898 Bay City MI   D6.2.1975 Cape Canaveral FL   BR/TR/5-9/165   d7.18

| 1924 | Phi N | 5 | 3 | 3 | 2 | 0 | 0 | 0 | 0 | 0-0 | 0 | 0 | .667 | .667 | .667 | 230 | 1 | 0-1 | 1.000 | 0 | 165 | 0 | /OL | | 0.0 |

EMMER, FRANK   Frank William   B2.17.1896 Crestline OH   D10.18.1963 Homestead FL   BR/TR/5-8/150   d4.25

1916	Cin N	42	89	8	13	3	1	0	2	7	0	27	.146	.208	.202	27	-8	1	.899	-0	109	63	S29,O2L/23		-0.7
1926	Cin N	80	224	22	44	7	6	0	18	13	1	30	.196	.244	.281	42	-19	1	.918	-9	101	99	S79		-2.1
Total	2	122	313	30	57	10	7	0	20	20	1	57	.182	.234	.259	38	-27	2	.913	-9	103	90	S108,O2L/32		-2.8

EMMERICH, BOB   Robert George   B8.1.1897 New York NY   D11.22.1948 Bridgeport CT   BR/TR/5-3/155   d9.22

| 1923 | Bos N | 13 | 24 | 3 | 2 | 0 | 0 | 0 | 2 | 2 | 0 | 3 | .083 | .154 | .083 | -37 | -5 | 1-1 | 1.000 | 0 | 101 | 148 | O8C | | -0.8 |

ENCARNACION, ANGELO   Angelo Benjamin   B4.18.1969 Santo Domingo, D.R.   BR/TR/5-8/180*   d5.2   [DL 1998 Ana A 107]

1995	Pit N	58	159	18	36	7	2	2	10	13-5	0	28	.226	.285	.333	61	-9	1-1	.979	6	95	143	C55		-0.7
1996	Pit N	7	22	3	7	2	0	0	1	0-0	0	5	.318	.318	.409	87	0	0-0	.951	-2	79	53	C7		-0.2
1997	Ana A	11	17	2	7	1	0	1	4	0-0	0	1	.412	.412	.647	170	2	2-0	.940	1	49	61	C11	107	0.1
Total	3	76	198	23	50	10	2	3	15	13-5	0	34	.253	.299	.369	73	-7	3-1	.971	5	89	126	C73		-0.8

ENCARNACION, EDWIN   Edwin Elpido   B1.7.1983 LaRomana, D.R.   BR/TR/6-1/195   d6.24

| 2005 | Cin N | 69 | 211 | 25 | 49 | 16 | 0 | 9 | 31 | 20-2 | 3 | 60 | .232 | .308 | .436 | 95 | -2 | 3-0 | .944 | 3 | 105 | 91 | 3b56 | | 0.1 |

ENCARNACION, JUAN   Juan De Dios   B3.8.1976 Las Matas de Farfan, D.R.   BR/TR/6-2/160(160-215)   d9.2

1997	Det A	11	33	3	7	1	1	5	3-0	2	12	.212	.316	.394	84	-1	3-1	1.000	-0	106	0	O10(0/2/10)		-0.1
1998	Det A	40	164	30	54	9	4	7	21	7-0	1	31	.329	.354	.561	133	7	7-4	.985	-5	68	145	O39(8/13/21)/D	29	0.1
1999	Det A	132	509	62	130	30	6	19	74	14-1	9	113	.255	.287	.450	83	-16	33-12	.968	1	100	123	O131(118/22/1)		-1.2
2000	Det A	141	547	75	158	25	6	14	72	29-1	7	90	.289	.330	.433	93	-8	16-4	.987	-5	100	68	O141C		-0.2
2001	Det A	120	417	52	101	19	7	12	52	25-1	6	93	.242	.292	.408	84	-11	9-5	.977	4	112	102	O116(0/56/63)/D		-2.0
2002	Cin N	83	321	43	89	11	2	16	51	26-0	1	63	.277	.330	.474	109	1	9-4	.977	-7	94	68	O82(0/59/31)		-0.2
	Fla N	69	263	34	69	11	3	8	34	20-0	3	50	.262	.317	.418	100	-2	12-5	.993	-0	99	91	O67(0/12/61)		-0.2
	Year	152	584	77	158	22	5	24	85	46-0	4	113	.271	.324	.449	105	-1	21-9	1.000	6	110	70	O155R		-0.4
2003	†Fla N	156	601	80	162	37	6	19	94	37-0	4	82	.270	.313	.446	100	-3	19-8	.976	-3	95	55	O85(9/0/77)	15	-1.7
2004	LA N	86	324	42	76	18	1	13	43	21-0	4	53	.235	.289	.417	81	-11	3-3	.976	-5	90	55	O48R		-0.5
	Fla N	49	160	21	38	12	1	3	19	17-2	3	33	.237	.320	.381	85	-3	2-1	.980	1	110	71	O133(9/0/125)		-0.2
	Year	135	484	63	114	30	2	16	62	38-2	7	86	.236	.299	.405	82	-14	5-4	.978	-2	100	61	O133(9/0/125)		-0.6
2005	Fla N	141	506	59	145	27	3	16	76	41-2	9	104	.287	.349	.447	114	9	6-5	.983	-9	88	54	O139(0/11/135)	44	-7.4
Total	9	1028	3845	501	1029	200	40	128	541	240-7	49	724	.268	.316	.440	96	-38	119-52	.983	-18	99	76	O1013(135/316/602),D2		-7.1

ENCARNACION, MARIO   Mario (Gonzalez)   B9.24.1975 Bani, D.R.   D10.3.2005 Danshui, Taiwan   BR/TR/6-2/210*   d8.26

2001	Col N	20	62	3	14	1	0	0	3	5-0	0	14	.226	.284	.242	32	-6	2-1	1.000	1	109	87	O20(14/0/6)		-0.5
2002	Chi N	3	7	0	0	0	0	0	0	2-0	0	3	.000	.222	.000	-33	-1	0-0	1.000	0	193	0	O2L		-0.0
Total	2	23	69	3	14	1	0	0	3	7-0	0	17	.203	.276	.217	26	-7	2-1	1.000	1	116	80	O22(16/0/6)		-0.5

ENDICOTT, BILL   William Franklin   B9.4.1918 Acorn MO   BL/TL/5-11.5/175   d4.21

| 1946 | StL N | 20 | 20 | 2 | 4 | 0 | 0 | 0 | 0 | 4-0 | 0 | 0 | .200 | .333 | .350 | 90 | 0 | 0 | 1.000 | 0 | 120 | 0 | O2L | | 0 |

ENGLE, CLYDE   Arthur Clyde "Hack"   B3.19.1884 Dayton OH   D12.26.1939 Boston MA   BR/TR/5-10/190   d4.12   OF(142/111/26)

1909	NY A	135	492	66	137	20	5	3	71	47	5		.278	.347	.358	122	13	18	.946	15	99	122	O134(119/16/0)		2
1910	NY A	5	13	0	3	0	0	0	0	2	0		.231	.333	.231	73	0	1	.857	-0	105	0	O3L		0
	Bos A	106	363	59	96	18	7	2	38	31	2		.264	.326	.369	115	6	12	.915	-2	108	100	3b51,2b27,O15(0/13/2),S7		0
	Year	111	376	59	99	18	7	2	38	33	2		.263	.326	.364	113	5	13	.915	-2	108	100	3b51,2b27,O18(3/13/2),S7		0
1911	Bos A	146	514	58	139	13	3	2	48	51	6		.270	.343	.319	86	-8	24	.975	-1	87	186	1b25,2b15,3b11,S2/OR		-1
1912	†Bos A	58	171	32	40	5	3	0	18	28	2		.234	.348	.298	81	-3	12	.987	-7	69	75	1b133,O2(0/1/1)		-1
1913	Bos A	143	498	75	144	17	12	3	50	53	5	41	.289	.363	.384	116	10	28	.976	-4	106	114	1b29,2b5,3b3/OR		-1
1914	Bos A	59	134	14	26	2	0	0	9	14	1	11	.194	.275	.209	46	-9	4-9	.976	-4	58	106	1b29,2b5,3b3/OR		-1
	Buf F	32	110	12	28	4	1	0	12	11	1	18	.255	.328	.309	73	-6	5	.889	-5	63	65	3b23,O9(3/0/7)		-3
1915	Buf F	141	501	56	131	22	8	3	71	34	3	43	.261	.312	.355	86	-18	24	.969	-7	100	56	O100(14/74/13),2b21,3b17/1		-0
1916	Cle A	11	26	1	4	0	0	0	1	0	0	6	.154	.154	.154	-7	-3	0	.810	-2	98	0	3b7,1b2/OR		-0
Total	8	836	2822	373	748	101	39	12	318	271	25	119	.265	.335	.341	97	-18	128-9	.959	-20	99	102	O276L,1b255,3b163,2b81,S9		-6

ENGLE, CHARLIE   Charlie August "Cholly"   B8.27.1903 New York NY   D10.12.1983 San Antonio TX   BR/TR/5-8/145   d9.14

1925	Phi A	1	0	0	0	0	0	0	0	0-0	0	0	—	—	—	—	0	0-0	—	0	0	0	/S		0
1926	Phi A	19	19	7	2	0	0	0	0	10	1	6	.105	.433	.105	43	-1	0-0	.930	1	111	147	S16		0
1930	Pit N	67	216	34	57	10	1	0	15	22	1	20	.264	.335	.319	59	-14	1	.975	-1	113	65	3b24,S23,2b10		-1
Total	3	87	235	41	59	10	1	0	15	32	2	26	.251	.346	.302	59	-15	1-0	.937	0	105	89	S40,3b24,2b10		-0

ENGLE, DAVE   Ralph David   B11.30.1956 San Diego CA   BR/TR/6-3/216*   [CalA78 3/66]   d4.14   C3   Col USC   OF(17/1/119)

1981	Min A	82	248	29	64	14	4	8	32	13-1	1	37	.258	.295	.407	95	-2	0-1	.980	1	106	83	O76R/3D		-0
1982	Min A	58	186	20	42	7	2	4	16	10-0	1	22	.226	.268	.349	66	-9	0-0	.985	3	115	158	O34(2/1/32),D20		-0
1983	Min A	120	374	46	114	22	4	8	43	28-1	1	39	.305	.350	.449	115	9	2-1	.973	-12	96	76	C73,D29,O4R		-0
1984	Min A☆	109	391	56	104	20	1	4	38	26-3	0	22	.266	.308	.353	79	-11	0-1	.981	-0	92	94	C86,D22		-0

YEAR	TM LG	G	AB	R	H	2B	3B	HR	RBI	BB-IB	HP	SO	AVG	OBP	SLG	AOPS	ABR	SB-CS	FA	FR	RNG	THR	GAMES AT POSITION	DL	BFW
1985	Min A	70	172	28	44	8	2	7	25	21-1	0	28	.256	.333	.448	106	1	2-2	.984	2	184	28	D38,C17,O3L		0.2
1986	Det A	35	86	6	22	7	0	4	7-0		0	13	.256	.312	.337	76	-3	0-0	1.000	-1	83	123	1b23,O4(2/0/2),C3,D5	38	-0.4
1987	Mon N	59	84	7	19	4	0	1	14	6-1	0	11	.226	.278	.310	53	-6	1-0	1.000	1	122	182	O11(9/0/2),C6,1b2/3		-0.5
1988	Mon N	34	37	4	8	3	0	0	1	5-0	0	5	.216	.310	.297	71	-1	0-0	1.000	0	65	96	C9,O4(1/0/3)/3		-0.1
1989	Mil A	27	65	5	14	3	0	2	8	4-0	0	13	.215	.261	.354	72	-3	0-0	.973	0	125	94	1b18,C3,D3		-0.1
Total 9		594	1643	201	431	88	13	31	181	120-7	3	190	.262	.311	.388	89	-26	5-5	.979	-7	99	83	C197,O136R,D118,1b43,3b3	38	-3.8

ENGLISH, CHARLIE   Charles Dewie B4.8.1910 Darlington SC D6.25.1999 Pasadena CA BR/TR/5-9.5/160 d7.23

YEAR	TM LG	G	AB	R	H	2B	3B	HR	RBI	BB-IB	HP	SO	AVG	OBP	SLG	AOPS	ABR	SB-CS	FA	FR	RNG	THR	GAMES AT POSITION	DL	BFW
1932	Chi A	24	63	7	20	3	1	1	8	3	0	7	.317	.348	.444	111	1	0-0	.821	-3	100	89	3b13/S		-0.1
1933	Chi A	3	9	2	4	2	0	0	1	1	0	1	.444	.500	.667	216	1	0-0	.923	-1	82	148	2b3		-0.1
1936	NY N	6	1	0	0	0	0	0	0	0	0	0	.000	.000	.000	-99	0	0	—	-0	0	0	/2		0.1
1937	Cin N	17	63	1	15	3	1	0	4	0	0	2	.238	.238	.317	52	-5	0	.958	2	112	106	3b15,2b2		0.0
Total 4		50	136	10	39	8	2	1	13	4	0	10	.287	.307	.397	90	-2	0-0	.897	-2	106	98	3b28,2b6/S		-0.2

ENGLISH, WOODY   Elwood George B3.2.1906 Fredonia OH D9.26.1997 Newark OH BR/TR/5-10/155 d4.26

YEAR	TM LG	G	AB	R	H	2B	3B	HR	RBI	BB-IB	HP	SO	AVG	OBP	SLG	AOPS	ABR	SB-CS	FA	FR	RNG	THR	GAMES AT POSITION	DL	BFW
1927	Chi N	87	334	46	97	14	4	1	28	16	1	26	.290	.325	.365	84	-8	1	.940	2	105	94	S84/3		0.3
1928	Chi N	116	475	68	142	22	4	1	34	30	2	28	.299	.343	.375	89	-8	4	.946	7	101	119	S114,3b2		1.1
1929	†Chi N	144	608	131	168	29	3	1	52	68	3	50	.276	.352	.339	72	-25	13	.955	14	102	116	S144		0.5
1930	Chi N	156	638	152	214	36	17	14	59	100	6	72	.335	.430	.511	125	31	3	.973	-11	88	126	S83,S78		2.9
1931	Chi N	156	634	117	202	38	8	2	53	68	7	80	.319	.391	.413	114	16	12	.965	1	96	78	S138,3b18		2.7
1932	†Chi N	127	522	70	142	23	7	3	47	55	2	73	.272	.344	.360	90	-6	5	.957	1	98	79	3b93,S38		0.1
1933	Chi N★	105	398	54	104	19	2	3	41	53	0	44	.261	.348	.342	98	1	5	.973	-8	92	68	3b103/S		-0.3
1934	Chi N	109	421	65	117	26	5	3	31	48	1	65	.278	.353	.385	99	1	6	.971	-1	76	89	S56,3b46,2b7		0.5
1935	Chi N	34	84	11	17	2	0	2	8	20	2	4	.202	.368	.298	81	-1	1	.868	-3	94	97	3b16,S12		-0.2
1936	Chi N	64	182	33	45	9	0	0	20	40	4	28	.247	.394	.297	86	0	1	.976	4	105	121	S42,3b17/2		0.7
1937	Bro N	129	378	45	90	16	2	1	42	65	5	55	.238	.350	.299	77	-9	4	.956	-14	90	76	S116,2b11		-1.5
1938	Bro N	34	72	9	18	2	0	0	7	8	1	11	.250	.333	.278	68	-3	2	.958	0	99	147	3b21,2b3,S3		-0.2
Total 12		1261	4746	801	1356	236	52	32	422	571	29	536	.286	.366	.378	95	-11	57	.957	-8	97	98	S826,3b400,2b22		6.6

ENGLISH, GIL   Gilbert Raymond B7.2.1909 Glenola NC D8.31.1996 Trinity NC BR/TR/5-11/180 d9.20

YEAR	TM LG	G	AB	R	H	2B	3B	HR	RBI	BB-IB	HP	SO	AVG	OBP	SLG	AOPS	ABR	SB-CS	FA	FR	RNG	THR	GAMES AT POSITION	DL	BFW
1931	NY N	3	8	0	0	0	0	0	0	1	0	3	.000	.111	.000	-69	-2	0	1.000	-0	86	0	3b3		-0.2
1932	NY N	59	204	22	46	7	5	2	19	5	1	20	.225	.244	.338	56	-14	0	.931	2	106	157	3b39,S23		-0.9
1936	Det A	1	1	0	0	0	0	0	0	0	0	1	.000	.000	.000	-99	0	0-0	1.000	0	111	0	/3		-0.9
1937	Det A	18	65	6	17	1	0	1	6	6	1	4	.262	.333	.323	65	-4	1-1	.962	-5	82	66	2b12,3b6		-0.7
	Bos N	79	269	25	78	5	2	2	37	23	1	27	.290	.348	.346	98	-1	3	.958	-5	101	114	3b71		-0.4
1938	Bos N	53	165	17	41	6	0	2	21	15	1	16	.248	.315	.321	84	-4	3	.956	-3	106	48	3b43,O3L,2b2,S2		-0.5
1944	Bro N	27	79	4	12	3	0	1	7	6	0	7	.152	.212	.228	24	-8	0	.918	-3	106	94	S13,3b11,2b2		-1.1
Total 6		240	791	74	194	22	7	8	90	56	3	78	.245	.298	.321	72	-33	5-1	.950	-14	101	104	3b174,S38,2b16,O3L		-3.8

ENNIS, DEL   Delmer B6.8.1925 Philadelphia PA D2.8.1996 Huntingdon Valley PA BR/TR/6-0/195* d4.28

YEAR	TM LG	G	AB	R	H	2B	3B	HR	RBI	BB-IB	HP	SO	AVG	OBP	SLG	AOPS	ABR	SB-CS	FA	FR	RNG	THR	GAMES AT POSITION	DL	BFW
1946	Phi N★	141	540	70	169	30	6	17	73	39	4	65	.313	.364	.485	144	28	5	.975	10	111	126	O138(138/0/1)		2.9
1947	Phi N	139	541	71	149	25	6	12	81	37	3	51	.275	.325	.410	98	-4	9	.979	4	103	112	O135(135/0/2)		-1.0
1948	Phi N	152	589	86	171	40	4	30	95	47	2	58	.290	.345	.525	135	26	2	.957	3	101	134	O151R		2.3
1949	Phi N	154	610	92	184	39	11	25	110	59	4	61	.302	.367	.525	140	33	2	.966	-1	97	114	O154L		2.0
1950	†Phi N	153	595	92	185	34	8	31	126	56	2	59	.311	.372	.551	142	34	2	.970	-3	99	87	O149(14/1/140)		2.0
1951	Phi N★	144	532	76	142	20	5	15	73	68	2	42	.267	.352	.408	105	5	4-2	.969	-2	97	109	O135(26/0/116)		2.5
1952	Phi N	151	592	90	171	30	10	20	107	47	0	65	.289	.341	.475	125	18	6-4	.970	-5	93	92	O149(120/0/31)		0.3
1953	Phi N	152	578	79	165	22	3	29	125	57	3	53	.285	.355	.484	117	13	1-3	.980	-5	94	108	O150L		-0.7
1954	Phi N	145	556	73	145	23	2	25	119	50	2	60	.261	.318	.444	98	-3	2-1	.957	-2	103	79	O142(72/0/71)/1		-1.3
1955	Phi N★	146	564	82	167	24	7	29	120	46-8	3	46	.296	.346	.518	129	22	4-2	.987	1	102	84	O145(143/0/3)		1.4
1956	Phi N	153	630	80	164	23	3	26	95	33-8	3	62	.260	.299	.430	95	-7	7-3	.962	-8	89	80	O153L		-2.5
1957	StL N	136	490	61	140	24	1	24	105	37-3	1	50	.286	.332	.494	117	11	1-3	.943	-17	77	35	O127(74/0/53)		-1.3
1958	StL N	106	329	22	86	18	1	3	47	15-3	1	35	.261	.290	.350	67	-15	0-1	.993	1	83	196	O84L		-2.0
1959	Cin N	5	12	1	4	0	0	0	1	2-1	0	2	.333	.429	.333	103	0	0-0	1.000	-0	99	0	O3L		0.0
	Chi A	26	96	10	21	6	0	2	7	4-0	0	10	.219	.250	.344	62	-5	0-0	.909	-3	65	146	O25L		-0.9
Total 14		1903	7254	985	2063	358	69	288	1284	597-23	31	719	.284	.340	.472	117	156	45-19	.969	-24	96	102	O1840(1291/1/568)/1		2.2

ENNIS, RUSS   Russell Elwood "Hack" B3.10.1897 Superior WI D1.21.1949 Superior WI BR/TR/5-11.5/160 d9.19

YEAR	TM LG	G	AB	R	H	2B	3B	HR	RBI	BB-IB	HP	SO	AVG	OBP	SLG	AOPS	ABR	SB-CS	FA	FR	RNG	THR	GAMES AT POSITION	DL	BFW
1926	Was A	1	0	0	0	0	0	0	0	—	—	—	—	0				0-0	—	-0	0	0	/C		0.0

ENRIGHT, GEORGE   George Albert B5.9.1954 New Britain CT BR/TR/5-11/175 [ChiA72 6/132] d8.8

YEAR	TM LG	G	AB	R	H	2B	3B	HR	RBI	BB-IB	HP	SO	AVG	OBP	SLG	AOPS	ABR	SB-CS	FA	FR	RNG	THR	GAMES AT POSITION	DL	BFW
1976	Chi A	2	1	0	0	0	0	0	0	0	0	0	.000	.000	.000	-99	0	0-0	1.000	-1	17	282	C2		-0.1

ENS, MUTZ   Anton B11.8.1884 St.Louis MO D6.28.1950 St.Louis MO BL/TL/6-1/180 d9.2 b-Jewel

YEAR	TM LG	G	AB	R	H	2B	3B	HR	RBI	BB-IB	HP	SO	AVG	OBP	SLG	AOPS	ABR	SB-CS	FA	FR	RNG	THR	GAMES AT POSITION	DL	BFW
1912	Chi A	3	6	0	0	0	0	0	0	0	0	0	.000	.000	.000	-99	-2	0	.857	-1	0	162	1b3		-0.2

ENS, JEWEL   Jewel Winklemeyer B8.24.1889 St.Louis MO D1.17.1950 Syracuse NY BR/TR/5-10.5/165 d4.29 M3/C13 b-Mutz

YEAR	TM LG	G	AB	R	H	2B	3B	HR	RBI	BB-IB	HP	SO	AVG	OBP	SLG	AOPS	ABR	SB-CS	FA	FR	RNG	THR	GAMES AT POSITION	DL	BFW
1922	Pit N	47	142	18	42	7	3	0	17	7	2	9	.296	.338	.387	85	-3	3-0	.951	-13	74	52	2b29,3b3,1b2/S		-1.4
1923	Pit N	12	29	3	8	1	1	0	5	0	0	3	.276	.276	.379	70	-1	2-0	.975	-0	135		1b4,3b3		-0.1
1924	Pit N	5	10	2	3	0	0	0	0	0	0	0	.300	.300	.300	60	-1	0-0	1.000	-0	71	51	1b5		-0.1
1925	Pit N	3	5	2	1	0	0	1	2	0	0	1	.200	.200	.800	133	0	0-0	1.000	-0	0		1b3		0.0
Total 4		67	186	25	54	8	4	1	24	7	2	16	.290	.323	.392	83	-5	5-0	.951	-14	74	52	2b29,1b14,3b6/S		-1.6

ENSBERG, MORGAN   Morgan Paul B8.26.1975 Redondo Beach CA BR/TR/6-2/210* [HouN98 9/272] d9.20 Col USC

YEAR	TM LG	G	AB	R	H	2B	3B	HR	RBI	BB-IB	HP	SO	AVG	OBP	SLG	AOPS	ABR	SB-CS	FA	FR	RNG	THR	GAMES AT POSITION	DL	BFW
2000	Hou N	4	7	0	2	0	0	0	0	0-0	0	1	.286	.286	.286	42	-1	0-0	.667	-1	55	0	/3		-0.1
2002	Hou N	49	132	14	32	7	2	3	19	18-0	3	25	.242	.346	.394	91	-2	2-0	.929	3	108	68	3b43		0.1
2003	Hou N	127	385	69	112	15	1	25	60	48-1	6	60	.291	.377	.530	127	15	7-2	.967	4	98	109	3b111/D		2.0
2004	†Hou N	131	411	51	113	20	3	10	66	36-1	0	46	.275	.330	.411	88	-8	6-4	.949	-6	83	123	3b118/S		-1.3
2005	†Hou N★	150	526	86	149	30	3	36	101	85-9	8	119	.283	.388	.557	144	36	6-7	.964	8	102	126	3b148		4.3
Total 5		461	1461	220	408	72	9	74	246	187-11	17	251	.279	.365	.493	118	40	21-13	.956	8	96	115	3b421/SD		5.0

ENWRIGHT, CHARLIE   Charles Massey B10.6.1887 Sacramento CA D1.19.1917 Sacramento CA BL/TR/5-10/? d4.19 Col St. Marys (CA)

YEAR	TM LG	G	AB	R	H	2B	3B	HR	RBI	BB-IB	HP	SO	AVG	OBP	SLG	AOPS	ABR	SB-CS	FA	FR	RNG	THR	GAMES AT POSITION	DL	BFW
1909	StL N	3	7	1	1	0	0	0	0	1	1	2	.143	.333	.143	10	-1	0	.444	-3	34	57	S2		-0.4

ENZENROTH, JACK   Clarence Herman B11.4.1885 Mineral Point WI D2.21.1944 Detroit MI BR/TR/5-7/160 d5.1 Col Michigan

YEAR	TM LG	G	AB	R	H	2B	3B	HR	RBI	BB-IB	HP	SO	AVG	OBP	SLG	AOPS	ABR	SB-CS	FA	FR	RNG	THR	GAMES AT POSITION	DL	BFW
1914	StL A	3	6	0	1	0	0	0	0	2	1	3	.167	.444	.167	88	0	0-1	.923	-1	96	41	C3		0.0
	KC F	26	67	7	12	4	1	0	5	5	0	19	.179	.236	.269	39	-7	0-0	.965	-2	91	105	C24		-0.8
1915	KC F	14	19	3	3	0	0	0	3	6	0	0	.158	.360	.158	50	-1	0	.973	1	112	130	C8		0.1
Total 2		43	92	10	16	4	1	0	8	13	1	22	.174	.283	.239	47	-8	0-1	.963	1	96	105	C35		-0.7

EPPARD, JIM   James Gerhard B4.27.1960 South Bend IN BL/TL/6-2/180* [OakA82 13/340] d9.8 Col California-Davis

YEAR	TM LG	G	AB	R	H	2B	3B	HR	RBI	BB-IB	HP	SO	AVG	OBP	SLG	AOPS	ABR	SB-CS	FA	FR	RNG	THR	GAMES AT POSITION	DL	BFW
1987	Cal A	8	9	2	3	0	0	0	0	0	0	3	.333	.455	.333	117	0	0-0	1.000	-0	55	0	/OR		0.0
1988	Cal A	56	113	7	32	3	1	0	14	11-0	0	15	.283	.347	.327	92	-1	0-0	.971	-1	116	0	O17L,D10,1b6		-0.1
1989	Cal A	12	12	0	3	0	0	0	2	1-0	0	4	.250	.308	.250	60	-1	0-0	1.000	-0	154	0	1b4		-0.1
1990	Tor A	6	5	0	1	0	0	0	1	2-0	1	2	.200	.333	.200	51	0	0-0	—	0			/H		0.0
Total 4		82	139	9	39	3	1	0	16	14-0	1	21	.281	.351	.317	90	-2	0-0	.972	0	112	0	O18(17/0/1),1b10,D10		0.0

EPPS, AUBREY   Aubrey Lee "Yo-Yo" B3.3.1912 Memphis TN D11.13.1984 Ackerman MS BR/TR/5-10/170 d9.29

YEAR	TM LG	G	AB	R	H	2B	3B	HR	RBI	BB-IB	HP	SO	AVG	OBP	SLG	AOPS	ABR	SB-CS	FA	FR	RNG	THR	GAMES AT POSITION	DL	BFW
1935	Pit N	1	4	1	3	0	0	0	3	0	0	0	.750	.750	1.250	414	2	0	.750	-1	43	0	/C		0.1

EPPS, HAL   Harold Franklin B3.26.1914 Athens GA D8.25.2004 Houston TX BL/TL/6-0/175 d9.9 Mil 1945-46

YEAR	TM LG	G	AB	R	H	2B	3B	HR	RBI	BB-IB	HP	SO	AVG	OBP	SLG	AOPS	ABR	SB-CS	FA	FR	RNG	THR	GAMES AT POSITION	DL	BFW
1938	StL N	17	50	8	15	0	0	1	3	2	0	4	.300	.327	.360	84	-1	2	.963	-1	103	0	O10C		-0.2
1940	StL N	11	15	6	3	0	0	0	1	2	0	3	.200	.200	.200	10	-2	0	.800	-0	99	0	O3C		-0.2
1943	StL A	8	35	2	6	1	0	0	3	2	0	1	.171	.216	.200	46									0.0
1944	StL A	22	62	15	11	1	0	0	3	14	1	14	.177	.338	.226	114	1	1-1	1.000	-1	91	0	O8C		0.0
	Phi N	67	229	27	60	8	0	0	13	18	1	18	.262	.316	.367	96	-3	0-5	.962	1	96	176	O18C		-0.3
	Year	89	291	42	71	9	0	0	16	32	2	19	.244	.321	.337	88	-5	2-1	.973	-2	96	79	O60(0/44/16)		-0.7
Total 4		125	391	58	99	9	1	1	21	37	1	43	.253	.329	.337	88	-5	2-2	.970	-3	96	81	O99(0/83/16)		-1.4

YEAR	TM LG	G	AB	R	H	2B	3B	HR	RBI	BB-IB	HP	SO	AVG	OBP	SLG	AOPS	ABR	SB-CS	FA	FR	RNG	THR	GAMES AT POSITION	DL	BFW

EPSTEIN, MIKE Michael Peter "Superjew" B4.4.1943 Bronx NY BL/TL/6-3.5/230* d9.16 Col California-Davis

																									-0.1
1966	Bal A	6	11	1	2	0	1	0	3	1-0	0	3	.182	.250	.364	75	0	0-0	1.000	.0	105	140	1b4		-0.1
1967	Bal A	9	13	0	2	0	0	0	0	3-0	0	5	.154	.313	.154	42	-1	0-0	1.000	-0	55	108	1b3		-0.2
	Was A	96	284	32	65	7	4	9	29	38-5	5	74	.229	.331	.377	114	5	1-4	.987	-1	104	127	1b80		-0.3
	Year	105	297	32	67	7	4	9	29	41-5	5	79	.226	.330	.367	110	4	1-4	.988	-1	102	126	1b83		0.2
1968	Was A	123	385	40	90	8	2	13	33	48-5	13	91	.234	.338	.366	118	9	1-1	.987	-1	103	97	1b110		3.3
1969	Was A	131	403	73	112	18	1	30	85	85-10	10	99	.278	.414	.551	177	46	2-5	.990	-4	91	105	1b118		0.5
1970	Was A	140	430	55	110	15	3	20	56	73-6	9	117	.256	.371	.444	131	20	2-3	.992	-5	88	105	1b122		-0.3
1971	Was A	24	85	6	21	1	1	1	9	12-1	4	31	.247	.366	.318	100	1	1-0	.992	-2	77	142	1b96		0.6
	†Oak A	104	329	43	77	13	0	18	51	62-5	8	71	.234	.368	.438	130	15	0-3	.995	-2	89	137	1b24		0.3
	Year	128	414	49	98	14	1	19	60	74-6	12	102	.237	.367	.413	124	16	1-3	.994	-3	86	138	1b120		3.1
1972	†Oak A	138	455	63	123	18	2	26	70	68-9	11	68	.270	.376	.490	165	38	0-1	.991	-1	77	79	1b25		-0.6
1973	Tex A	27	85	9	16	3	0	1	6	14-0	3	19	.188	.317	.259	68	-3	0-0	.993	1	97	82	1b86		-1.4
	Cal A	91	312	30	67	8	2	8	32	34-2	5	54	.215	.300	.330	84	-7	0-0	.993	-1	93	81	1b111		-2.0
	Year	118	397	39	83	11	2	9	38	48-2	8	73	.209	.304	.315	80	-10	0-0	.993	1	119	91	1b18		0.0
1974	Cal A	18	62	10	10	2	0	4	6	10-0	1	13	.161	.288	.387	98	0	0-0	.991	-13	95	108	1b823		5.0
Total	9	907	2854	362	695	93	16	130	380	448-43	70	645	.244	.358	.424	130	123	7-17	.991	-13	95	108	1b823		5.0

ERAUTT, JOE Joseph Michael "Stubby" B9.1.1921 Vibank SK, Can. D10.6.1976 Portland OR BR/TR/5-9/175* d5.9 b-Eddie Col Portland

																									-0.1
1950	Chi A	16	18	0	4	0	0	0	1	1-0	0	3	.222	.263	.222	26	-2	0-0	1.000	1	57	220	C5		0.0
1951	Chi A	16	25	3	4	1	0	0	3	1-0	1	2	.160	.276	.200	31	-2	0-0	.977	2	112	116	C12		-0.1
Total	2	32	43	3	8	1	0	0	4	1-0	1	5	.186	.271	.209	29	-4	0-0	.983	2	99	140	C17		

ERICKSON, HANK Henry Nels "Popeye" B11.11.1907 Chicago IL D12.13.1964 Louisville KY BR/TR/6-1/185 d4.17

1935	Cin N	37	88	9	23	3	2	1	4	6	2		.261	.323	.375	90	-1	0-	.972	2	93	155	C25		0.2

ERICKSON, MATT Matt B7.30.1975 Appleton WI BL/TR/5-11/190 [FlaN97 7/216] d7.9 Col Arkansas

2004	Mil N	4	6	1	1	0	0	0	1	0-0	0	1	.167	.167	.167	-13	-1	0-0	1.000	1	116	179	/2S		0.0

ERMER, CAL Calvin Coolidge B11.10.1923 Baltimore MD BR/TR/6-0.5/175 d9.26 M2/C4

1947	Was A	1	3	0	0	0	0	0	0	0	0	0	.000	.000	.000	-99	-1	0-0	1.000	0	101	0	/2		-0.1

ERNAGA, FRANK Frank John B8.22.1930 Susanville CA BR/TR/6-1/195* d5.24 Col UCLA

																									0.5
1957	Chi N	20	35	9	11	3	2	2	7	9-0	0	14	.314	.455	.686	204	6	0-0	.950	0	121	0	O10(3/0/7)		-0.2
1958	Chi N	9	8	0	1	0	0	0	0	0-0	0	2	.125	.125	.125	-34	-2	0-0	—	0			/H		0.3
Total	2	29	43	9	12	3	2	2	7	9-0	0	16	.279	.404	.581	163	4	0-0	.950	0	121	0	O10(3/0/7)		

ERSTAD, DARIN Darin Charles B6.4.1974 Jamestown ND BL/TL/6-2/210* [CalA95 1/1] d6.14 Col Nebraska

																									-0.7
1996	Cal A	57	208	34	59	5	1	4	20	17-1	0	29	.284	.333	.375	79	-1	7-3	.976	-1	106	67	O48(11/36/1)		-0.3
1997	Ana A	139	539	99	161	34	4	16	77	51-4	4	86	.299	.360	.466	114	11	23-8	.990	-6	82	88	O72(70/3/0),1b70,D2	15	0.3
1998	Ana A★	133	537	84	159	39	4	19	82	43-7	6	77	.296	.353	.486	114	11	20-6	.992	-2	87	99	1b78,O69(67/2/0),D2	15	-2.1
1999	Ana A	142	585	84	148	22	5	13	53	47-3	1	101	.253	.308	.374	73	-23	13-7	.999	12	96	91	1b78,O69(67/2/0),D2		3.9
2000	Ana A★	157	676	121	240	39	6	25	100	64-9	1	82	.355	.409	.541	135	37	28-8	.992	9	113	107	O136(112/30/0),D20,1b3		-0.7
2001	Ana A	157	631	89	163	35	4	9	63	62-7	10	113	.258	.331	.360	81	-15	24-10	.998	19	122	147	O143C,1b5,D4		1.1
2002	†Ana A	150	625	99	177	28	4	10	73	27-4	2	67	.283	.313	.389	87	-13	23-3	.998	4	114	69	O66C		-0.4
2003	Ana A	67	258	36	65	7	1	4	17	18-1	4	40	.252	.309	.333	73	-11	9-1	1.000	1	114	86	1b124	103	-1.3
2004	†Ana A	125	495	79	146	29	1	7	69	37-1	4	74	.295	.346	.400	97	-9	16-1	.996	-6	79	86	1b147,D5	36	-2.9
2005	†LA A	153	609	86	166	33	3	7	66	47-3	5	109	.273	.325	.371	86	-12	10-3	.997	-6	81	94	1b147,D5	169	-3.1
Total	10	1280	5163	810	1484	271	29	114	620	413-40	33	778	.287	.342	.417	97	-24	169-50	.995	29	112	116	O681(260/427/1),1b565,D46		

ERWIN, TEX Ross Emil B12.22.1885 Forney TX D4.5.1953 Rochester NY BL/TR/6-0/185 d8.26

																									0.0
1907	Det A	4	5	0	1	0	0	0	1	1	0		.200	.333	.200	68	0	0	.909	-0	94	134	C4		-0.8
1910	Bro N	81	202	15	38	3	1	1	10	24	1	12	.188	.278	.228	49	-13	3	.949	-1	94	111	C68		0.8
1911	Bro N	91	218	30	59	13	2	7	34	31	2	23	.271	.367	.445	132	10	5	.971	-7	79	109	C74		-0.6
1912	Bro N	59	133	14	28	3	0	2	14	18	0	16	.211	.305	.278	62	-7	1	.949	-2	92	94	C41		-0.2
1913	Bro N	20	31	6	8	1	0	0	3	4	0	1	.258	.343	.290	80	-1	0-1	.950	-2	90	57	C13		0.1
1914	Bro N	9	11	0	5	0	0	0	1	2	0	1	.455	.538	.455	192	1	1	1.000	-1	69	121	C4		0.3
	Cin N	12	35	5	11	3	0	1	7	2	0	3	.314	.351	.486	144	2	0	.962	0	107	74	C12		0.4
	Year	21	46	5	16	3	0	1	8	4	0	4	.348	.400	.478	157	3	1	.966	-0	102	81	C16		-0.4
Total	6	276	635	70	150	23	3	11	70	82	3	60	.236	.326	.334	90	-8	10-1	.957	-13	89	103	C216		

ESASKY, NICK Nicholas Andrew B2.24.1960 Hialeah FL BR/TR/6-3/205(200-215) [CinN78 1/17] d6.19 [DL 1991 Atl N 182, 1992 Atl N 85]

																									-0.7
1983	Cin N	85	302	41	80	10	5	12	46	27-1	3	99	.265	.328	.450	111	3	6-2	.935	-9	87	81	3b84		-2.1
1984	Cin N	113	322	30	62	10	5	10	45	52-3	0	103	.193	.301	.348	79	-9	1-2	.910	-8	94	67	3b82,1b25		0.3
1985	Cin N	125	413	61	108	21	0	21	66	41-3	4	102	.262	.332	.465	115	8	3-4	.946	-1	91	147	3b62,O54L,1b12		-0.9
1986	Cin N	102	330	35	76	17	2	12	41	47-0	1	97	.230	.325	.403	97	-1	0-2	.994	-9	63	102	1b93/3OL	32	-0.7
1987	Cin N	100	346	48	94	19	2	22	59	29-3	0	76	.272	.327	.529	118	7	0-0	.994	-6	76	95	1b116	43	-0.9
1988	Cin N	122	391	40	95	17	2	15	62	48-4	4	104	.243	.327	.412	108	5	7-2	.996	0	94	97	1b153/OL	23	1.1
1989	Bos A	154	564	79	156	26	5	30	108	66-9	3	117	.277	.355	.500	130	22	1-2	.996	0	94	97	1b153/OL	165	-0.6
1990	Atl N	9	35	2	6	0	0	0	0	4-0	0	14	.171	.256	.171	19	-4	0-0	.944	-1	81	102	1b9	530	-4.5
Total	8	810	2703	336	677	120	21	122	427	314-23	15	712	.250	.329	.446	110	31	18-14	.993	-36	78	96	1b478,3b230,O98L		

ESCALERA, NINO Saturnino Cuadrado B12.1.1929 Santurce, PR BL/TR/5-10/165 d4.17

1954	Cin N	73	69	15	11	1	1	1	5	11	1	15	.159	.234	.203	15	-9	1-0	.962	2	125	422	O14(1/3/10),1b8/S		-0.7

ESCALONA, FELIX Felix Eduardo B3.12.1979 Puerto Cabello, Venez BR/TR/6-0/185* d4.4

																									-1.0
2002	TB A	59	157	17	34	8	2	0	9	3-0	7	44	.217	.262	.293	49	-12	7-2	.945	-2	106	118	S26,2b25,3b4/D		0.0
2003	TB A	10	27	2	5	2	0	0	2	2-0	0	6	.185	.241	.259	33	-3	1-0	1.000	2	96	147	S8/23		-0.2
2004	NY A	5	8	1	0	0	0	0	0	0-0	1	2	.000	.111	.000	-68	-2	0-0	1.000	-0	100	64	S4/3		0.1
2005	NY A	10	14	0	4	1	0	0	2	1-0	1	4	.286	.375	.357	96	0	0-0	1.000	0	84	139	S5,3b3/12		-1.1
Total	4	84	206	20	43	11	2	0	13	6-0	9	56	.209	.261	.282	45	-17	8-2	.947	-1	101	123	S43,2b27,3b9/1D		

ESCHEN, JIM James Godrich B8.21.1891 Brooklyn NY D9.27.1960 Sloatsburg NY BR/TR/5-10.5/160 d7.10 s-Larry

1915	Cle A	15	42	11	10	2	0	0	2	5	0	9	.238	.319	.262	73	-1	0-0	.968	0	115	64	O10C		-0.2

ESCHEN, LARRY Lawrence Edward B9.22.1920 Suffern NY BR/TR/6-0/180 d6.16 f-Jim Col St. Lawrence

1942	Phi A	12	11	0	0	0	0	0	4	0	0	6	.000	.267	.000	-22	-2	0-0	.824	-2	48	0	S7/2		-0.4

ESCOBAR, ALEX Alexander Jose B9.6.1978 Valencia, Venez BR/TR/6-1/185* d5.8 [DL 2002 Cle A 183, 2005 Was N 183]

																									-0.2
2001	NY N	18	50	3	10	1	0	3	8	3-0	1	19	.200	.245	.400	67	-3	1-0	.935	1	88	375	O15(0/9/7)		0.1
2003	Cle A	28	99	16	27	2	0	5	14	7-1	1	33	.273	.324	.444	101	0	1-0	.969	3	111	201	O25R		-0.1
2004	Cle A	46	152	20	32	8	2	1	12	23-0	1	42	.211	.318	.309	67	-7	1-1	.991	7	103	364	O42(8/21/15),D3	366	-0.2
Total	3	92	301	39	69	11	2	9	34	33-1	2	94	.229	.309	.369	79	-10	3-1	.976	10	103	316	O82(8/30/47),D3		

ESCOBAR, ANGEL Angel Rubenque (Rivas) B5.12.1965 LaSabana, Venez BR/TR/6-0/160 d5.17

1988	SF N	3	3	1	1	0	0	0	0	0-0	0	0	.333	.333	.333	96	0	0-0	1.000	0	0	0	/S3		0.0

ESCOBAR, JOSE Jose Elias (Sanchez) B10.30.1960 Las Flores, Venez BR/TR/5-10/140 d4.13

1991	Cle A	10	15	0	3	0	0	0	1	1-0	0	4	.200	.250	.200	26	-2	0-0	1.000	-1	51	0	S5,2b4/3		-0.2

ESMOND, JIMMY James Joseph B10.8.1889 Albany NY D6.26.1948 Troy NY BR/TR/5-11/167 d4.20

																									-0.1
1911	Cin N	73	198	27	54	4	6	1	11	17	0	30	.273	.330	.369	99	-1	7	.918	-3	85	121	S44,3b14,2b2		-2.2
1912	Cin N	82	231	24	45	5	3	1	8	11	0	31	.195	.259	.255	42	-19	11	.930	-8	87	82	S74		-0.5
1914	Ind F	151	542	74	160	23	15	2	49	40	0	48	.295	.344	.404	93	-13	25	.919	-8	98	96	S151		0.1
1915	New F	155	569	79	147	20	11	4	62	59	1	54	.258	.329	.353	98	-12	18	.939	1	101	101	S424,3b14,2b2		-3.4
Total	4	461	1540	204	406	52	35	8	162	136	1	163	.264	.324	.358	88	-45	61	.929	-18	96	94	S424,3b14,2b2		

YEAR	TM	LG	G	AB	R	H	2B	3B	HR	RBI	BB-IB	HP	SO	AVG	OBP	SLG	AOPS	ABR	SB-CS	FA	FR	RNG	THR	GAMES AT POSITION	DL	BFW

ESPINO, JUAN Juan (Reyes) B3.16.1956 Bonao, D.R. BR/TR/6-1/190* d6.25

YEAR	TM	LG	G	AB	R	H	2B	3B	HR	RBI	BB-IB	HP	SO	AVG	OBP	SLG	AOPS	ABR	SB-CS	FA	FR	RNG	THR	GAMES AT POSITION	DL	BFW
1982	NY	A	3	2	1	0	0	0	0	0	0-0	0	1	.000	.000	.000	-99	-1	0-0	1.000	-0	0	0	C3		-0.1
1983	NY	A	10	23	1	6	0	0	0	3	0-0	0	5	.261	.280	.391	89	-1	0-0	1.000	-1	96	43	C10		-0.2
1985	NY	A	9	11	0	4	0	0	0	0	0-0	0	0	.364	.364	.364	102	0	0-0	1.000	0	108	0	C9		0.0
1986	NY	A	27	37	1	6	2	0	0	5	2-0	0	9	.162	.200	.216	15	-4	0-0	.987	0	84	50	C27		-0.4
Total	4		49	73	2	16	2	0	1	8	3-0	0	15	.219	.244	.288	47	-6	0-0	.993	-1	89	39	C49		-0.7

ESPINOZA, ALVARO Alvaro Alberto B2.19.1962 Valencia, Venez BR/TR/6-0/181(170-190) d9.14

YEAR	TM	LG	G	AB	R	H	2B	3B	HR	RBI	BB-IB	HP	SO	AVG	OBP	SLG	AOPS	ABR	SB-CS	FA	FR	RNG	THR	GAMES AT POSITION	DL	BFW
1984	Min	A	1	0	0	0	0	0	0	0	0-0	0	0	—	—	—	—	0	0-0	—	0	0	0	/S		0.0
1985	Min	A	32	57	5	15	0	0	0	9	1-0	1	9	.263	.288	.298	57	-3	0-1	.949	1	112	113	S31		-0.1
1986	Min	A	37	42	4	9	1	0	0	1	1-0	0	10	.214	.233	.238	28	-4	0-1	.941	-1	130	105	2b19,S18		-0.4
1988	NY	A	3	3	0	0	0	0	0	0	0-0	0	0	.000	.000	.000	-99	-1	0-0	1.000	-0	31	0	2b2/S		-0.1
1989	NY	A	146	503	51	142	23	1	0	41	14-1	1	60	.282	.301	.332	79	-15	3-3	.970	19	108	118	S146		1.4
1990	NY	A	150	438	31	98	12	2	2	20	16-0	5	54	.224	.258	.274	49	-31	1-2	.977	**23**	108	107	S150		0.2
1991	NY	A	148	480	51	123	23	2	5	33	16-0	2	57	.256	.282	.344	72	-20	1-2	.969	21	107	**129**	S147,3b2/P		1.2
1993	Cle	A	129	263	34	73	15	4	4	27	8-0	1	36	.278	.298	.380	82	-8	2-2	.937	-6	96	81	3b99,S35,2b2		-1.2
1994	Cle	A	90	231	27	55	13	0	1	19	6-0	1	33	.238	.258	.307	45	-19	1-3	.915	16	101	68	3b37,S36,2b20,1b3		-0.1
1995	†Cle	A	66	143	15	36	4	0	2	17	2-0	1	16	.252	.264	.322	51	-11	0-2	.966	-4	108	97	2b22,3b22,S19,1b2,D3		-1.3
1996	Cle	A	59	112	12	25	4	2	4	11	6-0	3	18	.223	.279	.402	70	-6	1-1	.947	1	79	73	3b20,1b18,S16,2b5/D		-0.5
	NY	N	48	134	19	41	7	2	4	16	4-0	0	19	.306	.324	.478	114	-7	0-2	.900	-3	93	40	3b38,S7,2b2/1		-0.1
1997	Sea	A	33	72	3	13	1	0	0	7	2-0	1	12	.181	.213	.194	7	-10	1-1	.965	2	84	57	S17,2b14/3		-0.6
Total	12		942	2478	252	630	105	9	22	201	76-1	16	324	.254	.279	.331	65	-126	13-19	.971	68	107	117	S624,3b219,2b86,1b24,D4/P	15	-1.6

ESPOSITO, SAMMY Samuel B12.15.1931 Chicago IL BR/TR/5-9/165* d9.28 Mil 1952-55 Col Indiana

YEAR	TM	LG	G	AB	R	H	2B	3B	HR	RBI	BB-IB	HP	SO	AVG	OBP	SLG	AOPS	ABR	SB-CS	FA	FR	RNG	THR	GAMES AT POSITION	DL	BFW
1952	Chi	A	1	4	0	1	0	0	0	0	0-0	0	2	.250	.250	.250	39	0	0-1	.500	-1	38	0	/S		-0.2
1955	Chi	A	3	4	3	0	0	0	0	0	1-0	0	0	.000	.200	.000	-41	-1	0-0	1.000	-1	0	0	3b2		-0.1
1956	Chi	A	81	184	30	42	8	2	3	25	41-0	2	19	.228	.371	.342	89	-1	1-2	.962	2	105	181	3b61,S19,2b3		0.0
1957	Chi	A	94	176	26	36	3	0	2	15	38-0	2	27	.205	.344	.256	66	-7	5-1	.960	10	109	143	3b53,S22,2b4/OC		0.5
1958	Chi	A	98	81	16	20	1	0	0	3	12-1	2	6	.247	.358	.284	81	-1	1-1	.979	5	125	74	3b63,S22,2b2/OL		0.5
1959	†Chi	A	69	66	12	11	1	0	1	5	11-1	0	16	.167	.282	.227	43	-5	0-1	.979	4	97	47	3b45,S14,2b2		-0.1
1960	Chi	A	57	77	14	14	5	0	1	11	10-1	0	20	.182	.273	.286	53	-5	0-0	.929	-8	94	96	3b37,S11,2b5		-1.3
1961	Chi	A	63	94	12	16	5	0	1	12	12-0	1	21	.170	.259	.255	40	-8	0-0	.976	-0	123	225	3b28,S20,2b11		-0.6
1962	Chi	A	75	81	14	19	1	0	0	4	17-1	0	13	.235	.367	.247	69	-3	0-1	.846	-8	65	46	3b41,S20,2b7		-1.0
1963	Chi	A	1	0	0	0	0	0	0	0	0-0	0		—	—	—	—	0	0-0	—	0			/R		0.0
	KC	A	18	25	3	5	1	0	0	2	3-0	0	3	.200	.276	.240	47	-2	0-0	1.000	-6	54	41	2b7,S4,3b3		-0.7
	Year		19	25	3	5	1	0	0	2	3-0	0	3	.200	.276	.240	47	-2	0-0	1.000	-6	54	41	2b7,S4,3b3		-0.7
Total	10		560	792	130	164	27	2	8	73	145-4	4	127	.207	.330	.277	66	-33	7-7	.957	-3	103	131	3b333,S133,2b41,O2(1/1/0)		-3.0

ESPY, CECIL Cecil Edward B1.20.1963 San Diego CA BB/TR/6-3/195(178-195) [ChiA80 1/8] d9.2

YEAR	TM	LG	G	AB	R	H	2B	3B	HR	RBI	BB-IB	HP	SO	AVG	OBP	SLG	AOPS	ABR	SB-CS	FA	FR	RNG	THR	GAMES AT POSITION	DL	BFW
1983	LA	N	20	11	4	3	1	0	0	1	1-0	0	2	.273	.333	.364	93	0	0-0	1.000	0	123	0	O15C		0.0
1987	Tex	A	14	8	1	0	0	0	0	0	1-0	0	3	.000	.111	.000	-67	-2	2-0	1.000	1	122	439	O8(5/0/3)		-0.1
1988	Tex	A	123	347	46	86	17	6	2	39	20-1	1	83	.248	.288	.349	76	-12	33-10	.972	2	99	223	O98(52/46/8),D12,S3,C2/12	15	-0.8
1989	Tex	A	142	475	65	122	12	7	3	31	38-2	2	99	.257	.313	.331	80	-13	45-20	.990	-1	100	87	O133(3/131/1),D3		-1.2
1990	Tex	A	52	71	10	9	0	0	1		10-0	0	20	.127	.235	.127	-4	-9	11-5	1.000	2	117	93	O39(4/28/9)/2D		-0.7
1991	†Pit	N	43	82	7	20	4	0	1	11	5-0	1	17	.244	.281	.329	74	-3	4-0	.966	-2	106	219	O35(2/25/11)		-0.1
1992	†Pit	N	112	194	21	50	7	3	1	20	15-2	2	40	.258	.310	.340	85	-4	6-3	.955	-3	91	38	O82(11/18/56)		-0.9
1993	Cin	N	40	60	6	14	2	0	0	5	14-0	0	13	.233	.368	.267	76	-1	2-2	.931	1	101	214	O18(18/0/1)		-0.1
Total	8		546	1248	160	304	43	16	7	108	104-5	3	277	.244	.301	.321	74	-44	103-40	.977	4	101	136	O428(95/263/89),D19,S3,2b2,C2/1	15	-3.9

ESSEGIAN, CHUCK Charles Abraham B8.9.1931 Boston MA BR/TR/5-11/202* d4.15 Col Stanford

YEAR	TM	LG	G	AB	R	H	2B	3B	HR	RBI	BB-IB	HP	SO	AVG	OBP	SLG	AOPS	ABR	SB-CS	FA	FR	RNG	THR	GAMES AT POSITION	DL	BFW
1958	Phi	N	39	114	15	28	5	2	5	16	12-0	0	34	.246	.317	.456	103	0	0-0	.952	-1	100	45	O30(28/2/0)		-0.3
1959	StL	N	17	39	2	7	1	0	1	5	1-0	0	13	.179	.200	.282	25	-4	0-0	1.000	0	74	225	O9L		-0.5
	†LA	N	24	46	6	14	6	0	1	5	4-1	0	11	.304	.360	.500	118	1	0-0	1.000	-1	81	0	O10(4/0/6)		0.0
	Year		41	85	8	21	8	1	1	10	5-1	0	24	.247	.289	.400	76	-3	0-0	1.000	-1	78	96	O19(13/0/6)		-0.5
1960	LA	N	52	79	8	17	3	0	3	11	8-1	0	24	.215	.284	.367	73	-3	0-0	.968	1	133	100	O18(13/0/5)		-0.2
1961	Bal	A	1	1	0	0	0	0	0	0	0-0	0	0	.000	.000	.000	-99	-1	0-0	—	0			/H		0.1
	KC	A	4	6	1	2	1	0	0	1	0-0	0	2	.333	.429	.500	145	0	0-0	1.000	0	199	0	/OL		0.6
	Cle	A	60	166	25	48	7	1	12	35	10-0	1	33	.289	.328	.560	138	8	0-0	.968	1	97	181	O49(16/19/16)		0.7
	Year		65	173	26	50	8	1	12	36	11-0	1	35	.289	.330	.555	137	8	0-0	.969	1	100	177	O50(17/19/16)		0.8
1962	Cle	A	106	336	59	92	12	0	21	50	42-2	2	68	.274	.363	.497	134	16	0-0	.994	-4	90	21	O90(88/1/1)		-1.3
1963	KC	A	101	231	23	52	9	0	5	27	19-0	1	48	.225	.285	.329	68	-10	0-0	.990	0	99	59	O53L		-0.8
Total	6		404	1018	139	260	45	4	47	150	97-4	9	233	.255	.323	.446	106	8	0-0	.981	-3	97	69	O260(212/22/28)		

ESSIAN, JIM James Sarkis B1.2.1951 Detroit MI BR/TR/6-2/195(187-205) d9.15 M1

YEAR	TM	LG	G	AB	R	H	2B	3B	HR	RBI	BB-IB	HP	SO	AVG	OBP	SLG	AOPS	ABR	SB-CS	FA	FR	RNG	THR	GAMES AT POSITION	DL	BFW
1973	Phi	N	2	3	0	0	0	0	0	0	0-0	0	1	.000	.000	.000	-97	-1	0-0	—	-0	0	0	/C		-0.1
1974	Phi	N	17	20	1	2	0	0	0	0	2-0	0	1	.100	.182	.100	-19	-3	0-0	.976	-2	50	90	C15/13		-0.1
1975	Phi	N	2	1	1	1	0	0	0	1	1-0	0	0	1.000	1.000	1.000	434	1	0-0	1.000	0	0	798	C2		0.1
1976	Chi	A	78	199	20	49	7	0	4	21	23-0	1	28	.246	.326	.281	79	-4	2-1	.974	0	124	128	C77,1b2/3		-0.1
1977	Chi	A	114	322	50	88	18	2	10	44	52-1	1	35	.273	.374	.435	120	11	1-4	.986	9	98	121	C111,3b2		1.5
1978	Oak	A	126	278	21	62	9	1	3	26	44-1	0	22	.223	.326	.295	81	-6	2-1	.981	7	70	163	C70,3b10,1b4,O4(3/0/1),D3		0.8
1979	Oak	A	98	313	34	76	16	0	8	40	25-1	0	29	.243	.295	.371	85	-7	0-1	.981	7	92	**158**	C119,1b3/2D		0.2
1980	Oak	A	87	285	19	66	11	0	5	29	30-0	1	18	.232	.302	.323	77	-9	1-3	.987	5	102	172	C68,D11/1		-0.2
1981	Chi	A	27	52	6	16	3	0	0	4	4-0	0	5	.308	.357	.365	110	1	0-1	.990	1	96	100	C25,3b2		0.2
1982	Sea	A	48	153	14	42	8	0	3	20	11-0	1	7	.275	.327	.386	92	-2	2-0	.994	-0	50	62	C48		-0.3
1983	Cle	A	48	93	11	19	4	0	2	11	16-0	0	8	.204	.315	.312	72	-3	0-1	.989	-1	96	125	C47/3	101	0.6
1984	Oak	A	63	136	17	32	9	0	2	10	23-0	1	17	.235	.348	.346	99	-1	1-1	.985	3	79	176	C59/3D	34	-0.3
Total	12		710	1855	194	453	85	3	33	207	231-3	6	171	.244	.327	.347	89	-21	9-13	.984	22	91	139	C642,3b18,D16,1b11,O4(3/0/1)/2	150	2.2

ESTALELLA, BOBBY Robert M B8.23.1974 Hialeah FL BR/TR/6-1/205(195-225) [PhiN92 23/641] d9.17 gf-Bobby Col Miami-Dade Kendall (FL) CC

YEAR	TM	LG	G	AB	R	H	2B	3B	HR	RBI	BB-IB	HP	SO	AVG	OBP	SLG	AOPS	ABR	SB-CS	FA	FR	RNG	THR	GAMES AT POSITION	DL	BFW
1996	Phi	N	7	17	5	6	0	0	2	4	1-0	0	6	.353	.389	.706	180	2	1-0	1.000	-0	309	81	C4		0.2
1997	Phi	N	13	29	9	10	1	0	4	9	7-0	1	7	.345	.472	.793	227	6	0-0	1.000	-3	214	34	C11		0.3
1998	Phi	N	47	165	16	31	6	1	8	20	13-0	1	49	.188	.247	.382	63	-10	0-0	.988	-10	77	55	C47		0.3
1999	Phi	N	9	18	2	3	0	0	1	4	0-0	0	7	.167	.318	.167	27	-2	0-1	.976	-1	56	61	C7		-1.7
2000	†SF	N	106	299	45	70	22	3	14	53	57-9	2	92	.234	.357	.468	114	8	3-0	.993	13	106	101	C106	24	-0.2
2001	SF	N	29	93	11	19	5	1	3	10	11-2	1	28	.204	.295	.376	76	-4	0-0	1.000	-2	107	82	C28		2.5
	NY	N	3	4	1	0	0	0	0	0	1-0	1	2	.000	.333	.000	-1	-1	0-0	1.000	1	111	0	C3		0.0
2002	Col	N	38	112	17	23	8	0	8	25	14-0	0	33	.205	.285	.491	92	-2	0-1	.995	-3	99	58	C38		0.0
2003	Col	N	46	140	17	28	7	0	7	21	19-0	1	55	.200	.294	.400	71	-6	2-0	.985	0	86	127	C46	84	-0.3
2004	Ari	N	7	14	2	2	0	0	2	4	0-0	0	6	.143	.143	.571	68	-1	0-0	1.000	-1	0	0	C6	49	-0.3
	Tor	A	5	13	1	3	0	0	0	2	3-0	1	5	.231	.412	.231	70	0	0-0	1.000	-0	37	0	C3,D2		-0.2
Total	9		310	904	126	195	49	5	48	147	130-11	7	290	.216	.315	.440	93	-10	6-2	.992	-2	100	84	C299,D2	265	0.3

ESTALELLA, BOBBY Roberto (Ventoza) B4.25.1911 Cardenas, Cuba D1.6.1991 Hialeah FL BR/TR/5-8/180 d9.7 gs-Bobby

YEAR	TM	LG	G	AB	R	H	2B	3B	HR	RBI	BB-IB	HP	SO	AVG	OBP	SLG	AOPS	ABR	SB-CS	FA	FR	RNG	THR	GAMES AT POSITION	DL	BFW
1935	Was	A	15	51	7	16	2	0	2	10	17	0	7	.314	.485	.471	153	6	1-0	.895	1	126	44	3b15		0.7
1936	Was	A	13	9	2	2	0	2	0	0	4	0	5	.222	.462	.667	186	1	0-0	—	0			/H		0.1
1939	Was	A	82	280	50	77	18	6	8	41	40	1	27	.275	.368	.468	121	9	2-3	.964	-3	97	59	O74(70/0/4)		0.1
1941	StL	A	46	83	7	20	6	1	0	14	18	0	13	.241	.376	.337	87	-1	0-0	1.000	0	78	0	O17(15/0/2)		-0.3
1942	Was	A	133	429	68	119	24	5	8	65	85	3	42	.277	.400	.413	130	22	5-2	.941	-5	94	26	3b78,O36(17/2/17)		1.9
1943	Phi	A	117	367	43	95	14	4	1	52	52	1	44	.259	.352	.409	123	11	1-3	.975	1	106	67	O97(95/1/1)		0.6
1944	Phi	A	140	506	54	151	17	9	7	60	59	2	60	.298	.374	.409	125	17	3-3	.988	-1	96	104	O128(5/103/25),1b6		1.2
1945	Phi	A	126	451	45	135	25	6	8	52	74	1	46	.299	.399	.435	142	27	1-6	.988	-6	92	91	O124(9/118/0)		1.7
1949	Phi	A	8	20	2	5	0	0	0	2	2	0	2	.250	.286	.250	44	-2	0-0	1.000	1	99	230	O6R		-0.1
Total	9		680	2196	279	620	106	33	44	308	350	8	246	.282	.383	.421	127	90	13-17	.982	-12	97	83	O482(211/224/55),3b93,1b6		5.9

YEAR	TM LG	G	AB	R	H	2B	3B	HR	RBI	BB-IB	HP	SO	AVG	OBP	SLG	AOPS	ABR	SB-CS	FA	FR	RNG	THR	GAMES AT POSITION	DL	BFW

ESTERBROOK, DUDE Thomas John B6.20.1857 Staten Is. NY D4.30.1901 Middletown NY BR/TR/5-11/167 d5.1 M1 OF(40/24/12)

1880	Buf N	64	253	20	61	12	1	0	35	0		15	.241	.241	.296	80	-5		.939	-2	147	86	1b47,O15(1/14/0),2b6/SC		-0.9
1882	Cle N	45	179	13	44	4	3	0	19	5		12	.246	.266	.302	85	-3		.893	7	133	263	O45(38/7/0)/1		0.3
1883	NY AA	97	407	55	103	9	7	0		15			.253	.280	.310	86	-7		.871	-6	84	92	3b97		-1.0
1884	†NY AA	112	477	110	150	29	11	1		12	10		.314	.345	.428	154	29		.885	-1	92	153	3b84,O4(1/0/3)		3.5
1885	NY N	88	359	48	92	14	5	2	44	4		28	.256	.264	.340	96	-3		.885	-1	92	153	3b84,O4(1/0/3)		-0.3
1886	NY N	123	473	62	125	20	6	3	43	8		43	.264	.277	.351	89	-8	13	.895	-6	89	69	3b123		-1.1
1887	NY AA	26	101	11	17	1	0	0	7	6	1		.168	.222	.178	13	-12	8	.950	-6	121	93	1b9,O7(0/3/5),S5,2b5		-1.5
1888	Ind N	64	246	21	54	8	0	0	17	2	2	20	.220	.232	.252	53	-13	11	.976	-3	89	97	1b61,3b3		-2.1
	Lou AA	23	93	9	21	6	0	0	7	3	2		.226	.265	.290	80	-2	5	.962	-0	120	74	1b23		-0.4
1889	Lou AA	11	44	8	14	3	0	0	9	5	1	2	.318	.400	.386	127	2	6	.931	-0	140	58	1b8,O2R/SM		0.1
1890	NY N	45	197	29	57	14	1	0	29	10	3	8	.289	.333	.371	105	1	12	.984	0	86	101	1b45		-0.2
1891	Bro N	3	8	1	3	0	0	0	0	0	1	1	.375	.444	.375	140	0	0	1.000	-1	0	0	O2R/2		0.0
Total	11	701	2837	387	741	120	34	6	210	70	20	129	.261	.284	.334	94	-21	55	.884	-8	92	102	3b419,1b194,O75L,2b12,S7/C		-3.6

ESTRADA, FRANK Francisco (Soto) B2.12.1948 Navojoa, Sonora, Mexico BR/TR/5-8/182 [NYN71*5/85] d9.14 Col Cuesta (CA) JC

1971	NY N	1	2	0	1	0	0	0	0	0-0			.500	.500	.500	184	0	0-0	1.000	-1	0	0	/C		0.0

ESTRADA, JOHNNY Johnny Pulado B6.27.1976 Hayward CA BB/TR/5-11/209* [PhiN97 17/506] d5.15 Col Sequoias (CA) [JC]

2001	Phi N	89	298	26	68	15	0	8	37	16-6	4	32	.228	.273	.359	66	-16	0-0	.993	-3	138	76	C89		-1.3
2002	Phi N	10	17	0	2	1	0	0	2	2-1	0	2	.118	.211	.176	6	-2	0-0	1.000	-3	53	0	C10		-0.3
2003	Atl N	16	36	2	11	0	0	0	2	3-3	0	3	.306	.359	.306	76	-1	0-0	1.000	-3	72	0	C14		-0.4
2004	†Atl N★	134	462	56	145	36	0	9	76	39-7	11	66	.314	.378	.450	113	11	0-0	.989	-1	90	65	C133		1.7
2005	†Atl N	105	357	31	93	26	0	4	39	20-6	3	38	.261	.303	.367	73	-14	0-0	.997	9	83	131	C104	16	0.2
Total	5	354	1170	115	319	78	0	21	156	77-20	21	141	.273	.326	.393	87	-22	0-0	.993	1	99	85	C350	16	-0.1

ETCHEBARREN, ANDY Andrew Auguste B6.20.1943 Whittier CA BR/TR/6-1/197* d9.26 C10

1962	Bal A	2	6	0	2	0	0	0	1	0-0	0	2	.333	.333	.333	85	0	0-0	.875	-2	67	0	C2		-0.2
1965	Bal A	5	6	1	1	0	0	0	4	0-0	0	2	.167	.167	.667	123	0	0-0	1.000	2	31	0	C5		0.2
1966	†Bal A☆	121	412	49	91	14	6	11	50	38-12	5	106	.221	.293	.364	89	-6	0-1	.989	-7	89	123	C121		-0.9
1967	Bal A☆	112	330	29	71	13	0	7	35	38-9	2	80	.215	.298	.318	83	-6	1-0	.989	-3	80	73	C110		-0.4
1968	Bal A	74	189	20	44	11	2	5	20	19-4	3	46	.233	.311	.392	112	3	0-0	.998	6	119	81	C70	36	1.4
1969	†Bal A	73	217	29	54	9	2	3	26	28-8	7	42	.249	.343	.348	81	-6	4-1	.984	-1	124	58	C76		1.1
1970	†Bal A	78	230	19	56	10	1	4	28	21-2	3	41	.243	.313	.348	81	-6	4-1	.986	2	152	126	C70		-0.3
1971	†Bal A	70	222	21	60	8	0	9	26	16-2	1	40	.270	.321	.428	110	2	1-4	.992	8	196	98	C70		0.7
1972	Bal A	71	188	11	38	6	1	2	21	17-2	3	43	.202	.276	.277	63	-8	0-2	.991	0	139	90	C51		0.1
1973	†Bal A	54	152	16	39	9	1	2	23	12-1	2	21	.257	.317	.368	93	-1	1-1	.991	8	177	58	C60		0.1
1974	†Bal A	62	180	13	40	8	0	2	15	6-0	1	26	.222	.249	.300	59	-10	1-0	.976	4	167	79	C60		-0.3
1975	Bal A	8	20	0	4	1	0	0	3	0-0	0	3	.200	.200	.250	28	-2	0-0	1.000	-1	79	125	C7	35	-0.2
	Cal A	31	100	10	28	0	1	3	17	14-1	0	19	.280	.365	.390	123	3	1-0	.981	-2	93	94	C31	56	0.2
	Year	39	120	10	32	1	1	3	20	14-1	0	22	.267	.341	.367	108	1	1-0	.980	-3	91	99	C38		0.0
1976	Cal A	103	247	15	56	9	1	0	21	24-0	4	37	.227	.305	.271	74	-7	0-2	.983	-3	82	128	C102		-0.7
1977	Cal A	80	114	11	29	2	2	0	14	12-0	0	19	.254	.320	.307	76	-4	3-1	.987	-4	74	86	C80	106	-0.5
1978	Mil A	4	5	1	2	1	0	0	3	1-0	0	2	.400	.500	.600	207	0	0-0	1.000	-2	0	112	C4	233	0.2
Total	15	948	2618	245	615	101	17	49	309	246-41	31	529	.235	.306	.343	88	-41	13-14	.987	10	129	96	C931		0.5

ETCHISON, BUCK Clarence Hampton B1.27.1915 Baltimore MD D1.24.1980 Cambridge MD BL/TL/6-1/190 d9.22

1943	Bos N	10	19	2	6	3	0	0	2	3-3	1	3	.316	.381	.474	148	1	0-0	.956	-1	72	211	1b6		0.0
1944	Bos N	109	308	30	66	16	0	8	33	33-1	1	50	.214	.292	.344	76	-10	1	.993	-2	89	102	1b85		-1.7
Total	2	119	327	32	72	19	0	8	35	35-1	1	52	.220	.298	.352	79	-9	1	.991	-3	88	107	1b91		-1.7

ETHERIDGE, BOBBY Bobby Lamar "Luke" B11.25.1942 Greenville MS BR/TR/5-9/178* d7.16 Col Mississippi St. [DL 1970 SD N 21]

1967	SF N	40	115	13	26	7	2	1	15	7-0	5	12	.226	.297	.348	86	-2	0-0	.925	-5	83	149	3b37		-0.8
1969	SF N	56	131	13	34	9	0	1	10	19-0	1	26	.260	.358	.351	100	1	0-0	.899	-3	99	91	3b39/S	21	-0.2
Total	2	96	246	26	60	16	2	2	25	26-0	6	38	.244	.330	.350	94	-1	0-0	.911	-8	91	119	3b76/S		-1.0

ETTEN, NICK Nicholas Raymond Thomas B9.19.1913 Spring Grove IL D10.18.1990 Hinsdale IL BL/TL/6-2/198 d9.8 Col Villanova

1938	Phi A	22	81	6	21	6	2	0	11	9		7	.259	.333	.383	81	-3	1-0	.987	-2	69	96	1b22		-0.6
1939	Phi A	43	155	20	39	11	2	3	29	16	0	11	.252	.322	.406	87	-3	0-0	.990	-3	77	79	1b41		-0.9
1941	Phi N	151	540	78	168	27	4	14	79	82	3	33	.311	.405	.454	147	37	9	.984	-3	96	92	1b150		2.1
1942	Phi N	139	459	37	121	21	3	8	41	67	0	26	.264	.357	.375	120	14	3	.985	0	105	93	1b135		0.2
1943	†NY A	154	583	78	158	35	5	14	107	76	0	31	.271	.355	.420	126	20	3-7	.989	-12	72	119	1b154		-0.3
1944	NY A	154	573	88	168	25	4	22	91	97	4	29	.293	.399	.466	142	35	4-2	.989	3	108	106	1b154		3.1
1945	NY A★	152	565	77	161	24	4	18	111	90	4	23	.285	.387	.437	133	26	2-3	.989	-11	79	121	1b152		0.8
1946	NY A	108	323	37	75	14	1	9	49	38	1	35	.232	.315	.365	88	-5	0-1	.991	-0	98	116	1b84		-0.9
1947	Phi N	14	41	5	10	4	0	1	8	5	0	4	.244	.326	.415	99	0	0-0	.990	1	141	46	1b11		0.1
Total	9	937	3320	426	921	167	25	89	526	480	12	199	.277	.371	.423	125	121	22-13	.988	-25	91	105	1b903		3.6

EUNICK, FRED Fernandas Bowen B4.22.1892 Baltimore MD D12.9.1959 Baltimore MD BR/TR/5-6/148 d8.29

1917	Cle A	1	2	0	0	0	0	0	0	0-0	0	0	.000	.000	.000	-93	-0		1.000	-0	107	0	/3		-0.1

EUSEBIO, TONY Raul Antonio Bare (b Raul Antonio Bare (Eusebio)) B4.27.1967 San Jose de los Llanos, D.R. BR/TR/6-2/210(180-210) d8.8

1991	Hou N	10	19	4	2	1	0	0	0	6-0	0	8	.105	.320	.158	41	-1	0-0	.981	1	139	74	C9		0.0
1994	Hou N	55	159	18	47	9	1	5	30	8-0	3	33	.296	.320	.459	108	1	0-1	.993	-3	90	152	C52		0.1
1995	Hou N	113	368	46	110	21	1	6	58	31-1	3	59	.299	.354	.410	109	5	0-2	.996	-4	95	79	C47	86	-0.3
1996	Hou N	58	152	15	41	7	2	1	19	18-2	0	20	.270	.343	.362	94	-1	0-1	.987	-2	86	62	C43		-0.4
1997	Hou N	60	164	12	45	2	0	1	18	19-1	4	27	.274	.364	.305	80	-4	0-1	.992	5	147	83	C54		0.0
1998	†Hou N	66	182	13	46	6	1	3	36	18-2	1	31	.253	.320	.313	70	-8	1-0	.994	8	162	78	C98	16	0.5
1999	†Hou N	103	323	31	88	15	0	4	33	40-4	6	67	.272	.353	.356	81	-8	0-0	.994	-8	99	58	C68		-0.5
2000	Hou N	74	218	24	61	18	0	7	33	25-2	4	45	.280	.361	.459	98	-3	0-0	.991	-2	117	70	C48	102	-0.2
2001	†Hou N	59	154	16	39	8	0	5	14	17-3	5	34	.253	.339	.403	84	-3	0-0	.992	-16	117	85	C522		-0.6
Total	9	598	1739	179	479	87	5	30	241	182-15	15	324	.275	.346	.383	91	-19	1-5	.992	-16	117	85	C522		

EUSTACE, FRANK Frank John B11.7.1873 New York NY D10.16.1932 Pottsville PA 5-9/160 d4.16

1896	Lou N	25	100	18	17	2	2	1	6		0	14	.170	.217	.260	26	-11	4	.841	-6	89	54	S22,2b3		-1.4

EVANS d6.1

1875	NH NA	1	4	1	2	0	0	0	1	0			.500	.500	.500	285	1	0-0	—	-0	0	0	/OL		0.1

EVANS, AL Alfred Hubert B9.28.1916 Kenly NC D4.6.1979 Wilson NC BR/TR/5-11/190* d9.13 Mil 1943-44

1939	Was A	7	21	2	7	0	0	0	1	5	0	7	.333	.462	.333	115	1	0-0	.964	0	137	120	C6		0.1
1940	Was A	14	25	1	8	0	0	0	7	6	0	7	.320	.452	.400	131	2	1-0	1.000	-1	76	57	C9		0.2
1941	Was A	53	159	16	44	8	4	1	19	9	0	18	.277	.315	.396	91	-3	0-0	.969	-1	97	113	C51		-0.2
1942	Was A	74	223	22	51	4	1	0	10	25	1	36	.229	.309	.256	60	-11	3-0	.961	-5	96	126	C67		-1.3
1944	Was A	14	22	5	2	0	0	0	2		0	6	.091	.167	.091	-27	-4	0-0	.933	-1	73	101	C8		-0.5
1945	Was A	51	150	19	39	11	2	2	19	17	1	22	.260	.339	.400	125	5	2-1	.973	-4	105	54	C41		0.3
1946	Was A	88	272	30	69	10	4	2	30	30	2	28	.254	.332	.342	94	-2	1-2	.966	-10	91	72	C81		-1.0
1947	Was A	99	319	17	77	8	3	2	23	28	1	25	.241	.303	.304	71	-13	2-1	.989	-1	94	117	C94		0.0
1948	Was A	93	228	19	59	6	3	2	28	38	1	19	.259	.367	.338	91	-2	1-1	.983	-2	112	154	C85		-1.1
1949	Was A	109	321	32	87	12	3	2	42	50	0	19	.271	.369	.346	92	-3	4-1	.992	-14	79	105	C107		-2.2
1950	Was A	90	289	24	68	8	3	2	30	29	2	21	.235	.309	.304	61	-18	0-0	.987	-10	65	68	C88		-0.2
1951	Bos A	12	24	1	3	1	0	0	2	4	0	7	.125	.250	.167	13	-3	0-0	1.000	0	130	0	C10		-0.2
Total	12	704	2053	188	514	70	23	13	211	243	7	206	.250	.332	.326	82	-51	14-9	.979	-49	91	101	C647		-6.8

EVANS, BARRY Barry Steven B11.30.1956 Atlanta GA BR/TR/6-1/180* [SDN77 2/34] d9.4 Col West Georgia

1978	SD N	24	90	7	24	1	1	0	4	4-1	0	10	.267	.295	.300	73	-4	0-0	.947	2	116	103	3b24		-0.3
1979	SD N	56	162	9	35	5	0	1	14	5-0	0	16	.216	.237	.265	40	-14	0-2	.952	4	114	151	3b53,S2/2		-1.2

YEAR	TM LG	G	AB	R	H	2B	3B	HR	RBI	BB-IB	HP	SO	AVG	OBP	SLG	AOPS	ABR	SB-CS	FA	FR	RNG	THR	GAMES AT POSITION	DL	BFW
1980	SD N	73	125	11	29	3	2	1	14	17-1	0	21	.232	.317	.312	84	-3	1-1	.983	-5	79	54	3b43,2b19,S4/1		-0.8
1981	SD N	54	93	11	30	5	0	1	7	9-2	0	9	.323	.371	.376	126	4	2-2	.969	-4	76	45	3b24,1b10,2b6,S2		-0.1
1982	NY A	17	31	2	8	3	0	0	2	6-0	1	6	.258	.395	.355	109	1	0-0	1.000	-1	87	73	2b8,3b6,S4	18	-0.1
Total	5	224	501	40	126	17	3	2	41	41-4	1	62	.251	.304	.309	77	-16	3-5	.960	-4	103	102		18	-2.4

EVANS, DARRELL Darrell Wayne B5.26.1947 Pasadena CA BL/TR/6-2/205* [OakA67 S7/132] d4.20 C1 Col Pasadena (CA) City

YEAR	TM LG	G	AB	R	H	2B	3B	HR	RBI	BB-IB	HP	SO	AVG	OBP	SLG	AOPS	ABR	SB-CS	FA	FR	RNG	THR	GAMES AT POSITION	DL	BFW
1969	Atl N	12	26	3	6	0	0	1	1	1-0	0	8	.231	.250	.231	38	-2	0-0	.917	-2	70	0	3b6		-0.4
1970	Atl N	12	44	4	14	1	1	0	9	7-0	1	5	.318	.423	.386	112	1	0-0	.941	1	120	0	3b12		0.2
1971	Atl N	89	260	42	63	11	1	12	38	39-4	1	54	.242	.338	.431	111	4	2-3	.937	7	111	115	3b72,O3L		1.1
1972	Atl N	125	418	67	106	12	0	19	71	90-4	4	58	.254	.384	.419	119	15	4-2	.941	14	114	92	3b123		3.0
1973	Atl N★	161	595	114	167	25	8	41	104	124-8	3	104	.281	.403	.556	153	46	6-3	.953	17	118	111	3b146,1b20		6.3
1974	Atl N	160	571	99	137	21	3	25	79	126-9	6	88	.240	.381	.419	120	20	4-2	.955	27	114	154	3b160		4.7
1975	Atl N	156	567	82	138	22	2	22	73	105-5	2	106	.243	.361	.406	110	10	12-3	.938	31	123	141	3b156,1b3		4.4
1976	Atl N	44	139	11	24	0	0	1	10	30-0	0	33	.173	.320	.194	46	-9	3-0	.994	1	96	84	1b36,3b7		-1.1
	SF N	92	257	42	57	9	1	10	36	42-4	0	73	.222	.329	.381	99	0	6-1	.991	8	138	88	1b83,3b5		0.4
	Year	136	396	53	81	9	1	11	46	72-4	0	71	.205	.326	.316	80	-9	9-1	.992	10	124	87	1b119,3b12		-0.7
1977	SF N	144	461	64	117	18	3	17	72	69-3	3	50	.254	.351	.416	106	5	9-6	.937	1	104	63	O81L,1b41,3b35		0.0
1978	SF N	159	547	82	133	24	2	20	78	105-12	2	64	.243	.360	.404	119	17	4-5	.952	5	101	99	3b155		2.0
1979	SF N	160	562	68	142	23	2	17	70	91-14	2	80	.253	.356	.391	112	12	6-7	.943	14	107	94	3b159		2.4
1980	SF N	154	556	69	147	23	0	20	78	83-6	2	65	.264	.356	.414	120	17	17-5	.946	12	107	118	3b140,1b14		3.0
1981	SF N	102	357	51	92	13	4	12	48	54-8	2	33	.258	.356	.417	123	12	2-3	.953	5	105	70	3b87,1b12		1.8
1982	SF N	141	465	64	119	20	4	16	61	77-7	2	64	.256	.360	.419	120	15	5-4	.933	4	94	93	3b84,1b49,S13		1.6
1983	SF N★	142	523	94	145	29	3	30	82	84-12	2	81	.277	.378	.516	150	37	5-4	.933	5	109	68	1b113,3b32,S9		3.6
1984	†Det A	131	401	60	93	11	1	16	63	77-10	0	70	.232	.353	.384	105	5	2-2	.997	3	135	102	D62,1b47,3b19		0.3
1985	Det A	151	505	81	125	17	0	40	94	86-12	1	85	.248	.356	.519	137	26	0-4	.984	13	143	95	1b113,D33,3b7		3.0
1986	Det A	151	507	78	122	15	0	29	85	91-5	1	105	.241	.356	.442	116	13	3-2	.998	13	141	108	1b105,D42,3b2		1.8
1987	†Det A	150	499	90	128	20	0	34	99	100-8	2	84	.257	.379	.501	137	30	6-5	.997	13	136	110	1b105,D44,3b7		3.3
1988	Det A	144	437	48	91	9	0	22	64	84-4	1	89	.208	.337	.380	104	4	1-4	.993	5	125	86	D72,1b65		0.1
1989	Atl N	107	276	31	57	6	1	11	39	41-6	0	46	.207	.303	.355	88	-4	0-1	.985	7	162	104	1b50,3b28		-0.1
Total	21	2687	8973	1344	2223	329	36	414	1354	1605-141	35	1410	.248	.361	.431	119	274	98-68	.946	207	110	110	3b1442,1b856,D253,O84L,S22		41.4

EVANS, DWIGHT Dwight Michael "Dewey" B11.3.1951 Santa Monica CA BR/TR/6-2/205(180-208) [BosA69 5/107] d9.16 C2

YEAR	TM LG	G	AB	R	H	2B	3B	HR	RBI	BB-IB	HP	SO	AVG	OBP	SLG	AOPS	ABR	SB-CS	FA	FR	RNG	THR	GAMES AT POSITION	DL	BFW
1972	Bos A	18	57	2	15	3	1	1	6	7-0	1	8	.263	.344	.404	115	1	0-0	1.000	1	82	240	O17(16/0/1)		0.1
1973	Bos A	119	282	46	63	13	1	10	32	40-2	1	52	.223	.320	.383	92	-2	5-0	.995	-0	101	67	O113(17/2/95),D2		-0.7
1974	Bos A	133	463	60	130	19	8	10	70	38-2	2	77	.281	.335	.421	110	5	4-4	.990	3	101	89	O122(1/3/120),D7		1.1
1975	†Bos A	128	412	61	113	24	6	13	56	47-3	4	60	.274	.353	.456	118	10	3-4	.987	19	130	116	O115R,D7		2.3
1976	Bos A	146	501	61	121	34	5	17	62	57-4	6	92	.242	.324	.431	108	6	6-7	.994	7	105	138	O145(0/8/140)/D		0.5
1977	Bos A	73	230	39	66	9	2	14	36	28-0	0	58	.287	.363	.526	135	14	4-2	.992	-1	100	48	O63(0/14/54),D6	44	0.5
1978	Bos A★	147	497	75	123	24	2	24	63	65-2	2	119	.247	.336	.449	108	6	8-5	.982	1	100	127	O142(0/3/140),D4		-0.1
1979	Bos A	152	489	69	134	24	1	21	58	69-7	1	76	.274	.364	.456	114	11	6-9	.988	5	103	136	O149R		0.5
1980	Bos A	148	463	72	123	37	5	18	60	64-6	5	98	.266	.358	.484	123	16	3-1	.982	-2	96	102	O144(0/1/144),D2		0.7
1981	Bos A★	108	412	84	122	19	4	22	71	85-1	1	85	.296	.415	.522	159	35	3-2	.993	6	109	108	O108(1/0/107)		3.6
1982	Bos A	162	609	122	178	37	7	32	98	112-1	1	125	.292	.402	.534	146	42	3-2	.973	-1	104	77	O161R/D		3.2
1983	Bos A	126	470	74	112	19	4	22	58	70-5	2	97	.238	.338	.436	104	3	3-0	.987	1	105	77	O99R,D21	19	-0.1
1984	Bos A	162	630	121	186	37	8	32	104	96-2	4	115	.295	.388	.532	145	42	3-1	.994	-4	97	72	O161R/D		2.9
1985	Bos A	159	617	110	162	29	1	29	78	114-4	5	105	.263	.378	.454	122	23	7-2	.990	-4	94	87	O152R,D7		1.2
1986	†Bos A	152	529	86	137	33	2	26	97	97-4	6	117	.259	.376	.476	130	25	3-3	.983	0	101	102	O149R/D		1.8
1987	Bos A★	154	541	109	165	37	2	34	123	106-6	3	98	.305	.417	.569	155	48	4-6	.982	-8	71	111	1b79,O77R,D4		2.8
1988	†Bos A	149	559	96	164	31	7	21	111	76-3	1	99	.293	.375	.487	134	27	5-1	.987	-6	101	91	O85(0/1/84),1b64,D6		1.6
1989	Bos A	146	520	82	148	27	3	20	100	99-1	3	84	.285	.397	.463	135	28	3-3	.981	-1	100	88	O77R,D69		2.3
1990	†Bos A	123	445	66	111	18	3	13	63	67-5	4	73	.249	.349	.391	103	3	3-4	—	0	0	0	D122	16	-0.2
1991	Bal A	101	270	35	73	9	1	6	38	54-2	2	54	.270	.393	.378	119	10	2-3	.984	-0	92	133	O67R,D21	27	0.7
Total	20	2606	8996	1470	2446	483	73	385	1384	1391-60	53	1697	.272	.370	.470	125	348	78-59	.987	24	103	103	O2146(35/32/2092),D282,1b143	106	24.7

EVANS, JOE Joseph Patton "Doc" B5.15.1895 Meridian MS D8.9.1953 Gulfport MS BR/TR/5-9/160 d7.3 Mil 1918 Col U. of Mississippi OF(172/85/54)

YEAR	TM LG	G	AB	R	H	2B	3B	HR	RBI	BB-IB	HP	SO	AVG	OBP	SLG	AOPS	ABR	SB-CS	FA	FR	RNG	THR	GAMES AT POSITION	DL	BFW
1915	Cle A	42	109	17	28	4	2	0	11	22	3	18	.257	.382	.330	111	3	6-1	.885	-0	118	21	3b30,2b2		0.4
1916	Cle A	33	82	4	12	1	0	0	1	7	0	12	.146	.213	.159	11	3	6-1	.915	3	120	67	3b28		-0.7
1917	Cle A	132	385	36	73	4	5	2	33	42	1	44	.190	.271	.242	53	-22	12	.939	1	107	111	3b127		-2.0
1918	Cle A	79	243	38	64	6	7	1	22	30	0	29	.263	.344	.358	102	1	7	.932	1	102	123	3b74		0.4
1919	Cle A	21	14	9	1	0	0	0	0	2	0	1	.071	.188	.071	-24	-2	1	.923	0	221	0	S6		0.0
1920	†Cle A	56	172	32	60	9	9	0	23	15	1	5	.349	.404	.506	136	8	6-2	.966	1	107	129	O43L,S6		0.8
1921	Cle A	57	153	36	51	11	0	0	21	19	1	5	.333	.410	.405	107	3	4-4	.933	3	105	162	O47L		0.3
1922	Cle A	75	145	35	39	6	2	0	22	8	0	4	.269	.307	.338	67	-7	11-2	.969	0	117	24	O49(30/17/3)		-0.8
1923	Was A	106	372	42	98	15	3	0	38	27	0	18	.263	.313	.320	70	-17	6-4	.982	-5	93	63	O72(2/65/5),3b21,1b5		-2.3
1924	StL A	77	209	30	53	3	3	0	19	24	0	12	.254	.330	.297	59	-13	4-4	.969	1	113	53	O49(38/1/10)		-1.6
1925	StL A	55	159	27	50	12	0	0	20	16	0	6	.314	.377	.390	90	-2	6-2	1.000	2	115	67	O47(12/2/36)		-0.2
Total	11	733	2043	306	529	71	31	3	210	212	3	152	.259	.329	.328	79	-51	67-16	.971	8	107	80	O307L,3b280,S12,1b5,2b2		-5.7

EVANS, STEVE Louis Richard B2.17.1885 Cleveland OH D12.28.1943 Cleveland OH BL/TL/5-10/175 d4.16

YEAR	TM LG	G	AB	R	H	2B	3B	HR	RBI	BB-IB	HP	SO	AVG	OBP	SLG	AOPS	ABR	SB-CS	FA	FR	RNG	THR	GAMES AT POSITION	DL	BFW
1908	NY N	2	2	0	1	0	0	0					.500	.500	.500	209	-0	0	—	-0	0	0	/OC		0.0
1909	StL N	143	498	67	129	17	6	2	56	66	14		.259	.362	.329	122	17	14	.947	-3	99	209	O141R,1b2		0.9
1910	StL N	151	506	73	122	21	8	2	73	78	31	63	.241	.376	.326	109	12	10	.968	-3	101	84	O141R,1b10		0.3
1911	StL N	154	547	74	161	24	13	5	71	46	19	52	.294	.369	.413	122	16	13	.972	-3	101	81	O150R		0.5
1912	StL N	135	491	59	139	23	9	6	72	36	17	51	.283	.353	.403	109	6	11	.942	-1	98	121	O134R		-0.1
1913	StL N	97	245	18	61	15	6	1	31	20	6	28	.249	.321	.371	99	0	5-5	.983	-1	109	63	O74(2/1/71)/1		-0.6
1914	Bro F	145	514	93	179	41	15	12	96	50	10	49	.348	.416	.556	165	39	18	.941	-1	101	80	O112(36/1/76),1b27		3.3
1915	Bro F	63	216	44	64	14	4	3	30	35	7	22	.296	.411	.440	140	11	7	.960	-1	93	103	O61R/1		0.7
	Bal F	88	340	50	107	20	6	1	37	28	7	34	.315	.379	.418	120	5	8	.925	-3	85	115	O88R,1b4		-0.2
	Year	151	556	94	171	34	10	4	67	63	14	56	.308	.392	.426	128	16	15	.940	-5	88	110	O149R,1b5		0.5
Total	8	978	3359	478	963	175	67	32	466	359	111	299	.287	.374	.407	125	106	86-5	.955	-16	99	112	O902(38/3/862),1b45		4.8

EVANS, TOM Thomas John B7.9.1974 Kirkland WA BR/TR/6-1/200(180-200) [TorA92 4/121] d9.2

YEAR	TM LG	G	AB	R	H	2B	3B	HR	RBI	BB-IB	HP	SO	AVG	OBP	SLG	AOPS	ABR	SB-CS	FA	FR	RNG	THR	GAMES AT POSITION	DL	BFW
1997	Tor A	12	38	7	11	2	0	1	10	7-0	1	10	.289	.341	.421	97	0	0-1	.917	2	122	56	3b12		0.1
1998	Tor A	7	10	0	0	0	0	0	0	1-0	0	2	.000	.091	.000	-73	-3	0-0	.889	-1	48	0	3b7		-0.3
2000	Tex A	23	54	10	15	4	0	0	5	5-0	1	13	.278	.394	.352	91	0	0-3	.909	1	108	140	3b21/1D		-0.3
Total	3	42	102	17	26	6	0	1	7	13-0	2	25	.255	.347	.343	78	-3	0-4	.910	2	106	95	3b40/D1	143	-0.2

EVANS, JAKE Uriah L. P. "Bloody Jake" B9.1856 Baltimore MD D1.16.1907 Baltimore MD TR/5-8/154 d5.1 ▲

YEAR	TM LG	G	AB	R	H	2B	3B	HR	RBI	BB-IB	HP	SO	AVG	OBP	SLG	AOPS	ABR	SB-CS	FA	FR	RNG	THR	GAMES AT POSITION	DL	BFW
1879	Tro N	72	280	30	65	9	5	0	17	5		18	.232	.246	.300	84	-4		.884	18	187	197	O72(2/7/64)		1.2
1880	Tro N	47	180	31	46	8	1	0	22	7		15	.256	.283	.311	96	-1		.906	-0	87	205	O47(0/6/41)/P		-0.1
1881	Tro N	83	315	35	76	11	5	0	28	14		30	.241	.274	.308	78	-8		.926	11	140	150	O83R		0.3
1882	Wor N	80	334	36	71	10	4	0	25	7		22	.213	.229	.266	57	-16		.910	17	195	44	O68(0/4/64),S11/32P		0.0
1883	Cle N	90	332	36	79	13	2	0	31	8		38	.238	.256	.289	66	-13		.902	3	144	34	O86R,S3,3b3/2P		-1.0
1884	Cle N	80	313	32	81	18	3	1	38	15		49	.259	.293	.345	97	-1		.917	8	125	115	O76(23/0/53),2b4,S2		0.5
1885	Bal AA	20	77	18	17	1	1	0	7	7	4		.221	.318	.260	85	-1		.894	1	140	277	O20R		0.0
Total	7	472	1831	215	435	70	21	1	168	63	4	172	.238	.264	.300	78	-44		.907	58	149	124	O452(25/17/411),S16,2b6,3b4,P3		0.9

EVERETT, CARL Carl Edward B6.3.1971 Tampa FL BB/TR/6-0/190(181-215) [NYA90 1/10] d7.1

YEAR	TM LG	G	AB	R	H	2B	3B	HR	RBI	BB-IB	HP	SO	AVG	OBP	SLG	AOPS	ABR	SB-CS	FA	FR	RNG	THR	GAMES AT POSITION	DL	BFW
1993	Fla N	11	19	0	2	0	0	0	0	1	0	9	.105	.150	.105	-29	-4	1-0	.857	-1	58	0	O8C		-0.5
1994	Fla N	16	51	7	11	1	0	2	6	3-0	1	15	.216	.259	.353	55	-4	4-0	1.000	1	102	234	O16(1/8/8)	18	-0.2
1995	NY N	79	289	48	75	13	1	12	54	39-2	2	67	.260	.352	.436	110	4	2-5	.981	2	96	165	O77(0/10/68)		0.2
1996	NY N	101	192	29	46	8	1	1	16	21-2	4	53	.240	.326	.307	72	-7	6-0	.935	4	126	162	O55(8/15/37)	15	-0.3
1997	NY N	142	443	58	110	28	3	14	57	32-3	7	102	.248	.308	.420	93	-6	17-9	.971	-1	98	120	O128(9/71/65)		-0.8
1998	†Hou N	133	467	72	138	34	4	15	76	44-2	3	102	.296	.359	.482	122	15	14-12	.987	6	106	162	O123(0/121/5),D2		2.0
1999	†Hou N	123	464	86	151	33	3	25	108	50-5	11	94	.325	.398	.571	145	33	27-7	.978	-4	89	167	O121(2/118/16),D2	21	3.1

YEAR	TM LG	G	AB	R	H	2B	3B	HR	RBI	BB-IB	HP	SO	AVG	OBP	SLG	AOPS	ABR	SB-CS	FA	FR	RNG	THR	GAMES AT POSITION	DL	BFW
2000	Bos A★	137	496	82	149	32	4	34	108	52-5	8	113	.300	.373	.587	135	25	11-4	.980	-3	90	184	O126C,D5		2.2
2001	Bos A	102	409	61	105	24	4	14	58	27-3	13	104	.257	.323	.438	98	-2	9-2	.974	-9	85	79	O93(0/84/9),D7	36	-0.9
2002	Tex A	105	374	47	100	16	0	16	62	33-4	6	77	.267	.333	.439	101	0	2-3	.969	-8	83	91	O83(18/33/39),D18	45	-1.1
2003	Tex A★	74	270	53	74	13	3	18	51	31-2	5	48	.274	.356	.544	125	10	4-1	.986	1	97	157	O72(40/15/33)/D		0.9
	Chi N	73	256	40	77	14	0	10	41	22-4	10	36	.301	.377	.473	118	7	4-3	.987	-1	98	112	O68(8/66/1),D3		0.7
	Year	147	526	93	151	27	3	28	92	53-6	15	84	.287	.366	.510	122	17	8-4	.986	1	97	136	O140(48/81/34),D4		1.6
2004	Mon N	39	127	8	32	10	0	2	14	8-2	5	19	.252	.319	.378	77	-4	0-0	.955	1	107	112	O33(19/0/14),D3	49	-0.5
	Chi A	43	154	21	41	7	1	5	21	8-1	5	26	.266	.320	.422	89	-3	1-0	1.000	1	65	2275	D41/OL		-0.4
2005	†Chi A	135	490	58	123	17	2	23	87	42-2	5	99	.251	.311	.435	93	-6	4-5	1.000	-2	78	82	D107,O22(14/0/8)		-1.5
Total 13		1313	4501	670	1234	250	26	191	759	413-37	84	964	.274	.344	.469	109	58	106-51	.977	-13	96	135	O1026(120/675/303),D187	184	2.9

EVERETT, ADAM   Jeffrey Adam B2.2.1977 Austell GA BR/TR/6-0/156(156-170) [BosA98 1/12] d8.30 Col South Carolina-Aiken

YEAR	TM LG	G	AB	R	H	2B	3B	HR	RBI	BB-IB	HP	SO	AVG	OBP	SLG	AOPS	ABR	SB-CS	FA	FR	RNG	THR	GAMES AT POSITION	DL	BFW
2001	Hou N	9	3	1	0	0	0	0	0	0-0	0	1	.000	.000	.000	-93	-1	1-0	.667	-0	89	214	S6		-0.1
2002	Hou N	40	88	11	17	3	0	0	4	12-1	1	19	.193	.297	.227	40	-8	3-0	.962	5	113	120	S34		0.0
2003	Hou N	128	387	51	99	18	3	8	51	28-6	1	66	.256	.320	.380	78	-13	8-1	.970	14	103	102	S128	53	1.1
2004	†Hou N	104	384	66	105	15	2	8	51	17-0	9	56	.273	.317	.385	79	-13	13-2	.977	11	102	97	S99		-0.5
2005	†Hou N	152	549	58	136	27	2	11	54	26-1	8	103	.248	.290	.364	70	-25	21-7	.978	36	102	107	S150	53	1.3
Total 5		433	1411	187	357	63	7	27	140	83-8	27	245	.253	.305	.365	72	-60	46-10	.973				S417		

EVERITT, BILL   William Lee "Wild Bill" B12.13.1868 Ft.Wayne IN D1.19.1938 Denver CO BL/TR/6-0.5/185 d4.18

YEAR	TM LG	G	AB	R	H	2B	3B	HR	RBI	BB-IB	HP	SO	AVG	OBP	SLG	AOPS	ABR	SB-CS	FA	FR	RNG	THR	GAMES AT POSITION	DL	BFW
1895	Chi N	**133**	550	129	194	16	10	3	88	33	4	42	.358	.399	.440	109	6	47	.854	-8	97	61	3b130,2b3		-1.4
1896	Chi N	**132**	575	130	184	16	13	2	46	41			.320	.367	.403	99	-2	46	.864	-6	92	83	3b83,O8(4/4/0)		-0.2
1897	Chi N	92	379	63	119	14	7	5	39	36	0		.314	.373	.364	113	11	28	.974	-3	96	**144**	1b149		0.7
1898	Chi N	149	596	102	190	15	6	0	69	53	3		.319	.377	.366	99	-1	30	.971	8	**140**	130	1b136		0.6
1899	Chi N	136	536	87	166	17	5	1	74	31	3		.310	.351	.366	99	-1	30	.979	-2	72	104	1b23		-0.6
1900	Chi N	23	91	10	24	4	0	0	17	3	0		.264	.287	.308	67	-4	2	.967	-4	69	68	1b33		-1.0
1901	Was A	33	115	14	22	3	2	0	8	15	3		.191	.301	.252	55	-6	7	.973	-26	108	129	1b341,3b310,O43(31/10/2),2b3		-1.9
Total 7		698	2842	535	902	85	43	11	341	212	15	85	.317	.368	.389	102	7	186							

EVERS, JOHNNY   John Joseph "Crab","Trojan" B7.21.1881 Troy NY D3.28.1947 Albany NY BL/TR/5-9/125 d9.1 M3/C7 HF1946 b-Joe

YEAR	TM LG	G	AB	R	H	2B	3B	HR	RBI	BB-IB	HP	SO	AVG	OBP	SLG	AOPS	ABR	SB-CS	FA	FR	RNG	THR	GAMES AT POSITION	DL	BFW
1902	Chi N	26	90	7	20	0	0	0	2	3	2		.222	.263	.222	51	-5	1	.990	1	112	81	2b18,S8		-0.4
1903	Chi N	124	464	70	136	27	7	0	52	19	3		.293	.325	.381	104	1	25	.937	-14	95	116	2b110,S11,3b2		-1.2
1904	Chi N	152	532	49	141	14	7	0	47	28	4		.265	.307	.318	93	-6	26	.943	28	**109**	125	2b152		2.5
1905	Chi N	99	340	44	94	11	2	1	37	27	2		.276	.333	.329	94	-2	19	.937	-1	94	137	2b99		-0.2
1906	†Chi N	154	533	65	136	17	6	1	51	36	5		.255	.305	.315	88	-8	49	.947	2	97	118	2b153/3		-0.6
1907	†Chi N	151	508	66	127	18	4	2	51	38	5		.250	.309	.313	89	-6	46	.964	27	113	126	2b151		2.5
1908	†Chi N	126	416	83	125	19	6	1	37	66	5		.300	.402	.375	143	25	36	.960	-1	99	122	2b122/OR		2.8
1909	Chi N	127	463	88	122	19	6	1	24	73	4		.263	.369	.337	116	13	28	.942	-1	100	79	2b126		1.7
1910	Chi N	125	433	87	114	11	7	0	28	108	2	18	.263	.413	.321	115	17	28	.950	-3	97	108	2b125		1.6
1911	Chi N	46	155	29	35	4	3	0	7	34	2	10	.226	.372	.290	86	-1	9	.975	-2	99	132	2b33,3b11		-0.3
1912	Chi N	143	478	73	163	23	11	1	63	74	2	18	.341	**.431**	.441	139	30	11-18	.959	6	104	122	2b136,M		3.7
1913	Chi N	136	446	81	127	20	5	3	49	50	3	14	.285	.361	.372	109	7	12	**.976**	6	99	**145**	2b139		2.7
1914	†Bos N	139	491	81	137	20	3	1	40	87	0	16	.279	.390	.338	118	17	7-8	.959	-2	95	112	2b82		0.5
1915	Bos N	83	278	38	73	4	1	1	22	50	0	19	.263	.375	.295	109	6	7-8	.951	-15	88	120	2b71		-2.0
1916	Bos N	71	241	33	52	4	1	0	15	40	1	13	.216	.330	.241	80	-3	4	.950	-4	97	129	2b24		0.1
1917	Bos N	24	83	5	16	0	0	0	13	2		8	.193	.302	.193	56	-2	1	.983	-1	108	78	2b49,3b7		-0.7
	Phi N	56	183	20	41	5	1	1	12	30	0	13	.224	.333	.279	85	-2	8	.973	-3	104	95	2b73,3b7		-0.7
	Year	80	266	25	57	5	1	1	12	43	0	21	.214	.324	.252	77	-5	9	.973	-3	104	95	2b73,3b7		-0.7
1922	Chi A	1	3	0	0	0	0	0	0	1	2	0	.000	.400	.000	12	0	0-0	1.000	-0	85	0	/2		-0.1
1929	Bos N	1	0	0	0	0	0	0	0		0		.000	.000	.000	0	0	0-0	.000	-1	0	0	/2		-0.0
Total 18		1784	6137	919	1659	216	70	12	538	778	39	142	.270	.356	.334	106	79	324-26	.955	58	101	119	2b1735,3b21,S19/OR		15.9

EVERS, JOE   Joseph Francis B9.10.1891 Troy NY D1.4.1949 Albany NY BR/TR/5-9/135 d4.24 b-Johnny

YEAR	TM LG	G	AB	R	H	2B	3B	HR	RBI	BB-IB	HP	SO	AVG	OBP	SLG	AOPS	ABR	SB-CS	FA	FR	RNG	THR	GAMES AT POSITION	DL	BFW
1913	NY N	1	0	0	0	0	0	0	0	0	0	0				0	0	0-0		0	0	0	/R		0.0

EVERS, TOM   Thomas Francis B3.31.1852 Troy NY D3.23.1925 Washington DC TL d5.25

YEAR	TM LG	G	AB	R	H	2B	3B	HR	RBI	BB-IB	HP	SO	AVG	OBP	SLG	AOPS	ABR	SB-CS	FA	FR	RNG	THR	GAMES AT POSITION	DL	BFW
1882	Bal AA	1	4	0	0	0	0	0		0			.000	.000	.000	-99	-1		.500	-2	0	0	/2		-0.3
1884	Was U	109	427	54	99	6	1	0		7			.232	.244	.251	52	-38		.869	15	103	83	2b109		-1.7
Total 2		110	431	54	99	6	1	0		7			.230	.242	.248	51	-39		.866	13	102	82	2b110		-2.0

EVERS, HOOT   Walter Arthur B2.8.1921 St.Louis MO D1.25.1991 Houston TX BR/TR/6-2/185* d9.16 Mil 1943-45 C1 Col Illinois

YEAR	TM LG	G	AB	R	H	2B	3B	HR	RBI	BB-IB	HP	SO	AVG	OBP	SLG	AOPS	ABR	SB-CS	FA	FR	RNG	THR	GAMES AT POSITION	DL	BFW
1941	Det A	1	4	0	1	0	0	0	0	0	0	2	.000	.000	.000	-91	0	0-0		0	0	0	/OR		-0.1
1946	Det A	81	304	42	81	8	4	4	33	34	2	43	.266	.344	.359	91	-3	7-1	.975	-5	96	38	O76(1/76/0)		-1.0
1947	Det A	126	460	67	136	24	5	10	67	45	6	49	.296	.366	.435	119	11	8-7	.978	3	103	123	O123C		1.1
1948	Det A★	139	538	81	169	33	6	10	103	51	4	31	.314	.378	.454	117	13	3-4	.973	-4	99	70	O123(81/42/2)		0.4
1949	Det A	132	432	68	131	21	6	7	72	70	2	38	.303	.403	.428	120	14	6-7	.994	8	108	133	O123(81/42/2)		1.3
1950	Det A★	143	526	100	170	35	**11**	21	103	71	4	40	.323	.408	.551	139	31	5-9	**.997**	3	96	129	O139(139/3/0)		1.9
1951	Det A	116	393	47	88	15	2	11	46	40	1	47	.224	.297	.356	76	-15	5-3	.976	-4	93	99	O108(66/45/1)		-2.4
1952	Det A	1	1	0	1	0	0	0	0	0	0	0	1.000	1.000	1.000	454	0	0-0		0	0	0	/H		0.0
	Bos A	106	401	53	105	17	4	14	59	29	4	55	.262	.318	.429	99	-2	5-2	.974	1	98	114	O105(90/12/20)		-0.8
	Year	107	402	53	106	17	4	14	59	29	4	55	.264	.320	.430	100	-2	5-2	.974	1	98	114	O105(90/12/20)		-1.6
1953	Bos A	99	300	39	72	10	1	11	31	23	3	41	.240	.301	.390	81	-9	2-1	.988	-3	97	52	O93(78/16/0)		-0.2
1954	Bos A	6	8	0	0	0	0	0	1	0	0	2	.000	.000	.000	-90	-2	0-0	1.000	-0	83	0	/OL		-0.1
	NY N	12	11	1	1	0	0	0	1	3	0	6	.091	.091	.091	12	-2	0-0	1.000	0	149	0	O4(2/2/0)		-0.5
	Det A	30	60	5	11	0	0	1	3	5	1	8	.183	.258	.250	40	-5	1-0	1.000	1	108	99	O24(17/2/6)		-0.5
1955	Bal A	60	185	21	44	10	1	6	30	19-0	0	28	.238	.307	.405	96	-2	2-1	.991	-2	103	28	O55(10/16/31)		0.1
	Cle A	39	66	10	19	7	1	2	9	3-0	0	12	.288	.314	.515	117	1	0-1	1.000	1	105	96	O25(15/9/2)		-0.4
	Year	99	251	31	63	17	2	8	39	22-0	0	40	.251	.309	.430	101	-1	2-2	.993	-1	103	44	O80(25/25/33)		0.0
1956	Cle A	3	0	1	0	0	0	0	0	1-0	0	0		1.000		180	0	0-0		0	0	0	/H		-0.2
	Bal A	48	112	20	27	3	0	1	4	24-0	0	18	.241	.375	.295	85	-1	1-0	.985	0	109	46	O36(3/2/34)		-0.2
	Year	51	112	21	27	3	0	1	4	25-0	0	18	.241	.380	.295	86	-1	1-0	.985	0	109	46	/H		0.0
Total 12		1142	3801	556	1055	187	44	98	565	415-0	27	420	.278	.353	.426	106	28	45-36	.983	-1	100	94	O1051(503/486/97)		-2.6

EWELL, GEORGE   George W. B2.1851 Philadelphia PA D10.20.1910 Philadelphia PA d6.26

YEAR	TM LG	G	AB	R	H	2B	3B	HR	RBI	BB-IB	HP	SO	AVG	OBP	SLG	AOPS	ABR	SB-CS	FA	FR	RNG	THR	GAMES AT POSITION	DL	BFW
1871	Cle NA	1	3	0	0	0	0	0		0			.000	.000	.000	-99	-1	0-0	1.000	0	0	0	/OR		0.0

EWING, REUBEN   Reuben (b Reuben Cohen) B11.30.1899 Odessa, Russia D10.5.1970 W.Hartford CT BR/TR/5-4.5/150 d6.21 Col Lebanon Valley

YEAR	TM LG	G	AB	R	H	2B	3B	HR	RBI	BB-IB	HP	SO	AVG	OBP	SLG	AOPS	ABR	SB-CS	FA	FR	RNG	THR	GAMES AT POSITION	DL	BFW
1921	StL N	3	1	0	0	0	0	0	0	0	0	0	.000	.000	.000	-99	0	0-0	1.000	0	258	0	/S		0.0

EWING, SAM   Samuel James B4.9.1949 Lewisburg TN BL/TL/6-3/200* [ChiA71*A1/5] d9.11 Col Tennessee

YEAR	TM LG	G	AB	R	H	2B	3B	HR	RBI	BB-IB	HP	SO	AVG	OBP	SLG	AOPS	ABR	SB-CS	FA	FR	RNG	THR	GAMES AT POSITION	DL	BFW
1973	Chi A	11	20	1	3	1	0	0	2	2-0	0	6	.150	.227	.200	20	-2	0-0	1.000	1	163	190	1b4		-0.2
1976	Chi A	19	41	3	9	2	1	0	3	2-0	0	8	.220	.256	.317	67	-2	0-0	1.000	-0	0	0	D12/1		-0.9
1977	Tor A	97	244	24	70	8	2	4	34	19-4	0	42	.287	.338	.385	95	-2	1-1	.957	-4	85	36	O46(15/0/31),D27,1b2		-0.4
1978	Tor A	40	56	3	10	0	2	0	9	5-2	0	9	.179	.242	.286	48	-4	0-0	1.000	0	118	0	O3R,D9		-1.7
Total 4		167	361	31	92	11	5	6	47	28-6	0	65	.255	.308	.352	81	-10	1-1	.959	-3	86	35	O49(15/0/34),D48,1b7		

EWING, BUCK   William B10.17.1859 Hoagland OH D10.20.1906 Cincinnati OH BR/TR/5-10/188 d9.9 M7 HF1939 b-John OF(9/34/193) ▲

YEAR	TM LG	G	AB	R	H	2B	3B	HR	RBI	BB-IB	HP	SO	AVG	OBP	SLG	AOPS	ABR	SB-CS	FA	FR	RNG	THR	GAMES AT POSITION	DL	BFW
1880	Tro N	13	45	1	8	1	0	0	5	1			.178	.196	.200	33	-3		.864	-3			C10,O4R		-0.6
1881	Tro N	67	272	40	68	14	7	0	25	7		8	.250	.269	.353	89	-4		.915	19			C44,S22,O2L/3		1.6
1882	Tro N	74	328	67	89	16	11	2	29	10		15	.271	.293	.405	127	10		.887	14	119	171	C63,O14(0/10/4),2b11,S4/3		2.4
1883	NY N	88	376	90	114	11	13	**10**	41	20		14	.303	.338	.481	147	20		.922	7			C80,O12(3/1/8),S3/3P		2.8
1884	NY N	94	382	90	106	15	**20**	3	41	28		22	.277	.327	.445	137	15		.933	14			C63,O14(1/3/10),3b8/S1P		2.9
1885	NY N	81	342	81	104	15	12	6	63	13		17	.304	.330	.471	159	20		.918	6			C50,O23(2/18/3),1b2		1.9
1886	NY N	73	275	59	85	11	7	4	31	16		17	.309	.347	.444	138	11	18	.863	-1	95	75	3b51,2b19,C8		1.7
1887	NY N	77	318	83	97	17	13	6	44	30	3	33	.305	.370	.497	146	20	26	.947	6			C78,3b21,S4,P2		3.8
1888	†NY N	103	415	83	127	18	15	6	58	24	1	28	.306	.348	.465	139	20	53	.937	16			C97,P3/OL		3.8
1889	†NY N	99	407	91	133	23	13	4	87	37			.327	.373	.477	139	20	34	.937						3.7

YEAR	TM LG	G	AB	R	H	2B	3B	HR	RBI	BB-IB	HP	SO	AVG	OBP	SLG	AOPS	ABR	SB-CS	FA	FR	RNG	THR	GAMES AT POSITION	DL	BFW
1890	NY P	83	352	98	119	19	15	8	72	39	1	12	.338	.406	.545	141	17	36	**.949**	8	100	111	C81/2PM		2.5
1891	NY N	14	49	8	17	2	1	0	18	5	0	5	.347	.407	.429	150	3	5	.881	-1	121	107	2b8,C6		0.2
1892	NY N	105	393	58	122	10	15	8	76	38	0	26	.310	.371	.473	157	25	42	.974	3	132	86	1b73,C30,2b2		2.8
1893	Cle N	116	500	117	172	28	15	6	122	41	0	18	.344	.394	.496	128	17	47	.927	-1	73	77	O112(0/1/112),2b5/1C		0.8
1894	Cle N	53	211	32	53	12	4	2	39	24	0	9	.251	.328	.374	66	-13	18	.912	-2	83	105	O52R/2		-1.3
1895	Cin N	105	434	90	138	24	13	5	94	30	1	22	.318	.363	.468	109	3	34	.976	8	139	110	1b105,M		0.9
1896	Cin N	69	263	41	73	14	4	1	38	29	0	13	.278	.349	.373	85	-6	41	.980	5	133	108	1b69,M		-0.1
1897	Cin N	1	3	1	0	0	0	0	0	0	1		.000	.500	.000	36	0		.800	-0	0		/1M		0.0
Total	18	1315	5363	1129	1625	250	178	71	883	392	9	294	.303	.351	.456	130	182	354	.931	104	91	116	C636,1b253,O235R,3b127,2b51,S34,P9		29.1

EWOLDT, ART Arthur Lee "Sheriff" B1.8.1894 Paullina IA D12.8.1977 Des Moines IA BR/TR/5-10/165 d9.17

| 1919 | Phi A | 9 | 32 | 2 | 7 | 0 | 2 | 1 | 0 | 2 | 1 | 0 | .219 | .242 | .250 | 38 | -3 | 0 | 1.000 | 0 | 99 | 0 | 3b9 | | -0.2 |

EZZELL, HOMER Homer Estell B2.28.1896 Victoria TX D8.3.1976 San Antonio TX BR/TR/5-10/158 d4.22

1923	StL A	88	279	31	68	6	0	0	14	15	2	20	.244	.287	.265	44	-23	4-3	.961	3	98	100	3b73,2b8		-1.5
1924	Bos A	90	277	35	75	8	4	0	32	14	2	21	.271	.311	.329	65	-16	12-5	.984	8	125	68	3b64,S21/C		-0.1
1925	Bos A	58	186	40	53	6	4	0	15	19	0	18	.285	.351	.360	81	-6	9-7	.916	-6	99	62	3b47,2b9		-0.9
Total	3	236	742	106	196	20	8	0	61	48	4	59	.264	.312	.313	61	-45	25-15	.957	5	106	80	3b184,S21,2b17/C		-2.5

FAATZ, JAY Jayson S. B10.24.1860 Weedsport NY D4.10.1923 Syracuse NY BR/TR/6-4/196 d8.22 M1

1884	Pit AA	29	112	18	27	2	3	0		1	4		.241	.274	.313	92	-1		.963	-1	64	108	1b29		-0.4
1888	Cle AA	120	470	73	124	10	2	0	51	12	21		.264	.312	.294	97	-1	64	**.989**	5	90	86	1b120		-0.9
1889	Cle N	117	442	50	102	12	5	2	38	17	10	28	.231	.275	.294	60	-26	27	.981	6	120	105	1b117		-2.7
1890	Buf P	32	111	18	21	0	2	1	16	9	8	5	.189	.297	.252	52	-7	2	.982	-2	48	89	1b32,M		-1.0
Total	4	298	1135	159	274	24	12	3	105	39	43	33	.241	.293	.292	77	-35	93	.982	5	95	96	1b298		-5.0

FABREGAS, JORGE Jorge B3.13.1970 Miami FL BL/TR/6-3/215(205-220) [CalA91 1/34] d4.24 Col Miami

1994	Cal A	43	127	12	36	3	0	0	16	7-1	0	18	.283	.321	.307	62	-7	2-1	.987	-2	85	88	C41		-0.6
1995	Cal A	73	227	18	56	10	0	1	22	17-0	0	28	.247	.298	.304	58	-14	0-2	.986	3	122	120	C73		-0.7
1996	Cal A	90	254	18	73	6	0	2	26	17-3	0	27	.287	.326	.335	68	-12	0-1	.989	0	81	105	C89/D		-0.7
1997	Ana A	21	38	2	3	1	0	0	3	3-0	0	3	.079	.146	.105	-33	-8	0-0	.989	1	196	54	C21		-0.5
	Chi A	100	322	31	90	10	1	7	48	11-0	1	43	.280	.302	.382	81	-11	1-1	.988	2	94	124	C92/1		-0.5
	Year	121	360	33	93	11	1	7	51	14-0	1	46	.258	.285	.353	68	-18	1-1	.988	3	107	115	C113/1		-0.8
1998	Ari N	50	151	8	30	4	0	1	15	13-1	1	26	.199	.263	.245	36	-14	0-0	.996	7	114	201	C41		-0.5
	NY N	20	32	3	6	0	0	0	5	1-0	0	6	.188	.212	.281	29	-4	0-0	.971	3	57	147	C12		0.0
	Year	70	183	11	36	4	0	2	20	14-1	1	32	.197	.255	.251	35	-18	0-0	.991	10	105	192	C53	30	-0.5
1999	Fla N	82	223	20	46	10	2	3	21	26-6	2	27	.206	.289	.309	56	-15	0-0	.989	7	139	144	C78		-0.4
	†Atl N	6	8	0	0	0	0	0	0	0-0	0	0	.000	.000	.000	-99	-2	0-0	1.000	0	0	0	C4/1		-0.1
	Year	88	231	20	46	10	2	3	21	26-6	2	27	.199	.282	.299	51	-18	0-0	.990	9	135	140	C82/1		-0.5
2000	KC A	43	142	13	40	4	0	3	17	8-1	0	11	.282	.320	.373	71	-7	1-0	.992	2	142	104	C39/D	43	-0.2
2001	Ana A	53	148	9	33	4	2	2	16	3-0	0	15	.223	.235	.318	44	-13	0-0	.990	6	105	120	C53	16	-0.4
2002	Ana A	35	88	8	17	1	0	0	8	6-1	0	6	.193	.245	.205	22	-10	0-0	.994	-0	71	82	C32		-0.8
	Mil N	30	67	5	11	3	0	3	14	2-0	0	7	.164	.178	.343	38	-7	0-0	1.000	2	139	112	C20		-0.5
Total	9	646	1827	153	441	56	5	23	211	114-13	4	217	.241	.284	.315	56	-124	4-5	.989	31	109	121	C595,1b2,D2	89	-5.7

FABRIQUE, BUNNY Albert La Verne B12.23.1887 Clinton MI D1.10.1960 Ann Arbor MI BB/TR/5-8.5/150 d10.4

1916	Bro N	2	2	0	0	0	0	0	0	0	0	1	.000	.000	.000	-97	-0	0	1.000	0	91	374	S2		0.0
1917	Bro N	25	88	8	18	3	0	1	3	8	0	9	.205	.271	.273	65	-3	0	.874	-5	85	80	S21		-0.8
Total	2	27	90	8	18	3	0	1	3	8	0	10	.200	.265	.267	62	-3	0	.878	-5	85	89	S23		-0.8

FAEDO, LENNY Leonardo Lago B5.13.1960 Tampa FL BR/TR/6-0/170* [MinA78 1/16] d9.6

1980	Min A	5	8	1	2	1	0	0	0	0-0	0	0	.250	.250	.375	64	0	0-0	.818	-3	49	15	S5		-0.3
1981	Min A	12	41	3	8	0	1	0	6	1-0	0	5	.195	.209	.244	30	-4	0-0	.971	2	107	113	S12		-0.1
1982	Min A	90	255	16	62	8	0	3	22	16-0	1	22	.243	.288	.310	63	-13	0-0	.967	-10	87	103	S88/D		-1.4
1983	Min A	51	173	16	48	7	0	1	18	4-1	0	19	.277	.291	.335	70	-7	0-0	.954	-17	85	66	S51	89	-1.9
1984	Min A	16	52	6	13	1	0	1	6	4-0	0	3	.250	.304	.327	71	-2	0-0	.968	-5	86	45	S15/D		-0.5
Total	5	174	529	42	133	17	1	5	52	25-1	1	49	.251	.284	.316	63	-26	1-0	.961	-32	87	85	S171,D2	89	-4.2

FAGIN, FRED Frederick H. B Cincinnati OH d6.25

| 1895 | StL N | 1 | 3 | 0 | 1 | 0 | 0 | 0 | | 2 | 0 | 0 | .333 | .333 | .333 | 73 | 0 | 0 | .636 | -1 | 74 | 172 | /C | | -0.1 |

FAHEY, FRANK Francis Raymond B1.22.1896 Milford MA D3.19.1954 Boston MA BB/TR/6-1/190 d4.25 Col Catholic America ▲

| 1918 | Phi A | 10 | 17 | 2 | 3 | 1 | 0 | 0 | 1 | 0 | 0 | 3 | .176 | .176 | .235 | 24 | -2 | 0 | 1.000 | -1 | 81 | | O5(4/1/0),P3 | | -0.2 |

FAHEY, HOWARD Howard Simpson "Cap", "Kid" B6.24.1892 Medford MA D10.24.1971 Clearwater FL BR/TR/5-7.5/145 d7.23 Col Dartmouth

| 1912 | Phi A | 5 | 8 | 0 | 0 | 0 | 0 | 0 | 0 | 0 | 0 | | .000 | .000 | .000 | -99 | -2 | 0 | 1.000 | -1 | 0 | 1059 | 3b2/2S | | -0.3 |

FAHEY, BILL William Roger B6.14.1950 Detroit MI BL/TR/6-0/200* [TexA70*S1/1] d9.26 C6 Col Detroit Mercy [DL 1978 Tex A 41]

1971	Was A	2	8	0	0	0	0	0	0	0-0	0	0	.000	.000	.000	-99	-2	0-0	.909	-0	85	186	C2		-0.3
1972	Tex A	39	119	8	20	2	0	1	10	12-0	1	23	.168	.250	.210	39	-9	4-0	.992	5	75	166	C39		-0.2
1974	Tex A	6	16	1	4	0	0	0	0	0-0	0	1	.250	.250	.250	45	-1	0-0	1.000	-1	0	59	C6		-0.2
1975	Tex A	21	37	3	11	1	0	0	3	1-0	0	10	.297	.316	.378	96	0	0-0	.983	-2	71	64	C21		0.2
1976	Tex A	38	80	12	20	2	0	1	9	11-0	1	6	.250	.348	.313	92	0	1-0	.993	1	99	94	C38	53	-0.2
1977	Tex A	37	68	3	15	4	0	0	5	1-0	0	8	.221	.232	.279	38	-6	0-0	1.000	-6	72	47	C34		-1.0
1979	SD N	73	209	14	60	9	1	3	19	21-5	0	17	.287	.348	.378	106	2	1-1	.994	-6	110	100	C68		-0.1
1980	SD N	93	241	18	62	4	0	1	22	21-6	0	16	.257	.314	.286	74	-8	2-0	.977	-7	92	102	C85		-1.3
1981	Det A	27	67	5	17	2	0	1	9	2-0	4	4	.254	.271	.328	71	-3	0-1	.981	1	93	95	C27	30	-0.2
1982	Det A	28	67	7	10	2	0	0	4	2-0	0	5	.149	.147	.179	-10	-10	0-0	1.000	1	103	158	C28	29	-0.7
1983	Det A	19	22	4	6	1	0	0	2	2-0	0	3	.273	.407	.318	105	1	0-0	1.000	0	630	0	C18	42	-0.2
Total	11	383	934	75	225	26	2	7	83	74-12	2	93	.241	.296	.296	69	-36	9-2	.989	-15	109	103	C366	195	-4.2

FAIN, FERRIS Ferris Roy "Burrhead" B5.29.1921 San Antonio TX D10.18.2001 Georgetown CA BL/TL/5-11/186* d4.15

1947	Phi A	136	461	70	134	28	6	7	71	95	2	34	.291	.414	.423	130	24	4-5	.985	-1	104	104	1b132		1.9
1948	Phi A	145	520	81	146	27	6	7	88	113	3	37	.281	.412	.396	115	18	10-5	.989	8	122	105	1b145		2.0
1949	Phi A	150	525	81	138	21	5	3	78	136	0	51	.263	.415	.339	104	12	8-1	.984	5	115	119	1b150		1.3
1950	Phi A★	151	522	83	147	25	4	10	83	133	3	26	.282	.430	.402	116	22	8-5	.987	11	**132**	113	1b151		2.5
1951	Phi A★	117	425	63	146	30	3	6	57	80	3	20	**.344**	.451	.471	144	33	0-3	.990	16	**159**	119	1b108,O11(1/0/10)		4.3
1952	Phi A☆	145	538	82	176	**43**	2	2	59	105	1	26	**.327**	**.438**	.429	133	32	3-5	.984	18	**148**	92	1b144		4.5
1953	Chi A★	128	446	73	114	48	2	6	52	108	4	28	.256	.405	.345	101	24	3-2	.989	9	125	86	1b127		0.9
1954	Chi A★	65	235	30	71	10	1	5	51	40	1	14	.302	.399	.417	121	9	5-1	.987	-4	75	105	1b64	66	0.2
1955	Det A	58	140	23	37	8	0	2	23	52-2	1	12	.264	.459	.364	128	11	2-1	.988	-0	104	113	1b44		0.8
	Cle A	56	118	9	30	3	0	0	8	42-1	1	13	.254	.451	.280	97	3	3-0	.992	3	120	91	1b51		0.4
	Year	114	258	32	67	11	0	2	31	94-3	2	25	.260	.455	.326	113	14	5-1	.990	3	112	102	1b95		1.2
Total	9	1151	3930	595	1139	213	30	48	570	904-3	18	261	.290	.424	.396	120	172	46-28	.987	63	124	105	1b1116,O11(1/0/10)	66	18.8

FAIR, BOBBY George T. B1.13.1856 Boston MA D2.12.1939 Roslindale MA 5-7.5/140 d7.29

| 1876 | NY N | 1 | 4 | 0 | 0 | 0 | 0 | 0 | 0 | 0 | 0 | | .000 | .000 | .000 | -99 | -1 | | .750 | -0 | 105 | 187 | /2 | | -0.1 |

FAIREY, JIM James Burke B9.22.1944 Orangeburg SC BL/TL/5-10/190(179-190) d4.14 Col Erskine

1968	LA N	99	156	17	31	3	1	1	10	9-0	0	32	.199	.241	.276	60	-9	1-1	.944	1	110	122	O63(40/2/23)		-1.1
1969	Mon N	20	49	6	14	1	0	1	6	1-0	0	7	.286	.300	.367	86	-1	0-2	.913	-1	90	163	O13(1/12/0)		-0.3
1970	Mon N	92	211	35	51	9	3	3	25	14-4	2	39	.242	.290	.355	73	-9	1-3	.978	-2	95	34	O59(33/30/4)		-1.4
1971	Mon N	92	200	19	49	8	1	1	19	12-5	0	23	.245	.285	.310	68	-9	3-3	.968	3	96	231	O58(56/2/1)	10	-0.9
1972	Mon N	86	141	9	33	7	0	1	15	10-2	0	21	.234	.285	.305	66	-6	1-3	.932	-2	85	56	O37(20/1/18)		-1.2
1973	LA N	10	9	0	2	0	0	0	1	1	0	0	.222	.300	.222	48	-1	0-0	—	0			/H		-0.1
Total	6	399	766	86	180	28	7	7	75	47-11	2	122	.235	.274	.317	66	-35	6-12	.957	-1	97	121	O230(150/47/46)	10	-5.0

FAIRLY, RON
Ronald Ray B7.12.1938 Macon GA BL/TL/5-10/181* d9.9 Col USC

YEAR	TM LG	G	AB	R	H	2B	3B	HR	RBI	BB-IB	HP	SO	AVG	OBP	SLG	AOPS	ABR	SB-CS	FA	FR	RNG	THR	GAMES AT POSITION	DL	BFW
1958	LA N	15	53	6	15	1	0	2	8	6-0	0	7	.283	.350	.415	100	0	0-0	.971	-2	94	0	O15(4/11/1)		-0.2
1959	†LA N	118	244	27	58	12	1	4	23	31-2	1	29	.238	.324	.344	73	-8	0-4	.963	-1	84	190	O88(7/23/62)		-1.4
1960	LA N	14	37	6	4	0	3	1	3	7-0	0	12	.108	.250	.351	59	-2	0-0	1.000	-1	75	105	O13(5/0/8)		-0.4
1961	LA N	111	245	42	79	15	2	10	48	48-0	1	22	.322	.434	.522	140	17	0-0	.989	1	96	177	Q71(6/15/53),1b23		1.4
1962	LA N	147	460	80	128	15	7	14	71	75-6	3	59	.278	.379	.433	126	19	1-1	.989	-10	57	79	1b120,O48(4/5/42)		0.1
1963	†LA N	152	490	62	133	21	0	12	77	58-7	1	69	.271	.347	.388	120	14	5-2	.995	-6	71	99	1b119,O45(16/22/10)		0.1
1964	LA N	150	454	62	116	19	5	10	74	65-6	2	55	.256	.349	.385	116	11	4-0	.987	-0	99	95	1b141		0.4
1965	†LA N	158	555	73	152	28	1	9	70	76-11	3	72	.274	.361	.377	117	16	2-0	.982	-5	95	72	O148(0/17/133),1b13		0.1
1966	†LA N	117	351	53	101	20	0	14	61	52-4	2	38	.288	.380	.464	146	24	3-2	.974	-9	77	36	O98(0/6/95),1b25		0.9
1967	LA N	153	486	45	107	19	0	10	55	54-9	1	51	.220	.295	.321	85	-9	1-4	.986	5	96	151	O97(1/0/97),1b68		-1.6
1968	LA N	141	441	32	103	15	1	4	43	41-10	4	61	.234	.301	.299	88	-6	0-2	.989	2	96	172	O105R,1b36		-1.5
1969	LA N	30	64	3	14	3	0	2	8	9-1	0	6	.219	.315	.328	86	-1	0-0	.981	1	137	65	1b12,O10(1/0/10)		-0.2
	Mon N	70	253	35	73	13	4	12	39	28-2	0	22	.289	.358	.514	141	13	1-0	.991	1	117	121	1b52,O21(3/18/0)	32	1.0
	Year	100	317	38	87	16	6	12	47	37-3	0	28	.274	.344	.476	132	13	1-0	.989	1	121	111	1b64,O31(4/18/10)		0.8
1970	Mon N	119	385	54	111	19	0	15	61	72-9	4	64	.288	.402	.455	130	20	10-2	.995	5	114	117	1b118,O4(2/2/0)	31	1.7
1971	Mon N	146	447	58	115	23	0	13	71	81-10	5	65	.257	.373	.396	118	15	1-3	.992	4	115	97	1b135,O10(10/1/0)		0.9
1972	Mon N	140	446	51	124	15	1	17	68	46-7	3	45	.278	.348	.430	118	11	3-4	.985	5	104	165	O70R,1b68		0.7
1973	Mon N★	142	413	70	123	13	1	17	49	86-11	3	33	.298	.422	.458	139	27	2-2	.974	-4	84	56	O121L,1b5		1.7
1974	Mon N	101	282	35	69	9	1	12	43	57-6	1	28	.245	.372	.411	113	7	2-1	.989	0	99	85	1b67,O20(19/0/1)		0.1
1975	StL N	107	229	32	69	13	2	7	37	45-9	3	22	.301	.421	.467	140	15	0-1	.980	1	114	92	1b56,O20(4/0/16)		1.2
1976	StL N	73	110	13	29	4	0	0	21	23-3	0	12	.264	.385	.300	96	1	0-0	.995	3	159	109	1b27		0.3
	Oak A	15	46	9	11	1	0	3	10	9-3	0	12	.239	.364	.457	145	3	0-0	1.000	0	97	88	1b15		0.2
1977	Tor A★	132	458	60	128	24	2	19	64	58-11	2	58	.279	.362	.465	122	15	0-4	.986	4	116	84	D58,1b40,O33(9/0/24)		1.2
1978	Cal A	91	235	23	51	15	0	10	40	25-2	1	31	.217	.289	.366	88	-5	0-1	.998	-3	72	91	1b78,D5		-1.3
Total	21	2442	7184	931	1913	307	33	215	1044	1052-129	40	877	.266	.360	.408	117	197	35-33	.991	-10	98	97	1b1218,O1037(212/120/727),D63	63	5.4

FALCH, ANTON
Anton C. B12.4.1860 Milwaukee WI D3.31.1936 Wauwatosa WI 6-6/220 d9.30

YEAR	TM LG	G	AB	R	H	2B	3B	HR	RBI	BB-IB	HP	SO	AVG	OBP	SLG	AOPS	ABR	SB-CS	FA	FR	RNG	THR	GAMES AT POSITION	DL	BFW
1884	Mil U	5	18	0	2	0	0	0					.111	.111	.111	-60	-4		.600	-0	101	0	O3L,C2		-0.4

FALK, BIBB
Bibb August "Jockey" B1.27.1899 Austin TX D6.8.1989 Austin TX BL/TL/6-0/175 d9.17 M1/C2 b-Chet Col Texas

YEAR	TM LG	G	AB	R	H	2B	3B	HR	RBI	BB-IB	HP	SO	AVG	OBP	SLG	AOPS	ABR	SB-CS	FA	FR	RNG	THR	GAMES AT POSITION	DL	BFW
1920	Chi A	7	17	1	5	1	1	0	2	0	0	5	.294	.294	.471	100	0	0-0	1.000	-0	93	0	O4R		-0.1
1921	Chi A	152	585	62	167	31	11	5	82	37	2	69	.285	.330	.402	87	-14	4-4	.958	-13	89	48	O149(148/1/0)		-3.7
1922	Chi A	131	483	58	144	27	1	12	79	27	0	55	.298	.335	.433	99	-2	2-6	.963	-9	91	62	O129(126/2/1)		-2.2
1923	Chi A	87	274	44	84	18	6	5	38	25	1	12	.307	.367	.471	121	7	5-5	.951	-3	97	69	O80L		-0.2
1924	Chi A	138	526	77	185	37	8	6	99	47	1	21	.352	.406	.487	134	26	6-6	.970	8	96	178	O134L		2.1
1925	Chi A	154	602	80	181	35	9	4	99	51	2	35	.301	.357	.409	99	-2	4-5	.992	-6	90	102	O153L		-1.9
1926	Chi A	155	566	86	195	43	4	8	108	66	2	22	.345	.415	.477	137	33	9-10	.978	8	107	109	O155L		2.7
1927	Chi A	145	535	76	175	35	6	9	83	52	4	19	.327	.391	.465	125	20	5-7	.978	18	115	146	O145L		2.4
1928	Chi A	98	286	42	83	18	4	1	37	25	0	16	.290	.347	.392	95	-2	5-1	.972	2	100	125	O78L		-0.5
1929	Cle A	125	426	65	133	30	7	13	93	42	0	14	.312	.374	.507	120	12	4-4	.943	-4	89	123	O120(61/0/61)		-0.2
1930	Cle A	82	191	34	62	12	1	4	36	23	0	8	.325	.397	.461	113	4	2-0	.967	0	98	111	O42(25/0/18)		0.2
1931	Cle A	79	161	30	49	13	1	2	28	17	0	13	.304	.371	.435	105	2	1-1	.949	-2	95	36	O33(2/0/31)		-0.2
Total	12	1353	4652	655	1463	300	59	69	784	412	12	279	.314	.372	.449	113	84	47-49	.967	-1	97	106	O1222(1107/3/115)		-1.6

FALLON, CHARLIE
Charles Augustus B3.7.1881 New York NY D6.10.1960 Kings Park NY BR/TR/5-6/? d6.30

YEAR	TM LG	G	AB	R	H	2B	3B	HR	RBI	BB-IB	HP	SO	AVG	OBP	SLG	AOPS	ABR	SB-CS	FA	FR	RNG	THR	GAMES AT POSITION	DL	BFW
1905	NY A	1	0	0	0	0	0	0										0-0	—	0			/R		0.0

FALLON, GEORGE
George Decatur "Flash" B7.8.1914 Jersey City NJ D10.25.1994 Lake Worth FL BR/TR/5-9/155 d9.27 Mil 1945

YEAR	TM LG	G	AB	R	H	2B	3B	HR	RBI	BB-IB	HP	SO	AVG	OBP	SLG	AOPS	ABR	SB-CS	FA	FR	RNG	THR	GAMES AT POSITION	DL	BFW
1937	Bro N	4	8	0	2	0	0	0	1	0	0	0	.250	.333	.375	91	0	0	.895	-0	87	56	2b4		0.4
1943	StL N	36	78	6	18	1	0	0	5	2	1	9	.231	.259	.244	44	-6	1	.968	9	122	133	2b36		-0.5
1944	†StL N	69	141	16	28	6	0	1	9	16	1	11	.199	.285	.262	54	-8	1	.973	1	86	104	2b38,S24,3b6		-0.4
1945	StL N	24	55	4	13	2	1	0	7	6	0	6	.236	.311	.309	71	-2	1	.948	-3	84	108	S20,2b4		-0.5
Total	4	133	282	26	61	10	1	1	21	25	2	26	.216	.285	.270	56	-16	2	.966	6	103	112	2b82,S44,3b6		-0.5

FALSEY, PETE
Peter James B4.24.1891 New Haven CT D5.23.1976 Los Angeles CA BL/TL/5-6.5/132 d7.16 Col Yale

YEAR	TM LG	G	AB	R	H	2B	3B	HR	RBI	BB-IB	HP	SO	AVG	OBP	SLG	AOPS	ABR	SB-CS	FA	FR	RNG	THR	GAMES AT POSITION	DL	BFW
1914	Pit N	3	1	0	0	0	0	0		0		1	.000	.000	.000	-99	-0		—	0			/H		0.0

FANEYTE, RIKKERT
Rikkert B5.31.1969 Amsterdam, Netherlands BR/TR/6-1/170* [SFN90 16/446] d8.29 Col Miami-Dade Kendall (FL) CC

YEAR	TM LG	G	AB	R	H	2B	3B	HR	RBI	BB-IB	HP	SO	AVG	OBP	SLG	AOPS	ABR	SB-CS	FA	FR	RNG	THR	GAMES AT POSITION	DL	BFW
1993	SF N	7	15	2	2	0	0	0		2-0	0	4	.133	.235	.133	-2	-2	0-0	1.000	0	112	0	O6(1/5/0)		-0.2
1994	SF N	19	26	1	3	3	0	0	4	1-0	0	11	.115	.207	.231	14	-3	0-0	.900	0	122	0	O6(0/2/4)		-0.3
1995	SF N	46	86	7	17	4	1	0	4	11-0	0	27	.198	.289	.267	49	-6	1-0	.981	1	97	239	O34(3/22/11)		-0.5
1996	Tex A	8	5	0	1	0	0	0	1	0-0	0	2	.200	.200	.200	1	-1	0-0	1.000	1	182	0	O6(2/4/0),D2		0.0
Total	4	80	132	10	23	7	1	0	9	16-0	0	42	.174	.264	.242	35	-12	1-0	.976	2	108	167	O52(6/33/15),D2		-1.0

FANNING, JIM
William James B9.14.1927 Chicago IL BR/TR/5-11/180* d9.11 M3/C1 Col Buena Vista

YEAR	TM LG	G	AB	R	H	2B	3B	HR	RBI	BB-IB	HP	SO	AVG	OBP	SLG	AOPS	ABR	SB-CS	FA	FR	RNG	THR	GAMES AT POSITION	DL	BFW
1954	Chi N	11	38	2	7	0	0	0	1	0	1	7	.184	.205	.184	2	-6	0-0	1.000	-1	51	111	C11		-0.7
1955	Chi N	5	10	0	0	0	0	0		1-0	0	2	.000	.091	.000	-73	-3	0-0	1.000	1	137	97	C5		-0.1
1956	Chi N	1	4	0	1	0	0	0		0		0	.250	.250	.250	36	0	0-0	.800	0	0	398	/C		0.0
1957	Chi N	47	89	3	16	2	0	0	4	4-1	1	17	.180	.223	.202	16	-11	0-0	.981	1	85	191	C35		-0.9
Total	4	64	141	5	24	2	0	0	5	6-1	1	26	.170	.209	.184	6	-20	0-0	.979	1	80	167	C52		-1.7

FANZONE, CARMEN
Carmen Ronald B8.30.1943 Detroit MI BR/TR/6-0/200* d7.21 Col Central Michigan

YEAR	TM LG	G	AB	R	H	2B	3B	HR	RBI	BB-IB	HP	SO	AVG	OBP	SLG	AOPS	ABR	SB-CS	FA	FR	RNG	THR	GAMES AT POSITION	DL	BFW
1970	Bos A	10	15	0	3	1	0	0	3	2-0	1	2	.200	.316	.267	63	-1	0-0	.750	-0	109	134	3b5		-0.1
1971	Chi N	12	43	5	8	2	0	2	5	2-0	0	7	.186	.222	.372	57	-3	0-0	1.000	0	84	0	O6(5/0/1),3b3,1b2		-0.3
1972	Chi N	86	222	26	50	11	0	8	42	35-6	3	45	.225	.333	.383	94	0	2-3	.923	2	112	137	3b36,1b21,2b13/SOL		0.0
1973	Chi N	64	150	22	41	7	0	6	22	20-1	0	38	.273	.357	.440	112	3	1-2	.922	-2	89	0	3b25,1b24,O6L		-0.1
1974	Chi N	65	158	13	30	6	0	4	22	15-1	2	27	.190	.264	.304	57	-9	0-1	.885	-0	99	127	3b35,2b10,1b7/OL		-1.1
Total	5	237	588	66	132	27	0	20	94	74-8	6	119	.224	.313	.372	86	-10	3-6	.896	0	104	101	3b104,1b54,2b23,O14(13/0/1)/S		-1.6

FARIES, PAUL
Paul Tyrrell B2.20.1965 Berkeley CA BR/TR/5-10/165* [SDN87 23/588] d9.6 Col Pepperdine

YEAR	TM LG	G	AB	R	H	2B	3B	HR	RBI	BB-IB	HP	SO	AVG	OBP	SLG	AOPS	ABR	SB-CS	FA	FR	RNG	THR	GAMES AT POSITION	DL	BFW
1990	SD N	14	37	4	7	1	0	0	2	7-1	1	7	.189	.279	.216	40	-3	0-1	1.000	2	94	83	2b7,S4/3		-0.1
1991	SD N	57	130	13	23	3	1	0	7	14-0	1	21	.177	.262	.215	35	-11	3-1	.988	6	115	129	2b36,3b12,S8	25	-0.4
1992	SD N	10	11	3	5	1	0	0	1	1-0	0	2	.455	.500	.545	192	1	0-0	1.000	-1	94	115	2b4,3b2/S		-0.3
1993	SF N	15	36	6	8	2	0	0	4	1-0	0	4	.222	.237	.333	54	-3	2-0	1.000	-1	107	94	2b7,S4/3		-0.3
Total	4	96	214	26	43	7	2	0	14	20-0	2	34	.201	.273	.252	47	-16	5-2	.992	6	110	116	2b54,S17,3b16	25	-0.8

FARISS, MONTY
Monty Ted B10.13.1967 Cordell OK BR/TR/6-4/200(180-205) [TexA88 1/6] d9.6 Col Oklahoma St.

YEAR	TM LG	G	AB	R	H	2B	3B	HR	RBI	BB-IB	HP	SO	AVG	OBP	SLG	AOPS	ABR	SB-CS	FA	FR	RNG	THR	GAMES AT POSITION	DL	BFW
1991	Tex A	19	31	6	8	1	0	1	6	7-0	0	11	.258	.395	.387	119	1	0-0	1.000	3	190	0	O8L,2b4,D4		0.4
1992	Tex A	67	166	13	36	7	1	3	21	17-0	2	51	.217	.297	.325	77	-5	0-2	1.000	-7	73	0	O49(28/10/12),2b17/1D	19	-1.4
1993	Fla N	18	29	3	5	2	1	0	2	5-0	0	13	.172	.294	.310	58	-2	0-0	1.000	-0	110	0	O8(1/0/7)		-0.2
Total	3	104	226	22	49	10	2	4	29	29-0	2	75	.217	.311	.332	80	-6	0-2	1.000	-4	91	0	O65(37/10/19),2b21,D8/1	19	-1.2

FARLEY, BOB
Robert Jacob B11.15.1937 Watsontown PA BL/TL/6-2/200* d4.15

YEAR	TM LG	G	AB	R	H	2B	3B	HR	RBI	BB-IB	HP	SO	AVG	OBP	SLG	AOPS	ABR	SB-CS	FA	FR	RNG	THR	GAMES AT POSITION	DL	BFW
1961	SF N	13	20	3	2	0	1	0		3-0	0	5	.100	.217	.100	-13	-3	0-0	1.000	-1	60	0	O3L/1		-0.4
1962	Chi A	35	53	7	10	1	1	1	4	13-0	0	13	.189	.348	.302	77	-3	0-1	.989	-1	70	102	1b14		-0.3
	Det A	36	50	9	8	2	0	1	4	14-0	0	10	.160	.338	.260	63	-2	0-0	.857	-3	35	0	O11R,1b6		-0.6
	Year	71	103	16	18	3	1	2	8	27-0	0	23	.175	.344	.282	70	-3	0-1	.974	-4	76	107	1b20,O11R		-0.9
Total	2	84	123	19	20	3	1	2	9	30-0	0	28	.163	.325	.252	58	-6	0-1	.975	-5	73	113	1b21,O14(3/0/11)		-1.3

FARLEY, TOM
Thomas T. B Chicago IL d6.24

YEAR	TM LG	G	AB	R	H	2B	3B	HR	RBI	BB-IB	HP	SO	AVG	OBP	SLG	AOPS	ABR	SB-CS	FA	FR	RNG	THR	GAMES AT POSITION	DL	BFW
1884	Was AA	14	52	5	11	4	0	0		1		1	.212	.241	.288	81	-1		.867	1	74	194	O14L		0.0

FARMER, ALEX
Alexander Johnson B5.9.1877 New York NY D3.5.1920 Bronx NY BR/TR/6-0/175 d9.1

YEAR	TM LG	G	AB	R	H	2B	3B	HR	RBI	BB-IB	HP	SO	AVG	OBP	SLG	AOPS	ABR	SB-CS	FA	FR	RNG	THR	GAMES AT POSITION	DL	BFW
1908	Bro N	12	30	1	5	1	0	0	2	1	0		.167	.194	.200	27	-3	0	.966	-0	85	58	C11		-0.2

YEAR	TM	LG	G	AB	R	H	2B	3B	HR	RBI	BB-IB	HP	SO	AVG	OBP	SLG	AOPS	ABR	SB-CS	FA	FR	RNG	THR	GAMES AT POSITION	DL	BFW
FARMER, JACK			Floyd Haskell		B7.14.1892		Granville TN			D5.21.1970			Columbia LA		BR/TR/6-0/180		d7.8		Col Cumberland							
1916	Pit	N	55	166	10	45	6	4	0	14	7		2	.24	.271	.309	.355	103	0	1	.929	-9	88	50	2b31,O15(8/0/7),S4/3		-1.1
1918	Cle	A	7	9	1	2	0	0	0	1	0		1	3	.222	.300	.222	53	0	2	.429	-1	63	0	O3(2/0/1)		-0.2
Total	2		62	175	11	47	6	4	0	15	7		3	27	.269	.308	.349	100	0	3	.929	-11	88	50	2b31,O18(10/0/8),S4/3		-1.3
FARMER, BILL			William		B12.27.1870		BR/TR/5-11.5/187		d5.1																	
1888	Pit	N	2	4	0	0	0	0	0	0	0		0	1	.000	.000	.000	-99	-1	0	.667	-0			/COR		-0.1
	Phi	AA	3	12	0	2	0	0	0	1	0		0		.167	.167	.167	7	-1	0	.960	0			C3		-0.1
Total	1		5	16	0	2	0	0	0	1	0		0	1	.125	.125	.125	-20	-2	0	.903	0			C4/OR		-0.2
FARRAR, SID			Sidney Douglas		B8.10.1859		Paris Hill ME		D5.7.1935		New York NY		TR/5-10/185		d5.1											
1883	Phi	N	**99**	377	41	88	19	8	0	29	4			37	.233	.241	.326	77	-9		.965	-0	96	69	1b99		-1.6
1884	Phi	N	111	428	62	105	16	6	1	45	9			25	.245	.261	.318	85	-7		.966	5	131	74	1b111		-1.1
1885	Phi	N	**111**	420	49	103	20	3	3	36	28			34	.245	.292	.329	103	2		.975	2	108	94	1b111		-0.5
1886	Phi	N	118	439	55	109	19	7	5	50	16			47	.248	.275	.358	90	-6	10	**.980**	3	99	75	1b118		-1.3
1887	Phi	N	116	443	83	125	20	9	4	72	42	10		29	.282	.358	.395	103	2	24	.977	3	108	90	1b116		-0.5
1888	Phi	N	**131**	508	53	124	24	7	1	53	31	13		38	.244	.304	.325	95	-2	24	.979	3	110	94	1b131		-1.1
1889	Phi	N	130	477	70	128	22	2	3	58	52	6		36	.268	.348	.342	86	-10	28	.978	-5	72	93	1b130		-2.3
1890	Phi	P	127	481	84	123	17	11	1	69	51	5		23	.256	.333	.343	79	-15	9	.973	-2	93	106	1b127		-2.3
Total	8		943	3573	497	905	157	53	18	412	233	34		269	.253	.305	.342	90	-45	92	.974	8	102	87	1b943		-10.7
FARRELL, DUKE			Charles Andrew		B8.31.1866		Oakdale MA		D2.15.1925		Boston MA		BB/TR/6-1/208		d4.21		C6		OF(48/22/39)							
1888	Chi	N	64	241	34	56	6	3	3	19	4		0	41	.232	.245	.320	73	-8	8	.874	-8			C33,O31(10/2/19)/1		-1.4
1889	Chi	N	101	407	66	107	19	7	11	75	41		1	21	.263	.332	.425	106	0	13	.910	-2			C76,O25(7/15/3)		0.4
1890	Chi	P	117	451	79	131	21	12	2	84	42		1	28	.290	.352	.404	98	-3	8	.929	30	115	127	C90,1b22,O10(0/2/8)		2.6
1891	Bos	AA	122	473	108	143	19	13	**12**	**110**	59		4	48	.302	.384	.474	148	28	21	.918	21	115	85	3b66,C37,O23(20/0/3),1b4		**4.4**
1892	Pit	N	**152**	605	96	130	10	13	8	77	46		5	53	.215	.276	.314	78	-19	20	.879	-9	96	97	3b133,O20(11/3/6)		-2.6
1893	Was	N	124	511	84	144	13	13	4	75	47		5	15	.282	.348	.382	96	-4	11	.923	2	77	161	C81,3b41,1b3		2.0
1894	†NY	N	116	404	50	116	20	12	5	70	38		3	18	.287	.353	.433	89	-9	9	.925	26	107	130	C105,3b5,1b4		2.0
1895	NY	N	90	312	38	90	16	9	1	58	38		3	18	.288	.371	.407	103	2	11	.941	2	112	112	C62,3b24,1b2		0.8
1896	NY	N	58	191	23	54	7	3	1	37	19		1	7	.283	.351	.366	92	-2	2	.954	-5	94	107	C34,S13,3b7		-0.3
	Was	N	37	130	18	39	7	3	1	30	7		2	3	.300	.345	.423	102	-0	2	1.000	-0	88	130	C18,3b14		0.1
	Year		95	321	41	93	14	6	2	67	26		3	10	.290	.349	.389	96	-2	4	.970	-5	92	115	C52,3b21,S13		-0.2
1897	Was	N	78	261	39	84	9	6	0	53	17		1		.322	.366	.402	103	1	8	.945	3	80	149	C63/1		0.8
1898	Was	N	99	338	47	106	12	6	1	53	34		4		.314	.383	.393	123	11	12	.929	-13	65	145	C61,1b28		0.3
1899	Was	N	5	12	2	4	1	0	0	1	2		0		.333	.429	.417	134	1	1	1.000	-0	74	142	C4		0.1
	Bro	N	80	254	40	76	10	7	2	55	35		7		.299	.399	.417	121	9	6	.948	6	91	115	C78		1.9
	Year		85	266	42	80	11	7	2	56	37		7		.301	.400	.417	122	10	7	.949	5	90	116	C82		2.0
1900	†Bro	N	76	273	33	75	11	5	0	39	11		3		.275	.310	.352	78	-9	3	.944	-4	94	97	C74		0.4
1901	Bro	N	80	284	38	84	10	6	1	31	7		3		.296	.320	.384	101	-1	7	.979	-1	80	129	C59,1b17		0.6
1902	Bro	N	74	264	14	64	5	2	0	24	12		2		.242	.281	.277	71	-9	6	.976	-1	84	124	C49,1b24		-0.6
1903	†Bos	A	17	52	5	21	5	1	0	8	5		1		.404	.466	.538	190	6	1	.960	1	118	114	C17		0.9
1904	Bos	A	68	198	11	42	9	2	0	15	15		4		.212	.281	.278	73	-5		.958	-1	128	91	C56		-0.1
1905	Bos	A	7	21	2	6	1	0	0	2	1		0		.286	.318	.333	105	0		1.000	1	146	119	C7		0.2
Total	18		1565	5682	829	1572	211	123	52	916	480		50	246	.277	.338	.385	100	-11	150	.938	49	96	127	C1004,3b290,O109L,1b106,S13		9.8
FARRELL, DOC			Edward Stephen		B12.26.1901		Johnson City NY		D12.20.1966		Livingston NJ		BR/TR/5-8/160		d6.15		Col Penn							
1925	NY	N	27	56	6	12	1	0	0	4	4		0	6	.214	.267	.232	30	-6	0-1	.900	1	130	50	S13,3b7/2		-0.4
1926	NY	N	67	171	19	49	10	1	2	23	12		2	17	.287	.341	.392	98	0	4	.950	-8	86	86	S53,2b3		-0.4
1927	NY	N	42	142	13	55	10	1	3	34	12		2	11	.387	.442	.535	161	13	0	.919	-0	105	93	S36,3b2		1.6
	Bos	N	110	424	44	124	13	2	1	58	14		0	21	.292	.315	.340	82	-12	4	.931	-8	103	70	S57,2b40,3b18		-1.2
	Year		152	566	57	179	23	3	4	92	26		2	32	.316	.348	.389	103	1	4	.926	-8	104	79	S93,2b40,3b20		0.4
1928	Bos	N*	134	483	36	104	14	2	3	43	26		5	26	.215	.263	.271	42	-43	3	.933	-17	96	79	S132/2		-4.5
1929	Bos	N	5	8	0	1	0	0	0	2	0		0	1	.125	.125	.125	-39	-2	0	—	-0	0	0	/2S		-0.2
	NY	N	63	178	18	38	6	0	0	16	9		0	17	.213	.251	.247	24	-22	2	.925	2	109	193	3b28,2b25,S4		-1.5
	Year		68	186	18	39	6	0	0	18	9		0	18	.210	.246	.242	22	-23	2	.925	2	109	193	3b28,2b26,S5		-1.7
1930	StL	N	23	61	3	13	1	1	0	6	4		0	2	.213	.262	.262	26	-8	1	.944	1	88	118	S15,2b6/1		-0.5
	Chi	N	46	113	21	33	6	0	1	16	9		0	5	.292	.344	.372	73	-5	0	.937	-1	101	87	S38/2		-0.2
	Year		69	174	24	46	7	1	1	22	13		0	7	.264	.316	.333	56	-12	1	.938	-1	97	95	S53,2b7/1		-0.7
1932	NY	A	26	63	4	11	1	1	0	4	2		1	8	.175	.212	.222	13	-9	0-0	.963	-1	90	120	2b16,S5,1b2/3		-0.8
1933	NY	A	44	93	16	25	0	0	0	6	16		0	6	.269	.376	.269	78	-2	0-0	.947	-4	77	94	S22,2b20		-0.4
1935	Bos	A	4	7	1	2	1	0	0	1	1		0		.286	.375	.429	101	0	0-0	.917	-1	81	78	2b4		0.0
Total	9		591	1799	181	467	63	8	10	213	109		10	120	.260	.306	.320	66	-96	14-1	.934	-36	97	82	S376,2b118,3b56,1b3		-8.5
FARRELL, JACK			John "Hartford Jack"		B1.2.1856		Hartford CT		D11.15.1916		Hartford CT		d10.27													
1874	Har	NA	3	13	3	5	0	0	0	1			0		.385	.429	.385	155	1	0-0	1.000	-0	0	0	O3C		0.1
FARRELL, JACK			John A. "Moose"		B7.5.1857		Newark NJ		D2.10.1914		Cedar Grove NJ		BR/TR/5-9/165		d5.1		M1							
1879	Syr	N	54	241	40	73	6	2	1	21	3			13	.303	.314	.357	135	9		.870	-19	93	65	2b54		-0.7
	Pro	N	12	51	5	13	2	0	0	5	0			0	.255	.255	.294	82	-1		.915	5	117	59	2b12		0.4
	Year		66	292	45	86	8	2	1	26	3			13	.295	.302	.346	125	8		.879	-14	98	85	2b66		-0.3
1880	Pro	N	80	339	46	92	12	5	3	36	10			9	.271	.292	.363	125	9		.887	-13	101	91	2b80		0.0
1881	Pro	N	84	345	69	82	16	5	2	36	29			23	.238	.297	.357	106	4		.881	-5	**103**	98	2b84,O3C,M		0.2
1882	Pro	N	**84**	366	67	93	21	6	2	31	16			23	.254	.285	.361	106	3		.875	-6	105	118	2b84		0.0
1883	Pro	N	95	420	92	128	24	11	3	61	15			21	.305	.329	.436	126	12		**.924**	25	117	136	2b95		**3.5**
1884	†Pro	N	111	469	70	102	13	6	1	37	35			44	.217	.272	.277	74	-13		.922	-8	98	104	2b109,3b3		-1.5
1885	Pro	N	68	257	27	53	7	1	1	19	10			25	.206	.236	.253	60	-11		.900	-13	92	57	2b68		-2.1
1886	Phi	N	17	60	7	11	0	1	0	3	3			11	.183	.222	.217	34	-5	1	.825	-5	112	32	2b17		-0.8
	Was	N	47	171	24	41	11	4	2	18	15			12	.240	.301	.386	116	4	12	.913	-2	100	59	2b47		0.3
	Year		64	231	31	52	11	5	2	21	18			23	.225	.281	.342	94	-1	13	.888	-7	103	51	2b64		-0.5
1887	Was	N	87	339	40	75	14	9	0	41	20	1		12	.221	.267	.316	65	-16	31	.876	-4	97	91	S48,2b40		-1.4
1888	Bal	AA	103	398	72	81	19	5	4	36	26	2			.204	.256	.307	82	-8	29	.902	9	101	80	S54,2b52		0.4
1889	Bal	AA	42	157	25	33	3	0	1	26	15	2		15	.210	.287	.248	52	-10	14	.891	-6	88	85	S42		-1.2
Total	11		884	3613	584	877	148	55	23	370	197	5		205	.243	.283	.333	94	-23	87	.899	-42	104	95	2b740,S144,3b3,O3C		-2.9
FARRELL, JACK			John J.		B6.16.1892		Chicago IL		D3.24.1918		Chicago IL		BB/TR/5-8/145		d4.16											
1914	Chi	F	156	524	58	123	23	4	0	35	52	3		65	.235	.307	.294	68	-32	12	.954	-4	102	107	2b155,S3		-3.5
1915	Chi	F	70	222	27	48	10	1	0	14	25	1		18	.216	.298	.270	64	-14	8	.941	-3	98	112	2b70/S		-1.7
Total	2		226	746	85	171	33	5	0	49	77	4		83	.229	.305	.287	67	-46	20	.950	-7	101	108	2b225,S4		-5.2
FARRELL, JOHN			John Sebastian		B12.4.1876		Covington KY		D5.13.1921		Kansas City MO		BR/TR/5-10/160		d4.26											
1901	Was	A	135	555	100	151	32	11	3	63	52	1			.272	.336	.386	101	1	25	.915	9	106	134	2b72,O62C/3		0.7
1902	StL	A	138	565	68	141	13	5	0	25	43	5			.250	.308	.290	88	-7	9	.947	32	119	146	2b118,S21		2.7
1903	StL	N	130	519	83	141	25	8	1	32	48	2			.272	.336	.356	100	1	17	.927	24	115	124	2b118,O12(2/10/0)		2.4
1904	StL	N	131	509	72	130	23	3	0	20	46	2			.255	.320	.312	100	1	16	.934	15	**109**	143	2b130		1.8
1905	StL	N	7	24	6	4	0	1	0	1	4	0			.167	.286	.250	62	-1	1	.892	-3	66	0	2b7		-0.5
Total	5		541	2172	329	567	93	28	4	141	193	10			.261	.324	.335	97	-5	68	.932	77	112	135	2b445,O74(2/72/0),S21/3		7.1
FARRELL, JOE			Joseph F.		B1857		Brooklyn NY		D4.17.1893		Brooklyn NY		BR/5-6/160		d5.1											
1882	Det	N	69	283	34	70	12	2	1	24	4			20	.247	.258	.314	83	-6		.816	-15	75	153	3b42,2b18,S9		-1.7
1883	Det	N	**101**	444	58	108	13	5	0	36	5			29	.243	.252	.295	69	-17		.845	13	123	92	3b101		-0.2
1884	Det	N	110	461	59	104	10	5	3	41	14			66	.226	.248	.289	73	-14		.842	-4	97	83	3b110/OL		-1.5
1886	Bal	AA	73	301	36	63	8	3	1	31	12			0	.209	.240	.266	60	-15	5	.870	-8	94	36	2b45,3b27/OC		-1.8
Total	4		353	1489	187	345	43	15	5	132	35			115	.232	.248	.291	71	-52	5	.840	-14	104	94	3b280,2b63,S9,O2(1/1/0)		-5.2

YEAR	TM	LG	G	AB	R	H	2B	3B	HR	RBI	BB-IB	HP	SO	AVG	OBP	SLG	AOPS	ABR	SB-CS	FA	FR	RNG	THR	GAMES AT POSITION	DL	BFW

FARRELL, KERBY Major Kerby B9.3.1913 Leapwood TN D12.17.1975 Nashville TN BL/TL/5-11/172 d4.24 M1/C6 Col Freed-Hardeman ▲

1943	Bos	N	85	280	11	75	14	1	0	21	16	0	15	.268	.307	.325	84	-6	1	.996	1	104	107	1b69,P5		-1.0
1945	Chi	A	103	396	44	102	11	3	0	34	24	0	18	.258	.300	.301	76	-13	4-9	.989	2	106	90	1b97		-2.0
Total 2			188	676	55	177	25	4	0	55	40	0	33	.262	.303	.311	80	-19	5-9	.992	2	105	97	1b166,P5		-3.0

FARRELL, BILL William d5.3

1882	Phi	AA	2	7	2	2	1	0	0		1	1			.286	.375	.429	160	1		—	-0	0	0	O2(0/1/1)/C		0.0
1883	Bal	AA	2	7	0	0	0	0	0		0	1			.000	.125	.000	-55	-1		.750	-1	88	203	S2		-0.1
Total 2			4	14	2	2	1	0	0		1	2			.143	.250	.214	52	0		.750	-1	88	203	S2,O2(0/1/1)/C		-0.1

FARROW, JOHN John Jacob B11.8.1853 Verplanck NY D12.31.1914 Perth Amboy NJ BL/TR d4.28

1873	Res	NA	12	48	2	8	1	0	0	3	0		3	.167	.167	.188	5	-5	0-0	.686	-3			C9,O4R/1S		-0.6
1874	Atl	NA	27	122	16	26	3	0	0	10	1		1	.213	.220	.238	53	-5	0-0	.694	-1			C16,2b12,O3(0/2/1)		-0.6
1884	Bro	AA	16	58	7	11	2	0	0		3		1	.190	.230	.224	48	-3	0-0	.915	-0			C16		-0.2
Total 2 NA			39	170	18	34	4	0	0	13	1		4	.200	.205	.224	38	-10	0-0	.691	-4			C25,2b12,O7(0/2/5)/S1		-1.2

FASANO, SAL Salvatore Frank B8.10.1971 Chicago IL BR/TR/6-2/230(220-245) [KCA93 37/1029] d4.3 Col Evansville

1996	KC	A	51	143	20	29	2	0	6	19	14-0	2	25	.203	.283	.343	57	-10	1-1	.984	7	138	87	C51		0.0
1997	KC	A	13	38	4	8	2	0	1	1	1-0	0	12	.211	.231	.342	45	-3	0-0	.982	-1	675	93	C12/D		-0.4
1998	KC	A	74	216	21	49	10	0	8	31	10-1	16	56	.227	.307	.384	76	-8	1-0	.996	-1	203	83	C70,1b5/3	48	-0.2
1999	KC	A	23	60	11	14	2	0	5	16	7-0	7	17	.233	.373	.517	121	2	0-1	1.000	7	181	47	C23		0.9
2000	†Oak	A	52	126	21	27	6	0	7	19	14-0	3	47	.214	.306	.429	85	-3	0-0	.981	-1	106	103	C52		-0.2
2001	Oak	A	11	21	2	1	0	0	0	0	1-0	1	12	.048	.130	.048	-50	-5	0-1	.952	-1	158	102	C9/D		-0.5
	KC	A	3	1	0	0	0	0	0	0	0-0	0	1	.000	.000	.000	-91	0	0-0	1.000	-0	0	0	C3		-0.1
	Year		14	22	2	1	0	0	0	0	1-0	1	13	.045	.125	.045	-51	-5	0-1	.955	-1	179	110	C12/D		-0.6
	Col	N	25	63	10	16	5	0	3	9	4-0	3	19	.254	.329	.476	87	-1	0-0	.982	7	179	110	C25		0.7
2002	Ana	N	2	1	0	0	0	0	0	0	0-0	0	1	.000	.000	.000	-99	0	0-0	1.000	2	42	1009	C2		0.1
2005	Bal	A	64	160	25	40	3	0	11	20	9-0	5	41	.250	.310	.475	104	0	0-0	.987	-8	68	66	C60/1D		-0.5
Total 8			318	829	114	184	30	0	41	115	60-1	37	230	.222	.302	.407	79	-28	2-2	.988	12	165	87	C307,1b6,D5/3	48	-0.2

FAUSETT, BUCK Robert Shaw "Leaky" B4.8.1908 Sheridan AR D5.2.1994 College Station TX BL/TR/5-10/170 d4.18 Col Texas A&M-Commerce ▲

| 1944 | Cin | N | 13 | 31 | 2 | 3 | 0 | 1 | 0 | 1 | 2 | | | .097 | .125 | .161 | -21 | -5 | 0 | 1.000 | 2 | 136 | 96 | 3b6,P2 | | -0.3 |

FAUTSCH, JOE Joseph Roamon B2.28.1887 Minneapolis MN D3.16.1971 New Hope MN BR/TR/5-10/162 d4.24

| 1916 | Chi | A | 1 | 1 | 0 | 0 | 0 | 0 | 0 | 0 | 0 | 0 | 0 | .000 | .000 | .000 | -99 | 0 | 0 | | 0 | | | /H | | 0.0 |

FAZIO, ERNIE Ernest Joseph B1.25.1942 Oakland CA BR/TR/5-7/165* d7.3 Col Santa Clara

1962	Hou	N	12	12	3	1	0	0	0	1	2-0	0	5	.083	.214	.083	-18	-2	0-0	.783	-1	101	38	S10		-0.3
1963	Hou	N	102	228	31	42	10	3	2	5	27-1	1	70	.184	.273	.281	64	-10	4-4	.972	-19	81	51	2b84/S3		-2.7
1966	KC	A	27	34	3	7	0	1	0	2	4-2	0	10	.206	.289	.265	62	-2	1-0	1.000	-1	103	84	2b10,S4		-0.2
Total 3			141	274	37	50	10	4	2	8	33-3	1	85	.182	.273	.270	60	-14	5-4	.974	-21	83	54	2b94,S15/3		-3.2

FEBLES, CARLOS Carlos Manuel B5.24.1976 Santa Cruz de El Seibo, D.R. BR/TR/5-11/185(170-185) d9.14

1998	KC	A	11	25	5	10	1	2	0	2	4-0	0	7	.400	.483	.600	172	1	2-1	1.000	-1	89	42	2b11		0.2
1999	KC	A	123	453	71	116	22	9	10	53	47-0	9	91	.256	.336	.411	86	-10	20-4	.979	3	103	112	2b122	27	0.2
2000	KC	A	100	339	59	87	12	1	2	29	36-1	10	48	.257	.345	.316	65	-17	17-6	.978	-7	98	111	2b99	60	-1.6
2001	KC	A	79	292	45	69	9	2	8	25	22-0	1	58	.236	.291	.363	65	-16	5-2	.981	-2	101	127	2b78	50	-1.3
2002	KC	A	119	351	44	86	16	4	4	26	41-0	7	63	.245	.336	.348	73	-13	16-5	.971	-2	103	105	2b116/S		-0.8
2003	KC	A	74	196	31	46	5	0	0	11	13-0	5	30	.235	.299	.260	46	-15	8-2	.989	-10	97	82	2b67/SD	18	-2.1
Total 6			506	1656	255	414	65	18	24	146	163-1	32	297	.250	.328	.354	72	-68	68-20	.979	-19	101	108	2b493,D4,S2	155	-5.4

FEDEROFF, AL Alfred "Whitey" B7.11.1924 Bairdford PA BR/TR/5-10.5/165* d9.27

1951	Det	A	2	4	0	0	0	0	0	0	0-0	0	0	.000	.000	.000	-99	-1	0-0	.889	0	148	0	/2		-0.1
1952	Det	A	74	231	14	56	4	2	0	14	16	1	13	.242	.294	.277	59	-13	1-0	.976	3	108	90	2b70,S7		-0.6
Total 2			76	235	14	56	4	2	0	14	16	1	13	.238	.290	.272	56	-14	1-0	.973	4	109	88	2b71,S7		-0.7

FEHRING, DUTCH William Paul "Bill" B5.31.1912 Columbus IN BB/TR/6-0/195 d6.25 Col Purdue

| 1934 | Chi | A | 1 | 1 | 0 | 0 | 0 | 0 | 0 | 0 | 0-0 | 0 | 1 | .000 | .000 | .000 | -97 | 0 | 0-0 | 1.000 | 0 | 0 | 0 | /C | | 0.0 |

FEINBERG, EDDIE Edward Isadore "Itzzy" B9.29.1917 Philadelphia PA D4.20.1986 Hollywood FL BB/TR/5-9/165 d9.11

1938	Phi	N	10	20	2	3	0	0	0	0	0	0	6	.150	.150	.150	-18	-3	0	.957	2	124	128	S4,O2(1/0/2)		-0.1
1939	Phi	N	6	18	2	4	1	0	0	0	2	0	7	.222	.300	.278	58	-1	0	.909	-3	64	92	2b4/S		-0.3
Total 2			16	38	2	7	1	0	0	0	2	0	13	.184	.225	.211	20	-4	0	.957	-1	116	120	S5,2b4,O2(1/0/2)		-0.4

FELDER, MIKE Michael Otis B11.18.1961 Vallejo CA BB/TR/5-8/160(160-175) [MilA81*3/74] d9.11 Col Contra Costa (CA) JC

1985	Mil	A	15	56	8	11	1	0	0	5	5-0	0	6	.196	.262	.214	32	-5	4-1	1.000	-1	84	111	O14C		-0.6
1986	Mil	A	44	155	24	37	2	4	1	13	13-1	0	16	.239	.289	.323	67	-8	16-2	1.000	1	115	0	O42(30/7/6)/D	33	-0.6
1987	Mil	A	108	289	48	77	5	7	2	31	28-0	0	23	.266	.329	.353	79	-9	34-8	.975	9	120	149	O99(80/22/0)/2D		0.1
1988	Mil	A	50	81	14	14	1	0	0	5	0-0	1	11	.173	.183	.185	3	-11	8-2	.976	-1	104	0	O28(12/11/5),D16/2	63	-1.2
1989	Mil	A	117	315	50	76	11	3	6	23	23-2	0	38	.241	.293	.324	74	-11	26-5	.985	6	108	158	O93(30/34/38),D11,2b10		-0.4
1990	Mil	A	121	237	38	65	7	3	2	27	22-0	0	17	.274	.330	.359	95	-2	20-9	.972	7	111	173	O109(61/15/44)/23D		0.4
1991	SF	N	132	348	51	92	10	6	0	18	30-2	1	31	.264	.325	.328	86	-7	21-6	.985	5	112	60	O107(45/38/44),3b3/2		-0.1
1992	SF	N	145	322	44	92	13	3	4	23	21-1	2	29	.286	.330	.382	107	2	14-4	.994	-4	94	52	O105(53/58/11),2b3		-0.1
1993	Sea	A	109	342	31	72	7	5	1	20	22-2	1	34	.211	.262	.269	42	-29	15-9	.987	0	89	190	O95(89/7/0),3b2,D6	20	-3.1
1994	Hou	N	58	117	10	28	2	2	0	13	4-0	0	12	.239	.264	.291	47	-10	3-0	.974	-1	83	136	O32(8/6/21)		-1.1
Total 10			899	2262	318	564	59	32	14	173	168-8	6	217	.249	.301	.322	73	-90	161-46	.984	20	105	117	O724(408/212/169),D38,2b17,3b6	131	-6.7

FELDERMAN, MARV Marvin Wilfred "Coonie" B12.20.1915 Bellevue IA D8.6.2000 Riverside CA BR/TR/6-1/187 d4.19 Mil 1943-45

| 1942 | Chi | N | 3 | 6 | 1 | 1 | 0 | 0 | 0 | 0 | 1 | 0 | 4 | .167 | .286 | .167 | 35 | 0 | | 1.000 | 0 | 60 | 198 | C2 | | 0.0 |

FELIX, GUS August Guenther B5.24.1895 Cincinnati OH D5.12.1960 Montgomery AL BR/TR/6-0/180 d4.19

1923	Bos	N	139	506	64	138	17	2	6	44	51	7	65	.273	.348	.350	88	-7	8-13	.950	-1	104	92	O123(121/6/0),2b5,3b4		-2.0
1924	Bos	N	59	204	25	43	7	1	1	10	18	0	16	.211	.275	.270	48	-15	0-3	.950	2	110	106	O51(11/38/2)		-1.7
1925	Bos	N	121	459	60	141	25	4	2	66	30	5	34	.307	.356	.405	103	2	5-5	.972	10	111	134	O114(42/74/3)		0.4
1926	Bro	N	134	432	64	121	21	7	3	53	51	3	32	.280	.360	.382	101	2	9	.956	-0	100	104	O125(53/74/0)		-0.5
1927	Bro	N	130	445	43	118	21	8	0	57	39	2	47	.265	.327	.348	81	-12	6	.947	-5	90	117	O119(117/4/0)		-2.6
Total 5			583	2046	256	561	91	25	12	230	189	17	194	.274	.341	.361	89	-30	28-21	.957	5	102	111	O532(344/196/5),2b5,3b4		-6.4

FELIX, JUNIOR Junior Francisco (Sanchez) B10.3.1967 Laguna Salada, D.R. BB/TR/5-11/165* d5.3

1989	†Tor	A	110	415	62	107	14	8	9	46	33-2	3	101	.258	.315	.395	101	-1	18-12	.966	0	100	116	O107(0/24/86),D2	27	-0.4
1990	Tor	A	127	463	73	122	23	7	15	65	45-0	2	99	.263	.328	.441	112	6	13-8	.966	-6	87	126	O125(0/28/99)/D	81	-0.3
1991	Cal	A	66	230	32	65	10	2	2	26	11-0	1	55	.283	.321	.370	91	-3	7-5	.977	-9	81	32	O65(0/63/2)		-1.3
1992	Cal	A	139	509	63	125	22	5	9	72	33-5	2	128	.246	.289	.361	82	-14	8-8	.983	1	99	128	O128(0/125/4),D8	15	-1.6
1993	Fla	N	57	214	25	51	11	1	7	22	10-1	1	50	.238	.276	.397	73	-9	2-1	.940	-4	90	79	O52(0/3/50)		-1.5
1994	Det	A	86	301	54	92	25	1	13	49	26-2	6	76	.306	.372	.525	127	13	1-6	.980	2	112	65	O81(5/2/75),D2	18	0.8
Total 6			585	2132	309	562	105	24	55	280	158-10	19	509	.264	.317	.413	99	-8	49-40	.972	-15	95	101	O558(5/245/316),D13	141	-4.3

FELIZ, PEDRO Pedro Julio B4.27.1975 Azua, D.R. BR/TR/6-1/195(180-205) d9.5

2000	SF	N	8	7	1	2	0	0	0	1				.286	.286	.286	48	-1	0-0	—	-1	0	0	3b4		-0.1
2001	SF	N	94	220	23	50	9	1	7	22	10-2	2	50	.227	.264	.373	67	-12	0-0	.908	-17	70	59	3b86/D		-2.8
2002	†SF	N	67	146	14	37	4	1	2	13	6-1	0	27	.253	.281	.336	67	-8	0-0	.966	-1	93	150	3b44/SOL		-0.9
2003	†SF	N	95	235	31	58	9	3	16	48	10-0	1	53	.247	.278	.515	100	-2	2-2	.972	5	123	136	3b49,O15(14/0/1),1b12		0.2
2004	SF	N	144	503	72	139	33	3	22	84	23-1	3	85	.276	.305	.485	91	-4	0-3	.991	5	105	117	3b70,3b51,S20,O4(2/0/2)		-2.2
2005	SF	N	156	569	69	142	30	4	20	81	38-1	1	102	.250	.295	.422	82	-16	0-0	.969	-1	104	131	3b79,O75L,1b15		-2.2
Total 6			564	1680	210	428	85	12	67	248	87-5	4	318	.255	.290	.439	86	-43	9-7	.958	-9	97	110	3b313,1b97,O95(92/0/3),S21/D		-6.1

FELLER, JACK Jack Leland B12.10.1936 Adrian MI BR/TR/5-10.5/185 d9.13

| 1958 | Det | A | 1 | 0 | 0 | 0 | 0 | 0 | 0 | 0 | 0-0 | | 0 | | | | | | 0-0 | 1.000 | 0 | 0 | 0 | /C | | 0.0 |

YEAR	TM LG	G	AB	R	H	2B	3B	HR	RBI	BB-IB	HP	SO	AVG	OBP	SLG	AOPS	ABR	SB-CS	FA	FR	RNG	THR	GAMES AT POSITION	DL	BFW
FELSCH, HAPPY	Oscar Emil B8.22.1891 Milwaukee WI D8.17.1964 Milwaukee WI BR/TR/5-11/175 d4.14 Def 1918																								
1915	Chi A	121	427	65	106	18	11	3	53	51	4	59	.248	.334	.363	105	2	16-18	.959	-6	99	56	O118(34/73/10)		-1.4
1916	Chi A	146	546	73	164	24	12	7	70	31	4	67	.300	.341	.427	129	16	13	.981	1	102	94	O141C		0.7
1917	†Chi A	152	575	75	177	17	10	6	102	33	6	52	.308	.352	.403	128	16	26	.985	15	117	107	O152C		2.2
1918	Chi A	53	206	16	52	2	5	1	20	15	1	13	.252	.306	.325	90	-4	6	.957	5	120	94	O53C		-0.3
1919	†Chi A	135	502	68	138	34	11	7	86	40	6	35	.275	.336	.428	113	8	19	.968	17	107	166	O135C		1.6
1920	Chi A	142	556	88	188	40	15	14	115	37	4	25	.338	.384	.540	143	31	8-13	.981	12	109	136	O142C		3.0
Total	6	749	2812	385	825	135	64	38	446	207	24	251	.293	.347	.427	123	69	88-31	.975	44	108	112	O741(34/696/10)		5.8
FELSKE, JOHN	John Frederick B5.30.1942 Chicago IL BR/TR/6-3/195* d7.26 M3/C3 Col Illinois																								
1968	Chi N	4	2	0	0	0	0	0	0	0-0	0	1	.000	.000	.000	-94	0	0-0	.833	0	0	0	C3		0.0
1972	Mil A	37	80	6	11	3	0	1	5	8-0	0	23	.138	.216	.213	28	-7	0-0	.972	-2	143	38	C23,1b8		-1.0
1973	Mil A	13	22	1	3	0	1	0	4	1-0	0	11	.136	.167	.227	12	-3	0-0	1.000	-1	107	75	C7,1b6		-0.4
Total	3	54	104	7	14	3	1	1	9	9-0	0	35	.135	.202	.212	23	-10	0-0	.969	-3	133	44	C33,1b14		-1.4
FENNELLY, FRANK	Francis John B2.18.1860 Fall River MA D8.4.1920 Fall River MA BR/TR/5-8/168 d5.1																								
1884	Was AA	62	257	52	75	17	7	2		20				.292	.343	.436	172	22		.863	13	117	78	S60,2b4		3.3
	Cin AA	28	122	42	43	5	8	2		11		2		.352	.415	.574	209	14		.813	-6	95	157	S28		0.8
	Year	90	379	94	118	22	15	4		31		2		.311	.367	.480	186	37		.849	7	110	109	S88,2b4		4.1
1885	Cin AA	**112**	454	82	124	14	17	10	**89**	38	3			.273	.333	.445	142	20		.873	-12	95	**135**	S112		1.0
1886	Cin AA	132	497	113	124	13	17	6	72	60	**18**			.249	.351	.380	125	15	32	.848	11	**113**	**130**	S132		2.6
1887	Cin AA	134	526	133	140	15	16	8	97	82	4			.266	.369	.401	112	9	74	.855	-11	101	96	S134		0.2
1888	Cin AA	120	448	64	88	8	7	2	56	63	1			.196	.297	.259	75	-12	43	.858	11	112	140	S112,2b4,O4(2/2/0)		0.3
	Phi AA	15	47	13	11	2	2	1	12	9	0			.234	.357	.426	151	3	5	.912	-1	91	121	S15		0.3
	Year	135	495	77	99	10	9	3	68	72	1			.200	.303	.275	82	-9	48	.863	10	110	138	S127,2b4,O4(2/2/0)		0.6
1889	Phi AA	**138**	513	70	132	20	5	1	64	65	3	78		.257	.344	.322	91	-3	15	.872	-20	95	106	S138		-1.6
1890	Bro AA	45	178	40	44	8	3	2	18	30				.247	.356	.360	115	4	6	.858	-5	103	56	S38,3b7		0.1
Total	7	786	3042	609	781	102	82	34	408	378	31	78		.257	.345	.378	118	72	175	.860	-19	104	116	S769,2b8,3b7,O4(2/2/0)		7.0
FENWICK, BOBBY	Robert Richard B12.10.1946 Naha, Okinawa BR/TR/5-9/165* [SFN67 S1/16] d4.26 Col Minnesota																								
1972	Hou N	36	50	7	9	3	0	0	4	3-1	0	13	.180	.226	.240	34	-4	0-1	.945	-1	100	174	2b17,S4,3b2		-0.5
1973	StL N	5	6	0	1	0	0	0	1	0-0	0	2	.167	.167	.167	-7	-1	0-0	.750	-2	23	227	2b3		-0.2
Total	2	41	56	7	10	3	0	0	5	3-1	0	15	.179	.220	.232	29	-5	0-1	.932	-2	91	180	2b20,S4,3b2		-0.7
FERGUSON, JOE	Joseph Vance B9.19.1946 San Francisco CA BR/TR/6-2/200(195-215) [LAN68 8/161] d9.12 C6 Col Pacific (CA)																								
1970	LA N	5	4	0	1	0	0	0	1	0-0	0	0	.250	.429	.250	112	0	0-0	1.000	0	63	0	C3		0.0
1971	LA N	36	102	13	22	3	0	2	7	12-1	1	15	.216	.304	.304	77	-3	1-0	.983	-2	110	84	C35		-0.4
1972	LA N	8	24	2	7	3	0	1	5	2-0	0	4	.292	.346	.542	151	2	0-0	1.000	1	141	176	C7,O2R		0.3
1973	LA N	136	487	84	128	26	0	25	88	87-9	1	81	.263	.369	.470	137	28	1-1	.996	6	113	84	C122,O20(5/1/14)	19	3.9
1974	†LA N	111	349	54	88	14	1	16	57	75-10	1	73	.252	.380	.436	134	19	2-2	.988	-1	125	103	C82,O32R		2.1
1975	LA N	66	202	15	42	2	1	5	35	35-5	1	47	.208	.325	.302	79	-5	2-1	.994	2	133	107	C35,O34(2/0/32)	89	-0.4
1976	LA N	54	185	24	41	7	0	6	18	25-1	1	41	.222	.318	.357	92	-2	2-0	.966	0	108	63	O39R,C17		-0.3
	StL N	71	189	22	38	8	4	4	21	32-3	1	40	.201	.317	.349	88	-3	4-2	.978	9	169	131	C48,O14R		0.8
	Year	125	374	46	79	15	4	10	39	57-4	2	81	.211	.317	.353	90	-4	6-2	.975	9	142	122	C65,O53R		0.5
1977	Hou N	132	421	59	108	21	3	16	61	85-7	1	79	.257	.379	.435	128	20	0-0	.985	-7	94	122	C122/1		1.9
1978	Hou N	51	150	20	31	5	0	7	22	37-6	1	30	.207	.363	.380	117	5	0-0	.994	0	98	104	C51		0.8
	†LA N	67	198	20	47	11	0	7	28	34-5	1	41	.237	.350	.399	109	4	1-2	.984	-2	129	64	C62,O3(2/0/1)		0.4
	Year	118	348	40	78	16	0	14	50	71-11	2	71	.224	.356	.391	112	9	1-2	.989	-2	115	82	C113,O3(2/0/1)		1.2
1979	LA N	122	363	54	95	14	0	20	69	70-6	1	68	.262	.380	.466	133	19	1-0	.981	-4	90	75	C67,O52(5/0/47)		1.6
1980	LA N	77	172	20	41	3	2	9	38	38-11	0	46	.238	.371	.436	129	8	2-2	.982	-2	83	56	C66/OR		0.8
1981	LA N	17	14	2	2	1	0	0	1	2-0	0	5	.143	.250	.214	34	-1	0-0	—	-0	0	0	/OR		-0.1
	Cal A	12	30	5	7	1	0	1	5	9-0	0	8	.233	.400	.367	124	2	0-0	.976	-0	99	168	C8,O4(3/0/1)		0.2
1982	Cal A	36	84	10	19	2	0	3	8	12-0	1	19	.226	.323	.357	86	-2	0-0	.993	4	76	154	C32,O2R		0.4
1983	Cal A	12	27	3	2	0	0	0	2	5-0	0	8	.074	.219	.074	-15	-4	0-0	.968	-1	72	98	C9,O3(1/0/2)	15	-0.6
Total	14	1013	3001	407	719	121	11	122	445	502-64	9	607	.240	.358	.409	117	87	22-12	.987	2	109	98	C766,O207(18/1/188)/1	146	11.4
FERGUSON, BOB	Robert Vavasour B1.31.1845 Brooklyn NY D5.3.1894 Brooklyn NY BB/TR/5-9.5/149 d5.18 M16/U10 OF(0/1/5) ▲																								
1871	Mut NA	**33**	158	30	38	6	1	0	25	3		2	.241	.255	.291	62	-6	4-5	.774	4	**145**	148	3b20,2b11,C5/PM		-0.2
1872	Atl NA	**37**	164	33	46	3	0	0	19	3		8	.280	.293	.299	70	-8	4-2	.807	**34**	**195**	141	3b37/CM		1.7
1873	Atl NA	51	228	36	59	3	5	0	25	4		8	.259	.272	.316	83	-3	1-2	.746	28	**164**	123	3b50,P4,M		1.6
1874	Atl NA	**56**	245	34	64	4	0	0	19	2		7	.261	.267	.278	85	-2	5-3	.760	2	120	43	3b55,C2/PM		-0.1
1875	Har NA	85	366	65	88	10	4	0	43	3		5	.240	.247	.290	82	-8	2-1	**.827**	9	91	106	3b85/PM		-0.1
1876	Har N	**69**	310	48	82	8	5	0	32	2		11	.265	.269	.323	89	-5		.826	2	96	105	3b69,M		0.0
1877	Har N	58	254	40	65	7	2	0	35	5		10	.256	.265	.299	86	-3		.841	17	**139**	102	3b56,P3,M		1.4
1878	Chi N	**61**	259	44	91	10	2	0	39	10		12	.351	**.375**	.405	147	13		.881	15	**124**	137	S57,2b4/CM		2.8
1879	Tro N	30	123	18	31	5	2	0	4	4		3	.252	.276	.325	104	1		.808	2	105	145	3b24,2b6,M		0.3
1880	Tro N	82	332	55	87	9	0	0	22	**24**		24	.262	.312	.289	100	0		.904	-5	94	105	2b82,M		-0.3
1881	Tro N	**85**	339	56	96	13	5	1	35	29		12	.283	.340	.360	114	6		.904	-13	91	108	2b85,M		-0.3
1882	Tro N	81	319	44	82	15	2	0	32	23		21	.257	.307	.317	106	4		.914	-12	90	144	2b79,S2,M		-0.5
1883	Phi N	86	329	39	85	9	2	0	27	18		21	.258	.297	.298	89	-3		.862	-11	101	74	2b86/PM		-1.0
1884	Pit AA	10	41	2	6	0	0	0	4			0	.146	.146	.146	-4	-5		.714	-3	0	0	O6(0/1/5),1b3/3M		-0.7
Total	5 NA	262	1161	198	295	26	10	0	131	15		22	.254	.264	.294	77	-27	16-12	.784	76	132	97	3b247,2b11,C8,P7		2.9
Total	9	562	2306	346	625	76	20	1	226	113	0	114	.271	.305	.323	102	8		.895	-7	94	95	2b342,3b150,S59,O6R,P4,1b3/C		2.0
FERMIN, FELIX	Felix Jose (Minaya) B10.9.1963 Mao Valverde, D.R. BR/TR/5-11/170(166-185) d7.8																								
1987	Pit N	23	68	6	17	0	0	0	4	4-1	1	9	.250	.301	.250	47	-5	0-0	.980	2	103	113	S23	36	-0.2
1988	Pit N	43	87	9	24	0	2	0	2	8-1	1	9	.276	.354	.322	97	0	3-1	.955	-7	86	86	S43		-0.4
1989	Cle A	156	484	50	115	9	1	0	21	41-0	4	27	.238	.302	.260	59	-26	6-4	.967	12	110	91	S153,2b2		-0.2
1990	Cle A	148	414	47	106	13	2	1	40	26-0	6	22	.256	.297	.304	69	-18	3-3	.975	5	105	90	S147/2		-0.3
1991	Cle A	129	424	30	111	13	2	0	31	26-0	3	27	.262	.307	.302	69	-18	5-4	.980	2	100	91	S129	19	-0.7
1992	Cle A	79	215	27	58	7	2	0	13	18-1	1	10	.270	.326	.321	84	-5	0-0	.971	-6	93	114	S55,3b17,2b7,1b2		-0.7
1993	Cle A	140	480	48	126	16	2	2	45	24-1	4	14	.262	.303	.317	67	-23	4-5	.960	-28	89	140	S140		-4.2
1994	Sea A	101	379	52	120	21	0	1	35	11-0	1	22	.317	.338	.380	84	-9	4-4	.974	-6	80	86	S77,2b25		-0.8
1995	†Sea A	73	200	21	39	6	0	0	6	6-0	1	6	.195	.222	.225	20	-24	2-0	.971	5	89	128	S46,2b29	21	-1.4
1996	Chi N	11	16	4	2	1	0	0	1	2-0	0	1	.125	.222	.188	9	-2	0-0	.875	-3	59	74	2b6,S2		-0.5
Total	10	903	2767	294	718	86	11	4	207	166-4	24	147	.259	.305	.303	66	-130	27-21	.971	-24	97	95	S815,2b70,3b17,1b2	76	-9.4
FERNANDES, ED	Edward Paul B3.11.1918 Oakland CA D11.27.1968 Hayward CA BB/TR/5-9/185 d6.9 Mil 1945																								
1940	Pit N	28	33	1	4	1	0	0	2	7		6	.121	.275	.152	21	-3	0-0	.981	-0	77	96	C27		-0.0
1946	Chi A	14	32	4	8	2	0	0	4	8		7	.250	.400	.313	105	1	0-0	.922	-1	77	117	C12		-0.3
Total	2	42	65	5	12	3	0	0	6	15		13	.185	.338	.231	61	-2	0-0	.952	-1	77	106	C39		-0.3
FERNANDEZ, FRANK	Frank B4.16.1943 Staten Island NY BR/TR/6-1/192* d9.12 Mil 1967																								
1967	NY A	9	28	1	6	2	0	1	7	.214	.281	.393	104	0	1-1	1.000	1	0	49	C7,O2R		0.1			
1968	NY A	51	135	15	23	6	1	7	30	35-2	1	50	.170	.341	.385	124	5	1-0	.989	4	104	123	C45,O4R		1.3
1969	NY A	89	229	34	51	6	1	12	29	65-3	3	68	.223	.399	.415	133	14	1-3	.994	1	106	123	C65,O14R		1.6
1970	Oak A	94	252	30	54	5	0	15	44	40-4	2	76	.214	.327	.413	106	2	1-1	.993	2	127	74	C76/OL		0.8
1971	Oak A	2	4	0	0	0	0	0	0	1-0	0	2	.000	.200	.000	-40	-1	0-0	1.000	-2	0	145	C2	24	-0.3
	Was A	18	30	1	3	0	0	1	4	4-0	0	10	.100	.194	.190	-2	-1	0-0	1.000	-3	73	311	O6(3/1/2)/C		-0.6
	Oak A	2	5	1	1	1	0	0	1	0-0	0	1	.200	.200	.400	68	0	0-0	1.000	-2	0	145	/C		0.0
	Year	22	39	2	4	1	0	1	5	5-0	0	13	.103	.196	.128	-4	-2	0-0	1.000	-5	73	311	O6(3/1/2),C4		-1.2
	Chi N	17	41	11	7	1	0	4	9	17-0	0	15	.171	.414	.488	135	3	0-0	.980	1	112	168	C16		0.5
1972	Chi N	3	3	0	0	0	0	0	0	0-0	0	1	.000	.000	.000	-90	-1	0-0	1.000	-0	0	0	/C		-0.1
Total	6	285	727	92	145	21	2	39	116	164-9	6	231	.199	.350	.420	113	18	4-4	.992	3	106	106	C214,O27(4/1/22)	24	3.0

YEAR	TM LG	G	AB	R	H	2B	3B	HR	RBI	BB-IB	HP	SO	AVG	OBP	SLG	AOPS	ABR	SB-CS	FA	FR	RNG	THR	GAMES AT POSITION	DL	BFW

FERNANDEZ, NANNY Froilan B10.25.1918 Wilmington CA D9.19.1996 Harbor City CA BR/TR/5-9/170* d4.14 Mil 1943-45

1942	Bos N	145	577	63	147	29	3	6	55	38	2	61	.255	.303	.347	92	-8	15	.914	2	102	83	3b98,O44(42/3/0)		-0.5
1946	Bos N	115	372	37	95	15	2	2	42	30	1	44	.255	.313	.323	79	-10	1	.940	1	104	92	3b81,S18,O14L		-1.1
1947	Bos N	83	209	16	43	4	0	2	21	22	0	20	.206	.281	.254	44	-17	2	.933	-7	95	79	S62,O8R,3b6		-2.3
1950	Pit N	65	198	23	51	11	0	6	27	19	1	17	.258	.326	.404	88	-4	2	.925	-3	99	57	3b52		-0.7
Total 4		408	1356	139	336	59	5	16	145	109	4	142	.248	.306	.334	80	-39	20	.925	-10	101	79	3b237,S80,O66(56/3/8)		-4.6

FERNANDEZ, CHICO Humberto (Perez) B3.2.1932 Havana, Cuba BR/TR/6-0/170* d7.14

1956	Bro N	34	66	11	15	2	0	9	3-1	0	10	.227	.261	.303	47	-5	2-3	.978	4	114	114	S25		0.0
1957	Phi N	149	500	42	131	14	4	5	51	31-5	1	64	.262	.302	.336	75	-19	18-5	.960	-23	86	79	S149		-2.8
1958	Phi N	148	522	38	120	18	5	6	51	37-3	2	48	.230	.280	.318	60	-31	12-6	.975	-14	94	87	S148		-3.3
1959	Phi N	45	123	15	26	5	1	0	3	10-0	1	11	.211	.269	.268	43	-10	2-1	.958	-1	87	120	S40,2b2		-0.8
1960	Det A	133	435	44	105	13	3	4	35	39-4	1	50	.241	.303	.313	66	-21	13-4	.947	-7	98	86	S130		-1.7
1961	Det A	133	435	41	108	15	4	3	40	36-4	0	45	.248	.305	.322	66	-21	8-5	.958	-9	94	91	S121,3b8		-2.1
1962	Det A	141	503	64	125	17	2	20	59	42-2	0	69	.249	.305	.410	88	-10	10-3	.960	-28	65	65	S138,3b2/1		-2.5
1963	Det A	15	49	3	7	1	0	0	2	6-0	1	11	.143	.236	.163	14	-6	0-1	.947	0	98	97	S14		-0.5
	NY N	58	145	12	29	6	0	1	9	9-2	1	30	.200	.244	.262	46	-10	3-0	.944	-9	87	80	S45,3b5,2b3		-1.7
Total 8		856	2778	270	666	91	19	40	259	213-21	4	338	.240	.292	.329	67	-133	68-28	.960	-87	92	84	S810,3b15,2b5/1		-15.4

FERNANDEZ, JOSE Jose Mayobanex (Rojas) B11.2.1974 LaVega, D.R. BR/TR/6-2/220* d7.3

1999	Mon N	8	24	0	5	2	0	0	1	1-0	0	7	.208	.240	.292	35	-2	0-0	.889	0	101	0	3b6.		-0.2
2001	Ana A	13	25	1	2	1	0	0	0	2-0	0	10	.080	.148	.120	-27	-5	0-1	.000	-0	0	0	1b2/3D		-0.5
Total 2		21	49	1	7	3	0	0	1	3-0	0	17	.143	.192	.204	3	-7	0-1	.889	-0	99	0	D7,3b7,1b2		-0.7

FERNANDEZ, CHICO Lorenzo Marto (Mosquera) B4.23.1939 Havana, Cuba BR/TR/5-10/160 d4.20

| | | | | | | | | | | | | | | | | | | | | | | | | | |
|1968|Bal A|24|18|0|2|0|0|0|1|1-0|0|4|.111|.158|.111|-17|-3|0-0|.923|-1|94|161|S7,2b4| |-0.3|

FERNANDEZ, TONY Octavio Antonio (Castro) (b Octavio Antonio Fernando (Castro)) B6.30.1962 San Pedro de Macoris, D.R. BB/TR/6-2/175(165-195) d9.2 [DL 1996 NY A 182]

1983	Tor A	15	34	5	9	1	1	0	2	2-0	1	2	.265	.324	.353	81	-1	0-1	1.000	-3	65	111	S13/D		-0.3
1984	Tor A	88	233	29	63	5	3	3	19	17-0	0	15	.270	.317	.356	83	-6	5-7	.974	14	107	115	S73,3b10/D		1.3
1985	†Tor A	161	564	71	163	31	10	2	51	43-2	2	41	.289	.340	.390	97	-2	13-6	.962	3	104	118	S160		2.4
1986	Tor A★	163	687	91	213	33	9	10	65	27-0	4	52	.310	.338	.428	104	3	25-12	**.983**	3	98	105	S163		2.4
1987	Tor A★	146	578	90	186	29	8	5	67	51-3	5	48	.322	.379	.426	111	10	32-12	.979	16	98	115	S146		4.1
1988	Tor A	154	648	76	186	41	4	5	70	45-3	4	65	.287	.335	.386	101	1	15-5	.981	10	103	109	S154		2.4
1989	†Tor A★	140	573	64	147	25	9	11	64	29-1	3	51	.257	.291	.389	93	-8	22-6	**.992**	16	107	104	S140	24	2.1
1990	Tor A	161	635	84	175	27	**17**	4	66	71-4	7	70	.276	.352	.391	106	6	26-13	.989	9	101	96	S161		2.7
1991	SD N	145	558	81	152	27	5	4	38	55-0	1	74	.272	.337	.360	93	-4	23-9	.972	10	104	**115**	S145		1.9
1992	SD N★	155	622	84	171	32	4	4	37	56-4	4	62	.275	.337	.359	96	-2	20-20	.983	-18	90	80	S154		-1.2
1993	NY N	48	173	20	39	5	2	1	14	25-0	1	19	.225	.323	.295	69	-7	6-2	.975	2	104	100	S48		0.0
	†Tor A	94	353	45	108	18	9	4	50	31-3	0	26	.306	.361	.442	113	6	15-8	.985	10	95	102	S94		2.2
1994	Cin N	104	366	50	102	18	6	8	50	44-8	5	40	.279	.361	.426	105	3	12-7	**.991**	0	98	92	3b93,S9,2b5		0.5
1995	†NY A	108	384	57	94	20	2	5	45	42-4	4	40	.245	.322	.346	76	-13	6-6	.976	-14	91	99	S103,2b4		-1.9
1997	†Cle A	120	409	55	117	21	1	11	44	22-0	2	47	.286	.323	.423	90	-7	6-6	.980	14	**105**	94	2b109,S10/D		1.1
1998	Tor A	138	486	71	156	36	2	9	72	45-5	1	53	.321	.387	.459	120	16	13-8	.975	-12	94	90	2b82,3b54/D		0.8
1999	Tor A★	142	485	73	159	41	0	6	75	77-11	10	62	.328	.427	.449	123	23	6-7	.939	-14	99	99	3b132,D9/2		0.8
2001	Mil N	28	64	6	18	0	0	1	3	7-0	0	9	.281	.352	.328	79	-2	1-2	.966	0	114	172	3b13		-0.2
	Tor A	48	59	5	18	4	0	1	12	1-0	1	8	.305	.323	.424	94	-1	0-1	—	0	0	0	D13		-0.2
Total 17		2158	7911	1057	2276	414	92	94	844	690-48	64	784	.288	.347	.399	101	15	246-138	.980	51	100	105	S1573,3b302,2b201,D26	224	20.9

FERRARA, AL Alfred John "The Bull" B12.22.1939 Brooklyn NY BR/TR/6-1/203* d7.30 Col Long Island-Brooklyn

1963	LA N	21	44	2	7	0	0	1	1	6-0	1	9	.159	.275	.227	50	-3	0-0	.950	0	105	145	O11(7/0/4)		-0.3
1965	LA N	41	81	5	17	2	1	1	10	9-0	1	20	.210	.297	.296	72	-3	0-0	.927	-1	102	9	O27(10/0/19)		-0.6
1966	†LA N	63	115	15	31	4	0	5	23	9-0	3	35	.270	.333	.435	123	3	0-0	.956	-1	109	0	O32(4/1/27)		0.1
1967	LA N	122	347	41	96	16	1	16	50	33-4	3	73	.277	.345	.467	142	18	0-1	.978	-7	89	17	O94(27/0/71)		0.5
1968	LA N	2	7	0	1	0	0	0	0	0-0	0	2	.143	.143	.143	-15	-1	0-0	.500	-1	35	0	O2L	144	-0.2
1969	SD N	138	366	39	95	22	1	14	56	45-5	7	69	.260	.349	.440	124	13	0-0	.958	-4	85	100	O96(95/1/0)		0.4
1970	SD N	138	372	44	103	15	4	13	51	46-2	11	63	.277	.372	.444	122	13	0-0	.968	-8	83	33	O96L		0.0
1971	SD N	17	17	0	2	1	0	0	2	5-1	0	5	.118	.318	.176	46	-1	0-0	1.000	-1	29	0	O2L		-0.2
	Cin N	32	33	2	6	0	0	1	5	3-0	1	10	.182	.270	.273	55	-2	0-0	1.000	0	137	0	O5L		-0.2
	Year	49	50	2	8	1	0	1	7	8-1	1	15	.160	.288	.240	52	-3	0-0	1.000	-0	92	0	O7L		-0.4
Total 8		574	1382	148	358	60	7	51	198	156-12	27	286	.259	.344	.423	119	37	0-1	.962	-22	89	46	O365(248/2/121)	144	-0.5

FERRARO, MIKE Michael Dennis B8.18.1944 Kingston NY BR/TR/5-11/175* d9.6 M2/C13

1966	NY A	10	28	4	5	0	0	0	3	3-0	1	3	.179	.281	.179	37	-2	0-0	.926	1	117	198	3b10		-0.2
1968	NY A	23	87	5	14	0	1	0	1	2-1	0	17	.161	.180	.184	11	-10	0-0	.975	4	134	77	3b22		-0.7
1969	Sea A	5	4	0	0	0	0	0	0	1-0	0	0	.000	.200	.000	-40	-1	0-0	—	0		/H		-0.1
1972	Mil A	124	381	19	97	18	1	2	29	17-1	0	41	.255	.284	.323	82	-9	0-5	.950	-17	83	77	3b115/S		-3.3
Total 4		162	500	28	116	18	2	2	30	23-2	1	61	.232	.265	.288	67	-22	0-5	.953	-12	94	85	3b147/S		-4.3

FERRELL, RICK Richard Benjamin B10.12.1905 Durham NC D7.27.1995 Bloomfield Hills MI BR/TR/5-10/160 d4.19 C8 HF1984 b-Wes Col Guilford

1929	StL A	64	144	21	33	6	1	0	20	32	1	10	.229	.373	.285	69	-5	1-2	.962	1	136	108	C45		-0.2
1930	StL A	101	314	43	84	18	4	1	41	46	1	10	.268	.363	.360	81	-8	1-4	.983	-4	117	**123**	C101		-0.6
1931	StL A	117	386	47	118	30	4	3	57	56	0	12	.306	.394	.427	112	9	2-3	.973	7	114	98	C108		2.0
1932	StL A	126	438	67	138	30	5	2	65	66	1	18	.315	.406	.420	108	9	5-5	.986	2	110	104	C120		1.6
1933	StL A	22	72	8	18	2	0	1	5	12	0	4	.250	.357	.319	76	-2	2-0	.991	2	131	108	C21		0.2
	Bos A★	118	421	50	125	19	4	3	72	58	2	19	.297	.385	.382	105	5	2-2	.990	2	81	118	C116		1.4
	Year	140	493	58	143	21	4	4	77	70	2	23	.290	.381	.373	100	2	4-2	.990	5	89	116	C137		1.6
1934	Bos A☆	132	437	50	130	29	4	1	48	66	0	20	.297	.390	.389	95	-1	0-0	**.990**	5	100	79	C128		1.1
1935	Bos A☆	133	458	54	138	34	4	3	61	65	0	15	.301	.388	.413	100	3	5-8	.979	13	116	142	C131		2.1
1936	Bos A★	121	410	59	128	27	5	8	55	65	0	17	.312	.406	.461	108	7	0-1	.987	9	88	93	C121		2.0
1937	Bos A	18	65	8	20	2	0	1	4	15	1	4	.308	.438	.385	100	1	0-0	.990	1	113	88	C18		0.3
	Was A☆	86	279	31	64	6	0	1	32	50	1	18	.229	.348	.262	59	-16	1-1	.987	-5	96	97	C84		-1.4
	Year	104	344	39	84	8	0	2	36	65	2	22	.244	.366	.285	68	-14	1-1	.988	-4	99	95	C102		-1.1
1938	Was A☆	135	411	55	120	24	5	1	58	75	1	17	.292	.401	.382	104	7	1-0	.981	-7	109	93	C131		0.8
1939	Was A	87	274	32	77	13	1	0	31	41	1	12	.281	.377	.336	90	-2	1-1	.976	-2	**145**	81	C83		0.1
1940	Was A	103	326	35	89	18	2	0	28	47	0	15	.273	.365	.340	90	-3	1-1	.980	-5	80	130	C99		-0.2
1941	Was A	21	66	8	18	5	0	0	13	15	0	4	.273	.407	.348	107	2	1-0	.980	-1	91	131	C21		-0.5
	StL A	100	321	30	81	14	3	2	52	52	0	22	.252	.357	.333	81	-7	2-1	.995	-4	93	92	C98		-0.5
	Year	121	387	38	99	19	3	2	36	67	0	26	.256	.366	.336	85	-6	3-1	.992	-5	93	99	C119		-0.3
1942	StL A	99	273	20	61	6	1	0	20	33	0	13	.223	.307	.253	57	-15	0-1	.986	3	87	91	C70		-0.7
1943	StL A	74	209	12	50	7	0	0	20	34	1	14	.239	.348	.273	81	-3	0-0	.987	3	72	113	C96		0.5
1944	Was A☆	99	339	14	94	11	0	0	25	46	0	13	.277	.364	.316	99	2	2-1	.981	2	87	93	C96		1.0
1945	Was A*	91	286	33	76	12	1	1	38	43	1	13	.266	.366	.325	110	6	2-4	.990	-1	110	81	C83		1.0
1947	Was A	37	99	10	30	11	0	0	12	14	0	7	.303	.389	.414	127	3	0-0	.994	2	97	151	C37		0.8
Total 18		1884	6028	687	1692	324	45	28	734	931	10	277	.281	.378	.363	95	-6	29-35	.984	24	102	104	C1806		11.5

FERRELL, WES Wesley Cheek B2.2.1908 Greensboro NC D12.9.1976 Sarasota FL BR/TR/6-2/195 d9.9 b-Rick ▲

1927	Cle A	1	0	0	0	0	0	0	0	0	0	0						-0	0	0	/P		0.0
1928	Cle A	2	4	0	1	0	0	0	0	0	0	0	.250	.250	.750	152	1	0-0	1.000	0	110	0	P2		0.0
1929	Cle A	47	93	12	22	5	3	1	12	6	0	28	.237	.283	.387	68	4	1-0	.973	3	121	106	P43		0.0
1930	Cle A	53	118	19	35	8	1	0	14	12	0	15	.297	.362	.415	93	8	0-0	.967	-3	65	0	P43		0.0
1931	Cle A	48	116	24	37	6	1	9	30	10	1	18	.319	.372	.621	149	17	0-0	.969	5	132	96	P40		0.0
1932	Cle A	55	128	14	31	5	2	2	18	6	0	21	.242	.276	.359	59	4	0-0	.986	0	101	148	P38		0.0
1933	Cle A☆	61	140	26	38	7	0	7	26	20	1	22	.271	.363	.471	114	3	0-0	**1.000**	2	111	183	P28,O13L		0.1
1934	Bos A	34	78	12	22	4	0	4	17	7	1	15	.282	.341	.487	104	8	1-0	.969	-3	64	104	P26		0.0
1935	Bos A	75	150	25	52	5	1	7	32	21	1	16	.347	.430	.533	138	20	0-0	.977	2	119	29	P41		0.0

YEAR	TM LG	G	AB	R	H	2B	3B	HR	RBI	BB-IB	HP	SO	AVG	OBP	SLG	AOPS	ABR	SB-CS	FA	FR	RNG	THR	GAMES AT POSITION	DL	BFW
1936	Bos A	61	135	20	36	6	1	5	24	14	0	10	.267	.336	.437	84	11	0-0	.962	-3	76	67	P39		0.0
1937	Bos A	18	33	7	12	2	0	1	9	7	0	3	.364	.475	.515	144	6	0-0	.964	2	152	570	P12		0.0
	Was A☆	53	106	7	27	5	0	0	16	9	0	18	.255	.313	.302	58	6	0-0	.975	-1	86	0	P25		0.0
	Year	71	139	14	39	7	0	1	25	16	0	21	.281	.355	.353	81	12	0-0	.971	1	103	148	P37		0.0
1938	Was A	26	49	6	11	2	0	1	6	15	0	7	.224	.406	.327	92	7	0-0	.976	1	114	163	P23		0.0
	NY A	5	12	1	2	1	0	0	1	1	0	4	.167	.231	.250	20	0	0-0	.917	1	159	884	P5		0.0
	Year	31	61	7	13	3	0	1	7	16	0	11	.213	.377	.311	79	7	0-0	.962	1	122	284	P28		0.0
1939	NY A	3	8	0	1	1	0	0	1	0	0	2	.125	.125	.250	-6	0	0-0	1.000	0	124	0	P3		0.0
1940	Bro N	2	2	0	0	0	0	0	0	0	0	2	.000	.000	.000	-94	0	0'	1.000	1	372	0	/P		0.0
1941	Bos N	4	4	2	2	0	0	1	2	1	0	1	.500	.600	1.250	430	2	0-0	1.000	-0	35	0	P4		0.0
Total	15	548	1176	175	329	57	12	38	208	129	0	185	.280	.351	.446	99	97	2-0	.975	1	104	104	P374,O13L		0.1

FERRELL, SERGIO   Sergio (Marrero) B1.29.1951 Santurce, PR BB/TR/5-7/145* d4.5

YEAR	TM LG	G	AB	R	H	2B	3B	HR	RBI	BB-IB	HP	SO	AVG	OBP	SLG	AOPS	ABR	SB-CS	FA	FR	RNG	THR	GAMES AT POSITION	DL	BFW
1974	Min A	24	57	12	16	0	2	0	3	8-0	1	6	.281	.379	.351	107	1	3-2	.855	-7	79	68	S20/2		-0.4
1975	Min A	32	81	14	20	3	1	0	2	3-0	1	11	.247	.279	.309	66	-4	3-4	.924	-1	119	133	S18,2b10,D2		-0.4
1978	NY N	37	33	8	7	0	1	0	1	4-0	1	7	.212	.316	.273	68	-1	1-0	.971	3	114	98	S29,2b3,3b2		0.3
1979	NY N	32	7	0	0	0	0	0	0	2-0	0	3	.000	.222	.000	-35	-1	0-2	.833	-0	48	0	3b12,S5,2b4		-0.2
Total	4	125	178	41	43	3	4	0	3	17-0	3	27	.242	.317	.303	76	-5	7-8	.922	-5	103	103	S72,2b18,3b14,D2		-0.7

FERRIS, HOBE   Albert Sayles B12.7.1877 Providence RI D3.18.1938 Detroit MI BR/TR/5-8/162 d4.26

YEAR	TM LG	G	AB	R	H	2B	3B	HR	RBI	BB-IB	HP	SO	AVG	OBP	SLG	AOPS	ABR	SB-CS	FA	FR	RNG	THR	GAMES AT POSITION	DL	BFW
1901	Bos A	**138**	523	68	131	16	15	2	63	23	6		.250	.290	.350	78	-18	13	.930	7	103	**130**	2b138/S		-0.8
1902	Bos A	134	499	57	122	16	14	8	63	21	1		.244	.276	.381	79	-18	11	.952	**24**	114	115	2b134		0.7
1903	†Bos A	**141**	525	69	132	19	7	9	66	25	1		.251	.287	.366	90	-8	11	.950	14	105	111	2b139,S2		0.8
1904	Bos A	156	563	50	120	23	10	3	63	23	1		.213	.245	.306	70	-20	7	.962	-0	98	107	2b156		-2.2
1905	Bos A	142	523	51	115	24	16	6	59	23	0		.220	.253	.361	93	-8	11	.960	15	**108**	111	2b142		0.9
1906	Bos A	130	495	47	121	25	13	2	44	10	2		.244	.262	.360	94	-6	8	.960	8	104	97	2b126,3b4		0.3
1907	Bos A	150	561	41	135	25	2	4	60	10	0		.241	.254	.314	82	-14	11	.967	8	102	94	2b150		-0.6
1908	StL A	148	555	54	150	26	7	2	74	14	2		.270	.291	.353	108	3	6	**.952**	14	103	**168**	3b148		2.3
1909	StL A	148	556	36	120	18	5	4	58	12	0		.216	.232	.288	69	-23	11	.937	7	103	103	3b114,2b34		-1.5
Total	9	1287	4800	473	1146	192	89	40	550	161	13		.239	.265	.341	84	-112	89	.954	96	104	109	2b1019,3b266,S3		-0.1

FETZER, WILLY   William McKinnon B6.24.1884 Concord NC D5.3.1959 Butner NC BL/TR/5-10.5/180 d9.4 Col Davidson

YEAR	TM LG	G	AB	R	H	2B	3B	HR	RBI	BB-IB	HP	SO	AVG	OBP	SLG	AOPS	ABR	SB-CS	FA	FR	RNG	THR	GAMES AT POSITION	DL	BFW
1906	Phi A	1	1	0	0	0	0	0	0	0-0	0		.000	.000	.000	-97	0		—	0			/H		0.0

FEWSTER, CHICK   Wilson Lloyd B11.10.1895 Baltimore MD D4.16.1945 Baltimore MD BR/TR/5-11/160 d9.19

YEAR	TM LG	G	AB	R	H	2B	3B	HR	RBI	BB-IB	HP	SO	AVG	OBP	SLG	AOPS	ABR	SB-CS	FA	FR	RNG	THR	GAMES AT POSITION	DL	BFW
1917	NY A	11	36	2	8	0	0	0	1	5	0	5	.222	.317	.222	64	-1	1	.919	-0	98	114	2b11		-0.1
1918	NY A	5	2	1	1	0	0	0	0	0	0	0	.500	.500	.500	197	0	0	—	-0	0	0	2b2		0.0
1919	NY A	81	244	38	69	9	3	1	15	34	7	36	.283	.386	.357	108	5	8	.946	4	81	236	O41(0/13/28),S24,2b4,3b2		0.8
1920	NY A	21	21	8	6	1	0	0	1	7	0	2	.286	.464	.333	110	1	0-1	.840	-1	91	66	S6,2b3		-0.2
1921	†NY A	66	207	44	58	19	0	1	19	28	6	43	.280	.382	.386	94	0	4-4	.974	-1	88	118	O43(7/35/1),2b15		-0.2
1922	NY A	44	132	20	32	4	1	1	9	16	0	23	.242	.324	.311	65	-7	2-4	.975	2	86	198	O38(35/4/0),2b2		-0.8
	Bos A	23	83	8	24	4	1	0	9	6	1	10	.289	.344	.361	85	-2	8-3	.959	2	113	78	3b23		0.2
	Year	67	215	28	56	8	2	1	18	22	1	33	.260	.332	.330	72	-9	10-7	.975	4	86	198	O38(35/4/0),3b23,2b2		-0.6
1923	Bos A	90	284	32	67	10	1	0	15	39	3	35	.236	.334	.278	62	-14	7-14	.938	-10	99	74	2b49,S37,3b3		-2.3
1924	Cle A	101	322	36	86	12	2	0	36	24	3	36	.267	.324	.317	65	-17	12-12	.961	-20	91	73	2b94,3b5		-3.5
1925	Cle A	93	294	39	73	16	1	1	38	36	0	25	.248	.330	.320	65	-15	6-9	.939	-11	93	83	2b83,3b10/OR		-2.4
1926	Bro N	105	337	53	82	16	3	2	24	45	5	49	.243	.341	.326	82	-7	9	.953	-12	90	66	2b103		-1.6
1927	Bro N	4	1	1	0	0	0	0	0	0	0	0	.000	.000	.000	-99	-0		—	0			/H		0.0
Total	11	644	1963	282	506	91	12	6	167	240	25	264	.258	.346	.326	77	-57	57-47	.945	-47	93	78	2b366,O123(42/52/30),S67,3b43		-9.9

FIALA, NEIL   Neil Stephen B8.24.1956 St.Louis MO BL/TR/6-1/185 [StLN77 32/720] d9.3 Col Southern Illinois

YEAR	TM LG	G	AB	R	H	2B	3B	HR	RBI	BB-IB	HP	SO	AVG	OBP	SLG	AOPS	ABR	SB-CS	FA	FR	RNG	THR	GAMES AT POSITION	DL	BFW
1981	StL N	3	3	0	0	0	0	0	0	0-0	0	1	.000	.000	.000	-96	-1	0-0	—	0			/H		-0.1
	Cin N	2	2	1	1	0	0	0	1	0-0	0	0	.500	.500	.500	185	0	0-0	—	0			/H		0.0
	Year	5	5	1	1	0	0	0	1	0-0	0	1	.200	.200	.200	13	-1	0-0	—	0					-0.1

FICK, ROBERT   Robert Charles John B3.15.1974 Torrance CA BL/TR/6-1/189(189-205) [DetA96 5/131] d9.19 Col Cal St.-Northridge OF(17/0/165)

YEAR	TM LG	G	AB	R	H	2B	3B	HR	RBI	BB-IB	HP	SO	AVG	OBP	SLG	AOPS	ABR	SB-CS	FA	FR	RNG	THR	GAMES AT POSITION	DL	BFW
1998	Det A	7	22	6	8	1	0	3	7	2-0	0	7	.364	.417	.818	208	3	1-0	.950	0	89	124	C3/1D		0.3
1999	Det A	15	41	6	9	0	0	3	10	7-0	0	6	.220	.327	.439	93	-1	1-0	1.000	1	98	0	C4,D8	155	0.0
2000	Det A	66	163	18	41	7	0	3	22	22-2	1	39	.252	.340	.374	83	-4	2-1	.984	-3	114	95	1b34,C16,D12	56	-0.8
2001	Det A	124	401	62	109	21	2	19	61	39-3	4	62	.272	.339	.476	115	8	0-3	.986	-4	80	61	C78,1b26,O8R,D8		0.6
2002	Det A★	148	556	66	150	36	2	17	63	46-4	7	90	.270	.331	.433	106	4	0-1	.963	9	101	**234**	O140R,D6		0.6
2003	†Atl N	126	409	52	110	26	1	11	80	42-4	2	47	.269	.335	.418	97	-2	1-0	.987	-8	78	102	1b115	16	-1.9
2004	TB A	76	214	12	43	5	2	6	26	20-2	2	32	.201	.273	.327	57	-14	0-0	.976	-1	121	0	D34,O21(13/0/8),1b10,C3		-1.8
	SD N	13	12	2	2	0	0	0	0	2-0	1	4	.167	.333	.167	37	-1	0-0	1.000	-0	143	0	/1		-0.1
2005	†SD N	93	230	25	61	10	2	3	30	26-2	1	33	.265	.340	.365	90	-3	0-2	.992	-2	80	121	1b29,C28,O13(4/0/9)/3D		-0.7
Total	8	668	2048	249	533	106	11	65	299	206-17	18	320	.260	.330	.418	98	-10	5-7	.987	-8	82·	99	1b216,O182R,C132,D72/3	227	-3.8

FIELD, JIM   James C. B4.24.1863 Philadelphia PA D5.13.1953 Atlantic City NJ 6-1/170 d6.2 ▲

YEAR	TM LG	G	AB	R	H	2B	3B	HR	RBI	BB-IB	HP	SO	AVG	OBP	SLG	AOPS	ABR	SB-CS	FA	FR	RNG	THR	GAMES AT POSITION	DL	BFW
1883	Col AA	75	291	31	75	10	6	1		7			.258	.275	.344	107	3		.938	-7	47	115	1b75		-0.9
1884	Col AA	105	417	74	97	9	7	4		23	12		.233	.292	.317	107	5		.958	-4	75	134	1b105		-0.6
1885	Pit AA	56	209	28	50	9	1	1	15	13	7		.239	.306	.306	95	0		.965	-0	99	123	1b56		-0.5
	Bal AA	38	144	16	30	3	2	0	10	13	1		.208	.278	.257	71	-4		.963	1	129	71	1b38		-0.6
	Year	94	353	44	80	12	3	1	25	26	8		.227	.295	.286	85	-4		.964	1	111	102	1b94		-1.1
1890	Roc AA	52	188	30	38	7	5	4	25	21	8		.202	.309	.356	104	1	8	.964	-4	61	92	1b51,P2		-0.7
1898	Was N	5	21	1	2	0	0	0	0	0	0		.095	.095	.095	-46	-4	1	.979	-0	86	0	1b5		-0.4
Total	5	331	1270	180	292	38	21	10	50	77	28		.230	.289	.317	97	1	9	.956	-15	77	112	1b330,P2		-3.8

FIELD, SAM   Samuel Jay B10.12.1848 Philadelphia PA D10.28.1904 Sinking Spring PA BR/TR/5-9.5/182 d5.19

YEAR	TM LG	G	AB	R	H	2B	3B	HR	RBI	BB-IB	HP	SO	AVG	OBP	SLG	AOPS	ABR	SB-CS	FA	FR	RNG	THR	GAMES AT POSITION	DL	BFW
1875	Cen NA	3	11	2	1	0	0	0	0				.091	.091	.091	-40	-1	0-0	.714	-1			C2/OR		-0.2
	Was NA	5	16	0	5	0	0	0	1			1	.313	.313	.313	122	0	1-0	.731	-2			C4/OR		-0.1
	Year	8	27	2	6	0	0	0	1			1	.222	.222	.222	58	-1	1-0	.723	-3			C6,O2R		-0.3
1876	Cin N	4	14	2	0	0	0	0	1				.000	.067	.000	-89	-3		.667	-3			C3,2b2		-0.5

FIELDER, CECIL   Cecil Grant B9.21.1963 Los Angeles CA BR/TR/6-3/240(220-261) [KCA82 S4/67] d7.20 s-Prince Col Nevada-Las Vegas

YEAR	TM LG	G	AB	R	H	2B	3B	HR	RBI	BB-IB	HP	SO	AVG	OBP	SLG	AOPS	ABR	SB-CS	FA	FR	RNG	THR	GAMES AT POSITION	DL	BFW
1985	†Tor A	30	74	6	23	4	0	4	16	6-0	0	16	.311	.358	.527	136	4	0-0	.979	0	117	144	1b25		0.3
1986	Tor A	34	83	7	13	2	0	4	13	6-0	1	27	.157	.222	.325	45	-7	0-0	1.000	-0	83	82	D22,1b7,3b2/OL		-0.8
1987	Tor A	82	175	30	47	7	1	14	32	20-2	1	48	.269	.345	.560	132	7	0-1	1.000	-1	74	136	D55,1b16,3b2		0.4
1988	Tor A	74	174	24	40	6	1	9	23	14-0	1	53	.230	.289	.431	98	-1	0-1	.991	0	113	92	D50,1b17,3b3,2b2		-0.4
1990	Det A★	159	573	104	159	25	1	**51**	**132**	90-11	5	182	.277	.377	**.592**	166	44	0-0	.989	5	114	107	1b143,D15		4.4
1991	Det A★	**162**	624	102	163	25	0	**44**	**133**	78-12	6	151	.261	.347	.513	133	27	0-0	.993	0	105	101	1b122,D42		1.7
1992	Det A	155	594	80	145	22	0	35	**124**	73-8	2	151	.244	.325	.458	117	12	0-0	.991	4	118	100	1b114,D43		0.7
1993	Det A★	154	573	80	153	23	0	30	117	90-15	4	125	.267	.368	.464	123	20	0-1	.991	-0	103	102	1b119,D36		0.7
1994	Det A	109	425	67	110	16	2	28	90	50-4	2	110	.259	.337	.504	112	6	0-0	.993	16	**162**	85	1b102,D7		1.2
1995	Det A	136	494	70	120	18	1	31	82	75-8	5	116	.243	.346	.472	111	7	0-1	.993	7	139	95	1b77,D58		0.5
1996	Det A	107	391	55	97	12	0	26	80	63-8	3	91	.248	.354	.478	108	5	2-0	.989	4	123	71	1b71,D36		0.1
	†NY A	53	200	30	52	8	0	13	37	24-4	2	48	.260	.342	.495	109	2	0-1	1.000	-0	71	103	D43,1b9		-0.1
	Year	160	591	85	149	20	0	39	117	87-12	5	139	.252	.350	.484	109	7	2-0	.990	4	117	75	1b80,D79		0.0
1997	†NY A	98	361	40	94	15	0	13	61	51-3	7	87	.260	.358	.410	102	2	0-0	1.000	1	130	129	D87,1b8		-0.2
1998	Ana A	103	381	48	92	16	1	17	68	52-1	2	98	.241	.335	.423	94	-3	0-1	.997	-2	84	101	1b72,D31		-1.3
	Cle A	14	35	1	5	1	0	0	0	1-0	1	13	.143	.189	.171	-5	-6	0-0	.933	0	121	51	D10,1b3		-0.6
	Year	117	416	49	97	17	1	17	68	53-1	4	111	.233	.324	.401	86	-9	0-1	.995	-2	85	99	1b75,D41		-1.9
Total	13	1470	5157	744	1313	200	7	319	1008	693-76	43	1316	.255	.345	.482	118	126	2-6	.992	33	117	97	1b905,D535,3b7,2b2/OL	62	6.6

FIELDER, PRINCE   Prince Semien B5.9.1984 Ontario CA BL/TR/6-0/260 d6.13 f-Cecil

YEAR	TM LG	G	AB	R	H	2B	3B	HR	RBI	BB-IB	HP	SO	AVG	OBP	SLG	AOPS	ABR	SB-CS	FA	FR	RNG	THR	GAMES AT POSITION	DL	BFW
2005	Mil N	39	59	2	17	4	0	2	10	2-0	0	17	.288	.306	.458	98	0	0-0	1.000	1	172	61	1b7,D5		0.0

YEAR	TM LG	G	AB	R	H	2B	3B	HR	RBI	BB-IB	HP	SO	AVG	OBP	SLG	AOPS	ABR	SB-CS	FA	FR	RNG	THR	GAMES AT POSITION	DL	BFW

FIELDS, BRUCE Bruce Alan B10.6.1960 Cleveland OH BL/TR/6-0/185* [DetA78 7/168] d9.3 C3

1986	Det A	16	43	4	12	1	0	6	1-0	0	6	.279	.283	.349	74	-2	1-1	.962	-1	102	0	O14L/D		-0.3
1988	Sea A	39	67	8	18	5	0	1	5	4-0	0	11	.269	.310	.388	90	-1	0-1	1.000	-2	79	0	O23(14/1/8),D6		-0.3
1989	Sea A	3	3	2	1	1	0	0	0	0-0	0	1	.333	.333	.667	170	0	0-0	—	-0	0	0	/OR		0.0
Total	3	58	113	14	31	7	1	1	11	5-0	0	18	.274	.300	.381	86	-3	1-2	.980	-2	89	0	O38(28/1/9),D7		-0.6

FIELDS, GEORGE George W. B7.1853 Waterbury CT D9.22.1933 Waterbury CT d5.2

| 1872 | Man NA | 18 | 86 | 17 | 19 | 3 | 1 | 0 | 14 | 0 | | 2 | .221 | .221 | .279 | 56 | -4 | 0-0 | .629 | -7 | 72 | 0 | 3b12,O5(1/0/4)/S | | -0.8 |

FIELDS, JOCKO John Joseph B10.20.1864 Cork, Ireland D10.14.1950 Jersey City NJ BR/TR/5-10/160 d5.31 OF(160/20/27)

1887	Pit N	43	164	26	44	9	2	0	17	7	2	13	.268	.306	.348	88	-2	7	.933	-0	100	0	O27(7/13/7),C14,1b3/3P		-0.2
1888	Pit N	45	169	22	33	7	2	1	15	8	0	19	.195	.232	.278	68	-6	9	.887	-4	118	0	O29(23/2/4),C14,3b3		-0.9
1889	Pit N	75	289	41	90	22	5	2	43	29	1	30	.311	.376	.443	142	17	7	.860	-5	64	103	O60(54/2/4),C16		1.1
1890	Pit P	126	526	101	148	18	20	9	86	57	3	52	.281	.355	.443	123	16	24	.879	-11	137	104	O80(76/3/1),2b30,C15,S4		0.4
1891	Pit N	23	75	10	18	3	0	0	5	10	1	13	.240	.337	.280	82	-1	-1	.897	-2	103	104	C15,S8		-0.2
	Phi N	8	30	4	7	2	1	0	5	4	0	2	.233	.324	.367	98	0	0	.769	-4	90	76	C8		-0.5
	Year	31	105	14	25	5	1	0	10	14	1	15	.238	.333	.305	87	-1	-1	.857	-6	98	94	C23,S8		-0.5
1892	NY N	21	66	8	18	4	2	0	5	9	1	10	.273	.368	.394	133	3	2	.917	-2	252	0	O11R,C10		0.1
Total	6	341	1319	212	358	65	32	12	176	124	8	139	.271	.338	.397	114	27	50	.883	-29	113	72	O207L,C92,2b30,S12,3b4,1b3/P		-0.0

FIGGA, MIKE Michael Anthony B7.31.1970 Tampa FL BR/TR/6-0/200* [NYA89 44/1140] d9.16 Col Central Florida CC [DL 1996 NYA 30]

1997	NY A	2	4	0	0	0	0	0	0	0-0	0	3	.000	.000	.000	-99	-2	0-0	1.000	-0	95	102	/CD		-0.1
1998	NY A	1	4	1	1	0	0	0	0	0-0	0	1	.250	.250	.250	32	0	0-0	1.000	-0	0	0	/C		-0.1
1999	NY A	2	0	0	0	0	0	0	0	0-0	0	0	—	—	—	—	0	0-0	1.000	0	0	0	C2		0.0
	Bal A	41	86	12	19	4	0	1	5	2-0	0	27	.221	.236	.302	38	-8	0-2	.973	-4	81	79	C41		-1.1
	Year	43	86	12	19	4	0	1	5	2-0	0	27	.221	.236	.302	38	-8	0-2	.973	-4	80	78	C43		-1.1
Total	3	46	94	13	20	4	0	1	5	2-0	0	31	.213	.227	.287	32	-9	0-2	.975	-5	75	73	C45/D	30	-1.3

FIGGINS, CHONE Desmond Dechone B1.22.1978 Leary GA BB/TR/5-8/155* [ColN97 4/132] d8.25 OF(19/148/10)

2002	†Ana A	15	12	6	2	1	0	0	1	0-0	0	5	.167	.167	.250	9	-2	2-1	.941	-0	95	102	2b8		-0.1
2003	Ana A	71	240	34	71	9	4	0	27	20-0	0	38	.296	.345	.367	93	-2	13-7	1.000	-3	104	52	O47(3/44/0),2b14,S8,D3		-0.4
2004	†Ana A	148	577	83	171	22	17	5	60	49-0	0	94	.296	.350	.419	104	2	34-13	.944	-6	94	71	3b92,O57(1/54/2),2b20,S13/D		0.1
2005	†LA A	158	642	113	186	25	10	8	57	64-1	0	101	.290	.352	.397	101	1	62-17	.989	-1	110	90	O72(15/50/8),3b56,2b42,S4,D7		1.1
Total	4	392	1471	236	430	57	31	13	145	133-1	0	238	.292	.349	.400	100	-1	111-38	.992	-9	106	69	O176C,3b148,2b84,S25,D11		0.7

FIGUEROA, BIEN Bienvenido B2.7.1964 Santo Domingo, D.R. BR/TR/5-10/170 [StLN86 5/130] d5.17 Col Florida St.

| 1992 | StL N | 12 | 11 | 1 | 2 | 1 | 0 | 0 | 4 | 1-0 | 0 | 1 | .182 | .250 | .273 | 49 | -1 | 0-0 | .938 | -1 | 81 | 0 | S9,2b3 | | -0.1 |

FIGUEROA, JESUS Jesus Maria (Figueroa) B2.20.1957 Santo Domingo, D.R. BL/TL/5-10/160 d4.22

| 1980 | Chi N | 115 | 198 | 20 | 50 | 5 | 0 | 1 | 11 | 14-0 | 2 | 16 | .253 | .308 | .293 | 63 | -9 | 2-1 | .979 | 2 | 92 | 222 | O57(22/36/1) | | -0.8 |

FIGUEROA, LUIS Luis R. B2.16.1974 Bayamon, D.R. BB/TR/5-9/152 d6.27

| 2001 | Pit N | 4 | 2 | 0 | 0 | 0 | 0 | 0 | 0 | 0-0 | 0 | 1 | .000 | .000 | .000 | -98 | -1 | 0-0 | 1.000 | 1 | 224 | 222 | 2b3 | | 0.0 |

FILE, SAM Samuel Lawrence B5.18.1922 Chester PA d9.10

| 1940 | Phi N | 7 | 13 | 0 | 1 | 0 | 0 | 1 | 0 | 0-0 | 0 | 2 | .077 | .077 | .077 | -60 | -3 | 0 | .850 | 0 | 126 | 99 | S6/3 | | -0.3 |

FILIPOWICZ, STEVE Stephen Charles "Flip" B6.28.1921 Donora PA D2.21.1975 Wilkes-Barre PA BR/TR/5-8/195 d9.3 Col Fordham

1944	NY N	15	41	10	8	2	1	0	7	3	0	7	.195	.250	.293	52	-3	0	1.000	-1	94	0	O10(6/4/0)/C		-0.4
1945	NY N	35	112	14	23	5	0	2	16	4	1	13	.205	.239	.304	50	-8	0	.935	-3	80	57	O31(27/2/2)		-1.3
1948	Cin N	7	26	0	9	0	1	0	3	2	0	1	.346	.393	.423	125	1	0	1.000	0	83	220	O7L		0.0
Total	3	57	179	24	40	7	2	2	26	9	1	21	.223	.265	.318	61	-10	0	.961	-4	84	67	O48(40/6/2)/C		-1.7

FIMPLE, JACK John Joseph B2.10.1959 Darby PA BR/TR/6-2/185* [CleA80 29/702] d7.30 Col Humboldt St.

1983	†LA N	54	148	16	37	8	1	2	22	11-0	0	39	.250	.300	.358	82	-4	1-0	.989	11	116	136	C54		1.0
1984	LA N	12	26	2	5	1	0	0	3	1-0	0	6	.192	.214	.231	27	-3	0-0	.983	-1	83	153	C12		-0.3
1986	LA N	13	13	2	1	0	0	0	2	6-1	0	6	.077	.350	.077	32	-1	0-0	1.000	0	133	107	C7/12		0.0
1987	Cal A	13	10	1	2	0	0	0	1	1-0	0	2	.200	.273	.200	29	-1	0-0	.913	-1	92	161	C13		-0.1
Total	4	92	197	21	45	9	1	2	28	19-1	0	53	.228	.292	.315	70	-9	1-0	.986	10	111	138	C86/21		0.6

FINIGAN, JIM James Leroy B8.19.1928 Quincy IL D5.16.1981 Quincy IL BR/TR/5-11/175* d4.25 Col St. Ambrose

1954	Phi A☆	136	487	57	147	25	6	7	51	64	0	66	.302	.381	.421	120	15	2-8	.948	6	107	114	3b136		1.8
1955	KC A★	150	545	72	139	30	7	9	68	61-6	3	49	.255	.333	.385	92	-7	1-3	.975	-5	95	93	2b90,3b59		-0.6
1956	KC A	91	250	29	54	7	2	2	30-1	1	28	.216	.298	.284	55	-16	3-1	.969	1	94	108	2b52,3b32		-1.2
1957	Det A	64	174	20	47	4	2	0	17	23-2	1	18	.270	.357	.316	84	-3	1-1	.954	-1	99	95	3b59,2b3		-0.4
1958	SF N	23	25	3	5	2	0	0	1	3-1	1	5	.200	.310	.280	59	-1	0-0	.917	-1	97	106	2b8,3b4		-0.2
1959	Bal A	48	119	14	30	6	0	1	10	9-0	0	10	.252	.300	.328	75	-4	1-0	.959	1	104	79	3b42,2b6,S2		-0.3
Total	6	512	1600	195	422	74	17	19	168	190-10	6	176	.264	.342	.367	92	-16	8-13	.948	0	108	105	3b332,2b159,S2		-0.9

FINLEY, BOB Robert Edward B11.25.1915 Ennis TX D1.2.1986 W.Covina CA BR/TR/6-1/200 d7.4 Col SMU

1943	Phi N	28	81	9	21	2	0	1	7	4	0	10	.259	.294	.321	81	-2	0	.962	2	89	160	C24		0.1
1944	Phi N	94	281	18	70	11	1	2	21	12	5	25	.249	.292	.306	71	-11	1	.967	-2	103	89	C74		-0.9
Total	2	122	362	27	91	13	1	2	28	16	5	35	.251	.292	.309	73	-13	1	.966	-1	100	106	C98		-0.8

FINLEY, STEVE Steven Allen B3.12.1965 Union City TN BL/TL/6-2/180(175-195) [BalA87 13/325] d4.3 Col Southern Illinois

1989	Bal A	81	217	35	54	5	2	2	25	15-1	1	30	.249	.298	.318	76	-7	17-3	.986	-2	102	24	O76(14/23/41),D3	52	-0.8
1990	Bal A	142	464	46	119	16	4	3	37	32-3	2	53	.256	.304	.328	80	-13	22-9	.977	2	112	52	O133(21/44/73),D2		-1.3
1991	Hou N	159	596	84	170	28	10	8	54	42-5	2	65	.285	.331	.406	113	9	34-18	.985	2	99	151	O153(1/124/69)		1.0
1992	Hou N	162	607	84	177	29	13	5	55	58-6	3	63	.292	.355	.407	120	16	44-9	.993	1	104	92	O160C		2.4
1993	Hou N	142	545	69	145	15	13	8	44	28-1	0	65	.266	.304	.385	86	-14	19-6	.988	3	98	178	O140C	19	-0.8
1994	Hou N	94	373	64	103	16	5	11	33	28-0	2	52	.276	.329	.434	102	0	13-7	.982	1	96	184	O92C	20	0.2
1995	SD N	139	562	104	167	23	8	10	44	59-5	3	62	.297	.366	.420	110	8	36-12	.977	-5	93	113	O138C		0.8
1996	†SD N	161	655	126	195	45	9	30	95	56-5	5	87	.298	.354	.531	136	32	22-8	.982	-2	101	84	O160C		3.3
1997	SD N★	143	560	101	146	26	5	28	92	43-2	3	92	.261	.313	.475	111	5	15-3	.989	6	108	152	O140C	16	1.4
1998	†SD N	159	619	92	154	40	6	14	67	45-0	3	103	.249	.301	.401	89	-12	12-3	.981	1	101	130	O157C		-0.8
1999	†Ari N	156	590	100	156	32	10	34	103	63-7	3	94	.264	.336	.525	113	9	8-4	.995	-0	106	60	O155C/D		1.0
2000	Ari N★	152	539	100	151	27	5	35	96	65-7	3	87	.280	.361	.544	121	16	12-6	.992	-2	99	117	O148C,D2		1.6
2001	†Ari N	140	495	66	136	27	4	14	73	47-9	1	67	.275	.337	.430	91	-7	11-7	.994	-1	103	89	O131C/P		-0.6
2002	†Ari N	150	505	82	145	24	4	25	89	65-7	3	73	.287	.370	.499	118	12	16-4	.994	0	107	58	O144C		1.6
2003	Ari N	147	516	82	148	24	10	22	70	57-4	2	94	.287	.363	.500	113	10	15-8	.982	-7	87	131	O103C		0.4
2004	Ari N	104	404	61	111	16	1	23	48	40-1	1	52	.275	.338	.490	104	2	8-4	.991	-5	90	101	O103C		-0.1
	†LA N	58	224	31	59	12	0	13	46	21-0	1	30	.263	.324	.491	109	2	1-3	.993	-0	108	0	O55C/D		0.2
	Year	162	628	92	170	28	1	36	94	61-1	2	82	.271	.333	.490	106	4	9-7	.992	-5	96	66	O158C/D		0.1
2005	†LA A	112	406	41	90	20	3	12	54	26-3	2	71	.222	.271	.374	71	-18	8-4	.985	1	104	101	O104C,D5	23	-1.5
Total	17	2401	8877	1368	2426	425	112	297	1125	790-66	51	1240	.273	.334	.447	106	50	313-118	.987	-8	101	106	O2329(36/2158/183),D14/P	130	8.0

FINLEY, BILL William James B10.4.1863 New York NY D10.6.1912 Asbury Park NJ 5-3/170 d7.12 Col Columbia/Manhattan

| 1886 | NY N | 13 | 44 | 2 | 8 | 0 | 0 | 0 | 5 | 1 | | 8 | .182 | .200 | .182 | 17 | -4 | 2 | .800 | -2 | 0 | 0 | O8(0/7/1),C8 | | -0.5 |

FINN, NEAL Cornelius Francis "Mickey" B1.24.1904 Brooklyn NY D7.7.1933 Allentown PA BR/TR/5-11/168 d4.21

1930	Bro N	87	273	42	76	13	0	3	30	26	4	18	.278	.350	.359	73	-11	3	.948	-5	92	138	2b81		-1.2
1931	Bro N	118	413	46	113	22	2	0	45	21	3	42	.274	.314	.337	75	-14	2	.975	0	97	93	2b112		-0.7
1932	Bro N	65	189	22	45	8	1	0	14	11	1	15	.238	.284	.286	55	-12	2	.933	-4	118	95	3b50,2b2/S		-0.7
1933	Phi N	51	169	15	40	4	1	0	13	10	2	14	.237	.287	.272	54	-10	2	.964	1	108	107	2b51		-0.7
Total	4	321	1044	125	274	44	5	3	102	68	10	89	.262	.314	.323	67	-47	9	.964	-1	98	111	2b246,3b50/S		-3.3

YEAR	TM LG	G	AB	R	H	2B	3B	HR	RBI	BB-IB	HP	SO	AVG	OBP	SLG	AOPS	ABR	SB-CS	FA	FR	RNG	THR	GAMES AT POSITION	DL	BFW

FINNEY, HAL Harold Wilson B7.30.1905 Lafayette AL D12.20.1991 Lafayette AL BR/TR/5-11/170 d6.24 b-Lou

YEAR	TM LG	G	AB	R	H	2B	3B	HR	RBI	BB-IB	HP	SO	AVG	OBP	SLG	AOPS	ABR	SB-CS	FA	FR	RNG	THR	GAMES AT POSITION	BFW
1931	Pit N	10	26	2	8	1	0	0	2	0	1	1	.308	.333	.346	84	-1	1	1.000	0	109	54	C6	0.0
1932	Pit N	31	33	14	7	3	0	0	4	3	1	4	.212	.297	.303	63	-2	0	.971	1	77	54	C11	0.0
1933	Pit N	56	133	17	31	4	1	1	18	3	0	19	.233	.250	.301	57	-8	0	.993	-2	75	62	C47	-0.8
1934	Pit N	5	0	3	0	0	0	0	0	0	0		—	1.000	—	188	0	0	—	.0	0	0	/C	0.0
1936	Pit N	21	35	3	0	0	0	0	3	0	0	8	.000	.000	.000	-98	-10	0	.956	0	87	88	C14	-0.9
Total	5	123	227	39	46	8	1	1	27	6	3	32	.203	.233	.260	37	-21	0	.983	-0	81	64	C79	-1.7

FINNEY, LOU Louis Klopsche B8.13.1910 Buffalo AL D4.22.1966 Lafayette AL BL/TR/6-0/180 d9.12 Def 1943-45 b-Hal

YEAR	TM LG	G	AB	R	H	2B	3B	HR	RBI	BB-IB	HP	SO	AVG	OBP	SLG	AOPS	ABR	SB-CS	FA	FR	RNG	THR	GAMES AT POSITION	BFW
1931	Phi A	9	24	7	9	0	0	0	3	6	1		.375	.516	.458	149	2	0-0	1.000	1	124	134	O8R	0.3
1933	Phi A	74	240	26	64	12	2	3	32	13	1	17	.267	.307	.371	78	-8	1-3	.947	2	112	106	O63(17/1/46)	-1.0
1934	Phi A	92	272	32	76	11	4	1	28	14	0	17	.279	.315	.360	77	-11	4-3	.943	-0	104	70	O54(12/4/40),1b15	-1.4
1935	Phi A	109	410	45	112	11	6	0	31	18	2	18	.273	.307	.329	65	-23	7-2	.943	-1	102	81	O76(5/0/72),1b18	-2.8
1936	Phi A	151	653	100	197	26	10	1	41	47	3	22	.302	.351	.377	81	-20	7-9	.990	-5	80	95	1b78,O73(22/21/32)	-3.4
1937	Phi A	92	379	53	95	14	9	1	20	20	0	16	.251	.288	.343	59	-26	2-5	.989	-4	104	89	O50,O39(2/37/0)/2	-3.4
1938	Phi A	122	454	61	125	21	12	10	48	39	0	25	.275	.333	.441	94	-7	5-8	.990	-5	59	59	1b64,O46(19/21/6)	-2.0
1939	Phi A	9	22	1	3	0	0	0	1	2	0	1	.136	.208	.136	-10	-4	0-0	1.000	0	112	0	O4(0/3/1)	-0.4
	Bos A	95	249	43	81	18	3	1	46	24	0	11	.325	.385	.434	105	2	2-5	.986	-5	60	101	1b32,O24(3/16/5)	-0.7
	Year	104	271	44	84	18	3	1	47	26	0	11	.310	.370	.410	96	-1	2-5	.986	-5	60	101	1b32,O28(3/19/6)	-1.1
1940	Bos A★	130	534	73	171	31	15	5	73	33	0	13	.320	.360	.463	107	4	5-2	.975	-1	100	167	O69R,1b51	-0.5
1941	Bos A	127	497	83	143	24	10	4	53	38	1	17	.288	.340	.400	93	-6	4-2	.945	-4	98	80	O92(1/0/91),1b24	-1.9
1942	Bos A	113	397	58	113	16	7	3	61	29	1	11	.285	.335	.383	98	-2	3-3	.976	-1	99	108	O95(3/1/92),1b2	-1.0
1944	Bos A	68	251	37	72	11	2	0	32	23	0	7	.287	.347	.347	100	0	1-0	.987	-5	65	101	1b59,O2(1/0/1)	-0.8
1945	Bos A	2	2	0	0	0	0	0	0	0	0	0	.000	.000	.000	-98	-1	0-0	—	0			/H	-0.1
	StL A	57	213	24	59	8	4	2	22	21	1	6	.277	.345	.380	105	1	0-0	.986	0	100	131	O36(24/0/13),1b22/3	-0.2
	Year	59	215	24	59	8	4	2	22	21	1	7	.274	.342	.377	103	1	0-0	.986	0	100	131	O36(24/0/13),1b22/3	-0.3
1946	StL A	16	30	0	9	0	0	0	3	2	0	4	.300	.344	.300	77	-1	0-0	.938	0	106	205	O7(4/0/3)	-0.1
1947	Phi N	4	4	0	0	0	0	0	0	0	0	0	.000	.000	.000	-99	-1	0	—	0			/H	-0.1
Total	15	1270	4631	643	1329	203	85	31	494	329	10	186	.287	.336	.388	88	-101	39-45	.961	-26	102	95	O688(113/104/479),1b415/32	-19.5

FIORE, MIKE Michael Gary Joseph B10.11.1944 Brooklyn NY BL/TL/6-0/185* d9.21

YEAR	TM LG	G	AB	R	H	2B	3B	HR	RBI	BB-IB	HP	SO	AVG	OBP	SLG	AOPS	ABR	SB-CS	FA	FR	RNG	THR	GAMES AT POSITION	BFW
1968	Bal A	6	17	2	1	0	0	0	0	4-0	1	5	.059	.273	.059	5	-2	0-0	.943	-0	110	238	1b5/OL	-0.3
1969	KC A	107	339	53	93	14	1	12	35	84-4	2	63	.274	.420	.428	136	22	4-4	.988	12	159	75	1b91,O13(3/8/2)	2.7
1970	KC A	25	72	6	13	2	0	0	4	13-0	0	24	.181	.306	.208	44	-5	1-1	.986	1	118	70	1b20	-0.6
	Bos A	41	50	5	7	0	0	0	4	8-1	0	14	.140	.254	.140	12	-6	0-0	1.000	0	133	45	1b17,O2(1/0/1)	-0.7
	Year	66	122	11	20	2	0	0	8	21-1	0	28	.164	.285	.180	30	-11	1-1	.991	1	122	63	1b37,O2(1/0/1)	-1.3
1971	Bos A	51	62	9	11	2	0	1	6	12-1	0	14	.177	.311	.258	58	-3	0-3	1.000	-0	91	105	1b12	-0.5
1972	StL N	17	10	0	1	0	0	0	1	2-0	0	3	.100	.250	.100	3	-1	0-0	1.000	-0	0	270	1b6/OR	-0.2
	SD N	7	6	0	0	0	0	0	0	1-1	0	3	.000	.143	.000	-61	-1	0-0	—	0			/H	-0.1
	Year	24	16	0	1	0	0	0	1	3-1	0	6	.063	.211	.063	-20	-2	0-0	1.000	-0	0	270	1b6/OR	-0.3
Total	5	254	556	75	126	18	1	13	50	124-7	3	115	.227	.369	.333	96	4	5-8	.988	12	144	81	1b151,O17(5/8/4)	0.3

FIORENTINO, JEFF Jeffrey Philip B4.14.1983 Pembrroke Pines FL BL/TR/6-1/190 d5.12 Col Florida Atlantic

YEAR	TM LG	G	AB	R	H	2B	3B	HR	RBI	BB-IB	HP	SO	AVG	OBP	SLG	AOPS	ABR	SB-CS	FA	FR	RNG	THR	GAMES AT POSITION	BFW
2005	Bal A	13	44	7	11	2	0	1	5	2-0	0	10	.250	.277	.364	70	-2	1-0	1.000	-0	107	0	O12C	-0.2

FIROVA, DAN Daniel Michael B10.16.1956 Refugio TX BR/TR/6-0/185* [SeaA80*S2/39] d9.1 Col Texas-Pan American

YEAR	TM LG	G	AB	R	H	2B	3B	HR	RBI	BB-IB	HP	SO	AVG	OBP	SLG	AOPS	ABR	SB-CS	FA	FR	RNG	THR	GAMES AT POSITION	BFW
1981	Sea A	13	2	0	0	0	0	0	0	0-0	0	1	.000	.000	.000	-96	-1	0-0	1.000	-1	0	123	C13	-0.1
1982	Sea A	3	5	0	0	0	0	0	0	0-0	0	0	.000	.000	.000	-97	-1	0-0	.900	-1	0		C3	-0.1
1988	Cle A	1	0	0	0	0	0	0	0	0-0	0	0	—	—	—		0	0-0	—	-0	0	0	/C	0.0
Total	3	17	7	0	0	0	0	0	0	0-0	0	1	.000	.000	.000	-96	-2	0-0	.944	-1	0	75	C17	-0.2

FISCHER, WILLIAM William Charles B3.2.1891 New York NY D9.4.1945 Richmond VA BL/TR/6-0/174 d6.11

YEAR	TM LG	G	AB	R	H	2B	3B	HR	RBI	BB-IB	HP	SO	AVG	OBP	SLG	AOPS	ABR	SB-CS	FA	FR	RNG	THR	GAMES AT POSITION	BFW
1913	Bro N	62	165	16	44	9	4	1	12	10	1	5	.267	.313	.388	97	-1	0-1	.974	-2	96	100	C51	0.1
1914	Bro N	43	105	12	27	1	2	0	8	8	0	12	.257	.310	.305	81	-3	1	.958	0	90	115	C30	0.0
1915	Chi F	105	292	30	96	15	4	4	50	24	2	19	.329	.384	.449	142	12	5	.972	-4	115	94	C80	1.5
1916	Chi N	65	179	15	35	9	2	1	14	11	1	8	.196	.246	.285	57	-9	2	.973	0	101	111	C56	-0.5
	Pit N	42	113	11	29	7	1	1	6	10	1	3	.257	.323	.363	109	2	1	.974	1	91	109	C35	0.7
	Year	107	292	26	64	16	3	2	20	21	2	11	.219	.276	.315	76	-8	3	.973	1	97	110	C91	0.2
1917	Pit N	95	245	25	70	9	2	3	25	27	1	19	.286	.359	.376	121	7	11	.961	-11	71	99	C69,1b2	0.2
Total	5	412	1099	109	301	50	15	10	115	90	6	66	.274	.332	.374	107	8	20-1	.969	-15	95	103	C321,1b2	2.0

FISCHLIN, MIKE Michael Thomas B9.13.1955 Sacramento CA BR/TR/6-1/165* [NYA75 7/163] d9.3 Col Cal St.-Sacramento

YEAR	TM LG	G	AB	R	H	2B	3B	HR	RBI	BB-IB	HP	SO	AVG	OBP	SLG	AOPS	ABR	SB-CS	FA	FR	RNG	THR	GAMES AT POSITION	BFW
1977	Hou N	13	15	0	3	0	0	0	0	2-0	0	4	.200	.200	.200	8	-2	0-0	1.000	-1	111	37	S12	-0.2
1978	Hou N	44	86	3	10	1	0	0	0	4-1	1	9	.116	.165	.128	-18	-14	1-0	.928	-9	75	66	S41	-2.2
1980	Hou N	1	0	0	0	0	0	0	0	0-0	0	0	1.000	.000	.000	-99	0	0-0	1.000	-0	0		/S	0.0
1981	Cle A	22	43	3	10	1	0	0	5	3-0	0	6	.233	.277	.256	56	-2	3-2	.955	-2	81	73	S19/2	-0.3
1982	Cle A	112	276	34	74	12	1	0	21	34-0	2	36	.268	.351	.319	86	-4	9-5	.970	-8	97	80	S101,3b8,2b6/C	-0.2
1983	Cle A	95	225	31	47	5	2	2	23	26-0	2	32	.209	.294	.276	56	-13	9-4	.965	6	100	106	2b71,S15,3b4/D	-0.2
1984	Cle A	85	133	17	30	4	2	1	14	12-0	1	20	.226	.290	.308	64	-7	2-2	.981	2	100	99	2b55,3b17,S15	-0.2
1985	Cle A	73	60	12	12	4	1	0	2	5-0	1	7	.200	.262	.300	54	-4	0-1	.990	10	120	120	2b31,S22,1b6,3b3,D5	0.7
1986	NY A	71	102	9	21	2	0	0	3	8-0	0	29	.206	.261	.225	35	-9	0-1	.955	-4	103	87	S42,2b27	-1.1
1987	Atl N	1	0	0	0	0	0	0	0	0-0	0	0	—	—	—		0	0-0	—	0			/R	0.0
Total	10	517	941	109	207	29	6	3	68	92-1	5	142	.220	.291	.273	57	-55	24-13	.959	-7	95	83	S268,2b191,3b32,1b6,D6/C	-3.7

FISHBURN, SAM Samuel E. B5.15.1893 Haverhill MA D4.11.1965 Bethlehem PA BR/TR/5-9/157 d5.30 Col Lehigh

YEAR	TM LG	G	AB	R	H	2B	3B	HR	RBI	BB-IB	HP	SO	AVG	OBP	SLG	AOPS	ABR	SB-CS	FA	FR	RNG	THR	GAMES AT POSITION	BFW
1919	StL N	9	6	0	2	1	0	0	2	0	0	0	.333	.333	.500	158	0	0	1.000	0	0		/12	0.1

FISHEL, JOHN John Alan B11.8.1962 Fullerton CA BR/TR/5-11/185 [HouN85 9/222] d7.14 Col Cal St.-Fullerton

YEAR	TM LG	G	AB	R	H	2B	3B	HR	RBI	BB-IB	HP	SO	AVG	OBP	SLG	AOPS	ABR	SB-CS	FA	FR	RNG	THR	GAMES AT POSITION	BFW
1988	Hou N	19	26	1	6	0	0	1	2	3-0	0	6	.231	.310	.346	92	0	1-0	1.000	-1	29	0	O6(5/0/2)	-0.2

FISHER, GUS August Harris B10.21.1885 Pottsboro TX D4.8.1972 Portland OR BL/TR/5-10/175 d4.18

YEAR	TM LG	G	AB	R	H	2B	3B	HR	RBI	BB-IB	HP	SO	AVG	OBP	SLG	AOPS	ABR	SB-CS	FA	FR	RNG	THR	GAMES AT POSITION	BFW
1911	Cle A	70	203	20	53	6	3	0	12	7	5		.261	.302	.320	73	-8	6	.956	2	92	118	C58/1	-0.1
1912	NY A	4	10	1	1	0	0	0	0	0	0		.100	.100	.100	-40	-2	0	1.000	1	98	95	C4	-0.1
Total	2	74	213	21	54	6	3	0	12	7	5		.254	.293	.310	68	-10	6	.958	2	92	117	C62/1	-0.2

FISHER, CHARLES Charles d6.15

YEAR	TM LG	G	AB	R	H	2B	3B	HR	RBI	BB-IB	HP	SO	AVG	OBP	SLG	AOPS	ABR	SB-CS	FA	FR	RNG	THR	GAMES AT POSITION	BFW
1889	Lou AA	1	2	0	1	0	0	0	0	0	0	0	.500	.500	.500	189	0	0	—	-0	0	0	/OL	0.0

FISHER, CHARLES Charles G. (b Charles G. Fish) B3.10.1852 Boxford MA D2.18.1917 Eagle AK BL/TR/5-8/143 d6.7

YEAR	TM LG	G	AB	R	H	2B	3B	HR	RBI	BB-IB	HP	SO	AVG	OBP	SLG	AOPS	ABR	SB-CS	FA	FR	RNG	THR	GAMES AT POSITION	BFW
1884	KC U	10	40	3	8	2	0	0		1			.200	.200	.250	41	-4		.711	0	134	0	3b9/S	-0.3
	CP U	1	3	1	2	0	0	0		1			.667	.750	.667	336	1		.500	-0			/3	0.0
	Year	11	43	4	10	2	0	0		1			.233	.250	.279	68	-3		.702	-1	123	0	3b10/S	-0.3

FISHER, SHOWBOAT George Aloys B1.16.1899 Wesley IA D5.15.1994 St.Cloud MN BL/TR/5-10/170 d4.24

YEAR	TM LG	G	AB	R	H	2B	3B	HR	RBI	BB-IB	HP	SO	AVG	OBP	SLG	AOPS	ABR	SB-CS	FA	FR	RNG	THR	GAMES AT POSITION	BFW
1923	Was A	13	23	4	6	2	0	0	2	4	0	0-0	.261	.370	.348	95	0	0-0	.750	0	75	318	O5R	0.0
1924	Was A	15	41	7	9	1	0	0	6	6	0	6	.220	.319	.244	48	-2	2-0	.933	-1	94	0	O11R	-0.4
1930	†StL N	92	254	49	95	18	6	8	61	25	1	21	.374	.432	.587	139	16	4	.962	-2	95	94	O67(24/0/42)	0.9
1932	StL N	18	22	2	4	0	0	0	2	1	0	3	.182	.250	.182	13	-1	0-0	1.000	0	112	0	O5L	-0.3
Total	4	138	340	62	114	21	6	8	71	37	1	35	.335	.402	.503	119	10	6-0	.946	-3	94	95	O88(29/0/58)	0.2

FISHER, GEORGE George Cresse B8.20.1855 Wilmington DE D1.29.1937 Oakland CA BL d8.9

YEAR	TM LG	G	AB	R	H	2B	3B	HR	RBI	BB-IB	HP	SO	AVG	OBP	SLG	AOPS	ABR	SB-CS	FA	FR	RNG	THR	GAMES AT POSITION	BFW
1884	Cle N	6	24	2	3	0	0	0		0		3	.125	.125	.125	-20	-3		.897	-2	76	88	2b6/C	-0.5
	Wil U	8	29	0	2	0	0	0		0		6	.069	.069	.069	-56	-6		.818	-1	0	0	O6(0/6/1),S2	-0.7
Total	1	14	53	2	5	0	0	0		0		9	.094	.094	.094	-40	-9		.818	-3	0	0	O6(0/6/1),2b6,S2/C	-1.2

YEAR	TM	LG	G	AB	R	H	2B	3B	HR	RBI	BB-IB	HP	SO	AVG	OBP	SLG	AOPS	ABR	SB-CS	FA	FR	RNG	THR	GAMES AT POSITION	DL	BFW

FISHER, HARRY Harry Devereux B1.3.1926 Newbury ON, Can. D9.20.1981 Waterloo ON, Can. BL/TR/6-0/180* d9.16 ▲

1951	Pit	N	3	3	0	0	0	0	0	0	0	0	0	.000	.000	.000	-97	-1	0-0	—	0			/H		-0.1
1952	Pit	N	15	15	0	5	1	0	0	1	0	0	3	.333	.333	.400	100	1	0-0	1.000	-1	31	0	P8		0.0
Total	2		18	18	0	5	1	0	0	1	0	0	3	.278	.278	.333	66	0	0-0	1.000	-1	31	0	P8		-0.1

FISHER, RED John Gus B6.22.1887 Pittsburgh PA D1.31.1940 Louisville KY BL/TR/5-9/176 d4.25

| 1910 | StL | A | 23 | 72 | 5 | 9 | 2 | 1 | 0 | 3 | 8 | 1 | | .125 | .222 | .181 | 28 | -6 | 5 | .935 | -1 | 91 | 82 | O19(14/0/5) | | -0.9 |

FISHER, NEWT Newton "Ike" B6.28.1871 Nashville TN D2.28.1947 Norwood Park IL BR/TR/5-9.5/171 d5.17 b-Bob

| 1898 | Phi | N | 9 | 26 | 0 | 3 | 1 | 0 | 0 | 0 | 0 | | | .115 | .148 | .154 | -14 | -4 | 1 | .844 | -1 | 114 | 37 | C8/3 | | -0.4 |

FISHER, BOB Robert Taylor B11.3.1886 Nashville TN D8.4.1963 Jacksonville FL BR/TR/5-9.5/170 d6.3 b-Newt

1912	Bro	N	82	257	27	60	10	3	0	26	14	0	32	.233	.273	.296	58	-16	7	.917	-11	94	83	S74/23		-2.2
1913	Bro	N	132	474	42	124	11	10	4	54	10	1	43	.262	.278	.352	77	-17	16-16	.923	-20	90	**128**	S131		-3.1
1914	Chi	N	15	50	5	15	2	2	0	5	3	0	4	.300	.340	.420	126	1	2	.943	-1	105	61	S15		0.2
1915	Chi	N	147	568	70	163	22	5	5	53	30	3	51	.287	.326	.370	110	6	9-20	.933	-19	95	56	S145		-1.0
1916	Cin	N	61	136	9	37	4	3	0	11	8	0	14	.272	.313	.346	104	0	7	.905	-8	91	72	S29,2b6/OL		-0.7
1918	StL	N	63	246	36	78	11	3	2	20	15	0	11	.317	.356	.411	138	11	7	.979	16	119	121	2b63		3.0
1919	StL	N	3	11	0	3	1	0	0	1	0	0	2	.273	.273	.364	96	0		.900	0	91	144	2b3		0.0
Total	7		503	1742	189	480	61	26	11	170	80	4	157	.276	.309	.359	96	-15	48-36	.925	-42	93	86	S394,2b73/OL3		-3.8

FISHER, WILBUR Wilbur McCullough B7.18.1894 Green Bottom WV D10.24.1960 Welch WV BL/TR/6-0/174 d6.13 Col Marshall

| 1916 | Pit | N | 1 | 0 | 0 | 0 | 0 | 0 | 0 | 0 | 0 | 0 | 0 | .000 | .000 | .000 | -99 | 0 | | — | 0 | | | /H | | 0.0 |

FISHER, CHEROKEE William Charles B12.1845 Philadelphia PA D9.26.1912 New York NY BR/TR/5-9/164 d5.6 OF NA(5/14/66) ▲

1871	Rok	NA	**25**	123	24	28	3	3	1	22	3		1	.228	.246	.325	65	-5	1-2	**.927**	4	**147**	**181**	P24,1b2/2		0.1
1872	Bal	NA	46	225	39	52	10	3	1	36	2		5	.231	.238	.316	66	-10	1-1	.761	-5	113	176	P19,O19(0/3/17),3b18		-0.9
1873	Ath	NA	51	253	50	66	4	3	1	37	4		5	.261	.272	.312	68	-12	2-2	.743	-4	192	285	O46(1/2/43),P13,2b3/1		-0.2
1874	Har	NA	52	241	28	54	7	0	0	31	2		7	.224	.230	.253	52	-13	2-3	.833	-4	76	154	P39,O12(0/3/9),3b7,S2		-0.6
1875	Phi	NA	41	177	26	41	3	1	0	11	1		6	.232	.236	.260	69	-6	4-3	.896	-3	71	34	P41,O5(4/1/0)		-0.1
1876	Cin	N	35	129	12	32	1	0	0	4	0		8	.248	.248	.256	80	-2		.793	-3	75		P28,O11(0/7/4)/S1		-0.2
1877	Chi	N	1	4	0	0	0	0	0	0	0		2	.000	.000	.000	-89	-1		.667	-0	127	0	/3		-0.1
1878	Pro	N	1	3	0	0	0	0	0	0	0		0	.000	.000	.000	-99	0		1.000	0	54	0	/P		0.0
Total	5 NA		215	1019	167	241	27	10	3	137	12		24	.237	.245	.291	64	-46	10-11	.862	-4	91	110	P136,O82R,3b25,2b4,1b3,S2		-1.7
Total	3		37	136	12	32	1	0	0	4	0		10	.235	.235	.243	68	-3		.803	-3	74		P29,O11(0/7/4)/31S		-0.3

FISK, CARLTON Carlton Ernest "Pudge" B12.26.1947 Bellows Falls VT BR/TR/6-2/220(200-235) [BosA67*1/4] d9.18 HF2000 Col New Hampshire

1969	Bos	A	2	5	0	0	0	0	0	0	0-0		2	.000	.000	.000	-96	-1	0-0	1.000	-1	0		/C		-0.3
1971	Bos	A	14	48	7	15	2	1	2	6	1-0		10	.313	.327	.521	127	1	0-0	.975	-1	147	134	C14		0.1
1972	Bos	A★	131	457	74	134	28	**9**	22	61	52-6	4	83	.293	.370	.538	159	33	5-2	.984	6	105	95	C131		5.1
1973	Bos	A★	135	508	65	125	21	0	26	71	37-2	10	99	.246	.309	.441	103	7	1-2	.983	11	134	72	C131,D3		1.9
1974	Bos	A*	52	187	36	56	12	1	11	26	24-2	2	23	.299	.383	.551	156	14	5-1	.980	6	128	79	C50,D2	119	2.3
1975	†Bos	A	79	263	47	87	14	4	10	52	27-4	2	32	.331	.395	.529	147	16	4-3	.979	5	138	76	C71,D6	77	2.4
1976	Bos	A★	134	487	76	124	17	5	17	58	56-3	6	71	.255	.336	.415	107	5	12-5	.984	20	**129**	86	C133/D		3.3
1977	Bos	A★	152	536	106	169	26	3	26	102	75-3	9	85	.315	.402	.521	136	29	7-6	.987	12	163	80	C151		4.6
1978	Bos	A★	157	571	94	162	39	5	20	88	71-6	7	83	.284	.366	.475	123	19	7-2	.980	11	98	80	C154/OLD		3.9
1979	Bos	A	91	320	49	87	23	2	10	42	10-0	6	38	.272	.304	.450	96	-3	3-0	.982	-5	94	40	D42,C39/OL	37	-0.6
1980	Bos	A	131	478	73	138	25	3	18	62	36-6	**13**	62	.289	.353	.467	117	11	11-5	.983	-5	99	78	C115,O5L,1b3,3b3,D5		1.2
1981	Chi	A★	96	338	44	89	12	0	7	45	38-3	12	37	.263	.354	.361	109	6	3-2	.990	2	79	95	C92/13OL		1.2
1982	Chi	A★	135	476	66	127	17	3	14	65	46-7	8	60	.267	.336	.403	102	2	17-2	.994	4	93	100	C133,1b2		1.4
1983	†Chi	A	138	488	85	141	26	4	26	86	46-5	6	88	.289	.355	.518	132	21	9-6	.991	5	102	78	C133,D2		3.1
1984	Chi	A	102	359	54	83	20	1	21	43	26-4	5	60	.231	.289	.468	101	-0	6-0	.987	-7	90	79	C90,D5	22	-0.2
1985	Chi	A★	153	543	85	129	23	1	37	107	52-12	17	81	.238	.320	.488	113	9	17-9	.989	7	92	117	C130,D28		2.0
1986	Chi	A	125	457	42	101	11	0	14	63	22-2	6	92	.221	.263	.337	61	-27	2-4	.991	-8	73	108	C71,O31L,D22		-1.8
1987	Chi	A	135	454	68	116	22	1	23	71	39-8	4	72	.256	.321	.460	102	1	1-4	.990	12	116	89	C122,1b9,O2L,D7		1.5
1988	Chi	A	76	253	37	70	8	1	19	50	37-9	5	40	.277	.377	.542	155	19	0-0	.995	-2	83	90	C74	78	2.2
1989	Chi	A	103	375	47	110	25	2	13	68	36-8	3	60	.293	.356	.475	136	18	1-0	**.993**	-6	103	98	C90,D13	51	1.7
1990	Chi	A	137	452	65	129	21	0	18	65	61-8	7	73	.285	.378	.451	134	22	7-2	.994	12	99	117	C106,D13,1b12		4.1
1991	Chi	A★	134	460	42	111	25	0	18	74	32-4	7	86	.241	.299	.413	97	-3	1-2	.993	8	104	**132**	C106,D13,1b12		0.9
1992	Chi	A	62	188	12	43	4	1	3	21	23-5	1	38	.229	.313	.309	76	-6	3-0	.993	-2	86	109	C54,D2	59	-0.4
1993	Chi	A	25	53	2	10	0	0	1	4	2-0	1	11	.189	.228	.245	29	-6	0-1	1.000	-6	44	37	C25		-1.1
Total	24		2499	8756	1276	2356	421	47	376	1330	849-105	143	1386	.269	.341	.457	116	181	128-58	.988	96	107	91	C2226,D166,O41L,1b27,3b4	443	38.5

FISLER, WES Weston Dickson "Icicle" B7.5.1841 Camden NJ D12.25.1922 Philadelphia PA TR/5-6/137 d5.20

1871	Ath	NA	**28**	147	43	41	8	2	0	16	3		2	.279	.293	.361	88	-2	6-3	**.972**	1	24	80	1b26,2b2		0.0
1872	Ath	NA	**47**	244	49	85	13	3	0	48	4		4	.348	.359	.426	140	11	3-0	.889	7	108	92	2b47		1.1
1873	Ath	NA	44	218	44	75	11	4	1	41	2		5	.344	.350	.445	125	4	3-1	.855	2	107	136	2b36,1b10		0.3
1874	Ath	NA	37	180	26	59	12	1	0	22	0		1	.328	.328	.406	123	4	2-0	.953	5	194	210	1b28,2b9/OR		0.7
1875	Ath	NA	58	268	54	74	13	3	0	31	4		4	.276	.287	.347	107	1	1-4	.958	2	66	145	1b46,O10(0/1/9),2b5		0.2
1876	Phi	N	59	278	42	80	15	1	1	30	2		4	.288	.293	.360	117	5		.911	3	133	100	O24(0/15/9),2b21,1b14/S		0.6
Total	5 NA		214	1057	216	334	57	13	1	158	13		13	.316	.324	.397	118	19	15-8	.951	16	92	142	1b110,2b99,O11(0/1/10)		2.3

FITZBERGER, CHARLIE Charles Casper B2.13.1904 Baltimore MD D1.25.1965 Baltimore MD BL/TL/6-1.5/170 d9.11

| 1928 | Bos | N | 7 | 7 | 0 | 2 | 0 | 0 | 0 | 3 | 0 | | 3 | .286 | .286 | .286 | 52 | -1 | 0 | — | 0 | | | /H | | -0.1 |

FITZGERALD, DENNIS Dennis S. B3.1865 , England D10.16.1936 New Haven CT 5-10/160 d4.17

| 1890 | Phi | AA | 2 | 8 | 0 | 2 | 0 | 0 | 0 | | 0 | | | .250 | .250 | .250 | 48 | -1 | 0 | .667 | -2 | 67 | 0 | S2 | | -0.2 |

FITZ GERALD, ED Edward Raymond B5.21.1924 Santa Ynez CA BR/TR/6-0/180* d4.19 C5 Col St. Marys (CA)

1948	Pit	N	102	262	31	70	9	1	1	35	32	1	37	.267	.349	.336	84	-5	3	.961	-3	104	100	C96		-0.3
1949	Pit	N	75	160	16	42	7	0	2	18	8	1	27	.262	.302	.344	71	-7	1	.974	-2	125	115	C56		-0.6
1950	Pit	N	6	15	1	1	0	0	0	0	0		3	.067	.067	.133	-47	-3	0	.950	-0	119	106	C5		-0.3
1951	Pit	N	55	97	8	22	6	0	0	13	7	1	10	.227	.286	.289	53	-6	1-1	.965	-1	106	94	C38		-0.7
1952	Pit	N	51	73	4	17	1	0	1	7	7	0	15	.233	.300	.288	62	-4	0-2	1.000	-1	80	82	C18,3b2		-0.5
1953	Pit	N	6	17	2	2	1	0	0	1	0		2	.118	.118	.176	-25	-3	0-0	1.000	-1	49	173	C5		-0.4
	Was	A	88	288	23	72	13	0	3	39	19	1	34	.250	.299	.326	70	-13	2-1	.989	0	103	79	C85		-0.8
1954	Was	A	115	360	33	104	13	5	4	40	33	2	22	.289	.349	.386	108	3	0-1	.973	-14	86	68	C107		-0.6
1955	Was	A	74	236	28	56	3	1	4	19	25-0	3	23	.237	.317	.309	73	-9	0-1	.982	-7	83	115	C72		-1.3
1956	Was	A	64	148	15	45	8	0	2	12	20-1	0	16	.304	.387	.399	108	3	0-0	.974	-2	85	116	C50		0.3
1957	Was	A	45	125	14	34	8	0	1	13	10-1	1	9	.272	.331	.360	90	-2	2-0	.963	-7	69	111	C37		-0.7
1958	Was A		58	114	7	30	3	0	0	11	8-0	1	15	.263	.309	.289	68	-5	0-0	.970	-6	54	52	C21,1b5		-1.0
1959	Was A		19	62	5	12	3	0	0	5	4-0	0	8	.194	.242	.242	34	-6	0-0	1.000	-0	57	176	C16		-0.5
	Cle	A	49	129	12	35	6	1	4	12-1		2	14	.271	.343	.357	96	0	0-0	.978	-1	90	152	C45	30	0.1
	Year		68	191	17	47	9	1	4	17	16-1	2	22	.246	.311	.319	76	-6	0-0	.984	-1	80	159	C61		-0.4
Total	12		807	2086	199	542	82	10	19	217	185-3	12	235	.260	.323	.336	80	-57	9-6	.975	-43	92	100	C651,1b5,3b2	30	-7.3

FITZGERALD, HOWIE Howard Chumney "Lefty" B5.16.1902 Eagle Lake TX D2.27.1959 Matthews TX BL/TL/5-11.5/163 d9.17 Col Texas

1922	Chi	N	10	24	3	8	1	0	0	4	.3		2	.333	.407	.375	101	0	1-0	.818	-1	81	0	O6R		-0.1
1924	Chi	N	7	19	1	3	0	0	0	2	0		2	.158	.158	-.158	-3	-0	0-0	1.000	-1	64	0	O5(0/1/4)		-0.4
1926	Bos	A	31	97	11	25	2	0	0	8	5		7	.258	.294	.278	52	-7	1-4	.882	-3	66	99	O23(21/0/2)		-1.3
Total	3		48	140	15	36	3	0	0	14	8		11	.257	.297	.279	52	-10	2-4	.878	-5	69	70	O34(21/1/12)		-1.8

FITZGERALD, JUSTIN Justin Howard B6.26.1891 San Mateo CA D1.18.1945 San Mateo CA BL/TR/5-8/160 d6.20 Col Santa Clara

1911	NY	N	16	37	6	10	1	0	0	6	4	0		.270	.341	.297	74	-1	4	1.000	-1	73	94	O9L		-0.2
1918	Phi	N	66	133	21	39	8	0	0	6	13	1	6	.293	.361	.353	110	2	3	.966	-4	84	48	O59(34/2/19)		-0.3
Total	2		82	170	27	49	9	0	0	12	17	1	6	.288	.356	.341	102	1	7	.971	-4	82	56	O68(43/2/19)		-0.5

YEAR	TM LG	G	AB	R	H	2B	3B	HR	RBI	BB-IB	HP	SO	AVG	OBP	SLG	AOPS	ABR	SB-CS	FA	FR	RNG	THR	GAMES AT POSITION	DL	BFW

FITZGERALD, MATTY Matthew William B8.31.1880 Albany NY D9.22.1949 Albany NY BR/TR/6-0/185 d9.15
1906	NY N	4	6	2	4	0	0	0	2	0	0		.667	.667	.667	309	1	1	1.000	0	161	0	C3		0.2
1907	NY N	7	15	1	2	1	0	0	1	0	0		.133	.133	.200	4	-2	0	.952	-1	129	93	C6		-0.2
Total	2	11	21	3	6	1	0	0	3	0	0		.286	.286	.333	91	-1	1	.967	-1	138	66	C9		0.0

FITZGERALD, MIKE Michael Patrick B3.28.1964 Savannah GA BR/TR/6-1/200 [StLN84 S1/20] d6.23 Col Middle Georgia JC
| 1988 | StL N | 13 | 46 | 4 | 9 | 1 | 0 | 0 | 1 | 0-0 | 1 | 9 | .196 | .213 | .217 | 23 | -5 | 0-0 | .990 | -1 | 54 | 128 | 1b12 | | -0.8 |

FITZGERALD, MIKE Michael Roy B7.13.1960 Long Beach CA BR/TR/5-11/190(185-198) [NYN78 6/133] d9.13 OF(15/0/15)
1983	NY N	8	20	1	2	0	0	1	2	3-1	0	6	.100	.217	.250	29	-2	0-0	.957	1	52	195	C8		-0.1
1984	NY N	112	360	20	87	15	1	2	33	24-7	1	71	.242	.288	.306	69	-15	1-0	.995	7	100	99	C107		-0.4
1985	Mon N	108	295	25	61	7	1	5	34	38-12	2	55	.207	.297	.288	69	-12	5-3	.987	-7	75	81	C108		-1.6
1986	Mon N	73	209	20	59	13	1	6	37	27-6	1	34	.282	.364	.440	122	7	3-2	.993	-5	69	78	C71		0.5
1987	Mon N	107	287	32	69	11	0	3	36	42-7	1	54	.240	.338	.310	71	-11	3-4	.981	-7	70	67	C104/12	65	0.5
1988	Mon N	63	155	17	42	6	1	5	23	19-0	0	22	.271	.347	.419	114	3	2-2	.979	2	57	81	C47,O4(3/0/1)	14	-1.5
1989	Mon N	100	290	33	69	18	2	7	42	35-3	2	61	.238	.322	.386	100	1	3-4	.984	-7	72	103	C77,3b8,O6L		-0.3
1990	Mon N	111	313	36	76	18	1	9	41	60-2	2	60	.243	.365	.393	113	9	8-1	.990	-4	74	85	C98,O6(1/0/5)		1.2
1991	Mon N	71	198	17	40	5	2	4	28	22-4	0	35	.202	.278	.308	67	-9	4-2	.994	2	62	112	C54,1b3,O3R	49	-0.5
1992	Cal A	95	189	19	40	4	0	6	17	22-0	0	34	.212	.294	.317	70	-8	2-2	.990	-7	93	96	C74,O11(5/0/6),3b3,1b2/2D		-1.2
Total	10	848	2316	220	545	95	9	48	293	292-42	9	432	.235	.321	.346	87	-37	31-20	.988	-26	76	89	C748,O30L,3b11,1b6,2b2/D	128	-3.2

FITZGERALD, RAY Raymond Francis B12.5.1904 Chicopee MA D9.6.1977 Westfield MA BR/TR/5-9/168 d4.18
| 1931 | Cin N | 1 | 1 | 0 | 0 | 0 | 0 | 0 | 0 | 0 | 0 | 0 | .000 | .000 | .000 | -99 | 0 | 0 | — | 0 | | | /H | | 0.0 |

FITZMAURICE, SHAUN Shaun Earle B8.25.1942 Worcester MA BR/TR/6-0/180 d9.9 Col Notre Dame
| 1966 | NY N | 9 | 13 | 2 | 2 | 0 | 0 | 0 | 0 | 2-0 | 0 | 6 | .154 | .267 | .154 | 21 | -1 | 1-0 | 1.000 | 1 | 126 | 417 | O5(2/3/0) | | 0.0 |

FITZPATRICK, ED Edward Henry B12.9.1889 Lewistown PA D10.23.1965 Bethlehem PA BR/TR/5-8/165 d4.17 Mil 1918
1915	Bos N	105	303	54	67	19	3	0	24	43	14	36	.221	.344	.304	101	4	13-8	.967	-1	94	102	2b71,O29(0/7/22)		0.3
1916	Bos N	83	216	17	46	8	0	1	18	15	5	26	.213	.280	.264	70	-7	5	.950	-10	81	97	2b46,O28(2/3/23)		-2.0
1917	Bos N	63	178	20	45	8	4	0	17	12	5	22	.253	.318	.343	109	2	4	.929	-11	86	25	2b22,O19(4/6/7),3b15		-1.0
Total	3	251	697	91	158	35	7	1	59	70	24	84	.227	.319	.301	94	-1	22-8	.956	-22	88	88	2b139,O76(6/16/52),3b15		-2.7

FITZSIMMONS, TOM Thomas William B4.6.1890 Oakland CA D12.20.1971 Oakland CA BR/TR/6-1/190 d6.12 Col St. Marys (CA)
| 1919 | Bro N | 4 | 4 | 1 | 0 | 0 | 0 | 0 | 0 | 1 | 0 | 0 | .000 | .200 | .000 | -36 | -1 | 0 | .500 | -1 | 36 | 0 | 3b4 | | -0.2 |

FLACK, MAX Max John B2.5.1890 Belleville IL D7.31.1975 Belleville IL BL/TL/5-7/148 d4.16
1914	Chi F	134	502	66	124	15	3	2	39	51	6	48	.247	.324	.301	75	-25	37	.973	-2	98	85	O133(112/0/23)		-3.5
1915	Chi F	141	523	88	164	20	14	3	45	40	2	21	.314	.366	.423	129	10	37	.969	5	97	137	O138(61/0/81)		0.9
1916	Chi N	141	465	65	120	14	3	3	20	42	0	43	.258	.320	.320	87	-6	24-19	.991	3	91	138	O136R		-1.3
1917	Chi N	131	447	65	111	18	7	1	21	51	0	34	.248	.325	.320	91	-3	17	.947	-5	97	97	O117(40/6/77)		-1.3
1918	†Chi N	123	478	74	123	17	10	4	41	56	6	19	.257	.343	.360	111	8	17	.978	-1	94	102	O121R		0.0
1919	Chi N	116	469	71	138	20	4	6	35	34	3	13	.294	.346	.392	121	12	18	.986	-0	94	109	O116R		0.6
1920	Chi N	135	520	85	157	30	6	4	49	52	7	15	.302	.373	.406	121	17	13-19	.967	-5	90	99	O132(0/1/131)		0.1
1921	Chi N	133	572	80	172	31	4	6	37	32	4	15	.301	.342	.400	96	-3	17-11	.989	-0	97	106	O130R		-1.4
1922	Chi N	17	54	7	12	1	0	0	6	2	0	4	.222	.250	.241	27	-6	2-1	.933	-2	101		O15R		-0.8
	StL N	66	267	46	78	12	1	2	21	31	1	11	.292	.368	.367	95	-1	3-5	.968	-3	94	62	O66(0/1/65)		-1.0
	Year	83	321	53	90	13	1	2	27	33	1	15	.280	.349	.346	83	-7	5-6	.961	-5	95	51	O81(0/1/80)		-1.8
1923	StL N	128	505	82	147	16	9	3	28	41	3	16	.291	.348	.376	93	-5	7-8	.951	-5	100	58	O121R		-2.0
1924	StL N	67	209	31	55	11	3	2	21	21	0	5	.263	.330	.373	90	-3	3-2	.971	2	99	162	O52R		-0.5
1925	StL N	79	241	23	60	11	3	2	28	21	0	9	.249	.309	.344	65	-13	5-3	.991	1	100	116	O59(5/0/54)		-1.5
Total	12	1411	5252	783	1461	212	72	35	391	474	32	253	.278	.342	.366	99	-18	200-71	.972	-10	96	103	O1336(218/8/1122)		-11.7

FLAGER, WALLY Walter Leonard B11.3.1921 Chicago Heights IL D12.16.1990 Keizer OR BL/TL/5-11/160 d4.17
1945	Cin N	21	52	5	11	1	0	0	6	8	0	5	.212	.317	.231	55	-3	0	.933	-4	85	58	S15		-0.6
	Phi N	49	168	21	42	4	1	0	2	15	1	15	.250	.323	.321	82	-4	1	.946	5	105	91	S48/2		0.4
	Year	70	220	26	53	5	1	0	2	21	1	20	.241	.321	.300	75	-7	1	.943	0	101	84	S63/2		-0.2

FLAGSTEAD, IRA Ira James "Pete" B9.22.1893 Montague MI D3.13.1940 Olympia WA BR/TR/5-9/165 d7.20 Mil 1918
1917	Det A	4	4	0	4	0	0	0	0	0	0	1	1.000	1.000	1.000	-99	-1	0	—	-0	0	0	O2R		-0.1
1919	Det A	97	287	43	95	22	3	5	41	35	7	39	.331	.416	.481	155	23	6	.951	1	93	127	O83R		2.0
1920	Det A	110	311	40	73	13	5	3	35	37	1	27	.235	.318	.338	76	-11	3-4	.967	3	105	113	O82(1/6/75)		-1.3
1921	Det A	85	259	40	79	16	2	0	31	21	6	21	.305	.371	.382	93	-2	8-4	.903	-7	90	33	S55,O12(6/2/5),2b8/3		-0.3
1922	Det A	44	91	21	28	5	3	3	8	14	2	16	.308	.411	.527	148	7	0-1	.967	0	96	132	O32(8/9/15)		0.5
1923	Det A	1	1	0	0	0	0	0	0	0	0	0	.000	.000	.000	-99	-0	0	—	0			/H		0.0
	Bos A	109	382	55	119	23	4	8	53	37	5	26	.312	.380	.455	119	10	7-10	.965	14	101	213	O102(0/3/99)/S		1.3
	Year	110	383	55	119	23	4	8	53	37	5	26	.311	.379	.454	118	10	7-10	.965	14	101	213	O102(0/3/99)/S		1.3
1924	Bos A	149	560	106	172	35	7	5	43	77	11	41	.307	.401	.421	112	14	10-13	.975	-10	94	64	O144(0/143/1)		-0.4
1925	Bos A	148	572	84	160	38	2	6	61	63	5	30	.280	.356	.385	88	-9	5-6	.976	14	108	154	O144C		-0.2
1926	Bos A	98	415	65	124	31	7	3	31	36	6	22	.299	.363	.429	110	6	4-6	.982	2	96	133	O98C		0.2
1927	Bos A	131	466	83	133	26	8	4	69	57	9	25	.285	.374	.401	103	3	12-2	.986	4	97	145	O129(0/128/1)		0.4
1928	Bos A	140	510	84	148	41	4	1	39	60	1	23	.290	.366	.392	101	3	12-9	.973	2	99	123	O135C		-0.1
1929	Bos A	14	36	9	11	2	0	0	3	5	0	7	.306	.390	.361	97	0	1-3	.955	-1	97	0	O13(13/1/0)		-0.2
	Was A	18	39	5	7	1	0	0	9	4	0	5	.179	.256	.205	20	-5	1-0	.971	4	103	353	O11(1/10/0)		-0.2
	Year	32	75	14	18	3	0	0	12	9	0	6	.240	.321	.280	57	-5	2-3	.965	2	103		O24(14/11/0)		-0.4
	Pit N	26	50	8	14	2	1	0	6	4	0	2	.280	.333	.360	70	-2	1	1.000	-0	103	0	O9(6/1/2)		-0.3
1930	Pit N	44	156	21	39	7	4	2	21	17	0	9	.250	.324	.385	70	-8	1	.961	-1	89	141	O40(21/15/5)		-1.0
Total	14	1218	4139	644	1202	262	50	40	450	467	53	288	.290	.370	.407	103	29	71-58	.974	25	99	134	O1036(56/695/288),S56,2b8/3		0.3

FLAHERTY, JOHN John Timothy B10.21.1967 New York NY BR/TR/6-1/205* d4.12 Col George Washington
1992	Bos A	35	66	3	13	2	0	2	3-0		1	6	.197	.229	.227	27	-7	0-0	.982	-6	107	83	C34		-1.2
1993	Bos A	13	25	3	3	2	0	0	2	2-0	1	6	.120	.214	.200	11	-3	0-0	1.000	-2	67	146	C13		-0.5
1994	Det A	34	40	2	6	1	0	0	4	1-0	0	11	.150	.167	.175	-10	-7	0-1	1.000	0	69	111	C33/D		-0.5
1995	Det A	112	354	39	86	22	1	11	40	18-0	3	47	.243	.284	.404	77	-13	0-0	.982	-12	88	80	C112		-1.7
1996	Det A	47	152	18	38	12	0	4	23	8-1	1	25	.250	.290	.408	74	-6	1-0	.981	-9	122	79	C46		-1.2
	†SD N	72	264	22	80	12	0	9	41	9-1	2	36	.303	.327	.451	108	2	2-3	.990	-8	96	111	C72		-0.2
1997	SD N	129	439	38	120	21	1	9	46	33-7	0	62	.273	.323	.387	91	-7	4-4	.987	-26	71	120	C124		-2.6
1998	TB A	91	304	21	63	11	0	3	24	22-0	1	46	.207	.261	.273	39	-28	0-5	.993	6	129	105	C91	25	-1.7
1999	TB A	117	446	53	124	19	0	14	71	19-0	6	64	.278	.310	.415	83	-13	0-2	.993	7	95	147	C115/D		0.1
2000	TB A	109	394	30	103	15	0	10	39	20-2	0	57	.261	.296	.376	70	-20	0-0	.993	-3	76	111	C108		-1.4
2001	TB A	78	248	20	59	17	1	4	29	10-1	1	33	.238	.269	.363	66	-13	1-0	.986	-7	89	77	C78		-1.5
2002	TB A	76	281	27	73	20	0	4	33	15-0	1	50	.260	.296	.374	79	-8	2-2	.992	-8	85	136	C75		-0.5
2003	†NY A	40	105	16	28	8	0	4	14	4-1	1	19	.267	.297	.457	97	-1	0-0	.991	-6	93	116	C40		-1.1
2004	NY A	47	127	11	32	9	0	6	16	5-2	1	25	.252	.286	.465	91	-2	0-2	.989	1	83	77	C46		0.0
2005	†NY A	47	127	10	21	5	0	2	11	6-0	1	26	.165	.206	.252	22	-15	0-0	.994	7	59	122	C45/1		-0.5
Total	14	1047	3372	309	849	176	3	80	395	175-15	19	514	.252	.290	.377	73	-141	10-19	.989	-67	90	109	C1032,D2/1	25	-14.5

FLAHERTY, MARTIN Martin John B9.24.1853 Worcester MA D6.10.1920 Providence RI BL/TL d8.18
| 1881 | Wor N | 1 | 2 | 0 | 0 | 0 | 0 | 0 | 0 | 0 | | 0 | .000 | .000 | .000 | -95 | 0 | | .000 | -1 | 0 | 0 | /O(1/1/0) | | -0.1 |

FLAHERTY, PAT Patrick Henry B1.31.1866 St.Louis MO D1.28.1946 Chicago IL BR/5-9/166 d7.11
| 1894 | Lou N | 39 | 150 | 15 | 43 | 6 | 3 | 0 | 15 | 9 | 1 | 7 | .287 | .331 | .360 | 71 | -7 | 2 | .852 | -2 | 99 | 117 | 3b39 | | -0.6 |

FLAHERTY, PATSY Patrick Joseph B6.29.1876 Mansfield PA D1.23.1968 Alexandria LA BL/TL/5-8/165 d9.8 ▲
1899	Lou N	7	24	3	5	1	0	0	6	3	0		.208	.296	.333	73	-1	0	.692	-1	71	0	P5,O2R		-0.1
1900	Pit N	4	9	0	1	0	0	0	0	1	0		.111	.200	.111	-13	-1	0	1.000	1	181	0	P4		0.0
1903	Chi A	40	102	7	14	4	0	0	5	5	0		.137	.178	.176	7	-3	4	.914	2	121	241	P40		0.0

YEAR	TM LG	G	AB	R	H	2B	3B	HR	RBI	BB-IB	HP	SO	AVG	OBP	SLG	AOPS	ABR	SB-CS	FA	FR	RNG	THR	GAMES AT POSITION	DL	BFW
1904	Chi A	5	12	1	4	1	0	0	0	4	0		.333	.500	.417	199	3	0	.880	1	129	0	P5		0.0
	Pit N	36	104	9	22	3	4	2	19	8	0		.212	.268	.375	95	-1	0	.965	4	132	146	P29,O2C		0.2
1905	Pit N	30	76	7	15	4	2	0	4	3	0		.197	.228	.303	56	-4	0	.894	2	133	69	P27,O2(0/1/1)		0.0
1907	Bos N	41	115	9	22	3	2	2	11	2	1		.191	.212	.304	62	-6	1	.907	3	126	316	P27,O8(6/0/2)		-0.1
1908	Bos N	32	86	8	12	0	2	0	5	6	0		.140	.196	.186	22	0	2	.961	2	114	152	P31		0.0
1910	Phi N	2	2	0	1	0	0	0	0	0	0		.500	.500	.500	186	0	0	—	0	0	0	/POC		0.0
1911	Bos N	38	94	9	27	3	2	2	20	8	0	11	.287	.343	.426	106	0	2	.933	-3	74	82	O19(1/11/7),P4		-0.3
Total	9	235	624	53	123	19	13	6	70	40	1	11	.197	.247	.298	63	-13	9	.921	10	124	173	P173,O34(7/15/12)		-0.3

FLAIR, AL   Albert Dell "Broadway"   B7.24.1916 New Orleans LA   D7.26.1988 New Orleans LA   BL/TL/6-4/195   d9.6   Mil 1942-45   Col Louisiana St.

YEAR	TM LG	G	AB	R	H	2B	3B	HR	RBI	BB-IB	HP	SO	AVG	OBP	SLG	AOPS	ABR	SB-CS	FA	FR	RNG	THR	GAMES AT POSITION	DL	BFW
1941	Bos A	10	30	3	6	2	1	0	2	1	0		.200	.226	.333	45	-3	1-1	1.000	-0	85	86	1b8		-0.3

FLANAGAN, CHARLIE   Charles James   B12.31.1891 Oakland CA   D1.8.1930 San Francisco CA   BR/TR/6-0/175   d7.9

| 1913 | StL A | 4 | 3 | 0 | 0 | 0 | 0 | 0 | 0 | 1 | 0 | | .000 | .250 | .000 | -26 | 0 | 0 | — | -0 | 0 | 0 | /3OL | | -0.1 |

FLANAGAN, ED   Edward J. "Sleepy"   B9.15.1861 Lowell MA   D11.10.1926 Lowell MA   6-1/190   d4.16

1887	Phi AA	19	80	12	20	5	0	1	10	3	1		.250	.286	.350	77	-3	3	.948	-1	82	100	1b19		-0.4
1889	Lou AA	23	88	11	22	7	3	0	8	7	0	11	.250	.305	.398	101	0	1	.953	-1	116	71	1b23		-0.3
Total	2	42	168	23	42	12	3	1	18	10	1	11	.250	.296	.375	89	-3	4	.951	-2	101	84	1b42		-0.7

FLANAGAN, STEAMER   James Paul   B4.20.1881 Kingston PA   D4.21.1947 Wilkes-Barre PA   BL/TL/6-1/185   d9.25   Col Notre Dame

| 1905 | Pit N | 7 | 25 | 7 | 7 | 3 | 1 | 0 | 3 | 1 | 0 | | .280 | .308 | .400 | 108 | 0 | 3 | 1.000 | 0 | 0 | 0 | O5C | | 0.0 |

FLANNERY, JOHN   John Michael   B1.25.1957 Long Beach CA   BR/TR/6-3/173   [AnaA75 9/193]   d9.2

| 1977 | Chi A | 7 | 2 | 1 | 0 | 0 | 0 | 0 | 0 | 1-0 | 0 | | .000 | .333 | .000 | 0 | 0 | 0-0 | 1.000 | 0 | 117 | 140 | S4/3D | | 0.0 |

FLANNERY, TIM   Timothy Earl   B9.29.1957 Tulsa OK   BL/TR/5-11/175(170-181)   [SDN78 6/135]   d9.3   C7   Col Chapman

1979	SD N	22	65	2	10	0	1	0	4	4-1	2	5	.154	.222	.185	14	-8	0-0	.991	3	113	132	2b21		-0.4
1980	SD N	95	292	15	70	12	0	0	25	18-4	0	30	.240	.283	.281	62	-15	2-2	.988	3	105	110	2b53,3b41		-1.2
1981	SD N	37	67	4	17	4	1	0	6	2-1	0	6	.254	.268	.343	81	-2	1-0	.967	-4	78	196	3b15,2b7		-0.6
1982	SD N	122	379	40	100	11	7	0	30	30-10	2	23	.264	.317	.330	88	-7	1-0	.974	-19	92	83	2b104,3b5,S2		-2.1
1983	SD N	92	214	24	50	7	3	3	19	20-8	5	23	.234	.309	.336	83	-5	2-2	.969	6	114	197	3b52,2b21,S7		0.1
1984	†SD N	86	128	24	35	3	3	2	10	12-1	3	17	.273	.347	.391	107	1	4-1	.944	-6	99	55	2b22,3b14,S14		-0.4
1985	SD N	126	384	50	108	14	3	1	40	58-1	9	39	.281	.386	.341	107	7	2-5	.977	-19	89	106	2b121/3		-0.8
1986	SD N	134	368	48	103	11	2	3	28	54-4	5	61	.280	.378	.345	103	4	3-6	.993	3	96	96	2b108,3b23,S8		1.1
1987	SD N	106	276	23	63	5	1	0	20	42-4	2	30	.228	.332	.254	101	-14	2-4	.972	-0	100	90	2b84,3b8,S2	25	-1.2
1988	SD N	79	170	16	45	5	4	0	19	24-1	4	32	.265	.365	.341	107	3	3-2	.972	5	93	121	3b51,2b2/S	24	-0.2
1989	SD N	73	130	9	30	5	0	0	8	13-0	1	20	.231	.299	.269	64	-6	2-0	.920	1	110	77	3b33/2	15	-0.5
Total	11	972	2473	255	631	77	25	9	209	277-35	32	293	.255	.335	.317	86	-42	22-22	.980	-38	96	95	2b544,3b243,S34	64	-6.2

FLASKAMPER, ROY   Raymond Harold "Flash"   B10.31.1901 St.Louis MO   D2.3.1978 San Antonio TX   BB/TR/5-7/140   d8.16

| 1927 | Chi A | 26 | 95 | 12 | 21 | 5 | 0 | 0 | 8 | 22 | 0 | 8 | .221 | .284 | .274 | 40 | -9 | 0-0 | .962 | -1 | 96 | 80 | S25 | | -0.7 |

FLEET, FRANK   Frank H.   B1848 New York NY   D6.13.1900 New York NY   d10.18 ▲

1871	Mut NA	1	6	1	2	0	0	0	1	0		0	.333	.333	.333	101	0	0-0	1.000	1	322	0	/P		0.0
1872	Eck NA	13	53	9	12	1	0	0	6	0		2	.226	.226	.245	53	-2	1-0	.800	2	107	56	3b10,2b2,O2(0/1/1)		0.0
1873	Res NA	22	89	11	23	1	0	0	10	1		3	.258	.267	.292	71	-2	0-2	.808	3	105	88	S9,2b8,P3,3b3/1		-0.1
1874	Atl NA	22	97	18	22	0	0	0	10	1		1	.227	.235	.227	55	-4	1-0	.759	-5			C13,2b11/OL		-0.7
1875	StL NA	4	16	1	1	0	0	0	1	0		0	.063	.063	.063	-62	-2	0-0	.900	0	124	479	P3/3OC		-0.1
	Atl NA	26	111	13	25	2	0	0	9	1		1	.225	.232	.243	75	-2	0-0	.719	-9			C11,2b10,S9,P2/3		-1.0
	Year	30	127	14	26	2	0	0	10	1		1	.205	.211	.220	57	-4	0-0	.719	-8			C11,2b10,S9,P5,3b2/OC		-1.0
Total	5 NA	88	372	53	85	6	0	0	37	3		7	.228	.235	.245	61	-12	2-2	.772	-7			2b31,C24,S18,3b15,P9,O4(1/2/1)/1		-1.9

FLEITAS, ANGEL   Angel Felix Husta   B11.10.1914 Los Abreus, Cuba   BR/TR/5-9/160   d7.5

| 1948 | Was A | 15 | 13 | 1 | 1 | 0 | 0 | 0 | 1 | 3 | 0 | 5 | .077 | .250 | .077 | -11 | -2 | 0-2 | .952 | 1 | 132 | 0 | S7 | | -0.2 |

FLEMING, LES   Leslie Harvey "Moe"   B8.7.1915 Singleton TX   D3.5.1980 Cleveland TX   BL/TL/5-10/185   d4.22   Col St. Marys (TX)

1939	Det A	8	16	0	0	0	0	0	1	0	0	4	.000	.000	.000	-93	-5	0-0	1.000	0	113	0	O3(1/0/2)		-0.5
1941	Cle A	2	8	0	2	1	0	0	0	0	0	0	.250	.250	.375	67	0	0-0	1.000	-0	70	171	1b2		-0.1
1942	Cle A	156	548	71	160	27	4	14	82	106	6	57	.292	.412	.432	146	40	6-8	.993	-7	84	116	1b156		1.7
1945	Cle A	42	140	18	46	10	2	3	22	11	1	5	.329	.382	.493	160	10	0-0	.938	-1	102	68	O33R,1b5		0.8
1946	Cle A	99	306	40	85	17	5	8	42	50	2	42	.278	.383	.444	140	18	1-0	.984	3	113	87	1b80/OR		1.8
1947	Cle A	103	281	39	68	14	2	4	43	53	0	42	.242	.362	.349	101	2	0-0	.989	3	115	123	1b77		0.3
1949	Pit N	24	31	0	8	2	0	0	7	6	1	2	.258	.395	.387	108	0	0-0	1.000	-1	0	105	1b5		-0.1
Total	7	434	1330	168	369	69	15	29	199	226	10	152	.277	.386	.417	131	65	7-8	.990	-3	98	110	1b325,O37(1/0/36)		3.9

FLEMING, TOM   Thomas Vincent "Sleuth"   B11.20.1873 Philadelphia PA   D12.26.1957 Boston MA   BL/TL/5-11/155   d9.19

1899	NY N	22	77	9	16	1	1	0	4	1	0		.208	.218	.247	28	-8	1	.909	1	177	0	O22C		-0.8
1902	Phi N	5	16	2	6	0	0	0	2	1	0		.375	.412	.375	143	1	0	1.000	1	396	0	O5R		0.1
1904	Phi N	3	6	0	0	0	0	0	0	0	0		.000	.000	.000	-99	-1	0	1.000	1	994	0	/OR		-0.1
Total	3	30	99	11	22	1	1	0	6	2	0		.222	.238	.253	39	-8	1	.920	2	242	0	O28(0/22/6)		-0.8

FLETCHER, ART   Arthur   B1.5.1885 Collinsville IL   D2.6.1950 Los Angeles CA   BR/TR/5-10.5/170   d4.15   M5/C19

1909	NY N	33	98	7	21	0	1	0	6	1	2		.214	.238	.235	46	-7	1	.893	-1	93	116	S22,2b7,3b6		-0.7
1910	NY N	51	125	12	28	2	1	0	13	4	0	9	.224	.248	.256	47	-9	9	.895	-5	82	90	S22,2b11,3b11		-1.4
1911	†NY N	112	326	73	104	17	8	1	37	30	14	29	.319	.400	.429	128	13	20	.926	5	102	88	S74,3b21,2b13		2.4
1912	†NY N	129	419	64	118	17	9	1	57	16	14	29	.282	.330	.372	89	-8	16	.927	15	108	131	S126,2b2/3		1.5
1913	†NY N	136	538	76	160	20	9	4	71	24	15	35	.297	.345	.390	109	5	32-18	.932	-6	102	96	S136		1.0
1914	NY N	135	514	62	147	26	4	3	79	22	13	8	.286	.332	.379	115	8	15	.922	6	105	101	S135		2.5
1915	NY N	149	562	59	143	17	7	3	74	6	14	36	.254	.280	.326	88	-11	12-18	.936	35	118	127	S149		3.3
1916	NY N	133	500	53	143	23	8	3	66	13	14	36	.286	.323	.382	122	11	15	.922	22	114	105	S133		4.7
1917	†NY N	151	557	70	145	24	5	4	56	23	19	26	.260	.312	.343	104	3	12	.956	28	114	119	S151		4.5
1918	NY N	124	468	51	123	20	2	0	47	18	15	26	.263	.311	.314	93	-4	12	.959	25	113	116	S124		3.3
1919	NY N	127	488	54	135	20	5	3	54	9	7		.277	.300	.357	98	-3	6	.944	25	119	95	S127		3.4
1920	NY N	41	171	21	44	7	2	0	24	1	5	15	.257	.282	.322	74	-6	3-2	.914	1	112	94	S41		-0.3
	Phi N	102	379	36	112	25	7	4	38	15	4	28	.296	.329	.430	112	5	4-6	.958	14	109	93	S102		2.6
	Year	143	550	57	156	32	9	4	62	16	9	43	.284	.315	.396	100	-1	7-8	.945	14	110	93	S143		2.3
1922	Phi N	110	396	46	111	20	5	7	53	21	5	14	.280	.325	.409	80	-12	3-2	.939	6	111	102	S106		0.4
Total	13	1533	5541	684	1534	238	77	32	675	203	141	348	.277	.319	.365	100	-15	160-46	.939	169	110	108	S1448,3b39,2b33		27.2

FLETCHER, DARRIN   Darrin Glen   B10.3.1966 Elmhurst IL   BL/TR/6-1/199*   [LAN87 6/144]   d9.10   f-Tom   Col Illinois

1989	LA N	5	8	1	4	0	0	1	2	1-0	0		.500	.556	.875	307	2	0-0	1.000	0	0	0	C5		0.3
1990	LA N	2	1	0	0	0	0	0	0	0-0	0		1.000	1.000	1.000	-99	0	0-0	—	-0	0	0	/C		-0.1
	Phi N	9	22	3	3	1	0	0	1	1-0	0		.136	.174	.182	-2	-3	0-0	1.000	-1	59	0	C6		-0.4
	Year	11	23	3	3	1	0	0	1	1-0	0	6	.130	.167	.174	-6	-3	0-0	1.000	-2	58	0	C7		-0.5
1991	Phi N	46	136	5	31	8	0	1	12	5-0	0	15	.228	.255	.309	58	-8	0-1	.992	0	99	80	C45		-0.6
1992	Mon N	83	222	13	54	10	2	2	26	14-3	2	40	.243	.289	.333	78	-7	0-0	.995	-7	63	109	C69	34	-1.2
1993	Mon N	133	396	33	101	20	1	9	60	34-2	6	40	.255	.320	.379	83	-9	0-0	.988	-6	73	73	C127		-0.7
1994	Mon N★	94	285	28	74	18	1	10	57	25-4	4	23	.260	.314	.435	95	-2	0-0	.996	-9	79	79	C81		-0.6
1995	Mon N	110	350	42	100	21	1	11	45	32-1	4	23	.286	.351	.446	105	3	0-1	.994	7	82	127	C98		1.5
1996	Mon N	127	394	41	105	22	0	12	57	27-4	6	21	.266	.321	.414	91	-6	0-0	.992	-11	70	88	C112		0.0
1997	Mon N	96	310	39	86	20	1	17	55	17-3	5	35	.277	.323	.513	117	6	1-1	.994	1	87	56	C83	15	1.1
1998	Tor A	124	407	37	115	23	1	9	52	25-7	6	39	.283	.328	.410	92	-5	0-0	.991	6	75	92	C121/D	15	-0.4
1999	Tor A	115	412	48	120	26	0	18	80	26-0	5	47	.291	.339	.485	106	3	0-0	.994	-8	85	87	C113	31	-0.4
2000	Tor A	122	416	43	133	19	1	20	58	20-3	5	26	.320	.355	.514	114	7	1-0	.994	-8	83	79	C117,D2	22	0.6
2001	Tor A	134	416	36	94	20	0	11	56	24-4	6	43	.226	.274	.353	63	-23	0-1	.995	-7	100	90	C36,D4		-2.2
2002	Tor A	45	127	8	28	6	0	3	22	4-0	0	13	.220	.239	.339	51	-9	0-0	.995	0	69	92	C36,D8	15	-0.9
Total	14	1245	3902	377	1048	214	8	124	583	255-31	49	399	.269	.318	.423	92	-51	2-6	.993	-51	82	87	C1143,D8	132	-3.8

YEAR	TM LG	G	AB	R	H	2B	3B	HR	RBI	BB-IB	HP	SO	AVG	OBP	SLG	AOPS	ABR	SB-CS	FA	FR	RNG	THR	GAMES AT POSITION	DL	BFW

FLETCHER, ELBIE Elburt Preston B3.18.1916 Milton MA D3.9.1994 Milton MA BL/TL/6-0/180 d9.16 Mil 1944-45

YEAR	TM LG	G	AB	R	H	2B	3B	HR	RBI	BB-IB	HP	SO	AVG	OBP	SLG	AOPS	ABR	SB-CS	FA	FR	RNG	THR	GAMES AT POSITION	DL	BFW
1934	Bos N	8	4	4	2	0	0	0	0	0	0	2	.500	.500	.500	182	0	1	.875	-0	0	287	/1		0.0
1935	Bos N	39	148	12	35	7	1	1	9	7	0	13	.236	.271	.318	63	-8	1	.997	2	117	75	1b39		-0.9
1937	Bos N	148	539	56	133	22	4	1	38	56	3	64	.247	.321	.308	79	-15	3	.993	-1	101	110	1b148		-3.0
1938	Bos N	147	529	71	144	24	7	6	48	60	4	40	.272	.351	.378	112	9	5	.990	8	127	93	1b146		0.4
1939	Bos N	35	106	14	26	2	0	0	6	19	1	5	.245	.365	.264	77	-2	1	.986	-6	39	123	1b31		-1.1
	Pit N	102	370	49	112	23	4	12	71	48	2	28	.303	.386	.484	134	19	3	.993	-5	82	104	1b101		0.5
	Year	137	476	63	138	25	4	12	77	67	3	33	.290	.381	.435	122	17	4	.991	-10	72	108	1b132		-0.6
1940	Pit N	147	510	94	139	22	7	16	104	119	9	54	.273	.418	.437	137	34	5	.993	5	111	97	1b147		2.5
1941	Pit N	151	521	95	150	29	13	11	74	118	2	54	.288	.421	.457	148	40	5	.991	10	128	93	1b151		3.6
1942	Pit N	145	506	86	146	22	5	7	57	105	6	60	.289	.417	.393	134	29	0	.992	11	131	92	1b144		2.8
1943	Pit N★	154	544	91	154	24	5	9	70	95	6	49	.283	.395	.395	124	22	1	.996	3	107	109	1b154		1.8
1946	Pit N	148	532	72	136	25	8	4	66	111	0	37	.256	.384	.355	108	11	4	.995	2	104	78	1b147		0.9
1947	Pit N	69	157	22	38	9	1	1	22	29	1	24	.242	.364	.331	83	-2	2	.986	-1	99	86	1b50		-0.4
1949	Bos N	122	413	57	108	19	3	11	51	84	8	65	.262	.396	.402	121	17	1	.991	1	102	99	1b121		1.4
Total	12	1415	4879	723	1323	228	58	79	616	851	42	495	.271	.384	.390	118	154	32	.993	30	110	97	1b1380		8.5

FLETCHER, GEORGE George Horace Elliott B4.21.1845 Brooklyn NY D6.18.1879 Brooklyn NY d6.21

YEAR	TM LG	G	AB	R	H	2B	3B	HR	RBI	BB-IB	HP	SO	AVG	OBP	SLG	AOPS	ABR	SB-CS	FA	FR	RNG	THR	GAMES AT POSITION	DL	BFW
1872	Eck NA	2	8	1	2	0	0	0	1	0			.250	.250	.250	64	0	0-0	.600	-0	0	0	O2R		0.0

FLETCHER, FRANK Oliver Frank B3.6.1891 Hildreth IL D10.7.1974 St.Petersburg FL BR/TR/5-10/165 d7.14

YEAR	TM LG	G	AB	R	H	2B	3B	HR	RBI	BB-IB	HP	SO	AVG	OBP	SLG	AOPS	ABR	SB-CS	FA	FR	RNG	THR	GAMES AT POSITION	DL	BFW
1914	Phi N	1	1	0	0	0	0	0	0	0		1	1.000	.000	.000	-94	0	0	—		0		/H		0.0

FLETCHER, SCOTT Scott Brian B7.30.1958 Fort Walton Beach FL BR/TR/5-11/173(150-173) [ChiN79 S1/6] d4.25 Col Georgia Southern

YEAR	TM LG	G	AB	R	H	2B	3B	HR	RBI	BB-IB	HP	SO	AVG	OBP	SLG	AOPS	ABR	SB-CS	FA	FR	RNG	THR	GAMES AT POSITION	DL	BFW
1981	Chi N	19	46	6	10	4	0	0	1	2-0	0	4	.217	.250	.304	53	-3	0-0	.972	4	108	131	2b13,S4/3		0.2
1982	Chi N	11	24	4	4	0	0	0	4	1-0	0	5	.167	.286	.167	28	-2	1-0	1.000	-1	100	70	S11		-0.2
1983	†Chi A	114	262	42	62	16	5	3	31	29-0	2	22	.237	.315	.370	85	-5	5-1	.965	23	116	122	S100,2b12,3b7/D		2.7
1984	Chi A	149	456	46	114	13	3	3	35	46-2	8	46	.250	.328	.311	75	-15	10-4	.973	14	107	108	S134,2b28,3b3		1.4
1985	Chi A	119	301	38	77	8	1	2	31	35-0	0	47	.256	.332	.309	74	-10	5-5	.934	3	89	97	3b55,S44,2b37,D2		-0.4
1986	Tex A	147	530	82	159	34	5	3	50	47-0	4	59	.300	.360	.400	104	4	12-11	.973	6	101	102	S136,3b12,2b7/D		2.3
1987	Tex A	156	588	82	169	28	4	5	63	61-3	5	66	.287	.358	.374	94	-3	13-12	.966	12	100	105	S155		2.2
1988	Tex A	140	515	59	142	19	4	0	47	62-1	12	34	.276	.364	.328	94	-1	8-5	.983	10	104	101	S139		1.9
1989	Tex A	83	314	47	75	14	1	0	22	38-1	2	41	.239	.323	.290	73	-10	1-0	.960	-14	78	86	S81/D	15	-1.8
	Chi A	59	232	30	63	11	1	1	21	26-0	1	19	.272	.344	.341	96	0	1-1	1.000	-5	102	103	2b53,S8		-0.3
	Year	142	546	77	138	25	2	1	43	64-1	3	60	.253	.332	.341	83	-10	2-1	.957	-18	76	88	S89,2b53/D		-2.1
1990	Chi A	151	509	54	123	18	3	4	56	45-3	3	63	.242	.304	.312	75	-17	1-3	.988	-6	96	115	2b151		-2.1
1991	Chi A	90	248	14	51	10	1	1	28	17-0	1	26	.206	.262	.266	48	-18	0-2	.992	-9	86	105	2b86,3b4		-2.5
1992	Mil A	123	386	53	106	18	3	3	51	30-1	7	33	.275	.335	.360	97	-1	17-10	.992	10	107	119	2b106,S22/3		1.3
1993	Bos A	121	480	81	137	31	5	5	45	37-1	5	35	.285	.341	.402	93	-4	16-3	.982	13	111	95	2b116,S2/3D		1.6
1994	Bos A	63	185	31	42	9	1	3	11	16-1	2	14	.227	.296	.335	59	-11	8-1	.996	5	111	107	2b53,D4	29	0.3
1995	Det A	67	182	19	42	8	0	1	17	19-0	1	27	.231	.312	.313	64	-9	1-0	1.000	5	107	131	2b63,S3/1D	21	-0.2
Total	15	1612	5258	688	1376	243	38	34	510	514-13	57	541	.262	.332	.342	84	-105	99-58	.971	78	101	104	S839,2b729,3b84,D11/1	80	6.4

FLICK, ELMER Elmer Harrison B1.11.1876 Bedford OH D1.9.1971 Bedford OH BL/TR/5-9/168 d4.26 HF1963

YEAR	TM LG	G	AB	R	H	2B	3B	HR	RBI	BB-IB	HP	SO	AVG	OBP	SLG	AOPS	ABR	SB-CS	FA	FR	RNG	THR	GAMES AT POSITION	DL	BFW
1898	Phi N	134	453	84	137	16	13	8	81	86	15		.302	.430	.448	158	41	23	.931	6	114	89	O133R		3.7
1899	Phi N	127	485	98	166	22	11	2	98	42	11		.342	.407	.445	138	27	31	.931	7	123	139	O125R		2.5
1900	Phi N	138	545	106	200	32	16	11	110	56	16		.367	.441	.545	173	56	35	.914	1	119	110	O138R		4.5
1901	Phi N	138	540	112	180	32	17	8	88	52	7		.333	.399	.500	157	39	30	.962	14	130	175	O138(1/0/137)		4.5
1902	Phi A	11	37	15	11	2	1	0	3	6	3		.297	.435	.405	128	2	4	.947	-0	70	0	O11R		0.1
	Cle A	110	424	70	126	19	11	2	61	47	3		.297	.371	.408	121	13	20	.929	-5	90	69	O110R		0.3
	Year	121	461	85	137	21	12	2	64	53	6		.297	.377	.408	121	15	24	.930	-5	88	63	O121R		0.4
1903	Cle A	140	523	81	155	23	16	2	51	51	8		.296	.368	.413	136	25	24	.955	-1	96	78	O140(6/0/134)		1.7
1904	Cle A	150	579	97	177	31	17	6	56	51	9		.306	.371	.449	160	40	38	.955	7	116	120	O145(0/6/139),2b6		4.5
1905	Cle A	132	500	72	154	29	18	4	64	53	8		.308	.383	.462	165	38	35	.939	-2	121	91	O131R/2		3.3
1906	Cle A	157	624	98	194	34	22	1	62	54	7		.311	.372	.441	156	40	39	.981	-1	70	111	O150(0/86/65),2b8		2.4
1907	Cle A	147	549	80	166	15	18	3	58	64	11		.302	.386	.412	153	35	41	.956	-1	115	162	O147(1/23/122)		3.0
1908	Cle A	9	35	4	8	1	1	0	2	3	0		.229	.289	.314	96	0	1	1.000	-0	103	416	O9R		-0.1
1909	Cle A	66	235	28	60	10	2	0	15	22	1		.255	.322	.315	97	0	9	.958	-2	56	63	O61(1/12/48)		-0.6
1910	Cle A	24	68	5	18	2	1	0	7	10	0		.265	.359	.368	126	2	1	.955	-2	94	0	O18R		-0.1
Total	13	1483	5597	950	1752	268	164	48	756	597	99		.313	.389	.445	149	358	330	.947	11	107	113	O1456(9/127/1320),2b15		29.7

FLICK, LEW Lewis Miller "Noisy" B2.18.1915 Bristol TN D12.7.1990 Weber City VA BL/TL/5-9/155 d9.28

YEAR	TM LG	G	AB	R	H	2B	3B	HR	RBI	BB-IB	HP	SO	AVG	OBP	SLG	AOPS	ABR	SB-CS	FA	FR	RNG	THR	GAMES AT POSITION	DL	BFW
1943	Phi A	1	5	2	3	0	0	0	0	0	0	0	.600	.600	.600	253	0	0-0	1.000	0	117	0	/OR		0.1
1944	Phi A	19	35	1	4	0	0	0	2	1	0	2	.114	.139	.114	-28	-6	1-0	1.000	-1	89	0	O6(0/1/5)		-0.7
Total	2	20	40	3	7	0	0	0	2	1	0	2	.175	.195	.175	6	-5	1-0	1.000	-1	95	0	O7(0/1/6)		-0.6

FLINN, DON Don Raphael B11.17.1892 Bluff Dale TX D3.9.1959 Waco TX BR/TR/6-1/185 d9.2

YEAR	TM LG	G	AB	R	H	2B	3B	HR	RBI	BB-IB	HP	SO	AVG	OBP	SLG	AOPS	ABR	SB-CS	FA	FR	RNG	THR	GAMES AT POSITION	DL	BFW
1917	Pit N	14	37	1	11	1	0	0	0	6			.297	.316	.378	109	0	1	1.000	1	122	77	O12(7/1/4)		0.1

FLINT, SILVER Frank Sylvester B8.3.1855 Philadelphia PA D1.14.1892 Chicago IL BR/TR/6-0/180 d5.4 M1

YEAR	TM LG	G	AB	R	H	2B	3B	HR	RBI	BB-IB	HP	SO	AVG	OBP	SLG	AOPS	ABR	SB-CS	FA	FR	RNG	THR	GAMES AT POSITION	DL	BFW
1875	RS NA	17	61	4	5	0	0	0	1	1		10	.082	.097	.082	-41	-8	2-0	.820	-3			C16,O2(1/0/1)/3		-0.9
1878	Ind N	63	254	23	57	7	0	0	18	2		15	.224	.230	.252	67	-8		.908	-3			C59,O9(5/0/4)		-0.9
1879	Chi N	79	324	46	92	22	6	1	41	6		44	.284	.297	.398	120	6		.915	5			C78/ORM		1.2
1880	Chi N	74	284	30	46	10	4	0	17	5		32	.162	.176	.225	34	-20		.934	7			C67,O13(0/4/10)		-1.1
1881	Chi N	80	306	46	95	18	0	1	34	6		39	.310	.324	.379	115	5		.938	-6			C80,O8R/1		0.1
1882	Chi N	81	331	48	83	18	8	4	44	2		50	.251	.255	.390	99	-2		.935	-1			C81,O10R		0.4
1883	Chi N	85	332	57	88	23	4	0	32	3		69	.265	.272	.358	83	-8		.877	-2			C83,O23R		-0.3
1884	Chi N	73	279	35	57	5	2	9	45	7		57	.204	.224	.333	67	-12		.884	-5			C73		-0.9
1885	†Chi N	68	249	27	52	8	2	1	17	2		52	.209	.215	.269	49	-15		.927	8			C68/OR		-0.2
1886	†Chi N	54	173	30	35	6	2	1	13	12		36	.202	.254	.277	54	-10	1	.893	9			C54,1b3		0.3
1887	Chi N	49	187	22	50	8	6	3	21	4	0	28	.267	.283	.422	83	-6	7	.909	5			C47,1b2		0.2
1888	Chi N	22	77	6	14	3	0	0	3	1	1	21	.182	.203	.221	33	-6	1	.926	1			C22		-0.3
1889	Chi N	15	56	6	13	1	0	1	9	3		18	.232	.271	.304	58	-4	1	.903	-2			C15		-0.4
Total	12	743	2852	376	682	129	34	21	294	53	1	461	.239	.253	.330	78	-80	10	.913	16			C727,O65(5/4/57),1b6		-1.9

FLOOD, CURT Curtis Charles B1.18.1938 Houston TX D1.20.1997 Los Angeles CA BR/TR/5-9/165* d9.9

YEAR	TM LG	G	AB	R	H	2B	3B	HR	RBI	BB-IB	HP	SO	AVG	OBP	SLG	AOPS	ABR	SB-CS	FA	FR	RNG	THR	GAMES AT POSITION	DL	BFW
1956	Cin N	5	1	0	0	0	0	0	0	0-0	0	1	1.000	.000	.000	-94	0	0-0	—				/H		0.0
1957	Cin N	3	3	2	1	0	0	1	1	0-0	0	0	.333	.333	1.333	299	1	0-0	—	-1	0	0	3b2/2		0.0
1958	StL N	121	422	50	110	17	2	10	41	31-1	4	56	.261	.317	.382	81	-12	2-12	.978	13	112	189	O120C/3		-0.8
1959	StL N	121	208	24	53	7	3	7	26	16-0	0	35	.255	.305	.418	86	-5	2-1	.967	-8	89	25	O106(2/103/1)/2		-1.6
1960	StL N	140	396	37	94	20	1	8	38	35-7	4	54	.237	.303	.354	73	-14	0-3	.993	1	104	84	O134(1/133/0)/3		-2.0
1961	StL N	132	335	53	108	15	5	2	21	35-2	3	33	.322	.391	.415	104	3	6-2	.984	8	110	196	O125C		1.0
1962	StL N	151	635	99	188	30	5	12	70	42-0	10	57	.296	.346	.416	95	-3	8-6	.990	7	117	118	O151C		-0.2
1963	StL N	158	662	112	200	34	9	5	63	42-3	2	57	.302	.345	.403	105	5	17-12	.988	8	110	116	O158C		0.9
1964	†StL N★	162	679	97	211	26	3	5	46	43-1	5	53	.311	.356	.378	98	0	8-11	.988	3	108	96	O162C		-0.4
1965	StL N	156	617	90	191	30	3	11	83	51-4	6	50	.310	.366	.421	111	11	9-3	.986	-1	102	79	O151C		0.7
1966	StL N★	160	626	64	167	21	5	10	78	26-0	4	56	.267	.298	.344	83	-15	14-7	1.000	0	108	45	O159C		-2.0
1967	†StL N	134	514	68	172	24	1	5	50	37-1	2	46	.335	.378	.414	129	20	2-2	.988	5	112	58	O126C	22	2.3
1968	†StL N★	150	618	71	186	17	4	5	60	33-2	5	58	.301	.339	.366	114	9	11-6	.983	9	111	116	O149C		1.6
1969	StL N	153	606	80	173	31	3	4	57	48-1	7	57	.285	.344	.366	99	0	9-7	.989	7	107	116	O150C/2		0.3
1971	Was A	13	35	4	7	0	0	0	2	5-0	0	9	.200	.300	.200	46	-2	0-1	.941	-2	76	0	O10C		-0.5
Total	15	1759	6357	851	1861	271	44	85	636	444-22	52	609	.293	.342	.389	99	-2	88-73	.987	50	107	106	O1697(3/1693/1),3b4,2b2	22	-0.7

FLOOD, TIM Timothy A. B3.13.1877 Montgomery City MO D6.15.1929 St.Louis MO BR/TR/5-9/160 d9.24

YEAR	TM LG	G	AB	R	H	2B	3B	HR	RBI	BB-IB	HP	SO	AVG	OBP	SLG	AOPS	ABR	SB-CS	FA	FR	RNG	THR	GAMES AT POSITION	DL	BFW
1899	StL N	10	31	0	9	0	0	0	4	3	0		.290	.371	.290	81	-1	1	.878	-1	107	97	2b10		-0.1
1902	Bro N	132	476	43	104	11	4	3	51	23	9		.218	.268	.277	68	-19	8	.942	-15	94	72	2b132/OL		-3.5

YEAR	TM LG	G	AB	R	H	2B	3B	HR	RBI	BB-IB	HP	SO	AVG	OBP	SLG	AOPS	ABR	SB-CS	FA	FR	RNG	THR	GAMES AT POSITION	DL	BFW
1903	Bro N	89	309	27	77	15	2	0	32	15	3		.249	.291	.311	73	-11	14	.924	-11	88	133	2b84,S2/OC		-2.0
Total	3	231	816	70	190	26	6	3	86	42	12		.233	.280	.290	70	-31	23	.933	-27	92	96	2b226,S2,O2(1/1/0)		-5.6

FLORA, KEVIN Kevin Scot B6.10.1969 Fontana CA BR/TR/6-0/180* [CalA87 2/57] d9.27

1991	Cal A	3	8	1	1	0	0	0	0	1-0	0	5	.125	.222	.125	-1	-1	1-0	.846	-2	40	56	2b3		-0.3
1995	Cal A	2	1	1	0	0	0	0	0	0-0	0	1	.000	.000	.000	-99	0	0-0	—	0			/D		0.0
	Phi N	24	75	12	16	3	0	2	7	4-0	0	22	.213	.253	.333	53	-5	1-0	1.000	-1	85	105	O20(5/15/0)		-0.6
Total	2	29	84	14	17	3	0	2	7	5-0	0	28	.202	.247	.310	46	-6	2-0	1.000	-3	85	105	O20(5/15/0),2b3/D		-0.9

FLORENCE, PAUL Paul Robert "Pep" B4.22.1900 Chicago IL D5.28.1986 Gainesville FL BB/TR/6-1/185 d5.22 Col Georgetown

1926	NY N	76	188	19	43	4	3	2	14	23	3	12	.229	.322	.314	73	-7	2	.937	-8	85	90	C76		-1.1

FLORES, GIL Gilberto (Garcia) B10.27.1952 Ponce, PR BR/TR/6-0/180* d5.8

1977	Cal A	104	342	41	95	19	4	1	26	23-2	1	39	.278	.325	.365	91	-4	12-10	.978	0	101	92	O85(41/45/9),D8		-0.7
1978	NY N	11	29	8	8	0	1	0	1	3-0	0	5	.276	.344	.345	95	0	1-0	.944	-1	97	0	O8(1/6/2)		-0.1
1979	NY N	70	93	9	18	1	1	1	10	8-0	1	17	.194	.262	.258	44	-7	2-0	.976	1	117	75	O32(0/6/28)		-0.7
Total	3	185	464	58	121	20	6	2	37	34-2	2	61	.261	.313	.343	82	-11	15-10	.976	0	103	83	O125(42/57/39),D8		-1.5

FLORES, JOSE Jose Carlos B6.28.1973 New York NY BR/TR/5-11/180* [PhiN94 34/954] d9.7 Col Texas

2002	Oak A	7	3	2	0	0	0	0	0	1-0	1	0	.000	.400	.000	20	0	1-1	—	-1	0	0	2b2/S		-0.1
2004	LA N	9	4	0	1	0	0	0	0	1-0	0	2	.250	.400	.250	75	0	0-0	—	-1	0	0	/23		-0.1
Total	2	16	7	2	1	0	0	0	0	2-0	1	2	.143	.400	.143	52	0	1-1	.000	-2	0	0	2b3/3S		-0.2

FLOWERS, DICKIE Charles Richard B1850 Philadelphia PA D10.5.1892 Philadelphia PA d6.3

1871	Tro NA	21	105	39	33	5	4	0	18	4		0	.314	.339	.438	120	2	8-2	.769	-2	95	142	S20/P2		0.1
1872	Ath NA	3	15	1	4	0	0	0	4	2		2	.267	.353	.267	93	0	0-0	.643	-1	85	0	S3		-0.1
Total	2 NA	24	120	40	37	5	4	0	22	6		2	.308	.341	.417	117	2	8-2	.757	-3	94	125	S23/2P		0.0

FLOWERS, JAKE D'Arcy Raymond B3.16.1902 Cambridge MD D12.27.1962 Clearwater FL BR/TR/5-11.5/170 d9.7 C9 Col Washington College

1923	StL N	13	32	0	3	1	0	0	2	2		7	.094	.147	.125	-28	-6	1-2	.971	-1	118	28	S7,2b2,3b2		-0.6
1926	†StL N	40	74	13	20	1	0	3	9	5	1	9	.270	.325	.405	92	-1	1	.984	-1	115	67	2b11,1b3/S		-0.2
1927	Bro N	67	231	26	54	5	5	2	20	21		15	.234	.300	.325	67	-11	3	.944	-7	89	81	S65/2		-1.1
1928	Bro N	103	339	51	93	11	6	4	44	47	2	30	.274	.366	.360	92	-3	10	.971	-2	91	81	2b94,S6		-0.3
1929	Bro N	46	130	16	26	6	0	1	16	22	0	18	.200	.316	.269	47	-10	9	.962	-7	84	69	2b39		-1.5
1930	Bro N	89	253	37	81	18	3	2	50	21	0	18	.320	.372	.439	96	-1	5	.949	-6	93	108	2b65/OR		-0.5
1931	Bro N	22	31	3	7	0	0	0	1	7		4	.226	.368	.226	64	-1	1	1.000	0	83	62	2b6/S		0.0
	†StL N	45	137	19	34	11	1	2	19	9		6	.248	.295	.387	79	-4	7	.971	3	103	109	S24,2b21/3		0.1
	Year	67	168	22	41	11	1	2	20	16		10	.244	.310	.357	77	-5	8	.991	4	100	117	2b27,S25/3		0.1
1932	StL N	67	247	35	63	11	1	2	18	31	1	18	.255	.341	.332	79	-6	7	.980	-0	89	99	3b54,S7,2b2		-0.4
1933	Bro N	78	210	28	49	11	2	2	22	24	0	15	.233	.312	.333	88	-3	13	.955	-9	85	61	S36,2b19,3b8/OR		-0.8
1934	Cin N	13	9	1	3	0	0	0	0	1	1	1	.333	.455	.333	117	0	1	—	0			/H		0.0
Total	10	583	1693	229	433	75	18	16	201	190	6	139	.256	.333	.350	80	-46	58-2	.967	-29	93	85	2b260,S147,3b65,1b3,O2R		-5.3

FLOYD, CLIFF Cornelius Clifford B12.5.1972 Chicago IL BL/TL/6-4/235(220-250) [MonN91 1/14] d9.18

1993	Mon N	10	31	3	7	0	1	2	9	.226	.226	.323	43	-3	0-0	1.000	-1	73	85	1b10		-0.4
1994	Mon N	100	334	43	94	19	4	4	41	24-0	3	63	.281	.332	.398	89	-5	10-3	.991	-1	90	93	1b77,O26(17/0/9)		-1.2
1995	Mon N	29	69	6	9	1	0	1	8	7-0	1	22	.130	.221	.188	9	-9	3-0	.987	-0	118	111	1b18,O4(2/1/1)	118	-1.0
1996	Mon N	117	227	29	55	15	4	6	26	30-1	5	52	.242	.340	.423	99	0	7-1	.960	-3	95	66	O85(69/16/7),1b2		-0.4
1997	†Fla N	61	137	23	32	9	1	6	19	24-0	2	33	.234	.354	.445	113	3	6-2	.970	2	106	222	O38(24/9/6),1b9	87	0.4
1998	Fla N	153	588	85	166	45	3	22	90	44-7	3	112	.282	.337	.481	120	16	27-14	.974	-2	92	103	O146(146/2/0),D3		0.9
1999	Fla N	69	251	37	76	19	1	11	49	30-5	2	47	.303	.379	.518	132	13	5-6	.952	-0	95	106	O62L,D3	101	0.9
2000	Fla N	121	420	75	126	30	0	22	91	50-5	8	82	.300	.378	.529	135	23	24-3	.951	-4	87	112	O108L/D	30	1.9
2001	Fla N★	149	555	123	176	44	4	31	103	59-19	10	101	.317	.390	.578	151	43	18-3	.972	3	104	87	O142L,D3		4.2
2002	Fla N	84	296	49	85	20	0	18	57	58-18	7	68	.287	.414	.537	158	26	10-5	.983	4	111	94	O80(20/0/60)/D		2.6
	Mon N	15	53	7	11	2	0	3	4	3-1	1	10	.208	.263	.415	74	-2	1-0	.941	-1	57	248	O13L		-0.4
	Year	99	349	56	96	22	0	21	61	61-19	8	78	.275	.394	.519	145	23	11-5	.980	3	84	70	O93(33/0/60)/D		2.2
	Bos A	47	171	30	54	21	0	7	18	15-0	2	28	.316	.374	.561	143	11	4-0	.977	-2	84	70	O26(21/0/6),D19		0.8
2003	NY N	108	365	57	106	25	2	18	68	51-2	3	66	.290	.376	.518	137	21	3-0	.971	4	104	153	O95L,D9	41	2.1
2004	NY N	113	396	55	103	26	4	18	63	47-6	11	103	.260	.352	.462	111	8	11-4	.988	-4	92	89	O106L/D	31	0.1
2005	NY N	150	550	85	150	22	3	34	98	63-13	11	98	.273	.358	.505	126	20	12-2	.993	8	103	**178**	O150L		2.8
Total	13	1326	4443	707	1250	298	21	202	737	508-77	69	894	.281	.361	.494	124	165	141-43	.973	3	98	117	O1081(975/28/89),1b116,D40	408	13.0

FLOYD, BUBBA Leslie Roe B6.23.1917 Dallas TX D12.15.2000 Dallas TX BR/TR/5-11/160 d6.16 Col SMU

1944	Det A	3	9	1	4	1	0	0	1		0	0	.444	.500	.556	191	1	0-0	1.000	-0	119	0	S3		0.1

FLOYD, BOBBY Robert Nathan B10.20.1943 Hawthorne CA BR/TR/6-0/181* d9.18 C2 Col UCLA

1968	Bal A	5	9	0	1	1	0	0	1	0-0	0	3	.111	.100	.222	-1	-1	0-0	1.000	1	105	190	S4		0.0
1969	Bal A	39	84	7	17	4	0	1	6	6-1	0	17	.202	.253	.250	41	-7	0-0	.984	5	123	152	2b15,S15,3b9		0.1
1970	Bal A	3	2	0	0	0	0	0	0	0-0	0	2	.000	.000	.000	-98	-1	0-0	1.000	-2	0	0	S2/2		-0.2
	KC A	14	43	5	14	4	0	0	9	4-0	0	9	.326	.375	.419	121	1	0-1	.880	0	111	104	S8,3b6		0.2
	Year	17	45	5	14	4	0	0	9	4-0	0	11	.311	.360	.400	111	1	0-1	.882	-1	106	100	S10,3b6/2		0.0
1971	KC A	31	66	8	10	3	0	2	7	7-0	0	21	.152	.233	.197	23	-7	0-0	.970	2	107	142	S15,2b8/3		-0.3
1972	KC A	61	134	9	24	3	0	0	5	5-0	0	29	.179	.209	.201	23	-13	1-0	.967	-11	68	64	3b30,S29,2b2		-2.6
1973	KC A	51	78	10	26	3	1	0	8	4-0	0	14	.333	.357	.397	107	1	1-1	1.000	-1	84	71	2b25,S24		0.0
1974	KC A	10	9	1	1	0	0	0	0	2-0	0	4	.111	.273	.111	13	-1	0-0	1.000	1	138	0	2b5,3b2/S		0.0
Total	7	214	425	40	93	18	1	0	26	28-1	0	99	.219	.264	.266	52	-28	2-2	.940	-5	100	111	S98,2b56,3b48		-2.6

FLUHRER, JOHN John Lister (aka Wm. G. Morris 1 Game in 1915) B1.3.1894 Adrian MI D7.17.1946 Columbus OH BR/TR/5-9/165 d9.5 Col Penn

1915	Chi N	6	6	0	2	0	0	0	1		0	0	.333	.429	.333	132	0	1	.500	-0	65	0	O2L		-0.3

FLYNN, ED Edward J. B1.25.1864 Chicago IL D8.28.1929 Chicago IL BL/5-9/165 d5.5 b-George

1887	Cle AA	7	27	5	5	1	0	0	4	1		0	.185	.214	.222	22	-3	3	.786	-1	73	0	3b6/OR		-0.3

FLYNN, GEORGE George A. "Dibby" B5.24.1871 Chicago IL D12.28.1901 Chicago IL 5-9/150 d4.17 b-Ed

1896	Chi N	29	106	15	27	1	2	0	4	11	2	9	.255	.336	.302	66	-5	12	.878	1	130	250	O29L		-0.7

FLYNN, JOHN John Anthony B9.7.1883 Providence RI D3.23.1935 Providence RI BR/TR/6-0.5/175 d4.22 f-Joe Col Holy Cross

1910	Pit N	96	332	32	91	10	2	6	52	30	1	47	.274	.336	.370	100	-1	6	.977	-3	93	107	1b93		-0.6
1911	Pit N	33	59	5	12	1	0	3	9	6	0	8	.203	.309	.237	52	-4	0	1.000	1	121	123	1b13/OR		-0.3
1912	Was A	20	71	9	12	4	1	0	5	7	1		.169	.253	.254	45	-5	2	.974	1	131	102	1b20		-0.4
Total	3	149	462	46	115	14	4	6	60	46	2	55	.249	.320	.335	85	-10	8	.978	-1	102	108	1b126/OR		-1.3

FLYNN, JOE Joseph Nicholas B12.29.1861 Providence RI D12.22.1933 Providence RI d4.18 s-John

1884	Phi U	52	209	38	52	9	4	4		11			.249	.286	.388	111	-4		.778	-12	90	176	O43(2/0/41),C10/1S		-1.3
	Bos U	9	31	4	7	2	0	0		2			.226	.273	.290	72	-2		.864	3			C7,O4(1/2/2)/1		0.1
	Year	61	240	42	59	11	4	4		13			.246	.285	.375	105	-6		.764	-9	111	158	O47(3/2/43),C17,1b2/S		-1.2

FLYNN, MIKE Michael J. B3.15.1872 Co. Kildare, Ireland D6.16.1941 Los Angeles CA d8.31

1891	Bos AA	1	2	0	0	0	0	0	0		0	1	.000	.000	.000	-99	-1	0	1.000	1	121	272	/C		0.0

FLYNN, DOUG Robert Douglas B4.18.1951 Lexington KY BR/TR/5-11/165(160-172) d4.9 Col Kentucky

1975	Cin N	89	127	17	34	7	0	1	20	11-2	0	13	.268	.324	.346	85	-2	3-0	.962	-4	80	53	3b40,2b30,S17		-0.3
1976	†Cin N	93	219	20	62	5	2	1	19	10-1	0	24	.283	.312	.338	83	-6	2-0	.988	-19	77	84	2b55,3b23,S20		-2.1
1977	Cin N	36	32	0	8	1	0	0	5	0-0	0	5	.250	.242	.344	56	-2	0-0	1.000	1	116	0	3b25,2b9,S4		-0.1
	NY N	90	282	14	54	6	1	0	14	11-2	0	24	.191	.220	.220	20	-33	1-3	.954	-16	78	75	S65,2b29,3b2		-4.4
	Year	126	314	14	62	7	1	0	19	11-2	0	29	.197	.223	.232	23	-35	1-3	.956	-15	80	78	S69,2b38,3b27		-4.5
1978	NY N	156	532	37	126	12	8	0	36	30-10	1	50	.237	.277	.289	61	-30	3-5	.986	-16	98	109	2b128,S60		-3.9
1979	NY N	157	555	35	135	19	5	4	61	17-7	0	46	.243	.265	.317	60	-33	0-4	.983	-8	93	104	2b148,S20		-3.5
1980	NY N	128	443	46	113	9	6	4	24	22-14	0	20	.255	.288	.312	69	-20	2-2	**.991**	-6	93	86	2b128,S3	17	-2.0

YEAR	TM LG	G	AB	R	H	2B	3B	HR	RBI	BB-IB	HP	SO	AVG	OBP	SLG	AOPS	ABR	SB-CS	FA	FR	RNG	THR	GAMES AT POSITION	DL	BFW
1981	NY N	**105**	325	24	72	12	4	1	20	11-8	0	19	.222	.247	.292	53	-22	1-2	.987	14	104	100	2b100,S5		-0.3
1982	Tex A	88	270	13	57	6	2	0	19	4-0	0	14	.211	.221	.248	30	-27	6-2	.989	-2	97	81	2b55,S35		-2.2
	Mon N	58	193	13	47	6	2	0	20	4-0	0	23	.244	.256	.295	53	-13	0-2	.983	-2	87	126	2b58		-1.3
1983	Mon N	143	452	44	107	18	4	0	26	19-8	0	38	.237	.267	.294	55	-28	2-1	.986	-13	93	94	2b107,S37		-3.5
1984	Mon N	124	366	23	89	12	1	0	17	12-6	0	41	.243	.267	.281	57	-22	0-0	.979	-19	93	102	2b88,S34		-3.6
1985	Mon N	9	6	0	1	0	0	0	0	0-0	0	0	.167	.167	.167	-7	-1	0-0	1.000	-1	64	0	2b6/S		-0.2
	Det A	32	51	2	13	2	1	0	2	0-0	0	3	.255	.250	.333	60	-3	0-0	.984	-0	90	186	2b20,S8,3b4		-0.2
Total	11	1308	3853	288	918	115	39	7	284	151-58	1	320	.238	.266	.294	56	-242	20-20	.986	-92	94	100	2b961,S309,3b94	17	-27.6

FLYNN, CLIPPER William B4.29.1849 Lansingburg NY D11.11.1881 Lansingburg NY TR/5-7/140 d5.9

YEAR	TM LG	G	AB	R	H	2B	3B	HR	RBI	BB-IB	HP	SO	AVG	OBP	SLG	AOPS	ABR	SB-CS	FA	FR	RNG	THR	GAMES AT POSITION	DL	BFW
1871	Tro NA	29	142	43	46	6	1	0	27	4		2	.338	.356	.394	114	2	3-3	.955	4	268	120	1b19,O8R/23		0.5
1872	Oly NA	9	40	4	9	1	0	0	2	0		0	.225	.225	.250	48	-2	0-0	.900	-1	95	103	1b9		-0.2
Total	2 NA	38	182	47	57	7	1	0	29	4		2	.313	.328	.363	101	0	3-3	.934	3	212	114	1b28,O8R/32		0.3

FOGARTY, JIM James G. B2.12.1864 San Francisco CA D5.20.1891 Philadelphia PA BR/TR/5-10.5/180 d5.1 M1 b-Joe Col St. Marys (CA) OF(0/312/373) ▲

YEAR	TM LG	G	AB	R	H	2B	3B	HR	RBI	BB-IB	HP	SO	AVG	OBP	SLG	AOPS	ABR	SB-CS	FA	FR	RNG	THR	GAMES AT POSITION	DL	BFW
1884	Phi N	97	378	42	80	12	6	1	37	20		54	.212	.251	.283	71	-12		.915	3	75	105	O78(0/72/6),3b14,2b4,S3/P		-1.0
1885	Phi N	**111**	427	49	99	13	6	0	39	30		37	.232	.282	.276	83	-7		.941	19	154	233	O88C,2b10,S8,3b5		0.9
1886	Phi N	77	280	54	82	13	5	3	47	42		16	.293	.385	.407	140	15	30	.953	-5	74	181	O60(0/1/59),2b13,S3,3b3/P		0.9
1887	Phi N	126	495	113	129	26	12	8	50	**82**	10	44	.261	.376	.410	112	10	102	.920	29	**176**	240	O123R,S2,3b2/2P		3.2
1888	Phi N	121	454	72	107	14	6	1	35	53	7	66	.236	.325	.300	95	-1	58	.930	-12	130	241	O117R,3b5/S		1.0
1889	Phi N	128	499	107	129	15	17	3	54	65	7	60	.259	.352	.375	95	-6	**99**	**.961**	18	**171**	129	O128C,P4		0.7
1890	Phi P	91	347	71	83	17	6	4	58	59	9	50	.239	.364	.357	91	3	36	.963	6	97	85	O91(0/23/68)/3M		0.1
Total	7	751	2880	508	709	110	55	20	320	351	33	327	.246	.335	.343	98	-4	325	.940	81	133	177	O685R,3b30,2b28,S17,P7		5.8

FOGARTY, JOE Joseph J. B San Francisco CA 5-9/158 d9.18 b-Jim

YEAR	TM LG	G	AB	R	H	2B	3B	HR	RBI	BB-IB	HP	SO	AVG	OBP	SLG	AOPS	ABR	SB-CS	FA	FR	RNG	THR	GAMES AT POSITION	DL	BFW
1885	StL N	2	8	1	1	0	0	0		1			.125	.125	.125	-20	-1		1.000	-0	0	0	O2L		-0.1

FOHL, LEE Leo Alexander B11.28.1876 Lowell OH D10.30.1965 Cleveland OH BL/TR/5-10/175 d8.29 M11/C1

YEAR	TM LG	G	AB	R	H	2B	3B	HR	RBI	BB-IB	HP	SO	AVG	OBP	SLG	AOPS	ABR	SB-CS	FA	FR	RNG	THR	GAMES AT POSITION	DL	BFW
1902	Pit N	1	3	0	0	0	0	0	0	0		1	.000	.000	.000	-97	-1	0	.875	0	118	105	/C		0.0
1903	Cin N	4	14	3	5	1	1	0	3	0		1	.357	.400	.571	158	1	0	.955	-0	132	115	C4		0.1
Total	2	5	17	3	5	1	1	0	3	0		1	.294	.333	.471	120	0	0	.933	-0	129	113	C5		0.1

FOILES, HANK Henry Lee B6.10.1929 Richmond VA BR/TR/6-0/195* d4.21 Col Virginia

YEAR	TM LG	G	AB	R	H	2B	3B	HR	RBI	BB-IB	HP	SO	AVG	OBP	SLG	AOPS	ABR	SB-CS	FA	FR	RNG	THR	GAMES AT POSITION	DL	BFW
1953	Cin N	5	13	1	2	0	0	0	1	0		1	.154	.214	.154	-2	-2	0-0	.909	-0	79	202	C3		-0.2
	Cle A	7	7	2	1	0	0	0	0	1		0	.143	.250	.143	9	-1	0-0	.933	0	72	297	C7		-0.1
1955	Cle A	62	111	13	29	9	0	1	7	17-3	0	18	.261	.354	.369	93	0	0-0	.988	9	123	133	C41		1.0
1956	Cle A	1	0	0	0	0	0	0	0	0-0	0	0	—	—	—	—	-0	0-0	—	-0	0	0	/C		0.0
	Pit N	79	222	24	47	10	2	7	25	17-4	0	56	.212	.266	.369	71	-10	0-1	.988	1	100	123	C73		-0.6
1957	Pit N★	109	281	32	76	10	4	9	36	37-5	0	53	.270	.352	.431	113	6	1-3	.981	-3	109	74	C109		0.7
1958	Pit N	104	264	31	54	10	2	8	30	45-10	1	53	.205	.322	.348	80	-7	0-1	.990	8	117	99	C103		0.5
1959	Pit N	53	80	10	18	3	0	3	4	7-2	0	16	.225	.287	.375	75	-3	0-0	1.000	4	132	72	C51		0.2
1960	KC A	6	7	1	4	0	0	0	1	3-0	0	1	.571	.700	.571	246	2	0-0	.900	-0	0	0	C2	31	0.2
	Cle A	24	68	9	19	1	0	1	6	7-0	0	5	.279	.347	.338	89	-1	0-0	.982	0	89	158	C22		0.0
	Det A	26	56	5	14	3	0	0	3	1-1	0	9	.250	.263	.304	51	-4	1-0	1.000	4	163	144	C22		0.1
	Year	56	131	15	37	4	0	1	10	11-1	0	15	.282	.338	.336	83	-3	1-0	.987	5	117	145	C46		0.3
1961	Bal N	43	124	18	34	6	0	6	19	12-1	0	27	.274	.336	.468	107	3	0-2	.995	-2	63	102	C38	61	0.2
1962	Cin N	43	131	17	36	6	1	7	25	13-3	0	39	.275	.340	.496	118	3	0-0	.981	-1	85	65	C41		0.4
1963	Cin N	1	3	0	0	0	0	0	0	1-1	0	2	.000	.250	.000	-21	0	1-0	1.000	-1	45	0	/C		-0.1
	LA A	41	84	8	18	1	1	4	10	8-1	1	13	.214	.290	.393	95	-1	0-0	.974	2	75	171	C30		0.2
1964	LA A	4	4	0	1	0	0	0	0	0-0	0	2	.250	.250	.250	44	0	0-0	—		0		/H		0.0
Total	11	608	1455	171	353	63	10	46	166	170-31	2	295	.243	.321	.392	92	-15	3-7	.986	23	104	105	C544	92	2.5

FOLEY, CURRY Charles Joseph B1.14.1856 Milltown, Ireland D10.20.1898 Boston MA TL/5-10/160 d5.13 ▲

YEAR	TM LG	G	AB	R	H	2B	3B	HR	RBI	BB-IB	HP	SO	AVG	OBP	SLG	AOPS	ABR	SB-CS	FA	FR	RNG	THR	GAMES AT POSITION	DL	BFW
1879	Bos N	35	146	16	46	3	1	0	17	3		4	.315	.329	.349	121	3		.857	-5	77	0	P21,O17(0/2/15),1b2		-0.2
1880	Bos N	80	332	44	97	13	2	2	31	8		14	.292	.309	.361	130	10		.953	-0	103	0	P36,O35R,1b25		0.5
1881	Buf N	**83**	375	58	96	20	2	1	25	7		27	.256	.270	.328	88	-5		.795	-4	99	215	O55(3/4/50),1b27,P10		-0.9
1882	Buf N	**84**	341	51	104	16	4	3	49	12		26	.305	.329	.402	131	11		.833	1	120	184	O84(0/1/84)/P		-0.3
1883	Buf N	23	111	23	30	5	3	0	6	4		12	.270	.296	.369	98	0		.885	-2	39	0	O23(1/21/1)/P		1.0
Total	5	305	1305	192	373	57	12	6	128	34		83	.286	.304	.362	114	19		.819	-10	101	148	O214(4/28/185),P69,1b54		0.1

FOLEY, MARV Marvis Edwin B8.29.1953 Stanford KY BL/TR/6-0/195* d9.11 C2 Col Kentucky

YEAR	TM LG	G	AB	R	H	2B	3B	HR	RBI	BB-IB	HP	SO	AVG	OBP	SLG	AOPS	ABR	SB-CS	FA	FR	RNG	THR	GAMES AT POSITION	DL	BFW
1978	Chi A	11	34	3	12	0	0	0	6	4-0	0	6	.353	.421	.353	118	1	0-1	.938	-3	45	86	C10		-0.2
1979	Chi A	34	97	6	24	3	0	2	10	7-1	0	5	.247	.294	.340	71	-4	0-0	.993	-3	76	96	C33		-0.6
1980	Chi A	68	137	14	29	5	0	4	15	9-3	0	22	.212	.263	.336	65	-7	0-0	.991	3	76	127	C64,1b3		-0.6
1982	Chi A	27	36	1	4	0	0	0	1	6-1	0	4	.111	.238	.111	-0	-5	0-0	.980	1	78	183	C15,3b2/1D	15	-0.4
1984	Tex A	63	115	13	25	2	0	6	19	15-1	3	24	.217	.306	.391	90	-2	0-0	.988	1	47	66	C36/13D		0.0
Total	5	203	419	37	94	10	0	12	51	41-6	3	61	.224	.292	.334	72	-17	0-1	.986	-2	67	106	C158,D5,1b5,3b3	15	-1.5

FOLEY, RAY Raymond Kirwin B6.23.1906 Naugatuck CT D3.22.1980 Vero Beach FL BL/TR/5-11/173 d7.4 Col Catholic America

YEAR	TM LG	G	AB	R	H	2B	3B	HR	RBI	BB-IB	HP	SO	AVG	OBP	SLG	AOPS	ABR	SB-CS	FA	FR	RNG	THR	GAMES AT POSITION	DL	BFW
1928	NY N	2	1	0	0	0	0	0	0	1		0	1	.000	.500	.000	41	0		1	—		0	/H		0.0

FOLEY, TOM Thomas J. B1847 Chicago IL D1.4.1896 LaGrange IL 5-9.5/157 d5.8

YEAR	TM LG	G	AB	R	H	2B	3B	HR	RBI	BB-IB	HP	SO	AVG	OBP	SLG	AOPS	ABR	SB-CS	FA	FR	RNG	THR	GAMES AT POSITION	DL	BFW
1871	Chi NA	18	84	18	22	3	0	1	13	3		2	.262	.287	.321	67	-4	1-4	.633	-5	58	0	O16(2/9/5),C4/3		-0.7

FOLEY, TOM Thomas Michael B9.9.1959 Columbus GA BL/TR/6-1/180(160-185) [CinN77 7/180] d4.9 C4

YEAR	TM LG	G	AB	R	H	2B	3B	HR	RBI	BB-IB	HP	SO	AVG	OBP	SLG	AOPS	ABR	SB-CS	FA	FR	RNG	THR	GAMES AT POSITION	DL	BFW
1983	Cin N	68	98	7	20	4	1	0	9	13-2	0	17	.204	.297	.265	55	-6	1-0	.983	1	94	102	S37,2b5		-0.2
1984	Cin N	106	277	26	70	8	3	5	27	24-7	0	36	.253	.310	.357	84	-6	3-2	.965	-9	91	73	S83,2b10/3		-0.8
1985	Cin N	43	92	7	18	5	1	0	6	6-1	0	16	.196	.245	.272	42	-7	1-0	.983	3	91	119	2b18,S15/3		-0.2
	Phi N	46	158	17	42	8	1	3	17	13-7	0	18	.266	.322	.373	91	-2	1-3	.981	0	95	97	S45		0.2
	Year	89	250	24	60	13	1	3	23	19-8	0	34	.240	.294	.336	73	-9	2-3	.978	3	99	113	S60,2b18/3		0.0
1986	Phi N	39	61	8	18	2	1	0	5	10-1	0	11	.295	.389	.361	106	1	0-1	.975	0	89	109	S24/23	22	0.3
	Mon N	64	202	18	52	13	2	1	18	20-5	0	26	.257	.320	.356	88	-3	8-3	.965	-1	78	61	S29,2b25,3b15		0.3
	Year	103	263	26	70	15	3	1	23	30-6	0	37	.266	.337	.357	92	-2	10-3	.970	-1	82	80	S53,2b6,3b16		0.3
1987	Mon N	106	280	35	82	18	3	5	28	11-0	1	40	.293	.322	.432	94	-1	6-10	.963	-1	95	115	S49,2b39,3b9	16	-0.1
1988	Mon N	127	377	33	100	21	3	5	43	30-10	1	49	.265	.319	.377	95	-2	2-7	.972	3	106	107	2b89,S32,3b9		0.3
1989	Mon N	122	375	34	86	19	2	7	39	45-4	3	53	.229	.314	.347	88	-5	2-3	.988	16	109	106	2b108,3b16,S14/P	17	1.3
1990	Mon N	73	164	11	35	2	1	0	12	12-2	0	22	.213	.266	.238	41	-14	0-1	.987	-2	107	148	S45,2b20,3b7/1		-1.4
1991	Mon N	86	168	12	35	11	1	0	15	14-4	1	30	.208	.269	.286	58	-9	2-0	.967	-2	91	90	S43,1b31,3b6,2b2		-1.1
1992	Mon N	72	115	7	20	3	1	0	5	8-2	1	21	.174	.230	.217	29	-11	3-0	.967	1	106	99	S33,2b13,1b12,3b4/OL		-0.9
1993	Pit N	86	194	18	49	11	1	3	22	11-1	0	26	.253	.287	.366	75	-7	0-1	.993	0	82	109	2b35,1b12,3b7,S6	16	-0.3
1994	Pit N	59	123	13	29	7	0	3	15	13-2	0	18	.236	.307	.366	74	-5	0-0	.986	8	113	112	2b17,3b14,S8,1b3	18	0.4
1995	Mon N	11	24	2	5	2	0	0	2	2-0	0	4	.208	.269	.292	46	-2	1-0	1.000	1	109	47	1b4,2b3	18	-0.1
Total	13	1108	2708	248	661	134	20	32	263	232-48	7	387	.244	.303	.344	78	-81	32-29	.972	18	96	104	S463,2b385,3b90,1b63/OLP	107	-2.6

FOLEY, WILL William Brown B11.15.1855 Chicago IL D11.12.1916 Chicago IL BR/TR/5-9.5/150 d8.23

YEAR	TM LG	G	AB	R	H	2B	3B	HR	RBI	BB-IB	HP	SO	AVG	OBP	SLG	AOPS	ABR	SB-CS	FA	FR	RNG	THR	GAMES AT POSITION	DL	BFW
1875	Chi NA	3	12	0	3	1	0	0	1	0		2	.250	.250	.333	100	0	0-0	.813	1	142	339	3b3		0.1
1876	Cin N	58	221	19	50	3	0	0	9	0		14	.226	.226	.258	71	-5		.804	-1	113	85	3b46,C20		-0.4
1877	Cin N	56	216	23	41	5	1	0	18	4		13	.190	.205	.222	39	-14		.836	7	117	113	3b56		-0.5
1878	Mil N	56	229	33	62	8	1	0	22	7		14	.271	.292	.349	103	0		.812	-8	84	131	3b53,C7		-0.6
1879	Cin N	56	218	22	46	5	1	0	25	2		16	.211	.218	.243	55	-10		.820	1	97	239	3b29,O25R,2b3		-0.6
1881	Det N	2	15	0	2	0	0	0	1	2		3	.133	.235	.133	18	-1		.769	-1	66	508	3b5		-0.2
1884	CP U	19	71	15	20	1	0	0	5	0			.282	.329	.324	99	-2		.804	1	77	129	3b19		-0.2
Total	6	250	970	112	221	22	10	0	75	20		60	.228	.243	.271	70	-32		.817	-2	101	137	3b208,C27,O25R,2b3		-2.6

FOLI, TIM Timothy John B12.8.1950 Culver City CA BR/TR/6-0/176* [NYN68 1/1] d9.11 C10

YEAR	TM LG	G	AB	R	H	2B	3B	HR	RBI	BB-IB	HP	SO	AVG	OBP	SLG	AOPS	ABR	SB-CS	FA	FR	RNG	THR	GAMES AT POSITION	DL	BFW
1970	NY N	5	11	0	4	0	0	0	0	0-0	0	1	.364	.364	.364	94	0	0-0	1.000	2	191	0	S2,3b2		0.2
1971	NY N	97	288	32	65	12	2	0	24	18-4	1	50	.226	.272	.281	57	-16	5-0	.964	5	91	111	2b58,3b36,S12/OC		-0.7

YEAR	TM LG	G	AB	R	H	2B	3B	HR	RBI	BB-IB	HP	SO	AVG	OBP	SLG	AOPS	ABR	SB-CS	FA	FR	RNG	THR	GAMES AT POSITION	DL	BFW
1972	Mon N	149	540	45	130	12	2	2	35	25-2	6	43	.241	.280	.281	59	-29	11-7	.966	18	106	104	S148/2		0.7
1973	Mon N	126	458	37	110	11	0	2	36	28-11	1	40	.240	.284	.277	54	-28	6-3	.960	18	107	108	S123,2b2/OC	29	0.5
1974	Mon N	121	441	41	112	10	3	0	39	28-0	3	27	.254	.300	.290	63	-22	8-2	.971	35	116	128	S120/3	16	2.8
1975	Mon N	152	572	64	136	25	2	1	29	36-5	2	49	.238	.284	.294	58	-33	13-3	.973	11	104	110	S151/2		-0.3
1976	Mon N	149	546	41	144	36	1	6	54	16-1	0	33	.264	.281	.366	80	-15	6-5	.975	17	105	108	S146/3		1.8
1977	Mon N	13	57	2	10	5	1	0	3	0-0	0	4	.175	.172	.298	25	-6	0-0	1.000	1	98	77	S13		-0.3
	SF N	104	368	30	84	17	3	4	27	11-1	0	16	.228	.247	.323	53	-26	2-4	.974	9	100	127	S102/23OL	30	-1.0
	Year	117	425	32	94	22	4	4	30	11-1	0	20	.221	.238	.320	49	-32	2-4	.977	8	100	121	S115/23OL		-1.4
1978	NY N	113	413	37	106	21	1	1	27	14-1	2	30	.257	.283	.320	70	-17	2-5	.966	-1	97	130	S112	26	-0.9
1979	NY N	3	7	0	0	0	0	0	0	0-0	0	0	.000	.000	.000	-99	-2	0-0	1.000	0	103	89	S3		-0.2
	†Pit N	133	525	70	153	23	1	1	65	28-0	9	14	.291	.335	.345	82	-12	6-5	.978	7	97	132	S132		0.8
	Year	136	532	70	153	23	1	1	65	28-0	9	14	.288	.330	.340	80	-14	6-5	.978	7	97	131	S135		0.6
1980	Pit N	127	495	61	131	22	0	3	38	19-1	6	23	.265	.296	.327	72	-18	11-7	.981	11	102	125	S125	15	0.6
1981	Pit N	86	316	32	78	12	2	0	20	17-0	1	10	.247	.285	.297	63	-16	7-7	.965	4	99	103	S81		-1.4
1982	†Cal A	150	480	46	121	14	2	3	56	14-1	2	22	.252	.273	.308	60	-28	2-4	.985	14	108	115	S139,2b8,3b2		0.0
1983	Cal A	88	330	29	83	10	0	2	29	5-1	1	18	.252	.263	.300	55	-21	2-3	.975	13	123	108	S74,3b13		-0.1
1984	NY A	61	163	8	41	11	0	0	16	2-0	1	16	.252	.265	.319	63	-8	0-0	.950	7	132	128	S28,2b21,3b10,1b2		0.1
1985	Pit N	19	37	1	7	0	0	0	2	4-1	0	2	.189	.268	.189	30	-3	0-0	.980	4	128	111	S13	24	0.1
Total	16	1696	6047	576	1515	241	20	25	501	265-29	35	399	.251	.283	.309	64	-300	81-55	.973	165	105	116	S1524,2b92,3b66,O3(1/2/0),1b2	140	2.6

FONDY, DEE Dee Virgil B10.31.1924 Slaton TX D8.19.1999 Redlands CA BL/TL/6-3/196* d4.17

YEAR	TM LG	G	AB	R	H	2B	3B	HR	RBI	BB-IB	HP	SO	AVG	OBP	SLG	AOPS	ABR	SB-CS	FA	FR	RNG	THR	GAMES AT POSITION	DL	BFW
1951	Chi N	49	170	23	46	7	2	3	20	11	1	20	.271	.319	.388	88	-3	5-6	.976	-3	89	95	1b44		-0.8
1952	Chi N	145	554	69	166	21	9	10	67	28	1	60	.300	.334	.424	108	3	13-11	.990	1	103	75	1b143		-0.2
1953	Chi N	150	595	79	184	24	11	18	78	44	1	106	.309	.358	.477	113	10	10-7	.987	4	111	75	1b149		0.4
1954	Chi N	141	568	77	162	30	4	9	49	35	1	84	.285	.326	.400	87	-11	20-5	.993	8	120	100	1b138		-0.8
1955	Chi N	150	574	69	152	23	8	17	65	35-6	2	87	.265	.307	.422	92	-9	8-9	.991	1	103	102	1b147		-1.8
1956	Chi N	137	543	52	146	22	9	9	46	20-5	0	74	.269	.290	.392	84	-14	9-7	.985	-4	92	88	1b133		-2.7
1957	Chi N	11	51	3	16	3	1	0	2	0-0	0	9	.314	.314	.412	94	-1	1-2	.991	-1	67	100	1b11		-0.3
	Pit N	95	323	42	101	13	2	2	35	25-0	1	59	.313	.360	.384	104	2	11-5	.982	-9	92	100	1b73		-0.5
	Year	106	374	45	117	16	3	2	37	25-0	1	68	.313	.354	.388	103	2	12-7	.983	-5	89	100	1b84		-0.8
1958	Cin N	89	124	23	27	1	1	1	11	5-0	0	27	.218	.246	.266	34	-12	7-1	.987	2	158	113	1b36,O22(7/0/15)		-1.0
Total	8	967	3502	437	1000	144	47	69	373	203-11	7	526	.286	.324	.413	95	-35	84-53	.988	5	104	90	1b874,O22(7/0/15)		-7.7

FONSECA, LEW Lewis Albert B1.21.1899 Oakland CA D11.26.1989 Ely IA BR/TR/5-10.5/180 d4.13 M3 Col St. Marys (CA) OF(99/15/5)

YEAR	TM LG	G	AB	R	H	2B	3B	HR	RBI	BB-IB	HP	SO	AVG	OBP	SLG	AOPS	ABR	SB-CS	FA	FR	RNG	THR	GAMES AT POSITION	DL	BFW
1921	Cin N	82	297	38	82	10	3	1	41	8	4	13	.276	.304	.340	74	-12	2-3	.961	-3	95	92	2b50,1b16,O16(14/0/2)		-1.6
1922	Cin N	81	291	55	105	20	3	4	45	14	0	18	.361	.390	.491	128	12	7-8	.970	9	103	117	2b71		2.0
1923	Cin N	65	237	33	66	11	4	3	28	9	2	16	.278	.310	.397	87	-5	4-0	.957	6	107	102	2b45,1b14		0.2
1924	Cin N	20	57	5	13	2	1	0	9	4	0	4	.228	.279	.298	55	-4	1-0	1.000	-1	94	72	2b10,1b6		-0.4
1925	Phi N	126	467	78	149	30	5	7	60	21	3	42	.319	.352	.450	95	-4	6-2	.956	-7	98	76	2b69,1b55		-1.1
1927	Cle A	112	428	60	133	20	7	2	40	12	2	17	.311	.333	.404	90	-9	12-4	.973	-2	101	89	2b96,1b13		-0.7
1928	Cle A	75	263	38	86	19	4	3	36	13	1	17	.327	.361	.464	114	5	4-2	1.000	5	122	143	1b56,3b15,S4/2		0.7
1929	Cle A	148	566	97	209	44	15	6	103	50	7	23	.369	.427	.532	140	35	19-11	.995	7	118	109	1b147		3.0
1930	Cle A	40	129	20	36	9	2	0	17	7	0	7	.279	.316	.380	73	-5	1-0	.980	1	154	64	1b28,3b6		-0.5
1931	Cle A	26	108	21	40	9	1	1	14	8	1	7	.370	.419	.500	133	5	3-2	.993	0	98	80	1b26		0.3
	Chi A	121	465	65	139	26	5	2	71	32	3	22	.299	.348	.389	99	-1	4-4	.974	-9	96	62	O95(80/15/0),2b21,1b2/3		-1.0
	Year	147	573	86	179	35	6	3	85	40	4	29	.312	.361	.410	106	-1	7-6	.974	-9	96	62	O95(80/15/0),1b28,2b21/3		-1.0
1932	Chi A	18	37	0	5	1	0	0	6	1	0	7	.135	.158	.162	-18	-7	0-0	1.000	1	92	362	O8(5/0/3)/PM		-0.5
1933	Chi A	23	59	8	12	2	0	2	15	7	0	6	.203	.288	.339	68	-3	1-0	1.000	2	172	149	1b12,M		-0.2
Total	12	937	3404	518	1075	203	50	31	485	186	23	199	.316	.355	.432	103	7	64-36	.994	10	112	104	1b375,2b363,O119L,3b22,S4/P		-0.1

FONTENOT, MIKE Michael Eugene B6.9.1980 Slidell LA BL/TR/5-8/165 d4.13 Col Louisiana St.

YEAR	TM LG	G	AB	R	H	2B	3B	HR	RBI	BB-IB	HP	SO	AVG	OBP	SLG	AOPS	ABR	SB-CS	FA	FR	RNG	THR	GAMES AT POSITION	DL	BFW
2005	Chi N	7	2	4	0	0	0	0	2	0-0	1	0	.000	.600	.000	73	0	0-0	—		0		/H		0.0

FONVILLE, CHAD Chad Everette B3.5.1971 Jacksonville NC BB/TR/5-6/155* [SFN92 11/299] d4.28 Col Louisburg (NC) JC

YEAR	TM LG	G	AB	R	H	2B	3B	HR	RBI	BB-IB	HP	SO	AVG	OBP	SLG	AOPS	ABR	SB-CS	FA	FR	RNG	THR	GAMES AT POSITION	DL	BFW
1995	Mon N	14	12	2	4	0	0	0	0	0-0	1	3	.333	.333	.333	74	0	0-2	—	0		0	2b2		-0.2
	†LA N	88	308	41	85	6	1	0	16	23-1	1	39	.276	.328	.302	73	-12	20-5	.971	-1	102	74	S38,2b36,O11(10/2/0)		-0.7
	Year	102	320	43	89	6	1	0	16	23-1	1	42	.278	.328	.303	72	-13	20-7	.971	-2	95	70	2b38,S38,O11(10/2/0)		-0.9
1996	LA N	103	201	34	41	4	1	0	13	17-1	0	31	.204	.266	.234	35	-19	7-2	.964	-10	92	159	O35(19/18/0),2b23,S20,3b2		-2.1
1997	LA N	9	14	1	2	0	0	0	1	2-0	0	3	.143	.250	.143	7	-2	0-1	.833	-4	47	0	2b3		-0.6
	Chi N	9	9	1	1	0	0	0	1	1-0	0	1	.111	.200	.111	-16	-2	2-0	1.000	-1	245	0	O3(1/2/0),2b2,S2/D		-0.1
1999	Bos A	3	2	1	0	0	0	0	0	2-0	0	0	.000	.500	.000	41	0	1-0	.900	1	85	142	2b2		0.1
Total	4	226	546	80	133	10	2	0	31	45-2	1	77	.244	.302	.269	56	-35	30-10	.964	-10	92	75	2b68,S60,O49(30/22/0),3b2/D		-3.6

FOOTE, BARRY Barry Clifton B2.16.1952 Smithfield NC BR/TR/6-3/210(205-220) [MonN70 1/3] d9.14 C3

YEAR	TM LG	G	AB	R	H	2B	3B	HR	RBI	BB-IB	HP	SO	AVG	OBP	SLG	AOPS	ABR	SB-CS	FA	FR	RNG	THR	GAMES AT POSITION	DL	BFW
1973	Mon N	6	6	0	4	0	1	0	4	0-0	0	0	.667	.667	1.000	343	2	0-0	—		0		/H		0.2
1974	Mon N	125	420	44	110	23	4	11	60	35-11	3	74	.262	.315	.414	100	-1	2-1	.984	11	109	113	C122		1.6
1975	Mon N	118	387	25	75	16	1	7	30	17-6	1	48	.194	.229	.295	42	-31	0-1	.985	5	121	83	C115		-2.3
1976	Mon N	105	350	32	82	12	2	7	27	17-3	1	32	.234	.272	.340	69	-15	2-1	.989	7	112	123	C96,3b2/1	16	-0.4
1977	Mon N	15	49	4	12	3	1	2	8	4-0	0	10	.245	.302	.469	105	0	0-0	.988	2	258	107	C13		0.2
	Phi N	18	32	3	7	1	0	1	3	3-0	0	6	.219	.286	.344	65	-2	0-0	.980	-1	113	54	C17		-0.2
	Year	33	81	7	19	4	1	3	11	7-0	0	16	.235	.295	.420	88	-2	0-0	.985	1	199	86	C30		0.0
1978	†Phi N	39	57	4	9	0	0	1	4	1-0	0	11	.158	.172	.211	6	-7	0-0	1.000	1	362	57	C17		-0.6
1979	Chi N	132	429	47	109	26	4	16	56	34-7	2	49	.254	.316	.427	92	-5	5-2	.979	3	115	104	C129		0.4
1980	Chi N	63	202	16	48	13	1	6	28	13-2	0	18	.238	.282	.401	82	-5	1-1	.992	5	121	114	C55	34	0.2
1981	Chi N	9	22	0	0	0	0	0	0	3-0	0	7	.000	.115	.000	-60	-5	0-0	1.000	-0	267	116	C8		-0.5
	†NY A	40	125	12	26	4	0	6	10	8-0	0	21	.208	.256	.384	83	-3	0-0	.996	8	82	117	C34/1D		0.6
1982	NY A	17	48	4	7	1	0	0	2	1-0	0	11	.146	.160	.250	12	-6	0-0	.973	-4	117	64	C17	31	-0.9
Total	10	687	2127	191	489	103	10	57	230	136-29	10	287	.230	.277	.368	75	-78	10-6	.985	37	124	104	C637,D4,1b2,3b2	81	-1.7

FORAN, JIM James H. B1848 NY D1.30.1928 Los Angeles CA 5-6.5/159 d5.4

YEAR	TM LG	G	AB	R	H	2B	3B	HR	RBI	BB-IB	HP	SO	AVG	OBP	SLG	AOPS	ABR	SB-CS	FA	FR	RNG	THR	GAMES AT POSITION	DL	BFW
1871	Kek NA	19	89	21	31	1	3	1	18	2		1	.348	.363	.461	132	3	1-0	.878	0	163	27	1b16,O4(3/1/0)		0.2

FORBES, P.J. Patrick Joseph B9.22.1967 Pittsburg KS BR/TR/5-10/160* [CalA90 20/556] d7.21 Col Wichita St.

YEAR	TM LG	G	AB	R	H	2B	3B	HR	RBI	BB-IB	HP	SO	AVG	OBP	SLG	AOPS	ABR	SB-CS	FA	FR	RNG	THR	GAMES AT POSITION	DL	BFW
1998	Bal A	9	10	0	2	0	0	0	2	0-0	0	2	.200	.200	.200	-49	-2	0-0	1.000	1	131	135	2b7/3S		-0.1
2001	Phi N	3	7	1	2	0	0	0	1	0-0	0	2	.286	.286	.286	51	-1	0-0	1.000	0	74	0	/2		-0.1
Total	2	12	17	1	3	0	0	0	3	0-0	0	2	.176	.176	.176	-8	-3	0-0	1.000	0	114	95	2b8/S3		-0.2

FORCE, DAVY David W. "Wee Davy","Tom Thumb" B7.27.1849 New York NY D6.21.1918 Englewood NJ BR/TR/5-4/130 d5.5 ▲

YEAR	TM LG	G	AB	R	H	2B	3B	HR	RBI	BB-IB	HP	SO	AVG	OBP	SLG	AOPS	ABR	SB-CS	FA	FR	RNG	THR	GAMES AT POSITION	DL	BFW
1871	Oly NA	32	162	45	45	9	4	0	29	4		0	.278	.295	.383	98	1	8-0	.844	18	136	104	S31/3		1.2
1872	Tro NA	25	130	40	53	11	0	0	21	4		0	.408	.412	.492	174	11	2-2	.871	4	105	227	3b16,S9		0.9
	Bal NA	19	95	29	41	2	2	0	14	1		0	.432	.438	.495	178	8	5-0	.846	4	100	0	3b19		0.8
	Year	44	225	69	94	13	2	0	33	2		0	.418	.423	.493	176	19	7-2	.857	7	102	107	3b35,S9		1.7
1873	Bal NA	49	233	77	85	10	1	0	30	9		1	.365	.388	.416	140	12	1-0	.830	7	101	26	3b34,S17,P3		1.2
1874	Chi N	59	294	61	92	9	0	2	26	3		1	.313	.320	.344	112	4	4-0	.802	9	111	100	3b42,S18/P		0.9
1875	Ath NA	77	386	78	120	22	5	0	49	7		5	.311	.323	.394	133	11	6-3	.887	11	100	162	S77,3b2		1.7
1876	Phi N	60	284	48	66	6	0	0	17	5		3	.232	.246	.254	67	-9		.898	20	122	75	S60,3b2		1.1
	NY N	1	3	0	0	0	0	0	0	0		0	.000	.000	.000	-99	-1		.833	0	105	0	/S		0.0
	Year	61	287	48	66	6	0	0	17	5		3	.230	.243	.251	66	-10		.897	20	122	74	S61,3b2		1.1
1877	StL N	58	225	24	59	5	3	0	22	11		15	.262	.297	.311	97	0		.914	6	102	80	S50,3b8		0.7
1879	Buf N	79	316	36	66	5	2	0	8	13		37	.209	.240	.237	57	-15		.929	7	101	164	S115,3b2		1.1
1880	Buf N	81	290	22	49	10	0	0	17	10		35	.169	.197	.203	35	-19		.939	26	121	108	2b53,S30		1.1
1881	Buf N	75	278	21	50	9	1	0	15	11		29	.180	.211	.219	36	-20		.937	25	130	66	2b51,S21,O3R/3		0.3
1882	Buf N	73	278	39	67	10	1	1	28	12		17	.241	.272	.295	81	-6		.908	7	106	74	S61,3b11/2		0.3
1883	Buf N	96	378	40	82	11	3	0	35	12		39	.217	.241	.262	52	-22		.884	-9	96	103	S78,3b13,2b7		-2.5
1884	Buf N	106	403	47	83	13	3	0	36	27		41	.206	.256	.253	59	-19		.898	-4	97	91	S105/2		-1.8
1885	Buf N	71	253	20	57	6	1	0	15	13		19	.225	.263	.257	66	-10		.882	0	105	115	2b42,S24,3b6		-0.6

YEAR	TM LG	G	AB	R	H	2B	3B	HR	RBI	BB-IB	HP	SO	AVG	OBP	SLG	AOPS	ABR	SB-CS	FA	FR	RNG	THR	GAMES AT POSITION	DL	BFW
1886	Was N	68	242	26	44	5	1	0	16	17		26	.182	.236	.211	39	-17	9	.909	18	124	119	S56,2b8,3b4		0.3
Total	5 NA	261	1300	330	436	63	12	0	167	25		7	.335	.348	.402	132	47	26-5	.865	52	107	133	S152,3b114,P4		6.7
Total	10	768	2950	323	623	80	15	1	209	131		261	.211	.245	.249	58	-138	9	.908	92	106	100	S564,2b163,3b46,O3R		-1.4

FORD, CURT Curtis Glenn B10.11.1960 Jackson MS BL/TR/5-10/150(150-165) [StLN81 4/85] d6.22 Col Jackson St.

YEAR	TM LG	G	AB	R	H	2B	3B	HR	RBI	BB-IB	HP	SO	AVG	OBP	SLG	AOPS	ABR	SB-CS	FA	FR	RNG	THR	GAMES AT POSITION	DL	BFW
1985	StL N	11	12	2	6	2	0	0	3	4-0	0	1	.500	.625	.667	263	3	1-0	.750	-1	71	0	O4(1/0/4)		0.3
1986	StL N	85	214	30	53	15	2	2	29	23-2	0	29	.248	.318	.364	89	-3	13-5	.975	4	105	169	O64(24/0/40)		0.0
1987	†StL N	89	228	32	65	9	5	3	26	14-0	1	32	.285	.325	.408	91	-3	11-8	.981	7	136	48	O75(15/2/61)	39	0.0
1988	StL N	91	128	11	25	6	0	1	18	8-1	0	26	.195	.239	.266	45	-9	6-1	.965	3	119	78	O40(24/3/13),1b7		-0.7
1989	Phi N	108	142	13	31	5	1	1	13	16-0	1	33	.218	.298	.289	70	-5	5-3	1.000	1	95	225	O52(26/2/25)/12		-0.5
1990	Phi N	22	18	0	2	0	0	0	0	1-0	0	5	.111	.158	.111	-25	-3	0-0	1.000	0	162	0	O3R		-0.3
Total	6	406	742	88	182	37	8	7	89	66-3	2	126	.245	.305	.345	79	-20	36-17	.977	14	116	118	O238(90/7/146),1b8/2	39	-1.2

FORD, DAN Darnell Glenn B5.19.1952 Los Angeles CA BR/TR/6-1/185(185-197) [OakA70 1/18] d4.12

YEAR	TM LG	G	AB	R	H	2B	3B	HR	RBI	BB-IB	HP	SO	AVG	OBP	SLG	AOPS	ABR	SB-CS	FA	FR	RNG	THR	GAMES AT POSITION	DL	BFW
1975	Min A	130	440	72	123	21	1	15	59	30-2	5	79	.280	.333	.434	114	7	6-7	.988	-11	88	40	O120(0/118/2),D3		-0.8
1976	Min A	145	514	87	137	24	7	20	86	36-2	10	118	.267	.323	.457	126	15	17-6	.968	-7	95	59	O139(1/0/139),D3		0.2
1977	Min A	144	453	66	121	25	4	11	60	41-3	10	79	.267	.338	.426	109	6	6-4	.964	-7	85	104	O137(1/3/135),D3		-0.7
1978	Min A	151	592	78	162	36	10	11	82	48-6	5	88	.274	.332	.424	109	6	7-7	.977	-15	88	59	O149(0/145/4)/D		-1.1
1979	†Cal A	142	569	100	166	25	5	21	101	40-0	3	86	.290	.333	.464	118	12	8-5	.977	6	113	99	O141(0/29/124)		1.1
1980	Cal A	65	226	22	63	11	0	7	26	19-1	2	45	.279	.339	.420	109	3	5-5	.940	-2	93	98	O45R,D15	63	-0.2
1981	Cal A	97	375	50	104	14	1	15	48	23-3	5	71	.277	.327	.440	118	8	2-2	.960	-7	94	42	O97R		-0.5
1982	Bal A	123	421	46	99	21	3	10	43	23-1	4	71	.235	.279	.371	78	-14	5-2	.975	5	116	76	O119R/D		-1.4
1983	†Bal A	103	407	63	114	30	4	9	55	29-1	3	55	.280	.328	.440	112	7	9-2	.987	-2	107	26	O103R	28	0.0
1984	Bal A	25	91	7	21	4	0	1	5	7-0	0	13	.231	.286	.308	65	-4	1-0	1.000	1	120	111	O15R,D8	125	-0.4
1985	Bal A	28	75	4	14	2	0	1	1	7-0	0	17	.187	.256	.253	41	-6	0-1	—	0	0	0	D28	121	-0.7
Total	11	1153	4163	598	1123	214	38	121	566	303-19	47	722	.270	.324	.427	108	40	61-37	.974	-38	98	67	O1065(2/295/783),D62	337	-4.5

FORD, ED Edgar L. B4.10.1862 Richmond VA D6.8.1931 Richmond VA 5-9.5/160 d10.9

YEAR	TM LG	G	AB	R	H	2B	3B	HR	RBI	BB-IB	HP	SO	AVG	OBP	SLG	AOPS	ABR	SB-CS	FA	FR	RNG	THR	GAMES AT POSITION	DL	BFW
1884	Ric AA	2	5	0	0	0	0	0	0	0-0	0		.000	.000	.000	-99	-1		.556	1	116	0	/S1		-0.1

FORD, HOD Horace Hills B7.23.1897 New Haven CT D1.29.1977 Winchester MA BR/TR/5-10/165 d9.8 Col Tufts

YEAR	TM LG	G	AB	R	H	2B	3B	HR	RBI	BB-IB	HP	SO	AVG	OBP	SLG	AOPS	ABR	SB-CS	FA	FR	RNG	THR	GAMES AT POSITION	DL	BFW
1919	Bos N	10	28	4	6	0	1	0	3	2	1	6	.214	.290	.286	77	-1	0-0	.946	2	133	122	S8,3b2		0.2
1920	Bos N	88	257	16	62	12	5	1	30	18	2	25	.241	.296	.339	86	-5	3-3	.972	11	116	73	2b59,S18,1b4		0.8
1921	Bos N	152	555	50	155	29	5	2	61	36	4	49	.279	.328	.360	87	-10	2-11	.973	4	103	84	2b119,S33		-0.3
1922	Bos N	143	515	58	140	23	9	2	60	30	4	36	.272	.317	.363	78	-18	2-1	.953	-0	99	84	S115,2b28		-0.4
1923	Bos N	111	380	27	103	16	7	2	50	31	0	30	.271	.326	.366	86	-8	1-1	.970	-8	97	106	2b95,S19		-1.1
1924	Phi N	145	530	58	144	27	5	3	53	27	0	40	.272	.309	.358	70	-22	1-9	.970	9	106	95	2b145		-1.2
1925	Bro N	66	216	32	59	11	0	1	15	26	2	15	.273	.357	.338	81	-5	0-3	.966	2	97	88	S66		0.2
1926	Cin N	57	197	14	55	6	1	0	18	14	3	12	.279	.336	.320	79	-5	1	.963	2	94	168	S57		0.3
1927	Cin N	115	409	45	112	16	2	1	46	33	2	34	.274	.331	.330	80	-11	0	.952	-6	96	129	S104,2b12		-0.5
1928	Cin N	149	506	49	122	17	4	0	54	47	2	31	.241	.308	.291	58	-31	1	.972	15	102	134	S149		0.0
1929	Cin N	148	529	68	146	14	6	3	50	41	1	25	.276	.329	.342	70	-26	8	.953	8	100	128	S108,2b42		-0.5
1930	Cin N	132	424	36	98	16	7	1	34	24	0	28	.231	.272	.309	42	-41	2	.974	5	99	107	S74,2b66		-2.5
1931	Cin N	84	175	18	40	8	1	0	13	13	1	13	.229	.286	.286	57	-11	0	.954	0	101	121	S73,2b3/3		-0.1
1932	StL N	1	2	0	0	0	0	0	0	0	0	0	.000	.000	.000	-97	-1	0	.750	—	45	235	/S		-0.1
	Bos N	40	95	9	26	5	2	0	6	6	1	9	.274	.324	.368	89	-2	0	.984	-1	96	118	2b20,S16,3b2		-0.1
	Year	41	97	9	26	5	2	0	6	6	1	9	.268	.317	.361	85	-2	0	.984	-1	96	118	2b20,S17,3b2		-0.2
1933	Bos N	5	15	0	1	0	0	0	1	3	0	1	.067	.222	.067	-16	-2	0	1.000	3	120	116	S5		0.1
Total	15	1446	4833	484	1269	200	55	16	494	351	24	354	.263	.316	.337	72	-199	21-28	.960	45	100	116	S846,2b589,3b5,1b4		-5.8

FORD, LEW Jon Lewis B8.12.1976 Beaumont TX BR/TR/6-0/190* [BosA99 12/379] d5.29 Col Dallas Baptist

YEAR	TM LG	G	AB	R	H	2B	3B	HR	RBI	BB-IB	HP	SO	AVG	OBP	SLG	AOPS	ABR	SB-CS	FA	FR	RNG	THR	GAMES AT POSITION	DL	BFW
2003	†Min A	34	73	16	24	7	1	3	9	8-0	1	9	.329	.402	.575	148	5	2-0	.923	-2	86	108	O25(8/13/6),D4	50	0.4
2004	†Min A	154	569	89	170	31	4	15	72	67-3	13	75	.299	.381	.446	113	13	20-2	.986	-1	100	101	O126(81/46/10),D26		1.1
2005	Min A	147	522	70	138	30	4	7	53	45-2	16	85	.264	.338	.377	89	-7	13-6	.972	-3	87	182	O95(18/63/16),D44		-1.2
Total	3	335	1164	175	332	68	9	25	140	120-5	30	169	.285	.364	.424	104	11	35-8	.976	-6	94	133	O246(107/122/32),D74	50	-0.1

FORD, TED Theodore Henry B2.7.1947 Vineland NJ BR/TR/5-10/180* [CleA66*1/11] d4.7

YEAR	TM LG	G	AB	R	H	2B	3B	HR	RBI	BB-IB	HP	SO	AVG	OBP	SLG	AOPS	ABR	SB-CS	FA	FR	RNG	THR	GAMES AT POSITION	DL	BFW
1970	Cle A	26	46	5	8	1	0	1	1	3-0	0	13	.174	.224	.261	32	-4	0-0	1.000	2	143	171	O12(2/1/10)		-0.3
1971	Cle A	74	196	15	38	6	0	2	14	9-0	0	34	.194	.229	.255	34	-17	2-2	1.000	5	116	144	O55(12/20/29)		-1.6
1972	Tex A	129	429	43	101	19	1	14	50	37-2	3	80	.235	.297	.382	106	2	4-3	.977	7	113	94	O119(16/0/104)		0.4
1973	Cle A	11	40	3	9	0	1	0	3	2-0	0	7	.225	.250	.275	50	-3	1-0	1.000	-4	27	0	O10(0/6/5)		-0.7
Total	4	240	711	66	156	26	2	17	68	51-2	3	134	.219	.272	.333	76	-22	7-5	.985	10	110	131	O196(30/27/148)		-2.2

FORDYCE, BROOK Brook Alexander B5.7.1970 New London CT BR/TR/6-1/190* [NYN89 3/84] d4.26

YEAR	TM LG	G	AB	R	H	2B	3B	HR	RBI	BB-IB	HP	SO	AVG	OBP	SLG	AOPS	ABR	SB-CS	FA	FR	RNG	THR	GAMES AT POSITION	DL	BFW
1995	NY N	4	2	1	1	0	0	0	1	1-0	0	0	.500	.667	1.000	344	1	0-0	—		0		/H		0.1
1996	Cin N	4	7	0	2	1	0	0	3	1-0	0	1	.286	.500	.429	146	1	0-0	1.000	1	223	112	C4		0.0
1997	Cin N	47	96	7	20	5	0	1	8	8-1	0	15	.208	.267	.292	46	-8	2-0	.983	-5	59	73	C30/D	20	-1.1
1998	Cin N	57	146	8	37	9	0	3	14	11-3	0	28	.253	.306	.377	77	-5	0-1	.978	-1	90	133	C54	30	-0.3
1999	Chi A	105	333	36	99	25	1	9	49	21-0	3	48	.297	.343	.459	101	0	2-0	.987	-10	96	93	C103		-0.3
2000	Chi A	40	125	18	34	7	1	5	21	6-0	2	23	.272	.313	.464	91	-2	0-0	1.000	8	139	116	C40	49	0.7
	Bal A	53	177	23	57	11	0	9	28	11-0	2	27	.322	.361	.542	132	8	0-0	.988	-8	68	50	C52		0.3
	Year	93	302	41	91	18	1	14	49	17-0	4	50	.301	.341	.507	114	5	0-0	.993	0	97	77	C92		1.0
2001	Bal A	95	292	30	61	18	0	5	19	21-1	3	56	.209	.268	.322	58	-18	1-2	.983	-13	64	93	C95		-2.5
2002	Bal A	56	130	7	30	8	0	1	8	9-0	4	19	.231	.301	.315	68	-6	1-0	.986	-8	54	76	C55		-1.1
2003	Bal A	108	348	28	95	12	2	6	31	19-1	7	44	.273	.311	.371	80	-11	2-3	.996	-8	79	83	C107		-1.2
2004	TB A	54	151	14	31	6	0	2	19	9-0	7	34	.205	.259	.285	43	-13	0-0	.990	-3	97	83	C51/D		-1.2
Total	10	623	1807	172	467	103	4	41	188	119-6	17	295	.258	.309	.388	81	-53	8-6	.988	-48	83	89	C591,D2	99	-6.6

FORSTER, TOM Thomas W. B5.1.1859 New York NY D7.17.1946 New York NY BR/TR/5-9/153 d8.4

YEAR	TM LG	G	AB	R	H	2B	3B	HR	RBI	BB-IB	HP	SO	AVG	OBP	SLG	AOPS	ABR	SB-CS	FA	FR	RNG	THR	GAMES AT POSITION	DL	BFW
1882	Det N	21	76	5	7	0	0	0	2	5		12	.092	.148	.092	-21	-10		.830	-8	81	51	2b21		-1.7
1884	Pit AA	35	126	10	28	5	0	0		7		0	.222	.263	.262	73	-3		.897	4	110	93	S28,3b6/2		0.2
1885	NY AA	57	213	28	47	7	2	0	18	17	1		.221	.281	.272	79	-4		.903	-5	95	95	2b52,O5(3/2/0)		-1.0
1886	NY AA	67	251	33	49	3	2	1	20	20	3		.195	.263	.235	61	-10	9	.891	-4	101	97	2b62,O4(2/2/0)/S		-1.0
Total	4	180	666	76	131	15	4	1	40	49		12	.197	.256	.236	59	-27	9	.885	-13	96	88	2b136,S29,O9(5/4/0),3b6		-3.2

FORSYTHE, ED Edward James B4.30.1887 Kingston NY D6.22.1956 Hoboken NJ BR/TR/5-10/155 d10.2

YEAR	TM LG	G	AB	R	H	2B	3B	HR	RBI	BB-IB	HP	SO	AVG	OBP	SLG	AOPS	ABR	SB-CS	FA	FR	RNG	THR	GAMES AT POSITION	DL	BFW
1915	Bal F	1	3	0	0	0	0	0	0	0-0	0		.000	.000	.000	-26	-1		.667	-0	112	0	/3		-0.1

FOSS, GEORGE George Dueward "Deeby" B6.13.1897 Register GA D11.10.1969 Brandon FL BR/TR/5-10.5/170 d4.16

YEAR	TM LG	G	AB	R	H	2B	3B	HR	RBI	BB-IB	HP	SO	AVG	OBP	SLG	AOPS	ABR	SB-CS	FA	FR	RNG	THR	GAMES AT POSITION	DL	BFW
1921	Was A	4	7	0	0	0	0	0	0	0-0	0	1	.000	.000	.000	-99	-2		.750	-0	89	536	/3		-0.2

FOSSE, RAY Raymond Earl B4.4.1947 Marion IL BR/TR/6-2/215* [CleA65 1/7] d9.8 [DL 1978 Mil A 179]

YEAR	TM LG	G	AB	R	H	2B	3B	HR	RBI	BB-IB	HP	SO	AVG	OBP	SLG	AOPS	ABR	SB-CS	FA	FR	RNG	THR	GAMES AT POSITION	DL	BFW
1967	Cle A	7	16	0	1	0	0	0	0	0-0	0	5	.063	.063	.063	-62	-3	0-0	1.000	2	75	275	C7		-0.1
1968	Cle A	1	0	0	0	0	0	0	0	0-0	0	0	—	—	—	—		0-0	1.000	-0	0		/C		0.0
1969	Cle A	37	116	11	20	3	0	2	9	8-1	1	29	.172	.230	.250	34	-11	1-0	.977	-3	48	142	C37	80	-1.2
1970	Cle A★	120	450	62	138	17	1	18	61	39-5	1	55	.307	.361	.469	122	13	1-5	.989	8	139	137	C120		2.6
1971	Cle A*	133	486	53	134	21	1	12	62	36-6	4	62	.276	.329	.397	96	-2	4-1	.988	1	96	112	C126,1b4		0.7
1972	Cle A	134	457	42	110	20	1	10	41	45-15	3	46	.241	.312	.354	92	-1	5-1	.985	7	108	90	C124,1b3		1.3
1973	†Oak A	143	492	37	126	23	2	7	52	25-4	1	62	.256	.291	.354	85	-11	2-2	.987	7	171	114	C141,D2		0.2
1974	†Oak A	69	204	20	40	8	3	4	23	11-1	2	31	.196	.241	.324	66	-10	1-1	.973	1	101	86	C68/D	77	-0.7
1975	†Oak A	82	136	14	19	3	2	0	14	16-0	1	16	.140	.192	.191	4	-15	0-1	.981	-8	69		C82/12		-1.9
1976	Cle A	90	276	26	83	9	1	3	30	20-1	0	20	.301	.347	.362	109	3	1-2	.987	3	103	85	C85,1b3/D	33	0.8
1977	Cle A	78	238	25	63	7	1	6	27	7-2	3	26	.265	.293	.378	84	-6	0-5	.983	3	66	128	C77/1D		-0.2
	Sea A	11	34	3	12	1	0	0	3	2-0	3	8	.353	.389	.441	126	1	0-1	.968	-2	205	0	C8,D2		-0.1
	Year	89	272	28	75	10	1	6	32	9-2	6	28	.276	.305	.386	90	-5	0-6	.982	1	78	117	C85,D3/1		-0.3
1979	Mil A	19	52	6	12	3	1	0	2	2-0	2	6	.231	.286	.327	65	-3	0-0	1.000	2	221	81	C13/1D		-0.1
Total	12	924	2957	299	758	117	13	61	324	203-35	18	363	.256	.306	.367	89	-48	15-19	.985	27	115	109	C889,1b13,D12/2	369	1.3

YEAR	TM LG	G	AB	R	H	2B	3B	HR	RBI	BB-IB	HP	SO	AVG	OBP	SLG	AOPS	ABR	SB-CS	FA	FR	RNG	THR	GAMES AT POSITION	DL	BFW

FOSTER, POP Clarence Francis B4.8.1878 New Haven CT D4.16.1944 Princeton NJ BR/TR/5-8.5/? d9.13 Col NYU

YEAR	TM LG	G	AB	R	H	2B	3B	HR	RBI	BB-IB	HP	SO	AVG	OBP	SLG	AOPS	ABR	SB-CS	FA	FR	RNG	THR	GAMES AT POSITION	DL	BFW
1898	NY N	32	112	10	30	6	1	0					.268	.268	.339	76	-4	0	.967	-3	39	0	O21(17/0/4),3b10,S2		-0.8
1899	NY N	84	301	48	89	9	7	3	57	20	4		.296	.348	.402	109	3	7	.949	-9	65	77	O84(1/0/84)/S3		-0.9
1900	NY N	31	84	19	22	3	1	0	11	11	0		.262	.347	.321	89	-1	0	1.000	1	65	218	O12(1/0/11),S7,2b5		0.0
1901	Was A	103	392	65	109	16	9	6	54	41	4		.278	.352	.411	113	7	10	.925	0	69	34	O102L,S2		0.1
	Chi A	12	35	4	10	2	2	1	6	4	0		.286	.359	.543	152	2	0	.909	-1	111	0	O9R		0.1
	Year	115	427	69	119	18	11	7	60	45	4		.279	.353	.422	116	9	10	.924	0	72	32	O111(102/0/9),S2		0.2
Total 4		262	924	146	260	36	20	10	137	76	8		.281	.341	.396	107	7	17	.938	-11	66	55	O228(121/0/108),S12,3b11,2b5		-1.5

FOSTER, EDDIE Edward Cunningham "Kid" B2.13.1887 Chicago IL D1.15.1937 Washington DC BR/TR/5-6.5/145 d4.14

YEAR	TM LG	G	AB	R	H	2B	3B	HR	RBI	BB-IB	HP	SO	AVG	OBP	SLG	AOPS	ABR	SB-CS	FA	FR	RNG	THR	GAMES AT POSITION	DL	BFW
1910	NY A	30	83	5	11	2	0	0	1	8	1		.133	.217	.157	16	-8	2	.909	-2	99	88	S22		-1.0
1912	Was A	154	618	98	176	34	9	2	70	53	4		.285	.345	.379	106	5	27	.920	10	108	105	3b154		1.9
1913	Was A	106	409	56	101	11	5	1	41	36	1	31	.247	.309	.306	78	-12	22	.901	2	106	146	3b105		-0.7
1914	Was A	157	616	82	174	16	10	2	50	60	2	47	.282	.348	.351	106	4	31-18	.929	-19	80	123	3b157		-1.1
1915	Was A	154	618	75	170	25	10	0	52	48	2	30	.275	.329	.348	101	-1	20-6	.919	-7	98	134	3b79,2b75		-0.2
1916	Was A	158	606	75	153	18	9	1	44	68	4	26	.252	.332	.317	96	-3	23-16	.929	-17	78	88	3b84,2b72		-1.8
1917	Was A	143	554	66	130	16	8	0	43	46	2	23	.235	.293	.292	80	-15	11	.935	-6	98	116	3b86,2b57		-2.0
1918	Was A	129	519	70	147	13	3	0	29	41	3	20	.283	.339	.320	101	0	12	.936	-3	100	133	3b127,2b2		0.1
1919	Was A	120	478	57	126	12	5	0	26	33	2	21	.264	.314	.310	76	-16	20	.946	7	109	85	3b115		-0.7
1920	Bos A	117	386	48	100	17	6	0	41	42	3	17	.259	.336	.334	82	-10	10-4	.957	9	110	138	3b88,2b21		0.2
1921	Bos A	120	412	51	117	18	6	0	35	57	0	15	.284	.371	.357	89	-5	13-7	.943	-10	99	115	3b94,2b22		
1922	Bos A	48	109	11	23	3	0	0	3	9	1	10	.211	.277	.239	36	-10	1-1	.886	-7	83	44	3b28,S3		-1.6
	StL A	37	144	29	44	4	0	0	12	20	1	8	.306	.394	.333	88	-1	3-1	.916	0	100	187	3b37		0.1
	Year	85	253	40	67	7	0	0	15	29	2	18	.265	.345	.292	67	-11	4-2	.905	-7	93	132	3b65,S3		-1.5
1923	StL A	27	100	9	18	2	0	0	4	7	1	7	.180	.241	.200	16	-12	0-0	.961	-4	81	125	3b20,b7		-1.6
Total 13		1500	5652	732	1490	191	71	6	451	528	25	**255**	.264	.329	.326	89	-84	195-53	.930	-48	98	119	3b1161,2b269,S25		-9.2

FOSTER, ELMER Elmer Ellsworth B8.15.1861 Minneapolis MN D7.22.1946 Deephaven MN BR/TL/5-10/178 d4.17

YEAR	TM LG	G	AB	R	H	2B	3B	HR	RBI	BB-IB	HP	SO	AVG	OBP	SLG	AOPS	ABR	SB-CS	FA	FR	RNG	THR	GAMES AT POSITION	DL	BFW
1886	NY AA	35	125	16	23	0	1	0	7	7	2		.184	.239	.200	41	-8	3	.853	-4	108	41	2b21,O14(9/5/0)		-1.0
1888	NY N	37	136	15	20	3	2	0	10	9	3	20	.147	.216	.199	33	-10	13	.852	-3	78	0	O37(16/21/0)/3		-1.4
1889	NY N	2	4	2	0	0	0	0	0	3	0	1	.000	.429	.000	25	0	2	1.000	0	0	0	O2C		0.0
1890	Chi N	27	105	20	26	4	2	5	23	9	3	21	.248	.325	.467	125	2	18	.986	2	46	0	O27C		0.3
1891	Chi N	4	16	3	3	0	0	1	1	1	0	2	.188	.235	.375	77	-1	1	.875	0	189	0	O4C		-0.1
Total 5		105	386	56	72	7	5	6	41	29	8	**44**	.187	.258	.277	44	-17	37	.883	-5	73	0	O84(25/59/0),2b21/3		-2.2

FOSTER, GEORGE George Arthur B12.1.1948 Tuscaloosa AL BR/TR/6-1/185(175-198) [SFN68*3/55] d9.10 Col El Camino (CA) JC

YEAR	TM LG	G	AB	R	H	2B	3B	HR	RBI	BB-IB	HP	SO	AVG	OBP	SLG	AOPS	ABR	SB-CS	FA	FR	RNG	THR	GAMES AT POSITION	DL	BFW
1969	SF N	9	5	1	2	0	0	0	1	0-0	0	1	.400	.400	.400	126	0	0-0	1.000	-0	87	0	O8R		0.0
1970	SF N	9	19	2	6	1	1	0	4	2-1	0	5	.316	.381	.632	168	2	0-0	1.000	-0	107	0	O7(6/0/1)		0.1
1971	SF N	36	105	11	28	5	0	3	8	6-1	0	27	.267	.304	.400	100	0	0-1	.980	-1	93	54	O30(24/0/7)		-0.4
	Cin N	104	368	39	86	18	4	10	50	23-2	7	93	.234	.289	.386	91	-5	7-6	.986	5	103	133	O102(1/101/1)		-0.4
	Year	140	473	50	114	23	4	13	58	29-3	7	120	.241	.292	.389	93	-6	7-7	.985	4	101	116	O132(25/101/8)		-0.8
1972	†Cin N	59	145	15	29	4	1	2	12	5-1	1	44	.200	.230	.283	48	-11	2-1	.973	-2	100	36	O47(2/1/44)		-1.5
1973	Cin N	17	39	6	11	3	0	4	9	4-0	0	7	.282	.349	.667	183	4	0-1	1.000	-0	81	148	O13(1/11/5)		0.3
1974	Cin N	106	276	31	73	18	0	7	41	30-5	4	52	.264	.343	.406	111	5	3-2	.989	-1	102	39	O98(6/45/69)		0.0
1975	†Cin N	134	463	71	139	24	4	23	78	40-11	3	73	.300	.356	.518	139	23	2-1	.990	10	112	118	O125(95/30/18)/1		2.7
1976	†Cin N★	144	562	86	172	21	9	29	**121**	52-4	4	89	.306	.364	.530	149	34	17-3	**.994**	5	106	89	O142(116/36/24)/1		3.6
1977	Cin N★	158	615	**124**	197	31	2	**52**	**149**	61-10	5	107	.320	.382	**.631**	164	**54**	6-4	.992	11	112	117	O158(136/32/1)		5.8
1978	Cin N★	158	604	97	170	26	3	**40**	**120**	70-16	7	138	.281	.360	.546	150	39	4-4	.971	-0	100	76	O157(154/11/0)		3.3
1979	†Cin N★	121	440	68	133	18	3	30	98	59-7	3	105	.302	.386	.561	156	34	0-2	.982	-2	93	78	O116L	21	2.7
1980	Cin N	144	528	79	144	21	5	25	93	75-14	1	99	.273	.362	.473	135	25	1-0	.997	3	107	58	O141L		2.3
1981	Cin N★	108	414	64	122	23	2	22	90	51-5	3	75	.295	.373	.519	153	29	4-0	.991	3	103	84	O108L		2.9
1982	NY N	151	550	64	136	23	2	13	70	50-9	2	123	.247	.309	.367	89	-8	1-1	.974	-6	105	106	O138L		-0.9
1983	NY N	157	601	74	145	19	2	28	90	38-5	4	111	.241	.289	.419	95	-7	1-1	.988	3	98	97	O153L		-1.2
1984	NY N	146	553	67	149	22	1	24	86	30-9	6	122	.269	.311	.443	112	6	2-2	.976	2	105	56	O141L		0.1
1985	NY N	129	452	57	119	24	1	21	77	46-5	2	87	.263	.331	.460	122	13	0-1	.976	-5	87	81	O123L		0.2
1986	NY N	72	233	28	53	6	1	13	38	21-1	0	53	.227	.289	.429	98	-2	1-1	.962	-2	87	102	O62L		-0.7
	Chi A	15	51	2	11	0	2	1	4	3-0	0	8	.216	.259	.353	62	-3	0-0	1.000	1	90	307	O11L,D3		-0.3
Total 18		1977	7023	986	1925	307	47	348	1239	666-106	52	1419	.274	.338	.480	127	232	51-31	.984	33	102	88	O1880(1534/267/178),D3,1b2	21	18.6

FOSTER, LEO Leonard Norris B2.2.1951 Covington KY BR/TR/5-11/165* [AtlN69 2/36] d7.9

YEAR	TM LG	G	AB	R	H	2B	3B	HR	RBI	BB-IB	HP	SO	AVG	OBP	SLG	AOPS	ABR	SB-CS	FA	FR	RNG	THR	GAMES AT POSITION	DL	BFW
1971	Atl N	9	10	1	1	0	0	0	0	0-0		1	.100	.100	.100	-94	-3	0-0	.900	-0	114	141	S3		-0.3
1973	Atl N	3	6	1	1	1	0	0	0	0-0		2	.167	.167	.333	33	-1	0-0	1.000	-1	24	115	/S		-0.1
1974	Atl N	72	112	16	22	2	0	1	5	9-0	0	22	.196	.254	.241	38	-9	1-2	.977	-3	98	91	S43,2b10,3b3/OR		-1.0
1976	NY N	24	59	11	12	2	0	1	15	8-1	0	5	.203	.299	.288	70	-2	3-0	.920	-1	101	82	3b9,S7,2b3		-0.2
1977	NY N	36	75	6	17	3	0	0	6	5-0	1	14	.227	.284	.267	50	-5	3-1	.968	-3	79	83	2b20,S8,3b2		-0.7
Total 5		144	262	35	52	8	0	2	26	22-1	1	44	.198	.262	.252	43	-20	7-3	.964	-9	97	90	S62,2b33,3b14/OR		-2.3

FOSTER, REDDY Oscar E. B8.1864 Richmond VA D12.19.1908 Richmond VA d6.3

YEAR	TM LG	G	AB	R	H	2B	3B	HR	RBI	BB-IB	HP	SO	AVG	OBP	SLG	AOPS	ABR	SB-CS	FA	FR	RNG	THR	GAMES AT POSITION	DL	BFW
1896	NY N	1	1	0	0	0	0	0	0	0	0		.000	.000	.000	-99	0	0	—	0			/H		0.0

FOSTER, BOB Robert d6.18

YEAR	TM LG	G	AB	R	H	2B	3B	HR	RBI	BB-IB	HP	SO	AVG	OBP	SLG	AOPS	ABR	SB-CS	FA	FR	RNG	THR	GAMES AT POSITION	DL	BFW
1884	Phi U	1	3	0	1	0	1	0		0			.333	.333	1.000	314	1		.625	-1			/C		-0.1
	Phi AA	4	11	4	2	0	0	0	3		0		.182	.357	.182	76	0		.885	-1			C4/OR		-0.1
Total 1		5	14	4	3	0	1	0	3		0		.214	.353	.357	124	1		.824	-2			C5/OR		-0.2

FOSTER, ROY Roy B7.29.1945 Bixby OK BR/TR/6-0/185* d4.7

YEAR	TM LG	G	AB	R	H	2B	3B	HR	RBI	BB-IB	HP	SO	AVG	OBP	SLG	AOPS	ABR	SB-CS	FA	FR	RNG	THR	GAMES AT POSITION	DL	BFW
1970	Cle A	139	477	66	128	26	0	23	60	54-4	**12**	75	.268	.357	.468	120	14	3-3	.965	-6	88	79	O131(114/0/17)		0.1
1971	Cle A	125	396	51	97	21	0	18	45	35-2	6	48	.245	.314	.439	102	1	6-1	.968	0	94	142	O107(46/0/64)		-0.4
1972	Cle A	73	143	19	32	4	0	4	13	21-2	2	23	.224	.325	.336	95	0	0-2	.966	-2	87	82	O45(15/0/31)		-0.5
Total 3		337	1016	136	257	51	0	45	118	110-8	20	146	.253	.336	.438	110	15	9-6	.967	-8	90	104	O283(175/0/112)		-0.8

FOTHERGILL, BOB Robert Roy "Fats" B8.16.1897 Massillon OH D3.20.1938 Detroit MI BR/TR/5-10.5/230 d4.18

YEAR	TM LG	G	AB	R	H	2B	3B	HR	RBI	BB-IB	HP	SO	AVG	OBP	SLG	AOPS	ABR	SB-CS	FA	FR	RNG	THR	GAMES AT POSITION	DL	BFW
1922	Det A	42	152	20	49	12	4	0	29	8	2	9	.322	.356	.454	113	3	1-5	.945	-5	73	53	O38(2/10/26)		-0.7
1923	Det A	101	241	34	76	18	2	1	49	12	4	19	.315	.358	.419	106	2	5-4	.977	-2	99	61	O68(45/20/3)		-0.4
1924	Det A	54	166	28	50	8	2	0	15	5	1	13	.301	.326	.386	84	-5	2-3	.968	-2	101	46	O45(43/0/2)		-1.0
1925	Det A	71	204	38	72	14	0	2	28	6	2	3	.353	.377	.451	111	3	3-2	.977	3	109	112	O59(40/16/4)		0.3
1926	Det A	110	387	63	142	31	7	3	73	33	2	31	.367	.421	.506	139	23	4-12	.961	-2	110	29	O103(76/19/9)		1.0
1927	Det A	143	527	93	189	38	9	9	114	47	2	31	.359	.413	.516	138	30	9-15	.961	-7	103	21	O137L		0.8
1928	Det A	111	347	49	110	26	3	3	63	24	3	19	.317	.366	.481	119	9	8-3	.959	-4	96	60	O90(70/0/20)		-0.1
1929	Det A	115	277	42	98	24	9	6	62	11	1	11	.354	.378	.570	140	15	3-1	.967	-1	109	38	O59(39/0/20)		1.0
1930	Det A	55	143	14	37	9	2	2	14	6	0	10	.259	.289	.406	72	-7	1-1	.947	-2	92	45	O38(32/0/6)		-1.0
	Chi A	52	135	10	40	9	0	0	24	4	2	8	.296	.326	.363	77	-5	0-0	.879	-2	95	85	O31(8/0/22)		-0.8
	Year	107	278	24	77	18	2	2	38	10	2	18	.277	.307	.385	75	-11	1-1	.913	-4	93	64	O69(40/0/28)		-1.8
1931	Chi A	108	312	25	88	9	4	3	56	17	2	17	.282	.323	.365	86	-8	2-2	.972	-1	109	33	O74(48/0/26)		-1.2
1932	Chi A	116	346	36	102	24	1	7	50	27	1	10	.295	.348	.431	107	4	4-4	.952	-6	87	70	O86(53/0/34)		-0.6
1933	Bos A	28	32	1	11	1	0	0	5	2	0	1	.344	.382	.375	102	0	0-0	1.000	-0	97	4	O4(1/0/3)		0.0
Total 12		1106	3269	453	1064	225	52	36	582	202	20	177	.325	.368	.459	115	64	42-52	.961	-30	101	49	O832(594/65/175)		-2.7

FOURNIER, JACK John Frank B9.28.1889 AuSable MI D9.5.1973 Tacoma WA BL/TR/6-0/195 d4.13

YEAR	TM LG	G	AB	R	H	2B	3B	HR	RBI	BB-IB	HP	SO	AVG	OBP	SLG	AOPS	ABR	SB-CS	FA	FR	RNG	THR	GAMES AT POSITION	DL	BFW
1912	Chi A	35	73	6	14	5	2	0	4		3		.192	.262	.315	69			.988	3	172	55	1b17		-0.1
1913	Chi A	68	172	20	40	8	5	1	23	21	2	23	.233	.323	.355	99	0	0	.990	3	105	72	1b29,O23(11/0/12)		0.1
1914	Chi A	109	379	44	118	14	9	6	44	31	3	44	.311	.368	.443	146	19	10-13	.978	4	127	69	1b97,O6(3/1/2)		2.0
1915	Chi A	126	422	86	136	20	18	5	77	64	**15**	37	.322	.429	**.491**	170	38	21-16	.986	1	104	105	1b65,O57(38/13/6)		3.6
1916	Chi A	105	313	36	75	13	9	3	44	36	5	40	.240	.328	.367	108	2	19	.976	-3	95	109	1b85/OL		-0.3
1917	Chi A	1	1	0	0	0	0	0	0	0			.000	.000	.000	-98	0	0	—	-0			/H		0.0
1918	NY A	27	100	9	35	6	1	0	12	7	0	7	.350	.393	.430	145	5	7	.976	-3	74	137	1b27		0.2

YEAR	TM LG	G	AB	R	H	2B	3B	HR	RBI	BB-IB	HP	SO	AVG	OBP	SLG	AOPS	ABR	SB-CS	FA	FR	RNG	THR	GAMES AT POSITION	DL	BFW
1920	StL N	141	530	77	162	33	14	3	61	42	**12**	42	.306	.370	.438	136	26	26-20	.983	0	106	101	1b138		2.2
1921	StL N	149	574	103	197	27	9	16	86	56	**8**	48	.343	.409	.505	144	38	20-22	.987	-4	89	89	1b149		2.0
1922	StL N	128	404	64	119	23	9	10	61	40	7	21	.295	.368	.470	120	12	6-8	.982	2	115	82	1b109/P		0.6
1923	Bro N	133	515	91	181	30	13	22	102	43	9	28	.351	.411	.588	165	47	11-4	.985	4	118	83	1b133		**4.2**
1924	Bro N	**154**	563	93	188	25	4	**27**	116	83	10	46	.334	.428	.536	162	54	7-5	.985	7	117	83	1b153		4.9
1925	Bro N	145	545	99	191	21	16	22	130	**86**	8	39	.350	.446	.569	162	54	4-6	.989	3	105	85	1b145		4.2
1926	Bro N	87	243	39	69	9	2	11	48	30	1	16	.284	.365	.473	126	9	0	.986	-2	84	40	1b64		0.3
1927	Bos N	122	374	55	106	18	2	10	53	44	6	16	.283	.368	.422	121	12	4	.989	-0	100	73	1b102		0.5
Total	15	1530	5208	822	1631	252	113	136	859	587	89	408	.313	.392	.483	143	313	146-94	.984	16	107	85	1b1313,O87(53/14/20)/P		24.4

FOUSER, BILL William C. B10.1855 Philadelphia PA D3.1.1919 Philadelphia PA d4.22

YEAR	TM LG	G	AB	R	H	2B	3B	HR	RBI	BB-IB	HP	SO	AVG	OBP	SLG	AOPS	ABR	SB-CS	FA	FR	RNG	THR	GAMES AT POSITION	DL	BFW
1876	Phi N	21	89	11	12	0	1	0	2	0		0	.135	.135	.157	-3	-10		.827	1	124	49	2b14,O7(0/1/6)/1		-0.7

FOUTZ, DAVE David Luther "Scissors" B9.7.1856 Carroll Co. MD D3.5.1897 Waverly MD BR/TR/6-2/161 d7.29 M4 b-Frank ▲

YEAR	TM LG	G	AB	R	H	2B	3B	HR	RBI	BB-IB	HP	SO	AVG	OBP	SLG	AOPS	ABR	SB-CS	FA	FR	RNG	THR	GAMES AT POSITION	DL	BFW
1884	StL AA	33	119	17	27	4	0	0		8	0		.227	.276	.261	73	-3		.940	1	108	**728**	P25,O14(0/3/11)		-0.1
1885	†StL AA	65	238	42	59	6	4	0	34	11	0		.248	.281	.307	82	-6		.899	6	**150**	207	P47,1b15,O4L		0.0
1886	StL AA	102	414	66	116	18	6	3	59	9	1		.280	.297	.389	109	8	17	.949	2	86	86	P59,O34R,1b11		0.0
1887	†StL AA	102	423	79	151	26	13	4	108	23	2		.357	.393	.508	136	17	22	.899	-4	49	0	O50R,P40,1b15		0.4
1888	Bro AA	140	563	91	156	20	13	3	99	28	2		.277	.314	.375	121	11	35	.895	2	103	125	O78(0/1/77),1b42,P23		0.5
1889	†Bro AA	**138**	553	118	152	19	8	6	113	64	3	23	.275	.353	.371	106	5	43	.979	-3	70	95	1b134,P12		-0.9
1890	†Bro N	**129**	509	106	154	25	5	3	98	52	1	25	.303	.368	.432	133	20	42	.978	-1	98	114	1b113,O13(4/9/1),P5		0.7
1891	Bro N	130	521	87	134	26	8	2	73	40	2	25	.257	.313	.349	93	-5	48	.976	-3	85	75	1b124,P6/S		-1.7
1892	Bro N	61	220	33	41	5	3	1	26	14	0	14	.186	.235	.250	-14	-14	19	.850	1	137	0	O29(11/7/11),P27,1b6		-1.0
1893	Bro N	**130**	557	91	137	20	10	7	67	32	0	34	.246	.287	.355	74	-25	39	.913	-7	75	36	O77(66/11/0),1b54,P6,M		-3.1
1894	Bro N	73	297	40	90	12	9	0	52	14	1	13	.303	.337	.404	84	-9	14	.976	-3	81	78	1b73/PM		-0.9
1895	Bro N	31	115	14	34	4	1	0	21	4	0	2	.296	.319	.348	78	-4	1	.879	-3	120	188	O20(7/2/11),1b8,M		-0.7
1896	Bro N	2	8	0	2	1	0	0	0	1	0		.250	.333	.375	92	0	0	1.000	1	1032	0	/OR1M		0.0
Total	13	1136	4537	784	1253	186	91	31	750	300	12	136	.276	.323	.378	101	-12	280	.977	-13	81	94	1b596,O320(92/33/196),P251/S		-6.8

FOUTZ, FRANK Frank Hayes B4.8.1877 Baltimore MD D12.25.1961 Lima OH BR/TR/5-11/165 d4.26 b-Dave

YEAR	TM LG	G	AB	R	H	2B	3B	HR	RBI	BB-IB	HP	SO	AVG	OBP	SLG	AOPS	ABR	SB-CS	FA	FR	RNG	THR	GAMES AT POSITION	DL	BFW
1901	Bal A	20	72	13	17	4	2	0	12	4	1		.236	.321	.403	96	0	0	.959	-0	107	69	1b20		-0.1

FOWLER, BOOB Joseph Chester "Gink" B11.11.1900 Waco TX D10.8.1988 Dallas TX BL/TR/5-11.5/180 d5.6 Col TCU

YEAR	TM LG	G	AB	R	H	2B	3B	HR	RBI	BB-IB	HP	SO	AVG	OBP	SLG	AOPS	ABR	SB-CS	FA	FR	RNG	THR	GAMES AT POSITION	DL	BFW
1923	Cin N	11	33	9	11	0	1	0	1	6	0	3	.333	.353	.485	121	1	0	.847	-2	88	115	S10		0.0
1924	Cin N	59	129	20	43	6	1	0	9	5	0	15	.333	.358	.395	103	1	2-2	.936	-4	96	87	S32,2b4,3b2		-0.1
1925	Cin N	6	5	0	2	1	0	0	2	0	0	1	.400	.400	.600	155	0	0-0	—	0	/H			0.0
1926	Bos A	2	8	1	1	0	0	0	1	0	0	0	.125	.125	.125	-36	-2	0-0	.800	-0	117	0	3b2		-0.2
Total	4	78	175	30	57	7	2	1	18	6	0	19	.326	.348	.406	102	0	3-2	.910	-6	94	94	S42,3b4,2b4		-0.3

FOX, ANDY Andrew Junipero B1.12.1971 Sacramento CA BL/TR/6-4/202* [NYA89 2/45] d4.7 OF(24/10/47)

YEAR	TM LG	G	AB	R	H	2B	3B	HR	RBI	BB-IB	HP	SO	AVG	OBP	SLG	AOPS	ABR	SB-CS	FA	FR	RNG	THR	GAMES AT POSITION	DL	BFW
1996	†NY A	113	189	26	37	4	0	3	13	20-0	1	28	.196	.276	.265	38	-19	11-3	.958	-3	87	71	2b72,3b31,S9/ORD		-1.6
1997	†NY A	22	31	13	7	1	0	0	1	7-0	0	9	.226	.368	.258		-1	2-1	1.000	4	132	124	3b11,2b5,S2,O2R,D2		0.3
1998	Ari N	139	502	67	139	21	6	9	44	43-0	18	97	.277	.355	.396	97	-2	14-7	.982	-13	83	73	2b60,O48(10/8/33),3b26,1b12		-1.3
1999	†Ari N	99	274	34	70	12	2	6	33	33-10	9	61	.255	.351	.380	85	-6	4-1	.958	-12	88	94	S82,3b12		-1.1
2000	Ari N	31	86	10	18	4	0	1	10	4-1	0	16	.209	.244	.291	33	-9	2-1	.952	-3	81	101	3b20,O6(1/1/4)/1	13	-1.1
	Fla N	69	164	19	40	4	2	3	10	18-3	3	37	.244	.330	.348	75	-7	8-3	.932	3	111	68	S33,O14(9/0/5),3b12,2b2		-0.1
	Year	100	250	29	58	8	2	4	20	22-4	3	53	.232	.302	.328	60	-16	10-4	.932	1	111	68	S33,3b32,O20(10/1/9),2b2/1		-1.2
2001	Fla N	54	81	8	15	0	1	3	7	15-1	2	17	.185	.327	.321	71	-4	1-0	.938	-2	94	122	S12,3b9,2b2,O2(1/1/0)	92	-0.4
2002	Fla N	133	435	55	109	14	5	4	41	49-6	10	94	.251	.338	.333	85	-11	31-7	.965	-6	90	101	S112,2b7,3b4/OR		-0.4
2003	Fla N	70	108	12	21	5	1	0	8	7-0	4	29	.194	.269	.259	40	-10	1-2	.923	-6	80	92	2b15,S9,3b5,1b2,O2L		-1.5
2004	Mon N	34	43	2	4	0	0	1	1	0-0	0	16	.093	.093	.163	-34	-9	0-0	1.000	-1	74	0	S5,2b3,3b3/1		-0.9
	Tex A	12	12	2	1	0	0	0	0	1-0	0	3	.083	.154	.083	-34	-2	0-0	1.000	1	137	131	2b3,3b2,O2(1/0/1)/D		-0.1
Total	9	776	1925	248	461	65	17	30	168	197-21	47	407	.239	.324	.338	73	-80	74-25	.956	-36	92	93	S264,2b169,3b135,O78R,1b16,D6	120	-8.2

FOX, CHARLIE Charles Francis "Irish" B10.7.1921 New York NY D2.16.2004 Stanford CA BR/TR/5-11/180 d9.24 Mil 1943-45 M7/C5

YEAR	TM LG	G	AB	R	H	2B	3B	HR	RBI	BB-IB	HP	SO	AVG	OBP	SLG	AOPS	ABR	SB-CS	FA	FR	RNG	THR	GAMES AT POSITION	DL	BFW
1942	NY N	3	7	1	3	0	0	0	1	0	2	.429	.500	.429	172	1	0	1.000	-1	67	0	C3		0.0

FOX, ERIC Eric Hollis B8.15.1963 Lemoore CA BB/TL/5-10/180* [SeaA86*S1/5] d7.7 Col Cal St.-Fresno

YEAR	TM LG	G	AB	R	H	2B	3B	HR	RBI	BB-IB	HP	SO	AVG	OBP	SLG	AOPS	ABR	SB-CS	FA	FR	RNG	THR	GAMES AT POSITION	DL	BFW
1992	†Oak A	51	143	24	34	5	2	3	13	13-0	0	29	.238	.299	.364	90	-3	3-4	.990	2	104	127	O43(20/19/16),D4		-0.2
1993	Oak A	29	56	5	8	1	0	1	5	2-0	0	7	.143	.172	.214	3	-8	0-2	1.000	1	112	0	O26(5/18/3),D2		-0.8
1994	Oak A	26	44	7	9	2	0	1	1	3-0	0	8	.205	.255	.318	51	-3	2-0	1.000	1	110	142	O24(0/16/8)		-0.2
1995	Tex A	10	15	2	0	0	0	0	0	3-0	0	4	.000	.167	.000	-50	-3	0-0	1.000	0	117	0	O8(3/2/3)/D		-0.3
Total	4	116	258	38	51	8	2	5	19	21-0	0	48	.198	.257	.302	55	-17	5-6	.995	4	108	91	O101(28/55/30),D7		-1.5

FOX, PETE Ervin B3.8.1909 Evansville IN D7.5.1966 Detroit MI BR/TR/5-11/165 d4.12

YEAR	TM LG	G	AB	R	H	2B	3B	HR	RBI	BB-IB	HP	SO	AVG	OBP	SLG	AOPS	ABR	SB-CS	FA	FR	RNG	THR	GAMES AT POSITION	DL	BFW
1933	Det A	128	535	82	154	26	13	7	57	23	2	38	.288	.320	.424	94	-8	9-6	.978	-5	100	56	O124(0/116/8)		-1.6
1934	†Det A	128	516	101	147	31	2	2	45	49	4	53	.285	.351	.364	85	-11	25-10	.974	4	101	137	O121(0/11/110)		-1.1
1935	†Det A	131	517	116	166	38	8	15	73	45	6	52	.321	.382	.513	134	25	14-4	.988	-1	100	87	O125(0/6/123)		1.7
1936	Det A	73	220	46	67	12	1	4	26	34	3	23	.305	.405	.423	104	3	1-3	.968	-1	107	59	O55(5/0/50)		-0.2
1937	Det A	148	628	116	208	39	8	12	82	41	0	43	.331	.372	.476	110	8	12-8	.976	-5	102	43	O143(11/27/106)		-0.4
1938	Det A	**155**	634	91	186	35	10	7	96	31	2	39	.293	.328	.413	80	-22	16-7	**.994**	-3	96	90	O155(1/0/154)		-3.0
1939	Det A	141	519	69	153	24	6	7	66	35	2	41	.295	.342	.405	84	-14	23-12	.970	8	**113**	126	O126R		-1.1
1940	†Det A	93	350	49	101	17	4	5	48	21	0	30	.289	.329	.403	81	-10	7-7	.967	0	103	90	O85(2/1/82)		-1.6
1941	Bos A	73	268	38	81	12	7	0	31	21	2	32	.302	.357	.399	98	-1	9-2	.977	-0	100	91	O62(8/5/49)		-0.4
1942	Bos A	77	256	42	67	15	5	3	42	20	1	28	.262	.323	.395	98	-1	8-7	.966	-5	90	44	O71(7/0/64)		-1.1
1943	Bos A	127	489	54	141	24	4	2	44	34	2	40	.288	.337	.346	104	2	22-8	.961	-4	95	104	O125(3/0/122)		-0.9
1944	Bos A☆	121	496	70	156	37	6	1	64	27	3	34	.315	.354	.419	122	13	10-5	.987	-1	98	88	O119R		0.5
1945	Bos A	66	208	21	51	4	1	0	20	11	4	18	.245	.296	.274	64	-10	2-2	.989	-3	84	99	O57R		-1.8
Total	13	1461	5636	895	1678	314	75	65	694	392	33	471	.298	.347	.415	98	-26	158-81	.977	-15	100	87	O1368(37/166/1170)		-11.0

FOX, PADDY George B. B12.1.1868 Pottstown PA D5.8.1914 Philadelphia PA d7.13

YEAR	TM LG	G	AB	R	H	2B	3B	HR	RBI	BB-IB	HP	SO	AVG	OBP	SLG	AOPS	ABR	SB-CS	FA	FR	RNG	THR	GAMES AT POSITION	DL	BFW
1891	Lou AA	6	19	1	2	0	0	0	2	1		.105	.261	.211	36	-2	0	.929	-1	69	0	3b6		-0.3
1899	Pit N	13	41	4	10	0	1	1	3	2	1	.244	.311	.366	86	-1	2	.971	2	153	204	1b9,C3		0.1
Total	2	19	60	5	12	0	2	1	5	5	3	.200	.294	.317	70	-3	2	.971	2	153	204	1b9,3b6,C3		-0.2

FOX, NELLIE Jacob Nelson B12.25.1927 St.Thomas PA D12.1.1975 Baltimore MD BL/TR/5-9/150(150-162) d6.8 C8 HF1997

YEAR	TM LG	G	AB	R	H	2B	3B	HR	RBI	BB-IB	HP	SO	AVG	OBP	SLG	AOPS	ABR	SB-CS	FA	FR	RNG	THR	GAMES AT POSITION	DL	BFW
1947	Phi A	7	3	2	0	0	0	0	0	1	0	0	.000	.250	.000	-26	-0	0-0	1.000	0	0	0	/2		-0.1
1948	Phi A	3	13	0	2	0	0	0	0	1	0	1	.154	.214	.154	-1	-2	1-0	.950	-2	53	36	2b3		-0.3
1949	Phi A	88	247	42	63	6	2	0	21	32	6	9	.255	.354	.296	75	-8	2-2	.982	-1	97	117	2b77		-0.5
1950	Chi A	130	457	45	113	12	7	0	30	35	2	17	.247	.304	.304	58	-31	4-3	.974	4	102	97	2b121		-2.0
1951	Chi A★	147	604	93	189	32	12	4	55	43	14	11	.313	.372	.425	118	14	9-12	.981	-9	96	103	2b147		1.2
1952	Chi A☆	152	648	76	**192**	25	10	0	39	34	3	14	.296	.334	.366	94	-7	5-5	**.985**	9	98	105	2b151		0.9
1953	Chi A	154	624	92	178	31	8	3	72	49	7	18	.285	.344	.375	91	-7	4-5	.983	3	95	87	2b154		0.6
1954	Chi A★	**155**	631	111	**201**	24	8	2	47	51	5	12	.319	.372	.391	106	6	16-9	**.989**	-2	96	99	2b155		1.6
1955	Chi A★	154	636	100	198	28	7	6	59	38-1	**17**	15	.311	.364	.406	109	4	7-9	.974	**31**	117	100	2b154		4.4
1956	Chi A★	**154**	649	109	192	20	10	4	52	44-1	6	14	.296	.347	.376	94	-10	8-4	**.986**	4	95	110	2b154		0.6
1957	Chi A★	**155**	619	110	**196**	27	8	6	61	75-2	16	13	.317	.403	.415	124	24	5-6	.986	**25**	**110**	**132**	2b155		6.1
1958	Chi A★	155	623	82	**187**	21	6	0	49	47-5	11	11	.300	.357	.353	99	-0	5-6	.985	-9	94	101	2b155		1.1
1959	†Chi A★	**156**	624	84	191	34	6	2	70	71-8	7	13	.306	.380	.389	114	15	5-6	**.988**	-8	102	89	2b156		1.8
1960	Chi A★	150	605	85	175	24	**10**	2	59	50-2	10	13	.289	.351	.372	97	-2	0-4	.985	19	**109**	**113**	2b149		2.8
1961	Chi A★	159	606	67	152	11	5	2	51	59-3	9	12	.251	.323	.295	69	-27	2-3	.982	2	100	92	2b159		-1.2
1962	Chi A★	157	621	79	166	27	7	2	54	38-0	7	12	.267	.314	.343	78	-20	1-2	**.990**	-5	102	96	2b154		-1.4
1963	Chi A★	137	539	54	140	19	0	2	42	24-1	7	17	.260	.299	.306	72	-21	0-4	**.988**	-3	99	94	2b134		-1.4
1964	Hou N	133	442	45	117	12	6	0	28	27-1	0	16	.265	.320	.319	86	-8	0-2	.977	-8	96	80	2b115		-0.8
1965	Hou N	21	41	3	11	0	0	0	1	0-0	1	5	.268	.286	.317	75	-1	0-0	1.000	1	119	120	3b6,1b2/2		-0.1
Total	19	2367	9232	1279	2663	355	112	35	790	719-24	142	216	.288	.348	.363	94	-81	76-80	.984	70	101	101	2b2295,3b6,1b2		14.5

FOX, JACK   John Paul B5.21.1885 Reading PA D6.28.1963 Reading PA BR/TR/5-10/185 d6.2

YEAR	TM LG	G	AB	R	H	2B	3B	HR	RBI	BB-IB	HP	SO	AVG	OBP	SLG	AOPS	ABR	SB-CS	FA	FR	RNG	THR	GAMES AT POSITION	DL	BFW
1908	Phi A	9	30	2	6	0	0	0	0	0	0		.200	.200	.200	28	-2	2	.923	-1	0	0	O8(0/1/7)		-0.4

FOX, BILL   William Henry B1.15.1872 Sturbridge MA D5.7.1946 Minneapolis MN BB/TR/5-10/160 d8.20 Col Holy Cross

YEAR	TM LG	G	AB	R	H	2B	3B	HR	RBI	BB-IB	HP	SO	AVG	OBP	SLG	AOPS	ABR	SB-CS	FA	FR	RNG	THR	GAMES AT POSITION	DL	BFW
1897	Was N	4	14	4	4	0	0	0	0	0			.286	.333	.286	65	-1		.700	-1	127	0	S2,2b2		-0.1
1901	Cin N	43	159	9	28	2	1	0	7	4	1		.176	.201	.201	18	-17	9	.948	4	106	115	2b43		-1.2
Total 2		47	173	13	32	2	1	0	7	5	1		.185	.212	.208	22	-18	9	.944	4	103	125	2b45,S2		-1.3

FOXX, JIMMIE   James Emory "Beast","Double X" B10.22.1907 Sudlersville MD D7.21.1967 Miami FL BR/TR/6-0/195 d5.1 C1 HF1951 OF(12/0/9) ▲

YEAR	TM LG	G	AB	R	H	2B	3B	HR	RBI	BB-IB	HP	SO	AVG	OBP	SLG	AOPS	ABR	SB-CS	FA	FR	RNG	THR	GAMES AT POSITION	DL	BFW
1925	Phi A	10	9	2	6	1	0	0	0	0	0	1	.667	.667	.778	249	2	0-0	—	0	0	0	/C		0.2
1926	Phi A	26	32	8	10	2	1	0	5	1	0	6	.313	.333	.438	95	0	1-0	1.000	1	105	128	C12,O3R		0.1
1927	Phi A	61	130	23	42	6	5	3	20	14	1	11	.323	.393	.515	127	5	2-1	.975	2	86	53	1b32,C5		0.2
1928	Phi A	118	400	85	131	29	10	13	79	60	1	43	.327	.416	.548	147	29	3-9	.940	0	104	92	3b60,1b30,C19		2.8
1929	†Phi A	149	517	123	183	23	9	33	118	103	2	70	.354	.463	.625	171	59	9-7	.995	-3	85	89	1b142,3b8		4.3
1930	†Phi A	153	562	127	188	33	13	37	156	93	0	66	.335	.429	.637	159	51	7-7	.990	-1	91	87	1b153		3.5
1931	†Phi A	139	515	93	150	32	10	30	120	73	1	84	.291	.380	.567	138	27	4-3	.993	-3	83	120	1b112,3b26/OL		1.3
1932	Phi A	154	585	151	213	33	9	58	169	116	0	96	.364	.469	.749	203	91	3-7	.994	-3	94	104	1b141,3b13		6.7
1933	Phi A☆	149	573	125	204	37	9	48	163	96	1	93	.356	.449	.703	199	82	2-2	.990	7	122	78	1b149/S		6.9
1934	Phi A★	150	539	120	180	28	6	44	130	111	1	75	.334	.449	.653	188	73	11-2	.993	4	112	107	1b140,3b9		6.1
1935	Phi A★	147	535	118	185	33	7	36	115	114	0	99	.346	.461	.636	182	70	6-4	.997	4	113	95	1b121,C26,3b2		5.9
1936	Bos A★	155	585	130	198	32	8	41	143	105	1	119	.338	.440	.631	153	49	13-4	.991	1	106	95	1b139,O16(11/0/5)/3		3.3
1937	Bos A★	150	569	111	162	24	6	36	127	99	1	96	.285	.392	.538	127	23	10-8	.994	11	129	91	1b150/C		1.8
1938	Bos A★	149	565	139	197	33	9	50	175	119	0	76	.349	.462	.704	180	72	5-4	.987	7	123	115	1b149		5.8
1939	Bos A☆	124	467	130	168	31	10	35	105	89	2	72	.360	.464	.694	185	62	4-3	.992	8	125	98	1b123/P		5.2
1940	Bos A★	144	515	106	153	30	4	36	119	101	0	87	.297	.412	.581	148	39	4-7	.990	0	132	101	1b95,C42/3		3.0
1941	Bos A★	135	487	87	146	27	8	19	105	93	0	103	.300	.412	.505	138	30	2-5	.992	8	125	95	1b124,3b5/OR		2.3
1942	Bos A	30	100	18	27	4	0	5	14	18	2	15	.270	.392	.460	134	5	0-0	.996	6	174	127	1b27		0.9
	Chi N	70	205	25	42	8	0	3	19	22	0	55	.205	.282	.288	69	-8	1	.983	-4	78	80	1b52/C		-1.8
1944	Chi N	15	20	0	1	1	0	0	2	2	0	5	.050	.136	.100	-33	-4	0	1.000	1	163	0	3b2/C		-0.2
1945	Phi N	89	224	30	60	11	1	7	38	23	0	39	.268	.336	.420	112	3	0	1.000	-1	113	63	1b40,3b14,P9		0.0
Total 20		2317	8134	1751	2646	458	125	534	1922	1452	13	1311	.325	.428	.609	161	760	87-73	.992	41	109	96	1b1919,3b141,C108,O21L,P10/S		58.3

FOY, JOE   Joseph Anthony B2.21.1943 New York NY D10.12.1989 Bronx NY BR/TR/6-0/215* d4.13

YEAR	TM LG	G	AB	R	H	2B	3B	HR	RBI	BB-IB	HP	SO	AVG	OBP	SLG	AOPS	ABR	SB-CS	FA	FR	RNG	THR	GAMES AT POSITION	DL	BFW
1966	Bos A	151	554	97	145	23	8	15	63	91-2	2	80	.262	.364	.413	112	12	2-5	.953	4	103	104	3b139,S13		1.6
1967	†Bos A	130	446	70	112	22	4	16	49	46-1	3	87	.251	.325	.426	111	7	8-6	.921	-11	90	71	3b118/OR		-0.6
1968	Bos A	150	515	65	116	18	2	10	60	84-5	4	91	.225	.336	.326	96	1	26-8	.935	2	105	132	3b147,O3L		-0.6
1969	KC A	145	519	72	136	19	2	11	71	74-4	5	75	.262	.354	.370	103	4	37-15	.964	-12	89	89	3b113,1b16,O16(2/13/1),S5,2b3		-0.6
1970	NY N	99	322	39	76	12	0	6	37	68-5	4	58	.236	.373	.329	89	-1	22-13	.937	-1	94	123	3b97		-0.2
1971	Was A	41	128	12	30	6	0	0	11	27-0	0	14	.234	.363	.297	94	1	4-1	.960	4	105	158	3b37,2b3/S		0.5
Total 6		716	2484	355	615	102	16	58	291	390-17	18	405	.248	.351	.372	103	24	99-48	.943	-14	98	104	3b651,O20(5/13/2),S19,1b16,2b6		1.3

FRANCO, JULIO   Julio Cesar (b Julio Cesar Robles (Franco)) B8.23.1958 Hato Mayor, D.R. BR/TR/6-0/190(155-200) d4.23 OF(4/0/1)

YEAR	TM LG	G	AB	R	H	2B	3B	HR	RBI	BB-IB	HP	SO	AVG	OBP	SLG	AOPS	ABR	SB-CS	FA	FR	RNG	THR	GAMES AT POSITION	DL	BFW
1982	Phi N	16	29	3	8	2	0	0	3	2-1	0	4	.276	.323	.310	75	-1	0-2	1.000	-3	84	42	S11,3b2		-0.4
1983	Cle A	149	560	68	153	24	8	8	80	27-1	2	50	.273	.306	.387	87	-12	32-12	.961	-3	97	95	S149		0.4
1984	Cle A	160	658	82	188	22	5	3	79	43-1	6	68	.286	.331	.348	88	-11	19-10	.955	3	101	114	S159/D		1.0
1985	Cle A	160	636	97	183	33	4	6	90	54-2	4	74	.288	.343	.381	100	1	13-9	.949	-15	98	94	S151,2b8/D		0.1
1986	Cle A	149	599	80	183	30	5	10	74	32-1	0	66	.306	.338	.422	108	5	10-7	.971	-3	104	90	S134,2b13,D3		1.6
1987	Cle A	128	495	86	158	24	3	8	52	57-2	3	56	.319	.389	.428	117	14	32-9	.963	-18	92	76	S111,2b9,D8	26	1.1
1988	Cle A	152	613	88	186	23	6	10	54	56-4	2	72	.303	.361	.409	113	11	25-11	.982	-2	102	87	2b151/D		1.4
1989	Tex A★	150	548	80	173	31	5	13	92	66-11	1	69	.316	.386	.462	137	28	21-3	.980	-5	92	76	2b140,D10		3.1
1990	Tex A★	157	582	96	172	27	1	11	69	82-3	2	83	.296	.383	.402	120	19	31-10	.975	0	98	96	2b152,D3		2.7
1991	Tex A☆	146	589	108	201	27	3	15	78	65-8	3	78	.341	.408	.474	146	39	36-9	.979	-33	84	76	2b146		1.4
1992	Tex A	35	107	19	25	7	0	2	8	15-2	0	17	.234	.328	.355	94	0	1-1	.906	-4	70	35	D15,2b9,O4(4/0/1)	129	-0.5
1993	Tex A	144	532	85	154	31	3	14	84	62-4	1	95	.289	.360	.438	118	15	9-3	—	0	0	0	D140		0.8
1994	Cle A	112	433	72	138	19	2	20	98	62-4	5	75	.319	.406	.510	137	26	8-1	.969	-1	79	91	D99,1b14		1.8
1996	†Cle A	112	432	72	139	20	1	14	76	61-2	3	82	.322	.407	.470	122	17	8-8	.990	3	114	113	1b97,D13	44	0.9
1997	Cle A	78	289	46	82	13	1	3	25	38-2	0	75	.284	.367	.367	89	-3	8-5	.983	6	111	106	D42,2b35/1		0.2
	Mil A	42	141	22	34	3	0	4	19	31-2	1	41	.241	.373	.348	91	-1	7-1	.992	1	119	178	D28,1b13		-0.1
	Year	120	430	68	116	16	1	7	44	69-4	1	116	.270	.369	.360	90	-4	15-6	.983	7	111	106	D70,2b35,1b14		0.1
1999	TB A	1	1	0	0	0	0	0	0	0-0	0	1	.000	.000	.000	-98	0	0-0	1.000	0	0	0	/1		0.0
2001	†Atl N	25	90	13	27	4	0	3	11	10-1	1	20	.300	.376	.444	110	2	0-0	.995	1	121	127	1b23		0.1
2002	†Atl N	125	338	51	96	13	1	6	30	39-3	1	75	.284	.357	.382	99	-1	5-1	.990	3	123	127	1b95,D2		-0.5
2003	†Atl N	103	197	28	58	12	2	5	31	25-5	0	43	.294	.372	.452	115	5	0-1	.998	1	107	120	1b75	15	0.1
2004	†Atl N	125	320	37	99	18	3	6	57	36-4	1	68	.309	.378	.441	111	6	4-2	.997	-0	98	116	1b84/D		0.0
2005	†Atl N	108	233	30	64	12	1	9	42	27-1	1	57	.275	.348	.451	98	2	4-0	.990	2	121	114	1b62,D4		0.0
Total 21		2377	8422	1263	2521	394	54	170	1152	890-64	37	1269	.299	.366	.419	112	161	273-105	.960	-66	98	95	S715,2b663,D371,O4L,3b2	214	15.2

FRANCO, MATT   Matthew Neil B8.19.1969 Santa Monica CA BL/TR/6-1/210* [ChiN87 7/166] d9.6 OF(34/0/8)

YEAR	TM LG	G	AB	R	H	2B	3B	HR	RBI	BB-IB	HP	SO	AVG	OBP	SLG	AOPS	ABR	SB-CS	FA	FR	RNG	THR	GAMES AT POSITION	DL	BFW
1995	Chi N	16	17	3	5	1	0	0	1	0-0	1	5	.294	.294	.353	70	-1		1.000	-1	64	0	2b3/13		-0.2
1996	NY N	14	31	3	6	1	0	1	2	1-0	1	5	.194	.235	.323	50	-2	0-0	.824	-0	116	0	3b8,1b2		-0.3
1997	NY N	112	163	21	45	5	0	5	21	13-4	0	23	.276	.330	.399	94	-2	1-0	.937	1	118	165	3b39,1b13/OLD		-0.1
1998	NY N	103	161	20	44	7	2	1	23	23-6	1	26	.273	.366	.360	95	-0	0-1	1.000	-2	95	122	1b19,O19(15/0/3),3b12,P2,D4	15	-0.3
1999	NY N	122	132	18	31	5	0	4	21	28-3	0	21	.235	.366	.364	90	-1	0-0	1.000	2	157	212	1b28,3b22,O3L/2D		0.0
2000	†NY N	101	134	9	32	4	0	2	14	21-3	0	22	.239	.340	.313	71	-6	0-0	.990	-1	109	104	1b28,3b22,O3L/2D		-0.7
2002	†Atl N	81	205	25	65	15	4	6	30	27-2	1	31	.317	.395	.517	142	12	1-0	.990	0	113	91	1b51,O4(2/0/2)		0.8
2003	†Atl N	112	134	11	33	5	0	3	15	11-0	0	26	.246	.299	.351	70	-6	0-1	.977	-2	82	135	1b15,O3(1/0/2),D3		-0.9
Total 8		661	977	110	261	43	6	22	117	124-18	2	158	.267	.349	.391	96	-6	2-2	.990	-2	105	103	1b140,3b95,O43L,D12,2b4,P2	15	-1.7

FRANCOEUR, JEFF   Jeffrey Braden B1.8.1984 Atlanta GA BR/TR/6-4/220 d7.7

YEAR	TM LG	G	AB	R	H	2B	3B	HR	RBI	BB-IB	HP	SO	AVG	OBP	SLG	AOPS	ABR	SB-CS	FA	FR	RNG	THR	GAMES AT POSITION	DL	BFW
2005	†Atl N	70	257	41	77	20	1	14	45	11-3	4	58	.300	.336	.549	124	8	3-2	.966	6	97	324	O67R		1.1

FRANCONA, TITO   John Patsy B11.4.1933 Aliquippa PA BL/TL/5-11/190(180-193) d4.17 s-Terry

YEAR	TM LG	G	AB	R	H	2B	3B	HR	RBI	BB-IB	HP	SO	AVG	OBP	SLG	AOPS	ABR	SB-CS	FA	FR	RNG	THR	GAMES AT POSITION	DL	BFW
1956	Bal A	139	445	62	115	16	4	9	57	51-4	1	60	.258	.334	.373	94	-5	11-5	.977	2	103	127	O122(1/41/97),1b21		-0.7
1957	Bal A	97	279	35	65	8	3	7	38	29-4	1	48	.233	.307	.358	88	-5	7-3	.992	-4	98	0	O73(28/2/55),1b4		-1.2
1958	Chi A	41	128	10	33	3	2	1	10	14-1	0	24	.258	.331	.336	86	-3	2-3	1.000	-1	85	121	O35(7/0/32)		-0.5
	Det A	45	69	11	17	5	0	0	10	15-3	0	16	.246	.381	.319	88	0	0-0	1.000	-1	97	0	O18(11/0/9)/1		-0.1
	Year	86	197	21	50	8	2	1	20	29-4	0	40	.254	.350	.330	86	-3	2-3	1.000	-2	88	87	O53(18/0/41)/1		-0.6
1959	Cle A	122	399	68	145	17	2	20	79	35-3	3	42	.363	.414	.566	174	40	2-0	.972	-4	95	51	O64(4/61/0),1b35		3.2
1960	Cle A	147	544	84	159	36	4	17	79	67-5	3	67	.292	.372	.460	128	23	4-1	.989	7	41		O138(138/0/1),1b13		1.4
1961	Cle A☆	155	592	87	178	30	6	16	85	56-3	4	52	.301	.363	.459	122	18	2-1	.987	-0	106	48	O138L,1b14		0.9
1962	Cle A	158	621	82	169	28	5	14	70	47-3	7	74	.272	.327	.401	99	-2	3-2	.986	0	105	119	1b158		-1.2
1963	Cle A	142	500	57	114	29	0	10	41	47-7	2	77	.228	.296	.346	80	-13	9-1	.986	-3	97	25	O122(121/0/1),1b11		-2.3
1964	Cle A	111	270	35	67	13	2	8	24	44-9	4	46	.248	.361	.400	113	6	1-3	.985	-8	67	60	O69(1/1/68),1b17		-0.8
1965	StL N	81	174	15	45	6	2	5	19	17-0	1	30	.259	.323	.402	95	-1	0-0	.972	-6	73		O34(1/0/34),1b13		-1.0
1966	StL N	83	156	14	33	4	1	4	17	7-1	1	27	.212	.250	.327	59	-9	0-0	.987	2	127	110	1b30,O9L		-1.0
1967	Phi N	27	73	7	15	1	0	0	3	7-1	0	10	.205	.272	.219	43	-5	0-0	1.000	2	123	106	1b24/OR		-0.6
	Atl N	82	254	28	63	5	1	6	25	20-2	1	34	.248	.304	.346	87	-5	1-0	.991	-0	97	87	1b56,O6(5/0/1)		-0.9
	Year	109	327	35	78	6	1	6	28	27-3	1	44	.239	.297	.318	77	-10	1-1	.993	1	104	92	1b80,O7(5/0/2)		-1.5
1968	Atl N	122	346	32	99	13	1	2	47	51-5	0	45	.286	.376	.347	118	11	3-0	.978	-6	93	54	O65L,1b33		0.2
1969	Atl N	51	88	5	26	1	0	2	22	13-2	0	10	.295	.371	.375	113	2	0-1	.957	0	101	152	O15L,1b7		0.1
	Oak A	32	85	12	29	6	1	3	20	12-2	1	16	.341	.418	.541	174	9	0-0	.988	-3	47	76	1b19/OL	30	0.5
1970	Oak A	32	33	2	3	0	0	1	6	6-1	0	6	.091	.231	.182	22	-4	0-0	1.000	4	141	131	1b6/OL		0.1
	Mil A	52	65	4	15	3	0	0	4	6-1	0	15	.231	.296	.277	59	-4	1-0	1.000	1	125	149	1b13		-0.3
	Year	84	98	6	18	3	0	1	10	12-2	0	21	.184	.273	.245	41	-8	1-0	1.000	5	129	144	1b19/OL		-0.3
Total 15		1719	5121	650	1395	224	34	125	656	544-59	32	694	.272	.343	.403	108	57	46-21	.984	-31	96	58	O911(546/105/299),1b475	30	-4.4

YEAR	TM LG	G	AB	R	H	2B	3B	HR	RBI	BB-IB	HP	SO	AVG	OBP	SLG	AOPS	ABR	SB-CS	FA	FR	RNG	THR	GAMES AT POSITION	DL	BFW

FRANCONA, TERRY Terry Jon B4.22.1959 Aberdeen SD BL/TL/6-1/190(175-190) [MonN80 1/22] d8.19 M6/C3 f-Tito Col Arizona

1981	†Mon N	34	95	11	26	0	1	1	8	5-1	1	6	.274	.317	.326	80	-3	1-0	1.000	1	86	243	O26(24/0/2)/1		-0.2
1982	Mon N	46	131	14	42	3	0	0	9	8-0	0	11	.321	.360	.344	94	-1	2-3	.936	-5	77	0	O33(30/1/3),1b16	102	-0.8
1983	Mon N	120	230	21	59	11	1	3	22	6-2	0	20	.257	.273	.352	73	-9	0-2	.978	0	106	102	O51(13/3/37),1b47		-1.3
1984	Mon N	58	214	18	74	19	2	1	18	5-3	1	12	.346	.360	.467	138	10	0-0	.994	6	142	117	O60(6/5/0/2)		-0.7
1985	Mon N	107	281	19	75	15	1	2	31	12-4	1	12	.267	.299	.349	85	-6	5-5	.988	4	119	95	1b57,O28(5/0/24)/3		-0.7
1986	Chi N	86	124	13	31	3	0	2	8	6-0	1	8	.250	.286	.323	64	-6	0-1	1.000	-6	110	0	O30(20/2/10),1b23		-0.9
1987	Cin N	102	207	16	47	5	0	3	12	10-1	1	12	.227	.266	.295	47	-16	2-0	.995	-6	153	116	1b57,O8(2/0/6)		-1.3
1988	Cle N	62	212	24	66	8	0	1	12	5-1	0	18	.311	.324	.363	90	-3	0-0	.977	1	109	90	D38,1b5,O5L		-0.4
1989	Mil A	90	233	26	54	10	1	3	23	8-3	0	20	.232	.255	.322	63	-12	2-1	.989	1	98	103	1b46,D23,O16R/P		-1.6
1990	Mil A	3	4	1	0	0	0	0	0	0-0	0	1	.000	.000	.000	-99	-1	0-0	1.000	-0	0	121	1b2/D		-0.1
Total	10	708	1731	163	474	74	6	16	143	65-15	5	119	.274	.300	.351	81	-47	12-12	.992	13	121	107	1b304,O203(104/6/100),D62/P3	184	-6.0

FRANK, CHARLIE Charles B5.30.1870 Mobile AL D5.24.1922 Memphis TN BL/TL/5-10/170 d8.18

1893	StL N	40	164	29	55	6	3	1	17	18	2	8	.335	.408	.427	122	5	8	.930	2	123	67	O40L		0.3
1894	StL N	80	319	52	89	12	7	4	42	44	3	13	.279	.372	.398	86	-7	14	.869	-4	80	124	O77(77/0/1),1b3,P2		-1.4
Total	2	120	483	81	144	18	10	5	59	62	5	21	.298	.384	.408	97	-2	22	.889	-2	95	104	O117(117/0/1),1b3,P2		-1.1

FRANK, FRED Frederick B3.11.1874 Louisa KY D3.27.1950 Ashland KY 5-9/162 d9.27

| 1898 | Cle N | 17 | 53 | 3 | 11 | 1 | 1 | 0 | 3 | 4 | 1 | | .208 | .276 | .264 | 56 | -3 | 1 | .915 | 2 | 121 | 374 | O17(0/6/11) | | -0.2 |

FRANK, MIKE Stephen Michael B1.14.1974 Pomona CA BL/TL/6-2/190 [CinN97 7/218] d6.19 Col Santa Clara

| 1998 | Cin N | 28 | 89 | 14 | 20 | 6 | 0 | 0 | 7 | 7-0 | 0 | 12 | .225 | .278 | .292 | 51 | -6 | 0-0 | 1.000 | 1 | 112 | 70 | O28(1/25/2) | 29 | -0.5 |

FRANKLIN d9.27

| 1884 | Was U | 3 | | 0 | 0 | 0 | 0 | 0 | 0 | | | | .000 | .000 | .000 | -99 | -1 | | 1.000 | 0 | 0 | 0 | /OC | | -0.1 |

FRANKLIN, MICAH Micah Ishanti B4.25.1972 San Francisco CA BB/TR/6-0/205 [NYN90 3/90] d5.13

| 1997 | StL N | 17 | 34 | 6 | 11 | 0 | 0 | 2 | 2 | 3-0 | 1 | 10 | .324 | .378 | .500 | 127 | 1 | 0-0 | 1.000 | -1 | 92 | 0 | O13(4/0/9) | | 0.0 |

FRANKLIN, MOE Murray Asher B4.1.1914 Chicago IL D3.16.1978 Harbor City CA BR/TR/6-0/175 d8.12 Mil 1943-45 Col Illinois

1941	Det A	13	10	1	3	1	0	0	2		0	2	.300	.417	.400	106	-1	0-0	.750	-1	77	167	S4/3		0.0
1942	Det A	48	154	24	40	7	0	2	16	7	2	5	.260	.301	.344	75	-5	0-0	.967	-3	88	73	S32,2b7		-0.6
Total	2	61	164	25	43	8	0	2	16	9	2	7	.262	.309	.348	77	-5	0-0	.961	-4	88	76	S36,2b7/3		-0.6

FRANKS, HERMAN Herman Louis B1.4.1914 Price UT BL/TR/5-10.5/187 d4.27 Mil 1942-45 M7/C10

1939	StL N	17	17	1	1	0	0	0	3		0	3	.059	.200	.059	-26	-3	0	.973	2	165	72	C13		-0.1
1940	Bro N	65	131	11	24	4	0	1	14	20	1	6	.183	.296	.237	46	-9	2	.990	6	120	84	C43		-0.1
1941	†Bro N	57	139	10	28	7	0	1	11	14	0	13	.201	.275	.273	52	-9	0	.986	3	152	85	C54/OR		-0.3
1947	Phi A	8	15	2	3	0	1	0	1	4	0	4	.200	.368	.333	94	0	0-0	1.000	-0	108	114	C4		0.0
1948	Phi A	40	98	10	22	7	1	1	14	16	2	11	.224	.345	.347	84	-2	0-0	.977	1	119	122	C27		0.1
1949	NY N	1	3	1	2	0	0	0	0	0	0	0	.667	.667	.667	259	1	0	1.000	0	0	0	/IC		0.1
Total	6	188	403	35	80	18	2	3	43	57	3	37	.199	.302	.275	57	-22	2-0	.985	11	132	93	C142/OR		-0.3

FRAZIER, LOU Arthur Louis B1.26.1965 St.Louis MO BB/TR/6-2/175* [HouN86 S1/5] d4.8 Col Scottsdale (AZ) CC

1993	Mon N	112	189	27	54	7	1	1	16	16-0	0	24	.286	.340	.349	82	-5	17-2	.986	-0	96	110	O60(52/7/2),1b8/2		-0.3
1994	Mon N	76	140	25	38	3	1	0	14	18-0	1	23	.271	.358	.307	75	-5	20-4	1.000	1	105	123	O36(31/5/0),2b6/1		-0.2
1995	Mon N	35	63	6	12	2	0	-0	3	8-0	2	12	.190	.297	.222	39	-5	4-0	.973	1	123	0	O25(10/11/5)/2		-0.4
	Tex A	49	99	19	21	2	0	0	8	7-0	2	20	.212	.278	.232	33	-10	9-1	.973	2	114	106	O47(43/6/0),D2		-0.7
1996	Tex A	30	50	5	13	2	1	0	5	8-0	1	10	.260	.373	.340	77	-2	4-2	.971	2	112	349	O15(12/3/0),D13/2		-0.1
1998	Chi A	7	7	0	0	0	0	0	0	2-0	1	6	.000	.222	.000	-36	-1	4-0	1.000	0	111	0	O3C		0.0
Total	5	309	548	82	138	16	3	1	46	59-0	6	95	.252	.330	.297	64	-28	58-9	.982	5	107	122	O186(148/35/7),D15,2b9,1b9		-1.7

FRAZIER, JOE Joseph Filmore B10.6.1922 Liberty NC BL/TR/6-0/195(180-200) d8.31 M2

1947	Cle A	9	14	1	1	0	0	0	1		0	4	.071	.133	.143	-24	-2	0-0	.857	-0	105	0	O5R		-0.3
1954	StL N	81	88	8	26	5	2	3	18	13	1	17	.295	.388	.500	129	4	0-0	.938	-1	96	0	O11(2/0/8)/1		0.3
1955	StL N	58	70	12	14	1	0	4	9	6-0	1	12	.200	.269	.386	72	-3	0-0	1.000	-1	102	0	O14(1/0/13)		-0.4
1956	StL N	14	19	1	4	0	0	1	4	3-0	0	3	.211	.318	.474	109	0	0-1	.800	-1	78	0	O3R		-0.1
	Cin N	10	17	2	4	0	0	1	2	1-0	0	7	.235	.278	.412	77	-1	0-0	—	-0	0	0	O4L		-0.1
	Year	24	36	3	8	2	0	2	6	4-0	0	10	.222	.300	.444	94	0	0-1	.800	-1	108	183	O7(4/0/3)		-0.2
	Bal A	45	74	7	19	6	0	1	12	11-2	1	6	.257	.356	.378	103	1	0-0	1.000	1	108	183	O19R		0.2
Total	4	217	282	31	68	15	2	10	45	35-2	3	46	.241	.328	.415	97	-1	0-1	.961	-1	101	73	O56(7/0/48)/1		-0.4

FREDERICK, JOHNNY John Henry B1.26.1902 Denver CO D6.18.1977 Tigard OR BL/TL/5-11/165 d4.18

1929	Bro N	148	628	127	206	**52**	6	24	75	39	5	34	.328	.372	.545	126	24	6	.975	1	103	93	O143C		1.7
1930	Bro N	142	616	120	206	44	11	17	76	46	3	34	.334	.383	.524	118	18	1	.990	4	103	103	O142C		1.4
1931	Bro N	146	611	81	165	34	8	17	71	31	6	46	.270	.312	.435	99	-3	2	.965	-2	101	84	O145C		-0.8
1932	Bro N	118	384	54	115	28	2	16	56	25	4	35	.299	.349	.508	130	16	1	.976	-4	94	74	O88(1/47/39)		0.8
1933	Bro N	147	556	65	171	22	7	7	64	36	5	14	.308	.355	.410	123	16	9	.971	-5	97	67	O138(10/26/102)		0.4
1934	Bro N°	104	307	51	91	20	1	4	35	33	3	13	.296	.370	.407	114	7	4	.957	2	88	193	O77(22/0/55)/1		0.5
Total	6	805	3102	498	954	200	35	85	377	210	26	176	.308	.357	.477	118	78	23	.974	-4	99	95	O733(33/503/196)/1		4.0

FREED, ED Edwin Charles B8.22.1919 Centre Valley PA D11.15.2002 Rock Hill SC BR/TR/5-6/165 d9.11 Mil 1943-45

| 1942 | Phi N | 13 | 33 | 3 | 10 | 3 | 1 | 0 | 1 | 4 | 0 | 3 | .303 | .378 | .455 | 151 | 2 | 1 | 1.000 | 0 | 75 | 308 | O11(3/7/1) | | 0.2 |

FREED, ROGER Roger Vernon B6.2.1946 Los Angeles CA D1.9.1996 Chino CA BR/TR/6-0/190(190-205) d9.18 Col Mt. San Antonio (CA) JC

1970	Bal A	4	13	0	2	0	0	1	3	3-0	0	4	.154	.294	.154	32	-1	0-0	1.000	-0	52	264	1b3/OR		-0.2
1971	Phi N	118	348	23	77	12	1	6	37	44-3	3	86	.221	.312	.313	78	-9	0-3	.989	-4	97	57	O106(7/0/99)/C		-2.0
1972	Phi N	73	129	10	29	4	0	6	18	23-2	1	39	.225	.344	.395	107	2	0-1	.971	3	110	178	O46(1/0/45)		0.3
1974	Cin N	6	6	1	2	0	0	1	3	1-0	1	1	.333	.429	.833	251	1	0-0	1.000	-0	0	0	/1		0.1
1976	Mon N	8	15	0	3	1	0	0	1	0-0	0	3	.200	.200	.267	30	-1	0-0	1.000	-0	54	40	1b3/OR		-0.2
1977	StL N	49	83	10	33	2	1	5	21	11-0	0	9	.398	.463	.627	192	11	0-0	1.000	-1	99	150	1b18,O6R		0.5
1978	StL N	52	92	3	22	6	0	2	20	8-0	0	17	.239	.297	.370	87	-2	1-0	.992	1	121	134	1b15,O6(3/0/3)		-0.3
1979	StL N	34	31	2	8	2	0	2	8	5-0	0	7	.258	.361	.516	134	2	0-0	.889	0	166	0	/1		0.1
Total	8	344	717	49	176	27	2	22	109	95-5	4	166	.245	.334	.381	100	3	1-4	.982	-3	97	80	O166(11/0/156),1b41/C		-1.3

FREEHAN, BILL William Ashley B11.29.1941 Detroit MI BR/TR/6-2/205* d9.26 Col Michigan

1961	Det A	4	10	1	4	0	0	0	4	1-0	0	1	.400	.455	.400	127	0	0-0	1.000	1	41	0	C3		0.2
1963	Det A	100	300	37	73	12	2	9	36	39-4	2	56	.243	.331	.387	98	0	2-0	.995	3	149	107	C73,1b19		0.6
1964	Det A☆	144	520	69	156	14	8	18	80	36-3	**8**	68	.300	.350	.462	123	15	5-1	.993	9	**194**	0	C141/1		3.2
1965	Det A★	130	431	45	101	.15	0	10	43	39-5	7	63	.234	.306	.339	83	-9	4-2	.996	5	137	84	C129		0.3
1966	Det A★	136	492	47	115	22	0	12	46	40-9	3	72	.234	.294	.352	83	-10	5-2	**.996**	4	136	68	C132,1b5		0.3
1967	Det A★	155	517	66	146	23	1	20	74	73-15	**20**	71	.282	.389	.447	143	32	1-2	.992	-4	101	79	C147,1b11		3.8
1968	†Det A★	155	540	73	142	24	2	25	84	65-4	**24**	64	.263	.366	.454	144	31	0-1	.994	10	107	96	C138,1b21/OR		5.2
1969	Det A★	143	489	61	128	16	3	16	49	53-6	8	55	.262	.342	.405	104	3	1-2	.992	4	92	120	C120,1b20		1.1
1970	Det A★	117	395	44	95	17	3	16	52	52-5	4	48	.241	.332	.420	106	3	0-3	**.997**	-10	125	110	C114	32	-0.3
1971	Det A★	148	516	57	143	26	4	21	71	54-9	14	48	.277	.353	.465	125	18	2-7	.996	-12	99	89	C144/OL		1.1
1972	†Det A★	111	374	51	98	18	2	10	56	48-0	6	51	.262	.354	.401	120	11	0-1	.989	4	85	114	C105/1		2.2
1973	Det A☆	110	380	33	89	10	1	6	29	40-2	11	30	.234	.323	.313	75	-11	0-0	**.995**	6	94	**128**	C98,1b7,D3		-0.1
1974	Det A	130	445	58	132	17	5	18	60	42-2	5	44	.297	.361	.479	136	20	2-0	.994	-8	97	81	1b65,C63/D		1.1
1975	Det A☆	120	427	42	105	13	4	14	47	32-3	6	56	.246	.306	.398	94	-4	2-0	.991	-1	100	102	C113,1b5		-0.1
1976	Det A	71	237	22	64	10	1	5	27	21-0	1	27	.270	.303	.384	98	-1	0-0	.983	2	90	62	C61,1b2,D3		0.3
Total	15	1774	6073	706	1591	241	35	200	758	626-67	114	753	.262	.340	.412	111	98	24-21	.993	13	115	96	C1581,1b157,D7,O2(1/0/1)	32	18.6

FREEL, RYAN Ryan Paul B3.8.1976 Jacksonville FL BR/TR/5-10/185* [TorA95 10/272] d4.4 Col Tallahassee (FL) CC

2001	Tor A	9	22	1	6	1	0	0	3	1-0	1	4	.273	.333	.318	71	-1	2-1	.969	1	123	112	2b7/OL		0.1
2003	Cin N	43	137	23	39	6	1	4	12	9-1	4	13	.285	.344	.431	106	1	9-4	1.000	-3	111	157	O24(5/20/0),2b11,3b2	36	-0.1
2004	Cin N	143	505	74	140	21	8	3	28	67-0	12	88	.277	.368	.368			1	37-10	.985	15	120	196	O89(12/42/46),3b56,2b15		1.8

YEAR	TM LG	G	AB	R	H	2B	3B	HR	RBI	BB-IB	HP	SO	AVG	OBP	SLG	AOPS	ABR	SB-CS	FA	FR	RNG	THR	GAMES AT POSITION	DL	BFW
2005	Cin N	103	369	69	100	19	3	4	21	51-0	8	59	.271	.371	.371	99	2	36-10	1.000	12	137	322	O51(25/18/13),2b48,3b10	51	1.9
Total	4	298	1033	167	285	47	12	11	64	128-1	24	164	.276	.369	.377	98	1	84-25	.992	26	123	226	O165(43/80/59),2b81,3b68	87	3.7

FREEMAN, JERRY   Frank Ellsworth "Buck"   B12.26.1879 Placerville CA   D9.30.1952 Los Angeles CA   BL/TR/6-2/220   d4.14

YEAR	TM LG	G	AB	R	H	2B	3B	HR	RBI	BB-IB	HP	SO	AVG	OBP	SLG	AOPS	ABR	SB-CS	FA	FR	RNG	THR	GAMES AT POSITION	DL	BFW
1908	Was A	154	531	45	134	15	5	1	45	36	3		.252	.304	.305	107	3	6	.975	-13	71	105	1b154		-1.4
1909	Was A	19	48	2	8	0	1	0	3	4	1		.167	.245	.208	46	-3	3	.956	-2	86	159	1b14/OL		-0.6
Total	2	173	579	47	142	15	6	1	48	40	4		.245	.299	.297	101	0	9	.974	-15	72	109	1b168/OL		-2.0

FREEMAN, JOHN   John Edward   B1.24.1901 Boston MA   D4.14.1958 Washington DC   BR/TR/5-8/160   d6.17   Col Holy Cross

YEAR	TM LG	G	AB	R	H	2B	3B	HR	RBI	BB-IB	HP	SO	AVG	OBP	SLG	AOPS	ABR	SB-CS	FA	FR	RNG	THR	GAMES AT POSITION	DL	BFW
1927	Bos A	4	2	0	0	0	0	0	0	0	0	0	.000	.000	.000	-99	-1	0-0	—	-0	0	0	O3(1/2/0)		-0.1

FREEMAN, BUCK   John Frank   B10.30.1871 Catasauqua PA   D6.25.1949 Wilkes-Barre PA   BL/TL/5-9/169   d6.27   ▲

YEAR	TM LG	G	AB	R	H	2B	3B	HR	RBI	BB-IB	HP	SO	AVG	OBP	SLG	AOPS	ABR	SB-CS	FA	FR	RNG	THR	GAMES AT POSITION	DL	BFW
1891	Was AA	5	18	1	4	1	0	0	1	2	0	2	.222	.300	.278	69	1	0	.769	-0	95	0	P5		0.0
1898	Was N	29	107	19	39	2	3	3	21	7	4		.364	.424	.523	171	9	2	.978	2	143	216	O29R		0.9
1899	Was N	155	588	107	187	19	25	25	122	23	18		.318	.362	.563	154	36	21	.944	-10	62	44	O155R,P2		1.7
1900	Bos N	117	418	58	126	19	13	6	65	25	10		.301	.365	.452	109	3	10	.950	-6	28	38	O91(16/3/72),1b19		-0.7
1901	Bos A	129	490	88	166	23	15	12	114	44	6		.339	.400	.520	157	37	17	.974	-5	84	115	1b128/2OR		2.7
1902	Bos A	138	564	75	174	38	19	11	121	32	6		.309	.352	.502	131	21	17	.944	-2	82	89	O138R		1.2
1903	†Bos A	141	567	74	163	39	20	13	104	30	4		.287	.328	.496	137	23	5	.933	-7	83	56	O141R		1.0
1904	Bos A	157	597	64	167	20	19	7	84	44	12		.280	.329	.412	126	16	7	.954	-7	80	102	O157R		0.2
1905	Bos A	130	455	59	109	20	8	3	49	46	5		.240	.316	.338	106	4	8	.973	-11	72	82	1b66,O57(0/1/56),3b2		-1.1
1906	Bos A	121	392	42	98	18	9	1	30	28	1		.250	.302	.349	104	1	5	.989	4	157	121	O65(0/3/62),1b43,3b4		0.2
1907	Bos A	4	12	1	2	0	0	1	2	3	0		.167	.333	.417	140	1	0	1.000	-0	0	0	O3R		0.0
Total	11	1126	4208	688	1235	199	131	82	713	272	66	2	.293	.346	.462	131	152	92	.950	-42	75	73	O837(16/7/814),1b256,P7,3b6/2		6.1

FREEMAN, LA VEL   La Vel Maurice   B2.18.1963 Oakland CA   BL/TL/5-9/170   [MilA83*1/26]   d4.7   Col Sacramento (CA) City

YEAR	TM LG	G	AB	R	H	2B	3B	HR	RBI	BB-IB	HP	SO	AVG	OBP	SLG	AOPS	ABR	SB-CS	FA	FR	RNG	THR	GAMES AT POSITION	DL	BFW
1989	Mil A	2	3	1	0	0	0	0	0	0-0	0	2	.000	.000	.000	-99	-1	0-0	—	0			D2		-0.1

FREEMAN, CHOO   Raphael   B10.20.1979 Pine Bluff AR   BR/TR/6-2/200*   [ColN98 1/36]   d6.4

YEAR	TM LG	G	AB	R	H	2B	3B	HR	RBI	BB-IB	HP	SO	AVG	OBP	SLG	AOPS	ABR	SB-CS	FA	FR	RNG	THR	GAMES AT POSITION	DL	BFW
2004	Col N	45	90	15	17	3	2	1	11	14-1	0	21	.189	.298	.300	49	-7	1-1	.986	-1	100	69	O41C		-0.7
2005	Col N	18	22	6	6	1	1	0	0	0-0	0	5	.273	.273	.409	66	-1	0-0	1.000	2	107	825	O6C		0.1
Total	2	63	112	21	23	4	3	1	11	14-1	0	26	.205	.294	.321	53	-8	1-1	.988	1	101	177	O47C		-0.6

FREESE, GENE   Eugene Lewis "Augie"   B1.8.1934 Wheeling WV   BR/TR/5-11/175(160-185)   d4.13   b-George   Col West Liberty St.

YEAR	TM LG	G	AB	R	H	2B	3B	HR	RBI	BB-IB	HP	SO	AVG	OBP	SLG	AOPS	ABR	SB-CS	FA	FR	RNG	THR	GAMES AT POSITION	DL	BFW
1955	Pit N	134	455	69	115	21	8	14	44	34-4	4	57	.253	.310	.426	94	-5	5-1	.943	-0	101	121	3b65,2b57		-0.1
1956	Pit N	65	207	17	43	9	0	3	14	16-3	3	45	.208	.273	.295	54	-13	2-1	.963	-3	95	32	3b47,2b26		-1.6
1957	Pit N	114	346	44	98	18	2	6	31	17-0	2	42	.283	.319	.399	95	-3	9-4	.924	-1	105	129	3b74,2b10,O10L		-0.4
1958	Pit N	17	18	1	3	0	0	1	2	1-0	0	2	.167	.211	.333	42	-2	0-0	.800	0	159	0	/3		-0.2
	StL N	62	191	28	49	11	1	6	16	10-0	1	32	.257	.294	.419	83	-5	1-1	.924	-18	66	54	S28,2b14,3b3		-2.1
	Year	79	209	29	52	11	1	7	18	11-0	1	34	.249	.286	.411	80	-7	1-1	.924	-18	66	54	S28,2b14,3b4		-2.3
1959	Phi N	132	400	60	107	14	5	23	70	43-4	5	61	.268	.343	.500	120	11	8-4	.916	-17	84	94	3b109,2b6		-0.6
1960	Chi A	127	455	60	124	32	6	17	79	29-2	1	65	.273	.312	.481	114	7	10-6	.946	-3	105	118	3b122		0.4
1961	†Cin N	152	575	78	159	27	2	26	87	27-5	0	78	.277	.307	.466	101	-2	8-2	.950	-14	90	84	3b151/2		-1.5
1962	Cin N	18	42	2	6	1	0	0	1	6-2	0	8	.143	.250	.167	14	-5	0-0	1.000	-3	53	56	3b10	126	-0.8
1963	Cin N	66	217	20	53	9	1	6	26	17-2	2	42	.244	.303	.378	93	-2	4-2	.930	-7	86	93	3b62/OR		-1.0
1964	Pit N	99	289	33	65	13	2	9	40	19-4	0	45	.225	.269	.377	81	-8	1-2	.920	-10	85	108	3b72		-1.9
1965	Pit N	43	80	6	21	4	0	0	8	6-1	0	2	.262	.326	.313	82	-2	0-2	.951	-2	94	42	3b19		-0.4
	Chi A	17	32	2	9	0	1	1	4	5-0	0	9	.281	.368	.438	140	2	0-0	.824	-4	65	76	3b8		-0.2
1966	Chi A	48	106	8	22	2	0	3	10	8-1	1	20	.208	.270	.311	71	-4	2-1	.894	1	121	121	3b34		-0.4
	Hou N	21	33	1	3	0	0	0	0	5-0	0	11	.091	.211	.091	-13	-5	1-0	.800	0	136	0	3b4,2b3/OL		-0.5
Total	12	1115	3446	429	877	161	28	115	432	243-28	20	535	.254	.305	.418	94	-36	51-26	.934	-80	94	98	3b781,2b117,S28,O12(11/0/1)	126	-11.3

FREESE, GEORGE   George Walter "Bud"   B9.12.1926 Wheeling WV   BR/TR/6-0/190*   d4.29   C2   b-Gene   Col West Virginia

YEAR	TM LG	G	AB	R	H	2B	3B	HR	RBI	BB-IB	HP	SO	AVG	OBP	SLG	AOPS	ABR	SB-CS	FA	FR	RNG	THR	GAMES AT POSITION	DL	BFW
1953	Det A	1	1	0	0	0	0	0	0	0-0	0	0	.000	.000	.000	-99	-1	0-0	—	0			/H		0.0
1955	Pit N	51	179	17	46	8	2	3	22	17-2	2	18	.257	.327	.374	87	-3	1-1	.936	-7	88	31	3b50		-1.0
1961	Chi N	9	7	0	2	0	0	1	1	1-0	0	4	.286	.375	.286	78	0	0-0	—	0			/H		0.0
Total	3	61	187	17	48	8	2	3	23	18-2	2	22	.257	.327	.369	86	-3	1-1	.936	-7	88	31	3b50		-1.0

FREGOSI, JIM   James Louis   B4.4.1942 San Francisco CA   BR/TR/6-1/190(187-205)   d9.14   M15

YEAR	TM LG	G	AB	R	H	2B	3B	HR	RBI	BB-IB	HP	SO	AVG	OBP	SLG	AOPS	ABR	SB-CS	FA	FR	RNG	THR	GAMES AT POSITION	DL	BFW
1961	LA A	11	27	7	6	0	0	0	3	1-0	0	4	.222	.250	.222	25	-3	0-0	.944	-1	98	59	S11		-0.3
1962	LA A	58	175	15	51	3	4	3	23	18-1	0	27	.291	.356	.406	108	2	2-1	.943	1	103	107	S52		0.7
1963	LA A	154	592	83	170	29	12	9	50	36-3	0	104	.287	.325	.422	115	10	2-2	.964	5	105	100	S151		2.8
1964	LA A★	147	505	86	140	22	9	18	72	72-2	4	87	.277	.369	.463	145	32	8-3	.966	10	108	111	S137		5.6
1965	Cal A	161	602	66	167	19	7	15	64	54-4	4	107	.277	.337	.407	114	10	14	103	100	S160		3.7
1966	Cal A★	162	611	78	154	32	7	13	67	67-1	2	89	.252	.325	.391	109	8	17-8	.959	19	111	128	S162/1		4.4
1967	Cal A★	151	590	75	171	23	6	9	56	49-2	5	77	.290	.349	.395	124	17	9-6	.965	-2	100	89	S151		3.1
1968	Cal A★	159	614	77	150	21	13	9	49	60-4	5	101	.244	.315	.365	109	6	9-4	.962	-12	95	108	S159		1.0
1969	Cal A★	161	580	78	151	22	6	12	47	93-7	1	86	.260	.361	.381	113	13	9-2	.972	-6	97	100	S160		2.8
1970	Cal A★	158	601	95	167	33	5	22	82	69-3	3	92	.278	.353	.459	127	22	0-2	.973	7	101	117	S150,1b6		4.6
1971	Cal A	107	347	31	81	15	1	5	33	39-6	1	61	.233	.317	.326	89	-4	2-1	.938	-3	108	76	S74,1b18,O7L	24	0.0
1972	NY N	101	340	31	79	15	4	5	32	38-2	1	71	.232	.311	.344	87	-6	0-1	.935	-7	82	68	3b85,S6,1b3		-1.4
1973	NY N	45	124	7	29	4	1	0	11	20-3	0	25	.234	.340	.282	75	-3	1-2	.906	-7	73	111	S17,3b17,1b3/OL		-1.0
	Tex A	45	157	25	42	6	2	6	16	12-0	1	31	.268	.318	.446	119	3	0-1	1.000	0	103	104	1b47,3b32		-0.5
1974	Tex A	78	230	31	60	5	0	12	34	22-4	0	41	.261	.324	.439	121	5	0-1	.985	1	123	96	1b54,D13,3b4		-0.1
1975	Tex A	77	191	25	50	5	0	7	33	20-4	1	39	.262	.329	.398	107	2	0-1	.995	1	88	113	1b26,D18,3b5		-0.2
1976	Tex A	58	133	17	31	7	0	2	12	23-1	0	33	.233	.342	.331	97	1	2-0	1.000	1	164	78	1b5,D3	20	0.0
1977	Tex A	13	28	4	7	1	0	1	5	3-0	0	4	.250	.313	.393	93	0	0-0	1.000	2	70	98	1b15/3		0.2
	Pit N	36	56	10	16	1	1	3	16	13-1	0	10	.286	.408	.500	141	4	2-0	.981	-1	70	98	1b15/3		0.2
1978	Pit N	20	20	3	4	1	0	1	6	6-0	0	8	.200	.385	.250	77	0	0-0	.667	-1	87	0	3b5,1b2/2		-0.1
Total	18	1902	6523	844	1726	264	78	151	706	715-48	32	1097	.265	.338	.398	113	119	76-40	.963	6	102	106	S1396,1b190,3b183,D34,O8L/2	44	25.5

FREIBURGER, VERN   Vern Donald   B12.19.1923 Detroit MI   D2.27.1990 Palm Springs CA   BR/TL/6-1/170   d9.6

YEAR	TM LG	G	AB	R	H	2B	3B	HR	RBI	BB-IB	HP	SO	AVG	OBP	SLG	AOPS	ABR	SB-CS	FA	FR	RNG	THR	GAMES AT POSITION	DL	BFW
1941	Cle A	2	8	0	1	0	0	0	1	0	0	2	.125	.125	.125	-35	-2	0-0	.947	1	223	120	1b2		-0.1

FREIGAU, HOWARD   Howard Earl "Ty"   B8.1.1902 Dayton OH   D7.18.1932 Chattanooga TN   BR/TR/5-10.5/160   d9.13   Col Ohio Wesleyan

YEAR	TM LG	G	AB	R	H	2B	3B	HR	RBI	BB-IB	HP	SO	AVG	OBP	SLG	AOPS	ABR	SB-CS	FA	FR	RNG	THR	GAMES AT POSITION	DL	BFW
1922	StL N	3	1	0	0	0	0	0	0	0	0	0	.000	.000	.000	-99	-0	0-0	1.000	1	154	290	S2/3		0.0
1923	StL N	113	358	30	94	18	1	1	35	25	2	36	.263	.314	.327	71	-15	5-4	.929	-6	100	82	S87,2b16,1b9/3OL		-1.2
1924	StL N	98	376	35	101	17	6	2	39	19	1	24	.269	.306	.362	80	-12	10-3	.958	-2	92	132	3b98,S2		-0.6
1925	StL N	9	26	2	4	0	0	0	2	1	0	1	.154	.214	.154	-4	-4	0-0	.936	1	111	133	S7/2		-0.2
	Chi N	117	476	77	146	22	10	8	71	30	1	31	.307	.349	.445	100	-1	10-6	.913	-4	103	114	3b96,S17,1b7		0.2
	Year	126	502	79	150	22	10	8	71	32	1	32	.299	.342	.430	94	-6	10-6	.913	-3	103	114	3b96,S24,1b7/2		-0.0
1926	Chi N	140	508	51	137	27	7	3	51	43	0	42	.270	.327	.368	86	-10	6	.966	-2	95	97	3b135,S2/OC		-0.4
1927	Chi N	30	86	12	20	5	0	0	6	8	1	10	.233	.313	.291	62	-4	0-0	.883	-1	107	82	3b30		-0.3
1928	Bro N	17	34	6	7	2	0	0	3	1	0	3	.206	.229	.265	29	-4	0	.810	-3	61	0	3b10/S		-0.9
	Bos N	52	109	11	28	8	1	1	17	9	1	14	.257	.319	.376	86	-2	1	.938	-8	82	58	S14,2b11		-1.5
	Year	69	143	17	35	10	1	1	20	10	1	17	.245	.299	.350	72	-6	1	.938	-11	81	57	S15,2b11,3b10		-1.5
Total	7	579	1974	224	537	99	25	15	258	161	6	161	.272	.322	.370	82	-52	32-13	.940	-24	96	108	3b371,S132,2b28,1b16,O2(1/1/0)		-4.0

FREIRE, ALEJANDRO   Alejandro   B8.23.1974 Caracas, Venez   BR/TR/6-2/225   d8.9

YEAR	TM LG	G	AB	R	H	2B	3B	HR	RBI	BB-IB	HP	SO	AVG	OBP	SLG	AOPS	ABR	SB-CS	FA	FR	RNG	THR	GAMES AT POSITION	DL	BFW
2005	Bal A	25	65	7	16	3	0	1	4	6-0	1	17	.246	.319	.338	75	-2	0-0	.991	-1	68	95	1b16/OLD		-0.4

FRENCH, CHARLIE   Charles Calvin   B10.12.1883 Indianapolis IN   D3.30.1962 Indianapolis IN   BL/TR/5-6/140   d5.23

YEAR	TM LG	G	AB	R	H	2B	3B	HR	RBI	BB-IB	HP	SO	AVG	OBP	SLG	AOPS	ABR	SB-CS	FA	FR	RNG	THR	GAMES AT POSITION	DL	BFW
1909	Bos A	51	167	15	42	3	1	0	13	15	3		.251	.324	.281	90	-1	8	.921	-5	103	106	2b28,S23		-0.7
1910	Bos A	9	40	4	8	1	0	0	0	1	0		.200	.220	.225	38	-3	0	.889	-0	115	106	2b8		-0.4
	Chi A	45	170	17	28	1	1	0	4	10	3		.165	.224	.182	29	-14	5	.930	-9	77	76	2b28,O16R		-2.7
	Year	54	210	21	36	2	1	0	7	11	3		.171	.223	.190	31	-17	5	.919	-9	87	84	2b36,O16R		-3.1
Total	2	105	377	36	78	5	2	0	20	26	6		.207	.269	.231	58	-18	13	.920	-15	93	93	2b64,S23,O16R		-3.8

YEAR	TM	LG	G	AB	R	H	2B	3B	HR	RBI	BB-IB	HP	SO	AVG	OBP	SLG	AOPS	ABR	SB-CS	FA	FR	RNG	THR	GAMES AT POSITION	DL	BFW

FRENCH, PAT   Frank Alexander   B9.22.1893 Dover NH   D7.13.1969 Bath ME   BR/TR/6-1/180   d7.2   Col Maine

1917	Phi	A	3	2	0	0	0	0	0	0	0	0	.000	.000	.000	-99	0	0-0	1.000	0	133	0	/OR		-0.1

FRENCH, RAY   Raymond Edward   B1.9.1895 Alameda CA   D4.3.1978 Alameda CA   BR/TR/5-9.5/158   d9.17

1920	NY	A	2	2	0	0	0	0	0	0	1	0	1	.000	.000	.000	-97	-1	0-0	.500	-1	0	0	/S		-0.1
1923	Bro	N	43	73	14	16	2	1	0	7	4	0	7	.219	.269	.274	45	-6	0-0	.874	1	109	127	S30		-0.2
1924	Chi	A	37	112	13	20	4	0	0	11	10	0	13	.179	.246	.214	20	-14	3-1	.927	-2	113	64	S28,2b3		-1.2
Total	3		82	187	29	36	6	1	0	19	14	1	21	.193	.252	.235	28	-21	3-1	.897	-1	110	92	S59,2b3		-1.5

FRENCH, JIM   Richard James   B8.13.1941 Warren OH   BL/TR/5-7/182*   d9.12   Col Ohio U.

1965	Was	A	13	37	4	11	0	0	1	7	9-1	0	5	.297	.435	.378	135	2	1-0	.974	-0	140	142	C13		0.3
1966	Was	A	10	24	0	5	1	0	0	3	4-0	0	5	.208	.321	.250	67	-1	0-1	.979	-2	58	143	C10	35	-0.3
1967	Was	A	6	16	0	1	0	0	0	1	3-1	0	4	.063	.211	.063	-16	-2	0-0	.968	-2	35	69	C6		-0.4
1968	Was	A	59	165	9	32	5	0	1	10	19-0	1	19	.194	.277	.242	46	-7	1-2	.984	-1	84	146	C53		-0.7
1969	Was	A	63	158	14	29	6	3	2	13	41-6	0	15	.184	.348	.297	88	-1	1-0	.989	8	96	190	C63		1.0
1970	Was	A	69	166	20	35	3	1	1	13	38-2	0	23	.211	.358	.259	76	-3	0-1	.973	-4	137	139	C62/OL		-0.6
1971	Was	A	14	41	6	6	2	0	0	4	7-0	0	7	.146	.271	.195	35	-3	0-2	.985	-1	144	110	C14		-0.5
Total	7		234	607	53	119	17	4	5	51	121-10	1	78	.196	.328	.262	74	-15	3-6	.982	-3	107	152	C221/OL	35	-1.2

FRENCH, WALTER   Walter Edward "Piggy","Fitz"   B7.12.1899 Moorestown NJ   D5.13.1984 Mountain Home AR   BL/TR/5-7.5/155   d9.15   Col Army

1923	Phi	A	16	39	7	9	3	0	0	7		0	7	.231	.318	.308	64	-2	0-1	1.000	-0	83	108	O10C		-0.3
1925	Phi	A	67	100	20	37	9	0	0	14	1	0	9	.370	.376	.460	104	1	1-1	.971	1	101	179	O19(3/0/16)		0.0
1926	Phi	A	112	397	51	121	18	7	1	36	18	3	24	.305	.340	.393	86	-10	2-3	.971	-0	98	107	O99(0/1/98)		-1.8
1927	Phi	A	109	326	48	99	10	5	0	41	16	1	14	.304	.338	.365	78	-11	9-1	.956	2	115	66	O94(8/5/81)		-1.4
1928	Phi	A	48	74	9	19	4	0	0	7	2	1	5	.257	.286	.311	65	-5	1-1	1.000	1	128	77	O19(8/0/11)		-0.5
1929	†Phi	A	45	45	7	12	1	0	1	9	2	0	3	.267	.298	.356	65	-3	0-0	1.000	0	120	0	O10(6/1/3)		-0.3
Total	6		397	981	142	297	45	12	2	109	44	5	62	.303	.336	.379	81	-30	13-7	.968	4	106	93	O251(25/17/209)		-4.3

FRENCH, BILL   William   B Baltimore MD   d4.14   ▲

1873	Mar	NA	5	18	3	4	0	0	1	0			0	.222	.222	.222	42	-1	0-0	.905	-0	0	0	1b2,O2R/P3		-0.1

FREY, LONNY   Linus Reinhard "Junior"   B8.23.1910 St.Louis MO   BL/TR (BB 1933-38)/5-10/160   d8.29   Mil 1944-45

1933	Bro	N	34	135	25	43	5	3	0	12	13	0	13	.319	.378	.400	128	5	4	.896	-11	85	52	S34		-0.3
1934	Bro	N	125	490	77	139	24	5	8	57	52	5	54	.284	.358	.402	109	7	11	.945	10	107	121	S109,3b13		2.4
1935	Bro	N	131	515	88	135	35	11	11	77	66	5	68	.262	.352	.437	113	11	6	.937	-1	101	103	S127,2b4		1.9
1936	Bro	N	148	524	63	146	29	4	4	60	71	4	56	.279	.369	.372	99	3	7	.918	-32	89	73	S117,2b30/OC		-1.8
1937	Chi	N	78	198	33	55	9	3	1	22	33	-0	15	.278	.381	.369	100	2	6	.938	-13	75	65	S30,2b13,3b9,O5(4/1/0)		-0.9
1938	Cin	N	124	501	76	133	26	6	4	36	49	0	50	.265	.331	.365	94	-4	4	.964	-7	98	110	2b121,S3		-0.3
1939	†Cin	N★	125	484	95	141	29	9	11	55	72	4	46	.291	.387	.452	124	19	5	.976	14	105	106	2b124		4.0
1940	†Cin	N	150	563	102	150	23	6	8	54	80	3	48	.266	.361	.371	101	4	22	.977	15	105	132	2b150		2.8
1941	Cin	N★	146	543	78	138	29	5	6	59	72	3	37	.254	.345	.359	98	0	16	.970	-4	98	111	2b145		0.6
1942	Cin	N	141	523	66	139	23	4	2	39	87	2	38	.266	.373	.344	111	11	9	.977	5	103	119	2b140		2.7
1943	Cin	N★	144	586	78	154	20	8	2	43	76	0	56	.263	.347	.334	99	1	7	.985	13	103	122	2b144		2.3
1946	Cin	N	111	333	46	82	10	3	3	24	63	1	31	.246	.368	.321	100	3	5	.963	1	103	107	2b65,O28(3/13/12)		0.7
1947	Chi	N	24	43	4	9	0	0	0	3	4	0	6	.209	.277	.209	32	-4	0	1.000	-1	95	77	2b9		-0.5
	†NY	A	24	28	10	5	2	0	0	2	10	1	1	.179	.410	.250	87	1	3-0	.923	0	114	158	2b8		0.3
1948	NY	A	1	0	1	0	0	0	0	0	0	0	0	—	—	—		0	0-0	—	0			/R		0.0
	NY	N	29	51	6	13	1	0	1	6	4	0	6	.255	.309	.333	73	-2	0	.920	-2	90	76	2b13		-0.3
Total	14		1535	5517	848	1482	263	69	61	549	752	28	525	.269	.359	.374	104	57	105-0	.973	-0	101	115	2b966,S420,O34(7/15/12),3b22		13.6

FRIAS, HANLEY   Hanley (Acevedo)   B12.5.1973 Villa Altagracia, D.R.   BB/TR/6-0/160(160-173)   d6.21

1997	Tex	A	14	26	4	5	1	0	0	1		0	4	.192	.222	.231	17	-3	0-0	1.000	-5	50	38	S12/2		-0.7
1998	Ari	N	15	23	4	3	0	1	0	2	0-0	0	5	.130	.130	.348	20	-3	0-0	1.000	-8	82	149	2b3,b2,S2	105	-0.3
1999	†Ari	N	69	150	27	41	3	2	1	16	29-2	0	18	.273	.391	.340	87	-2	4-3	.965	-9	83	73	S53,2b8		-0.8
2000	Ari	N	75	112	18	23	5	0	2	6	17-0	0	18	.205	.310	.304	54	-8	2-2	.938	-3	94	135	S21,2b15,3b7		-0.9
Total	4		173	311	53	72	9	3	4	25	47-2	0	45	.232	.332	.318	65	-16	6-5	.962	-17	82	83	S88,2b27,3b9	105	-2.7

FRIAS, PEPE   Jesus Maria (Andujar)   B7.14.1948 San Pedro de Macoris, D.R.   BR/TR (BB 1976p, 1977-7)/5-10/159(150-165)   d4.6

1973	Mon	N	100	225	19	52	10	1	0	22	10-2	1	24	.231	.266	.284	51	-15	1-3	.950	2	111	101	S46,2b44,3b6/OR		-0.8
1974	Mon	N	75	112	12	24	4	1	0	7	7-3	0	10	.214	.258	.268	45	-8	1-0	.962	7	107	98	S30,3b27,2b15,O3(1/0/2)		0.2
1975	Mon	N	51	64	4	8	2	0	0	4	3-0	0	13	.125	.162	.156	-10	-10	0-1	.938	-0	90	107	S29,3b11,2b7		-0.8
1976	Mon	N	76	113	7	28	5	0	0	8	4-3	0	14	.248	.271	.292	58	-6	0-1	.957	-2	95	105	2b35,S35,3b4/OC		-0.5
1977	Mon	N	53	70	10	18	4	1	0	5	0-0	0	10	.257	.257	.271	43	-6	1-0	.978	0	103	138	2b16,S14/3		-0.5
1978	Mon	N	73	15	5	4	2	1	0	5	0-0	0	5	.267	.267	.533	119	-0	0-0	1.000	-5	79	91	2b61,S3		-0.4
1979	Atl	N	140	475	41	123	18	4	1	44	20-5	2	36	.259	.290	.320	63	-25	3-2	.954	8	104	93	S137		-0.3
1980	Tex	A	116	227	27	55	5	1	0	10	4-0	1	23	.242	.256	.273	47	-17	5-1	.947	-16	77	91	S106,3b7,2b2		-2.6
	LA	N	14	9	1	2	1	0	0	0	0-0	0	0	.222	.222	.333	55	-1	0-0	.933	-1	82	106	S11		-0.1
1981	LA	N	25	36	6	9	1	0	0	3	1-1	0	5	.250	.282	.278	64	-2	0-0	.906	-8	63	41	S15,2b6/3		-0.9
Total	9		723	1346	132	323	49	8	1	108	49-14	5	136	.240	.267	.290	53	-90	12-8	.951	-14	96	93	S426,2b186,3b57,O5(1/1/3)		-6.7

FRIBERG, BERNIE   Bernard Albert (b Gustaf Bernhard Friberg)   B8.18.1899 Manchester NH   D12.8.1958 Lynn MA   BR/TR/5-11/178   d8.20   OF(84/52/62)

1919	Chi	N	8	20	0	4	1	0	0	1	0	0	4	.200	.200	.250	35	-2	0-1	1.000	-0	110	0	O7(2/5/0)		-0.2
1920	Chi	N	50	114	11	24	5	1	0	7	6	0	20	.211	.250	.272	49	-8	2-2	.963	4	105	84	2b24,O24(15/8/3)		-0.5
1922	Chi	N	97	296	51	92	8	2	0	23	37	2	37	.311	.391	.351	91	-2	8-10	.972	0	87	147	O74(8/11/55),1b6,3b5,2b3		-0.8
1923	Chi	N	146	547	91	174	27	11	12	88	45	2	49	.318	.372	.473	122	16	13-19	.955	10	105	136	3b146		3.0
1924	Chi	N	142	495	67	138	19	3	5	62	66	5	53	.279	.369	.360	95	-0	19-27	.954	5	105	90	3b142		0.9
1925	Chi	N	44	152	12	39	5	3	1	16	14	1	22	.257	.327	.349	72	-7	0-1	.889	-3	93	93	3b26,O12L,1b6,S2		-0.9
	Phi	N	91	304	41	82	12	1	5	22	39	0	35	.270	.353	.365	77	-10	1-1	.965	-1	102	78	2b77,3b14/PC		-0.7
	Year		135	456	53	121	17	4	6	38	53	1	57	.265	.344	.360	75	-16	1-2	.965	-3	102	78	2b77,3b40,O12L,1b6,S2/PC		-1.6
1926	Phi	N	144	478	38	128	21	3	1	51	57	0	77	.268	.346	.331	79	-12	2	.976	22	107	94	2b144		1.3
1927	Phi	N	111	335	31	78	8	2	1	28	41	3	49	.233	.322	.278	61	-17	3	.959	20	118	129	3b103,2b5		0.9
1928	Phi	N	52	94	11	19	3	0	1	7	12	0	16	.202	.292	.266	45	-7	0	.908	0	95	50	S31,3b5,2b3,O3(2/1/0),1b2		-0.5
1929	Phi	N	128	455	74	137	21	10	7	55	49	1	54	.301	.370	.437	93	-5	1	.923	-18	86	65	S73,O40(18/19/4),2b8,1b2		-1.7
1930	Phi	N	105	331	62	113	21	1	4	42	47	1	35	.341	.425	.447	104	5	1	.953	-1	102	77	2b44,O35(27/8/0),S12,3b8		0.3
1931	Phi	N	103	353	33	92	19	5	1	26	33	0	25	.261	.324	.351	75	-12	1	.955	6	103	95	2b64,3b25,1b5,S3		-0.1
1932	Phi	N	61	154	17	37	8	2	0	14	19	0	23	.240	.324	.318	66	-7	0	.957	-5	98	78	2b56		-0.9
1933	Bos	A	17	41	5	13	3	0	0	9	6	1	3	.317	.404	.390	112	1	0	.950	1	113	123	2b6,3b5,S2		0.2
Total	14		1299	4169	544	1170	181	44	38	471	471	16	498	.281	.356	.373	87	-67	51-60	.953	41	107	103	3b479,2b434,O195L,S123,1b21/CP		0.3

FRIDLEY, JIM   James Riley "Big Jim"   B9.6.1924 Philippi WV   D2.28.2003 Port Charlotte FL   BR/TR/6-2/205*   d4.15   Col West Virginia

1952	Cle	A	62	175	23	44	2	4	6	16	14	2	40	.251	.311	.331	84	-5	3-3	.978	-1	97	98	O54(37/0/20)		-0.9
1954	Bal	A	85	240	25	59	8	5	4	36	21	2	41	.246	.311	.371	93	-4	0-1	.985	-2	99	25	O67(64/0/3)		-1.0
1958	Cin	N	5	9	2	2	0	0	0	1	0-0	0	2	.222	.222	.444	67	-0	0-0	1.000	-0	49	0	O2L		-0.1
Total	3		152	424	50	105	12	5	8	53	35-0	3	83	.248	.309	.356	89	-9	3-4	.982	-3	98	54	O123(103/0/23)		-2.0

FRIEL, PAT   Patrick Henry   B6.11.1860 Lewisburg (now In West Virginia) VA   D1.15.1924 Providence RI   BB/5-11/170   d7.13   b-Bill

1890	Syr	AA	62	261	51	65	8	2	3	21	17	3		.249	.302	.330	99	-1	34	.913	-4	72	87	O62(13/0/49)		-0.5
1891	Phi	AA	2	8	2	2	0	0	0	0	0	0		.250	.250	.375	78	-0	0	1.000	-0	0	0	O2R		0.0
Total	2		64	269	53	67	8	2	3	21	17	3	0	.249	.301	.331	96	-1	34	.914	-4	71	85	O64(13/0/51)		-0.5

FRIEL, BILL   William Edward   B4.1.1876 Renovo PA   D12.24.1959 St.Louis MO   BL/TR/5-10/165   d5.3   C1/U1   b-Pat   Col Niagara   OF(6/27/39)

1901	Mil	A	106	376	51	100	13	7	4	35	23	1		.266	.310	.370	92	-5	15	.866	-6	107	119	3b61,O29(5/23/1),2b9,S6		-0.9
1902	StL	A	80	267	26	64	9	2	2	20	14	2		.240	.283	.311	65	-13	4	.921	-6	97	168	O33(1/0/32),2b25,1b10,3b8,S3/PC		-1.9
1903	StL	A	97	351	46	80	11	8	0	25	23	2		.228	.279	.305	77	-10	4	.915	-11	92	69	2b63,3b24,O9(0/4/6)		-2.1
Total	3		283	994	123	244	33	17	6	80	60	5		.245	.292	.331	80	-28	23	.924	-24	91	70	2b97,3b93,O71R,1b10,S9/CP		-4.9

YEAR	TM LG	G	AB	R	H	2B	3B	HR	RBI	BB-IB	HP	SO	AVG	OBP	SLG	AOPS	ABR	SB-CS	FA	FR	RNG	THR	GAMES AT POSITION	DL	BFW

FRIEND, FRANK   Frank B. (b Lawrence Lentz Freund) B7.5.1875 Jeffersonville IN D11.5.1933 Jeffersonville IN   TR/5-10/180 d8.2

| 1896 | Lou N | 2 | 5 | 1 | 1 | 0 | 0 | 0 | 1 | | 0 | 1 | .200 | .333 | .200 | 44 | 0 | 0-0 | 1.000 | 0 | 76 | 149 | C2 | | 0.0 |

FRIEND, OWEN   Owen Lacey "Red" B3.21.1927 Granite City IL   BR/TR/6-1/180*   d10.2   Mil 1951-52   C1

1949	StL A	2	8	1	3	0	0	1	0		0	0	.375	.375	.375	95	0	0-0	1.000	1	140	57	2b2		0.1
1950	StL A	119	372	48	88	15	2	8	50	40	1	68	.237	.312	.352	67	-3	2-1	.961	-3	112	74	2b93,3b24,S3		-1.6
1953	Det A	31	96	10	17	4	0	3	10	6		9	.177	.233	.313	47	-8	0-1	.947	-0	98	101	2b26		-0.6
	Cle A	34	68	7	16	2	0	2	13	5		16	.235	.288	.353	74	-3	0-0	1.000	5	115	152	2b19,S8/3		0.3
	Year	65	164	17	33	6	0	5	23	11		25	.201	.256	.329	58	-11	0-1	.964	5	104	118	2b45,S8/3		-0.3
1955	Bos A	14	42	3	11	3	0	0	11	4-0		11	.262	.326	.333	71	-2	0-0	.951	1	114	73	S14/2		0.0
	Chi N	6	10	0	1	0	0	0	0	0-0		3	.100	.100	.100	-47	-2	0-0	1.000	-1	67	0	3b2/S		-0.3
1956	Chi N	2	2	0	0	0	0	0	0	0-0		0	.000	.000	.000	-99	-1	0-0	—	0			/H		-0.1
Total	5	208	598	69	136	24	2	13	76	55-0	2	109	.227	.295	.339	63	-35	2-2	.963	3	110	86	2b141,3b27,S26		-2.2

FRIERSON, BUCK   Robert Lawrence B7.29.1917 Chicota TX D6.26.1996 Paris TX   BR/TR/6-3/195   d9.9

| 1941 | Cle A | 5 | 11 | 2 | 3 | 1 | 0 | 0 | 2 | 1 | | 0 | 1 | .273 | .333 | .364 | 89 | 0 | 0-0 | 1.000 | -0 | 57 | | O3(2/0/1) | | -0.1 |

FRINK, FRED   Frederick Ferdinand B8.25.1911 Macon GA D5.19.1995 Miami Springs FL   BR/TR/6-1/180   d7.1   Col Illinois

| 1934 | Phi N | 2 | 0 | 0 | 0 | 0 | 0 | 0 | 0 | | | 0 | | | | | | | — | 0 | | 0 | /OC | | 0.0 |

FRISBEE, CHARLIE   Charles Augustus "Bunt" B2.2.1874 Dows IA D11.7.1954 Iowa Falls IA   BB/TR/5-9/175   d6.22   Col Grinnell

1899	Bos N	42	152	22	50	4	2	0	20	9	2		.329	.374	.382	98	-1	10	.875	-2	155	73	O40(0/36/4)		-0.4
1900	NY N	4	13	2	2	1	0	0	3	2	0		.154	.267	.231	40	-1	0	.400	-2	84	0	O4R		-0.3
Total	2	46	165	24	52	5	2	0	23	11	2		.315	.365	.370	94	-2	10	.849	-3	141	66	O44(0/36/8)		-0.7

FRISCH, FRANKIE   Frank Francis "The Fordham Flash" B9.9.1898 Bronx NY D3.12.1973 Wilmington DE   BB/TR/5-11/165   d6.14   M16/C1   HF1947   Col Fordham

1919	NY N	54	190	21	43	3	2	2	24	4	0	14	.226	.242	.295	62	-10	15	.972	3	101	61	2b29,3b20/S		-0.7
1920	NY N	110	440	57	123	10	10	4	77	20	0	18	.280	.311	.375	97	-4	34-11	.967	10	116	134	3b109,S2		0.1
1921	†NY N	153	618	121	211	31	17	8	100	42	3	28	.341	.384	.485	128	24	49-13	.936	8	112	105	2b85,3b53/S		4.5
1922	†NY N	132	514	101	168	16	13	5	51	47	3	13	.327	.387	.438	111	9	31-17	.975	8	105	104	2b135,3b17		2.1
1923	†NY N	151	641	116	223	32	10	12	111	46	4	12	.348	.395	.485	133	30	29-12	.973	0	98	106	2b153,3b17		3.5
1924	†NY N	145	603	121	198	33	15	7	69	56	2	24	.328	.387	.468	132	28	22-9	.972	28	106	117	2b143,S10,3b2		6.0
1925	NY N	120	502	89	166	26	6	11	48	32	3	14	.331	.374	.472	119	14	21-12	.931	4	111	49	3b46,2b42,S39		2.4
1926	NY N	135	545	75	171	29	4	5	44	33	0	16	.314	.353	.409	106	4	23	.975	10	108	99	2b127,3b7		1.7
1927	StL N	153	617	112	208	31	11	10	78	43	7	10	.337	.387	.472	125	22	48	.979	49	120	124	2b153/S		7.2
1928	†StL N	141	547	107	164	29	9	10	86	64	1	17	.300	.374	.441	110	9	29	.976	-5	100	92	2b139		0.8
1929	StL N	138	527	93	176	40	12	5	74	53	2	12	.334	.397	.484	116	14	24	.970	-6	94	89	2b121,3b13/S		1.1
1930	†StL N	133	540	121	187	46	9	10	114	55	0	16	.346	.407	.520	118	18	15	.969	22	108	106	2b123,3b10		3.9
1931	†StL N	131	518	96	161	24	4	4	82	45	2	13	.311	.368	.396	101	2	28	.974	11	103	113	2b129		2.1
1932	StL N	115	486	59	142	26	2	3	60	25	0	13	.292	.327	.372	85	-10	18	.971	16	103	111	2b75,3b37,S4		1.2
1933	StL N★	147	585	74	177	32	6	4	66	48	3	16	.303	.358	.398	110	9	18	.982	-6	90	88	2b132,S15,M		1.4
1934	†StL N★	140	550	74	168	30	6	3	75	45	1	10	.305	.359	.398	96	-2	11	.977	3	95	117	2b115,3b25,M		0.9
1935	StL N☆	103	354	52	104	16	2	1	55	33	1	16	.294	.356	.359	89	-4	2	.982	-5	95	112	2b88,3b5,M		-0.4
1936	StL N	93	303	40	83	10	0	1	26	36	1	10	.274	.353	.317	82	-6	2	.965	-13	94	79	2b60,3b22/SM		-1.5
1937	StL N	17	32	3	7	2	0	0	4	1	0	2	.219	.242	.281	41	-3	0	1.000	-1	89	0	2b5,M		-0.3
Total	19	2311	9112	1532	2880	466	138	105	1244	728	31	272	.316	.369	.432	110	144	419-74	.974	135	102	104	2b1762,3b459,S75		37.3

FRISK, EMIL   John Emil B10.15.1874 Kalkaska MI D1.27.1922 Seattle WA   BL/TR/6-1/190   d9.2 ▲

1899	Cin N	9	25	5	7	1	0	0	2	1		1	.280	.357	.320	85	1	0	.950	-0	87	0	P9		0.0
1901	Det A	20	48	10	15	3	0	1	7	3	1		.313	.365	.438	117	1	0	.851	2	168	0	P11,O2(0/1/1)		0.1
1905	StL A	124	429	58	112	11	6	3	36	42	11		.261	.342	.336	122	12	7	.923	-7	121	70	O115R		0.0
1907	StL A	5	4	0	1	0	0	0	0		1		.250	.400	.250	108	0	0	—	0			/H		0.0
Total	4	158	506	73	135	15	6	4	45	48	13		.267	.346	.344	119	14	7	.918	-5	119	69	O117(0/1/116),P20		0.1

FRITZ, HARRY   Harry Koch "Dutchman" B9.30.1890 Philadelphia PA D11.4.1974 Columbus OH   BR/TR/5-8/170   d9.29

1913	Phi A	5	13	1	0	0	0	0	0	1		4	.000	.188	.000	-45	-2	0	.846	-1	71	0	3b5		-0.3
1914	Chi F	65	174	16	37	5	1	0	13	18	3	18	.213	.297	.253	54	-14	2	.912	-6	89	152	3b46,S9/2		-1.9
1915	Chi F	79	236	27	59	8	4	3	26	13	3	27	.250	.298	.356	89	-9	4	.964	-5	90	101	3b70,2b6/S		-1.3
Total	3	149	423	44	96	13	5	3	39	33	7	49	.227	.294	.303	70	-25	6	.941	-12	89	116	3b121,S10,2b7		-3.5

FRITZ, LARRY   Lawrence Joseph B2.14.1949 E.Chicago IN   BL/TL/6-2/225   [NYN69 S3/57]   d5.30   Col Arizona St.

| 1975 | Phi N | 1 | 1 | 0 | 0 | 0 | 0 | 0 | 0 | 0-0 | | 0 | .000 | .000 | .000 | -95 | 0 | 0-0 | — | 0 | | | /H | | 0.0 |

FROBEL, DOUG   Douglas Steven B6.6.1959 Ottawa ON, Can.   BL/TR/6-4/196(193-205)   d9.5

1982	Pit N	16	34	5	7	2	0	2	3	1-0		11	.206	.229	.441	80	-1	1-1	1.000	0	117	0	O12R		-0.2
1983	Pit N	32	60	10	17	4	1	3	11	4-0		17	.283	.328	.533	131	2	1-1	.964	-2	91	0	O24(18/0/6)		0.0
1984	Pit N	126	276	33	56	9	3	12	28	24-2		84	.203	.271	.388	83	-8	7-5	.956	9	121	168	O112R		-0.4
1985	Pit N	53	109	14	22	5	0	4	7	19-5		24	.202	.320	.248	61	-5	4-3	.941	-1	86	101	O36(20/0/16)		-0.8
	Mon N	12	23	3	3	1	0	1	4	2-0		6	.130	.200	.304	41	-2	0-0	.923	-0	114	0	O6(1/2/3)		-0.2
	Year	65	132	17	25	6	0	1	11	21-5		30	.189	.301	.258	58	-7	4-3	.938	-1	92	86	O42(21/2/19)		-1.0
1987	Cle A	29	40	5	4	0	0	2	5	5-1		13	.100	.196	.250	18	-5	0-0	1.000	-1	63	0	O12(2/2/7),D5		-0.6
Total	5	268	542	70	109	21	4	20	58	55-8	2	155	.201	.276	.365	77	-19	13-10	.957	5	108	115	O202(41/4/156),D5		-2.2

FROELICH, BEN   William Palmer B11.12.1887 Pittsburgh PA D9.1.1916 Pittsburgh PA   BR/TR   d7.2

| 1909 | Phi N | 1 | 1 | 0 | 0 | 0 | 0 | 0 | 0 | | | 0 | .000 | .000 | .000 | -99 | 0 | 0 | — | 0 | 0 | 0 | /C | | 0.0 |

FRY, JERRY   Jerry Ray B2.29.1956 Salinas CA   BR/TR/6-0/185   [MonN74 2/33]   d9.4

| 1978 | Mon N | 4 | 9 | 0 | 0 | 0 | 0 | 0 | 0 | 1-0 | | 5 | .000 | .100 | .000 | -70 | -2 | 0-0 | 1.000 | -1 | 27 | 0 | C4 | | -0.3 |

FRYE, JEFF   Jeffrey Dustin B8.31.1966 Oakland CA   BR/TR/5-9/165*   [TexA88 30/765]   d7.9   Col Southeastern Oklahoma   OF(9/8/18)   [DL 1993 Tex A 182, 1998 Bos A 181]

1992	Tex A	67	199	24	51	9	1	1	12	16-0	3	27	.256	.320	.327	84	-4	1-3	.978	2	101	94	2b67		-0.1
1994	Tex A	57	205	37	67	20	3	0	18	29-0	1	23	.327	.408	.454	122	9	6-1	.983	-6	95	87	2b54/3D	15	0.5
1995	Tex A	90	313	38	87	15	2	4	29	24-0	5	45	.278	.335	.377	83	-8	3-3	.975	7	106	102	2b83	30	0.2
1996	Bos A	105	419	74	120	27	2	4	41	54-0	5	57	.286	.372	.389	92	-3	18-4	.983	14	106	92	2b100,O5(2/1/2),S3/D		1.7
1997	Bos A	127	404	56	126	36	2	3	51	27-1	2	44	.312	.352	.433	103	3	19-8	.991	8	99	114	2b80,3b18,O13(5/5/3),D11,S3/1		1.4
1999	Bos A	41	114	14	32	3	0	1	12	14-1	1	11	.281	.362	.333	77	-4	2-2	.980	-6	77	63	2b26,3b7,S2,D2	77	-0.8
2000	Bos A	69	239	35	69	13	0	1	13	28-0	1	38	.289	.364	.356	82	-6	1-3	.991	-5	91	69	2b52,O15(1/2/13),3b3,D3		-0.9
	Col N	37	87	14	31	6	0	0	8	8-0	1	16	.356	.412	.425	92	4	4-0	.989	2	106	118	2b27/3		0.3
2001	Tor A	74	175	24	24	6	1	2	15	12-0	2	15	.246	.305	.326	65	-9	2-1	.995	3	104	117	2b47,3b27,S2/OL	8	-0.4
Total	8	667	2155	316	626	135	11	16	194	212-2	22	279	.290	.357	.386	91	-22	56-25	.984	18	100	96	2b536,3b57,O34R,D18,S10/1	493	1.9

FRYMAN, TRAVIS   David Travis B3.25.1969 Lexington KY   BR/TR/6-1/194(180-195)   [DetA87 1/30]   d7.7

1990	Det A	66	232	32	69	11	1	9	27	17-0	1	51	.297	.348	.470	125	7	3-3	.915	1	109	142	3b48,S17/D		0.9
1991	Det A	149	557	65	144	36	3	21	91	40-0	5	149	.259	.309	.447	105	2	12-5	.946	-20	86	77	3b85,S71		-1.2
1992	Det A★	161	659	87	175	31	4	20	96	45-0	6	144	.266	.316	.416	103	0	8-4	.970	-1	107	98	S137,3b26		1.0
1993	Det A★	151	607	98	182	37	5	22	97	77-1	4	128	.300	.379	.486	131	28	9-4	.953	-5	106	112	S81,3b69/D		3.0
1994	Det A★	114	464	66	122	34	5	18	85	45-1	5	128	.263	.326	.474	104	2	2-2	.955	-1	105	67	3b114		0.1
1995	Det A	144	567	79	156	21	5	15	81	63-4	3	100	.275	.347	.409	97	-3	4-2	.979	27	127	137	3b144		2.4
1996	Det A★	157	616	90	165	32	3	22	100	57-2	4	118	.268	.329	.437	93	-8	4-3	.978	23	122	94	3b128,S29		1.6
1997	Det A	154	595	90	163	27	2	22	102	46-5	5	123	.274	.334	.409	84	0	16-3	.978	14	111	84	3b153		1.5
1998	†Cle A	146	557	74	160	33	2	28	96	44-0	3	125	.287	.340	.504	112	9	10-8	.963	-3	98	94	3b144,S3,D2		0.6
1999	†Cle A	85	322	45	82	16	2	10	48	25-1	1	57	.255	.309	.410	78	-12	2-1	.969	-1	99	88	3b85	79	-1.2
2000	Cle A★	155	574	93	184	38	2	22	106	32-2	3	111	.321	.392	.516	125	23	1-1	.978	-1	97	71	3b154/1D	62	2.1
2001	†Cle A	98	334	34	88	15	0	3	38	30-1	3	63	.263	.327	.335	73	-12	1-2	.944	-10	78	88	3b96/SD	15	-2.2
2002	Cle A	118	397	42	86	14	3	11	55	40-1	2	82	.217	.292	.350	68	-19	0-0	.960	-6	93	139	3b113	156	-2.3
Total	13	1698	6481	895	1776	345	40	223	1022	602-19	41	1369	.274	.336	.443	103	15	72-38	.965	17	103	95	3b1359,S339,D7/1	156	6.3

YEAR	TM LG	G	AB	R	H	2B	3B	HR	RBI	BB-IB	HP	SO	AVG	OBP	SLG	AOPS	ABR	SB-CS	FA	FR	RNG	THR	GAMES AT POSITION	DL	BFW

FUENTES, MIKE Michael Jay B7.11.1958 Miami FL BR/TR/6-3/190* [MonN81 2/44] d9.2 Col Florida St.

1983	Mon N	6	4	1	0	0	0	0	0-0	0		2	.250	.250	.250	39	0	0-0	—	0			/H		-0.1
1984	Mon N	3	4	0	1	0	0	0	1-0	0		2	.250	.400	.250	90	0	0-0	1.000	0	221	0	/OL		0.0
Total	2	9	8	1	2	0	0	0	1-0	0		4	.250	.333	.250	66	0	0-0	1.000	0	221	0	/OL		-0.1

FUENTES, TITO Rigoberto (Peat) B1.4.1944 Havana, Cuba BB/TR (BR 1965-67, 70p)/5-11/175* d8.18

1965	SF N	26	72	12	15	1	0	0	1	5-1	1	14	.208	.269	.222	39	-6	0-1	.919	-6	82	54	S18,2b7/3		-1.2
1966	SF N	133	541	63	141	21	3	9	40	9-1	3	57	.261	.276	.360	73	-21	6-3	.957	2	100	106	S76,2b60		-0.8
1967	SF N	133	344	27	72	12	1	5	29	27-9	0	61	.209	.266	.294	61	-18	4-3	.980	17	108	128	2b130,S5		0.9
1969	SF N	67	183	28	54	4	3	1	14	15-1	1	25	.295	.350	.366	103	0	2-4	.925	-4	109	145	3b36,S30	24	-0.2
1970	SF N	123	435	49	116	13	7	2	32	36-3	3	52	.267	.323	.343	80	-13	4-5	.966	-0	105	87	2b78,S36,3b24		-0.7
1971	†SF N	152	630	83	172	28	6	4	52	18-2	6	46	.273	.299	.356	86	-14	12-2	.973	2	101	98	2b152		0.0
1972	SF N	152	572	64	151	33	6	7	53	39-3	3	56	.264	.310	.379	95	-5	16-5	.964	-16	95	92	2b152		-1.0
1973	SF N	160	656	78	182	25	5	6	63	45-0	7	62	.277	.328	.358	87	-11	12-6	.993	-6	98	97	2b160/3		-0.6
1974	SF N	108	390	33	97	15	2	0	22	22-0	3	32	.249	.293	.297	63	-20	7-3	.979	2	100	111	2b103		-1.1
1975	SD N	146	565	57	158	21	3	4	43	25-2	3	51	.280	.309	.349	89	-11	8-8	.970	1	107	107	2b142		0.8
1976	SD N	135	520	48	137	18	0	2	36	18-0	1	38	.263	.287	.310	76	-19	5-3	.971	11	108	108	2b127		0.1
1977	Det A	151	615	83	190	19	10	5	51	38-1	2	61	.309	.348	.397	98	-2	4-4	.970	8	101	118	2b151/D		1.3
1978	Oak A	13	43	5	6	1	0	0	2	1-0	0	6	.140	.159	.163	-10	-6	0-0	.944	-6	57	61	2b13		-1.3
Total	13	1499	5566	610	1491	211	46	45	438	298-23	33	561	.268	.307	.347	82	-146	80-47	.974	13	102	105	2b1275,S165,3b62/D	24	-3.8

FUHRMAN, OLLIE Alfred George B7.20.1896 Jordan MN D1.11.1969 Peoria IL BB/TR/5-11/185 d4.13

| 1922 | Phi A | 6 | 6 | 1 | 2 | 1 | 0 | 0 | 0 | 0-0 | 0 | | .333 | .333 | .500 | 112 | 0 | 0-0 | 1.000 | 0 | 59 | 0 | C4 | | 0.0 |

FULGHUM, DOT James Lavoisier B7.4.1900 Valdosta GA D11.11.1967 Miami FL BR/TR/5-8.5/165 d9.15

| 1921 | Phi A | 2 | 2 | 0 | 0 | 0 | 0 | 0 | 1 | 0-0 | 0 | 1 | .000 | .333 | .000 | -9 | 0 | 0-0 | — | -0 | 0 | 0 | /S | | 0.0 |

FULLER, NIG Charles F. B3.30.1879 Toledo OH D11.12.1947 Toledo OH BR/TR/5-11/165 d7.1

| 1902 | Bro N | 3 | 9 | 0 | 0 | 0 | 0 | 0 | 0 | 1-0 | 0 | | .000 | .000 | .000 | -99 | -2 | 0 | 1.000 | -1 | 66 | 47 | C3 | | -0.3 |

FULLER, FRANK Frank Edward "Rabbit" B1.1.1893 Detroit MI D10.29.1965 Warren MI BB/TR/5-7/150 d4.14

1915	Det A	14	32	6	4	0	0	0	2	9		7	.156	.341	.156	47	-2	2-3	.962	-3	93	41	2b9/S		-0.6
1916	Det A	20	10	2	1	0	0	0	1	1		4	.100	.182	.100	-15	-1	3	.846	1	166	323	2b8/S		-0.1
1923	Bos A	6	21	3	5	0	0	0	0	1		1	.238	.273	.238	35	-2	1-1	.952	0	100	50	2b6		-0.2
Total	3	40	63	11	11	0	0	0	3	11		12	.175	.297	.175	35	-5	6-4	.938	-2	104	73	2b23,S2		-0.9

FULLER, HARRY Henry W. B12.5.1862 Cincinnati OH D12.12.1895 Cincinnati OH 5-8/160 d9.19 b-Shorty

| 1891 | StL AA | 1 | 2 | 0 | 0 | 0 | 0 | 0 | 0 | 0-0 | 0 | | | .000 | .000 | .000 | -87 | 0 | 0 | 1.000 | -1 | 0 | 0 | /3 | | -0.1 |

FULLER, JIM James Hardy B11.28.1950 Bethesda MD BR/TR/6-3/215* [BalA70*S2/41] d9.10. Col San Diego Mesa (CA) JC

1973	Bal A	9	26	2	3	0	0	2	4	1-0	0	17	.115	.148	.346	35	-3	0-0	1.000	2	161	396	O5R,1b2/D		-0.1
1974	Bal A	64	189	17	42	11	0	7	28	8-2	3	68	.222	.265	.392	89	-3	1-0	.960	1	109	75	O59(4/0/56),1b4,D2		-0.5
1977	Hou N	34	100	5	16	6	0	2	9	10-1	1	45	.160	.243	.280	43	-8	0-1	.983	4	102	285	O27(26/0/1)/1		-0.6
Total	3	107	315	24	61	17	0	11	41	19-3	4	130	.194	.249	.352	70	-14	1-1	.969	7	109	160	O91(30/0/62),1b7,D3		-1.2

FULLER, JOHN John Edward B1.29.1950 Lynwood CA BL/TL/6-2/180 [AtlN68 11/235] d5.9

| 1974 | Atl N | 3 | 3 | 1 | 1 | 0 | 0 | 0 | 0 | 0-0 | 0 | 0 | .333 | .333 | .333 | 84 | 0 | 0-0 | 1.000 | 0 | 337 | 0 | /OC | | 0.0 |

FULLER, VERN Vernon Gordon B3.1.1944 Menomonie WI BR/TR/6-1/170(160-190) d9.5

1964	Cle A	2	1	0	0	0	0	0	0	0-0	0		.000	.000	.000	-99	0	0	—	0			/H	141	0.0
1966	Cle A	16	47	7	11	2	1	2	2	7-0	2	6	.234	.357	.447	129	2	0-0	1.000	-3	70	141	2b16		0.0
1967	Cle A	73	206	18	46	10	0	7	21	19-0	4	55	.223	.300	.374	98	0	2-3	.986	-3	92	114	2b64,S2		0.2
1968	Cle A	97	244	14	59	8	2	0	18	24-2	4	49	.242	.316	.291	88	-3	2-2	.988	-18	83	79	2b73,3b23,S4		-1.9
1969	Cle A	108	254	25	60	11	1	4	22	20-2	2	53	.236	.295	.335	74	-9	2-1	.978	6	94	101	2b102,3b7		0.3
1970	Cle A	29	33	3	6	2	0	1	2	3-0	0	9	.182	.250	.333	57	-2	0-0	.919	-1	78	80	2b16,3b4/1		-0.3
Total	6	325	785	67	182	33	4	14	65	73-4	12	172	.232	.305	.338	87	-12	6-6	.982	-19	88	101	2b271,3b34,S6/1	141	-1.7

FULLER, SHORTY William Benjamin B10.10.1867 Cincinnati OH D4.11.1904 Cincinnati OH BR/TR/5-6/157 d7.19 b-Harry

1888	Was N	49	170	11	31	5	2	0	12	10		14	.182	.232	.235	53	-9	6	.845	-2	103	101	S47,2b2		-0.9
1889	StL AA	140	517	91	117	18	6	0	51	52	5	56	.226	.303	.284	60	-29	38	.913	-2	93	101	S140		-2.3
1890	StL AA	130	526	118	146	9	9	1	40	73	11		.278	.377	.335	96	-3	60	.870	-0	92	105	S130		0.1
1891	StL AA	135	576	105	122	14	7	2	61	67	4	28	.212	.298	.271	55	-37	42	.857	-4	96	111	S102,2b38		-3.2
1892	NY N	141	508	74	116	11	4	1	48	52	0	24	.228	.300	.272	74	-15	37	.888	3	94	91	S141		-0.5
1893	NY N	130	474	78	112	14	8	0	51	60	2	21	.236	.325	.300	66	-23	26	.911	9	103	91	S130		-0.6
1894	†NY N	95	377	82	104	14	4	2	47	52	2	16	.276	.367	.350	74	-15	32	.881	-11	91	108	S91,O2R,3b2/2		-1.6
1895	NY N	126	458	82	103	11	3	0	32	64	2	34	.225	.323	.262	53	-30	15	.913	33	114	114	S126		0.8
1896	NY N	18	72	10	12	0	0	0	7	14	1	5	.167	.310	.167	28	-7	4	.874	-2	100	103	S18		-0.5
Total	9	964	3678	651	863	96	43	6	349	444	28	198	.235	.322	.289	67	-168	260	.890	26	98	102	S925,2b41,3b2,O2R		-8.7

FULLIS, CHICK Charles Philip B2.27.1904 Girardville PA D3.28.1946 Ashland PA BR/TR/5-9/175 d4.13

1928	NY N	11	1	5	0	0	0	0	0	0		1	.000	.500	.000	41	0	0	—	0			/H		0.0
1929	NY N	86	274	67	79	11	1	7	29	30	3	26	.288	.365	.412	92	-3	7	.962	-9	84	48	O78(33/46/1)		-1.5
1930	NY N	13	6	2	0	0	0	0	0	0	0		.000	.000	.000	-99	-2	1	—	0	0	0	O2(1/1/0)		-0.2
1931	NY N	89	302	61	99	15	2	3	28	23	4	13	.328	.383	.421	119	9	13	.988	-4	90	97	O68(1/65/0),2b9		0.3
1932	NY N	96	235	35	70	14	3	1	21	11	1	12	.298	.332	.396	97	-1	1	.990	-4	91	31	O55(36/19/0)/2		-0.7
1933	Phi N	151	647	91	200	31	6	1	45	36	5	34	.309	.350	.380	96	-2	18	.977	2	100	140	O151C/3		-0.3
1934	Phi N	28	102	8	23	6	0	0	12	10	1	4	.225	.301	.284	51	-7	2	.956	-2	89	65	O27(24/3/0)		-0.9
	†StL N	69	199	21	52	9	1	0	26	14	0	11	.261	.310	.317	64	-10	4	.969	-2	99	57	O56(8/48/0)		-1.3
	Year	97	301	29	75	15	1	0	38	24	1	15	.249	.307	.306	59	-17	6	.966	-3	96	59	O83(32/51/0)		-2.2
1936	StL N	47	89	15	25	6	1	0	6	7	0	11	.281	.333	.371	90	-1	0	1.000	2	109	115	O26(2/15/9)		0.0
Total	8	590	1855	305	548	92	14	12	167	132	14	113	.295	.347	.380	92	-17	46	.977	-16	95	91	O463(105/348/10),2b10/3		-4.6

FULLMER, BRAD Bradley Ryan B1.17.1975 Chatsworth CA BL/TR/6-0/215(190-220) [MonN93 2/60] d9.2

1997	Mon N	19	40	4	12	2	0	3	8	2-1	1	7	.300	.349	.575	138	2	0-0	.982	0	138	116	1b8,O2L		0.2
1998	Mon N	140	505	58	138	44	2	13	73	39-4	2	70	.273	.327	.446	104	3	6-6	.985	-7	86	79	1b137		-1.7
1999	Mon N	100	347	38	96	34	2	9	47	22-6	2	35	.277	.321	.464	100	-1	2-3	.991	-8	67	66	1b94		-1.7
2000	Tor A	133	482	76	142	29	1	32	104	30-3	6	68	.295	.340	.558	119	12	3-1	1.000	0	683	0	D129/1		0.5
2001	Tor A	146	522	71	143	31	2	18	83	38-8	6	88	.274	.326	.444	99	-1	5-2	1.000	0	158	131	D135/1		-0.7
2002	†Ana A	130	429	75	124	35	6	19	59	32-6	5	44	.289	.357	.531	135	21	10-3	.995	-3	51	122	D94,1b29		1.2
2003	Ana A	63	206	32	63	9	2	9	35	26-4	2	31	.306	.387	.500	137	12	5-4	1.000	-0	92	123	D41,1b19	94	0.7
2004	Tex A	76	258	41	60	19	1	11	33	27-1	3	30	.233	.310	.442	90	-4	1-2	1.000	-1	0	282	D66,1b4	71	-0.8
Total	8	807	2789	395	778	203	16	114	442	216-33	37	373	.279	.336	.486	111	44	32-21	.989	-19	78	84	D465,1b293,O2L	165	-2.3

FULMER, CHICK Charles John B2.12.1851 Philadelphia PA D2.15.1940 Philadelphia PA BR/TR/6-0/158 d6.5 U1 b-Washington

1871	Rok NA	16	63	11	17	1	3	0	3	5		1	.270	.324	.381	106	1	0-0	.770	2	110	107	S16/1		0.1
1872	Mut NA	36	165	29	50	1	1	1	15	3			.303	.315	.339	108	2	1-1	.752	-5	81	3b22,S14		-0.3
1873	Phi NA	49	236	42	66	11	3	1	38	2		4	.280	.286	.364	88	-4	3-1	.801	18	123	144	S49,P2/C1		0.9
1874	Phi NA	57	258	49	72	3	2	0	37	2		5	.279	.285	.306	86	-5	0-2	.793	3	109	127	S32,3b25		-0.3
1875	Phi NA	69	295	50	65	6	1	0	24	0		6	.220	.220	.247	60	-12	10-4	.835	-2	99	74	S53,3b17		-1.3
1876	Lou N	66	267	28	73	9	5	1	29	1		10	.273	.276	.356	93	-4		.861	-5	105	104	S66		-0.6
1879	Buf N	76	306	30	82	11	5	0	28	5		34	.268	.280	.337	100	-1		.905	18	110	171	2b76		1.9
1880	Buf N	11	44	3	7	0	0	0	2	4			.159	.196	.159	21	-4		.882	-1	80	40	2b11		-0.4
1882	Cin AA	79	324	54	91	13	4	0	27	10			.281	.302	.346	112	3		.897	-16	85	81	S79		-0.9
1883	Cin AA	92	362	52	92	13	5	5	52	12			.254	.278	.359	98	-2		.863	-0	94	155	S92		0.1
1884	Cin AA	31	114	13	20	2	1	0		0			.175	.183	.211	27	-9		.786	-8	85	115	S29,O2(0/1/1)/3		-1.6
	StL AA	1	5	0	0	0	0	0		0			.000	.000	.000	-97	-1		.778	-1	69	0	/2		-0.2
	Year	32	119	13	20	2	1	0		0			.168	.175	.202	22	-10		.786	-9	85	115	S29,O2(0/1/1)/32		-1.8

YEAR	TM LG	G	AB	R	H	2B	3B	HR	RBI	BB-IB	HP	SO	AVG	OBP	SLG	AOPS	ABR	SB-CS	FA	FR	RNG	THR	GAMES AT POSITION	DL	BFW
Total	5 NA	227	1017	181	270	22	10	2	117	12		19	.265	.274	.313	84	-18	14-8	.807	16	109	118	S164,3b64,P2,1b2/C		-0.9
Total	6	356	1422	180	365	48	20	6	145	31	0	48	.257	.273	.331	92	-18		.867	-13	91	116	S266,2b88,O2(0/1/1)/3		-1.7

FULMER, CHRIS Christopher B7.4.1858 Tamaqua PA D11.9.1931 Tamaqua PA BR/TR/5-8/165 d8.4

YEAR	TM LG	G	AB	R	H	2B	3B	HR	RBI	BB-IB	HP	SO	AVG	OBP	SLG	AOPS	ABR	SB-CS	FA	FR	RNG	THR	GAMES AT POSITION	DL	BFW
1884	Was U	48	181	39	50	9	0	0		11			.276	.318	.326	99	-5		.937	2			C34,O16(0/7/9),1b5		-0.1
1886	Bal AA	80	270	54	66	9	3	1	30	48	2		.244	.363	.311	115	8	29	.949	-5			C68,O12(6/5/1)/P		0.8
1887	Bal AA	56	201	52	54	11	4	0	32	36	1		.269	.382	.363	115	7	35	.913	-7			C48,O8L		0.3
1888	Bal AA	52	166	20	31	5	1	0	10	21	2		.187	.286	.229	67	-5	10	.903	-14			C45,O7(2/1/4)		-1.4
1889	Bal AA	16	58	11	15	3	1	0	13	6	1	12	.259	.338	.345	93	0	2	.938	-3	0	0	O14(0/11/3),C2		-0.3
Total	5	252	876	176	216	37	9	1	85	122	6	12	.247	.343	.313	102	5	76	.929	-25			C197,O57(16/24/17),1b5/P		-0.7

FULMER, WASHINGTON Washington Fayette B6.15.1840 Philadelphia PA D12.8.1907 Philadelphia PA d7.19 b-Chick

YEAR	TM LG	G	AB	R	H	2B	3B	HR	RBI	BB-IB	HP	SO	AVG	OBP	SLG	AOPS	ABR	SB-CS	FA	FR	RNG	THR	GAMES AT POSITION	DL	BFW
1875	Atl NA	1	4	1	2	0	0	0	1	0		0	.500	.500	.500	285	1	0-0	.750	-0	0	0	/OC		0.0

FULTZ, DAVE David Lewis B5.29.1875 Staunton VA D10.29.1959 DeLand FL BR/TR/5-11/170 d7.1 Col Brown OF(34/510/10)

YEAR	TM LG	G	AB	R	H	2B	3B	HR	RBI	BB-IB	HP	SO	AVG	OBP	SLG	AOPS	ABR	SB-CS	FA	FR	RNG	THR	GAMES AT POSITION	DL	BFW
1898	Phi N	19	55	7	10	2	2	0	5	6	0		.182	.262	.291	61	-3	1	.871	-1	59	244	O14(8/3/3),2b3/S		-0.5
1899	Phi N	2	5	0	2	0	0	0	0	0	0		.400	.400	.400	124	0	1	.750	-1	80	0	/2S		-0.1
	Bal N	57	210	31	62	3	2	0	18	13	2		.295	.342	.329	80	-6	17	.940	-7	0	0	O31(14/14/3),3b20,2b2/1		-1.4
	Year	59	215	31	64	3	2	0	18	13	2		.298	.343	.330	81	-6	18	.940	-8	0	0	O31(14/14/3),3b20,2b3/S1		-1.5
1901	Phi A	132	561	95	164	17	9	0	52	32	3		.292	.334	.355	87	-11	36	.935	-8	93	33	O106(11/95/0),2b18,S9		-2.1
1902	Phi A	129	506	109	153	20	5	1	49	62	2		.302	.381	.368	104	5	44	.961	-9	120	33	O114C,2b16		-0.9
1903	NY A	79	295	39	66	12	1	0	25	25	5		.224	.288	.271	67	-11	29	.933	-2	131	97	O77(1/73/3),3b2		-1.7
1904	NY A	97	339	32	93	17	4	2	32	24	1		.274	.324	.366	113	5	17	.976	1	80	84	O90C		0.2
1905	NY A	129	422	49	98	13	3	0	42	39	7		.232	.308	.277	77	-10	44	.966	-7	30	65	O122(0/121/1)		-2.5
Total	7	644	2393	369	648	84	26	3	223	201	20		.271	.332	.331	89	-31	189	.952	-34	82	53	O554C,2b40,3b22,S11/1		-9.0

FUNDERBURK, MARK Mark Clifford B5.16.1957 Charlotte NC BR/TR/6-4/226* [MinA76 16/370] d9.4 Col Louisburg (NC) JC

YEAR	TM LG	G	AB	R	H	2B	3B	HR	RBI	BB-IB	HP	SO	AVG	OBP	SLG	AOPS	ABR	SB-CS	FA	FR	RNG	THR	GAMES AT POSITION	DL	BFW
1981	Min A	8	15	2	3	1	0	2		2-0	1		.200	.278	.267	59	-1	0-0	1.000	-1	39	302	O6L/D		-0.2
1985	Min A	23	70	7	22	7	1	2	13	5-0	0	12	.314	.351	.529	131	3	0-1	1.000	-0	102	0	D15,O5L/1		0.2
Total	2	31	85	9	25	8	1	2	15	7-0	0	13	.294	.337	.482	119	2	0-1	1.000	-1	65	178	D16,O11L/1		0.0

FUNK, LIZ Elias Calvin B10.28.1904 LaCygne KS D1.16.1968 Norman OK BL/TL/5-8.5/160 d4.26 Col Oklahoma

YEAR	TM LG	G	AB	R	H	2B	3B	HR	RBI	BB-IB	HP	SO	AVG	OBP	SLG	AOPS	ABR	SB-CS	FA	FR	RNG	THR	GAMES AT POSITION	DL	BFW
1929	NY A	1	0	0	0	0	0	0	0	0	0	0						0-0		0			/R		0.0
1930	Det A	140	527	74	145	26	11	4	65	29	5	39	.275	.319	.389	77	-20	12-6	.965	1	102	86	O129(0/128/1)		-2.2
1932	Chi A	122	440	59	114	21	5	2	40	43	0	19	.259	.325	.343	78	-14	17-15	.979	6	101	156	O120(4/115/1)		-1.2
1933	Chi A	10	9	1	2	0	0	0	0	1	0	0	.222	.300	.222	42	-1	0-0	—	-0	0	0	O2(1/1/0)		-0.1
Total	4	273	976	134	261	47	16	6	105	73	5	58	.267	.322	.367	77	-35	29-21	.972	7	101	119	O251(5/244/2)		-3.5

FURCAL, RAFAEL Rafael B8.24.1980 Loma de Cabrera, D.R. BB/TR/5-10/165(150-165) d4.4

YEAR	TM LG	G	AB	R	H	2B	3B	HR	RBI	BB-IB	HP	SO	AVG	OBP	SLG	AOPS	ABR	SB-CS	FA	FR	RNG	THR	GAMES AT POSITION	DL	BFW
2000	†Atl N	131	455	87	134	20	4	4	37	73-0	3	80	.295	.394	.382	99	2	40-14	.950	5	104	98	S110,2b31	15	1.9
2001	Atl N	79	324	39	89	19	0	4	30	24-1	1	56	.275	.321	.370	79	-10	22-6	.970	0	98	108	S79	93	-0.1
2002	Atl N	154	636	95	175	31	8	8	47	43-0	3	114	.275	.323	.387	89	-14	27-15	.963	10	105	123	S150,2b4		0.8
2003	Atl N★	156	664	130	194	35	10	15	61	60-2	1	76	.292	.352	.443	107	6	25-2	.959	4	106	112	S155		2.6
2004	†Atl N	143	563	103	157	24	5	14	59	58-4	1	71	.279	.344	.414	95	-4	29-6	.962	15	111	127	S131/2		2.4
2005	†Atl N	154	616	100	175	31	12	12	58	62-3	1	78	.284	.348	.429	100	0	46-10	.965	31	117	124	S152		4.8
Total	6	817	3258	554	924	160	38	57	292	320-10	12	475	.284	.348	.409	96	-20	189-53	.965	66	108	117	S777,2b36	108	12.4

FURILLO, CARL Carl Anthony "Skoonj","The Reading Rifle" B3.8.1922 Stony Creek Mills PA D1.21.1989 Stony Creek Mills PA BR/TR/6-0/190(190-203) d4.16

YEAR	TM LG	G	AB	R	H	2B	3B	HR	RBI	BB-IB	HP	SO	AVG	OBP	SLG	AOPS	ABR	SB-CS	FA	FR	RNG	THR	GAMES AT POSITION	DL	BFW
1946	Bro N	117	335	29	95	18	6	3	35	31	1	20	.284	.346	.400	110	4		.984	9	117	102	O112(5/103/4)		1.0
1947	†Bro N	124	437	61	129	24	7	8	88	34	1	7	.295	.347	.437	103	1	7	.977	1	101	111	O121(28/93/2)		-0.2
1948	Bro N	108	364	55	108	20	4	4	44	43	2	32	.297	.374	.407	108	5	6	.983	7	106	178	O104(0/96/12)		0.9
1949	†Bro N	142	549	95	177	27	10	18	106	37	3	29	.322	.368	.506	127	19	4	.965	2	105	102	O142R		1.6
1950	Bro N	153	620	99	189	30	6	18	106	41	5	40	.305	.353	.460	110	7	8	.971	0	93	164	O153R		0.3
1951	Bro N	158	667	93	197	32	4	16	91	43	7	33	.295	.344	.427	104	3	8-7	.986	12	107	165	O157R		1.0
1952	†Bro N☆	134	425	52	105	18	1	8	59	31	4	33	.247	.304	.351	80	-12	1-4	.988	2	103	111	O131R		-1.5
1953	†Bro N☆	132	479	82	165	38	6	21	92	34	4	32	.344	.393	.580	146	32	1-1	.988	1	97	117	O131R		2.7
1954	Bro N	150	547	56	161	23	1	19	96	49	5	35	.294	.356	.444	104	4	2-4	.972	4	111	79	O149(3/5/145)		0.1
1955	†Bro N	140	523	83	164	24	3	26	95	43-5	7	43	.314	.371	.520	130	23	4-5	.981	-3	96	87	O140(6/1/139)		1.3
1956	†Bro N	149	523	66	150	30	0	21	83	57-15	1	41	.289	.357	.467	111	10	1-1	.984	-7	89	82	O146(9/3/143)		-0.3
1957	Bro N	119	395	61	121	17	4	12	66	29-4	5	33	.306	.358	.461	108	5	0-2	.988	-5	87	100	O107(1/0/106)		-0.4
1958	LA N	122	411	54	119	19	3	18	83	35-2	2	28	.290	.343	.482	113	7	0-2	.975	-9	89	55	O119(1/7/116)		-0.6
1959	†LA N	50	93	8	27	4	0	0	13	7-2	0	11	.290	.333	.333	75	-3	0-0	.920	-3	77	0	O25R	32	-0.6
1960	LA N	8	10	1	2	0	1	0	1	0-0	0	2	.200	.200	.400	56	-1	0-0	1.000	-0	103	0	O2R		-0.1
Total	15	1806	6378	895	1910	324	56	192	1058	514-28	47	436	.299	.355	.458	112	104	48-26	.979	12	100	111	O1739(53/308/1408)	32	5.1

FURMANIAK, J.J. Jason Joseph B7.31.1979 Naperville IL BR/TR/6-3/190 d9.13 Col Lewis

YEAR	TM LG	G	AB	R	H	2B	3B	HR	RBI	BB-IB	HP	SO	AVG	OBP	SLG	AOPS	ABR	SB-CS	FA	FR	RNG	THR	GAMES AT POSITION	DL	BFW
2005	Pit N	13	26	3	5	1	1	0	4	4-0	0	4	.192	.300	.308	60	-2	0-0	.960	-3	61	24	2b9,S2		-0.4

FUSSELBACK, EDDIE Edward L. B7.17.1856 Philadelphia PA D4.14.1926 Philadelphia PA BR/5-6/156 d5.3 ▲

YEAR	TM LG	G	AB	R	H	2B	3B	HR	RBI	BB-IB	HP	SO	AVG	OBP	SLG	AOPS	ABR	SB-CS	FA	FR	RNG	THR	GAMES AT POSITION	DL	BFW
1882	StL AA	35	136	13	31	2	0	0	5				.228	.255	.243	66	-5		.853	2			C19,O15(4/0/11),P4		-0.1
1884	Bal U	68	303	60	86	16	3	1	3				.284	.294	.366	89	-13		.912	14			C54,3b6,S5,O4(1/2/1)		0.5
1885	Phi AA	5	19	2	6	1	0	0	2		0		.316	.316	.368	109	0		.911	0			C5		0.1
1888	Lou AA	1	4	0	1	0	0	0	1	0	0		.250	.250	.250	62	0	0	1.000	1	769	0	/OR		0.0
Total	4	109	462	75	124	19	3	1	3	8	0		.268	.281	.329	84	-18	0	.901	16			C78,O20(5/2/13),3b6,S5,P4		0.5

FUSSELMAN, LES Lester Leroy B3.7.1921 Pryor OK D5.21.1970 Cleveland OH BR/TR/6-1/195* d4.16 Col Western Illinois

YEAR	TM LG	G	AB	R	H	2B	3B	HR	RBI	BB-IB	HP	SO	AVG	OBP	SLG	AOPS	ABR	SB-CS	FA	FR	RNG	THR	GAMES AT POSITION	DL	BFW
1952	StL N	32	63	5	10	3	0	1	3	0	0	9	.159	.159	.254	13	-8	0-0	.991	2	145	90	C32		-0.5
1953	StL N	11	8	1	2	1	0	0	0	0	0	0	.250	.250	.375	60	0	0-0	1.000	1	91	181	C11		0.1
Total	2	43	71	6	12	4	0	1	3	0	0	9	.169	.169	.268	18	-8	0-0	.992	3	137	104	C43		-0.4

GABLER, BILL William Louis "Gabe" B8.4.1930 St.Louis MO BL/TR/6-1/190 d9.16

YEAR	TM LG	G	AB	R	H	2B	3B	HR	RBI	BB-IB	HP	SO	AVG	OBP	SLG	AOPS	ABR	SB-CS	FA	FR	RNG	THR	GAMES AT POSITION	DL	BFW
1958	Chi N	3	3	0	0	0	0	0	0	0	0	3	.000	.000	.000	-99	-1	0-0	—	0			/H		-0.1

GABRIELSON, LEN Leonard Gary B2.14.1940 Oakland CA BL/TR/6-4/210(205-220) d9.9 f-Len Col USC

YEAR	TM LG	G	AB	R	H	2B	3B	HR	RBI	BB-IB	HP	SO	AVG	OBP	SLG	AOPS	ABR	SB-CS	FA	FR	RNG	THR	GAMES AT POSITION	DL	BFW
1960	Mil N	4	3	0	0	0	0	0		1-0	0		.000	.250	.000	-27	-1	0-0	—	-0	0	0	/OL		-0.1
1963	Mil N	46	120	14	26	5	0	3	15	8-1	0	23	.217	.264	.333	72	-4	1-1	1.000	-0	114	0	O22(18/6/1),1b16,3b3		-0.7
1964	Mil N	24	38	0	7	2	0	0	1	1-0	0	8	.184	.205	.237	24	-4	1-0	1.000	-1	52	197	1b12,O2R		-0.5
	Chi N	89	272	22	67	11	2	5	23	19-1	1	37	.246	.298	.357	80	-7	9-4	.984	-1	96	105	O68(1/12/58),1b8		-1.2
	Year	113	310	22	74	13	2	5	24	20-1	1	45	.239	.287	.342	74	-11	10-4	.984	-1	96	103	O70(1/12/60),1b20		-1.7
1965	Chi N	28	48	4	12	0	0	3	5	7-2	0	16	.250	.345	.438	116	1	0-0	1.000	-2	74	0	O14(0/2/12)/1		-0.2
	SF N	88	269	36	81	6	5	4	26	26-5	2	48	.301	.365	.405	114	5	4-0	.975	-1	96	79	O77(70/0/9),1b5		0.3
	Year	116	317	40	93	6	5	7	31	33-7	2	64	.293	.362	.410	114	6	4-2	.977	-1	93	66	O91(70/2/21),1b6		0.1
1966	SF N	94	240	27	52	7	0	4	16	21-3	2	51	.217	.278	.296	58	-13	0-1	.948	-7	73	26	O67(61/0/9),1b6		-2.5
1967	Cal A	11	12	2	1	0	0	0	2	2-0	1	2	.083	.214	.083	-9	-2	0-0	—	-0	0	0	/OL		0.0
	LA N	90	238	20	62	10	3	7	29	15-3	1	41	.261	.307	.416	114	3	3-1	.980	-1	89	179	O68(47/1/26)		1.0
1968	LA N	108	304	38	82	16	1	10	35	32-4	1	47	.270	.337	.428	139	14	1-1	.976	-1	92	116	O86(57/0/30)		-0.9
1969	LA N	83	178	13	48	5	1	1	18	12-1	0	25	.270	.313	.326	85	-4	1-2	.981	-4	78	40	O47(13/0/34),1b2		-1.1
1970	LA N	43	42	6	8	0	0	1	6	1-0	0	15	.190	.205	.238	20	-5	0-0	1.000	0	82	0	O2R/1		-0.5
Total	9	708	1764	178	446	64	13	37	176	145-20	4	315	.253	.309	.366	94	-17	20-12	.977	-14	89	89	O455(269/21/183),1b51,3b3		-5.7

GABRIELSON, LEN Leonard Hilbourne B9.8.1915 Oakland CA D11.14.2000 Stanford CA BL/TL/6-3/210 d4.21 s-Len

YEAR	TM LG	G	AB	R	H	2B	3B	HR	RBI	BB-IB	HP	SO	AVG	OBP	SLG	AOPS	ABR	SB-CS	FA	FR	RNG	THR	GAMES AT POSITION	DL	BFW
1939	Phi N	5	18	3	4	0	0	0	1	2	0	3	.222	.300	.222	43	-1	0-0	.977	2	289	66	1b5		0.0

GAEDEL, EDDIE Edward Carl (b Edward Carl Gaedele) B6.8.1925 Chicago IL D6.18.1961 Chicago IL BR/TL/3-7/ 65 d8.19

YEAR	TM LG	G	AB	R	H	2B	3B	HR	RBI	BB-IB	HP	SO	AVG	OBP	SLG	AOPS	ABR	SB-CS	FA	FR	RNG	THR	GAMES AT POSITION	DL	BFW
1951	StL A	1	0	0	0	0	0	0	0	1	0	0	—	1.000	—	-182	0	0-0	—	0			/H		0.0

YEAR	TM LG	G	AB	R	H	2B	3B	HR	RBI	BB-IB	HP	SO	AVG	OBP	SLG	AOPS	ABR	SB-CS	FA	FR	RNG	THR	GAMES AT POSITION	DL	BFW

GAETTI, GARY　Gary Joseph　B8.19.1958 Centralia IL　BR/TR/6-0/200(180-205)　[MinA79 S1/11]　d9.20　C2　Col Northwest Missouri　OF(13/0/1)

YEAR	TM LG	G	AB	R	H	2B	3B	HR	RBI	BB-IB	HP	SO	AVG	OBP	SLG	AOPS	ABR	SB-CS	FA	FR	RNG	THR	GAMES AT POSITION	DL	BFW
1981	Min A	9	26	4	5	0	0	2	3	0-0	0	6	.192	.192	.423	69	-1	0-0	1.000	2	125	76	3b8/D		0.0
1982	Min A	145	508	59	117	25	4	25	84	37-2	3	107	.230	.280	.443	94	-6	0-4	.963	-6	93	115	3b142,S2/D		-1.6
1983	Min A	157	584	81	143	30	3	21	78	54-2	4	121	.245	.309	.414	94	-5	7-1	.967	9	103	124	3b154,S3/D		0.3
1984	Min A	162	588	55	154	29	4	5	65	44-1	4	81	.262	.315	.330	83	-15	11-5	.960	15	111	95	3b154,O8L,S2		-0.2
1985	Min A	160	560	71	138	31	6	20	63	37-3	7	89	.246	.301	.409	87	-11	13-5	.962	18	110	113	3b156,O4L/1D		0.6
1986	Min A	157	596	91	171	34	1	34	108	52-4	6	108	.287	.347	.518	129	23	14-15	.956	17	112	128	3b156,S2/2OL		3.4
1987	†Min A	154	584	95	150	36	2	31	109	37-7	3	92	.257	.303	.485	101	-1	10-7	.973	1	93	99	3b150,D2		-0.2
1988	Min A★	133	468	66	141	29	2	28	88	36-5	5	85	.301	.353	.551	146	28	7-4	.977	-1	88	132	3b115,S2,D5	15	2.7
1989	Min A★	130	498	63	125	11	4	19	75	25-5	3	87	.251	.286	.404	88	-10	6-2	.973	9	102	110	3b125,1b2,D3	18	-0.1
1990	Min A	154	577	61	132	27	5	16	85	36-1	3	101	.229	.274	.376	76	-20	6-1	.959	9	107	133	3b151,1b2,S2		-1.0
1991	Cal A	152	586	58	144	22	1	18	66	33-3	8	104	.246	.293	.379	85	-14	5-5	.965	16	105	139	3b152		0.1
1992	Cal A	130	456	41	103	13	2	12	48	21-4	6	79	.226	.267	.342	69	-21	3-1	.927	14	117	161	3b67,1b44,D17		-1.1
1993	Cal A	20	50	3	9	2	0	0	4	5-0	1	12	.180	.250	.220	2	-8	1-0	.857	-1	92	213	3b7,1b6,D5		-0.6
	KC A	82	281	37	72	18	1	14	46	16-0	8	75	.256	.309	.477	103	0	0-3	.974	10	113	132	3b72,1b18/D		0.8
	Year	102	331	40	81	20	1	14	50	21-0	8	87	.245	.303	.438	92	-5	1-3	.970	9	112	135	3b79,1b24,D6		0.2
1994	KC A	90	327	53	94	15	3	12	57	19-3	2	63	.287	.328	.462	97	-3	0-2	.982	10	113	113	3b85,1b9	15	0.6
1995	KC A	137	514	76	134	27	0	35	96	47-6	8	91	.261	.329	.518	115	9	3-3	.954	-1	101	104	3b123,1b11,D6		0.7
1996	†StL N	141	522	71	143	27	4	23	80	35-6	8	97	.274	.326	.473	108	4	2-2	.970	-15	90	83	3b133,1b14	16	-1.0
1997	StL N	148	502	63	126	24	1	17	69	36-3	6	88	.251	.305	.404	85	-13	7-3	.978	6	107	115	3b132,1b20/P		-0.6
1998	StL N	91	306	39	81	23	1	11	43	31-1	5	39	.265	.339	.454	108	4	1-1	.985	-3	102	105	3b83,1b3/P2OR		0.1
	†Chi N	37	128	21	41	11	0	8	27	12-1	5	23	.320	.397	.594	152	10	0-0	.979	2	109	33	3b36		1.2
	Year	128	434	60	122	34	1	19	70	43-2	10	62	.281	.356	.495	121	14	1-1	.983	-1	104	83	3b119,1b3/P2OR		1.3
1999	Chi N	113	280	22	57	9	1	9	46	21-0	2	51	.204	.260	.339	51	-22	0-1	.962	3	112	72	3b81,1b8/SP		-1.8
2000	Bos A	5	10	0	0	0	0	0	1	0-0	0	3	.000	.000	.000	-97	-3	0-0	—				D5		-0.3
Total	20	2507	8951	1130	2280	443	39	360	1341	634-57	96	1602	.255	.308	.434	96	-72	96-65	.965	114	104	114	3b2282,1b138,D48,O14L,S14,P3,2b2	64	2.0

GAFFKE, FABIAN　Fabian Sebastian　B8.5.1913 Milwaukee WI　D2.8.1992 Milwaukee WI　BR/TR/5-10/185　d9.9

YEAR	TM LG	G	AB	R	H	2B	3B	HR	RBI	BB-IB	HP	SO	AVG	OBP	SLG	AOPS	ABR	SB-CS	FA	FR	RNG	THR	GAMES AT POSITION	DL	BFW
1936	Bos A	15	55	5	7	2	0	1	3	4	1	5	.127	.200	.218	3	-9	0-0	1.000	-0	94	87	O15(5/0/10)		-0.9
1937	Bos A	54	184	32	53	10	4	6	34	15	1	25	.288	.342	.484	102	-1	1-2	.965	-1	96	81	O50(16/1/33)		-0.5
1938	Bos A	15	10	2	1	0	0	0	1	3	0	2	.100	.308	.100	6	-1	0-0	—	0	0	0	O2R/C		-0.1
1939	Bos A	1	1	0	0	0	0	0	0	0	0	0	.000	.000	.000	-96	0	0-0	—		0		/H		0.0
1941	Cle A	4	4	0	1	0	0	0	0	2	0	1	.250	.500	.250	109	0	0-0	1.000	-0	84	0	O2C		0.0
1942	Cle A	40	67	4	11	2	0	0	3	6	1	13	.164	.243	.194	25	-7	1-0	1.000	-0	111	0	O16(5/1/10)		0.0
Total	6	129	321	43	73	14	4	7	42	30	2	47	.227	.297	.361	67	-18	2-2	.979	-2	98	66	O85(26/4/55)/C		-2.3

GAGLIANO, PHIL　Philip Joseph　B12.27.1941 Memphis TN　BR/TR/6-1/185*　d4.16　b-Ralph　OF(34/0/31)

YEAR	TM LG	G	AB	R	H	2B	3B	HR	RBI	BB-IB	HP	SO	AVG	OBP	SLG	AOPS	ABR	SB-CS	FA	FR	RNG	THR	GAMES AT POSITION	DL	BFW
1963	StL N	10	5	1	2	0	0	0	1	1-0	0	1	.400	.500	.400	149	-0	0-0	1.000	1	80	0	2b3/3		0.1
1964	StL N	40	58	5	15	4	0	1	9	3-0	0	10	.259	.290	.379	81	-1	0-1	.918	0	116	98	2b12,O2(1/0/1)/13		-0.1
1965	StL N	122	363	46	87	14	2	8	53	40-0	1	45	.240	.312	.355	81	-8	2-1	.960	2	96	104	2b57,O25(4/0/23),3b19		-0.4
1966	StL N	90	213	23	54	8	2	2	15	24-1	1	29	.254	.329	.338	86	-3	2-1	.982	-2	91	96	3b41,1b8,O5L/2		-0.6
1967	†StL N	73	217	20	48	7	0	2	21	19-3	1	26	.221	.283	.281	64	-10	0-0	.972	-12	81	65	2b27,3b25,1b4,S2		-2.2
1968	†StL N	53	105	13	24	4	2	0	13	7-0	1	13	.229	.281	.305	77	-3	0-0	.982	1	103	97	2b17,3b10,O5(4/0/1)		-0.2
1969	StL N	62	128	7	29	2	0	1	10	14-0	0	12	.227	.303	.266	60	-7	0-0	.989	1	82	104	2b20,1b9,3b9,O2R		-0.7
1970	StL N	18	32	0	6	0	0	0	2	1-0	0	3	.188	.212	.188	4	-4	0-1	1.000	9	47	119	3b6,1b3,2b2		-0.6
	Chi N	26	40	5	6	0	0	0	5	5-0	0	5	.150	.244	.150	7	-5	0-0	1.000	-1	106	39	2b16/13		-0.6
	Year	44	72	5	12	0	0	0	7	6-0	0	8	.167	.231	.167	8	-9	0-1	.980	-3	108	50	2b18,3b7,1b4		-1.2
1971	Bos A	47	68	11	22	5	0	0	13	11-0	0	5	.324	.412	.397	123	3	0-0	1.000	-3	78	0	O11(7/0/4),2b7,3b4		0.0
1972	Bos A	52	82	9	21	4	1	0	10	10-0	1	13	.256	.333	.329	93	0	1-0	.962	1	144	475	O12L,3b5,2b4,1b2		0.1
1973	†Cin N	63	69	8	20	2	0	0	7	13-2	0	16	.290	.402	.319	107	2	0-0	.824	-2	79	103	3b7,2b4/1OL		0.0
1974	Cin N	46	31	2	2	0	0	0	1	7-0	1	7	.065	.370	.065	27	-2	0-0	1.000	-0	0	0	2b2/13		-0.2
Total	12	702	1411	150	336	50	7	14	159	163-7	4	184	.238	.316	.313	77	-38	5-4	.969	-17	94	85	2b172,3b130,O63L,1b30,S2		-5.4

GAGLIANO, RALPH　Ralph Michael　B10.8.1946 Memphis TN　BL/TR/5-11/170　d9.21　b-Phil

YEAR	TM LG	G	AB	R	H	2B	3B	HR	RBI	BB-IB	HP	SO	AVG	OBP	SLG	AOPS	ABR	SB-CS	FA	FR	RNG	THR	GAMES AT POSITION	DL	BFW
1965	Cle A	1	0	0	0	0	0	0	0	0-0	0	0	—	—	—	0	0	0-0	—		0		/R	142	0.0

GAGNE, GREG　Gregory Carpenter　B11.12.1961 Fall River MA　BR/TR/5-11/172(172-185)　[NYA79 5/129]　d6.5

YEAR	TM LG	G	AB	R	H	2B	3B	HR	RBI	BB-IB	HP	SO	AVG	OBP	SLG	AOPS	ABR	SB-CS	FA	FR	RNG	THR	GAMES AT POSITION	DL	BFW
1983	Min A	10	27	2	3	1	0	0	3	0-0	0	6	.111	.103	.148	-24	-5	0-0	.923	-8	49	33	S10		-1.2
1984	Min A	2	1	0	0	0	0	0	0	0-0	0	0	.000	.000	.000	-95	-0	0-0	—	0			/H		-0.2
1985	Min A	114	293	37	66	15	3	2	23	20-0	3	57	.225	.279	.317	60	-16	10-4	.968	3	104	86	S106,D5	22	-0.3
1986	Min A	156	472	63	118	22	6	12	54	30-0	6	108	.250	.301	.398	86	-10	12-10	.959	-14	92	101	S155,2b4		-1.0
1987	†Min A	137	437	68	116	28	7	10	40	25-0	4	84	.265	.310	.430	90	-7	6-6	.970	19	111	102	S136,O4(0/3/1)/2D		2.3
1988	Min A	149	461	70	109	20	6	14	48	27-2	7	110	.236	.288	.397	87	-10	15-7	.970	-12	93	94	S146,O2C/23		-1.0
1989	Min A	149	460	69	125	29	7	9	48	17-0	2	108	.272	.298	.424	96	-4	11-4	.971	-9	95	76	S146/DC		-0.2
1990	Min A	138	388	38	91	22	3	7	38	24-0	1	76	.235	.280	.361	73	-15	8-8	.976	-4	102	77	S135/OCD		-1.1
1991	†Min A	139	408	52	108	23	8	8	42	26-0	3	72	.265	.310	.395	90	-6	11-9	.984	4	105	96	S137/D		0.6
1992	Min A	146	439	53	108	23	0	7	39	19-0	2	84	.246	.280	.346	72	-17	6-7	.973	9	109	116	S141		1.1
1993	KC A	159	540	66	151	32	3	10	57	33-1	0	93	.280	.319	.406	88	-10	10-12	.986	12	101	99	S159		1.1
1994	KC A	107	375	39	97	23	3	7	51	27-0	4	79	.259	.314	.392	77	-13	10-17	.977	13	106	102	S106		0.4
1995	KC A	120	430	58	110	25	4	6	49	38-2	2	60	.256	.316	.374	78	-14	3-5	.969	12	115	119	S118,D2	21	0.5
1996	†LA N	128	428	48	109	13	2	10	55	50-11	2	93	.255	.333	.364	90	-6	4-2	.966	14	106	113	S127	33	1.7
1997	LA N	144	514	49	129	29	3	9	57	31-4	5	120	.251	.298	.354	75	-21	2-5	.971	-25	89	71	S143		-3.6
Total	15	1798	5673	712	1440	296	50	111	604	367-20	40	1121	.254	.302	.382	82	-154	108-96	.972	26	101	95	S1765,D11,O8(0/7/1),2b6/3	76	-0.7

GAGNIER, ED　Edward James　B4.16.1883 Paris, France　D9.13.1946 Detroit MI　BR/TR/5-9/170　d4.14

YEAR	TM LG	G	AB	R	H	2B	3B	HR	RBI	BB-IB	HP	SO	AVG	OBP	SLG	AOPS	ABR	SB-CS	FA	FR	RNG	THR	GAMES AT POSITION	DL	BFW
1914	Bro F	94	337	22	63	12	2	0	25	13	1	24	.187	.219	.234	24	-43	8	.933	-1	93	108	S88,3b6		-3.9
1915	Bro F	20	50	8	13	1	0	0	4	10	1	5	.260	.393	.280	92	0	2	.930	2	117	114	S13,2b6		0.2
	Buf F	1	2	0	0	0	0	0	0	0	0	0	.000	.000	.000	-98	-1	0	.800	1	44	0	/2		-0.1
	Year	21	52	8	13	1	0	0	4	10	1	5	.250	.381	.269	85	-1	2	.930	2	117	114	S13,2b6		0.1
Total	2	115	389	30	76	13	2	0	29	23	2	29	.195	.244	.239	33	-44	10	.931	1	96	109	S101,2b7,3b6		-3.8

GAGNON, CHICK　Harold Dennis　B9.27.1897 Millbury MA　D4.30.1970 Wilmington DE　BR/TR/5-7.5/158　d6.27　Col Holy Cross

YEAR	TM LG	G	AB	R	H	2B	3B	HR	RBI	BB-IB	HP	SO	AVG	OBP	SLG	AOPS	ABR	SB-CS	FA	FR	RNG	THR	GAMES AT POSITION	DL	BFW
1922	Det A	10	4	2	1	0	0	0	0	0	0	2	.250	.250	.250	32	0	0-0	—	1	0	0	/S3		-0.1
1924	Was A	4	5	1	1	0	0	0	1	0	0	0	.200	.200	.200	3	-1	0-0	1.000	0	116	0	S2		0.0
Total	2	14	9	3	2	0	0	0	1	0	0	2	.222	.222	.222	16	-1	0-0	1.000	1	97	0	S3/3		-0.1

GAINER, DEL　Dellos Clinton "Sheriff"　B11.10.1886 Montrose WV　D1.29.1947 Elkins WV　BR/TR/6-0/180　d10.2　Mil 1918

YEAR	TM LG	G	AB	R	H	2B	3B	HR	RBI	BB-IB	HP	SO	AVG	OBP	SLG	AOPS	ABR	SB-CS	FA	FR	RNG	THR	GAMES AT POSITION	DL	BFW
1909	Det A	2	5	0	1	0	0	0	0	0	0		.200	.200	.200	25	-0	1	.929	-0	132	0	1b2		-0.1
1911	Det A	70	248	32	75	11	4	2	25	20	5		.302	.366	.403	109	3	10	.975	-4	85	107	1b69		-0.2
1912	Det A	52	179	28	43	5	6	0	20	18	3		.240	.320	.330	90	-3	15	.986	-3	76	99	1b50/OC		-0.7
1913	Det A	105	363	47	97	16	8	3	25	30	6	45	.267	.333	.372	108	3	10	.988	-5	82	95	1b103		-0.5
1914	Det A	1	0	0	0	0	0	0	0	0	0		—	—	—	0	0	0	1.000	-0	0		/1		0.0
	Bos A	38	84	11	20	9	2	2	13	8	1	14	.238	.312	.464	133	3	2-2	.981	-2	91	44	1b18,2b11/OC		0.1
	Year	39	84	11	20	9	2	2	13	8	1	14	.238	.312	.464	133	3	2-2	.982	-2	88	43	1b19,2b11/OC		0.1
1915	†Bos A	82	200	30	59	5	8	1	29	21	3	31	.295	.371	.415	139	9	7-2	.988	2	114	99	1b56,O6(0/5/1)		1.1
1916	†Bos A	56	142	14	36	6	0	3	18	10	0	24	.254	.303	.359	98	-1	5	.997	1	107	94	1b48,2b2		-0.1
1917	Bos A	52	172	28	53	16	2	2	19	15	3	21	.308	.374	.424	145	9	1	.989	-1	96	123	1b50		0.8
1919	Bos A	47	118	9	28	6	0	0	13	13	1	15	.237	.318	.297	82	-2	5	.978	-0	98	67	1b21,O18L		-0.4
1922	StL N	43	97	19	26	7	4	2	23	14	0	6	.268	.360	.485	122	3	0-2	.979	-5	91	68	1b26,O10(6/4/0)		0.1
Total	10	548	1608	218	438	75	36	14	185	149	22	156	.272	.342	.390	113	24	55-6	.985	-11	91	96	1b444,O36(24/11/1),2b13		0.1

GAINER, JAY　Johnathan Keith　B10.8.1966 Panama City FL　BL/TL/6-0/190　[SDN90 24/655]　d5.14　Col South Alabama

YEAR	TM LG	G	AB	R	H	2B	3B	HR	RBI	BB-IB	HP	SO	AVG	OBP	SLG	AOPS	ABR	SB-CS	FA	FR	RNG	THR	GAMES AT POSITION	DL	BFW
1993	Col N	23	41	4	7	0	0	3	6	4-0	0	12	.171	.244	.390	57	-3	1-1	.982	-1	40	49	1b7		-0.5

YEAR	TM LG	G	AB	R	H	2B	3B	HR	RBI	BB-IB	HP	SO	AVG	OBP	SLG	AOPS	ABR	FA	FR	RNG	THR	GAMES AT POSITION	DL	BFW

GAINES, JOE Arnesta Joe B11.22.1936 Bryan TX BR/TR/6-1/190* d6.29

1960	Cin N	11	15	2	3	0	0	0	1	0-0	0	1	.200	.200	.200	10	-2	1.000	-0	97	0	O3(1/1/2)		-0.2
1961	Cin N	5	3	2	0	0	0	0	0	2-0	0	1	.000	.400	.000	18	0	.500	-1	44	0	O3(1/2/0)		-0.1
1962	Cin N	64	52	12	12	3	0	1	7	8-0	0	16	.231	.333	.346	80	-1	1.000	-0	96	0	O13(11/0/2)		-0.2
1963	Bal A	66	126	24	36	4	1	6	20	20-0	0	39	.286	.381	.476	145	8	.945	-2	94	97	O39(34/4/2)		0.5
1964	Bal A	16	26	2	4	0	0	1	2	3-0	0	7	.154	.241	.269	42	-2	.846	0	149	0	O5L		-0.2
	Hou N	89	307	37	78	9	7	7	34	27-0	3	69	.254	.318	.397	106	2	.957	-3	96	69	O81(1/0/81)		-1.4
1965	Hou N	100	229	21	52	8	1	6	31	18-0	3	59	.227	.290	.349	86	-5	.913	-6	86	29	O65(26/0/39)		-0.3
1966	Hou N	11	13	4	1	1	0	0	0	3-0	0	5	.077	.250	.154	17	-1	.500	-1	27	0	O3(1/0/2)		-0.2
Total	7	362	771	104	186	25	9	21	95	81-0	5	197	.241	.316	.379	99	-1	.934	-13	93	39	O212(80/7/128)		-2.5

GAINEY, TY Telmanch B12.25.1960 Cheraw SC BL/TR/6-1/190* [HouN79 2/34] d4.24 [DL 1988 Hou N 182]

1985	Hou N	13	37	4	6	1	0	0	2-0		0	9	.162	.244	.162	16	-4	.913	-1	97	0	O9(0/8/1)		-0.6
1986	Hou N	26	50	6	15	3	1	1	6	6-0	0	19	.300	.375	.450	133	2	1.000	0	115	0	O19(7/14/3)		0.3
1987	Hou N	18	24	1	3	0	0	0	1	2-0	0	9	.125	.192	.125	-14	-4	1.000	1	145	0	O6L		-0.4
Total	3	57	111	12	24	3	1	1	7	10-0	0	37	.216	.293	.288	62	-6	.968	-0	113	0	O34(13/22/4)	182	-0.7

GALAN, AUGIE August John B5.23.1912 Berkeley CA D12.28.1993 Fairfield CA (BL 1943p, 44-49)/6-0/175 d4.29 C1 OF(1000/335/38)

1934	Chi N	66	192	31	50	6	2	5	22	16	0	15	.260	.317	.391	90	-3	.961	-5	86	79	2b43,3b3/S		-0.6
1935	†Chi N	154	646	133	203	41	11	12	79	87		4	53	.314	.399	.467	131	32	**22**	.978	4	102	106	O154L		2.6
1936	Chi N★	145	575	74	152	26	4	8	81	67	3	50	.264	.344	.365	89	-7	16	.987	-0	99	86	O145(8/139/0)		-1.1
1937	Chi N	147	611	104	154	24	10	18	78	79	1	48	.252	.339	.412	99	-1	**23**	.980	8	110	84	O140(133/6/1),2b8,S2		-0.1
1938	†Chi N	110	395	52	113	16	9	6	69	49	2	17	.286	.368	.418	112	7	8.	.987	3	98	68	O145L		0.5
1939	Chi N	148	549	104	167	36	8	6	71	75	4	26	.304	.392	.432	119	18	8	.970	-3	98	68	O145L		0.7
1940	Chi N	68	209	33	48	14	2	3	22	37		0	23	.230	.346	.359	96	0	.984	-0	95	149	O54(31/24/0),2b2		-0.2
1941	Chi N	65	120	18	25	3	0	1	13	22	0	10	.208	.331	.258	70	-4	0	.959	-2	85	113	O31(17/11/4)		0.0
	†Bro N	17	27	3	7	3	0	0	4	3	0	1	.259	.333	.370	94	0	0	1.000	1	99	279	O6C		-0.7
	Year	82	147	21	32	6	0	1	17	25	0	11	.218	.331	.279	74	-4		.967	-1	87	139	O37(17/17/4)		-0.4
1942	Bro N	69	209	24	55	16	0	0	22	24	0	12	.263	.339	.340	97	0	2	.990	-2	97	51	O55(20/26/10),1b4,2b3		3.6
1943	Bro N★	139	495	83	142	26	3	9	67	**103**	2	39	.287	.412	.406	136	30	6	.981	10	111	101	O124(88/97/0),1b13		4.5
1944	Bro N★	151	547	96	174	43	9	12	93	**101**	2	23	.318	.426	.495	162	51	4	.988	1	103	91	O147(126/25/2),2b2		2.6
1945	Bro N	152	576	114	177	36	7	9	92	114	2	27	.307	.423	.441	142	40	13	.935	-5	96	94	O60L,3b19,1b12		1.8
1946	Bro N	99	274	53	85	22	5	3	38	68	2	21	.310	.451	.460	157	26	0	.988	-3	102	24	O118(118/1/1)		1.4
1947	Cin N	124	392	60	123	18	2	6	61	94	2	19	.314	**.449**	.416	132	26	0	.967	-2	96	0	O18(1/0/17)		0.7
1948	Cin N	54	77	18	22	3	2	2	16	26	1	4	.286	.471	.455	157	9	0	1.000	-0	156	0	1b3/OR		-0.2
1949	NY N	22	17	0	1	1	0	0	2	5		0	3	.059	.273	.118	8	-2	0	1.000	-0	107	0	O9(7/0/2)		0.2
	Phi A	12	26	4	9	2	0	0	9	4	2	.346	.486	.385	136	2	0-0	1.000	-0	107	0	O8(1/7/0)		
Total	16	1742	5937	1004	1706	336	74	100	830	979	25	393	.287	.390	.419	122	224	123-0	.981	-4	102	87	O1359L,1b98,3b62,2b58,S3		15.3

GALARRAGA, ANDRES Andres Jose "The Big Cat" (b Andres Jose Padovani (Galarraga)) B6.18.1961 Caracas, Venez BR/TR/6-3/235(209-265) d8.23 [DL 1999 Atl N 182]

1985	Mon N	24	75	9	14	1	0	2	4	3-0	1	18	.187	.228	.280	44	-6	1-2	.995	4	166	93	1b23		-0.5
1986	Mon N	105	321	39	87	13	0	10	42	30-5	3	79	.271	.338	.405	105	2	6-5	.995	-11	57	88	1b102	55	-1.6
1987	Mon N	147	551	72	168	40	3	13	90	41-13	**10**	127	.305	.361	.459	112	11	7-10	.993	-2	93	89	1b146		-0.3
1988	Mon N★	157	609	99	**184**	**42**	8	29	92	39-9	10	153	.302	.352	.540	146	35	13-4	.991	-7	87	118	1b156		1.9
1989	Mon N	152	572	76	147	30	1	23	85	48-10	**13**	158	.257	.327	.434	114	10	12-5	.992	-4	88	98	1b147		-0.4
1990	Mon N	155	579	65	148	29	0	20	87	40-8	4	169	.256	.306	.409	99	-2	10-1	.993	-8	82	95	1b154		-2.1
1991	Mon N	107	375	34	82	13	2	9	33	23-5	2	86	.219	.268	.336	69	-17	5-6	.991	3	112	101	1b105	39	-2.3
1992	StL N	95	325	38	79	14	2	10	39	11-0	8	69	.243	.282	.391	92	-5	5-4	.991	-3	96	124	1b90	44	-1.6
1993	Col N★	120	470	71	174	35	4	22	98	24-12	6	73	**.370**	.403	.602	143	29	2-4	.990	7	122	85	1b119	44	2.4
1994	Col N	103	417	77	133	21	0	31	85	19-8	6	93	.319	.356	.592	122	13	8-3	.992	-5	83	94	1b103	14	-0.1
1995	†Col N	143	554	89	155	29	3	31	106	32-6	13	146	.280	.331	.511	93	-6	12-2	.991	3	111	107	1b142		-1.3
1996	Col N	159	626	119	190	39	3	**47**	**150**	40-3	17	157	.304	.357	.601	120	17	18-8	.992	-2	99	108	1b159/3		0.2
1997	Col N★	154	600	120	191	31	3	-41	**140**	54-2	17	141	.318	.389	.585	123	21	15-8	.991	-5	98	**131**	1b154		2.7
1998	†Atl N★	153	555	103	169	27	1	44	121	63-11	25	146	.305	.397	.595	158	48	7-6	.992	-7	79	108	1b149,D2		-0.3
2000	†Atl N	141	494	67	149	25	1	28	100	36-5	17	126	.302	.369	.526	124	17	3-5	.988	-8	79	106	1b132/D		-0.8
2001	Tex A	72	243	33	57	16	0	10	34	18-1	9	68	.235	.310	.424	88	2	1-0	.995	0	101	112	D39,1b25		-0.2
	SF N	49	156	17	45	12	1	7	35	13-1	3	49	.288	.351	.513	128	6	0-3	.984	-5	58	130	1b41		-0.9
2002	Mon N	104	292	30	76	12	0	9	40	30-6	9	81	.260	.344	.394	93	-4	2-2	.981	2	116	87	1b89	24	-0.5
2003	†SF N	110	272	36	82	15	0	12	42	19-1	5	61	.301	.352	.489	115	5	1-3	.994	-4	74	116	1b69,D2		0.1
2004	Ana A	7	10	1	3	1	0	0	2	0-0	1	3	.300	.364	.600	151	1	0-0	1.000	0	141	245	/1D		-0.3
Total	19	2257	8096	1195	2333	444	32	399	1425	583-106	178	2003	.288	.347	.499	116	171	128-81	.991	-52	93	105	1b2106,D48/3	402	-5.3

GALATZER, MILT Milton B5.4.1907 Chicago IL D1.29.1976 San Francisco CA BL/TL/5-10/168 d6.25

1933	Cle A	57	160	19	38	2	1	1	17	23	0	21	.237	.333	.281	61	-9	2-3	.975	0	95	116	O40(11/4/25),1b5		-1.1
1934	Cle A	49	196	29	53	10	-2	0	15	21	1	8	.270	.344	.342	76	-7	3-2	.980	1	93	179	O49(3/0/46)		-0.8
1935	Cle A	93	259	45	78	9	3	0	19	35	2	8	.301	.389	.359	93	-1	4-5	.934	-4	88	118	O81(8/18/56)		-1.0
1936	Cle A	49	97	12	23	4	1	0	6	13	1	8	.237	.318	.299	54	-7	1-2	.964	-0	98	92	O42(6/9/27)/P1		-0.7
1939	Cin N	3	5	0	0	0	0	0	0	0	0	1	.000	.000	.000	-99	-1	0	1.000	-0	0	0	1b2		-0.2
Total	5	251	717	105	192	25	7	1	57	92	4	46	.268	.354	.326	75	-25	10-12	.959	-3	92	131	O212(28/31/154),1b8/P		-3.8

GALL, JOHN John Christopher B4.2.1978 Stanford CA BR/TR/6-0/195 d7.26 Col Stanford

2005	†StL N	22	37	5	10	3	0	2	10	1-0	0	8	.270	.282	.514	103	0	0-0	1.000	-0	64	301	O10L		0.0

GALLAGHER, AL Alan Mitchell Edward George Patrick Henry B10.19.1945 San Francisco CA BR/TR/6-0/180* [SFN65 1/14] d4.7 Col Santa Clara

1970	SF N	109	282	31	75	15	2	4	28	30-4	0	37	.266	.335	.376	91	-3	2-1	.971	-4	92	83	3b91		-0.7
1971	†SF N	136	429	47	119	18	5	5	57	40-10	2	57	.277	.340	.378	105	3	2-1	.951	-7	93	99	3b128		-0.5
1972	SF N	82	233	19	52	3	1	2	18	33-4	1	39	.223	.317	.270	69	-9	2-1	.974	-3	92	64	3b69		-1.3
1973	SF N	5	9	1	2	0	0	0	1	0-0	1	0	.222	.300	.222	45	-1	0-0	.833	-1	20	0	3b5		-0.2
	Cal A	110	311	16	85	6	1	0	26	35-3	1	31	.273	.345	.299	90	-3	1-3	.961	1	99	77	3b98/2S		-0.3
Total	4	442	1264	114	333	42	9	11	130	138-21	5	164	.263	.335	.337	91	-13	7-6	.961	-9	94	83	3b391/S2		-3.0

GALLAGHER, SHORTY Charles William B4.30.1872 Detroit MI D6.23.1924 Detroit MI d8.13

1901	Cle A	2	4	0	0	0	0	0	0	0	0		.000	.000	.000	-99	-1	0	.667	-0	0	0	O2R		-0.1

GALLAGHER, DAVE David Thomas B9.20.1960 Trenton NJ BR/TR/6-0/184(165-185) [CleA80 S1/8] d4.12 Col Mercer Co. (NJ) CC

1987	Cle A	15	36	2	4	1	1	0	1	2-0	0	5	.111	.158	.194	-7	-6	2-0	.972	1	106	180	O14C		-0.4
1988	Chi A	101	347	59	105	15	3	5	31	29-3	0	40	.303	.354	.406	113	6	5-4	1.000	-2	94	109	O95(5/78/17),D2		0.3
1989	Chi A	161	601	74	160	22	6	1	46	46-1	2	79	.266	.320	.314	81	-15	5-6	.993	-1	99	93	O160(1/138/27)/D		-1.9
1990	Chi A	45	75	5	21	3	1	0	5	3-0	1	9	.280	.316	.347	87	-1	0-1	.981	-1	93	84	O37(14/22/1),D4	29	-0.3
	Bal A	23	51	7	11	1	0	0	2	4-0	0	3	.216	.268	.235	44	-4	1-1	.980	4	136	202	O20(17/2/1),D2		-0.1
	Year	68	126	12	32	4	1	0	7	7-0	1	12	.254	.296	.302	70	-5	1-2	.980	3	111	132	O57(31/24/2),D6		-0.4
1991	Cal A	90	270	32	79	17	0	1	30	24-0	2	43	.293	.355	.367	100	1	2-4	1.000	4	111	149	O76(22/13/48)	44	-0.1
1992	NY N	98	175	20	42	11	1	1	21	19-0	1	16	.240	.307	.331	85	-1	4-5	.982	1	115	180	O72(19/39/20),1b9		0.3
1993	NY N	99	201	34	55	12	2	6	28	20-1	1	18	.274	.338	.443	109	2	1-1	1.000	2	98	91	O77(71/5/7)/1		-0.8
1994	Atl N	89	152	27	34	5	0	2	14	22-2	1	22	.224	.326	.296	61	-8	0-2	.989	1	120	41	O77(75/1/1)/D		0.1
1995	Phi N	62	157	12	50	12	0	1	12	16-0	0	20	.318	.379	.414	109	3	0-0	1.000	-1	102	35	O56(5/21/28)	20	0.0
	Cal A	11	16	1	3	1	0	0	0	1-0	0	4	.188	.278	.250	39	-1	0-0	1.000	-1	113	460	O6(2/3/1)/D	93	-0.8
Total	9	794	2081	273	564	100	10	17	190	187-7	7	251	.271	.331	.353	90	-26	20-24	.993	13	102	120	O699(166/396/173),D12,1b10	93	-2.8

GALLAGHER, JIM James E. B Findlay OH D3.29.1894 Scranton PA d9.4

1886	Was N	1	5	1	1	0	0	0	0	0		2	.200	.200	.200	24	0	0	.875	0	140	0	/S		0.0

GALLAGHER, JOHN John Carroll B2.18.1892 Pittsburgh PA D3.30.1952 Norfolk VA BR/TR/5-10.5/156 d8.20 Col Georgetown

1915	Bal F	40	126	11	25	4	2	0	4	5		0	.198	.229	.230	28	-14	1	.945	-1	104	70	2b37,S5/3		-1.6

GALLAGHER, JACKIE John Laurence B1.28.1902 Providence RI D9.10.1984 Gladwyne PA BL/TR/5-10/175 d8.24

1923	Cle A	1	1	1	1	0	1	0	0	0		0	1.000	1.000	1.000	428	0	0-0	—	-0	0	0	/OL		0.0

YEAR	TM LG	G	AB	R	H	2B	3B	HR	RBI	BB-IB	HP	SO	AVG	OBP	SLG	AOPS	ABR	SB-CS	FA	FR	RNG	THR	GAMES AT POSITION	DL	BFW

GALLAGHER, JOE Joseph Emmett "Muscles" B3.7.1914 Buffalo NY D2.25.1998 Houston TX BR/TR/6-2/210 d4.20 Mil 1941-45 Col Manhattan

1939	NY A	14	41	8	10	1	2	9	3	1	1	9	.244	.311	.439	91	-1	1-0	1.000	0	97	138	O12R		-0.1
	StL A	71	266	41	75	7	2	9	40	17	1	42	.282	.327	.462	98	-1	0-1	.944	1	96	170	O79(56/0/23)		-0.5
	Year	85	307	49	85	17	3	11	49	20	2	50	.277	.325	.459	97	-3	0-1	.950	1	96	166	O79(56/0/23)		-0.6
1940	StL A	23	70	14	19	3	1	2	8	4	0	12	.271	.311	.429	88	-2	2-0	.966	1	85	95	O15L		-0.3
	Bro N	57	110	10	29	6	1	3	16	2	1	14	.264	.283	.418	86	-3	1-0	.941	-1	93	75	O20(3/0/17)		-0.5
Total	2	165	487	73	133	26	5	16	73	26	3	76	.273	.314	.446	93	-8	4-1	.950	-1	94	142	O114(74/0/40)		-1.4

GALLAGHER, GIL Lawrence Kirby B9.5.1896 Washington DC D1.6.1957 Washington DC BB/TR/5-8/155 d9.13

| 1922 | Bos N | 7 | 22 | 1 | 1 | 1 | 0 | 0 | 2 | 1 | 0 | 7 | .045 | .087 | .091 | -57 | -5 | 0-0 | .893 | -1 | 120 | 0 | S6 | | -0.6 |

GALLAGHER, BOB Robert Collins B7.7.1948 Newton MA BL/TL/6-3/185* [LAN68 17/377] d5.17 gf-Shano Collins Col Stanford

1972	Bos A	7	5	0	0	0	0	0	0	0-0	0	3	.000	.000	.000	-94	-1	0-0	—	0			/H		-0.1
1973	Hou N	71	148	16	39	3	1	2	10	3-1	0	27	.264	.275	.338	70	-7	0-1	1.000	2	125	44	O42(15/12/16)/1		-0.6
1974	Hou N	102	87	13	15	2	0	0	3	12-1	0	23	.172	.280	.195	36	-7	1-0	.978	-1	102	0	O62(5/4/53),1b4		-0.9
1975	NY N	33	15	5	2	1	0	0	0	1-0	0	3	.133	.188	.200	8	-2	0-0	.900	0	151	0	O16(10/1/5)		-0.2
Total	4	213	255	34	56	6	1	2	13	16-2	1	56	.220	.266	.275	52	-17	1-1	.985	2	118	24	O120(30/17/74),1b5		-1.8

GALLAGHER, WILLIAM William Howard B2.4.1874 Boston MA D3.11.1950 Worcester MA d8.19

| 1896 | Phi N | 14 | 49 | 9 | 15 | 2 | 0 | 0 | 6 | 10 | 1 | 0 | .306 | .433 | .347 | 108 | 2 | 0 | .894 | -2 | 99 | 87 | S14 | | 0.0 |

GALLAGHER, BILL William John B Philadelphia PA TL d5.2 ▲

1883	Bal AA	16	61	9	10	3	1	0		3			.164	.203	.246	43	-4		.824	-1	135	508	O9(1/0/8),P7,S4		-0.3
	Phi N	2	8	1	0	0	0	0		0		4	.000	.000	.000	-99	-2		1.000	-0	0	0	O2C		-0.2
1884	Phi U	3	11	1	1	0	0	0		0			.091	.091	.091	-48	-2		.800	-0	107	0	P3		0.0
Total	2	21	80	11	11	3	1	0	0	3		4	.138	.169	.200	16	-8		.850	-2	113	425	O11(1/2/8),P10,S4		-0.5

GALLE, STAN Stanley Joseph (b Stanley Joseph Galazewski) B2.7.1919 Milwaukee WI BR/TR/5-7/165 d4.14 Mil 1942-45

| 1942 | Was A | 13 | 18 | 3 | 2 | 0 | 0 | 0 | 1 | 1 | 0 | 0 | .111 | .158 | .111 | -24 | -3 | 0-0 | .857 | -0 | 76 | 0 | 3b3 | | -0.4 |

GALLEGO, MIKE Michael Anthony B10.31.1960 Whittier CA BR/TR/5-8/160(160-175) [OakA81 2/33] d4.11 C2 Col UCLA

1985	Oak A	76	77	13	16	5	1	1	9	12-0	1	14	.208	.319	.338	87	-1	1-1	.991	-2	93	133	2b42,S21,3b12		-0.1
1986	Oak A	20	37	2	10	2	0	0	4	1-0	0	6	.270	.289	.324	72	-2	0-2	.986	5	135	72	2b19,3b2/S		0.3
1987	Oak A	72	124	18	31	6	0	2	14	12-0	1	21	.250	.319	.347	82	-3	0-1	.968	7	116	160	2b31,3b24,S17		0.3
1988	†Oak A	129	277	38	58	8	0	2	20	34-0	1	53	.209	.298	.260	60	-14	2-3	.993	-12	92	85	2b83,S42,3b16	46	0.6
1989	†Oak A	133	357	45	90	14	2	3	30	35-0	6	43	.252	.327	.328	88	-5	7-5	.967	10	102	136	S94,2b41,3b/D		-2.3
1990	†Oak A	140	389	36	80	13	2	3	34	35-0	6	50	.206	.277	.272	57	-23	5-5	.990	-2	109	104	2b83,S38,3b27/ORD		-2.1
1991	Oak A	159	482	67	119	15	4	12	49	67-3	5	84	.247	.343	.369	103	3	6-9	.989	-15	99	81	2b135,S55		-0.7
1992	NY A	53	173	24	44	7	1	3	14	20-0	4	22	.254	.343	.358	98	0	0-1	.990	1	98	101	2b40,S14	113	0.3
1993	NY A	119	403	63	114	20	1	10	54	50-0	4	65	.283	.364	.412	112	8	3-2	.976	26	124	123	S55,2b52,3b27/D	15	3.8
1994	NY A	89	306	39	73	17	1	6	41	38-1	4	46	.239	.327	.359	81	-8	0-1	.970	16	114	125	S72,2b26	20	1.2
1995	Oak A	43	120	11	28	0	0	6	9-0	1	24	.233	.292	.233	41	-11	0-1	.960	-1	107	91	2b18,S14,3b12	84	-1.0
1996	†StL N	51	143	12	30	2	0	0	4	12-1	1	31	.210	.276	.224	34	-14	0-0	.985	1	101	126	2b43,3b7/S	102	-1.0
1997	StL N	27	43	6	7	2	0	0	1	1-0	0	6	.163	.178	.209	2	-6	0-0	.962	3	110	99	2b11,S10,3b7		-0.3
Total	13	1111	2931	374	700	111	12	42	282	326-5	32	465	.239	.320	.328	80	-76	24-31	.986	38	105	103	2b624,S434,3b137,D3/OR	380	-0.1

GALLIGAN, JOHN John T. B6.1865 Easton PA D8.22.1937 Bronx NY 5-10/160 d9.2

| 1889 | Lou AA | 31 | 120 | 6 | 20 | 0 | 2 | 0 | 1 | | 1 | 17 | .167 | .213 | .200 | 18 | -13 | 1 | .915 | 1 | 112 | 62 | O31L | | -1.2 |

GALLOWAY, CHICK Clarence Edward B8.4.1896 Clinton SC D11.7.1969 Clinton SC BR/TR/5-8/160 d9.9 Col Presbyterian

1919	Phi A	17	63	2	9	0	0	4	1	0	8	.143	.156	.143	-16	-10	0	.969	2	93	153	S17		-0.8
1920	Phi A	98	298	28	60	9	3	0	18	22	1	22	.201	.259	.252	35	-29	2-2	.928	3	101	67	S84,2b4,3b3		-2.0
1921	Phi A	131	465	42	123	28	5	3	47	29	2	43	.265	.310	.366	72	-21	12-7	.922	-25	91	98	S110,3b20/2		-3.1
1922	Phi A	155	571	83	185	26	9	6	69	39	1	39	.324	.368	.433	105	4	10-19	.952	6	100	95	S155		2.1
1923	Phi A	134	504	64	140	18	9	2	62	37	0	30	.278	.327	.361	80	-16	12-10	.944	2	99	105	S134		0.0
1924	Phi A	129	464	41	128	16	4	2	48	23	1	23	.276	.311	.341	67	-24	11-12	.952	-4	96	103	S129		-1.4
1925	Phi A	149	481	52	116	11	4	3	71	59	0	28	.241	.324	.299	55	-33	16-9	.954	-4	96	105	S148		-1.9
1926	Phi A	133	408	38	98	13	6	0	49	31	1	20	.240	.295	.301	53	-29	8-7	.935	-16	85	78	S133		-3.2
1927	Phi A	77	181	25	48	10	4	0	22	18	0	9	.265	.332	.365	76	-7	1-3	.946	-1	94	74	S61,3b7		-0.3
1928	Det A	53	148	17	39	5	2	1	17	15	0	3	.264	.331	.345	77	-5	7-3	.914	-2	84	94	S22,3b21/1OL		-0.4
Total	10	1076	3583	391	946	136	46	17	407	274	6	225	.264	.317	.342	69	-170	79-72	.943	-39	95	95	S993,3b51,2b5/OL1		-11.0

GALLOWAY, JIM James Cato "Bad News" B9.16.1887 Iredell TX D5.3.1950 Fort Worth TX BB/TR/6-3/187 d8.24

| 1912 | StL N | 21 | 54 | 4 | 10 | 2 | 0 | 0 | 4 | 8 | | 8 | .185 | .254 | .222 | 32 | -5 | 2 | .971 | 2 | 116 | 91 | 2b16/S | | -0.3 |

GALVIN, JIM James Joseph B8.11.1907 Somerville MA D9.30.1969 Marietta GA BR/TR/5-11.5/180 d9.27

| 1930 | Bos A | 2 | 2 | 0 | 0 | 0 | 0 | 0 | 0 | 0 | 0 | 0 | .000 | .000 | .000 | -99 | -1 | 0-0 | — | 0 | | | /H | | -0.1 |

GALVIN, JOHN John A. B8.1842 Brooklyn NY D4.20.1904 Brooklyn NY 5-7/178 d5.7

| 1872 | Atl NA | 1 | 4 | 0 | 0 | 0 | 0 | 0 | 0 | 0 | 0 | 0 | .000 | .000 | .000 | -85 | -1 | 0-0 | .200 | -2 | 0 | 0 | /2 | | -0.2 |

GAMBLE, JOHN John Robert B2.10.1948 Reno NV BR/TR/5-10/165* [LAN66 2/39] d9.7

1972	Det A	6	3	0	0	0	0	0	0	0-0	0	0	.000	.000	.000	-97	-1	0-0	1.000	0	77	0	/S		-0.1
1973	Det A	7	0	1	0	0	0	0	0	0-0	0	0					0	0-0	—	0			/R		0.0
Total	2	13	3	1	0	0	0	0	0	0-0	0	0	.000	.000	.000	-97	-1	0-0	1.000	0	77	0	/S		-0.1

GAMBLE, LEE Lee Jesse B6.28.1910 Renovo PA D10.5.1994 Punxsutawney PA BL/TR/6-1/170 d9.15

1935	Cin N	2	4	2	2	1	0	0		0	0	.500	.600	.750	269	1	1	1.000	-0	101	0	O2L		0.1
1938	Cin N	53	75	13	24	3	1	0	5	0		6	.320	.320	.387	96	-1	0	1.000	0	114	0	O9L		-0.1
1939	†Cin N	72	221	24	59	7	2	0	14	9	0	14	.267	.296	.317	64	-12	5	.989	-3	78	150	O56(55/1/0)		-1.8
1940	Cin N	38	42	12	6	1	0	0	2	0	0	1	.143	.143	.167	-15	-7	0	1.000	1	135	190	O10(2/0/8)		-0.6
Total	4	165	342	51	91	12	3	0	21	10	0	21	.266	.287	.319	64	-19	6	.993	-2	88	134	O77(68/1/8)		-2.4

GAMBLE, OSCAR Oscar Charles B12.20.1949 Ramer AL BL/TR/5-11/165(160-187) [ChiN68 16/363] d8.27

1969	Chi N	24	71	6	16	1	1	1	5	10-1	0	12	.225	.321	.310	69	-3	0-2	.913	-2	86	76	O24(1/23/0)		-0.7
1970	Phi N	88	275	31	72	12	4	1	19	27-3	1	37	.262	.330	.345	83	-7	5-4	.956	-1	103	96	O74(0/47/28)		-1.0
1971	Phi N	92	280	24	62	11	1	6	23	21-2	1	35	.221	.275	.332	72	-11	5-2	.970	-3	91	80	O80(54/1/26)		-1.9
1972	Phi N	74	135	17	32	5	2	1	13	19-0	1	16	.237	.331	.326	86	-2	0-1	1.000	0	93	0	O35R/1		-0.4
1973	Cle A	113	390	56	104	11	3	20	44	34-1	3	37	.267	.329	.464	119	8	3-4	.971	-1	107	46	D70,O37(2/1/35)		0.4
1974	Cle A	135	454	74	132	16	4	19	59	48-10	5	51	.291	.363	.469	130	23	5-6	1.000	0	89	138	O82(81/0/1),D29		1.9
1975	Cle A	121	348	60	91	16	3	15	45	53-4	2	39	.261	.361	.454	129	14	11-5	.987	1	93	144	O82(81/0/1),D29		1.1
1976	†NY A	110	340	43	79	13	1	17	57	38-4	4	38	.232	.317	.426	117	7	5-3	.981	2	98	139	O104R/D		0.4
1977	Chi A	137	408	75	121	22	2	31	83	54-7	6	54	.297	.386	.588	161	35	1-2	.987	-4	87	35	D79,O49(5/7/38)		2.7
1978	SD N	126	375	46	103	15	3	7	47	51-11	6	45	.275	.366	.387	122	10	1-2	.979	2	95	154	O107(39/0/70)		0.9
1979	Tex A	64	161	27	54	6	0	8	32	37-11	1	15	.335	.458	.522	166	18	2-1	1.000	2	115	153	D37,O21R	27	1.7
	NY A	36	113	21	44	4	1	11	32	13-1	0	13	.389	.452	.735	217	18	0-0	.943	-4	96	164	O27(25/2/0),D6		1.7
	Year	100	274	48	98	10	1	19	64	50-12	1	28	.358	.456	.609	187	36	2-1	.969	-2	104	159	O48(25/2/21),D43		3.4
1980	†NY A	78	194	40	54	10	2	14	50	28-4	4	21	.278	.376	.567	158	16	2-0	1.000	-2	89	74	O49(36/0/14),D20	40	1.2
1981	†NY A	80	189	24	45	0	0	10	27	35-2	1	23	.238	.357	.439	131	9	0-2	1.000	1	73	0	O43(16/0/27),D33		0.7
1982	NY A	108	316	49	86	21	2	18	57	58-2	4	47	.272	.387	.522	150	24	6-3	1.000	5	111	332	D74,O29(1/0/28)		2.6
1983	NY A	74	180	26	47	10	2	7	25	25-1	3	25	.261	.361	.456	127	7	3-1	.942	0	113	49	O32(2/0/30),D21		0.5
1984	NY A	54	125	17	23	2	0	10	25	25-0	1	18	.184	.318	.440	112	2	0-1	1.000	-1	73	164	D28,O12R	48	-0.4
1985	NY A	70	148	20	30	5	0	8	34	34-3	1	20	.203	.353	.318	82	-2	0-0	—	0	0	0	D48	115	11.4
Total	17	1584	4502	656	1195	188	31	200	666	610-62	43	546	.265	.356	.454	126	168	47-37	.977	1	98	113	O818(274/81/469),D561/1		

GAMMONS, DAFF John Ashley B3.17.1876 New Bedford MA D9.24.1963 E.Greenwich RI BR/TR/5-11/170 d4.23 Col Harvard

| 1901 | Bos N | 28 | 93 | 10 | 18 | 0 | 1 | 0 | 10 | 3 | 3 | | .194 | .242 | .204 | 30 | -8 | 5 | .880 | -3 | 203 | 0 | O23(20/0/3),2b2/3 | | -1.2 |

YEAR	TM LG	G	AB	R	H	2B	3B	HR	RBI	BB-IB	HP	SO	AVG	OBP	SLG	AOPS	ABR	SB-CS	FA	FR	RNG	THR	GAMES AT POSITION	DL	BFW

GANDIL, CHICK Arnold B1.19.1887 St.Paul MN D12.13.1970 Calistoga CA BR/TR/6-1.5/190 d4.14

1910	Chi A	77	275	21	53	7	3	2	21	24	4		.193	.267	.262	69	-10	12	.989	6	130	107	1b74,O2L		-0.6
1912	Was A	117	443	59	135	20	15	4	81	27	4		.305	.350	.431	122	10	19	.990	2	98	91	1b117		0.9
1913	Was A	148	550	61	175	25	8	1	72	36	3	33	.318	.363	.398	120	13	22	.990	8	115	123	1b145		1.8
1914	Was A	145	526	48	136	24	10	3	75	44	7	44	.259	.324	.359	101	0	30-19	.991	23	156	126	1b145		2.1
1915	Was A	136	485	53	141	20	15	4	64	29	7	33	.291	.340	.406	121	9	20-13	.986	-1	96	105	1b134		0.5
1916	Cle A	146	533	51	138	26	9	0	72	36	5	48	.259	.312	.341	91	-7	13	.995	8	118	99	1b145		-0.3
1917	†Chi A	149	553	57	151	9	7	0	57	30	5	36	.273	.316	.315	91	-8	16	.995	-6	81	103	1b149		-2.0
1918	Chi A	114	439	49	119	18	4	0	55	27	4	19	.271	.319	.330	95	-4	9	.992	-3	86	107	1b114		-1.0
1919	†Chi A	115	441	54	128	24	7	1	60	20	3	20	.290	.325	.383	98	-3	10	.997	-4	79	124	1b115		-1.0
Total	9	1147	4245	449	1176	173	78	11	557	273	42	233	.277	.327	.362	103	0	151-32	.992	35	107	110	1b1138,O2L		0.4

GANDY, BOB Robert Brinkley "String" B8.25.1893 Jacksonville FL D6.19.1945 Jacksonville FL BL/TR/6-3/180 d10.5

1916	Phi N	1	2	0	0	0	0	0	0	0	0	1	.000	.000	.000	-97	0		1.000	0	124	0	/OC		-0.1

GANLEY, BOB Robert Stephen B4.23.1875 Lowell MA D10.9.1945 Lowell MA BL/TL/5-7/156 d9.1

1905	Pit N	32	127	12	40	1	2	0	7	8	0		.315	.356	.354	109	1	3	1.000	-2	76	0	O32(0/6/27)		-0.2
1906	Pit N	137	511	63	132	7	6	0	31	41	2		.258	.316	.295	87	-8	19	.965	-3	96	137	O134(0/12/122)		-1.9
1907	Was A	154	605	73	167	10	5	1	35	54	2		.276	.337	.314	117	13	40	.940	7	112	98	O154(62/13/78)		1.2
1908	Was A	150	549	61	131	19	9	1	36	45	2		.239	.299	.311	107	4	30	.964	4	74	21	O150L		0.0
1909	Was A	19	63	5	16	3	0	0	5	1	0		.254	.266	.302	83	-1	4	1.000	-2	0	0	O17(11/5/1)		-0.5
	Phi A	80	274	32	54	4	2	0	9	28	0		.197	.272	.226	56	-13	16	.980	4	90	98	O77C		-1.5
	Year	99	337	37	70	7	2	0	14	29	0		.208	.270	.240	61	-15	20	.982	2	77	84	O94(11/82/1)		-2.0
Total	5	572	2129	246	540	44	24	2	123	177	6		.254	.313	.300	97	-4	112	.962	9	90	79	O564(223/113/228)		-2.9

GANNON, BILLY William G. B1876 New Haven CT D4.26.1927 Fort Worth TX 5-9/170 d9.9

1901	Chi N	15	61	2	9	0	0	0	1	4	0		.148	.161	.148	-11	-9	5	1.000	-0	128	0	O15R		-1.0

GANT, RON Ronald Edwin B3.2.1965 Victoria TX BR/TR/6-0/192(172-200) [AtlN83 4/100] d9.6 OF(1184/299/9) [DL 1994 Cin N 52]

1987	Atl N	21	83	9	22	4	0	2	9	1-0	0	11	.265	.271	.386	70	-4	4-2	.972	2	104	131	2b20		-0.1
1988	Atl N	146	563	85	146	28	8	19	60	46-4	3	118	.259	.317	.439	111	7	19-10	.963	4	105	104	2b122,3b22		1.5
1989	Atl N	75	260	26	46	8	3	9	25	20-0	1	63	.177	.237	.335	61	-15	9-6	.887	-1	102	99	3b53,O14(2/14/0)		-1.7
1990	Atl N	152	575	107	174	34	3	32	84	50-0	1	86	.303	.357	.539	136	27	33-16	.978	-0	104	84	O146(38/113/3)		2.7
1991	†Atl N	154	561	101	141	35	3	32	105	71-8	5	104	.251	.338	.496	125	19	34-15	.983	-8	95	86	O148C		1.2
1992	†Atl N★	153	544	74	141	22	6	17	80	45-5	7	101	.259	.321	.415	102	0	32-10	.986	-6	95	73	O147(138/23/0)		-0.6
1993	†Atl N	157	606	113	166	27	4	36	117	67-2	2	117	.274	.345	.510	123	19	26-9	.962	-13	89	42	O117L		2.5
1995	†Cin N★	119	410	79	113	19	4	29	88	74-5	3	108	.276	.386	.554	144	27	23-8	.985	1	103	106	O116L		1.3
1996	†StL N	122	419	74	103	14	2	30	82	73-5	3	98	.246	.359	.504	125	15	13-4	.978	5	106	61	O128L/D	34	-1.8
1997	StL N	139	502	68	115	21	4	17	62	58-3	1	162	.229	.310	.388	81	-15	14-6	.977	1	105	49	O104L	20	0.1
1998	StL N	121	383	60	92	17	1	26	67	51-2	2	92	.240	.331	.493	114	7	8-0	.971	-4	89	63	O133L,D2		0.1
1999	Phi N	138	516	107	134	27	5	17	77	85-0	1	112	.260	.364	.430	99	1	13-3	.993	4	102	87	O084L		0.3
2000	Phi N	89	343	54	87	16	2	20	38	36-1	1	73	.254	.324	.487	102	0	5-4	.968	4	116	80	O21L,D12		0.3
	Ana A	34	82	15	19	3	1	6	16	20-0	0	18	.232	.379	.512	120	3	1-2	.977	2	127	103	O21L,D12		-0.5
2001	Col N	59	171	31	44	8	2	8	22	24-2	0	56	.257	.345	.468	90	-2	3-1	.965	-1	102	67	O51L		-0.3
	†Oak A	34	81	15	21	5	1	2	13	11-0	0	24	.259	.344	.420	101	0	2-0	1.000	-3	24	0	D20,O11L		-0.3
2002	SD N	102	309	58	81	14	1	18	59	36-1	2	59	.262	.338	.489	130	4	4-6	.980	4	108	137	O80(78/1/5),D4	27	1.1
2003	Oak A	17	41	4	6	0	0	1	4	2-0	1	5	.146	.182	.220	6	-6	0-0	1.000	-1	81	0	O9(8/0/1),D6		-0.7
Total	16	1832	6449	1080	1651	302	50	321	1008	770-38	32	1411	.256	.336	.468	111	94	243-102	.978	-15	100	74	O1464L,2b142,3b75,D45	133	5.3

GANTENBEIN, JOE Joseph Steven "Sep" B8.25.1916 San Francisco CA D8.2.1993 Novato CA BL/TR/5-9/168 d4.20

1939	Phi A	111	348	47	101	14	4	4	36	32	2	22	.290	.353	.388	91	-5	1-5	.948	-28	84	51	2b76,3b14,S5		-2.7
1940	Phi A	75	197	21	47	6	2	4	23	11	1	21	.239	.282	.350	64	-11	1-0	.930	-4	95	144	3b45,1b6,S3/OL		-1.3
Total	2	186	545	68	148	20	6	8	59	43	3	43	.272	.328	.374	82	-16	2-5	.948	-32	84	51	2b76,3b59,S8,1b6/OL		-4.0

GANTNER, JIM James Elmer B1.5.1953 Fond Du Lac WI BL/TR/6-0/175* [MilA74 12/270] d9.3 C2 Col Wisconsin-Oshkosh

1976	Mil A	26	69	6	17	4	0	0	7	6-0	1	11	.246	.316	.261	71	-2	1-0	.982	-4	82	77	3b24,D2		-0.6
1977	Mil A	14	47	4	14	1	0	1	2	2-0	0	5	.298	.327	.383	92	-1	2-1	.902	1	116	129	3b14		0.0
1978	Mil A	43	97	14	21	1	0	1	8	5-0	2	10	.216	.269	.258	49	-7	2-0	.980	2	114	96	2b21,3b15/1S		-0.4
1979	Mil A	70	208	29	59	10	3	2	22	16-1	2	17	.284	.336	.389	96	-1	3-5	.952	1	93	125	3b42,2b22,S3/P		-0.3
1980	Mil A	132	415	47	117	21	3	4	40	30-5	2	29	.282	.330	.376	96	-2	11-10	.958	-3	107	135	3b69,2b66/S		1.7
1981	†Mil A	107	352	35	94	14	1	2	33	29-5	3	29	.267	.325	.330	94	-2	3-6	.982	10	108	116	2b131		1.6
1982	†Mil A	132	447	48	132	17	2	4	43	26-3	2	36	.295	.335	.369	99	-1	6-3	.984	8	106	110	2b158		2.0
1983	Mil A	161	603	85	170	23	8	11	74	38-5	6	46	.282	.329	.401	108	5	5-6	.984	10	100	107	2b153		0.7
1984	Mil A	153	613	61	173	27	1	3	56	30-0	4	51	.282	.314	.344	86	-12	6-5	.985	10	100	107	2b153		-0.9
1985	Mil A	143	523	63	133	15	4	5	44	33-7	3	42	.254	.300	.327	72	-21	11-8	.988	6	107	103	2b124,3b24/S		-0.5
1986	Mil A	139	497	58	136	25	1	7	38	26-2	6	50	.274	.313	.370	84	-11	13-7	.985	-2	94	100	2b135,3b3/SD		-1.2
1987	Mil A	81	265	37	72	14	0	4	30	19-2	5	22	.272	.331	.370	83	-6	6-2	.984	2	113	112	2b57,3b38/D	38	-0.1
1988	Mil A	155	539	67	149	28	2	0	47	34-1	3	50	.276	.322	.336	84	-11	20-8	.986	-5	98	100	2b154/3		-0.2
1989	Mil A	116	409	51	112	18	3	0	34	21-2	10	33	.274	.321	.333	86	-7	20-6	.987	18	110	122	2b114,D2	47	1.6
1990	Mil A	88	323	36	85	8	5	0	25	29-0	1	19	.263	.328	.319	82	-6	18-3	.982	-9	97	97	2b80,3b9	66	-1.2
1991	Mil A	140	526	63	149	27	4	2	47	27-5	3	34	.283	.320	.361	90	-8	4-6	.976	0	92	98	3b90,2b59		-1.1
1992	Mil A	101	256	22	63	12	1	1	18	12-2	0	17	.246	.278	.313	67	-12	6-2	.994	2	101	119	2b68,3b31,1b2,D2	15	-0.8
Total	17	1801	6189	726	1696	262	38	47	568	383-40	52	501	.274	.319	.351	87	-107	137-78	.985	52	105	109	2b1449,3b360,D8,S7,1b3/P	166	1.6

GANZEL, CHARLIE Charles William B6.18.1862 Waterford WI D4.7.1914 Quincy MA BR/TR/6-0/161 d9.27 b-John s-Babe OF(25/5/71)

1884	StP U	7	23	2	5	0	0	0		0			.217	.217	.217	59	-2		.956	0			C6/OC		-0.
1885	Phi N	34	125	15	21	3	1	0	6	4		13	.168	.194	.208	31	-10		.888	0			C33/OC		-0.
1886	Phi N	1	3	0	0	0	0	0	0	0			1.000	.000	.000	-99	-1	0	.600	-1			/C		-0.
	Det N	57	213	28	58	7	2	1	31	7		22	.272	.295	.338	89	-3	5	.911	3			C46,O7L,1b5		0.
	Year	58	216	28	58	7	2	1	31	7		23	.269	.291	.333	87	-4	5	.903	2			C51,O4L,1b2/3		0.
1887	†Det N	57	227	40	59	6	5	0	20	8	1		.260	.288	.330	69	-10	3	.913	7			C45,O7L,1b5		-0.
1888	Det N	95	386	45	96	13	5	4	46	14		15	.249	.277	.316	88	-6	12	.900	-1	102	62	2b49,C28,3b9,O5R,S3/1		-0.
1889	Bos N	73	275	30	73	5	1	4	43	15	2	11	.265	.308	.324	72	-12	13	.927	7			C39,O26(0/1/25),1b7,S6/3		-0.
1890	Bos N	38	163	21	44	7	3	0	24	5	2	6	.270	.300	.350	83	-5	1	.958	8	127	92	C22,O15(1/0/14),S3/2		-0.
1891	Bos N	70	263	33	68	18	5	1	29	12	5	13	.259	.304	.376	87	-6	7	.956	12	128	90	C59,O13(5/1/7)		-0.
1892	†Bos N	54	198	25	53	9	3	0	25	18	1	12	.268	.332	.343	95	-1	7	.933	2	133	86	C51,O2(1/1/0)/1		-0.
1893	Bos N	73	281	50	75	10	2	1	48	22	2	9	.267	.325	.327	68	-14	6	.952	3	130	92	C40,O23(6/0/18),1b10		-0.
1894	Bos N	70	266	51	74	7	6	3	56	19	0	6	.278	.326	.383	65	-17	1	.897	0	120	91	C59,1b7,O3(1/0/2),S2/2		-0.
1895	Bos N	81	280	38	73	2	5	1	52	15	1	6	.261	.324	.314	60	-18	1	.963	20	129	83	C77,S2,1b2		0.
1896	Bos N	47	179	28	47	2	0	1	18	9	1	6	.263	.305	.291	54	-12	2	.989	9	113	118	C41,1b3,S2		-0.
1897	Bos N	30	105	15	28	4	3	0	14	4	1		.267	.300	.362	70	-5	2	.942	5	153	89	C27,1b2		0.
Total	14	787	2987	421	774	91	45	10	412	162	18	121	.259	.301	.330	73	-122	60	.937	74	128	91	C579,O100R,2b51,1b40,S18,3b11		0.

GANZEL, BABE Foster Pirie B5.22.1901 Malden MA D2.6.1978 Jacksonville FL BR/TR/5-10.5/172 d9.19 f-Charlie

1927	Was A	13	48	7	21	1	1	3	17	7	0	3	.438	.509	.667	206	8	0-0	.944	-1	101	74	O13(4/9/0)		0
1928	Was A	10	26	2	2	1	0	0	4	1	0	4	.077	.111	.115	-41	-5	0-0	1.000	0	92	200	O7(4/2/2)		-0.
Total	2	23	74	9	23	2	1	3	21	8	0	7	.311	.378	.473	122	3	0-0	.957	-0	99	108	O20(8/11/2)		0

GANZEL, JOHN John Henry B4.7.1874 Kalamazoo MI D1.14.1959 Orlando FL BR/TR/6-0.5/195 d4.21 M2 b-Charlie

1898	Pit N	15	45	6	6	0	0	0	2	4	1		.133	.220	.133	2	-6	0	.963	-1	59	84	1b12		-0.
1900	Chi N	78	284	29	78	14	4	4	32	10	7		.275	.316	.394	99	-1	5	.980	-4	77	94	1b78		-0.
1901	NY N	138	526	42	113	13	3	6	26	20	9		.215	.256	.262	52	-33	9	.986	2	99	80	1b138		-3.
1903	NY A	129	476	62	132	25	7	3	71	30	12		.277	.336	.378	107	5	9	.988	7	117	110	1b129		1
1904	NY A	130	465	50	121	16	10	6	48	24	5	13	.260	.309	.376	111	5	13	.988	-1	87	108	1b118,2b9/S		-0
1907	Cin N	145	531	61	135	20	16	2	64	29	3		.254	.297	.364	102	-1	9	.990	1	97	123	1b143		-0

YEAR	TM LG	G	AB	R	H	2B	3B	HR	RBI	BB-IB	HP	SO	AVG	OBP	SLG	AOPS	ABR	SB-CS	FA	FR	RNG	THR	GAMES AT POSITION	DL	BFW
1908	Cin N	112	388	32	97	16	10	1	53	19	2		.250	.289	.351	107	1	6	**.990**	-2	91	109	1b108,M		-0.3
Total	7	747	2715	281	682	104	50	18	336	136		43	.251	.298	.346	93	-30	48	.987	2	96	104	1b726,2b9/S		-3.8

GARABITO, EDDY　Eddy Jorge B12.2.1976 Manrreza, D.R.　BB/TR/5-8/190　d5.27

YEAR	TM LG	G	AB	R	H	2B	3B	HR	RBI	BB-IB	HP	SO	AVG	OBP	SLG	AOPS	ABR	SB-CS	FA	FR	RNG	THR	GAMES AT POSITION	DL	BFW
2005	Col N	42	88	15	27	5	0	1	8	8-0	3	12	.307	.384	.398	92	-1	3-2	.986	-2	86	106	2b18,S2		-0.2

GARAGIOLA, JOE　Joseph Henry B2.12.1926 St.Louis MO　BL/TR/6-0/190*　d5.26

YEAR	TM LG	G	AB	R	H	2B	3B	HR	RBI	BB-IB	HP	SO	AVG	OBP	SLG	AOPS	ABR	SB-CS	FA	FR	RNG	THR	GAMES AT POSITION	DL	BFW
1946	†StL N	74	211	21	50	4	1	3	22	23	0	25	.237	.312	.308	73	-8	0	.990	0	148	71	C70		-0.4
1947	StL N	77	183	20	47	10	4	3	25	40	3	14	.257	.398	.415	111	5	0	.987	2	127	64	C74		1.0
1948	StL N	24	56	9	6	1	0	2	7	12	1	9	.107	.275	.232	36	-5	0	.990	3	352	107	C23		-0.1
1949	StL N	81	241	25	63	4	0	3	26	31	1	19	.261	.348	.357	85	-4	0	.984	4	128	85	C80		0.5
1950	StL N	34	88	8	28	6	1	2	20	10	0	7	.318	.388	.477	120	3	0	1.000	-1	142	71	C30	74	0.3
1951	StL N	27	72	9	14	3	2	2	9	9	0	7	.194	.284	.375	75	-3	0-0	1.000	-1	121	44	C23		-0.3
	Pit N	72	212	24	54	8	2	9	35	32	2	20	.255	.358	.439	110	3	4-1	.986	-5	96	79	C61		0.2
	Year	99	284	33	68	11	4	11	44	41	2	27	.239	.339	.423	101	1	4-1	**.989**	-6	102	70	C84		-0.1
1952	Pit N	118	344	35	94	15	4	8	54	50	2	24	.273	.369	.410	113	7	0-1	.978	-1	78	**126**	C105		1.1
1953	Pit N	27	73	9	17	5	0	2	14	10	2	11	.233	.341	.384	89	-1	1-0	.989	-3	66	97	C22		-0.2
	Chi N	74	228	21	62	9	4	1	21	21	1	23	.272	.336	.360	80	-7	0-0	.988	-1	88	116	C68		-0.4
	Year	101	301	30	79	14	4	3	35	31	3	34	.262	.337	.365	82	-7	1-0	.988	-3	83	112	C90		-0.6
1954	Chi N	63	153	16	43	5	0	5	21	28	4	12	.281	.403	.412	112	4	0-0	.982	-7	56	95	C55	36	0.0
	NY N	5	11	1	3	2	0	0	1	1	0	2	.273	.308	.455	102	0	0-0	1.000	-0	86	0	C3		0.0
	Year	68	164	17	46	7	0	5	22	29	4	14	.280	.397	.415	112	5	0-0	.983	-7	58	89	C58		0.0
Total	9	676	1872	198	481	82	16	42	255	267	16	173	.257	.354	.385	96	-6	5-2	.986	-9	112	91	C614	110	1.7

GARBARK, MIKE　Nathaniel Michael (b Nathaniel Michael Garbach) B2.3.1916 Houston TX　D8.31.1994 Charlotte NC　BR/TR/6-0/200　d4.18　b-Bob　Col Villanova

YEAR	TM LG	G	AB	R	H	2B	3B	HR	RBI	BB-IB	HP	SO	AVG	OBP	SLG	AOPS	ABR	SB-CS	FA	FR	RNG	THR	GAMES AT POSITION	DL	BFW
1944	NY A	89	299	23	78	9	4	1	33	25	1	27	.261	.320	.328	82	-7	0-1	.988	6	116	92	C85		0.4
1945	NY A	60	176	23	38	5	3	1	26	23	1	12	.216	.310	.295	73	-6	0-1	.972	-1	76	156	C59		-0.4
Total	2	149	475	46	116	14	7	2	59	48	2	39	.244	.316	.316	79	-13	0-2	.982	6	100	117	C144		0.0

GARBARK, BOB　Robert Michael (b Robert Michael Garbach) B11.13.1909 Houston TX　D8.15.1990 Meadville PA　BR/TR/5-11/178　d9.3　b-Mike

YEAR	TM LG	G	AB	R	H	2B	3B	HR	RBI	BB-IB	HP	SO	AVG	OBP	SLG	AOPS	ABR	SB-CS	FA	FR	RNG	THR	GAMES AT POSITION	DL	BFW
1934	Cle A	5	11	1	0	0	0	0	1	1	0	3	.000	.083	.000	-76	-3	0-0	1.000	-1	103	0	C5		-0.4
1935	Cle A	6	18	4	6	1	0	0	4	5	0	1	.333	.478	.389	124	1	0-0	1.000	1	138	109	C6		0.2
1937	Chi N	1	0	0	0	0	0	0	0	0	0	0	.000	.000	.000	-96	0	0	—	0			/H		0.0
1938	Chi N	23	54	2	14	0	0	0	5	1	0	5	.259	.273	.259	46	-4	0	1.000	1	125	97	C20/1		-0.3
1939	Chi N	24	21	1	3	0	0	0	0	1	0	3	.143	.143	.143	-23	-4	0	1.000	0	134	88	C21		-0.3
1944	Phi A	18	23	2	6	2	0	0	2	1	0	0	.261	.292	.348	83	-1	0-0	1.000	-0	74	73	C15		-0.1
1945	Bos A	68	199	21	52	6	0	0	17	18	2	10	.261	.329	.291	79	-5	0-1	.993	-2	108	83	C67		-0.4
Total	7	145	327	31	81	9	0	0	28	26	2	17	.248	.307	.275	64	-16	0-1	.996	-2	112	85	C134/1		-1.3

GARBEY, BARBARO　Barbaro (Garbey) B12.4.1956 Santiago de Cuba, Cuba　BR/TR/5-10/170*　d4.3　OF(25/2/16)

YEAR	TM LG	G	AB	R	H	2B	3B	HR	RBI	BB-IB	HP	SO	AVG	OBP	SLG	AOPS	ABR	SB-CS	FA	FR	RNG	THR	GAMES AT POSITION	DL	BFW
1984	†Det A	110	327	45	94	17	1	5	52	17-2	2	35	.287	.325	.391	98	-1	6-7	.989	-3	112	134	1b65,3b20,D17,O10(8/1/1),2b3		-0.9
1985	Det A	86	237	27	61	9	1	6	29	15-1	2	37	.257	.305	.380	88	-4	3-2	.991	-2	114	130	3b37,O24(10/1/14),D21/3		-0.9
1988	Tex A	30	62	4	12	2	0	0	5	4-0	0	11	.194	.239	.226	31	-6	0-0	.900	1	90	0	O8(7/0/1),1b7,3b3,D7		-0.5
Total	3	226	626	76	167	28	2	11	86	36-3	5	83	.267	.309	.371	87	-11	9-9	.990	-4	119	129	1b109,D45,O42L,3b24,2b3	34	-2.3

GARBOWSKI, ALEX　Alexander B6.25.1925 Yonkers NY　BR/TR/6-1/185　d4.16

YEAR	TM LG	G	AB	R	H	2B	3B	HR	RBI	BB-IB	HP	SO	AVG	OBP	SLG	AOPS	ABR	SB-CS	FA	FR	RNG	THR	GAMES AT POSITION	DL	BFW
1952	Det A	2	0	0	0	0	0	0	0	0	0		—	—	—		0	0-0		0		0	/R		0.0

GARCIA, KIKO　Alfonso Rafael B10.14.1953 Martinez CA　BR/TR/5-11/180*　[BalA71 3/69]　d9.11

YEAR	TM LG	G	AB	R	H	2B	3B	HR	RBI	BB-IB	HP	SO	AVG	OBP	SLG	AOPS	ABR	SB-CS	FA	FR	RNG	THR	GAMES AT POSITION	DL	BFW
1976	Bal A	11	32	2	7	1	1	1	4	0-0	0	4	.219	.219	.406	85	-1	2-1	1.000	-0	94	137	S11		1.0
1977	Bal A	65	131	20	29	6	0	2	10	6-0	0	31	.221	.255	.313	57	-8	2-3	.966	14	121	189	S61,2b2		1.0
1978	Bal A	79	186	17	49	6	4	0	13	7-0	0	43	.263	.287	.339	81	-6	7-1	.945	8	111	122	S74,2b3		0.9
1979	†Bal A	126	417	54	103	15	9	5	24	32-0	2	87	.247	.303	.362	82	-12	11-9	.955	-10	88	117	S113,2b25,3b2,O2L		-1.1
1980	Bal A	111	311	27	62	8	0	1	27	24-0	0	57	.199	.255	.235	36	-28	8-4	.974	5	97	105	S96,2b27/OL	15	-1.3
1981	†Hou N	48	136	9	37	6	1	0	15	10-3	1	16	.272	.324	.331	92	-1	2-2	.950	3	105	89	S28,3b13,2b9	11	0.4
1982	Hou N	34	76	5	16	5	0	1	5	3-1	0	15	.211	.241	.316	59	-4	1-0	.946	3	110	137	S21,3b2/2	15	0.1
1983	Phi N	84	118	22	34	7	1	2	9	9-2	1	20	.288	.344	.415	110	2	1-2	.970	8	102	86	2b52,S22,3b10		1.1
1984	Phi N	57	60	6	14	2	0	0	5	4-1	0	11	.233	.281	.267	54	-4	0-0	.965	-1	102	30	S30,3b23/2		-0.4
1985	Phi N	4	3	0	0	0	0	0	0	0-0	0	1	.000	.000	.000	-98	-1	0-0	1.000	-1	69	0	S3/3		-0.2
Total	10	619	1470	162	351	56	16	12	112	95-7	4	285	.239	.286	.323	70	-63	34-22	.961	29	101	119	S459,2b120,3b51,O3L	41	0.5

GARCIA, AMAURY　Amaury Miguel (Paula) B5.20.1975 Santo Domingo, D.R.　BR/TR/5-10/160　d7.5

YEAR	TM LG	G	AB	R	H	2B	3B	HR	RBI	BB-IB	HP	SO	AVG	OBP	SLG	AOPS	ABR	SB-CS	FA	FR	RNG	THR	GAMES AT POSITION	DL	BFW
1999	Fla N	10	24	6	6	0	1	2	2	3-0	1	11	.250	.333	.583	133	1	0-0	.932	3	142	114	2b8		0.4

GARCIA, CARLOS　Carlos Jesus (Guerrero) B10.15.1967 Tachira, Venez　BR/TR/6-1/185(185-205)　d9.20　.C1

YEAR	TM LG	G	AB	R	H	2B	3B	HR	RBI	BB-IB	HP	SO	AVG	OBP	SLG	AOPS	ABR	SB-CS	FA	FR	RNG	THR	GAMES AT POSITION	DL	BFW
1990	Pit N	4	4	1	2	0	0	0	0	0-0	0	2	.500	.500	.500	182	0	0-0	1.000	0	136	201	S3		0.1
1991	Pit N	12	24	2	6	0	2	0	1	1-0	0	8	.250	.280	.417	94	-1	0-0	.947	0	105	155	S9,3b2/2		-0.4
1992	†Pit N	22	39	4	8	1	0	0	4	0-0	0	9	.205	.195	.231	23	-4	0-0	.977	0	101	169	2b14,S8		-0.4
1993	Pit N	141	546	77	147	25	5	12	47	31-2	9	67	.269	.316	.399	91	-8	18-11	.983	-20	90	99	2b140,S3		-2.2
1994	Pit N★	98	412	49	114	15	2	6	28	16-2	4	67	.277	.309	.367	74	-16	18-9	.978	18	114	**122**	2b98		0.7
1995	Pit N	104	367	41	108	24	2	6	50	25-5	2	55	.294	.340	.420	97	-1	8-4	.982	7	104	114	2b92,S15		1.1
1996	Pit N	101	390	66	111	18	4	6	44	23-3	4	58	.285	.329	.397	88	-7	16-6	.985	7	110	81	2b77,S19,3b14	17	0.5
1997	Tor A	103	350	29	77	18	2	3	23	15-0	2	60	.220	.253	.309	46	-28	11-3	.981	-10	91	89	2b96,S5,3b4	31	-3.1
1998	Ana N	19	35	4	5	1	0	0	0	3-0	1	11	.143	.231	.171	7	-5	2-0	.978	2	109	133	2b11,S5,D3		-0.1
1999	SD N	6	11	1	2	0	0	0	0	1-0	0	3	.182	.250	.182	13	-2	0-0	.778	-1	67	0	3b4/1		-0.2
Total	10	610	2178	274	580	102	17	33	197	115-12	22	340	.266	.307	.374	79	-72	73-33	.982	5	100	104	2b529,S67,3b24,D3/1	99	-3.6

GARCIA, DAMASO　Damaso Domingo (Sanchez) B2.7.1955 Moca, D.R.　BR/TR/6-0/170(155-185)　d6.24　[DL 1987 Atl N 148]

YEAR	TM LG	G	AB	R	H	2B	3B	HR	RBI	BB-IB	HP	SO	AVG	OBP	SLG	AOPS	ABR	SB-CS	FA	FR	RNG	THR	GAMES AT POSITION	DL	BFW
1978	NY A	18	41	5	8	0	0	1	2-0	6		.195	.227	.195	22	-4	1-0	.959	-1	88	129	2b16,S3		-0.5
1979	NY A	11	38	3	10	1	0	0	4	0-0	1	2	.263	.263	.289	50	-3	2-0	.902	-4	90	65	S10/3		-0.5
1980	Tor A	140	543	50	151	30	7	4	46	12-2	3	55	.278	.296	.381	81	-15	13-13	.980	7	105	104	2b138/D		-0.3
1981	Tor A	64	250	24	63	8	1	1	9-1	0	32		.252	.277	.304	64	-12	13-3	.972	-19	85	68	2b62/D	44	-2.8
1982	Tor A	147	597	89	185	32	3	5	42	21-1	5	44	.310	.338	.399	93	-5	54-20	.980	6	105	100	2b141,D4		1.3
1983	Tor A	131	525	84	161	23	6	3	38	24-3	2	34	.307	.336	.390	94	-5	31-17	.981	-14	90	85	2b130		-1.1
1984	Tor A★	152	633	79	180	32	5	4	46	16-1	9	46	.284	.310	.374	85	-13	46-12	.980	-16	92	102	2b149/D		-1.5
1985	†Tor A★	146	600	70	169	25	4	8	65	15-2	4	41	.282	.302	.377	83	-16	28-15	.981	-15	89	105	2b143		-2.3
1986	Tor A	122	424	57	119	22	0	6	46	13-0	4	32	.281	.306	.375	83	-11	9-6	.985	-0	97	104	2b106,D11/1		-0.6
1988	Atl N	21	60	3	7	1	0	1	4	3-0	0	10	.117	.159	.183	-2	-8	1-0	.984	-3	91	59	2b13		-1.2
1989	Mon N	80	203	26	55	9	1	3	18	15-1	0	24	.271	.317	.369	95	-1	6-2	.972	7	113	97	2b62/3	19	0.7
Total	11	1032	3914	490	1108	183	27	36	323	130-11	27	322	.283	.309	.371	83	-93	203-90	.980	-54	96	97	2b960,D18,S13,3b2/1	211	-8.8

GARCIA, DANIEL　Daniel Joseph B4.12.1980 Riverside CA　BR/TR/6-0/180*　[NYN01 5/162]　d9.2　Col Pepperdine

YEAR	TM LG	G	AB	R	H	2B	3B	HR	RBI	BB-IB	HP	SO	AVG	OBP	SLG	AOPS	ABR	SB-CS	FA	FR	RNG	THR	GAMES AT POSITION	DL	BFW
2003	NY N	19	56	5	12	0	2	6	2-0	3		.214	.274	.357	67	-3	0-0	.950	-2	96	83	2b17/OL		-0.4
2004	NY N	58	138	23	32	7	1	3	17	22-2	9	34	.232	.372	.362	93	0	3-0	.969	-7	86	75	2b44		-0.5
Total	2	77	194	28	44	9	1	5	23	24-2	12	45	.227	.345	.361	87	-3	3-0	.964	-9	89	77	2b61/OL		-0.9

GARCIA, DANNY　Daniel Raphael B4.29.1954 Brooklyn NY　BL/TL/6-1/182　[KCA75 11/249]　d4.26　Col Baruch

YEAR	TM LG	G	AB	R	H	2B	3B	HR	RBI	BB-IB	HP	SO	AVG	OBP	SLG	AOPS	ABR	SB-CS	FA	FR	RNG	THR	GAMES AT POSITION	DL	BFW
1981	KC A	12	14	4	2	0	0	0	0	0-0	0	3	.143	.143	.143	-17	-2	0-0	1.000	-1	70	0	O6(1/0/5),1b2		-0.3

GARCIA, FREDDY　Freddy Adrian (Felix) B8.1.1972 LaRomana, D.R.　BR/TR/6-2/190(190-224)　d5.2　[DL 2000 Sea A 75]

YEAR	TM LG	G	AB	R	H	2B	3B	HR	RBI	BB-IB	HP	SO	AVG	OBP	SLG	AOPS	ABR	SB-CS	FA	FR	RNG	THR	GAMES AT POSITION	DL	BFW
1995	Pit N	42	57	5	8	1	1	9	8-0	0	17		.140	.246	.193	17	-7	0-1	1.000	-3	97	0	O10L,3b8		-0.4
1997	Pit N	20	40	4	6	1	0	3	5	2-0	1	17	.150	.190	.400	49	-3	0-0	.842	-3	60	70	3b10,1b2		0.6
1998	Pit N	56	172	28	44	11	1	9	26	18-3	2	45	.256	.332	.488	112	3	0-2	.949	5	116	113	3b47,1b4		0.7
1999	Pit N	55	130	16	30	5	0	6	18	11-2	0	41	.231	.252	.408	63	-8	0-0	.977	-0	113	0	O24(17/0/7),3b9,D2		-0.9
	Atl N	2	2	1	1	0	0	1	1	1-0	0	1	.500	.667	2.000	544	1	0-0	—	-0	0	0	/1OL		0.1
	Year	57	132	17	31	5	0	7	24	5-0	0	42	.235	.261	.432	71	-7	0-0	.977	-1	110		O25(18/0/7),3b9,D2/1		-0.8
Total	4	175	401	53	89	18	2	19	56	33-3	3	121	.222	.283	.419	79	-14	0-3	.938	5	112	132	3b74,O35(28/0/7),1b7,D2	75	-1.1

YEAR	TM LG	G	AB	R	H	2B	3B	HR	RBI	BB-IB	HP	SO	AVG	OBP	SLG	AOPS	ABR	SB-CS	FA	FR	RNG	THR	GAMES AT POSITION	DL	BFW

GARCIA, GUILLERMO Guillermo Antonio (Morel) B4.4.1972 Santiago, D.R. BR/TR/6-3/215* d7.19

YEAR	TM LG	G	AB	R	H	2B	3B	HR	RBI	BB-IB	HP	SO	AVG	OBP	SLG	AOPS	ABR	SB-CS	FA	FR	RNG	THR	GAMES AT POSITION	DL	BFW
1998	Cin N	12	36	3	7	2	0	2	4	2-0	0	13	.194	.237	.417	67	-2	0-0	.988	2	65	258	C11		0.1
1999	Fla N	4	4	0	1	0	0	0	0	0-0	0	2	.250	.250	.250	29	0	0-0	1.000	0	0	0	C3		0.0
Total	2	16	40	3	8	2	0	2	4	2-0	0	15	.200	.238	.400	63	-2	0-0	.988	2	62	246	C14		0.1

GARCIA, KARIM Gustavo Karim B10.29.1975 Ciudad Obregon, Sonora, Mexico BL/TL/6-0/200(172-210) d9.2

YEAR	TM LG	G	AB	R	H	2B	3B	HR	RBI	BB-IB	HP	SO	AVG	OBP	SLG	AOPS	ABR	SB-CS	FA	FR	RNG	THR	GAMES AT POSITION	DL	BFW
1995	LA N	13	20	1	4	0	0	0	0	0-0	0	4	.200	.200	.200	6	-3	0-0	1.000	2	92	1007	O5(2/0/3)		-0.1
1996	LA N	1	1	0	0	0	0	0	0	0-0	0	1	.000	.000	.000	-99	0	0-0	—	0			/H		0.0
1997	LA N	15	39	5	5	0	0	1	8	6-1	0	14	.128	.239	.205	21	-5	0-0	1.000	-1	72	0	O12(12/0/2)	10	-0.6
1998	Ari N	113	333	39	74	10	8	9	43	18-1	0	78	.222	.260	.381	66	-19	5-4	.975	3	109	98	O81(35/0/55),D6		-1.2
1999	Det A	96	288	38	69	10	3	14	32	20-1	0	67	.240	.288	.441	81	-10	2-4	.958	2	102	137	O81(35/0/55),D6		-0.4
2000	Det A	8	17	1	3	0	0	0	0	0-0	0	4	.176	.176	.176	-10	-3	0-0	1.000	-1	74	0	O7R/D		-0.5
	Bal A	8	16	0	0	0	0	0	0	0-0	0	6	.000	.000	.000	-99	-5	0-0	1.000	0	85	0	O9(2/0/7),D5		-0.9
	Year	16	33	1	3	0	0	0	0	0-0	0	10	.091	.091	.091	-55	-8	0-0	1.000	-1	85	0	O18(6/0/13),1b2		0.3
2001	Cle A	20	45	8	14	3	0	5	9	3-0	1	13	.311	.360	.711	168	4	0-0	.905	0	59	485	O18(6/0/13),1b2		-0.1
2002	NY A	2	5	1	1	0	0	0	0	0-0	0	1	.200	.200	.200	7	-1	0-0	1.000	-0	44	0	O2(1/0/1)		0.3
	Cle A	51	197	29	59	8	0	16	52	6-0	0	40	.299	.317	.584	131	7	0-3	.990	-1	99	66	O51(1/3/48)		0.2
	Year	53	202	30	60	8	0	16	52	6-0	0	41	.297	.314	.574	128	7	0-3	.990	-1	98	65	O53(2/3/49)	46	-1.0
2003	Cle A	24	93	8	18	1	0	5	14	5-1	1	20	.194	.238	.366	57	-6	0-0	.905	-3	71	158	O23(0/7/17)/D		-0.7
	†NY A	52	151	17	46	5	0	6	21	9-1	0	32	.305	.342	.457	110	2	0-2	.981	4	112	202	O50(13/3/37)/D	15	-1.3
	Year	76	244	25	64	6	0	11	35	14-2	1	52	.262	.302	.422	90	-5	0-2	.968	1	98	187	O73(13/10/54),D2		-0.6
2004	NY N	62	192	24	45	7	2	7	22	10-0	0	35	.234	.272	.401	73	-9	3-0	.968	-2	101	0	O51R		
	Bal A	23	66	9	14	0	0	3	11	4-1	0	15	.212	.247	.348	56	-5	0-0	1.000	-2	84	0	O19(0/15/7)/1	71	-7.0
Total	10	488	1463	180	352	44	13	66	212	81-6	2	330	.241	.279	.424	81	-53	10-13	.970	-0	99	118	O424(72/35/341),D13,1b3		

GARCIA, JESSE Jesus Jesse B9.24.1973 Corpus Christi TX BR/TR/5-10/171* [BalA93 26/735] d4.5

YEAR	TM LG	G	AB	R	H	2B	3B	HR	RBI	BB-IB	HP	SO	AVG	OBP	SLG	AOPS	ABR	SB-CS	FA	FR	RNG	THR	GAMES AT POSITION	DL	BFW
1999	Bal A	17	29	6	6	0	0	2	2	2-0	0	3	.207	.258	.414	70	-2	0-0	1.000	-1	96	156	S7,2b6,3b2/D		-0.2
2000	Bal A	14	17	2	1	0	0	0	0	2-0	0	2	.059	.158	.059	-44	-4	0-0	1.000	2	162	114	2b6,S5		-0.1
2001	Atl N	22	5	3	1	0	0	0	0	0-0	0	1	.200	.200	.200	4	-1	6-2	1.000	-0	82	192	2b4,S2		0.0
2002	Atl N	39	61	6	12	1	0	0	5	0-0	0	14	.197	.197	.213	10	-8	0-1	.986	5	118	123	2b21,S5,O4(2/0/2)		-0.3
2003	†Atl N	13	10	6	4	0	1	0	2	0-0	0	1	.400	.400	.600	157	1	0-1	1.000	-0	95	100	2b6,S3,3b2		0.0
2004	Atl N	50	115	14	29	4	1	1	10	1-0	0	16	.252	.265	.330	52	-9	1-2	.963	4	115	104	S25,2b11,3b3		-0.3
2005	SD N	16	36	4	6	0	0	2	4	3-1	0	11	.167	.231	.333	48	-3	0-0	1.000	-2	72	68	S13,2b2		-0.5
Total	7	171	273	41	59	5	2	5	23	8-1	1	48	.216	.241	.304	41	-26	7-6	.978	6	100	113	S60,2b56,3b7,O4(2/0/2)/D		-1.4

GARCIA, LEO Leonardo Antonio (Peralta) B11.6.1962 Santiago, D.R. BL/TL/5-8/165* d4.6

YEAR	TM LG	G	AB	R	H	2B	3B	HR	RBI	BB-IB	HP	SO	AVG	OBP	SLG	AOPS	ABR	SB-CS	FA	FR	RNG	THR	GAMES AT POSITION	DL	BFW
1987	Cin N	31	30	8	6	0	0	1	2	4-0	0	8	.200	.286	.300	56	-2	3-1	1.000	0	121		O14(0/13/1)		-0.1
1988	Cin N	23	28	2	4	1	0	0	0	4-1	0	5	.143	.250	.179	24	-3	0-1	1.000	0	103		O9(2/4/3)		-0.3
Total	2	54	58	10	10	1	0	1	2	8-1	0	13	.172	.269	.241	41	-5	3-2	1.000	0	113		O23(2/17/4)		-0.4

GARCIA, LUIS Luis Carlos B9.22.1975 Hermosillo, Sonora, Mexico BR/TR/6-3/200 [ChiA94 19/537] d4.10

YEAR	TM LG	G	AB	R	H	2B	3B	HR	RBI	BB-IB	HP	SO	AVG	OBP	SLG	AOPS	ABR	SB-CS	FA	FR	RNG	THR	GAMES AT POSITION	DL	BFW
2002	Bal A	6	3	0	1	0	0	0	0	0-0	0	1	.333	.333	.333	82	0	0-0	1.000	0	132	0	O2(0/1/1)		0.0

GARCIA, LUIS Luis Rafael B5.20.1975 San Francisco de Macoris, D.R. BR/TR/6-0/175 d4.5

YEAR	TM LG	G	AB	R	H	2B	3B	HR	RBI	BB-IB	HP	SO	AVG	OBP	SLG	AOPS	ABR	SB-CS	FA	FR	RNG	THR	GAMES AT POSITION	DL	BFW
1999	Det A	9	9	0	1	0	0	0	0	0-0	0	2	.111	.111	.222	-18	-2	0-0	1.000	-2	37	0	S7/2		-0.3

GARCIA, PEDRO Pedro Modesto (Delfi) B4.17.1950 Guayama, PR BR/TR/5-10/175* d4.6

YEAR	TM LG	G	AB	R	H	2B	3B	HR	RBI	BB-IB	HP	SO	AVG	OBP	SLG	AOPS	ABR	SB-CS	FA	FR	RNG	THR	GAMES AT POSITION	DL	BFW
1973	Mil A	160	580	67	142	32	5	15	54	40-4	5	119	.245	.296	.395	95	-5	11-10	.970	-21	96	91	2b160		-1.7
1974	Mil A	141	452	46	90	15	4	12	54	26-4	5	67	.199	.248	.330	66	-22	8-5	.970	-9	96	101	2b140		-2.3
1975	Mil A	98	302	40	68	15	2	6	38	18-1	2	59	.225	.271	.348	74	-11	12-6	.985	10	109	99	2b94/D	23	0.6
1976	Mil A	41	106	12	23	7	1	1	9	4-0	2	23	.217	.257	.330	73	-4	2-2	.971	-3	96	113	2b39		-0.5
	Det A	77	227	21	45	10	2	3	20	9-0	4	40	.198	.239	.300	56	-13	2-3	.958	8	108	110	2b77		-0.2
	Year	118	333	33	68	17	3	4	29	13-0	6	63	.204	.244	.309	61	-17	4-5	.962	5	104	111	2b116		-0.7
1977	Tor A	41	130	10	27	10	1	0	9	5-0	3	21	.208	.254	.300	59	-9	0-0	.971	-3	94	91	2b34,D4		-1.0
Total	5	558	1797	196	395	89	15	37	184	102-9	21	329	.220	.267	.348	75	-64	35-26	.971	-18	100	98	2b544,D5	23	-5.1

GARCIA, CHICO Vinicio Uzcanga B12.24.1924 Veracruz, Veracruz, Mexico BR/TR/5-8/170 d4.24

YEAR	TM LG	G	AB	R	H	2B	3B	HR	RBI	BB-IB	HP	SO	AVG	OBP	SLG	AOPS	ABR	SB-CS	FA	FR	RNG	THR	GAMES AT POSITION	DL	BFW
1954	Bal A	39	62	4	7	0	1	0	2	6-0	0	3	.113	.211	.177	9	-8	0-0	.962	2	93	115	2b24		-0.5

GARCIAPARRA, NOMAR Anthony Nomar B7.23.1973 Whittier CA BR/TR/6-0/180(167-190) [BosA94 1/12] d8.31 Col Georgia Tech

YEAR	TM LG	G	AB	R	H	2B	3B	HR	RBI	BB-IB	HP	SO	AVG	OBP	SLG	AOPS	ABR	SB-CS	FA	FR	RNG	THR	GAMES AT POSITION	DL	BFW
1996	Bos A	24	87	11	21	2	3	4	16	4-0	0	14	.241	.272	.471	82	-3	5-0	.988	-4	80	69	S22/2D		-0.4
1997	Bos A★	153	684	122	209	44	11	30	98	35-2	6	92	.306	.342	.534	122	19	22-9	.971	3	103	106	S153	19	3.4
1998	†Bos A	143	604	111	195	37	8	35	122	33-1	8	62	.323	.362	.584	139	32	12-6	.962	-11	96	80	S143		3.0
1999	†Bos A★	135	532	103	190	42	4	27	104	51-7	8	39	.357	.418	.603	152	43	14-3	.972	-4	92	87	S134	14	4.7
2000	Bos A★	140	529	104	197	51	3	21	96	61-20	2	50	.372	.434	.599	155	47	5-2	.971	-3	100	77	S136/D	161	5.0
2001	Bos A	21	83	13	24	3	0	4	8	7-0	1	9	.289	.352	.470	114	2	0-1	.968	1	98	100	S21		0.4
2002	Bos A★	156	635	101	197	56	5	24	120	41-4	6	63	.310	.352	.528	129	26	5-2	.965	19	109	103	S154		5.4
2003	†Bos A★	156	658	120	198	37	13	28	105	39-1	11	61	.301	.345	.524	121	18	19-5	.971	7	106	82	S156	66	3.7
2004	Bos A	38	156	24	50	7	3	5	21	8-2	4	16	.321	.367	.500	124	3	2-0	.957	-8	82	79	S37/D		-0.1
	Chi N	43	165	28	49	14	0	4	20	16-0	2	14	.297	.364	.455	107	2	2-1	.982	-5	79	70	S42		0.0
2005	Chi N	62	230	28	65	12	0	9	30	12-0	2	24	.283	.320	.452	97	-1	0-0	.934	-4	100	16	3b34,S26	106	-0.3
Total	10	1071	4363	765	1395	305	50	191	740	307-37	50	444	.320	.367	.544	130	188	86-29	.968	-8	99	89	S1024,3b34,D3/2	366	24.8

GARDELLA, AL Alfred Stephan B1.11.1918 New York NY BL/TL/5-10/172 d5.17 b-Danny

YEAR	TM LG	G	AB	R	H	2B	3B	HR	RBI	BB-IB	HP	SO	AVG	OBP	SLG	AOPS	ABR	SB-CS	FA	FR	RNG	THR	GAMES AT POSITION	DL	BFW
1945	NY N	16	26	2	2	0	0	0	4	3-0	0	3	.077	.226	.077	-14	-4	0	.961	-1	82	39	1b9/OC		-0.5

GARDELLA, DANNY Daniel Lewis B2.26.1920 New York NY D3.6.2005 Yonkers NY BL/TL/5-7.5/160* d5.14 b-Al

YEAR	TM LG	G	AB	R	H	2B	3B	HR	RBI	BB-IB	HP	SO	AVG	OBP	SLG	AOPS	ABR	SB-CS	FA	FR	RNG	THR	GAMES AT POSITION	DL	BFW
1944	NY N	47	112	20	28	2	2	6	14	11	1	13	.250	.323	.464	120	2	0	.912	1	101	167	O25(11/4/10)		0.1
1945	NY N	121	430	54	117	10	1	18	71	46	5	55	.272	.349	.426	113	7	2	.954	-4	89	87	O94(85/0/9),1b15		-0.3
1950	StL N	1	1	0	0	0	0	0	0	0-0	0	0	.000	.000	.000	-95	0	0	—	0			/H		0.0
Total	3	169	543	74	145	12	3	24	85	57	6	68	.267	.343	.433	114	9	2	.943	-3	92	105	O119(96/4/19),1b15		-0.2

GARDENHIRE, RON Ronald Clyde B10.24.1957 Butzbach, W.Germany BR/TR/6-0/175* [NYN79 6/132] d9.1 M4/C11 Col Texas

YEAR	TM LG	G	AB	R	H	2B	3B	HR	RBI	BB-IB	HP	SO	AVG	OBP	SLG	AOPS	ABR	SB-CS	FA	FR	RNG	THR	GAMES AT POSITION	DL	BFW
1981	NY N	27	48	2	13	1	0	0	3	5-2	0	9	.271	.340	.292	81	-1	2-2	.969	0	99	84	S18,2b6/3		0.1
1982	NY N	141	384	29	92	17	1	3	33	23-2	0	55	.240	.279	.313	66	-18	5-6	.956	7	105	92	S135/23		0.0
1983	NY N	17	32	1	2	0	0	1	1-0	0	4	.063	.091	.063	-57	-7	0-0	1.000	-1	101	66	S15		-0.8
1984	NY N	74	207	20	51	7	1	1	10	9-1	0	43	.246	.276	.304	64	-10	6-1	.947	-1	88	67	S49,2b18,3b7	41	-0.6
1985	NY N	26	39	5	7	2	1	0	2	8-0	0	11	.179	.319	.282	71	-1	0-0	.911	-1	110	71	S13,2b5,3b2	86	-0.1
Total	5	285	710	57	165	27	3	4	49	46-5	0	122	.232	.277	.296	61	-37	13-9	.955	4	101	84	S230,2b30,3b11	127	-1.4

GARDNER, ALEX Alexander B4.28.1861 Toronto ON, Can. D6.18.1926 Danvers MA BR d5.10

YEAR	TM LG	G	AB	R	H	2B	3B	HR	RBI	BB-IB	HP	SO	AVG	OBP	SLG	AOPS	ABR	SB-CS	FA	FR	RNG	THR	GAMES AT POSITION	DL	BFW
1884	Was AA	1	3	0	0	0	0	0	0	0-0	0	0	.000	.000	.000	-99	-1		.600	-2			/C		-0.2

GARDNER, ART Arthur Junior B9.21.1952 Madden MS BL/TL/5-11/175(165-180) [HouN71 2/36] d9.2

YEAR	TM LG	G	AB	R	H	2B	3B	HR	RBI	BB-IB	HP	SO	AVG	OBP	SLG	AOPS	ABR	SB-CS	FA	FR	RNG	THR	GAMES AT POSITION	DL	BFW
1975	Hou N	13	31	3	6	0	0	0	2	1-1	1	8	.194	.242	.194	24	-3	1-0	1.000	-0	98	0	O8(3/1/4)		-0.4
1977	Hou N	66	65	7	10	0	0	0	3	3-1	1	15	.154	.203	.154	-3	-10	0-0	1.000	1	102	110	O26(14/9/4)		-1.0
1978	SF N	7	3	2	0	0	0	0	0	0-0	0	2	.000	.000	.000	-99	-1	0-1	—	0			/H		-0.1
Total	3	86	99	12	16	0	0	0	5	4-2	2	25	.162	.210	.162	2	-14	1-1	1.000	1	101	72	O34(17/10/8)		-1.5

GARDNER, EARLE Earle McClurkin B1.24.1884 Sparta IL D3.2.1943 Sparta IL BR/TR/5-11/160 d9.18

YEAR	TM LG	G	AB	R	H	2B	3B	HR	RBI	BB-IB	HP	SO	AVG	OBP	SLG	AOPS	ABR	SB-CS	FA	FR	RNG	THR	GAMES AT POSITION	DL	BFW
1908	NY A	20	75	7	16	2	0	0	4	1	0		.213	.234	.240	53	-4	0	.947	1	96	184	2b20		-0.3
1909	NY A	22	85	12	28	4	0	0	15	3	0		.329	.352	.376	129	3	4	.945	-6	85	39	2b22		-0.4
1910	NY A	86	271	36	66	4	2	1	24	21	2		.244	.303	.284	79	-7	9	.936	0	97	145	2b70		-0.6
1911	NY A	102	357	36	94	13	2	0	39	20	5		.263	.312	.311	69	-15	14	.959	3	105	134	2b101		-1.1
1912	NY A	43	160	14	45	3	1	0	26	5	1		.281	.303	.313	72	-6	11	.922	-8	98	122	2b256		-1.3
Total	5	273	948	105	249	26	6	1	108	50	8		.263	.305	.304	76	-29	38	.944	-8	98	122	2b256		-3.7

YEAR	TM LG	G	AB	R	H	2B	3B	HR	RBI	BB-IB	HP	SO	AVG	OBP	SLG	AOPS	ABR	SB-CS	FA	FR	RNG	THR	GAMES AT POSITION	DL	BFW

GARDNER, GID   Franklin Washington   B5.6.1859 Boston MA   D8.1.1914 Cambridge MA   ?/165   d8.23   OF(16/36/69) ▲

1879	Tro N	2	6	1	1	0	0	0	0			0	.167	.167	.167	11	0		.429	-1	68	0	P2		0.0
1880	Cle N	10	32	0	6	1	1	0	4	2		4	.188	.235	.281	76	-1		.850	-0	111	0	P9/OC		0.0
1883	Bal AA	42	161	28	44	10	3	1	18				.273	.346	.391	133	7		.837	-3	72	0	O35C,2b4,3b3,P2		0.2
1884	Bal AA	41	173	32	37	6	8	2	14		2		.214	.280	.376	108	1		.860	0	131	0	O40(1/0/39),1b2		0.1
	CP U	38	149	22	38	10	2	0	10				.255	.302	.349	98	-4		.872	-1	28	0	O29(15/0/14),3b8/P2		-0.6
	Bal U	1	4	0	1	0	0	0	0				.250	.250	.250	47	0		.714	-0	55	476	/S		-0.1
	Year	39	153	22	39	10	2	0	10				.255	.301	.346	96	-5		.872	-2	28	0	O29(15/0/14),3b8/P2S		-0.7
1885	Bal AA	44	170	22	37	5	4	0	17	12	0		.218	.269	.294	79	-4		.891	-1	105	85	2b39,O5R/1P		-0.3
1887	Ind N	18	63	8	11	1	0	1	8	12	0	11	.175	.307	.238	55	-3	7	1.000	-3	67	0	O11R,2b7		-0.4
1888	Was N	1	3	0	1	0	0	0	1		1	1	.333	.500	.333	182	0	0	.750	0	107	263	/S		0.0
	Phi N	1	3	0	2	0	0	0	1		0	0	.667	.667	.667	309	1	0	1.000	-0	45	0	/2		0.0
	Was N	1	1	0	0	0	0	0	0		0	0	.000	.000	.000	-99	0	0	1.000	-0	0	0	/2		-0.1
	Year	3	7	0	3	0	0	0	1	1	1	1	.429	.500	.429	204	1	0	1.000	-1	27	0	2b2/S		-0.1
Total	7	199	765	113	178	33	18	4	30	69	2	16	.233	.298	.339	99	-3	7	.855	-8	85	0	O121R,2b53,P15,3b11,1b3,S2		-1.2

GARDNER, JEFF   Jeffrey Scott   B2.4.1964 Newport Beach CA   BL/TR/5-11/165*   d9.10

1991	NY N	13	37	3	6	0	0	0	1	4-0	0	6	.162	.238	.162	16	-4	0-0	.818	-3	91	55	S8,2b3		-0.7
1992	SD N	15	19	0	2	0	0	0	0	1-0	0	6	.105	.150	.105	-26	-3	0-0	1.000	2	136	100	2b11		-0.1
1993	SD N	140	404	53	106	21	7	1	24	45-0	1	69	.262	.337	.356	85	-8	2-6	.983	-11	92	73	2b133/3S		-1.5
1994	Mon N	18	32	4	7	0	1	0	1	3-0	1	5	.219	.286	.281	48	-3	0-0	.714	-5	22	0	3b9,2b4		-0.7
Total	4	186	492	60	121	21	8	1	26	53-0	1	88	.246	.319	.327	74	-18	2-6	.984	-16	94	73	2b151,3b10,S9		-3.0

GARDNER, RAY   Raymond Vincent   B10.25.1901 Frederick MD   D5.3.1968 Frederick MD   BR/TR/5-8/145   d4.16

1929	Cle A	82	256	28	67	3	2	1	24	29		0	16	.262	.337	.301	63	-14	10-13	.952	11	108	107	S82		0.3
1930	Cle A	33	13	7	1	0	0	0	1	0		0	0	.077	.077	.077	-9	-3	0-1	.861	3	165	39	S22,2b5/3		0.0
Total	2	115	269	35	68	3	2	1	25	29		0	16	.253	.326	.290	57	-17	10-14	.945	15	111	104	S104,2b5/3		0.3

GARDNER, BILLY   William Frederick "Shotgun"   B7.19.1927 Waterford CT   BR/TR/6-0/180*   d4.22   M6/C5

1954	NY N	62	108	10	23	5	0	1	7	6	1	19	.213	.261	.287	42	-9	0-1	.987	5	127	52	3b30,2b13,S5		-0.4
1955	NY N	59	187	26	38	10	1	3	17	13-0	2	16	.203	.261	.316	52	-13	0-0	.940	-2	102	109	S38,3b10,2b4		-1.2
1956	Bal A	144	515	53	119	16	2	11	50	29-1	7	53	.231	.281	.334	67	-28	5-5	.974	-10	99	84	2b132,S25,3b6		-2.8
1957	Bal A	154	644	79	169	36	3	6	55	53-2	8	67	.262	.326	.356	92	-7	10-7	.987	8	106	93	2b148,S9		1.2
1958	Bal A	151	560	32	126	28	2	3	33	34-4	3	55	.225	.271	.298	60	-31	2-3	.985	-15	92	107	2b151,S13		-3.7
1959	Bal A	140	401	34	87	13	2	6	27	38-9	1	61	.217	.284	.304	64	-20	2-1	.976	23	112	127	2b139/S3		1.2
1960	Was A	145	592	71	152	26	5	9	56	43-0	6	76	.257	.313	.363	84	-15	0-4	.973	-1	104	92	2b145,S13		-0.7
1961	Min A	45	154	13	36	9	0	1	11	10-1	0	14	.234	.280	.312	55	-10	0-0	.973	-7	89	110	2b41,3b2		-1.4
	†NY A	41	99	11	21	5	0	1	2	6-0	3	18	.212	.278	.293	56	-6	0-0	.952	1	105	136	3b33,2b6		-0.5
	Year	86	253	24	57	14	0	2	13	16-1	3	32	.225	.279	.304	56	-16	0-0	.975	-6	88	108	2b47,3b35		-1.9
1962	NY A	4	1	0	0	0	0	0	0	0-0	0	1	.000	.000	.000	-99	0	0-0	1.000	1	0	0	/23		0.0
	Bos A	53	199	22	54	9	2	0	12	10-0	1	39	.271	.310	.337	72	-8	0-1	.963	-6	86	83	2b38,3b7,S4		-1.1
	Year	57	200	23	54	9	2	0	12	10-0	1	40	.270	.308	.335	71	-8	0-1	.963	-5	85	82	2b39,3b8,S4		-1.1
1963	Bos A	36	84	4	16	2	1	0	1	4-1	0	19	.190	.236	.238	32	-8	0-0	.989	3	104	113	2b21,3b2		-0.3
Total	10	1034	3544	356	794	159	18	41	271	246-18	33	439	.224	.277	.292	327	70	-155	19-22	.978	-1	101	100	2b839,S108,3b92		-9.7

GARDNER, LARRY   William Lawrence   B5.13.1886 Enosburg Falls VT   D3.11.1976 St.George VT   BL/TR/5-8/165   d6.25   Col Vermont

1908	Bos A	3	10	0	3	1	0	0	1		0		.300	.300	.400	124	0	0	.571	-2	44	0	3b3		-0.2
1909	Bos A	19	37	7	11	1	2	0	5	4	1		.297	.381	.432	153	2	1	.800	-3	94	0	3b8,S5		0.0
1910	Bos A	113	413	56	117	12	10	2	36	41	4		.283	.354	.375	125	12	8	.944	-9	101	73	2b113		0.4
1911	Bos A	138	492	80	140	17	8	4	44	64	5		.285	.373	.376	110	9	27	.962	-1	99	88	3b72,2b62		3.3
1912	†Bos A	143	517	88	163	24	18	3	86	56	1		.315	.383	.449	140	20	25	.930	-1	99	88	3b143		2.2
1913	Bos A	131	473	64	133	17	10	0	63	47	1	34	.281	.347	.359	104	2	18	.943	-15	89	72	3b130		-0.9
1914	Bos A	155	553	50	143	23	19	3	68	35	0	39	.259	.303	.385	107	1	16-23	.942	-1	103	96	3b153		-0.7
1915	†Bos A	127	430	51	111	14	6	1	55	39	5	24	.258	.327	.326	98	-1	11-12	.933	-7	96	91	3b127		-0.7
1916	†Bos A	148	493	47	152	19	7	2	62	48	2	27	.308	.372	.387	128	17	12	.953	-12	93	97	3b147		0.9
1917	Bos A	146	501	53	133	23	7	1	61	54	3	37	.265	.341	.345	110	7	16	.937	-7	101	91	3b146		0.5
1918	Phi A	127	463	50	132	22	6	1	52	43	0	22	.285	.346	.365	113	7	9	.964	13	110	126	3b127		2.6
1919	Cle A	139	524	67	157	29	7	2	79	39	3	29	.300	.352	.393	103	2	7	.946	-5	101	106	3b139		0.1
1920	†Cle A	154	597	72	185	31	11	3	118	53	1	25	.310	.367	.414	103	3	3-20	.976	-1	101	133	3b154		0.0
1921	Cle A	153	586	101	187	32	14	3	120	65	4	16	.319	.391	.437	109	9	3-3	.950	1	101	84	3b152		1.8
1922	Cle A	137	470	74	134	31	3	2	68	49	2	21	.285	.355	.377	90	-5	9-8	.951	-6	96	96	3b128		-0.4
1923	Cle A	52	79	4	20	5	1	0	12	12	0	7	.253	.352	.342	83	-2	0-1	.962	3	135	79	3b19		0.2
1924	Cle A	38	50	3	10	0	0	0	4	5	0	1	.200	.273	.200	23	-6	0-1	.875	-2	127	248	3b8,2b6		-0.8
Total	17	1923	6688	867	1931	301	129	27	934	654	32	282	.289	.355	.384	109	76	165-68	.948	-31	100	95	3b1656,2b181,S5		8.9

GARIBALDI, ART   Arthur Edward   B8.21.1907 San Francisco CA   D10.19.1967 Sacramento CA   BR/TR/5-8/165   d6.20

| 1936 | StL N | 71 | 232 | 30 | 64 | 12 | 0 | 1 | 20 | 16 | 0 | 30 | .276 | .323 | .341 | 79 | -7 | 3 | .925 | -7 | 83 | 42 | 3b46,2b24 | | -1.0 |

GARKO, RYAN   Ryan F.   B1.2.1981 Pittsburgh PA   BR/TR/6-2/225   d9.18   Col Stanford

| 2005 | Cle A | 1 | 1 | 0 | 0 | 0 | 0 | 0 | 0 | | 0 | 1 | .000 | .000 | .000 | -99 | 0 | 0-0 | — | 0 | | | /D | | 0.0 |

GARMS, DEBS   Debs C. "Tex"   B6.26.1907 Bangs TX   D12.16.1984 Glen Rose TX   BL/TR/5-8.5/165   d8.10   Col Howard Payne

1932	StL A	34	134	20	38	7	1	1	8	17	0	7	.284	.364	.373	86	-2	4-3	.953	-1	92	114	O33(0/32/1)		-0.4
1933	StL A	78	189	35	60	10	2	4	24	30	2	21	.317	.416	.455	123	8	2-5	.960	-0	93	131	O47(28/17/3)		0.4
1934	StL A	91	232	25	68	14	4	0	31	27	2	19	.293	.372	.388	89	-3	0-0	.942	-3	99	44	O56(42/1/13)		-0.9
1935	StL A	10	15	1	4	0	0	0	2	2	0	2	.267	.353	.267	59	-1	0-0	.800	-0	90	0	O2R		-0.1
1937	Bos N	125	478	60	124	15	4	0	37	37	3	33	.259	.317	.337	85	-11	2-7	.977	-6	99	17	O81(64/15/2),3b36		-2.0
1938	Bos N	117	428	62	135	19	1	0	47	34	4	22	.315	.371	.364	114	10	4	.985	-3	91	114	O63(51/2/12),3b54/2		0.5
1939	Bos N	132	513	68	153	24	9	2	37	39	2	20	.298	.346	.392	107	4	2	.964	1	96	75	O96(25/0/73),3b37		0.1
1940	Pit N	103	358	76	127	23	7	5	57	23	1	6	.355	.395	.500	147	22	3	.964	3	104	144	3b64,O19(8/4/8)		2.6
1941	Pit N	83	220	25	58	9	3	3	42	22	1	12	.264	.331	.373	98	-1	0	.911	-6	86	22	3b29,O24(23/0/1)		-0.8
1943	†StL N	90	249	26	64	10	2	0	22	13	2	8	.257	.299	.313	74	-9	1	.940	-4	106	69	O47(18/0/29),3b23/S		-1.6
1944	†StL N	73	149	17	30	3	0	0	5	13	0	8	.201	.265	.221	37	-12	1	1.000	-4	96	0	O23(3/2/18),3b21		-1.8
1945	StL N	74	146	23	49	7	2	0	18	31	0	3	.336	.452	.411	137	10	0	.964	-4	83	96	3b32,O10(1/0/9)		0.6
Total	12	1010	3111	438	910	141	39	17	328	288	16	161	.293	.355	.379	103	15	18-8	.966	-28	96	75	O501(263/73/171),3b296/S2		-3.4

GARNER, PHIL   Philip Mason   B4.30.1949 Jefferson City TN   BR/TR/5-10/177*   [OakA71*A1/3]   d9.10   M13/C3   Col Tennessee

1973	Oak A	9	5	0	0	0	0	0	0	0-0	0	3	.000	.000	.000	-99	-1	0-0	1.000	-1	45	198	3b9		-0.3
1974	Oak A	30	28	4	5	1	0	0	1	1-0	0	5	.179	.207	.214	23	-3	1-1	.955	-2	83	65	3b19,S8,2b3,D2		-0.5
1975	†Oak A	160	488	46	120	21	5	6	54	30-1	5	65	.246	.295	.346	83	-12	4-6	.968	-2	102	98	2b160/S		-0.6
1976	Oak A★	159	555	54	145	29	12	8	74	36-1	2	71	.261	.307	.400	111	5	35-13	.975	-10	98	92	2b159		0.9
1977	Pit N	153	585	99	152	35	10	17	77	55-4	2	65	.260	.325	.441	100	-1	32-9	.971	-3	103	185	3b107,2b50,S12		0.1
1978	Pit N	154	528	66	138	25	9	10	66	66-12	5	71	.261	.345	.400	103	3	27-14	.976	7	98	110	2b81,3b81,S4		1.5
1979	†Pit N	150	549	76	161	32	8	11	59	55-15	3	74	.293	.359	.441	111	9	17-8	.981	1	102	132	2b83,3b78,S14		1.6
1980	Pit N★	151	548	62	142	27	6	5	58	46-12	2	53	.259	.315	.358	85	-10	32-7	.976	16	106	124	2b151/S		1.9
1981	Pit N★	56	181	22	46	6	2	1	20	21-1	0	21	.254	.327	.326	83	-4	4-6	.968	-8	89	94	2b50	15	-1.1
	†Hou N	31	113	13	27	3	1	0	6	15-1	0	11	.239	.326	.283	79	-3	6-2	.982	4	108	104	2b31		0.4
	Year	87	294	35	73	9	3	1	26	36-2	0	32	.248	.326	.310	81	-6	10-8	.973	-4	96	98	2b81		-0.7
1982	Hou N	155	588	65	161	33	8	13	83	40-4	3	92	.274	.320	.423	116	10	24-13	.980	1	98	112	2b136,3b18		2.1
1983	Hou N	154	567	76	135	24	2	14	79	63-8	5	84	.238	.317	.362	94	-5	18-12	.945	3	106	93	3b154		-0.5
1984	Hou N	128	374	60	104	17	6	4	45	43-2	4	63	.278	.355	.388	117	9	3-2	.979	19	115	140	3b82,2b35		3.0
1985	Hou N	135	463	65	124	23	10	6	51	34-3	2	76	.268	.317	.400	103	0	20-8	.932	-10	90	74	3b123,2b15		-1.2
1986	†Hou N	107	313	43	83	14	3	9	41	30-2	1	45	.265	.329	.415	108	3	12-6	.896	-1	97	120	3b84,2b7		0.2
1987	Hou N	43	112	15	25	9	0	2	15	8-1	0	20	.223	.268	.348	66	-6	1-0	.976	1	92	63	3b36,2b2		-0.5
	LA N	70	126	14	24	4	0	2	8	20-7	0	24	.190	.300	.270	54	-8	5-1	.923	3	109	95	3b46,2b12,S2		-0.4
	Year	113	238	29	49	9	0	5	23	28-8	0	44	.206	.288	.307	60	-14	6-1	.947	4	101	79	3b82,2b14,S2		-0.9

YEAR	TM LG	G	AB	R	H	2B	3B	HR	RBI	BB-IB	HP	SO	AVG	OBP	SLG	AOPS	ABR	SB-CS	FA	FR	RNG	THR	GAMES AT POSITION	DL	BFW
1988	SF N	15	13	0	2	0	0	0	1	1-0	0	3	.154	.214	.154	8	-2	0-1	—	-0	0	0	3b2	142	-0.3
Total	16	1860	6136	780	1594	299	82	109	738	564-74	34	842	.260	.323	.389	99	-16	225-105	.974	17	99	107	2b975,3b839,S42,D2	157	6.3

GARR, RALPH   Ralph Allen "Road Runner"   B12.12.1945 Monroe LA   BL/TR/5-11/197(185-197)   [AtlN67 3/52]   d9.3 Col Grambling St.

YEAR	TM LG	G	AB	R	H	2B	3B	HR	RBI	BB-IB	HP	SO	AVG	OBP	SLG	AOPS	ABR	SB-CS	FA	FR	RNG	THR	GAMES AT POSITION	DL	BFW
1968	Atl N	11	7	3	2	0	0	0	0	1-0	0	0	.286	.375	.286	100	0	1-0	—	0			/H		0.0
1969	Atl N	22	27	6	6	1	0	0	2	2-1	0	4	.222	.276	.259	50	-2	1-1	.857	-1	57	0	O7L		-0.4
1970	Atl N	37	96	18	27	3	0	0	8	5-1	0	12	.281	.314	.313	65	-5	5-2	1.000	0	111	0	O21(1/8/12)		-0.5
1971	Atl N	154	639	101	219	24	6	9	44	30-1	2	68	.343	.372	.441	122	18	30-14	.968	9	96	130	O153L		2.0
1972	Atl N	134	554	87	180	22	0	12	53	25-2	6	41	.325	.359	.430	114	10	25-9	.962	-3	92	82	O131(70/13/59)		0.2
1973	Atl N	148	668	94	200	32	6	11	55	22-5	2	64	.299	.323	.415	96	-5	35-11	.968	-4	95	63	O148(21/0/127)		-1.4
1974	Atl N★	143	606	87	**214**	24	**17**	11	54	28-10	2	52	**.353**	.383	.503	142	30	26-16	.967	-5	92	79	O139(107/0/80)		1.7
1975	Atl N	151	625	74	174	26	**11**	6	31	44-**17**	3	50	.278	.327	.384	94	-6	14-9	.966	-1	96	100	O148L		-1.7
1976	Chi A	136	527	63	158	22	6	4	36	17-2	2	41	.300	.322	.387	107	2	14-5	.978	-5	93	80	O125(35/41/57),D6		-0.8
1977	Chi A	134	543	78	163	29	7	10	54	27-4	0	44	.300	.333	.435	107	4	12-7	.987	0	96	115	O126(125/0/1),D2		-0.1
1978	Chi A	118	443	67	122	18	9	3	29	24-1	1	41	.275	.314	.377	92	-6	7-5	.959	-2	101	75	O109L,D9		-1.3
1979	Chi A	102	307	34	86	10	2	9	39	17-0	1	19	.280	.318	.414	96	-3	2-4	.951	-4	91	76	O67L,D17		-1.0
	Cal A	6	24	0	3	0	0	0	0	0-0	0	3	.125	.125	.125	-33	-5	0-0	—	0			D6		-0.5
	Year	108	331	34	89	10	2	9	39	17-0	1	22	.269	.305	.393	87	-7	2-4	.951	-4	91	76	O67L,D23		-1.5
1980	Cal A	21	42	5	8	1	0	0	3	4-2	0	6	.190	.261	.214	32	-4	0-0	.750	-2	129	0	O2(1/0/1),D8		-0.4
Total	13	1317	5108	717	1562	212	64	75	408	246-46	19	445	.306	.339	.416	106	28	172-83	.968	-16	95	88	O1176(844/62/337),D48		-4.2

GARRETT, ADRIAN   Henry Adrian "Pat"   B1.3.1943 Brooksville FL   BL/TR/6-3/185*   d4.13 Mil 1971 C5 b-Wayne

YEAR	TM LG	G	AB	R	H	2B	3B	HR	RBI	BB-IB	HP	SO	AVG	OBP	SLG	AOPS	ABR	SB-CS	FA	FR	RNG	THR	GAMES AT POSITION	DL	BFW
1966	Atl N	4	3	0	0	0	0	0	0	0-0	0	2	.000	.000	.000	-99	-1	0-0	—	-0	0	0	/OR		-0.1
1970	Chi N	3	3	0	0	0	0	0	0	0-0	0	3	.000	.000	.000	-89	-1	0-0	—	0			/H		-0.1
1971	Oak A	14	21	1	3	0	0	1	2	5-1	0	7	.143	.308	.286	70	-1	0-0	1.000	0	121	0	O5(4/0/1)		-0.3
1972	Oak A	14	11	0	0	0	0	0	0	1-0	0	4	.000	.083	.000	-77	-2	0-0	1.000	0	117	0	O2L		-0.2
1973	Chi N	36	54	7	12	0	0	3	8	4-1	0	18	.222	.267	.389	76	-2	1-0	1.000	0	94	0	O7(3/0/4),C6		-0.2
1974	Chi N	10	8	0	0	0	0	0	0	1-0	0	1	.000	.111	.000	-64	-2	0-0	1.000	1	0	0	C3/1OL		-0.1
1975	Chi N	16	21	1	2	0	0	1	6	1-0	0	8	.095	.130	.143	2	-3	0-0	1.000	1	211	163	1b4		0.0
	Cal A	37	107	17	28	5	0	6	18	14-0	0	28	.262	.344	.477	140	6	3-0	1.000	0	130	126	D23,1b10,O2R/C		0.5
1976	Cal A	29	48	4	6	3	0	0	3	5-0	0	16	.125	.204	.188	17	-5	0-0	.974	-3	84	34	C15/1D		-0.9
Total	8	163	276	30	51	8	0	11	37	31-2	0	87	.185	.263	.333	71	-11	4-0	.959	-2	70	112	D27,C25,O18(10/0/8),1b16		-1.5

GARRETT, WAYNE   Ronald Wayne   B12.3.1947 Brooksville FL   BL/TR/5-11/183(160-185)   [AtlN65 6/104]   d4.12 Mil 1971 b-Adrian

YEAR	TM LG	G	AB	R	H	2B	3B	HR	RBI	BB-IB	HP	SO	AVG	OBP	SLG	AOPS	ABR	SB-CS	FA	FR	RNG	THR	GAMES AT POSITION	DL	BFW
1969	†NY N	124	400	38	87	11	3	1	39	40-3	3	75	.218	.290	.268	57	-23	4-2	.951	-11	85	97	3b72,2b47,S9		-3.3
1970	NY N	114	366	74	93	17	4	12	45	81-6	2	60	.254	.390	.421	116	12	5-1	.944	-12	82	51	3b70,2b45/S		0.3
1971	NY N	56	202	20	43	2	0	1	11	28-2	1	31	.213	.310	.238	58	-10	1-3	.967	-2	94	94	3b53,2b9		-1.4
1972	NY N	111	298	41	69	13	3	2	29	70-3	0	58	.232	.374	.315	100	3	3-2	.960	1	98	113	3b82,2b22		0.6
1973	†NY N	140	504	76	129	20	3	16	58	72-4	1	74	.256	.348	.403	109	7	6-5	.942	4	103	**165**	3b130,S9,2b6		1.2
1974	NY N	151	522	55	117	14	3	13	53	89-7	2	96	.224	.337	.337	90	-5	4-6	.955	2	97	193	3b144,S9		-0.4
1975	NY N	107	274	49	73	8	3	6	34	50-4	1	45	.266	.379	.383	116	3	3-2	.966	5	101	193	3b94,S3/2		1.6
1976	NY N	80	251	36	56	8	1	4	26	52-5	1	26	.223	.359	.311	95	1	7-5	.948	5	105	127	3b64,2b10/S		0.6
	Mon N	59	177	15	43	4	1	2	11	30-7	0	20	.243	.353	.311	85	-2	2-2	.982	6	108	91	2b54,3b2		0.7
	Year	139	428	51	99	12	2	6	37	82-12	1	46	.231	.356	.311	91	-1	9-7	.949	11	104	125	3b66,2b64/S		1.3
1977	Mon N	68	159	17	43	6	1	2	22	30-7	1	18	.270	.385	.358	104	3	2-2	1.000	3	112	28	3b49/2		0.4
1978	Mon N	49	69	6	12	0	0	1	3	2-8	1	10	.174	.260	.217	35	-6	0-0	.969	-1	97	104	3b19		-0.8
	StL N	33	63	11	21	4	0	1	10	11-1	0	16	.333	.432	.444	146	5	1-0	.927	-1	91	202	3b19		0.4
	Year	82	132	17	33	4	0	2	13	19-2	1	26	.250	.344	.326	88	-1	1-0	.959	-2	94	159	3b32		-0.4
Total	10	1092	3285	438	786	107	22	61	340	561-50	12	529	.239	.350	.341	94	-6	38-30	.956	2	97	119	3b792,2b195,S32	67	-0.1

GARRIDO, GIL   Gil Gonzalo   B6.26.1941 Panama City, Pan   BR/TR/5-8/160*   d4.24

YEAR	TM LG	G	AB	R	H	2B	3B	HR	RBI	BB-IB	HP	SO	AVG	OBP	SLG	AOPS	ABR	SB-CS	FA	FR	RNG	THR	GAMES AT POSITION	DL	BFW
1964	SF N	14	25	1	2	0	0	0	0	2-0	0	7	.080	.148	.080	-33	-4	0-0	.969	-3	97	60	S14		-0.7
1968	Atl N	18	53	5	11	0	0	0	2	2-1	0	2	.208	.228	.208	34	-4	0-0	.987	2	107	152	S17		-0.1
1969	†Atl N	82	227	18	50	5	1	0	10	16-3	0	11	.220	.272	.251	47	-16	0-0	.973	-19	87	83	S81		-2.9
1970	Atl N	101	367	38	97	5	4	1	19	15-3	0	16	.264	.290	.308	58	-23	0-2	.975	-4	100	84	S80,2b26		-1.7
1971	Atl N	79	125	8	27	3	0	0	12	15-1	0	12	.216	.300	.240	51	-8	0-1	.961	-5	91	114	S32,3b28,2b18		-0.9
1972	Atl N	40	75	11	20	1	0	0	7	11-1	0	6	.267	.368	.280	79	-1	1-1	.989	-1	108	81	2b21,S10,3b3		-0.1
Total	6	334	872	81	207	14	5	1	51	61-9	1	54	.237	.286	.268	53	-56	2-4	.974	-29	94	92	S234,2b65,3b31		-6.4

GARRIOTT, CECIL   Virgil Cecil   B8.15.1916 Harristown IL   D2.20.1990 Lake Elsinore CA   BL/TR/5-8/165   d9.4 Col Millikin

YEAR	TM LG	G	AB	R	H	2B	3B	HR	RBI	BB-IB	HP	SO	AVG	OBP	SLG	AOPS	ABR	SB-CS	FA	FR	RNG	THR	GAMES AT POSITION	DL	BFW
1946	Chi N	6	5	1	0	0	0	0	0	0-0	0	0	.000	.167	.000	-52	-1	0-0	—	0			/H		-0.1

GARRISON, FORD   Robert Ford "Rocky","Snapper"   B8.29.1915 Greenville SC   D6.6.2001 Largo FL   BR/TR/5-10.5/180   d4.22 Mil 1945 C1

YEAR	TM LG	G	AB	R	H	2B	3B	HR	RBI	BB-IB	HP	SO	AVG	OBP	SLG	AOPS	ABR	SB-CS	FA	FR	RNG	THR	GAMES AT POSITION	DL	BFW
1943	Bos A	36	129	13	36	5	1	0	11	5	0	14	.279	.306	.357	92	-2	0-1	.988	-0	100	76	O32(26/6/0)		-0.5
1944	Bos A	13	49	5	12	3	0	0	2	6	0	4	.245	.327	.306	82	-1	0-0	.969	-0	114	0	O12R		-0.2
	Phi A	121	449	58	121	13	2	4	37	22	2	40	.269	.307	.334	84	-11	10-4	.987	5	114	63	O119(95/0/24)		-1.3
	Year	134	498	63	133	16	2	4	39	28	2	44	.267	.309	.331	84	-12	10-4	.985	5	114	56	O131(95/0/36)		-1.5
1945	Phi A	6	23	3	7	1	0	1	6	4	0	3	.304	.407	.478	157	2	1-0	1.000	9	202	161	O5L		0.2
1946	Phi A	9	37	1	4	0	0	0	0	0	0	6	.108	.108	.108	-40	-7	0-0	1.000	-1	65	0	O8L		-1.0
Total	4	185	687	80	180	22	3	6	56	37	2	67	.262	.302	.329	81	-19	11-5	.986	4	109	63	O176(134/6/36)		-2.8

GARRISON, WEBSTER   Webster Leotis   B8.24.1965 Marrero LA   BR/TR/5-11/170   [TorA83 2/37]   d8.2

YEAR	TM LG	G	AB	R	H	2B	3B	HR	RBI	BB-IB	HP	SO	AVG	OBP	SLG	AOPS	ABR	SB-CS	FA	FR	RNG	THR	GAMES AT POSITION	DL	BFW
1996	Oak A	5	9	0	0	0	0	0	0	0-0	0	3	.000	.100	.000	-73	-2	0-0	.875	-1	67	66	2b3/1		-0.3

GARRITY, HANK   Francis Joseph   B2.4.1908 Boston MA   D9.1.1962 Boston MA   BR/TR/6-1/185   d7.26 Col Holy Cross

YEAR	TM LG	G	AB	R	H	2B	3B	HR	RBI	BB-IB	HP	SO	AVG	OBP	SLG	AOPS	ABR	SB-CS	FA	FR	RNG	THR	GAMES AT POSITION	DL	BFW
1931	Chi A	8	14	0	3	1	0	0	2	1	0	2	.214	.267	.286	48	-1	0-0	.941	-1	61	142	C7		-0.1

GARVEY, STEVE   Steven Patrick   B12.22.1948 Tampa FL   BR/TR/5-10/190*   [LAN68 S1/13]   d9.1 Col Michigan St.

YEAR	TM LG	G	AB	R	H	2B	3B	HR	RBI	BB-IB	HP	SO	AVG	OBP	SLG	AOPS	ABR	SB-CS	FA	FR	RNG	THR	GAMES AT POSITION	DL	BFW
1969	LA N	3	3	0	1	0	0	0	0	0-0	0	1	.333	.333	.333	93	0	0-0	—	0			/H		0.0
1970	LA N	34	93	8	25	5	0	1	6	6-0	0	17	.269	.310	.355	82	-3	1-1	.943	5	130	100	3b27/2	33	0.2
1971	LA N	81	225	27	51	12	1	7	26	21-2	0	33	.227	.290	.382	94	-2	1-2	.939	12	123	110	3b79		1.0
1972	LA N	96	294	36	79	14	2	9	30	19-3	1	36	.269	.312	.422	109	3	4-2	.902	8	112	155	3b85,1b3		1.1
1973	LA N	114	349	37	106	17	3	8	50	11-4	3	42	.304	.328	.438	115	5	0-2	.993	-7	62	108	1b76,O10(8/0/2)		-0.9
1974	†LA N★	156	642	95	200	32	3	21	111	31-4	3	66	.312	.342	.469	131	23	5-4	.995	-12	64	95	1b156		-0.3
1975	LA N★	160	659	85	210	38	6	18	95	33-6	3	66	.319	.351	.476	134	27	11-2	**.995**	-11	70	85	1b160		0.4
1976	LA N★	162	631	85	200	37	4	13	80	50-11	1	69	.317	.363	.450	133	28	19-8	**.998**	-15	62	**110**	1b162		-0.1
1977	†LA N★	162	646	91	192	25	3	33	115	38-10	1	90	.297	.335	.498	120	15	9-6	**.995**	-16	57	122	1b160		1.1
1978	†LA N★	162	639	89	**202**	36	9	21	113	40-9	1	70	.316	.353	.499	137	29	10-5	.994	-8	77	103	1b161		1.2
1979	LA N★	162	648	92	204	32	1	28	110	37-16	2	59	.315	.351	.497	132	26	3-6	.995	-3	89	78	1b162		1.1
1980	LA N★	163	658	78	**200**	27	1	26	106	36-6	3	67	.304	.341	.467	127	21	6-11	**.999**	-0	78	106	1b110		-0.7
1981	†LA N★	110	431	63	122	23	1	10	64	25-6	1	49	.283	.322	.411	112	5	3-5	**.999**	-4	78	104	1b110		-0.6
1982	LA N★	162	625	66	176	35	1	16	86	20-10	3	86	.282	.301	.418	103	0	5-3	.995	5	109	93	1b158		-0.1
1983	SD N	100	388	76	114	22	0	14	59	29-11	3	39	.294	.344	.459	125	13	4-1	**1.000**	-2	92	101	1b100	65	-0.1
1984	†SD N★	161	617	72	175	27	3	8	86	24-3	1	64	.284	.307	.373	91	-9	1-2	**1.000**	-2	92	101	1b159		-2.2
1985	SD N★	162	654	80	184	34	6	17	81	35-7	3	67	.281	.318	.430	109	5	0-0	.997	-8	83	109	1b162		-3.9
1986	SD N	155	557	58	142	22	0	21	81	23-5	1	72	.255	.284	.408	91	-10	1-2	.994	-18	54	87	1b148	134	-0.9
1987	SD N	27	76	5	16	2	0	1	9	1-0	1	10	.211	.231	.276	35	-7	0-0	1.000	-0	89	76	1b20	232	-6.1
Total	19	2332	8835	1143	2599	440	43	272	1308	479-113	29	1003	.294	.329	.446	117	167	83-62	.996	-79	78	99	1b2059,3b191,O10(8/0/2)/2	232	-6.1

GASPAR, ROD   Rodney Earl   B4.3.1946 Long Beach CA   BB/TR/5-11/165*   d4.8 Col Cal St.-Long Beach

YEAR	TM LG	G	AB	R	H	2B	3B	HR	RBI	BB-IB	HP	SO	AVG	OBP	SLG	AOPS	ABR	SB-CS	FA	FR	RNG	THR	GAMES AT POSITION	DL	BFW
1969	†NY N	118	215	26	49	6	1	1	14	25-2	2	19	.228	.313	.279	66	-9	7-3	.983	8	99	308	O91(22/16/64)		-0.4
1970	NY N	11	14	4	0	0	0	0	0	0-0	0	4	.000	.067	.000	-80	-4	1-0	1.000	1	138	0	O8(0/4/5)		-0.3
1971	SD N	16	17	1	2	0	0	0	2	3-0	0	5	.118	.250	.118	8	-2	0-1	1.000	0	42	0	O2L		-0.3
1974	SD N	33	14	4	3	0	0	0	1	5-0	0	1	.214	.389	.214	76	0	0-0	1.000	1	143	0	O8(2/5/1),1b2		0.0
Total	4	178	260	35	54	6	1	1	17	33-2	2	29	.208	.301	.250	55	-15	8-4	.986	9	101	271	O109(26/25/70),1b2		-1.0

YEAR	TM LG	G	AB	R	H	2B	3B	HR	RBI	BB-IB	HP	SO	AVG	OBP	SLG	AOPS	ABR	SB-CS	FA	FR	RNG	THR	GAMES AT POSITION	DL	BFW

GASTALL, TOM Thomas Everett B6.13.1932 Fall River MA D9.20.1956 Riviera Beach MD BR/TR/6-2/187* d6.21 Col Boston U.

YEAR	TM LG	G	AB	R	H	2B	3B	HR	RBI	BB-IB	HP	SO	AVG	OBP	SLG	AOPS	ABR	SB-CS	FA	FR	RNG	THR	GAMES AT POSITION	DL	BFW
1955	Bal A	20	27	4	4	1	0	0	0	3-0	0	5	.148	.233	.185	15	-3	0-0	.967	-1	77	0	C15		-0.4
1956	Bal A	32	56	3	11	2	0	0	4	3-0	1	8	.196	.246	.232	30	-6	0-0	1.000	1	84	87	C20		-0.4
Total	2	52	83	7	15	3	0	0	4	6-0	1	13	.181	.242	.217	25	-9	0-0	.990	-0	82	58	C35		-0.8

GASTFIELD, ED Edward B8.1.1865 Chicago IL D12.1.1899 Chicago IL BR/5-9.5/155 d8.13

YEAR	TM LG	G	AB	R	H	2B	3B	HR	RBI	BB-IB	HP	SO	AVG	OBP	SLG	AOPS	ABR	SB-CS	FA	FR	RNG	THR	GAMES AT POSITION	DL	BFW
1884	Det N	23	82	6	6	1	0	0	2	2		34	.073	.095	.085	-45	-13		.827	4			C19,O2R,1b2		-0.7
1885	Det N	1	3	0	0	0	0	0	0	0		2	.000	.000	.000	-99	-1		.714	-1			/C		-0.1
	Chi N	1	3	0	0	0	0	0	0	0		1	.000	.000	.000	-88	-1		1.000	1			/C		0.0
	Year	2	6	0	0	0	0	0	0	0		3	.000	.000	.000	-93	-1		.889	0			C2		-0.1
Total	2	25	88	6	6	1	0	0	2	2		37	.068	.089	.080	-49	-15		.832	4			C21,1b2,O2R		-0.8

GASTON, ALEX Alexander Nathaniel B3.12.1893 New York NY D2.8.1979 Marina Del Ray CA BR/TR/5-9/170 d9.26 b-Milt

YEAR	TM LG	G	AB	R	H	2B	3B	HR	RBI	BB-IB	HP	SO	AVG	OBP	SLG	AOPS	ABR	SB-CS	FA	FR	RNG	THR	GAMES AT POSITION	DL	BFW
1920	NY N	4	10	2	1	0	0	0	1	1	0	2	.100	.182	.100	-18	-2	0-0	.917	-1	107	52	C3		-0.2
1921	NY N	20	22	1	5	1	1	0	3	1	0	9	.227	.261	.364	63	-1	0-0	.950	-0	125	0	C11		-0.1
1922	NY N	16	26	1	5	0	0	0	1	0	0	3	.192	.192	.192	-1	-4	1-0	1.000	0	119	32	C13		-0.3
1923	NY N	22	39	3	8	2	0	0	5	0	1	6	.205	.225	.333	46	-3	0-0	.957	0	160	115	C21		-0.2
1926	Bos A	98	301	37	67	5	3	0	21	21	4	28	.223	.282	.259	43	-26	3-0	.981	-15	62	86	C98		-3.4
1929	Bos A	55	116	14	26	5	2	2	9	6	0	8	.224	.262	.353	58	-8	1-0	.986	1	103	126	C49		-0.5
Total	6	215	514	58	112	13	6	3	40	29	5	56	.218	.266	.284	45	-44	5-0	.979	-15	83	91	C195		-4.7

GASTON, CITO Clarence Edwin B3.17.1944 San Antonio TX BR/TR/6-4/210* d9.14 M9/C10

YEAR	TM LG	G	AB	R	H	2B	3B	HR	RBI	BB-IB	HP	SO	AVG	OBP	SLG	AOPS	ABR	SB-CS	FA	FR	RNG	THR	GAMES AT POSITION	DL	BFW
1967	Atl N	9	25	1	3	0	1	0	1	0-0	0	5	.120	.120	.200	-10	-4	1-0	.800	-2	45	239	O7(0/6/1)		-0.6
1969	SD N	129	391	20	90	11	7	2	28	24-0	1	117	.230	.275	.309	66	-19	1-0	.959	2	100	179	O113C		-2.2
1970	SD N★	146	584	92	186	26	9	29	93	41-2	2	142	.318	.364	.543	145	34	4-1	.975	-5	97	87	O142(1/142/0)		2.5
1971	SD N	141	518	57	118	13	9	17	61	24-1	2	121	.228	.264	.386	88	-13	1-0	.982	-7	81	101	O133(6/126/1)		-2.5
1972	SD N	111	379	30	102	14	0	7	44	22-2	2	76	.269	.313	.361	98	-2	0-2	.977	-1	90	149	O94(18/7/73)		-1.9
1973	SD N	133	476	51	119	18	4	16	57	20-3	1	88	.250	.281	.405	96	-7	0-0	.947	-3	89	153	O119(1/0/118)	16	-1.0
1974	SD N	106	267	19	57	11	0	6	33	16-2	1	51	.213	.259	.322	65	-14	0-0	.992	4	107	170	O63(18/0/50)		-1.3
1975	Atl N	64	141	17	34	4	0	6	15	17-3	0	33	.241	.321	.397	96	-1	1-0	.974	-0	102	96	O35(2/17/17)/1		-0.3
1976	Atl N	69	134	15	39	4	0	4	25	13-1	0	21	.291	.354	.410	110	2	1-0	.977	-2	85	58	O28(25/0/3),1b2		-0.1
1977	Atl N	56	85	6	23	4	0	3	21	5-0	0	19	.271	.301	.424	85	-2	1-0	1.000	0	90	0	O9(7/0/2),1b5		-0.2
1978	Atl N	60	118	5	27	1	0	1	9	3-0	0	20	.229	.244	.263	39	-10	0-0	.957	-1	114	0	O29(13/11/17),1b4		-1.3
	Pit N	2	2	1	1	0	0	0	0	0-0	0	0	.500	.500	.500	171	0	0-0	—	-0	0	0	/OL		0.0
	Year	62	120	6	28	1	0	1	9	3-0	0	20	.233	.248	.267	41	-10	0-0	.957	-1	112	0	O30(14/1/17),1b4		-1.3
Total	11	1026	3120	314	799	106	30	91	387	185-14	9	693	.256	.298	.397	95	-36	13-7	.970	-11	93	125	O773(92/412/282),1b12	16	-8.3

GATES, BRENT Brent Robert B3.14.1970 Grand Rapids MI BB/TR/6-1/180(180-191) [OakA91 1/26] d5.5 Col Minnesota

YEAR	TM LG	G	AB	R	H	2B	3B	HR	RBI	BB-IB	HP	SO	AVG	OBP	SLG	AOPS	ABR	SB-CS	FA	FR	RNG	THR	GAMES AT POSITION	DL	BFW
1993	Oak A	139	535	64	155	29	2	7	69	56-4	4	75	.290	.357	.391	108	7	7-3	.981	-5	102	88	2b139		0.9
1994	Oak A	64	233	29	66	11	1	2	24	21-1	1	32	.283	.337	.365	90	-3	3-3	.974	-11	86	72	2b63/1	51	-0.9
1995	Oak A	136	524	60	133	24	4	5	56	46-2	0	84	.254	.308	.344	75	-20	3-3	.982	11	107	91	2b132/1D		-0.3
1996	Oak A	64	247	26	65	19	2	2	30	18-0	2	35	.263	.316	.381	77	-9	1-1	.973	-1	100	105	2b63		-0.3
1997	†Sea A	65	151	18	36	8	0	3	20	14-0	0	21	.238	.298	.351	70	-7	0-0	.934	-4	90	90	3b32,2b21,S5/1OLD	106	-0.7
1998	Min A	107	333	31	83	15	0	3	42	36-0	2	46	.249	.324	.321	68	-15	3-3	.961	-7	90	48	3b77,2b21/1SD		-2.0
1999	Min A	110	306	40	78	13	2	3	38	34-1	1	56	.255	.328	.340	48	-15	1-3	.972	-3	98	146	3b61,2b47,1b5/SD		-1.6
Total	7	685	2329	268	616	119	11	25	279	225-8	10	349	.264	.327	.357	81	-62	18-13	.980	-19	102	89	2b486,3b170,1b9,S7,D7/OL	157	-5.5

GATES, JOE Joseph Daniel B10.3.1954 Gary IN BL/TR/5-7/175* d9.12 Col Manatee (FL) CC

YEAR	TM LG	G	AB	R	H	2B	3B	HR	RBI	BB-IB	HP	SO	AVG	OBP	SLG	AOPS	ABR	SB-CS	FA	FR	RNG	THR	GAMES AT POSITION	DL	BFW
1978	Chi A	8	24	6	6	0	0	0	1	4-0	1	6	.250	.379	.250	79	0	1-0	.972	-1	109	73	2b8		-0.1
1979	Chi A	16	16	5	1	0	1	0	1	2-0	0	3	.063	.167	.188	-5	-3	1-1	.966	1	126	88	2b8/3D		-0.1
Total	2	24	40	11	7	0	1	0	2	6-0	1	9	.175	.298	.225	46	-3	2-1	.969	0	115	78	2b16/D3		-0.2

GATES, MIKE Michael Grant B9.20.1956 Culver City CA BL/TR/6-0/165* [MonN79 7/166] d5.6 Col Pepperdine

YEAR	TM LG	G	AB	R	H	2B	3B	HR	RBI	BB-IB	HP	SO	AVG	OBP	SLG	AOPS	ABR	SB-CS	FA	FR	RNG	THR	GAMES AT POSITION	DL	BFW
1981	Mon N	1	2	1	1	0	0	0	0	1-0	0	1	.500	.500	1.500	436	1	0-0	1.000	0	135	0	/2		0.1
1982	Mon N	36	121	16	28	2	3	0	8	9-0	0	19	.231	.280	.298	61	-7	0-0	1.000	-2	94	106	2b36		-0.8
Total	2	37	123	17	29	2	4	0	9	9-0	0	20	.236	.284	.317	67	-6	0-0	1.000	-2	94	105	2b37		-0.7

GATHRIGHT, JOEY Joey Renard B4.22.1982 Hattiesburg MS BL/TR/5-10/175* [TBA01 32/949] d6.25

YEAR	TM LG	G	AB	R	H	2B	3B	HR	RBI	BB-IB	HP	SO	AVG	OBP	SLG	AOPS	ABR	SB-CS	FA	FR	RNG	THR	GAMES AT POSITION	DL	BFW
2004	TB A	19	52	11	13	0	0	0	1	2-0	3	14	.250	.316	.250	51	-1	6-1	1.000	-1	86	0	O16(4/11/1)/D		-0.4
2005	TB A	76	203	29	56	7	3	0	13	10-0	2	39	.276	.316	.340	77	-7	20-5	.984	6	123	106	O70C		0.3
Total	2	95	255	40	69	7	3	0	14	12-0	5	53	.271	.316	.322	72	-11	26-6	.986	5	116	85	O86(4/81/1)/D		-0.1

GATINS, FRANK Frank Anthony B3.6.1871 Johnstown PA D11.8.1911 Johnstown PA d9.21

YEAR	TM LG	G	AB	R	H	2B	3B	HR	RBI	BB-IB	HP	SO	AVG	OBP	SLG	AOPS	ABR	SB-CS	FA	FR	RNG	THR	GAMES AT POSITION	DL	BFW
1898	Was N	17	58	6	13	2	0	0	5	3	1		.224	.274	.259	53	-4	2	.790	-5	91	94	S17		-0.7
1901	Bro N	50	197	21	45	7	2	1	21	5	2		.228	.255	.299	59	-11	6	.919	-8	69	104	3b46,S5		-1.7
Total	2	67	255	27	58	9	2	1	26	8	3		.227	.259	.290	58	-15	8	.919	-12	69	104	3b46,S22		-2.4

GAUDET, JIM James Jennings B6.3.1955 New Orleans LA BR/TR/6-0/185* [KCA76 6/138] d9.10 Col Tulane

YEAR	TM LG	G	AB	R	H	2B	3B	HR	RBI	BB-IB	HP	SO	AVG	OBP	SLG	AOPS	ABR	SB-CS	FA	FR	RNG	THR	GAMES AT POSITION	DL	BFW
1978	KC A	3	8	0	0	0	0	0	0	0-0	1	3	.000	.000	.000	-97	-2	0-0	.938	1	0	0	C3		-0.1
1979	KC A	3	6	0	1	0	0	0	1	0-0	0	1	.167	.167	.167	-10	-1	0-0	1.000	1	32	0	C3		0.0
Total	2	6	14	0	1	0	0	0	1	0-0	1	4	.071	.071	.071	-59	-3	0-0	.966	1	13	0	C6		-0.1

GAULE, MIKE Michael John B8.4.1869 Baltimore MD D1.24.1918 Baltimore MD BL/TL/6-2/? d6.15

YEAR	TM LG	G	AB	R	H	2B	3B	HR	RBI	BB-IB	HP	SO	AVG	OBP	SLG	AOPS	ABR	SB-CS	FA	FR	RNG	THR	GAMES AT POSITION	DL	BFW
1889	Lou AA	1	2	0	0	0	0	0	0	0	0	1	.000	.000	.000	-99	-1	0	.000	-1	0	0	/OC		-0.1

GAUTREAU, DOC Walter Paul "Punk" B7.26.1901 Cambridge MA D8.23.1970 Salt Lake City UT BR/TR/5-4/129 d6.22 Col Holy Cross

YEAR	TM LG	G	AB	R	H	2B	3B	HR	RBI	BB-IB	HP	SO	AVG	OBP	SLG	AOPS	ABR	SB-CS	FA	FR	RNG	THR	GAMES AT POSITION	DL	BFW
1925	Phi A	4	7	0	0	0	0	0	0	0-0	0	3	.000	.000	.000	-94	-2	0-0	.933	1	109	85	2b4		-0.1
	Bos N	68	279	45	73	13	3	0	23	35	1	13	.262	.346	.330	81	-7	11-7	.976	-9	94	93	2b68		-1.3
1926	Bos N	79	266	36	71	9	4	0	8	35	2	24	.267	.356	.331	94	-1	17	.942	-19	83	94	2b74		-1.8
1927	Bos N	87	236	38	58	12	2	0	20	25	1	20	.246	.321	.314	76	-7	11	.965	-6	98	61	2b57		-1.1
1928	Bos N	23	18	3	5	0	1	0	1	4	0	3	.278	.409	.389	116	1	1	.750	-1	89	206	2b4/S		0.0
Total	4	261	806	122	207	34	10	0	52	99	4	63	.257	.341	.324	83	-16	40-7	.960	-34	91	85	2b207/S		-4.3

GAUTREAUX, SID Sidney Allen "Pudge" B5.4.1912 Schriever LA D4.19.1980 Morgan City LA BB/TR/5-8/190 d4.15

YEAR	TM LG	G	AB	R	H	2B	3B	HR	RBI	BB-IB	HP	SO	AVG	OBP	SLG	AOPS	ABR	SB-CS	FA	FR	RNG	THR	GAMES AT POSITION	DL	BFW
1936	Bro N	75	71	8	19	3	0	0	16	9	1	7	.268	.358	.310	80	-1	0	.963	-0	78	73	C15		-0.1
1937	Bro N	11	10	0	1	1	0	0	2	1	0	1	.100	.182	.200	4	-1	0	—	0			/H		-0.1
Total	2	86	81	8	20	4	0	0	18	10	1	8	.247	.337	.296	71	-2	0	.963	-0	78	73	C15		-0.2

GAVERN d6.15

YEAR	TM LG	G	AB	R	H	2B	3B	HR	RBI	BB-IB	HP	SO	AVG	OBP	SLG	AOPS	ABR	SB-CS	FA	FR	RNG	THR	GAMES AT POSITION	DL	BFW
1874	Atl NA	1	4	1	0	0	0	0	0	0			.000	.000	.000	-99	-1	0-0	.750	1	237	0	/2		0.0

GAZELLA, MIKE Michael B10.13.1895 Olyphant PA D9.11.1978 Odessa TX BR/TR/5-7.5/165 d7.2 Col Lafayette

YEAR	TM LG	G	AB	R	H	2B	3B	HR	RBI	BB-IB	HP	SO	AVG	OBP	SLG	AOPS	ABR	SB-CS	FA	FR	RNG	THR	GAMES AT POSITION	DL	BFW
1923	NY A	8	13	2	1	0	1	0	1	2	0	3	.077	.200	.077	-25	-2	0-0	1.000	-0	121	0	S4,2b3,3b2		-0.3
1926	†NY A	66	168	21	39	6	0	0	20	25	1	24	.232	.335	.268	60	-9	2-2	.913	-6	93	79	3b45,S11		-1.1
1927	NY A	54	115	17	32	8	4	0	9	23	1	16	.278	.403	.417	117	4	4-1	.961	-6	82	95	3b44,S6		0.0
1928	NY A	32	56	11	13	0	0	0	2	6	1	7	.232	.317	.232	48	-4	2-1	.969	-2	95	52	3b16,2b4,S3		-0.5
Total	4	160	352	51	85	14	4	0	32	56	3	50	.241	.350	.304	73	-11	8-4	.940	-14	89	81	3b107,S24,2b6		-1.9

GEAR, DALE Dale Dudley B2.2.1872 Lone Elm KS D9.23.1951 Topeka KS BR/TR/5-11/165 d8.15 Col Kansas ▲

YEAR	TM LG	G	AB	R	H	2B	3B	HR	RBI	BB-IB	HP	SO	AVG	OBP	SLG	AOPS	ABR	SB-CS	FA	FR	RNG	THR	GAMES AT POSITION	DL	BFW
1896	Cle N	4	15	5	6	1	0	0	3	1			.400	.438	.600	163	1		.857	-1	70	0	P3/1		0.0
1897	Cle N	7	24	3	4	1	0	0	3	3	1		.167	.286	.208	30	-2	2	.750	0	342	0	O6C		-0.2
1901	Was A	58	199	17	47	9	2	0	20	4			.236	.251	.302	54	-13	2	.944	3	159	350	O35(12/1/22),P24		-0.7
Total	3	69	238	25	57	11	2	0	26	8	1		.239	.267	.311	59	-14	4	.900	2	191	290	O41(12/7/22),P27/1		-0.9

GEARHART, GARY Lloyd William B8.10.1923 New Lebanon OH D4.2.2001 Dayton OH BR/TL/5-11/180 d4.18

YEAR	TM LG	G	AB	R	H	2B	3B	HR	RBI	BB-IB	HP	SO	AVG	OBP	SLG	AOPS	ABR	SB-CS	FA	FR	RNG	THR	GAMES AT POSITION	DL	BFW
1947	NY N	73	179	26	44	9	0	6	17	17	1	30	.246	.315	.397	87	-4	1	.961	-1	91	133	O44(17/28/0)		-0.7

YEAR	TM LG	G	AB	R	H	2B	3B	HR	RBI	BB-IB	HP	SO	AVG	OBP	SLG	AOPS	ABR	SB-CS	FA	FR	RNG	THR	GAMES AT POSITION	DL	BFW

GEARY, HUCK Eugene Francis Joseph B1.22.1917 Buffalo NY D1.27.1981 Cuba NY BL/TR/5-10.5/170 d7.17 Mil 1944-45 [DL 1946 Pit N 115]

1942	Pit N	9	22	3	5	0	0	0	2	2	0	3	.227	.292	.227	52	-1	0	.939	-1	77	142	S8		-0.2
1943	Pit N	46	166	17	25	4	0	1	13	18	0	6	.151	.234	.193	23	-16	3	.956	-3	94	102	S46		-1.7
Total	2	55	188	20	30	4	0	1	15	20	0	9	.160	.240	.197	26	-17	3	.954	-3	92	107	S54	115	-1.9

GEDEON, ELMER Elmer John B4.15.1917 Cleveland OH D4.20.1944 St.Pol, France BR/TR/6-4/196 d9.18 Col Michigan

| 1939 | Was A | 5 | 15 | 1 | 3 | 0 | 0 | 1 | 2 | 0 | 0 | 5 | .200 | .294 | .200 | 31 | -2 | 0-0 | 1.000 | 0 | 127 | 0 | O5(0/4/1) | | -0.1 |

GEDEON, JOE Elmer Joseph B12.5.1893 Sacramento CA D5.19.1941 San Francisco CA BR/TR/6-0/167 d5.13

1913	Was A	29	71	3	13	1	3	0	6	1	1	6	.183	.205	.282	41	-6	3	.929	1	95	167	O15(14/0/1),3b7,2b2,S2/P		-0.5
1914	Was A	4	2	0	0	0	0	0	1	0	1	1	.000	.333	.000	1	0	0	.667	-0	100	0	O4(0/1/3)		-0.1
1916	NY A	122	435	50	92	14	4	0	27	40	3	61	.211	.282	.262	62	-20	14	.955	-13	95	114	2b122		-3.5
1917	NY A	33	117	15	28	7	0	0	8	7	1	13	.239	.288	.299	78	-3	4	.983	1	93	93	2b31		-0.2
1918	StL A	123	441	39	94	14	3	1	41	27	8	29	.213	.271	.265	64	-20	8	.977	16	107	86	2b123		-0.3
1919	StL A	120	437	57	111	13	4	0	27	50	7	35	.254	.340	.302	79	-11	4	.975	-3	96	90	2b118		-1.2
1920	StL A	153	606	95	177	33	6	0	61	55	4	36	.292	.355	.366	89	-9	1-3	.964	-27	88	102	2b153		-3.3
Total	7	584	2109	259	515	82	20	1	171	180	25	181	.244	.311	.303	75	-69	34-3	.969	-26	96	98	2b549,O19(14/1/4),3b7,S2/P		-9.1

GEDMAN, RICH Richard Leo B9.26.1959 Worcester MA BL/TR/6-0/215(205-222) d9.7

1980	Bos A	9	24	2	5	0	0	0	0	0-0	1	.208	.208	.208	14	-3	0-0	.867	-0	66	0	C2,D4		-0.3
1981	Bos A	62	205	22	59	15	0	5	26	9-1	1	31	.288	.317	.434	109	2	0-0	.990	-7	72	105	C59		-0.2
1982	Bos A	92	289	30	72	17	2	4	26	10-2	1	37	.249	.279	.363	71	-12	0-1	.977	-7	80	82	C86		-1.6
1983	Bos A	81	204	21	60	16	1	2	18	15-6	1	37	.294	.345	.412	100	0	0-1	.980	-5	60	66	C68		-0.3
1984	Bos A	133	449	54	121	26	4	24	72	29-8	1	72	.269	.312	.506	117	9	0-0	.977	-5	91	136	C125		0.9
1985	Bos A★	144	498	66	147	30	5	18	80	50-11	3	79	.295	.362	.484	124	17	2-0	.983	13	125	125	C139		3.5
1986	†Bos A★	135	462	49	119	29	0	16	65	37-13	4	61	.258	.315	.424	99	-1	1-0	.994	18	153	126	C134		2.2
1987	Bos A	52	151	11	31	8	0	1	13	10-2	1	24	.205	.250	.278	40	-13	0-0	.976	-1	147	94	C51	82	-1.0
1988	†Bos A	95	299	33	69	14	0	9	39	18-2	3	49	.231	.279	.368	77	-10	0-1	.992	4	118	117	C93/D	24	-0.1
1989	Bos A	93	260	24	55	9	0	4	16	23-1	1	47	.212	.273	.292	56	-15	0-1	.981	-8	74	99	C91		-1.9
1990	Bos A	10	15	3	3	0	0	0	0	5-0	0	6	.200	.429	.200	77	0	0-0	1.000	3	73	114	C9		0.1
	Hou N	40	104	4	21	7	0	1	10	15-6	0	24	.202	.300	.298	68	-4	0-1	.976	6	76	91	C43		-0.6
1991	StL N	46	94	7	10	1	0	3	8	4-0	0	15	.106	.140	.213	-1	-13	0-1	.976	4	66	27	C40		0.2
1992	StL N	41	105	5	23	4	0	1	8	11-1	0	22	.219	.291	.286	66	-5	0-0	.988	4	66	27	C40		-0.3
Total	13	1033	3159	331	795	176	12	88	382	236-53	16	509	.252	.304	.399	90	-48	3-4	.984	15	103	108	C979,D5	106	0.7

GEDNEY, COUNT Alfred W. B5.10.1849 Brooklyn NY D3.26.1922 Hackensack NJ 5-9/140 d4.27 ▲

1872	Tro NA	9	47	14	20	3	0	3	18	0		0	.426	.426	.681	232	7	1-0	.933	-1	0	0	O9C		0.4
	Eck NA	18	71	5	13	1	0	0	6	0		3	.183	.183	.197	20	-5	2-2	.881	1	0	0	O18L		-0.3
	Year	27	118	19	33	4	0	3	24	0		3	.280	.280	.390	115	3	3-2	.892	0	0	0	O27(18/9/0)		0.1
1873	Mut NA	53	225	41	60	5	5	1	24	6		4	.267	.286	.347	88	-3	1-0	.852	14	134	313	O53L		0.9
1874	Ath NA	54	222	49	61	4	1	1	34	7		11	.275	.297	.315	89	-4	2-2	.822	0	44	188	O51L,1b4		-0.2
1875	Mut NA	68	267	30	55	12	2	0	17	0		8	.206	.206	.266	60	-11	2-3	.843	11	70	91	O67(67/0/1),P2		0.2
Total	4 NA	202	832	139	209	25	8	5	99	13		26	.251	.263	.319	83	-17	8-7	.846	26	72	162	O198(189/9/1),1b4,P2		1.0

GEER, BILLY William Henry Harrison (b George Harrison Geer) TR/5-8/160 d10.15

1874	Mut NA	2	8	0	2	0	0	0	1	0		0	.250	.250	.250	59	0	0-0	.889	2	482	1500	O2(1/1/0)		0.1
1875	NH NA	37	164	20	40	4	1	0	9	1		4	.244	.248	.280	96	1	2-2	.765	1	205	476	O17(4/11/3),2b13,S6/13		0.0
1878	Cin N	61	237	31	52	13	2	0	20	10		18	.219	.251	.291	86	-2		.867	-4	93	118	S60,2b2		-0.3
1880	Wor N	2	6	0	0	0	0	0	0	0		0	.000	.000	.000	-92	-1		1.000	-0	0	0	/ORS		0.0
1884	Phi U	9	36	7	9	2	1	0		4			.250	.325	.361	117	0		.772	0	121	52	S9		0.0
	Bro AA	107	391	68	82	15	7	0		38	1		.210	.281	.284	84	-5		.870	17	109	122	S107,P2,2b2		1.3
1885	Lou AA	14	51	2	6	2	0	0	3	2	1		.118	.167	.157	3	-5		.872	-0	96	47	S14		-0.5
Total	2 NA	39	172	20	42	4	1	0	10	1		4	.244	.249	.279	93	1	2-2	.791	2	244	620	O19(5/12/3),2b13,S6/31		0.1
Total	4	193	721	108	149	32	10	0	23	54	2	18	.207	.264	.279	79	-13		.864	13	104	111	S191,2b4,P2/OR		0.4

GEHRIG, LOU Henry Louis "The Iron Horse" B6.19.1903 New York NY D6.2.1941 Riverdale NY BL/TL/6-0/200 d6.15 HF1939 Col Columbia

1923	NY A	13	26	6	11	4	1	1	9	2	0	5	.423	.464	.769	217	4	0-0	.933	-1	82	104	1b9		0.3
1924	NY A	10	12	2	6	1	0	0	5	1	0	3	.500	.538	.583	190	2	0-0	1.000	0	138	0	1b2/OR		0.2
1925	NY A	126	437	73	129	23	10	20	68	46	2	49	.295	.365	.531	127	15	6-3	.989	-9	70	82	1b114,O6(2/0/4)		-0.2
1926	†NY A	155	572	135	179	47	20	16	112	105	1	73	.313	.420	.549	154	48	6-5	.991	-8	76	79	1b155		2.7
1927	†NY A	155	584	149	218	52	18	47	175	109	3	84	.373	.474	.765	224	109	10-8	.992	-7	83	99	1b155		8.4
1928	†NY A	154	562	139	210	47	13	27	142	95	4	69	.374	.467	.648	197	83	4-11	.989	-9	80	96	1b154		5.9
1929	NY A	154	553	127	166	32	10	35	126	122	5	68	.300	.431	.584	170	63	4-3	.994	-4	87	108	1b154		4.5
1930	NY A	154	581	143	220	42	17	41	174	101	3	63	.379	.473	.721	207	99	12-14	.989	2	102	86	1b153/OL		7.7
1931	NY A	155	619	163	211	31	15	46	184	117	0	56	.341	.446	.662	199	91	17-12	.991	-10	68	101	1b154/OR		6.0
1932	†NY A	156	596	138	208	42	9	34	151	108	3	38	.349	.451	.621	184	79	4-11	.987	-6	80	83	1b152		5.1
1933	NY A	152	593	138	198	41	12	32	139	92	1	42	.334	.424	.605	181	70	9-13	.993	-3	81	85	1b152		4.7
1934	NY A★	154	579	128	210	40	6	49	165	109	2	31	.363	.465	.706	213	100	9-5	.994	1	99	107	1b153/S		7.9
1935	NY A★	149	535	125	176	26	10	30	119	132	5	38	.329	.466	.583	180	72	8-7	.990	0	100	89	1b149		5.3
1936	NY A★	155	579	167	205	37	7	49	152	130	4	46	.354	.478	.696	193	91	3-4	.994	-4	98	99	1b155		6.6
1937	†NY A★	157	569	138	200	37	9	37	159	127	4	49	.351	.473	.643	177	74	4-3	.989	-6	84	92	1b157		4.8
1938	†NY A★	157	576	115	170	32	6	29	114	107	5	75	.295	.410	.523	133	32	6-1	.991	-1	97	117	1b157		1.5
1939	NY A★	8	28	2	4	0	0	0	1	5	0	1	.143	.273	.143	9	-4	0-0	.971	-1	86	90	1b8		-0.5
Total	17	2164	8001	1888	2721	534	163	493	1995	1508	45	790	.340	.447	.632	182	1028	102-100	.991	-59	86	95	1b2137,O9(3/0/6)/S		70.9

GEHRINGER, CHARLIE Charles Leonard "The Mechanical Man" B5.11.1903 Fowlerville MI D1.21.1993 Bloomfield Hills MI BL/TR/5-11/180 d9.22 Mil 1942-45 C1 HF1949 Col Michigan

1924	Det A	5	13	2	6	0	0	0	1	1	0	2	.462	.462	.462	141	1	1-1	.967	2	139	90	2b5		0.3
1925	Det A	8	18	3	3	0	0	0	0	2	0	0	.167	.250	.167	7	-3	0-1	1.000	3	151	199	2b6		0.0
1926	Det A	123	459	62	127	19	17	1	48	30	1	42	.277	.322	.399	86	-12	9-7	.973	-6	94	89	2b112,3b6		-1.5
1927	Det A	133	508	110	161	29	11	4	61	52	2	31	.317	.383	.441	112	9	17-8	.965	17	108	110	2b121		2.9
1928	Det A	154	603	108	193	29	16	6	74	69	6	22	.320	.395	.451	120	19	15-9	.962	-0	99	103	2b154		2.2
1929	Det A	155	634	131	215	45	19	13	106	64	6	17	.339	.405	.532	139	36	27-10	.975	-8	96	82	2b154		3.3
1930	Det A	154	610	144	201	47	15	16	98	69	7	17	.330	.404	.534	133	32	19-15	.979	-4	91	102	2b78,1b9		3.6
1931	Det A	101	383	67	119	24	5	4	53	29	0	15	.311	.359	.431	103	1	13-4	.979	-4	91	100	2b102		0.3
1932	Det A	152	618	112	184	44	11	19	107	68	3	34	.298	.370	.497	118	16	9-8	.967	2	97	110	2b152		2.4
1933	Det A★	155	628	103	204	42	6	12	105	68	3	27	.325	.393	.468	125	24	5-4	.981	5	102	117	2b155		3.6
1934	†Det A★	154	601	134	214	50	7	11	127	99	3	25	.356	.450	.517	149	50	11-8	.981	7	103	101	2b154		6.0
1935	†Det A★	150	610	123	201	32	8	19	108	79	3	16	.330	.409	.502	139	37	11-4	.985	-2	99	104	2b149		4.6
1936	Det A★	154	641	144	227	60	12	15	116	83	4	13	.354	.431	.555	141	44	4-1	.974	16	103	116	2b142		4.8
1937	Det A★	144	564	133	209	42	1	14	96	90	1	25	.371	.458	.520	143	43	11-4	.986	-0	100	100	2b140		3.2
1938	Det A★	152	568	133	174	32	5	20	107	113	4	21	.306	.425	.486	121	23	14-1	.976	1	100	107	2b152		3.1
1939	Det A	118	406	86	132	29	6	16	86	68	1	16	.325	.423	.544	135	23	4-3	.972	-19	89	101	2b138		1.0
1940	†Det A	139	515	108	161	33	3	10	81	101	3	26	.313	.428	.447	116	18	10-0	.982	0	95	77	2b116		-0.8
1941	Det A	127	436	65	96	19	4	3	46	95	3	26	.220	.363	.303	71	-15	1-2	.976	-5	93	90	2b3		1.0
1942	Det A	45	45	6	12	0	0	1	7	4	1	3	.267	.365	.333	90	0	0-0	1.000	1	97	0	2b3		0.0
Total	19	2323	8860	1774	2839	574	146	184	1427	1186	50	372	.320	.404	.480	123	346	181-90	.976	27	99	100	2b2206,1b9,3b6		45.1

GEIER, PHIL Philip Louis "Little Phil" B11.3.1875 Washington DC D9.25.1967 Spokane WA BL/TR/5-7/145 d8.17 OF(14/167/98)

1896	Phi N	17	56	12	13	0	1	0	6	6		1	.232	.317	.268	56	-4	3	.813	-1	85	0	O12(2/0/10),2b3,C2		-0.4
1897	Phi N	92	316	51	88	6	2	1	35	56		19	.278	.392	.320	91	0	19	.932	-5	185	87	O45(2/3/40),2b37,S6,3b2		-0.4
1900	Cin N	30	113	18	29	1	4	0	10	7		1	.257	.306	.336	79	-4	3	.941	0	128	0	O27(0/9/18),3b2		-0.5
1901	Phi A	50	211	42	49	5	2	0	23	24		1	.232	.314	.275	61	-11	7	.934	-5	76	65	O50(6/14/30),S2/3		-1.7
	Mil A	11	39	4	7	2	1	0	1	5		0	.179	.273	.256	50	-1	4	1.000	5	276	574	O8C,3b3		-0.3
	Year	61	250	46	56	6	3	0	24	29		1	.224	.307	.272	60	-13	11	.941	-5	96	116	O58(6/22/30),3b4,S2		-2.0
1904	Bos N	149	580	70	141	17	2	1	27	56		1	.243	.314	.284	88	-6	18	.933	-4	120	198	O137(4/133/0),3b7,2b5/S		-1.7
Total	5	349	1315	197	327	30	12	2	102	154		10	7	.249	.332	.294	81	-28	54	.932	-15	125	136	O279C,2b45,3b15,S9,C2		-5.0

YEAR	TM LG	G	AB	R	H	2B	3B	HR	RBI	BB-IB	HP	SO	AVG	OBP	SLG	AOPS	ABR	SB-CS	FA	FR	RNG	THR	GAMES AT POSITION	DL	BFW

GEIGER, GARY Gary Merle B4.4.1937 Sand Ridge IL D4.24.1996 Murphysboro IL BL/TR/6-0/168* d4.15

1958	Cle A	91	195	28	45	3	1	6	27-0		3	43	.231	.330	.272	70	-7	2-2	.986	3	114	99	O53(1/44/8),3b2/P		-0.7
1959	Bos A	120	335	45	82	10	4	11	48	27-0		55	.245	.289	.397	83	-9	9-3	.989	1	100	100	O95(46/61/1)		-1.2
1960	Bos A	77	245	32	74	13	3	9	33	23-0	3	38	.302	.369	.490	126	9	2-2	1.000	5	104	230	O66(5/7/59)		
1961	Bos A	140	499	82	116	21	6	18	64	87-4	4	91	.232	.349	.407	99	1	3	102	173	O137C		67	1.1
1962	Bos A	131	466	67	116	18	4	16	54	67-3	2	66	.249	.344	.408	99	0	18-11	.987	-1	100	137	O129C		-0.4
1963	Bos A	121	399	67	105	13	5	16	44	36-2	3	63	.263	.327	.441	110	5	9-4	.984	8	115	196	O95(2/89/4),1b6		1.0
1964	Bos A	5	13	3	5	0	1	0	2	2-0		2	.385	.467	.538	170	1	0-0	1.000	0	111	0	O4(0/1/3)		0.1
1965	Bos A	24	45	5	9	3	0	1	2	13-1	0	10	.200	.379	.333	98	1	3-0	.970	0	117		O16(5/10/1)		0.1
1966	Atl N	78	126	23	33	5	3	4	10	21-1	1	29	.262	.367	.444	124	5	0-1	.982	-1	74	226	O49(5/33/15)	94	0.2
1967	Atl N	69	117	17	19	1	1	1	5	20-0		35	.162	.285	.214	45	-8	1-1	.980	-2	81	120	O38(6/26/7)		-1.2
1969	Hou N	93	125	19	28	4	1	0	16	24-2	1	34	.224	.351	.272	78	-2	2-1	.968	1	103	153	O65(47/5/14)		-0.3
1970	Hou N	5	4	0	1	0	0	0	0	0-0		0	.250	.250	.250	36	0	0-0	1.000	0	101	0	O2R		0.0
Total	12	954	2569	388	633	91	29	77	283	341-13	17	466	.246	.337	.394	98	-4	62-29	.986	17	102	155	O749(117/542/114),1b6,3b2/P	161	-1.1

GEIS, BILL William J. (b William J. Geiss) B7.15.1858 Chicago IL D9.18.1924 Chicago IL 5-10/164 d5.1 b-Emil

| 1884 | Det N | 75 | 283 | 22 | 50 | 11 | 4 | 2 | 16 | 6 | | 60 | .177 | .194 | .265 | 46 | -17 | | .862 | -7 | 95 | 86 | 2b73/OR1P | | -2.0 |

GEISS, EMIL Emil August B3.20.1867 Chicago IL D10.4.1911 Chicago IL BR/TR/5-11/170 d5.18 b-Bill ▲

| 1887 | Chi N | 3 | 12 | 0 | 1 | 0 | 0 | 0 | | | | 7 | .083 | .083 | .083 | -47 | -2 | 0 | .571 | -1 | 58 | 0 | /21P | | -0.3 |

GELBERT, CHARLIE Charles Magnus B1.26.1906 Scranton PA D1.13.1967 Easton PA BR/TR/5-11/170 d4.16 Col Lebanon Valley

1929	StL N	146	512	60	134	29	8	3	65	51		46	.262	.329	.367	71	-23	8	.948	8	101	100	S146		0.0
1930	†StL N	139	513	92	156	39	11	3	72	43	2	41	.304	.360	.441	89	-8	6	.947	5	97	104	S139		1.0
1931	†StL N	131	447	61	129	29	5	1	62	54		31	.289	.365	.383	97	1	7	.959	9	101	105	S130		1.9
1932	StL N	122	455	60	122	28	9	1	45	39	3	30	.268	.330	.376	87	-8	3	.945	-3	94	87	S122		-0.1
1935	StL N	62	168	24	49	7	2	2	21	17	0	18	.292	.357	.393	97	0	0	.978	1	103	187	3b37,S21,2b3		0.5
1936	StL N	93	280	33	64	15	2	3	27	25	0	26	.229	.292	.329	67	-13	2	.965	4	110	150	3b60,S28,2b8		-0.5
1937	Cin N	43	114	12	22	4	0	1	13	15	0	12	.193	.287	.254	51	-8	1	.968	-0	93	85	S37,2b9/3		-0.5
	Det A	20	47	4	4	2	0	0	1	4	0	11	.085	.157	.128	-27	-9	0-0	.934	-1	102	101	S16		-0.9
1939	Was A	68	188	36	48	7	5	3	29	30	1	11	.255	.361	.394	100	1	2-0	.970	-2	104	100	S28,3b20/2		0.1
1940	Was A	22	54	7	20	7	1	0	7	4	1	3	.370	.424	.537	157	5	0-0	.920	-4	81	42	S12,P2/2		0.1
	Bos A	30	91	9	18	2	0	0	8	8	0	16	.198	.263	.220	25	-10	0-0	.926	3	122	97	3b29/S		-0.6
	Year	52	145	16	38	9	1	0	15	12	1	19	.262	.323	.338	72	-6	0-0	.926	-1	122	97	3b29,S13,P2/2		-0.5
Total	8	876	2869	398	766	169	43	17	350	290	7	245	.267	.336	.374	82	-73	34-0	.951	22	98	98	S680,3b147,2b22,P2		1.0

GENINS, FRANK C. Frank "Frenchy" B11.2.1866 St.Louis MO D9.30.1922 St.Louis MO TR d7.5

1892	Cin N	35	110	12	20	4	0	0	2	12	0	12	.182	.262	.218	46	-7	7	.901	3	115	119	S17,O14(7/7/0),3b4		-0.4
	StL N	15	51	5	10	1	0	0	4	1	0	11	.196	.212	.216	31	-4	3	.821	-6	75	94	S14/OR		-0.9
	Year	50	161	17	30	5	0	0	1	13	0	23	.186	.247	.217	42	-11	10	.868	-3	97	108	S31,O15(7/7/1),3b4		-1.3
1895	Pit N	73	252	43	63	8	0	2	24	22	2	14	.250	.315	.306	64	-13	19	.931	-7	24		O29(14/3/12),3b16,2b16,S8,1b2		-1.7
1901	Cle A	26	101	15	23	5	0	0	9	8	0		.228	.284	.277	58	-5	3	.940	1	94	125	O26C		-0.5
Total	3	149	514	75	116	18	0	2	44	43	2	37	.226	.288	.272	56	-29	32	.934	-9	66	48	O70(21/36/13),S39,3b20,2b16,1b2		-3.5

GENOVESE, GEORGE George Michael B2.22.1922 Staten Island NY BL/TR/5-6.5/160 d4.29

| 1950 | Was A | 3 | 1 | 1 | 0 | 0 | 0 | 0 | 1 | | | 0 | .000 | .500 | .000 | 39 | 0 | 0-0 | — | 0 | | | /H | | 0.0 |

GENTILE, JIM James Edward "Diamond Jim" B6.3.1934 San Francisco CA BL/TL/6-4/215* d9.10

1957	Bro N	4	6	1	1	0	0	1	1	1-0	0	1	.167	.286	.667	133	0	0-0	1.000	-0	0	292	1b2		0.0
1958	LA N	12	30	0	4	1	0	0	4	4-1	0	6	.133	.235	.167	9	-4	0-0	.981	-1	48	145	1b8		-0.5
1960	Bal A★	138	384	67	112	17	0	21	98	68-5	7	72	.292	.403	.500	146	28	0-0	.993	-6	75	110	1b124		1.6
1961	Bal A★	148	486	96	147	25	2	46	141	96-5	11	106	.302	.423	.646	189	65	1-1	.989	-0	99	116	1b144		5.5
1962	Bal A★	152	545	80	137	21	1	33	87	77-16	6	101	.251	.346	.475	128	22	1-0	.988	4	110	103	1b150		1.7
1963	Bal A	145	496	65	123	16	1	24	72	76-9	6	101	.248	.353	.429	123	17	1-0	.995	8	118	114	1b143		1.8
1964	KC A	136	439	71	110	10	0	28	71	84-6	4	122	.251	.372	.465	128	20	0-0	.988	1	100	82	1b128		1.2
1965	KC A	38	118	14	29	5	0	10	22	9-1	1	26	.246	.305	.542	138	5	0-0	.981	-2	86	98	1b35		0.2
	Hou N	81	227	22	55	11	1	7	31	34-7	5	72	.242	.352	.392	118	7	0-0	.993	-0	98	85	1b68		0.3
1966	Hou N	49	144	16	35	6	1	7	18	21-3	4	39	.243	.355	.444	129	6	0-0	.989	2	113	86	1b43		0.6
	Cle A	33	47	2	6	1	0	2	4	5-1	0	18	.128	.212	.277	39	-4	0-0	.944	-0	105	76	1b9		-0.5
Total	9	936	2922	434	759	113	6	179	549	475-54	45	663	.260	.368	.486	137	162	3-1	.990	3	101	103	1b854		11.9

GENTILE, SAM Samuel Christopher B10.12.1916 Charlestown MA D5.4.1998 Everett MA BL/TR/5-11/180 d4.24 Mil 1944-45 Col St. Johns

| 1943 | Bos N | 8 | 4 | 1 | 1 | 0 | 0 | 0 | 1 | 0 | 0 | 0 | .250 | .400 | .500 | 162 | 0 | 0 | — | 0 | | | /H | | 0.0 |

GENTRY, HARVEY Harvey William B5.27.1926 Winston-Salem NC BL/TR/6-0/170 d4.14 b-Rufe

| 1954 | NY N | 5 | 4 | 0 | 1 | 0 | 0 | 0 | 1 | 1 | 0 | 0 | .250 | .400 | .250 | 73 | 0 | 0-0 | — | 0 | | | /H | | 0.0 |

GEORGE, ALEX Alex Thomas M. B9.27.1938 Kansas City MO BL/TR/5-11.5/170 d9.16

| 1955 | KC A | 5 | 10 | 0 | 1 | 0 | 0 | 0 | | 1-0 | 0 | 7 | .100 | .182 | .100 | -22 | -2 | 0-0 | .917 | -1 | 62 | 55 | S5 | | -0.3 |

GEORGE, GREEK Charles Peter B12.25.1912 Waycross GA D8.15.1999 Metairie LA BR/TR/6-2/200 d6.30 Col Oglethorpe

1935	Cle A	2	0	0	0	0	0	0	0	0	0	0	—	—	—		0	0-0	1.000	0	0	0	/C		0.0
1936	Cle A	23	77	3	15	3	0	0	5	9		16	.195	.279	.234	28	-9	0-0	.994	8	122	122	C22		0.1
1938	Bro N	7	20	0	4	0	1	0	2	0		4	.200	.200	.300	35	-2	0	1.000	1	72	170	C7		-0.1
1941	Chi N	35	64	4	10	2	0	0	6	2		10	.156	.182	.188	4	-6	0-0	.973	1	91	150	C18		-0.7
1945	Phi A	51	138	8	24	4	1	0	11	17		29	.174	.265	.217	41	-10	0-0	.972	-5	87	62	C46		-1.4
Total	5	118	299	15	53	9	2	0	24	28	0	59	.177	.248	.221	29	-29	0-0	.983	5	97	94	C94		-2.1

GERAGHTY, BEN Benjamin Raymond B7.19.1912 Jersey City NJ D6.18.1963 Jacksonville FL BR/TR/5-11/175 d4.17 Col Villanova

1936	Bro N	51	129	11	25	4	0	0	9	8		16	.194	.241	.225	26	-14	4	.922	-7	83	60	S31,2b9,3b5		-1.8
1943	Bos N	8	1	0	0	0	0	0	0	0		0	.000	.000	.000	-99	0	0	1.000	0	139	0	/2S3		0.0
1944	Bos N	11	16	3	4	0	0	0		1		2	.250	.294	.250	52	-1	0	1.000	-1	131	0	2b4,3b3		-0.2
Total	3	70	146	16	29	4	0	0	9	9	0	18	.199	.245	.226	28	-15	4	.922	-8	92	59	S32,2b14,3b9		-2.0

GERBER, CRAIG Craig Stuart B1.8.1959 Chicago IL BL/TR/6-0/175 [AnaA81 20/496] d4.11 Col Cal Poly-San Luis Obispo

| 1985 | Cal A | 65 | 91 | 8 | 24 | 1 | 2 | 0 | 6 | 2-0 | 0 | 3 | .264 | .277 | .319 | 63 | -5 | 0-3 | .970 | 9 | 128 | 145 | S53,3b9/2D | | 0.6 |

GERBER, WALLY Walter "Spooks" B8.18.1891 Columbus OH D6.19.1951 Columbus OH BR/TR/5-10/152 d9.23 Mil 1918

1914	Pit N	17	54	5	13	1	1	0	5	2		5	.241	.281	.296	75	-2	0	.921	1	115	122	S7		0.0
1915	Pit N	56	144	8	28	2	0	0	7	9	2	16	.194	.252	.208	40	-10	6-1	.930	1	97	72	3b23,S21,2b2		-0.7
1917	StL A	14	39	2	12	1	1	0	2	3	0	2	.308	.357	.385	131	1	1	.939	0	115	45	S12,2b2		0.2
1918	StL A	56	171	10	41	4	0	0	10	19		11	.240	.316	.263	77	-4	2	.922	-10	95	88	S56		-1.1
1919	StL A	140	462	43	105	14	6	1	37	49	5	36	.227	.308	.290	67	-20	1	.940	-9	99	82	S140		-2.0
1920	StL A	154	584	70	163	26	2	2	60	58	2	32	.279	.346	.341	80	-15	4-13	.939	7	106	104	S154		-0.1
1921	StL A	114	436	55	121	12	9	2	48	34	1	19	.278	.337	.360	73	-18	4-7	.943	-1	94	111	S113		-0.8
1922	StL A	153	604	81	161	22	8	1	51	52	1	34	.267	.326	.334	70	-27	6-4	.944	-1	94	127	S153		-1.1
1923	StL A	154	605	85	170	26	3	1	62	54	2	50	.281	.342	.339	75	-21	4-6	.950	7	97	111	S154		0.2
1924	StL A	148	496	61	135	20	4	0	55	43	9	34	.272	.341	.329	69	-22	4-5	.946	-6	94	107	S147		-1.3
1925	StL A	72	246	29	67	13	1	0	19	26	1	15	.272	.344	.333	69	-11	1-2	.949	5	104	94	S71		0.0
1926	StL A	131	411	37	111	8	0	0	42	40	5	22	.270	.339	.290	62	-22	0-2	.944	2	99	127	S129		-0.8
1927	StL A	142	438	44	98	13	9	0	45	35	2	25	.224	.284	.295	49	-35	3-6	.946	9	102	110	S141/3		-0.2
1928	StL A	6	18	1	5	1	0	0		1	0	3	.278	.316	.333	69	-1	0-0	.783	-2	91	158	S6		-1.2
	Bos A	104	300	21	64	6	1	0	28	32	0	31	.213	.289	.240	41	-25	6-1	.955	27	124	94	S103		1.2
	Year	110	318	22	69	7	1	0	28	33	0	34	.217	.291	.245	43	-26	6-1	.948	26	122	97	S109		1.0
1929	Bos A	61	91	6	15	3	1	0	5	8	0	12	.165	.232	.220	17	-12	1-0	.937	5	102	38	S30,2b22		-0.4
Total	15	1522	5099	558	1309	172	46	7	476	465	33	357	.257	.323	.313	67	-245	43-47	.943	36	100	106	S1447,2b26,3b24		-8.1

YEAR	TM LG	G	AB	R	H	2B	3B	HR	RBI	BB-IB	HP	SO	AVG	OBP	SLG	AOPS	ABR	SB-CS	FA	FR	RNG	THR	GAMES AT POSITION	DL	BFW

GEREN, BOB   Robert Peter   B9.22.1961 San Diego CA   BR/TR/6-3/221(200-228)   [SDN79 1/24]   d5.17 C3

1988	NY A	10	10	0	1	0	0	0	4	2-0	0	3	.100	.250	.100	2	-1	0-0	1.000	-0	124	0	C10		-0.1
1989	NY A	65	205	26	59	5	1	9	27	12-0	1	44	.288	.329	.454	120	4	0-0	.991	5	189	81	C60,D2		1.2
1990	NY A	110	277	21	59	7	0	8	31	13-1	5	73	.213	.259	.325	62	-15	0-0	.993	1	101	142	C107/D		-0.9
1991	NY A	64	128	7	28	3	0	2	12	9-0	0	31	.219	.270	.289	54	-8	0-1	.989	-3	87	98	C63		-0.9
1993	SD N	58	145	8	31	6	0	3	6	13-4	0	28	.214	.278	.317	59	-9	0-0	.993	1	80	133	C49/13		-0.5
Total	5	307	765	62	178	21	1	22	76	49-5	6	179	.233	.283	.349	74	-29	0-1	.992	3	116	115	C289,D3/31		-1.2

GERHARDT, JOE   John Joseph "Move Up Joe"   B2.14.1855 Washington DC   D3.11.1922 Middletown NY   BR/TR/6-0/160   d9.1 M2

1873	Was NA	13	57	6	12	3	0	0	9	0		6	.211	.211	.263	41	-4	0-1	.710	-4	91	123	S13		-0.6
1874	Bal NA	14	61	10	19	0	1	0	6	0		1	.311	.311	.344	111	1	0-0	.750	1	125	94	S14		0.1
1875	Mut NA	58	252	29	54	7	3	0	20	0		2	.214	.214	.266	62	-10	0-5	.753	0	109	67	3b47,2b13/SOL		-1.2
1876	Lou N	65	292	33	76	10	3	2	18	3		5	.260	.268	.336	85	-7		.944	4	133	83	1b54,2b5,S3,O2L,3b2		-0.5
1877	Lou N	59	250	41	76	6	5	1	35	5		8	.304	.318	.380	101	-2		.888	19	121	150	2b57/OCS1		1.7
1878	Cin N	60	259	46	77	7	2	0	28	7		14	.297	.316	.340	127	8		.906	6	102	118	2b60		1.6
1879	Cin N	79	313	22	62	12	3	1	39	3		19	.198	.206	.265	57	-14		.908	4	94	100	2b55,3b16,1b8/S		-0.7
1881	Det N	80	297	35	72	13	6	0	36	7		31	.242	.260	.327	80	-7		.908	6	94	153	2b79/3		0.2
1883	Lou AA	78	319	56	84	11	9	0		14			.263	.294	.354	116	7		.906	18	112	133	2b106		2.4
1884	Lou AA	106	404	39	89	7	8	0	40	13	5		.220	.254	.277	76	-10		.920	23	113	164	2b106		1.5
1885	NY N	112	399	43	62	12	2	0	33	24		47	.155	.203	.195	30	-30		.911	9	98	151	2b112		-1.6
1886	NY N	123	426	44	81	11	7	0	40	22		63	.190	.230	.249	45	-29	8	.924	9	96	105	2b123		-1.4
1887	NY N	1	4	0	0	0	0	0	0	0	0	0	.000	.000	.000	-99	-1	0	1.000	0	108	0	/3		-0.1
	NY AA	85	307	40	68	13	2	0	27	24	1		.221	.280	.277	58	-16	15	.896	9	104	116	2b84/3		-0.4
1890	Bro AA	99	369	34	75	10	4	2	40	30	3		.203	.270	.268	61	-19	9	.938	33	122	133	2b99		1.5
	StL AA	37	125	15	32	0	0	1	11	9	3		.256	.321	.280	68	-6	5	.955	6	101	64	2b20,3b17,M		0.1
	Year	136	494	49	107	10	4	3	51	39	7		.217	.283	.271	63	-25	14	.940	38	119	122	2b119,3b17		1.6
1891	Lou AA	2	6	0	0	0	0	0	0	1	0		.000	.143	.000	-59	-1	0	.833	-1	98	0	2b2		-0.2
Total	3 NA	85	370	45	85	10	4	0	35	0		8	.230	.230	.278	67	-13	0-6	.753	2	109	67	3b47,S28,2b13/OL		-1.7
Total	12	986	3770	448	854	112	51	7	347	162	13	187	.227	.261	.289	72	-127	37	.913	144	105	131	2b880,1b63,3b38,S5,O3(2/1/0)		4.1

GERHART, KEN   Harold Kenneth   B5.19.1961 Charleston SC   BR/TR/6-0/190*   [BalA82 5/130]   d9.14 Col Middle Tennessee

1986	Bal A	20	69	4	16	2	0	1	7	4-0	0	18	.232	.267	.304	58	-4	0-1	.971	-2	84	0	O20(6/14/0)		-0.7
1987	Bal A	92	284	41	69	10	2	14	34	17-0	1	53	.243	.286	.440	91	-5	9-2	.973	-4	93	64	O91(53/42/0)	53	-1.0
1988	Bal A	103	262	27	51	10	1	9	23	21-0	2	57	.195	.256	.344	69	-12	7-3	.975	-2	97	75	O93(30/57/10),D3	12	-1.5
Total	3	215	615	72	136	22	3	24	64	42-0	3	128	.221	.271	.384	78	-21	16-6	.974	-8	94	63	O204(89/113/10),D3	65	-3.2

GERKEN, GEORGE   George Herbert "Pickles"   B7.28.1903 Chicago IL   D10.23.1977 Arcadia CA   BR/TR/5-11.5/175   d4.19

1927	Cle A	6	14	1	3	0	0	0	2	1	0	3	.214	.267	.214	26	-2	0-0	.917	0	105	250	O5(2/3/0)		-0.1
1928	Cle A	38	115	16	26	7	2	0	9	12	1	22	.226	.305	.322	64	-6	3-4	.940	-1	99	89	O34(14/16/4)		-1.0
Total	2	44	129	17	29	7	2	0	11	13	1	25	.225	.301	.310	60	-8	3-4	.937	-1	100	106	O39(16/19/4)		-1.1

GERLACH, JOHNNY   John Glenn   B5.11.1917 Shullsburg WI   D8.28.1999 Madison WI   BR/TR/5-9/165   d9.3 Col Wisconsin-Madison

1938	Chi A	9	25	2	7	0	0	0	4	0		2	.280	.379	.280	66	-1	0-0	.949	1	97	197	S8		0.0
1939	Chi A	3	2	0	2	0	0	0	0	0		0	1.000	1.000	1.000	402	1	0-0	1.000	0	140	0	/3		0.1
Total	2	12	27	2	9	0	0	0	4	0		2	.333	.419	.333	89	0	0-0	.949	1	97	197	S8/3		0.1

GERMAN, ESTEBAN   Esteban (Guridi)   B1.26.1978 Haina, D.R.   BR/TR/5-10/180(165-180)   d5.21

2002	Oak A	9	35	4	7	0	0	0	4	4-0	1	11	.200	.300	.200	37	-3	1-0	.978	1	95	111	2b8		-0.2
2003	Oak A	5	4	0	1	0	0	0	1	0-0	0	1	.250	.250	.250	32	0	0-0	1.000	1	149	110	2b5		0.1
2004	Oak A	31	60	9	15	1	1	0	7	4-0	0	13	.250	.297	.300	57	-4	0-1	.935	2	91	159	3b15,2b10,D2	27	-0.2
2005	Tex A	5	4	3	3	1	0	0	1	0-0	0	1	.750	.750	1.000	347	1	2-0	.917	2	267	268	/23		0.4
Total	4	50	103	16	26	2	1	0	9	8-0	1	26	.252	.313	.291	60	-6	3-1	.980	6	129	145	2b24,3b16,D2	27	0.1

GERNERT, DICK   Richard Edward   B9.28.1928 Reading PA   BR/TR/6-3/210*   d4.16 C2 Col Temple

1952	Bos A	102	367	58	89	20	2	19	67	35	5	83	.243	.317	.463	107	2	4-1	.987	-1	97	113	1b99		-0.2
1953	Bos A	139	494	73	125	15	1	21	71	88	5	82	.253	.371	.415	106	7	0-7	.986	-2	97	107	1b136		-0.6
1954	Bos A	14	23	2	6	2	0	0	1	6	0	4	.261	.414	.348	99	0	1.000	-1	31	110	1b6		-0.1	
1955	Bos A	7	20	4	4	2	0	0	1	1-0	0	5	.200	.238	.300	40	-2	0-0	.974	-0	105	54	1b5		-0.2
1956	Bos A	106	306	53	89	11	0	16	68	56-1	2	57	.291	.399	.484	119	10	1-0	.985	4	81	146	O50L,1b37		0.9
1957	Bos A	99	316	45	75	13	3	14	58	39-3	3	62	.237	.324	.430	99	-1	1-1	.989	-0	107	123	1b71,O16L		-0.6
1958	Bos A	122	431	59	102	19	1	20	69	59-4	2	78	.237	.330	.425	100	0	2-0	.991	7	127	103	1b114		0.1
1959	Bos A	117	298	41	78	14	1	11	42	52-3	6	49	.262	.369	.426	113	7	1-2	.995	6	130	101	1b75,O25(21/0/7)		0.8
1960	Chi A	52	96	8	24	3	0	0	11	10-0	1	19	.250	.321	.281	67	-4	1-0	.987	3	144	103	1b18,O5L		-0.1
	Det A	21	50	6	15	4	0	1	5	4-0	0	5	.300	.352	.440	110	1	0-0	1.000	-1	65	160	1b13,O6L		0.1
1961	Det A	6	5	1	1	0	0	0	1	1-0	0	2	.200	.333	.800	187	1	0-0	—	0			/H		0.1
	†Cin N	40	63	4	19	1	0	0	7	7-1	0	9	.302	.361	.317	84	-1	0-0	.993	3	156	74	1b21		-0.3
1962	Hou N	10	24	1	5	0	0	0	1	5-0	0	7	.208	.345	.208	57	-1	0-0	1.000	-1	39	151	1b9		-0.3
Total	11	835	2493	357	632	104	8	103	402	363-12	17	462	.254	.351	.426	104	19	10-11	.990	16	112	108	1b604,O102(98/0/7)		-0.3

GERONIMO, CESAR   Cesar Francisco (Zorrilla)   B3.11.1948 Santa Cruz de El Seibo, D.R.   BL/TL/6-2/170(164-175)   d4.16

1969	Hou N	28	8	2	2	1	0	0	0	0-0	0	3	.250	.250	.375	74	0	0-0	1.000	-0	45	0	O9(4/1/4)		-0.1
1970	Hou N	47	42	5	9	0	0	2	2	2-0	1	5	.243	.293	.243	49	-3	0-0	.920	0	129	0	O26(12/5/10)		-0.3
1971	Hou N	94	82	13	18	2	2	1	6	5-0	0	31	.220	.264	.329	69	-4	2-2	.977	-1	76	50	O64(47/3/15)		-0.7
1972	†Cin N	120	255	32	70	9	7	4	29	24-3	3	74	.275	.344	.412	120	6	2-7	.982	3	102	179	O106(0/21/91)		0.3
1973	†Cin N	139	324	35	68	14	3	4	33	23-3	2	74	.210	.266	.309	62	-18	5-5	.992	4	106	135	O130(0/104/26)		-1.8
1974	Cin N	150	474	73	133	17	8	7	54	46-11	2	96	.281	.345	.395	109	5	9-5	.987	11	113	169	O145C		1.3
1975	†Cin N	148	501	69	129	25	5	6	53	48-8	4	97	.257	.327	.363	90	-7	13-5	.993	11	113	134	O148C		0.2
1976	†Cin N	149	486	59	149	24	11	2	49	56-13	6	95	.307	.382	.414	123	17	22-5	.985	-2	107	45	O146C		1.5
1977	Cin N	149	492	54	131	22	4	10	52	35-13	5	89	.266	.321	.388	87	-9	10-4	.992	7	113	102	O147C		-0.3
1978	Cin N	122	296	28	67	15	1	5	27	43-10	3	67	.226	.329	.334	86	-4	8-3	.981	2	108	77	O115C		-0.5
1979	†Cin N	123	356	30	85	17	4	4	38	37-11	2	56	.239	.312	.343	79	-10	1-1	.993	6	109	144	O118C		-0.4
1980	Cin N	103	145	16	37	5	0	2	9	14-3	0	24	.255	.319	.331	84	-3	2-1	1.000	0	102	72	O86C		-0.2
1981	†KC A	59	118	14	29	0	2	2	13	11-2	0	16	.246	.305	.331	85	-3	6-1	.980	3	114	141	O44(10/32/3)/D	24	0.4
1982	KC A	53	119	14	32	6	3	4	23	8-2	1	25	.269	.305	.471	111	1	2-0	1.000	3	132	106	O35(9/3/26)	18	-0.6
1983	KC A	38	87	2	18	4	2	0	4	2-0	2	13	.207	.242	.253	36	-8	0-1	.986	3	103	67	O25(4/2/19)	42	-1.5
Total	15	1522	3780	460	977	161	50	51	392	354-83	31	746	.258	.325	.368	93	-40	82-40	.988	48	109	113	O1376(87/1079/225)/D	42	-1.5

GERTENRICH, LOU   Louis Wilhelm   B5.4.1875 Chicago IL   D10.20.1933 Chicago IL   BR/TR/5-8/175   d9.15

1901	Mil A	2	3	1	1	0	0	0	0	0	0		.333	.333	.333	90	0	0	—	-0	0	0	/OR		0.0
1903	Pit N	1	3	0	0	0	0	0	0	0	0		.000	.000	.000	-97	-1	0	1.000	-0	0	0	/OR		-0.1
Total	2	3	6	1	1	0	0	0	0	0	0		.167	.167	.167	-6	-1	0	1.000	-0	0	0	O2R		-0.1

GERUT, JODY   Joseph Diego   B9.18.1977 Elmhurst IL   BL/TL/6-0/190*   [ColN98 2/71]   d4.26 Col Stanford

2003	Cle A	127	480	66	134	33	2	22	75	35-4	7	70	.279	.336	.494	116	10	4-5	.984	2	98	138	Q113(36/14/63),D11		0.6
2004	Cle A	134	481	72	121	31	5	11	51	54-4	7	59	.252	.334	.405	99	-3	13-6	.986	-1	100	83	O131(2/12/118),D	16	-0.8
2005	Cle A	44	138	12	38	9	1	1	12	18-1	0	14	.275	.357	.377	100	1	1-1	1.000	-4	80	49	O38(17/0/21),D3	40	-0.5
	Chi N	11	14	1	1	0	0	0	0	2-0	0	3	.071	.188	.143	-11	-2	0-0	1.000	1	219	0	O5(4/0/1)	53	-0.3
	Pit N	4	18	2	4	0	0	0	2	0-0	0	3	.222	.222	.278	30	-2	0-0	1.000	0	39	0	O4R		-0.5
	Year	15	32	3	5	0	0	0	2	2-0	0	6	.156	.206	.219	11	-4	0-0	1.000	-0	94	0	O9(4/0/5)		-0.5
Total	3	320	1131	153	298	73	8	34	140	109-9	14	149	.263	.334	.434	102	4	18-12	.987	-3	97	98	O291(59/26/207),D15	109	-1.2

GESSLER, DOC   Henry Homer "Brownie"   B12.23.1880 Greensburg PA   D12.24.1924 Greensburg PA   BL/TL/5-10/180   d4.23 M1 Col Ohio U.

1903	Det A	29	105	9	25	5	4	0	12	3	2		.238	.273	.362	92	-1	1	.974	-1	40	153	O28R		-0.3
	Bro N	49	154	20	38	8	5	0	18	17	12		.247	.366	.338	104	2	9	.984	-2	71	64	O43(0/2/41)		-0.1
1904	Bro N	104	341	41	99	18	4	2	28	30	14		.290	.365	.384	131	13	13	.920	3	144	64	O88(14/72/2)/12		1.3
1905	Bro N	126	431	48	125	17	4	3	46	38	14		.290	.366	.369	129	18	26	.973	2	115	89	1b107,O12(1/1/10)		1.8

YEAR	TM LG	G	AB	R	H	2B	3B	HR	RBI	BB-IB	HP	SO	AVG	OBP	SLG	AOPS	ABR	SB-CS	FA	FR	RNG	THR	GAMES AT POSITION	DL	BFW
1906	Bro N	9	33	3	8	1	2	0	4	3	1		.242	.324	.394	134	1	3	.946	1	153	89	1b9		0.2
	†Chi N	34	83	8	21	3	0	0	10	12	1		.253	.354	.289	95	0	4	1.000	1	193	0	O21(0/19/2)/1		0.0
	Year	43	116	11	29	4	2	0	14	15	2		.250	.346	.319	104	1	7	1.000	1	193	0	O21(0/19/2),1b10		0.2
1908	Bos A	128	435	55	134	13	14	3	63	51	11		.308	.394	.423	161	31	19	.950	-4	60	111	O126R		2.4
1909	Bos A	111	396	57	115	24	1	0	46	31	8		.290	.354	.356	122	11	16	.933	1	138	34	O109R		0.9
	Was A	17	54	10	13	2	1	0	8	12	3		.241	.406	.315	134	4	4	1.000	-0	54	226	O16R/1		0.3
	Year	128	450	67	128	26	2	0	54	43	11		.284	.361	.351	123	15	20	.940	1	128	58	O125R/1		1.2
1910	Was A	145	487	58	126	17	12	2	50	62	16		.259	.361	.355	131	20	18	.953	-1	87	126	O144R		1.4
1911	Was A	128	450	65	127	19	5	4	78	74	20		.282	.406	.373	120	19	29	.943	-8	78	96	O126(2/0/124)/1		0.4
Total	8	880	2969	370	831	127	50	14	363	333	92		.280	.370	.370	128	118	142	.945	-9	95	91	O713(17/94/602),1b120/2		8.3

GETTIG, CHARLIE   Charles Henry B12.1870 Baltimore MD D4.11.1935 Baltimore MD BR/5-10/172 d8.5 OF(3/1/21) ▲

YEAR	TM LG	G	AB	R	H	2B	3B	HR	RBI	BB-IB	HP	SO	AVG	OBP	SLG	AOPS	ABR	SB-CS	FA	FR	RNG	THR	GAMES AT POSITION	DL	BFW
1896	NY N	6	9	1	3	0	0	0		0			.333	.333	.444	107	1	0	1.000	0	144	0	P4		0.0
1897	NY N	22	75	8	15	6	0	0	12	6	2		.200	.277	.280	49	-5	3	.556	-6	37	0	3b7,2b6,O3L,S3,P3		-1.0
1898	NY N	64	196	30	49	6	2	0	26	15	2		.250	.310	.301	78	-6	5	.833	-4	56	0	O21(0/1/20),P17,2b12,S9,3b4,1b2/C		-0.8
1899	NY N	34	97	7	24	3	0	0	9	7	1		.247	.305	.278	63	-5	4	.833	-3	99	0	P18,3b8,2b3,1b3/OR		-0.8
Total	4	126	377	48	91	16	2	0	47	28	5		0	.241	.302	.294	68	-15	12	.879	-13	116	43	P42,O25R,2b21,3b19,S12,1b5/C		-2.2

GETTINGER, TOM   Lewis Thomas Leyton (b Lewis Thomas Leyton Gittinger) B12.11.1868 Frederick MD D7.26.1943 Pensacola FL BL/TL/5-10/180 d9.21

YEAR	TM LG	G	AB	R	H	2B	3B	HR	RBI	BB-IB	HP	SO	AVG	OBP	SLG	AOPS	ABR	SB-CS	FA	FR	RNG	THR	GAMES AT POSITION	DL	BFW
1889	StL AA	4	16	2	7	0	0	0		2	0	1	.438	.500	.625	194	2	0	.750	-1	0	0	O4(1/3/0)		0.0
1890	StL AA	58	227	31	54	7	5	3	30	20	1		.238	.302	.352	81	-7	9	.886	-4	88	52	O58L		-1.1
1895	Lou N	63	260	28	70	11	5	2	32	8	2	15	.269	.296	.373	77	-10	5	.910	-4	54	42	O63(0/34/29),P2		-1.4
Total	3	125	503	61	131	18	10	6	64	30	3	16	.260	.306	.372	82	-15	14	.897	-9	68	45	O125(59/37/29),P2		-2.5

GETTIS, BYRON   Byron Earl B3.13.1980 Centreville IL BR/TR/6-0/240 d5.27

YEAR	TM LG	G	AB	R	H	2B	3B	HR	RBI	BB-IB	HP	SO	AVG	OBP	SLG	AOPS	ABR	SB-CS	FA	FR	RNG	THR	GAMES AT POSITION	DL	BFW
2004	KC A	21	39	7	7	1	1	0		8-1	1	14	.179	.327	.256	57	-2	0-1	.930	2	122	211	O21(11/0/10)		-0.2

GETTMAN, JAKE   Jacob John B10.25.1875 Frank, Russia D10.4.1956 Denver CO BB/TL/5-11/185 d8.20

YEAR	TM LG	G	AB	R	H	2B	3B	HR	RBI	BB-IB	HP	SO	AVG	OBP	SLG	AOPS	ABR	SB-CS	FA	FR	RNG	THR	GAMES AT POSITION	DL	BFW
1897	Was N	36	143	28	45	7	3	3	29	7	3		.315	.359	.469	118	3	8	.981	-2	63	0	O36R		0.0
1898	Was N	142	567	75	157	16	5	5	47	29	6		.277	.319	.349	92	-8	32	.926	2	96	80	O139(6/19/114),1b3		-1.2
1899	Was N	19	62	5	13	1	0	0	2	4	0		.210	.258	.226	33	-6	4	1.000	0	53	0	O16(6/10/0),1b2		-0.6
Total	3	197	772	108	215	24	8	8	78	40	9		.278	.322	.361	92	-11	44	.941	1	87	60	O191(12/29/150);1b5		-1.8

GETZ, GUS   Gustave "Gee-Gee" B8.3.1889 Pittsburgh PA D5.28.1969 Red Bank NJ BR/TR/5-11/165 d8.15

YEAR	TM LG	G	AB	R	H	2B	3B	HR	RBI	BB-IB	HP	SO	AVG	OBP	SLG	AOPS	ABR	SB-CS	FA	FR	RNG	THR	GAMES AT POSITION	DL	BFW
1909	Bos N	40	148	6	33	2	0	0	9	1	0		.223	.228	.236	42	-11	2	.934	3	122	65	3b36,2b2,S2		-0.8
1910	Bos N	54	144	14	28	0	1	0	7	6	1	10	.194	.232	.208	27	-14	2	.915	5	117	141	3b22,2b13,O8(4/1/3),S4		-1.0
1914	Bro N	55	210	13	52	8	1	0	20	2	0	15	.248	.255	.295	62	-11	9	.949	12	123	159	3b55		0.3
1915	Bro N	130	477	39	123	10	5	2	46	8	3	14	.258	.275	.312	76	-16	19-15	.951	6	113	77	3b128,S2		-0.8
1916	†Bro N	40	96	9	21	1	2	0	8	0	0	5	.219	.219	.271	49	-6	9	.913	-3	81	0	3b20,S7,1b3		-1.0
1917	Cin N	7	14	2	4	0	0	0	3	0	0	0	.286	.412	.286	121	1	0	.875	-2	40	124	2b4,3b3		-0.2
1918	Cle A	6	15	2	2	1	0	0	4	0	0	1	.133	.350	.200	60	0	1	.941	-0	98	0	3b5		-0.1
	Pit N	7	10	0	2	0	0	0	0	0	0	1	.200	.200	.200	21	-1	0	.875	-0	96	334	3b2		-0.1
Total	7	339	1114	85	265	22	9	2	93	24	5	46	.238	.257	.279	60	-58	41-15	.942	21	114	93	3b271,2b19,S15,O8(4/1/3),1b3		-3.7

GEYGAN, CHAPPIE   James Edward B6.3.1903 Ironton OH D3.15.1966 Columbus OH BR/TR/5-11/170 d7.16

YEAR	TM LG	G	AB	R	H	2B	3B	HR	RBI	BB-IB	HP	SO	AVG	OBP	SLG	AOPS	ABR	SB-CS	FA	FR	RNG	THR	GAMES AT POSITION	DL	BFW
1924	Bos A	33	82	7	21	5	4	0	2	16	0		.256	.307	.366	73	-4	0-2	.952	2	99	94	S32		0.0
1925	Bos A	3	11	0	2	0	0	0	0	0	0	2	.182	.182	.182	-8	-2	0-0	.813	-2	69	55	S3		-0.3
1926	Bos A	4	10	0	3	0	0	0	1	0		1	.300	.364	.300	77	0	0-0	.800	-1	89	0	3b3		-0.1
Total	3	40	103	7	26	5	2	0	4	5	2	19	.252	.300	.340	65	-6	0-2	.938	-0	96	90	S35,3b3		-0.4

GHARRITY, PATSY   Edward Patrick B3.13.1892 Parnell IA D10.10.1966 Beloit WI BR/TR/5-10/170 d5.16 C7

YEAR	TM LG	G	AB	R	H	2B	3B	HR	RBI	BB-IB	HP	SO	AVG	OBP	SLG	AOPS	ABR	SB-CS	FA	FR	RNG	THR	GAMES AT POSITION	DL	BFW
1916	Was A	39	92	8	21	5	1	0	9	8	1	18	.228	.297	.304	81	-2	1	1.000	-2	103	107	C16,1b16		-0.4
1917	Was A	76	176	15	50	5	1	0	18	14	1	18	.284	.337	.313	99	0	7	.980	1	116	84	1b46,C5/OR		0.0
1918	Was A	4	4	0	1	1	0	0	2	0		1	.250	.250	.500	129	0	0	—	0		0	/H		0.0
1919	Was A	111	347	35	94	19	4	2	43	25	3	39	.271	.325	.366	95	-3	4	.969	-0	88	98	C60,O33(30/2/1),1b7		0.0
1920	Was A	131	428	51	105	18	3	3	44	37	1	52	.245	.307	.322	69	-20	6-5	.965	-2	89	126	C121,1b7/OL		-1.2
1921	Was A	121	387	62	120	19	8	7	55	45	3	44	.310	.386	.455	120	12	4-3	.977	6	137	104	C115		2.3
1922	Was A	96	273	40	70	16	6	5	45	36	4	30	.256	.351	.414	104	2	3-3	.981	5	97	122	C87		1.1
1923	Was A	93	251	26	52	9	4	3	33	22	2	27	.207	.276	.311	57	-17	6-2	.986	1	97	114	C35,1b33		-1.5
1929	Was A	3	2	0	0	0	0	0	0	1	0	2	.000	.333	.000	-7	0	0-0	—	0		0	/H		0.0
1930	Was A	2	1	0	0	0	0	0	0	0	0		.000	.000	.000	-99	0	0-0	1.000	0	0	0	/1		0.0
Total	10	676	1961	237	513	92	26	20	249	188	14	231	.262	.331	.366	90	-28	32-13	.974	8	105	114	C439,1b110,O35(31/2/2)		0.3

GIAMBI, JASON   Jason Gilbert B1.8.1971 W.Covina CA BL/TR/6-3/235(200-235) [OakA92 2/58] d5.8 b-Jeremy Col Cal St.-Long Beach

YEAR	TM LG	G	AB	R	H	2B	3B	HR	RBI	BB-IB	HP	SO	AVG	OBP	SLG	AOPS	ABR	SB-CS	FA	FR	RNG	THR	GAMES AT POSITION	DL	BFW
1995	Oak A	54	176	27	45	7	0	6	25	28-0	3	31	.256	.364	.398	104	2	2-1	.960	0	100	88	3b30,1b26,D2		0.0
1996	Oak A	140	536	84	156	40	1	20	79	51-3	5	95	.291	.355	.481	111	9	0-1	.993	5	110	95	1b45,O45(44/0/1),3b39,D12		0.7
1997	Oak A	142	519	66	152	41	2	20	81	55-3	6	89	.293	.362	.495	123	18	0-1	.982	-2	80	124	O68L,1b51,D25		0.7
1998	Oak A	153	562	92	166	28	0	27	110	81-7	5	102	.295	.384	.489	128	25	2-2	.990	-11	76	100	1b146,D7		0.1
1999	Oak A	158	575	115	181	36	1	33	123	105-6	7	106	.315	.422	.553	152	50	1-1	.995	-16	53	103	1b142,D15/3		1.9
2000	†Oak A★	152	510	108	170	29	1	43	137	137-6	9	96	.333	.476	.647	185	77	2-0	.995	-8	74	101	1b124,D24		5.1
2001	†Oak A★	154	520	109	178	47	2	38	120	129-24	13	83	.342	.477	.660	196	84	2-0	.992	-4	89	107	1b136,D17		6.3
2002	†NY A★	155	560	120	176	34	1	41	122	109-4	15	112	.314	.435	.598	173	66	2-2	.995	-7	64	77	1b92,D63		4.5
2003	NY A★	156	535	97	134	25	0	41	107	129-9	21	140	.250	.412	.527	148	45	2-1	.995	-13	35	94	1b85,D69		1.9
2004	NY A	80	264	33	55	9	0	12	40	47-1	8	62	.208	.342	.379	89	-3	0-1	.990	-7	47	47	1b47,D28	65	-1.5
2005	†NY A	139	417	74	113	14	0	32	87	108-5	19	109	.271	.440	.535	157	42	0-0	.988	-9	46	90	1b78,D60		2.3
Total	11	1483	5174	925	1526	310	8	313	1031	979-68	111	1025	.295	.413	.539	148	415	13-10	.992	-73	69	98	1b972,D322,O113(112/0/1),3b70	65	22.0

GIAMBI, JEREMY   Jeremy Dean B9.30.1974 San Jose CA BL/TL/6-0/200(185-218) [KCA96 6/169] d9.1 b-Jason Col Cal St.-Fullerton

YEAR	TM LG	G	AB	R	H	2B	3B	HR	RBI	BB-IB	HP	SO	AVG	OBP	SLG	AOPS	ABR	SB-CS	FA	FR	RNG	THR	GAMES AT POSITION	DL	BFW
1998	KC A	18	58	6	13	4	0	2	8	11-0	0	9	.224	.343	.397	89	-1	0-1	1.000	0	82	191	O9L,D7		-0.1
1999	KC A	90	288	34	82	13	1	9	34	40-5	3	67	.285	.373	.368	88	-4	0-1	.991	-4	92	94	D48,1b26,O5L	40	-1.1
2000	†Oak A	104	260	42	66	10	2	10	50	32-2	3	61	.254	.338	.423	94	-3	0-0	.966	-2	91	99	O55(6/0/49),D21,1b15	16	-0.8
2001	†Oak A	124	371	64	105	26	0	12	57	63-1	4	83	.283	.391	.450	121	15	0-1	.943	-9	62	38	D60,O47(11/0/37),1b10	24	-0.1
2002	Oak A	42	157	26	43	7	0	8	17	27-0	1	40	.274	.390	.471	129	8	0-0	.984	-4	84	0	O40L,D2		0.2
	Phi N	82	156	32	38	10	0	12	28	52-2	1	54	.244	.435	.538	170	18	1-0	.989	-4	76	119	1b21,O20(2/0/18),D8		1.2
2003	Bos A	50	127	15	25	5	0	5	15	26-0	2	42	.197	.342	.354	81	-3	1-0	.944	0	113	0	D30,O11(9/0/2)	83	-0.4
Total	6	510	1417	219	372	75	3	52	209	251-10	16	356	.263	.377	.430	110	30	1-3	.963	-23	81	48	O187(82/0/106),D176,1b72	163	-1.1

GIANNELLI, RAY   Raymond John B2.5.1966 Brooklyn NY BL/TR/6-0/195* [TorA88 38/992] d5.4 Col New York Tech

YEAR	TM LG	G	AB	R	H	2B	3B	HR	RBI	BB-IB	HP	SO	AVG	OBP	SLG	AOPS	ABR	SB-CS	FA	FR	RNG	THR	GAMES AT POSITION	DL	BFW
1991	Tor A	9	24	2	4	1	0	0	5-0		9	.167	.310	.208	45	-2	1-0	.923	-2	78	149	3b9		-0.4
1995	StL N	9	11	0	1	0	0	0	3-0		4	.091	.286	.091	5	-1	0-0	1.000	0	123	0	1b2,O2(1/0/1)		-0.2
Total	2	18	35	2	5	1	0	0	8-0		13	.143	.302	.171	32	-3	1-0	.923	-3	78	149	3b9,O2(1/0/1),1b2		-0.6

GIANNINI, JOE   Joseph Francis B9.8.1888 San Francisco CA D9.26.1942 San Francisco CA BL/TR/5-8/155 d8.7 Col San Francisco

YEAR	TM LG	G	AB	R	H	2B	3B	HR	RBI	BB-IB	HP	SO	AVG	OBP	SLG	AOPS	ABR	SB-CS	FA	FR	RNG	THR	GAMES AT POSITION	DL	BFW
1911	Bos A	2	2	0	1	0	0	0	0	0			.500	.500	1.000	317	1	0	.500	-1	108	0	/S		0.0

GIARRATANO, TONY   Anthony James B11.29.1982 Queens NY BB/TR/6-0/180 d6.1 Col Tulane

YEAR	TM LG	G	AB	R	H	2B	3B	HR	RBI	BB-IB	HP	SO	AVG	OBP	SLG	AOPS	ABR	SB-CS	FA	FR	RNG	THR	GAMES AT POSITION	DL	BFW
2005	Det A	15	42	4	6	1	0	0	4	5-0	0	7	.143	.234	.167	21	-5	1-0	.949	-1	109	63	S13		-0.4

GIBBONS, JAY   Jay Jonathan B3.2.1977 Rochester MI BL/TL/6-0/200* [TorA98 14/411] d4.6 Col Cal St.-Los Angeles

YEAR	TM LG	G	AB	R	H	2B	3B	HR	RBI	BB-IB	HP	SO	AVG	OBP	SLG	AOPS	ABR	SB-CS	FA	FR	RNG	THR	GAMES AT POSITION	DL	BFW
2001	Bal A	73	225	27	53	10	0	15	36	17-0	4	39	.236	.301	.480	107	1	0-1	1.000	2	114	183	O28L,D28,1b7	64	0.0
2002	Bal A	136	490	71	121	29	1	28	69	45-3	2	66	.247	.311	.482	113	8	1-3	.994	-2	97	105	O92R,1b30,D12		-0.3
2003	Bal A	160	625	80	173	39	2	23	100	49-11	3	89	.277	.330	.456	106	5	0-1	.983	-2	97	105	O144R,1b13,D5		-0.6
2004	Bal A	97	346	36	85	14	1	10	47	29-0	5	64	.246	.303	.379	78	-12	0-1	.984	1	89	140	O66R,D16,1b14	61	-1.6
2005	Bal A	139	488	72	135	33	3	26	79	28-3	1	56	.277	.317	.516	116	10	0-0	.986	3	106	165	O71R,D42,1b22		0.5
Total	5	605	2174	286	567	125	7	102	331	168-17	11	314	.261	.315	.466	105	12	2-6	.988	1	98	122	O401(28/0/373),D103,1b86	125	-2.0

GIBBONS, JOHN John Michael B6.8.1962 Great Falls MT BR/TR/5-11/187* [NYN80 1/24] d4.11 M2/C3

YEAR	TM LG	G	AB	R	H	2B	3B	HR	RBI	BB-IB	HP	SO	AVG	OBP	SLG	AOPS	ABR	SB-CS	FA	FR	RNG	THR	GAMES AT POSITION	DL	BFW
1984	NY N	10	31	1	2	0	0	0	1	3-1	1	11	.065	.171	.065	-32	-6	0-0	.983	-1	85	144	C9	33	-0.7
1986	NY N	8	19	4	9	4	0	1	1	3-1	0	5	.474	.545	.842	283	5	0-0	1.000	-0	110	39	C8		0.5
Total 2		18	50	5	11	4	0	1	2	6-2	1	16	.220	.316	.360	89	-1	0-0	.990	-1	95	102	C17	33	-0.2

GIBBS, JAKE Jerry Dean B11.7.1938 Grenada MS BL/TR/6-0/185* d9.11 Col U. of Mississippi

YEAR	TM LG	G	AB	R	H	2B	3B	HR	RBI	BB-IB	HP	SO	AVG	OBP	SLG	AOPS	ABR	SB-CS	FA	FR	RNG	THR	GAMES AT POSITION	DL	BFW
1962	NY A	2	0	0	0	0	0	0	0	0-0	0	0					0	0-0	—	-0	0	0	/3		0.0
1963	NY A	4	8	1	2	0	0	0	0	0-0	0	1	.250	.250	.250	41	-1	0-0	1.000	-1	0	0	/C		-0.2
1964	NY A	3	6	1	1	0	0	0	0	0-0	0	2	.167	.167	.167	-7	-1	0-0	1.000	-1	0	0	C2		-0.1
1965	NY A	37	68	6	15	1	0	2	7	4-0	1	20	.221	.267	.324	70	-3	0-0	.991	0	94	131	C21		-0.2
1966	NY A	62	182	19	47	6	0	3	20	19-2	0	16	.258	.327	.341	96	-1	5-2	.988	6	172	96	C54	35	0.9
1967	NY A	116	374	33	87	7	1	4	25	28-1	1	57	.233	.291	.289	75	-12	7-6	.975	-1	97	129	C99		-0.9
1968	NY A	124	423	31	90	12	3	3	29	27-5	6	68	.213	.270	.277	68	-17	9-8	.991	6	165	91	C121		-0.7
1969	NY A	71	219	18	49	9	2	0	18	23-9	0	30	.224	.294	.283	65	-10	3-4	.990	8	170	68	C66		0.0
1970	NY A	49	153	23	46	9	2	8	26	7-1	1	14	.301	.331	.542	144	8	2-0	.987	2	171	62	C44		1.2
1971	NY A	70	206	23	45	9	0	5	21	12-1	1	23	.218	.270	.335	74	-8	2-2	.986	5	143	37	C51		-1.1
Total 10		538	1639	157	382	53	8	25	146	120-19	15	231	.233	.289	.321	80	-45	28-22	.986	15	146	89	C459/3	35	-1.1

GIBRALTER, STEVE Stephan Benson B10.9.1972 Dallas TX BR/TR/6-0/190* [CinN90 6/162] d6.1 [DL 1997 Cin N 181]

YEAR	TM LG	G	AB	R	H	2B	3B	HR	RBI	BB-IB	HP	SO	AVG	OBP	SLG	AOPS	ABR	SB-CS	FA	FR	RNG	THR	GAMES AT POSITION	DL	BFW
1995	Cin N	4	3	0	1	0	0	0	0	0-0	0	0	.333	.333	.333	76	0	0-0	1.000	0	91	0	O2C	1	0.0
1996	Cin N	2	2	0	0	0	0	0	0	0-0	0	2	.000	.000	.000	-98	-1	0-0	.000	-1	0	0	O2(1/1/0)		-0.1
Total 2		6	5	0	1	0	0	0	0	0-0	0	2	.200	.200	.200	6	-1	0-0	.500	-1	40	0	O4(1/3/0)	182	-0.1

GIBSON, CHARLIE Charles Ellsworth "Gibby" B11.17.1879 Sharon PA D11.22.1954 Sharon PA BR/TR/6-0/160 d9.23

YEAR	TM LG	G	AB	R	H	2B	3B	HR	RBI	BB-IB	HP	SO	AVG	OBP	SLG	AOPS	ABR	SB-CS	FA	FR	RNG	THR	GAMES AT POSITION	DL	BFW
1905	StL A	1	3	0	0	0	0	0	0	0-0	0	0	.000	.000	.000	-99	-1	0	1.000	-0	75	166	/C		-0.1

GIBSON, CHARLIE Charles Griffin B11.21.1899 LaGrange GA D12.18.1990 LaGrange GA BR/TR/5-8/160 d5.30 Col Auburn-Montgomery

YEAR	TM LG	G	AB	R	H	2B	3B	HR	RBI	BB-IB	HP	SO	AVG	OBP	SLG	AOPS	ABR	SB-CS	FA	FR	RNG	THR	GAMES AT POSITION	DL	BFW
1924	Phi A	12	15	1	2	0	0	0	0	0-0	0	0	.133	.235	.133	-2	-2	0	.870	-1	100	128	C12		-0.3

GIBSON, DERRICK Derrick Lamont B2.5.1975 Winter Haven FL BR/TR/6-2/244* [ColN93 13/380] d9.8

YEAR	TM LG	G	AB	R	H	2B	3B	HR	RBI	BB-IB	HP	SO	AVG	OBP	SLG	AOPS	ABR	SB-CS	FA	FR	RNG	THR	GAMES AT POSITION	DL	BFW
1998	Col N	7	21	4	9	1	0	0	2	1-0	1	4	.429	.478	.476	126	1	0-0	.929	1	100	523	O7L		0.2
1999	Col N	10	28	2	5	1	0	2	6	0-0	1	7	.179	.207	.429	44	-3	0-0	.944	2	112	447	O10R		-0.1
Total 2		17	49	6	14	2	0	2	8	1-0	2	11	.286	.327	.449	78	-2	0-0	.938	3	106	482	O17(7/0/10)		0.1

GIBSON, FRANK Frank Gilbert B9.27.1890 Omaha NE D4.27.1961 Austin TX BB/TR (BL 1913)/6-0.5/172 d4.22

YEAR	TM LG	G	AB	R	H	2B	3B	HR	RBI	BB-IB	HP	SO	AVG	OBP	SLG	AOPS	ABR	SB-CS	FA	FR	RNG	THR	GAMES AT POSITION	DL	BFW
1913	Det A	23	57	8	8	1	0	0	2	3	1	9	.140	.197	.158	4	-7	2	.914	-6	78	82	C19,O2R		-1.2
1921	Bos N	63	125	14	33	5	4	2	13	3	2	17	.264	.292	.416	99	-3	0-0	.979	1	113	104	C41		0.0
1922	Bos N	66	164	15	49	7	2	3	20	10	0	27	.299	.339	.421	99	-1	4-1	.981	-0	98	99	C29,1b20		0.0
1923	Bos N	41	50	13	15	1	0	0	5	7	1	7	.300	.386	.320	92	0	0-2	.923	-1	89	64	C20		-0.2
1924	Bos N	90	229	25	71	15	6	1	30	10	1	23	.310	.342	.441	113	3	1-1	.972	-2	83	118	C46,1b10,3b2		0.4
1925	Bos N	104	316	36	88	23	5	2	50	15	1	28	.278	.313	.402	89	-2	3-3	.968	-2	113	85	C86,1b2		-0.2
1926	Bos N	24	47	3	16	4	0	0	7	4	1	6	.340	.392	.426	132	2	0	1.000	1	85	151	C13		0.4
1927	Bos N	60	167	7	37	1	2	0	19	3	0	10	.222	.235	.251	33	-17	2	.965	-2	100	125	C47		-1.7
Total 8		471	1155	121	317	57	19	8	146	55	5	127	.274	.310	.377	86	-29	12-7	.967	-11	100	102	C301,1b32,3b2,O2R		-2.5

GIBSON, GEORGE George C. "Moon" B7.22.1880 London ON, Can. D1.25.1967 London ON, Can. BR/TR/5-11.5/190 d7.2 M7/C3

YEAR	TM LG	G	AB	R	H	2B	3B	HR	RBI	BB-IB	HP	SO	AVG	OBP	SLG	AOPS	ABR	SB-CS	FA	FR	RNG	THR	GAMES AT POSITION	DL	BFW
1905	Pit N	46	135	14	24	2	2	2	14	15	2		.178	.270	.267	59	-7	2	.966	4	129	90	C44		0.1
1906	Pit N	81	259	8	46	6	1	0	20	16	0		.178	.225	.208	34	-20	1	.971	-1	118	94	C81		-1.5
1907	Pit N	113	382	28	84	8	7	3	35	18	3		.220	.261	.301	75	-13	2	.972	7	132	91	C109/1		0.5
1908	Pit N	143	486	37	111	19	4	2	45	19	2		.228	.260	.296	78	-14	4	.973	-2	124	71	C140		-0.2
1909 †	Pit N	150	510	42	135	25	9	2	52	44	2		.265	.326	.361	104	2	9	.983	17	148	91	C150		3.7
1910	Pit N	143	482	53	125	22	6	3	44	47	6	31	.259	.333	.349	93	-4	7	.984	10	123	90	C143		2.1
1911	Pit N	100	311	32	65	12	2	0	19	29	1	16	.209	.281	.260	50	-21	3	.979	6	116	92	C98		-0.7
1912	Pit N	95	300	23	72	14	3	2	35	20	1	16	.240	.290	.327	69	-14	0	.990	2	132	86	C94		-0.3
1913	Pit N	48	118	6	33	4	2	0	12	10	1	8	.280	.341	.347	101	0	2-1	.986	-5	84	58	C48		-0.2
1914	Pit N	102	274	19	78	9	5	0	30	27	5	27	.285	.359	.354	117	7	4	.974	-4	108	94	C101		1.1
1915	Pit N	120	351	23	88	15	6	1	30	31	1	25	.251	.313	.336	98	-1	5-2	.965	2	90	95	C118		1.3
1916	Pit N	33	84	4	17	2	0	0	4	3	1	7	.202	.239	.274	57	-5	0	.989	3	94	118	C29		0.1
1917	NY N	35	82	1	14	3	0	0	5	7	0	2	.171	.236	.207	38	-6	1	.986	1	107	69	C35		-0.3
1918	NY N	4	2	0	1	1	0	0	0	0	0		.500	.500	1.000	360	1	0	1.000	-0	56	230	C4		0.1
Total 14		1213	3776	295	893	142	49	15	345	286	26	132	.236	.295	.312	81	-95	40-3	.977	39	121	88	C1194/1		5.8

GIBSON, RUSS John Russell B5.6.1939 Fall River MA BR/TR/6-1/195* d4.14

YEAR	TM LG	G	AB	R	H	2B	3B	HR	RBI	BB-IB	HP	SO	AVG	OBP	SLG	AOPS	ABR	SB-CS	FA	FR	RNG	THR	GAMES AT POSITION	DL	BFW
1967 †	Bos A	49	138	8	28	7	0	1	15	12-3	0	31	.203	.263	.275	56	-7	0-0	1.000	-3	168	88	C48		-0.9
1968	Bos A	76	231	15	52	11	1	3	20	8-1	0	38	.225	.247	.320	68	-9	1-2	.983	-2	82	104	C74/1	22	-1.0
1969	Bos A	85	287	21	72	9	1	3	27	15-1	1	25	.251	.289	.321	68	-13	1-1	.979	-7	108	122	C83		-1.7
1970	SF N	24	69	3	16	6	0	0	6	7-1	0	12	.232	.303	.319	67	-3	0-0	.971	-3	67	139	C23		-0.3
1971	SF N	25	57	2	11	1	1	1	7	2-0	0	13	.193	.220	.298	46	-4	0-0	.965	-3	170	78	C22		-0.7
1972	SF N	5	12	0	2	0	0	0	3	0-0	0	4	.167	.167	.333	38	-1	0-0	1.000	-0	30	87	C5		-0.3
Total 6		264	794	49	181	34	4	8	78	44-6	1	123	.228	.267	.311	64	-37	2-3	.983	-19	111	108	C255/1	22	-4.9

GIBSON, KIRK Kirk Harold B5.28.1957 Pontiac MI BL/TL/6-3/215(210-225) [DetA78 1/12] d9.8 C3 Col Michigan St.

YEAR	TM LG	G	AB	R	H	2B	3B	HR	RBI	BB-IB	HP	SO	AVG	OBP	SLG	AOPS	ABR	SB-CS	FA	FR	RNG	THR	GAMES AT POSITION	DL	BFW
1979	Det A	12	38	3	9	3	0	1	4	1-0	0	3	.237	.256	.395	70	-2	3-3	1.000	-2	75	0	O10(7/1/2)		-0.4
1980	Det A	51	175	23	46	2	1	9	16	10-0	1	45	.263	.303	.440	99	-1	4-7	.992	-2	100	32	O49C/D	110	-0.5
1981	Det A	83	290	41	95	11	3	9	40	18-1	2	64	.328	.369	.479	138	13	17-5	.973	-4	97	23	O67(8/26/37),D9		0.9
1982	Det A	69	266	34	74	16	2	8	35	25-2	1	41	.278	.341	.444	113	5	9-7	.994	-2	94	91	O64C,D4	85	-0.1
1983	Det A	128	401	60	91	12	9	15	51	53-3	1	96	.227	.320	.414	103	1	14-3	.975	-1	101	58	D66,O54(29/22/4)		1.5
1984 †	Det A	149	531	92	150	23	10	27	91	63-6	8	103	.282	.363	.516	140	30	29-9	.954	-11	90	48	O139(0/1/140),D6		2.0
1985	Det A	154	581	96	167	37	5	29	97	71-16	5	137	.287	.364	.518	140	33	30-4	.963	-12	95	10	O144(0/20/127),D8	40	0.8
1986	Det A	119	441	84	118	11	2	28	86	68-4	7	107	.268	.371	.492	133	21	34-6	.990	-12	83	25	O114(0/1/114),D4	29	2.2
1987 †	Det A	128	487	95	135	25	3	24	79	71-8	5	117	.277	.372	.489	132	24	26-7	.974	1	104	67	O148(148/1/0)		4.4
1988 †	LA N	150	542	106	157	28	1	25	76	73-14	7	120	.290	.377	.483	151	38	31-4	.964	3	107	82	O70(62/15/0)	98	-0.1
1989	LA N	71	253	35	54	8	2	9	28	35-5	2	55	.213	.312	.368	95	-1	12-3	.980	1	102	64	O81(11/70/0)	54	-0.3
1990	LA N	89	315	59	82	20	0	8	38	39-0	3	65	.260	.345	.400	107	4	26-2	.995	0	103	99	O94(91/0/3),D30		-0.3
1991	KC A	132	462	81	109	17	6	16	55	69-3	6	103	.236	.341	.403	105	4	18-4	.976	-5	87	61	O13R		-0.1
1992	Pit N	16	56	6	11	0	0	2	5	3-0	0	12	.196	.237	.304	52	-4	3-1	1.000	-0	103	0	D76,O32(2/30/0)		-0.1
1993	Det A	116	403	62	105	18	6	13	62	44-4	4	87	.261	.337	.432	106	2	15-6	.988	-1	93	145	D56,O38(0/23/15)		0.8
1994	Det A	98	330	71	91	17	2	23	72	42-3	3	69	.276	.358	.548	129	14	4-5	.988	-1	93	84	D63/OR		1.9
1995	Det A	70	227	37	59	12	2	9	35	33-3	1	61	.260	.353	.449	109	4	9-2	—	0	0	0	O13R		-0.3
Total 17		1635	5798	1155	1553	260	54	255	870	718-72	61	1285	.268	.352	.463	123	185	284-78	.976	-47	96	55	O1239(477/325/456),D327	416	11.9

GIBSON, WHITEY Leighton P. B10.6.1868 Lancaster PA D10.12.1907 Talmage PA TR/5-9/178 d5.2

YEAR	TM LG	G	AB	R	H	2B	3B	HR	RBI	BB-IB	HP	SO	AVG	OBP	SLG	AOPS	ABR	SB-CS	FA	FR	RNG	THR	GAMES AT POSITION	DL	BFW
1888	Phi AA	1	3	0	0	0	0	0	0				.000	.000	.000	-99	-1	0	1.000	1			/C		0.0

GIEBEL, JOE Joseph Henry B11.30.1891 Washington DC D3.17.1981 Silver Spring MD BR/TR/5-10.5/175 d9.30

YEAR	TM LG	G	AB	R	H	2B	3B	HR	RBI	BB-IB	HP	SO	AVG	OBP	SLG	AOPS	ABR	SB-CS	FA	FR	RNG	THR	GAMES AT POSITION	DL	BFW
1913	Phi A	1	3	0	1	0	0	0	0	0	0	1	.333	.333	.333	97	0	0	1.000	-0	107	0	/C		0.0

GIGON, NORM Norman Phillip B5.12.1938 Teaneck NJ BR/TR/6-0/195 Col Colby

YEAR	TM LG	G	AB	R	H	2B	3B	HR	RBI	BB-IB	HP	SO	AVG	OBP	SLG	AOPS	ABR	SB-CS	FA	FR	RNG	THR	GAMES AT POSITION	DL	BFW
1967	Chi N	34	70	8	12	3	1		4	6-0	2	14	.171	.234	.286	47	-5	0-0	.982	1	128	104	2b12,O4R/3		-0.4

GIL, GERONIMO Geronimo B8.7.1975 Estacion Lagunas, Oaxaca, Mexico BR/TR/6-2/195(195-234) d9.8

YEAR	TM LG	G	AB	R	H	2B	3B	HR	RBI	BB-IB	HP	SO	AVG	OBP	SLG	AOPS	ABR	SB-CS	FA	FR	RNG	THR	GAMES AT POSITION	DL	BFW
2001	Bal A	17	58	3	17	2	0	0	6	5-0	2	7	.293	.369	.328	91	0	0-0	.985	3	93	99	C17		0.4
2002	Bal A	125	422	33	98	19	0	12	45	21-1	3	88	.232	.270	.363	70	-20	2-2	.995	1	106	115	C125		-1.1
2003	Bal A	54	169	22	40	4	0	3	16	12-0	3	34	.237	.299	.314	62	-9	0-0	.984	4	72	85	C53		-0.2
2004	Bal A	12	32	1	9	2	0	0	4	3-1	0	5	.281	.343	.344	81	-1	0-0	1.000	1	112	188	C11		-0.5
2005	Bal A	64	125	7	24	3	0	4	17	5-0	1	23	.192	.220	.312	40	-11	0-0	.993	12	91	112	C62	61	-0.5
Total 5		272	806	66	188	30	0	19	88	46-2	6	157	.233	.279	.341	66	-41	2-2	.992	12	96	110	C268	61	-1.3

YEAR	TM LG	G	AB	R	H	2B	3B	HR	RBI	BB-IB	HP	SO	AVG	OBP	SLG	AOPS	ABR	SB-CS	FA	FR	RNG	THR	GAMES AT POSITION	DL	BFW

GIL, JERRY Jerry Bienvenido B10.14.1982 San Pedro de Macoris, D.R. BR/TR/6-3/185 d8.22 [DL 2005 Ari N 62, 2005 Ari N 24]

2004	Ari N	29	86	3	15	2	1	0	8	0-0	1	33	.174	.182	.221	4	-12	2-0	.955	2	102	110	S28		-0.8

GIL, BENJI Romar Benjamin (Aguilar) B10.6.1972 Tijuana, Baja California, Mexico BR/TR/6-2/182(182-210) [TexA91 1/19] d4.5

1993	Tex A	22	57	3	7	0	0	0	2	5-0	0	22	.123	.194	.123	-13	-9	1-2	.954	4	123	76	S22		-0.4
1995	Tex A	130	415	36	91	20	3	9	46	26-0	1	147	.219	.266	.347	56	-28	2-4	.974	18	110	113	S130		-0.1
1996	Tex A	5	5	0	2	0	0	0	1	1-0	0	1	.400	.500	.400	124	0	0-1	.923	0	107	0	S5		0.0
1997	Tex A	110	317	35	71	13	2	5	31	17-0	1	96	.224	.263	.325	50	-24	1-2	.963	18	117	108	S106,D4	51	0.1
2000	Ana A	110	301	28	72	14	1	6	23	30-0	5	59	.239	.317	.352	68	-15	10-6	.957	-1	102	101	S94,2b7,1b3,D6		-0.9
2001	Ana A	104	260	33	77	15	4	8	39	14-0	0	57	.296	.330	.477	108	2	3-4	.945	5	101	101	S44,2b21,1b18,D14/OC		0.8
2002	†Ana A	61	130	11	37	8	1	3	20	5-0	0	33	.285	.307	.431	96	-1	2-1	.990	3	98	90	2b26,S14,1b10,D10	54	0.3
2003	Ana A	62	125	12	24	5	1	1	9	4-1	0	33	.192	.214	.272	49	-13	5-1	.979	1	107	114	2b28,S20,1b5,3b4,D2		-0.9
Total 8		604	1610	158	381	75	12	32	171	102-1	7	448	.237	.283	.358	64	-88	24-21	.962	48	110	106	S435,2b82,1b36,D36,3b4/OC	105	-1.1

GIL, GUS Tomas Gustavo (Guillen) B4.19.1939 Caracas, Venez BR/TR/5-10/180* d4.11

1967	Cle A	51	96	11	11	4	0	0	5	9-0	1	18	.115	.198	.156	6	-11	0-0	1.000	-3	83	74	2b49/1		-1.3
1969	Sea A	92	221	20	49	7	0	0	17	16-0	0	28	.222	.272	.253	49	-15	0-0	.942	1	121	116	3b38,2b18,S12		-1.3
1970	Mil A	64	119	12	22	4	0	1	12	21-4	0	12	.185	.303	.244	54	-7	2-0	.978	-5	71	66	2b38,3b14		-1.0
1971	Mil A	14	32	3	5	1	0	0	3	10-1	0	5	.156	.357	.188	59	-1	1-0	.977	1	109	58	2b6,3b5		0.0
Total 4		221	468	46	87	16	0	1	37	56-5	1	63	.186	.272	.226	43	-34	5-0	.987	-6	84	69	2b113,3b58,S12/1	36	-3.6

GILBERT, SHAWN Albert Shawn B3.12.1965 Camden NJ BR/TR/5-9/185(170-185) [MinA87 12/295] d6.2 Col Cal St.-Fresno

1997	NY N	29	22	3	3	0	0	1	1	1-0	0	8	.136	.174	.273	15	-3	1-0	.875	-2	20	97	2b8,S6,3b3/OL	18	-0.4
1998	NY N	3	3	1	0	0	0	0	0	0-0	0	1	.000	.000	.000	-99	-1	0-0	—	-0	0	0	/3		-0.1
	StL N	4	2	0	1	0	0	0	0	0-0	0	1	.500	.500	.500	165	0	1-0	1.000	-0	0	0	2b2		0.0
	Year	7	5	1	1	0	0	0	0	0-0	0	2	.200	.200	.200	6	-1	1-0	1.000	-1	0	0	2b2/3		-0.1
2000	LA N	15	20	5	3	1	0	1	3	2-0	0	7	.150	.227	.350	45	-2	0-0	.941	1	123	297	O14(8/4/2)		-0.1
Total 3		51	47	9	7	1	0	2	4	3-0	0	17	.149	.200	.298	27	-6	2-0	.941	-1	118	285	O15(9/4/2),2b10,S6,3b4	18	-0.6

GILBERT, ANDY Andrew B7.18.1914 Bradenville PA D8.29.1992 Davis CA BR/TR/6-0/203 d9.14 Mil 1943-45 C4

1942	Bos A	6	11	0	1	0	0	0	1	1-0	0	3	.091	.167	.091	-26	-2	0-0	1.000	-0	93	0	O5C		-0.2
1946	Bos A	2	1	1	0	0	0	0	0	0-0	0	0	.000	.000	.000	-95	-0	0-0	—	-0	0	0	/OC		0.0
Total 2		8	12	1	1	0	0	0	1	1-0	0	3	.083	.154	.083	-31	-2	0-0	1.000	-0	89	0	O6C		-0.2

GILBERT, CHARLIE Charles Mader B7.8.1919 New Orleans LA D8.13.1983 New Orleans LA BL/TL/5-9/165 d4.16 Mil 1944-45 b-Tookie f-Larry

1940	Bro N	57	142	23	35	9	1	2	8	8	0	13	.246	.287	.366	74	-5	0	.960	1	101	135	O43C		-0.6
1941	Chi N	39	86	11	24	2	1	0	12	11	0	6	.279	.361	.326	98	-1	1	1.000	-1	106	0	O22(0/21/1)		-0.1
1942	Chi N	74	179	18	33	6	3	0	7	25	0	24	.184	.284	.251	60	-9	1	.981	0	93	149	O47(3/44/0)		-1.1
1943	Chi N	8	20	1	3	0	0	0	0	3	0	3	.150	.261	.150	20	-2	0	1.000	0	84	230	O6(3/3/0)		-0.2
1946	Chi N	15	13	2	1	0	0	0	1	1	0	4	.077	.143	.077	-38	-2	0	1.000	1	82	2356	O2C		-0.2
	Phi N	88	260	34	63	5	2	1	17	25	2	18	.242	.314	.288	73	-9	3	1.000	5	108	138	O69(8/16/46)		-0.7
	Year	103	273	36	64	5	2	1	18	26	2	22	.234	.306	.278	68	-12	3	1.000	6	108	163	O71(8/18/46)		-0.9
1947	Phi N	83	152	20	36	5	2	2	10	13	1	14	.237	.301	.336	72	-7	1	.961	2	104	168	O37(18/7/12)		-0.6
Total 6		364	852	109	195	27	9	5	55	86	3	82	.229	.302	.299	70	-34	7	.982	8	102	138	O226(32/136/59)		-3.5

GILBERT, BUDDY Drew Edward B7.26.1935 Knoxville TN BL/TR/6-3/200 d9.9 Col Tennessee

1959	Cin N	7	20	4	3	0	0	2	3	3-0	0	4	.150	.261	.450	82	-1	0-0	1.000	0	125	0	O6R		-0.1

GILBERT, TOOKIE Harold Joseph B4.4.1929 New Orleans LA D6.23.1967 New Orleans LA BL/TR/6-2.5/185* d5.5 b-Charlie f-Larry

1950	NY N	113	322	40	71	12	2	4	32	43	1	36	.220	.314	.307	64	-16	3	.988	0	102	105	1b111		-1.9
1953	NY N	70	160	12	27	3	0	3	16	22	0	21	.169	.269	.244	34	-16	1-0	.995	-1	92	96	1b44		-1.8
Total 2		183	482	52	98	15	2	7	48	65	1	57	.203	.299	.286	54	-32	4-0	.991	-1	99	102	1b155		-3.7

GILBERT, HARRY Harry H. B7.7.1868 Pottstown PA D12.23.1909 Pottstown PA d6.23 b-John

1890	Pit N	2	8	1	2	0	0	0	0	0	0	3	.250	.250	.250	52	-1	0	1.000	-0	109	132	2b2		-0.1

GILBERT, JOHN John G. B1.8.1864 Pottstown PA D11.12.1903 Pottstown PA d6.23 b-Harry

1890	Pit N	2	8	0	0	0	0	0	0	0	0	2	.000	.000	.000	-99	-2	0	—	-0	81	118	S2		-0.2

GILBERT, JACK John Robert "Jackrabbit" B9.4.1875 Rhinecliff NY D7.7.1941 Albany NY d9.11

1898	Was N	2	5	0	1	0	0	0	1	1	1		.200	.429	.200	82	0	1	.500	0	514	0	O2(0/1/1)		0.0
	NY N	1	4	0	1	0	0	0	0	0	0		.250	.250	.250	45	0	1	.500	-1	0	0	/OR		-0.1
	Year	3	9	0	2	0	0	0	1	1	1		.222	.364	.222	70	0	2	.500	-2	280	0	O3(0/1/2)		-0.1
1904	Pit N	25	87	13	21	0	0	0	3	12	3		.241	.353	.241	82	-1	3	.857	-4	0	0	O25L		-0.7
Total 2		28	96	13	23	0	0	0	4	13	4		.240	.354	.240	81	-1	5	.821	-5	29	0	O28(25/1/2)		-0.8

GILBERT, LARRY Lawrence William B12.3.1891 New Orleans LA D2.17.1965 New Orleans LA BL/TL/5-9/158 d4.14 s-Charlie s-Tookie

1914	†Bos N	72	224	32	60	6	1	5	25	26	1	34	.268	.347	.371	114	4	3	.979	1	79	158	O60(3/6/51)		0.2
1915	Bos N	45	106	11	16	4	0	0	4	11	0	13	.151	.231	.189	29	-9	4-1	.941	0	83	171	O27(2/0/26)		-1.0
Total 2		117	330	43	76	10	1	5	29	37	1	47	.230	.310	.312	88	-5	7-1	.969	1	80	162	O87(5/6/77)		-0.8

GILBERT, MARK Mark David B8.22.1956 Atlanta GA BB/TR/6-0/175 [ChiN78 14/351] d7.21 Col Florida St.

1985	Chi A	7	22	3	6	1	0	0	3	4-0	0	5	.273	.385	.318	91	-0	0-0	1.000	-1	92	0	O7(2/5/1)		-0.1

GILBERT, PETE Peter B9.6.1867 Baltic CT D1.1.1912 Springfield MA TR/5-8/180 d9.6

1890	Bal AA	29	100	25	28	2	1	1	18	10	3		.280	.363	.350	105	1	12	.899	0	96	126	3b29		0.1
1891	Bal AA	139	513	81	118	15	7	3	72	37	28	77	.230	.317	.304	77	-16	31	.862	2	105	151	3b139		-1.0
1892	Bal N	4	15	0	3	0	0	0	0	1	0	3	.200	.250	.200	35	-1	1	.889	1	147	0	3b4		0.0
1894	Bro N	6	25	1	2	0	0	1	1	1	1	3	.080	.148	.080	-47	-6	2	.938	1	126	0	2b3,3b3		-0.4
	Lou N	28	108	13	33	3	1	1	14	5	1	4	.306	.353	.380	82	-3	2	.742	-7	83	100	3b28		-0.7
	Year	34	133	14	35	3	1	1	15	6	1	7	.263	.315	.323	58	-9	4	.766	-6	86	126	3b31,2b3		-1.1
Total 4		206	761	120	184	20	9	5	105	54	35	87	.242	.321	.311	76	-25	48	.851	-3	101	141	3b203,2b3		-2.0

GILBERT, WALLY Walter John B12.19.1900 Oscoda MI D9.7.1958 Duluth MN BR/TR/6-0/180 d8.18 Col Valparaiso

1928	Bro N	39	153	26	31	4	0	3	14	9	1	8	.203	.274	.229	33	-15	2	.965	0	101	103	3b39		-1.2
1929	Bro N	143	569	88	173	31	4	3	58	42	7	29	.304	.359	.388	87	-11	7	.956	9	104	77	3b142		0.6
1930	Bro N	150	623	92	183	34	5	3	67	47	2	33	.294	.345	.379	76	-24	7	.944	9	110	112	3b150		-0.5
1931	Bro N	145	552	60	147	25	6	0	46	39	6	33	.266	.322	.333	77	-18	3	.948	8	107	95	3b145		-0.5
1932	Cin N	114	420	35	90	18	2	1	40	20	1	23	.214	.252	.274	43	-35	2	.929	-7	102	92	3b111	Bal N	-3.7
Total 5		591	2317	301	624	112	17	7	214	162	17	131	.269	.322	.341	71	-103	21	.947	19	106	95	3b587		-5.3

GILBERT, BILLY William Oliver B6.21.1876 Tullytown PA D8.8.1927 New York NY BR/TR/5-4/153 d4.25

1901	Mil A	127	492	77	133	14	7	0	43	31	9		.270	.320	.327	84	-10	19	.936	-3	98	113	2b127		-1.1
1902	Bal A	129	445	74	109	12	3	2	38	45	9		.245	.327	.299	71	-16	38	.907	-3	94	114	S129		-1.4
1903	NY N	128	413	62	104	9	0	1	40	41	20		.252	.348	.281	77	-10	37	.935	6	98	107	2b128		-0.2
1904	NY N	146	478	57	121	13	3	1	54	46	17		.253	.340	.299	94	-1	33	.947	20	105	128	2b115		0.6
1905	†NY N	115	376	45	93	11	3	0	24	41	9		.247	.341	.293	84	-5	11	.947	20	101	122	2b146		1.6
1906	NY N	104	307	44	71	6	1	0	27	42	9		.231	.341	.257	85	-3	22	.940	22	113	105	2b98		2.2
1908	StL N	89	276	12	59	7	0	0	20	20	3		.214	.274	.239	67	-10	6	.952	5	96	86	2b89		-0.4
1909	StL N	12	29	4	5	0	0	0	1	4	3		.172	.333	.172	61	-1	1	.922	-1	107	29	2b12		-0.1
Total 8		850	2816	375	695	72	17	4	237	270	72		.247	.328	.289	81	-56	167	.942	53	102	111	2b715,S129		1.2

GILBREATH, ROD Rodney Joe B9.24.1952 Laurel MS BR/TR (BB 1975p)/6-2/185(170-185) [AtlN70 3/69] d6.17

1972	Atl N	18	38	2	9	1	0	0	2	2-0	1	10	.237	.293	.263	54	-2	1-1	1.000	1	84	86	2b7,3b4		-0.1
1973	Atl N	29	74	10	21	2	1	0	2	6-1	1	10	.284	.341	.338	74	-2	2-1	.960	-0	97	112	3b22		-0.2
1974	Atl N	3	6	2	2	0	0	0	0	2-0	0	1	.333	.500	.333	132	0	0-0	1.000	-0	95	83	2b2		-0.2
1975	Atl N	90	202	24	49	3	1	2	16	24-0	1	26	.243	.323	.297	72	-7	5-5	.980	1	99	97	2b52,3b10/S		-0.6
1976	Atl N	116	383	57	96	11	8	1	32	42-1	4	36	.251	.325	.340	76	-8	7-7	.975	6	101	110	2b104,3b7/S		0.4

YEAR	TM LG	G	AB	R	H	2B	3B	HR	RBI	BB-IB	HP	SO	AVG	OBP	SLG	AOPS	ABR	SB-CS	FA	FR	RNG	THR	GAMES AT POSITION	DL	BFW
1977	Atl N	128	407	47	99	15	2	8	43	45-6	2	79	.243	.320	.349	72	-16	3-9	.978	-6	90	77	2b122/3		-1.8
1978	Atl N	116	326	22	80	13	3	3	31	26-3	0	51	.245	.300	.331	69	-13	7-6	.968	-7	106	94	3b62,2b39		-2.
Total	7	500	1436	164	356	45	15	14	125	147-11	9	212	.248	.320	.329	75	-47	25-29	.978	-6	94	89	2b326,3b106,S2		-4.

GILE, DON Donald Loren "Bear" B4.19.1935 Modesto CA BR/TR/6-6/220* d9.25 Col Arizona

YEAR	TM LG	G	AB	R	H	2B	3B	HR	RBI	BB-IB	HP	SO	AVG	OBP	SLG	AOPS	ABR	SB-CS	FA	FR	RNG	THR	GAMES AT POSITION	DL	BFW
1959	Bos A	3	10	1	2	1	0	0	1	0-0	1	2	.200	.250	.300	55	-1	0-0	1.000	-0	100	0	C3		-0.
1960	Bos A	29	51	6	9	1	1	1	4	1-0	0	13	.176	.189	.294	29	-5	0-0	1.000	-2	75	201	C15,1b11		-0.
1961	Bos A	8	18	2	5	0	0	1	1	1-0	0	5	.278	.316	.444	98	0	0-0	.958	-1	55	68	1b6/C		-0.
1962	Bos A	18	41	3	2	0	0	1	3	3-0	1	15	.049	.133	.122	-30	-8	0-0	.990	-1	61	120	1b14		-1.0
Total	4	58	120	12	18	2	1	3	9	5-0	2	35	.150	.194	.258	21	-14	0-0	.982	-4	59	92	1b31,C19		-2.

GILES, BRIAN Brian Jeffrey B4.27.1960 Manhattan KS BR/TR/6-1/165(162-175) [NYN78 3/55] d9.12

YEAR	TM LG	G	AB	R	H	2B	3B	HR	RBI	BB-IB	HP	SO	AVG	OBP	SLG	AOPS	ABR	SB-CS	FA	FR	RNG	THR	GAMES AT POSITION	DL	BFW
1981	NY N	9	7	0	0	0	0	0	0	0-0	0	3	.000	.000	.000	-99	-2	0-0	1.000	1	110	277	2b2,S2		0.
1982	NY N	45	138	14	29	5	0	3	10	12-1	0	29	.210	.270	.312	63	-7	6-1	.992	8	102	99	2b45,S2		0.
1983	NY N	145	400	39	98	15	0	2	27	36-1	2	77	.245	.308	.298	70	-16	17-10	.980	8	104	111	2b140,S12		-0.
1985	Mil A	34	58	6	10	1	0	1	1	7-0	0	16	.172	.262	.241	39	-5	2-1	.963	1	98	70	S20,2b13,D2		-0.
1986	Chi A	9	11	0	3	0	0	0	1	0-0	0	2	.273	.273	.273	47	-1	0-0	1.000	2	120	304	2b7/S	42	0.
1990	Sea A	45	95	15	22	6	0	4	11	15-0	0	24	.232	.336	.421	109	1	2-1	.978	3	92	134	S37,2b2/3D		0.
Total	6	287	709	74	162	27	0	10	50	70-2	2	151	.228	.298	.309	69	-30	27-13	.985	23	103	111	2b209,S74,D3/3	42	0.

GILES, BRIAN Brian Stephen B1.20.1971 El Cajon CA BL/TL/5-11/200* [CleA89 17/437] d9.16 b-Marcus

YEAR	TM LG	G	AB	R	H	2B	3B	HR	RBI	BB-IB	HP	SO	AVG	OBP	SLG	AOPS	ABR	SB-CS	FA	FR	RNG	THR	GAMES AT POSITION	DL	BFW
1995	Cle A	6	9	6	5	0	0	1	3	0-0	0	1	.556	.556	.889	263	2	0-0	1.000	1	91	1304	O3R/D		0.
1996	†Cle A	51	121	26	43	14	1	5	27	19-4	0	13	.355	.434	.612	163	13	3-0	1.000	1	128	0	D21,O16(11/0/5)		1.
1997	†Cle A	130	377	62	101	15	3	17	63	63-2	1	50	.268	.368	.459	112	7	13-3	.972	-1	96	113	O115(82/20/25),D9		1.
1998	†Cle A	112	350	56	94	19	0	16	66	73-8	3	75	.269	.396	.460	118	13	10-5	.978	5	107	119	O101(95/3/6),D6	36	1.
1999	Pit N	141	521	109	164	33	3	39	115	95-7	3	80	.315	.418	.614	157	54	6-2	.990	-6	93	104	O138(8/108/25),D3		4.
2000	Pit N★	156	559	111	176	37	7	35	123	114-13	7	69	.315	.432	.594	157	54	6-0	.982	-2	93	145	O155(46/72/39)		4.
2001	Pit N★	160	576	116	178	37	7	37	95	90-14	4	67	.309	.404	.590	149	44	13-6	.969	-7	96	69	O159(124/61/0)		3.
2002	Pit N	153	497	95	148	37	5	38	103	135-24	7	74	.298	.450	.622	180	63	15-6	.973	-3	88	138	O151(151/3/0)		2.
2003	Pit N	105	388	70	116	30	4	16	70	85-11	6	48	.299	.430	.521	145	31	0-3	.992	3	108	60	O105(99/16/0)	26	2.
	SD N	29	104	23	31	4	2	4	18	20-1	2	10	.298	.414	.490	150	9	4-0	.966	1	105	116	O29L		3.
	Year	134	492	93	147	34	6	20	88	105-12	8	58	.299	.427	.514	146	40	4-3	.987	4	107	72	O134(128/16/0)		1.
2004	SD N	159	609	97	173	33	7	23	94	89-6	4	80	.284	.374	.475	125	24	10-3	.979	2	106	81	O159R		1.
2005	†SD N	158	545	92	164	38	8	15	83	119-9	2	64	.301	.423	.483	145	44	13-5	.988	3	109	60	O155(1/17/143)	62	30.
Total	11	1360	4656	863	1393	297	47	246	858	902-99	43	352	.299	.413	.542	146	352	93-33	.981	-5	100	100	O1286(646/300/405),D40		

GILES, MARCUS Marcus William B5.18.1978 San Diego CA BR/TR/5-8/175* [AtlN96 53/1512] d4.17 b-Brian Col Grossmont (CA) JC

YEAR	TM LG	G	AB	R	H	2B	3B	HR	RBI	BB-IB	HP	SO	AVG	OBP	SLG	AOPS	ABR	SB-CS	FA	FR	RNG	THR	GAMES AT POSITION	DL	BFW
2001	†Atl N	68	244	36	64	10	2	9	31	28-0	0	37	.262	.338	.430	96	-2	2-5	.978	-1	105	92	2b62		-0.
2002	†Atl N	68	213	27	49	10	1	8	23	25-3	2	41	.230	.315	.399	90	-4	1-1	.977	4	107	117	2b52,3b8	48	5.
2003	†Atl N★	145	551	101	174	49	2	21	69	59-2	11	80	.316	.390	.526	138	33	14-4	.982	18	120	91	2b139	60	2.
2004	†Atl N	102	379	61	118	22	2	8	48	36-0	9	70	.311	.378	.443	112	8	17-4	.975	12	113	122	2b97		2.
2005	†Atl N	152	577	104	168	45	4	15	63	64-1	5	108	.291	.365	.461	112	12	16-4	.984	8	112	101	2b149/3	108	11.
Total	5	535	1964	329	573	136	11	61	234	212-6	27	336	.292	.366	.465	115	47	50-17	.980	41	113	103	2b499,3b9		

GILHAM, GEORGE George Louis B9.17.1899 Shamokin PA D4.25.1937 Lansdowne PA BR/TR/5-11/164 d9.24

YEAR	TM LG	G	AB	R	H	2B	3B	HR	RBI	BB-IB	HP	SO	AVG	OBP	SLG	AOPS	ABR	SB-CS	FA	FR	RNG	THR	GAMES AT POSITION	DL	BFW
1920	StL N	1	3	0	0	0	0	0	0	0-0	0	1	.000	.000	.000	-99	-1	0-0	.750	-1	60	187	/C		-0
1921	StL N	1	1	0	0	0	0	0	0	0-0	0	0	.000	.000	.000	-99	0	0-0	—				/H		-0
Total	2	2	4	0	0	0	0	0	0	0-0	0	1	.000	.000	.000	-99	-1	0-0	.750	-1	60	187	/C		-0

GILHOOLEY, FRANK Frank Patrick "Flash" B6.10.1892 Toledo OH D7.11.1959 Toledo OH BL/TR/5-8/155 d9.18 Col St. Johns

YEAR	TM LG	G	AB	R	H	2B	3B	HR	RBI	BB-IB	HP	SO	AVG	OBP	SLG	AOPS	ABR	SB-CS	FA	FR	RNG	THR	GAMES AT POSITION	DL	BFW
1911	StL N	1	0	0	0	0	0	0	0	—	—	—	—	—	—	—	—	0	0	—	-0	0	0	/OR		0
1912	StL N	13	49	5	11	0	0	0	2	3	0	8	.224	.269	.224	37	-4	0	1.000	-1	76	72	O11C		-0
1913	NY A	24	85	10	29	2	1	0	14	4	1	9	.341	.378	.388	124	2	6	.977	-0	112	56	O24R		-0
1914	NY A	1	3	0	2	0	0	0	0	1	0	1	.667	.750	.667	327	1	0	—	0	0		/OR		-0
1915	NY A	1	4	0	0	0	0	0	0	0	0	1	.000	.000	.000	-99	-1	0	1.000	0	81	0	/OR		-0
1916	NY A	58	223	40	62	5	3	1	10	37	0	17	.278	.383	.341	115	6	16	.971	0	95	121	O57(0/2/55)		0
1917	NY A	54	165	14	40	6	1	0	8	30	1	13	.242	.362	.291	99	2	6	.933	-1	102	81	O46R		-0
1918	NY A	112	427	59	118	13	5	1	23	53	1	24	.276	.358	.337	107	5	7	.961	-1	101	98	O111(0/4/107)		0
1919	Bos A	48	112	14	27	4	0	0	1	12	0	8	.241	.315	.277	71	-4	2	.922	-1	92	120	O33(30/2/1)		-1
Total	9	312	1068	142	289	30	10	2	58	140	4	80	.271	.357	.323	102	7	37	.957	-3	99	97	O285(30/19/236)		-1

GILKEY, BERNARD Otis Bernard B9.24.1966 St.Louis MO BR/TR/6-0/190(170-200) d9.4

YEAR	TM LG	G	AB	R	H	2B	3B	HR	RBI	BB-IB	HP	SO	AVG	OBP	SLG	AOPS	ABR	SB-CS	FA	FR	RNG	THR	GAMES AT POSITION	DL	BFW
1990	StL N	18	64	11	19	5	2	1	3	8-0	0	5	.297	.375	.484	134	3	6-1	.961	2	128	157	O18(18/1/0)		0
1991	StL N	81	268	28	58	7	2	5	20	39-0	1	33	.216	.316	.313	77	-7	14-8	.994	6	109	146	O74L	27	2
1992	StL N	131	384	56	116	19	4	7	43	39-1	1	52	.302	.364	.427	128	14	18-12	.978	7	108	192	O111(110/0/1)		2
1993	StL N	137	557	99	170	40	5	16	70	56-2	4	66	.305	.370	.481	127	23	15-10	.969	-3	84	178	O134(133/0/2),1b3	15	1
1994	StL N	105	380	52	96	22	1	6	45	39-2	10	65	.253	.336	.363	83	-8	15-8	.983	-1	90	146	O102L	19	1
1995	StL N	121	480	73	143	33	4	17	69	42-3	5	70	.298	.358	.490	119	13	12-6	.986	3	100	138	O118L		5
1996	NY N	153	571	108	181	44	3	30	117	73-7	4	125	.317	.393	.562	158	49	17-9	.982	18	112	209	O151L		5
1997	NY N	145	518	85	129	31	1	18	78	70-1	6	111	.249	.338	.417	103	4	7-11	.989	6	94	181	O136(136/1/0),D2	16	-0
1998	NY N	82	264	33	60	15	0	4	28	32-1	4	66	.227	.317	.330	74	-10	5-1	.992	4	91	201	O77(76/1/4)		-0
	Ari N	29	101	8	25	0	0	1	5	11-0	1	14	.248	.327	.277	61	-6	4-2	.981	1	98	169	O27L		-0
	Year	111	365	41	85	15	0	5	33	43-1	5	80	.233	.320	.315	70	-15	9-3	.989	5	96	192	O104(103/1/4)		-0
1999	†Ari N	94	204	28	60	16	1	8	39	29-2	2	42	.294	.379	.500	121	8	2-2	.969	-1	104	105	O53(15/0/40)		-0
2000	Ari N	38	73	6	8	1	0	2	6	7-2	0	16	.110	.185	.205	-1	-12	0-0	1.000	0	101	112	O17(2/0/16)		-0
	Bos A	36	91	11	21	5	1	1	9	10-0	1	22	.231	.327	.341	68	-4	0-0	1.000	1	117	97	O22(7/0/16),D8		-0
2001	Atl N	69	106	8	29	6	0	2	14	11-0	1	31	.274	.339	.387	89	-2	0-1	.983	-1	104	0	O36(28/0/8)/D	18	-0
Total	12	1239	4061	606	1115	244	24	118	546	466-21	42	708	.275	.352	.434	110	65	115-71	.983	45	100	166	O1076(997/3/87),D11,1b3	95	

GILKS, BOB Robert James B7.2.1864 Cincinnati OH D8.21.1944 Brunswick GA BR/TR/5-8/178 d8.25 OF(181/56/21) ▲

YEAR	TM LG	G	AB	R	H	2B	3B	HR	RBI	BB-IB	HP	SO	AVG	OBP	SLG	AOPS	ABR	SB-CS	FA	FR	RNG	THR	GAMES AT POSITION	DL	BFW
1887	Cle AA	22	83	12	26	2	0	0	13	3		2	.313	.352	.337	96	0	5	.881	*3	132	337	P13,1b6,O3(0/2/1)/2		0
1888	Cle AA	119	484	59	111	14	4	1	63	7		3	.229	.245	.281	70	-17	16	.899	1	75	63	O87(57/27/3),3b28,S4,P4/2		-1
1889	Cle N	53	210	17	50	5	2	0	18	7	3	20	.238	.273	.281	56	-13	6	1.000	1	104	0	O29(2/26/1),S13,1b10/2		-1
1890	Cle N	130	544	65	116	10	3	0	41	32	6	38	.213	.265	.243	49	-36	17	.941	3	97	43	O123(121/1/1),P4,S3,2b2		-3
1893	Bal N	15	64	10	17	2	0	0	7	0	1	3	.266	.277	.297	52	-5	3	.969	3	203	182	O15(1/0/15)		-0
Total	5	339	1385	163	320	33	9	1	142	49	15	61	.231	.265	.270	60	-71	60	.937	11	98	63	O257L,3b28,P21,S20,1b16,2b5		-0

GILL, JIM James Clifford B7.1866 D4.10.1923 Beaver Falls PA d6.27

YEAR	TM LG	G	AB	R	H	2B	3B	HR	RBI	BB-IB	HP	SO	AVG	OBP	SLG	AOPS	ABR	SB-CS	FA	FR	RNG	THR	GAMES AT POSITION	DL	BFW
1889	StL AA											2	.250	.333	.375	90	0		1.000	-1	0	0	/OC2		-0

GILL, JOHNNY John Wesley "Patcheye" B3.27.1905 Nashville TN D12.26.1984 Nashville TN BL/TR/6-2/190 d8.28

YEAR	TM LG	G	AB	R	H	2B	3B	HR	RBI	BB-IB	HP	SO	AVG	OBP	SLG	AOPS	ABR	SB-CS	FA	FR	RNG	THR	GAMES AT POSITION	DL	BFW
1927	Cle A	21	60	8	13	3	0	1	4	7	2	13	.217	.319	.317	65	-3	1-1	1.000	0	84	153	O17(14/3/0)		-
1928	Cle A	2	2	0	0	0	0	0	0	0	0	1	.000	.000	.000	-99	-1	0-0	—				/H		-
1931	Was A	8	30	2	8	2	1	0	5	1	1	6	.267	.313	.400	86	-1	0-1	1.000	2	128	220	O8R		-
1934	Was A	13	53	7	13	3	0	2	7	2	1	9	.245	.286	.415	82	-2	0-0	1.000	-1	103	0	O13(2/0/11)		-
1935	Chi N	3	3	2	1	1	0	0	1	0	0	0	.333	.333	.667	161	0		—				/H		-
1936	Chi N	71	174	20	44	8	0	7	28	13	1	19	.253	.309	.420	92	-2	1-2	.938	-1	95	104	O41(35/1/5)		-
Total	6	118	322	39	79	17	1	10	45	23	5	43	.245	.306	.398	84	-9	1-2	.968	1	99	111	O79(51/4/24)		-

GILL, WARREN Warren Darst "Doc" B12.21.1878 Ladoga IN D11.26.1952 Laguna Beach CA BR/TR/6-1/175 d8.26 Col Washington-St. Louis

YEAR	TM LG	G	AB	R	H	2B	3B	HR	RBI	BB-IB	HP	SO	AVG	OBP	SLG	AOPS	ABR	SB-CS	FA	FR	RNG	THR	GAMES AT POSITION	DL	BFW
1908	Pit N	27	76	10	17	0	1	0	6		0	4	.224	.366	.250	97	1		1.000	-3	47	103	1b25		-

GILLEN, SAM Samuel (b Samuel Gilleland) B11.14.1867 Pittsburgh PA D5.13.1905 Pittsburgh PA 5-8/? d8.19

YEAR	TM LG	G	AB	R	H	2B	3B	HR	RBI	BB-IB	HP	SO	AVG	OBP	SLG	AOPS	ABR	SB-CS	FA	FR	RNG	THR	GAMES AT POSITION	DL	BFW
1893	Pit N	3	6	0	0	0	0	0	0		0	1	.000	.000	.000	-99	-2	0	.750	-0	106	189	S3		
1897	Phi N	75	270	32	70	10	3	0	27	35	4		.259	.353	.319	80	-6	2	.896	-23	88	24	S69,3b6		
Total	2	78	276	32	70	10	3	0	27	35	4	1	.254	.346	.312	76	-8	2	.892	-23	88	28	S72,3b6		

YEAR	TM LG	G	AB	R	H	2B	3B	HR	RBI	BB-IB	HP	SO	AVG	OBP	SLG	AOPS	ABR	SB-CS	FA	FR	RNG	THR	GAMES AT POSITION	DL	BFW

GILLEN, TOM Thomas J. B5.18.1862 Philadelphia PA D1.26.1889 Philadelphia PA 5-8/160 d4.18

1884	Phi U	29	116	5	18	2	0	0		1			.155	.162	.172	2	-18		.895	-5			C27,O3L		-1.8
1886	Det N	2	10	2	4	0	0	0	4	0		1	.400	.400	.400	139	0	0	.889	-1			C2		
Total	2	31	126	7	22	2	0	0	4	1		1	.175	.181	.190	14	-18		.895	-6			C29,O3L		-1.8

GILLENWATER, CARDEN Carden Edison B5.13.1917 Riceville TN D5.10.2000 Largo FL BR/TR/6-1/178 d9.22

1940	StL N	7	25	1	4	1	0	0	5	0	0	2	.160	.160	.200	-1	-3	0	1.000	-0	99	0	O7(5/2/0)		-0.4
1943	Bro N	8	17	1	3	0	0	0	2	2	0	3	.176	.263	.176	28	-2	0	1.000	0	73	328	O4(2/1/1)		-0.2
1945	Bos N	144	517	74	149	20	2	7	72	73	3	70	.288	.379	.375	110	10	13	.979	17	110	194	O140C		2.2
1946	Bos N	99	224	30	51	10	1	1	14	39	0	27	.228	.342	.295	81	-4	3	.979	4	111	104	O78(11/67/0)		-0.3
1948	Was A	77	221	23	54	10	4	3	21	39	0	36	.244	.358	.367	96	-1	4-2	.974	-1	101	75	O67(1/65/1)		-0.3
Total	5	335	1004	129	261	41	7	11	114	153	3	138	.260	.359	.348	96	0	20-2	.979	19	108	145	O296(19/275/2)		1.0

GILLESPIE, JOHN John William B NY BL/TR d10.1

| 1890 | Buf P | 1 | 3 | 0 | 0 | 0 | 0 | 0 | 0 | 0 | | 2 | .000 | .000 | .000 | -99 | -1 | 0 | .250 | -0 | 391 | 0 | /OR | | -0.1 |

GILLESPIE, PAUL Paul Allen B9.18.1920 Sugar Valley GA D8.11.1970 Anniston AL BL/TR/6-3/195 d9.11

1942	Chi N	5	16	3	4	0	0	2	4	1	0	2	.250	.294	.625	172	1	0	1.000	-1	119	99	C4		0.1
1944	Chi N	9	26	2	7	1	0	1	2	3	0	3	.269	.345	.423	116	1	0	.903	-1	101	200	C7		0.0
1945	†Chi N	75	163	12	47	6	0	3	25	18	2	9	.288	.366	.380	110	3	2	.989	3	145	86	C45/OR		0.8
Total	3	89	205	17	58	7	0	6	31	22	2	14	.283	.358	.405	115	5	2	.978	1	137	103	C56/OR		0.9

GILLESPIE, PETE Peter Patrick B11.30.1851 Carbondale PA D5.5.1910 Carbondale PA BL/TR/6-1.5/178 d5.1

1880	Tro N	82	346	50	84	20	5	2	24	17		35	.243	.278	.347	105	2		.905	6	72	136	O82L		0.3
1881	Tro N	84	348	43	96	14	3	0	41	9		24	.276	.294	.333	92	-4		.933	3	70	145	O84L		-0.6
1882	Tro N	74	298	46	82	5	4	2	33	9		14	.275	.296	.339	108	3		.827	-6	53	25	O74L		-0.4
1883	NY N	98	411	64	129	23	12	1	62	9		27	.314	.329	.436	131	14		.897	6	50	169	O98(97/1/0)		1.6
1884	NY N	101	413	75	109	7	4	2	44	19		35	.264	.296	.315	90	-5		.893	-3	39	28	O101(100/0/1)		-1.0
1885	NY N	102	420	67	123	17	6	0	52	15		32	.293	.317	.362	121	9		.942	4	63	93	O102L		0.2
1886	NY N	97	396	65	108	13	8	0	58	16		30	.273	.301	.346	95	-3	17	.901	-12	31	0	O97(95/1/1)		-1.6
1887	NY N	76	295	40	78	9	3	3	37	12	5	21	.264	.304	.346	84	-6	37	.946	2	119	49	O76L/3		-0.5
Total	8	714	2927	450	809	108	45	10	351	106	5	218	.276	.303	.354	104	10	54	.903	7	60	82	O714(710/2/2)/3		-2.0

GILLIAM, JIM James William "Junior" B10.17.1928 Nashville TN D10.8.1978 Inglewood CA BB/TR/5-10.5/175* d4.14 C14 Negro Lg 1945-51 OF(207/5/26)

1953	†Bro N	151	605	125	168	31	17	6	63	100	3	38	.278	.383	.415	106	8	21-14	.976	1	97	106	2b149		1.9
1954	Bro N	146	607	107	171	28	8	13	52	76	2	30	.282	.361	.418	100	1	8-7	.977	-14	92	97	2b143,O4(4/0/2)		-0.3
1955	†Bro N	147	538	110	134	20	8	7	40	70-4	6	37	.249	.341	.355	83	-12	15-15	.968	-6	98	102	2b99,O46(41/4/7)		1.6
1956	†Bro N☆	153	594	102	178	23	8	6	43	95-6	4	39	.300	.399	.396	107	11	21-9	.981	11	107	103	2b102,O56(53/0/7)		2.7
1957	Bro N	149	617	89	154	26	4	2	37	64-0	4	31	.250	.323	.314	66	-27	26-10	.986	6	93	101	2b148,O2L		-0.8
1958	LA N	147	555	81	145	25	5	2	43	78-1	0	22	.261	.352	.335	81	-13	18-11	.987	8	101	91	O75(71/1/5),3b44,2b32		-0.8
1959	†LA N★	145	553	91	156	18	4	3	34	96-4	0	25	.282	.387	.345	91	-2	23-10	.958	-1	94	87	3b132,2b8,O3(3/0/1)		-0.2
1960	LA N	151	557	96	138	20	2	5	40	96-1	3	28	.248	.359	.318	82	-9	12-9	.960	15	110	106	3b130,2b30		0.8
1961	LA N	144	439	74	107	26	3	4	32	79-2	0	34	.244	.358	.344	81	-9	8-4	.956	14	114	101	3b74,2b71,O11L		1.0
1962	LA N	160	588	83	159	24	1	4	43	93-0	2	35	.270	.370	.335	97	3	17-11	.981	5	103	100	2b113,3b90/O(1/0/1)		1.7
1963	†LA N	148	525	77	148	27	4	6	49	60-2	2	28	.282	.354	.383	122	17	19-5	.985	7	99	102	2b119,3b55		3.7
1964	LA N	116	334	44	76	8	3	2	27	42-2	3	21	.228	.318	.287	78	-9	4-4	.936	-12	86	67	3b86,2b25,O2R		-2.1
1965	†LA N	111	372	54	104	19	4	4	39	53-5	4	31	.280	.374	.382	123	14	9-5	.960	-1	96	138	3b80,O22(21/0/1),2b5		1.2
1966	†LA N	88	235	30	51	9	0	1	16	34-3	0	17	.217	.315	.268	70	-8	2-1	.953	-5	87	84	3b70,1b2,2b2		-1.4
Total	14	1956	7119	1163	1889	304	71	65	558	1036-30	33	416	.265	.360	.355	92	-35	203-111	.979	28	97	100	2b1046,3b761,O222L,1b2		5.8

GILLIGAN, BARNEY Andrew Bernard B1.3.1856 Cambridge MA D4.1.1934 Lynn MA BR/TR/5-6.5/130 d9.25

1875	Atl NA	2	8	2	2	0	0	0	0	0			.250	.250	.250	85	0	0-0	1.000	-0			/COR		0.0
1879	Cle N	52	205	20	35	6	2	0	11	0		13	.171	.171	.220	28	-16		.870	-0			C27,O23(21/2/0),S2		-1.5
1880	Cle N	30	99	9	17	4	3	1	13	6		12	.172	.219	.303	77	-2		.969	6			C23,O4C,S4		0.4
1881	Pro N	46	183	19	40	7	2	0	20	9		24	.219	.255	.279	69	-6		.930	-1			C36,S10/OC		-0.6
1882	Pro N	56	201	32	45	7	6	0	26	4		26	.224	.239	.318	77	-5		.932	6			C54,S2		0.5
1883	Pro N	74	263	34	52	13	3	0	24	26		32	.198	.270	.270	63	-11		.900	9			C74		0.3
1884	†Pro N	82	294	47	72	13	2	1	38	35		41	.245	.325	.313	104	3		.928	13			C81/31		2.0
1885	Pro N	71	252	25	54	7	3	0	12	23		33	.214	.280	.266	80	-5		.872	-2			C65,S5/OL2		-0.1
1886	Was N	81	273	23	52	9	2	0	17	39		35	.190	.292	.238	68	-8	6	.925	-6			C71,O14(1/6/7)/S3		-0.8
1887	Was N	28	90	7	18	2	0	1	6	5	0	18	.200	.242	.256	41	-7	2	.874	-3			C26,S3/OC		-0.7
1888	Det N	1	5	1	1	0	0	0	0	0	0	1	.200	.200	.200	28	0	0	.875	0			/C		0.0
Total	10	521	1865	215	386	68	23	3	167	147	0	235	.207	.265	.273	71	-57	8	.912	21			C458,O44(23/14/7),S27,3b2/21		-0.5

GILLIS, GRANT Grant B1.24.1901 Grove Hill AL D2.4.1981 Thomasville AL BR/TR/5-10/165 d9.19 Col Alabama

1927	Was A	10	36	8	8	1	0	2	2	0	0	2	.222	.263	.361	61	-2	0-0	1.000	-1	82	131	S10		-0.2
1928	Was A	24	87	13	22	5	1	0	10	4	3	5	.253	.309	.333	69	-4	0-1	.910	-7	79	52	S16,2b5,3b3		-0.9
1929	Bos A	28	73	5	18	4	0	0	11	6	0	8	.247	.304	.301	58	-5	0-1	.956	-3	98	81	2b25		-0.7
Total	3	62	196	26	48	12	2	2	23	12	3	13	.245	.299	.327	63	-11	0-2	.948	-11	94	82	2b30,S26,3b3		-1.8

GILMAN, JIMMY James Joseph B6.14.1870 D12.21.1912 Cleveland OH TR d7.10

| 1893 | Cle N | 2 | 7 | 1 | 2 | 0 | 0 | 0 | 1 | 0 | 0 | 2 | .286 | .286 | .286 | 49 | -1 | 0 | .667 | -1 | 88 | 0 | 3b2 | | -0.1 |

GILMAN, PIT Pitkin Clark B3.14.1864 Laporte OH D8.17.1950 Elyria OH BL/TL/?/170 d9.18

| 1884 | Cle N | 2 | 10 | 0 | 1 | 0 | 0 | 0 | 0 | 0 | | 3 | .100 | .100 | .100 | -36 | -2 | | 1.000 | 0 | 0 | 0 | O2L | | -0.1 |

GILMORE, GROVER Ernest Grover B11.1.1888 Chicago IL D11.25.1919 Sioux City IA BL/TL/5-9.5/170 d4.18

1914	KC F	139	530	91	152	25	5	1	32	37	3	108	.287	.337	.358	93	-14	23	.973	-1	92	107	O132(0/10/122)		-2.3
1915	KC F	119	411	53	117	22	15	1	47	26	13	50	.285	.347	.418	120	3	19	.979	5	109	107	O119R		0.2
Total	2	258	941	144	269	47	20	2	79	63	16	158	.286	.341	.385	105	-11	42	.976	4	100	107	O251(0/10/241)		-2.1

GILMORE, JIM James B5.1853 Baltimore MD D11.18.1928 Baltimore MD d4.26

| 1875 | Was NA | 3 | 12 | 2 | 3 | 0 | 0 | 0 | 0 | 0 | | 3 | .250 | .250 | .250 | 77 | 0 | 0-0 | .667 | -1 | | | C2/3OR | | -0.1 |

GILROY d9.7

1874	Chi NA	8	38	4	8	1	0	0	7	1		3	.211	.231	.237	50	-2	0-0	.816	-1			C8		-0.2
1875	Ath NA	2	6	0	1	0	0	0	0	0		3	.167	.167	.167	15	-1	0-0	.800	1			/COR		0.0
Total	2 NA	10	44	4	9	1	0	0	7	1		3	.205	.222	.227	45	-3	0-0	.814	0			C9/OR		-0.2

GINN, TINSLEY Tinsley Rucker B9.26.1891 Royston GA D8.30.1931 Atlanta GA BL/TR/5-9/180 d6.27 Col Georgia

| 1914 | Cle A | 2 | 1 | 0 | 0 | 0 | 0 | 0 | 0 | 0 | 0 | 0 | .000 | .000 | .000 | -96 | 0 | | — | 0 | 0 | 0 | O2 | | 0.0 |

GINSBERG, JOE Myron Nathan B10.11.1926 New York NY BL/TR/5-11/180* d9.15

1948	Det A	11	36	7	13	0	0	1	3		0	1	.361	.410	.361	103	0	0-0	.943	-1	104	43	C11		0.0
1950	Det A	36	95	12	22	6	0	0	12	11	1	6	.232	.318	.295	56	-6	1-0	.981	-2	147	68	C31		-0.6
1951	Det A	102	304	44	79	10	2	8	37	43	2	21	.260	.355	.385	100	0	0-2	.978	-4	76	108	C95		0.1
1952	Det A	113	307	26	68	13	2	6	36	51	3	21	.221	.338	.336	87	-4	1-1	.984	-1	97	86	C101		-0.7
1953	Det A	18	53	6	16	2	0	0	3	10	1	2	.302	.422	.340	109	2	0-0	.988	-1	83	187	C15		0.1
	Cle A	46	109	10	31	4	0	0	10	14	1	4	.284	.371	.321	91	-1	0-0	.966	-3	91	52	C39		-0.2
	Year	64	162	16	47	6	0	0	13	24	2	5	.290	.388	.327	97	1	0-0	.974	-4	88	97	C54		-0.1
1954	Cle A	3	2	0	1	0	1	0	1	0	1	1	.500	.667	1.500	473	1	0-0	1.000	0	0	0	/C		0.1
1956	KC A	71	195	15	48	8	1	1	23	23-3	0	17	.246	.323	.313	69	-8	1-1	.989	-1	81	120	C57		-0.7
	Bal A	15	28	0	2	0	0	0	2	2-0	0	4	.071	.129	.071	-48	-6	0-0	1.000	-0	83	89	C8		0.1
	Year	86	223	15	50	8	1	1	14	25-3	0	21	.224	.299	.283	56	-14	1-1	.990	-2	81	117	C65		-0.6
1957	Bal A	85	175	15	48	8	2	1	18	18-1	2	19	.274	.342	.360	100	0	2-1	.986	1	116	100	C66		0.2
1958	Bal A	61	109	4	23	1	0	3	16	13-1	2	14	.211	.302	.303	72	-4	0-0	.994	3	154	51	C39		-0.3
1959	Bal A	65	166	14	30	2	1	0	14	21-3	0	13	.181	.268	.211	35	-15	1-0	.993	3	143	159	C62		-0.9
1960	Bal A	14	30	1	8	0	0	0	6	6-1	0	1	.267	.389	.300	92	-1	0-0	.940	-1	71	42	C14		-0.1

YEAR	TM LG	G	AB	R	H	2B	3B	HR	RBI	BB-IB	HP	SO	AVG	OBP	SLG	AOPS	ABR	SB-CS	FA	FR	RNG	THR	GAMES AT POSITION	DL	BFW
	Chi A	28	75	8	19	4	0	0	9	10-0	1	8	.253	.345	.307	80	-2	1-0	.993	4	74	64	C25		0.3
	Year	42	105	11	27	5	0	0	15	16-1	1	9	.257	.358	.305	83	-2	1-0	.976	2	73	57	C39		0.2
1961	Chi A	6	3	0	0	0	0	0	0	1-0	0	2	.000	.250	.000	-27	-1	0-0	1.000	0	0	0	C2		0.0
	Bos N	19	24	1	6	0	0	0	5	0-0	0	2	.250	.250	.250	33	-2	0-0	1.000	-2	35	173	C6		-0.4
	Year	25	27	1	6	0	0	0	5	1-0	0	4	.222	.250	.222	27	-3	0-0	1.000	-2	31	155	C8		-0.4
1962	NY N	2	5	0	0	0	0	0	0	0-0	0	1	.000	.000	.000	-98	-1	0-0	1.000	1	0	0	C2		0.0
Total	13	695	1716	168	414	59	8	20	182	226-9	14	135	.241	.332	.320	79*	-47	7-5	.983	-13	100	98	C574		-3.4

GINTER, KEITH Keith Michael B5.5.1976 Norwalk CA BR/TR/5-10/190* [HouN98 10/302] d9.20 Col Texas Tech

YEAR	TM LG	G	AB	R	H	2B	3B	HR	RBI	BB-IB	HP	SO	AVG	OBP	SLG	AOPS	ABR	SB-CS	FA	FR	RNG	THR	GAMES AT POSITION	DL	BFW
2000	Hou N	5	8	3	2	0	0	1	3	1-0	0	3	.250	.300	.625	125	0	0-0	1.000	-0	84	145	2b2		0.0
2001	Hou N	1	1	0	0	0	0	0	0	0-0	0	0	.000	.000	.000	-93	0	0-0	—	0			/H		0.0
2002	Hou N	7	5	1	1	1	0	0	0	2-0	1	1	.200	.500	.400	135	1	0-0	.875	1	144	345	3b4/S		0.2
	Mil N	21	76	6	18	8	0	1	8	15-0	0	14	.237	.363	.382	100	0	0-0	.961	-4	75	67	3b21		-0.3
	Year	28	81	7	19	9	0	1	8	17-0	1	15	.235	.374	.383	102	1	0-0	.949	-3	80	85	3b25/S		-0.1
2003	Mil N	127	358	51	92	15	2	14	44	37-1	17	87	.257	.352	.427	103	2	1-1	.991	-19	89	95	2b53,3b40,S2,O2L		-1.4
2004	Mil N	113	386	47	101	23	2	19	60	37-2	6	100	.262	.333	.479	106	3	8-1	.973	-17	85	75	2b53,3b47,O2R,D2		-1.1
2005	Oak A	51	137	12	22	5	0	3	25	13-0	1	25	.161	.234	.263	33	-13	0-0	.975	2	101	118	2b25,3b12,O2L,D9	34	-1.1
Total	6	325	971	120	236	52	4	38	140	105-3	25	230	.243	.329	.422	95	-7	9-2	.981	-37	89	85	2b134,3b124,D11,O6(4/0/2),S3	34	-3.6

GIONFRIDDO, AL Albert Francis B3.8.1922 Dysart PA D3.14.2003 Solvang CA BL/TL/5-6/165 d9.23

YEAR	TM LG	G	AB	R	H	2B	3B	HR	RBI	BB-IB	HP	SO	AVG	OBP	SLG	AOPS	ABR	SB-CS	FA	FR	RNG	THR	GAMES AT POSITION	DL	BFW
1944	Pit N	4	6	0	1	0	0	0	1	1-0	0	1	.167	.286	.167	28	-1	0	1.000	-0	94	0	/OC		-0.1
1945	Pit N	122	409	74	116	18	9	2	42	60	1	22	.284	.377	.386	108	6	12	.964	-7	91	73	O106(13/82/11)		-0.5
1946	Pit N	64	102	11	26	2	2	0	10	14	0	5	.255	.345	.314	85	-2	1	.944	-0	101	99	O33(8/13/12)		-0.3
1947	Pit N	1	1	0	0	0	0	0	0	0	0	0	.000	.000	.000	-97	0	0	—	0			/H		0.0
	†Bro N	37	62	10	11	2	1	0	6	16	0	11	.177	.346	.242	57	-3	2	.938	-1	96	89	O17(11/0/6)		-0.5
	Year	38	63	10	11	2	1	0	6	16	0	11	.175	.342	.238	54	-4	2	.938	-1	96	89	O17(11/0/6)		-0.5
Total	4	228	580	95	154	22	12	2	58	91	1	39	.266	.366	.355	97	-0	15	.959	-8	93	78	O157(32/96/29)		-1.4

GIORDANO, TOMMY Thomas Arthur "T-Bone" (b Carmine Arthur Giordano) B10.9.1925 Newark NJ BR/TR/6-0/175 d9.11

YEAR	TM LG	G	AB	R	H	2B	3B	HR	RBI	BB-IB	HP	SO	AVG	OBP	SLG	AOPS	ABR	SB-CS	FA	FR	RNG	THR	GAMES AT POSITION	DL	BFW
1953	Phi A	11	40	6	7	2	1	2	5	5	0	6	.175	.267	.375	69	-2	0-1	.984	0	101	117	2b11		-0.1

GIOVANOLA, ED Edward Thomas B3.4.1969 Los Gatos CA BL/TR/5-10/175(170-188) [AtlN90 7/183] d9.10 Col Santa Clara

YEAR	TM LG	G	AB	R	H	2B	3B	HR	RBI	BB-IB	HP	SO	AVG	OBP	SLG	AOPS	ABR	SB-CS	FA	FR	RNG	THR	GAMES AT POSITION	DL	BFW
1995	Atl N	13	14	2	1	0	0	0	0	3-0	0	5	.071	.235	.071	-14	-2	0-0	1.000	-1	61	57	2b7,3b3/S		-0.3
1996	Atl N	43	82	10	19	2	0	0	7	8-0	1	13	.232	.304	.256	48	-6	1-0	.983	1	89	112	S25,3b6,2b5		-0.3
1997	Atl N	14	8	0	2	0	0	0	0	2-1	0	1	.250	.400	.250	74	0	0-0	1.000	-0	94	0	3b8/2S		0.0
1998	SD N	92	139	19	32	3	3	1	9	22-0	1	22	.230	.335	.317	78	-4	1-2	.965	12	127	66	3b37,2b36/S		0.8
1999	SD N	56	58	10	11	0	1	0	3	9-0	0	8	.190	.294	.224	38	-6	2-0	.938	4	124	0	3b25,2b19,S7/P		-0.1
Total	5	218	301	41	65	5	4	1	19	44-1	1	49	.216	.316	.269	57	-18	4-2	.964	15	119	66	3b79,2b68,S35/P		0.1

GIPSON, CHARLES Charles Wells B12.16.1972 Orange CA BR/TR/6-2/180(180-195) [SeaA91 63/1493] d3.31 Col Cypress (CA) JC OF(142/62/82)

YEAR	TM LG	G	AB	R	H	2B	3B	HR	RBI	BB-IB	HP	SO	AVG	OBP	SLG	AOPS	ABR	SB-CS	FA	FR	RNG	THR	GAMES AT POSITION	DL	BFW
1998	Sea A	44	51	11	12	1	0	0	2	5-1	1	9	.235	.316	.255	51	-4	2-1	.973	2	121	229	O36(14/11/13),3b4		-0.2
1999	Sea A	55	80	16	18	5	2	0	9	6-0	1	13	.225	.287	.338	59	-5	3-4	.960	9	105	895	O28(8/9/15),3b17,2b3,S3,D4	52	0.3
2000	Sea A	59	29	7	9	1	1	0	3	4-0	0	9	.310	.394	.414	107	0	2-3	1.000	1	136	0	O48(14/8/29),3b5,S5/D		0.0
2001	†Sea A	94	64	16	14	2	2	0	5	4-0	2	20	.219	.282	.313	61	-1	4-1	1.000	-1	94	82	O65(41/14/11),D11,3b9,S6/2		-0.6
2002	Sea A	79	72	22	17	5	2	0	8	9-0	1	14	.236	.329	.361	86	-1	4-0	.971	2	114	121	O73(57/5/13),3b4		-0.1
2003	NY A	18	10	3	2	0	0	0	2	1-0	0	2	.200	.273	.200	28	-1	2-1	1.000	0	88	0	O8C,D3		0.1
2004	TB A	5	4	1	2	0	0	0	0	0-0	0	1	.500	.500	.500	166	0	1-0	1.000	0	122	265	S2,O2(1/2/0)/D		-0.2
2005	Hou N	19	11	2	2	1	0	0	1	1-0	0	3	.182	.250	.273	37	-1	1-0	1.000	-1	74	0	O13(7/5/1)		-0.2
Total	8	373	321	78	76	15	7	0	30	30-1	5	71	.237	.311	.327	68	-16	16-11	.981	11	104	193	O273L,3b39,D20,S16,2b4	52	-0.7

GIRARDI, JOE Joseph Elliott B10.14.1964 Peoria IL BR/TR/5-11/195* [ChiN86 5/116] d4.4 C1 Col Northwestern

YEAR	TM LG	G	AB	R	H	2B	3B	HR	RBI	BB-IB	HP	SO	AVG	OBP	SLG	AOPS	ABR	SB-CS	FA	FR	RNG	THR	GAMES AT POSITION	DL	BFW
1989	†Chi N	59	157	15	39	10	0	1	14	11-5	2	26	.248	.304	.331	77	-4	2-1	.981	9	107	121	C59		0.8
1990	Chi N	133	419	36	113	24	2	1	38	17-11	3	50	.270	.300	.344	72	-16	8-3	.985	-8	137	103	C133		-1.6
1991	Chi N	21	47	3	9	2	0	0	6	6-1	0	6	.191	.283	.234	45	-3	0-0	.972	1	92	96	C21	111	-0.2
1992	Chi N	91	270	19	73	3	1	1	12	19-3	1	38	.270	.320	.300	75	-9	0-2	.991	-3	131	114	C86	67	-0.9
1993	Col N	86	310	35	90	14	5	3	31	24-0	3	41	.290	.346	.397	84	-6	6-6	.989	-3	92	111	C84	15	-0.2
1994	Col N	93	330	47	91	9	4	4	34	21-1	2	48	.276	.321	.364	67	-16	3-3	.992	8	98	118	C93		-2.0
1995	†Col N	125	462	63	121	17	2	8	55	29-0	2	76	.262	.308	.359	59	-27	3-3	.988	-1	104	87	C122		-2.0
1996	†NY A	124	422	55	124	22	3	2	45	30-1	5	55	.294	.346	.374	83	-11	13-4	.996	2	78	99	C120,D2		0.0
1997	†NY A	112	398	38	105	23	1	1	50	26-1	2	53	.264	.311	.334	69	-18	2-3	.994	12	106	104	C111/D		0.1
1998	†NY A	78	254	31	70	11	4	3	31	14-1	2	38	.276	.317	.386	86	-6	2-4	.995	12	97	79	C78		0.9
1999	†NY A	65	209	23	50	16	1	2	27	10-0	0	25	.239	.271	.354	60	-13	3-1	.984	3	72	98	C65		-0.5
2000	Chi N☆	106	363	47	101	15	4	6	40	32-3	3	61	.278	.339	.375	82	-10	1-0	.993	-10	96	134	C103		-1.3
2001	Chi N	78	229	22	58	10	1	3	25	21-4	0	50	.253	.315	.345	73	-9	0-1	1.000	-1	93	147	C71	15	-0.6
2002	Chi N	90	234	19	53	10	1	1	13	16-3	0	35	.226	.275	.291	52	-18	1-0	.990	-6	91	103	C88	135	-1.9
2003	StL N	16	23	1	3	0	0	0	1	3-0	0	4	.130	.231	.130	-2	-4	0-0	.958	-4	98	0	C13	135	-0.8
Total	15	1277	4127	454	1100	186	26	36	422	279-34	25	607	.267	.315	.350	71	-170	44-31	.991	11	103	105	C1247,D3	343	-8.6

GIULIANI, TONY Angelo John B11.24.1912 St.Paul MN D10.8.2004 St.Paul MN BR/TR/5-11/175 d4.18

YEAR	TM LG	G	AB	R	H	2B	3B	HR	RBI	BB-IB	HP	SO	AVG	OBP	SLG	AOPS	ABR	SB-CS	FA	FR	RNG	THR	GAMES AT POSITION	DL	BFW
1936	StL A	71	198	17	43	1	0	0	13	11	0	13	.217	.258	.232	21	-25	0-0	.966	2	109	47	C66		-1.8
1937	StL A	19	53	16	16	1	0	0	3	3	0	3	.302	.339	.321	67	-3	0-0	.986	-1	90	95	C19		-0.3
1938	Was A	46	115	10	25	4	0	0	15	8	0	7	.217	.268	.252	33	-12	1-0	1.000	-1	109	92	C46		-1.0
1939	Was A	54	172	20	43	6	2	0	18	4	0	7	.250	.267	.308	50	-14	0-1	.979	2	151	85	C50		-0.9
1940	Bro N	1	1	0	0	0	0	0	0	0	0	1	.000	.000	.000	-94	0	0	1.000	-0	0	0	/C		0.0
1941	Bro N	3	2	0	0	0	0	0	0	0	0	0	.000	.000	.000	-96	-1	0	1.000	1	0	0	C3		0.0
1943	Was A	49	133	5	30	4	1	0	20	12	0	14	.226	.290	.271	67	-6	0-1	.962	-1	119	81	C49		-0.6
Total	7	243	674	58	157	18	3	0	69	38	0	41	.233	.274	.269	42	-61	1-2	.976	1	119	75	C234		-4.6

GLADD, JIM James Walter B10.2.1922 Ft.Gibson OK D11.8.1977 Long Beach CA BR/TR/6-2/190 d9.9

YEAR	TM LG	G	AB	R	H	2B	3B	HR	RBI	BB-IB	HP	SO	AVG	OBP	SLG	AOPS	ABR	SB-CS	FA	FR	RNG	THR	GAMES AT POSITION	DL	BFW
1946	NY N	4	11	0	1	0	0	0	1	0	0	4	.091	.167	.091	-26	-2	0-0	1.000	2	89	74	C4		0.0

GLADDEN, DAN Clinton Daniel B7.7.1957 San Jose CA BR/TR/5-11/180* d9.5 Col Cal St.-Fresno

YEAR	TM LG	G	AB	R	H	2B	3B	HR	RBI	BB-IB	HP	SO	AVG	OBP	SLG	AOPS	ABR	SB-CS	FA	FR	RNG	THR	GAMES AT POSITION	DL	BFW
1983	SF N	18	63	6	14	2	0	1	9	5-0	0	11	.222	.275	.302	63	-3	4-3	1.000	2	125	0	O18(0/17/1)		-0.2
1984	SF N	86	342	71	120	17	2	4	31	33-2	2	37	.351	.410	.447	145	22	31-16	.988	4	105	164	O85C		2.7
1985	SF N	142	502	64	122	15	8	7	41	40-1	7	78	.243	.307	.347	86	-11	32-15	.975	-7	97	41	O124(14/111/1)		-1.9
1986	SF N	102	351	55	97	16	1	4	29	39-3	5	59	.276	.357	.362	104	3	27-10	.987	5	113	141	O89C	49	1.0
1987	†Min A	121	438	69	109	21	2	8	38	38-2	3	72	.249	.312	.361	75	-16	25-9	.987	7	110	136	O111(105/8/2),D4		-1.0
1988	Min A	141	576	91	155	32	6	11	62	46-4	4	74	.269	.325	.403	100	0	28-8	.991	12	113	151	O140L/23P		1.1
1989	Min A	121	461	69	136	23	3	8	46	23-3	5	53	.295	.331	.410	102	1	23-7	.966	4	110	122	O117(116/2/0)/PD	36	0.4
1990	Min A	136	534	64	147	27	6	5	40	26-2	6	67	.275	.314	.376	87	-10	25-9	.980	9	110	146	O133(133/1/0),D2		-0.3
1991	†Min A	126	461	65	114	14	6	6	52	36-1	5	60	.247	.306	.356	79	-14	15-9	.988	0	102	63	O126L	25	-1.1
1992	Det A	113	417	57	106	20	1	7	42	30-0	2	64	.254	.304	.357	84	-9	4-2	.987	1	98	130	O108(95/17/0),D2	31	-1.1
1993	Det A	91	356	52	95	16	2	13	56	21-0	5	50	.267	.312	.433	98	-3	8-5	.986	4	104	173	O86(69/18/0),D5	50	-0.1
Total	11	1197	4501	663	1215	203	40	74	446	337-18	42	625	.270	.324	.382	94	-40	222-93	.984	40	107	122	O1137(798/349/4),D15,P2/32	191	-1.1

GLADMON, BUCK James Henry B11.1863 Washington DC D1.13.1890 Washington DC d7.7

YEAR	TM LG	G	AB	R	H	2B	3B	HR	RBI	BB-IB	HP	SO	AVG	OBP	SLG	AOPS	ABR	SB-CS	FA	FR	RNG	THR	GAMES AT POSITION	DL	BFW
1883	Phi N	1	4	1	0	0	0	0	0	0		2	.000	.000	.000	-99	-1		1.000	-0	74	0	/3		-0.1
1884	Was AA	56	224	17	35	5	3	1		3	3		.156	.178	.219	33	-15		.796	-5	94	70	3b53,O2R/S		-1.8
1886	Was N	44	152	17	21	5	3	1	15	12		30	.138	.201	.230	33	-12	5	.830	-2	92	154	3b44		-1.2
Total	3	101	380	35	56	10	6	2	15	15		32	.147	.186	.221	31	-28	5	.812	-7	93	105	3b98,O2R/S		-3.1

GLADU, ROLAND Roland Edouard B5.10.1911 Montreal QC, Can. D7.26.1994 Montreal QC, Can. BL/TL/5-8.5/185 d4.18

YEAR	TM LG	G	AB	R	H	2B	3B	HR	RBI	BB-IB	HP	SO	AVG	OBP	SLG	AOPS	ABR	SB-CS	FA	FR	RNG	THR	GAMES AT POSITION	DL	BFW
1944	Bos N	21	66	5	16	2	1	1	7	3	0	8	.242	.275	.348	72	-3	0	.891	-2	74	244	3b15,O3L		-0.5

GLANVILLE, DOUG Douglas Metunwa B8.25.1970 Hackensack NJ BR/TR/6-2/180* [ChiN91 1/12] d6.9 Col Penn

YEAR	TM LG	G	AB	R	H	2B	3B	HR	RBI	BB-IB	HP	SO	AVG	OBP	SLG	AOPS	ABR	SB-CS	FA	FR	RNG	THR	GAMES AT POSITION	DL	BFW
1996	Chi N	49	83	10	20	5	1	1	10	3-0	0	11	.241	.264	.361	62	-5	2-0	.973	-0	97	95	O35(19/9/8)		-0.5
1997	Chi N	146	474	79	142	22	5	4	35	24-0	1	46	.300	.333	.392	87	-10	19-11	.989	9	108	166	O138(120/30/1)		-0.4

YEAR	TM LG	G	AB	R	H	2B	3B	HR	RBI	BB-IB	HP	SO	AVG	OBP	SLG	AOPS	ABR	SB-CS	FA	FR	RNG	THR	GAMES AT POSITION	DL	BFW
1998	Phi N	158	678	106	189	28	7	8	49	42-1	6	89	.279	.325	.376	84	-17	23-6	.995	-1	97	142	O158C		-1.3
1999	Phi N	150	628	101	204	38	6	11	73	48-1	6	82	.325	.376	.457	109	9	34-2	.980	6	107	163	O148C		2.2
2000	Phi N	154	637	89	175	27	6	8	52	31-1	2	76	.275	.307	.374	72	-29	31-8	.990	4	108	103	O150C		-1.9
2001	Phi N	153	634	74	166	24	3	14	55	19-1	4	91	.262	.285	.375	73	-29	28-6	.991	6	114	96	O150C		-1.6
2002	Phi N	138	422	49	105	16	3	6	29	25-4	2	57	.249	.292	.344	75	-19	19-2	1.000	-5	89	123	O117C		-1.9
2003	Tex A	52	195	22	53	5	0	4	14	6-1	0	25	.272	.294	.359	66	-10	4-0	1.000	-3	94	46	O52C		-1.1
	†Chi N	28	51	2	12	0	0	1	2	2-0	0	4	.235	.259	.294	44	-4	0-1	1.000	2	136	188	O18(3/15/1)	53	-0.2
2004	Phi N	87	162	21	34	1	0	2	14	8-1	0	21	.210	.244	.265	32	-17	8-0	1.000	2	121	0	O68(13/56/0)		-1.3
Total	9	1115	3964	553	1100	166	32	59	333	208-10	21	502	.277	.315	.380	80	-131	168-36	.991	21	105	121	O1034(155/885/10)	53	-8.0

GLASSCOCK, JACK John Wesley "Pebbly Jack" B7.22.1857 Wheeling WV D2.24.1947 Wheeling WV BR/TR/5-8/160 d5.1 M2

YEAR	TM LG	G	AB	R	H	2B	3B	HR	RBI	BB-IB	HP	SO	AVG	OBP	SLG	AOPS	ABR	SB-CS	FA	FR	RNG	THR	GAMES AT POSITION	DL	BFW
1879	Cle N	80	325	31	68	9	3	0	29	6		24	.209	.224	.255	58	-14		.919	-9	86	63	2b66,3b14		-1.8
1880	Cle N	77	296	37	72	13	3	0	27	2		21	.243	.248	.307	89	-3		.891	5	100	114	S77		0.5
1881	Cle N	85	335	49	86	9	5	0	33	15		8	.257	.289	.313	94	-2		.911	9	105	123	S79,2b6		1.0
1882	Cle N	84	358	66	104	27	9	4	46	13		9	.291	.315	.450	147	19		.900	24	118	174	S83/3		4.1
1883	Cle N	96	383	67	110	19	6	0	46	13		23	.287	.311	.368	107	3		.922	18	107	119	S93,2b3		2.0
1884	Cle N	72	281	45	70	4	4	1	22	25		16	.249	.310	.302	91	-3		.893	26	115	96	S69,2b3,P2		2.2
	Cin U	38	172	48	72	9	5	2		8			.419	.444	.564	189	14		.889	1	104	81	S36,2b2		1.4
1885	StL N	111	446	66	125	18	3	1	40	29		10	.280	.324	.341	123	13		.917	21	112	98	S110/2		3.5
1886	StL N	121	486	96	158	29	7	3	40	38		13	.325	.374	.432	154	34	38	.906	15	107	124	S120/OR		4.6
1887	Ind N	122	483	91	142	18	7	0	40	41	10	8	.294	.361	.360	105	6	62	.906	39	122	135	S122/P		4.0
1888	Ind N	113	442	63	119	17	3	1	45	14	7	17	.269	.302	.328	99	-1	48	.901	14	106	110	S110,2b3/P		1.6
1889	Ind N	134	582	128	205	40	3	7	85	31	5	10	.352	.390	.467	136	27	57	.915	38	118	129	S132,2b2/PM		5.8
1890	NY N	124	512	91	172	32	9	1	66	41	9	8	.336	.395	.439	143	28	54	.910	23	101	102	S124		4.8
1891	NY N	97	369	46	89	12	6	0	55	36	5	11	.241	.317	.306	85	-6	29	.913	1	91	126	S97		-0.2
1892	StL N	139	566	83	151	27	5	3	72	44	7	19	.267	.327	.348	110	7	26	.916	6	102	87	S139,M		1.9
1893	StL N	48	195	32	56	8	1	1	26	25	5	3	.287	.382	.354	96	0	20	.907	-5	96	100	S48		-0.2
	Pit N	66	293	49	100	7	11	1	74	17	4	4	.341	.385	.451	124	8	16	.934	10	103	153	S66		1.8
	Year	114	488	81	156	15	12	2	100	42	9	7	.320	.384	.412	113	9	36	.923	5	100	131	S114		1.6
1894	Pit N	87	335	47	94	10	7	1	65	32	4	4	.281	.350	.361	73	-15	18	.933	3	99	121	S86		-0.6
1895	Lou N	18	74	9	25	1	1	1	6	3	3	1	.338	.387	.446	122	3	1	.900	1	102	91	S13,1b5		0.3
	Was N	25	100	20	23	2	0	0	10	7	3	3	.230	.300	.250	43	-8	3	.895	6	118	84	S25		-0.1
	Year	43	174	29	48	3	1	1	16	10	6	4	.276	.337	.333	76	-6	4	.897	7	112	86	S38,1b5		0.2
Total	17	1737	7033	1164	2041	313	98	27	827	440	62	212	.290	.337	.374	112	110	372	.910	246	108	117	S1629,2b86,3b15,1b5,P5/OR		36.6

GLAUS, TROY Troy B8.3.1976 Tarzana CA BR/TR/6-5/229(225-245) [CalA97 1/3] d7.31 Col UCLA

YEAR	TM LG	G	AB	R	H	2B	3B	HR	RBI	BB-IB	HP	SO	AVG	OBP	SLG	AOPS	ABR	SB-CS	FA	FR	RNG	THR	GAMES AT POSITION	DL	BFW
1998	Ana A	48	165	19	36	9	0	1	23	15-0	0	51	.218	.280	.291	49	-12	1-0	.941	0	102	99	3b48		-1.1
1999	Ana A	154	551	85	132	29	0	29	79	71-1	6	143	.240	.331	.450	97	-3	5-1	.954	-6	97	99	3b153/D		-0.6
2000	Ana A★	159	563	120	160	37	1	47	102	112-6	2	163	.284	.404	.604	147	43	14-11	.933	12	117	115	3b156,S6,D4		4.9
2001	Ana A	161	588	100	147	38	2	41	108	107-7	6	158	.250	.367	.531	131	29	10-3	.953	-16	92	79	3b159,S2,D2		1.5
2002	†Ana A	156	569	99	142	24	1	30	111	88-4	6	144	.250	.352	.453	115	14	10-3	.950	-2	100	128	3b156,S2		1.3
2003	Ana A★	91	319	53	79	17	2	16	50	46-4	1	73	.248	.343	.464	144	7	7-2	.923	-8	91	79	3b87,D4	69	0.1
2004	†Ana A	58	207	47	52	11	1	18	42	31-3	5	52	.251	.355	.575	143	13	2-3	.950	-2	84	68	D39,3b19	109	0.8
2005	Ari N	149	538	78	139	29	1	37	97	84-2	7	145	.258	.363	.522	124	20	4-2	.946	8	110	92	3b145/D		2.9
Total	8	976	3500	601	887	194	8	219	612	554-27	31	929	.253	.358	.501	120	111	53-25	.945	-14	102	100	3b923,D51,S10	178	9.8

GLAVIANO, TOMMY Thomas Giatano "Rabbit" B10.26.1923 Sacramento CA D1.19.2004 Sacramento CA BR/TR/5-9/175* d4.19

YEAR	TM LG	G	AB	R	H	2B	3B	HR	RBI	BB-IB	HP	SO	AVG	OBP	SLG	AOPS	ABR	SB-CS	FA	FR	RNG	THR	GAMES AT POSITION	DL	BFW
1949	StL N	87	258	32	69	16	1	6	36	41	6	35	.267	.380	.407	106	4	0	.929	7	113	106	3b73,2b7		1.1
1950	StL N	115	410	92	117	29	2	11	44	90	6	74	.285	.421	.446	122	19	6	.935	2	106	71	3b106,2b5/S		2.1
1951	StL N	54	104	20	19	4	0	1	4	26	2	18	.183	.356	.250	66	-4	3-0	.972	-2	87	0	O17(2/14/1),2b9		-0.5
1952	StL N	80	162	30	39	5	1	3	19	27	5	26	.241	.366	.340	97	1	0-0	.934	2	105	70	3b52/2		0.2
1953	Phi N	53	74	17	15	1	2	3	5	24	2	20	.203	.410	.392	111	3	2-0	.892	-2	82	82	3b14,2b12/S		0.1
Total	5	389	1008	191	259	55	6	24	108	208	21	173	.257	.395	.395	108	23	11-0	.931	6	107	82	3b245,2b34,O17(2/14/1),S2		3.0

GLAVINE, MIKE Michael Patrick B1.24.1973 Concord MA BL/TL/6-3/210 [CleA95 22/614] d9.14 b-Tom Col Northeastern

YEAR	TM LG	G	AB	R	H	2B	3B	HR	RBI	BB-IB	HP	SO	AVG	OBP	SLG	AOPS	ABR	SB-CS	FA	FR	RNG	THR	GAMES AT POSITION	DL	BFW
2003	NY N	6	7	0	1	0	0	0	0	0-0	0	1	.143	.143	.143	-26	-1	0-0	1.000	0	157	109	1b3		-0.1

GLEASON, HARRY Harry Gilbert B3.28.1875 Camden NJ D10.21.1961 Camden NJ BR/TR/5-6/160 d9.27 b-Kid

YEAR	TM LG	G	AB	R	H	2B	3B	HR	RBI	BB-IB	HP	SO	AVG	OBP	SLG	AOPS	ABR	SB-CS	FA	FR	RNG	THR	GAMES AT POSITION	DL	BFW
1901	Bos A	1	1	0	1	0	0	0	0	0	0		1.000	1.000	1.000	464	0	1	.667	0	195	1796	/3		0.1
1902	Bos A	71	240	30	54	5	5	2	25	10	3		.225	.265	.313	58	-15	6	.930	-3	98	174	3b35,O23(8/15/0),2b4		-1.7
1903	Bos A	6	13	3	2	1	0	0	2	0	0		.154	.154	.231	13	-1	0	.750	-1	92	0	3b2		-0.2
1904	StL A	46	155	10	33	7	1	0	6	4	3		.213	.247	.271	68	-6	1	.908	-4	109	132	S20,3b20,2b5/OC		-1.0
1905	StL A	150	535	45	116	11	5	1	57	34	4		.217	.269	.262	72	-18	23	.911	-15	95	64	3b144,2b7		-3.2
Total	5	274	944	88	206	24	11	3	90	48	10		.218	.263	.276	67	-40	31	.914	-22	95	99	3b202,O24(8/16/0),S20,2b16		-6.0

GLEASON, JACK John Day B7.14.1854 St.Louis MO D9.4.1944 St.Louis MO BR/TR/?/170 d10.2 b-Bill

YEAR	TM LG	G	AB	R	H	2B	3B	HR	RBI	BB-IB	HP	SO	AVG	OBP	SLG	AOPS	ABR	SB-CS	FA	FR	RNG	THR	GAMES AT POSITION	DL	BFW
1877	StL N	1	4	0	1	0	0	0	0	0		1	.250	.250	.250	61	0		—	-0	0	0	/OC		0.0
1882	StL AA	78	331	53	84	10	1	2		27			.254	.310	.308	105	2		.768	3	105	134	3b73,O6R/2		0.6
1883	StL AA	9	34	2	8	0	0	0		4			.235	.316	.235	76	-1		.833	1	186	0	O9L/3		0.0
	Lou AA	84	355	69	106	11	4	2		25			.299	.345	.369	140	18		.795	-32	62	66	3b83/S		-1.1
	Year	93	389	71	114	11	4	2		29			.293	.342	.357	134	17		.798	-31	64	65	3b84,O9L/S		-1.1
1884	StL U	92	395	90	128	30	2	4		23			.324	.361	.441	137	7		.768	-4	105	146	3b92		0.4
1885	StL N	2	7	0	1	0	0	0	0	0		1	.143	.143	.143	-8	-1		.857	-0	77	0	3b2		-0.1
1886	Phi AA	77	299	39	56	8	7	1	31	16	11		.187	.255	.271	64	-13	8	.797	-6	98	162	3b77		-1.6
Total	6	343	1425	253	384	59	14	9	31	95	11	2	.269	.320	.349	112	12	8	.781	-39	93	125	3b328,O16(9/1/6)/S2		-1.8

GLEASON, ROY Roy William B4.9.1943 Melrose Park IL BB/TR/6-5.5/225 d9.3

YEAR	TM LG	G	AB	R	H	2B	3B	HR	RBI	BB-IB	HP	SO	AVG	OBP	SLG	AOPS	ABR	SB-CS	FA	FR	RNG	THR	GAMES AT POSITION	DL	BFW
1963	LA N	8	1	3	1	1	0	0	0	0-0	0	0	1.000	1.000	2.000	795	1	0-0	—	0			/H		0.1

GLEASON, BILL William G. "Will" B11.12.1858 St.Louis MO D7.21.1932 St.Louis MO BR/TR/5-8/170 d5.2 U1 b-Jack

YEAR	TM LG	G	AB	R	H	2B	3B	HR	RBI	BB-IB	HP	SO	AVG	OBP	SLG	AOPS	ABR	SB-CS	FA	FR	RNG	THR	GAMES AT POSITION	DL	BFW
1882	StL AA	79	347	63	100	11	6	1		6			.288	.300	.363	118	5		.833	-10	106	112	S79		1.6
1883	StL AA	98	425	81	122	21	9	2	42	15			.287	.311	.393	119	8		.871	-2	93	129	S98		0.7
1884	StL AA	110	472	97	127	21	7	1		27	12		.269	.325	.350	116	9		.867	-21	89	87	S110/3		-0.8
1885	†StL AA	112	472	79	119	9	5	3	53	29	15		.252	.316	.311	94	-3		.869	-42	80	63	S112		-3.8
1886	†StL AA	125	524	97	141	18	5	0	61	43	7		.269	.333	.323	101	1	19	.853	-30	86	113	S125		-2.2
1887	†StL AA	135	598	135	172	19	1	0	76	41	8		.288	.342	.323	78	-20	23	.875	-11	98	85	S135		-2.2
1888	Phi AA	123	499	55	112	10	2	0	61	12	9		.224	.256	.253	63	-21	27	.858	-14	94	118	S121/31		-2.9
1889	Lou AA	16	58	6	14	2	0	0	5	4	1		.241	.302	.276	66	-2	1	.822	-1	107	63	S16		-0.3
Total	8	798	3395	613	907	111	35	7	298	177	52	1	.267	.313	.327	95	-23	70	.860	-110	92	99	S796,3b2/1		-9.9

GLEASON, KID William J. B10.26.1866 Camden NJ D1.2.1933 Philadelphia PA BB/TR/5-7/158 d4.20 M5/C16 b-Harry OF(14/15/13) ▲

YEAR	TM LG	G	AB	R	H	2B	3B	HR	RBI	BB-IB	HP	SO	AVG	OBP	SLG	AOPS	ABR	SB-CS	FA	FR	RNG	THR	GAMES AT POSITION	DL	BFW
1888	Phi N	24	83	4	17	2	0	0	5	3	0	16	.205	.233	.229	45	-5	3	.841	-3	72	112	P24/OR		-0.2
1889	Phi N	30	99	11	25	5	0	0	8	8	0	12	.253	.308	.303	65	-5	1	.862	-1	109	61	P29,O3C,2b2		-0.1
1890	Phi N	63	224	22	47	3	0	0	17	12	0	21	.210	.250	.223	37	-18	10	.937	-2	93	118	P60,2b2		-0.2
1891	Phi N	65	214	31	53	5	2	0	17	20	2	17	.248	.318	.290	75	-7	6	.896	-5	84	65	P53,O9(1/8/0),S4		-0.5
1892	StL N	66	233	35	50	4	2	3	25	34	0	23	.215	.315	.288	87	-3	7	.934	4	112	122	P47,O10(3/2/6),2b9/1		0.1
1893	StL N	59	199	25	51	6	4	0	20	19	2	8	.256	.327	.327	74	-8	2	.907	-1	103	112	P48,O11(5/0/6)/S		-0.3
1894	StL N	9	28	9	7	1	0	1	4	2	0	1	.250	.300	.321	50	-3	0	.885	1	146	0	P8/1		0.0
	†Bal N	26	86	22	30	5	1	0	17	7	0	2	.349	.398	.430	95	-1	3	.900	-2	65	91	P21/1		-0.1
	Year	35	114	25	37	6	2	1	18	9	0	3	.325	.374	.404	85	-3	1	.894	-1	85	68	P29,1b2		-0.1
1895	†Bal N	112	421	90	130	14	12	0	74	33	2	18	.309	.366	.399	95	-5	19	.899	-16	96	99	2b85,3b12,P9,O4L		-1.3
1896	NY N	133	541	79	162	17	5	4	89	42	2	13	.299	.352	.372	93	-5	46	.938	7	101	72	2b130,3b3/OC		0.6
1897	NY N	132	543	86	172	16	4	1	106	27	3		.317	.353	.364	93	-6	44	.933	-3	95	98	2b133,S3		-0.2
1898	NY N	150	570	78	126	8	5	0	62	39	6		.221	.278	.253	54	-34	21	.938	18	104	94	2b144,S6		-0.9
1899	NY N	147	580	73	154	14	5	0	60	24	0		.266	.295	.307	67	-27	29	.946	29	105	93	2b147		0.7
1900	NY N	111	420	60	104	11	3	0	29	17	2		.248	.280	.295	62	-23	23	.931	13	104	101	2b111/S		-0.5

YEAR	TM LG	G	AB	R	H	2B	3B	HR	RBI	BB-IB	HP	SO	AVG	OBP	SLG	AOPS	ABR	SB-CS	FA	FR	RNG	THR	GAMES AT POSITION	DL	BFW
1901	Det A	135	547	82	150	16	12	3	75	41	2		.274	.327	.364	87	-11	32	.925	4	**107**	113	2b135		-0.5
1902	Det A	118	441	42	109	11	4	1	38	25	3		.247	.292	.297	62	-23	17	.941	6	99	132	2b118		-1.5
1903	Phi N	106	412	65	117	19	6	1	49	23	3		.284	.326	.367	101	-1	12	.959	-3	97	85	2b102,O4C		-0.3
1904	Phi N	153	587	61	161	23	6	0	42	37	2		.274	.319	.334	106	4	17	.942	4	99	84	2b152/3		1.0
1905	Phi N	155	608	95	150	17	7	1	50	45	3		.247	.302	.303	83	-13	16	.947	-11	95	99	2b155		-2.3
1906	Phi N	135	494	47	112	17	2	0	34	36	1		.227	.281	.269	71	-17	17	.947	-26	92	90	2b135		-4.8
1907	Phi N	36	126	11	18	3	0	0	6	7	2		.143	.200	.167	15	-12	3	.979	-2	88	90	2b26,1b4,S4/OC		-1.6
1908	Phi N	2	1	0	0	0	0	0	0	0	0		.000	.000	.000	-97	0	0	1.000	0	99	0	/2OL		0.0
1912	Chi A	1	2	0	1	0	0	0	0	0	0		.500	.500	.500	192	0	0	1.000	-0	83	0	/2		0.0
Total	22	1968	7459	1022	1946	216	81	15	824	501	38	131	.261	.311	.318	78	-223	329	.938	10	99	96	2b1585,P299,O45C,S19,3b16,1b7		-12.9

GLEASON, BILLY William Patrick B9.6.1894 Chicago IL D1.9.1957 Holyoke MA BR/TR/5-6.5/157 d9.25

YEAR	TM LG	G	AB	R	H	2B	3B	HR	RBI	BB-IB	HP	SO	AVG	OBP	SLG	AOPS	ABR	SB-CS	FA	FR	RNG	THR	GAMES AT POSITION	DL	BFW
1916	Pit N	1	2	0	0	0	0	0	0	0	0	0	.000	.000	.000	-99	0	0	1.000	-0	75	0	/2		-0.1
1917	Pit N	13	42	3	7	1	0	0	5	5	0	5	.167	.255	.190	36	-3	1	.978	-3	88	62	2b13		-0.7
1921	StL A	26	74	6	19	0	1	0	8	6	2	6	.257	.329	.284	54	-5	0-1	.960	-3	94	96	2b25		-0.8
Total	3	40	118	9	26	1	1	0	8	11	2	11	.220	.298	.246	47	-8	1-1	.966	-6	92	83	2b39		-1.6

GLEESON, JIM James Joseph "Gee Gee" B3.5.1912 Kansas City MO D5.1.1996 Kansas City MO BB/TR/6-1/191 d4.25 C2 Col Rockhurst

YEAR	TM LG	G	AB	R	H	2B	3B	HR	RBI	BB-IB	HP	SO	AVG	OBP	SLG	AOPS	ABR	SB-CS	FA	FR	RNG	THR	GAMES AT POSITION	DL	BFW
1936	Cle A	41	139	26	36	9	2	4	12	18	0	17	.259	.344	.439	91	-2	2-1	.958	-2	100	32	O33(4/0/30)		-0.6
1939	Chi N	111	332	43	74	19	6	4	45	39	0	46	.223	.308	.352	76	-11	7	.957	-3	98	68	O91(13/12/66)		-2.0
1940	Chi N	129	485	76	152	39	11	5	61	54	6	52	.313	.389	.470	139	27	4	.983	-1	92	139	O123(32/82/13)		2.1
1941	Cin N	102	301	47	70	10	0	3	34	45	4	30	.233	.340	.296	80	-6	7	.981	-5	98	16	O84(22/15/50)		-1.6
1942	Cin N	9	20	3	4	0	0	0	2	2	1	2	.200	.304	.200	49	-1	0	.889	-0	77	238	O5R		-0.2
Total	5	392	1277	195	336	77	19	16	154	158	13	147	.263	.350	.391	101	7	20-1	.972	-12	96	82	O336(71/109/164)		-2.3

GLEICH, FRANK Frank Elmer "Inch" B3.7.1894 Columbus OH D3.27.1949 Columbus OH BL/TR/5-11/175 d9.17

YEAR	TM LG	G	AB	R	H	2B	3B	HR	RBI	BB-IB	HP	SO	AVG	OBP	SLG	AOPS	ABR	SB-CS	FA	FR	RNG	THR	GAMES AT POSITION	DL	BFW
1919	NY A	5	4	0	1	0	0	0	1	1	0	0	.250	.400	.250	84	-1	0	.000	-1	0	0	O4(3/1/0)		-0.1
1920	NY A	24	41	6	5	0	0	0	3	6	0	10	.122	.234	.122	-4	-6	0-0	.864	-2	93	0	O15(9/4/2)		-0.8
Total	2	29	45	6	6	0	0	0	4	7	0	10	.133	.250	.133	4	-6	0-0	.826	-3	85	0	O19(12/5/2)		-0.9

GLENALVIN, BOB Robert J. (b Edward A. Dowling) B1.17.1867 Indianapolis IN D3.24.1944 Detroit MI BB/TR/5-9/160 d7.12

YEAR	TM LG	G	AB	R	H	2B	3B	HR	RBI	BB-IB	HP	SO	AVG	OBP	SLG	AOPS	ABR	SB-CS	FA	FR	RNG	THR	GAMES AT POSITION	DL	BFW
1890	Chi N	66	250	43	67	10	3	4	26	19	7	31	.268	.344	.380	105	1	30	.928	-8	96	86	2b66		-0.4
1893	Chi N	16	61	11	21	3	1	0	12	7	0	3	.344	.412	.426	125	2	7	.928	-3	89	55	2b16		0.0
Total	2	82	311	54	88	13	4	4	38	26	7	34	.283	.352	.389	109	3	37	.928	-11	95	80	2b82		-0.4

GLENN, ED Edward C. "Mouse" B9.19.1860 Richmond VA D2.10.1892 Richmond VA BR/TR/5-10/160 d8.5

YEAR	TM LG	G	AB	R	H	2B	3B	HR	RBI	BB-IB	HP	SO	AVG	OBP	SLG	AOPS	ABR	SB-CS	FA	FR	RNG	THR	GAMES AT POSITION	DL	BFW
1884	Ric AA	43	175	26	43	2	4	1		5	1		.246	.271	.320	93	-2		.833	5	64	150	O43L		0.2
1886	Pit AA	71	277	32	53	6	5	0	26	17	1		.191	.241	.249	54	-15	19	.865	-0	82	101	O71L		-1.6
1888	KC AA	3	8	0	0	0	0	0	0	0	0		.000	.200	.000	-32	-1	1	.857	-0	0	0	O3L		-0.1
	Bos N	20	65	8	10	0	2	0	3	2	2		.154	.203	.215	33	-5	0	.957	1	55	283	O19L/3		-0.5
Total	3	137	525	66	106	8	11	1	29	24	6	8	.202	.245	.265	62	-23	20	.867	6	71	142	O136L/3		-2.0

GLENN, ED Edward D. B10.1875 OH D12.6.1911 Ludlow KY BR/TR d9.7

YEAR	TM LG	G	AB	R	H	2B	3B	HR	RBI	BB-IB	HP	SO	AVG	OBP	SLG	AOPS	ABR	SB-CS	FA	FR	RNG	THR	GAMES AT POSITION	DL	BFW
1898	Was N	1	4	0	0	0	0	0	0	0	0	0	.000	.000	.000	-99	-1	0	1.000	-0	86	0	/S		-0.1
	NY N	2	4	1	1	0	0	0	0	3	0	0	.250	.571	.250	142	1	1	.750	-1	47	0	S2		-0.1
	Year	3	8	1	1	0	0	0	0	3	0	0	.125	.364	.125	42	0	1	.857	-2	61	0	S3		-0.2
1902	Chi N	2	7	0	0	0	0	0	0	1	0	0	.000	.125	.000	-63	-1	0	1.000	-0	115	0	S2		-0.2
Total	2	5	15	1	1	0	0	0	0	4	0	0	.067	.263	.067	-2	-1	1	.923	-2	85	0	S5		-0.4

GLENN, HARRY Harry Melville "Husky" B6.9.1890 Shelburn IN D10.12.1918 St.Paul MN BR/TR/6-1/200 d4.14

YEAR	TM LG	G	AB	R	H	2B	3B	HR	RBI	BB-IB	HP	SO	AVG	OBP	SLG	AOPS	ABR	SB-CS	FA	FR	RNG	THR	GAMES AT POSITION	DL	BFW
1915	StL N	6	16	1	5	0	0	0	1	3	0	0	.313	.421	.313	123	1	0	.929	-1	109	55	C5		0.0

GLENN, JOHN John B7.10.1928 Moultrie GA BR/TR/6-3/180 d6.16

YEAR	TM LG	G	AB	R	H	2B	3B	HR	RBI	BB-IB	HP	SO	AVG	OBP	SLG	AOPS	ABR	SB-CS	FA	FR	RNG	THR	GAMES AT POSITION	DL	BFW
1960	StL N	32	31	4	8	0	1	0	5	0-0	0	9	.258	.250	.323	53	-2	0-0	1.000	-1	90	0	O28(19/5/4)		-0.4

GLENN, JOHN John W. B1849 Rochester NY D11.10.1888 Sandy Hill (now Hudson Falls) NY BR/TR/5-8.5/169 d5.13

YEAR	TM LG	G	AB	R	H	2B	3B	HR	RBI	BB-IB	HP	SO	AVG	OBP	SLG	AOPS	ABR	SB-CS	FA	FR	RNG	THR	GAMES AT POSITION	DL	BFW
1871	Oly NA	26	120	25	37	3	2	0	21	3		1	.308	.325	.367	104	1	1-1	.860	1	112	**443**	O26(1/0/25)		0.3
1872	Oly NA	9	39	6	6	0	0	0	3	1		0	.154	.175	.154	2	-4	0-1	.800	3	313	725	O9L		-0.1
	Nat NA	1	4	0	2	0	0	0	0	0		0	.500	.500	.500	179	0	0	.667	-0	0	0	/OC		0.0
	Year	10	43	6	8	0	0	0	3	1		0	.186	.205	.186	21	-4	0-1	.791	3	281	651	O10(9/1/0)		-0.1
1873	Was NA	39	186	39	49	9	2	1	22	3		0	.263	.275	.349	87	-2	3-1	.915	-2	45	81	1b39		-0.3
1874	Chi NA	55	237	33	67	9	0	0	32	5		4	.283	.298	.321	97	0	2-2	.918	0	135	81	1b37,O19(2/1/17)		0.1
1875	Chi NA	69	308	46	75	8	0	0	27	3		6	.244	.251	.269	80	-6	10-2	.898	-3	37	69	O44(39/7/1),1b29		-0.5
1876	Chi N	66	276	55	84	9	2	0	32	12		6	.304	.333	.351	115	3		.881	-1	54	60	O56L,1b15		-0.1
1877	Chi N	50	202	31	46	6	1	0	20	8		16	.228	.257	.267	58	-10		.948	0	99	83	O36(36/0/1),1b14		-1.1
Total	5 NA	199	894	149	236	29	4	1	105	15		11	.264	.276	.309	87	-11	16-7	.918	-1	65	87	1b105,O99(51/9/43)		-0.5
Total	2	116	478	86	130	15	3	0	52	20		22	.272	.301	.316	90	-7		.904	0	72	69	O92(92/0/1),1b29		-1.2

GLENN, JOE Joseph Charles "Gabby" (b Joseph Charles Gurzensky) B11.19.1908 Dickson City PA D5.6.1985 Tunkhannock PA BR/TR/5-11/175 d9.15

YEAR	TM LG	G	AB	R	H	2B	3B	HR	RBI	BB-IB	HP	SO	AVG	OBP	SLG	AOPS	ABR	SB-CS	FA	FR	RNG	THR	GAMES AT POSITION	DL	BFW
1932	NY A	6	16	2	2	0	0	0	1	1	1	5	.125	.222	.125	-8	-3	0-0	1.000	-1	72	0	C5		-0.3
1933	NY A	5	21	1	3	0	0	0	1	0	0	3	.143	.143	.143	-26	-4	0-0	1.000	-1	155	0	C5		-0.4
1935	NY A	17	43	7	10	4	0	0	6	4	1	10	.233	.298	.326	65	-2	0-0	.984	0	146	99	C16		-0.1
1936	NY A	44	129	21	35	7	0	1	20	20	1	35	.271	.373	.349	82	-3	1-1	.970	2	159	120	C44		0.2
1937	NY A	25	53	6	15	2	2	0	4	10	0	11	.283	.397	.396	100	0	0-0	.978	3	143	116	C24		0.4
1938	NY A	41	123	10	32	7	2	0	25	10	0	14	.260	.316	.350	67	-1	1-0	.974	1	129	69	C40		-0.4
1939	StL A	88	286	29	78	13	1	4	29	31	0	40	.273	.344	.367	80	-8	4-4	.968	-13	75	**140**	C82		-1.6
1940	Bos A	22	47	3	6	1	0	0	4	5	0	7	.128	.212	.149	-5	-7	0-0	.961	-2	107	83	C19		-0.8
Total	8	248	718	77	181	34	5	5	89	81	2	91	.252	.330	.334	69	-34	6-5	.972	-10	114	110	C235		-1.2

GLOAD, ROSS Ross Peter B4.5.1976 Brooklyn NY BL/TL/6-2/210(185-210) [FlaN97 13/396] d8.31 Col South Florida

YEAR	TM LG	G	AB	R	H	2B	3B	HR	RBI	BB-IB	HP	SO	AVG	OBP	SLG	AOPS	ABR	SB-CS	FA	FR	RNG	THR	GAMES AT POSITION	DL	BFW
2000	Chi N	18	31	4	6	0	1	1	3	3-0	0	10	.194	.257	.355	55	-2	0-0	1.000	-1	95	0	O8(7/0/1),1b2		-0.3
2002	Col N	26	31	4	8	1	0	1	4	3-0	0	7	.258	.324	.387	79	-1	0-0	1.000	1	202	47	1b4,O2L		0.0
2004	Chi A	110	234	28	75	16	0	7	44	20-1	2	37	.321	.375	.479	118	7	0-3	1.000	-1	77	74	1b42,O39(17/1/22),D13		0.0
2005	Chi A	28	42	2	7	2	0	0	5	2-0	0	9	.167	.205	.214	11	-5	0-0	.987	-1	61	113	1b24,O3(2/0/1)	83	-0.7
Total	4	182	338	38	96	19	1	9	56	28-1	2	63	.284	.339	.426	95	-1	0-3	.997	-2	78	87	1b72,O52(28/1/24),D13	83	-1.0

GLOCKSON, NORM Norman Stanley B6.15.1894 Blue Island IL D8.5.1955 Maywood IL BR/TR/6-2/200 d9.16

YEAR	TM LG	G	AB	R	H	2B	3B	HR	RBI	BB-IB	HP	SO	AVG	OBP	SLG	AOPS	ABR	SB-CS	FA	FR	RNG	THR	GAMES AT POSITION	DL	BFW
1914	Cin N	7	12	0	0	0	0	0	0	0	0	6	.000	.077	.000	-74	-3	0	.923	-1	102	92	C7		-0.3

GLOSSOP, AL Alban B7.12.1914 Christopher IL D7.2.1991 Walnut Creek CA BB/TR/6-0/170 d9.23 Mil 1944-45

YEAR	TM LG	G	AB	R	H	2B	3B	HR	RBI	BB-IB	HP	SO	AVG	OBP	SLG	AOPS	ABR	SB-CS	FA	FR	RNG	THR	GAMES AT POSITION	DL	BFW
1939	NY N	10	32	3	6	0	0	1	3	2	0	2	.188	.278	.281	50	-2	0	.980	2	128	121	2b10		0.0
1940	NY N	27	91	16	19	3	0	4	8	10	1	16	.209	.294	.374	82	-2	1	.952	2	113	53	2b24		0.1
	Bos N	60	148	17	35	2	1	3	14	17	0	22	.236	.315	.324	81	-4	1	.938	4	120	112	2b18,3b18/S		0.3
	Year	87	239	33	54	5	1	7	22	27	1	38	.226	.307	.343	82	-6	2	.947	6	116	76	2b42,3b18/S		0.3
1942	Phi N	121	454	33	102	15	1	4	40	29	1	35	.225	.273	.289	68	-20	3	.961	10	103	104	2b118/3		-2.0
1943	Bro N	87	217	28	37	9	0	3	21	28	1	27	.171	.268	.253	51	-13	0	.927	-9	103	92	S33,2b24,3b17/OR		-0.3
1946	Chi N	4	10	2	0	0	0	0	0	3	0	3	.000	.231	.000	-32	-2	0	1.000	-2	61	0	2b2,S2		-0.3
Total	5	309	952	99	199	29	2	15	86	89	5	105	.209	.280	.291	66	-43	5	.954	8	105	93	2b196,S36,3b36/OR		-2.3

GLYNN, BILL William Vincent B7.30.1925 Sussex NJ BL/TL/6-0/190* d9.16

YEAR	TM LG	G	AB	R	H	2B	3B	HR	RBI	BB-IB	HP	SO	AVG	OBP	SLG	AOPS	ABR	SB-CS	FA	FR	RNG	THR	GAMES AT POSITION	DL	BFW
1949	Phi N	8	10	0	2	0	0	0	0	0	0	8	.200	.200	.200	8	-1	0	1.000	0	159	0	/1		-0.1
1952	Cle A	44	92	15	25	5	0	2	7	5	0	16	.272	.309	.391	101	0	1-0	.973	-0	106	105	1b32		-0.1
1953	Cle A	147	411	60	100	14	2	3	30	44	5	65	.243	.324	.349	79	-15	1-3	**.993**	3	108	**138**	1b135,O2(1/0/1)		-1.9
1954	Cle A	111	171	19	43	7	0	5	19	12	0	21	.251	.297	.380	84	-5	3-2	.987	1	113	111	1b96/OR		-0.7
Total	4	310	684	94	170	26	2	10	56	61	5	105	.249	.314	.336	79	-21	5-5	.989	4	109	126	1b264,O3(1/0/2)		-2.8

YEAR	TM LG	G	AB	R	H	2B	3B	HR	RBI	BB-IB	HP	SO	AVG	OBP	SLG	AOPS	ABR	SB-CS	FA	FR	RNG	THR	GAMES AT POSITION	DL	BFW

GOCHNAUR, JOHN John Peter B9.12.1875 Altoona PA D9.27.1929 Altoona PA BR/TR/5-9/160 d9.29

1901	Bro N	3	11	1	4	0	0	0	2	1	0		.364	.417	.364	124	0	1	1.000	0	105	0	S3		0.0
1902	Cle A	127	459	45	85	16	4	0	37	38	0		.185	.247	.237	36	-40	7	.933	-5	103	109	S127		-3.9
1903	Cle A	134	438	48	81	16	4	0	48	48	0		.185	.265	.240	53	-23	10	.869	-23	97	101	S134		-4.4
Total 3		264	908	94	170	32	8	0	87	87	0		.187	.258	.240	45	-63	18	.901	-28	100	104	S264		-8.3

GODAR, JOHN John Michael B10.25.1864 Cincinnati OH D6.23.1949 Park Ridge IL BR/TR/5-9/170 d7.8

1892	Bal N	5	14	2	3	0	0	0	1	2	1	1	.214	.353	.214	70	0	1	1.000	0	188	0	O5R		0.0

GODBY, DANNY Danny Ray B11.4.1946 Logan WV BR/TR/6-0/185 d8.10 Col Bowling Green

1974	StL N	13	13	2	2	0	0	0	1	3-1	0	4	.154	.294	.154	33	-1	0-0	1.000	1	152	520	O4(2/0/2)		0.0

GODDARD, JOE Joseph Harold B7.23.1950 Beckley WV BR/TR/5-11/190 [SDN71 8/173] d7.31 Col Marshall

1972	SD N	12	35	0	7	2	0	0	2	5-0	0	9	.200	.300	.257	64	-1	0-0	.973	-5	38	88	C12		-0.6

GODWIN, TYRELL Carlton Tyrell B7.10.1979 Wilmington NC BL/TR/6-0/200 d5.27 Col North Carolina

2005	Was N	3	3	0	0	0	0	0	0	0-0	0	1	.000	.000	.000	-99	-1	0-0	—	0			/H		-0.1

GODWIN, JOHN John Henry "Bunny" B3.10.1877 E.Liverpool OH D5.5.1956 E.Liverpool OH BR/TR/6-0/190 d8.14

1905	Bos A	15	43	4	14	1	0	0	10	3	3		.326	.408	.349	139	2	3	.950	-0	0	0	O7(5/2/0),2b5		0.2
1906	Bos A	66	193	11	36	2	1	0	15	6	1		.187	.215	.207	32	-15	6	.907	1	107	218	3b27,S14,O10(0/1/9),2b3/1		-1.5
Total 2		81	236	15	50	3	1	0	25	9	4		.212	.253	.233	53	-13	9	.907	0	107	218	3b27,O17(5/3/9),S14,2b8/1		-1.3

GOEBEL, ED Wilbur Edwin B9.1.1898 Brooklyn NY D8.12.1959 Brooklyn NY BR/TR/5-11/170 d5.13

1922	Was A	37	59	13	16	1	0	1	3	6	0		.271	.358	.339	87	-1	1-1	1.000	1	120	70	O16(2/1/13)		-0.1

GOECKEL, BILLY William John B9.3.1871 Wilkes-Barre PA D11.1.1922 Philadelphia PA BR/TL/5-11/162 d8.10 Col Penn

1899	Phi N	37	141	17	37	3	1	0	16	1	3		.262	.283	.298	61	-8	6	.978	-3	61	57	1b36		-1.0

GOFF, JERRY Jerry Leroy B4.12.1964 San Rafael CA BL/TR/6-3/207* [SeaA86 3/63] d5.15 Col California-Davis

1990	Mon N	52	119	14	27	1	0	3	7	21-4	0	36	.227	.343	.311	84	-2	0-2	.963	-7	82	62	C38,1b3,3b3		-0.8
1992	Mon N	3	3	0	0	0	0	0	0	0-0	0	3	.000	.000	.000	-99	-1	0-0	—	0			/H		-0.1
1993	Pit N	14	37	5	11	2	0	2	6	8-1	0	9	.297	.422	.514	150	3	0-0	.984	-2	129	98	C14		0.2
1994	Pit N	8	25	0	2	0	0	0	1	0-0	0	11	.080	.080	.080	-57	-0	0-0	.950	-2	124	87	C7		-0.7
1995	Hou N	12	26	2	4	2	0	1	3	4-0	0	13	.154	.267	.346	64	-1	0-0	1.000	4	49	159	C11		0.3
1996	Hou N	1	4	1	2	0	0	1	2	0-0	0	1	.500	.500	1.250	370	1	0-0	1.000	0	68	0	/C		0.2
Total 6		90	214	22	46	5	0	7	19	33-5	0	73	.215	.320	.336	80	-6	0-2	.974	-6	92	84	C71,3b3,1b3		-0.9

GOGGIN, CHUCK Charles Francis B7.7.1945 Pompano Beach FL BB/TR/5-11/175* d9.8 Col Broward (FL) CC

1972	Pit N	5	7	2	2	0	0	0	1	0-0	0	1	.286	.375	.286	91	-0	0-0	1.000	-0	129	0	/2		0.0
1973	Pit N	1	1	1	1	0	0	0	0	0-0	0	0	1.000	1.000	1.000	465	0	0-0	1.000	0	0	0	/C		0.0
	Atl N	64	90	18	26	5	0	0	7	9-0	0	19	.289	.350	.344	88	-1	0-1	.938	-7	93	88	2b19,O6(5/0/1),S5/C		-0.7
	Year	65	91	19	27	5	0	0	7	9-0	0	19	.297	.356	.352	91	-1	0-1	.938	-7	93	88	2b19,O6(5/0/1),S5,C2		-0.7
1974	Bos A	2	1	0	0	0	0	0	0	0-0	0	1	.000	.000	.000	-93	-0	0-0	.667	0	158	601	2b2		0.0
Total 3		72	99	19	29	5	0	0	7	10-0	0	21	.293	.355	.343	89	-1	0-1	.927	-7	99	101	2b22,O6(5/0/1),S5,C2	19	-0.7

GOLDEN, MIKE Michael Henry B9.11.1851 Shirley MA D1.11.1929 Rockford IL BR/TR/5-8/168 d5.4 ▲

1875	Wes NA	13	46	6	6	0	0	0	1	0			.130	.130	.130	-9	-4	0-0	.844	-1	76	0	P13		0.0
	Chi NA	39	155	16	40	3	0	0	14	2			.258	.268	.277	89	-2	3-2	.833	-1	120	133	O27(25/0/2),P14		0.0
	Year	52	201	22	46	3	0	0	15	2			.229	.236	.244	66	-7	3-2	.833	-1	81	0	P27,O27(25/0/2)		0.0
1878	Mil N	55	214	16	44	6	3	0	20	3			.206	.217	.262	53	-11		.831	-3	96	135	O39(0/25/14),P22/1		-1.1

GOLDMAN, JONAH Jonah John B8.29.1906 New York NY D8.17.1980 Palm Beach FL BR/TR/5-7/170 d9.22 Col Syracuse

1928	Cle A	7	21	5	5	1	0	0	2	3	0	0	.238	.333	.286	63	-1	0-0	.878	-1	111	45	S7		-0.1
1930	Cle A	111	306	32	74	18	0	1	44	28	3	25	.242	.312	.310	56	-20	3-5	.945	15	108	102	S93,3b20		0.3
1931	Cle A	30	62	-0	8	1	0	0	3	4	0	6	.129	.182	.145	-12	-10	1-1	.947	10	140	100	S30		0.1
Total 3		148	389	33	87	20	0	1	49	35	3	31	.224	.293	.283	46	-31	4-6	.941	25	114	98	S130,3b20		0.3

GOLDSBERRY, GORDON Gordon Frederick B8.30.1927 Sacramento CA D2.23.1996 Laguna Hills CA BL/TL/6-0/170* d4.20

1949	Chi A	39	145	25	36	3	2	1	13	18		9	.248	.331	.317	74	-6	2-0	.990	-1	93	95	1b38		-0.7
1950	Chi A	82	127	19	34	8	2	2	25	26		18	.268	.392	.409	108	3	0-2	.989	5	167	128	1b40,O3(1/0/2)		0.5
1951	Chi A	10	11	4	1	0	0	0	1	2		2	.091	.231	.091	-11	-2	0-0	1.000	1	225	144	1b8		-0.1
1952	StL A	86	227	30	52	9	3	3	17	34		37	.229	.330	.335	83	-5	0-2	.983	-2	93	96	1b72,O2L		-1.0
Total 4		217	510	78	123	20	7	6	56	80		66	.241	.344	.343	85	-10	2-4	.987	3	112	104	1b158,O5(3/0/2)		-1.3

GOLDSBY, WALT Walton Hugh B12.31.1861 Marion LA D1.11.1914 Dallas TX BL/?/197 d5.28

1884	StL AA	5	20	2	4	0	0	0	1	0			.200	.200	.200	30	-2		.800	-1	0	0	O5(1/4/0)		-0.3
	Was AA	6	24	4	9	0	0	0	3	1	0		.375	.400	.375	174	2		.909	1	182	0	O6(1/3/2)		0.2
	Ric AA	11	40	4	9	1	0	0	4	1	1		.225	.262	.250	69	-1		.737	0	117	687	O11(2/6/3)		-0.1
	Year	22	84	10	22	1	0	0	8	2	1		.262	.287	.274	87	-1		.800	-0	104	306	O22(4/13/5)		-0.2
1886	Was N	6	18	0	4	1	0	0	1	2			.222	.300	.278	83	0		.818	-1	0	0	O6(0/5/1)		-0.1
1888	Bal AA	45	165	-13	39	1	1	0	14	8	4		.236	.288	.255	76	-4	17	.903	-3	47	0	O45L		-0.8
Total 3		73	267	23	65	3	1	0	23	12	3		.243	.289	.262	80	-5	17	.858	-4	62	96	O73(49/18/6)		-1.1

GOLDSMITH, WALLY Warren M. B10.1848 Baltimore MD D9.16.1915 Washington DC 5-7/146 d5.4

1871	Kek NA	19	88	8	18	1	0	0	12	4		2	.205	.239	.216	31	-8	0-0	.767	-10	70	36	S14,3b8,C2		-1.2
1872	Oly NA	9	41	4	10	2	0	0	5	0		0	.244	.244	.293	68	-1	0-0	.679	-2	80	72	S5,2b4		-0.2
1873	Mar NA	1	4	0	0	0	0	0	0	0		0	.000	.000	.000	-99	-1	0-0	.667	-1	118	0	/2		-0.1
1875	Wes NA	13	51	3	6	0	0	0	1	0		2	.118	.118	.118	-17	-6	0-0	.814	-1	90	172	3b13		-0.6
Total 4 NA		42	184	15	34	3	0	0	18	4		4	.185	.202	.201	24	-16	0-0	.694	-13	73	117	3b21,S19,2b5,C2		-2.1

GOLDSTEIN, LONNIE Leslie Elmer B5.13.1918 Austin TX BL/TL/6-2.5/190 d9.11 Mil 1945-46

1943	Cin N	5	5	1	1	0	0	0	0	0		0	.200	.429	.200	85	-0	0	1.000	-0	0	0	1b2		0.0
1946	Cin N	6	5	1	0	0	0	0	0	1		0	.000	.167	.000	-53	-1	0	—	0			/H		-0.1
Total 2		11	10	2	1	0	0	0	0	3		2	.100	.308	.100	20	-1	0	1.000	-0	0	0	1b2		-0.1

GOLDY, PURNAL Purnal William B11.28.1937 Camden NJ BR/TR/6-5/205* d4.12 Col Temple

1962	Det A	20	70	8	16	1	1	3	12	0-0	1	12	.229	.236	.400	66	-4	0-0	.964	-1	86	107	O15R		-0.6
1963	Det A	9	8	1	2	0	0	0	0	0-0	0	4	.250	.250	.250	39	-1	0-0	—	0			/H		-0.1
Total 2		29	78	9	18	1	1	3	12	0-0	1	16	.231	.237	.385	64	-5	0-0	.964	-1	86	107	O15R		-0.7

GOLETZ, STAN Stanley "Stash" B5.21.1918 Crescent OH D6.7.1997 Temple TX BL/TL/6-3/200 d9.9 Mil 1942-45 Col Ohio St.

1941	Chi A	5	5	0	3	0	0	0	1	0-0	0	1	.600	.600	.600	221	1	0-0	—	0			/H		0.1

GOLIAT, MIKE Mike Mitchel B11.5.1921 Yatesboro PA D1.13.2004 Seven Hills OH BR/TR/6-0/180* d8.3

1949	Phi N	55	189	24	40	6	3	3	19	20	1	32	.212	.290	.323	66	-10		.969	-5	99	91	2b50,1b5		-1.2
1950	†Phi N	145	483	49	113	19	6	13	64	53	3	75	.234	.314	.366	80	-16	3	.972	-15	98	89	2b145		-2.2
1951	Phi N	41	138	14	31	2	1	4	15	9	1	18	.225	.277	.341	66	-7	0-1	.968	-8	89	87	2b37,3b2		-1.4
	StL A	5	11	0	2	0	0	0	1	0		1	.182	.182	.182	-1	-2		1.000	0	101	97	2b2		-0.1
1952	StL A	3	4	0	0	0	0	0	0	1		0	.000	.200	.000	-40	-1		1.000	1	103	287	2b3		0.0
Total 4		249	825	87	186	21	10	20	99	83	5	127	.225	.300	.348	73	-36	3-1	.971	-27	97	90	2b237,1b5,3b2		-4.9

GOLVIN, WALT Walter George B2.1.1894 Hershey NE D6.11.1973 Gardena CA BL/TL/6-0/165 d4.15

1922	Chi N	2	2	0	0	0	0	0	0	0		0	.000	.000	.000	-98	-1	0-0	1.000	-0	0	0	1b2		-0.1

GOMES, JONNY Jonny Johnson B11.22.1980 Petaluma CA BR/TR/6-1/200* [TBA01 18/529] d9.12 Col Santa Rosa (CA) JC

2003	TB A	8	15	1	2	1	0	0	0	0-0		6	.133	.188	.200	2	-2	0-0	—	0			D8		-0.2
2004	TB A	5	14	0	1	0	0	0	1	1-0		6	.071	.133	.071	-46	-3	0-0	—	0			D4		-0.3
2005	TB A	101	348	61	98	13	6	21	54	39-1	14	113	.282	.372	.534	142	21	9-5	.963	5	107	267	O50(14/0/36),D49		2.0
Total 3		114	377	62	101	14	6	21	55	40-1	15	125	.268	.357	.504	130	16	9-5	.963	5	107	267	D61,O50(14/0/36)		1.5

YEAR	TM LG	G	AB	R	H	2B	3B	HR	RBI	BB-IB	HP	SO	AVG	OBP	SLG	AOPS	ABR	SB-CS	FA	FR	RNG	THR	GAMES AT POSITION	DL	BFW
GOMEZ, ALEXIS	Alexis De Jesus B8.6.1978 Loma de Cabrera, D.R. BL/TL/6-2/180* d6.16																								0.0
2002	KC A	5	10	0	2	0	0	0	0	0-0	0	2	.200	.200	.200	6	-1	0-0	1.000	1	115	909	O2R		-0.2
2004	KC A	13	29	1	8	1	0	0	4	2-0	0	8	.276	.323	.310	66	-1	0-0	.955	0	124	0	O12(6/2/5)		-0.2
2005	Det A	9	16	2	3	0	0	0	1	2-0	0	2	.188	.278	.188	28	-2	0-0	1.000	0	94	0	O9(6/3/0)		-0.2
Total	3	27	55	3	13	1	0	0	5	4-0	0	12	.236	.288	.255	44	-4	0-0	.972	1	114	107	O23(12/5/7)		-0.4
GOMEZ, CHRIS	Christopher Cory B6.16.1971 Los Angeles CA BR/TR/6-1/195(183-195) [DetA92 3/84] d7.19 Col Cal St.-Long Beach																								
1993	Det A	46	128	11	32	7	1	0	11	9-0	1	17	.250	.304	.320	68	-6	2-2	.963	-1	104	105	S29,2b17/D		-0.5
1994	Det A	84	296	32	76	19	0	8	53	33-0	3	64	.257	.336	.402	88	-5	5-3	.981	-24	84	58	S57,2b30		-2.1
1995	Det A	123	431	49	96	20	2	11	50	41-0	3	96	.223	.292	.355	68	-21	4-1	.973	-2	104	92	S97,2b31,D2		-1.3
1996	Det A	48	128	21	31	5	0	1	16	18-0	1	20	.242	.340	.305	65	-6	1-1	.970	4	101	111	S47		0.0
	†SD N	89	328	32	86	16	1	3	29	39-1	6	64	.262	.349	.345	88	-4	2-2	.967	-7	96	101	S89		-0.4
1997	SD N	150	522	62	132	19	2	5	54	53-1	5	114	.253	.326	.326	76	-18	5-8	.978	-4	101	84	S150		-1.2
1998	†SD N	145	449	55	120	32	3	4	39	51-7	5	87	.267	.346	.379	98	0	1-3	.980	9	101	120	S143		1.8
1999	SD N	76	234	20	59	8	1	1	15	27-3	1	49	.252	.331	.308	68	-11	1-2	.961	1	98	115	S75	59	-0.5
2000	SD N	33	54	4	12	0	0	0	3	7-0	0	5	.222	.306	.222	41	-5	0-0	.928	2	109	122	S17,2b3	101	-0.2
2001	SD N	40	112	6	21	3	0	0	7	9-0	0	14	.188	.244	.214	23	-13	1-0	.937	-11	74	82	S36,2b8		-2.2
	TB A	58	189	31	57	16	0	8	36	8-0	2	24	.302	.332	.513	122	6	3-0	.968	-11	85	80	S58		0.0
2002	TB A	130	461	51	122	31	3	10	46	21-0	1	58	.265	.305	.410	90	-7	1-3	.980	-1	98	104	S130		0.0
2003	†Min A	58	175	14	44	9	3	1	16	7-1	0	13	.251	.279	.354	64	-10	2-1	.989	-7	96	89	2b23,3b18,S17	28	-1.5
2004	Tor A	109	341	41	96	11	4	1	37	28-0	2	41	.282	.337	.346	75	-12	3-2	.969	-3	100	94	S77,1b19,3b5,2b3/D		-1.0
2005	Bal A	89	219	27	61	11	0	1	18	27-1	1	28	.279	.359	.342	88	-3	2-1	.993	-1	87	118	1b42,2b18,3b17,S10,D6		-0.5
Total	13	1278	4067	456	1045	207	17	56	429	378-14	37	683	.257	.324	.358	80	-115	33-29	.972	-58	97	97	S1032,2b133,1b61,3b40,D14	188	-9.6
GOMEZ, CHILE	Jose Luis (Gonzales) B5.23.1909 Mazatlan, Sonora, Mexico D12.1.1992 Nuevo Laredo, Tamaulipas, Mexico BR/TR/5-10/165 d7.27																								
1935	Phi N	67	222	24	51	3	1	0	16	17	0	34	.230	.285	.243	39	-19	2	.948	9	104	44	S36,2b32		-0.5
1936	Phi N	108	332	24	77	4	1	0	28	14	1	32	.232	.265	.250	36	-30	0	.948	11	116	84	2b71,S40		-1.3
1942	Was A	25	73	8	14	2	2	0	6	9	0	7	.192	.280	.274	57	-4	1-0	.973	-2	97	88	2b23/3		-0.5
Total	3	200	627	56	142	9	3	0	50	40	1	73	.226	.274	.250	39	-53	3-0	.954	18	114	103	2b126,S76/3		-2.3
GOMEZ, LEO	Leonardo (Velez) B3.2.1966 Canovanas, PR BR/TR/6-0/208(180-208) d9.17																								
1990	Bal A	12	39	3	9	0	0	1	8	8-0	0	7	.231	.362	.231	71	-1	0-0	.886	-2	88	92	3b12		-0.3
1991	Bal A	118	391	40	91	17	2	16	45	40-0	1	82	.233	.302	.409	100	-1	1-1	.972	-13	89	99	3b105,D10,1b3		-1.4
1992	Bal A	137	468	62	124	24	0	17	64	63-4	8	78	.265	.356	.425	116	12	2-3	.951	-10	93	82	3b137		0.2
1993	Bal A	71	244	30	48	7	0	10	25	32-1	3	60	.197	.295	.348	70	-11	0-1	.951	6	110	137	3b70/D	55	-0.5
1994	Bal A	84	285	46	78	20	0	15	56	41-0	3	55	.274	.366	.502	116	7	0-0	.975	-1	94	108	3b78/1D		0.6
1995	Bal A	53	127	16	30	5	0	4	12	18-1	1	23	.236	.336	.370	83	-3	0-1	.978	2	105	54	3b44,1b3,D5	63	-0.1
1996	Chi N	136	362	44	86	19	0	17	56	53-0	7	94	.238	.344	.431	100	1	1-4	.972	-1	97	110	3b124,1b8/S	118	-0.1
Total	7	611	1916	241	466	92	2	79	259	255-6	25	399	.243	.336	.417	101	4	4-10	.962	-18	96	100	3b570,D21,1b15/S	118	-1.6
GOMEZ, LUIS	Luis (Sanchez) B8.19.1951 Guadalajara, Jalisco, Mexico BR/TR/5-9/150* d4.28 Col UCLA																								
1974	Min A	82	168	18	35	1	0	0	3	12-0	1	16	.208	.261	.214	37	-14	2-3	.960	6	103	103	S74,2b2/D		-0.1
1975	Min A	89	72	7	10	0	0	0	5	4-0	0	12	.139	.182	.139	-8	-10	0-2	.975	-4	77	99	S70,2b6,D7		-1.2
1976	Min A	38	57	5	11	1	0	0	3	3-0	0	3	.193	.233	.211	30	-5	1-0	.988	1	96	146	S24,2b8,3b4/OCD		0.0
1977	Min A	32	65	6	16	4	2	0	11	4-0	0	9	.246	.290	.369	79	-2	0-2	.983	2	102	70	2b19,S7,3b4/OCD		-2.3
1978	Tor A	153	413	39	92	7	3	0	32	34-1	0	41	.223	.280	.254	51	-27	2-10	.976	-7	92	105	S153		-1.1
1979	Tor A	59	163	11	39	7	0	0	11	6-0	0	17	.239	.266	.282	47	-12	1-0	1.000	-1	82	202	3b22,2b20,S15		-2.0
1980	Atl N	121	278	18	53	6	0	0	24	17-2	1	27	.191	.239	.212	27	-27	0-4	.968	-3	105	101	S119		-0.9
1981	Atl N	35	35	4	7	0	0	0	1	6-0	1	4	.200	.317	.200	49	-2	0-1	.895	-7	77	42	S21,3b9,2b3/P		-7.8
Total	8	609	1251	108	263	26	5	0	90	86-3	5	129	.210	.261	.239	41	-99	6-22	.970	-10	97	105	S483,2b58,3b39,D11,O2C/P		-7.8
GOMEZ, PRESTON	Pedro (Martinez) B4.20.1923 Preston, Cuba BR/TR/5-11/170 d5.5 M7/C13																								
1944	Was A	8	7	2	2	1	0	0	2	0-0	0	4	.286	.286	.429	107	0	0-0	1.000	-1	0	0	2b2,S2		-0.1
GOMEZ, RANDY	Randell Scott B2.4.1957 San Mateo CA BR/TR/5-10/185 [SFN80 25/624] d8.21 Col Utah																								
1984	SF N	14	30	0	5	1	0	0	0	8-0	0	3	.167	.342	.200	57	-1	0-0	.951	-2	42	49	C14		-0.2
GONDER, JESSE	Jesse Lemar B1.20.1936 Monticello AR D11.14.2004 Oakland CA BL/TR/5-10/190* d9.23																								
1960	NY A	7	7	1	2	0	0	1	3	1-0	0	1	.286	.333	.714	199	1	0-0	1.000	0	36	0	/C		0.1
1961	NY A	15	12	2	4	1	0	0	3	3-1	0	1	.333	.467	.417	146	1	0-0	—	0			/H		0.1
1962	Cin N	4	4	0	0	0	0	0	0	0-0	0	3	.000	.000	.000	-97	-1	0-0	—	0			/H		-0.1
1963	Cin N	31	32	5	10	2	0	3	5	1-0	0	12	.313	.333	.656	172	3	0-0	1.000	0	38	0	C7		0.3
	NY N	42	126	12	38	4	0	3	15	6-0	0	25	.302	.328	.405	110	1	1-2	.978	-9	121	60	C31		-0.7
	Year	73	158	17	48	6	0	6	20	7-0	0	37	.304	.329	.456	122	4	1-2	.981	-9	113	55	C38		-0.4
1964	NY N	131	341	28	92	11	4	7	35	29-5	2	65	.270	.329	.370	99	0	0-0	.979	0	75	157	C97		0.4
1965	NY N	53	105	6	25	4	0	4	9	11-4	0	20	.238	.308	.390	100	0	0-0	.992	1	41	217	C31		0.2
	Mil N	31	53	2	8	2	0	1	5	4-0	0	9	.151	.211	.245	28	-5	0-0	.989	6	138	254	C13		0.1
	Year	84	158	8	33	6	0	5	14	15-4	0	29	.209	.276	.342	75	-5	0-0	.991	7	72	229	C44		0.3
1966	Pit N	59	160	13	36	3	1	7	16	12-7	2	39	.225	.287	.387	85	-4	0-0	.978	-2	96	105	C52		-0.4
1967	Pit N	22	36	4	5	1	0	0	3	5-3	2	5	.139	.279	.167	30	-3	0-0	.971	-1	41	32	C18		-0.4
Total	8	395	876	73	220	28	2	26	94	72-20	6	184	.251	.310	.377	94	-7	1-2	.981	-5	83	132	C250		-0.4
GONZALES, DAN	Daniel David B9.30.1953 Whittier CA BL/TR/6-1/195(180-195) [DetA72*2/43] d4.7 Col Fullerton (CA) JC																								
1979	Det A	7	18	1	4	1	0	0	2	0-0	0	2	.222	.222	.278	33	-2	1-0	1.000	-1	50	0	O3R/D		-0.2
1980	Det A	2	7	1	1	0	0	0	0	0-0	0	1	.143	.143	.143	-21	-1	0-0	.750	-0	148	0	/OLD		-0.1
Total	2	9	25	2	5	1	0	0	2	0-0	0	3	.200	.200	.240	18	-3	1-0	.857	-1	73	0	O4(1/0/3),D2		-0.3
GONZALES, LARRY	Lawrence Christopher B3.28.1967 West Covina CA BR/TR/6-3/200 [CalA88 22/559] d6.13 Col Hawaii-Manoa																								
1993	Cal A	2	2	0	1	1	0	0	1	1-0	0	0	.500	.667	.500	212	0	0-0	1.000	0	0	0	C2		0.1
GONZALES, RENE	Rene Adrian B9.3.1960 Austin TX BR/TR/6-3/201(180-220) [MonN82 5/123] d7.27 Col Cal St.-Los Angeles OF(1/0/2)																								
1984	Mon N	29	30	5	7	1	0	0	2	2-0	1	5	.233	.303	.267	64	-1	0-0	.957	-4	77	76	S27		-0.5
1986	Mon N	11	26	1	3	0	0	0	0	2-0	0	7	.115	.179	.115	-17	-4	0-2	1.000	-0	97	91	S6,3b5		-0.5
1987	Bal A	37	60	14	16	2	1	1	7	3-0	0	11	.267	.302	.383	82	-2	1-0	.963	3	105	62	3b29,2b6/S		0.1
1988	Bal A	92	237	13	51	6	0	2	15	13-0	3	32	.215	.263	.266	50	-16	2-0	.966	13	129	164	3b80,2b14,S2/1OR		-0.2
1989	Bal A	71	166	16	36	4	0	1	11	12-0	0	30	.217	.268	.259	51	-11	5-3	.978	-4	98	126	2b54,3b17/S		-1.5
1990	Bal A	67	103	13	22	3	1	1	12	12-0	0	14	.214	.296	.291	66	-5	1-2	.994	1	105	98	2b43,3b16,S9/OR		-0.3
1991	†Tor A	71	118	16	23	9	0	1	6	12-0	4	22	.195	.289	.246	48	-8	0-0	.973	0	84	88	S36,3b26,2b11,1b2		-0.3
1992	Cal A	104	329	47	91	17	1	7	38	41-1	4	46	.277	.363	.398	112	7	7-4	.954	2	103	102	3b53,3b42,1b13,S8	54	0.9
1993	Cal A	118	335	34	84	17	0	2	31	49-2	1	45	.251	.346	.319	78	-8	5-5	.956	0	102	151	3b79,1b31,S5,2b4/P		-1.0
1994	Cle A	22	23	6	8	1	1	1	3	5-0	0	5	.348	.448	.609	172	3	2-0	.952	2	157	0	3b13,1b4,S4/2		0.5
1995	Cal A	30	18	1	6	1	0	0	3	0-0	0	4	.333	.333	.556	127	1	0-0	1.000	-1	65	0	3b18,2b6/SD		0.0
1996	†Tex A	51	92	19	20	4	0	2	5	10-0	0	11	.217	.288	.326	53	-7	0-0	.989	-1	74	106	1b23,3b15,S10,2b5/OL		-0.3
1997	Col N	12	2	1	1	0	0	0	1	0-0	0	0	.500	.500	.500	133	-1	0-0	—	-0	0	0	/3		0.0
Total	13	705	1539	185	368	59	4	19	136	161-3	13	230	.239	.315	.320	74	-51	23-16	.957	16	113	129	3b352,2b186,S110,1b74,O3R/DP	54	-3.4
GONZALEZ, ADRIAN	Adrian B5.8.1982 San Diego CA BL/TL/6-2/220* [FlaN00 1/1] d4.18																								
2004	Tex A	16	42	5	7	1	0	1	7	2-0	0	6	.238	.273	.381	65	-2	0-0	.990	-0	92	148	1b11/D		-0.3
2005	Tex A	43	150	17	34	7	1	6	17	10-2	0	37	.227	.272	.407	75	-6	0-0	.978	0	115	93	D32,1b10/OR		-0.8
Total	2	59	192	24	44	10	1	7	24	12-2	0	43	.229	.272	.401	73	-8	0-0	.985	-0	102	124	D33,1b21/OR		-1.1
GONZALEZ, ALEX	Alexander B2.15.1977 Cagua, Venez BR/TR/6-0/170(170-200) d8.25																								
1998	Fla N	25	86	11	13	2	0	3	7	9-0	1	30	.151	.240	.279	38	-8	0-0	.978	-7	83	101	S25		-1.3
1999	Fla N★	136	560	81	155	28	8	14	59	15-0	12	113	.277	.308	.430	90	-12	3-5	.955	-8	95	99	S135	34	-1.1
2000	Fla N	109	385	35	77	17	4	7	42	13-0	2	77	.200	.229	.319	39	-39	7-1	.957	1	104	100	S104		-2.8
2001	Fla N	145	515	57	129	36	1	9	48	30-6	10	107	.250	.303	.377	77	-18	2-2	.960	5	101	114	S142	134	-0.2
2002	Fla N	42	151	15	34	7	1	2	18	12-1	4	24	.225	.296	.325	70	-8	3-1	.984	3	99	120	S42		-0.1

YEAR	TM LG	G	AB	R	H	2B	3B	HR	RBI	BB-IB	HP	SO	AVG	OBP	SLG	AOPS	ABR	SB-CS	FA	FR	RNG	THR	GAMES AT POSITION	DL	BFW
2003	†Fla N	150	528	52	135	33	6	18	77	33-13	13	106	.256	.313	.443		99	-3	0-4	.976	4	96	117	S150		1.1
2004	Fla N	159	561	67	130	30	3	23	79	27-9	4	126	.232	.270	.419		79	-21	3-1	.976	-1	95	109	S158		-1.0
2005	Fla N	130	435	45	115	30	0	5	45	31-10	5	81	.264	.319	.368		85	-10	5-3	.974	16	101	122	S124		1.6
Total	8	896	3221	363	788	183	23	81	375	170-39	51	672	.245	.291	.391		78	-119	23-17	.968	14	98	111	S880	168	-3.8

GONZALEZ, ALEX   Alexander Scott   B4.8.1973 Miami FL   BR/TR/6-0/190(170-200)   [TorA91 14/380]   d4.4

YEAR	TM LG	G	AB	R	H	2B	3B	HR	RBI	BB-IB	HP	SO	AVG	OBP	SLG	AOPS	ABR	SB-CS	FA	FR	RNG	THR	GAMES AT POSITION	DL	BFW
1994	Tor A	15	53	7	8	1	0	1	4-0	1	17	.151	.224	.245		21	-6	3-0	.918	1	113	62	S15		28	-0.3
1995	Tor A	111	367	51	89	19	4	10	42	44-1	1	114	.243	.322	.398	87	-8	4-4	.957	-29	77	68	S97,3b9,D3		-2.9
1996	Tor A	147	527	64	124	30	5	14	64	45-0	5	127	.235	.300	.391	74	-23	16-6	.973	28	109	126	S147		1.7
1997	Tor A	126	426	46	102	23	2	12	35	34-1	5	94	.239	.302	.387	78	-14	15-6	.986	9	97	102	S125	31	0.3
1998	Tor A	158	568	70	136	28	1	13	51	28-1	6	121	.239	.281	.361	66	-30	21-6	.976	-7	93	99	S158		-2.2
1999	Tor A	38	154	22	45	13	0	2	12	16-0	3	23	.292	.370	.416	98	0	4-2	.980	12	120	130	S37/D	140	1.4
2000	Tor A	141	527	68	133	31	2	15	69	43-0	4	113	.252	.313	.404	77	-19	4-4	.975	-8	97	97	S141	14	-1.5
2001	Tor A	154	636	79	161	25	5	17	76	43-0	7	149	.253	.303	.388	80	-20	18-11	.987	33	118	122	S154		2.4
2002	Chi N	142	513	58	127	27	5	18	61	46-7	3	136	.248	.312	.425	95	-8	5-3	.965	1	90	93	S142	15	0.4
2003	†Chi N	152	536	71	122	37	0	20	59	47-1	6	123	.228	.295	.409	80	-17	3-3	.984	26	104	109	S150		1.9
2004	Chi N	37	129	15	28	10	0	3	8	4-0	0	26	.217	.241	.364	52	-9	1-1	.967	0	85	91	S37	74	-0.7
	Mon N	35	133	19	32	7	0	4	16	8-0	1	32	.241	.289	.383	69	-6	1-1	.960	-2	93	113	S33		-0.6
	SD N	11	23	2	4	1	1	0	3	2-0	0	6	.174	.240	.304	41	-2	0-0	1.000	-2	81	89	S11		-0.3
	Year	83	285	36	64	18	1	7	27	14-0	1	64	.225	.263	.368	59	-18	2-2	.967	-4	88	101	S81		-1.6
2005	TB A	109	349	47	94	20	1	9	38	26-1	3	74	.269	.323	.410	97	-2	2-1	.945	-10	95	56	3b98,S12	20	-1.0
Total	12	1455	4941	619	1205	274	27	137	535	390-12	45	1155	.244	.303	.393	79	-164	97-48	.975	51	99	104	S1259,3b107,D4	322	-1.4

GONZALEZ, TONY   Andres Antonio (Gonzalez)   B8.28.1936 Central Cunagua, Cuba   BL/TR/5-9/170*   d4.12

YEAR	TM LG	G	AB	R	H	2B	3B	HR	RBI	BB-IB	HP	SO	AVG	OBP	SLG	AOPS	ABR	SB-CS	FA	FR	RNG	THR	GAMES AT POSITION	DL	BFW
1960	Cin N	39	99	10	21	5	1	3	14	4-0	1	27	.212	.248	.374	67	-5	1-0	.957	-1	94	87	O31(1/0/30)		-0.7
	Phi N	78	241	27	72	17	5	6	33	11-0	3	47	.299	.337	.485	122	7	2-2	.981	2	105	137	O67(3/61/5)		0.6
	Year	117	340	37	93	22	6	9	47	15-0	4	74	.274	.311	.453	106	2	3-2	.975	1	102	122	O98(4/61/35)		-0.1
1961	Phi N	126	426	58	118	16	8	12	58	49-7	6	66	.277	.358	.437	112	7	15-5	.984	-5	95	77	O118(1/86/34)		-0.1
1962	Phi N	118	437	76	132	16	4	20	63	40-5	9	82	.302	.371	.494	134	21	17-8	1.000	2	103	109	O114(0/114/1)		2.1
1963	Phi N	155	555	78	170	36	12	4	66	53-5	8	68	.306	.372	.436	134	26	13-8	.986	-5	88	118	O151(56/107/9)		1.6
1964	Phi N	131	421	55	117	25	3	4	40	44-7	6	74	.278	.352	.380	108	7	0-5	.996	0	105	74	O119(6/114/0)		0.2
1965	Phi N	108	370	48	109	19	1	13	41	31-3	3	52	.295	.351	.457	129	14	3-4	.983	-5	91	57	O104(53/60/2)		0.5
1966	Phi N	132	384	53	110	20	4	6	40	26-1	5	40	.286	.335	.406	105	3	2-6	.986	4	108	104	O121(73/47/4)		0.1
1967	Phi N	149	508	74	172	23	9	9	59	47-14	5	58	.339	.396	.472	147	32	10-9	.993	8	112	125	O143(105/29/16)		3.4
1968	Phi N	121	416	45	110	13	4	3	38	40-3	7	42	.264	.335	.337	104	3	6-5	.979	-4	97	58	O117(19/98/4)		-0.6
1969	SD N	53	182	17	41	4	0	2	8	19-2	1	24	.225	.309	.280	68	-7	1-0	.975	4	127	71	O49(40/11/3)		-0.6
	†Atl N	89	320	51	94	15	2	10	50	27-1	5	22	.294	.354	.447	123	10	3-1	.989	-1	105	21	O82(35/49/0)		0.7
	Year	142	502	68	135	19	2	12	58	46-3	6	46	.269	.338	.386	104	3	4-1	.983	4	113	54	O131(75/60/3)		0.1
1970	Atl N	123	430	57	114	18	2	7	55	46-10	3	45	.265	.345	.365	86	-7	3-5	.987	-8	94	16	O119(3/116/0)		-2.0
	Cal A	26	92	9	28	2	0	1	12	2-0	1	11	.304	.326	.359	91	-1	3-2	.960	-2	86	137	O24(0/23/1)		-0.4
1971	Cal A	111	314	32	77	9	2	3	38	28-5	3	28	.245	.310	.315	84	-7	0-1	.987	-3	94	81	O88(67/18/9)		-1.6
Total	12	1559	5195	690	1485	238	57	103	615	467-63	71	706	.286	.350	.413	114	103	79-61	.987	-12	100	83	O1447(462/933/118)		3.2

GONZALEZ, DENNY   Denio Mariano (Manzueta)   B7.22.1963 Sabana Grande de Boya, D.R.   BR/TR/5-11/185*   d8.6

YEAR	TM LG	G	AB	R	H	2B	3B	HR	RBI	BB-IB	HP	SO	AVG	OBP	SLG	AOPS	ABR	SB-CS	FA	FR	RNG	THR	GAMES AT POSITION	DL	BFW
1984	Pit N	26	82	9	15	3	1	0	4	7-1	0	21	.183	.247	.244	38	-7	1-1	1.000	-1	113	183	3b11,S10,O3L		-0.8
1985	Pit N	35	124	11	28	4	0	4	12	13-2	0	27	.226	.299	.355	83	-3	2-4	.894	-5	72	85	3b21,O13L,2b6		-1.0
1987	Pit N	5	7	1	0	0	0	0	1	0-0	0	2	.000	.125	.000	-63	-2	0-0	1.000	-1	33	0	/S		-0.2
1988	Pit N	24	32	5	6	1	0	0	1	6-0	0	10	.188	.316	.219	57	-2	0-0	1.000	0	68	105	S14,2b4,3b2		-0.1
1989	Cle A	8	17	3	5	1	0	1	9	0-0	1	4	.294	.333	.353	92	0	0-0	.000	-0	0	0	/3D		0.0
Total	5	98	262	29	54	9	1	5	18	27-3	1	64	.206	.283	.294	62	-14	3-5	.925	-7	87	118	3b35,S25,O16L,2b10,D6		-2.1

GONZALEZ, EUSEBIO   Eusebio Miguel (Lopez) "Papo"   B7.13.1892 Havana, Cuba   D2.14.1976 Havana, Cuba   BR/TR/5-10/165   d7.26

YEAR	TM LG	G	AB	R	H	2B	3B	HR	RBI	BB-IB	HP	SO	AVG	OBP	SLG	AOPS	ABR	SB-CS	FA	FR	RNG	THR	GAMES AT POSITION	DL	BFW
1918	Bos A	3	5	2	2	0	1	0	1	0-0	0	1	.400	.571	.800	319	1	0-0	1.000	-0	95	0	S2/3		0.1

GONZALEZ, FERNANDO   Jose Fernando (Quinones)   B6.19.1950 Arecibo, PR   BR/TR/5-10/170(165-178)   d9.15

YEAR	TM LG	G	AB	R	H	2B	3B	HR	RBI	BB-IB	HP	SO	AVG	OBP	SLG	AOPS	ABR	SB-CS	FA	FR	RNG	THR	GAMES AT POSITION	DL	BFW
1972	Pit N	3	2	0	0	0	0	0	0	0-0	0	2	.000	.000	.000	-99	-1	0-0	.500	0	468	0	/3		0.0
1973	Pit N	37	49	5	11	0	1	1	5	1-0	1	11	.224	.255	.327	61	-3	0-0	.923	-1	77	0	3b5		-0.4
1974	KC A	9	21	1	3	1	0	0	2	0-0	0	4	.143	.143	.190	-5	-3	1-0	1.000	0	71	97	3b8/D		-0.3
	NY A	51	121	11	26	5	1	1	7	7-0	0	7	.215	.258	.298	60	-7	0-0	.982	-0	90	92	2b42,3b7,S3		-0.5
	Year	60	142	12	29	6	1	1	9	7-0	0	11	.204	.242	.282	50	-9	1-0	.982	-0	90	92	2b42,3b15,S3/D		-0.8
1977	Pit N	80	181	17	50	10	0	4	27	13-6	0	21	.276	.320	.398	89	-3	3-3	.972	-5	92	79	3b37,O16(15/0/1),2b6,S2		-0.9
1978	Pit N	9	21	2	4	1	0	0	0	1-0	0	3	.190	.227	.238	29	-2	0-0	.923	-4	65	0	2b4,3b3		-0.7
	SD N	101	320	27	80	10	2	2	29	18-3	0	32	.250	.286	.313	74	-13	4-4	.982	7	108	132	2b94		-0.2
	Year	110	341	29	84	11	2	2	29	19-3	0	35	.246	.282	.308	70	-15	4-4	.981	2	106	127	2b98,3b3		-0.9
1979	SD N	114	323	22	70	13	3	9	34	18-11	0	34	.217	.258	.359	71	-15	0-0	.976	-9	93	94	2b103,3b3		-2.0
Total	6	404	1038	85	244	40	7	17	104	58-20	1	114	.235	.274	.336	71	-47	8-7	.979	-13	98	107	2b249,3b64,O16(15/0/1),S5/D		-5.0

GONZALEZ, JOSE   Jose Rafael (Gutierrez)   B11.23.1964 Puerto Plata, D.R.   BR/TR/6-2/196*   d9.2

YEAR	TM LG	G	AB	R	H	2B	3B	HR	RBI	BB-IB	HP	SO	AVG	OBP	SLG	AOPS	ABR	SB-CS	FA	FR	RNG	THR	GAMES AT POSITION	DL	BFW
1985	LA N	23	11	6	3	2	0	0	0	1-0	0	3	.273	.333	.455	121	0	1-1	1.000	-0	99	0	O18(5/6/8)		0.0
1986	LA N	57	93	15	20	5	1	2	6	7-0	0	29	.215	.270	.355	76	-4	3-0	.924	-3	102	0	O57(0/49/8)		-0.7
1987	LA N	19	16	2	3	2	0	0	1	0-0	0	2	.188	.222	.313	45	-1	5-0	1.000	2	153	278	O16(8/5/3)		0.2
1988	†LA N	37	24	7	2	1	0	0	0	2-0	0	10	.083	.154	.125	-20	-4	3-0	.938	-1	104	0	O24(9/9/9)		-0.4
1989	LA N	95	261	31	70	11	2	3	18	23-5	0	53	.268	.326	.360	98	-1	9-3	1.000	5	105	216	O87(4/55/34)		0.4
1990	LA N	106	99	15	23	5	3	2	8	6-1	1	27	.232	.280	.404	89	-2	3-1	1.000	-0	99	53	O81(43/18/25)		-0.3
1991	LA N	42	28	3	0	0	0	0	0	2-0	0	9	.000	.067	.000	-81	-7	0-0	1.000	1	127	0	O27(12/1/15)		-0.7
	Pit N	16	20	2	2	0	0	1	3	0-0	1	6	.100	.095	.250	-5	-3	0-0	1.000	2	146	307	O14(3/6/5)		-0.1
	Year	58	48	5	2	0	0	1	3	2-0	1	15	.042	.078	.104	-49	-10	0-0	1.000	2	103	66	O41(15/7/20)		-0.8
	Cle A	33	69	10	11	2	1	1	4	11-0	1	27	.159	.284	.261	51	-5	0-0	.981	-0	103	66	O32(5/10/17)		-0.4
1992	Cal A	33	55	4	10	2	0	2	7-1	0	20	.182	.270	.218	39	-4	0-1	1.000	-0	96	101	O22(11/5/8)/D		-0.6
Total	8	461	676	95	144	30	7	9	42	60-7	2	186	.213	.277	.318	68	-31	33-9	.972	5	106	116	O378(100/164/132)/D		-2.6

GONZALEZ, JUAN   Juan Alberto (Vazquez)   B10.20.1969 Arecibo, PR   BR/TR/6-3/220(175-220)   d9.1

YEAR	TM LG	G	AB	R	H	2B	3B	HR	RBI	BB-IB	HP	SO	AVG	OBP	SLG	AOPS	ABR	SB-CS	FA	FR	RNG	THR	GAMES AT POSITION	DL	BFW
1989	Tex A	24	60	6	9	3	0	1	7	6-0	0	17	.150	.227	.250	34	-5	0-0	.964	0	112	0	O24(1/24/0)		-0.6
1990	Tex A	25	90	11	26	7	1	4	12	2-0	2	18	.289	.316	.522	131	3	0-1	1.000	-1	93	0	O16(1/12/4),D9		0.2
1991	Tex A	142	545	78	144	34	1	27	102	42-7	5	118	.264	.321	.479	121	14	4-4	.981	-2	97	82	O136(92/93/8),D4	18	0.8
1992	Tex A	155	584	77	152	24	2	43	109	35-1	5	143	.260	.304	.529	134	21	0-1	.975	2	103	111	O148(31/123/1),D4		2.2
1993	Tex A★	140	536	105	166	33	1	46	118	37-7	13	99	.310	.368	.632	169	49	4-1	.985	-1	105	66	O129L,D10		4.2
1994	Tex A	107	422	57	116	18	4	19	85	30-10	7	66	.275	.330	.472	103	0	6-4	.991	3	103	117	O107L		-0.1
1995	Tex A	90	352	57	104	20	2	27	82	17-3	0	66	.295	.324	.594	129	12	0-0	1.000	-0	70	347	D83,O5L	57	0.7
1996	†Tex A	134	541	89	170	33	2	47	144	45-12	3	82	.314	.368	.643	141	31	2-0	.988	-8	81	85	O102R,D32	24	1.5
1997	Tex A	133	533	87	158	24	3	42	131	33-7	3	107	.296	.335	.589	128	26	0-0	.971	1	96	143	D69,O64R	31	1.0
1998	†Tex A★	154	606	110	193	50	2	45	157	46-9	6	126	.318	.366	.630	146	40	2-1	.982	-4	94	96	O116R,D38		2.7
1999	†Tex A	144	562	114	183	36	1	39	128	51-7	4	105	.326	.378	.601	138	32	3-3	.983	-7	89	78	O131R,D14		1.6
2000	Det A	115	461	69	133	30	2	22	67	32-3	2	84	.289	.337	.505	110	6	1-2	.992	-3	95	46	O66R,D48		-0.3
2001	†Cle A★	140	532	97	173	34	1	35	140	41-5	6	94	.325	.370	.590	145	34	1-0	.987	4	103	143	O119R,D21		3.0
2002	Tex A	70	277	38	78	21	1	8	35	17-1	1	56	.282	.324	.451	101	0	2-0	.992	5	100	247	O62R,D8	98	0.2
2003	Tex A	82	327	49	96	17	1	24	70	14-1	4	73	.294	.329	.572	123	10	1-1	1.000	5	93	329	O57R,D24	71	1.0
2004	KC A	33	127	17	35	4	1	5	17	9-1	1	19	.276	.326	.441	98	-1	0-0	.948	-0	89	160	O29R,D4	135	-0.3
2005	Cle A	1	1	0	0	0	0	0	0	0-0	0	0	.000	.000	.000	-99	-0	0-0	—	0			/H	181	0.0
Total	17	1689	6556	1061	1936	388	25	434	1404	457-74	62	1273	.295	.343	.561	131	265	26-19	.983	-5	97	113	O1311(366/252/759),D368	615	17.9

GONZALEZ, JULIO   Julio Cesar (Hernandez)   B12.25.1952 Caguas, PR   BR/TR/5-11/165*   d4.8

YEAR	TM LG	G	AB	R	H	2B	3B	HR	RBI	BB-IB	HP	SO	AVG	OBP	SLG	AOPS	ABR	SB-CS	FA	FR	RNG	THR	GAMES AT POSITION	DL	BFW
1977	Hou N	110	383	34	94	18	3	1	27	19-1	4	45	.245	.287	.316	67	-19	3-3	.921	-15	86	90	S63,2b45		-2.6
1978	Hou N	70	223	24	52	3	1	0	16	8-1	1	31	.233	.263	.269	52	-15	6-1	.983	-13	89	83	2b54,S17,3b4		-2.6
1979	Hou N	68	181	16	45	5	2	0	10	5-0	3	14	.249	.280	.298	62	-10	2-1	.987	4	104	97	2b32,S21,3b9		-0.3
1980	Hou N	40	52	5	6	1	0	0	1	1-1	0	8	.115	.132	.135	-28	-9	1-0	1.000	1	89	152	S16,3b11,2b2		-0.8

YEAR	TM LG	G	AB	R	H	2B	3B	HR	RBI	BB-IB	HP	SO	AVG	OBP	SLG	AOPS	ABR	SB-CS	FA	FR	RNG	THR	GAMES AT POSITION	DL	BFW
1981	StL N	20	22	2	7	1	0	1	3	1-0	0	3	.318	.348	.500	132	1	0-0	1.000	0	147	115	S5,2b4,3b2		0.1
1982	StL N	42	87	9	21	3	2	1	7	1-0	1	24	.241	.258	.356	68	-4	1-1	.907	-2	93	39	3b21,2b9/S		-0.7
1983	Det A	12	21	0	3	1	0	0	2	1-0	0	7	.143	.182	.190	3	-3	0-0	.889	0	129	36	S6,2b5/3		-0.2
Total	7	370	969	90	228	33	4	6	66	36-3	2	132	.235	.269	.297	58	-59	13-6	.976	-25	100	98	2b151,S129,3b48		-7.1

GONZALEZ, LUIS Luis Alberto B6.26.1979 Maracay, Venez BR/TR/5-11/170(170-200) d4.6 OF(21/0/18)

YEAR	TM LG	G	AB	R	H	2B	3B	HR	RBI	BB-IB	HP	SO	AVG	OBP	SLG	AOPS	ABR	SB-CS	FA	FR	RNG	THR	GAMES AT POSITION	DL	BFW
2004	Col N	102	322	42	94	17	2	12	40	15-1	4	67	.292	.330	.469	92	-4	1-5	.994	0	107	109	2b40,O29(20/0/11),3b18,S10/D		-0.4
2005	Col N	128	404	51	118	25	0	9	44	20-0	6	63	.292	.333	.421	84	-9	3-4	1.000	-3	104	80	2b83,S17,3b12,1b10,O8(1/0/7)		-0.9
Total	2	230	726	93	212	42	2	21	84	35-1	10	130	.292	.332	.442	88	-13	4-9	.998	-3	105	90	2b123,O37L,3b30,S27,1b10/D		-1.3

GONZALEZ, LUIS Luis Emilio B9.3.1967 Tampa FL BL/TR/6-2/185(180-200) [HouN88 4/90] d9.4 Col South Alabama

YEAR	TM LG	G	AB	R	H	2B	3B	HR	RBI	BB-IB	HP	SO	AVG	OBP	SLG	AOPS	ABR	SB-CS	FA	FR	RNG	THR	GAMES AT POSITION	DL	BFW
1990	Hou N	12	21	1	4	2	0	0	2-1	0	5	.190	.261	.286	52	-1	0-0	1.000	2	170	218	3b4,1b2		0.1
1991	Hou N	137	473	51	120	28	9	13	69	40-4	8	101	.254	.320	.433	117	9	10-7	.984	14	114	85	O133L	15	1.5
1992	Hou N	122	387	40	94	19	3	10	55	24-3	2	52	.243	.289	.385	93	-5	7-7	.993	14	129	108	O111L	15	0.5
1993	Hou N	154	540	82	162	34	3	15	72	47-7	10	83	.300	.361	.457	123	18	20-9	.978	15	124	95	O149L		2.9
1994	Hou N	112	392	57	107	29	4	8	67	49-6	3	57	.273	.353	.449	109	7	15-13	.991	6	112	77	O111L		0.7
1995	Hou N	56	209	35	54	10	4	6	35	18-3	3	30	.258	.322	.431	104	0	1-3	.980	-1	101	62	O55L		-0.3
	Chi N	77	262	34	76	19	4	7	34	39-5	3	33	.290	.384	.473	126	11	5-5	.978	8	126	111	O76(74/6/0)		1.5
	Year	133	471	69	130	29	8	13	69	57-8	6	63	.276	.357	.454	117	12	6-8	.978	7	115	90	O131(129/6/0)		1.2
1996	Chi N	146	483	70	131	30	4	15	79	61-8	4	49	.271	.354	.443	106	5	9-6	.988	-0	96	79	O139L,1b2		0.0
1997	†Hou N	152	550	78	142	31	2	10	68	71-7	5	67	.258	.345	.376	93	-4	10-7	.982	1	98	105	O146L/1		-0.9
1998	Det A	154	547	84	146	35	5	23	71	57-7	8	62	.267	.340	.475	109	7	12-7	.988	-7	86	99	O132(132/3/0),D19		-0.5
1999	†Ari N★	153	614	112	**206**	45	4	26	111	66-6	7	63	.336	.403	.549	138	37	9-5	.983	-1	97	107	O148L,D4		2.8
2000	Ari N	**162**	618	106	192	47	2	31	114	78-6	12	85	.311	.392	.544	130	31	2-4	.990	-2	103	42	O162L		2.1
2001	†Ari N★	**162**	609	128	198	36	7	57	142	100-24	14	83	.325	.429	.688	171	67	1-1	**1.000**	-0	100	77	O161L		5.8
2002	Ari N★	148	524	90	151	19	3	28	103	97-8	5	76	.288	.400	.496	127	21	9-2	.985	-1	105	48	O146L		1.6
2003	Ari N★	156	579	92	176	46	4	26	104	94-17	3	67	.304	.402	.532	131	30	5-3	.989	-2	92	100	O154L		2.1
2004	Ari N	105	379	69	98	28	5	17	48	68-11	2	58	.259	.373	.493	114	10	2-2	.965	-6	93	36	O104L/D	63	-0.1
2005	Ari N★	155	579	90	157	37	0	24	79	78-12	11	99	.271	.366	.459	110	11	4-1	.989	-4	93	79	O152L		0.2
Total	16	2163	7766	1210	2214	495	63	316	1251	989-135	100	1061	.285	.369	.487	121	254	121-82	.986	30	103	82	O2079(2077/9/0),D24,1b5,3b4	93	20.0

GONZALEZ, MIKE Miguel Angel (Cordero) B9.24.1890 Havana, Cuba D2.19.1977 Havana, Cuba BR/TR/6-1/200 d9.28 M2/C13

YEAR	TM LG	G	AB	R	H	2B	3B	HR	RBI	BB-IB	HP	SO	AVG	OBP	SLG	AOPS	ABR	SB-CS	FA	FR	RNG	THR	GAMES AT POSITION	DL	BFW
1912	Bos N	1	2	0	0	0	0	0	1	0	1	.000	.333	.000	-5	0	0	.875	0	135	278	/C		0.0
1914	Cin N	95	176	19	41	6	0	0	10	13	2	16	.233	.293	.267	65	-7	2	.954	6	110	130	C83		0.4
1915	StL N	51	97	12	22	2	2	0	10	8	3	9	.227	.306	.289	80	-2	4-2	.992	4	118	88	C32,1b8		0.4
1916	StL N	118	331	33	79	15	4	0	29	28	3	18	.239	.304	.308	89	-4	5	.981	4	82	119	C93,1b13		0.8
1917	StL N	106	290	28	76	8	1	1	28	22	1	24	.262	.316	.307	94	-2	12	.977	2	119	118	C68,1b18/OR		0.6
1918	StL N	117	349	33	88	13	4	3	20	39	0	30	.252	.327	.338	107	4	14	.978	-6	82	109	C100,O5(1/1/3),1b2		0.7
1919	NY N	58	158	18	30	6	0	0	8	20	3	9	.190	.293	.228	58	-7	3	.962	-3	102	76	C52,1b4		-0.6
1920	NY N	11	13	1	3	0	0	0	0	3	0	1	.231	.375	.231	77	0	1-0	1.000	-0	120	94	C8		0.0
1921	NY N	13	24	3	9	1	0	0	0	1	0	0	.375	.400	.417	116	1	0-0	.981	-1	80	171	1b6,C2		0.1
1924	StL N	120	402	34	119	27	1	3	53	24	1	22	.296	.337	.391	96	-2	1-5	.986	-3	98	86	C119		0.3
1925	StL N	22	71	9	22	3	0	0	4	6	2	2	.310	.380	.352	86	-1	1-2	.982	3	134	75	C22		-0.1
	Chi N	70	197	26	52	13	1	3	18	13	2	15	.264	.316	.386	77	-7	2-1	.989	3	136	94	C50,1b9		-0.2
	Year	92	268	35	74	16	1	3	22	19	4	17	.276	.333	.377	80	-8	3-3	**.989**	9	173	82	C78		-0.2
1926	Chi N	80	253	24	63	13	3	1	23	13	1	17	.249	.288	.336	67	-12	5	.994	7	156	109	C36		0.5
1927	Chi N	39	108	15	26	4	1	1	15	10	1	8	.241	.311	.324	70	-5	1	.990	4	105	95	C45		0.7
1928	Chi N	49	158	12	43	9	2	1	21	12	0	7	.272	.324	.373	83	-4	2	.983	8	178	95	C45		0.5
1929	†Chi N	60	167	15	40	3	0	0	18	18	1	14	.240	.317	.257	44	-14	1	.992	6	127	103	C60		-0.5
1931	StL N	15	19	1	2	0	0	0	3	0	0	3	.105	.105	.105	-42	-4	0	1.000	0	120	196	C12		-0.2
1932	StL N	17	14	0	2	0	0	0	3	0	0	2	.143	.143	.143	-22	-2	0	1.000	1	51	244	C7		-0.2
Total	17	1042	2829	283	717	123	19	13	263	231	20	198	.253	.314	.324	81	-68	52-10	.980	40	117	101	C868,1b60,O6(1/1/4)		2.9

GONZALEZ, ORLANDO Orlando Eugene B11.15.1951 Havana, Cuba BL/TL/6-2/180* [CleA74 18/410] d6.7 Col Miami

YEAR	TM LG	G	AB	R	H	2B	3B	HR	RBI	BB-IB	HP	SO	AVG	OBP	SLG	AOPS	ABR	SB-CS	FA	FR	RNG	THR	GAMES AT POSITION	DL	BFW
1976	Cle A	28	68	5	17	2	0	0	4	5-0	0	7	.250	.301	.279	71	-2	1-2	.992	-1	89	68	1b15,O7(3/0/4),D2		-0.5
1978	†Phi N	26	26	1	5	0	0	0	1	0-0	1	1	.192	.222	.192	16	-3	0-0	1.000	0	135	0	O11(1/0/10),1b3		-0.3
1980	Oak A	25	70	10	17	0	0	1	0	9-0	0	8	.243	.329	.243	63	-3	0-2	.990	1	113	85	1b11,O2L,D8		-0.4
Total	3	79	164	16	39	2	0	1	5	15-0	1	16	.238	.302	.250	59	-8	1-4	.991	1	98	74	1b29,O20(6/0/14),D10		-1.2

GONZALEZ, PEDRO Pedro (Olivares) B12.12.1937 San Pedro de Macoris, D.R. BR/TR/6-0/176* d4.11

YEAR	TM LG	G	AB	R	H	2B	3B	HR	RBI	BB-IB	HP	SO	AVG	OBP	SLG	AOPS	ABR	SB-CS	FA	FR	RNG	THR	GAMES AT POSITION	DL	BFW
1963	NY A	14	26	3	5	1	0	0	0	0-0	0	5	.192	.192	.231	18	-3	0-1	.963	-2	59	62	2b7		-0.5
1964	†NY A	80	112	18	31	8	1	0	5	7-0	2	22	.277	.331	.366	92	-1	3-4	.992	1	157	122	1b31,O20(5/0/15),3b9,2b6		-0.1
1965	NY A	7	5	0	2	1	0	0	0	0-0	0	2	.400	.400	.600	181	0	0-0	—	0			/H		0.1
	Cle A	116	400	38	101	14	3	5	39	18-7	3	57	.253	.288	.340	78	-13	7-4	.980	8	98	91	2b112,O3R,3b2		0.5
	Year	123	405	38	103	15	3	5	39	18-7	3	59	.254	.289	.343	79	-12	7-4	.980	8	98	91	2b112,O3R,3b2		0.6
1966	Cle A	110	352	21	82	19	2	2	17	15-1	2	54	.233	.268	.287	60	-19	8-5	.984	9	98	107	2b104/3OR		-0.2
1967	Cle A	80	189	19	43	6	1	8	12	10-1	1	36	.228	.275	.376	73	-9	4-6	.971	-5	91	101	2b64,1b4,3b4,S3		-1.2
Total	5	407	1084	99	264	39	6	8	70	52-8	8	176	.244	.282	.313	70	-44	22-20	.980	11	95	98	2b293,1b35,O24(5/0/19),3b16,S3		-1.4

GONZALEZ, RAUL Victor Raul B12.27.1973 Santurce, PR BR/TR/5-8/190* [KCA90 17/477] d5.25

YEAR	TM LG	G	AB	R	H	2B	3B	HR	RBI	BB-IB	HP	SO	AVG	OBP	SLG	AOPS	ABR	SB-CS	FA	FR	RNG	THR	GAMES AT POSITION	DL	BFW
2000	Chi N	3	2	0	0	0	0	0	0	0-0	0	2	.000	.000	.000	-99	-1	0-0	—	-0	0	0	O2L		-0.1
2001	Cin N	11	14	0	3	0	0	0	1	0-0	0	3	.214	.267	.214	25	-2	0-0	1.000	0	105	0	O2L		-0.2
2002	Cin N	10	23	4	6	1	0	0	1	2-0	0	5	.261	.320	.304	66	-1	2-0	1.000	0	93	360	O6(1/5/0)		0.0
	NY N	30	81	9	21	2	0	3	11	4-0	0	17	.259	.291	.395	87	-2	2-2	1.000	1	112	92	O24(11/13/4)		-0.2
	Year	40	104	13	27	3	0	3	12	6-0	0	22	.260	.297	.375	82	-4	4-2	1.000	1	108	147	O30(12/18/4)		-0.2
2003	NY N	107	217	28	50	12	2	2	21	27-1	1	34	.230	.317	.332	73	-8	3-0	.993	5	120	116	O88(45/25/40)		-0.4
2004	Cle A	7	11	0	1	0	0	0	0	0-0	0	4	.091	.091	.091	-54	-3	0-0	1.000	0	166	0	O4(1/0/3)		-0.2
Total	5	168	348	41	81	15	2	5	33	34-1	1	65	.233	.301	.330	69	-17	7-2	.995	7	117	119	O126(62/43/47)		-1.1

GONZALEZ, WIKI Wiklenman Vicente B5.17.1974 Aragua, Venez BR/TR/5-11/203* d8.14

YEAR	TM LG	G	AB	R	H	2B	3B	HR	RBI	BB-IB	HP	SO	AVG	OBP	SLG	AOPS	ABR	SB-CS	FA	FR	RNG	THR	GAMES AT POSITION	DL	BFW
1999	SD N	30	83	7	21	2	1	3	12	1-0	1	8	.253	.271	.410	74	-4	0-0	.992	3	417	155	C17		0.0
2000	SD N	95	284	25	66	15	1	5	30	30-4	3	31	.232	.311	.345	70	-13	1-2	.991	2	102	115	C87		-0.6
2001	SD N	64	160	16	44	6	0	8	27	11-1	4	28	.275	.335	.463	112	2	2-0	.989	-4	92	126	C47/D	30	0.1
2002	SD N	56	164	16	36	8	1	1	20	27-3	1	24	.220	.330	.299	78	-5	0-0	.985	0	134	112	C54	76	-0.2
2003	SD N	24	65	1	13	5	0	0	10	5-1	1	13	.200	.264	.277	47	-5	0-0	.993	-1	61	105	C23/P		-0.5
2005	Sea A	14	45	7	12	5	0	0	2	2-0	0	3	.267	.298	.378	84	-1	0-0	1.000	3	226	104	C14	47	0.3
Total	6	283	801	72	192	41	3	17	101	76-9	10	107	.240	.312	.362	80	-26	3-2	.990	3	138	118	C242/PD	153	-0.9

GOOCH, CHARLIE Charles Furman B6.5.1902 Smyrna TN D5.30.1982 Lanham MD BR/TR/5-9/170 d4.18

YEAR	TM LG	G	AB	R	H	2B	3B	HR	RBI	BB-IB	HP	SO	AVG	OBP	SLG	AOPS	ABR	SB-CS	FA	FR	RNG	THR	GAMES AT POSITION	DL	BFW
1929	Was A	39	57	6	16	2	1	0	7	3	0	8	.281	.359	.351	83	-1	0	.970	-1	218	65	1b7,3b7/S		-0.2

GOOCH, JOHNNY John Beverley B11.9.1897 Smyrna TN D5.15.1975 Nashville TN BB/TR/5-11/175 d9.9 C3

YEAR	TM LG	G	AB	R	H	2B	3B	HR	RBI	BB-IB	HP	SO	AVG	OBP	SLG	AOPS	ABR	SB-CS	FA	FR	RNG	THR	GAMES AT POSITION	DL	BFW
1921	Pit N	13	38	2	9	0	0	0	3	3	0	3	.237	.293	.237	41	-3	1-0	.985	2	149	106	C13		0.0
1922	Pit N	105	353	45	116	15	3	1	42	39	5	15	.329	.403	.397	106	5	1-0	.970	-3	95	87	C103		0.9
1923	Pit N	66	202	16	56	10	2	1	20	17	1	13	.277	.336	.361	82	-5	2-1	.975	4	133	81	C66		0.3
1924	Pit N	70	224	26	65	6	5	0	25	16	2	12	.290	.343	.362	88	-4	1-3	.988	1	142	71	C69		-0.1
1925	†Pit N	79	215	24	64	8	4	0	30	20	0	16	.298	.357	.372	81	-6	1-0	.968	1	125	73	C76		0.1
1926	Pit N	86	218	19	59	15	1	1	42	20	3	14	.271	.340	.362	85	-4	1	.980	0	119	72	C80		0.2
1927	†Pit N	101	291	22	75	17	2	1	48	19	1	21	.258	.305	.351	70	-12	0	.974	5	133	74	C91		-0.2
1928	Pit N	31	80	7	19	2	1	0	5	3	0	6	.237	.265	.287	43	-7	0	.957	1	81	119	C31		0.0
	Bro N	42	101	9	32	1	0	0	12	7	0	9	.317	.361	.366	92	-1	0	.969	-1	77	85	C38		-0.4
	Year	73	181	16	51	3	1	0	17	10	0	15	.282	.319	.331	70	-9	0	.964	0	79	102	C69		-0.4
1929	Bro N	1	1	0	0	0	0	0	0	0	0	0	.000	.000	.000	-99	0	0	—	0			/H		0.0
	Cin N	92	287	22	86	13	5	0	34	24	1	10	.300	.356	.380	86	-6	4	.975	5	108	117	C86		0.4
	Year	93	288	22	86	13	5	0	34	24	1	10	.299	.355	.378	86	-6	4	.975	5	108	117	C86		0.4
1930	Cin N	82	276	29	67	10	3	2	30	27	2	15	.243	.308	.322	57	-19	0	.955	-5	91	101	C79		-1.7

YEAR	TM LG	G	AB	R	H	2B	3B	HR	RBI	BB-IB	HP	SO	AVG	OBP	SLG	AOPS	ABR	SB-CS	FA	FR	RNG	THR	GAMES AT POSITION	DL	BFW
1933	Bos A	37	77	6	14	1	1	0	2	11		0	7	.182	.284	.221	36	-7	0-0	.991	2	82	176	C26		-0.4
Total	11	805	2363	227	662	98	29	7	293	206		15	141	.280	.342	.355	79	-69	11-5	.973	12	113	90	C758		-1.1

GOODCH, LEE Lee Currin B2.23.1890 Oxford NC D5.18.1966 Raleigh NC BR/TR/6-0/190 d8.17 Col Wake Forest

YEAR	TM LG	G	AB	R	H	2B	3B	HR	RBI	BB-IB	HP	SO	AVG	OBP	SLG	AOPS	ABR	SB-CS	FA	FR	RNG	THR	GAMES AT POSITION	DL	BFW
1915	Cle A	2	2	0	1	0	0	0	0	0		0	0	.500	.500	.500	196	0	0	—	0			/H		0.0
1917	Phi A	17	59	4	17	2	0	1	8	4		0	10	.288	.333	.373	117	1	0	.893	-2	87	45	O16R		-0.2
Total	2	19	61	4	18	2	0	1	8	4		0	10	.295	.338	.377	120	1	0	.893	-2	87	45	O16R		-0.2

GOOD, GENE Eugene J. B12.13.1882 Roxbury MA D8.6.1947 Boston MA BL/TR/5-6/130 d4.12

YEAR	TM LG	G	AB	R	H	2B	3B	HR	RBI	BB-IB	HP	SO	AVG	OBP	SLG	AOPS	ABR	SB-CS	FA	FR	RNG	THR	GAMES AT POSITION	DL	BFW
1906	Bos N	34	119	4	18	0	0	0	0	13	2			.151	.246	.151	25	-10	2	.873	-3	114	88	O34(24/10/0)		-1.7

GOOD, WILBUR Wilbur David "Lefty" B9.28.1885 Punxsutawney PA D12.30.1963 Brooksville FL BL/TL/5-11.5/180 d8.18 ▲

YEAR	TM LG	G	AB	R	H	2B	3B	HR	RBI	BB-IB	HP	SO	AVG	OBP	SLG	AOPS	ABR	SB-CS	FA	FR	RNG	THR	GAMES AT POSITION	DL	BFW
1905	NY A	5	8	2	3	0	0	0	0	0	0			.375	.375	.375	124	1	0	.889	0	120	15	P5		0.0
1908	Cle A	46	154	23	43	1	3	1	14	13	4			.279	.351	.344	126	4	7	.845	-8	0	0	O42(2/17/23)		-0.7
1909	Cle A	94	318	33	68	6	5	0	17	28	9			.214	.296	.264	74	-9	13	.953	2	119	90	O80R		-1.2
1910	Bos N	23	86	15	29	5	4	0	11	6	2	13		.337	.394	.488	150	5	5	.969	3	100	207	O83(0/22/1)		0.7
1911	Bos N	43	165	21	44	9	4	0	15	12	0	22		.267	.316	.358	82	-4	3	.945	5	102	192	O43(0/41/2)		-0.3
	Chi N	58	145	27	39	5	4	2	21	11	2	17		.269	.329	.400	103	0	10	.928	-4	90	56	O40(3/34/3)		-0.7
	Year	101	310	48	83	14	7	2	36	23	2	39		.268	.322	.377	92	-4	13	.938	1	97	132	O83(3/75/5)		-1.0
1912	Chi N	39	35	7	5	0	0	0	1	3	0	7		.143	.211	.143	-2	-5	3	1.000	1	112	229	O10(5/4/1)		-0.4
1913	Chi N	49	91	11	23	3	2	1	12	11	1	16		.253	.340	.363	100	0	5-2	.974	-1	107	39	O26(3/1/22)		-0.1
1914	Chi N	154	580	70	158	24	7	2	43	53	7	74		.272	.341	.348	105	4	31	.930	-0	99	106	O154R		-0.4
1915	Chi N	128	498	66	126	18	9	2	27	34	5	65		.253	.307	.337	95	-4	19-17	.936	-1	101	98	O125(0/1/125)		-1.4
1916	Phi N	75	136	25	34	4	3	1	15	8	3	13		.250	.306	.346	96	-1	7	.983	0	98	101	O46(9/1/36)		-0.3
1918	Chi A	35	148	24	37	9	4	0	11	11	3	16		.250	.315	.365	104	0	1	.982	3	120	77	O35(1/33/1)		0.0
Total	11	749	2364	324	609	84	44	9	187	190	26	243		.258	.322	.342	98	-8	104-19	.942	-1	96	99	O624(23/154/448),P5		-4.8

GOODENOUGH, BILL William B. B1863 NY D5.24.1905 St.Louis MO BL/6-1/170 d8.31

YEAR	TM LG	G	AB	R	H	2B	3B	HR	RBI	BB-IB	HP	SO	AVG	OBP	SLG	AOPS	ABR	SB-CS	FA	FR	RNG	THR	GAMES AT POSITION	DL	BFW
1893	StL N	10	31	4	5	1	0	0	2	3	3	4		.161	.297	.194	31	-3	2	.880	-1	69	0	O10C		-0.3

GOODFELLOW, MIKE Michael J. B10.3.1866 Port Jervis NY D2.12.1920 Newark NJ BR/TR/6-0/180 d6.13

YEAR	TM LG	G	AB	R	H	2B	3B	HR	RBI	BB-IB	HP	SO	AVG	OBP	SLG	AOPS	ABR	SB-CS	FA	FR	RNG	THR	GAMES AT POSITION	DL	BFW
1887	StL AA	1	4	0	0	0	0	0	0	0				.000	.000	.000	-90	-1	0	.800	-0			/C		-0.1
1888	Cle AA	68	269	24	66	7	0	0	29	11	3			.245	.283	.271	80	-6	7	.863	-4	75	39	O62(11/0/52),C4,1b3/S		-0.9
Total	2	69	273	24	66	7	0	0	29	11	3			.242	.279	.267	77	-7	7	.863	-4			O62(11/0/52),C5,1b3/S		-1.0

GOODMAN, IVAL Ival Richard "Goodie" B7.23.1908 Northview MO D11.25.1984 Cincinnati OH BL/TR/5-11/170 d4.16

YEAR	TM LG	G	AB	R	H	2B	3B	HR	RBI	BB-IB	HP	SO	AVG	OBP	SLG	AOPS	ABR	SB-CS	FA	FR	RNG	THR	GAMES AT POSITION	DL	BFW
1935	Cin N	148	592	86	159	23	18	12	72	35	4	50		.269	.314	.429	101	-3	14	.960	5	108	111	O146(2/0/144)		-0.7
1936	Cin N	136	489	81	139	15	14	17	71	38	9	53		.284	.347	.476	128	16	6	.972	-2	110	44	O120(1/1/118)		0.7
1937	Cin N	147	549	86	150	25	14	12	55	55	7	58		.273	.347	.428	115	11	10	.974	3	109	92	O141(7/1/133)		0.5
1938	Cin N★	145	568	103	166	27	10	30	92	53	15	51		.292	.348	.533	149	37	3	.988	3	108	77	O142R		3.0
1939	†Cin N★	124	470	85	152	37	16	7	84	54	7	32		.323	.401	.516	144	30	2	.981	7	105	144	O123R		2.9
1940	†Cin N	136	519	78	134	20	6	12	63	60	0	54		.258	.335	.389	98	-1	9	.970	-7	97	56	O135R		-1.7
1941	Cin N	42	149	14	40	5	2	1	12	16	1	15		.268	.343	.349	95	-1	1	.966	-1	110	29	O40R		-0.5
1942	Cin N	87	226	21	55	18	1	0	15	24	1	32		.243	.319	.332	91	-2	0	.991	1	95	142	O57R		-0.5
1943	Chi N	80	225	31	72	10	5	3	45	24	2	20		.320	.390	.449	144	13	4	.968	-4	95	36	O61(55/10/0)		0.6
1944	Chi N	62	141	24	37	8	1	1	16	23	3	15		.262	.377	.355	107	3	0	1.000	-3	89	0	O35(23/14/0)		-0.2
Total	10	1107	3928	609	1104	188	85	95	525	382	49	380		.281	.352	.445	120	103	49	.975	1	105	82	O1000(88/26/892)		4.1

GOODMAN, JAKE Jacob B9.14.1853 Lancaster PA D3.9.1890 Reading PA 6-1.5/? d5.2

YEAR	TM LG	G	AB	R	H	2B	3B	HR	RBI	BB-IB	HP	SO	AVG	OBP	SLG	AOPS	ABR	SB-CS	FA	FR	RNG	THR	GAMES AT POSITION	DL	BFW
1878	Mil N	60	252	28	62	4	3	1	27	7			33	.246	.266	.298	80	-6		.944	-4	71	52	1b60		-1.2
1882	Pit AA	10	41	5	13	2	2	0		2			2	.317	.349	.463	180	3		.962	1	177	0	1b10		0.3
Total	2	70	293	33	75	6	5	1	27	9			33	.256	.278	.321	92	-3		.946	-3	85	45	1b70		-0.9

GOODMAN, BILLY William Dale B3.22.1926 Concord NC D10.1.1984 Sarasota FL BL/TR/5-11/165* d4.19 C3 OF(68/0/43)

YEAR	TM LG	G	AB	R	H	2B	3B	HR	RBI	BB-IB	HP	SO	AVG	OBP	SLG	AOPS	ABR	SB-CS	FA	FR	RNG	THR	GAMES AT POSITION	DL	BFW
1947	Bos A	12	11	1	2	0	0	0	1	1	0	2		.182	.250	.182	20	-1	0-0	1.000	0	146	0	/OR		-0.1
1948	Bos A	127	445	65	138	27	4	1	66	74	5	44		.310	.414	.387	108	10	5-3	.993	-3	91	107	1b117,2b2,3b2		0.3
1949	Bos A★	122	443	54	132	23	3	0	56	58	2	21		.298	.382	.363	91	-4	2-0	.992	-1	95	121	1b117		-0.7
1950	Bos A	110	424	91	150	25	3	4	68	52	2	25		.354	.427	.455	115	12	2-4	.991	-2	99	55	O45L,3b27,1b21,2b5/S		0.5
1951	Bos A	141	546	92	162	34	4	0	50	79	2	37		.297	.388	.374	97	1	7-4	.995	-2	72	102	1b62,2b44,O38(2/0/36)/3		-0.1
1952	Bos A	138	513	79	157	27	3	4	56	48	4	23		.306	.370	.394	94	4	8-2	.975	23	113	118	2b103,1b23,3b5,O4L		3.4
1953	Bos A★	128	514	71	161	33	5	2	41	57	2	11		.313	.384	.409	108	8	1-4	.974	-1	102	104	2b112,1b20		1.3
1954	Bos A	127	489	71	148	25	4	1	36	51	2	15		.303	.370	.376	95	-2	3-3	.979	6	110	108	2b72,1b27,O13L,3b12		0.7
1955	Bos A	149	599	100	176	31	2	0	52	99-1	3	44		.294	.394	.352	94	1	5-5	.969	-21	93	84	2b143,1b5/OR		-1.0
1956	Bos A	105	399	61	117	22	8	2	38	40-1	0	22		.293	.356	.404	90	-6	0-3	.966	-8	100	94	2b95		-0.8
1957	Bos A	18	16	1	1	1	0	0		2-0		1		.063	.167	.125	-18	-3	0-0	—	0			/H		-0.3
	Bal A	73	263	36	81	10	3	3	33	31-1	3	18		.308	.362	.403	117	6	0-2	.961	-7	87	100	3b54,O9(4/0/5),1b8,2b5,S5		-0.2
	Year	91	279	37	82	11	3	3	33	23-1	3	19		.294	.351	.387	106	2	0-2	.961	-7	87	100	3b54,O9(4/0/5),1b8,2b5,S5		-0.5
1958	Chi A	116	425	41	127	15	5	0	40	37-1	2	21		.299	.355	.358	100	1	1-0	.954	-11	97	79	3b111,1b3/2S		-1.1
1959	†Chi A	104	268	21	67	14	1	1	28	19-0	2	20		.250	.304	.321	73	-10	3-0	.950	-0	106	95	3b74,2b3		-1.0
1960	Chi A	30	77	5	18	4	0	0	6	12-1	0	8		.234	.337	.286	71	-3	0-0	.982	4	136	73	3b20,2b7		0.2
1961	Chi A	41	51	4	13	4	0	1	10	7-0	0	6		.255	.339	.392	98	0	0-0	.944	-0	106	89	3b7,1b2/2		0.0
1962	Hou N	82	161	12	41	4	1	0	10	12-2	0	11		.255	.306	.292	66	-8	0-0	.972	-4	93	56	2b31,3b17/1		-1.1
Total	16	1623	5644	807	1691	299	44	19	591	669-7	29	329		.300	.376	.378	98	5	37-30	.972	-27	102	99	2b624,1b406,3b330,O111L,S7		0.0

GOODSON, ED James Edward B1.25.1948 Pulaski VA BL/TR (BB 1975p)/6-3/185* [SFN68 S1/3] d9.5 Col East Tennessee

YEAR	TM LG	G	AB	R	H	2B	3B	HR	RBI	BB-IB	HP	SO	AVG	OBP	SLG	AOPS	ABR	SB-CS	FA	FR	RNG	THR	GAMES AT POSITION	DL	BFW
1970	SF N	7	11	1	3	0	0	0	0	0-0	0	2		.273	.273	.273	47	-1	0-0	.941	0	163	67	1b2		-0.1
1971	SF N	20	42	4	8	1	0	0	0	2-0	0	4		.190	.227	.214	26	-4	0-0	1.000	0	106	39	1b14		-0.5
1972	SF N	58	150	15	42	1	1	6	30	8-2	1	12		.280	.319	.420	107	1	0-0	.991	2	132	32	1b42		-0.8
1973	SF N	102	384	37	116	20	1	12	53	15-4	2	44		.302	.331	.453	111	4	0-1	.911	-8	97	76	3b93	43	-0.4
1974	SF N	98	298	25	81	15	0	6	48	18-6	3	22		.272	.320	.383	92	-4	1-0	.997	-2	73	100	1b73,3b8		-1.1
1975	SF N	39	121	10	25	7	0	1	8	7-2	0	14		.207	.248	.298	55	-5	0-1	.993	2	125	95	1b16,3b13	20	-0.9
	Atl N	47	76	5	16	2	0	1	8	2-0	0	8		.211	.228	.276	39	-7	0-0	.990	-0	100	88	1b13/3		-0.8
	Year	86	197	15	41	9	0	2	16	9-2	0	22		.208	.240	.284	44	-15	0-1	.992	2	115	92	1b29,3b14		-1.7
1976	LA N	83	118	8	27	4	0	3	17	8-2	0	19		.229	.273	.339	75	-4	0-0	.833	-4	93	85	3b16,1b3,O2L/2	15	-0.9
1977	†LA N	61	66	3	11	1	0	1	5	3-2	1	10		.167	.203	.227	15	-8	0-1	1.000	0	94	203	1b13,3b4		-0.9
Total	8	515	1266	108	329	51	2	30	170	63-18	6	135		.260	.297	.374	84	-32	1-3	.994	-9	99	79	1b176,3b135,O2L/2	78	-5.6

GOODWIN, PEP Claire Vernon B12.19.1891 Pocatello ID D2.15.1972 Oakland CA BL/TR/5-10.5/160 d4.16 Col California-Davis

YEAR	TM LG	G	AB	R	H	2B	3B	HR	RBI	BB-IB	HP	SO	AVG	OBP	SLG	AOPS	ABR	SB-CS	FA	FR	RNG	THR	GAMES AT POSITION	DL	BFW
1914	KC F	112	374	38	88	15	6	1	32	27	2	23		.235	.290	.316	68	-24	4	.907	-7	119	89	S67,3b40/1		-2.7
1915	KC F	81	229	22	54	5	1	0	16	15	3	23		.236	.291	.266	60	-16	6	.906	-5	97	82	S42,2b23		-2.0
Total	2	193	603	60	142	20	7	1	48	42	5	46		.235	.291	.297	65	-40	10	.907	-12	106	86	S109,3b40,2b23/1		-4.7

GOODWIN, CURTIS Curtis La Mar B9.30.1972 Oakland CA BL/TL/5-11/180* [BalA91 12/316] d6.2

YEAR	TM LG	G	AB	R	H	2B	3B	HR	RBI	BB-IB	HP	SO	AVG	OBP	SLG	AOPS	ABR	SB-CS	FA	FR	RNG	THR	GAMES AT POSITION	DL	BFW
1995	Bal A	87	289	40	76	11	3	4	24	15-0	2	53		.263	.301	.332	64	-16	22-4	.990	-1	104	26	O84C,D3	15	-1.2
1996	Cin N	49	136	20	31	3	0	0	5	19-0	0	34		.228	.323	.250	53	-9	15-6	.970	-4	85	0	O42(9/28/6)		-1.2
1997	Cin N	85	265	27	67	11	0	1	12	24-0	1	53		.253	.316	.306	63	-14	22-13	1.000	4	116	82	O71(32/41/1)		-1.0
1998	Col N	119	159	27	39	7	0	1	16	16-0	0	40		.245	.313	.308	53	-10	5-1	.983	1	112	35	O91(14/74/7)		-0.9
1999	Chi N	89	157	15	38	6	1	0	13	13-1	0	38		.242	.298	.293	51	-12	2-4	.983	4	112	123	O76(36/42/0)		-0.9
	Tor A	2	8	0	0	0	0	0	0	0-0	0	2		.000	.000	.000	-98	-2	0-0	1.000	0	1	142	821	O2C		-0.1
Total	5	431	1014	129	251	38	4	3	56	87-1	3	221		.248	.307	.302	57	-63	66-28	.988	5	107	59	O366(91/271/14),D3	15	-5.3

GOODWIN, DANNY Danny Kay B9.2.1953 St.Louis MO BL/TR/6-1/195* [AnaA75 1/1] d9.3 Col Southern A&M

YEAR	TM LG	G	AB	R	H	2B	3B	HR	RBI	BB-IB	HP	SO	AVG	OBP	SLG	AOPS	ABR	SB-CS	FA	FR	RNG	THR	GAMES AT POSITION	DL	BFW
1975	Cal A	4	10	0	1	0	0	0	0	0-0	0	5		.100	.100	.100	-47	-2	0-0	—	0			D3		-0.2
1977	Cal A	35	91	5	19	6	1	1	11	5-1	0	19		.209	.250	.330	58	-5	0-0	—	0	0		D30		-0.6
1978	Cal A	24	58	9	16	5	0	2	10	10-0	1	13		.276	.377	.466	142	4	0-0	—	0	0		D15		0.3
1979	Min A	58	159	22	46	8	5	1	27	11-1	3	23		.289	.338	.497	116	3	0-0	1.000	-1	55	104	D51,1b8		0.0
1980	Min A	55	115	12	23	5	0	1	11	17-0	2	32		.200	.301	.270	54	-7	0-0	1.000	0	109	74	D38,1b13		-0.8

YEAR	TM LG	G	AB	R	H	2B	3B	HR	RBI	BB-IB	HP	SO	AVG	OBP	SLG	AOPS	ABR	SB-CS	FA	FR	RNG	THR	GAMES AT POSITION	DL	BFW
1981	Min A	59	151	18	34	6	1	2	17	16-2	0	32	.225	.298	.318	73	-5	3-1	.992	-2	76	76	1b40/OLD		-1.0
1982	Oak A	17	52	6	11	2	1	2	8	2-0	0	13	.212	.236	.404	76	-2	0-0	—	0	0		D15		-0.3
Total	7	252	636	72	150	32	8	13	81	61-4	0	137	.236	.301	.373	83	-14	3-1	.994	-3	80	79	D150,1b61/OL		-2.6

GOODWIN, TOM Thomas Jones B7.27.1968 Fresno CA BL/TR/6-1/175(165-195) [LAN89 1/22] d9.1 Col Cal St.-Fresno

YEAR	TM LG	G	AB	R	H	2B	3B	HR	RBI	BB-IB	HP	SO	AVG	OBP	SLG	AOPS	ABR	SB-CS	FA	FR	RNG	THR	GAMES AT POSITION	DL	BFW
1991	LA N	16	7	3	1	0	0	0	0	0-0	0	1	.143	.143	.143	-20	-1	1-1	1.000	1	167	0	O5(2/4/0)		-0.1
1992	LA N	57	73	15	17	1	1	0	3	6-0	0	10	.233	.291	.274	62	-4	7-3	1.000	-0	92	0	O45(35/9/2)		-0.6
1993	LA N	30	17	6	5	1	0	0	1	1-0	0	4	.294	.333	.353	89	-0	1-2	1.000	-0	93	0	O12(6/4/2)		-0.1
1994	KC A	2	2	0	0	0	0	0	0	0-0	0	0	.000	.000	.000	-95	-1	0-0	1.000	0	146	0	/ORD		-0.1
1995	KC A	133	480	72	138	16	3	4	28	38-0	5	72	.287	.346	.358	82	-13	50-18	.990	-7	90	82	O130(37/95/1),D2		-1.5
1996	KC A	143	524	80	148	14	4	1	35	39-0	2	79	.282	.334	.330	69	-25	66-22	.984	-6	94	77	O136(75/81/0),D5		-2.4
1997	KC A	97	367	51	100	13	4	2	22	19-0	2	51	.272	.311	.346	69	-17	34-10	.996	-4	96	61	O96C		-1.6
	Tex A	53	207	39	49	13	2	0	17	25-1	1	37	.237	.319	.319	64	-11	16-6	.986	3	110	118	O51(5/49/0)		-0.6
	Year	150	574	90	149	26	6	2	39	44-1	3	88	.260	.314	.336	67	-28	50-16	.992	-2	101	81	O147(5/145/0)		-2.2
1998	†Tex A	154	520	102	151	13	3	2	33	73-0	2	90	.290	.378	.338	84	-9	38-20	.992	4	109	61	O150C/D		-0.3
1999	†Tex A	109	405	63	105	12	6	3	33	40-0	0	61	.259	.324	.341	66	-21	39-11	.989	5	96	61	O107C	54	-1.9
2000	Col N	91	317	65	86	8	8	5	47	50-2	1	76	.271	.368	.394	76	-11	39-7	.986	-1	107	62	O88C		-0.4
	LA N	56	211	29	53	3	1	1	11	18-0	0	41	.251	.310	.289	55	-15	16-3	1.000	3	114	65	O55(10/48/0)		-0.9
	Year	147	528	94	139	11	9	6	58	68-2	1	117	.263	.346	.352	69	-25	55-10	.992	2	110	63	O143(10/136/0)		-1.3
2001	LA N	105	286	51	66	8	5	4	22	23-0	0	58	.231	.286	.336	64	-17	22-8	.994	-5	94	26	O78(70/8/0)	19	-1.9
2002	†SF N	78	154	23	40	5	2	1	17	14-0	0	25	.260	.321	.338	80	-6	16-2	.990	3	129	0	O53(28/22/7)		-0.1
2003	†Chi N	87	171	26	49	10	0	1	12	11-0	0	33	.287	.328	.363	79	-5	19-5	1.000	-3	92	0	O57(17/27/15)	27	-0.6
2004	Chi N	77	105	11	21	8	0	0	3	8-0	0	22	.200	.254	.276	37	-10	5-0	1.000	-0	102	0	O28(14/8/7)	18	-0.1
Total	14	1288	3846	636	1029	125	39	24	284	365-3	13	660	.268	.332	.339	72	-166	369-118	.991	-20	100	59	O1092(237/858/35),D9	118	-14.0

GOOLSBY, RAY Raymond Daniel "Ox" B9.5.1919 Florala AL D11.13.1999 Apopka FL BR/TR/6-1/185 d4.18

YEAR	TM LG	G	AB	R	H	2B	3B	HR	RBI	BB-IB	HP	SO	AVG	OBP	SLG	AOPS	ABR	SB-CS	FA	FR	RNG	THR	GAMES AT POSITION	DL	BFW
1946	Was A	3	4	0	0	0	0	0	1	0-0	0	1	.000	.200	.000	-43	-1	0-0	1.000	-0	65	0	/OL		-0.1

GOOSSEN, GREG Gregory Bryant B12.14.1945 Los Angeles CA BR/TR/6-1.5/210* d9.3

YEAR	TM LG	G	AB	R	H	2B	3B	HR	RBI	BB-IB	HP	SO	AVG	OBP	SLG	AOPS	ABR	SB-CS	FA	FR	RNG	THR	GAMES AT POSITION	DL	BFW
1965	NY N	11	31	2	9	0	0	1	2	1-0	0	5	.290	.313	.387	99	0	0-0	.979	-1	90	52	C8		-0.1
1966	NY N	13	32	1	6	2	0	1	5	1-0	1	11	.188	.235	.344	60	-2	0-0	1.000	-5	55	119	C11		-0.7
1967	NY N	37	69	2	11	1	0	0	3	4-0	1	26	.159	.216	.174	13	-8	0-0	.973	-0	38	97	C23		-0.8
1968	NY N	38	106	4	22	7	0	0	6	10-0	2	21	.208	.288	.274	69	-3	0-0	.992	2	131	94	1b31/C		-0.4
1969	Sea A	52	139	19	43	8	1	10	30	14-0	3	29	.309	.385	.597	172	13	1-1	.993	1	111	55	1b31,O2L		1.2
1970	Mil A	21	47	3	12	3	0	1	3	10-0	2	12	.255	.407	.383	119	2	0-0	.990	-2	57	77	1b15		0.0
	Was A	21	36	2	8	3	0	0	1	2-0	0	8	.222	.256	.306	59	-2	0-0	1.000	-0	51	0	O5L,1b2		-0.3
	Year	42	83	5	20	6	0	1	4	12-0	2	20	.241	.347	.349	96	0	0-0	.992	-2	81	101	1b17,O5L		-0.3
Total	6	193	460	33	111	24	1	13	44	42-0	9	112	.241	.316	.383	99	0	1-1	.992	-4	113	79	1b79,C43,O7L		-1.1

GORBOUS, GLEN Glen Edward B7.8.1930 Drumheller AL, Can. D6.12.1990 Calgary AL, Can. BL/TR/6-2/175* d4.11

YEAR	TM LG	G	AB	R	H	2B	3B	HR	RBI	BB-IB	HP	SO	AVG	OBP	SLG	AOPS	ABR	SB-CS	FA	FR	RNG	THR	GAMES AT POSITION	DL	BFW
1955	Cin N	8	18	2	6	3	0	0	4	3-0	0	1	.333	.429	.500	137	1	0-0	.857	-0	115	0	O5L		0.1
	Phi N	91	224	25	53	9	1	4	23	21-3	0	17	.237	.301	.339	71	-9	0-3	.984	7	111	226	O57(0/4/53)		-0.6
	Year	99	242	27	59	12	1	4	27	24-3	0	18	.244	.311	.351	77	-8	0-3	.971	6	111	207	O62(5/4/53)		-0.5
1956	Phi N	15	33	1	6	0	0	0	1	0-0	0	1	.182	.182	.182	-2	-5	0-0	1.000	-1	84	0	O8R		-0.6
1957	Phi N	3	2	1	1	0	0	1	1	0-0	0	0	.500	.667	1.000	163	1	0-0	—	0			/H		0.1
Total	3	117	277	29	66	13	1	4	29	25-3	0	19	.238	.300	.336	70	-12	0-3	.973	6	109	190	O70(5/4/61)		-1.0

GORDON, JOE Joseph Lowell "Flash" B2.18.1915 Los Angeles CA D4.14.1978 Sacramento CA BR/TR/5-10/180* d4.18 Mil 1944-45 M5/C1 Col Oregon

YEAR	TM LG	G	AB	R	H	2B	3B	HR	RBI	BB-IB	HP	SO	AVG	OBP	SLG	AOPS	ABR	SB-CS	FA	FR	RNG	THR	GAMES AT POSITION	DL	BFW
1938	†NY A	127	458	83	117	24	7	25	97	56	3	72	.255	.340	.502	109	3	11-3	.960	21	116	115	2b126		3.0
1939	†NY A★	151	567	92	161	32	5	28	111	75	2	57	.284	.370	.506	124	19	11-10	.967	8	102	135	2b151		3.3
1940	NY A★	155	616	112	173	32	10	30	103	52	3	57	.281	.340	.511	122	8	18-8	.975	14	105	116	2b155		3.8
1941	†NY A★	156	588	104	162	26	7	24	87	72	4	80	.276	.358	.466	118	14	10-9	.958	9	102	134	2b131,1b30		2.7
1942	†NY A★	147	538	88	173	29	4	18	103	79	1	95	.322	.409	.491	156	42	12-6	.966	6	98	146	2b147		5.8
1943	†NY A☆	152	543	82	135	28	5	17	69	98	2	75	.249	.365	.413	126	21	4-7	.969	25	107	117	2b152		5.6
1946	NY A★	112	376	35	79	15	0	11	47	49	4	72	.210	.308	.338	79	-10	2-5	.974	18	109	120	2b108		1.3
1947	Cle A★	155	562	89	153	27	6	29	93	57	1	49	.272	.346	.496	136	24	7-3	.978	-6	101	106	2b155		2.8
1948	†Cle A★	144	550	96	154	21	4	32	124	77	3	68	.280	.371	.507	136	26	5-2	.971	-8	100	103	2b144,S2		2.5
1949	Cle A★	148	541	74	136	18	3	20	84	83	3	44	.251	.355	.407	103	2	5-6	.980	-17	97	115	2b145		-0.7
1950	Cle A	119	368	59	87	12	1	19	57	56	2	44	.236	.340	.429	99	-2	4-1	.969	-18	91	88	2b105		-1.3
Total	11	1566	5707	914	1530	264	52	253	975	759	29	702	.268	.357	.466	121	155	89-60	.970	51	103	118	2b1519,1b30,S2		28.8

GORDON, KEITH Keith Bradley B1.22.1969 Bethesda MD BR/TR/6-1/205 [CinN90 2/47] d7.9 Col Wright St.

YEAR	TM LG	G	AB	R	H	2B	3B	HR	RBI	BB-IB	HP	SO	AVG	OBP	SLG	AOPS	ABR	SB-CS	FA	FR	RNG	THR	GAMES AT POSITION	DL	BFW
1993	Cin N	3	6	0	1	0	0	0	0	0-0	0	2	.167	.167	.167	-10	-1	0-0	1.000	-0	89	0	O2L		-0.1

GORDON, MIKE Michael William B9.11.1953 Leominster MA BB/TR/6-3/215* d4.7 [ChiN72 3/63]

YEAR	TM LG	G	AB	R	H	2B	3B	HR	RBI	BB-IB	HP	SO	AVG	OBP	SLG	AOPS	ABR	SB-CS	FA	FR	RNG	THR	GAMES AT POSITION	DL	BFW
1977	Chi N	8	23	0	1	0	0	0	2	2-0	0	8	.043	.120	.043	-49	-5	0-0	.970	-3	55	38	C8		-0.8
1978	Chi N	4	5	0	1	0	0	0	0	3-1	1	2	.200	.556	.200	106	1	0-0	1.000	0	81	0	C4		0.1
Total	2	12	28	0	2	0	0	0	2	5-1	1	10	.071	.235	.071	-11	-4	0-0	.979	-3	62	28	C12		-0.7

GORDON, SID Sidney B8.13.1917 Brooklyn NY D6.17.1975 New York NY BR/TR/5-10/185* d9.11 Mil 1944-45 Col Long Island-Brooklyn

YEAR	TM LG	G	AB	R	H	2B	3B	HR	RBI	BB-IB	HP	SO	AVG	OBP	SLG	AOPS	ABR	SB-CS	FA	FR	RNG	THR	GAMES AT POSITION	DL	BFW
1941	NY N	9	31	4	8	1	1	0	4	6	0	1	.258	.378	.355	105	-1		1.000	-1	97	0	O9(3/6/0)		0.0
1942	NY N	6	19	4	6	1	0	2	3	3	0	2	.316	.409	.421	142	1	0-1	.913	1	109	0	3b6		0.2
1943	NY N	131	474	50	119	9	11	9	63	43	1	32	.251	.315	.373	98	-4	2	.941	2	106	117	3b53,1b41,O28L,2b3		-0.6
1946	NY N	135	450	64	132	15	4	5	45	60	3	27	.293	.380	.378	115	11	1	.995	-1	95	91	O101L,3b30		0.4
1947	NY N	130	437	57	119	19	8	13	57	50	0	21	.272	.347	.442	107	4	2	.971	-1	96	142	O124L,3b2		-0.6
1948	NY N☆	142	521	100	156	26	4	30	107	74	3	39	.299	.390	.537	146	35	8	.948	-3	97	99	3b115,O23(18/0/2)		3.0
1949	NY N★	141	489	87	139	26	2	26	90	95	3	37	.284	.404	.505	142	33	1	.958	-18	84	79	3b123,O15(3/0/12)/1		1.4
1950	Bos N	134	481	78	146	33	4	27	103	78	2	31	.304	.403	.557	160	44	2	.990	3	105	87	O123L,3b10		3.6
1951	Bos N	150	550	96	158	28	1	29	109	80	5	32	.287	.383	.500	146	37	2-0	.984	-5	101	38	O122(103/0/23),3b34		2.4
1952	Bos N	144	522	69	151	22	2	25	75	77	3	49	.289	.384	.483	144	33	0-4	.996	-1	98	88	O142L,3b2		2.1
1953	Mil N	140	464	67	127	22	4	19	75	71	2	42	.274	.372	.461	123	18	1-1	.977	2	106	99	O137L		1.2
1954	Pit N	131	363	38	111	12	0	12	49	67	0	24	.306	.405	.438	124	16	0-0	.977	2	100	165	O73(8/0/66),3b40		1.5
1955	Pit N	16	47	2	8	1	0	0	1	2-0	0	6	.170	.204	.191	6	-6	0-0	1.000	2	132	238	3b8,O4L		-0.5
	NY N	66	144	19	35	6	1	7	25	25-2	0	15	.243	.349	.444	110	3	0-0	1.000	6	110	121	3b31,O17(12/0/5)		0.7
	Year	82	191	21	43	7	1	7	26	27-2	0	21	.225	.317	.382	86	-4	0-0	1.000	7	115	149	3b39,O21(16/0/5)		0.2
Total	13	1475	4992	735	1415	220	43	202	805	731-2	22	356	.283	.377	.466	130	225	19-5	.985	-10	100	98	O918(806/6/108),3b454,1b42,2b3		14.8

GORE, GEORGE George F. "Piano Legs" B5.3.1857 Saccarappa ME D9.16.1933 Utica NY BL/TR/5-11/195 d5.1 M1

YEAR	TM LG	G	AB	R	H	2B	3B	HR	RBI	BB-IB	HP	SO	AVG	OBP	SLG	AOPS	ABR	SB-CS	FA	FR	RNG	THR	GAMES AT POSITION	DL	BFW
1879	Chi N	63	266	43	70	17	4	0	32	8			.263	.285	.357	104	1		.872	-3	73	0	O54(0/48/6),1b9		-0.4
1880	Chi N	77	322	70	116	23	2	4	47	21		10	.360	.399	.463	180	27		.879	2	100	142	O74(0/73/1),1b7		2.5
1881	Chi N	73	309	86	92	18	9	1	44	27		23	.298	.354	.424	137	13		.874	1	110	114	O72C/31		1.0
1882	Chi N	84	367	99	117	15	7	3	51	29		19	.319	.369	.422	146	19		.842	3	122	143	O84C		1.7
1883	Chi N	92	392	105	131	30	9	2	52	27		13	.334	.377	.472	144	20		.867	9	130	117	O92C		2.2
1884	Chi N	103	422	104	134	18	4	5	34	61		26	.318	.404	.415	146	24		.868	-1	116	141	O103(0/103/1)		1.8
1885	†Chi N	109	441	115	138	21	13	5	57	68		25	.313	.405	.454	156	28		.884	-5	83	80	O109(1/108/0)		1.8
1886	†Chi N	118	444	150	135	20	12	6	63	102		30	.304	.434	.444	146	28	23	.876	-6	85	124	O118(0/115/3)		1.6
1887	NY N	111	459	95	133	16	5	1	49	42	7	18	.290	.358	.353	103	5	39	.889	0	103	210	O111C		0.1
1888	†NY N	64	254	37	56	4	2	0	17	30	2	31	.220	.308	.291	93	-1	11	.836	-10	37	0	O64(42/21/1)		-1.2
1889	†NY N	120	488	132	149	21	7	5	54	84	8	23	.305	.416	.420	134	26	28	.864	-8	92	122	O120(0/118/2)		1.2
1890	NY P	93	399	132	127	24	8	10	55	77	5	23	.318	.432	.499	136	22	28	.877	-13	62	87	O93(52/33/10)		0.5
1891	NY N	130	528	103	150	22	7	2	48	74	7	34	.284	.379	.364	122	19	19	.909	-11	78	86	O130(1/127/3)		0.3
1892	NY N	53	193	47	49	11	2	0	19	46	3	16	.254	.412	.332	117	11	20	.932	0	93	107	O53(0/50/3)		0.7
	StL N	20	73	9	15	0	1	0	4	18	0	6	.205	.363	.233	85	0	2	.844	-2	99	0	O20C,M		-0.3
	Year	73	266	56	64	11	3	0	15	67	3	22	.241	.399	.305	116	11	22	.908	-1	95	79	O73(0/70/3)		0.4
Total	14	1310	5357	1327	1612	262	94	46	618	717	30	332	.301	.386	.411	134	242	170	.876	-42	93	109	O1297(96/1175/31),1b17/3		13.5

YEAR	TM LG	G	AB	R	H	2B	3B	HR	RBI	BB-IB	HP	SO	AVG	OBP	SLG	AOPS	ABR	SB-CS	FA	FR	RNG	THR	GAMES AT POSITION	DL	BFW
GORINSKI, BOB	Robert John B1.7.1952 Latrobe PA BR/TR/6-3/215 [MinA70 1/22] d4.10																								
1977	Min A	54	118	14	23	4	1	3	22	5-0	0	29	.195	.226	.322	48	-9	1-0	.936	-3	87	0	O37(30/0/7),D9		-1.3
GORMAN, HERB	Herbert Allen B12.18.1924 San Francisco CA D4.5.1953 San Diego CA BL/TL/5-11/180 d4.19																								
1952	StL N	1	1	0	0	0	0	0	0	0-0	0	0	.000	.000	.000	-99	0	0-0	—		0		/H		0.0
GORMAN, HOWIE	Howard Paul "Lefty" B5.14.1913 Pittsburgh PA D4.29.1984 Harrisburg PA BL/TL/6-2/160 d8.7																								
1937	Phi N	13	19	3	4	1	0	0	1	1-0	0	1	.211	.250	.263	37	-2	1-1	.500	-1	26	0	O7R		-0.3
1938	Phi N	1	1	0	0	0	0	0	0	0-0	0	0	.000	.000	.000	-99	0	0	—		0		/H		0.0
Total	2	14	20	3	4	1	0	0	1	1-0	0	1	.200	.238	.250	30	-2	1	.500	-1	26	0	O7R		-0.3
GORMAN, JACK	John F. "Stooping Jack" B1859 St.Louis MO D9.9.1889 St.Louis MO d7.1 ▲																								
1883	StL AA	1	4	0	0	0	0	0	0				.000	.000	.000	-95	-1		.667	0	349	0	/OL		-0.1
1884	KC U	8	31	3	4	1	0	0	0				.129	.129	.161	-14	-5		.579	-1	64	0	3b4,O4L		-0.6
	Pit AA	8	27	3	4	0	1	0	1		0		.148	.179	.222	30	-2		.750	-1	120	1	P3,O3(0/1/2),3b2		-0.2
Total	2	17	62	6	8	1	1	0	1		0		.129	.143	.177	0	-8		.933	-2	128	302	O8(5/1/2),3b6,P3		-0.9
GORMAN, TOM	Thomas B St.Louis MO BL/TL d6.10																								
1884	KC U	25	106	22	34	4	2	0				4	.321	.345	.396	143	3		.954	-1	56	70	1b24/OL		-0.1
GORYL, JOHNNY	John Albert B10.21.1933 Cumberland RI BR/TR/5-10/175* d9.20 M2/C13																								
1957	Chi N	9	38	7	8	2	0	0	1	5-0	1	9	.211	.318	.263	59	-2	0-1	.952	-0	90	243	3b9		-0.3
1958	Chi N	83	219	27	53	9	3	4	14	27-2	2	34	.242	.331	.365	85	-4	0-1	.931	7	105	154	3b44,2b35		0.4
1959	Chi N	25	48	1	9	3	1	1	6	5-0	0	3	.188	.264	.354	63	-3	1-1	.973	1	127	23	2b11,3b4		-0.2
1962	Min A	37	26	6	5	0	1	2	2	2-0	0	6	.192	.250	.500	93	-1	0-0	.923	1	177	75	2b4/S		0.0
1963	Min A	64	150	29	43	5	3	9	24	15-4	1	29	.287	.353	.540	144	8	0-0	.958	-8	87	87	2b34,3b11,S7		0.4
1964	Min A	58	114	9	16	0	2	0	1	10-2	1	25	.140	.216	.175	10	-14	1-0	.975	4	109	64	2b28,3b13		-0.9
Total	6	276	595	79	134	19	10	16	48	64-8	5	106	.225	.305	.371	83	-16	2-3	.960	4	109	76	2b112,3b81,S8		-0.6
GOSGER, JIM	James Charles B11.6.1942 Port Huron MI BL/TL/5-11/185* d5.4 Col St. Clair Co. (MI) CC																								
1963	Bos A	19	16	3	1	0	0	0	0	3-0	0	5	.063	.211	.063	-19	-3	0-0	.818	0	168	0	O4(0/2/2)		-0.3
1965	Bos A	81	324	45	83	15	4	9	35	29-1	2	61	.256	.318	.410	100	0	3-1	.975	5	116	104	O81(0/61/22)		0.2
1966	Bos A	40	126	16	32	4	0	5	17	15-0	0	20	.254	.333	.405	101	0	0-0	.985	-3	95	0	O32(0/29/4)		-0.4
	KC A	88	272	34	61	14	1	5	27	37-1	2	53	.224	.321	.338	93	-1	5-3	.994	1	107	67	O77(47/33/1)		-0.4
	Year	128	398	50	93	18	1	10	44	52-1	2	73	.234	.325	.359	96	-1	5-4	.991	-2	103	47	O109(47/62/5)		-0.8
1967	KC A	134	356	31	86	14	5	5	36	53-8	0	69	.242	.337	.351	108	5	5-7	.981	4	112	97	O113(54/30/40)		0.3
1968	Oak A	88	150	7	27	1	1	0	5	17-8	0	21	.180	.262	.200	44	-10	4-0	1.000	5	111	176	O64(39/26/4)		-0.8
1969	Sea A	39	55	4	6	2	1	1	1	6-0	0	11	.109	.197	.236	21	-6	2-1	1.000	1	113	102	O26(1/24/1)		-0.6
	NY N	10	15	0	2	2	0	0	1	1-1	0	6	.133	.188	.267	25	-1	0-0	1.000	-0	78	0	O5(4/1/0)		-0.2
1970	Mon N	91	274	38	72	11	2	5	37	35-3	1	35	.263	.348	.372	93	-2	5-3	1.000	1	104	149	O71(21/50/4),1b19		-0.4
1971	Mon N	51	102	7	16	2	2	0	6	9-0	1	17	.157	.230	.216	27	-10	1-1	.952	1	96	79	O23(20/6/1),1b6		-1.1
1973	NY N	38	92	9	22	2	0	0	10	9-2	0	16	.239	.304	.261	59	-5	0-1	1.000	-3	85	0	O35(21/18/0)		-0.9
1974	NY N	26	33	3	3	0	0	0	1	3-1	0	2	.091	.167	.091	-27	-6	0-0	1.000	-2	68	0	O24(9/11/4)		-0.7
Total	10	705	1815	197	411	67	16	30	177	217-25	6	316	.226	.309	.331	83	-39	25-18	.985	10	107	92	O555(216/291/83),1b25	30	-5.4
GOSLIN, GOOSE	Leon Allen B10.16.1900 Salem NJ D5.15.1971 Bridgeton NJ BL/TR/5-11.5/185 d9.16 HF1968																								
1921	Was A	14	50	8	13	1	1	1	6	6	1	5	.260	.351	.380	91	-1	0-0	1.000	1	123	55	O14(1/0/14)		-0.1
1922	Was A	101	358	44	116	19	7	3	53	25	3	26	.324	.373	.441	117	8	4-4	.932	-3	103	70	O92(88/0/5)		-0.2
1923	Was A	150	600	86	180	29	18	9	99	40	3	53	.300	.347	.453	115	9	7-2	.957	4	97	141	O149L		0.1
1924	†Was A	154	579	100	199	30	17	12	129	68	9	29	.344	.421	.516	145	39	15-14	.960	4	111	74	O154L		2.8
1925	†Was A	150	601	116	201	34	20	18	113	53	6	50	.334	.394	.547	140	33	27-8	.971	14	112	139	O150(140/20/0)		3.5
1926	Was A	147	568	105	201	26	15	17	108	63	7	38	.354	.425	.542	155	45	8-8	.964	14	107	168	O147(86/61/0)		4.6
1927	Was A	148	581	96	194	37	15	13	120	50	5	23	.334	.392	.516	136	29	21-6	.955	-2	106	51	O148(146/2/0)		1.6
1928	Was A	135	456	80	173	36	10	17	102	46	3	19	**.379**	.442	.614	176	51	16-3	.962	8	109	123	O125(125/0/2)		4.9
1929	Was A	145	553	82	159	28	7	18	91	66	2	33	.288	.366	.461	111	9	11-3	.968	-6	98	50	O142L		-0.7
1930	Was A	47	188	34	51	11	5	7	38	19	2	14	.271	.344	.495	110	2	3-2	.937	-4	83	61	O47L		-0.5
	StL A	101	396	81	129	25	7	30	100	48	1	35	.326	.400	.652	156	32	14-9	.973	9	111	163	O101L		2.9
	Year	148	584	115	180	36	12	37	138	67	3	54	.308	.382	.601	142	35	17-11	.964	5	103	133	O148L		2.4
1931	StL A	151	591	114	194	42	10	24	105	80	4	41	.328	.412	.555	147	41	9-6	.960	2	101	127	O151L		3.2
1932	StL A	150	572	88	171	28	9	17	104	92	2	35	.299	.398	.469	117	16	12-9	.951	5	102	139	O149(148/1/0)/3		1.1
1933	†Was A	132	549	97	163	35	10	10	64	42	1	32	.297	.348	.452	112	7	5-2	.965	5	100	140	O128(3/0/125)		0.4
1934	†Det A	151	614	106	187	38	7	13	100	65	2	38	.305	.373	.453	112	11	5-4	.953	0	98	124	O149(145/0/4)		0.2
1935	†Det A	147	590	88	172	34	6	9	109	56	2	31	.292	.355	.415	102	1	5-4	.965	-0	108	51	O144(128/0/18)		-0.6
1936	Det A★	147	572	122	180	33	8	24	125	85	0	50	.315	.403	.526	127	25	14-4	.955	-4	95	93	O144L		1.3
1937	Det A	79	181	30	43	11	1	4	35	35	2	18	.238	.367	.376	86	-3	0-1	.954	-2	97	45	O40(39/0/1)/1		-0.7
1938	Was A	38	57	16	9	2	0	2	8	8	0	5	.158	.262	.316	47	-5	0-0	1.000	0	114	0	O13(12/0/1)		-0.5
Total	18	2287	8656	1483	2735	500	173	248	1609	949	55	585	.316	.387	.500	128	349	176-89	.960	44	103	108	O2187(1949/84/170)/13		23.3
GOSS, HOWIE	Howard Wayne B11.1.1934 Wewoka OK D7.31.1996 Reno NV BR/TR/6-4/204* d4.10 Col Bakersfield (CA) JC																								
1962	Pit N	89	111	19	27	6	0	2	10	9-2	1	36	.243	.306	.351	76	-4	5-2	.985	0	99	87	O66(47/18/6)		-0.5
1963	Hou N	133	411	37	86	18	2	9	44	31-2	0	128	.209	.264	.328	74	-14	4-6	.993	4	109	97	O123C		-1.6
Total	2	222	522	56	113	24	2	11	54	40-2	1	164	.216	.273	.333	75	-18	9-8	.991	5	107	95	O189(47/141/6)		-2.1
GOSSETT, DICK	John Star B8.21.1891 Dennison OH D10.6.1962 Massillon OH BR/TR/5-11/185 d4.30																								
1913	NY A	39	105	9	17	2	0	0	9	10	3	22	.162	.254	.181	28	-9	1	.972	-6	66	116	C38		-1.4
1914	NY A	10	21	3	3	0	0	0	1	5	1	5	.143	.333	.143	44	-1	0	.977	-1	87	54	C10		-0.1
Total	2	49	126	12	20	2	0	0	10	15	4	27	.159	.269	.175	31	-10	1	.973	-7	70	104	C48		-1.5
GOTAY, JULIO	Julio Enrique (Sanchez) B6.9.1939 Fajardo, PR BR/TR/6-0/180* d8.6																								
1960	StL N	3	8	1	3	0	0	0	0	0-0	0	2	.375	.375	.375	98	0	1-0	.750	-1	60	0	S2/3		-0.1
1961	StL N	10	45	5	11	4	0	0	5	3-1	0	5	.244	.292	.333	59	-2	0-0	.804	-4	83	90	S10		-0.6
1962	StL N	127	369	47	94	12	1	2	27	27-6	6	47	.255	.316	.309	62	-19	7-3	.956	11	109	108	S120,2b8,O2L/3		0.2
1963	Pit N	4	2	0	1	0	0	0	0	0-0	0	0	.500	.500	.500	188	0	0-0	.667	-0	0	0	/2		0.0
1964	Pit N	3	2	1	1	0	0	0	0	1-0	0	0	.500	.667	.500	235	1	0-0	—		0		/H		0.1
1965	Cal A	40	77	6	19	4	0	1	3	4-2	1	5	.247	.284	.338	78	-2	0-0	.961	-2	122	85	2b23,3b9/S		-0.1
1966	Hou N	4	5	0	0	0	0	0	0	0-0	0	1	.000	.000	.000	-99	0	0-0	1.000	0	221	0	/3		-0.1
1967	Hou N	77	234	30	66	10	2	2	15	15-1	2	30	.282	.329	.368	103	1	1-1	.971	-2	90	90	2b30,S20,3b3		0.3
1968	Hou N	75	165	9	41	3	0	1	11	4-0	1	21	.248	.271	.285	68	-7	1-2	.982	6	95	113	2b48/3		0.4
1969	Hou N	46	81	7	21	5	0	0	9	7-1	0	13	.259	.318	.321	81	-2	2-1	.987	5	108	138	2b16/3		0.4
Total	10	389	988	106	257	38	3	6	70	61-11	10	127	.260	.309	.323	75	-31	12-7	.944	10	106	101	S153,2b126,3b17,O2L		0.6
GOTAY, RUBEN	Ruben A. B12.25.1982 Rio Piedras, PR BB/TR/5-11/160(160-175) [KCA00 31/914] d8.3 Col Indian Hills (IA) CC																								
2004	KC A	44	152	17	41	7	1	3	16	9-0	2	36	.270	.315	.375	80	-5	0-0	.983	-9	86	100	2b42		-1.2
2005	KC A	86	282	32	64	14	2	5	29	22-0	4	51	.227	.288	.344	73	-11	2-2	.980	4	103	84	2b81,D2		-0.4
Total	2	130	434	49	105	21	5	6	45	31-0	6	87	.242	.297	.355	76	-16	2-3	.981	-5	97	90	2b123,D2		-1.6
GOULD, CHARLIE	Charles Harvey B8.21.1847 Cincinnati OH D4.9.1917 Flushing NY BR/TR/6-0/172 d5.5 M2																								
1871	Bos NA	**31**	151	38	43	9	2	0	32	3			1	.285	.299	.411	98	-1	6-2	.906	-4	62	160	1b30/OR		-0.2
1872	Bos NA	45	212	40	54	9	**8**	0	32	2			3	.255	.262	.373	88	-5	0-0	.933	-0	116	251	1b44,O2R		-0.3
1874	Bal NA	33	143	19	32	6	0	0	14	2			6	.224	.224	.266	60	-6	1-0	.951	0	68	86	1b32/C		0.0
1875	NH NA	27	109	9	29	4	1	0	8	1			2	.266	.273	.321	121	3	0-1	.946	-4	58	69	1b26/CORM		0.0
1876	Cin N	61	258	27	66	13	0	0	11	6			11	.252	.269	.279	97	2		.939	1	122	114	1b61,P2,M		-0.1
1877	Cin N	24	91	5	25	2	1	0	13	5			2	.275	.313	.319	112	2		.922	-1	78	100	1b24/OL		0.0
Total	4 NA	136	615	106	158	28	11	2	86	8			8	.257	.266	.348	90	-9	7-3	.934	-7	81	154	1b132,O4R,C2		-0.9
Total	2	85	349	32	90	15	1	0	24	11			16	.258	.281	.289	101	4		.934	0	123	110	1b85,P2/OL		0.0

GOULISH, NICK
Nicholas Edward B11.13.1917 Punxsutawney PA D5.15.1984 Youngstown OH BL/TL/6-1/179 d4.19

YEAR	TM LG	G	AB	R	H	2B	3B	HR	RBI	BB-IB	HP	SO	AVG	OBP	SLG	AOPS	ABR	SB-CS	FA	FR	RNG	THR	GAMES AT POSITION	DL	BFW
1944	Phi N	1	1	0	0	0	0	0	0	0	0	0	.000	.000	.000	-99	0	0	—	0			7/H		0.0
1945	Phi N	13	11	4	3	0	0	0	2	1	0	3	.273	.333	.273	72	0	0	1.000	-0	69	0	O2(1/0/1)		-0.1
Total	2	14	12	4	3	0	0	0	2	1	0	3	.250	.308	.250	58	0	0	1.000	-0	69	0	O2(1/0/1)		-0.1

GOUZZIE, CLAUDE
Claude B1873 , France D9.21.1907 Denver CO BR/TR/5-9/170 d7.22

YEAR	TM LG	G	AB	R	H	2B	3B	HR	RBI	BB-IB	HP	SO	AVG	OBP	SLG	AOPS	ABR	SB-CS	FA	FR	RNG	THR	GAMES AT POSITION	DL	BFW
1903	StL A	1	1	0	0	0	0	0	0	0	0	0	.000	.000	.000	-99	0	0	1.000	0	149	0	/2		0.0

GOWDY, HANK
Henry Morgan B8.24.1889 Columbus OH D8.1.1966 Columbus OH BR/TR/6-2/182 d9.13 Mil 1917-19 M1/C18

YEAR	TM LG	G	AB	R	H	2B	3B	HR	RBI	BB-IB	HP	SO	AVG	OBP	SLG	AOPS	ABR	SB-CS	FA	FR	RNG	THR	GAMES AT POSITION	DL	BFW
1910	NY N	7	14	1	3	0	0	0	2	2	0	3	.214	.313	.286	75	0	1	.943	0	152	52	1b5		0.0
1911	NY N	4	4	1	1	0	0	0	2	0	0	0	.250	.500	.500	175	1	0	1.000	-0	-0	0	1b2		0.0
	Bos N	29	97	9	28	4	2	0	16	4	1	19	.289	.324	.371	87	-2	2	.966	-2	88	56	1b26/C		-0.4
	Year	33	101	10	29	5	2	0	16	6	1	19	.287	.333	.376	92	-1	2	.969	-2	83	53	1b28/C		-0.4
1912	Bos N	44	96	16	26	6	1	3	10	16	2	13	.271	.386	.448	126	4	3	.926	-3	91	108	C22,1b7		0.3
1913	Bos N	3	5	0	3	1	0	0	2	3	0	2	.600	.750	.800	336	2	0	1.000	-1	108	93	C2		0.2
1914	†Bos N	128	366	42	89	17	6	3	46	48	4	40	.243	.337	.347	104	3	14	.968	3	133	93	C115,1b9		1.6
1915	Bos N	118	316	27	78	15	3	2	30	41	3	34	.247	.339	.332	108	5	10-4	.974	6	138	104	C114		2.3
1916	Bos N	118	349	32	88	14	1	1	34	24	6	33	.252	.311	.307	94	-2	8	.980	15	171	93	C116		2.6
1917	Bos N	49	154	12	33	7	0	0	14	15	1	13	.214	.288	.260	73	-4	2	.969	1	110	120	C49		0.1
1919	Bos N	78	219	18	61	8	1	1	22	19	1	16	.279	.339	.338	108	3	5	.977	3	101	113	C74/1		1.3
1920	Bos N	80	214	14	52	11	2	0	18	20	2	15	.243	.314	.313	84	-4	6-1	.980	10	114	130	C74		1.3
1921	Bos N	64	164	17	49	7	2	2	17	16	2	11	.299	.368	.402	110	3	2	.981	-0	110	107	C53		0.6
1922	Bos N	92	221	23	70	11	1	1	27	24	3	15	.317	.391	.389	107	4	2-1	.971	-0	99	131	C72/1		0.7
1923	Bos N	23	48	5	6	1	1	0	5	15	2	5	.125	.354	.188	48	-3	1-1	.982	-1	80	98	C15		-0.3
	†NY N	53	122	13	40	6	3	1	18	21	0	9	.328	.427	.451	133	7	2-0	.986	-3	149	59	C43		0.4
	Year	76	170	18	46	7	4	1	23	36	2	14	.271	.404	.376	109	5	3-1	.985	-4	128	71	C58		0.4
1924	†NY N	87	191	25	62	9	1	4	37	26	2	11	.325	.411	.445	133	10	1-0	.982	1	110	89	C78		1.6
1925	NY N	47	114	14	37	4	3	3	19	12	0	7	.325	.389	.491	128	5	0-0	1.000	1	92	112	C41		0.7
1929	Bos N	10	16	1	7	0	0	0	3	0	0	2	.438	.438	.438	122	1	0	1.000	0	101	68	C9		0.1
1930	Bos N	16	25	0	5	1	0	0	2	3	1	1	.200	.310	.240	37	-2	0	.972	0	100	85	C15		-0.2
Total	17	1050	2735	270	738	124	27	21	322	311	30	247	.270	.351	.358	105	31	59-7	.975	31	124	104	C893,1b51		13.2

GRABARKEWITZ, BILLY
Billy Cordell B1.18.1946 Lockhart TX BR/TR/5-10/170* [LAN66 12/239] d4.22 Col St. Marys (TX)

YEAR	TM LG	G	AB	R	H	2B	3B	HR	RBI	BB-IB	HP	SO	AVG	OBP	SLG	AOPS	ABR	SB-CS	FA	FR	RNG	THR	GAMES AT POSITION	DL	BFW
1969	LA N	34	65	4	6	1	1	0	5	4-1	0	19	.092	.145	.138	-22	-11	1-0	.954	-6	87	46	S18,3b6,2b3		-1.6
1970	LA N★	156	529	92	153	20	8	17	84	95-8	6	149	.289	.399	.454	134	30	19-9	.959	-10	103	116	3b97,S50,2b20		2.6
1971	LA N	44	71	9	16	5	0	0	6	19-0	0	16	.225	.389	.296	101	2	1-2	1.000	4	110	127	2b13,3b10/S	72	0.7
1972	LA N	53	144	17	24	4	0	4	16	18-1	2	53	.167	.265	.278	56	-8	3-0	.902	-3	88	32	3b24,2b19,S2	15	-1.0
1973	Cal A	61	129	27	21	6	1	3	9	28-0	1	27	.163	.316	.295	78	-3	2-2	.965	-3	94	95	2b18,3b12/SOLD		-0.5
	Phi N	25	66	12	19	2	0	2	7	12-0	1	18	.288	.397	.409	120	2	3-1	.960	3	105	134	2b20,3b3/OR		0.6
1974	Phi N	34	30	7	4	0	0	1	2	5-0	0	10	.133	.257	.233	36	-3	3-1	1.000	-0	93	34	O5L/3		-0.3
	Chi N	53	125	21	31	3	2	1	12	21-2	1	28	.248	.358	.328	90	-1	1-2	.954	-2	100	34	2b45,S7,3b6		-0.1
	Year	87	155	28	35	3	2	2	14	26-2	1	38	.226	.339	.310	79	-4	4-3	.954	-3	100	34	2b45,3b7,S7,O5L		-0.4
1975	Oak A	6	2	0	0	0	0	0	0	0-0	0	1	.000	.000	.000	-99	-1	0-0	.833	0	107	0	3b4/D		0.0
Total	7	466	1161	189	274	41	12	28	141	202-12	10	321	.236	.351	.364	100	7	33-17	.952	-17	101	105	3b159,2b142,S79,O7(6/0/1),D6	87	0.4

GRABER, ROD
Rodney Blaine B6.20.1930 Massillon OH BL/TL/5-11/175 d9.9

YEAR	TM LG	G	AB	R	H	2B	3B	HR	RBI	BB-IB	HP	SO	AVG	OBP	SLG	AOPS	ABR	SB-CS	FA	FR	RNG	THR	GAMES AT POSITION	DL	BFW
1958	Cle A	4	8	0	1	0	0	0	0	1-0	0	2	.125	.222	.125	-2	-1	0-0	1.000	0	119	0	O2C		-0.1

GRABOWSKI, JASON
Jason William B5.24.1976 New Haven CT BL/TR/6-3/200* [TexA97 2/75] d9.22 Col Connecticut

YEAR	TM LG	G	AB	R	H	2B	3B	HR	RBI	BB-IB	HP	SO	AVG	OBP	SLG	AOPS	ABR	SB-CS	FA	FR	RNG	THR	GAMES AT POSITION	DL	BFW
2002	Oak A	4	8	3	3	1	1	0	1	3-0	0	1	.375	.545	.750	241	2	0-0	1.000	0	96	0	O4L		0.2
2003	Oak A	8	8	0	0	0	0	0	0	1-0	0	5	.000	.111	.000	-67	-2	0-0	1.000	0	185	0	O3R/3D		-0.2
2004	†LA N	113	173	18	38	7	0	7	20	19-0	0	50	.220	.297	.382	75	-7	0-0	.977	-2	90	0	O31(30/0/3),1b3,D3		-1.0
2005	LA N	65	112	14	18	0	0	4	12	10-1	0	29	.161	.228	.268	30	-12	1-0	.974	-2	85	78	O32(28/0/4),1b3	20	-1.5
Total	4	190	301	35	59	8	1	11	33	33-1	0	85	.196	.275	.339	59	-19	1-0	.978	-4	90	33	O70(62/0/10),1b6,D4/3	20	-2.5

GRABOWSKI, JOHNNY
John Patrick "Nig" B1.7.1900 Ware MA D5.23.1946 Albany NY BR/TR/5-10/185 d7.11

YEAR	TM LG	G	AB	R	H	2B	3B	HR	RBI	BB-IB	HP	SO	AVG	OBP	SLG	AOPS	ABR	SB-CS	FA	FR	RNG	THR	GAMES AT POSITION	DL	BFW
1924	Chi A	20	56	10	14	3	0	0	3	2	0	4	.250	.276	.304	51	-4	0-0	.972	1	77	158	C19		-0.3
1925	Chi A	21	46	5	14	4	1	0	10	2	0	4	.304	.333	.435	99	0	0-1	.983	0	172	85	C21		0.1
1926	Chi A	48	122	6	32	1	1	1	11	8	0	15	.262	.286	.311	58	-8	0-1	.973	-1	129	91	C38/1		-0.8
1927	†NY A	70	195	29	54	2	4	0	25	20	2	15	.277	.350	.328	79	-6	0-0	.984	2	104	67	C68		-0.1
1928	NY A	75	202	21	48	7	1	1	21	10	0	21	.238	.274	.297	51	-15	0-0	.987	0	94	81	C75		-1.0
1929	NY A	22	59	4	12	1	0	0	3	0	0	6	.203	.242	.220	21	-7	1-0	.943	-1	112	71	C22		-0.6
1931	Det A	40	136	9	32	7	1	1	14	6	0	19	.235	.268	.324	53	-10	0-0	.984	0	76	123	C39		-0.7
Total	7	296	816	84	206	25	8	3	86	47	2	84	.252	.295	.314	60	-50	1-2	.979	1	103	91	C282/1		-3.4

GRACE, JOE
Joseph Laverne B1.5.1914 Gorham IL D9.18.1969 Murphysboro IL BL/TR/6-1/180 d9.24 Mil 1942-45

YEAR	TM LG	G	AB	R	H	2B	3B	HR	RBI	BB-IB	HP	SO	AVG	OBP	SLG	AOPS	ABR	SB-CS	FA	FR	RNG	THR	GAMES AT POSITION	DL	BFW
1938	StL A	12	47	7	16	1	0	0	4	2	0	3	.340	.367	.362	83	-1	0-1	.933	-1	75	126	O12R		-0.3
1939	StL A	74	207	35	63	11	2	3	22	19	0	24	.304	.363	.420	98	-1	3-2	.968	1	82	265	O53(10/22/21)		-0.2
1940	StL A	80	229	45	59	14	2	5	25	26	1	23	.258	.336	.402	88	-4	2-2	.958	-2	89	153	O51(3/0/48),C12		-0.8
1941	StL A	115	362	53	112	17	4	6	60	57	5	31	.309	.410	.428	118	12	1-3	.983	0	95	157	O88R,C9		0.6
1946	StL A	48	161	21	37	7	2	1	13	16	2	20	.230	.307	.317	71	-6	1-3	.967	-3	99	159	O43R		-0.7
	Was A	77	321	39	97	17	4	2	31	24	4	19	.302	.358	.399	118	7	1-4	.959	-1	101	65	O74(60/0/14)		-0.1
	Year	125	482	60	134	24	6	3	44	40	6	39	.278	.341	.371	101	0	2-7	.962	0	100	96	O117(60/0/57)		-0.8
1947	Was A	78	234	25	58	9	4	3	17	35	1	15	.248	.348	.359	99	0	1-2	.976	2	109	87	O67(56/3/8)		-0.2
Total	6	484	1561	225	442	76	18	20	172	179	13	135	.283	.362	.393	102	7	9-17	.969	-1	97	135	O388(129/25/234),C21		-1.7

GRACE, MARK
Mark Eugene B6.28.1964 Winston-Salem NC BL/TL/6-2/190* [ChiN85 24/624] d5.2 Col San Diego St.

YEAR	TM LG	G	AB	R	H	2B	3B	HR	RBI	BB-IB	HP	SO	AVG	OBP	SLG	AOPS	ABR	SB-CS	FA	FR	RNG	THR	GAMES AT POSITION	DL	BFW
1988	Chi N	134	486	65	144	23	4	7	57	60-5	0	43	.296	.371	.403	110	13	3-3	.987	-4	92	93	1b133		-0.1
1989	†Chi N	142	510	74	160	28	3	13	79	80-13	1	42	.314	.405	.457	137	28	14-7	.996	12	128	95	1b142	18	3.2
1990	Chi N	157	589	72	182	32	1	9	82	59-5	5	54	.309	.372	.413	109	10	15-6	.992	25	156	103	1b153		2.6
1991	Chi N	160	619	87	169	28	5	8	58	70-7	1	53	.273	.346	.373	99	1	3-4	.995	17	134	95	1b160		0.5
1992	Chi N	158	603	72	185	37	5	9	79	72-8	1	36	.307	.380	.430	126	24	6-1	.998	6	112	102	1b157		2.1
1993	Chi N★	155	594	86	193	39	4	14	98	71-14	1	32	.325	.393	.475	133	31	8-4	.997	1	101	112	1b154		1.8
1994	Chi N	106	403	55	120	23	3	6	44	48-5	0	41	.298	.370	.414	105	4	0-1	.993	-1	98	108	1b103		-0.6
1995	Chi N★	143	552	97	180	51	3	16	92	65-9	2	46	.326	.395	.516	139	34	6-2	.995	1	102	81	1b143		2.2
1996	Chi N	142	547	88	181	39	1	9	75	62-8	1	41	.331	.396	.455	121	19	2-3	.997	0	100	110	1b141	17	0.3
1997	Chi N★	151	555	87	177	32	5	13	78	88-3	2	45	.319	.409	.465	125	25	2-4	.995	5	108	79	1b148	15	1.5
1998	†Chi N	158	595	92	184	39	3	17	89	93-8	3	56	.309	.401	.471	125	26	4-7	.994	0	99	63	1b156		1.0
1999	Chi N	161	593	107	183	44	5	16	91	83-4	2	44	.309	.390	.481	121	22	3-4	.994	-4	91	90	1b160		0.5
2000	Chi N	143	510	75	143	41	1	11	82	95-11	1	26	.280	.394	.429	111	14	1-2	.997	5	109	87	1b140	19	-0.4
2001	†Ari N	145	476	66	142	31	2	15	78	67-6	4	36	.298	.386	.466	112	11	1-0	.995	-4	81	112	1b135		-1.6
2002	†Ari N	124	298	43	75	19	0	7	48	46-6	1	30	.252	.351	.386	89	-4	2-0	.990	-5	71	101	1b98/P		-1.6
2003	Ari N	66	135	13	27	5	0	3	16	16-2	0	15	.200	.279	.304	49	-10	0-0	.993	-0	92	97	1b39/D	26	-0.8
Total	16	2245	8065	1179	2445	511	45	173	1146	1075-114	34	642	.303	.383	.442	118	248	70-48	.995	54	107	95	1b2162/DP	95	12.3

GRACE, MIKE
Michael Lee B6.14.1956 Pontiac MI BR/TR/6-0/175 [CinN74 2/47] d4.18

YEAR	TM LG	G	AB	R	H	2B	3B	HR	RBI	BB-IB	HP	SO	AVG	OBP	SLG	AOPS	ABR	SB-CS	FA	FR	RNG	THR	GAMES AT POSITION	DL	BFW
1978	Cin N	5	3	1	0	0	0	0	0	0-0	0	2	.000	.000	.000	-99	-1	0-0	1.000	0	219	0	3b2		0.0

GRACE, EARL
Robert Earl B2.24.1907 Barlow KY D12.22.1980 Phoenix AZ BL/TR/6-0/175 d4.23

YEAR	TM LG	G	AB	R	H	2B	3B	HR	RBI	BB-IB	HP	SO	AVG	OBP	SLG	AOPS	ABR	SB-CS	FA	FR	RNG	THR	GAMES AT POSITION	DL	BFW
1929	Chi N	27	80	7	20	1	0	2	7	9	1	7	.250	.333	.338	67	-4	0	1.000	3	133	113	C27		0.0
1931	Chi N	7	9	2	1	0	0	1	4	1	0	1	.111	.385	.111	39	-1	0	1.000	0	78	0	C2		0.0
	Pit N	47	150	8	42	6	1	1	20	13	0	5	.280	.337	.353	87	-3	0	.974	-1	99	82	C45		-0.1
	Year	54	159	10	43	6	1	2	21	17	0	6	.270	.341	.340	84	-3	0	.976	1	98	78	C47		-0.1
1932	Pit N	115	390	41	107	17	5	8	55	54	1	23	.274	.305	.405	91	-7	0	.998	-3	83	68	C114		-0.3
1933	Pit N	93	291	22	84	13	1	3	44	26	1	23	.289	.349	.371	106	3	0	.980	-1	78	72	C88		0.8
1934	Pit N	95	289	27	78	17	1	4	24	20	0	9	.270	.334	.377	83	-7	0	.982	-7	67	60	C83/1		-0.9

YEAR	TM LG	G	AB	R	H	2B	3B	HR	RBI	BB-IB	HP	SO	AVG	OBP	SLG	AOPS	ABR	SB-CS	FA	FR	RNG	THR	GAMES AT POSITION	DL	BFW
1935	Pit N	77	224	19	59	8	1	3	29	32	0	17	.263	.355	.348	87	-3	1	.990	4	83	103	C69		0.5
1936	Phi N	86	221	20	55	11	0	4	32	34	1	20	.249	.352	.353	82	-4	0	.976	-3	94	71	C65		-0.4
1937	Phi N	80	223	19	47	10	1	6	29	33	0	15	.211	.313	.345	73	-8	0	.990	-2	136	69	C64		-0.6
Total	8	627	1877	169	493	83	10	31	251	185	6	130	.263	.331	.367	86	-33	1	.987	-10	91	75	C557/1		-1.0

GRADY, JOHN   John J.   B6.18.1860 Lowell MA   D7.15.1893 Lowell MA   5-7/150 d5.10

YEAR	TM LG	G	AB	R	H	2B	3B	HR	RBI	BB-IB	HP	SO	AVG	OBP	SLG	AOPS	ABR	SB-CS	FA	FR	RNG	THR	GAMES AT POSITION	DL	BFW
1884	Alt U	9	36	5	11	3	0	0		2			.306	.342	.389	120	0		.909	-1	121	27	1b8/OC		-0.2

GRADY, MIKE   Michael William   B12.23.1869 Kennett Square PA   D12.3.1943 Kennett Square PA   BR/TR/5-11/190 d4.24   OF(14/7/29)

YEAR	TM LG	G	AB	R	H	2B	3B	HR	RBI	BB-IB	HP	SO	AVG	OBP	SLG	AOPS	ABR	SB-CS	FA	FR	RNG	THR	GAMES AT POSITION	DL	BFW
1894	Phi N	61	190	45	69	13	6	0	40	14	7	13	.363	.427	.516	129	9	3	.878	-11	91	82	C45,1b11,O2(1/0/1)		0.1
1895	Phi N	46	123	21	40	3	1	1	23	14	3	8	.325	.407	.390	106	2	5	.926	-9	93	37	C38,O5(3/0/2)/31		-0.4
1896	Phi N	72	242	49	77	20	7	1	44	16	9	19	.318	.382	.471	126	9	10	.942	-6	104	104	C61,3b7		0.7
1897	Phi N	4	13	1	2	0	0	0	0	1	0		.154	.214	.154	-2	-2	0	1.000	0	111	124	C3		-0.1
	StL N	84	326	49	91	11	3	8	57	26	10		.279	.351	.405	101	0	7	.974	-1	105	106	1b84/OR		0.0
	Year	88	339	50	93	11	3	8	57	27	10		.274	.346	.395	97	-2	7	.974	-1	105	106	1b84,C3/OR		-0.1
1898	NY N	93	287	64	85	19	5	3	49	38	11		.296	.399	.429	142	18	20	.944	-6	91	109	C57,O30(7/7/16),1b7,S3		1.4
1899	NY N	87	315	49	106	18	8	2	54	29	7		.337	.405	.463	143	19	20	.940	-8	86	116	C44,3b35,O4R,1b4		1.4
1900	NY N	83	251	36	55	8	4	0	27	34			.219	.331	.283	74	-7	9	.932	-4	110	82	C41,1b12,S11,3b7,O5R,2b2		-0.7
1901	Was A	94	347	57	99	17	10	9	56	27	8		.285	.351	.470	128	12	14	.975	8	173	104	1b59,C30,O3L		1.9
1904	StL N	101	323	44	101	15	11	5	43	31	2		.313	.376	.474	169	26	6	.955	-18	81	65	C77,1b11,2b3/3		1.6
1905	StL N	100	311	41	89	20	7	4	41	33	3		.286	.360	.434	141	16	15	.956	-11	84	85	C71,1b20		1.2
1906	StL N	97	280	33	70	11	3	2	27	48	5		.250	.369	.332	124	11	5	.983	-11	72	97	C60,1b38		0.5
Total	11	922	3008	489	884	155	67	35	461	311	73	40	.294	.374	.425	126	113	114	.946	-74	91	87	C527,1b247,3b51,O50R,S14,2b5		7.6

GRAF, FRED   Frederick Gottlieb   B8.25.1889 Canton OH   D10.4.1979 Chattanooga TN   BR/TR/5-10.5/164 d5.14

YEAR	TM LG	G	AB	R	H	2B	3B	HR	RBI	BB-IB	HP	SO	AVG	OBP	SLG	AOPS	ABR	SB-CS	FA	FR	RNG	THR	GAMES AT POSITION	DL	BFW
1913	StL A	4	5	1	2	1	0	0	2	3	0	3	.400	.625	.600	266	2	0	1.000	-0	109	363	3b4		0.2

GRAFF, LOUIS   Louis George "Chappie"   B7.25.1866 Philadelphia PA   D4.16.1955 Bryn Mawr PA   TR d6.23

YEAR	TM LG	G	AB	R	H	2B	3B	HR	RBI	BB-IB	HP	SO	AVG	OBP	SLG	AOPS	ABR	SB-CS	FA	FR	RNG	THR	GAMES AT POSITION	DL	BFW
1890	Syr AA	1	5	0	2	1	0	0	3	0			.400	.400	.600	217	1	0	.333	-2	75	0	/C		-0.1

GRAFF, MILT   Milton Edward   B12.30.1930 Jefferson Center PA   D8.2.2005 Rockdale TX   BL/TR/5-7.5/158* d4.16   C1   Col Penn St.

YEAR	TM LG	G	AB	R	H	2B	3B	HR	RBI	BB-IB	HP	SO	AVG	OBP	SLG	AOPS	ABR	SB-CS	FA	FR	RNG	THR	GAMES AT POSITION	DL	BFW
1957	KC A	56	155	16	28	4	3	0	10	15-0	0	10	.181	.260	.245	39	-13	2-5	.988	-1	102	105	2b53		-1.3
1958	KC A	5	1	0	0	0	0	0	0	0-0	0	0	.000	.000	.000	-98	-0	0-0	1.000	-0	0	0	/2		0.0
Total	2	61	156	16	28	4	3	0	10	15-0	0	10	.179	.259	.244	38	-13	2-5	.988	-1	102	104	2b54		-1.3

GRAFFANINO, TONY   Anthony Joseph   B6.6.1972 Amityville NY   BR/TR/6-1/195(175-195)   [AtlN90 10/264] d4.19

YEAR	TM LG	G	AB	R	H	2B	3B	HR	RBI	BB-IB	HP	SO	AVG	OBP	SLG	AOPS	ABR	SB-CS	FA	FR	RNG	THR	GAMES AT POSITION	DL	BFW
1996	Atl N	22	46	7	8	1	0	2	4-0		1	13	.174	.250	.239	29	-5	0-0	.969	1	110	121	2b18		-0.3
1997	†Atl N	104	186	33	48	9	1	8	20	26-1	1	46	.258	.344	.446	106	2	6-4	.982	7	118	97	2b75,3b2,S2/1		1.1
1998	†Atl N	105	289	32	61	14	1	5	22	24-0	1	68	.211	.275	.318	56	-19	1-4	.971	13	114	99	2b93,S2/3		-0.4
1999	TB A	39	130	20	41	9	4	2	19	9-0	1	22	.315	.364	.492	114	2	3-2	.990	8	129	108	2b17,S17/3		1.1
2000	TB A	13	20	8	6	1	0	0	1	1-0	1	2	.300	.364	.350	83	0	0-0	1.000	2	114	127	2b6,3b3/S		0.2
	†Chi A	57	148	25	40	5	1	2	16	21-0	1	25	.270	.363	.358	81	-4	7-4	.966	6	108	127	S21,2b19,3b12,D3		0.4
	Year	70	168	33	46	6	1	2	17	22-0	2	27	.274	.363	.357	82	-4	7-4	.973	8	124	119	2b25,S22,3b15,D3		0.6
2001	Chi A	74	145	23	44	9	0	2	15	16-0	1	29	.303	.370	.407	100	1	4-1	.923	4	106	93	3b38,2b20,S5,O3L/1D		0.6
2002	Chi A	70	229	35	60	12	4	6	31	22-1	2	38	.262	.329	.428	96	1	2-1	.952	2	101	93	3b35,2b25,S8		0.2
2003	Chi A	90	250	51	65	15	3	7	23	24-1	3	37	.260	.331	.428	95	-2	8-0	.968	9	106	101	S36,2b29,3b20,1b2,D3		1.1
2004	KC A	75	278	37	73	11	0	3	26	27-0	2	35	.263	.332	.335	75	-10	10-2	.988	19	114	136	2b75	91	-0.3
2005	KC A	59	191	29	57	5	2	3	18	22-1	2	28	.298	.377	.393	112	4	3-1	.987	-7	84	55	2b22,1b22,3b17/SD		-0.3
	†Bos A	51	188	39	60	12	1	4	20	9-1	2	23	.319	.355	.457	108	2	4-1	.987	-2	98	86	2b51		0.3
	Year	110	379	68	117	17	3	7	38	31-2	4	51	.309	.366	.425	111	6	7-2	.987	-9	94	77	2b73,1b22,3b17/SD		0.0
Total	10	759	2100	339	563	103	18	42	213	205-5	20	369	.268	.336	.394	90	-30	48-20	.980	61	112	111	2b450,3b129,S93,1b26,D10,O3L	126	5.4

GRAHAM, MOONLIGHT   Archibald Wright   B11.9.1876 Fayetteville NC   D8.25.1965 Chisholm MN   BL/TR/5-10.5/170 d6.29   Col Maryland-Baltimore Co.

YEAR	TM LG	G	AB	R	H	2B	3B	HR	RBI	BB-IB	HP	SO	AVG	OBP	SLG	AOPS	ABR	SB-CS	FA	FR	RNG	THR	GAMES AT POSITION	DL	BFW
1905	NY N	1	0	0	0	0	0	0									0			0	0	0	/OR		0.0

GRAHAM, SKINNY   Arthur William   B8.12.1909 Somerville MA   D7.10.1967 Cambridge MA   BL/TR/5-7/162 d9.14

YEAR	TM LG	G	AB	R	H	2B	3B	HR	RBI	BB-IB	HP	SO	AVG	OBP	SLG	AOPS	ABR	SB-CS	FA	FR	RNG	THR	GAMES AT POSITION	DL	BFW
1934	Bos A	13	47	7	11	2	1	0	3	6	0	13	.234	.321	.319	61	-3	2-2	1.000	-1	83	113	O13(0/4/9)		-0.4
1935	Bos A	8	10	1	3	0	0	1	1	1	0	3	.300	.364	.300	69	0	1-0	1.000	-0	89	0	O2R		0.0
Total	2	21	57	8	14	2	1	0	4	7	0	16	.246	.328	.316	62	-3	3-2	1.000	-1	84	103	O15(0/4/11)		-0.4

GRAHAM, BERNIE   Bernard W.   B1860 Beloit WI   D10.30.1886 Mobile AL   BL   d7.11

YEAR	TM LG	G	AB	R	H	2B	3B	HR	RBI	BB-IB	HP	SO	AVG	OBP	SLG	AOPS	ABR	SB-CS	FA	FR	RNG	THR	GAMES AT POSITION	DL	BFW
1884	CP U	1	5	2	1	0	0	0		0			.200	.200	.200	22	-1		1.000	-0	0	0	/OL		-0.1
	Bal U	41	167	21	45	11	0	0		2			.269	.278	.335	77	-9		.814	-1	94	115	O40(0/25/15)/1		-1.1
	Year	42	172	23	46	11	0	0		2			.267	.276	.331	76	-10		.816	-2	92	112	O41(1/25/15)/1		-1.2

GRAHAM, BERT   Bert "B.G."   B4.3.1886 Tilton IL   D6.19.1971 Cottonwood AZ   BB/TR/5-11.5/187 d9.9

YEAR	TM LG	G	AB	R	H	2B	3B	HR	RBI	BB-IB	HP	SO	AVG	OBP	SLG	AOPS	ABR	SB-CS	FA	FR	RNG	THR	GAMES AT POSITION	DL	BFW
1910	StL A	8	26	1	3	2	1	0	5	1	0		.115	.148	.269	32	-2	0	.964	1	146	0	1b5,2b2		-0.1

GRAHAM, CHARLIE   Charles Henry   B4.24.1878 Santa Clara CA   D8.29.1948 San Francisco CA   BR/TR/6-0/190 d4.16   Col Santa Clara

YEAR	TM LG	G	AB	R	H	2B	3B	HR	RBI	BB-IB	HP	SO	AVG	OBP	SLG	AOPS	ABR	SB-CS	FA	FR	RNG	THR	GAMES AT POSITION	DL	BFW
1906	Bos A	30	90	10	21	1	4	0	8	7	0	1	.233	.330	.278	91	0	1	.963	2	88	128	C27		0.5

GRAHAM, DAN   Daniel Jay   B7.19.1954 Ray AZ   BL/TR/6-1/212*   [MinA75 5/109] d6.8   Col La Verne

YEAR	TM LG	G	AB	R	H	2B	3B	HR	RBI	BB-IB	HP	SO	AVG	OBP	SLG	AOPS	ABR	SB-CS	FA	FR	RNG	THR	GAMES AT POSITION	DL	BFW
1979	Min A	2	4	0	0	0	0	0	0	0-0	0	2	.000	.000	.000	-96	-1	0-0	—	0			/D		-0.1
1980	Bal A	86	266	32	74	7	1	15	54	14-0	0	40	.278	.310	.481	116	4	0-0	.981	1	106	99	C73,3b9/ORD		0.8
1981	Bal A	55	142	7	25	3	0	2	11	13-1	0	32	.176	.244	.239	40	-11	0-0	.975	-3	93	153	C40,3b4,D6		-1.4
Total	3	143	412	39	99	10	1	17	65	27-1	0	72	.240	.284	.393	89	-8	0-0	.979	-2	102	116	C113,3b13,D9/OR		-0.7

GRAHAM, TINY   Dawson Francis   B9.9.1892 Nashville TN   D12.29.1962 Nashville TN   BR/TR/6-2/185 d8.30

YEAR	TM LG	G	AB	R	H	2B	3B	HR	RBI	BB-IB	HP	SO	AVG	OBP	SLG	AOPS	ABR	SB-CS	FA	FR	RNG	THR	GAMES AT POSITION	DL	BFW
1914	Cin N	25	61	5	14	1	0	0	3	3	0	10	.230	.266	.246	51	-4	1	.961	-2	87	142	1b25		-0.6

GRAHAM, PEACHES   George Frederick   B3.23.1877 Aledo IL   D7.25.1939 Long Beach CA   BR/TR/5-9/180 d9.14   s-Jack

YEAR	TM LG	G	AB	R	H	2B	3B	HR	RBI	BB-IB	HP	SO	AVG	OBP	SLG	AOPS	ABR	SB-CS	FA	FR	RNG	THR	GAMES AT POSITION	DL	BFW
1902	Cle A	2	6	0	2	0	0	0	1	1	0		.333	.429	.333	118	0	0	1.000	0	123	0	/2		0.0
1903	Chi N	1	2	0	0	0	0	0	0	0	0		.000	.000	.000	-99	0	0	1.000	0	220	0	/P		0.0
1908	Bos N	75	215	22	59	5	0	0	22	23	6		.274	.347	.298	112	5	4	.955	-5	91	99	C62,2b5		0.6
1909	Bos N	92	267	27	64	6	0	0	17	24			.240	.302	.285	79	-7	7	.948	-3	83	113	C76,O6(1/0/3)/S3		-0.5
1910	Bos N	110	291	31	82	13	2	0	21	33	2	15	.282	.359	.340	100	1	5	.966	-10	82	111	C87,3b2/1OR		-0.1
1911	Bos N	33	88	7	24	6	1	0	12	14	0	5	.273	.373	.364	98	0	2	.912	-7	75	97	C26		-0.4
	Chi N	36	71	6	17	3	0	0	8	11	3	8	.239	.365	.282	82	-1	2	.972	5	149	89	C28		0.1
	Year	69	159	13	41	9	1	0	20	25	3	13	.258	.369	.327	92	0	4	.937	-7	108	93	C54		-0.3
1912	Phi N	24	59	6	17	1	0	1	4	8	0	5	.288	.373	.356	94	0	1	.944	-2	88	107	C19		-0.1
Total	7	373	999	99	265	34	6	1	85	114	11	33	.265	.347	.314	95	-2	21	.953	-29	89	106	C298,O7(1/0/4),2b6,3b3/1SP		-0.4

GRAHAM, BARNEY   James B   Philadelphia PA   d9.4

YEAR	TM LG	G	AB	R	H	2B	3B	HR	RBI	BB-IB	HP	SO	AVG	OBP	SLG	AOPS	ABR	SB-CS	FA	FR	RNG	THR	GAMES AT POSITION	DL	BFW
1889	Phi AA	4	18	0	3	0	0	0	0	0	0		.167	.167	.167	-5	-3	0	.933	1	155	151	3b4		-0.1

GRAHAM, JACK   John Bernard   B12.24.1916 Minneapolis MN   D12.30.1998 Los Alamitos CA   BL/TL/6-2/200 d4.16   f-Peaches

YEAR	TM LG	G	AB	R	H	2B	3B	HR	RBI	BB-IB	HP	SO	AVG	OBP	SLG	AOPS	ABR	SB-CS	FA	FR	RNG	THR	GAMES AT POSITION	DL	BFW
1946	Bro N	2	5	0	1	0	0	0	0	0	0		.200	.200	.200	14	-1	0	1.000	0	104	0	1b2		-0.1
	NY N	100	270	34	59	6	4	14	47	23	1	37	.219	.282	.426	99	-3	1	.949	-1	97	125	O62(1/0/60),1b7		-0.6
	Year	102	275	34	60	6	4	14	47	23	1	37	.218	.281	.422	97	-4	1	.949	-1	97	125	O62(1/0/60),1b9		-0.7
1949	StL A	137	500	71	119	22	1	24	79	61	4	62	.238	.326	.430	95	-6	0-1	.984	-6	88	77	1b136		-1.7
Total	2	239	775	105	179	28	5	38	126	84	5	99	.231	.310	.427	96	-10	1-1	.985	-6	88	75	1b145,O62(1/0/60)		-2.4

GRAHAM, LEE   Lee Willard   B9.22.1959 Summerfield FL   BL/TL/5-10/170   [BosA77 26/641] d9.3

YEAR	TM LG	G	AB	R	H	2B	3B	HR	RBI	BB-IB	HP	SO	AVG	OBP	SLG	AOPS	ABR	SB-CS	FA	FR	RNG	THR	GAMES AT POSITION	DL	BFW
1983	Bos A	5	6	2	0	0	0	0	0	0	0		.000	.000	.000	-93	-2	0-1	1.000	1	125	923	O3(0/2/1)		-0.1

GRAHAM, ROY   Roy Vincent   B2.22.1895 San Francisco CA   D4.26.1933 Manila, Philippines   BR/TR/5-10.5/175 d5.28

YEAR	TM LG	G	AB	R	H	2B	3B	HR	RBI	BB-IB	HP	SO	AVG	OBP	SLG	AOPS	ABR	SB-CS	FA	FR	RNG	THR	GAMES AT POSITION	DL	BFW
1922	Chi A	5	3	0	0	0	0	0	0	1	0		.000	.400	.000	12	0	0-0	1.000	-0	0	0	C3		0.0
1923	Chi A	36	82	3	16	2	0	0	6	9	2	6	.195	.290	.220	36	-7	0-0	.949	-5	71	79	C33		-1.1
Total	2	41	85	3	16	2	0	0	6	10	2	6	.188	.296	.212	35	-7	0-0	.950	-5	69	77	C36		-1.1

YEAR	TM LG	G	AB	R	H	2B	3B	HR	RBI	BB-IB	HP	SO	AVG	OBP	SLG	AOPS	ABR	SB-CS	FA	FR	RNG	THR	GAMES AT POSITION	DL	BFW
GRAHAM, WAYNE	Wayne Leon B4.6.1937 Yoakum TX BR/TR/6-0/200* d4.10 Col Texas																								
1963	Phi N	10	22	1	4	0	0	0	0	3-0	0	1	.182	.280	.182	36	-2	0-0	.857	-1	71	0	O6L		-0.3
1964	NY N	20	33	1	3	1	0	0	0	0-0	0	5	.091	.091	.121	-42	-6	0-0	1.000	-3	58	0	3b11		-1.0
Total	2	30	55	2	7	1	0	0	0	3-0	0	6	.127	.172	.145	-9	-8	0-0	1.000	-4	58	0	3b11,O6L		-1.3
GRAMMAS, ALEX	Alexander Peter B4.3.1926 Birmingham AL BR/TR/6-0/178* d4.13 M3/C26 Col Mississippi St.																								
1954	StL N	142	401	57	106	17	4	2	29	40	5	29	.264	.335	.342	77	-13	6-1	.966	22	113	118	S142/3		2.1
1955	StL N	128	366	32	88	19	2	3	25	33-9	3	36	.240	.308	.328	69	-16	4-1	.968	4	98	102	S126		-0.1
1956	StL N	6	12	1	3	0	0	0	1	1-0	0	2	.250	.308	.250	52	-1	0-0	1.000	0	117	60	S5		0.0
	Cin N	77	140	17	34	11	0	0	16	16-1	1	18	.243	.323	.321	70	-5	0-1	.968	0	101	117	.3b58,S12,2b5		-0.5
	Year	83	152	18	37	11	0	0	17	17-1	1	20	.243	.322	.316	69	-6	0-1	.968	0	101	117	3b58,S17,2b5		-0.5
1957	Cin N	73	99	14	30	4	0	0	8	10-0	0	6	.303	.364	.343	86	-1	1-3	.966	-0	93	39	S42,2b20,3b9		-0.1
1958	Cin N	105	216	25	47	8	0	0	12	34-1	2	24	.218	.329	.255	54	-13	2-2	.993	-2	100	116	S61,3b38,2b14		-1.2
1959	StL N	131	368	43	99	14	2	3	30	38-6	1	26	.269	.337	.342	77	-11	3-3	.964	6	102	104	S130		0.5
1960	StL N	102	196	20	48	4	1	4	17	12-1	1	15	.245	.290	.337	66	-9	0-1	.972	7	99	74	S46,2b38,3b13		0.1
1961	StL N	89	170	23	36	10	1	0	21	19-3	1	21	.212	.293	.282	49	-12	0-1	.960	13	113	109	S65,2b18,3b3		0.5
1962	StL N	21	18	0	2	0	0	0	1	1-1	0	6	.111	.158	.111	-24	-3	0-0	.933	-2	90	54	S16,2b2		-0.4
	Chi N	23	60	3	14	3	0	0	3	2-0	1	7	.233	.270	.283	47	-4	1-1	1.000	1	108	127	S13,2b3/3		-0.3
	Year	44	78	3	16	3	0	0	4	3-1	1	13	.205	.244	.244	29	-8	1-1	.978	-1	102	103	S29,2b5/3		-0.7
1963	Chi N	16	27	1	5	0	0	0	0	0-0	0	3	.185	.185	.185	7	-3	0-0	.955	-2	66	27	S13		-0.8
Total	10	913	2073	236	512	90	10	12	163	206-22	15	193	.247	.318	.317	67	-91	17-14	.968	45	104	103	S671,3b123,2b100		-0.2
GRANDERSON, CURTIS	Curtis B3.16.1981 Blue Island IL BL/TR/6-1/185* [DetA02 3/80] d9.13 Col Illinois-Chicago																								
2004	Det A	9	25	2	6	1	1	0	3-0		0	8	.240	.321	.360	80	-1	0-0	1.000	0	90	287	O8C		-0.1
2005	Det A	47	162	18	44	6	3	8	20	10-0	0	43	.272	.314	.494	113	2	1-1	1.000	5	120	91	O45(20/41/0)		0.6
Total	2	56	187	20	50	7	4	8	20	13-0	0	51	.267	.315	.476	109	1	1-1	1.000	5	116	118	O53(20/49/0)		0.5
GRANEY, JACK	John Gladstone B6.10.1886 St.Thomas ON, Can. D4.20.1978 Louisiana MO BL/TL/5-9/180 d4.30																								
1908	Cle A	2	0	0	0	0	0	0	0	0	0	—	—	—	—	—	0	0	—	-0	0	0	P2		0.0
1910	Cle A	116	454	62	107	13	9	1	31	37	0		.236	.293	.311	88	-7	18	.949	-2	99	85	O114(53/43/18)		-1.8
1911	Cle A	146	527	84	142	25	5	1	45	66	11		.269	.363	.342	96	0	21	.927	3	105	104	O142(139/1/2)		-0.3
1912	Cle A	78	264	44	64	13	2	0	20	50	2		.242	.367	.307	90	0	9	.958	4	105	119	O75L		0.1
1913	Cle A	148	517	56	138	18	12	3	68	48	5	55	.267	.335	.366	102	0	27	.970	3	103	81	O148(144/0/4)		-0.7
1914	Cle A	130	460	63	122	17	10	1	39	67	3	46	.265	.362	.352	111	8	20-18	.935	5	118	86	O127L		0.6
1915	Cle A	116	404	42	105	20	7	1	56	59	2	29	.260	.357	.351	110	7	12-15	.972	1	105	117	O115(107/1/8)		0.3
1916	Cle A	155	589	106	142	41	14	5	54	102	2	72	.241	.355	.384	115	14	10	.959	1	97	109	O154L		0.9
1917	Cle A	146	535	87	122	29	7	3	35	94	4	49	.228	.348	.325	98	3	16	.959	-11	92	65	O145L		-1.6
1918	Cle A	70	177	24	42	7	4	0	9	28	3	13	.237	.351	.322	94	0	3	.975	-4	94	37	O125L		-0.6
1919	Cle A	128	461	79	108	22	8	1	30	105	3	39	.234	.380	.323	93	1	7	.961	3	108	98	O125L		-0.1
1920	†Cle A	62	152	31	45	11	1	0	13	27	3	21	.296	.412	.382	108	4	4-2	.941	-1	97	82	O47(44/2/1)		0.1
1921	Cle A	68	107	19	32	3	0	2	18	20	1	9	.299	.414	.383	103	2	1-1	.933	-3	98	0	O32(17/11/5)		-0.2
1922	Cle A	37	58	6	9	0	0	0	2	9	1	12	.155	.279	.155	16	-7	0-0	.862	-1	90	75	O13(2/4/7)		-0.9
Total	14	1402	4705	706	1178	219	79	18	420	712	40	345	.250	.354	.342	100	25	148-36	.953	-0	103	91	O1282(1176/62/46),P2		-4.2
GRANT, EDDIE	Edward Leslie "Harvard Eddie" B5.21.1883 Franklin MA D10.5.1918 Argonne Forest, France BL/TR/5-11.5/168 d8.4 Col Harvard																								
1905	Cle A	2	8	1	3	0	0	0		0	0		.375	.375	.375	136	0	0	.833	-1	92	63	2b2		-0.1
1907	Phi N	74	268	26	65	4	3	0	19	10	1		.243	.272	.280	74	-9	10	.916	-4	93	63	3b74		-1.2
1908	Phi N	147	598	69	146	13	8	0	32	35	3		.244	.289	.293	83	-12	27	.930	-2	99	138	3b134,S13		-1.2
1909	Phi N	154	631	75	170	18	4	1	37	35	3		.269	.311	.315	94	-6	28	.957	3	101	98	3b154		0.1
1910	Phi N	152	579	70	155	15	5	1	67	39	1	54	.268	.315	.316	81	-15	25	.935	-12	87	101	3b152		-2.4
1911	Cin N	136	458	49	102	12	7	1	53	51	0	47	.223	.301	.286	67	-21	28	.953	-5	97	129	3b122,S11		-2.2
1912	Cin N	96	255	37	61	6	1	2	20	18	1	27	.239	.292	.294	62	-14	11	.948	0	103	92	S56,3b15		-0.9
1913	Cin N	27	94	12	20	1	0	0	9	11	0	10	.213	.295	.223	49	-6	7-4	.929	-1	98	126	3b26		-0.6
	†NY N	27	20	8	4	1	0	0	1	2	0	2	.200	.273	.250	49	-1	1-1	1.000	3	269	0	3b5,2b3/S		0.2
	Year	54	114	20	24	2	0	0	10	13	0	12	.211	.291	.228	49	-7	8-40	.940	2	114	114	3b31,2b3/S		-0.4
1914	NY N	88	282	34	78	7	1	0	29	23	1	21	.277	.333	.309	94	-2	11	.948	-3	108	115	3b52,S21,2b16		-1.7
1915	NY N	87	192	18	40	2	1	0	10	9	1	20	.208	.248	.229	47	-13	5-6	.970	-2	90	70	3b35,2b9/1S		-1.7
Total	10	990	3385	399	844	79	30	5	277	233	11	181	.249	.300	.295	78	-99	153-11	.942	-21	97	108	3b769,S103,2b30/1		-10.2
GRANT, JIMMY	James Charles B10.6.1918 Racine WI D7.8.1970 Rochester MN BL/TR/5-8/166 d9.8																								
1942	Chi A	12	36	0	6	1	0	0	1	5	0	6	.167	.268	.250	47	-3	0-0	.944	0	93	164	3b10		-0.2
1943	Chi A	58	197	23	51	9	2	4	22	18	0	34	.259	.321	.386	106	1	4-3	.893	-2	109	113	3b51		-0.1
	Cle A	15	22	3	3	2	0	0	1	4	0	7	.136	.269	.227	49	-1	0-0	.941	1	142	0	3b5		0.0
	Year	73	219	26	54	11	2	4	23	22	0	41	.247	.315	.370	101	0	4-3	.897	-1	112	104	3b56		-0.1
1944	Cle A	61	99	12	27	4	3	1	12	11	2	20	.273	.357	.404	122	3	1-0	.926	-4	98	47	2b20,3b4		0.0
Total	3	146	354	38	87	16	6	5	36	38	2	67	.246	.322	.367	101	0	5-3	.907	-4	108	110	3b70,2b20		-0.3
GRANT, TOM	Thomas Raymond B5.28.1957 Worcester MA BL/TR/6-2/190 [ChiN79 16/402] d6.17 Col New Haven																								
1983	Chi N	16	20	2	3	1	0	0	2	3-0	0	4	.150	.261	.200	28	-2	0-0	1.000	0	72	316	O10(5/0/5)		-0.2
GRANTHAM, GEORGE	George Farley "Boots" B5.20.1900 Galena KS D3.16.1954 Kingman AZ BL/TR/5-10/170 d9.20 Col Northern Arizona																								
1922	Chi N	7	23	3	4	1	0	3	1	0		.174	.208	.304	30	-3	2-0	1.000	-1	52	149	3b5		-0.3
1923	Chi N	152	570	81	160	36	8	8	70	71	0	92	.281	.360	.414	104	5	43-28	.942	4	101	106	2b150		1.2
1924	Chi N	127	469	85	148	19	6	12	60	55	2	63	.316	.390	.458	125	18	21-21	.911	-1	101	108	2b118,3b6		1.8
1925	†Pit N	114	359	74	117	24	6	8	52	50	3	29	.326	.413	.493	122	14	14-4	.989	-4	82	123	1b102		0.5
1926	Pit N	141	449	66	143	27	13	6	70	60	1	42	.318	.400	.490	131	21	6	.990	-2	92	106	1b132		1.1
1927	†Pit N	112	531	96	162	33	11	8	66	74	6	39	.305	.396	.454	119	17	9	.953	-22	88	101	2b124,1b29		-0.4
1928	Pit N	124	440	93	142	24	9	10	85	59	4	37	.323	.408	.486	128	19	9	.986	1	109	86	1b119/23		1.3
1929	Pit N	110	349	85	107	23	10	12	90	93	1	38	.307	.454	.533	140	27	10	.967	-0	96	125	2b76,O19L,1b12		2.5
1930	Pit N	146	552	120	179	34	14	18	99	81	2	66	.324	.413	.534	126	25	5	.958	-12	101	82	2b141,1b4		1.5
1931	Pit N	127	465	91	142	26	6	10	46	71	2	50	.305	.400	.452	130	23	5	.985	-22	63	100	1b78,2b51		-0.4
1932	Cin N	126	493	81	144	29	6	6	39	56	2	21	.292	.364	.412	112	10	4	.959	-25	95	70	2b115,1b10		-0.9
1933	Cin N	87	260	32	53	14	3	4	28	38	2	21	.204	.310	.327	83	-5	4	.948	-8	95	93	2b72,1b12		-1.0
1934	NY N	32	29	5	7	2	0	1	4	8	0	6	.241	.405	.414	123	1	0	1.000	0	82	71	1b4,3b2		0.1
Total	13	1444	4989	912	1508	292	93	105	712	717	25	526	.302	.392	.461	122	172	132-53	.949	-92	97	97	2b848,1b502,O19L,3b14		7.0
GRASSO, MICKEY	Newton Michael B5.10.1920 Newark NJ D10.15.1975 Miami FL BR/TR/6-0/195* d9.18 [DL 1954 Was A 141]																								
1946	NY N	7	22	1	3	0	0	0	3	0	3	.136	.136	.136	-22	-4	0-0	.967	0	106	184	C7		-0.3
1950	Was A	75	195	25	56	4	1	1	22	25	2	31	.287	.374	.333	86	-3	1-1	.942	-1	74	138	C69		-0.1
1951	Was A	52	175	16	36	3	0	1	14	14	1	17	.206	.268	.240	39	-15	0-0	.967	-3	102	108	C49		-1.6
1952	Was A	115	361	22	78	9	0	0	27	29	1	36	.216	.276	.241	46	-27	1-0	.970	4	116	75	C114		-1.7
1953	Was A	61	196	13	41	7	0	2	22	9	1	20	.209	.251	.276	43	-16	0-0	.984	2	105	85	C59		-1.2
1954	†Cle A	4	6	1	2	0	0	1	1	1	1	1	.333	.500	.833	256	1	0-0	.833	-1	68	191	C4		0.1
1955	NY N	8	2	0	0	0	0	0	3-0	0	0	.000	.600	.000	77	0	0-0	.900	-0	0	0	C8		0.0
Total	7	322	957	78	216	23	1	5	87	81-0	7	108	.226	.291	.268	53	-64	2-1	.964	-0	101	99	C310	141	-4.8
GRAULICH, LEW	Lewis B1862 Philadelphia PA d9.17																								
1891	Phi N	7	26	2	8	0	0	0	3	1	0	2	.308	.333	.308	85	-1		.640	-3	94	46	C4,1b3		-0.3
GRAVES, FRANK	Frank Norris B11.2.1860 Cincinnati OH BR/6-0/163 d5.10																								
1886	StL N	43	138	7	21	2	0	0	9	7		48	.152	.193	.167	11	-14	11	.885	0			C41,O3C/P		-1.0
GRAVES, JOE	Joseph Ebenezer B2.26.1906 Marblehead MA D12.22.1980 Salem MA BR/TR/5-10/160 d9.26 b-Sid																								
1926	Chi N	2	5	0	0	0	0	0	0	0	1	.000	.000	.000	-99	-0	0-0	.250	-1	42	470	3b2		-0.3
GRAVES, SID	Samuel Sidney "Whitey" B11.30.1901 Marblehead MA D12.26.1983 Biddeford ME BR/TR/6-0/170 d7.23 b-Joe Col Bowdoin																								
1927	Bos N	7	20	5	5	1	1	0	2	0	0	1	.250	.250	.400	78	-1	1	.857	0	78	405	O5C		-0.1

YEAR	TM LG	G	AB	R	H	2B	3B	HR	RBI	BB-IB	HP	SO	AVG	OBP	SLG	AOPS	ABR	SB-CS	FA	FR	RNG	THR	GAMES AT POSITION	DL	BFW

GRAY, GARY Gary George B9.21.1952 New Orleans LA BR/TR/6-0/203(180-215) [TexA74 18/408] d6.23 Col Southeastern Oklahoma

YEAR	TM LG	G	AB	R	H	2B	3B	HR	RBI	BB-IB	HP	SO	AVG	OBP	SLG	AOPS	ABR	SB-CS	FA	FR	RNG	THR	GAMES AT POSITION	DL	BFW
1977	Tex A	1	2	0	0	0	0	0	0	0-0	0	0	1.000	.000	.000	-99	-1	0-0	—	-0	0	0	/OL		-0.1
1978	Tex A	17	50	4	12	1	0	2	6	1-0	0	12	.240	.255	.380	76	-2	0-0	—	0	0	0	D11		-0.2
1979	Tex A	16	42	4	10	0	0	0	1	2-0	0	8	.238	.273	.238	39	-4	1-1	—	0	0	0	D13		-0.4
1980	Cle A	28	54	4	8	1	0	2	4	3-1	0	13	.148	.193	.278	27	-6	0-0	1.000	-0	148	50	1b6,O6L,D9		-0.6
1981	Sea A	69	208	27	51	7	1	13	31	4-1	0	44	.245	.257	.476	103	-1	2-0	.993	-2	78	119	1b34,D15,O4L		-0.6
1982	Sea A	80	269	26	69	14	2	7	29	24-0	2	59	.257	.322	.401	94	-2	1-1	.984	-3	82	77	1b60,D14		-0.9
Total 6		211	625	65	150	23	3	24	71	34-2	2	137	.240	.281	.402	86	-16	5-2	.988	-6	82	91	1b100,D62,O11L		-2.8

GRAY, REDDY James W. B8.1863 Allegheny (now part of Pittsburgh) PA D1.31.1938 Pittsburgh PA TR d10.9

YEAR	TM LG	G	AB	R	H	2B	3B	HR	RBI	BB-IB	HP	SO	AVG	OBP	SLG	AOPS	ABR	SB-CS	FA	FR	RNG	THR	GAMES AT POSITION	DL	BFW
1884	Pit AA	1	2	0	1	0	0	0	0			0	.500	.500	.500	230				-0	138	0	/3		0.0
1890	Pit P	2	9	3	2	0	0	1	3	0	0	2	.222	.222	.556	114	0	0	.813	-1	67	0	2b2		-0.1
	Pit	1	3	0	0	0	0	0	0				1.000	.000	.000	-99	-1	0	.571	-1	57	210	/S		-0.2
1893	Pit N	2	9	0	4	1	0	0	2	0	0	1	.444	.444	.556	168	1	0	.800	-2	20	0	S2		-0.1
Total 3		6	23	3	7	1	0	1	5	0	0	4	.304	.304	.478	119	0	0	.667	-4	35	86	S3,2b2/3		-0.4

GRAY, LORENZO Lorenzo B3.4.1958 Mound Bayou MS BR/TR/6-1/180* [ChiA76 8/176] d7.8

YEAR	TM LG	G	AB	R	H	2B	3B	HR	RBI	BB-IB	HP	SO	AVG	OBP	SLG	AOPS	ABR	SB-CS	FA	FR	RNG	THR	GAMES AT POSITION	DL	BFW
1982	Chi A	17	28	4	8	1	0	0	2	0-0	0		.286	.333	.321	80	-1	1-0	.864	-3	59	122	3b16		-0.3
1983	Chi A	41	78	18	14	3	0	1	4	8-0	0	16	.179	.256	.256	40	-6	1-0	.940	-2	89	65	3b31,D7		-0.9
Total 2		58	106	22	22	4	0	1	6	8-0	0	20	.208	.276	.274	50	-7	2-0	.921	-5	81	79	3b47,D7		-1.2

GRAY, MILT Milton Marshall B2.21.1914 Louisville KY D6.30.1969 Quincy FL BR/TR/6-1/170 d5.27

YEAR	TM LG	G	AB	R	H	2B	3B	HR	RBI	BB-IB	HP	SO	AVG	OBP	SLG	AOPS	ABR	SB-CS	FA	FR	RNG	THR	GAMES AT POSITION	DL	BFW
1937	Was A	2	6	0	0	0	0	0	0	0-0	0	1	.000	.000	.000	-99	-2	0-0	1.000	0	84	0	C2		-0.2

GRAY, PETE Peter J. (b Peter Wyshner) B3.6.1915 Nanticoke PA D6.30.2002 Nanticoke PA BL/TL/6-1/169 d4.17

YEAR	TM LG	G	AB	R	H	2B	3B	HR	RBI	BB-IB	HP	SO	AVG	OBP	SLG	AOPS	ABR	SB-CS	FA	FR	RNG	THR	GAMES AT POSITION	DL	BFW
1945	StL A	77	234	26	51	6	2	0	13	13	0	11	.218	.259	.261	49	-16	5-6	.959	2	117	59	O61(35/29/0)		-1.9

GRAY, DICK Richard Benjamin B7.11.1931 Jefferson PA BR/TR/5-11/165* d4.15 Col Waynesburg

YEAR	TM LG	G	AB	R	H	2B	3B	HR	RBI	BB-IB	HP	SO	AVG	OBP	SLG	AOPS	ABR	SB-CS	FA	FR	RNG	THR	GAMES AT POSITION	DL	BFW
1958	LA N	58	197	25	49	5	6	9	30	19-0	4	30	.249	.327	.472	105	1	1-1	.929	11	117	157	3b55		1.1
1959	LA N	21	52	4	8	1	0	2	4	6-0	0	12	.154	.241	.288	38	-5	0-0	1.000	0	105	133	3b11		-0.5
	StL N	36	51	9	16	1	0	1	6	6-0	0	8	.314	.386	.392	101	0	3-0	.958	-5	64	71	S13,3b6,2b2/OL		-0.3
	Year	57	103	17	24	2	0	3	10	12-1	0	20	.233	.313	.340	69	-4	3-0	.935	-4	98	103	3b17,S13,2b2/OL		-0.8
1960	StL N	9	5	1	0	0	0	0	1	2-0	0	2	.000	.250	.000	-13	-1	0-0	1.000	1	143	320	2b4/3		0.0
Total 3		124	305	43	73	7	6	12	41	33-1	4	52	.239	.321	.420	91	-5	4-1	.930	7	114	147	3b73,S13,2b6/OL		0.3

GRAY, STAN Stanley Oscar B12.10.1888 Ladonia TX D10.11.1964 Snyder TX BR/TR/6-0.5/184 d9.17

YEAR	TM LG	G	AB	R	H	2B	3B	HR	RBI	BB-IB	HP	SO	AVG	OBP	SLG	AOPS	ABR	SB-CS	FA	FR	RNG	THR	GAMES AT POSITION	DL	BFW
1912	Pit N	6	20	4	5	0	1	0	2	0	0	3	.250	.250	.350	64	-1	0	1.000	-1	0	94	1b4		-0.2

GRAY, BILL William Tolan B4.15.1871 Philadelphia PA D12.8.1932 Philadelphia PA 5-11/175 d5.14 OF(8/7/9)

YEAR	TM LG	G	AB	R	H	2B	3B	HR	RBI	BB-IB	HP	SO	AVG	OBP	SLG	AOPS	ABR	SB-CS	FA	FR	RNG	THR	GAMES AT POSITION	DL	BFW
1890	Phi N	34	128	20	31	8	4	0	21	6	2	3	.242	.287	.367	88	-3	5	1.000	-6	170	0	O10(6/3/1),3b8,2b8,C7/1		-0.7
1891	Phi N	23	75	11	18	0	0	0	7	3	3	10	.240	.296	.240	55	-4	3	.804	-5	92	66	C11,O10(0/4/6),S3/3		-0.8
1895	Cin N	52	181	24	55	17	4	1	29	15	2	0	.304	.364	.459	107	2	4	.906	-3	97	162	3b27,2b16,S5,C5/OL		0.0
1896	Cin N	46	121	15	25	2	1	0	17	19	0	11	.207	.314	.240	44	-10	6	.927	1	126	123	2b12,C11,S8,O3(1/0/2),1b2/3		-0.6
1898	Pit N	137	528	56	121	17	5	0	67	28	12		.229	.283	.240	63	-26	5	.879	-21	88	86	3b137		-4.2
Total 5		292	1033	126	250	44	14	1	141	71	19	32	.242	.303	.315	72	-41	23	.879	-34	87	97	3b174,2b36,C34,O24R,S16,1b3		-6.3

GREBECK, CRAIG Craig Allen B12.29.1964 Johnstown PA BR/TR/5-7/148(148-160) d4.13 Col Cal St.-Dominguez Hills

YEAR	TM LG	G	AB	R	H	2B	3B	HR	RBI	BB-IB	HP	SO	AVG	OBP	SLG	AOPS	ABR	SB-CS	FA	FR	RNG	THR	GAMES AT POSITION	DL	BFW
1990	Chi A	59	119	7	20	3	1	1	9	8-0	2	24	.168	.227	.235	32	-11	0-0	.987	1	112	65	3b35,S16,2b6/D		-1.0
1991	Chi A	107	224	37	63	16	3	6	31	38-0	1	40	.281	.386	.460	136	13	1-3	.933	-3	108	151	3b49,2b36,S26		1.1
1992	Chi A	88	287	24	77	21	2	3	35	30-0	3	34	.268	.341	.387	105	3	0-3	.980	2	111	89	S85,3b7,O2(1/0/1)	57	1.0
1993	†Chi A	72	190	25	43	5	0	1	12	26-0	0	26	.226	.319	.268	61	-10	1-2	.983	10	106	151	S46,2b16,3b14		0.3
1994	Chi A	35	97	17	30	5	0	0	5	12-0	1	5	.309	.391	.361	97	0	0-0	.982	-5	78	50	2b14,S14,3b7	40	0.3
1995	Chi A	53	154	19	40	12	0	1	18	21-0	1	23	.260	.360	.357	91	-1	0-0	.961	4	118	106	S31,3b18,2b8		0.5
1996	Fla N	50	95	8	20	1	0	1	9	4-1	1	14	.211	.245	.253	34	-9	0-0	.985	5	100	160	2b29,S2/3	40	-0.3
1997	Ana A	63	126	12	34	9	0	1	6	18-1	0	11	.270	.359	.365	90	-1	0-1	1.000	-5	94	124	2b26,S20,3b15,O3L,D2		-0.4
1998	Tor A	102	301	33	77	17	2	2	27	39-0	4	42	.256	.337	.346	76	-10	2-2	.975	1	101	76	2b91,S6,3b4	15	-0.5
1999	Tor A	34	113	18	41	7	0	0	10	15-0	2	13	.363	.443	.425	122	5	0-0	.959	-6	85	65	2b17,D10,S4,3b2	93	0.0
2000	Tor A	66	241	38	71	19	0	3	23	25-0	2	33	.295	.364	.411	93	-2	0-0	.968	4	109	87	2b56,S8		0.5
2001	Bos A	23	41	1	2	1	0	0	2	5-0	0	9	.049	.191	.073	-55	-9	0-0	1.000	-3	87	47	S23	143	-1.1
Total 12		752	1988	239	518	116	8	19	187	228-2	19	274	.261	.340	.356	86	-32	4-11	.981	7	101	93	2b299,S281,3b152,D13,O5(4/0/1)	388	-0.2

GREEN, ANDY Andrew Mulligan B7.7.1977 Lexington KY BR/TR/5-9/165(165-180) [AriN00 24/729] d6.12 Col Kentucky

YEAR	TM LG	G	AB	R	H	2B	3B	HR	RBI	BB-IB	HP	SO	AVG	OBP	SLG	AOPS	ABR	SB-CS	FA	FR	RNG	THR	GAMES AT POSITION	DL	BFW
2004	Ari N	46	109	13	22	2	1	1	4	5-0	1	17	.202	.241	.266	30	-12	1-1	.918	3	121	38	3b18,2b14,O9L		-0.8
2005	Ari N	17	31	5	7	1	0	0	2	7-0	0	3	.226	.359	.258	65	-1	0-0	1.000	0	94	131	2b5,S2,O2L		-0.1
Total 2		63	140	18	29	3	1	1	6	12-0	1	20	.207	.271	.264	38	-13	1-1	.981	4	90	108	2b19,3b18,O11L,S2		-0.9

GREEN, SCARBOROUGH Bertrum Scarborough B6.9.1974 Creve Coeur MO BB/TR/5-10/170* [StLN92 10/279] d8.2

YEAR	TM LG	G	AB	R	H	2B	3B	HR	RBI	BB-IB	HP	SO	AVG	OBP	SLG	AOPS	ABR	SB-CS	FA	FR	RNG	THR	GAMES AT POSITION	DL	BFW
1997	StL N	20	31	5	3	0	0	0	0	2-0	0	5	.097	.152	.097	-33	-6	0-0	.952	0	101	209	O19(7/12/0)		-0.6
1999	Tex A	18	13	4	4	0	0	0	0	1-0	0	2	.308	.357	.308	68	-1	0-1	1.000	-0	84	0	O9(3/4/3),D4		-0.1
2000	Tex A	79	124	21	29	1	1	0	9	10-0	0	26	.234	.291	.258	40	-12	10-6	1.000	8	114	393	O65(3/41/23),D6		-0.4
Total 3		117	168	30	36	1	1	0	10	13-0	0	33	.214	.271	.232	29	-19	10-7	.993	8	110	333	O93(13/57/26),D10		-1.1

GREEN, DAVID David Alejandro (Casaya) B12.4.1960 Managua, Nicaragua BR/TR/6-3/170* d9.4

YEAR	TM LG	G	AB	R	H	2B	3B	HR	RBI	BB-IB	HP	SO	AVG	OBP	SLG	AOPS	ABR	SB-CS	FA	FR	RNG	THR	GAMES AT POSITION	DL	BFW
1981	StL N	21	34	6	5	1	0	0	2	6-1	0	5	.147	.275	.176	29	-3	0-1	.970	0	103	126	O18C		-0.4
1982	†StL N	76	166	21	47	7	1	2	23	8-2	1	29	.283	.315	.373	91	-2	11-3	.991	1	102	134	O68(7/46/19)	15	-0.1
1983	StL N	146	422	52	120	14	10	8	69	26-1	1	76	.284	.325	.422	106	1	34-16	.991	-1	94	130	O136(20/19/100)		-0.4
1984	StL N	126	452	49	121	14	4	15	65	20-4	1	105	.268	.297	.416	102	-2	17-9	.991	-2	96	114	1b117,O14(0/6/8)	22	-1.1
1985	SF N	106	294	36	73	10	4	5	20	22-3	1	58	.248	.301	.347	85	-7	6-5	.987	-2	93	94	1b78,O12(1/0/11)		-1.4
1987	StL N	14	30	4	8	2	1	1	2	2-0	0	5	.267	.313	.500	108	0	0-1	.882	0	104	206	O10(1/0/9),1b3		0.0
Total 6		489	1398	168	374	48	18	31	180	84-11	4	278	.268	.308	.394	96	-13	68-35	.972	-3	98	131	O258(29/89/147),1b198	37	-3.4

GREEN, DANNY Edward B11.6.1876 Burlington NJ D11.9.1914 Camden NJ BL/TR d8.17

YEAR	TM LG	G	AB	R	H	2B	3B	HR	RBI	BB-IB	HP	SO	AVG	OBP	SLG	AOPS	ABR	SB-CS	FA	FR	RNG	THR	GAMES AT POSITION	DL	BFW
1898	Chi N	47	188	26	59	4	3	4	27	7	1		.314	.342	.431	121	4	12	.970	4	148	331	O47(8/2/37)		0.5
1899	Chi N	117	475	90	140	12	11	6	56	35	7		.295	.352	.404	110	5	18	.947	1	125	261	O115(9/0/106)		0.0
1900	Chi N	103	389	63	116	21	5	5	49	17	7		.298	.339	.416	112	5	28	.938	0	73	56	O102(3/60/39)		-0.1
1901	Chi A	133	537	82	168	16	12	6	61	40			.313	.364	.421	132	21	31	.932	7	96	161	O133C		2.1
1902	Chi A	129	481	77	150	16	11	0	62	53	7		.312	.388	.391	122	17	35	.942	-3	66	124	O129(18/2/110)		0.7
1903	Chi A	135	499	75	154	26	7	6	62	47	6		.309	.375	.425	146	30	29	.933	2	111	216	O133R		2.7
1904	Chi A	147	536	83	142	16	10	2	62	63	9		.265	.352	.343	125	18	28	.964	1	81	133	O146R		1.4
1905	Chi A	112	379	56	92	13	6	0	44	53	6		.243	.345	.309	112	8	11	.914	-8	83	138	O107(0/7/100)		-0.4
Total 8		923	3484	552	1021	124	65	29	423	315	46		.293	.359	.391	124	108	192	.941	3	94	167	O912(38/204/671)		6.9

GREEN, PUMPSIE Elijah Jerry B10.27.1933 Oakland CA BB/TR/6-0/175* d7.21

YEAR	TM LG	G	AB	R	H	2B	3B	HR	RBI	BB-IB	HP	SO	AVG	OBP	SLG	AOPS	ABR	SB-CS	FA	FR	RNG	THR	GAMES AT POSITION	DL	BFW
1959	Bos A	50	172	30	46	3	1		10	29-0	2	22	.233	.350	.320	81	-3	4-2	.972	4	106	115	2b45/S		0.4
1960	Bos A	133	260	36	63	10	3	3	21	44-2	1	47	.242	.350	.338	85	-4	3-4	.982	-13	87	62	2b69,S41		-1.3
1961	Bos A	88	219	33	57	12	3	6	27	42-3	0	32	.260	.376	.425	112	5	4-2	.940	-3	107	98	S57,2b7		0.8
1962	Bos A	56	91	12	21	2	1	2	11	11-0	0	18	.231	.308	.341	74	-3	1-0	.953	-6	77	77	2b18,S5		-0.8
1963	NY N	17	54	8	15	1	2	1	5	12-0	0	13	.278	.409	.426	139	3	0-2	.857	1	126	82	3b16		0.4
Total 5		344	796	119	196	31	12	13	74	138-5	3	132	.246	.357	.364	94	-2	12-10	.975	-17	93	88	2b139,S104,3b16	38	-0.5

GREEN, GARY Gary Allan B1.14.1962 Pittsburgh PA BR/TR/6-3/175* [SDN84 1/27] d9.14 f-Fred Col Oklahoma St.

YEAR	TM LG	G	AB	R	H	2B	3B	HR	RBI	BB-IB	HP	SO	AVG	OBP	SLG	AOPS	ABR	SB-CS	FA	FR	RNG	THR	GAMES AT POSITION	DL	BFW
1986	SD N	13	33	2	7	1	0	0	1	2-0	0		.212	.235	.242	33	-3	0-0	1.000	2	109	141	S13		0.0
1989	SD N	15	27	4	7	1	0	0	1	1-0	0	1	.259	.286	.370	86	0	0-1	.921	2	133	189	S11/3		0.2
1990	Tex A	62	88	10	19	3	0	0	8	6-0	0	18	.216	.263	.250	45	-7	1-1	.972	7	111	119	S58		0.3
1991	Tex A	8	20	0	3	1	0	0	1	1-0	0	6	.150	.190	.200	8	-3	0-0	.968	1	112	124	S8	39	-0.1
1992	Cin N	8	12	3	4	1	0	0	2	0-0	0	3	.333	.333	.417	108	0	0-0	1.000	-3	32	0	S6/3		-0.3
Total 5		106	180	19	40	9	0	0	11	9-0	0	38	.222	.258	.272	49	-13	1-2	.970	9	109	126	S96,3b2	39	0.1

YEAR	TM LG	G	AB	R	H	2B	3B	HR	RBI	BB-IB	HP	SO	AVG	OBP	SLG	AOPS	ABR	SB-CS	FA	FR	RNG	THR	GAMES AT POSITION	DL	BFW

GREEN, GENE Gene Leroy B6.26.1933 Los Angeles CA D5.23.1981 St.Louis MO BR/TR/6-2/205* d9.10

1957	StL N	6	15	0	3	1	0	0	2	0-0	0	3	.200	.188	.267	23	-2	0-0	1.000	-1	49	0	O3R		-0.2
1958	StL N	137	442	47	124	18	3	13	55	37-4	1	48	.281	.333	.423	96	-3	2-1	.956	5	101	192	O75(0/1/75),C48		0.2
1959	StL N	30	74	8	14	6	0	1	3	5-1	0	18	.189	.241	.311	43	-6	0-0	.944	5	102	521	O19R,C11		-0.2
1960	Bal A	1	4	0	1	0	0	0	0-0		0	0	.250	.250	.250	36	0	0-0	1.000	0	1763	0	/OR		0.0
1961	Was A	110	364	52	102	16	3	18	62	35-5	1	65	.280	.341	.489	122	10	0-2	.986	-17	69	72	C79,O21R		-0.5
1962	Cle A	66	143	16	40	4	1	11	28	8-0	0	21	.280	.316	.552	133	5	0-0	.964	1	107	135	O33(3/0/30),1b2		0.4
1963	Cle A	43	78	4	16	3	0	2	7	4-0	2	22	.205	.259	.321	63	-4	0-0	1.000	-2	65	115	O18(1/0/17)		-0.7
	Cin N	15	31	3	7	1	0	1	3	0-0	1	6	.226	.250	.355	70	-1	0-0	.932	-3	44	51	C8		-0.4
Total	7	408	1151	130	307	49	7	46	160	89-10	5	185	.267	.318	.441	101	-1	2-3	.963	-11	94	190	O170(4/1/166),C146,1b2		-1.4

GREEN, JIM James F. B5.22.1854 Windham Co. CT D12.12.1912 Cleveland OH d7.19

1884	Was U	10	36	4	5	1	0	0			0		.139	.139	.167	-8	-6		.818	0	119	0	3b9/OR		-0.5

GREEN, JOE Joseph Henry (aka Joseph Henry Greene) B9.17.1897 Philadelphia PA D2.4.1972 Bryn Mawr PA BR/TR/6-2/170 d7.2

1924	Phi A	1	1	0	0	0	0	0	0-0	0	0	.000	.000	.000	-99	0	0-0	—	0		/H		0.0

GREEN, LENNY Leonard Charles B1.6.1933 Detroit MI BL/TL/5-11/170(161-177) d8.25

1957	Bal A	19	33	2	6	1	1	1	5	1-0	0	4	.182	.206	.364	56	-2	0-1	.950	-1	101	0	O15(3/12/2)		-0.4
1958	Bal A	69	91	10	21	4	0	0	4	9-0	0	10	.231	.297	.275	63	-4	0-2	.965	3	131	57	O53(28/30/6)		-0.4
1959	Bal A	27	24	3	7	0	1	0	2	1-0	1	3	.292	.346	.417	111	0	0-0	1.000	1	90	625	O23(20/0/5)		0.1
	Was A	88	190	29	46	6	1	2	15	20-0	0	15	.242	.314	.316	74	-7	9-5	.979	1	97	143	O58(21/13/27)		-0.9
	Year	115	214	32	53	6	1	3	17	21-0	1	18	.248	.318	.327	78	-6	9-5	.981	1	96	191	O81(41/13/32)		-0.8
1960	Was A	127	330	62	97	16	7	5	33	43-4	6	25	.294	.383	.430	121	11	21-8	.991	2	110	76	O100(20/92/0)		1.1
1961	Min A	156	600	92	171	28	7	9	50	81-2	6	50	.285	.374	.400	102	4	17-11	.978	-4	105	34	O153(56/141/4)		-0.5
1962	Min A	158	619	97	168	33	3	14	63	88-2	8	36	.271	.367	.402	104	7	8-4	.995	6	108	102	O156(88/146/0)		0.7
1963	Min A	145	280	41	67	10	1	4	27	31-1	2	21	.239	.315	.325	80	-7	11-5	.988	-4	101	22	O119(15/118/0)		-1.4
1964	Min A	26	15	3	0	0	0	0	0	0-0	0	6	.000	.211	.000	-35	-3	0-1	1.000	-0	72	0	O7(6/1/0)		-0.3
	LA A	39	92	13	23	2	0	2	4	10-0	1	8	.250	.327	.337	96	-1	2-0	.977	-1	94	78	O23(11/13/0)		0.2
	Bal A	14	21	0	4	0	0	0	1	7-1	0	3	.190	.393	.190	69	0	1-0	1.000	2	195	0	O8(2/6/0)		0.9
	Year	79	128	16	27	2	0	2	5	21-1	1	17	.211	.325	.273	72	-4	3-1	.985	1	113	61	O38(19/20/0)		0.2
1965	Bos A	119	373	69	103	24	6	7	24	48-0	3	43	.276	.361	.429	117	10	8-2	.980	-0	106	52	O95(12/86/0)		-0.5
1966	Bos A	85	133	18	32	6	0	1	12	15-1	2	19	.241	.325	.308	76	-3	0-1	.978	-1	84	227	O27(4/23/0)		-0.5
1967	Det A	58	151	22	42	8	1	1	13	9-0	0	17	.278	.317	.364	99	0	1-1	.983	-2	93	0	O44(43/2/0)		0.0
1968	Det A	6	4	0	1	0	0	0	0	1-1	0	0	.250	.400	.250	98	0	0-0	—	-0	0	0	O2L		0.0
Total	12	1136	2956	461	788	138	27	47	253	368-12	29	260	.267	.351	.379	99	5	78-41	.984	2	105	71	O883(331/683/44)		-2.1

GREEN, NICK Nicholas Anthony B9.10.1978 Pensacola FL BR/TR/6-0/180* [AtlN98 32/971] d5.15 Col Georgia Perimeter JC [DL 2002 Atl N 23]

2004	†Atl N	95	264	40	72	15	3	3	26	12-1	4	63	.273	.312	.386	79	-9	1-2	.977	5	109	107	2b75,b5/OR		-0.1
2005	TB A	111	318	53	76	15	2	5	29	33-0	11	86	.239	.329	.346	83	-7	3-1	.988	-25	84	70	2b91,3b13/OR		-2.7
Total	2	206	582	93	148	30	5	8	55	45-1	15	149	.254	.321	.364	81	-16	4-3	.983	-20	95	86	2b166,3b18,O2R	23	-2.8

GREEN, DICK Richard Larry B4.21.1941 Sioux City IA BR/TR/5-10/180* d9.9

1963	KC A	13	37	5	10	2	1	0	4	2-0	1	10	.270	.317	.405	98	0	0-0	.941	3	138	85	S6,2b4		0.3
1964	KC A	130	435	48	115	14	5	11	37	27-3	3	87	.264	.311	.395	92	-5	3-3	.990	13	112	82	2b120		1.8
1965	KC A	133	474	64	110	15	1	15	55	50-1	3	110	.232	.308	.363	92	-5	0-2	.980	-7	101	87	2b126		-0.3
1966	KC A	140	507	58	127	24	3	9	62	27-4	7	101	.250	.297	.363	92	-6	6-1	.979	-6	101	92	2b137,3b2		0.1
1967	KC A	122	349	26	69	12	4	5	37	30-1	0	68	.198	.260	.298	67	-15	6-3	.946	-4	88	61	3b59,2b50/1S		-1.7
1968	Oak A	76	202	19	47	6	0	6	26	18-1	0	41	.233	.307	.351	104	1	3-1	.974	7	107	113	2b61/C3		1.4
1969	Oak A	136	483	61	133	25	6	12	64	53-3	8	94	.275	.353	.427	123	15	2-3	.986	-4	99	111	2b131		2.0
1970	Oak A	135	384	34	73	7	0	4	29	38-5	3	73	.190	.267	.240	42	-31	3-0	.978	-3	99	96	2b127,3b5/C		-2.7
1971	†Oak A	144	475	58	116	14	1	12	49	51-14	3	83	.244	.320	.354	93	-5	1-1	.986	3	97	114	2b143/S		0.9
1972	†Oak A	26	42	1	12	1	1	0	3	3-0	1	5	.286	.348	.357	115	1	0-1	.964	-1	105	95	2b26	117	0.1
1973	†Oak A	133	332	33	87	17	0	3	42	21-0	2	63	.262	.308	.340	87	-6	0-2	.988	-0	102	123	2b133/S3		0.0
1974	†Oak A	100	287	20	61	8	2	2	22	22-0	0	50	.213	.269	.275	60	-15	2-3	.983	8	105	111	2b100	66	-0.2
Total	12	1288	4007	427	960	145	23	80	422	345-34	32	785	.240	.303	.347	87	-71	26-20	.983	8	101	102	2b1158,3b68,S9,C2/1	183	1.7

GREEN, SHAWN Shawn David B11.10.1972 Des Plaines IL BL/TL/6-4/195* [TorA91 1/16] d9.28

1993	Tor A	3	6	0	0	0	0	0	0	0-0	0	1	.000	.000	.000	-98	-2	0-0	1.000	-0	62	0	O2R/D		-0.2
1994	Tor A	14	33	1	3	1	0	0	1	1-0	0	8	.091	.118	.121	-38	-7	1-0	1.000	0	68	325	O14(10/0/5)		-0.7
1995	Tor A	121	379	52	109	31	4	15	54	20-3	3	68	.288	.326	.509	114	6	1-2	.973	5	107	135	O109R		0.5
1996	Tor A	132	422	52	118	32	3	11	45	33-3	4	75	.280	.342	.448	99	-1	5-1	.992	8	111	124	O91(45/0/46),D35		0.2
1997	Tor A	135	429	57	123	22	4	16	53	36-4	1	99	.287	.340	.469	109	5	14-3	.984	4	106	116	O90(10/0/32),D35		1.0
1998	Tor A	158	630	106	175	33	4	35	100	50-2	5	142	.278	.334	.510	115	6	35-12	.979	1	100	132	O157(0/32/128)		1.8
1999	Tor A★	153	614	134	190	45	4	42	123	66-4	11	117	.309	.384	.588	141	39	20-7	.997	5	112	47	O152R		3.4
2000	LA N	162	610	98	164	44	4	24	99	90-9	8	121	.269	.367	.472	116	17	24-5	.980	-9	88	88	O161(0/1/161)		0.3
2001	LA N	161	619	121	184	31	4	49	125	72-10	5	107	.297	.372	.598	155	49	20-4	.982	-2	100	77	O159(0/2/159)/1		4.0
2002	LA N★	158	582	110	166	31	1	42	114	93-22	5	112	.285	.385	.558	158	47	8-5	.994	3	106	66	O157R,D2		4.1
2003	LA N	160	611	84	171	49	2	19	85	68-2	6	112	.280	.355	.460	114	14	6-2	.982	-7	88	91	O157R,D2		-0.1
2004	†LA N	157	590	92	157	28	1	28	86	71-6	8	114	.266	.352	.459	109	8	5-2	.995	-5	98	46	O155(0/41/135)		-1.3
2005	Ari N	158	581	87	166	37	4	22	73	62-6	5	95	.286	.355	.477	112	11	8-4	1.000	-5	98	0	1b111,O52R,D3		0.7
Total	13	1672	6106	1046	1726	384	31	303	958	662-71	65	1171	.283	.356	.505	122	198	147-47	.987	-7	100	89	O1492(55/78/1389),1b112,D43		11.7

GREENBERG, ADAM Adam Daniel B2.21.1981 New Haven CT BL/TL/5-9/180 d7.9 Col North Carolina

2005	Chi N	1	0	0	0	0	0	0	0	0-0	1	0	—	1.000	—	187	0	0-0	—	0		/H	18	0.0

GREENBERG, HANK Henry Benjamin "Hammerin' Hank" B1.1.1911 New York NY D9.4.1986 Beverly Hills CA BR/TR/6-3.5/210 d9.14 Mil 1941-45 HF1956

1930	Det A	1	1	0	0	0	0	0	0	0-0	0	0	.000	.000	.000	-98	-0	0-0	—	0		/H		0.0
1933	Det A	117	449	59	135	33	3	12	87	46	1	78	.301	.367	.468	118	11	6-2	.988	1	103	129	1b117		0.2
1934	†Det A	153	593	118	201	63	7	26	139	63	2	93	.339	.404	.600	156	49	9-5	.990	1	101	102	1b153		3.3
1935	†Det A	152	619	121	203	46	16	36	170	87	0	91	.328	.411	.628	171	64	4-3	.992	6	114	118	1b152		5.0
1936	Det A	12	46	10	16	6	2	1	16	9	0	6	.348	.455	.630	165	7	1-0	.992	1	136	135	1b12		0.4
1937	Det A☆	154	594	137	200	49	14	40	183	102	3	101	.337	.436	.668	171	65	8-3	.992	5	115	98	1b154		5.1
1938	Det A★	155	556	144	175	23	4	58	146	119	3	92	.315	.438	.683	167	58	7-5	.991	7	118	103	1b155		4.5
1939	Det A★	138	500	112	156	42	7	33	112	91	2	95	.312	.420	.622	152	40	8-3	.993	-2	90	97	1b136		2.4
1940	†Det A★	148	573	129	195	50	8	41	150	93	1	75	.340	.433	.670	166	57	6-3	.954	-1	95	133	O148L		4.5
1941	Det A	19	67	12	18	5	1	2	12	16	0	12	.269	.410	.463	118	-2	1-0	.914	-3	86	0	O19L		-0.1
1945	†Det A★	78	270	47	84	20	2	13	60	42	1	40	.311	.404	.544	164	23	3-1	1.000	-5	89	48	O72L		1.5
1946	Det A	142	523	91	145	29	5	44	127	80	0	88	.277	.373	.604	160	41	5-1	.989	2	100	99	1b140		3.9
1947	Pit N	125	402	71	100	13	2	25	74	104	4	73	.249	.408	.478	131	22	0	.992	1	104	86	1b119		1.9
Total	13	1394	5193	1051	1628	379	71	331	1276	852	16	844	.313	.412	.605	157	437	58-26	.991	11	106	104	1b1138,O239L		32.6

GREENE, ALTAR Altar Alphonse B11.9.1954 Detroit MI BL/TR/5-11/190 d7.23 Col Northwood

1979	Det A	29	59	9	8	1	0	0	6	10-1	0	15	.136	.257	.305	50	-4	0-1	1.000	1	203	0	O15,O6(4/0/2)		-0.4

GREENE, CHARLIE Charles Patrick B1.23.1971 Miami FL BR/TR/6-2/185(170-190) [SDN91 19/497] d9.15 Col Miami-Dade Kendall (FL) CC

1996	NY N	2	1	0	0	0	0	0	0	0-0	0	1	.000	.000	.000	-99	-0	0-0	1.000	0		/C		0.0
1997	Bal A	5	2	0	0	0	0	0	0	0-0	0	0	.000	.000	.000	-99	-1	0-0	1.000	0		C4		-0.1
1998	Bal A	13	21	1	4	0	0	0	1	0-0	0	8	.190	.190	.238	11	-3	0-0	1.000	3	499	45	C13		0.1
1999	Mil N	32	42	4	8	1	0	0	5	5-0	0	11	.190	.271	.214	26	-5	0-0	.991	-1	70	82	C31		-0.5
2000	Tor A	3	9	0	1	0	0	0	2	0-0	0	5	.111	.111	.111	-42	-2	0-0	1.000	0	0	0	C3		-0.2
Total	5	55	75	5	13	2	0	0	9	5-0	0	25	.173	.222	.200	10	-11	0-0	.995	2	177	62	C52		-0.7

GREENE, JUNE Julius Foust B6.25.1899 Ramseur NC D3.19.1974 Glendora CA BL/TR/6-2.5/185 d4.20 ▲

1928	Phi N	11	6	0	3	0	0	0	3	0-0	1	1	.500	.667	.500	202	2	0	1.000	4	429	0	/P		0.0
1929	Phi N	21	19	1	4	1	0	0	5	1-0	0	4	.211	.286	.263	35	0	0	1.000	1	128	0	P5		0.0
Total	2	32	25	1	7	1	0	0	5	1-0	1	5	.280	.400	.320	79	2	0	1.000	1	166	0	P6		0.0

YEAR	TM	LG	G	AB	R	H	2B	3B	HR	RBI	BB-IB	HP	SO	AVG	OBP	SLG	AOPS	ABR	SB-CS	FA	FR	RNG	THR	GAMES AT POSITION	DL	BFW

GREENE, KHALIL Khalil Thabit B10.21.1979 Butler PA BR/TR/5-11/210* [SDN02 1/13] d9.3 Col Clemson

YEAR	TM	LG	G	AB	R	H	2B	3B	HR	RBI	BB-IB	HP	SO	AVG	OBP	SLG	AOPS	ABR	SB-CS	FA	FR	RNG	THR	GAMES AT POSITION	DL	BFW
2003	SD	N	20	65	8	14	4	1	2	6	4-0	1	19	.215	.271	.400	79	-2	0-1	.963	0	100	96	S20		-0.1
2004	SD	N	139	484	67	132	31	4	15	65	53-10	8	94	.273	.349	.446	111	8	4-2	.965	-6	98	103	S136		1.2
2005	†SD	N	121	436	51	109	30	2	15	70	25-3	6	93	.250	.296	.431	93	-6	5-0	.971	-12	94	86	S121	37	-0.8
Total	3		280	985	126	255	65	7	32	141	82-13	15	206	.259	.321	.437	101	0	9-3	.968	-18	96	95	S277	37	0.3

GREENE, PADDY Patrick Joseph "Patsy" (aka Patrick Foley in 1902) B3.20.1875 Providence RI D10.20.1934 Providence RI BR/TR/5-8/150 d9.10 Col Villanova

YEAR	TM	LG	G	AB	R	H	2B	3B	HR	RBI	BB-IB	HP	SO	AVG	OBP	SLG	AOPS	ABR	SB-CS	FA	FR	RNG	THR	GAMES AT POSITION	DL	BFW
1902	Phi	N	19	65	6	11	1	0	1	2	1			.169	.206	.185	21	-6	2	.912	0	104	78	3b19		-0.6
1903	NY	A	4	13	1	4	1	0	0	0	0			.308	.308	.385	100	0	0	1.000	1	191	0	3b2/S		0.1
	Det	A	1	3	0	0	0	0	0	0	0			.000	.000	.000	-99	-1	0	.750	-1	0	0	/3		-0.2
	Year		5	16	1	4	1	0	0	0	0			.250	.250	.313	65	-1	0	.933	0	135	0	3b3/S		-0.1
Total	2		24	81	7	15	2	0	1	2	1			.185	.214	.210	30	-7	2	.916	1	109	64	3b22/S		-0.7

GREENE, TODD Todd Anthony B5.8.1971 Augusta GA BR/TR/5-10/208* [CalA93 12/327] d7.30 Col Georgia Southern

YEAR	TM	LG	G	AB	R	H	2B	3B	HR	RBI	BB-IB	HP	SO	AVG	OBP	SLG	AOPS	ABR	SB-CS	FA	FR	RNG	THR	GAMES AT POSITION	DL	BFW
1996	Cal	A	29	79	9	15	1	0	2	9	4-0	1	11	.190	.238	.278	30	-9	2-0	1.000	0	83	142	C26/D		-0.6
1997	Ana	A	34	124	24	36	6	0	9	24	7-1	0	25	.290	.328	.556	125	4	2-0	1.000	-3	108	78	C26,D8	39	0.3
1998	Ana	A	29	71	3	18	4	0	1	7	2-0	0	14	.254	.274	.352	60	-4	0-0	1.000	-2	68	0	C12,1b3,D4	127	-0.6
1999	Ana	A	97	321	36	78	20	0	14	42	12-0	3	63	.243	.275	.436	78	-12	1-4	.974	-5	67	54	D44,O30(5/0/25),C12		-2.0
2000	Tor	A	34	85	11	20	2	0	5	10	5-0	0	18	.235	.278	.435	74	-4	0-0	1.000	-1	27	0	D23,C2/OL	14	-0.5
2001	NY	A	35	96	9	20	4	0	1	11	3-0	1	21	.208	.240	.281	36	-9	0-0	1.000	-6	46	78	C34,D2		-1.3
2002	Tex	A	42	112	15	30	5	0	10	19	2-0	1	23	.268	.282	.580	119	2	0-0	.989	3	55	98	C15,1b15/OLD		0.5
2003	Tex	A	62	205	25	47	10	1	10	20	2-0	2	47	.229	.243	.434	90	-10	0-0	.987	-8	72	160	C51,1b2,D3	15	-1.4
2004	Col	N	75	195	23	55	14	0	10	35	13-4	0	38	.282	.325	.508	99	0	0-0	.989	-14	91	70	C53	24	-1.1
2005	Col	N	38	126	10	32	4	0	7	23	7-0	1	21	.254	.299	.452	81	-4	0-0	.975	-14	60	63	C33	72	-1.6
Total	10		475	1414	165	351	70	1	69	200	57-5	9	287	.248	.281	.446	81	-46	5-4	.991	-48	77	104	C252,D89,O44(19/0/25),1b20	291	-8.3

GREENE, WILLIE Willie Louis B9.23.1971 Milledgeville GA BL/TR/5-11/192(160-192) [PitN89 1/18] d9.1

YEAR	TM	LG	G	AB	R	H	2B	3B	HR	RBI	BB-IB	HP	SO	AVG	OBP	SLG	AOPS	ABR	SB-CS	FA	FR	RNG	THR	GAMES AT POSITION	DL	BFW
1992	Cin	N	29	93	10	25	4	1	2	13	10-0	0	23	.269	.337	.430	114	-4	0-2	.948	-2	83	155	3b25		-0.1
1993	Cin	N	15	50	7	8	1	1	2	5	2-0	0	19	.160	.189	.340	39	-5	0-0	.978	2	105	145	S10,3b5	44	-0.2
1994	Cin	N	16	37	5	8	2	0	0	3	6-1	0	14	.216	.318	.270	58	-2	0-0	.958	-1	104	64	3b13/OL		-0.3
1995	Cin	N	8	19	1	2	0	0	0	0	3-0	0	7	.105	.227	.105	-9	-3	0-0	1.000	-0	106	113	3b7		-0.3
1996	Cin	N	115	287	48	70	5	5	19	63	36-6	0	88	.244	.327	.495	111	3	0-1	.927	10	121	129	3b74,O10(9/0/1),1b2/S		-0.3
1997	Cin	N	151	495	62	125	22	5	26	91	78-5	1	111	.253	.354	.459	109	7	6-0	.934	-11	90	43	3b103,O39(6/0/33),1b7,S3	15	1.3
1998	Cin	N	111	356	57	96	18	1	14	49	56-2	3	80	.270	.372	.444	113	8	6-3	.936	-2	93	161	3b76,O28(9/0/22),S2/D		0.6
	Bal	A	24	40	8	6	1	0	1	5	13-0	0	10	.150	.358	.250	63	-2	1-0	.941	-1	72	132	O14(1/0/13)/D		-0.3
1999	Tor	A	81	226	22	46	7	0	12	41	20-0	0	56	.204	.266	.394	65	-13	0-0	.917	-2	62	0	D51,3b7,O3R		-1.7
2000	Chi	N	105	299	34	60	15	2	10	37	36-3	2	69	.201	.289	.365	65	-17	4-0	.967	5	108	124	3b90	27	-1.0
Total	9		655	1902	254	446	76	12	86	307	260-16	6	477	.234	.326	.423	93	-22	17-6	.943	-1	100	107	3b400,O95(26/0/72),D53,S16,1b9	86	-2.3

GREENGRASS, JIM James Raymond B10.24.1927 Addison NY BR/TR/6-1/200* d9.9

YEAR	TM	LG	G	AB	R	H	2B	3B	HR	RBI	BB-IB	HP	SO	AVG	OBP	SLG	AOPS	ABR	SB-CS	FA	FR	RNG	THR	GAMES AT POSITION	DL	BFW
1952	Cin	N	18	68	10	21	2	1	5	24	7	0	12	.309	.373	.588	163	5	0-0	.965	-1	110	0	O17(4/13/0)		0.4
1953	Cin	N	154	606	86	173	24	7	20	100	47	3	83	.285	.340	.444	102	0	6-4	.983	3	110	0	O153L		-0.6
1954	Cin	N	139	542	79	152	27	4	27	95	41	0	81	.280	.329	.494	109	5	0-3	.968	3	105	101	O137L		-0.2
1955	Cin	N	13	39	1	4	2	0	0	1	9-0	0	9	.103	.271	.154	16	-5	0-0	1.000	1	125	111	O11L		-0.4
	Phi	N	94	323	43	88	20	2	12	37	33-2	1	43	.272	.339	.458	112	6	0-2	.988	3	106	151	O83(5/0/79),3b2		0.4
	Year		107	362	44	92	22	2	12	38	42-2	1	52	.254	.331	.425	100	1	0-2	.990	4	108	146	O94(16/0/79),3b2		0.0
1956	Phi	N	86	215	24	44	9	2	5	25	28-3	0	43	.205	.294	.335	71	-9	0-0	.991	-0	105	63	O62R		-1.1
Total	5		504	1793	243	482	82	16	69	282	165-5	4	271	.269	.330	.448	102	2	6-9	.980	8	108	94	O463(310/13/141),3b2		-1.5

GREENWELL, MIKE Michael Lewis B7.18.1963 Louisville KY BL/TR/6-0/200(170-205) [BosA82 3/72] d9.5 C1

YEAR	TM	LG	G	AB	R	H	2B	3B	HR	RBI	BB-IB	HP	SO	AVG	OBP	SLG	AOPS	ABR	SB-CS	FA	FR	RNG	THR	GAMES AT POSITION	DL	BFW
1985	Bos	A	17	31	10	10	1	0	4	8	3-1	0	4	.323	.382	.742	191	4	1-0	1.000	-1	74	0	O17(16/0/3)		0.2
1986	†Bos	A	31	35	4	11	2	0	4	5-0	0	7	.314	.400	.371	111	1	0-0	1.000	2	153	257	O15(8/0/7),D3		0.3
1987	Bos	A	125	412	71	135	31	6	19	89	35-1	6	40	.328	.386	.570	146	27	5-4	.971	1	98	141	O91(64/0/28),D15/C		2.2
1988	†Bos	A★	158	590	86	192	39	8	22	119	87-18	9	38	.325	.416	.531	157	49	16-8	.981	3	104	75	O147(143/0/8),D11		4.7
1989	Bos	A★	145	578	87	178	36	0	14	95	56-15	3	44	.308	.370	.443	121	18	13-5	.967	-10	76	136	O139L,D5	15	0.5
1990	†Bos	A	159	610	71	181	30	6	14	73	65-12	4	43	.297	.367	.434	118	15	8-7	.977	-3	87	130	O159L		0.6
1991	Bos	A	147	544	76	163	26	6	9	83	43-6	3	35	.300	.350	.419	107	5	15-5	.989	0	96	120	O143L/D		0.2
1992	Bos	A	49	180	16	42	2	0	2	18	18-1	2	19	.233	.307	.278	61	-9	2-3	1.000	-1	102	36	O41L,D6	120	-1.3
1993	Bos	A	146	540	77	170	38	6	13	72	54-12	4	46	.315	.379	.480	122	18	5-4	.993	-1	98	77	O134L,D10	15	1.0
1994	Bos	A	95	327	60	88	25	1	11	45	38-6	4	26	.269	.348	.453	101	1	2-2	.993	0	86	119	O84L,D6	8	-0.2
1995	†Bos	A	120	481	67	143	25	4	15	76	38-4	2	35	.297	.349	.459	106	3	9-5	.972	-7	81	133	O118L,D2	21	-0.8
1996	Bos	A	77	295	35	87	20	1	7	44	18-3	2	27	.295	.336	.441	94	-3	4-0	.973	3	96	188	O76(75/1/1)	82	-0.2
Total	12		1269	4623	657	1400	275	38	130	726	460-79	39	364	.303	.368	.463	119	129	80-43	.981	-15	92	121	O1164(1124/1/47),D59/C	261	7.2

GREENWOOD, BILL William F. B1857 Philadelphia PA D5.2.1902 Philadelphia PA BB/TL/5-7.5/180 d9.16

YEAR	TM	LG	G	AB	R	H	2B	3B	HR	RBI	BB-IB	HP	SO	AVG	OBP	SLG	AOPS	ABR	SB-CS	FA	FR	RNG	THR	GAMES AT POSITION	DL	BFW
1882	Phi	AA	7	30	8	9	1	0	0	1	1			.300	.323	.333	114	-1	0	.909	-1	0	0	O7R,2b2		-0.1
1884	Bro	AA	92	385	52	83	8	3	3		10	1		.216	.237	.275	66	-15		.900	-9	103	0	2b92/S		-1.9
1887	Bal	AA	118	495	114	130	16	6	0	65	54	1		.263	.336	.319	88	-5	71	.928	10	102	69	2b117/OL		0.7
1888	Bal	AA	115	409	69	78	13	1	0	29	30	6		.191	.256	.227	57	-18	46	.913	-17	102	54	2b86,S28/OR		-3.0
1889	Col	AA	118	414	62	93	7	10	3	49	58	5	71	.225	.327	.312	86	-6	37	.914	-2	95	84	2b118		-0.3
1890	Roc	AA	124	437	76	97	11	6	2	41	48	8		.222	.310	.288	83	-8	40	.921	1	100	114	2b123/S		-0.2
Total	6		574	2170	381	490	56	26	8	185	201	21	71	.226	.298	.287	78	-52	194	.916	-18	100	85	2b538,S30,O9(1/0/8)		-4.8

GREER, BRIAN Brian Keith B5.14.1959 Lynwood CA BR/TR/6-3/210* [SDN77 1/8] d9.13

YEAR	TM	LG	G	AB	R	H	2B	3B	HR	RBI	BB-IB	HP	SO	AVG	OBP	SLG	AOPS	ABR	SB-CS	FA	FR	RNG	THR	GAMES AT POSITION	DL	BFW
1977	SD	N	1	1	0	1	0	0	0	0	0-0	0	0	1.000	1.000	1.000	-99	0	0-0	—	0			/H		0.0
1979	SD	N	4	3	0	0	0	0	0	0	0-0	0	1	.000	.000	.000	-99	-1	0-0	1.000	-0	102	0	O4C		-0.1
Total	2		5	4	0	1	0	0	0	0	0-0	0	1	.250	.250	.250	-99	-1	0-0	1.000	-0	102	0	O4C		-0.1

GREER, ED Edward C. B1865 Philadelphia PA D2.4.1890 Philadelphia PA BR d6.24

YEAR	TM	LG	G	AB	R	H	2B	3B	HR	RBI	BB-IB	HP	SO	AVG	OBP	SLG	AOPS	ABR	SB-CS	FA	FR	RNG	THR	GAMES AT POSITION	DL	BFW
1885	Bal	AA	56	211	32	42	7	0	0	21	8	2		.199	.235	.232	49	-12		.908	-1	74	61	O47(2/38/7),C12		-1.2
1886	Bal	AA	11	38	2	5	1	0	0	4	2	0		.132	.175	.158	5	-4	4	.875	-1	207	0	O9L,C2		-0.4
	Phi	AA	71	264	33	51	5	3	1	20	8	2		.193	.223	.246	46	-17	12	.921	6	86	145	O70(0/66/4)/C		-1.2
	Year		82	302	35	56	6	3	1	24	10	2		.185	.217	.235	41	-21	16	.919	6	96	133	O79(9/66/4),C3		-1.6
1887	Phi	AA	3	11	1	2	0	0	0	0	0	0		.182	.182	.182	2	-1	2	.857	0	238	0	O3C		-0.1
	Bro	AA	91	327	49	83	13	2	2	48	25	6		.254	.318	.324	79	-9	33	.921	2	64	35	O76L,C16		-0.6
	Year		94	338	50	85	13	2	2	48	25	6		.251	.314	.320	76	-11	35	.918	2	70	34	O79(76/3/0),C16		-0.7
Total	3		232	851	117	183	26	5	3	93	43	10		.215	.261	.268	58	-43	51	.916	7	80	76	O205(87/107/11),C31		-3.5

GREER, RUSTY Thurman Clyde B1.21.1969 Fort Rucker AL BL/TL/6-0/195* [TexA90 10/279] d5.16 Col Montevallo [DL 2003 Tex A 183, 2004 Tex A 183]

YEAR	TM	LG	G	AB	R	H	2B	3B	HR	RBI	BB-IB	HP	SO	AVG	OBP	SLG	AOPS	ABR	SB-CS	FA	FR	RNG	THR	GAMES AT POSITION	DL	BFW
1994	Tex	A	80	277	36	87	16	1	10	46	46-2	2	46	.314	.410	.487	130	15	0-0	.976	-4	101	41	O73(11/23/53),1b9		0.7
1995	Tex	A	131	417	58	113	21	2	13	61	55-1	1	66	.271	.355	.424	99	0	3-1	.982	-2	95	121	O125(51/4/101),1b3		-0.7
1996	†Tex	A	139	542	96	180	41	6	18	100	62-4	3	86	.332	.397	.530	125	23	9-0	.984	2	105	62	O137(136/1/0)/1D		1.9
1997	Tex	A	157	601	112	193	42	4	26	87	83-4	8	87	.321	.405	.531	133	32	9-5	.965	-1	101	66	O153(148/19/1),D2		2.4
1998	†Tex	A	155	598	107	183	31	5	16	108	80-1	4	93	.306	.386	.455	113	14	2-4	.990	-1	100	66	O154(154/2/0)		0.6
1999	†Tex	A	147	556	107	167	41	3	20	101	96-2	5	67	.300	.405	.493	121	22	2-2	.983	-6	97	32	O145L/D		0.9
2000	Tex	A	105	394	65	117	34	3	8	65	51-1	3	61	.297	.377	.459	110	8	4-1	.985	-4	99	51	O97L,D2	43	0.9
2001	Tex	A	62	245	38	67	23	0	7	29	27-1	1	32	.273	.342	.453	106	3	1-2	.962	-1	106	54	O60L/D	118	0.0
2002	Tex	A	51	199	24	59	9	2	1	17	19-0	0	17	.296	.356	.377	93	-2	1-0	.947	-5	71	0	O26(22/0/6),D22/1	117	-0.8
Total	9		1027	3829	643	1166	258	25	119	614	519-16	22	555	.305	.387	.478	117	115	31-15	.979	-21	99	65	O970(824/49/161),D29,1b14	644	5.1

GREGG, TOMMY William Thomas B7.29.1963 Boone NC BL/TL/6-1/190* [PitN85 7/164] d9.14 Col Wake Forest

YEAR	TM	LG	G	AB	R	H	2B	3B	HR	RBI	BB-IB	HP	SO	AVG	OBP	SLG	AOPS	ABR	SB-CS	FA	FR	RNG	THR	GAMES AT POSITION	DL	BFW
1987	Pit	N	10	8	3	2	1	0	0	0-0	0	2	.250	.250	.375	62	0	0-0	1.000	-0	83	0	O4(1/2/2)		-0.1
1988	Pit	N	14	15	4	3	1	0	1	3	0-0	0	2	.200	.235	.467	102	-0	0-1	1.000	-0	71	0	O6(5/0/1)		-0.1
	Atl	N	11	29	1	10	3	0	0	4	2-1	0	2	.345	.387	.448	134	1	0-0	1.000	2	142	242	O7(5/3/0)		0.3
	Year		25	44	5	13	4	0	1	7	2-1	0	4	.295	.333	.455	125	1	0-1	1.000	2	122	174	O13(10/3/1)		0.2
1989	Atl	N	102	276	24	67	8	0	6	23	18-2	0	45	.243	.288	.337	77	-9	3-4	.967	-4	81	51	O48(7/2/41),1b37	43	-1.9

YEAR	TM LG	G	AB	R	H	2B	3B	HR	RBI	BB-IB	HP	SO	AVG	OBP	SLG	AOPS	ABR	SB-CS	FA	FR	RNG	THR	GAMES AT POSITION	DL	BFW
1990	Atl N	124	239	18	63	13	1	5	32	20-4	1	39	.264	.322	.389	90	-3	4-3	.987	1	123	101	1b50,O20(7/0/12)		-0.6
1991	†Atl N	72	107	13	20	8	1	1	4	12-2	1	24	.187	.275	.308	60	-5	2-2	1.000	0	91		O14(9/0/5),1b13	42	-0.7
1992	Atl N	18	19	1	5	0	0	1	1	1-0	0	7	.263	.300	.421	96	0	1-0	1.000	1	188	0	O9(2/4/4)	106	0.1
1993	Cin N	10	12	1	2	0	0	0	1	0-0	0	3	.167	.154	.167	-10	-2	0-0	1.000	-1	50	0	O4(3/0/1)		-0.3
1995	Fla N	72	156	20	37	5	0	6	20	16-1	2	33	.237	.313	.385	82	-4	3-1	1.000	-2	97	0	O38(6/4/30),1b2	21	-0.8
1997	†Atl N	13	19	1	5	2	0	0	0	1-0	0	2	.263	.300	.368	73	-1	1-1	1.000	-1	37	0	O6(5/0/1)/1		-0.2
Total	9	446	880	86	214	41	2	20	88	71-10	4	158	.243	.301	.363	81	-23	14-12	.981	-4	92	32	O156(50/15/97),1b103	212	-4.3

GREGORIO, TOM   Thomas Andrew   B5.5.1977 Brooklyn NY   BR/TR/6-2/200   [AnaA99 27/821]   d9.5   Col Troy St.

| 2003 | Ana A | 12 | 19 | 1 | 3 | 0 | 0 | 0 | 2 | 1-0 | 1 | 8 | .158 | .238 | .158 | 8 | -3 | 0-0 | .979 | -0 | 121 | 129 | C12 | | -0.2 |

GREMMINGER, ED   Lorenzo Edward "Battleship"   B3.30.1874 Canton OH   D5.26.1942 Canton OH   BR/TR/6-1/200   d4.21

1895	Cle N	20	78	10	21	1	0	0	15	5	0	13	.269	.313	.282	51	-6	0	.873	-1	95	119	3b20		-0.5
1902	Bos N	140	522	55	134	20	12	1	65	39	5		.257	.314	.347	103	1	7	.951	2	94	83	3b140		0.7
1903	Bos N	140	511	57	135	24	9	5	56	31	5		.264	.313	.376	100	-2	12	.935	16	106	132	3b140		1.7
1904	Det A	83	309	18	66	13	3	1	28	14	4		.214	.257	.285	73	-9	3	.950	-13	78	38	3b83		-2.4
Total	4	383	1420	140	356	58	24	7	164	89	14	13	.251	.301	.340	92	-16	22	.940	4	95	93	3b383		-0.5

GREMP, BUDDY   Lewis Edward   B8.5.1919 Denver CO   D1.30.1995 Manteca CA   BR/TR/6-1/175   d9.13   Mil 1942-45

1940	Bos N	4	9	0	2	0	0	0	2	0	0	0	.222	.222	.222	24	-1	0	1.000	-0	80	117	1b3		-0.1
1941	Bos N	37	75	7	18	3	0	0	10	5	0	3	.240	.287	.280	63	-4	0	.977	-3	59	115	1b21,2b6,C3		-0.9
1942	Bos N	72	207	12	45	11	0	3	19	13	1	21	.217	.267	.314	71	-8	1	.991	1	108	10	1b62/3		-1.3
Total	3	113	291	19	65	14	0	3	31	18	1	24	.223	.271	.302	67	-13	1	.988	-3	96	38	1b86,2b6,C3/3		-2.3

GREY, REDDY   Romer Carl (b Romer Carl Gray)   B4.8.1875 Zanesville OH   D11.9.1934 Altadena CA   BL/TL/5-11/175   d5.28

| 1903 | Pit N | 1 | 3 | 1 | 1 | 0 | 0 | 0 | 1 | 1 | 0 | 0 | .333 | .500 | .333 | 135 | 0 | 0 | 1.000 | -0 | 0 | 0 | /OL | | 0.0 |

GRICH, BOBBY   Robert Anthony   B1.15.1949 Muskegon MI   BR/TR/6-2/190*   [BalA67 1/19]   d6.29

1970	Bal A	30	95	11	20	1	3	0	8	9-0	0	21	.211	.279	.284	55	-6	1-1	.915	2	101	49	S20,2b9/3		-0.2
1971	Bal A	7	30	7	9	0	1	0	6	5-0	0	8	.300	.400	.400	126	1	1-0	1.000	3	149	73	S5,2b2		0.5
1972	Bal A★	133	460	66	128	21	3	12	50	53-3	7	96	.278	.358	.415	126	16	13-6	.950	-6	97	126	S81,2b45,1b16,3b8		2.4
1973	†Bal A	162	581	82	146	29	7	12	50	107-3	7	91	.251	.373	.387	114	16	17-9	.995	27	114	129	2b162		5.4
1974	†Bal A	160	582	92	153	29	6	19	82	90-6	20	117	.263	.376	.431	136	32	17-11	.979	16	108	114	2b160		6.0
1975	Bal A	150	524	81	136	26	4	13	57	107-4	8	88	.260	.389	.399	131	29	14-10	.985	6	101	103	2b140,3b2,D2		6.5
1976	Bal A	144	518	93	138	31	4	13	54	86-1	3	99	.266	.373	.417	139	30	14-6	.985	6	101	103	2b140,3b2,D2		4.8
1977	Cal A	52	181	24	44	6	0	7	23	37-4	1	40	.243	.369	.392	113	5	6-6	.983	-3	89	74	S52	116	0.6
1978	Cal A	144	487	68	122	16	2	6	42	75-1	7	83	.251	.353	.329	97	2	4-3	.983	0	96	82	2b144		1.0
1979	†Cal A	153	534	78	157	30	5	30	101	59-10	7	84	.294	.365	.537	144	33	1-0	.984	-1	93	102	2b153		3.9
1980	Cal A★	150	498	60	135	22	2	14	62	84-2	4	108	.271	.377	.408	118	16	3-7	.989	4	102	91	2b146,1b3		2.6
1981	Cal A	100	352	56	107	14	2	22	61	40-4	4	71	.304	.378	.543	162	28	2-4	.983	18	113	122	2b100	59	5.2
1982	†Cal A	145	506	74	132	28	5	19	65	82-3	8	109	.261	.371	.449	123	19	3-3	.986	17	108	120	2b142/D		4.2
1983	Cal A	120	387	65	113	17	0	16	62	76-2	7	62	.292	.414	.460	142	27	2-4	.969	18	122	106	2b118/S		4.9
1984	Cal A	116	363	60	93	15	1	18	58	57-3	2	70	.256	.357	.452	123	13	2-5	.982	-3	99	120	2b91,1b25,3b21		1.2
1985	Cal A	144	479	74	116	17	3	13	53	81-3	3	77	.242	.355	.372	99	2	3-5	.997	12	110	135	2b116,1b16,3b15,D6		1.8
1986	Cal A	98	313	42	84	18	0	9	30	39-1	3	54	.268	.354	.412	109	5	1-3	.980	-9	95	106	2b87,1b11,3b2	34	-0.1
Total	17	2008	6890	1033	1833	320	47	224	864	1087-50	86	1278	.266	.371	.424	124	268	104-83	.984	126	106	112	2b1765,S159,1b71,3b49,D9	209	50.7

GRIESENBECK, TIM   Carlos Phillipe Timothy   B12.10.1897 San Antonio TX   D3.25.1953 San Antonio TX   BR/TR/5-10.5/190   d9.11   Col Texas A&M-Commerce

| 1920 | StL N | 5 | 3 | 1 | 1 | 0 | 0 | 0 | 0 | 0 | 0 | 0 | .333 | .333 | .333 | 95 | 0 | 0-0 | 1.000 | 0 | 0 | 0 | C3 | | 0.0 |

GRIEVE, BEN   Benjamin   B5.4.1976 Arlington TX   BL/TR/6-4/230(200-230)   [OakA94 1/2]   d9.3   f-Tom

1997	Oak A	24	93	12	29	6	0	3	24	13-1	1	25	.312	.402	.473	127	4	0-0	1.000	-2	78	63	O24R		0.1
1998	Oak A★	155	583	94	168	41	6	18	89	85-3	9	123	.288	.386	.458	120	21	2-2	.993	-10	88	64	O151R,D3		0.3
1999	Oak A	148	486	80	129	21	0	28	86	63-2	8	108	.265	.358	.481	115	11	4-0	.988	-2	96	77	O137(131/0/8),D4		0.5
2000	†Oak A	158	594	92	166	40	1	27	104	73-2	3	130	.279	.359	.487	114	13	3-0	.988	-10	84	73	O144L,D12		-0.2
2001	TB A	154	542	72	143	30	2	11	72	87-2	8	159	.264	.372	.387	103	6	7-1	.984	0	106	55	O120(56/0/64),D32		0.1
2002	TB A	136	482	62	121	30	0	19	64	69-5	8	121	.251	.353	.432	110	9	8-2	.988	0	103	79	O118R,D16		0.3
2003	TB A	55	165	28	38	7	0	4	17	32-1	6	41	.230	.371	.345	94	0	0-0	.947	-0	86	175	D37,O10R	107	-0.2
2004	Mil N	108	234	28	61	15	0	7	29	39-5	0	65	.261	.364	.415	100	1	0-0	.964	-3	102	0	O65R		-0.4
	Chi N	15	16	2	4	2	0	1	6	0-0	2	5	.250	.316	.563	122	1	0-0	1.000	0	104	0	O4(1/0/3)/D		-0.4
	Year	123	250	30	65	17	0	8	35	39-5	2	70	.260	.361	.424	102	2	0-0	.965	-3	102	0	O69(1/0/68)/D		-0.4
2005	Chi N	23	20	1	5	0	0	1	5	1-0	0	7	.250	.400	.250	73	-1	0-0	—	0	0	0	/OL		-0.1
Total	9	976	3215	471	864	192	5	118	492	466-22	45	784	.269	.367	.442	111	65	24-5	.986	-27	95	65	O774(333/0/443),D105	107	0.4

GRIEVE, TOM   Thomas Alan   B3.4.1948 Pittsfield MA   BR/TR/6-2/190*   [TexA66 1/6]   d7.5   s-Ben

1970	Was A	47	116	12	23	5	1	3	10	14-0	1	38	.198	.290	.336	75	-4	0-0	.939	-4	82	0	O39(15/1/24)		-1.0
1972	Tex A	64	142	12	29	2	1	3	11	11-1	2	39	.204	.271	.296	71	-6	1-3	.985	1	89	216	O49(45/3/5)		-0.8
1973	Tex A	66	123	22	38	6	0	7	21	7-0	1	26	.309	.348	.528	150	7	1-0	1.000	-3	92	0	O59(34/10/19)/D		0.3
1974	Tex A	84	259	30	66	10	4	9	32	20-1	2	48	.255	.311	.429	114	4	0-0	1.000	3	99	232	D40,O38(31/0/7)/1		0.4
1975	Tex A	118	369	46	102	17	1	14	61	22-0	0	74	.276	.316	.442	114	5	0-2	.990	-4	83	73	O63(46/2/16),D45		-0.4
1976	Tex A	149	546	57	139	23	3	20	81	35-5	4	119	.255	.301	.418	108	3	4-1	.983	2	107	110	D96,O52(45/0/8)		0.1
1977	Tex A	79	236	24	53	9	0	7	30	13-1	3	57	.225	.273	.352	68	-11	1-0	.976	-3	76	136	O60(30/0/32),D13	41	-1.7
1978	NY N	54	101	5	21	3	0	2	8	9-0	0	23	.208	.273	.297	61	-6	0-1	.979	3	120	195	O26(2/0/24),1b2		-0.4
1979	StL N	9	15	1	3	1	0	0	0	4-1	0	1	.200	.368	.267	75	0	0-0	.875	-1	89	0	O5L		-0.1
Total	9	670	1907	200	474	65	10	65	254	135-9	13	424	.249	.301	.401	100	-7	7-7	.982	-4	91	113	O391(253/16/135),D195,1b3	41	-3.6

GRIFFEY, KEN   George Kenneth Jr. "Junior"   B11.21.1969 Donora PA   BL/TL/6-3/205(195-220)   [SeaA87 1/1]   d4.3   f-Ken

1989	Sea A	127	455	61	120	23	0	16	61	44-8	2	83	.264	.329	.420	107	4	16-7	.969	0	95	184	O127C	27	0.4
1990	Sea A★	155	597	91	179	28	7	22	80	63-12	2	81	.300	.366	.481	134	27	16-11	.980	-11	87	108	O151C,D2		1.4
1991	Sea A★	154	548	76	179	42	1	22	100	71-21	1	82	.327	.399	.527	155	44	18-6	.989	3	96	202	O152C/D		4.6
1992	Sea A★	142	565	83	174	39	4	27	103	44-15	5	67	.308	.361	.535	147	34	10-5	.997	-2	97	105	O137C,D3	16	3.1
1993	Sea A★	156	582	113	180	38	3	45	109	96-25	6	91	.309	.408	.617	166	59	17-9	.991	-7	89	159	O150C,D19/1		5.1
1994	Sea A★	111	433	94	140	24	4	40	90	56-19	2	73	.323	.402	.674	167	43	11-3	.983	1	91	239	O103(0/103/1),D9	80	4.2
1995	†Sea A★	72	260	52	67	7	0	17	42	52-6	0	53	.258	.379	.481	121	9	4-2	.990	6	115	157	O70C,D2	23	1.5
1996	Sea A★	140	545	125	165	26	2	49	140	78-13	7	104	.303	.392	.628	153	44	16-1	.993	5	109	122	O137C,D5		4.8
1997	†Sea A★	157	608	125	185	34	3	56	147	76-23	8	121	.304	.382	.646	164	56	15-4	.985	4	106	122	O153(1/153/0),D4		6.0
1998	Sea A★	161	633	120	180	33	3	56	146	76-11	7	121	.284	.365	.611	147	47	20-5	.988	8	108	107	O158(1/158/1)/1D		5.0
1999	Sea A★	160	606	123	173	26	3	48	134	91-17	7	108	.285	.384	.576	142	38	24-7	.978	-1	101	106	O158C,D6		3.9
2000	Cin N★	145	520	100	141	22	3	40	118	94-17	9	117	.271	.387	.556	132	26	6-4	.987	2	106	103	O141C		2.8
2001	Cin N	111	364	57	104	20	2	22	65	44-6	4	72	.286	.365	.533	122	12	2-0	.985	-10	89	0	O90C,D2	47	0.3
2002	Cin N	70	197	17	52	8	0	8	23	28-6	2	39	.264	.358	.426	107	2	1-2	.971	-5	78	139	O55(1/54/1)	74	-0.4
2003	Cin N	53	166	34	41	12	1	13	26	27-5	1	44	.247	.370	.566	147	12	1-0	.989	-2	89	159	O43C,D3	110	1.0
2004	Cin N★	83	300	49	76	18	0	20	60	44-3	2	67	.253	.351	.513	123	10	1-0	.994	-2	94	104	O77(0/76/1)/D	76	0.7
2005	Cin N	128	491	85	148	30	0	35	92	54-3	2	93	.301	.369	.576	149	35	0-1	.990	-4	96	94	O124C,D2		3.2
Total	17	2125	7870	1405	2304	430	36	536	1536	1038-210	74	1416	.293	.377	.561	144	497	178-67	.986	-16	98	127	O2015(3/2013/4),D62,1b2	453	47.8

GRIFFEY, KEN   George Kenneth Sr.   B4.10.1950 Donora PA   BL/TL/6-0/200(185-210)   [CinN69 29/680]   d8.25   C7   s-Ken

1973	†Cin N	25	86	19	33	5	1	3	14	6-0	0	15	.384	.424	.570	180	9	4-2	1.000	-0	62	53	O21R		0.5
1974	Cin N	88	227	24	57	9	5	2	19	27-2	1	43	.251	.333	.361	96	-1	9-4	1.000	1	102	120	O70(2/0/68)		-0.3
1975	†Cin N	132	463	95	141	15	9	4	46	67-2	1	67	.305	.391	.402	119	14	16-7	.967	-8	87	73	O119R		0.1
1976	†Cin N★	148	562	111	189	28	9	6	74	62-0	1	65	.336	.401	.450	138	30	34-11	.979	-3	98	86	O144R		2.5
1977	Cin N☆	154	585	117	186	35	8	12	57	69-2	1	84	.318	.389	.467	126	23	17-8	.990	4	108	108	O154(0/13/142)		2.1
1978	Cin N	158	614	90	177	33	8	10	63	54-6	3	70	.288	.346	.417	112	7	23-5	.969	-1	101	108	O154(0/13/142)		0.4
1979	Cin N	95	380	62	120	27	4	8	32	36-3	1	39	.316	.374	.471	130	16	12-5	.984	-3	94	103	O93(0/8/92)	24	1.0
1980	Cin N★	146	544	89	160	28	10	13	85	62-4	1	77	.294	.370	.454	130	23	23-7	.978	-3	106	111	O138(0/2/138)		1.8
1981	Cin N	101	396	65	123	21	6	2	34	39-6	1	42	.311	.370	.409	123	12	12-4	.989	5	109	123	O99C		1.9
1982	NY A	127	484	70	134	23	2	12	54	39-1	0	58	.277	.329	.407	103	2	10-4	.983	4	108	96	O125(0/26/102)		0.1

YEAR	TM LG	G	AB	R	H	2B	3B	HR	RBI	BB-IB	HP	SO	AVG	OBP	SLG	AOPS	ABR	SB-CS	FA	FR	RNG	THR	GAMES AT POSITION	DL	BFW
1983	NY A	118	458	60	140	21	3	11	46	34-3	2	45	.306	.355	.437	120	12	6-1	.992	1	98	99	1b101,O14(2/12/1),D2	31	0.8
1984	NY A	120	399	44	109	20	1	7	56	29-2	1	32	.273	.321	.381	97	-1	2-2	.974	-0	105	124	O82(38/35/9),1b27,D2		-0.6
1985	NY A	127	438	68	120	28	4	10	69	41-4	0	51	.274	.331	.425	109	5	7-7	.970	5	109	128	O110(106/5/1)/1D		0.5
1986	NY A	59	198	33	60	7	0	9	26	15-0	1	24	.303	.349	.475	124	6	2-2	.971	2	103	167	O51(50/2/1),D2		0.6
	Atl N	80	292	36	90	15	3	12	32	20-4	0	43	.308	.351	.503	127	10	12-7	.986	-2	95	20	O77L/1		0.5
1987	Atl N	122	399	65	114	24	1	14	64	46-11	1	54	.286	.358	.456	110	7	4-7	.995	-3	90	97	O107(107/1/0),1b3	5	-0.2
1988	Atl N	69	193	21	48	5	0	2	19	17-2	0	26	.249	.307	.306	74	-6	1-3	.969	-4	79	83	O42(41/0/2),1b11		-1.3
	Cin N	25	50	5	14	1	0	2	4	2-1	0	5	.280	.308	.420	103	0	0-0	.986	0	106	16	1b10		-0.1
	Year	94	243	26	62	6	0	4	23	19-3	0	31	.255	.307	.329	80	-6	1-3	.969	-3	79	83	O42(41/0/2),1b21		-1.4
1989	Cin N	106	236	26	62	8	3	8	30	29-3	1	42	.263	.346	.424	115	5	4-2	.987	-6	79	74	O58(58/0/1),1b9		-0.3
1990	Cin N	46	63	6	13	2	0	1	8	2-0	1	5	.206	.235	.286	43	-5	2-1	.979	1	113	60	1b9,O6(5/0/1)		-0.5
	Sea A	21	77	13	29	2	0	3	18	10-0	1	3	.377	.443	.519	168	7	0-0	.963	-2	73	93	O20L		0.5
1991	Sea A	30	85	10	24	7	0	1	9	13-0	1	13	.282	.380	.400	117	3	0-0	1.000	-3	75	0	O26L/D		-0.1
Total	19	2097	7229	1129	2143	364	77	152	859	719-51	14	898	.296	.359	.431	118	180	200-83	.981	-17	99	91	O1703(532/203/989),1b172,D14	211	9.9

GRIFFIN, ALFREDO
Alfredo Claudino (b Alfredo Claudino Baptist (Griffin)) B10.6.1957 Santo Domingo, D.R. BB/TR/5-11/165(151-167) d9.4 C8

YEAR	TM LG	G	AB	R	H	2B	3B	HR	RBI	BB-IB	HP	SO	AVG	OBP	SLG	AOPS	ABR	SB-CS	FA	FR	RNG	THR	GAMES AT POSITION	DL	BFW
1976	Cle A	12	4	0	1	0	0	0	0	0-0	0	2	.250	.250	.250	47	0	0-1	.750	-1	51	0	S6,D4		-0.2
1977	Cle A	14	41	5	6	1	0	0	3	3-0	0	5	.146	.205	.171	4	-6	2-2	.940	-3	86	86	S13/D		-0.8
1978	Cle A	5	4	1	2	1	0	0	0	2-0	0	1	.500	.667	.750	300	1	0-0	.917	1	123	439	S2		0.3
1979	Tor A	153	624	81	179	22	10	2	31	40-0	1	59	.287	.333	.364	87	-12	21-16	.956	11	105	112	S153		1.3
1980	Tor A	155	653	63	166	26	15	2	41	24-2	4	58	.254	.283	.349	70	-29	18-23	.955	4	101	113	S155		-1.3
1981	Tor A	101	388	30	81	19	6	0	21	17-1	1	38	.209	.243	.289	50	-26	8-12	.937	-12	92	96	S97,3b4/2		-3.2
1982	Tor A	162	539	57	130	18	8	1	48	22-0	0	48	.241	.269	.314	55	-34	10-8	.968	12	100	98	S162		-0.6
1983	Tor A	162	528	62	132	22	9	4	47	27-0	3	44	.250	.289	.348	70	-23	8-11	.965	-5	93	92	S157,2b5/D		-1.4
1984	Tor A★	140	419	53	101	8	2	4	30	4-0	1	33	.241	.248	.298	44	-30	11-3	.962	-17	86	99	S115,2b21,D5		-3.4
1985	Oak A	162	614	75	166	18	7	2	64	20-1	0	50	.270	.290	.332	76	-23	24-9	.960	-10	97	85	S162		-1.4
1986	Oak A	162	594	74	169	23	6	4	51	35-6	2	52	.285	.323	.364	94	-6	33-16	.966	-8	95	83	S162		0.4
1987	Oak A	144	494	69	130	23	5	3	60	28-2	4	41	.263	.306	.348	79	-16	26-13	.963	9	100	91	S137/2		0.8
1988	†LA N	95	316	39	63	8	3	1	27	24-7	2	30	.199	.259	.253	49	-21	7-5	.965	5	101	94	S93	64	-1.1
1989	LA N	136	506	49	125	27	2	0	29	29-2	2	57	.247	.287	.308	71	-19	10-7	.975	-3	93	113	S131	20	-1.6
1990	LA N	141	461	38	97	11	3	1	35	29-11	2	65	.210	.258	.254	43	-37	6-3	.959	12	104	95	S139		-1.6
1991	LA N	109	350	27	85	6	2	0	27	22-5	1	49	.243	.286	.271	60	-19	5-4	.961	21	115	89	S109	41	0.9
1992	†Tor A	63	150	21	35	7	0	0	10	9-0	1	19	.233	.273	.280	54	-9	3-1	.981	-4	93	55	S48,2b16		-1.0
1993	†Tor A	46	95	15	20	3	0	0	13	2-1	0	11	.211	.235	.242	28	-10	0-0	.960	-2	70	74	S20,2b11,3b6	25	-1.0
Total	18	1962	6780	759	1688	245	78	24	527	338-37	25	664	.249	.285	.319	67	-319	192-134	.961	9	98	96	S1861,2b55,D11,3b10	150	-14.7

GRIFFIN, DOUG
Douglas Lee B6.4.1947 South Gate CA BR/TR/6-0/170(150-170) [AnaA65 14/538] d9.11

YEAR	TM LG	G	AB	R	H	2B	3B	HR	RBI	BB-IB	HP	SO	AVG	OBP	SLG	AOPS	ABR	SB-CS	FA	FR	RNG	THR	GAMES AT POSITION	DL	BFW
1970	Cal A	18	55	2	7	1	0	0	4	6-1	0	5	.127	.213	.145	1	-8	0-0	.964	-1	115	141	2b11,3b8		-0.9
1971	Bos A	125	483	51	118	23	2	3	27	31-3	2	45	.244	.291	.319	68	-20	11-5	.986	6	102	104	2b124	27	-0.5
1972	Bos A	129	470	43	122	12	1	2	35	45-6	2	48	.260	.325	.302	83	-9	9-2	.978	-3	92	91	2b129	23	-0.2
1973	Bos A	113	396	43	101	14	5	1	33	21-0	3	42	.255	.293	.323	70	-16	7-5	.990	-6	92	100	2b113	50	-1.5
1974	Bos A	93	310	35	83	12	4	0	33	28-3	2	21	.266	.329	.330	85	-6	2-8	.979	-13	98	82	2b99/S	62	-1.6
1975	†Bos A	100	287	21	69	6	0	1	29	18-0	1	29	.240	.288	.272	56	-17	2-2	.967	-14	91	83	2b99/S		-2.7
1976	Bos A	49	127	14	24	2	0	0	4	9-0	1	14	.189	.248	.205	30	-11	2-1	.989	-12	84	62	2b44,D2		-2.2
1977	Bos A	5	6	0	0	0	0	0	0	0-0	0	0	.000	.000	.000	-90	-2	0-0	1.000	-0	99	125	2b3		-0.2
Total	8	632	2136	209	524	70	12	7	165	158-13	12	204	.245	.299	.299	68	-89	33-23	.981	-43	95	92	2b614,3b8,D2,S2	162	-9.8

GRIFFIN, PUG
Francis Arthur B4.24.1896 Lincoln NE D10.12.1951 Colorado Springs CO BR/TR/5-11.5/187 d7.27

YEAR	TM LG	G	AB	R	H	2B	3B	HR	RBI	BB-IB	HP	SO	AVG	OBP	SLG	AOPS	ABR	SB-CS	FA	FR	RNG	THR	GAMES AT POSITION	DL	BFW
1917	Phi A	18	25	4	5	1	0	1	3	1	0	9	.200	.231	.360	81	-1	1	1.000	1	161	55	1b3		0.0
1920	NY N	5	4	0	1	0	0	0	0	1	0	2	.250	.400	.250	90	0	0-0	1.000	-0	56	0	O2(0/1/1)		0.0
Total	2	23	29	4	6	1	0	1	3	2	0	11	.207	.258	.345	83	-1	1-0	1.000	0	161	55	1b3,O2(0/1/1)		0.0

GRIFFIN, IVY
Ivy Moore B11.16.1896 Thomasville AL D8.25.1957 Gainesville GA BL/TR/5-11/180 d9.9 Col Auburn-Montgomery

YEAR	TM LG	G	AB	R	H	2B	3B	HR	RBI	BB-IB	HP	SO	AVG	OBP	SLG	AOPS	ABR	SB-CS	FA	FR	RNG	THR	GAMES AT POSITION	DL	BFW
1919	Phi A	17	68	5	20	2	0	6	3	1	0	10	.294	.333	.382	99	0	0	.989	4	182	106	1b17		0.3
1920	Phi A	129	467	46	111	15	1	0	20	17	11	49	.238	.281	.274	47	-36	3-3	.990	5	118	101	1b127,2b2		-3.4
1921	Phi A	39	103	14	33	4	2	0	13	5	3	6	.320	.369	.398	95	-1	1-2	.973	-2	82	69	1b27		-0.5
Total	3	185	638	65	164	21	5	0	39	25	15	65	.257	.301	.306	60	-37	4-5	.988	7	119	97	1b171,2b2		-3.6

GRIFFIN, JOHN-FORD
John-Ford David B11.19.1979 Sarasota FL BL/TL/6-2/215 d9.6 Col Florida St.

YEAR	TM LG	G	AB	R	H	2B	3B	HR	RBI	BB-IB	HP	SO	AVG	OBP	SLG	AOPS	ABR	SB-CS	FA	FR	RNG	THR	GAMES AT POSITION	DL	BFW
2005	Tor A	7	13	3	4	2	0	1	6	0-0	0	4	.308	.308	.692	147	1	0-0	—		0		D4		0.1

GRIFFIN, MIKE
Michael Joseph B3.20.1865 Utica NY D4.10.1908 Utica NY BL/TR/5-7/160 d4.16 M1

YEAR	TM LG	G	AB	R	H	2B	3B	HR	RBI	BB-IB	HP	SO	AVG	OBP	SLG	AOPS	ABR	SB-CS	FA	FR	RNG	THR	GAMES AT POSITION	DL	BFW
1887	Bal AA	136	532	142	160	32	13	3	94	55	8		.301	.375	.427	131	25	94	.924	-15	58	21	O136(1/135/0)		0.4
1888	Bal AA	137	542	103	139	21	11	0	46	55	5		.256	.331	.336	117	12	46	.938	5	123	117	O137C		1.2
1889	Bal AA	137	531	152	148	21	14	4	48	91	3	29	.279	.387	.394	120	17	39	.910	-12	81	108	O109C,S25,2b5		0.2
1890	Phi P	115	489	127	140	29	6	6	54	64	7	19	.286	.377	.407	107	6	30	.954	13	148	223	O54(1/100/13)		1.2
1891	Bro N	134	521	106	139	36	9	3	65	57	1	31	.267	.340	.388	113	9	65	.960	20	147	191	O134(2/132/0)		2.2
1892	Bro N	129	452	103	125	17	11	3	66	68	4	36	.277	.376	.383	134	22	49	.986	9	122	166	O127(0/126/1),S2		2.1
1893	Bro N	95	362	85	103	21	7	6	59	59	8	23	.285	.396	.431	126	16	30	.965	7	121	243	O93C,2b2		1.4
1894	Bro N	108	406	123	145	29	4	5	76	78	4	14	.357	.465	.485	139	35	39	.966	4	77	113	O107C		2.4
1895	Bro N	132	524	140	174	38	7	4	65	93	10	30	.332	.442	.454	143	44	27	.969	12	117	287	O132C/S		3.8
1896	Bro N	122	493	101	152	27	9	4	51	48	9	25	.308	.380	.424	118	15	23	.961	1	47	23	O122C		0.7
1897	Bro N	134	534	136	169	25	11	2	56	81	10		.316	.416	.416	127	27	16	.956	3	68	161	O134C		1.8
1898	Bro N	134	537	88	161	18	6	2	44	60	12	15	.300	.379	.367	114	12	15	.974	6	107	154	O134C,M		0.9
Total	12	1513	5923	1406	1755	314	108	42	720	809	77	207	.296	.388	.407	124	240	473	.956	52	102	149	O1480(7/1461/14),S28,2b7		18.3

GRIFFIN, THOMAS
Thomas William B1.1857 Titusville PA D4.17.1933 Rockford IL d9.27

YEAR	TM LG	G	AB	R	H	2B	3B	HR	RBI	BB-IB	HP	SO	AVG	OBP	SLG	AOPS	ABR	SB-CS	FA	FR	RNG	THR	GAMES AT POSITION	DL	BFW
1884	Mil U	11	41	5	9	2	0	0	3				.220	.273	.268	118	0		.918	-2	31	0	1b11		-0.2

GRIFFIN, SANDY
Tobias Charles B10.24.1858 Fayetteville NY D6.4.1926 Syracuse NY BR/TR/5-10/160 d5.26 M1

YEAR	TM LG	G	AB	R	H	2B	3B	HR	RBI	BB-IB	HP	SO	AVG	OBP	SLG	AOPS	ABR	SB-CS	FA	FR	RNG	THR	GAMES AT POSITION	DL	BFW
1884	NY N	16	62	7	11	2	0	0	6	1		19	.177	.190	.210	25	-5		.842	-2	78	227	O16(0/5/11)		-0.6
1890	Roc AA	107	407	85	125	28	4	5	53	50	4		.307	.388	.432	153	30	21	.856	-21	38	25	O107C/2		0.5
1891	Was AA	20	69	15	19	4	2	0	10	10	4	3	.275	.398	.391	132	4	2	.939	-2	35	138	O20C,M		0.1
1893	StL N	23	92	9	18	1	1	0	9	16	0	2	.196	.315	.228	45	-7	2	.906	-2	50	0	O23L		-0.9
Total	4	166	630	116	173	35	7	5	78	77	8	24	.275	.361	.376	120	22	25	.873	-26	43	49	O166(23/132/11)/2		-0.9

GRIFFITH, BERT
Bartholomew Joseph "Buck" B3.3.1896 St.Louis MO D5.5.1973 Bishop CA BR/TR/5-11/185 d4.13 gs-Matt Williams

YEAR	TM LG	G	AB	R	H	2B	3B	HR	RBI	BB-IB	HP	SO	AVG	OBP	SLG	AOPS	ABR	SB-CS	FA	FR	RNG	THR	GAMES AT POSITION	DL	BFW
1922	Bro N	106	325	45	100	22	8	2	35	5	2	11	.308	.322	.443	96	-3	5-7	.981	0	102	77	O77(0/8/69),1b6		-1.0
1923	Bro N	79	248	23	73	8	4	2	37	13	1	16	.294	.332	.383	91	-4	1-2	.949	-5	96	19	O62(51/9/3)		-1.3
1924	Was A	6	8	1	1	0	0	0	0	0		1	.125	.125	.125	-37	-2	0-0	1.000	0	165	0	O2C		-0.1
Total	3	191	581	69	174	30	12	4	72	18	3	29	.300	.324	.413	92	-9	6-9	.968	-4	100	51	O141(51/19/72),1b6		-2.4

GRIFFITH, DERRELL
Robert Derrell B12.12.1943 Anadarko OK BL/TR/6-0/168* d9.26

YEAR	TM LG	G	AB	R	H	2B	3B	HR	RBI	BB-IB	HP	SO	AVG	OBP	SLG	AOPS	ABR	SB-CS	FA	FR	RNG	THR	GAMES AT POSITION	DL	BFW
1963	LA N	1	2	0	0	0	0	0	0	0-0	0		.000	.000	.000	-99	-1	0-0	—	-1	0	0	/2		-0.1
1964	LA N	78	238	27	69	16	2	4	23	5-0	1	21	.290	.307	.424	112	3	5-1	.769	-8	95	70	3b35,O29(6/0/23)		-0.6
1965	LA N	22	41	3	7	0	0	0	2	0-0	0	9	.171	.171	.244	16	-5	0-0	1.000	0	114	0	O11(10/0/1)		-0.6
1966	LA N	23	15	3	1	0	0	0	2	2-2	0	1	.067	.176	.067	-32	-3	0-0	1.000	0	107	0	O7(5/1/2)		-0.3
Total	4	124	296	33	77	16	2	5	27	7-2	1	33	.260	.280	.378	90	-6	5-1	.970	-8	100	37	O47(21/1/26),3b35/2		-1.6

GRIFFITH, TOMMY
Thomas Herman B10.26.1889 Prospect OH D4.13.1967 Cincinnati OH BL/TR/5-10/175 d8.28

YEAR	TM LG	G	AB	R	H	2B	3B	HR	RBI	BB-IB	HP	SO	AVG	OBP	SLG	AOPS	ABR	SB-CS	FA	FR	RNG	THR	GAMES AT POSITION	DL	BFW
1913	Bos N	37	127	16	32	4	1	1	12	9	0	6	.252	.301	.323	77	-4	1-7	.886	-0	93	152	O35R		-0.9
1914	Bos N	16	48	3	5	0	0	0	1	2	0	6	.104	.140	.104	-27	-8	0-0	.931	3	82	307	O14(1/0/14)		-0.6
1915	Cin N	160	583	59	158	31	16	4	85	41	2	34	.300	.355	.436	136	24	6-24	.952	-14	85	160	O160(2/0/160)		-0.7
1916	Cin N	155	595	50	158	28	7	2	61	36	2	37	.266	.310	.346	104	2	16	.967	2	90	140	O155R		0.6
1917	Cin N	115	363	45	98	18	7	1	45	19	1	23	.270	.308	.366	111	4	5	.974	7	103	155	O100R		-0.6
1918	Cin N	118	427	47	119	10	4	6	48	39	1	30	.279	.326	.321	99	1	8	.969	3	107	104	O118R		-0.3
1919	Bro N	125	484	65	136	18	4	6	57	23	1	32	.281	.315	.372	104	1	8	.954	-2	93	111	O125R		-0.8

YEAR	TM LG	G	AB	R	H	2B	3B	HR	RBI	BB-IB	HP	SO	AVG	OBP	SLG	AOPS	ABR	SB-CS	FA	FR	RNG	THR	GAMES AT POSITION	DL	BFW
1920	†Bro N	93	334	41	87	9	4	2	30	15	0	18	.260	.292	.329	76	-11	3-3	.972	-7	86	68	O92R		-2.5
1921	Bro N	129	455	66	142	21	6	12	71	36	1	13	.312	.364	.464	113	9	3-3	.972	7	95	169	O124R		0.6
1922	Bro N	99	329	44	104	17	8	4	49	23	0	10	.316	.361	.453	110	4	7-1	.952	2	101	120	O82R		0.0
1923	Bro N	131	481	70	141	21	9	8	66	50	1	19	.293	.361	.424	109	7	8-2	.927	-7	87	100	O127R		-0.9
1924	Bro N	140	482	43	121	19	5	3	67	34	0	19	.251	.300	.330	71	-20	0-5	.965	-7	94	65	O139R		-3.9
1925	Bro N	7	4	2	0	0	0	0	0	3	0	2	.000	.429	.000	20	0	1-0	1.000	0	145	0	O2R		0.0
	Chi N	76	235	38	67	12	1	1	27	21	1	11	.285	.346	.434	97	-1	2-4	.937	-2	92	117	O60(4/4/53)		-0.8
	Year	83	239	40	67	12	1	1	27	24	1	13	.280	.348	.427	96	-1	3-4	.938	-2	93	116	O62(4/4/55)		-0.8
Total	13	1401	4947	589	1383	208	72	52	619	351	9	262	.280	.328	.382	102	7	70-49	.956	-15	93	112	O1333(7/4/1326)		-10.8

GRIGGS, ART Arthur Carle B12.10.1884 Topeka KS D12.19.1938 Los Angeles CA BR/TR/5-11/185 d5.2 Col Pittsburgh

YEAR	TM LG	G	AB	R	H	2B	3B	HR	RBI	BB-IB	HP	SO	AVG	OBP	SLG	AOPS	ABR	SB-CS	FA	FR	RNG	THR	GAMES AT POSITION	DL	BFW
1909	StL A	108	364	38	102	17	5	0	43	24	3		.280	.330	.354	125	10	11	.982	-2	110	84	1b49,O41(36/2/3),2b8/S		0.5
1910	StL A	123	416	28	98	22	5	2	30	25	1		.236	.281	.327	96	-3	11	.878	-1	98	60	O49(6/0/43),2b41,1b17,S3,3b3		-0.7
1911	Cle A	27	68	7	17	3	2	1	7	5	0		.250	.301	.397	93	-1	1	.949	-1	104	76	2b11,O4(1/0/3),3b3/1		-0.1
1912	Cle A	89	273	29	83	16	7	0	39	33	1		.304	.381	.414	123	9	10	.986	1	102	93	1b71		0.8
1914	Bro F	40	112	10	32	6	1	1	15	5	2	11	.286	.328	.384	94	-3	1	.980	-3	61	71	1b27/OL		-0.6
1915	Bro F	27	38	4	11	1	0	1	2	3	2	7	.289	.372	.395	117	0	0	1.000	1	146	104	1b5/OR		0.1
1918	Det A	28	99	11	36	8	0	0	16	10	0	5	.364	.422	.444	168	9	2	.986	-3	55	64	1b25		0.6
Total	7	442	1370	127	379	73	20	5	152	105	9	23	.277	.332	.370	115	21	36	.983	-8	94	85	1b195,O96(44/2/50),2b60,3b6,S4		0.6

GRIGSBY, DENVER Denver Clarence B3.25.1901 Jackson KY D11.10.1973 Sapulpa OK BL/TR/5-9/155 d8.29

YEAR	TM LG	G	AB	R	H	2B	3B	HR	RBI	BB-IB	HP	SO	AVG	OBP	SLG	AOPS	ABR	SB-CS	FA	FR	RNG	THR	GAMES AT POSITION	DL	BFW
1923	Chi N	24	72	8	21	5	2	0	5	7	1	5	.292	.363	.417	105	1	1-3	1.000	-1	102	47	O22(6/1/16)		-0.2
1924	Chi N	124	411	58	123	18	2	3	48	31	6	47	.299	.357	.375	95	-1	10-19	.974	5	100	134	O121(108/5/8)		-1.0
1925	Chi N	51	137	20	35	5	0	0	20	19	0	12	.255	.346	.292	64	-7	1-1	.966	0	96	115	O39(21/15/3)		-0.9
Total	3	199	620	86	179	28	4	3	73	57	7	64	.289	.355	.361	89	-7	12-23	.975	4	99	120	O182(135/21/27)		-2.1

GRIM, JOHN John Helm B8.9.1867 Lebanon KY D7.28.1961 Indianapolis IN BR/TR/6-2/175 d9.29 OF(2/0/12)

YEAR	TM LG	G	AB	R	H	2B	3B	HR	RBI	BB-IB	HP	SO	AVG	OBP	SLG	AOPS	ABR	SB-CS	FA	FR	RNG	THR	GAMES AT POSITION	DL	BFW
1888	Phi N	2	7	0	1	0	0	0	0	0	0	0	.143	.143	.143	-8	-1	0	—	-1	0	0	/OR2		-0.2
1890	Roc AA	50	192	30	51	6	9	2	34	7	2		.266	.299	.422	121	-4	3	.851	-5	78	122	S21,C15,3b8,2b4,O3R,1b2/P		0.0
1891	Mil AA	29	119	14	28	5	1	1	14	2	0	5	.235	.248	.319	52	-9	1	.926	4	120	76	C16,3b10,2b3		-0.3
1892	Lou N	97	370	40	90	16	4	1	36	13	6	24	.243	.280	.316	87	-7	18	.940	-9	90	102	C69,1b11,2b10,O8(1/0/7)/S3		-0.9
1893	Lou N	99	415	68	111	19	8	3	54	12	9	24	.267	.303	.372	86	-10	15	.952	-5	105	112	C92,1b3,2b2/ORS		-0.5
1894	Lou N	109	412	66	123	27	7	7	71	18	10	15	.299	.343	.449	96	-4	14	.927	10	99	126	C78,2b24,1b7/3		1.1
1895	Bro N	94	333	55	93	17	5	0	45	13	7	9	.279	.320	.360	82	-9	10	.947	8	132	114	C92/OL1		0.6
1896	Bro N	81	281	32	75	13	1	2	35	12	6	14	.267	.311	.342	76	-10	7	.939	-1	105	103	C77,1b5		-0.3
1897	Bro N	80	290	26	72	10	1	0	25	1	3		.248	.259	.290	47	-23	3	.947	-1	89	129	C77		-1.5
1898	Bro N	52	178	17	50	5	1	0	11	8	3		.281	.323	.320	85	-4	1	.950	-4	93	102	C52		-0.3
1899	Bro N	15	47	3	13	1	0	0	7	1	2		.277	.320	.298	68	-2	0	.966	1	89	112	C12		0.0
Total	11	708	2644	351	707	119	37	16	332	87	48	77	.267	.303	.359	82	-76	83	.943	-3	104	112	C580,2b44,1b29,S23,3b20,O14R/P		-2.3

GRIMES, ROY Austin Roy "Bummer" B9.11.1893 Bergholz OH D9.13.1954 Hanover Twp. OH BR/TR/6-1/176 d7.5 twb-Ray

YEAR	TM LG	G	AB	R	H	2B	3B	HR	RBI	BB-IB	HP	SO	AVG	OBP	SLG	AOPS	ABR	SB-CS	FA	FR	RNG	THR	GAMES AT POSITION	DL	BFW
1920	NY N	26	57	5	9	1	0	0	3	3	0	8	.158	.200	.175	8	-7	1-1	.948	-2	106	48	2b21		-0.9

GRIMES, ED Edward Adelbert B9.8.1905 Chicago IL D10.5.1974 Chicago IL BR/TR/5-10/165 d4.19

YEAR	TM LG	G	AB	R	H	2B	3B	HR	RBI	BB-IB	HP	SO	AVG	OBP	SLG	AOPS	ABR	SB-CS	FA	FR	RNG	THR	GAMES AT POSITION	DL	BFW
1931	StL A	43	57	9	15	1	2	0	5	9	0	3	.263	.364	.351	86	-1	1-0	.892	-2	91	0	3b22,2b4,S3		-0.2
1932	StL A	31	68	7	16	0	1	0	13	6	0	12	.235	.297	.265	44	-6	0-1	.891	1	119	148	3b18,2b2/S		-0.4
Total	2	74	125	16	31	1	3	0	18	15	0	15	.248	.329	.304	63	-7	1-1	.891	-1	107	86	3b40,2b6,S4		-0.6

GRIMES, OSCAR Oscar Ray Jr. B4.13.1915 Minerva OH D5.19.1993 Westlake OH BR/TR/5-11/178 d9.28 f-Ray

YEAR	TM LG	G	AB	R	H	2B	3B	HR	RBI	BB-IB	HP	SO	AVG	OBP	SLG	AOPS	ABR	SB-CS	FA	FR	RNG	THR	GAMES AT POSITION	DL	BFW
1938	Cle A	4	10	2	2	0	1	0	2	2	0		.200	.333	.400	85	0	0-0	1.000	-1	58	123	2b2/1		-0.1
1939	Cle A	119	364	51	98	20	5	4	56	56	1	61	.269	.368	.385	96	-1	8-3	.968	-10	91	81	2b48,1b43,S37,3b3		-0.8
1940	Cle A	11	13	3	0	0	0	0	0	0	0	5	.000	.000	.000	-99	-4	0-0	.958	1	164	132	1b4/3		-0.3
1941	Cle A	77	244	28	58	9	3	4	24	39	1	47	.238	.345	.348	88	-4	4-0	.995	-4	75	104	1b62,2b13/3		-1.2
1942	Cle A	51	84	10	15	2	0	0	2	13	0	17	.179	.289	.202	42	-6	3-2	.944	1	83	98	2b24,3b8/1S		-0.9
1943	NY A	9	20	4	3	0	0	0	1	3	0	7	.150	.261	.150	21	-2	0-0	1.000	0	105	224	S3/1		-0.2
1944	NY A	116	387	44	108	17	8	5	46	59	2	57	.279	.377	.403	119	11	6-0	.945	-11	90	79	3b97,S20		0.4
1945	NY A*	142	480	64	127	19	7	4	45	97	6	73	.265	.395	.358	114	14	7-6	.937	7	105	136	3b141/1		2.3
1946	NY A	14	39	1	8	1	0	0	4	1	0	7	.205	.225	.231	27	-4	0-1	.895	-1	72	75	S7,2b5		-0.5
	Phi A	59	191	28	50	5	0	1	20	27	1	29	.262	.356	.304	86	-2	2-0	.958	-9	85	99	2b43,3b6,S4		-0.9
	Year	73	230	29	58	6	0	1	24	28	1	36	.252	.336	.291	76	-6	2-1	.957	-10	86	97	2b48,S11,3b6		-1.4
Total	9	602	1832	235	469	73	24	18	200	297	11	303	.256	.363	.352	98	2	30-12	.940	-32	100	109	3b257,2b135,1b113,S72		-2.2

GRIMES, RAY Oscar Ray Sr. B9.11.1893 Bergholz OH D5.25.1953 Minerva OH BR/TR/5-11/168 d9.24 twb-Roy s-Oscar

YEAR	TM LG	G	AB	R	H	2B	3B	HR	RBI	BB-IB	HP	SO	AVG	OBP	SLG	AOPS	ABR	SB-CS	FA	FR	RNG	THR	GAMES AT POSITION	DL	BFW
1920	Bos A	1	4	1	1	0	0	0	0	0	0	0	.250	.400	.250	78	0	0-0	1.000	-0	0	283	/1		0.0
1921	Chi N	147	530	91	170	38	6	6	79	70	6	55	.321	.406	.449	126	24	5-8	.993	-5	83	86	1b147		0.8
1922	Chi N	138	509	99	180	45	12	14	99	75	6	33	.354	.442	.572	157	47	7-7	.987	-2	96	106	1b138		3.2
1923	Chi N	64	216	32	71	7	2	2	36	24	2	17	.329	.401	.407	114	5	5-0	.991	-1	91	99	1b62		0.1
1924	Chi N	51	177	33	53	6	5	5	34	28	2	15	.299	.401	.475	132	9	4-2	.982	-8	42	95	1b50		-0.2
1926	Phi N	32	101	13	30	5	0	0	15	6	1	13	.297	.343	.347	82	-2	0	.981	0	112	121	1b28		-0.4
Total	6	433	1537	269	505	101	25	27	263	204	17	133	.329	.413	.480	132	83	21-17	.989	-16	85	98	1b426		3.5

GRIMM, CHARLIE Charles John "Jolly Cholly" B8.28.1898 St.Louis MO D11.15.1983 Scottsdale AZ BL/TL/5-11.5/173 d7.30 M19/C4

YEAR	TM LG	G	AB	R	H	2B	3B	HR	RBI	BB-IB	HP	SO	AVG	OBP	SLG	AOPS	ABR	SB-CS	FA	FR	RNG	THR	GAMES AT POSITION	DL	BFW
1916	Phi A	12	22	0	2	0	0	0	2	0	0	4	.091	.167	.091	-24	-3	0	.875	-1	91	0	O7(3/1/3)		-0.5
1918	StL N	50	141	11	31	7	0	0	12	6	2	15	.220	.262	.270	64	-6	2	.971	-3	65	115	1b42,O2R/3		-1.2
1919	Pit N	14	44	6	14	1	3	0	6	2	0	4	.318	.348	.477	141	2	1	.968	3	29	17	1b13		-0.1
1920	Pit N	148	533	38	121	13	7	2	54	30	4	40	.227	.273	.289	60	-28	7-8	.995	4	108	106	1b148		-3.1
1921	Pit N	151	562	62	154	21	17	7	71	31	2	38	.274	.314	.409	88	-12	6-8	.994	-7	78	94	1b150		-3.0
1922	Pit N	154	593	64	173	28	13	0	76	43	3	15	.292	.343	.383	86	-13	6-10	.994	-3	84	94	1b154		-2.7
1923	Pit N	152	563	78	194	29	13	7	99	41	0	43	.345	.389	.480	125	20	6-9	.995	3	103	111	1b152		1.0
1924	Pit N	151	542	53	156	25	12	2	63	37	3	22	.288	.336	.392	92	-6	3-6	.995	-3	87	121	1b151		-2.1
1925	Chi N	141	519	73	159	29	5	10	76	38	0	29	.306	.354	.439	100	0	4-3	.989	-0	99	112	1b139		-0.9
1926	Chi N	147	524	58	145	30	6	8	82	49	3	25	.277	.342	.403	99	-1	3	.988	-6	81	119	1b147		-1.6
1927	Chi N	147	543	68	169	29	6	2	74	45	3	21	.311	.367	.398	105	3	5	.990	2	105	96	1b147		-0.3
1928	Chi N	147	547	67	161	25	5	5	62	39	1	20	.294	.342	.386	91	-8	7	.993	-2	86	122	1b147		-1.9
1929	†Chi N	120	463	66	138	28	3	10	91	42	1	26	.298	.358	.436	95	-3	3	.992	-1	94	116	1b120		-1.1
1930	Chi N	114	429	58	124	27	2	6	65	41	6	26	.289	.359	.403	83	-10	1	.995	0	96	98	1b113		-1.6
1931	Chi N	146	531	65	176	33	11	4	66	53	1	29	.331	.393	.458	126	21	1	.993	9	119	108	1b144		0.8
1932	†Chi N	149	570	66	175	42	2	7	80	35	2	22	.307	.349	.425	108	7	2	.993				1b149,M		0.2
1933	Chi N	107	384	38	95	15	2	3	37	23	0	15	.247	.290	.320	74	-13	1	.996	9	125	119	1b104,M		-1.5
1934	Chi N	75	267	24	79	8	1	5	47	16	1	12	.296	.338	.390	96	-2	1	.995	1	98	75	1b74,M		-0.8
1935	Chi N	2	8	0	0	0	0	0	0	0	0	1	.000	.000	.000	-99	-2	0	1.000	-0	65	236	1b2,M		-0.3
1936	Chi N	39	132	13	33	4	0	1	16	5	0	9	.250	.277	.303	55	-9	0	1.000	5	150	128	1b35,M		-0.6
Total	20	2166	7917	908	2299	394	108	79	1077	578	31	410	.290	.341	.397	95	-61	57-44	.993	5	97	106	1b2131,O9(3/1/5)/3		-21.3

GRIMSHAW, MYRON Myron Frederick B11.30.1875 St.Johnsville NY D12.11.1936 Canajoharie NY BB/TR/6-1/173 d4.25

YEAR	TM LG	G	AB	R	H	2B	3B	HR	RBI	BB-IB	HP	SO	AVG	OBP	SLG	AOPS	ABR	SB-CS	FA	FR	RNG	THR	GAMES AT POSITION	DL	BFW
1905	Bos A	85	285	39	68	8	2	4	35	21	1		.239	.293	.323	94	-2	4	.980	-5	74	126	1b74		-1.0
1906	Bos A	110	428	46	124	16	12	0	48	23	4		.290	.332	.383	124	10	5	.987	-2	90	83	1b110		0.7
1907	Bos A	64	181	19	37	7	2	0	33	16	1		.204	.273	.265	72	-5	6	.980	-4	84	127	1b20,O18(1/0/17),S2		-1.1
Total	3	259	894	104	229	31	16	4	116	60	6		.256	.307	.340	104	3	15	.984	-11	84	103	1b204,O18(1/0/17),S2		-1.4

GRISSOM, MARQUIS Marquis Deon B4.17.1967 Atlanta GA BR/TR/5-11/190(188-210) [MonN88 3/76] d8.22 Col Florida A&M

YEAR	TM LG	G	AB	R	H	2B	3B	HR	RBI	BB-IB	HP	SO	AVG	OBP	SLG	AOPS	ABR	SB-CS	FA	FR	RNG	THR	GAMES AT POSITION	DL	BFW
1989	Mon N	26	74	16	19	2	0	1	2	12	0	21	.257	.360	.324	95	0	1-0	.943	-3	69	104	O23(1/22/1)		-0.3
1990	Mon N	98	288	42	74	14	2	3	29	27-2	0	40	.257	.320	.351	88	-5	22-2	.988	0	100	106	O87(18/35/40)	32	-0.2
1991	Mon N	148	558	73	149	23	9	6	39	34-0	1	89	.267	.310	.373	92	-8	76-17	.984	8	108	194	O138(3/125/11)		1.0
1992	Mon N	159	653	99	180	39	6	14	66	42-6	5	81	.276	.322	.418	109	7	78-13	.983	-7	97	78	O157C		1.2
1993	Mon N★	157	630	104	188	27	2	19	95	52-6	3	76	.298	.351	.438	106	5	53-10	.984	0	102	97	O157C		1.5

YEAR	TM LG	G	AB	R	H	2B	3B	HR	RBI	BB-IB	HP	SO	AVG	OBP	SLG	AOPS	ABR	SB-CS	FA	FR	RNG	THR	GAMES AT POSITION	DL	BFW
1994	Mon N★	110	475	96	137	25	4	11	45	41-4	1	66	.288	.344	.427	99	-1	36-6	.985	9	118	117	O109C		1.5
1995	†Atl N	139	551	80	142	23	3	12	42	47-4	3	61	.258	.317	.376	79	-17	29-9	.994	3	104	132	O136C		-0.9
1996	†Atl N	158	671	106	207	32	10	23	74	41-6	3	73	.308	.349	.489	112	9	28-11	.997	-3	94	127	O158C		1.0
1997	†Cle A	144	558	74	146	27	6	12	66	43-1	6	89	.262	.317	.396	83	-15	22-13	.992	-2	99	97	O124C	15	-1.4
1998	Mil N	142	542	57	147	28	1	10	60	24-2	2	78	.271	.304	.382	78	-19	13-8	.991	-2	100	95	O137C		-1.9
1999	Mil N	154	603	92	161	27	1	20	83	49-4	0	109	.267	.320	.415	84	-16	24-6	.987	-8	100	12	O149C		-1.9
2000	Mil N	146	595	67	145	18	2	14	62	39-2	0	99	.244	.288	.351	61	-38	20-10	.992	-12	95	33	O142C		-4.5
2001	LA N	135	448	56	99	17	1	21	60	16-0	2	107	.221	.250	.404	70	-24	7-5	1.000	-3	94	100	O123(26/95/3),D2		-2.7
2002	LA N	111	343	57	95	21	4	17	60	22-2	2	68	.277	.321	.510	125	9	5-1	.978	-4	92	103	O102(36/72/2)		0.5
2003	†SF N	149	587	82	176	33	3	20	79	20-0	2	82	.300	.322	.468	102	0	11-3	.977	-6	101	38	O148C		-0.3
2004	SF N	145	562	78	157	26	2	22	90	37-5	1	83	.279	.333	.450	94	-6	3-1	.994	-4	100	42	O142C		-0.8
2005	SF N	44	137	8	29	4	0	2	15	7-0	1	18	.212	.248	.285	38	-13	1-1	.986	-5	82	0	O36(1/34/1)		-1.8
Total	17	2165	8275	1187	2251	386	56	227	967	553-44	31	1240	.272	.318	.415	91	-132	429-116	.988	-38	100	88	O2088(85/1962/58),D2	103	-10.0

GROAT, DICK   Richard Morrow B11.4.1930 Wilkinsburg PA BR/TR/5-11.5/180* d6.19 Mil 1953-54 Col Duke

YEAR	TM LG	G	AB	R	H	2B	3B	HR	RBI	BB-IB	HP	SO	AVG	OBP	SLG	AOPS	ABR	SB-CS	FA	FR	RNG	THR	GAMES AT POSITION	DL	BFW
1952	Pit N	95	384	38	109	6	1	1	29	19	1	27	.284	.319	.313	74	-14	2-4	.952	5	99	91	S94		-0.5
1955	Pit N	151	521	45	139	28	2	4	51	38-11	1	26	.267	.317	.351	74	-16	0-2	.961	17	105	106	S149		1.2
1956	Pit N	142	520	40	142	19	3	0	37	35-3	0	25	.273	.317	.321	74	-19	0-3	.954	7	104	82	S141,3b2		-0.1
1957	Pit N	125	501	58	158	30	5	7	54	27-1	3	28	.315	.350	.437	114	10	0-1	.968	4	106	94	S123,3b2		2.4
1958	Pit N★	151	584	67	175	36	9	3	66	23-7	4	32	.300	.328	.408	97	-4	2-2	.975	9	102	126	S149		1.7
1959	Pit N★	147	593	74	163	22	7	5	51	32-2	2	35	.275	.312	.361	80	-18	0-2	.964	2	103	110	S145		-0.4
1960	†Pit N★	138	573	85	186	26	4	2	50	39-0	4	35	.325	.371	.394	125	9	0-2	.966	14	109	123	S136		3.3
1961	Pit N	148	596	71	164	25	6	6	55	40-0	1	44	.275	.320	.367	82	-16	0-4	.957	12	108	126	S144/3		0.8
1962	Pit N★	161	678	76	199	34	3	2	61	31-1	3	61	.294	.325	.365	85	-15	2-1	.956	16	104	125	S161		1.5
1963	StL N★	158	631	85	201	43	11	6	73	56-2	1	58	.319	.377	.450	126	24	3-1	.964	-8	97	103	S158		1.5
1964	†StL N★	161	636	70	186	35	6	1	70	44-3	0	42	.292	.335	.371	92	-5	2-3	.949	-6	103	102	S160		3.2
1965	StL N	153	587	55	149	26	5	0	52	56-2	1	50	.254	.316	.315	73	-19	1-1	.962	-7	100	99	S148,3b2		0.1
1966	Phi N	155	584	58	152	21	4	2	53	40-6	5	38	.260	.311	.320	77	-18	2-1	.974	21	108	99	S139,3b20/1		-1.4
1967	Phi N	10	26	3	3	0	0	0	1	4-0	0	1	.115	.233	.115	3	-3	0-0	.947	3	125	149	S6	31	0.0
	SF N	34	70	4	12	1	1	0	4	6-1	0	1	.171	.237	.214	30	-6	0-0	.912	-5	84	113	S24/2		-1.2
	Year	44	96	7	15	1	1	0	5	10-1	0	2	.156	.236	.188	23	-10	0-0	.925	-3	95	122	S30/2		-1.2
Total	14	1929	7484	829	2138	352	67	39	707	490-39	31	512	.286	.330	.366	89	-111	14-27	.961	82	104	108	S1877,3b27/21	31	12.1

GROH, HEINIE   Henry Knight B9.18.1889 Rochester NY D8.22.1968 Cincinnati OH BR/TR/5-8/158 d4.12 M1 b-Lew

YEAR	TM LG	G	AB	R	H	2B	3B	HR	RBI	BB-IB	HP	SO	AVG	OBP	SLG	AOPS	ABR	SB-CS	FA	FR	RNG	THR	GAMES AT POSITION	DL	BFW
1912	NY N	27	48	8	13	2	1	0	3	8	0	7	.271	.375	.354	97	0	6	.887	0	103	124	2b12,S7,3b6		0.1
1913	NY N	4	2	0	0	0	0	0	0	0	0	0	.000	.000	.000	-99	-1	0	1.000	0	0	0	3b2/S		0.0
	Cin N	117	397	51	112	19	5	3	48	38	4	36	.282	.351	.378	109	5	24-17	.963	11	108	91	2b113,S4		1.8
	Year	121	399	51	112	19	5	3	48	38	4	37	.281	.349	.376	107	5	24-17	.963	11	108	91	2b113,S5,3b2		1.8
1914	Cin N	139	455	59	131	18	4	2	32	64	13	28	.288	.391	.358	120	15	24	.936	-5	100	108	2b134,S2		1.4
1915	Cin N	160	587	72	170	32	9	3	50	50	9	33	.290	.354	.390	123	17	12-17	.969	12	106	183	3b131,2b29		3.3
1916	Cin N	149	553	85	149	24	14	2	28	84	4	34	.269	.370	.374	132	25	13	.957	14	109	179	3b110,2b33,S5		4.8
1917	Cin N	156	599	91	182	39	11	1	53	71	8	30	.304	.385	.411	150	40	15	.966	9	104	104	3b154,2b2		5.8
1918	Cin N	126	493	86	158	28	3	1	37	54	7	24	.320	.395	.396	144	30	11	.969	5	93	164	3b126,M		4.1
1919	†Cin N	122	448	79	139	17	11	5	63	56	4	26	.310	.392	.431	151	30	21	.971	-2	90	147	3b121		3.4
1920	Cin N	145	550	86	164	28	12	0	49	60	8	29	.298	.375	.393	122	19	16-19	.969	-4	91	129	3b144/S		1.7
1921	Cin N	97	357	54	118	19	6	0	48	36	4	17	.331	.398	.417	122	13	22-14	.950	3	100	164	3b97		2.1
1922	†NY N	115	426	63	113	21	3	3	51	53	5	21	.265	.353	.350	81	-10	5-6	.965	4	107	169	3b110		0.0
1923	†NY N	123	465	91	135	22	5	4	48	60	6	22	.290	.379	.385	103	5	3-4	.975	4	105	96	3b118		1.5
1924	†NY N	145	559	82	157	32	3	2	46	52	11	29	.281	.354	.360	94	-2	8-6	.983	7	112	103	3b145		1.4
1925	NY N	25	65	7	15	4	0	0	4	6	0	3	.231	.296	.292	53	-4	0-0	.909	-4	68	46	3b16,2b2		-0.7
1926	NY N	12	35	2	8	2	0	0	3	2	0	3	.229	.270	.286	50	-2	0	.950	-0	99	88	3b7		-0.2
1927	†Pit N	14	35	2	10	1	0	0	2	4	0	2	.286	.324	.314	67	-2	0	.958	0	100	0	3b12		-0.1
Total	16	1676	6074	918	1774	308	87	26	566	696	83	345	.292	.373	.384	119	178	180-83	.967	55	101	139	3b1299,2b325,S20		30.4

GROH, LEW   Lewis Carl "Silver" B10.16.1883 Rochester NY D10.20.1960 Rochester NY BR/TR d8.2 b-Heinie

YEAR	TM LG	G	AB	R	H	2B	3B	HR	RBI	BB-IB	HP	SO	AVG	OBP	SLG	AOPS	ABR	SB-CS	FA	FR	RNG	THR	GAMES AT POSITION	DL	BFW
1919	Phi A	2	4	0	0	0	0	0	0	0	0	2	.000	.000	.000	-99	-1	0	1.000	-0	85	0	/3		-0.1

GROSKLOSS, HOWDY   Howard Hoffman B4.9.1907 Pittsburgh PA BR/TR/5-9/176 d6.23 Col Amherst

YEAR	TM LG	G	AB	R	H	2B	3B	HR	RBI	BB-IB	HP	SO	AVG	OBP	SLG	AOPS	ABR	SB-CS	FA	FR	RNG	THR	GAMES AT POSITION	DL	BFW
1930	Pit N	2	3	0	1	0	0	0	1	0	0	0	.333	.333	.333	62	0	0	.000	-1	0	0	/S		-0.1
1931	Pit N	53	161	13	45	7	2	0	20	11	0	16	.280	.326	.348	62	-4	1	.981	-2	97	145	2b39,S3		-0.4
1932	Pit N	17	20	1	2	0	0	0	0	0	0	3	.100	.100	.100	-47	-4	0	.800	-1	60	0	/S		-0.5
Total	3	72	184	14	48	7	2	0	21	11	0	19	.261	.303	.321	68	-8	1	.981	-4	97	145	2b39,S5		-1.0

GROSS, EMIL   Emil Michael B3.3.1858 Chicago IL D8.24.1921 Eagle River WI BR/TR/6-0/190 d8.13

YEAR	TM LG	G	AB	R	H	2B	3B	HR	RBI	BB-IB	HP	SO	AVG	OBP	SLG	AOPS	ABR	SB-CS	FA	FR	RNG	THR	GAMES AT POSITION	DL	BFW
1879	Pro N	30	132	31	46	9	5	0	24	4		8	.348	.368	.492	183	12		.897	-3			C30		0.9
1880	Pro N	87	347	43	90	18	3	1	34	16		15	.259	.292	.337	116	7		.866	-18			C87		-0.8
1881	Pro N	51	182	15	50	9	4	1	24	13		11	.275	.323	.385	124	5		.893	-5			C50/OR		0.2
1883	Phi N	57	231	39	71	25	7	1	25	12		18	.307	.342	.489	163	19		.789	-23			C55,O2(1/1/0)		0.0
1884	CP U	23	95	13	34	6	2	4		6			.358	.396	.589	197	8		.860	-3			C15,O9(6/0/3)		0.6
Total	5	248	987	141	291	67	21	7	107	51		52	.295	.329	.427	146	51		.859	-50			C237,O12(7/1/4)		0.9

GROSS, TURKEY   Ewell B2.21.1896 Mesquite TX D1.11.1936 Dallas TX BR/TR/6-0/165 d4.14

YEAR	TM LG	G	AB	R	H	2B	3B	HR	RBI	BB-IB	HP	SO	AVG	OBP	SLG	AOPS	ABR	SB-CS	FA	FR	RNG	THR	GAMES AT POSITION	DL	BFW
1925	Bos A	9	32	2	3	0	1	0	2	2	1	2	.094	.171	.156	-16	-6	0-0	.976	1	119	78	S9		-0.4

GROSS, GABE   Gabriel Jordan B10.21.1979 Baltimore MD BL/TR/6-3/210* [TorA01 1/15] d8.7 Col Auburn

YEAR	TM LG	G	AB	R	H	2B	3B	HR	RBI	BB-IB	HP	SO	AVG	OBP	SLG	AOPS	ABR	SB-CS	FA	FR	RNG	THR	GAMES AT POSITION	DL	BFW
2004	Tor A	44	129	18	27	4	0	3	16	19-0	0	31	.209	.311	.310	59	-8	2-2	1.000	5	110	271	O38L,D7		-0.4
2005	Tor A	40	92	11	23	4	1	1	7	10-0	0	21	.250	.324	.348	75	-3	1-1	.981	-0	92	127	O37(19/0/20),D2		-0.5
Total	2	84	221	29	50	8	1	4	23	29-0	0	52	.226	.316	.326	66	-11	3-3	.992	4	102	206	O75(57/0/20),D9		-0.9

GROSS, GREG   Gregory Eugene B8.1.1952 York PA BL/TL/5-11/175(160-180) [HouN70 4/80] d9.5 C4

YEAR	TM LG	G	AB	R	H	2B	3B	HR	RBI	BB-IB	HP	SO	AVG	OBP	SLG	AOPS	ABR	SB-CS	FA	FR	RNG	THR	GAMES AT POSITION	DL	BFW
1973	Hou N	14	39	5	9	2	1	0	1	2-1	1	7	.231	.302	.333	77	-1	2-1	1.000	0	52	199	O9(4/2/3)		-0.2
1974	Hou N	156	589	78	185	21	8	0	36	76-4	1	39	.314	.393	.377	122	20	12-20	.994	5	101	139	O151(56/0/143)		1.3
1975	Hou N	132	483	67	142	14	10	0	41	63-1	0	37	.294	.373	.364	114	10	2-2	.958	-0	91	158	O121(60/0/61)	17	0.3
1976	Hou N	128	426	52	122	12	3	0	27	64-3	0	39	.286	.375	.329	111	9	2-6	.978	0	95	158	O115R		0.2
1977	Chi N	115	239	43	77	10	4	5	32	33-4	0	19	.322	.397	.460	118	7	0-1	.991	-1	92	82	O71(45/25/9)		0.4
1978	Chi N	124	347	34	92	12	7	1	39	33-5	0	19	.265	.323	.349	80	-9	3-1	.979	-5	87	104	O111(40/70/12)		-1.6
1979	Phi N	111	174	21	58	6	3	0	15	29-4	1	5	.333	.422	.402	123	7	5-2	.978	2	95	163	O73(49/19/11)		0.8
1980	†Phi N	127	154	19	37	8	2	0	12	24-1	1	7	.240	.346	.312	80	1	1-1	.973	-1	84	166	O91(58/14/26)/1		-0.6
1981	†Phi N	83	102	14	23	6	1	0	7	15-4	0	7	.225	.319	.304	75	-3	2-2	.982	5	106	376	O55(13/5/38)		0.1
1982	Phi N	119	134	14	40	4	0	0	10	19-3	0	10	.299	.386	.328	98	1	4-3	.983	2	108	172	O71(50/12/19)		0.2
1983	†Phi N	136	245	25	74	12	3	0	29	34-4	1	16	.302	.385	.392	114	6	3-5	.991	-5	87	26	O110(77/27/25)/1		-0.2
1984	Phi N	112	202	19	65	9	1	0	16	24-1	1	11	.322	.393	.376	116	6	1-0	.986	4	130	101	O48(30/1/20),1b28		0.8
1985	Phi N	93	169	21	44	5	2	0	14	32-1	0	11	.260	.374	.314	93	0	1-0	1.000	-0	77	166	O52(46/0/9),1b8		-0.2
1986	Phi N	87	101	11	25	5	0	0	8	21-7	0	11	.248	.379	.297	87	-0	1-0	1.000	2	122	102	O27(21/1/6),1b5/P		0.1
1987	Phi N	114	133	14	38	4	1	1	12	25-4	1	12	.286	.393	.353	99	1	0-0	1.000	-3	75	166	O50(49/0/1),1b11		-0.3
1988	Phi N	98	133	10	27	1	0	0	5	16-1	1	9	.203	.291	.211	46	-9	0-0	1.000	-1	87	138	O37(20/0/19),1b14		-1.2
1989	Hou N	60	75	2	15	0	0	0	6	6-1	0	8	.200	.310	.200	50	-4	0-0	.929	-1	84	0	O12(5/0/7),1b6/P		-0.7
Total	17	1809	3745	449	1073	130	46	7	308	523-51	8	250	.287	.372	.351	103	38	39-44	.982	3	94	133	O1204(623/176/524),1b74,P2	48	-0.8

GROSS, WAYNE   Wayne Dale B1.14.1952 Riverside CA BL/TR/6-2/210(205-221) [OakA73 9/215] d8.21 Col Cal Poly-Pomona

YEAR	TM LG	G	AB	R	H	2B	3B	HR	RBI	BB-IB	HP	SO	AVG	OBP	SLG	AOPS	ABR	SB-CS	FA	FR	RNG	THR	GAMES AT POSITION	DL	BFW
1976	Oak A	10	18	0	4	0	0	0	1	2-0	1		.222	.300	.222	57	-1	0-0	.966	-1	54	99	1b3,O2R,D3		-0.2
1977	Oak A☆	146	485	66	113	21	1	22	63	86-6	5	84	.233	.343	.416	110	10	5-4	.932	-26	80	93	3b145/1		-1.8
1978	Oak A	118	285	18	57	10	2	7	23	40-2	1	63	.200	.308	.323	82	-6	0-2	.917	-8	88	131	3b106,1b15		-1.8
1979	Oak A	138	442	54	99	19	1	14	50	72-9	1	62	.224	.332	.367	93	-2	4-3	.943	-6	88	74	3b120,1b18,O2L		-1.1
1980	Oak A	113	366	45	103	20	3	14	61	44-9	1	68	.281	.355	.467	133	17	5-3	.948	-17	78	79	3b99,1b10/D		-0.1
1981	†Oak A	82	243	24	50	7	1	10	31	34-0	2	28	.206	.300	.366	97	-1	2-1	.946	-2	97	59	3b73,1b2/D		-0.4

GROSS (continued)

YEAR	TM LG	G	AB	R	H	2B	3B	HR	RBI	BB-IB	HP	SO	AVG	OBP	SLG	AOPS	ABR	SB-CS	FA	FR	RNG	THR	GAMES AT POSITION	DL	BFW
1982	Oak A	129	386	43	97	14	0	9	41	53-0	2	50	.251	.342	.358	96	0	3-1	.970	-1	93	117	3b108,1b16/D		-0.3
1983	Oak A	137	339	34	79	18	0	12	36	36-4	3	52	.233	.311	.392	98	-1	3-5	.996	-10	64	88	1b74,3b67/PD		-1.6
1984	Bal A	127	342	53	74	9	1	22	64	68-4	1	69	.216	.346	.442	119	10	1-2	.937	-0	108	75	3b117,1b3/D		0.8
1985	Bal A	103	217	31	51	8	0	11	18	46-0	1	48	.235	.369	.424	119	7	1-1	.933	-0	98	137	3b67,D10,1b9		0.5
1986	Oak A	3	2	0	0	0	0	0	0	1-0	0	0	.000	.333	.000	0	0	0-0	.000	-0	0	0	/3		-0.1
Total	11	1106	3125	373	727	126	9	121	396	482-34	20	496	.233	.337	.395	105	33	24-22	.941	-71	90	93	3b903,1b151,D18,O4(2/0/2)/P		-6.1

GROSSART, GEORGE George Albert B4.11.1880 Meadville PA D4.18.1902 Pittsburgh PA d6.7

YEAR	TM LG	G	AB	R	H	2B	3B	HR	RBI	BB-IB	HP	SO	AVG	OBP	SLG	AOPS	ABR	SB-CS	FA	FR	RNG	THR	GAMES AT POSITION	DL	BFW
1901	Bos N	7	26	4	3	0	0	0	0				.115	.115	.115	-30	-4	0	1.000	0	0	0	O7L		-0.5

GROTE, JERRY Gerald Wayne B10.6.1942 San Antonio TX BR/TR/5-10/190* d9.21 Col Trinity (TX)

YEAR	TM LG	G	AB	R	H	2B	3B	HR	RBI	BB-IB	HP	SO	AVG	OBP	SLG	AOPS	ABR	SB-CS	FA	FR	RNG	THR	GAMES AT POSITION	DL	BFW
1963	Hou N	3	5	0	1	0	0	0	1	1-0	0	1	.200	.286	.200	61	0	0-0	1.000	-1	93	0	C3		-0.1
1964	Hou N	100	298	26	54	9	3	3	24	20-5	4	75	.181	.240	.262	44	-23	0-2	.985	-1	71	121	C98		-2.1
1966	NY N	120	317	26	75	12	3	2	31	40-8	3	81	.237	.327	.315	82	-6	4-3	.981	-2	117	85	C115,3b2		-0.4
1967	NY N	120	344	25	67	8	0	4	23	14-8	1	65	.195	.226	.253	38	-28	2-2	.990	2	115	126	C119		-2.4
1968	NY N★	124	404	29	114	18	0	3	31	44-11	3	81	.282	.357	.349	112	8	1-5	.994	7	124	95	C115		2.2
1969	†NY N	113	365	38	92	12	3	6	40	32-5	1	59	.252	.313	.351	84	-8	2-1	.991	19	140	138	C112		1.6
1970	NY N	126	415	38	106	14	1	2	34	36-8	1	39	.255	.313	.308	67	-19	2-1	.991	15	155	85	C125		0.1
1971	NY N	125	403	35	109	25	0	2	35	40-4	2	47	.270	.339	.347	95	-1	1-4	.990	3	101	64	C122		0.7
1972	NY N	64	205	15	43	5	1	3	21	26-8	3	27	.210	.304	.288	71	-7	1-0	.998	4	174	111	C59,3b3/OR		0.0
1973	†NY N	84	285	17	73	10	2	1	32	13-1	1	23	.256	.290	.316	68	-13	0-0	.995	10	130	76	C81,3b2	60	-0.1
1974	NY N★	97	319	25	82	8	1	5	36	33-4	2	33	.257	.326	.335	87	-5	0-1	.988	0	117	94	C94		-0.1
1975	NY N	119	386	28	114	14	5	2	39	38-8	1	23	.295	.357	.373	107	4	0-1	.995	6	101	111	C111		1.5
1976	NY N	101	323	30	88	14	2	4	28	38-4	1	19	.272	.350	.365	108	4	1-2	.993	10	104	99	C95,O2(1/0/1)		1.9
1977	NY N	42	115	8	31	3	1	0	7	9-1	2	12	.270	.333	.313	77	-4	0-0	1.000	-3	87	87	C28,3b11		-0.5
	†LA N	18	27	3	7	0	0	0	4	2-1	0	5	.259	.310	.259	54	-2	0-1	1.000	3	64	96	C16,3b2		0.1
	Year	60	142	11	38	3	1	0	11	11-2	2	17	.268	.329	.303	72	-5	0-1	1.000	0	81	89	C44,3b13		-0.4
1978	†LA N	41	70	5	19	5	0	0	9	10-1	0	5	.271	.354	.343	98	0	0-0	.985	4	80	28	C32,3b7	38	0.6
1981	KC A	22	56	4	17	3	1	1	9	3-0	1	2	.304	.344	.446	128	2	1-0	1.000	-1	79	58	C22		0.2
	LA N	2	2	0	0	0	0	0	0	0-0	0	1	.000	.000	.000	-99	-1	0-0	1.000	0	0	0	/C		0.0
Total	16	1421	4339	352	1092	160	22	39	404	399-77	26	600	.252	.316	.326	82	-99	15-23	.991	75	117	98	C1348,3b27,O3(1/0/2)	98	3.3

GROTEWOLD, JEFF Jeffrey Scott B12.8.1965 Madera CA BL/TR/6-0/215* d4.12 Col San Diego

YEAR	TM LG	G	AB	R	H	2B	3B	HR	RBI	BB-IB	HP	SO	AVG	OBP	SLG	AOPS	ABR	SB-CS	FA	FR	RNG	THR	GAMES AT POSITION	DL	BFW
1992	Phi N	72	65	7	13	2	0	3	5	9-0	1	16	.200	.307	.369	91	-1	0-0	1.000	-0	0	0	C2,O2L/1		-0.1
1995	KC A	15	36	4	10	1	0	1	6	9-0	0	7	.278	.422	.389	110	1	0-0	.750	-0	0	257	D11/1		0.0
Total	2	87	101	11	23	3	0	4	11	18-0	1	23	.228	.350	.376	98	0	0-0	.833	-0	0	171	D11,1b2,O2L,C2		-0.1

GROTH, JOHNNY John Thomas B7.23.1926 Chicago IL BR/TR/6-0/182* d9.5

YEAR	TM LG	G	AB	R	H	2B	3B	HR	RBI	BB-IB	HP	SO	AVG	OBP	SLG	AOPS	ABR	SB-CS	FA	FR	RNG	THR	GAMES AT POSITION	DL	BFW
1946	Det A	4	9	1	0	0	0	0	0	0-0	0	3	.000	.000	.000	-94	-2	0-0	1.000	0	105	0	O4C		-0.3
1947	Det A	2	4	1	1	0	0	0	0	0		2		.250	.500	.250	109	0	0-0	1.000	0	133	0	/OL		0.0
1948	Det A	6	17	3	8	3	0	1	5	1	0	1	.471	.500	.824	242	3	0-0	.900	0	78	341	O4C		0.3
1949	Det A	103	348	60	102	19	5	11	73	65	2	27	.293	.407	.471	132	18	3-7	.966	-2	95	122	O99C		1.0
1950	Det A	157	566	95	173	30	8	12	85	95	2	27	.306	.407	.451	116	16	1-5	.985	-18	84	65	O157C		-0.7
1951	Det A	118	428	41	128	29	1	3	49	31	2	32	.299	.349	.393	100	0	1-1	.993	-5	90	109	O112C		-0.8
1952	Det A	141	524	56	149	22	4	4	51	51	0	39	.284	.348	.357	96	-3	2-10	.986	-5	88	135	O139(2/137/0)		-1.5
1953	StL A	141	557	65	141	27	4	10	57	42	2	53	.253	.308	.370	81	-16	5-6	.991	12	109	146	O141C		-1.2
1954	Chi A	125	422	41	116	20	0	7	60	42	2	37	.275	.341	.372	93	-4	3-9	.988	1	102	66	O125(9/116/2)		-1.3
1955	Chi A	32	77	13	26	7	0	2	11	6-1	0	13	.338	.376	.506	135	4	1-0	1.000	1	107	79	O26C		0.4
	Was A	63	183	22	40	4	5	2	17	18-0	0	18	.219	.286	.328	69	-9	2-0	.984	-0	102	64	O48(12/40/1)		-1.2
	Year	95	260	35	66	11	5	4	28	24-1	0	31	.254	.313	.381	89	-5	3-0	.989	0	104	69	O74(12/66/1)		-0.8
1956	KC A	95	244	22	63	13	3	5	37	30-2	1	31	.258	.335	.398	94	-2	1-2	1.000	-1	86	168	O84(13/56/18)		-0.7
1957	KC A	55	59	10	15	0	0	0	2	7-0	0	6	.254	.333	.254	62	-3	0-0	.974	-1	107	0	O50(9/3/38)		-0.5
	Det A	38	103	11	30	10	0	0	16	6-0	1	7	.291	.333	.388	95	0	0-0	1.000	1	113	0	O36(12/25/0)		-0.1
	Year	93	162	21	45	10	0	0	18	13-0	1	13	.278	.333	.340	83	-3	0-0	.991	-0	111	0	O86(21/28/38)		-0.6
1958	Det A	88	146	24	41	5	2	2	11	13-0	0	19	.281	.340	.384	92	-2	0-1	.990	1	105	73	O80(52/19/10)		-0.4
1959	Det A	55	102	12	24	7	1	1	10	7-0	1	14	.235	.284	.353	70	-4	0-0	.983	0	114	0	O41(11/18/13)		-0.5
1960	Det A	25	19	3	7	1	0	0	2	3-0	1	4	.368	.455	.421	135	1	0-1	1.000	-1	67	0	O8(0/7/1)		0.0
Total	15	1248	3808	480	1064	197	31	60	486	419-3	11	329	.279	.352	.395	99	-3	19-42	.987	-20	96	99	O1155(121/964/83)		-7.5

GROVER, ROY Roy Arthur B1.17.1892 Snohomish WA D2.7.1978 Milwaukie OR BR/TR/5-8/150 d9.13

YEAR	TM LG	G	AB	R	H	2B	3B	HR	RBI	BB-IB	HP	SO	AVG	OBP	SLG	AOPS	ABR	SB-CS	FA	FR	RNG	THR	GAMES AT POSITION	DL	BFW
1916	Phi A	20	77	8	21	1	2	0	7	6	0	10	.273	.325	.338	104	-3	5	.952	-3	78	81	2b20		-0.3
1917	Phi A	141	482	45	108	15	7	0	34	43	3	53	.224	.292	.284	77	-14	12	.960	6	105	81	2b139		-0.6
1918	Phi A	22	56	8	13	1	0	0	2	5	0	6	.232	.295	.250	53	-3	0	.915	-5	83	58	2b12,3b3		-0.9
1919	Was A	24	75	6	14	0	0	0	7	6	1	10	.187	.256	.187	25	-7	2	.947	-5	75	66	2b24		-1.3
	Year	46	131	14	27	1	0	0	9	11	1	16	.206	.273	.214	37	-11	2	.936	-10	78	62	2b36,3b3		-2.2
Total	3	207	690	67	156	17	9	0	50	60	4	79	.226	.292	.277	72	-24	19	.956	-7	98	78	2b195,3b3		-3.1

GRUBB, HARVEY Harvey Harrison B9.18.1890 Lexington NC D1.25.1970 Corpus Christi TX BR/TR/6-0/165 d9.27

YEAR	TM LG	G	AB	R	H	2B	3B	HR	RBI	BB-IB	HP	SO	AVG	OBP	SLG	AOPS	ABR	SB-CS	FA	FR	RNG	THR	GAMES AT POSITION	DL	BFW
1912	Cle A	1	0	0	0	0	0	0	0	0	1		—	1.000	—	187	0	0-0	1.000	0	0	0	/3		0.0

GRUBB, JOHNNY John Maywood B8.4.1948 Richmond VA BL/TR/6-3/188(175-188) [SDN71*A1/24] d9.10 Col Florida St. OF(389/408/280)

YEAR	TM LG	G	AB	R	H	2B	3B	HR	RBI	BB-IB	HP	SO	AVG	OBP	SLG	AOPS	ABR	SB-CS	FA	FR	RNG	THR	GAMES AT POSITION	DL	BFW
1972	SD N	7	21	4	7	1	0	1	0	1-0	0	3	.333	.364	.476	147	1	0-1	1.000	0	124	0	O6C		0.1
1973	SD N	113	389	52	121	22	3	8	37	37-2	2	50	.311	.373	.445	137	20	9-3	.988	1	98	181	O102(1/102/0),3b2		1.9
1974	SD N★	140	444	53	127	20	4	8	42	46-2	4	47	.286	.355	.403	118	11	4-0	.976	5	113	112	O122(8/114/0),3b2		1.4
1975	SD N	144	553	72	149	36	2	4	38	59-4	5	59	.269	.342	.363	104	4	2-7	.991	-13	90	33	O139C		-1.6
1976	SD N	109	384	54	109	22	1	5	27	65-10	4	53	.284	.391	.385	132	20	1-2	.974	-7	95	44	O98(63/15/30),1b9,3b3	32	0.9
1977	Cle A	34	93	8	28	3	3	2	14	19-2	1	18	.301	.425	.462	146	7	0-3	1.000	0	94	109	O28(27/0/1),D4	104	0.5
1978	Cle A	113	378	54	100	16	6	14	61	59-5	2	60	.265	.365	.450	130	16	5-1	.973	4	96	204	O110(108/0/6),D3		1.7
	Tex A	21	33	8	13	3	0	1	6	11-0	0	5	.394	.545	.576	214	6	1-1	1.000	1	88	382	O13(8/0/5),D3		0.7
	Year	134	411	62	113	19	6	15	67	70-5	2	65	.275	.381	.460	137	22	6-2	.974	5	95	216	O123(116/0/11),D3		2.4
1979	Tex A	102	289	42	79	14	0	10	37	34-3	1	44	.273	.350	.426	109	4	2-4	.986	-0	89	164	O82(38/29/25),D6	26	0.1
1980	Tex A	110	274	40	76	12	1	9	32	42-5	2	35	.277	.374	.427	123	10	2-3	.952	-4	86	124	O77(19/3/60),D8		0.3
1981	Tex A	67	199	26	46	9	1	2	26	23-0	2	25	.231	.316	.332	91	-2	0-3	.990	-5	83	50	O58(2/0/56)		-1.2
1982	Tex A	103	308	35	86	13	3	3	26	39-2	6	37	.279	.368	.370	109	6	0-3	.965	-4	90	85	O77(41/0/40),D18	21	-0.3
1983	Det A	57	134	20	34	5	2	4	22	28-1	2	21	.254	.388	.410	123	6	0-0	1.000	-2	86	66	O26(2/0/24),D18	48	0.6
1984	†Det A	86	176	25	47	5	0	8	17	36-5	2	36	.267	.395	.432	129	9	1-0	1.000	-1	96	0	O36(27/0/9),D33		0.6
1985	Det A	78	155	19	38	7	1	5	25	24-0	1	25	.245	.342	.400	105	2	0-1	1.000	-1	95	0	D33,O18(14/0/4)	15	-0.1
1986	Det A	81	210	32	70	13	1	13	51	28-0	2	28	.333	.412	.590	170	21	0-1	1.000	1	106	122	D52,O19(10/0/10)	38	1.9
1987	†Det A	59	114	9	23	6	0	2	13	15-0	0	16	.202	.290	.307	62	-6	0-0	1.000	-24	108	75	O31(21/0/10),D16/3	26	-0.7
Total	16	1424	4154	553	1153	207	29	99	475	566-41	36	558	.278	.364	.413	121	135	27-33	.981	-24	95	106	O1042C,D191,1b9,3b8	310	6.4

GRUBE, FRANK Franklin Thomas "Hans" B1.7.1905 Easton PA D7.2.1945 New York NY BR/TR/5-9/190 d5.12 Col Lafayette

YEAR	TM LG	G	AB	R	H	2B	3B	HR	RBI	BB-IB	HP	SO	AVG	OBP	SLG	AOPS	ABR	SB-CS	FA	FR	RNG	THR	GAMES AT POSITION	DL	BFW
1931	Chi A	88	265	24	58	11	2	1	24	22	2	22	.219	.284	.294	55	-18	2-2	.977	-10	65	87	C81		-2.2
1932	Chi A	93	277	36	78	16	2	0	31	33	2	13	.282	.362	.354	92	-2	6-1	.957	-5	84	125	C92		0.0
1933	Chi A	85	256	23	59	13	0	0	23	38	2	20	.230	.334	.281	67	-10	1-1	.984	-9	85	82	C83		-1.4
1934	StL A	65	170	22	49	10	0	0	11	24	1	11	.288	.379	.347	82	-3	2-1	.963	2	99	81	C55		0.1
1935	StL A	3	6	3	2	1	0	0	0	0	0	1	.333	.333	.500	108	0	0-0	1.000	0	64	0	C3		0.0
	Chi A	9	19	1	7	2	0	0	6	3	0	3	.368	.455	.474	137	1	0-0	.944	1	132	109	C9		0.3
	Year	12	25	4	9	3	0	0	6	3	0	3	.360	.429	.480	131	1	0-0	.955	1	119	88	C12		0.3
1936	Chi A	33	93	6	15	2	0	1	11	6	3	4	.161	.235	.204	9	-14	0-0	.991	3	125	127	C32		-0.4
1941	StL A	18	39	1	6	2	0	0	1	2	0	4	.154	.195	.205	6	-5	0-0	.951	1	121	183	C18		-0.1
Total	7	394	1125	121	274	59	5	1	107	131	7	88	.244	.326	.308	67	-51	12-5	.970	-18	88	102	C373		-4.5

GRUBER, KELLY Kelly Wayne B2.26.1962 Houston TX BR/TR/6-0/185* [CleA80 1/10] d4.20

YEAR	TM LG	G	AB	R	H	2B	3B	HR	RBI	BB-IB	HP	SO	AVG	OBP	SLG	AOPS	ABR	SB-CS	FA	FR	RNG	THR	GAMES AT POSITION	DL	BFW
1984	Tor A	15	16	1	1	0	0	0	2	0-0	0	5	.063	.063	.250	-17	-3	0-0	.933	2	180	0	3b12,O2R/S		0.0
1985	Tor A	5	13	1	3	0	0	0	1	0-0	0	3	.231	.231	.231	26	-1	0-0	1.000	-0	101	0	3b5/2		-0.2

YEAR	TM LG	G	AB	R	H	2B	3B	HR	RBI	BB-IB	HP	SO	AVG	OBP	SLG	AOPS	ABR	SB-CS	FA	FR	RNG	THR	GAMES AT POSITION	DL	BFW
1986	Tor A	87	143	20	28	4	1	5	15	5-0	0	27	.196	.220	.343	50	-11	2-5	.940	-2	112	64	3b42,2b14,D14,O9(4/2/3),S5		-1.4
1987	Tor A	138	341	50	80	14	3	12	36	17-2	2	70	.235	.283	.399	77	-13	12-2	.948	-3	102	75	3b119,S21,2b7,O2C/D		-1.3
1988	Tor A	158	569	75	158	33	5	16	81	38-1	7	92	.278	.328	.438	112	8	23-5	.971	26	118	125	3b156,2b7,O2C/SD		3.8
1989	†Tor A☆	135	545	83	158	24	4	18	73	30-0	3	60	.290	.328	.448	119	11	10-5	.945	19	116	76	3b119,O16(3/0/14)/SD	15	2.8
1990	Tor A★	150	592	92	162	36	6	31	118	48-2	8	94	.274	.330	.512	131	23	14-2	.955	-3	97	86	3b145,O6R/D		2.2
1991	†Tor A	113	429	58	108	18	2	20	65	31-5	6	70	.252	.308	.443	102	0	12-7	.962	5	101	80	3b111,D2	41	0.5
1992	†Tor A	120	446	42	102	16	3	11	43	26-3	4	72	.229	.275	.352	72	-18	7-7	.949	-1	93	52	3b120	25	-2.1
1993	Cal A	18	65	10	18	3	0	3	9	2-0	1	11	.277	.309	.462	101	0	0-0	.938	5	128	106	3b17/OLD	125	0.5
Total	10	939	3159	431	818	148	24	117	443	190-13	36	504	.259	.307	.432	101	-4	80-33	.955	46	106	84	3b846,O38(8/6/25),2b29,S29,D21	206	4.8

GRUDZIELANEK, MARK Mark James B6.30.1970 Milwaukee WI BR/TR/6-1/185* [MonN91 11/295] d4.28 Col Trinidad St. (CO) JC

1995	Mon N	78	269	27	66	12	2	1	20	14-4	7	47	.245	.300	.316	60	-15	8-3	.987	5	105	92	S34,3b31,2b13		-0.6
1996	Mon N★	153	657	99	201	34	4	6	49	26-3	9	83	.306	.340	.397	92	-8	33-7	.959	-6	97	89	S153		0.2
1997	Mon N	156	649	76	177	54	3	4	51	23-0	10	76	.273	.307	.384	81	-19	25-9	.955	-3	98	110	S156		-0.7
1998	Mon N	105	396	51	109	15	1	8	41	21-1	9	50	.275	.323	.379	87	-8	11-5	.950	-8	96	89	S105		-0.8
	LA N	51	193	11	51	6	0	2	21	5-1	2	23	.264	.286	.326	65	-11	7-0	.962	13	116	113	S51		0.7
	Year	156	589	62	160	21	1	10	62	26-2	11	73	.272	.311	.362	80	-19	18-5	.954	4	103	97	S156		-0.1
1999	LA N	123	488	72	159	23	5	7	46	31-1	10	65	.326	.376	.436	111	8	6-6	.973	-10	94	95	S119	33	0.6
2000	LA N	148	617	101	172	35	6	7	49	45-0	9	81	.279	.335	.389	87	-13	12-3	.976	2	99	106	2b148/S		-0.2
2001	LA N	133	539	83	146	21	3	13	55	28-0	11	83	.271	.317	.393	88	-11	4-4	.984	-6	95	96	2b133	16	-1.1
2002	LA N	150	536	56	145	23	0	9	50	22-4	3	89	.271	.301	.364	82	-19	4-1	.989	-11	99	90	2b147/D		-2.2
2003	†Chi N	121	481	73	151	38	1	3	38	30-0	11	64	.314	.366	.416	102	3	6-2	.986	17	97	123	2b121	30	2.5
2004	Chi N	81	257	32	79	17	1	6	23	15-0	1	32	.307	.347	.432	97	-1	1-1	.985	6	99	77	2b76	70	0.7
2005	†StL N	137	528	64	155	30	3	8	59	26-3	7	81	.294	.334	.407	92	-7	8-6	.990	21	116	133	2b137		2.0
Total	11	1436	5610	745	1611	303	29	74	502	286-17	89	774	.287	.330	.391	89	-101	125-47	.984	21	101	106	2b775,S619,3b31/D	149	1.1

GRYSKA, SIG Sigmund Stanley B11.4.1914 Chicago IL D8.27.1994 Hines IL BR/TR/5-11.5/173 d9.28

1938	StL A	7	21	3	10	2	1	0	4	3	0	3	.476	.542	.667	202	4	0-0	.912	-0	90	108	S7		0.3
1939	StL A	18	49	4	13	2	0	0	8	6	0	10	.265	.345	.306	66	-2	3-1	.873	-3	97	47	S14		-0.4
Total	2	25	70	7	23	4	1	0	12	9	0	13	.329	.405	.414	107	2	3-1	.887	-3	95	68	S21		-0.1

GUBANICH, CREIGHTON Creighton Wade B3.27.1972 Belleville NJ BR/TR/6-3/200 [OakA90 6/181] d4.16

| 1999 | Bos A | 18 | 47 | 4 | 13 | 2 | 1 | 1 | 11 | 3-0 | 2 | 13 | .277 | .346 | .426 | 92 | -1 | 0-0 | .979 | -3 | 78 | 100 | C14/3D | | -0.3 |

GUDAT, MARV Marvin John B8.27.1903 Goliad TX D3.1.1954 Los Angeles CA BL/TL/5-11/162 d5.21 Col UCLA ▲

1929	Cin N	9	10	0	2	0	0	0	0	0	0	0	.200	.200	.200	-1	0	0	.800	-1	66	0	P7		0.0
1932	†Chi N	60	94	15	24	4	1	1	15	16	1	10	.255	.369	.351	96	0	0	.933	-2	77	0	O14(5/1/9),1b8/P		-0.3
Total	2	69	104	15	26	4	1	1	15	16	1	10	.255	.345	.337	87	0	0	.933	-3	77	0	O14(5/1/9),1b8,P8		-0.3

GUERRA, MIKE Fermin (Romero) B10.11.1912 Havana, Cuba D10.9.1992 Miami Beach FL BR/TR/5-9/162* d9.19

1937	Was A	1	3	0	0	0	0	0	0	0	0	2	.000	.000	.000	-99	-1	0-0	.750	-0	0	0	/C		-0.1
1944	Was A	75	210	29	59	7	2	1	29	13	0	14	.281	.323	.348	96	-2	8-2	.960	-3	82	75	C58/OL		-0.1
1945	Was A	56	138	11	29	1	1	1	15	10	1	12	.210	.268	.254	57	-8	4-1	.990	3	119	76	C38		-0.3
1946	Was A	41	83	3	21	2	1	0	4	5	0	6	.253	.295	.301	71	-4	1-0	.938	-2	94	150	C27		-0.4
1947	Phi A	72	209	20	45	2	2	0	18	10	0	15	.215	.251	.244	37	-19	1-2	.964	1	145	130	C62		-1.4
1948	Phi A	53	142	18	30	4	2	1	23	18	0	13	.211	.300	.289	57	-9	2-3	.973	-1	120	95	C47		-0.8
1949	Phi A	98	298	41	79	14	1	3	31	37	0	26	.265	.346	.349	87	-5	3-0	.982	-3	101	111	C95		-0.3
1950	Phi A	87	252	25	71	10	4	2	26	16	0	12	.282	.325	.377	81	-9	1-0	.990	-5	87	78	C78		-0.9
1951	Bos A	10	32	1	5	0	0	0	2	6	0	5	.156	.289	.156	21	-3	1-0	1.000	-6	116	39	C10		-0.3
	Was A	72	214	20	43	2	1	1	20	16	0	18	.201	.257	.234	34	-21	4-4	.977	-8	95	89	C66		-2.6
	Year	82	246	21	48	2	1	1	22	22	0	23	.195	.261	.224	32	-24	5-4	.982	-8	98	81	C76		-2.9
Total	9	565	1581	168	382	42	14	9	168	131	1	123	.242	.300	.303	65	-81	25-12	.975	-16	104	96	C482/OL		-7.2

GUERRERO, JUAN Juan Antonio B2.1.1967 Los Llanos, D.R. BR/TR/5-11/160 d4.9

| 1992 | Hou N | 79 | 125 | 8 | 25 | 7 | 2 | 1 | 14 | 10-2 | 1 | 32 | .200 | .261 | .288 | 59 | -7 | 1-0 | .980 | -6 | 82 | 61 | S19,3b12,O3L,2b2 | | -1.3 |

GUERRERO, MARIO Mario Miguel (Abud) B9.28.1949 Santo Domingo, D.R. BR/TR/5-10/155* d4.8

1973	Bos A	66	219	19	51	5	2	0	11	10-0	2	21	.233	.272	.274	51	-15	2-2	.974	0	100	126	S46,2b24		-0.9
1974	Bos A	93	284	18	70	6	2	0	23	13-0	2	22	.246	.282	.282	59	-15	3-1	.969	-3	99	99	S93		-0.9
1975	StL A	64	184	17	44	9	0	0	11	10-1	2	7	.239	.281	.288	57	-11	0-0	.955	7	115	86	S64		0.3
1976	Cal A	83	268	24	76	12	0	1	18	7-2	3	12	.284	.304	.340	96	-2	0-0	.973	-9	91	83	2b41,S41,D7		-0.5
1977	Cal A	86	244	17	69	8	2	1	28	4-1	0	16	.283	.292	.344	76	-9	0-0	.985	-1	95	91	S31,D19,2b12		-0.7
1978	Oak A	143	505	27	139	18	4	3	38	15-2	6	35	.275	.302	.345	86	-11	0-5	.958	-24	82	80	S142	36	-2.4
1979	Oak A	46	166	12	38	5	0	0	18	6-0	0	7	.229	.253	.259	41	-14	0-1	.952	-2	98	100	S43		-1.1
1980	Oak A	116	381	32	91	16	2	2	23	19-2	1	32	.239	.273	.307	64	-20	3-3	.962	-36	80	71	S116		-4.5
Total	8	697	2251	166	578	79	12	7	170	84-8	16	152	.257	.285	.312	69	-97	8-12	.961	-67	91	87	S576,2b77,D26	36	-10.7

GUERRERO, PEDRO Pedro B6.29.1956 San Pedro de Macoris, D.R. BR/TR/6-0/195(176-199) d9.22 OF(216/108/239)

1978	LA N	5	8	3	5	0	1	0	1	0-0	0	1	.625	.625	.875	314	2	0-0	1.000	-0	77	0	1b4		0.2
1979	LA N	25	62	7	15	2	0	2	9	1-1	0	14	.242	.250	.371	70	-3	2-0	1.000	-1	92	0	O12(4/1/9),1b8,3b3		-0.4
1980	LA N	75	183	27	59	9	1	7	31	12-3	0	31	.322	.359	.497	142	10	2-1	.987	-4	97	44	O40(3/25/15),2b12,3b3,1b2	23	0.5
1981	†LA N★	98	347	46	104	17	2	12	48	34-3	2	57	.300	.365	.464	140	18	5-9	.974	1	97	66	O75(0/8/70),3b21/1		1.4
1982	LA N	150	575	87	175	27	5	32	100	65-16	5	89	.304	.378	.536	158	44	22-5	.976	0	95	119	O137(0/44/105),3b24		4.3
1983	†LA N★	160	584	87	174	28	6	32	103	72-12	2	110	.298	.373	.531	149	38	23-7	.934	3	98	93	3b157,1b2		4.2
1984	LA N	144	535	85	162	29	4	16	72	49-7	1	105	.303	.358	.462	130	21	9-7	.917	-7	93	100	3b76,O58(1/20/38),1b16	15	1.0
1985	†LA N✷	137	487	99	156	22	2	33	87	83-14	6	68	.320	.422	.577	182	56	12-4	.974	4	98	87	O81(71/10/1),3b44,1b12		5.8
1986	LA N★	31	61	7	15	3	0	5	10	2-0	1	19	.246	.281	.541	130	2	0-0	1.000	-1	78	240	O10L,1b4	137	0.1
1987	LA N★	152	545	89	184	25	2	27	89	74-18	4	85	.338	.416	.539	156	46	9-7	.971	-2	85	87	O109L,1b40		3.6
1988	LA N	59	215	24	64	7	1	5	35	25-2	1	33	.298	.374	.409	130	9	2-1	.895	-6	84	32	3b45,1b15,O2(1/0/1)	54	0.2
	StL N	44	149	16	40	7	1	5	30	21-7	2	26	.268	.358	.430	125	6	2-0	1.000	-1	95	74	1b37,O7L		0.3
	Year	103	364	40	104	14	2	10	65	46-9	3	59	.286	.367	.418	128	15	4-1	.998	-7	104	71	1b52,3b45,O9(8/0/1)		0.5
1989	StL N★	162	570	60	177	42	1	17	117	79-13	4	84	.311	.391	.477	144	37	2-0	.990	-13	71	101	1b160		1.4
1990	StL N	136	498	42	140	31	1	13	80	44-14	1	70	.281	.334	.426	109	6	1-1	.989	-8	83	86	1b132	15	-1.1
1991	StL N	115	427	41	116	12	1	8	70	37-2	1	46	.272	.326	.361	93	-4	4-2	.985	-9	80	105	1b112	42	-2.2
1992	StL N	43	146	10	32	6	1	1	16	11-3	0	25	.219	.270	.295	62	-7	2-2	.988	-7	29	93	1b28,O10L	121	-1.9
Total	15	1536	5392	730	1618	267	29	215	898	609-115	32	862	.300	.370	.480	138	281	97-47	.988	-51	82	94	1b573,O541R,3b373,2b12	407	17.4

GUERRERO, VLADIMIR Vladimir B2.9.1976 Nizao Bani, D.R. BR/TR/6-3/205(165-220) d9.19 b-Wilton

1996	Mon N	9	27	2	5	0	0	1	1	0-0	0	3	.185	.185	.296	24	-3	0-0	1.000	-0	94	0	O8(0/1/7)		-0.4
1997	Mon N	90	325	44	98	22	2	11	40	19-2	7	39	.302	.350	.483	118	8	3-4	.929	1	97	165	O85(0/1/84)	61	0.4
1998	Mon N	159	623	108	202	37	7	38	109	42-13	7	95	.324	.371	.589	152	44	11-9	.951	2	109	86	O157R		3.7
1999	Mon N★	160	610	102	193	37	5	42	131	55-14	7	62	.316	.378	.600	148	43	14-7	.948	5	108	143	O160R		3.7
2000	Mon N★	154	571	101	197	28	11	44	123	58-23	8	74	.345	.410	.664	165	55	9-10	.969	3	103	129	O151R,D2		4.5
2001	Mon N★	159	599	107	184	45	4	34	108	60-24	9	88	.307	.377	.566	141	37	37-16	.965	5	103	136	O158R		3.5
2002	Mon N★	161	614	106	206	37	2	39	111	84-32	6	70	.336	.417	.593	159	51	40-20	.969	-1	95	130	O161R		4.3
2003	Mon N	112	394	71	130	20	3	25	79	63-22	6	53	.330	.426	.586	158	36	9-5	.970	3	104	140	O112R	46	3.2
2004	†Ana A★	156	612	124	206	39	2	39	126	52-14	8	74	.337	.391	.598	161	54	15-3	.973	8	111	140	O143R,D13		5.2
2005	†LA A★	141	520	95	165	29	1	61-26		48		37	.394	.565			42	13-1	.988	5	104	117	O120R,D19	20	3.8
Total	10	1301	4895	860	1586	294	38	305	936	494-170	66	606	.324	.391	.587	151	367	151-75	.963	28	104	129	O1255(0/2/1253),D34	127	31.9

GUERRERO, WILTON Wilton B10.24.1974 Don Gregorio, D.R. BB/TR (BR 1996)/6-0/175(145-175) d9.3 b-Vladimir OF(81/21/27)

1996	LA N	5	2	1	0	0	0	0	0	0-0	0	2	.000	.000	.000	-99	-1	0-0	—	0			/H		-0.1
1997	LA N	111	357	39	104	10	9	4	32	8-1	0	52	.291	.305	.403	90	-8	6-5	.989	-18	88	50	2b90,S5		-2.2
1998	LA N	64	180	21	51	4	3	0	7	4-0	1	33	.283	.299	.339	72	-8	5-2	.968	-5	84	10	2b32,S14,O7(6/1/0)		-1.1
	Mon N	52	222	29	63	10	6	2	20	10-0	0	30	.284	.313	.410	91	-4	3-0	.975	-10	88	74	2b52		-1.1
	Year	116	402	50	114	14	9	2	27	14-0	1	63	.284	.307	.378	83	-12	8-2	.972	-15	87	80	2b84,S14,O7(6/1/0)		-2.2
1999	Mon N	132	315	42	92	15	7	2	31	13-0	2	38	.292	.324	.403	86	-8	7-6	.931	-14	87	66	2b54,O22L,D5		-2.1

YEAR	TM LG	G	AB	R	H	2B	3B	HR	RBI	BB-IB	HP	SO	AVG	OBP	SLG	AOPS	ABR	SB-CS	FA	FR	RNG	THR	GAMES AT POSITION	DL	BFW
2000	Mon N	127	288	30	77	7	2	2	23	19-0	0	41	.267	.312	.326	61	-18	8-1	.967	3	111	126	O75(42/13/24)/2D		-1.5
2001	Cin N	60	142	16	48	5	1	1	9	3-0	0	17	.338	.352	.408	91	-2	5-2	.927	-5	84	108	S16,2b11,O6L,3b4/D		-0.5
2002	Cin N	59	78	9	19	1	1	0	4	6-0	0	13	.244	.298	.282	55	-6	2-1	1.000	0	121	118	O2b10,S7,3b3		-0.5
	Mon N	44	62	3	12	1	0	0	1	1-1	0	19	.194	.206	.210	11	-8	5-0	1.000	-2	100	362	O12(4/5/3),2b7,3b2		-0.9
	Year	103	140	12	31	2	1	0	5	7-1	0	32	.221	.259	.250	36	-14	7-1	1.000	-2	100	89	2b17,O12(4/5/3),S7,3b5		-1.4
2004	KC A	24	32	7	7	0	0	1	1	0-0	0	4	.219	.219	.281	29	-4	1-0	.960	-2	107	52	2b8,S3,O3(1/2/0),1b2,3b2,D2		-0.4
Total	8	678	1678	197	473	53	30	11	127	64-2	3	249	.282	.308	.369	76	-67	42-17	.974	-52	89	66	2b265,O125L,S45,D14,3b11,1b2		-10.4

GUEVARA, GIOMAR Giomar Antonio (Diaz) B10.23.1972 Miranda, Venez BB/TR/5-8/150* d9.19

1997	Sea A	5	4	0	0	0	0	0	0	0-0	0	2	.000	.000	.000	-99	-1	1-0	.875	1	166	0	2b2/SD		0.0
1998	Sea A	11	13	4	3	2	0	0	4	4-0	0	4	.231	.444	.385	118	-1	0-0	1.000	-0	124	116	2b5,S5	154	0.1
1999	Sea A	10	12	2	3	0	0	0	2	0-0	0	2	.250	.250	.417	67	-1	0-0	.870	-1	96	55	S9		-0.1
Total	3	26	29	6	6	2	0	0	6	4-0	0	8	.207	.324	.345	73	-1	1-0	.900	-1	85	57	S15,2b7,D2	154	0.0

GUIEL, AARON Aaron Colin B10.5.1972 Vancouver BC, Can. BL/TR/5-10/190* [AnaA92 21/580] d6.22

2002	KC A	70	240	30	56	13	0	4	38	19-1	4	61	.233	.296	.338	62	-13	1-5	.952	0	99	139	O61(0/1/61),D2		-1.7
2003	KC A	99	354	63	98	30	0	15	52	27-0	13	63	.277	.346	.489	110	6	3-5	.985	6	105	177	O89(1/1/87),D2		0.6
2004	KC A	42	135	15	21	4	0	5	13	17-0	3	42	.156	.263	.296	46	-11	1-1	.966	3	122	151	O39(38/0/1),D2	65	-0.9
2005	KC A	33	109	18	32	5	0	4	7	6-1	5	21	.294	.355	.450	120	3	1-0	.985	-1	99	74	O30(0/24/7)		0.3
Total	4	244	838	126	207	52	0	28	110	69-2	25	187	.247	.319	.409	87	-15	6-11	.973	8	105	149	O219(39/26/156),D6	65	-1.7

GUILLEN, CARLOS Carlos Alfonso B9.30.1975 Maracay, Venez BB/TR/6-1/180(180-205) d9.6

1998	Sea A	10	39	9	13	1	1	0	5	3-0	0	9	.333	.381	.410	105	0	2-0	1.000	2	118	86	2b10		0.3
1999	Sea A	5	19	2	3	0	0	1	3	1-0	0	6	.158	.200	.316	29	-2	0-0	.938	2	130	58	S3,2b2	176	0.0
2000	†Sea A	90	288	45	74	15	2	7	42	28-0	2	53	.257	.324	.396	83	-8	1-3	.911	-5	96	63	3b68,S23	14	-1.0
2001	Sea A	140	456	72	118	21	4	5	53	53-0	1	89	.259	.333	.355	88	-7	4-1	.980	-21	87	110	S137/D		-1.8
2002	Sea A	134	475	73	124	24	6	9	56	46-4	1	91	.261	.326	.394	94	-5	4-5	.966	-23	83	91	S130,D3		-1.9
2003	Sea A	109	388	63	107	19	3	7	52	52-2	1	64	.276	.359	.394	105	5	4-4	.963	-11	82	137	S76,3b32/D	25	-0.1
2004	Det A☆	136	522	97	166	37	10	20	97	52-3	2	87	.318	.379	.542	142	32	12-5	.974	17	109	105	S135		5.6
2005	Det A	87	334	48	107	15	4	5	23	24-3	1	45	.320	.368	.434	116	7	2-3	.978	0	109	97	S75,D10	61	1.2
Total	8	711	2521	409	712	132	30	54	331	259-12	9.	444	.282	.349	.423	106	22	29-21	.972	-39	94	106	S579,3b100,D15,2b12	276	2.3

GUILLEN, JOSE Jose Manuel B5.17.1976 San Cristobal, D.R. BR/TR/5-11/195(185-196) d4.1

1997	Pit N	143	498	58	133	20	5	14	70	17-0	8	88	.267	.300	.412	83	-15	1-2	.963	-4	93	95	O136(0/4/134)		-2.6
1998	Pit N	153	573	60	153	38	2	14	84	21-0	6	100	.267	.298	.414	85	-14	3-5	.968	7	103	166	O151(0/2/149)		-1.6
1999	Pit N	40	120	18	32	6	0	1	18	10-1	0	21	.267	.321	.342	68	-6	0-0	.952	-1	98	51	O37R		-0.8
	TB A	47	168	24	41	10	0	2	13	10-1	7	36	.244	.312	.339	65	-9	0-0	.966	-1	88	156	O47R		-1.1
2000	TB A	105	316	40	80	16	5	10	41	18-1	13	65	.253	.320	.430	89	-7	3-1	.978	-0	99	117	O99(0/1/98)	8	-1.0
2001	TB A	41	135	14	37	5	0	3	11	6-2	3	26	.274	.317	.378	84	-3	2-3	.969	8	129	309	O36R,D4	72	0.2
2002	Ari N	54	131	13	30	4	0	4	15	7-1	2	25	.229	.277	.351	61	-8	3-4	1.000	-0	95	106	O27(2/2/34)		-1.1
	Cin N	31	109	12	27	3	0	4	16	7-0	1	18	.248	.299	.385	79	-4	1-1	.980	-1	87	169	O27(4/0/26)/D		-0.6
	Year	85	240	25	57	7	0	8	31	14-1	3	43	.237	.287	.367	68	-12	4-5	.990	-1	91	135	O64(6/2/60)/D		-1.7
2003	Cin N	91	315	52	106	21	1	23	63	17-1	9	63	.337	.385	.629	167	30	1-3	.957	7	114	181	O78(22/1/63)		3.1
	†Oak A	45	170	25	45	7	1	8	23	7-1	5	32	.265	.311	.459	100	-1	0-0	.942	-7	75	0	O44(10/4/33)/D		-0.9
2004	Ana N	148	565	88	166	28	3	27	104	37-5	15	92	.294	.352	.497	123	18	5-4	.979	4	103	124	O136(135/0/4),D10		1.5
2005	Was N	148	551	81	156	32	2	24	76	31-6	19	102	.283	.338	.479	120	15	1-1	.978	7	111	122	O142(2/0/140),D2		1.4
Total	9	1046	3651	485	1006	190	19	134	534	188-19	88	668	.276	.324	.448	101	-4	21-24	.970	18	101	131	O970(175/14/801),D18	80	-3.5

GUILLEN, OZZIE Oswaldo Jose (Barrios) B1.20.1964 Ocumare Del Tuy, Venez BL/TR/5-11/150(150-165) d4.9 M2/C3

1985	Chi A	150	491	71	134	21	9	1	33	12-1	1	36	.273	.291	.358	74	-19	7-4	.980	4	95	93	S150		-0.1
1986	Chi A	159	547	58	137	19	4	2	47	12-1	1	52	.250	.265	.311	55	-36	8-4	.970	18	111	102	S157/D		-0.1
1987	Chi A	149	560	64	156	22	7	2	51	22-2	1	52	.279	.303	.354	72	-23	25-8	.975	19	112	124	S149		1.3
1988	Chi A*	156	566	58	148	16	7	0	39	25-3	2	40	.261	.294	.314	71	-24	25-13	.977	41	123	111	S156		3.0
1989	Chi A	155	597	63	151	20	8	1	54	15-3	0	48	.253	.270	.318	67	-29	36-15	.973	18	109	102	S155		0.2
1990	Chi A★	160	516	61	144	21	4	1	58	26-8	1	37	.279	.312	.341	85	-11	13-17	.977	6	103	103	S159		0.3
1991	Chi A★	154	524	52	143	20	3	3	49	11-1	0	38	.273	.284	.340	74	-20	21-15	.970	0	101	103	S149		-1.0
1992	Chi A	12	40	5	8	4	0	0	7	1-0	0	5	.200	.214	.300	45	-3	1-0	1.000	1	106	90	S12	166	-0.1
1993	†Chi A	134	457	44	128	23	4	4	50	10-0	1	41	.280	.292	.374	80	-15	5-4	.972	-10	95	103	S133		-1.5
1994	Chi A	100	365	46	105	9	5	1	39	14-2	0	35	.288	.311	.348	71	-17	5-4	.959	-22	82	82	S99		-3.0
1995	Chi A	122	415	50	103	20	3	1	41	13-1	0	25	.248	.270	.318	55	-29	6-7	.976	-8	96	75	S120/D		-2.9
1996	Chi A	150	499	62	131	24	8	4	45	10-0	0	27	.263	.273	.367	64	-30	6-5	.981	-22	88	76	S146,O2L		-3.9
1997	Chi A	142	490	59	120	21	6	4	52	22-1	0	24	.245	.275	.337	61	-30	5-3	.974	-21	89	88	S139		-3.9
1998	Bal A	12	16	.2	1	0	0	0	0	1-0	0	2	.063	.118	.063	-52	-4	0-1	.933	-0	113	48	S6/3		-0.4
	†Atl N	83	264	35	73	15	1	1	22	24-0	1	25	.277	.337	.352	83	-6	1-4	.977	-6	86	74	S71,2b2/13		-0.8
1999	†Atl N	92	232	21	56	16	0	1	20	15-2	0	17	.241	.284	.323	55	-16	4-2	.965	-1	100	110	S53,3b11,1b5,2b2		-1.3
2000	TB A	63	107	22	26	4	0	2	12	6-0	0	7	.243	.283	.336	57	-7	1-0	.948	1	108	85	S42,3b11,1b6,2b5,O2L,D2	166	-0.4
Total	16	1993	6686	773	1764	275	69	28	639	239-25	7	511	.264	.287	.338	68	-319	169-108	.974	17	101	97	S1896,3b19,1b6,2b5,O2L,D2	166	-14.6

GUINDON, BOBBY Robert Joseph B9.4.1943 Brookline MA BL/TL/6-2/185 d9.19

| 1964 | Bos A | 5 | 8 | 0 | 1 | 1 | 0 | 0 | 1 | 1-0 | 0 | 1 | .125 | .222 | .250 | 30 | -1 | 0-0 | 1.000 | -0 | 0 | 0 | /1OL | | -0.1 |

GUINEY, BEN Benjamin Franklin B11.16.1858 Detroit MI D12.5.1930 Detroit MI BB/TR/6-0/170 d9.4

1883	Det N	1	5	1	1	0	0	0	0	0		1	.200	.200	.200	23	0		.000	-1	0	0	/OC		-0.1
1884	Det N	2	7	0	0	0	0	0	0	0		3	.000	.000	.000	-99	-2	0-0	.750	-1			C2		-0.2
Total	2	3	12	1	1	0	0	0	0	0		4	.083	.083	.083	-51	-2		.750	-2			C2/OC		-0.3

GUINTINI, BEN Benjamin John B1.13.1919 Los Banos CA D12.2.1998 Roseville CA BR/TR/6-1.5/190* d4.21

1946	Pit N	2	3	0	0	0	0	0	0	0-0	0	0	.000	.000	.000	-98	-1	0-0	1.000	0	112	0	/OR		-0.1
1950	Phi A	3	4	0	0	0	0	0	0	0-0	0	1	.000	.000	.000	-99	-1	0-0	1.000	1	0	2754	/OL		-0.1
Total	2	5	7	0	0	0	0	0	0	0-0	.0	1	.000	.000	.000	-99	-2	0-0	1.000	1	56	1377	O2(1/0/1)		-0.2

GUISTO, LOU Louis Joseph B1.16.1895 Napa CA D10.15.1989 Napa CA BR/TR/5-11/193 d9.10 Mil 1917-18 Col St. Marys (CA)

1916	Cle A	6	19	2	3	0	0	0	2	4	0	3	.158	.304	.158	37	-1	1	1.000	-0	85	88	1b6		-0.2
1917	Cle A	73	200	9	37	4	2	0	29	25	2	18	.185	.282	.225	51	-11	3	.989	-1	93	144	1b59		-1.6
1921	Cle A	2	2	0	1	0	0	0	1	0	0	1	.500	.500	.500	153	0	0-0	1.000	0	337	0	/1		0.0
1922	Cle A	35	84	7	21	10	1	0	9	2	.1	7	.250	.276	.393	72	-4	0-0	.995	1	108	103	1b24		-0.4
1923	Cle A	40	144	17	26	5	0	0	18	15	1	15	.181	.262	.215	27	-15	1-1	.988	1	116	104	1b40		-1.7
Total	5	156	449	35	88	19	3	0	59	46	4	44	.196	.277	.252	47	-31	5-1	.990	1	103	121	1b130		-3.9

GULAN, MIKE Michael Watts B12.18.1970 Steubenville OH BR/TR/6-1/192(192-211) [StLN92 2/53] d5.14 Col Kent St.

1997	StL N	5	9	2	0	0	0	0	1	1-0	0	5	.000	.100	.000	-71	-2	0-0	1.000	0	39	428	3b3		-0.3
2001	Fla N	6	6	1	0	0	0	0	0	2-0	0	2	.000	.250	.000	-28	-1	0-0	1.000	0	110	0	/3		-0.1
Total	2	11	15	3	0	0	0	0	1	3-0	0	7	.000	.167	.000	-52	-3	0-0	1.000	-0	69	245	3b4		-0.4

GULDEN, BRAD Bradley Lee B6.10.1956 New Ulm MN BL/TR/5-11/180* [LAN75 17/408] d9.22

1978	LA N	3	4	0	0	0	0	0	0	0-0	0	2	.000	.000	.000	-99	-1	0-0	1.000	1	0	0	C3		0.0
1979	NY A	40	92	10	15	4	0	0	6	9-0	0	16	.163	.238	.207	21	-10	0-1	.995	8	102	138	C40		-0.2
1980	NY A	2	3	1	1	0	0	0	1	0-0	0	1	.333	.333	1.333	339	1	0-0	1.000	-0	0	0	C2		0.1
1981	Sea A	8	16	0	3	2	0	0	1	0-0	0	3	.188	.188	.313	40	-1	0-0	1.000	2	95	85	C6		0.1
1982	Mon N	5	6	1	0	0	0	0	0	1-0	0	1	.000	.143	.000	-55	-1	0-0	1.000	-0	23	233	C2		-0.1
1984	Cin N	107	292	31	66	8	4	0	33	33-2	2	35	.226	.307	.308	70	-11	2-2	.975	-2	87	111	C100		-1.0
1986	SF N	17	22	2	2	0	0	0	1	2-2	0	5	.091	.167	.091	-28	-4	0-0	1.000	1	120	62	C10		-0.4
Total	7	182	435	45	87	14	2	5	45	45-4	2	61	.200	.277	.276	53	-27	2-5	.975	9	92	115	C163		-1.5

GULLEY, TOM Thomas Jefferson B12.25.1899 Garner NC D11.24.1966 St.Charles AR BL/TR/5-11/178 d8.24 Col Mississippi College

| 1923 | Cle A | 2 | 3 | 1 | 1 | 0 | 0 | 0 | 0 | 0 | 0 | 0 | .333 | .333 | .667 | 159 | -0 | | 1.000 | -0 | 85 | 0 | /OC | | 0.0 |
| 1924 | Cle A | 8 | 20 | 4 | 3 | 0 | 1 | 0 | 1 | 3 | 0 | 2 | .150 | .261 | .250 | 32 | -2 | 0-0 | .933 | -0 | 118 | 0 | O5(0/2/3) | | -0.3 |

YEAR	TM LG	G	AB	R	H	2B	3B	HR	RBI	BB-IB	HP	SO	AVG	OBP	SLG	AOPS	ABR	SB-CS	FA	FR	RNG	THR	GAMES AT POSITION	DL	BFW
1926	Chi A	16	35	5	8	3	1	0	8	5	0	2	.229	.325	.371	84	-1	0-0	1.000	-0	113	0	O12R		-0.2
Total	3	26	58	10	12	4	2	0	9	8	0	4	.207	.303	.345	69	-3	0-0	.971	-1	114	0	O18(0/3/15)		-0.5

GULLIC, TED   Tedd Jasper B1.2.1907 Koshkonong MO D1.28.2000 West Plains MO   BR/TR/6-2/175   d4.15

YEAR	TM LG	G	AB	R	H	2B	3B	HR	RBI	BB-IB	HP	SO	AVG	OBP	SLG	AOPS	ABR	SB-CS	FA	FR	RNG	THR	GAMES AT POSITION	DL	BFW
1930	StL A	92	308	39	77	7	5	4	44	27	0	43	.250	.310	.344	64	-18	0-0	.967	0	85	153	O82R,1b3		-2.2
1933	StL A	104	304	34	74	18	3	5	35	15	1	38	.243	.281	.372	67	-15	3-1	.988	10	100	249	O36(14/16/7),3b33,1b14		-0.6
Total	2	196	612	73	151	25	8	9	79	42	1	81	.247	.296	.358	65	-33	7-1	.975	10	89	180	O118(14/16/89),3b33,1b17		-2.8

GULLIVER, GLENN   Glenn James B10.15.1954 Detroit MI   BL/TR/5-11/175*   [DetA76 8/170]   d7.17   Col Eastern Michigan

YEAR	TM LG	G	AB	R	H	2B	3B	HR	RBI	BB-IB	HP	SO	AVG	OBP	SLG	AOPS	ABR	SB-CS	FA	FR	RNG	THR	GAMES AT POSITION	DL	BFW
1982	Bal A	50	145	24	29	7	0	1	5	37-0	0	18	.200	.363	.269	77	-2	0-0	.970	2	106	74	3b50		-0.1
1983	Bal A	23	47	5	10	3	0	0	2	9-0	0	5	.213	.333	.277	73	-1	0-1	1.000	3	116	119	3b21		0.1
Total	2	73	192	29	39	10	0	1	7	46-0	0	23	.203	.356	.271	76	-3	0-1	.978	5	108	84	3b71		0.0

GUNKLE, FRED   Frederick William B10.26.1857 Reading PA D12.21.1936 Long Beach CA   d5.17

YEAR	TM LG	G	AB	R	H	2B	3B	HR	RBI	BB-IB	HP	SO	AVG	OBP	SLG	AOPS	ABR	SB-CS	FA	FR	RNG	THR	GAMES AT POSITION	DL	BFW
1879	Cle N	1	3	1	0	0	0	0		0	0		.000	.000	.000	-99	-1		1.000	-2	0	0	/ORC		-0.2

GUNNING, HY   Hyland B8.6.1888 Maplewood NJ D3.28.1975 Togus ME   BL/TR/6-1.5/189   d8.8   Col Princeton

YEAR	TM LG	G	AB	R	H	2B	3B	HR	RBI	BB-IB	HP	SO	AVG	OBP	SLG	AOPS	ABR	SB-CS	FA	FR	RNG	THR	GAMES AT POSITION	DL	BFW
1911	Bos A	4	9	0	1	0	0	0	2	2-0	0		.111	.273	.111	9	-1	0	1.000	-1	0	0	1b4		-0.2

GUNNING, TOM   Thomas Francis B3.4.1862 Newmarket NH D3.17.1931 Fall River MA   BR/TR/5-10/160   d7.26   U2   Col Boston College

YEAR	TM LG	G	AB	R	H	2B	3B	HR	RBI	BB-IB	HP	SO	AVG	OBP	SLG	AOPS	ABR	SB-CS	FA	FR	RNG	THR	GAMES AT POSITION	DL	BFW
1884	Bos N	12	45	4	5	1	1	0	2	1		12	.111	.130	.178	-4	-5		.914	-3			C12		-0.7
1885	Bos N	48	174	17	32	3	0	0	15	5		29	.184	.207	.201	34	-13		.877	-5			C48		-1.3
1886	Bos N	27	98	15	22	2	1	0	7	3		19	.224	.248	.265	58	-5	3	.892	-7			C27		-0.9
1887	Phi N	28	104	22	27	6	1	1	16	5	2	6	.260	.306	.365	81	-3	18	.895	5			C28		0.4
1888	Phi AA	23	92	18	18	0	0	0	5	2	3		.196	.237	.196	40	-6	14	.894	-1			C23		-0.5
1889	Phi AA	8	24	3	6	0	1	1	1	0		4	.250	.250	.458	101	0	3	.838	-1			C8		-0.1
Total	6	146	537	79	110	12	4	2	46	16	5	70	.205	.235	.253	50	-32	38	.887	-11			C146		-3.1

GUNSON, JOE   Joseph Brook B3.23.1863 Philadelphia PA D11.15.1942 Philadelphia PA   BR/TR/5-6/160   d6.14

YEAR	TM LG	G	AB	R	H	2B	3B	HR	RBI	BB-IB	HP	SO	AVG	OBP	SLG	AOPS	ABR	SB-CS	FA	FR	RNG	THR	GAMES AT POSITION	DL	BFW
1884	Was U	45	166	15	23	2	0	0		3			.139	.154	.151	-8	-27		.915	6			C33,O18(0/10/9)		-1.7
1889	KC AA	34	122	15	24	3	1	0	12	3		17	.197	.228	.238	31	-12	2	.862	-6			C32/OL3		-1.3
1892	Bal N	89	314	35	67	10	5	0	32	16	7	17	.213	.267	.277	63	-15	2	.921	-3	95	109	C67,O20(10/3/7),1b2/2		-1.3
1893	StL N	40	151	20	41	5	0	0	15	6	5	6	.272	.321	.305	66	-7	0	.927	2	87	101	C35,O5(1/0/4)		-0.2
	Cle N	21	73	11	19	1	0	0	9	6	0	0	.260	.316	.274	54	-5	0	.942	3	114	111	C20		-0.1
	Year	61	224	31	60	6	0	0	24	12	5	6	.268	.320	.295	62	-12	0	.932	4	96	105	C55,O5(1/0/4)		-0.3
Total	4	229	826	96	174	21	6	0	68	34	14	40	.211	.254	.251	45	-66	4	.912	0	96	107	C187,O44(12/13/20),1b2/23		-4.6

GUST, ERNIE   Ernest Herman Frank "Red" B1.24.1888 Bay City MI D10.26.1945 Maupin OR   BR/TR/6-0/170   d8.17

YEAR	TM LG	G	AB	R	H	2B	3B	HR	RBI	BB-IB	HP	SO	AVG	OBP	SLG	AOPS	ABR	SB-CS	FA	FR	RNG	THR	GAMES AT POSITION	DL	BFW
1911	StL A	3	12	0	0	0	0	0	0	0	0	0	.000	.000	.000	-99	-3	0	1.000	-0	94	123	1b3		-0.4

GUSTINE, FRANKIE   Frank William B2.20.1920 Hoopeston IL D4.1.1991 Davenport IA   BR/TR/6-0/180*   d9.13   C1

YEAR	TM LG	G	AB	R	H	2B	3B	HR	RBI	BB-IB	HP	SO	AVG	OBP	SLG	AOPS	ABR	SB-CS	FA	FR	RNG	THR	GAMES AT POSITION	DL	BFW
1939	Pit N	22	70	5	13	3	0	0	3	9		4	.186	.278	.229	38	-6	0	.896	2	125	74	3b22		-0.3
1940	Pit N	133	524	59	147	32	7	1	55	35	2	39	.281	.328	.374	94	-4	7	.941	-8	100	103	2b130		-0.4
1941	Pit N	121	463	46	125	24	7	1	46	28	1	38	.270	.313	.359	89	-8	5	.954	-2	105	73	2b104,3b15		-0.3
1942	Pit N	115	388	34	89	11	4	2	35	29	2	27	.229	.286	.294	68	-16	5	.954	-14	101	84	2b108,S2,3b2/C		-2.5
1943	Pit N	112	414	40	120	21	3	0	43	32	0	36	.290	.341	.355	98	-1	12	.938	-4	103	101	S68,2b40/1		0.3
1944	Pit N	127	405	42	93	18	3	2	42	33	0	41	.230	.288	.304	64	-20	4	.938	-23	94	73	S116,2b11/3		-3.5
1945	Pit N	128	478	67	134	27	5	2	66	37	2	33	.280	.335	.370	92	-5	8	.930	-14	93	98	S104,2b29/C		-1.0
1946	Pit N★	131	495	60	128	23	6	8	52	42	3	52	.259	.318	.378	95	-5	2	.967	8	**108**	92	2b113,S13,3b7		1.0
1947	Pit N★	**156**	616	102	183	30	6	9	67	63	2	65	.297	.364	.409	102	3	5	.944	16	**110**	122	3b156		1.8
1948	Pit N★	131	449	68	120	19	2	9	42	42	2	62	.267	.333	.379	90	-6	5	.947	13	**115**	114	3b118		0.6
1949	Chi N	76	261	29	59	13	4	4	27	18	1	22	.226	.279	.352	70	-12	3	.931	0	98	106	3b55,2b16		-1.1
1950	StL A	9	19	1	3	1	0	0	2	3	0	8	.158	.273	.211	24	-2	0-1	.857	-1	70	219	3b6		-0.3
Total	12	1261	4582	553	1214	222	47	38	480	369	15	427	.265	.322	.359	87	-82	60-1	.955	-27	103	90	2b551,3b382,S303,C2/1		-5.7

GUTH, BUCKY   Charles Henry B8.18.1947 Baltimore MD   BR/TR/6-1/180   [AtlN69 20/466]   d9.12   Col West Virginia

YEAR	TM LG	G	AB	R	H	2B	3B	HR	RBI	BB-IB	HP	SO	AVG	OBP	SLG	AOPS	ABR	SB-CS	FA	FR	RNG	THR	GAMES AT POSITION	DL	BFW
1972	Min A	3	3	1	0	0	0	0	0	0-0	0	0	.000	.000	.000	-95	-1	0-0	1.000	-0	125	0	/S		-0.1

GUTIERREZ, CESAR   Cesar Dario "Cocoa" B1.26.1943 Coro, Venez D1.22.2005 Maracaibo, Venez   BR/TR/5-9/155*   d4.16

YEAR	TM LG	G	AB	R	H	2B	3B	HR	RBI	BB-IB	HP	SO	AVG	OBP	SLG	AOPS	ABR	SB-CS	FA	FR	RNG	THR	GAMES AT POSITION	DL	BFW
1967	SF N	18	21	4	3	0	0	0	0	1-0	1	4	.143	.217	.143	5	-3	1-0	.946	1	105	124	S15/2		-0.1
1969	SF N	15	23	4	5	1	0	0	0	6-1	0	2	.217	.379	.261	83	0	1-0	.882	-2	105	0	3b7,S4		-0.1
	Det A	17	49	5	12	1	0	0	0	5-0	0	3	.245	.315	.265	61	-2	1-2	.946	0	100	75	S16		-0.1
1970	Det A	135	415	40	101	11	6	0	22	18-6	1	39	.243	.275	.299	58	-25	4-3	.957	-22	86	77	S135		-3.5
1971	Det A	38	37	8	7	0	0	0	4	0-0	1	3	.189	.211	.189	13	-4	0-0	.971	0	103	49	S14,3b5,2b2	41	-0.3
Total	4	223	545	61	128	13	6	0	26	30-7	3	51	.235	.277	.281	55	-34	7-5	.955	-22	89	77	S184,3b12,2b3	41	-4.1

GUTIERREZ, FRANKLIN   Franklin Rafael B2.21.1983 Caracas, Venez   BR/TR/6-2/180   d8.31

YEAR	TM LG	G	AB	R	H	2B	3B	HR	RBI	BB-IB	HP	SO	AVG	OBP	SLG	AOPS	ABR	SB-CS	FA	FR	RNG	THR	GAMES AT POSITION	DL	BFW
2005	Cle A	7	1	2	0	0	0	0	0	0-0	0	0	.000	.500	.000	52	0	0-0	1.000	0	115	0	O2C,D3		0.0

GUTIERREZ, JACKIE   Joaquin Fernando B6.27.1960 Cartagena, Colombia   BR/TR/5-11/175(145-180)   d9.6

YEAR	TM LG	G	AB	R	H	2B	3B	HR	RBI	BB-IB	HP	SO	AVG	OBP	SLG	AOPS	ABR	SB-CS	FA	FR	RNG	THR	GAMES AT POSITION	DL	BFW
1983	Bos A	5	10	2	3	0	0	0	1	1	0	1	.300	.364	.300	79	-0	0-0	.938	-1	61	50	S4		-0.1
1984	Bos A	151	449	55	118	12	3	2	29	15-0	0	49	.263	.284	.316	63	-23	12-5	.949	-25	84	68	S150		-3.4
1985	Bos A	103	275	33	60	5	2	2	21	12-0	0	37	.218	.250	.273	42	-23	10-2	.943	-3	98	85	S99		-1.6
1986	Bal A	61	145	8	27	3	0	0	4	3-0	1	27	.186	.207	.207	14	-18	3-1	.990	-5	85	107	S2b53,3b6/D	74	-0.5
1987	Bal A	3	1	0	0	0	0	0	0	0-0	0	0	.000	.000	.000	-99	0	0-0	—	-0	0	0	/23		-0.1
1988	Phi N	33	77	8	19	4	0	0	9	2-0	0	9	.247	.259	.299	60	-4	0-0	.919	-3	104	76	S22,3b13		-0.1
Total	6	356	957	106	227	24	5	4	63	33-0	1	123	.237	.261	.285	50	-68	25-9	.945	-38	90	74	S275,2b54,3b20/D	74	-7.8

GUTIERREZ, RICKY   Ricardo B5.23.1970 Miami FL   BR/TR/6-1/175(175-195)   [BalA88 1/28]   d4.13

YEAR	TM LG	G	AB	R	H	2B	3B	HR	RBI	BB-IB	HP	SO	AVG	OBP	SLG	AOPS	ABR	SB-CS	FA	FR	RNG	THR	GAMES AT POSITION	DL	BFW
1993	SD N	133	438	76	110	10	5	5	26	50-0	5	97	.251	.334	.331	78	-13	4-3	.971	-3	92	83	S117,2b6,O5(3/0/2),3b4		-0.8
1994	SD N	90	275	27	66	11	2	1	28	32-1	2	54	.240	.321	.305	67	-13	2-6	.925	-11	91	77	S78,2b7		-2.0
1995	Hou N	52	156	22	43	6	0	0	12	10-3	1	33	.276	.321	.314	74	-6	5-0	.956	-6	88	70	S44,3b2		-0.8
1996	Hou N	89	218	28	62	8	1	1	15	23-3	3	42	.284	.359	.344	94	-1	6-1	.953	-9	85	90	S74,3b6,2b5		-0.5
1997	†Hou N	102	303	33	79	14	4	3	34	21-2	3	50	.261	.315	.363	79	-10	5-2	.967	-3	97	116	S64,3b22,2b9	35	-0.8
1998	†Hou N	141	491	55	128	24	3	2	46	54-5	6	84	.261	.337	.334	81	-12	13-7	.976	14	103	111	S141		1.2
1999	†Hou N	85	268	33	70	7	5	1	25	37-4	2	45	.261	.354	.336	77	-9	2-5	.971	-6	94	83	S80/3	70	-1.0
2000	Chi N	125	449	73	124	19	2	11	56	66-0	7	58	.276	.375	.401	98	1	8-2	**.986**	-13	88	82	S121	28	-0.2
2001	Chi N	147	528	76	153	23	3	10	66	40-0	10	56	.290	.345	.402	97	-2	4-3	.971	-8	91	81	S144		0.1
2002	Cle A	94	353	38	97	13	0	4	38	20-0	7	45	.275	.325	.346	77	-11	0-1	.976	12	109	103	2b93/D	64	0.4
2003	Cle A	16	50	2	13	0	0	0	3	3-0	1	5	.260	.309	.320	68	-2	0-0	.929	-3	102	71	S9,3b7	164	-0.5
2004	NY N	24	63	2	11	2	0	0	5	6-0	0	6	.175	.257	.206	23	-7	0-0	1.000	0	111	115	2b18,3b2		-0.1
	Bos A	21	40	6	11	1	0	0	3	2-0	0	6	.275	.310	.300	57	-3	1-0	1.000	0	102	127	2b14,S6		-0.1
Total	12	1119	3632	471	967	141	25	38	357	364-20	48	586	.266	.338	.350	82	-88	50-30	.967	-35	93	89	S878,2b152,3b44,O5(3/0/2)/D	361	-5.6

GUTTERIDGE, DON   Donald Joseph B6.19.1912 Pittsburg KS   BR/TR/5-10.5/165   d9.7   M2/C14   Col Pittsburg St. (KS)

YEAR	TM LG	G	AB	R	H	2B	3B	HR	RBI	BB-IB	HP	SO	AVG	OBP	SLG	AOPS	ABR	SB-CS	FA	FR	RNG	THR	GAMES AT POSITION	DL	BFW
1936	StL N	23	91	13	29	3	4	3	16	1	0	14	.319	.326	.538	130	3	3	.967	0	94	109	3b23		0.3
1937	StL N	119	447	66	121	26	10	7	61	25	1	66	.271	.311	.421	95	-5	12	.978	0	93	**133**	3b105,S8		0.0
1938	StL N	142	552	61	141	21	15	9	64	29	0	49	.255	.293	.397	83	-15	14	.945	-7	98	132	3b73,S68		-1.5
1939	StL N	148	524	71	141	27	4	7	54	27	3	70	.269	.309	.376	78	-17	5	.934	-19	79	107	3b143,S2		-3.2
1940	StL N	69	108	19	29	8	0	3	14	5	0	15	.269	.301	.398	86	-2	3	.877	-4	79	90	3b39		-0.6
1942	StL A	147	616	90	157	27	11	1	50	59	0	54	.255	.320	.339	84	-14	16-13	.973	2	102	98	2b145,3b2		-2.2
1943	StL A	132	538	77	147	35	6	1	36	50	0	46	.273	.335	.366	103	2	10-9	.958	-29	85	69	2b132		-2.2
1944	†StL A	148	603	89	148	27	3	3	36	51	0	63	.245	.304	.342	80	-17	20-8	.957	-10	96	94	2b146		-1.8
1945	StL A	143	543	72	129	24	3	2	49	43	1	46	.238	.295	.304	70	-21	9-6	.970	-17	91	83	2b128,O14L		-3.4
1946	†Bos A	22	47	8	11	3	0	1	6	2	0	7	.234	.265	.362	70	-2	0-1	1.000	-1	125	136	2b9,3b8		-0.3
1947	Bos A	54	131	20	22	2	0	2	5	17	0	13	.168	.264	.229	35	-12	3-1	.938	-2	96	85	2b20,3b19		-1.3
1948	Pit N	4	2	0	0	0	0	0	0	0	0	0	.000	.000	.000	-98	-1	0	—	0			/H		-0.1
Total	12	1151	4202	586	1075	200	64	39	391	309	5	444	.256	.308	.362	84	-101	95-<u>37</u>	.964	-86	94	87	2b580,3b412,S78,O14L		-14.4

YEAR	TM LG	G	AB	R	H	2B	3B	HR	RBI	BB-IB	HP	SO	AVG	OBP	SLG	AOPS	ABR	SB-CS	FA	FR	RNG	THR	GAMES AT POSITION	DL	BFW
GUZMAN, CRISTIAN	Cristian B3.21.1978 Santo Domingo, D.R. BB/TR/6-0/195(188-205) d4.6																								
1999	Min A	131	420	47	95	12	3	1	26	22-0	3	90	.226	.267	.276	38	-41	9-7	.959	-5	100	101	S131	15	-3.5
2000	Min A	156	631	89	156	25	**20**	8	54	46-1	2	101	.247	.299	.388	68	-34	28-10	.967	-17	90	94	S151/D		-3.4
2001	Min A★	118	493	80	149	28	**14**	10	51	21-0	5	78	.302	.337	.477	105	2	25-8	.959	-10	100	85	S118	35	0.3
2002	†Min A	148	623	80	170	31	6	9	59	17-2	2	79	.273	.292	.385	76	-23	12-13	.981	-17	87	98	S147/D		-3.0
2003	†Min A	143	534	78	143	15	**14**	3	53	30-0	5	79	.268	.311	.365	75	-21	18-9	.980	-30	88	78	S141		-3.8
2004	†Min A	145	576	84	158	31	4	8	46	30-4	1	64	.274	.309	.384	78	-20	10-5	.983	9	102	115	S145		0.0
2005	Was N	142	456	39	100	19	6	4	31	25-6	1	76	.219	.260	.314	53	-34	7-4	.973	-23	88	99	S142		-4.7
Total	7	983	3733	497	971	161	67	43	320	191-13	19	567	.260	.298	.374	72	-171	109-56	.972	-93	93	96	S975,D2	50	-18.1
GUZMAN, EDWARDS	Edwards B9.11.1976 Bayamon, PR BL/TR/5-11/205* [SFN95 50/1363] d4.6																								
1999	SF N	14	15	0	0	0	0	0	0	0-0	0	4	.000	.000	.000	-99	-5	0-0	1.000	1	150	0	3b5/C		-0.4
2001	SF N	61	115	8	28	6	0	3	7	5-2	0	16	.243	.273	.374	70	-6	0-0	.990	-4	149	91	C26,1b7,3b7,2b3,O2L		-0.9
2003	Mon N	52	146	15	35	5	0	1	14	5-2	0	17	.240	.263	.295	45	-12	0-0	.956	-5	95	91	3b28,1b13,C4,D3		-1.7
Total	3	127	276	23	63	11	0	4	21	10-4	0	37	.228	.253	.312	47	-23	0-0	.969	-7	100	84	3b40,C31,1b20,D3,2b3,O2L		-3.0
GUZMAN, FREDDY	Freddy Antonio B1.20.1981 Santo Domingo, D.R. BB/TR/5-10/165 d8.17 [DL 2005 SD N 183]																								
2004	SD N	20	76	8	16	3	0	0	1	13	.211	.250	.250	31	-8	5-2	.960	2	122	254	O17C		-0.5		
GWOSDZ, DOUG	Douglas Wayne "Eye Chart" B6.20.1960 Houston TX BR/TR/5-11/180* [SDN78 2/40] d8.17																								
1981	SD N	16	24	1	4	0	0	0	3	3-2	0	6	.167	.241	.250	49	-2	0-0	1.000	2	328	130	C13		0.1
1982	SD N	7	17	1	3	0	0	0	0	2-1	0	7	.176	.263	.176	27	-2	0-0	1.000	2	443	0	C7		0.1
1983	SD N	39	55	7	6	1	0	1	4	7-0	0	19	.109	.210	.182	10	-7	0-0	.971	-2	137	53	C32		-0.9
1984	SD N	7	8	0	2	0	0	0	1	2-0	0	5	.250	.400	.250	86	0	0-0	.963	2	114	98	C6		0.2
Total	4	69	104	9	15	3	0	1	8	14-3	0	37	.144	.242	.202	27	-11	0-0	.981	4	228	67	C58		-0.5
GWYNN, TONY	Anthony Keith B5.9.1960 Los Angeles CA BL/TL/5-11/199(185-225) [SDN81 3/58] d7.19 b-Chris Col San Diego St.																								
1982	SD N	54	190	33	55	12	2	1	17	14-0	0	16	.289	.337	.389	110	2	8-3	.991	-2	100	29	O52(23/28/13)	15	0.0
1983	SD N	86	304	34	94	12	2	1	37	23-5	0	21	.309	.355	.372	106	2	7-4	.994	4	102	153	O81(26/6/54)	78	0.2
1984	†SD N★	158	606	88	213	21	10	5	71	59-13	2	23	.351	.410	.444	139	33	33-18	.989	9	112	103	O156(0/1/156)		3.6
1985	SD N★	154	622	90	197	29	5	6	46	45-4	2	33	.317	.364	.408	117	14	14-11	.989	11	112	129	O152R		1.6
1986	SD N★	160	642	**107**	**211**	33	7	14	59	52-11	3	35	.329	.381	.467	136	31	37-9	.989	14	113	147	O160R		4.2
1987	SD N★	157	589	119	218	36	13	7	54	82-26	3	35	.370	.447	.511	160	55	56-12	.981	4	104	123	O156R		5.8
1988	SD N	133	521	64	163	22	5	7	70	51-13	0	40	.313	.373	.415	129	20	26-11	.982	-3	94	122	O133(0/32/102)	21	1.7
1989	SD N★	158	604	82	203	27	7	4	62	56-16	1	30	.336	.389	.424	133	27	40-16	.984	1	97	153	O157(0/86/73)		3.0
1990	SD N★	141	573	79	177	29	10	4	72	44-20	1	23	.309	.357	.415	111	9	17-8	.985	6	107	104	O141R		1.1
1991	SD N★	134	530	69	168	27	11	4	62	34-8	0	19	.317	.355	.432	117	11	8-8	.990	5	108	78	O134R		1.1
1992	SD N★	128	520	77	165	27	3	6	41	46-12	0	16	.317	.371	.415	121	15	3-6	.982	4	104	102	O127R		1.4
1993	SD N★	122	489	70	175	41	3	7	59	36-11	1	19	.358	.398	.497	138	28	14-1	.981	2	107	90	O121(0/4/121)		2.6
1994	†SD N★	†110	419	79	**165**	35	1	12	64	48-16	2	19	**.394**	**.454**	.568	171	47	5-0	.985	-2	99	81	O106(0/1/105)	35	3.9
1995	SD N★	135	535	82	**197**	33	1	9	90	35-10	1	15	.368	.404	.484	138	30	17-5	.992	2	103	89	O133R		2.6
1996	†SD N★	116	451	67	159	27	2	3	50	39-12	1	17	.353	.400	.441	129	20	11-4	.989	-10	87	27	O111R	35	0.6
1997	SD N★	149	592	97	220	49	2	17	119	43-12	3	28	.372	.409	.547	160	52	12-5	.983	-10	83	77	O143R,D3	19	3.5
1998	†SD N★	127	461	65	148	35	0	16	69	35-6	1	18	.321	.364	.501	136	24	3-1	.993	-11	75	74	O116R,D3	50	0.8
1999	SD N★	111	411	59	139	27	0	10	62	29-5	2	14	.338	.381	.477	126	16	7-2	.993	-8	83	67	O104R,D2	50	0.4
2000	SD N	36	127	17	41	12	0	1	17	9-2	1	4	.323	.364	.441	111	3	0-1	1.000	-4	66	66	O26R,D6	114	-0.2
2001	SD N☆	71	102	5	33	9	1	1	17	10-1	0	9	.324	.384	.461	127	4	1-0	1.000	-9	72	254	O17R/D	71	0.7
Total	20	2440	9288	1383	3141	543	85	135	1138	790-203	24	434	.338	.388	.459	133	443	319-125	.987	12	100	102	O2326(49/158/2144),D15	403	38.3
GWYNN, CHRIS	Christopher Karlton B10.13.1964 Los Angeles CA BL/TL/6-0/210(200-220) [LAN85 1/10] d8.14 b-Tony Col San Diego St.																								
1987	LA N	17	32	2	7	1	0	0	2	1-0	0	7	.219	.242	.250	32	-3	0-0	1.000	-1	83	0	O10L		-0.4
1988	LA N	12	11	1	2	0	0	0	1	1-0	0	2	.182	.250	.182	27	-1	0-0	—	-0	0	0	O4L		-0.4
1989	LA N	32	68	8	16	4	1	0	7	2-0	0	9	.235	.254	.324	66	-3	1-0	1.000	-0	86	132	O19(14/5/2)	102	-0.4
1990	LA N	101	141	19	40	7	1	5	22	7-2	0	28	.284	.311	.418	103	0	0-1	1.000	-2	80	64	O44(32/5/8)		-0.3
1991	LA N	94	139	18	35	5	1	5	22	10-1	1	23	.252	.301	.410	101	0	1-0	1.000	-2	76	132	O41(31/2/14)		-0.2
1992	KC A	34	84	10	24	3	2	1	7	3-0	0	10	.286	.303	.405	96	-1	0-0	1.000	-2	91	0	O19(5/0/14),D2	118	-0.3
1993	KC A	103	287	36	86	14	4	1	25	24-5	1	34	.300	.354	.387	93	-3	0-1	.994	3	102	135	O83(66/0/19)/1D		-0.3
1994	LA N	58	71	9	19	0	0	3	13	7-0	0	7	.268	.333	.394	94	-1	0-2	1.000	-1	75	0	O20(19/0/1)		-0.3
1995	†LA N	67	84	8	18	3	2	1	10	6-1	1	23	.214	.272	.333	64	-5	0-0	1.000	0	109	0	O17(12/0/5),1b2	21	-0.5
1996	†SD N	81	90	8	16	4	0	1	10	10-0	0	28	.178	.260	.256	38	-8	0-0	1.000	-1	90	0	O29(5/0/24)/1	36	-0.9
Total	10	599	1007	119	263	36	11	17	118	71-9	3	171	.261	.308	.369	84	-25	2-4	.997	-5	91	84	O286(198/12/87),D7,1b4	277	-3.8
GYSELMAN, DICK	Richard Renald B4.6.1908 San Francisco CA D9.20.1990 Seattle WA BR/TR/6-2/170 d4.20																								
1933	Bos N	58	155	10	37	6	2	0	12	7	0	21	.239	.272	.303	70	-7	0	.926	2	110	72	3b42,2b5/S		-0.4
1934	Bos N	24	36	7	6	1	1	0	4	2	0	11	.167	.211	.250	25	-4	0	.739	-3	67	0	3b15,2b2		-0.7
Total	2	82	191	17	43	7	3	0	16	9	0	32	.225	.260	.293	61	-11	0	.901	-1	104	62	3b57,2b7/S		-1.1
HAAD, YAMID	Yamid Salcedo B9.2.1977 Cartagena, Colombia BR/TR/6-2/204* d7.5																								
1999	Pit N	1	1	0	0	0	0	0	0	0-0	0	0	.000	.000	.000	-99	0	0-0	—	0			/H		0.0
2005	SF N	17	28	0	2	1	0	0	1	3-0	0	7	.071	.156	.107	-27	-5	0-0	.957	0	107	232	C16		-0.5
Total	2	18	29	0	2	1	0	0	1	3-0	0	7	.069	.152	.103	-29	-5	0-0	.957	0	107	232	C16		-0.5
HAAS, BERT	Berthold John B2.8.1914 Naperville IL D6.23.1999 Tampa FL BR/TR/5-11/180* d9.9 Mil 1944-45																								
1937	Bro N	16	25	2	10	3	0	0	2	1	0	1	.400	.423	.520	152	2	0	1.000	-0	109	0	O4R,1b3		0.1
1938	Bro N	1	0	0	0	0	0	0	0	0	0	0	—	—	—	—	0	0	—	0			/H		0.0
1942	Cin N	**154**	585	59	140	21	6	6	54	59	1	54	.239	.310	.326	86	-10	6	.925	-14	91	**125**	3b146,1b6,O2L		-2.1
1943	Cin N	101	332	39	87	17	6	4	44	22	0	26	.262	.308	.386	101	-1	6	.993	6	169	142	1b44,3b23,O18C		0.3
1946	Cin N	140	535	57	141	24	7	3	50	33	3	42	.264	.310	.351	91	-9	22	.994	-2	93	**141**	1b140,3b6		-1.7
1947	Cin N★	135	482	58	138	17	7	3	67	42	1	27	.286	.346	.369	91	-7	9	.956	-6	108	47	O69(8/58/0),1b53		-1.7
1948	Phi N	95	333	35	94	9	2	4	34	36	1	25	.282	.354	.357	91	-2	8	.892	-7	85	101	3b54,1b35		-1.0
1949	Phi N	2	1	0	0	0	0	0	0	1	0	1	.000	.500	.000	47	0	0	—	0			/H		0.0
	NY N	54	104	12	27	2	3	1	10	5	0	8	.260	.294	.365	76	-4	0	.983	-2	97	95	1b23,3b11		-0.7
	Year	56	105	12	27	2	3	1	10	6	0	9	.257	.297	.362	76	-4	0	.983	-2	97	95	1b23,3b11		-0.7
1951	Chi A	23	43	1	7	0	1	1	2	5	0	4	.163	.250	.279	44	-4	0-0	1.000	-0	99	80	1b7,O4(1/0/3)/3		-0.4
Total	9	721	2440	263	644	93	32	22	263	204	7	188	.264	.323	.355	91	-35	51-0	.991	-26	95	120	1b311,3b241,O97(11/76/7)		-7.2
HAAS, EDDIE	George Edwin B5.26.1935 Paducah KY BL/TR/5-11/178* d9.8 M1/C5 [DL 1959 Mil N 145]																								
1957	Chi N	14	24	1	5	1	0	0	4	1-0	0	5	.208	.231	.250	32	-2	0-0	1.000	1	65	0	O4(3/1/0)		-0.3
1958	Mil N	9	14	2	5	0	0	0	1	2-0	0	1	.357	.438	.357	124	1	0-0	1.000	-0	99	0	O3(0/2/1)		0.0
1960	Mil N	32	32	4	7	2	0	1	5	5-0	0	14	.219	.324	.375	98	0	0-0	1.000	-0	58	0	O2(1/0/1)		0.0
Total	3	55	70	7	17	3	0	1	10	8-0	0	20	.243	.316	.329	80	-1	0-0	1.000	0	74	0	O9(4/3/2)	145	-0.3
HAAS, MULE	George William B10.15.1903 Montclair NJ D6.30.1974 New Orleans LA BL/TR/6-1/175 d8.15 C7																								
1925	Pit N	4	3	1	0	0	0	0	0	1-0	0	0	.000	.000	.000	-94	-1	0-0	1.000	0	142	0	O2(0/1/1)		-0.1
1928	Phi A	91	332	41	93	21	4	6	39	23	2	20	.280	.331	.422	94	-4	2-3	.974	-3	91	110	O82(10/69/4)		-1.1
1929	†Phi A	139	578	115	181	41	9	16	82	34	4	38	.313	.356	.498	113	9	0-4	.982	-4	97	68	O139(1/139/0)		-0.7
1930	†Phi A	132	532	91	159	33	7	2	68	43	1	33	.299	.352	.398	86	-11	2-2	.976	7	106	121	O131C		-0.8
1931	†Phi A	102	440	82	142	29	7	8	56	30	0	29	.323	.366	.475	113	7	0-0	.989	-1	98	75	O102C		0.3
1932	Phi A	143	558	91	170	28	6	5	65	62	2	49	.305	.376	.405	99	0	1-0	.987	1	106	54	O137(0/108/29)		-0.3
1933	Chi A	146	585	97	168	33	4	1	51	65	2	41	.287	.360	.362	96	-1	1-0	.983	-10	90	85	O146C		-1.5
1934	Chi A	106	351	54	94	16	3	2	40	47	0	22	.268	.354	.348	79	-10	1-0	.991	-5	92	72	O89(0/85/4)		-1.6
1935	Chi A	92	327	44	95	22	1	2	40	37	1	17	.291	.363	.382	90	-4	4-1	.989	-1	102	58	O84(0/22/64)		-0.8
1936	Chi A	119	408	75	116	26	2	0	46	64	1	29	.284	.383	.358	81	-10	1-1	.989	-5	91	79	O96(2/1/94),1b7		-1.8
1937	Chi A	54	111	8	23	5	1	0	15	16	1	10	.207	.313	.288	52	-8	0-0	.975	0	127	103	1b32,O2R		-1.0
1938	Phi A	40	78	7	16	3	0	0	12	12	0	10	.205	.311	.231	39	-7	0-0	1.000	-1	100	0	O12(0/5/7),1b6		-0.8
Total	12	1168	4303	706	1257	254	45	43	496	433	13	299	.292	.359	.402	90	-40	12-16	.984	-20	97	80	O1022(13/809/205),1b45		-9.7

YEAR	TM LG	G	AB	R	H	2B	3B	HR	RBI	BB-IB	HP	SO	AVG	OBP	SLG	AOPS	ABR	SB-CS	FA	FR	RNG	THR	GAMES AT POSITION	DL	BFW

HABERER, EMIL Emil Karl B2.2.1878 Cincinnati OH D10.19.1951 Louisville KY BR/TR/6-1/204 d7.9

YEAR	TM LG	G	AB	R	H	2B	3B	HR	RBI	BB-IB	HP	SO	AVG	OBP	SLG	AOPS	ABR	SB-CS	FA	FR	RNG	THR	GAMES AT POSITION	DL	BFW
1901	Cin N	6	18	2	3	0	1	0	3	0			.167	.286	.278	68	-1	0	.545	-2	84	0	3b3,1b2		-0.2
1903	Cin N	5	13	1	1	0	0	0	2	0			.077	.200	.077	-18	-2	0	.933	-1	92	53	C4		-0.3
1909	Cin N	5	16	1	3	1	0	0	2	0			.188	.188	.250	36	-1	0	.895	-1	81	59	C4		-0.3
Total	3	16	47	4	7	1	1	0	3	5	0		.149	.231	.213	31	-4	0	.912	-4	86	56	C8,3b3,1b2		-0.8

HACH, IRV Irvin William "Major" B6.6.1873 Louisville KY D8.13.1936 Louisville KY BR/TR d7.1

| 1897 | Lou N | 16 | 51 | 5 | 11 | 2 | 0 | 0 | 3 | 5 | 3 | | .216 | .322 | .255 | 55 | -3 | 1 | .889 | -2 | 97 | 88 | 2b9,3b7 | | -0.3 |

HACK, STAN Stanley Camfield "Smiling Stan" B12.6.1909 Sacramento CA D12.15.1979 Dixon IL BL/TR/6-0/170 d4.12 M4/C3

1932	†Chi N	72	178	32	42	5	6	2	19	17	1	16	.236	.306	.365	80	-6	5	.913	-4	100	60	3b51		-0.8
1933	Chi N	20	60	10	21	3	1	1	2	8	3	3	.350	.451	.483	167	6	4	.983	4	113	320	3b17		1.1
1934	Chi N	111	402	54	116	16	6	1	21	45	2	42	.289	.363	.366	98	0	11	.949	8	107	77	3b109		1.1
1935	†Chi N	124	427	75	133	23	9	4	64	65	3	17	.311	.406	.436	125	19	14	.942	5	112	128	3b111,1b7		2.6
1936	Chi N	149	561	102	167	27	4	6	78	89	2	39	.298	.396	.392	110	13	17	.950	-13	87	82	3b140,1b11		0.4
1937	Chi N	154	582	106	173	27	6	2	63	83	3	42	.297	.388	.375	104	7	16	.968	-11	89	129	3b150,1b4		0.2
1938	†Chi N★	152	609	109	195	34	11	4	67	94	0	39	.320	.411	.432	128	29	16	.954	7	100	103	3b152		4.0
1939	Chi N★	156	641	112	191	28	6	8	56	65	2	35	.298	.364	.398	103	4	17	.956	-8	91	54	3b156		0.1
1940	Chi N	149	603	101	191	38	6	8	40	75	3	24	.317	.395	.439	132	30	21	.954	10	103	122	3b148/1		4.5
1941	Chi N★	151	586	111	186	33	5	7	45	99	1	40	.317	.417	.427	143	39	10	.954	-14	92	78	3b150/1		3.1
1942	Chi N	140	553	91	166	36	3	6	39	94	0	40	.300	.402	.409	143	36	9	.965	-12	92	75	3b139		3.1
1943	Chi N★	144	533	78	154	24	4	3	35	82	0	27	.289	.384	.366	119	17	5	.960	-5	98	48	3b136		1.4
1944	Chi N	98	383	65	108	16	1	3	32	53	0	21	.282	.369	.352	104	5	5	.939	5	108	55	3b75,1b18		1.0
1945	†Chi N★	150	597	110	193	29	7	2	43	99	1	30	.323	.420	.405	133	33	12	.975	20	105	115	3b146,1b5		5.3
1946	Chi N	92	323	55	92	13	4	0	26	83	0	32	.285	.431	.350	125	18	3	.968	-2	97	45	3b90		1.6
1947	Chi N	76	240	28	65	11	2	0	12	41	0	19	.271	.377	.333	94	0	1	.962	8	115	97	3b66		0.7
Total	16	1938	7278	1239	2193	363	81	57	642	1092	21	466	.301	.394	.397	120	250	165					3b1836,1b47		29.4

HACKER, RICH Richard Warren B10.6.1947 Belleville IL BB/TR (BR 1971p)/6-0/160 [NYN67 S8/154] d7.2 C9 Col Southern Illinois

| 1971 | Mon N | 16 | 33 | 2 | 4 | 1 | 0 | 0 | 2 | 3-0 | | 12 | .121 | .194 | .152 | -1 | -1 | 0-0 | .984 | 4 | 129 | 119 | S16 | | 0.1 |

HACKETT, JIM James Joseph "Sunny Jim" B10.1.1877 Jacksonville IL D3.28.1961 Douglas MI BR/TR/6-2/185 d9.14 ▲

1902	StL N	6	21	2	6	1	0	0	4	2	0		.286	.348	.333	115	0	1	.833	-1	92	0	P4,O2R		-0.1
1903	StL N	99	351	24	80	13	8	0	36	19	2		.228	.272	.311	68	-16	2	.972	-6	78	132	1b89,P7		-2.2
Total	2	105	372	26	86	14	8	0	40	21	2		.231	.276	.312	70	-16	3	.972	-7	78	132	1b89,P11,O2R		-2.3

HACKETT, MERT Mortimer Martin B11.11.1859 Cambridge MA D2.22.1938 Cambridge MA BR/TR/5-10.5/175 d5.2 b-Walter

1883	Bos N	46	179	20	42	8	6	2	24	1		48	.235	.239	.380	82	-5		.909	-2			C44,O4(0/3/1)		-0.3
1884	Bos N	72	268	28	55	13	2	1	20	2		66	.205	.211	.280	53	-14		.928	7			C71/3		-0.1
1885	Bos N	34	115	9	21	7	1	0	4	2		28	.183	.197	.261	49	-6		.901	4			C34		0.1
1886	KC N	62	230	18	50	8	3	3	25	4		59	.217	.231	.317	61	-12	1	.926	-13			C52,O13(0/6/7)		-1.9
1887	Ind N	42	147	12	35	6	3	2	10	7		24	.238	.282	.361	80	-4	4	.938	-6			C40,O2(1/0/1)/1		-0.6
Total	5	256	939	87	203	42	15	8	83	16	2	225	.216	.231	.318	65	-41	5	.921	-10			C241,O19(1/9/9)/13		-2.8

HACKETT, WALTER Walter Henry B8.15.1857 Cambridge MA D10.2.1920 Cambridge MA d4.17 b-Mert

1884	Bos U	103	415	71	101	19	0	1		7			.243	.256	.296	68	-28		.855	12	99	79	S103		-1.2
1885	Bos N	35	125	8	23	3	0	0	9	3		22	.184	.203	.208	34	-9		.893	-7	85	61	2b20,S15		-1.5
Total	2	138	540	79	124	22	0	1	9	10		22	.230	.244	.276	61	-37		.852	4	97	81	S118,2b20		-2.7

HADLEY, KENT Kent William B12.17.1934 Pocatello ID D3.10.2005 Pocatello ID BL/TL/6-3/190* d9.14 Col USC

1958	KC A	3	11	1	2	0	0	0	0-0				.182	.182	.182	0	-2	0-0	1.000	-1	0	45	1b2		-0.2
1959	KC A	113	288	40	73	11	1	10	39	24-0	1	74	.253	.310	.403	93	-3	1-2	.989	-2	93	101	1b95		-1.0
1960	NY A	55	64	8	13	2	0	4	11	6-0	0	19	.203	.271	.422	90	-1	0-0	.991	-1	77	95	1b24		-0.3
Total	3	171	363	49	88	13	1	14	50	30-0	1	97	.242	.300	.399	90	-6	1-2	.989	-3	88	99	1b121		-1.5

HAEFFNER, BILL William Bernhard B7.8.1894 Philadelphia PA D1.27.1982 Springfield PA BR/TR/5-9/165 d6.29

1915	Phi A	3	4	0	1	0	0	0	0	0			.250	.250	.250	51	0	0	1.000	-1	34	199	C3		-0.1
1920	Pit N	54	175	8	34	4	1	0	14	8		14	.194	.230	.229	31	-16	1-1	.972	-3	96	78	C52		-1.6
1928	NY N	2	1	0	0	0	0	0	0	0			.000	.000	.000	-99	0		.750	-0	0		C2		0.0
Total	3	59	180	8	35	4	1	0	14	8		15	.194	.229	.228	30	-16	1-1	.968	-4	94	78	C57		-1.7

HAFEY, CHICK Charles James B2.12.1903 Berkeley CA D7.2.1973 Calistoga CA BR/TR/6-0/185 d8.28 HF1971

1924	StL N	24	91	10	23	5	2	2	22	4	1	8	.253	.292	.418	90	-2	1-0	.927	0	99	133	O24(16/7/1)		-0.3
1925	StL N	93	358	36	108	25	2	5	57	10	0	29	.302	.321	.425	87	-8	3-7	.955	1	107	90	O88(25/5/58)		-1.4
1926	†StL N	78	225	30	61	19	2	4	38	11	2	36	.271	.311	.427	93	-2	2	.974	-0	99	96	O64(28/0/36)		-0.7
1927	StL N	103	346	62	114	26	5	18	63	36	5	41	.329	.401	.590	157	28	12	.980	5	89	199	O94(71/3/22)		2.5
1928	†StL N	138	520	101	175	46	6	27	111	40	2	53	.337	.386	.604	152	38	8	.965	-1	97	114	O133(117/0/16)		2.6
1929	StL N	134	517	101	175	47	9	29	125	45	2	42	.338	.394	.632	148	37	7	.966	2	105	93	O130L		2.6
1930	†StL N	120	446	108	150	39	12	26	107	46	7	51	.336	.407	.652	146	32	12	.976	-2	89	147	O116L		1.9
1931	†StL N	122	450	94	157	35	8	16	95	39	3	43	.349	.404	.569	153	34	11	.983	-5	93	66	O118L		2.2
1932	Cin N	83	253	34	87	19	3	2	36	22	1	20	.344	.403	.466	137	15	4	.965	-0	98	133	O65L		1.1
1933	Cin N★	144	568	77	172	34	6	7	62	40	2	44	.303	.351	.421	121	16	3	.987	6	102	149	O144(59/85/0)		1.7
1934	Cin N	140	535	75	157	29	6	18	67	52	3	63	.293	.359	.471	123	18	4	.967	-1	104	68	O140(18/122/0)		1.2
1935	Cin N	15	59	10	20	6	1	1	9	4	2	5	.339	.400	.525	151	4	1	.912	-3	82	0	O15C		0.1
1937	Cin N	89	257	39	67	11	5	9	41	23	1	42	.261	.324	.447	113	3	2	.971	-2	93	107	O64(20/44/0)		0.0
Total	13	1283	4625	777	1466	341	67	164	833	372	33	477	.317	.372	.526	133	213	70-7	.971	1	98	113	O1195(783/281/133)		13.5

HAFEY, BUD Daniel Albert B8.6.1912 Berkeley CA D7.27.1986 Sacramento CA BR/TR/6-0/185 d4.21 b-Tom

1935	Chi A	2	0	1	0	0	0	0	0	0	0		—	—	—	—	0	0-0					/R		0.0
	Pit N	58	184	29	42	11	2	6	16	16	0	48	.228	.290	.408	83	-5		.970	3	110	128	O47(1/36/10)		-0.3
1936	Pit N	39	118	19	25	6	1	4	13	10	0	27	.212	.273	.381	73	-5	0	.932	-1	97	126	O29(0/18/10)		-0.7
1939	Cin N	6	13	1	2	1	0	0	1	0	0	4	.154	.214	.231	19	-1	1	1.000	-0	97	0	O4L		-0.2
	Phi N	18	51	3	9	1	0	0	3	3	0	12	.176	.222	.196	14	-6	1	1.000	1	116	94	O13(3/1/9),P2		-0.6
	Year	24	64	4	11	2	0	0	4	4	0	16	.172	.221	.203	15	-8	2	1.000	1	112	73	O17(7/1/9),P2		-0.8
Total	3	123	366	53	78	19	3	10	33	30	0	91	.213	.273	.363	68	-17	2-0	.963	3	106	117	O93(8/55/29),P2		-1.8

HAFEY, TOM Thomas Francis "Heave-O", "The Arm" B7.12.1913 Berkeley CA D10.2.1996 El Cerrito CA BR/TR/6-1/180 d7.21 b-Bud

1939	NY N	70	256	37	62	10	1	6	26	10	0	44	.242	.271	.359	67	-13	1	.960	-0	99	84	3b70		-1.1
1944	StL A	8	14	1	5	2	0	0	2	1	0	4	.357	.400	.500	148	1	0-0	1.000	0	117	0	O4(3/0/1)/1		0.1
Total	2	78	270	38	67	12	1	6	28	11	0	48	.248	.278	.367	72	-12	1-0	.960	0	99	84	3b70,O4(3/0/1)/1		-1.0

HAFNER, TRAVIS Travis Lee B6.3.1977 Jamestown ND BL/TR/6-3/240* [TexA96 31/923] d8.6 Col Cowley Co. (KS) CC

2002	Tex A	23	62	6	15	4	1	1	6	8-1	0	15	.242	.329	.387	87	-1	0-1	.909	0	188	0	D13,1b3		-0.2
2003	Cle A	91	291	35	74	19	3	14	40	22-2	10	81	.254	.327	.485	111	4	2-1	.985	-3	77	152	D43,1b42	16	-0.4
2004	Cle A	140	482	96	150	41	3	28	109	68-7	17	111	.311	.410	.583	162	48	3-2	1.000	1	150	50	D128,1b11		3.9
2005	Cle A	137	486	94	148	42	0	33	108	79-7	9	123	.305	.408	.595	169	53	0-0	1.000	1	401	0	D130/1	18	4.4
Total	4	391	1321	231	387	106	7	76	263	177-17	36	330	.293	.388	.550	150	104	5-4	.986	-1	101	123	D314,1b57	34	7.7

HAGUE, JOE Joe Clarence B4.25.1944 Huntington WV D11.5.1994 San Antonio TX BL/TL/6-0/198* d9.19 Col Texas

1968	StL N	7	17	2	4	0	0	1	2-0		9	.235	.316	.412	119	0	0-0	.800	-1	76	0	O3R,1b2		-0.1
1969	StL N	40	100	8	17	2	1	2	8	12-1	0	23	.170	.259	.270	48	-7	0-2	.939	-1	110	0	O17(1/0/16),1b9		-1.1
1970	StL N	139	451	58	122	16	4	14	68	63-3	1	87	.271	.358	.417	105	4	2-1	.994	-3	97	103	1b82,O52(6/0/47)		-0.7
1971	StL N	129	380	46	86	9	3	16	54	58-10	2	69	.226	.330	.392	99	0	0-3	.996	1	107	97	1b91,O36R		-1.0
1972	StL N	27	76	8	18	5	1	3	11	17-2	0	18	.237	.368	.447	134	4	0-1	1.000	1	78	99	1b22,O3R		0.1
	†Cin N	69	138	17	34	7	1	4	20	20-5	0	18	.246	.340	.399	115	3	1-1	1.000	0	74	99	1b22,O19R		0.2
	Year	96	214	25	52	12	2	7	31	37-7	0	36	.243	.350	.416	123	7	1-2	1.000	0	76	99	1b44,O22R		0.3

YEAR	TM LG	G	AB	R	H	2B	3B	HR	RBI	BB-IB	HP	SO	AVG	OBP	SLG	AOPS	ABR	SB-CS	FA	FR	RNG	THR	GAMES AT POSITION	DL	BFW
1973	Cin N	19	33	2	5	2	0	0	1	5-0	0	5	.152	.256	.212	35	-3	1-0	1.000	-1	65	0	O5R,1b4	62	-0.4
Total	6	430	1195	141	286	41	10	40	163	177-21	3	222	.239	.336	.391	100	1	4-8	.996	-6	97	98	1b232,O135(7/0/129)	62	-3.0

HAGUE, BILL   William L. (b William L. Haug)   B1852 Philadelphia PA   BR/TR/5-9/164   d5.4

YEAR	TM LG	G	AB	R	H	2B	3B	HR	RBI	BB-IB	HP	SO	AVG	OBP	SLG	AOPS	ABR	SB-CS	FA	FR	RNG	THR	GAMES AT POSITION	DL	BFW
1875	StL NA	62	260	24	57	2	0	0	22	2		9	.219	.225	.227	63	-8	3-4	.781	2	107	58	3b62/1		-0.7
1876	Lou N	67	294	31	78	8	0	1	22	2		10	.265	.270	.303	77	-9		.754	-27	66	101	3b67/S		-3.0
1877	Lou N	59	263	38	70	7	1	1	24	7		18	.266	.285	.312	75	-9		.843	-19	65	65	3b59		-2.4
1878	Pro N	62	250	21	51	3	0	0	25	5		34	.204	.220	.216	44	-15		.925	19	133	64	3b62		0.6
1879	Pro N	51	209	20	47	3	1	0	21	3		19	.225	.236	.249	61	-9		.822	4	114	35	3b51		-0.3
Total	4	239	1016	110	246	21	2	2	92	17		81	.242	.255	.273	66	-42		.843	-23	93	69	3b239/S		-5.1

HAHN, DON   Donald Antone   B11.16.1948 San Francisco CA   BR/TR/6-1/185*   [SFN66 17/337]   d4.8

YEAR	TM LG	G	AB	R	H	2B	3B	HR	RBI	BB-IB	HP	SO	AVG	OBP	SLG	AOPS	ABR	SB-CS	FA	FR	RNG	THR	GAMES AT POSITION	DL	BFW
1969	Mon N	4	9	0	1	0	0	0	2	0-0	0	5	.111	.111	.111	-37	-2	0-0	1.000	0	60	728	O3C		-0.2
1970	Mon N	82	149	22	38	6	0	0	8	27-1	2	27	.255	.374	.309	86	-1	4-2	.986	1	91	195	O61(42/14/9)		-0.2
1971	NY N	98	178	16	42	5	1	1	11	21-1	1	32	.236	.317	.292	75	-5	2-3	.973	1	111	68	O80C		-0.7
1972	NY N	17	37	0	6	0	0	0	1	4-0	0	12	.162	.244	.162	18	-4	0-0	1.000	-2	49	0	O10(0/1/9)		-0.7
1973	†NY N	93	262	22	60	10	0	2	21	22-2	0	43	.229	.285	.290	61	-14	2-1	.989	-2	106	45	O87(4/83/2)		-1.8
1974	NY N	110	323	34	81	14	1	4	28	37-5	1	34	.251	.328	.337	87	-5	2-0	.987	-2	94	142	O106(0/104/2)		-1.0
1975	Phi N	9	5	0	0	0	0	0	0	0-0	0	2	.000	.000	.000	-95	-1	0-0	1.000	1	110	943	O7(1/4/2)		-0.1
	StL N	7	8	3	1	0	0	0	0	1-0	0	1	.125	.222	.125	-2	-1	0-0	1.000	-0	73	0	O4(1/2/1)		-0.2
	SD N	34	26	7	6	1	2	0	3	10-0	0	2	.231	.444	.423	152	3	1-0	1.000	1	104	142	O26(17/11/0)		0.3
	Year	50	39	10	7	1	2	0	3	11-0	0	5	.179	.360	.308	89	0	1-0	1.000	1	99	212	O37(19/17/3)		0.0
Total	7	454	997	104	235	38	4	7	74	122-9	4	158	.236	.319	.303	75	-30	11-6	.985	-2	99	113	O384(65/302/25)		-4.6

HAHN, DICK   Richard Frederick   B7.24.1916 Canton OH   D11.5.1992 Orlando FL   BR/TR/5-11/176   d9.7

| 1940 | Was A | 1 | 3 | 0 | 0 | 0 | 0 | 0 | 0 | 0-0 | 0 | 0 | .000 | .000 | .000 | -99 | -1 | 0-0 | 1.000 | 0 | 0 | 543 | /C | | -0.1 |

HAHN, ED   William Edgar   B8.27.1875 Nevada OH   D11.29.1941 Des Moines IA   BL/TR/?/160   d8.31

1905	NY A	43	160	32	51	5	0	0	11	25	5		.319	.426	.350	132	8	1	.957	1	99	85	O43(20/10/13)		0.7
1906	NY A	11	22	2	2	1	0	0	1	3	2		.091	.259	.136	23	-2	2	1.000	-0	0	0	O7(3/4/0)		-0.2
	†Chi A	130	484	80	110	7	5	0	27	69	9		.227	.335	.262	90	-1	21	.949	-5	128	97	O130(55/0/75)		-1.4
	Year	141	506	82	112	8	5	0	28	72	11		.221	.331	.257	86	-4	23	.952	-5	123	93	O137(58/4/75)		-1.6
1907	Chi A	156	592	87	151	9	7	0	45	84	12		.255	.359	.294	112	14	17	.990	-4	121	143	O156R		0.3
1908	Chi A	122	447	58	112	12	8	0	21	39	13		.251	.329	.313	111	7	11	.965	-12	29	62	O118(18/14/86)		-1.3
1909	Chi A	76	287	30	52	6	0	1	16	31	3		.181	.268	.213	54	-14	9	.990	-7	31	51	O76R		-2.8
1910	Chi A	15	53	2	6	2	0	0	1	7	0		.113	.217	.151	16	-5	0	.933	-2	83	0	O15R		-0.9
Total	6	553	2045	291	484	42	20	1	122	258	44		.237	.335	.278	97	7	61	.970	-29	86	92	O545(96/28/421)		-5.6

HAIGH, ED   Edward E.   B2.7.1867 Philadelphia PA   D2.13.1953 Atlantic City NJ   d8.14

| 1892 | StL N | 1 | 4 | 0 | 1 | 0 | 0 | 0 | 0 | 0 | | | .250 | .250 | .250 | 54 | 0 | 0 | — | -0 | 0 | 0 | /OR | | 0.0 |

HAINES, HINKEY   Henry Luther   B12.23.1898 Red Lion PA   D1.9.1979 Sharon Hill PA   BR/TR/5-10/170   d4.20   Col Penn St.

| 1923 | †NY A | 28 | 25 | 9 | 4 | 2 | 0 | 0 | 3 | 4 | | 5 | .160 | .276 | .240 | 36 | -2 | 3-1 | 1.000 | 1 | 133 | 151 | O14(2/8/4) | | -0.1 |

HAIRSTON, JERRY   Jerry Wayne Jr.   B5.29.1976 Des Moines IA   BR/TR/5-10/175(172-185)   [BalA97 11/345]   d9.11   b-Scott f-Jerry gf-Sammy   Col Southern Illinois

1998	Bal A	6	7	2	0	0	0	0	0	0-0	0	1	.000	.000	.000	-99	-2	0-0	.750	-2	38	89	2b4		-0.3
1999	Bal A	50	175	26	47	12	1	4	17	11-0	3	24	.269	.323	.417	90	-3	9-4	1.000	8	101	140	2b50		0.7
2000	Bal A	49	180	27	46	5	0	5	19	11-0	6	22	.256	.353	.367	87	-3	8-5	.981	6	104	126	2b49		0.5
2001	Bal A	159	532	65	124	25	5	8	47	44-0	13	73	.233	.305	.344	75	-19	29-11	.976	4	101	94	2b156		-0.5
2002	Bal A	122	426	55	114	25	3	5	32	34-0	7	55	.268	.329	.376	93	-4	21-6	.982	2	102	98	2b119		0.6
2003	Bal A	58	218	25	59	12	2	2	21	23-0	6	25	.271	.353	.372	93	-1	14-5	.980	1	96	104	2b48,D9	106	0.3
2004	Bal A	86	287	43	87	19	1	2	24	29-1	8	29	.303	.378	.397	105	4	13-8	.991	3	102	107	O52(10/15/27),D21,2b12/3	84	0.4
2005	Chi N	114	380	51	99	25	2	4	30	31-0	12	46	.261	.336	.368	82	-9	8-9	.983	25	96	109	O62(20/48/1),2b44/S	15	-0.6
Total	8	644	2205	292	576	123	14	30	190	193-1	55	275	.261	.334	.371	87	-37	102-48	.980	25	101	105	2b482,O114(30/63/28),D30/S3	205	1.1

HAIRSTON, JERRY   Jerry Wayne Sr.   B2.16.1952 Birmingham AL   BB/TR/5-10/180(170-196)   [ChiA70 3/54]   d7.26   b-Johnny f-Sammy s-Jerry s-Scott

1973	Chi A	60	210	25	57	11	1	0	23	33-0	1	30	.271	.371	.333	97	1	0-0	.944	1	105	154	O33L,1b19,D8		-0.1
1974	Chi A	45	109	8	25	7	0	0	8	13-0	0	18	.229	.311	.294	73	-3	0-2	.926	-3	70	81	O22(19/0/3),D10	15	-0.8
1975	Chi A	69	219	26	62	8	0	0	23	46-3	1	23	.283	.407	.320	107	6	1-0	.951	-5	95	136	O59(57/0/3),D8		0.1
1976	Chi A	44	119	20	27	2	2	0	10	24-0	1	19	.227	.352	.277	87	-1	1-1	.973	-0	106	42	O40(1/0/39)		-0.3
1977	Chi A	13	26	3	8	2	0	0	4	5-0	0	7	.308	.419	.385	121	1	0-0	1.000	0	97	0	O11(6/6/0)		0.1
	Pit N	51	52	5	10	2	0	2	6	6-0	0	10	.192	.271	.346	63	-3	0-0	.923	-1	81	0	O14(6/0/8)/2		-0.4
1981	Chi A	9	25	5	7	1	0	1	6	2-0	1	4	.280	.345	.440	131	1	0-0	1.000	1	104	208	O7(4/2/1)		0.0
1982	Chi A	85	90	11	21	5	0	5	18	9-0	0	15	.233	.294	.456	104	0	0-0	1.000	1	104	68	O36(22/7/7),D2		0.1
1983	†Chi A	101	126	17	37	9	1	5	22	23-4	1	16	.294	.397	.500	141	8	0-1	.968	-2	84	88	O32(19/11/3),D4		0.6
1984	Chi A	115	227	41	59	13	2	5	19	41-3	1	29	.260	.373	.401	109	5	2-1	.967	-2	90	106	O37(22/13/3),D20		0.1
1985	Chi A	95	140	9	34	8	0	2	20	29-3	2	18	.243	.371	.343	96	1	0-0	1.000	-0	88	0	D29,O5L		-0.3
1986	Chi A	101	225	32	61	15	0	5	26	26-3	1	26	.271	.348	.404	101	1	0-0	1.000	-2	61	83	D29,1b19,O11(9/0/2)		-0.1
1987	Chi A	66	126	14	29	8	0	5	20	25-2	1	25	.230	.357	.413	102	1	0-0	1.000	1	143	0	O13L,D13,1b7		-0.1
1988	Chi A	2	2	0	0	0	0	0	0	0-0	0	0	.000	.000	.000	-99	-1	0-0	—	0			/H		0.0
1989	Chi A	3	3	0	1	0	0	0	0	0-0	0	1	.333	.333	.333	90	0	0-0	—	0			D2		0.0
Total	14	859	1699	216	438	91	6	30	205	282-18	8	240	.258	.362	.371	102	17	4-5	.963	-6	97	107	O320(216/39/69),D125,1b45/2	15	-0.4

HAIRSTON, JOHNNY   John Louis   B8.27.1944 Birmingham AL   BR/TR/6-2/200   [ChiN65 11/325]   d9.6   b-Jerry f-Sammy   Col Southern A&M

| 1969 | Chi N | 3 | 4 | 1 | 1 | 0 | 0 | 0 | 0 | 0-0 | 0 | 2 | .250 | .250 | .250 | 36 | 0 | 0-0 | 1.000 | 0 | | | /COL | | 0.0 |

HAIRSTON, SAMMY   Samuel Harding   B1.20.1920 Crawford MS   D10.31.1997 Birmingham AL   BR/TR/5-10.5/187   d7.21   C1   s-Jerry s-Johnny gs-Jerry gs-Scott   Negro Lg 1944-50

| 1951 | Chi A | 4 | 5 | 1 | 2 | 1 | 0 | 0 | 1 | 2 | 0 | 0 | .400 | .571 | .600 | 222 | 1 | 0-0 | 1.000 | -0 | 0 | 0 | C2 | | 0.1 |

HAIRSTON, SCOTT   Scott Alexander   B5.25.1980 Fort Worth TX   BR/TR/6-0/190*   [AriN01 3/98]   d5.7   b-Jerry f-Jerry gf-Sammy   Col Central Arizona JC

2004	Ari N	101	339	39	84	15	6	13	29	21-0	1	88	.248	.293	.442	81	-11	3-3	.972	-2	95	85	2b85,O3(0/2/0)		-1.0
2005	Ari N	15	20	0	2	1	0	0	0	0-0	0	6	.100	.100	.150	-34	-4	0-0	1.000	-0	96	0	O4(4/1/0),D2	31	-0.4
Total	2	116	359	39	86	16	6	13	29	21-0	1	94	.240	.283	.426	75	-15	3-3	.972	-2	95	85	2b85,O7(6/1/2),D2	31	-1.4

HAJDUK, CHET   Chester   B7.21.1918 Chicago IL   BR/TR/6-0/195   d4.16

| 1941 | Chi A | 1 | 1 | 0 | 0 | 0 | 0 | 0 | 0 | 0-0 | 0 | 0 | .000 | .000 | .000 | -99 | 0 | 0-0 | — | 0 | | | /H | | 0.0 |

HAJEK, DAVE   David Vincent   B10.14.1967 Roseville CA   BR/TR/5-10/165*   d9.15   Col Cal Poly-Pomona

1995	Hou N	5	2	0	0	0	0	0	0	1-0	0	1	.000	.333	.000	-3	0	1-0	—	0			/H		0.0
1996	Hou N	8	10	3	3	1	0	0	0	2-0	0	0	.300	.417	.400	126	1	0-0	1.000	1	158	0	3b3,2b2		0.1
Total	2	13	12	3	3	1	0	0	0	3-0	0	1	.250	.400	.333	104	1	1-0	1.000	1	158	0	3b3,2b2		0.1

HALAS, GEORGE   George Stanley   B2.2.1895 Chicago IL   D10.31.1983 Chicago IL   BB/TR/6-0/164   d5.6   Col Illinois

| 1919 | NY A | 12 | 22 | 0 | 2 | 0 | 0 | 0 | 0 | 0 | 0 | 8 | .091 | .091 | .091 | -49 | -4 | 0 | 1.000 | -0 | 101 | 0 | O6(0/1/5) | | -0.5 |

HALDEMAN, JOHN   John Avery   B12.2.1855 Pewee Valley KY   D9.17.1899 Louisville KY   BL/TR/5-10/175   d7.3   Col Washington and Lee

| 1877 | Lou N | 1 | 4 | 0 | 0 | 0 | 0 | 0 | 0 | 0 | | 0 | .000 | .000 | .000 | -85 | -1 | | .571 | -1 | 116 | 0 | /2 | | -0.2 |

HALE, ODELL   Arvel Odell "Bad News"   B8.10.1908 Hosston LA   D6.9.1980 El Dorado AR   BR/TR/5-10/175   d8.1

1931	Cle A	25	92	14	26	2	4	1	5	8	0	8	.283	.340	.424	94	-1	2-0	.918	-4	87	35	3b15,2b10/S		-0.3
1933	Cle A	98	351	49	97	19	8	10	64	30		37	.276	.333	.462	104	0	2-3	.954	-2	99	102	2b73,3b21		0.3
1934	Cle A	143	563	82	170	44	6	13	101	48	0	50	.302	.357	.471	110	7	8-12	.956	26	109	113	2b137,3b5		1.9
1935	Cle A	150	589	80	179	37	11	16	101	52	0	55	.304	.361	.486	115	11	15-13	.938	6	109	87	3b149/2		3.2
1936	Cle A	153	620	126	196	50	13	14	87	64		43	.316	.380	.506	116	14	8-5	.946	17	108	103	3b148,2b3		0.9
1937	Cle A	154	561	74	150	32	4	8	82	56	1	41	.267	.335	.371	77	-20	9-6	.963	-11	90	81	2b73,3b2		-1.1
1938	Cle A	130	496	69	138	32	2	8	69	44	1	39	.278	.338	.399	86	-12	8-1	.963	-11	89	80	2b127		-0.4
1939	Cle A	108	253	36	79	16	2	4	48	25	0	18	.312	.374	.439	111	4	4-5	.966	-11	85	83	2b73,3b2		-0.4
1940	Cle A	48	50	3	11	3	1	0	6	5	0	7	.220	.291	.320	60	-3	0-0	.700	-1	86	0	3b3		-0.4
1941	Bos A	12	24	5	5	2	0	1	3	3		4	.208	.296	.417	85	-1	0-0	.857	-3	43	0	3b6/2		-0.3

YEAR	TM LG	G	AB	R	H	2B	3B	HR	RBI	BB-IB	HP	SO	AVG	OBP	SLG	AOPS	ABR	SB-CS	FA	FR	RNG	THR	GAMES AT POSITION	DL	BFW
	NY N	41	102	13	20	3	0	0	9	18	0	13	.196	.317	.225	53	-6	1	.964	0	90	95	2b29		-0.4
Total	10	1062	3701	551	1071	240	51	73	573	353	3	315	.289	.352	.441	100	-7	57-45	.959	40	99	94	2b518,3b439/S		7.0

HALE, GEORGE   George Wagner "Ducky" B8.3.1894 Dexter KS D11.1.1945 Wichita KS BR/TR/5-10/160 d8.24

YEAR	TM LG	G	AB	R	H	2B	3B	HR	RBI	BB-IB	HP	SO	AVG	OBP	SLG	AOPS	ABR	SB-CS	FA	FR	RNG	THR	GAMES AT POSITION	DL	BFW
1914	StL A	6	11	1	2	0	0	0	0	0	0	3	.182	.182	.182	10	-1	0	.895	-1	97	184	C6		-0.2
1916	StL A	4	1	0	0	0	0	0	0	0	1	1	1.000	.500	.000	54	0	0	1.000	0	0	0	C3		0.0
1917	StL A	38	61	4	12	2	1	0	8	10	0	12	.197	.310	.262	78	-1	0	.927	-0	92	121	C28		0.0
1918	StL A	12	30	0	4	1	0	0	1	1	0	5	.133	.161	.167	4	-4	0	.981	1	90	94	C11		-0.2
Total	4	60	103	5	18	3	1	0	9	11	1	21	.175	.261	.223	49	-6	0	.940	0	91	118	C48		-0.4

HALE, JOHN   John Steven B8.5.1953 Fresno CA BL/TR/6-2/195* [LAN71 14/337] d9.8

YEAR	TM LG	G	AB	R	H	2B	3B	HR	RBI	BB-IB	HP	SO	AVG	OBP	SLG	AOPS	ABR	SB-CS	FA	FR	RNG	THR	GAMES AT POSITION	DL	BFW
1974	LA N	4	4	2	4	1	0	0	2	0-0	0	0	1.000	1.000	1.250	546	2	0-0	—	-0	0	0	O3R		0.2
1975	LA N	71	204	20	43	7	0	6	22	26-4	2	15	.211	.303	.333	81	-5	1-2	.977	-2	99	53	O68(0/35/42)		-1.0
1976	LA N	44	91	4	14	2	1	0	8	16-1	2	14	.154	.291	.198	42	-6	4-1	.983	-1	86	132	O37(0/11/27)		-0.9
1977	LA N	79	108	10	26	4	1	2	11	15-1	0	28	.241	.331	.352	84	-2	2-1	.986	-2	92	38	O73(25/13/37)		-0.6
1978	Sea A	107	211	24	36	8	0	4	22	34-1	0	64	.171	.283	.265	56	-12	3-4	.988	-3	103	20	O98(27/24/47),D3		-1.8
1979	Sea A	54	63	6	14	3	0	2	7	12-4	0	26	.222	.342	.365	90	0	0-0	1.000	0	80	0	O42(34/0/9),D2		-0.4
Total	6	359	681	66	137	25	2	14	72	103-11	4	183	.201	.307	.305	72	-23	10-8	.985	-11	95	45	O321(86/83/165),D5		-4.5

HALE, BOB   Robert Houston B11.7.1933 Sarasota FL BL/TL/5-10/195* d7.4

YEAR	TM LG	G	AB	R	H	2B	3B	HR	RBI	BB-IB	HP	SO	AVG	OBP	SLG	AOPS	ABR	SB-CS	FA	FR	RNG	THR	GAMES AT POSITION	DL	BFW
1955	Bal A	67	182	13	65	7	1	0	29	5-0	1	19	.357	.376	.407	119	4	0-2	.974	2	133	71	1b44		0.3
1956	Bal A	85	207	18	49	10	1	1	24	11-0	1	10	.237	.274	.309	60	-13	0-2	.975	-1	106	84	1b51		-1.6
1957	Bal A	42	44	2	11	0	0	0	7	2-1	0	2	.250	.265	.250	50	-3	0-0	1.000	-0	62	44	1b5		-0.4
1958	Bal A	19	20	2	7	2	0	0	3	2-0	0	1	.350	.409	.450	144	1	0-0	1.000	1	373	253	1b2		0.2
1959	Bal A	40	54	2	10	3	0	0	7	2-1	0	6	.185	.214	.241	25	-6	0-0	1.000	-1	59	117	1b8		-0.7
1960	Cle A	70	70	2	21	7	0	0	12	3-1	0	6	.300	.312	.400	99	0	0-0	.944	0	279	68	1b5		0.0
1961	Cle A	42	36	1	6	0	0	0	6	1-0	1	7	.167	.200	.167	2	-5	0-0	—	0			/H		-0.5
	NY A	11	13	2	2	0	0	1	1	0-0	0	1	.154	.154	.385	41	-1	0-0	1.000	0	84	74	1b5		-0.1
	Year	53	49	2	8	0	0	1	7	1-0	1	8	.163	.189	.224	12	-6	0-0	1.000	0	84	74	1b5		-0.6
Total	7	376	626	41	171	29	2	2	89	26-3	3	51	.273	.299	.335	76	-23	0-4	.977	2	119	82	1b120		-2.8

HALE, SAMMY   Samuel Douglas B9.10.1896 Glen Rose TX D9.6.1974 Wheeler TX BR/TR/5-8.5/160 d4.20

YEAR	TM LG	G	AB	R	H	2B	3B	HR	RBI	BB-IB	HP	SO	AVG	OBP	SLG	AOPS	ABR	SB-CS	FA	FR	RNG	THR	GAMES AT POSITION	DL	BFW
1920	Det A	76	116	13	34	3	3	1	14	5	0	15	.293	.322	.397	92	-2	2-0	.886	-1	110	97	3b16,O4C/2		-0.2
1921	Det A	9	2	0	0	0	0	0	0	0	0	1	.000	.000	.000	-99	-1	0-1	—	0			/H		-0.1
1923	Phi A	115	434	68	125	22	8	3	51	17	8	31	.288	.327	.396	89	-9	8-3	.916	-14	96	88	3b107		-1.6
1924	Phi A	80	261	41	83	14	2	2	17	17	3	19	.318	.367	.410	99	-2	3-2	.948	-2	103	112	3b55,O5(4/0/1)/S		0.0
1925	Phi A	110	391	62	135	30	11	8	63	17	2	27	.345	.376	.540	122	11	7-4	.919	-4	97	113	3b96/2		1.2
1926	Phi A	111	327	49	92	22	9	4	43	13	1	36	.281	.311	.440	89	-7	1-4	.947	0	96	142	3b77/OR		-0.4
1927	Phi A	131	501	77	157	24	8	5	81	32	3	32	.313	.358	.423	97	-4	11-3	.961	1	94	189	3b128		0.6
1928	Phi A	88	314	38	97	20	9	4	58	9	3	21	.309	.344	.468	106	1	2-0	.932	8	111	126	3b79		1.4
1929	Phi A	101	379	51	105	14	3	1	40	12	2	18	.277	.303	.338	62	-22	6-2	.956	-6	94	79	3b99/2		-2.1
1930	StL A	62	190	21	52	8	1	2	25	8	0	18	.274	.303	.358	65	-11	1-1	.947	-1	101	68	3b47		-0.9
Total	10	883	2915	422	880	157	54	30	392	130	22	218	.302	.339	.425	89	-45	41-20	.939	-19	98	120	3b704,O10(4/4/2),2b3/S		-2.1

HALE, CHIP   Walter William B12.2.1964 San Jose CA BL/TR/5-11/191(180-191) [MinA87 17/425] d8.27 Col Arizona

YEAR	TM LG	G	AB	R	H	2B	3B	HR	RBI	BB-IB	HP	SO	AVG	OBP	SLG	AOPS	ABR	SB-CS	FA	FR	RNG	THR	GAMES AT POSITION	DL	BFW
1989	Min A	28	67	6	14	3	0	0	4	1-0	0	6	.209	.214	.254	31	-5	0-0	.980	-2	115	108	2b16,3b9,D2		-0.8
1990	Min A	1	2	0	0	0	0	0	2	0-0	0	1	.000	.000	.000	-94	-1	0-0	1.000	1	200	279	/2		0.1
1993	Min A	69	186	25	62	6	1	3	27	18-0	6	17	.333	.408	.425	123	7	2-1	.952	-1	104	98	2b21,3b19,D19/1S		0.6
1994	Min A	67	118	13	31	9	0	1	11	16-1	1	14	.263	.350	.364	86	-2	0-2	.964	4	139	70	3b21,D10,1b7,2b5/OR		0.1
1995	Min A	69	103	10	27	4	0	2	18	11-1	0	20	.262	.333	.359	80	-3	0-0	1.000	-1	102	89	D27,2b7,3b5,1b3		-0.5
1996	Min A	85	87	8	24	5	0	1	16	10-2	0	6	.276	.347	.368	81	-2	0-0	1.000	0	101	66	2b14,D10,1b6,3b3,O3R		-0.2
1997	LA N	14	12	0	1	0	0	0	0	2-0	0	4	.083	.214	.083	-20	-2	0-0	1.000	0	0	0	3b2		-0.2
Total	7	333	575	62	159	27	1	7	78	58-4	7	68	.277	.346	.363	87	-9	2-3	.969	2	110	106	D68,2b64,3b59,1b7,O4R/S		-0.9

HALEY, J.   J. TR d6.22

YEAR	TM LG	G	AB	R	H	2B	3B	HR	RBI	BB-IB	HP	SO	AVG	OBP	SLG	AOPS	ABR	SB-CS	FA	FR	RNG	THR	GAMES AT POSITION	DL	BFW
1880	Tro N	2	7	0	0	0	0	0	1			2	.000	.125	.000	-51	-1		.750	-2			C2		-0.3

HALEY, RAY   Raymond Timothy "Pat" B1.23.1891 Danbury IA D10.8.1973 Bradenton FL BR/TR/5-11/180 d4.21 Mil 1918-19 Col Western Illinois

YEAR	TM LG	G	AB	R	H	2B	3B	HR	RBI	BB-IB	HP	SO	AVG	OBP	SLG	AOPS	ABR	SB-CS	FA	FR	RNG	THR	GAMES AT POSITION	DL	BFW
1915	Bos A	5	7	2	1	1	0	0	1		0	1	.143	.250	.286	62	0	0	1.000	0	123	113	C4		0.0
1916	Bos A	1	1	0	0	0	0	0	0		0	1	.000	.000	.000	-99	0	0	—	0			/H		0.0
	Phi A	34	108	8	25	5	0	0	4	6	1	19	.231	.278	.278	70	-4	0	.982	-1	60	171	C33		-0.2
	Year	35	109	8	25	5	0	0	4	6	1	20	.229	.276	.275	69	-4	0	.982	-1	60	171	C33		-0.2
1917	Phi A	41	98	7	27	2	1	0	11	4	1	12	.276	.311	.316	93	-1	2	.947	-5	72	91	C34		-0.5
Total	3	81	214	17	53	8	1	0	15	11	2	32	.248	.291	.294	80	-5	2	.970	-6	67	136	C71		-0.7

HALL, ALBERT   Albert B3.7.1958 Birmingham AL BB/TR/5-11/155* [AtlN77 6/134] d9.12

YEAR	TM LG	G	AB	R	H	2B	3B	HR	RBI	BB-IB	HP	SO	AVG	OBP	SLG	AOPS	ABR	SB-CS	FA	FR	RNG	THR	GAMES AT POSITION	DL	BFW
1981	Atl N	6	2	1	0	0	0	0	0	1-0	0	1	1.000	.333	.000	1	0	0-0	—	-0	0	0	O2(1/0/1)		0.0
1982	Atl N	5	1	1	0	0	0	0	0	0-0	0	1				—	0	0-0	—	0	0	0	/R		0.0
1983	Atl N	10	8	2	0	0	0	0	0	2-0	0	2	.000	.200	.000	-37	-1	1-1	.750	-1	62	0	O4(4/1/0)		-0.3
1984	Atl N	87	142	25	37	6	1	1	9	10-0	0	18	.261	.309	.338	76	-4	6-4	.932	-0	92	148	O66(48/2/17)		-0.7
1985	Atl N	54	47	5	7	0	1	0	3	9-1	0	12	.149	.286	.191	34	-4	1-1	.900	1	63	621	O13(6/6/3)		-0.4
1986	Atl N	16	50	6	12	2	0	0	1	5-0	0	6	.240	.309	.280	61	-3	8-3	.900	-0	109	95	O14R		-0.3
1987	Atl N	92	292	54	83	20	4	3	24	38-3	2	36	.284	.369	.411	103	3	33-10	.981	-2	93	132	O69(0/68/1)	16	0.6
1988	Atl N	85	231	27	57	7	1	1	15	21-1	2	35	.247	.314	.299	74	-7	15-10	.973	-2	97	278	O63(1/63/0)	59	-0.6
1989	Pit N	20	33	4	6	2	1	0	1	3-0	0	5	.182	.250	.303	59	-2	3-0	.909	-1	71	0	O12(5/1/6)		-0.3
Total	9	375	805	125	202	37	8	5	53	89-5	4	115	.251	.328	.335	80	-18	67-29	.958	-3	93	182	O243(65/141/42)	75	-2.3

HALL, AL   Archibald W. B Worcester MA D2.10.1885 Warren PA d5.1

YEAR	TM LG	G	AB	R	H	2B	3B	HR	RBI	BB-IB	HP	SO	AVG	OBP	SLG	AOPS	ABR	SB-CS	FA	FR	RNG	THR	GAMES AT POSITION	DL	BFW
1879	Tro N	67	306	30	79	7	3	0	14	3		13	.258	.265	.301	92	-2		.842	2	114	150	O67(2/63/2)		-0.3
1880	Cle N	3	8	1	1	0	0	0	0	0			.125	.125	.125	-15	-1		1.000	-1	0	0	O3L		-0.2
Total	2	70	314	31	80	7	3	0	14	3		13	.255	.262	.296	90	-3		.843	1	111	146	O70(5/63/2)		-0.5

HALL, CHARLIE   Charles Walter "Doc" B8.24.1863 Toulon IL D6.24.1921 Tacoma WA 5-10/158 d5.3

YEAR	TM LG	G	AB	R	H	2B	3B	HR	RBI	BB-IB	HP	SO	AVG	OBP	SLG	AOPS	ABR	SB-CS	FA	FR	RNG	THR	GAMES AT POSITION	DL	BFW
1887	NY AA	3	12	1	1	0	0	0	0				.083	.214	.083	-16	-2	1	1.000	-0	0	0	O3C		-0.2

HALL, GEORGE   George William B3.29.1849 Stepney, England D6.11.1923 Ridgewood NY BL/5-7/142 d5.5

YEAR	TM LG	G	AB	R	H	2B	3B	HR	RBI	BB-IB	HP	SO	AVG	OBP	SLG	AOPS	ABR	SB-CS	FA	FR	RNG	THR	GAMES AT POSITION	DL	BFW
1871	Oly NA	32	136	31	40	3	3	2	17	8		0	.294	.333	.404	117	4	2-1	.913	6	81	0	O32(1/31/0)		0.6
1872	Bal NA	53	250	69	84	17	6	1	37	3		1	.336	.344	.464	140	10	8-1	.836	-3	71	191	O52(3/51/0)/1		0.6
1873	Bal NA	35	168	44	58	6	4	0	31	2		1	.345	.353	.429	132	6	0-0	.865	2	59	0	O35C		0.6
1874	Bos NA	47	222	58	64	10	8	1	34	1		0	.288	.291	.419	118	3	2-0	.811	-3	73	174	O47(20/21/7)		0.1
1875	Ath NA	77	358	71	107	10	12	4	62	3		4	.299	.305	.427	136	10	8-5	.887	4	63	87	O77(74/0/3)/1		1.4
1876	Phi N	60	268	51	98	7	13	5	45	8		2	.366	.384	.545	208	29	0-0	.801	-2	68	109	O60(59/0/1)		2.0
1877	Lou N	61	269	53	87	15	8	0	26	12		19	.323	.352	.439	125	6		.900	-5	60	56	O61L		-0.3
Total	5 NA	244	1134	273	353	46	33	8	181	17		6	.311	.321	.431	130	33	20-7	.865	6	68	102	O243(98/138/10),1b2		3.3
Total	2	121	537	104	185	22	21	5	71	20		23	.345	.368	.492	162	35		.837	-7	64	82	O121(120/0/1)		1.7

HALL, IRV   Irvin Gladstone B10.7.1918 Alberton (now Daniels) MD BR/TR/5-10.5/160 d4.20

YEAR	TM LG	G	AB	R	H	2B	3B	HR	RBI	BB-IB	HP	SO	AVG	OBP	SLG	AOPS	ABR	SB-CS	FA	FR	RNG	THR	GAMES AT POSITION	DL	BFW
1943	Phi A	151	544	37	139	15	4	0	54	22	6	42	.256	.292	.298	73	-21	10-7	.948	-9	98	88	S148/23		-1.9
1944	Phi A	143	559	60	150	20	8	0	45	31	2	46	.268	.309	.333	85	-13	2-5	.980	-8	99	62	2b97,S40,1b4		-1.4
1945	Phi A	151	616	62	161	17	5	0	50	35	6	42	.261	.307	.305	78	-18	3-10	.978	20	110	103	2b151		0.8
1946	Phi A	63	185	19	46	6	2	0	19	9	1	18	.249	.287	.303	65	-9	1-1	.973	-5	92	66	2b40,S7		-1.3
Total	4	508	1904	178	496	58	19	0	168	97	15	148	.261	.302	.311	77	-61	16-23	.977	-1	104	85	2b289,S195,1b4/3		-3.8

HALL, JIM   James D1.30.1886 Brooklyn NY d5.20

YEAR	TM LG	G	AB	R	H	2B	3B	HR	RBI	BB-IB	HP	SO	AVG	OBP	SLG	AOPS	ABR	SB-CS	FA	FR	RNG	THR	GAMES AT POSITION	DL	BFW
1872	Atl NA	13	57	9	18	0	1	0	6	1		1	.316	.328	.351	93	-1	0-0	.750	-4	90	105	2b13		-0.4
1874	Atl NA	2	9	0	1	0	0	0	0	0		0	.111	.111	.111	-32	-1	0-0	.857	-1	50	0	2b2/OR		-0.2
1875	Wes NA	1	3	0	1	0	1	0	1	0		0	.333	.333	1.000	327	1	0-0	.000	-0	0	0	/OL		0.0
Total	3 NA	16	69	9	20	0	2	0	7	1		1	.290	.300	.348	89	-1	0-0	.758	-5	86	95	2b15,O2(1/0/1)		-0.6

HALL, JIMMIE Jimmie Randolph B3.17.1938 Mt.Holly NC BL/TR/6-0/175* d4.9

YEAR	TM	LG	G	AB	R	H	2B	3B	HR	RBI	BB-IB	HP	SO	AVG	OBP	SLG	AOPS	ABR	SB-CS	FA	FR	RNG	THR	GAMES AT POSITION	DL	BFW
1963	Min	A	156	497	88	129	21	5	33	80	63-4	0	101	.260	.342	.521	136	23	3-3	.982	11	113	151	O143(87/93/16)		2.8
1964	Min	A★	149	510	61	144	20	3	25	75	44-3	1	112	.282	.338	.480	125	16	5-2	.985	6	107	143	O137C		1.9
1965	†Min	A	148	522	81	149	25	4	20	86	51-6	5	79	.285	.342	.464	124	16	14-7	.976	-5	93	116	O141(6/140/6)		0.8
1966	Min	A	120	356	52	85	7	4	20	47	33-5	0	66	.239	.302	.449	106	2	1-2	.978	2	104	111	O103(69/27/12)		-0.2
1967	Cal	A	129	401	54	100	8	3	16	55	42-7	0	65	.249	.318	.404	117	8	4-1	.990	0	104	86	O120(2/6/116)		0.1
1968	Cal	A	46	126	15	27	3	0	1	8	16-3	0	19	.214	.303	.262	75	-3	1-0	.981	-3	89	0	O39(4/2/33)		-1.0
	Cle	A	53	111	4	22	4	0	1	8	10-3	0	19	.198	.264	.261	61	-5	1-0	.983	5	139	72	O29(20/6/4)		-0.3
	Year		99	237	19	49	7	0	2	16	26-6	0	38	.207	.285	.262	68	-9	2-0	.982	0	109	29	O68(24/8/37)		-1.3
1969	Cle	A	4	10	1	0	0	0	0	0	2-1	0	3	.000	.167	.000	-49	-2	1-0	1.000	-0	86	0	O3(2/1/0)		-0.2
	NY	A	80	212	21	50	8	5	3	26	19-1	0	34	.236	.296	.363	87	-5	8-3	.963	-6	84	29	O50(9/19/22),1b7		-1.3
	Year		84	222	22	50	8	5	3	26	21-2	0	37	.225	.290	.347	81	-7	9-3	.966	-6	55	0	O53(11/20/22),1b7		-1.5
	Chi	N	11	24	1	5	1	0	0	1	1-0	0	5	.208	.240	.250	33	-2	0-0	1.000	-1	55	0	O5(1/4/0)		-0.4
1970	Chi	N	28	32	2	3	1	0	0	4	4-1	0	12	.094	.194	.125	-11	-5	0-0	1.000	0	100	0	O8(2/7/0)		-0.4
	Atl	N	39	47	7	10	2	0	2	4	2-1	0	14	.213	.245	.383	62	-3	0-0	1.000	-0	85	128	O28(19/1/8)		-0.9
	Year		67	79	9	13	3	0	2	5	6-2	0	26	.165	.224	.278	31	-8	0-0	1.000	-1	89	91	O36(21/8/8)		
Total	8		963	2848	387	724	100	24	121	391	287-35	2	529	.254	.321	.434	112	40	38-18	.982	6	103	108	O806(221/443/217),1b7		1.3

HALL, JOE Joseph Geroy B3.6.1966 Paducah KY BR/TR/6-0/180* [StLN88 10/262] d4.5 Col Southern Illinois

YEAR	TM	LG	G	AB	R	H	2B	3B	HR	RBI	BB-IB	HP	SO	AVG	OBP	SLG	AOPS	ABR	SB-CS	FA	FR	RNG	THR	GAMES AT POSITION	DL	BFW
1994	Chi	A	17	28	6	11	3	0	1	9	2-0	0	4	.393	.452	.607	172	3	0-0	.917	-1	93	0	O9(7/0/2),D2	68	0.2
1995	Det	A	7	15	2	2	0	0	0	0	2-0	0	3	.133	.235	.133	-1	-2	0-0	1.000	1	135	369	O5L,D2		-0.1
1997	Det	A	2	4	1	2	1	0	0	3	0-0	0	0	.500	.500	.750	221	1	0-0	1.000	-0	60	0	/OR		0.0
Total	3		26	47	9	15	4	0	1	12	4-0	0	7	.319	.385	.468	120	2	0-0	.960	0	106	132	O15(12/0/3),D4	68	0.1

HALL, MEL Melvin B9.16.1960 Lyons NY BL/TL/6-1/205(185-223) [ChiN78 2/39] d9.3

YEAR	TM	LG	G	AB	R	H	2B	3B	HR	RBI	BB-IB	HP	SO	AVG	OBP	SLG	AOPS	ABR	SB-CS	FA	FR	RNG	THR	GAMES AT POSITION	DL	BFW
1981	Chi	N	10	11	1	1	0	0	1	2	1-0	0	4	.091	.167	.364	45	-1	0-0		-1	0		O3(1/2/0)		-0.2
1982	Chi	N	24	80	6	21	3	2	0	4	5-1	2	17	.262	.318	.350	85	-2	0-1	.939	-0	82	322	O22(0/21/1)		-0.3
1983	Chi	N	112	410	60	116	23	5	17	56	42-6	3	101	.283	.352	.488	125	14	6-6	.988	-4	89	153	O112(5/108/0)	46	0.8
1984	Chi	N	48	150	25	42	11	3	4	22	12-3	0	23	.280	.329	.473	115	3	2-1	.961	0	94	190	O46(5/5/40)		0.1
	Cle	A	83	257	43	66	13	1	7	30	35-5	2	55	.257	.344	.397	104	3	1-1	.993	2	105	69	O69(64/1/6),D9		0.1
1985	Cle	A	23	66	7	21	6	0	0	12	8-0	0	12	.318	.387	.409	120	2	0-1	1.000	-3	65	0	O15(15/0/1),D5	150	-0.1
1986	Cle	A	140	442	68	131	29	2	18	77	33-8	2	65	.296	.346	.493	128	16	6-2	.972	-1	97	93	O126(123/0/14),D7		1.1
1987	Cle	A	142	485	57	136	21	4	18	76	20-6	1	68	.280	.309	.439	95	-5	5-4	.989	6	118	40	O122L,D14		-0.5
1988	Cle	A	150	515	69	144	32	4	6	71	28-12	0	50	.280	.312	.392	94	-4	7-3	.967	-2	105	139	O141(135/7/3),D6	30	-1.0
1989	NY	A	113	361	54	94	9	0	17	58	21-4	0	37	.260	.295	.427	104	0	0-0	.993	1	105	70	O75(46/0/31),D34	16	-0.3
1990	NY	A	113	360	41	93	23	2	12	46	6-2	2	46	.258	.272	.433	94	-5	0-0	.973	-5	77	67	D54,O50(36/0/15)		-1.3
1991	NY	A	141	492	67	140	23	2	19	80	26-6	3	40	.285	.321	.455	112	6	0-1	.987	0	97	111	O120(62/1/65),D10		0.2
1992	NY	A	152	583	67	163	36	3	15	81	29-4	1	53	.280	.310	.429	107	3	4-2	.990	1	99	109	O136(99/0/37),D11		-0.5
1996	SF	N	25	25	3	3	0	0	0	5	1-0	0	4	.120	.148	.120	-2	-1	0-0		-1	0		O4(3/0/1)		-0.5
Total	13		1276	4237	568	1171	229	25	134	620	267-57	16	575	.276	.318	.437	106	25	31-22	.981	-6	99	94	O1041(716/145/214),D150	242	-1.9

HALL, DICK Richard Wallace B9.27.1930 St.Louis MO BR/TR/6-6/200(199-220) d4.15 Col Swarthmore ▲

YEAR	TM	LG	G	AB	R	H	2B	3B	HR	RBI	BB-IB	HP	SO	AVG	OBP	SLG	AOPS	ABR	SB-CS	FA	FR	RNG	THR	GAMES AT POSITION	DL	BFW
1952	Pit	N	26	80	6	11	1	0	0	2	1-0	0	17	.138	.159	.150	-14	-12	0-1	.972	0	105	79	O14(0/12/2),3b5		-1.4
1953	Pit	N	7	24	2	4	0	0	0	1	1	0	3	.167	.200	.167	-3	-4	1-1	.978	2	112	113	2b7		-0.1
1954	Pit	N	112	310	38	74	8	4	2	27	33	0	46	.239	.304	.310	64	-17	3-0	.956	3	113	75	O102(42/44/18)		-1.8
1955	Pit	N	21	40	3	7	1	0	1	3	6-0	0	5	.175	.283	.275	50	-3	0-0	1.000	-2	39	0	P15,O3(1/3/0)		-0.1
1956	Pit	N	33	29	5	10	0	0	1	1	5-0	0	7	.345	.441	.345	118	1	0-0	1.000	-1	58	0	P19/1	41	0.0
1957	Pit	N	10	1	0	0	0	0	0	0	0-0	0	1	.000	.000	.000	-99	0	0-0	—	-0	0	0	P8	30	0.0
1959	Pit	N	2	2	0	0	0	0	0	0	0-0	0	0	.000	.000	.000	-99	0	0-0	1.000	-2	69	0	P2		0.0
1960	KC	A	32	56	5	6	0	0	0	4	0-0	0	15	.107	.107	.107	-24	-2	1-0	.925	-1	97	46	P29		0.0
1961	Bal	A	30	36	4	5	0	0	0	1	3-0	0	13	.139	.205	.139	-6	0	0-0	.970	1	118	74	P29		0.0
1962	Bal	A	44	24	3	4	1	0	0	1	4-0	0	9	.167	.286	.208	38	1	0-0	1.000	-0	91	73	P43		0.0
1963	Bal	A	48	28	7	13	1	0	1	4	0-0	0	8	.464	.464	.607	205	8	1-0	1.000	-0	90	105	P45		0.0
1964	Bal	A	45	16	1	2	0	0	0	3	1-0	0	3	.125	.176	.125	-14	0	0-0	1.000	-1	51	217	P48		0.0
1965	Bal	A	49	15	1	5	2	0	0	4	1-0	1	4	.333	.412	.467	146	3	0-0	.923	-1	51	217	P48		0.0
1966	Bal	A	32	12	0	2	0	0	0	2	0-0	0	1	.167	.231	.167	17	0	0-0	1.000	-0	95	0	P32		0.0
1967	Phi	N	48	14	1	1	0	0	0	0	5-0	0	5	.071	.071	.071	-58	-1	0-0	1.000	1	147	121	P48		0.0
1968	Phi	N	32	3	0	1	0	0	0	0	0-0	0	1	.333	.333	.333	101	0	0-0	1.000	-0	80	0	P32		0.0
1969	†Bal	A	39	7	1	2	0	0	0	2	1-0	0	1	.286	.375	.286	86	1	1-0	1.000	-1	61	296	P39		0.0
1970	†Bal	A	32	12	2	1	0	0	0	1	0-0	0	3	.083	.083	.083	-53	-1	0-0	1.000	-2	34	0	P32		0.0
1971	†Bal	A	27	5	0	2	1	0	0	0	0-0	0	1	.400	.400	.600	179	1	0-0	.800	-1	44	0	P27		0.0
Total	19		669	714	79	150	15	4	4	56	61-0	2	147	.210	.271	.259	44	-27	6-2	.976	-3	85	77	P495,O119(43/59/20),2b7,3b5/1	71	-3.4

HALL, BOB Robert Prill B12.20.1878 Baltimore MD D12.1.1950 Wellesley MA TR/5-10/158 d4.18

YEAR	TM	LG	G	AB	R	H	2B	3B	HR	RBI	BB-IB	HP	SO	AVG	OBP	SLG	AOPS	ABR	SB-CS	FA	FR	RNG	THR	GAMES AT POSITION	DL	BFW
1904	Phi	N	46	163	11	26	4	0	0	17	14	0		.160	.226	.184	28	-13	5	.843	-9	92	98	3b20,S15,1b11		-2.4
1905	NY	N	1	3	1	1	0	0	0	0	0	1		.333	.333	.333	97	0	0	—	0	0	0	/OR		0.0
	Bro	N	56	203	21	48	4	1	2	15	11	1		.236	.279	.296	77	-6	8	.939	2	97	117	O42(24/12/7),2b7,1b3		-0.7
	Year		57	206	22	49	4	1	2	15	11	1		.238	.280	.296	77	-6	8	.939	2	97	117	O43(24/12/8),2b7,1b3		-0.7
Total	2		103	369	33	75	8	1	2	32	25	1		.203	.256	.247	55	-19	13	.000	-7	97	117	O43(24/12/8),3b20,S15,1b14,2b7		-3.1

HALL, RUSS Robert Russell B9.29.1871 Shelbyville KY D7.1.1937 Los Angeles CA BL/TL/5-10/170 d4.15

YEAR	TM	LG	G	AB	R	H	2B	3B	HR	RBI	BB-IB	HP	SO	AVG	OBP	SLG	AOPS	ABR	SB-CS	FA	FR	RNG	THR	GAMES AT POSITION	DL	BFW
1898	StL	N	39	143	13	35	2	1	0	10	7	1		.245	.285	.273	59	-8	1	.835	-12	91	81	S35,3b3/OR		-1.7
1901	Cle	A	1	4	2	2	0	0	0	0	0	0		.500	.500	.500	185	0	0	.500	-1	60	0	/S		-0.1
Total	2		40	147	15	37	2	1	0	10	7	1		.252	.290	.279	62	-8	1	.824	-13	90	79	S36,3b3/OR		-1.8

HALL, TOBY Toby Jason B10.21.1975 Tacoma WA BR/TR/6-3/205(205-240) [TBA97 9/294] d9.15 Col Nevada-Las Vegas

YEAR	TM	LG	G	AB	R	H	2B	3B	HR	RBI	BB-IB	HP	SO	AVG	OBP	SLG	AOPS	ABR	SB-CS	FA	FR	RNG	THR	GAMES AT POSITION	DL	BFW
2000	TB	A	4	12	1	2	0	0	1	1	1-0	0	6	.167	.231	.417	60	-1	0-0	1.000	1	0	0	C4		0.0
2001	TB	A	49	188	28	56	16	0	4	30	4-0	3	16	.298	.321	.447	102	0	2-2	.986	3	124	87	C46		0.6
2002	TB	A	85	330	37	85	19	1	6	42	17-3	1	27	.258	.293	.376	79	-11	0-1	.989	-5	112	114	C83		-1.0
2003	TB	A	130	463	50	117	23	0	12	47	23-4	7	40	.253	.296	.380	79	-15	0-1	.988	-2	128	84	C130		-0.8
2004	TB	A	119	404	33	103	21	0	8	60	24-1	5	41	.255	.300	.366	76	-15	0-2	.992	-2	128	84	C135,1b2		-1.0
2005	TB	A	135	432	28	124	20	0	5	48	16-5	1	39	.287	.315	.368	85	-10	0-0	.989	1	130	107	C125,1b2		-0.1
Total	6		522	1829	179	487	99	1	36	228	85-9	21	163	.266	.303	.381	82	-52	2-6	.989	-5	130	107	C517,1b2		-2.3

HALL, BILL William B12.28.1979 Tupelo MS BR/TR/6-0/175(175-195) [MilN98 6/176] d9.1

YEAR	TM	LG	G	AB	R	H	2B	3B	HR	RBI	BB-IB	HP	SO	AVG	OBP	SLG	AOPS	ABR	SB-CS	FA	FR	RNG	THR	GAMES AT POSITION	DL	BFW
2002	Mil	N	19	36	3	7	1	1	1	5	3-0	0	13	.194	.256	.361	63	-2	0-1	.949	-3	77	74	S13,3b2		-0.5
2003	Mil	N	52	142	23	37	9	2	5	20	7-0	1	28	.261	.298	.458	94	-2	1-2	.956	-0	105	126	2b18,S18/3		0.0
2004	Mil	N	126	390	43	93	20	3	9	53	20-1	1	119	.238	.276	.374	66	-21	12-6	.959	1	84	100	2b50,S37,3b11		-1.5
2005	Mil	N	146	501	69	146	39	6	17	62	39-2	1	103	.291	.342	.495	116	11	18-6	.976	-8	94	86	S66,3b59,2b23		1.1
Total	4		343	1069	138	283	69	12	32	140	69-3	3	263	.265	.310	.442	93	-14	31-15	.964	-10	99	92	S134,2b91,3b73		-0.9

HALL, BILL William Lemuel B7.30.1928 Moultrie GA D1.1.1986 Moultrie GA BL/TR/5-11/165* d4.18

YEAR	TM	LG	G	AB	R	H	2B	3B	HR	RBI	BB-IB	HP	SO	AVG	OBP	SLG	AOPS	ABR	SB-CS	FA	FR	RNG	THR	GAMES AT POSITION	DL	BFW
1954	Pit	N	5	7	0	0	0	0	0	0	0-0	0	0	.000	.000	.000	-99	-2	0-0	1.000	-0	0	0	/C		-0.2
1956	Pit	N	1	3	0	0	0	0	0	0	0-0	0	0	.000	.000	.000	-99	-1	0-0	1.000	1	0	0	/C		0.0
1958	Pit	N	51	116	15	33	6	0	1	15	15-8	0	13	.284	.366	.362	96	0	0-0	.982	5	114	140	C51		0.7
Total	3		57	126	15	33	6	0	1	15	15-8	0	14	.262	.340	.333	81	-2	0-0	.983	6	109	133	C53		0.5

HALLER, TOM Thomas Frank B6.23.1937 Lockport IL D11.26.2004 Los Angeles CA BL/TR/6-4/195(195-210) d4.11 C3 Col Illinois

YEAR	TM	LG	G	AB	R	H	2B	3B	HR	RBI	BB-IB	HP	SO	AVG	OBP	SLG	AOPS	ABR	SB-CS	FA	FR	RNG	THR	GAMES AT POSITION	DL	BFW
1961	SF	N	30	62	5	9	1	0	2	8	9-0	1	23	.145	.260	.258	41	-5	0-1	1.000	-1	61	74	C25		-0.6
1962	†SF	N	99	272	53	71	13	1	18	55	51-1	4	59	.261	.384	.515	142	18	1-4	.992	-0	145	76	C91		2.0
1963	SF	N	98	298	32	76	8	1	14	44	34-5	2	45	.255	.332	.430	120	8	4-6	.994	-4	130	97	C85,O7(1/0/6)		0.7
1964	SF	N	117	388	43	98	14	3	16	48	55-10	5	51	.253	.345	.428	115	9	4-2	.989	1	86	86	C113,O3(1/0/2)		1.6
1965	SF	N	134	422	40	106	4	3	16	49	47-15	8	67	.251	.335	.389	101	1	0-0	.987	2	140	56	C133		0.9
1966	SF	N☆	142	471	74	113	19	2	27	67	53-11	6	74	.240	.323	.461	112	8	1-3	.991	-4	100	63	C136,1b4		0.9
1967	SF	N★	141	455	54	114	23	5	14	49	62-9	4	76	.251	.344	.415	118	12	0-0	.997	1	101	89	C136/OR		1.9
1968	LA	N★	144	474	37	135	27	5	4	53	46-13	2	76	.285	.345	.388	131	19	1-4	.994	12	113	133	C139		4.1

The Batter Register

YEAR	TM LG	G	AB	R	H	2B	3B	HR	RBI	BB-IB	HP	SO	AVG	OBP	SLG	AOPS	ABR	SB-CS	FA	FR	RNG	THR	GAMES AT POSITION	DL	BFW
1969	LA N	134	445	46	117	18	3	6	39	48-13	2	58	.263	.337	.357	101	1	0-3	.992	-2	83	90	C132		0.4
1970	LA N	112	325	47	93	16	6	10	47	32-7	2	35	.286	.351	.465	122	9	3-0	.993	-6	76	77	C106		0.8
1971	LA N	84	202	23	54	5	0	5	32	25-8	2	30	.267	.346	.366	110	3	0-2	.978	2	75	104	C67		0.8
1972	†Det A	59	121	7	25	5	2	2	13	15-4	0	14	.207	.292	.331	83	-3	0-1	1.000	6	53		C36		0.2
Total	12	1294	3935	461	1011	153	31	134	504	477-96	35	593	.257	.340	.414	114	80	14-30	.992	3	105	86	C1199,O11(2/0/9),1b4		13.7

HALLIDAY, NEWT Newton Schurz B6.18.1896 Chicago IL D4.6.1918 Great Lakes IL BR/TR/6-1/175 d8.19

| 1916 | Pit N | 1 | 1 | 0 | 0 | 0 | 0 | 0 | 0 | 0 | 0 | 1 | .000 | .000 | .000 | -99 | 0 | | 1.000 | 0 | 603 | 0 | /1 | | 0.0 |

HALLIGAN, JOCKO William E. B12.8.1868 Avon NY D2.13.1945 Buffalo NY BL/5-9/166 d5.13

1890	Buf P	57	211	28	53	9	2	3	33	20	1	19	.251	.319	.355	87	-3	7	.824	-7	137	52	O43(1/5/37),C16		-0.8
1891	Cin N	61	247	43	77	13	6	3	44	24		25	.312	.375	.449	139	12	5	.856	-5	59	58	O61R		0.5
1892	Cin N	26	101	14	29	4	0	2	12	12	0	9	.287	.363	.386	128	4	3	.875	-1	95	115	O26R		0.1
	Bal N	46	178	38	48	4	7	2	43	30	2	24	.270	.381	.404	134	8	8	.861	-6	118	117	O22(1/0/21),1b19,C5		0.1
	Year	72	279	52	77	8	7	4	55	42	2	33	.276	.375	.398	132	12	11	.869	-7	105	116	O48(1/0/47),1b19,C5		0.2
Total	3	190	737	123	207	30	15	10	132	86	4	77	.281	.359	.403	121	21	23	.848	-20	94	74	O152(2/5/145),C21,1b19		-0.1

HALLINAN, ED Edward S. B8.23.1888 San Francisco CA D8.24.1940 San Francisco CA BR/TR/5-9/168 d5.13 Col Santa Clara

1911	StL A	52	169	13	35	3	1	0	14	14	0		.207	.268	.237	43	-13	4	.902	-5	94	164	S34,2b15,3b3		-1.6
1912	StL A	28	86	11	19	2	0	0	1	5	1		.221	.272	.244	50	-6	3	.866	-5	87	166	S26		-0.9
Total	2	80	255	24	54	5	1	0	15	19	1		.212	.269	.239	45	-19	7	.887	-10	91	165	S60,2b15,3b3		-2.5

HALLINAN, JIMMY James H. B5.27.1849 , Ireland D10.28.1879 Chicago IL BL/TL/5-9/172 d7.26

1871	Kek NA	5	25	7	5	0	0	0	2	2			.200	.259	.240	34	-2	1-1	.475	-7	54	0	S5		-0.6
1875	Wes NA	13	51	12	14	2	1	0	3	0		1	.275	.275	.353	110	0	2-2	.742	-4	74	91	S13		-0.4
	Mut NA	44	203	29	58	6	3	3	21	1		2	.286	.289	.389	127	4	2-2	.765	-11	89	36	S43/3OR		-0.7
	Year	57	254	41	72	8	4	3	24	1		3	.283	.286	.382	123	5	4-4	.761	-15	86	48	S56/3OR		-1.1
1876	NY N	54	240	45	67	7	6	2	36	2		4	.279	.285	.383	139	11		.764	-17	102	57	S50,2b4,O2R		-0.3
1877	Cin N	16	73	18	27	1	1	0	7	1		1	.370	.378	.411	167	6		.854	-5	69	111	2b16		0.1
	Chi N	19	89	17	25	4	1	0	11	4		2	.281	.312	.348	96	-1		.800	-1	30	177	O19R		-0.2
	Year	35	162	35	52	5	2	0	18	5		3	.321	.341	.377	124	4		.800	-7	30	177	O19R,2b16		-0.1
1878	Chi N	16	67	14	19	3	0	0	2	5		6	.284	.333	.328	111	1		.789	-5	67	0	O11L,2b5		-0.4
	Ind N	3	12	0	3	2	0	0	1	0		1	.250	.250	.417	134	1		.667	-1	0	0	O3(2/1/0)		0.0
	Year	19	79	14	22	5	0	0	3	5		8	.278	.321	.342	114	2		.760	-5	53	0	O14(13/1/0),2b5		-0.4
Total	2 NA	62	279	48	77	8	4	3	26	3		3	.276	.284	.366	114	2	5-5	.728	-22	83	44	S61/OR3		-1.7
Total	3	108	481	94	141	17	8	2	57	12		15	.293	.310	.374	129	18		.728	-29	102	57	S50,O35(13/1/21),2b25		-0.8

HALLMAN, BILL William Harry B3.15.1876 Philadelphia PA D4.23.1950 Philadelphia PA BL/TL/5-8/165 d4.25

1901	Mil A	139	549	70	135	27	6	2	47	41	2		.246	.301	.328	78	-16	12	.905	-1	121	144	O139(49/15/75)		-2.1
1903	Chi A	63	207	29	43	7	4	0	18	31	3		.208	.320	.280	85	-2	11	.953	2	111	0	O57(51/0/6)		-0.3
1906	Pit N	23	89	12	24	3	1	1	6	15	0		.270	.375	.360	124	3	3	.935	-1	107	0	O23(8/15/0)		0.1
1907	Pit N	94	302	39	67	6	2	0	15	33	3		.222	.305	.255	74	-8	21	.966	-1	87	41	O84(14/28/45)		-1.4
Total	4	319	1147	150	269	43	13	3	86	120			.235	.311	.303	82	-23	47	.933	-1	109	73	O303(122/58/126)		-3.7

HALLMAN, BILL William Wilson B3.31.1867 Pittsburgh PA D9.11.1920 Philadelphia PA BR/TR/5-8/160 d4.23 M1 OF(3/4/35)

1888	Phi N	18	63	5	13	4	1	0	6	1	0	12	.206	.219	.302	61	-3	1	.898	-4			C10,2b4,O3L/S3		-0.6
1889	Phi N	119	462	67	117	21	8	2	60	36	4	54	.253	.313	.346	77	-17	20	.895	3	98	S106,2b13/C		-0.9
1890	Phi P	84	356	59	95	16	7	1	37	33	5	56	.267	.338	.360	84	-9	6	.885	-3	100	397	O34(0/3/32),C26,2b14,3b10,S2		-0.8
1891	Phi AA	141	587	112	166	21	13	6	69	38	5	56	.283	.332	.394	107	2	18	.930	-4	96	93	2b141		0.2
1892	Phi N	138	586	106	171	27	10	2	84	32	5	52	.292	.335	.382	117	10	19	.936	-28	87	108	2b138		-1.1
1893	Phi N	132	596	119	183	28	7	5	76	51	5	27	.307	.367	.403	104	3	22	.950	-13	97	97	2b120,1b12		-0.4
1894	Phi N	122	519	111	162	19	9	6	69	37	5	15	.312	.364	.383	82	-15	37	.932	-19	87	114	2b122		-2.2
1895	Phi N	124	539	94	169	26	5	1	91	34	4	20	.314	.359	.386	92	-7	16	.943	4	105	116	2b122,S3		0.2
1896	Phi N	120	469	82	150	21	3	2	83	45	2	23	.320	.382	.390	105	5	16	.945	4	100	116	2b120/P		1.2
1897	Phi N	31	126	16	33	3	0	0	15	8	4		.262	.326	.286	64	-6	1	.958	-8	80	91	2b31		-1.1
	StL N	80	302	32	67	7	2	0	26	24	4		.222	.288	.258	46	-24	12	.940	5	104	117	2b78,1b3,M		-1.3
	Year	111	428	48	100	10	2	0	41	32	8		.234	.299	.266	51	-30	13	.945	-3	97	109	2b109,1b3		-2.4
1898	Bro N	134	509	57	124	10	7	2	63	29	5		.244	.291	.303	70	-21	9	.944	-4	108	90	2b124,3b10		-1.8
1901	Cle A	5	19	2	4	0	0	0	3	2			.211	.286	.211	41	-1	0	.815	-3	66	47	S5		-0.4
	Phi N	123	445	46	82	13	5	0	38	26	4		.184	.236	.236	36	-37	13	.971	-4	100	72	2b90,3b33		-3.9
1902	Phi N	73	254	14	63	8	4	0	35	14	0		.248	.287	.311	46	-5	9	.932	-1	102	84	2b72		-0.5
1903	Phi N	63	198	20	42	11	2	0	17	16	0		.212	.271	.288	61	-10	2	.932	-3	103	65	2b22,3b19,1b9,O4(0/1/3),S3		-1.2
Total	14	1507	6030	942	1641	235	83	21	772	426	53	283	.272	.326	.349	85	-135	201	.941	-79			2b1139,3b145,S120,041R,C37,1b24/P		-14.6

HALPIN, JIM James Nathaniel B10.4.1863 , England D1.4.1893 Boston MA d6.15

1882	Wor N	2	8	0	0	0	0	0		2			.000	.000	.000	-98	-2		.625	-1	53	0	3b2		-0.3
1884	Was U	46	168	24	31	3	0	0		2			.185	.194	.202	21	-21		.809	-5	88	65	S39,3b7		-2.3
1885	Det N	15	54	3	7	2	0	0	1	1			.130	.145	.167	1	-6		.846	-1	106	61	S15		-0.6
Total	3	63	230	27	38	5	0	0	1	3			.165	.176	.187	12	-29		.821	-7	93	64	S54,3b9		-3.2

HALT, AL Alva William B11.23.1890 Sandusky OH D1.22.1973 Sandusky OH BR/TR/6-0/180 d5.29

1914	Bro F	80	261	26	61	6	2	3	25	13	0	39	.234	.270	.307	57	-21	11	.890	-10	88	110	S71,2b3/OC		-2.8
1915	Bro F	151	524	41	131	22	7	3	64	39	4	79	.250	.307	.336	81	-22	20	.930	6	106	138	3b111,S40		-1.1
1918	Cle A	26	69	9	12	0	0	0	1	9	0	12	.174	.269	.203	39	-5	4	.971	1	97	49	3b14,2b4,S4,1b2		-0.4
Total	3	257	854	76	204	30	9	6	90	61	4	130	.239	.293	.316	70	-48	35	.933	-4	105	130	3b125,S115,2b7,1b2/OC		-4.3

HALTER, SHANE Shane David B11.8.1969 LaPlata MD BR/TR/6-0/180(160-195) [KCA91 5/132] d4.6 Col Texas OF(28/15/24)

1997	KC A	74	123	16	34	5	1	2	10	10-0	2	28	.276	.341	.382	86	-3	4-3	1.000	4	92	96	O32(10/9/17),2b18,3b12,S5,D4		-0.7
1998	KC A	86	204	17	45	12	0	2	13	12-0	1	38	.221	.265	.309	47	-16	2-5	.964	5	116	90	S66,O9(6/0/3),3b8,2b6/1P		-0.8
1999	NY N	7	0	0	0	0	0	0	0	0-0	0	0	—	—	—		0	0-0	—	-0	0	0	O2(0/1/1)/S		0.0
2000	Det A	105	238	26	62	12	2	3	27	14-0	1	49	.261	.302	.366	69	-12	5-2	.937	8	104	184	3b55,1b29,S17,2b10,O8(2/5/3),C2/P		-0.4
2001	Det A	136	450	53	128	32	7	12	65	37-2	7	100	.284	.344	.467	115	10	3-3	.924	14	129	102	3b74,S62,1b8/D		2.6
2002	Det A	122	410	46	98	22	6	10	39	39-1	4	92	.239	.309	.395	89	-7	0-4	.962	4	113	69	S81,3b30,O8L,2b4/1D		0.2
2003	Det A	114	360	33	78	5	2	12	30	27-0	0	77	.217	.269	.342	63	-21	2-3	.985	8	125	154	3b50,S27,2b24,1b12,O2L,D1		-1.1
2004	Ana A	46	114	10	23	5	1	2	7-0	1	0	30	.202	.248	.351	56	-8	1-1	.878	1	111	52	3b33,2b6,1b4,S3,D3	22	-0.7
Total	6	690	1899	201	468	93	18	45	197	146-3	15	414	.246	.303	.385	81	-57	17-21	.964	36	111	92	S262,3b262,2b68,061L,1b55,D14,C2,P222		-0.9

HAM, RALPH Ralph A. B3.1849 Troy NY D2.13.1905 Troy NY 5-8/158 d5.6

| 1871 | Rok NA | 25 | 113 | 25 | 28 | 4 | 0 | 0 | 12 | 1 | | | .248 | .254 | .283 | 57 | -5 | 6-2 | .723 | -6 | 215 | 232 | O19L,3b7,S2 | | -0.7 |

HAMBURG, CHARLIE Charles M. (b Charles M. Hambrick) B11.22.1863 Louisville KY D5.18.1931 Union NJ 6-0/175 d4.18

| 1890 | †Lou AA | 133 | 485 | 93 | 132 | 22 | 2 | 3 | 77 | 69 | 6 | | .272 | .370 | .344 | 113 | 12 | 46 | .946 | -3 | 72 | 69 | O133L | | 0.4 |

HAMBY, JIM James Sanford "Cracker" B7.29.1897 Wilkesboro NC D10.21.1991 Springfield IL BR/TR/6-0/170 d9.20

1926	NY N	1	3	0	0	0	0	0	0	0	0		.000	.000	.000	-99	-1	0	.600	-1	48	0	/C		-0.2
1927	NY N	21	52	6	10	0	1	0	5	7	0		.192	.288	.231	40	-4	1	.904	-1	119	151	C19		-0.4
Total	2	22	55	6	10	0	1	0	5	7	0		.182	.274	.218	33	-5	1	.885	-2	115	142	C20		-0.6

HAMELIN, BOB Robert James B11.29.1967 Elizabeth NJ BL/TL/6-0/235* [KCA88 2/48] d9.12 Col UCLA

1993	KC A	16	49	2	11	3	0	2	5	5	0	15	.224	.309	.408	85	-1	0-0	.986	-1	90	88	1b15		-0.3
1994	KC A	101	312	64	88	25	1	24	65	56-3	1	62	.282	.388	.599	144	21	4-3	.992	0	106	57	D70,1b24		1.4
1995	KC A	72	208	20	35	7	1	7	25	26-1	6	56	.168	.278	.313	53	-15	0-1	1.000	2	171	180	D56,1b8		-1.7
1996	KC A	89	239	31	61	14	1	9	40	54-2	1	58	.255	.391	.435	110	6	5-2	.984	0	109	108	D47,1b33		0.4
1997	Det A	110	318	47	86	15	0	18	52	48-3	1	72	.270	.366	.487	121	11	2-1	1.000	1	38	31	D95,1b7	28	0.1
1998	Mil N	109	146	15	32	6	0	7	22	16-1	1	30	.219	.295	.404	82	-4	0-1	.992	-5	35	93	1b51/D		-1.2
Total	6	497	1272	179	313	70	3	67	209	206-10	11	293	.246	.350	.464	108	18	11-8	.990	-5	87	92	D269,1b138	28	-1.3

YEAR	TM LG	G	AB	R	H	2B	3B	HR	RBI	BB-IB	HP	SO	AVG	OBP	SLG	AOPS	ABR	SB-CS	FA	FR	RNG	THR	GAMES AT POSITION	DL	BFW

HAMILTON, DARRYL Darryl Quinn B12.3.1964 Baton Rouge LA BL/TR/6-1/180(180-192) [MilA86 11/269] d6.3 Col Nicholls St.

1988	Mil A	44	103	14	19	4	0	1	11	12-0	1	9	.184	.274	.252	48	-7	7-3	1.000	1	109	54	O37(8/6/23),D3		-0.7
1990	Mil A	89	156	27	46	5	0	1	18	9-0	0	12	.295	.333	.346	91	-2	10-3	.992	3	123	32	O72(41/6/25),D9		0.1
1991	Mil A	122	405	64	126	15	6	1	57	33-2	0	38	.311	.361	.385	109	5	16-6	.996	-5	95	45	O117(25/55/49)	24	-0.1
1992	Mil A	128	470	67	140	19	7	5	62	45-0	1	42	.298	.356	.400	114	4	41-14	1.000	2	100	121	O124(30/32/74)	18	1.2
1993	Mil A	.135	520	74	161	21	1	9	48	45-5	3	62	.310	.367	.406	109	7	21-13	.992	11	117	117	O129(31/49/70)/D	15	1.4
1994	Mil A	36	141	23	37	10	1	1	13	15-1	1	17	.262	.331	.369	77	-5	3-0	1.000	-4	74	122	O32C,D4	78	-0.7
1995	Mil A	112	398	54	108	20	6	5	44	47-3	3	35	.271	.350	.389	88	-7	11-1	.989	-2	99	78	O109C,D2		-0.5
1996	†Tex A	148	627	94	184	29	4	6	51	54-4	2	66	.293	.348	.381	80	-19	15-5	1.000	-6	103	22	O147C	22	-1.2
1997	†SF N	125	460	78	124	23	3	5	43	61-1	0	61	.270	.354	.365	91	-5	15-10	.980	-8	96	19	O118C		-0.1
1998	SF N	97	367	65	108	19	2	1	26	59-0	2	53	.294	.393	.365	107	7	9-8	1.000	-9	87	67	O96C		0.0
	Col N	51	194	30	65	9	1	5	25	23-1	1	20	.335	.406	.469	107	3	4-1	.990	-4	91	33	O48C		-0.1
	Year	148	561	95	173	28	3	6	51	82-1	3	73	.308	.398	.401	107	10	13-9	.997	-13	88	56	O144C		-1.3
1999	Col N	91	337	63	102	11	3	4	24	38-0	1	21	.303	.374	.389	75	-12	4-5	1.000	-2	105	23	O82C		0.6
	†NY N	55	168	19	57	8	1	5	21	19-0	1	18	.339	.410	.488	132	9	2-3	1.000	-3	92	83	O52C		-0.7
	Year	146	505	82	159	19	4	9	45	57-0	2	39	.315	.386	.422	91	-5	6-8	1.000	-4	100	45	O134C		-0.1
2000	†NY N	43	105	20	29	4	1	1	6	14-0	0	20	.276	.358	.362	88	-2	2-0	1.000	-2	81	66	O33(17/11/8)	123	-0.5
2001	NY N	52	126	15	27	7	1	1	6	19-3	2	20	.214	.322	.310	71	-5	3-1	1.000	1	103	99	O37(24/11/3)	18	-0.5
Total	13	1328	4577	707	1333	204	37	51	454	493-20	17	494	.291	.360	.385	95	-24	163-73	.995	-27	100	63	O1233(176/854/252),D19	298	-4.0

HAMILTON, JEFF Jeffrey Robert B3.19.1964 Flint MI BR/TR/6-3/207* [LAN82 29/733] d6.28

1986	LA N	71	147	22	33	5	0	5	19	2-1	0	43	.224	.232	.361	66	-8	0-0	.968	5	105	90	3b66,S2		-0.4
1987	LA N	35	83	5	18	3	0	0	1	7-2	1	22	.217	.286	.253	45	-7	0-1	.935	6	122	119	3b31/S	52	-0.1
1988	†LA N	111	309	34	73	14	2	6	33	10-1	4	51	.236	.268	.353	79	-10	0-2	.941	0	96	60	3b105,S2/1	36	-1.0
1989	LA N	151	548	45	134	35	1	12	56	20-5	3	71	.245	.272	.378	86	-12	0-0	.951	-1	88	133	3b147/P2S		-1.4
1990	LA N	7	24	1	3	0	0	0	1	0-0	0	4	.125	.125	.125	-32	-4	0-0	1.000	1	108	234	3b7	166	-0.4
1991	LA N	41	94	4	21	4	0	1	14	4-0	0	21	.223	.255	.298	56	-6	0-0	.928	0	101	56	3b33/S	79	-0.6
Total	6	416	1205	111	282	61	3	24	124	43-9	8	211	.234	.263	.349	74	-47	0-3	.948	11	96	104	3b389,S7/2P1	333	-3.9

HAMILTON, TOM Thomas Ball "Ham" B9.29.1925 Altoona KS D11.29.1973 Tyler TX BL/TR/6-4/213* d9.4 Col Texas

1952	Phi A	9	10	1	2	0	0	0	1	1	0	1	.200	.273	.300	56	-1	0-0	1.000	-0	0	79	1b5		-0.1
1953	Phi A	58	56	8	11	2	0	0	5	7	0	11	.196	.286	.232	40	-5	0-0	1.000	0	105	0	1b7,O2R		-0.5
Total	2	67	66	9	13	3	0	0	6	8	0	12	.197	.284	.242	42	-6	0-0	1.000	0	72	25	1b12,O2R		-0.6

HAMILTON, BILLY William Robert "Sliding Billy" B2.16.1866 Newark NJ D12.16.1940 Worcester MA BL/TR/5-6/165 d7.31 HF1961

1888	KC AA	35	129	21	34	4	0	0	11	4	4		.264	.307	.357	106	0	19	.961	-8	82	0	O35(3/0/32)		0.0
1889	KC AA	137	534	144	161	17	12	3	77	87	14	41	.301	.413	.395	123	19	111	.857	-8	75	93	O137(7/0/130)		0.8
1890	Phi N	123	496	133	161	13	9	2	49	83	9	37	.325	.430	.399	139	29	102	.882	3	107	88	O123L		2.6
1891	Phi N	133	527	141	179	23	7	2	60	102	7	28	.340	.453	.421	151	42	111	.907	7	81	191	O133L		4.0
1892	Phi N	139	554	132	183	21	7	3	53	81	8	29	.330	.423	.410	152	40	57	.919	12	113	151	O139(138/1/0)		3.7
1893	Phi N	82	355	110	135	22	7	5	44	63	13	7	.380	.490	.524	169	41	43	.937	1	55	196	O82(19/63/0)		3.0
1894	Phi N	132	558	198	225	25	15	4	90	128	10	19	.403	.522	.523	156	66	100	.962	2	67	74	O132C		4.5
1895	Phi N	123	517	166	201	22	6	7	74	96	7	30	.389	.490	.495	154	50	97	.913	-4	60	114	O123(3/120/0)		3.1
1896	Bos N	131	524	153	192	24	10	3	55	110	2	29	.366	.478	.468	141	39	83	.934	-12	45	47	O131(6/125/0)		1.6
1897	†Bos N	127	507	152	174	17	5	3	61	105	6		.343	.461	.414	124	26	66	.962	-6	55	0	O126C		1.4
1898	Bos N	110	417	110	154	16	5	3	50	87	1		.369	.480	.453	159	39	54	.904	-17	53	64	O110C		0.0
1899	Bos N	84	297	63	92	7	1	1	33	72	1		.310	.446	.350	109	9	19	.952	-4	88	58	O81(2/78/1)		1.1
1900	Bos N	136	520	103	173	20	5	1	47	107	3		.333	.449	.396	119	21	32	.947	-0	76	130	O136C		1.1
1901	Bos N	102	348	71	100	11	2	3	38	64	4		.287	.404	.356	111	9	20	.945	-0	56	138	O99(0/98/1)		0.4
Total	14	1594	6283	1697	2164	242	95	40	742	1189	90	220	.344	.455	.432	139	430	914	.926	-28	73	102	O1587(434/989/164)		27.2

HAMLIN, KEN Kenneth Lee B5.18.1935 Detroit MI BR/TR/5-10/170* d6.17 Col Western Michigan

1957	Pit N	2	1	0	0	0	0	0	0	0-0	0	0	.000	.000	.000	-99	-0	0-0	1.000	-0	0	0	/S		0.0
1959	Pit N	3	8	1	1	0	0	0	0	2-0	0	1	.125	.300	.125	19	-1	0-0	1.000	-0	89	155	S3		-0.1
1960	KC A	140	428	51	96	10	2	2	24	44-1	1	48	.224	.297	.271	55	-27	1-1	.955	-40	85	70	S139		-5.8
1961	LA A	42	19	4	19	3	0	1	5	11-2	1	9	.209	.298	.275	49	-6	0-0	.963	8	109	129	S87,2b2		0.4
1962	Was A	98	292	29	74	12	0	3	22	22-0	0	22	.253	.303	.325	70	-12	7-7	.963	-10	94	100	S87,2b2		-1.7
1965	Was A	117	362	45	99	21	1	4	22	33-1	1	45	.273	.333	.370	102	2	8-2	.976	-21	86	74	2b77,S47/3		-1.1
1966	Was A	66	158	13	34	7	1	1	16	13-1	0	21	.215	.267	.291	63	-7	1-0	.963	4	112	115	2b50/3		0.0
Total	7	468	1340	143	323	53	4	11	89	125-5	3	146	.241	.304	.311	71	-51	17-11	.959	-59	90	87	S316,2b129,3b2		-8.3

HAMMOCK, ROB Robert Wade B3.13.1977 Macon GA BR/TR/5-11/180* [AriN98 23/703] d4.11 Col Georgia

2003	Ari N	65	195	30	55	10	2	8	28	17-3	2	44	.282	.343	.477	103	1	3-2	.993	15	83	105	C36,O17(5/0/12),3b16/D		1.7
2004	Ari N	62	195	22	47	16	2	4	18	13-6	0	39	.241	.287	.405	72	-8	3-3	.997	1	87	134	C46,O12L/3	73	-0.5
Total	2	127	390	52	102	26	4	12	46	30-9	2	83	.262	.315	.441	88	-7	6-5	.995	16	85	122	C82,O29(17/0/12),3b17/D	73	1.2

HAMMOND, STEVE Steven Benjamin B5.9.1957 Atlanta GA BL/TR/6-2/190 d6.28 b-Chris Col Florida St.

| 1982 | KC A | 46 | 126 | 14 | 29 | 5 | 1 | 1 | 11 | 4-0 | 0 | 18 | .230 | .252 | .310 | 53 | -8 | 0-1 | 1.000 | 4 | 121 | 130 | O37R/D | | -0.7 |

HAMMOND, JACK Walter Charles "Wobby" B2.26.1891 Amsterdam NY D3.4.1942 Kenosha WI BR/TR/5-11/170 d4.15 Col Colgate

1915	Cle A	35	84	9	18	2	1	0	4	1	0	19	.214	.224	.262	44	-6	0-1	.957	-5	87	80	2b19		-1.2
1922	Cle A	1	4	1	1	0	0	0	0	0	0	0	.250	.250	.250	30	0	0-0	.333	-1	41	0	/2		-0.2
	Pit N	9	11	3	3	0	0	0	0	1	0	0	.273	.333	.273	57	-1	0-0	1.000	0	83	156	2b4		0.0
Total	2	45	99	13	22	2	1	0	4	2	0	19	.222	.238	.263	45	-7	0-1	.943	-6	85	86	2b24		-1.4

HAMMONDS, JEFFREY Jeffrey Bryan B3.5.1971 Plainfield NJ BR/TR/6-0/195(195-220) [BalA92 1/4] d6.25 Col Stanford

1993	Bal A	33	105	10	32	8	0	3	19	2-1	2	16	.305	.312	.467	103	0	4-0	.961	1	104	138	O23(14/0/10),D8	30	0.
1994	Bal A	68	250	45	74	18	2	8	31	17-1	2	39	.296	.339	.480	104	1	5-0	.962	2	110	103	O66(9/0/58)	43	0.
1995	Bal A	57	178	18	43	9	1	4	23	9-0	1	30	.242	.279	.371	67	-4	4-2	.989	0	109	36	O46R,D5	47	-1.
1996	Bal A	71	248	38	56	10	1	9	27	23-1	4	53	.226	.301	.383	72	-11	3-3	.980	-5	105	63	O70(64/1/11)/D	37	-1.
1997	†Bal A	118	397	71	105	19	3	21	55	32-1	3	73	.264	.323	.486	111	4	15-1	.980	1	107	66	O114(31/40/54),D4		-1.
1998	Bal A	63	171	36	46	12	1	6	28	26-1	1	38	.269	.369	.456	117	5	7-2	.980	-2	95	67	O53(7/24/29),D7	38	-0.
	Cin N	26	86	14	26	4	1	0	11	13-0	0	18	.302	.390	.372	102	1	1-1	.985	3	117	207	O25C		-0.
1999	Cin N	123	262	43	73	13	0	17	41	27-0	1	64	.279	.347	.523	113	4	3-6	1.000	5	111	118	O106(46/21/53)	17	-0.
2000	Col N★	122	454	94	152	24	2	20	106	44-4	5	83	.335	.395	.529	107	6	14-7	.991	-4	89	109	O118(32/9/85)	123	-0.
2001	Mil N	49	174	20	43	11	1	6	21	14-1	2	42	.247	.314	.425	92	-2	5-3	.982	-3	95	78	O46C		-1.
2002	Mil N	128	448	47	115	26	5	9	41	52-0	2	86	.257	.332	.397	96	-4	4-5	.992	-7	94	42	O125(2/78/55)	50	-1.
2003	Mil N	10	38	2	6	2	0	0	3	3-0	0	7	.158	.220	.289	31	-4	0-0	1.000	1	91	0	O10R		-0.
	†SF N	36	94	13	20	10	0	3	10	13-0	1	21	.277	.370	.479	118	3	1-0	1.000	-1	95	70	O30(17/14/4)		-0.
	Year	46	132	22	32	12	0	4	13	16-0	1	28	.242	.329	.424	94	-1	1-0	1.000	-1	94	50	O40(17/14/14)	6	-0.
2004	SF N	40	95	14	20	5	0	3	6	15-0	2	22	.211	.336	.358	77	-3	1-0	1.000	2	106	207	O28(7/1/20)		-0.
2005	Was N	13	32	3	7	0	1	0	2	2-1	1	4	.219	.286	.250	45	-3	0-0	1.000	0	117	0	O11(10/0/1)/D	17	-0.
Total	13	957	3032	475	824	172	17	110	423	292-11	30	596	.272	.338	.449	99	-12	67-30	.985	-3	101	84	O871(239/259/436),D26	408	-3.

HAMNER, GRANNY Granville Wilbur B4.26.1927 Richmond VA D9.12.1993 Philadelphia PA BR/TR/5-10/163(160-185) d9.14 Mil 1945 b-Garvin ▲

1944	Phi N	21	77	6	19	1	0	0	9	7	0	7	.247	.275	.260	53	-5	0	.933	5	132	131	S21		0.
1945	Phi N	14	41	3	7	2	0	0	6	1	0	3	.171	.190	.220	14	-5	0	.861	0	103	97	S13		-0.
1946	Phi N	2	7	0	1	0	0	0	1	0	0	1	.143	.143	.143	-19	-1	0	.857	-1	101	98	S2		-0.
1947	Phi N	2	7	1	2	0	0	0	1	0	0	0	.286	.375	.286	81	0	0	1.000	0	94	80	S2		0.
1948	Phi N	129	446	42	116	16	5	3	48	22	2	39	.260	.298	.350	76	-16	7	.967	-10	93	97	2b8,S37,3b3		-2.
1949	Phi N	154	662	83	174	32	5	6	53	25	0	47	.263	.290	.353	74	-27	6	.961	-3	104	111	S154		-2.
1950	†Phi N	157	637	78	172	27	5	11	82	39	2	35	.270	.314	.380	83	-18	2	.944	-3	103	101	S157		-1.
1951	Phi N	150	589	61	150	17	9	9	72	19	0	32	.255	.290	.363	76	-23	10-5	.958	-2	102	99	S150		-1.
1952	Phi N★	151	596	74	164	30	5	17	87	27	1	51	.275	.307	.428	103	-1	7-3	.951	-2	106	113	S151		0.
1953	Phi N★	154	609	90	168	30	8	21	92	32	2	28	.276	.313	.455	98	-5	2-1	.970	-6	108	108	2b93,S71		0.
1954	Phi N★	152	596	83	178	39	11	13	89	53	0	41	.299	.351	.466	104	10	1-2	.978	-20	94	95	2b152/S		0.

YEAR	TM LG	G	AB	R	H	2B	3B	HR	RBI	BB-IB	HP	SO	AVG	OBP	SLG	AOPS	ABR	SB-CS	FA	FR	RNG	THR	GAMES AT POSITION	DL	BFW
1955	Phi N	104	405	57	104	12	4	5	43	41-1	1	30	.257	.323	.343	79	-12	0-1	.960	-27	87	82	2b82,S32		-3.2
1956	Phi N	122	401	42	90	24	3	4	42	30-5	0	42	.224	.276	.329	64	-21	2-0	.937	-13	95	102	S110,2b11,P3		-2.5
1957	Phi N	133	502	59	114	19	5	10	62	34-3	0	42	.227	.274	.345	68	-24	3-1	.963	-33	82	72	2b125,S5/P		-4.9
1958	Phi N	35	133	18	40	7	3	2	18	8-0	0	16	.301	.341	.444	107	1	0-0	.984	-3	102	165	3b22,2b11,S3		-0.1
1959	Phi N	21	64	10	19	4	0	2	6	5-1	0	5	.297	.348	.453	109	1	0-1	.947	-3	104	51	S15/3	118	-0.1
	Cle A	27	67	4	11	1	1	1	3	1-0	0	8	.164	.174	.254	17	-8	0-0	.960	-2	81	62	S10,2b7,3b5	33	-1.0
1962	KC A	3	0	0	0	0	0	0	0	0-0	0	0	—	—	—	—	—	0-0	1.000	0	157	0	P3		0.0
Total 17		1531	5839	711	1529	272	62	104	708	351-10	6	432	.262	.303	.383	84	-154	35-14	.946	-123	101	103	S934,2b568,3b31,P7	151	-17.9

HAMNER, GARVIN Wesley Garvin B3.18.1924 Richmond VA D12.15.2003 Richmond VA BR/TR/5-11/172 d4.17 b-Granny

YEAR	TM LG	G	AB	R	H	2B	3B	HR	RBI	BB-IB	HP	SO	AVG	OBP	SLG	AOPS	ABR	SB-CS	FA	FR	RNG	THR	GAMES AT POSITION	DL	BFW
1945	Phi N	32	101	12	20	3	0	0	5	7	0	9	.198	.250	.228	34	-9	2	.962	-4	103	75	2b21,S9/3		-1.1

HAMPTON, IKE Isaac Bernard B8.22.1951 Camden SC BB/TR (BR 1978-79)/6-1/185(165-185) d9.12

YEAR	TM LG	G	AB	R	H	2B	3B	HR	RBI	BB-IB	HP	SO	AVG	OBP	SLG	AOPS	ABR	SB-CS	FA	FR	RNG	THR	GAMES AT POSITION	DL	BFW
1974	NY A	4	4	0	0	0	0	0	1	0-0	0	1	1.000	1.000	1.000	-99	-1	0-0	1.000	-0	30	0	/C		-0.1
1975	Cal A	31	66	8	10	3	0	0	4	7-0	1	19	.152	.243	.197	27	-6	0-0	.947	-9	100	125	C28,S2/3		-1.5
1976	Cal A	3	2	0	0	0	0	0	0	0-0	0	0	.000	.000	.000	-99	-1	0-0	1.000	0	0	0	C2/S		0.0
1977	Cal A	52	44	5	13	1	0	3	9	2-0	1	10	.295	.340	.523	136	2	0-0	.968	-4	85	98	C47,D2		-0.1
1978	Cal A	19	14	2	3	0	1	1	4	2-0	0	7	.214	.313	.571	148	1	1-0	.905	-1	52	81	C13/1D		0.0
1979	Cal A	4	5	0	2	0	0	0	0	0-0	0	1	.400	.400	.400	120	0	0-0	1.000	0	211	0	1b2		0.0
Total 6		113	135	15	28	4	1	4	18	11-0	2	38	.207	.275	.341	75	-5	1-0	.953	-14	89	110	C91,D6,1b3,S3/3		-1.7

HAMRIC, BERT Odbert Herman B3.1.1928 Clarksburg WV D8.8.1984 Springboro OH BL/TR/6-0/165(165-180) d4.24

YEAR	TM LG	G	AB	R	H	2B	3B	HR	RBI	BB-IB	HP	SO	AVG	OBP	SLG	AOPS	ABR	SB-CS	FA	FR	RNG	THR	GAMES AT POSITION	DL	BFW
1955	Bro N	2	1	0	0	0	0	0	0	0-0	0	1	.000	.000	.000	-97	-1	0-0	—		0		/H		0.0
1958	Bal A	8	8	0	1	0	0	0	0	0-0	0	6	.125	.125	.125	-33	-1	0-0	—		0		/H		-0.2
Total 2		10	9	0	1	0	0	0	0	0-0	0	7	.111	.111	.111	-41	-1	0-0	—		0				-0.2

HAMRICK, RAY Raymond Bernard B8.1.1921 Nashville TN BR/TR/5-11.5/160 d8.14 Mil 1944-46

YEAR	TM LG	G	AB	R	H	2B	3B	HR	RBI	BB-IB	HP	SO	AVG	OBP	SLG	AOPS	ABR	SB-CS	FA	FR	RNG	THR	GAMES AT POSITION	DL	BFW
1943	Phi N	44	160	12	32	3	1	0	9	8	0	28	.200	.238	.231	37	-14	0	.960	-8	96	53	2b31,S12		-2.0
1944	Phi N	74	292	22	60	10	1	1	23	23	2	34	.205	.268	.257	50	-20	1	.948	13	114	122	S74		0.0
Total 2		118	452	34	92	13	2	1	32	31	2	62	.204	.258	.248	46	-34	1	.946	6	111	111	S86,2b31		-2.0

HANCKEN, BUDDY Morris Medlock B8.30.1914 Birmingham AL BR/TR/6-1/175 d5.14 C5 Col Birmingham-Southern

YEAR	TM LG	G	AB	R	H	2B	3B	HR	RBI	BB-IB	HP	SO	AVG	OBP	SLG	AOPS	ABR	SB-CS	FA	FR	RNG	THR	GAMES AT POSITION	DL	BFW
1940	Phi A	1	0	0	0	0	0	0	0	0-0	0	0	—	—	—	—	—	0-0	1.000	-0	0	0	/C		0.0

HANCOCK, FRED Fred James B3.28.1920 Allenport PA D3.12.1986 Clearwater FL BR/TR/5-8/170 d4.26

YEAR	TM LG	G	AB	R	H	2B	3B	HR	RBI	BB-IB	HP	SO	AVG	OBP	SLG	AOPS	ABR	SB-CS	FA	FR	RNG	THR	GAMES AT POSITION	DL	BFW
1949	Chi A	39	52	7	7	2	1	0	9	8	1	9	.135	.262	.212	27	-6	0-1	.978	-2	83	140	S27,3b3/OR		-0.7

HANCOCK, GARRY Ronald Garry B1.23.1954 Tampa FL BL/TL/6-0/175(175-190) [CleA76*S1/17] d7.16 Col South Carolina-Aiken

YEAR	TM LG	G	AB	R	H	2B	3B	HR	RBI	BB-IB	HP	SO	AVG	OBP	SLG	AOPS	ABR	SB-CS	FA	FR	RNG	THR	GAMES AT POSITION	DL	BFW
1978	Bos A	38	80	10	18	4	0	0	4	1-0	0	12	.225	.232	.262	36	-3	1-0	1.000	2	105	355	O19(4/5/10),D13		-0.5
1980	Bos A	46	115	9	33	6	0	4	19	3-0	0	11	.287	.300	.443	97	-1	0-3	.963	-1	81	185	O27(6/20/1),D12		-0.4
1981	Bos A	26	45	4	7	3	0	0	3	2-1	0	4	.156	.191	.222	18	-5	0-0	1.000	1	74	566	O8(0/5/3),D4		-0.4
1982	Bos A	11	14	3	0	0	0	0	0	1-0	0	1	.000	.067	.000	-75	-3	0-0	1.000	1	58	0	O7R		-0.4
1983	Oak A	101	256	29	70	7	3	8	30	5-4	1	13	.273	.289	.418	97	-3	2-0	.981	-1	107	115	O67(26/1/40),1b27,D9		-0.6
1984	Oak A	51	60	2	13	2	0	0	8	0-0	0	1	.217	.217	.250	31	-6	0-0	1.000	0	131	0	O18(9/2/9),1b4/PD	31	-0.6
Total 6		273	570	57	141	21	3	12	64	12-5	1	42	.247	.262	.358	70	-25	2-3	.982	1	98	177	O146(45/33/70),D43,1b31/P	31	-2.9

HANDIBOE, MIKE Aloysius James "Coalyard Mike" B7.21.1887 Washington DC D1.31.1953 Savannah GA BL/TL/5-10/155 d9.8

YEAR	TM LG	G	AB	R	H	2B	3B	HR	RBI	BB-IB	HP	SO	AVG	OBP	SLG	AOPS	ABR	SB-CS	FA	FR	RNG	THR	GAMES AT POSITION	DL	BFW
1911	NY A	5	15	0	1	0	0	0	0	0-0	0	3	.067	.176	.067	-29	-3	0	1.000	-0	108	0	O4(2/0/2)		-0.3

HANDLEY, GENE Eugene Louis B11.25.1914 Kennett MO BR/TR/5-10.5/165 d4.16 b-Lee Col Bradley

YEAR	TM LG	G	AB	R	H	2B	3B	HR	RBI	BB-IB	HP	SO	AVG	OBP	SLG	AOPS	ABR	SB-CS	FA	FR	RNG	THR	GAMES AT POSITION	DL	BFW
1946	Phi A	89	251	31	63	8	5	0	21	22	0	25	.251	.311	.323	78	-8	8-3	.947	-16	80	71	2b68,3b4/S		-2.1
1947	Phi A	36	90	10	23	2	1	0	8	10	0	2	.256	.330	.300	74	-3	1-0	.973	-6	92	98	2b17,3b10/S		-0.8
Total 2		125	341	41	86	10	6	0	29	32	0	27	.252	.316	.317	77	-11	9-3	.952	-21	82	76	2b85,3b14,S2		-2.9

HANDLEY, LEE Lee Elmer "Jeep" B7.31.1913 Clarion IA D4.8.1970 Pittsburgh PA BR/TR/5-7/160 d4.15 b-Gene Col Bradley

YEAR	TM LG	G	AB	R	H	2B	3B	HR	RBI	BB-IB	HP	SO	AVG	OBP	SLG	AOPS	ABR	SB-CS	FA	FR	RNG	THR	GAMES AT POSITION	DL	BFW
1936	Cin N	24	78	10	24	1	0	2	8	7	0	16	.308	.365	.397	112	-1	3	.926	-1	95	67	2b16,3b7		0.2
1937	Pit N	127	480	59	120	21	12	3	37	37	1	40	.250	.305	.363	81	-14	5	.950	-14	91	91	2b126/3		-2.0
1938	Pit N	139	570	91	153	25	8	6	51	53	1	31	.268	.332	.372	93	-6	7	.948	11	115	115	3b136		1.0
1939	Pit N	101	376	43	107	14	5	1	42	32	1	20	.285	.341	.356	89	-6	17	.936	-3	102	82	3b100		-0.6
1940	Pit N	98	302	50	85	7	4	1	19	27	0	16	.281	.340	.341	89	-4	7	.925	0	101	99	3b80,2b2		-0.1
1941	Pit N	124	459	59	132	18	4	0	33	35	1	22	.288	.338	.344	93	-5	16	.947	1	105	92	3b114		-0.6
1944	Pit N	40	86	7	19	2	0	0	5	3	0	5	.221	.247	.244	37	-7	1	.947	1	92	101	2b19,3b11,S3		0.1
1945	Pit N	98	312	39	93	16	2	1	32	20	1	16	.298	.340	.372	94	-2	3	.947	11	116	95	3b79		-0.6
1946	Pit N	116	416	43	99	8	7	1	28	29	1	20	.238	.289	.298	65	-21	4	.958	12	122	82	3b102,2b3		0.9
1947	Phi N	101	277	17	70	10	3	0	42	24	0	18	.253	.312	.310	68	-13	1	.975	0	101	62	3b83,2b3/S		-0.9
Total 10		968	3356	418	902	122	45	15	297	267	3	204	.269	.323	.345	84	-78	68	.949	18	110	92	3b713,2b169,S4		-3.3

HANEBRINK, HARRY Harry Aloysius B11.12.1927 St.Louis MO D9.9.1996 Bridgeton MO BL/TR/6-0/165(165-185) d5.3

YEAR	TM LG	G	AB	R	H	2B	3B	HR	RBI	BB-IB	HP	SO	AVG	OBP	SLG	AOPS	ABR	SB-CS	FA	FR	RNG	THR	GAMES AT POSITION	DL	BFW
1953	Mil N	51	80	8	19	1	1	1	8	6	0	8	.237	.291	.313	61	-5	1-0	.979	2	106	149	2b21/3		-0.2
1957	Mil N	6	7	0	2	0	0	0	0	1-0	0	2	.286	.375	.286	87	0	0-0	1.000	0	181	0	3b2		0.0
1958	†Mil N	63	133	14	25	3	0	4	10	13-2	2	9	.188	.270	.301	56	-9	0-1	.982	1	101	145	O33(24/0/9),3b7		-1.0
1959	Phi N	57	97	10	25	3	1	1	7	2-0	0	12	.258	.273	.340	61	-6	0-0	.889	-3	77	164	2b15,3b9/OR		-0.9
Total 4		177	317	32	71	7	2	6	25	22-2	2	31	.224	.279	.315	60	-20	1-1	.949	-1	99	153	2b36,O34(24/0/10),3b19		-2.1

HANEY, FRED Fred Girard "Pudge" B4.25.1898 Albuquerque NM D11.9.1977 Beverly Hills CA BR/TR/5-6/170 d4.18 M10/C1

YEAR	TM LG	G	AB	R	H	2B	3B	HR	RBI	BB-IB	HP	SO	AVG	OBP	SLG	AOPS	ABR	SB-CS	FA	FR	RNG	THR	GAMES AT POSITION	DL	BFW
1922	Det A	81	213	41	75	7	4	0	25	32	1	14	.352	.439	.423	129	11	3-8	.937	3	114	130	3b53,1b11,S2		1.3
1923	Det A	142	503	85	142	13	4	4	67	45	5	23	.282	.347	.348	85	-11	13-5	.955	-2	94	74	2b69,3b55,S16		-0.5
1924	Det A	86	256	54	79	11	4	1	30	39	0	13	.309	.400	.371	101	2	7-4	.933	1	117	90	3b59,S4,2b3		0.8
1925	Det A	114	398	84	111	15	3	0	40	66	2	29	.279	.384	.332	84	-6	11-1	.953	-1	99	107	3b106		0.1
1926	Bos A	138	462	47	102	15	7	0	52	74	1	28	.221	.330	.284	63	-24	13-6	.957	8	110	113	3b137		-0.7
1927	Bos A	47	116	23	32	4	1	3	12	25	0	14	.276	.404	.405	113	3	4-1	.936	-3	81	66	3b34/OC		0.3
	Chi N	4	3	0	0	0	0	0	0	0-0	0	0	.000	.000	.000	-99	-1	0	—		0		/H		-0.1
1929	StL N	10	26	4	3	1	1	0	2	1	1	2	.115	.179	.231	1	-1	0	.958	1	110	191	3b6		-0.3
Total 7		622	1977	338	544	66	21	8	228	282	10	123	.275	.368	.342	87	-30	51-25	.949	7	106	110	3b450,2b72,S22,1b11/OC		0.9

HANEY, TODD Todd Michael B7.30.1965 Waco TX BR/TR/5-9/165* [SeaA87 38/958] d9.9 Col Texas

YEAR	TM LG	G	AB	R	H	2B	3B	HR	RBI	BB-IB	HP	SO	AVG	OBP	SLG	AOPS	ABR	SB-CS	FA	FR	RNG	THR	GAMES AT POSITION	DL	BFW
1992	Mon N	7	10	0	3	1	0	0	1	0-0	0	0	.300	.300	.400	97	0	0-0	1.000	-1	93	80	2b5		-0.1
1994	Chi N	17	37	6	6	0	0	1	2	3-0	1	4	.162	.238	.243	28	-4	2-1	.979	-0	95	139	2b11,3b3		-0.4
1995	Chi N	25	73	11	30	8	0	0	7	7-0	0	11	.411	.463	.603	178	9	0-0	.978	4	125	124	2b17,3b4		1.3
1996	Chi N	49	82	11	11	1	0	0	3	5-0	0	15	.134	.200	.146	-6	-13	1-0	.978	4	129	124	2b23,3b4,S3		-0.7
1998	NY N	3	3	0	0	0	0	0	0	1-0	0	0	.000	.250	.000	-28	-1	0-0	—	-1	0	0	/2OL		-0.1
Total 5		101	205	28	50	10	0	3	12	18-0	1	29	.244	.305	.337	69	-9	3-1	.979	7	118	124	2b57,3b11,S3/OL		-0.0

HANEY, LARRY Wallace Larry B11.19.1942 Charlottesville VA BR/TR/6-2/195(165-195) d7.27 C14 s-Chris

YEAR	TM LG	G	AB	R	H	2B	3B	HR	RBI	BB-IB	HP	SO	AVG	OBP	SLG	AOPS	ABR	SB-CS	FA	FR	RNG	THR	GAMES AT POSITION	DL	BFW
1966	Bal A	20	56	3	9	1	0	3	5	1-0	0	15	.161	.190	.232	21	-6	0-0	.985	1	147	92	C20		-0.4
1967	Bal A	58	164	13	44	11	0	3	20	6-0	1	28	.268	.294	.390	101	0	1-0	.991	-1	103	139	C57		0.2
1968	Bal A	38	89	5	21	3	1	1	5	0-0	0	19	.236	.236	.326	69	-4	0-0	.994	1	89	186	C32		-0.3
1969	Sea A	22	59	3	15	3	0	2	7	6-0	0	12	.254	.323	.407	104	0	1-1	.956	-3	50	69	C20		-0.1
	Oak A	53	86	8	13	4	0	2	12	7-1	1	19	.151	.221	.267	38	-7	0-0	.994	-5	102	114	C53		-1.1
	Year	75	145	11	28	7	0	4	19	13-1	1	31	.193	.262	.324	66	-7	1-1	.979	-8	84	105	C73		-1.3
1970	Oak A	2	2	0	0	0	0	0	0	0-0	0	1	.000	.000	.000	-99	-1	0-0	1.000	-0	37	0	/C		0.0
1972	Oak A	4	5	0	0	0	0	0	0	0-0	0	1	.000	.000	.000	-99	-1	0-0	.800	-1	0	0	C4/2		-0.2
1973	Oak A	2	2	0	1	0	0	0	0	0-0	0	0	.500	.500	.500	191	0	0-0	1.000	0	0	0	C2		0.0
	StL N	2	1	0	0	0	0	0	0	0-0	0	1	.000	.000	.000	-99	-1	0-0	1.000	-0	0	0	C2		0.0
1974	†Oak A	76	121	12	20	4	0	2	18	6-5	0	18	.165	.185	.248	21	-12	1-0	.992	2	152	94	C73,3b3,1b2		-0.9
1975	Oak A	47	26	3	5	0	0	1	2	1-0	0	4	.192	.222	.308	49	-2	0-0	1.000	0	115	59	C43,3b4		-0.1
1976	Oak A	88	177	12	40	2	0	0	10	13-0	1	26	.226	.280	.237	55	-10	0-1	.974	0	82	106	C87		-0.7
1977	Mil A	46	127	7	29	2	0	0	9	5-0	1	30	.228	.254	.244	38	-11	0-0	.985	5	118	84	C63		-0.4

YEAR	TM LG	· G	AB	R	H	2B	3B	HR	RBI	BB-IB	HP	SO	AVG	OBP	SLG	AOPS	ABR	SB-CS	FA	FR	RNG	THR	GAMES AT POSITION	DL	BFW
1978	Mil A	4	5	0	1	0	0	0	1	0-0	0	1	.200	.200	.200	13	-1	0-0	1.000	-0	0	0	C4		-0.1
Total	12	480	919	68	198	30	1	12	73	44-1	3	175	.215	.252	.289	57	-54	3-2	.985	-1	105	108	C461,3b7,1b2/2		-4.2

HANFORD, CHARLIE Charles Joseph B6.3.1881 Tunstall, England D7.19.1963 Trenton NJ BR/TR/5-6.5/145 d4.13

YEAR	TM LG	· G	AB	R	H	2B	3B	HR	RBI	BB-IB	HP	SO	AVG	OBP	SLG	AOPS	ABR	SB-CS	FA	FR	RNG	THR	GAMES AT POSITION	DL	BFW
1914	Buf F	**155**	597	83	174	28	13	12	90	32	4	81	.291	.332	.442	107	-6	37	.973	7	104	114	O155C		-1.0
1915	Chi F	77	179	27	43	4	5	0	22	12	2	28	.240	.295	.318	77	-9	10	.971	-2	105	41	O43(10/1/32)		-1.4
Total	2	232	776	110	217	32	18	12	112	44	6	109	.280	.323	.414	101	-15	47	.972	5	104	100	O198(10/156/32)		-2.4

HANKINS, JAY Jay Nelson B11.7.1935 St.Louis Co. MO BL/TR/5-7/170* d4.15 Col Missouri

YEAR	TM LG	· G	AB	R	H	2B	3B	HR	RBI	BB-IB	HP	SO	AVG	OBP	SLG	AOPS	ABR	SB-CS	FA	FR	RNG	THR	GAMES AT POSITION	DL	BFW
1961	KC A	76	173	23	32	0	3	3	6	8-0	1	17	.185	.225	.272	32	-18	2-0	.970	-3	95	32	O65(23/31/14)		-2.3
1963	KC A	10	34	2	6	0	1	1	4	0-0	0	3	.176	.176	.324	35	-3	0-1	.952	0	102	199	O9C		-0.4
Total	2	86	207	25	38	0	4	4	10	8-0	1	20	.184	.218	.280	32	-21	2-1	.967	-3	96	56	O74(23/40/14)		-2.7

HANKINSON, FRANK Frank Edward B4.29.1856 New York NY D4.5.1911 Palisades Park NJ BR/TR/5-11/168 d5.1 OF(26/8/1) ▲

YEAR	TM LG	· G	AB	R	H	2B	3B	HR	RBI	BB-IB	HP	SO	AVG	OBP	SLG	AOPS	ABR	SB-CS	FA	FR	RNG	THR	GAMES AT POSITION	DL	BFW
1878	Chi N	58	240	38	64	8	3	1	27	5		36	.267	.282	.338	96	-2		.875	8	110	**135**	3b57/P		0.7
1879	Chi N	44	171	14	31	4	0	0	8	2		14	.181	.191	.205	29	-13		.933	7	139	105	P26,O14(10/4/0),3b5		-0.1
1880	Cle N	69	263	32	55	7	4	1	19	1		23	.209	.212	.278	66	-9		.844	-10	77	127	3b56,O12(10/2/0),P4		-1.8
1881	Tro N	**85**	321	34	62	15	0	1	19	10		41	.193	.218	.249	44	-20		.870	5	99	**161**	3b84/S		-1.1
1883	NY N	94	337	40	74	13	6	2	30	19		38	.220	.261	.312	74	-10		.870	-2	93	75	3b93/OR		-0.9
1884	NY N	105	389	44	90	16	7	2	43	23	1	59	.231	.274	.324	85	-7		.871	1	94	61	3b105/OC		-0.4
1885	NY AA	94	362	43	81	12	2	2	44	12	1		.224	.251	.285	72	-11		**.906**	21	**123**	67	3b94/P		1.0
1886	NY AA	136	522	66	126	14	5	2	63	49	0		.241	.306	.299	98	2	10	.873	27	**118**	**139**	3b136		2.7
1887	NY AA	127	512	79	137	29	11	1	71	38	0		.268	.318	.373	97	-2	19	.864	9	**109**	120	3b127		0.7
1888	KC AA	37	155	20	27	4	1	0	20	11	0		.174	.229	.232	45	-10	2	.947	-2	105	54	2b13,S9,O7(6/1/0),3b7,1b2		-1.0
Total	10	849	3272	410	747	122	39	13	344	170	1	211	.228	.267	.301	77	-82	31	.875	63	105	109	3b764,O35L,P32,2b13,S10,1b2		-0.2

HANLON, NED Edward Hugh B8.22.1857 Montville CT D4.14.1937 Baltimore MD BL/TR/5-9.5/170 d5.1 M19 HF1996

YEAR	TM LG	· G	AB	R	H	2B	3B	HR	RBI	BB-IB	HP	SO	AVG	OBP	SLG	AOPS	ABR	SB-CS	FA	FR	RNG	THR	GAMES AT POSITION	DL	BFW
1880	Cle N	73	280	30	69	10	3	0	32	11		30	.246	.275	.304	98	0		.804	-6	50	135	O69(67/2/0),S4		-1.0
1881	Det N	76	305	63	85	14	8	2	28	22		11	.279	.327	.397	122	7		.897	-6	77	134	O74(2/72/0),S2		-0.1
1882	Det N	82	347	68	80	18	6	5	38	26		25	.231	.284	.360	105	3		.887	-10	100	**201**	O82C/2		0.9
1883	Det N	100	413	65	100	13	2	1	40	34		44	.242	.300	.291	84	-6		.874	12	132	123	O114C		-0.9
1884	Det N	**114**	450	86	119	18	6	5	39	40		52	.264	.324	.364	124	15		.863	1	95	71	O105C		2.1
1885	Det N	105	424	93	128	18	8	1	29	47		18	.302	.372	.389	146	23		.929	-7	72	118	O126C/2		2.0
1886	Det N	**126**	494	105	116	6	4	4	60	57		39	.235	.314	.296	83	-9	50	.904	1	86	110	O118(1/117/0)		-1.9
1887	†Det N	118	471	79	129	13	7	4	69	30	2	24	.274	.330	.357	84	-11	69	.919	-3	88	87	O109C		-1.2
1888	Det N	109	459	64	122	6	8	5	39	15	4	32	.266	.295	.346	103	0	38	.919	-3	82	52	O116C,M		-1.0
1889	Pit N	116	461	81	110	14	10	2	37	58		25	.239	.326	.325	91	-4	53	.911	-4	70	98	O118C,M		0.2
1890	Pit P	118	472	106	131	16	6	1	44	80	6	24	.278	.389	.343	105	10	65	.881	-1	137	32	O119(39/80/0)/SM		-0.5
1891	Pit N	119	455	87	121	12	8	0	60	48	4	30	.266	.341	.327	97	-1	54	.786	-1	106	0	O11(8/2/1),M		-0.5
1892	Bal N	11	43	3	7	1	1	0	2	3		3	.163	.217	.233	35	-4	0	.891	-13	85	106	O1251(119/1130/1),2b13,S7		-3.1
Total	13	1267	5074	930	1317	159	79	30	517	471	18	357	.260	.325	.340	102	23	329							

HANLON, BILL William Joseph "Big Bill" B6.24.1876 Los Angeles CA D11.23.1905 Los Angeles CA BR/6-0/175 d4.16 Col St. Marys (CA)

YEAR	TM LG	· G	AB	R	H	2B	3B	HR	RBI	BB-IB	HP	SO	AVG	OBP	SLG	AOPS	ABR	SB-CS	FA	FR	RNG	THR	GAMES AT POSITION	DL	BFW
1903	Chi N	8	21	4	2	0	0	0	4				.095	.296	.095	14	-2	1	.980	-0	86	54	1b8		-0.2

HANNA, JOHN John B11.3.1863 Philadelphia PA D11.7.1930 Philadelphia PA d5.23

YEAR	TM LG	· G	AB	R	H	2B	3B	HR	RBI	BB-IB	HP	SO	AVG	OBP	SLG	AOPS	ABR	SB-CS	FA	FR	RNG	THR	GAMES AT POSITION	DL	BFW
1884	Was AA	23	76	8	5	0	0	0		6			.066	.134	.066	-37	-11		.874	-0			C18,O6(1/1/4)		-0.9
	Ric AA	22	67	6	13	2	1	0		0	1		.194	.206	.254	50	-4		.924	3			C21/S		0.1
	Year	45	143	14	18	2	1	0		6	1		.126	.167	.154	6	-14		.900	2			C39,O6(1/1/4)/S		-0.8

HANNAH, TRUCK James Harrison B6.5.1889 Larimore ND D4.27.1982 Fountain Valley CA BR/TR/6-1/190 d4.15

YEAR	TM LG	· G	AB	R	H	2B	3B	HR	RBI	BB-IB	HP	SO	AVG	OBP	SLG	AOPS	ABR	SB-CS	FA	FR	RNG	THR	GAMES AT POSITION	DL	BFW
1918	NY A	90	250	24	55	6	0	2	21	51	4	25	.220	.361	.268	88	0	5	.974	4	121	99	C88		1.2
1919	NY A	75	227	14	54	8	3	1	20	22	3	19	.238	.313	.313	76	-7	0	**.984**	-6	103	82	C73/1		-0.8
1920	NY A	79	259	24	64	11	1	2	25	24	1	35	.247	.313	.320	66	-13	2-0	.961	-2	113	67	C78		-0.7
Total	3	244	736	62	173	25	4	5	66	97	8	79	.235	.330	.300	76	-20	7-0	.973	-5	113	83	C239/1		-0.3

HANNIFAN, PAT Patrick James B4.20.1866 Halifax NS, Can. D11.5.1908 Springfield MA BB/TL d4.29

YEAR	TM LG	· G	AB	R	H	2B	3B	HR	RBI	BB-IB	HP	SO	AVG	OBP	SLG	AOPS	ABR	SB-CS	FA	FR	RNG	THR	GAMES AT POSITION	DL	BFW
1897	Bro N	10	20	4	5	0	0	0	4	3			.250	.375	.250	71	-1	4	.867	0	302	774	O3(1/2/0),2b2		0.0

HANNIFIN, JACK John Joseph B2.25.1883 Holyoke MA D10.27.1945 Northampton MA BR/TR/5-11/167 d4.19

YEAR	TM LG	· G	AB	R	H	2B	3B	HR	RBI	BB-IB	HP	SO	AVG	OBP	SLG	AOPS	ABR	SB-CS	FA	FR	RNG	THR	GAMES AT POSITION	DL	BFW
1906	Phi N	1	1	0	1	0	0	0	0	0-0	0		1.000	1.000	1.000	511	0	0	—		0		/H		0.0
	NY N	10	30	4	6	0	1	0	3	2	0		.200	.250	.267	60	-2	1	.903	-0	98	107	S6,3b3/2		-0.2
1907	NY N	56	149	16	34	7	3	1	15	15	1		.228	.303	.336	97	-1	6	.996	-2	80	40	1b29,3b10,S9,O2(0/1/1)		-0.3
1908	NY N	1	2	0	0	0	0	0	0	0-0	0		.000	.000	.000	-95	-0	0	—	-0	0	0	/OR		-0.1
	Bos N	90	257	30	53	6	2	2	22	28	0		.206	.284	.268	78	-6	7	.930	5	113	342	3b35,2b22,S15,O7(2/1/2)		-0.1
	Year	91	259	30	53	6	2	2	22	28	0		.205	.282	.266	77	-6	7	.930	5	113	342	3b35,2b22,S15,O8(2/1/3)		-0.2
Total	3	158	439	50	94	13	6	4	40	45	1		.214	.289	.292	84	-9	14	.937	2	106	302	3b48,S30,1b29,2b23,O10(2/2/4)		-0.6

HANSEN, DAVE David Andrew B11.24.1968 Long Beach CA BL/TR/6-0/195(180-195) [LAN86 2/47] d9.16

YEAR	TM LG	· G	AB	R	H	2B	3B	HR	RBI	BB-IB	HP	SO	AVG	OBP	SLG	AOPS	ABR	SB-CS	FA	FR	RNG	THR	GAMES AT POSITION	DL	BFW
1990	LA N	5	7	0	1	0	0	0	1	0-0	0	0	.143	.143	.143	-22	-0	0-0	.500	-1	48	0	3b2		-0.2
1991	LA N	53	56	3	15	4	0	1	5	2-0	0	12	.268	.293	.393	93	-1	1-0	1.000	2	124	81	3b21/S		0.2
1992	LA N	132	341	30	73	11	0	6	22	34-3	1	49	.214	.286	.299	67	-15	0-2	**.968**	6	107	78	3b108		-1.0
1993	LA N	84	105	13	38	3	0	4	30	21-3	0	13	.362	.465	.505	170	12	0-1	.927	0	106	42	3b18		1.2
1994	LA N	40	44	3	15	3	0	0	5	5-0	0	5	.341	.408	.409	121	2	0-0	.857	-1	84	0	3b7	19	-0.1
1995	†LA N	100	181	19	52	10	1	1	14	28-4	1	28	.287	.384	.359	105	3	0-0	.933	-4	85	91	3b58		-0.9
1996	†LA N	80	104	7	23	1	0	0	6	11-1	0	22	.221	.293	.231	44	-8	0-0	.962	-5	78	94	3b51,1b4/2		0.2
1997	Chi N	90	151	19	47	8	2	3	21	31-1	1	32	.311	.429	.450	127	8	1-2	.922	-5	78	94	3b35,1b4/2		0.1
1999	LA N	100	107	14	27	8	1	2	17	26-0	2	20	.252	.404	.402	111	4	0-0	.982	-2	100	129	1b20,3b13,O2R,D2		0.9
2000	LA N	102	121	18	35	6	2	8	26	26-0	1	32	.289	.415	.570	153	11	0-1	.980	0	136	121	1b16,3b16,O3L,D5	26	0.3
2001	LA N	92	140	13	33	10	0	2	20	32-5	0	29	.236	.371	.350	96	1	0-0	.984	4	105	86	1b25,3b21/D		0.0
2002	LA N	96	120	15	35	6	0	2	17	14-3	0	22	.292	.363	.392	109	1	1-0	1.000	-0	85	40	1b27,3b11,D4		-0.1
2003	SD N	110	135	13	33	4	1	2	15	23-3	0	25	.244	.358	.333	99	1	1-0	1.000	1	136	149	1b20,3b11/2D		0.6
2004	Sea A	57	78	14	22	5	0	2	12	18-3	0	16	.282	.412	.423	126	4	0-0	1.000	2	167	31	1b7,3b6,D8		0.6
	SD N	29	28	1	4	0	0	0	0	3-0	0	6	.143	.226	.143	-2	-4	0-0	1.000	-2	75	135	1b7,3b2	23	-0.7
2005	Sea A	60	75	5	13	0	0	2	11	9-1	0	19	.173	.256	.253	41	-7	1-0	1.000	-0	99	78	3b371,1b143,D28,O5(3/0/2),2b2/S	68	-0.1
Total	15	1230	1793	187	466	79	6	35	222	283-27	6	332	.260	.360	.369	99	9	5-7	.947	-0	99	78	3b371,1b143,D28,O5(3/0/2),2b2/S		-0.1

HANSEN, DOUG Douglas William B12.16.1928 Los Angeles CA D9.16.1999 Orem UT BR/TR/6-0/180 d9.4

YEAR	TM LG	· G	AB	R	H	2B	3B	HR	RBI	BB-IB	HP	SO	AVG	OBP	SLG	AOPS	ABR	SB-CS	FA	FR	RNG	THR	GAMES AT POSITION	DL	BFW
1951	Cle N	3	0	2	0	0	0	0	0	0-0	0	0	—	—	—		0	0-0	—	0			/R		0.0

HANSEN, JED Jed Ramon B8.19.1972 Tacoma WA BR/TR/6-1/195(180-195) [KCA94 2/50] d7.29 Col Stanford

YEAR	TM LG	· G	AB	R	H	2B	3B	HR	RBI	BB-IB	HP	SO	AVG	OBP	SLG	AOPS	ABR	SB-CS	FA	FR	RNG	THR	GAMES AT POSITION	DL	BFW
1997	KC A	34	94	11	29	6	1	1	14	13-0	1	29	.309	.394	.426	112	2	3-2	.993	-2	99	90	2b31		0.2
1998	KC A	4	3	0	0	0	0	0	0	0-0	0	3	.000	.000	.000	-96	-1	0-0	1.000	-1	0	0	2b2		-0.2
1999	KC A	49	79	16	16	1	0	3	5	10-0	0	32	.203	.289	.329	56	-6	0-1	.989	-1	79	130	2b21,S10,3b4,O2C/1D		-0.5
Total	3	87	176	27	45	7	1	4	19	23-0	1	64	.256	.342	.375	83	-5	3-3	.991	-3	90	105	2b54,S10,3b4,D3,O2C/1		-0.5

HANSEN, BOB Robert Joseph B5.26.1948 Boston MA BL/TL/6-0/195* [MilA69 21/499] d5.10 Col Massachusetts

YEAR	TM LG	· G	AB	R	H	2B	3B	HR	RBI	BB-IB	HP	SO	AVG	OBP	SLG	AOPS	ABR	SB-CS	FA	FR	RNG	THR	GAMES AT POSITION	DL	BFW
1974	Mil A	58	88	8	26	4	1	2	9	8-0	0	16	.295	.319	.432	115	1	2-1	1.000	-0	0	0	D18,1b3		0.0
1976	Mil A	24	61	4	10	1	0	4	6-0		0	8	.164	.239	.180	24	-6	0-0	—	0	0	0	D14/1		-0.7
Total	2	82	149	12	36	5	1	2	13	9-0	0	24	.242	.285	.329	78	-5	2-1	1.000	-0	0	0	D32,1b4		-0.7

HANSEN, RON Ronald Lavern B4.5.1938 Oxford NE BR/TR/6-3/200* d4.15 C9

YEAR	TM LG	· G	AB	R	H	2B	3B	HR	RBI	BB-IB	HP	SO	AVG	OBP	SLG	AOPS	ABR	SB-CS	FA	FR	RNG	THR	GAMES AT POSITION	DL	BFW
1958	Bal A	12	19	1	0	0	0	0	0	1-0	0	7	.000	.048	.000	-90	-5	0-0	.943	-1	101	87	S12		-0.6
1959	Bal A	2	4	0	0	0	0	0	0	1-0	0	1	.000	.200	.000	-41	-1	0-0	.889	0	124	107	S2		-0.1
1960	Bal A★	153	530	72	135	22	5	22	86	69-5	1	94	.255	.342	.440	111	8	3-3	.964	12	98	117	S153		3.2
1961	Bal A	155	533	51	132	13	2	12	51	66-2	1	96	.248	.329	.347	85	-11	1-3	.959	12	102	131	S149,2b7		1.3
1962	Bal A	71	196	12	34	7	0	3	17	30-3	1	36	.173	.289	.255	51	-2	1-1	.983	28	**115**	**122**	S144	30	-1.2
1963	Chi A	144	482	55	109	17	2	13	67	78-2	1	74	.226	.330	.351	94	-2	1-0							3.9

YEAR	TM LG	G	AB	R	H	2B	3B	HR	RBI	BB-IB	HP	SO	AVG	OBP	SLG	AOPS	ABR	SB-CS	FA	FR	RNG	THR	GAMES AT POSITION	DL	BFW
1964	Chi A	158	575	85	150	25	3	20	68	73-7	6	73	.261	.347	.419	116	14	1-0	.975	18	108	129	S158		4.7
1965	Chi A	**162**	587	61	138	23	4	11	66	60-8	2	73	.235	.304	.344	91	-8	1-1	.969	13	**110**	114	S161/2		2.1
1966	Chi A	23	74	3	13	1	0	0	4	15-3	1	10	.176	.322	.189	55	-4	0-1	.946	-9	98	127	S23		-0.2
1967	Chi A	157	498	35	116	20	0	8	51	64-11	0	51	.233	.317	.321	94	-2	0-3	.964	2	106	**116**	S157	130	-0.2
1968	Was A	86	275	28	51	12	0	8	28	35-5	2	49	.185	.281	.316	84	-5	0-0	.963	0	114	100	S81,3b5		1.3
	Chi A	40	87	7	20	3	0	1	4	11-0	0	12	.230	.317	.299	86	-1	0-0	.959	2	125	114	3b29,S7,2b2		1.4
	Year	126	362	35	71	15	0	9	32	46-5	2	61	.196	.290	.312	84	-6	0-0	.963	13	115	99	S88,3b34,2b2		0.2
1969	Chi A	85	185	15	48	6	1	2	22	18-0	1	25	.259	.327	.335	82	-4	2-0	.967	1	101	106	2b26,1b21,S8,3b7		1.6
1970	NY A	59	91	13	27	4	0	4	14	19-0	1	9	.297	.420	.473	153	8	0-1	.983	0	106	88	S15,3b11/2		-0.2
1971	NY A	61	145	6	30	3	0	2	20	9-2	0	27	.207	.245	.269	50	-10	0-1	.918	-3	97	190	3b30,2b9,S3	25	0.9
1972	KC A	16	30	2	4	0	0	0	2	3-1	0	6	.133	.212	.133	4	-4	0-0	.944	4	134	54	S6,3b4/2		-1.3
Total 15		1384	4311	446	1007	156	17	106	501	551-49	19	643	.234	.320	.351	92	-40	5-4	.968	95	106	117	S1143,3b86,2b47,1b21	185	15.4

HANSKI, DON Donald Thomas (b Donald Thomas Hanyzewski) B2.27.1916 LaPorte IN D9.2.1957 Worth IL BL/TL/5-11/180 d5.6 Mil 1945

YEAR	TM LG	G	AB	R	H	2B	3B	HR	RBI	BB-IB	HP	SO	AVG	OBP	SLG	AOPS	ABR	SB-CS	FA	FR	RNG	THR	GAMES AT POSITION	DL	BFW
1943	Chi A	9	21	1	5	1	0	0	2	0-0	0	5	.238	.238	.286	53	-1	0-0	.952	0	105	135	1b5/P		-0.2
1944	Chi A	2	1	0	0	0	0	0	0	0-0	0	0	.000	.000	.000	-99	0	0-0	—	-0	105	135	P2		0.0
Total 2		11	22	1	5	1	0	0	2	0-0	0	5	.227	.227	.273	46	-1	0-1	.952	-0	105	135	1b5,P3		-0.2

HANSON, HARRY Harry Francis B1.17.1896 Elgin IL D10.5.1966 Savannah GA BR/TR/5-11/? d7.14

1913	NY A	1	2	0	0	0	0	0	0	0-0	0	0	.000	.000	.000	-99	-1	0	1.000	-0	62	201	/C		-0.1

HAPPENNY, CLIFF John Clifford B5.18.1901 Waltham MA D12.29.1988 Coral Springs FL BR/TR/5-11/165 d7.2 Col Illinois

1923	Chi A	32	86	7	19	5	0	0	3		1	13	.221	.256	.279	41	-8	0-0	.947	-1	124	133	2b19,S9,3b2		-0.7

HARBRIDGE, BILL William Arthur "Yaller Bill" B3.29.1855 Philadelphia PA D3.17.1924 Philadelphia PA BL/TL/?/162 d5.15 OF(13/112/47)

YEAR	TM LG	G	AB	R	H	2B	3B	HR	RBI	BB-IB	HP	SO	AVG	OBP	SLG	AOPS	ABR	SB-CS	FA	FR	RNG	THR	GAMES AT POSITION	DL	BFW
1875	Har NA	53	208	32	50	3	3	0	26	9		3	.240	.272	.284	89	-3	2-4	.871	2			C31,O13R,2b11,1b3/S		
1876	Har N	30	106	11	23	2	1	0	6	3		2	.217	.239	.255	59	-5		.799	1			C24,O6(0/2/4),1b2		-0.2
1877	Har N	41	167	18	37	5	2	0	8	3		6	.222	.235	.275	68	-5		.881	-6			C32,O5(0/3/2),2b4/3		-0.3
1878	Chi N	54	240	32	71	12	0	0	37	6		13	.296	.313	.346	109	-8		.878	-6			C53,O8(4/3/1)		-0.9
1879	Chi N	4	18	2	2	0	0	0	1	0		5	.111	.111	.111	-25	-2		.571	-1	125	0	O4(1/3/0)		-0.3
1880	Tro N	9	27	3	10	0	1	0	2	0		3	.370	.370	.444	166	2		.887	0			C9/O(0/1/1)		0.2
1882	Tro N	32	123	11	23	1	1	0	13	10		17	.187	.248	.211	52	-6		.836	-5	57	81	O23C,1b6,C3		-1.1
1883	Phi N	73	280	32	62	12	3	0	21	24		20	.221	.283	.286	81	-4		.796	-12	72	50	O44(8/36/0),S11,2b9,C7,3b5		-1.5
1884	Cin U	82	341	59	95	12	5	2		25			.279	.328	.361	100	-10		.906	4	129	79	O80(0/41/39),S3,1b2		-0.6
Total 8		325	1302	168	323	44	13	2	88	71		66	.248	.287	.306	86	-28		.849	-24			O171C,C128,S14,2b13,1b10,3b6		-4.8

HARDESTY, SCOTT Scott Durbin B1.26.1870 Bellville OH D10.29.1944 Fostoria OH d8.17

1899	NY N	22	72	4	16	0	0	0	4				.222	.243	.222	29	-7	2	.895	4	117	118	S20,1b2		-0.2

HARDGROVE, PAT William Henry B5.10.1895 Palmyra KS D1.26.1973 Jackson MS BR/TR/5-10/158 d6.8 Mil 1918

1918	Chi A	2	2	0	0	0	0	0	0	0-0	0	0	.000	.000	.000	-99	0	0		0			/H		-0.1

HARDIE, LOU Louis W. B8.24.1864 New York NY D3.5.1929 Oakland CA BR/5-11/180 d5.22

YEAR	TM LG	G	AB	R	H	2B	3B	HR	RBI	BB-IB	HP	SO	AVG	OBP	SLG	AOPS	ABR	SB-CS	FA	FR	RNG	THR	GAMES AT POSITION	DL	BFW
1884	Phi N	3	8	0	3	2	0	0	0			2	.375	.375	.625	219	1		.857	-2			C3		-0.1
1886	Chi N	16	51	4	9	0	0	0	3	4		10	.176	.236	.176	24	-5	1	.964	0			C13,O2R/3		-0.3
1890	Bos N	47	185	17	42	8	0	3	17	18		36	.227	.296	.319	73	-7	4	.886	1	127	103	C25,O15(6/4/6),3b7/S1		-0.4
1891	Bal AA	15	56	7	13	0	3	0	1	8		8	.232	.328	.339	90	-1	3	1.000	1	36	0	O15(0/3/12)		0.0
Total 4		81	300	28	67	10	3	3	21	30		56	.223	.294	.307	71	-12	8	.910	-0	127	103	C41,O32(6/7/20),3b8/1S		-0.8

HARDIN, BUD William Edgar B6.14.1922 Shelby NC D7.28.1997 Rancho Santa Fe CA BR/TR/5-10/165 d4.15

1952	Chi N	3	7	1	1	0	0	0	0	0-0	0	0	.143	.143	.143	-20	-1	0-0	1.000	-0	100	153	S2/2	47	-0.1

HARDING, ED Edward H. A. "Jumbo" B1862 MO 5-9.5/213 d10.5

1886	StL AA	1	3	0	1	0	0	0	1	0		0	.333	.333	.667	201	0	0	.889	1			/C		0.1

HARDTKE, JASON Jason Robert B9.15.1971 Milwaukee WI BB/TR/5-10/175* [CleA90 3/81] d9.8

YEAR	TM LG	G	AB	R	H	2B	3B	HR	RBI	BB-IB	HP	SO	AVG	OBP	SLG	AOPS	ABR	SB-CS	FA	FR	RNG	THR	GAMES AT POSITION	DL	BFW
1996	NY N	19	57	3	11	5	0	0	6	2-0	1	12	.193	.233	.281	37	-5	0-0	1.000	-3	85	102	2b18		-0.7
1997	NY N	30	56	9	15	2	0	2	4	4-1	0	6	.268	.323	.411	97	-5	1-1	.981	-6	70	93	2b21/3		-0.6
1998	Chi N	18	21	2	5	0	0	0	2	2-0	0	6	.238	.304	.238	44	-2	0-0	1.000	-0	101	0	3b7/ORD		-0.2
Total 3		67	134	14	31	7	0	2	16	8-1	1	24	.231	.283	.328	63	-7	1-1	.991	-9	78	98	2b39,3b8/DOR		-1.5

HARDY, CARROLL Carroll William B5.18.1933 Sturgis SD BR/TR/6-0/185* d4.15 Col Colorado

YEAR	TM LG	G	AB	R	H	2B	3B	HR	RBI	BB-IB	HP	SO	AVG	OBP	SLG	AOPS	ABR	SB-CS	FA	FR	RNG	THR	GAMES AT POSITION	DL	BFW
1958	Cle A	27	49	10	10	3	0	1	6	6-0	1	14	.204	.298	.327	75	-1	1-2	1.000	2	114	270	O17(0/16/1)	30	-0.1
1959	Cle A	32	53	12	11	1	0	0	2	3-0	0	7	.208	.250	.226	33	-5	1-1	1.000	1	133	0	O15(1/14/0)		-0.4
1960	Cle A	29	18	7	2	1	0	0	1	2-0	0	2	.111	.200	.167	0	-3	0-0	1.000	0	117	0	O17(4/9/5)		-0.3
	Bos A	73	145	26	34	5	2	2	15	17-0	1	40	.234	.313	.338	74	-5	3-2	.968	2	110	115	O59(44/8/14)		-0.5
	Year	102	163	33	36	6	2	2	16	19-0	1	42	.221	.301	.319	67	-8	3-2	.973	2	111	98	O76(48/17/19)		-0.8
1961	Bos A	85	281	46	74	20	2	3	36	26-0	1	53	.263	.330	.381	77	-5	4-2	.961	0	95	157	O76(20/38/21)		-0.8
1962	Bos A	115	362	52	78	13	5	8	36	54-1	2	68	.215	.318	.345	77	-11	3-7	.991	0	100	130	O105(3/45/64)		-1.8
1963	Hou N	15	44	5	10	3	0	0	3	3-0	0	7	.227	.277	.295	69	-2	1-0	.947	0	95	154	O10L		-0.2
1964	Hou N	46	157	13	29	1	1	2	12	8-0	2	30	.185	.232	.242	36	-14	1-0	.990	4	122	119	O41(5/33/4)		-1.3
1967	Min N	11	8	1	3	0	0	0	2	1-0	0	1	.375	.444	.750	229	1	0-0	—	-0	0	0	O4(1/0/3)		0.1
Total 8		433	1117	172	251	47	10	17	113	120-1	7	222	.225	.302	.330	72	-45	13-14	.981	10	105	131	O344(88/163/112)	30	-5.3

HARDY, J.J. James Jerry B8.19.1982 Tucson AZ BR/TR/6-2/180 d4.4

2005	Mil N	124	372	46	92	22	1	9	50	44-7	1	48	.247	.327	.384	86	-7	0-0	.975	-24	82	77	S119		-2.3

HARDY, JACK John Doolittle B6.23.1877 Cleveland OH D10.20.1921 Cleveland OH BR/TR/6-0/185 d8.29

YEAR	TM LG	G	AB	R	H	2B	3B	HR	RBI	BB-IB	HP	SO	AVG	OBP	SLG	AOPS	ABR	SB-CS	FA	FR	RNG	THR	GAMES AT POSITION	DL	BFW
1903	Cle A	5	19	1	3	1	0	0	1	1		0	.158	.200	.211	24	-2	1	1.000	-1	0	0	O5R		-0.3
1907	Chi N	1	4	0	1	0	0	0	0	1		0	.250	.250	.250	53	0	0	.909	-0	158	76	/C		0.0
1909	Was A	10	24	3	4	0	0	0	4	1		0	.167	.200	.167	17	-2	0	.974	-1	83	32	C9/2		-0.4
1910	Was A	7	8	1	2	0	0	0	0	0		0	.250	.250	.250	59	0	0	.933	0	119	104	C4/OL		0.0
Total 4		23	55	5	10	1	0	0	5	2		0	.182	.211	.200	28	-4	1	.953	-2	102	54	C14,O6(1/0/5)/2		-0.7

HARE, SHAWN Shawn Robert B3.26.1967 St.Louis MO BL/TL/6-2/190* d9.6 Col Central Michigan

YEAR	TM LG	G	AB	R	H	2B	3B	HR	RBI	BB-IB	HP	SO	AVG	OBP	SLG	AOPS	ABR	SB-CS	FA	FR	RNG	THR	GAMES AT POSITION	DL	BFW
1991	Det A	9	19	0	1	1	0	0	0	2-0	0	1	.053	.143	.105	-30	-3	0-0	1.000	1	124	387	O6R,D2		-0.3
1992	Det A	15	26	0	3	1	0	0	5	2-0	0	5	.115	.172	.154	-6	-4	0-0	1.000	0	104	0	O9(3/0/7),1b4	63	-0.4
1994	NY N	22	40	7	9	1	0	2	2	4-0	0	11	.225	.295	.300	56	-3	0-0	1.000	0	119	0	O14L		-0.3
1995	Tex A	18	24	2	6	1	0	0	2	4-0	0	5	.250	.357	.292	69	-1	0-0	1.000	0	86	283	O9(4/0/5)/1D		-0.1
Total 4		64	109	9	19	4	1	0	9	12-0	0	22	.174	.254	.229	31	-11	0-0	1.000	2	109	117	O38(21/0/18),1b5,D5	63	-1.1

HARGIS, GARY Gary Lynn B11.2.1956 Minneapolis MN BR/TR/5-11/165 [PitN74 2/35] d9.29

1979	Pit N	1	0	0	0	0	0	0	0	0-0	0	0					0	0-0	—	0			/R		0.0

HARGRAVE, BUBBLES Eugene Franklin B7.15.1892 New Haven IN D2.23.1969 Cincinnati OH BR/TR/5-10.5/174 d9.18 b-Pinky

YEAR	TM LG	G	AB	R	H	2B	3B	HR	RBI	BB-IB	HP	SO	AVG	OBP	SLG	AOPS	ABR	SB-CS	FA	FR	RNG	THR	GAMES AT POSITION	DL	BFW
1913	Chi N	3	3	0	1	0	0	0	1	0		0	.333	.333	.333	91	0	0	1.000	0	86	151	C2		0.0
1914	Chi N	23	36	3	8	0	0	0	2	0		4	.222	.222	.278	48	-2	2	.930	-3	82	61	C16		-0.5
1915	Chi N	15	19	2	3	0	1	0	2	1		5	.158	.200	.263	40	-2	0	1.000	-0	79	147	C9		-0.2
1921	Cin N	93	263	28	76	17	8	1	38	12		15	.289	.327	.426	102	0	4-2	.973	-1	109	62	C73		0.4
1922	Cin N	98	320	49	101	22	10	7	57	26		18	.316	.371	.512	128	12	7-4	.982	-2	114	76	C87		0.4
1923	Cin N	118	378	54	126	23	9	10	78	44	**12**	22	.333	.419	.521	150	29	4-5	.988	4	106	110	C109		1.5
1924	Cin N	98	312	42	94	19	10	3	33	30		21	.301	.370	.455	122	10	2-2	.983	0	96	91	C91		1.5
1925	Cin N	87	273	28	82	13	6	3	33	25	1	23	.300	.361	.414	100	7	4-3	.979	-7	75	73	C84		-0.2
1926	Cin N	105	326	42	115	22	6	9	62	25		17	**.353**	.406	.525	153	24	2	.988	-7	109	62	C93		2.2
1927	Cin N	102	305	36	94	18	3	6	35	31		17	.308	.376	.387	108	5	0	.988	-7	83	63	C92		0.4
1928	Cin N	65	190	19	56	12	3	0	23	13		14	.295	.353	.389	95	-1	4	**.991**	2	103	99	C57		0.4
1930	NY A	45	108	11	30	7	0	0	7	6		15	.278	.339	.343	77	-3	0-0	.992	-3	83	84	C34		-0.5
Total 12		852	2533	314	786	155	58	29	376	217	32	165	.310	.368	.451	119	72	29-16	.983	-25	99	82	C747		8.8

YEAR	TM LG	G	AB	R	H	2B	3B	HR	RBI	BB-IB	HP	SO	AVG	OBP	SLG	AOPS	ABR	SB-CS	FA	FR	RNG	THR	GAMES AT POSITION	DL	BFW

HARGRAVE, PINKY William McKinley B1.31.1896 New Haven IN D10.3.1942 Ft.Wayne IN BB/TR (BR 1923-26)/5-8.5/180 d5.18 b-Bubbles

YEAR	TM LG	G	AB	R	H	2B	3B	HR	RBI	BB-IB	HP	SO	AVG	OBP	SLG	AOPS	ABR	SB-CS	FA	FR	RNG	THR	GAMES AT POSITION	DL	BFW
1923	Was A	33	59	4	17	2	0	0	8	2	0	6	.288	.311	.322	70	-3	0-0	.917	-2	56	131	3b8,C5/OL		-0.4
1924	Was A	24	33	3	5	1	1	0	5	1	0	4	.152	.176	.242	8	-5	0-0	1.000	-0	122	51	C8		-0.5
1925	Was A	5	6	0	3	0	0	0	1	0		2	.500	.571	.500	177	1	0-0	1.000	0	194		/C		0.1
	StL A	67	225	34	64	15	2	8	43	13	1	13	.284	.326	.476	97	-3	2-0	.981	-5	83	106	C62		-0.3
	Year	72	231	34	67	15	2	8	43	14	1	15	.290	.333	.476	99	-2	2-0	.981	-5	81	108	C63		-0.2
1926	StL A	92	235	20	66	16	3	7	37	10	3	38	.281	.319	.464	98	-2	3-0	.977	1	128	132	C58		0.3
1928	Det A	121	320	38	88	13	5	10	63	32	1	28	.275	.343	.441	103	0	4-1	.977	-9	92	80	C88		-0.3
1929	Det A	76	185	26	61	12	0	3	26	20	2	24	.330	.401	.443	117	6	2-2	.973	-4	72	129	C48		0.4
1930	Det A	55	137	18	39	8	0	5	18	20	1	12	.285	.380	.453	108	2	2-0	.984	-4	67	74	C40		0.1
	Was A	10	31	3	6	2	2	1	7	3	0	1	.194	.265	.484	85	-1	1-0	1.000	1	131	107	C9		0.1
	Year	65	168	21	45	10	2	6	25	23	1	13	.268	.359	.458	104	1	3-0	.987	-3	79	80	C49		0.2
1931	Was A	40	80	6	26	8	0	1	9	19	0	12	.325	.393	.463	124	3	1-0	.978	-1	112	80	C25		0.5
1932	Bos N	82	217	20	57	14	3	4	33	24	0	18	.263	.336	.410	103	1	1	.957	0	201	59	C25		-0.7
1933	Bos N	45	73	5	13	0	0	0	6	5	1	7	.178	.241	.178	23	-7	1	.976	-24	105	99	C442,3b8/OL		-0.4
Total 10		650	1601	177	445	91	16	39	265	140	9	165	.278	.339	.428	98	-8	17-3	.976	-24	105	99	C442,3b8/OL		

HARGREAVES, CHARLIE Charles Russell B12.14.1896 Trenton NJ D5.9.1979 Neptune NJ BR/TR/6-0/170 d6.27

YEAR	TM LG	G	AB	R	H	2B	3B	HR	RBI	BB-IB	HP	SO	AVG	OBP	SLG	AOPS	ABR	SB-CS	FA	FR	RNG	THR	GAMES AT POSITION	DL	BFW
1923	Bro N	20	57	5	16	0	0	0	4	1	0	2	.281	.293	.281	54	-4	0-0	.921	-3	75	75	C15		-0.6
1924	Bro N	15	27	4	11	2	0	0	5	1	0	1	.407	.429	.481	148	2	0-1	1.000	-1	84	70	C9		0.1
1925	Bro N	45	83	9	23	3	1	0	13	6	0	1	.277	.326	.337	72	-4	1-1	.986	1	72	196	C18,1b2		-0.2
1926	Bro N	85	208	14	52	13	2	2	23	19	1	10	.250	.316	.361	83	-5	1	.986	3	78	148	C70		0.2
1927	Bro N	46	133	9	38	3	1	0	11	14	2	7	.286	.362	.323	85	-2	1	.985	1	78	125	C44		0.2
1928	Bro N	20	61	3	12	2	0	0	5	6	1	6	.197	.269	.230	32	-6	1	.979	1	73	109	C20		-0.4
	Pit N	79	260	15	74	8	2	1	32	12	1	9	.285	.319	.342	70	-12	1	.962	-5	80	105	C77		-1.1
	Year	99	321	18	86	10	2	1	37	18	2	15	.268	.309	.321	63	-18	2	.966	-4	79	106	C97		-1.5
1929	Pit N	102	328	33	88	12	5	1	44	16	2	12	.268	.306	.345	60	-22	1	.981	4	99	101	C101		-1.1
1930	Pit N	11	31	4	7	1	0	0	2	2	0	1	.226	.273	.258	29	-4	0	1.000	4	103	156	C11		0.1
Total 8		423	1188	96	321	44	11	4	139	77	6	49	.270	.318	.336	69	-57	6-2	.977	5	85	119	C365,1b2		-2.8

HARGROVE, MIKE Dudley Michael "The Human Rain Delay" B10.26.1949 Perryton TX BL/TL/6-0/195* [TexA72 25/572] d4.7 M14/C2 Col Northwestern Oklahoma

YEAR	TM LG	G	AB	R	H	2B	3B	HR	RBI	BB-IB	HP	SO	AVG	OBP	SLG	AOPS	ABR	SB-CS	FA	FR	RNG	THR	GAMES AT POSITION	DL	BFW
1974	Tex A	131	415	57	134	18	6	4	66	49-4	4	42	.323	.395	.424	140	24	0-0	.987	8	140	84	1b91,D32,O6L		2.5
1975	Tex A★	145	519	82	157	22	2	11	62	79-10	4	66	.303	.395	.416	132	26	4-3	.964	1	94	29	O96L,1b48,D12		1.8
1976	Tex A	151	541	80	155	30	1	7	58	97-13	6	64	.287	.397	.384	128	26	2-3	.993	0	106	89	1b141,D5		1.5
1977	Tex A	153	525	98	160	28	4	18	69	103-7	6	59	.305	.420	.476	143	38	2-5	.993	3	92	117	1b152		2.4
1978	Tex A	146	494	63	124	24	1	7	40	107-8	5	47	.251	.388	.346	108	13	2-5	.987	10	132	90	1b140,D4		1.4
1979	SD N	52	125	15	24	5	0	0	8	25-3	5	15	.192	.325	.232	59	-6	0-2	.986	-1	92	97	1b37		-1.0
	Cle A	100	338	60	110	21	4	10	56	63-5	5	40	.325	.433	.500	152	29	2-3	.993	-0	109	67	O65L,1b28,D7		2.3
1980	Cle A	160	589	86	179	22	2	11	85	111-10	8	36	.304	.415	.404	126	29	4-2	.993	-5	84	83	1b160		1.4
1981	Cle A	94	322	43	102	21	0	2	49	60-5	5	16	.317	.424	.401	142	23	5-4	.989	5	121	81	1b88,D4		2.3
1982	Cle A	160	591	67	160	26	1	4	65	101-3	5	58	.271	.377	.338	99	5	0-6	.996	8	115	83	1b153,D5		0.3
1983	Cle A	134	469	57	134	21	4	3	57	78-5	5	40	.286	.388	.367	106	8	0-6	.994	4	117	104	1b124		0.9
1984	Cle A	133	352	44	94	14	2	2	44	53-3	0	38	.267	.361	.335	93	-1	0-2	.991	4	117	104	1b124		-0.3
1985	Cle A	107	284	31	81	14	1	1	27	39-2	0	29	.285	.370	.352	100	2	1-0	.991	5	126	98	1b85		0.3
Total 12		1666	5564	783	1614	266	28	80	686	965-75	53	550	.290	.396	.391	121	216	24-37	.991	44	113	94	1b1378,O167L,D70		15.8

HARKNESS, TIM Thomas William B12.23.1937 Lachine QC, Can. BL/TL/6-2/182* d9.12

YEAR	TM LG	G	AB	R	H	2B	3B	HR	RBI	BB-IB	HP	SO	AVG	OBP	SLG	AOPS	ABR	SB-CS	FA	FR	RNG	THR	GAMES AT POSITION	DL	BFW
1961	LA N	5	8	4	4	2	0	0		3-0	0	1	.500	.636	.750	245	2	1-0	1.000	0	87	142	1b2		0.2
1962	LA N	92	62	9	16	2	0	2	7	10-1	1	20	.258	.370	.387	110	1	1-0	.986	-1	75	103	1b59		0.0
1963	NY N	123	375	35	79	12	3	10	41	36-5	7	79	.211	.290	.339	80	-10	4-3	.986	16	164	85	1b106	44	0.2
1964	NY N	39	117	11	33	2	1	2	13	9-1	1	18	.282	.336	.368	101	1	1-1	.993	3	147	139	1b32	44	0.4
Total 4		259	562	59	132	18	4	14	61	58-7	9	118	.235	.315	.356	90	-7	7-4	.989	19	150	98	1b199		

HARLEY, DICK Richard Joseph B9.25.1872 Philadelphia PA D4.3.1952 Philadelphia PA BL/TR/5-10.5/165 d6.2 Col Georgetown

YEAR	TM LG	G	AB	R	H	2B	3B	HR	RBI	BB-IB	HP	SO	AVG	OBP	SLG	AOPS	ABR	SB-CS	FA	FR	RNG	THR	GAMES AT POSITION	DL	BFW
1897	StL N	90	333	43	96	6	4	3	36	36	12		.288	.378	.357	97	1	23	.901	1	158	139	O90(1/89/0)		-0.4
1898	StL N	142	549	74	135	6	5	0	42	34	22		.246	.316	.275	68	-22	13	.926	8	129	60	O141(135/5/1)		-2.5
1899	Cle N	142	567	70	142	15	7	1	50	40	13		.250	.315	.307	76	-18	15	.924	8	128	94	O142(140/0/2)		-2.0
1900	Cin N	5	21	2	9	1	0	0	5	1	0		.429	.455	.476	161	2	4	1.000	1	0	0	O5L		0.1
1901	Cin N	133	535	69	146	13	2	4	27	31	9		.273	.323	.327	95	-3	37	.898	-4	118	43	O133L		-1.5
1902	Det A	125	491	59	138	9	8	2	44	36	12		.281	.345	.344	90	-7	20	.930	1	96	31	O125L		-1.2
1903	Chi N	104	386	72	89	9	1	0	33	45	11		.231	.328	.259	70	-13	27	.923	2	124	62	O103R		-1.5
Total 7		741	2882	389	755	59	27	10	236	223	79		.262	.332	.312	83	-61	139	.918	14	123	68	O739(539/94/106)		-9.0

HARLOW, LARRY Larry Duane B11.13.1951 Colorado Springs CO BL/TL/6-2/176* d9.20 Col Mesa (AZ) CC

YEAR	TM LG	G	AB	R	H	2B	3B	HR	RBI	BB-IB	HP	SO	AVG	OBP	SLG	AOPS	ABR	SB-CS	FA	FR	RNG	THR	GAMES AT POSITION	DL	BFW
1975	Bal A	4	3	1	1	0	0	0	0	0-0	0	1	.333	.333	.333	94	0	0-0	1.000	-0	67	0	O4(2/2/0)		0.0
1977	Bal A	46	48	4	10	0	1	0	0	5-0	0	8	.208	.283	.250	49	-3	6-1	.887	-3	95	91	O38(0/37/1)		-0.5
1978	Bal A	147	460	67	112	25	1	8	26	55-3	1	72	.243	.324	.354	97	-1	14-11	.979	-4	97	91	O138(0/135/3)/P		-0.7
1979	Bal A	38	41	5	11	1	0	0	1	7-0	0	4	.268	.375	.293	86	0	1-3	.970	-1	94	0	O31(0/12/22)/D		-0.3
	†Cal A	62	159	22	37	8	2	0	14	25-0	2	34	.233	.344	.308	80	-3	1-3	.975	2	102	128	O58(11/33/15)		-0.4
	Year	100	200	27	48	9	2	0	15	32-0	2	38	.240	.350	.305	81	-4	2-6	.974	1	100	89	O89(11/45/37)/D		-0.7
1980	Cal A	109	301	47	83	13	4	4	27	48-1	1	61	.276	.376	.385	111	7	3-2	.976	13	123	179	O94(5/32/59)/1D		1.6
1981	Cal A	43	82	13	17	1	0	0	4	16-0	1	25	.207	.337	.220	63	-3	1-1	.981	-2	91	56	O39(21/7/13)		-0.6
Total 6		449	1094	159	271	48	8	12	72	156-4	4	175	.248	.343	.339	93	-3	26-21	.971	5	104	108	O402(39/258/113),D2/1P		-0.9

HARMAN, BILL William Bell B1.2.1919 Bridgewater VA BR/TR/6-4/200 d6.17 Mil 1942 Col Virginia ▲

YEAR	TM LG	G	AB	R	H	2B	3B	HR	RBI	BB-IB	HP	SO	AVG	OBP	SLG	AOPS	ABR	SB-CS	FA	FR	RNG	THR	GAMES AT POSITION	DL	BFW
1941	Phi N	15	14	1	1	0	0	0	0	0-0	0	3	.071	.071	.071	-62	-3		1.000	-1	75	0	P5,C5		-0.2

HARMON, CHUCK Charles Byron B4.23.1924 Washington IN BR/TR/6-2/175* d4.17 Negro Lg 1947 Col Toledo

YEAR	TM LG	G	AB	R	H	2B	3B	HR	RBI	BB-IB	HP	SO	AVG	OBP	SLG	AOPS	ABR	SB-CS	FA	FR	RNG	THR	GAMES AT POSITION	DL	BFW
1954	Cin N	94	286	39	68	7	3	2	25	17	1	27	.238	.277	.304	52	-21	7-3	.961	4	103	164	3b67,1b3		-1.7
1955	Cin N	96	198	31	50	6	3	5	28	26-0	1	24	.253	.345	.389	90	-2	9-9	.935	2	91	63	3b39,O32(32/2/0),1b4		-0.3
1956	Cin N	13	4	2	0	0	0	0	0	0-0	0	2	.000	.000	.000	-94	-1	1-0	1.000	0	155	0	O6(1/1/4),1b2		-0.1
	StL N	20	15	2	0	0	0	0	0	2-0	0	2	.000	.118	.000	-65	-4	0-0	1.000	-4	102	0	O11(3/4/5),1b2/3		-0.4
	Year	33	19	4	0	0	0	0	0	2-0	0	2	.000	.095	.000	-70	-5	1-0	1.000	-0	117	0	O17(4/5/9),1b4/3		-0.5
1957	StL N	9	3	2	1	0	1	0	1	0-0	0	0	.333	.333	1.000	236	0	1-0	1.000	0	126	0	O25(21/2/2),3b5,1b2		-0.4
	Phi N	57	86	14	22	2	1	0	5	1-0	0	4	.256	.264	.302	53	-6	7-2	1.000	2	145	0	O33(21/3/9),3b5,1b2		-0.3
	Year	66	89	16	23	2	2	0	6	1-0	0	4	.258	.267	.326	60	-6	8-2	1.000	2	143	0	O33(21/3/9),3b5,1b2		0.1
Total 4		289	592	90	141	15	8	7	59	46-0	4	57	.238	.294	.326	62	-34	25-14	.952	8	99	133	3b112,O82(57/10/18),1b13		-2.8

HARMON, TERRY Terry Walter B4.12.1944 Toledo OH BR/TR/6-2/180* [PhiN65 5/85] d7.23 Col Ohio U.

YEAR	TM LG	G	AB	R	H	2B	3B	HR	RBI	BB-IB	HP	SO	AVG	OBP	SLG	AOPS	ABR	SB-CS	FA	FR	RNG	THR	GAMES AT POSITION	DL	BFW
1967	Phi N	2	0	0	0	0	0	0	0	0-0	0	0	—	—	—	—	-1	0-0	—	0			/R		0.0
1969	Phi N	87	201	25	48	8	1	0	16	22-1	3	31	.239	.323	.289	74	-6	1-2	.968	7	105	130	S38,2b19,3b2	23	0.6
1970	Phi N	71	129	16	32	2	4	0	7	12-1	1	22	.248	.315	.326	74	-5	6-3	.989	-10	76	72	S35,2b14,3b2		-1.2
1971	Phi N	79	221	27	45	4	2	0	12	20-0	4	45	.204	.279	.240	49	-15	3-2	.986	4	111	111	2b58,S9,3b3,1b2		-0.7
1972	Phi N	73	218	35	62	8	2	0	13	29-0	2	28	.284	.372	.367	108	3	3-2	.996	6	114	112	2b50,S15,3b5		1.5
1973	Phi N	72	148	17	31	3	0	0	8	13-3	1	14	.209	.278	.230	41	-12	1-0	.988	-1	84	92	2b43,S19/3		-1.0
1974	Phi N	27	15	5	2	0	0	0	0	3-0	0	3	.133	.278	.133	17	-2	0-0	1.000	-1	41	71	S7,2b5		-0.2
1975	Phi N	48	72	14	13	1	2	0	5	9-0	1	13	.181	.280	.250	46	-5	0-0	.989	-5	86	68	S25,2b7/3		-0.8
1976	†Phi N	42	61	12	18	4	1	0	6	10-0	0	10	.295	.328	.393	100	0	3-3	.960	-3	85	64	S19,2b13,3b5		-0.1
1977	Phi N	46	60	13	11	1	0	2	6	6-0	1	9	.183	.265	.300	50	-4	0-2	.982	3	132	175	2b28,S16,3b3		-0.1
Total 10		547	1125	164	262	31	12	4	72	117-5	13	175	.233	.311	.292	69	-45	17-11	.989	1	106	107	2b237,S183,3b22,1b2	23	-2.0

HARPER, BRIAN Brian David B10.16.1959 Los Angeles CA BR/TR/6-2/195(195-208) [CalA77 4/85] d9.29 OF(78/0/38)

YEAR	TM LG	G	AB	R	H	2B	3B	HR	RBI	BB-IB	HP	SO	AVG	OBP	SLG	AOPS	ABR	SB-CS	FA	FR	RNG	THR	GAMES AT POSITION	DL	BFW
1979	Cal A	1	2	0	0	0	0	0	0	0-0	0	0	.000	.000	.000	-99	-1	0-0	—			0	/D		-0.1
1981	Cal A	4	11	1	3	0	0	0	1	0-0	0	0	.273	.250	.273	57	-1	1-0	.833	-0	125	0	O2(1/0/1)/D		-0.1
1982	Pit N	20	29	4	8	1	0	2	4	1-1	0	5	.276	.300	.517	119	1	0-0	1.000	-0	104	0	O8R		0.0
1983	Pit N	61	131	16	29	4	1	7	20	2-0	1	18	.221	.232	.427	79	-5	0-0	.982	3	82	0	O35(33/0/2)/1		-0.9

YEAR	TM LG	G	AB	R	H	2B	3B	HR	RBI	BB-IB	HP	SO	AVG	OBP	SLG	AOPS	ABR	SB-CS	FA	FR	RNG	THR	GAMES AT POSITION	DL	BFW
1984	Pit N	46	112	4	29	4	0	2	11	5-0	2	11	.259	.300	.348	82	-3	0-0	.981	1	101	150	O37(34/0/4),C2	47	-0.3
1985	†StL N	43	52	5	13	4	0	0	8	2-0	0	3	.250	.273	.327	69	-2	0-0	1.000	-1	109	0	O13(7/0/6),3b6,C2/1		-0.3
1986	Det A	19	36	2	5	1	0	0	3	3-0	0	3	.139	.200	.167	3	-5	0-0	.929	0	100		O11R,C2,1b2,D6		-0.5
1987	Oak A	11	17	1	4	1	0	0	3	0-0	0	4	.235	.222	.294	42	-1	0-0		-0	0		/OLD		-0.1
1988	Min A	60	166	15	49	11	4	3	20	10-1	3	12	.295	.344	.428	112	3	0-3	.991	-5	123	100	C48,3b2,D5		-0.1
1989	Min A	126	385	43	125	24	0	8	57	13-3	6	16	.325	.353	.449	118	9	2-4	.978	-4	112	96	C101,D19,O3R,1b2,3b2		0.8
1990	Min A	134	479	61	141	42	3	6	54	19-2	7	27	.294	.328	.432	105	3	3-2	.985	9	86	130	C120,D11,3b3,1b2		1.9
1991	†Min A	123	441	54	137	28	1	10	69	14-3	6	22	.311	.336	.447	111	4	1-2	.988	-5	73	78	C119/1OLD		0.7
1992	Min A	140	502	58	154	25	0	9	73	26-7	7	22	.307	.343	.410	108	5	0-1	.984	-3	79	108	C133,D2		1.0
1993	Min A	147	530	52	161	26	1	12	73	29-9	9	29	.304	.347	.425	106	4	1-3	.988	-12	77	113	C134,D7		1.0
1994	Mil A	64	251	23	73	15	0	4	32	9-1	3	18	.291	.318	.398	81	-7	0-2	.981	1	58	118	D36,C25,O3(1/0/3)		0.0
1995	Oak A	2	7	0	0	0	0	0	0	0-0	0	0	1.000	.000	.000		-2	0-0		0	0		C2	58	-0.7
Total	16	1001	3151	339	931	186	7	63	428	133-27	44	188	.295	.329	.419	102	4	8-17	.985	-21	85	106	C688,O114L,D97,3b13,1b9	105	1.0

HARPER, GEORGE George Washington B6.24.1892 Arlington KY D8.18.1978 Magnolia AR BL/TR/5-8/167 d4.15

YEAR	TM LG	G	AB	R	H	2B	3B	HR	RBI	BB-IB	HP	SO	AVG	OBP	SLG	AOPS	ABR	SB-CS	FA	FR	RNG	THR	GAMES AT POSITION	DL	BFW
1916	Det A	44	56	4	9	1	0	0	3	5	0	8	.161	.230	.179	22	-5		.938	-2	86	0	O14(2/4/8)		-0.8
1917	Det A	47	117	6	24	3	0	0	12	11	1	15	.205	.290	.231	59	-5	2	.980	-2	97	51	O31(0/3/28)		-1.0
1918	Det A	69	227	19	55	2	0	2	16	18	1	14	.242	.301	.282	79	-6	3	.956	-3	104	54	O64(0/1/63)		-1.0
1922	Cin N	128	430	67	146	22	8	2	68	35	6	22	.340	.397	.442	118	13	11-10	.955	-1	98	105	O109(1/5/103)		0.2
1923	Cin N	61	125	14	32	4	2	3	16	11	0	9	.256	.316	.392	88	-3	0-2	.967	-1	91	100	O22(9/17/3)		-0.6
1924	Cin N	28	74	7	20	3	0	0	3	13	2	5	.270	.393	.311	92	0	1-3	.964	0	98	129	O22(12/10/0)		-0.2
	Phi N	109	411	68	121	26	6	16	55	38	5	23	.294	.361	.504	115	9	10-11	.991	3	103	101	O109(0/3/107)		0.2
	Year	137	485	75	141	29	6	16	58	51	7	28	.291	.366	.475	113	10	11-14	.986	3	102	106	O131(12/13/107)		0.2
1925	Phi N	132	495	86	173	35	7	18	97	28	6	32	.349	.391	.558	128	20	10-8	.971	4	103	117	O126(36/61/33)		1.5
1926	Phi N	56	194	32	61	6	7	5	38	16	0	7	.314	.367	.505	126	6	6	.942	-3	102	39	O55(44/8/8)		0.0
1927	NY N	145	483	85	160	19	6	16	87	84	5	27	.331	.435	.495	149	38	7	.975	-2	101	75	O142R		2.5
1928	NY N	19	57	11	13	1	0	2	7	10	1	4	.228	.353	.351	84	-1	1	.957	2	100	210	O18R		-0.1
	†StL N	99	272	41	83	8	2	17	58	51	2	15	.305	.418	.537	145	19	2	.988	2	90	157	O84R		1.5
	Year	118	329	52	96	9	2	19	65	61	3	19	.292	.407	.505	135	18	3	.982	4	92	167	O102R		1.4
1929	Bos N	136	457	65	133	25	5	16	68	69	4	27	.291	.389	.433	108	8	5	.972	2	106	82	O130(119/1/10)		0.0
Total	11	1073	3398	505	1030	158	43	91	528	389	35	208	.303	.380	.455	118	93	58-34	.970	0	100	95	O933(223/113/607)		1.8

HARPER, TERRY Terry Joe B8.19.1955 Douglasville GA BR/TR/6-4/195* [AtlN73 16/370] d9.12

YEAR	TM LG	G	AB	R	H	2B	3B	HR	RBI	BB-IB	HP	SO	AVG	OBP	SLG	AOPS	ABR	SB-CS	FA	FR	RNG	THR	GAMES AT POSITION	DL	BFW
1980	Atl N	21	54	3	10	2	1	0	3	6-0	1	5	.185	.279	.259	50	-4	2-1	.968	-1	104	0	O18(15/1/3)		-0.5
1981	Atl N	40	73	9	19	1	0	2	8	11-0	0	17	.260	.353	.356	103	1	5-1	.976	1	107	129	O27(9/0/18)		0.2
1982	†Atl N	48	150	16	43	3	0	2	16	14-0	1	28	.287	.347	.347	94	-1	7-4	.987	1	98	133	O41(29/1/16)	53	-0.2
1983	Atl N	80	201	19	53	13	1	3	26	20-0	1	43	.264	.332	.383	91	-2	6-5	.952	1	101	140	O60(28/2/32)		-0.4
1984	Atl N	40	102	4	16	3	1	0	8	4-0	1	21	.157	.194	.206	12	-12	4-1	1.000	4	121	150	O29(28/0/1)		-1.0
1985	Atl N	138	492	58	130	15	2	17	72	44-4	3	76	.264	.327	.407	99	-1	9-9	.978	-4	87	107	O131(129/0/2)	22	-1.0
1986	Atl N	106	265	26	68	12	0	8	30	29-2	1	39	.257	.330	.392	95	-2	3-6	.970	-5	74	110	O83(66/0/25)		-1.2
1987	Det A	31	64	4	13	3	0	3	10	9-0	1	8	.203	.301	.391	85	-1	1-0	.952	-1	104	0	D15,O14(1/0/13)		-1.2
	Pit N	36	66	8	19	3	0	1	7	7-1	0	11	.288	.356	.379	94	0	0-1	1.000	-1	94	0	O20(10/0/11)		-0.3
Total	8	540	1467	147	371	55	6	36	180	144-7	8	248	.253	.321	.371	88	-22	37-28	.976	-4	92	108	O423(315/4/121),D15	75	-4.8

HARPER, TOMMY Tommy B10.14.1940 Oak Grove LA BR/TR/5-10/168* d4.9 C18 Col San Francisco St. OF(683/258/348)

YEAR	TM LG	G	AB	R	H	2B	3B	HR	RBI	BB-IB	HP	SO	AVG	OBP	SLG	AOPS	ABR	SB-CS	FA	FR	RNG	THR	GAMES AT POSITION	DL	BFW
1962	Cin N	6	23	1	4	0	0	0	1	2-0	0	6	.174	.240	.174	13	-3	1-0	.929	-2	64	97	3b6		-0.4
1963	Cin N	129	408	67	106	12	3	10	37	44-1	3	72	.260	.335	.377	102	2	12-1	.983	5	117	91	O118(1/23/94)/3		0.3
1964	Cin N	102	317	42	77	5	2	4	22	39-1	5	56	.243	.326	.309	78	-2	24-3	.994	5	109	79	O92(88/4/0),3b2		-0.4
1965	Cin N	159	646	126	166	28	3	18	64	78-0	5	127	.257	.340	.393	99	2	35-6	.983	5	109	72	O159(156/5/0),3b2/2		0.3
1966	Cin N	149	553	85	154	22	5	5	31	57-4	3	85	.278	.348	.363	91	-5	29-10	.996	0	105	53	O147(73/25/95)		-1.0
1967	Cin N	103	365	55	82	17	3	7	22	43-1	0	51	.225	.306	.345	77	-10	23-8	.995	7	123	89	O100(2/4/97)	59	-0.7
1968	Cle A	130	235	26	51	15	2	6	26	26-2	1	56	.217	.295	.374	104	1	11-7	.984	-4	99	0	O115(67/7/46),2b2		-0.8
1969	Sea A	148	537	78	126	10	2	9	41	95-2	1	90	.235	.349	.311	87	-6	73-18	.959	-6	92	83	2b59,3b59,O26(3/22/1)		0.0
1970	Mil A★	154	604	104	179	35	4	31	82	77-5	4	107	.296	.377	.522	146	39	38-16	.943	13	113	87	3b128,2b22,O13(8/5/2)		5.6
1971	Mil A	152	585	79	151	26	3	14	52	65-4	1	92	.258	.333	.385	104	3	25-3	.975	-6	97	40	O90(77/13/2),3b70/2		-0.3
1972	Bos A	144	556	92	141	29	2	14	49	67-1	9	104	.254	.341	.388	111	10	25-7	.985	-6	99	46	O144C		0.4
1973	Bos A	147	566	92	159	23	3	17	71	61-2	1	93	.281	.351	.422	110	8	54-14	.985	1	96	136	O143(139/5/0)/D		0.8
1974	Bos A	118	443	66	105	15	3	5	24	46-2	2	65	.237	.312	.318	77	-13	28-12	.982	-4	88	48	O61L,D51		-2.0
1975	Cal A	89	285	40	68	10	1	3	31	38-5	2	51	.239	.329	.312	89	-1	19-8	.992	-1	65	127	D57,1b19,O9(2/0/7)		-0.5
	†Oak A	34	69	11	22	4	0	2	7	5-0	1	9	.319	.373	.464	138	3	7-0	.963	-2	36	81	1b16,O9(5/1/4),3b2,D3		0.2
	Year	123	354	51	90	14	1	5	38	43-5	3	60	.254	.337	.342	98	0	26-8	.978	-3	51	104	D60,1b35,O18(7/1/11),3b2		-0.3
1976	Bal A	46	77	8	18	5	0	1	7	10-0	0	16	.234	.318	.338	99	0	4-3	1.000	0	0	0	D27/1OL		-0.1
Total	15	1810	6269	972	1609	256	36	146	567	753-30	35	1080	.257	.338	.379	100	20	408-116	.986	6	105	70	O1227L,3b270,D139,2b85,1b36	59	1.4

HARRAH, TOBY Colbert Dale B10.26.1948 Sissonville WV BR/TR/6-0/180(165-190) d9.5 M1/C8

YEAR	TM LG	G	AB	R	H	2B	3B	HR	RBI	BB-IB	HP	SO	AVG	OBP	SLG	AOPS	ABR	SB-CS	FA	FR	RNG	THR	GAMES AT POSITION	DL	BFW
1969	Was A	8	1	4	0	0	0	0	0	0-0	0	0	.000	.000	.000	-99	-0	0-0	—	-0	0	0	/S		0.0
1971	Was A	127	383	45	88	11	3	2	22	40-3	0	48	.230	.300	.290	72	-14	10-9	.955	-4	98	108	S116,3b7		-0.8
1972	Tex A★	116	374	47	97	14	3	1	31	34-1	0	31	.259	.316	.321	94	-3	16-7	.960	-8	95	91	S106		0.3
1973	Tex A	118	461	64	120	16	1	10	50	46-2	2	49	.260	.328	.364	99	-1	10-3	.951	3	112	81	S76,3b52	23	0.3
1974	Tex A	161	573	94	149	23	2	21	74	50-2	2	65	.260	.319	.417	114	9	15-14	.963	6	96	105	S158,3b3	36	1.2
1975	Tex A☆	151	522	81	153	24	1	20	93	98-3	1	71	.293	.403	.458	145	36	23-9	.963	17	112	101	S118,3b28,2b21		3.3
1976	Tex A★	155	584	64	152	21	1	15	67	91-5	3	59	.260	.360	.377	114	14	8-5	.955	2	101	92	S146,3b5,D4		6.9
1977	Tex A	159	539	90	142	25	5	27	87	109-7	10	73	.263	.393	.479	135	32	27-5	.963	-21	89	72	3b159/S		3.6
1978	Tex A	139	450	56	103	17	3	12	59	83-3	2	66	.229	.349	.360	100	3	31-8	.965	-2	91	93	3b91,S49		1.2
1979	Cle A	149	527	99	147	25	1	20	77	89-2	8	60	.279	.389	.444	124	22	20-9	.940	-42	64	81	3b127,S33,D9		0.9
1980	Cle A	160	561	100	150	22	4	11	72	98-3	7	60	.267	.379	.380	109	12	17-2	.971	5	99	83	3b156,S2,D3		-1.8
1981	Cle A	103	361	64	105	12	4	5	44	57-8	1	44	.291	.382	.388	125	14	12-1	.949	-11	90	63	3b101,S3/D		1.7
1982	Cle A☆	162	602	100	183	29	4	25	78	84-7	12	52	.304	.398	.490	142	38	17-3	.971	-15	89	76	3b159,2b3,S2		0.5
1983	Cle A	138	526	81	140	23	1	9	55	75-1	7	49	.266	.363	.365	98	2	16-10	.971	-5	95	100	3b137/2D		2.4
1984	NY A	88	253	40	55	9	4	1	26	42-2	2	28	.217	.331	.296	85	-6	3-0	.968	-5	97	140	3b74,2b4/ORD	27	-0.5
1985	Tex A	126	396	65	107	18	1	9	44	113-2	4	60	.270	.432	.389	126	23	11-4	.989	-6	97	86	2b122,S2/D	17	-0.5
1986	Tex A	95	289	36	63	18	2	7	41	44-0	2	53	.218	.322	.367	86	-5	2-5	.982	-14	84	83	2b93	15	-1.6
Total	17	2155	7402	1115	1954	307	40	195	918	1153-51	63	868	.264	.365	.395	114	176	238-94	.963	-94	90	83	3b1099,S813,2b244,D21/OR	118	19.2

HARRELL, JOHN John Robert B11.27.1947 Long Beach CA BR/TR/6-2/190 [SFN66 31/605] d10.1 Col West Valley (CA) CC

YEAR	TM LG	G	AB	R	H	2B	3B	HR	RBI	BB-IB	HP	SO	AVG	OBP	SLG	AOPS	ABR	SB-CS	FA	FR	RNG	THR	GAMES AT POSITION	DL	BFW
1969	SF N	2	6	0	3	0	0	0	2	0-0	0	1	.500	.625	.500	221	1	0-0	1.000	-0	0	0	C2		0.1

HARRELL, BILLY William B7.18.1928 Norristown PA BR/TR/6-1.5/180* d9.2 Negro Lg 1951 Col Siena

YEAR	TM LG	G	AB	R	H	2B	3B	HR	RBI	BB-IB	HP	SO	AVG	OBP	SLG	AOPS	ABR	SB-CS	FA	FR	RNG	THR	GAMES AT POSITION	DL	BFW
1955	Cle A	13	19	2	8	0	0	1	1	3-0	0	3	.421	.500	.421	144	1	1-0	.926	-0	106	30	S11		0.2
1957	Cle A	22	57	6	15	1	1	1	5	4-0	0	7	.263	.311	.368	86	-1	3-1	.893	-4	86	67	S14,3b6/2		-0.4
1958	Cle A	101	229	36	50	4	0	7	19	15-2	2	36	.218	.271	.328	66	-12	12-2	.986	-5	111	151	3b46,S45,2b7/OR		-0.7
1961	Bos A	37	37	10	6	2	0	0	1	1-0	0	8	.162	.184	.216	6	-5	1-0	1.000	2	109	250	3b10,S7,1b3		-1.2
Total	4	173	342	54	79	7	1	8	26	23-2	2	54	.231	.283	.327	68	-17	17-3	.933	-8	93	72	S77,3b62,2b8,1b3/OR		-1.7

HARRELSON, BUD Derrel McKinley B6.6.1944 Niles CA BB/TR (BR 1965, 1975p)/5-11/160* d9.2 M2/C7 Col San Francisco St.

YEAR	TM LG	G	AB	R	H	2B	3B	HR	RBI	BB-IB	HP	SO	AVG	OBP	SLG	AOPS	ABR	SB-CS	FA	FR	RNG	THR	GAMES AT POSITION	DL	BFW
1965	NY N	19	37	3	4	1	0	0	2	2-0	0	11	.108	.154	.189	-4	-5	0-0	.955	-1	92	74	S18		-0.6
1966	NY N	33	99	20	22	2	4	0	4	13-1	0	23	.222	.313	.323	79	-3	7-3	.993	6	111	152	S29		0.7
1967	NY N	151	540	59	137	16	4	1	28	48-0	1	64	.254	.317	.304	80	-13	12-13	.958	15	107	102	S149		1.4
1968	NY N	111	402	38	88	7	3	0	14	29-2	1	68	.219	.273	.251	60	-21	4-5	.972	-0	94	105	S106		-1.5
1969	†NY N	123	395	42	95	11	6	0	24	54-7	2	54	.241	.341	.306	81	-9	1-3	.969	1	94	113	S119		0.6
1970	NY N★	157	564	72	137	18	6	1	42	95-4	3	74	.243	.351	.309	78	-14	23-4	.971	-26	80	97	S156		0.6
1971	NY N★	142	547	55	138	16	6	0	32	53-0	2	79	.252	.319	.303	78	-15	28-7	.978	15	96	104	S140		2.1
1972	NY N	115	418	54	90	10	4	0	24	58-4	3	57	.215	.313	.266	68	-16	12-4	.970	-9	90	79	S115		2.1
1973	†NY N	106	356	35	92	12	3	0	20	48-4	1	49	.258	.348	.309	84	-6	5-1	.979	-10	91	82	S103	22	-1.1
1974	NY N	106	331	48	75	10	0	1	13	71-1	2	39	.227	.366	.266	79	-5	9-4	.968	20	106	121	S97	48	2.8
1975	NY N	34	73	16	16	2	0	0	3	12-2	0	13	.219	.329	.247	60	-3	0-0	.941	-2	86	129	S34	97	-0.2

YEAR	TM LG	G	AB	R	H	2B	3B	HR	RBI	BB-IB	HP	SO	AVG	OBP	SLG	AOPS	ABR	SB-CS	FA	FR	RNG	THR	GAMES AT POSITION	DL	BFW
1976	NY N	118	359	34	84	12	4	1	26	63-5	2	56	.234	.351	.298	90	-11	9-3	.962	-11	87	73	S117		0.2
1977	NY N	107	269	25	48	6	2	1	12	27-1	1	28	.178	.255	.227	32	-27	5-4	.984	-2	92	92	S98		-2.1
1978	Phi N	71	103	16	22	1	0	0	9	18-0	1	21	.214	.331	.223	56	-5	5-2	.972	12	127	199	2b43,S15		0.9
1979	Phi N	53	71	7	20	6	0	0	7	13-0	1	14	.282	.395	.366	106	2	2-3	.990	1	97	103	2b25,S17,3b9/OL		0.4
1980	Tex A	87	180	26	49	6	0	1	9	29-0	1	23	.272	.373	.322	95	0	4-4	.952	11	104	119	S87,2b2	46	1.7
Total	16	1533	4744	539	1120	136	45	7	267	633-31	22	653	.236	.327	.288	75	-142	127-60	.969	21	94	100	S1400,2b70,3b9/OL	213	3.2

HARRELSON, KEN Kenneth Smith "Hawk" B9.4.1941 Woodruff SC BR/TR/6-2/190* d6.9

YEAR	TM LG	G	AB	R	H	2B	3B	HR	RBI	BB-IB	HP	SO	AVG	OBP	SLG	AOPS	ABR	SB-CS	FA	FR	RNG	THR	GAMES AT POSITION	DL	BFW
1963	KC A	79	226	16	52	10	1	6	23	23-3	0	58	.230	.299	.363	81	-6	1-1	.980	-6	65	90	1b34,O28L		-1.7
1964	KC A	49	139	15	27	5	0	1	7	13-0	0	34	.194	.263	.381	74	-5	0-1	.977	4	110	193	O24L,1b15		-0.4
1965	KC A	150	483	61	115	17	3	23	66	66-3	1	112	.238	.329	.429	116	10	9-7	.992	-4	87	93	1b125,O4(3/0/1)		-0.5
1966	KC A	63	210	24	47	5	0	5	22	27-3	0	59	.224	.312	.319	85	-4	9-2	.985	2	119	87	1b58,O3(3/0/1)		-0.7
	Was A	71	250	25	62	8	1	7	28	26-1	1	53	.248	.321	.372	100	4	4-1	.991	-3	86	102	1b70		-1.2
	Year	134	460	49	109	13	1	12	50	53-5	1	112	.237	.317	.348	93	-4	13-3	.989	-1	101	95	1b128,O3(3/0/1)		-0.4
1967	Was A	26	79	10	16	0	0	3	10	7-1	0	15	.203	.261	.316	75	-3	1-0	.996	0	110	108	1b23		0.9
	KC A	61	174	23	53	11	0	6	30	17-1	0	17	.305	.361	.471	151	11	8-2	.992	-2	84	68	1b45		-0.7
	†Bos A	23	80	9	16	4	1	3	14	5-2	0	12	.200	.247	.387	79	-2	1-1	.929	-3	74	77	O23R/1		-0.2
	Year	110	333	42	85	15	1	12	54	29-4	0	44	.255	.311	.414	115	6	10-3	.993	-4	93	81	1b69,O23R		3.1
1968	Bos A★	150	535	79	147	17	4	35	**109**	69-9	2	90	.275	.356	.518	154	35	2-6	1.000	4	110	111	O132R,1b19		-0.1
1969	Bos A	10	46	6	10	1	0	3	8	4-0	0	6	.217	.275	.435	93	-1	0-1	.991	1	138	145	1b10		0.1
	Cle A	149	519	83	115	13	4	27	84	95-6	2	96	.222	.341	.418	109	7	17-8	.985	1	105	66	O144(7/0/137),1b16		0.0
	Year	159	565	89	125	14	4	30	92	99-6	2	102	.221	.336	.419	108	7	17-9	.985	2	105	66	O144(7/0/137),1b26	148	0.0
1970	Cle A	17	39	3	11	1	0	1	6	6-0	0	4	.282	.378	.385	106	1	0-0	1.000	-1	111	179	1b13		-1.2
1971	Cle A	52	161	20	32	2	0	5	14	24-3	0	21	.199	.301	.304	66	-2	1-0	.988	-6	95	95	1b40,O7(5/0/2)	148	-1.8
Total	9	900	2941	374	703	94	14	131	421	382-33	6	577	.239	.325	.414	109	36	53-30	.990	-6	95	95	1b469,O365(70/0/296)		-1.8

HARRINGTON, ANDY Andrew Matthew B2.12.1903 Mountain View CA D1.26.1979 Boise ID BR/TR/5-11/170 d4.18 Col St. Marys (CA)

YEAR	TM LG	G	AB	R	H	2B	3B	HR	RBI	BB-IB	HP	SO	AVG	OBP	SLG	AOPS	ABR	SB-CS	FA	FR	RNG	THR	GAMES AT POSITION	DL	BFW
1925	Det A	1	1	0	0	0	0	0	0	0-0	0	0	.000	.000	.000	-99	0	0-0	—	0			/H		0.0

HARRINGTON, MICKEY Charles Michael B10.8.1934 Hattiesburg MS BR/TR/6-4/205 d7.10 Col Southern Mississippi

YEAR	TM LG	G	AB	R	H	2B	3B	HR	RBI	BB-IB	HP	SO	AVG	OBP	SLG	AOPS	ABR	SB-CS	FA	FR	RNG	THR	GAMES AT POSITION	DL	BFW
1963	Phi N	1	0	0	0	0	0	0	0	0-0	0	0	—	—	—	—	0	0-0	—	0			/R		0.0

HARRINGTON, JERRY Jeremiah Peter B8.12.1869 Keokuk IA D4.16.1913 Keokuk IA BR/TR/5-11/220 d4.30

YEAR	TM LG	G	AB	R	H	2B	3B	HR	RBI	BB-IB	HP	SO	AVG	OBP	SLG	AOPS	ABR	SB-CS	FA	FR	RNG	THR	GAMES AT POSITION	DL	BFW
1890	Cin N	65	236	25	58	7	1	1	23	15	3	29	.246	.299	.297	74	-8	4	.957	11	123	90	C65		0.7
1891	Cin N	92	333	25	76	10	5	2	41	19	1	34	.228	.272	.306	68	-15	4	.908	-8	90	96	C92/3		-1.4
1892	Cin N	22	61	6	13	1	0	0	3	6	0	9	.213	.284	.230	56	-3	0	.989	2	115	91	C22/1		0.0
1893	Lou N	10	36	4	4	1	0	0	6	3	0	9	.111	.179	.139	-16	-6	0	.853	-3	101	72	C10		-0.7
Total	4	189	666	60	151	19	6	3	73	43	4	73	.227	.278	.287	64	-32	8	.932	1	105	92	C189/13		-1.4

HARRINGTON, JOE Joseph C. B12.21.1869 Fall River MA D9.13.1933 Fall River MA BR/TR/5-8.5/162 d9.10

YEAR	TM LG	G	AB	R	H	2B	3B	HR	RBI	BB-IB	HP	SO	AVG	OBP	SLG	AOPS	ABR	SB-CS	FA	FR	RNG	THR	GAMES AT POSITION	DL	BFW
1895	Bos N	18	65	21	18	0	2	2	13	7	1	5	.277	.356	.431	95	-1	3	.912	-1	99	96	2b18		-0.1
1896	Bos N	54	199	26	40	5	3	1	25	19	1	17	.201	.274	.271	42	-18	2	.819	-6	104	107	3b49,S4/2		-2.0
Total	2	72	264	47	58	5	5	3	38	26	2	22	.220	.295	.311	55	-19	5	.819	-8	104	107	3b49,2b19,S4		-2.1

HARRIS, CANDY Alonzo B9.17.1947 Selma AL BB/TR/6-0/160 d4.13

YEAR	TM LG	G	AB	R	H	2B	3B	HR	RBI	BB-IB	HP	SO	AVG	OBP	SLG	AOPS	ABR	SB-CS	FA	FR	RNG	THR	GAMES AT POSITION	DL	BFW
1967	Hou N	6	1	0	0	0	0	0	0	0-0	0	1	.000	.000	.000	-99	0	0-0	—	0			/H	25	0.0

HARRIS, SPENCER Anthony Spencer B8.12.1900 Duluth MN D7.3.1982 Minneapolis MN BL/TL/5-9/145 d4.14

YEAR	TM LG	G	AB	R	H	2B	3B	HR	RBI	BB-IB	HP	SO	AVG	OBP	SLG	AOPS	ABR	SB-CS	FA	FR	RNG	THR	GAMES AT POSITION	DL	BFW
1925	Chi A	56	92	12	26	2	0	1	13	14	1	13	.283	.383	.337	89	-1	1-3	.957	-0	94	141	O27(1/12/17)		-0.3
1926	Chi A	80	222	36	56	11	3	2	27	20	1	15	.252	.317	.356	78	-8	8-3	.949	-1	95	101	O63(7/11/48)		-1.2
1929	Was A	6	14	1	3	1	0	0	1	0	0	3	.214	.214	.286	27	-2	1-0	1.000	-0	94	0	O4C		-0.2
1930	Phi A	22	49	4	9	1	0	0	5	5	0	2	.184	.259	.204	18	-6	0-0	.958	1	97	242	O13(10/1/2)		-0.6
Total	4	164	377	53	94	15	3	3	46	39	2	33	.249	.323	.329	70	-17	10-6	.954	-1	95	124	O107(18/28/67)		-2.3

HARRIS, GAIL Boyd Gail B10.15.1931 Abingdon VA BL/TL/6-0/195* d6.3

YEAR	TM LG	G	AB	R	H	2B	3B	HR	RBI	BB-IB	HP	SO	AVG	OBP	SLG	AOPS	ABR	SB-CS	FA	FR	RNG	THR	GAMES AT POSITION	DL	BFW
1955	NY N	79	263	27	61	9	0	12	36	20-3	2	46	.232	.289	.403	82	-8	0-0	.982	-0	105	106	1b75		-1.2
1956	NY N	12	38	2	5	0	1	1	1	3-1	0	10	.132	.233	.263	33	-4	0-0	.975	0	113	128	1b11		-0.5
1957	NY N	90	225	28	54	7	3	9	31	16-2	6	28	.240	.305	.418	93	-3	1-0	.985	-2	96	119	1b61		-0.8
1958	Det A	134	451	63	123	18	4	20	83	36-3	4	60	.273	.328	.481	113	6	1-2	.986	2	108	88	1b122		0.1
1959	Det A	114	349	39	77	4	3	9	39	29-3	6	49	.221	.290	.327	66	-17	0-1	.992	3	106	87	1b93		-2.0
1960	Det A	8	5	0	0	0	0	0	0	2-1	0	1	.000	.286	.000	-15	-1	0-0	1.000	0	134	101	1b5		-0.1
Total	6	437	1331	159	320	38	15	51	190	106-13	20	194	.240	.304	.406	88	-27	2-3	.986	3	105	98	1b367		-4.5

HARRIS, BRENDAN Brendan Michael B8.26.1980 Albany NY BR/TR/6-1/200* [ChiN01 5/138] d7.6 Col William and Mary

YEAR	TM LG	G	AB	R	H	2B	3B	HR	RBI	BB-IB	HP	SO	AVG	OBP	SLG	AOPS	ABR	SB-CS	FA	FR	RNG	THR	GAMES AT POSITION	DL	BFW
2004	Chi N	3	9	0	2	1	0	0	1	1-0	1	1	.222	.300	.333	62	0	0-0	.889	0	84	0	3b3		0.0
	Mon N	20	50	4	8	2	0	1	2	2-0	1	11	.160	.208	.260	19	-6	0-0	.972	-6	73	49	2b11,3b4		-1.2
	Year	23	59	4	10	3	0	1	3	3-0	1	12	.169	.222	.271	26	-7	0-0	.972	-6	73	49	2b11,3b7		-1.2
2005	Was N	4	9	1	3	1	0	1	3	0-0	1	0	.333	.400	.778	213	1	0-0	1.000	1	112	101	2b2/3		0.2
Total	2	27	68	5	13	4	0	2	6	3-0	2	12	.191	.247	.338	48	-5	0-0	.977	-5	78	56	2b13,3b8		-1.0

HARRIS, CHARLIE Charles Jenkins B10.21.1877 Macon GA D3.14.1963 Gainesville FL BR/TR/5-8/200 d5.26 Col Mercer

YEAR	TM LG	G	AB	R	H	2B	3B	HR	RBI	BB-IB	HP	SO	AVG	OBP	SLG	AOPS	ABR	SB-CS	FA	FR	RNG	THR	GAMES AT POSITION	DL	BFW
1899	Bal N	30	68	16	19	3	0	0	1	3	1		.279	.319	.324	73	-3	4	.872	-3	92	106	3b21,O3(2/0/1),2b2/S		-0.5

HARRIS, DAVE David Stanley "Sheriff" B7.14.1900 Summerfield NC D9.18.1973 Atlanta GA BR/TR/5-11/170 d4.14

YEAR	TM LG	G	AB	R	H	2B	3B	HR	RBI	BB-IB	HP	SO	AVG	OBP	SLG	AOPS	ABR	SB-CS	FA	FR	RNG	THR	GAMES AT POSITION	DL	BFW
1925	Bos N	92	340	49	90	8	7	5	36	27	0	44	.265	.321	.374	84	-10	6-4	.962	7	110	142	O90(87/4/0)		-0.9
1928	Bos N	7	17	2	2	1	0	0	0	2	0	6	.118	.211	.176	2	-2	0	.833	-1	105	0	O6L		-0.3
1930	Chi A	33	86	16	21	2	1	5	13	7	1	22	.244	.309	.465	96	-1	0-0	1.000	-0	107	62	O23L/2		-0.3
	Was A	73	205	40	65	19	8	4	44	28	0	35	.317	.399	.546	137	12	6-3	.983	4	99	190	O59(19/12/28)		1.1
	Year	106	291	56	86	21	9	9	57	35	1	57	.296	.373	.522	125	11	6-3	.988	4	101	152	O82(42/12/28)/2		1.2
1931	Was A	77	231	49	72	14	8	5	50	49	1	38	.312	.434	.506	146	18	7-6	.950	-1	100	76	O34(7/8/20)		0.7
1932	Was A	81	156	26	51	7	4	6	29	19	1	34	.327	.400	.538	143	10	4-4	.932	-0	100	127	O34(7/8/20)		-0.2
1933	†Was A	82	177	33	46	9	2	5	38	25	2	26	.260	.358	.418	106	2	3-1	.964	-3	103	31	O45(4/11/32),1b6,3b2		-0.4
1934	Was A	97	235	28	59	14	3	3	37	39	1	40	.251	.358	.362	89	-3	2-3	.973	2	99	169	O64(15/1/49),3b5		0.9
Total	7	542	1447	243	406	74	33	32	247	196	5	245	.281	.368	.444	112	26	28-21	.963	8	103	122	O381(164/36/186),3b7,1b6/2		0.9

HARRIS, DONALD Donald B11.12.1967 Waco TX BR/TR/6-1/185* [TexA89 1/5] d9.4 Col Texas Tech

YEAR	TM LG	G	AB	R	H	2B	3B	HR	RBI	BB-IB	HP	SO	AVG	OBP	SLG	AOPS	ABR	SB-CS	FA	FR	RNG	THR	GAMES AT POSITION	DL	BFW
1991	Tex A	18	8	4	3	0	0	1	2	1-0	0	3	.375	.444	.750	228	1	1-0	1.000	-0	88	0	O12(2/7/5),D3		0.0
1992	Tex A	24	33	3	6	1	0	0	0	0-0	1	15	.182	.182	.212	10	-4	1-0	.974	2	125	150	O24(5/15/5)		-0.2
1993	Tex A	40	76	10	15	2	0	1	8	6-0	1	18	.197	.253	.263	41	-7	0-1	.943	-2	78	213	O38(1/27/11),D3		-0.1
Total	3	82	117	17	24	3	0	2	11	6-0	1	36	.205	.248	.282	46	-10	2-1	.959	-0	93	176	O74(8/49/21),D6		-1.1

HARRIS, FRANK Frank W. B11.2.1858 Pittsburgh PA D11.26.1939 E.Moline IL BR/TR d4.17

YEAR	TM LG	G	AB	R	H	2B	3B	HR	RBI	BB-IB	HP	SO	AVG	OBP	SLG	AOPS	ABR	SB-CS	FA	FR	RNG	THR	GAMES AT POSITION	DL	BFW
1884	Alt U	24	95	10	25	2	1	0		3			.263	.286	.305	78	-5		.941	1	160	13	1b17,O8(4/3/1)		-0.6

HARRIS, BILLY James William B11.24.1943 Hamlet NC BL/TR/6-0/176* [CleA66 27/531] d6.16 Col North Carolina-Wilmington

YEAR	TM LG	G	AB	R	H	2B	3B	HR	RBI	BB-IB	HP	SO	AVG	OBP	SLG	AOPS	ABR	SB-CS	FA	FR	RNG	THR	GAMES AT POSITION	DL	BFW
1968	Cle A	38	94	10	20	5	1	0	3	8-0	0	22	.213	.275	.287	72	-3	2-0	.970	2	119	90	2b27,3b10/S		0.0
1969	KC A	5	7	1	2	1	0	0	0	0-0	0	1	.286	.286	.429	96	0	0-0	1.000	0	213	0	/2	53	0.0
Total	2	43	101	11	22	6	1	0	3	8-0	0	23	.218	.275	.297	74	-3	2-0	.971	2	121	88	2b28,3b10/S	53	0.0

HARRIS, JOHN John Thomas B9.13.1954 Portland OR BL/TL/6-3/205* [AnaA76 29/638] d9.26 Col Lubbock Christian

YEAR	TM LG	G	AB	R	H	2B	3B	HR	RBI	BB-IB	HP	SO	AVG	OBP	SLG	AOPS	ABR	SB-CS	FA	FR	RNG	THR	GAMES AT POSITION	DL	BFW
1979	Cal A	1	2	0	0	0	0	0	0	0-0	0	0	.000	.000	.000	-99	0	0-0	1.000	-0	0	0	/1		-0.
1980	Cal A	20	41	8	12	5	0	2	7	7-0	0	4	.293	.388	.561	161	4	0-1	1.000	-0	38	51	1b10,O3L		-0.
1981	Cal A	36	77	13	19	4	0	1	8	5-0	0	11	.247	.275	.403	92	-1	0-0	.976	-3	88	124	1b11,O10L/D		-0.
Total	3	56	120	13	31	9	0	3	15	12-0	0	15	.258	.313	.450	114	3	0-1	.987	-3	61	85	1b22,O13L/D		-0.

HARRIS, JOE Joseph "Moon" B5.20.1891 Plum Borough PA D12.10.1959 Renton PA BR/TR/5-9/170 d6.9 Mil 1918

YEAR	TM LG	G	AB	R	H	2B	3B	HR	RBI	BB-IB	HP	SO	AVG	OBP	SLG	AOPS	ABR	SB-CS	FA	FR	RNG	THR	GAMES AT POSITION	DL	BFW
1914	NY A	2	1	0	0	0	0	0	0	0-0	1	1	.000	.800	.000	143	1	0	1.000	-0	0	0	/1OL		2.
1917	Cle A	112	369	40	112	22	4	0	65	55	3	32	.304	.398	.385	129	16	11	.985	9	144	107	1b95,O5R,3b2		2.
1919	Cle A	62	184	30	69	16	1	1	46	33	1	21	.375	.472	.489	160	18	2	.988	2	122	92	1b46,S4		2.

YEAR	TM LG	G	AB	R	H	2B	3B	HR	RBI	BB-IB	HP	SO	AVG	OBP	SLG	AOPS	ABR	SB-CS	FA	FR	RNG	THR	GAMES AT POSITION	DL	BFW
1922	Bos A	119	408	53	129	30	9	6	54	30	1	15	.316	.364	.478	119	10	2-6	.953	6	102	139	O83(71/0/12),1b21		0.6
1923	Bos A	142	483	82	162	28	11	13	76	52	5	27	.335	.406	.520	142	29	7-3	.968	-1	106	71	O132L,1b9		1.7
1924	Bos A	133	491	82	148	36	9	3	77	81	5	25	.301	.406	.430	115	15	6-1	.993	5	111	104	1b128,O3L		1.2
1925	Bos A	8	19	4	3	0	1	1	2	5	0	5	.158	.333	.421	90	0	0-0	1.000	-1	31	48	1b6		-0.1
	†Was A	100	300	60	97	21	9	12	59	51	5	28	.323	.430	.573	156	27	6-3	.989	4	121	106	1b58,O41(16/0/25)		2.3
	Year	108	319	64	100	21	10	13	61	56	5	33	.313	.424	.564	152	26	6-3	.990	3	113	101	1b64,O41(16/0/25)		2.2
1926	Was A	92	257	43	79	13	9	5	55	37	5	9	.307	.405	.486	135	14	2-3	.994	-0	84	80	1b36,O35(3/0/32)		0.8
1927	†Pit N	129	411	57	134	27	9	5	73	48	4	19	.326	.402	.472	125	16	0	.990	2	105	96	1b116,O3L		1.0
1928	Pit N	16	23	2	9	2	1	0	2	4	1	2	.391	.500	.565	171	3	0	1.000	1	218	206	1b6		0.4
	Bro N	55	89	8	21	6	1	1	8	14	0	4	.236	.340	.360	84	-2	0	.958	-1	76	164	O16(6/0/10)		-0.3
	Year	71	112	10	30	8	2	1	10	18	1	6	.268	.374	.402	103	1	0	.958	1	76	164	O16(6/0/10),1b6		0.1
Total	10	970	3035	461	963	201	64	47	517	413	31	188	.317	.404	.472	131	147	36-16	.989	28	117	100	1b522,O319(235/0/84),S4,3b2		12.2

HARRIS, LENNY Leonard Anthony B10.28.1964 Miami FL BL/TR/5-10/205(195-235) [CinN83 5/108] d9.7 Col Miami-Dade North (FL) CC OF(157/3/161)

YEAR	TM LG	G	AB	R	H	2B	3B	HR	RBI	BB-IB	HP	SO	AVG	OBP	SLG	AOPS	ABR	SB-CS	FA	FR	RNG	THR	GAMES AT POSITION	DL	BFW
1988	Cin N	16	43	7	16	1	0	0	8	5-0	0	4	.372	.420	.395	136	2	4-1	1.000	1	127	0	3b10,2b6		0.4
1989	Cin N	61	188	17	42	4	0	2	11	9-0	1	20	.223	.263	.277	53	-12	10-6	.980	5	91	112	2b32,S17,3b16		-0.6
	LA N	54	147	19	37	6	1	1	15	11-0	1	13	.252	.308	.327	83	-3	4-3	1.000	-5	76	94	O21(20/0/1),2b14,3b8/S		-1.0
	Year	115	335	36	79	10	1	3	26	20-0	2	33	.236	.283	.299	66	-16	14-9	.975	-1	87	115	2b46,3b24,O21(20/0/1),S18		-1.6
1990	LA N	137	431	61	131	16	4	2	29	29-2	1	31	.304	.348	.374	101	0	15-10	.959	-0	101	109	2b46,3b24,O2(0/1/1)/S		0.1
1991	LA N	145	429	59	123	16	1	3	38	37-5	5	32	.287	.349	.350	99	0	12-3	.943	7	95	116	3b94,2b44,S20/OL		1.1
1992	LA N	135	347	28	94	11	0	0	30	24-3	1	24	.271	.318	.303	78	-0	19-7	.963	17	108	99	2b81,3b33,O15(7/0/8),S10		1.1
1993	LA N	107	160	20	38	6	1	2	11	15-4	0	15	.237	.305	.325	72	-7	3-1	.987	-0	107	65	3b35,3b17,S3,O2R		1.1
1994	Cin N	66	100	13	31	3	1	0	14	5-0	0	13	.310	.340	.360	84	-3	7-2	.846	1	128	132	3b15,1b4,O3R,2b2		-0.5
1995	†Cin N	101	197	32	41	8	3	2	16	14-0	0	20	.208	.259	.310	49	-15	10-1	.939	7	145	114	3b24,1b23,O8(4/0/4)/2		-0.1
1996	Cin N	125	302	33	86	17	2	5	32	21-1	1	31	.285	.330	.404	92	-4	14-6	1.000	3	102	138	O37(23/1/18),3b24,1b16,2b8		-0.8
1997	Cin N	120	238	32	65	13	1	3	28	18-1	2	18	.273	.327	.374	82	-6	4-3	.977	-2	88	58	O42(26/0/17),2b20,3b13,1b11		-0.2
1998	Cin N	57	122	12	36	8	0	0	10	8-2	1	9	.295	.338	.361	85	-2	1-3	.929	0	100	153	O32(13/0/20)/P		-0.9
	NY N	75	168	18	39	7	0	6	17	9-1	1	12	.232	.272	.381	73	-8	5-2	.988	2	112	119	O65(21/1/53),3b10,2b2/1D		-0.4
	Year	132	290	30	75	15	0	6	27	17-3	2	21	.259	.300	.372	78	-10	6-5	.968	2	108	131	O97(34/1/73),3b10,2b2/P1D		-0.7
1999	Col N	91	158	15	47	12	0	0	13	6-0	0	6	.297	.323	.373	60	-9	1-1	.924	5	114	157	2b24,O14(3/0/11),3b2,D2		-1.1
	†Ari N	19	29	2	11	1	0	1	7	0-0	0	1	.379	.367	.517	123	1	1-0	1.000	-0	65	352	3b5,O2R		-0.3
	Year	110	187	17	58	13	0	1	20	6-0	0	7	.310	.330	.396	68	-8	2-1	.924	5	114	157	2b24,O16(3/0/13),3b7,D2		0.1
2000	Ari N	36	85	9	16	1	1	1	13	3-1	0	5	.188	.209	.259	18	-11	5-0	.909	-3	80	33	3b20,O3R		-1.3
	†NY N	76	138	22	42	6	3	3	13	17-1	0	17	.304	.381	.457	117	3	8-1	.854	1	100	57	3b16,O11(6/0/5),1b10,2b3/D		0.5
	Year	112	223	31	58	7	4	4	26	20-2	0	22	.260	.317	.381	78	-8	13-1	.880	-2	88	57	3b36,O14(6/0/8),1b10,2b3/D		-0.8
2001	NY N	110	135	12	30	5	1	0	9	8-0	0	9	.222	.266	.274	43	-12	3-2	.875	-2	55	0	3b11,O8(5/0/3),1b7/2D		-1.4
2002	Mil N	122	197	23	60	8	2	3	17	14-1	2	19	.305	.355	.411	106	0	4-1	1.000	0	112	0	O16L,3b14,1b12,D2		0.0
2003	Chi N	75	131	11	24	3	0	1	7	13-3	0	20	.183	.255	.229	27	-14	1-0	.948	-1	90	86	3b14,1b12,D2		-1.5
	†Fla N	13	14	3	4	0	0	0	1	3-0	0	2	.286	.412	.286	90	0	0	1.000	0	130	0	O4(2/0/2)		-1.5
	Year	88	145	14	28	3	0	1	8	16-3	0	21	.193	.272	.234	34	-14	1-0	.948	-1	90	86	3b35,O6(3/0/3),1b2		-1.5
2004	Fla N	79	95	7	20	5	0	1	17	3-0	0	8	.211	.232	.295	38	-9	0-0	1.000	-1	91	0	O14(8/0/6),3b3,D2		-1.0
2005	Fla N	83	70	5	22	4	0	1	13	7-1	1	11	.314	.385	.414	116	2	0-1	—	-0	0	0	3b2,O2(1/0/1)/1D		0.1
Total	18	1903	3924	460	1055	161	21	37	369	279-26	17	337	.269	.318	.349	80	-117	131-54	.937	32	99	103	3b485,O304R,2b300,1b87,S52,D12/P		-7.3

HARRIS, NED Robert Ned B7.9.1916 Ames IA D12.18.1976 W.Palm Beach FL BL/TL/5-11/175 d4.20 Mil 1944-45 Col Brewton-Parker

YEAR	TM LG	G	AB	R	H	2B	3B	HR	RBI	BB-IB	HP	SO	AVG	OBP	SLG	AOPS	ABR	SB-CS	FA	FR	RNG	THR	GAMES AT POSITION	DL	BFW
1941	Det A	26	61	11	13	3	1	1	4	6	0	13	.213	.284	.344	59	-4	1-0	1.000	-1	78	0	O12L		-0.5
1942	Det A	121	398	53	108	16	10	9	45	49	0	35	.271	.351	.430	110	5	5-4	.944	-7	88	73	O104R		-0.9
1943	Det A	114	354	43	90	14	3	6	32	47	1	29	.254	.343	.362	99	0	6-8	.961	-3	96	87	O96(4/6/86)		-1.2
1946	Det A	1	1	0	0	0	0	0	0	0	0	0	.000	.000	.000	-94	-0	0-0	—	0			/H		0.0
Total	4	262	814	107	211	33	14	16	81	102	1	77	.259	.342	.393	101	1	12-12	.955	-12	91	76	O212(16/6/190)		-2.6

HARRIS, BUCKY Stanley Raymond B11.8.1896 Port Jervis NY D11.8.1977 Bethesda MD BR/TR/5-9.5/156 d8.28 M29 HF1975

YEAR	TM LG	G	AB	R	H	2B	3B	HR	RBI	BB-IB	HP	SO	AVG	OBP	SLG	AOPS	ABR	SB-CS	FA	FR	RNG	THR	GAMES AT POSITION	DL	BFW
1919	Was A	8	28	0	6	2	0	0	4	1	1	3	.214	.267	.286	56	-2	0	.925	0	100	105	2b8		-0.2
1920	Was A	136	506	76	152	26	6	1	68	41	21	36	.300	.377	.381	104	5	16-17	.958	-12	95	91	2b134		-0.7
1921	Was A	154	584	82	169	22	8	0	54	54	18	39	.289	.367	.354	89	2	29-9	.959	12	103	116	2b154		1.2
1922	Was A	154	602	95	162	24	8	2	40	52	14	38	.269	.341	.346	84	-14	25-11	.970	31	104	134	2b154		2.2
1923	Was A	145	532	60	150	21	13	2	70	50	13	29	.282	.358	.382	100	0	23-16	.961	19	103	136	2b144/S		2.1
1924	†Was A	143	544	88	146	28	9	1	58	56	7	41	.268	.344	.358	84	-13	20-10	.968	-12	86	136	2b143,M		-1.9
1925	†Was A	144	551	91	158	30	3	1	66	64	9	21	.287	.370	.358	87	-8	14-12	.970	5	94	129	2b144,M		-0.1
1926	Was A	141	537	94	152	39	9	1	63	58	9	41	.283	.363	.395	100	1	16-11	.963	-11	93	90	2b141,M		-0.6
1927	Was A	128	475	98	127	20	3	1	55	66	5	33	.267	.363	.328	81	-10	18-3	.972	2	97	94	2b128,M		-0.2
1928	Was A	99	358	34	73	11	5	0	28	27	2	26	.204	.264	.263	39	-33	5-2	.970	11	104	110	2b96/3ORM		-1.9
1929	Det A	7	11	3	1	0	0	0	0	2	0	2	.091	.231	.091	-14	-2	1-0	.900	-0	131	0	2b4/SM		-0.2
1931	Det A	4	8	1	1	1	0	0	0	1	0	1	.125	.222	.250	21	-1	0-0	1.000	-0	96	79	2b3,M		-0.1
Total	12	1263	4736	722	1297	224	64	9	506	472	99	310	.274	.352	.354	86	-85	167-91	.965	44	98	116	2b1253,S2/OR3		-0.4

HARRIS, VIC Victor Lanier B3.27.1950 Los Angeles CA BB/TR/6-0/170* [OakA70*S1/9] d7.21 Col Los Angeles Valley (CA) JC

YEAR	TM LG	G	AB	R	H	2B	3B	HR	RBI	BB-IB	HP	SO	AVG	OBP	SLG	AOPS	ABR	SB-CS	FA	FR	RNG	THR	GAMES AT POSITION	DL	BFW
1972	Tex A	61	186	8	26	5	1	0	6	12-1	0	39	.140	.192	.177	11	-21	7-3	.960	-9	91	76	2b58/S		-3.1
1973	Tex A	152	555	71	138	14	7	8	44	55-1	2	81	.249	.317	.342	89	-9	13-12	.977	-4	108	63	O113(2/111/7),3b25,2b18		-1.7
1974	Chi N	62	200	18	39	6	3	0	11	29-3	0	26	.195	.294	.255	53	-12	9-3	.943	-9	92	54	2b56		-1.8
1975	Chi N	51	56	6	10	0	0	0	5	6-0	0	7	.179	.254	.179	22	-6	0-0	.900	-0	76	0	O11(9/2/0),3b7,2b5	88	-0.7
1976	StL N	97	259	21	59	12	3	1	19	16-0	1	55	.228	.275	.309	64	-13	1-2	.945	-1	99	104	2b37,O35(9/25/1),3b12/S		-1.3
1977	SF N	69	165	28	43	12	0	2	14	19-1	0	36	.261	.332	.370	89	-2	2-1	.973	-6	88	104	2b27,S11,3b9,O3(0/2/1)		-0.6
1978	SF N	53	100	8	15	4	0	1	11	11-1	0	24	.150	.230	.220	28	-10	0-0	.934	-4	96	59	S22,2b10,O6(4/2/1)		-1.3
1980	Mil A	34	89	8	19	4	1	1	7	12-0	0	13	.213	.304	.315	72	-3	4-1	.967	-1	106	52	O31(4/5/22),3b2/2		-0.5
Total	8	579	1610	168	349	57	15	13	121	160-7	3	281	.217	.287	.295	65	-76	36-22	.954	-33	93	77	2b212,O199(28/147/32),3b55,S35	88	-11.0

HARRIS, WILLIE William Charles B6.22.1978 Cairo GA BL/TR/5-9/175* [BalA99 24/727] d9.2 Col Kennesaw St.

YEAR	TM LG	G	AB	R	H	2B	3B	HR	RBI	BB-IB	HP	SO	AVG	OBP	SLG	AOPS	ABR	SB-CS	FA	FR	RNG	THR	GAMES AT POSITION	DL	BFW
2001	Bal A	9	24	3	3	1	0	0	0	0-0	0	7	.125	.125	.167	-25	-4	0-0	1.000	1	97	271	O8C		-0.4
2002	Chi A	49	163	14	38	4	0	2	12	9-0	0	21	.233	.270	.294	49	-12	8-0	.985	5	100	90	2b38,O6C		-0.4
2003	Chi A	79	137	19	28	3	1	0	5	10-0	0	28	.204	.259	.241	32	-14	12-2	.977	3	110	229	O61C,2b12		-0.8
2004	Chi A	129	409	68	107	15	2	2	27	51-0	1	79	.262	.343	.323	73	-15	19-7	.990	4	103	95	2b92,O30(1/29/0),D2	25	-0.5
2005	†Chi A	56	121	17	31	2	1	1	8	13-0	1	25	.256	.333	.314	71	-5	10-3	.986	-2	94	116	2b32,S5,D9		-0.4
Total	5	322	854	121	207	25	4	5	52	83-0	2	160	.242	.309	.299	59	-50	49-12	.988	10	101	98	2b174,O105(1/104/0),D11,S5	25	-2.5

HARRISON, CHUCK Charles William B4.25.1941 Abilene TX BR/TR/5-10/190* d9.15 Col Texas Tech

YEAR	TM LG	G	AB	R	H	2B	3B	HR	RBI	BB-IB	HP	SO	AVG	OBP	SLG	AOPS	ABR	SB-CS	FA	FR	RNG	THR	GAMES AT POSITION	DL	BFW
1965	Hou N	15	45	2	9	4	0	1	9	8-0	0	9	.200	.321	.356	97	0	0-0	.983	-0	94	96	1b12		-0.1
1966	Hou N	119	434	52	111	23	2	9	52	37-4	2	69	.256	.316	.380	100	0	2-0	.992	3	105	74	1b114		-0.4
1967	Hou N	70	177	13	43	7	3	2	26	13-0	0	30	.243	.292	.350	87	-4	0-0	.987	-1	95	61	1b59		-0.8
1969	KC A	75	213	18	47	5	1	3	18	16-2	1	20	.221	.276	.296	60	-12	1-2	.993	1	104	64	1b55		-1.7
1971	KC A	49	143	9	31	4	0	2	21	11-2	0	19	.217	.266	.287	59	-8	0-0	.992	-0	99	100	1b39		-1.2
Total	5	328	1012	94	241	43	6	17	126	85-8	3	147	.238	.297	.343	83	-24	3-2	.991	2	102	74	1b279		-4.2

HARRISON, BEN Ben d9.27

YEAR	TM LG	G	AB	R	H	2B	3B	HR	RBI	BB-IB	HP	SO	AVG	OBP	SLG	AOPS	ABR	SB-CS	FA	FR	RNG	THR	GAMES AT POSITION	DL	BFW
1901	Was A	1	2	0	0	0	0	0	0	0	1	0	.000	.333	.000	-2	-0	0	—	-0	0	0	/OL		0.0

HARRISON, RIT Washington Ritter B9.16.1849 Waterbury CT D11.7.1888 Bridgeport CT d5.20

YEAR	TM LG	G	AB	R	H	2B	3B	HR	RBI	BB-IB	HP	SO	AVG	OBP	SLG	AOPS	ABR	SB-CS	FA	FR	RNG	THR	GAMES AT POSITION	DL	BFW
1875	NH NA	1	4	0	2	1	0	0	0	0	0	0	.500	.500	.750	376	1	0-1	.333	-2			/CS		-0.1

HARSHANEY, SAM Samuel B4.24.1910 Madison IL D2.1.2001 San Antonio TX BR/TR/6-0/180 d9.28

YEAR	TM LG	G	AB	R	H	2B	3B	HR	RBI	BB-IB	HP	SO	AVG	OBP	SLG	AOPS	ABR	SB-CS	FA	FR	RNG	THR	GAMES AT POSITION	DL	BFW
1937	StL A	5	11	0	1	1	0	0	0	3	0	3	.091	.286	.182	20	-1	0-0	.905	-0	94	181	C4		-0.1
1938	StL A	11	24	2	7	0	0	0	3	0	0	2	.292	.370	.292	68	-1	0-0	.975	-3	78	109	C10		-0.1
1939	StL A	42	145	15	35	2	0	0	15	9	1	8	.241	.290	.255	40	-13	0-1	.994	-3	78	135	C36		-1.4
1940	StL A	3	1	0	0	0	0	0	0	1	0	0	.000	.000	.000	41	0	0-0	—	0	0	0	C2		0.0
Total	4	61	181	17	43	3	0	0	15	16	1	10	.238	.303	.254	43	-15	0-1	.983	-4	79	135	C52		-1.6

YEAR	TM LG	G	AB	R	H	2B	3B	HR	RBI	BB-IB	HP	SO	AVG	OBP	SLG	AOPS	ABR	SB-CS	FA	FR	RNG	THR	GAMES AT POSITION	DL	BFW
HART, BO	Bodhi J. B9.27.1976 Creswell OR BR/TR/5-11/170* [StLN99 33/1002] d6.19 Col Gonzaga																								-1.3
2003	StL N	77	296	46	82	13	5	4	28	12-0	6	64	.277	.317	.395	86	-7	3-1	.989	-9	90	78	2b69,S3		-0.1
2004	StL N	11	13	0	2	0	0	0	2	1-0	0	3	.154	.214	.154	-2	-2	0-0	1.000	1	112	255	2b4/S		-0.1
Total	2	88	309	46	84	13	5	4	30	13-0	6	67	.272	.313	.385	82	-9	3-1	.989	-8	91	85	2b73,S4		-1.4
HART, BURT	James Burton B6.28.1870 Brown Co. MN D1.29.1921 Sacramento CA BB/6-3/200 d6.6																								-0.6
1901	Bal A	58	206	33	64	3	5	0	23	20	4		.311	.383	.374	106	2	7	.976	-8	.30	83	1b58		
HART, HUB	James Henry B2.2.1878 Everett MA D10.10.1960 Fort Wayne IN BL/TR/5-11/170 d7.16 Col Georgetown																								-0.3
1905	Chi A	11	20	3	2	0	0	0	4	3	0		.100	.217	.100	2	-2	0	1.000	-1	120	26	C7		-0.5
1906	Chi A	17	37	1	6	0	0	0	0	2	0		.162	.205	.162	16	-4	0	.935	-2	125	55	C15		-0.1
1907	Chi A	29	70	6	19	1	0	0	7	5	1		.271	.329	.286	100	0	1	.956	-3	110	92	C25		-0.1
Total	3	57	127	10	27	1	0	0	11	10	1		.213	.275	.220	59	-6	1	.957	-5	116	73	C47		-0.9
HART, MIKE	James Michael B12.20.1951 Kalamazoo MI BB/TR/6-3/185 [MonN72 11/245] d6.12 Col Alma																								0.0
1980	Tex A	5	4	1	1	0	0	0	1-0	0	1	.250	.400	.250	85	0	0-0	1.000	-1	33	0	O2C		0.0
HART, JIM RAY	James Ray B10.30.1941 Hookerton NC BR/TR/5-11/185* d7.7																							70	0.0
1963	SF N	7	20	4	4	1	0	0	2	3-1	2	6	.200	.360	.250	80	0	0-0	1.000	-0	74	107	3b7		2.5
1964	SF N	153	566	71	162	15	6	31	81	47-4	4	94	.286	.342	.498	132	22	5-2	.937	2	100	108	3b149,O6(1/0/5)		2.5
1965	SF N	160	591	91	177	30	6	23	96	47-3	2	75	.299	.349	.487	130	23	6-4	.919	-9	91	76	3b144,O15(14/0/1)		1.4
1966	SF N★	156	578	88	165	23	4	33	93	48-6	3	75	.285	.342	.510	130	23	2-5	.941	-2	104	98	3b139,O17(16/0/1)		1.8
1967	SF N	158	578	98	167	26	7	29	99	77-11	4	100	.289	.373	.509	153	41	1-1	.937	-13	98	75	3b89,O72L		2.5
1968	SF N	136	480	67	124	14	3	23	78	46-10	3	74	.258	.323	.444	130	16	3-1	.925	-11	80	97	O68L,3b3		0.3
1969	SF N	95	236	27	60	9	0	3	26	28-1	5	49	.254	.343	.331	91	-2	0-0	.908	-13	76	22	3b56,O18L		-0.9
1970	SF N	76	255	30	72	12	1	8	37	30-6	3	29	.282	.360	.431	113	5	0-0	.833	0	76	610	3b3,O3L	23	-0.9
1971	†SF N	31	39	5	10	0	2	2	5	6-0	1	10	.304	.356	.410	118	1	0-1	.886	-8	56	61	3b20		0.0
1972	SF N	24	79	10	24	5	0	5	8	6-0	1	9	.304	.360	.557	155	5	0-1	.600	0	269	0	/3		-0.3
1973	SF N	5	3	0	0	0	0	1	3	3-0	0	1	.000	.429	.000	48	0	0-2	—	0	0	0	D106		0.0
	NY A	114	339	29	86	13	2	13	52	36-7	0	45	.254	.324	.419	111	4	0-2	.929	-56	93	87	D4		0.1
1974	NY A	10	19	1	1	0	0	0	1	1-0	0	7	.053	.182	.053	-3	-3	0-0	—	0	0	0	D110		-0.4
Total	12	1125	3783	518	1052	148	29	170	578	380-49	28	573	.278	.345	.467	128	135	17-17	.929	-56	93	87	3b683,O264(257/0/7),D110	93	6.1
HART, JASON	Jason Wyatt B9.5.1977 Walnut Creek CA BR/TR/6-4/237* [OakA98 5/135] d8.18 Col Missouri St.																								0.0
2002	Tex A	10	15	2	4	3	0	0	2-0	0	7	.267	.353	.467	112	0	0-0	1.000	-0	97	0	O7L,1b2		0.0
HART, COREY	Jon Corey B3.24.1982 Bowling Green KY BR/TR/6-6/200* [MilN00 11/321] d5.25																								0.0
2004	Mil N	1	1	0	0	0	0	0	0-0	1	0	1.000	1.000	1.000	-99	0	0-0	—	0			/H		-0.4
2005	Mil N	21	57	9	11	2	1	2	7	6-0	0	11	.193	.270	.368	65	-3	2-0	.966	-1	84	133	O16(2/11/3)		-0.4
Total	2	22	58	9	11	2	1	2	7	6-0	0	12	.190	.266	.362	62	-3	2-0	.966	-1	84	133	O16(2/11/3)		-0.4
HART, MIKE	Michael Lawrence B2.17.1958 Milwaukee WI BL/TL/5-11/185* [SeaA79 13/313] d5.8 Col Wisconsin-Madison																								-0.3
1984	Min A	13	29	0	5	0	0	5	1-0	0	4	.172	.194	.172	4	-4	0-0	1.000	1	127	166	O11(8/0/3)		-0.6
1987	Bal A	34	76	7	12	2	0	4	12	6-0	0	19	.158	.217	.342	47	-6	1-4	1.000	1	113	0	O32(4/29/1)		0.2
Total	2	47	105	7	17	2	0	4	17	7-0	0	21	.162	.211	.295	35	-10	1-5	1.000	3	117	42	O43(12/29/4)		-0.4
HART, TOM	Thomas Henry "Bushy" B6.15.1869 Canaan NY D9.17.1939 Gardner MA 5-7/160 d4.15																								-0.2
1891	Was AA	8	24	1	3	0	0	2	2		1	.125	.192	.125	-9	-3	1	1.000	1	81	203	C5,O3C		
HART, BILL	William Woodrow B3.4.1913 Wiconisco PA D7.29.1968 Lykens PA BR/TR/6-0/175 d9.18																								0.0
1943	Bro N	8	19	3	3	0	0	1	1	0	2	.158	.200	.158	4	-2	0	1.000	2	127	112	3b6/S		-1.1
1944	Bro N	29	90	8	16	4	2	0	4	9	0	7	.178	.253	.267	47	-7	1	.941	-6	95	44	S25,3b2		-1.0
1945	Bro N	58	161	27	37	6	2	3	27	14	0	21	.230	.291	.348	78	-6	7	.913	-5	78	111	3b39,S8		-2.1
Total	3	95	270	35	56	10	4	3	32	24	0	30	.207	.272	.307	63	-15	8	.924	-9	83	111	3b47,S34		
HARTFORD, BRUCE	Bruce Daniel B5.14.1892 Chicago IL D5.25.1975 Los Angeles CA BR/TR/6-0.5/190 d6.3																								-0.
1914	Cle A	8	22	5	4	1	0	0	4	0	9	.182	.308	.227	59	-1	0	.913	-2	99	0	S8		
HARTJE, CHRIS	Christian Henry B3.25.1915 San Francisco CA D6.26.1946 Seattle WA BR/TR/5-10.5/165 d9.9																								-0.
1939	Bro N	9	16	2	5	1	0	0	5	0	0	.313	.353	.375	92	0	0	.909	-1	90	0	C8		
HARTLEY, GROVER	Grover Allen "Slick" B7.2.1888 Osgood IN D10.19.1964 Daytona Beach FL BR/TR/5-11/175 d5.13 C10																								0.2
1911	NY N	11	18	1	4	2	0	1	1	0	1	.222	.263	.333	64	-1	1	.962	2	149	84	C10		0.
1912	NY N	25	34	3	8	2	1	0	7	0	1	4	.235	.257	.353	64	-2	2	.960	2	146	75	C25		0.2
1913	NY N	23	19	4	6	0	0	0	1	0	2	.316	.350	.316	90	0	4-1	.978	2	138	54	C21/1		-1.2
1914	StL F	86	212	24	61	13	2	1	25	12	1	26	.288	.329	.382	89	-6	4	.956	-8	81	93	C32,2b13,1b9,3b3,O2C		0.
1915	StL F	120	394	47	108	21	6	1	50	42	8	21	.274	.356	.365	98	-5	10	.972	-4	102	91	C113/1		0.
1916	StL A	89	222	19	50	8	0	0	12	30		24	.225	.325	.261	80	-4	4	.875	0	102	244	C4/S3		0.
1917	StL A	19	13	2	3	0	0	0	2		1	.231	.333	.231	75	0	0	1.000	-0	112	100	C3		0.
1924	NY N	4	7	1	2	1	0	0	1		3	.286	.375	.429	118	0	1-0	1.000	-0	93	140	C37,1b8		-0.
1925	NY N	46	95	9	30	1	0	0	8	8	1	3	.316	.375	.347	89	-1	2-0	1.000	0	90	72	C13		-0.
1926	NY N	13	21	0	1	0	0	0	5		0	1	.048	.231	.048	-22	-4	0	1.000	0	94	0	C13		-1.
1927	Bos A	103	244	23	67	11	0	1	31	22	1	14	.275	.337	.332	76	-8	1-0	.967	-14	60	70	C86		0.
1929	Cle A	24	33	2	9	0	0	1	8	2	0	2	.273	.314	.333	64	-2	0-0	1.000	-1	85	0	C13		0.
1930	Cle A	1	4	0	3	0	0	0	1	0		0	.750	.750	.750	271	1	0-0	.750	-1	46	0	/C		0.
1934	StL A	5	3	0	1	1	0	0	1	1		0	.333	.500	.667	183	0	0-0	1.000	0	0	0	C2		-2.
Total	14	569	1319	135	353	60	11	3	144	127	15	97	.268	.339	.337	85	-32	29-1	.968	-23	90	86	C435,1b19,2b13,3b4,O2C/S		
HARTLEY, CHICK	Walter Scott B8.22.1880 Philadelphia PA D7.18.1948 Philadelphia PA BR/TR/5-8/180 d6.4																								-0.
1902	NY N	1	4	0	0	0	0	0		0		.000	.000	.000	-99	-0	0	1.000	-0	0	0	/OL		
HARTMAN, FRED	Frederick Orrin "Dutch" B4.25.1868 Allegheny (now part of Pittsburgh) PA D11.11.1938 McKeesport PA BR/TR/5-8/170 d7.26																								-0.
1894	Pit N	49	182	41	58	4	7	2	20	16	5	11	.319	.389	.451	103	-2	12	.876	-2	99	77	3b49		-0.
1897	StL N	125	519	60	158	21	8	2	67	26	10		.304	.350	.387	96	-4	18	.867	-1	106	83	3b125		0
1898	NY N	123	475	57	129	16	11	2	88	25	4		.272	.313	.364	97	-4	11	.882	8	107	87	3b123		0.
1899	NY N	51	177	25	42	3	5	1	17	12	10		.237	.322	.328	81	-5	2	.883	-2	94	132	3b51		0.
1901	Chi A	120	473	77	146	23	3	3	89	25	9		.309	.355	.431	120	12	31	.894	-6	98	96	3b119		0.
1902	StL N	114	416	30	90	10	3	0	52	14	5		.216	.251	.255	58	-21	14	.908	-4	102	59	3b105,S4,1b3		-1
Total	6	582	2242	297	623	77	47	10	333	118	43	11	.278	.326	.368	95	-22	88	.886	-7	102	86	3b572,S4,1b3		
HARTMAN, J C	J C B4.15.1934 Cottonton AL BR/TR/6-0/175* d7.21 Negro Lg 1952-55																								-0.
1962	Hou N	51	148	11	33	5	0	0	5	4-0	1	16	.223	.248	.257	39	-13	1-1	.972	5	97	122	S48		-1
1963	Hou N	39	90	2	11	1	0	0	3	2-1	1	13	.122	.151	.133	-19	-14	1-0	.950	0	99	104	S32		-1
Total	2	90	238	13	44	6	0	0	8	6-1	2	29	.185	.211	.210	18	-27	2-1	.964	5	98	115	S80		
HARTNETT, GABBY	Charles Leo B12.20.1900 Woonsocket RI D12.20.1972 Park Ridge IL BR/TR/6-1/195 d4.12 M3/C3 HF1955 Col Dean (MA) JC																								-0
1922	Chi N	31	72	4	14	1	1	0	4	6		8	.194	.256	.236	27	-8	1-0	.982	4	128	167	C27		-0
1923	Chi N	85	231	28	62	12	2	8	39	25	3	22	.268	.347	.442	107	2	4-0	.994	5	118	75	C39,1b31		2
1924	Chi N	111	354	56	106	17	7	16	67	39	5	37	.299	.377	.523	137	19	10-2	.963	-1	116	118	C105		2
1925	Chi N	117	398	61	115	28	3	24	67	36	2	77	.289	.351	.555	126	14	1-5	.958	10	143	124	C110		2
1926	Chi N	93	284	35	78	25	3	8	41	32	2	37	.275	.352	.468	118	8	0	.978	9	180	121	C88		2
1927	Chi N	127	449	56	132	32	5	10	80	44	2	42	.294	.361	.454	117	11	2	.973	6	163	101	C126		2
1928	Chi N	120	388	61	117	26	9	14	57	65	2	32	.302	.404	.523	143	26	3	.989	15	184	112	C118		0
1929	†Chi N	25	22	2	6	1	1	1	9	5	0		.273	.407	.591	144	2	1	1.000	0	0	0	/C		4
1930	Chi N	141	508	84	172	31	3	37	122	55	1	62	.339	.404	.630	144	35	0	.989	3	131	89	C136		2
1931	Chi N	116	380	53	107	32	1	8	70	52	1	48	.282	.371	.354	112	9	3	.981	4	120	98	C105		2
1932	†Chi N	121	406	52	110	25	3	12	52	51	1	59	.271	.354	.436	112	9	1	.982	10	194	104	C117/1		2
1933	Chi N★	140	490	55	135	21	4	16	88	37	0	51	.276	.326	.433	115	9	1	.989	11	145	95	C140		2

YEAR	TM LG	G	AB	R	H	2B	3B	HR	RBI	BB-IB	HP	SO	AVG	OBP	SLG	AOPS	ABR	SB-CS	FA	FR	RNG	THR	GAMES AT POSITION	DL	BFW
1934	Chi N★	130	438	58	131	21	1	22	90	37	3	46	.299	.358	.502	130	18	0	**.996**	11	**120**	**143**	C129		3.5
1935	†Chi N★	116	413	67	142	32	6	13	91	41	1	46	.344	.404	.545	152	31	1	.984	11	109	**135**	C110		4.7
1936	Chi N★	121	424	49	130	25	6	7	64	30	6	36	.307	.361	.443	113	8	0	**.991**	9	121	106	C114		2.2
1937	Chi N★	110	356	47	126	21	6	12	82	43	0	19	.354	.424	.548	156	28	0	**.996**	0	121	102	C103		3.4
1938	†Chi N☆	88	299	40	82	19	1	10	59	48	3	17	.274	.380	.445	123	11	1	**.995**	-0	109	80	C83,M		1.6
1939	Chi N	97	306	36	85	18	2	12	59	37	1	32	.278	.358	.467	118	8	0	.992	-3	134	90	C86,M		1.0
1940	Chi N	37	64	3	17	3	0	1	12	8	0	7	.266	.347	.359	97	0	1	.951	-0	98	84	C22/1M		0.1
1941	NY N	64	150	20	45	5	0	5	26	12	1	14	.300	.356	.433	119	3	0	.994	-1	114	68	C34		0.4
Total	20	1990	6432	867	1912	396	64	236	1179	703	35	697	.297	.370	.489	126	242	28-7	.984	106	138	108	C1793,1b33		44.3

HARTNETT, PAT   Patrick J. "Happy" B10.20.1863 Boston MA D4.10.1935 Boston MA 6-1/175 d4:18

YEAR	TM LG	G	AB	R	H	2B	3B	HR	RBI	BB-IB	HP	SO	AVG	OBP	SLG	AOPS	ABR	SB-CS	FA	FR	RNG	THR	GAMES AT POSITION	DL	BFW
1890	StL AA	14	53	6	10	2	1	0	4	6				.189	.283	.264	54	-3	1	.954	-1	89	28	1b14		-0.5

HARTS, GREG   Gregory Rudolph B4.21.1950 Atlanta GA d9.15

| 1973 | NY N | 3 | 2 | 0 | 1 | 0 | 0 | 0 | 0 | 0-0 | | | | .500 | .500 | .500 | 179 | 0 | 0-0 | — | 0 | | | /H | | 0.0 |

HARTSEL, TOPSY   Tully Frederick B6.26.1874 Polk OH D10.14.1944 Toledo OH BL/TL/5-5/155 d9.14

1898	Lou N	22	71	11	23	0	0	0	9	11	1		.324	.422	.324	116	2	2	.931	-1	78	159	O21R		0.0
1899	Lou N	30	75	8	18	1	1	1	7	11	1		.240	.345	.320	83	-1	1	.927	-1	70	135	O22(7/0/15)		-0.3
1900	Cin N	18	64	10	21	3	1	2	5	8	0		.328	.403	.484	148	4	7	.957	-4	0	O18L		0.0
1901	Chi N	140	558	111	187	25	16	7	54	74	1		.335	.414	.475	163	48	41	.951	-2	88	63	O140(131/0/9)		3.6
1902	Phi A	**137**	545	**109**	154	20	12	5	58	**87**	2		.283	.383	.391	110	11	**47**	.955	-1	100	55	O137L		0.1
1903	Phi A	98	373	65	116	19	14	5	26	49			.311	.391	.477	152	5	13	.968	-4	59	0	O96(94/2/0)		1.7
1904	Phi A	147	534	79	135	17	12	2	25	75	2		.253	.347	.341	112	10	19	.959	-3	94	50	O147(122/25/0)		-0.1
1905	†Phi A	150	538	88	148	22	8	0	28	**121**	1		.275	**.409**	.346	138	33	37	.939	-9	35	27	O149(134/15/0)		1.6
1906	Phi A	144	533	96	136	21	9	1	30	**88**	2		.255	.363	.334	115	14	31	.969	1	82	127	O144L		0.7
1907	Phi A	143	507	93	142	23	6	3	29	**106**	0		.280	**.405**	.367	143	33	20	.967	-11	60	50	O143L		1.5
1908	Phi A	129	460	73	112	16	6	4	29	**93**			.243	.371	.330	120	16	15	.960	-4	41	50	O129L		0.6
1909	Phi A	83	267	30	72	4	4	1	18	48	0		.270	.381	.326	121	9	3	.966	-3	0	O74(72/0/2)		0.2
1910	†Phi A	90	285	45	63	10	3	0	22	58	0		.221	.353	.277	99	3	11	.945	-2	94	86	O83L		-0.3
1911	Phi A	25	38	8	9	2	0	0	1	8	2		.237	.396	.289	94	1	0	.941	1	92	248	O9L		0.1
Total	14	1356	4848	826	1336	182	92	31	341	837	12		.276	.384	.370	128	208	247	.956	-42	67	57	O1312(1223/42/47)		9.4

HARTSFIELD, ROY   Roy Thomas "Spec" B10.25.1925 Chattahoochee GA BR/TR/5-9/165* d4.28 M3/C5

1950	Bos N	107	419	62	116	15	2	7	24	27	1	61	.277	.322	.372	88	-9	7	.949	-18	93	73	2b96		-2.1
1951	Bos N	120	450	63	122	11	2	6	31	41	1	73	.271	.333	.344	89	-7	7-2	.969	-5	92	97	2b114		-0.6
1952	Bos N	38	107	13	28	4	3	0	4	5	0	12	.262	.295	.355	82	-3	0-0	.950	-3	94	54	2b29		-0.8
Total	3	265	976	138	266	30	7	13	59	73	2	146	.273	.324	.358	88	-19	14-2	.959	-28	93	82	2b239		-3.5

HARTUNG, CLINT   Clinton Clarence "Floppy","The Hondo Hurricane" B8.10.1922 Hondo TX BR/TR/6-4/215(200-215) d4.15 ▲

1947	NY N	34	94	13	29	4	4	4	13	3		21	.309	.330	.543	127	3	0	1.000	-2	85	126	P23,O7L		-0.1
1948	NY N	43	56	5	10	1	1	0	3	7		24	.179	.270	.232	37	-5	0	1.000	-0	102	60	P36		0.0
1949	NY N	38	63	7	12	0	0	4	7	4		21	.190	.239	.381	64	4	0	.957	2	130	55	P33		0.0
1950	NY N	32	43	7	13	2	1	3	10	1		13	.302	.318	.605	136	2	0	.939	-2	197	0	P20,O2(1/0/1)/1		0.1
1951	†NY N	21	44	4	9	1	0	0	2	1	0	9	.205	.222	.227	21	-5	0-0	1.000	-0	82	157	O12R		-0.5
1952	NY N	28	78	6	17	2	1	3	8	9		24	.218	.299	.385	88	-2	0-0	.932	0	94	156	O24(3/0/22)		-0.2
Total	6	196	378	42	90	10	6	14	43	25	0	112	.238	.285	.407	84	4	0-0	.972	1	118	69	P112,O45(11/0/35)/1		-0.7

HARTZELL, ROY   Roy Allen B7.6.1881 Golden CO D11.6.1961 Golden CO BL/TR/5-8.5/155 d4.17 OF(213/32/307)

1906	StL A	113	404	43	86	7	0	0	24	19	10		.213	.266	.230	58	-19	21	.889	-3	**101**	**122**	3b103,S6,2b2		-2.2
1907	StL A	60	220	20	52	3	5	0	13	11	4		.236	.285	.295	85	-4	7	.911	-1	96	130	3b38,2b12,S2,O2R		-0.4
1908	StL A	115	422	41	112	5	6	2	32	19	3		.265	.302	.320	101	-1	24	.943	-2	164	208	O82(0/4/78),S18,3b7,2b4		-0.7
1909	StL A	152	595	64	161	12	5	0	32	29	7		.271	.312	.308	103	0	14	.940	6	188	193	O85R,S65/2		0.5
1910	StL A	151	542	52	118	13	5	2	30	49	6		.218	.290	.271	81	-12	18	.929	7	107	132	3b89,S38,O23R		-0.2
1911	NY A	144	527	67	156	17	11	3	91	63	4		.296	.375	.387	106	5	22	.936	-12	87	103	3b124,S12,O8(2/0/8)		-0.3
1912	NY A	125	416	50	113	10	11	1	38	64	1		.272	.370	.356	102	2	20	.906	-2	91	50	3b56,O56(0/13/43),S10,2b2		0.0
1913	NY A	141	490	60	127	18	1	0	38	67	4	40	.259	.353	.300	91	-2	26	.942	3	101	100	2b81,O31(4/11/16),3b21,S4		0.2
1914	NY A	137	481	55	112	15	9	1	32	68	6	38	.233	.335	.308	94	-2	22-25	.973	-4	100	80	O128(91/3/34),2b5		-1.6
1915	NY A	119	387	39	97	11	2	3	60	57	3	37	.251	.351	.313	99	2	7-19	.963	-4	96	72	O107(105/0/2),2b5,3b2		-1.3
1916	NY A	33	64	12	12	1	0	0	7	9	1	3	.188	.297	.203	49	-4	1	1.000	-1	95	50	O18(11/1/16)		-0.6
Total	11	1293	4548	503	1146	112	55	12	393	455	49	118	.252	.327	.309	93	-35	182-44	.959	-10	123	126	O550R,3b440,S155,2b112		-6.6

HARVEL, LUTHER   Luther Raymond "Red" B9.30.1905 Cambria IL D4.10.1986 Kansas City MO BR/TR/5-11/180 d7.31

| 1928 | Cle A | 40 | 136 | 12 | 30 | 6 | 1 | 0 | 12 | 4 | 4 | 17 | .221 | .264 | .279 | 42 | -12 | 1-1 | .948 | -1 | 92 | 153 | O39C | | -1.4 |

HARVEY, ZAZA   Ervin King B1.5.1879 Saratoga CA D6.3.1954 Santa Monica CA BL/TL/6-0/190 d5.3 ▲

1900	Chi N	2	3	0	0	0	0	0	0	0			.000	.000	.000	-99	-1	0	1.000	-0	0	0	/P		0.0
1901	Chi N	17	40	11	10	3	1	0	3	2	1		.250	.302	.375	89	2	1	.930	-2	133	248	P16		0.0
	Cle A	45	170	21	60	5	5	1	24	9	2		.353	.392	.459	141	9	15	.890	2	121	276	O45(21/0/24)		0.8
	Year	62	210	32	70	8	6	1	27	11	3		.333	.375	.443	131	8	16	.890	2	121	276	O45(21/0/24),P16		0.8
1902	Cle A	12	46	5	16	2	0	0	5	3	0		.348	.388	.391	121	1	1	1.000	1	136	340	O12R		0.1
Total	3	76	259	37	86	10	6	1	32	14	3		.332	.373	.429	127	11	17	.907	4	124	289	O57(21/0/36),P17		0.9

HARVEY, KEN   Kenneth Eugene B3.1.1978 Los Angeles CA BR/TR/6-2/240* [KCA99 5/151] d9.18 Col Nebraska

2001	KC A	4	12	1	3	1	0	0	4	0-0		4	.250	.250	.333	47	-1	0-1	1.000	-0	72	60	1b3/D		-0.2
2003	KC A	135	485	50	129	30	0	13	64	29-4	5	94	.266	.313	.408	83	-12	2-3	.988	6	132	94	1b99,D32		-1.6
2004	KC A★	120	456	47	131	20	4	13	55	28-2	6	89	.287	.338	.421	97	-3	1-1	.994	5	125	114	1b73,D41,O4L	15	-0.8
2005	KC A	12	45	4	10	3	0	1	5	3-0	0	13	.222	.271	.356	69	-2	0-0	1.000	-1	0	47	1b5,D7	137	-0.2
Total	4	271	998	102	273	54	1	27	126	60-6	13	200	.274	.322	.411	88	-18	3-5	.991	8	125	101	1b180,D81,O4L	152	-2.9

HASBROOK, ZIGGY   Robert Lyndon "Ziggy" (b Robert Lyndon Hasbrouck) B11.21.1893 Grundy Center IA D2.9.1976 Garland TX BR/TR/6-1/180 d9.6

1916	Chi A	9	8	1	1	0	0	0	0	2			.125	.222	.125	4	-1	0	1.000	1	234	93	1b7		0.0
1917	Chi A	2	1	1	0	0	0	0	0	0			.000	.000	.000	-98	-0	0	1.000	1	205	763	/2		0.0
Total	2	11	9	2	1	0	0	0	0	1			.111	.200	.111	-6	-1	0	1.000	1	234	93	1b7/2		0.0

HASELMAN, BILL   William Joseph B5.25.1966 Long Branch NJ BR/TR/6-3/223(205-223) [TexA87 1/23] d9.3 C1 Col UCLA [DL 1992 Tex A 28]

1990	Tex A	7	13	0	2	0	0	0	3	1-0		5	.154	.214	.154	5		0-0	1.000	-1	0	0	/CD		-0.1
1992	Sea A	8	19	1	5	0	0	0	0	0-0		7	.263	.263	.263	47	-1	0-0	1.000	-1	280	142	C5,O2L		-0.2
1993	Sea A	58	137	21	35	8	0	5	16	12-0	1	19	.255	.316	.423	96	-1	2-1	.992	-3	67	77	C49,O2R,D4		-0.1
1994	Sea A	38	83	11	16	7	1	1	8	3-0	1	11	.193	.230	.337	43	-7	1-0	.982	-3	72	113	C33,O2R,D3		-0.8
1995	†Bos A	64	152	22	37	6	1	5	23	17-0	2	30	.243	.322	.395	84	-4	0-2	.989	4	103	101	C48,D11/13		0.2
1996	Bos A	77	237	33	65	13	1	8	34	19-3	1	52	.274	.331	.439	91	-4	4-2	.994	9	91	92	C69,1b2,D2		0.9
1997	Bos A	67	212	22	50	15	0	6	26	15-2	2	44	.236	.290	.392	75	-8	0-2	.983	-4	66	113	C66		-0.8
1998	Tex A	40	105	11	33	6	0	5	17	3-0	0	17	.314	.327	.543	116	2	0-0	.995	-2	75	68	C36,D2	39	0.1
1999	Det A	48	143	13	39	8	0	4	14	10-1	0	26	.273	.320	.413	84	-4	2-0	.996	-1	113	83	C39,D9		-0.2
2000	Tex A	62	193	23	53	18	0	6	26	15-0	1	36	.275	.329	.461	98	-1	0-1	.989	-1	95	95	C62		0.1
2001	Tex A	47	130	12	37	6	0	3	18	11-0	1	27	.285	.331	.400	89	-2	0-1	1.000	-6	82	128	C47		-0.6
2002	Tex A	69	179	16	44	7	0	3	18	11-1	2	25	.246	.297	.335	66	-9	0-0	.991	-1	87	76	C67,D2	82	-1.6
2003	Bos A	1	0	0	0	0	0	0	0	0		1	.000	.000	.000	-96	-1	0	1.000	-0	0	13	C2,D2		-0.1
Total	13	589	1606	185	416	94	3	47	210	114-7	11	300	.259	.311	.409	83	-42	9-9	.991	-17	87	95	C524,D38,O6(2/0/4),1b3/3	149	-3.2

HASENMAYER, DON   Donald Irvin B4.4.1927 Roslyn PA BR/TR/5-10.5/180 d5.2 Mil 1945

1945	Phi N	5	18	1	2	0	0	0	0	1		4	.111	.200	.111	-13	-3	0	.920	1	130	40	2b4/3		-0.1
1946	Phi N	6	12	0	1	0	0	0	0	0		2	.083	.083	.167	-31	-2	0	1.000	1	128	449	3b3		-0.1
Total	2	11	30	1	3	0	0	0	0	1		6	.100	.156	.133	-19	-5	0	1.000	3	142	295	3b4,2b4		-0.2

YEAR	TM LG	G	AB	R	H	2B	3B	HR	RBI	BB-IB	HP	SO	AVG	OBP	SLG	AOPS	ABR	SB-CS	FA	FR	RNG	THR	GAMES AT POSITION	DL	BFW

HASLIN, MICKEY Michael Joseph (b Michael Joseph Haslinsky) B10.25.1909 Wilkes-Barre PA D3.7.2002 Wilkes-Barre PA BR/TR/5-8/165 d9.7

YEAR	TM LG	G	AB	R	H	2B	3B	HR	RBI	BB-IB	HP	SO	AVG	OBP	SLG	AOPS	ABR	SB-CS	FA	FR	RNG	THR	GAMES AT POSITION	DL	BFW
1933	Phi N	26	89	3	21	2	0	0	9	3	0	5	.236	.261	.258	43	-6	1	.956	-2	104	76	2b26		-0.8
1934	Phi N	72	166	28	44	8	2	1	11	16	0	13	.265	.330	.355	74	-6	1	.941	-3	100	115	3b26,2b21,S4		-0.7
1935	Phi N	110	407	53	108	17	3	3	52	19	1	25	.265	.300	.344	66	-20	5	.931	-2	96	98	S87,3b11,2b9		-1.4
1936	Phi N	16	64	6	22	1	1	0	6	3	0	5	.344	.373	.391	96	0	0	.938	-3	97	93	2b12,3b5		-0.3
	Bos N	36	104	14	29	1	2	2	11	5	0	9	.279	.312	.385	93	-2	0	.892	-3	65	0	3b17,2b7		-0.4
	Year	52	168	20	51	2	3	2	17	8	0	14	.304	.335	.387	95	-2	0	.854	-6	71	40	3b22,2b19		-0.7
1937	NY N	27	42	8	8	1	0	0	5	9	0	3	.190	.333	.214	51	-2	1	.920	5	148	96	S9,2b4,3b4		0.3
1938	NY N	31	102	13	33	3	0	3	15	4	2	4	.324	.361	.441	119	2	0	.902	-1	117	0	3b15,2b13		-3.0
Total 6		318	974	125	265	33	8	9	109	59	3	64	.272	.316	.350	74	-34	8	.927	-9	100	99	S100,2b92,3b78		-3.0

HASNEY, PETE Peter James B5.26.1865 , England D5.24.1908 Philadelphia PA d9.13

YEAR	TM LG	G	AB	R	H	2B	3B	HR	RBI	BB-IB	HP	SO	AVG	OBP	SLG	AOPS	ABR	SB-CS	FA	FR	RNG	THR	GAMES AT POSITION	DL	BFW
1890	Phi AA	2	7	1	1	0	0	0	1	0		0	.143	.250	.143	16	-1	0	.000	-1	0	0	O2R		-0.2

HASSAMAER, BILL William Louis "Roaring Bill" B7.26.1864 St.Louis MO D5.29.1910 St.Louis MO 6-0/180 d4.19 OF(3/0/140)

YEAR	TM LG	G	AB	R	H	2B	3B	HR	RBI	BB-IB	HP	SO	AVG	OBP	SLG	AOPS	ABR	SB-CS	FA	FR	RNG	THR	GAMES AT POSITION	DL	BFW
1894	Was N	118	494	106	159	33	17	4	90	41	1	20	.322	.375	.482	108	5	16	.916	3	104	144	O68(3/0/65),3b31,2b14,S4		0.5
1895	Was N	86	363	42	101	18	4	1	60	26	0	13	.278	.326	.358	77	-13	8	.964	-6	40	39	O75R,1b10/S3		-1.7
	Lou N	23	96	7	20	2	2	0	14	3	0	4	.208	.232	.271	31	-10	0	.980	3	153	86	1b21/2S		-0.6
	Year	109	459	49	121	20	6	1	74	29	0	17	.264	.307	.340	68	-23	8	.964	-3	40	39	O75R,1b31,S2/32		-2.3
1896	Lou N	30	106	8	26	5	0	2	14	14	0	7	.245	.333	.349	83	-2	1	.938	6	195	116	1b29		0.3
Total 3		257	1059	163	306	58	23	7	178	84	1	44	.289	.342	.407	89	-20	25	.938	6	71	90	O143R,1b60,3b32,2b15,S6		-1.5

HASSETT, BUDDY John Aloysius B9.5.1911 New York NY D8.23.1997 Westwood NJ BL/TL/5-11/180 d4.14 Mil 1943-46 Col Manhattan

YEAR	TM LG	G	AB	R	H	2B	3B	HR	RBI	BB-IB	HP	SO	AVG	OBP	SLG	AOPS	ABR	SB-CS	FA	FR	RNG	THR	GAMES AT POSITION	DL	BFW
1936	Bro N	156	635	79	197	29	11	3	82	35	4	17	.310	.350	.405	102	0	5	.983	5	114	71	1b156		-0.9
1937	Bro N	137	556	71	169	31	6	1	53	20	5	19	.304	.334	.387	94	-5	13	.984	10	129	92	1b131,O7(1/6/1)		-0.8
1938	Bro N	115	335	49	98	11	6	0	40	32	1	19	.293	.356	.361	95	-2	3	.945	-2	102	0	O71(71/0/2),1b8		-0.9
1939	Bro N	147	590	72	182	15	3	2	60	29	1	14	.308	.342	.354	94	-7	13	.985	10	139	116	1b123,O23R		-2.8
1940	Bos N	124	458	59	107	19	4	0	27	25	0	16	.234	.273	.293	59	-27	4	.979	9	146	119	1b98,O13R		-0.1
1941	Bos N	118	405	59	120	9	4	1	33	36	0	16	.296	.354	.346	102	1	10	.991	7	129	111	1b99		-0.8
1942	†NY A	132	538	80	153	16	6	5	48	32	1	16	.284	.325	.364	95	-6	5-5	.991	11	126	137	1b132		-0.8
Total 7		929	3517	469	1026	130	40	12	343	209	11	116	.292	.333	.362	92	-46	53-5	.985	49	130	105	1b747,O114(72/6/39)		-7.1

HASSEY, RON Ronald William B2.27.1953 Tucson AZ BL/TR/6-2/200* [CleA76 18/422] d4.23 C5 Col Arizona

YEAR	TM LG	G	AB	R	H	2B	3B	HR	RBI	BB-IB	HP	SO	AVG	OBP	SLG	AOPS	ABR	SB-CS	FA	FR	RNG	THR	GAMES AT POSITION	DL	BFW
1978	Cle A	25	74	5	15	0	0	2	9	5-0	1	7	.203	.256	.284	54	-5	2-0	.993	4	94	91	C24		0.0
1979	Cle A	75	223	20	64	14	0	4	32	19-2	1	19	.287	.339	.404	100	0	1-0	.992	3	76	82	C68,1b2/D		0.6
1980	Cle A	130	390	43	124	18	4	8	65	49-3	1	51	.318	.390	.446	129	17	0-2	.993	-9	86	114	C113,1b3,D7		1.1
1981	Cle A	61	190	8	44	4	0	1	25	17-0	2	11	.232	.297	.268	66	-8	0-1	.991	9	126	155	C56,1b5/D		0.2
1982	Cle A	113	323	33	81	18	0	5	34	53-5	1	32	.251	.356	.353	96	1	3-2	.993	1	67	116	C105,1b2,D2		0.6
1983	Cle A	117	341	48	92	21	0	6	42	38-2	2	35	.270	.342	.384	97	0	2-2	.995	2	106	95	C113/D		-0.6
1984	Cle A	48	149	11	38	5	1	0	19	15-2	1	21	.255	.321	.302	73	-5	1-0	1.000	1	108	69	C6,1b4	58	0.3
	Chi N	19	33	5	11	0	0	2	5	4-1	0	6	.333	.405	.515	145	2	0-1	1.000	-3	80	64	C69,1b2,D2		1.5
1985	NY A	92	267	31	79	16	1	13	42	28-4	3	21	.296	.369	.509	140	15	0-0	.985	-9	102	76	C51,D3		0.2
1986	NY A	64	191	23	57	14	0	6	29	24-1	1	16	.298	.381	.466	130	9	1-1	1.000	5	178	107	D34,C11		1.6
	Chi A	49	150	22	53	11	1	3	20	22-2	1	11	.353	.437	.500	150	12	0-0	.988	-4	113	81	C62,D37		1.8
	Year	113	341	45	110	25	1	9	49	46-3	2	27	.323	.406	.481	139	21	1-1	1.000	1	75	67	C24,D18	66	-0.5
1987	Chi A	49	145	15	31	9	0	3	12	17-2	2	11	.214	.303	.338	68	-6	0-0	.994	-3	134	75	C91,D9		-0.3
1988	†Oak A	107	323	32	83	15	0	7	45	30-1	4	42	.257	.323	.368	98	-1	2-0	.991	1	92	99	C78/1D		-0.3
1989	†Oak A	97	268	29	61	12	0	5	23	24-2	1	45	.228	.290	.328	77	-8	1-0	.997	5	178	63	C59,D15,1b3		-0.4
1990	†Oak A	94	254	18	54	7	0	5	22	27-3	1	29	.213	.288	.299	68	-11	0-0	.989	-6	75	74	C34		-0.8
1991	Mon N	52	119	5	27	8	0	1	14	13-1	0	16	.227	.301	.319	76	-3	1-1	.993	-3	100	93			4.3
Total 14		1192	3440	348	914	172	7	71	438	385-31	21	378	.266	.340	.382	100	9	14-10	.993	-3	100	93	C946,D96,1b23	124	4.3

HASSLER, JOE Joseph Frederick B4.7.1905 Ft.Smith AR D9.4.1971 Duncan OK BR/TR/6-0/165 d5.26

YEAR	TM LG	G	AB	R	H	2B	3B	HR	RBI	BB-IB	HP	SO	AVG	OBP	SLG	AOPS	ABR	SB-CS	FA	FR	RNG	THR	GAMES AT POSITION	DL	BFW
1928	Phi A	28	34	5	9	2	0	0	3	2	0	4	.265	.306	.324	64	-2	0-1	.879	-2	89	79	S28		-0.3
1929	Phi A	4	4	1	0	0	0	0	0	0	0	2	.000	.000	.000	-97	-1	0-0	.600	-1	82	0	S2		-0.2
1930	StL A	5	8	3	2	0	0	0	1	0	0	1	.250	.250	.250	26	-1	0-0	1.000	1	126	312	S3		0.0
Total 3		37	46	9	11	2	0	0	4	2	0	7	.239	.271	.283	43	-4	0-1	.875	-2	93	100	S33		-0.5

HASSON, GENE Charles Eugene B7.20.1915 Connellsville PA D7.30.2003 Pomona CA BL/TL/6-0/197 d9.9

YEAR	TM LG	G	AB	R	H	2B	3B	HR	RBI	BB-IB	HP	SO	AVG	OBP	SLG	AOPS	ABR	SB-CS	FA	FR	RNG	THR	GAMES AT POSITION	DL	BFW
1937	Phi A	28	98	12	30	6	3	3	14	13	0	14	.306	.387	.520	129	4	0-0	1.000	-3	51	126	1b28		-0.1
1938	Phi A	19	69	10	19	6	2	1	12	12	0	7	.275	.383	.464	114	2	0-0	.958	-2	51	100	1b19		-0.3
Total 2		47	167	22	49	12	5	4	26	25	0	21	.293	.385	.497	123	6	0-0	.985	-6	51	116	1b47		-0.4

HASTINGS, SCOTT Winfield Scott B8.10.1847 Hillsboro OH D8.14.1907 Sawtelle (now part of Los Angeles) CA BR/TR/5-8/161 d5.6 M2

YEAR	TM LG	G	AB	R	H	2B	3B	HR	RBI	BB-IB	HP	SO	AVG	OBP	SLG	AOPS	ABR	SB-CS	FA	FR	RNG	THR	GAMES AT POSITION	DL	BFW
1871	Rok NA	25	118	27	30	6	4	0	20	2		2	.254	.267	.373	85	-2	11-2	.856	-1			C23,2b2,O2(2/1/0)/1M		0.0
1872	Cle NA	22	115	34	45	4	0	0	16	3		2	.391	.407	.426	165	10	5-1	.797	-7			C12,O8(0/3/5),2b6,M		0.2
	Bal NA	13	62	16	19	3	1	0	4	1		2	.306	.317	.387	111	0	0-1	.905	-3			C13,2b2/OC		0.2
	Year	35	177	50	64	7	1	0	20	4		1	.362	.376	.412	145	10	5-2	.854	-4			C19,O12C/2		0.4
1873	Bal NA	30	145	41	41	4	0	0	30	4		1	.283	.302	.310	83	-3	4-2	.901	0			C39,O26(0/12/14)/2S		-0.2
1874	Har NA	52	247	60	80	11	2	0	30	4		1	.324	.334	.385	124	6	10-5	.753	-10			C46,O29(1/15/15),2b3		-0.3
1875	Chi N	65	287	43	73	9	0	0	30	9		14	.254	.277	.286	95	-1	13-11	.815	-4			C20/OC		0.3
1876	Lou N	67	283	36	73	6	1	0	21	5		11	.258	.271	.286	73	-10		.872	-9	102	203	O65C,C5		-1.9
1877	Cin N	20	71	7	10	1	0	0	3	3		6	.141	.176	.155	6	-7		.791	-7			C20/OC		-1.3
Total 5 NA		207	974	221	288	37	7	0	115	23		26	.296	.312	.348	108	10	43-22	.824	-10			C152,O78(3/44/34),2b15/S1		0.2
Total 2		87	354	43	83	7	1	0	24	8		17	.234	.251	.260	61	-17		.872	-16			O66C,C25		-3.2

HATCHER, CHRIS Christopher Kenneth B1.7.1969 Anaheim CA BR/TR/6-3/220 [HouN90 3/88] d9.6 Col Iowa

YEAR	TM LG	G	AB	R	H	2B	3B	HR	RBI	BB-IB	HP	SO	AVG	OBP	SLG	AOPS	ABR	SB-CS	FA	FR	RNG	THR	GAMES AT POSITION	DL	BFW
1998	KC A	8	15	0	1	0	0	0	1	1-0	0	7	.067	.125	.067	-46	-3	0-0	1.000	-1	82	0	O5L		-0.4

HATCHER, MICKEY Michael Vaughn B3.15.1955 Cleveland OH BR/TR/6-2/200(184-200) [LAN77 5/124] d8.3 C9 Col Oklahoma OF(345/88/146)

YEAR	TM LG	G	AB	R	H	2B	3B	HR	RBI	BB-IB	HP	SO	AVG	OBP	SLG	AOPS	ABR	SB-CS	FA	FR	RNG	THR	GAMES AT POSITION	DL	BFW
1979	LA N	33	93	9	25	4	1	0	5	7-0	1	12	.269	.327	.366	90	-1	1-3	.974	1	109	72	O19(1/1/18),3b17		-0.2
1980	LA N	57	84	9	19	2	0	1	5	2-1	0	12	.226	.244	.286	49	-6	0-2	1.000	2	85	106	O25(4/0/21),3b18		-0.6
1981	Min A	99	377	36	96	23	2	3	37	15-2	0	29	.255	.285	.350	78	-11	3-1	.992	-2	100	55	O91(5/86/0),1b7,3b2/D		-1.5
1982	Min A	84	277	23	69	13	2	3	26	8-1	0	27	.249	.269	.343	65	-14	0-2	.988	2	87	250	O47(26/1/21),D29,3b5		-1.6
1983	Min A	106	375	50	119	15	3	9	47	14-0	1	19	.317	.342	.445	111	4	2-0	.979	7	130	102	O56(10/0/48),D39,1b7/3	39	0.7
1984	Min A	152	576	61	174	35	5	6	69	37-3	2	34	.302	.342	.406	102	2	0-1	.974	8	115	155	O100L,D37,1b17/3	15	-1.2
1985	Min A	116	444	46	125	28	0	3	49	16-1	2	23	.282	.308	.365	79	-13	0-0	.991	5	112	102	O97(96/0/1),D11,1b4		-1.0
1986	Min A	115	317	40	88	13	3	3	32	19-2	0	26	.278	.315	.366	83	-8	2-1	.971	1	90	283	O46L,D28,1b22,3b3		-0.2
1987	LA N	101	287	51	81	19	1	7	42	20-4	1	19	.282	.328	.429	102	0	0-3	1.000	1	90	189	O29(8/0/21),1b25,3b3	15	-0.2
1988	†LA N	88	191	22	56	8	0	1	25	7-3	2	7	.293	.322	.351	97	-1	0-0	.961	-0	93	252	O48(39/0/10),3b16,1b5/P	30	-0.2
1989	LA N	94	224	18	66	9	2	2	25	13-3	1	16	.295	.328	.379	106	1	1-2	1.000	-2	79	120	1b25,3b10,O10L		-1.5
1990	LA N	85	132	12	28	3	1	0	13	6-1	1	22	.212	.248	.250	39	-11	0-0	.983	26	105	139	O575L,1b149,D145,3b125/P	99	-6.7
Total		1130	3377	348	946	172	38		375	164-21	13	246	.280	.313	.377	80	-58	11-15	.983	26	105	139	O575L,1b149,D145,3b125/P	99	-6.7

HATCHER, BILLY William Augustus B10.4.1960 Williams AZ BR/TR/5-9/175(175-190) [ChiN81*6/131] d9.10 C8 Col Yavapai (AZ) JC

YEAR	TM LG	G	AB	R	H	2B	3B	HR	RBI	BB-IB	HP	SO	AVG	OBP	SLG	AOPS	ABR	SB-CS	FA	FR	RNG	THR	GAMES AT POSITION	DL	BFW
1984	Chi N	8	9	1	1	0	0	0		1-1	0	0	.111	.200	.111	-10	-1	2-0	1.000	0	55	682	O4L	15	-1.0
1985	Chi N	53	163	24	40	12	1	2	10	8-0	3	12	.245	.290	.368	76	-5	2-4	.988	-3	86	79	O44(16/27/3)	15	-1.0
1986	†Hou N	127	419	55	108	15	4	6	36	22-1	5	52	.258	.302	.356	83	-11	38-14	.983	0	99	115	O121(39/95/9)	15	-1.0
1987	Hou N	141	564	96	167	28	3	11	63	42-1	4	70	.296	.352	.415	107	6	53-9	.986	6	204	204	O140(51/94/6)		-0.
1988	Hou N	145	530	79	142	25	4	7	52	31-4	8	56	.268	.321	.370	103	2	32-13	.983	-1	100	86	O142(124/25/0)		-0.
1989	Hou N	108	395	49	90	15	3	4	44	30-2	1	53	.228	.281	.304	70	-16	22-6	.991	0	107	18	O104(96/11/0)		-0.
	Pit N	27	86	10	21	4	0	1	7	0-0	1	8	.244	.253	.326	66	-4	2-1	1.000	-4	100	15	O20(2/10/9)		-2.
	Year	135	481	59	111	19	3	4	51	30-2	2	62	.231	.277	.308	70	-20	24-7	.992	-4	100	15	O124(98/21/9)		-0.
1990	†Cin N	139	504	68	139	28	5	5	25	33-5	6	42	.276	.327	.381	91	-6	30-10	.997	7	109	129	O131(76/69/0)		-1.
1991	Cin N	138	442	45	116	25	2	4	41	26-4	1	55	.262	.312	.360	85	-5	11-9	.981	0	107	66	O121(81/54/0)	17	-1.
1992	Cin N	43	94	10	27	3	0	2	10	5-0	1	16	.287	.314	.340	97	-1	0-0	.967	-2	95	0	O23L		-0.

YEAR	TM LG	G	AB	R	H	2B	3B	HR	RBI	BB-IB	HP	SO	AVG	OBP	SLG	AOPS	ABR	SB-CS	FA	FR	RNG	THR	GAMES AT POSITION	DL	BFW
1993	Bos A	75	315	37	75	16	2	1	23	17-1	3	41	.238	.283	.311	62	-16	4-6	.968	-4	91	103	O75(63/13/0)		-2.4
1994	Bos A	136	508	71	146	24	3	9	57	28-4	11	46	.287	.336	.400	92	-6	14-7	.993	-11	86	87	O130(0/129/2),2b2		-1.5
	Phi N	43	134	15	33	5	1	2	13	6-0	0	14	.246	.271	.343	60	-8	4-1	.968	0	104	98	O43R/D		-1.2
1995	Tex A	6	12	2	1	1	0	0	0	1-0	0	1	.083	.154	.167	-4	-16	-2	1.000	1	93	208	O40(7/26/11)		-0.7
Total	12	1233	4339	586	1146	210	30	54	399	267-23	55	476	.264	.312	.364	85	-86	218-87	.986	-8	98	105	O1143(583/553/87),D2,2b2	62	-10.5

HATFIELD, FRED   Fred James   B3.18.1925 Lanett AL   D5.22.1998 Tallahassee FL   BL/TR/6-1/171*   d8.31   C2

YEAR	TM LG	G	AB	R	H	2B	3B	HR	RBI	BB-IB	HP	SO	AVG	OBP	SLG	AOPS	ABR	SB-CS	FA	FR	RNG	THR	GAMES AT POSITION	DL	BFW
1950	Bos A	10	12	3	3	0	0	0	2	3	0	1	.250	.400	.250	63	-1	0-0	1.000	2	152	320	3b3		0.1
1951	Bos A	80	163	23	28	4	2	0	14	22	1	27	.172	.274	.258	40	-14	1-0	.959	14	139	170	3b49		0.0
1952	Bos A	19	25	6	8	1	1	1	3	4	1	2	.320	.433	.560	162	2	0-3	1.000	2	137	0	3b17		0.3
	Det A	112	441	42	104	12	2	2	25	35	5	52	.236	.301	.286	63	-22	2-2	.968	10	107	124	3b107,S9		-1.3
	Year	131	466	48	112	13	3	3	28	39	6	54	.240	.309	.300	69	-20	2-5	.971	12	109	116	3b124,S9		-1.0
1953	Det A	109	311	41	79	11	1	3	19	40	1	34	.254	.341	.325	81	-7	3-5	.978	5	110	99	3b54,2b28/S		-0.1
1954	Det A	81	218	31	64	12	0	2	25	28	4	24	.294	.385	.376	112	5	4-2	.972	-6	98	84	2b54,3b15		0.3
1955	Det A	122	413	51	96	15	3	8	33	61-6	5	49	.232	.337	.341	85	-8	3-2	.975	-5	103	109	2b92,3b16,S14		-0.5
1956	Det A	8	12	2	3	0	0	0	2	2-0	1	1	.250	.400	.250	75	0	0-0	1.000	-1	83	48	2b4		-0.1
	Chi A	106	321	46	84	9	1	7	33	37-3	8	36	.262	.349	.361	88	-5	1-0	.961	0	101	124	3b100,S3		-0.5
	Year	114	333	48	87	9	1	7	35	39-3	9	37	.261	.351	.357	87	-5	1-0	.961	-1	101	124	3b100,2b4,S3		-0.6
1957	Chi A	69	114	14	23	3	0	0	8	15-1	5	20	.202	.316	.228	52	-7	1-0	.951	3	117	192	3b44		-0.4
1958	Cle A	3	8	0	1	0	0	0	1	1-0	0	1	.125	.222	.125	-2	-1	0-0	1.000	1	140	0	3b2		-0.1
	Cin N	3	1	0	0	0	0	0	0	0-0	0	0	.000	.000	.000	-95	0	0-0	—	-0	0	0	/23		-0.1
Total	9	722	2039	259	493	67	10	25	165	248-10	33	247	.242	.332	.321	78	-58	15-14	.962	25	111	129	3b408,2b179,S27		-2.4

HATFIELD, GIL   Gilbert "Colonel"   B1.27.1855 Hoboken NJ   D5.26.1921 Hoboken NJ   TR/5-9.5/168   d9.24 b-John ▲

YEAR	TM LG	G	AB	R	H	2B	3B	HR	RBI	BB-IB	HP	SO	AVG	OBP	SLG	AOPS	ABR	SB-CS	FA	FR	RNG	THR	GAMES AT POSITION	DL	BFW
1885	Buf N	1	30	1	4	0	1	0	0			11	.133	.133	.200	6	-3		.913	-0	112	0	3b8,2b3		-0.3
1887	NY N	2	7	3	3	1	0	0	3	0		0	.429	.429	.571	184	1	0	1.000	0	76	0	3b2		0.1
1888	†NY N	28	105	7	19	1	0	0	9	2	0	18	.181	.211	.190	29	-8	0	.813	-2	76	0	3b14,S13/OC2		-0.2
1889	NY N	32	125	21	23	2	0	1	12	9	2	15	.184	.250	.224	33	-12	9	.858	1	98	74	S24,P6,3b2		-0.7
1890	NY P	71	287	32	80	13	6	2	37	17	4	19	.279	.328	.387	83	-9	12	.836	-15	98	71	3b42,S27,P3/OC		-1.8
1891	Was AA	134	500	83	128	11	8	1	48	50	9	39	.256	.335	.316	90	-5	43	.869	13	104	99	S105,3b27,P4,O3(1/0/2)		0.9
1893	Bro N	34	120	24	35	3	3	2	19	17	2	5	.292	.388	.417	119	4	9	.875	-6	84	33	3b34		-0.2
1895	Lou N	5	16	3	3	0	0	0	1	1	1	1	.188	.278	.188	23	-2	0	.889	-0	94	0	3b3,S2		-0.2
Total	8	317	1190	173	295	31	18	6	129	96	20	109	.248	.315	.319	79	-34	81	.850	-10	100	93	S171,3b132,P13,O5(1/2/2),2b4		-3.2

HATFIELD, JOHN   John Van Buskirk   B7.20.1847 NJ   D2.20.1909 Long Island City NY   5-10/165   d5.18   M2 b-Gil

YEAR	TM LG	G	AB	R	H	2B	3B	HR	RBI	BB-IB	HP	SO	AVG	OBP	SLG	AOPS	ABR	SB-CS	FA	FR	RNG	THR	GAMES AT POSITION	DL	BFW
1871	Mut NA	33	168	41	43	3	2	0	22	4		0	.256	.273	.298	70	-5	10-3	.853	1	65	0	O24L,2b7,3b2		-0.1
1872	Mut NA	56	288	76	93	15	2	1	47	9		6	.323	.343	.399	136	15	12-5	.847	4	102	151	2b55/1M		1.1
1873	Mut NA	52	255	54	78	5	6	2	46	3		2	.306	.314	.398	110	2	2-0	.743	-9	79	91	3b45,2b12/ORM		-0.6
1874	Mut NA	63	292	47	66	12	1	0	29	7		12	.226	.244	.274	64	-11	4-0	.874	6	36	0	O58L,3b7,P3/1S		-0.2
1875	Mut NA	1	4	1	2	1	0	0	1	0		0	.500	.500	.750	312	1	0-0	1.000	-0	0	0	/OL		0.1
1876	NY N	1	4	0	1	0	0	0	0	0		0	.250	.250	.250	77	0		.833	-0	126	0	/2		0.0
Total	5 NA	205	1007	219	282	36	11	3	145	23		20	.280	.296	.347	98	2	28-8	.868	3	44		O84(83/0/1),2b74,3b54,P3,1b2/S		0.3

HATTEBERG, SCOTT   Scott Allen   B12.14.1969 Salem OR   BL/TR/6-1/205(192-210)   [BosA91 1/43]   d9.8   Col Washington St.

YEAR	TM LG	G	AB	R	H	2B	3B	HR	RBI	BB-IB	HP	SO	AVG	OBP	SLG	AOPS	ABR	SB-CS	FA	FR	RNG	THR	GAMES AT POSITION	DL	BFW
1995	Bos A	2	2	1	1	0	0	0	0	0-0	0	1	.500	.500	.500	156	1	0-0	1.000	1	0	0	C2		0.1
1996	Bos A	10	11	3	2	1	0	0	0	3-0	0	2	.182	.357	.273	61	-1	0-0	1.000	-0	43	89	C10		0.0
1997	Bos A	114	350	46	97	23	1	10	44	40-2	2	70	.277	.354	.434	102	2	0-1	.983	-14	69	90	C106/D		-0.5
1998	†Bos A	112	359	46	99	23	1	12	43	43-3	5	58	.276	.359	.446	106	4	0-0	.993	8	94	114	C108		1.8
1999	†Bos A	30	80	12	22	5	0	1	11	18-0	1	14	.275	.410	.375	100	1	0-0	.993	-1	105	105	C23,D6		0.3
2000	Bos A	92	230	21	61	15	0	8	36	38-3	0	39	.265	.367	.435	100	1	0-0	.993	1	51	105	C23,D6	112	0.3
2001	Bos A	94	278	34	68	19	0	3	25	33-0	4	26	.245	.332	.345	79	-7	1-1	.981	-6	47	117	C48,D20/3		-0.4
2002	†Oak A	136	492	58	138	22	4	15	61	68-1	6	56	.280	.374	.433	115	12	0-0	.994	9	147	120	1b91,D42		-2.4
2003	†Oak A	147	541	63	137	34	0	12	61	66-0	9	53	.253	.342	.383	91	-5	0-1	.992	2	105	100	1b128,D15		1.2
2004	Oak A	152	550	87	156	30	0	15	82	72-5	5	48	.284	.367	.420	107	8	0-0	.993	-1	101	114	1b148,D2		-1.5
2005	Oak A	134	464	52	119	19	0	7	59	51-4	4	54	.256	.334	.343	80	-12	0-1	.985	-2	117	119	D79,1b53		-0.6
Total	11	1023	3357	423	900	191	6	88	422	432-18	36	420	.268	.356	.403	98	3	1-5	.992	-21	114	112	1b420,C369,D173/3	112	-3.9

HATTON, GRADY   Grady Edgebert   B10.7.1922 Beaumont TX   BL/TR/5-9/175*   d4.16   M3/C3   Col Texas

YEAR	TM LG	G	AB	R	H	2B	3B	HR	RBI	BB-IB	HP	SO	AVG	OBP	SLG	AOPS	ABR	SB-CS	FA	FR	RNG	THR	GAMES AT POSITION	DL	BFW
1946	Cin N	116	436	56	118	18	3	14	69	66-2	2	53	.271	.369	.422	129	18	6	.941	-16	92	**90**	3b116,O2L		0.1
1947	Cin N	146	524	91	147	24	8	16	77	81	2	50	.281	.377	.448	119	16	7	.938	-8	93	72	3b136		0.7
1948	Cin N	133	458	58	110	17	2	9	44	72	5	50	.240	.343	.345	90	-5	7	.932	4	100	103	3b123,2b3,S2/OL		-0.2
1949	Cin N	137	537	71	141	38	5	11	69	62	3	48	.263	.342	.413	101	1	4	**.975**	-3	98	98	3b136		-0.2
1950	Cin N	130	438	67	114	17	1	11	54	70	3	39	.260	.366	.379	96	0	6	.954	-1	93	76	3b126/2S		-0.2
1951	Cin N	96	331	41	84	9	3	4	37	33	1	32	.254	.321	.335	76	-11	4-2	.972	5	101	126	3b87,O2L		-0.7
1952	Cin N☆	128	433	48	92	14	1	9	57	66	2	60	.212	.319	.312	76	-13	5-4	**.990**	-9	91	86	3b120		-1.7
1953	Cin N	83	159	22	37	3	1	7	22	29	0	24	.233	.351	.396	94	-1	0-1	.991	-4	88	105	2b35,1b10,3b5		-0.4
1954	Cin N	1	1	0	0	0	0	0	0	0	0	0	.000	.000	.000	-97	0	0-0	—	0			/H		0.0
	Chi A	13	30	3	5	1	0	0	3	5	0	3	.167	.278	.200	34	-3	1-0	1.000	0	82	68	3b10,1b3		-0.3
	Year	99	302	40	85	12	3	5	33	58	2	25	.281	.399	.391	106	5	1-1	.966	6	111	116	3b93/1S		1.1
1955	Bos A	126	380	48	93	11	4	4	49	76-3	2	28	.245	.367	.326	81	-7	0-1	**.969**	5	**108**	52	3b113,1b4/S		0.8
1956	Bos A	5	5	0	2	0	0	0	2	0-0	1	0	.400	.400	.400	100	0	0-0	.976	4	**107**	106	3b111/2		-0.4
	StL N	44	73	10	18	1	0	2	7	13-0	0	7	.247	.360	.315	84	-1	1-0	.951	-2	100	100	2b13/3		0.0
	Bal A	27	61	4	9	1	0	1	3	13-1	0	6	.148	.297	.213	40	-5	0-0	1.000	-2	99	42	2b15,3b12		-0.7
1960	Chi N	28	38	3	13	0	0	0	7	2-1	1	5	.342	.381	.342	104	0	0-0	.931	-1	108	58	2b8		0.0
Total	12	1312	4206	562	1068	166	33	91	533	646-5	13	430	.254	.354	.374	96	-6	42-9	.956	-28	98	95	3b956,2b196,1b14,O5L,S4		-3.1

HAUGER, ARTHUR   John Arthur   B11.18.1893 Delhi OH   D8.2.1944 Redwood City CA   BL/TR/5-11/168   d7.17

YEAR	TM LG	G	AB	R	H	2B	3B	HR	RBI	BB-IB	HP	SO	AVG	OBP	SLG	AOPS	ABR	SB-CS	FA	FR	RNG	THR	GAMES AT POSITION	DL	BFW
1912	Cle A	15	18	0	1	0	0	0	0				.056	.105	.056	-52	-4	0	1.000	-0	111	0	O5(1/2/2)		-0.4

HAUSER, ARNOLD   Arnold George "Peewee","Stub"   B9.25.1888 Chicago IL   D5.22.1966 Aurora IL   BR/TR/5-6/145   d4.21

YEAR	TM LG	G	AB	R	H	2B	3B	HR	RBI	BB-IB	HP	SO	AVG	OBP	SLG	AOPS	ABR	SB-CS	FA	FR	RNG	THR	GAMES AT POSITION	DL	BFW
1910	StL N	119	375	37	77	4	2	2	36	49	9	39	.205	.312	.251	67	-14	15	.931	-7	101	62	S117/3		-1.8
1911	StL N	136	515	61	124	11	8	3	46	26	7	67	.241	.286	.311	69	-24	24	.918	-13	98	93	S134,3b2		-2.9
1912	StL N	133	479	73	124	14	7	1	42	39	3	69	.259	.319	.324	78	-15	26	.934	8	**109**	96	S132		0.2
1913	StL N	22	45	3	13	0	0	0	9	2	1	2	.289	.347	.422	121	1	1-2	.848	-3	84	78	S8,2b4		-0.2
1915	Chi F	23	54	6	11	1	0	0	4	5	1	7	.204	.283	.222	46	-5	2	.851	-0	90	141	S16,3b6		-0.8
Total	5	433	1468	180	349	33	20	6	137	121	22	184	.238	.305	.300	72	-57	68-2	.924	-17	102	87	S407,3b9,2b4		-5.5

HAUSER, JOE   Joseph John "Unser Choe"   B1.12.1899 Milwaukee WI   D7.11.1997 Sheboygan WI   BL/TL/5-10.5/175   d4.18

YEAR	TM LG	G	AB	R	H	2B	3B	HR	RBI	BB-IB	HP	SO	AVG	OBP	SLG	AOPS	ABR	SB-CS	FA	FR	RNG	THR	GAMES AT POSITION	DL	BFW
1922	Phi A	111	368	61	119	21	5	9	43	30	2	37	.323	.378	.481	119	10	1-5	.986	-3	92	92	1b94		-0.1
1923	Phi A	146	537	93	165	21	9	17	94	69	12	52	.307	.398	.475	127	22	6-6	.990	-3	93	99	1b146		0.8
1924	Phi A	149	562	97	162	31	8	27	115	56	5	52	.288	.358	.516	123	15	7-5	.993	-3	92	116	1b146		0.3
1926	Phi A	91	234	31	44	10	0	8	36	39	1	35	.192	.312	.341	66	-11	1-1	.996	0	93	91	1b65		-1.5
1928	Phi A	95	300	61	78	19	5	16	59	52	0	45	.260	.369	.517	127	12	4-2	.986	-5	75	83	1b88		0.1
1929	Cle A	37	48	8	12	1	1	3	9	4	1	8	.250	.321	.500	104	0	0-0	.986	0	137	39	1b8		0.0
Total	6	629	2044	351	580	103	28	80	356	250	21	229	.284	.368	.479	117	48	19-19	.990	-13	90	98	1b547		-0.4

HAUSMANN, GEORGE   George John   B2.11.1916 St.Louis MO   D6.16.2004 Boerne TX   BR/TR/5-5/145   d4.18

YEAR	TM LG	G	AB	R	H	2B	3B	HR	RBI	BB-IB	HP	SO	AVG	OBP	SLG	AOPS	ABR	SB-CS	FA	FR	RNG	THR	GAMES AT POSITION	DL	BFW
1944	NY N	131	466	70	124	20	4	1	30	40		29	.266	.324	.333	85	-9	3	.960	-1	98	90	2b122		-0.4
1945	NY N	154	623	98	174	15	8	2	45	73	1	46	.279	.356	.339	92	-5	7	.968	2	103	76	2b154		0.6
1949	NY N	16	47	5	6	0	1	0	3	7	1	12	.128	.241	.170	12	-6	0	.984	1	114	104	2b13		-0.5
Total	3	301	1136	173	304	35	13	3	78	120	1	77	.268	.338	.329	86	-20	10	.965	2	101	83	2b289		-0.3

HAUTZ, CHARLIE   Charles A.   B2.5.1852 St.Louis MO   D1.24.1929 St.Louis MO   BR/5-7/150   d5.4   U3

YEAR	TM LG	G	AB	R	H	2B	3B	HR	RBI	BB-IB	HP	SO	AVG	OBP	SLG	AOPS	ABR	SB-CS	FA	FR	RNG	THR	GAMES AT POSITION	DL	BFW
1875	RS NA	19	83	5	25	3	0	0	4	0		9	.301	.301	.337	134	3	5-1	.921	-1	80	74	1b19		0.3
1884	Pit AA	7	24	1	5	0	0	0		3	0		.208	.296	.208	68	-1		.980	1	64	121	1b5,O2C		-0.1

YEAR	TM LG	G	AB	R	H	2B	3B	HR	RBI	BB-IB	HP	SO	AVG	OBP	SLG	AOPS	ABR	SB-CS	FA	FR	RNG	THR	GAMES AT POSITION	DL	BFW

HAWES, ROY Roy Lee B7.5.1926 Shiloh IL BL/TL/6-2/190 d9.23
| 1951 | Was A | 3 | 6 | 0 | 1 | 0 | 0 | 0 | 0 | 0-0 | | 0 | 1 | .167 | .167 | .167 | -10 | -1 | 0-0 | 1.000 | -0 | 0 | 0 | /1 | | -0.1 |

HAWES, BILL William Hildreth B11.17.1853 Nashua NH D6.16.1940 Lowell MA BR/TR/5-10/155 d5.1
1879	Bos N	38	155	19	31	3	3	0	9	2		13	.200	.210	.258	52	-8		.828	-2	141	279	O34(1/7/26),C5		-0.9
1884	Cin U	79	349	80	97	7	4	4		5			.278	.288	.355	87	-17		.827	-7	51		O58(22/9/28),1b21		-2.4
Total	2	117	504	99	128	10	7	4	9	7		13	.254	.264	.325	77	-25		.827	-9	84	103	O92(23/16/54),1b21,C5		-3.3

HAWKES, THORNY Thorndike Proctor B10.15.1852 Danvers MA D2.2.1929 Danvers MA BR/TR/5-8/135 d5.1
1879	Tro N	64	250	24	52	6	1	0	20	4		14	.208	.220	.240	55	-11		.896	15	116	93	2b64		0.6
1884	Was AA	38	151	16	42	4	2	0		4	0		.278	.297	.331	118	3		.917	1	96	53	2b38,O2C		0.5
Total	2	102	401	40	94	10	3	0	20	8		14	.234	.249	.274	79	-8		.903	15	109	79	2b102,O2C		1.1

HAWKS, CHICKEN Nelson Louis B2.3.1896 San Francisco CA D5.26.1973 San Rafael CA BL/TL/5-11/167 d4.14 Col Santa Clara
1921	NY A	41	73	16	21	2	3	2	15	5	0	12	.288	.333	.479	103	0	0-1	.970	-1	105	0	O15(5/10/0)		-0.2
1925	Phi N	105	320	52	103	15	5	5	45	32	2	33	.322	.387	.447	103	2	3-6	.986	-0	102	90	1b90		-0.4
Total	2	146	393	68	124	17	8	7	60	37	2	45	.316	.377	.453	103	2	3-7	.986	-1	102	90	1b90,O15(5/10/0)		-0.6

HAWORTH, HOWIE Homer Howard "Cully" B8.27.1893 Newberg OR D1.28.1953 Troutdale OR BL/TR/5-10.5/165 d8.14
| 1915 | Cle A | 7 | 7 | 0 | 1 | 0 | 0 | 0 | 1 | 0 | | 2 | .143 | .333 | .143 | 42 | 0 | | .917 | -1 | 107 | 64 | C5 | | -0.1 |

HAWPE, BRAD Bradley Bonte B6.22.1979 Fort Worth TX BL/TL/6-3/200* [ColN00 11/317] d5.1 Col Louisiana St.
2004	Col N	42	105	12	26	3	2	9	11-3	1	34	.248	.322	.400	76	-4	1-1	.982	-1	96	56	O34(2/0/32)		-0.6
2005	Col N	101	305	38	80	10	3	9	47	43-3	0	70	.262	.350	.403	85	-6	2-2	.981	3	96	220	O89R	52	-0.7
Total	2	143	410	50	106	13	5	12	56	54-6	1	104	.259	.343	.402	83	-10	3-3	.982	3	96	178	O123(2/0/121)	52	-1.3

HAYDEN, JACK John Francis B10.21.1880 Bryn Mawr PA D8.3.1942 Haverford PA BL/TL/5-9/170 d4.26 Col Villanova
1901	Phi A	51	211	35	56	6	4	0	17	18	0		.265	.323	.332	78	-6	4	.841	-4	168	0	O50(30/4/16)		-1.2
1906	Bos A	85	322	22	80	6	4	1	14	17	3		.248	.292	.301	86	-6	6	.973	-3	61	41	O85R		-1.4
1908	Chi N	11	45	3	9	2	0	0	2	1	0		.200	.217	.244	45	-3	1	1.000	-1	0	0	O11R		-0.5
Total	3	147	578	60	145	14	8	1	33	36	3		.251	.298	.308	80	-15	11	.929	-8	91	24	O146(30/4/112)		-3.1

HAYES, CHARLIE Charles Dewayne B5.29.1965 Hattiesburg MS BR/TR/6-0/207(190-224) [SFN83 4/96] d9.11 OF(4/0/1)
1988	SF N	7	11	0	1	0	0	0	0-0		3	.091	.091	.091	-50	-2	0-0	1.000	-1	98	0	O4(3/0/1),3b3		-0.3
1989	SF N	3	5	0	1	0	0	0	0-0		1	.200	.200	.200	15	-1	0-0	1.000	-1	39	0	3b3		-0.1
	Phi N	84	299	26	77	15	1	8	43	11-1	0	49	.258	.281	.395	92	-4	3-1	.910	4	109	109	3b82		0.0
	Year	87	304	26	78	15	1	8	43	11-1	0	50	.257	.280	.391	91	-5	3-1	.911	4	108	107	3b85		-0.1
1990	Phi N	152	561	56	145	20	0	10	57	28-3	2	91	.258	.293	.348	76	-19	4-4	.957	19	114	139	3b146,1b4/2		-1.8
1991	Phi N	142	460	34	106	23	1	12	53	16-3	1	75	.230	.257	.363	73	-18	3-3	.958	2	101	123	3b138,1b4		-1.5
1992	NY A	142	509	52	131	19	2	18	66	28-0	3	100	.257	.297	.409	97	-5	3-5	.963	-9	93	117	3b139,1b4		2.1
1993	Col N	157	573	89	175	45	2	25	98	43-6	5	82	.305	.355	.522	113	12	11-6	.954	8	105	79	3b154/S		-0.2
1994	Col N	113	423	46	122	23	4	10	50	36-4	3	71	.288	.348	.433	87	-7	3-6	.944	6	109	95	3b110		-0.5
1995	Col N	141	529	58	146	30	3	11	85	50-2	4	88	.276	.340	.406	96	-2	5-1	.963	-5	91	114	3b124		-0.8
1996	Pit N	128	459	51	114	21	2	10	62	36-4	0	78	.248	.301	.368	73	-18	0-0	1.000	2	101	144	3b19		0.0
	†NY A	20	67	7	19	3	0	2	13	1-0	0	12	.284	.294	.418	77	-3	0-0	.947	-5	91	126	3b98,2b5		-0.8
1997	†NY A	100	353	39	91	16	0	11	53	40-2	1	66	.258	.332	.397	91	-5	3-2	.989	-3	87	89	3b46,1b45,D2		-0.3
1998	SF N	111	329	39	94	8	0	12	62	34-0	5	61	.286	.351	.419	107	3	2-1	.940	-9	85	36	3b55,1b20/OLD	19	-2.6
1999	SF N	95	264	33	54	9	1	6	48	33-0	1	41	.205	.292	.314	58	-18	3-1	.976	-5	100	62	3b59,1b57/D		-1.7
2000	Mil N	121	370	46	93	17	0	9	46	57-4	1	84	.251	.348	.370	84	-8	1-1	.976	-0	82	149	3b11,1b2/D		-0.5
2001	Hou N	31	50	4	10	2	0	4		7-1	0	16	.200	.293	.240	39	-4	0-0	.954	11	101	108	3b1328,1b132,D6,2b6,O5L,S3	19	-9.1
Total	14	1547	5262	580	1379	251	16	144	740	420-30	21	918	.262	.316	.398	88	-99	47-31							

HAYES, FRANKIE Franklin Witman "Blimp" B10.13.1914 Jamesburg NJ D6.22.1955 Point Pleasant NJ BR/TR/6-0/185 d9.21
1933	Phi A	3	5	0	0	0	0	0	0	0-0	0	2	.000	.000	.000	-99	-1	0-0	.889	0	0	0	C3		-0.1
1934	Phi A	92	248	24	56	10	0	6	30	20	1	44	.226	.286	.339	63	-15	2-1	.955	-10	85	94	C89		-1.9
1936	Phi A	144	505	59	137	25	2	10	67	46	2	58	.271	.335	.388	79	-18	4-0	.971	-5	89	79	C56		-3.1
1937	Phi A	60	188	24	49	11	1	10	38	29	1	34	.261	.359	.489	114	4	0-0	.975	-14	75	94	C90		0.2
1938	Phi A	99	316	56	92	19	3	11	55	54	1	51	.291	.396	.475	120	11	2-3	.978	-16	72	102	C114		0.1
1939	Phi A☆	124	431	66	122	28	5	20	83	40	3	55	.283	.348	.510	119	10	4-1	.971	-14	64	78	C134,1b2		0.2
1940	Phi A★	136	465	73	143	23	4	16	70	61	1	56	.308	.389	.477	126	19	9-3	.971	-14	64	94	C123		1.3
1941	Phi A★	126	439	66	123	27	4	12	63	62	0	56	.280	.369	.442	117	11	2-0	1.000	-3	68	134	C20		0.9
1942	Phi A	21	63	8	15	4	0	0	5	9	0	8	.238	.333	.302	80	-1	1-1	.971	-4	79	74	C51		-0.4
	StL A	56	159	14	40	6	0	2	17	28	0	39	.252	.364	.327	94	0	0-0	.979	-5	74	90	C71		-0.4
	Year	77	222	22	55	10	0	2	22	37	0	47	.248	.355	.320	90	-1	1-1	.983	-9	76	87	C76/1		-0.8
1943	StL A	88	250	16	47	7	0	5	30	37	1	36	.188	.295	.276	66	-10	6-2							-1.6
1944	Phi A★	155	581	62	144	18	6	13	78	57	0	59	.248	.315	.367	96	-5	2-1	.982	-3	72	116	C155/1		0.1
1945	Phi A	32	110	12	25	2	1	3	14	18	0	14	.227	.336	.345	98	-1	1-0	.994	5	84	86	C119		0.3
	Cle A★	119	385	39	91	15	6	6	43	53	4	66	.236	.335	.353	104	3	2-1	.989	5	86	97	C151		1.5
	Year	151	495	51	116	17	7	9	57	71	4	80	.234	.335	.352	103	3	2-1	.989	5	86	97	C151		1.8
1946	Cle A★	51	156	11	40	12	0	3	18	21	0	26	.256	.345	.391	112	4	1-3	.981	-4	89	50	C50		0.4
	Chi A	53	179	15	38	6	0	2	16	29	0	33	.212	.322	.279	72	-6	1-1	.979	-1	83	111	C52		-0.5
	Year	104	335	26	78	18	0	5	34	50	0	59	.233	.332	.331	90	-3	2-4	.980	-2	102	90	C102		-0.1
1947	Bos A	5	13	0	2	0	0	0	1	0		1	.154	.154	.154	-13	-2	0-0	.917	0	129	92	C4		-0.2
Total	14	1364	4493	545	1164	213	32	119	628	564	13	627	.259	.343	.400	100	3	30-20	.977	-112	77	95	C1311,1b4		-3.2

HAYES, MIKE John Edward B1.1855 New York NY D5.25.1904 New York NY 5-7.5/170 d9.9
| 1876 | NY N | 5 | 21 | 1 | 3 | 0 | 2 | 0 | | 2 | 0 | | .143 | .143 | .333 | 63 | -1 | | .882 | 0 | 0 | 0 | O5L | | -0.1 |

HAYES, JACKIE John J. B6.27.1861 Brooklyn NY D4.25.1905 Brooklyn NY TR/5-8/175 d5.2 OF(4/75/24)
1882	Wor N	78	326	27	88	22	4	4	54	6		26	.270	.283	.399	113	5		.855	-11	101	59	O58(0/55/3),C15,3b5/S		-0.6
1883	Pit AA	85	351	41	92	23	5	3		15			.262	.292	.382	120	4		.911	-16			C62,O18(0/15/3),S5,1b5/2		-0.2
1884	Pit AA	33	124	11	28	6	1	0		4	1		.226	.256	.290	79	-3		.912	-1			C24,1b5,O3R/2		-0.1
	Bro AA	16	51	4	12	3	0	0		3	1		.235	.274	.294	86	-1		.946	4			C14,O2(1/1/0)		0.4
	Year	49	175	15	40	9	1	0		7	1		.229	.262	.291	81	-3		.900	-4			C42		0.3
1885	Bro AA	42	137	10	18	3	0	0	10	5	3		.131	.179	.153	6	-14		.926	-2			C14,O12(1/4/7)/2		-1.3
1886	Was N	26	89	8	17	3	0	3	9	4		23	.191	.226	.326	71	-3	0	.250	-3			C14,1b5,O5(1/1/3)/2		-0.4
1887	Bal AA	8	28	2	4	1	0	0		3			.143	.143	.250	9	-3	0	.867	-3	0	78	O6R,S3,C2/2		-0.5
1890	Bro P	12	42	3	8	0	0	0	5	2		4	.190	.227	.190	11	-6	0	.906	-34			O174,O103C,1b10,S9,3b8,2b4		-0.7
Total	7	300	1148	106	267	63	10	10	81	39		53	.233	.260	.331	87	-16	0							-3.4

HAYES, JACKIE Minter Carney B7.19.1906 Clanton AL D2.9.1983 Birmingham AL BR/TR/5-10.5/165 d8.5 Col Alabama
1927	Was A	10	29	2	7	0	0	0	2	1	0		.241	.267	.241	33	-3	0-0	.969	-0	103	30	S8/3		-0.2
1928	Was A	60	210	30	54	7	0	0	22	5		10	.257	.274	.319	56	-14	3-0	.974	7	102	120	2b41,S15,3b2		-0.4
1929	Was A	123	424	52	117	20	3	2	57	24		29	.276	.316	.351	71	-19	4-5	.945	5	114	168	3b63,2b57,S2		-0.9
1930	Was A	51	166	25	47	7	2	1	20	7		8	.283	.312	.367	71	-8	2-3	.981	-5	84	81	2b19,3b8,S3		-0.3
1931	Was A	38	108	11	24	2	1	0	8	6		4	.222	.263	.259	38	-10	2-0	.962	-4	81	72	2b29,3b9,1b8		-1.2
1932	Chi A	117	475	53	122	20	5	2	54	30		36	.257	.302	.333	69	-23	2-3	.981	6	107	104	2b138		-1.3
1933	Chi A	138	535	65	138	23	5	2	47	55		25	.258	.331	.331	79	-16	4-3	.980	-10	93	77	2b61		-1.2
1934	Chi A	62	226	19	58	9	1	1	31	23		20	.257	.325	.319	65	-12	3-1	.966	-5	99	90	2b85		-1.2
1935	Chi A	89	329	45	89	14	0	4	45	29		24	.271	.327	.347	72	-14	3-1	.979	13	113	118	2b89,S13,3b2		1.1
1936	Chi A	108	417	53	130	34	3	5	84	35		15	.312	.366	.444	96	-3	4-2	.984	23	109	123	2b143		-1.0
1937	Chi A	143	573	63	129	29	9	1	79	41		37	.225	.282	.300	47	-48	1-6	.976	-2	101	121	2b61		-0.9
1938	Chi A	62	238	25	78	21	2	1	20	24		6	.328	.389	.445	106	3	3-2	.974	3	101	126	2b69		-0.9
1939	Chi A	72	269	34	67	12	1	0	31	27		11	.249	.316	.301	59	-13	0-0	.981	-1	100	123	2b15		-0.5
1940	Chi A	18	41	2	8	0	0	0	5	1		2	.195	.233	.244	23	-5	0-0	.973	0	98	94	2b15		-8.
Total	14	1091	4040	494	1069	196	33	20	493	309	9	241	.265	.318	.344	70	-188	34-31	.976	43	104	111	2b904,3b95,S51,1b8		

YEAR	TM LG	G	AB	R	H	2B	3B	HR	RBI	BB-IB	HP	SO	AVG	OBP	SLG	AOPS	ABR	SB-CS	FA	FR	RNG	THR	GAMES AT POSITION	DL	BFW

HAYES, VON Von Francis B8.31.1958 Stockton CA BL/TR/6-5/185* [CleA79 7/163] d4.14 Col St. Marys (CA) OF(207/398/555)

1981	Cle A	43	109	21	28	8	2	1	17	14-1	2	10	.257	.346	.394	115	3	8-1	.939	1	111	236	D21,O13(12/0/1),3b5		0.4
1982	Cle A	150	527	65	132	25	3	14	82	42-3	4	63	.250	.310	.389	90	-8	32-13	.981	5	111	95	O139(14/7/123),3b5,1b4		-0.7
1983	†Phi N	124	351	45	93	9	5	6	32	36-7	3	55	.265	.337	.370	97	-2	20-12	.972	-2	95	130	O103(3/39/77)	8	-0.7
1984	Phi N	152	561	85	164	27	6	16	67	59-4	0	84	.292	.359	.447	124	18	48-13	.988	-4	101	24	O148(14/116/36)		1.8
1985	Phi N	152	570	76	150	30	4	13	70	61-6	0	99	.263	.332	.409	102	2	21-8	.984	8	111	98	O146(66/123/14)		0.8
1986	Phi N	158	610	107	186	46	2	19	98	74-9	1	77	.305	.379	.480	131	28	24-12	.990	1	102	99	1b134,O31(24/6/3)		2.3
1987	Phi N	158	556	84	154	36	5	21	84	121-12	0	77	.277	.404	.473	128	28	16-7	.990	-5	88	94	1b144,O32(5/29/3)		1.5
1988	Phi N	104	367	43	100	28	2	6	45	49-5	1	59	.272	.355	.409	117	10	20-9	.990	1	97	98	1b85,O16(4/12/2),3b3	49	0.7
1989	Phi N★	154	540	93	140	27	2	26	78	101-14	4	103	.259	.376	.461	139	32	28-7	.980	5	99	140	O128(0/13/124),1b30,3b10		3.7
1990	Phi N	129	467	70	122	14	3	17	73	87-16	4	81	.261	.375	.413	119	15	16-7	.979	-1	100	85	O127(45/4/81)	15	1.2
1991	Phi N	77	284	43	64	15	1	0	21	31-1	3	42	.225	.303	.285	69	-11	9-2	.990	6	121	72	O72(20/49/6)	83	-0.5
1992	Cal A	94	307	35	69	17	1	4	29	37-4	0	54	.225	.305	.326	77	-9	11-6	.983	-2	101	19	O85R,1b4,D5		-1.4
Total	12	1495	5249	767	1402	282	36	143	696	712-82	22	804	.267	.354	.416	113	106	253-97	.983	14	105	90	O1040R,1b401,D26,3b23	155	9.1

HAYES, BILL William Ernest B10.24.1957 Cheverly MD BR/TR/6-0/195* [ChiN78 1/13] d9.30 C1 Col Indiana St.

1980	Chi N	4	9	0	2	1	0	0	0	0-0	0	3	.222	.222	.333	49	-1	0-0	1.000	-1	69	329	C3		-0.1
1981	Chi N	1	0	0	0	0	0	0	0	0-0	0	0	—	—	—	—	0	0-0	—	-0	0	0	/C		0.0
Total	2	5	9	0	2	1	0	0	0	0-0	0	3	.222	.222	.333	49	-1	0-0	1.000	-1	66	313	C4		-0.1

HAYWORTH, RED Myron Claude B5.14.1916 High Point NC BR/TR/6-1.5/200 d4.21 b-Ray Col Oak Ridge Mil. Inst. [JC]

1944	†StL A	90	270	20	60	11	1	1	25	10	1	13	.222	.253	.281	50	-18	0-0	.967	-2	94	77	C87		-1.6
1945	StL A	56	160	7	31	4	0	0	17	7	0	6	.194	.228	.219	28	-15	0-2	.992	1	108	69	C55		-1.2
Total	2	146	430	27	91	15	1	1	42	17	1	19	.212	.243	.258	42	-33	0-2	.976	-0	99	74	C142		-2.8

HAYWORTH, RAY Raymond Hall B1.29.1904 High Point NC D9.25.2002 Salisbury NC BR/TR/6-0/180 d6.27 C2 b-Red Col Oak Ridge Mil. Inst. [JC]

1926	Det A	12	11	1	3	0	0	0	5	1	0	.273	.333	.273	59	-1	0-0	1.000	-1	115	0	C8		0.0
1929	Det A	14	43	5	11	0	0	0	4	3	0	8	.256	.304	.256	45	-4	0-0	.951	-1	75	146	C14		-0.1
1930	Det A	77	227	24	63	15	4	0	22	20	0	19	.278	.336	.379	79	-7	0-2	.977	-11	65	83	C76		-0.4
1931	Det A	88	273	28	70	10	3	0	25	19	1	27	.256	.307	.315	62	-16	0-1	.973	-1	78	125	C88		-1.3
1932	Det A	109	338	41	99	20	2	2	44	31	1	22	.293	.354	.382	87	-6	1-1	.991	3	92	102	C106		-1.1
1933	Det A	134	425	37	104	14	3	1	45	35	0	28	.245	.302	.299	59	-26	0-0	.994	-6	61	121	C133		0.2
1934	†Det A	54	167	20	49	5	2	0	27	16	0	22	.293	.355	.347	82	-5	0-2	.984	4	153	106	C54		-2.3
1935	Det A	51	175	22	54	14	2	0	22	9	0	14	.309	.342	.411	98	-1	0-0	.996	8	138	148	C48		0.2
1936	Det A	81	250	31	60	10	0	1	30	39	2	18	.240	.347	.292	59	-15	0-0	.988	-4	123	73	C81		0.9
1937	Det A	30	78	9	21	0	2	1	8	14	2	15	.269	.394	.333	83	-1	0-0	.992	2	101	87	C28		-1.3
1938	Det A	8	19	1	4	0	0	0	5	3	0	4	.211	.318	.211	33	-2	1-0	.971	1	281	0	C7		0.2
	Bro N	5	4	0	0	0	0	0	0	1	0	1	.000	.200	.000	-40	-1	0-0	1.000	0	0	0	C3		0.0
1939	Bro N	21	26	0	4	0	0	0	0	7	0	7	.154	.267	.154	34	-2	0-0	1.000	1	108	55	C18		-0.1
	NY N	5	13	1	3	0	0	0	0	0	0	1	.231	.231	.231	24	-1	0-0	1.000	1	113	210	C5		-0.1
	Year	26	39	1	7	0	0	0	0	7	0	8	.179	.256	.231	31	-4	0-0	1.000	2	110	105	C23		0.0
1942	StL A	1	1	0	1	0	0	0	0	0	0	0	1.000	1.000	1.000	456	0	0-0	—	0			/H		-0.1
1944	Bro N	7	10	1	0	0	0	0	0	2	0	1	.000	.167	.000	-51	-2	0	1.000	1	99	135	C6		-0.1
1945	Bro N	2	0	0	0	0	0	0	0	0	0	0	.000	.333	.000	-3	0	0-0	1.000	0	0	0	C2		0.0
Total	15	699	2062	221	546	92	16	5	238	198	6	188	.265	.331	.332	71	-90	2-6	.987	-3	95	106	C677		-5.3

HAZEWOOD, DRUNGO Drungo La Rue B9.2.1959 Mobile AL BR/TR/6-3/210 [BalA77 1/19] d9.19

| 1980 | Bal A | 6 | 5 | 1 | 0 | 0 | 0 | 0 | 0 | 0-0 | 0 | 4 | .000 | .000 | .000 | -99 | -1 | 0-0 | 1.000 | -0 | 36 | 0 | O3R | | -0.2 |

HAZLE, BOB Robert Sidney "Hurricane" B12.9.1930 Laurens SC D4.25.1992 Columbia SC BL/TR/6-0/190* d9.8

1955	Cin N	6	13	0	3	0	0	0	0	0-0	0	3	.231	.231	.231	22	-1	0-0	1.000	1	149	333	O3L		0.0
1957	†Mil N	41	134	26	54	12	0	7	27	18-4	1	15	.403	.477	.649	214	23	1-3	.906	-5	84	37	O40R		1.6
1958	Mil N	20	56	6	10	0	0	0	5	9-0	1	4	.179	.303	.179	34	-5	0-0	1.000	-1	106	0	O20R		-0.7
	Det A	43	58	5	14	2	0	2	5	5-0	0	13	.241	.302	.379	80	-2	0-0	1.000	-0	94	0	O12(8/0/4)		-0.2
Total	3	110	261	37	81	14	0	9	37	32-4	2	35	.310	.390	.467	135	15	1-3	.951	-4	95	42	O75(11/0/64)		0.7

HAZLETON, DOC Willard Carpenter B8.28.1876 Strafford VT D3.10.1941 Burlington VT BR d4.17 Col Tufts

| 1902 | StL N | 7 | 23 | 0 | 3 | 0 | 0 | 0 | 2 | 1 | .130 | .231 | .130 | 12 | -2 | 0 | .973 | 0 | 109 | 209 | 1b7 | | -0.3 |

HEALY, FRAN Francis Xavier B9.6.1946 Holyoke MA BR/TR/6-5/210* d9.3 Col American International

1969	KC A	6	10	0	4	1	0	0	0	5	0	.400	.400	.500	148	1	0-0	1.000	0	124	C5		0.1
1971	SF N	47	93	10	26	3	0	2	11	15-0	0	24	.280	.380	.376	116	3	1-0	.966	-3	55	106	C22		0.1
1972	SF N	45	99	12	15	4	0	1	8	13-2	1	24	.152	.257	.222	36	-8	0-1	.995	4	114	172	C43		-0.3
1973	KC A	95	279	25	77	15	2	6	34	31-0	0	56	.276	.348	.409	105	2	3-4	.979	-1	117	112	C92/D		0.4
1974	KC A	139	445	59	112	24	2	9	53	62-1	0	73	.252	.343	.375	101	3	16-8	.977	-8	86	90	C138		0.2
1975	KC A	56	188	16	48	5	2	2	18	14-1	1	19	.255	.307	.335	79	-6	4-3	.982	-3	109	64	C51,D4		-0.6
1976	KC A	8	24	2	3	0	0	0	1	4-0	0	10	.125	.250	.125	12	-3	2-0	1.000	1	71	117	C6/D		-0.1
	NY A	46	120	10	32	3	0	0	9	9-0	0	17	.267	.318	.292	80	-3	3-1	.983	2	289	94	C31,D9		0.1
	Year	54	144	12	35	3	0	0	10	13-0	0	27	.243	.306	.264	68	-6	5-1	.987	3	245	99	C37,D10		0.0
1977	NY A	27	67	10	15	5	0	0	7	6-0	0	13	.224	.288	.299	60	-3	1-0	.971	-3	114	62	C26		-0.5
1978	NY A	1	1	0	0	0	0	0	0	0-0	0	1	.000	.000	.000	-99	0	0-0	—	-0	0	0	/C		-0.1
Total	9	470	1326	144	332	60	6	20	141	154-4	2	242	.250	.329	.350	90	-14	30-17	.980	-10	112	98	C415,D15		-0.7

HEALY, FRANCIS Francis Xavier Paul B6.29.1910 Holyoke MA D2.12.1997 Springfield MA BR/TR/5-9.5/175 d4.29

1930	NY N	7	2	2	0	0	0	0	0	0-0	0	0	.000	.000	.000	-99	-1	0	—	0	0	0	/C		
1931	NY N	6	7	1	1	0	0	0	0	0-0	0	0	.143	.143	.143	-24	-1	0	1.000	0	0	0	C4		-0.1
1932	NY N	14	32	5	8	2	0	0	4	2-0	0	8	.250	.294	.313	65	-2	0	.960	1	113	110	C11		0.0
1934	StL N	15	13	1	4	1	0	0	1	0-0	0	2	.308	.308	.385	79	0	0	1.000	1	0	0	C2/3OR		0.0
Total	4	42	54	9	13	3	0	0	5	2-0	0	10	.241	.268	.296	51	-4	0	.969	1	91	89	C18/OR3		-0.2

HEALY, THOMAS Thomas Fitzgerald B10.30.1895 Altoona PA D1.15.1974 Cleveland OH BR/TR/6-0/172 d7.13 Col Pittsburgh

1915	Phi A	23	77	11	17	1	0	0	5	6	4	.221	.310	.234	65	-3	0-4	.933	4	116	107	3b17/S		0.0
1916	Phi A	6	23	4	6	1	0	0	2	1	1	.261	.320	.391	119	0	0-1	.947	0	100	77	3b6		0.1
Total	2	29	100	15	23	2	1	0	7	7	5	.230	.313	.270	77	-3	1-4	.936	4	112	100	3b23/S		0.1

HEARD, CHARLIE Charles B1.30.1872 Philadelphia PA D2.20.1945 Philadelphia PA BR/TR/6-2/190 d7.14 ▲

| 1890 | Pit N | 12 | 43 | 2 | 8 | 2 | 0 | 0 | 1 | 0 | 15 | .186 | .205 | .233 | 31 | -4 | 0 | .600 | -2 | 0 | 0 | O6(1/0/5),P6 | | -0.3 |

HEARN, ED Edward John B8.23.1960 Stuart FL BR/TR/6-3/215* [PhiN78 4/101] d5.17

1986	NY N	49	136	16	36	5	0	4	10	12-0	1	19	.265	.322	.390	98	-1	0-1	.987	-11	106	53	C45		-1.1
1987	KC A	6	17	2	5	2	0	0	4	4-0	0	2	.294	.429	.412	121	1	0-0	1.000	-1	126	59	C5		0.0
1988	KC A	7	18	1	4	2	0	0	1	0-0	0	1	.222	.222	.333	53	-1	0-0	1.000	-1	99	0	C4,D2	169	0.0
Total	3	62	171	19	45	9	0	4	14	16-0	1	22	.263	.324	.386	96	-1	0-1	.989	-14	108	50	C54,D2	150	-0.2

HEARNE, ED Edmund B9.17.1888 Ventura CA D9.8.1952 Los Angeles CA BR/TR/5-9/160 d6.9

| 1910 | Bos A | 2 | 0 | 0 | 0 | 0 | 0 | 0 | 0 | 0 | .000 | .000 | .000 | -98 | 0 | 0 | 1.000 | 1 | 140 | 326 | S2 | 319 | -1.3 |

| 1910 | Bos A | 2 | 0 | 0 | 0 | 0 | 0 | 0 | 0 | 0 | 0 | .000 | .000 | .000 | -98 | 0 | 0 | 1.000 | 1 | 140 | 326 | S2 | | 0.0 |

HEARNE, HUGHIE Hugh Joseph B4.18.1873 Troy NY D9.22.1932 Troy NY BR/TR/5-8/182 d8.29

1901	Bro N	2	5	1	2	0	0	0	0	0	0	.400	.400	.400	129	0	0	1.000	-0	70	179	C2		0.0
1902	Bro N	66	231	22	65	10	0	0	28	16	3	.281	.336	.325	103	2	3	.966	-11	78	89	C65		-0.4
1903	Bro N	26	57	8	16	3	2	0	7	3	1	.281	.328	.404	111	1	2	.960	-1	76	137	C17,1b2		0.1
Total	3	94	293	31	83	13	2	0	35	19	4	.283	.335	.341	105	3	5	.965	-12	77	100	C84,1b2		-0.3

HEARRON, JEFF Jeffrey Vernon B11.19.1961 Long Beach CA BR/TR/6-1/195* [TorA83 4/89] d8.25 Col Texas

1985	†Tor A	4	7	0	1	0	0	0	0	0-0	0	2	.143	.143	.143	-21	-1	0-0	1.000	1	74	280	C4		0.0
1986	Tor A	12	23	2	5	1	0	0	4	3-0	0	5	.217	.308	.261	55	-1	0-0	.980	-1	102	38	C12		-0.2
Total	2	16	30	2	6	1	0	0	4	3-0	0	7	.200	.297	.233	38	-2	0-0	.985	-0	96	94	C16		-0.2

YEAR	TM LG	G	AB	R	H	2B	3B	HR	RBI	BB-IB	HP	SO	AVG	OBP	SLG	AOPS	ABR	SB-CS	FA	FR	RNG	THR	GAMES AT POSITION	DL	BFW

HEATH, JEFF John Geoffrey B4.1.1915 Ft.William ON, Can. D12.9.1975 Seattle WA BL/TR/5-11.5/200 d9.13

																									0.1
1936	Cle A	12	41	6	14	3	1	8	3	0		4	.341	.386	.634	147	2	1-0	1.000	-1	61	151	O12(10/2/0)		0.1
1937	Cle A	20	61	8	14	1	4	0	8	0		9	.230	.230	.377	50	-6	0-1	1.000	0	O14(2/0/12)		O14(2/0/12)		-0.7
1938	Cle A	126	502	104	172	31	18	21	112	33	0	55	.343	.393	.602	146	31	3-1	.974	4	109	58	O122(113/0/9)		2.2
1939	Cle A	121	431	64	126	31	7	14	69	41	0	64	.292	.354	.494	119	11	8-4	.964	2	104	93	O90L		0.8
1940	Cle A	100	356	55	78	16	3	14	50	40	0	62	.219	.298	.399	81	-12	5-3	.971	2	104	93	O108L		-1.4
1941	Cle A★	151	585	89	199	32	20	24	123	50	0	69	.340	.396	.586	165	50	18-12	.949	-5	86	144	O151(25/0/126)		3.4
1942	Cle A	147	568	82	158	37	13	10	76	62	1	66	.278	.350	.442	130	21	9-9	.980	4	104	102	O146(145/0/2)		1.5
1943	Cle A★	118	424	58	116	22	6	18	79	63	1	58	.274	.369	.481	157	30	5-8	.968	-3	103	44	O111(107/3/4)		2.1
1944	Cle A✱	60	151	20	50	5	2	5	33	18	0	12	.331	.402	.490	160	12	0-1	.952	0	96	134	O37(31/5/1)		1.0
1945	Cle A✱	102	370	60	113	16	7	15	61	56	1	39	.305	.398	.508	169	33	3-1	.973	-6	97	32	O101L		2.2
1946	Was A	48	166	23	47	12	3	4	27	36	0	36	.283	.411	.464	153	14	0-4	.969	-2	92	97	O47L		0.3
	StL A	86	316	46	87	20	4	12	57	37	1	37	.275	.353	.478	124	10	0-2	.962	-2	94	103	O83L		1.1
	Year	134	482	69	134	32	7	16	84	73	1	73	.278	.374	.473	134	23	0-6	.965	-3	93	101	O130L		1.2
1947	StL A	141	491	81	123	20	7	27	85	88	1	87	.251	.366	.485	133	22	2-1	.991	1	103	76	O106(99/7/0)		2.8
1948	Bos N	115	364	64	116	26	5	20	76	51	0	46	.319	.404	.582	167	34	2	.983	-1	95	86	O31(26/0/5)		0.9
1949	Bos N	36	111	17	34	7	0	9	23	15	0	26	.306	.389	.613	174	11	0	.983	-1	95	86	O31(26/0/5)		17.2
Total	14	1383	4937	777	1447	279	102	194	887	593	10	670	.293	.370	.509	140	263	56-47	.972	-8	100	85	O1299(1127/17/159)		17.2

HEATH, KELLY Kelly Mark B9.4.1957 Plattsburgh NY BR/TR/5-7/155 [KCA77 7/177] d4.20 Col Louisburg (NC) JC

																									0.0
1982	KC A	1	1	0	0	0	0	0	0	0-0	0	0	.000	.000	.000	-99	0	0-0	1.000	1	212	436	/2		0.0

HEATH, MIKE Michael Thomas B2.5.1955 Tampa FL BR/TR/5-11/190(175-200) [NYA73 2/37] d6.3 OF(79/1/142)

																									-0.4
1978	†NY A	33	92	6	21	3	1	0	8	4-0	1	9	.228	.265	.283	56	-6	0-0	.970	1	164	54	C33		-0.4
1979	Oak A	74	258	19	66	8	0	3	27	17-1	3	18	.256	.304	.322	74	-10	1-0	.978	-1	103	165	O46(23/0/23),C22,3b7,D3		-1.1
1980	Oak A	92	305	27	74	10	2	1	33	16-2	0	28	.243	.280	.298	62	-17	3-3	.986	14	191	96	C47,D31,O8(4/0/4)		-0.2
1981	†Oak A	84	301	26	71	7	1	8	30	13-1	1	36	.236	.269	.346	79	-10	3-3	.973	-6	114	117	C90,O10(9/0/2),3b5		0.1
1982	Oak A	101	318	43	77	18	4	3	39	27-3	0	36	.242	.298	.352	81	-8	3-4	.973	-1	105	98	C80,O24(1/0/23),3b2,D2		-0.1
1983	Oak A	96	345	45	97	17	0	6	33	18-4	1	59	.281	.318	.383	97	-2	3-4	.986	-5	93	118	C108,O45(13/0/32),3b2/S		-0.9
1984	Oak A	140	475	49	118	21	5	13	64	26-2	1	72	.248	.287	.396	93	-7	7-4	.986	-5	93	118	C112,O35(16/0/24),3b13		0.5
1985	Oak A	138	436	71	109	18	6	13	55	41-0	1	63	.250	.313	.408	104	1	7-7	.981	-2	129	97	C112,O35(16/0/24),3b13		-0.7
1986	StL N	65	190	19	39	8	1	4	25	23-4	1	36	.205	.293	.321	70	-8	2-3	.967	-0	139	73	C63,O2(1/0/1)		-0.2
	Det A	30	98	11	26	3	0	4	11	4-0	1	17	.265	.291	.418	91	-2	4-1	.987	-2	128	57	C29/3		0.9
1987	†Det A	93	270	34	76	16	0	8	33	21-0	3	42	.281	.339	.430	106	3	1-5	.989	6	124	117	C67,O24(4/1/20),1b4,3b4,S2/2D		0.0
1988	Det A	86	219	24	54	7	2	5	18	18-0	1	32	.247	.307	.365	90	-3	1-0	.984	2	141	63	C75,O9R		0.7
1989	Det A	122	396	38	104	16	2	10	43	24-2	4	71	.263	.308	.389	98	-2	7-1	.986	2	95	124	C117,3b4,O3L/D		0.0
1990	Det A	122	370	46	100	18	2	7	38	19-0	4	71	.270	.311	.386	93	-4	7-6	.980	-1	80	96	C117,O3R/SD	86	-1.3
1991	Atl N	49	139	14	29	3	1	1	12	7-5	1	26	.209	.250	.266	43	-11	0-0	.991	-4	69	121	C45	131	-3.8
Total	14	1325	4212	462	1061	173	27	86	469	278-24	22	616	.252	.300	.367	87	-86	54-40	.981	11	115	103	C1083,O215R,D40,3b38,1b4,S4/2	131	-3.8

HEATH, MICKEY Minor Wilson B10.30.1903 Toledo OH D7.30.1986 Dallas TX BL/TL/6-0/175 d4.18

																									-0.2
1931	Cin N	7	26	2	7	0	0	3	2	0	0	5	.269	.321	.269	64	-1	0	1.000	-0	87	128	1b7		-1.1
1932	Cin N	39	134	14	27	1	3	0	15	20	1	23	.201	.310	.254	55	-8	0	.991	1	114	94	1b39		-1.3
Total	2	46	160	16	34	1	3	0	18	22	1	28	.213	.311	.256	57	-9	0	.992	1	110	99	1b46		-1.3

HEATH, TOMMY Thomas George B8.18.1913 Akron CO D2.26.1967 Los Gatos CA BR/TR/5-10/185 d4.23

																									-0.3
1935	StL A	47	93	10	22	3	0	0	9		0	13	.237	.372	.269	65	-4		.982	-0	119	45	C37		0.0
1937	StL A	17	43	4	10	1	0	2	1	3	10	0	3	.233	.377	.395	94	0	0-1	1.000	-1	88	55	C14		-0.2
1938	StL A	70	194	22	44	13	0	2	22	35	0	24	.227	.345	.325	69	-8	0-1	.986	3	81	121	C65		-0.5
Total	3	134	330	36	76	16	2	3	34	65	0	40	.230	.357	.318	71	-12	0-1	.987	2	91	93	C116		-0.5

HEATH, BILL William Chris B3.10.1939 Yuba City CA BL/TR/5-8/175* d10.3 Col USC

																									0.0
1965	Chi A	1	1	0	0	0	0	0	0	0-0	0	0	.000	.000	.000	-99	0	0-0	—	0			/H		0.1
1966	Hou N	55	123	12	37	6	0	0	8	9-1	1	11	.301	.353	.350	103	1	1-0	.995	-2	83	163	C37		0.0
1967	Hou N	9	11	0	1	0	0	0	0	4-0	0	3	.091	.333	.091	28	-1	0-0	1.000	1	23	303	C5		-0.5
	Det A	20	32	0	4	0	0	0	1	0-0	0	4	.125	.152	.125	-17	-5	0-0	1.000	0	29	0	C7		-0.1
1969	Chi A	27	32	1	5	0	1	0	1	12-2	0	4	.156	.378	.219	65	-1	0-0	.979	-0	100	153	C9	23	-0.1
Total	4	112	199	13	47	6	1	0	13	26-3	1	22	.236	.326	.276	73	-6	1-0	.993	-1	77	151	C58	23	-0.5

HEATHCOTE, CLIFF Clifton Earl B1.24.1898 Glen Rock PA D1.18.1939 York PA BL/TL/5-10.5/160 d6.4 Col Penn St.

																									-1.7
1918	StL N	88	348	37	90	12	3	4	32	20	1	40	.259	.301	.345	100	-1	12	.934	-8	97	50	O87(3/84/0)		-0.9
1919	StL N	114	401	53	112	13	4	1	29	20	1	41	.279	.315	.339	103	2	27	.967	-2	101	80	O101(1/85/17),1b2		0.2
1920	StL N	133	489	55	139	18	8	3	56	25	1	31	.284	.320	.372	102	0	21-14	.964	10	105	151	O129(0/74/57)		-1.4
1921	StL N	62	156	18	38	6	2	0	9	10	1	9	.244	.293	.308	61	-9	7-5	.926	-3	92	94	O51(1/40/10)		-0.4
1922	StL N	34	98	11	24	5	2	0	14	9	1	15	.245	.315	.337	71	-4	0-2	.950	2	123	58	O32C		-1.2
	Chi N	76	243	37	68	8	7	1	34	18	0	19	.280	.330	.383	82	-7	5-2	.971	-0	106	63	O92(0/53/40)		-1.6
	Year	110	341	48	92	13	9	1	48	27	1	19	.270	.325	.370	79	-11	5-4	.980	-4	105	111	O112(1/0/111)		-2.6
1923	Chi N	117	393	48	98	14	3	1	27	25	2	22	.249	.298	.308	60	-23	32-17	.979	-2	104	57	O111(1/20/90)		-1.2
1924	Chi N	113	392	66	121	19	7	0	30	28	1	26	.309	.356	.393	100	0	26-24	.979	8	105	141	O99(3/8/88)		-1.1
1925	Chi N	109	380	57	100	14	5	5	39	39	7	26	.263	.343	.366	80	-11	15-11	.985	9	105	123	O133(13/13/110)		0.2
1926	Chi N	139	510	98	141	33	6	3	53	58	2	30	.276	.353	.412	104	4	18	.987	7	104	182	O57(0/9/49)		0.5
1927	Chi N	83	228	28	67	12	4	2	25	20	3	12	.294	.359	.408	105	2	6	.973	1	93	172	O39(7/13/20)		0.0
1928	Chi N	67	137	26	39	8	0	3	18	17	1	17	.285	.364	.409	103	1	1	.985	1	107	70	O52(1/6/45)		-0.3
1929	†Chi N	82	224	45	70	17	0	2	31	25	1	17	.313	.384	.415	98	1	9	.985	1	100	111	O35(0/3/32)		-0.1
1930	Chi N	70	150	30	39	10	1	9	18	18	1	15	.260	.343	.520	104	2	4	.986	0	100	111	O59R		0.6
1931	Cin N	90	252	24	65	15	6	0	28	32	0	16	.258	.342	.365	96	-1	3	.989	11	120	166	O59R		-0.1
1932	Chi N	8	3	3	0	0	0	0	0	0	0	0	.000	.000	.000	-99	-1	0	—	0			/H		-0.2
	Phi N	30	39	7	11	2	0	1	5	3	0	3	.282	.333	.410	88	-1	0	.962	-1	88	160	1b7		-0.3
	Year	38	42	10	11	2	0	1	5	3	0	3	.262	.311	.381	78	-1	0	.962	-1	88	160	1b7		-0.3
Total	15	1415	4443	643	1222	206	55	42	448	367	22	325	.275	.333	.375	92	-50	191-75	.971	35	104	109	O1157(31/408/728),1b9		-9.7

HEBNER, RICHIE Richard Joseph B11.26.1947 Boston MA BL/TR/6-1/197(188-210) [PitN66 1/15] d9.23 C4* OF(5/0/27)

																									0.0
1968	Pit N	2	1	0	0	0	0	0	0	0-0	0	0	.000	.000	.000	-99	0	0-0	.944	2	98	147	3b124/1		2.2
1969	Pit N	129	459	72	138	23	4	8	47	53-10	8	53	.301	.380	.420	128	19	4-1	.940	1	107	112	3b117		1.2
1970	†Pit N	120	420	60	122	24	8	11	46	42-5	1	58	.290	.362	.464	121	12	2-3	.949	-4	93	126	3b108		0.8
1971	†Pit N	112	388	50	105	17	8	17	67	32-1	3	68	.271	.326	.487	128	13	2-2	.969	-11	94	92	3b121		2.1
1972	†Pit N	124	427	63	128	24	4	19	72	52-7	6	54	.300	.378	.508	154	31	0-0	.939	-12	95	69	3b139		0.7
1973	Pit N	144	509	73	138	28	4	25	74	56-12	4	60	.271	.346	.477	129	22	0-3	.937	-13	93	123	3b141		0.7
1974	†Pit N	146	550	97	160	21	6	18	68	60-5	6	53	.291	.363	.449	131	22	0-3	.946	-16	88	83	3b126		-2.1
1975	†Pit N	128	472	65	116	16	4	15	57	43-6	10	44	.246	.319	.392	97	-3	0-0	.953	-13	92	76	3b126		-0.2
1976	Pit N	132	434	60	108	21	3	8	51	47-2	8	39	.249	.325	.366	95	-2	7-8	.991	3	122	130	1b103,3b13/2	23	1.1
1977	†Phi N	118	397	67	113	17	4	18	62	61-4	12	34	.285	.381	.484	124	15	7-8	.991	-5	80	116	1b117,3b19/2		0.8
1978	†Phi N	137	435	61	123	22	3	17	71	53-16	4	58	.283	.369	.464	130	19	4-7	.940	-8	96	111	3b134,1b6		-0.3
1979	NY N	136	473	54	127	25	2	10	79	59-6	8	59	.268	.354	.393	108	7	3-1	.998	-2	98	71	1b61,3b32,D5		-0.1
1980	Det A	104	341	48	91	10	7	12	82	30-1	2	45	.290	.360	.466	123	10	0-3	.995	-4	76	81	1b61,D11		-1.2
1981	Det A	78	226	19	51	8	2	5	28	27-5	1	28	.226	.311	.345	86	-4	1-2	.990	-2	122	64	1b40,D20		0.8
1982	Det A	68	179	25	49	6	0	8	18	25-2	0	21	.274	.364	.441	114	5	1-1	.964	-0	99	207	O21R,1b4/3		-0.1
	Pit N	25	70	6	21	2	0	2	12	5-0	0	3	.300	.347	.414	107	1	4-0	.967	-9	68	20	3b40,1b7,O7(2/0/5)		-0.1
1983	Pit N	78	162	23	43	4	1	5	26	17-4	1	28	.265	.332	.395	100	3	0-0	.963	0	115	109	3b14,1b3,O3(2/0/1)		-0.1
1984	†Chi N	44	81	12	27	6	0	3	18	10-2	1	15	.333	.407	.444	128	3	1-0	.963	4	120	133	1b27,3b8	50	-0.1
1985	Chi N	83	120	10	26	4	1	3	20	7-1	1	15	.217	.266	.308	55	-7	0-1	.991	1	80	163	1b12,3b7/OL	73	-0.1
Total	18	1908	6144	865	1694	273	57	203	890	687-95	74	741	.276	.352	.438	119	161	38-40	.946	-86	95	103	3b1262,1b415,D36,O32R,2b2	73	-0.1

HECHINGER, MIKE Michael Vincent B2.14.1890 Chicago IL D8.13.1967 Chicago IL BR/TR/6-0/175 d9.27

																									0.
1912	Chi N	2	3	0	0	0	0	0	0	0	0	0	.000	.000	.000	14	0	0	1.000	0	177	71	C2		0.
1913	Chi N	2	2	0	0	0	0	0	0	0	0	0	.000	.000	.000	-99	-1	0	—	0			/H		

YEAR	TM LG	G	AB	R	H	2B	3B	HR	RBI	BB-IB	HP	SO	AVG	OBP	SLG	AOPS	ABR	SB-CS	FA	FR	RNG	THR	GAMES AT POSITION	DL	BFW
	Bro N	9	11	1	2	1	0	0	0	0	0	2	.182	.182	.273	28	-1	0	1.000	-1	78	81	C4		-0.2
	Year	11	13	1	2	1	0	0	0	0	0	2	.154	.154	.231	9	-2	0	1.000	-1	78	81	C4		-0.3
Total 2		11	16	1	2	1	0	0	0	2	0	2	.125	.222	.188	16	-2	0	1.000	-0	130	76	C6		-0.3

HECKER, GUY Guy Jackson B4.3.1856 Youngsville PA D12.3.1938 Wooster OH BR/TR/6-0/190 d5.2 M1/U1 ▲

YEAR	TM LG	G	AB	R	H	2B	3B	HR	RBI	BB-IB	HP	SO	AVG	OBP	SLG	AOPS	ABR	SB-CS	FA	FR	RNG	THR	GAMES AT POSITION	DL	BFW
1882	Lou AA	78	340	62	94	14	4	3	5				.276	.287	.368	126	9		.958	5	132	163	1b66,P13,O2C		0.5
1883	Lou AA	81	332	59	90	6	6	1	12				.271	.297	.334	111	8		.933	6	109	167	P53,O23(9/14/0),1b10		0.4
1884	Lou AA	78	316	53	94	14	8	4	42	10	2		.297	.323	.430	150	17		.951	5	108	128	P75,O5(4/1/0)		0.3
1885	Lou AA	70	297	48	81	9	2	2	35	5	1		.273	.287	.337	97	-2		.927	4	122	53	P53,1b17,O3L		0.0
1886	Lou AA	84	343	76	117	14	5	4	48	32	3		.341	.402	.446	157	22	25	.875	-3	101	229	P49,1b22,O17(6/0/11)		0.3
1887	Lou AA	91	370	89	118	21	6	4	50	31	6		.319	.381	.441	126	13	48	.954	-3	29	136	1b43,P34,O16L		-0.1
1888	Lou AA	56	211	32	48	9	2	0	29	11	6		.227	.285	.289	86	-3	20	.936	-4	46	79	1b30,P26/OL		-0.8
1889	Lou AA	81	327	42	93	17	5	1	36	18	6	27	.284	.333	.376	104	1	17	.969	0	103	106	1b65,P19/OR		-0.4
1890	Pit N	86	340	43	77	13	9	0	38	19	9	17	.226	.285	.318	86	-7	13	.962	2	136	58	1b69,P14,O7(5/1/1),M		-0.8
Total 9		705	2876	504	812	117	47	19	278	143	33	44	.282	.324	.376	118	55	123	.934	13	111	118	P336,1b322,O75(44/18/13)		-0.6

HEEP, DANNY Daniel William B7.3.1957 San Antonio TX BL/TL/5-11/185* [HouN78 2/37] d8.31 Col St. Marys (TX)

YEAR	TM LG	G	AB	R	H	2B	3B	HR	RBI	BB-IB	HP	SO	AVG	OBP	SLG	AOPS	ABR	SB-CS	FA	FR	RNG	THR	GAMES AT POSITION	DL	BFW
1979	Hou N	14	14	0	2	0	0	0	2	1-1	0	4	.143	.176	.143	-5	-2	0-0	1.000	1	256	0	O2L		-0.1
1980	†Hou N	33	87	6	24	8	0	0	6	8-0	1	9	.276	.340	.368	107	1	0-0	.990	-2	58	55	1b22		-0.2
1981	Hou N	33	96	6	24	3	0	0	11	10-2	1	11	.250	.321	.281	76	-3	0-0	.990	-2	61	80	1b22/OR		-0.2
1982	Hou N	85	198	16	47	14	1	4	22	21-3	1	31	.237	.311	.379	101	0	0-2	1.000	-3	103	85	O39(1/0/39),1b16	15	-0.7
1983	NY N	115	253	30	64	12	0	8	21	29-6	1	40	.253	.326	.395	101	1	3-3	1.000	-3	82	118	O61(11/19/31),1b14		-0.6
1984	NY N	99	199	36	46	9	2	1	22	27-3	1	22	.231	.319	.312	81	-4	3-1	.967	2	118	36	O48(25/0/23),1b10		-0.6
1985	NY N	95	271	26	76	17	0	7	42	27-1	1	27	.280	.341	.421	116	6	2-2	.977	3	96	21	O78(45/7/31),1b4		0.0
1986	†NY N	86	195	24	55	8	2	5	33	30-5	1	31	.282	.379	.421	123	7	1-4	.988	-1	95	61	O56(44/0/13)		0.3
1987	LA N	60	98	7	16	4	0	0	8	8-0	0	10	.163	.226	.204	15	-12	1-0	.962	1	91	219	O22(17/0/6),1b6		-1.2
1988	†LA N	95	149	14	36	2	0	0	11	22-0	1	13	.242	.341	.255	76	-4	2-0	1.000	1	122	97	O32(17/0/16),1b12/P		-0.2
1989	Bos A	113	320	36	96	17	0	5	49	29-4	1	26	.300	.356	.400	107	4	0-1	.989	-5	83	51	O75(17/0/59),1b19,D9		-0.4
1990	†Bos A	41	69	3	12	1	1	0	8	7-0	1	14	.174	.256	.217	33	-6	0-0	1.000	1	121	178	O14(11/0/13),1b5/PD	66	-0.5
1991	Atl N	14	12	4	5	1	0	0	3	1-0	0	4	.417	.462	.500	161	1	0-1	1.000	-0	-0		/1OL		0.1
Total 13		883	1961	208	503	96	6	30	229	220-25	9	242	.257	.330	.357	94	-11	12-14	.986	-12	97	70	O429(181/26/232),1b131,D15,P2	81	-4.6

HEFFERNAN, BERT Bertram Alexander B3.3.1965 Centereach NY BL/TR/5-10/185 [MilA88 9/237] d5.13 Col Clemson

YEAR	TM LG	G	AB	R	H	2B	3B	HR	RBI	BB-IB	HP	SO	AVG	OBP	SLG	AOPS	ABR	SB-CS	FA	FR	RNG	THR	GAMES AT POSITION	DL	BFW
1992	Sea A	8	11	0	1	1	0	0	0	0-0	0	1	.091	.091	.182	-25	-2	0-0	1.000	0	55	90	C5/D		-0.2

HEFFNER, DON Donald Henry "Jeep" B2.8.1911 Rouzerville PA D8.1.1989 Pasadena CA BR/TR/5-10/155 d4.17 M1/C8

YEAR	TM LG	G	AB	R	H	2B	3B	HR	RBI	BB-IB	HP	SO	AVG	OBP	SLG	AOPS	ABR	SB-CS	FA	FR	RNG	THR	GAMES AT POSITION	DL	BFW
1934	NY A	72	241	29	63	8	3	0	25	25	0	18	.261	.331	.320	73	-10	1-1	.971	-9	88	115	2b68		-1.4
1935	NY A	10	36	3	11	3	1	0	8	4	0	1	.306	.375	.444	118	1	0-0	.980	-1	93	89	2b10		0.1
1936	NY A	19	48	7	11	2	1	0	6	6	0	5	.229	.315	.313	57	-3	0-0	.971	2	123	138	3b8,2b5,S3		0.0
1937	NY A	60	201	23	50	6	5	0	21	19	0	19	.249	.314	.328	62	-13	1-4	.980	-6	78	116	2b38,S13,3b3/1OR		-1.6
1938	StL A	141	473	47	116	23	3	2	69	65	4	53	.245	.341	.319	67	-23	1-1	.971	-5	88	96	2b141		-1.7
1939	StL A	110	375	45	100	10	2	1	35	48	3	30	.267	.350	.312	69	-16	1-7	.944	-0	105	68	S73,2b32		-1.1
1940	StL A	126	487	52	115	23	2	3	53	39	2	37	.236	.295	.310	56	-32	5-5	.977	16	111	108	2b125		-0.9
1941	StL A	110	399	48	93	14	2	0	17	38	2	27	.233	.303	.278	53	-27	5-6	.974	-0	105	81	2b105		-2.1
1942	StL A	19	36	2	6	2	0	0	3	1	0	4	.167	.189	.222	15	-4	0-0	.906	2	108	31	2b6,1b4		-0.4
1943	StL A	18	33	2	4	1	0	0	2	2	0	2	.121	.171	.152	-5	-4	0-0	.974	-1	81	80	2b13/1		-0.5
	Phi A	52	178	17	37	6	0	0	8	18	1	12	.208	.284	.242	55	-10	3-2	.978	-7	94	82	2b47/1		-1.6
	Year	70	211	19	41	7	0	0	10	20	1	14	.194	.267	.227	45	-14	3-2	.978	-8	92	82	2b60,1b2		-2.1
1944	Det A	6	19	0	4	1	0	0	1	5	0	1	.211	.375	.263	40	-5	0-0	.962	0	98	122	2b5		0.0
Total 11		743	2526	275	610	99	19	6	248	270	9	218	.241	.317	.303	61	-141	18-26	.973	-11	97	97	2b595,S89,3b11,1b7/OR		-11.2

HEGAN, JIM James Edward B8.3.1920 Lynn MA D6.17.1984 Lynn MA BR/TR/6-2/195* d9.9 Mil 1943-45 C21 s-Mike

YEAR	TM LG	G	AB	R	H	2B	3B	HR	RBI	BB-IB	HP	SO	AVG	OBP	SLG	AOPS	ABR	SB-CS	FA	FR	RNG	THR	GAMES AT POSITION	DL	BFW
1941	Cle A	16	47	4	15	2	0	1	5	4	0	7	.319	.373	.426	116	1	0-0	.973	0	104	113	C16		0.2
1942	Cle A	68	170	10	33	5	0	0	11	11	0	31	.194	.243	.224	34	-15	1-3	.977	5	118	88	C66		-0.8
1946	Cle A	88	271	29	64	11	5	0	17	17	1	44	.236	.284	.314	71	-12	1-4	.991	5	123	121	C87		-0.3
1947	Cle A☆	135	378	38	94	14	5	4	42	41	1	49	.249	.324	.344	88	-7	3-1	.989	7	174	86	C133		0.8
1948	†Cle A	144	472	60	117	21	6	14	61	48	1	79	.248	.317	.407	94	-7	1-0	.990	22	151	81	C142		2.2
1949	Cle A★	152	468	54	105	19	5	8	55	49	0	89	.224	.298	.338	69	-23	1-0	.990	13	143	96	C152		-0.2
1950	Cle A★	131	415	53	91	16	5	14	58	42	0	52	.219	.291	.383	74	-20	1-0	.993	9	97	82	C129		0.8
1951	Cle A★	133	416	60	99	17	5	6	43	38	1	52	.238	.302	.346	79	-14	0-3	.991	2	97	96	C107		0.1
1952	Cle A☆	112	333	39	75	17	2	4	41	29	0	47	.225	.287	.324	75	-12	0-2	.987	-0	95	76	C106		-0.6
1953	Cle A	112	299	37	65	10	1	9	37	25	1	41	.217	.280	.348	71	-14	1-2	.976	10	114	90	C137		-1.0
1954	†Cle A	139	423	56	99	12	7	11	40	34	0	48	.234	.289	.374	80	-14	0-1	.994	8	114	69	C111		0.2
1955	Cle A	116	304	30	67	5	2	9	40	34-5	0	33	.220	.293	.339	69	-15	0-1	.997	9	90	65	C118		-0.2
1956	Cle A	122	315	42	70	15	2	9	34	49-6	2	54	.222	.327	.340	75	-11	1-1	.985	9	79	58	C58		0.3
1957	Cle A	58	148	14	32	7	0	4	15	16-1	1	23	.216	.291	.345	74	-5	0-1	1.000	2	103	119	C45		-0.7
1958	Det A	45	130	14	25	6	0	1	7	10-1	0	20	.192	.250	.262	38	-11	0-0	.996	1	89	93	C25		-0.7
	Phi N	25	59	5	13	6	0	0	6	4-0	0	16	.220	.270	.322	57	-4	0-0	.991	1	72	217	C25		-0.5
	Year	25	51	1	10	1	0	0	3	3-1	0	10	.196	.232	.216	22	-6	0-1	.990	2	112	135	C21		-0.2
1959	SF N	21	30	0	4	1	0	0	1	1-0	0	10	.133	.161	.167	-13	-5	0-1	.975	3	88	185	C46		-0.7
	Year	46	81	1	14	2	0	0	4	4-1	0	20	.173	.207	.198	10	-11	0-2	.983	-1	55	162	C22		-0.3
1960	Chi N	24	43	4	9	1	0	0	5	1-0	1	10	.209	.244	.372	67	-2	0-0	.977	117	121	93	C1629		-0.7
Total 17		1666	4772	550	1087	187	46	92	525	456-14	4	742	.228	.295	.344	74	-196	15-24	.990	117	121	93	C1629		-0.7

HEGAN, MIKE James Michael B7.21.1942 Cleveland OH BL/TL/6-1/190* d9.13 Mil 1967 f-Jim Col Holy Cross

YEAR	TM LG	G	AB	R	H	2B	3B	HR	RBI	BB-IB	HP	SO	AVG	OBP	SLG	AOPS	ABR	SB-CS	FA	FR	RNG	THR	GAMES AT POSITION	DL	BFW
1964	†NY A	5	5	0	0	0	0	0	0	1-0	0	2	.000	.167	.000	-48	-1	0-0	1.000	1	369	157	1b2		0.0
1966	NY A	13	39	7	8	0	1	0	2	7-0	0	2	.205	.326	.256	73	-1	1-1	.991	0	110	69	1b13		-0.2
1967	NY A	68	118	12	16	4	1	1	3	20-1	1	40	.136	.266	.212	44	-8	7-1	1.000	-1	95	123	1b54,O10R		-1.2
1969	Sea A✶	95	267	54	78	9	6	8	37	62-1	1	61	.292	.427	.461	149	21	6-5	.955	3	100	159	O64(2/1/61),1b19		2.0
1970	Mil A	148	476	70	116	21	2	11	52	67-3	0	116	.244	.336	.366	94	-2	9-7	.994	10	127	98	1b139,O8(2/0/6)		-0.3
1971	Mil A	46	122	19	27	4	1	4	11	26-2	0	19	.221	.356	.369	107	2	1-1	1.000	4	130	64	1b45		-0.3
	†Oak A	65	55	5	13	3	0	0	3	5-0	0	13	.236	.300	.291	-69	-2	1-0	1.000	0	113	112	1b47,O2(1/0/1)		-0.3
	Year	111	177	24	40	7	1	4	14	31-2	0	32	.226	.340	.345	96	0	2-1	1.000	4	125	97	1b92,O2(1/0/1)		-0.3
1972	†Oak A	98	79	13	26	3	1	1	5	7-1	0	20	.329	.375	.430	149	8	1-0	1.000	1	90	150	1b64,O3R		0.4
1973	Oak A	75	71	8	13	2	0	1	6	7-1	0	17	.183	.237	.254	40	-6	0-0	.988	-3	87		1b56,O3(2/0/1),D3		-1.1
	NY A	37	131	12	36	3	1	6	14	7-1	0	34	.275	.309	.466	119	2	0-0	.992	1	114	82	1b37		-1.1
	Year	112	202	20	49	5	2	7	19	12-2	0	51	.243	.284	.391	92	-3	0-0	.991	-2	88	84	1b93,O3(2/0/1),D3		-1.1
1974	NY A	18	53	3	12	2	0	2	9	9-0	1	9	.226	.317	.377	100	1	0-1	1.000	0	92	73	1b17		-0.1
	Mil A	89	190	21	45	7	1	7	32	33-4	2	34	.237	.347	.395	114	4	0-4	.996	-2	70	87	D37,1b34,O17(4/0/13)		-0.2
	Year	107	243	24	57	9	1	7	41	38-4	2	43	.235	.340	.391	111	4	1-5	.996	-2	48	101	D37,1b17,O17(4/0/13)		-0.1
1975	Mil A	93	203	19	51	11	0	6	22	31-3	0	42	.251	.347	.379	106	3	1-1	.984	1	95	44	O42(33/0/9),1b27,D5		0.0
1976	Mil A	80	218	30	54	4	3	5	31	25-1	1	54	.248	.324	.362	104	1	0-0	1.000	3	103	0	D40,O20(5/0/15),1b10		-0.2
1977	Mil A	35	53	9	9	0	0	2	3	10-1	1	17	.170	.313	.283	64	-3	0-0	.992	-0	68	0	O8L,1b6,D7		-0.3
Total 12		965	2080	281	504	73	18	53	229	311-19	7	489	.242	.341	.371	103	15	28-21	.995	15	112	97	1b553,O177(57/1/119),D92		-1.1

HEGMAN, BOB Robert Hilmer B2.26.1958 Springfield MN BR/TR/6-1/180 [KCA80 15/380] d8.8 Col St. Cloud St.

YEAR	TM LG	G	AB	R	H	2B	3B	HR	RBI	BB-IB	HP	SO	AVG	OBP	SLG	AOPS	ABR	SB-CS	FA	FR	RNG	THR	GAMES AT POSITION	DL	BFW
1985	KC A	1	0	0	0	0	0	0	0	0-0	0	0	—				0	0-0	—	-0	0	0	/2		0.0

HEIDEMANN, JACK Jack Seale B7.11.1949 Brenham TX BR/TR/6-0/178* [CleA67 1/11] d5.2

YEAR	TM LG	G	AB	R	H	2B	3B	HR	RBI	BB-IB	HP	SO	AVG	OBP	SLG	AOPS	ABR	SB-CS	FA	FR	RNG	THR	GAMES AT POSITION	DL	BFW
1969	Cle A	3	3	0	0	0	0	0	0	0-0	0	2	.000	.250	.000	-24	0	0-0	1.000	0	118	0	S3		0.0
1970	Cle A	133	445	44	94	14	2	6	37	34-8	2	88	.211	.265	.292	53	-29	2-4	.961	-8	90	98	S132		-2.4
1971	Cle A	81	240	16	50	7	0	0	9	12-0	2	46	.208	.251	.237	36	-20	1-3	.977	-14	85	70	S81		-2.9
1972	Cle A	10	20	0	3	0	0	0	0	2-0	1	5	.150	.261	.150	24	-2	0-0	.964	-2	95	0	S10	58	-0.4
1974	Cle A	12	11	2	1	0	0	0	0	1-0	0	2	.091	.091	.091	-48	-2	0-0	1.000	-2	30	0	3b6,S4/12		-0.4
	StL N	47	70	8	19	1	0	0	5	5-0	0	14	.271	.320	.286	65	-2	1-0	.967	-9	68	73	S45/3		-1.0
1975	NY N	61	145	12	31	4	0	1	16	17-3	0	28	.214	.291	.290	65	-7	1-0	.951	-9	75	70	S44,3b4/2		-1.2

YEAR	TM LG	G	AB	R	H	2B	3B	HR	RBI	BB-IB	HP	SO	AVG	OBP	SLG	AOPS	ABR	SB-CS	FA	FR	RNG	THR	GAMES AT POSITION	DL	BFW
1976	NY N	5	12	0	1	0	0	0	0	0-0	0	0	.083	.083	.083	-55	-2	0-0	1.000	-1	69	87	S3/2		-0.3
	Mil A	69	146	11	32	1	0	2	10	7-0	0	24	.219	.253	.267	54	-9	1-3	.962	-8	68	35	3b40,2b24/D		-1.8
1977	Mil A	5	1	1	0	0	0	0	0	1-0	0	0	.000	.500	.000	50	0	0-0	1.000	1	292	1287	/2D		0.1
Total	8	426	1093	94	231	27	4	9	75	78-11	6	203	.211	.264	.268	54	-74	0-0	.965	-52	85	83	S322,3b51,2b28,D4/1	58	-10.3

HEIDRICK, EMMET R. Emmet "Snags" B7.9.1876 Queenstown PA D1.20.1916 Clarion PA BL/TR/6-0/185 d9.14

YEAR	TM LG	G	AB	R	H	2B	3B	HR	RBI	BB-IB	HP	SO	AVG	OBP	SLG	AOPS	ABR	SB-CS	FA	FR	RNG	THR	GAMES AT POSITION	DL	BFW
1898	Cle N	19	76	10	23	2	2	0	8	3	0		.303	.329	.382	105	0	3	.850	-0	195	181	O19(1/12/7)		-0.1
1899	StL N	146	591	109	194	21	14	2	82	34	3		.328	.368	.421	114	9	55	.925	3	153	106	O145(0/2/143)		0.4
1900	StL N	85	339	51	102	6	8	2	45	18	1		.301	.338	.383	100	-2	22	.959	13	181	136	O83C		0.5
1901	StL N	118	502	94	170	24	12	6	67	21	1		.339	.366	.470	149	29	32	.945	-3	99	53	O118C		2.1
1902	StL A	110	447	75	129	19	10	3	56	34	0		.289	.339	.396	105	2	17	.940	-3	109	142	O109C/PS3		-0.6
1903	StL A	120	461	55	129	20	15	1	42	19	1		.280	.310	.395	113	6	19	.954	-4	130	155	O119C/C		0.1
1904	StL A	133	538	66	147	14	10	1	36	16	0		.273	.294	.342	107	2	35	.963	7	149	155	O130C		0.2
1908	StL A	26	93	8	20	2	2	1	6	1	0		.215	.223	.312	73	-3	3	.957	-0	120	153	O25(2/23/0)		-0.5
Total	8	757	3047	468	914	108	73	16	342	146	6		.300	.333	.399	114	43	186	.946	18	137	126	O748(3/596/150)/C3SP		2.1

HEIFER, FRANK Franklin "Heck" B1.18.1854 Reading PA D8.29.1893 Reading PA 5-10.5/175 d6.3

YEAR	TM LG	G	AB	R	H	2B	3B	HR	RBI	BB-IB	HP	SO	AVG	OBP	SLG	AOPS	ABR	SB-CS	FA	FR	RNG	THR	GAMES AT POSITION	DL	BFW
1875	Bos NA	11	50	11	14	0	3	0	5	0	0		.280	.280	.400	129	1	0-0	.885	-2	0	56	1b9,O6(4/1/1),P2		-0.1

HEILEMAN, CHINK John George B8.10.1872 Cincinnati OH D7.19.1940 Cincinnati OH BR/TR/5-8/155 d7.8

YEAR	TM LG	G	AB	R	H	2B	3B	HR	RBI	BB-IB	HP	SO	AVG	OBP	SLG	AOPS	ABR	SB-CS	FA	FR	RNG	THR	GAMES AT POSITION	DL	BFW
1901	Cin N	5	15	1	2	1	0	0	1	0	0		.133	.133	.200	-4	-2	0-0	.667	-1	73	487	3b4/2		-0.3

HEILMANN, HARRY Harry Edwin "Slug" B8.3.1894 San Francisco CA D7.9.1951 Southfield MI BR/TR/6-1/195 d5.16 Mil 1918 C1 HF1952

YEAR	TM LG	G	AB	R	H	2B	3B	HR	RBI	BB-IB	HP	SO	AVG	OBP	SLG	AOPS	ABR	SB-CS	FA	FR	RNG	THR	GAMES AT POSITION	DL	BFW
1914	Det A	68	182	25	41	8	1	2	18	22	2	29	.225	.316	.313	86	-3	1-8	.870	-4	63	151	O31(2/29/0),1b16,2b6		-1.2
1916	Det A	136	451	57	127	30	11	2	73	42	5	40	.282	.349	.410	124	12	9	.952	-10	80	98	O77(5/6/66),1b30,2b9		-0.3
1917	Det A	150	556	57	156	22	11	5	86	41	3	54	.281	.333	.387	120	11	11	.960	-2	91	103	O123(0/28/95),1b27		0.2
1918	Det A	79	286	34	79	10	6	5	39	35	2	10	.276	.359	.406	136	12	13	.957	-3	88	115	O40R,1b37,2b2		0.7
1919	Det A	140	537	74	172	30	15	8	93	37	2	41	.320	.366	.477	139	25	7	.979	-10	82	80	1b140		1.2
1920	Det A	145	543	66	168	28	5	9	89	39	2	32	.309	.358	.429	111	7	3-7	.985	2	101	69	1b122,O22R		0.3
1921	Det A	149	602	114	237	43	14	19	139	53	2	37	.394	.444	.606	162	61	2-6	.962	-11	94	51	O147R,1b3		3.4
1922	Det A	118	455	92	162	27	10	21	92	58	3	28	.356	.432	.598	172	48	8-4	.948	-11	85	47	O115R,1b5		2.7
1923	Det A	144	524	121	211	44	11	18	115	74	5	40	.403	.481	.632	195	76	9-7	.960	-1	104	74	O130(6/0/124),1b12		6.0
1924	Det A	153	570	107	197	45	16	10	114	78	4	41	.346	.428	.533	149	43	13-5	.970	7	97	150	O147R,1b4		3.7
1925	Det A	150	573	97	225	40	11	13	134	67	1	27	.393	.457	.569	161	55	6-6	.970	-6	100	59	O148R		3.4
1926	Det A	141	502	90	184	41	8	9	103	67	4	19	.367	.445	.534	153	42	6-7	.972	-0	94	126	O134R		2.9
1927	Det A	141	505	106	201	50	9	14	120	72	2	16	.398	.475	.616	179	63	11-5	.966	-9	87	76	O135R		4.1
1928	Det A	151	558	83	183	38	10	14	107	57	0	45	.328	.390	.507	132	26	7-3	.971	-1	92	131	O125R,1b25		1.4
1929	Det A	125	453	86	156	41	7	15	120	50	2	39	.344	.412	.565	148	34	5-6	.966	-6	95	71	O114R,1b2		1.7
1930	Cin N	142	459	79	153	43	6	19	91	64	1	50	.333	.416	.577	144	35	2	.955	12	120	121	O106R,1b19		3.3
1932	Cin N	15	31	3	8	2	0	0	6	0	0	2	.258	.258	.323	57	-2	0	.981	-0	84	51	1b6		-0.3
Total	17	2147	7787	1291	2660	542	151	183	1539	856	40	550	.342	.410	.520	148	545	113-64	.962	-52	94	95	O1594(13/63/1518),1b448,2b17		33.2

HEIM, VAL Val Raymond B11.4.1920 Plymouth WI d8.31 Mil 1942-45

YEAR	TM LG	G	AB	R	H	2B	3B	HR	RBI	BB-IB	HP	SO	AVG	OBP	SLG	AOPS	ABR	SB-CS	FA	FR	RNG	THR	GAMES AT POSITION	DL	BFW
1942	Chi A	13	45	6	9	1	1	0	3	3	0	5	.200	.294	.267	60	-2	1-0	.958	-1	94	0	O12(9/0/3)		-0.4

HEINE, BUD William Henry B9.22.1900 Elmira NY D9.2.1976 Ft.Lauderdale FL BL/TR/5-8/145 d10.1 Col St. Bonaventure

YEAR	TM LG	G	AB	R	H	2B	3B	HR	RBI	BB-IB	HP	SO	AVG	OBP	SLG	AOPS	ABR	SB-CS	FA	FR	RNG	THR	GAMES AT POSITION	DL	BFW
1921	NY N	1	2	0	0	0	0	0	0	0-0	0	0	.000	.000	.000	-99	-1	0-0	1.000	-0	106	0	/2		-0.1

HEINTZ, CHRIS Christopher John B8.6.1974 Syosset NY BR/TR/6-1/210 d9.10 Col South Florida

YEAR	TM LG	G	AB	R	H	2B	3B	HR	RBI	BB-IB	HP	SO	AVG	OBP	SLG	AOPS	ABR	SB-CS	FA	FR	RNG	THR	GAMES AT POSITION	DL	BFW
2005	Min A	8	25	1	5	3	0	0	2	1-0	0	6	.200	.231	.320	43	-2	0-0	1.000	1	118	66	C8		0.0

HEINTZELMAN, TOM Thomas Kenneth B11.3.1946 St.Charles MO BR/TR/6-1/180* [StLN68 7/151] d8.12 f-Ken

YEAR	TM LG	G	AB	R	H	2B	3B	HR	RBI	BB-IB	HP	SO	AVG	OBP	SLG	AOPS	ABR	SB-CS	FA	FR	RNG	THR	GAMES AT POSITION	DL	BFW
1973	StL N	23	29	5	9	0	0	0	3	3-2	0	1	.310	.375	.310	91	0	0-0	1.000	0	107	120	2b6		0.0
1974	StL N	38	74	10	17	4	0	1	6	9-0	0	14	.230	.313	.324	79	-2	0-0	.978	-2	97	102	2b28,3b2/S		-0.3
1977	SF N	2	2	0	0	0	0	0	0	0-0	0	0	.000	.000	.000	-99	-1	0-0	—				/H		-0.1
1978	SF N	27	35	2	8	1	0	2	6	2-0	0	5	.229	.270	.429	96	-1	0-0	1.000	2	152	73	2b5,3b3,1b2		0.2
Total	4	90	140	17	34	5	0	3	12	14-2	0	22	.243	.312	.343	83	-4	0-0	.984	0	104	102	2b39,3b5,1b2/S		-0.2

HEINZMAN, JACK John Peter B9.27.1863 New Albany IN D11.10.1914 Louisville KY BR/TR d10.2

YEAR	TM LG	G	AB	R	H	2B	3B	HR	RBI	BB-IB	HP	SO	AVG	OBP	SLG	AOPS	ABR	SB-CS	FA	FR	RNG	THR	GAMES AT POSITION	DL	BFW
1886	Lou AA	1	5	1	0	0	0	0	0	0-0	0		.000	.000	.000	-95	-1	0	1.000	-0	0	0	/1		-0.1

HEISE, BOB Robert Lowell B5.12.1947 San Antonio TX BR/TR/6-0/175* d9.12 Col Solano (CA) CC

YEAR	TM LG	G	AB	R	H	2B	3B	HR	RBI	BB-IB	HP	SO	AVG	OBP	SLG	AOPS	ABR	SB-CS	FA	FR	RNG	THR	GAMES AT POSITION	DL	BFW
1967	NY N	16	62	7	20	4	0	0	3	3-0	0	1	.323	.354	.387	114	1	0-1	.973	3	102	84	2b12,S3,3b2		0.5
1968	NY N	6	23	3	5	0	0	0	1	1-0	0	2	.217	.250	.217	41	-2	0-0	.929	-5	36	126	S6/2		-0.8
1969	NY N	4	10	1	3	1	0	0	0	3-1	0	2	.300	.462	.400	140	1	0-0	1.000	-2	52	0	S3		-0.1
1970	SF N	67	154	15	36	5	1	1	22	5-0	0	13	.234	.256	.299	49	-12	0-1	.915	-3	112	107	S33,3b2b,3b2		-1.1
1971	SF N	13	11	2	0	0	0	0	0	0-0	0	1	.000	.000	.000	-99	-3	0-0	.833	-1	67	120	S3,3b2/2		-0.4
	Mil A	68	189	10	48	7	0	0	7	7-1	0	15	.254	.279	.291	63	-10	1-1	.961	4	110	142	S51,3b11,2b3/OL		-0.9
1972	Mil A	95	271	23	72	10	1	0	12	12-1	2	14	.266	.301	.310	84	-6	1-1	.990	-5	97	98	2b49,3b24,S9		-1.2
1973	Mil A	49	98	8	20	2	0	0	4	4-0	0	4	.204	.235	.224	30	-9	1-0	.956	-5	92	62	S29,3b9,1b4,2b4,D2		-0.9
1974	StL N	3	7	0	1	0	0	0	0	0-0	0	0	.143	.143	.143	-20	-1	0-0	1.000	2	107	102	2b17,3b6,S3		0.3
	Cal A	29	75	7	20	7	0	0	6	5-0	0	10	.267	.313	.360	98	0	0-1	1.000	2	117	105	3b45,2b14,S4/1		-0.9
1975	Bos A	63	126	12	27	3	0	0	21	4-0	2	6	.214	.246	.238	36	-11	0-1	.940	-3	57	3b22,S9/2		26	-0.3
1976	Bos A	32	56	5	15	2	0	0	5	1-0	1	2	.268	.293	.304	67	-3	0-1	1.000	2	94	132	2b21,S21,3b12/1		-0.7
1977	KC A	54	62	11	16	2	1	0	5	2-0	0	8	.258	.292	.323	67	-3	3-7	.945	-9	99	110	S174,2b154,3b135,1b6,D2/OL	26	-4.9
Total	11	499	1144	104	283	43	3	1	86	47-3	6	77	.247	.280	.293	63	-57								

HEIST, AL Alfred Michael B10.5.1927 Brooklyn NY BR/TR/6-2/185* d7.17 C3

YEAR	TM LG	G	AB	R	H	2B	3B	HR	RBI	BB-IB	HP	SO	AVG	OBP	SLG	AOPS	ABR	SB-CS	FA	FR	RNG	THR	GAMES AT POSITION	DL	BFW
1960	Chi N	41	102	11	28	5	3	1	6	10-0	0	12	.275	.339	.412	106	1	3-1	.985	-0	98	100	O33(1/32/0)		-0.1
1961	Chi N	109	321	48	82	14	3	7	37	39-0	1	51	.255	.337	.383	90	-4	3-3	.978	2	104	146	O99C	32	-0.5
1962	Hou N	27	72	4	16	1	0	0	3	3-0	1	9	.222	.263	.236	38	-6	0-0	.974	-1	89	88	O23C	32	-0.8
Total	3	177	495	63	126	20	6	8	46	52-0	2	72	.255	.327	.368	86	-9	6-4	.979	0	101	128	O155(1/154/0)		-1.4

HEITMULLER, HEINIE William Frederick B5.25.1883 San Francisco CA D10.8.1912 Los Angeles CA BR/TR/6-2/215 d4.26 Col California-Davis

YEAR	TM LG	G	AB	R	H	2B	3B	HR	RBI	BB-IB	HP	SO	AVG	OBP	SLG	AOPS	ABR	SB-CS	FA	FR	RNG	THR	GAMES AT POSITION	DL	BFW
1909	Phi A	64	210	36	60	9	8	0	15	18	3		.286	.351	.405	136	8	7	.927	-0	54	132	O61(54/7/0)		0.5
1910	Phi A	31	111	11	27	2	2	0	7	7	0		.243	.288	.297	84	-2	6	.981	-0	104	56	O28(15/11/2)		-0.5
Total	2	95	321	47	87	11	10	0	22	25	3		.271	.330	.368	118	6	13	.943	-0	70	108	O89(69/18/2)		0.0

HELD, WOODIE Woodson George B3.25.1932 Sacramento CA BR/TR/5-11/180(170-185) d9.5 OF(113/276/111)

YEAR	TM LG	G	AB	R	H	2B	3B	HR	RBI	BB-IB	HP	SO	AVG	OBP	SLG	AOPS	ABR	SB-CS	FA	FR	RNG	THR	GAMES AT POSITION	DL	BFW
1954	NY A	4	3	2	0	0	0	0	2	1-0	0	1	.000	.400	.000	17	0	0-0	1.000	-0	86	140	S4/3		0.0
1957	NY A	1	1	0	0	0	0	0	0	0-0	0	0	.000	.000	.000	-99	0	0-0	—				/H		0.0
	KC A	92	326	48	78	14	3	20	50	37-1	3	81	.239	.321	.485	116	6	4-0	.996	9	110	180	O92C		1.2
	Year	93	327	48	78	14	3	20	50	37-1	3	81	.239	.320	.483	115	5	4-0	.996	9	110	180	O92C		1.2
1958	KC A	47	131	13	28	2	0	4	16	10-0	2	28	.214	.276	.321	64	-7	0-1	1.000	-1	96	55	O41C,3b4/S		-1.0
	Cle A	67	144	12	28	4	1	3	17	15-0	4	36	.194	.285	.299	64	-14	1-3	.982	-0	105	113	O84(7/78/0),S15,3b8		-1.8
	Year	114	275	25	56	6	1	7	33	25-0	6	64	.204	.281	.309	64	-21	1-2	.962	-10	92	71	S103,3b40,O6C,2b3		0.6
1959	Cle A	143	525	82	132	19	3	29	71	46-1	2	118	.251	.313	.465	115	8	1-2	.967	9	102	120	S109	45	2.8
1960	Cle A	109	376	45	97	15	1	21	67	44-5	3	111	.258	.342	.471	122	11	0-0	.960	-15	94	99	S144		1.8
1961	Cle A	146	509	67	136	23	5	23	78	69-11	3	111	.267	.354	.468	122	16	0-0	.960	-5	101	125	S133,3b5/OC		1.8
1962	Cle A	139	466	55	116	12	2	19	78	73-5	11	107	.249	.362	.406	110	9	5-1	.982	2	103	95	2b96,O35(12/12/12),S5,3b3		2.2
1963	Cle A	133	416	61	103	19	4	17	61	61-10	8	96	.248	.352	.435	121	13	2-2	.966	2	103	114	2b52,O41(5/19/18),3b30		0.8
1964	Cle A	118	364	50	86	13	0	18	49	49-3	7	88	.236	.327	.451	107	4	1-1	.963	1	104	101	O106(57/43/50),3b5,2b4,S2		1.0
1965	Was A	122	332	46	82	16	2	16	54	49-1	5	74	.247	.345	.452	108	8	1-0	1.000	-3	77	219	O10L,2b5,S3,3b3		-0.5
1966	Bal A	56	82	6	17	3	1	1	7	12-0	0	30	.207	.309	.305	72	-1	0-0	.974	1	102	150	2b9,3b5,O2L		-0.1
1967	Bal A	26	41	4	6	1	0	1	6	6-0	1	12	.146	.286	.293	72	-1	0-0	1.000	0	117	123	3b19,O17(8/10/1),S13,2b3		-0.1
	Cal A	58	141	15	31	3	0	4	17	18-0	2	41	.220	.317	.326	94	-1	0-2	.979	0	119	0	O19(10/10/1),S13,2b12		0.0
	Year	84	182	19	37	4	0	5	23	24-0	3	53	.203	.310	.319	88	-2	0-2	.962	1	118	0	2b5,S5,3b5,O3(0/1/2)		-0.8
1968	Cal A	33	45	4	5	1	0	0	0	5-0	2	15	.111	.231	.133	13	-5	0-0	1.000	-3	118				

YEAR	TM LG	G	AB	R	H	2B	3B	HR	RBI	BB-IB	HP	SO	AVG	OBP	SLG	AOPS	ABR	SB-CS	FA	FR	RNG	THR	GAMES AT POSITION	DL	BFW
	Chi A	40	54	5	9	1	0	0	2	5-0	1	14	.167	.246	.185	33	-4	0-0	1.000	1	113	227	O33(9/3/23),3b5/2		-0.5
	Year	73	99	9	14	2	0	0	2	10-0	3	29	.141	.239	.162	24	-9	0-0	1.000	-2	112	212	O36(9/4/25),3b10,2b6,S5		-1.3
1969	Chi A	56	63	9	9	2	0	3	6	13-3	1	19	.143	.299	.317	69	-2	0-0	1.000	1	79	0	O18(3/11/5),S3,3b3/2		-0.2
Total	14	1390	4019	524	963	150	22	179	559	508-45	56	944	.240	.331	.421	109	-51	14-11	.960	1	97	104	S539,O448C,2b179,3b132	67	7.9

HELF, HANK Henry Hartz B8.26.1913 Austin TX D10.27.1984 Austin TX BR/TR/6-1/196 d5.5 Mil 1944-45

YEAR	TM LG	G	AB	R	H	2B	3B	HR	RBI	BB-IB	HP	SO	AVG	OBP	SLG	AOPS	ABR	SB-CS	FA	FR	RNG	THR	GAMES AT POSITION	DL	BFW
1938	Cle A	6	13	1	1	0	0	0	1	1-0	0	1	.077	.143	.077	-44	-3	0-0	.947	0	68	230	C5		-0.2
1940	Cle A	1	1	0	0	0	0	0	0	0-0	0	0	.000	.000	.000	-99	-0	0-0	1.000	-0	0	0	/C		0.0
1946	StL A	71	182	17	35	11	0	6	21	9	1	40	.192	.234	.352	59	-11	0-1	.965	3	74	152	C69		-0.5
Total	3	78	196	18	36	11	0	6	22	10	1	41	.184	.227	.332	51	-14	0-1	.964	3	73	156	C75		-0.7

HELFAND, ERIC Eric James B3.25.1969 Erie PA BL/TR/6-0/195* [OakA90 2/65] d9.4 Col Arizona St.

YEAR	TM LG	G	AB	R	H	2B	3B	HR	RBI	BB-IB	HP	SO	AVG	OBP	SLG	AOPS	ABR	SB-CS	FA	FR	RNG	THR	GAMES AT POSITION	DL	BFW
1993	Oak A	8	13	1	3	0	0	0	1	0-0	1	.231	.231	.231	26	-1	0-0	1.000	3	63	185	C5		0.2
1994	Oak A	7	6	1	1	0	0	0	1	0-0	1	.167	.167	.167	-15	-1	0-0	1.000	2	0	0	C6		0.1
1995	Oak A	38	86	9	14	2	1	0	7	11-0	1	25	.163	.265	.209	27	-9	0-0	.994	-4	88	97	C36		-1.1
Total	3	53	105	11	18	2	1	0	9	11-0	1	27	.171	.256	.210	25	-11	0-0	.996	1	83	101	C47		-0.8

HELFRICH, TY Emory Wilbur B10.9.1890 Pleasantville NJ D3.18.1955 Pleasantville NJ BR/TR/5-10/178 d6.30 Col Lafayette

YEAR	TM LG	G	AB	R	H	2B	3B	HR	RBI	BB-IB	HP	SO	AVG	OBP	SLG	AOPS	ABR	SB-CS	FA	FR	RNG	THR	GAMES AT POSITION	DL	BFW
1915	Bro F	43	104	12	25	6	0	0	5	15	0	21	.240	.336	.298	80	-4	2	.912	-2	113	38	2b34/OR		-0.5

HELLINGS B Philadelphia PA d7.19

YEAR	TM LG	G	AB	R	H	2B	3B	HR	RBI	BB-IB	HP	SO	AVG	OBP	SLG	AOPS	ABR	SB-CS	FA	FR	RNG	THR	GAMES AT POSITION	DL	BFW
1875	Atl NA	1	4	0	1	0	0	0	0	0	0	.250	.250	.250	85	0	0-0	.750	-0	98	0	/2		0.0

HELLMAN, TONY Anthony Joseph B1861 Cincinnati OH D3.29.1898 Cincinnati OH 5-9/175 d10.10

YEAR	TM LG	G	AB	R	H	2B	3B	HR	RBI	BB-IB	HP	SO	AVG	OBP	SLG	AOPS	ABR	SB-CS	FA	FR	RNG	THR	GAMES AT POSITION	DL	BFW
1886	Bal AA	1	3	0	0	0	0	0	0	0	0	.000	.000	.000	-99	-1	0	1.000	0			/C		0.0

HELMS, TOMMY Tommy Vann B5.5.1941 Charlotte NC BR/TR/5-10/175* d9.23 M2/C9

YEAR	TM LG	G	AB	R	H	2B	3B	HR	RBI	BB-IB	HP	SO	AVG	OBP	SLG	AOPS	ABR	SB-CS	FA	FR	RNG	THR	GAMES AT POSITION	DL	BFW
1964	Cin N	2	1	0	0	0	0	0	0	0-0	1	.000	.000	.000	-97	0	0-0	—	0			/H		0.0
1965	Cin N	21	42	4	16	2	2	0	6	3-1	1	7	.381	.435	.524	158	3	1-0	.973	-0	85	100	S8,3b2/2		0.4
1966	Cin N	138	542	72	154	23	1	9	49	24-2	2	31	.284	.315	.380	85	-10	3-4	.961	-7	87	71	3b113,2b20		-1.8
1967	Cin N★	137	497	40	136	27	4	2	35	24-8	0	41	.274	.305	.356	80	-12	5-10	.978	-20	86	90	2b88,S46		-2.5
1968	Cin N★	127	507	35	146	28	2	2	47	12-6	2	27	.288	.305	.363	94	-4	5-6	.979	5	100	99	2b127,S2/3		1.3
1969	Cin N	126	480	39	129	18	1	1	40	18-5	1	33	.269	.296	.317	68	-21	4-6	.975	-5	99	101	2b125,S4		-3.6
1970	†Cin N	150	575	42	136	21	1	1	45	21-4	0	33	.237	.262	.282	46	-45	2-2	.983	1	101	116	2b148,S12	21	-1.9
1971	Cin N	150	547	40	141	26	1	3	52	26-5	1	33	.258	.289	.325	76	-18	3-4	.990	26	110	136	2b149		1.8
1972	Hou N	139	518	45	134	20	5	5	60	24-8	0	27	.259	.291	.346	84	-12	4-3	.979	29	108	126	2b139		2.7
1973	Hou N	146	543	44	156	28	2	4	61	32-12	0	21	.287	.325	.368	93	-6	1-1	.988	2	103	105	2b145		0.6
1974	Hou N	137	452	32	126	21	1	5	50	23-7	1	27	.279	.313	.363	93	-6	5-4	.985	11	105	126	2b133		1.4
1975	Hou N	64	135	7	28	2	0	1	14	10-1	1	8	.207	.265	.222	40	-11	0-0	.988	4	119	89	2b42,3b3/S	23	-0.6
1976	Pit N	62	87	10	24	5	1	1	13	10-0	1	5	.276	.350	.391	110	1	0-0	.921	-1	103	188	3b22,2b11/S		0.1
1977	Pit N	15	12	0	0	0	0	0	0	0-0	0	3	.000	.000	.000	-97	-0	0-0	—	0			/H		-0.4
	Bos A	21	59	5	16	2	0	1	9	4-1	1	4	.271	.328	.356	78	-2	0-0	1.000	-1	25	0	D13,3b2/2		-0.4
Total	14	1435	4997	414	1342	223	21	34	477	231-60	15	301	.269	.300	.342	79	-146	33-40	.983	42	102	112	2b1129,3b143,S74,D13	44	-2.9

HELMS, WES Wesley Ray B5.12.1976 Gastonia NC BR/TR/6-4/230* [AtlN94 10/286] d9.5 [DL 1999 Atl N 30]

YEAR	TM LG	G	AB	R	H	2B	3B	HR	RBI	BB-IB	HP	SO	AVG	OBP	SLG	AOPS	ABR	SB-CS	FA	FR	RNG	THR	GAMES AT POSITION	DL	BFW
1998	Atl N	7	13	2	4	1	0	0	2	0-0	0	4	.308	.308	.615	136	1	0-0	.750	-1	41	0	3b4		
2000	Atl N	6	5	0	1	0	0	0	0	0-0	0	2	.200	.200	.200	1	-1	0-0	.833	1	161	472	3b5		-0.1
2001	Atl N	100	216	28	48	10	3	10	36	21-2	1	56	.222	.293	.435	84	-6	1-1	.991	0	94	105	1b77,3b17/OL		-1.1
2002	†Atl N	85	210	20	51	16	0	6	22	11-2	1	57	.243	.283	.405	83	-6	1-1	.987	-3	133	130	1b45,3b24,O9(5/0/4)	31	-1.3
2003	Mil N	134	476	56	124	21	0	23	67	43-3	10	131	.261	.330	.450	103	1	0-1	.945	-16	88	79	3b130	16	-1.4
2004	Mil N	92	274	24	72	13	1	4	28	24-1	5	60	.263	.331	.361	79	-8	0-1	.904	-9	87	91	3b66,1b10	40	-1.8
2005	Mil N	95	168	18	50	13	1	4	24	14-0	5	30	.298	.356	.458	113	3	0-1	.964	1	98	106	3b35,1b16,D3		0.3
Total	7	519	1362	148	350	74	5	48	179	113-8	22	340	.257	.320	.424	93	-16	2-5	.936	-28	88	81	3b281,1b148,O10(6/0/4),D3	117	-5.4

HELTON, TODD Todd Lynn B8.20.1973 Knoxville TN BL/TL/6-2/206(190-220) [ColN95 1/8] d8.2 Col Tennessee

YEAR	TM LG	G	AB	R	H	2B	3B	HR	RBI	BB-IB	HP	SO	AVG	OBP	SLG	AOPS	ABR	SB-CS	FA	FR	RNG	THR	GAMES AT POSITION	DL	BFW
1997	Col N	35	93	13	26	3	0	5	11	8-0	0	11	.280	.337	.484	91	-1	0-1	1.000	1	63	223	O15(13/0/2),1b8		-0.2
1998	Col N	152	530	78	167	37	1	25	97	53-5	0	54	.315	.380	.530	113	12	0-1	.995	16	140	129	1b146		1.4
1999	Col N	159	578	114	185	39	5	35	113	68-6	6	77	.320	.395	.587	115	14	7-6	.993	3	107	109	1b156		0.3
2000	Col N★	160	580	138	216	59	2	42	147	103-22	4	61	.372	.463	.698	154	53	5-3	.995	19	145	111	1b160		5.4
2001	Col N★	159	587	132	197	54	2	49	146	98-15	5	104	.336	.432	.685	152	50	7-5	.999	13	133	108	1b157		4.6
2002	Col N★	156	553	107	182	39	4	30	109	99-21	5	91	.329	.429	.577	148	40	5-1	.995	7	119	101	1b156		3.4
2003	Col N★	160	583	135	209	49	5	33	117	111-21	0	72	.358	.458	.630	159	57	0-4	.993	20	153	102	1b159		5.9
2004	Col N	154	547	115	190	49	2	32	96	127-19	3	72	.347	.469	.620	159	57	3-0	.997	20	154	90	1b153		6.2
2005	Col N	144	509	92	163	45	2	20	79	106-22	9	80	.320	.445	.534	135	34	3-0	.996	14	137	99	1b144		3.5
Total	9	1279	4560	924	1535	373	24	271	915	773-131	40	622	.337	.433	.607	141	316	33-23	.996	112	136	106	1b1239,O15(13/0/2)	15	30.5

HELTZEL, HEINIE William Wade B12.21.1913 York PA D5.1.1998 York PA BR/TR/5-10/150 d7.27

YEAR	TM LG	G	AB	R	H	2B	3B	HR	RBI	BB-IB	HP	SO	AVG	OBP	SLG	AOPS	ABR	SB-CS	FA	FR	RNG	THR	GAMES AT POSITION	DL	BFW
1943	Bos N	29	86	6	13	3	0	0	5	7	0	13	.151	.215	.186	17	-9	0	.880	-1	116	85	3b29		-1.1
1944	Phi N	11	22	1	4	1	0	0	2	1	0	3	.182	.280	.227	45	-2	0	.919	-2	80	27	S10		-0.3
Total	2	40	108	7	17	4	0	0	5	9	0	16	.157	.229	.194	23	-11	0	.880	-3	116	85	3b29,S10		-1.4

HEMINGWAY, ED Edson Marshall B5.8.1893 Sheridan MI D7.5.1969 Grand Rapids MI BB/TR/5-11.5/165 d9.17

YEAR	TM LG	G	AB	R	H	2B	3B	HR	RBI	BB-IB	HP	SO	AVG	OBP	SLG	AOPS	ABR	SB-CS	FA	FR	RNG	THR	GAMES AT POSITION	DL	BFW
1914	StL A	3	5	0	0	0	0	0	1	0	0	1	.000	.167	.000	-51	-1	-1	1.000	-0	64	0	3b3		-0.1
1917	NY N	7	25	3	8	1	1	0	1	2	0	5	.320	.370	.440	153	1	1	.958	1	110	205	3b7		0.3
1918	Phi N	33	108	7	23	4	1	0	12	7	1	9	.213	.267	.269	59	-5	4	.955	-1	104	67	2b25,3b3/1		-0.6
Total	3	43	138	10	31	5	2	0	13	10	1	11	.225	.282	.290	71	-5	7	.955	0	104	67	2b25,3b13/1		-0.4

HEMOND, SCOTT Scott Mathew B11.18.1965 Taunton MA BR/TR/6-0/205* [OakA86 1/12] d9.9 Col South Florida OF(8/1/3)

YEAR	TM LG	G	AB	R	H	2B	3B	HR	RBI	BB-IB	HP	SO	AVG	OBP	SLG	AOPS	ABR	SB-CS	FA	FR	RNG	THR	GAMES AT POSITION	DL	BFW
1989	Oak A	4	0	2	0	0	0	0	0	0-0	0	0					0	0-0					R3		0.0
1990	Oak A	7	13	0	2	0	0	0	1	0-0	0	5	.154	.154	.154	-14	-2	0-0	1.000	-1	70	0	3b7/2		-0.4
1991	Oak A	23	23	4	5	0	0	0	0	1-0	0	7	.217	.250	.217	32	-2	1-2	.947	-1	216	88	C8,2b7,3b2/SD		-0.3
1992	Chi A	8	13	1	3	0	0	0	1	3-0	0	7	.231	.367	.308	67	-1	1-0	1.000	0	65	150	C8,S3,3b2,O2(1/0/1)/D	88	-0.2
	Year	25	40	8	24	0	0	0	2	4-0	0	13	.225	.289	.275	63	-2	1-0	1.000	-1	64	147	C9,D5,O4(3/0/1),S3,3b3		0.0
1993	Oak A	91	215	31	55	16	0	6	26	32-0	1	55	.256	.353	.414	112	5	14-5	.991	-3	91	104	C75,O6(4/1/1)/12D		0.8
1994	Oak A	91	198	23	44	11	0	3	20	16-0	0	51	.222	.280	.323	60	-12	7-6	1.000	-6	169	84	C39,2b25,3b12,1b7,O2(1/0/1),D3		-1.5
1995	StL N	57	118	11	17	1	0	3	9	12-0	2	31	.144	.233	.229	22	-14	0-0	.985	0	98	186	C38,2b6		-1.1
Total	7	298	607	79	132	30	0	12	58	65-0	3	162	.217	.295	.326	68	-27	23-13	.991	-11	111	119	C169,2b40,3b24,D15,O12L,1b8,S4	88	-2.7

HEMP, DUCKY William H. B12.27.1867 St.Louis MO D3.6.1923 St.Louis MO d10.6

YEAR	TM LG	G	AB	R	H	2B	3B	HR	RBI	BB-IB	HP	SO	AVG	OBP	SLG	AOPS	ABR	SB-CS	FA	FR	RNG	THR	GAMES AT POSITION	DL	BFW
1887	Lou AA	1	3	1	1	0	0	0	0	0	.333	.500	.667	219	1	0	.000	-1	0	0	/OR		0.0
1890	Pit N	21	81	9	19	0	2	0	4	8	1	12	.235	.311	.284	83	-2	3	.867	1	155	343	O21(2/14/5)		-0.1
	Syr AA	9	33	1	5	1	0	0	1	0	1	.152	.176	.182	6	-4	1	.947	3	302	635	O9(2/7/0)		-0.1
Total	2	31	117	11	25	2	2	0	5	9	2	12	.214	.281	.265	67	-5	4	.877	3	192	416	O31(4/21/6)		-0.2

HEMPHILL, BRET Bret Ryan B12.17.1971 Santa Clara CA BB/TR/6-3/200 [AnaA94 14/377] d6.28 Col Cal St.-Fullerton

YEAR	TM LG	G	AB	R	H	2B	3B	HR	RBI	BB-IB	HP	SO	AVG	OBP	SLG	AOPS	ABR	SB-CS	FA	FR	RNG	THR	GAMES AT POSITION	DL	BFW
1999	Ana A	12	21	3	3	0	0	0	2	4-0	0	4	.143	.269	.143	12	-3	0-0	.955	-1	103	202	C12		-0.3

HEMPHILL, CHARLIE Charles Judson "Eagle Eye" B4.20.1876 Greenville MI D6.22.1953 Detroit MI BL/TL/5-9/160 d6.27 b-Frank

YEAR	TM LG	G	AB	R	H	2B	3B	HR	RBI	BB-IB	HP	SO	AVG	OBP	SLG	AOPS	ABR	SB-CS	FA	FR	RNG	THR	GAMES AT POSITION	DL	BFW
1899	StL N	11	37	4	9	0	1	0	3	6	1		.243	.364	.324	87	0	0	.750	-2	140	274	O10C		-0.3
	Cle N	55	202	23	56	3	5	2	23	6	1		.277	.301	.371	91	-4	3	.859	-5	84	40	O54R		-1.1
	Year	66	239	27	65	3	6	2	26	12	2		.272	.312	.364	90	-5	3	.837	-7	93	79	O64(0/10/54)		-1.4
1901	Bos A	136	545	71	142	10	10	3	62	39	2		.261	.312	.332	80	-16	11	.925	-9	136	0	O136(0/2/134)		-2.4
1902	Cle A	25	94	14	25	2	0	0	11	5	0		.266	.303	.287	67	-4	4	.860	-2	108	0	O19(17/1/1)		-0.7
	StL A	103	416	67	132	14	11	6	58	44	1		.317	.383	.447	131	18	23	.952	-6	111	229	O101(1/31/71),2b2		0.9
	Year	128	510	81	157	16	11	6	69	49	1		.308	.369	.418	120	14	27	.935	-6	110	190	O120(18/32/72),2b2		0.2
1903	StL A	105	383	36	94	6	3	3	29	23	2		.245	.292	.300	80	-10	16	.961	2	150	144	O104(4/18/82)		-1.3
1904	StL A	114	438	47	112	13	2	2	45	35	0		.256	.311	.308	102	2	23	.926	-5	95	151	O108(6/26/76)/2		-1.0

YEAR	TM LG	G	AB	R	H	2B	3B	HR	RBI	BB-IB	HP	SO	AVG	OBP	SLG	AOPS	ABR	SB-CS	FA	FR	RNG	THR	GAMES AT POSITION	DL	BFW
1906	StL A	**154**	585	90	169	19	12	4	62	43	0		.289	.338	.383	131	19	33	.961	-5	84	25	O154(0/114/40)		0.8
1907	StL A	153	603	66	156	20	9	0	38	51	2		.259	.319	.322	105	3	14	.957	-7	60	44	O153(0/134/19)		-1.2
1908	NY A	142	505	62	150	12	9	0	44	59	3		.297	.357	.356	136	22	42	.937	-4	82	41	O142(4/130/8)		1.4
1909	NY A	73	181	23	44	5	1	0	10	32	0		.243	.357	.282	101	2	10	.976	1	117	82	O45(13/32/0)		0.1
1910	NY A	102	351	49	84	9	4	0	21	55	5		.239	.350	.288	95	1	19	.971	-4	96	77	O94(0/63/31)		-0.8
1911	NY A	69	201	32	57	4	2	1	15	37	1		.284	.397	.338	99	2	9	.952	-5	93	49	O55(0/46/9)		-0.6
Total	11	1242	4541	580	1230	117	68	22	421	435	17		.271	.337	.341	106	35	207	.944	-44	98	90	O1175(45/607/525),2b3		-6.2

HEMPHILL, FRANK   Frank Vernon B5.13.1878 Greenville MI   D11.16.1950 Chicago IL   BR/TR/5-11/165   d4.17   b-Charlie

		G	AB	R	H	2B	3B	HR	RBI	BB-IB	HP	SO	AVG	OBP	SLG	AOPS	ABR	SB-CS	FA	FR	RNG	THR	GAMES AT POSITION		BFW
1906	Chi A	13	40	0	3	0	0	0	2	9	2		.075	.275	.075	11	-3	1	.970	-0	48	0	O13L		-0,5
		1	3	0	0	0	0	0	0	0	0		.000	.000	.000	-99	-1	0	1.000	0	0	0	/OL		-0.1
1909	Was A	5	4	0	1	0	0	0	0	0			.000	.259	.070	5	-4	1	.971	-9	45	0	O14L		-0.6
Total	2	14	43	0	3	0	0	0	2	9	2		.070	.259	.070										

HEMSLEY, ROLLIE   Ralston Burdett B6.24.1907 Syracuse OH   D7.31.1972 Washington DC   BR/TR/5-10/170   d4.19   Mil 1944-45   C3

		G	AB	R	H	2B	3B	HR	RBI	BB-IB	HP	SO	AVG	OBP	SLG	AOPS	ABR	SB-CS	FA	FR	RNG	THR	GAMES AT POSITION		BFW
1928	Pit N	50	133	14	36	1	3	0	18	4	0	10	.271	.292	.331	60	-8	-1	.962	-1	79	105	C49		-0.7
1929	Pit N	88	235	31	68	13	7	0	37	11	0	22	.289	.321	.404	77	-10	1	.954	5	98	114	C80		0.0
1930	Pit N	104	324	45	82	19	6	2	45	22	0	21	.253	.301	.367	60	-22	3	.979	4	96	103	C98		-1.0
1931	Pit N	10	35	3	6	3	0	0	1	3	0	3	.171	.237	.257	33	-3	0	1.000	0	96	62	C9		-0.3
	Chi N	66	204	28	63	17	4	3	31	17	0	30	.309	.362	.475	121	6	4	.975	4	125	113	C53		1.3
	Year	76	239	31	69	20	4	3	32	20	0	33	.289	.344	.444	109	3	4	.978	4	120	105	C62		1.0
1932	†Chi N	60	151	27	36	10	3	4	20	10	0	16	.238	.286	.424	89	-3	2	.974	3	195	73	C47/OC		0.2
1933	Cin N	49	116	9	22	8	0	0	7	6	0	9	.190	.230	.259	40	-9	0	.970	2	98	101	C41		-0.5
	StL A	32	95	7	23	2	1	1	15	11	0	12	.242	.321	.316	65	-5	0-0	.965	-1	112	81	C27		-0.4
1934	StL A★	123	431	47	133	31	7	2	52	29	2	37	.309	.355	.427	93	-5	6-2	.973	23	106	**135**	C114,O6L		2.4
1935	StL A★	144	504	57	146	32	7	0	48	44	2	41	.290	.349	.381	85	-11	3-2	.979	11	118	86	C141		0.8
1936	StL A☆	116	377	43	99	24	2	3	39	46	2	30	.263	.343	.353	70	-17	2-3	.969	-5	98	66	C114		-1.5
1937	StL A	100	334	30	74	12	3	3	28	25	0	29	.222	.276	.302	45	-29	0-0	.969	-5	91	116	C94,1b2		-2.7
1938	Cle A	26	203	27	60	11	3	2	28	23	0	14	.296	.367	.409	96	-1	1-1	.980	6	88	117	C58		0.8
1939	Cle A☆	107	395	58	104	17	4	2	36	26	0	26	.263	.309	.342	69	-20	2-4	.984	7	111	101	C106		-0.7
1940	Cle A★	119	416	46	111	20	5	4	42	22	0	25	.267	.304	.368	75	-17	1-3	**.994**	12	146	104	C117		0.2
1941	Cle A	98	288	29	69	10	5	2	24	18	0	19	.240	.284	.330	65	-16	2-0	.980	1	114	91	C96		-1.0
1942	Cin N	36	115	7	13	1	2	0	7	4	0	11	.113	.143	.157	-12	-17	0	.982	5	95	77	C34		-1.0
	NY A	31	85	12	25	3	1	0	15	5	0	9	.294	.333	.353	95	-1	1-0	.991	3	192	82	C29		0.3
1943	NY A	62	180	12	43	6	3	2	24	13	0	9	.239	.290	.339	83	-5	0-1	.981	1	107	97	C76		-0.3
1944	NY A★	81	284	23	76	12	5	2	26	9	0	13	.268	.290	.366	84	-7	0-2	.977	7	95	170	C45		0.0
1946	Phi N	49	139	7	31	4	1	0	11	9	0	10	.223	.270	.266	54	-9	0	.977	1	0	0	C2		0.0
1947	Phi N	2	3	0	1	0	0	0	1	0	0		.333	.333	.333	80	0	0	1.000	0	0	0	C2		0.0
Total	19	1593	5047	562	1321	261	72	31	555	357		4	395	.262	.311	.360	74	-209	29-18	.978	82	114	101	C1482,O7(6/1/0),1b2	-4.0

HEMUS, SOLLY   Solomon Joseph B4.17.1923 Phoenix AZ   BL/TR/5-9/175*   d4.27   M3/C4

		G	AB	R	H	2B	3B	HR	RBI	BB-IB	HP	SO	AVG	OBP	SLG	AOPS	ABR	SB-CS	FA	FR	RNG	THR	GAMES AT POSITION		BFW
1949	StL N	20	3	8	1	1	0	0	2	7	0	3	.333	.450	.364	115	1	0	.981	1	105	72	2b16		0.3
1950	StL N	11	15	1	2	1	0	0	0	4	1		.133	.235	.200	15	-2	0	1.000	1	135	179	3b5		-0.1
1951	StL N	120	420	68	118	18	9	2	32	75	4	31	.281	.395	.381	109	9	7-7	.965	12	**111**	108	S105,2b12		2.7
1952	StL N	151	570	**105**	153	28	8	15	52	96	**20**	55	.268	.392	.425	126	26	1-5	.964	9	105	96	S150,2b3		3.9
1953	StL N	154	585	110	163	32	11	14	61	86	**12**	40	.279	.382	.443	114	16	2-1	.944	-9	95	76	S66,3b27,2b12		3.5
1954	StL N	124	214	43	65	15	3	2	27	55	1	22	.304	.453	.430	131	15	5-1	.956	-3	95	100	3b43,2b10,S2		1.1
1955	StL N	96	206	36	50	10	4	3	21	27-0	2	22	.243	.335	.383	91	-1	1-0	—	0			/H		-0.5
1956	StL N	8	5	1	1	0	0	0	2	1-0	1	6	.200	.429	.200	77	0	0-0	—	0			/H		0.0
	Phi N	78	187	24	54	10	4	5	24	28-2	7	21	.289	.397	.465	134	11	1-1	.974	-18	74	61	2b49/3		-0.4
	Year	86	192	25	55	10	4	5	26	29-2	8	21	.286	.398	.458	133	11	1-1	.974	-18	74	61	2b49/3		-0.4
1957	Phi N	70	108	8	20	6	1	0	5	20-4	2	21	.185	.323	.259	61	-5	1-1	.980	-4	78	81	2b24		-0.8
1958	Phi N	105	334	53	95	14	3	6	36	51-6	**8**	34	.284	.390	.416	116	10	3-1	.969	-17	90	84	2b85/3		0.2
1959	StL N	24	17	2	4	2	0	1	8	8-0	1	2	.235	.500	.353	124	2	0-0	1.000	1	188	0	/23M		0.2
Total	11	961	2694	459	736	137	41	51	263	456-12	62	247	.273	.390	.411	115	81	21-18	.962	-21	104	102	S471,2b212,3b80		9.9

HENDERSON, DAVE   David Lee B7.21.1958 Merced CA   BR/TR/6-2/220*   [SeaA77 1/26]   d4.9

		G	AB	R	H	2B	3B	HR	RBI	BB-IB	HP	SO	AVG	OBP	SLG	AOPS	ABR	SB-CS	FA	FR	RNG	THR	GAMES AT POSITION	DL	BFW
1981	Sea A	59	126	17	21	3	0	6	13	16-1	1	24	.167	.264	.333	68	-5	2-1	1.000	3	101	150	O58(2/33/31)		-0.4
1982	Sea A	104	324	47	82	17	1	14	48	36-2	0	67	.253	.327	.441	105	2	2-5	.985	5	100	179	O101(2/99/2)	15	0.5
1983	Sea A	137	484	50	130	24	5	17	55	28-3	1	93	.269	.306	.444	101	-1	9-3	.982	7	100	203	O97(0/88/11),D10	19	0.3
1984	Sea A	112	350	42	98	23	0	14	43	19-0	2	56	.280	.320	.466	115	7	5-5	.988	8	109	203	O80(0/88/11),D10		-1.3
1985	Sea A	139	502	70	121	28	2	14	68	48-2	3	104	.241	.310	.388	89	-7	6-1	.986	-4	95	92	O138(1/126/27)		1.2
1986	Sea A	103	337	51	93	19	4	14	44	37-4	0	95	.276	.350	.481	122	10	1-3	.979	5	105	208	O80(0/51/31),D22		-0.5
	†Bos A	36	51	8	10	3	0	1	3	2-0	0	15	.196	.226	.314	45	-4	1-0	.981	3	126	256	O32C		1.1
	Year	139	388	59	103	22	4	15	47	39-4	0	110	.265	.335	.459	112	6	2-3	.980	8	109	**216**	O112(0/83/31),D22		1.1
1987	Bos A	75	184	30	43	10	0	8	25	22-0	0	48	.234	.313	.418	90	-3	1-1	.958	-2	101	0	O64(5/29/30)/D		0.2
	SF N	15	21	2	5	2	0	0	1	8-0	0	5	.238	.448	.333	116	1	2-0	1.000	0	78	319	O9(1/8/1)		3.1
1988	†Oak A	146	507	100	154	38	1	24	94	47-1	4	92	.304	.363	.525	151	35	2-4	.982	0	103	79	O149C,D2		5.
1989	†Oak A	152	579	77	145	24	3	15	80	54-1	3	131	.250	.315	.380	99	-1	8-5	.977	-5	99	63	O116(1/110/5),D6	31	1.6
1990	†Oak A	127	450	65	122	28	0	20	63	40-1	1	105	.271	.331	.467	125	14	3-1	.988	2	101	139	O140(4/135/1)/2D		-0.3
1991	Oak A★	150	572	86	158	33	4	25	85	58-3	4	113	.276	.346	.465	129	23	6-6	.997	2	101	130	O12(0/9/3),D4	142	-1.2
1992	Oak A	20	63	1	9	1	0	0	2	2-0	0	16	.143	.169	.159	-8	-9	0-0	.991	7	112	164	O76(2/60/14),D28	24	-0.2
1993	Oak A	107	382	37	84	19	0	20	53	32-0	0	113	.220	.275	.427	92	-7	0-3	.962	-1	91	154	O40(17/6/17),D16	13	-0.7
1994	KC A	56	198	27	49	14	1	5	31	16-1	1	28	.247	.304	.404	77	-7	2-0	.984	28	102	129	O1388(36/1157/229),D99/2	244	5.
Total	14	1538	5130	710	1324	286	17	197	708	465-19	22	1105	.258	.320	.436	108	48	50-38	.984	28	102	129	O1388(36/1157/229),D99/2	244	5.

HENDERSON, KEN   Kenneth Joseph B6.15.1946 Carroll IA   BB/TR/6-2/180*   d4.23

		G	AB	R	H	2B	3B	HR	RBI	BB-IB	HP	SO	AVG	OBP	SLG	AOPS	ABR	SB-CS	FA	FR	RNG	THR	GAMES AT POSITION	DL	BFW
1965	SF N	63	73	10	14	1	1	1	9	9-4	0	19	.192	.277	.233	45	-5	1-1	.980	1	100	143	O48(5/31/16)		-0.
1966	SF N	11	29	4	9	1	1	1	1	2-0	1	3	.310	.375	.517	141	2	0-0	.917	-2	67	0	O10(1/7/4)		-1.
1967	SF N	65	179	15	34	3	0	4	14	19-0	2	52	.190	.274	.274	58	-10	0-1	.947	-1	94	108	O52(8/33/18)		-1.
1968	SF N	3	3	1	1	0	0	0	0	2-0	0	1	.333	.600	.333	186	1	0-0	1.000	-0	83	0	O2(1/1/0)		-1.
1969	SF N	113	374	42	84	14	4	6	44	42-2	5	64	.225	.308	.332	81	-9	6-4	.969	4	100	146	O146(113/25/35)	28	2.
1970	SF N	148	554	104	163	35	4	17	88	87-9	5	78	.294	.394	.460	130	27	20-3	.966	-3	104	33	O138(109/14/26)/1		1.
1971	†SF N	141	504	80	133	26	6	15	65	84-12	2	66	.264	.370	.429	111	6	14-7	.974	9	105	178	O123(95/26/2)		-0.
1972	SF N	130	439	60	113	21	2	18	51	38-6	2	66	.257	.317	.437	111	4	3-4	.972	-3	97	32	O44(8/36/0),D26	82	-0.
1973	Chi A	73	262	32	68	13	0	6	32	27-2	1	49	.260	.330	.378	96	-1	3-4	.987	-4	103	58	O162C		-0.
1974	Chi A	162	602	76	176	35	5	20	95	66-9	2	112	.292	.360	.467	134	17	12-7	.990	1	107	71	O137C/D		-0.
1975	Chi A	140	513	65	129	20	3	9	53	74-14	4	65	.251	.347	.355	98	1	5-3	.987	-10	92	31	O122(0/20/115)		-1.
1976	Atl N	133	435	52	114	19	0	13	61	62-7	1	68	.262	.352	.395	107	4	2-1	.983	-6	91	0	O65(0/8/61),D3	54	-1.
1977	Tex A	75	244	23	63	14	0	5	23	18-4	5	37	.258	.317	.377	87	-4	2-1	1.000	-0	113	0	O7R	28	-1.
1978	NY N	7	22	2	5	2	0	1	4	4-1	0	4	.227	.346	.455	125	1	0-1	1.000	-2	99	0	O38(0/30/9)		-1.
	Cin N	64	144	10	24	6	1	3	19	23-3	1	32	.167	.278	.285	58	-8	0-0	1.000	-2	101	0	O45(0/30/16)		-1.
	Year	71	166	12	29	8	1	4	23	27-4	0	36	.175	.287	.307	67	-7	0-1	1.000	-0	96	0	O2(1/0/1)	51	-1.
1979	Cin N	10	13	1	3	1	0	0	2	0-0	1	2	.231	.231	.308	46	-1	0-0	.950	-2	83	0	O23(14/9/0)		-0.
	Chi N	62	81	11	19	2	0	2	9	15-1	1	16	.235	.361	.333	82	-1	0-0	.955	-2	84	0	O25(15/9/0)		-0.
	Year	72	94	12	22	3	0	2	11	15-1	2	18	.234	.345	.330	78	-2	0-0	.944	1	90	214	O22(15/0/9)	33	-0.
1980	Chi N	44	82	7	16	3	0	2	9	17-3	0	19	.195	.333	.305	73	-2	0-0	.977	-17	100	83	O1252(434/544/360),D30,3b3/1	276	-1.
Total	16	1444	4553	595	1168	216	26	122	576	589-77	30	763	.257	.343	.396	106	51	86-42	.977	-17	100	83	O1252(434/544/360),D30,3b3/1	276	-1.

HENDERSON, RICKEY   Rickey Henley B12.25.1958 Chicago IL   BR/TL/5-10/195(180-195)   [OakA76 4/96]   d6.24

		G	AB	R	H	2B	3B	HR	RBI	BB-IB	HP	SO	AVG	OBP	SLG	AOPS	ABR	SB-CS	FA	FR	RNG	THR	GAMES AT POSITION		BFW
1979	Oak A	89	351	49	96	13	3	1	26	34-0	2	39	.274	.338	.336	88	-5	33-11	.973	1	106	78	O88(62/32/1)		-0.
1980	Oak A★	158	591	111	179	22	4	9	53	117-7	5	54	.303	.420	.399	134	37	**100**-26	.984	14	111	121	O157(157/1/0)/D		5
1981	†Oak A★	108	423	**89**	**135**	18	7	6	35	64-4	2	68	.319	.408	.437	150	30	**56**-22	.979	15	**128**	87	O107(107/1/0)		4
1982	Oak A★	149	536	119	143	24	4	10	51	**116**-1	2	94	.267	.398	.382	120	22	**130**-42	.977	4	112	21	O144(138/10/0),D4		3
1983	Oak A★	145	513	105	150	25	7	9	48	**103**-8	4	80	.292	.414	.421	138	34	**108**-19	.992	8	114	81	O142(138/10/0)/D		4
1984	Oak A★	142	502	113	147	27	4	16	58	86-1	5	81	.293	.399	.458	146	36	**66**-18	.969	8	114	74	O140(140/6/0)		4

YEAR	TM LG	G	AB	R	H	2B	3B	HR	RBI	BB-IB	HP	SO	AVG	OBP	SLG	AOPS	ABR	SB-CS	FA	FR	RNG	THR	GAMES AT POSITION	DL	BFW
1985	NY A★	143	547	**146**	172	28	5	24	72	99-1	3	65	.314	.419	.516	158	49	**80**-10	.980	10	**117**	79	O141(6/141/0)/D	14	**6.9**
1986	NY A★	153	608	**130**	160	31	5	28	74	89-2	2	81	.263	.358	.469	124	22	**87**-18	.986	4	110	50	O146(11/138/0),D5		3.6
1987	NY A★	95	358	78	104	17	3	17	37	80-1	2	52	.291	.423	.497	144	27	41-8	.980	5	120	79	O69(34/39/0),D24	61	3.4
1988	NY A	140	554	118	169	30	2	6	50	82-1	3	54	.305	.394	.399	124	23	**93**-13	.965	4	110	86	O136(135/3/0),D3		3.8
1989	NY A	65	235	41	58	13	1	3	22	56-0	1	29	.247	.392	.349	112	8	25-8	.993	2	110	78	O65L		1.0
	†Oak A	85	306	72	90	13	2	9	35	70-5	1	39	.294	.425	.438	149	25	52-6	.985	4	112	62	O82L,D3		3.6
	Year	150	541	**113**	148	26	3	12	57	**126**-5	2	68	.274	.411	.399	133	33	**77**-14	.988	6	111	69	O147L,D3		3.6
1990	†Oak A★	136	489	**119**	159	33	3	28	61	97-2	4	60	.325	**.439**	.577	**189**	**64**	65-10	.983	7	115	65	O118L,D15		**4.6**
1991	Oak A★	134	470	105	126	17	1	18	57	98-7	5	73	.268	.400	.423	136	29	**58**-18	.970	7	105	160	O119L,D10		**7.7**
1992	†Oak A	117	396	77	112	18	3	15	46	95-5	6	56	.283	.426	.457	155	36	48-11	.984	5	104	130	O108L,D6	15	3.7
1993	Oak A	90	318	77	104	19	1	17	47	85-6	2	46	.327	.469	.553	184	45	31-6	.974	6	115	110	O74L,D16	36	4.5
	†Tor A	44	163	37	35	3	1	4	12	35-1	2	19	.215	.356	.319	83	-3	22-2	.975	-4	85	39	O44L		4.9
	Year	134	481	114	139	22	2	21	59	120-7	4	65	.289	.432	.474	148	41	53-8	.974	2	104	83	O118L,D16		-0.4
1994	Oak A	87	296	66	77	13	0	6	20	72-1	5	45	.260	.411	.365	111	11	22-7	.977	5	119	90	O71(66/10/0),D13		4.5
1995	Oak A	112	407	67	122	31	1	9	54	72-2	1	66	.300	.407	.447	129	22	32-10	.988	-2	92	87	O90L,D19	16	1.4
1996	†SD N	148	465	110	112	17	2	9	29	125-2	10	90	.241	.410	.344	107	14	37-15	.975	-5	96	40	O134(114/10/17)		1.8
1997	†SD N	88	288	63	79	11	0	6	27	71-2	4	62	.274	.422	.375	119	13	29-4	.959	3	112	87	O78(55/17/8),D2	15	0.7
	Ana N	32	115	21	21	3	0	2	7	26-0	2	23	.183	.343	.261	60	-6	16-4	1.000	0	111	0	O19,O13(11/2/0)		1.8
1998	Oak A	152	542	101	128	16	1	14	57	**118**-0	5	114	.236	.376	.347	91	-2	**66**-13	.988	2	110	34	O151(142/24/0)		-0.5
1999	†NY N	121	438	89	138	30	0	12	42	82-1	2	82	.315	.423	.466	131	26	37-14	.988	-8	88	0	O116L/D		0.5
2000	NY N	31	96	17	21	1	0	0	2	25-1	2	20	.219	.387	.229	65	-4	5-2	.946	-3	82	0	O29L	19	1.6
	†Sea A	92	324	58	77	13	2	4	30	63-0	2	55	.238	.362	.327	79	-8	31-9	.984	-1	111	0	O88L		-0.7
2001	SD N	123	379	70	86	17	3	8	42	81-0	3	84	.227	.366	.351	94	0	25-7	.982	-3	90	80	O104L/D		-0.3
2002	Bos A	72	179	40	40	6	1	5	16	38-0	4	47	.223	.369	.352	92	0	8-2	.946	-2	88	152	O54(49/4/1),D5		-0.3
2003	LA N	30	72	7	15	1	0	2	5	11-0	2	16	.208	.321	.306	67	-3	3-0	.955	-1	73	108	O18L		-0.5
Total	25	3081	10961	2295	3055	510	66	297	1115	2190-61	98	1694	.279	.401	.419	127	542	1406-335	.979	84	108	73	O2826(2421/448/27),D149	176	70.2

HENDERSON, STEVE   Stephen Curtis B11.18.1952 Houston TX BR/TR/6-2/190* [CinN74 5/119] d6.16 C4 Col Prairie View A&M

YEAR	TM LG	G	AB	R	H	2B	3B	HR	RBI	BB-IB	HP	SO	AVG	OBP	SLG	AOPS	ABR	SB-CS	FA	FR	RNG	THR	GAMES AT POSITION	DL	BFW
1977	NY N	99	350	67	104	16	6	12	65	43-2	1	79	.297	.372	.480	132	16	6-3	.980	4	111	68	O97L		1.6
1978	NY N	157	587	83	156	30	9	10	65	60-3	2	109	.266	.333	.399	107	5	13-7	.968	8	103	137	O155L		0.7
1979	NY N	98	350	42	107	16	3	6	39	38-6	4	58	.306	.380	.440	126	13	13-5	.990	4	106	80	O94L		1.4
1980	NY N	143	513	75	149	17	8	8	58	62-3	3	90	.290	.368	.402	117	13	23-12	.981	7	113	71	O136L	48	1.5
1981	Chi N	82	287	32	84	9	5	5	35	42-7	2	61	.293	.382	.411	119	9	5-7	.951	-3	98	58	O77L	74	0.1
1982	Chi N	92	257	23	60	12	4	2	29	22-3	0	64	.233	.293	.335	73	-10	6-5	.956	1	99	99	O70L		-1.3
1983	Sea A	121	436	50	128	32	3	10	54	44-2	0	82	.294	.356	.450	116	10	10-14	.970	-2	85	192	O112L,D6		0.4
1984	Sea A	109	325	42	85	12	3	10	35	38-4	1	62	.262	.341	.409	107	4	2-4	.958	-3	91	131	O53L,D51	15	-0.3
1985	Oak A	85	193	25	58	8	3	3	31	18-0	0	34	.301	.358	.420	121	6	0-0	.953	-3	86	106	O58(47/0/11)/D		0.1
1986	Oak A	11	26	2	2	1	0	0	3	0-0	0	5	.077	.074	.115	-52	-6	0-0	.800	-1	67	0	O7L/D		-0.7
1987	Oak A	46	114	14	33	7	0	3	9	12-1	0	19	.289	.357	.430	115	3	0-0	.943	-4	72	0	O31(5/0/28),D9		-0.3
1988	Hou N	42	46	4	10	2	0	0	5	7-1	0	14	.217	.321	.261	72	-1	1-1	1.000	5	133	398	O8(4/0/4)/1		-0.3
Total	12	1085	3484	459	976	162	49	68	428	386-32	13	677	.280	.352	.413	112	61	79-58	.968	12	100	104	O898(856/0/43),D68/1	137	3.1

HENDRICK, GEORGE   George Andrew B10.18.1949 Los Angeles CA BR/TR/6-3/195(195-207) [OakA68*1/1] d6.4 C5

YEAR	TM LG	G	AB	R	H	2B	3B	HR	RBI	BB-IB	HP	SO	AVG	OBP	SLG	AOPS	ABR	SB-CS	FA	FR	RNG	THR	GAMES AT POSITION	DL	BFW
1971	Oak A	42	114	8	27	4	1	0	8	3-0	1	20	.237	.254	.289	55	-7	0-1	.981	-2	86	56	O36(18/16/10)		-1.2
1972	†Oak A	58	121	10	22	1	1	4	15	3-0	1	22	.182	.205	.306	54	-8	3-2	1.000	-2	97	0	O41(5/28/12)		-1.3
1973	Cle A	113	440	64	118	18	0	21	61	25-1	2	71	.268	.308	.452	110	4	7-6	.988	-5	85	0	O110(0/107/3)	46	-1.3
1974	Cle A★	139	495	65	138	23	1	19	67	33-4	1	73	.279	.322	.444	120	11	6-4	.989	-5	96	91	O133(2/131/0)/D		0.3
1975	Cle A	149	551	72	146	20	3	25	81	51-6	0	82	.265	.323	.448	126	16	4-4	.987	2	96	128	O146(136/13/3),D3		0.9
1976	SD N	152	541	75	168	25	2	23	81	61-8	2	74	.311	.381	.492	147	36	11-6	.983	8	109	115	O142(24/131/9)		4.2
1977	SD N	36	111	9	27	4	0	3	8	12-0	0	16	.243	.317	.360	96	-1	1-1	.986	-1	96	55	O33(1/26/6)		-0.3
	StL N	102	382	55	110	27	1	17	67	28-1	2	44	.288	.337	.497	132	15	1-0	.996	-2	98	85	O101(2/87/12)		1.3
	Year	138	493	64	137	31	1	20	75	40-1	2	60	.278	.332	.467	124	15	2-1	.994	-3	98	78	O134(3/113/18)		1.0
1979	StL N	140	493	67	148	27	1	16	75	49-5	0	62	.300	.359	.456	120	14	2-3	.993	3	92	**177**	O138(0/14/124)		1.0
1980	StL N★	150	572	73	173	33	2	25	109	32-9	4	67	.302	.342	.498	126	19	6-1	.994	-2	99	81	O149(0/54/121)		1.2
1981	StL N	101	394	67	112	19	3	18	61	41-7	4	44	.284	.356	.485	131	16	4-2	.983	-7	90	71	O101(0/51/59)		0.6
1982	†StL N	136	515	65	145	20	5	19	104	37-8	1	80	.282	.323	.450	113	7	3-2	.980	-8	93	61	O134R		-0.8
1983	StL N☆	144	529	73	168	33	3	18	97	51-15	2	76	.318	.373	.493	139	29	3-4	.992	-1	117	99	O134R		1.9
1984	StL N	120	441	57	122	28	1	9	69	32-2	1	75	.277	.324	.406	107	4	0-2	.990	-6	85	115	O116R/1		-0.9
1985	Pit N	69	256	23	59	15	0	2	25	18-1	0	42	.230	.278	.313	66	-12	1-0	.971	0	111	46	O65R		-1.6
	Cal A	16	41	5	5	1	0	2	6	4-1	0	8	.122	.196	.293	33	-4	0-0	1.000	-0	85	140	O12R/D		-0.5
1986	†Cal A	102	283	45	77	13	1	14	47	26-5	1	41	.272	.332	.473	118	7	1-1	.968	2	108	129	O93(0/2/92),1b7,D4		-0.5
1987	Cal A	65	162	14	39	10	0	5	25	14-1	0	18	.241	.301	.395	85	-4	0-0	.967	-4	84	42	O45(37/0/11),1b9,D5	48	-0.9
1988	Cal A	69	127	12	31	1	0	3	19	7-1	1	20	.244	.283	.323	73	-5	0-1	.933	0	109	0	O24(20/0/4),1b12,D3		-0.7
Total	18	2048	7129	941	1980	343	27	267	1111	567-77	22	1013	.278	.329	.446	116	139	59-47	.985	-46	96	89	O1813(246/749/897),1b121,D17	94	1.3

HENDRICK, HARVEY   Harvey "Gink" B11.9.1897 Mason TN D10.29.1941 Covington TN BL/TR/6-2/190 d4.20 Col Vanderbilt OF(128/21/86)

YEAR	TM LG	G	AB	R	H	2B	3B	HR	RBI	BB-IB	HP	SO	AVG	OBP	SLG	AOPS	ABR	SB-CS	FA	FR	RNG	THR	GAMES AT POSITION	DL	BFW
1923	†NY A	37	66	9	18	3	1	3	12	2	0	8	.273	.294	.485	101	-1	3-0	.947	-0	78	179	O13(11/2/0)		-0.1
1924	NY A	40	76	7	20	0	0	1	11	2	1	7	.263	.291	.303	53	-6	1-0	.975	1	117	60	O17(15/0/2)		-0.6
1925	Cle A	25	28	2	8	1	2	0	9	3	0	5	.286	.355	.464	106	0	0-0	1.000	1	117	46	1b3		0.0
1927	Bro N	128	458	55	142	18	11	4	50	24	4	40	.310	.350	.424	106	2	29	.969	-3	88	88	O64(15/0/64),1b53/2		-0.8
1928	Bro N	126	425	83	135	15	10	11	59	54	2	34	.318	.397	.478	129	19	16	.913	0	103	115	3b91,O17(6/11/0)		2.3
1929	Bro N	110	384	69	136	25	6	14	82	31	1	20	.354	.404	.560	139	23	14	.975	1	98	107	O42(30/2/10),1b39,3b7,S4		1.7
1930	Bro N	68	167	29	43	10	1	5	28	20	2	19	.257	.344	.419	84	-4	2	.947	0	96	164	O42(36/6/0),1b7		-0.6
1931	Bro N	1	1	0	0	0	0	0	0	0	0	0	.000	.000	.000	-99	-0		—	0			/H		0.0
	Cin N	137	530	74	167	32	9	1	75	53	2	40	.315	.379	.415	121	17	3	.987	-6	87	**121**	1b137		0.0
	Year	138	531	74	167	32	9	1	75	53	2	40	.315	.379	.414	120	16	3	.987	-6	87	**121**	1b137		-0.1
1932	StL N	28	72	8	18	2	0	1	5	5	0	9	.250	.299	.319	64	-4	0	.987	-6	87	121	1b137		-0.1
	Cin N	94	398	56	120	30	3	4	40	23	1	29	.302	.341	.422	107	4	3	.986	-4	91	100	3b12,O5R		-0.5
	Year	122	470	64	138	32	3	5	45	28	1	38	.294	.335	.406	100	0	3	.986	-5	91	100	1b94		-0.9
1933	Chi N	69	189	30	55	13	3	4	23	13	3	17	.291	.346	.455	128	7	4	.983	-1	99	114	1b94,3b12,O5R		-1.4
1934	Phi N	59	116	12	34	8	0	0	19	9	0	15	.293	.344	.362	79	-3	0	.962	-2	98	121	O12(11/0/1),1b7,3b7		0.2
Total	11	922	2910	434	896	157	46	48	413	239	16	243	.308	.364	.443	113	54	75-0	.986	-15	95	106	1b378,O220L,3b118,S4/2		-0.6

HENDRICKS, ELROD   Elrod Jerome "Ellie" B12.22.1940 Charlotte Amalie, V.I.   D12.21.2005 Glen Burnie MD BL/TR/6-1/175* d4.13 C28

YEAR	TM LG	G	AB	R	H	2B	3B	HR	RBI	BB-IB	HP	SO	AVG	OBP	SLG	AOPS	ABR	SB-CS	FA	FR	RNG	THR	GAMES AT POSITION	DL	BFW
1968	Bal A	79	183	19	37	8	1	7	23	19-2	1	51	.202	.279	.372	96	-1	0-0	.991	-1	88	99	C53		0.0
1969	†Bal A	105	295	36	72	5	0	12	38	39-5	2	44	.244	.333	.383	100	0	0-1	**.998**	8	**156**	99	C87,1b4		1.2
1970	†Bal A	106	322	32	78	9	0	12	41	33-4	4	44	.242	.317	.382	91	-4	0-1	.986	-5	109	102	C90,1b3		-0.2
1971	†Bal A	101	316	33	79	14	1	9	42	39-5	2	38	.250	.334	.386	103	2	0-0	.986	-5	112	97	C95		0.1
1972	Chi N	33	84	6	13	4	0	1	4	12-2	0	19	.155	.258	.202	37	-6	0-1	.986	1	163	136	C28		-0.5
	Chi N	17	43	7	5	1	0	2	6	13-6	0	8	.116	.321	.279	65	-2	0-1	.978	2	75	101	C16		-0.9
1973	†Bal A	41	101	9	18	5	1	3	15	10-4	1	22	.178	.257	.337	66	-5	0-0	.971	1	93	82	C38/D		-0.2
1974	†Bal A	66	159	18	33	8	2	3	8	17-4	1	25	.208	.283	.340	82	-4	0-0	1.000	-6	95	82	C54/1D		-0.9
1975	Bal A	85	223	32	48	8	2	8	38	34-5	1	40	.215	.319	.377	102	1	0-1	**.995**	1	109	99	C83		0.5
1976	Bal A	28	79	2	11	1	0	1	4	7-1	0	13	.139	.209	.190	18	-8	0-0	.971	-7	66	77	C27		-1.6
	†NY A	26	53	6	12	1	0	3	6	3-0	1	10	.226	.263	.415	99	-1	0-1	1.000	-0	136	53	C18		0.0
	Year	54	132	8	23	2	0	4	10	10-1	1	23	.174	.231	.280	51	-9	0-1	.982	-7	91	68	C45		-1.6
1977	NY A	10	11	1	3	1	0	1	5	0-0	0	2	.273	.273	.636	140	1	0-0	1.000	0	146	0	C6		-0.2
1978	Bal A	13	18	4	6	1	0	1	3	3-2	0	5	.333	.429	.556	185	2	0-0	.955	0	104	81	C6/PD		0.3
1979	Bal A	1	1	0	0	0	0	0	0	0-0	0	1	.000	.000	.000	-99	-0	0-0	.500	-1	11	0	/C		-0.1
Total	12	711	1888	205	415	66	7	62	230	229-40	12	319	.220	.306	.361	90	-25	1-5	.990	-10	118	96	C602,1b8,D3/P		-1.4

HENDRICKS, JACK   John Charles B4.9.1875 Joliet IL D5.13.1943 Chicago IL BL/TL/5-11.5/160 d6.12 M7 Col Butler/North Central

YEAR	TM LG	G	AB	R	H	2B	3B	HR	RBI	BB-IB	HP	SO	AVG	OBP	SLG	AOPS	ABR	SB-CS	FA	FR	RNG	THR	GAMES AT POSITION	DL	BFW
1902	NY N	8	26	1	6	2	0	0	4				.231	.286	.308	84	0	2	.929	-0	92	0	O7R		-0.1
	Chi N	2	7	0	4	0	1	0	0	0	0		.571	.571	.857	350	2	0	1.000	0	0	0	O2R		0.2

YEAR	TM LG	G	AB	R	H	2B	3B	HR	RBI	BB-IB	HP	SO	AVG	OBP	SLG	AOPS	ABR	SB-CS	FA	FR	RNG	THR	GAMES AT POSITION	DL	BFW
	Year	10	33	1	10	2	1	0	0	2	0		.303	.343	.424	138	1	2	.950	-0	68	0	O9R		0.1
1903	Was A	32	112	10	20	1	3	0	4	13	0		.179	.264	.241	51	-7	3	.891	-3	33	122	O32R		-1.1
Total	2	42	145	11	30	3	4	0	4	15	0		.207	.281	.283	70	-5	5	.909	-3	43	87	O41R		-1.0

HENDRYX, TIM   Timothy Green   B1.31.1891 LeRoy IL   D8.14.1957 Corpus Christi TX   BR/TR/5-9/170   d9.4

YEAR	TM LG	G	AB	R	H	2B	3B	HR	RBI	BB-IB	HP	SO	AVG	OBP	SLG	AOPS	ABR	SB-CS	FA	FR	RNG	THR	GAMES AT POSITION	DL	BFW
1911	Cle A	4	7	0	2	0	0	0	0	0	0		.286	.286	.286	59	0	0	1.000	0	84	0	3b3		0.0
1912	Cle A	23	70	9	17	2	4	1	14	8	1		.243	.329	.429	113	1	3	1.000	-1	99	34	O22C		-0.2
1915	NY A	13	40	4	8	2	0	0	1	4	1	2	.200	.289	.250	61	-2	0-3	.968	0	102	118	O12C		-0.3
1916	NY A	15	62	10	18	7	1	0	5	8	1		.290	.380	.435	142	4	4	1.000	-1	85	62	O15R		0.2
1917	NY A	125	393	43	98	14	7	5	44	62	5	45	.249	.359	.359	118	10	6	.955	2	104	111	O107(0/30/77)		0.6
1918	StL A	88	219	22	61	14	3	0	33	37	2	35	.279	.388	.370	133	11	5	.982	-4	94	52	O65(28/20/18)		0.5
1920	Bos A	99	363	54	119	21	5	0	73	42	2	27	.328	.400	.413	121	13	7-9	.964	-12	87	48	O98C		-0.8
1921	Bos A	49	137	10	33	8	2	0	22	24	2	13	.241	.362	.328	79	-3	1-1	.958	-3	100	41	O41(2/2/37)		-0.8
Total	8	416	1291	152	356	68	22	6	192	185	14	128	.276	.372	.376	115	34	26-13	.966	-19	96	70	O360(30/184/147),3b3		-0.8

HENGEL, DAVE   David Lee   B12.18.1961 Oakland CA   BR/TR/6-0/195*   [SeaA83 3/61]   d9.3   Col California-Davis

YEAR	TM LG	G	AB	R	H	2B	3B	HR	RBI	BB-IB	HP	SO	AVG	OBP	SLG	AOPS	ABR	SB-CS	FA	FR	RNG	THR	GAMES AT POSITION	DL	BFW
1986	Sea A	21	63	3	12	1	0	1	6	1-0	1	13	.190	.215	.254	27	-7	0-0	1.000	-1	63	215	D11,O8(6/0/2)		-0.8
1987	Sea A	10	19	2	6	0	0	1	4	0-0	0	4	.316	.316	.474	100	0	0-0	.875	-1	81	0	O7(2/0/7)/D		-0.1
1988	Sea A	26	60	3	10	1	0	2	7	1-0	0	15	.167	.177	.283	26	-6	0-0	.952	-0	103	0	O12(4/0/8),D12		-0.7
1989	Cle A	12	25	2	3	1	0	0	2	2-0	0	4	.120	.185	.160	-2	-3	0-0	1.000	-1	71	199	O9L,D3	18	-0.4
Total	4	69	167	10	31	3	0	4	18	4-0	1	36	.186	.208	.275	31	-16	0-0	.962	-2	81	108	O36(21/0/17),D27	18	-2.0

HENGLE, MOXIE   Emery J.   B10.7.1857 Chicago IL   D12.11.1924 River Forest IL   BR/5-8/144   d4.20

YEAR	TM LG	G	AB	R	H	2B	3B	HR	RBI	BB-IB	HP	SO	AVG	OBP	SLG	AOPS	ABR	SB-CS	FA	FR	RNG	THR	GAMES AT POSITION	DL	BFW
1884	CP U	19	74	9	15	2	1	0		3			.203	.234	.257	49	-7		.840	-5	79	39	2b19		-1.0
	StP U	9	33	2	5	1	0	0		3			.152	.152	.242	32	-4		.923	3	106	106	2b9		-0.1
	Year	28	107	11	20	3	2	0		3			.187	.209	.252	46	-10		.870	-2	87	59	2b28		-1.1
1885	Buf N	7	26	2	4	0	0	0	0	1		2	.154	.185	.154	10	-3		.864	-2	49	52	2b5,O3(0/2/1)		-0.4
Total	2	35	133	13	24	3	2	0	0	4		2	.180	.204	.233	38	-14		.869	-4	82	58	2b33,O3(0/2/1)		-1.5

HENLEY, GAIL   Gail Curtice   B10.15.1928 Wichita KS   BL/TR/5-9/180   d4.13   Col USC

YEAR	TM LG	G	AB	R	H	2B	3B	HR	RBI	BB-IB	HP	SO	AVG	OBP	SLG	AOPS	ABR	SB-CS	FA	FR	RNG	THR	GAMES AT POSITION	DL	BFW
1954	Pit N	14	30	7	9	1	0	1	4				.300	.382	.433	114	1	0-0	1.000	0	102	173	O9(1/0/8)		0.1

HENLEY, BOB   Robert Clifton   B1.30.1973 Mobile AL   BR/TR/6-2/205   [MonN91 26/685]   d7.19   [DL 1999 Mon N 182, 2000 Mon N 181]

YEAR	TM LG	G	AB	R	H	2B	3B	HR	RBI	BB-IB	HP	SO	AVG	OBP	SLG	AOPS	ABR	SB-CS	FA	FR	RNG	THR	GAMES AT POSITION	DL	BFW
1998	Mon N	41	115	16	35	8	1	3	18	11-0	5	26	.304	.377	.470	125	5	3-0	.995	-2	96	114	C35	35	0.5

HENLINE, BUTCH   Walter John   B12.20.1894 Ft.Wayne IN   D10.9.1957 Sarasota FL   BR/TR/5-10/175   d4.13   U4

YEAR	TM LG	G	AB	R	H	2B	3B	HR	RBI	BB-IB	HP	SO	AVG	OBP	SLG	AOPS	ABR	SB-CS	FA	FR	RNG	THR	GAMES AT POSITION	DL	BFW
1921	NY N	1	1	0	0	0	0	0	0	0	0	1	.000	.000	.000	-99	-0	0-0	—	0			/H		0.0
	Phi N	33	111	8	34	2	0	0	8	2	0	6	.306	.319	.324	65	-5	1-0	.987	3	81	142	C32		0.0
	Year	34	112	8	34	2	0	0	8	2	0	7	.304	.316	.321	64	-6	1-0	.987	3	81	142	C32		1.1
1922	Phi N	125	430	57	136	20	4	14	64	36	8	33	.316	.380	.479	110	6	2-2	.983	-3	82	99	C119		-0.1
1923	Phi N	111	330	45	107	14	3	7	46	37	9	33	.324	.407	.448	112	8	7-5	.978	-16	76	95	C96/OL		0.1
1924	Phi N	115	289	41	82	18	4	5	35	27	1	15	.284	.361	.426	98	0	1-2	.973	-2	90	106	C83,O2(1/1/0)		0.1
1925	Phi N	93	263	43	80	12	5	8	48	24	8	16	.304	.380	.479	108	3	3-1	.956	-3	103	96	C68/OL		-0.1
1926	Phi N	99	283	32	80	14	1	2	30	21	3	18	.283	.339	.360	84	-6	1	.970	-7	81	87	C77,1b4,O2L		-0.1
1927	Bro N	67	177	12	47	10	3	1	18	17	2	10	.266	.337	.373	90	-1	6	.947	1	78	146	C60		-0.
1928	Bro N	55	132	12	28	3	1	2	8	17	0	9	.212	.302	.295	58	-8	2	.976	-1	76	97	C45		-0.
1929	Bro N	27	62	5	15	2	0	1	7	9	0	7	.242	.338	.323	66	-3	0	.967	-1	60	143	C21		-0.
1930	Chi A	3	8	1	1	0	0	0	2	0	0	3	.125	.125	.125	-38	-2	0-0	1.000	1	121	113	C3		-0.
1931	Chi A	11	15	2	1	1	0	0	2	2	0	4	.067	.176	.133	-19	-3	0-0	.889	-1	80	81	C4		-0.
Total	11	740	2101	258	611	96	21	40	268	192	38	156	.291	.361	.414	96	-12	18-10	.971	-30	83	106	C608,O6(5/1/0),1b4		-0.

HENNESSEY, LES   Lester Baker   B12.12.1893 Lynn MA   D11.20.1976 New York NY   BR/TR/6-0/190   d6.4   Col Lafayette

YEAR	TM LG	G	AB	R	H	2B	3B	HR	RBI	BB-IB	HP	SO	AVG	OBP	SLG	AOPS	ABR	SB-CS	FA	FR	RNG	THR	GAMES AT POSITION	DL	BFW
1913	Det A	14	22	2	3	0	0	0	3	3	0	6	.136	.240	.136	11	-2	2	.880	-2	98	0	2b10		-0.

HENRICH, FRITZ   Frank Wilde   B5.8.1899 Cincinnati OH   D5.1.1959 Philadelphia PA   BL/TL/5-10/160   d4.19   Col St. Josephs (PA)

YEAR	TM LG	G	AB	R	H	2B	3B	HR	RBI	BB-IB	HP	SO	AVG	OBP	SLG	AOPS	ABR	SB-CS	FA	FR	RNG	THR	GAMES AT POSITION	DL	BFW
1924	Phi N	90	90	4	19	4	0	4	2	4	0	12	.211	.228	.256	26	-9	0-0	.978	-1	92	92	O32(12/14/10)		-1.

HENRICH, BOBBY   Robert Edward   B12.24.1938 Lawrence KS   BR/TR/6-1/185*   d5.3

YEAR	TM LG	G	AB	R	H	2B	3B	HR	RBI	BB-IB	HP	SO	AVG	OBP	SLG	AOPS	ABR	SB-CS	FA	FR	RNG	THR	GAMES AT POSITION	DL	BFW
1957	Cin N	29	10	8	2	0	0	0	1	1-0	0		.200	.250	.200	28	-1	0-0	.875	1	188	0	S7,O6(4/2/0),3b2/2		0.
1958	Cin N	5	3	2	0	0	0	0	0	0-0	0		2.000	.000	.000	-95	-1	0-0	1.000	-0	114	0	S2		-0.
1959	Cin N	14	3	3	0	0	0	0	0	0-0	0	1	.000	.000	.000	-97	-1	0-0	.929	1	138	0	S5/3		-0.
Total	3	48	16	13	2	0	0	0	1	1-0	0	7	.125	.167	.125	-17	-3	0-0	.929	1	138	0	S14,O6(4/2/0),3b3/2		-0.

HENRICH, TOMMY   Thomas David "The Clutch","Old Reliable"   B2.20.1913 Massillon OH   BL/TL/6-0/180*   d5.11   Mil 1942-45   C4

YEAR	TM LG	G	AB	R	H	2B	3B	HR	RBI	BB-IB	HP	SO	AVG	OBP	SLG	AOPS	ABR	SB-CS	FA	FR	RNG	THR	GAMES AT POSITION	DL	BFW
1937	NY A	67	206	39	66	14	5	8	42	35	0	17	.320	.419	.553	142	14	4-0	.970	-1	87	137	O59(30/0/29)		1.
1938	†NY A	131	471	109	127	24	7	22	91	92	2	32	.270	.391	.490	120	16	6-2	.984	-1	95	120	O130R		0.
1939	NY A	99	347	64	96	18	4	9	57	51	1	23	.277	.371	.429	106	4	7-0	.991	1	102	99	O88(1/38/50)/1		1.
1940	NY A	90	293	57	90	28	5	10	53	48	2	30	.307	.408	.539	149	23	1-2	.969	-3	95	99	O139(0/19/121)		0.
1941	†NY A	144	538	106	149	27	5	31	85	81	3	40	.277	.377	.519	137	28	3-1	.987	1	97	119	O119R,1b7		0.
1942	NY A★	127	483	77	129	30	5	13	67	58	5	42	.267	.352	.431	122	14	4-4	.992	-0	103	100	O111R,1b41		0.
1946	NY A	150	565	92	142	25	4	19	83	87	7	63	.251	.358	.411	113	12	5-2	.983	3	105	138	O132(0/8/125),1b6		2.
1947	†NY A★	142	550	109	158	35	13	16	98	71	3	54	.287	.372	.485	139	28	3-2	.978	-1	102	108	O102(6/3/96),1b46		3.
1948	†NY A	146	588	138	181	42	14	25	100	76	4	42	.308	.391	.554	151	41	2-3	.958	-5	94	89	O61R,1b52		2.
1949	†NY A☆	115	411	90	118	20	3	24	85	86	5	34	.287	.416	.526	148	31	2-2	.987	-4	38	79	1b34		0.
1950	NY A★	73	151	20	41	6	8	6	34	27	0	6	.272	.382	.536	137	8	0-1	.981	-9	98	117	O1017(38/92/894),1b189		15
Total	11	1284	4603	901	1297	269	73	183	795	712	34	383	.282	.382	.491	132	219	37-19	.981	-9	98	117	O1017(38/92/894),1b189		15

HENRIKSEN, OLAF   Olaf "Swede"   B4.26.1888 Kirkerup, Denmark   D10.17.1962 Norwood MA   BL/TL/5-7.5/158   d8.11

YEAR	TM LG	G	AB	R	H	2B	3B	HR	RBI	BB-IB	HP	SO	AVG	OBP	SLG	AOPS	ABR	SB-CS	FA	FR	RNG	THR	GAMES AT POSITION	DL	BFW
1911	Bos A	27	93	17	34	1	9	0	8	14	0		.366	.449	.409	141	6	4	.953	0	113	80	O25(5/0/20)		0
1912	†Bos A	44	56	20	18	3	1	0	8	14	0		.321	.457	.411	142	4	0	.909	-1	85	0	O11(0/1/10)		0
1913	Bos A	31	40	8	15	1	0	0	2	7	0	5	.375	.468	.400	151	3	3	1.000	-0	102	0	O7(6/1/0)		0
1914	Bos A	63	95	16	25	2	1	1	5	22	1	12	.263	.407	.337	124	4	5-4	.947	-1	101	105	O25(9/4/12)		0
1915	†Bos A	73	92	9	18	2	0	1	18	18	1	7	.196	.333	.261	80	-1	1-5	.967	1	94	0	O29(8/11/10)		0
1916	†Bos A	68	99	13	20	2	2	0	11	19	1	15	.202	.331	.263	78	-2	2	1.000	0	106	74	O31(14/7/9)		0
1917	Bos A	15	12	1	1	0	0	0	1	3	0	4	.083	.267	.083	7	-1	0	—	0			/H		0
Total	7	321	487	84	131	12	7	1	48	97	3	43	.269	.392	.329	112	13	15-9	.966	-2	104	64	O128(42/24/61)		0

HENRY, SNAKE   Frederick Marshall   B7.19.1895 Waynesville NC   D10.12.1987 Wendell NC   BL/TL/6-0/170   d9.15

YEAR	TM LG	G	AB	R	H	2B	3B	HR	RBI	BB-IB	HP	SO	AVG	OBP	SLG	AOPS	ABR	SB-CS	FA	FR	RNG	THR	GAMES AT POSITION	DL	BFW
1922	Bos N	18	66	5	13	4	1	0	5	2	0	8	.197	.221	.288	32	-7	2-2	.995	1	130	52	1b18		-0
1923	Bos N	11	9	1	1	0	0	0	2	1	0	1	.111	.200	.111	-17	-2	0-0	—	0			/H		-0
Total	2	29	75	6	14	4	1	0	7	3	0	9	.187	.218	.267	26	-9	2-2	.995	1	130	52	1b18		-0

HENRY, GEORGE   George Washington   B8.10.1863 Philadelphia PA   D12.30.1934 Lynn MA   BR/TR/5-9/180   d4.27

YEAR	TM LG	G	AB	R	H	2B	3B	HR	RBI	BB-IB	HP	SO	AVG	OBP	SLG	AOPS	ABR	SB-CS	FA	FR	RNG	THR	GAMES AT POSITION	DL	BFW
1893	Cin N	21	83	11	23	3	0	0	13	11	2	12	.277	.375	.313	82	-2	2	.965	3	151	119	O21(10/0/11)		0

HENRY, JOHN   John Michael   B9.2.1863 Springfield MA   D6.11.1939 Hartford CT   TL   d8.13   ▲

YEAR	TM LG	G	AB	R	H	2B	3B	HR	RBI	BB-IB	HP	SO	AVG	OBP	SLG	AOPS	ABR	SB-CS	FA	FR	RNG	THR	GAMES AT POSITION	DL	BFW
1884	Cle N	9	26	2	4	0	0	0	0			12	.154	.154	.154	-3	-3		1.000	1	128	0	P5,O4R		0
1885	Bal AA	10	34	4	9	3	0	0	3	1	0		.265	.286	.353	102	0		.931	2	153	320	P9/OL		0
1886	Was N	4	14	3	5	0	0	0	0			3	.357	.357	.357	127	1	0	.833	-0	52	0	P4		-0
1890	NY N	37	144	19	35	6	0	0	16	7	1	12	.243	.283	.285	65	-7	12	.870	-3	61	71	O37(34/1/3),P18		-0
Total	4	60	218	28	53	9	0	0	19	8		27	.243	.273	.284	66	-9	12	.867	-0	69	66	O42(35/1/7),P18		-0

HENRY, JOHN   John Park "Bull"   B12.26.1889 Amherst MA   D11.24.1941 Fort Huachuca AZ   BR/TR/6-0/180   d7.8   Col Amherst

YEAR	TM LG	G	AB	R	H	2B	3B	HR	RBI	BB-IB	HP	SO	AVG	OBP	SLG	AOPS	ABR	SB-CS	FA	FR	RNG	THR	GAMES AT POSITION	DL	BFW
1910	Was A	28	87	2	13	1	1	0	5	2	0		.149	.169	.184	11	-9	2	.989	3	101	131	C18,1b10		-0
1911	Was A	85	261	24	53	5	0	0	21	25	0		.203	.273	.222	39	-21	8	.969	9	106	118	C51,1b30		-0
1912	Was A	66	191	23	37	4	1	0	9	31			.194	.309	.225	53	-10	10	.977	13	132	111	C65		-0
1913	Was A	96	273	26	61	8	4	1	26	30		43	.223	.299	.293	75	-7	8-5	.982	7	114	103	C96		-0
1914	Was A	92	261	22	44	7	4	0	20	37		47	.169	.274	.226	49	-16	7-3	.980	5	105	97	C92		-0

YEAR	TM LG	G	AB	R	H	2B	3B	HR	RBI	BB-IB	HP	SO	AVG	OBP	SLG	AOPS	ABR	SB-CS	FA	FR	RNG	THR	GAMES AT POSITION	DL	BFW
1915	Was A	95	277	20	61	9	2	1	22	36	6	28	.220	.323	.278	78	-6	10-2	.972	8	114	92	C94		1.1
1916	Was A	117	305	28	76	12	3	0	46	49	6	40	.249	.364	.308	103	4	12	.981	-0	99	92	C116		1.4
1917	Was A	65	163	10	31	6	0	0	18	24	2	16	.190	.302	.227	62	-6	1	.988	1	87	90	C59		-0.1
1918	Bos N	43	102	6	21	2	0	0	4	10	1	15	.206	.282	.225	58	-5	0	.964	-2	96	102	C38		-0.4
Total	9	687	1920	161	397	54	15	2	171	244	21	189	.207	.303	.254	65	-77	55-5	.978	43	107	100	C629,1b40		1.6

HENRY, RON Ronald Baxter B8.7.1936 Chester PA BR/TR/6-1/180* d4.15

YEAR	TM LG	G	AB	R	H	2B	3B	HR	RBI	BB-IB	HP	SO	AVG	OBP	SLG	AOPS	ABR	SB-CS	FA	FR	RNG	THR	GAMES AT POSITION	DL	BFW
1961	Min A	20	28	1	4	0	0	0	3	2-0	0	7	.143	.194	.143	-6	-4	0-0	1.000	-1	70	0	C5/1		-0.5
1964	Min A	22	41	4	5	1	1	2	5	2-0	0	17	.122	.163	.341	36	-4	0-0	.984	1	137	182	C13		-0.3
Total	2	42	69	5	9	1	1	2	8	4-0	0	24	.130	.176	.261	18	-8	0-0	.988	-0	116	124	C18/1		-0.8

HENSON, DREW Drew Daniel B2.13.1980 San Diego CA BR/TR/6-5/222* [NYA98 3/97] d9.5

YEAR	TM LG	G	AB	R	H	2B	3B	HR	RBI	BB-IB	HP	SO	AVG	OBP	SLG	AOPS	ABR	SB-CS	FA	FR	RNG	THR	GAMES AT POSITION	DL	BFW
2002	NY A	3	1	1	0	0	0	0	0	0-0	0	1	.000	.000	.000	-99	0	0-0	—		0		D2		0.0
2003	NY A	5	8	2	1	0	0	0	0	0-0	0	2	.125	.125	.125	-34	-2	0-0	1.000	0	80	0	3b3		-0.1
Total	2	8	9	3	1	0	0	0	0	0-0	0	3	.111	.111	.111	-42	-2	0-0	1.000	0	80	0	3b3,D2		-0.1

HERMAN, BABE Floyd Caves B6.26.1903 Buffalo NY D11.27.1987 Glendale CA BL/TL/6-4/190 d4.14 C1

YEAR	TM LG	G	AB	R	H	2B	3B	HR	RBI	BB-IB	HP	SO	AVG	OBP	SLG	AOPS	ABR	SB-CS	FA	FR	RNG	THR	GAMES AT POSITION	DL	BFW
1926	Bro N	137	496	64	158	35	11	11	81	44	1	53	.319	.375	.500	136	24	8	.986	1	107	69	1b101,O35(6/0/29)		1.7
1927	Bro N	130	412	65	112	26	9	14	73	39	1	41	.272	.336	.481	116	8	4	.980	1	107	81	1b105/OL		0.2
1928	Bro N	134	486	64	165	37	6	12	91	38	2	36	.340	.390	.514	136	26	1	.937	-8	86	97	O127R		0.8
1929	Bro N	146	569	105	217	42	13	21	113	55	0	45	.381	.436	.612	160	53	21	.941	-15	83	70	O141R,1b2		2.4
1930	Bro N	153	614	143	241	48	11	35	130	66	4	56	.393	.455	.678	171	72	18	.978	-21	78	52	O153R		3.4
1931	Bro N	151	610	93	191	43	16	18	97	50	0	65	.313	.365	.525	137	30	17	.960	-1	90	132	O150R		1.9
1932	Cin N	148	577	87	188	38	19	16	87	60	0	45	.326	.389	.541	152	42	7	.969	13	117	113	O146R		4.5
1933	Chi N	137	508	77	147	36	13	16	93	50	0	57	.289	.353	.502	142	27	6	.957	-6	92	96	O131R		1.4
1934	Chi N	125	467	65	142	34	5	14	84	35	0	71	.304	.353	.488	125	16	1	.971	-11	84	68	O113R,1b7		-0.2
1935	Pit N	26	81	8	19	8	1	0	7	3	1	10	.235	.271	.358	65	-4	0	.958	-2	79	110	O15L,1b3		-0.7
	Cin N	92	349	44	117	23	5	10	58	35	0	25	.335	.396	.516	147	24	5	.976	-0	98	95	O76L,1b14		1.7
	Year	118	430	52	136	31	6	10	65	38	1	35	.316	.373	.486	131	19	5	.974	-3	95	97	O91L,1b17		1.0
1936	Cin N	119	380	59	106	25	2	13	71	39	1	36	.279	.348	.458	123	12	4	.967	-3	99	47	O92(91/0/1),1b4		0.4
1937	Det A	17	20	2	6	3	0	0	3	1	0	6	.300	.364	.450	102	0	2-0	1.000	-0	93	0	O3R		0.0
1945	Bro N	37	34	6	9	1	0	1	9	5	0	7	.265	.350	.382	107	0	0	—	-0	0	0	O3R		0.0
Total	13	1552	5603	882	1818	399	110	181	997	520	11	553	.324	.383	.532	144	330	94-0	—	-0	0	0	O1185(191/0/994),1b236		17.5

HERMAN, BILLY William Jennings Bryan B7.7.1909 New Albany IN D9.5.1992 W.Palm Beach FL BR/TR/5-11/180 d8.29 Mil 1944-45 M4/C16 HF1975

YEAR	TM LG	G	AB	R	H	2B	3B	HR	RBI	BB-IB	HP	SO	AVG	OBP	SLG	AOPS	ABR	SB-CS	FA	FR	RNG	THR	GAMES AT POSITION	DL	BFW
1931	Chi N	25	98	14	32	7	0	0	16	13	0	16	.327	.405	.398	115	3	2	.939	-2	90	93	2b25		0.3
1932	†Chi N	154	656	102	206	42	7	1	51	40	5	33	.314	.358	.404	105	6	14	.961	12	105	112	2b154		2.8
1933	Chi N	153	619	82	173	35	2	0	44	45	4	34	.279	.332	.342	93	-4	5	.956	29	103	129	2b153		3.7
1934	Chi N	113	456	79	138	21	6	3	42	34	3	31	.303	.355	.395	102	2	6	.975	9	102	102	2b111		1.7
1935	†Chi N	154	666	113	227	57	6	7	83	42	3	29	.341	.383	.476	128	28	6	.964	16	103	135	2b154		5.2
1936	Chi N	153	632	101	211	57	7	5	93	59	1	30	.334	.392	.470	128	27	5	.975	17	97	128	2b153		5.2
1937	Chi N	138	564	106	189	35	11	8	65	56	1	22	.335	.396	.479	131	26	2	.954	15	103	115	2b137		4.9
1938	†Chi N	152	624	86	173	34	7	1	56	59	2	31	.277	.342	.359	90	-7	3	.981	22	103	120	2b151		2.4
1939	Chi N	156	623	111	191	34	18	7	70	66	5	31	.307	.378	.453	120	18	9	.967	-4	99	92	2b156		2.4
1940	Chi N	135	558	77	163	24	4	5	57	47	0	30	.292	.347	.376	101	1	1	.974	20	107	111	2b135		3.0
1941	Chi N	11	36	4	7	0	1	0	9		0	5	.194	.356	.250	75	-1	0	.898	-3	67	81	2b11		-0.4
	†Bro N	133	536	77	156	30	4	3	41	58	1	38	.291	.361	.379	104	5	1	.970	-26	89	92	2b133		-1.4
	Year	144	572	81	163	30	5	3	41	67	1	43	.285	.361	.371	103	4	1	.964	-29	87	91	2b144		-1.8
1942	Bro N	155	571	76	146	34	2	2	65	72	0	52	.256	.339	.333	95	-1	6	.973	-10	90	117	2b153,1b3		-0.2
1943	Bro N	153	585	76	193	41	2	2	100	66	0	26	.330	.398	.417	135	30	4	.971	-17	88	88	2b117,3b37		2.0
1946	Bro N	47	184	24	53	8	4	0	22	26	0	10	.288	.376	.375	112	4	2	.945	-2	98	180	3b29,2b16		0.3
	Bos N	75	252	32	77	23	1	3	28	43	1	13	.306	.409	.440	139	16	1	.956	-12	85	99	2b44,1b22,3b5		0.5
	Year	122	436	56	130	31	5	3	50	69	1	23	.298	.395	.413	128	19	3	.968	-14	85	88	2b60,3b34,1b22		0.8
1947	Pit N	15	47	3	10	4	0	0	6	2	0	7	.213	.245	.298	42	-4	0	1.000	-5	60	38	2b10,1b2,M		-0.8
Total	15	1922	7707	1163	2345	486	82	47	839	737	26	428	.304	.367	.407	112	149	67	.967	59	98	111	2b1813,3b71,1b27		31.6

HERMANN, AL Albert Bartel B3.28.1899 Milltown NJ D8.20.1980 Lewes DE BR/TR/6-0/180 d7.13 Col Colgate

YEAR	TM LG	G	AB	R	H	2B	3B	HR	RBI	BB-IB	HP	SO	AVG	OBP	SLG	AOPS	ABR	SB-CS	FA	FR	RNG	THR	GAMES AT POSITION	DL	BFW
1923	Bos N	31	93	2	22	4	0	0	11	0	0	7	.237	.237	.280	37	-9	3-2	.957	-4	100	49	2b15,3b5,1b4		-1.2
1924	Bos N	1	1	0	0	0	0	0	0	0	0	1	.000	.000	.000	-99	0	0-0	—	0		/H		0.0
Total	2	32	94	2	22	4	0	0	11	0	0	8	.234	.234	.277	36	-9	3-2	.957	-4	100	49	2b15,3b5,1b4		-1.2

HERMANSEN, CHAD Chad Bruce B9.10.1977 Salt Lake City UT BR/TR/6-2/185* [PitN95 1/10] d9.7

YEAR	TM LG	G	AB	R	H	2B	3B	HR	RBI	BB-IB	HP	SO	AVG	OBP	SLG	AOPS	ABR	SB-CS	FA	FR	RNG	THR	GAMES AT POSITION	DL	BFW
1999	Pit N	19	60	5	14	3	0	1	1	7-1	1	19	.233	.324	.333	66	-3	2-2	1.000	-3	76	0	O18(3/9/6)		-0.6
2000	Pit N	33	108	12	20	4	1	2	8	6-0	0	37	.185	.226	.296	31	-12	0-0	.979	-6	63	112	O31(0/27/4)		-1.7
2001	Pit N	22	55	5	9	1	0	2	5	1-0	0	18	.164	.179	.291	18	-7	0-1	1.000	0	96	112	O20(0/6/15)		-1.0
2002	Pit N	65	194	22	40	11	1	7	15	17-0	1	68	.206	.272	.381	71	-9	7-5	.982	-0	94	187	O60(2/59/2)		-1.0
	Chi N	35	43	3	9	3	0	1	3	5-0	0	14	.209	.292	.349	71	-2	0-0	.895	-1	84	0	O21(4/9/9)	41	-0.4
	Year	100	237	25	49	14	1	8	18	22-0	1	82	.207	.276	.376	71	-11	7-5	.970	-1	92	154	O81(6/68/11)		-1.4
2003	LA N	11	25	2	4	1	0	0	2	2-0	0	9	.160	.222	.200	12	-3	0-0	1.000	-0	98	0	O6L		-0.4
2004	Tor A	4	7	0	0	0	0	0	0	0-0	0	3	.000	.000	.000	-95	-2	0-0	1.000	0	103	0	O4L	47	-0.4
Total	6	189	492	49	96	23	2	13	34	38-1	2	168	.195	.255	.329	51	-38	9-8	.980	-10	84	110	O160(19/110/36)	88	-5.1

HERMANSKI, GENE Eugene Victor B5.11.1920 Pittsfield MA BL/TR/5-11.5/185* d8.15 Mil 1943-45 Col Seton Hall

YEAR	TM LG	G	AB	R	H	2B	3B	HR	RBI	BB-IB	HP	SO	AVG	OBP	SLG	AOPS	ABR	SB-CS	FA	FR	RNG	THR	GAMES AT POSITION	DL	BFW
1943	Bro N	18	60	6	18	2	1	0	12	11	1	7	.300	.417	.367	127	3	1	.976	2	102	238	O17(11/0/6)		0.4
1946	Bro N	64	110	15	22	2	2	0	8	17	1	10	.200	.313	.255	61	-5	2	.938	-3	94	0	O34(12/4/17)		-1.0
1947	†Bro N	79	189	36	52	7	1	7	39	28	3	7	.275	.377	.434	111	4	5	.982	2	100	138	O66(64/1/3)		0.2
1948	Bro N	133	400	63	116	22	7	15	60	64	2	46	.290	.391	.493	133	20	15	.971	6	105	161	O119(6/0/113)		2.2
1949	†Bro N	87	224	48	67	12	3	8	42	47	2	21	.299	.431	.487	140	15	12	.980	2	102	128	O77(64/0/13)		1.3
1950	Bro N	94	289	36	86	17	3	7	34	36	3	26	.298	.381	.450	115	7	2	.989	5	116	97	O78(76/0/3)		0.7
1951	Bro N	31	80	8	20	4	0	1	5	10	0	12	.250	.333	.338	79	-2	0-2	.977	1	100	117	O19(18/0/1)		-0.4
	Chi N	75	231	28	65	12	1	3	20	35	4	42	.273	.372	.370	98	2	3-2	.966	2	103	147	O63(3/0/60)		0.0
	Year	106	311	36	85	16	1	4	25	45	4	54	.273	.364	.362	93	0	3-0	.969	3	102	140	O82(21/0/61)		-0.4
1952	Chi N	99	275	28	70	6	0	4	34	29	2	32	.255	.330	.320	80	-7	2-4	.981	4	112	110	O76(3/0/73)		-0.5
1953	Chi N	18	40	1	6	1	0	0	1	4	0	7	.150	.227	.175	7	-6	1-0	1.000	-0	106	0	O13(3/0/10)		-0.6
	Pit N	41	62	7	11	0	0	1	4	8	1	14	.177	.282	.226	35	-6	0-0	1.000	0	121	0	O13(5/0/8)		-0.6
	Year	59	102	8	17	1	0	1	5	12	1	21	.167	.261	.206	24	-12	1-0	1.000	0	114	0	O26(8/0/18)		-1.2
Total	9	739	1960	276	533	85	18	46	259	289	22	212	.272	.372	.404	107	27	43-2	.977	21	106	124	O575(265/5/311)		2.1

HERMIDA, JEREMY Jeremy Ryan B1.30.1984 Atlanta GA BL/TR/6-4/200 d8.31

YEAR	TM LG	G	AB	R	H	2B	3B	HR	RBI	BB-IB	HP	SO	AVG	OBP	SLG	AOPS	ABR	SB-CS	FA	FR	RNG	THR	GAMES AT POSITION	DL	BFW
2005	Fla N	23	41	9	12	3	0	1	9	12-3	1	9	.293	.383	.634	170	4	2-0	1.000	0	122	0	O14(4/0/10)		0.4

HERMOSO, REMY Angel Remigio B10.1.1946 Carabobo, Venez BR/TR/5-8/155(152-175) d9.14 [DL 1975 Cle A 35]

YEAR	TM LG	G	AB	R	H	2B	3B	HR	RBI	BB-IB	HP	SO	AVG	OBP	SLG	AOPS	ABR	SB-CS	FA	FR	RNG	THR	GAMES AT POSITION	DL	BFW
1967	Atl N	11	26	3	8	0	0	0	2-0	0	4	.308	.357	.308	93	0	1-0	.952	-2	95	86	S9,2b2		-0.1
1969	Mon N	28	74	6	12	0	0	0	5-0	1	10	.162	.225	.162	10	-9	3-1	.968	1	116	141	2b18,S6		-0.7
1970	Mon N	4	1	0	0	0	0	0	0-0	0	0	.000	.000	.000	-99	0	0-0	1.000	0	301	0	/23		0.0
1974	Cle A	48	122	15	27	3	1	0	5	7-0	0	7	.221	.262	.262	52	-8	2-2	.967	3	113	102	2b45	102	-0.3
Total	4	91	223	24	47	3	1	0	8	14-0	1	21	.211	.259	.233	42	-17	6-3	.968	3	113	113	2b66,S15/3	137	-1.1

HERNANDEZ, ALEX Alexander (Vargas) B5.28.1977 San Juan, PR BL/TL/6-4/190* [PitN95 4/97] d9.1

YEAR	TM LG	G	AB	R	H	2B	3B	HR	RBI	BB-IB	HP	SO	AVG	OBP	SLG	AOPS	ABR	SB-CS	FA	FR	RNG	THR	GAMES AT POSITION	DL	BFW
2000	Pit N	20	60	4	12	3	1	0	4	0-0	0	13	.200	.200	.300	24	-7	1-1	.992	-1	38	130	1b12,O5(3/0/2)		-0.9
2001	Pit N	7	11	0	1	0	0	0	0	0-0	0	2	.091	.091	.091	-51	-3	0-0	1.000	0	62	633	O4R,1b2	60	-0.2
Total	2	27	71	4	13	3	1	0	5	0-0	0	15	.183	.183	.268	12	-10	1-1	.992	-1	37	136	1b14,O9(3/0/6)	60	-1.1

HERNANDEZ, ANDERSON Anderson Mejia B10.30.1982 Santo Domingo, D.R. BB/TR/5-9/170 d9.18

YEAR	TM LG	G	AB	R	H	2B	3B	HR	RBI	BB-IB	HP	SO	AVG	OBP	SLG	AOPS	ABR	SB-CS	FA	FR	RNG	THR	GAMES AT POSITION	DL	BFW
2005	NY N	6	18	1	1	0	0	0	0	1-0	0	4	.056	.105	.056	-58	-4	0-1	1.000	-0	122	31	2b5,S2		-0.5

YEAR	TM LG	G	AB	R	H	2B	3B	HR	RBI	BB-IB	HP	SO	AVG	OBP	SLG	AOPS	ABR	SB-CS	FA	FR	RNG	THR	GAMES AT POSITION	DL	BFW

HERNANDEZ, CARLOS Carlos Alberto (Almeida) B5.24.1967 San Felix, Venez BR/TR/5-11/218(185-218) d4.20 [DL 1999 SD N 181, 2001 StL N 190]

1990	LA N	10	20	2	4	1	0	0	1	0-0	0	2	.200	.200	.250	24	-2	0-0	1.000	0	537	185	C10		-0.2
1991	LA N	15	14	1	3	1	0	0	1	0-0	1	5	.214	.250	.286	56	-1	1-0	.966	-0	121	113	C13/3		0.0
1992	LA N	69	173	11	45	4	0	3	17	11-1	4	21	.260	.316	.335	86	-3	0-1	.979	1	87	84	C63		-0.1
1993	LA N	50	99	6	25	5	0	2	7	2-0	0	11	.253	.267	.364	71	-5	0-0	.966	1	92	79	C43		-0.2
1994	LA N	32	64	6	14	4	0	2	6	1-0	0	14	.219	.231	.344	50	-5	0-0	1.000	1	80	136	C27	18	-0.3
1995	LA N	45	94	3	14	1	0	2	8	7-0	1	25	.149	.216	.223	17	-12	0-0	1.000	1	177	133	C41		-0.3
1996	LA N	13	14	1	4	0	0	0	2	'2-0	0	2	.286	.375	.286	82	0	0-0	1.000	1	282	88	C9	28	0.1
1997	SD N	50	134	15	42	7	1	3	14	3-0	0	27	.313	.328	.448	107	1	0-2	.989	1	83	192	C44,1b4	33	0.3
1998	†SD N	129	390	34	102	15	0	9	52	16-2	9	54	.262	.305	.369	82	-12	2-2	.992	6	112	80	C122/1		0.1
2000	SD N	58	191	16	48	11	0	2	25	16-1	3	26	.251	.316	.340	'71	-8	1-3	.987	-0	80	126	C54/1	35	-0.6
	†StL N	17	51	7	14	4	0	1	10	5-0	1	9	.275	.345	.412	90	-1	1-0	.963	-2	46	174	C16		-0.2
	Year	75	242	23	62	15	0	3	35	21-1	4	35	.256	.322	.355	75	-9	2-3	.982	-3	73	137	C70/1		-0.8
Total	10	488	1244	102	315	51	1	24	141	63-4	19	196	.253	.298	.354	76	-48	5-8	.985	15	109	112	C442,1b6/3	485	-1.4

HERNANDEZ, CARLOS Carlos Eduardo B12.12.1975 Caracas, Venez BR/TR/5-9/175* d5.26

1999	Hou N	16	14	4	2	0	0	0	1	0-0	0	0	.143	.143	.143	-28	-3	3-1	1.000	2	191	238	2b7,S2		0.0
2000	Sea A	2	1	0	0	0	0	0	0	0-0	0	1	.000	.000	.000	-99	0	0-1	1.000	-0	0	0	3b2	31	-0.1
Total	2	18	15	4	2	0	0	0	1	0-0	0	1	.133	.133	.133	-33	-3	3-2	1.000	2	191	238	2b7,3b2,S2	31	-0.1

HERNANDEZ, CESAR Cesar Dario (Perez) B9.28.1966 Yamasa, D.R. BR/TR/6-0/160 [MonN85 D1/1] d7.19

1992	Cin N	34	51	6	14	4	0	0	4	0-0	0	10	.275	.275	.353	74	-2	3-1	.952	1	95	442	O18(12/6/1)		-0.1
1993	Cin N	27	24	3	2	0	0	0	1	1-0	0	8	.083	.120	.083	-44	-5	1-2	.970	4	155	394	O23(17/7/0)		-0.2
Total	2	61	75	9	16	4	0	0	5	1-0	0	18	.213	.224	.267	35	-7	4-3	.963	5	124	419	O41(29/13/1)		-0.3

HERNANDEZ, ENZO Enzo Octavio B2.12.1949 Valle de Guanape, Venez BR/TR/5-8/150* d4.17

1971	SD N	143	549	58	122	9	3	0	12	54-1	3	34	.222	.295	.250	59	-29	21-5	.955	-5	95	88	S143		-1.5
1972	SD N	114	329	33	64	11	2	1	15	22-6	2	25	.195	.243	.249	44	-25	24-3	.963	-7	97	88	S107,O3(2/0/1)		-1.7
1973	SD N	70	247	26	55	2	1	0	9	17-0	0	14	.223	.273	.239	47	-19	15-4	.977	1	97	106	S67	40	-0.9
1974	SD N	147	512	55	119	19	2	0	34	38-2	0	36	.232	.285	.277	61	-28	37-10	.966	-2	101	67	S145		-0.8
1975	SD N	116	344	37	75	12	2	0	19	26-0	2	25	.218	.275	.265	54	-22	20-4	.965	1	102	116	S111		-0.6
1976	SD N	113	340	31	87	13	3	1	24	32-4	0	16	.256	.319	.321	89	-5	12-7	.964	7	111	111	S101		1.4
1977	SD N	7	3	1	0	0	0	0	0	0-0	0	0	.000	.000	.000	-99	-1	0-0	1.000	0	101	0	S7	149	-0.1
1978	LA N	4	3	0	0	0	0	0	0	0-0	0	1	.000	.000	.000	-99	-1	0-0	—	-1	0	0	S2	189	-0.2
Total	8	714	2327	241	522	66	13	2	113	189-13	5	151	.224	.283	.266	59	-130	129-33	.964	-5	100	92	S683,O3(2/0/1)	189	-4.4

HERNANDEZ, JACKIE Jacinto (Zulueta) B9.11.1940 Central Tinguaro, Cuba BR/TR/6-0/175(163-175) d9.14

1965	Cal A	6	6	2	2	1	0	0	1	0-0	0	1	.333	.333	.500	137	-1	1-0	1.000	-1	76	0	S2/3		0.0
1966	Cal A	58	23	19	1	0	0	0	2	1-0	0	4	.043	.080	.043	-64	-5	1-1	.857	1	100	0	3b11,2b8,S8,O3(0/1/2)		-0.4
1967	Min A	29	28	1	4	0	0	0	3	0-0	0	6	.143	.143	.143	-14	-4	0-0	.974	0	85	50	S15,3b13		-0.3
1968	Min A	83	199	13	35	3	0	2	17	9-2	2	52	.176	.218	.221	32	-17	5-2	.927	4	100	127	S79/1		-0.8
1969	KC A	145	504	54	112	14	2	4	40	38-1	2	111	.222	.278	.282	57	-30	17-7	.954	-13	89	76	S144		-2.7
1970	KC A	83	238	14	55	4	1	2	10	15-0	2	50	.231	.281	.282	56	-15	1-3	.951	-8	90	89	S77		-1.6
1971	†Pit N	88	233	30	48	7	3	3	26	17-2	0	45	.206	.257	.300	58	-14	0-2	.950	7	112	101	S75,3b9		0.1
1972	Pit N	72	176	12	33	7	1	1	14	9-1	0	43	.188	.227	.256	37	-15	0-0	.929	-1	102	106	S68,3b4		-1.0
1973	Pit N	54	73	8	18	1	2	0	8	4-2	0	12	.247	.286	.315	68	-4	0-0	.940	-0	99	114	S49		-0.1
Total	9	618	1480	153	308	37	9	12	121	93-8	6	324	.208	.256	.270	49	-104	25-15	.945	-11	96	95	S517,3b38,2b8,O3(0/1/2)/1		-6.8

HERNANDEZ, JOSE Jose Antonio (Figueroa) B7.14.1969 Rio Piedras, PR BR/TR/6-1/180* d8.9 OF(59/50/7)

1991	Tex A	45	98	8	18	2	1	0	4	3-0	0	31	.184	.208	.224	20	-11	0-1	.975	3	110	75	S44/3		-0.6
1992	Cle A	3	4	0	0	0	0	0	0	0-0	0	2	.000	.000	.000	-99	-1	0-0	.857	0	108	0	S3		-0.1
1994	Chi N	56	132	18	32	2	3	1	9	8-0	1	29	.242	.291	.326	60	-8	2-2	.938	3	87	0	3b28,S21,2b8/OC		-0.5
1995	Chi N	93	245	37	60	11	4	13	40	13-3	0	69	.245	.281	.482	97	-3	1-0	.961	3	99	115	S43,2b29,3b20		0.4
1996	Chi N	131	331	52	80	14	1	10	41	24-4	1	97	.242	.293	.381	74	-13	4-0	.948	-6	95	109	S87,3b43/2OC		-1.2
1997	Chi N	121	183	33	50	8	5	7	26	14-2	0	42	.273	.323	.486	105	0	2-5	.922	-4	72	83	3b47,S21,2b20,O6L/1D		-0.3
1998	†Chi N	149	488	76	124	23	7	23	75	40-3	1	140	.254	.311	.471	99	-3	4-6	.958	7	106	38	3b72,O54(31/31/2),S45,1b3,2b2		0.5
1999	Chi N	99	342	57	93	12	2	15	43	40-3	5	101	.272	.357	.450	103	1	7-2	.971	6	110	103	S92,O20(6/14/2)/1		1.3
	†Atl N	48	166	22	42	8	0	4	19	12-3	0	44	.253	.302	.373	71	-1	4-1	.964	-1	100	110	S45/1OL		-0.5
	Year	147	508	79	135	20	2	19	62	52-6	5	145	.266	.339	.425	92	-7	11-3	.969	5	107	105	S137,O21(7/14/2),1b2		0.8
2000	Mil N	124	446	51	109	22	1	11	59	41-3	6	125	.244	.315	.372	74	-19	3-7	.950	8	107	137	3b95,S37,O2L	21	-0.9
2001	Mil N	152	542	67	135	26	2	25	78	39-8	2	185	.249	.300	.443	91	-10	5-4	.972	-1	104	93	S150,O2(1/1/0)		4.0
2002	Mil N★	152	525	72	151	24	2	24	73	52-5	4	188	.288	.356	.478	121	13	3-5	.973	17	107	108	S149		4.4
2003	Col N	69	257	33	61	6	1	8	27	27-0	0	95	.237	.308	.362	65	-13	1-1	.983	-5	93	104	3b17,S5,O2C/2		-0.4
	Chi N	23	69	6	13	3	1	2	9	3-0	0	26	.188	.222	.348	45	-6	0-0	.968	2	97	209	3b75,S74,O2C/12		0.1
	Pit N	58	193	19	43	9	1	3	21	16-0	1	56	.223	.282	.326	59	-12	1-0	.955	13	138	146	3b58		-1.6
	Year	150	519	58	117	18	3	13	57	46-0	1	177	.225	.287	.347	61	-31	2-1	.957	10	130	159	3b75,S74,O2C/12		-1.9
2004	†LA N	95	211	32	61	12	1	13	29	26-6	1	61	.289	.370	.540	133	10	3-1	.980	3	106	91	2b50,S13,3b12,O9L,1b8		1.5
2005	Cle A	84	234	28	54	7	0	6	31	14-0	2	66	.231	.277	.338	66	-12	1-3	.995	-2	112	114	1b45,3b21,O6(3/0/3),2b4/SD	21	-1.4
Total	14	1502	4466	611	1126	189	32	165	584	372-40	24	1351	.252	.312	.420	88	-95	41-38	.969	49	104	105	S825,3b414,2b115,O104L,1b60,D2	21	0.6

HERNANDEZ, KEITH Keith B10.20.1953 San Francisco CA BL/TL/6-0/195(175-205) [StLN71 42/783] d8.30 [DL 1991 Cle A 182]

1974	StL N	14	34	3	10	1	2	0	2	7-0	0	8	.294	.415	.441	139	2	0-0	.973	-2	18	112	1b9		-0.1
1975	StL N	64	188	20	47	8	2	3	20	17-2	0	26	.250	.309	.362	83	-5	0-0	.996	1	105	80	1b56		-0.8
1976	StL N	129	374	54	108	21	5	7	46	49-5	3	53	.289	.376	.428	125	4	4-2	.990	16	164	101	1b110		2.3
1977	StL N	161	560	90	163	41	4	15	91	79-11	1	88	.291	.379	.459	125	22	7-7	.992	-4	112	127	1b158		1.6
1978	StL N	159	542	90	138	32	4	11	64	82-11	2	68	.255	.351	.389	108	9	13-5	.994	15	137	119	1b160		0.0
1979	StL N★	161	610	**116**	210	**48**	11	11	105	80-5	1	78	**.344**	.417	.513	151	46	11-6	.995	15	137	119	1b160		5.3
1980	StL N★	159	595	**111**	191	39	8	16	99	86-4	4	73	.321	**.408**	.494	144	39	14-8	.995	6	117	120	1b157		3.7
1981	StL N	103	376	65	115	27	4	8	48	61-6	2	67	.306	.401	.463	139	23	12-5	.997	5	126	130	1b98,O3L		2.8
1982	†StL N	160	579	79	173	33	6	7	94	100-19	2	67	.299	.397	.413	125	26	19-11	.994	5	117	121	1b158,O4(2/0/2)		0.4
1983	StL N	55	218	34	62	15	4	3	26	24-5	0	30	.284	.352	.431	116	5	1-1	.991	3	123	135	1b54		0.4
	NY N	95	320	43	98	8	3	9	37	64-9	2	42	.306	.424	.434	139	21	8-4	.993	10	139	115	1b90		3.3
	Year	150	538	77	160	23	7	12	63	88-14	2	72	.297	.396	.433	130	26	9-5	.992	12	133	123	1b144		4.0
1984	NY N★	154	550	83	171	31	0	15	94	97-12	1	89	.311	.409	.449	144	39	2-3	.994	17	**133**	104	1b157		4.4
1985	NY N	158	593	87	183	34	4	10	91	77-15	2	59	.309	.384	.430	132	28	3-3	**.996**	18	138	108	1b149		4.0
1986	†NY N	149	551	94	171	34	1	13	83	94-9	4	69	.310	.413	.446	140	40	2-1	.993	16	**134**	96	1b154		2.1
1987	NY N★	154	587	87	170	28	2	18	89	81-8	4	104	.290	.377	.436	120	20	0-2	.998	9	125	110	1b93		2.5
1988	†NY N	95	348	43	96	16	0	11	55	31-3	1	57	.276	.333	.417	120	9	2-1	.994	-1	88	62	1b58	56	-0.1
1989	NY N	75	215	18	50	8	0	4	19	27-3	2	39	.233	.324	.326	90	-2	0-3	.991	-1	80	87	1b42	107	-1.1
1990	Cle A	43	130	7	26	2	0	1	8	14-3	1	17	.200	.283	.238	47	-9	0-0	.994	-2	80	109	1b42,O7(5/0/2)	402	-1.6
Total	17	2088	7370	1124	2182	426	60	162	1071	1070-130	32	1012	.296	.384	.436	128	323	98-63	.994	133	123	109	1b2014,O7(5/0/2)	402	33.8

HERNANDEZ, LEO Leonardo Jesus B11.6.1959 Santa Lucia, Venez BR/TR/5-11/170(170-200) d9.19

1982	Bal A	2	2	0	0	0	0	0	0	0-0	0	2	.000	.000	.000	-99	-1	0-0	—	0		/H		-0.1
1983	Bal A	64	203	21	50	6	1	6	26	12-1	0	19	.246	.287	.374	82	-6	1-0	.922	-8	89	26	3b64		-0.5
1985	Bal A	12	21	0	1	0	0	0	0	0-0	0	4	.048	.048	.048	-75	-5	0-0	1.000	0	0	0	/1OLD		-0.3
1986	NY A	7	22	2	5	2	0	1	4	1-0	0	8	.227	.261	.455	91	0	0-0	1.000	-1	95	0	3b7/2		-0.1
Total	4	85	248	23	56	8	1	7	30	13-1	0	33	.226	.263	.351	68	-12	1-0	.927	-9	90	24	3b71,D8/2OL1		-2.1

HERNANDEZ, MICHEL Michel B8.12.1978 LaHabana, Cuba BR/TR/6-0/210 d9.6

2003	NY A	5	4	0	1	0	0	0	1	0-0	0	0	.250	.400	.250	78	0	0-0	1.000	-0	81	0	C5		0.0

HERNANDEZ, PEDRO Pedro Julio (b Pedro Julio Montas (Hernandez)) B4.4.1959 LaRomana, D.R. BR/TR/6-1/160* d9.8

1979	Tor A	3	0	1	0	0	0	0	0	0-0	0	0						0-0	—	0		R2		-0.0
1982	Tor A	8	9	1	0	0	0	0	0	0-0	0	5	.000	.000	.000	-92	-2	0-0	—	-1	0	0	3b2/OLD		-0.1
Total	2	11	9	2	0	0	0	0	0	0-0	0	5	.000	.000	.000	-92	-2	0-0	.000	-1	0	0	D3,3b2/OL		-0.1

YEAR TM LG	G	AB	R	H	2B	3B	HR	RBI	BB-IB	HP	SO	AVG	OBP	SLG	AOPS	ABR	SB-CS	FA	FR	RNG	THR	GAMES AT POSITION	DL	BFW

HERNANDEZ, TOBY Rafael Tobias (Alvarado) B11.30.1958 Calabozo, Venez BR/TR/6-1/160 d6.22

YEAR TM LG	G	AB	R	H	2B	3B	HR	RBI	BB-IB	HP	SO	AVG	OBP	SLG	AOPS	ABR	SB-CS	FA	FR	RNG	THR	GAMES AT POSITION	DL	BFW
1984 Tor A	3	2	1	1	0	0	0	0-0	0	0	.500 .500 .500	171	0	0-0	1.000	-0	0	0	C3		0.0

HERNANDEZ, RAMON Ramon Jose (Marin) B5.20.1976 Caracas, Venez BR/TR/6-0/210(210-227) d6.29

YEAR TM LG	G	AB	R	H	2B	3B	HR	RBI	BB-IB	HP	SO	AVG	OBP	SLG	AOPS	ABR	SB-CS	FA	FR	RNG	THR	GAMES AT POSITION	DL	BFW
1999 Oak A	40	136	13	38	7	0	3	21	18-0	1	11	.279 .363 .397	98	0	1-0	.980	5	79	89	C40	32	0.7
2000 †Oak A	143	419	52	101	19	0	14	62	38-1	7	64	.241 .311 .387	77	-15	1-0	.984	2	108	84	C142		-0.5
2001 †Oak A	136	453	55	115	25	0	15	60	37-3	6	68	.254 .316 .408	89	-7	1-1	.989	15	98	111	C135,1b2		1.6
2002 †Oak A	136	403	51	94	20	0	7	42	43-1	5	64	.233 .313 .335	73	-15	0-0	.992	11	156	91	C135		0.5
2003 †Oak A★	140	483	70	132	24	1	21	78	33-2	12	79	.273 .331 .458	106	4	0-0	.991	11	104	109	C139		2.3
2004 SD N	111	384	45	106	23	0	18	63	35-0	5	45	.276 .341 .477	115	8	1-0	.992	2	109	94	C108		1.7
2005 †SD N	99	369	36	107	19	2	12	58	18-0	1	40	.290 .322 .450	106	1	1-0	.988	36	110	95	C97	35	-0.2
Total 7	805	2647	322	693	137	3	90	384	222-7	37	371	.262 .325 .418	94	-24	5-1	.989				C796,1b2	58	125	6.1

HERNANDEZ, RUDY Rodolfo (Acosta) B10.18.1951 Empalme, Sonora, Mexico BR/TR/5-9/150 d9.6

YEAR TM LG	G	AB	R	H	2B	3B	HR	RBI	BB-IB	HP	SO	AVG	OBP	SLG	AOPS	ABR	SB-CS	FA	FR	RNG	THR	GAMES AT POSITION	DL	BFW
1972 Chi A	8	21	0	4	0	0	0	1	0-0	0	3	.190 .190 .190	13	-2	0-0	1.000	-0	91	92	S6		-0.2

HERNANDEZ, CHICO Salvador Jose (Ramos) B1.3.1916 Havana, Cuba D1.3.1986 Havana, Cuba BR/TR/6-0/195 d4.16

YEAR TM LG	G	AB	R	H	2B	3B	HR	RBI	BB-IB	HP	SO	AVG	OBP	SLG	AOPS	ABR	SB-CS	FA	FR	RNG	THR	GAMES AT POSITION	DL	BFW
1942 Chi N	47	118	6	27	5	0	0	7	11	0	13	.229 .295 .271	69	-5	0	.975	-2	108	88	C43		-0.5
1943 Chi N	43	126	10	34	4	0	0	9	9	1	9	.270 .324 .302	82	-3	0	.981	-2	132	72	C41		-0.3
Total 2	90	244	16	61	9	0	0	16	20	1	22	.250 .309 .287	76	-8	0	.978	-4	120	80	C84		-0.8

HERNDON, LARRY Larry Darnell B11.3.1953 Sunflower MS BR/TR/6-3/195(188-200) [StLN71 3/54] d9.4 C7

YEAR TM LG	G	AB	R	H	2B	3B	HR	RBI	BB-IB	HP	SO	AVG	OBP	SLG	AOPS	ABR	SB-CS	FA	FR	RNG	THR	GAMES AT POSITION	DL	BFW
1974 StL N	12	1	3	1	0	0	0	0	0-0	0	0	1.000 1.000 1.000	461	0	0-0	1.000	0	112	0	/OC		0.0
1976 SF N	115	337	42	97	11	3	2	23	23-0	2	45	.288 .337 .356	94	-3	12-10	.967	-1	99	144	O110C		-0.7
1977 SF N	49	109	13	26	4	3	1	5	5-1	1	20	.239 .278 .358	69	-5	4-2	.957	2	121	106	O44C		-0.4
1978 SF N	151	471	52	122	15	9	1	32	35-2	1	71	.259 .311 .335	84	-12	13-8	.974	-2	107	40	O149C	68	-1.5
1979 SF N	132	354	35	91	14	5	7	36	29-5	1	70	.257 .313 .384	97	-3	8-6	.963	-1	97	147	O122(40/84/12)		-0.7
1980 SF N	139	493	54	127	17	11	8	49	19-1	1	91	.258 .284 .385	89	-11	8-8	.959	-5	95	91	O122(53/53/28)		-2.2
1981 SF N	96	364	48	105	15	8	5	41	20-2	1	55	.288 .325 .415	113	4	15-6	.977	4	110	97	O93(82/7/10)		0.5
1982 Det A	157	614	92	179	21	13	23	88	38-3	1	92	.292 .332 .480	120	13	12-9	.983	0	94	113	O155L,D3		0.6
1983 Det A	153	603	88	182	28	9	20	92	46-6	3	95	.302 .351 .478	129	23	9-3	.951	-5	95	57	O133L,D19		1.2
1984 †Det A	125	407	52	114	18	5	7	43	32-1	2	63	.280 .333 .400	103	1	6-2	.986	-4	87	97	O117L,D4		-0.6
1985 Det A	137	442	45	108	12	7	12	37	33-1	1	79	.244 .298 .385	86	-11	2-1	.976	3	104	88	O136L		-1.3
1986 Det A	106	283	33	70	13	1	8	37	27-2	1	40	.247 .310 .385	89	-4	2-1	.988	-2	101	41	O83L,D18		-0.9
1987 †Det A	89	225	32	73	13	2	9	47	23-0	1	35	.324 .378 .520	143	14	1-0	.989	2	102	142	O57(32/0/26),D23		1.3
1988 Det A	76	174	16	39	5	0	4	20	23-0	1	37	.224 .313 .322	83	-4	0-1	1.000	0	108	5	D53,O15L		-0.6
Total 14	1537	4877	605	1334	186	76	107	550	353-24	16	793	.274 .322 .409	103	2	92-57	.972	-8	99	92	O1337(847/448/76),D120	68	-5.3

HERNON, TOM Thomas H. B11.4.1866 E.Bridgewater MA D2.4.1902 New Bedford MA BR/TR/5-7.5/156 d9.13

YEAR TM LG	G	AB	R	H	2B	3B	HR	RBI	BB-IB	HP	SO	AVG	OBP	SLG	AOPS	ABR	SB-CS	FA	FR	RNG	THR	GAMES AT POSITION	DL	BFW
1897 Chi N	4	16	2	1	0	0	0	2	0	0		.063 .063 .063	-64	-4	1	1.000	-0	0	0	O4L		-0.4

HERR, JOE Joseph B3.1867 MO BR/TR/5-9.5/179 d4.16

YEAR TM LG	G	AB	R	H	2B	3B	HR	RBI	BB-IB	HP	SO	AVG	OBP	SLG	AOPS	ABR	SB-CS	FA	FR	RNG	THR	GAMES AT POSITION	DL	BFW
1887 Cle AA	11	44	6	12	2	0	0	6	6	0		.273 .360 .318	93	0	2	.729	-3	76	50	3b11		-0.2
1888 †StL AA	43	172	21	46	7	1	3	43	11	3		.267 .323 .372	110	1	9	.872	-6	80	75	S28,O11(4/4/3),3b4		-0.4
1890 StL AA	12	41	5	9	2	1	0	1	5	3		.220 .347 .317	84	-1	2	.793	-5	45	40	2b7,O4C/3		-0.5
Total 3	66	257	32	67	11	2	3	50	22	6		.261 .333 .354	102	0	13	.872	-14	80	75	S28,3b16,O15(4/8/3),2b7		-1.1

HERR, TOM Thomas Mitchell B4.4.1956 Lancaster PA BB/TR/6-0/185(175-196) d8.13

YEAR TM LG	G	AB	R	H	2B	3B	HR	RBI	BB-IB	HP	SO	AVG	OBP	SLG	AOPS	ABR	SB-CS	FA	FR	RNG	THR	GAMES AT POSITION	DL	BFW
1979 StL N	14	10	4	2	0	0	0	1	2-0	0	2	.200 .333 .200	48	-1	1-0	1.000	1	108	147	2b6		0.1
1980 StL N	76	222	29	55	12	5	0	15	16-5	1	21	.248 .299 .347	77	-7	9-2	.984	3	102	131	2b58,S14		0.1
1981 StL N	103	411	50	110	14	9	0	46	39-3	1	30	.268 .329 .345	88	-6	23-7	.992	3	113	118	2b103		0.6
1982 †StL N	135	493	83	131	19	4	0	36	57-2	2	56	.266 .341 .320	85	-8	25-12	.987	9	110	130	2b128		0.9
1983 StL N	89	313	43	101	14	4	2	31	43-2	1	27	.323 .403 .412	127	13	6-8	.986	-2	103	115	2b86	80	1.4
1984 StL N	145	558	67	154	23	2	4	49	49-2	2	56	.276 .335 .346	94	-4	13-7	.992	9	105	117	2b144		1.4
1985 †StL N★	159	596	97	180	38	3	8	110	80-5	2	55	.302 .379 .416	125	24	31-3	.985	-25	93	121	2b158		1.4
1986 StL N	152	559	48	141	30	4	2	61	73-10	5	75	.252 .342 .331	87	-7	22-8	.988	-15	95	141	2b152		-1.2
1987 †StL N	141	510	73	134	29	0	2	83	68-3	3	62	.263 .346 .331	80	-11	19-4	.989	-11	94	120	2b137	18	-1.2
1988 StL N	15	50	4	13	0	0	1	3	11-3	0	4	.260 .393 .320	105	1	3-0	.984	-5	81	103	2b15		-0.3
Min A	86	304	42	80	16	0	1	21	40-1	0	47	.263 .349 .326	87	-3	10-3	.988	-3	95	116	2b73,S2,D3	55	-0.3
1989 Phi N	151	561	65	161	25	6	2	37	54-2	3	63	.287 .352 .364	105	5	10-7	.990	11	107	94	2b144		2.1
1990 Phi N	119	447	39	118	21	3	4	50	36-4	2	47	.264 .320 .351	85	-9	7-1	.991	0	98	130	2b114		-0.5
NY N	27	100	9	25	5	0	1	10	14-0	0	11	.250 .342 .330	86	-1	0-0	.979	-4	83	118	2b26		-0.5
Year	146	547	48	143	26	3	5	60	50-4	2	58	.261 .324 .347	85	-11	7-1	.989	-4	95	128	2b140		-1.0
1991 NY N	70	155	17	30	7	0	1	14	32-4	0	21	.194 .328 .258	68	-5	7-2	1.000	4	96	130	2b57/OC		0.1
SF N	32	60	6	15	1	1	0	7	13-1	0	7	.250 .384 .300	97	1	2-0	1.000	4	83	66	2b15,3b3		-0.3
Year	102	215	23	45	8	1	1	21	45-5	0	28	.209 .344 .270	76	-5	9-2	1.000	0	93	117	2b72,3b3/OC		-0.2
Total 13	1514	5349	676	1450	254	41	28	574	627-47	22	584	.271 .347 .350	94	-18	188-64	.989	-29	100	121	2b1416,S16,3b3,D3/OC	153	3.8

HERRERA, JOSE Jose Concepcion (Ontiveros) "Loco" B4.8.1942 San Lorenzo, Venez BR/TR/5-8/165* d6.3

YEAR TM LG	G	AB	R	H	2B	3B	HR	RBI	BB-IB	HP	SO	AVG	OBP	SLG	AOPS	ABR	SB-CS	FA	FR	RNG	THR	GAMES AT POSITION	DL	BFW
1967 Hou N	5	4	0	1	0	0	0	1	0-0	0	1	.250 .250 .250	45	0	0-0	—	0			/H		0.0
1968 Hou N	27	100	9	24	5	0	0	7	4-0	0	12	.240 .269 .290	69	-4	0-2	.958	-1	82	85	O17(5/0/12),2b7		-0.7
1969 Mon N	47	126	7	36	5	0	2	12	3-0	0	14	.286 .302 .373	88	-3	1-2	.980	-2	90	127	O31(20/13/0),2b2/3		-0.6
1970 Mon N	1	1	0	0	0	0	0	0	0-0	0	1	1.000 .000 .000	-99	0	0-0	—	0			/H		0.0
Total 4	80	231	16	61	10	0	2	20	7-0	0	28	.264 .286 .333	79	-7	1-4	.973	-3	87	112	O48(25/13/12),2b9/3		-1.3

HERRERA, JOSE Jose Ramon (Catalino) B8.30.1972 Santo Domingo, D.R. BL/TL/6-0/165* d8.12

YEAR TM LG	G	AB	R	H	2B	3B	HR	RBI	BB-IB	HP	SO	AVG	OBP	SLG	AOPS	ABR	SB-CS	FA	FR	RNG	THR	GAMES AT POSITION	DL	BFW
1995 Oak A	33	70	9	17	1	0	2	6	0	0	11	.243 .299 .314	64	-4	1-3	.956	1	98	231	O25(0/22/5),D5		-0.4
1996 Oak A	108	320	44	86	15	1	6	30	20-1	3	59	.269 .318 .378	76	-12	8-2	.970	-0	110	35	O100(0/18/92)/D		-1.4
Total 2	141	390	53	103	16	3	6	32	26-1	3	70	.264 .314 .367	74	-16	9-5	.967	0	108	70	O125(0/40/97),D6		-1.8

HERRERA, PANCHO Juan Francisco (Willavicencio) B6.16.1934 Santiago de Cuba, Cuba D4.28.2005 Miami FL BR/TR/6-3/220* d4.15 Negro Lg 1954

YEAR TM LG	G	AB	R	H	2B	3B	HR	RBI	BB-IB	HP	SO	AVG	OBP	SLG	AOPS	ABR	SB-CS	FA	FR	RNG	THR	GAMES AT POSITION	DL	BFW
1958 Phi N	29	63	5	17	3	0	1	6	7-0	1	15	.270 .347 .365	92	0	1-2	.980	0	88	101	3b16,1b11		-0.1
1960 Phi N	145	512	61	144	26	6	17	71	51-6	5	136	.281 .348 .455	119	14	2-3	.988	8	117	89	1b134,2b17		1.5
1961 Phi N	126	400	56	103	17	2	13	51	55-4	4	120	.257 .351 .408	102	3	5-1	.993	5	115	103	1b115		0.2
Total 3	300	975	122	264	46	8	31	128	113-10	10	271	.271 .349 .430	110	17	8-6	.990	13	117	96	1b260,2b17,3b16		1.6

HERRERA, MIKE Ramon B12.19.1897 Havana, Cuba D2.3.1978 Havana, Cuba BR/TR/5-6/147 d9.22

YEAR TM LG	G	AB	R	H	2B	3B	HR	RBI	BB-IB	HP	SO	AVG	OBP	SLG	AOPS	ABR	SB-CS	FA	FR	RNG	THR	GAMES AT POSITION	DL	BFW
1925 Bos A	10	39	2	15	0	0	0	8	2	0	2	.385 .415 .385	104	1	1-0	.958	2	128	45	2b10		0.3
1926 Bos A	74	237	20	61	14	1	0	19	15	1	13	.257 .304 .325	66	-12	0-5	.962	6	109	83	2b48,3b16,S4		-0.5
Total 2	84	276	22	76	14	1	0	27	17	1	15	.275 .320 .333	72	-12	1-5	.961	8	112	76	2b58,3b16,S4		-0.2

HERRING, LEFTY Silas Clarke B3.4.1880 Philadelphia PA D2.11.1965 Massapequa NY BL/TL/5-11/160 d5.16

YEAR TM LG	G	AB	R	H	2B	3B	HR	RBI	BB-IB	HP	SO	AVG	OBP	SLG	AOPS	ABR	SB-CS	FA	FR	RNG	THR	GAMES AT POSITION	DL	BFW
1899 Was A	2	1	1	1	0	0	0	1	0	0		1.000 1.000 1.000	454	1	0	1.000	0	198	0	P2		0.0
1904 Was A	15	46	3	8	1	0	0	2	7	0		.174 .283 .196	54	-2	0	.991	1	162	125	1b10,O5C		-0.1
Total 2	17	47	4	9	1	0	0	2	8	0		.191 .309 .213	67	-1	0	.991	2	162	125	1b10,O5C,P2		-0.1

HERRMANN, ED Edward Martin B8.27.1946 San Diego CA BL/TR/6-1/210* d9.1 gf-Marty

YEAR TM LG	G	AB	R	H	2B	3B	HR	RBI	BB-IB	HP	SO	AVG	OBP	SLG	AOPS	ABR	SB-CS	FA	FR	RNG	THR	GAMES AT POSITION	DL	BFW
1967 Chi A	2	3	1	2	1	0	0	1	1-1	0	0	.667 .750 1.000	429	1	0-0	1.000	1	0	337	C2		0.3
1969 Chi A	102	290	31	67	8	0	8	31	30-0	8	35	.231 .319 .341	81	-7	0-2	.983	-5	105	80	C92		-0.9
1970 Chi A	96	297	42	84	9	0	19	52	31-3	3	41	.283 .356 .505	130	12	0-1	.988	0	60	105	C88		1.6
1971 Chi A	101	294	32	63	6	0	11	35	44-12	2	48	.214 .317 .347	87	-5	2-0	.995	7	94	118	C97	24	0.8
1972 Chi A	116	354	23	88	9	0	10	40	43-19	4	37	.249 .333 .359	105	3	0-0	.989	0	108	143	C112		0.9
1973 Chi A	119	379	42	85	17	1	10	39	31-3	7	55	.224 .291 .354	79	-11	0-0	.984	3	74	96	C114,D2		-0.3
1974 Chi A★	107	367	32	95	13	1	10	39	16-6	0	49	.259 .288 .381	89	-6	1-0	.987	-1	105	105	C107	16	-0.2
1975 NY A	80	200	16	51	9	0	6	30	16-5	0	23	.255 .309 .410	103	0	0-0	.979	7	138	83	D35,C24		0.8
1976 Cal A	29	46	5	8	0	0	1	8	7-2	0	8	.174 .278 .370	96	0	0-0	.954	-8	55	105	C27		-0.8
Hou N	79	265	14	54	6	1	3	25	22-2	4	40	.204 .273 .268	49	-15	0-0	.987	-2	76	106	C79		-1.4

YEAR	TM LG	G	AB	R	H	2B	3B	HR	RBI	BB-IB	HP	SO	AVG	OBP	SLG	AOPS	ABR	SB-CS	FA	FR	RNG	THR	GAMES AT POSITION	DL	BFW
1977	Hou N	56	158	7	46	7	0	1	17	15-1	1	18	.291	.352	.354	99	0	1-1	.990	4	73	81	C49		0.6
1978	Hou N	16	36	1	4	1	0	0	0	3-1	0	3	.111	.179	.139	-11	-5	0-0	1.000	-3	76	73	C14		-0.8
	Mon N	19	40	1	7	1	0	0	3	1-0	0	4	.175	.195	.200	11	-5	0-0	.977	-4	45	88	C12		-0.9
	Year	35	76	2	11	2	0	0	3	4-1	0	7	.145	.188	.171	1	-10	0-0	.991	-6	62	80	C26		-1.7
Total	11	922	2729	247	654	92	4	80	320	260-55	29	361	.240	.310	.364	.90	-38	6-8	.987	2	88	106	C817,D37	40	-0.3

HERRNSTEIN, JOHN John Ellett B3.31.1938 Hampton VA BL/TL/6-3/215* d9.15 Col Michigan

										1-0			.200	.333	.200	48	0	0-0	—	-0	0	0	/OR		0.0
1962	Phi N	6	5	0	1	0	0	0	1	1-0	0	5	.167	.231	.417	83	0	0-0	1.000	0	259	0	O2L/1		0.0
1963	Phi N	15	12	1	2	0	0	1	1	22-0	2	67	.234	.288	.360	83	-7	1-2	.977	-6	102	0	O69(63/4/3),1b68		-2.0
1964	Phi N	125	303	38	71	12	4	6	25	2-1	1	18	.200	.227	.259	37	-7	0-0	.984	0	94	127	1b18,O14(11/2/1)		-0.9
1965	Phi N	63	85	8	17	2	0	1	5	0-0	0	7	.100	.100	.100	-44	-2	0-0	1.000	-0	83	0	O2L		-0.2
1966	Phi N	4	10	0	1	0	0	0	1	0-0	0	8	.176	.300	.176	36	-1	0-0	.975	-1	0	109	1b4/OL		-0.3
	Chi N	9	17	3	3	0	0	0	1	3-0	0	7	.222	.222	.222	24	-2	0-0	1.000	9	131	0	O5L		-0.2
	Atl N	17	18	2	4	0	0	0	2	0-0	0	22	.178	.229	.178	15	-5	0-0	1.000	-1	105	0	O8L,1b4		-0.7
	Year	30	45	5	8	0	0	0	3	3-0	0	22	.178	.229	.178	15	-5	0-0	1.000	-1	105	0	O8L,1b4		-3.6
Total	5	239	450	52	99	14	4	8	34	29-1	3	115	.220	.270	.322	67	-19	1-2	.983	-7	101	55	O94(84/6/5),1b91		

HERRSCHER, RICK Richard Franklin B11.3.1936 St.Louis MO BR/TR/6-2.5/187 d8.1 Col SMU

| 1962 | NY N | 35 | 50 | 5 | 11 | 3 | 0 | 1 | 6 | 5-0 | 0 | 11 | .220 | .291 | .340 | 68 | -2 | 0-0 | 1.000 | 1 | 133 | 110 | 1b10,3b6,O4(3/0/1),S3 | | -0.1 |

HERSH, EARL Earl Walter B5.21.1932 Ebbvale MD BL/TL/6-0/205 d9.4 Col West Chester

| 1956 | Mil N | 7 | 13 | 0 | 3 | 3 | 0 | 0 | 0 | 0-0 | 0 | 5 | .231 | .231 | .462 | 85 | 0 | 0-0 | .000 | -1 | 0 | 0 | O2L | | -0.1 |

HERSHBERGER, MIKE Norman Michael B10.9.1939 Massillon OH BR/TR/5-10/175* d9.5 Col Cincinnati

1961	Chi A	15	55	9	17	3	0	0	5	2-0	0	2	.309	.333	.364	88	-1	1-1	1.000	1	94	248	O13(1/9/3)		-0.1
1962	Chi A	148	427	54	112	14	2	4	46	37-0	3	36	.262	.324	.333	78	-13	10-6	.984	-1	100	112	O135(1/52/90)		-2.0
1963	Chi A	135	476	64	133	26	4	3	45	39-1	4	39	.279	.338	.361	98	0	9-3	.976	-1	94	173	O119(1/73/67)		-0.6
1964	Chi A	141	452	55	104	15	3	2	31	48-1	4	47	.230	.308	.290	70	-18	8-6	.984	-1	96	128	O134(0/64/85)		-2.7
1965	KC A	150	494	43	114	15	5	5	48	37-5	5	42	.231	.289	.312	72	-19	7-3	.988	5	100	167	O144(5/9/134)		-2.3
1966	KC A	146	538	55	136	27	7	2	57	47-3	3	37	.253	.313	.340	92	-5	13-5	.977	9	109	168	O143(12/3/130)		-0.5
1967	KC A	142	480	55	122	25	1	1	49	38-2	7	40	.254	.314	.317	91	-4	10-3	.982	8	101	218	O130(10/0/122)		-0.4
1968	Oak A	99	246	23	67	9	2	5	32	21-4	1	22	.272	.327	.386	122	6	8-3	.978	1	102	117	O90(71/6/27)		0.5
1969	Oak A	51	129	11	26	2	0	1	10	10-0	0	15	.202	.259	.240	42	-10	1-2	.980	-4	81	0	O35(16/8/13)	60	-1.8
1970	Mil A	49	98	7	23	5	0	1	6	10-0	0	8	.235	.306	.316	72	-4	1-2	.946	-2	81	65	O35R	78	-0.8
1971	Chi A	74	177	22	46	9	0	2	15	30-3	4	23	.260	.377	.345	103	3	6-2	.960	-6	84	34	O59(0/58/2)		-0.5
Total	11	1150	3572	398	900	150	22	26	344	319-19	31	311	.252	.316	.328	85	-65	74-36	.980	9	98	146	O1037(117/282/708)	138	-11.2

HERSHBERGER, WILLARD Willard McKee "Bill" B5.28.1910 Lemoncove CA D8.3.1940 Boston MA BR/TR/5-10.5/167 d4.19

1938	Cin N	49	105	12	29	3	1	0	12	5	1	6	.276	.315	.324	78	-3	1	.960	-1	126	81	C39/2		-0.3
1939	†Cin N	63	174	23	60	9	2	0	32	9	2	4	.345	.384	.420	115	4	1	.987	-1	109	99	C60		0.6
1940	Cin N	48	123	6	38	4	2	0	26	6	2	6	.309	.351	.374	99	0	0	.985	-1	117	47	C37		0.0
Total	3	160	402	41	127	16	5	0	70	20	5	16	.316	.356	.381	101	1	2	.980	-3	116	79	C136/2		0.3

HERTWECK, NEAL Neal Charles B11.22.1931 St.Louis MO BL/TL/6-1.5/175 d9.27 Col Missouri

| 1952 | StL N | 2 | 6 | 0 | 0 | 0 | 0 | 0 | 1 | 0 | 0 | 1 | .000 | .143 | .000 | -57 | -1 | 0-0 | 1.000 | -0 | 78 | 241 | 1b2 | | -0.2 |

HERTZ, STEVE Stephen Allan B2.26.1945 Fairfield OH BR/TR/6-1/195 d4.21

| 1964 | Hou N | 5 | 4 | 2 | 0 | 0 | 0 | 0 | 0 | 0-0 | 0 | 3 | .000 | .000 | .000 | -99 | -1 | 0-0 | 1.000 | 0 | 0 | 0 | 3b2 | | -0.1 |

HERZOG, BUCK Charles Lincoln B7.9.1885 Baltimore MD D9.4.1953 Baltimore MD BR/TR/5-11/160 d4.17 M3 Col Maryland-Baltimore Co. OF(28/0/4)

1908	NY N	64	160	38	48	8	2	0	11	36	7		.300	.448	.363	152	13	16	.921	-0	107	189	2b42,S12,3b4/OL		1.6
1909	NY N	42	130	16	24	2	0	0	8	13	1		.185	.264	.200	43	-8	10	.914	-3	90	106	O29(26/0/4),2b6,3b4/S		-1.5
1910	Bos N	106	380	51	95	20	3	3	32	30	15	34	.250	.329	.342	92	-3	13	.915	8	116	111	3b105		0.7
1911	Bos N	79	294	53	91	19	5	5	41	33	10	21	.310	.398	.459	129	12	26	.934	3	106	85	S74,3b4		2.1
	†NY N	69	247	37	66	14	4	1	26	14	7	19	.267	.325	.368	91	-3	22	.926	7	110	83	3b65,2b3/S		0.6
	Year	148	541	90	157	33	9	6	67	47	17	40	.290	.365	.418	112	9	48	.935	10	106	85	S75,3b69,2b3		2.7
1912	†NY N	140	482	72	127	20	9	2	47	57	7	34	.263	.350	.355	90	-6	37	.942	20	117	126	3b140		1.8
1913	†NY N	96	290	46	83	15	3	3	31	22	6	12	.286	.349	.390	110	4	23-15	.947	2	97	205	3b84,2b2		0.8
1914	Cin N	138	498	54	140	14	8	1	40	42	9	27	.281	.348	.347	104	3	46	.939	33	113	118	S137,1b2,M		4.8
1915	Cin N	155	579	61	153	14	10	1	42	34	8	21	.264	.314	.328	93	-6	35-16	.945	30	108	141	S153,1b2,M		4.0
1916	Cin N	79	281	30	75	14	2	1	24	21	5	12	.267	.329	.342	109	4	15-12	.931	-4	94	99	S65,3b12/OLM		0.5
	NY N	77	280	40	73	10	4	0	25	22	5	24	.261	.326	.325	106	2	19-16	.978	12	105	117	2b44,3b27,S9		1.8
	Year	156	561	70	148	24	6	1	49	43	10	36	.264	.327	.333	107	6	34-28	.926	8	97	105	S74,2b44,3b39/OL		2.3
1917	†NY N	114	417	69	98	10	8	2	31	31	13	36	.235	.308	.312	93	-3	12	.948	-9	95	128	2b113		-1.1
1918	Bos N	118	473	57	108	12	6	0	26	29	5	28	.228	.280	.279	74	-15	14	.961	2	104	91	2b99,1b12,S7		-1.2
1919	Bos N	73	275	27	77	8	5	1	25	13	6	11	.280	.327	.356	110	3	16	.953	-15	91	80	2b70/1		-0.3
	Chi N	52	193	15	53	4	4	0	17	10	8	7	.275	.336	.337	102	1	12	.987	-4	99	75	2b52		-1.5
	Year	125	468	42	130	12	9	1	42	23	14	18	.278	.331	.348	106	3	28	.967	-18	94	78	2b122/1		-2.8
1920	Chi N	91	305	39	59	9	2	0	19	20	8	21	.193	.261	.236	43	-22	8-9	.938	-4	93	87	2b59,3b28/1		10.6
Total	13	1493	5284	705	1370	191	75	20	445	427	120	307	.259	.329	.335	96	-24	320-68	.954	80	98	108	2b490,3b473,S459,O31L,1b18		

HERZOG, WHITEY Dorrel Norman Elvert B11.9.1931 New Athens IL BL/TL/5-11/182* d4.17 M18/C4

1956	Was A	117	421	49	103	13	7	4	35	35-0	0	74	.245	.302	.337	69	-21	8-5	.980	-4	93	125	O103(15/84/7),1b5		-3.0
1957	Was A	36	78	7	13	3	0	0	4	13-0	2	12	.167	.301	.205	41	-6	1-2	.981	-1	101	0	O28(2/26/0)		-0.9
1958	Was A	8	5	0	0	0	0	0	0	1-0	0	5	.000	.167	.000	-51	-1	0-0	1.000	0	138	0	O7(0/5/2)		-0.1
	KC A	88	96	11	23	1	2	0	9	16-1	0	21	.240	.345	.292	77	-3	0-3	.968	-0	127	0	O44(29/12/3),1b22		-0.5
	Year	96	101	11	23	1	2	0	9	17-1	0	26	.228	.336	.277	71	-4	0-3	.972	-1	128	0	O51(29/17/5),1b22		-0.6
1959	KC A	38	123	25	36	7	1	1	9	34-0	0	23	.293	.446	.390	129	8	1-0	.985	0	99	90	O69(29/0/42),1b2	81	0.7
1960	KC A	83	252	43	67	10	2	8	38	40-2	0	32	.266	.364	.417	111	5	0-1	1.000	9	99	99	O98(27/0/73)	39	0.1
1961	Bal A	113	323	39	94	11	6	5	35	50-1	1	41	.291	.387	.409	117	9	1-4	.978	-7	86	31	O70(13/1/59)		-0.4
1962	Bal A	99	263	34	70	13	1	7	35	41-1	3	36	.266	.369	.403	116	7	2-3	.978	2	110	109	O70(13/1/59)		0.5
1963	Det A	52	53	5	8	2	1	2	6	11-3	1	17	.151	.303	.226	51	-7	0-0	.976	-1	31	55	1b7,O4(1/1/2)		-0.5
Total	8	634	1614	213	414	60	20	25	172	241-8	7	261	.257	.354	.365	96	-5	13-18	.982	-11	98	82	O450(117/137/206),1b37	120	-4.1

HESS, OTTO Otto C. B10.10.1878 Bern, Switzerland D2.25.1926 Tucson AZ BL/TL/6-1/170 d8.3 ▲

1902	Cle A	7	14	2	1	0	0	0	1	2	0		.071	.188	.071	-27	-1	0	.870	1	124	0	P7		0.0
1904	Cle A	34	100	4	12	2	1	0	5	3	0		.120	.146	.160	-3	-12	0	.951	1	92	0	P21,O12(7/5/0)		-0.3
1905	Cle A	54	173	15	44	8	1	2	13	7	2		.254	.291	.347	101	0	2	.950	3	165	297	O28(27/0/1),P26		0.1
1906	Cle A	53	154	13	31	5	2	0	11	2	0		.201	.212	.260	48	-10	1	.949	-2	85	165	P43,O5C		-0.1
1907	Cle A	19	30	4	4	0	0	0	4	0	0		.133	.278	.133	31	-1	0	.941	-1	90	0	P17,O2L		-0.3
1908	Cle A	9	14	0	0	0	0	0	0	0	0		.000	.000	.000	-78	-3	0	1.000	-0	140	0	P4,O4R		-0.3
1912	Bos N	33	94	10	23	4	4	0	10	0	0	26	.245	.245	.372	66	3	0	.951	-4	74	145	P33		0.0
1913	Bos N	35	83	9	26	0	1	2	11	7	0	15	.313	.367	.410	119	4	0	.945	1	103	141	P29		0.0
1914	Bos N	31	47	5	11	1	0	0	1	0	0	11	.234	.250	.319	69	-2	0	.947	1	140	293	P14,1b5		-0.1
1915	Bos N	5	5	1	2	1	0	0	1	0	0	2	.400	.400	.600	210	1	0	.800	-0	106	0	P4/1		0.0
Total	10	280	714	63	154	21	9	5	58	27	4	54	.216	.248	.291	63	-18	4	.941	0	94	105	P198,O51(36/10/5),1b6		-0.6

HESS, TOM Thomas (b Thomas Heslin) B8.15.1875 Brooklyn NY D12.15.1945 Albany NY TR d6.6

| 1892 | Bal N | 1 | 2 | 0 | 0 | 0 | 0 | 0 | 0 | 0 | 0 | | .000 | .000 | .000 | -97 | -1 | 0 | — | 0 | 0 | 0 | /C | | 0.0 |

HESSMAN, MIKE Michael Steven B3.5.1978 Fountain Valley CA BR/TR/6-5/210* [AtlN96 15/452] d8.22

2003	Atl N	19	21	2	6	2	0	2	5-1		0	6	.286	.423	.667	179	3	0-0	.800	-1	123	0	O8(7/0/1),1b4,3b3		0.2
2004	Atl N	29	69	8	9	3	0	2	5	1-0	1	24	.130	.155	.261	5	-10	0-0	.962	1	57	72	1b16,3b7,O3L		-1.0
Total	2	48	90	10	15	5	0	4	8	6-1	1	30	.167	.227	.356	47	-7	0-0	.970	0	56	82	1b20,O11(10/0/1),3b10		-0.8

HETLING, GUS August Julius B11.21.1885 St.Louis MO D10.13.1962 Wichita KS BR/TR/5-10/165 d10.6

| 1906 | Det A | 2 | 7 | 0 | 1 | 0 | 0 | 0 | 0 | 0 | 0 | | .143 | .143 | .143 | -10 | -1 | 0 | 1.000 | -0 | 59 | 0 | 3b2 | | -0.1 |

YEAR	TM LG	G	AB	R	H	2B	3B	HR	RBI	BB-IB	HP	SO	AVG	OBP	SLG	AOPS	ABR	SB-CS	FA	FR	RNG	THR	GAMES AT POSITION	DL	BFW

HEUBEL, GEORGE George A. B1849 Paterson NJ D1.22.1896 Philadelphia PA 5-11.5/178 d5.20 U2

1871	Ath NA	17	75	18	23	4	2	0	13	2		0	.307	.325	.413	112	1	1-0	.758	0	160	0	O16R/1		0.2
1872	Oly NA	5	23	2	3	0	0	0	1	0		0	.130	.130	.130	-21	-3	0-0	.800	-1	0	0	O5C		-0.3
1876	NY N	1	4	0	0	0	0	0	0	0		0	.000	.000	.000	-99	-1		.750	-0	0	0	/1		-0.1
Total	2 NA	22	98	20	26	4	2	0	14	2		0	.265	.280	.347	83	-2	1-0	.767	-0	124	0	O21(0/5/16)/1		-0.1

HEVING, JOHNNIE John Aloysius B4.29.1896 Covington KY D12.24.1968 Salisbury NC BR/TR/6-0/175 d9.24 b-Joe

1920	StL A	1	1	0	0	0	0	0	0	0	0	0	.000	.000	.000	-97	0	0-0	—	0			/H		0.0
1924	Bos A	45	109	15	31	5	1	0	11	10	0	7	.284	.345	.349	79	-3	0-0	.969	2	101	148	C29		0.0
1925	Bos A	45	119	14	20	7	0	0	6	12	0	7	.168	.244	.227	20	-15	0-1	.958	-0	74	102	C34		-1.2
1928	Bos A	82	158	11	41	7	2	0	11	11	0	10	.259	.308	.329	69	-7	1-1	.967	-5	78	107	C62		-1.0
1929	Bos A	76	188	26	60	4	3	0	23	8	2	7	.319	.354	.372	89	-7	1-2	.988	4	110	123	C55		0.4
1930	Bos A	75	220	15	61	5	3	0	17	11	0	14	.277	.312	.327	65	-12	2-0	.987	1	155	88	C71		-0.7
1931	†Phi A	42	113	8	27	3	2	1	12	6	0	8	.239	.277	.327	55	-8	0-0	.993	3	126	65	C40		-0.3
1932	Phi A	33	77	14	21	6	1	0	10	7	0	6	.273	.333	.377	81	-2	0-0	1.000	0	110	34	C28		-0.1
Total	8	399	985	103	261	37	12	1	90	65	2	59	.265	.312	.330	66	-51	4-4	.981	3	112	100	C319		-2.9

HEYDON, MIKE Michael Edward "Ed" B7.15.1874 MO D10.13.1913 Indianapolis IN BL/TR/6-0/? d10.12

1898	Bal N	3	9	2	1	0	0	0	1	2	1		.111	.333	.111	28	-1	0	.917	-0	95	131	C3		-0.1
1899	Was N	3	3	0	0	0	0	0	0	2	0		.000	.400	.000	14	-1	0	.833	-0	85	147	C2		-0.1
1901	StL N	16	43	2	9	1	1	1	6	5	0		.209	.292	.349	90	-1	2	.941	-2	97	69	C13/OC		-0.2
1904	Chi A	4	10	0	1	1	0	0	1	1	1		.100	.250	.200	45	0	1	1.000	1	153	123	C4		0.1
1905	Was A	77	245	20	47	7	4	1	26	21	2		.192	.261	.265	70	-9	5	.955	9	101	113	C77		0.9
1906	Was A	49	145	14	23	7	1	0	10	14	1		.159	.237	.221	46	-9	2	.937	-6	80	124	C49		-1.1
1907	Was A	62	164	14	30	3	0	0	9	25	3		.183	.302	.201	66	-4	3	.961	-9	85	92	C57		-0.9
Total	7	214	619	52	111	19	6	3	59	70	8		.179	.271	.239	64	-24	12	.952	-7	92	108	C205/OC		-1.3

HIATT, JACK Jack E B7.27.1942 Bakersfield CA BR/TR/6-2/190* d9.7 C1

1964	LA A	9	16	2	6	0	0	0	2	2-0	0	7	.375	.444	.375	145	1	0-0	.889	0	45	0	C3,1b2		0.1
1965	SF N	40	67	5	19	4	0	1	7	12-2	0	14	.284	.392	.388	118	2	0-0	.987	-2	79	95	C21,1b7		0.0
1966	SF N	18	23	2	7	2	0	0	1	4-0	0	5	.304	.407	.391	120	1	0-0	.982	1	180	109	1b7		0.2
1967	SF N	73	153	24	42	6	0	6	26	27-1	0	37	.275	.387	.431	136	8	0-0	.990	-2	90	109	1b36,C3,O2L		0.5
1968	SF N	90	224	14	52	10	2	4	34	41-4	1	61	.232	.351	.348	111	5	0-0	.994	0	109	97	C58,1b10		1.1
1969	SF N	69	194	18	38	6	0	7	34	48-5	0	58	.196	.352	.325	93	0	0-0	.992	-3	45	0	C60,1b3		0.4
1970	Mon N	17	43	4	14	2	0	0	7	14-0	0	14	.326	.491	.372	135	4	0-0	.961	-3	45	0	C12,1b2	39	0.4
	Chi N	66	178	19	43	12	1	2	22	31-2	0	48	.242	.352	.354	80	-4	0-0	.990	6	87	100	C63,1b2		0.1
	Year	83	221	23	57	14	1	2	29	45-2	0	62	.258	.382	.357	91	-1	0-0	.986	3	80	84	C75,1b4		0.5
1971	Hou N	69	174	16	48	8	1	1	16	35-2	2	39	.276	.401	.351	119	7	0-1	.991	-2	87	90	C65/1		0.6
1972	Hou N	10	25	2	5	3	0	0	0	5-2	0	5	.200	.333	.320	89	0	0-0	1.000	-4	76	87	C10		0.7
	Cal A	22	45	4	13	0	1	1	5	5-0	0	11	.289	.360	.400	133	2	0-0	1.000	-6	129	52	C17	53	-0.4
Total	9	483	1142	96	287	51	5	22	154	224-18	4	295	.251	.374	.363	109	26	0-1	.990	-9	102	95	C312,1b70,O2L	92	2.8

HIATT, PHIL Philip Farrell B5.1.1969 Pensacola FL BR/TR/6-3/200* [KCA90 8/234] d4.7 Col Louisiana Tech

1993	KC A	81	238	30	52	12	1	7	36	16-0	7	82	.218	.285	.366	69	-11	6-3	.909	-3	98	55	3b70,D9		-1.3
1995	KC A	52	113	11	23	6	0	4	12	9-0	0	37	.204	.262	.363	59	-7	1-0	.957	2	105	195	O47(1/2/45),D2	15	-0.6
1996	Det A	7	21	3	4	0	1	0	1	2-0	0	11	.190	.261	.286	38	-2	0-0	1.000	1	135	161	3b3,O2(1/0/1)/D		-0.1
2001	LA N	30	50	6	12	3	0	2	6	3-1	0	19	.240	.283	.420	83	-1	0-0	1.000	-3	49	64	3b17,1b6		-0.5
Total	4	170	422	50	91	21	2	13	55	30-1	7	149	.216	.278	.367	67	-21	7-3	.920	-3	93	93	3b90,O49(2/2/46),D12,1b6	15	-2.5

HIBBS, JIM James Kerr B9.10.1944 Klamath Falls OR BR/TR/6-0/190 [LAN66*S3/50] d4.12 Col Stanford

1967	Cal A	3	3	0	0	0	0	0	0	0	0	2	.000	.000	.000	-99	-1	0-0	—	0			/H		-0.1

HICKEY, EDDIE Edward A. B8.18.1872 Cleveland OH D3.25.1941 Tacoma WA d9.3

1901	Chi N	10	37	4	6	0	0	0	3	2	1		.162	.225	.162	14	-4	1	.743	-2	93	183	3b10		-0.6

HICKEY, MIKE Michael Francis B12.25.1871 Chicopee MA D6.11.1918 Springfield MA BR/TR/5-10.5/150 d9.14 Col Holy Cross

1899	Bos N	1	3	0	1	0	0	0	0	0	0		.333	.333	.333	76	0	0	.889	0	139	0	/2		0.0

HICKMAN, CHARLIE Charles Taylor "Cheerful Charlie","Piano Legs" B3.4.1876 Taylortown (Dunkard Twp.) PA D4.19.1934 Morgantown WV BR/TR/5-9/180 d9.8 Col West Virginia OF(46/3/242) ▲

1897	†Bos N	2	3	1	2	0	0	1	2	0	0		.667	.667	1.667	476	2	0	1.000	0	55	1809	P2		0.0
1898	Bos N	19	58	4	15	2	0	0	7	1	1		.259	.283	.293	62	-3	0	1.000	-1	101	0	O7(6/1/0),1b6,P6		-0.3
1899	Bos N	19	63	15	25	2	7	0	15	2	2		.397	.433	.651	178	6	1	.941	-3	72	235	P11,O7(6/1/0)/1		0.0
1900	NY N	127	473	65	148	19	17	9	91	17	17		.313	.359	.482	137	21	10	.842	-4	99	105	3b20,O7R		1.7
1901	NY N	112	406	44	113	20	6	4	62	15	7		.278	.315	.387	107	3	5	.904	-3	132	59	O50(6/1/44),S23,3b15,P9,2b7,1b2		-0.1
1902	Bos A	28	108	13	32	5	2	3	16	3	4		.296	.339	.463	118	2	1	.939	-1	51	0	O27L		-0.1
	Cle A	102	426	61	161	31	11	8	94	12	5		.378	.399	.559	170	38	8	.966	-7	87	110	1b98,2b3/P		2.7
	Year	130	534	74	193	36	13	11	110	15	7		.361	.387	.539	159	39	8	.966	-8	87	110	1b98,O27L,2b3/P		2.6
1903	Cle A	131	522	64	154	31	11	12	97	17	6		.295	.325	.466	137	22	14	.972	-7	84	112	1b125,2b7		1.3
1904	Cle A	86	337	34	97	22	10	4	45	13	2		.288	.318	.448	142	15	9	.943	1	112	56	2b45,1b40/OL		1.6
	Det A	42	144	18	35	6	6	2	22	11	0		.243	.297	.410	126	4	3	.970	-2	91	99	1b39		0.1
	Year	128	481	52	132	28	16	6	67	24	2		.274	.312	.437	137	18	12	.969	-2	89	100	1b79,2b45/OL		1.7
1905	Det A	59	213	21	47	12	3	2	20	12	5		.221	.278	.333	93	-2	3	.940	3	136	238	O47R,1b12		-0.2
	Was A	88	360	48	112	25	9	2	46	9	2		.311	.332	.447	152	19	3	.922	6	119	83	2b85,1b3		2.8
	Year	147	573	69	159	37	12	4	66	21	7		.277	.311	.405	129	16	6	.922	9	123	83	2b85,O47R,1b15		2.6
1906	Was A	120	451	53	128	25	5	9	57	14	4		.284	.311	.421	135	16	9	.955	-1	100	70	O95R,1b18,3b5/2		1.2
1907	Was A	60	198	20	55	9	3	1	23	14	4		.278	.338	.369	136	8	4	.965	-2	87	84	1b30,O18R,2b3/P		0.5
	Chi A	21	23	1	6	2	0	0	1	0	0		.261	.370	.348	134	1	0	.667	-1	0	0	O3R		0.1
	Year	81	221	21	61	11	3	1	24	18	4		.276	.342	.367	135	9	4	.965	-2	87	84	1b30,O21R,2b3/P		0.6
1908	Cle A	65	197	16	46	6	1	2	16	9	1		.234	.271	.305	86	-3	2	.907	-1	150	121	O28R,1b20/2		-0.6
Total	12	1081	3982	478	1176	217	91	59	614	153	58		.295	.331	.440	133	149	72	.968	-22	90	106	1b394,O290R,2b152,3b140,P30,S23		10.7

HICKMAN, JIM David James B5.19.1892 Johnson City TN D12.30.1958 Brooklyn NY BR/TR/5-7.5/170 d9.17 Mil 1918

1915	Bal F	20	81	7	17	4	1	1	7	4	1	14	.210	.256	.321	60	-6	5	.963	4	101	242	O20C		-0.4
1916	Bro N	9	5	3	1	0	0	0	0	2	0		.200	.429	.200	94	0	1	1.000	0	141	0	O3(2/1/0)		0.0
1917	Bro N	114	370	46	81	15	4	6	36	17	0	66	.219	.253	.330	76	-12	14	.942	6	99	169	O101(26/71/3)		-1.3
1918	Bro N	53	167	14	39	4	1	1	16	8	3	31	.234	.281	.359	95	-2	5	.914	-1	92	132	O46(0/10/42)		-0.6
1919	Bro N	57	104	14	20	3	1	0	11	6	0	17	.192	.236	.240	43	-7	2	.962	1	107	95	O29(4/6/22)		-0.9
Total	5	253	727	84	158	26	13	8	70	37	4	128	.217	.259	.322	74	-27	27	.941	9	99	158	O199(32/108/67)		-3.2

HICKMAN, JIM James Lucius B5.10.1937 Henning TN BR/TR/6-4/205* d4.14

1962	NY N	140	392	54	96	18	2	13	46	47-2	3	96	.245	.328	.401	94	-3	4-4	.971	3	110	89	O124(7/84/33)		-0.6
1963	NY N	146	494	53	113	21	6	17	51	44-1	1	120	.229	.291	.399	96	-4	0-5	.963	-3	100	119	O82(19/42/22),3b59		-1.2
1964	NY N	139	409	48	105	14	1	11	57	36-4	2	90	.257	.319	.377	98	-1	0-1	.976	5	113	118	O113(39/89/19)/3		-0.1
1965	NY N	141	369	32	87	18	0	15	40	27-3	2	76	.236	.294	.407	98	-2	3-1	.965	-1	104	76	O91(35/44/16),1b30,3b14		-0.8
1966	NY N	58	160	15	38	7	0	4	16	13-0	1	34	.237	.299	.356	83	-4	2-1	.965	-1	105	221	O45(16/8/23),1b17	86	-0.1
1967	LA N	65	98	7	16	6	1	0	10	14-1	0	28	.163	.268	.245	52	-6	1-1	1.000	3	125	145	O37(13/13/12),1b2,3b2/P		-0.5
1968	Chi N	75	188	22	42	6	3	5	23	18-2	1	38	.223	.290	.367	92	-2	1-1	.975	2	110	70	O66(3/20/49)		-0.4
1969	Chi N	134	338	38	80	11	2	21	54	47-3	0	74	.237	.326	.467	107	3	2-1	.981	-5	89	85	O125(5/9/116)		-0.7
1970	Chi N★	149	514	102	162	33	4	32	115	93-8	1	99	.315	.419	.582	148	38	0-1	.974	6	97	165	O79(2/53/28),1b74		3.5
1971	Chi N	117	383	50	98	13	2	19	60	50-7	3	61	.256	.342	.449	108	5	3-1	.982	-2	90	78	O69(1/3/66),1b44	15	-0.4
1972	Chi N	115	368	65	100	15	2	17	64	52-3	2	62	.272	.364	.462	120	11	3-1	.992	7	153	110	1b77,O27(1/0/26)		1.2
1973	Chi N	92	201	27	49	11	3	3	20	42-2	1	44	.244	.368	.373	113	6	1-0	.988	-1	108	76	1b51,O13(3/0/11)		0.1
1974	StL N	50	60	5	16	1	0	2	9	6-1	0	10	.267	.353	.367	101	-2	0-0	.986	1	153	220	1b14/3		0.7
Total	13	1421	3974	518	1002	163	25	159	560	491-36	15	832	.252	.335	.426	106	33	17-19	.976	21	102	104	O871(144/365/421),1b309,3b77/P	101	-0.7

HICKS, BUDDY Clarence Walter B2.15.1927 Belvedere CA BB/TR/5-10/170 d4.17

1956	Det A	26	47	5	10	2	0	0	5	5	0	2	.213	.260	.255	36	-4	0-1	1.000	-1	117	86	S16,2b6/3		-0.4

YEAR	TM LG	G	AB	R	H	2B	3B	HR	RBI	BB-IB	HP	SO	AVG	OBP	SLG	AOPS	ABR	SB-CS	FA	FR	RNG	THR	GAMES AT POSITION	DL	BFW
HICKS, JIM	James Edward B5.18.1940 East Chicago IN BR/TR/6-3/205(185-205) d10.2 Col Illinois																						/R		0.0
1964	Chi A	2	0	0	0	0	0	0	0	0-0	0						0	0-0	—	0			/R		-0.1
1965	Chi A	13	19	2	5	1	0	1	2	0-0	0	9	.263	.263	.474	112	0	0-0	.750	-1	51	0	O5(3/0/2)		-0.3
1966	Chi A	18	26	3	5	0	1	0	1	1-0	0	5	.192	.222	.269	43	-2	0-0	1.000	-0	133	0	O10(2/0/8),1b2		-0.2
1969	StL N	19	44	5	8	0	2	1	3	4-0	0	14	.182	.250	.341	64	-3	0-0	1.000	1	111	216	O15R		-0.6
	Cal A	37	48	6	4	0	0	3	8	13-1	0	18	.083	.274	.271	57	-3	0-1	.981	-2	92	0	O10(4/3/3),1b8		0.0
1970	Cal A	4	4	0	1	0	0	0	0	0-0	0	2	.250	.250	.250	39	0	0-0	—	0			/H		-1.2
Total	5	93	141	16	23	1	3	5	14	18-1	0	48	.163	.256	.319	64	-8	0-1	.981	-1	105	100	O40(9/3/28),1b10		
HICKS, NAT	Nathan Woodhull B4.19.1845 Hempstead NY D4.21.1907 Hoboken NJ BR/TR/6-1/186 d4.22 M2																								
1872	Mut NA	**56**	267	54	82	12	2	0	32	6		3	.307	.322	.367	119	8	3-0	.875	5			C54,O3R		0.9
1873	Mut NA	28	120	12	29	1	2	1	14	8		4	.242	.289	.308	78	-3	2-1	.778	2			C28		-0.1
1874	Phi NA	58	266	51	73	8	1	0	30	5		4	.274	.288	.312	89	-4	3-2	.823	7			C57,O4C/2M		0.3
1875	Mut NA	62	269	32	67	10	0	0	22	2		10	.249	.255	.286	83	-5	1-0	.819	5			C60,O5(0/1/4),M		0.1
1876	NY N	45	188	20	44	4	1	0	15	3		4	.234	.246	.266	81	-2		.741	-6			C45		-0.6
1877	Cin N	8	32	3	6	0	0	0	3	1		2	.188	.212	.188	30	-2		.868	0			C8		-0.2
Total	4 NA	204	922	149	251	31	5	1	98	21		17	.272	.288	.320	94	-4	9-3	.828	19			C199,O12(0/5/7)/2		1.2
Total	2	53	220	23	50	4	1	0	18	4		6	.227	.241	.255	73	-4		.757	-6			C53		-0.8
HICKS, JOE	William Joseph B4.7.1933 Ivy VA BL/TR/6-0/180* d9.18 Col Virginia																								
1959	Chi A	6	7	0	3	0	0	0	1	1-0	0	1	.429	.500	.429	160	1	0-1	1.000	1	83	951	O4(1/2/1)		0.1
1960	Chi A	36	47	3	9	1	0	2	6	6-0	1	3	.191	.291	.213	40	-4	0-1	1.000	-2	65	0	O14(3/11/0)		-0.7
1961	Was A	12	29	2	5	0	0	1	1	0-0	0	4	.172	.172	.276	18	-4	0-1	1.000	-0	105	194	O7(3/0/4)		-0.4
1962	Was A	102	174	20	39	4	2	6	14	15-0	0	34	.224	.286	.374	76	-7	3-1	.962	-0	106	58	O42(5/22/16)		-0.8
1963	NY N	56	159	16	36	6	1	5	22	7-0	3	31	.226	.272	.371	82	-4	0-2	.966	-1	103	40	O41(5/33/5)		-0.8
Total	5	212	416	41	92	11	3	12	39	29-0	4	73	.221	.278	.349	72	-18	3-6	.970	-2	100	71	O108(17/68/26)		-2.6
HIDALGO, RICHARD	Richard Jose B6.28.1975 Caracas, Venez BR/TR/6-3/190(190-220) d9.1																								
1997	†Hou N	19	62	8	19	5	0	2	6	4-0	1	18	.306	.358	.484	122	2	1-0	1.000	-3	77	0	O19(1/17/1)		0.0
1998	†Hou N	74	211	31	64	15	0	7	35	17-0	2	37	.303	.355	.474	120	6	3-3	.978	0	103	85	O72(9/57/14)	52	0.6
1999	Hou N	108	383	49	87	25	2	15	56	56-2	4	73	.227	.328	.420	90	-6	8-5	.991	9	101	238	O108(97/30/3)	56	0.0
2000	Hou N	153	558	118	175	42	3	44	122	56-3	21	110	.314	.391	.636	144	38	13-6	.984	14	**122**	77	O150(36/125/37)		4.8
2001	†Hou N	146	512	70	141	29	3	19	80	54-3	16	107	.275	.356	.455	102	-3	3-5	.991	6	104	139	O144(23/128/37)		0.6
2002	Hou N	114	388	54	91	17	4	15	48	43-1	6	85	.235	.319	.415	88	-9	6-2	.995	3	108	90	O110(0/1/110)	17	-1.0
2003	Hou N	141	514	91	159	43	4	28	88	58-8	8	104	.309	.385	.572	139	30	9-7	.987	14	105	**249**	O137R/D	15	3.6
2004	Hou N	58	199	21	51	15	2	4	30	17-4	2	53	.256	.309	.412	83	-5	1-2	.982	3	115	131	O56R		-0.7
	NY N	86	324	46	74	11	1	21	52	27-3	5	76	.228	.296	.463	95	-5	3-2	.977	2	92	180	O86(5/0/83)		-1.2
	Year	144	523	67	125	26	3	25	82	44-7	7	129	.239	.301	.444	90	-10	4-4	.979	5	101	162	O142(5/0/139)		-1.3
2005	Tex A	88	308	43	68	12	0	16	43	26-1	4	74	.221	.289	.416	82	-9	1-2	.989	1	106	61	O85(0/3/83)/D	59	-1.3
Total	9	987	3459	531	929	214	19	171	560	358-25	67	737	.269	.345	.490	110	45	48-34	.987	50	106	142	O967(171/361/561),D2	199	6.1
HIETPAS, JOE	Joseph Carl B5.1.1979 Appleton WI BR/TR/6-3/220 [NYN01 16/492] d10.3 Col Northwestern																								
2004	NY N	1	0	0	0	0	0	0	0								0		1.000	0	0	0	/C		0.0
HIGBEE, MAHLON	Mahlon Jesse B8.16.1901 Louisville KY D4.7.1968 Depauw IN BR/TR/5-11/165 d9.27																								
1922	NY N	3	10	2	4	0	0	1	5	0		2	.400	.400	.700	177	1	0-0	1.000	-0	57	0	O3(2/0/1)		0.0
HIGBY	d9.18																								
1872	Atl NA	1	4	0	0	0	0	0	0	0		0	.000	.000	.000	-85	-1	0-0	.667	-0	0	0	/OR		-0.1
HIGDON, BILL	William Travis B4.27.1924 Camp Hill AL D8.30.1986 Pascagoula MS BL/TR/6-1/193 d9.10 Col Auburn-Montgomery																								
1949	Chi A	11	23	3	7	3	0	0	1	6	0	3	.304	.448	.435	139	2	1-0	1.000	-0	71	314	O6C		0.2
HIGGINS, KEVIN	Kevin Wayne B1.22.1967 San Gabriel CA BL/TR/5-11/185 [SDN89 12/312] d5.29 Col Arizona St.																								
1993	SD N	71	181	17	40	4	1	0	13	16-0	3	17	.221	.294	.254	48	-13	0-1	.983	2	82	98	C59,3b4,1b3,O3(1/0/2)/2		-0.9
HIGGINS, MARK	Mark Douglas B7.9.1963 Miami FL BR/TR/6-2/210 [CleA84 S1/8] d9.7 Col New Orleans																								
1989	Cle A	6	10	1	1	0	0	0	1	0		6	.100	.182	.100	-18	-2	0-0	1.000	0	146	39	1b5		-0.1
HIGGINS, PINKY	Michael Franklin "Mike" B5.27.1909 Red Oak TX D3.21.1969 Dallas TX BR/TR/6-1/185 d6.25 Mil 1945 M8 Col Texas																								
1930	Phi A	14	24	1	6	2	0	0	4	0		5	.250	.357	.333	73	-1	0-0	1.000	-1	86	0	3b5,2b2/S		-0.2
1933	Phi A	**152**	567	85	178	34	12	13	99	61	2	53	.314	.383	.485	127	22	2-7	.947	-6	96	80	3b152		1.8
1934	Phi A☆	144	543	89	179	37	6	16	90	56	0	70	.330	.392	.508	136	28	9-2	.914	-15	89	116	3b144		1.8
1935	Phi A	133	524	69	155	32	4	23	94	42	2	62	.296	.350	.504	120	12	6-2	.947	-12	87	75	3b131		0.6
1936	Phi A★	146	550	89	159	32	2	12	80	67	0	61	.289	.366	.420	96	-3	7-4	.941	-11	94	93	3b145		-0.9
1937	Bos A	153	570	88	172	33	5	9	106	76	1	55	.302	.385	.425	100	2	2-6	.935	-21	81	94	3b152		-0.8
1938	Bos A	139	524	77	159	29	5	5	106	71	1	55	.303	.388	.406	95	-2	10-9	.914	-10	95	**112**	3b138		-1.5
1939	Det A	132	489	57	135	23	2	8	76	56	2	41	.276	.353	.380	81	-13	7-4	.914	-8	92	90	3b130		-0.8
1940	†Det A	131	480	70	130	24	3	13	76	61	3	31	.271	.357	.415	91	-6	4-2	.928	-7	91	66	3b129		-0.8
1941	Det A	147	540	79	161	28	3	11	73	67	2	45	.298	.377	.422	101	2	5-4	.946	-2	101	51	3b145		-0.5
1942	Det A	143	499	65	133	34	2	11	79	72	3	21	.267	.362	.409	108	7	3-7	.926	-15	87	92	3b137		-0.5
1943	Det A	138	523	62	145	20	1	10	84	57	1	31	.277	.349	.377	104	4	2-5	.940	-10	88	88	3b138		-0.6
1944	Det A★	148	543	79	161	32	4	7	76	81	4	34	.297	.392	.409	122	20	4-4	.954	-9	93	79	3b146		1.2
1946	Det A	18	60	2	13	3	1	0	8	5	0	6	.217	.277	.300	58	-3	0-1	.949	-2	85	71	3b17		-0.1
	†Bos A	64	200	18	55	11	1	2	28	24	1	24	.275	.356	.370	97	0	0-2	.947	-1	99	125	3b59		-0.7
	Year	82	260	20	68	14	2	2	36	29	1	30	.262	.338	.354	88	-3	0-3	.947	-2	96	114	3b76		-0.7
Total	14	1802	6636	930	1941	374	51	140	1075	800	22	590	.292	.370	.428	106	69	61-59	.935	-127	91	87	3b1768,2b2/S		-1.2
HIGGINS, BOB	Robert Stone B9.23.1886 Fayetteville TN D5.25.1941 Chattanooga TN BR/TR/5-8/176 d9.13																								
1909	Cle A	8	23	0	2	0	0	0	0	0	0		.087	.087	.087	-43	-4	0	1.000	2	119	101	C8		-0.
1911	Bro N	4	10	1	3	0	0	0	2	1	0		.300	.364	.300	90	0	1	.933	-0	98	85	C2/3		0.
1912	Bro N	1	2	0	0	0	0	0	0	0	0	1	.000	.000	.000	-99	-1	0	.750	-0	73	0	/C		-0.
Total	3	13	35	1	5	0	0	0	2	1	0		.143	.167	.143	-6	-5	1	.970	2	111	91	C11/3		-0.
HIGGINS, BILL	William Edward B9.8.1861 Wilmington DE D4.25.1919 Wilmington DE TR/5-9/155 d8.9																								
1888	Bos N	14	54	5	10	1	0	0	4	1	0	3	.185	.200	.204	28	-4	1	.906	2	104	210	2b14		-0.
1890	StL AA	67	258	39	65	6	2	0	35	24	0		.252	.316	.291	69	-11	7	.951	13	105	122	2b67		0.
	Syr AA	1	4	1	1	1	0	0	1	0	0		.250	.250	.500	135	0	0	1.000	1	122	188	/2		0.
	Year	68	262	40	66	7	2	0	36	24	0		.252	.315	.294	70	-11	7	.952	14	105	123	2b68		0.
Total	2	82	316	45	76	8	2	0	40	25	0	3	.241	.296	.278	64	-15	8	.943	16	105	139	2b82		0.
HIGGINSON, BOBBY	Robert Leigh B8.18.1970 Philadelphia PA BL/TR/5-11/195(180-195) [DetA92 12/336] d4.26 Col Temple																								
1995	Det A	131	410	61	92	17	5	14	43	62-3	5	107	.224	.329	.393	88	-7	6-4	.985	6	102	159	O123(65/0/67),D2		-0.
1996	Det A	130	440	75	141	35	0	26	81	65-7	1	66	.320	.404	.577	145	33	6-3	.963	-3	93	112	O123(63/19/57),D4	27	2.
1997	Det A	146	546	94	163	30	5	27	101	70-2	3	85	.299	.379	.520	133	27	12-7	.972	9	99	**217**	O143(104/2/57),D2	15	2.
1998	Det A	157	612	92	174	37	4	25	85	63-2	6	101	.284	.355	.480	114	12	3-3	.982	3	97	159	O153(17/0/136),D2		0.
1999	Det A	107	377	51	90	18	0	12	46	64-2	2	66	.239	.351	.382	86	-7	4-6	.983	-2	102	**215**	O88R,D17	31	-1.
2000	Det A	154	597	104	179	44	4	30	102	74-6	2	99	.300	.377	.538	130	28	15-3	.979	10	99	215	O145L,D10	16	3.
2001	Det A	147	541	84	150	28	6	17	71	80-3	2	65	.277	.367	.445	117	15	20-12	.976	7	107	110	O142L,D5	32	0.
2002	Det A	119	444	50	125	24	1	10	63	41-3	6	45	.282	.345	.417	107	5	12-5	.973	6	98	210	O117L/D	26	-1.
2003	Det A	130	469	61	110	13	4	14	52	59-3	3	73	.235	.320	.369	86	-10	8-8	.981	-2	102	57	O118(0/1/117),D8		-1.
2004	Det A	131	448	63	110	24	2	12	64	70-5	7	84	.246	.353	.388	98	1	5-2	.975	2	95	170	O115R,D10	150	-0.
2005	Det A	10	26	1	2	0	0	0	1	2-0	0	5	.077	.111	.077	-50	-6	0-0	1.000	-0	99	150	O7(1/0/6)/D	297	6.
Total	11	1362	4910	736	1336	270	33	187	709	649-36	37	796	.272	.358	.455	111	91	91-53	.977	33	99	150	O1274(654/22/643),D62		
HIGH, ANDY	Andrew Aird "Handy Andy" B11.21.1897 Ava IL D2.22.1981 Sylvania OH BL/TR/5-6/155 d4.12 C2 b-Charlie b-Hugh																								
1922	Bro N	153	579	82	164	27	10	6	65	59	4	26	.283	.354	.396	94	-5	3-12	.958	-3	102	106	3b130,S22/2		-0.
1923	Bro N	123	426	51	115	23	9	3	37	47	1	13	.270	.344	.387	95	-2	4-1	.969	-4	97	90	3b80,S45,2b5		0.

YEAR	TM LG	G	AB	R	H	2B	3B	HR	RBI	BB-IB	HP	SO	AVG	OBP	SLG	AOPS	ABR	SB-CS	FA	FR	RNG	THR	GAMES AT POSITION	DL	BFW
1924	Bro N	144	582	98	191	26	13	6	61	57	2	16	.328	.390	.448	128	24	3-6	.964	-9	91	62	2b133,S17/3		1.8
1925	Bro N	44	115	11	23	4	1	0	6	14	0	5	.200	.287	.252	40	-10	0-1	.938	-4	87	86	2b11,3b11,S3		-1.3
	Bos N	60	219	31	63	11	1	4	28	24	1	2	.288	.361	.402	104	2	3-5	.979	-5	94	72	3b60/2		-0.1
	Year	104	334	42	86	15	2	4	34	38	1	7	.257	.335	.350	80	-9	3-6	.963	-9	91	78	3b71,2b12,S3		-1.4
1926	Bos N	130	476	55	141	17	10	2	66	39	1	9	.296	.351	.387	108	5	4	.962	-11	97	99	3b81,2b49		0.0
1927	Bos N	113	384	59	116	15	9	4	46	26	2	11	.302	.350	.419	114	6	4	.915	-19	76	61	3b89,2b8,S2		-0.8
1928	†StL N	111	368	58	105	14	3	6	37	37	3	10	.285	.355	.389	93	-4	2	.935	-16	85	87	3b73,2b19		-1.4
1929	StL N	146	603	95	178	32	4	10	63	38	3	18	.295	.340	.411	84	-16	7	.967	-14	90	98	3b123,2b22		-2.0
1930	†StL N	72	215	34	60	12	2	2	29	23	0	6	.279	.349	.381	74	-9	1	.990	-6	81	63	3b48,2b3		-1.1
1931	†StL N	63	131	20	35	6	1	0	19	24	2	4	.267	.389	.328	91	0	0	1.000	-2	85	176	3b23,2b19		-0.1
1932	Cin N	84	191	16	36	4	2	0	12	23	0	6	.188	.276	.230	39	-16	1	.950	-6	89	32	3b46,2b12		-2.1
1933	Cin N	24	43	1	9	2	0	1	6	5	0	1	.209	.292	.326	77	-1	0	.966	1	115	82	3b11,2b2		0.0
1934	Phi N	47	68	4	14	2	0	0	7	9	0	3	.206	.299	.235	40	-6	1	.906	-2	74	184	3b14,2b2		-0.7
Total	13	1314	4400	618	1250	195	65	44	482	425	19	130	.284	.350	.388	94	-32	33-25	.956	-100	91	90	3b790,2b287,S89		-7.5

HILL, CHARLIE Charles Edwin B12.1.1898 Ava IL D9.11.1960 Oak Grove OR BL/TR/5-9/170 d9.5 b-Andy b-Hugh Col St.Louis

YEAR	TM LG	G	AB	R	H	2B	3B	HR	RBI	BB-IB	HP	SO	AVG	OBP	SLG	AOPS	ABR	SB-CS	FA	FR	RNG	THR	GAMES AT POSITION	DL	BFW
1919	Phi A	11	29	2	2	0	0	0	1	3	1	4	.069	.182	.069	-28	-5	2	.944	-0	97	81	O9(0/1/8)		-0.6
1920	Phi A	17	65	7	20	2	1	1	6	3	4	6	.308	.375	.415	108	1	0-2	.882	-1	84	128	O17(0/2/15)		-0.2
Total	2	28	94	9	22	2	1	1	7	6	5	10	.234	.314	.309	68	-4	2-2	.904	-2	88	112	O26(0/3/23)		-0.8

HIGH, HUGH Hugh Jenken "Bunny" B10.24.1887 Pottstown PA D11.16.1962 St.Louis MO BL/TL/5-7.5/155 d4.11 b-Andy b-Charlie

YEAR	TM LG	G	AB	R	H	2B	3B	HR	RBI	BB-IB	HP	SO	AVG	OBP	SLG	AOPS	ABR	SB-CS	FA	FR	RNG	THR	GAMES AT POSITION	DL	BFW
1913	Det A	87	183	18	42	6	1	0	16	28	1	24	.230	.335	.273	80	-3	6	.982	2	105	108	O52(3/43/7)		-0.5
1914	Det A	84	184	25	49	5	3	0	17	26	2	11	.266	.363	.326	104	2	7-6	.959	-6	88	31	O53(13/39/1)		-0.8
1915	NY A	119	427	51	110	19	7	1	43	62	3	47	.258	.356	.342	109	7	22-13	.981	-5	97	60	O117(44/71/1)		-0.6
1916	NY A	116	377	44	99	13	4	1	28	47	3	44	.263	.349	.326	101	2	13	.950	-2	97	98	O110(107/2/1)		-0.5
1917	NY A	103	365	37	86	11	6	1	19	48	3	31	.236	.329	.307	93	-2	8	.986	-3	88	108	O100(99/1/0)		-1.1
1918	NY A	7	10	1	0	0	0	0	0	1	0	1	.000	.091	.000	-71	-2	0	1.000	1	103	257	O4(2/1/1)		-0.2
Total	6	516	1546	176	386	54	21	3	123	212	12	168	.250	.345	.318	98	4	56-19	.972	-14	95	85	O436(268/157/11)		-3.7

HIGHAM, DICK Richard B7.24.1851 Ipswich, England D3.18.1905 Chicago IL BL/TR/5-8.5/171 d6.1 M1/U2

YEAR	TM LG	G	AB	R	H	2B	3B	HR	RBI	BB-IB	HP	SO	AVG	OBP	SLG	AOPS	ABR	SB-CS	FA	FR	RNG	THR	GAMES AT POSITION	DL	BFW
1871	Mut NA	21	94	21	34	3	1	0	9	2		0	.362	.375	.415	139	6	3-2	.747	-5	93	86	2b12,O8R/C		0.1
1872	Bal NA	50	245	72	84	10	1	2	37	2		3	.343	.348	.416	128	7	4-5	.847	-2			C25,O24(0/2/22),2b5,3b2/1		0.4
1873	Mut NA	49	244	57	77	5	4	0	34	2		1	.316	.321	.369	105	1	2-2	.750	-9	34	202	O19(0/1/18),2b18,C17		-0.6
1874	Mut NA	65	333	58	87	14	3	1	38	4		0	.261	.270	.330	89	-5	5-3	.852	6			C48,O33(0/3/31)/2M		0.3
1875	Chi NA	42	208	44	49	5	3	0	12	0		0	.236	.236	.288	80	-4	6-2	.821	-5			C24,O14(0/3/11),2b13		-0.8
	Mut NA	15	64	12	25	5	0	0	10	1			.391	.391	.469	187	5	0-0	.739	-4			C8,2b6/O3R,1b2		0.1
	Year	57	272	56	74	10	3	0	22	0		1	.272	.272	.331	106	1	6-2	.802	-9			C32,2b19,O17(0/3/14),1b2		-0.7
1876	Har N	67	312	59	102	21	2	0	35	2		7	.327	.331	.407	134	10		.869	1	168	62	O59R,C13/S2		1.0
1878	Pro N	62	281	60	90	22	1	1	29	5		16	.320	.332	.416	145	14		.811	2	168	158	O62R/C		1.5
1880	Tro N	1	5	1	1	0	0	0	0	0		0	.200	.200	.200	34	0		-1	0	0	0	/ORC		-0.2
Total	5 NA	242	1188	264	356	42	12	3	140	10		5	.300	.306	.363	108	10	20-14	.836	-18			C123,O101(0/9/93),2b55,1b3,3b2		-0.5
Total	3	130	598	120	193	43	3	1	64	7		23	.323	.331	.410	138	24		.834	2			O122R,C15/2S		2.3

HILAND, JOHN John William B9.1860 Baltic CT D4.10.1901 Philadelphia PA BL/TL/5-8.5/165 d8.20

YEAR	TM LG	G	AB	R	H	2B	3B	HR	RBI	BB-IB	HP	SO	AVG	OBP	SLG	AOPS	ABR	SB-CS	FA	FR	RNG	THR	GAMES AT POSITION	DL	BFW
1885	Phi N	3	9	0	0	0	0	0	0	0		4	.000	.000	.000	-99	-2		.833	-1	59	0	2b3		-0.3

HILDEBRAND d8.29

YEAR	TM LG	G	AB	R	H	2B	3B	HR	RBI	BB-IB	HP	SO	AVG	OBP	SLG	AOPS	ABR	SB-CS	FA	FR	RNG	THR	GAMES AT POSITION	DL	BFW
1902	Chi N	1	4	1	0	0	0	0	0	1		0	.000	.200	.000	-39	-1	0	1.000	-0	0	0	/OR		-0.1

HILDEBRAND, GEORGE George Albert B9.6.1878 San Francisco CA D5.30.1960 Reseda CA BR/TR/5-8/170 d4.17 U22

YEAR	TM LG	G	AB	R	H	2B	3B	HR	RBI	BB-IB	HP	SO	AVG	OBP	SLG	AOPS	ABR	SB-CS	FA	FR	RNG	THR	GAMES AT POSITION	DL	BFW
1902	Bro N	11	41	3	9	1	0	0	5	3		1	.220	.289	.244	64	-2	0	1.000	2	135	0	O11L		0.0

HILDEBRAND, PALMER Palmer Marion "Pete" B12.23.1884 Shauck OH D1.25.1960 N.Canton OH BR/TR/5-10/170 d5.14

YEAR	TM LG	G	AB	R	H	2B	3B	HR	RBI	BB-IB	HP	SO	AVG	OBP	SLG	AOPS	ABR	SB-CS	FA	FR	RNG	THR	GAMES AT POSITION	DL	BFW
1913	StL N	26	55	3	9	2	0	1	2	10		2	.164	.207	.200	17	-6	1-2	.968	-1	81	103	C22/OL		-0.6

HILL, AARON Aaron Walter B3.21.1982 Visalia CA BR/TR/5-11/195 d5.20 Col LSU

YEAR	TM LG	G	AB	R	H	2B	3B	HR	RBI	BB-IB	HP	SO	AVG	OBP	SLG	AOPS	ABR	SB-CS	FA	FR	RNG	THR	GAMES AT POSITION	DL	BFW
2005	Tor A	105	361	49	99	25	3	3	40	34-0	5	41	.274	.342	.385	89	-5	2-1	.949	11	112	142	3b35,D34,2b22,S16		0.7

HILL, BELDEN Belden L. B8.24.1864 Kewanee IL D10.22.1934 Cedar Rapids IA BR/TR/6-0/? d8.27

YEAR	TM LG	G	AB	R	H	2B	3B	HR	RBI	BB-IB	HP	SO	AVG	OBP	SLG	AOPS	ABR	SB-CS	FA	FR	RNG	THR	GAMES AT POSITION	DL	BFW
1890	Bal AA	9	30	3	5	2	0	0	2	3		3	.167	.306	.233	56	-1	6	.857	0	79	126	3b9		-0.1

HILL, DONNIE Donald Earl B11.12.1960 Pomona CA BB/TR/5-10/160* [OakA81 S1/1] d7.25 Col Arizona St.

YEAR	TM LG	G	AB	R	H	2B	3B	HR	RBI	BB-IB	HP	SO	AVG	OBP	SLG	AOPS	ABR	SB-CS	FA	FR	RNG	THR	GAMES AT POSITION	DL	BFW
1983	Oak A	53	158	20	42	7	0	2	15	4-0	0	21	.266	.280	.348	77	-5	1-1	.961	-3	95	80	S53		-0.4
1984	Oak A	73	174	21	40	6	0	2	16	5-0	0	12	.230	.249	.299	55	-11	1-1	.949	-13	81	80	S66,2b4,3b2,D2	15	-2.0
1985	Oak A	123	393	45	112	13	2	3	48	23-2	0	33	.285	.321	.351	91	-5	9-4	.973	-29	90	68	2b122		-2.7
1986	Oak A	108	339	37	96	16	4	4	29	23-1	0	38	.283	.329	.378	99	-9	5-2	.984	-9	92	74	2b68,3b33,S2,D3		-0.7
1987	Chi A	111	410	57	98	14	6	9	46	30-1	1	35	.239	.290	.368	72	-18	1-0	.987	-11	98	95	2b84,3b32/D	30	-2.4
1988	Chi A	83	221	17	48	6	1	2	20	26-1	0	21	.217	.296	.281	64	-11	3-1	.975	-3	96	108	2b59,3b12,D5		-1.2
1990	Cal A	103	352	36	93	18	2	3	32	29-1	1	27	.264	.319	.352	90	-3	1-2	.990	10	115	125	2b60,S24,3b21,1b3/PD	17	0.7
1991	Cal A	77	209	36	50	8	1	1	20	30-1	0	21	.239	.335	.301	77	-6	1-0	.971	10	103	111	2b39,S29,1b3		0.7
1992	Min A	25	51	7	15	3	0	0	2	5-0	1	6	.294	.368	.353	99	0	0-0	.944	-0	118	170	S10,2b7,3b5/OR	39	0.1
Total	9	756	2307	276	594	91	14	26	228	175-7	3	225	.257	.308	.343	81	-62	22-11	.980	-50	97	90	2b443,S184,3b105,D12,1b6/ORP	101	-7.9

HILL, GLENALLEN Glenallen B3.22.1965 Santa Cruz CA BR/TR/6-2/210(210-230) [TorA83 9/219] d7.31

YEAR	TM LG	G	AB	R	H	2B	3B	HR	RBI	BB-IB	HP	SO	AVG	OBP	SLG	AOPS	ABR	SB-CS	FA	FR	RNG	THR	GAMES AT POSITION	DL	BFW
1989	Tor A	19	52	4	15	0	0	1	7	3-0	0	12	.288	.327	.346	91	-1	2-1	.964	-1	92	0	O16(3/0/13),D3		-0.3
1990	Tor A	84	260	47	60	11	3	12	32	18-0	0	62	.231	.281	.435	95	-3	8-3	.983	-1	95	99	O60(27/1/34),D20	15	-0.6
1991	Tor A	35	99	14	25	5	2	3	11	7-0	0	24	.253	.296	.434	97	-1	2-2	.967	0	119	0	D16,O13(9/0/4)		-0.2
	Cle A	37	122	15	32	3	0	5	14	16-0	0	30	.262	.345	.410	108	1	4-2	.978	1	115	0	O33(12/26/1)/D	28	0.2
	Year	72	221	29	57	8	2	8	25	23-0	0	54	.258	.324	.421	103	0	6-4	.975	1	116	0	O46(21/26/5),D17		0.1
1992	Cle A	102	369	38	89	16	1	18	49	20-0	4	73	.241	.287	.436	101	-2	9-6	.956	-2	93	114	O59(50/1/8),D34	29	-0.7
1993	Cle A	66	174	19	39	7	2	5	25	11-1	1	50	.224	.268	.374	72	-8	7-3	.940	-3	93	44	O39(9/0/30),D18		-1.2
	Chi N	31	87	14	30	7	0	10	22	6-0	0	21	.345	.387	.770	202	12	1-0	.957	2	117	145	O21(18/0/4)		1.3
1994	Chi N	89	269	48	80	12	1	10	38	29-0	0	57	.297	.365	.461	114	6	19-6	.987	-3	97	0	O78(31/44/7)		0.3
1995	SF N	132	497	71	131	29	4	24	86	39-4	1	98	.264	.317	.483	110	-6	25-5	.959	-6	88	105	O125(0/1/124)		-0.3
1996	SF N	89	379	56	106	26	0	19	67	33-3	6	95	.280	.344	.499	122	12	6-3	.960	-6	86	92	O98R	70	0.2
1997	†SF N	128	398	47	104	28	4	11	64	19-0	4	87	.261	.297	.435	92	-6	7-4	.947	-6	95	31	O97R,D7		-1.6
1998	Sea A	74	259	37	75	20	2	12	33	14-1	3	45	.290	.332	.521	117	-3	1-1	.965	-3	98	58	O71L		0.1
	†Chi N	48	131	26	46	5	0	8	23	14-1	0	34	.351	.414	.573	157	10	0-0	.984	3	116	170	O34(28/0/6)		1.1
1999	Chi N	99	253	43	76	9	1	20	55	22-1	0	61	.300	.353	.581	132	11	5-1	.955	-4	81	92	O62(37/0/26),D4	15	0.5
2000	Chi N	64	168	23	44	4	1	11	29	10-2	2	43	.262	.303	.494	98	-2	0-1	.955	1	89	210	O29L,D9	8	-0.2
	†NY A	40	132	22	44	5	0	16	29	9-0	1	33	.333	.378	.735	176	14	0-0	1.000	-0	107	0	D24,O12L		1.1
2001	Ana A	16	66	4	9	0	0	1	2	0-0	0	20	.136	.136	.182	-17	-11	0-0	—	0	0	0	D16	38	-1.2
Total	13	1162	3715	528	1005	187	21	186	586	270-13	20	845	.271	.321	.482	111	43	96-38	.964	-28	94	77	O847(336/73/452),D152	203	-1.5

HILL, HERMAN Herman Alexander B10.12.1945 Tuskegee AL D12.14.1970 Valencia, Venez BL/TR/6-2/190* d9.2

YEAR	TM LG	G	AB	R	H	2B	3B	HR	RBI	BB-IB	HP	SO	AVG	OBP	SLG	AOPS	ABR	SB-CS	FA	FR	RNG	THR	GAMES AT POSITION	DL	BFW
1969	Min A	16	2	4	0	0	0	0	0	0-0	0	1	1.000	.000	.000	-97	-1	1-2	—	-0	0	0	O2C		-0.1
1970	Min A	27	22	8	2	0	0	0	0	0-0	0	6	.091	.091	.091	-49	-5	0-0	1.000	1	117	277	O14(2/10/2)		-0.4
Total	2	43	24	12	2	0	0	0	0-0	0	7	.083	.083	.083	-53	-6	1-2	1.000	1	106	251	O16(2/12/2)		-0.5

HILL, HUGH Hugh Ellis B7.21.1879 Ringgold GA D9.6.1958 Cincinnati OH BL/TR/5-11.5/168 d5.1 b-Bill

YEAR	TM LG	G	AB	R	H	2B	3B	HR	RBI	BB-IB	HP	SO	AVG	OBP	SLG	AOPS	ABR	SB-CS	FA	FR	RNG	THR	GAMES AT POSITION	DL	BFW
1903	Cle A	1	1	0	0	0	0	0	0	0	0	0	.000	.000	.000	-99	0	0	—	—	0		/H		0.0
1904	StL N	23	93	13	21	2	1	3	4	2		0	.226	.242	.366	91	-2	3	1.000	0	67	122	O23L		-0.3
Total	2	24	94	13	21	2	1	3	4	2		0	.223	.240	.362	89	-2	3	1.000	0	67	122	O23L		-0.3

HILL, HUNTER Hunter Benjamin B6.21.1879 Austin TX D2.22.1959 Austin TX BR/TR d7.1

YEAR	TM LG	G	AB	R	H	2B	3B	HR	RBI	BB-IB	HP	SO	AVG	OBP	SLG	AOPS	ABR	SB-CS	FA	FR	RNG	THR	GAMES AT POSITION	DL	BFW
1903	StL A	86	317	30	77	11	3	0	25	8	1		.243	.264	.297	70	-12	2	.923	1	99	113	3b86		-1.0
1904	StL A	58	219	19	47	3	0	0	14	6	3		.215	.246	.228	54	-12	4	.826	-18	70	56	3b56/OL		-3.3
	Was A	77	290	18	57	6	1	0	17	11	1		.197	.228	.224	44	-19	10	.895	-3	98	57	3b71,O5R		-2.3

YEAR	TM LG	G	AB	R	H	2B	3B	HR	RBI	BB-IB	HP	SO	AVG	OBP	SLG	AOPS	ABR	SB-CS	FA	FR	RNG	THR	GAMES AT POSITION	DL	BFW
	Year	135	509	37	104	9	1	0	31	17	4		.204	.236	.226	48	-31	14	.864	-21	85	57	3b127,O6(1/0/5)		-5.6
1905	Was A	104	374	37	78	12	1		24	32	4		.209	.278	.254	72	-11	10	.908	-1	100	109	3b103		-1.0
Total	3	325	1200	104	259	32	5	1	80	57	9		.216	.257	.253	62	-54	26	.895	-21	94	89	3b316,O6(1/0/5)		-7.6

HILL, JESSE   Jesse Terrill   B1.20.1907 Yates MO   D8.31.1993 Pasadena CA   BR/TR/5-9/165   d4.17   Col USC

YEAR	TM LG	G	AB	R	H	2B	3B	HR	RBI	BB-IB	HP	SO	AVG	OBP	SLG	AOPS	ABR	SB-CS	FA	FR	RNG	THR	GAMES AT POSITION	DL	BFW
1935	NY A	107	392	69	115	20	3	4	33	42	0	23	.293	.362	.390	100	0	14-4	.951	2	102	117	O94L		-0.2
1936	Was A	85	233	50	71	19	5	0	34	29	1	33	.305	.384	.429	106	3	11-0	.967	-2	86	124	O60(54/4/2)		0.1
1937	Was A	33	92	24	20	2	1	1	4	13	0	16	.217	.314	.293	57	-6	2-1	.986	1	122	0	O21(3/18/0)		-0.5
	Phi A	70	242	32	71	12	3	1	37	31	0	20	.293	.374	.380	82	-2	16-3	.954	-3	98	69	O68(6/83/0)		-0.4
	Year	103	334	56	91	14	4	2	41	44	0	36	.272	.357	.356	82	-8	18-4	.964	-2	104	51	O89(6/83/0)		-0.9
Total	3	295	959	175	277	53	12	6	108	115	1	91	.289	.366	.388	95	-5	43-8	.959	-2	100	94	O243(154/87/2)		-1.0

HILL, KOYIE   Koyie Dolan   B3.9.1979 Tulsa OK   BB/TR/6-0/190*   [LAN00 4/117]   d9.5   Col Wichita St.

YEAR	TM LG	G	AB	R	H	2B	3B	HR	RBI	BB-IB	HP	SO	AVG	OBP	SLG	AOPS	ABR	SB-CS	FA	FR	RNG	THR	GAMES AT POSITION	DL	BFW
2003	LA N	3	3	0	1	1	0	0	0	0-0	0	2	.333	.333	.667	156	0	0-0	—	0			/H		0.0
2004	Ari N	13	36	3	9	1	0	1	6	2-1	0	14	.250	.289	.361	63	-2	1-0	.984	-3	65	203	C11	47	-0.4
2005	Ari N	34	78	6	17	5	0	0	6	11-0	0	27	.218	.308	.282	56	-5	0-1	1.000	-3	105	78	C32		-0.7
Total	3	50	117	9	27	7	0	1	12	13-1	0	35	.231	.303	.316	60	-7	1-1	.995	-6	94	113	C43	47	-1.1

HILL, MARC   Marc Kevin   B2.18.1952 Elsberry MO   BR/TR/6-3/210(200-240)   [StLN70 10/234]   d9.28   C2

YEAR	TM LG	G	AB	R	H	2B	3B	HR	RBI	BB-IB	HP	SO	AVG	OBP	SLG	AOPS	ABR	SB-CS	FA	FR	RNG	THR	GAMES AT POSITION	DL	BFW
1973	StL N	1	3	0	0	0	0	0	0	0-0	0	1	.000	.000	.000	-99	-1	0-0	1.000	-0	49	0	/C		-0.1
1974	StL N	10	21	2	5	1	0	0	2	4-1	0	5	.238	.360	.286	82	0	0-0	1.000	2	432	45	C9		0.2
1975	SF N	72	182	14	39	4	0	5	23	25-5	0	27	.214	.305	.319	72	-7	0-0	.994	3	89	137	C60/3		-0.1
1976	SF N	54	131	11	24	5	0	3	15	10-2	1	19	.183	.243	.290	50	-9	0-1	.995	-0	108	73	C49/1	61	-0.8
1977	SF N	108	320	28	80	10	0	9	50	34-6	0	34	.250	.316	.366	84	-7	0-1	.989	1	94	102	C102		-0.5
1978	SF N	117	358	20	87	15	1	3	36	45-8	1	39	.243	.329	.316	84	-7	1-2	.986	1	99	109	C116,1b2		-0.2
1979	SF N	63	169	20	35	3	0	3	15	26-5	0	25	.207	.308	.278	67	-7	0-1	.991	-4	96	145	C58/1	40	-0.9
1980	SF N	17	41	1	7	2	0	0	0	1-0	0	7	.171	.190	.220	15	-5	0-0	.972	-0	85	101	C14		-0.5
	Sea A	29	70	8	16	2	1	2	9	3-0	0	10	.229	.260	.371	70	-3	0-0	.991	1	151	111	C29		-0.2
1981	Chi A	16	6	0	0	0	0	0	0	0-0	0	1	.000	.000	.000	-99	-2	0-0	1.000	-1	0	91	C14/13		-0.1
1982	Chi A	53	88	9	23	2	0	3	13	6-0	1	13	.261	.313	.386	91	-1	0-0	.993	1	102	114	C49/13		0.1
1983	Chi A	58	133	11	30	6	1	1	11	9-2	0	21	.226	.275	.293	54	-8	0-1	.991	0	123	96	C55/1D		-0.7
1984	Chi A	77	193	15	45	10	1	5	20	9-0	2	26	.233	.275	.373	73	-7	0-1	.991	-2	108	77	C72,1b2		-0.7
1985	Chi A	40	75	5	10	2	0	0	4	12-0	1	9	.133	.253	.160	15	-9	0-0	.985	-0	101	56	C37/3		-0.8
1986	Chi A	22	19	2	3	0	0	0	0	1-0	1	3	.158	.238	.158	10	-2	0-0	1.000	4	110	139	C22		0.1
Total	14	737	1809	146	404	62	3	34	198	185-29	6	243	.223	.295	.317	69	-75	1-7	.990	2	106	104	C687,1b9,3b4,D2	101	-5.4

HILL, OLIVER   Oliver Clinton   B10.16.1909 Powder Springs GA   D9.20.1970 Decatur GA   BL/TR/5-11/178   d4.19

YEAR	TM LG	G	AB	R	H	2B	3B	HR	RBI	BB-IB	HP	SO	AVG	OBP	SLG	AOPS	ABR	SB-CS	FA	FR	RNG	THR	GAMES AT POSITION	DL	BFW
1939	Bos N	2	2	1	1	0	0	0	0	0-0	0	0	.500	.500	1.000	317	1			0			/H		0.1

HILL, BOBBY   William Robert   B4.3.1978 San Jose CA   BB/TR/5-10/180*   [ChiN00 2/43]   d5.10   Col Miami

YEAR	TM LG	G	AB	R	H	2B	3B	HR	RBI	BB-IB	HP	SO	AVG	OBP	SLG	AOPS	ABR	SB-CS	FA	FR	RNG	THR	GAMES AT POSITION	DL	BFW
2002	Chi N	59	190	26	48	7	2	4	20	17-4	4	42	.253	.327	.374	87	-5	6-1	.991	-2	84	98	2b55/S		-0.4
2003	Chi N	5	4	0	1	0	0	0	0	1-0	0	2	.250	.400	.250	73	0	0-0	1.000	-1	0	0	2b2		-0.1
	Pit N	1	3	1	1	0	0	0	0	1-0	0	0	.333	.500	.333	122	0	0-0	1.000	-0	96	0	/2		0.0
	Year	6	7	1	2	0	0	0	0	2-0	0	2	.286	.444	.286	94	0	0-0	1.000	-1	52	0	2b3		-0.1
2004	Pit N	126	233	28	62	7	2	2	27	20-2	12	39	.266	.353	.339	81	-6	0-3	.994	1	111	115	2b40,3b25		-0.4
2005	Pit N	58	93	12	25	6	0	0	11	9-0	2	17	.269	.343	.333	80	-2	0-0	.977	-2	90	119	3b24/2		-0.4
Total	4	249	523	67	137	20	4	6	58	48-6	18	100	.262	.343	.350	83	-13	6-4	.989	-5	93	103	2b99,3b49/S		-1.3

HILLEBRAND, HOMER   Homer Hiller Henry   B10.10.1879 Freeport IL   D1.20.1974 Elsinore (now Lake Elsinore) CA   BR/TL/5-8/165   d4.24   Col Princeton ▲

YEAR	TM LG	G	AB	R	H	2B	3B	HR	RBI	BB-IB	HP	SO	AVG	OBP	SLG	AOPS	ABR	SB-CS	FA	FR	RNG	THR	GAMES AT POSITION	DL	BFW
1905	Pit N	39	110	9	26	3	2	0	7	6	1		.236	.282	.302	72	-4	1	.978	-3	62	95	1b16,P10,O7(1/0/6),C3		-0.8
1906	Pit N	7	21	1	5	1	0	0	3	1	0		.238	.273	.286	71	-1		1.000	1	125	442	P7		0.0
1908	Pit N	1	0	0	0	0	0	0	0	0	0		—	—	—		0	0	—	-0	0	0	/P		0.0
Total	3	47	131	10	31	4	2	0	10	7	1		.237	.281	.298	71	0	1	.984	-2	92	204	P18,1b16,O7(1/0/6),C3		-0.8

HILLENBRAND, SHEA   Shea Matthew   B7.27.1975 Mesa AZ   BR/TR/6-1/200*   [BosA96 10/301]   d4.2   Col Mesa (AZ) CC   [DL 1999 Bos A 34]

YEAR	TM LG	G	AB	R	H	2B	3B	HR	RBI	BB-IB	HP	SO	AVG	OBP	SLG	AOPS	ABR	SB-CS	FA	FR	RNG	THR	GAMES AT POSITION	DL	BFW
2001	Bos A	139	468	52	123	20	2	12	49	13-3	7	61	.263	.291	.391	78	-16	3-4	.941	-2	92	78	3b129,1b6/D		-1.8
2002	Bos A★	156	634	94	186	43	4	18	83	25-4	12	95	.293	.330	.459	106	4	4-2	.943	4	102	113	3b156		0.9
2003	Bos A	49	185	20	56	17	0	3	38	7-1	4	26	.303	.335	.443	101	1	1-0	.958	-1	87	64	3b29,1b28,D2		-0.2
	Ari N	85	330	40	88	18	1	17	59	17-3	2	44	.267	.302	.482	94	-4	0-0	.989	-5	76	75	1b56,3b34	20	-1.4
2004	Ari N	148	562	68	174	36	3	15	80	24-2	12	49	.310	.348	.464	102	1	2-0	.989	-5	90	93	1b131,3b17		-1.4
2005	Tor A★	152	594	91	173	36	2	18	82	26-2	22	79	.291	.343	.449	103	3	5-1	.991	-4	115	124	1b67,3b54,D33	54	-0.7
Total	5	729	2773	365	800	170	12	83	391	112-15	59	354	.288	.327	.448	98	-11	15-7	.942	-13	95	94	3b419,1b288,D36		-4.6

HILLER, CHUCK   Charles Joseph   B10.1.1934 Johnsburg IL   D10.20.2004 St.Pete Beach FL   BL/TR/5-11/170*   d4.11   C10   Col St. Thomas (MN)

YEAR	TM LG	G	AB	R	H	2B	3B	HR	RBI	BB-IB	HP	SO	AVG	OBP	SLG	AOPS	ABR	SB-CS	FA	FR	RNG	THR	GAMES AT POSITION	DL	BFW
1961	SF N	70	240	38	57	12	1	2	12	32-0	1	30	.237	.328	.321	76	-7	4-4	.973	-19	82	75	2b67		-2.1
1962	†SF N	161	602	94	166	22	2	3	48	55-3	8	49	.276	.341	.334	84	-11	5-4	.964	-9	97	110	2b161		-0.4
1963	SF N	111	417	44	93	10	2	6	33	20-0	1	23	.223	.261	.300	62	-21	3-2	.963	-14	95	78	2b109		-3.0
1964	SF N	80	205	21	37	8	1	1	17	17-0	1	23	.180	.243	.244	38	-17	1-1	.977	1	100	101	2b60/3		-0.1
1965	SF N	7	7	1	1	0	0	1	0	0-0	0	1	.143	.143	.571	88	0	0-0	1.000	-0	72	0	2b2		-1.1
	NY N	100	286	24	68	11	1	5	21	14-2	1	24	.238	.275	.336	74	-11	1-1	.959	-4	102	94	2b80,O4(3/0/1),3b2		-1.1
	Year	107	293	25	69	11	1	6	22	14-2	1	25	.235	.272	.341	74	-11	1-1	.959	-5	102	93	2b82,O4(3/0/1),3b2		-1.2
1966	NY N	108	254	25	71	8	2	2	14	15-0	5	22	.280	.332	.350	92	-3	0-0	.981	12	119	126	2b45,3b14,O9L		1.2
1967	NY N	25	54	0	5	3	0	0	3	2-0	0	11	.093	.125	.148	-22	-9	0-2	.968	2	115	123	2b14	38	-0.6
	Phi N	31	43	4	13	1	0	0	2	2-0	0	4	.302	.333	.326	88	-1	0-2	.947	-2	74	37	2b6		-0.
	Year	56	97	4	18	4	0	0	5	4-0	0	15	.186	.218	.227	27	-9	0-2	.963	0	103	99	2b20		-0.5
1968	Pit N	11	13	2	5	1	0	0	1	0-0	0	0	.385	.385	.462	155	1	0-0	.857	-0	68	0	2b2		0.
Total	8	704	2121	253	516	76	9	20	152	157-5	18	187	.243	.299	.316	72	-79	14-14	.967	-31	97	96	2b546,3b17,O13(12/0/1)	38	-7.5

HILLER, HOB   Harvey Max   B5.12.1893 E.Mauch Chunk PA   D12.27.1956 Lehighton PA   BR/TR/5-8/162   d4.22

YEAR	TM LG	G	AB	R	H	2B	3B	HR	RBI	BB-IB	HP	SO	AVG	OBP	SLG	AOPS	ABR	SB-CS	FA	FR	RNG	THR	GAMES AT POSITION	DL	BFW
1920	Bos A	17	29	4	5	1	1	0	2	2	0	5	.172	.226	.276	34	-3	0-3	.905	1	116	113	3b6,S5,2b2/OR		-0.3
1921	Bos A	1	1	0	0	0	0	0	0	0	0	0	.000	.000	.000	-99	0	0-3	—	0			/H		0.
Total	2	18	30	4	5	1	1	0	2	2	0	5	.167	.219	.267	29	-3	0-3	.905	1	116	113	3b6,S5,2b2/OR		-0.

HILLEY, ED   Edward Garfield "Whitey"   B6.17.1879 Cleveland OH   D11.14.1956 Cleveland OH   BR/TR/5-10.5/170   d9.29

YEAR	TM LG	G	AB	R	H	2B	3B	HR	RBI	BB-IB	HP	SO	AVG	OBP	SLG	AOPS	ABR	SB-CS	FA	FR	RNG	THR	GAMES AT POSITION	DL	BFW
1903	Phi A	3	3	1	1	0	0	0	0	1	0		.333	.500	.333	147	0	0	.800	-0	35	655	/3		0.

HILLIS, MACK   Malcolm David   B7.23.1901 Cambridge MA   D6.16.1961 Cambridge MA   BR/TR/5-10/165   d9.13

YEAR	TM LG	G	AB	R	H	2B	3B	HR	RBI	BB-IB	HP	SO	AVG	OBP	SLG	AOPS	ABR	SB-CS	FA	FR	RNG	THR	GAMES AT POSITION	DL	BFW
1924	NY A	1	1	1	0	0	0	0	0	0-0	0	0	.000	.000	.000	-99	0	0-0	—	-0	0	0	/2		-0.
1928	Pit N	11	36	6	9	2	3	1	7	0-0	0	6	.250	.250	.556	101	-1	1	.973	-1	96		2b8/3		-0.
Total	2	12	37	7	9	2	3	1	7	0-0	0	6	.243	.243	.541	96	-1	1-0	.973	-1	109	94	2b9/3		-0.

HILLY, PAT   William Edward (b William Edward Hilgerink)   B2.24.1887 Fostoria OH   D7.25.1953 Eureka MO   BR/TR/5-11/180   d5.7   Col Dayton

YEAR	TM LG	G	AB	R	H	2B	3B	HR	RBI	BB-IB	HP	SO	AVG	OBP	SLG	AOPS	ABR	SB-CS	FA	FR	RNG	THR	GAMES AT POSITION	DL	BFW
1914	Phi N	8	10	2	3	0	0	0	0			5	.300	.364	.300	92	0	0	1.000	0	138	0	O4R		0.

HILTON, DAVE   John David   B9.15.1950 Uvalde TX   BR/TR/5-11/185*   [SDN71*1/1]   d9.10   C2   Col Rice

YEAR	TM LG	G	AB	R	H	2B	3B	HR	RBI	BB-IB	HP	SO	AVG	OBP	SLG	AOPS	ABR	SB-CS	FA	FR	RNG	THR	GAMES AT POSITION	DL	BFW
1972	SD N	13	47	2	10	2	1	0	5	3-0	0	6	.213	.260	.298	63	-3	1-0	.939	-3	73	43	3b13		-0.
1973	SD N	70	234	21	46	9	0	5	16	19-6	1	35	.197	.260	.299	59	-14	2-1	.970	-10	94	120	3b47,2b23		-2.
1974	SD N	74	217	17	52	8	2	1	12	13-1	0	28	.240	.281	.309	69	-10	3-5	.948	-5	91	117	3b55,2b15		-1.
1975	SD N	4	8	0	0	0	0	0	0	0-0	0	0	.000	.000	.000	-99	-2	0-0	.900	1	142	0	3b4	58	-0.
Total	4	161	506	40	108	19	3	6	33	35-7	1	69	.213	.265	.298	61	-29	6-6	.954	-16	91	107	3b119,2b38	58	-4.

HIMES, JACK   John Herb   B9.22.1878 Bryan OH   D12.16.1949 Joliet IL   BL/TR/6-2/180   d9.18

YEAR	TM LG	G	AB	R	H	2B	3B	HR	RBI	BB-IB	HP	SO	AVG	OBP	SLG	AOPS	ABR	SB-CS	FA	FR	RNG	THR	GAMES AT POSITION	DL	BFW
1905	StL N	12	41	3	6	0	0	0	0	0		4	.146	.167	.146	-7	-5	0	1.000	-0	74	0	O11(1/0/11)		-0.
1906	StL N	40	155	10	42	5	2	0	14	7	1		.271	.307	.329	102	0	4	.977	4	197	158	O40(0/32/8)		-0.
Total	2	52	196	13	48	5	2	0	14	8	1		.245	.289	.291	79	-5	4	.981	4	172	126	O51(1/32/19)		-0.

HINCH, A.J. Andrew Jay B5.15.1974 Waverly IA BR/TR/6-1/207* [OakA96 3/75] d4.1 Col Stanford

YEAR	TM	LG	G	AB	R	H	2B	3B	HR	RBI	BB-IB	HP	SO	AVG	OBP	SLG	AOPS	ABR	SB-CS	FA	FR	RNG	THR	GAMES AT POSITION	DL	BFW
1998	Oak	A	120	337	34	78	10	0	9	35	30-0	4	89	.231	.296	.341	68	-17	3-0	.986	-8	112	99	C118		-1.6
1999	Oak	A	76	205	26	44	4	1	7	24	11-0	2	41	.215	.260	.346	55	-15	6-2	.987	-10	101	73	C73		-1.9
2000	Oak	A	6	8	1	2	0	0	0	0	1-0	0	1	.250	.333	.250	52	-1	0-0	.900	-1	131	174	C5/D		-0.2
2001	KC	A	45	121	10	19	3	0	6	15	8-1	3	26	.157	.226	.331	40	-11	1-1	.987	-1	125	62	C43,D2		-0.9
2002	KC	A	72	197	25	49	7	1	7	27	18-0	3	35	.249	.321	.401	80	-6	3-3	.989	-5	80	62	C68		-0.6
2003	Det	A	27	74	7	15	3	1	3	11	3-0	2	18	.203	.247	.392	70	-4	0-0	.983	-7	54	59	C27	42	-0.9
2004	Phi	N	4	11	1	2	1	0	0	0	3-0	0	5	.182	.182	.273	15	-1	0-0	1.000	1	156	321	C4		-0.1
Total	7		350	953	104	209	28	3	32	112	71-1	14	214	.219	.280	.356	64	-55	13-6	.987	-31	101	81	C338,D3	42	-6.2

HINCHMAN, HARRY Harry Sibley B8.4.1878 Philadelphia PA D1.19.1933 Toledo OH BB/TR/5-11/165 d7.29 b-Bill

YEAR	TM	LG	G	AB	R	H	2B	3B	HR	RBI	BB-IB	HP	SO	AVG	OBP	SLG	AOPS	ABR	SB-CS	FA	FR	RNG	THR	GAMES AT POSITION	DL	BFW
1907	Cle	A	15	51	3	11	3	1	0	9	5	0		.216	.286	.314	90	0	2	.904	3	135	106	2b15		0.3

HINCHMAN, BILL William White B4.4.1883 Philadelphia PA D2.20.1963 Columbus OH BR/TR/5-11/190 d9.24 C1 b-Harry OF(330/61/357)

YEAR	TM	LG	G	AB	R	H	2B	3B	HR	RBI	BB-IB	HP	SO	AVG	OBP	SLG	AOPS	ABR	SB-CS	FA	FR	RNG	THR	GAMES AT POSITION	DL	BFW
1905	Cin	N	17	51	10	13	4	1	0	10	13	1		.255	.415	.373	122	2	4	.905	-2	65	251	O12L,3b4/1		0.0
1906	Cin	N	18	54	7	11	1	1	0	1	8	0		.204	.306	.259	73	-1	2	.963	1	153	415	O16(8/0/8)		-0.2
1907	Cle	A	152	514	62	117	19	9	1	50	47	15		.228	.311	.305	96	-1	15	.958	-1	99	73	O148(128/14/8),1b4/2		-1.1
1908	Cle	A	137	464	55	107	23	8	6	59	38	9		.231	.301	.353	112	6	9	.975	-9	146	45	O75(23/1/51),S51,1b4		-0.5
1909	Cle	A	139	457	57	118	20	13	2	53	41	9		.258	.331	.372	117	9	22	.918	0	107	27	O131(87/38/6),S6		0.2
1915	Pit	N	156	577	72	177	33	14	5	77	48	8	75	.307	.368	.438	146	32	17-17	.969	2	103	96	O156(6/0/151)		2.5
1916	Pit	N	152	555	64	175	18	16	4	76	54	2	61	.315	.378	.427	146	30	10	.962	-5	107	54	O124(23/0/101),1b31		2.1
1917	Pit	N	69	244	27	46	5	2	2	29	33	1	27	.189	.288	.275	71	-8	5	.945	-1	102	84	O48(41/8/0),1b20		-1.3
1918	Pit	N	50	111	10	26	5	2	0	13	15	2		.234	.336	.315	96	0	1	1.000	2	77	245	O40(2/0/32),1b3		0.1
1920	Pit	N	18	16	0	3	0	0	0	1	1	1		.188	.278	.188	34	-1	0-0	—	0			/H		-0.1
Total	10		908	3043	364	793	128	69	20	369	298	48	174	.261	.336	.368	118	68	85-17	.954	-13	108	79	O750R,1b63,S57,3b4/2		1.7

HINES, HUNKEY Henry Fred B9.29.1867 Elgin IL D1.2.1928 Rockford IL BR/TR/5-7/165 d5.16

YEAR	TM	LG	G	AB	R	H	2B	3B	HR	RBI	BB-IB	HP	SO	AVG	OBP	SLG	AOPS	ABR	SB-CS	FA	FR	RNG	THR	GAMES AT POSITION	DL	BFW
1895	Bro	N	2	8	3	2	0	0	0	1	2	0		.250	.400	.250	76	0	0	1.000	-0	0	0	O2R		0.0

HINES, MIKE Michael P. B9.1862, Ireland D3.14.1910 Taunton MA BR/TL/5-10/176 d5.1

YEAR	TM	LG	G	AB	R	H	2B	3B	HR	RBI	BB-IB	HP	SO	AVG	OBP	SLG	AOPS	ABR	SB-CS	FA	FR	RNG	THR	GAMES AT POSITION	DL	BFW
1883	Bos	N	63	231	38	52	13	1	0	16	7		36	.225	.248	.290	61	-11		.887	6			C59,O7(0/2/5)		0.1
1884	Bos	N	35	132	16	23	3	0	0	3	3		24	.174	.193	.197	23	-12		.919	4			C35		-0.4
1885	Bos	N	14	56	11	13	4	0	0	4	4		5	.232	.283	.304	93	0		.857	-2	49	0	O14R		-0.2
	Bro	AA	3	13	1	1	0	1	0	1	0	0		.077	.077	.231	-6	-2		1.000	-1			C3		-0.2
	Pro	N	1	3	0	0	0	0	0	0	0		2	.000	.000	.000	-99	-1		.636	-1			/C		-0.1
1888	Bos	N	4	16	3	2	0	1	0	2	2	0		.125	.222	.250	49	-1	0	1.000	-1	0	0	O3(2/0/1)/C		-0.2
Total	4		120	451	69	91	20	3	6	26	16	0	67	.202	.229	.259	51	-27	0	.896	5			C99,O24(2/2/20)		-1.0

HINES, PAUL Paul A. B3.1.1852 VA D7.10.1935 Hyattsville MD BR/TR/5-9.5/173 d4.20 OF NA(41/85/0) OF(27/1218/7)

YEAR	TM	LG	G	AB	R	H	2B	3B	HR	RBI	BB-IB	HP	SO	AVG	OBP	SLG	AOPS	ABR	SB-CS	FA	FR	RNG	THR	GAMES AT POSITION	DL	BFW
1872	Nat	NA	11	49	9	11	1	0	0	5	0		0	.224	.224	.245	38	-4	0-0	.862	-3	95	0	1b9,3b2/C		-0.5
1873	Was	NA	39	181	33	60	6	3	1	29	1		0	.331	.335	.414	125	6	0-1	.798	-0	79	0	O36L,2b2/C		0.4
1874	Chi	NA	59	271	47	80	10	2	0	34	4		4	.295	.305	.347	108	2	4-1	.877	3	73	157	O50(1/50/0),2b11,S2		0.4
1875	Chi	NA	69	308	45	101	14	4	0	36	1		0	.328	.330	.399	151	15	6-9	.889	7	108	258	O39(4/35/0),2b30/CS		1.5
1876	Chi	N	64	305	62	101	21	3	2	59	1		3	.331	.333	.439	139	11		.923	4	75	209	O64C/2		1.1
1877	Chi	N	60	261	44	73	11	7	0	23	1		8	.280	.282	.375	94	-3		.806	-10	45	66	O49(24/18/7),2b11		-1.3
1878	Pro	N	62	257	42	92	13	4	4	50	2		10	.358	.363	.486	178	20		.849	1	95	161	O61C/S		1.7
1879	Pro	N	85	409	81	146	25	10	2	52	8		16	.357	.369	.482	181	35		.867	5	124	149	O85C		3.2
1880	Pro	N	85	374	64	115	20	2	3	35	13		17	.307	.331	.396	150	20		.927	3	91	251	O75C,2b6,1b4		1.9
1881	Pro	N	80	361	65	103	27	5	2	31	13		12	.285	.310	.404	125	11		.897	-2	69	65	O78C,2b4/1		0.5
1882	Pro	N	84	379	73	117	28	10	4	34	10		14	.309	.326	.467	151	21		.861	-2	86	117	O82C,1b2		1.4
1883	Pro	N	97	442	94	132	32	4	4	45	18		23	.299	.326	.416	120	11		.905	5	106	72	O89C,1b9		1.1
1884	†Pro	N	114	490	94	148	36	10	3	41	44		28	.302	.360	.435	151	31		.895	-3	87	174	O108C,1b7/P		2.1
1885	Pro	N	98	411	63	111	20	4	1	35	19		18	.270	.302	.345	112	6		.865	2	104	127	O92C,1b4/S32		0.4
1886	Was	N	121	487	80	152	30	8	9	56	35		21	.312	.358	.462	160	36	21	.899	0	108	33	O92(1/91/0),3b15,1b10,S5,2b3		2.9
1887	Was	N	123	478	83	147	32	5	10	72	46	8	24	.308	.380	.458	141	30	46	.886	-16	72	143	O109C,1b7,2b5,S4		0.9
1888	Ind	N	133	513	60	144	26	3	4	58	41	8	45	.281	.343	.366	124	16	31	.912	-8	63	67	O125C,1b6,S2		0.3
1889	Ind	N	121	486	77	148	27	1	6	72	49	5	22	.305	.374	.401	114	10	34	.964	3	121	108	1b109,O12C		0.3
1890	Pit	N	31	121	11	22	1	0	0	9	11	1	7	.182	.256	.190	34	-10	6	.973	-2	219	69	1b17,O14C		-0.8
	Bos	N	69	273	41	72	12	3	2	48	32	4	20	.264	.350	.352	97	-1	9	.881	-11	36	96	O69(2/68/0)/1		-1.3
	Year		100	394	52	94	13	3	2	57	43	5	27	.239	.321	.302	80	-9	15	.871	-9	45	108	O83(2/82/0),1b18		-2.1
1891	Was	AA	54	206	25	58	7	5	0	31	21	10	16	.282	.376	.364	117	6	6	.856	-3	99	197	O47C,1b8		0.0
Total	4 NA		178	809	134	252	31	9	1	104	6		6	.311	.317	.376	122	19	10-11	.857	6	86	143	O125C,2b43,1b9,S3,C3,3b2		1.8
Total	16		1481	6253	1083	1881	368	84	56	751	366	36	304	.301	.343	.413	133	250	153	.887	-29	86	125	O1251C,1b185,2b31,3b16,S13/P		14.4

HINKLE, GORDIE Daniel Gordon B4.3.1905 Toronto OH D3.19.1972 Houston TX BR/TR/6-0/185 d4.19

YEAR	TM	LG	G	AB	R	H	2B	3B	HR	RBI	BB-IB	HP	SO	AVG	OBP	SLG	AOPS	ABR	SB-CS	FA	FR	RNG	THR	GAMES AT POSITION	DL	BFW
1934	Bos	A	27	75	7	13	6	1	0	9	7	0	23	.173	.244	.280	33	-8	0-0	.992	3	110	73	C26		-0.3

HINSHAW, GEORGE George Addison B10.23.1959 Los Angeles CA BR/TR/6-0/185* [SDN80 11/265] d9.19 Col La Verne

YEAR	TM	LG	G	AB	R	H	2B	3B	HR	RBI	BB-IB	HP	SO	AVG	OBP	SLG	AOPS	ABR	SB-CS	FA	FR	RNG	THR	GAMES AT POSITION	DL	BFW
1982	SD	N	6	15	1	4	0	0	0	1	3-1	0	5	.267	.389	.267	92	0	0-0	1.000	0	90	261	O6(1/0/5)		0.0
1983	SD	N	7	16	1	7	1	0	0	4	0-0	0	4	.438	.438	.500	164	1	1-0	1.000	-1	60	0	3b5		0.1
Total	2		13	31	2	11	1	0	0	5	3-1	0	9	.355	.412	.387	129	1	1-0	1.000	-1	90	261	O6(1/0/5),3b5		0.1

HINSKE, ERIC Eric Scott B8.5.1977 Menasha WI BL/TR/6-2/225* [ChiN98 17/496] d4.1 Col Arkansas-Monticello

YEAR	TM	LG	G	AB	R	H	2B	3B	HR	RBI	BB-IB	HP	SO	AVG	OBP	SLG	AOPS	ABR	SB-CS	FA	FR	RNG	THR	GAMES AT POSITION	DL	BFW
2002	Tor	A	151	566	99	158	38	2	24	84	77-5	2	138	.279	.365	.481	119	17	13-1	.946	-8	97	55	3b148		1.2
2003	Tor	A	124	449	74	109	45	3	12	69	59-1	1	104	.243	.329	.437	97	-1	12-2	.930	-7	97	61	3b124		-0.5
2004	Tor	A	155	570	66	140	23	3	15	69	54-2	4	109	.246	.312	.375	75	-22	12-8	.978	-8	93	89	3b153/D		-2.8
2005	Tor	A	147	477	79	125	31	2	15	68	46-4	8	121	.262	.333	.430	97	-1	8-4	.993	3	113	94	1b100,D43		-0.9
Total	4		577	2062	318	532	137	10	66	284	236-12	15	472	.258	.335	.430	96	-7	45-15	.952	-21	96	69	3b425,1b100,D44	31	-3.0

HINSON, PAUL James Paul B5.9.1904 Vanleer TN D9.23.1960 Muskogee OK BR/TR/5-10/150 d4.19

YEAR	TM	LG	G	AB	R	H	2B	3B	HR	RBI	BB-IB	HP	SO	AVG	OBP	SLG	AOPS	ABR	SB-CS	FA	FR	RNG	THR	GAMES AT POSITION	DL	BFW
1928	Bos	A	3	0	1	0	0	0	0	0	0	0		—	—	—		0	0-0	—	0			/R		0.0

HINTON, CHUCK Charles Edward B5.3.1934 Rocky Mount NC BR/TR/6-1/197(180-197) d5.14 Col Shaw OF(525/201/299)

YEAR	TM	LG	G	AB	R	H	2B	3B	HR	RBI	BB-IB	HP	SO	AVG	OBP	SLG	AOPS	ABR	SB-CS	FA	FR	RNG	THR	GAMES AT POSITION	DL	BFW
1961	Was	A	106	339	51	88	13	5	6	34	40-1	1	81	.260	.337	.381	93	-3	22-5	.963	1	100	91	O92(72/0/20)		-0.4
1962	Was	A	151	542	73	168	25	6	17	75	47-0	0	66	.310	.361	.472	124	18	28-10	.988	-4	88	95	O136(54/28/67),2b12/S		1.0
1963	Was	A	150	566	80	152	20	12	15	55	64-2	1	79	.269	.340	.426	115	11	25-9	.989	1	111	91	O125(86/7/45),3b19,1b6,S2		0.6
1964	Was	A★	138	514	71	141	26	7	11	57	57-7	1	77	.274	.346	.414	112	9	17-6	.985	7	110	103	O131(131/1/1),3b2		1.0
1965	Cle	A	133	431	59	110	17	6	18	54	53-5	1	65	.255	.336	.448	120	11	17-3	.966	-3	94	137	O72(33/43/4),1b40,2b23/3		0.8
1966	Cle	A	123	348	46	89	9	3	12	50	35-2	1	66	.256	.323	.402	108	3	10-6	.973	-1	99	113	O104(53/57/11),1b6,2b2		-0.2
1967	Cle	A	147	498	55	122	19	3	10	37	43-5	1	100	.245	.304	.355	94	-4	6-8	.976	-1	103	64	O136(26/53/92),2b5		-0.3
1968	Cal	A	116	267	28	52	10	3	7	23	24-3	0	61	.195	.259	.333	82	-7	3-1	.987	4	148	112	1b48,O37(10/6/23),3b13,2b9		-1.5
1969	Cle	A	94	121	18	31	3	2	3	19	8-2	1	22	.256	.303	.388	91	-2	2-0	.941	-2	106	0	O40(28/4/9),3b14		-0.7
1970	Cle	A	107	195	24	62	4	0	9	29	25-1	0	34	.318	.392	.477	133	9	0-2	.994	-4	61	81	1b40,O35(17/0/22),C4,2b3,3b2		0.2
1971	Cle	A	88	147	11	33	5	1	1	14	20-2	0	34	.224	.317	.374	87	-2	0-0	1.000	-4	75	166	1b20,O20(15/0/5),C5		-0.8
Total	11		1353	3968	518	1048	152	47	113	443	416-27	7	685	.264	.332	.412	108	43	130-50	.979	-7	101	95	O928L,1b160,2b54,3b51,C9,S3		-0.5

HINTON, JOHN John Robert "Red" B6.20.1876 Pittsburg PA D7.19.1920 Braddock PA BR/TR/6-0/200 d6.3

YEAR	TM	LG	G	AB	R	H	2B	3B	HR	RBI	BB-IB	HP	SO	AVG	OBP	SLG	AOPS	ABR	SB-CS	FA	FR	RNG	THR	GAMES AT POSITION	DL	BFW
1901	Bos	N	4	13	0	1	0	0	0	2	0	0		.077	.200	.077	-17	-2		.750	-2	69	0	3b4		-0.3

HINZO, TOMMY Thomas Lee B6.18.1964 San Diego CA BB/TR/5-10/170* [CleA86 7/161] d7.16 Col Arizona

YEAR	TM	LG	G	AB	R	H	2B	3B	HR	RBI	BB-IB	HP	SO	AVG	OBP	SLG	AOPS	ABR	SB-CS	FA	FR	RNG	THR	GAMES AT POSITION	DL	BFW
1987	Cle	A	67	257	31	66	9	3	3	21	10-0	2	47	.265	.296	.358	72	-11	9-4	.973	1	110	96	2b67		-0.5
1989	Cle	A	18	17	4	5	0	0	0	0	2-0	0	6	.000	.105	.000	-67	-4	1-2	.867	-4	64	42	2b6/SD	18	-0.8
Total	2		85	274	35	71	9	3	3	21	12-0	2	53	.248	.284	.336	64	-15	10-6	.968	-2	107	93	2b73/DS	18	-1.3

HISER, GENE Gene Taylor B12.11.1948 Baltimore MD BL/TL/5-11/175* [ChiN70 1/19] d8.20 Col Maryland-Baltimore Co.

YEAR	TM	LG	G	AB	R	H	2B	3B	HR	RBI	BB-IB	HP	SO	AVG	OBP	SLG	AOPS	ABR	SB-CS	FA	FR	RNG	THR	GAMES AT POSITION	DL	BFW
1971	Chi	N	17	29	4	6	0	0	0	4	4-0	0	8	.207	.303	.207	41	-2	1-0	1.000	0	111	0	O9(0/4/5)		-0.2
1972	Chi	N	32	46	2	9	1	0	0	4	6-0	0	8	.196	.288	.196	24	-4	1-0	1.000	1	95	250	O15(4/2/9)		-0.3

YEAR	TM LG	G	AB	R	H	2B	3B	HR	RBI	BB-IB	HP	SO	AVG	OBP	SLG	AOPS	ABR	SB-CS	FA	FR·RNG	THR	GAMES AT POSITION	DL	BFW
1973	Chi N	100	109	15	19	3	0	1	6	11-1	1	17	.174	.254	.229	33	-10	4-5	.980	-4 81	0	O64(25/22/18)		-1.7
1974	Chi N	12	17	2	4	1	0	0	1	0-0	0	3	.235	.235	.294	45	-1	0-0	1.000	0 107	0	O8(6/1/1)		-0.2
1975	Chi N	45	62	11	15	3	0	0	6	11-1	0	7	.242	.351	.290	77	-1	0-1	1.000	0 117	0	O18(7/6/5)/1		-0.2
Total	5	206	263	64	53	7	0	1	18	32-2	1	43	.202	.289	.240	46	-18	6-6	.992	-3 95	46	O114(42/35/38)/1		-2.6

HISLE, LARRY   Larry Eugene   B5.5.1947 Portsmouth OH   BR/TR/6-2/195*   [PhiN65 2/38]   d4.10   C4

YEAR	TM LG	G	AB	R	H	2B	3B	HR	RBI	BB-IB	HP	SO	AVG	OBP	SLG	AOPS	ABR	SB-CS	FA	FR·RNG	THR	GAMES AT POSITION	DL	BFW
1968	Phi N	7	11	1	4	1	0	0	1	1-0	0	1	.364	.417	.455	162	0	0-0	1.000	0 112	0	O6C		0.1
1969	Phi N	145	482	75	128	23	5	20	56	48-8	5	152	.266	.338	.459	124	15	18-8	.977	7 111 137	O140(1/139/0)		2.0
1970	Phi N	126	405	52	83	22	4	10	44	53-2	3	139	.205	.299	.353	76	-14	5-5	.978	1 107 72	O121(0/86/36)		-1.8
1971	Phi N	36	76	7	15	3	0	0	3	6-1	0	22	.197	.256	.237	40	-6	1-0	.962	2 123 157	O27(19/8/0)		-0.5
1973	Min A	143	545	88	148	25	6	15	64	64-2	4	128	.272	.351	.422	112	10	11-4	.975	1 102 110	O143(49/93/3)		0.7
1974	Min A	143	510	68	146	20	7	19	79	48-5	8	112	.286	.353	.465	131	20	12-6	.979	-5 97 44	O137(74/52/26)		0.9
1975	Min A	80	255	37	80	9	2	11	51	27-3	1	39	.314	.376	.494	144	15	17-3	.976	-3 93 49	O58(37/26/9),D14	54	1.2
1976	Min A	155	581	81	158	19	5	14	96	56-4	4	93	.272	.335	.394	112	9	31-18	.984	11 109 142	O154(135/5/18)		1.2
1977	Min A★	141	546	95	165	36	3	28	**119**	56-5	6	106	.302	.369	.533	145	35	21-10	.974	-6 90 110	O134(68/65/6),D6		2.6
1978	Mil A★	142	520	96	151	24	0	34	115	67-3	5	90	.290	.374	.533	152	36	10-6	.978	-5 87 100	O87(67/22/1),D51		2.7
1979	Mil A	26	96	18	27	7	0	3	14	11-2	0	19	.281	.352	.448	115	2	1-0	1.000	0 77 254	D15,O10L	111	0.2
1980	Mil A	17	60	16	17	0	0	6	16	14-2	1	7	.283	.421	.583	178	7	1-1	—	0	D17	120	0.6
1981	Mil A	27	87	11	20	4	0	2	11	6-0	2	17	.230	.289	.414	107	0	0-0	—	0	D24	97	0.0
1982	Mil A	9	31	7	4	0	0	2	5	5-0	0	13	.129	.250	.323	59	-2	0-0	—	0	D8	150	-0.2
Total	14	1197	4205	652	1146	193	32	166	674	462-37	39	941	.273	.347	.452	123	128	128-61	.978	2 101 103	O1017(460/502/99),D135	532	9.7

HITCHCOCK, JIM   James Franklin   B6.28.1911 Inverness AL   D6.23.1959 Montgomery AL   BR/TR/5-11/175   d8.24   b-Billy   Col Auburn-Montgomery

YEAR	TM LG	G	AB	R	H	2B	3B	HR	RBI	BB-IB	HP	SO	AVG	OBP	SLG	AOPS	ABR	SB-CS	FA	FR·RNG	THR	GAMES AT POSITION	DL	BFW
1938	Bos N	28	76	2	13	0	0	0	7	2	0	11	.171	.192	.171	1	-11	1	.881	-4 93 109	S24,3b2		-1.3

HITCHCOCK, BILLY   William Clyde   B7.31.1916 Inverness AL   D4.14   Mil 1943-45   M5/C7   b-Jim   Col Auburn-Montgomery

YEAR	TM LG	G	AB	R	H	2B	3B	HR	RBI	BB-IB	HP	SO	AVG	OBP	SLG	AOPS	ABR	SB-CS	FA	FR·RNG	THR	GAMES AT POSITION	DL	BFW
1942	Det A	85	280	27	59	8	1	0	29	26	1	21	.211	.280	.246	45	-20	2-2	.944	-3 93 86	S80/3		-1.9
1946	Det A	3	3	0	0	0	0	0	0	1	0	0	.000	.250	.000	-25	0	0-0	1.000	0 122	0	/2		0.0
	Was A	98	354	27	75	8	3	0	25	26	1	52	.212	.268	.251	48	-26	2-4	.966	-10 94 78	S53,3b46		-3.6
	Year	101	357	27	75	8	3	0	25	27	1	52	.210	.268	.249	48	-26	2-4	.966	-10 94 78	S53,3b46/2		-3.6
1947	StL A	80	275	25	61	2	2	1	28	21	0	34	.222	.277	.255	47	-20	3-0	.977	6 101 97	2b46,3b17,S7,1b5		-1.1
1948	Bos A	49	124	15	37	3	2	1	20	7	1	9	.298	.341	.379	87	-3	0-0	.951	3 109 114	2b15,3b15		0.1
1949	Bos A	55	147	22	30	6	1	0	9	17	1	11	.204	.291	.259	43	-12	2-3	.993	-5 75 95	1b29,2b8		-1.8
1950	Phi A	115	399	35	109	22	5	1	54	45	1	32	.273	.347	.361	83	-10	3-1	.967	-0 104 105	2b107/S		-0.4
1951	Phi A	77	222	27	68	10	4	1	36	21	2	23	.306	.371	.401	107	2	2-0	.929	5 116 161	3b45,2b23/1		0.8
1952	Phi A	119	407	45	100	8	4	1	56	39	4	45	.246	.318	.292	66	-18	1-1	.942	-1 101 109	3b104,1b13		-2.1
1953	Det A	22	38	8	8	0	0	0	3	3	0	3	.211	.268	.211	31	-4	0-0	.929	-0 103 50	3b12/2S		-0.4
Total	9	703	2249	231	547	67	22	5	257	206	10	230	.243	.310	.299	65	-111	15-11	.938	-4 105 111	3b240,2b201,S142,1b48		-10.4

HOAG, MYRIL   Myril Oliver   B3.9.1908 Davis CA   D7.28.1971 High Springs FL   BR/TR/5-11/180   d4.15   Mil 1943

YEAR	TM LG	G	AB	R	H	2B	3B	HR	RBI	BB-IB	HP	SO	AVG	OBP	SLG	AOPS	ABR	SB-CS	FA	FR·RNG	THR	GAMES AT POSITION	DL	BFW
1931	NY A	44	28	6	4	2	0	0	3	1	0	8	.143	.172	.214	1	-4	0-0	1.000	2 162 337	O23(11/2/10)/3		-0.3
1932	†NY A	46	54	18	20	5	0	1	7	7	0	13	.370	.443	.519	156	5	1-1	.962	2 97 371	O35(27/2/9)/1		0.5
1934	NY A	97	251	45	67	8	2	3	34	21	0	21	.267	.324	.351	79	-9	1-3	.974	-0 113 144	O86(29/17/50)		-0.7
1935	NY A	48	110	13	28	4	1	1	13	12	0	19	.255	.328	.336	76	-4	4-2	.986	2 120 88	O37(2/3/32)/3		-0.3
1936	NY A	45	156	23	47	9	4	3	34	7	3	16	.301	.343	.468	102	-1	3-1	.955	-2 95 64	O39(2/26/12)		-0.3
1937	†NY A	106	362	48	109	19	8	4	66	33	3	33	.301	.364	.423	97	-2	4-7	.955	-2 96 96	O99(24/9/70)		-1.0
1938	†NY A	85	267	28	74	14	3	0	48	25	2	31	.277	.344	.352	75	-10	4-3	.965	-2 94 91	O70(31/13/28)		-1.4
1939	StL A★	129	482	58	142	23	4	10	75	24	1	35	.295	.329	.421	89	-10	9-5	.971	-2 89 153	O117(11/49/60)/P		-1.5
1940	StL A	76	191	20	50	11	0	3	26	13	0	30	.262	.309	.366	73	-8	2-0	.971	-1 85 132	O46(1/1/44)		-1.0
1941	StL A	1	1	0	0	0	0	0	0	0	0	0	.000	.000	.000	-97	0	0-0	—	0	/H		0.0
	Chi A	106	380	30	97	13	3	1	44	27	1	29	.255	.306	.313	65	-20	6-10	.957	-5 94 71	O99(75/25/0)		-3.2
	Year	107	381	30	97	13	3	1	44	27	1	29	.255	.306	.312	65	-20	6-10	.957	-5 94 71	O99(75/25/0)		-3.2
1942	Chi A	113	412	47	99	18	2	2	37	36	0	21	.240	.301	.308	73	-15	17-8	.972	2 98 146	O112(41/81/0)		-1.6
1944	Chi A	17	48	5	11	1	0	0	4	10	0	1	.229	.362	.250	77	-1	1-3	.969	-0 87 173	O14(0/13/1)		-0.2
	Cle A	67	277	33	79	9	3	1	27	25	1	23	.285	.347	.350	103	1	6-4	.947	-5 87 131	O66C		-0.6
	Year	84	325	38	90	10	3	1	31	35	1	24	.277	.349	.335	99	0	7-7	.950	-5 87 137	O80(0/79/1)		-0.8
1945	Cle A	40	128	10	27	5	3	0	11	9	1	18	.211	.279	.297	70	-5	1-2	.987	1 96 152	O33(0/27/6),P2		-0.7
Total	13	1020	3147	384	854	141	33	28	401	252	12	298	.271	.328	.364	83	-83	59-49	.965	-7 96 123	O876(254/334/322),P3,3b2/1		-12.3

HOAK, DON   Donald Albert "Tiger"   B2.5.1928 Roulette PA   D10.9.1969 Pittsburgh PA   BR/TR/6-0/175(165-185)   d4.18   C1

YEAR	TM LG	G	AB	R	H	2B	3B	HR	RBI	BB-IB	HP	SO	AVG	OBP	SLG	AOPS	ABR	SB-CS	FA	FR·RNG	THR	GAMES AT POSITION	DL	BFW
1954	Bro N	88	261	41	64	9	5	7	26	25	4	39	.245	.318	.398	83	-7	8-3	.950	3 103 100	3b75		-0.3
1955	†Bro N	94	279	50	67	13	3	5	19	46-0	1	50	.240	.350	.362	87	-4	9-5	.960	15 120 112	3b78		1.1
1956	Chi N	121	424	51	91	18	4	5	37	41-0	1	46	.215	.283	.311	61	-23	8-3	.949	-13 80 87	3b110		-3.7
1957	Cin N★	149	529	78	155	**39**	2	19	89	74-5	4	54	.293	.381	.482	122	20	8-15	**.971**	-1 93 105	3b149/2		1.5
1958	Cin N	114	417	51	109	30	0	6	50	43-4	2	36	.261	.333	.376	83	-8	6-8	.964	1 99 133	3b112/S		-1.0
1959	Pit N	**155**	564	60	166	29	3	8	65	71-4	4	75	.294	.374	.399	108	9	9-2	.961	-8 106 128	3b155		1.8
1960	†Pit N	**155**	553	97	156	24	9	16	79	74-9	1	74	.282	.366	.445	120	17	3-2	.948	4 107 136	3b155		2.1
1961	Pit N	145	503	72	150	27	7	12	61	73-8	3	53	.298	.388	.451	122	19	4-2	.953	-4 95 107	3b143		1.5
1962	Pit N	121	411	63	99	14	8	5	48	49-5	1	49	.241	.320	.350	81	-11	4-2	**.969**	-1 101 92	3b116		-1.2
1963	Phi N	115	377	35	87	11	3	6	24	27-1	1	52	.231	.282	.324	75	-13	5-5	.958	10 110 90	3b106		-0.3
1964	Phi N	6	4	0	0	0	0	0	0	0-0	0	2	.000	.000	.000	-99	-1	0-0	—	0	/H		-0.1
Total	11	1263	4322	598	1144	214	44	89	498	523-36	22	530	.265	.345	.396	98	-2	64-47	.959	24 101 111	3b1199/S2		1.4

HOBBS, BILL   William Lee "Smokey"   B5.7.1893 Grants Lick KY   D1.5.1945 Hamilton OH   BR/TR/5-9.5/155   d8.9

YEAR	TM LG	G	AB	R	H	2B	3B	HR	RBI	BB-IB	HP	SO	AVG	OBP	SLG	AOPS	ABR	SB-CS	FA	FR·RNG	THR	GAMES AT POSITION	DL	BFW
1913	Cin N	4	4	0	0	0	0	0	0	0	0	3	.000	.000	.000	-99	-1	0	1.000	0 199	0	/23		-0.1
1916	Cin N	6	11	1	2	1	0	0	1	2	0	0	.182	.308	.273	81	-1	1	.947	4 160 127	S6		0.4
Total	2	10	15	1	2	1	0	0	1	2	0	3	.133	.235	.200	32	-1	1	.947	4 160 127	S6/32		0.3

HOBLITZEL, DICK   Richard Carleton "Doc" (b Hoblitzell)   B10.26.1888 Waverly WV   D11.14.1962 Parkersburg WV   BL/TL/6-0/172   d9.5   Mil 1918-20   Col Pittsburgh

YEAR	TM LG	G	AB	R	H	2B	3B	HR	RBI	BB-IB	HP	SO	AVG	OBP	SLG	AOPS	ABR	SB-CS	FA	FR·RNG	THR	GAMES AT POSITION	DL	BFW
1908	Cin N	32	114	8	29	3	2	0	8	7	2		.254	.309	.316	102	0	2	.985	2 123 79	1b32		0.1
1909	Cin N	142	517	59	159	23	11	4	67	44	2		.308	.364	.418	144	25	17	.982	-3 95 111	1b142		2.1
1910	Cin N	155	611	85	170	24	13	4	70	47	2	32	.278	.332	.380	112	7	28	.984	-7 80 71	1b148,2b7		-0.3
1911	Cin N	158	622	81	180	19	13	11	91	42	8	44	.289	.342	.415	116	7	32	.990	2 102 92	1b158		0.5
1912	Cin N	148	558	73	164	32	12	2	85	48	2	28	.294	.352	.405	110	7	23	.985	2 107 90	1b147		0.5
1913	Cin N	137	502	59	143	23	7	3	62	35	2	26	.285	.334	.376	103	1	18-12	.988	-5 82 105	1b134		-0.7
1914	Cin N	78	248	31	52	8	4	0	26	26	1	26	.210	.287	.298	72	-9	7	.988	-4 74 107	1b75		-1.7
	Bos A	69	229	31	73	10	3	0	33	19	6	21	.319	.386	.389	133	10	12-12	.979	-5 74 80	1b68		0.1
1915	†Bos A	124	399	54	113	15	12	2	61	38	4	26	.283	.351	.396	128	12	9-14	.987	-1 95 100	1b117		0.6
1916	†Bos A	130	417	57	108	17	1	0	39	47	3	28	.259	.338	.305	93	-2	10	.989	-8 93 97	1b118		-0.7
1917	Bos A	120	420	49	108	19	7	1	47	46	4	22	.257	.336	.343	108	1	9	.990	-8 73 97	1b118		-0.7
1918	Bos A	25	69	4	11	3	0	0	4	8	2	9	.159	.266	.174	33	-5	3	.996	1 118 171	1b19		-0.5
Total	11	1318	4706	591	1310	194	88	27	593	407	38	256	.278	.341	.374	111	60	173-38	.987	-28 91 96	1b1284,2b7		-0.5

HOBSON, BUTCH   Clell Lavern   B8.17.1951 Tuscaloosa AL   BR/TR/6-1/193*   [BosA73 8/185]   d9.7   M3   Col Alabama

YEAR	TM LG	G	AB	R	H	2B	3B	HR	RBI	BB-IB	HP	SO	AVG	OBP	SLG	AOPS	ABR	SB-CS	FA	FR·RNG	THR	GAMES AT POSITION	DL	BFW
1975	Bos A	2	4	1	1	0	0	0	0	0-0	0	2	.250	.250	.250	38	0	0-0	1.000	0 131	0	/3		0.0
1976	Bos A	76	269	34	63	7	5	8	34	15-1	0	62	.234	.272	.387	83	-7	0-1	.936	-6 97 87	3b76		-1.5
1977	Bos A	159	593	77	157	33	5	30	112	27-4	4	162	.265	.300	.489	100	-2	5-4	.946	-18 88 92	3b159		-2.3
1978	Bos A	147	512	65	128	26	2	17	80	50-3	0	122	.250	.312	.408	93	-5	1-0	.899	-8 98 98	3b133,D14		-1.5
1979	Bos A	146	528	74	138	26	1	28	93	30-2	0	78	.261	.298	.496	105	1	3-2	.935	-16 90 64	3b142/2		-1.8
1980	Bos A	93	324	35	74	6	0	11	39	25-2	0	69	.228	.281	.349	69	-15	1-1	.910	1 107 46	3b57,D36	30	-1.6
1981	Cal A	85	268	27	63	7	4	4	36	15-1	0	60	.235	.321	.336	90	-3	1-1	.929	-6 87 92	3b83,D2		-1.1
1982	NY A	30	58	2	10	2	0	0	3	1-0	0	14	.172	.183	.207	8	-7	0-0	.951	-1 76 78	D15,1b11	19	-0.9
Total	8	738	2556	314	634	107	23	98	397	183-12	5	569	.248	.297	.423	91	-38	11-9	.926	-53 93 83	3b651,D67,1b11/2	49	-10.7

YEAR	TM LG	G	AB	R	H	2B	3B	HR	RBI	BB-IB	HP	SO	AVG	OBP	SLG	AOPS	ABR	SB-CS	FA	FR	RNG	THR	GAMES AT POSITION	DL	BFW

HOCK, ED   Edward Francis   B3.27.1899 Franklin Furnace OH   D11.21.1963 Portsmouth OH   BL/TL/5-10.5/165   d7.8

1920	StL N	1	0	0	0	0	0	0	0	0	0	—	—	—	—	0	0-0	—	-0	0	0	/OL		0.0
1923	Cin N	2	0	0	0	0	0	0	0	0	0	—	—	—	—	0	0-0	—	0			/R		0.0
1924	Cin N	16	10	7	1	0	0	0	0	1	1	2	.100	.182	.100	-23	-2	0-0	1.000	0	178	0	O2(1/2/0)		-0.1
Total	3	19	10	7	1	0	0	0	0	1	1	2	.100	.182	.100	-23	-2	0-0	1.000	0	164	0	O3(2/2/0)		-0.1

HOCKETT, ORIS   Oris Leon "Brown"   B9.29.1909 Amboy IN   D3.23.1969 Torrance CA   BL/TR/5-9/182   d9.4

1938	Bro N	21	70	8	23	5	1	1	8	4	0	9	.329	.365	.471	126	2	0	.893	-2	75	91	O17(4/13/0)		0.0
1939	Bro N	9	13	3	3	0	0	0	1	1	0	1	.231	.286	.231	39	-1	0	1.000	-1	41	1401	/OL		-0.1
1941	Cle A	2	6	0	2	0	0	0	1	2	0	0	.333	.500	.333	131	1	0-0	1.000	-1	56	0	O2C		0.0
1942	Cle A	148	601	85	150	22	7	7	48	45	3	45	.250	.305	.344	88	-13	12-12	.980	-3	94	109	O145(0/2/144)		-2.6
1943	Cle A	141	601	70	166	33	4	2	51	45	4	45	.276	.331	.354	107	4	13-18	.960	-4	95	113	O139(35/81/26)		-1.0
1944	Cle A☆	124	457	47	132	29	5	1	50	35	0	27	.289	.339	.381	110	5	8-9	.986	-6	96	58	O110(45/65/1)		-0.7
1945	Chi A	106	417	46	122	23	4	2	55	27	3	30	.293	.340	.381	112	6	10-9	.982	-2	98	79	O106C		-0.1
Total	7	551	2165	259	598	112	21	13	214	159	10	157	.276	.329	.365	103	4	43-48	.974	-16	95	96	O520(85/269/171)		-4.5

HOCKING, DENNY   Dennis Lee   B4.2.1970 Torrance CA   BB/TR (BR 1998p)/5-10/183(174-188)   [MinA89 52/1314]   d9.10   Col El Camino (CA) JC   OF(85/51/101)

1993	Min A	15	36	7	5	1	0	0	0	6-0	0	8	.139	.262	.167	18	-4	1-0	.971	-1	79	169	S12/2		-0.4
1994	Min A	11	31	3	10	3	0	0	2	0-0	0	4	.323	.323	.419	89	-1	2-0	1.000	-1	100	116	S10		0.0
1995	Min A	9	25	4	5	0	2	0	3	2-1	0	2	.200	.259	.360	59	-2	1-0	.971	-1	110	116	S6		0.0
1996	Min A	49	127	16	25	6	0	1	10	8-0	0	24	.197	.243	.268	29	-14	3-3	.985	1	99	183	O33R,S6,2b2/1D	98	-1.4
1997	Min A	115	253	28	65	12	4	2	26	18-0	1	51	.257	.308	.360	72	-11	3-5	.975	3	90	130	S44,3b39,O20(7/2/12),2b15/1D		-0.4
1998	Min A	110	198	32	40	6	1	3	15	16-1	0	44	.202	.259	.288	42	-18	2-1	1.000	-6	99	88	2b47,S28,O24(17/1/7),3b11,1b2,D2		-2.1
1999	Min A	136	386	47	103	18	2	7	41	22-1	3	54	.267	.307	.378	71	-18	11-7	.987	-9	84	87	S61,2b56,O38(17/11/13),3b6,1b2		-2.1
2000	Min A	134	373	52	111	24	4	4	47	48-1	0	77	.298	.373	.416	94	-2	7-5	1.000	-4	97	261	O51(16/21/19),2b47,3b16,S15,1b12/D		-0.4
2001	Min A	112	327	34	82	16	3	2	25	29-1	2	67	.251	.315	.339	69	-14	6-1	.983	-3	93	105	S47,2b17,O16(6/5/5),1b11,3b6,D9		-1.4
2002	†Min A	102	260	28	65	13	0	2	25	24-0	1	44	.250	.310	.323	68	-12	0-2	.963	-15	91	82	2b56,S25,3b16,1b6,O6(0/1/4)		-2.3
2003	†Min A	83	188	22	45	10	2	3	22	15-0	0	37	.239	.291	.362	70	-8	0-1	1.000	-1	90	93	2b25,3b24,S17,1b10,O8(2/2/4),D2	17	-0.8
2004	Col N	55	94	7	19	2	0	0	4	7-0	0	20	.202	.257	.223	23	-11	0-1	.975	5	162	0	O30(20/8/4),S13,2b8,3b2		-0.5
2005	KC A	23	60	14	16	1	0	0	5	10-0	0	10	.267	.371	.283	83	-1	0-1	.976	6	120	123	2b13/3S		0.5
Total	13	954	2358	294	591	112	17	25	226	205-5	7	442	.251	.310	.344	67	-116	36-27	.983	-21	91	94	2b287,S285,O225R,3b121,1b45,D16	115	-11.3

HODAPP, JOHNNY   Urban John   B9.26.1905 Cincinnati OH   D6.14.1980 Cincinnati OH   BR/TR/6-0/185   d8.19

1925	Cle A	37	130	12	31	5	1	0	14	11	0	7	.238	.298	.292	50	-10	2-3	.960	-2	109	98	3b37		-0.6
1926	Cle A	3	5	0	1	0	0	0	0	0	0	1	.200	.200	.200	5	-1	0-0	.750	-1	73	0	3b3		-0.1
1927	Cle A	79	240	25	73	15	3	5	40	14	0	23	.304	.343	.454	105	1	2-2	.935	1	108	120	3b67,1b4		0.4
1928	Cle A	116	449	51	145	31	6	2	73	20	0	20	.323	.352	.432	104	2	2-1	.944	2	109	102	3b101,1b13		0.9
1929	Cle A	90	294	30	96	12	7	4	51	15	1	14	.327	.361	.456	105	1	3-3	.977	8	115	68	2b72		1.0
1930	Cle A	154	635	111	225	51	8	9	121	32	1	29	.354	.386	.502	119	18	6-5	.970	10	106	97	2b154		2.9
1931	Cle A	122	468	71	138	19	4	2	56	27	2	23	.295	.336	.365	80	-14	1-5	.969	15	110	95	2b121		0.8
1932	Cle A	7	16	2	2	0	0	0	0	0	0	2	.125	.125	.188	-19	-3	0-0	1.000	-1	97	0	2b7		-0.3
	Chi A	68	176	21	40	8	0	3	20	11	0	3	.227	.273	.324	58	-12	1-0	.967	-5	94	0	O31(29/0/2),2b5,3b4		-1.6
	Year	75	192	23	42	9	0	3	20	11	0	5	.219	.261	.313	51	-15	1-0	.967	-6	94	0	O31(29/0/2),2b12,3b4		-1.9
1933	Bos N	115	413	55	129	27	5	3	54	33	1	14	.312	.365	.424	109	6	1-1	.960	-0	99	100	2b101,1b10		1.1
Total	9	791	2826	378	880	169	34	28	429	163	5	136	.311	.350	.425	98	-12	18-20	.967	32	106	92	2b460,3b212,O31(29/0/2),1b27		4.3

HODERLEIN, MEL   Melvin Anthony   B6.26.1923 Mt.Carmel OH   D5.21.2001 Mt.Carmel OH   BB/TR/5-10/185*   d8.16

1951	Bos A	9	14	1	5	1	0	1	6	1	0	2	.357	.550	.571	185	2	0-1	1.000	0	87	217	2b3,3b3		0.2
1952	Was A	72	208	16	56	8	2	0	17	18	2	22	.269	.333	.327	87	-4	2-0	.978	-6	97	100	2b58		-0.7
1953	Was A	23	47	5	9	0	0	0	5	6	0	9	.191	.283	.191	31	-5	0-0	.953	-2	96	97	2b11,S2		-0.5
1954	Was A	14	25	0	4	1	0	0	1	1	0	4	.160	.192	.200	8	-3	0-0	.939	0	106	123	S6,2b5		-0.3
Total	4	118	294	22	74	10	3	0	24	31	2	37	.252	.327	.306	78	-10	2-1	.973	-8	97	103	2b77,S8,3b3		-1.3

HODES, CHARLIE   Charles   B1848 New York NY   D2.14.1875 Brooklyn NY   TR/5-11.5/175   d5.8

1871	Chi NA	28	130	32	36	4	1	2	25	7		0	.277	.314	.369	86	-4	3-0	.796	3			C20,3b10,O4(0/3/1)/S		0.0
1872	Tro NA	13	62	17	15	3	0	0	10	1		0	.242	.254	.290	66	-2	0-0	.759	-0	108	0	S5,O4C,C3/3		-0.2
1874	Atl NA	21	81	8	12	3	0	0	7	0		2	.148	.148	.185	7	-7	0-0	.825	-4	40	0	O18(0/13/5),C3,2b3/1		-0.9
Total	3 NA	62	273	57	63	10	1	2	42	8		2	.231	.253	.297	63	-13	3-0	.820	-2			O26(0/20/6),C26,3b11,S6,2b3/1		-1.1

HODGE, GOMER   Harold Morris   B4.3.1944 Rutherfordton NC   BB/TR/6-2/185   d4.6

| 1971 | Cle A | 80 | 83 | 3 | 17 | 3 | 1 | 0 | 9 | 4-1 | 2 | 19 | .205 | .256 | .277 | 47 | -6 | 0-0 | 1.000 | -1 | 63 | 132 | 1b3,3b3,2b2 | | -0.7 |

HODGES, BERT   Edward Burton   B5.25.1917 Knoxville TN   D1.8.2001 Knoxville TN   BL/TR/5-11/170   d4.14

| 1942 | Phi N | 8 | 11 | 0 | 2 | 0 | 0 | 0 | 1 | 0 | 0 | 2 | .182 | .250 | .182 | 29 | -1 | 0 | 1.000 | -0 | 91 | 0 | 3b2 | | -0.1 |

HODGES, GIL   Gilbert Raymond (b Gilbert Ray Hodge)   B4.4.1924 Princeton IN   D4.2.1972 West Palm Beach FL   BR/TR/6-1.5/200*   d10.3   Mil 1944-45 M9 Col St. Josephs (IN)

1943	Bro N	1	2	0	0	0	0	0	0	1	0	2	.000	.333	.000	0	0	1	.600	-0	82	438	/3		-0.1
1947	†Bro N	28	77	9	12	3	1	1	7	14	0	19	.156	.286	.260	44	-6	0	.958	-1	97	153	C24		-0.6
1948	Bro N	134	481	48	120	18	5	11	70	43	0	61	.249	.311	.376	82	-13	7	.986	-2	92	114	1b96,C38		-1.6
1949	†Bro N★	156	596	94	170	23	4	23	115	66	4	64	.285	.360	.453	112	10	10	.995	-4	82	114	1b156		0.0
1950	Bro N☆	153	561	98	159	26	2	32	113	73	1	73	.283	.367	.508	125	20	6	.994	-1	92	114	1b153		1.4
1951	Bro N★	158	582	118	156	25	3	40	103	93	5	99	.268	.374	.527	137	31	9-7	.992	7	111	120	1b158		3.2
1952	†Bro N☆	153	508	87	129	27	1	32	102	107	2	90	.254	.386	.500	142	33	2-4	.992	4	106	114	1b153		3.1
1953	†Bro N★	141	520	101	157	22	7	31	122	75	3	84	.302	.393	.550	139	31	1-4	.993	7	115	108	1b127,O24(18/0/6)		2.7
1954	Bro N★	154	579	106	176	23	5	42	130	74	1	84	.304	.373	.579	142	35	3-3	.995	7	109	94	1b154		3.1
1955	†Bro N★	150	546	75	158	24	5	27	102	80-3	3	91	.289	.377	.500	128	24	2-1	.991	2	106	112	1b139,O16(9/1/6)		1.8
1956	†Bro N★	153	550	86	146	29	4	32	87	76-10	2	87	.265	.354	.507	119	16	3-3	.992	1	104	112	1b138,O30(22/0/8)/C		0.7
1957	Bro N★	150	579	94	173	28	7	27	98	63-6	2	91	.299	.366	.511	122	19	5-3	.990	3	103	99	1b150,3b2/2		1.3
1958	LA N	141	475	68	123	15	1	22	64	52-3	0	87	.259	.334	.434	98	-2	8-2	.992	3	100	130	1b122,3b15,O9(4/0/5)/C		-0.4
1959	†LA N★	124	413	57	114	19	2	25	80	58-6	3	92	.276	.367	.513	123	14	3-2	.992	-0	91	88	1b113,3b4		0.9
1960	LA N	101	197	22	39	8	1	8	30	26-1	1	37	.198	.291	.371	76	-7	0-1	.995	1	92	106	1b92,3b10		-1.0
1961	LA N	109	215	25	52	4	0	8	31	24-1	0	43	.242	.323	.372	76	-8	3-1	.998	-0	85	83	1b100		-1.1
1962	NY N	54	127	15	32	1	0	9	17	15-1	0	27	.252	.331	.472	111	2	0-0	.986	2	140	74	1b47		0.3
1963	NY N	11	22	2	5	0	0	0	3	2	0	6	.227	.320	.227	60	-1	0-0	1.000	2	185	129	1b10	14	0.0
Total	18	2071	7030	1105	1921	295	48	370	1274	943-31	25	1137	.273	.359	.487	119	198	63-31	.992	32	101	108	1b1908,O79(53/1/25),C64,3b32/2	73	13.7

HODGES, RON   Ronald Wray   B6.22.1949 Rocky Mount VA   BL/TR/6-1/185*   [NYN72*S2/47]   d6.13   Col Appalachian St.

1973	†NY N	45	127	5	33	2	0	1	18	11-2	0	19	.260	.314	.299	73	-5	0-1	.992	2	156	86	C40		-0.1
1974	NY N	59	136	16	30	4	0	4	14	19-3	1	11	.221	.310	.338	84	-3	0-0	.953	-7	81	63	C44		-0.8
1975	NY N	9	34	3	7	1	0	2	4	1-0	0	6	.206	.229	.412	77	-1	0-0	1.000	-1	79	137	C9		-0.2
1976	NY N	56	155	21	35	6	0	4	24	27-2	0	16	.226	.339	.342	99	-8	0-0	.976	-8	119	72	C52	15	-0.5
1977	NY N	66	117	6	31	4	0	1	9	9-1	0	17	.265	.317	.325	75	-4	0-2	.992	-2	82	122	C27		-0.6
1978	NY N	47	102	9	26	4	1	0	7	10-0	1	11	.255	.322	.314	82	-2	1-2	.982	9	82	152	C30		0.1
1979	NY N	59	86	4	14	4	0	0	5	19-3	0	16	.163	.311	.209	47	-5	0-0	.980	-0	99	137	C22		-0.5
1980	NY N	36	42	4	10	2	0	0	5	10-0	0	13	.238	.377	.286	91	0	1-1	.982	-2	88	196	C9	93	0.3
1981	NY N	35	43	5	13	2	0	1	6	5-2	1	6	.302	.375	.419	125	2	1-0	1.000	-2	56	102	C7		0.0
1982	NY N	80	228	26	56	12	1	5	27	41-6	0	40	.246	.358	.373	105	3	4-3	.980	9	96	100	C74		0.7
1983	NY N	110	250	20	65	12	0	0	21	49-6	2	42	.260	.383	.308	95	2	0-3	.971	-9	86	93	C96		-0.5
1984	NY N	64	106	5	22	3	0	1	11	23-0	1	18	.208	.351	.264	77	-1	1-1	.979	-1	81	99	C35		-0.2
Total	12	666	1426	119	342	56	2	19	147	224-26	4	217	.240	.342	.322	88	-14	10-13	.978	-22	97	99	C445	108	-2.3

HODGIN, RALPH   Elmer Ralph   B2.10.1916 Greensboro NC   BL/TR/5-10/170   d4.19   Mil 1945

1939	Bos N	32	48	4	10	1	0	0	4	7	0	4	.208	.255	.229	33	-5	0	1.000	-0	108	0	O9(2/0/7)		-0.5
1943	Chi A	117	407	52	128	22	8	1	50	20	6	24	.314	.356	.415	125	11	3-5	.945	-2	111	70	3b56,O42(17/0/25)		0.7
1944	Chi A	121	465	56	137	25	7	1	65	23	6	11	.295	.333	.385	106	2	3-1	.942	7	112	143	3b82,Q33L		0.9
1946	Chi A	87	258	32	65	10	1	0	25	19	2	6	.252	.308	.298	73	-10	0-1	.983	-2	93	73	O57(49/0/8)		-1.7

YEAR	TM LG	G	AB	R	H	2B	3B	HR	RBI	BB-IB	HP	SO	AVG	OBP	SLG	AOPS	ABR	SB-CS	FA	FR	RNG	THR	GAMES AT POSITION	DL	BFW
1947	Chi A	59	180	26	53	10	3	1	24	13	3	4	.294	.352	.400	113	3	1-0	.990	0	103	66	O41(40/0/1)	64	0.0
1948	Chi A	114	331	28	88	11	5	1	34	21	0	11	.266	.310	.338	75	-14	0-3	.970	3	102	146	O79(39/2/40)		-1.6
Total 6		530	1689	198	481	79	24	4	188	97	17	63	.285	.330	.367	98	-13	7-10	.985	6	102	86	O261(180/2/81),3b138	64	-2.2

HODGSON, PAUL Paul Joseph Denis B4.14.1960 Montreal QC, Can. BR/TR/6-2/190 d8.31

YEAR	TM LG	G	AB	R	H	2B	3B	HR	RBI	BB-IB	HP	SO	AVG	OBP	SLG	AOPS	ABR	SB-CS	FA	FR	RNG	THR	GAMES AT POSITION	DL	BFW
1980	Tor A	20	41	5	9	0	1	1	5	3-0		12	.220	.273	.341	65	-2	0-1	1.000	-1	80	126	O11(10/1/0),D3		-0.4

HOELSKOETTER, ART Arthur "Holley","Hoss" (aka Arthur H. Hostetter) B9.30.1882 St.Louis MO D8.3.1954 St.Louis MO BR/TR/6-2/? d9.10 OF(1/7/13) ▲

YEAR	TM LG	G	AB	R	H	2B	3B	HR	RBI	BB-IB	HP	SO	AVG	OBP	SLG	AOPS	ABR	SB-CS	FA	FR	RNG	THR	GAMES AT POSITION	DL	BFW
1905	StL N	24	83	7	20	2	1	0	5	3	0		.241	.267	.289	68	-4	1	.972	1	108	128	3b20,2b3/P		-0.2
1906	StL N	94	317	21	71	6	3	0	14	4	2		.224	.238	.262	58	-17	2	.943	-0	110	113	3b53,S16,P12,O12(1/1/11)/2		-1.6
1907	StL N	119	397	21	98	6	3	2	28	27	2		.247	.298	.292	88	-6	5	.927	2	109	96	2b73,1b27,C8,O8(0/6/2),P2,3b2		-0.4
1908	StL N	62	155	10	36	7	1	0	6	6	1		.232	.265	.290	81	-4	1	.948	-6	67	112	C41,3b2/12		-0.6
Total 4		299	952	59	225	21	8	2	53	40	5		.236	.271	.282	75	-31	9	.924	-2	94	94	2b78,3b77,C49,1b28,O20R,S16,P15		-2.8

HOEY, JACK John Bernard B11.10.1881 Watertown MA D11.14.1947 Waterbury CT BL/TL/5-9/185 d6.27 Col Holy Cross

YEAR	TM LG	G	AB	R	H	2B	3B	HR	RBI	BB-IB	HP	SO	AVG	OBP	SLG	AOPS	ABR	SB-CS	FA	FR	RNG	THR	GAMES AT POSITION	DL	BFW
1906	Bos A	94	361	27	88	8	4	0	24	14	1		.244	.274	.288	76	-11	10	.915	-7	59	0	O94L		-2.6
1907	Bos A	39	96	7	21	2	1	0	8	1	0		.219	.227	.260	56	-5	2	.857	-4	0	0	O21(17/4/0)		-1.1
1908	Bos A	13	43	5	7	0	0	0	3	0	0		.163	.163	.163	6	-5	1	1.000	1	189	0	O11R		-0.5
Total 3		146	500	39	116	10	5	0	35	15	1		.232	.256	.272	66	-21	13	.913	-10	60	0	O126(111/4/11)		-4.2

HOFFERTH, STEW Stewart Edward B1.27.1913 Logansport IN D3.7.1994 Valparaiso IN BR/TR/6-2/195 d4.19

YEAR	TM LG	G	AB	R	H	2B	3B	HR	RBI	BB-IB	HP	SO	AVG	OBP	SLG	AOPS	ABR	SB-CS	FA	FR	RNG	THR	GAMES AT POSITION	DL	BFW
1944	Bos N	66	180	14	36	8	0	1	26	11	0	5	.200	.246	.261	41	-14	0	.984	-1	63	112	C47		-1.3
1945	Bos N	50	170	13	40	2	0	3	15	14	1	11	.235	.297	.300	66	-8	1	.980	4	102	140	C45		-0.1
1946	Bos N	20	58	3	12	1	1	0	10	3	0	6	.207	.246	.259	43	-5	0	1.000	-1	78	48	C15		-0.6
Total 3		136	408	30	88	11	1	4	51	28	1	22	.216	.268	.277	52	-27	1	.985	2	82	115	C107		-2.0

HOFFMAN, DUTCH Clarence Casper "Red" B1.28.1904 Freeburg IL D12.6.1962 Belleville IL BR/TR/6-0/175 d4.23

YEAR	TM LG	G	AB	R	H	2B	3B	HR	RBI	BB-IB	HP	SO	AVG	OBP	SLG	AOPS	ABR	SB-CS	FA	FR	RNG	THR	GAMES AT POSITION	DL	BFW
1929	Chi A	107	337	27	87	16	5	3	37	24	0	28	.258	.307	.362	73	-15	6-3	.984	-0	106	45	O88(2/74/12)		-1.8

HOFFMAN, DANNY Daniel John B3.2.1880 Canton CT D3.14.1922 Manchester CT BL/TL/5-9/175 d4.20

YEAR	TM LG	G	AB	R	H	2B	3B	HR	RBI	BB-IB	HP	SO	AVG	OBP	SLG	AOPS	ABR	SB-CS	FA	FR	RNG	THR	GAMES AT POSITION	DL	BFW
1903	Phi A	74	248	29	61	5	7	2	22	6	1		.246	.267	.347	79	-7	7	.950	-0	57	0	O62(43/0/19)/P		-1.2
1904	Phi A	53	204	31	61	7	5	3	24	5	4		.299	.329	.426	131	6	9	.936	-0	87	70	O51(14/14/23)		0.4
1905	†Phi A	120	459	66	120	10	10	1	35	33	1		.261	.312	.333	103	0	46	.942	-3	93	141	O118(14/102/2)		-1.0
1906	Phi A	7	22	4	5	0	0	0	3	0	0		.227	.320	.227	70	-1	1	1.000	3	240	0	O7C		-1.1
	NY A	100	320	34	82	10	6	0	23	27	2		.256	.318	.325	92	-3	32	.938	-3	67	46	O98C		-1.1
	Year	107	342	38	87	10	6	0	23	30	2		.254	.318	.319	91	-3	33	.943	-3	80	43	O105C		-0.4
1907	NY A	136	517	81	131	10	3	5	46	42	13		.253	.325	.313	96	-1	30	.953	4	116	90	O135C		0.6
1908	StL A	99	363	41	91	9	7	1	25	23	5		.251	.304	.322	103	1	17	.962	9	168	270	O99(6/46/47)		1.0
1909	StL A	110	387	44	104	6	7	2	26	41	7		.269	.349	.336	125	12	24	.968	1	75	194	O110(0/109/1)		1.0
1910	StL A	106	380	20	90	11	5	0	27	34	4		.237	.306	.292	93	-3	16	.960	-2	97	92	O106(0/102/4)		-1.1
1911	StL A	24	81	11	17	3	2	0	7	12	2		.210	.326	.296	77	-2	3	.908	2	113	145	O23C		-0.2
Total 9		829	2981	361	762	71	52	14	235	226	39		.256	.316	.328	101	2	185	.951	8	100	122	O809(77/636/96)/P		-3.0

HOFFMAN, TEX Edward Adolph B11.30.1893 San Antonio TX D5.19.1947 New Orleans LA BL/TR/5-9/195 d7.11

YEAR	TM LG	G	AB	R	H	2B	3B	HR	RBI	BB-IB	HP	SO	AVG	OBP	SLG	AOPS	ABR	SB-CS	FA	FR	RNG	THR	GAMES AT POSITION	DL	BFW
1915	Cle A	9	13	1	2	0	0	0	5	1			.154	.214	.154	10	-1	0	.750	-1	59	0	3b3		-0.3

HOFFMAN, GLENN Glenn Edward B7.7.1958 Orange CA BR/TR/6-2/190* [BosA76 2/46] d4.12 M1/C7 b-Trevor

YEAR	TM LG	G	AB	R	H	2B	3B	HR	RBI	BB-IB	HP	SO	AVG	OBP	SLG	AOPS	ABR	SB-CS	FA	FR	RNG	THR	GAMES AT POSITION	DL	BFW
1980	Bos A	114	312	37	89	15	4	4	42	19-2	2	41	.285	.326	.397	93	-3	2-4	.946	-3	103	85	3b110,S5,2b2		-0.8
1981	Bos A	78	242	28	56	10	0	1	20	12-0	1	25	.231	.271	.285	57	-14	0-1	.960	3	102	108	S78/3		-0.4
1982	Bos A	150	469	53	98	23	2	7	49	30-5	5	69	.209	.262	.311	54	-30	0-4	.972	16	104	112	S150		-0.1
1983	Bos A	143	473	56	123	24	1	4	41	30-1	2	76	.260	.306	.340	72	-18	1-1	.962	-6	96	93	S143		-0.9
1984	Bos A	64	74	8	14	4	0	0	4	5-0	0	10	.189	.241	.243	33	-7	0-1	.957	-1	88	99	S56,3b4,2b2		-0.8
1985	Bos A	96	279	40	77	17	2	6	34	25-0	1	40	.276	.343	.416	103	2	2-2	.975	5	99	115	S93,2b3,3b3	27	1.4
1986	Bos A	12	23	1	5	2	0	0	1	2-0	1	3	.217	.269	.304	59	-1	0-0	.923	-5	53	72	S11/3	76	-0.3
1987	Bos A	21	55	5	11	3	0	0	5	3-0	2	9	.200	.267	.255	38	-5	0-0	.984	2	122	103	S16,3b3,2b2		-0.1
	LA N	40	132	10	29	5	0	0	10	7-1	2	23	.220	.270	.258	42	-11	0-1	.966	-1	90	87	S40		-0.9
1989	Cal A	48	104	9	22	3	0	1	13	3-1	1	13	.212	.241	.269	44	-8	0-2	.982	-1	92	101	S23,3b18,2b4/1D		-0.8
Total 9		766	2163	247	524	106	9	23	210	136-9	20	309	.242	.291	.331	68	-95	5-16	.966	9	99	103	S615,3b140,2b13/D1	-103	-3.7

HOFFMAN, IZZY Harry C. B1.5.1875 Bridgeport NJ D11.13.1942 Philadelphia PA BL/TL/5-9/160 d4.14

YEAR	TM LG	G	AB	R	H	2B	3B	HR	RBI	BB-IB	HP	SO	AVG	OBP	SLG	AOPS	ABR	SB-CS	FA	FR	RNG	THR	GAMES AT POSITION	DL	BFW
1904	Was A	10	30	1	3	1	0	0	1	4			.100	.156	.133	-8	-4	0	1.000	1	110	365	O9C		-0.4
1907	Bos N	19	86	17	24	3	1	0	3	6	0		.279	.326	.337	108	1	2	.897	-2	143	133	O19(3/1/16)		-0.2
Total 2		29	116	18	27	4	1	0	4	8	0		.233	.282	.284	79	-3	2	.939	-1	133	201	O28(3/10/16)		-0.6

HOFFMAN, JOHN John Edward "Pork Chop" B10.31.1943 Aberdeen SD D12.27.2001 Seattle WA BL/TR/6-0/195* d7.30

YEAR	TM LG	G	AB	R	H	2B	3B	HR	RBI	BB-IB	HP	SO	AVG	OBP	SLG	AOPS	ABR	SB-CS	FA	FR	RNG	THR	GAMES AT POSITION	DL	BFW
1964	Hou N	6	15	1	1	0	0	0	0	1-0		7	.067	.125	.067	-47	-3	0-0	1.000	-2	38	0	C5		-0.5
1965	Hou N	2	6	1	2	0	0	0	1	0-0		3	.333	.333	.333	95	0	0-0	1.000	0	55	0	C2		0.0
Total 2		8	21	2	3	0	0	0	1	1-0		10	.143	.182	.143	-8	-3	0-0	1.000	-2	42	0	C7		-0.5

HOFFMAN, LARRY Lawrence Charles B7.18.1878 Chicago IL D12.29.1948 Chicago IL BR/TR/5-8/175 d7.4

YEAR	TM LG	G	AB	R	H	2B	3B	HR	RBI	BB-IB	HP	SO	AVG	OBP	SLG	AOPS	ABR	SB-CS	FA	FR	RNG	THR	GAMES AT POSITION	DL	BFW
1901	Chi N	6	22	2	7	1	0	0	6	0	1		.318	.348	.364	110	0	1	.800	-1	75	0	3b5/2		-0.1

HOFFMAN, HICKEY Otto Charles B10.27.1856 Cleveland OH D10.27.1915 Peoria IL d5.10

YEAR	TM LG	G	AB	R	H	2B	3B	HR	RBI	BB-IB	HP	SO	AVG	OBP	SLG	AOPS	ABR	SB-CS	FA	FR	RNG	THR	GAMES AT POSITION	DL	BFW
1879	Cle N	1	4	0	0	0	0	0		0			.000	.000	.000	-99	-1		.857	0			C2/OR		-0.1

HOFFMAN, RAY Raymond Lamont B6.14.1917 Detroit MI BL/TR/6-0.5/175 d8.30

YEAR	TM LG	G	AB	R	H	2B	3B	HR	RBI	BB-IB	HP	SO	AVG	OBP	SLG	AOPS	ABR	SB-CS	FA	FR	RNG	THR	GAMES AT POSITION	DL	BFW
1942	Was A	7	19	2	1	0	0	0	2	1		1	.053	.100	.053	-57	-4	0-0	.815	1	135	0	3b6		-0.4

HOFFMEISTER, JESSE Jesse H. B6.1872 Toledo OH D1.14.1933 Des Moines IA TR d7.24

YEAR	TM LG	G	AB	R	H	2B	3B	HR	RBI	BB-IB	HP	SO	AVG	OBP	SLG	AOPS	ABR	SB-CS	FA	FR	RNG	THR	GAMES AT POSITION	DL	BFW
1897	Pit N	48	188	33	58	6	9	3	36	8	0		.309	.337	.484	120	3	6	.792	-10	82	129	3b48		-0.5

HOFMAN, SOLLY Arthur Frederick "Circus Solly" B10.29.1882 St.Louis MO D3.10.1956 St.Louis MO BR/TR/6-0/160 d7.28 OF(77/557/79)

YEAR	TM LG	G	AB	R	H	2B	3B	HR	RBI	BB-IB	HP	SO	AVG	OBP	SLG	AOPS	ABR	SB-CS	FA	FR	RNG	THR	GAMES AT POSITION	DL	BFW
1903	Pit N	3	2	1	0	0	0	0	0	0	0		.000	.000	.000	-97	-1	0	—	-0	0	0	O2(1/1/0)		-0.1
1904	Chi N	7	26	7	7	0	0	1	4	1	0		.269	.296	.385	110	0	2	1.000	0	296	560	O6(1/3/2)/S		0.0
1905	Chi N	86	287	43	68	14	4	1	38	20	1		.237	.289	.324	79	-8	15	.955	2	99	81	2b59,1b9,S9,S9,3b3,3b03(0/2/1)		-0.6
1906	†Chi N	64	195	30	50	2	3	2	20	20	1		.256	.326	.328	98	-1	13	.976	-1	84	205	O23(1/17/6),1b21,S9,2b4,3b4		-0.2
1907	Chi N	134	470	67	126	11	3	1	36	41	3		.268	.328	.311	94	-3	29	.938	-3	126	170	O69(12/23/35),S42,1b18,3b4,2b3		-0.9
1908	†Chi N	120	411	55	100	15	5	2	42	33	6		.243	.309	.319	96	-1	15	.955	-3	128	65	O50(0/50/2),1b37,2b22,3b9		-0.9
1909	Chi N	153	527	60	150	21	4	2	58	53	1		.285	.351	.351	115	10	20	.965	-2	71	115	O153(0/143/11)		0.1
1910	†Chi N	136	477	83	155	24	16	3	86	65	34		.325	.406	.461	154	33	29	.975	-0	97	124	O110(0/110/1),1b24/3		2.8
1911	Chi N	143	512	66	129	17	2	2	70	66	3		.252	.341	.305	81	-11	30	.968	-11	89	67	O107(2/107/0),1b36		-3.0
1912	Chi N	36	125	28	34	11	0	0	18	22	1	13	.272	.385	.360	105	2	5	.987	2	99	158	O27C,1b9		0.2
	Pit N	17	53	7	15	4	1	0	2	5	0	6	.283	.345	.396	104	0	0	1.000	2	113	153	O15C		0.1
	Year	53	178	35	49	15	1	0	20	27	1	19	.275	.374	.371	105	3	5	.991	3	104	150	O42C,1b9		0.3
1913	Pit N	28	83	11	19	5	2	0	7	8	1	6	.229	.297	.337	84	-2	3-3	.951	-0	96	92	3b11,1b22,O21(10/10/1)/S		-0.2
1914	Bro F	147	515	65	148	26	12	5	83	54	2	41	.287	.357	.412	110	-1	34	.961	3	91	157	O82(46/20/18),1b11,3b4,2b2/S		-2.5
1915	Buf F	109	346	29	81	10	6	0	27	30	1	28	.234	.295	.298	66	-21	12	.961	3	91	157	O6C		0.1
1916	NY A	6	27	0	8	3	1	0	2	1	0	2	.296	.321	.407	116	0	1	1.000	1	107	206	O4L		0.2
	Chi N	5	16	2	5	1	0	0	2	2	0	2	.313	.389	.563	172	1	0	1.000	0	89	234	O4C		0.2
Total 14		1194	4072	554	1095	162	60	19	495	421	15	171	.269	.340	.352	102	-3	208-3	.967	-10	98	128	O702C,2b198,1b187,S63,3b25		-5.2

HOFMAN, BOBBY Robert George B10.5.1925 St.Louis MO D4.5.1994 Chesterfield MO BR/TR/5-11/175(170-185) d4.19 C10

YEAR	TM LG	G	AB	R	H	2B	3B	HR	RBI	BB-IB	HP	SO	AVG	OBP	SLG	AOPS	ABR	SB-CS	FA	FR	RNG	THR	GAMES AT POSITION	DL	BFW
1949	NY N	19	48	4	10	0	0	3	5	1	6		.208	.296	.208	38	-4	0	.939	0	119	103	2b16		-0.3
1952	NY N	32	63	11	18	2	2	4	8	1	10		.286	.375	.476	134	3	0-0	.964	-0	104	93	2b21,3b2/1		0.4
1953	NY N	74	169	21	45	7	2	12	34	12	1	23	.266	.315	.544	117	3	1-1	.918	-3	123	2b17	3b23,2b17		-0.4
1954	NY N	71	125	12	28	5	0	8	30	17	1	15	.224	.317	.456	99	0	0-0	.994	-5	51	140	1b21,2b10,3b8		-0.1
1955	NY N	96	207	32	55	7	2	10	28	22-2	1	31	.266	.336	.464	110	3	0-2	1.000	-3	69	101	1b24,C19,2b19,3b5		-0.1
1956	NY N	47	56	1	10	1	0	0	2	6-0	1	8	.179	.270	.196	28	-6	0-0	1.000	0	135	0	C7,3b7,1b3,2b2		-0.4

YEAR	TM LG	G	AB	R	H	2B	3B	HR	RBI	BB-IB	HP	SO	AVG	OBP	SLG	AOPS	ABR	SB-CS	FA	FR	RNG	THR	GAMES AT POSITION	DL	BFW
1957	NY N	2	2	0	0	0	0	0	0	0-0	0	1	.000	.000	.000	-99	-1	0-0	—	0			/H		-0.1
Total	7	341	670	81	166	22	6	32	101	70-2	5	94	.248	.322	.442	100	-2	1-3	.969	-7	104	93	2b85,1b49,3b45,C26		-0.7

HOFMANN, FRED Fred "Bootnose" B6.10.1894 St.Louis MO D11.19.1964 St.Helena CA BR/TR/5-11.5/175 d9.26 C13

1919	NY A	1	1	0	0	0	0	0	0	0-0	0	0	.000	.000	.000	-99	0	0-0	1.000	0	0	446	/C		0.0
1920	NY A	15	24	3	7	0	0	0	1	1-0	1	2	.292	.346	.292	68	0	0-0	.905	-2	84	33	C14		-0.3
1921	NY A	23	62	7	11	1	1	1	5	5-0	1	13	.177	.250	.274	33	-7	0-0	.952	-1	110	81	C18/1		-0.6
1922	NY A	37	91	13	27	5	3	2	10	9-0	0	12	.297	.360	.484	116	2	0-0	.962	-2	133	60	C29		-0.6
1923	†NY A	72	238	24	69	10	4	3	26	18-0	4	27	.290	.350	.403	96	-2	2-1	.979	-3	124	55	C70		0.1
1924	NY A	62	166	17	29	6	1	1	11	12-0	2	15	.175	.239	.241	24	-20	2-1	.991	2	111	112	C54		-1.4
1925	NY A	3	2	0	0	0	0	0	0	0-0	0	0	.000	.000	.000	-99	-1	0-0	1.000	0	0	930	/C		-0.1
1927	Bos A	87	217	20	59	19	1	0	24	21-0	2	26	.272	.342	.369	86	-4	2-0	.943	-10	66	77	C81		-0.8
1928	Bos A	78	199	14	45	8	1	0	16	11-0	1	25	.226	.270	.276	45	-16	0-1	.982	-1	82	135	C71		-1.3
Total	9	378	1000	98	247	49	11	7	93	77-0	11	120	.247	.308	.339	68	-49	6-3	.969	-16	98	89	C339/1		-4.4

HOGAN, HARRY Harry Sweet B11.1.1876 Syracuse NY D1.24.1934 Syracuse NY d8.13

1901	Cle A	1	4	0	0	0	0	0	0	0-0	0		.000	.000	.000	-99	-1	0-0	—	-0	0	0	/OR		-0.1

HOGAN, SHANTY James Francis B3.21.1906 Somerville MA D4.7.1967 Boston MA BR/TR/6-1/240 d6.23

1925	Bos N	9	21	2	6	1	0	0	3	1-0	0	3	.286	.318	.429	97	0	0-0	1.000	-0	98	0	O5(2/0/3)		-0.1
1926	Bos N	4	14	1	4	1	0	1	5	0-0	0	0	.286	.286	.500	119	0	0-0	.852	-1	76	113	C4		0.0
1927	Bos N	71	229	24	66	17	1	3	32	9-0	3	23	.288	.324	.410	104	1	2	.985	1	99	128	C61		0.6
1928	NY N	131	411	48	137	25	2	10	71	42-0	8	25	.333	.406	.477	129	19	0	.978	-3	140	56	C124		2.3
1929	NY N	102	317	19	95	13	0	5	45	25-0	6	22	.300	.362	.388	86	-6	1	.979	1	139	52	C93		0.0
1930	NY N	122	389	60	132	26	2	13	75	21-0	3	24	.339	.378	.517	116	10	2	.982	-2	103	89	C96		1.3
1931	NY N	123	396	42	119	17	1	12	65	29-0	4	29	.301	.354	.439	115	8	1	.996	5	144	88	C113		1.9
1932	NY N	140	502	36	144	18	2	8	77	26-0	1	22	.287	.323	.378	90	-8	0	.983	-5	98	93	C136		-0.5
1933	Bos N	96	328	15	83	7	0	3	30	13-0	3	9	.253	.288	.302	75	-12	0	.997	2	188	89	C95		-0.4
1934	Bos N	92	279	20	73	5	2	4	34	16-0	6	13	.262	.316	.337	81	-8	0	.986	-1	111	125	C90		-0.4
1935	Bos N	59	163	9	49	8	0	2	25	21-0	4	8	.301	.394	.387	120	6	0	.990	-5	88	79	C56		0.5
1936	Was A	19	65	8	21	4	0	1	7	11-0	0	2	.323	.421	.431	117	2	0-1	.989	1	91	81	C19		0.4
1937	Was A	21	66	4	10	4	0	0	5	5-0	1	3	.152	.222	.212	10	-9	0-1	.979	1	97	170	C21		-0.7
Total	13	989	3180	288	939	146	12	61	474	220-0	38	188	.295	.348	.406	101	3	6-2	.985	-6	124	89	C908,O5(2/0/3)		4.9

HOGAN, KENNY Kenneth Sylvester B10.9.1902 Cleveland OH D1.2.1980 Cleveland OH BL/TR/5-9/145 d10.2

1921	Cin N	1	2	0	0	0	0	0	0	0-0	0	1	.000	.000	.000	-99	0	0-0	—	-0	0	0	/OC		-0.1
1923	Cle A	1	0	0	0	0	0	0	0	0-0	0		—	—	—		0	0-0	—	0			/R		0.0
1924	Cle A	2	1	0	0	0	0	0	0	0-0	0	0	.000	.000	.000	-99	0	0-0	—	0			/H		0.0
Total	3	4	3	0	0	0	0	0	0	0-0	0	1	.000	.000	.000	-99	-1	0-0	.000	-0	0	0	/OC		-0.1

HOGAN, MARTY Martin F. B10.25.1869 Wednesbury, England D8.15.1923 Youngstown OH BR/TR/5-8/145 d8.6

1894	Cin N	6	23	4	3	0	0	0	3	1-0	0	4	.130	.167	.130	-27	-5	2	.846	-0	109	0	O6R		-0.4
	StL N	29	100	11	28	3	4	0	13	3-0	1	13	.280	.308	.390	67	-6	7	.887	1	121	517	O29(1/1/28)		-0.5
	Year	35	123	15	31	3	4	0	16	4-0	1	17	.252	.281	.341	49	-11	9	.879	1	119	423	O35(1/1/34)		-0.9
1895	StL N	5	18	2	3	1	0	0	2	3-0	0		.167	.286	.222	33	-2	2	.833	0	235	0	O5C		-0.1
Total	2	40	141	17	34	4	4	0	18	7-0	1	17	.241	.282	.326	47	-13	11	.869	1	137	355	O40(1/6/34)		-1.0

HOGAN, EDDIE Mortimer Edward B1862 IL D3.17.1923 Chicago IL BR d9.27

1884	Mil U	11	37	6	3	1	0	0		7-0			.081	.227	.108	-9	-4		.806	6	306	377	O11R		0.2
1887	NY AA	32	120	22	24	6	1	0	30	3-0	3		.200	.373	.267	84	0	12	.750	-6	108	88	O29(1/2/26),S4/3		-0.5
1888	Cle AA	78	269	60	61	16	6	0	24	50-0	10		.227	.368	.331	128	13	30	.896	-4	65	34	O78(26/0/52),S4/3		0.8
Total	3	121	426	88	88	23	7	0		60-0			.207	.357	.293	108	9	42	.844	-4	100	83	O118(27/2/89),S4/3		0.5

HOGAN, WILLIE William Henry B9.14.1884 N.San Juan CA D9.28.1974 San Jose CA BR/TR/5-10/175 d4.12 b-George Col Santa Clara

1911	Phi A	7	19	1	2	1	0	0		1-0	0		.105	.105	.158	-27	-3	0	.900	1	89	297	O6L		-0.3
	StL A	123	443	53	115	17	8	2	62	43-0	2		.260	.328	.348	92	-5	18	.929	11	116	133	O117(115/0/2),1b5		0.1
	Year	130	462	54	117	18	8	2	64	43-0	2		.253	.320	.340	87	-8	18	.928	12	115	139	O123(121/0/2),1b5		-0.2
1912	StL A	108	360	32	77	10	2	1	36	34-0	1		.214	.284	.261	58	-20	17	.972	10	118	108	O100(91/5/4),1b5		-1.4
Total	2	238	822	86	194	28	10	3	100	77-0	3		.236	.304	.305	75	-28	35	.947	22	116	125	O223(212/5/6),1b5		-1.6

HOGG, WILLY Wilbert George "Sonny" B4.21.1913 Detroit MI D11.5.1973 Detroit MI BR/TR/5-11.5/162 d6.1

1934	Bro N	1	0	0	0	0	0	0	0	0-0	0		.000	.000	.000	-99	0	0	—	-0	0	0	/3		0.0

HOGRIEVER, GEORGE George C. B3.17.1869 Cincinnati OH D1.26.1961 Appleton WI BR/TR/5-8/160 d4.24

1895	Cin N	69	239	61	65	8	7	2	34	36-0	3	17	.272	.374	.389	93	-2	41	.934	0	100	134	O66(10/48/8),2b3		-0.5
1901	Mil A	54	221	25	52	10	2	0	16	30-0	1		.235	.329	.299	79	-5	7	.901	-2	36	51	O54(49/5/0)		-1.0
Total	2	123	460	86	117	18	9	2	50	66-0	4	17	.254	.353	.346	87	-7	48	.920	-2	68	93	O120(59/53/8),2b3		-1.5

HOHMAN, BILL William Henry B11.27.1903 Brooklyn MD D10.29.1968 Baltimore MD BR/TR/6-0/178 d8.24

1927	Phi N	7	18	1	5	0	0	0		3-0	0	3	.278	.350	.278	69	-1	0	.917	0	102	226	O6L		-0.1

HOHNHORST, EDDIE Edward Hicks B1.31.1885 Covington KY D3.28.1916 Covington KY BL/TL/6-1/175 d9.10

1910	Cle A	18	63	8	20	3	1	0	6	4-0	0		.317	.358	.397	135	2	3	.972	-1	77	117	1b18		0.1
1912	Cle A	15	54	5	11	1	0	0	2	2-0	0		.204	.232	.222	29	-5	5	.963	-1	90	120	1b15		-0.7
Total	2	33	117	13	31	4	1	0	8	6-0	0		.265	.301	.316	83	-3	8	.968	-2	83	118	1b33		-0.6

HOILES, CHRIS Christopher Allen B3.20.1965 Bowling Green OH BR/TR/6-0/213(195-215) [DetA86 19/489] d4.25 Col Eastern Michigan

1989	Bal A	6	9	0	1	1	0	0	1	1-0	0	3	.111	.200	.222	19	-1	0-0	1.000	1	90	214	C3,D3		0.0
1990	Bal A	23	63	7	12	3	0	1	6	5-1	0	12	.190	.250	.286	51	-4	0-0	1.000	-1	90	214	C7,1b6,D7		-0.6
1991	Bal A	107	341	36	83	15	0	11	31	29-1	1	61	.243	.304	.384	93	-4	0-2	.998	-7	112	93	C89,D13,1b2		-0.8
1992	Bal A	96	310	49	85	10	1	20	40	55-2	2	60	.274	.384	.506	144	19	0-2	.994	-9	80	63	C95/D		-0.8
1993	Bal A	126	419	80	130	28	0	29	82	69-4	5	94	.310	.416	.585	159	37	1-1	.993	10	122	102	C124,D2	57	1.5
1994	Bal A	99	332	45	82	10	0	19	53	63-2	5	73	.247	.371	.449	105	4	2-0	.989	12	133	77	C98	21	5.3
1995	Bal A	114	352	53	88	15	1	19	58	67-3	4	80	.250	.373	.460	114	9	1-0	.996	3	101	110	C107,D6		2.1
1996	†Bal A	127	407	64	105	13	0	25	73	57-1	9	97	.258	.356	.474	110	6	0-1	.992	-10	79	86	C126/1	15	1.7
1997	†Bal A	99	320	45	83	15	0	12	49	51-3	10	86	.259	.375	.419	111	7	1-0	1.000	-2	78	72	C87,1b4/3D	31	0.3
1998	Bal A	97	267	36	70	12	0	15	56	38-0	1	50	.262	.358	.476	118	7	0-1	.995	-4	55	112	C83,1b6,D6	31	1.1
Total	10	894	2820	415	739	122	2	151	449	435-17	44	616	.262	.366	.467	118	80	5-7	.994	-8	96	90	C819,D46,1b19/3	124	11.3

HOLBERT, AARON Aaron Keith B1.9.1973 Torrance CA BR/TR/6-0/160(160-180) [StLN90 1/18] d4.14 b-Ray

1996	StL N	1	3	0	0	0	0	0	0	0-0	0	0	.000	.000	.000	-99	-1	0-0	1.000	-1	62	0	/2		-0.1
2005	Cin N	22	27	3	6	3	0	0	2	3-1	0	8	.222	.290	.333	68	-1	1-0	.950	1	90	133	2b4,1b2,3b2		-0.1
Total	2	23	30	3	6	3	0	0	2	3-1	0	8	.200	.265	.300	52	-2	1-0	.952	1	86	113	2b5,3b2,1b2		-0.1

HOLBERT, RAY Ray Arthur B9.25.1970 Torrance CA BR/TR/6-0/175* [SDN88 3/58] d5.2 b-Aaron

1994	SD N	5	5	1	1	0	0	0	4	0-0	0	0	.200	.200	.200	5	-1	0-0	—	-0	0	0	/S		-0.1
1995	SD N	63	73	11	13	2	1	2	5	8-1	2	20	.178	.277	.315	57	-5	4-0	.940	0	103	113	S30,2b7/OR	33	-0.2
1998	Atl N	8	15	2	2	0	0	0	1	2-0	0	4	.133	.222	.133	0	-2	0-0	.952	1	112	132	S7		-0.1
	Mon N	2	5	0	0	0	0	0	0	0-0	0	1	.000	.000	.000	-99	-1	0-0	1.000	-0		0	/2		-0.2
	Year	10	20	2	2	0	0	0	1	2-0	0	5	.100	.174	.100	-24	-4	0-0	.952	1	112	132	S7/2		-0.3
1999	KC A	34	100	14	28	6	0	3	20	14-0	1	20	.280	.330	.310	63	-6	7-4	.987	-7	81	111	S22,2b11/3		-1.0
2000	KC A	3	4	0	1	0	0	0	0	0-0	0	2	.250	.250	.250	26	0	0-0	1.000	-0	94	402	/23S		0.0
Total	5	115	202	28	45	5	1	2	11	18-1	2	51	.223	.290	.287	51	-15	11-4	.962	-6	94	116	S61,2b20,3b2/OR	33	-1.6

HOLBERT, BILL William Henry B3.14.1855 Baltimore MD D3.20.1935 Laurel MD BR/TR/?/197 d9.5 M1/U1 OF(12/19/38)

1876	Lou N	12	43	3	11	0	0	0	7				.256	.256	.256	60	-2		.843	6			C12		0.3
1878	Mil N	45	173	10	32	2	0	0	12	3			14	.185	.199	.197	28	-13		.818	-5	229	76	O30R,C21		-0.7
1879	Syr N	59	229	11	46	0	0	0	21	1			20	.201	.204	.201	39	-14		.897	-0			C56,O4(0/3/1),M		-1.2

YEAR	TM LG	G	AB	R	H	2B	3B	HR	RBI	BB-IB	HP	SO	AVG	OBP	SLG	AOPS	ABR	SB-CS	FA	FR	RNG	THR	GAMES AT POSITION	DL	BFW
	Tro N	4	15	1	4	0	0	0	2	0		1	.267	.267	.267	82	0		.893	1			C4		0.0
	Year	63	244	12	50	0	0	0	23	1		21	.205	.208	.205	41	-15		.897	1			C60,O4(0/3/1)		-1.2
1880	Tro N	60	212	18	40	5	1	0	8	9		18	.189	.222	.222	48	-11		.911	11			C58,O3R		0.2
1881	Tro N	46	180	16	49	3	0	0	14	3		13	.272	.284	.289	77	-5		.918	7			C43,O3R		0.3
1882	Tro N	71	251	24	46	5	0	0	23	11		22	.183	.218	.203	38	-17		.892	15			C58,3b12,O3C		0.3
1883	NY AA	73	299	26	71	9	1	0					.237	.240	.274	62	-13		.920	33			C68,O5C/2		2.2
1884	†NY AA	65	255	28	53	5	0	0		7	2		.208	.235	.227	53	-13		.920	21			C59,O5(4/0/1)/S		1.2
1885	NY AA	56	202	13	35	3	0	0	13	8	0		.173	.205	.188	26	-17		.900	11			C39,O13(8/5/0),3b5		-0.3
1886	NY AA	48	171	8	35	4	2	0	13	6	0		.205	.232	.251	56	-9	4	.922	16			C45,O3C/S		0.9
1887	NY AA	69	255	20	58	4	3	0	32	7	0		.227	.248	.267	46	-19	12	.894	2			C60,1b8,S2/2		-1.0
1888	Bro AA	15	50	4	6	1	0	0	1	2	1		.120	.170	.140	-0	-6	0	.926	1			C15		-0.3
Total	12	623	2335	182	486	41	7	0	144	58	3	91	.208	.228	.232	47	-139	16	.907	128			C538,O69R,3b17,1b8,S4,2b2		1.9

HOLBROOK, SAMMY James Marbury B7.17.1910 Meridian MS D4.10.1991 Jackson MS BR/TR/5-11/189 d4.25

| 1935 | Was A | 52 | 135 | 20 | 35 | 2 | 2 | 2 | 25 | 30 | | 4 | 16 | .259 | .408 | .348 | 101 | 2 | 0-0 | .952 | -12 | 77 | 47 | C47 | | -0.7 |

HOLDEN, JOE Joseph Francis "Socks" B6.4.1913 St.Clair PA D5.10.1996 St.Clair PA BL/TR/5-8/175 d6.14

1934	Phi N	10	14	1	1	0	0	0	0	0		2	.071	.071	.071	-54	-3	0	1.000	1	98	282	C6		-0.1
1935	Phi N	6	9	0	1	0	0	0	0	0		3	.111	.111	.111	-36	-2	1	1.000	-0	0	0	C4		-0.2
1936	Phi N	1	1	0	0	0	0	0	0	0		0	.000	.000	.000	-91	0		—	0			/H		0.0
Total	3	17	24	1	2	0	0	0	0	0		5	.083	.083	.083	-49	-5	1	1.000	1	68	197	C10		-0.3

HOLDEN, BILL William Paul B9.7.1889 Birmingham AL D9.14.1971 Pensacola FL BR/TR/6-0/170 d9.11

1913	NY A	18	53	6	16	3	1	0	8	8		5	.302	.393	.396	131	3	2	.977	2	102	192	O16C		0.4
1914	NY A	50	165	12	30	3	2	0	12	16		26	.182	.254	.224	44	-12	2-4	.981	-1	106	52	O45(3/37/6)		-1.8
	Cin N	11	28	2	6	0	0	0	1	3		5	.214	.290	.214	49	-2	0	1.000	-0	86	112	O10(7/3/1)		-0.2
Total	2	79	246	20	52	6	3	0	21	27		36	.211	.289	.260	64	-12	2-4	.981	-1	103	93	O71(10/56/7)		-1.6

HOLDSWORTH, JIM James "Long Jim" B7.14.1850 New York NY D3.22.1918 New York NY BR/TR d5.14

1872	Cle NA	22	110	19	33	5	0	0	11	1		2	.300	.306	.345	106	1	3-2	.765	-2	78	200	S22		-0.1
	Eck NA	3	11	1	3	1	0	0	0	0		0	.273	.273	.364	111	0	0-0	.833	1	123		S3		0.1
	Year	25	121	20	36	6	0	0	11	1		2	.298	.303	.347	106	2	3-2	.774	-0	84	175	S25		0.0
1873	Mut NA	53	232	46	75	4	8	0	28	0		0	.323	.323	.409	117	4	1-0	.770	-14	75	92	S53		-0.9
1874	Phi NA	57	285	60	97	8	9	0	37	1		0	.340	.343	.432	142	11	1-2	.694	-22	60	119	3b31,S21,O6(0/3/3),2b2/1		-1.0
1875	Mut NA	71	324	45	92	12	1	0	23	1		3	.284	.286	.327	107	1	3-3	.780	-4	148	128	O45(0/43/2),S26		-0.3
1876	NY N	52	241	23	64	3	2	0	19	1		2	.266	.269	.295	101	1		.902	-1	118	46	O49C,2b3		-0.2
1877	Har N	55	260	26	66	5	2	0	20	2		8	.254	.260	.288	81	-5		.833	-4	108	62	O55C		-1.0
1882	Tro N	1	3	0	0	0	0	0	0	0		1	.000	.000	.000	-99	-1		1.000	1	443		/OC		0.0
1884	Ind AA	5	18	1	2	0	0	0		2			.111	.200	.111	4	-2		.929	1	103	613	O5C		-0.1
Total 4 NA	206	962	171	300	30	18	0	99	3		9	.312	.314	.380	120	17	8-7	.747	-40	81	117	S125,O51(0/46/5),3b31,2b2/1		-2.2
Total 4	113	522	50	132	8	4	0	39	5		11	.253	.260	.284	85	-7		.875	-3	115	78	O110C,2b3		-1.3

HOLKE, WALTER Walter Henry "Union Man" B12.25.1892 St.Louis MO D10.12.1954 St.Louis MO BB/TL/6-1.5/185 d10.6 Def 1918 C1

1914	NY N	2	6	0	2	0	0	0	0	0		0	.333	.333	.333	102	0	0	.950	0	210	120	1b2		0.0
1916	NY N	34	111	16	39	4	0	0	13	6		1	16	.351	.390	.423	158	7	10	.997	0	85	92	1b34		0.7
1917	†NY N	153	527	55	146	12	7	2	55	34		5	54	.277	.327	.338	107	4	13	.989	-6	83	121	1b153		-0.6
1918	NY N	88	326	38	82	17	4	1	27	10		1	26	.252	.276	.337	88	-6	10	.990	5	120	107	1b88		-0.3
1919	Bos N	137	518	48	151	14	6	0	48	21		5	25	.292	.325	.342	105	2	19	.993	6	115	108	1b136		0.5
1920	Bos N	144	551	53	162	15	11	3	64	28		1	31	.294	.329	.377	107	3	4-11	.991	-3	92	91	1b143		-0.7
1921	Bos N	150	579	60	151	15	10	3	63	17		2	41	.261	.284	.337	67	-30	8-11	.997	2	100	94	1b150		-4.0
1922	Bos N	105	395	35	115	9	4	0	46	14		1	23	.291	.317	.334	71	-18	6-8	.993	-4	81	81	1b105		-2.8
1923	Phi N	147	562	64	175	31	4	7	70	16		0	37	.311	.330	.418	86	-12	7-9	.991	-2	93	103	1b146/P		-2.3
1924	Phi N	148	563	60	169	23	6	6	64	25		0	33	.300	.330	.394	83	-14	3-8	.993	4	109	96	1b148		-2.2
1925	Phi N	39	86	11	21	5	0	1	17	3		0	6	.244	.270	.372	50	-7	0-0	.994	1	126	103	1b23		-0.6
	Cin N	65	232	24	65	8	4	1	20	17		0	12	.280	.329	.362	78	-8	1-3	.997	1	103	128	1b65		-1.1
	Year	104	318	35	86	13	4	2	37	20		0	18	.270	.314	.355	69	-15	1-3	.996	3	108	123	1b88		-1.7
Total	11	1212	4456	464	1278	153	58	24	487	191	16	304	.287	.318	.363	89	-79	81-50	.993	5	99	102	1b1193/P		-13.4

HOLLAHAN, BILL William James "Happy" B11.22.1896 New York NY D11.27.1965 New York NY BR/TR/5-8/165 d9.27

| 1920 | Was A | 3 | 4 | 0 | 1 | 0 | 0 | 0 | 1 | 1 | | 0 | .250 | .400 | .250 | 77 | 0 | 1-0 | 1.000 | -0 | 54 | 0 | 3b3 | | 0.0 |

HOLLAND, DUTCH Robert Clyde B10.12.1903 Middlesex NC D6.16.1967 Lumberton NC BR/TR/6-1/190 d8.16 Col North Carolina St.

1932	Bos N	39	156	15	46	11	1	1	18	12		0	20	.295	.345	.397	103	1	0	.990	-0	97	108	O39L		-0.2
1933	Bos N	13	31	3	8	0	0	0	3	3		0	8	.258	.324	.355	102	0	1	.867	-1	88	0	O7L		-0.1
1934	Cle A	50	128	19	32	12	1	2	13	13		0	11	.250	.319	.406	85	-3	0-0	.957	-2	85	48	O31(15/0/16)		-0.7
Total	3	102	315	37	86	26	2	3	34	28		0	39	.273	.332	.397	95	-2	1-0	.969	-4	92	78	O77(61/0/16)		-1.0

HOLLAND, WILL Willard A. B1862 Georgetown DE D7.19.1930 Philadelphia PA 5-10/180 d7.10

| 1889 | Bal AA | 40 | 143 | 13 | 27 | 1 | 2 | 0 | 16 | 9 | | 2 | 28 | .189 | .247 | .224 | 34 | -13 | 4 | .853 | -11 | 85 | 73 | S39/OL | | -1.9 |

HOLLANDSWORTH, TODD Todd Mathew B4.20.1973 Dayton OH BL/TL/6-2/215(193-215) [LAN91 3/80] d4.25

1995	†LA N	41	103	16	24	2	0	5	13	10-2		1	29	.233	.304	.398	91	-2	2-1	.938	-1	96	65	O37(9/25/3)	99	-0.3
1996	†LA N	149	478	64	139	26	4	12	59	41-1		1	93	.291	.348	.437	113	8	21-6	.978	-2	94	100	O99(80/30/4)	35	0.5
1997	LA N	106	296	39	73	20	2	4	31	17-2		0	60	.247	.286	.368	75	-12	5-5	.984	6	125	45	O51(48/10/1)	115	-0.6
1998	LA N	55	175	23	47	6	4	3	20	9-0		1	42	.269	.308	.400	89	-4	4-3	.957	-1	105	36	O51(48/10/1)	40	-0.6
1999	LA N	92	261	39	74	12	0	9	32	24-1		1	61	.284	.345	.448	104	1	5-2	.984	1	98	163	O77(9/68/1)		-0.8
2000	LA N	81	261	42	61	12	0	8	24	30-2		1	61	.234	.314	.372	76	-10	11-4	.987	-1	87	223	O48(31/4/18)		0.1
	Col N	56	167	39	54	8	0	11	23	11-1		0	38	.323	.365	.569	106	1	7-3	.988	1	86	0	O56(9/3/44)/1		-0.7
	Year	137	428	81	115	20	0	19	47	41-3		1	99	.269	.333	.449	89	-8	18-7	.987	2	93	188	O125(40/72/19)		-0.7
2001	Col N	33	117	21	43	15	1	6	19	8-2		0	20	.368	.408	.667	142	8	5-0	.981	-1	90	111	O31(25/12/5)	149	0.7
2002	Col N	95	298	39	88	21	1	11	48	26-4		1	71	.295	.352	.483	107	2	7-8	.973	-0	94	140	O90(74/1/20)	16	-0.3
	Tex A	39	132	16	34	6	0	5	19	14-0		0	27	.258	.327	.417	94	-1	1-0	1.000	-3	89	0	O38(25/16/4)		-0.4
2003	†Fla N	93	228	32	58	23	3	3	20	22-4		0	55	.254	.317	.421	95	-2	2-3	.983	3	111	143	O64(61/0/3)/D	18	-0.1
2004	Chi N	57	148	28	47	6	2	8	22	17-3		1	26	.318	.392	.547	135	8	1-1	1.000	2	110	115	O36(4/0/32),1b3,D3	98	0.8
2005	Chi N	107	268	23	68	17	2	5	35	18-1		1	53	.254	.301	.388	77	-9	4-4	.980	-6	80	55	O95(92/0/6)/1		-1.8
	Atl N	24	35	3	6	0	0	1	1	5-0		0	13	.171	.275	.257	40	-3	0-1	1.000	-1	86	0	O9(6/0/3)/1		-0.4
	Year	131	303	26	74	17	2	6	36	23-1		1	66	.244	.298	.373	73	-12	4-5	.982	-6	80	51	O104(98/0/9),1b2		-2.2
Total	11	1028	2967	424	816	174	21	91	366	252-23	9	649	.275	.332	.440	99	-15	75-41	.980	0	99	99	O884(613/218/118),1b18,D4	570	-3.4

HOLLE, GARY Gary Charles B8.11.1954 Albany NY BR/TL/6-6/210 [MilA76 13/292] d6.2 Col Siena

| 1979 | Tex A | 5 | 6 | 0 | 1 | 1 | 0 | 0 | 0 | 1 | | 0 | 0-0 | .167 | .286 | .333 | 67 | 0 | 1.000 | -0 | 0 | 128 | /1 | | -0.1 |

HOLLIDAY, BUG James Wear B2.8.1867 St.Louis MO D2.15.1910 Cincinnati OH BR/TR/5-11/151 d4.17 U1 OF(211/598/92)

1889	Cin AA	135	563	107	181	28	7	19	104	43		2	59	.321	.372	.497	142	28	46	.923	-9	112	107	O135C		1.2
1890	Cin N	131	518	93	140	18	14	4	75	49		7	36	.270	.341	.382	111	6	50	.948	-5	89	118	O131C		-0.3
1891	Cin N	111	442	74	141	21	10	9	84	37		3	28	.319	.376	.473	145	24	30	.939	-8	78	107	O111(49/62/0)		1.0
1892	Cin N	152	602	114	177	23	16	13	91	57		1	39	.294	.356	.450	145	31	43	.933	-4	83	120	O152(1/78/77)/P		1.7
1893	Cin N	126	500	108	155	24	15	5	89	73		3	22	.310	.401	.428	117	14	32	.944	-12	67	90	O125(1/125/0)/1		-0.5
1894	Cin N	123	521	126	196	24	8	13	123	41		2	20	.376	.424	.528	124	19	33	.912	-1	107	116	O121(111/5/8)/1		0.7
1895	Cin N	32	127	25	38	9	2	0	20	10		1	9	.299	.350	.402	90	-2	6	.940	-2	74	109	O32(5/27/0)		-0.5
1896	Cin N	29	84	17	27	4	0	1	8	9		1	4	.321	.394	.369	95	0	1	.925	-2	45	0	O16(10/3/3),1b5/SP		-0.2
1897	Cin N	61	195	50	61	9	4	2	20	20		0	10	.313	.399	.431	112	4	9	.940	-3	44	37	O42(32/6/4),S4,2b3,1b3		-0.2
1898	Cin N	30	106	21	25	2	1	0	7	14		0		.236	.325	.274	67	-4	5	.969	-1	28	118	O28(2/26/0)		-0.7
Total	10	930	3658	735	1141	162	72	65	621	360	20	211	.312	.377	.449	125	120	252	.934	-45	84	104	O893C,1b10,S5,2b3,P2		2.3

YEAR	TM LG	G	AB	R	H	2B	3B	HR	RBI	BB-IB	HP	SO	AVG	OBP	SLG	AOPS	ABR	SB-CS	FA	FR	RNG	THR	GAMES AT POSITION	DL	BFW

HOLLIDAY, MATT Matthew Thomas B1.15.1980 Stillwater OK BR/TR/6-4/235* [ColN98 7/210] d4.16

YEAR	TM LG	G	AB	R	H	2B	3B	HR	RBI	BB-IB	HP	SO	AVG	OBP	SLG	AOPS	ABR	SB-CS	FA	FR	RNG	THR	GAMES AT POSITION	DL	BFW
2004	Col N	121	400	65	116	31	3	14	57	31-0	6	86	.290	.349	.488	101	1	3-3	.963	-5	94	67	O115L		-0.8
2005	Col N	125	479	68	147	24	7	19	87	36-1	7	79	.307	.361	.505	109	6	14-3	.972	1	104	72	O123L	40	0.4
Total 2		246	879	133	263	55	10	33	144	67-1	13	165	.299	.356	.497	105	7	17-6	.968	-4	99	70	O238L	40	-0.4

HOLLINGSHEAD, HOLLY John Samuel (aka Samuel John Holly) B1.17.1853 Washington DC D10.6.1926 Washington DC d4.20 M2/U1

YEAR	TM LG	G	AB	R	H	2B	3B	HR	RBI	BB-IB	HP	SO	AVG	OBP	SLG	AOPS	ABR	SB-CS	FA	FR	RNG	THR	GAMES AT POSITION	DL	BFW
1872	Nat NA	9	44	12	14	1	1	0	6	1		0	.318	.333	.386	103	-1	0-0	.778	-4	70	45	2b9		-0.3
1873	Was NA	30	136	25	35	2	2	0	22	0		5	.257	.257	.301	68	-5	0-0	.824	2	119	0	O30C,2b2		-0.2
1875	Was NA	19	81	8	20	1	1	0	5	1		2	.247	.256	.284	91	-1	2-1	.826	2	202	126	O19(4/13/3),M		0.2
Total 3	NA	58	261	45	69	4	4	0	33	2		7	.264	.270	.310	81	-7	2-1	.824	1	150	47	O49(4/43/3),2b11		-0.3

HOLLINS, DAMON Damon Jamall B6.12.1974 Fairfield CA BR/TL/5-11/180* [AtlN92 4/117] d4.24 [DL 2003 Atl N 29]

YEAR	TM LG	G	AB	R	H	2B	3B	HR	RBI	BB-IB	HP	SO	AVG	OBP	SLG	AOPS	ABR	SB-CS	FA	FR	RNG	THR	GAMES AT POSITION	DL	BFW
1998	Atl N	3	6	0	1	0	0	0	0	0-0	0	1	.167	.167	.167	-12	-1	0-0	1.000	-0	67	0	O3(2/0/1)		-0.1
	LA N	5	9	1	2	0	0	0	2	0-0	0	2	.222	.222	.222	18	-1	0-1	1.000	-0	103	0	O4(1/0/3)		-0.2
	Year	8	15	1	3	0	0	0	2	0-0	0	3	.200	.200	.200	6	-2	0-1	1.000	-0	89	0	O7(3/0/4)		-0.3
2004	Atl N	7	22	3	8	2	0	0	5	0-0	0	4	.364	.364	.455	109	0	0-0	1.000	0	84	337	O6(6/0/1)		0.0
2005	TB A	120	342	44	85	17	1	13	46	23-0	1	63	.249	.296	.418	90	-6	8-1	.977	8	110	165	O116(8/80/48)		0.3
Total 3		135	379	48	96	19	1	13	53	23-0	1	70	.253	.296	.412	88	-8	8-2	.979	8	108	167	O129(17/80/53)	29	0.0

HOLLINS, DAVE David Michael B5.25.1966 Buffalo NY BB/TR/6-1/207(195-232) [SDN87 6/146] d4.12 Col South Carolina-Aiken

YEAR	TM LG	G	AB	R	H	2B	3B	HR	RBI	BB-IB	HP	SO	AVG	OBP	SLG	AOPS	ABR	SB-CS	FA	FR	RNG	THR	GAMES AT POSITION	DL	BFW
1990	Phi N	72	114	14	21	0	0	5	15	10-3	1	28	.184	.252	.316	56	-7	0-0	.932	-3	86	0	3b30/1		-1.1
1991	Phi N	56	151	18	45	10	2	6	21	17-1	3	26	.298	.378	.510	149	10	1-1	.922	-2	94	37	3b36,1b6	21	0.8
1992	Phi N	156	586	104	158	28	4	27	93	76-4	19	110	.270	.369	.469	137	30	9-6	.954	-18	84	83	3b156/1		1.4
1993	†Phi N★	143	543	104	148	30	4	18	93	85-5	5	109	.273	.372	.442	120	18	2-3	.914	-29	79	40	3b143	17	-1.0
1994	Phi N	44	162	28	36	7	1	4	26	23-0	4	32	.222	.328	.352	77	-5	1-0	.887	-13	61	31	3b43/OR	79	-1.7
1995	Phi N	65	205	46	47	12	2	7	25	53-4	5	39	.229	.393	.410	114	7	1-1	.988	-6	67	109	1b61	15	-0.5
	Bos A	5	13	2	2	0	0	0	1	4-0	0	7	.154	.353	.154	37	-1	0-0	1.000	0	111	0	O2R,D3	54	-0.1
1996	Min A	121	422	71	102	26	0	13	53	71-5	10	102	.242	.364	.396	90	-4	6-4	.953	0	102	82	3b116/SD		-0.3
	Sea A	28	94	17	33	3	0	3	25	13-2	1	35	.351	.438	.479	133	6	0-2	.961	2	105	122	3b28/1		0.6
	Year	149	516	88	135	29	0	16	78	84-7	13	117	.262	.377	.411	98	2	6-6	.955	2	103	90	3b144,D3/S1		0.3
1997	Ana A	149	572	101	165	29	2	16	85	62-2	8	124	.288	.363	.430	106	7	16-6	.922	-8	94	76	3b135,1b14		0.0
1998	Ana A	101	363	60	88	16	2	11	39	44-2	7	69	.242	.334	.388	86	-2	11-3	.929	-2	94	99	3b91,1b7,D2	49	-0.7
1999	Tor A	27	99	12	22	5	0	2	6	5-0	0	22	.222	.260	.333	49	-8	0-0	—	0	0	0	D23	33	-0.9
2001	Cle A	2	5	0	1	0	0	0	0	1-0	0	2	.200	.333	.200	44	0	0-0	—	0	0	0	D2		0.0
2002	Phi N	14	17	1	2	0	0	0	0	0-0	1	3	.118	.167	.118	-23	-3	0-1	1.000	-0	45	106	1b5		0.0
Total 12		983	3346	578	870	166	17	112	482	464-28	66	687	.260	.358	.420	106	43	47-27	.933	-80	89	70	3b778,1b96,D33,O3R/S	410	-3.9

HOLLMIG, STAN Stanley Ernest "Hondo" B1.2.1926 Fredericksburg TX D12.4.1981 San Antonio TX BR/TR/6-2.5/190* d4.19 Col Texas A&M-Commerce

YEAR	TM LG	G	AB	R	H	2B	3B	HR	RBI	BB-IB	HP	SO	AVG	OBP	SLG	AOPS	ABR	SB-CS	FA	FR	RNG	THR	GAMES AT POSITION	DL	BFW
1949	Phi N	81	251	28	64	11	6	2	26	20		2	43	.255	.315	.371	85	-6	1	.958	-4	88	87	O66R	-1.2
1950	Phi N	11	12	1	3	2	0	0	1	0		0	3	.250	.250	.417	73	0	0	1.000	0	127	0	O3(2/0/1)	0.0
1951	Phi N	2	2	0	0	0	0	0	0	0		0	0	.000	.000	.000	-99	-1	0	—	0	0	0	/H	-0.1
Total 3		94	265	29	67	13	6	2	27	20		2	46	.253	.310	.370	84	-7	1-0	.959	-4	89	85	O69(2/0/67)	-1.3

HOLLOCHER, CHARLIE Charles Jacob B6.11.1896 St.Louis MO D8.14.1940 Frontenac MO BL/TR/5-7/154 d4.16

YEAR	TM LG	G	AB	R	H	2B	3B	HR	RBI	BB-IB	HP	SO	AVG	OBP	SLG	AOPS	ABR	SB-CS	FA	FR	RNG	THR	GAMES AT POSITION	DL	BFW
1918	†Chi N	131	509	72	161	23	6	2	38	47		4	30	.316	.379	.397	133	22	26	.929	-22	90	75	S131	1.0
1919	Chi N	115	430	51	116	14	5	3	26	44		3	19	.270	.347	.347	108	6	16	.941	6	105	107	S115	2.2
1920	Chi N	80	301	53	96	17	2	0	22	41		3	15	.319	.406	.389	126	13	20-14	.954	9	102	89	S80	2.9
1921	Chi N	140	558	71	161	28	8	3	37	43		2	13	.289	.342	.384	91	-6	5-16	.963	6	105	95	S137	1.0
1922	Chi N	152	592	90	201	37	8	3	69	58		5	5	.340	.403	.444	116	17	19-29	.965	6	98	101	S152	2.0
1923	Chi N	66	260	46	89	14	2	1	28	26		4	5	.342	.410	.423	120	9	9-10	.963	-4	96	96	S65	1.0
1924	Chi N	76	286	28	70	12	4	2	21	18		1	7	.245	.292	.336	67	-14	4-11	.969	2	102	94	S71	-0.7
Total 7		760	2936	411	894	145	35	14	241	277		26	94	.304	.370	.392	110	47	99-80	.954	-9	100	94	S751	9.4

HOLLY, ED Edward William (b Edward William Ruthlavy) B7.6.1879 Chicago IL D11.27.1973 Williamsport PA BR/TR/5-10/165 d7.18

YEAR	TM LG	G	AB	R	H	2B	3B	HR	RBI	BB-IB	HP	SO	AVG	OBP	SLG	AOPS	ABR	SB-CS	FA	FR	RNG	THR	GAMES AT POSITION	DL	BFW
1906	StL N	10	34	1	2	0	0	0	7	5		0	.059	.179	.059	-27	-5	0	.939	-2	73	214	S10		-0.7
1907	StL N	150	545	55	125	18	5	1	40	36		5	.229	.283	.279	79	-14	16	.927	9	105	86	S147,2b3		0.0
1914	Pit F	100	350	28	86	9	4	0	26	17		0	52	.246	.281	.294	57	-28	14	.942	-3	95	87	S94,O2(1/0/1)/2	-2.5
1915	Pit F	16	42	8	11	2	0	0	5	5		1	2	.262	.354	.310	88	-1	3	.865	-4	77	106	S11,3b3	-0.5
Total 4		276	971	92	224	29	7	1	78	63		6	58	.231	.282	.278	67	-48	33	.931	1	99	92	S262,2b4,3b3,O2(1/0/1)	-3.7

HOLM, WATTIE Roscoe Albert B12.28.1901 Peterson IA D5.19.1950 Everly IA BR/TR/5-9.5/160 d4.15 Col Iowa

YEAR	TM LG	G	AB	R	H	2B	3B	HR	RBI	BB-IB	HP	SO	AVG	OBP	SLG	AOPS	ABR	SB-CS	FA	FR	RNG	THR	GAMES AT POSITION	DL	BFW
1924	StL N	81	293	40	86	10	4	0	23	8		2	16	.294	.317	.355	81	-9	1-4	.988	1	101	140	O64(1/63/0),C9,3b4	-1.1
1925	StL N	13	58	10	12	1	1	0	2	3		0	4	.207	.246	.259	28	-6	1-0	.976	1	127	50	O13(3/0/11)	-0.6
1926	†StL N	55	144	18	41	5	1	0	21	18		0	14	.285	.364	.333	85	-2	3	.962	-2	102	25	O39(26/0/13)	-0.7
1927	StL N	110	419	55	120	27	8	3	66	24		1	29	.286	.327	.411	93	-5	4	.967	-8	93	31	O97(55/25/18),3b9	-1.9
1928	†StL N	102	386	61	107	24	6	3	47	32		1	17	.277	.334	.394	88	-7	1	.918	-17	81	61	3b83,O7R	-1.8
1929	StL N	64	176	21	41	5	6	0	14	12		0	8	.233	.282	.330	50	-15	1	.944	2	116	90	O44(6/4/34)/3	-1.5
1932	StL N	11	17	2	3	1	0	0	1	3		1	1	.176	.333	.235	55	-1	0	1.000	-0	110	0	O4(2/0/2)	-0.1
Total 7		436	1493	207	410	73	26	6	174	100		5	86	.275	.322	.370	81	-45	11-4	.970	-22	103	65	O268(93/92/85),3b97,C9	-7.7

HOLM, BILLY William Frederick Henry B7.21.1912 Chicago IL D7.27.1977 East Chicago IN BR/TR/5-10.5/168 d9.24

YEAR	TM LG	G	AB	R	H	2B	3B	HR	RBI	BB-IB	HP	SO	AVG	OBP	SLG	AOPS	ABR	SB-CS	FA	FR	RNG	THR	GAMES AT POSITION	DL	BFW
1943	Chi N	7	15	0	1	0	0	0	2			4	.067	.176	.067	-29	-2	0	1.000	1	152	83	C7		-0.2
1944	Chi N	54	132	10	18	2	0	0	6	16		1	19	.136	.235	.152	10	-16	1	.979	-2	97	92	C50	-1.6
1945	Bos A	58	135	12	25	2	1	0	9	23		3	17	.185	.317	.215	54	-7	1-1	.980	-3	105	113	C57	-0.8
Total 3		119	282	22	44	4	1	0	15	41		4	40	.156	.272	.177	30	-25	2-1	.981	-4	104	102	C114	-2.6

HOLMAN, GARY Gary Richard B1.25.1944 Long Beach CA BL/TL/6-1/200* d6.26 Col USC

YEAR	TM LG	G	AB	R	H	2B	3B	HR	RBI	BB-IB	HP	SO	AVG	OBP	SLG	AOPS	ABR	SB-CS	FA	FR	RNG	THR	GAMES AT POSITION	DL	BFW
1968	Was A	75	85	10	25	5	1	0	7	13-1	0	15	.294	.388	.376	137	5	0-0	1.000	2	112	44	1b33,O10(3/0/8)		0.6
1969	Was A	41	31	1	5	1	0	0	2	4-0	0	7	.161	.257	.194	29	-3	0-0	1.000	-1	0	58	1b11,O3(1/0/2)	-0.4
Total 2		116	116	11	30	6	1	0	9	17-1	0	22	.259	.353	.328	107	2	0-0	1.000	1	90	47	1b44,O13(4/0/10)	0.2

HOLMES, FRED Frederick C. B7.1.1878 Chicago IL D2.13.1956 Norwood Park IL BR/TR/5-7/145 d8.23

YEAR	TM LG	G	AB	R	H	2B	3B	HR	RBI	BB-IB	HP	SO	AVG	OBP	SLG	AOPS	ABR	SB-CS	FA	FR	RNG	THR	GAMES AT POSITION	DL	BFW
1903	NY A	1	0	0	0	0	0	0	0	1			—	1.000	—	-207	0	0	.833	-0	0	0	/1		0.0
1904	Chi N	1	3	1	1	1	0	0	0	0			.333	.333	.667	206	0	0	1.000	0	99	118	/C	0.0
Total 2		2	3	1	1	1	0	0	0	1			.333	.500	.667	255	0	0	1.000	-0	99	118	/C1	0.0

HOLMES, DUCKY Howard Elbert B7.8.1883 Dayton OH D9.18.1945 Dayton OH BR/TR/5-10/160 d4.18 U1

YEAR	TM LG	G	AB	R	H	2B	3B	HR	RBI	BB-IB	HP	SO	AVG	OBP	SLG	AOPS	ABR	SB-CS	FA	FR	RNG	THR	GAMES AT POSITION	DL	BFW
1906	StL N	9	27	2	5	0	0	0	2	2		1	.185	.267	.185	43	-2	0	.979	-1	78	91	C9		-0.2

HOLMES, DUCKY James William B1.28.1869 Des Moines IA D8.6.1932 Truro IA BL/TR/5-6/170 d8.8 OF(564/37/285) ▲

YEAR	TM LG	G	AB	R	H	2B	3B	HR	RBI	BB-IB	HP	SO	AVG	OBP	SLG	AOPS	ABR	SB-CS	FA	FR	RNG	THR	GAMES AT POSITION	DL	BFW
1895	Lou N	40	161	33	60	10	2	3	20	12	3	9	.373	.426	.516	152	13	9	.780	-6	180	99	O29(0/3/26),S8,3b4,P2		0.5
1896	Lou N	47	141	22	38	3	2	0	18	13	7	5	.270	.360	.319	83	-3	8	.790	-7	142	81	O33(0/26/7),P2/S2	-0.9
1897	Lou N	2	4	0	0	0	0	0	0	1			.000	.200	.000	-46	-1	0	1.000	1	101	420	/S	-0.9
	NY N	80	310	52	82	8	6	1	45	18	4		.265	.313	.339	74	-13	30	.905	-9	78	92	O78L/S	-2.5
	Year	82	314	52	82	8	6	1	45	19	4		.261	.312	.334	73	-13	30	.905	-8	78	92	O78L,S2	-2.5
1898	StL N	23	101	9	24	1	1	0	2	2	1		.238	.260	.267	50	-7	4	.900	1	183	367	O22(11/2/9)	-0.7
	Bal N	113	442	54	126	10	9	1	64	23	9		.285	.333	.355	96	-4	25	.935	2	79	116	O113L	-1.1
	Year	136	543	63	150	11	10	1	64	25	10		.276	.320	.339	87	-11	29	.930	3	96	158	O135(124/2/9)	-1.8
1899	Bal N	138	553	80	177	31	7	4	66	39	15		.320	.381	.423	114	11	50	.927	3	96	113	O138(137/0/1)	0.5
1901	Det A	131	537	90	158	28	10	4	62	37	6		.294	.347	.406	103	2	35	.907	-2	107	129	O131(2/0/131)	-0.5
1902	Det A	92	362	50	93	15	4	2	33	28	5		.257	.319	.337	80	-9	16	.950	4	131	195	O92(1/0/91)	-0.1
1903	Was A	71		13	16	3	1	1	8	5	1		.279	.338	.338	85	-1	10	.912	1	302	0	O14(0/3/11),3b4,2b2	-0.1
	Chi A	86	344	53	96	7	0	6	18	25	4		.279	.338	.328	104	2	25	.965	3	156	0	O82L,3b3	0.1
	Year	107	415	66	112	10	1	6	26	30	5		.270	.327	.330	101	1	35	.956	4	179	0	O96(82/3/11),3b7,2b2	0.0
1904	Chi A	68	251	42	78	11	6	1	19	14	3		.311	.354	.438	156	15	13	.975	1	110	174	O63(53/2/8)	1.3
1905	Chi A	92	328	42	66	15	2	0	22	19	7		.201	.258	.259	67	-12	11	.936	-4	105	48	O89(87/1/1)	-2.4
Total 10		933	3605	540	1014	142	58	17	375	236	64	14	.281	.336	.367	99	-7	236	.924	-7	117	110	O884L,3b11,S11,P4,2b3	-6.7

YEAR TM LG	G	AB	R	H	2B	3B	HR	RBI	BB-IB	HP	SO	AVG	OBP	SLG	AOPS	ABR	SB-CS	FA	FR	RNG	THR	GAMES AT POSITION	DL	BFW
HOLMES, TOMMY Thomas Francis "Kelly" B3.29.1917 Brooklyn NY BL/TL/5-10/180* d4.14 M2																						
1942 Bos N	141	558	56	155	24	4	4	41	64	1	10	.278	.353	.357	110	8	2	.990	5	105	117	O140(0/137/3)		1.1
1943 Bos N	152	629	75	170	33	10	5	41	58	2	11	.270	.334	.378	107	5	7	.993	-2	94	114	O152(2/149/1)		-0.2
1944 Bos N	155	631	93	195	42	6	13	73	61	2	11	.309	.372	.456	127	23	-4	.991	-2	97	95	O155(2/154/0)		1.7
1945 Bos N*	154	636	125	224	47	6	28	117	70	4	9	.352	.420	.577	175	64	15	.983	-2	98	89	O154(32/2/121)		5.1
1946 Bos N	149	568	80	176	35	6	6	79	58	3	14	.310	.377	.424	126	20	7	.987	5	104	115	O146R		2.2
1947 Bos N	150	618	90	191	33	9	9	53	44	5	16	.309	.360	.416	108	7	3	.989	6	109	90	O147R		0.7
1948 †Bos N★	139	585	85	190	35	7	6	61	46	1	20	.325	.375	.439	122	18	1	.983	-2	99	74	O137R		1.1
1949 Bos N	117	380	47	101	20	4	8	59	39	2	6	.266	.337	.403	103	1	1	.987	6	112	114	O103R		0.4
1950 Bos N	105	322	44	96	20	1	9	51	33	4	8	.298	.370	.450	122	11	0	1.000	1	104	100	O88R		0.9
1951 Bos N	27	29	1	5	2	0	0	5	3	0	4	.172	.250	.241	35	-3	0-0	1.000	-0	65	0	O3(2/0/1),M		-0.3
1952 †Bro N	31	36	2	4	1	0	0	4	4	0	4	.111	.200	.139	-4	-5	0-0	1.000	-0	89	300	O6R		-0.5
Total 11	1320	4992	698	1507	292	47	88	581	480	24	122	.302	.366	.432	122	149	40-0	.989	16	102	101	O1231(38/442/753)		12.2
HOLT, RED James Emmett Madison B7.25.1894 Dayton TN D2.2.1961 Birmingham AL BL/TL/5-11/175 d9.5																						
1925 Phi A	27	88	13	24	7	0	1	8	12	0	9	.273	.360	.386	84	-2	0-0	.986	-0	98	103	1b25		-0.3
HOLT, JIM James William B5.27.1944 Graham NC BL/TR/6-0/195(170-195) d4.17																						
1968 Min A	70	106	9	22	2	1	0	8	4-2	0	20	.208	.236	.245	44	-7	0-1	.973	-1	85	145	O38(23/2/14)/1		-1.1
1969 Min A	12	14	3	5	0	0	1	2	0-0	0	5	.357	.357	.571	152	1	0-0	1.000	-1	44	0	O5(1/0/4)/1		0.0
1970 †Min A	142	319	37	85	9	3	3	40	17-3	0	32	.266	.300	.342	76	-11	3-1	.995	2	111	36	O130(76/52/4),1b2		-1.4
1971 Min A	126	340	35	88	11	3	1	29	16-4	1	28	.259	.292	.318	71	-14	5-1	.986	0	104	75	O106(12/86/12),1b3		-1.7
1972 Min A	10	27	6	12	1	0	1	6	0-0	0	1	.444	.429	.593	197	3	0-0	.917	0	92	236	O7(2/0/5)/1		0.3
1973 Min A	132	441	52	131	25	3	11	58	29-4	2	43	.297	.341	.442	115	8	0-3	.990	5	105	94	O102(80/3/21),1b33		0.5
1974 Min A	79	197	24	50	11	0	0	16	14-2	1	16	.254	.302	.310	75	-6	0-0	.996	5	137	128	1b67,O5(2/0/3)		-0.5
†Oak A	30	42	1	6	0	0	0	0	1-0	1	9	.143	.182	.143	-6	-6	0-0	1.000	1	143	81	1b17,D3		-0.6
Year	109	239	25	56	11	0	0	16	15-2	2	25	.234	.282	.280	63	-11	0-0	.996	6	138	122	1b84,O5(2/0/3),D3		-1.1
1975 †Oak A	102	123	7	27	3	0	2	16	11-2	2	11	.220	.292	.293	68	-5	0-0	.991	0	117	102	1b52,O2L/CD		-0.7
1976 Oak A	4	7	0	2	2	0	0	2	1-0	0	2	.286	.375	.571	182	1	0-0	—	0			D2		0.1
Total 9	707	1616	174	428	64	10	19	177	93-17	7	166	.265	.305	.352	84	-36	8-6	.988	12	104	76	O395(198/143/63),1b177,D9/C		-5.1
HOLT, ROGER Roger Boyd B4.8.1956 Daytona Beach FL BB/TR/5-11/165 [NYA77 4/101] d10.4 Col Florida																						
1980 NY A	2	6	0	1	0	0	0	1	1-0	0	2	.167	.286	.167	28	-1	0-0	1.000	1	150	0	2b2		0.0
HONAN, MARTY Martin Weldon B5.29.1869 Chicago IL D8.20.1908 Chicago IL d10.3																						
1890 Chi N	1	3	0	0	0	0	0	1	0	0	2	.000	.000	.000	-96	-1	0	.857	-1	105	0	/C		-0.1
1891 Chi N	5	12	1	2	0	1	0	3	1	0	3	.167	.231	.333	64	-1	0	.963	1	141	170	C5		0.1
Total 2	6	15	1	2	0	1	0	4	1	0	5	.133	.188	.267	32	-2	0	.941	0	133	134	C6		0.0
HOOD, ABIE Albie Larrison B1.31.1903 Sanford NC D10.14.1988 Chesapeake VA BL/TR/5-7/152 d7.15																						
1925 Bos N	5	21	2	6	2	0	1	2	1	0	0	.286	.318	.524	122	1	0-0	.920	-3	64	68	2b5		-0.2
HOOD, WALLY Wallace James Sr. B2.9.1895 Whittier CA D5.2.1965 Hollywood CA BR/TR/5-11.5/160 d4.15 s-Wally																						
1920 Bro N	7	14	4	2	1	0	0	1	4	0	4	.143	.333	.214	58	0	2-0	.944	1	125	126	O5(0/2/3)		0.0
Pit N	2	1	1	0	0	0	0	0	1	0	0	.000	.500	.000	50	0	1-0	—	0			/H		0.0
Year	9	15	5	2	1	0	0	1	5	0	4	.133	.350	.200	59	0	3-0	.944	1	125	126	O5(0/2/3)		-0.3
1921 Bro N	56	65	16	17	1	2	1	4	9	1	14	.262	.360	.385	94	0	2-2	.957	-1	99	0	O20(3/9/7)		0.0
1922 Bro N	2	0	2	0	0	0	0	0	0	0	0	—	—	—	—	0	0-0	—	0			/R		0.0
Total 3	67	80	23	19	2	2	1	5	14	1	18	.237	.358	.350	88	0	5-2	.951	-1	109	48	O25(3/11/10)		-0.3
HOOKS, ALEX Alexander Marcus B8.29.1906 Edgewood TX D6.19.1993 Edgewood TX BL/TL/6-1/183 d4.17 Col SMU																						
1935 Phi A	15	44	4	10	3	0	1	6	1-0	0	10	.227	.277	.295	48	-3	0-0	1.000	0	93	127	1b10		-0.4
HOOPER, HARRY Harry Bartholomew B8.24.1887 Bell Station CA D12.18.1974 Santa Cruz CA BL/TR/5-10/168 d4.16 HF1971 Col St. Marys (CA)																						
1909 Bos A	81	255	29	72	3	4	0	12	16	5		.282	.337	.325	107	2	15	.952	4	149	143	O74(62/4/8)		0.3
1910 Bos A	155	584	81	156	9	10	2	27	62	8		.267	.346	.327	108	7	40	.938	9	107	139	O155(9/4/142)		0.9
1911 Bos A	130	524	93	163	20	6	4	45	73	4		.311	.399	.395	123	20	38	.954	6	105	131	O130R		1.8
1912 †Bos A	147	590	98	143	20	12	2	53	66	7		.242	.326	.327	83	-13	29	.964	1	100	105	O147R		-2.0
1913 Bos A	148	586	100	169	29	12	4	40	60	5	51	.288	.359	.399	119	14	26	.968	8	110	114	O147(1/9/137)/P		1.4
1914 Bos A	142	530	85	137	23	15	1	41	58	4	47	.258	.336	.364	110	6	19-14	.973	10	113	128	O140(0/1/139)		0.9
1915 †Bos A	149	566	90	133	20	13	2	51	89	3	36	.235	.342	.327	103	4	22-20	.972	5	111	125	O149R		0.3
1916 †Bos A	151	575	75	156	20	11	1	37	80	1	35	.271	.361	.350	113	11	27-11	.966	5	111	144	O151R		1.1
1917 Bos A	151	559	89	143	21	11	3	45	80	6	40	.256	.355	.349	116	13	21	.971	-4	94	94	O126R		0.1
1918 †Bos A	126	474	81	137	26	13	1	44	75	4	25	.289	.391	.405	142	27	24	.963	-0	100	94	O126R		2.2
1919 Bos A	128	491	76	131	25	6	3	49	79	5	28	.267	.374	.360	113	13	23	.979	6	110	102	O128R		1.2
1920 Bos A	139	536	91	167	30	17	7	53	88	2	27	.312	.411	.470	139	33	16-18	.963	5	106	116	O139(2/0/137)		2.7
1921 Chi A	108	419	74	137	26	5	8	58	55	1	21	.327	.406	.470	125	17	13-7	.975	-3	95	83	O108R		0.6
1922 Chi A	152	602	111	183	35	8	11	80	68	5	33	.304	.379	.444	114	14	16-12	.962	5	106	112	O149R		0.5
1923 Chi A	145	576	87	166	32	4	10	65	68	7	22	.288	.370	.410	106	7	18-18	.960	-6	95	77	O143R		-1.3
1924 Chi A	130	476	107	156	27	8	10	62	65	4	26	.328	.413	.481	134	26	16-13	.986	10	112	128	O123R		-1.1
1925 Chi A	127	442	62	117	23	5	6	55	54	5	21	.265	.351	.380	90	-6	12-8	.976	4	102	127	O124R		-1.1
Total 17	2309	8785	1429	2466	389	160	75	817	1136	76	412	.281	.368	.387	114	195	375-121	.966	68	106	112	O2284(74/18/2192)/P		12.0
HOOPER, KEVIN Kevin James B12.7.1976 Lawrence KS BR/TR/5-10/160 d7.9 Col Wichita St.																						
2005 Det A	6	5	0	1	0	0	0	0	0	0	0	.200	.200	.200	7	-1	0-0	1.000	-0	110	0	O3L,S2/2		-0.1
HOOPER, MIKE Michael H. B2.7.1850 Baltimore MD D12.2.1917 Baltimore MD 5-6/165 d6.27																						
1873 Mar NA	3	14	3	3	1	0	0	2	0			.214	.214	.286	62	0	0-0	.833	-2	0	0	O2L/C		-0.1
HOOVER, CHARLIE Charles E. B9.21.1865 Mound City IL BL/TR/5-8/170 d10.9																						
1888 KC AA	3	10	0	3	0	0	0	1	0	0		.300	.300	.300	87	0	0	.857	-0			C3		0.4
1889 KC AA	71	258	44	64	2	5	1	25	29	2	38	.248	.329	.306	76	-9	9	.916	-4			C66,3b4,O3L		-0.8
Total 2	74	268	44	67	2	5	1	26	29	2	38	.250	.328	.306	77	-9	9	.913	-4			C69,3b4,O3L		-0.6
HOOVER, PAUL Paul Chester B4.14.1976 Columbus OH BR/TR/6-1/210* [TBA97 23/714] d9.8 Col Kent St.																						
2001 TB A	3	4	1	1	0	0	0	0	0	0	1	.250	.250	.250	33	0	0-0	1.000	-1	82	0	C2		-0.1
2002 TB A	5	17	1	3	0	0	0	2	0-0	0	5	.176	.176	.176	-6	-3	0-0	1.000	-2	52	308	C4		-0.4
Total 2	8	21	2	4	0	0	0	2	0-0	0	6	.190	.190	.190	2	-3	0-0	1.000	-3	59	238	C6		-0.5
HOOVER, JOE Robert Joseph B4.15.1915 Brawley CA D9.2.1965 Los Angeles CA BR/TR/5-11/175 d4.21 Col Pomona (CA) JC																						
1943 Det A	144	575	78	140	15	8	4	38	36	1	101	.243	.289	.318	72	-22	6-5	.944	-8	90	144	S144		-2.1
1944 Det A	120	441	60	104	20	2	0	29	35	6	66	.236	.301	.290	66	-19	7-10	.932	15	102	131	S119/2		0.1
1945 †Det A	74	222	33	57	10	5	1	17	21	1	35	.257	.324	.360	92	-2	6-2	.944	-4	89	102	S68		-0.3
Total 3	338	1238	178	301	45	15	5	84	92	8	202	.243	.300	.316	73	-43	19-17	.939	3	94	109	S331/2		-1.9
HOOVER, BUSTER William James B4.12.1863 Philadelphia PA D4.16.1924 Jersey City NJ BR/TR/6-1/178 d4.17																						
1884 Phi U	63	275	76	100	20	8	0		12			.364	.390	.495	180	19		.780	0	141	113	O37L,S15,1b6,2b6/3		1.1
Phi N	10	42	6	8	1	0	1	4	4		9	.190	.261	.286	75	-1		.929	-1	59	0	O10(6/4/0)		-0.2
1886 Bal AA	40	157	25	34	2	6	0	10	16	2		.217	.297	.306	91	-2	15	.839	-3	43	0	O40C		-0.1
1892 Cin N	14	51	7	9	0	0	0	2	5	0	4	.176	.250	.176	30	-4	1	.966	1	131	422	O14(12/1/2)		-0.1
Total 4	127	525	114	151	23	14	1	16	37	2	13	.288	.337	.390	129	12	16	.840	-2	93	101	O101(55/45/2),S15,2b6,1b6/3		0.8
HOPKINS, DON Donald B1.9.1952 West Point MS BL/TR/6-0/175* d4.8																						
1975 †Oak A	82	6	25	1	0	0	0	0	2-0	0	0	.167	.375	.167	59	0	21-9	1.000	0	113	0	D20,O5(1/2/2)/R		0.0
1976 Oak A	3	0	0	0	0	0	0	0	0	0	0						0-1	—	0			H2		0.0
Total 2	85	6	25	1	0	0	0	0	2-0	0	0	.167	.375	.167	59	0	21-10	1.000	0	113	0	D20,O5(1/2/2)		0.0

YEAR	TM LG	G	AB	R	H	2B	3B	HR	RBI	BB-IB	HP	SO	AVG	OBP	SLG	AOPS	ABR	SB-CS	FA	FR	RNG	THR	GAMES AT POSITION	DL	BFW

HOPKINS, GAIL Gail Eason B2.19.1943 Tulsa OK BL/TR/5-10/200* d6.29 Col Pepperdine

1968	Chi A	29	37	4	8	2	0	0	2	6-1	0	1	.216	.326	.270	81	-1	0-0	1.000	-1	32	79	1b7		-0.2
1969	Chi A	124	373	52	99	13	3	8	46	50-1	1	28	.265	.351	.381	101	1	2-1	.994	-2	91	103	1b101		-0.8
1970	Chi A	116	287	32	82	8	1	6	29	28-5	1	19	.286	.346	.383	99	0	0-0	.987	-1	101	115	1b77,C8		-0.6
1971	KC A	103	295	35	82	16	1	9	47	37-9	4	13	.278	.364	.431	126	11	3-1	.990	2	114	118	1b83		0.8
1972	KC A	53	71	1	15	2	0	0	5	7-1	0	4	.211	.282	.239	56	-4	0-0	.990	-2	34	86	1b13/3		-0.7
1973	KC A	74	138	17	34	6	1	2	16	29-2	2	15	.246	.380	.348	100	2	1-2	1.000	0	101	68	D36,1b10		0.0
1974	LA N	15	18	1	4	0	0	0	0	3-2	0	1	.222	.333	.222	60	-1	0-0	1.000	1	0	0	C2,1b2		0.0
Total	7	514	1219	142	324	47	6	25	145	160-21	8	83	.266	.352	.376	103	8	6-4	.991	-2	98	108	1b293,D36,C10/3		-1.5

HOPKINS, BUCK John Winton "Sis" B1.3.1883 Grafton VA D10.2.1929 Phoebus VA BL/TL/5-10/165 d7.22

| 1907 | StL N | 15 | 44 | 7 | 6 | 3 | 0 | 0 | 3 | 10 | | 3 | .136 | .333 | .205 | 71 | 0 | 2 | .875 | -3 | 0 | 0 | O15C | | -0.5 |

HOPKINS, MARTY Meredith Hilliard B2.22.1907 Wolfe City TX D11.20.1963 Dallas TX BR/TR/5-11/175 d4.17 Col Texas

1934	Phi N	10	25	6	3	2	0	0	3	7	0	5	.120	.313	.200	36	-2		1.000	-0	93	189	3b9		-0.2
	Chi A	67	210	22	45	7	0	2	28	42	1	26	.214	.348	.276	61	-11	0-3	.957	5	116	32	3b63		-0.5
1935	Chi A	59	144	20	32	3	0	2	17	36	0	23	.222	.378	.285	72	-4	1-0	.960	-4	102	31	3b49,2b5		-0.7
Total	2	136	379	48	80	12	0	4	48	85	1	54	.211	.357	.274	63	-17	1-3	.960	0	110	61	3b121,2b5		-1.4

HOPKINS, MIKE Michael Joseph "Skinner" B11.1.1872 Glasgow, Scotland D2.5.1952 Pittsburgh PA BR/TR/5-8/160 d8.24

| 1902 | Pit N | 1 | 2 | 0 | 1 | 0 | 0 | 0 | 0 | | 0 | 0 | 1.000 | 1.000 | 1.500 | 648 | 1 | 0 | 1.000 | 0 | 189 | /C | | 0.1 |

HOPP, JOHNNY John Leonard "Hippity" B7.18.1916 Hastings NE D6.1.2003 Scottsbluff NE BL/TL/5-10/175* d9.18 C2

1939	StL N	6	4	1	2	0	0	0	2	1	0	1	.500	.600	.750	246	1		1.000	0	342	258	1b2		0.1
1940	StL N	80	152	24	41	7	4	1	14	9	1	21	.270	.315	.388	88	-3	3	.967	2	125	44	O39(12/27/0),1b10		-0.2
1941	StL N	134	445	83	135	25	11	4	50	50	1	50	.303	.378	.436	121	13	15	.982	-1	107	60	O91(58/23/10),1b39		0.5
1942	†StL N	95	314	41	81	16	7	3	37	36	0	40	.258	.334	.382	102	1	14	.983	-4	85	116	1b88		-1.2
1943	†StL N	91	241	33	54	10	2	2	25	24	1	42	.224	.297	.307	71	-9	8	.950	1	113	23	O52(40/12/0),1b27		-1.3
1944	†StL N	139	527	106	177	35	9	11	72	58	2	47	.336	.404	.499	150	36	15	.997	-8	98	19	O131(1/130/0),1b6		2.5
1945	StL N	124	446	67	129	22	8	3	44	49	3	24	.289	.363	.395	108	5	14	.980	2	**113**	56	O104(2/26/89),1b15		0.1
1946	Bos N★	129	445	71	148	28	8	3	48	34	5	34	.333	.386	.440	133	19	21	.981	-2	94	96	1b68,O58(1/57/0)		1.4
1947	Bos N	134	430	74	124	20	8	2	32	58	2	30	.288	.376	.358	98	-1	13	.980	-6	100	25	O125(0/123/2)		-0.7
1948	Pit N	120	392	64	109	15	12	1	31	40	0	25	.278	.345	.385	95	-3	5	1.000	-3	95	52	O80(1/71/8),1b25		-0.9
1949	Pit N	20	55	5	12	3	1	0	3	7	0	3	.218	.306	.309	64	-3	0	.929	-1	88	166	O7(2/0/5),1b6		-0.4
	Bro N	8	14	0	0	0	0	0	0	0	0	3	.000	.000	.000	-96	-4	0	1.000	1	105	393	O4(1/0/3),1b2		-0.3
	Pit N	85	316	50	106	11	4	5	36	30	0	26	.335	.393	.443	121	9	9	.994	-0	113	79	1b71,O9(2/0/7)		0.7
	Year	113	385	55	118	14	5	5	39	37	0	32	.306	.367	.408	105	3	9	.990	0	102	110	1b79,O20(5/0/15)		-0.0
1950	Pit N	106	318	51	108	24	5	8	47	43	1	17	.340	.420	.522	141	21	7	.990	-4	75	98	1b70,O7(2/2/3)		1.4
	†NY A	19	27	9	9	1	0	1	8	8	0	1	.333	.486	.593	180	4	0-1	1.000	0	71	23	1b12,O6L		0.3
1951	†NY A	46	63	9	13	1	0	2	4	9	0	11	.206	.306	.317	71	-3	2-0	.992	-2	55	83	1b25		-0.4
1952	NY A	15	25	4	4	0	0	0	2	2	·1	3	.160	.250	.160	17	-3	2-0	1.000	1	119	156	1b12		-0.2
	Det A	42	46	5	10	1	0	0	3	6	0	7	.217	.308	.239	53	-3	0-0	1.000	0	91	0	O4L/1		-0.3
	Year	57	71	9	14	1	0	0	5	8	1	10	.197	.287	.211	41	-6	2-0	1.000	0	115	150	1b13,O4L		-0.5
Total	14	1393	4260	698	1262	216	74	46	458	464	19	378	.296	.368	.414	113	79	128-1	.985	-23	104	44	O717(132/471/127),1b479		1.1

HORAN, SHAGS Joseph Patrick B9.6.1895 St.Louis MO D2.13.1969 Torrance CA BR/TR/5-10/170 d7.14

| 1924 | NY A | 22 | 31 | 4 | 9 | 0 | 0 | 1 | 7 | 2 | 0 | 1 | .290 | .313 | .323 | 64 | -2 | 0-0 | 1.000 | 0 | 89 | 156 | O14(4/1/9) | | -0.2 |

HORN, SAM Samuel Lee B11.2.1963 Dallas TX BL/TL/6-5/250(215-250) [BosA82 1/16] d7.25

1987	Bos A	46	158	31	44	7	0	14	34	17-0	2	55	.278	.356	.589	140	9	0-1	—	0	0	0	D40		0.7
1988	Bos A	24	61	4	9	0	0	2	8	11-3	0	20	.148	.274	.246	46	-4	0-0	—	0	0	0	D16		-0.5
1989	Bos A	33	54	1	8	2	0	0	4	8-1	0	16	.148	.258	.185	25	-5	0-0	1.000	-0	0	0	D14,1b2	50	-0.6
1990	Bal A	79	246	30	61	13	0	14	45	32-1	6	62	.248	.332	.472	126	8	0-0	.970	-1	93	95	D63,1b10	21	0.5
1991	Bal A	121	317	45	74	16	0	23	61	41-4	3	99	.233	.326	.502	130	12	0-0	—	0	0	0	D102		0.9
1992	Bal A	63	162	13	38	10	1	5	19	21-2	1	60	.235	.324	.401	99	0	0-0	—	0	0	0	D46		-0.1
1993	Cle A	12	33	8	15	1	0	4	8	1-0	1	5	.455	.472	.848	250	7	0-0	—	0	0	0	D11		0.6
1995	Tex A	11	9	0	1	0	0	0	0	1-0	0	6	.111	.200	.111	-16	-2	0-0	—	0			/D		-0.2
Total	8	389	1040	132	250	49	1	62	179	132-11	7	323	.240	.328	.468	118	25	0-1	.972	-1	88	90	D293,1b12	71	1.3

HORNER, BOB James Robert B8.6.1957 Junction City KS BR/TR/6-1/210(195-220) [AtlN78 1/1] d6.16 Col Arizona St.

1978	Atl N	89	323	50	86	17	1	23	63	24-2	2	44	.266	.313	.539	123	9	0-0	.956	10	110	108	3b89		1.8
1979	Atl N	121	487	66	153	15	1	33	98	22-6	2	74	.314	.346	.552	134	20	0-2	.930	-7	96	74	3b82,1b45	15	0.9
1980	Atl N	124	463	81	124	14	1	35	89	27-3	1	50	.268	.307	.529	129	14	3-1	.935	11	**115**	124	3b121/1		2.5
1981	Atl N	79	300	42	83	10	0	15	42	32-3	1	39	.277	.345	.460	127	10	2-3	.938	-11	89	92	3b79		-0.3
1982	†Atl N★	140	499	85	130	24	1	32	97	66-3	4	75	.261	.350	.501	133	22	3-5	.970	-14	86	92	3b137		0.5
1983	Atl N	104	386	75	117	25	·1	20	68	50-2	1	63	.303	.383	.528	140	22	4-2	.958	-10	83	113	3b104/1	48	1.1
1984	Atl N	32	113	19	31	8	0	3	19	14-2	0	17	.274	.349	.425	110	2	0-0	.965	2	108	121	3b32	138	0.0
1985	Atl N	130	483	61	129	25	3	27	89	50-4	1	57	.267	.333	.499	124	14	1-1	1.000	-8	93	134	1b87,3b40		0.0
1986	Atl N	141	517	70	141	22	0	27	87	52-8	2	72	.273	.336	.472	117	11	1-4	.995	0	98	**123**	1b139		0.1
1988	StL N	60	206	15	53	9	1	3	33	32-6	1	23	.257	.348	.354	104	2	0-0	.990	1	106	98	1b57	105	-0.1
Total	10	1020	3777	560	1047	169	8	218	685	369-39	16	512	.277	.340	.499	127	126	14-18	.946	-27	96	97	3b684,1b330	306	6.8

HORNSBY, ROGERS Rogers "Rajah" B4.27.1896 Winters TX D1.5.1963 Chicago IL BR/TR/5-11/175 d9.10 M14/C3 HF1942 OF(6/1/13)

1915	StL N	18	57	5	14	2	0	0	4	2	0	6	.246	.271	.281	67	-2	0-2	.922	-2	82	163	S18		-0.4
1916	StL N	139	495	63	155	17	15	6	65	40	4	63	.313	.369	.444	150	28	17	.928	-0	112	56	3b83,S45,1b15/2		3.7
1917	StL N	145	523	86	171	24	**17**	8	66	45	4	34	.327	.385	**.484**	170	42	17	.939	19	112	**129**	S144		7.8
1918	StL N	115	416	51	117	19	11	5	60	40	3	43	.281	.349	.416	138	18	8	.933	9	**113**	113	S109,O3(0/1/2)		3.8
1919	StL N	**138**	512	68	163	15	9	8	71	48	7	41	.318	.384	.430	**154**	34	17	.933	9	106	106	3b72,S37,2b25,1b5		5.1
1920	StL N	149	589	96	**218**	**44**	20	9	**94**	60	3	50	**.370**	**.431**	**.559**	190	69	12-15	.962	7	**104**	94	2b149		7.9
1921	StL N	154	592	131	**235**	44	18	21	**126**	60	7	48	**.397**	**.458**	**.639**	191	79	13-13	.969	-2	100	87	2b142,O6L,S3,3b3/1		7.7
1922	StL N	154	623	141	**250**	46	14	**42**	**152**	65	1	50	**.401**	**.459**	**.722**	210	100	17-12	**.967**	-7	90	95	2b154		8.9
1923	StL N	107	424	89	163	32	10	17	83	55	3	29	**.384**	**.459**	**.627**	188	56	3-7	.962	-16	92	86	2b96,1b10		3.8
1924	StL N	143	536	**121**	**227**	43	14	25	94	**89**	2	32	**.424**	**.507**	**.696**	223	99	5-12	.965	-3	100	105	2b143		9.3
1925	StL N	138	504	133	203	41	10	**39**	**143**	83	2	39	**.403**	**.489**	**.756**	208	85	5-3	.954	-14	91	122	2b136,M		6.8
1926	†StL N	134	527	96	167	34	5	11	93	61	0	39	.317	.388	.463	123	19	3	.962	-31	94	100	2b134,M		-0.8
1927	NY N	155	568	**133**	205	32	9	26	125	**86**	4	38	.361	**.448**	.586	176	64	9	.972	2	107	106	2b155,M		6.8
1928	Bos N	140	486	99	188	42	7	21	94	**107**	1	41	**.387**	**.498**	**.632**	204	83	5	.973	-23	97	85	2b140,M		6.1
1929	†Chi N	**156**	602	**156**	229	47	8	**39**	149	87	1	65	.380	.459	**.679**	178	76	0	.973	-3	103	112	2b156		6.8
1930	Chi N	42	104	15	32	5	1	2	18	12	1	2	.308	.385	.433	96	0	0	.916	-3	99	104	2b25,M		-0.2
1931	Chi N	100	357	64	118	37	1	16	90	56	0	23	.331	.421	.574	162	34	1	.951	-8	103	58	2b69,3b26,M		3.0
1932	Chi N	19	58	10	13	2	0	1	7	10	2	4	.224	.357	.310	82	-1	0	1.000	-4	86	0	O10R,3b6,M		-0.5
1933	StL N	46	83	9	27	6	0	2	21	12	2	6	.325	.423	.470	147	6	1	.967	-3	86	90	2b17		0.4
	StL A	11	9	2	3	1	0	1	2	2	0	1	.333	.455	.778	208	1	0-0	—	0			/HM		0.1
1934	StL A	24	23	2	7	2	0	1	11	7	1	4	.304	.484	.522	147	2	0-0	1.000	0	123	397	/3ORM		0.2
1935	StL A	10	24	1	5	3	0	0	3	3	0	6	.208	.296	.333	60	-1	0-0	1.000	-0	50	31	1b3,2b2/3M		-0.2
1936	StL A	2	5	1	2	0	0	0	2	1	0	0	.400	.500	.400	121	0	0-0	1.000	0	0	0	/1M		0.0
1937	StL A	20	56	7	18	3	1	1	11	7	0	5	.321	.397	.429	107	1	0-0	.947	-3	93	90	2b17,M		-0.1
Total	23	2259	8173	1579	2930	541	169	301	1584	1038	48	679	.358	.434	.577	176	892	135-64	.965	-77	99	98	2b1561,S356,3b192,1b35,O20R		86.0

HORNUNG, JOE Michael Joseph "Ubbo Ubbo" B6.12.1857 Carthage NY D10.30.1931 Howard Beach NY BR/TR/5-8.5/164 d5.1 U2 OF(1051/1/5)

1879	Buf N	78	319	46	85	18	7	0	38	2		27	.266	.271	.367	105	1		.844	-1	69	57	O77(76/0/1)/1		-0.4
1880	Buf N	**85**	342	47	89	8	11	1	42	8		29	.266	.282	.368	115	4		.874	1	77	62	O67L,1b18,2b5/P		0.0
1881	Bos N	83	324	39	78	12	8	2	25	5		25	.241	.252	.346	90	-4		.948	2	86	149	O83(83/1/0)		0.2
1882	Bos N	85	388	67	117	14	11	1	50	2		25	.302	.305	.402	124	9		.932	12	75	114	O84L/1		1.6
1883	Bos N	98	446	**107**	124	25	13	8	66	8		54	.278	.291	.446	117	7		**.936**	7	67	96	O98L/3		1.0
1884	Bos N	115	518	119	139	27	10	7	51	17		80	.268	.292	.400	116	8		.916	2	60	33	O110L,1b6		0.6

YEAR	TM LG	G	AB	R	H	2B	3B	HR	RBI	BB-IB	HP	SO	AVG	OBP	SLG	AOPS	ABR	SB-CS	FA	FR	RNG	THR	GAMES AT POSITION	DL	BFW
1885	Bos N	25	109	14	22	4	1	1	7	1		20	.202	.209	.284	61	-5		.919	-2	23	0	O25L		-0.7
1886	Bos N	94	424	67	109	12	2	2	40	10		62	.257	.274	.309	79	-11	16	.948	5	62	33	O94L		-0.8
1887	Bos N	98	437	85	118	10	6	5	49	17	3	28	.270	.302	.355	81	-13	41	.935	12	128	87	O98L		-0.3
1888	Bos N	107	431	61	103	11	7	3	53	16	2	39	.239	.269	.318	84	-9	29	.947	-7	57	0	O107(106/0/1)		-1.8
1889	Bal AA	135	533	73	122	13	9	1	78	22	7	72	.229	.269	.293	59	-32	34	.913	12	126	179	O134(134/0/1)/3		-2.0
1890	NY N	120	513	62	122	18	5	0	65	12	2	37	.238	.258	.292	60	-29	39	.931	-1	94	109	O77(76/0/2),1b36,3b5,S2		-3.1
Total	12	1123	4784	787	1230	172	90	31	564	120	14	498	.257	.277	.350	90	-74	159	.922	51	82	83	O1054L,1b62,3b7,2b5,S2/P		-5.7

HORTON, TONY Anthony Darrin B12.6.1944 Santa Monica CA BR/TR/6-3/210(195-210) d7.31

YEAR	TM LG	G	AB	R	H	2B	3B	HR	RBI	BB-IB	HP	SO	AVG	OBP	SLG	AOPS	ABR	SB-CS	FA	FR	RNG	THR	GAMES AT POSITION	DL	BFW
1964	Bos A	36	126	9	28	5	0	1	8	3-0	0	20	.222	.238	.286	44	-10	0-0	1.000	1	112	205	O24L,1b8		-1.1
1965	Bos A	60	163	23	48	8	1	7	23	18-1	0	36	.294	.361	.485	131	7	0-2	.980	-2	90	91	1b44		0.2
1966	Bos A	6	22	0	3	0	0	0	2	0-0	0	5	.136	.136	.136	-19	-3	0-0	1.000	1	136	163	1b6		-0.3
1967	Bos A	21	39	2	12	3	0	0	9	0-0	0	5	.308	.300	.385	96	0	0-0	.929	-1	95	97	1b6		-0.2
	Cle A	106	363	35	102	13	4	10	44	18-3	4	52	.281	.321	.421	117	6	3-0	.991	-5	74	95	1b94		-0.4
	Year	127	402	37	114	16	4	10	53	18-3	4	57	.284	.319	.418	114	6	3-0	.987	-6	75	95	1b100		-0.6
1968	Cle A	133	477	57	119	29	3	14	59	34-5	3	56	.249	.302	.411	117	9	3-1	.992	-4	79	93	1b128		-0.4
1969	Cle A	159	625	77	174	25	4	27	93	37-3	3	91	.278	.319	.461	113	3	3-3	.989	2	101	95	1b157		-0.4
1970	Cle A	115	413	48	111	19	3	17	59	28-6	5	54	.269	.321	.453	107	3	3-2	.994	4	106	116	1b112		-0.3
Total	7	636	2228	251	597	102	15	76	297	140-17	13	319	.268	.313	.430	109	20	12-8	.990	-5	91	99	1b555,O24L		-2.9

HORTON, WILLIE Willie Wattison B10.18.1942 Arno VA BR/TR/5-11/209(190-210) d9.10 C2

YEAR	TM LG	G	AB	R	H	2B	3B	HR	RBI	BB-IB	HP	SO	AVG	OBP	SLG	AOPS	ABR	SB-CS	FA	FR	RNG	THR	GAMES AT POSITION	DL	BFW
1963	Det A	15	43	6	14	2	1	1	4	0-0	0	8	.326	.326	.488	120	1	2-0	1.000	-1	78	0	O9(8/0/1)		0.0
1964	Det A	25	80	6	13	1	3	1	10	11-2	1	20	.162	.272	.287	55	-5	0-0	.943	-2	88	0	O23(20/0/3)		-0.9
1965	Det A★	143	512	69	140	20	2	29	104	48-9	6	101	.273	.340	.490	132	21	5-9	.988	3	104	85	O141(111/0/34)/3		1.4
1966	Det A	146	526	72	138	22	6	27	100	44-4	3	103	.262	.321	.481	125	15	1-1	.979	-4	97	48	O137(129/0/20)		0.4
1967	Det A	122	401	47	110	20	3	19	67	36-0	4	80	.274	.338	.481	137	18	0-0	.971	1	99	79	O110(109/0/1)		1.4
1968	†Det A★	143	512	68	146	20	2	36	85	49-8	8	110	.285	.352	.543	165	39	0-3	.973	-6	88	70	O139L		2.8
1969	Det A	141	508	66	133	17	1	28	91	52-10	3	93	.262	.332	.465	117	10	3-3	.972	5	112	78	O136(135/0/3)		0.7
1970	Det A★	96	371	53	113	18	2	17	69	28-6	2	43	.305	.354	.501	133	15	0-1	.982	3	96	172	O96(96/0/2)	69	1.3
1971	Det A	119	450	64	130	25	1	22	72	37-8	7	75	.289	.349	.496	132	18	1-5	.963	-7	85	113	O118(106/0/29)		0.4
1972	†Det A	108	333	44	77	9	5	11	36	27-5	3	47	.231	.293	.387	98	-2	0-0	1.000	-4	86	96	O98(81/0/30)	15	-1.2
1973	†Det A★	111	411	42	130	19	3	17	53	23-5	7	57	.316	.362	.501	133	17	1-4	.942	-9	89	31	O107L/D	18	0.1
1974	Det A	72	238	32	71	8	1	15	47	21-3	3	36	.298	.361	.529	144	14	0-1	.947	-4	91	48	O64L/D	83	0.6
1975	Det A	159	615	62	169	13	1	25	92	44-11	0	109	.275	.319	.421	104	1	1-2	—	0	0	0	D159		-0.4
1976	Det A	114	401	40	105	17	0	14	56	49-7	2	63	.262	.342	.409	115	9	0-0	—	0	0	0	D105	39	0.6
1977	Det A	4	1	0	0	0	0	0	0	0-0	0	0	.250	.250	.250	35	0	0-0	1.000	-0	49	0	/OL		-0.1
	Tex A	139	519	55	150	23	3	15	75	42-5	0	117	.289	.337	.432	108	5	2-3	.938	-1	89	0	D128,O10L		0.0
	Year	140	523	55	151	23	3	15	75	42-5	0	117	.289	.337	.430	107	5	2-3	.941	-1	85	0	D128,O11L		-0.1
1978	Cle A	50	169	15	42	7	0	5	22	15-4	1	25	.249	.314	.379	95	-1	3-0	—	0	0	0	D48		-0.2
	Oak A	32	102	16	32	8	0	3	19	9-2	0	15	.314	.369	.480	144	6	0-1	.333	-0	104	0	D27/OL		0.5
	Tor A	33	122	12	25	6	0	3	19	4-0	0	29	.205	.228	.328	54	-8	0-0	—	0	0	0	D30		-0.9
	Year	115	393	38	99	21	0	11	60	28-6	1	69	.252	.303	.389	94	-4	3-1	.697	-0	104	0	D105/OL		-0.6
1979	Sea A	162	646	77	180	19	5	29	106	42-4	4	112	.279	.326	.458	107	3	1-1	—	0	0	0	D162		-0.2
1980	Sea A	97	335	32	74	10	1	8	36	39-2	4	70	.221	.306	.328	74	-12	0-4	—	0	0	0	D92	48	-1.6
Total	18	2028	7298	873	1993	284	40	325	1163	620-95	58	1313	.273	.332	.457	119	164	20-38	.972	-26	95	79	O1190(1117/0/123),D753/3	272	4.7

HOSEY, DWAYNE Dwayne Samuel B3.11.1967 Sharon PA BB/TR/5-10/175* [ChiA87 13/323] d9.1 Col Pasadena (CA) City

YEAR	TM LG	G	AB	R	H	2B	3B	HR	RBI	BB-IB	HP	SO	AVG	OBP	SLG	AOPS	ABR	SB-CS	FA	FR	RNG	THR	GAMES AT POSITION	DL	BFW
1995	†Bos A	24	68	20	23	8	1	3	7	8-0	0	16	.338	.408	.618	157	6	6-0	1.000	0	103	111	O21(2/19/1)/D		0.7
1996	Bos A	28	78	13	17	2	1	3	7-0	0	17	.218	.282	.333	54	-6	6-3	.984	3	121	156	O26(7/20/0),D2		-0.3
Total	2	52	146	33	40	10	3	4	10	15-0	0	33	.274	.342	.466	102	0	12-3	.991	3	113	136	O47(9/39/1),D3		0.4

HOSEY, STEVE Steven Bernard B4.2.1969 Oakland CA BR/TR/6-3/215* [SFN89 1/14] d8.29 Col Cal St.-Fresno

YEAR	TM LG	G	AB	R	H	2B	3B	HR	RBI	BB-IB	HP	SO	AVG	OBP	SLG	AOPS	ABR	SB-CS	FA	FR	RNG	THR	GAMES AT POSITION	DL	BFW
1992	SF N	21	56	6	14	1	0	1	6	0-0	0	15	.250	.241	.321	64	-3	1-1	.960	-2	81	0	O18R		-0.6
1993	SF N	3	2	0	1	1	0	0	1	1-0	0	1	.500	.667	1.000	350	1	0-0	—	-0	0	0	/OR		0.1
Total	2	24	58	6	15	2	0	1	7	1-0	0	16	.259	.262	.345	77	-2	1-1	.960	-2	80	0	O19R		-0.5

HOSLEY, TIM Timothy Kenneth B5.10.1947 Spartanburg SC BR/TR/5-10/195(175-195) d9.8

YEAR	TM LG	G	AB	R	H	2B	3B	HR	RBI	BB-IB	HP	SO	AVG	OBP	SLG	AOPS	ABR	SB-CS	FA	FR	RNG	THR	GAMES AT POSITION	DL	BFW
1970	Det A	7	12	1	2	0	0	1	2	0-0	0	6	.167	.154	.417	55	-1	0-0	1.000	1	135	348	C4		0.0
1971	Det A	7	16	2	3	0	0	2	6	0-0	0	1	.188	.188	.563	101	0	0-0	1.000	1	126	0	C4/1		0.0
1973	Oak A	13	14	3	3	0	0	0	2	2-0	0	3	.214	.313	.214	53	-1	0-0	.952	-1	0	68	C13		-0.1
1974	Oak A	11	7	3	2	0	0	0	1	1-0	0	2	.286	.333	.286	98	0	0-0	1.000	1	87	0	C8/1		0.1
1975	Chi N	62	141	22	36	7	0	6	20	27-3	2	25	.255	.382	.433	120	5	1-1	.968	0	107	90	C53		0.7
1976	Oak A	37	55	4	9	2	0	1	4	8-0	0	12	.164	.270	.255	56	-3	0-0	.968	0	78	58	C37		-0.2
	Chi N	1	0	0	0	0	0	0	0	0-0	0	0	.000	.000	.000	-92	0	0-0	—	0			/H		0.0
1977	Oak A	39	78	5	15	0	0	1	10	16-0	1	13	.192	.333	.231	59	-4	0-0	.955	2	69	100	C19,D12,1b3		-0.2
1978	Oak A	13	23	1	7	2	0	0	3	1-0	1	6	.304	.360	.391	117	1	0-0	.962	0	66	131	C6/D		0.1
1981	Oak A	18	21	2	2	0	0	1	5	2-0	0	5	.095	.174	.238	18	-2	0-0	.750	-0	0	0	/1D		-0.3
Total	9	208	368	43	79	11	0	12	53	57-3	4	73	.215	.324	.342	87	-5	1-1	.968	3	89	91	C144,D17,1b6		0.1

HOSTETLER, CHUCK Charles Cloyd B9.22.1903 McClellantown PA D2.18.1971 Fort Collins CO BL/TR/6-0/175 d4.18

YEAR	TM LG	G	AB	R	H	2B	3B	HR	RBI	BB-IB	HP	SO	AVG	OBP	SLG	AOPS	ABR	SB-CS	FA	FR	RNG	THR	GAMES AT POSITION	DL	BFW
1944	Det A	90	265	42	79	9	2	0	20	21	0	31	.298	.350	.347	94	-2	4-4	.985	-1	96	109	O65(1/4/61)		-0.7
1945	†Det A	42	44	3	7	3	0	0	2	7	0	8	.159	.275	.227	43	-3	0-0	.889	1	82	0	O8(6/1/1)		-0.4
Total	2	132	309	45	86	12	2	0	22	28	0	39	.278	.338	.330	87	-5	4-4	.979	-1	95	102	O73(7/5/62)		-1.1

HOSTETLER, DAVE David Alan B3.27.1956 Pasadena CA BR/TR/6-4/215* [MonN78 4/87] d9.15 Col USC

YEAR	TM LG	G	AB	R	H	2B	3B	HR	RBI	BB-IB	HP	SO	AVG	OBP	SLG	AOPS	ABR	SB-CS	FA	FR	RNG	THR	GAMES AT POSITION	DL	BFW
1981	Mon N	5	6	1	3	0	0	1	1	0-0	0	2	.500	.500	1.000	307	1	0-0	1.000	-0	0	303	1b2		0.1
1982	Tex A	113	418	53	97	12	3	22	67	42-3	1	113	.232	.300	.433	104	1	2-2	.990	-9	70	105	1b109,D3		-1.6
1983	Tex A	94	304	31	67	9	2	11	46	42-1	5	103	.220	.323	.372	92	-3	0-2	1.000	-0	0	0	D88,1b2		-0.7
1984	Tex A	37	82	7	18	2	1	3	10	13-0	0	27	.220	.326	.378	91	-1	0-0	1.000	0	104	102	1b14,D13		-0.2
1988	Pit N	6	8	0	2	0	0	0	0	0-0	0	3	.250	.250	.250	44	-1	0-0	.944	0	241	0	1b4/C		-0.1
Total	5	255	818	92	187	23	6	37	124	97-4	6	248	.229	.313	.407	99	-3	2-4	.990	-10	73	104	1b131,D104/C		-2.5

HOTALING, PETE Peter James "Monkey" B12.16.1856 Mohawk NY D7.3.1928 Cleveland OH BL/TR/5-8/166 d5.1

YEAR	TM LG	G	AB	R	H	2B	3B	HR	RBI	BB-IB	HP	SO	AVG	OBP	SLG	AOPS	ABR	SB-CS	FA	FR	RNG	THR	GAMES AT POSITION	DL	BFW
1879	Cin N	**81**	369	64	103	20	9	1	27	12		17	.279	.302	.390	133	14		.843	0	107	116	O69(0/67/2),C8,2b6,3b3		1.1
1880	Cle N	78	325	40	78	17	8	0	41	10		30	.240	.263	.342	105	2		.896	-5	76	131	O78(2/76/0),C2		-0.7
1881	Wor N	77	317	51	98	15	3	1	35	18		12	.309	.346	.385	123	8		.862	-4	107	61	O74(2/72/1),C3		0.1
1882	Bos N	84	378	64	98	16	5	0	28	16		21	.259	.289	.328	97	-1		.865	0	84	139	O84(0/84/1)		-0.3
1883	Cle N	**100**	417	54	108	20	8	0	30	12		31	.259	.280	.345	90	-5		.829	-2	101	149	O100C		-0.9
1884	Cle N	102	408	69	99	16	6	3	27	28		50	.243	.291	.333	93	-4		.849	-1	113	144	O102(3/99/0)/2		-0.7
1885	Bro AA	94	370	73	95	9	5	1	34	49	4		.257	.350	.316	111	7		.893	-1	107	105	O94C		0.3
1887	Cle AA	126	505	108	151	28	13	3	94	53	7		.299	.373	.424	126	19	43	.903	-1	112	94	O126C		1.2
1888	Cle AA	98	403	67	101	7	6	0	55	26	7		.251	.307	.298	97	-1	35	.878	-10	64	187	O98C		-1.3
Total	9	840	3492	590	931	148	63	9	371	224	18	161	.267	.314	.353	108	39	78	.869	-23	97	126	O825(7/816/4),C13,2b7,3b3		-1.2

HOTTMAN, KEN Kenneth Roger B5.7.1948 Stockton CA BR/TR/5-11/190 [ChiA68 S2/22] d9.11 Col Sacramento (CA) City

YEAR	TM LG	G	AB	R	H	2B	3B	HR	RBI	BB-IB	HP	SO	AVG	OBP	SLG	AOPS	ABR	SB-CS	FA	FR	RNG	THR	GAMES AT POSITION	DL	BFW
1971	Chi A	6	16	1	2	0	0	0	1	0-0	0	2	.125	.176	.125	-13	-2	0-0	1.000	-1	65	0	O5L		-0.4

HOUCK, SADIE Sargent Perry B3.1856 Washington DC D5.26.1919 Washington DC BR/TR/5-7/151 d5.1

YEAR	TM LG	G	AB	R	H	2B	3B	HR	RBI	BB-IB	HP	SO	AVG	OBP	SLG	AOPS	ABR	SB-CS	FA	FR	RNG	THR	GAMES AT POSITION	DL	BFW
1879	Bos N	80	356	69	95	24	9	2	49	4		11	.267	.275	.402	117	6		.814	-10	144	168	O47(1/5/42),S33		-0.2
1880	Bos N	12	47	2	7	0	0	0	2	0		6	.149	.149	.149	1	-5		.786	-2	35	0	O12(0/2/10)		-0.6
	Pro N	49	184	27	37	7	7	1	22	3		6	.201	.214	.332	85	-3		.873	-1	82	0	O49(38/0/12/2)		-0.7
	Year	61	231	29	44	7	7	1	24	3		12	.190	.201	.294	68	-8		.855	-3	73	0	O61(38/14/12)		-1.3
1881	Det N	75	308	43	86	16	1	1	36	6		18	.279	.293	.380	106	1		.868	1	97	166	S75		0.5
1883	Det N	**101**	416	52	105	18	12	0	40	9		18	.252	.268	.353	91	-5		.852	4	103	122	S101		0.2
1884	Phi AA	**108**	472	93	140	19	14	0		7	8		.297	.318	.396	124	10		**.893**	22	112	117	S108/2		3.2
1885	Phi AA	93	388	74	99	10	9	0	54	10			.255	.286	.327	88	-7		.863	19	114	117	S93		1.3
1886	Bal AA	81	260	29	50	8	1	0	17	4	4		.192	.216	.231	41	-18	25	.849	-6	86	25	S55,2b5,OC		-2.0

YEAR	TM LG	G	AB	R	H	2B	3B	HR	RBI	BB-IB	HP	SO	AVG	OBP	SLG	AOPS	ABR	SB-CS	FA	FR	RNG	THR	GAMES AT POSITION	DL	BFW
	Was N	52	195	14	42	6	0	0	14	2		28	.215	.223	.231	41	-14	4	.858	2	107	59	S51/2		-1.0
1887	NY AA	10	33	3	5	1	0	0	0	3	1		.152	.243	.182	20	-3	2	.831	2	137	106	S10/2		-0.1
Total	8	641	2659	406	666	106	58	4	234	48	20	75	.250	.269	.338	91	-38	31	.863	31	104	111	S526,O109(39/20/54),2b8		0.6

HOUK, RALPH Ralph George "Major" B8.9.1919 Lawrence KS BR/TR/5-11/193* d4.26 M20/C4

YEAR	TM LG	G	AB	R	H	2B	3B	HR	RBI	BB-IB	HP	SO	AVG	OBP	SLG	AOPS	ABR	SB-CS	FA	FR	RNG	THR	GAMES AT POSITION	DL	BFW
1947	†NY A	41	92	7	25	3	1	0	12	11	1	5	.272	.356	.326	91	-1	0-0	.987	0	88	81	C41		0.1
1948	NY A	14	29	3	8	2	0	0	3	0	0		.276	.276	.345	65	-2	0-0	1.000	3	132	146	C14		0.1
1949	NY A	5	7	0	4	0	0	0	1	0	0		.571	.571	.571	203	1	0-0	.889	-1	49	0	C5		0.0
1950	NY A	10	9	0	1	0	0	0	1	0	0	2	.111	.111	.222	-17	-2	0-0	.929	0	0	0	C9		-0.1
1951	NY A	3	5	0	1	0	0	0	2	0	0	1	.200	.200	.200	9	-1	0-0	1.000	-0	0	447	C3		-0.1
1952	†NY A	9	6	0	2	0	0	0	0	1	0	0	.333	.429	.333	121	0	0-0	.917	0	0	0	C9		0.1
1953	NY A	8	9	2	2	0	0	0	1	0	0	1	.222	.222	.222	21	-1	0-0	1.000	0	0	0	C8		-0.1
1954	NY A	1	1	0	0	0	0	0	0	0	0	0	.000	.000	.000	-99	0	0-0	—	0			/H		0.0
Total	8	91	158	12	43	6	1	0	20	12	1	10	.272	.327	.323	79	-6	0-0	.981	2	81	87	C89		0.0

HOUSE, FRANK Henry Franklin "Pig" B2.18.1930 Bessemer AL D3.13.2005 Birmingham AL BL/TR/6-2/190* d7.21 Mil 1952-53

YEAR	TM LG	G	AB	R	H	2B	3B	HR	RBI	BB-IB	HP	SO	AVG	OBP	SLG	AOPS	ABR	SB-CS	FA	FR	RNG	THR	GAMES AT POSITION	DL	BFW
1950	Det A	5	5	1	2	0	0	0	1	0	0		.400	.400	.600	148	0	0-0	1.000	0	0	0	C5		0.0
1951	Det A	18	41	3	9	2	0	1	4	6	0	2	.220	.319	.341	78	-1	1-1	.957	-0	74	152	C18		-0.1
1954	Det A	114	352	35	88	12	1	9	38	31	1	34	.250	.307	.366	87	-7	2-1	.992	2	131	121	C107		-0.1
1955	Det A	102	328	37	85	11	1	15	53	22-4	3	25	.259	.308	.436	102	-2	0-0	.987	-1	100	115	C93		0.2
1956	Det A	94	321	44	77	6	2	10	44	21-0	3	19	.240	.290	.364	72	-15	1-1	.986	-3	133	101	C88		-1.3
1957	Det A	106	348	31	90	9	0	7	36	35-13	1	26	.259	.327	.345	82	-8	1-1	.997	8	147	80	C97		0.4
1958	KC A	90	202	16	51	6	3	4	24	12-2	1	13	.252	.295	.371	81	-6	1-0	.992	-4	122	84	C55		-0.7
1959	KC A	98	347	32	82	14	3	1	30	20-6	2	23	.236	.282	.303	59	-20	0-3	.982	-4	105	65	C95		-2.1
1960	Cin N	23	28	0	5	2	0	0	3	0	0	2	.179	.179	.250	16	-3	0-0	1.000	1	132	108	C8		-0.2
1961	Det A	17	22	3	5	1	1	0	3	4-0	0	2	.227	.333	.364	87	0	0-0	.974	-1	73	76	C14		-0.1
Total	10	653	1994	202	494	64	11	47	235	151-25	11	147	.248	.302	.362	80	-62	6-7	.988	-3	121	96	C580		-4.0

HOUSE, J.R. James Rodger B11.11.1979 Charleston WV BR/TR/5-10/202(202-215) [PitN99 5/152] d9.27

YEAR	TM LG	G	AB	R	H	2B	3B	HR	RBI	BB-IB	HP	SO	AVG	OBP	SLG	AOPS	ABR	SB-CS	FA	FR	RNG	THR	GAMES AT POSITION	DL	BFW
2003	Pit N	1	1	0	1	0	0	0	0	0-0	0	0	1.000	1.000	1.000	420	0	0-0	—	0			/H		0.0
2004	Pit N	5	9	1	1	0	0	0	0	0-0	0	2	.111	.111	.222	-17	-2	0-0	1.000	0	0	0	C3		-0.1
Total	2	6	10	1	2	1	0	0	0	0-0	0	2	.200	.200	.300	27	-2	0-0	1.000	0	0	0	C3		-0.1

HOUSEHOLDER, CHARLIE Charles F. B1856 Harrisburg PA D12.26.1908 Harrisburg PA BR/TR/5-7/150 d4.20

YEAR	TM LG	G	AB	R	H	2B	3B	HR	RBI	BB-IB	HP	SO	AVG	OBP	SLG	AOPS	ABR	SB-CS	FA	FR	RNG	THR	GAMES AT POSITION	DL	BFW
1884	CP U	83	310	32	74	12	5	1		12			.239	.267	.319	78	-18		.796	-4	78	107	3b41,O40L,S3,P2		-2.0

HOUSEHOLDER, CHARLIE Charles W. B2.8.1854 Philadelphia PA D9.3.1913 Philadelphia PA BL/TL/5-11/158 d5.2

YEAR	TM LG	G	AB	R	H	2B	3B	HR	RBI	BB-IB	HP	SO	AVG	OBP	SLG	AOPS	ABR	SB-CS	FA	FR	RNG	THR	GAMES AT POSITION	DL	BFW
1882	Bal AA	**74**	307	42	78	10	7	1		4			.254	.264	.342	111	4		.971	3	111	83	1b74,C3		-0.4
1884	Bro AA	76	273	28	66	15	3	3		12	2		.242	.279	.352	104	1		.959	-4	132	87	1b40,C31,O6(2/2/1)/2		-0.4
Total	2	150	580	70	144	25	10	4		16	2		.248	.271	.347	108	5		.967	-1	118	84	1b114,C34,O6(2/2/1)/2		-0.4

HOUSEHOLDER, ED Edward H. B10.12.1869 Pittsburgh PA D7.3.1924 Los Angeles CA BL/TL/5-9.5/180 d4.17

YEAR	TM LG	G	AB	R	H	2B	3B	HR	RBI	BB-IB	HP	SO	AVG	OBP	SLG	AOPS	ABR	SB-CS	FA	FR	RNG	THR	GAMES AT POSITION	DL	BFW
1903	Bro N	12	43	9	9	2	0	0		2			.209	.244	.209	31	-4		.967	1	60	250	O12C		-0.4

HOUSEHOLDER, PAUL Paul Wesley B9.4.1958 Columbus OH BB/TR/6-0/180(180-200) [CinN76 2/47] d8.26

YEAR	TM LG	G	AB	R	H	2B	3B	HR	RBI	BB-IB	HP	SO	AVG	OBP	SLG	AOPS	ABR	SB-CS	FA	FR	RNG	THR	GAMES AT POSITION	DL	BFW
1980	Cin N	20	45	3	11	1	1	0	7	1-0	0	13	.244	.261	.311	60	-3	1-0	1.000	0	81	234	O14(0/1/13)		-0.3
1981	Cin N	23	69	12	19	4	0	2	9	10-0	0	16	.275	.367	.420	123	2	3-1	1.000	-1	95	77	O19(1/6/13)		0.2
1982	Cin N	138	417	40	88	11	5	9	34	30-5	2	77	.211	.265	.326	65	-21	17-11	.992	8	106	182	O131(0/9/123)		-0.5
1983	Cin N	123	380	40	97	24	4	6	43	44-5	1	60	.255	.335	.387	96	-1	12-12	**.991**	2	109	80	O112(6/36/80)	22	-0.5
1984	Cin N	14	12	3	1	1	0	0	0	3-1	0	3	.083	.267	.167	23	-1	1-1	1.000	1	121	670	O10(3/1/6)		0.0
	StL N	13	14	1	2	0	0	0	0	0-0	0	3	.143	.143	.143	-20	-2	0-0	1.000	-1	64	0	O8(4/1/4)		-0.3
	Year	27	26	4	3	1	0	0	0	3-1	0	6	.115	.207	.154	3	-3	1-1	1.000	1	92	327	O18(7/2/10)		-0.3
1985	Mil A	95	299	41	76	15	0	11	34	27-0	1	60	.258	.320	.418	101	0	1-2	.986	2	105	90	O91(7/32/59),D3		-0.2
1986	Mil A	26	78	4	17	3	1	1	16	7-0	1	16	.218	.284	.321	64	-4	1-2	1.000	-1	89	87	O22(12/5/8),D3		-0.6
1987	Hou N	14	12	2	1	1	0	0	0	4-0	0	7	.083	.313	.167	33	-1	0-0	1.000	-1	64	0	O7(0/6/1)		-0.1
Total	8	466	1326	146	313	60	11	29	144	126-11	6	250	.236	.304	.363	84	-31	36-29	.991	10	104	123	O414(33/97/307),D6	22	-3.8

HOUSEMAN, JOHN John Franklin B1.10.1870 , Netherlands D11.4.1922 Chicago IL ?/160 d9.11

YEAR	TM LG	G	AB	R	H	2B	3B	HR	RBI	BB-IB	HP	SO	AVG	OBP	SLG	AOPS	ABR	SB-CS	FA	FR	RNG	THR	GAMES AT POSITION	DL	BFW
1894	Chi N	4	15	5	6	3	1	0	4	5		3	.400	.571	.733	201	3	2	.950	1	107	129	S3/2		0.3
1897	StL N	80	278	34	68	6	6	0	21	28	7		.245	.329	.309	70	-12	16	.918	-1	102	61	2b41,O33(7/7/19),S5,3b3		-1.0
Total	2	84	293	39	74	9	7	0	25	33	8	3	.253	.344	.331	79	-9	18	.916	-0	102	69	2b42,O33(7/7/19),S8,3b3		-0.7

HOUSER, BEN Benjamin Franklin B11.30.1883 Shenandoah PA D1.15.1952 Augusta ME BL/TL/6-1/185 d5.2

YEAR	TM LG	G	AB	R	H	2B	3B	HR	RBI	BB-IB	HP	SO	AVG	OBP	SLG	AOPS	ABR	SB-CS	FA	FR	RNG	THR	GAMES AT POSITION	DL	BFW
1910	Phi A	34	69	9	13	3	2	0	7	7	0		.188	.263	.290	74	-2	0	1.000	-0	72	142	1b26		-0.3
1911	Bos N	20	71	11	18	1	0	1	9	8	0	6	.254	.329	.310	73	-2	2	.988	1	112	111	1b20		-0.2
1912	Bos N	108	332	38	95	17	3	8	52	22	1	29	.286	.332	.428	105	1	1	.986	-3	84	103	1b83		-0.4
Total	3	162	472	58	126	21	5	9	68	37	1	35	.267	.322	.390	96	-3	3	.989	-3	86	110	1b129		-0.9

HOUSIE, WAYNE Wayne Tyrone B5.20.1965 Hampton VA BB/TR/5-9/165* [DetA86*8/199] d9.17 Col Riverside (CA) CC

YEAR	TM LG	G	AB	R	H	2B	3B	HR	RBI	BB-IB	HP	SO	AVG	OBP	SLG	AOPS	ABR	SB-CS	FA	FR	RNG	THR	GAMES AT POSITION	DL	BFW
1991	Bos A	11	8	2	2	1	0	0	0	1-0	0	3	.250	.333	.375	91	0	1-0	1.000	-1	58	0	O4C,D2		0.0
1993	NY N	18	16	2	3	1	0	0	1	1-0	0	1	.188	.235	.250	30	-2	0-0	—	-0	0	0	O2R		-0.2
Total	2	29	24	4	5	2	0	0	1	2-0	0	4	.208	.269	.292	51	-2	1-0	1.000	-1	45	0	O6(0/4/2),D2		-0.2

HOUSTON, TYLER Tyler Sam B1.17.1971 Las Vegas NV BL/TR/6-1/210(205-218) [AtlN89 1/2] d4.3

YEAR	TM LG	G	AB	R	H	2B	3B	HR	RBI	BB-IB	HP	SO	AVG	OBP	SLG	AOPS	ABR	SB-CS	FA	FR	RNG	THR	GAMES AT POSITION	DL	BFW
1996	Atl N	33	27	3	6	2	1	1	8	1-0	0	9	.222	.250	.481	82	-1	0-0	1.000	-0	59	55	1b11		-0.1
	Chi N	46	115	18	39	7	0	2	19	8-1	0	18	.339	.382	.452	115	3	3-2	.986	-5	66	101	C27,3b9,2b2/1OL		0.0
	Year	79	142	21	45	9	1	3	27	9-1	0	27	.317	.358	.458	108	2	3-2	.986	-5	66	101	C27,1b12,3b9,2b2/OL		-0.1
1997	Chi N	72	196	15	51	10	0	2	28	9-1	0	35	.260	.290	.342	63	-11	1-0	.986	-1	71	69	C41,3b12,1b2/2S		-0.9
1998	†Chi N	95	255	26	65	7	1	9	33	13-1	0	53	.255	.290	.396	76	-10	2-2	.993	-3	78	91	C63,3b12,1b7	29	-1.0
1999	Chi N	100	249	26	58	9	1	9	27	28-4	0	67	.233	.309	.386	75	-10	1-1	.901	-10	88	83	3b63,C18,1b2/OR		-1.9
	Cle A	13	27	2	4	1	0	1	3	3-0	0	11	.148	.233	.296	32	-3	0-0	1.000	-0	102	101	3b10/C		-0.3
2000	Mil N	101	284	30	71	15	0	18	43	17-3	0	72	.250	.292	.493	94	-5	2-1	.982	2	99	116	1b35,3b28,C23	17	-0.4
2001	Mil N	75	235	36	68	7	0	12	38	18-1	1	46	.289	.343	.472	110	3	0-0	.928	-2	102	107	3b62,1b3	78	0.1
2002	Mil N	76	255	25	77	15	2	7	33	14-3	4	41	.302	.347	.459	114	3	1-0	.947	-13	79	58	3b72/1		-0.9
	LA N	35	65	9	13	5	1	0	7	2-0	0	21	.200	.224	.308	43	-6	0-0	.981	-2	50	115	1b12,3b2		-0.8
	Year	111	320	34	90	20	3	7	40	16-3	4	62	.281	.323	.428	101	-2	1-0	.943	-15	80	57	3b74,1b13		-1.7
2003	Phi N	54	97	7	27	6	0	2	14	6-1	0	19	.278	.320	.402	94	-1	0-0	.936	-1	92	0	3b21/1	59	-0.2
Total	8	700	1805	197	479	84	6	63	253	119-15	5	408	.265	.312	.423	89	-38	10-6	.930	-36	94	81	3b291,C173,1b75,2b3,O2(1/0/1)/S	229	-6.4

HOUTZ, LEFTY Fred Fritz B9.4.1875 Connersville IN D2.15.1959 St.Marys OH BL/TL/5-10/170 d7.23

YEAR	TM LG	G	AB	R	H	2B	3B	HR	RBI	BB-IB	HP	SO	AVG	OBP	SLG	AOPS	ABR	SB-CS	FA	FR	RNG	THR	GAMES AT POSITION	DL	BFW
1899	Cin N	5	17	1	4	0	1	0	4	0	0		.235	.381	.353	100	0	1	1.000	3	399	773	O5(1/4/0)		0.3

HOVLEY, STEVE Stephen Eugene B12.18.1944 Ventura CA BL/TL/5-10/188(175-188) [AnaA66 35/665] d6.26 Col Stanford

YEAR	TM LG	G	AB	R	H	2B	3B	HR	RBI	BB-IB	HP	SO	AVG	OBP	SLG	AOPS	ABR	SB-CS	FA	FR	RNG	THR	GAMES AT POSITION	DL	BFW
1969	Sea A	91	329	41	91	14	3	3	20	30-3	1	34	.277	.338	.365	98	-1	10-4	.989	4	106	136	O84(3/35/49)		0.0
1970	Mil A	40	135	17	38	9	0	0	16	17-1	1	11	.281	.366	.348	98	1	5-1	.958	-0	110	45	O38(0/4/38)		-0.1
	Oak A	72	100	8	19	1	0	0	1	5-1	0	11	.190	.239	.200	20	-11	3-0	1.000	1	113	66	O42(10/26/7)		-1.1
	Year	112	235	25	57	10	0	0	17	22-2	1	22	.243	.310	.285	66	-10	8-1	.977	1	111	54	O80(10/30/45)		-1.2
1971	Oak A	24	27	3	3	2	0	0	3	7-0	1	6	.111	.306	.185	45	-1	2-0	1.000	1	129	285	O11(4/3/4)		0.0
1972	KC A	105	196	24	53	5	1	3	24	24-2	1	29	.270	.351	.352	111	3	3-3	.982	3	102	184	O68(5/25/39)		0.4
1973	KC A	104	232	29	59	8	1	2	24	33-2	0	34	.254	.346	.323	83	-4	6-4	.975	1	103	113	O79(4/25/53),D15		-0.6
Total	8	436	1019	122	263	39	5	8	88	116-9	4	128	.258	.343	.334	88	-13	29-12	.982	10	106	125	O322(26/118/190),D15		-1.4

HOWARD, CHRIS Christopher Hugh B2.27.1966 San Diego CA BR/TR/6-2/200(200-220) [SeaA88 41/1056] d9.15 Col Louisiana-Lafayette

YEAR	TM LG	G	AB	R	H	2B	3B	HR	RBI	BB-IB	HP	SO	AVG	OBP	SLG	AOPS	ABR	SB-CS	FA	FR	RNG	THR	GAMES AT POSITION	DL	BFW
1991	Sea A	9	6	1	1	0	0	0	0	1-0	0	2	.167	.286	.333	70	0	0-0	1.000	-1	218	265	C9		-0.1
1993	Sea A	4	1	0	0	0	0	0	0	0-0	0	0	.000	.000	.000	-98	0	0-0	1.000	-0	19	0	C4		-0.1
1994	Sea A	9	25	1	5	1	0	0	2	1-0	1	6	.200	.250	.240	29	-3	0-0	1.000	0	0	86	C9		-0.2
Total	3	22	32	2	6	1	0	0	2	2-0	1	8	.188	.250	.250	33	-3	0-0	1.000	-2	67	136	C22		-0.4

YEAR	TM LG	G	AB	R	H	2B	3B	HR	RBI	BB-IB	HP	SO	AVG	OBP	SLG	AOPS	ABR	SB-CS	FA	FR	RNG	THR	GAMES AT POSITION	DL	BFW

HOWARD, DAVE David Austin "Del" B5.1.1889 Washington DC D1.26.1956 Dallas TX BR/TR/5-11/165 d5.8 Col Cornell

YEAR	TM LG	G	AB	R	H	2B	3B	HR	RBI	BB-IB	HP	SO	AVG	OBP	SLG	AOPS	ABR	SB-CS	FA	FR	RNG	THR	GAMES AT POSITION	DL	BFW
1912	Was A	1	0	0	0	0	0	0	0	0	0		—	—	—	—	39	-4	0	0	—		/R		0.0
1915	Bro F	24	36	5	8	1	0	0	1	1	0	8	.222	.243	.250	39	-4	0	.925	1	134	0	2b12,O2(0/1/1)/3S		-0.2
Total	2	25	36	6	8	1	0	0	1	1	0	8	.222	.243	.250	39	-4	0	.925	1	134	0	2b12,O2(0/1/1)/3S		-0.2

HOWARD, DAVID David Wayne B2.26.1967 Sarasota FL BB/TR/6-0/175* [KCA86 32/774] d4.14 f-Bruce Col Manatee (FL) CC OF(20/25/28)

YEAR	TM LG	G	AB	R	H	2B	3B	HR	RBI	BB-IB	HP	SO	AVG	OBP	SLG	AOPS	ABR	SB-CS	FA	FR	RNG	THR	GAMES AT POSITION	DL	BFW
1991	KC A	94	236	20	51	7	0	1	17	16-0	1	45	.216	.267	.258	46	-17	3-2	.962	6	111	80	S63,2b26/3ORD		-0.7
1992	KC A	74	219	19	49	6	2	1	18	15-0	0	43	.224	.271	.283	54	-14	3-4	.976	1	97	116	S74,O2C	75	-0.9
1993	KC A	15	24	5	8	0	1	0	2	2-0	0	5	.333	.370	.417	108	0	1-0	.927	1	114	46	2b7,S3,3b2/OC	92	0.1
1994	KC A	46	83	9	19	4	0	1	13	11-0	0	23	.229	.309	.313	61	-5	3-2	1.000	5	113	43	3b25,S15,2b3/OLPD		0.1
1995	KC A	95	255	23	62	13	4	0	19	24-1	1	41	.243	.310	.325	64	-14	6-1	.994	12	105	102	2b41,S33,O30(11/16/8)/1D	21	0.2
1996	KC A	143	420	51	92	14	5	4	48	40-0	4	74	.219	.291	.305	51	-32	5-6	.982	13	109	136	S135,2b3,1b2/OC		-0.9
1997	KC A	80	162	24	39	8	1	1	13	10-1	1	31	.241	.287	.321	57	-10	2-2	.973	5	102	138	2b34,O23(5/2/17),S9,3b7,D5	18	-0.4
1998	StL N	46	102	15	25	1	1	2	12	12-2	1	22	.245	.322	.333	74	-4	0-0	1.000	-0	120	52	2b19,S16,3b14,O2(0/2/1)	102	-0.3
1999	StL N	52	82	3	17	4	0	1	6	7-3	2	27	.207	.286	.293	46	-7	0-2	.966	-2	91	44	S13,1b9,2b9,O5(3/1/1),3b4	74	-0.9
Total	9	645	1583	169	362	57	14	11	148	137-7	9	311	.229	.291	.303	56	-103	23-19	.976	41	108	116	S361,2b142,O66R,3b53,1b12,D9/P	382	-3.7

HOWARD, DOUG Douglas Lynn B2.6.1948 Salt Lake City UT BR/TR/6-3/185* [AnaA70 8/183] d9.6 Col Brigham Young

YEAR	TM LG	G	AB	R	H	2B	3B	HR	RBI	BB-IB	HP	SO	AVG	OBP	SLG	AOPS	ABR	SB-CS	FA	FR	RNG	THR	GAMES AT POSITION	DL	BFW
1972	Cal A	11	38	4	10	1	0	0	1	1-0	0	3	.263	.300	.289	80	-1	0-0	1.000	-1	63	373	O8L/13		-0.2
1973	Cal A	8	21	2	2	0	0	0	1	1-0	0	6	.095	.130	.095	-36	-4	0-0	1.000	-0	81	0	O6L/13		-0.5
1974	Cal A	22	39	5	9	0	1	0	5	2-0	0	1	.231	.268	.282	62	-2	0-0	1.000	-1	59	0	O8(2/6/0),1b5,D3		-0.3
1975	StL N	17	29	1	6	0	0	1	0	0-0	0	7	.207	.207	.310	40	-3	0-0	1.000	1	172	115	1b7		-0.2
1976	Cle A	39	90	7	19	4	0	0	13	3-2	1	13	.211	.237	.256	47	-6	1-1	.991	1	110	96	1b32,O2R,D4		-0.8
Total	5	97	217	19	46	5	1	1	22	7-2	2	30	.212	.239	.258	46	-16	2-1	.994	0	118	99	1b46,O24(16/6/2),D7,3b2		-2.0

HOWARD, ELSTON Elston Gene B2.23.1929 St.Louis MO D12.14.1980 New York NY BR/TR/6-2/200(196-208) d4.14 C11 Negro Lg 1948-50

YEAR	TM LG	G	AB	R	H	2B	3B	HR	RBI	BB-IB	HP	SO	AVG	OBP	SLG	AOPS	ABR	SB-CS	FA	FR	RNG	THR	GAMES AT POSITION	DL	BFW
1955	†NY A	97	279	33	81	8	7	10	43	20-5	1	36	.290	.336	.477	120	5	0-0	.978	5	98	191	O75(62/0/15),C9		0.7
1956	†NY A	98	290	35	76	8	3	5	34	21-6	1	30	.262	.312	.362	81	-9	0-1	.990	0	94	174	O65(62/0/5),C26		-1.1
1957	†NY A☆	110	356	33	90	13	4	8	44	16-6	0	43	.253	.283	.379	81	-11	2-5	.961	-3	66	177	O71(69/0/2),C32,1b2		-1.8
1958	†NY A☆	103	376	45	118	19	5	11	66	22-6	0	60	.314	.348	.479	131	14	1-1	.997	0	98	119	C67,O24(17/0/8),1b5		1.6
1959	†NY A☆	125	443	59	121	24	6	18	73	20-4	3	57	.273	.306	.476	116	7	0-1	.985	-2	86	96	1b50,C43,O28(18/0/10)		0.2
1960	†NY A★	107	323	29	79	11	3	6	39	28-7	0	43	.245	.298	.353	82	-9	3-0	.987	3	152	102	C91/OL		-0.2
1961	†NY A★	129	446	64	155	17	5	21	77	28-6	3	65	.348	.387	.549	156	33	0-3	.993	10	**196**	92	C111,1b9		4.5
1962	†NY A★	136	494	63	138	23	5	21	91	31-1	1	76	.279	.318	.474	115	8	1-1	.995	8	**229**	95	C129		2.2
1963	†NY A★	135	487	75	140	21	6	28	85	35-4	6	68	.287	.342	.528	141	25	0-0	.994	2	**203**	71	C132		3.4
1964	†NY A★	150	550	63	172	27	3	15	84	48-12	5	73	.313	.371	.455	127	21	1-1	**.998**	13	178	87	C146		4.2
1965	NY A☆	110	391	38	91	15	1	9	45	24-3	1	65	.233	.278	.345	77	-13	0-0	.991	2	106	105	C95,1b5/OL	32	-0.7
1966	NY A	126	410	38	105	19	2	6	35	37-9	1	65	.256	.317	.356	97	-1	0-0	.985	3	145	72	C100,1b13		0.6
1967	NY A	66	199	13	39	6	0	3	17	12-3	2	36	.196	.247	.271	56	-11	0-0	.984	0	104	79	C48/1		-1.0
	†Bos A	42	116	9	17	3	0	1	11	9-3	1	24	.147	.211	.198	21	-11	0-0	.996	3	109	-73	C41		-0.7
	Year	108	315	22	56	9	0	4	28	21-6	3	60	.178	.233	.244	42	-23	0-0	.990	3	106	76	C89/1		-1.7
1968	Bos A	71	203	22	49	4	0	5	18	22-7	1	45	.241	.317	.335	93	-1	1-1	.995	-6	73	83	C68		-0.5
Total	14	1605	5363	619	1471	218	50	167	762	373-82	26	786	.274	.322	.427	108	49	9-14	.993	37	**156**	92	C1138,O265(230/0/40),1b85	32	11.4

HOWARD, FRANK Frank Oliver "Hondo","The Capital Punisher" B8.8.1936 Columbus OH BR/TR/6-7/255(205-285) d9.10 M2/C20 Col Ohio St.

YEAR	TM LG	G	AB	R	H	2B	3B	HR	RBI	BB-IB	HP	SO	AVG	OBP	SLG	AOPS	ABR	SB-CS	FA	FR	RNG	THR	GAMES AT POSITION	DL	BFW
1958	LA N	8	29	3	7	1	0	1	2	1-0	0	11	.241	.267	.379	66	-1	0-0		0	90	178	O8(3/0/5)		-0.2
1959	LA N	9	21	3	3	1	0	1	6	2-0	0	9	.143	.217	.381	52	-2	0-0	1.000	0	101	0	O6(4/0/2)		-0.2
1960	LA N	117	448	54	120	15	2	23	77	32-1	3	108	.268	.320	.464	105	2	0-1	.984	-5	90	83	O115(22/0/94),1b4		-0.8
1961	LA N	92	267	36	79	12	2	15	45	21-3	1	50	.296	.347	.517	116	6	0-1	.934	-2	85	134	O65(20/0/46),1b7		-0.1
1962	LA N	141	493	80	146	25	6	31	119	39-10	1	108	.296	.346	.560	148	31	1-0	.972	2	88	189	O131(9/0/128)		2.4
1963	†LA N	123	417	58	114	16	1	28	64	33-2	4	116	.273	.330	.518	151	26	1-2	.960	-3	105	51	O111(6/0/107)		1.6
1964	LA N	134	433	60	98	13	2	24	69	51-10	0	113	.226	.303	.432	114	7	0-0	.979	-8	93	24	O122R		-0.9
1965	Was A	149	516	53	149	22	6	21	84	55-2	2	112	.289	.358	.477	138	25	0-0	.981	-5	90	65	O138(138/0/5)		1.4
1966	Was A	146	493	52	137	19	4	18	71	53-6	1	104	.278	.348	.442	127	17	1-1	.982	0	102	66	O135L		1.1
1967	Was A	149	519	71	133	20	2	36	89	60-7	5	155	.256	.338	.511	154	34	0-1	.986	-6	88	55	O141(141/0/3),1b4		2.3
1968	Was A★	158	598	79	164	28	3	**44**	106	54-12	6	141	.274	.338	**.552**	173	49	0-0	.955	-1	83	161	O107L,1b55		4.5
1969	Was A★	161	592	111	175	17	2	48	111	102-19	5	96	.296	.402	.574	180	65	1-0	.974	-16	73	36	O114(108/0/6),1b70		4.0
1970	Was A★	161	566	90	160	15	1	**44**	126	132-29	2	125	.283	.416	.546	172	61	1-2	.973	-9	83	83	O120(114/0/6),1b48		3.0
1971	Was A★	153	549	60	153	25	2	26	83	77-20	2	121	.279	.367	.474	144	32	1-0	.993	-5	79	119	O100(95/0/5),1b68		3.0
1972	Tex A	95	287	28	70	9	0	9	31	42-8	1	55	.244	.341	.369	116	6	0-0	.981	-6	83	77	1b66,O21(20/0/1)		-0.6
	Det A	14	33	1	8	1	0	1	7	4-0	0	8	.242	.324	.364	101	0	0-0	.952	0	121	84	1b10/OL		0.0
	Year	109	320	29	78	10	0	10	38	46-8	1	63	.244	.340	.369	114	6	0-0	.978	-6	88	78	1b76,O22(21/0/1)		-0.6
1973	Det A	85	227	26	58	9	1	12	29	24-4	0	28	.256	.327	.463	113	3	0-1	.923	-0	0	0	D76,1b2		0.0
Total	16	1895	6488	864	1774	245	35	382	1119	782-135	33	1460	.273	.352	.499	143	361	8-9	.975	-53	89	91	O1435(923/0/530),1b334,D76		21.8

HOWARD, DEL George Elmer B12.24.1877 Kenney IL D12.24.1956 Seattle WA BL/TR/6-0/180 d4.15 b-Ivan OF(137/34/85)

YEAR	TM LG	G	AB	R	H	2B	3B	HR	RBI	BB-IB	HP	SO	AVG	OBP	SLG	AOPS	ABR	SB-CS	FA	FR	RNG	THR	GAMES AT POSITION	DL	BFW
1905	Pit N	123	435	56	127	18	5	2	63	27	8		.292	.345	.370	110	6	19	.978	-5	85	133	1b90,O28(1/0/27)/P		-0.2
1906	Bos N	147	545	46	142	19	8	1	54	26	10		.261	.306	.330	101	-1	17	.911	-12	128	106	O87L,2b45,S14,1b2		-1.9
1907	Bos N	50	187	20	51	4	2	1	13	11	5		.273	.330	.332	108	-1	11	.969	-1	140	131	O45L,2b3		-0.2
	†Chi N	51	148	10	34	2	2	0	13	6	2		.230	.269	.270	65	-6	3	.972	-3	88	132	1b33,O8(0/3/6)		-1.1
	Year	101	335	30	85	6	4	1	26	17	7		.254	.304	.304	88	-5	14	.961	-4	121	113	O53(45/3/6),1b33,2b3		-1.3
1908	†Chi N	96	315	42	88	7	3	1	26	23	5		.279	.338	.330	109	3	11	.965	-3	101	46	O81(4/31/52),1b5		-0.3
1909	Chi N	69	203	25	40	4	2	1	24	18	6		.197	.282	.251	64	-8	6	.980	-0	101	120	1b57		-1.1
Total	5	536	1833	199	482	54	22	6	193	111	36		.263	.318	.326	98	-5	67	.946	-23	115	77	O249L,1b187,2b48,S14/P		-4.8

HOWARD, IVAN Ivan Chester B10.12.1882 Kenney IL D3.30.1967 Medford OR BB/TR/5-10/170 d4.25 b-Del

YEAR	TM LG	G	AB	R	H	2B	3B	HR	RBI	BB-IB	HP	SO	AVG	OBP	SLG	AOPS	ABR	SB-CS	FA	FR	RNG	THR	GAMES AT POSITION	DL	BFW
1914	StL A	81	209	21	51	6	2	0	20	28	3	42	.244	.342	.292	94	0	14-10	.936	-4	93	75	3b34,1b28,O3(1/1/1)/S		-0.5
1915	StL A	113	324	43	90	10	7	2	43	43	3	48	.278	.368	.370	126	11	29-12	.992	8	132	93	1b48,3b23,O17(5/1/11),2b2,S2		2.0
1916	Cle A	81	246	20	46	11	5	0	23	30	9	34	.187	.298	.272	68	-9	9	.970	6	116	62	2b65,1b7		-0.2
1917	Cle A	27	39	7	4	0	0	0	3				-5	.103	.167	.103	-17	-5	1	.833	-0	86	414	3b6,2b4,O4C	-0.7
Total	4	302	818	91	191	27	14	2	89	15	129		.233	.331	.308	92	-3	53-22	.990	9	125	68	1b83,2b71,3b63,O24(6/6/12),S3		0.6

HOWARD, LARRY Lawrence Rayford B6.6.1945 Columbus OH BR/TR/6-3/200* d8.9

YEAR	TM LG	G	AB	R	H	2B	3B	HR	RBI	BB-IB	HP	SO	AVG	OBP	SLG	AOPS	ABR	SB-CS	FA	FR	RNG	THR	GAMES AT POSITION	DL	BFW
1970	Hou N	31	88	11	27	6	0	2	16	10-3	0	23	.307	.378	.443	124	3	0-0	.993	-2	192	120	C26,1b2/OR		0.2
1971	Hou N	24	64	6	15	3	0	2	14	3-0	0	17	.234	.265	.375	83	-2	0-1	.992	3	149	122	C22		0.2
1972	Hou N	54	157	16	35	7	0	2	13	17-3	0	30	.223	.299	.306	74	-5	0-0	.980	-6	79	80	C53/OL		-0.9
1973	Hou N	20	48	3	8	3	0	0	4	5-2	0	12	.167	.245	.229	32	-4	0-0	.989	-1	99	152	C22		-0.5
	Atl N	4	8	0	1	0	0	0	0	2-0	0	3	.125	.300	.125	20	-1	0-0	1.000	-0	88	0	C2		0.0
	Year	24	56	3	9	3	0	0	4	7-2	0	15	.161	.254	.214	31	-5	0-0	.990	-2	98	135	C24		-0.6
Total	4	133	365	36	86	19	0	6	47	37-8	0	85	.236	.305	.337	81	-9	0-0	.986	-6	118	104	C123,O2(1/0/1),1b2		-1.1

HOWARD, MATT Matthew Christopher B9.22.1967 Fall River MA BR/TR/5-10/170 [LAN89 34/890] d5.17 Col Pepperdine

YEAR	TM LG	G	AB	R	H	2B	3B	HR	RBI	BB-IB	HP	SO	AVG	OBP	SLG	AOPS	ABR	SB-CS	FA	FR	RNG	THR	GAMES AT POSITION	DL	BFW
1996	NY A	35	54	9	11	1	1	0	9	2-0	0	8	.204	.228	.278	28	-6	1-0	.976	-8	72	54	2b30,3b6		-1.2

HOWARD, MIKE Michael Fredric B4.2.1958 Seattle WA BB/TR/6-2/185* [LAN76 6/139] d9.12

YEAR	TM LG	G	AB	R	H	2B	3B	HR	RBI	BB-IB	HP	SO	AVG	OBP	SLG	AOPS	ABR	SB-CS	FA	FR	RNG	THR	GAMES AT POSITION	DL	BFW
1981	NY N	14	24	4	4	1	0	0	3	4-0	0	6	.167	.276	.208	42	-2	2-0	.952	1	114	313	O14(6/1/7)		0.0
1982	NY N	33	39	5	7	0	0	1	3	6-0	1	7	.179	.298	.256	58	-2	2-0	1.000	2	111	272	O22(9/7/8),2b3		0.0
1983	NY N	1	3	0	1	0	0	0	0	0-0	0	1	.333	.333	.333	86	0	0-0	—	-1	0	0	/OR		-0.1
Total	3	48	66	9	12	1	0	1	7	10-0	1	14	.182	.291	.242	54	-4	4-0	.980	3	106	274	O37(15/8/16),2b3		-0.1

HOWARD, PAUL Paul Joseph "Del" B5.20.1884 Boston MA D8.29.1968 Miami FL BR/TR/5-8/170 d9.16

YEAR	TM LG	G	AB	R	H	2B	3B	HR	RBI	BB-IB	HP	SO	AVG	OBP	SLG	AOPS	ABR	SB-CS	FA	FR	RNG	THR	GAMES AT POSITION	DL	BFW
1909	Bos A	6	15	2	3	1	0	0	2	3	1		.200	.368	.267	99	0	0	1.000	-0	228	0	O6(4/0/2)		0.0

HOWARD, RYAN Ryan James B11.19.1979 St.Louis MO BL/TL/6-4/230* [PhiN01 5/140] d9.1 Col Missouri St.

YEAR	TM LG	G	AB	R	H	2B	3B	HR	RBI	BB-IB	HP	SO	AVG	OBP	SLG	AOPS	ABR	SB-CS	FA	FR	RNG	THR	GAMES AT POSITION	DL	BFW
2004	Phi N	19	39	5	11	5	0	2	5	2-0	0	13	.282	.333	.564	122	1	0-0	1.000	1	133	164	1b8		0.1
2005	Phi N	88	312	52	90	17	2	22	63	33-8	2	100	.288	.356	.567	133	14	0-1	.993	-4	78	82	1b84		0.3
Total	2	107	351	57	101	22	2	24	68	35-8	2	113	.288	.354	.567	132	15	0-1	.994	-3	82	89	1b92		0.4

YEAR	TM LG	G	AB	R	H	2B	3B	HR	RBI	BB-IB	HP	SO	AVG	OBP	SLG	AOPS	ABR	SB-CS	FA	FR	RNG	THR	GAMES AT POSITION	DL	BFW
HOWARD, STEVE	Steven Bernard B12.7.1963 Oakland CA BR/TR/6-2/205 [OakA83*8/186] d6.16																								
1990	Oak A	21	52	5	12	4	0	0	1	4-1	0	17	.231	.286	.308	68	-2	0-0	.933	-2	71	0	O14(4/3/8),D7		-0.4
HOWARD, THOMAS	Thomas Sylvester B12.11.1964 Middletown OH BB/TR (BL 1996-98)/6-2/205* [SDN86 1/11] d7.3 Col Ball St.																								
1990	SD N	20	44	4	12	1	0	0	0	0	0	11	.273	.273	.318	61	-2	0-1	.950	-1	92	0	O13(9/2/2)		-0.4
1991	SD N	106	281	30	70	12	3	4	22	24-4	1	57	.249	.309	.356	84	-6	10-7	.995	4	113	92	O86(34/41/14)		-0.4
1992	SD N	5	3	1	1	0	0	0	0	0-0	0	0	.333	.333	.333	88	0	0-0	—	0			/H		0.0
	Cle A	117	358	36	99	15	2	2	32	17-1	0	60	.277	.308	.346	84	-8	15-8	.990	-2	96	90	O97(68/22/13),D2		-1.2
1993	Cle A	74	178	26	42	7	0	3	23	12-0	0	42	.236	.278	.326	63	-10	5-1	.977	2	106	129	O47(9/11/28),D7		-0.8
	Cin N	38	141	22	39	8	3	4	13	12-0	0	21	.277	.331	.461	109	1	5-6	.987	2	103	180	O37(27/12/0)		0.2
1994	Cin N	83	178	24	47	11	0	5	24	10-1	0	30	.264	.302	.410	84	-5	4-2	.965	1	106	83	O57(41/7/12)		-0.5
1995	†Cin N	113	281	42	85	15	2	3	26	20-0	1	37	.302	.350	.402	97	-1	17-8	.985	-0	58	68	O82(36/39/14)		-0.2
1996	Cin N	121	360	50	98	19	10	6	42	17-3	0	51	.272	.307	.431	91	-6	6-5	.982	1	97	146	O103(51/40/32)	19	-0.8
1997	†Hou N	107	255	24	63	16	1	3	22	26-1	3	48	.247	.323	.353	80	-7	1-2	1.000	0	93	163	O62(10/41/18)		-0.8
1998	LA N	47	76	9	14	4	0	2	4	3-0	0	15	.184	.215	.316	39	-7	1-0	1.000	1	102	207	O29(11/13/6)/D		-0.6
1999	StL N	98	195	16	57	10	0	6	28	17-0	2	26	.292	.353	.436	97	-1	1-1	.987	-2	100	0	O48(3/0/45)/D		-0.4
2000	StL N	86	133	13	28	4	1	0	14	21-1	0	34	.211	.255	.391	59	-9	1-0	.960	-2	75	101	O27(6/0/22)/1D		-1.1
Total	11	1015	2483	297	655	123	22	44	264	165-10	11	432	.264	.311	.384	84	-61	66-41	.986	4	100	106	O688(305/228/206),D14/1	19	-7.0
HOWARD, WILBUR	Wilbur Leon B1.8.1949 Lowell NC BB/TR/6-2/175* [MilA68 19/441] d9.4																								
1973	Mil A	16	39	3	8	0	0	0	1	2-1	0	10	.205	.244	.205	28	-4	0-1	.969	2	135	268	O12(5/0/7)/D		-0.2
1974	Hou N	64	111	19	24	4	0	2	5	5-0	0	18	.216	.250	.306	58	-7	4-5	1.000	2	103	137	O50(43/4/3)		-0.2
1975	Hou N	121	392	62	111	16	8	0	21	21-3	1	67	.283	.324	.365	98	-3	32-11	.995	2	101	112	O95(53/34/12)		-0.8
1976	Hou N	94	191	26	42	7	2	1	18	7-1	0	28	.220	.245	.293	58	-12	7-5	.961	1	107	65	O63(37/11/20),2b2		-1.5
1977	Hou N	87	187	22	48	6	0	2	13	5-1	0	30	.257	.276	.321	65	-10	11-1	.990	2	109	68	O62(46/15/4),2b4		-0.8
1978	Hou N	84	148	17	34	4	1	1	13	5-0	3	22	.230	.268	.291	60	-9	6-2	1.000	-3	78	103	O38(30/5/4),C3/2	20	-1.2
Total	6	466	1068	149	267	37	11	6	71	45-6	6	175	.250	.283	.322	73	-45	60-25	.987	7	103	105	O320(214/69/50),2b7,C3/D	20	-4.7
HOWARTH, JIM	James Eugene B3.7.1947 Biloxi MS BL/TL/5-11/175* d9.5 Col Mississippi St.																								
1971	SF N	7	13	3	3	1	0	0	2	3-0	0	3	.231	.375	.308	96	0	0-0	1.000	0	144	0	O6(2/1/3)		0.0
1972	SF N	74	119	16	28	4	1	0	7	16-1	0	18	.235	.326	.294	76	-3	3-2	1.000	-1	97	0	O25(8/17/0),1b4		-0.6
1973	SF N	65	90	8	18	1	1	0	7	7-0	0	8	.200	.258	.233	35	-8	0-0	1.000	0	102	79	O33(5/21/7)/1		-0.9
1974	SF N	6	4	0	0	0	0	0	0	0-0	0	0	.000	.000	.000	-96	-1	0-0	—	-0	0	0	/OL		-0.1
Total	4	152	226	27	49	6	1	1	16	26-1	0	29	.217	.298	.265	58	-12	3-2	1.000	-1	103	36	O65(16/39/10),1b5		-1.6
HOWE, ART	Arthur Henry B12.15.1946 Pittsburgh PA BR/TR/6-2/190* d7.10 M14/C5 Col Wyoming [DL 1983 Hou N 182]																								
1974	†Pit N	29	74	10	18	4	1	1	5	9-0	0	13	.243	.321	.365	95	0	0-0	.937	1	110	216	3b20,S2		0.0
1975	Pit N	63	146	13	25	9	1	0	10	15-3	1	15	.171	.248	.253	39	-12	1-0	.938	4	102	61	3b42,S3		-1.6
1976	Hou N	21	29	0	4	1	0	0	0	6-1	0	6	.138	.286	.172	35	-2	0-0	.938	0	90	99	3b8,2b2		-0.2
1977	Hou N	125	413	44	109	23	7	8	58	41-6	5	60	.264	.336	.412	108	4	0-1	.985	-1	101	89	2b96,3b19,S11		0.8
1978	Hou N	119	420	46	123	33	3	7	55	34-3	1	41	.293	.343	.436	126	4	2-3	.977	-9	92	81	2b107,3b11/1		1.1
1979	Hou N	118	355	32	88	15	2	6	33	36-5	1	37	.248	.316	.352	88	-6	3-1	.991	11	106	96	2b68,3b59,1b3		0.8
1980	†Hou N	110	321	34	91	12	5	10	46	34-6	1	29	.283	.350	.445	133	13	0-0	.986	-1	108	97	1b77,3b25,S5,2b3		1.7
1981	†Hou N	103	361	43	107	22	4	3	36	41-7	0	23	.296	.365	.404	126	13	1-3	.966	5	107	118	3b98,1b2		1.7
1982	Hou N	110	365	29	87	15	1	5	38	41-15	1	45	.238	.315	.326	87	-6	2-0	.972	8	111	118	3b72,1b35	38	-0.1
1984	StL N	89	139	17	30	5	0	2	12	18-1	0	18	.216	.300	.295	71	-5	0-2	.979	3	117	121	3b45,1b11,2b8,S5		-0.3
1985	StL N	4	3	0	0	0	0	0	0	0-0	0	0	.000	.000	.000	-99	-1	0-0	1.000	1	0	572	/13		0.0
Total	11	891	2626	268	682	139	23	43	293	275-47	9	287	.260	.329	.379	103	12	10-10	.965	14	106	108	3b400,2b284,1b130,S26	220	3.0
HOWE, SHORTY	John B New York NY d6.17																								
1890	NY N	19	64	4	11	0	0	0	4	3	1	2	.172	.221	.172	15	-7	3	.887	2	111	44	2b18/3		-0.4
1893	NY N	1	5	1	3	0	0	0	2	0	0	0	.600	.600	.600	218	1	1	.400	-1	69	0	/3		0.0
Total	2	20	69	5	14	0	0	0	6	3	1	2	.203	.247	.203	30	-6	4	.887	0	111	44	2b18,3b2		-0.4
HOWELL, DIXIE	Homer Elliott B4.24.1920 Louisville KY D10.5.1990 Binghamton NY BR/TR/5-11/195* d5.6																								
1947	Pit N	76	214	23	59	11	0	4	25	27	0	34	.276	.357	.383	94	-1	1	.974	-4	91	85	C74		-0.1
1949	Cin N	64	172	17	42	6	1	2	18	8	2	21	.244	.286	.326	63	-10	0	.987	3	117	138	C56		-0.4
1950	Cin N	82	224	30	50	9	1	2	22	32	2	31	.223	.326	.299	65	-11	0	.986	-5	74	83	C81		-1.1
1951	Cin N	77	207	22	52	6	1	2	18	15	0	34	.251	.302	.319	66	-10	0-2	.987	0	80	87	C73		-0.7
1952	Cin N	17	37	4	7	1	1	2	4	3	0	9	.189	.250	.432	86	-1	0-0	.981	1	83	165	C16		0.0
1953	Bro N	1	1	0	0	0	0	0	0	0	0	1	.000	.000	.000	-98	0	0-0	—	0			/H		0.0
1955	Bro N	16	42	1	14	0	0	5	1-0		0	7	.262	.273	.357	66	-2	0-0	.981	-1	128	50	C13		-0.2
1956	Bro N	7	13	0	3	0	0	1	1-1		0	5	.231	.267	.385	72	0	0-0	1.000	-0	104	0	C6		0.0
Total	8	340	910	98	224	39	4	12	93	87-1	4	140	.246	.314	.337	73	-35	1-2	.984	-5	90	95	C319		-2.5
HOWELL, JACK	Jack Robert B8.18.1961 Tucson AZ BL/TR/6-0/201(185-201) d5.20 Col Arizona OF(88/1/23)																								
1985	Cal A	43	137	19	27	4	0	5	18	16-2	0	33	.197	.279	.336	68	-6	1-1	.931	-2	98	132	3b42		-0.9
1986	†Cal A	63	151	26	41	14	2	4	21	19-0	0	28	.272	.349	.470	123	5	2-0	.977	-1	95	77	3b39,O8(7/0/1),D2		0.4
1987	Cal A	138	449	64	110	18	5	23	64	57-4	2	118	.245	.331	.461	111	6	4-3	.987	2	97	76	O89(78/0/15),3b48,2b13		0.4
1988	Cal A	154	500	59	127	32	2	16	63	46-8	6	130	.254	.323	.422	110	7	2-6	.953	-12	96	74	3b152,O2(1/1/0)		-0.7
1989	Cal A	144	474	56	108	19	4	20	52	52-9	3	125	.228	.308	.411	103	1	0-3	.974	23	121	123	3b142,O4(1/0/3)		2.3
1990	Cal A	105	316	35	72	19	1	8	33	46-5	1	61	.228	.326	.370	96	0	3-0	.939	-0	99	102	3b102/1S	17	0.0
1991	Cal A	32	81	11	17	2	0	2	7	11-0	0	21	.210	.304	.309	70	-3	1-1	.968	5	132	62	2b12,3b8,O5(1/0/4),1b3/D	24	0.1
	SD N	58	160	24	33	3	1	6	16	18-1	0	33	.206	.287	.350	76	-6	0-0	.985	6	114	106	3b54		0.0
1996	Cal A	66	126	20	34	4	1	8	21	10-0	0	30	.270	.324	.508	104	0	0-1	.884	-2	97	111	3b43,1b2/2D	33	-0.2
1997	Ana A	77	174	25	45	7	0	14	34	13-2	1	36	.259	.305	.540	116	3	1-0	.976	-2	80	134	3b24,D22,1b12		0.0
1998	Hou N	24	38	4	11	5	0	1	7	4-0	0	12	.289	.357	.500	126	2	0-0	1.000	1	145	66	1b10,3b2	131	0.2
1999	Hou N	37	33	2	7	2	0	1	1	8-0	0	9	.212	.366	.364	87	0	0-0	1.000	1	179	307	1b5,3b3,D2	107	0.0
Total	11	941	2639	345	632	129	16	108	337	300-31	12	626	.239	.318	.423	103	9	14-15	.958	19	105	107	3b659,O108L,1b33,D31,2b26/S	312	1.6
HOWELL, RED	Murray Donald "Porky" B1.29.1909 Atlanta GA D10.1.1950 Travelers Rest SC BR/TR/6-0/215 d4.24																								
1941	Cle A	11	7	0	2	0	0	0	2	4	1	2	.286	.545	.286	132	1	0-0	—	0			/H		0.1
HOWELL, PAT	Patrick O'Neal B8.31.1968 Mobile AL BB/TR/5-11/155 [NYN87 9/238] d7.10																								
1992	NY N	31	75	9	14	1	0	0	1	2-0	1	15	.187	.218	.200	19	-8	4-2	.985	2	129	0	O28C		-0.7
HOWELL, ROY	Roy Lee B12.18.1953 Lompoc CA BL/TR/6-1/190* [TexA72 1/4] d9.9																								
1974	Tex A	13	44	2	11	1	0	1	3	2-0	0	10	.250	.283	.341	81	-1	0-0	.906	-1	105	41	3b12		-0.2
1975	Tex A	125	383	43	96	15	2	10	51	39-6	3	79	.251	.322	.379	99	-1	2-2	.933	-2	100	**159**	3b115,D5		-0.3
1976	Tex A	140	491	55	124	28	2	8	53	30-8	1	106	.253	.295	.367	92	-6	1-0	.926	-6	98	95	3b130,D8		-1.3
1977	Tex A	7	17	0	0	0	0	0	0	2-0	0	4	.000	.105	.000	-68	-4	0-0	1.000	-0	135	0	O2L/13D		-0.5
	Tor A★	96	364	41	115	11	1	10	44	42-2	1	76	.316	.386	.451	126	15	4-1	.953	-4	94	67	3b87,D8		1.0
	Year	103	381	41	115	11	1	10	44	44-2	1	80	.302	.374	.430	117	11	4-1	.954	-4	94	67	3b88,D10,O2L/1		0.5
1978	Tor A	140	551	67	149	28	3	8	61	44-3	1	78	.270	.325	.376	95	-4	0-1	.950	8	106	97	3b131,O5R/D		0.2
1979	Tor A	138	511	60	126	28	4	15	72	42-4	6	91	.247	.310	.405	90	-8	1-4	.952	4	105	103	3b133,D4	16	-0.7
1980	Tor A	142	528	51	142	28	9	10	57	50-8	5	92	.269	.335	.413	100	0	0-0	.958	-14	92	79	3b138,D2		-1.6
1981	†Mil A	76	244	37	58	13	1	6	33	23-4	2	39	.238	.306	.361	95	-4	0-0	.948	-4	93	97	3b53,D13,1b3/OR		-0.6
1982	†Mil A	98	300	31	78	11	2	4	38	21-2	0	39	.260	.305	.350	85	-7	0-2	.933	-0	117	43	D84,1b4,O2R		-1.0
1983	Mil A	69	194	23	54	9	6	4	25	15-0	0	29	.278	.330	.448	120	4	1-3	.960	1	284	217	D54,1b2		0.3
1984	Mil A	68	164	12	38	5	1	4	17	8-1	4	32	.232	.284	.348	76	-6	0-1	.907	0	107	0	1b34,D4,3b8		-0.2
Total	11	1112	3791	422	991	183	31	80	454	318-38	23	675	.261	.321	.389	97	-18	9-14	.944	-18	99	99	3b846,D189,1b14,O10(2/0/8)	16	-5.4
HOWERTON, BILL	William Ray "Hopalong" B12.12.1921 Lompoc CA D12.18.2001 Blakely PA BL/TR/5-11/185* d9.11 Col St. Marys (CA)																								
1949	StL N	9	13	4	4	0	0	1	1	3-0	0	2	.308	.308	.385	91	0	0	.900	0	123	0	O6(2/3/1)		-0.1
1950	StL N	110	313	50	88	20	8	10	59	47	0	60	.281	.375	.492	120	10	0	.969	-5	96	31	O94(32/54/11)		0.1
1951	StL N	24	65	10	17	4	1	1	4	10	0	12	.262	.360	.400	104	1	0-1	.949	-5	106	132	O17(3/0/14)		0.0
	Pit N	80	219	29	60	12	2	11	37	26	0	44	.274	.351	.498	122	7	1-0	.950	-6	83	76	O53(4/38/11),3b4		0.0

YEAR	TM LG	G	AB	R	H	2B	3B	HR	RBI	BB-IB	HP	SO	AVG	OBP	SLG	AOPS	ABR	SB-CS	FA	FR	RNG	THR	GAMES AT POSITION	DL	BFW
	Year	104	284	39	77	16	3	12	41	36	0	56	.271	.353	.475	118	7	1-1	.950	-5	89	91	O70(7/38/25),3b4		0.0
1952	Pit N	13	25	3	8	1	1	0	4	6	0	5	.320	.452	.440	144	2	0-0	.900	-2	92	0	O5(0/2/3)/3		0.0
	NY N	11	15	2	1	1	0	0	1	3	0	2	.067	.222	.133	1	-2	0-0	1.000	-0	99	0	O3(0/1/2)		-0.2
	Year	24	40	5	9	2	1	0	5	9	0	7	.225	.367	.325	92	0	0-0	.938	-2	95	0	O8(0/3/5)/3		-0.2
Total	4	247	650	95	178	39	12	22	106	92	0	125	.274	.364	.472	117	18	1-1	.958	-12	94	53	O178(41/98/42),3b5		0.0

HOWITT, DANN Dann Paul John B2.13.1964 Battle Creek MI BL/TR/6-5/205* [OakA86 18/457] d9.15 Col Cal St.-Fullerton

YEAR	TM LG	G	AB	R	H	2B	3B	HR	RBI	BB-IB	HP	SO	AVG	OBP	SLG	AOPS	ABR	SB-CS	FA	FR	RNG	THR	GAMES AT POSITION	DL	BFW
1989	Oak A	3	3	0	0	0	0	0	0	0-0	0	2	.000	.000	.000	-99	-1	0-0	1.000	-0	0	0	/1OR		-0.1
1990	Oak A	14	22	3	3	0	1	0	1	3-0	0	12	.136	.240	.227	33	-2	0-0	1.000	1	207	0	O11R,1b5/3		-0.1
1991	Oak A	21	42	5	7	1	0	1	3	1-0	0	12	.167	.182	.262	24	-5	0-0	1.000	1	126	0	O20(5/7/10)/1		-0.4
1992	Oak A	22	48	1	6	0	0	1	2	5-1	0	4	.125	.208	.188	12	-6	0-0	.951	3	109	311	O19(4/5/12),1b4/D		-0.4
	Sea A	13	37	6	10	4	1	1	8	3-0	0	5	.270	.302	.514	130	1	1-1	1.000	1	107	135	O11(10/0/1)		0.1
	Year	35	85	7	16	4	1	2	10	8-1	0	9	.188	.250	.329	65	-4	1-1	.970	3	108	235	O30(14/5/13),1b4/D		-0.3
1993	Sea A	32	76	6	16	3	1	2	8	4-0	0	18	.211	.250	.355	59	-5	0-0	1.000	1	110	85	O29(16/6/12),D2		-0.5
1994	Chi N	10	14	4	5	3	0	0	0	1-0	0	7	.357	.400	.571	148	1	0-0	1.000	-0	82	0	O7(1/1/5),1b4		0.1
Total	6	115	242	25	47	11	3	5	22	17-1	0	60	.194	.243	.326	57	-17	1-1	.987	5	116	126	O98(36/19/52),1b15,D3/3		-1.3

HOWLEY, DAN Daniel Philip "Howling Dan","Dapper Dan" B10.16.1885 Weymouth MA D3.10.1944 Weymouth MA BR/TR/6-0/187 d5.15 M6/C3

YEAR	TM LG	G	AB	R	H	2B	3B	HR	RBI	BB-IB	HP	SO	AVG	OBP	SLG	AOPS	ABR	SB-CS	FA	FR	RNG	THR	GAMES AT POSITION	DL	BFW
1913	Phi N	26	32	5	4	2	0	0	2	4	0	4	.125	.222	.188	17	-3	3	.954	1	111	52	C22		-0.1

HOWSER, DICK Richard Dalton B5.14.1936 Miami FL D6.17.1987 Kansas City MO BR/TR/5-8/155* d4.11 M8/C8 Col Florida St.

YEAR	TM LG	G	AB	R	H	2B	3B	HR	RBI	BB-IB	HP	SO	AVG	OBP	SLG	AOPS	ABR	SB-CS	FA	FR	RNG	THR	GAMES AT POSITION	DL	BFW
1961	KC A★	158	611	108	171	29	6	3	45	92-0	5	38	.280	.377	.362	97	2	37-9	.950	-13	95	79	S157		0.7
1962	KC A	83	286	53	68	8	3	6	34	38-0	1	8	.238	.326	.350	79	-8	19-2	.962	-5	95	79	S72	46	-0.3
1963	KC A	15	41	4	8	0	0	0	1	7-1	0	3	.195	.313	.195	44	-3	0-0	.957	-2	81	100	S10		-0.4
	Cle A	49	162	25	40	5	0	1	10	22-0	0	18	.247	.333	.296	80	-4	9-3	.950	-11	76	66	S44		-1.0
	Year	64	203	29	48	5	0	1	11	29-1	0	21	.236	.329	.276	72	-7	9-3	.951	-13	77	73	S54		-1.4
1964	Cle A	162	637	101	163	23	4	3	52	76-1	2	39	.256	.335	.319	84	-11	20-7	.974	1	96	98	S162		0.6
1965	Cle A	107	307	47	72	8	4	1	6	57-0	1	25	.235	.354	.283	83	-4	17-4	.977	-3	87	90	S73,2b17		0.3
1966	Cle A	67	140	18	32	9	1	2	4	15-0	0	23	.229	.299	.350	87	-2	2-4	.986	-12	75	66	2b26,S26		-1.2
1967	NY A	63	149	18	40	6	0	0	10	25-0	2	15	.268	.381	.309	110	-5	1-4	.990	-5	87	122	2b22,3b12,S3	46	-0.1
1968	NY A	85	150	24	23	2	1	0	3	35-0	2	17	.153	.321	.180	57	-6	0-1	.982	7	133	118	2b29,3b2/S		0.4
Total	8	789	2483	398	617	90	17	16	165	367-2	13	186	.248	.346	.318	86	-32	105-34	.963	-42	92	85	S548,2b94,3b14	92	-1.0

HOY, DUMMY William Ellsworth B5.23.1862 Houcktown OH D12.15.1961 Cincinnati OH BL/TR/5-6/160 d4.20

YEAR	TM LG	G	AB	R	H	2B	3B	HR	RBI	BB-IB	HP	SO	AVG	OBP	SLG	AOPS	ABR	SB-CS	FA	FR	RNG	THR	GAMES AT POSITION	DL	BFW
1888	Was N	136	503	77	138	10	8	2	29	69	11	48	.274	.374	.338	137	27	82	.897	7	117	148	O136(0/136/1)		2.9
1889	Was N	127	507	98	139	11	6	0	39	75	6	30	.274	.374	.320	101	5	35	.890	-4	121	80	O127(1/126/0)		-0.3
1890	Buf P	122	493	107	147	17	8	1	53	94	8	36	.298	.418	.371	122	25	39	.912	4	104	172	O122C/2		2.0
1891	StL AA	139	559	134	163	13	5	5	64	117	12	25	.292	.424	.360	108	10	59	.911	-2	107	62	O139C		0.3
1892	Was N	152	593	108	167	19	8	3	75	86	4	23	.282	.376	.356	125	23	60	.884	-15	66	55	O152(3/150/0)		-0.2
1893	Was N	130	564	106	138	12	6	0	45	66	13	9	.245	.337	.287	68	-23	48	.892	-4	119	148	O130C		-2.9
1894	Cin N	128	503	118	153	23	13	6	71	90	12	19	.304	.421	.431	102	5	28	.895	0	138	55	O128C		-0.2
1895	Cin N	107	429	93	119	21	12	3	55	52	6	8	.277	.363	.403	94	-4	50	.883	-5	86	163	O107(62/41/4)		-1.4
1896	Cin N	121	443	120	132	23	7	4	57	65	13	13	.298	.403	.409	107	7	50	.946	3	84	78	O120C		0.2
1897	Cin N	128	497	87	145	24	6	2	42	54	12		.292	.375	.376	92	-4	37	.934	5	55	147	O128C		-0.6
1898	Lou N	148	582	104	177	15	16	6	66	49	9		.304	.367	.416	126	18	37	.946	2	92	119	O148C		1.0
1899	Lou N	155	636	117	194	17	13	5	49	62	10		.305	.376	.396	112	11	33	.928	-11	87	128	O155C		-0.9
1901	Chi A	132	527	112	155	28	11	2	60	86	14		.294	.407	.400	128	27	27	.958	-3	92	164	O132C		1.6
1902	Cin N	72	279	48	81	15	2	2	20	41	4		.290	.389	.380	125	11	11	.933	-5	43	42	O72C		0.3
Total	14	1797	7115	1429	2048	248	121	40	725	1006	134	211	.288	.386	.374	110	138	596	.915	-25	95	113	O1796(66/1727/5)/2		1.8

HRBEK, KENT Kent Alan B5.21.1960 Minneapolis MN BL/TR/6-4/235(215-260) [MinA78 17/432] d8.24

YEAR	TM LG	G	AB	R	H	2B	3B	HR	RBI	BB-IB	HP	SO	AVG	OBP	SLG	AOPS	ABR	SB-CS	FA	FR	RNG	THR	GAMES AT POSITION	DL	BFW
1981	Min A	24	67	5	16	5	0	1	7	5-1	1	9	.239	.301	.358	84	-1	0-0	1.000	-2	49	126	1b13,D8		-0.4
1982	Min A★	140	532	82	160	21	4	23	92	54-12	1	80	.301	.363	.485	127	19	3-1	.993	1	100	102	1b138,D2		1.2
1983	Min A	141	515	75	153	41	5	16	84	57-5	3	71	.297	.366	.489	129	22	4-6	.990	-1	100	97	1b137,D2		1.2
1984	Min A	149	559	80	174	31	3	27	107	65-15	4	87	.311	.383	.522	141	33	1-1	.990	-4	92	94	1b148/D		1.9
1985	Min A	158	593	78	165	31	2	21	93	67-12	2	87	.278	.351	.444	110	9	1-1	.995	1	102	91	1b156,D2		0.1
1986	Min A	149	550	85	147	27	1	29	91	71-9	6	81	.267	.353	.478	121	17	2-2	.992	-1	95	110	1b147/D		0.7
1987	†Min A	143	477	85	136	20	1	34	90	84-12	0	60	.285	.389	.545	140	29	5-2	.996	-10	69	103	1b137/D		1.0
1988	Min A	143	510	75	159	31	0	25	76	67-7	0	54	.312	.387	.520	148	35	0-3	.997	-5	78	109	1b105,D37		2.0
1989	Min A	109	375	59	102	17	0	25	84	53-4	1	35	.272	.360	.517	137	18	3-0	.995	3	109	89	1b89,D18	41	1.5
1990	Min A	143	492	61	141	26	0	22	79	69-8	7	45	.287	.377	.474	130	22	5-2	.997	3	103	98	1b120,D20/3		1.6
1991	†Min A	132	462	72	131	20	1	20	89	67-4	0	48	.284	.373	.461	124	16	4-4	.994	3	108	111	1b128		0.9
1992	Min A	112	394	52	96	20	0	15	58	71-9	1	56	.244	.357	.409	110	8	5-2	.997	1	99	91	1b104,D8	45	0.1
1993	Min A	123	392	60	95	11	0	25	83	71-6	1	57	.242	.357	.467	119	11	4-2	.995	2	107	103	1b115,D2	15	0.4
1994	Min A	81	274	34	74	11	0	10	53	37-6	1	28	.270	.353	.420	99	0	0-0	.997	-1	96	85	1b72,D4	26	-0.6
Total	14	1747	6192	903	1749	312	18	293	1086	838-110	26	798	.282	.367	.481	126	238	37-26	.994	-10	96	100	1b1609,D106/3	127	11.6

HRINIAK, WALT Walter John B5.22.1943 Natick MA BL/TR/5-11/180* d9.10 C21

YEAR	TM LG	G	AB	R	H	2B	3B	HR	RBI	BB-IB	HP	SO	AVG	OBP	SLG	AOPS	ABR	SB-CS	FA	FR	RNG	THR	GAMES AT POSITION	DL	BFW
1968	Atl N	9	26	4	9	0	0	0	3	0-0	1	3	.346	.346	.346	108	0	0-0	.967	1	43	0	C9		0.1
1969	Atl N	7	7	0	1	0	0	0	0	2-0	0	1	.143	.333	.143	37	0	0-0	1.000	0	0	0	C6	25	0.0
	SD N	31	66	4	15	0	0	0	1	8-1	2	11	.227	.329	.227	60	-3	0-0	.981	-2	72	84	C19	15	-0.4
	Year	38	73	4	16	0	0	0	1	10-1	2	12	.219	.329	.219	58	-4	0-0	.982	-2	65	58	C25		-0.4
Total	2	47	99	4	25	0	0	0	4	10-1	2	15	.253	.333	.253	70	-3	0-0	.977	-1	59	42	C34	40	-0.3

HUBBARD, AL Allen (aka Al West For 1 Game in 1883) B12.9.1860 Westfield MA D12.14.1930 Newton MA d9.13 Col Yale

YEAR	TM LG	G	AB	R	H	2B	3B	HR	RBI	BB-IB	HP	SO	AVG	OBP	SLG	AOPS	ABR	SB-CS	FA	FR	RNG	THR	GAMES AT POSITION	DL	BFW
1883	Phi AA	2	6	2	2	0	0	0		2	1		.333	.429	.333	136	0		.750	-1	45	0	/SC		0.0

HUBBARD, GLENN Glenn Dee B9.25.1957 Hahn Air Force Base, W.Germany BR/TR/5-7/170(150-180) [AtlN75 20/473] d7.14 C7

YEAR	TM LG	G	AB	R	H	2B	3B	HR	RBI	BB-IB	HP	SO	AVG	OBP	SLG	AOPS	ABR	SB-CS	FA	FR	RNG	THR	GAMES AT POSITION	DL	BFW
1978	Atl N	44	163	15	42	4	0	2	13	10-1	2	20	.258	.309	.319	68	-7	2-1	.979	2	101	107	2b44	32	-0.2
1979	Atl N	97	325	34	75	12	0	3	29	27-2	1	43	.231	.290	.295	57	-19	0-6	.968	-0	100	95	2b91		-1.7
1980	Atl N	117	431	55	107	21	3	9	43	49-2	0	69	.248	.322	.374	93	-3	7-5	.978	21	113	130	2b117		2.5
1981	Atl N	99	361	39	85	13	5	6	33	33-2	2	59	.235	.302	.349	84	-8	4-2	.991	-4	105	82	2b98		-0.7
1982	†Atl N	145	532	75	132	25	1	9	59	59-5	3	62	.248	.324	.350	87	-8	4-3	.983	19	109	125	2b144		1.9
1983	Atl N★	148	517	65	136	24	6	12	70	56-4	4	71	.263	.334	.402	97	-1	3-8	.985	25	110	112	2b148		3.0
1984	Atl N	120	397	53	93	27	2	9	43	55-6	4	61	.234	.331	.380	93	-2	4-1	.988	14	111	107	2b117		2.0
1985	Atl N	142	439	51	102	21	0	5	39	56-2	4	54	.232	.321	.314	75	-13	4-3	.989	60	131	131	2b140		5.6
1986	Atl N	143	408	42	94	16	1	4	36	66-14	4	74	.230	.340	.304	76	-11	3-2	.976	40	118	138	2b142		3.7
1987	Atl N	141	443	69	117	33	2	5	38	77-17	6	57	.264	.378	.381	99	4	1-1	.986	28	118	123	2b139		3.8
1988	†Oak A	105	294	35	75	12	2	3	33	33-0	3	50	.255	.334	.340	93	-2	1-3	.987	1	99	104	2b104/D	11	0.1
1989	Oak A	53	131	12	26	6	0	3	12	19-0	0	21	.198	.296	.313	75	-4	2-0	.968	7	109	142	2b48,D3	15	0.5
Total	12	1354	4441	545	1084	214	22	70	448	539-53	33	640	.244	.328	.349	85	-74	35-35	.983	212	112	117	2b1332,D4	58	20.5

HUBBARD, MIKE Michael Wayne B2.16.1971 Lynchburg VA BR/TR/6-1/200(180-205) [ChiN92 8/219] d7.13 Col James Madison

YEAR	TM LG	G	AB	R	H	2B	3B	HR	RBI	BB-IB	HP	SO	AVG	OBP	SLG	AOPS	ABR	SB-CS	FA	FR	RNG	THR	GAMES AT POSITION	DL	BFW
1995	Chi N	15	23	2	4	0	0	0	1	2-0	0	2	.174	.240	.174	11	-3	0-0	.971	-3	80	98	C9		-0.6
1996	Chi N	21	38	1	4	0	0	1	4	0-0	0	15	.105	.103	.184	-25	-7	0-0	1.000	1	623	41	C14		-0.6
1997	Chi N	29	64	4	13	0	0	1	2	2-1	0	21	.203	.227	.250	24	-7	0-0	.992	1	89	70	C20/3		-0.5
1998	Mon N	32	55	3	8	1	0	1	3	0-0	1	17	.145	.161	.218	-2	-8	0-0	1.000	-6	32	129	C24/2		-0.6
2000	Atl N	2	1	0	0	0	0	0	0	0-0	0	1	.000	.000	.000	-99	0	0-0	1.000	0	0	0	/C		0.0
2001	Tex A	5	11	1	3	1	0	1	1	0-0	0	4	.273	.273	.636	126	0	0-0	1.000	-4	40	99	C5	116	-0.1
Total	6	104	192	11	32	2	0	4	11	4-1	1	60	.167	.187	.240	11	-25	0-0	.994	-9	158	88	C73/23	116	-3.1

HUBBARD, TRENIDAD Trenidad Aviel (b Trent Hubbard) B5.11.1964 Chicago IL BR/TR/5-9/185(180-203) [HouN86 12/302] d7.7 Col Southern A&M

YEAR	TM LG	G	AB	R	H	2B	3B	HR	RBI	BB-IB	HP	SO	AVG	OBP	SLG	AOPS	ABR	SB-CS	FA	FR	RNG	THR	GAMES AT POSITION	DL	BFW
1994	Col N	18	25	3	7	1	1	3	3-0	0	4	.280	.357	.520	107	0	0-0	1.000	-1	53	0	O5(2/3/0)		-0.1
1995	†Col N	24	58	13	18	4	0	3	9	8-0	0	12	.310	.394	.534	111	1	2-1	1.000	-2	57	146	O16(4/14/0)		-0.1
1996	Col N	45	60	12	13	5	1	1	12	9-0	1	22	.217	.329	.383	70	-2	2-0	1.000	1	121	0	O19(3/16/0)		-0.1
	SF N	10	29	3	6	0	1	1	2	2-0	0	5	.207	.258	.379	67	-2	0-0	1.000	2	134	229	O9(8/1/0)	17	0.0
	Year	55	89	15	19	5	2	2	14	11-0	1	27	.213	.307	.382	68	-4	2-0	1.000	2	126	93	O28(11/17/0)		-0.1

YEAR	TM LG	G	AB	R	H	2B	3B	HR	RBI	BB-IB	HP	SO	AVG	OBP	SLG	AOPS	ABR	SB-CS	FA	FR	RNG	THR	GAMES AT POSITION	DL	BFW
1997	Cle A	7	12	3	3	1	0	0	0	1-0	0	3	.250	.308	.333	65	-1	2-0	1.000	-1	44	0	O6(5/1/0)		-0.1
1998	LA N	94	208	29	62	9	1	7	18	18-0	3	46	.298	.358	.452	118	5	9-5	.991	-1	97	90	O81(34/46/4)/3	38	0.4
1999	LA N	82	105	23	33	5	0	1	13	13-1	0	24	.314	.387	.390	103	1	4-3	.980	-1	97	76	O51(29/19/3)/C2		0.0
2000	Atl N	61	81	15	15	2	1	1	6	11-0	1	20	.185	.290	.272	43	-7	2-1	1.000	-1	89	68	O44(36/0/10)		-0.9
	Bal N	31	27	3	5	0	1	0	0	0-0	0	3	.185	.185	.259	11	-4	2-1	.929	-1	73	188	O24(11/0/14),D6		-0.4
2001	KC A	5	12	2	3	0	1	0	0	0-0	0	2	.250	.250	.417	65	-1	0-0	1.000	-1	38	0	O3(0/2/1)		-0.1
2002	SD N	89	129	16	27	5	0	1	7	14-0	0	28	.209	.285	.271	55	-9	9-6	.981	-1	91	129	O57(16/16/26),3b6,2b4/D		-1.1
2003	Chi N	10	16	2	4	1	0	0	2	4-0	1	3	.250	.429	.313	95	0	1-0	1.000	-1	69	0	O4(0/4/1)		0.0
Total 10		476	762	124	196	33	7	16	72	83-1	6	166	.257	.333	.382	85	-19	33-17	.989	-7	91	93	O319(148/122/59),D7,3b7,2b5/C	55	-2.5

HUBBS, KEN Kenneth Douglas B12.23.1941 Riverside CA D2.13.1964 Provo UT BR/TR/6-2/180* d9.10

YEAR	TM LG	G	AB	R	H	2B	3B	HR	RBI	BB-IB	HP	SO	AVG	OBP	SLG	AOPS	ABR	SB-CS	FA	FR	RNG	THR	GAMES AT POSITION	DL	BFW
1961	Chi N	10	28	4	5	1	0	0	4	0-0	0	3	.179	.179	.393	46	-2	0-0	1.000	-2	84	43	2b8		-0.4
1962	Chi N	160	661	90	172	24	9	5	49	35-0	3	129	.260	.299	.346	71	-29	3-7	.983	4	107	93	2b159		-1.3
1963	Chi N	154	566	54	133	19	3	8	47	39-2	2	93	.235	.285	.322	71	-21	8-9	.974	19	116	111	2b152		1.1
Total 3		324	1255	148	310	44	13	14	98	74-2	5	230	.247	.290	.336	70	-52	11-16	.979	21	111	101	2b319		-0.6

HUBER, CLARENCE Clarence Bill "Gilly" B10.27.1896 Tyler TX D2.22.1965 Laredo TX BR/TR/5-10/165 d9.17

YEAR	TM LG	G	AB	R	H	2B	3B	HR	RBI	BB-IB	HP	SO	AVG	OBP	SLG	AOPS	ABR	SB-CS	FA	FR	RNG	THR	GAMES AT POSITION	DL	BFW
1920	Det A	11	42	4	9	2	1	0	5	0	0	5	.214	.214	.310	39	-4	0-0	.907	1	103	0	3b11		-0.3
1921	Det A	1	0	0	0	0	0	0	0	0	0	0	—	—	—	—		0-0	1.000	-0	0	0	/3		
1925	Phi N	124	436	46	124	28	5	5	54	17	0	33	.284	.311	.406	75	-17	3-5	.947	-9	94	72	3b120		-1.9
1926	Phi N	118	376	45	92	17	7	1	34	42	2	29	.245	.324	.335	74	-13	9	.956	9	111	110	3b115		0.0
Total 4		254	854	95	225	47	13	6	93	59	2	67	.263	.313	.370	73	-34	12-5	.948	1	102	85	3b247		-2.0

HUBER, JUSTIN Justin Patrick B7.1.1982 Melbourne, Victoria, Australia BR/TR/6-2/200 d6.21

YEAR	TM LG	G	AB	R	H	2B	3B	HR	RBI	BB-IB	HP	SO	AVG	OBP	SLG	AOPS	ABR	SB-CS	FA	FR	RNG	THR	GAMES AT POSITION	DL	BFW
2005	KC A	25	78	6	17	3	0	0	6	3-0	0	20	.218	.271	.256	45	-6	0-0	.978	-1	75	99	1b19,D4		-0.9

HUBER, OTTO Otto B3.12.1914 Garfield NJ D4.9.1989 Passaic NJ BR/TR/5-10/165 d6.10

YEAR	TM LG	G	AB	R	H	2B	3B	HR	RBI	BB-IB	HP	SO	AVG	OBP	SLG	AOPS	ABR	SB-CS	FA	FR	RNG	THR	GAMES AT POSITION	DL	BFW
1939	Bos N	11	22	2	6	1	0	0	3	0	0	1	.273	.273	.318	63	-1	0	1.000	-0	99	0	2b4,3b4		-0.1

HUCKABY, KEN Kenneth Paul B1.27.1971 San Leandro CA BR/TR/6-1/205* [LAN91 22/585] d10.6 Col San Joaquin Delta (CA) JC

YEAR	TM LG	G	AB	R	H	2B	3B	HR	RBI	BB-IB	HP	SO	AVG	OBP	SLG	AOPS	ABR	SB-CS	FA	FR	RNG	THR	GAMES AT POSITION	DL	BFW
2001	Ari N	1	1	0	0	0	0	0	0	0-0	0	1	.000	.000	.000	-94	0	0-0	1.000	0	0	0	/C		0.0
2002	Tor A	88	273	29	67	6	1	3	22	9-1	0	44	.245	.270	.308	51	-20	0-0	.989	0	115	97	C88		-1.4
2003	Tor A	5	11	1	2	1	0	0	2	0-0	0	2	.182	.182	.273	17	-1	0-0	1.000	0	35	0	C4		-0.1
2004	Tex A	8	25	2	4	1	0	0	3	0-0	0	10	.160	.250	.200	19	-3	0-0	1.000	2	0	0	C8		0.0
	Bal A	8	12	1	2	0	0	0	0	0-0	0	5	.167	.167	.250	7	-2	0-0	1.000	-1	0	0	C8		-0.2
	Tex A	8	13	1	1	1	0	0	0	2-0	0	2	.077	.200	.154	-6	-2	0-0	.939	-1	0	0	C8		-0.2
	Year	24	50	4	7	3	0	0	3	5-0	0	12	.140	.218	.200	10	-7	0-0	.983	1	78	100	C24		-0.4
2005	Tor A	35	87	8	18	4	0	0	6	5-0	0	19	.207	.250	.253	33	-8	0-0	.987	-2	123	160	C35		-0.8
Total 5		153	422	42	94	14	1	3	30	19-1	0	78	.223	.256	.282	41	-36	0-0	.991	-1	97	93	C152		-2.7

HUDGENS, DAVE David Mark B12.5.1956 Oroville CA BL/TL/6-2/210 d9.4 C4 Col Arizona St.

YEAR	TM LG	G	AB	R	H	2B	3B	HR	RBI	BB-IB	HP	SO	AVG	OBP	SLG	AOPS	ABR	SB-CS	FA	FR	RNG	THR	GAMES AT POSITION	DL	BFW
1983	Oak A	6	7	0	1	0	0	0	0	0-0	0	3	.143	.143	.143	-22	-1	0-0	1.000	0	0	0	1b3/D		-0.1

HUDGENS, JIMMY James Price B8.24.1902 Newburg MO D8.26.1955 St.Louis MO BL/TR/6-0/180 d9.14

YEAR	TM LG	G	AB	R	H	2B	3B	HR	RBI	BB-IB	HP	SO	AVG	OBP	SLG	AOPS	ABR	SB-CS	FA	FR	RNG	THR	GAMES AT POSITION	DL	BFW
1923	StL N	6	12	2	3	0	0	0	3		0	3	.250	.400	.333	97	0	0-0	1.000	-0	210	0	1b3/2		0.0
1925	Cin N	3	7	0	3	1	1	0	1		0	1	.429	.500	.857	245	2	0-0	1.000	-0	71	103	1b3		0.1
1926	Cin N	17	20	2	5	2	0	0	1	1	0	0	.250	.286	.300	59	-1	0-0	1.000	1	129	50	1b6		-0.1
Total 3		26	39	4	11	3	1	0	5	1	0	4	.282	.364	.410	107	1	0-0	1.000	-0	138	50	1b12/2		0.0

HUDLER, REX Rex Allen B9.2.1960 Tempe AZ BR/TR/6-0/180(180-202) [NYA78 1/18] d9.9 OF(124/65/64) [DL 1987 Bal A 71]

YEAR	TM LG	G	AB	R	H	2B	3B	HR	RBI	BB-IB	HP	SO	AVG	OBP	SLG	AOPS	ABR	SB-CS	FA	FR	RNG	THR	GAMES AT POSITION	DL	BFW
1984	NY A	9	7	2	1	1	0	0	0	1-0	1	5	.143	.333	.286	76	0	0-0	1.000	-2	72	44	2b9		-0.2
1985	NY A	20	51	4	8	1	0	0	1	1-0	0	9	.157	.173	.196	1	-7	0-1	.977	4	115	124	2b16/1S		-0.3
1986	Bal A	14	1	1	0	0	0	0	0	0-0	0	0	.000	.000	.000	-99	0	1-0	.800	-2	36	0	2b13/3		-0.2
1988	Mon N	77	216	38	59	14	2	4	14	10-6	0	34	.273	.303	.412	99	-1	29-7	.978	-5	103	120	2b41,S27,O4(2/0/2)		0.1
1989	Mon N	92	155	21	38	7	0	6	13	6-2	1	23	.245	.278	.406	92	-2	15-4	.958	-5	99	113	2b38,O23(14/5/4),S18		-0.5
1990	Mon N	4	3	1	1	0	0	0	0	0-0	0	1	.333	.333	.333	87	0		0				/H		0.0
	StL N	89	217	30	61	11	2	7	22	12-1	2	31	.281	.323	.447	109	2	18-10	.979	5	108	108	O45(17/3/27),2b10,1b6,3b6/S		0.6
	Year	93	220	31	62	11	2	7	22	12-1	2	32	.282	.323	.445	109	2	18-10	.979	5	108	108	O45(17/3/27),2b10,1b6,3b6/S		0.6
1991	StL N	101	207	21	47	10	2	1	15	10-1	0	29	.227	.260	.309	60	-12	12-8	.981	0	99	154	O58(28/21/10),1b12,2b5		-1.3
1992	StL N	61	98	17	24	4	0	3	5	2-0	1	23	.245	.265	.378	83	-3	2-6	.957	-1	108	89	2b16,O12(5/1/7),1b8	53	-0.6
1994	Cal A	56	124	17	37	8	0	8	20	6-0	0	28	.298	.326	.556	121	3	2-2	.971	3	109	149	2b22,O18L,3b4/1D	17	0.6
1995	Cal A	84	223	30	59	16	0	6	27	10-1	5	48	.265	.310	.417	88	-4	13-5	.986	4	104	120	2b52,O22(18/4/1),1b2,D3		0.4
1996	Cal A	92	302	60	94	20	3	16	40	9-0	5	54	.311	.337	.556	119	4	14-5	.982	-5	91	106	2b53,O21(8/14/0),1b7,D8		0.5
1997	Phi N	50	122	17	27	4	0	5	10	6-1	1	28	.221	.264	.377	66	-7	1-0	.962	1	104	76	O35(11/16/8),2b6	84	-0.6
1998	Phi N	25	41	2	5	1	0	0	2	4-0	1	12	.122	.200	.146	-7	-7	0-0	1.000	1	145	0	O9(3/1/5)/1		-0.6
Total 13		774	1767	261	461	96	10	56	169	77-12	14	325	.261	.296	.422	95	-31	107-43	.975	-1	102	115	2b281,O247L,S47,1b38,D15,3b11	225	-2.1

HUDSON, JOHNNY John Wilson "Mr. Chips" B6.30.1912 Bryan TX D11.7.1970 Bryan TX BR/TR/5-10/160 d6.20

YEAR	TM LG	G	AB	R	H	2B	3B	HR	RBI	BB-IB	HP	SO	AVG	OBP	SLG	AOPS	ABR	SB-CS	FA	FR	RNG	THR	GAMES AT POSITION	DL	BFW
1936	Bro N	6	12	1	2	0	0	0	2		0	1	.167	.286	.167	24	-1	0	.889	-2	68	49	S4/2		-0.3
1937	Bro N	13	27	3	5	4	0	0	2	3	0	9	.185	.267	.333	61	-1	0	.867	-3	83	49	S11/2		-0.4
1938	Bro N	135	498	59	130	21	5	2	37	39	0	76	.261	.315	.335	77	-16	7	.963	-0	99	100	2b132,S3		-0.8
1939	Bro N	109	343	46	87	17	3	2	32	30	2	36	.254	.317	.338	74	-13	5	.959	-13	93	105	S50,2b45/3		-2.0
1940	Bro N	85	179	13	39	4	3	0	19	9	0	26	.218	.255	.274	43	-14	0	.921	-4	97	67	S38,2b27/3		-1.6
1941	Chi N	50	99	8	20	4	0	0	6	3	0	15	.202	.225	.242	33	-9	3	.907	-1	83	97	S17,2b13,3b10		-0.9
1945	NY N	28	11	2	0	0	0	0	0	1	0	1	.000	.083	.000	-75	-3	0	.875	1	112	406	3b5,2b2		-0.2
Total 7		426	1169	138	283	50	11	4	96	87	2	164	.242	.296	.314	65	-57	17	.962	-23	99	99	2b221,S123,3b17		-6.2

HUDSON, ORLANDO Orlando Thill B12.12.1977 Darlington SC BB/TR/6-0/175* [TorA97 43/1280] d7.24 Col Spartanburg Methodist (SC) JC

YEAR	TM LG	G	AB	R	H	2B	3B	HR	RBI	BB-IB	HP	SO	AVG	OBP	SLG	AOPS	ABR	SB-CS	FA	FR	RNG	THR	GAMES AT POSITION	DL	BFW
2002	Tor A	54	192	20	53	10	5	4	23	11-0	2	27	.276	.319	.443	97	-2	0-1	.986	9	104	139	2b52		1.0
2003	Tor A	142	474	54	127	21	6	9	57	39-1	5	87	.268	.328	.395	87	-9	5-4	.984	45	123	112	2b139		3.9
2004	Tor A	135	489	73	132	32	7	12	58	51-0	4	98	.270	.341	.438	96	-2	7-3	.984	33	118	104	2b133		3.5
2005	Tor A	131	461	62	125	25	5	10	63	30-1	3	65	.271	.315	.412	88	-8	7-1	.991	28	112	102	2b130	23	2.6
Total 4		462	1616	209	437	88	23	35	201	131-2	14	277	.270	.328	.418	92	-21	19-9	.986	116	116	110	2b454	23	11.0

HUELSMAN, FRANK Frank Elmer B6.5.1874 St.Louis MO D6.9.1959 Affton MO BR/TR/6-2/210 d10.3

YEAR	TM LG	G	AB	R	H	2B	3B	HR	RBI	BB-IB	HP	SO	AVG	OBP	SLG	AOPS	ABR	SB-CS	FA	FR	RNG	THR	GAMES AT POSITION	DL	BFW
1897	StL N	2	7	0	2	1	0	0	0		0		.286	.286	.429	89	0	0	.000	-1	0	0	O2L		-0.1
1904	Chi A	3	6	0	1	1	0	0	0		0		.167	.167	.333	58	0	0	.000	-1	0	0	/OC		-0.1
	Det A	4	18	1	6	1	0	0	4		0		.333	.368	.389	144	1	1	1.000	-0	0	0	O4L		0.0
	Chi A	1	1	0	0	0	0	0	0		0		.000	.000	.000	-99	0						/H		0.0
	StL A	20	68	6	15	2	1	0	1	6	2		.221	.303	.279	90	0	0	—	-2	0	0	O18R		-0.3
	Was A	84	303	21	75	19	4	2	30	24	5		.248	.313	.356	113	5	6	.960	-1	80	76	O84(82/2/0)		0.0
	Year	112	396	28	97	23	5	2	35	31	7		.245	.311	.343	110	5	7	.960	-4	65	62	O107(86/3/18)		-0.4
1905	Was A	121	421	48	114	28	8	3	62	31	8		.271	.333	.397	136	17	11	.929	-7	56	67	O116(115/0/1)		0.4
Total 3		235	824	76	213	52	13	5	97	62	15		.258	.322	.371	123	23	18	.941	-12	60	64	O225(203/3/19)		-0.1

HUFF, AUBREY Aubrey Lewis B12.20.1976 Marion OH BL/TR/6-4/221* [TBA98 5/162] d8.2 Col Miami

YEAR	TM LG	G	AB	R	H	2B	3B	HR	RBI	BB-IB	HP	SO	AVG	OBP	SLG	AOPS	ABR	SB-CS	FA	FR	RNG	THR	GAMES AT POSITION	DL	BFW
2000	TB A	39	122	12	35	7	0	4	14	5-1	1	18	.287	.318	.443	92	-2	0-0	.939	-2	94	52	3b37		-0.4
2001	TB A	111	411	42	102	25	1	8	45	23-2	0	72	.248	.288	.372	73	-17	1-3	.918	-4	95	104	3b73,D20,1b19		-2.3
2002	TB A	113	454	67	142	25	0	23	59	37-7	1	55	.313	.364	.520	135	22	4-1	.987	-4	70	98	D53,1b45,3b14		1.1
2003	TB A	**162**	636	91	198	47	3	34	107	53-17	8	80	.311	.367	.555	143	39	2-3	.970	-7	86	87	O102R,D33,1b22,3b8		2.2
2004	TB A	157	600	92	178	27	2	29	104	56-6	6	74	.297	.360	.493	123	20	5-1	.943	-4	88	88	3b86,1b38,D34,O9(8/0/1)		1.1
2005	TB A	154	575	70	150	26	2	22	92	49-13	5	88	.261	.321	.428	101	0	8-7	.986	3	112	114	O97R,D33,1b25,3b4		-0.6
Total 6		736	2798	374	805	157	8	120	421	223-46	21	387	.288	.342	.478	116	62	20-15	.929	-18	90	88	3b222,O208(8/0/200),D173,1b149		1.1

HUFF, MIKE Michael Kale B8.11.1963 Honolulu HI BR/TR/6-1/190* [LAN85 16/402] d8.7 Col Northwestern

YEAR	TM LG	G	AB	R	H	2B	3B	HR	RBI	BB-IB	HP	SO	AVG	OBP	SLG	AOPS	ABR	SB-CS	FA	FR	RNG	THR	GAMES AT POSITION	DL	BFW
1989	LA N	12	25	4	5	1	0	1	2	3-0	1	6	.200	.310	.360	92	0	1-0	1.000	0	122	0	O9(7/1/2)		0.0
1991	Cle A	51	146	28	35	6	1	2	10	25-0	1	30	.240	.364	.336	95	0	11-2	.990	-1	97	145	O48(8/39/5),2b2		0.0
	Chi A	51	97	14	26	4	1	1	15	12-2	2	18	.268	.357	.361	102	1	3-2	.986	-1	104	48	O48(9/14/35),2b2,D2	15	-0.1

YEAR	TM LG	G	AB	R	H	2B	3B	HR	RBI	BB-IB	HP	SO	AVG	OBP	SLG	AOPS	ABR	SB-CS	FA	FR	RNG	THR	GAMES AT POSITION	DL	BFW
	Year	102	243	42	61	10	2	3	25	37-2	6	48	.251	.361	.346	98	1	14-4	.988	-2	100	102	O96(17/53/40),2b4,D2		-0.1
1992	Chi A	60	115	13	24	5	0	0	8	10-1	1	24	.209	.273	.252	50	-8	1-2	1.000	-0	99	89	O56(10/3/45),/D	76	-1.0
1993	Chi A	43	44	4	8	2	0	1	6	9-0	1	15	.182	.321	.295	72	-1	1-0	1.000	-1	98	0	O43(31/8/7)		-0.2
1994	Tor A	80	207	31	63	15	3	3	25	27-2	3	27	.304	.392	.449	115	6	2-1	.992	2	106	111	O76(57/19/8)	15	0.6
1995	Tor A	61	138	14	32	9	1	1	9	22-0	1	21	.232	.337	.333	76	-4	1-1	.980	1	105	133	O55(9/33/15)	34	-0.3
1996	Tor A	11	29	5	5	0	0	0	1	1-0	0	5	.172	.200	.241	11	-4	0-0	1.000	-1	104	0	O9(1/4/4),3b3		-0.5
Total	7	369	801	113	198	42	7	9	75	109-5	13	146	.247	.344	.351	88	-10	19-9	.991	-0	103	94	O344(132/121/121),2b4,3b3,D3	140	-1.5

HUFFMAN, BEN Benjamin Franklin B7.18.1914 Rileyville VA D2.22.2005 Luray VA BL/TR/5-11.5/175 d4.23 Col Bridgewater (VA)

| 1937 | StL A | 76 | 176 | 18 | 48 | 9 | 0 | 1 | 24 | 10 | 3 | 7 | .273 | .323 | .341 | 67 | -9 | 1-0 | .970 | -6 | 84 | 77 | C42 | | -1.2 |

HUG, ED Edward Ambrose B7.14.1880 Fayetteville OH D5.11.1953 Cincinnati OH BR/TR d7.6

| 1903 | Bro N | 1 | 0 | 0 | 0 | 0 | 0 | 0 | 0 | 0 | 0 | — | -1.000 | — | — | -199 | 0 | 0 | — | 0 | 0 | 0 | /C | | 0.0 |

HUGGINS, MILLER Miller James "Hug","Mighty Mite" B3.27.1878 Cincinnati OH D9.25.1929 New York NY BB/TR/5-6.5/140 d4.15 M17 HF1964 Col Cincinnati

1904	Cin N	140	491	96	129	12	7	2	30	88		2	.263	.377	.328	108	9	13	.945	-2	101	78	2b140		0.9
1905	Cin N	149	564	117	154	11	8	1	38	103	7		.273	.392	.326	103	8	27	.945	37	116	108	2b149		4.7
1906	Cin N	146	545	81	159	11	7	0	26	71	3		.292	.376	.338	118	14	41	.948	22	107	128	2b146		4.0
1907	Cin N	156	561	64	139	12	4	1	31	83	1		.248	.346	.289	95	1	28	.961	4	99	134	2b156		0.6
1908	Cin N	135	498	65	119	14	5	0	23	58	2		.239	.321	.287	97	0	30	.959	6	102	116	2b135		0.8
1909	Cin N	57	159	18	34	3	1	0	6	28	1		.214	.335	.245	81	-2	11	.933	4	113	130	2b31,3b15		0.3
1910	StL N	151	547	101	145	15	6	1	36	116	6	46	.265	.399	.320	114	19	34	.963	6	107	81	2b151		2.7
1911	StL N	138	509	106	133	19	2	1	24	96	6	52	.261	.385	.312	99	6	37	.961	11	111	100	2b136		1.9
1912	StL N	120	431	82	131	15	4	0	29	87	1	31	.304	.422	.357	117	17	35	.943	-7	99	96	2b114		1.1
1913	StL N	121	382	74	109	12	0	0	27	92	7	49	.285	.432	.317	117	18	23-19	.977	4	102	91	2b147,M		2.3
1914	StL N	148	509	85	134	17	4	1	24	105	7	63	.263	.396	.318	115	18	32	.964	-8	98	109	2b147,M		1.3
1915	StL N	107	353	57	85	5	2	2	24	74	3	68	.241	.377	.283	101	6	13-12	.957	6	111	110	2b105,M		1.3
1916	StL N	18	9	2	3	0	0	0	1	3	1	3	.333	.500	.333	159	1	0	1.000	0	2	149	2b7,M		0.4
Total	13	1586	5558	948	1474	146	50	9	318	1003	47	312	.265	.382	.314	107	115	324-31	.956	84	105	105	2b1530,3b15		22.3

HUGHES, JOE Joseph Thompson B2.21.1880 Pardoe PA D3.13.1951 Cleveland OH BR/TR/5-10/165 d8.30 Col Geneva

| 1902 | Chi N | 1 | 3 | 0 | 0 | 0 | 0 | 0 | 0 | 0 | 0 | | .000 | .000 | .000 | -99 | -1 | 0 | — | -0 | 0 | 0 | /OR | | -0.1 |

HUGHES, KEITH Keith Wills B9.12.1963 Bryn Mawr PA BL/TL/6-3/210* d5.19

1987	NY A	4	4	0	0	0	0	0	0	0-0	0	2	.000	.000	.000	-99	-1	0-0	—	0			/H		-0.1
	Phi N	37	76	8	20	2	0	0	10	7-1	1	11	.263	.333	.289	65	-4	0-0	.963	-2	88	0	O19(13/0/6)		-0.6
1988	Bal A	41	108	10	21	4	2	2	14	16-1	0	27	.194	.294	.324	76	-3	1-0	.969	1	95	220	O31R/D		-0.3
1990	NY N	8	0	0	0	0	0	0	0	0-0	0		.000	.000	.000	-99	-2	0-0	1.000	-0	0	0	O5(4/1/0)		-0.2
1993	Cin N	3	4	0	0	0	0	0	0	0-0	0	4	.000	.000	.000	-99	-1	0-0	—	-0	0	0	O2L		-0.1
Total	4	93	201	18	41	6	2	2	24	23-1	1	44	.204	.286	.284	57	-11	1-0	.969	-0	95	138	O57(19/1/37)/D		-1.3

HUGHES, BOBBY Robert E. B3.10.1971 Burbank CA BR/TR/6-4/237* [MilA92 2/50] d4.2 Col USC

1998	Mil N	85	218	28	50	7	2	9	29	16-1	1	54	.229	.284	.404	77	-8	1-2	.995	-2	81	74	C72,O3R		-0.7
1999	Mil N	48	101	10	26	2	0	3	8	5-0	0	28	.257	.292	.366	65	-6	0-0	.988	-2	105	103	C44/D	68	-0.6
Total	2	133	319	38	76	9	2	12	37	21-1	1	82	.238	.287	.392	73	-14	1-2	.993	-4	88	83	C116,O3R/D	68	-1.3

HUGHES, ROY Roy John "Jeep","Sage" B1.11.1911 Cincinnati OH D3.5.1995 Asheville NC BR/TR/5-10.5/167 d4.16

1935	Cle A	82	266	40	78	15	3	0	14	18	1	17	.293	.340	.372	83	-7	13-3	.987	1	106	99	2b40,S29/3		0.0
1936	Cle A	152	638	112	188	35	9	0	63	57	4	40	.295	.356	.378	81	-19	20-9	.973	7	95	96	2b152		-0.2
1937	Cle A	104	346	57	96	12	6	1	40	40	0	22	.277	.352	.355	78	-11	11-6	.939	11	103	59	3b58,2b32		0.4
1938	StL A	58	96	16	27	3	0	2	13	12	0	11	.281	.361	.375	85	-2	3-0	.957	3	98	105	2b21,3b5,S2		0.2
1939	StL A	17	23	6	2	0	0	0	1	4	0	4	.087	.222	.087	-18	-4	0-0	1.000	1	108	129	2b6/S		-0.3
	Phi N	65	237	22	54	5	1	1	16	21	0	18	.228	.291	.270	53	-16	4	.984	-4	92	64	2b65		-1.6
1940	Phi N	1	0	0	0	0	0	0	0	0	0		—	—	—	—	0	0	1.000	0	0	0	/2		0.0
1944	Chi N	126	478	86	137	16	6	1	28	35	1	30	.287	.337	.351	94	-4	16	.951	14	111	163	3b66,S52		1.4
1945	†Chi N	69	222	34	58	8	1	0	8	16	0	18	.261	.311	.306	73	-8	6	.931	-2	93	130	S36,2b21,3b9,1b2		-0.7
1946	Phi N	89	276	23	65	11	3	0	22	19	1	15	.236	.287	.283	64	-14	7	.942	-8	93	82	S34,3b31,2b7/1		-2.1
Total	9	763	2582	396	705	105	27	5	205	222	7	175	.273	.332	.340	78	-85	80-18	.980	22	97	91	2b345,3b170,S154,1b3		-2.9

HUGHES, TERRY Terry Wayne B5.13.1949 Spartanburg SC BR/TR/6-1/185* [ChiN67 1/2] d9.2

1970	Chi N	2	3	0	1	0	0	0	0	0-0	0		.333	.333	.333	71	0	0-0	—	-0	0	0	/3OR		-0.1
1973	StL N	11	14	1	3	1	0	0	1	1-0	0	4	.214	.267	.286	53	-1	0-0	1.000	-0	110	277	3b5/1		-0.1
1974	Bos A	41	69	5	14	2	0	1	6	6-0	2	18	.203	.282	.275	58	-4	0-0	.958	-1	90	105	3b36/D		-0.5
Total	3	54	86	6	18	3	0	1	7	7-0	2	22	.209	.281	.279	58	-5	0-0	.961	-1	91	118	3b42/D1OR		-0.7

HUGHES, TOM Thomas Franklin B8.6.1907 Emmet AR D8.10.1989 Beaumont TX BL/TR/6-1/190 d9.9 Col Texas

| 1930 | Det A | 17 | 59 | 8 | 22 | 3 | 2 | 0 | 5 | 4 | 0 | 8 | .373 | .413 | .508 | 130 | 2 | 0-1 | .897 | -2 | 83 | 0 | O16(4/12/0) | | -0.1 |

HUGHES, BILL William R. B11.25.1866 Blandinsville IL D8.25.1943 Santa Ana CA BL/TL d9.28 ▲

1884	Was U	14	49	5	6	0	0	0	2				.122	.157	.122	-15	-8		.955	-0	82	33	1b9,O6(0/1/5)		-0.9
1885	Phi AA	4	16	3	3	1	1	0	1	1	1		.188	.278	.375	99	0		1.000	-0	0	0	O2R,P2		0.0
Total	2	18	65	8	9	1	1	0	1	3	1		.138	.188	.185	15	-8		.955	-1	82	33	1b9,O8(0/1/7),P2		-0.9

HUHN, EMIL Emil Hugo "Hap" B3.10.1892 North Vernon IN D9.5.1925 Camden SC BR/TR/6-0/180 d4.10

1915	New F	124	415	34	94	18	1	1	41	28	2	40	.227	.279	.282	61	-29	13	.985	-1	93	121	1b101,C16		-3.4
1916	Cin N	37	94	4	24	3	2	0	3	2	0	11	.255	.271	.330	86	-2	0	.989	-0	82	105	C18,1b14/OR		-0.3
1917	Cin N	23	51	2	10	1	2	0	3	2	0	5	.196	.226	.294	62	-3	1	.969	-1	88	110	C15/1		-0.3
Total	3	184	560	40	128	22	5	1	47	32	2	56	.229	.273	.291	65	-34	14	.986	-3	95	119	1b116,C49/OR		-3.9

HULEN, BILLY William Franklin B3.12.1870 Dixon CA D10.2.1947 Santa Rosa CA BL/TL/5-8/148 d5.2

1896	Phi N	88	339	87	90	18	7	0	38	55	0	20	.265	.368	.360	93	-1	23	.874	-19	85	101	S73,O12C,2b2		-1.5
1899	Was N	19	68	10	10	1	0	0	3	10	0		.147	.256	.162	16	-8	5	.902	-1	111	26	S19		-0.7
Total	2	107	407	97	100	19	7	0	41	65	0	20	.246	.350	.327	81	-9	28	.880	-20	90	86	S92,O12C,2b2		-2.2

HULETT, TIM Timothy Craig B1.12.1960 Springfield IL BR/TR/6-0/195(180-199) [ChiA80*S1/3] d9.15 Col South Florida

1983	Chi A	6	5	0	1	0	0	0	0	0-0	0		.200	.200	.200	10	-1	1-0	.875	-1	76	56	2b6		-0.1
1984	Chi A	8	7	1	0	0	0	0	0	1-0	0	4	.000	.125	.000	-59	-2	1-0	1.000	3	116	0	3b4,2b3		0.2
1985	Chi A	141	395	52	106	19	4	5	37	30-1	4	81	.268	.324	.375	87	-7	6-4	.924	3	103	118	3b115,2b28/OL		-0.4
1986	Chi A	150	520	53	120	16	5	17	44	21-0	1	91	.231	.260	.379	69	-25	4-1	.951	2	96	72	3b89,2b66		-2.0
1987	Chi A	68	240	20	52	10	0	7	28	10-1	0	41	.217	.246	.346	54	-17	0-2	.953	-1	103	136	3b61,2b8		-1.8
1989	Bal A	33	97	12	27	5	0	3	18	10-0	0	17	.278	.343	.423	119	2	0-0	.976	-1	99	92	2b23,3b11		0.2
1990	Bal A	53	153	16	39	7	1	3	16	15-0	0	41	.255	.321	.373	96	-1	1-0	.961	9	135	101	3b24,2b16,D15/S	64	0.9
1991	Bal A	79	206	29	42	9	0	7	18	13-0	1	49	.204	.255	.350	68	-10	0-1	.976	-5	99	125	3b39,2b26,D15/S		-1.6
1992	Bal A	57	142	11	41	7	2	2	21	10-1	1	31	.289	.340	.408	105	1	0-1	.935	11	147	168	3b27,D13,2b10,S5	16	1.1
1993	Bal A	85	260	40	78	15	0	2	23	23-1	3	56	.300	.361	.381	96	-1	1-2	.963	15	126	202	3b75,S8,2b4,D2		1.4
1994	Bal A	36	92	11	21	2	1	2	15	12-0	0	24	.228	.314	.337	65	-5	0-0	.992	13	127	187	2b23,3b9,S6	13	0.8
1995	StL N	4	11	0	2	0	0	0	0	3-0	0	3	.182	.182	.182	-4	-2	0-0	.941	3	227	274	2b2/S		0.1
Total	12	720	2128	245	529	90	13	48	220	145-4	10	438	.249	.298	.371	79	-68	14-11	.947	51	109	125	3b454,2b215,D38,S21/OL	93	-1.2

HULSE, DAVID David Lindsey B2.25.1968 San Angelo TX BL/TL/5-11/170* [TexA90 13/360] d8.11 Col Schreiner

1992	Tex A	32	92	14	28	4	0	2	2	3-0	0	18	.304	.326	.348	92	-1	3-1	.984	-2	96	0	O31(0/29/2)/D		-0.3
1993	Tex A	114	407	71	118	9	10	1	29	26-1	1	57	.290	.333	.369	92	-7	29-9	.988	-5	95	56	O112C,D2	18	-0.7
1994	Tex A	77	310	58	79	8	4	1	19	21-0	2	53	.255	.305	.316	60	-19	18-2	.978	-8	90	0	O76C/D		-2.1
1995	Mil A	119	339	46	85	11	6	3	47	18-2	0	60	.251	.285	.345	60	-21	15-3	.984	-10	84	34	O115(67/52/17)	33	-1.1
1996	Mil A	81	117	18	26	3	0	0	8	8-0	0	16	.222	.272	.248	31	-12	4-1	.990	-0	105	42	O68(24/37/11),D4		-1.1
Total	5	423	1265	207	336	35	20	5	103	76-3	3	204	.266	.307	.337	69	-60	69-16	.985	-24	92	31	O402(91/306/30),D8	51	-7.1

YEAR	TM LG	G	AB	R	H	2B	3B	HR	RBI	BB-IB	HP	SO	AVG	OBP	SLG	AOPS	ABR	SB-CS	FA	FR	RNG	THR	GAMES AT POSITION	DL	BFW
HULSWITT, RUDY						Rudolph Edward B2.23.1877 Newport KY D1.16.1950 Louisville KY BR/TR/5-8.5/165 d6.16 C3																		
1899	Lou N	1	0	0	0	0	0	0	0		0		—	—	—		0	0	.333	-2	42	0	/S		-0.1
1902	Phi N	128	497	59	135	11	7	0	38	30	2		.272	.316	.322	97	-3	12	.917	8	97	78	S125,3b3		1.0
1903	Phi N	138	519	56	128	22	9	1	58	28	2		.247	.288	.329	78	-17	10	.906	-1	88	83	S138		-1.2
1904	Phi N	113	406	36	99	11	4	1	36	16	2		.244	.276	.298	80	-11	8	.912	-11	89	95	S113		-1.9
1908	Cin N	119	386	27	88	5	7	1	28	30	2		.228	.287	.285	85	-7	7	.936	-8	95	100	S118/2		-1.3
1909	StL N	82	289	21	81	8	3	0	29	19	1		.280	.329	.329	111	3	7	.930	-7	96	61	S65,2b12		-0.2
1910	StL N	63	133	9	33	7	2	0	14	13	1	10	.248	.320	.331	93	-1	5	.854	-2	93	33	S30,2b2		-1.1
Total	7	644	2230	208	564	64	32	3	203	136	11	10	.253	.299	.314		-36	49	.915	-30	95	83	S590,2b15,3b3		-4.8
HUMMEL, JOHN						John Edwin "Silent John" B4.4.1883 Bloomsburg PA D5.18.1959 Springfield MA BR/TR/5-11/160 d9.12 Col Bloomsburg OF(145/26/125)																		
1905	Bro N	30	109	19	29	3	4	0	7	9	0		.266	.322	.367	114	1	6	.962	2	100	120	2b30		0.4
1906	Bro N	97	286	29	57	6	4	1	21	36	0		.199	.289	.259	77	-7	10	.953	2	102	151	2b50,O21(15/1/4),1b15		-0.7
1907	Bro N	107	342	41	80	12	3	3	31	26	0		.234	.294	.313	98	-2	8	.951	9	115	102	2b44,O33(22/3/9),1b12,S8		0.6
1908	Bro N	154	594	51	143	11	12	4	41	34	2		.241	.284	.320	97	-5	20	.973	12	172	284	O95(92/4/2),2b43,S9,1b8		0.2
1909	Bro N	146	542	54	152	15	9	4	52	22	2		.280	.311	.363	113	4	16	.987	-11	50	77	5b4,2b38,S36,O17(0/6/11)		-0.8
1910	Bro N	153	578	67	141	21	13	5	74	57	2	81	.244	.314	.351	97	-4	21	.965	-18	94	96	2b153		-2.3
1911	Bro N	137	477	54	129	21	11	5	58	67	0	66	.270	.360	.392	115	10	16	.972	-4	96	105	2b127,1b4,S2		0.8
1912	Bro N	122	411	55	116	21	7	5	54	49	0	55	.282	.359	.404	113	8	7	.969	-5	98	73	2b58,O44R,1b11		0.2
1913	Bro N	67	198	20	48	7	7	2	24	13	1	23	.242	.292	.379	88	-4	4-1	.938	1	97	195	O28(3/0/25),S17,1b6,2b3		-0.3
1914	Bro N	73	208	25	55	8	9	0	20	16	0	25	.264	.317	.389	107	1	5	.982	-1	91	68	1b36,O19(5/4/11),2S		-0.2
1915	Bro N	53	100	6	23	2	3	0	8	6	0	11	.230	.274	.310	75	-3	1-1	1.000	-2	105		O21(2/1/18),1b11/S		-0.2
1918	NY A	22	61	9	18	1	2	0	4	11	1	8	.295	.411	.377	135	3	5	.960	-3	91	0	O15(6/7/1),1b3/2		0.0
Total	12	1161	3906	421	991	128	84	29	394	346	11	269	.254	.312	.352	103	2	119-2	.963	-17	99	98	2b548,O293L,1b160,S74		-2.8
HUMMEL, TIM						Timothy Robert B11.18.1978 Goshen NY BR/TR/6-2/190(190-205) [ChiA00 2/52] d8.26 Col Old Dominion																		
2003	Cin N	26	84	9	19	5	0	2	10	8-0	0	13	.226	.290	.357	72	-4	0-0	.894	-3	90	0	3b20,S2/2		-0.7
2004	Cin N	56	110	10	24	4	0	1	7	8-2	2	17	.218	.281	.282	48	-9	1-0	.941	3	113	118	3b32,1b13/2S		-0.6
Total	2	82	194	19	43	9	0	3	17	16-2	2	30	.222	.285	.314	58	-13	1-0	.922	-1	103	64	3b52,1b13,S3,2b2		-1.3
HUMPHREY, AL						Albert B2.28.1886 Ashtabula OH D5.13.1961 Ashtabula OH BL/TR/5-11/180 d9.1																		
1911	Bro N	8	27	4	5	0	0	0	3	0	0	7	.185	.267	.185	29	-3	0	.923	-1	82	0	O8(0/7/1)		-0.5
HUMPHREY, TERRY						Terryal Gene B8.4.1949 Chickasha OK BR/TR/6-3/190* [MonN69 39/873] d9.5 Col Los Angeles (CA) City																		
1971	Mon N	9	26	1	5	1	0	0	1	9-0	0	4	.192	.192	.231	19	-3	0-0	.981	1	64	179	C9		-0.1
1972	Mon N	69	215	13	40	6	1	0	9	16-4	2	38	.186	.248	.237	19	-17	4-1	.986	-5	123	161	C65		-2.1
1973	Mon N	43	90	5	15	2	0	1	9	5-0	0	16	.167	.206	.222	19	-10	0-1	1.000	3	177	150	C35		-0.6
1974	Mon N	20	52	3	10	3	0	0	3	4-0	0	9	.192	.246	.250	38	-4	0-0	.990	5	84	299	C17		0.1
1975	Det A	18	41	0	10	0	0	0	1	2-0	0	6	.244	.279	.244	47	-3	0-0	1.000	-3	66	86	C18	79	-0.6
1976	Cal A	71	196	17	48	10	0	1	19	13-0	5	30	.245	.306	.311	87	-3	0-1	.980	-2	73	127	C71		-0.3
1977	Cal A	123	304	17	69	11	0	2	34	21-0	4	58	.227	.283	.283	58	-18	0-1	.989	2	78	**138**	C123		-1.2
1978	Cal A	53	114	11	25	4	1	1	9	6-0	2	21	.219	.264	.298	62	-6	0-1	.978	0	69	89	C52/3		-0.5
1979	Cal A	9	17	2	1	0	0	0	0	1-0	0	2	.059	.111	.059	-54	-4	0-0	.983	3	47	126	C9	70	-0.1
Total	9	415	1055	69	223	39	1	6	85	68-4	13	175	.211	.265	.267	51	-68	5-5	.986	3	91	141	C399/32	149	-5.4
HUMPHREYS, MIKE						Michael Butler B4.10.1967 Dallas TX BR/TR/6-0/185* [SDN88 15/370] d7.29 Col Texas Tech																		
1991	NY A	25	40	9	8	0	0	0	3	9-0	0	7	.200	.347	.200	55	-2	2-0	1.000	-1	90	0	O9(8/0/2),3b6,D7		-0.3
1992	NY A	4	10	0	1	0	0	0	0	0-0	0	1	.100	.100	.100	-44	-2	0-0	1.000	1	189	847	O2L/D		-0.1
1993	NY A	25	35	6	6	2	1	0	1	4-0	0	11	.171	.250	.371	68	-2	2-1	1.000	-2	69	0	O21(11/5/7),D3		-0.4
Total	3	54	85	15	15	2	1	0	4	13-0	0	19	.176	.283	.259	51	-6	4-1	1.000	-2	88	91	O32(21/5/9),D11,3b6		-0.8
HUMPHRIES, JOHN						John Henry B11.12.1861 N.Gower ON, Can. D11.29.1933 Salinas CA BL/TL/6-0/185 d7.7 Col Cornell																		
1883	NY N	29	107	5	12	1	0	0	4	1		22	.112	.120	.121	-26	-16		.815	-4			C20,O12(0/1/11)		-1.7
1884	Was AA	49	193	23	34	2	0	0		9	1		.176	.217	.187	37	-12		.890	-6			C35,O12(1/3/8),1b4		-1.5
	NY N	20	64	6	6	0	0	0	2	9		19	.094	.205	.094	-2	-7		.896	7			C20		0.1
Total	2	98	364	34	52	3	0	0	6	19		41	.143	.188	.151	9	-35		.876	-4			C75,O24(1/4/19),1b4		-3.1
HUNDLEY, RANDY						Cecil Randolph B6.1.1942 Martinsville VA BR/TR/6-0/175(160-175) d9.27 C1 s-Todd																		
1964	SF N	2	1	0	0	0	0	0	0	0-0	0	1	.000	.000	.000	-98	0	0-0	—	-1	0	0	C2		-0.1
1965	SF N	6	15	0	1	0	0	0	0	0-0	0	4	.067	.067	.067	-61	-3	0-0	1.000	2	62	140	C6		-0.1
1966	Chi N	149	526	50	124	22	3	19	63	35-3	3	113	.236	.285	.397	87	-10	1-3	.986	-11	99	**113**	C149		-1.5
1967	Chi N	152	539	68	144	25	3	14	60	44-6	2	75	.267	.322	.403	102	2	2-4	.996	-4	132	76	C152		0.4
1968	Chi N	160	553	41	125	18	4	7	65	39-6	4	69	.226	.280	.311	73	-18	1-0	.995	-7	148	105	C160		-1.9
1969	Chi N★	151†	522	67	133	15	4	18	64	61-7	3	90	.255	.334	.391	91	-5	2-3	.992	17	125	123	C151		1.9
1970	Chi N	73	250	13	61	5	0	7	36	16-0	0	52	.244	.288	.348	62	-14	0-1	.990	6	177	99	C73	79	-0.5
1971	Chi N	9	21	1	7	1	0	0	2	0-0	0	2	.333	.333	.381	89	0	0-0	.979	3	109	172	C8	134	0.3
1972	Chi N	114	357	23	78	12	0	5	30	22-10	1	62	.218	.261	.294	53	-22	1-0	**.995**	6	87	87	C113		-1.2
1973	Chi N	124	368	35	83	11	1	10	43	30-8	1	51	.226	.283	.342	68	-17	5-6	.993	16	120	105	C122		0.3
1974	Min A	32	88	2	17	2	0	0	3	4-0	1	12	.193	.228	.216	27	-8	0-0	.965	1	80	204	C28		-0.7
1975	SD N	74	180	7	37	5	1	2	14	19-1	1	29	.206	.284	.278	61	-10	0-0	.970	1	100	100	C51		-0.7
1976	Chi N	13	18	3	3	2	0	0	1	1-0	0	4	.167	.200	.278	35	-2	0-0	.923	-0	44	88	C9	143	-0.2
1977	Chi N	2	4	0	0	0	0	0	0	0-0	0	1	.000	.000	.000	-90	-1	0-0	1.000	1	0	102	C2		-0.1
Total	14	1061	3442	311	813	118	13	82	381	271-41	13	565	.236	.292	.350	76	-108	12-17	.990	29	122	105	C1026	356	-4.1
HUNDLEY, TODD						Todd Randolph B5.27.1969 Martinsville VA BB/TR (BL 1999p, 2000p)/5-11/185(170-199) [NYN87 2/39] d5.18 f-Randy [DL 2004 LA N 183]																		
1990	NY N	36	67	8	14	6	0	0	2	6-0	0	18	.209	.274	.299	57	-4	0-0	.988	-1	109	49	C36		-0.4
1991	NY N	21	60	5	8	0	1	1	7	6-0	1	14	.133	.221	.217	24	-6	0-0	1.000	-5	88	101	C20		-1.1
1992	NY N	123	358	32	75	17	0	7	32	19-4	4	76	.209	.256	.316	62	-19	3-0	.996	1	89	86	C121		-1.2
1993	NY N	130	417	40	95	17	2	11	53	23-7	2	62	.228	.269	.357	68	-21	1-1	.988	-4	81	89	C123		-1.8
1994	NY N	91	291	45	69	10	1	16	42	25-4	3	73	.237	.303	.443	93	-5	2-1	.990	-1	128	88	C82		0.0
1995	NY N	90	275	39	77	11	0	15	51	42-5	5	64	.280	.382	.484	132	14	1-0	.987	-4	123	70	C89	40	1.5
1996	NY N★	153	540	85	140	32	1	41	112	79-15	3	146	.259	.356	.550	142	32	1-3	.992	-2	116	72	C150		3.8
1997	NY N★	132	417	78	114	21	2	30	86	83-16	3	116	.273	.394	.549	152	34	2-3	.987	-10	113	62	C122/D		3.0
1998	NY N	53	124	8	20	4	0	3	12	16-0	1	54	.161	.261	.266	41	-11	1-1	.898	1	92	104	O34L,C2	117	-1.1
1999	LA N	114	376	49	78	14	0	24	55	44-3	4	113	.207	.295	.436	87	0	3-0	.979	-10	68	107	C108		-1.2
2000	LA N	90	299	49	85	16	0	24	70	45-6	2	69	.284	.375	.579	145	21	0-1	.979	-12	64	106	C84/D	34	1.3
2001	Chi N	79	246	23	46	10	0	12	31	25-0	3	89	.187	.268	.374	66	-14	0-0	.993	-3	69	73	C70	37	-1.2
2002	Chi N	92	266	32	56	8	0	16	35	32-3	3	80	.211	.301	.421	91	-6	0-0	.984	6	71	105	C79/D	23	0.4
2003	Chi N	21	33	2	6	1	0	2	11	8-0	0	12	.182	.341	.394	94	0	0-1	.982	-2	72	123	C10	121	-0.2
Total	14	1225	3769	495	883	167	7	202	599	453-63	34	988	.234	.320	.443	102	5	14-11	.988	-46	94	85	C1096,O34L,D3	555	1.8
HUNGLING, BERNIE						Bernard Herman "Bud" B3.5.1896 Dayton OH D3.30.1968 Dayton OH BR/TR/6-2/180 d4.14																		
1922	Bro N	39	102	9	23	1	2	1	13	6	0	20	.225	.269	.304	48	-8	2-0	.968	-1	77	86	C36		-0.7
1923	Bro N	2	6	0	0	0	0	0	0	0	0	2	.000	.000	.000	-99	-1	0-1	.667	-1	47	0	/C		-0.2
1930	StL A	10	31	4	10	2	0	0	2	5	0	3	.323	.417	.387	102	0	0-1	1.000	-2	92	39	C10		-0.1
Total	3	51	137	13	33	3	2	1	15	11	0	25	.241	.297	.314	57	-9	2-2	.968	-4	80	75	C47		-1.0
HUNNEFIELD, BILL						William Fenton "Wild Bill" B1.5.1899 Dedham MA D8.28.1976 Nantucket MA BB/TR/5-10/165 d4.17 Col Northeastern																		
1926	Chi A	131	470	81	129	26	4	3	48	37	1	28	.274	.329	.366	84	-12	24-9	.931	-5	97	94	S98,3b17,2b15		-0.3
1927	Chi A	112	365	45	104	25	1	0	36	25	1	24	.285	.332	.375	85	-8	15-13	.933	-17	93	97	S79,2b17/3		-1.7
1928	Chi A	94	333	42	98	8	3	2	24	26	3	24	.294	.351	.354	87	-6	16-6	.967	-10	94	99	2b82,S3/3		-1.2
1929	Chi A	47	127	13	23	5	0	0	9	7	0	15	.181	.224	.220	15	-16	5-2	.969	-2	101	107	2b29,3b4,S2		-1.6
1930	Chi A	31	81	11	22	2	0	0	5	4	1	10	.272	.314	.333	67	-4	1-1	.932	-6	74	88	S22/1		-0.8
1931	Cle A	21	71	13	17	4	1	0	4	9	0	4	.239	.325	.324	67	-3	3-1	.853	-6	84	73	S21/2		-0.7
	Bos N	11	21	4	6	1	0	0	1	0	0	2	.286	.286	.286	56	-1	0	.864	1	118	0	3b5,2b4		-0.9
	NY N	64	196	23	53	16	9	0	17	9	0	16	.270	.302	.311	67	-10	3	.951	-2	96	96	2b56,S5		-0.9

YEAR	TM LG	G	AB	R	H	2B	3B	HR	RBI	BB-IB	HP	SO	AVG	OBP	SLG	AOPS	ABR	SB-CS	FA	FR	RNG	THR	GAMES AT POSITION	DL	BFW
	Year	75	217	25	59	5	0	1	18	9	0	18	.272	.301	.309	66	-11	3	.951	-2	97	95	2b60,3b5,S5		-1.0
Total	6	511	1664	230	452	75	9	9	144	117	6	111	.272	.322	.344	76	-60	67-32	.925	-48	93	92	S230,2b204,3b28/1		-7.3

HUNT, RANDY James Randall B1.3.1960 Prattville AL BR/TR/6-0/185* [StLN81 S1/2] d6.4 Col Alabama

YEAR	TM LG	G	AB	R	H	2B	3B	HR	RBI	BB-IB	HP	SO	AVG	OBP	SLG	AOPS	ABR	SB-CS	FA	FR	RNG	THR	GAMES AT POSITION	DL	BFW
1985	StL N	14	19	1	3	0	0	0	1	0-0	0	5	.158	.158	.158	-12	-3	0-1	1.000	-0	149	0	C13		-0.3
1986	Mon N	21	48	4	10	0	0	2	5	5-2	0	16	.208	.283	.333	70	-2	0-0	.960	2	77	84	C21		0.0
Total	2	35	67	5	13	0	0	2	6	5-2	0	21	.194	.250	.284	48	-5	0-1	.967	1	96	62	C34		-0.3

HUNT, KEN Kenneth Lawrence B7.13.1934 Grand Forks ND D6.8.1997 Gardena CA BR/TR/6-1/205* d9.10

YEAR	TM LG	G	AB	R	H	2B	3B	HR	RBI	BB-IB	HP	SO	AVG	OBP	SLG	AOPS	ABR	SB-CS	FA	FR	RNG	THR	GAMES AT POSITION	DL	BFW
1959	NY A	6	12	2	4	1	0	0	1	0-0	0	3	.333	.308	.417	108	0	0-0	1.000	0	121	0	O5R		0.0
1960	NY A	25	22	4	6	2	0	0	1	4-0	1	5	.273	.407	.364	117	1	0-0	.957	-0	103	0	O24(17/5/2)		-0.9
1961	LA A	149	479	70	122	29	3	25	84	49-1	4	120	.255	.325	.484	103	1	8-2	.950	-6	96	88	O134(8/108/23)/2		-0.1
1962	LA A	13	11	4	2	0	0	1	1	1-0	0	5	.182	.250	.455	88	0	1-0	.867	-1	0		1b3	117	-1.1
1963	LA A	59	142	17	26	6	1	5	16	15-2	0	49	.183	.261	.345	72	-6	0-1	.972	-2	93	38	O50(22/2/27)		-1.1
	Was A	7	20	1	4	0	0	1	4	2-1	0	6	.200	.273	.350	73	-1	0-0	1.000	0	112	0	O5(1/3/1)		-0.1
	Year	66	162	18	30	6	1	6	20	17-3	0	55	.185	.263	.346	73	-6	0-1	.976	-2	95	34	O55(23/5/28)		-1.2
1964	Was A	51	96	9	13	4	0	0	14	14-0	1	35	.135	.243	.208	28	-9	0-1	1.000	0	101	47	O37(4/33/0)		-1.2
Total	6	310	782	107	177	42	4	33	111	85-4	5	222	.226	.303	.417	89	-14	9-4	.964	-10	97	65	O255(52/151/58),1b3/2	117	-3.4

HUNT, JOEL Oliver Joel "Jodie" B10.11.1905 Texico NM D7.24.1978 Teague TX BR/TR/5-10/165 d4.27 Col Texas A&M-Commerce

YEAR	TM LG	G	AB	R	H	2B	3B	HR	RBI	BB-IB	HP	SO	AVG	OBP	SLG	AOPS	ABR	SB-CS	FA	FR	RNG	THR	GAMES AT POSITION	DL	BFW
1931	StL N	4	1	2	0	0	0	0	0	0-0	0	1	.000	.000	.000	-96	0	0	—	-0	0	0	/OR		0.0
1932	StL N	12	21	0	4	1	0	0	3	4	0	3	.190	.320	.238	51	-1	0	1.000	0	124	0	O5R		-0.1
Total	2	16	22	2	4	1	0	0	3	4	0	4	.182	.308	.227	45	-1	0	1.000	0	121	0	O6R		-0.1

HUNT, DICK Richard M. B1847 NY D11.20.1895 New York NY 5-9/145 d5.7

YEAR	TM LG	G	AB	R	H	2B	3B	HR	RBI	BB-IB	HP	SO	AVG	OBP	SLG	AOPS	ABR	SB-CS	FA	FR	RNG	THR	GAMES AT POSITION	DL	BFW
1872	Eck NA	11	46	10	15	1	1	0	4	1	0		.326	.340	.391	146	3	0-1	.583	-1	257	0	O9(0/1/8),2b2		0.2

HUNT, RON Ronald Kenneth B2.23.1941 St.Louis MO BR/TR/6-0/185(170-186) d4.16

YEAR	TM LG	G	AB	R	H	2B	3B	HR	RBI	BB-IB	HP	SO	AVG	OBP	SLG	AOPS	ABR	SB-CS	FA	FR	RNG	THR	GAMES AT POSITION	DL	BFW
1963	NY N	143	533	64	145	28	4	10	42	40-0	13	50	.272	.334	.396	109	7	5-4	.967	12	108	93	2b142/3		3.3
1964	NY N★	127	475	59	144	19	6	6	42	29-4	11	30	.303	.357	.406	117	11	6-2	.979	2	103	107	2b109,3b12		2.3
1965	NY N	57	196	21	47	12	1	1	10	14-2	6	19	.240	.309	.327	82	-4	2-7	.979	-2	101	58	2b46,3b6	85	-0.4
1966	NY N★	132	479	63	138	19	2	3	33	41-2	11	34	.288	.356	.355	101	3	8-10	.970	13	112	98	2b123/S3		2.5
1967	LA N	110	388	44	102	17	3	3	33	39-3	10	24	.263	.344	.345	107	5	2-1	.980	-12	92	91	2b90,3b8		0.1
1968	SF N	148	529	79	132	19	0	2	28	78-2	25	47	.250	.371	.297	103	9	6-6	.972	-11	101	82	2b147		1.1
1969	SF N	128	478	72	125	23	3	4	31	51-0	25	51	.262	.361	.341	99	7	9-2	.979	-7	106	91	2b125/3		0.6
1970	SF N	117	367	70	103	17	1	6	41	44-1	26	29	.281	.394	.381	110	9	1-2	.968	-22	82	75	2b85,3b16		-0.8
1971	Mon N	152	520	89	145	20	3	5	38	58-1	50	41	.279	.402	.358	115	18	5-7	.979	-8	97	78	2b133,3b19		1.7
1972	Mon N	129	443	56	112	20	0	0	18	51-4	26	29	.253	.363	.298	88	-2	9-2	.982	9	105	84	2b122,3b5		1.7
1973	Mon N	113	401	61	124	14	0	0	18	52-3	24	17	.309	.418	.344	110	11	10-7	.982	-7	94	104	2b102,3b14	24	1.0
1974	Mon N	115	403	66	108	15	0	0	26	55-0	14	17	.268	.375	.305	87	-3	2-5	.941	-3	103	104	3b75,2b31/S		-0.6
	StL N	12	23	1	4	0	0	0	3	3-0	2	2	.174	.321	.174	41	-2	0-0	1.000	-0	100	104	2b5		-0.2
	Year	127	426	67	112	15	0	0	29	58-0	16	19	.263	.372	.298	85	-5	2-5	.941	-3	103	104	3b75,2b36/S		-0.8
Total	12	1483	5235	745	1429	223	23	39	370	555-22	243	382	.273	.368	.347	104	65	65-55	.976	-34	101	87	2b1260,3b158,S2	109	12.3

HUNTER, BRIAN Brian Lee B3.5.1971 Portland OR BR/TR/6-3/180* [HouN89 2/35] d6.27

YEAR	TM LG	G	AB	R	H	2B	3B	HR	RBI	BB-IB	HP	SO	AVG	OBP	SLG	AOPS	ABR	SB-CS	FA	FR	RNG	THR	GAMES AT POSITION	DL	BFW
1994	Hou N	6	24	2	6	1	0	0	1	0-0	0	6	.250	.280	.292	52	-2	2-1	.938	0	92	300	O6C		-0.1
1995	Hou N	78	321	52	97	14	5	2	28	21-0	2	52	.302	.346	.396	102	0	24-7	.955	4	106	204	O74C	18	0.7
1996	Hou N	132	526	74	145	27	2	5	35	17-0	2	92	.276	.297	.363	80	-17	35-9	.960	3	102	184	O127C	28	-0.9
1997	Det A	162	658	112	177	29	7	4	45	66-1	1	121	.269	.334	.353	81	-18	74-18	.990	-5	97	95	O162C		-2.1
1998	Det A	142	595	67	151	29	3	4	36	36-0	2	94	.254	.298	.333	63	-33	42-12	.988	5	105	124	O139C		-0.3
1999	Det A	18	55	8	13	2	1	0	0	5-0	1	11	.236	.311	.309	58	-4	0-3	1.000	2	120	100	O18C		-2.5
	Sea A	121	484	71	112	11	5	4	34	32-0	1	80	.231	.277	.300	49	-40	44-5	.985	8	111	189	O121(119/19/0)	15	-2.8
	Year	139	539	79	125	13	6	4	34	37-0	2	91	.232	.280	.301	50	-43	44-8	.988	10	112	178	O139(119/37/0)		-1.1
2000	Col N	72	200	36	55	4	1	3	13	21-0	1	31	.275	.347	.320	57	-13	15-3	.981	3	115	558	O25(9/16/0)		0.1
	Cin N	32	40	11	9	1	0	0	1	6-0	0	9	.225	.319	.250	47	-3	5-0	.971	3	115	192	O88(36/50/12)		-1.0
	Year	104	240	47	64	5	1	3	14	27-0	1	40	.267	.342	.308	57	-15	20-3	.979	3	110	161	O41(22/18/5)/D	18	0.2
2001	Phi N	83	145	22	40	6	0	2	16	16-0	1	25	.276	.344	.359	87	-2	14-3	1.000	3	110	150	O88C	37	0.0
2002	Hou N	98	201	32	54	16	3	3	26	16-0	1	39	.269	.329	.423	92	-3	5-0	1.000	2	105	150	O32(5/14/15)		-0.9
2003	Hou N	56	98	13	23	6	1	0	13	6-0	1	21	.235	.278	.316	54	-7	0-0	.944	22	80	85			
Total	10	1000	3347	500	882	146	28	25	241	243-1	13	581	.264	.319	.346	72	-142	260-61	.980	22	103	152	O896(182/715/32)/D	116	-8.0

HUNTER, BRIAN Brian Ronald B3.4.1968 Torrance CA BR/TL/6-0/180(195-225) [AtlN87 8/194] d5.31 Col Cerritos (CA) JC

YEAR	TM LG	G	AB	R	H	2B	3B	HR	RBI	BB-IB	HP	SO	AVG	OBP	SLG	AOPS	ABR	SB-CS	FA	FR	RNG	THR	GAMES AT POSITION	DL	BFW
1991	†Atl N	97	271	32	68	16	1	12	50	17-0	1	48	.251	.296	.450	101	-1	0-2	.988	-1	102	97	1b85,O6(5/0/1)		-0.7
1992	†Atl N	102	238	34	57	13	2	14	41	21-3	0	50	.239	.292	.487	113	3	1-2	.997	5	118	81	1b92,O6(1/0/5)		0.3
1993	Atl N	37	80	4	11	3	1	0	8	2-1	0	15	.138	.153	.200	-5	-12	0-0	.994	0	99	143	1b29,O2R	30	-1.4
1994	Pit N	76	233	28	53	15	1	11	47	15-2	0	55	.227	.270	.442	81	-7	0-0	.991	1	113	115	1b59,O5L		-1.1
	Cin N	9	23	6	7	1	0	4	10	2-0	0	1	.304	.346	.870	208	3	0-0	1.000	0	114	0	O5(1/0/4)/1		0.3
	Year	85	256	34	60	16	1	15	57	17-2	0	56	.234	.277	.480	92	-4	0-0	.991	1	113	113	1b60,O10(6/0/4)	53	-0.8
1995	Cin N	40	79	9	17	6	0	1	9	11-1	1	21	.215	.312	.329	70	-3	2-1	.983	-0	85		1b41,O29(29/0/2),D2		-0.7
1996	Sea A	75	198	21	53	10	0	7	28	15-2	4	43	.268	.327	.424	89	-4	0-1	.991	-0	43	85	1b23,O4(3/0/1)		-0.5
1998	StL N	62	112	11	23	9	1	4	13	7-0	1	23	.205	.258	.411	73	-5	1-1	.938	2	115	152	O25(16/0/11),1b10/D		-0.1
1999	†Atl N	114	181	28	45	12	1	6	30	31-1	1	40	.249	.367	.425	101	1	0-1	.991	2	115	100	1b101,O8L		0.1
2000	Atl N	2	2	1	1	0	0	1	1	0-0	0	0	.500	.500	2.000	495	1	0-0	—	0			/H		-0.7
	Phi N	85	138	13	29	5	0	7	22	20-1	0	39	.210	.310	.399	78	-5	0-1	.994	1	106	64	1b40,O9(6/0/3)/D		-0.6
	Year	87	140	14	30	5	0	8	23	20-1	0	39	.214	.313	.421	84	-4	0-1	.994	1	106	64	1b40,O9(6/0/3)/D		-0.6
Total	9	699	1555	187	364	90	7	67	259	141-11	11	335	.234	.298	.430	89	-28	4-9	.991	10	104	99	1b481,O99(74/0/29),D4	83	-4.9

HUNTER, EDDIE Edison Franklin B2.6.1905 Bellevue KY D3.14.1967 Colerain OH BR/TR/5-7.5/150 d8.5

YEAR	TM LG	G	AB	R	H	2B	3B	HR	RBI	BB-IB	HP	SO	AVG	OBP	SLG	AOPS	ABR	SB-CS	FA	FR	RNG	THR	GAMES AT POSITION	DL	BFW
1933	Cin N	1	0	1	0	0	0	0	0	—	0	0	—	—	—		0	0	—	-0	0	0	/3		0.0

HUNTER, NEWT Frederick Creighton B1.5.1880 Chillicothe OH D10.26.1963 Columbus OH BR/TR/6-0/180 d4.12 C5

YEAR	TM LG	G	AB	R	H	2B	3B	HR	RBI	BB-IB	HP	SO	AVG	OBP	SLG	AOPS	ABR	SB-CS	FA	FR	RNG	THR	GAMES AT POSITION	DL	BFW
1911	Pit N	65	209	35	53	10	6	2	24	25	4	43	.254	.345	.388	101	0	9	.989	-2	81	159	1b61		-0.3

HUNTER, GEORGE George Henry B7.8.1887 Buffalo NY D1.11.1968 Harrisburg PA BB/TL/5-8.5/165 d5.4 twb-Bill ▲

YEAR	TM LG	G	AB	R	H	2B	3B	HR	RBI	BB-IB	HP	SO	AVG	OBP	SLG	AOPS	ABR	SB-CS	FA	FR	RNG	THR	GAMES AT POSITION	DL	BFW
1909	Bro N	44	123	8	28	7	0	0	8	9	1		.228	.286	.285	80	-3	1	.871	-2	40	165	O23(4/1/18),P16		-0.5
1910	Bro N	1	0	0	0	0	0	0	0	0	0	0	—	—	—		0		—	-0	0	0	/OR		0.0
Total	2	45	123	8	28	7	0	0	8	9	1		.228	.286	.285	80	-3	1	.871	-2	40	164	O24(4/1/19),P16		-0.5

HUNTER, BILLY Gordon William B6.4.1928 Punxsutawney PA BR/TR/6-0/180* d4.14 M2/C14 Col Indiana (PA)

YEAR	TM LG	G	AB	R	H	2B	3B	HR	RBI	BB-IB	HP	SO	AVG	OBP	SLG	AOPS	ABR	SB-CS	FA	FR	RNG	THR	GAMES AT POSITION	DL	BFW
1953	StL A★	154	567	50	124	18	1	1	37	24	2	45	.219	.253	.259	38	-51	3-1	.970	14	108	91	S152		-2.4
1954	Bal A	125	411	28	100	9	5	2	27	21	2	38	.243	.281	.304	66	-22	5-4	.948	0	96	96	S124		-1.3
1955	NY A	98	255	14	58	7	1	3	20	15-2	0	18	.227	.269	.298	54	-18	9-2	.958	-1	104	123	S98		-1.0
1956	NY A	39	75	8	21	3	4	0	11	2-0	0	11	.280	.299	.427	93	-2	0-1	1.000	7	102	164	S32,3b4	32	0.6
1957	KC A	116	319	39	61	10	4	8	29	27-2	3	43	.191	.259	.323	58	-20	1-2	.974	-6	105	100	2b64,S35,3b17		-2.1
1958	KC A	22	58	6	9	2	1	2	11	5-0	0	7	.155	.222	.310	44	-5	1-1	.933	2	88	110	S12,2b8/3		-0.5
	Cle A	76	190	21	37	10	2	0	9	17-1	1	37	.195	.263	.268	48	-13	4-1	.948	-7	90	103	S87,2b8,3b3		-2.0
	Year	98	248	27	46	12	3	2	20	22-1	1	44	.185	.254	.278	47	-18	5-2	.946	-8	90	103	S99,2b8,3b3		-2.5
Total	6	630	1875	166	410	58	18	16	144	111-5	8	192	.219	.264	.294	53	-131	23-12	.958	6	100	103	S528,2b72,3b24	32	-8.2

HUNTER, BUDDY Harold James B8.9.1947 Omaha NE BR/TR/5-10/170* [BosA69 3/61] d7.1 Col Nebraska

YEAR	TM LG	G	AB	R	H	2B	3B	HR	RBI	BB-IB	HP	SO	AVG	OBP	SLG	AOPS	ABR	SB-CS	FA	FR	RNG	THR	GAMES AT POSITION	DL	BFW
1971	Bos A	8	9	2	2	1	0	0	0	2-0	0	1	.222	.364	.333	92	0	0-0	1.000	-1	97	42	2b6		-0.1
1973	Bos A	13	7	3	3	1	0	2	3	0-1	1	1	.429	.636	.571	228	2	0-0	1.000	1	50	604	3b3,2b2/D		0.3
1975	Bos A	1	1	0	0	0	0	0	0	0-0	0	1	.000	.000	.000	-92	0	0-0	.750	-0	61	264	/2		0.0
Total	3	22	17	5	5	2	0	2	5	2-1	1	3	.294	.478	.412	144	2	0-0	.968	-0	103	122	2b9,3b5/D		0.2

HUNTER, HERB Herbert Harrison B12.25.1896 Boston MA D7.25.1970 Orlando FL BL/TR/6-0.5/165 d4.29

YEAR	TM LG	G	AB	R	H	2B	3B	HR	RBI	BB-IB	HP	SO	AVG	OBP	SLG	AOPS	ABR	SB-CS	FA	FR	RNG	THR	GAMES AT POSITION	DL	BFW
1916	NY N	21	28	3	7	0	0	1	4	0-0	0	5	.250	.250	.357	90	-1	0-1	1.000	-0	71	0	3b6,1b2		-0.1
	Chi N	2	4	0	0	0	0	0	0	0-0	0	0	.000	.000	.000	-90	-1	0-0	.750	-0	110	0	/3		-0.1

YEAR	TM LG	G	AB	R	H	2B	3B	HR	RBI	BB-IB	HP	SO	AVG	OBP	SLG	AOPS	ABR	SB-CS	FA	FR	RNG	THR	GAMES AT POSITION	DL	BFW
	Year	23	32	3	7	0	1	0	4	0	0	5	.219	.219	.313	65	-2	0	.941	-0	79	0	3b7,1b2		-0.2
1917	Chi N	3	3	0	0	0	0	0	0	0	0	0	.000	.000	.000	-93	-1	0	1.000	-0	0	0	/23		-0.1
1920	Bos A	4	12	2	1	0	0	0	1	0	0	1	.083	.154	.083	-38	-2	0	.857	-0	70	234	O4(3/1/0)		-0.3
1921	StL N	9	2	3	0	0	0	0	1	0	0	0	.000	.333	.000	-4	-0	0-3	1.000	-0	0	632	/1		-0.1
Total	4	39	49	8	8	0	1	0	4	2	0	6	.163	.196	.224	24	-5	0-3	.905	-1	86	0	3b8,O4(3/1/0),1b3/2		-0.7

HUNTER, LEM Robert Lemuel B1.16.1863 Warren OH D11.9.1956 W.Lafayette OH d9.1

| 1883 | Cle N | 1 | 4 | 1 | 1 | 0 | 0 | 0 | | | 0 | | .250 | .250 | .250 | 53 | 0 | | — | -0 | 0 | 0 | /ORP | | 0.0 |

HUNTER, TORII Torii Kedar B7.18.1975 Pine Bluff AR BR/TR/6-2/205(201-220) [MinA93 1/20] d8.22

1997	Min A	1	0	0	0	0	0	0		0-0	0		—	—	—		0	0-0	—	0			/R		0.0
1998	Min A	6	17	0	4	1	0	0	2	2-0	0	6	.235	.316	.294	59	-1	0-1	1.000	-1	59	0	O6C		-0.3
1999	Min A	135	384	52	98	17	2	9	35	26-1	6	72	.255	.309	.380	72	-17	10-6	.997	2	104	98	O130(16/107/14)		-1.4
2000	Min A	99	336	44	94	14	7	5	44	18-2	2	68	.280	.318	.408	77	-13	4-3	.989	11	113	257	O99(1/98/0)		-0.1
2001	Min A	148	564	82	147	32	5	27	92	29-1	8	125	.261	.306	.479	97	-4	9-6	.992	19	121	164	O147C	15	1.5
2002	†Min A★	148	561	89	162	37	4	29	94	35-3	5	118	.289	.334	.524	120	14	23-8	.992	3	99	94	O146C/D		1.6
2003	†Min A	154	581	83	145	31	4	26	102	50-7	5	106	.250	.312	.451	95	-5	6-7	.991	3	107	73	O151C,D3		-0.2
2004	†Min A★	138	520	79	141	37	0	23	81	40-4	7	101	.271	.330	.475	104	3	21-7	.988	-3	98	80	O126C,D10	18	0.3
2005	Min A	98	372	63	100	24	1	14	56	34-3	6	65	.269	.337	.452	105	3	23-7	.987	-2	90	191	O93C,D5	65	0.5
Total	9	927	3335	492	891	193	23	133	506	234-20	39	661	.267	.321	.458	97	-20	96-45	.991	27	105	128	O898(17/874/14),D19	98	1.9

HUNTER, BILL William Ellsworth B7.8.1887 Buffalo NY D4.10.1934 Buffalo NY BL/TL/5-7.5/155 d8.6 twb-George

| 1912 | Cle A | 21 | 55 | 6 | 9 | 2 | 0 | 2 | 10 | 1 | 0 | | .164 | .303 | .200 | 43 | -4 | 0 | 1.000 | -1 | 100 | 44 | O16C | | -0.5 |

HUNTER, BILL William F. B1855 St.Thomas ON, Can. BR/5-7.5/160 d5.2

| 1884 | Lou AA | 2 | 7 | 1 | 1 | 0 | 0 | 0 | | | 0 | | .143 | .143 | .143 | -7 | -1 | | .667 | -2 | | | C2 | | -0.2 |

HUNTZ, STEVE Stephen Michael B12.3.1945 Cleveland OH BB/TR/6-1/204(185-204) d9.19 Col Villanova [DL 1965 StL N 142]

1967	StL N	3	6	1	1	0	0	0	0	1-0	0	2	.167	.286	.167	33	0	0-0	1.000	-2	40	0	2b2		-0.2
1969	StL N	71	139	13	27	4	0	3	13	27-7	0	34	.194	.325	.288	72	-4	0-0	.945	-4	93	113	S52,2b12,3b6		-0.4
1970	SD N	106	352	54	77	8	0	11	37	66-1	0	69	.219	.341	.335	86	-5	0-3	.958	6	115	109	S57,3b51		0.4
1971	Chi A	35	86	10	18	3	1	2	6	7-0	0	9	.209	.266	.337	69	-4	1-0	1.000	-2	95	83	2b14,S7,3b6		-0.4
1975	SD N	22	53	3	8	4	0	0	4	7-2	1	8	.151	.250	.226	35	-5	0-0	.939	2	116	257	3b16,2b2		-0.3
Total	5	237	636	81	131	19	1	16	60	108-10	1	122	.206	.320	.314	76	-18	1-3	.955	0	106	111	S116,3b79,2b30	142	-0.9

HUPPERT, DAVE David Blain B4.17.1957 South Gate CA BR/TR/6-1/190* d9.15 C1

1983	Bal A	2	0	0	0	0	0	0	0	0-0	0	0	—	—	—		0	0-0	1.000	0	0	0	C2		0.0
1985	Mil A	15	21	1	1	0	0	0	1	2-0	0	7	.048	.130	.048	-49	-4	0-0	.960	-1	78	74	C15		-0.5
Total	2	17	21	1	1	0	0	0	1	2-0	0	7	.048	.130	.048	-49	-4	0-0	.962	-0	74	70	C17		-0.5

HURDLE, CLINT Clinton Merrick B7.30.1957 Big Rapids MI BL/TR/6-3/195* [KCA75 1/9] d9.18 M4/C6 OF(97/0/238)

1977	KC A	9	26	5	8	0	0	2	7	2-0	0	7	.308	.357	.538	139	1	0-0	1.000	0	121	0	O9R		0.1
1978	†KC A	133	417	48	110	25	5	7	56	56-1	1	84	.264	.348	.398	107	6	1-3	.958	-5	93	102	O78(41/0/42),1b52/3D		-0.6
1979	KC A	59	171	16	41	10	3	3	30	28-4	1	24	.240	.343	.386	96	0	0-1	.968	-2	96	60	O50(30/0/20)/3D		-0.4
1980	†KC A	130	395	50	116	31	2	10	60	34-5	2	61	.294	.349	.458	119	11	0-0	.960	-2	99	91	O126R		0.3
1981	†KC A	28	76	12	25	3	1	4	15	13-3	1	10	.329	.427	.553	181	8	0-0	1.000	2	119	57	O28(2/0/26)	75	0.9
1982	Cin N	19	34	2	7	1	0	0	1	2-2	1	6	.206	.270	.235	42	-3	0-1	.950	1	90	258	O17(17/0/1)		-0.3
1983	NY N	13	33	3	6	2	0	0	2	2-0	1	10	.182	.229	.242	31	-3	0-0	.800	-1	123	181	3b9/OR		-0.4
1985	NY N	43	82	7	16	4	0	3	7	13-3	1	20	.195	.313	.354	88	-1	0-1	1.000	-3	84	105	C17,O10(2/0/8)		-0.5
1986	StL N	78	154	18	30	5	1	3	15	26-0	1	38	.195	.311	.299	70	-6	0-0	.994	1	102	139	1b39,O10(5/0/5),C5,3b4		-0.7
1987	NY N	3	3	1	1	0	0	0	0	0-0	1	1	.333	.333	.333	81	0	0-0	1.000	-0	0	0	/1		0.0
Total	10	515	1391	162	360	81	12	32	193	176-18	7	261	.259	.341	.403	105	13	1-6	.965	-9	98	90	O329R,1b92,C22,3b15,D5	75	-1.6

HURLEY, JERRY Jeremiah B4.1875 New York NY D12.27.1919 New York NY BR/TR d9.23

1901	Cin N	9	21	1	1	0	0	0	0	1	1		.048	.130	.048	-51	-4	1	.938	-0	120	74	C7		-0.4
1907	Bro N	1	2	0	0	0	0	0	1		0		.000	.333	.000	5	0	0	1.000	-0	107	113	/C		0.0
Total	2	10	23	1	1	0	0	0	2	1		.043	.154	.043	-44	-4	1	.943	-0	118	79	C8		-0.4

HURLEY, JERRY Jeremiah Joseph B6.15.1863 Boston MA D9.17.1950 Boston MA BR/TR/6-0/190 d5.1 Col Boston U.

1889	Bos N	1	4	0	0	0	0	0	0	0	0	0	.000	.000	.000	-94	-1	0	—	-1	0	0	/ORC		-0.1
1890	Pit P	8	22	5	6	1	0	0	2	2	0	5	.273	.333	.318	81	0	0	.906	-2	102	50	C7/OL		0.0
1891	Cin AA	24	66	10	14	3	2	0	6	12	0	13	.212	.333	.318	80	-2	2	.862	-4	89	51	C24/OR1		-0.3
Total	3	33	92	15	20	4	2	0	8	14	0	18	.217	.321	.304	73	-3	2	.870	-4	92	51	C32,O3(1/0/2)/1		-0.4

HURLEY, DICK William H. B1847 Honesdale PA 5-7/160 d4.18

| 1872 | Oly NA | 2 | 7 | 0 | 0 | 0 | 0 | 0 | 0 | | | 1 | .000 | .000 | .000 | -99 | -2 | 0-0 | .667 | -0 | 0 | 0 | O2R | | -0.1 |

HURST, DON Frank O'Donnell B8.12.1905 Maysville KY D12.6.1952 Los Angeles CA BL/TL/6-0/215 d5.13 Col Ohio St.

1928	Phi N	107	396	73	113	23	4	19	64	68	1	40	.285	.391	.508	129	18	3	.989	5	119	87	1b104		1.5
1929	Phi N	154	589	100	179	29	4	31	125	80	2	36	.304	.390	.525	117	15	10	.985	5	117	88	1b154		0.9
1930	Phi N	119	391	78	128	19	3	17	78	46	2	22	.327	.401	.522	113	9	6	.984	-2	103	91	1b96,O7C		0.1
1931	Phi N	137	489	63	149	37	5	11	91	64	1	28	.305	.386	.468	119	16	8	.986	11	139	90	1b135		1.4
1932	Phi N	150	579	109	196	41	4	24	143	65	7	27	.339	.412	.547	139	34	10	.993	-2	92	81	1b150		1.8
1933	Phi N	147	550	58	147	27	8	8	76	48	1	32	.267	.327	.389	92	-5	3	.985	8	128	106	1b142		-1.1
1934	Phi N	40	130	16	34	9	0	2	21	12	0	7	.262	.324	.377	77	-4	1	.994	-1	84	113	1b34		-0.8
	Chi N	51	151	13	30	6	0	3	12	8	0	18	.199	.239	.291	42	-13	0	.986	-3	72	131	1b48		-2.0
	Year	91	281	29	64	14	0	5	33	20	0	25	.228	.279	.331	60	-16	1	.990	-4	77	123	1b82		-2.8
Total	7	905	3275	510	976	190	28	115	610	391	15	210	.298	.375	.478	113	70	41	.987	21	113	93	1b863,O7C		1.8

HURST, JIMMY Jimmy O'Neal B3.1.1972 Tuscaloosa AL BR/TR/6-6/225 [ChiA90 12/321] d9.10 Col Three Rivers (MO) CC

| 1997 | Det A | 13 | 17 | 1 | 3 | 1 | 0 | 1 | 1 | 2-0 | 0 | 6 | .176 | .263 | .412 | 73 | -1 | 3-0 | 1.000 | -0 | 97 | 0 | O12(1/1/10)/D | | -0.1 |

HUSKEY, BUTCH Robert Leon B11.10.1971 Anadarko OK BR/TR/6-3/244* [NYN89 7/190] d9.8

1993	NY N	13	41	2	6	1	0	0	3	1-1	0	13	.146	.159	.171	-10	-6	0-0	.923	1	113	104	3b13		-0.6
1995	NY N	28	90	8	17	1	0	3	11	10-0	0	16	.189	.267	.300	52	-7	1-0	.925	3	124	52	3b27/OL		-0.3
1996	NY N	118	414	43	115	16	2	15	60	27-3	0	77	.278	.319	.435	102	-1	1-2	.984	-4	85	104	1b75,O40R,3b6		-1.2
1997	NY N	142	471	61	135	26	2	24	81	25-5	1	84	.287	.319	.503	118	9	8-5	.968	1	110	97	O92(30/0/72),1b22,3b15,D4	26	0.5
1998	NY N	113	369	43	93	18	0	13	59	26-3	1	66	.252	.300	.407	87	-8	7-6	.978	0	96	131	O103R/D	29	-1.3
1999	Sea A	74	262	44	76	9	0	15	49	27-0	0	45	.290	.353	.496	116	5	3-1	1.000	-1	109	32	O53(30/0/24),1b10/3D		0.2
	†Bos A	45	124	18	33	6	0	7	28	7-1	0	20	.266	.305	.484	94	-2	0-0	1.000	-0	61	449	D37,O4(2/0/2),3b2		-0.4
	Year	119	386	62	109	15	0	22	77	34-1	0	65	.282	.338	.492	108	3	3-1	1.000	-1	106	60	O57(32/0/26),D44,1b10,3b3		-0.2
2000	Min A	64	215	22	48	13	0	5	27	25-1	2	49	.223	.306	.353	63	-12	0-2	.975	2	123	196	D39,O15R,1b9		-1.3
	Col N	45	92	18	32	8	0	4	18	16-1	0	14	.348	.432	.565	124	4	1-1	1.000	0	103	88	O23(15/0/8),1b8		0.3
Total	7	642	2078	259	555	98	4	86	336	164-15	4	384	.267	.318	.442	97	-18	21-17	.976	3	104	104	O331(78/0/264),1b124,D88,3b64	55	-4.1

HUSON, JEFF Jeffrey Kent B8.15.1964 Scottsdale AZ BL/TR/6-3/180(170-185) d9.2 Col Wyoming OF(10/3/3) [DL 1994 Tex A 64]

1988	Mon N	20	42	7	13	2	0	0	3	4-2	0	3	.310	.370	.357	104	0	2-1	.932	-1	102	76	S15,2b2/3OC		0.0
1989	Mon N	32	74	1	12	5	0	0	2	6-3	0	14	.162	.225	.230	30	-7	3-0	.886	1	99	96	S20,2b9/3		-0.4
1990	Tex A	145	396	57	95	12	2	0	28	46-0	2	54	.240	.320	.280	70	-15	12-4	.960	6	97	117	S119,3b36,2b12		-0.1
1991	Tex A	119	268	36	57	8	3	2	26	39-0	0	32	.213	.312	.287	68	-11	8-3	.965	1	103	72	S116,2b2/3	23	-0.3
1992	Tex A	123	318	49	83	14	3	4	24	41-2	1	43	.261	.342	.362	102	2	18-6	.968	-3	99	113	S82,2b47,O2C/D		0.6
1993	Tex A	23	45	3	6	1	1	0	2	1-0	0	10	.133	.133	.200	-12	-7	0-0	.909	-3	129	143	S12,2b5,3b2,D2	122	-0.4
1995	Bal A	66	161	24	40	4	2	1	19	15-1	0	20	.248	.315	.317	64	-9	5-4	1.000	0	95	191	S12,3b33,2b21/SD		-0.8
1996	Bal A	17	28	5	9	1	0	0	2	1-0	0	3	.321	.333	.357	78	-1	0-0	.973	-0	86	133	2b12,3b3/OR	58	0.0
1997	Mil A	84	143	12	29	3	0	0	11	5-0	2	15	.203	.238	.224	22	-1	3-0	.989	-3	91	86	2b32,1b21,O9(8/0/1),3b2,D4		-1.8
1998	Sea A	31	49	8	8	1	0	1	4	5-0	1	6	.163	.241	.245	27	-5	1-1	1.000	-0	84	64	2b8,3b8,1b7/SORD		-1.0
1999	Ana A	97	225	21	59	7	1	0	18	16-0	0	27	.262	.307	.302	65	-15	10-1	.993	-3	105	98	2b41,S22,3b9,1b8,O2L,D7		-1.3

YEAR	TM LG	G	AB	R	H	2B	3B	HR	RBI	BB-IB	HP	SO	AVG	OBP	SLG	AOPS	ABR	SB-CS	FA	FR	RNG	THR	GAMES AT POSITION	DL	BFW
2000	Chi N	70	130	19	28	7	1	0	11	13-1		9	.215	.287	.285	46	-11	2-1	1.000	-3	83	52	3b18,2b17,S17/1		-1.2
Total	12	827	1879	242	439	65	13	8	150	191-9	6	228	.234	.304	.295	64	-96	64-21	.956	-7	100	98	S405,2b208,3b114,1b37,D18,O16L	267	-6.7

HUSTA, CARL   Carl Lawrence "Sox" B4.8.1902 Egg Harbor City NJ D11.6.1951 Kingston NY BR/TR/5-11/176 d9.24

YEAR	TM LG	G	AB	R	H	2B	3B	HR	RBI	BB-IB	HP	SO	AVG	OBP	SLG	AOPS	ABR	SB-CS	FA	FR	RNG	THR	GAMES AT POSITION	DL	BFW
1925	Phi A	6	22	2	3	0	0	0	2	2	0	3	.136	.208	.136	-11	-4	0-0	.976	1	100	96	S6		-0.2

HUSTON, HARRY   Harry Emanuel Kress B10.14.1883 Bellefontaine OH D10.13.1969 Blackwell OK BR/TR/5-9/168 d9.3 Col Kansas

YEAR	TM LG	G	AB	R	H	2B	3B	HR	RBI	BB-IB	HP	SO	AVG	OBP	SLG	AOPS	ABR	SB-CS	FA	FR	RNG	THR	GAMES AT POSITION	DL	BFW
1906	Phi A	2	4	0	0	0	0	0	0	1	0		.000	.200	.000	-37	-1	0-0		0	75	81	C2		-0.1

HUSTON, WARREN   Warren Llewellyn B10.31.1913 Newtonville MA D8.30.1999 Wareham MA BR/TR/6-0/170 d6.24 Col Springfield

YEAR	TM LG	G	AB	R	H	2B	3B	HR	RBI	BB-IB	HP	SO	AVG	OBP	SLG	AOPS	ABR	SB-CS	FA	FR	RNG	THR	GAMES AT POSITION	DL	BFW
1937	Phi A	38	54	5	7	3	0	0	3	2	0	9	.130	.161	.185	-13	-10	0-1	.918	4	117	153	2b16,S15,3b2		-0.5
1944	Bos N	33	55	7	11	1	0	0	1	8	1	5	.200	.313	.218	49	-3	0-0	.979	2	121	43	3b20,2b5,S4		-0.1
Total	2	71	109	12	18	4	0	0	4	10	1	14	.165	.242	.202	19	-13	0-1	.964	6	124	106	3b22,2b21,S19		-0.6

HUTCHESON, JOE   Joseph Johnson "Slug","Poodles" B2.5.1905 Springtown TX D2.23.1993 Tyler TX BL/TR/6-2/200 d7.8 Col North Texas

YEAR	TM LG	G	AB	R	H	2B	3B	HR	RBI	BB-IB	HP	SO	AVG	OBP	SLG	AOPS	ABR	SB-CS	FA	FR	RNG	THR	GAMES AT POSITION	DL	BFW
1933	Bro N	55	184	19	43	4	1	6	21	15	1	13	.234	.295	.364	91	-3	1	.989	2	92	194	O45R		-0.3

HUTCHINSON, ED   Edwin Forrest B5.19.1867 Pittsburgh PA D7.19.1934 Colfax CA BL/TR/5-11/175 d6.17

YEAR	TM LG	G	AB	R	H	2B	3B	HR	RBI	BB-IB	HP	SO	AVG	OBP	SLG	AOPS	ABR	SB-CS	FA	FR	RNG	THR	GAMES AT POSITION	DL	BFW
1890	Chi N	4	17	0	1	1	0	0	0	0	0	0	.059	.059	.118	-47	-3	0	1.000	3	227	164	2b4		0.0

HUTSON, ROY   Roy Lee B2.27.1902 Luray MO D5.20.1957 LaMesa CA BL/TR/5-9/165 d9.20

YEAR	TM LG	G	AB	R	H	2B	3B	HR	RBI	BB-IB	HP	SO	AVG	OBP	SLG	AOPS	ABR	SB-CS	FA	FR	RNG	THR	GAMES AT POSITION	DL	BFW
1925	Bro N	7	8	1	4	0	0	0	1	0		1	.500	.556	.500	177	1	0-0	1.000	0	114	0	O4(3/0/1)		0.1

HUTTO, JIM   James Neamon B10.17.1947 Norfolk VA BR/TR/5-11/195* [BosA65 7/135] d4.17

YEAR	TM LG	G	AB	R	H	2B	3B	HR	RBI	BB-IB	HP	SO	AVG	OBP	SLG	AOPS	ABR	SB-CS	FA	FR	RNG	THR	GAMES AT POSITION	DL	BFW
1970	Phi N	57	92	7	17	2	0	3	12	5-0	0	20	.185	.222	.304	42	-8	0-0	1.000	0	102	197	O22(16/0/6),1b12,C5/3		-0.9
1975	Bal A	4	5	0	0	0	0	0	0	0-0	0	2	.000	.000	.000	-99	-1	0-0	1.000	-1	34	0	C3		-0.2
Total	2	61	97	7	17	2	0	3	12	5-0	0	22	.175	.212	.289	35	-9	0-0	1.000	-1	102	197	O22(16/0/6),1b12,C8/3		-1.1

HUTTON, TOM   Thomas George B4.20.1946 Los Angeles CA BL/TL/5-11/180* d9.16

YEAR	TM LG	G	AB	R	H	2B	3B	HR	RBI	BB-IB	HP	SO	AVG	OBP	SLG	AOPS	ABR	SB-CS	FA	FR	RNG	THR	GAMES AT POSITION	DL	BFW
1966	LA N	3	2	0	0	0	0	0	0	0-0	0	0	.000	.000	.000	-99	-1	0-0	1.000	-0	0	0	1b3		-0.1
1969	LA N	16	48	2	13	0	0	0	4	5-0	0	7	.271	.340	.271	78	-1	0-0	.993	4	217	88	1b16		0.2
1972	Phi N	134	381	40	99	16	2	4	38	56-4	0	24	.260	.354	.344	97	1	5-8	.992	4	106	90	1b87,O48(5/4/39)		-0.5
1973	Phi N	106	247	31	65	11	0	5	29	32-6	0	31	.263	.346	.368	96	0	3-1	.998	4	122	117	1b71		-0.1
1974	Phi N	96	208	32	50	6	3	4	30	30-8	0	13	.240	.331	.356	89	-3	2-2	.996	-2	87	108	1b39,O33L		-0.9
1975	Phi N	113	165	24	41	6	0	3	24	27-1	0	10	.248	.352	.339	89	-2	2-5	.994	5	148	132	1b71,O12R		-0.2
1976	†Phi N	95	124	15	25	5	1	1	13	27-0	0	11	.202	.342	.282	76	-3	1-2	1.000	3	125	92	1b72/OR		-0.3
1977	†Phi N	107	81	12	25	3	0	2	11	12-3	0	10	.309	.394	.420	114	2	1-1	.993	2	183	102	1b73,O9(7/0/2)		0.3
1978	Tor A	64	173	19	44	9	0	2	9	19-0	0	11	.254	.328	.341	87	-3	1-2	1.000	-2	91	63	1b17,O5(3/1/1)		-0.8
	Mon N	39	59	4	12	3	0	0	5	10-2	0	5	.203	.319	.254	62	-3	0-0	1.000	3	221	64	1b25,O9R		0.0
1979	Mon N	86	83	14	21	2	1	1	13	10-0	0	7	.253	.333	.337	83	-2	0-0	1.000	-1	71	182	1b7,O4(1/0/3)/P		-0.5
1980	Mon N	62	55	2	12	0	0	0	5	4-0	0	1	.218	.267	.255	47	-4	0-0	1.000	-1	90	90	1b9,O2(1/0/1)		-0.5
1981	Mon N	31	29	1	3	0	0	0	2	2-0	0	1	.103	.161	.103	-23	-5	0-0	1.000	0	0	0	/P		-0.5
Total	12	952	1655	196	410	63	7	22	186	234-24	0	140	.248	.339	.334	87	-24	15-21	.995	17	126	103	1b499,O178(82/5/91)/P		-3.9

HYATT, HAM   Robert Hamilton B11.1.1884 Buncombe Co. NC D9.11.1963 Liberty Lake WA BL/TR/6-1/185 d4.15

YEAR	TM LG	G	AB	R	H	2B	3B	HR	RBI	BB-IB	HP	SO	AVG	OBP	SLG	AOPS	ABR	SB-CS	FA	FR	RNG	THR	GAMES AT POSITION	DL	BFW
1909	†Pit N	49	67	9	20	3	4	0	7	3	0		.299	.329	.463	134	2	1	.933	3	583	592	O6(5/0/1),1b2		0.5
1910	Pit N	74	175	19	46	5	6	1	30	8	3	14	.263	.306	.377	94	-3	3	.986	-0	95	99	1b38,O4(0/3/1)		-0.4
1912	Pit N	46	97	13	28	3	1	0	22	6	0	8	.289	.330	.340	85	-2	2	.955	-2	83	48	O15(0/1/14),1b3		-0.5
1913	Pit N	63	81	8	27	6	2	4	16	3	2	8	.333	.372	.605	184	8	0	1.000	-0	42	46	1b5,O5(1/0/5)		0.8
1914	Pit N	74	79	2	17	3	1	1	15	7	2	14	.215	.295	.316	86	-1	1	.980	-2	0	39	1b7/C		-0.3
1915	StL N	106	295	23	79	8	9	2	46	28	3	24	.268	.337	.376	116	5	3-3	.991	-4	69	98	1b64,O25(0/1/26)		-0.2
1918	NY A	53	131	11	30	8	0	2	10	8	0	8	.229	.273	.336	82	-3	1	1.000	0	94	99	O25(21/2/2),1b5		-0.5
Total	7	465	925	85	247	36	23	10	146	63	10	76	.267	.321	.388	108	6	11-3	.989	-5	76	102	1b124,O80(27/7/49)/C		-0.6

HYERS, TIM   Timothy James B10.3.1971 Atlanta GA BL/TL/6-1/195* [TorA90 2/71] d4.4

YEAR	TM LG	G	AB	R	H	2B	3B	HR	RBI	BB-IB	HP	SO	AVG	OBP	SLG	AOPS	ABR	SB-CS	FA	FR	RNG	THR	GAMES AT POSITION	DL	BFW
1994	SD N	52	118	13	30	3	0	0	7	9-0	0	15	.254	.307	.280	56	-8	3-0	.986	0	103	82	1b41,O2R	49	-0.9
1995	SD N	6	5	0	0	0	0	0	0	0-0	0	1	.000	.000	.000	-99	-1	0-0	1.000	0	1166	0	/1		-0.1
1996	Det A	17	26	1	2	1	0	0	0	4-2	0	5	.077	.200	.115	-17	-5	0-0	1.000	-1	36	145	1b9/OLD		-0.5
1999	Fla N	58	81	8	18	4	1	2	12	14-0	0	11	.222	.333	.370	83	-2	0-0	1.000	-1	92	0	O15(12/0/4),1b14/D		-0.4
Total	4	133	230	22	50	8	1	2	19	27-2	0	32	.217	.298	.287	54	-16	3-0	.990	-1	91	90	1b65,O18(13/0/6),D3	49	-1.9

HYNES, PAT   Patrick J. B3.12.1884 St.Louis MO D3.12.1907 St.Louis MO TL d9.27 ▲

YEAR	TM LG	G	AB	R	H	2B	3B	HR	RBI	BB-IB	HP	SO	AVG	OBP	SLG	AOPS	ABR	SB-CS	FA	FR	RNG	THR	GAMES AT POSITION	DL	BFW
1903	StL N	1	3	0	0	0	0	0	0	0	0		.000	.000	.000	-99	0	0	.500	-1	0	0	/P		0.0
1904	StL A	66	254	23	60	7	3	0	15	3	1		.236	.248	.287	74	-9	3	.901	-9	16	0	O63R,P5		-2.2
Total	2	67	257	23	60	7	3	0	15	3	1		.233	.245	.284	71	-9	3	.901	-9	16	0	O63R,P6		-2.2

HYZDU, ADAM   Adam Davis B12.6.1971 San Jose CA BR/TR/6-2/220* [SFN90 1/15] d9.8

YEAR	TM LG	G	AB	R	H	2B	3B	HR	RBI	BB-IB	HP	SO	AVG	OBP	SLG	AOPS	ABR	SB-CS	FA	FR	RNG	THR	GAMES AT POSITION	DL	BFW
2000	Pit N	12	18	2	7	2	0	1	4	0-0	0	4	.389	.389	.667	159	2	0-0	1.000	-0	92	0	O5(1/0/4)		0.1
2001	Pit N	51	72	7	15	1	0	5	9	4-0	1	18	.208	.260	.431	72	-4	0-1	1.000	-0	96	0	O27(8/1/18),1b4		-0.5
2002	Pit N	59	155	24	36	6	0	11	34	21-0	1	44	.232	.324	.484	111	1	0-0	1.000	-2	90	82	O50(10/36/13)/1		-0.1
2003	Pit N	51	63	16	13	5	0	1	8	10-0	1	21	.206	.320	.333	71	-2	0-0	1.000	0	98	103	O34(3/20/11)		-0.3
2004	Bos A	10	3	3	2	1	0	0	2	1-0	0	2	.300	.364	.800	180	1	0-0	1.000	0	84	0	O14(11/0/4),D2		0.1
2005	SD N	17	20	1	3	1	0	0	3	3-0	0	4	.150	.250	.200	24	-2	1-0	1.000	2	126	338	O12(11/3/0)		-0.1
	†Bos A	12	16	1	4	1	0	0	2	0-0	0	5	.250	.333	.313	69	-1	0-0	.909	1	89	0	O12(3/5/5)		-0.1
Total	6	219	354	54	81	18	0	19	61	41-0	3	96	.229	.311	.441	94	-5	1-1	.995	-2	94	78	O154(47/65/55),1b5,D2		-0.9

IBANEZ, RAUL   Raul Javier B6.2.1972 New York NY BL/TR/6-2/200* [SeaA92 36/1006] d8.1 Col Miami-Dade Kendall (FL) CC

YEAR	TM LG	G	AB	R	H	2B	3B	HR	RBI	BB-IB	HP	SO	AVG	OBP	SLG	AOPS	ABR	SB-CS	FA	FR	RNG	THR	GAMES AT POSITION	DL	BFW
1996	Sea A	4	5	0	0	0	0	0	0	0-0	0	1	.000	.167	.000	-53	-1	0-0	—	0			D2		-0.1
1997	Sea A	11	26	3	4	0	1	1	4	0-0	0	6	.154	.154	.346	26	-3	0-0	1.000	-1	76	0	O8(2/0/6)/D		-0.4
1998	Sea A	37	98	12	25	7	1	2	12	5-0	0	22	.255	.291	.408	79	-3	0-0	.988	1	120	42	O17(6/0/12),1b16/D	90	-0.7
1999	Sea A	87	209	23	54	7	0	9	27	17-1	0	32	.258	.301	.421	86	-5	5-1	.978	0	111	40	O57(22/0/39),1b3,D4	16	-0.9
2000	†Sea A	92	140	21	32	8	0	2	15	14-1	1	25	.229	.301	.329	61	-8	2-0	.967	17	147		O42(17/2/24),D33,1b10/3	14	-0.2
2001	KC A	104	279	44	78	11	5	13	54	32-2	0	51	.280	.353	.495	109	3	0-2	.989	-3	87	101	O55(42/0/16),1b49,D36		0.0
2002	KC A	137	497	70	146	37	2	24	103	40-5	2	76	.294	.346	.537	116	11	5-3	.989	3	87	115	O131(128/0/5),1b22,D12		-0.3
2003	KC A	157	608	95	179	33	5	18	90	49-5	3	81	.294	.345	.454	103	2	8-4	.988	1	95	115	O112(110/0/3),1b10,D2	37	1.1
2004	Sea A	123	481	67	146	31	1	16	62	36-5	3	72	.304	.353	.472	104	13	9-4	.982	2	94	195	O101,O58(55/0/3),1b4		1.0
2005	Sea A	162	614	92	177	32	2	20	89	71-6	3	89	.288	.355	.436	117	16	9-4	.984	2	99	124	O156(4/0/152),D3,1b3/C	157	-1.1
Total	10	914	2957	427	836	166	21	105	456	264-25	12	465	.283	.341	.460	106	25	30-16	.984						

IGUCHI, TADAHITO   Tadahito B12.4.1974 Tokyo, Japan BR/TR/5-10/185 d4.4 Col Aoyama Gakuin

YEAR	TM LG	G	AB	R	H	2B	3B	HR	RBI	BB-IB	HP	SO	AVG	OBP	SLG	AOPS	ABR	SB-CS	FA	FR	RNG	THR	GAMES AT POSITION	DL	BFW
2005	†Chi A	135	511	74	142	25	6	15	71	47-0	6	114	.278	.342	.438	102	1	15-5	.978	-14	96	104	2b133		-0.4

INCAVIGLIA, PETE   Peter Joseph B4.2.1964 Pebble Beach CA BR/TR/6-1/230(220-235) [MonN85 1/8] d4.8 Col Oklahoma St.

YEAR	TM LG	G	AB	R	H	2B	3B	HR	RBI	BB-IB	HP	SO	AVG	OBP	SLG	AOPS	ABR	SB-CS	FA	FR	RNG	THR	GAMES AT POSITION	DL	BFW
1986	Tex A	153	540	82	135	21	2	30	88	55-2	4	185	.250	.320	.463	108	5	3-2	.921	-11	80	88	O114(1/0/112),D36		-1.2
1987	Tex A	139	509	85	138	26	4	27	80	48-1	1	168	.271	.332	.497	116	11	9-3	.945	-6	89	99	O132L,D6		0.0
1988	Tex A	116	418	59	104	19	3	22	54	39-3	7	153	.249	.321	.467	115	8	6-4	.989	3	92	129	O93L,D21		0.7
1989	Tex A	133	453	48	107	27	4	21	81	32-6	6	136	.236	.293	.453	106	2	5-7	.973	-3	93	108	O125(120/10/0),D5	15	-0.6
1990	Tex A	153	529	59	123	27	0	24	85	45-5	9	146	.233	.302	.420	100	1	3-4	.974	2	98	138	O54(50/0/4),D41	45	-1.4
1991	Det A	97	337	38	72	12	1	11	38	36-0	1	92	.214	.290	.353	76	-12	1-3	.975	-3	89	60	O98(57/0/48)		0.9
1992	Hou N	113	349	31	93	22	1	11	44	25-2	1	99	.266	.319	.430	115	6	2-2	.970	6	108	163	O97(89/0/8)		0.5
1993	†Phi N	116	368	60	101	16	3	24	89	21-1	6	82	.274	.318	.530	126	11	1-1	.971	-2	100	63	O63L		-1.3
1994	Phi N	80	244	28	56	10	1	13	32	16-2	1	82	.230	.278	.439	82	-8	1-0	.979	-3	89	60	O71(70/0/2)		0.1
1996	Phi N	99	269	33	63	7	2	16	42	30-2	3	82	.234	.318	.454	100	1	2-0	.969	-3	86	116	O75(74/0/1)		0.1
	†Bal A	12	33	4	10	2	0	2	5	12-0	0	12	.303	.344	.545	115	1	0-0	1.000	0	85	275	O7L,D4	6	-0.6
1997	Bal A	48	138	18	34	4	0	7	19	11-2	5	43	.246	.314	.384	84	-4	0-0	.952	-1	95	0	D26,O18(4/0/14)		-0.6
	NY A	5	16	1	4	0	0	0	2	0-0	0	4	.250	.250	.250	31	-2	0-0	—	0			D5		-0.8
	Year	53	154	19	38	4	0	7	21	11-2	5	46	.247	.303	.370	75	-5	0-0	.952	-0	0		D31,O18(4/0/14)		-0.3
1998	Det A	7	14	0	1	0	0	0	1	0-1	0	5	.071	.133	.071	-44	-3	0-0		0	0		/OLD		-0.3

YEAR	TM LG	G	AB	R	H	2B	3B	HR	RBI	BB-IB	HP	SO	AVG	OBP	SLG	AOPS	ABR	SB-CS	FA	FR	RNG	THR	GAMES AT POSITION	DL	BFW
	†Hou N	13	16	0	2	1	0	0	2	1-0	0	4	.125	.176	.188	-4	-2	0-0	1.000	-0	92	0	O3L	15	-0.3
Total	12	1284	4233	546	1043	194	21	206	655	360-21	45	1277	.246	.310	.448	104	11	33-26	.966	-17	93	120	O1021(825/37/189),D150	81	-4.8

INFANTE, ALEXIS Fermin Alexis (Carpio) B12.4.1961 Barquisimeto, Venez BR/TR/5-10/175(175-188) d9.27

YEAR	TM LG	G	AB	R	H	2B	3B	HR	RBI	BB-IB	HP	SO	AVG	OBP	SLG	AOPS	ABR	SB-CS	FA	FR	RNG	THR	GAMES AT POSITION	DL	BFW
1987	Tor A	1	0	0	0	0	0	0	0	0-0	0							0-0	—		0		/R		0.0
1988	Tor A	19	15	7	3	0	0	0	0	2-0	0	4	.200	.294	.200	41	-1	0-0	.909	-2	66	0	3b9,S2,D7		-0.3
1989	Tor A	20	12	1	2	0	0	0	0	0-0	0	5	.167	.167	.167	-6	-2	1-0	1.000	-1	90	100	S9,3b4/2D		-0.2
1990	Atl N	20	28	3	1	1	0	0	0	0-0	1	7	.036	.069	.071	-58	-6	0-0	.964	1	98	105	2b10,3b4,S3		-0.5
Total	4	60	55	11	6	1	0	0	0	2-0	1	12	.109	.155	.127	-20	-9	1-0	.933	-2	80	0	3b17,S14,2b11,D11		-1.0

INFANTE, OMAR Omar Rafael B12.26.1981 Puerto La Cruz, Venez BR/TR/6-0/150(150-175) d9.7

YEAR	TM LG	G	AB	R	H	2B	3B	HR	RBI	BB-IB	HP	SO	AVG	OBP	SLG	AOPS	ABR	SB-CS	FA	FR	RNG	THR	GAMES AT POSITION	DL	BFW
2002	Det A	18	72	4	24	3	0	1	6	3-0	0	10	.333	.360	.417	110	7	0-1	.935	2	118	91	S16,2b2		0.3
2003	Det A	69	221	24	49	6	1	0	8	18-0	0	37	.222	.278	.258	45	-18	6-3	.962	16	125	124	S63,3b4,2b2		0.3
2004	Det A	142	503	69	133	27	9	16	55	40-3	1	112	.264	.317	.449	101	-1	13-7	.976	3	101	111	2b105,S23,3b10,O5C		0.8
2005	Det A	121	406	36	90	28	2	9	43	16-0	2	73	.222	.254	.367	64	-22	8-0	.988	12	98	116	2b69,S50		-0.1
Total	4	350	1202	133	296	64	12	26	112	77-3	3	232	.246	.291	.384	79	-40	27-11	.981	33	100	116	2b178,S152,3b14,O5C		1.3

INGE, BRANDON Charles Brandon B5.19.1977 Lynchburg VA BR/TR/5-11/185* [DetA98 2/57] d4.3 Col Virginia Commonwealth

YEAR	TM LG	G	AB	R	H	2B	3B	HR	RBI	BB-IB	HP	SO	AVG	OBP	SLG	AOPS	ABR	SB-CS	FA	FR	RNG	THR	GAMES AT POSITION	DL	BFW
2001	Det A	79	189	13	34	11	0	0	15	9-0	0	41	.180	.215	.238	20	-22	1-4	.989	7	145	140	C79	42	-1.6
2002	Det A	95	321	27	65	15	3	7	24	24-0	4	101	.202	.266	.333	60	-19	1-3	.998	-2	117	72	C94/D	15	-1.5
2003	Det A	104	330	32	67	15	3	8	30	24-0	5	79	.203	.265	.339	61	-20	4-4	.996	4	77	180	C104		-0.9
2004	Det A	131	408	43	117	15	7	13	64	32-0	4	72	.287	.340	.453	110	5	5-4	.935	7	116	119	3b73,C39,O26(7/19/2)	19	1.3
2005	Det A	160	616	75	161	31	9	16	72	63-1	3	140	.261	.330	.419	101	1	7-6	.957	24	116	149	3b160,O2(1/1/0)		2.4
Total	5	569	1864	190	444	87	22	44	205	152-1	16	433	.238	.299	.379	81	-56	18-21	.994	35	102	145	C316,3b233,O28(8/20/2)/D	76	-0.3

INGERTON, SCOTTY William John B4.19.1886 Peninsula OH D6.15.1956 Cleveland OH BR/TR/6-1/172 d4.12

YEAR	TM LG	G	AB	R	H	2B	3B	HR	RBI	BB-IB	HP	SO	AVG	OBP	SLG	AOPS	ABR	SB-CS	FA	FR	RNG	THR	GAMES AT POSITION	DL	BFW
1911	Bos N	136	521	63	130	24	4	5	61	39		68	.250	.304	.340	74	-19	6	.942	13	104	58	3b58,O43(43/0/2),1b17,2b11,S4		-0.7

INGRAHAM, CHARLIE Charles W. B4.8.1860 IL D2.18.1906 Chicago IL 5-11/170 d7.4

YEAR	TM LG	G	AB	R	H	2B	3B	HR	RBI	BB-IB	HP	SO	AVG	OBP	SLG	AOPS	ABR	SB-CS	FA	FR	RNG	THR	GAMES AT POSITION	DL	BFW
1883	Bal AA	1	4	0	1	0	0	0	0				.250	.250	.250	60	0		.833	-1			/C		-0.1

INGRAM, GAREY Garey Lamar B7.25.1970 Columbus GA BR/TR/5-11/180* [LAN89 44/1146] d5.15 Col Middle Georgia JC [DL 1996 LA N 1]

YEAR	TM LG	G	AB	R	H	2B	3B	HR	RBI	BB-IB	HP	SO	AVG	OBP	SLG	AOPS	ABR	SB-CS	FA	FR	RNG	THR	GAMES AT POSITION	DL	BFW
1994	LA N	26	78	10	22	1	0	3	8	7-3	0	22	.282	.341	.410	100	0	0-0	.982	1	100	104	2b23		0.2
1995	LA N	44	55	5	11	2	0	0	3	9-0	0	8	.200	.313	.236	51	-4	3-0	.750	-0	100	0	3b12,2b7,O4L		-0.3
1997	LA N	12	9	2	4	0	0	1	1	1-0	0	3	.444	.500	.444	160	1	1-0	1.000	-0	87	0	O7(6/1/0)		0.1
Total	3	82	142	17	37	3	0	3	12	17-3	0	33	.261	.340	.345	85	-3	4-0	.985	1	100	109	2b30,3b12,O11(10/1/0)	1	-0.0

INGRAM, MEL Melvin David B7.4.1904 Asheville NC D10.28.1979 Medford OR BR/TR/5-11.5/175 d7.24 Col Gonzaga

YEAR	TM LG	G	AB	R	H	2B	3B	HR	RBI	BB-IB	HP	SO	AVG	OBP	SLG	AOPS	ABR	SB-CS	FA	FR	RNG	THR	GAMES AT POSITION	DL	BFW
1929	Pit N	3	0	1	0	0	0	0	0	0	0	0	—	—	—	0	0	0-0			0		/R		0.0

INGRAM, RICCARDO Riccardo Benay B9.10.1966 Douglas GA BR/TR/6-0/205* [DetA87 4/105] d6.26 Col Georgia Tech

YEAR	TM LG	G	AB	R	H	2B	3B	HR	RBI	BB-IB	HP	SO	AVG	OBP	SLG	AOPS	ABR	SB-CS	FA	FR	RNG	THR	GAMES AT POSITION	DL	BFW
1994	Det A	12	23	3	5	0	0	2	1-0		0	2	.217	.240	.217	22	-3	0-1	1.000	0	94	224	O8(7/1/0)/D		-0.3
1995	Min A	4	8	0	1	0	0	0	1	2-0	0	1	.125	.300	.125	16	-1	0-0	—	0			D3		-0.1
Total	2	16	31	3	6	0	0	3	3-0	0	3	.194	.257	.194	21	-4	0-1	1.000	0	94	224	O8(7/1/0),D4		-0.4

IORG, DANE Dane Charles B5.11.1950 Eureka CA BL/TR/6-0/180* [PhiN71 D1/22] d4.9 b-Garth Col Brigham Young OF(223/0/124)

YEAR	TM LG	G	AB	R	H	2B	3B	HR	RBI	BB-IB	HP	SO	AVG	OBP	SLG	AOPS	ABR	SB-CS	FA	FR	RNG	THR	GAMES AT POSITION	DL	BFW
1977	Phi N	12	30	3	5	1	0	0	2	1-0	0	3	.167	.194	.200	5	-4	0-0	.986	-0	95	108	1b9		-0.5
	StL N	30	32	2	10	1	0	0	4	5-0	0	4	.313	.395	.344	104	1	0-1	.875	-3	107	0	O7(4/0/3)		0.0
	Year	42	62	5	15	2	0	0	6	6-0	0	7	.242	.304	.274	57	-4	0-1	.986	-0	95	108	1b9,O7(4/0/3)		-0.5
1978	StL N	35	85	6	23	4	1	0	4	4-1	0	10	.271	.300	.341	80	-2	0-0	1.000	2	93	326	O25(8/0/18)		-0.1
1979	StL N	79	179	12	52	11	1	1	21	12-1	1	28	.291	.337	.380	94	-1	1-2	.964	-3	81	78	O39(22/0/20),1b10		-0.7
1980	StL N	105	251	33	76	23	1	3	36	20-2	0	34	.303	.349	.438	114	6	1-1	.991	-3	96	45	O63(49/0/14),1b5/3		-0.5
1981	StL N	75	217	23	71	11	2	2	39	7-0	0	9	.327	.344	.424	113	3	2-0	.963	-6	82	0	O57(46/0/14),1b8,3b2		-0.5
1982	†StL N	102	238	17	70	14	1	0	34	23-3	0	23	.294	.352	.361	98	0	0-1	.971	-1	99	50	O63(47/0/17),1b10,3b2		-0.4
1983	StL N	58	116	4	31	9	1	0	11	10-2	1	15	.267	.321	.362	91	-1	1-0	.974	-1	115	0	O22(10/0/13),1b11	29	-0.3
1984	StL N	15	28	3	4	2	0	0	3	2-1	0	6	.143	.200	.214	17	-3	0-0	1.000	1	47	159	1b6,O5(3/0/2)		-0.3
	†KC A	78	235	27	60	16	2	5	30	13-3	0	15	.255	.287	.404	90	-4	0-1	.995	-2	86	109	1b43,O22(18/0/4)/3D		-0.9
1985	†KC A	64	130	7	29	9	1	1	21	8-2	0	16	.223	.268	.331	62	-7	0-1	1.000	-2	90	0	O32(13/0/19),1b2/3D	15	-1.0
1986	SD N	90	106	10	24	2	1	2	11	2-0	0	21	.226	.239	.321	55	-7	0-0	1.000	-3	31	84	1b10,3b6,O3L,P2		-1.1
Total	10	743	1647	149	455	103	11	14	216	107-15	2	180	.276	.317	.378	91	-19	5-7	.977	-18	95	57	O338L,1b114,3b13,D7,P2	44	-5.8

IORG, GARTH Garth Ray B10.12.1954 Arcata CA BR/TR/5-11/170* [NYA73 8/181] d4.9 C2 b-Dane OF(13/1/0)

YEAR	TM LG	G	AB	R	H	2B	3B	HR	RBI	BB-IB	HP	SO	AVG	OBP	SLG	AOPS	ABR	SB-CS	FA	FR	RNG	THR	GAMES AT POSITION	DL	BFW
1978	Tor A	19	49	3	8	0	0	0	3	3-0	1	6	.163	.218	.163	11	-6	0-0	.966	2	108	124	2b18		-0.3
1980	Tor A	80	222	24	55	10	1	2	14	12-0	0	39	.248	.286	.329	65	-11	2-1	.988	11	118	137	2b32,3b20,O14(13/1/0),1b11/SD		0.1
1981	Tor A	70	215	17	52	11	0	0	10	7-1	1	31	.242	.269	.293	58	-12	2-3	.963	0	107	92	2b64,3b17,S2/1D		-1.0
1982	Tor A	129	417	45	119	20	5	1	36	12-2	4	38	.285	.307	.365	78	-13	3-2	.946	1	103	84	3b100,2b30/D		-1.2
1983	Tor A	122	375	40	103	22	5	2	39	13-3	1	45	.275	.304	.376	80	-11	7-0	.976	-6	108	69	3b85,2b39/S		-1.4
1984	Tor A	121	247	24	56	10	3	1	25	5-0	1	16	.227	.244	.304	49	-18	1-3	.945	0	97	127	3b112,2b7,S2/D		-2.0
1985	†Tor A	131	288	33	90	22	1	7	37	21-3	0	26	.313	.358	.469	121	3	3-6	.951	-2	108	114	3b104,2b23		0.5
1986	Tor A	137	327	30	85	19	1	3	44	20-0	1	47	.260	.303	.352	76	-11	3-0	.955	-19	99	68	3b90,2b52,S2		-2.8
1987	Tor A	122	310	35	65	11	0	4	30	21-0	2	52	.210	.262	.284	44	-25	2-2	.982	-13	90	71	3b73,2b28,D5		-3.3
Total	9	931	2450	251	633	125	16	20	238	114-9	11	298	.258	.292	.347	72	-98	23-17	.955	-25	105	101	3b556,2b338,O14L,1b12,D10,S8		-11.4

IOTT, HAPPY Frederick Bidds "Happy Jack","Biddo" (b Frederick Hoyot) B7.7.1876 Houlton ME D2.17.1941 Island Falls ME BR/TR/5-10/175 d9.16

YEAR	TM LG	G	AB	R	H	2B	3B	HR	RBI	BB-IB	HP	SO	AVG	OBP	SLG	AOPS	ABR	SB-CS	FA	FR	RNG	THR	GAMES AT POSITION	DL	BFW
1903	Cle A	3	10	1	2	0	0	0	0	0			.200	.333	.200	64	0	1	.875	-0	0	0	O3C		-0.1

IRELAN, HAL Harold "Grump" B8.5.1890 Burnettsville IN D7.16.1944 Carmel IN BB/TR/5-7/165 d4.23

YEAR	TM LG	G	AB	R	H	2B	3B	HR	RBI	BB-IB	HP	SO	AVG	OBP	SLG	AOPS	ABR	SB-CS	FA	FR	RNG	THR	GAMES AT POSITION	DL	BFW
1914	Phi N	67	165	16	39	8	0	1	16	21	1	22	.236	.326	.303	82	-3	3	.909	4	112	67	2b44,S3,1b2,3b2		0.2

IRELAND, TIM Timothy Neal B3.14.1953 Oakland CA BR/TR (BB 1981)/6-0/180* [MonN73 25/563] d9.20 Col Chabot (CA) JC

YEAR	TM LG	G	AB	R	H	2B	3B	HR	RBI	BB-IB	HP	SO	AVG	OBP	SLG	AOPS	ABR	SB-CS	FA	FR	RNG	THR	GAMES AT POSITION	DL	BFW
1981	KC A	4	0	1	0	0	0	0	0	0-0	0	0	—	—	—			0-1	1.000	-0	0	0	1b4		-0.1
1982	KC A	7	7	2	1	0	0	0	0	1-0	0	1	.143	.250	.143	11	-1	0-0	1.000	-0	145	119	2b4,O2R/3		-0.1
Total	2	11	7	3	1	0	0	0	0	1-0	0	1	.143	.250	.143	11	-1	0-1	1.000	-0	145	119	2b4,1b4,O2R/3	24	-0.2

IRVIN, MONTE Monford B2.25.1919 Columbia AL BR/TR/6-1/195* d7.8 HF1973 Negro Lg 1937-48 Mil 1943-45

YEAR	TM LG	G	AB	R	H	2B	3B	HR	RBI	BB-IB	HP	SO	AVG	OBP	SLG	AOPS	ABR	SB-CS	FA	FR	RNG	THR	GAMES AT POSITION	DL	BFW
1949	NY N	36	76	7	17	3	2	0	7	17	0	11	.224	.366	.316	84	-1	0	1.000	1	89	379	O10R,1b5,3b2		0.0
1950	NY N	110	374	61	112	19	5	15	66	52	5	41	.299	.392	.497	131	18	3	.979	3	126	136	1b59,O49(20/0/30)/3		1.7
1951	†NY N	151	558	94	174	19	11	24	121	89	9	44	.312	.415	.514	147	40	12-2	.996	5	94	94	O112(89/0/27),1b39		3.7
1952	NY N*	46	126	10	39	2	1	4	21	10	1	11	.310	.365	.437	120	3	0-1	1.000	-1	83	147	O32(30/1/1)		0.9
1953	NY N	124	444	72	146	21	5	21	97	55	3	34	.329	.406	.541	142	28	2-0	.973	4	109	107	O113(102/0/13)	98	2.5
1954	†NY N	135	432	62	113	13	3	19	64	70	2	23	.262	.363	.438	108	6	7-4	.976	2	106	86	O128(126/0/2)/13		0.0
1955	NY N	51	150	16	38	7	1	1	17	17-0	3	15	.253	.337	.333	80	-4	3-0	.961	2	108	121	O45(44/0/4)		-0.4
1956	Chi N	111	339	44	92	13	3	15	50	41-5	0	41	.271	.346	.460	118	8	1-0	.991	10	125	108	O96L		1.3
Total	8	764	2499	366	731	97	31	99	443	351-5	23	220	.293	.383	.475	126	98	28-7	.983	27	106	102	O585(507/1/87),1b104,3b7	98	8.8

IRWIN, ARTHUR Arthur Albert "Doc","Sandy" B2.14.1858 Toronto ON, Can. D7.16.1921, At Sea Atlantic Ocean N.Y. To Boston BL/TR/5-8.5/158 d5.1 M8/U1 b-John

YEAR	TM LG	G	AB	R	H	2B	3B	HR	RBI	BB-IB	HP	SO	AVG	OBP	SLG	AOPS	ABR	SB-CS	FA	FR	RNG	THR	GAMES AT POSITION	DL	BFW
1880	Wor N	85	352	53	91	19	4	1	35	11		27	.259	.281	.344	102	0		.895	29	126	134	S82,3b3/C		3.2
1881	Wor N	50	206	27	55	8	2	0	24	7		4	.267	.291	.325	88	-3		.851	-7	97	65	S50		-0.8
1882	Wor N	84	333	30	73	12	4	0	30	14		34	.219	.251	.279	68	-12		.837	17	131	93	3b51,S33		0.6
1883	Pro N	98	406	67	116	22	7	0	44	12		38	.286	.306	.374	103	1		.856	-8	98	127	S94,2b4		-0.4
1884	†Pro N	102	404	73	97	14	3	2	44	28		52	.240	.289	.304	89	-4		.881	-10	96	109	S102/P		-1.0
1885	Pro N	59	218	16	39	2	1	0	14	14		29	.179	.228	.197	40	-14		.875	2	109	94	S58/32		-0.9
1886	Phi N	101	373	51	87	6	6	0	34	35		39	.233	.299	.282	77	-10	24	.891	-4	102	82	S100/3		-0.9
1887	Phi N	100	374	65	95	14	8	2	56	48		3	.254	.344	.350	88	-6	19	.892	-14	87	96	S100		-1.4
1888	Phi N	125	448	51	98	12	4	0	28	33		56	.219	.277	.263	69	-15	19	.900	10	102	96	S122,2b3		-0.1
1889	Phi N	18	73	9	16	5	0	0	10	6		6	.219	.278	.288	54	-5	6	.845	-3	90	101	S18		-0.1
	Was N	85	313	49	73	10	5	0	32	42		37	.233	.324	.297	80	-8	9	.895	12	107	108	S85/P2M		-0.7
	Year	103	386	58	89	15	5	0	42	48		43	.231	.317	.295		-13	15	.888	8	104	107	S103/P2		-0.1

YEAR	TM LG	G	AB	R	H	2B	3B	HR	RBI	BB-IB	HP	SO	AVG	OBP	SLG	AOPS	ABR	SB-CS	FA	FR	RNG	THR	GAMES AT POSITION	DL	BFW
1890	Bos P	96	354	60	92	17	1	0	45	57	1	29	.260	.364	.314	77	-10	16	.878	2	**106**	115	S96		-0.4
1891	Bos AA	6	17	1	2	0	0	0	0	2	2	1	.118	.286	.118	16	-2	0	.778	-1	90	330	S6,M		-0.2
1894	Phi N	1	0	0	0	0	0	0	0	0	0	0	—	—	—	0	0	0	—				/SM		0.0
Total	13	1010	3871	552	934	141	45	5	396	309	10	378	.241	.299	.305	81	-88	93	.881	30	103	106	S947,3b56,2b9,P2/C		-2.1

IRWIN, CHARLIE Charles Edwin B2.15.1869 Clinton IL D9.21.1925 Chicago IL BL/TR/5-10/160 d9.3

YEAR	TM LG	G	AB	R	H	2B	3B	HR	RBI	BB-IB	HP	SO	AVG	OBP	SLG	AOPS	ABR	SB-CS	FA	FR	RNG	THR	GAMES AT POSITION	DL	BFW
1893	Chi N	21	82	-14	25	6	2	0	13	10	2	1	.305	.394	.427	120	3	4	.910	2	94	112	S21		0.4
1894	Chi N	130	504	85	149	25	9	8	100	64	10	23	.296	.386	.429	91	-8	35	.819	-4	93	130	3b68,S62		-0.6
1895	Chi N	3	10	4	2	0	0	0	0	2	0	1	.200	.333	.200	37	-1	0	.900	-1	84	113	S3		-0.1
1896	Cin N	127	476	77	141	16	6	1	67	26	4	17	.296	.338	.361	79	-16	31	**.931**	7	98	**162**	3b127		-0.6
1897	Cin N	**134**	505	89	146	26	6	0	74	47	9		.289	.360	.364	86	-10	27	.940	-6	90	117	3b134		-1.1
1898	Cin N	136	501	77	120	14	5	3	55	31	10		.240	.297	.305	68	-22	18	.940	12	105	104	3b136		-0.8
1899	Cin N	90	314	42	73	4	8	1	52	26	2		.232	.295	.306	64	-17	26	.909	-10	84	47	3b78,S6,2b3/1		-2.3
1900	Cin N	87	333	59	91	15	6	1	44	14	6		.273	.314	.363	89	-6	9	.931	-8	91	137	3b61,S16,O6(1/0/5),2b3		-1.1
1901	Cin N	67	260	25	62	12	2	0	25	14	3		.238	.285	.300	75	-8	13	.893	4	105	126	3b67		-0.3
	Bro N	65	242	25	52	13	2	0	20	14	4		.215	.269	.285	59	-12	4	.956	-4	82	68	3b65		-1.4
	Year	132	502	50	114	25	4	0	45	28	7		.227	.277	.293	67	-21	17	.921	-0	94	97	3b132		-1.7
1902	Bro N	131	458	59	125	14	0	2	43	39	12		.273	.346	.317	104	4	13	.927	-9	89	136	3b130/S		-0.1
Total	10	991	3685	556	986	145	46	16	493	287	62	42	.268	.331	.345	82	-93	180	.921	-16	94	118	3b866,S109,O6(1/0/5),2b6/1		-8.0

IRWIN, JOHN John B7.21.1861 Toronto ON, Can. D2.28.1934 Boston MA BL/TR/5-10/168 d5.31 b-Arthur

YEAR	TM LG	G	AB	R	H	2B	3B	HR	RBI	BB-IB	HP	SO	AVG	OBP	SLG	AOPS	ABR	SB-CS	FA	FR	RNG	THR	GAMES AT POSITION	DL	BFW
1882	Wor N	1	4	0	0	0	0	0	0	0		2	.000	.000	.000	-98	-1		.636	-1	0	171	/1		-0.2
1884	Bos U	105	432	81	101	22	6	1		15			.234	.260	.319	76	-26		.780	4	103	73	3b105		-1.8
1886	Phi AA	3	13	4	3	1	0	0	1	0	0		.231	.231	.308	67	-1	0	.714	-1	58	0	S2/3		-0.1
1887	Was N	8	31	6	11	2	0	2	3	3	1	6	.355	.429	.613	198	4	6	.875	-2	77	67	S5,3b4		0.3
1888	Was N	37	126	14	28	5	2	0	8	5	2	18	.222	.263	.294	83	-2	15	.860	-2	102	58	S27,3b10		-0.3
1889	Was N	58	228	42	66	11	4	0	25	25	4	14	.289	.370	.373	115	6	10	.868	4	104	116	3b58		0.7
1890	Buf P	77	308	62	72	11	4	0	34	43	2	19	.234	.335	.295	75	-8	18	.883	8	106	105	3b64,1b12/2		0.0
1891	Bos AA	19	72	6	16	2	0	0	15	6	0	9	.222	.282	.306	69	-3	6	.882	-0	166	0	O17(9/0/9),3b2/S		-0.3
	Lou AA	14	55	7	15	1	0	0	7	5	1	6	.273	.344	.327	93	0	1	.795	-5	77	47	3b14		-0.4
	Year	33	127	13	31	3	3	0	22	11	1	15	.244	.309	.315	80	-4	7	.882	-5	166	0	O17(9/0/9),3b16/S		-0.7
Total	8	322	1269	222	312	55	19	3	93	102	12	74	.246	.308	.326	87	-31	56	.829	4	101	88	3b258,S35,O17(9/0/9),1b13/2		-2.1

IRWIN, TOMMY Thomas Andrew B12.20.1912 Altoona PA D4.25.1996 Altoona PA BR/TR/5-11/165 d10.1 Col North Carolina-Asheville

YEAR	TM LG	G	AB	R	H	2B	3B	HR	RBI	BB-IB	HP	SO	AVG	OBP	SLG	AOPS	ABR	SB-CS	FA	FR	RNG	THR	GAMES AT POSITION	DL	BFW
1938	Cle A	3	9	1	1	0	0	0	0	0		3	.111	.333	.111	16	-1	0-0	1.000	0	110	121	S3		-0.1

IRWIN, WALT Walter Kingsley B9.23.1897 Henrietta PA D8.18.1976 Spring Lake MI BR/TR/5-10.5/170 d4.24

YEAR	TM LG	G	AB	R	H	2B	3B	HR	RBI	BB-IB	HP	SO	AVG	OBP	SLG	AOPS	ABR	SB-CS	FA	FR	RNG	THR	GAMES AT POSITION	DL	BFW
1921	StL N	4	1	1	0	0	0	0	0	0		1	.000	.000	.000	-99	0	0-0	—	0			/H		0.0

IRWIN, ED William Edward B1882 Philadelphia PA D2.5.1916 Philadelphia PA BR/TR d5.18

YEAR	TM LG	G	AB	R	H	2B	3B	HR	RBI	BB-IB	HP	SO	AVG	OBP	SLG	AOPS	ABR	SB-CS	FA	FR	RNG	THR	GAMES AT POSITION	DL	BFW
1912	Det A	1	3	0	2	0	0	0	2	0		0	.667	.667	2.000	675	2	0	.500	-1	72	0	/3		0.1

ISALES, ORLANDO Orlando (Pizarro) B12.22.1959 Santurce, PR BR/TR/5-9/175 d9.11

YEAR	TM LG	G	AB	R	H	2B	3B	HR	RBI	BB-IB	HP	SO	AVG	OBP	SLG	AOPS	ABR	SB-CS	FA	FR	RNG	THR	GAMES AT POSITION	DL	BFW
1980	Phi N	3	5	1	2	0	1	0	1	0		1-0	.400	.500	.800	241	1	0-0	1.000	-0	105	0	O2R		0.1

ISBELL, FRANK William Frank "Bald Eagle" B8.21.1875 Delevan NY D7.15.1941 Wichita KS BL/TR/5-11/190 d5.1 OF(15/33/54) ▲

YEAR	TM LG	G	AB	R	H	2B	3B	HR	RBI	BB-IB	HP	SO	AVG	OBP	SLG	AOPS	ABR	SB-CS	FA	FR	RNG	THR	GAMES AT POSITION	DL	BFW
1898	Chi N	45	159	17	37	4	0	0	8	3	1		.233	.252	.258	46	-12	3	.956	-4	103	0	O28(4/12/11),P13,3b3,2b3,S2		-1.3
1901	Chi A	**137**	556	93	143	15	8	3	70	36	7		.257	.311	.329	79	-16	**52**	.980	13	**139**	109	1b137,2b2/PS3		-0.5
1902	Chi A	137	515	62	130	14	4	4	59	14	3		.252	.276	.318	68	-24	38	.986	10	125	128	1b133,S4/PC		-1.6
1903	Chi A	**138**	546	52	132	25	9	2	59	12	6		.242	.266	.332	82	-13	26	.984	4	122	99	1b117,3b19,2b2/SOR		-1.1
1904	Chi A	96	314	27	66	10	3	1	34	16	3		.210	.255	.271	69	-11	19	.986	-1	137	102	1b57,2b27,O5R,S4		-1.4
1905	Chi A	94	341	55	101	21	11	4	45	15	5		.296	.335	.440	151	18	15	.964	1	100	198	2b43,O41(2/5/34),1b9,S2		1.8
1906	†Chi A	143	549	71	153	18	11	0	57	30	7		.279	.324	.352	115	8	37	.949	-18	97	93	2b132,O14(4/7/3)/PC		-1.0
1907	Chi A	125	486	60	118	19	7	0	41	22	4		.243	.281	.311	92	-6	22	.957	9	106	114	2b119,O5L/PS		0.4
1908	Chi A	84	320	31	79	15	3	1	49	19	4		.247	.297	.322	103	1	18	.990	0	111	114	1b65,2b18		0.0
1909	Chi A	120	433	33	97	17	6	0	33	23	1		.224	.265	.291	79	-12	23	.994	2	105	106	1b101,O9C,2b5		-1.4
Total	10	1119	4219	501	1056	158	62	13	455	190	41		.250	.289	.326	89	-67	253	.986	16	126	111	1b619,2b351,O103R,3b23,P17,S15,C2		-6.1

IVIE, MIKE Michael Wilson B8.8.1952 Atlanta GA BR/TR/6-3/205(200-215) [SDN70 1/1] d9.4

YEAR	TM LG	G	AB	R	H	2B	3B	HR	RBI	BB-IB	HP	SO	AVG	OBP	SLG	AOPS	ABR	SB-CS	FA	FR	RNG	THR	GAMES AT POSITION	DL	BFW
1971	SD N	6	17	0	8	0	0	0	3	1-1	1	1	.471	.526	.471	197	2	0-0	1.000	-2	33	95	C6		0.1
1974	SD N	12	34	1	3	0	0	1	3	2-0	0	5	.088	.139	.176	-13	-5	0-0	.986	-0	85	105	1b11		-0.7
1975	SD N	111	377	36	94	16	2	8	46	20-2	4	63	.249	.291	.366	88	-8	4-4	.989	-4	122	117	1b78,3b61/C	15	-1.8
1976	SD N	140	405	51	118	19	5	7	70	30-8	5	41	.291	.345	.415	126	12	6-6	.995	1	105	100	1b135,C2,3b2		0.4
1977	SD N	134	489	66	133	29	2	9	66	39-4	2	57	.272	.326	.395	103	1	3-2	.992	-4	99	91	1b105,3b25		-0.9
1978	SF N	117	318	34	98	14	3	11	55	27-6	2	45	.308	.363	.475	138	15	3-0	.995	-8	54	77	1b76,O22L		0.4
1979	SF N	133	402	58	115	18	3	27	89	47-7	1	80	.286	.359	.547	155	29	5-1	.995	-2	89	77	1b98,O24L,3b4/2	17	2.3
1980	SF N	79	286	21	69	16	1	4	25	19-2	0	40	.241	.288	.346	79	-9	1-2	.993	-5	72	79	1b72		-2.0
1981	SF N	7	17	1	5	2	0	0	3	0-0	0	2	.294	.278	.412	102	0	0-0	1.000	1	150	63	1b5		0.0
	Hou N	19	42	2	10	3	0	0	6	2-0	0	11	.238	.267	.310	69	-2	0-1	.989	2	172	78	1b10	111	-0.1
	Year	26	59	3	15	5	0	0	9	2-0	0	12	.254	.270	.339	78	-2	0-1	.992	3	165	74	1b15		-0.1
1982	Hou N	7	6	0	2	0	0	0	0	1-0	0	1	.333	.429	.333	125	0	0-0	—	0	0		/H		-0.2
	Det A	80	259	35	60	12	1	14	38	24-3	2	51	.232	.299	.448	102	0	0-0	1.000	-0	82	76	1b12		-0.4
1983	Det A	12	42	4	9	4	0	0	7	2-1	0	6	.214	.244	.310	54	-3	0-0					D79	143	-0.4
Total	11	857	2694	309	724	133	17	81	411	214-34	17	402	.269	.324	.421	112	32	22-16	.993	-22	80	89	1b602,3b92,D79,O46L,C9/2		-2.9

IZQUIERDO, HANK Enrique Roberto (Valdes) B3.20.1931 Matanzas, Cuba BR/TR/5-11/175 d8.9

YEAR	TM LG	G	AB	R	H	2B	3B	HR	RBI	BB-IB	HP	SO	AVG	OBP	SLG	AOPS	ABR	SB-CS	FA	FR	RNG	THR	GAMES AT POSITION	DL	BFW
1967	Min A	16	26	4	7	2	0	0	2	1-0		2	.269	.296	.346	83	-1	0-0	.986	2	125	115	C16		0.2

IZTURIS, CESAR Cesar D. B2.10.1980 Barquisimeto, Venez BB/TR/5-9/175* d6.23 b-Macier

YEAR	TM LG	G	AB	R	H	2B	3B	HR	RBI	BB-IB	HP	SO	AVG	OBP	SLG	AOPS	ABR	SB-CS	FA	FR	RNG	THR	GAMES AT POSITION	DL	BFW
2001	Tor A	46	134	19	36	6	2	2	9	2-0	0	15	.269	.279	.388	72	-6	8-1	.988	1	108	103	2b41,S6		-0.2
2002	LA N	135	439	43	102	24	2	2	31	14-1	0	39	.232	.253	.303	52	-34	7-7	.979	-12	91	103	S128/2D		-3.9
2003	LA N	158	558	47	140	21	6	1	40	25-8	0	70	.251	.282	.315	57	-37	10-5	.977	18	104	106	S158		-0.7
2004	†LA N	159	670	90	193	32	9	4	62	43-2	0	70	.288	.330	.381	84	-17	25-8	.985	-12	92	105	S159		-1.4
2005	LA N*	106	444	48	114	19	2	2	31	25-1	4	51	.257	.302	.322	64	-24	8-8	.977	8	110	94	S106	56	-0.9
Total	5	604	2245	247	585	102	21	10	173	109-12	4	245	.261	.295	.338	67	-118	58-30	.980	2	99	103	S557,2b42/D	56	-7.1

IZTURIS, MAICER Maicer B9.12.1980 Barquisimeto, Venez BB/TR/5-8/150* d8.27 b-Cesar

YEAR	TM LG	G	AB	R	H	2B	3B	HR	RBI	BB-IB	HP	SO	AVG	OBP	SLG	AOPS	ABR	SB-CS	FA	FR	RNG	THR	GAMES AT POSITION	DL	BFW
2004	Mon N	32	107	10	22	5	2	1	4	10-1	2	20	.206	.286	.318	54	-8	4-0	.937	1	117	110	S23,2b10		-0.4
2005	†LA A	77	191	18	47	8	4	1	15	17-2	0	21	.246	.306	.346	75	-7	9-3	.911	-3	105	96	3b45,S29/2OC	53	-0.7
Total	2	109	298	28	69	13	6	2	19	27-3	2	41	.232	.299	.336	67	-15	13-3	.958	-2	97	81	S52,3b45,2b11/OC	53	-1.1

JABLONSKI, RAY Raymond Leo "Jabbo" B12.17.1926 Chicago IL D11.25.1985 Chicago IL BR/TR/5-10/183* d4.14

YEAR	TM LG	G	AB	R	H	2B	3B	HR	RBI	BB-IB	HP	SO	AVG	OBP	SLG	AOPS	ABR	SB-CS	FA	FR	RNG	THR	GAMES AT POSITION	DL	BFW
1953	StL N	**157**	604	64	162	23	5	21	112	34	2	61	.268	.308	.427	89	-12	2-2	.932	-18	93	86	3b157		-3.0
1954	StL N★	152	611	80	181	33	4	12	104	49	2	42	.296	.345	.419	99	-1	9-4	.925	-10	**99**	90	3b149/1		-1.1
1955	Cin N	74	221	28	53	9	0	9	28	13-1	3	35	.240	.289	.403	77	-8	0-1	.872	-6	84	64	3b28,O28L		-1.5
1956	Cin N	130	407	42	104	25	1	15	66	37-6	7	57	.256	.324	.432	96	-1	2-4	.970	-20	80	59	3b127/2		-2.3
1957	NY N	107	305	37	88	15	1	9	57	31-2	0	47	.289	.346	.433	110	5	0-2	.941	2	111	84	3b70,1b6/OL		0.5
1958	SF N	82	230	28	53	15	1	12	46	17-2	2	50	.230	.287	.461	97	2	2-0	.946	-8	87	20	3b57		-1.0
1959	StL N	60	87	11	22	4	0	3	14	8-0	0	19	.253	.313	.402	84	-2	1-0	.900	-2	93	106	3b19/S		-0.4
	KC A	25	65	4	17	1	0	2	8	3-0	0	11	.262	.294	.369	79	-2	0-0	.947	-2	85	121	3b17		-0.2
1960	KC A	21	32	3	7	1	0	0	3	4-0	0	5	.219	.297	.250	52	-2	0-0	.944	1	129	0	3b6		-0.2
Total	8	808	2562	297	687	126	11	83	438	196-11	15	330	.268	.320	.423	94	-25	16-13	.936	-62	93	81	3b630,O29L,1b7/S2		-9.4

JACKLITSCH, FRED Frederick Lawrence B5.24.1876 Brooklyn NY D7.18.1937 Brooklyn NY BR/TR/5-9/180 d6.6

YEAR	TM LG	G	AB	R	H	2B	3B	HR	RBI	BB-IB	HP	SO	AVG	OBP	SLG	AOPS	ABR	SB-CS	FA	FR	RNG	THR	GAMES AT POSITION	DL	BFW
1900	Phi N	5	11	0	2	1	0	0	3	0	2		.182	.182	.273	25	-1		1.000	-1	68	61	C3		-0.2
1901	Phi N	33	120	14	30	4	1	0	24	12	2		.250	.328	.333	90	-1	2	.971	-0	98	107	C30/3		0.2
1902	Phi N	38	114	8	23	0	0	0	8	9	3		.202	.278	.237	59	-5	2	.927	-9	75	96	C29/OC		-1.2
1903	Bro N	60	176	31	47	8	3	1	21	33	2		.267	.389	.364	118	6	4	.975	-13	65	112	C53/2OC		-0.1

YEAR	TM LG	G	AB	R	H	2B	3B	HR	RBI	BB-IB	HP	SO	AVG	OBP	SLG	AOPS	ABR	SB-CS	FA	FR	RNG	THR	GAMES AT POSITION	DL	BFW
1904	Bro N	26	77	8	18	3	1	0	8	7	3		.234	.322	.299	94	0	7	.957	-6	85	129	1b11,2b8,C5		-0.6
1905	NY A	1	3	1	0	0	0	0	1	1	0		.000	.250	.000	-17	0	0	1.000	-0	119	105	/C		0.0
1907	Phi N	73	202	19	43	7	0	0	17	27	2		.213	.312	.248	76	-4	7	.984	13	123	113	C58,1b6/OR		1.6
1908	Phi N	37	86	6	19	3	0	0	7	14	1		.221	.337	.256	87	0	3	.976	5	134	104	C30		0.8
1909	Phi N	20	32	6	10	1	1	0	1	10			.313	.476	.406	173	4	1	.964	-1	101	101	C11/2		0.4
1910	Phi N	25	51	7	10	3	0	0	2	5	0	9	.196	.268	.255	51	-3	0	.989	2	105	119	C13,1b2/23		0.0
1914	Bal F	122	337	40	93	21	4	2	48	52	2	66	.276	.376	.380	102	-1	7	.988	4	110	102	C118		1.3
1915	Bal F	49	135	20	32	9	4	2	13	31	2	25	.237	.387	.348	104	1	2	.992	-4	101	83	C45/S		0.0
1917	Bos N	1	0	0	0	0	0	0	0	0	0		—	—	—		0	0	1.000	-0	0	0	/C		0.0
Total	13	490	1344	160	327	64	12	5	153	201	17	100	.243	.349	.320	95	-4	35	.978	-11	103	103	C397,1b19,2b11,O3(0/2/1),3b2/S		2.2

JACKSON, CHARLIE Charles Herbert "Lefty" B2.7.1894 Granite City IL D5.27.1968 Radford VA BL/TL/5-9/150 d8.20 Mil 1918

YEAR	TM LG	G	AB	R	H	2B	3B	HR	RBI	BB-IB	HP	SO	AVG	OBP	SLG	AOPS	ABR	SB-CS	FA	FR	RNG	THR	GAMES AT POSITION	DL	BFW
1915	Chi A	1	1	0	0	0	0	0	0	0	0	1	.000	.000	.000	-97	0	0	—				/H		0.0
1917	Pit N	41	121	7	29	3	2	0	1	10	1	22	.240	.303	.298	82	-2	4	.986	2	106	122	O36(20/1/15)		-0.3
Total	2	42	122	7	29	3	2	0	1	10	1	23	.238	.301	.295	80	-2	4	.986	2	106	122	O36(20/1/15)		-0.3

JACKSON, CHUCK Charles Leo B3.19.1963 Seattle WA BR/TR/6-0/185* [HouN84 7/175] d5.26 Col Hawaii-Manoa [DL 1990 SF N 80]

YEAR	TM LG	G	AB	R	H	2B	3B	HR	RBI	BB-IB	HP	SO	AVG	OBP	SLG	AOPS	ABR	SB-CS	FA	FR	RNG	THR	GAMES AT POSITION	DL	BFW
1987	Hou N	35	71	3	15	3	0	1	6	7-0	0	19	.211	.282	.296	55	-5	1-1	.957	3	137	177	3b16,O13(1/12/0)/S		-0.2
1988	Hou N	46	83	7	19	5	1	1	8	7-4	0	16	.229	.286	.349	86	-2	1-1	.908	1	107	170	3b32,S3,O3(0/1/2)		-0.1
1994	Tex A	1	2	0	0	0	0	0	0	0-0	0	1	.000	.000	.000	-99	-1	0-0	—	-0	0	0	/3		-0.1
Total	3	82	156	10	34	8	1	2	14	14-4	0	35	.218	.281	.321	69	-8	2-2	.928	3	117	171	3b49,O16(1/13/2),S4	80	-0.4

JACKSON, CONOR Conor Sims B5.7.1982 Austin TX BR/TR/6-3/225 d7.28 Col California

YEAR	TM LG	G	AB	R	H	2B	3B	HR	RBI	BB-IB	HP	SO	AVG	OBP	SLG	AOPS	ABR	SB-CS	FA	FR	RNG	THR	GAMES AT POSITION	DL	BFW
2005	Ari N	40	85	8	17	3	0	2	8	12-0	1	11	.200	.303	.306	59	-5	0-0	.973	-1	103	116	1b20/OL		-0.8

JACKSON, DAMIAN Damian Jacques B8.16.1973 Los Angeles CA BR/TR/5-11/185(160-185) [CleA91 44/1148] d9.12 Col Laney (CA) JC OF(73/37/18)

YEAR	TM LG	G	AB	R	H	2B	3B	HR	RBI	BB-IB	HP	SO	AVG	OBP	SLG	AOPS	ABR	SB-CS	FA	FR	RNG	THR	GAMES AT POSITION	DL	BFW
1996	Cle A	5	10	2	3	2	0	0	1	1-0	0	4	.300	.364	.500	116	0	0-0	1.000	3	191	266	S5		0.3
1997	Cle A	8	9	2	1	0	0	0	0	0-0	1	1	.111	.200	.111	-15	-2	1-0	1.000	-0	91	111	S5/2		-0.1
	Cin N	12	27	6	6	2	1	0	2	4-1	0	7	.222	.323	.481	105	0	1-1	1.000	0	93	68	S6,2b3		0.1
1998	Cin N	13	38	4	12	5	0	0	7	6-0	0	4	.316	.400	.447	124	2	2-0	.972	-1	87	60	S10,O3(0/3/1)		0.2
1999	SD N	133	388	56	87	20	2	9	39	53-3	3	105	.224	.320	.356	77	-14	34-10	.940	7	105	110	S100,2b21,O3(2/0/1)		0.4
2000	SD N	138	470	68	120	27	6	6	37	62-2	3	108	.255	.345	.377	88	-8	28-6	.955	13	115	100	S88,2b36,O17L		1.5
2001	SD N	122	440	67	106	21	6	4	38	44-2	6	128	.241	.316	.343	77	-16	23-6	.986	0	99	98	2b118,S3,O2C		-0.7
2002	Det N	81	245	31	63	20	1	6	25	21-0	3	36	.257	.320	.359	84	-5	12-3	.981	-7	96	99	2b56,S6,O6(3/3/0),3b2,D5	40	-0.7
2003	†Bos A	109	161	34	42	7	0	1	13	8-0	0	28	.261	.294	.323	61	-9	16-8	.960	-1	106	54	2b38,O38(13/13/12),S18,3b3,1b2,D9	15	-0.7
2004	†SD N	7	15	1	1	0	0	1	1	3-2	0	6	.067	.222	.267	25	-2	0-0	.957	2	129	222	2b5		-0.8
	KC A	14	15	1	2	2	0	0	2	1-0	0	6	.133	.188	.267	16	-2	0-0	1.000	1	88	0	O5(1/1/3)/2SD		0.1
2005	†SD N	118	275	44	70	9	0	5	23	30-1	5	45	.255	.335	.342	83	-7	15-2	1.000	-2	112	181	O52(37/15/1),2b35,S26,3b8		-0.4
Total	10	760	2093	316	513	115	16	28	188	233-11	20	478	.245	.335	.355	80	-63	132-36	.982	14	100	100	2b314,S268,O126L,D16,3b13,1b2	55	-0.3

JACKSON, DARRIN Darrin Jay B8.22.1962 Los Angeles CA BR/TR/6-0/185(170-198) [ChiN81 2/28] d6.17

YEAR	TM LG	G	AB	R	H	2B	3B	HR	RBI	BB-IB	HP	SO	AVG	OBP	SLG	AOPS	ABR	SB-CS	FA	FR	RNG	THR	GAMES AT POSITION	DL	BFW
1985	Chi N	5	11	0	1	0	0	0	0	0-0	0	3	.091	.091	.091	-45	-2	0-0	1.000	-1	82	0	O4C		-0.3
1987	Chi N	7	5	2	4	1	0	0	0	0-0	0	1	.800	.800	1.000	359	2	0-0	1.000	-0	46	0	O5(2/3/0)		0.2
1988	Chi N	100	188	29	50	11	3	6	20	5-1	1	28	.266	.287	.452	105	0	4-1	.983	10	104	45	O74(11/46/20)		0.0
1989	Chi N	45	83	7	19	4	0	1	8	6-1	0	17	.229	.281	.313	65	-4	1-2	.970	4	124	231	O39(10/9/20)		-0.1
	SD N	25	87	10	18	3	0	3	12	7-4	0	17	.207	.260	.345	73	-3	0-2	.954	-0	95	154	O24C		-0.5
	Year	70	170	17	37	7	0	4	20	13-5	0	34	.218	.270	.329	68	-7	1-4	.962	3	109	191	O63(10/33/20)		-0.6
1990	SD N	58	113	10	29	3	0	3	9	5-1	0	24	.257	.286	.363	77	-4	3-0	.985	-1	99	68	O39(4/30/5)		-0.4
1991	SD N	122	359	51	94	12	1	21	49	27-2	2	66	.262	.315	.476	116	6	5-3	.992	2	113	39	O98(21/79/0)/P		0.7
1992	SD N	155	587	72	146	23	5	17	70	26-4	4	106	.249	.283	.392	88	-12	14-3	.996	14	108	205	O153(5/152/2)		-0.4
1993	Tor A	46	176	15	38	8	0	5	19	8-0	1	53	.216	.250	.347	57	-11	0-2	.989	-4	83	63	O46(0/10/37)		-1.7
	NY N	31	87	4	17	1	0	1	7	2-0	0	22	.195	.211	.241	22	-10	0-0	1.000	2	98	301	O26(10/16/0)	44	-0.8
1994	Chi A	104	369	43	115	17	3	10	51	27-3	3	56	.312	.362	.455	111	5	7-1	.996	3	117	31	O102(0/16/92)		0.5
1997	Min A	49	130	19	33	2	1	3	21	4-0	0	21	.254	.272	.354	62	-8	2-0	.990	2	101	216	O44C		-0.5
	Mil A	26	81	7	22	7	0	2	15	2-0	0	10	.272	.289	.432	84	-2	2-1	1.000	3	117	155	O26(21/9/3)		0.0
	Year	75	211	26	55	9	1	5	36	6-0	0	31	.261	.279	.384	70	-10	4-1	.994	4	107	193	O70(21/53/3)		-0.5
1998	Mil N	114	204	20	49	13	1	4	20	9-0	1	37	.240	.276	.373	67	-10	1-1	.982	-1	95	89	O94(55/43/5),D2	7	-1.2
1999	Chi A	73	149	22	41	9	1	4	16	3-0	1	20	.275	.288	.430	79	-5	4-1	.972	3	118	82	O64(46/25/3),D3	17	-0.3
Total	12	960	2629	311	676	114	15	80	317	131-16	11	480	.257	.293	.403	87	-58	43-17	.989	27	107	117	O838(185/510/187),D5/P	68	-4.0

JACKSON, GEORGE George Christopher "Hickory" B10.14.1882 Springfield MO D11.25.1972 Cleburne TX BR/TR/6-0.5/180 d8.2

YEAR	TM LG	G	AB	R	H	2B	3B	HR	RBI	BB-IB	HP	SO	AVG	OBP	SLG	AOPS	ABR	SB-CS	FA	FR	RNG	THR	GAMES AT POSITION	DL	BFW
1911	Bos N	39	147	28	51	11	2	0	25	12	2	21	.347	.404	.449	128	6	12	.929	-2	98	75	O39(38/1/0)		0.3
1912	Bos N	110	397	55	104	13	5	4	48	38	10	72	.262	.342	.350	88	-6	22	.943	1	96	119	O107(96/11/0)		-1.0
1913	Bos N	3	10	2	3	0	0	0	0	0	0	2	.300	.300	.300	70	0	0	.875	0	90	254	O3C		0.0
Total	3	152	554	85	158	24	7	4	73	50	12	95	.285	.357	.375	98	0	34	.938	-1	96	111	O149(134/15/0)		-0.7

JACKSON, HENRY Henry Everett B6.23.1861 Union City IN D9.14.1932 Chicago IL BR/TR/6-2/185 d9.13

YEAR	TM LG	G	AB	R	H	2B	3B	HR	RBI	BB-IB	HP	SO	AVG	OBP	SLG	AOPS	ABR	SB-CS	FA	FR	RNG	THR	GAMES AT POSITION	DL	BFW
1887	Ind N	10	38	1	10	1	0	0	3	0	0	12	.263	.263	.289	55	-2	1	.933	-1	82	112	1b10		-0.4

JACKSON, JIM James Benner B11.28.1877 Philadelphia PA D10.9.1955 Philadelphia PA BR/TR/5-6.5/165 d4.26 Col Penn

YEAR	TM LG	G	AB	R	H	2B	3B	HR	RBI	BB-IB	HP	SO	AVG	OBP	SLG	AOPS	ABR	SB-CS	FA	FR	RNG	THR	GAMES AT POSITION	DL	BFW
1901	Bal A	99	364	42	91	17	3	2	50	20	1		.250	.291	.330	69	-14	11	.971	2	32	34	O96(35/59/2)		-1.7
1902	NY N	37	116	14	21	5	1	0	15	16	0		.181	.280	.241	62	-5	6	.899	-2	88	0	O36(32/2/2)		-0.9
1905	Cle A	109	426	60	109	12	4	2	31	34	4		.256	.317	.317	100	0	15	.951	4	135	115	O106(104/0/2),3b3		-0.2
1906	Cle A	105	374	44	80	13	2	0	38	38	2		.214	.290	.259	73	-10	25	.975	-7	37	75	O104(103/1/0)		-2.6
Total	4	350	1280	160	301	47	10	4	134	108	7		.235	.298	.297	79	-31	57	.959	-2	71	69	O342(274/62/6),3b3		-5.4

JACKSON, JOE Joseph Jefferson "Shoeless Joe" B7.16.1889 Pickens Co. SC D12.5.1951 Greenville SC BL/TR/6-1/200 d8.25 Def 1918

YEAR	TM LG	G	AB	R	H	2B	3B	HR	RBI	BB-IB	HP	SO	AVG	OBP	SLG	AOPS	ABR	SB-CS	FA	FR	RNG	THR	GAMES AT POSITION	DL	BFW
1908	Phi A	5	23	0	3	0	0	0	3	0	0		.130	.130	.130	-14	-3	0	.875	-0	221	0	O5C		-0.4
1909	Phi A	5	17	3	3	0	0	0	3	0	1		.176	.222	.176	26	-1	0	.833	-1	0	0	O4(3/1/0)		-0.3
1910	Cle A	20	75	15	29	2	5	1	11	8	0		.387	.446	.587	220	10	4	.977	-0	103	67	O20(0/15/5)		0.9
1911	Cle A	147	571	126	233	45	19	7	83	56	8		.408	.468	.590	192	71	41	.958	5	98	129	O147(0/47/100)		6.5
1912	Cle A	154	572	121	226	44	26	3	90	54	12		.395	.458	.579	190	67	35	.950	14	118	144	O150(0/19/131)		7.1
1913	Cle A	148	528	109	197	39	17	7	71	80	5	26	.373	.460	.551	190	63	26	.930	1	95	126	O148R		5.9
1914	Cle A	122	453	61	153	22	13	3	45	41	5	34	.338	.399	.464	153	29	22-15	.967	2	107	91	O119(0/31/88)		2.6
1915	Cle A	83	303	42	99	16	9	3	45	28	3	11	.327	.389	.469	154	19	10-10	.961	-2	100	113	O50(5/0/44),1b30		1.4
	Chi A	45	158	21	43	4	5	2	36	24	3	12	.272	.378	.399	129	6	6-10	.947	-2	89	101	O45(19/26/0)		-0.1
	Year	128	461	63	142	20	14	5	81	52	6	23	.308	.385	.445	145	25	16-20	.953	-4	94	107	O95(24/26/44),1b30		1.3
1916	Chi A	155	592	91	202	40	21	3	78	46	5	25	.341	.393	.495	165	44	24-14	.975	-4	94	94	O155(131/1/23)		3.6
1917	†Chi A	146	538	91	162	20	17	5	75	57	7	25	.301	.375	.429	142	27	13	.984	6	111	84	O145(134/0/11)		2.8
1918	Chi A	17	65	9	23	2	2	1	20	8			.354	.425	.492	175	6	3	1.000	4	100	45	O17(14/0/3)		0.5
1919	†Chi A	139	516	79	181	31	14	7	96	60		10	.351	.422	.506	159	42	9	.967	-3	92	109	O139(133/0/6)		3.3
1920	Chi A	146	570	105	218	42	20	12	121	56		14	.382	.444	.589	172	59	9-12	.965	-3	101	71	O145L		4.5
Total	13	1332	4981	873	1772	307	168	54	785	519	59	158	.356	.423	.517	169	439	202-61	.962	13	101	102	O1289(584/145/559),1b30		38.3

JACKSON, KEN Kenneth Bernard B8.21.1963 Shreveport LA BR/TR/5-9/170 [PhiN82 S1/17] d9.12 Col Angelina (TX) JC

YEAR	TM LG	G	AB	R	H	2B	3B	HR	RBI	BB-IB	HP	SO	AVG	OBP	SLG	AOPS	ABR	SB-CS	FA	FR	RNG	THR	GAMES AT POSITION	DL	BFW
1987	Phi N	8	16	1	4	2	0	0	2	1-1	1	4	.250	.333	.375	84	0	0-0	.955	-1	94	33	S8		-0.1

JACKSON, LOU Louis Clarence B7.26.1935 Riverton LA D5.27.1969 Tokyo, Japan BL/TR/5-10/168* d7.23 Col Grambling St.

YEAR	TM LG	G	AB	R	H	2B	3B	HR	RBI	BB-IB	HP	SO	AVG	OBP	SLG	AOPS	ABR	SB-CS	FA	FR	RNG	THR	GAMES AT POSITION	DL	BFW
1958	Chi N	24	35	5	6	2	1	1	6	1-0	0	9	.171	.194	.371	46	-3	0-1	1.000	-1	84	0	O12(4/4/6)		-0.4
1959	Chi N	6	4	2	1	0	0	0	0	0-0	0	3	.250	.250	.250	34	-0	0-0	—	0			/H		0.0
1964	Bal A	4	8	0	3	0	0	0	0	0-0	0	1	.375	.375	.375	110	0	0-0	1.000	0	223	0	/OL		0.0
Total	3	34	47	7	10	2	1	1	6	1-0	0	13	.213	.229	.362	55	-3	0-1	1.000	-1	107	0	O13(5/4/6)		-0.4

JACKSON, RANDY Ransom Joseph "Handsome Ransom" B2.10.1926 Little Rock AR BR/TR/6-1.5/180* d5.2 Col Texas

YEAR	TM LG	G	AB	R	H	2B	3B	HR	RBI	BB-IB	HP	SO	AVG	OBP	SLG	AOPS	ABR	SB-CS	FA	FR	RNG	THR	GAMES AT POSITION	DL	BFW
1950	Chi N	34	111	13	25	4	3	6	7	6	1	25	.225	.271	.396	74	-5	4	.911	-4	95	48	3b27		-0.9
1951	Chi N	145	557	78	153	24	6	16	76	47	1	44	.275	.332	.425	101	-1	14-3	.956	7	103	86	3b143		0.8
1952	Chi N	116	379	44	88	8	5	9	34	27	1	42	.232	.285	.351	75	-15	6-5	.958	-2	104	79	3b104/OL		-1.8

YEAR	TM LG	G	AB	R	H	2B	3B	HR	RBI	BB-IB	HP	SO	AVG	OBP	SLG	AOPS	ABR	SB-CS	FA	FR	RNG	THR	GAMES AT POSITION	DL	BFW
1953	Chi N	139	498	61	142	22	8	19	66	42	0	61	.285	.341	.476	108	4	8-4	.949	4	104	79	3b133		0.7
1954	Chi N★	126	484	77	132	17	6	19	67	44	2	55	.273	.340	.450	102	0	2-1	.955	-4	99	85	3b124		-0.5
1955	Chi N★	138	499	73	132	13	7	21	70	58-6	2	38	.265	.340	.445	107	4	0-2	.949	-12	92	102	3b134		-0.8
1956	†Bro N	101	307	37	84	15	7	8	53	28-3	2	38	.274	.333	.446	101	0	2-1	.993	22	129	164	3b80		2.2
1957	Bro N	48	131	7	26	1	0	2	16	9-0	0	20	.198	.246	.252	32	-13	0-0	.976	0	93	144	3b34	68	-1.3
1958	LA N	35	65	8	12	3	0	1	4	5-1	0	10	.185	.243	.277	36	-6	0-0	.964	5	137	207	3b17		-0.1
	Cle A	29	91	7	22	3	1	4	13	3-0	0	18	.242	.266	.429	90	-2	0-0	.901	1	112	77	3b24		-0.1
1959	Cle A	3	7	0	1	0	0	0	0	0-0	0	1	.143	.143	.143	-22	-1	0-0	1.000	-0	82	0	3b2		-0.2
	Chi N	41	74	7	18	5	1	1	10	11-1	0	10	.243	.341	.378	92	0	0-0	.941	-2	86	76	3b22/OL		-0.2
Total 10		955	3203	412	835	115	44	103	415	281-11	7	382	.261	.320	.421	94	-35	36-16	.955	16	103	96	3b844,O2L	68	-2.2

JACKSON, REGGIE Reginald Martinez B5.18.1946 Wyncote PA BL/TL/6-0/200(195-208) [OakA66 1/2] d6.9 HF1993 Col Arizona St.

YEAR	TM LG	G	AB	R	H	2B	3B	HR	RBI	BB-IB	HP	SO	AVG	OBP	SLG	AOPS	ABR	SB-CS	FA	FR	RNG	THR	GAMES AT POSITION	DL	BFW
1967	KC A	35	118	13	21	4	1	6	10-0		5	46	.178	.269	.305	72	-4	1-1	.933	-3	89	44	O34(19/3/14)		-1.0
1968	Oak A	154	553	82	138	13	6	29	74	50-5	5	171	.250	.316	.452	137	22	14-4	.959	6	108	169	O151(1/9/147)		2.2
1969	Oak A★	152	549	123	151	36	3	47	118	114-20	12	142	.275	.410	.608	189	70	13-5	.964	-2	99	116	O150(0/10/144)		6.3
1970	Oak A	149	426	57	101	21	2	23	66	75-11	8	135	.237	.359	.458	128	18	26-17	.956	-3	100	97	O145(0/3/145)		1.0
1971	†Oak A★	150	567	87	157	29	3	32	80	63-5	6	161	.277	.352	.508	145	32	16-10	.977	6	103	156	O135(0/92/43)		3.3
1972	†Oak A★	135	499	72	132	25	2	25	75	59-7	8	125	.265	.350	.473	151	31	9-8	.971	-8	95	84	O145(0/1/144),D3	15	2.0
1973	Oak A★	151	539	99	158	28	2	32	117	76-11	7	111	.293	.383	.531	164	47	22-8	.971	-1	106	42	O145(0/1/144),D3		4.1
1974	Oak A★	148	506	90	146	25	1	29	93	86-20	4	105	.289	.391	.514	170	49	25-5	.968	6	115	83	O127(0/3/126),D19		5.3
1975	Oak A★	157	593	91	150	39	3	36	104	67-5	3	133	.253	.329	.511	138	28	17-8	.965	5	109	107	O147R,D9		2.7
1976	Bal A	134	498	84	138	27	2	27	91	54-7	4	108	.277	.351	.502	157	35	28-7	.964	1	104	87	O121(0/16/111),D11		3.5
1977	†NY A★	146	525	93	150	39	2	32	110	74-4	3	129	.286	.375	.550	150	38	17-3	.949	-4	97	66	O127R,D18		3.0
1978	†NY A*	139	511	82	140	13	5	27	97	58-2	9	133	.274	.356	.477	135	23	14-11	.986	-3	97	77	O104R,D35		1.4
1979	NY A★	131	465	78	138	24	2	29	89	65-3	2	107	.297	.382	.544	150	33	9-8	.986	1	104	74	O125R,D3	24	2.6
1980	†NY A★	143	514	94	154	22	4	41	111	83-15	2	122	.300	.398	.597	172	52	1-2	.962	-9	94	45	O94R,D46		4.0
1981	†NY A★	94	334	33	79	17	1	15	54	46-2	1	82	.237	.330	.428	119	8	0-3	.974	-2	93	73	O61R,D33	9	0.1
1982	†Cal A★	153	530	92	146	17	1	39	101	85-12	2	156	.275	.375	.532	145	34	0-2	.972	-17	75	64	O139R,D5		-2.3
1983	Cal A*	116	397	43	77	14	1	14	49	52-5	4	140	.194	.290	.340	74	-14	0-2	.986	-4	74	121	D62,O47R		-1.0
1984	Cal A★	143	525	67	117	17	2	25	81	55-7	3	141	.223	.300	.406	93	-6	8-4	1.000	-0	107	0	D134,O3R		0.7
1985	Cal A	143	460	64	116	27	0	27	85	78-12	1	138	.252	.360	.487	130	21	1-2	.944	-8	75	120	O81R,D52		1.0
1986	†Cal A	132	419	65	101	12	2	18	58	92-11	3	115	.241	.379	.408	116	13	1-1	.833	1	99	698	D79,O20R		-1.1
1987	Oak A	115	336	42	74	14	1	15	43	33-0	4	97	.220	.297	.402	89	-6	2-1	1.000	-2	83	0	D79,O20R		
Total 21		2820	9864	1551	2584	463	49	563	1702	1375-164	96	2597	.262	.356	.490	139	524	228-115	.967	-34	99	92	O2102(20/186/1939),D630	48	38.7

JACKSON, SONNY Roland Thomas B7.9.1944 Washington DC BL/TR/5-9/155* d9.27 C8

YEAR	TM LG	G	AB	R	H	2B	3B	HR	RBI	BB-IB	HP	SO	AVG	OBP	SLG	AOPS	ABR	SB-CS	FA	FR	RNG	THR	GAMES AT POSITION	DL	BFW
1963	Hou N	1	3	0	0	0	0	0	0	0-0	0	1	.000	.000	.000	-99	-1	0-0	.833	1	306	0	/S		0.0
1964	Hou N	9	23	3	8	1	0	0	1	2-0	0	3	.348	.400	.391	131	1	0-0	.870	-3	72	32	S7		-0.2
1965	Hou N	10	23	1	3	0	0	0	1	1-0	0	1	.130	.167	.130	-16	-4	1-1	.969	-2	74	74	S8/3		-0.5
1966	Hou N	150	596	80	174	6	5	3	25	42-0	3	53	.292	.341	.334	95	-4	49-14	.951	-3	98	81	S150		1.2
1967	Hou N	129	520	67	123	18	3	0	25	36-1	0	45	.237	.285	.283	66	-24	22-9	.943	-9	93	80	S128	21	-2.1
1968	Atl N	105	358	37	81	8	2	1	19	25-6	3	35	.226	.282	.268	66	-15	16-6	.952	-15	100	68	S99	32	-2.3
1969	†Atl N	98	318	41	76	3	5	1	27	35-2	2	33	.239	.317	.289	71	-12	12-7	.961	-9	93	100	S97		-1.1
1970	Atl N	103	328	60	85	14	3	0	20	45-1	1	27	.259	.347	.320	76	-9	11-4	.933	-13	92	83	S87		-1.2
1971	Atl N	149	547	58	141	20	5	2	25	35-1	1	45	.258	.302	.324	73	-19	7-6	.980	-7	85	87	O145C	25	-3.4
1972	Atl N	60	126	20	30	6	3	0	8	7-0	0	9	.238	.278	.333	67	-6	1-0	.976	4	117	101	S17,O10(0/9/1),3b6		-1.4
1973	Atl N	117	206	29	43	5	2	0	12	22-0	1	13	.209	.283	.252	47	-14	6-3	.981	-1	94	56	O56(48/4/4),S36		-1.4
1974	Atl N	5	7	0	3	0	0	0	0	0-0	0	4	.429	.429	.429	135	0	0-0	1.000	0	131	0	/OR		
Total 12		936	3055	396	767	81	28	7	162	250-11	11	265	.251	.308	.303	73	-107	126-51	.949	-57	96	81	S630,O212(48/158/6),3b7	78	-11.0

JACKSON, RON Ronald Harris B10.22.1933 Kalamazoo MI BR/TR/6-7/225* d6.15 Col Western Michigan

YEAR	TM LG	G	AB	R	H	2B	3B	HR	RBI	BB-IB	HP	SO	AVG	OBP	SLG	AOPS	ABR	SB-CS	FA	FR	RNG	THR	GAMES AT POSITION	DL	BFW
1954	Chi A	40	93	10	26	4	0	4	10	6	2	20	.280	.333	.452	111	1	2-1	.988	-3	55	74	1b35		-0.3
1955	Chi A	40	74	10	15	1	1	2	7	8-2	0	22	.203	.277	.324	61	-5	1-0	.988	-1	77	93	1b29		-0.2
1956	Chi A	22	56	7	12	3	0	1	4	10-1	0	13	.214	.333	.321	73	-2	1-0	1.000	-1	114	116	1b19		-0.2
1957	Chi A	13	60	4	19	3	0	2	8	1-1	0	12	.317	.328	.467	114	1	0-0	.992	-1	62	87	1b13		-0.1
1958	Chi A	61	146	19	34	4	0	7	21	18-0	2	46	.233	.323	.404	101	0	2-0	.997	-2	76	98	1b38		0.0
1959	Chi A	10	14	3	3	1	0	1	2	1-0	0	5	.214	.313	.500	121	0	0-0	1.000	-0	53	127	1b5		-0.3
1960	Bos A	10	31	4	7	2	0	0	0	1-0	0	11	.226	.250	.290	44	-2	0-0	.973	-0	97	134	1b9		-0.3
Total 7		196	474	54	116	18	1	17	52	45-4	4	129	.245	.315	.395	92	-7	6-1	.992	-7	76	96	1b148		-1.9

JACKSON, RON Ronnie Damien B5.9.1953 Birmingham AL BR/TR/6-0/205(205-217) [AnaA71 2/37] d9.12 C8 OF(51/1/4)

YEAR	TM LG	G	AB	R	H	2B	3B	HR	RBI	BB-IB	HP	SO	AVG	OBP	SLG	AOPS	ABR	SB-CS	FA	FR	RNG	THR	GAMES AT POSITION	DL	BFW
1975	Cal A	13	39	2	9	2	0	0	2	2-0	1	10	.231	.268	.282	60	-2	1-1	.947	0	97	160	O9L,3b3/D		-0.3
1976	Cal A	127	410	44	93	18	3	8	40	30-1	7	58	.227	.289	.344	91	-6	5-4	.950	4	100	109	3b114,2b7,O4(3/0/1),D6		-0.3
1977	Cal A	106	292	38	71	15	2	8	28	24-2	1	42	.243	.301	.390	90	-4	3-2	.990	2	121	109	1b43,3b30,D20,O3L/S		-0.5
1978	Cal A	105	387	49	115	18	6	6	57	16-1	9	31	.297	.337	.421	116	7	2-3	.994	-5	116	86	1b75,3b31/ORD	32	0.8
1979	Min A	159	583	85	158	40	5	14	68	51-5	9	59	.271	.337	.429	101	2	3-1	.994	13	128	125	1b157/S3OL		0.8
1980	Min A	131	396	48	105	29	3	5	42	28-5	3	41	.265	.316	.391	87	-7	1-8	.991	0	109	80	1b36,O7(6/0/1),3b2/D		-1.2
1981	Min A	54	175	12	46	9	0	4	28	10-0	1	15	.263	.305	.383	92	-2	2-2	.988	0	90	103	1b29		-0.2
	Det A	31	95	12	27	8	1	1	12	8-0	0	11	.284	.337	.421	114	2	4-1	1.000	-0	90	103	1b29		-0.2
	Year	85	270	29	73	17	1	5	40	18-0	1	26	.270	.316	.396	99	0	6-3	.993	-0	101	89	1b65,O7(6/0/1),D6,3b3		
1982	†Cal A	53	142	15	47	6	0	2	19	10-0	2	12	.331	.381	.415	118	4	0-1	.994	-2	89	140	1b37,3b9		-0.0
1983	Cal A	102	348	41	80	16	1	8	39	27-2	3	33	.230	.291	.351	76	-12	2-2	.957	2	110	103	3b38,1b35,D16,O15(14/0/1)		-1.0
1984	Cal A	33	91	5	15	2	1	0	5	7-1	0	13	.165	.222	.209	21	-10	0-0	.990	-1	90	103	1b21,3b9/OL		-0.0
	Bal A	12	28	0	8	2	0	0	2	0-0	0	4	.286	.286	.357	78	-1	0-0	.960	2	94	344	3b10		-0.0
	Year	45	119	5	23	4	1	0	7	7-1	0	17	.193	.236	.244	34	-11	0-0	.990	0	90	103	1b21,3b19/OL		
Total 10		926	2986	356	774	165	22	56	342	213-17	35	329	.259	.314	.385	93	-29	23-27	.993	18	116	112	1b552,3b250,O56L,D51,2b7,S2	32	-5.

JACKSON, RYAN Ryan Dewitte B11.15.1971 Orlando FL BL/TL/6-2/195(185-205) [FlaN94 7/180] d3.31 Col Duke

YEAR	TM LG	G	AB	R	H	2B	3B	HR	RBI	BB-IB	HP	SO	AVG	OBP	SLG	AOPS	ABR	SB-CS	FA	FR	RNG	THR	GAMES AT POSITION	DL	BFW
1998	Fla N	111	260	26	65	15	1	5	30	20-0	1	73	.250	.305	.373	82	-7	1-1	.973	-5	82	90	1b44,O32(10/0/23),D5		-1.
1999	Sea A	32	68	4	16	3	0	0	10	6-0	1	19	.235	.299	.279	51	-5	3-3	.989	-0	97	94	1b29/OL		-1.
2001	Det A	79	118	19	25	4	2	2	11	5-0	1	26	.212	.250	.331	52	-9	3-1	1.000	-2	128	114	1b35,O34(19/0/15),D5		-1.
2002	Det A	4	6	0	2	1	0	0	1	0-0	0	2	.333	.429	.833	233	1	0-0	1.000	-0	73	0	O3(2/1/0)		0.
Total 4		226	452	49	108	23	4	7	52	32-0	3	120	.239	.292	.354	72	-20	7-5	.983	-7	95	96	1b108,O70(32/1/38),D10		-3.

JACKSON, SAM Samuel B3.24.1849 Ripon, England D8.4.1930 Clifton Springs NY BR/TR/5-5.5/160 d5.9

YEAR	TM LG	G	AB	R	H	2B	3B	HR	RBI	BB-IB	HP	SO	AVG	OBP	SLG	AOPS	ABR	SB-CS	FA	FR	RNG	THR	GAMES AT POSITION	DL	BFW
1871	Bos NA	16	76	17	17	5	3	0	11	1	.	4	.224	.234	.368	68	-3	0-1	.818	-1	110	22	2b14/SOC		-0.
1872	Atl NA	4	12	0	2	0	0	0	0	0	.	0	.167	.167	.167	2	-2	0-0	.667	-1	317	0	O3L/23		-0.
Total 2 NA		20	88	17	19	5	3	0	11	1	.	4	.216	.225	.341	58	-5	0-1	.810	-2	108	0	2b15,O4(3/1/0)/3S		-0.

JACKSON, TRAVIS Travis Calvin "Stonewall" B11.2.1903 Waldo AR D7.27.1987 Waldo AR BR/TR/5-10.5/160 d9.27 C4 HF1982

YEAR	TM LG	G	AB	R	H	2B	3B	HR	RBI	BB-IB	HP	SO	AVG	OBP	SLG	AOPS	ABR	SB-CS	FA	FR	RNG	THR	GAMES AT POSITION	DL	BFW
1922	NY N	3	8	1	0	0	0	0	0	0	0	2	.000	.000	.000	-99	-2	0-0	.909	0	120	113	S3		-0
1923	†NY N	96	327	45	90	12	7	4	37	22	2	40	.275	.321	.391	88	-7	3-3	.943	3	112	86	S60,3b31/2		0
1924	NY N	151	596	81	180	26	8	11	76	21	2	56	.302	.326	.428	103	0	6-7	.937	0	102	107	S151		1
1925	NY N	112	411	51	117	15	7	9	59	24	2	43	.285	.327	.397	87	-9	8-3	.942	-2	99	95	S110		0
1926	NY N	111	385	64	126	24	8	8	51	20-1	1	51	.327	.362	.494	130	15	2	.962	-1	97	111	S108/OR		2
1927	NY N	127	469	67	149	29	4	14	98	32	1	30	.318	.363	.486	126	16	8	.952	26	113	116	S124,3b2		5
1928	NY N	150	537	73	145	35	6	14	77	56	2	46	.270	.339	.436	101	4	8	.952	28	111	125	S149		4
1929	NY N	149	551	92	162	21	12	21	94	64	0	56	.294	.367	.490	111	7	10	.969	15	107	123	S149		3
1930	NY N	116	431	70	146	27	8	13	82	32	1	25	.339	.386	.529	126	14	6	.956	9	109	91	S115		3
1931	NY N	145	555	65	172	26	10	5	71	36	6	23	.310	.353	.420	110	6	13	.970	10	102	88	S145		2
1932	NY N	52	195	23	50	17	1	4	38	13	2	16	.256	.310	.415	93	-2	5	.925	-4	99	52	S52		-0
1933	†NY N	53	122	11	30	5	0	0	12	8	1	11	.246	.292	.287	67	-5	2	.890	2	96	175	S21,3b21		-0
1934	NY N★	137	523	75	140	26	7	16	101	37	2	71	.268	.316	.436	102	-1	1	.945	10	109	87	S130,3b9		0
1935	NY N	128	511	74	154	20	12	9	80	29	1	64	.301	.340	.440	110	5	3	.947	-9	92	70	3b128		0
1936	†NY N	126	465	41	107	8	1	7	53	18	1	56	.230	.260	.297	50	-34	0	.952	-2	101	61	3b116,S9		-3
Total 15		1656	6086	833	1768	291	86	135	929	412	10	565	.291	.337	.433	102	4	71-13	.952	90	105	105	S1326,3b307/OR2		22

YEAR	TM LG	G	AB	R	H	2B	3B	HR	RBI	BB-IB	HP	SO	AVG	OBP	SLG	AOPS	ABR	SB-CS	FA	FR	RNG	THR	GAMES AT POSITION	DL	BFW

JACKSON, BO   Vincent Edward   B11.30.1962 Bessemer AL   BR/TR/6-1/225(222-235)   [KCA86 4/105]   d9.2   Col Auburn-Montgomery   [DL 1992 Chi A 182]

1986	KC A	25	82	9	17	2	1	2	9	7-0	2	34	.207	.286	.329	65	-4	3-1	.886	-3	67	133	O23R/D		-0.8
1987	KC A	116	396	46	93	17	2	22	53	30-0	5	158	.235	.296	.455	93	-6	10-4	.955	-7	82	132	O113(95/21/3)/D		-1.6
1988	KC A	124	439	63	108	16	4	25	68	25-6	1	146	.246	.287	.472	107	1	27-6	.973	3	100	162	O121(103/5/15),D2	31	0.5
1989	KC A★	135	515	86	132	15	6	32	105	39-8	3	172	.256	.310	.495	124	13	26-9	.967	4	100	172	O110(110/1/0),D24	15	1.5
1990	Chi A	111	405	74	110	16	4	28	78	44-2	2	128	.272	.342	.523	142	21	15-9	.952	2	102	154	O97(36/61/0),D10	39	2.1
1991	Chi A	23	71	8	16	4	0	3	14	12-1	0	25	.225	.333	.408	107	1	0-1	—	0	0	0	D21	147	0.0
1993	†Chi A	85	284	32	66	9	0	16	45	23-1	0	106	.232	.289	.433	93	-5	0-2	.989	4	108	190	O47(28/0/19),D36		-0.5
1994	Cal A	75	201	23	56	7	0	13	43	20-2	1	72	.279	.344	.507	115	4	1-0	.964	-0	104	110	O46(43/0/3),D9		0.2
Total	8	694	2393	341	598	86	14	141	415	200-20	14	841	.250	.309	.474	111	25	82-32	.962	2	96	154	O557(415/88/63),D104	414	1.4

JACKSON, BILL   William Riley   B4.4.1881 Pittsburgh PA   D9.24.1958 Peoria IL   BL/TL/5-11.5/160   d4.30

1914	Chi F	26	25	2	1	0	0	0	1	3		5	.040	.143	.040	-52	-6	0	.917	1	152	178	O6(2/2/2),1b4		-0.6
1915	Chi F	50	98	15	16	1	0	1	12	14		15	.163	.268	.204	36	-10	3	.983	0	109	71	1b36/OC		-1.2
Total	2	76	123	17	17	1	0	1	13	17		20	.138	.243	.171	18	-16	3	.984	1	105	76	1b40,O7(2/3/2)		-1.8

JACOBS, JAKE   Lamar Gary   B6.9.1937 Youngstown OH   BR/TR/6-0/175*   d9.13   Col Ohio U.

1960	Was A	6	2	0	0	0	0	0	0	0-0	0	0	.000	.000	.000	-99	-1	0-0	—	0			/H		-0.1
1961	Min A	4	8	0	2	0	0	0	0	0-0	0	2	.250	.250	.250	32	-1	0-0	1.000	-1	49	0	O3C		-0.1
Total	2	10	10	0	2	0	0	0	0	0-0	0	2	.200	.200	.200	7	-1	0-0	1.000	-1	49	0	O3C		-0.2

JACOBS, MIKE   Michael James   B10.30.1980 Chula Vista CA   BL/TR/6-2/200   d8.21   Col Grossmont (CA) JC

2005	NY N	30	100	19	31	7	0	11	23	10-0	1	27	.310	.375	.710	181	11	0-0	.984	-3	59	108	1b28		0.6

JACOBS, MIKE   Morris Elmore   B12.1877 Louisville KY   D3.21.1949 Louisville KY   d7.16

1902	Chi N	5	19	1	4	0	0	0	2	0			.211	.211	.211	31	-2	0	.880	-1	87	66	S5		-0.3

JACOBS, OTTO   Otto Albert   B4.19.1889 Chicago IL   D11.19.1955 Chicago IL   BR/TR/5-9/180   d6.13

1918	Chi A	29	73	4	15	3	1	0	3	5		9	.205	.256	.274	59	-4	0	.955	-2	119	83	C21		-0.5

JACOBS, RAY   Raymond Frederick   B1.2.1902 Salt Lake City UT   D4.5.1952 Los Angeles CA   BR/TR/6-0/160   d4.20

1928	Chi N	2	2	0	0	0	0	0	0	0		1	.000	.000	.000	-99	-1	0	—	0			/H		-0.1

JACOBS, SPOOK   Robert Forrest Vandergrift   B11.4.1925 Cheswold DE   BR/TR/5-8.5/155*   d4.13

1954	Phi A	132	508	63	131	11	1	0	26	60		22	.258	.336	.283	71	-19	17-3	.974	-16	88	91	2b131		-2.4
1955	KC A	13	23	7	6	0	0	0	1	3-0	1	1	.261	.370	.261	71	-1	1-2	1.000	-2	78	109	2b7		-0.2
1956	KC A	32	97	13	21	3	0	0	5	15-1	0	5	.216	.321	.247	52	-6	4-1	.968	-2	92	116	2b31		-0.5
	Pit N	11	37	4	6	2	0	0	1	2-0	1	4	.162	.225	.216	20	-4	0-2	.926	-3	79	71	2b11		-0.8
Total	3	188	665	87	164	16	1	0	33	80-1	2	32	.247	.329	.274	65	-30	22-8	.971	-22	88	94	2b180		-3.9

JACOBSEN, BUCKY   Larry William   B8.31.1975 Riverton WY   BR/TR/6-4/220   [MilA97 7/217]   d7.16   Col Lewis-Clark St.   [DL 2005 Sea A 140]

2004	Sea A	42	160	17	44	9	0	9	28	14-0	1	47	.275	.335	.500	120	4	0-0	.984	-1	97	73	1b21,D20		0.1

JACOBSON, MERWIN   Merwin John William "Jake"   B3.7.1894 New Britain CT   D1.13.1978 Baltimore MD   BL/TL/5-11.5/165   d9.8

1915	NY N	8	24	0	2	0	0	0	1			5	.083	.120	.083	-40	-4	0	.909	0	90	164	O5(0/2/3)		-0.5
1916	Chi N	4	13	2	3	0	0	0	1			4	.231	.286	.231	54	-1	2	1.000	0	120	0	O4R		-0.1
1926	Bro N	110	288	41	71	9	2	0	23	36		24	.247	.330	.292	70	-11	5	.975	-0	106	61	O86(2/53/32)		-1.6
1927	Bro N	11	6	4	0	0	0	0	1	0		1	.000	.000	.000	-99	-2	0	1.000	0	142	0	O3R		-0.2
Total	4	133	331	47	76	9	2	0	24	38		34	.230	.309	.269	59	-18	7	.973	-0	106	64	O98(2/55/42)		-2.4

JACOBSON, BABY DOLL   William Chester   B8.16.1890 Cable IL   D1.16.1977 Orion IL   BR/TR/6-3/215   d4.14   Mil 1918

1915	Det A	37	65	5	14	6	2	0	4	5	1	14	.215	.282	.369	90	-1	0-2	.983	-1	69	103	1b10,O7(3/5/0)		-0.3
	StL A	34	115	13	24	6	1	1	9	10	4	26	.209	.295	.304	82	-2	3-3	.981	-1	105	55	O32(3/3/26)		-0.6
	Year	71	180	18	38	12	3	1	13	15	5	40	.211	.290	.328	84	-4	3-5	.984	-1	104	70	O39(6/8/26),1b10		-0.9
1917	StL A	148	529	53	131	23	7	4	55	31	4	67	.248	.294	.340	97	-4	10	.975	3	108	95	O131(0/54/77),1b11		-1.1
1919	StL A	120	455	70	147	31	8	4	51	24		47	.323	.362	.453	125	14	9	.949	-3	107	61	O106(17/73/16),1b8		0.4
1920	StL A	154	609	97	216	34	14	9	122	46	2	37	.355	.402	.501	134	29	11-7	.979	10	116	94	O154(0/120/34)/1		2.7
1921	StL A	151	599	90	211	38	14	5	90	42	3	30	.352	.398	.487	118	16	8-8	.982	-1	107	39	O142(0/141/1),1b10		0.7
1922	StL A	145	555	88	176	22	16	9	102	46	9	36	.317	.379	.463	114	11	19-6	.969	-1	108	62	O137(11/125/1),1b7		0.5
1923	StL A	147	592	76	183	29	6	8	81	29	2	45	.309	.343	.419	95	-7	6-6	.974	4	111	61	O146C		-1.0
1924	StL A	152	579	103	184	41	12	19	97	35	4	45	.318	.361	.528	120	13	6-8	.986	10	119	48	O152C		1.4
1925	StL A	142	540	103	184	30	9	15	76	45	1	26	.341	.392	.513	122	16	8-11	.965	-4	90	120	O139C		0.4
1926	StL A	50	182	18	52	15	1	2	21	9	0	14	.286	.319	.412	86	-4	1-2	.964	-3	94	47	O50C		-1.0
	Bos A	98	394	44	120	36	1	6	69	22	2	22	.305	.344	.447	109	4	4-1	.980	-9	85	68	O98(6/57/36)		-1.0
1927	Bos A	45	155	11	38	9	3	0	24	5	2	12	.245	.288	.342	61	-1	5-3	.975	-13	88	62	O148(6/107/36)		-2.0
	Cle A	32	103	13	26	5	0	0	13	6	1	4	.252	.300	.301	56	-7	0-0	.979	-0	99	94	O39L		-1.2
	Phi A	17	35	3	8	3	0	1	5	0	0	3	.229	.229	.400	57	-2	0-0	1.000	-1	69	0	O14(9/2/3)		-1.0
	Year	94	293	27	72	17	3	1	42	11	3	19	.246	.280	.334	59	-19	1-0	.959	-3	99	63	O84(48/33/3)		-0.4
Total	11	1472	5507	787	1714	328	94	83	819	355	39	410	.311	.357	.450	111	66	86-54	.973	1	106	71	O1378(88/1098/194),1b47		-2.6
																									-1.5

JACOBY, BROOK   Brook Wallace   B11.23.1959 Philadelphia PA   BR/TR/5-11/195(175-195)   [AtlN79*7/153]   d9.13   Col Ventura (CA) JC

1981	Atl N	11	10	0	2	0	0	0	1	0-0		3	.200	.200	.200	14	-1	0-0	1.000	2	229	695	3b3		0.0
1983	Atl N	4	8	0	0	0	0	0	0	0-0		1	.000	.000	.000	-93	-2	0-0	1.000	-1	63	0	3b2		-0.3
1984	Cle A	126	439	64	116	19	3	7	40	32-0	5	73	.264	.314	.369	88	-7	3-2	.951	-23	81	71	3b126/S		-0.8
1985	Cle A	161	606	72	166	26	3	20	87	48-3	6	120	.274	.324	.426	105	3	2-3	.958	-8	98	78	3b161/2	42	-3.3
1986	Cle A★	158	583	83	168	30	4	17	80	56-5	0	137	.288	.350	.441	105	12	5-5	.941	-12	100	79	3b158		-0.2
1987	Cle A	155	540	73	162	26	4	32	69	75-2	3	73	.300	.387	.541	141	33	2-3	.946	-5	94	65	3b144,1b7,D4		2.4
1988	Cle A	152	552	59	133	25	0	9	49	48-2	1	101	.241	.300	.335	76	-17	2-3	.975	2	103	91	3b151		-1.6
1989	Cle A	147	519	49	141	26	5	13	64	62-3	3	90	.272	.348	.416	114	10	2-5	.955	-14	92	64	3b144,D3		-0.5
1990	Cle A★	155	553	77	162	24	4	14	75	63-6	2	58	.293	.365	.427	121	17	1-4	.981	-15	90	86	3b99,1b78		-0.4
1991	Cle A	66	231	14	54	9	1	4	24	16-2	1	32	.234	.289	.333	71	-10	0-1	.988	1	95	63	1b55,3b15	17	-1.3
	Oak A	56	188	14	40	12	0	0	20	11-1	1	22	.213	.255	.277	54	-13	2-0	.982	-6	78	92	3b52,1b3		-1.9
	Year	122	419	28	94	21	1	4	44	27-3	2	54	.224	.274	.308	63	-22	2-1	.987	-6	85	97	3b67,1b58		-3.2
1992	Cle A	120	291	30	76	7	0	4	36	28-2	1	54	.261	.324	.326	85	-6	0-3	.957	-1	105	115	3b111,1b10		-0.5
Total	11	1311	4520	535	1220	204	24	120	545	439-26	16	764	.270	.334	.405	103	19	16-25	.958	-82	95	80	3b1166,1b153,D7/2S	59	-8.7

JACOBY, HARRY   Harry M.   B Philadelphia PA   D7.22.1900 Philadelphia PA   d5.2

1882	Bal AA	31	121	17	21	1	1		7				.174	.219	.223	53	-5		.776	7	112	83	3b19,O13R		0.2
1885	Bal AA	11	43	4	6	2	0	0	1	2	0		.140	.178	.186	15	-4		.896	-5	75	46	2b11		-0.8
Total	2	42	164	21	27	3	1	1	2		0		.165	.208	.213	43	-9		.776	3	112	83	3b19,O13R,2b11		-0.6

JAHA, JOHN   John Emil   B5.27.1966 Portland OR   BR/TR/6-1/222(195-240)   [MilA84 14/358]   d7.9

1992	Mil A	47	133	17	30	3	1	2	10	12-1	2	30	.226	.291	.308	71	-5	10-0	1.000	-1	89	87	1b38/OLD		-0.7
1993	Mil A	153	515	78	136	21	0	19	70	51-4	8	109	.264	.337	.416	103	2	13-9	.992	7	121	92	1b150/23		-0.4
1994	Mil A	84	291	45	70	14	0	12	39	32-3	10	75	.241	.332	.412	87	-5	3-3	.989	-2	96	103	1b73/D11		-1.4
1995	Mil A	88	316	59	99	20	2	20	65	36-0	4	66	.313	.389	.579	140	18	2-1	.997	3	113	122	1b81,D6		1.5
1996	Mil A	148	543	108	163	28	1	34	118	85-1	5	118	.300	.398	.543	130	26	3-1	.992	1	108	113	1b85,D63	49	1.3
1997	Mil A	46	162	25	40	7	0	11	26	25-1	1	40	.247	.354	.494	114	4	1-0	.992	-1	82	125	1b27,D10		1.5
1998	Mil N	73	216	29	45	6	1	7	38	49-3	6	66	.208	.366	.343	87	-2	0-0	.992	-4	75	107	1b57,D8	120	0.0
1999	Oak A★	142	457	93	126	23	0	35	111	101-2	9	129	.276	.414	.556	149	39	2-0	1.000	-5	64	134	1b57,D8	63	-1.3
2000	Oak A	33	97	14	17	1	0	3	13	33-0	3	38	.175	.398	.216	63	-3	1-0	—	0	0	0	D30	123	3.0
2001	Oak A	12	45	2	4	1	0	0	6	0		15	.089	.192	.156	-6	-7	0-0	—	0	0	0	D12	71	-0.4
Total	10	826	2775	470	730	126	5	141	490	430-15	50	686	.263	.373	.465	114	67	36-17	.993	1	104	107	1b519,D279/32OL	426	0.8

JAHN, ART   Arthur Charles   B12.2.1895 Struble IA   D1.9.1948 Little Rock AR   BR/TR/6-0/180   d7.2

1925	Chi N	58	226	30	68	10	8	0	37	11	1	20	.301	.336	.416	90	-4	2-2	.985	0	98	91	O58L		-0.9
1928	NY N	10	29	3	8	1	0	1	7	2	0	5	.276	.323	.414	91	0	0	1.000	1	108	148	O8(7/1/0)		-0.1

YEAR	TM LG	G	AB	R	H	2B	3B	HR	RBI	BB-IB	HP	SO	AVG	OBP	SLG	AOPS	ABR	SB-CS	FA	FR	RNG	THR	GAMES AT POSITION	DL	BFW
	Phi N	36	94	8	21	4	0	0	11	4	2	11	.223	.270	.266	39	-8	0	.978	-1	97	48	O29(2/0/27)		-1.1
	Year	46	123	15	29	5	0	1	18	6	2	16	.236	.282	.301	51	-9	0	.985	-0	100	77	O37(9/1/27)		-1.2
Total	2	104	349	45	97	15	8	1	55	17	3	36	.278	.317	.375	76	-12	2-2	.985	-0	99	86	O95(67/1/27)		-2.1

JAMES, ART Arthur B8.2.1952 Detroit MI BL/TL/6-0/170 [DetA72*6/112] d4.10 Col Macomb (MI) CC

| 1975 | Det A | 11 | 40 | 2 | 9 | 2 | 0 | 0 | 1 | 1-0 | 0 | 3 | .225 | .244 | .275 | 44 | -3 | 1-2 | 1.000 | 2 | 149 | 0 | O11(0/4/7) | | -0.2 |

JAMES, BERT Berton Hulon "Jesse" B7.7.1886 Coopertown TN D1.2.1959 Adairville KY BL/TR/5-11/175 d9.18

| 1909 | StL N | 6 | 21 | 1 | 6 | 0 | 0 | 0 | 4 | 0 | | | .286 | .400 | .286 | 120 | 1 | 1 | .909 | 0 | 119 | 477 | O6R | | 0.1 |

JAMES, CHARLIE Charles Wesley B12.22.1937 St.Louis MO BR/TR/6-1/195* d8.2 Col Missouri

1960	StL N	43	50	5	9	1	0	2	5	1-0	0	12	.180	.196	.320	35	-5	0-0	.917	-1	84	94	O37(23/7/9)		-0.6
1961	StL N	108	349	43	89	19	2	4	44	15-1	3	59	.255	.288	.355	64	-18	2-2	.962	-5	96	41	O90(39/4/56)		-2.8
1962	StL N	129	388	50	107	13	4	8	59	10-1	4	58	.276	.301	.392	77	-13	3-4	.988	-5	89	85	O116(17/1/104)		-2.6
1963	StL N	116	347	34	93	14	2	10	45	10-0	1	64	.268	.291	.406	91	-5	2-1	.994	4	115	70	O101(82/1/25)		-0.6
1964	†StL N	88	233	24	52	9	1	5	17	11-1	1	58	.223	.261	.335	61	-12	0-0	.963	-2	89	90	O60(46/0/14)		-1.8
1965	Cin N	26	39	2	8	0	0	0	2	1-0	0	9	.205	.225	.205	21	-4	0-0	.909	-0	103	97	O7(3/0/4)		-0.5
Total	6	510	1406	158	358	56	9	29	172	48-3	10	260	.255	.283	.369	71	-57	7-7	.976	-8	97	70	O411(210/13/212)		-8.9

JAMES, CLEO Cleo Joel B8.31.1940 Clarksdale MS BR/TR/5-10/176* d4.15 Col Riverside (CA) CC

1968	LA N	10	10	2	2	1	0	0	0-0		0	6	.200	.200	.300	52	-1	0-0	1.000	-0	94	0	O2L		-0.1
1970	Chi N	100	176	33	37	7	2	3	14	17-5	5	24	.210	.298	.324	59	-10	5-0	.979	1	97	170	O48(1/35/14),3b2		-0.1
1971	Chi N	54	150	25	43	7	0	6	13	10-0	6	16	.287	.353	.373	93	-1	6-2	.960	1	103	154	O22(14/8/1)		-0.7
1973	Chi N	44	45	9	5	0	0	0	1-0		0	6	.111	.130	.111	-3	-4	5-0	.988	1	96	161	O162(22/126/17),3b2		-1.9
Total	4	208	381	69	87	15	2	5	27	28-5	11	52	.228	.299	.318	63	-20	16-2	.988	1	96	161	O162(22/126/17),3b2		-1.9

JAMES, DION Dion B11.9.1962 Philadelphia PA BL/TL/6-1/170(170-185) [MilA80 1/25] d9.16

1983	Mil A	11	20	1	2	0	0	0	1	2-0	0	2	.100	.182	.100	-21	-3	1-0	1.000	-0	78	220	O9(4/8/1),D2		-0.4
1984	Mil A	128	387	52	114	19	5	1	30	32-1	3	41	.295	.351	.377	106	4	10-10	.989	3	106	104	O118(2/30/93)		0.1
1985	Mil A	18	49	5	11	1	0	0	3	6-0	0	6	.224	.309	.245	54	-3	0-0	.996	-3	67	0	O11C,D3	124	-0.6
1987	Atl N	134	494	80	154	37	6	10	61	70-2	2	63	.312	.397	.472	125	21	10-8	.987	-8	92	55	O120(86/49/3)		1.1
1988	Atl N	132	386	46	99	17	5	3	30	58-5	1	59	.256	.353	.350	99	2	9-9	.987	-4	93	82	O120(86/49/3)		-0.7
1989	Atl N	63	170	15	44	7	0	1	11	25-2	1	23	.259	.355	.318	92	0	1-3	1.000	1	106	0	O46(26/1/23),1b8		-0.2
	Cle A	71	245	26	75	11	0	4	29	24-4	0	26	.306	.368	.400	114	5	1-4	.976	1	115	57	O37(26/10/0),D27,1b2		0.3
1990	Cle A	87	248	28	68	15	2	1	22	27-3	1	23	.274	.347	.363	99	1	5-3	.996	-4	87	84	O46(8/12/27),D5		-0.6
1992	NY A	67	145	24	38	8	0	3	17	22-0	1	15	.262	.359	.379	108	3	1-0	1.000	-4	77	44	O46(8/12/27),D5		-0.2
1993	NY A	115	343	62	114	21	2	7	36	31-1	2	31	.332	.390	.466	133	17	0-0	.966	-8	82	82	O103(91/14/1),1D		0.6
1995	†NY A	85	209	22	60	6	1	2	26	20-2	0	16	.287	.346	.354	84	-5	4-1	.968	-2	77	0	O29(23/0/6),D27,1b6		-0.8
1996	NY A	6	12	1	2	0	0	0	1-0		0	2	.167	.231	.167	3	-2	1-0	1.000	-1	56	0	O4(3/0/1)/D		-0.2
Total	11	917	2708	362	781	142	21	32	266	318-20	11	307	.288	.364	.392	107	40	43-38	.986	-29	93	64	O682(322/242/155),D76,1b52	124	-1.6

JAMES, CHRIS Donald Chris B10.4.1962 Rusk TX BR/TR/6-1/190(190-202) d4.23 Col Blinn (TX) JC OF(322/51/229)

1986	Phi N	16	46	5	13	3	0	1	5	1-0	0	13	.283	.298	.413	91	-1	0-0	1.000	-1	90	0	O11(4/7/0)	76	-0.2
1987	Phi N	115	358	48	105	20	6	17	54	27-0	2	67	.293	.344	.525	123	10	3-1	.990	2	109	78	O108(96/16/5)		0.9
1988	Phi N	150	566	57	137	24	1	19	66	31-2	3	73	.242	.283	.389	90	-9	7-4	.989	-2	110	124	O116(8/27/101),3b31		-1.5
1989	Phi N	45	179	14	37	4	0	2	19	4-0	0	23	.207	.223	.263	39	-15	3-1	.985	-2	89	155	O37L,3b11		-2.0
	SD N	87	303	41	80	13	2	11	46	22-2	1	45	.264	.314	.429	111	3	2-1	.987	1	101	75	O79(50/0/29),3b6		0.2
	Year	132	482	55	117	17	2	13	65	26-2	1	68	.243	.281	.367	84	-12	5-2	.986	-1	97	101	O116(87/0/29),3b17		-1.8
1990	Cle A	140	528	62	158	32	4	12	70	31-4	4	71	.299	.341	.443	118	12	4-3	1.000	0	95	124	D124,O14(12/1/1)		0.7
1991	Cle A	115	437	31	104	16	2	5	41	18-2	1	61	.238	.273	.318	63	-23	3-4	1.000	1	103	86	D60,O39(25/0/18),1b15	27	-2.8
1992	SF N	111	248	25	60	10	4	5	32	14-2	2	45	.242	.285	.375	91	-4	2-3	.974	2	109	82	O62(60/0/2)	17	-0.5
1993	Hou N	65	129	19	33	10	1	6	19	15-2	1	34	.256	.333	.488	122	4	2-0	.958	4	121	195	O34(16/0/18)		0.7
	Tex A	8	31	5	11	1	0	3	7	3-0	0	6	.355	.412	.677	193	4	0-0	1.000	-0	105	0	O7(4/0/4)		0.3
1994	Tex A	52	133	28	34	8	4	7	19	20-0	3	38	.256	.361	.534	127	5	0-0	1.000	-2	87	75	O48(1/0/47)	42	0.1
1995	KC A	26	58	6	18	3	0	2	7	6-0	1	10	.310	.373	.466	117	2	1-0	1.000	1	130	0	O14,O5L	66	0.1
	Bos A	16	24	2	4	1	0	0	1	1-0	0	4	.167	.200	.208	6	-3	0-0	1.000	1	141	0	O8(4/0/4),D6	15	-0.3
	Year	42	82	8	22	4	0	2	8	7-0	1	14	.268	.326	.390	85	-2	1-0	1.000	1	137	0	D20,O13(9/0/4)		-0.2
Total	10	946	3040	343	794	145	24	90	386	193-14	21	490	.261	.307	.413	98	-15	27-17	.987	3	105	98	O568L,D204,3b48,1b15	243	-4.3

JAMES, SKIP Philip Robert B10.21.1949 Elmhurst IL BL/TL/6-0/190* [SFN71 5/114] d9.12 Col Kansas

1977	SF N	10	15	3	4	1	0	0	3	2-0	0	3	.267	.353	.333	85	0	0-0	1.000	1	134	53	1b9		0.0
1978	SF N	41	21	5	2	1	0	0	3	4-0	0	5	.095	.240	.143	10	-2	1-0	1.000	1	143	92	1b27		-0.2
Total	2	51	36	8	6	2	0	0	6	6-0	0	8	.167	.286	.222	42	-2	1-0	1.000	1	139	77	1b36		-0.2

JAMES, BERNIE Robert Byrne B9.2.1905 Angleton TX D8.1.1994 San Antonio TX BB/TR/5-9.5/150 d5.6

1929	Bos N	46	101	12	31	3	2	0	9	9	1	13	.307	.369	.376	89	-2	3	.940	-7	74	75	2b32/OC		-0.7
1930	Bos N	8	11	1	2	1	0	0	1	0	0	1	.182	.182	.273	8	-2		.941	0	118	53	2b7		-0.1
1933	NY N	60	125	22	28	2	1	1	10	8	1	12	.224	.271	.280	58	-7	5	.948	1	105	78	2b26,S6,3b5		-0.4
Total	3	114	237	35	61	6	3	1	20	17	2	26	.257	.310	.321	70	-11	8	.944	-5	91	75	2b65,3b5,OC		-1.2

JAMIESON, CHARLIE Charles Devine "Cuckoo" B2.7.1893 Paterson NJ D10.27.1969 Paterson NJ BL/TL/5-8.5/165 d9.20 ▲

1915	Was A	17	68	9	19	3	2	0	7	6		9	.279	.338	.382	113	1	0	1.000	3	111	232	O17L		0.3
1916	Was A	64	145	16	36	4	0	0	13	18	0	18	.248	.331	.276	83	-2	5	.913	0	105	105	O41(24/2/15),1b4/P		-0.4
1917	Was A	20	35	4	6	2	0	0	2	6	0	5	.171	.293	.229	60	-1	0	.875	-1	104	0	O9L/P		-0.3
	Phi A	85	345	41	92	6	2	0	27	37	2	36	.267	.341	.296	96	-1	8	.937	-4	86	104	O83R		-1.1
	Year	105	380	45	98	8	2	0	29	43	2	41	.258	.336	.289	92	-2	8	.930	-5	87	96	O92(9/0/83)/P		-1.4
1918	Phi A	110	416	50	84	11	2	0	11	54	2	30	.202	.297	.238	61	-18	11	.970	-2	94	101	O102(0/1/101),P5		-2.9
1919	Cle A	26	17	3	6	2	1	0	2	0	0	2	.353	.353	.588	153	1	2	.750	-0	58	0	P4,O3(0/2/1)		0.0
1920	†Cle A	108	370	69	118	17	7	1	40	41	1	26	.319	.388	.411	108	5	2-9	.966	2	100	122	O98(93/5/0),1b4		0.1
1921	Cle A	140	536	94	166	33	10	1	46	67	1	27	.310	.387	.414	103	3	8-4	.974	3	100	107	O144(141/2/1),P2		-0.2
1922	Cle A	145	567	87	183	29	11	3	57	54	6	37	.323	.388	.429	112	11	15-9	.978	5	109	95	O152L		0.3
1923	Cle A	152	644	130	222	36	12	2	51	80	4	15	.345	.422	.447	129	31	18-14	.974	2	106	72	O139L		2.2
1924	Cle A	143	594	98	213	34	8	3	54	47	2	15	.359	.407	.458	121	19	21-12	.974	-5	108	101	O135L		1.0
1925	Cle A	138	557	109	165	24	5	4	42	72	5	22	.296	.380	.379	92	-5	14-18	.955	1	100	108	O135L		-1.3
1926	Cle A	143	555	89	166	33	7	2	45	53	5	22	.299	.361	.395	96	-3	9-7	.960	1	100	108	O143L		-1.2
1927	Cle A	127	489	73	151	23	6	0	36	64	5	14	.309	.394	.380	101	4	7-9	.969	4	100	96	O127L		-0.4
1928	Cle A	112	433	63	133	18	4	1	37	56	1	12	.307	.388	.374	100	2	3-12	.984	16	111	195	O111L		0.6
1929	Cle A	102	364	56	106	22	1	0	26	50	1	12	.291	.378	.357	87	-4	2-13	.980	-3	93	84	O93L		-1.5
1930	Cle A	103	366	64	110	22	1	1	52	36	8	20	.301	.368	.374	85	-7	5-2	.955	-4	90	106	O95(93/2/0)		-1.5
1931	Cle A	28	43	7	13	2	1	0	4	5	0	1	.302	.375	.395	97	0	1-1	.833	-1	82	0	O7(6/1/0)		-0.2
1932	Cle A	16	16	0	1	1	0	0	0	2	1	3	.063	.211	.125	-10	-3	0-0	1.000	1	87	739	O2R		-0.2
Total	18	1779	6560	1062	1990	322	80	18	552	748	35	345	.303	.378	.385	101	35	131-110	.967	29	101	108	O1638(1408/34/203),P13,1b8		-7.0

JANOWICZ, VIC Victor Felix B2.26.1930 Elyria OH D2.27.1996 Columbus OH BR/TR/5-9/185* d5.31 Col Ohio St.

1953	Pit N	42	123	10	31	3	1	2	8	5	1	31	.252	.287	.341	63	-7	0-1	.937	-9	59	111	C35		-1.0
1954	Pit N	41	73	10	11	3	0	2	7	1	3	23	.151	.235	.192	13	-9	0-0	.904	0	106	98	3b18/OL		-1.5
Total	2	83	196	20	42	6	1	4	15	6	4	54	.214	.267	.286	44	-16	0-1	.937	-9	59	111	C35,3b18/OL		-2.5

JANSEN, RAY Raymond William B1.16.1889 St.Louis MO D3.19.1934 St.Louis MO BR/TR/5-11/155 d9.30

| 1910 | StL A | 1 | 5 | 0 | 4 | 0 | 0 | 0 | 0 | 0 | 0 | | .800 | .800 | .800 | 428 | 2 | 0 | .700 | -0 | 122 | 0 | /3 | | 0.2 |

JANTZEN, HEINIE Walter C. B4.9.1890 Chicago IL D4.1.1948 Hines IL BR/TR/5-11.5/170 d6.29

| 1912 | StL A | 31 | 119 | 10 | 22 | 0 | 1 | 1 | 8 | 4 | 1 | | .185 | .218 | .227 | 28 | -12 | 3 | 1.000 | 3 | 111 | 132 | O31R | | -1.1 |

JANVRIN, HAL Harold Chandler "Childe Harold" B8.27.1892 Haverhill MA D3.1.1962 Boston MA BR/TR/5-11.5/168 d7.9 Mil 1918 OF(17/4/1)

1911	Bos A	9	27	2	4	1	0	1	3	4			.148	.258	.185	25	-3	0	.733	-2	75	0	3b5,1b4		-0.5
1913	Bos A	87	276	18	57	5	1	3	25	23	2	27	.207	.272	.264	56	-16	17	.923	-10	97	49	S48,3b19,2b8,1b6		-2.4
1914	Bos A	145	492	65	117	18	6	1	51	38	3	50	.238	.296	.305	81	-12	29-20	.919	-18	89	78	2b59,1b57,S20,3b6		-3.4

YEAR	TM LG	G	AB	R	H	2B	3B	HR	RBI	BB-IB	HP	SO	AVG	OBP	SLG	AOPS	ABR	SB-CS	FA	FR	RNG	THR	GAMES AT POSITION	DL	BFW
1915	†Bos A	99	316	41	85	9	1	0	37	14	8	27	.269	.317	.304	88	-5	8-14	.917	-17	90	73	S64,3b20,2b8		-2.2
1916	†Bos A	117	310	32	69	11	4	0	26	32	2	32	.223	.299	.284	75	-9	6	.921	-12	81	130	S59,2b39,1b4,3b4		-2.0
1917	Bos A	55	127	21	25	3	0	0	8	11	1	13	.197	.266	.220	49	-8	2	.940	-0	107	137	2b38,S10/1		-0.8
1919	Was A	61	208	17	37	4	1	1	13	19	2	17	.178	.253	.221	34	-18	8	.927	-22	75	65	2b56,S2		-4.3
	Stl N	7	14	1	3	1	0	0	1	2	0	2	.214	.313	.286	86	0	1	1.000	-1	38	0	2b2/S3		-0.1
1920	Stl N	87	270	33	74	8	4	1	28	17	0	19	.274	.317	.344	93	-3	5-6	.926	-1	82	120	S27,1b25,O20(16/4/0),2b6		-0.5
1921	Stl N	18	32	5	9	1	0	0	5	1	0	0	.281	.303	.313	65	-2	1-0	.968	0	94	126	1b9/2		-0.2
	Bro N	44	92	8	18	4	0	0	14	7	0	6	.196	.253	.239	30	-9	3-1	.922	-4	91	46	S17,2b10,1b8,3b5/OR		-1.2
	Year	62	124	13	27	5	0	0	19	8	0	6	.218	.265	.258	38	-11	4-1	.922	-4	81	65	1b17,S17,2b11,3b5/OR		-1.4
1922	Bro N	30	57	7	17	3	1	0	1	4	0	4	.298	.344	.386	88	-1	0-0	.889	-3	111	60	2b15,S4,3b2/1OL		-0.3
Total	10	759	2221	250	515	68	18	6	210	171	19	197	.232	.292	.287	70	-86	79-41	.907	-90	87	92	S252,2b242,1b115,3b62,O22L		-17.9

JARVIS, ROY Leroy Gilbert B6.27.1926 Shawnee OK D1.13.1990 Oklahoma City OK BR/TR/5-9/160 d4.30 Mil 1944-46

YEAR	TM LG	G	AB	R	H	2B	3B	HR	RBI	BB-IB	HP	SO	AVG	OBP	SLG	AOPS	ABR	SB-CS	FA	FR	RNG	THR	GAMES AT POSITION	DL	BFW
1944	Bro N	1	1	0	0	0	0	0	0	0	0	1	.000	.000	.000	-99	-0		1.000	-0	0	0	/C		0.0
1946	Pit N	2	4	0	1	0	0	0	0	1	0	0	.250	.400	.250	84	0	0	.800	-1	44	0	/C		-0.1
1947	Pit N	18	45	4	7	1	0	1	4	6	0	1	.156	.255	.244	32	-4	0	.967	-1	94	100	C15		-0.4
Total	3	21	50	4	8	1	0	1	4	7	0	7	.160	.263	.240	34	-4	0	.955	-1	88	90	C17		-0.5

JATA, PAUL Paul B9.4.1949 Astoria NY BR/TR/6-1/190 [DetA67 5/95] d4.19

YEAR	TM LG	G	AB	R	H	2B	3B	HR	RBI	BB-IB	HP	SO	AVG	OBP	SLG	AOPS	ABR	SB-CS	FA	FR	RNG	THR	GAMES AT POSITION	DL	BFW
1972	Det A	32	74	8	17	2	0	3	7-0	0	0	14	.230	.296	.257	63	-3	0-1	.991	0	104	72	1b12,O10(5/0/5)/C		-0.5

JAVIER, AL Ignacio Alfredo (b Ignacio Alfredo Wilkes (Javier)) B2.4.1954 San Pedro de Macoris, D.R. BR/TR/5-11/170 d9.9

YEAR	TM LG	G	AB	R	H	2B	3B	HR	RBI	BB-IB	HP	SO	AVG	OBP	SLG	AOPS	ABR	SB-CS	FA	FR	RNG	THR	GAMES AT POSITION	DL	BFW
1976	Hou N	8	24	1	5	0	0	0	0	2-1	0	5	.208	.269	.208	40	-2	0-0	1.000	-1	57	0	O7(4/0/4)		-0.4

JAVIER, JULIAN Manuel Julian (Liranzo) B8.9.1936 San Francisco de Macoris, D.R. BR/TR/6-1/175* d5.28 s-Stan

YEAR	TM LG	G	AB	R	H	2B	3B	HR	RBI	BB-IB	HP	SO	AVG	OBP	SLG	AOPS	ABR	SB-CS	FA	FR	RNG	THR	GAMES AT POSITION	DL	BFW
1960	Stl N	119	451	55	107	19	8	4	21	21-1	1	72	.237	.273	.341	62	-25	19-4	.962	17	**109**	102	2b119		0.4
1961	Stl N	113	445	58	124	14	3	2	41	30-1	2	51	.279	.326	.337	70	-19	11-4	.966	4	106	102	2b113		-0.4
1962	Stl N	155	598	97	157	25	5	7	39	47-0	1	73	.263	.316	.356	73	-20	26-9	.977	-3	99	105	2b151,S4	30	-1.0
1963	Stl N★	161	609	82	160	27	9	9	46	24-1	6	86	.263	.296	.381	86	-12	18-10	.969	-9	95	100	2b161		-0.7
1964	†Stl N	155	535	66	129	19	5	12	65	30-7	1	82	.241	.282	.363	74	-19	9-7	.966	3	100	104	2b154		-0.7
1965	Stl N	77	229	34	52	6	4	2	23	8-2	3	44	.227	.260	.314	56	-14	5-5	.975	-5	98	103	2b69	46	-1.5
1966	Stl N	147	460	52	105	13	5	7	31	26-1	1	63	.228	.269	.324	64	-23	11-5	.981	4	104	114	2b145		-0.8
1967	†Stl N	140	520	68	146	16	3	14	64	25-3	1	92	.281	.314	.404	106	-2	6-7	.965	-18	93	87	2b138		-0.6
1968	†Stl N★	139	519	54	135	25	4	4	52	24-2	1	61	.260	.291	.347	93	-6	10-3	.976	-25	88	89	2b139		-2.0
1969	Stl N	143	493	59	139	28	2	10	42	40-11	1	74	.282	.336	.408	107	4	8-4	.967	-19	98	86	2b141		-0.5
1970	Stl N	139	513	62	129	16	3	2	42	24-6	1	70	.251	.284	.306	57	-32	6-4	.980	16	**113**	92	2b137		-0.7
1971	Stl N	90	259	32	67	6	4	3	28	9-3	2	33	.259	.286	.347	76	-9	5-1	.978	-4	95	90	2b80/3		-0.8
1972	†Cin N	44	91	3	19	2	0	2	12	6-0	0	11	.209	.255	.297	60	-5	1-0	.896	-3	94	154	3b19,2b5/1		-0.9
Total	13	1622	5722	722	1469	216	55	78	506	314-39	21	812	.257	.296	.355	78	-180	135-63	.972	-40	100	99	2b1552,3b20,S4/1	76	-9.9

JAVIER, STAN Stanley Julian Antonio (De Javier) B1.9.1964 San Francisco de Macoris, D.R. BB/TR/6-0/185(180-202) d4.15 f-Julian OF(465/691/492)

YEAR	TM LG	G	AB	R	H	2B	3B	HR	RBI	BB-IB	HP	SO	AVG	OBP	SLG	AOPS	ABR	SB-CS	FA	FR	RNG	THR	GAMES AT POSITION	DL	BFW
1984	NY A	7	7	1	1	0	0	0	0	0-0	0	1	.143	.143	.143	-21	-1	0-0	1.000	-1	53	0	O5(0/3/3)		-0.2
1986	Oak A	59	114	13	23	8	0	0	8	16-0	1	27	.202	.305	.272	63	-5	8-0	1.000	3	120	50	O51(3/49/0),D2		
1987	Oak A	81	151	22	28	3	1	2	9	19-3	0	33	.185	.276	.258	46	-12	3-2	.983	2	105	138	O71(8/52/15),1b6/D	29	-1.1
1988	†Oak A	125	397	49	102	13	3	2	35	32-1	2	63	.257	.313	.320	81	-10	20-1	.980	2	102	108	O115(69/45/29),1b4,D2	15	-0.7
1989	†Oak A	112	310	42	77	12	3	1	28	31-1	1	45	.248	.317	.316	82	-7	12-2	.991	5	113	65	O107(23/28/72)/12	15	-0.3
1990	Oak A	19	33	4	8	0	2	0	3	3-0	0	6	.242	.306	.364	90	-1	0-0	1.000	1	130	0	O13(4/4/5),D2		
	LA N	104	276	56	84	9	4	3	24	37-2	0	44	.304	.384	.399	119	8	15-7	1.000	6	123	51	O87(9/70/12)		1.4
1991	LA N	121	176	21	36	5	3	1	11	16-0	0	36	.205	.268	.284	57	-10	7-1	.986	-1	95	43	O69(49/7/18),1b2		-1.3
1992	LA N	56	58	6	11	3	0	1	5	6-2	1	11	.190	.277	.293	62	-3	1-2	1.000	-1	83	0	O27(15/2/11)		-0.5
	Phi N	74	276	36	72	14	1	0	24	31-0	2	43	.261	.338	.319	87	-3	17-1	.986	11	127	189	O74(27/49/1)		1.1
	Year	130	334	42	83	17	1	1	29	37-2	3	54	.249	.327	.314	83	-6	18-3	.987	10	121	165	O101(42/51/12)		0.6
1993	Cal A	92	237	33	69	10	4	3	28	27-1	1	33	.291	.362	.405	104	1	12-2	.981	-4	96	55	O64(36/16/16),1b12,2b2/D		-0.2
1994	Oak A	109	419	75	114	23	0	10	44	49-1	2	76	.272	.349	.399	100	1	24-7	.986	1	104	55	O108(12/102/1)/13		0.5
1995	Oak A	130	442	81	123	20	2	8	56	49-3	4	63	.278	.353	.387	98	-1	36-5	**1.000**	9	**118**	49	O124(32/101/1)/3		1.3
1996	SF N	71	274	44	74	25	0	2	22	25-0	2	51	.270	.336	.383	91	-3	14-2	.984	4	119	53	O71(0/53/18)	91	0.3
1997	†SF N	142	440	69	126	16	4	8	50	56-1	5	70	.286	.368	.395	104	4	25-3	.977	0	112	28	O130(5/46/94),1b3		0.5
1998	SF N	135	417	63	121	13	5	4	49	65-4	1	63	.290	.385	.374	107	6	21-5	.986	-7	98	0	O121(6/29/95)		-0.1
1999	SF N	112	333	49	92	15	1	3	30	29-4	1	55	.276	.335	.354	80	-10	13-6	.976	-1	98	76	O94(51/3/42)		-1.3
	†Hou N	20	64	12	21	4	1	0	4	9-0	0	8	.328	.405	.422	113	2	3-1	1.000	-0	94	106	O18(7/6/10)/D		0.1
	Year	132	397	61	113	19	2	3	34	38-4	1	63	.285	.347	.365	86	-8	16-7	.980	-1	97	80	O112(58/9/52)/D		-1.2
2000	†Sea A	105	342	61	94	18	5	5	40	42-2	0	64	.275	.351	.401	92	-4	4-3	.993	-4	85	124	O88(47/13/38),1b3,D4		-1.2
2001	†Sea A	89	281	44	82	14	1	4	33	36-1	2	47	.292	.375	.391	109	5	11-1	.993	-1	105	25	O76(62/13/11),1b6,D2	17	0.4
Total	17	1763	5047	781	1358	225	40	57	503	578-26	25	839	.269	.345	.363	93	-43	246-51	.988	23	107	66	O1513C,1b38,D15,2b3,3b2	167	-1.1

JEANES, TEX Ernest Lee B12.19.1900 Maypearl TX D4.5.1973 Longview TX BR/TR/6-0/176 d4.20 Col Trinity (TX)

YEAR	TM LG	G	AB	R	H	2B	3B	HR	RBI	BB-IB	HP	SO	AVG	OBP	SLG	AOPS	ABR	SB-CS	FA	FR	RNG	THR	GAMES AT POSITION	DL	BFW
1921	Cle A	5	3	2	2	1	0	0	1	0	0	0	.667	.750	1.000	338	1	0-0	1.000	1	49	854	O5(1/2/1)		0.2
1922	Cle A	1	1	0	0	0	0	0	0	1	0	0	.000	.500	.000	39	0	0-0	—	-0	0	0	/POL		0.0
1925	Was A	15	19	2	5	1	0	1	4	3	0	2	.263	.364	.474	113	0	1-0	1.000	1	90	0	O13(1/10/2)		0.0
1926	Was A	21	30	6	7	2	0	0	3	0	0	3	.233	.233	.300	39	-3	0-0	1.000	-1	133	0	O14(3/10/1)		-0.2
1927	NY N	11	20	5	6	0	0	0	2	2	0	2	.300	.364	.300	79	-1	0	1.000	1	123	166	O6(4/0/2)/P		0.0
Total	5	53	73	15	20	4	0	1	11	7	0	7	.274	.338	.370	85	-3	1-0	1.000	1	114	102	O39(10/22/6),P2		0.0

JEFFCOAT, HAL Harold Bentley B9.6.1924 W.Columbia SC BR/TR/5-10.5/185(185-198) d4.20 b-George ▲

YEAR	TM LG	G	AB	R	H	2B	3B	HR	RBI	BB-IB	HP	SO	AVG	OBP	SLG	AOPS	ABR	SB-CS	FA	FR	RNG	THR	GAMES AT POSITION	DL	BFW
1948	Chi N	134	473	53	132	16	4	4	42	24	1	68	.279	.315	.355	85	-12	8	.976	3	102	146	O119C		-1.2
1949	Chi N	108	363	43	89	18	6	2	26	20	1	48	.245	.286	.344	70	-17	12	.963	0	97	148	O101(1/68/32)		-1.9
1950	Chi N	66	179	21	42	13	1	2	18	6	0	23	.235	.259	.352	60	-11	7	.967	0	91	177	O53(12/11/31)		-1.2
1951	Chi N	113	278	64	76	20	2	4	27	16	1	23	.273	.315	.403	90	-4	8-4	.989	5	102	175	O87(14/39/34)		-0.1
1952	Chi N	102	297	29	65	17	2	4	30	15	1	40	.219	.259	.330	61	-16	7-2	.996	10	108	209	O95C		-0.8
1953	Chi N	106	183	22	43	3	1	4	22	21	0	26	.235	.314	.328	66	-9	5-0	.973	5	113	116	O100(2/99/0)		-0.6
1954	Chi N	56	31	13	8	2	1	1	6	1	0	7	.258	.265	.484	94	-1	2-0	.889	1	112	69	P43,O3C		0.0
1955	Chi N	52	23	3	4	0	0	1	1	2-0	0	9	.174	.240	.304	43	1	0-0	.903	1	144	85	P50		0.0
1956	Cin N	49	54	5	8	2	0	0	5	3-0	0	20	.148	.193	.185	2	-1	0-1	.969	3	**148**	178	P38		0.0
1957	Cin N	53	69	13	14	3	1	4	11	5-0	1	20	.203	.267	.449	82	6	0-0	.958	-1	90	202	P37		0.0
1958	Cin N	50	9	2	5	0	0	0	1	1-0	0	2	.556	.600	.556	198	2	0-0	1.000	2	158	219	P49/OC		0.1
1959	Cin N	17	1	1	1	1	0	0	0	0-0	0	0	1.000	1.000	2.000	655	1	0-0	1.000	0	57	378	P17		0.1
	Stl N	12	3	0	0	0	0	0	0	0-0	0	3	.000	.000	.000	-94	-0	0-0	1.000	-0	104	0	P11		0.0
	Year	29	4	1	1	1	0	0	0	0-0	0	3	.250	.250	.500	90	0	0-0	1.000	-0	78	208	P28		0.0
Total	12	918	1963	249	487	95	18	26	188	114-0	5	254	.248	.291	.355	73	-62	49-7	.978	29	102	160	O559(29/435/97),P245		-5.7

JEFFERIES, GREGG Gregory Scott B8.1.1967 Burlingame CA BB/TR/5-10/185(170-185) [NYN85 1/20] d9.6

YEAR	TM LG	G	AB	R	H	2B	3B	HR	RBI	BB-IB	HP	SO	AVG	OBP	SLG	AOPS	ABR	SB-CS	FA	FR	RNG	THR	GAMES AT POSITION	DL	BFW
1987	NY N	6	6	0	3	1	0	0	2	0-0	0	0	.500	.500	.667	214	1	0-0	—			0	/H		0.1
1988	†NY N	29	109	19	35	8	2	6	17	8-0	0	10	.321	.364	.596	180	11	5-1	.979	-2	81	181	3b20,2b10		1.0
1989	NY N	141	508	72	131	28	2	12	56	39-8	1	46	.258	.314	.392	106	3	21-6	.975	-26	78	66	2b123,3b20		-1.8
1990	NY N	153	604	96	171	**40**	3	15	68	46-2	5	40	.283	.337	.434	111	9	11-2	.976	-1	88	86	2b118,3b34		-1.3
1991	NY N	136	486	59	132	19	2	9	62	47-2	2	38	.272	.336	.374	91	1	26-5	.982	-15	87	42	2b77,3b51	16	-0.9
1992	KC A	152	604	66	172	36	3	10	75	43-4	1	29	.285	.329	.404	102	1	19-9	.939	2	106	87	3b146/2D		0.4
1993	Stl N★	142	544	89	186	24	3	16	83	62-7	2	32	.342	.408	.485	140	33	46-9	.993	-7	84	110	1b140/2		2.0
1994	Stl N	103	397	52	129	27	1	12	55	45-12	1	26	.325	.391	.489	129	18	12-5	.993	-7	77	111	1b102		0.3
1995	Phi N	114	480	69	147	31	4	11	55	35-5	0	26	.306	.349	.448	109	6	9-5	.996	-7	76	112	1b59,O55L	15	-0.6
1996	Phi N	104	404	59	118	17	3	7	51	36-6	1	21	.292	.348	.401	97	-1	20-6	.998	5	108	94	1b53,O51L	60	-0.9
1997	Phi N	130	476	68	122	25	3	11	48	53-7	2	27	.256	.333	.391	90	-7	12-6	.986	1	101	109	O124L	15	-1.0
1998	Phi N	125	483	65	142	22	3	8	48	29-4	1	27	.294	.331	.402	93	-6	11-3	.994	-4	82	100	O121L		-1.0
	Ana A	19	72	5	25	6	0	1	10	0-0	0	5	.347	.347	.472	108	1	1-0	1.000	0	113	0	O15L,1b3		-1.3
1999	Det A	70	205	22	41	8	0	6	18	13-1	4	11	.200	.258	.327	-17		3-4	1.000	0	239	41	D45,1b3,3b2,2b2,O2L	47	-1.9

YEAR	TM LG	G	AB	R	H	2B	3B	HR	RBI	BB-IB	HP	SO	AVG	OBP	SLG	AOPS	ABR	SB-CS	FA	FR	RNG	THR	GAMES AT POSITION	DL	BFW
2000	Det A	41	142	18	39	8	0	2	14	16-1	0	10	.275	.344	.373	84	-3	0-2	.994	-3	122	116	1b20,2b14,3b6/OLD	124	-0.7
Total	14	1465	5520	761	1593	300	27	126	663	472-59	24	348	.289	.349	.421	106	50	196-63	.994	-62	87	108	1b380,0369L,2b346,3b277,D48	277	-3.1

JEFFERSON, REGGIE   Reginald Jirod   B9.25.1968 Tallahassee FL   BL/TL (BB 1991-93)/6-4/215*   [CinN86 3/72]   d5.18

YEAR	TM LG	G	AB	R	H	2B	3B	HR	RBI	BB-IB	HP	SO	AVG	OBP	SLG	AOPS	ABR	SB-CS	FA	FR	RNG	THR	GAMES AT POSITION	DL	BFW
																									0.0
1991	Cin N	5	7	1	1	0	0	1	1	1-0	0	2	.143	.250	.571	119	0	0-0	1.000	0	113	346	1b2		0.0
	Cle A	26	101	10	20	3	0	2	12	3-0	0	22	.198	.219	.287	39	-9	0-0	.993	2	133	122	1b26	16	-0.3
1992	Cle A	24	89	8	30	6	2	1	6	1-0	1	17	.337	.352	.483	133	3	0-0	.993	0	110	66	1b15,D7	89	0.3
1993	Cle A	113	366	35	91	11	2	10	34	28-7	5	78	.249	.310	.372	82	-10	1-3	.976	-0	111	87	D88,1b15		-1.7
1994	Sea A	63	162	24	53	11	0	8	32	17-5	1	32	.327	.392	.543	135	9	0-0	.981	1	156	143	D32,1b13,O2L	20	0.7
1995	†Bos A	46	121	21	35	8	0	5	26	9-1	0	24	.289	.333	.479	107	1	0-0	1.000	1	152	127	D32,1b7,O2L	71	0.0
1996	Bos A	122	386	67	134	30	4	19	74	25-5	3	89	.347	.388	.593	142	24	0-0	.969	0	89	44	D49,O45L,1b16		1.7
1997	Bos A	136	489	74	156	33	1	13	67	24-5	7	93	.319	.358	.470	112	8	1-2	.975	-1	81	108	D119,1b12	75	0.5
1998	Bos A	62	196	24	60	16	1	8	31	21-2	1	40	.306	.374	.520	127	8	0-0	1.000	0	278	57	D58,1b2	11	-0.6
1999	Bos A	83	206	21	57	13	1	5	17	17-0	2	54	.277	.338	.422	89	-3	0-0	.986	5	129	100	D433,1b115,O49L	282	0.1
Total	9	680	2123	285	637	131	11	72	300	146-25	20	451	.300	.349	.474	111	31	2-5	.986	5	129	100	D433,1b115,O49L		

JEFFERSON, STAN   Stanley   B12.4.1962 New York NY   BB/TR/5-11/175*   [NYN83 1/20]   d9.7   Col Bethune-Cookman

YEAR	TM LG	G	AB	R	H	2B	3B	HR	RBI	BB-IB	HP	SO	AVG	OBP	SLG	AOPS	ABR	SB-CS	FA	FR	RNG	THR	GAMES AT POSITION	DL	BFW
																									-0.1
1986	NY N	14	24	6	5	1	0	1	3	2-0	1	8	.208	.296	.375	86	-1	0-0	1.000	-0	98	0	O7(1/7/0)		-1.9
1987	SD N	116	422	59	97	8	7	8	29	39-2	2	92	.230	.296	.339	71	-19	34-11	.987	-0	103	50	O107(61/83/0)	39	-1.6
1988	SD N	49	111	16	16	1	2	1	4	9-0	1	21	.144	.211	.216	25	-11	5-1	1.000	-3	84	0	O38(10/27/0)		-0.3
1989	NY A	10	12	1	1	0	0	0	1	0-0	0	4	.083	.083	.083	-53	-2	0-1	1.000	-1	53	0	O7(0/2/6)/D		0.1
	Bal A	35	127	19	33	7	0	4	20	4-0	1	22	.260	.284	.409	97	-1	9-3	.988	1	106	125	O32(1/8/26),D2		-0.2
	Year	45	139	20	34	7	0	4	21	4-0	1	26	.245	.267	.381	84	-4	10-4	.988	1	102	116	O39(1/10/32),D3		-0.5
1990	Bal A	10	19	1	0	0	0	0	0	2-0	0	5	.000	.095	.000	-73	-5	0-0	1.000	-1	93	0	O5(0/3/5)/D		0.4
	Cle A	49	98	21	27	8	0	2	10	8-0	2	18	.276	.333	.418	112	2	8-4	.985	2	103	247	O34(23/11/1),D5		-0.1
	Year	59	117	22	27	8	0	2	10	10-0	2	26	.231	.295	.350	82	-3	9-4	.987	2	102	212	O39(23/14/6),D6		-0.5
1991	Cin N	13	19	2	1	0	0	0	1	0-0	1	6	.053	.100	.053	-54	-4	2-0	1.000	-1	56	0	O5(4/1/1)		-0.5
Total	6	296	832	125	180	25	9	16	67	65-2	7	177	.216	.276	.326	66	-41	60-20	.990	-2	99	76	O235(100/142/39),D9	39	-4.4

JEFFRIES, IRV   Irvine Franklin   B9.10.1905 Louisville KY   D6.8.1982 Louisville KY   BR/TR/5-10/175   d4.30   Col Kentucky

YEAR	TM LG	G	AB	R	H	2B	3B	HR	RBI	BB-IB	HP	SO	AVG	OBP	SLG	AOPS	ABR	SB-CS	FA	FR	RNG	THR	GAMES AT POSITION	DL	BFW
																									-0.6
1930	Chi A	40	97	14	23	3	0	2	11	3	2	2	.237	.275	.330	54	-7	1-2	.976	-1	97	135	3b20,S13		-1.2
1931	Chi A	79	223	29	50	10	0	2	16	14	0	9	.224	.270	.296	52	-16	3-0	.949	1	102	42	3b61,2b6,S5/OC		-0.2
1934	Phi N	56	175	28	43	6	0	4	19	15	1	10	.246	.305	.349	66	-8	2	.962	3	101	147	2b52/3		-2.0
Total	3	175	495	71	116	19	0	8	46	32	3	21	.234	.284	.321	58	-31	6-2	.955	3	100	60	3b82,2b58,S18/OC		

JELIC, CHRIS   Christopher John   B12.16.1963 Bethlehem PA   BR/TR/5-11/180   [KCA85 2/45]   d9.30   Col Pittsburgh

YEAR	TM LG	G	AB	R	H	2B	3B	HR	RBI	BB-IB	HP	SO	AVG	OBP	SLG	AOPS	ABR	SB-CS	FA	FR	RNG	THR	GAMES AT POSITION	DL	BFW
1990	NY N	4	11	2	1	0	0	0	0	1-0	0	3	.091	.091	.364	19	-1	0-0	1.000	-1	22	0	O4L		-0.2

JELINCICH, FRANK   Frank Anthony "Jelly"   B9.3.1917 San Jose CA   D6.27.1992 Rochester MN   BR/TR/6-2/198   d9.6   Mil 1942-45

YEAR	TM LG	G	AB	R	H	2B	3B	HR	RBI	BB-IB	HP	SO	AVG	OBP	SLG	AOPS	ABR	SB-CS	FA	FR	RNG	THR	GAMES AT POSITION	DL	BFW
1941	Chi N	4	8	0	1	0	0	0	2	1	0	2	.125	.222	.125	-1	-1	0-0	1.000	-0	45	0	O2L		-0.1

JELKS, GREG   Gregory Dion   B8.16.1961 Cherokee AL   BR/TR/6-2/190   d8.20   Col Gadsden St. (AL) CC

YEAR	TM LG	G	AB	R	H	2B	3B	HR	RBI	BB-IB	HP	SO	AVG	OBP	SLG	AOPS	ABR	SB-CS	FA	FR	RNG	THR	GAMES AT POSITION	DL	BFW
1987	Phi N	10	11	2	1	1	0	0	0	3-0	0	4	.091	.286	.182	26	-1	0-0	.750	-0	67	0	3b4,1b2/OL		-0.2

JELTZ, STEVE   Larry Steven   B5.28.1959 Paris, France   BB/TR (BR 1983-85)/5-11/180(170-190)   [PhiN80 9/221]   d7.17   Col Kansas

YEAR	TM LG	G	AB	R	H	2B	3B	HR	RBI	BB-IB	HP	SO	AVG	OBP	SLG	AOPS	ABR	SB-CS	FA	FR	RNG	THR	GAMES AT POSITION	DL	BFW
																									-0.
1983	Phi N	13	8	0	1	0	1	0	1	1-0	0	2	.125	.222	.375	63	-1	0-0	1.000	-1	43	201	2b4,S2,3b2		-0.
1984	Phi N	28	68	7	14	0	1	1	7	7-1	0	11	.206	.276	.279	57	-4	2-1	.992	7	123	61	S27/3		-1.
1985	Phi N	89	196	17	37	4	1	0	12	26-4	0	55	.189	.283	.219	42	-15	1-1	.958	-3	98	87	S86		-1.
1986	Phi N	145	439	44	96	11	4	0	36	65-9	1	97	.219	.320	.262	60	-22	6-3	.967	-5	100	100	S114/OL		-1.
1987	Phi N	114	293	37	68	9	6	0	12	39-4	1	54	.232	.324	.304	65	-14	1-2	.971	-6	91	97	S114/OL		-1.
1988	Phi N	148	379	39	71	11	4	0	27	59-8	0	58	.187	.295	.237	54	-21	3-0	.976	-4	97	93	S148		0.
1989	Phi N	116	263	28	64	7	3	4	25	45-6	1	44	.243	.356	.338	99	1	4-2	.985	3	90	59	S63,3b30,2b23/OC		-1.
1990	KC A	74	103	11	16	4	0	0	6	21-1	0	21	.155	.200	.194	11	-12	1-1	.977	-9	92	92	2b34,S23,O13(1/1/11),3b3,D3		-5.
Total	8	727	1749	183	367	46	20	5	130	248-32	3	342	.210	.308	.268	61	-88	18-10	.971	-9	97	90	S604,2b61,3b36,O15(2/2/11),D3		-5.

JENKINS, GEOFF   Geoffrey Scott   B7.21.1974 Olympia WA   BL/TR/6-1/204*   [MilA95 1/9]   d4.24   Col USC

YEAR	TM LG	G	AB	R	H	2B	3B	HR	RBI	BB-IB	HP	SO	AVG	OBP	SLG	AOPS	ABR	SB-CS	FA	FR	RNG	THR	GAMES AT POSITION	DL	BFW
																									-1.
1998	Mil N	84	262	33	60	12	1	9	28	20-4	2	61	.229	.288	.385	74	-11	1-3	.968	0	92	134	O81(81/0/1)		2
1999	Mil N	135	447	70	140	43	3	21	82	35-7	7	87	.313	.371	.564	132	22	5-1	.974	11	109	187	O128L	22	2
2000	Mil N	135	512	100	155	36	4	34	94	33-6	15	135	.303	.360	.588	136	26	11-1	.975	7	101	145	O131L	47	2
2001	Mil N	105	397	60	105	21	1	20	63	36-7	8	120	.264	.334	.474	109	5	4-2	.986	6	107	115	O104L	104	0
2002	Mil N	67	243	35	59	17	1	10	29	22-1	6	60	.243	.320	.444	103	0	1-2	.992	3	97	142	O123L/D	41	2
2003	Mil N☆	124	487	81	144	30	2	28	95	58-10	12	152	.296	.375	.538	136	26	0-0	1.000	3	94	117	O156L		-0
2004	Mil N	157	617	81	163	36	6	27	93	46-10	12	152	.264	.325	.473	103	1	3-1	.996	-3	94	117	O156L		2
2005	Mil N	148	538	87	157	42	1	25	86	56-9	19	138	.292	.375	.513	130	26	25-10	.984	11	115	128	O144R,D2	214	9
Total	8	955	3503	554	983	237	19	174	570	306-54	75	873	.281	.349	.508	119	95	25-10	.985	41	103	140	O933(789/0/145),D3		

JENKINS, JOHN   John Robert   B7.7.1896 Bosworth MO   D8.3.1968 Columbia MO   BR/TR/5-8/160   d8.5

YEAR	TM LG	G	AB	R	H	2B	3B	HR	RBI	BB-IB	HP	SO	AVG	OBP	SLG	AOPS	ABR	SB-CS	FA	FR	RNG	THR	GAMES AT POSITION	DL	BFW
1922	Chi A	5	3	0	0	0	0	0	1	0	0	2	.000	.000	.000	-99	-1	0-0	.000	-1	0	0	/2S		-0

JENKINS, JOE   Joseph Daniel   B10.12.1890 Shelbyville TN   D6.21.1974 Fresno CA   BR/TR/5-11/170   d4.30   Mil 1918

YEAR	TM LG	G	AB	R	H	2B	3B	HR	RBI	BB-IB	HP	SO	AVG	OBP	SLG	AOPS	ABR	SB-CS	FA	FR	RNG	THR	GAMES AT POSITION	DL	BFW
1914	StL A	19	32	0	4	1	1	0	4	0	0	11	.125	.152	.219	12	-4	2	.931	-3	79	34	C9		-0
1917	Chi A	10	9	0	1	0	0	0	0	2	0	5	.111	.111	.111	-32	-1	0	—	0	0	0	/C		-0
1919	Chi A	11	19	0	3	1	0	0	1	1	0	1	.158	.200	.211	15	-2	1	.824	-1	121	102	C4		-0
Total	3	40	60	0	8	2	1	0	3	2	0	17	.133	.161	.200	6	-7	3	.891	-4	93	58	C14		-0

JENKINS, TOM   Thomas Griffith "Tut"   B4.10.1898 Camden AL   D5.3.1979 Weymouth MA   BL/TR/6-1.5/174   d9.15

YEAR	TM LG	G	AB	R	H	2B	3B	HR	RBI	BB-IB	HP	SO	AVG	OBP	SLG	AOPS	ABR	SB-CS	FA	FR	RNG	THR	GAMES AT POSITION	DL	BFW
1925	Bos A	15	64	9	19	2	1	0	5	3	1	4	.297	.338	.359	77	-2	0-0	.938	-2	94	0	O15L		-0
1926	Bos A	21	50	3	9	1	0	0	6	3	0	7	.180	.226	.240	22	-6	0-0	1.000	-1	96	0	O13(12/1/0)		-0
	Phi A	6	23	3	4	2	0	0	0	3	0	2	.174	.174	.261	12	-3	0-0	1.000	0	115	0	O6(5/0/1)		-1
	Year	27	73	6	13	3	1	0	6	3	0	9	.178	.211	.247	19	-9	0-0	1.000	-1	102	0	O19(17/1/1)		-1
1929	StL A	21	22	1	4	0	1	0	4	0	0	8	.182	.308	.273	49	-2	0-0	1.000	-0	66	0	O2R		-1
1930	StL A	2	8	1	2	1	1	0	3	0	0	1	.250	.250	.625	110	0	0-0	1.000	-0	98	0	O2R		-0
1931	StL A	81	230	20	61	7	2	3	25	17	0	25	.265	.316	.352	73	-10	1-3	.952	-2	89	119	O58R		-1
1932	StL A	25	62	5	20	1	0	0	5	1	0	6	.323	.333	.339	70	-3	0-0	.939	1	111	197	O12R		-3
Total	6	171	459	42	119	14	6	3	44	28	1	53	.259	.303	.336	64	-26	1-3	.958	-4	95	86	O109(32/2/75)		

JENNINGS, ALAMAZOO   Alfred Gorden   B11.30.1850 Newport KY   D11.2.1894 Cincinnati OH   d8.15   U2

YEAR	TM LG	G	AB	R	H	2B	3B	HR	RBI	BB-IB	HP	SO	AVG	OBP	SLG	AOPS	ABR	SB-CS	FA	FR	RNG	THR	GAMES AT POSITION	DL	BFW
1878	Mil N	2	6	0	0	0	0	0		1	0		.000	.333	.000	16	0		.429	-2			/C		-0

JENNINGS, HUGHIE   Hugh Ambrose "Ee-Yah"   B4.2.1869 Pittston PA   D2.1.1928 Scranton PA   BR/TR/5-8.5/165   d6.1   M16/C5   HF1945   Col Mansfield

YEAR	TM LG	G	AB	R	H	2B	3B	HR	RBI	BB-IB	HP	SO	AVG	OBP	SLG	AOPS	ABR	SB-CS	FA	FR	RNG	THR	GAMES AT POSITION	DL	BFW
1891	Lou AA	88	351	51	103	19	8	1	58	17	9	35	.293	.342	.376	107	1	12	.891	6	100	118	S68,1b17,3b3		-0
1892	Lou N	152	594	65	133	16	4	2	61	30	9	30	.224	.272	.274	71	-21	28	.907	15	105	111	S152		-0
1893	Lou N	23	88	6	12	3	0	0	9	3	1		.136	.174	.170	-9	-14	0	.899	4	109	102	S23		-0
	Bal N	16	55	6	14	0	1	0	6	4	3	3	.255	.339	.309	71	-2	0	.886	3	79	70	S15/OR		-0
	Year	39	143	12	26	3	1	0	15	7	4	6	.182	.240	.224	25	-16	0	.895	1	98	91	S38/OR		-0
1894	†Bal N	128	501	134	168	28	16	4	109	37	**27**	17	.335	.411	.479	107	7	37	**.928**	33	112	129	S128		6
1895	†Bal N	**131**	529	159	204	41	7	4	125	24	**32**	17	.386	.444	.512	142	35	53	**.940**	37	102	**147**	S131		6
1896	†Bal N	130	521	125	209	27	9	0	121	19	**51**	11	.401	.472	.488	151	43	70	**.928**	31	107	**138**	S130		8
1897	†Bal N	117	439	133	156	26	9	2	79	42	**46**		.355	.463	.469	146	36	60	.933	23	105	128	S115,2b27/OR		4
1898	†Bal N	143	534	135	175	25	11	1	87	78	**46**		.328	.454	.421	149	44	28	.929	1	96	97	S11,1b4		2
1899	Bro N	16	41	7	7	0	2	0	6	9	2		.171	.346	.268	68	-2	4	.825	-5	64	80	2b2		0
	Bal N	2	8	2	3	0	0	0	1	0	0		.375	.375	.875	227	1	0	1.000	-0	239	0	2b2		
	Bro N	51	175	35	57	3	6	0	34	13	17		.326	.424	.434	133	9	14	.987	-5	110	90	1b46/2S		
	Year	69	224	44	67	3	12	0	42	22	19		.299	.408	.420	124	8	18	.982	5	119	111	1b112,2b2		-0
1900	†Bro N	115	441	61	120	18	6	1	69	31	20		.272	.348	.354	100	2	13	.979	-3	85	57	1b80/2S		-0
1901	Phi N	82	302	38	79	21	2	1	39	25	12		.262	.330	.355	111	4	20	.983	2	118	81	1b69,S5,2b4		-0
1902	Phi N	78	290	32	79	13	4	1	32	14	11		.272	.348	.407	87	-7	31	.982	-3	89	64	1b50,S12,2b3		-0
1903	Bro N	6	17	3	4	0	0	0	1	1	1		.235	.316	.235	60	-1	1	1.000	-0	0	0	O4(1/0/3)		-0

YEAR	TM LG	G	AB	R	H	2B	3B	HR	RBI	BB-IB	HP	SO	AVG	OBP	SLG	AOPS	ABR	SB-CS	FA	FR	RNG	THR	GAMES AT POSITION	DL	BFW
1907	Det A	1	4	0	1	1	0	0	0	0	0		.250	.250	.500	133	0	0	.750	-1	99	0	/2SM		-0.1
1909	Det A	2	4	1	2	0	0	0	2	0	0		.500	.500	.500	207	0	0	1.000	0	182	477	1b2,M		0.1
1910	Det A	1	0	0	0	0	0	0	0	0	0		—	—	—	—	0	0	—	0			/RM		0.0
1912	Det A	1	1	0	0	0	0	0	0	0	0		.000	.000	.000	-99	0	0	—	0			/HM		0.0
1918	Det A	1	0	0	0	0	0	0	0	0	0		—	—	—	—	0	0	1.000	0	-0	0	/1M		0.0
Total	18	1284	4895	992	1526	232	88	18	840	347	287	116	.312	.391	.406	118	135	359	.922	146	103	122	S897,1b331,2b38,O6(1/0/5),3b3		26.8

JENNINGS, DOUG James Douglas B9.30.1964 Atlanta GA BL/TL/5-10/170(165-195) [CalA84*2/31] d4.8 Col Brevard (FL) CC

1988	Oak A	71	101	9	21	6	0	1	15	21-1	2	28	.208	.346	.297	87	0	0-1	1.000	-0	107	119	O23(16/0/7),1b14,D2	34	-0.2
1989	Oak A	4	4	0	0	0	0	0	0	0-0	0	2	.000	.000	.000	-99	-1	0-0	1.000	-0	76	0	O3L		-0.1
1990 †Oak A	64	156	19	30	7	2	2	14	17-0	1	48	.192	.275	.301	65	-7	0-3	.984	-3	90	46	O45(33/0/15),1b4,D8		-0.1
1991	Oak A	8	9	0	1	0	0	0	0	2-0	0	2	.111	.273	.111	11	-1	0-1	1.000	0	41	153	1b10		-1.3
1993	Chi N	42	52	8	13	3	1	2	8	3-0	2	10	.250	.316	.462	106	0	0-0	1.000	1	151	0	O6L		-0.1
Total	5	189	322	36	65	16	3	5	37	43-1	6	90	.202	.302	.317	76	-9	0-5	.991	-4	98	63	O77(58/0/22),1b28,D10	34	-1.8

JENNINGS, ROBIN Robin Christopher B4.11.1972 Singapore, Singapore BL/TL/6-2/205* [ChiN91 33/865] d4.18 Col Manatee (FL) CC [DL 1998 Chi N 69]

1996	Chi N	31	58	7	13	5	0	0	4	3-0	1	9	.224	.274	.310	52	-4	1-0	1.000	1	109	319	O11R		-0.3
1997	Chi N	9	18	1	3	1	0	0	2	0-0	0	2	.167	.158	.222	1	-3	0-0	1.000	-1	72	0	O5(4/2/0)		-0.3
1999	Chi N	5	5	0	1	0	0	0	0	0-0	0	2	.200	.200	.200	2	-1	0-0	—	0			/H	77	-0.1
2001	Oak A	20	52	4	13	3	0	0	4	2-0	0	6	.250	.273	.308	54	-3	0-0	1.000	-1	67	154	O13(3/0/12),1b6,D2		-0.5
	Col N	1	3	0	0	0	0	0	0	0-0	0	1	.000	.000	.000	-83	-1	0-0	.000	-1	0	0	/OL		-0.1
	Cin N	27	77	10	22	5	2	3	14	5-1	0	11	.286	.329	.519	108	1	0-0	.893	1	89	233	O15R,1b8		0.0
	Year	28	80	10	22	5	2	3	14	5-1	0	12	.275	.318	.500	100	0	0-0	.862	0	83	217	O16(1/0/15),1b8		-0.1
Total	4	93	213	22	52	14	2	3	24	10-1	1	31	.244	.279	.371	66	-11	1-0	.942	0	84	204	O45(8/2/38),1b14,D2	146	-1.3

JENNINGS, BILL William Lee B9.28.1925 St.Louis MO BR/TR/6-2/175 d7.19 Col Washington-St.Louis

1951	StL A	64	195	20	35	10	2	0	13	26		0	42	.179	.276	.251	42	-16	1-0	.953	-8	91	74	S64		-2.0

JENSEN, WOODY Forrest Docenus B8.11.1907 Bremerton WA D10.5.2001 Wichita KS BL/TL/5-10.5/160 d4.20 Col Western Washington

1931	Pit N	73	267	43	65	5	4	3	17	10	2	18	.243	.276	.326	62	-16	4	.974	3	116	51	O67(64/3/0)		-1.7
1932	Pit N	7	5	0	0	0	0	0	0	0	0	2	.000	.000	.000	-99	-1	0	—	0			/OL		-0.1
1933	Pit N	70	196	29	58	7	3	0	15	8	2	13	.296	.330	.362	98	-1	1	.980	-1	106	30	O40L		-0.4
1934	Pit N	88	283	34	82	13	4	0	27	4	2	13	.290	.304	.364	76	-10	2	.993	-0	107	23	O66(46/17/4)		-1.3
1935	Pit N	143	627	97	203	28	7	8	62	15	4	14	.324	.344	.429	103	1	9	.977	-6	93	59	O140(138/0/2)		-1.3
1936	Pit N	153	696	98	197	34	10	10	58	16	6	19	.283	.305	.404	87	-15	2	.975	-2	104	52	O153(152/1/0)		-2.5
1937	Pit N	124	509	77	142	23	9	5	45	15	1	29	.279	.301	.389	86	-12	2	.963	-2	103	58	O120(88/32/0)		-2.0
1938	Pit N	68	125	12	25	4	0	0	10	1	1	3	.200	.213	.232	22	-14	0	.900	-4	85	0	O38(15/21/2)		-1.9
1939	Pit N	12	12	0	2	0	0	0	1	0	0	0	.167	.167	.167	-10	-2	0	1.000	1	0	1636	O3(0/1/2)		-0.1
Total	9	738	2720	392	774	114	37	26	235	69	18	100	.285	.307	.382	84	-70	20	.972	-12	102	50	O628(544/75/10)		-11.3

JENSEN, JACKIE Jack Eugene B3.9.1927 San Francisco CA D7.14.1982 Charlottesville VA BR/TR/5-11/190* d4.18 Col California-Davis

1950 †NY A	45	70	13	12	2	1	1	5	7	1	0	.171	.247	.300	41	-5	4-0	.947	0	120	0	O23(17/0/7)		-0.7
1951	NY A	56	168	30	50	8	1	8	25	18	1	18	.298	.369	.500	138	8	8-2	.974	2	101	158	O48(21/27/1)		0.9
1952	NY A	7	19	3	2	1	1	0	2	4	0	4	.105	.261	.263	49	-1	1-0	1.000	-1	77	0	O5C		-0.2
	Was A★	144	570	80	163	29	5	10	80	63	3	40	.286	.360	.407	117	13	17-6	.977	3	102	135	O143(0/7/142)		1.4
	Year	151	589	83	165	30	6	10	82	67	3	44	.280	.357	.402	115	12	18-6	.978	2	101	132	O148(0/12/142)		1.2
1953	Was A	147	552	87	147	32	8	10	84	73	5	51	.266	.357	.408	109	8	18-8	.983	-8	95	65	O146(0/1/145)		-0.5
1954	Bos A	152	580	92	160	25	7	25	117	79	2	52	.276	.359	.472	115	12	22-7	.986	-11	88	90	O151(8/106/44)		-0.3
1955	Bos A★	152	574	95	158	27	6	26	116	89-8	3	63	.275	.369	.479	118	15	16-7	.977	-4	96	90	O150R		0.6
1956	Bos A	151	578	80	182	23	11	20	97	89-5	1	43	.315	.405	.497	123	20	11-3	.962	-5	93	108	O151R		1.1
1957	Bos A	145	544	82	153	29	2	23	103	75-3	2	66	.281	.367	.469	121	17	8-5	.960	1	97	149	O144(4/0/143)		1.3
1958	Bos A★	154	548	83	157	31	0	35	122	99-7	0	65	.286	.396	.535	144	37	9-4	.981	-3	95	102	O153(2/0/153)		3.0
1959	Bos A	148	535	101	148	31	0	28	112	88-3	0	67	.277	.372	.492	131	25	20-5	.982	8	113	141	O146(0/7/142)		3.1
1961	Bos A	137	498	64	131	21	2	13	66	66-2	3	69	.263	.353	.392	96	-1	9-8	.986	7	105	137	O131(2/0/129)		-0.4
Total	11	1438	5236	810	1463	259	45	199	929	750-28	23	546	.279	.369	.460	119	146	143-55	.977	-10	98	112	O1391(54/153/1207)		9.3

JENSEN, MARCUS Marcus Christian B12.14.1972 Oakland CA BB/TR/6-4/204* [SFN90 1/33] d4.14

1996	SF N	9	19	4	4	1	0	0	4	8-0	0	7	.211	.444	.263	95	1	0-0	.955	1	154	166	C7		0.2
1997	SF N	30	74	5	11	2	0	1	3	7-1	0	23	.149	.222	.216	16	-9	0-0	.983	-7	113	134	C28		-1.5
	Det A	8	11	1	2	0	0	0	1	1-0	0	5	.182	.250	.182	15	-1	0-0	.964	0	0	0	C8		-0.1
1998	Mil N	2	0	0	0	0	0	0	0	0-0	0	0	.000	.000	.000	-98	-1	0-0	1.000	0	0	0	/C		-0.1
1999	StL N	16	34	5	8	5	0	1	1	6-1	0	12	.235	.350	.471	103	0	0-0	.988	3	185	130	C14		0.4
2000	Min A	52	139	16	29	7	1	3	14	24-0	0	36	.209	.325	.338	64	-7	0-1	.993	1	153	81	C49/D		-0.4
2001	Bos A	1	4	0	1	0	0	0	0	0-0	0	1	.250	.250	.250	32	0	0-0	1.000	0	0	321	/C		0.1
	Tex A	11	25	0	4	1	0	0	2	0-0	0	9	.160	.160	.200	-6	-4	0-0	1.000	-2	70	97	C11		-0.6
	Year	12	29	0	5	1	0	0	2	0-0	0	10	.172	.172	.207	-1	-4	0-0	1.000	-1	61	127	C12		-0.5
2002	Mil N	16	35	2	4	0	1	1	4	4-2	0	11	.114	.200	.200	9	-5	0-0	.976	2	155	175	C15		-0.3
Total	7	145	343	33	63	16	1	6	29	50-4	0	106	.184	.287	.289	48	-26	0-1	.985	-1	135	113	C134/D		-2.3

JESSEE, DAN Daniel Edward B2.22.1901 Olive Hill KY D4.30.1970 Venice FL BL/TR/5-10/165 d8.14 Col Pacific (OR)

1929	Cle A	1	0	0	0	0	0	0	0	0-0	0	0	—	—	—	—	0	0-0	—	0			/R		0.0

JESTADT, GARRY Garry Arthur B3.19.1947 Chicago IL BR/TR/6-2/188* [ChiN65 7/121] d9.17

1969	Mon N	6	6	1	0	0	0	0	1	0-0	0	0	.000	.000	.000	-99	-2	0-0	.667	-2	0	0	/S		-0.2
1971	Chi N	3	3	0	0	0	0	0	0	0-0	0	0	.000	.000	.000	-87	-1	0-0	—	-0	0	0	/3		-0.1
	SD N	75	189	17	55	13	0	0	13	11-0	0	24	.291	.328	.360	102	0	1-3	.935	2	129	65	3b49,2b23/S		0.2
	Year	78	192	17	55	13	0	0	13	11-0	0	24	.286	.324	.354	98	-1	1-3	.935	1	128	64	3b50,2b23/S		0.1
1972	SD N	92	256	15	63	5	1	6	22	13-2	0	21	.246	.281	.344	83	-7	0-0	.944	-17	80	80	2b48,3b25,S3		-2.3
Total	3	176	454	33	118	18	1	6	36	24-2	0	45	.260	.296	.344	87	-10	1-3	.942	-16	111	81	3b75,2b71,S5		-2.4

JETER, DEREK Derek Sanderson B6.26.1974 Pequannock NJ BR/TR/6-3/195* [NYA92 1/6] d5.29

1995	NY A	15	48	5	12	4	1	0	11	3-0	0	11	.250	.294	.375	73	-2	0-0	.962	-4	83	81	S15		-0.4
1996 †NY A	157	582	104	183	25	6	10	78	48-1	9	102	.314	.370	.430	103	3	14-7	.969	-2	96	80	S157		1.3
1997 †NY A	159	654	116	190	31	7	10	70	74-0	10	125	.291	.370	.405	104	5	23-12	.975	-6	96	88	S159		1.2
1998 †NY A★	149	626	127	203	25	8	19	84	57-1	5	119	.324	.384	.481	129	26	30-6	.986	-22	88	97	S148	15	1.9
1999 †NY A★	158	627	134	219	37	9	24	102	91-5	12	116	.349	.438	.552	154	56	19-8	.978	-32	83	83	S158		3.4
2000 †NY A★	148	593	119	201	31	4	15	73	68-4	12	99	.339	.416	.481	128	29	22-4	.961	-36	79	80	S148	14	0.7
2001 †NY A	150	614	110	191	35	3	21	74	56-3	10	99	.311	.377	.480	123	22	27-3	.974	-27	81	78	S150	6	1.0
2002 †NY A★	157	644	124	191	26	0	18	75	73-2	7	114	.297	.373	.421	112	13	32-3	.977	-40	80	73	S156/D		-0.9
2003 †NY A	119	482	87	156	25	3	10	52	43-2	13	88	.324	.393	.450	124	18	11-5	.968	-31	80	70	S118	42	-0.2
2004 †NY A★	154	643	111	188	44	1	23	78	46-1	14	99	.292	.352	.471	112	12	23-4	.981	-4	92	101	S154		2.1
2005 †NY A	159	654	122	202	25	5	19	70	77-3	11	117	.309	.389	.450	122	23	14-5	.979	9	102	95	S157/D		4.3
Total 11	1525	6167	1159	1936	308	47	169	763	636-22	103	1089	.314	.386	.461	125	215-57		.975	-194	88	85	S1520,D2	77	14.4

JETER, JOHNNY John B10.24.1944 Shreveport LA BR/TR/6-1/180* d6.14 s-Shawn Col Grambling St.

1969	Pit N	28	29	7	9	1	1	1	6	3-1	0	15	.310	.375	.517	151	0	2-1	1.000	-0	79	186	O20(16/1/4)		0.1
1970 †Pit N	85	126	27	30	3	2	2	12	13-1	1	34	.238	.314	.341	76	-5	9-5	1.000	-1	90	96	O56(35/10/11)		-0.7
1971	SD N	18	75	8	24	4	1	3	15	2-0	0	16	.320	.338	.413	119	2	2-0	.967	2	87	66	O17C		0.4
1972	SD N	110	326	25	72	4	7	7	21	18-4	2	92	.221	.266	.316	70	-15	11-5	.987	-1	109	20	O91C		-1.9
1973	Chi N	89	300	38	72	14	4	7	26	9-0	1	74	.240	.260	.383	77	-11	4-3	.955	-3	97	63	O72(19/27/29),D3		-1.8
1974	Cle A	6	17	3	6	1	0	0	1	1-0	0	6	.353	.389	.412	131	1	1-2	.833	-1	57	0	O5(1/1/0)		-0.1
Total	6	336	873	108	213	27	10	18	69	46-6	3	237	.244	.283	.360	81	-26	28-16	.975	-4	98	55	O262(75/147/44),D3		-4.0

JETER, SHAWN Shawn Darrell B6.28.1966 Shreveport LA BL/TR/6-2/185 [TorA85 7/183] d6.13 f-Johnny

1992	Chi A	13	18	1	2	1	0	0	0	0-0	0	7	.111	.111	.111	-38	-3	0-0	.909	-0	114	0	O8(1/1/6),D3		-0.4

YEAR	TM LG	G	AB	R	H	2B	3B	HR	RBI	BB-IB	HP	SO	AVG	OBP	SLG	AOPS	ABR	SB-CS	FA	FR	RNG	THR	GAMES AT POSITION	DL	BFW

JETHROE, SAM Samuel "Jet" B1.20.1918 E.St.Louis IL D6.16.2001 Erie PA BB/TR/6-1/178* d4.18 Negro Lg 1938-48

																									0.6
1950	Bos N	141	582	100	159	28	8	18	58	52	5	93	.273	.338	.442	110	7	35	.969	3	98	148	O141C		2.0
1951	Bos N	148	572	101	160	29	10	18	65	57	11	88	.280	.356	.460	127	21	35-5	.974	-2	94	142	O140(13/127/2)		-1.4
1952	Bos N	151	608	79	141	23	7	13	58	68	9	112	.232	.311	.357	90	-8	28-9	.970	-4	102	66	O151(1/150/0)		0.0
1954	Pit N	2	1	0	0	0	0	0	0	0	0	0	.000	.000	.000	-99	0	0-0	1.000	0	153	0	/OR		1.2
Total	4	442	1763	280	460	80	25	49	181	177	25	293	.261	.337	.418	108	20	98-14	.971	-3	98	117	O433(14/418/3)		

JEWETT, NAT Nathan W. B12.25.1842 New York NY D2.23.1914 Bronx NY 5-6/137 d7.4

| | | | | | | | | | | | | | | | | | | | | | | | | | -0.2 |
| 1872 | Eck NA | 2 | 8 | 1 | 1 | 0 | 0 | 0 | 0 | 0 | | | .125 | .125 | .125 | -27 | -1 | 0-0 | .700 | -2 | | | C2 | | |

JIMENEZ, HOUSTON Alfonso (Gonzales) B10.30.1957 Mexico City, Distrito Federal, Mexico BR/TR/5-8/144* d6.13

																									-0.7
1983	Min A	36	86	5	15	5	1	0	4	4-0	0	11	.174	.207	.256	27	-9	0-1	.969	-1	97	110	S36		-3.1
1984	Min A	108	298	28	60	11	1	0	19	15-0	0	34	.201	.238	.245	33	-27	0-1	.959	-12	94	104	S107		0.0
1987	Pit N	5	6	0	0	0	0	0	0	1-0	0	2	.000	.143	.000	-57	-1	0-0	1.000	1	0	0	2b2,S2		0.0
1988	Cle A	9	21	1	1	0	0	0	1	0-0	0	2	.048	.048	.048	-71	-5	0-0	.973	5	173	84	2b7,S2		0.0
Total	4	158	411	34	76	16	2	0	29	20-0	0	49	.185	.221	.234	25	-42	0-2	.962	-7	96	107	S147,2b9		-3.8

JIMENEZ, D'ANGELO D'Angelo B12.21.1977 Santo Domingo, D.R. BB/TR/6-0/160(160-215) d9.15 [DL 2000 NY A 142]

																									0.1
1999	NY A	7	20	3	8	2	0	0	4	3-0	0	4	.400	.478	.500	152	2	0-0	1.000	-0	101	295	3b6/2		0.8
2001	SD N	86	308	45	85	19	0	3	33	39-4	0	68	.276	.355	.367	95	-1	2-3	.948	4	107	91	S85		0.8
2002	SD N	87	321	39	77	11	4	3	33	34-1	0	63	.240	.311	.327	78	-12	4-2	.975	17	110	123	2b54,3b32/P		0.8
	Chi A	27	108	22	31	4	3	1	11	16-0	1	10	.287	.384	.407	107	1	2-1	.988	5	109	147	2b17,S10/3		-0.7
2003	Chi A	73	271	35	69	11	5	7	26	32-1	0	46	.255	.332	.410	91	-4	4-3	.977	-6	90	99	2b68,3b2		0.7
	Cin N	73	290	34	84	13	2	7	31	34-0	1	43	.290	.365	.421	110	5	7-4	.990	-2	99	105	2b73,3b2		-0.9
2004	Cin N	152	563	76	152	28	3	12	67	82-1	2	99	.270	.364	.394	98	1	13-7	.990	-18	93	77	2b146,S5		-0.5
2005	Cin N	35	105	14	24	7	0	0	5	14-0	0	23	.229	.319	.295	65	-5	2-1	.983	-1	93	99	2b27		1.1
Total	6	540	1986	268	530	95	17	33	210	254-7	5	356	.267	.350	.382	95	-13	34-21	.985	-1	97	97	2b386,S100,3b43/P	142	

JIMENEZ, ELVIO Felix Elvio (Rivera) B1.6.1940 San Pedro de Macoris, D.R. BR/TR/5-9/170 d10.4 b-Manny

| | | | | | | | | | | | | | | | | | | | | | | | | | 0.0 |
| 1964 | NY A | 1 | 6 | 0 | 2 | 0 | 0 | 0 | 0 | 0-0 | 0 | 0 | .333 | .333 | .333 | 85 | 0 | 0-0 | 1.000 | 0 | 153 | 0 | /OL | | |

JIMENEZ, MANNY Manuel Emilio (Rivera) B11.19.1938 San Pedro de Macoris, D.R. BL/TR/6-1/195* d4.11 b-Elvio

																									-0.8
1962	KC A	139	479	48	144	24	2	11	69	31-3	11	34	.301	.354	.428	105	-5	0-1	.985	-5	82	109	O122(116/0/6)		-0.1
1963	KC A	60	157	12	44	9	0	0	15	16-2	5	14	.280	.361	.338	93	0	0-1	.960	2	91	233	O40(33/0/8)		-0.5
1964	KC A	95	204	19	46	7	0	12	38	15-1	5	24	.225	.293	.436	97	-1	0-0	.939	-2	83	146	O49(46/0/4)		-0.6
1966	KC A	13	35	1	4	0	1	0	1	6-0	0	4	.114	.244	.171	22	-4	0-0	.909	-1	55	182	O12(8/0/4)		-0.2
1967	Pit N	50	56	3	14	2	0	2	10	1-0	1	4	.250	.276	.393	89	-1	0-0	1.000	-1	69	0	O6L		0.4
1968	Pit N	66	66	7	20	1	1	1	11	6-0	5	15	.303	.403	.394	142	4	0-0	.857	-1	87	0	O5L		-0.1
1969	Chi N	6	6	0	1	0	0	0	0	0-0	0	2	.167	.167	.167	-6	-1	0-0	—	0			/H		-1.9
Total	7	429	1003	90	273	43	4	26	144	75-6	27	97	.272	.337	.401	100	1	0-2	.966	-7	83	138	O234(214/0/22)		

JIMERSON, CHARLTON Charlton Maxwell B9.22.1979 San Leandro CA BR/TR/6-3/210 d9.14 Col Miami

| | | | | | | | | | | | | | | | | | | | | | | | | | 0.0 |
| 2005 | Hou N | 1 | 0 | 0 | 0 | 0 | 0 | 0 | 0 | 0-0 | 0 | 0 | | | | | — | -0 | 0 | 0 | /OC | | |

JOHNS, KEITH Robert Keith B7.19.1971 Callahan FL BR/TR/6-1/175 [StLN92 6/167] d5.23 Col U. of Mississippi

| | | | | | | | | | | | | | | | | | | | | | | | | | 0.1 |
| 1998 | Bos A | 2 | 0 | 0 | 0 | 0 | 0 | 0 | 0 | 1-0 | 0 | 0 | — | 1.000 | — | 187 | 0 | 0-0 | 1.000 | 0 | 150 | 755 | /2D | | |

JOHNS, TOMMY Thomas Pearce B9.7.1851 Baltimore MD D4.13.1927 Baltimore MD d5.14

| | | | | | | | | | | | | | | | | | | | | | | | | | -0.1 |
| 1873 | Mar NA | 1 | 4 | 0 | 0 | 0 | 0 | 0 | 0 | 0-0 | 0 | 0 | .000 | .000 | .000 | -99 | -1 | 0-0 | .000 | -1 | 0 | 0 | /OL | | |

JOHNS, PETE William R. B1.17.1889 Cleveland OH D8.9.1964 Cleveland OH BR/TR/5-10/165 d8.25

																									-0.7
1915	Chi A	28	100	7	21	1	0	0	14	4	1	11	.210	.275	.250	56	-6	2-7	.943	0	102	112	3b28		-1.0
1918	StL A	46	89	5	16	1	1	0	11	4	0	6	.180	.215	.213	30	-8	0	.990	-1	177	60	1b10,S4,3b4,O4(1/3/0),2b2		-1.7
Total	2	74	189	12	37	3	2	0	22	12	1	17	.196	.248	.233	44	-14	2-7	.929	-0	100	105	3b32,1b10,O4(1/3/0),S4,2b2		

JOHNSON, ABBIE Albert J. B1.19.1874 Ontario, Can D11.28.1960 Detroit MI 5-9.5/165 d9.1

																									-0.8
1896	Lou N	25	87	10	20	2	1	0	14	4	0	6	.230	.264	.276	44	-7	0	.937	-3	87	84	2b25		-1.4
1897	Lou N	49	165	16	40	6	1	0	23	13	1	6	.242	.302	.291	59	-10	2	.882	-9	92	67	2b34,S12		-2.2
Total	2	74	252	26	60	8	2	0	37	17	1	6	.238	.289	.286	54	-17	2	.904	-12	90	74	2b59,S12		

JOHNSON, ALEX Alexander B12.7.1942 Helena AR BR/TR/6-0/205* d7.25

																									0.4
1964	Phi N	43	109	18	33	7	1	4	18	6-1	1	26	.303	.345	.495	135	5	1-2	.980	1	105	60	O35(34/0/1)		0.3
1965	Phi N	97	262	27	77	9	3	8	28	15-3	2	60	.294	.337	.443	120	6	4-4	.966	0	102	89	O82(76/9/1)		-1.1
1966	StL N	25	86	7	16	0	1	2	6	5-1	0	18	.186	.231	.279	41	-7	1-1	.962	-2	65	139	O22L		-0.5
1967	StL N	81	175	20	39	9	2	1	12	9-0	3	26	.223	.271	.314	68	-7	6-3	.970	5	113	231	O57(5/6/48)		0.4
1968	Cin N	149	603	79	188	32	6	2	58	26-4	3	71	.312	.342	.395	114	10	16-6	.947	-0	103	86	O140(140/0/1)		0.5
1969	Cin N	139	523	86	165	18	4	17	88	25-1	9	69	.315	.350	.463	122	14	11-8	.927	-2	101	71	O132L		1.9
1970	Cal A★	156	614	85	202	26	6	14	86	35-9	7	68	.329	.370	.459	132	25	17-2	.959	-0	98	112	O156(155/0/1)	97	-1.7
1971	Cal A	65	242	19	63	8	0	2	21	15-3	1	40	.260	.308	.318	84	-6	5-2	.926	-7	76	81	O61L		-2.4
1972	Cle A	108	356	31	85	10	1	8	37	22-10	1	40	.239	.283	.340	82	-9	6-8	.955	-5	88	59	O95L		-0.6
1973	Tex A	158	624	62	179	26	3	8	68	32-5	2	82	.287	.322	.377	100	-2	10-5	.987	1	94	148	D116,O41(40/1/0)		-0.2
1974	Tex A	114	453	57	132	14	3	4	41	28-4	4	59	.291	.338	.362	104	2	20-9	.956	4	108	114	O81L,D32		-0.2
	NY A	10	28	3	6	1	0	1	2	0-0	0	3	.214	.214	.357	63	-2	0-0	—	-0	0	0	/OLD		0.0
	Year	124	481	60	138	15	3	5	43	28-4	4	62	.287	.331	.362	102	0	20-9	.956	4	107	113	O82L,D36		-0.2
1975	NY A	52	119	15	31	5	1	1	15	7-1	0	21	.261	.297	.345	83	-3	2-3	1.000	-1	83	0	D28,O7(5/0/2)		-2.3
1976	Det A	125	429	41	115	15	2	6	45	19-1	2	49	.268	.298	.354	88	-8	14-10	.954	-5	90	111	O90L,D19		-2.1
Total	13	1322	4623	550	1331	180	33	78	525	244-43	36	626	.288	.326	.392	105	18	113-63	.953	-10	97	100	O1000(937/16/54),D199	97	-5.1

JOHNSON, TONY Anthony Clair B6.23.1956 Memphis TN BR/TR/6-3/195* [MonN77 26/631] d9.27 Col LeMoyne-Owen (TN)

																									0.0
1981	Mon N	2	1	0	0	0	0	0	0	0-0	0	0	.000	.000	.000	-97	0	0-0	—	-0	0	0	/OL		-0.1
1982	Tor A	70	98	17	23	2	1	3	14	11-1	0	26	.235	.309	.367	79	-3	3-13	.979	2	108	176	O28(25/2/2),D28		0.0
Total	2	72	99	17	23	2	1	3	14	11-1	0	26	.232	.306	.364	77	-3	3-13	.979	2	107	175	O29(26/2/2),D28		

JOHNSON, BEN Benjamin Joseph B6.18.1981 Memphis TN BR/TR/6-1/200 d6.26

| | | | | | | | | | | | | | | | | | | | | | | | | | 0.0 |
| 2005 | †SD N | 31 | 75 | 10 | 16 | 8 | 1 | 3 | 13 | 11-1 | 0 | 23 | .213 | .310 | .467 | 106 | 1 | 0-2 | .962 | 0 | 115 | 0 | O29(13/9/11) | | |

JOHNSON, BOB Bobby Earl B7.31.1959 Dallas TX BR/TR/6-3/195* [TexA77 9/217] d9.1

																									0.0
1981	Tex A	6	18	2	5	0	0	2	4	1-0	0	3	.278	.316	.611	170	1	0-0	1.000	-0	118	0	C5/1		-0.0
1982	Tex A	20	56	4	7	2	0	2	7	3-0	1	22	.125	.183	.268	23	-6	0-1	1.000	0	146	122	C14,1b3		-0.0
1983	Tex A	72	175	18	37	6	1	5	16	16-0	1	55	.211	.280	.343	72	-7	3-0	1.000	4	137	75	C62,1b10		-0.0
Total	3	98	249	24	49	8	1	9	27	20-0	2	80	.197	.261	.345	67	-12	3-1	1.000	4	138	81	C81,1b14		

JOHNSON, BRIAN Brian David B1.8.1968 Oakland CA BR/TR/6-2/210* [NYA89 16/415] d4.5 Col Stanford

																									0.0
1994	SD N	36	93	7	23	4	1	3	16	5-0	0	21	.247	.283	.409	81	-3	0-0	1.000	3	66	178	C24,1b5		-0.0
1995	SD N	68	207	20	52	9	0	3	29	11-2	1	39	.251	.287	.338	68	-10	0-0	.993	2	111	87	C55,1b2		-0.0
1996	†SD N	82	243	18	66	13	1	8	35	4-2	4	36	.272	.290	.432	93	-4	0-0	.989	-3	95	88	C66/13		-1.3
1997	Det A	45	139	13	33	6	1	2	18	5-1	0	19	.237	.262	.338	56	-10	1-0	.987	-10	80	66	C43,D2		1.1
	†SF N	56	179	19	50	7	2	11	27	14-7	2	26	.279	.333	.525	124	5	0-1	.995	-3	132	81	C95/OL	33	0.1
1998	SF N	99	308	34	73	8	1	13	34	28-4	5	67	.237	.310	.396	89	-6	0-2	.995	4	147	82	C39	48	-0.0
1999	Cin N	45	117	12	27	7	0	5	18	9-1	0	31	.231	.286	.419	73	-5	0-0	.995	4	58	59	C37		-1.3
2000	KC A	37	125	9	26	6	0	4	18	4-0	0	25	.208	.229	.352	43	-11	0-0	.991	-2	68	90	C37		-0.0
2001	LA N	3	4	0	1	0	0	0	0	0-0	0	4	.250	.250	.250	32	0	0-0	1.000	0	0	0	C2		-0.0
Total	8	471	1415	132	351	60	6	49	196	80-16	12	268	.248	.291	.403	81	-44	1-3	.993	-5	108	91	C416,1b10,D2/OL3	81	-2.6

JOHNSON, CALEB Caleb Clark B5.23.1844 Fulton IL D3.7.1925 Sterling IL d5.20

| | | | | | | | | | | | | | | | | | | | | | | | | | 0.0 |
| 1871 | Cle NA | 16 | 67 | 10 | 15 | 1 | 0 | 0 | 7 | 0 | | 1 | .224 | .224 | .239 | 35 | -5 | 1-0 | .736 | -4 | 81 | 88 | 2b10,O6R | | |

JOHNSON, CHARLIE Charles Cleveland "Home Run" B3.12.1885 Slatington PA D8.28.1940 Marcus Hook PA BL/TL/5-9/150 d9.21

| | | | | | | | | | | | | | | | | | | | | | | | | | 0.0 |
| 1908 | Phi N | 6 | 16 | 2 | 4 | 0 | 1 | 0 | 2 | 1 | | 1 | .250 | .333 | .375 | 122 | 0 | 0 | 1.000 | -0 | 0 | 0 | O4(1/3/0) | | |

JOHNSON, CHARLES
Charles Edward B7.20.1971 Fort Pierce FL BR/TR/6-2/220* [FlaN92 1/28] d5.6 Col Miami

YEAR	TM	LG	G	AB	R	H	2B	3B	HR	RBI	BB-IB	HP	SO	AVG	OBP	SLG	AOPS	ABR	SB-CS	FA	FR	RNG	THR	GAMES AT POSITION	DL	BFW
1994	Fla	N	4	11	5	5	1	0	1	4	1-0	0	4	.455	.462	.818	227	2	0-0	1.000	1	0	106	C4		0.3
1995	Fla	N	97	315	40	79	15	1	11	39	46-2	0	71	.251	.351	.410	99	0	0-2	.992	3	145	122	C97		0.9
1996	Fla	N	120	386	34	84	13	1	13	37	40-6	2	91	.218	.292	.358	73	-16	1-0	.995	19	203	114	C120	23	0.9
1997	†Fla	N★	124	416	43	104	26	1	19	63	60-6	3	109	.250	.347	.454	113	9	0-2	1.000	13	153	128	C123	35	2.9
1998	Fla	N	31	113	13	25	5	0	7	23	16-0	0	30	.221	.315	.451	106	1	0-1	.990	-6	112	80	C31		-0.4
	LA	N	102	346	31	75	13	0	12	35	29-1	1	99	.217	.279	.358	70	-17	0-1	.992	5	154	107	C100		-0.5
	Year		133	459	44	100	18	0	19	58	45-1	1	129	.218	.289	.381	78	-16	0-2	.992	-1	144	101	C131		-0.9
1999	Bal	A	135	426	58	107	19	0	16	54	55-2	4	107	.251	.340	.413	95	-3	0-1	.994	5	128	97	C135		0.9
2000	Bal	A	84	286	52	84	16	0	21	55	32-0	0	69	.294	.364	.570	138	16	2-0	.994	-8	119	72	C83/D		1.2
	†Chi	A	44	135	24	44	8	0	10	36	20-0	1	37	.326	.411	.607	142	11	0-0	.987	-7	144	97	C43		0.5
	Year		128	421	76	128	24	0	31	91	52-0	1	106	.304	.379	.582	142	27	2-0	.992	-16	127	80	C126/D		1.7
2001	Fla	N★	128	451	51	117	32	0	18	75	38-2	4	133	.259	.321	.450	100	-1	0-0	.996	4	128	110	C125		1.1
2002	Fla	N	83	244	18	53	19	0	6	36	31-7	2	61	.217	.301	.369	83	-7	0-0	.994	0	106	135	C82	27	-0.2
2003	Col	N	108	356	49	82	20	0	20	61	49-2	1	84	.230	.320	.455	88	-6	1-3	.993	-5	143	114	C107		-0.4
2004	Col	N	109	305	42	72	20	0	13	47	49-1	5	91	.236	.350	.430	89	-4	2-1	.988	-5	74	91	C91		-0.3
2005	TB	A	19	46	5	9	4	0	0	5	9-0	0	11	.196	.327	.283	66	-2	0-0	.959	-5	59	148	C19		-0.6
Total	12		1188	3836	465	940	211	4	167	570	475-29	25	997	.245	.330	.433	97	-17	6-10	.993	13	136	109	C1160/D	85	6.4

JOHNSON, CLIFF
Clifford B7.22.1947 San Antonio TX BR/TR/6-4/225(212-225) [HouN66 5/83] d9.13

YEAR	TM	LG	G	AB	R	H	2B	3B	HR	RBI	BB-IB	HP	SO	AVG	OBP	SLG	AOPS	ABR	SB-CS	FA	FR	RNG	THR	GAMES AT POSITION	DL	BFW
1972	Hou	N	5	4	0	1	0	0	0	0	2-0	0	0	.250	.500	.250	122	0	0-0	1.000	1	0	0	/C		0.1
1973	Hou	N	7	20	6	6	2	0	2	6	1-0	1	7	.300	.364	.700	190	2	0-0	1.000	-0	68	169	1b5		0.2
1974	Hou	N	83	171	26	39	4	1	10	29	33-1	3	45	.228	.357	.439	129	7	0-1	.978	-3	66	82	C28,1b21		0.4
1975	Hou	N	122	340	52	94	16	1	20	65	46-5	5	64	.276	.370	.506	152	24	1-0	.991	-14	70	84	1b47,C41/OL		0.9
1976	Hou	N	108	318	36	72	21	2	10	49	62-6	4	59	.226	.359	.399	125	13	0-0	.977	-14	54	104	C66,O20L,1b16		0.0
1977	Hou	N	51	144	22	43	8	0	10	23	23-2	4	30	.299	.400	.563	151	15	0-1	.946	1	85	205	O34(33/0/4),1b10		1.4
	†NY	A	56	142	24	42	8	0	12	31	20-0	6	23	.296	.405	.606	172	15	0-1	1.000	2	721	108	D25,C15,1b11		1.6
1978	†NY	A	76	174	20	32	9	1	6	19	30-5	1	32	.184	.307	.351	86	-3	0-0	.975	-5	101	72	D39,C22/1		-0.8
1979	NY	A	28	64	11	17	6	0	2	6	10-4	0	7	.266	.360	.453	121	2	0-0	1.000	-1	92	99	D22,C4		0.1
	Cle	A	72	240	37	65	10	0	18	61	24-1	5	39	.271	.343	.538	135	11	2-0	—	-0	0	0	D62/C		0.9
	Year		100	304	48	82	16	0	20	67	34-5	5	46	.270	.347	.520	132	14	2-0	1.000	-1	85	91	D84,C5		1.0
1980	Cle	A	54	174	25	40	3	1	6	28	25-5	0	35	.230	.320	.362	87	-3	0-1	—	-0	0	0	D45		-0.5
	Chi	A	68	196	28	46	8	0	10	34	29-5	1	35	.235	.335	.429	103	1	0-0	.992	-6	53	90	1b46,O3L/C		-0.8
1981	†Oak	A	84	273	40	71	8	0	17	59	28-2	3	60	.260	.329	.476	136	12	5-3	1.000	-1	24	41	D68,1b9		0.9
1982	Oak	A	73	214	19	51	10	0	7	31	26-2	2	41	.238	.324	.383	97	0	1-2	.987	1	134	88	D48,1b11		0.9
1983	Tor	A	142	407	59	108	23	1	22	76	67-8	5	69	.265	.373	.489	127	17	0-1	1.000	0	98	106	D130,1b6	27	-0.2
1984	Tor	A	127	359	51	109	23	1	16	61	50-4	3	62	.304	.390	.507	141	22	0-1	1.000	-1	0	0	D109,1b2		1.3
1985	Tex	A	82	296	31	76	17	1	12	56	31-2	3	44	.257	.330	.443	108	4	0-0	—	0	0	0	D82		1.8
	†Tor	A	24	73	4	20	0	0	1	10	9-0	0	15	.274	.349	.315	83	-2	0-0	.947	-1	57	225	D21,1b3	38	0.1
	Year		106	369	35	96	17	1	13	66	40-2	3	59	.260	.334	.417	103	2	0-0	.947	-1	57	225	D103,1b3		-0.3
1986	Tor	A	107	336	48	84	12	1	15	55	52-1	4	57	.250	.355	.426	109	5	0-1	1.000	0	124	244	D95/1		-0.2
Total	15		1369	3945	539	1016	188	10	196	699	568-53	54	719	.258	.355	.459	125	142	9-12	.993	-40	72	97	D746,1b189,C179,O58(57/0/4)	80	7.3

JOHNSON, DAN
Daniel Ryan B8.10.1979 Coon Rapids MN BL/TR/6-2/220 d5.27 Col Nebraska

YEAR	TM	LG	G	AB	R	H	2B	3B	HR	RBI	BB-IB	HP	SO	AVG	OBP	SLG	AOPS	ABR	SB-CS	FA	FR	RNG	THR	GAMES AT POSITION	DL	BFW
2005	Oak	A	109	375	54	103	21	0	15	58	50-1	1	52	.275	.355	.451	113	8	0-1	.994	-3	87	118	1b101,D5		-0.4

JOHNSON, DARRELL
Darrell Dean B8.25.1928 Horace NE D5.3.2004 Fairfield CA BR/TR/6-1/180* d4.20 M8/C8

YEAR	TM	LG	G	AB	R	H	2B	3B	HR	RBI	BB-IB	HP	SO	AVG	OBP	SLG	AOPS	ABR	SB-CS	FA	FR	RNG	THR	GAMES AT POSITION	DL	BFW
1952	StL	A	29	78	9	22	2	1	0	9	11	0	4	.282	.371	.333	94	0	0-0	.990	1	103	137	C22		0.2
	Chi	A	22	37	3	4	0	0	0	1	5	0	9	.108	.214	.108	-8	-5	1-0	.955	2	89	125	C21		-0.3
	Year		51	115	12	26	2	1	0	10	16	0	13	.226	.321	.261	62	-6	1-0	.974	2	98	132	C43		-0.1
1957	NY	A	21	46	4	10	1	0	1	8	3-0	1	10	.217	.275	.304	61	-3	0-0	1.000	3	115	176	C20		0.1
1958	NY	A	5	16	1	4	0	0	0	1	1-0	0	2	.250	.250	.250	39	-1	0-0	1.000	1	108	229	C4		-0.1
1960	StL	N	8	2	0	0	0	0	0	0	1-0	0	0	.000	.333	.000	1	0	0-0	1.000	0	60	0	C8		-0.1
1961	Phi	N	21	61	4	14	1	0	0	3	3-0	1	8	.230	.277	.246	41	-5	0-0	.982	1	71	223	C21		0.0
	†Cin	N	20	54	3	17	2	0	1	6	1-0	0	2	.315	.321	.407	92	-1	0-0	1.000	2	59	184	C20		-0.3
	Year		41	115	7	31	3	0	1	9	4-0	1	10	.270	.298	.322	65	-6	0-0	.991	3	65	204	C41		0.2
1962	Cin	N	2	4	0	0	0	0	0	0	2-1	0	0	.000	.333	.000	-2	0	0-0	1.000	1	44	220	C2		-0.1
	Bal	A	6	22	0	4	0	0	0	1	0-0	0	4	.182	.182	.182	-2	-3	0-0	1.000	-2	70	171	C6		0.1
Total	6		134	320	24	81	6	2	2	28	26-1	2	39	.234	.294	.278	57	-18	1-0	.988	8	85	171	C124		-0.6

JOHNSON, DAVEY
David Allen B1.30.1943 Orlando FL BR/TR/6-1/180(170-182) d4.13 M14 Col Texas A&M-Commerce

YEAR	TM	LG	G	AB	R	H	2B	3B	HR	RBI	BB-IB	HP	SO	AVG	OBP	SLG	AOPS	ABR	SB-CS	FA	FR	RNG	THR	GAMES AT POSITION	DL	BFW
1965	Bal	A	20	47	5	8	1	0	0	1	5-0	0	6	.170	.245	.234	38	-4	3-0	.929	1	113	61	3b9,2b3,S2		-0.2
1966	†Bal	A	131	501	47	129	20	3	7	56	31-3	1	64	.257	.298	.351	88	-8	3-4	.971	-4	98	95	2b126,S3		-0.1
1967	Bal	A	148	510	62	126	30	3	10	64	59-10	4	82	.247	.325	.376	109	7	4-5	.981	-2	96	97	2b144,3b3		1.8
1968	Bal	A★	145	504	50	122	24	4	9	56	44-5	5	80	.242	.308	.359	102	1	7-3	.978	-5	99	103	2b127,S34		1.1
1969	†Bal	A★	142	511	52	143	34	1	7	57	57-2	3	52	.280	.351	.391	108	7	1-3	.990	1	98	118	2b142,S2		1.5
1970	†Bal	A★	149	530	68	149	27	1	10	53	66-8	0	68	.281	.360	.392	106	6	2-1	.990	1	98	118	2b149,S2		1.8
1971	†Bal	A★	142	510	67	144	26	1	18	72	51-5	5	55	.282	.351	.443	123	16	3-1	.984	4	100	125	2b140		3.1
1972	Bal	A	118	376	31	83	22	3	5	32	52-8	4	68	.221	.320	.335	92	-2	1-1	.990	10	103	127	2b116		1.7
1973	Atl	N★	157	559	84	151	25	0	43	99	81-9	3	93	.270	.370	.546	140	31	5-3	.966	-17	94	97	2b156		2.6
1974	Atl	N	136	454	56	114	18	0	15	62	75-6	3	59	.251	.358	.390	106	6	1-2	.993	-4	116	113	1b73,2b71		0.0
1975	Atl	N	1	1	0	1	0	0	0	1	0-0	0	0	1.000	1.000	2.000	695	1	0-0	—	0			/H		0.1
1977	†Phi	N	78	156	23	50	9	1	8	36	23-1	2	20	.321	.408	.545	147	11	1-1	1.000	-1	79	112	1b43,2b9,3b6	16	1.0
1978	Phi	N	44	89	14	17	2	0	2	14	10-0	2	19	.191	.284	.281	58	-5	0-0	.930	-3	92	105	2b15,3b9,1b7		-0.8
	Chi	N	24	49	5	15	1	1	2	6	5-0	2	9	.306	.393	.490	130	2	0-0	.839	-1	108	57	3b12		0.1
	Year		68	138	19	32	3	1	4	20	15-0	4	28	.232	.323	.355	85	-3	0-0	.844	-4	94	35	3b21,2b15,1b7		-0.7
Total	13		1435	4797	564	1252	242	18	136	609	559-57	40	675	.261	.340	.404	110	69	33-25	.980	-20	98	111	2b1198,1b123,S43,3b39	16	13.7

JOHNSON, DERON
Deron Roger B7.17.1938 San Diego CA D4.23.1992 Poway CA BR/TR/6-2/209* d9.20 C13 OF(216/1/32)

YEAR	TM	LG	G	AB	R	H	2B	3B	HR	RBI	BB-IB	HP	SO	AVG	OBP	SLG	AOPS	ABR	SB-CS	FA	FR	RNG	THR	GAMES AT POSITION	DL	BFW
1960	NY	A	6	4	0	2	1	0	0	0	0-0	0	0	.500	.500	.750	247	-1	0-0	.750	-1	99	0	3b5		0.0
1961	NY	A	13	19	1	2	0	0	0	0	2-0	0	5	.105	.182	.105	-20	-3	0-0	1.000	2	158	0	3b8		0.0
	KC	A	83	283	31	61	11	3	8	42	14-1	1	44	.216	.252	.360	61	-17	0-1	.948	5	97	146	O59(28/1/30),3b19,1b3		-1.6
	Year		96	302	32	63	11	3	8	44	16-1	1	49	.209	.247	.344	57	-20	0-1	.948	6	97	146	O59(28/1/30),3b27,1b3		-1.8
1962	KC	A	17	19	1	2	1	0	0	3	3-0	0	8	.105	.227	.158	6	-3	0-0	1.000	-1	0	0	1b2,3b2,O2R		-0.3
1964	Cin	N	140	477	63	130	24	4	21	79	37-0	2	98	.273	.326	.472	118	11	4-3	.990	4	107	99	1b131,O10L/3		0.7
1965	Cin	N	159	616	92	177	30	7	32	130	52-9	2	97	.287	.340	.515	129	23	0-4	.948	-12	85	96	3b159		0.9
1966	Cin	N	142	505	75	130	25	3	24	81	39-5	2	87	.257	.309	.461	103	2	1-2	.980	-8	95	68	O106L,1b71,3b18		-1.4
1967	Cin	N	108	361	39	81	18	1	13	53	22-2	2	104	.224	.270	.388	78	-10	0-1	.997	-4	86	84	1b81,3b24		-2.1
1968	Atl	N	127	342	29	71	11	1	8	33	35-2	3	79	.208	.285	.316	80	-8	0-1	.996	-3	87	120	1b81,3b21		-1.9
1969	Phi	N	138	475	51	121	19	4	17	80	60-4	0	111	.255	.333	.419	114	9	4-2	1.000	-10	79	28	O72L,3b50,1b18		-0.7
1970	Phi	N	159	574	66	147	28	3	27	93	72-7	0	132	.256	.338	.456	114	10	0-0	.995	-10	71	83	1b154,3b3		-1.2
1971	Phi	N	158	582	74	154	29	0	34	95	72-8	2	146	.265	.347	.490	134	26	0-1	.995	-4	100	111	1b136,3b22		1.2
1972	Phi	N	96	230	19	49	4	1	9	31	26-4	3	69	.213	.298	.357	84	-5	0-1	.982	-3	82	98	1b62		1.2
1973	Phi	N	12	36	3	6	2	0	1	5	5-0	1	10	.167	.279	.306	62	-2	0-0	.976	-3	101	137	1b10	16	-1.4
	†Oak	A	131	464	61	114	14	2	19	81	59-7	1	116	.246	.330	.407	112	7	0-0	.976	-2	101	137	1b91		-0.3
1974	Oak	A	50	174	16	34	1	2	11	34	11-2	0	37	.195	.239	.345	72	-8	1-0	.991	-2	66	70	1b28,D23	15	-1.3
	Mil	A	49	152	14	23	0	0	6	18	21-2	0	41	.151	.253	.289	56	-9	0-1	.833	-4	144	300	D46,1b2		-1.1
	Bos	A	11	25	0	3	0	0	0	1	0-0	0	6	.120	.115	.120	-29	-4	0-0	—	0			D8		-0.5
	Year		110	351	30	60	4	2	13	43	32-4	0	84	.171	.237	.305	57	-21	1-0	.983	-6	69	80	D77,1b30		-2.9
1975	Chi	A	148	555	66	129	25	1	18	72	48-0	1	117	.232	.292	.378	88	-10	2-0	.994	-2	80	82	D93,1b55		0.2
	Bos	A	3	15	1	2	0	0	0	0	0-0	0	6	.400	.667	.400	313	3	0-0	1.000	-1	0	134	1b2/D		-1.9
	Year		151	565	68	135	25	1	19	75	50-0	1	117	.239	.300	.388	92	-7	2-0	.994	-1	0	134	1b2/D		0.2
1976	Bos	A	15	38	3	5	1	1	0	5	5-1	0	9	.132	.233	.211	27	-4	0-1	1.000	-1	40	110	1b5,D9		-0.5
Total	16		1765	5941	706	1447	247	33	245	923	585-54	20	1318	.244	.311	.420	102	9	11-18	.993	-53	85	97	1b880,3b332,D287,O249L	31	-13.4

YEAR	TM LG	G	AB	R	H	2B	3B	HR	RBI	BB-IB	HP	SO	AVG	OBP	SLG	AOPS	ABR	SB-CS	FA	FR	RNG	THR	GAMES AT POSITION	DL	BFW

JOHNSON, DON Donald Spore "Pep" B12.7.1911 Chicago IL D4.6.2000 Laguna Beach CA BR/TR/6-0/170 d9.26 f-Ernie Col Oregon St.

1943	Chi N	10	42	5	8	2	0	0	4		0	4	.190	.227	.238	35	-4	0	.957	2	105	126	2b10		-0.1
1944	Chi N☆	154	608	50	169	37	1	2	71	28	1	48	.278	.311	.352	87	-11	8	.947	-1	100	94	2b154		-0.4
1945	†Chi N✱	138	557	94	168	23	2	2	58	32	3	34	.302	.343	.361	98	-2	9	.975	-5	108	111	2b138		2.0
1946	Chi N	83	314	37	76	10	1	1	19	26	2	39	.242	.306	.290	71	-12	6	.981	-9	96	72	2b83		-1.8
1947	Chi N	120	402	33	104	17	2	3	26	24	1	45	.259	.302	.333	71	-18	2	.970	-2	100	108	2b108,3b6		-1.4
1948	Chi N	6	12	0	3	0	0	0	0	0	0	1	.250	.250	.250	37	-1	1	1.000	-1	53	235	2b2,3b2		-0.2
Total	6	511	1935	219	528	89	6	8	175	112	8	171	.273	.315	.337	83	-48	26	.966	4	102	95	2b495,3b8		-1.9

JOHNSON, ED Edwin Cyril B3.31.1899 Morganfield KY D7.3.1975 Morganfield KY BL/TR/5-9/160 d9.26

| 1920 | Was A | 4 | 13 | 1 | 3 | 0 | 0 | 0 | 2 | 3 | 0 | 2 | .231 | .375 | .231 | 65 | 0 | 0 | .625 | -2 | 66 | 0 | O4R | | -0.2 |

JOHNSON, ELMER Elmer Ellsworth "Hickory" B6.12.1884 Beard IN D10.31.1966 Hollywood FL BR/TR/5-9/185 d4.24

| 1914 | NY N | 11 | 12 | 0 | 2 | 1 | 0 | 0 | 4 | 5 | 0 | 3 | .167 | .231 | .250 | 44 | -1 | 0 | .947 | -1 | 119 | 70 | C11 | | -0.1 |

JOHNSON, ERIK Erik Anthony B10.11.1965 Oakland CA BR/TR/5-11/175* [SFN87 18/464] d7.8 Col California-Santa Barbara

1993	SF N	4	5	1	2	2	0	0	0	0-0	0	1	.400	.400	.800	219	-1	0-0	1.000	-1	0	0	2b2/3S		0.0
1994	SF N	5	13	0	2	0	0	0	0	0-0	0	4	.154	.154	.154	-20	-2	0-0	1.000	0	95	317	2b2/S		-0.2
Total	2	9	18	1	4	2	0	0	0	0-0	0	5	.222	.222	.333	45	-1	0-0	1.000	-0	78	259	2b4,S2/3		-0.2

JOHNSON, ERNIE Ernest Rudolph B4.29.1888 Chicago IL D5.1.1952 Monrovia CA BL/TR/5-9/151 d8.5 s-Don

1912	Chi A	21	42	7	11	0	1	0	5	1	0		.262	.279	.310	70	-2	0	.984	2	112	91	S16		0.1
1915	StL F	152	512	58	123	18	10	7	67	46	2	35	.240	.305	.355	81	-21	32	.942	16	102	117	S152		0.6
1916	StL A	74	236	29	54	9	3	0	19	30	3	23	.229	.323	.292	89	-2	13	.936	-3	106	90	S60,3b12		-0.1
1917	StL A	80	199	28	49	6	2	2	20	12	2	16	.246	.296	.327	93	-3	13	.924	9	105	51	S39,2b18,3b14		1.0
1918	StL A	29	34	7	9	1	0	0	0	0	1	2	.265	.286	.294	77	-1	4	.821	-2	100	47	S11/3		-0.3
1921	Chi A	142	613	93	181	28	7	1	51	29	1	24	.295	.328	.369	78	-21	22-13	.947	21	112	115	S141		1.4
1922	Chi A	144	603	85	153	17	3	0	56	40	4	30	.254	.304	.292	56	-39	21-18	.952	-1	101	103	S141		-2.5
1923	Chi A	12	53	5	10	2	0	0	1	3	1	5	.189	.246	.226	25	-6	2-1	.922	-2	89	137	S12		-0.6
	†NY A	19	38	6	17	1	1	0	8	1	0	1	.447	.462	.605	176	4	0-0	.977	-1	80	97	S15/3		0.3
	Year	31	91	11	27	3	1	1	9	4	1	6	.297	.333	.385	88	-2	2-1	.944	-3	85	121	S27/3		-0.3
1924	NY A	64	119	24	42	4	3	2	12	11	1	7	.353	.412	.597	158	9	1-6	.955	-1	102	94	2b27,S9,3b2		-1.0
1925	NY A	76	170	30	48	5	1	5	17	8	1	10	.282	.315	.412	85	-5	6-3	.955	-8	95	100	2b34,S28,3b2		-0.4
Total	10	813	2619	372	697	91	36	19	256	181	15	153	.266	.317	.350	80	-87	114-41	.944	31	103	105	S624,2b79,3b32		

JOHNSON, FRANK Frank Herbert B7.22.1942 El Paso TX BR/TR/6-1/155* d9.7

1966	SF N	15	32	2	7	0	0	0	2	2-0	0	7	.219	.265	.219	35	-3	0-1	1.000	-1	91	0	O13(8/2/7)		-0.5
1967	SF N	8	10	3	3	0	0	0	0	1-0	0	2	.300	.364	.300	93	0	0-0	.889	0	152	0	O3(2/1/1)		-1.3
1968	SF N	67	174	11	33	2	0	1	7	12-2	1	23	.190	.246	.218	40	-13	1-0	.944	1	105	73	3b36,O8(4/5/0),S5,2b3		-0.2
1969	SF N	7	10	2	1	0	0	0	0	0-0	0	1	.100	.100	.100	-44	-2	0-0	1.000	0	115	0	O7(5/1/1)		-0.4
1970	SF N	67	161	25	44	1	2	3	31	19-3	2	18	.273	.357	.360	94	-1	1-1	.979	-0	100	110	O33(29/1/4),1b27		-1.3
1971	SF N	32	49	4	4	1	0	0	5	3-0	0	9	.082	.132	.102	-33	-9	0-0	.975	-2	28	73	1b9,O4(3/0/1)		-0.7
Total	6	196	436	47	92	4	2	4	43	37-5	3	60	.211	.277	.257	52	-28	2-2	.979	-2	103	56	O68(51/10/14),1b36,3b36,S5,2b3		-3.7

JOHNSON, GARY Gerald Clyde B10.29.1975 Palo Alto CA BL/TL/6-3/210 [AnaA99 19/581] d4.26 Col Brigham Young/California

| 2003 | Ana A | 5 | 8 | 1 | 3 | 1 | 0 | 0 | 0 | 1-0 | 0 | 3 | .375 | .444 | .500 | 155 | 1 | 0-0 | 1.000 | 0 | 139 | 0 | O4(2/0/2) | | 0.1 |

JOHNSON, HOWARD Howard Michael B11.29.1960 Clearwater FL BB/TR/5-11/178(175-195) [DetA79*S1/12] d4.14 OF(99/86/36)

1982	Det A	54	155	23	49	5	0	4	14	16-1	1	30	.316	.384	.426	121	5	7-4	.901	-7	70	111	3b33,D10,O9(3/1/5)		-0.3
1983	Det A	27	66	11	14	0	0	3	5	7-0	1	10	.212	.297	.348	79	-2	0-0	.851	-1	63	67	3b21,D2		-0.4
1984	†Det A	116	355	43	88	14	1	12	50	40-1	1	67	.248	.324	.394	98	-1	10-6	.944	-11	87	101	3b108,S9/1O(1/1/0)D		-1.3
1985	NY N	126	389	38	94	18	4	11	46	34-10	0	78	.242	.300	.393	95	-4	6-4	.941	-10	85	131	3b45,S34/OL		-1.6
1986	†NY N	88	220	30	54	14	0	10	39	31-8	1	64	.245	.341	.445	118	6	8-1	.903	-2	106	191	3b45,S34/OL	21	0.7
1987	NY N	157	554	93	147	22	1	36	99	83-18	5	113	.265	.364	.504	133	27	32-10	.938	-16	91	95	3b140,S38,O2L		1.5
1988	†NY N	148	495	85	114	21	1	24	68	86-25	1	104	.230	.343	.422	125	18	23-7	.951	-13	83	95	3b143,S31		1.1
1989	NY N★	153	571	104	164	41	3	36	101	77-8	1	126	.287	.369	.559	170	52	41-8	.910	-40	69	75	3b143,S21		1.7
1990	NY N	154	590	89	144	37	3	23	90	69-12	1	100	.244	.319	.434	106	5	34-8	.913	-2	92	92	3b92,S73		3.4
1991	NY N★	156	564	108	146	34	4	38	117	78-12	1	120	.259	.342	.535	146	34	30-16	.927	-3	89	70	3b104,O30R,S28		-1.0
1992	NY N	100	350	48	78	19	0	7	43	55-5	2	79	.223	.329	.337	91	-2	22-5	.981	-9	88	105	O98(16/84/1)	64	0.3
1993	NY N	72	235	32	56	8	2	7	26	43-3	0	43	.238	.354	.379	98	1	6-4	.944	2	104	105	3b67	94	-0.9
1994	Col N	93	227	30	48	10	2	10	40	39-2	0	73	.211	.323	.405	77	-8	11-3	.979	-1	95	66	O62L/1		-0.8
1995	Chi N	87	169	26	33	4	1	7	22	34-0	1	46	.195	.330	.355	82	-4	1-1	.926	-4	98	94	3b34,O13L,2b8,1b3/S	179	4.6
Total	14	1531	4940	760	1229	247	22	228	760	692-105	17	1053	.249	.340	.446	118	127	231-77	.929	-114	87	94	3b1031,S273,O217L,D16,2b8,1b5		

JOHNSON, SPUD John Ralph B1860 Can BL/TL/5-9/175 d4.18

1889	Col AA	116	459	91	130	14	10	2	79	39	12	47	.283	.355	.370	112	8	34	.879	-4	108	76	O69R,3b44,1b2/S		0.4
1890	Col AA	135	538	106	186	23	18	1	113	48	10		.346	.409	.461	168	46	43	.926	-13	55	24	O135(96/0/39)		2.7
1891	Cle N	80	327	49	84	8	3	1	46	22	8	23	.257	.319	.309	80	-9	16	.872	-4	84	46	O79R/1		-1.3
Total	3	331	1324	246	400	45	31	4	238	109	30	70	.302	.368	.392	125	45	93	.899	-21	75	42	O283(96/0/187),3b44,1b3/S		

JOHNSON, KEITH Keith B4.17.1971 Hanford CA BR/TR/5-11/200 [LAN92 4/115] d4.17 Col Pacific (CA)

| 2000 | Ana A | 6 | 4 | 2 | 2 | 0 | 0 | 0 | 0 | 0-0 | 0 | 0 | .500 | .667 | .500 | 196 | 1 | 0-0 | 1.000 | 1 | 0 | 0 | 1b3,2b2/S | | 0.2 |

JOHNSON, KELLY Kelly Andrew B2.22.1981 Austin TX BL/TR/6-1/205 d5.29

| 2005 | †Atl N | 87 | 290 | 46 | 70 | 12 | 3 | 9 | 40 | 40-1 | 1 | 75 | .241 | .334 | .397 | 89 | -5 | 2-1 | 1.000 | 7 | 114 | 135 | O79L/D | | -0. |

JOHNSON, LANCE Kenneth Lance B7.6.1963 Cincinnati OH BL/TL/5-11/160* [StLN84 6/139] d7.10 Col South Alabama

1987	†StL N	33	59	4	13	2	1	0	7	4-1	0	6	.220	.270	.288	47	-5	6-1	.931	-2	89	0	O25(3/6/17)		-0.
1988	Chi A	33	124	11	23	4	1	0	6	6-0	0	11	.185	.223	.234	28	-12	6-2	.970	-5	76	71	O31C/D		-1.
1989	Chi A	50	180	28	54	8	2	0	16	17-0	0	24	.300	.360	.367	107	2	16-3	.983	1	119	0	O45(42/8/0)/D		0.
1990	Chi A	151	541	76	154	18	9	1	51	33-2	1	45	.285	.325	.370	93	-7	36-22	.973	-3	100	73	O148(6/148/0)/D		-1.
1991	Chi A	159	588	72	161	14	13	0	49	26-2	1	58	.274	.304	.342	80	-19	26-11	.995	6	105	136	O157(0/157/2)		0.
1992	Chi A	157	567	67	158	15	12	3	47	34-4	1	33	.279	.318	.363	92	-9	41-14	.987	-1	98	121	O157C		1.
1993	†Chi A	147	540	75	168	18	14	0	47	36-1	0	33	.311	.354	.396	103	1	35-7	.980	9	114	90	O146C		1.
1994	Chi A	106	412	56	114	11	14	3	54	26-5	2	23	.277	.321	.393	84	-12	26-6	1.000	7	119	19	O103C/D		0.
1995	Chi A	142	607	98	186	18	12	10	57	32-2	1	31	.306	.341	.445	102	-1	40-6	.991	-1	98	119	O140C/D		3.
1996	NY N★	160	682	117	227	31	21	9	69	33-8	1	40	.333	.362	.479	127	22	50-12	.971	-1	105	111	O157C		0.
1997	NY N	72	265	43	82	10	6	1	24	33-2	0	21	.309	.385	.404	112	5	15-10	.975	-1	100	125	O66C	45	0
	Chi N	39	145	17	44	6	2	4	15	9-1	0	10	.303	.342	.455	104	0	5-2	.963	-1	109	0	O39C/D		0.
	Year	111	410	60	126	16	8	5	39	42-3	0	31	.307	.370	.422	109	5	20-12	.971	-2	103	83	O105C/D		0.
1998	†Chi N	85	304	51	85	8	4	2	21	26-1	0	22	.280	.335	.352	79	-10	10-6	.975	-4	91	112	O78C	77	-1
1999	Chi N	95	335	46	87	11	6	1	21	37-0	0	20	.260	.332	.337	71	-15	13-3	.988	6	115	132	O91C	72	-0
2000	NY A	18	30	6	9	1	0	0	0	0-0	0	7	.300	.300	.333	61	-2	2-0	1.000	-1	51	0	O4(2/0/2),D2	194	-1
Total	14	1447	5379	767	1565	175	117	34	486	352-29	7	384	.291	.334	.386	94	-62	327-105	.983	13	104	96	O1387(53/1327/21),D8		

JOHNSON, LAMAR Lamar B9.2.1950 Bessemer AL BR/TR/6-2/225(207-232) [ChiA68 3/54] d5.18 C9

1974	Chi A	10	29	1	10	0	0	2	2-0		0	3	.345	.333	.345	96	0	0-0	1.000	-0	67	159	1b7,D3		-0
1975	Chi A	8	30	2	6	3	0	1	2	1-0	0	5	.200	.226	.400	73	-1	0-0	.960	-1	63	82	1b6,D2		-0
1976	Chi A	82	222	29	71	11	1	4	33	19-1	2	37	.320	.372	.432	136	10	2-1	.983	-1	100	87	D35,1b34/OL		0
1977	Chi A	118	374	52	113	12	5	18	65	24-3	0	53	.302	.342	.505	128	13	1-1	.990	2	113	86	D68,1b45		0
1978	Chi A	148	498	52	136	23	2	8	72	43-2	2	46	.273	.329	.376	98	-1	6-5	.992	4	114	91	1b108,D36		1
1979	Chi A	133	479	60	148	19	3	12	74	41-1	2	56	.309	.363	.449	118	13	8-2	.990	5	129	102	1b80,D66		0
1980	Chi A	147	541	51	150	26	3	13	81	47-5	0	53	.277	.331	.409	103	2	2-3	.990	4	121	108	1b36,D2		0
1981	Chi A	41	134	10	37	6	0	1	15	5-1	0	14	.276	.298	.351	89	-2	0-0	.982	-2	56	59	D77,1b12		-0
1982	Tex A	105	324	37	84	11	0	7	38	31-0	1	46	.259	.326	.358	92	-1	1-1	.989	9	112	92	1b422,D326/OL		-0
Total	9	792	2631	294	755	122	12	64	381	211-13	7	307	.287	.338	.415	109	30	22-19	.989	9	112	92	1b422,D326/OL		

YEAR	TM	LG	G	AB	R	H	2B	3B	HR	RBI	BB-IB	HP	SO	AVG	OBP	SLG	AOPS	ABR	SB-CS	FA	FR	RNG	THR	GAMES AT POSITION	DL	BFW

JOHNSON, LARRY Larry Doby B8.17.1950 Cleveland OH BR/TR/6-0/185* [CleA68 9/186] d10.3

1972	Cle	A	1	2	0	1	0	0	0	0	0-0	0	1	.500	.500	.500	191		0-0	1.000	0	0	0	/C		
1974	Cle	A	1	0	1	0	0	0	0	0	0-0	0		—	—	—		0	0-0	—	0			/R		0.1
1975	Mon	N	1	3	0	1	1	0	0	0	1-0	0	1	.333	.500	.667	211	0	0-0	1.000	0			/C		0.0
1976	Mon	N	6	13	0	2	1	0	0	1	1-0	0	2	.154	.154	.231	8	-2	0-0	1.000	-0	54	0	C5		0.0
1978	Chi	A	3	8	0	1	0	0	0	0	1-0	0	4	.125	.222	.125	0	-1	0-0	.857	-1	57	70	C5		-0.2
Total	5		12	26	1	5	2	0	0	1	2-0	0	8	.192	.250	.269	45	-2	0-0	.975	-1	47	120	C2/D		-0.3

JOHNSON, LOU Louis Brown "Slick" B9.22.1934 Lexington KY BR/TR/5-11/175* d4.17 Col Kentucky St.

1960	Chi	N	34	68	6	14	2	1	0	5	5-1	1	19	.206	.270	.265	48	-5	3-1	1.000	4	122	257	O25(8/4/13)		-0.2
1961	LA	N	1	0	0	0	0	0	0	0	0-0	0	0	—	—	—		0	0-0	—	-0	0	0	/OL		0.0
1962	Mil	N	61	117	22	33	4	5	2	13	11-0	1	27	.282	.349	.453	116	2	6-1	1.000	-0	101	47	O55(38/20/1)		0.2
1965	†LA	N	131	468	57	121	24	1	12	58	24-8	16	81	.259	.315	.391	105	3	15-6	.985	-2	99	45	O128(124/11/3)		-0.5
1966	†LA	N	152	526	71	143	20	2	17	73	21-4	14	75	.272	.316	.414	110	6	8-10	.985	4	107	86	O148(104/2/65)		-0.1
1967	LA	N	104	330	39	89	14	1	11	41	24-5	7	52	.270	.330	.418	124	10	4-3	.976	3	105	128	O91(81/1/11)		0.8
1968	Chi	N	62	205	14	50	14	3	1	14	6-2	7	23	.244	.289	.356	87	-3	3-1	.970	-5	97	0	O57(1/0/56)		-1.3
	Cle	A	65	202	25	52	11	1	5	23	9-2	4	24	.257	.298	.396	112	2	6-1	.989	2	101	166	O57(41/0/20)		0.3
1969	Cal	A	67	133	10	27	8	0	0	9	10-1	3	19	.203	.272	.263	53	-8	5-1	.935	-1	102	86	O44(23/0/23)		-1.0
Total	8		677	2049	244	529	97	14	48	232	110-23	53	320	.258	.311	.389	103	7	50-24	.981	5	103	85	O606(421/38/192)	42	-1.8

JOHNSON, MARK Mark Landon B9.12.1975 Wheat Ridge CO BL/TR/6-0/185(185-200) [ChiA94 1/26] d9.14

1998	Chi	A	7	23	2	2	0	0	0	1	2-0	0	8	.087	.125	.261	-3	-4	0-0	1.000	0	219	99	C7		-0.3
1999	Chi	A	73	207	27	47	11	0	4	16	36-0	1	58	.227	.344	.338	75	-7	3-1	.993	2	117	92	C72,D2		0.0
2000	Chi	A	75	213	29	48	11	0	3	23	27-0	1	40	.225	.315	.319	59	-13	3-2	.992	6	103	161	C74/D		-0.3
2001	Chi	A	61	173	21	43	6	1	5	18	23-1	2	31	.249	.338	.382	86	-3	2-1	.992	3	126	103	C61		0.3
2002	Chi	A	86	263	31	55	8	1	4	18	30-1	3	52	.209	.297	.293	56	-17	0-0	.994	-3	105	116	C85		-1.4
2003	Oak	A	13	27	3	3	1	0	0	3	3-0	1	4	.111	.219	.148	2	-4	0-0	1.000	2	108	85	C13		-0.2
2004	Mil	N	7	11	1	1	0	0	0	2	3-1	0	2	.091	.267	.091	4	-2	0-0	.952	-2	45	138	C5		-0.3
Total	7		322	917	114	199	37	4	16	81	123-3	9	195	.217	.313	.318	63	-50	8-4	.993	8	113	118	C317,D3		-2.2

JOHNSON, MARK Mark Patrick B10.17.1967 Worcester MA BL/TL/6-4/230* [PitN90 20/537] d4.26 Col Dartmouth

1995	Pit	N	79	221	32	46	6	1	13	28	37-2	2	66	.208	.326	.421	93	-2	5-2	.986	-4	82	101	1b70		-1.2
1996	Pit	N	127	343	55	94	24	0	13	47	44-3	2	64	.274	.361	.458	111	7	6-4	.994	6	126	92	1b100/OL		0.5
1997	Pit	N	78	219	30	47	10	0	4	29	43-1	2	78	.215	.345	.315	74	-7	1-1	.992	1	106	102	1b63/D		-1.1
1998	Ana	A	10	14	1	1	0	0	0	0	0-0	0	6	.071	.071	.071	-62	-3	0-0	1.000	-0	78	121	1b5,D2		-0.3
2000	NY	N	21	22	2	4	0	0	1	6	5-0	0	9	.182	.333	.318	70	-1	0-0	1.000	1	0	113	1b4/OLD		-0.1
2001	NY	N	71	118	17	30	6	1	6	23	16-1	0	31	.254	.338	.475	116	3	0-2	.991	-3	93	110	1b21,O19(12/0/7),D3		-0.3
2002	NY	N	42	51	5	7	4	0	1	4	9-0	0	18	.137	.267	.275	48	-4	0-0	.989	-0	97	84	1b15/OL		-0.5
Total	7		428	988	142	229	50	2	38	137	154-7	9	272	.232	.338	.402	93	-7	12-9	.991	-0	105	98	1b278,O22(15/0/7),D7		-3.0

JOHNSON, NICK Nicholas Robert B9.19.1978 Sacramento CA BL/TL/6-3/224* [NYA96 3/89] d8.21 [DL 2000 NY A 181]

2001	NY	A	23	67	6	13	2	0	2	8	4	15	.194	.308	.313	64	-3	0-0	1.000	-1	67	44	1b15,D6		-0.5
2002	†NY	A	129	378	56	92	15	0	15	58	48-5	12	98	.243	.347	.402	99	1	1-3	.988	2	114	95	1b78,D50,O2L	25	-0.6
2003	†NY	A	96	324	60	92	19	0	14	47	70-4	8	57	.284	.422	.472	138	23	5-2	.991	-2	87	92	1b60,D34	70	1.3
2004	Mon	N	73	251	35	63	16	0	7	33	40-2	3	58	.251	.359	.398	92	-1	6-3	.994	-3	88	118	1b73	98	-1.0
2005	Was	N	131	453	66	131	35	3	15	74	80-8	12	87	.289	.408	.479	141	32	3-8	.996	4	113	101	1b129	403	2.3
Total	5		452	1473	223	391	87	3	53	220	245-19	39	315	.265	.383	.437	117	52	15-16	.993	1	102	100	1b355,D90,O2L		1.5

JOHNSON, OTIS Otis L. B11.5.1883 Fowler IN D11.9.1915 Johnson City NY BB/TR/5-9/185 d4.12

| 1911 | NY | A | 71 | 209 | 21 | 49 | 9 | 6 | 3 | 36 | 39 | 3 | | .234 | .363 | .378 | 100 | 1 | 12 | .907 | -8 | 94 | 116 | S47,2b15,3b3 | | -0.4 |

JOHNSON, PAUL Paul Oscar B9.2.1896 N.Grosvenor Dale CT D2.14.1973 McAllen TX BR/TR/5-8/160 d9.13

1920	Phi	A	18	72	6	15	0	0	0	5	4	0	8	.208	.250	.208	22	-8	1-1	.933	-2	76	97	O18(13/4/1)		-1.1
1921	Phi	A	48	127	17	40	6	2	1	10	9	0	17	.315	.360	.417	97	-1	0-2	.969	-3	91	28	O32(6/24/2)		-0.6
Total	2		66	199	23	55	6	2	1	15	13	0	25	.276	.321	.342	71	-9	1-3	.958	-5	86	53	O50(19/28/3)		-1.7

JOHNSON, RANDY Randall Glenn B6.10.1956 Escondido CA BR/TR/6-1/190* [NYN78 11/263] d4.27 Col San Jose St.

1982	Atl	N	27	46	5	11	5	0	0	6	6-1	2	4	.239	.345	.348	94	0	0-1	.955	2	123	102	2b13,3b4		
1983	Atl	N	86	144	22	36	3	0	1	17	20-3	1	27	.250	.345	.292	73	-4	1-3	.991	8	110	204	3b53,2b4		0.2
1984	Atl	N	91	294	28	82	13	0	5	30	21-6	1	21	.279	.329	.374	91	-3	4-7	.939	6	117	110	3b81	19	0.2
Total	3		204	484	55	129	21	0	6	53	47-10	4	52	.267	.336	.347	86	-7	5-11	.956	16	115	136	3b138,2b17	19	0.4

JOHNSON, RANDY Randall Stuart B8.15.1958 Miami FL BL/TL/6-2/195* [ChiA79*3/62] d7.5 Col Miami-Dade Kendall (FL) CC

1980	Chi	A	12	20	0	4	0	0	0	3	2-0	1	4	.200	.280	.200	41	-2	0-0	—	-0	0	0	/1OLD		-0.2
1982	Min	A	89	234	26	58	10	0	10	33	30-2	0	46	.248	.325	.419	102	1	0-0	1.000	-0	71	0	D67,O2R		-0.2
Total	2		101	254	26	62	10	0	10	36	32-2	1	50	.244	.321	.402	97	-1	0-0	1.000	-0	85	0	D71,O3(1/0/2)/1		-0.4

JOHNSON, REED Reed Cameron B12.8.1976 Riverside CA BR/TR/5-10/180* [TorA99 17/523] d4.17 Col Cal St.-Fullerton

2003	Tor	A	114	412	79	121	21	2	10	52	20-1	20	67	.294	.353	.427	102	1	5-3	.977	-7	82	104	O111(53/5/71)		-1.0
2004	Tor	A	141	537	68	145	25	2	10	61	28-2	12	98	.270	.320	.380	77	-18	6-3	.989	0	98	121	O137(57/33/53),D4		-2.1
2005	Tor	A	142	398	55	107	21	6	8	58	22-1	16	82	.269	.332	.412	91	-5	5-6	.990	-3	94	88	O139(118/9/35)		-1.2
Total	3		397	1347	202	373	67	10	28	171	70-4	48	247	.277	.334	.404	89	-22	16-12	.986	-10	92	106	O387(228/47/159),D4		-4.3

JOHNSON, FOOTER Richard Allan "Treads" B2.15.1932 Dayton OH BL/TL/5-11/175 d6.15 Col Duke

| 1958 | Chi | N | 8 | 5 | 1 | 0 | 0 | 0 | 0 | 1 | 1.000 | .000 | .000 | -99 | -1 | 0-0 | — | 0 | | | /H | | -0.1 |

JOHNSON, BOB Robert Lee "Indian Bob" B11.26.1905 Pryor OK D7.6.1982 Tacoma WA BR/TR/6-0/180 d4.12 b-Roy OF(1592/162/24)

1933	Phi	A	142	535	103	155	44	4	21	93	85	0	74	.290	.387	.505	133	28	8-3	.952	-0	97	111	O142(127/1/15)		1.9
1934	Phi	A	141	547	111	168	26	6	34	92	58	4	60	.307	.375	.563	144	32	12-8	.967	9	107	147	O139L		3.0
1935	Phi	A★	147	582	103	174	29	5	28	109	78	2	76	.299	.384	.510	130	26	2-4	.946	4	106	107	O147L		1.9
1936	Phi	A	153	566	91	165	29	14	25	121	88	2	71	.292	.389	.525	126	22	6-6	.962	5	108	114	O131(131/1/0),2b22/1		1.7
1937	Phi	A	138	477	91	146	32	6	25	108	98	1	65	.306	.425	.556	148	38	9-7	.976	8	106	135	O133(129/6/0),2b2		3.6
1938	Phi	A★	152	563	115	176	27	9	30	113	87	2	73	.313	.406	.552	142	36	9-8	.963	8	106	145	O150(29/122/0),2b3/3		3.5
1939	Phi	A☆	150	544	115	184	30	9	23	114	99	1	59	.338	.440	.553	156	49	15-5	.967	9	108	145	O150(135/14/0)/2		4.8
1940	Phi	A	138	512	93	137	25	4	31	103	83	4	64	.268	.374	.514	130	23	8-2	.962	6	102	149	O136(116/13/8)		2.2
1941	Phi	A	149	552	98	152	30	4	22	107	95	1	75	.275	.385	.478	130	26	6-4	.990	7	105	161	O122(118/4/0),1b28		2.2
1942	Phi	A	149	550	78	160	35	7	13	80	82	1	61	.291	.384	.451	135	26	3-2	.963	5	102	157	O149(148/0/1)		2.5
1943	Was	A★	117	438	65	116	22	8	7	63	64	3	50	.265	.362	.400	127	16	11-5	.996	8	106	153	O88L,3b19,1b10		2.0
1944	Bos	A★	144	525	106	170	40	8	17	106	95	4	67	.324	.431	.528	175	57	2-7	.977	5	91	203	O142L		5.3
1945	Bos	A★	143	525	71	148	27	7	12	74	63	1	56	.280	.358	.425	124	16	5-3	.975	4	101	122	O140(140/1/0)		1.2
Total	13		1863	6920	1239	2051	396	95	288	1283	1075	24	851	.296	.393	.506	139	397	96-64	.968	79	104	143	O1769L,1b39,2b28,3b20		35.7

JOHNSON, BOB Robert Wallace B3.4.1936 Omaha NE BR/TR/5-10/175* d4.19

1960	KC	A	76	146	12	30	6	1	0	9	19-1	1	23	.205	.301	.253	51	-10	2-0	.947	0	96	91	S30,2b27,3b11		-0.6
1961	Was	A	61	224	27	66	13	1	6	28	19-2	1	26	.295	.350	.442	113	4	4-2	.956	-0	109	89	S57,2b2,3b2		0.9
1962	Was	A	135	466	58	134	20	2	12	43	32-1	1	50	.288	.334	.416	102	0	9-6	.944	-3	97	93	3b72,S50,2b3/OL		0.0
1963	Bal	A	82	254	34	75	10	0	8	32	18-0	1	35	.295	.347	.429	120	7	5-1	.987	2	107	122	2b50,1b8,S7,3b5		1.4
1964	Bal	A	93	210	18	52	8	3	9	29	9-1	1	37	.248	.281	.348	74	-8	0-1	.964	-9	80	65	S18,1b15,2b15/3OL		-1.7
1965	Bal	A	87	273	36	66	13	2	5	27	15-2	1	34	.242	.282	.359	80	-1	1-0	.996	-9	75	84	1b34,S23,3b13,2b5		-1.8
1966	Bal	A	71	157	13	34	5	0	1	10	12-1	1	24	.217	.276	.268	58	-8	0-1	.966	-2	102	105	2b20,1b17,3b3		-1.0
1967	Bal	A	4	3	1	1	0	0	0	1	0	.333	.500	.333	152	0	0-0		—	0		/H		-1.0
	NY	N	90	230	26	80	8	3	5	27	12-0	1	29	.348	.377	.474	145	13	1-1	.987	-1	95	107	2b39,1b23,S14/3		1.5
1968	Cin	N	16	15	2	4	0	0	0	3	2-0	1	4	.267	.313	.267	71	-1	0-0	.500	-1	92	0	S2/1		-0.2
	Atl	N	59	187	15	49	5	1	0	11	10-3	1	20	.262	.298	.299	80	-5	0-0	.948	5	116	114	3b48,2b6		0.0
1969	StL	N	75	202	17	53	5	1	0	12	11-3	1	22	.262	.299	.297	79	-5	0-0	.948	4	116	114	3b48,2b4,S2/1		-0.2
	Oak	A	51	67	5	23	1	0	1	9	3-1	1	4	.343	.375	.403	124	1	0-0	1.000	0	125	176	1b7,2b2		0.2

YEAR	TM LG	G	AB	R	H	2B	3B	HR	RBI	BB-IB	HP	SO	AVG	OBP	SLG	AOPS	ABR	SB-CS	FA	FR	RNG	THR	GAMES AT POSITION	DL	BFW
1970	Oak A	30	46	6	8	1	0	1	2	3-0	1	2	.174	.235	.261	39	-4	2-1	.952	1	137	86	3b6/1		-0.3
Total	11	874	2307	254	628	88	11	44	230	156-12	10	291	.272	.320	.377	95	-20	24-12	.956	-17	100	82	S201,2b167,3b166,1b107,O2L		-1.8

JOHNSON, RON Ronald David B3.23.1956 Long Beach CA BR/TR/6-3/215* [KCA78 24/595] d9.12 Col Cal St.-Fresno

																									0.0
1982	KC A	8	14	2	4	2	0	0	0	4-0	0	3	.286	.444	.429	140	1	0-0	.976	-0	74	80	1b7		-0.3
1983	KC A	9	27	2	7	0	0	0	1	3-0	0	1	.259	.333	.259	65	-1	0-0	.971	1	64	134	1b7,C2		-0.1
1984	Mon N	5	5	0	1	0	0	0	1	0-0	0	2	.200	.200	.200	13	-1	0-0	1.000	-0	0	0	1b2/OR		-0.4
Total	3	22	46	4	12	2	0	0	2	7-0	0	6	.261	.358	.304	84	-1	0-0	.974	-2	64	107	1b16,C2/OR		

JOHNSON, RONDIN Rondin Allen B12.16.1958 Bremerton WA BB/TR/5-10/160 [KCA80 6/146] d9.3 Col Washington

																									0.1
1986	KC A	11	31	1	8	0	0	0	3	2-0	0	3	.258	.258	.323	56	-2	0-0	1.000	3	135	94	2b11		

JOHNSON, RONTREZ Rontrez Demon B12.8.1976 Marshall TX BR/TR/5-10/180 [BosA95 16/438] d3.31

																									-0.1
2003	KC A	8	3	3	1	0	0	0	0	0-0	0	2	.333	.333	.333	72	0	0-0	.000	-1	0	0	O6C,D2		

JOHNSON, ROY Roy Cleveland B2.23.1903 Pryor OK D9.10.1973 Tacoma WA BL/TR/5-9/175 d4.18 b-Bob

																									1.1
1929	Det A	148	640	128	201	45	14	10	69	67	0	60	.314	.379	.475	118	17	20-16	.928	6	103	153	O146(91/37/23)		-1.4
1930	Det A	125	462	84	127	30	13	2	35	40	0	46	.275	.333	.409	85	-11	17-10	.936	5	106	153	O118(7/2/110)		0.4
1931	Det A	151	621	107	173	37	19	8	55	72	2	51	.279	.355	.438	104	3	33-21	.960	11	105	165	O150(0/5/148)		-0.8
1932	Det A	49	195	33	49	14	2	3	22	20	1	26	.251	.324	.390	81	-6	7-2	.929	-1	103	78	O48R		0.2
	Bos A	94	349	70	104	24	4	11	47	44	1	41	.298	.378	.484	125	14	13-4	.930	-8	86	85	O85(14/16/56)		1.0
	Year	143	544	103	153	38	6	14	69	64	2	67	.281	.359	.450	109	7	20-6	.930	-9	92	82	O133(14/16/104)		1.1
1933	Bos A	133	483	88	151	30	7	10	95	55	4	36	.313	.387	.466	126	19	13-10	.922	9	104	116	O125(26/10/95)		-0.4
1934	Bos A	143	569	85	182	43	10	7	119	54	3	36	.320	.379	.467	109	8	11-5	.948	-5	92	102	O137L		0.0
1935	Bos A	145	553	70	174	33	9	3	66	74	3	34	.315	.398	.423	105	7	11-12	.944	2	91	184	O142L		-0.5
1936	†NY A	63	147	21	39	8	2	1	19	21	1	14	.265	.361	.367	83	-4	3-1	.944	-0	105	74	O33(28/0/3)		-0.4
1937	NY A	12	51	5	15	3	0	0	6	3	0	2	.294	.333	.353	73	-2	1-0	.840	-2	85	0	O12L		0.0
	Bos N	85	260	24	72	8	3	3	22	38	0	29	.277	.369	.365	110	5	5	.965	-1	98	105	O63L/3		-0.7
	Bos N	7	29	2	5	0	0	0	1	1	0	5	.172	.200	.172	4	-4	1	.769	-2	67	0	O7L		
Total	10	1155	4359	717	1292	275	83	58	556	489	12	380	.296	.369	.437	107	46	135-81	.938	6	99	131	O1066(527/70/483)/3		-1.4

JOHNSON, ROY Roy Edward B6.27.1959 Parkin AR BL/TL/6-4/205(205-220) [MonN80 5/125] d7.3 Col Tennessee St.

																									-0.3
1982	Mon N	17	32	2	7	2	0	0	2	1-0	0	6	.219	.235	.281	44	-2	1-0	1.000	-0	108	0	O11(0/9/3)		-0.2
1984	Mon N	16	33	2	5	2	0	1	2	7-0	1	10	.152	.300	.303	73	-1	0-0	.938	-1	87	0	O10(9/0/1)		-0.2
1985	Mon N	3	5	0	0	0	0	0	0	0-0	0	3	.000	.000	.000	-99	-1	0-0	—	-0	0	0	O3(0/1/2)		-0.7
Total	3	36	70	4	12	4	0	1	4	8-0	1	19	.171	.253	.271	48	-4	1-0	.971	-2	90	0	O24(9/10/6)		

JOHNSON, STAN Stanley Lucius B2.12.1937 Dallas TX BL/TL/5-10/180* d9.18 Col San Francisco

																									-0.1
1960	Chi A	5	6	1	1	0	0	1	1	0-0	0	1	.167	.167	.667	116	0	0-1	1.000	-0	70	0	O2L		-0.1
1961	KC A	3	3	1	0	0	0	0	0	2-0	0	1	.000	.400	.000	17	0	0-0	—	-0	0	0	O2R		-0.2
Total	2	8	9	2	1	0	0	1	1	2-0	0	2	.111	.273	.444	89	0	0-1	1.000	-1	30	0	O4(2/0/2)		

JOHNSON, TIM Timothy Evald B7.22.1949 Grand Forks ND BL/TR/6-1/170(170-185) d4.24 M1/C4

																									-3.4
1973	Mil A	136	465	39	99	10	2	0	32	29-2	1	93	.213	.259	.243	43	-36	6-3	.962	-13	94	100	S135		-0.2
1974	Mil A	93	245	25	60	7	7	0	25	11-1	1	48	.245	.278	.331	75	-9	4-3	.970	-1	106	94	S64,2b26/3OLD		-1.4
1975	Mil A	38	85	12	12	1	0	0	2	6-0	0	17	.141	.198	.153	0	-11	3-0	1.000	-4	105	91	2b11,3b11,S10,1b2,D3	77	-1.3
1976	Mil A	105	273	25	75	4	3	0	14	19-0	2	32	.275	.327	.311	89	-4	4-1	.980	-14	93	76	2b100,3b17/1S		-0.6
1977	Mil A	30	33	5	2	1	0	0	2	5-1	0	10	.061	.179	.091	-22	-6	1-0	.929	-2	18	0	2b10,S6,3b4/OLD	49	-0.2
1978	Mil A	3	3	1	0	0	0	0	0	2-0	0	0	.000	.400	.000	21	0	0-1	1.000	-2	0	0	S2		-0.1
	Tor A	68	79	9	19	2	0	0	3	8-0	1	16	.241	.315	.266	65	-3	0-1	.975	1	95	57	S49,2b13		-0.3
	Year	71	82	10	19	2	0	0	3	10-0	1	16	.232	.319	.256	63	-4	0-1	.975	-2	89	53	S51,2b13		-0.5
1979	Tor A	43	86	6	16	2	-1	0	4	8-0	0	15	.186	.255	.233	32	-8	0-1	.958	3	87	138	2b25,3b9,1b7		-0.5
Total	7	516	1269	116	283	27	13	0	84	88-4	5	231	.223	.274	.265	55	-77	18-9	.965	-31	97	95	S267,2b185,3b42,1b10,D8,O2L	126	-7.7

JOHNSON, WALLACE Wallace Darnell B12.25.1956 Gary IN BB/TR/5-11/185(170-185) [MonN79 6/140] d9.8 C5 Col Indiana St.

																									0.0
1981	†Mon N	11	9	2	2	0	0	0	3	1-1	0	1	.222	.300	.444	106	-1	1-1	1.000	0	135	388	/2		-0.6
1982	Mon N	36	57	5	11	0	2	0	5	5-0	0	5	.193	.258	.263	44	-5	4-1	.952	-2	71	90	2b13		0.1
1983	Mon N	3	2	1	1	0	0	0	0	0-0	0	0	.500	.667	.500	228	-1	1-0	—	0			/H		-0.1
	SF N	7	8	0	1	0	0	0	1	0-0	0	0	.125	.125	.125	-31	-1	0-0	1.000	0	73	168	/2		0.0
	Year	10	10	1	2	0	0	0	1	0-0	0	0	.200	.273	.200	34	-1	1-0	1.000	0	73	168	/2		-0.1
1984	Mon N	17	24	3	5	0	0	0	4	5-0	0	4	.208	.345	.208	61	-1	0-0	.968	1	134	126	1b4		-0.5
1986	Mon N	61	127	13	36	3	1	1	10	7-0	0	9	.283	.321	.346	84	-3	6-3	.991	-0	98	89	1b27		-0.4
1987	Mon N	75	85	7	21	5	0	1	14	7-0	0	14	.247	.298	.341	68	-4	5-0	.972	-1	44	91	1b13/2		0.2
1988	Mon N	86	94	3	29	5	1	0	3	12-1	0	15	.309	.387	.383	116	3	0-2	.989	1	77	92	1b78		-0.4
1989	Mon N	85	114	9	31	3	1	2	17	7-0	0	12	.272	.309	.368	93	-1	1-0	.972	-1	77	92	1b7	15	-0.5
1990	Mon N	47	49	6	8	1	0	0	5	7-2	1	6	.163	.281	.245	48	-3	1-0	1.000	-1	0	285	1b78,2b16	15	-0.2
Total	9	428	569	52	145	17	6	5	59	52-4	1	58	.255	.316	.332	80	-14	19-7	.983	-5	86	98	1b78,2b16		-2.3

JOHNSON, BILL William F. "Sleepy Bill" B9.1862 NJ D7.17.1942 Chester PA BL/TL/?/167 d6.27

																									-0.1
1884	Phi U	1	4	0	0	0	0	0	0	0			.000	.000	.000	-99	-1		—	-0	0	0	/OL		-0.5
1887	Ind N	11	42	3	8	0	0	0		1		6	.190	.209	.190	12	-5	5	.765	-1	120	0	O11R		0.2
1890	Bal AA	24	95	15	28	2	3	0	6	7	1		.295	.350	.379	110	1	8	.865	3	151	347	O24R		1.1
1891	Bal AA	129	480	101	130	13	14	2	79	89	4	55	.271	.389	.369	116	13	32	.877	3	120	103	O129(60/24/46)		-0.3
1892	Bal N	4	15	2	2	0	0	0	2	2	0		.133	.235	.133	12	-2	0	.667	-1	0	0	O4(1/0/3)		-0.1
Total	5	169	636	121	168	15	17	2	90	98	6	61	.264	.368	.351	105	6	45	.867	3	121	128	O169(62/24/84)		

JOHNSON, BILL William Lawrence B10.18.1892 Chicago IL D11.5.1950 Los Angeles CA BL/TR/5-11/170 d9.22

																									-0.1
1916	Phi A	4	15	1	4	1	0	0	1	0	0		.267	.267	.333	84	0	0	1.000	-1	70	0	O4C		-1.1
1917	Phi A	48	109	7	19	2	2	1	8	8	1	14	.174	.237	.257	51	-7	4	.900	-2	70	142	O30(2/1/27)		-1.2
Total	2	52	124	8	23	3	2	1	9	8	1	18	.185	.241	.266	55	-7	4	.909	-2	70	129	O34(2/5/27)		

JOHNSON, BILLY William Russell "Bull" B8.30.1918 Montclair NJ BR/TR/5-10/180* d4.22 Mil 1944-46

																									2.0
1943	†NY A	155	592	70	166	24	6	5	94	53	4	30	.280	.344	.367	107	5	3-5	.966	13	106	120	3b155		0.5
1946	NY A	85	296	51	77	14	5	4	35	31	2	42	.260	.334	.382	98	-1	1-0	.955	5	108	97	3b74		-1.1
1947	†NY A★	132	494	67	141	19	8	10	95	44	6	43	.285	.351	.417	114	8	1-2	.952	-17	81	54	3b132		0.9
1948	NY A	127	446	59	131	20	6	12	64	41	4	30	.294	.358	.446	114	7	0-0	.947	-3	94	122	3b118		-0.8
1949	NY A	113	329	48	82	11	3	8	56	48	2	44	.249	.348	.374	91	-5	1-0	.951	-3	93	95	3b81,1b21/2		-0.9
1950	NY A	108	327	44	85	16	2	6	40	42	1	30	.260	.346	.376	87	-6	1-0	.958	-3	94	113	3b100,1b5		-0.9
1951	NY A	15	40	5	12	3	0	0	4	7	0		.300	.404	.375	116	1	0-1	.960	-2	83	0	3b13		1.0
	StL N	124	442	52	116	23	1	14	64	46	6	49	.262	.340	.414	101	1	5-3	.976	10	115	106	3b124		-0.2
1952	StL N	94	282	23	71	10	2	2	34	34	3	21	.252	.339	.323	84	-5	1-0	.951	4	112	79	3b89		0.1
1953	StL N	11	5	0	1	0	0	0	1	0	0	1	.200	.333	.400	90	0	0-0	1.000	1	172	206	3b11		1.4
Total	9	964	3253	419	882	141	33	61	487	347	28	290	.271	.346	.391	102	5	13-11	.959	10	100	98	3b897,1b26/2		

JOHNSON, RUSS William Russell B2.22.1973 Baton Rouge LA BR/TR/5-10/180* [HouN94 S1/30] d4.8 Col Louisiana St.

																									-0.2
1997	†Hou N	21	60	7	18	1	0	2	9	6-0	0	14	.300	.364	.417	107	-2	1-1	.963	-2	93	99	3b14,2b3		0.1
1998	Hou N	8	13	2	3	1	0	0	0	1-0	1	5	.231	.333	.308	72	0	1-0	1.000	1	174	0	3b5/2		0.8
1999	†Hou N	83	156	24	44	10	0	3	23	20-0	0	31	.282	.358	.442	104	1	2-3	1.000	-4	109	201	S5,3b4,2b3		-0.0
2000	Hou N	26	45	4	8	1	0	0	3	2-0	0	5	.178	.213	.178	-0	-7	4-1	.967	9	135	108	3b49,2b18,S11		0.3
	TB A	74	185	28	47	8	0	2	17	25-0	0	30	.254	.344	.330	73	1	1-0	.922	-4	91	116	3b36,2b33,S6,D2	15	0.5
2001	TB A	85	248	32	73	19	2	4	33	34-0	1	57	.294	.380	.435	117	8	2-2	.984	-5	99	87	3b57,S2/2D	73	0.3
2002	TB A	45	111	15	24	7	0	1	12	16-1	1	26	.216	.320	.288	65	-5	5-2	1.000	-2	50	0	3b8,1b7,O3R/2D		-0.2
2005	NY A	22	14	4	5	0	0	0	1	0-0	0	4	.222	.300	.333	68	-1	0-0	1.000	-2	0	0	3b8,1b7,O3R	88	-0.3
Total	7	364	836	117	221	46	2	14	97	105-1	5	173	.264	.348	.374	89	-10	16-10	.957	0	103	120	3b179,2b75,S26,D10,1b7,O3R	88	

JOHNSTON, GREG Gregory Bernard B2.12.1955 Los Angeles CA BL/TL/6-0/175* [SFN75 12/272] d7.27 Col Citrus (CA) JC

																									-0.1
1979	SF N	42	74	5	15	2	0	1	7	2-0	0	17	.203	.224	.270	37	-7	0-0	.966	1	118	110	O17(13/1/5)		-0.2
1980	Min A	14	27	3	5	3	0	0	1	2-0	0	6	.185	.233	.296	43	-2	0-0	1.000	-0	106	0	O14C		-0.2

YEAR	TM LG	G	AB	R	H	2B	3B	HR	RBI	BB-IB	HP	SO	AVG	OBP	SLG	AOPS	ABR	SB-CS	FA	FR	RNG	THR	GAMES AT POSITION	DL	BFW
1981	Min A	7	16	2	2	0	0	0	0	2-0	0	5	.125	.222	.125	2	-2	0-0	1.000	0	76	307	O6C		-0.2
Total	3	63	117	10	22	5	0	1	8	6-0	0	26	.188	.226	.256	33	-11	0-0	.985	1	105	115	O37(13/21/5)		-1.1

JOHNSTON, JIMMY   James Harle B12.10.1889 Cleveland TN D2.14.1967 Chattanooga TN BR/TR/5-10/160 d5.3 C1 b-Doc OF(72/112/177)

YEAR	TM LG	G	AB	R	H	2B	3B	HR	RBI	BB-IB	HP	SO	AVG	OBP	SLG	AOPS	ABR	SB-CS	FA	FR	RNG	THR	GAMES AT POSITION	DL	BFW
1911	Chi A	1	2	0	0	0	0	0	2	0	0		.000	.000	.000	-99	-1	0	1.000	-0	100	0	/OC		-0.1
1914	Chi A	50	101	9	23	3	2	1	8	4	1	9	.228	.264	.327	76	-4	3	.929	4	119	246	O28(2/22/4),2b4		-0.1
1916	†Bro N	118	425	58	107	13	8	1	26	35	3	38	.252	.313	.327	94	-3	22-19	.964	4	104	119	O106(8/45/55)		-0.9
1917	Bro N	103	330	33	89	10	4	0	25	23	2	28	.270	.321	.324	96	-2	16	.958	0	103	90	O66(37/24/5),1b14,S4,2b3,3b3		-0.6
1918	Bro N	123	484	54	136	16	8	0	27	33	1	31	.281	.328	.347	106	3	22	.956	4	98	121	O96(20/5/75),1b21,3b4/2		0.2
1919	Bro N	117	405	56	114	11	4	1	23	29	3	26	.281	.334	.336	100	0	11	.960	-2	105	84	2b87,O14(1/8/6),1b2/S		-0.1
1920	†Bro N	155	635	87	185	17	12	1	52	43	2	23	.291	.338	.361	98	-2	19-15	.934	-7	96	88	3b146,O7R,S3		-0.7
1921	Bro N	152	624	104	203	41	14	5	56	45	1	26	.325	.372	.460	115	14	28-16	.935	7	103	120	3b150,S3		3.0
1922	Bro N	138	567	110	181	20	7	4	49	38	2	17	.319	.364	.400	98	-2	18-9	.947	0	97	105	2b62,S50,3b26		0.8
1923	Bro N	151	625	111	203	29	11	4	60	53	0	15	.325	.378	.424	115	14	16-13	.948	14	99	92	2b84,S52,3b14		3.5
1924	Bro N	86	315	51	94	11	2	2	29	27	1	10	.298	.356	.365	97	-1	5-6	.939	-4	93	80	S63,3b10,1b4/OR		0.1
1925	Bro N	123	431	63	128	13	3	2	43	45	4	15	.297	.369	.355	88	-6	7-5	.886	-20	75	66	3b81,O20(2/0/18),1b8,S2		-2.2
1926	Bos N	23	57	7	14	1	0	1	5	10	0	3	.246	.358	.316	91	0	2	.865	-3	89	128	3b14,2b2/OL		-0.2
	NY N	37	69	11	16	0	0	0	5	6	0	5	.232	.293	.232	43	-5	0	1.000	-2	60	0	O14(1/7/6)		-0.8
	Year	60	126	18	30	1	0	1	10	16	0	8	.238	.324	.270	64	-6	2	1.000	-5	62	0	O15(2/7/6),3b14,2b2		-1.0
Total	13	1377	5070	754	1493	185	75	22	410	391	20	246	.294	.347	.374	100	5	169-83	.926	-4	93	88	3b448,O354R,2b243,S178,1b49		1.9

JOHNSTON, JOHNNY   John Thomas B3.28.1890 Longview TX D3.7.1940 San Diego CA BL/TR/5-11/172 d4.10

YEAR	TM LG	G	AB	R	H	2B	3B	HR	RBI	BB-IB	HP	SO	AVG	OBP	SLG	AOPS	ABR	SB-CS	FA	FR	RNG	THR	GAMES AT POSITION	DL	BFW
1913	StL A	111	380	37	85	14	4	2	27	42	4	51	.224	.308	.297	79	-9	11	.965	10	107	152	O107L		-0.5

JOHNSTON, REX   Rex David B11.8.1937 Colton CA BB/TR/6-1.5/202 d4.15 Col USC

YEAR	TM LG	G	AB	R	H	2B	3B	HR	RBI	BB-IB	HP	SO	AVG	OBP	SLG	AOPS	ABR	SB-CS	FA	FR	RNG	THR	GAMES AT POSITION	DL	BFW
1964	Pit N	14	7	1	0	0	0	0	0	3-1	0	5	.000	.300	.000	-7	-1	0-0	1.000	-0	52	0	O8(6/2/0)		-0.1

JOHNSTON, DICK   Richard Frederick B4.6.1863 Kingston NY D4.4.1934 Detroit MI BR/TR/5-8/155 d8.12

YEAR	TM LG	G	AB	R	H	2B	3B	HR	RBI	BB-IB	HP	SO	AVG	OBP	SLG	AOPS	ABR	SB-CS	FA	FR	RNG	THR	GAMES AT POSITION	DL	BFW
1884	Ric AA	39	146	23	41	5	5	2		2	0		.281	.291	.425	132	4		.865	8	143	254	O37C,S2		1.0
1885	Bos N	26	111	17	26	4	1	1	23	0		15	.234	.234	.369	96	-1		.842	1	174	306	O26C		0.0
1886	Bos N	109	413	48	99	18	9	1	57	3		70	.240	.245	.334	77	-13	11	.892	14	133	117	O109C		-0.3
1887	Bos N	127	507	87	131	13	20	5	77	16	0	35	.258	.281	.393	84	-14	52	.933	23	151	209	O127C		0.3
1888	Bos N	135	585	102	173	31	18	12	68	15	1	33	.296	.314	.472	144	26	35	.898	4	141	67	O135C		2.5
1889	Bos N	132	539	80	123	16	4	5	67	41	2	60	.228	.285	.301	60	-32	34	.917	-8	87	139	O132C		-3.9
1890	Bos P	2	9	0	1	0	0	0	0	0	0	1	.111	.111	.111	-38	-2	0	.800	0	313	0	O2C		-0.1
	NY P	77	306	37	74	9	7	1	43	18	2	25	.242	.288	.327	59	-20	7	.897	-0	123	106	O76(12/62/2),S2		-1.9
	Year	79	315	37	75	9	7	1	43	18	2	26	.238	.284	.321	56	-22	7	.894	-0	127	104	O78(12/64/2),S2		-2.0
1891	Cin AA	99	376	59	83	11	2	6	51	38	5	44	.221	.301	.309	69	-17	12	.895	-2	115	102	O99(0/99/1)		-2.0
Total	8	746	2992	453	751	109	68	33	386	133	10	283	.251	.285	.366	86	-69	151	.903	40	128	137	O743(12/729/3),S4		-4.4

JOHNSTON, DOC   Wheeler Roger B9.9.1887 Cleveland TN D2.17.1961 Chattanooga TN BL/TL/6-0/170 d10.3 b-Jimmy

YEAR	TM LG	G	AB	R	H	2B	3B	HR	RBI	BB-IB	HP	SO	AVG	OBP	SLG	AOPS	ABR	SB-CS	FA	FR	RNG	THR	GAMES AT POSITION	DL	BFW
1909	Cin N	3	10	1	0	0	0	0	1	0	0		.000	.000	.000	-99	-2	0	1.000	0	142	0	1b3		-0.2
1912	Cle A	43	164	22	46	7	4	1	11	11	0		.280	.326	.390	101	-1	8	.991	-1	76	142	1b41		-0.3
1913	Cle A	133	530	74	135	19	12	2	39	35	7	65	.255	.309	.347	89	-9	19	.989	-1	92	105	1b133		-1.4
1914	Cle A	104	340	43	83	15	1	0	23	28	5	46	.244	.311	.294	79	-8	14-9	.987	-7	65	86	1b90,O2C		-1.9
1915	Pit N	147	543	71	144	19	12	5	64	38	13	40	.265	.328	.372	113	8	26-17	.991	-12	61	84	1b147		-0.9
1916	Pit N	114	404	33	86	10	10	0	39	20	7	42	.213	.262	.287	68	-16	17	.987	-3	87	71	1b110		-2.5
1918	Cle A	74	273	30	62	12	2	0	25	26	3	19	.227	.301	.286	70	-9	12	.989	-3	83	58	1b73		-1.6
1919	Cle A	102	331	42	101	17	3	1	33	25	3	18	.305	.359	.384	102	1	21	.984	-4	89	117	1b98		-0.5
1920	†Cle A	147	535	68	156	24	10	2	71	28	5	32	.292	.333	.385	87	-11	13-7	.992	-1	95	105	1b147		-1.5
1921	Cle A	118	384	53	114	20	7	2	46	29	4	15	.297	.353	.401	90	-6	2-9	.988	-2	95	110	1b116		-1.6
1922	Phi A	71	260	41	65	11	7	1	29	24	1	15	.250	.316	.358	73	-11	7-6	.990	-5	74	73	1b65		-1.6
Total	11	1056	3774	478	992	154	68	14	381	264	48	292	.263	.319	.351	88	-64	139-48	.989	-37	83	94	1b1023,O2C		-14.4

JOHNSTON, FRED   Wilfred Ivy B7.9.1899 Charlotte NC D7.14.1959 Tyler TX BR/TR/5-11.5/170 d6.29 Col North Carolina St.

YEAR	TM LG	G	AB	R	H	2B	3B	HR	RBI	BB-IB	HP	SO	AVG	OBP	SLG	AOPS	ABR	SB-CS	FA	FR	RNG	THR	GAMES AT POSITION	DL	BFW
1924	Bro N	4	4	1	1	0	0	0	0	0	0		.250	.250	.250	4	-0		.667	-0	123	0	/23		-0.1

JOHNSTONE, JAY   John William B11.20.1945 Manchester CT BL/TR/6-1/175(175-190) d7.30 OF(258/521/572)

YEAR	TM LG	G	AB	R	H	2B	3B	HR	RBI	BB-IB	HP	SO	AVG	OBP	SLG	AOPS	ABR	SB-CS	FA	FR	RNG	THR	GAMES AT POSITION	DL	BFW
1966	Cal A	61	254	35	67	12	4	3	17	11-1	1	36	.264	.297	.378	95	-3	3-3	.975	-2	96	52	O61(41/12/13)		-0.9
1967	Cal A	79	230	18	48	7	1	2	10	5-0	0	37	.209	.226	.274	49	-16	3-2	.973	3	118	95	O63(0/62/1)		-1.7
1968	Cal A	41	115	11	30	4	1	0	3	5-0	0	15	.261	.303	.313	90	-2	2-1	.984	2	100	233	O29(1/21/7)		-0.1
1969	Cal A	148	540	64	146	20	5	10	59	38-5	5	75	.270	.321	.381	101	-1	3-9	.983	3	104	139	O144C		-0.4
1970	Cal A	119	320	34	76	10	5	11	39	24-6	1	53	.237	.290	.403	93	-5	1-0	.981	-1	99	124	O100(2/88/10)	21	-0.8
1971	Chi A	124	388	53	101	14	1	16	40	38-4	3	50	.260	.329	.425	110	5	10-5	.968	-2	95	136	O119(11/92/23)		0.0
1972	Oak A	23	28	1	3	1	0	0	3	2-0	0	4	.107	.167	.143	-13	-4	0-1	1.000	1	204		O7(3/1/3),2b2,D4		-2.1
1973	Phi N	64	200	30	59	10	4	6	30	24-4	0	28	.295	.371	.475	129	8	5-5	.968	-2	88	109	O59(31/1/40)		-0.4
1974	Phi N	122	350	50	115	19	2	7	54	42-7	0	39	.329	.397	.454	130	16	7-3	.976	3	95	181	O101(0/3/100)		0.2
1975	†Phi N	129	440	62	140	38	4	5	53	41-5	2	39	.318	.373	.457	131	19	5-5	.982	8	121	88	O122(2/0/120),1b6		1.5
1976	†Phi N	112	363	64	103	18	4	15	59	38-3	2	38	.284	.349	.479	115	8	3-7	1.000	4	103	146	O91(4/0/87),1b19		2.2
1977	Phi N	35	56	3	10	2	0	0	4	6-0	0	9	.179	.258	.214	33	-5	0-2	.988	4	161	173	1b8,O7(3/0/4)		0.5
1978	†NY A	36	65	6	17	0	0	1	6	4-0	3	10	.262	.329	.308	83	-1	0-1	1.000	-0	110	0	O22(8/0/14),D5		-0.7
1979	NY A	23	48	7	10	1	0	1	7	2-0	0	7	.208	.240	.292	43	-4	1-0	1.000	1	127	0	O19(14/4/1),D3		-0.3
	SD N	75	201	10	59	8	2	0	32	18-3	0	21	.294	.348	.353	99	0	1-3	.985	-0	80	142	O45(35/7/4),1b22		-0.4
1980	LA N	109	251	31	77	15	2	2	20	24-1	2	29	.307	.372	.406	120	8	3-2	.965	3	101	202	O61(5/0/57)		0.8
1981	†LA N	61	83	8	17	3	0	3	6	7-0	1	15	.205	.267	.349	77	-3	0-1	.957	1	93	334	O16(8/0/8),1b2		-0.3
1982	LA N	21	13	1	1	1	0	0	2	5-1	0	2	.077	.316	.154	42	-1	0-0	—	0			/H		-0.1
	Chi N	98	269	39	67	13	1	10	43	40-8	0	41	.249	.343	.416	108	4	0-2	.982	4	106	140	O86(34/0/58)		0.3
	Year	119	282	40	68	14	1	10	45	45-9	0	43	.241	.341	.404	106	4	0-2	.982	4	106	140	O86(34/0/58)		0.2
1983	Chi N	86	140	16	36	7	0	6	22	20-6	3	24	.257	.362	.436	115	3	1-1	.935	-1	90	127	O44(36/0/8)		0.1
1984	Chi N	52	73	8	21	2	2	0	3	7-4	1	18	.288	.350	.370	94	-1	0-0	1.000	-2	64	0	O15(7/1/8)	33	-0.3
1985	†LA N	17	15	0	2	1	0	0	2	1-1	0	2	.133	.188	.200	9	-2	0-0	—	0			/H	112	-0.2
Total	20	1748	4703	578	1254	215	38	102	534	429-61	22	632	.267	.329	.394	102	9	50-54	.979	21	101	128	O1308R,1b57,D12,2b2	166	-3.5

HOK, STAN   Stanley Edward "Tucker" B5.3.1926 Buffalo NY D3.6.1972 Buffalo NY BR/TR/6-0/190* d4.13

YEAR	TM LG	G	AB	R	H	2B	3B	HR	RBI	BB-IB	HP	SO	AVG	OBP	SLG	AOPS	ABR	SB-CS	FA	FR	RNG	THR	GAMES AT POSITION	DL	BFW
1954	Phi N	3	3	1	0	0	0	0	0	0	0	2	.000	.000	.000	-99	-1	0-0		0			/H		-0.1
	Chi A	3	12	1	2	0	0	0	2	1	0	1	.167	.231	.167	10	-2	0-0	1.000	0	101	180	3b3		-0.1
1955	Chi A	6	4	3	1	0	0	1	2	1-0	0	1	.250	.333	1.000	260	1	0-0	.857	-0	112	0	3b3/OL		0.1
Total	2	12	19	4	3	0	0	1	4	2-0	0	5	.158	.227	.316	47	-2	0-0	.941	0	105	116	3b6/OL		-0.1

HOLLEY, SMEAD   Smead Powell "Guinea","Smudge" B1.14.1902 Wesson AR D11.17.1991 Alameda CA BL/TR/6-3.5/210 d4.17

YEAR	TM LG	G	AB	R	H	2B	3B	HR	RBI	BB-IB	HP	SO	AVG	OBP	SLG	AOPS	ABR	SB-CS	FA	FR	RNG	THR	GAMES AT POSITION	DL	BFW
1930	Chi A	152	616	76	193	38	12	16	114	28	3	52	.313	.346	.492	114	10	3-1	.950	-0	93	146	O151(68/0/83)		-0.1
1931	Chi A	54	110	15	33	11	0	3	28	7	2	4	.300	.353	.482	125	4	0-0	.857	-3	76	60	O23(8/0/15)		0.0
1932	Chi A	12	42	3	15	3	0	0	7	3	1	6	.357	.413	.429	127	2	1-0	.923	-1	63	158	O11(7/0/4)		0.1
	Bos A	137	531	57	164	27	5	18	99	27	2	29	.309	.345	.480	115	3	0-5	.943	-3	90	131	O126(120/0/6),C5		-0.3
	Year	149	573	60	179	30	5	18	106	30	3	35	.312	.350	.476	116	10	1-5	.942	-4	88	133	O137(127/0/10),C5		-0.2
1933	Bos A	118	411	47	116	32	4	9	65	24	2	20	.282	.325	.445	103	1	1-1	.955	-9	92	134	O102(87/0/15)		-0.8
Total	4	473	1710	188	521	111	21	46	313	89	10	105	.305	.343	.475	112	25	5-7	.944	-8	90	134	O413(290/0/123),C5		-0.8

ONES   B Johnstown PA d7.14

YEAR	TM LG	G	AB	R	H	2B	3B	HR	RBI	BB-IB	HP	SO	AVG	OBP	SLG	AOPS	ABR	SB-CS	FA	FR	RNG	THR	GAMES AT POSITION	DL	BFW
1884	Was AA	4	17	5	5	0	0	0		1	0		.294	.333	.294	120	0		1.000	0	0	0	O4L		0.0

ONES   d4.30

YEAR	TM LG	G	AB	R	H	2B	3B	HR	RBI	BB-IB	HP	SO	AVG	OBP	SLG	AOPS	ABR	SB-CS	FA	FR	RNG	THR	GAMES AT POSITION	DL	BFW
1885	NY AA	1	4	0	1	0	0	0	0	0	0		.250	.250	.250	61	0		1.000	1	156	0	/3		0.1

YEAR	TM LG	G	AB	R	H	2B	3B	HR	RBI	BB-IB	HP	SO	AVG	OBP	SLG	AOPS	ABR	SB-CS	FA	FR	RNG	THR	GAMES AT POSITION	DL	BFW

JONES, ANDRUW   Andruw Rudolf   B4.23.1977 Willemstad, Curacao   BR/TR/6-1/210(185-210)   d8.15

1996	†Atl N	31	106	11	23	7	1	5	13	7-0	0	29	.217	.265	.443	78	-4	3-0	.975	6	141	256	O29(0/12/20)		0.2
1997	†Atl N	153	399	60	92	18	1	18	70	56-2	4	107	.231	.329	.416	93	-4	20-11	.977	17	**126**	**202**	O147(2/57/95)		1.0
1998	†Atl N	159	582	89	158	33	8	31	90	40-8	4	129	.271	.321	.515	117	11	27-4	.995	20	118	**215**	O159C		3.6
1999	†Atl N	162	592	97	163	35	5	26	84	76-11	9	103	.275	.365	.483	113	13	24-12	.981	17	**122**	145	O162C		3.1
2000	†Atl N★	161	656	122	199	36	6	36	104	59-0	9	100	.303	.366	.541	127	25	21-6	.996	5	110	91	O161C		3.2
2001	†Atl N★	161	625	104	157	25	2	34	104	56-3	3	142	.251	.312	.461	96	-6	11-4	.987	11	**117**	111	O161C		0.8
2002	†Atl N★	154	560	91	148	34	0	35	94	83-4	10	135	.264	.366	.512	133	15	8-3	.993	-1	106	56	O154C/D		2.6
2003	†Atl N★	156	595	101	165	28	2	36	116	53-2	5	125	.277	.338	.513	119	15	4-3	.993	4	104	128	O154C		1.4
2004	†Atl N	154	570	85	149	34	4	29	91	71-9	3	147	.261	.345	.488	112	10	6-3	.993	4	94	131	O159C		2.5
2005	†Atl N★	160	586	95	154	24	3	**51**	128	64-13	15	112	.263	.347	.575	134	27	5-3	.995	-4	94	130	O1441(2/1334/115)/D		20.2
Total	10	1451	5271	855	1408	274	32	301	894	565-52	62	1129	.267	.342	.503	116	112	129-52	.990	77	112	130			

JONES, CHARLIE   Charles Claude "Casey"   B6.2.1876 Butler PA   D4.2.1947 Two Harbors MN   BR/TR/6-1/165   d5.2   Col Grove City

1901	Bos A	10	41	6	6	2	0	0	6	1	0		.146	.167	.195	0	-6	2	.929	-2	0	0	O10(0/8/2)		-0.7
1904	Chi A	5	17	2	4	0	1	0	1	1	0		.235	.278	.353	103	0	0	1.000	1	411	0	O5C		0.1
1905	Was A	142	544	68	113	18	4	2	41	31	3		.208	.254	.267	68	-21	24	.971	14	153	161	O142C		-1.5
1906	Was A	131	497	56	120	11	1	3	42	24	5		.241	.283	.326	95	-5	34	.961	5	124	181	O128C/2		-0.7
1907	Was A	121	437	48	116	14	10	0	37	22	2		.265	.304	.343	115	5	26	.967	-2	43	58	O72(0/70/2)		-0.2
1908	StL A	74	263	37	61	11	2	0	17	14	3		.232	.279	.289	84	-5	14	.963	2	182	107	O72(0/70/2)		-0.7
Total	6	483	1799	217	420	56	28	5	144	93	13		.233	.276	.304	87	-32	100	.966	17	122	130	O468(12/443/12),2b6,1b4,S2		-3.7

JONES, CHARLIE   Charles F.   B10.24.1861 New York NY   D9.15.1922 New York NY   d6.28

1884	Bro AA	25	90	10	16	1	0	0		5	0		.178	.221	.189	35	-6		.871	-5	94	75	2b13,3b11,O2(1/0/1)		-1.0

JONES, CHARLEY   Charles Wesley "Baby" (b Benjamin Wesley Rippay)   B4.30.1850 Alamance Co. NC   BR/TR/5-11.5/202   d5.4   U2

1875	Wes NA	12	47	4	13	2	4	0	10	0		5	.277	.277	.489	152	2	1-1	.800	-2	103	0	O12L		0.1
	Har NA	1	4	1	0	0	0	0	0	0		0	.000	.000	.000	-95	-1	0-0	.667	-0	0	0	/OC		-0.1
	Year	13	51	5	13	2	4	0	10	0		6	.255	.255	.451	133	1	1-1	.778	-2	93	0	O13(12/1/0)		0.0
1876	Cin N	64	276	40	79	17	4	4	38	7		17	.286	.304	.420	162	21		.857	1	99	69	O64(10/53/1)		1.6
1877	Cin N	17	69	16	21	3	3	1	10	4		8	.304	.342	.478	175	6		.920	1	95	70	1b10,O8(5/3/0)		0.5
	Chi N	2	8	1	3	1	0	0	1	1		0	.375	.444	.500	176	1		1.000	1	251	0	O2C		0.1
	Cin N	38	163	36	51	8	7	1	26	10		17	.313	.353	.466	175	15		.845	12	163	102	O48(43/5/0),1b10		2.0
	Year	57	240	53	75	12	10	2	38	15		25	.313	.353	.471	175	22		.896	4	53	42	O61(51/10/0)		2.6
1878	Cin N	61	261	50	81	11	7	3	39	4		17	.310	.321	.441	163	18		.904	4	71	98	O83L		1.7
1879	Bos N	83	355	**85**	112	22	10	9	**62**	**29**		38	.315	.367	.510	182	32		.826	-4	66	0	O66(66/1/0)		3.0
1880	Bos N	66	280	44	84	15	3	5	37	11		27	.300	.326	.429	159	17		.876	-0	69	58	O90(16/75/0)		0.9
1883	Cin AA	90	391	84	115	15	12	10	80	20			.294	.328	.471	146	18		.887	-1	52	0	O112L		1.3
1884	Cin AA	112	472	117	148	19	17	7	71	37	10		.314	**.376**	.470	166	34		.891	11	114	161	O112L		2.3
1885	Cin AA	112	487	108	157	19	17	5	35	21	9		.322	.362	.462	156	29		.879	2	107	24	O127L		1.3
1886	Cin AA	127	500	87	135	22	10	6	68	61	6		.270	.356	.390	130	18	3	.900	1	106	151	O41(41/1/0)		0.4
1887	Cin AA	41	153	28	48	7	4	2	40	19	3		.314	.400	.451	134	7	7	.917	4	182	246	O62(6/50/7),P2/1		-0.2
	NY AA	62	247	30	63	11	3	3	29	12	6		.255	.306	.360	89	-4	8	.910	5	**152**	**208**	O103(47/51/7),P2/1		-0.5
	Year	103	400	58	111	18	7	5	69	31	9		.278	.343	.395	107	4	15	.910	5	152	208	O6L		-0.2
1888	KC AA	6	25	2	4	1	0	0	5	1	0		.160	.192	.240	36	-2	1	.750	-1	98	0	O6L		-0.1
Total	11	881	3687	728	1101	170	98	56	542	237	34	**124**	.299	.347	.443	150	210	19	.882	43	98	79	O872(624/246/8),1b11,P2		19.

JONES, CHRIS   Christopher Carlos   B12.16.1965 Utica NY   BR/TR/6-2/205(205-219)   [CinN84 3/59]   d4.21

1991	Cin N	52	89	14	26	1	2	2	6	2-0	0	31	.292	.304	.416	98	-1	2-1	1.000	-1	82	99	O26(18/3/9)		-0.
1992	Hou N	54	63	7	12	2	1	1	4	7-0	0	21	.190	.271	.302	65	-3	3-0	.931	-3	77	0	O43(17/5/25)		-0.
1993	Col N	86	209	29	57	11	4	6	31	10-1	0	48	.273	.305	.450	85	-5	9-4	.983	-2	92	71	O70(16/52/4)		-0.
1994	Col N	21	40	6	12	2	1	0	2	2-1	0	14	.300	.333	.400	77	-1	0-1	.941	-2	70	0	O14(4/13/0)		-0.
1995	NY N	79	182	33	51	6	2	8	31	13-1	1	45	.280	.327	.467	111	2	2-1	.976	2	111	117	O52(25/0/28),1b5		-0.
1996	NY N	89	149	22	36	7	0	4	18	12-1	2	42	.242	.307	.369	81	-4	1-0	.957	-2	104	0	O66(17/8/44),1b5		-0.
1997	SD N	92	152	24	37	9	0	7	25	16-0	2	45	.243	.322	.441	104	1	7-2	.951	1	97	176	O61(24/19/25)	19	-0.
1998	Ari N	20	31	3	6	1	0	0	3	3-0	0	9	.194	.265	.226	31	-3	0-0	1.000	-0	107	0	O8(1/0/7)		-1
	SF N	43	90	14	17	2	1	2	10	8-0	0	28	.189	.250	.300	48	-7	2-1	.941	-2	84	77	O37(6/0/31),D2		-0
	Year	63	121	17	23	3	1	2	13	11-0	0	37	.190	.254	.281	43	-11	2-1	.956	-2	89	61	O37(6/0/31),D2		-0
2000	Mil N	12	16	3	3	2	0	0	1	1-0	0	4	.188	.235	.313	37	-2	0-0	1.000	0	157	0	O2R		-0
Total	9	548	1021	155	257	43	11	30	131	74-4	5	287	.252	.303	.404	86	-23	26-10	.967	-8	95	77	O371(127/100/168),1b10,D2	19	-3

JONES, CHRIS   Christopher Dale   B7.13.1957 Los Angeles CA   BL/TL/6-0/183*   [HouN79 25/625]   d6.8   Col San Diego St.

1985	Hou N	31	25	0	5	0	0	0	1	3-0	0	7	.200	.286	.200	39	-2	0-0	1.000	1	161	0	O15(2/9/4)		-0
1986	SF N	3	1	0	0	0	0	0	0	0-0	0	0	.000	.000	.000	-99	-0	1-0	—	0		0	/H		-0
Total	2	34	26	0	5	0	0	0	1	3-0	0	7	.192	.276	.192	34	-2	1-0	1.000	1	161	0	O15(2/9/4)		-0

JONES, CLARENCE   Clarence Woodrow   B11.7.1941 Zanesville OH   BL/TL/6-2/205(185-205)   d4.20   C15

1967	Chi N	53	135	13	34	7	0	2	16	14-3	0	33	.252	.314	.348	88	-2	0-0	.978	-3	95	0	O31(2/0/29),1b13		-0
1968	Chi N	5	2	0	0	0	0	0	0	2-0	0	1	.000	.500	.000	56	0	1-0	1.000	-0	0	0	O/1		-0
Total	2	58	137	13	34	7	0	2	16	16-3	0	34	.248	.318	.343	88	-2	0-0	.978	-3	95	0	O31(2/0/29),1b14		-0

JONES, CLEON   Cleon Joseph   B8.4.1942 Plateau AL   BR/TL/6-0/200(185-200)   d9.14   Col Alabama A&M

1963	NY N	6	15	1	2	0	0	0	1	0-0	0	4	.133	.133	.133	-23	-2	0-0	1.000	-0	82	0	O5(1/5/0)		-0
1965	NY N	30	74	2	11	1	0	1	9	2-0	1	23	.149	.171	.203	5	-10	1-0	.979	1	92	184	O129(3/107/35)		-0
1966	NY N	139	495	74	136	16	4	8	57	30-2	3	62	.275	.318	.372	94	-5	16-8	.979	1	102	115	O129(3/107/35)		-1
1967	NY N	129	411	46	101	10	5	5	30	19-6	4	57	.246	.282	.331	77	-14	12-8	.977	-1	99	83	O139(117/28/18)		-0
1968	NY N	147	509	63	151	29	4	14	55	31-3	5	98	.297	.341	.452	136	22	23-12	.963	-2	99	82	O122(121/1/0),1b15		3
1969	†NY N★	137	483	92	164	25	4	12	75	64-11	7	60	.340	.422	.482	149	35	16-8	.991	5	112	62	O130(125/6/1)		0
1970	NY N	134	506	71	140	25	8	10	63	57-2	5	87	.277	.352	.417	105	4	12-3	.981	3	**112**	51	O132(132/1/0)		-1
1971	NY N	136	505	63	161	24	6	14	69	53-6	3	87	.319	.382	.473	142	29	6-5	.986	1	94	152	O84(71/5/14),1b20		-1
1972	NY N	106	375	39	92	15	1	5	52	30-4	4	83	.245	.305	.331	83	-8	1-6	.967	-2	95	98	O92(73/13/8)	36	-1
1973	†NY N	92	339	48	88	13	0	11	48	28-6	3	51	.260	.315	.395	98	-1	1-1	.970	-2	101	99	O120(117/3/3)		-0
1974	NY N	124	461	62	130	23	1	13	60	38-3	6	79	.282	.343	.421	114	8	3-3	1.000	-2	50	0	O12L	50	-0
1975	NY N	21	50	2	12	1	0	0	3	3-0	0	5	.240	.283	.260	53	-3	0-0	1.000	-2	49	0	O8L,D3		-0
1976	Chi A	12	40	2	8	1	0	0	3	5-0	1	5	.200	.304	.225	56	-2	0-0	.978	-2	102	92	O1111(802/273/103),1b35,D3	86	-0
Total	13	1213	4263	565	1196	183	33	93	524	360-42	40	702	.281	.339	.404	110	53	91-48	.978	7	102	92	O1111(802/273/103),1b35,D3		

JONES, COBE   Coburn Dyas   B8.21.1907 Denver CO   D6.3.1969 Denver CO   BB/TR/5-7/155   d9.27   Col Colorado

1928	Pit N	1	2	0	1	0	0	0	0	0	0	0	.500	.500	.500	156	0	0	1.000	-0	89	0	/S		0
1929	Pit N	25	63	6	16	5	1	0	4	1	0	5	.254	.266	.365	53	-5	1	.919	-6	69	80	S15		-0
Total	2	26	65	6	17	5	1	0	4	1	0	5	.262	.273	.369	56	-5	1	.921	-6	70	78	S16		-0

JONES, DARRYL   Darryl Lee   B6.5.1951 Meadville PA   BR/TR/5-10/175   [NYA72 5/110]   d6.6   b-Lynn   Col Westminster (PA)

1979	NY A	18	47	6	12	6	0	0	2	6-0	0	9	.255	.286	.404	85	-1	0-0	1.000	0	103		D15,O2(1/0/1)		-0

JONES, DAVY   David Jefferson "Kangaroo"   B6.30.1880 Cambria WI   D3.30.1972 Mankato MN   BL/TR/5-10/165   d9.15   Col Northern Illinois

1901	Mil A	14	52	12	9	0	3	0	5	11	1		.173	.328	.346	91	0	4	.911	0	0	0	O14L		-0
1902	StL A	15	49	4	11	1	1	0	3	6	0		.224	.309	.286	67	-2	5	.973	-3	212	662	O15R		-0
	Chi N	64	243	41	74	12	3	0	14	38	0		.305	.399	.379	144	15	12	.955	-4	32	45	O64(0/47/17)		-0
1903	Chi N	130	497	64	140	18	3	1	62	53	1		.282	.352	.326	99	1	15	.970	1	82	79	O130(0/97/33)		-0
1904	Chi N	98	336	44	82	11	5	3	39	41	2		.244	.330	.333	105	3	14	.932	-9	68	0	O83(0/82/1)		-0
1906	Det A	84	323	41	84	12	2	0	24	41	1		.260	.347	.310	103	3	21	.981	3	96	122	O83(0/82/1)		-0
1907	†Det A	126	491	101	134	10	6	0	27	60	4		.273	.357	.318	111	9	30	.971	13	92	52	O125(121/4/0)		-0
1908	†Det A	56	121	17	25	2	1	0	10	13	0		.207	.284	.240	68	-4	11	.960	2	139	196	O32(4/26/2)		-0
1909	†Det A	69	204	44	57	2	0	0	10	28	1		.279	.369	.309	110	4	12	.982	-2	56	65	O57(42/13/2)		-0
1910	Det A	113	377	77	100	6	6	0	24	51			.265	.362	.313	105	4	25	.956	2	104	97	O101(95/6/0)		-0

YEAR	TM LG	G	AB	R	H	2B	3B	HR	RBI	BB-IB	HP	SO	AVG	OBP	SLG	AOPS	ABR	SB-CS	FA	FR	RNG	THR	GAMES AT POSITION	DL	BFW
1911	Det A	98	341	78	93	10	0	0	19	41	2		.273	.354	.302	80	-7	25	.950	1	96	108	O92L		-1.0
1912	Det A	99	316	54	93	5	2	0	24	38	0		.294	.370	.323	102	2	16	.962	-0	88	122	O81(72/5/4)		-0.2
1913	Chi A	12	21	2	6	0	0	0	0	9	0	0	.286	.500	.286	132	2	1	.867	-0	79	197	O9L		0.2
1914	Pit F	97	352	58	96	9	8	2	24	42	3	16	.273	.355	.361	96	-7	15	.970	6	123	73	O93L		-0.6
1915	Pit F	14	49	6	16	0	1	0	4	6	0		.327	.400	.367	118	1	1	.926	-1	102	60	O13L		-0.1
1918	Det A	1	2	0	0	0	0	0	0	0	0	1	.000	.000	.000	-99	-1	0	1.000	0	0	0	/O(1/1/0)		-0.1
Total	15	1090	3774	643	1020	98	40	9	289	478	22	17	.270	.356	.325	102	23	207	.962	15	89	89	O1007(556/282/171)		-1.1

JONES, DAX Dax Xenos B8.4.1970 Pittsburgh PA BR/TR/6-0/180 [SFN91 8/219] d7.11 Col Creighton

| 1996 | SF N | 34 | 58 | 7 | 10 | 0 | 2 | 0 | 8 | 0-1 | 0 | 12 | .172 | .269 | .293 | 50 | -5 | 2-2 | 1.000 | 2 | 124 | 117 | O33(0/29/4) | | -0.3 |

JONES, FIELDER Fielder Allison B8.13.1871 Shinglehouse PA D3.13.1934 Portland OR BL/TR/5-11/180 d4.18 M10

1896	Bro N	104	395	82	140	10	8	3	46	48	2	15	.354	.427	.443	137	24	18	.928	-4	71	170	O103R		1.3
1897	Bro N	135	548	134	172	15	10	1	49	61	9		.314	.392	.383	111	12	48	.941	3	113	210	O135(2/0/133)		0.7
1898	Bro N	146	596	89	181	15	9	1	69	46	8		.304	.362	.364	108	7	36	.946	-8	84	142	O144(0/4/144),S2		-0.7
1899	Bro N	102	365	75	104	8	2	2	38	54	9		.285	.390	.334	97	2	18	.946	-5	74	52	O96(2/89/6)		-0.8
1900	†Bro N	136	552	106	171	26	4	4	54	57	6		.310	.383	.393	108	8	33	.957	-1	82	61	O136C		-0.1
1901	Chi A	133	521	120	162	16	5	3	65	84	5		.311	.412	.365	120	21	38	.937	-2	112	134	O133(0/5/128)		1.2
1902	Chi A	135	532	98	171	16	5	0	54	57	3		.321	.390	.370	117	15	33	.972	10	142	322	O135C		1.8
1903	Chi.A	136	530	71	152	18	5	0	45	47	3		.287	.348	.340	112	10	21	**.985**	-1	73	78	O136C		0.2
1904	Chi A	149	547	72	133	14	5	3	42	53	5		.243	.316	.303	100	2	25	.977	2	92	104	O149C,M		-0.3
1905	Chi A	153	568	91	139	17	12	2	38	73	4		.245	.335	.327	115	12	20	.970	7	129	153	O153C,M		1.3
1906	†Chi A	144	496	77	114	22	4	2	34	83	5		.230	.346	.302	106	9	26	**.988**	3	125	143	O144C,M		0.6
1907	Chi A	154	559	72	146	18	1	0	47	67	5		.261	.345	.297	109	10	17	.973	-1	91	143	O154C,M		0.1
1908	Chi A	149	529	92	134	11	7	1	50	86	6		.253	.366	.306	121	18	26	.968	-4	101	125	O149C,M		0.8
1914	StL F	5	3	0	1	0	0	0	0	1	0		.333	.500	.333	123	0	0		-0			/HM		0.0
1915	StL F	7	6	1	0	0	0	0	0	0	0		.000	.000	.000	-95	-2	0	1.000	-0	82	0	O3(0/1/2),M		-0.2
Total	15	1788	6747	1180	1920	206	75	21	631	817	76	15	.285	.368	.347	112	148	359	.964	0	101	143	O1770(4/1255/516),S2		5.9

JONES, FRANK Frank M. B8.25.1858 Princeton IL D2.4.1936 Marietta OH BL d7.2

| 1884 | Det N | 2 | 8 | 0 | 1 | 0 | 0 | 0 | | 1 | 0 | | .125 | .125 | .125 | -22 | -1 | | .667 | -1 | 83 | 0 | /SOR | | -0.2 |

JONES, DEACON Grover William B4.18.1934 White Plains NY BL/TR/5-10/185* d9.8 C11 Col Ithaca

1962	Chi A	18	28	3	9	2	0	0	8	4-2	1	6	.321	.394	.393	117	1	0-0	.962	-0	92	63	1b6		0.0
1963	Chi A	17	16	4	3	0	1	1	2	2-1	1	2	.188	.316	.500	127	0	0-0	1.000	0	145	531	/1		0.1
1966	Chi A	5	5	0	2	0	0	0	0-0		1		.400	.400	.400	140	0	0-0	—	0			1b		0.0
Total	3	40	49	7	14	2	1	1	10	6-3	1	8	.286	.368	.429	122	1	0-0	.966	-0	100	131	1b7		0.1

JONES, HAL Harold Marion B4.9.1936 Louisiana MO BR/TR/6-2/194* d4.25

1961	Cle A	12	35	2	6	0	0	2	4	2-0	0	12	.171	.216	.343	48	-3	0-0	.974	-2	42	147	1b10		-0.6
1962	Cle A	5	16	2	5	1	0	0	1	0-0	1	4	.313	.353	.375	99	0	0-0	.969	-0	99	30	1b4		0.0
Total	2	17	51	4	11	1	0	2	5	2-0	1	16	.216	.259	.353	64	-3	0-0	.973	-2	59	112	1b14		-0.6

JONES, HENRY Henry Monroe B5.10.1857 NY D5.31.1955 Manistee MI BB/5-6/149 d8.20

| 1884 | Det N | 34 | 127 | 24 | 28 | 3 | 1 | 0 | | 3 | 16 | | .220 | .308 | .260 | 86 | -1 | | .897 | -1 | 95 | 45 | 2b16,O11R,S7 | | -0.1 |

JONES, HOWIE Howard "Cotton" (b Howard Painter) B3.1.1897 Irwin PA D7.15.1972 Jeannette PA BL/TL/5-11/165 d9.5

| 1921 | StL N | 3 | 2 | 0 | 0 | 0 | 0 | 0 | 0 | 0 | 0 | 1 | .000 | .000 | .000 | -99 | -1 | 0-0 | — | -0 | 0 | 0 | /OL | | -0.1 |

JONES, JACQUE Jacque Dewayne B4.25.1975 San Diego CA BL/TL/5-10/176(176-205) [MinA96 2/37] d6.9 Col USC

1999	Min A	95	322	54	93	24	2	9	44	17-1	4	63	.289	.329	.460	94	-3	3-4	.980	9	117	175	O93(1/82/19)		0.5
2000	Min A	154	523	66	149	26	5	19	76	26-4	0	111	.285	.319	.463	89	-11	7-5	.994	7	112	119	O147(90/63/1)		-0.6
2001	Min A	149	475	57	131	25	0	14	49	39-2	3	92	.276	.335	.417	91	-6	12-9	.983	4	108	100	O140(137/2/2),D5		-0.7
2002	†Min A	149	577	96	173	37	2	27	85	37-2	5	129	.300	.341	.511	119	15	6-7	.986	13	119	136	O143L,D3		2.1
2003	†Min A	136	517	76	157	33	1	16	69	21-2	4	105	.304	.333	.464	104	3	13-1	.977	-0	108	34	O110(90/0/11),D29	16	0.0
2004	Min A	151	555	69	141	22	1	24	80	40-2	10	117	.254	.315	.427	89	-11	13-10	.994	2	108	52	O142(0/2/141),D3		-1.6
2005	Min A	142	523	74	130	22	4	23	73	51-12	5	120	.249	.319	.438	97	-3	13-4	.986	1	99	125	O132(0/10/123),D9		-0.6
Total	7	976	3492	492	974	189	15	132	476	231-25	28	737	.279	.327	.455	98	-16	67-40	.986	37	110	104	O898(461/159/297),D49	16	-0.9

JONES, DALTON James Dalton B12.10.1943 McComb MS BL/TR/6-1/180* d4.17 OF(12/0/8)

1964	Bos A	118	374	37	86	16	4	6	39	22-2	1	38	.230	.274	.342	67	-17	6-3	.959	-7	87	74	2b85/S3		-1.8
1965	Bos A	112	367	41	99	13	5	5	37	28-0	2	45	.270	.325	.373	92	-4	8-1	.930	0	108	86	3b81,2b8		-0.2
1966	Bos A	115	252	26	59	11	5	4	23	22-4	2	27	.234	.303	.365	83	-6	1-2	.962	-11	82	74	2b70,3b3		-1.3
1967	†Bos A	89	159	18	46	6	2	3	25	11-3	0	23	.289	.333	.409	110	2	0-1	.912	-3	107	113	3b30,2b19/1		-0.1
1968	Bos A	111	354	38	83	13	0	5	29	17-0	1	53	.234	.271	.314	72	-12	1-1	.996	-10	85	120	1b56,2b26,3b8		-2.8
1969	Bos A	111	336	50	74	18	3	3	33	39-3	2	36	.220	.303	.318	71	-12	1-1	.992	-2	105	91	1b81,3b9/2		-2.2
1970	Det A	89	191	29	42	7	0	6	21	33-4	1	33	.220	.333	.351	89	-2	1-1	.985	-4	90	90	2b35,3b18,1b10		-0.5
1971	Det A	83	138	15	35	5	0	5	11	9-1	1	21	.254	.304	.399	94	-2	1-3	1.000	-5	72		O16(10/0/8),3b13,1b3/2		-0.9
1972	Det A	7	7	0	0	0	0	0	0	0-0	0	2	.000	.000	.000	-97	-2	0-0	1.000	0			/H		-0.2
	Tex A	72	151	14	24	2	0	4	19	10-1	0	31	.159	.207	.252	39	-12	1-0	.979	-4	76	68	3b23,2b17,1b7,O2L		-1.8
	Year	79	158	14	24	2	0	4	19	10-1	0	33	.152	.199	.241	32	-14	1-0	.979	-4	76	68	3b23,2b17,1b7,O2L		-2.0
Total	9	907	2329	268	548	91	19	41	237	191-18	11	309	.235	.295	.343	79	-67	20-13	.967	-45	85	76	2b262,3b186,1b158,O18L/S		-11.8

JONES, JAKE James Murrell B11.23.1920 Epps LA D12.13.2000 Delhi LA BR/TR/6-3/197 d9.20 Mil 1942-45

1941	Chi A	3	11	0	0	0	0	0	0	0	0	4	.000	.000	.000	-99	-1	0-0	1.000	-1	0	0	1b3		-0.4
1942	Chi A	7	20	2	3	1	0	0	0	2	0	2	.150	.227	.200	21	-2	1-0	.961	-1	60	51	1b5		-0.3
1946	Chi A	24	79	10	21	5	1	3	13	2	0	13	.266	.284	.468	112	0	0-0	.986	-3	40	108	1b20		-0.4
1947	Chi A	45	171	15	41	7	1	3	20	13	1	25	.240	.297	.345	81	-5	1-0	.988	-1	100	115	1b43		-0.7
	Bos A	109	404	50	95	14	3	16	76	41	3	60	.235	.310	.403	91	-6	5-4	.991	-3	91	108	1b109		-1.4
	Year	154	575	65	136	21	4	19	96	54	4	85	.237	.306	.386	88	-11	6-4	.990	-3	94	110	1b152		-2.1
1948	Bos A	36	105	3	21	4	0	1	8	11	0	26	.200	.276	.267	43	-9	1-0	.993	2	122	114	1b31		-0.8
Total	5	224	790	80	181	31	5	23	117	69	4	130	.229	.294	.368	80	-25	8-4	.989	-6	91	108	1b211		-4.0

JONES, JIM James Tilford "Sheriff" B12.25.1876 London KY D5.6.1953 London KY BR/TR/5-10/162 d6.29 Col Centre ▲

1897	Lou N	2	4	2	1	1	0	0	0	1	0		.250	.400	.500	141	0		—	-0	0	0	/P		0.0
1901	NY N	21	91	10	19	4	3	0	5	4	1		.209	.250	.319	67	-4	2	.900	-0	137	124	O20R/P		-0.5
1902	NY N	67	249	16	59	11	1	0	19	13	0		.237	.275	.289	75	-4	8	.897	-2	94	82	O67(49/3/15)		-1.5
Total	3	90	344	28	79	16	4	0	24	18	1		.230	.270	.299	74	-11	9	.898	-3	105	92	O87(49/3/35),P2		-2.0

JONES, JASON Jason Dewey B10.17.1976 Marietta GA BB/TR/6-3/210 [TexA99 13/405] d7.23 Col Kennesaw St.

| 2003 | Tex A | 40 | 107 | 11 | 23 | 6 | 0 | 3 | 11 | 10-0 | 3 | 21 | .215 | .298 | .355 | 67 | -5 | 0-1 | .978 | 1 | 97 | 241 | O27(14/0/13),1b3,D6 | | -0.5 |

JONES, JEFF Jeffrey Raymond B10.22.1957 Philadelphia PA BR/TR/6-2/200 [CinN79 20/516] d4.4 Col Iowa

| 1983 | Cin N | 16 | 44 | 6 | 10 | 3 | 0 | 1 | 13 | 11-0 | 1 | 13 | .227 | .379 | .295 | 90 | 0 | 2-0 | 1.000 | 0 | 109 | 109 | O13(8/0/5)/1 | | 0.1 |

JONES, BINKY John Joseph B7.11.1899 St.Louis MO D5.13.1961 St.Louis MO BR/TR/5-9/154 d4.15

| 1924 | Bro N | 10 | 37 | 4 | 4 | 0 | 0 | 0 | 3 | 0 | 0 | 0 | .108 | .108 | .135 | -36 | -7 | 0-0 | .898 | -1 | 90 | 109 | S10 | | -0.8 |

JONES, JOHN John William "Skins" B5.13.1901 Coatesville PA D11.3.1956 Baltimore MD BL/TL/5-11/185 d9.26 Col Penn St.

1923	Phi A	1	4	0	1	0	0	0		0	0	1	.250	.250	.250	31	0	0-0	1.000	-0	105	0	/OC		-0.1
1932	Phi A	4	6	0	1	0	0	0		0	0	3	.167	.167	.167	-13	-1	0-0	1.000	-0	89	0	/OR		-0.1
Total	2	5	10	0	2	0	0	0		0	0	4	.200	.200	.200	4	-1	0-0	1.000	-0	101	0	O2(0/1/1)		-0.1

JONES, CHIPPER Larry Wayne B4.24.1972 DeLand FL BB/TR/6-4/210(185-210) [AtlN90 1/1] d9.11 [DL 1994 Atl N 131]

1993	Atl N	8	3	2	2	1	0	0		0	0	1	.667	.750	1.000	355	0	0-0	1.000	-1	48	0	S3		0.1
1995	†Atl N	140	524	87	139	22	3	23	86	73-1	0	99	.265	.353	.450	106	5	8-4	.931	5	97	104	3b123,O20(15/0/5)		0.6
1996	†Atl N★	157	598	114	185	32	5	30	110	87-0	0	88	.309	.393	.530	134	31	14-1	.947	-30	75	94	3b118,S38/OR	5	0.8
1997	†Atl N★	157	597	100	176	41	3	21	111	76-8	0	88	.295	.371	.479	120	19	20-5	.955	-25	81	76	3b152,O5(3/0/3)		-0.3

(continued from previous page)

YEAR	TM LG	G	AB	R	H	2B	3B	HR	RBI	BB-IB	HP	SO	AVG	OBP	SLG	AOPS	ABR	SB-CS	FA	FR	RNG	THR	GAMES AT POSITION	DL	BFW
1998	†Atl N★	160	601	123	188	29	5	34	107	96-1	1	93	.313	.404	.547	150	46	16-6	.971	-5	89	111	3b158		4.2
1999	†Atl N	157	567	116	181	41	1	45	110	126-18	2	94	.311	.404	.566	145	67	25-3	.950	-34	76	42	3b156/S		3.6
2000	†Atl N★	156	579	118	180	38	1	36	111	95-10	2	64	.311	.404	.566	145	42	14-7	.944	-4	100	91	3b152,S6		3.8
2001	†Atl N★	159	572	113	189	33	5	38	102	98-20	2	82	.330	.427	.605	162	56	9-10	.945	-25	83	51	3b149,O8L/D		2.9
2002	†Atl N	158	548	90	179	35	1	26	100	107-23	2	89	.327	.435	.536	159	50	8-2	.975	-6	94	81	O149L/D		3.9
2003	†Atl N	153	555	103	169	33	2	27	106	94-13	1	83	.305	.402	.517	139	36	2-2	.968	-14	74	97	3b96,O29L,D7		1.5
2004	†Atl N	137	472	69	117	20	1	30	96	84-8	4	96	.248	.362	.485	117	13	2-0	.975	-5	100	78	3b96,O29L,D7	19	0.8
2005	†Atl N	109	358	66	106	30	0	21	72	72-5	0	56	.296	.412	.556	147	28	5-1	.980	-6	92	101	3b101	42	2.3
Total	12	1651	5974	1101	1811	355	27	331	1111	1009-107	14	933	.303	.401	.538	141	394	123-41	.954	-154	87	78	3b1205,O364(356/0/9),S48,D9	197	24.2

JONES, LEVIN Levin B Baltimore MD d5.14

YEAR	TM LG	G	AB	R	H	2B	3B	HR	RBI	BB-IB	HP	SO	AVG	OBP	SLG	AOPS	ABR	SB-CS	FA	FR	RNG	THR	GAMES AT POSITION	DL	BFW
1873	Mar NA	1	4	0	3	0	0	0	1	0		0	.750	.750	.750	452	2	0-0	.800	-0	0	0	/OC		0.1
1874	Bal NA	2	7	0	1	0	0	0	1	0		0	.143	.143	.143	-8	-1	0-0	.875	-0			/COR		-0.1
Total	2 NA	3	11	0	4	0	0	0	2	0		0	.364	.364	.364	140	1	0-0	.800	-1			O2(0/1/1)/C		0.0

JONES, LYNN Lynn Morris B1.1.1953 Meadville PA BR/TR/5-9/175* [CinN74 10/239] d4.13 C5 b-Darryl Col Thiel

YEAR	TM LG	G	AB	R	H	2B	3B	HR	RBI	BB-IB	HP	SO	AVG	OBP	SLG	AOPS	ABR	SB-CS	FA	FR	RNG	THR	GAMES AT POSITION	DL	BFW
1979	Det A	95	213	33	63	8	0	4	26	17-0	1	22	.296	.349	.390	96	-0	9-6	.980	-0	102	73	O84(20/42/25),D6		-0.3
1980	Det A	30	55	9	14	2	2	0	6	10-0	0	5	.255	.364	.364	99	0	1-0	1.000	1	125	0	O17(4/4/9),D6	86	0.1
1981	Det A	71	174	19	45	5	0	2	19	18-1	1	10	.259	.328	.322	86	-3	1-2	.989	-1	88	146	O60(9/0/52),D4		-0.7
1982	Det A	58	139	15	31	3	1	0	14	7-0	0	14	.223	.259	.259	43	-11	0-2	1.000	1	102	103	O56(5/2/49)/D		-1.3
1983	Det A	49	64	9	17	1	2	0	6	3-0	0	6	.266	.299	.344	78	-2	1-0	.968	1	102	198	O31(9/1/22),D6		-0.2
1984	†KC A	47	103	11	31	6	0	1	10	4-0	1	9	.301	.330	.388	98	0	1-3	.962	1	84	81	O45(13/7/29)	86	-0.7
1985	†KC A	110	152	12	32	7	0	0	9	8-0	3	15	.211	.261	.257	43	-12	0-1	.983	-1	100	60	O100(57/21/32),D2		-1.5
1986	KC A	67	47	1	6	2	0	0	1	6-0	1	5	.128	.226	.170	10	-6	0-0	.971	-3	82	0	O62(37/8/19)/2D		-0.9
Total	8	527	947	109	239	34	5	7	91	73-1	6	86	.252	.308	.321	73	-13	13-14	.975	-3	96	78	O455(154/85/237),D28/2	172	-5.5

JONES, MACK Mack F. "Mack the Knife" B11.6.1938 Atlanta GA D6.8.2004 Atlanta GA BL/TR/6-1/180(180-204) d7.13

YEAR	TM LG	G	AB	R	H	2B	3B	HR	RBI	BB-IB	HP	SO	AVG	OBP	SLG	AOPS	ABR	SB-CS	FA	FR	RNG	THR	GAMES AT POSITION	DL	BFW
1961	Mil N	28	104	13	24	3	2	0	12	12-2	2	28	.231	.322	.298	70	-4	4-4	1.000	-4	70	103	O26C		-1.0
1962	Mil N	91	333	51	85	17	4	10	36	44-3	7	100	.255	.354	.420	110	6	5-1	.973	-10	84	39	O91(0/9/85)		-1.0
1963	Mil N	93	228	36	50	11	4	3	22	26-5	7	59	.219	.317	.342	91	-2	8-4	.978	-4	97	24	O80(12/69/0)		-0.8
1965	Mil N	143	504	78	132	18	7	31	75	29-1	9	122	.262	.313	.510	127	15	8-2	.980	-8	93	0	O133(31/119/0)		0.4
1966	Atl N	118	417	60	110	14	1	23	66	39-4	8	85	.264	.335	.468	120	11	16-10	.981	-5	103	13	O112(1/112/3)/1		0.3
1967	Atl N	140	454	72	115	23	4	17	50	64-4	9	108	.253	.355	.434	127	18	10-6	.985	-3	95	98	O126(26/100/0)		-0.3
1968	Cin N	103	234	40	59	9	1	10	34	28-3	5	46	.252	.341	.427	123	7	2-3	.988	-7	77	29	O60(24/34/3)		2.2
1969	Mon N	135	455	73	123	23	5	22	79	67-8	15	110	.270	.379	.488	141	27	6-7	.959	2	105	88	O129(125/5/0)		0.8
1970	Mon N	108	271	51	65	11	3	14	32	59-0	13	74	.240	.398	.458	129	14	5-3	.968	-2	96	59	O87(85/2/0)		-0.5
1971	Mon N	43	91	11	15	3	0	3	9	15-1	2	24	.165	.296	.297	67	-4	1-0	.952	0	101	76	O27L		1.3
Total	10	1002	3091	485	778	132	31	133	415	383-31	77	756	.252	.347	.444	120	88	65-40	.976	-40	95	53	O871(331/476/91)/1		

JONES, RED Morris E. B11.2.1911 Timpson TX D6.30.1974 Lincoln CA BL/TR/6-3/190 d4.16

YEAR	TM LG	G	AB	R	H	2B	3B	HR	RBI	BB-IB	HP	SO	AVG	OBP	SLG	AOPS	ABR	SB-CS	FA	FR	RNG	THR	GAMES AT POSITION	DL	BFW
1940	StL N	12	11	0	1	0	0	0	0	1-0	0	2	.091	.167	.091	-26	-2	0	1.000	0	139	0	/OL		-0.2

JONES, RICKY Ricky Miron B6.4.1958 Tupelo MS BR/TR/6-3/186 [BalA80 15/390] d9.3 Col West Georgia

YEAR	TM LG	G	AB	R	H	2B	3B	HR	RBI	BB-IB	HP	SO	AVG	OBP	SLG	AOPS	ABR	SB-CS	FA	FR	RNG	THR	GAMES AT POSITION	DL	BFW
1986	Bal A	16	33	2	6	2	0	0	4	6-0	0	8	.182	.308	.242	53	-2	0-0	1.000	4	124	105	2b11,3b6		0.3

JONES, BOB Robert Oliver B10.11.1949 Elkton MD BL/TL/6-2/195(170-215) [TexA67 36/665] d10.1 C2

YEAR	TM LG	G	AB	R	H	2B	3B	HR	RBI	BB-IB	HP	SO	AVG	OBP	SLG	AOPS	ABR	SB-CS	FA	FR	RNG	THR	GAMES AT POSITION	DL	BFW
1974	Tex A	2	5	0	0	0	0	0	0	0-0	0	1	.000	.000	.000	-99	-1	0-0	1.000	0	143	0	O2L		-0.1
1975	Tex A	9	11	2	1	0	0	0	0	3-0	0	3	.091	.286	.091	11	-1	0-0	1.000	0	123	0	O5(3/1/1)/D		-0.4
1976	Cal A	78	166	22	35	6	0	6	17	14-3	1	30	.211	.273	.355	89	-3	3-0	.990	1	91	182	O62(17/25/21),D2		0.0
1977	Cal A	14	17	3	3	0	0	1	3	4-0	0	5	.176	.318	.353	90	0	0-0	—	0			D6		0.4
1981	Tex A	10	34	4	9	1	0	3	7	1-0	0	7	.265	.286	.559	145	2	0-1	1.000	3	106	601	O10(1/0/9)		-0.4
1983	Tex A	41	72	5	16	4	0	1	11	5-1	2	17	.222	.284	.319	69	-3	0-2	1.000	-0	103	155	O22(11/0/11),b15,D4		-0.5
1984	Tex A	64	143	14	37	4	0	4	22	10-1	1	19	.259	.308	.371	85	-3	1-1	1.000	-3	81	22	O30(8/1/22),D10,1b4	18	-0.9
1985	Tex A	83	134	14	30	2	0	5	23	11-1	1	30	.224	.284	.351	72	-5	0-0	.909	-1	100		O9(5/0/4),1b2		-0.5
1986	Tex A	13	21	1	2	0	0	0	3	2-0	0	5	.095	.174	.095	-24	-4	0-0							
Total	9	314	603	65	133	17	0	20	86	50-6	5	117	.221	.282	.348	78	-18	5-4	.992	1	97	152	O151(53/27/73),D34,1b22	18	-2.5

JONES, BOB Robert Walter "Ducky" B12.2.1889 Clayton CA D8.30.1964 San Diego CA BL/TR/6-0/170 d4.11

YEAR	TM LG	G	AB	R	H	2B	3B	HR	RBI	BB-IB	HP	SO	AVG	OBP	SLG	AOPS	ABR	SB-CS	FA	FR	RNG	THR	GAMES AT POSITION	DL	BFW
1917	Det A	46	77	16	12	1	2	0	2	4	0	8	.156	.198	.221	28	-7	3	.938	-1	114	19	2b18,3b8		-0.9
1918	Det A	74	287	43	79	14	4	0	21	17	2	16	.275	.320	.352	107	-7	1	.947	-5	93	48	3b63,1b6/O		-0.2
1919	Det A	127	439	37	114	18	6	1	57	34	1	39	.260	.314	.335	84	-10	11	.944	-22	85	71	3b67,2b5/S		-3.0
1920	Det A	81	265	35	66	6	3	1	18	22	1	13	.249	.309	.306	65	-14	3-4	.942	0	100	65	3b67,2b5/S		-1.2
1921	Det A	141	554	82	168	23	9	1	72	37	2	24	.303	.348	.383	87	-12	8-9	.950	9	**106**	45	3b141		0.4
1922	Det A	124	455	65	117	10	6	3	44	36	2	18	.257	.314	.325	69	-22	8-5	**.962**	10	**105**	95	3b119		-0.4
1923	Det A	100	372	51	93	15	4	1	40	29	1	13	.250	.306	.320	66	-19	7-6	.954	7	107	100	3b97		-1.4
1924	Det A	110	393	52	107	27	4	0	47	20	1	20	.272	.308	.361	73	-17	1-5	.956	-2	100	76	3b106		-0.5
1925	Det A	50	148	18	35	6	0	0	15	9	0	5	.236	.280	.277	42	-13	1-1	.985	6	119	66	3b46		-0.5
Total	9	853	2990	399	791	120	38	7	316	208	8	156	.265	.314	.337	75	-113	49-30	.953	3	101	72	3b774,2b23,1b6/SO		-7.9

JONES, RON Ronald Glen B6.11.1964 Seguin TX BL/TR/5-10/200(195-214) d8.26 Col Wharton Co. (TX) JC

YEAR	TM LG	G	AB	R	H	2B	3B	HR	RBI	BB-IB	HP	SO	AVG	OBP	SLG	AOPS	ABR	SB-CS	FA	FR	RNG	THR	GAMES AT POSITION	DL	BFW
1988	Phi N	33	124	15	36	6	1	8	26	2-0	0	14	.290	.295	.548	136	5	0-0	1.000	2	115	65	O32R		0.6
1989	Phi N	12	31	7	9	0	0	2	4	9-1	0	9	.290	.450	.484	167	3	1-0	1.000	2	142	191	O12(3/0/10)	166	0.6
1990	Phi N	24	58	5	16	2	0	3	7	9-0	0	9	.276	.373	.466	129	2	0-1	—	0			/H	95	0.1
1991	Phi N	28	26	0	4	2	0	0	3	2-0	0	9	.154	.214	.231	25	-3	0-0	1.000	-1	82	94	O16(8/0/8)	56	-0.4
Total	4	97	239	27	65	10	1	13	40	22-1	0	33	.272	.330	.485	128	7	1-1	1.000	3	111	95	O60(11/0/50)	317	0.9

JONES, ROSS Ross A. B1.14.1960 Miami FL BR/TR/6-2/185* [LAN80 1/9] d4.2 Col Miami

YEAR	TM LG	G	AB	R	H	2B	3B	HR	RBI	BB-IB	HP	SO	AVG	OBP	SLG	AOPS	ABR	SB-CS	FA	FR	RNG	THR	GAMES AT POSITION	DL	BFW
1984	NY N	17	10	2	1	0	0	0	1	3-0	0	4	.100	.308	.200	46	-1	0-0	.833	-1	90	92	S6/23		-0.1
1986	Sea A	11	21	0	2	0	0	0	0	0-0	0	4	.095	.095	.095	-47	-4	0-1	1.000	-0	79	53	S4,2b3,3b2/D		-0.5
1987	KC A	39	114	10	29	4	2	0	10	5-0	1	15	.254	.285	.325	61	-7	1-0	.974	1	112	65	S36,2b3		-0.2
Total	3	67	145	12	32	5	2	0	11	8-0	1	23	.221	.261	.283	46	-12	1-1	.971	-0	109	65	S46,2b7,3b3/D		-0.8

JONES, RUPPERT Ruppert Sanderson B3.12.1955 Dallas TX BL/TL/5-10/175(170-189) [KCA73 3/57] d8.1

YEAR	TM LG	G	AB	R	H	2B	3B	HR	RBI	BB-IB	HP	SO	AVG	OBP	SLG	AOPS	ABR	SB-CS	FA	FR	RNG	THR	GAMES AT POSITION	DL	BFW
1976	KC A	28	51	9	11	1	1	1	7	3-0	0	16	.216	.259	.333	72	-2	0-2	1.000	-1	87	0	O17(2/7/9),D3		-0.5
1977	Sea A★	160	597	85	157	26	8	24	76	55-3	2	120	.263	.324	.454	111	7	13-9	.981	9	114	99	O155C,D4	34	1.5
1978	Sea A	129	472	48	111	24	3	6	46	55-2	0	85	.235	.312	.337	83	-10	22-6	.985	6	107	116	O128C		-0.2
1979	Sea A	162	622	109	166	29	9	21	78	86-4	3	78	.267	.356	.444	112	12	33-12	.989	4	102	121	O161C	85	1.7
1980	NY A	83	328	38	73	11	3	9	42	34-3	5	50	.223	.299	.357	81	-9	18-8	.988	3	103	119	O104C		0.4
1981	SD N	105	397	53	99	34	1	4	39	43-2	0	66	.249	.318	.370	105	3	11-11	.984	-2	105	42	O114C	15	1.6
1982	SD N★	116	424	69	120	20	2	12	61	62-11	1	90	.283	.373	.425	131	20	18-15	.984	1	106	67	O111C,1b5		-0.5
1983	SD N	133	335	42	78	12	3	12	49	35-4	0	58	.233	.305	.394	95	-3	11-11	.981	1	106	0	O73(61/24/0),D2		1.2
1984	†Det A	79	215	26	61	12	1	12	37	21-0	0	47	.284	.346	.516	136	10	2-4	1.000	5	112	104	O73(31/18/31),D43		1.3
1985	Cal A	125	389	66	90	17	2	21	67	57-2	1	82	.231	.328	.447	110	6	10-3	.981	-6	93	68	O121(28/10/96)		-0.4
1986	†Cal A	126	393	73	90	21	3	17	49	64-5	3	87	.229	.339	.427	109	-1	2-1	.965	-3	91	94	O66(52/3/21),D3		-0.6
1987	Cal A	85	192	25	47	8	2	8	28	20-2	1	38	.245	.316	.432	99	-1	2-1	.986	-3	91	99	O66(52/3/21),D3		4.8
Total	12	1331	4415	643	1103	215	38	147	579	534-38	12	817	.250	.330	.416	106	39	143-84	.986	28	105	99	O1205(174/917/157),D55,1b5	134	

JONES, JACK Ryerson L. "Ri","Angel Sleeves" B Cincinnati OH BR/TR d8.13

YEAR	TM LG	G	AB	R	H	2B	3B	HR	RBI	BB-IB	HP	SO	AVG	OBP	SLG	AOPS	ABR	SB-CS	FA	FR	RNG	THR	GAMES AT POSITION	DL	BFW
1883	Lou AA	2	7	1	2	0	0	0		0			.000	.000	.000	-99	-2		.500	-1	0	0	O2C/S		-0.2
1884	Cin U	69	272	36	71	5	1	2	12				.261	.292	.309	76	-16		.858	-1	109	146	S41,2b19,3b10		-1.4
Total	2	71	279	37	71	5	1	2	12				.254	.285	.301	73	-18		.857	-2	109	143	S42,2b19,3b10,O2C		-1.6

JONES, TERRY Terry Lee B2.15.1971 Birmingham AL BB/TR/5-10/165* [ColN93 40/1136] d9.8 Col North Alabama

YEAR	TM LG	G	AB	R	H	2B	3B	HR	RBI	BB-IB	HP	SO	AVG	OBP	SLG	AOPS	ABR	SB-CS	FA	FR	RNG	THR	GAMES AT POSITION	DL	BFW
1996	Col N	12	10	1	3	0	0	0	1	0-0	0	1	.300	.273	.300	48	-1	0-0	1.000	-0	91	0	O4C		-0.1
1998	Mon N	60	212	30	46	7	2	1	15	21-1	0	46	.217	.288	.283	52	-15	16-4	.988	5	121	113	O60C		-0.7
1999	Mon N	17	63	4	17	1	0	0	3	3-0	0	14	.270	.303	.317	60	-4	1-2	1.000	3	134	235	O17(5/12/0)		-0.1
2000	Mon N	108	168	30	42	8	2	0	13	10-1	0	32	.250	.292	.321	54	-12	7-2	.970	3	111	163	O78(55/26/7)	16	-0.9

YEAR	TM LG	G	AB	R	H	2B	3B	HR	RBI	BB-IB	HP	SO	AVG	OBP	SLG	AOPS	ABR	SB-CS	FA	FR	RNG	THR	GAMES AT POSITION	DL	BFW
2001	Mon N	30	77	8	20	5	0	0	2	2-0	0	11	.260	.278	.325	56	-5	3-0	.977	2	109	195	O22(10/13/2)	142	-0.3
Total 5		227	530	78	128	21	5	1	34	36-2	0	106	.242	.289	.306	54	-37	27-8	.984	13	117	151	O181(70/115/9)	158	-2.1

JONES, TOM Thomas B1.22.1877 Honesdale PA D6.19.1923 Danville PA BR/TR/6-1/195 d8.25

YEAR	TM LG	G	AB	R	H	2B	3B	HR	RBI	BB-IB	HP	SO	AVG	OBP	SLG	AOPS	ABR	SB-CS	FA	FR	RNG	THR	GAMES AT POSITION	DL	BFW
1902	Bal A	37	159	22	45	8	4	0	14	2	0		.283	.292	.384	83	-5	1	.955	-2	110	94	1b37/2		-0.6
1904	StL A	156	625	53	152	15	10	2	68	15	8		.243	.270	.309	88	-11	16	.988	1	107	87	1b134,2b23,O4R		-1.5
1905	StL A	135	504	44	122	16	2	0	48	30	4		.242	.290	.282	86	-8	19	.985	7	119	92	1b135		-0.4
1906	StL A	144	539	51	136	22	6	0	30	24	5		.252	.290	.315	94	-5	27	.985	11	129	101	1b143		0.4
1907	StL A	155	549	52	137	17	3	0	34	34	4		.250	.298	.291	88	-7	24	.983	2	106	101	1b155		-0.9
1908	StL A	155	549	43	135	14	2	1	50	30	4		.246	.290	.284	86	-9	18	.986	-2	93	118	1b155		-1.5
1909	StL A	97	337	30	84	9	3	0	29	18	6		.249	.299	.294	94	-3	13	.989	7	121	120	1b95,3b2		0.3
	†Det A	44	153	13	43	9	0	0	18	5	3		.281	.317	.340	103	0	9	.984	3	131	104	1b44		0.3
	Year	141	490	43	127	18	3	0	47	23	9		.259	.305	.308	97	-2	22	.988	9	124	115	1b139,3b2		0.6
1910	Det A	135	432	32	110	12	4	1	45	35	10		.255	.325	.308	92	-3	22	.985	-4	89	81	1b135		-1.1
Total 8		1058	3847	340	964	122	34	4	336	193	44		.251	.293	.303	90	-51	149	.984	22	109	100	1b1033,2b24,O4R,3b2		-5.0

JONES, TRACY Tracy Donald B3.31.1961 Hawthorne CA BR/TR/6-3/220(180-220) [CinN83*S1/1] d4.7 Col Loyola Marymount

YEAR	TM LG	G	AB	R	H	2B	3B	HR	RBI	BB-IB	HP	SO	AVG	OBP	SLG	AOPS	ABR	SB-CS	FA	FR	RNG	THR	GAMES AT POSITION	DL	BFW
1986	Cin N	46	86	16	30	3	0	2	10	9-1	0	5	.349	.406	.453	133	4	7-1	1.000	2	125	82	O24(23/3/0),1b2	76	0.6
1987	Cin N	117	359	53	104	17	3	10	44	23-0	3	40	.290	.333	.437	100	-1	31-8	.990	0	109	36	O95(56/34/17)		0.0
1988	Cin N	37	83	9	19	1	0	1	9	8-2	1	6	.229	.304	.277	66	-4	9-0	.955	-0	105	0	O25(3/0/23)	42	-0.3
	Mon N	53	141	20	47	5	1	2	15	12-1	1	12	.333	.390	.426	127	5	9-6	1.000	-4	73	99	O43(26/9/15)		0.1
	Year	90	224	29	66	6	1	3	24	20-3	2	18	.295	.358	.371	105	2	18-6	.980	-4	85	63	O68(29/9/38)		-0.2
1989	SF N	40	97	5	18	4	0	0	12	5-3	1	14	.186	.233	.227	33	-9	2-1	1.000	-4	69	0	O30(9/5/22)		-1.5
	Det A	46	158	41	41	10	0	3	26	16-1	1	16	.259	.326	.380	102	1	1-1	.986	-1	102	0	O36(34/0/3),D8	46	-0.2
1990	Det A	50	118	15	27	4	1	4	9	6-0	3	13	.229	.283	.381	83	-3	1-1	.952	1	91	237	O27L,D20		-0.4
	Sea A	25	86	8	26	4	0	2	15	3-0	2	12	.302	.341	.419	110	1	0-1	1.000	-1	92	0	O18(18/1/0),D5		-0.1
	Year	75	204	23	53	8	1	6	24	9-0	5	25	.260	.307	.397	94	-2	1-2	.973	-1	91	126	O45(45/1/0),D25	56	-0.5
1991	Sea A	79	175	30	44	8	1	3	24	18-2	1	25	.251	.321	.360	89	-3	2-0	1.000	-0	108	46		30	-0.4
Total 6		493	1303	173	356	56	6	27	164	100-10	13	140	.273	.329	.388	96	-9	62-19	.988	-9	98	46	O334(231/52/83),D70,1b2	250	-2.2

JONES, NIPPY Vernal Leroy B6.29.1925 Los Angeles CA D10.3.1995 Sacramento CA BR/TR/6-1/185* d6.8

YEAR	TM LG	G	AB	R	H	2B	3B	HR	RBI	BB-IB	HP	SO	AVG	OBP	SLG	AOPS	ABR	SB-CS	FA	FR	RNG	THR	GAMES AT POSITION	DL	BFW
1946	†StL N	16	12	3	4	0	0	0	1	2	0	2	.333	.429	.333	113	0	0	.800	0	127	319	2b3		0.1
1947	StL N	23	73	6	18	4	1	0	5	2	0	10	.247	.267	.342	58	-5	0	.935	-2	103	57	2b13,O2R		-0.6
1948	StL N	132	481	58	122	21	9	10	81	36	1	45	.254	.307	.397	84	-12	2	.986	-8	78	107	1b128		-2.5
1949	StL N	110	380	51	114	20	2	8	62	16	1	20	.300	.330	.426	97	-3	1	.984	-7	74	113	1b98		-1.3
1950	StL N	13	26	0	6	1	0	0	6	3	0	1	.231	.310	.269	52	-2	0	.983	-0	79	147	1b8		-0.2
1951	StL N	80	300	20	79	12	0	3	41	9	1	13	.263	.287	.333	66	-15	1-2	.991	-0	100	115	1b71	90	-1.8
1952	Phi N	8	30	1	5	0	0	0	5	0	0	4	.167	.167	.267	1	-4	0-0	.976	0	123	125	1b8		-0.4
1957	†Mil N	30	79	5	21	2	1	2	8	3-1	0	7	.266	.293	.392	88	-2	0-0	.994	0	103	90	1b20/OR		-0.3
Total 8		412	1381	146	369	60	12	25	209	71-1	3	102	.267	.304	.382	81	-43	4-2	.987	-17	84	111	1b333,2b16,O3R	90	-7.0

JONES, BILL William B Syracuse NY d5.17

YEAR	TM LG	G	AB	R	H	2B	3B	HR	RBI	BB-IB	HP	SO	AVG	OBP	SLG	AOPS	ABR	SB-CS	FA	FR	RNG	THR	GAMES AT POSITION	DL	BFW
1882	Bal AA	4	15	1	1	0	0	0		0			.067	.067	.067	-59	-2		1.000	1	248	0	O2(0/1/1),C2		-0.2
1884	Phi U	4	14	2	2	0	0	0	1				.143	.200	.143	6	-2		.862	-1			C4/OR		-0.3
Total 2		8	29	3	3	0	0	0	1				.103	.133	.103	-25	-4		.857	-1			C6,O3(0/1/2)		-0.5

JONES, BILL William Dennis "Midget" B4.8.1887 Hartland NB, Can. D10.10.1946 Boston MA BL/TR/5-6.5/157 d6.20

YEAR	TM LG	G	AB	R	H	2B	3B	HR	RBI	BB-IB	HP	SO	AVG	OBP	SLG	AOPS	ABR	SB-CS	FA	FR	RNG	THR	GAMES AT POSITION	DL	BFW
1911	Bos N	24	51	6	11	2	1	0	3	15		7	.216	.394	.294	87	0	1	.867	-1	97	127	O18C		-0.2
1912	Bos N	3	2	0	1	0	0	0	2	0		1	.500	.500	.500	171	0	0	—	0			/H		0.0
Total 2		27	53	6	12	2	1	0	5	15	0	8	.226	.397	.302	89	0	1	.867	-1	97	127	O18C		-0.2

JONES, TEX William Roderick B8.4.1885 Marion KS D2.26.1938 Wichita KS BR/TR/6-0/192 d4.13

YEAR	TM LG	G	AB	R	H	2B	3B	HR	RBI	BB-IB	HP	SO	AVG	OBP	SLG	AOPS	ABR	SB-CS	FA	FR	RNG	THR	GAMES AT POSITION	DL	BFW
1911	Chi A	9	31	4	6	1	0	0	4	3	0		.194	.265	.226	39	-3	1	1.000	3	198	153	1b9		0.0

JONES, TIM William Timothy B12.1.1962 Sumter SC BL/TR/5-10/175* [StLN85 2/46] d7.26 Col The Citadel

YEAR	TM LG	G	AB	R	H	2B	3B	HR	RBI	BB-IB	HP	SO	AVG	OBP	SLG	AOPS	ABR	SB-CS	FA	FR	RNG	THR	GAMES AT POSITION	DL	BFW
1988	StL N	31	52	2	14	0	0	0	3	4-0	1	10	.269	.321	.269	70	-2	4-1	.955	3	110	121	S9,2b8/3		0.2
1989	StL N	42	75	11	22	6	0	0	7	7-1	1	8	.293	.353	.373	107	1	1-0	1.000	-3	102	58	2b12,S12,3b5/COL		-0.1
1990	StL N	67	128	9	28	7	1	1	12	12-1	1	20	.219	.291	.313	65	-6	3-4	.944	-0	110	96	S29,2b19,3b6/P		-0.5
1991	StL N	16	24	1	4	2	0	0	2	2-1	0	6	.167	.222	.250	35	-2	0-1	1.000	-5	70	95	S14,2b4		-0.7
1992	StL N	67	145	9	29	4	0	0	3	11-1	0	29	.200	.256	.228	39	-12	5-2	.972	-9	85	156	S34,2b28,3b2/OC	33	-1.9
1993	StL N	29	61	13	16	6	0	0	1	9-0	1	8	.262	.366	.361	96	0	2-2	.976	2	120	94	S21,2b7		0.3
Total 6		252	485	45	113	25	1	1	28	45-4	4	81	.233	.300	.295	62	-21	15-10	.964	-13	98	98	S119,2b78,3b14,O2(1/1/0)/PC	33	-2.7

JONES, WILLIE Willie Edward "Puddin' Head" B8.16.1925 Dillon SC D10.18.1983 Cincinnati OH BR/TR/6-1/192* d9.10

YEAR	TM LG	G	AB	R	H	2B	3B	HR	RBI	BB-IB	HP	SO	AVG	OBP	SLG	AOPS	ABR	SB-CS	FA	FR	RNG	THR	GAMES AT POSITION	DL	BFW
1947	Phi N	18	62	5	14	0	1	0	10	7	0	7	.226	.304	.258	53	-4	2	.909	1	110	90	3b17		-0.4
1948	Phi N	17	60	9	20	2	0	2	9	3	0	5	.333	.365	.467	126	2	0	.926	1	95	34	3b17		0.3
1949	Phi N	149	532	71	130	35	1	19	77	65	1	66	.244	.328	.421	102	2	3	.948	-6	98	63	3b145		-0.5
1950	†Phi N★	157	610	100	163	28	6	25	88	61	3	40	.267	.337	.456	108	5	5	.954	-5	95	95	3b157		0.0
1951	Phi N★	148	564	79	161	28	5	22	81	60	4	47	.285	.358	.470	123	18	6-2	.966	-8	91	95	3b147		1.0
1952	Phi N	147	541	60	135	12	3	18	72	53	6	36	.250	.323	.383	96	-4	5-3	.969	5	97	135	3b147		0.1
1953	Phi N	149	481	61	108	16	2	19	70	85	1	45	.225	.342	.385	90	-6	1-1	.975	1	93	124	3b147		-0.5
1954	Phi N	142	535	64	145	28	3	12	56	61	0	54	.271	.342	.402	94	-4	4-1	.968	2	96	95	3b141		-0.2
1955	Phi N	146	516	65	133	20	3	16	81	77-5	3	51	.258	.352	.401	103	4	6-2	.960	-7	84	86	3b146		-0.3
1956	Phi N	149	520	88	144	20	4	17	78	92-6	1	49	.277	.383	.429	121	19	5-4	.973	-1	89	91	3b149		1.8
1957	Phi N	133	440	58	96	19	2	9	47	61-3	0	41	.218	.310	.332	76	-14	1-0	.966	-7	83	87	3b126		-2.2
1958	Phi N	118	398	52	108	15	1	14	60	49-4	2	45	.271	.351	.420	105	-4	1-2	.967	-14	82	60	3b110/1		-1.1
1959	Phi N	47	160	23	43	9	1	7	24	19-2	0	14	.269	.343	.469	113	3	0-0	.975	-2	93	72	3b46		0.1
	Cle A	11	18	1	4	1	0	0	1	1-0	1	1	.222	.263	.278	51	-1	0-0	.929	1	125	295	3b4		0.0
	Cin N	72	233	33	58	12	1	7	31	28-1	1	26	.249	.330	.399	91	-3	0-2	.966	-3	84	86	3b68		-0.6
1960	Cin N	79	149	16	40	7	0	3	27	31-3	0	16	.268	.388	.376	110	4	1-0	.962	-5	83	79	3b46/2		0.0
1961	Cin N	9	7	1	0	0	0	0	0	2-0	0	3	.000	.222	.000	-34	-1	0-0	.000	-0	0	0	/3		-0.2
Total 15		1691	5826	786	1502	252	33	190	812	755-24	22	541	.258	.343	.410	102	24	40-17	.963	-47	91	93	3b1614/21		-2.7

JONNARD, BUBBER Clarence James B11.23.1897 Nashville TN D8.23.1977 New York NY BR/TR/6-1/185 d10.1 C6 twb-Claude

YEAR	TM LG	G	AB	R	H	2B	3B	HR	RBI	BB-IB	HP	SO	AVG	OBP	SLG	AOPS	ABR	SB-CS	FA	FR	RNG	THR	GAMES AT POSITION	DL	BFW
1920	Chi A	2	5	0	0	0	0	0	0	0	1		.000	.000	.000	-99	-1	0-0	.857	-0	0	142	/C		-0.1
1922	Pit N	10	21	4	5	0	1	0	2	2	0	4	.238	.304	.333	64	-1	0-0	.974	1	124	85	C10		0.0
1926	Phi N	19	34	3	4	1	0	0	2	3	0	4	.118	.189	.147	-8	-5	0-0	.949	-1	89	116	C15		-0.5
1927	Phi N	53	143	18	42	9	0	1	14	7	0	7	.294	.327	.336	77	-5	0-0	.967	-7	82	82	C41		-1.0
1929	StL N	18	31	1	3	0	0	0	2	0	0	6	.097	.097	.097	-51	-8	0-0	.957	1	128	81	C18		-0.6
1935	Phi N	1	1	0	0	0	0	0	0	0	0	0	.000	.000	.000	-91	0	0	1.000	-0	0	0	/C		-0.6
Total 6		103	235	26	54	7	1	0	20	12	0	23	.230	.267	.268	41	-20	0-0	.960	-6	93	88	C86		-2.2

JOOST, EDDIE Edwin David B6.5.1916 San Francisco CA BR/TR/6-0/175* d9.11 Def 1944 M1

YEAR	TM LG	G	AB	R	H	2B	3B	HR	RBI	BB-IB	HP	SO	AVG	OBP	SLG	AOPS	ABR	SB-CS	FA	FR	RNG	THR	GAMES AT POSITION	DL	BFW
1936	Cin N	13	26	1	4	1	0	0	1	2	0	5	.154	.214	.192	-11	-3	0	.947	-0	114	127	S7,2b5		-0.3
1937	Cin N	6	12	0	1	0	0	0	0	0	0	3	.083	.083	.083	-57	-3	0	.875	-0	110	83	2b6		-0.3
1939	Cin N	42	143	23	36	6	3	0	14	12	0	15	.252	.310	.336	73	-6	1	.957	-2	92	104	2b32,S6		-0.6
1940	†Cin N	88	278	24	60	7	2	1	24	32	2	40	.216	.301	.266	57	-16	4	.960	-2	98	117	S78,2b7,3b4		-1.2
1941	Cin N	152	537	67	136	25	4	4	40	69	2	59	.253	.340	.337	91	-5	9	.942	-8	93	105	S147,2b4,1b2/3		-0.2
1942	Cin N	142	562	65	126	30	3	6	41	62	5	57	.224	.307	.320	84	-11	4	.933	-15	94	109	S130,2b15		-1.5
1943	Bos N	124	421	34	78	16	3	2	20	68	0	80	.185	.299	.252	61	-19	5	.945	3	122	88	3b67,2b60,S4		-1.3
1945	Bos N	35	141	16	35	7	1	0	9	13	0	7	.248	.312	.312	73	-5	0	.945	-7	80	92	2b19,3b16		-1.1
1947	Phi A	151	540	76	111	22	3	13	64	114	4	110	.206	.348	.330	87	-5	6-6	.956	-0	99	97	S151		-1.1
1948	Phi A	135	509	99	127	22	2	16	55	119	1	87	.250	.393	.386	110	12	2-4	.973	7	98	113	S135		2.6
1949	Phi A★	144	525	128	138	25	3	23	81	149	4	80	.263	.429	.453	138	38	2-1	.969	7	99	110	S144		5.1
1950	Phi A	131	476	79	111	12	3	18	58	103	3	68	.233	.373	.384	96	-1	5-1	.956	-5	98	109	S131		0.3
1951	Phi A	140	553	65	160	28	5	19	78	106	6	70	.289	.409	.461	132	29	10-8	.974	7	100	112	S140		4.3

YEAR	TM LG	G	AB	R	H	2B	3B	HR	RBI	BB-IB	HP	SO	AVG	OBP	SLG	AOPS	ABR	SB-CS	FA	FR	RNG	THR	GAMES AT POSITION	DL	BFW
1952	Phi A☆	146	540	94	132	26	3	20	75	122	5	94	.244	.388	.415	116	17	5-8	.962	-5	100	87	S146		2.0
1953	Phi A	51	177	39	44	6	0	6	15	45	0	24	.249	.401	.384	109	5	3-2	.958	-8	90	92	S51		0.1
1954	Phi A	19	47	7	17	3	0	1	9	10	0	10	.362	.474	.489	163	5	0-1	.963	-1	92	65	S9,3b5/2M		0.4
1955	Bos A	55	119	15	23	2	0	5	17	17-2	1	21	.193	.299	.336	65	-6	0-0	.932	1	112	144	S20,2b17,3b2		-0.3
Total	17	1574	5606	874	1339	238	35	134	601	1043-2	33	827	.239	.361	.366	99	26	61-31	.958	-28	97	106	S1299,2b166,3b95,1b2		8.3

JORDAN, DUTCH Adolf Otto B1.5.1880 Pittsburgh PA D12.23.1972 W.Allegheny PA BR/TR/5-10/185 d4.25

YEAR	TM LG	G	AB	R	H	2B	3B	HR	RBI	BB-IB	HP	SO	AVG	OBP	SLG	AOPS	ABR	SB-CS	FA	FR	RNG	THR	GAMES AT POSITION	DL	BFW
1903	Bro N	78	267	27	63	11	1	0	21	19	1		.236	.289	.285	66	-12	9	.928	-12	91	73	2b54,3b18,O4(1/0/3)/1		-2.3
1904	Bro N	87	252	21	45	10	2	0	19	13	2		.179	.225	.234	43	-17	7	.958	-19	82	77	2b70,3b11,1b4		-3.8
Total	2	165	519	48	108	21	3	0	40	32	3		.208	.258	.260	55	-29	16	.945	-31	86	75	2b124,3b29,1b5,O4(1/0/3)		-6.1

JORDAN, BUCK Baxter Byerly B1.16.1907 Cooleemee NC D3.18.1993 Salisbury NC BL/TR/6-0/170 d9.15

YEAR	TM LG	G	AB	R	H	2B	3B	HR	RBI	BB-IB	HP	SO	AVG	OBP	SLG	AOPS	ABR	SB-CS	FA	FR	RNG	THR	GAMES AT POSITION	DL	BFW
1927	NY N	5	5	0	1	0	0	0	0	0	0	3	.200	.200	.200	7	-1	0	—	0			/H		-0.1
1929	NY N	2	2	1	1	0	0	0	0	0	0	0	.500	.500	1.000	262	1	0	1.000	-0	0	592	/1		0.0
1931	Was A	9	18	3	4	2	0	0	1	1	0	3	.222	.263	.333	56	-1	0	.978	-1	0	95	1b7		-0.2
1932	Bos N	49	212	-27	68	12	3	2	29	4	0	5	.321	.333	.434	109	2	1	.991	-2	89	115	1b49		-0.5
1933	Bos N	152	588	77	168	29	9	4	46	34	2	22	.286	.327	.386	112	8	4	.991	-3	104	150	1b150		-1.0
1934	Bos N	124	489	68	152	26	9	2	58	35	1	17	.311	.358	.413	114	10	3	.989	-3	92	93	1b117		-0.5
1935	Bos N	130	470	62	131	24	5	3	35	19	0	17	.279	.307	.383	91	-7	3	.983	-2	97	79	1b95,3b8,O2R		-1.4
1936	Bos N	138	555	81	179	27	5	3	66	45	2	22	.323	.375	.405	118	15	2	.993	1	104	**129**	1b136		0.3
1937	Bos N	8	8	1	2	0	0	0	0	0	0	0	.250	.250	.250	40	-1	0	—	0			/H		-0.1
	Cin N	98	316	45	89	14	3	1	28	25	0	14	.282	.334	.354	92	-4	6	.989	-1	96	91·	1b76		-1.1
	Year	106	324	46	91	14	3	1	28	25	0	14	.281	.332	.352	91	-4	6	.989	-1	96	91	1b76		-1.2
1938	Cin N	9	7	0	2	0	0	0	0	2	0	0	.286	.444	.286	107	0	0	—	0			/H		0.0
	Phi N	87	310	31	93	18	1	0	18	17	0	4	.300	.336	.365	95	-2	1	.973	0	98	126	3b58,1b17		-0.2
	Year	96	317	31	95	18	1	0	18	19	0	4	.300	.339	.363	96	-2	1	.973	0	98	126	3b58,1b17		-0.2
Total	10	811	2980	396	890	153	35	17	281	182	5	109	.299	.340	.391	106	20	20-0	.990	-8	98	102	1b648,3b66,O2R		-4.8

JORDAN, BRIAN Brian O'Neal B3.29.1967 Baltimore MD BR/TR/6-1/205(205-225) [StLN88 1/30] d4.8 Col Richmond

YEAR	TM LG	G	AB	R	H	2B	3B	HR	RBI	BB-IB	HP	SO	AVG	OBP	SLG	AOPS	ABR	SB-CS	FA	FR	RNG	THR	GAMES AT POSITION	DL	BFW
1992	StL N	55	193	17	40	9	4	5	22	10-1	4	48	.207	.250	.373	76	-7	7-2	.991	-1	92	133	O53(27/9/21)	30	-1.0
1993	StL N	67	223	33	69	10	6	10	44	12-0	4	35	.309	.351	.543	137	10	6-6	.973	-2	96	101	O65(23/37/12)		0.7
1994	StL N	53	178	14	46	8	2	5	15	16-0	1	40	.258	.320	.410	89	-3	4-3	.991	5	114	165	O46(18/9/22)/1	33	0.5
1995	StL N	131	490	83	145	20	4	22	81	22-4	11	79	.296	.339	.488	113	7	24-9	.996	2	107	45	O126(0/13/116)		2.5
1996	†StL N	140	513	82	159	36	1	17	104	29-4	7	84	.310	.349	.483	118	13	22-5	.994	11	**120**	103	O136(0/13/128)/1	14	-0.8
1997	StL N	47	145	17	34	5	0	0	10	10-1	6	21	.234	.311	.269	53	-10	6-1	1.000	1	112	84	O44(0/14/30)	117	-0.8
1998	StL N	150	564	100	178	34	7	25	91	40-1	9	66	.316	.368	.534	135	27	17-5	.970	-2	102	118	O141(0/33/123)/3D		2.5
1999	†Atl N★	153	576	100	163	28	4	23	115	51-2	9	81	.283	.346	.465	105	3	13-8	.990	2	101	94	O150R		-0.2
2000	†Atl N	133	489	71	129	26	0	17	77	38-1	5	80	.264	.320	.421	87	-11	10-2	.990	6	111	87	O130R	15	-0.9
2001	†Atl N	148	560	82	165	32	3	25	97	31-3	5	80	.295	.334	.496	111	7	3-2	.991	10	112	117	O144(0/1/144),D2		1.0
2002	LA N	128	471	65	134	27	3	18	80	34-3	6	86	.285	.338	.469	120	10	2-2	.982	2	99	134	O125(121/0/4),D2	15	0.1
2003	LA N	66	224	28	67	9	0	6	28	23-3	4	30	.299	.372	.420	110	4	1-1	.990	-3	91	35	O62(54/14/3),D2	96	-0.5
2004	Tex A	61	212	27	47	13	1	5	23	16-2	1	25	.222	.275	.363	63	-12	2-2	.990	3	99	175	O62(45/0/17)	59	-1.5
2005	†Atl N	76	231	25	57	8	2	3	24	14-0	3	46	.247	.295	.338	65	-12	2-0	1.000	3	99	175	O62(45/0/17)	59	-1.5
Total	14	1408	5069	744	1433	265	37	181	811	346-25	73	819	.283	.334	.457	105	26	119-48	.988	38	106	102	O1328(289/143/944),D27,1b2/3	462	1.4

JORDAN, SLATS Clarence Veasey B9.27.1878 Baltimore MD D12.7.1953 Catonsville MD BL/TL/6-1/190 d9.28

YEAR	TM LG	G	AB	R	H	2B	3B	HR	RBI	BB-IB	HP	SO	AVG	OBP	SLG	AOPS	ABR	SB-CS	FA	FR	RNG	THR	GAMES AT POSITION	DL	BFW
1901	Bal A	1	3	0	0	0	0	0	0	0	0		.000	.000	.000	-96	-1	0	.867	-1	0	0	/1		-0.0
1902	Bal A	1	4	0	0	0	0	0	0	0	0		.000	.000	.000	-96	-1	0	—	-0	0	0	/OR		-0.0
Total	2	2	7	0	0	0	0	0	0	0	0		.000	.000	.000	-96	-2	0	.000	-1	0	0	/OR1		-0.0

JORDAN, JIMMY James William "Lord" B1.13.1908 Tucapau (now Startex) SC D12.4.1957 Gastonia NC BR/TR/5-9/157 d4.20

YEAR	TM LG	G	AB	R	H	2B	3B	HR	RBI	BB-IB	HP	SO	AVG	OBP	SLG	AOPS	ABR	SB-CS	FA	FR	RNG	THR	GAMES AT POSITION	DL	BFW
1933	Bro N	70	211	16	54	12	1	0	17	4	1	6	.256	.270	.322	71	-8	3	.969	6	113	77	S51,2b11		0.1
1934	Bro N	97	369	34	98	17	2	0	43	9	1	32	.266	.285	.322	66	-19	1	.956	-6	102	52	S51,2b41,3b9		-1.1
1935	Bro N	94	295	26	82	7	0	0	30	9	1	17	.278	.302	.302	64	-15	3	.983	19	121	103	2b46,S28,3b5		-0.4
1936	Bro N	115	398	26	93	15	1	2	28	15	0	21	.234	.262	.291	48	-30	1	.970	-17	86	78	2b98,S9,3b6		-4.1
Total	4	376	1273	102	327	51	4	2	118	37	2	76	.257	.279	.308	60	-72	8	.969	2	98	93	2b196,S139,3b20		-4.1

JORDAN, KEVIN Kevin Wayne B10.9.1969 San Francisco CA BR/TR/6-1/207(193-207) [NYA90 20/542] d8.8 Col Nebraska

YEAR	TM LG	G	AB	R	H	2B	3B	HR	RBI	BB-IB	HP	SO	AVG	OBP	SLG	AOPS	ABR	SB-CS	FA	FR	RNG	THR	GAMES AT POSITION	DL	BFW
1995	Phi N	24	54	6	10	1	0	2	6	2-1	1	9	.185	.228	.315	41	-5	0-0	.984	5	127	139	2b9/3		0.1
1996	Phi N	43	131	15	37	10	0	3	12	5-0	1	20	.282	.309	.427	93	-2	2-1	1.000	1	68	93	1b30,2b7/3	105	-0.4
1997	Phi N	84	177	19	47	8	0	6	30	3-0	0	26	.266	.273	.412	79	-6	0-1	.987	-4	59	73	1b25,3b12,2b6/D		-1.1
1998	Phi N	112	250	23	69	13	0	2	27	8-1	2	30	.276	.303	.352	72	-11	0-0	1.000	2	100	103	1b24,2b22,3b6,D8		-1.0
1999	Phi N	120	347	36	99	17	3	4	51	24-1	6	34	.285	.339	.386	83	-9	0-0	.943	2	96	115	3b62,2b33,1b13		-0.4
2000	Phi N	109	337	30	74	16	2	5	36	17-0	1	41	.220	.257	.323	46	-29	0-1	.988	-4	101	70	2b47,3b39,1b9		-3.0
2001	Phi N	68	113	9	27	5	0	1	13	14-2	1	20	.239	.323	.310	68	-5	0-0	.948	-2	43	67	1b10,2b10,3b10		-0.9
Total	7	560	1409	138	363	70	5	23	175	73-5	11	181	.258	.297	.363	70	-67	2-3	.977	4	110	104	2b134,3b131,1b111,D9	105	-6.7

JORDAN, MIKE Michael Henry "Mitty" B2.7.1863 Lawrence MA D9.25.1940 Lawrence MA 5-7.5/155 d8.21

YEAR	TM LG	G	AB	R	H	2B	3B	HR	RBI	BB-IB	HP	SO	AVG	OBP	SLG	AOPS	ABR	SB-CS	FA	FR	RNG	THR	GAMES AT POSITION	DL	BFW
1890	Pit N	37	125	8	12	1	0	0	6	15	3	19	.096	.210	.104	-9	-16	5	.947	4	161	0	O37(29/8/0)		-1.7

JORDAN, RICKY Paul Scott B5.26.1965 Richmond CA BR/TR/6-3/209(185-210) [PhiN83 1/22] d7.17

YEAR	TM LG	G	AB	R	H	2B	3B	HR	RBI	BB-IB	HP	SO	AVG	OBP	SLG	AOPS	ABR	SB-CS	FA	FR	RNG	THR	GAMES AT POSITION	DL	BFW
1988	Phi N	69	273	41	84	15	1	11	43	7-2	0	39	.308	.324	.491	128	8	1-1	.992	-4	75	74	1b69		-0.1
1989	Phi N	144	523	63	149	22	3	12	75	23-5	5	62	.285	.317	.407	107	3	4-3	.993	-9	71	100	1b140		-1.4
1990	Phi N	92	324	32	78	21	0	5	44	13-6	5	39	.241	.277	.352	73	-12	2-0	.995	-7	68	114	1b84	21	-2.2
1991	Phi N	101	301	38	82	21	3	9	49	14-2	1	49	.272	.304	.452	112	4	0-2	.987	-6	75	75	1b72	35	-0.6
1992	Phi N	94	276	33	84	19	0	4	34	5-0	0	44	.304	.313	.417	106	1	3-0	.995	-5	74	91	1b54,O11L		-0.7
1993	†Phi N	90	159	21	46	4	1	5	18	8-1	1	32	.289	.324	.421	97	-2	0-0	.993	-7	45	108	1b49		-0.8
1994	Phi N	72	220	29	62	14	2	8	37	6-1	1	32	.282	.303	.473	90	-2	0-0	1.000	-1	32	114	1b9,D2	121	-0.9
1996	Sea A	15	28	4	7	0	0	1	4	1-0	2	6	.250	.290	.357	65	-2	0-0	1.000	-1	57	90	1b510,O11L,D2	177	-8.2
Total	8	677	2104	261	592	116	10	55	304	77-17	15	303	.281	.308	.424	103	-1	10-6	.993	-44	66	95	1b510,O11L,D2	177	-8.2

JORDAN, SCOTT Scott Allan B5.27.1963 Waco TX BR/TR/6-0/178 [CleA85 4/89] d9.2 Col Georgia Tech

YEAR	TM LG	G	AB	R	H	2B	3B	HR	RBI	BB-IB	HP	SO	AVG	OBP	SLG	AOPS	ABR	SB-CS	FA	FR	RNG	THR	GAMES AT POSITION	DL	BFW
1988	Cle A	7	9	0	1	0	0	0	1	0-0		3	.111	.111	.111	-36	-2	0-0	1.000	0	109	0	O6(0/5/1)		-0.0

JORDAN, TOM Thomas Jefferson B9.5.1919 Lawton OK BR/TR/6-1.5/195 d9.4

YEAR	TM LG	G	AB	R	H	2B	3B	HR	RBI	BB-IB	HP	SO	AVG	OBP	SLG	AOPS	ABR	SB-CS	FA	FR	RNG	THR	GAMES AT POSITION	DL	BFW
1944	Chi A	14	45	2	12	1	1	0	3	1	0		.267	.283	.333	77	-2	0-0	.947	-1	130	94	C14		-0.0
1946	Chi A	10	15	1	4	2	1	0	0	0	0	1	.267	.267	.533	124	0	0-0	1.000	0	65	0	C2		-0.0
	Cle A	14	35	2	7	1	0	1	3	3	0	1	.200	.263	.314	65	-2	1-1	.974	-3	86	141	C18		-0.0
	Year	24	50	3	11	3	1	1	3	3	0	2	.220	.264	.380	83	-2	1-1	.980	-3	82	111	C15		-0.0
1948	StL A	1	1	0	0	0	0	0	0	0	0		.000	.000	.000	-97	0	0-0	—	0			/H		-0.0
Total	3	39	96	5	23	4	2	1	6	4	0	2	.240	.270	.354	78	-4	1-1	.963	-4	108	102	C29		-0.0

JORDAN, TIM Timothy Joseph B2.14.1879 New York NY D9.13.1949 Bronx NY BL/TL/6-1/170 d8.10

YEAR	TM LG	G	AB	R	H	2B	3B	HR	RBI	BB-IB	HP	SO	AVG	OBP	SLG	AOPS	ABR	SB-CS	FA	FR	RNG	THR	GAMES AT POSITION	DL	BFW
1901	Was A	6	20	2	4	1	0	0	2	3	0		.200	.304	.250	56	-1	0	.941	-1	66	61	1b6		-0.0
1903	NY A	2	8	1	1	0	0	0	0	0	0		.125	.125	.125	-23	-1	0	.889	-1	0	327	1b2		-0.0
1906	Bro N	129	450	67	118	20	8	**12**	78	59	3		.262	.352	.422	153	28	16	.978	-9	79	71	1b126		2.0
1907	Bro N	147	485	43	133	15	8	4	53	74	1		.274	.371	.363	141	20	10	.980	-6	89	97	1b143		1.7
1908	Bro N	148	515	58	127	18	5	**12**	60	59	2		.247	.328	.371	128	17	9	.982	-15	61	81	1b146		0.1
1909	Bro N	103	330	47	90	20	3	3	36	59	2		.273	.386	.379	142	20	13	.983	-9	57	75	1b95		1.3
1910	Bro N	5	5	1	1	0	0	1	3	2	0		.200	.200	.800	195	0	2	—	0			/H		0.0
Total	7	540	1813	220	474	74	24	32	232	254	9		.261	.355	.382	139	89	48	.980	-40	72	83	1b518		2.1

YEAR	TM LG	G	AB	R	H	2B	3B	HR	RBI	BB-IB	HP	SO	AVG	OBP	SLG	AOPS	ABR	SB-CS	FA	FR	RNG	THR	GAMES AT POSITION	DL	BFW

JORGENS, ART Arndt Ludwig B5.18.1905 Modum, Norway D3.1.1980 Evanston IL BR/TR/5-9/160 d4.26 b-Orville

YEAR	TM LG	G	AB	R	H	2B	3B	HR	RBI	BB-IB	HP	SO	AVG	OBP	SLG	AOPS	ABR	SB-CS	FA	FR	RNG	THR	GAMES AT POSITION	DL	BFW
1929	NY A	18	34	6	11	3	0	0	4	6	0	7	.324	.425	.412	125	2	0-4	.979	-0	103	74	C15		0.1
1930	NY A	16	30	7	11	3	0	0	1	2	0	4	.367	.406	.467	126	1	0-0	.960	-1	104	101	C16		0.1
1931	NY A	46	100	12	27	1	2	0	14	9	0	3	.270	.330	.320	76	-4	0-1	.962	-3	104	66	C40		-0.5
1932	NY A	56	151	13	33	7	1	2	19	14	0	11	.219	.285	.318	59	-10	0-0	.967	-1	107	80	C56		-0.8
1933	NY A	21	50	9	11	3	0	2	13	12	0	3	.220	.371	.400	111	1	1-0	.982	1	185	22	C19		0.4
1934	NY A	58	183	14	38	6	1	0	20	23	0	24	.208	.296	.251	45	-15	2-0	.984	3	109	69	C56		-0.8
1935	NY A	36	84	6	20	2	0	0	8	12	0	10	.238	.333	.262	59	-5	0-0	1.000	4	134	77	C33		0.1
1936	NY A	31	66	5	18	3	1	0	5	2	0	3	.273	.294	.348	60	-5	0-0	.990	2	150	92	C30		-0.1
1937	NY A	13	23	3	3	1	0	0	3	2	0	5	.130	.200	.174	-5	-4	0-0	1.000	0	121	69	C11		-0.3
1938	NY A	9	17	3	4	2	0	0	2	3	0	3	.235	.350	.353	77	0	0-0	.923	0	105	142	C8		-0.3
1939	NY A	3	0	1	0	0	0	0	0	0	0	0	—	—	—		0	0-0	1.000	0	0	0	C2		0.0
Total 11		307	738	79	176	31	5	4	89	85	0	73	.238	.317	.310	66	-39	3-5	.978	7	120	73	C286		-1.8

JORGENSEN, PINKY Carl B11.21.1914 Laton CA D5.2.1996 Santa Cruz CA BR/TR/6-1/195 d9.14 Col St. Marys (CA)

YEAR	TM LG	G	AB	R	H	2B	3B	HR	RBI	BB-IB	HP	SO	AVG	OBP	SLG	AOPS	ABR	SB-CS	FA	FR	RNG	THR	GAMES AT POSITION	DL	BFW
1937	Cin N	6	14	1	4	0	0	0	1	1	0	2	.286	.333	.286	73	-1	0	.875	0	80	362	O4L		-0.1

JORGENSEN, SPIDER John Donald B11.3.1919 Folsom CA D11.6.2003 Rancho Cugamonga CA BL/TR/5-9/155* d4.15 Col Sacramento (CA) City

YEAR	TM LG	G	AB	R	H	2B	3B	HR	RBI	BB-IB	HP	SO	AVG	OBP	SLG	AOPS	ABR	SB-CS	FA	FR	RNG	THR	GAMES AT POSITION	DL	BFW
1947	†Bro N	129	441	57	121	29	8	5	67	58	1	45	.274	.360	.410	100	1	4	.949	-3	98	123	3b128		-0.2
1948	Bro N	31	90	15	27	6	2	1	13	16	1	13	.300	.411	.444	127	4	1	.887	-6	74	82	3b24		-0.1
1949	†Bro N	53	134	15	36	5	1	1	14	23	0	13	.269	.376	.343	90	-1	0	.946	-2	90	84	3b36		-0.3
1950	Bro N	2	2	0	0	0	0	0	1	1	0	0	.000	.333	.000	-4	0	0	1.000	-0	104	0	/3		0.0
	NY N	24	37	5	5	0	0	0	4	5	0	2	.135	.238	.135	1	-5	0	.913	0	110	85	3b5		-0.5
	Year	26	39	5	5	0	0	0	5	6	0	2	.128	.244	.128	1	-6	0	.917	0	110	79	3b6		-0.5
1951	NY N	28	51	5	12	0	0	2	8	3	1	2	.235	.291	.353	72	-2	0-0	1.000	-1	95	0	O11R/3		-0.3
Total 5		267	755	97	201	40	11	9	107	106	3	75	.266	.359	.384	95	-3	5-0	.940	-11	94	109	3b195,O11R		-1.4

JORGENSEN, MIKE Michael B8.16.1948 Passaic NJ BL/TL/6-0/195* [NYN66 4/61] d9.10 M1

YEAR	TM LG	G	AB	R	H	2B	3B	HR	RBI	BB-IB	HP	SO	AVG	OBP	SLG	AOPS	ABR	SB-CS	FA	FR	RNG	THR	GAMES AT POSITION	DL	BFW
1968	NY N	8	14	0	2	1	0	0	0	0-0	0	4	.143	.143	.214	6	-2	0-0	1.000	-0	49	134	1b4		-0.3
1970	NY N	76	87	15	17	3	1	3	4	10-1	0	23	.195	.278	.356	68	-4	2-2	.992	2	112	77	1b50,O10(0/9/1)		-0.5
1971	NY N	45	118	16	26	1	1	5	11	11-1	3	24	.220	.303	.373	91	-2	1-2	.951	-2	95	0	O31(4/25/4)/1		-0.5
1972	Mon N	113	372	48	86	12	3	13	47	53-7	4	75	.231	.332	.384	102	2	12-13	.995	-1	115	104	1b76,O28(2/26/0)		-0.9
1973	Mon N	138	413	49	95	16	2	9	47	64-4	3	49	.230	.336	.344	86	-6	16-7	.995	4	112	93	1b91,O29(28/1/0)		-1.0
1974	Mon N	131	287	45	89	16	1	11	59	70-5	2	39	.310	.444	.488	153	25	3-5	.998	6	121	98	1b123,O11(9/2/0)		2.5
1975	Mon N	144	445	58	116	18	0	18	67	79-8	7	75	.261	.378	.422	117	13	3-3	.994	5	114	114	1b133,O6(5/1/0)		0.8
1976	Mon N	125	343	36	87	13	0	6	23	52-9	0	48	.254	.349	.344	93	-1	7-1	.989	3	136	104	1b81,O41(25/0/16)		-0.4
1977	Mon N	19	20	3	4	1	0	0	3	0-0	0	4	.200	.304	.250	52	-1	0-0	1.000	1	283	61	1b5		0.0
	Oak A	66	203	18	50	4	1	8	32	25-2	2	44	.246	.329	.394	99	0	3-2	.989	2	121	77	1b48,O20(6/1/13),D2	51	-0.1
1978	Tex A	96	97	20	19	3	0	1	9	18-1	0	10	.196	.319	.258	64	-4	3-1	.994	5	144	94	1b78,O9(2/4/4)/D		-0.1
1979	Tex A	90	157	21	35	7	0	6	16	14-1	2	29	.223	.293	.382	82	-4	0-2	.988	3	129	103	1b60,O20(4/7/9),D2	30	-0.4
1980	NY N	119	321	43	82	11	0	7	43	46-6	0	55	.255	.349	.355	98	1	0-3	.995	-1	88	70	1b72,O31(9/0/22)		-0.7
1981	NY N	86	122	8	25	5	2	3	15	12-1	0	24	.205	.270	.352	77	-4	4-0	.991	1	88	76	1b40,O19(4/0/15)		-0.5
1982	NY N	120	114	16	29	6	0	2	14	21-3	0	24	.254	.370	.360	105	2	2-0	.991	-2	57	140	1b56,O16(1/0/15)		-0.2
1983	NY N	38	24	5	6	3	0	1	3	2-0	1	4	.250	.333	.500	129	1	0-1	1.000	-0	92	143	1b19		0.0
	Atl N	57	48	5	12	1	0	1	8	8-0	0	8	.250	.351	.333	86	-1	0-0	1.000	0	89	169	1b19,O6L		-0.1
	Year	95	72	10	18	4	0	2	11	10-0	1	12	.250	.345	.389	100	0	0-0	1.000	0	90	156	1b38,O6L		-0.1
1984	Atl N	31	26	4	7	1	0	0	5	3-1	0	6	.269	.333	.308	79	-1	0-1	1.000	-1	0	0	1b8,O4(1/0/3)		-0.2
	StL N	59	98	5	24	4	2	1	12	10-1	0	17	.245	.315	.357	90	-1	0-0	.991	1	123	164	1b39		-0.2
	Year	90	124	9	31	5	2	1	17	13-2	0	23	.250	.319	.347	87	-2	0-1	.992	1	115	153	1b47,O4(1/0/3)		-0.4
1985	†StL N	72	112	14	22	6	0	0	11	31-0	1	27	.196	.375	.250	79	-1	2-1	.994	-2	78	133	1b49,O2L		-0.5
Total 17		1633	3421	429	833	132	13	95	426	532-51	25	589	.243	.347	.373	99	12	58-44	.994	23	114	102	1b1052,O283(108/76/102),D5	81	-3.3

JORGENSEN, RYAN Ryan Wayne B5.4.1979 Jacksonville FL BR/TR/6-2/220 d8.8 Col Louisiana St.

YEAR	TM LG	G	AB	R	H	2B	3B	HR	RBI	BB-IB	HP	SO	AVG	OBP	SLG	AOPS	ABR	SB-CS	FA	FR	RNG	THR	GAMES AT POSITION	DL	BFW
2005	Fla N	4	4	0	0	0	0	0	0	0-0	0	3	.000	.000	.000	-99	-1	0-0	1.000	-1	32	0	C3		-0.2

JORGENSEN, TERRY Terry Allen B9.2.1966 Kewaunee WI BR/TR/6-4/208* [MinA87 2/35] d9.10 Col Wisconsin-Oshkosh

YEAR	TM LG	G	AB	R	H	2B	3B	HR	RBI	BB-IB	HP	SO	AVG	OBP	SLG	AOPS	ABR	SB-CS	FA	FR	RNG	THR	GAMES AT POSITION	DL	BFW
1989	Min A	10	23	1	4	1	0	0	2	4-0	0	5	.174	.296	.217	44	-2	0-0	.958	1	120	223	3b9		0.0
1992	Min A	22	58	5	18	1	0	0	5	3-0	1	11	.310	.349	.328	89	-1	1-2	1.000	3	111	127	1b13,3b9,S2		0.1
1993	Min A	59	152	15	34	7	0	1	12	10-0	0	21	.224	.270	.289	50	-11	1-0	.982	6	115	113	3b45,1b9,S6		-0.5
Total 3		91	233	21	56	9	0	1	19	17-0	1	37	.240	.292	.292	59	-14	2-2	.975	10	117	152	3b63,1b22,S8		-0.4

JOSE, FELIX Domingo Felix Andujar (b Domingo Felix Andujar (Jose)) B5.2.1965 Santo Domingo, D.R. BB/TR/6-1/190(184-221) d9.2

YEAR	TM LG	G	AB	R	H	2B	3B	HR	RBI	BB-IB	HP	SO	AVG	OBP	SLG	AOPS	ABR	SB-CS	FA	FR	RNG	THR	GAMES AT POSITION	DL	BFW
1988	Oak A	8	6	2	2	1	0	0	0	1-0	0	1	.333	.333	.500	134	0	1-0	1.000	1	235	0	O6(1/0/5)		0.1
1989	Oak A	20	57	3	11	2	0	0	5	4-0	0	13	.193	.246	.228	35	-5	0-1	.974	1	109	174	O19(4/0/16)		-0.5
1990	Oak A	101	341	42	90	12	0	8	39	16-0	5	65	.264	.306	.370	92	-5	8-2	.977	3	111	87	O92(26/24/53),D7		-0.3
	StL N	25	85	12	23	4	1	3	13	8-0	0	16	.271	.333	.447	112	1	4-4	1.000	-2	90	0	O23(1/2/21)		-0.2
1991	StL N★	154	568	69	173	40	6	8	77	50-8	2	113	.305	.360	.438	123	18	20-12	.990	-2	90	130	O153R		1.2
1992	StL N	131	509	62	150	22	3	14	75	40-8	1	100	.295	.347	.432	122	14	28-12	.979	3	102	119	O127R		1.6
1993	KC A	149	499	64	126	24	3	6	43	36-5	1	95	.253	.303	.349	70	-21	31-13	.977	-8	96	66	O144(0/10/136)/D	23	1.6
1994	KC A	99	366	56	111	28	1	11	55	35-6	2	75	.303	.362	.475	109	3	5-10	.982	-3	96	94	O98R	12	-3.2
1995	KC A	9	30	2	4	1	0	0	1	2-0	0	9	.133	.188	.167	-7	-5	0-0	1.000	2	108	417	O7R		-0.4
2000	NY A	20	29	4	7	0	0	1	5	2-0	0	9	.241	.281	.345	61	-2	0-1	.929	-0	103	0	O14(6/0/8),D2	29	-0.3
2002	Ari N	13	19	5	5	0	0	2	4	4-0	0	8	.263	.360	.579	141	1	0-0	1.000	-1	70	0	O14(0/1/0/4)		0.0
2003	Ari N	18	18	1	6	0	0	0	1	6-1	0	3	.333	.500	.556	162	2	0-0	—	-0	0	0	/ORD		0.2
Total 11		747	2527	322	708	135	14	54	324	203-28	9	507	.280	.334	.409	102	3	102-57	.980	-6	97	101	O689(39/36/629),D11	64	-2.2

JOSEPH, RICK Ricardo Emelindo (Harrigan) B8.24.1939 San Pedro de Macoris, D.R. D9.8.1979 Santiago, D.R. BR/TR/6-1/195(190-210) d6.18

YEAR	TM LG	G	AB	R	H	2B	3B	HR	RBI	BB-IB	HP	SO	AVG	OBP	SLG	AOPS	ABR	SB-CS	FA	FR	RNG	THR	GAMES AT POSITION	DL	BFW
1964	KC A	17	54	3	12	2	0	0	1	3-0	0	11	.222	.263	.259	45	-4	0-1	.981	-1	76	123	1b12,3b3		-0.6
1967	Phi N	17	41	4	9	2	0	1	5	4-0	0	10	.220	.289	.341	79	-1	0-0	1.000	1	139	87	1b13		-0.1
1968	Phi N	66	155	20	34	5	0	3	12	16-2	1	35	.219	.295	.310	82	-3	0-1	.992	1	96	91	1b30,3b14/OL		-0.4
1969	Phi N	99	264	35	72	15	0	6	37	22-2	1	57	.273	.329	.398	106	2	2-1	.956	-2	95	111	3b58,1b17/2		-0.1
1970	Phi N	71	119	7	27	2	1	3	10	6-1	0	28	.227	.264	.336	61	-7	0-0	.917	-6	71	0	O12L,1b10,3b9		-0.1
Total 5		270	633	69	154	26	1	13	65	51-5	2	141	.243	.300	.349	84	-13	2-3	.933	-6	93	137	3b84,1b82,O13L/2		-2.7

JOSEPHSON, DUANE Duane Charles B6.3.1942 New Hampton IA D1.30.1997 New Hampton IA BR/TR/6-0/195* d9.15 Col Northern Iowa [DL 1973 Bos A 9]

YEAR	TM LG	G	AB	R	H	2B	3B	HR	RBI	BB-IB	HP	SO	AVG	OBP	SLG	AOPS	ABR	SB-CS	FA	FR	RNG	THR	GAMES AT POSITION	DL	BFW
1965	Chi A	4	9	2	1	0	0	0	0	2-0	0	4	.111	.273	.111	14	-1	0-0	1.000	1	60	0	C4		0.0
1966	Chi A	11	38	3	9	1	0	0	3	3-0	0	3	.237	.293	.263	65	-2	0-0	.974	2	105	226	C11		0.1
1967	Chi A	62	189	11	45	5	1	1	9	6-0	0	24	.238	.262	.291	65	-9	0-3	1.000	-4	103	102	C59	24	-1.3
1968	Chi A★	128	434	35	107	16	6	6	45	18-2	6	52	.247	.284	.353	92	-6	2-4	.990	16	95	118	C122		1.7
1969	Chi A	52	162	19	39	6	2	1	20	13-0	1	17	.241	.296	.321	71	-6	0-0	.984	-2	80	111	C47	62	-0.7
1970	Chi A	96	285	28	90	12	1	4	41	24-2	3	24	.316	.370	.407	112	5	0-1	.985	-9	76	77	C84	21	-0.1
1971	Bos A	91	306	38	75	14	1	10	39	22-4	0	35	.245	.294	.395	88	-2	6-0	.989	-2	99	55	C87		-0.1
1972	Bos A	26	82	11	22	4	1	1	7	4-0	1	11	.268	.310	.378	98	0	0-2	.980	-4	95	58	1b16,C6	64	-0.7
Total 8		470	1505	147	388	58	12	23	164	92-8	11	174	.258	.303	.358	89	-25	4-10	.989	-3	94	95	C420,1b16	180	-1.3

YEAR	TM LG	G	AB	R	H	2B	3B	HR	RBI	BB-IB	HP	SO	AVG	OBP	SLG	AOPS	ABR	SB-CS	FA	FR	RNG	THR	GAMES AT POSITION	DL	BFW

JOSHUA, VON Von Everett B5.1.1948 Oakland CA BL/TL/5-10/170* d9.2 C4 Col Chabot (CA) JC/Laney (CA) JC

1969	LA N	14	8	2	2	0	0	0	0	0-0	0	2	.250	.250	.250	43	-1	1-0	.800	-1	74	0	O8(7/0/2)		-0.1
1970	LA N	72	109	23	29	1	3	1	8	6-2	0	24	.266	.302	.358	80	-4	2-2	.941	-0	104	61	O41(21/10/16)		-0.6
1971	LA N	11	7	2	0	0	0	0	0	0-0	0	1	.000	.000	.000	-99	-2	0-0	1.000	1	317	0	O5(4/1/0)		-0.1
1973	LA N	75	159	19	40	4	1	2	17	8-2	1	29	.252	.288	.327	74	-6	7-2	.984	-3	82	77	O46(42/1/4)	27	-1.1
1974	†LA N	81	124	11	29	5	1	1	16	7-5	1	17	.234	.276	.315	69	-6	3-2	.943	-5	67	0	O35(12/17/6)		-1.2
1975	SF N	129	507	75	161	25	10	7	43	32-0	1	75	.318	.359	.448	119	11	20-10	.993	1	98	141	O117C		1.0
1976	SF N	42	156	13	41	5	2	0	2	4-2	0	20	.263	.280	.321	68	-7	1-3	.948	-5	76	133	O35(3/33/0)		-1.5
	Mil A	107	423	44	113	13	5	5	28	18-3	0	58	.267	.295	.357	93	-6	8-10	.982	-5	99	131	O105(26/82/0)/D		-1.0
1977	Mil A	144	536	58	140	25	7	9	49	21-4	0	74	.261	.286	.384	81	-16	12-9	.970	-11	90	86	O140C		-2.8
1979	LA N	94	142	22	40	7	1	3	14	7-1	0	23	.282	.315	.408	98	-1	1-1	.967	-0	103	95	O46(11/10/28)		-0.2
1980	SD N	53	63	8	15	2	1	2	7	5-1	0	15	.238	.294	.397	98	-1	0-1	1.000	0	120	0	O12(3/8/1),1b2	18	-0.1
Total	10	822	2234	277	610	87	31	30	184	108-20	3	338	.273	.306	.380	91	-39	55-40	.975	-20	93	104	O590(129/419/57),1b2/D	45	-7.7

JOURDAN, TED Theodore Charles B9.5.1895 New Orleans LA D9.23.1961 New Orleans LA BL/TL/6-0/175 d9.18 Mil 1918

1916	Chi A	3	2	0	0	0	0	0	1	0-0	0	1	.000	.333	.000	1	0	2					/H		0.0
1917	Chi A	17	34	2	5	0	1	0	2	1	0	3	.147	.171	.206	15	-4	0	.973	-0	101	47	1b14		-0.5
1918	Chi A	7	10	1	1	0	0	0	1	0	0	0	.100	.100	.100	-39	-2	0	1.000	-0	0	0	1b2		-0.2
1920	Chi A	48	150	16	36	5	2	0	8	17	5	17	.240	.337	.300	70	-6	3-2	.982	-4	71	163	1b40		-1.0
Total	4	75	196	19	42	5	3	0	11	19	5	21	.214	.300	.270	56	-12	5-2	.981	-4	74	140	1b56		-1.7

JOY, POP Aloysius C. B6.11.1860 Washington DC D6.28.1937 Washington DC d6.3

1884	Was U	36	130	12	28	0	0	0		2			.215	.227	.215	36	-14		.966	0	69	112	1b36		-1.5

JOYCE, GEORGE George W. B1847 Washington DC D11.9.1895 Washington DC d8.14

1886	Was N	1	0	0	0	0	0	0	0	0			—	—	—	—	0	0	—	-0	0	0	/OC		0.0

JOYCE, BILL William Michael "Scrappy Bill" B9.21.1865 St.Louis MO D5.8.1941 St.Louis MO BL/TR/5-11/185 d4.19 M3

1890	Bro P	133	489	121	123	18	18	1	78	123	12	77	.252	.413	.368	103	7	43	.811	-13	97	90	3b133		-0.3
1891	Bos AA	65	243	76	75	9	15	3	51	63	5	27	.309	.460	.506	179	29	36	.849	-0	104	124	3b64/1		2.5
1892	Bro N	97	372	89	91	15	12	6	45	82	8	55	.245	.392	.398	144	25	23	.862	-20	76	56	3b94,O3L		0.6
1894	Was N	99	355	103	126	25	14	17	89	87	12	33	.355	.496	.648	179	52	21	.866	4	100	126	3b99		4.3
1895	Was N	127	479	110	149	26	13	17	97	96	14	56	.311	.440	.526	150	41	29	.846	-4	93	78	3b127		3.1
1896	Was N	81	310	85	97	16	10	8	51	67	12	20	.313	.452	.506	152	28	32	.888	-5	108	76	3b48,2b33		2.1
	NY N	49	165	36	61	9	2	5	43	34	10	14	.370	.502	.539	180	24	13	.883	2	102	55	3b49,M		2.2
	Year	130	475	121	158	25	12	13	94	101	22	34	.333	.470	.518	162	52	45	.885	-3	105	65	3b97,2b33		4.3
1897	NY N	110	389	111	118	15	13	3	64	81	17		.303	.444	.432	135	27	35	.851	-6	90	124	3b107,1b2,M		1.9
1898	NY N	145	508	91	131	20	9	10	91	88	18		.258	.386	.392	127	23	34	.966	8	142	91	1b130,3b14,2b2,M		2.9
Total	8	906	3310	822	971	153	106	70	609	721	108	282	.293	.435	.467	144	256	266	.851	-35	95	91	3b735,1b133,2b35,O3L		19.3

JOYNER, WALLY Wallace Keith B6.16.1962 Atlanta GA BL/TL/6-2/203(185-207) [CalA83 3/67] d4.8 Col Brigham Young

1986	†Cal A★	154	593	82	172	27	3	22	100	57-8	2	58	.290	.348	.457	120	16	5-2	.989	6	113	113	1b152		1.3
1987	Cal A	149	564	100	161	33	1	34	117	72-12	5	64	.285	.366	.528	139	33	8-2	.993	-8	83	114	1b149		1.6
1988	Cal A	158	597	81	176	31	2	13	85	55-14	6	51	.295	.356	.419	120	17	8-2	.995	10	122	107	1b156		1.7
1989	Cal A	159	593	78	167	30	2	16	79	46-7	6	58	.282	.335	.420	115	11	3-2	.997	-3	90	114	1b159		-0.4
1990	Cal A	83	310	35	83	15	0	8	41	41-4	1	34	.268	.350	.394	111	6	2-1	.995	4	116	104	1b83	84	0.4
1991	Cal A	143	551	79	166	34	3	21	96	52-4	1	66	.301	.360	.488	133	24	2-0	.994	6	112	108	1b141		2.0
1992	KC A	149	572	66	154	36	2	9	66	55-4	4	50	.269	.336	.386	99	0	11-5	.993	13	131	113	1b145,D4		0.3
1993	KC A	141	497	83	145	36	3	15	65	66-13	4	67	.292	.375	.467	118	14	5-9	.994	19	145	102	1b140		1.8
1994	KC A	97	363	52	113	20	3	8	57	47-3	0	43	.311	.386	.449	110	7	3-2	.991	2	108	100	1b86,D11	18	0.0
1995	KC A	131	465	69	144	28	0	12	83	69-10	2	65	.310	.394	.447	118	15	3-2	.998	11	132	116	1b126,D2	39	1.4
1996	†SD N	121	433	59	120	29	1	8	65	69-8	3	71	.277	.377	.404	112	11	5-3	.997	1	100	96	1b131	15	0.1
1997	SD N	135	455	59	149	29	2	13	83	51-5	2	51	.327	.390	.486	138	27	3-5	.996	0	100	80	1b127		1.5
1998	†SD N	131	439	58	131	30	1	12	80	51-8	1	44	.298	.370	.453	125	17	1-2	.993	-1	93	114	1b105/D		0.4
1999	SD N	110	323	34	80	14	2	5	43	58-6	2	54	.248	.363	.350	89	-4	0-1	.995	4	112	122	1b55,D7	39	-0.8
2000	†Atl N	119	224	24	63	12	0	5	32	31-3	1	31	.281	.365	.402	96	0	0-0	.992	2	119	110	1b39,D9		-0.2
2001	Ana A	53	148	14	36	5	1	3	14	13-0	1	18	.243	.304	.351	71	-6	1-1	.997	-1	90	108	1b39,D9		-1.0
Total	16	2033	7127	973	2060	409	26	204	1106	833-109	38	825	.289	.362	.440	117	188	60-39	.994	63	111	108	1b1913,D34	195	10.1

JUDE, FRANK Frank B1884 Libby MN D5.4.1961 Brownsville TX BR/TR/5-7/150 d7.9

1906	Cin N	80	308	31	64	6	4	1	31	16	6		.208	.261	.263	61	-15	7	.965	-0	152	44	O80R		-2.1

JUDGE, JOE Joseph Ignatius B5.25.1894 Brooklyn NY D3.11.1963 Washington DC BL/TL/5-8.5/155 d9.20 C2

1915	Was A	12	41	7	17	2	0	0	9	4	3	6	.415	.500	.463	185	5	2-3	.990	-0	82	149	1b10,O2R		0.4
1916	Was A	103	336	42	74	10	8	0	28	54	3	44	.220	.333	.298	91	-2	18	.986	4	112	94	1b103		-0.7
1917	Was A	102	393	62	112	15	15	2	30	50	2	40	.285	.369	.415	141	19	17	.988	-1	95	103	1b100		1.7
1918	Was A	130	502	56	131	23	7	1	46	49	4	32	.261	.332	.341	105	3	20	.985	0	94	94	1b130		1.4
1919	Was A	135	521	83	150	33	12	2	31	81	2	35	.288	.386	.409	124	20	23	.992	-7	76	88	1b133		1.5
1920	Was A	126	493	103	164	19	15	5	51	65	5	34	.333	.416	.462	136	27	12-12	.996	-3	90	105	1b152		0.7
1921	Was A	153	622	87	187	26	11	7	72	68	3	35	.301	.372	.412	105	5	21-6	.996	5	107	122	1b147		0.5
1922	Was A	148	591	84	174	32	15	10	81	50	5	20	.294	.355	.450	114	10	5-15	.996	8	126	131	1b140		1.7
1923	Was A	113	405	56	127	24	6	2	63	58	5	21	.314	.406	.417	123	17	11-7	.993	-2	89	118	1b112		1.5
1924	†Was A	140	516	71	167	38	9	3	79	53	6	21	.324	.393	.450	121	17	13-8	.993	3	106	117	1b109		1.9
1925	†Was A	112	376	65	118	31	5	8	66	51	5	21	.314	.406	.487	128	18	7-12	.993	3	106	117	1b112		1.6
1926	Was A	134	453	70	132	25	11	7	92	53	1	25	.291	.367	.442	113	4	10-5	.996	-6	77	80	1b136		-1.2
1927	Was A	137	522	68	161	29	11	2	71	45	2	22	.308	.366	.418	104	3	5-9	.996	1	99	106	1b149		0.0
1928	Was A	153	542	78	166	31	10	3	93	80	7	19	.306	.396	.417	115	15	16-4	.996	3	105	103	1b142		0.3
1929	Was A	143	543	83	171	35	8	6	71	73	9	33	.315	.397	.442	115	15	12-5	.998	2	101	111	1b117		1.2
1930	Was A	126	442	83	144	29	11	10	80	.60	3	29	.326	.410	.509	131	22	13-6	.994	1	115	78	1b15		-0.7
1931	Was A	35	74	11	21	3	0	0	9	8	0	1	.284	.354	.324	79	-2	0-0	.997	1	102	123	1b78		-1.1
1932	Was A	82	291	45	75	16	3	0	29	37	0	19	.258	.343	.364	84	-6	3-3	.994	0	100	110	1b28		-1.2
1933	Bro N	42	112	7	24	2	1	0	9	7	0	10	.214	.261	.250	48	-8	1	.989	0	100	110	1b28		-0.5
	Bos A	35	108	20	32	8	1	0	22	13	0	4	.296	.372	.389	103	1	2-1	1.000	0	89	95	1b29		0.2
1934	Bos A	10	15	3	5	1	0	0	2	2	0	1	.333	.412	.467	118	1	0	1.000	0	82	49	1b2		0.0
Total	20	2171	7898	1184	2352	433	159	71	1034	965	51	478	.298	.378	.420	115	188	213-92	.993	15	99	104	1b2084,O2R		8.5

JUDNICH, WALLY Walter Franklin B1.24.1916 San Francisco CA D7.10.1971 Glendale CA BL/TL/6-1/205 d4.16 Mil 1943-45

1940	StL A	137	519	97	157	27	7	24	89	54	0	71	.303	.368	.520	125	18	8-5	.989	-5	94	68	O133C		0.9
1941	StL A	146	546	90	155	40	6	14	83	80	2	45	.284	.377	.456	116	14	5-5	.980	2	102	95	O140C		1.6
1942	StL A	132	457	78	143	22	6	17	82	76	4	41	.313	.413	.499	153	35	3-2	.991	-6	97	43	O122C		2.3
1946	StL A	142	511	60	134	23	4	15	72	60	0	54	.262	.340	.411	104	3	0-4	.995	0	137(6/131/1)			O137(6/131/1)		0.8
1947	StL A	144	500	58	129	24	3	18	64	60	2	62	.258	.338	.426	109	5	2-5	.989	-6	84	100	1b129,O15(0/14/1)		-0.4
1948	†Cle A	79	218	36	56	13	3	2	29	56	1	23	.257	.411	.372	112	7	2-3	.970	-5	85	121	O49(0/35/14),1b20		-0.6
1949	Pit N	10	35	5	8	1	0	1	1	6	0	2	.229	.250	.257	35	-3	0	1.000	0	112	0	O8C		-0.1
Total	7	790	2786	424	782	150	29	90	420	385	7	298	.281	.369	.452	119	79	20-24	.988	-14	100	71	O604(6/583/16),1b149		3.5

JUDY, LYLE Lyle Leroy "Punch" B11.15.1913 Lawrenceville IL D1.15.1991 Ormond Beach FL BR/TR/5-10/150 d9.17

1935	StL N	8	11	2	0	0	0	0	0	2	0	2	.000	.154	.000	-53	-2	2	1.000	0	80	142	2b5		-0.2

JUELICH, RED John Samuel B9.20.1916 St.Louis MO D12.25.1970 St.Louis MO BR/TR/5-11.5/170 d5.30

1939	Pit N	17	46	5	11	0	2	0	4	2	1	4	.239	.271	.326	61	-3		.935	-3	84	81	2b10,3b2		-0.5

JUMONVILLE, GEORGE George Benedict B5.16.1917 Mobile AL D12.12.1996 Mobile AL BR/TR/6-0/175 d9.13

1940	Phi N	11	34	3	3	0	0	0	1	6	1	6	.088	.139	.088	-38	-7	0	.952	-2	79	58	S10/3		-0.5
1941	Phi N	6	7	1	3	0	0	1	2	0	0		.429	.429	.857	266	1	0	1.000	0	178	0	/2S		-0.0
Total	2	17	41	4	6	0	0	1	2	1	1	6	.146	.186	.220	-24	-6	0	.953	-2	81	56	S11/23		-0.5

YEAR	TM LG	G	AB	R	H	2B	3B	HR	RBI	BB-IB	HP	SO	AVG	OBP	SLG	AOPS	ABR	SB-CS	FA	FR	RNG	THR	GAMES AT POSITION	DL	BFW

JURAK, ED Edward James B10.24.1957 Los Angeles CA BR/TR/6-2/185(165-187) [BosA75 3/63] d6.30

1982	Bos A	12	21	3	7	0	0	0	7	2-0	0	4	.333	.375	.333	96	0	0-0	.923	1	127	76	3b11/OC		0.1
1983	Bos A	75	159	19	44	8	4	0	18	18-1	1	25	.277	.350	.377	94	-1	1-2	.943	5	104	100	S38,1b19,3b12/2D		0.4
1984	Bos A	47	66	6	16	3	1	1	7	12-0	0	12	.242	.359	.364	96	0	0-2	1.000	2	158	104	1b19,2b14,3b9,S2		0.1
1985	Bos A	26	13	4	3	0	0	0	0	1-0	0	3	.231	.286	.231	42	-1	0-0	.833	1	119	0	3b7,S3/1OLD		0.0
1988	Oak A	3	1	1	0	0	0	0	0	0-0	0	1	.000	.000	.000	-99	0	0-0	—	-0	0	0	/3D		0.0
1989	SF N	30	42	2	10	0	0	0	1	5-0	0	5	.238	.319	.238	63	-2	0-0	.875	-1	97	143	S6,3b5,2b4,O2(1/0/1)/1		-0.3
Total	6	193	302	35	80	11	5	1	33	38-1	1	49	.265	.346	.344	88	-4	1-4	.941	7	103	98	S49,3b45,1b40,2b19,D8,O4(2/1/1)		0.3

JURGES, BILLY William Frederick B5.9.1908 Bronx NY D3.3.1997 Clearwater FL BR/TR/5-11/175 d5.4 M2/C6

1931	Chi N	88	293	34	59	15	5	0	23	25		41	.201	.264	.287	47	-22	2	.963	9	122	121	3b54,2b33,S3		-1.0
1932	†Chi N	115	396	40	100	24	4	2	52	19	1	26	.253	.288	.348	71	-17	1	.964	30	119	116	S108,3b5		2.1
1933	Chi N	143	487	49	131	17	6	5	50	26	5	39	.269	.313	.359	92	-6	3	.958	23	108	114	S143		2.8
1934	Chi N	100	358	43	88	15	2	8	33	19	3	34	.246	.289	.366	76	-13	1	.966	-1	98	107	S98		-0.6
1935	Chi N	146	519	69	125	33	1	1	59	42	5	39	.241	.304	.314	66	-24	3	.964	25	107	132	S146		1.2
1936	Chi N	118	429	51	120	25	1	1	42	23	3	25	.280	.321	.350	79	-12	4	.960	14	104	120	S116		1.0
1937	Chi N☆	129	450	53	134	18	10	1	65	42	6	41	.298	.365	.389	101	1	2	.975	-13	91	97	S128		-0.3
1938	†Chi N	137	465	53	114	18	3	1	47	58	5	53	.245	.335	.303	75	-14	3	.953	-5	97	100	S136		-0.9
1939	NY N☆	138	543	84	155	21	11	6	63	47	6	34	.285	.349	.398	99	-1	3	.965	20	107	102	S137		2.8
1940	NY N✳	63	214	23	54	3	3	2	36	25	6	14	.252	.347	.322	85	-4	2	.967	3	100	100	S63		0.4
1941	NY N	134	471	50	138	25	2	5	61	47	3	36	.293	.361	.386	108	6	0	.957	6	107	105	S134		2.3
1942	NY N	127	464	45	119	7	1	2	30	43	3	42	.256	.324	.289	79	-12	1	.978	6	103	95	S124		0.4
1943	NY N	136	481	46	110	8	2	4	29	53	4	38	.229	.310	.279	70	-18	2	.955	4	96	69	S99,3b28		-0.6
1944	NY N	85	246	28	52	2	1	1	23	23	0	20	.211	.279	.240	47	-17	4	.961	5	115	75	3b61,S10/2		-1.1
1945	NY N	61	176	22	57	3	1	3	24	24	0	11	.324	.405	.403	123	6	2	.937	2	110	38	S10/2		0.9
1946	Chi N	82	221	26	49	9	2	0	17	43	1	28	.222	.351	.281	82	-3	3	.976	-1	103	68	S73,3b7,2b2		0.0
1947	Chi N	14	40	5	8	2	0	1	2	9	0	9	.200	.347	.325	83	-1	0	.925	-1	103	137	S14		-0.1
Total	17	1816	6253	721	1613	245	55	43	656	568	51	530	.258	.325	.335	82	-151	36	.964	126	103	104	S1540,3b199,2b36		9.3

JUST, JOE Joseph Erwin (b Joseph Erwin Juszczak) B1.8.1916 Milwaukee WI D11.22.2003 Franklin WI BR/TR/5-11/185 d5.13

1944	Cin N	11	11	0	2	0	0	0	0	1	2	.182	.250	.182	24	-1	0	.923	-0	95	0	C10		-0.1
1945	Cin N	14	34	2	5	0	0	0	2	4	0	7	.147	.237	.147	8	-4	0	.947	-1	84	73	C14		-0.5
Total	2	25	45	2	7	0	0	0	2	4		9	.156	.240	.156	12	-5	0	.941	-1	87	56	C24		-0.6

JUSTICE, DAVID David Christopher B4.14.1966 Cincinnati OH BL/TL/6-3/200* [AtlN85 4/94] d5.24 Col Thomas More

1989	Atl N	16	51	7	12	3	0	1	3	3-1	1	9	.235	.291	.353	81	-1	2-1	1.000	-2	80	0	O16(3/0/13)		-0.4
1990	Atl N	127	439	76	124	23	2	28	78	64-4	0	92	.282	.373	.535	139	24	11-6	.981	-3	89	92	1b69,O61R		1.6
1991	†Atl N	109	396	67	109	25	1	21	87	65-9	3	81	.275	.377	.503	138	22	8-8	.968	-1	93	109	O106R		1.7
1992	†Atl N	144	484	78	124	19	5	21	72	79-8	2	85	.256	.359	.446	120	15	2-4	.976	7	112	85	O140R		1.7
1993	†Atl N★	157	585	90	158	15	4	40	120	78-12	3	90	.270	.357	.515	128	22	3-5	.985	-0	102	74	O157R		1.8
1994	Atl N★	104	352	61	110	16	2	19	59	69-5	2	45	.313	.427	.531	143	25	2-4	.947	-2	100	83	O120R		1.7
1995	†Atl N	120	411	73	104	17	2	24	78	73-5	2	68	.253	.365	.479	116	11	4-2	.984	3	104	97	O120R		0.8
1996	Atl N	40	140	23	45	9	0	6	25	21-1	1	22	.321	.409	.514	135	8	1-1	1.000	4	118	115	O40R		0.9
1997	†Cle A✳	139	495	84	163	31	1	33	101	80-11	0	79	.329	.418	.596	156	43	3-5	.984	-6	81	64	O78(74/0/5),D61		2.8
1998	†Cle A	146	540	94	151	39	2	21	88	76-7	0	98	.280	.363	.476	113	12	9-3	1.000	-1	95	0	D123,O21(19/0/2)		0.5
1999	†Cle A	133	429	75	123	18	0	21	88	94-11	2	90	.287	.413	.476	121	18	1-3	.977	-2	89	119	O93(79/0/15),D34		0.8
2000	Cle A	68	249	46	66	14	1	21	58	38-2	0	49	.265	.361	.582	129	11	1-1	.977	-2	95	72	O47(25/2/23),D20		0.5
	†NY A	78	275	43	84	17	0	20	60	39-1	1	42	.305	.391	.585	145	19	1-0	.985	4	116	177	O60(43/1/25),D18		2.0
	Year	146	524	89	150	31	1	41	118	77-3	1	91	.286	.377	.584	138	30	2-1	.982	4	106	129	O107(68/3/48),D38		2.5
2001	†NY A	111	381	58	92	16	1	18	51	54-5	0	83	.241	.333	.430	99	0	1-2	.981	4	121	308	D85,O25(16/0/11)		-0.2
2002	†Oak A	118	398	54	106	18	3	11	49	70-3	1	66	.266	.376	.410	110	8	4-1	.985	-3	92	74	O75(53/0/23),D37		0.1
Total	14	1610	5625	929	1571	280	24	305	1017	903-85	18	999	.279	.378	.500	127	237	53-46	.978	1	100	95	O1141(312/3/842),D378,1b69		15.8

JUTZE, SKIP Alfred Henry B5.28.1946 Bayside NY BR/TR/5-11/190* [StLN68*S4/74] d9.1 Col Central Connecticut

1972	StL N	21	71	1	17	2	0	0	5	1-0	0	16	.239	.247	.268	47	-5	0-1	.964	0	135	242	C17		-0.5
1973	Hou N	90	278	18	62	6	0	0	18	19-5	1	37	.223	.273	.245	45	-21	0-1	.984	-8	93	92	C86		-2.7
1974	Hou N	8	13	0	3	0	0	0	1	1-0	0	1	.231	.267	.231	48	-1	0-0	1.000	-2	105	196	C7		-0.2
1975	Hou N	51	93	9	21	2	0	0	6	2-0	1	4	.226	.242	.247	39	-8	1-0	.986	-6	82	49	C47		-1.3
1976	Hou N	42	92	7	14	2	3	0	6	4-0	0	16	.152	.186	.239	22	-10	0-0	.986	-3	76	108	C42		-1.3
1977	Sea A	42	109	10	24	2	0	3	15	7-1	0	12	.220	.267	.321	60	-6	0-4	.984	-5	61	107	C40		-1.1
Total	6	254	656	45	141	14	3	3	51	34-6	1	86	.215	.253	.259	44	-51	1-6	.983	-24	87	106	C239		-7.1

KADING, JACK John Frederick B11.17.1884 Waukesha WI D6.2.1964 Chicago IL BR/TR/6-3/190 d9.12

1910	Pit N	8	23	5	7	2	1	0	4	4	0	5	.304	.407	.478	149	2	0	1.000	1	166	124	1b8		0.3
1914	Chi F	3	3	0	0	0	0	0	0	0	0	0	.000	.000	.000	-99	-1	0	—	0			/H		-0.1
Total	2	11	26	5	7	2	1	0	4	4	0	5	.269	.367	.423	123	1	0	1.000	1	166	124	1b8		0.2

KAFORA, JAKE Frank Jacob "Tomatoes" B10.16.1888 Chicago IL D3.23.1928 Chicago IL BR/TR/6-0/180 d10.5

1913	Pit N	1	1	1	0	0	0	0	1		0	1	.000	.500	.000	52	0	1	1.000	-0	43	0	/C		0.0
1914	Pit N	21	23	2	3	0	0	0	2	6	0	6	.130	.200	.130	-1	-3	0	1.000	-1	98	55	C17		-0.3
Total	2	22	24	3	3	0	0	0	3	7	0	7	.125	.222	.125	4	-3	0	1.000	-1	95	52	C18		-0.3

KAHDOT, IKE Isaac Leonard "Chief" B10.22.1899 Georgetown OK D3.31.1999 Oklahoma City OK BR/TR/5-5.5/145 d9.5 Col Haskell

| 1922 | Cle A | 4 | 2 | 0 | 0 | 0 | 0 | 0 | 0 | 0 | 0 | 0 | .000 | .000 | .000 | -99 | -1 | 0-0 | 1.000 | 0 | 160 | 0 | 3b2 | | 0.0 |

KAHL, NICK Nicholas Alexander B4.10.1879 Coulterville IL D7.13.1959 Sparta IL BR/TR/5-9/185 d5.2

| 1905 | Cle A | 40 | 135 | 16 | 29 | 4 | 1 | 0 | 21 | 4 | 2 | | .215 | .248 | .259 | 60 | -6 | 1 | .940 | -3 | 106 | 37 | 2b32/SOC | | -1.1 |

KAHLE, BOB Robert Wayne B11.23.1915 New Castle IN D12.16.1988 Inglewood CA BR/TR/6-0/170 d4.21

| 1938 | Bos N | 8 | 3 | 2 | 1 | 0 | 0 | 0 | 0 | | 0 | 0 | .333 | .333 | .333 | 93 | 0 | 0 | — | 0 | | | /H | | 0.0 |

KAHN, OWEN Owen Earle "Jack" B6.5.1905 Richmond VA D1.17.1981 Richmond VA BR/TR/5-11/160 d5.24 Col William and Mary

| 1930 | Bos N | 1 | 0 | 1 | 0 | 0 | 0 | 0 | 0 | 0 | 0 | 0 | | | | | 0 | 0 | — | 0 | | | /R | | 0.0 |

KAHOE, MIKE Michael Joseph B9.3.1873 Yellow Springs OH D5.14.1949 Akron OH BR/TR/6-0/185 d9.22

1895	Cin N	3	4	0	0	0	0	0	0	0	0	0	.000	.000	.000	-96	-1	0	1.000	-0	122	0	C3		-0.1
1899	Cin N	14	42	2	7	1	1	0	4	0	0		.167	.167	.238	10	-5	1	.957	2	131	117	C13		-0.2
1900	Cin N	52	175	18	33	3	3	1	9	4	2		.189	.215	.257	31	-17	3	.963	5	117	98	C51/S		-0.8
1901	Cin N	4	13	0	4	0	0	0	1	0		.308	.357	.308	100	0	1	1.000	-1	98	64	C4		-0.1
	Chi N	67	237	21	53	12	2	1	21	8		.224	.249	.304	62	-12	5	.974	3	95	99	C63,1b6		-0.2
	Year	71	250	21	57	12	2	1	21	9		.228	.255	.304	64	-12	5	.974	3	95	97	C67,1b6		-0.3
1902	Chi N	7	18	0	4	1	0	0	2	0		.222	.222	.278	56	-1	0	.875	-1	114	81	C4,3b2/S		-0.1
	StL A	55	197	21	48	9	2	2	28	6	1	.244	.270	.340	69	-9	4	.967	0	115	80	C53		-0.3
1903	StL A	77	244	26	46	7	5	0	23	11		.189	.227	.258	46	-16	1	.971	2	119	79	C71,O2(0/1/1)		-0.8
1904	StL A	72	236	9	51	6	1	0	12	8		.216	.242	.250	59	-11	4	.968	-3	95	113	C69		-0.9
1905	Phi N	16	51	2	13	2	0	0	2	0		.255	.269	.294	70	-2	1	.975	1	116	98	C15		0.1
1907	Chi N	5	10	0	4	0	0	0	0	4	0	.400	.400	.400	142	0	1	1.000	-1	79	76	C3/1		0.0
	Was A	17	47	3	9	1	0	0	1	0		.191	.191	.213	31	-4	0	.976	-1	90	130	C15		-0.4
1908	Was A	17	27	1	5	1	0	0	1	0		.185	.185	.222	35	-2	0	.983	2	129	62	C11		0.1
1909	Was A	4	8	0	1	0	0	0	0	0		.125	.125	.125	-2	0	0	.867	-1	92	131	C3		-0.2
Total	11	410	1309	103	278	43	14	4	105	39	4	0	.212	.237	.276	52	-81	21	.968	9	108	95	C378,1b7,O2(0/1/1),3b2,S2		-3.9

KAISER, AL Alfred Edward "Deerfoot" B8.3.1886 Cincinnati OH D4.11.1969 Cincinnati OH BR/TR/5-9/165 d4.18

1911	Chi N	26	84	16	21	0	5	0	7	7	0	12	.250	.308	.369	89	-2	6	.905	-3	74	99	O22(1/21/0)		-0.7
	Bos N	66	197	20	40	5	2	2	15	10	2	26	.203	.249	.279	44	-16	4	.922	-1	99	86	O58(35/21/2)		-2.0
	Year	92	281	36	61	5	7	2	22	17	2	38	.217	.267	.306	57	-18	10	.918	-4	92	90	O80(36/42/2)		-2.7
1912	Bos N	4	13	0	0	0	0	0	0	0	0	3	.000	.000	.000	-98	-4	0	.900	0	94	167	O4L		-0.4

YEAR	TM	LG	G	AB	R	H	2B	3B	HR	RBI	BB-IB	HP	SO	AVG	OBP	SLG	AOPS	ABR	SB-CS	FA	FR	RNG	THR	GAMES AT POSITION	DL	BFW
1914	Ind	F	59	187	22	43	10	0	1	16	17	2	41	.230	.301	.299	58	-13	6	.918	-3	112	42	O50(40/10/0)/1		-2.0
Total	3		155	481	58	104	15	7	3	38	34	4	82	.216	.274	.295	53	-35	16	.917	-7	100	73	O134(80/52/2)/1		-5.1

KALAHAN, JOHN   John Joseph B9.30.1878 Philadelphia PA D6.20.1952 Philadelphia PA   BR/TR/6-0/165   d9.29

| 1903 | Phi | A | 1 | 5 | 0 | 0 | 0 | 0 | 0 | 0 | 0 | 0 | | .000 | .000 | .000 | -96 | -1 | 0 | 1.000 | -0 | 106 | 118 | /C | | -0.2 |

KALBFUS, CHARLIE   Charles Henry "Skinny" B12.28.1864 Washington DC D11.18.1941 Washington DC   BR/TR/5-11/145   d4.18

| 1884 | Was | U | 1 | 5 | 1 | 1 | 0 | 0 | 0 | 0 | 0 | 0 | | .200 | .200 | .200 | 22 | -1 | 0 | | | | | /OR | | -0.1 |

KALIN, FRANK   Frank Bruno "Fats" (b Frank Bruno Kalinkiewicz) B10.3.1917 Steubenville OH D1.12.1975 Weirton WV   BR/TR/6-0/200   d9.25   Mil 1943-45

1940	Pit	N	3	3	0	0	0	0	0	1	2	0	0	.000	.400	.000	19	0	1	.667	-1	67	0	O2(1/0/1)		-0.1
1943	Chi	A	4	4	0	0	0	0	0	0	0	0	0	.000	.000	.000	-99	-1	0-0		0			/H		-0.1
Total	2		7	7	0	0	0	0	0	1	2	0	0	.000	.222	.000	-34	-1	0-0	.667	-1	67	0	O2(1/0/1)		-0.2

KALINE, AL   Albert William B12.19.1934 Baltimore MD   BR/TR/6-2/180*   d6.25   HF1980   OF(16/484/2040)

1953	Det	A	30	28	9	7	0	1	1	2	1	1	5	.250	.300	.357	78	-1	1-0	1.000	0	92	239	O20(5/11/4)		-0.1
1954	Det	A	138	504	42	139	18	3	4	43	22	0	45	.276	.305	.347	80	-16	9-5	.971	7	108	157	O135R		-1.4
1955	Det	A★	152	588	121	**200**	24	8	27	102	82-12	5	57	**.340**	.421	.546	163	54	6-8	.979	13	115	150	O152R		4.9
1956	Det	A★	153	617	96	194	32	10	27	128	70-4	1	55	.314	.383	.530	139	33	7-1	.984	**12**	110	**156**	O153(1/12/142)		3.9
1957	Det	A★	149	577	83	170	29	4	23	90	43-7	3	38	.295	.343	.478	120	14	11-9	.985	5	108	113	O145(5/21/137)		3.7
1958	Det	A★	146	543	84	170	34	7	16	85	54-6	2	47	.313	.374	.490	127	21	7-4	.994	20	**119**	192	O145R		3.3
1959	Det	A★	136	511	86	167	19	2	27	94	72-**12**	4	42	.327	.410	**.530**	149	37	10-4	.989	2	110	44	O136(0/122/15)		3.3
1960	Det	A★	147	551	77	153	29	4	15	68	65-3	3	47	.278	.354	.426	100	7	19-4	.987	-4	103	56	O142C		-0.1
1961	Det	A★	153	586	116	190	**41**	7	19	82	66-2	4	42	.324	.393	.515	138	33	14-1	.990	13	**123**	81	O147(1/22/141)/3	57	3.0
1962	Det	A★	100	398	78	121	16	6	29	94	47-3	1	39	.304	.376	.593	152	28	4-0	.983	5	121	140	O100R		1.8
1963	Det	A★	145	551	89	172	24	3	27	101	54-**12**	4	48	.312	.375	.514	142	31	6-4	.992	-5	98	54	O140(0/2/140)		2.6
1964	Det	A*	146	525	77	154	31	5	17	68	75-6	3	51	.293	.383	.469	134	27	4-1	.990	7	119	74	O136R		1.4
1965	Det	A★	125	399	72	112	18	2	18	72	72-11	0	49	.281	.388	.471	142	25	6-0	.985	-8	90	36	O112(0/62/51)/3		3.8
1966	Det	A★	142	479	85	138	29	1	29	88	81-7	5	66	.288	.392	.534	161	42	5-5	**.993**	1	103	93	O136(0/86/53)		5.1
1967	Det	A*	131	458	94	141	28	2	25	78	83-10	1	47	.308	.411	.541	176	47	8-2	.983	7	107	182	O130(0/1/130)	30	5.1
1968	†Det	A	102	327	49	94	14	1	10	53	55-7	3	39	.287	.392	.428	145	21	6-4	.978	-0	115	26	O74(4/0/75),1b22	36	1.7
1969	Det	A	131	456	74	124	17	0	21	69	54-4	1	61	.272	.346	.447	117	10	1-2	.966	-0	101	109	O118R,1b9		0.3
1970	Det	A	131	467	64	130	24	4	16	71	77-5	1	49	.278	.377	.450	127	20	2-2	.988	4	111	60	O91R,1b52		1.6
1971	Det	A★	133	405	69	119	19	2	15	54	82-9	7	57	.294	.416	.462	144	28	4-6	**1.000**	-2	96	80	O129(0/3/128),1b5	15	2.1
1972	†Det	A	106	278	46	87	11	2	10	32	28-5	2	33	.313	.374	.475	128	17	1-0	.991	-1	91	110	O84R,1b11		1.3
1973	Det	A	91	310	40	79	13	0	10	45	29-4	3	28	.255	.320	.394	95	-2	4-1	1.000	-1	108	31	O63R,1b36		-0.8
1974	Det	A★	147	558	71	146	28	2	13	64	65-2	1	75	.262	.337	.389	105	5	2-2	—	-1	0	0	D146		0.1
Total	22		2834	10116	1622	3007	498	75	399	1583	1277-**131**	55	1020	.297	.376	.480	134	481	137-65	.986	69	108	101	O2488R,D146,1b135,3b2	138	43.3

KAMM, WILLIE   William Edward B2.2.1900 San Francisco CA D12.21.1988 Belmont CA   BR/TR/5-10.5/170   d4.18

1923	Chi	A	149	544	57	159	39	9	6	87	62	1	82	.292	.366	.430	110	8	18-13	.960	8	106	104	3b149		2.4
1924	Chi	A	147	528	58	134	28	6	3	93	64	2	59	.254	.337	.364	83	-13	10-9	**.971**	9	105	119	3b146		0.4
1925	Chi	A	152	509	82	142	32	4	6	83	**90**	4	36	.279	.391	.393	105	8	11-13	**.957**	-0	102	108	3b152		1.5
1926	Chi	A	143	480	63	141	24	10	0	62	77	4	24	.294	.396	.385	108	9	12-4	.978	16	**110**	72	3b142		3.4
1927	Chi	A	148	540	85	146	32	13	0	59	70	0	18	.270	.354	.378	92	-5	8-9	.972	3	96	75	3b146		0.5
1928	Chi	A	**155**	552	70	170	30	12	1	84	73	2	22	.308	.391	.411	112	13	17-9	**.977**	-0	89	113	3b155		2.2
1929	Chi	A	147	523	72	140	33	4	3	63	75	3	26	.268	.363	.371	90	-5	12-5	.978	4	98	97	3b145		0.9
1930	Chi	A	112	331	49	89	21	6	3	47	51	1	20	.269	.368	.396	97	0	5-4	.939	13	**111**	79	3b106		1.7
1931	Chi	A	18	59	9	15	4	1	0	9	7	0	6	.254	.333	.356	86	0	1-1	.938	1	94	119	3b18		1.1
	Cle	A	114	410	68	121	31	4	0	66	64	1	13	.295	.392	.390	100	3	13-9	.947	4	100	139	3b114		1.1
	Year		132	469	77	136	35	5	0	75	71	1	19	.290	.384	.386	99	3	14-10	.945	5	**99**	**136**	3b132		1.3
1932	Cle	A	148	524	76	150	34	9	3	83	75	3	36	.286	.379	.403	96	-1	6-3	**.984**	3	99	79	3b131		-0.2
1933	Cle	A	133	447	59	126	17	2	1	47	54	0	27	.282	.359	.336	81	-10	6-3	.978	9	109	107	3b118		0.7
1934	Cle	A	121	386	52	104	23	3	0	42	62	1	38	.269	.372	.345	82	-6	7-1	.978	9	109	107	3b118		-0.2
1935	Cle	A	6	18	2	6	0	0	0	1	0	0	1	.333	.333	.333	72	-1	0-1	.875	-1	69	0	3b4		-0.2
Total	13		1693	5851	802	1643	348	85	29	826	824	22	405	.281	.372	.384	97	-1	126-84	.967	77	102	99	3b1674		15.7

KAMPOURIS, ALEX   Alexis William B11.13.1912 Sacramento CA D5.29.1993 Sacramento CA   BR/TR/5-8/155   d7.31   Mil 1944-45

1934	Cin	N	19	66	6	13	1	0	0	3	3	2	18	.197	.254	.212	27	-7	2	.946	-1	105	73	2b16		-0.7
1935	Cin	N	148	499	46	123	26	5	7	62	32	2	84	.246	.295	.361	77	-17	8	.957	-3	95	115	2b141,S6		-1.0
1936	Cin	N	122	355	43	85	10	4	5	46	24	1	46	.239	.289	.332	72	-16	3	.969	22	**115**	119	2b119/OL		1.3
1937	Cin	N	146	458	62	114	21	4	17	71	60	5	65	.249	.342	.424	112	8	2	.973	9	100	97	2b146		2.6
1938	Cin	N	21	74	13	19	1	0	2	7	10	1	13	.257	.353	.351	97	0	1	.972	13	108	120	2b79		0.1
	NY	N	82	268	35	66	9	5	3	37	27	1	50	.246	.314	.343	81	-7	0	.972	13	107	115	2b100		1.1
	Year		103	342	48	85	10	5	5	44	37	2	63	.249	.340	.345	84	-7	1	.973	11	111	97	2b62,3b11		1.2
1939	NY	N	74	201	23	50	12	5	2	29	30	1	41	.249	.349	.403	101	1	0	.987	-1	102	91	2b15		0.6
1941	Bro	N	16	51	8	16	4	2	2	9	11	0	4	.314	.444	.588	181	6	0	1.000	1	104	167	2b9		0.2
1942	Bro	N	10	21	3	5	2	1	0	4	0	0	4	.238	.238	.429	92	0	0	.970	1	99	167	2b9		0.3
1943	Bro	N	19	44	9	10	4	1	0	4	1	0	6	.227	.452	.364	136	4	0	.946	-3	86	73	2b18		0.1
	Was	A	51	145	24	30	4	2	2	13	30	5	25	.207	.361	.276	91	0	7-1	.936	-2	92	204	3b33,2b10/OR		5.8
Total	9		708	2182	272	531	94	20	45	284	244	20	360	.243	.325	.367	91	-28	22-1	.964	47	103	105	2b636,3b44,S6,O2(1/0/1)		5.8

KANE, FRANK   Francis Thomas "Sugar" (aka Frank Thomas Kiley in 1915) B3.9.1895 Whitman MA D12.2.1962 Brockton MA   BL/TR/5-11.5/175   d9.13

1915	Bro	F	3	10	2	2	0	1	0	2	0	0	0	.200	.200	.400	67	-1	0	1.000	1	107	304	O2L		0.0
1919	NY	A	1	1	0	0	0	0	0	0	0	0	0	.000	.000	.000	-99	-1	0	—	0	0	0	/H		0.0
Total	2		4	11	2	2	0	1	0	2	0	0	0	.182	.182	.364	52	-1	0	1.000	1	107	304	O2L		0.0

KANE, JIM   James Joseph "Shamus" B11.27.1881 Scranton PA D10.2.1947 Omaha NE   BL/TL/6-2/225   d4.21

| 1908 | Pit | N | 55 | 145 | 16 | 35 | 3 | 3 | 0 | 22 | 12 | 0 | | .241 | .299 | .303 | 93 | -1 | 5 | .966 | -2 | 98 | 118 | 1b40 | | -0.5 |

KANE, JOHN   John Francis B9.24.1882 Chicago IL D1.28.1934 St.Anthony ID   BR/TR/5-6/138   d4.11

1907	Cin	N	79	262	40	65	9	4	3	19	22	8		.248	.325	.347	106	2	20	.959	-2	98	0	O42(38/0/4),3b25,S6,2b2		-0.9
1908	Cin	N	130	455	61	97	11	7	3	23	43	13		.213	.299	.288	90	-4	30	**.981**	2	96	53	O127(0/120/7)/2		-0.5
1909	Cin	N	20	45	6	4	1	0	0	5	2	1		.089	.146	.111	-20	-6	2	.917	2	238	0	O8(6/1/1),S3,3b3,2b2		-0.5
1910	†Chi	N	32	62	11	15	0	0	1	12	9	0	10	.242	.338	.290	84	-1	2	1.000	-2	100	0	O18(9/9/1),2b6,3b4,S2		-2.0
Total	4		261	824	118	181	21	11	7	59	76	22	10	.220	.303	.297	89	-9	53	.975	-0	101	36	O195(53/130/13),3b32,2b11,S11		-3.9

KANE, JOHN   John Francis B2.19.1900 Chicago IL D7.25.1956 Chicago IL   BB/TR/5-10.5/162   d9.3

| 1925 | Chi | A | 14 | 56 | 6 | 10 | 0 | 1 | 0 | 3 | 3 | 1 | 3 | .179 | .193 | .196 | -1 | -9 | 0-0 | .935 | 1 | 116 | 125 | S8,2b6 | | -0.7 |

KANE, TOM   Thomas Joseph "Sugar" B12.15.1906 Chicago IL D11.26.1973 Chicago IL   BR/TR/5-10.5/160   d8.3

| 1938 | Bos | N | 2 | 2 | 0 | 0 | 0 | 0 | 0 | 0 | 2 | 0 | 0 | .000 | .500 | .000 | 53 | 0 | 0 | 1.000 | -1 | 67 | 0 | 2b2 | | 0.0 |

KANE, JERRY   William Jeremiah B4.4.1866 Collinsville IL D6.16.1949 E.St.Louis IL   BR/TR/6-0/175   d5.2

| 1890 | StL | AA | 8 | 25 | 3 | 5 | 0 | 0 | 0 | 2 | 0 | | | .200 | .200 | .200 | 31 | -2 | 0 | .907 | -1 | 57 | 46 | 1b5,C4 | | -0.3 |

KANEHL, ROD   Roderick Edwin "Hot Rod" B4.1.1934 Wichita KS D12.14.2004 Palm Springs CA   BR/TR/6-1/180*   d4.15   OF(42/56/7)

1962	NY	N	133	351	52	87	10	2	4	27	23-2	1	36	.248	.296	.322	65	-18	8-6	.944	12	111	123	2b62,3b30,O20(10/7/3),1b3,S2		-0.1
1963	NY	N	109	191	26	46	6	0	1	9	5-0	2	26	.241	.268	.288	59	-10	6-3	.974	-2	115	202	O58(30/26/4),3b13,2b12,1b3		-0.5
1964	NY	N	98	254	25	59	7	1	1	11	7-0	1	18	.232	.256	.280	52	-17	3-1	.988	10	103	83	2b34,O25(2/23/0),3b19,1b2		-2.0
Total	3		340	796	103	192	23	3	6	47	35-2	4	80	.241	.277	.300	60	-45	17-10	.950	21	104	105	2b108,O103C,3b62,1b8,S2		-2.7

KAPLER, GABE   Gabriel Stefan B8.31.1975 Hollywood CA   BR/TR/6-2/208(190-208)   [DetA95 57/1488]   d9.20   Col Moorpark (CA) JC

1998	Det	A	7	25	3	6	1	0	1	0	1-0	0	4	.240	.231	.280	32	-3	2-0	1.000	-1	101	0	O6R/D		-0.4
1999	Det	A	130	416	60	102	22	4	18	49	42-2	0	74	.245	.315	.447	91	-7	11-5	.981	-2	101	52	O128(0/114/32),D2	36	-0.4
2000	Tex	A	116	444	59	134	32	1	14	66	42-2	0	57	.302	.360	.473	108	6	8-4	.969	3	109	77	O133C/D	21	0.8
2001	Tex	A	134	483	77	129	29	1	17	72	61-2	0	70	.267	.348	.437	103	4	23-6	.997	5	106	241	O64(31/23/18)/1D	22	-0.5
2002	Tex	A	72	196	25	51	12	1	9	17	8-0	0	30	.260	.285	.472	63	-11	5-2	.977	5	106	241	O64(31/23/18)/1D		

YEAR	TM LG	G	AB	R	H	2B	3B	HR	RBI	BB-IB	HP	SO	AVG	OBP	SLG	AOPS	ABR	SB-CS	FA	FR	RNG	THR	GAMES AT POSITION	DL	BFW
	Col N	40	119	12	37	4	3	2	17	8-0	1	23	.311	.359	.445	100	-1	6-2	1.000	2	106	152	O38(15/1/23)		0.1
2003	Col N	39	67	10	15	2	0	0	4	8-1	0	18	.224	.307	.254	43	-5	2-0	.970	2	94	304	O29(15/2/13)		-0.4
	†Bos A	68	158	29	46	11	1	4	23	14-0	1	23	.291	.349	.449	104	1	4-2	.932	-2	82	199	O61(25/8/30)/1		-0.2
2004	†Bos A	136	290	51	79	14	1	6	33	15-0	2	49	.272	.311	.390	77	-10	5-4	.978	-1	98	112	O127(18/17/101),D2		-1.4
2005	Bos A	36	97	15	24	7	0	1	9	3-0	2	15	.247	.282	.351	64	-5	1-0	1.000	0	109	0	O36(8/12/22)	15	-0.5
Total	8	778	2295	341	622	133	13	62	290	202-5	10	363	.271	.330	.421	91	-31	67-25	.980	5	101	110	O738(112/394/285),D7,1b2	94	-2.8

KAPPEL, HEINIE   Henry B9.1863 Philadelphia PA D8.27.1905 Philadelphia PA BR/TR/5-8/160 d5.22 b-Joe

YEAR	TM LG	G	AB	R	H	2B	3B	HR	RBI	BB-IB	HP	SO	AVG	OBP	SLG	AOPS	ABR	SB-CS	FA	FR	RNG	THR	GAMES AT POSITION	DL	BFW
1887	Cin AA	23	78	11	22	3	2	0	15	2	1		.282	.309	.372	87	-2	3	.667	-2	93	74	3b9,O7(2/0/5),2b6/S		-0.3
1888	Cin AA	36	143	18	37	4	4	1	15	2	1		.259	.274	.364	98	-1	20	.790	-11	93	95	S25,2b10/3		-1.0
1889	Col AA	46	173	25	47	7	5	3	21	21	1	28	.272	.354	.422	127	6	10	.791	-1	94	45	S23,3b23		0.5
Total	3	105	394	54	106	14	11	4	51	25	3	28	.269	.318	.391	109	3	33	.796	-14	94	68	S49,3b33,2b16,O7(2/0/5)		-0.8

KAPPEL, JOE   Joseph B4.27.1857 Philadelphia PA D7.8.1929 Philadelphia PA BR/5-11/175 d5.26 b-Heinie

YEAR	TM LG	G	AB	R	H	2B	3B	HR	RBI	BB-IB	HP	SO	AVG	OBP	SLG	AOPS	ABR	SB-CS	FA	FR	RNG	THR	GAMES AT POSITION	DL	BFW
1884	Phi N	4	15	1	1	0	0	0	0	0		2	.067	.067	.067	-61	-3		.727	-4			C4		-0.6
1890	Phi AA	56	208	29	50	8	1	1	22	20	1		.240	.310	.303	81	-5	12	.851	-4	146	0	O23(11/8/5),S18,3b11,C3,2b2		-0.7
Total	2	60	223	30	51	8	1	1	22	20	1	2	.229	.295	.287	73	-8	12	.851	-7			O23(11/8/5),S18,3b11,C7,2b2		-1.3

KARKOVICE, RON   Ronald Joseph B8.8.1963 Union NJ BR/TR/6-1/215* [ChiA82 1/14] d8.17

YEAR	TM LG	G	AB	R	H	2B	3B	HR	RBI	BB-IB	HP	SO	AVG	OBP	SLG	AOPS	ABR	SB-CS	FA	FR	RNG	THR	GAMES AT POSITION	DL	BFW
1986	Chi A	37	97	13	24	7	0	4	13	9-0	1	37	.247	.315	.443	101	0	1-0	.996	8	87	132	C37		1.0
1987	Chi A	39	85	7	6	0	0	2	7	7-0	2	40	.071	.160	.141	-19	-15	3-0	.982	6	444	100	C37/D		-0.7
1988	Chi A	46	115	10	20	4	0	3	9	7-0	1	30	.174	.228	.287	43	-9	4-2	.995	6	169	121	C46		-0.1
1989	Chi A	71	182	21	48	9	2	3	24	10-0	1	56	.264	.306	.385	96	-1	0-0	.986	12	152	135	C68,D2		1.4
1990	Chi A	68	183	30	45	10	0	6	20	16-1	1	52	.246	.308	.399	99	-1	2-0	.994	9	193	102	C64,D2		0.6
1991	Chi A	75	167	25	41	13	0	5	22	15-1	1	42	.246	.310	.413	101	0	0-0	.988	6	129	115	C69/OL		0.9
1992	Chi A	123	342	39	81	12	1	13	50	30-1	1	89	.237	.302	.392	94	-4	10-4	.990	0	109	85	C119/OR	45	0.4
1993	†Chi A	128	403	60	92	17	1	20	54	29-1	6	126	.228	.287	.424	91	-7	2-2	.994	19	**166**	124	C127·	16	1.9
1994	Chi A	77	207	33	44	9	1	11	29	36-2	0	68	.213	.325	.425	94	-2	0-3	.993	-1	141	70	C76	25	0.1
1995	Chi A	113	323	44	70	14	1	13	51	39-0	5	84	.217	.306	.387	83	-8	2-3	.991	-4	95	123	C113		-0.6
1996	Chi A	111	355	44	78	22	0	10	38	24-2	1	93	.220	.270	.366	62	-22	0-0	.993	11	133	118	C111		-0.4
1997	Chi A	51	138	10	25	3	0	6	18	11-0	3	32	.181	.248	.333	54	-10	0-0	.996	-4	120	72	C51		-1.1
Total	12	939	2597	336	574	120	6	96	335	233-8	26	749	.221	.289	.383	80	-79	24-14	.992	62	147	109	C918,D5,O2(1/0/1)	86	3.4

KARLON, BILL   William John "Hank" B1.21.1909 Palmer MA D12.7.1964 Ware MA BR/TR/6-1/190 d4.28

YEAR	TM LG	G	AB	R	H	2B	3B	HR	RBI	BB-IB	HP	SO	AVG	OBP	SLG	AOPS	ABR	SB-CS	FA	FR	RNG	THR	GAMES AT POSITION	DL	BFW
1930	NY A	2	5	0	0	0	0	0	0	0		1	.000	.000	.000	-99	-2	0-0	1.000	-0	74	0	/OL		-0.2

KAROW, MARTY   Martin Gregory (b Martin Gregory Karowsky) B7.18.1904 Braddock PA D4.27.1986 Bryan TX BR/TR/5-10.5/170 d6.21 Col Ohio St.

YEAR	TM LG	G	AB	R	H	2B	3B	HR	RBI	BB-IB	HP	SO	AVG	OBP	SLG	AOPS	ABR	SB-CS	FA	FR	RNG	THR	GAMES AT POSITION	DL	BFW
1927	Bos A	6	10	2	2	0	0	0	0	0		2	.200	.200	.200	29	-1	0-0	1.000	0	95	318	S3,3b2		0.0

KARROS, ERIC   Eric Peter B11.4.1967 Hackensack NJ BR/TR/6-4/222(205-226) [LAN88 6/140] d9.1 Col UCLA

YEAR	TM LG	G	AB	R	H	2B	3B	HR	RBI	BB-IB	HP	SO	AVG	OBP	SLG	AOPS	ABR	SB-CS	FA	FR	RNG	THR	GAMES AT POSITION	DL	BFW
1991	LA N	14	14	0	1	0	0	0	1	1-0	0	6	.071	.133	.143	-23	-2	0-0	1.000	-0	74	225	1b10		-0.3
1992	LA N	149	545	63	140	30	1	20	88	37-3	2	103	.257	.304	.426	106	3	2-4	.993	8	**116**	93	1b143		0.0
1993	LA N	158	619	74	153	27	2	23	80	34-1	2	82	.247	.287	.409	89	-13	0-1	.992	9	118	97	1b157		-1.8
1994	LA N	111	406	51	108	21	1	14	46	29-1	0	53	.266	.310	.426	97	-3	2-0	.991	6	129	96	1b109		0.1
1995	†LA N	143	551	83	164	29	3	32	105	61-4	4	115	.298	.369	.535	146	36	4-4	.995	0	96	94	1b143		2.2
1996	†LA N	154	608	84	158	29	1	34	111	53-2	1	121	.260	.316	.479	114	9	8-0	.990	1	102	109	1b154		-0.2
1997	LA N	**162**	628	86	167	28	0	31	104	61-2	2	116	.266	.329	.459	112	8	15-7	.992	-2	95	74	1b162		-0.7
1998	LA N	139	507	59	150	20	1	23	87	47-1	3	93	.296	.355	.475	123	16	7-2	.991	5	111	115	1b136,D2		0.9
1999	LA N	153	578	74	176	40	0	34	112	53-0	2	119	.304	.362	.550	134	28	8-5	.991	9	126	93	1b151	24	2.3
2000	LA N	155	584	84	146	29	0	31	106	63-2	4	122	.250	.321	.459	100	-2	4-3	.995	14	129	103	1b153/D		-0.2
2001	LA N	121	438	42	103	22	0	15	63	41-2	3	101	.235	.303	.388	82	-12	3-1	.996	-2	90	93	1b119	24	-2.4
2002	LA N	142	524	52	142	26	1	13	73	37-1	6	74	.271	.323	.399	98	-5	4-2	**.997**	11	**131**	77	1b142		-0.6
2003	†Chi N	114	336	37	96	16	1	12	40	28-1	0	46	.286	.340	.446	101	1	1-1	.992	-2	83	117	1b97		-1.0
2004	Oak A	40	103	8	20	6	0	2	11	7-1	0	16	.194	.243	.311	44	-9	0-0	.989	3	174	110	1b22,D10		-0.8
Total	14	1755	6441	797	1724	324	11	284	1027	552-21	31	1167	.268	.325	.454	108	54	59-30	.993	68	112	98	1b1698,D13	48	-2.5

KARST, JOHN   John Gottlieb "King" B10.15.1893 Philadelphia PA D5.21.1976 Cape May Court House NJ BL/TR/5-11.5/175 d10.6 Col Penn

YEAR	TM LG	G	AB	R	H	2B	3B	HR	RBI	BB-IB	HP	SO	AVG	OBP	SLG	AOPS	ABR	SB-CS	FA	FR	RNG	THR	GAMES AT POSITION	DL	BFW
1915	Bro N	1	0	0	0	0	0	0	0	0		0					0	0	1.000	0	149	2105	/3		0.0

KASKO, EDDIE   Edward Michael B6.27.1932 Linden NJ BR/TR/6-0/180* d4.18 M4

YEAR	TM LG	G	AB	R	H	2B	3B	HR	RBI	BB-IB	HP	SO	AVG	OBP	SLG	AOPS	ABR	SB-CS	FA	FR	RNG	THR	GAMES AT POSITION	DL	BFW
1957	StL N	134	479	59	131	16	5	1	35	33-7	0	53	.273	.319	.334	75	-17	6-1	.961	-0	**106**	102	3b120,S13/2		-1.6
1958	StL N	104	259	20	57	8	1	2	21	21-6	0	25	.220	.277	.282	47	-20	1-2	.961	-1	97	103	S77,2b12/3		-1.6
1959	Cin N	118	329	39	93	14	1	2	31	14-5	0	38	.283	.309	.350	74	-12	2-2	.976	10	105	117	S84,3b31,2b2		0.4
1960	Cin N	126	479	56	140	21	1	6	51	46-0	6	37	.292	.359	.378	101	2	9-9	.966	10	120	146	3b86,2b33,S15		1.5
1961	†Cin N★	126	469	64	127	22	4	2	27	32-1	4	36	.271	.320	.335	74	-17	4-3	.964	-10	91	90	S112,3b12,2b6		-1.7
1962	Cin N	134	533	74	148	26	2	4	41	35-1	5	44	.278	.326	.356	81	-13	3-3	.941	-4	95	89	3b114,S21		-1.8
1963	Cin N	76	199	25	48	9	0	3	10	21-4	0	29	.241	.311	.332	83	-4	0-2	.959	2	93	87	3b48,S15/2		-0.2
1964	Hou N	133	448	45	109	16	1	0	22	37-8	1	52	.243	.302	.283	70	-17	4-6	**.978**	13	108	105	S128,3b2		0.5
1965	Hou N	68	215	18	53	7	1	1	10	11-1	4	20	.247	.296	.302	74	-8	1-3	.976	-5	94	83	S59,3b2	58	-1.0
1966	Bos A	58	136	11	29	7	0	1	12	15-0	0	19	.213	.291	.287	61	-6	1-0	.976	7	117	71	S20,3b10,2b8	27	0.3
Total	10	1077	3546	411	935	146	13·	22	261	265-33	20	353	.264	.317	.331	76	-112	31-31	.971	22	100	101	S544,3b426,2b63	85	-5.2

KATA, MATT   Matthew John B3.14.1978 Avon Lake OH BB/TR/6-1/180(180-195) [AriN99 9/268] d6.15 Col Vanderbilt

YEAR	TM LG	G	AB	R	H	2B	3B	HR	RBI	BB-IB	HP	SO	AVG	OBP	SLG	AOPS	ABR	SB-CS	FA	FR	RNG	THR	GAMES AT POSITION	DL	BFW
2003	Ari N	78	288	42	74	16	5	7	29	25-0	1	53	.257	.315	.420	84	-7	3-2	.988	2	95	88	2b52,3b23,S6		-0.2
2004	Ari N	42	162	17	40	9	2	2	13	13-2	0	29	.247	.301	.364	67	-8	4-1	.989	8	112	99	2b38,3b3/S	127	0.3
2005	Ari N	30	31	6	6	2	1	0	0	5-0	0	5	.194	.306	.323	62	-2	0-0	1.000	2	131	274	2b7		0.0
	Phi N	10	6	1	1	0	0	0	0	0-0	0	2	.167	.167	.167	-12	-1	0-0	—	-1	0	0	2b3/SORD		-0.2
	Year	40	37	7	7	2	1	0	0	5-0	0	6	.189	.286	.297	51	-3	0-1	1.000	1	111	232	2b10/SORD		-0.2
Total	3	160	487	66	121	27	8	9	42	43-2	1	88	.248	.308	.392	76	-18	7-4	.989	12	103	99	2b100,3b26,S8/DOR	127	-0.1

KATT, RAY   Raymond Frederick B5.9.1927 New Braunfels TX D10.19.1999 New Braunfels TX BR/TR/6-2/200* d9.16 C3 Col Texas A&M-Commerce

YEAR	TM LG	G	AB	R	H	2B	3B	HR	RBI	BB-IB	HP	SO	AVG	OBP	SLG	AOPS	ABR	SB-CS	FA	FR	RNG	THR	GAMES AT POSITION	DL	BFW
1952	NY N	9	27	4	6	0	0	1	1	1	0	5	.222	.250	.222	32	-3	0-0	1.000	1	249	53	C8		-0.1
1953	NY N	8	29	2	5	1	0	0	1	1	0	4	.172	.200	.207	6	-4	0-0	.975	-0	112	141	C8		-0.4
1954	NY N	86	200	26	51	7	1	9	33	19	0	29	.255	.314	.435	94	0	1-0	.973	-3	146	89	C82		-0.4
1955	NY N	124	326	27	70	7	2	7	28	22-4	2	38	.215	.268	.313	54	-23	0-0	.987	-5	115	89	C122		-2.3
1956	NY N	37	101	10	23	4	0	7	14	6-1	1	16	.228	.278	.475	98	-1	0-1	.978	1	117	125	C37		0.1
	StL N	47	158	11	41	4	0	6	20	6-1	1	24	.259	.289	.399	83	-4	0-1	.984	-2	94	61	C47		0.5
	Year	84	259	21	64	8	0	13	34	12-2	2	40	.247	.285	.429	89	-5	0-2	.982	-1	103	87	C84		-0.5
1957	NY N	72	165	11	38	3	1	2	17	15-1	2	35	.230	.294	.297	62	-9	1-0	.981	-3	128	101	C68		-0.9
1958	StL N	19	41	1	7	1	0	1	4	4-0	0	6	.171	.239	.268	34	-4	0-0	.971	-1	69	51	C14		-0.4
1959	StL N	15	24	0	7	2	0	0	2	1-0	0	0	.292	.292	.375	71	-1	0-0	.976	-0	106	81	C14		-0.4
Total	8	417	1071	92	248	29	4	32	120	74-7	6	164	.232	.283	.356	69	-52	2-5	.981	-12	121	89	C400		-4.8

KAUFF, BENNY   Benjamin Michael B1.5.1890 Pomeroy OH D11.17.1961 Columbus OH BL/TL/5-8/157 d4.20 Mil 1918

YEAR	TM LG	G	AB	R	H	2B	3B	HR	RBI	BB-IB	HP	SO	AVG	OBP	SLG	AOPS	ABR	SB-CS	FA	FR	RNG	THR	GAMES AT POSITION	DL	BFW
1912	NY A	5	11	4	3	0	0	0	1		0		.273	.429	.273	96	-1		1.000	-1	76	0	O4C		0.0
1914	Ind F	154	571	**120**	211	**44**	13	8	95	72	8	55	**.370**	**.447**	.534	150	37	**75**	1.000	9	107	123	O154(33/54/68)		3.7
1915	Bro F	136	483	92	165	23	11	12	83	85	6	50	.342	.446	**.509**	170	43	55	.959	11	103	**161**	O136C		**4.7**
1916	NY N	154	552	71	146	22	15	9	74	68	3	65	.264	.348	.408	139	26	40-26	.976	-4	91	117	O154C		1.2
1917	†NY N	153	559	89	172	24	11	5	68	59	5	54	.308	.379	.388	140	29	30	.976	-11	96	57	O153(3/150/0)		0.9
1918	NY N	67	270	41	85	19	4	2	39	16	1	30	.315	.355	.437	144	14	9	.952	-5	93	118	O67C		0.5
1919	NY N	135	491	73	136	27	7	10	67	39	3	45	.277	.334	.422	128	16	21	.950	-6	92	103	O134C		0.1
1920	NY N	55	157	31	43	13	3	3	26	25	2	14	.274	.380	.446	138	9	3-7	.960	-6	76	120	O51C		-0.2
Total	8	859	3094	521	961	169	57	49	454	367	28	313	.311	.389	.450	146	174	234-33	.960	-12	95	112	O853(36/750/68)		10.9

YEAR	TM LG	G	AB	R	H	2B	3B	HR	RBI	BB-IB	HP	SO	AVG	OBP	SLG	AOPS	ABR	SB-CS	FA	FR	RNG	THR	GAMES AT POSITION	DL	BFW

KAUFFMAN, DICK   Howard Richard   B6.22.1888 E.Lewisburg PA   D4.16.1948 Mifflinburg PA   BB/TR/6-3/190   d9.17   Col Susquehanna

1914	StL A	7	15	1	4	1	0	0	2	0	0	3	.267	.267	.333	83	0	0	.967	-1	0	0	1b7		-0.2
1915	StL A	37	124	9	32	8	2	0	14	5	2	27	.258	.298	.355	99	-1	0-3	.984	-1	90	135	1b32/OR		-0.4
Total	2	44	139	10	36	9	2	0	16	5	2	30	.259	.295	.353	97	-1	0-3	.982	-2	81	121	1b39/OR		-0.6

KAUFMANN, TONY   Anthony Charles   B12.16.1900 Chicago IL   D6.4.1982 Elgin IL   BR/TR/5-11/165   d9.23   C4 ▲

1921	Chi N	2	5	0	2	1	0	0	0	0	0	1	.400	.400	.600	161	1	0-0	1.000	-1	29	0	P2		0.0
1922	Chi N	38	45	4	9	2	1	1	4	2	0	14	.200	.234	.356	49	1	0-0	.933	-1	79	0	P37		0.0
1923	Chi N	33	74	10	16	2	0	2	10	7	0	17	.216	.284	.324	60	3	0-0	.962	-1	85	124	P33		0.0
1924	Chi N	35	76	6	24	5	0	1	14	3	0	10	.316	.342	.421	102	6	0-0	.981	-2	75	123	P34		0.0
1925	Chi N	31	78	8	15	7	0	2	13	2	0	17	.192	.213	.359	42	2	0-0	.981	-0	93	210	P31		0.0
1926	Chi N	30	60	9	15	2	0	1	7	2	0	10	.250	.274	.333	62	2	1	1.000	-2	81	87	P26		0.0
1927	Chi N	9	16	2	5	0	0	1	6	4	0	4	.313	.450	.500	154	3	0-0	1.000	2	155	176	P9		0.0
	Phi N	8	7	1	1	0	0	1	2	0	0	1	.143	.143	.571	83	0	0-0	1.000	-0	72	0	P5/OL		0.0
	StL N	1	0	0	0	0	0	0	0	0	0	0	—	—	—	—	0	0	—	0	0	0	/P		0.0
	Year	18	23	3	6	0	0	2	8	4	0	5	.261	.370	.522	136	1	0-0	1.000	1	133	130	P15/OL		0.0
1928	StL N	5	0	0	0	0	0	0	0	0	0	0	—	—	—	—	0	0	1.000	-0	86	0	P4		0.0
1929	NY N	39	32	18	1	0	0	0	1	6	0	4	.031	.184	.031	-43	-7	3	.964	1	131	0	O16(4/8/4)		-0.7
1930	StL N	2	3	1	1	0	0	0	0	1	0	1	.333	.500	.333	103	0	0-0	1.000	-0	50	0	P2		0.0
1931	StL N	20	18	1	2	0	0	0	1	1	0	3	.111	.158	.111	-26	-2	0-0	.929	-0	107	0	P15/OL		0.0
1935	StL N	7	0	2	0	0	0	0	0	0	0	0	—	—	—	—	0	0	1.000	0	119	0	P3		0.0
Total	12	260	414	62	91	19	1	9	57	28	0	82	.220	.269	.336	57	8	4-0	.972	-5	86	107	P202,O18(6/8/4)		-0.7

KAVANAGH, CHARLIE   Charles Hugh "Silk"   B6.9.1893 Chicago IL   D9.6.1973 Reedsburg WI   BR/TR/5-9/165   d6.11

| 1914 | Chi A | 6 | 5 | 0 | 1 | 0 | 0 | 0 | 1 | 2 | 0 | 2 | .200 | .333 | .200 | 62 | 0 | 0 | — | | 0 | | /H | | 0.0 |

KAVANAGH, LEO   Leo Daniel   B8.9.1894 Chicago IL   D8.10.1950 Chicago IL   BR/TR/5-9/180   d4.22

| 1914 | Chi F | 5 | 11 | 0 | 3 | 0 | 0 | 1 | 1 | 0 | 0 | 0 | .273 | .333 | .273 | 70 | -1 | 0 | 1.000 | -0 | 76 | 123 | S5 | | -0.1 |

KAVANAGH, MARTY   Martin Joseph   B6.13.1891 Harrison NJ   D7.28.1960 Taylor MI   BR/TR/6-0/187   d4.18

1914	Det A	128	439	60	109	21	6	4	35	41	4	42	.248	.318	.351	98	-1	16-14	.929	-11	102	79	2b115,1b4		-1.3
1915	Det A	113	332	55	98	14	13	4	49	42	2	44	.295	.378	.452	141	16	8-8	.987	-11	88	70	1b44,2b42,S2,O2L/3		0.3
1916	Det A	58	78	6	11	4	0	0	5	9	1	15	.141	.239	.192	29	-7	0-0	1.000	-1	98	69	O11(1/0/10),2b2/3		-0.9
	Cle A	19	44	4	11	2	1	1	10	2	0	5	.250	.283	.409	102	0	0	.894	-1	123	55	2b9/13		-0.1
	Year	77	122	10	22	6	1	1	15	11	1	20	.180	.254	.270	55	-7	0-0	1.000	-2	98	69	O11(1/0/10),2b11,3b2/1		-1.0
1917	Cle A	14	14	1	0	0	0	0	0	3	0	2	.000	.176	.000	-43	-2	0	1.000	-1	68	107	1b12		-0.2
1918	Cle A	13	38	4	8	2	0	0	6	7	1	7	.211	.348	.263	77	-1	1	.967	-1	68	107	1b12		-0.3
	StL N	12	44	6	8	1	0	1	8	3	0	1	.182	.234	.273	56	-2	1	1.000	-2	95	0	O8R,2b4		-0.5
	Det A	13	44	2	12	3	0	0	9	11	0	6	.273	.418	.341	135	3	0	.964	-2	73	76	1b12		0.1
Total	5	370	1033	138	257	47	20	10	122	118	8	122	.249	.330	.362	104	6	26-22	.926	-28	101	71	2b172,1b73,O23(3/2/18),3b3,S2		-2.9

KAVANAUGH   d9.11

| 1872 | Eck NA | 5 | 23 | 3 | 6 | 1 | 0 | 0 | 4 | 0 | 0 | 0 | .261 | .261 | .304 | 86 | 0 | 0-0 | .921 | -0 | 0 | 0 | 1b4,O2R | | 0.0 |

KAY, BILL   Walter Brocton "King Bill"   B2.14.1878 New Castle VA   D12.3.1945 Roanoke VA   BL/TR/6-2/180   d8.12   Col Roanoke

| 1907 | Was A | 25 | 60 | 8 | 20 | 1 | 1 | 0 | 7 | 0 | 0 | | .333 | .333 | .383 | 139 | 2 | 0 | 1.000 | 0 | 74 | 0 | O12(0/1/11) | | 0.2 |

KAZAK, EDDIE   Edward Terrance (b Edward Terrance Tkaczuk)   B7.18.1920 Steubenville OH   D12.15.1999 Austin TX   BR/TR/6-0/175*   d9.29

1948	StL N	6	22	1	6	3	0	0	2	0	0	2	.273	.273	.409	78	-1	0	.900	-0	92	221	3b6		-0.1
1949	StL N★	92	326	43	99	15	3	6	42	29	1	17	.304	.362	.423	105	2	0	.926	-2	103	132	3b80,2b5		-0.8
1950	StL N	93	207	21	53	2	5	2	23	18	1	19	.256	.319	.357	74	-8	0	.936	1	107	83	3b48		-0.4
1951	StL N	11	33	2	6	2	0	0	4	5	0	5	.182	.289	.242	44	-2	0-0	.933	-1	85	46	3b10		-0.1
1952	StL N	3	2	1	0	0	0	0	0	0	0	0	.000	.000	.000	-99	-1	0-0	1.000	0	143	0	/3		-0.4
	Cin N	13	15	1	1	0	1	0	0	0	0	2	.067	.067	.200	-29	-3	0-0	.667	-1	54	0	3b3/1		-0.5
	Year	16	17	2	1	0	1	0	0	0	0	2	.059	.059	.176	-37	-3	0-0	.750	-1	78	0	3b4/1		-0.5
Total	5	218	605	69	165	22	6	11	71	52	2	45	.273	.332	.383	87	-13	0-0	.927	-4	102	114	3b148,2b5/1		-1.8

KAZANSKI, TED   Theodore Stanley   B1.25.1934 Hamtramck MI   BR/TR/6-1/175*   d6.25

1953	Phi N	95	360	39	78	17	5	2	27	26	3	53	.217	.275	.308	52	-26	1-1	.949	-18	85	93	S95		-3.5
1954	Phi N	39	104	7	14	2	0	1	8	4	0	14	.135	.164	.183	-9	-17	0-1	.945	-4	95	111	S38		-2.0
1955	Phi N	9	12	1	1	0	0	1	1	0	0	5	.083	.154	.333	25	-1	0-0	1.000	0	94	77	S4,3b4		-0.1
1956	Phi N	117	379	35	80	11	4	4	34	20-6	1	41	.211	.251	.277	43	-31	0-2	.979	-16	88	97	2b116/S		-4.2
1957	Phi N	62	185	15	49	7	1	3	11	17-1	0	20	.265	.327	.362	88	-3	1-1	.968	-2	88	100	3b36,2b22,S3		-0.5
1958	Phi N	95	289	21	66	12	2	3	35	22-2	4	34	.228	.291	.315	62	-16	2-3	.988	-13	89	100	2b59,S22,3b16		-2.6
Total	6	417	1329	118	288	49	9	14	116	90-9	8	163	.217	.269	.299	51	-94	4-8	.981	-53	89	99	2b197,S163,3b56		-12.9

KEARNEY, BOB   Robert Henry   B10.3.1956 San Antonio TX   BR/TR/6-0/190*   [SFN77 14/348]   d9.25   Col Texas

1979	SF N	2	0	0	0	0	0	0	0	1-0	0	0	—	1.000	—	212	0	0-0	—	-0	0	0	/C		0.0
1981	Oak A	1	0	0	0	0	0	0	0	0-0	0	0	—	—	—	—	0	0-0	—	-0	0	0	/C		0.0
1982	Oak A	22	71	7	12	3	0	0	5	3-0	2	10	.169	.218	.211	21	-8	0-0	.970	4	102	132	C22		-0.3
1983	Oak A	108	298	33	76	11	0	8	32	21-1	4	50	.255	.312	.372	93	-3	1-4	.982	2	116	105	C101,D3		0.1
1984	Sea A	133	431	39	97	24	1	7	43	18-0	2	72	.225	.257	.334	63	-22	7-5	.988	7	106	118	C133		-1.0
1985	Sea A	108	305	24	74	14	1	6	27	11-1	4	59	.243	.277	.354	71	-13	1-1	.995	5	114	119	C108		0.8
1986	Sea A	81	204	23	49	10	0	6	25	12-1	0	35	.240	.281	.377	77	-7	0-2	.989	13	89	175	C79		0.8
1987	Sea A	24	47	5	8	4	1	0	1	1-0	0	9	.170	.188	.298	25	-5	0-0	.981	4	270	103	C24		0.8
Total	8	479	1356	131	316	66	3	27	133	67-3	12	235	.233	.274	.346	70	-58	9-12	.987	34	113	124	C469,D3		1.8

KEARNS, AUSTIN   Austin Ryan   B5.20.1980 Lexington KY   BR/TR/6-3/220(220-245)   [CinN98 1/7]   d4.17

2002	Cin N	107	372	66	117	24	3	13	56	54-3	6	81	.315	.407	.500	137	20	6-3	.983	5	111	117	O103(13/6/95)	34	2.7
2003	Cin N	82	292	39	77	11	0	15	58	41-1	5	68	.264	.364	.455	118	8	5-2	.990	4	113	100	O80(0/40/51)	82	1.7
2004	Cin N	64	217	28	50	10	2	9	32	28-0	1	71	.230	.321	.419	91	-3	2-1	.975	-2	103	27	O60(0/1/60)	105	0.5
2005	Cin N	112	387	62	93	26	1	18	67	48-2	8	107	.240	.333	.452	108	5	0-0	.988	9	117	135	O107(0/2/107)	221	0.9
Total	4	365	1268	195	337	71	6	55	213	171-6	20	327	.266	.360	.461	116	30	13-6	.985	17	112	103	O350(13/49/313)	221	3.8

KEARNS, TEDDY   Edward Joseph   B1.1.1900 Trenton NJ   D12.21.1949 Trenton NJ   BR/TR/5-11/180   d10.1

1920	Phi A	1	1	0	0	0	0	0	0	0	0	0	.000	.000	.000	-99	-1	0-0	—	0			/H		0.0
1924	Chi N	4	16	0	4	0	1	0	1	1	0	1	.250	.294	.375	77	-1	0-0	1.000	0	96	98	1b4		-0.1
1925	Chi N	3	2	0	1	0	0	0	0	0	0	0	.500	.500	.500	154	0	0-0	1.000	-0	0	265	1b3		-0.1
Total	3	8	19	0	5	0	1	0	2	1	0	1	.263	.300	.368	76	-1	0-0	1.000	0	86	116	1b7		-0.2

KEARNS, TOM   Thomas J. "Dasher"   B11.9.1859 Rochester NY   D12.7.1938 Buffalo NY   BR/TR/5-7/160   d8.26

1880	Buf N	2	7	0	0	0	0	0	0	0	0		.000	.000	.000	-98	-1		.667	-2			C2		-0.1
1882	Det N	4	13	2	4	2	0	0	1	0			.308	.308	.462	143	1		.733	-2	86	0	2b4		-0.1
1884	Det N	21	79	9	16	0	1	0	7	2		10	.203	.222	.228	45	-5		.810	-8	80	58	2b21		-1.1
Total	3	27	99	11	20	2	1	0	8	2		14	.202	.218	.242	48	-5		.801	-12			2b25,C2		-1.4

KEARSE, EDDIE   Edward Paul "Truck"   B2.23.1916 San Francisco CA   D7.15.1968 Eureka CA   BR/TR/6-1/195   d6.13

| 1942 | NY A | 11 | 26 | 2 | 5 | 0 | 0 | 0 | 2 | 3 | 0 | 2 | .192 | .276 | .192 | 34 | -2 | 1-0 | 1.000 | 2 | 184 | 143 | C11 | | 0.1 |

KEATING, CHICK   Walter Francis   B8.8.1891 Philadelphia PA   D7.13.1959 Philadelphia PA   BR/TR/5-9.5/155   d9.26

1913	Chi N	2	5	1	1	0	0	0	0	1	0		.200	.200	.400	69	0	0	1.000	-1	26	0	S2		-0.1
1914	Chi N	20	30	3	3	0	1	0	0	6	0	9	.100	.250	.167	25	-3	0	.951	-0	97	72	S14		-0.2
1915	Chi N	4	8	1	0	0	0	0	0	0	0	3	.000	.000	.000	-99	-2	1	.750	-1	82	0	S2		-0.2
1926	Phi N	4	2	0	0	0	0	0	0	0	0	1	.000	.000	.000	-95	-1	0	1.000	-1	86	0	2b2,S2/3		-0.1
Total	4	30	45	5	4	1	1	0	0	6	0	13	.089	.196	.156	4	-6	1	.903	-3	86	50	S20,2b2/3		-0.6

KEATLEY, GREG   Gregory Steven   B9.12.1953 Princeton WV   BR/TR/6-2/200   [ChiN76 5/103]   d9.27   Col South Carolina-Aiken

| 1981 | KC A | 2 | 0 | 0 | 0 | 0 | 0 | 0 | 0 | 0 | 0 | 0 | — | — | — | — | 0 | 0-0 | 1.000 | 0 | 0 | 0 | C2 | | 0.0 |

YEAR	TM LG	G	AB	R	H	2B	3B	HR	RBI	BB-IB	HP	SO	AVG	OBP	SLG	AOPS	ABR	SB-CS	FA	FR	RNG	THR	GAMES AT POSITION	DL	BFW

KEEDY, PAT Charles Patrick B1.10.1958 Birmingham AL BR/TR/6-4/205(204-223) [CalA79 5/119] d9.10 Col Auburn-Montgomery

1985	Cal A	3	4	1	2	0	1	1	1	0-0	0		.500 .500 1.500	527	2	0-1	—	-1	0	0	3b2/OL		0.1
1987	Chi A	17	41	6	7	1	0	2	2	2-0	0	14	.171 .209 .341	41	-4	1-0	.943	4	131	113	3b11,1b2/2SOLD		0.0
1989	Cle A	9	14	3	3	2	0	0	1	2-0	0	5	.214 .313 .357	87	0	0-0	1.000	1	85	0	O3L,3b2/1SD		0.1
Total	3	29	59	10	12	4	0	3	4	4-0	0	19	.203 .254 .424	77	-2	1-1	.929	5	140	154	3b15,O5L,1b3,D2,S2/2		0.2

KEELER, WILLIE William Henry "Wee Willie","Hit 'Em Where They Ain't" (b O'Kelleher) B3.3.1872 Brooklyn NY D1.1.1923 Brooklyn NY BL/TL/5-4.5/140 d9.30 HF1939

1892	NY N	14	53	7	17	3	0	0	6	3	1	3	.321 .368 .377	128	3	2	.878	-2	77	52	3b14		0.0
1893	NY N	7	24	5	8	2	1	1	7	5	0	1	.333 .448 .625	183	3	3	.667	-3	0	0	O3C,2b2,S2		0.0
	Bro N	20	80	14	25	1	1	1	9	4	1	4	.313 .353 .387	101	0	2	.833	-2	96	83	3b12,O8L		-0.2
	Year	27	104	19	33	3	2	2	16	9	1	5	.317 .377 .442	121	3	5	.833	-5	96	83			-0.2
1894	†Bal N	**129**	590	165	219	27	22	5	94	40	18	6	.371 .427 .517	121	19	32	.938	2	116	81	O128R/2		1.1
1895	†Bal N	**131**	565	162	213	24	15	4	78	37	14	12	.377 .429 .494	134	28	47	.964	10	107	126	O131R/2		2.5
1896	†Bal N	126	544	153	210	22	13	4	82	37	7	9	.386 .432 .496	142	33	67	.969	3	110	144	O126(2/0/124)		2.5
1897	†Bal N	129	564	145	**239**	27	19	0	74	35	7		**.424** .464 .539	164	52	64	.970	-2	65	61	O129R		3.7
1898	Bal N	129	561	126	**216**	7	2	1	44	31	3		**.385** .420 .410	136	26	28	.961	-1	78	53	O128R/3		1.7
1899	Bro N	141	570	**140**	216	12	13	1	61	37	9		.379 .425 .410	137	29	45	.979	-0	102	74	O141R		2.0
1900	†Bro N	136	563	106	**204**	13	12	4	68	30	7		.362 .402 .449	127	19	41	.940	6	121	82	O136R/2		1.6
1901	Bro N	136	595	123	202	18	12	2	43	21	7		.339 .369 .420	125	17	23	**.985**	-2	111	99	O125R,3b10,2b3		0.9
1902	Bro N	133	559	86	186	20	5	0	38	21	7		.333 .363 .386	131	19	19	**.978**	0	78	119	O133R		1.4
1903	NY A	132	512	95	160	14	7	0	32	32	13		.313 .368 .367	114	10	24	.935	-8	74	120	O128(0/5/123),3b4		-0.4
1904	NY A	143	543	78	186	14	8	2	40	35	7		.343 .390 .409	146	28	21	.935	-3	103	**188**	O142R		2.1
1905	NY A	149	560	81	169	14	4	4	38	43	5		.302 .357 .363	115	10	19	.968	1	116	29	O137(3/0/134),2b12,3b3		0.6
1906	NY A	152	592	96	180	8	3	2	33	40	5		.304 .353 .338	106	4	23	.987	-2	83	75	O152(1/0/151)		-0.5
1907	NY A	107	423	50	99	2	0	2	17	15	3		.234 .265 .255	61	-19	7	.969	-2	96	145	O107R		-2.9
1908	NY A	91	323	38	85	3	1	1	14	31	5		.263 .337 .288	102	2	14	.936	-1	90	65	O88(2/0/86)		-0.3
1909	NY A	99	360	44	95	7	5	1	32	24	10		.264 .327 .319	104	2	10	.968	-6	74	69	O95R		-0.9
1910	NY N	19	10	5	3	0	0	0	3	0		1	.300 .462 .300	123	1	1	1.000	-0	84	0	O2(1/1/0)		0.1
Total	19	2123	8591	1719	2932	241	145	33	810	524	129	36	.341 .388 .415	125	285	495	.960	-12	96	96	O2039(17/9/2013),3b44,2b19,S2		15.0

KEELY, BOB Robert William B8.22.1909 St.Louis MO D5.20.2001 Sarasota FL BR/TR/6-0/175 d7.25 C12

1944	StL N	1	0	0	0	0	0	0	0	0	0	0	—	—	—	—	0	0	1.000	0	0	0	/C		0.0
1945	StL N	1	1	0	0	0	0	0	0	0	0	0	.000 .000 .000	-98	0	0	1.000	-0	0	0	/C		0.0
Total	2	2	1	0	0	0	0	0	0	0	0	0	.000 .000 .000	-98	0	0	1.000	0	0	0	C2		0.0

KEEN, BILL William Brown "Buster" B8.16.1892 Oglethorpe GA D7.16.1947 South Point OH BR/TR/6-0/181 d8.8

| 1911 | Pit N | 6 | 7 | 0 | 0 | 0 | 0 | 0 | 0 | 1 | 0 | 4 | .000 .125 .000 | -61 | -2 | 0 | 1.000 | -0 | 0 | 0 | /1 | | -0.2 |

KEENAN, JIM James William B2.10.1858 New Haven CT D9.21.1926 Cincinnati OH BR/TR/5-10/186 d5.17 OF(0/1/12) ▲

1875	NH NA	5	13	1	1	0	0	0		1			.077 .077 .077	-53	-2	0-0	.800	-4			C3,3b2/OL		-0.5
1880	Buf N	2	7	1	1	0	0	0	0	1		1	.143 .250 .143	36	0		.947	2			C2		0.1
1882	Pit AA	25	96	10	21	7	0	1		1			.219 .227 .323	87	-1		.906	-0			C22,O3(0/1/2)/S		0.1
1884	Ind AA	68	249	36	73	14	4	3	16		3		.293 .343 .418	151	15		.923	-2			C59,1b6,O2R/SP		1.6
1885	Cin AA	36	132	16	35	2	2	1	15	8	0		.265 .307 .333	100	0		.926	0			C33,1b4/P		0.2
1886	Cin AA	44	148	31	40	4	3	3	24	18	2		.270 .357 .399	132	6	0	.915	0			C30,O7R,3b5,1b4,P2		0.7
1887	Cin AA	47	174	19	44	4	1	0	17	11	1		.253 .301 .287	63	-9	7	.934	8			C38,1b11		0.1
1888	Cin AA	85	313	38	73	9	4	1	40	22	5		.233 .284 .323	93	-4	9	.946	3			C69,1b16		0.3
1889	Cin AA	87	300	52	86	10	11	6	60	48	6	35	.287 .395 .453	137	15	18	.962	4			C66,1b21/3		1.9
1890	Cin N	54	202	21	28	4	2	3	19	19	1	36	.139 .216 .223	28	-19	5	.950	9	124	105	C50,1b2/OR3		-0.5
1891	Cin N	75	252	30	51	7	5	4	33	33	3	39	.202 .302 .317	80	-7	2	.974	-4	133	89	1b41,C34/3		-1.1
Total	10	523	1873	254	452	61	36	22	208	177	21	111	.241 .314 .348	99	-4	41	.935	18	_111_	_93_	C403,1b105,O13R,3b8,P4,S2		3.4

KEERL, GEORGE George Henry B4.10.1847 Baltimore MD D9.9.1923 Menominee MI BR/TR/5-7/145 d5.4

| 1875 | Chi NA | 6 | 23 | 2 | 3 | 0 | 0 | 0 | 3 | 0 | | 2 | .130 .130 .130 | -9 | -2 | 0-0 | .815 | -2 | 98 | 0 | 2b6 | | -0.4 |

KEESEY, JIM James Ward B10.27.1902 Perryville MD D9.5.1951 Boise ID BR/TR/6-0.5/170 d9.6

1925	Phi A	5	5	1	2	0	0	1	0	2	0	2	.400 .400 .400	97	0	0-0	1.000	-0	0	0	1b2		0.0
1930	Phi A	11	12	2	3	1	0	0	2	1	0	2	.250 .308 .333	60	-1	0-0	.909	-0	0	233	1b3		-0.1
Total	2	16	17	3	5	1	0	1	2	3	0	4	.294 .333 .353	71	-1	0-0	.923	-1	0	179	1b5		-0.1

KEISTER, BILL William Hoffman "Wagon Tongue" B8.17.1874 Baltimore MD D8.19.1924 Baltimore MD BL/TR/5-5.5/168 d5.20

1896	Bal N	15	58	8	14	3	0	0	5	3	2	5	.241 .302 .293	56	-4	4	.923	-4	80	47	2b8,3b6		-0.6
1898	Bos N	10	30	5	5	2	0	0	4	0	0		.167 .167 .233	14	-3	0	1.000	2	111	170	S4,2b4/OR		-0.2
1899	Bal N	136	523	96	172	22	16	3	73	16	16		.329 .368 .449	117	10	33	.895	-21	95	79	S90,2b46/OL		-0.4
1900	StL N	126	497	78	149	26	10	1	72	25	11		.300 .347 .398	106	4	32	.927	-2	116	59	2b116,S7,3b3		-1.2
1901	Bal A	115	442	78	145	20	**21**	2	93	18	8		.328 .365 .482	128	14	24	.851	-21	93	71	S112		-0.3
1902	Was A	119	483	82	145	33	9	9	90	14	7		.300 .329 .462	117	9	27	.912	-3	108	172	O65(0/12/53),2b40,3b14,S2		0.4
1903	Phi N	100	400	53	128	27	7	3	63	14	6		.320 .352 .445	131	14	11	.940	5	167	30	O100R		1.4
Total	7	621	2433	400	758	133	63	18	400	90	50	5	.312 .349 .440	116	44	131	.870	-64	94	74	S215,2b214,O167(1/12/154),3b23		-0.9

KELIHER, MICKEY Maurice Michael B1.11.1890 Washington DC D9.7.1930 Washington DC BL/TL/6-0/175 d9.10

1911	Pit N	3	7	0	0	0	0	0	0	0		5	.000 .000 .000	-96	-2	0	.875	0	142	164	1b3		-0.2
1912	Pit N	2	0	1	0	0	0	0	0	0			—	—	—	—	0	0			/R		0.0
Total	2	5	7	1	0	0	0	0	0	0		5	.000 .000 .000	-96	-2	0	.875	0	142	164	1b3		-0.2

KELL, SKEETER Everett Lee B10.11.1929 Swifton AR BR/TR/5-9/160 d4.19 b-George Col Arkansas-Monticello

| 1952 | Phi A | 75 | 213 | 24 | 47 | 8 | 3 | 0 | 17 | 14 | 2 | 25 | .221 .275 .286 | 53 | -14 | 5-1 | .963 | -6 | 101 | 79 | 2b68 | | -1.6 |

KELL, GEORGE George Clyde B8.23.1922 Swifton AR BR/TR/5-9/175* d9.28 HF1983 b-Skeeter Col Arkansas St.

1943	Phi A	1	5	1	1	0	1	0	1	0		0-0	.200 .200 .600	131	0	0-0	1.000	0	116	0	/3		0.0
1944	Phi A	139	514	51	138	15	3	0	44	22	1	23	.268 .300 .309	75	-18	5-2	.958	-2	95	103	3b139		-1.9
1945	Phi A	147	567	50	154	30	3	4	56	27	1	15	.272 .306 .356	92	-8	2-0	**.964**	22	**114**	106	3b147		1.7
1946	Phi A	26	87	3	26	6	1	0	11	10		6	.299 .378 .391	116	2	0-0	.979	4	107	80	3b26		0.6
	Det A	105	434	67	142	19	9	4	41	30		14	.327 .371 .440	119	10	3-2	.984	1	93	102	3b105/1		1.1
	Year	131	521	70	168	25	10	4	52	40		20	.322 .372 .432	118	12	3-2	**.983**	5	**96**	**98**	3b131/1		1.7
1947	Det A★	152	588	75	188	29	5	5	93	61		16	.320 .387 .412	118	16	9-11	.962	16	**110**	93	3b152		3.1
1948	Det A☆	92	368	47	112	24	3	2	44	33		15	.304 .364 .402	102	2	2-2	.969	-7	82	92	3b92		-0.6
1949	Det A★	134	522	97	179	38	9	3	59	71	3	13	**.343** .424 .467	136	29	7-5	.975	-3	97	76	3b134		2.5
1950	Det A★	157	641	114	**218**	**56**	6	8	101	66		18	.340 .403 .484	122	23	3-3	**.982**	-2	99	96	3b157		1.9
1951	Det A★	147	598	92	**191**	**36**	3	2	59	61	4	18	.319 .386 .400	112	12	10-3	**.960**	7	**103**	109	3b147		2.0
1952	Det A	39	152	11	45	8	0	2	17	15		13	.296 .359 .368	102	1	0-1	.959	-1	96	79	3b39		0.0
	Bos A★	75	276	41	88	15	2	6	40	31	1	10	.319 .390 .453	124	10	0-1	.959	-5	93	83	3b73		0.5
	Year	114	428	52	133	23	2	7	57	46	1	23	.311 .379 .423	117	11	0-2	.959	-5	94	82	3b112		0.5
1953	Bos A★	134	460	68	141	41	2	12	73	52	5	22	.307 .383 .483	126	18	5-2	.972	-12	90	83	3b124,O7L		0.6
1954	Bos A	26	93	15	24	3	0	0	15	10		3	.258 .361 .290	72	-3	0-0	.920	-3	89	96	3b25		-0.6
	Chi A★	71	233	25	66	10	0	5	48	18		12	.283 .323 .391	95	-2	1-1	.996	-7	41	111	1b32,3b31,O2(2/0/1)		-1.1
	Year	97	326	40	90	13	0	5	58	33		15	.276 .334 .362	88	-5	1-1	.936	-10	90	96	3b56,1b32,O2(2/0/1)		-1.7
1955	Chi A	128	429	44	134	24	1	8	81	51-2		36	.312 .389 .429	118	13	2-2	**.976**	-15	85	46	3b105,1b24/OL		-0.3
1956	Chi A	21	80	7	25	6	0	1	11	8-0		6	.313 .371 .412	106	1	0-0	1.000	-2	81	0	3b18,1b4		0.0
	Bal A★	102	345	45	90	17	6	8	37	25-3		31	.261 .313 .391	93	-5	0-1	.974	-3	91	105	3b97,1b2/2		-0.9
	Year	123	425	52	115	23	6	9	48	33-3		37	.271 .324 .395	96	-4	0-1	**.978**	-5	89	89	3b115,1b6/2		-1.1
1957	Bal A★	99	310	28	92	19	0	9	44	25-2	2	16	.297 .352 .413	116	6	2-0	.979	-4	92	134	3b80,1b22		0.1
Total	15	1795	6702	881	2054	385	50	78	870	621-7	36	287	.306 .367 .414	111	107	51-36	.969	-16	97	93	3b1692,1b85,O10(10/0/1)/2		8.5

KELLEHER, DUKE Albert Aloysius B9.30.1893 New York NY D9.28.1947 Staten Island NY TR/5-7/180 d8.18 Col Princeton

| 1916 | NY N | 1 | 0 | 0 | 0 | 0 | 0 | 0 | 0 | 0 | 0 | 0 | — | — | — | — | 0 | 0 | — | -0 | 0 | 0 | /C | | 0.0 |

YEAR	TM LG	G	AB	R	H	2B	3B	HR	RBI	BB-IB	HP	SO	AVG	OBP	SLG	AOPS	ABR	SB-CS	FA	FR	RNG	THR	GAMES AT POSITION	DL	BFW

KELLEHER, FRANKIE Francis Eugene B8.22.1916 San Francisco CA D4.13.1979 Stockton CA BR/TR/6-1/195 d7.18 Mil 1944-45 Col St.Marys (CA)

																								-0.6
1942	Cin N	38	110	13	20	3	1	3	12	16	0	20	.182	.286	.309	74	-4	0	.986	-1	100	47	O30L		-0.2
1943	Cin N	9	10	1	0	0	0	0	0	2	0	0	.000	.167	.000	-51	-2	0	1.000	-0	94	0	/OR		-0.2
Total	2	47	120	14	20	3	1	3	12	18	0	20	.167	.275	.283	64	-6	0	.986	-1	100	45	O31(30/0/1)		-0.8

KELLEHER, JOHN John Patrick B9.13.1893 Brookline MA D8.21.1960 Brighton MA BR/TR/5-11/150 d7.31

																								0.1
1912	StL N	8	12	0	4	1	0	0	0	0	0	2	.333	.333	.417	107	0	0	1.000	0	109	360	3b3		-0.2
1916	Bro N	2	3	0	0	0	0	0	0	0	0	0	.000	.000	.000	-97	-1	0	1.000	-1	54	0	/S3		0.6
1921	Chi N	95	301	31	93	11	7	4	47	16	1	16	.309	.346	.432	104	1	2-5	.947	3	108	103	3b37,2b27,1b11,S11/OL		-0.7
1922	Chi N	63	193	23	50	7	1	0	20	15	1	14	.259	.316	.306	60	-1	5-7	.932	2	110	123	3b46,S7,1b4		-0.4
1923	Chi N	66	193	27	59	10	0	6	21	14	0	9	.306	.353	.451	110	3	2-4	.975	-7	86	74	1b22,S14,3b11,2b6		0.0
1924	Bos N	1	1	0	0	0	0	0	0	0	0	1	.000	.000	.000	-99	0	0-0	—	0			/H		-0.6
Total	6	235	703	81	206	29	8	10	89	45	2	42	.293	.337	.400	92	-8	9-16	.954	-2	106	117	3b98,1b37,2b33,S33/OL	

KELLEHER, MICK Michael Dennis B7.25.1947 Seattle WA BR/TR/5-9/176(165-176) [StLN69 3/68] d9.1 C4 Col Puget Sound

																								0.0
1972	StL N	23	63	5	10	2	1	0	1	6-0	0	15	.159	.232	.222	30	-6	0-0	.984	3	92	107	S23		-0.2
1973	StL N	43	38	4	7	2	0	0	2	4-1	1	11	.184	.279	.237	44	-3	0-0	.955	-1	97	91	S42		-0.2
1974	Hou N	19	57	4	9	0	0	0	2	5-0	0	10	.158	.226	.158	9	-7	1-1	.944	3	122	105	S18		0.0
1975	StL N	7	4	0	0	0	0	0	0	0-0	0	1	.000	.000	.000	-96	-1	0-0	.909	1	129	94	S7		-0.9
1976	Chi N	124	337	28	77	12	1	0	22	15-3	2	32	.228	.264	.270	48	-23	0-4	.980	5	106	97	S101,3b22,2b5		0.4
1977	Chi N	63	122	14	28	5	2	0	11	9-2	1	12	.230	.288	.303	53	-8	0-0	.976	6	116	94	2b40,S14/3	16	0.7
1978	Chi N	68	95	8	24	1	0	0	6	7-0	0	11	.253	.304	.263	53	-6	4-1	1.000	8	129	110	3b37,2b17,S10		-0.6
1979	Chi N	73	142	14	36	4	1	0	10	7-0	2	9	.254	.296	.296	57	-8	2-0	.966	13	106	108	3b32,2b29,S14		-0.5
1980	Chi N	105	96	12	14	1	1	0	4	9-1	0	17	.146	.217	.177	11	-12	1-3	.974	5	109	98	3b39,2b11,S9		0.0
1981	Det A	61	77	10	17	4	0	0	6	7-0	0	10	.221	.282	.273	59	-4	0-0	.930	-1	82	68	3b39,2b11,S9		-0.2
1982	Det A	2	1	0	0	0	0	0	0	0-0	0	0	.000	.000	.000	-99	0	0-0	1.000	0	285	0	/23		0.0
	Cal A	34	49	9	8	1	0	1	5	5-0	1	5	.163	.255	.184	22	-5	1-1	.965	1	100	81	S28,3b6		-0.2
	Year	36	50	9	8	1	0	1	5	5-0	1	5	.160	.250	.180	20	-5	1-1	.965	1	100	81	S28,3b7/2		
Total	11	622	1081	108	230	32	6	2	65	74-7	7	133	.213	.266	.253	43	-83	9-10	.976	43	105	95	S283,3b169,2b160	16	-1.5

KELLER, CHARLIE Charles Ernest "King Kong" B9.12.1916 Middletown MD D5.23.1990 Frederick MD BL/TR/5-10/190* d4.22 Mer 1944-45 C2 b-Hal Col Maryland-Baltimore Co.

																								1.9
1939	†NY A	111	398	87	133	21	6	11	83	81	0	49	.334	.447	.500	144	31	6-3	.969	-4	96	64	O105(47/0/58)		2.3
1940	NY A★	138	500	102	143	18	15	21	93	106	0	65	.286	.411	.508	142	34	8-2	.967	-3	104	44	O136(65/0/71)		4.0
1941	†NY A★	140	507	102	151	24	10	33	122	102	1	65	.298	.416	.580	163	48	6-4	.980	2	108	59	O137L		4.2
1942	†NY A	152	544	106	159	24	9	26	108	114	2	61	.292	.417	.513	164	50	14-2	.985	-2	98	83	O141L		4.0
1943	†NY A*	141	512	97	139	15	11	31	86	106	0	60	.271	.396	.525	167	45	7-5	.994	2	105	70	O141L		1.6
1945	NY A	44	163	26	49	7	4	10	34	31	0	21	.301	.412	.577	178	16	0-2	1.000	3	112	97	O44L		3.1
1946	NY A★	150	538	98	148	29	10	30	101	113	4	101	.275	.405	.533	158	46	1-4	.979	-3	101	40	O149(146/0/3)		1.1
1947	NY A*	45	151	36	36	6	1	13	36	41	1	18	.238	.404	.550	165	15	0-0	.967	-1	97	75	O43L		-0.4
1948	NY A	83	247	41	66	15	2	6	44	41	0	25	.267	.372	.417	111	5	1-1	.977	-4	97	23	O66L		-0.2
1949	NY A	60	116	17	29	4	1	3	16	25	2	15	.250	.392	.379	104	2	2-0	.976	-3	83	0	O31(29/0/2)		0.4
1950	Det A	50	51	7	16	1	3	2	16	13	0	6	.314	.453	.569	155	5	0-0	1.000	-0	101	0	O6(1/0/5)		0.2
1951	Det A	54	62	6	16	2	0	3	21	11	0	12	.258	.370	.435	117	2	0-0	1.000	1	127	-	O8(4/0/4)		0.0
1952	NY A	2	1	0	0	0	0	0	0	1	0	0	.000	.000	.000	-99	-0	0-0	—	0			/OL		0.0
Total	13	1170	3790	725	1085	166	72	189	760	784	10	499	.286	.410	.518	152	299	45-23	.980	-12	102	58	O1019(876/0/143)		22.2

KELLER, HAL Harold Kefauver B7.7.1927 Middletown MD BL/TR/6-1/200* d9.13 b-Charlie Col Maryland-Baltimore Co.

																								0.0
1949	Was A	3	3	1	1	0	0	0	0	0	0	0	.333	.333	.333	78	-1	0-0	—	0			/H		-0.2
1950	Was A	11	28	1	6	3	0	1	5	2	0	2	.214	.267	.429	79	-1	0-0	1.000	-1	71	0	C8		-0.2
1952	Was A	11	23	2	4	2	0	0	0	1	0	1	.174	.208	.261	31	-2	0-0	.967	-1	93	62	C11		-0.4
Total	3	25	54	4	11	5	0	1	5	3	0	3	.204	.246	.352	60	-3	0-0	.982	-1	82	30	C19	

KELLERT, FRANK Frank William B7.6.1924 Oklahoma City OK D11.19.1976 Oklahoma City OK BR/TR/6-2.5/185* d4.18 Col Oklahoma St.

																								-0.1
1953	StL A	2	4	0	0	0	0	0	0	0	0	0	.000	.000	.000	-98	-1	0-0	1.000	-0	0	0	/1		-0.4
1954	Bal A	10	34	3	7	2	0	0	1	5	0	4	.206	.308	.265	62	-2	0-0	1.000	-1	33	75	1b9		0.4
1955	†Bro N	39	80	12	26	4	2	4	19	9-0	0	10	.325	.385	.575	149	6	0-1	.983	-0	97	64	1b22		-0.9
1956	Chi N	71	129	10	24	3	1	4	17	12-1	0	22	.186	.254	.318	54	-9	0-0	.991	2	122	100	1b27		-1.0
Total	4	122	247	25	57	9	3	8	37	26-1	0	36	.231	.301	.389	85	-6	0-1	.990	-0	97	82	1b59	

KELLETT, RED Donald Stafford B7.15.1909 Brooklyn NY D11.3.1970 Ft.Lauderdale FL BR/TR/6-0/185 d7.2 Col Penn

| | | | | | | | | | | | | | | | | | | | | | | | | -0.2 |
| 1934 | Bos A | 9 | 9 | 0 | 0 | 0 | 0 | 0 | 0 | 0 | 0 | 5 | .000 | .100 | .000 | 5 | 0 | 0-0 | .778 | -0 | 103 | 0 | S4,2b2/3 | |

KELLEY, JOE Joseph James B12.9.1871 Cambridge MA D8.14.1943 Baltimore MD BR/TR/5-11/190 d7.27 M5/C1 HF1971. OF(1131/328/8)

																								-0.3
1891	Bos N	12	45	7	11	1	0	3	2	0	0	7	.244	.277	.311	63	-2	0	.852	-0	104	0	O12(12/1/0)		-0.4
1892	Pit N	56	205	26	49	7	7	0	28	17	0	21	.239	.297	.341	93	-3	8	.919	2	151	215	O56C		-0.3
	Bal N	10	33	3	7	0	0	0	4	4	1	7	.212	.316	.212	59	-1	2	.824	-2	0	0	O10C		-0.7
	Year	66	238	29	56	7	7	0	32	21	1	28	.235	.300	.324	88	-4	10	.908	-0	132	188	O66C		1.6
1893	Bal N	125	502	120	153	27	16	9	76	77	4	44	.305	.401	.476	131	22	33	.940	6	104	85	O125(18/107/1)		3.4
1894	†Bal N	129	507	165	199	48	20	6	111	107	5	36	.393	.502	.602	158	55	46	.951	2	74	60	O129L		2.6
1895	†Bal N	131	518	148	189	26	19	10	134	77	10	29	.365	.456	.546	154	44	54	.946	1	101	125	O131(130/1/0)		3.8
1896	†Bal N	131	519	148	189	31	19	8	100	91	12	19	.364	.460	.543	164	54	87	.958	3	107	70	O131(129/0/2)		2.3
1897	†Bal N	131	505	113	183	31	9	5	118	70	7		.362	.447	.489	147	39	44	.959	-0	84	93	O130L,S3,3b2		1.5
1898	Bal N	124	464	71	149	18	15	2	110	56	3		.321	.398	.438	137	23	24	.969	2	111	118	O122(39/83/0),3b2		2.1
1899	Bro N	143	538	108	175	21	14	6	93	70	7		.325	.410	.450	133	26	31	.977	10	120	124	O143L		1.4
1900	†Bro N	121	454	90	145	23	17	6	91	53	6		.319	.398	.485	135	21	26	.959	1	115	71	O77L,1b32,3b13		1.9
1901	Bro N	120	492	77	151	22	12	4	65	40	3		.307	.363	.425	124	15	18	.975	7	126	107	O116L,3b8,1b5		0.9
1902	Bal A	60	222	50	69	17	7	1	34	34	1		.311	.405	.464	134	12	12	.973	0	119	146	O48(1/47/0),3b8,1b5		1.1
	Cin N	40	156	24	50	9	2	1	12	15	0		.321	.380	.423	135	7	3	.971	4	183	178	O20(18/2/0),2b10,3b9,S2,M		0.5
1903	Cin N	105	383	85	121	22	4	3	45	51	6		.316	.402	.418	120	12	18	.947	-4	90	0	O67(61/6/0),S12,2b11,3b8,1b6,M		1.0
1904	Cin N	123	449	75	126	21	13	0	63	49	6		.281	.359	.385	119	11	15	.988	0	99	105	1b117,O6(0/3/3)/2M		-0.9
1905	Cin N	90	321	43	89	7	6	1	37	27	7		.277	.346	.374	96	1	8	.974	-2	99	0	O85(84/0/1),1b2,M		-1.9
1906	Cin N	129	465	43	106	19	11	1	53	44	6		.228	.300	.323	90	-6	9	.966	-4	87	136	O122L,1b3/S3		0.3
1908	Bos N	73	228	25	59	8	2	2	17	27	2		.259	.342	.338	119	6	5	.938	-0	93	75	O51(38/12/1),1b11,M		
Total	17	1853	7006	1421	2220	358	194	65	1194	911	82	163	.317	.402	.451	132	334	443	.955	24	102	93	O1465L,1b291,3b48,2b22,S18		20.6

KELLEY, MIKE Michael Joseph B12.2.1875 Templeton MA D6.6.1955 Minneapolis MN BR/TR/6-0/210 d7.15

| | | | | | | | | | | | | | | | | | | | | | | | | -1.0 |
| 1899 | Lou N | 76 | 282 | 48 | 68 | 11 | 2 | 3 | 33 | 21 | 6 | | .241 | .307 | .326 | 74 | -10 | 10 | .974 | -0 | 104 | 88 | 1b76 | |

KELLIHER, FRANK Francis Mortimer "Yucka" B5.23.1899 Somerville MA D3.4.1956 Somerville MA BL/TL/5-9.5/175 d9.19

| | | | | | | | | | | | | | | | | | | | | | | | | 0.0 |
| 1919 | Was A | 1 | 1 | 0 | 0 | 0 | 0 | 0 | 0 | 0 | 0 | 0 | .000 | .000 | .000 | -99 | 0 | 0 | — | 0 | | | /H | |

KELLOGG, NATE Nathaniel Monroe B9.28.1858 Rochester IA D7.19.1923 Brooklyn NY 5-9/175 d8.27

| | | | | | | | | | | | | | | | | | | | | | | | | -0.3 |
| 1885 | Det N | 5 | 17 | 4 | 2 | 1 | 0 | 0 | 0 | 1 | | | 5 | .118 | .167 | .176 | 11 | -2 | | .783 | -2 | 75 | 65 | S5 | |

KELLOGG, BILL William Dearstyne B5.25.1884 Albany NY D12.12.1971 Baltimore MD BR/TR/5-10/153 d4.14

| | | | | | | | | | | | | | | | | | | | | | | | | -1.3 |
| 1914 | Cin N | 71 | 126 | 14 | 22 | 0 | 1 | 0 | 7 | 14 | | | 28 | .175 | .262 | .190 | 34 | -10 | 7 | .988 | -1 | 87 | 104 | 1b38,2b11,O2C/3 | |

KELLY, RED Albert Michael B11.15.1884 Union IL D2.4.1961 Zephyrhills FL BR/TR/5-11.5/165 d6.18 Col Notre Dame

| | | | | | | | | | | | | | | | | | | | | | | | | -0.3 |
| 1910 | Chi A | 14 | 45 | 6 | 7 | 0 | 1 | 0 | 1 | 7 | | | 2 | .156 | .296 | .200 | 58 | -2 | 0 | 1.000 | -0 | 103 | 58 | O14R | |

KELLY, CHARLIE Charles H. d6.14

																								-0.1
1883	Phi N	2	7	1	1	0	0	0	0	0			3	.143	.143	.429	71	0		.700	-0	93	270	3b2		-0.2
1886	Phi AA	1	3	0	0	0	0	0	0	0			0	.000	.000	.000	-99	-1	0	.333	-1	68	0	/S		-0.3
Total	2	3	10	1	1	0	0	0	0	0			3	.100	.100	.300	19	-1	0	.700	-2	93	270	3b2/S	

KELLY, PAT Dale Patrick B8.27.1955 Santa Maria CA BR/TR/6-3/210 [AnaA73 3/55] d5.28

| | | | | | | | | | | | | | | | | | | | | | | | | 0.1 |
| 1980 | Tor A | 3 | 7 | 0 | 2 | 0 | 0 | 0 | 0 | 0-0 | 0 | 4 | .286 | .286 | .286 | 55 | 0 | 0-0 | 1.000 | 1 | 0 | 0 | C3 | |

YEAR	TM LG	G	AB	R	H	2B	3B	HR	RBI	BB-IB	HP	SO	AVG	OBP	SLG	AOPS	ABR	SB-CS	FA	FR	RNG	THR	GAMES AT POSITION	DL	BFW

KELLY, GEORGE George Lange "Highpockets" B9.10.1895 San Francisco CA D10.13.1984 Burlingame CA BR/TR/6-4/190 d8.18 Mil 1918 C11 HF1973 b-Ren OF(27/16/19)

1915	NY N	17	38	2	6	0	0	1	4	1	0	9	.158	.179	.237	27	-4	0-1	.983	0	96	31	1b9,O4C		-0.5
1916	NY N	49	76	4	12	2	1	0	3	6	0	24	.158	.220	.211	34	-6	0-1	.981	-2	38	73	1b13,O7(0/2/5)/3		-0.9
1917	NY N	11	7	0	0	0	0	0	0	0	0	3	.000	.000	.000	-99	-2	0	1.000	1	66	1005	O4(3/0/1)/P12		-0.1
	Pit N	8	23	2	2	0	1	0	0	1	0	9	.087	.125	.174	-9	-3	0	.971	-1	58	73	1b8		-0.5
	Year	19	30	2	2	0	1	0	0	1	0	12	.067	.097	.133	-30	-5	0	.972	-0	56	98	1b9,O4(3/0/1)/P2		-0.6
1919	NY N	32	107	12	31	6	2	1	14	3	1	15	.290	.315	.411	119	2	1	.994	-3	61	108	1b32		-0.1
1920	NY N	155	590	69	157	22	11	11	94	41	6	92	.266	.320	.397	106	3	6-16	.994	4	109	**120**	1b155		-0.1
1921	†NY N	149	587	95	181	42	9	**23**	122	40	3	73	.308	.356	.528	131	24	4-12	.990	12	**138**	**136**	1b149		2.2
1922	†NY N	151	592	96	194	33	8	17	107	30	3	65	.328	.363	.497	119	14	12-3	.993	9	**129**	122	1b151		1.4
1923	†NY N	145	560	82	172	23	5	16	103	47	1	64	.307	.362	.452	115	11	14-7	.993	-6	78	102	1b145		-0.3
1924	†NY N	144	571	91	185	37	9	21	**136**	38	5	52	.324	.371	.531	143	33	7-2	.993	-3	89	108	1b125,O14(5/9/0),2b5/3		2.2
1925	NY N	147	586	87	181	29	3	20	99	35	2	54	.309	.350	.471	112	9	5-2	.981	16	107	113	2b108,1b25,O17(8/0/9)		2.4
1926	NY N	136	499	70	151	24	4	13	80	36	2	52	.303	.352	.445	115	9	4	**.993**	7	118	101	1b114,2b18		0.9
1927	Cin N	61	222	27	60	16	4	5	21	11	1	23	.270	.308	.446	103	0	1	.992	-1	117	138	1b49,2b13,O2L		-0.4
1928	Cin N	116	402	46	119	33	7	3	58	28	2	35	.296	.345	.435	104	2	2	.991	8	141	133	1b99,O13(9/0/4)		0.3
1929	Cin N	147	577	73	169	45	9	5	103	33	1	61	.293	.332	.428	91	-9	7	.993	5	112	111	1b147		-1.3
1930	Cin N	51	188	18	54	10	1	5	35	7	0	20	.287	.313	.431	81	-6	1	.993	3	111	95	1b50		-0.7
	Chi N	39	166	22	55	6	1	3	19	7	1	16	.331	.362	.434	91	-3	0	.998	5	130	79	1b39		-0.2
	Year	90	354	40	109	16	2	8	54	14	1	36	.308	.336	.432	86	-9	1	.995	4	120	89	1b89		-0.9
1932	Bro N	64	202	23	49	9	1	4	22	22	0	27	.243	.317	.356	82	-5	0	.984	-2	95	100	1b62/OC		-1.2
Total	16	1622	5993	819	1778	337	76	148	1020	386	28	694	.297	.342	.452	110	69	65-43	.992	49	111	113	1b1373,2b145,O62L,3b2/P		3.1

KELLY, PAT Harold Patrick B7.30.1944 Philadelphia PA D10.2.2005 Chambersburg PA BL/TL/6-1/185* d9.6 Mil 1967

1967	Min A	8	1	0	0	0	0	0	0	0-0	1	0	.000	.000	.000	-93	0	0-0		0			/H		0.0
1968	Min A	12	35	2	4	2	0	1	2	3-0	1	10	.114	.205	.257	37	-3	0-2	.955	1	114	183	O10(2/5/4)		-0.4
1969	KC A	112	417	61	110	20	4	8	32	49-3	5	70	.264	.348	.388	104	3	40-13	.980	7	110	157	O107(2/44/63)		1.1
1970	KC A	136	452	56	106	16	1	6	38	76-3	2	105	.235	.347	.314	83	-7	34-16	.963	7	118	103	O118(1/3/115)		-0.5
1971	Chi A	67	213	32	62	6	3	3	22	36-4	1	29	.291	.394	.390	120	7	14-9	.991	3	97	198	O61(0/1/61)		0.7
1972	Chi A	119	402	57	105	14	7	5	24	55-1	4	69	.261	.355	.368	113	8	32-9	.968	-3	89	111	O109R		0.4
1973	Chi A★	144	550	77	154	24	5	1	44	65-1	2	91	.280	.355	.347	96	-1	22-15	.978	-2	96	100	O141(0/3/138)/D		-1.1
1974	Chi A	122	424	60	119	16	3	4	21	46-0	2	58	.281	.354	.361	103	3	18-11	.976	-4	83	56	D67,O53(1/0/52)		-0.5
1975	Chi A	133	471	73	129	21	7	9	45	58-2	2	69	.274	.353	.406	113	9	18-10	**.991**	-1	103	45	O115R,D14		0.2
1976	Chi A	107	311	42	79	20	3	5	34	45-1	3	45	.254	.349	.386	116	8	15-7	.950	-2	87	67	D63,O26(14/0/12)		0.5
1977	Bal A	120	360	50	92	13	0	10	49	53-6	4	75	.256	.353	.375	106	5	25-7	.984	-7	95	27	O109(91/1/33)/D		-0.3
1978	Bal A	100	274	38	75	12	1	11	40	34-1	2	58	.274	.357	.445	132	12	10-8	.969	-6	86	64	O80(73/1/7),D2		0.3
1979	†Bal A	68	153	29	44	11	0	9	25	20-1	1	25	.288	.367	.536	147	11	4-5	1.000	-2	90	0	O24(23/0/1),D18		0.6
1980	Bal A	89	200	38	52	10	1	3	26	34-0	0	54	.260	.363	.365	103	2	16-2	1.000	0	88	205	O36(34/2/0),D30		0.4
1981	Cle A	48	75	8	16	4	0	1	16	14-2	1	9	.213	.333	.307	87	-1	2-4	1.000	0	113	0	D18,O8(3/0/5)		-0.2
Total	15	1385	4338	620	1147	189	35	76	418	588-25	29	768	.264	.354	.377	107	56	250-118	.978	-9	96	96	O997(244/60/715),D214		1.2

KELLY, JIM James Robert (Also Played Under Real Name of Robert John Taggert in 1918) B2.1.1884 Bloomfield NJ D4.10.1961 Kingsport TN BL/TR/5-10.5/180 d4.24

1914	Pit N	32	44	4	10	2	1	0	3	4	2	7	.227	.261	.318	75	-2	0	1.000	0	114	105	O7(1/0/6)		-0.2
1915	Pit F	148	524	68	154	12	17	4	50	35	2	46	.294	.340	.405	110	-4	38	.952	13	**117**	138	O148(14/4/133)		0.2
1918	Bos N	35	146	19	48	1	4	0	4	9	0	5	.329	.376	.390	140	6	4	.955	-1	109	49	O35L		0.5
Total	3	215	714	91	212	15	22	4	57	46	4	58	.297	.343	.396	114	0	42	.954	13	115	119	O190(50/4/139)		0.5

KELLY, TOM Jay Thomas B8.15.1950 Graceville MN BL/TL/5-11/188 [MilA68 8/178] d5.11 M16/C4

1975	Min A	49	127	11	23	5	0	1	11	15-0	0	22	.181	.262	.244	45	-9	0-0	.985	1	105	85	1b43,O2(1/0/1)		-1.2

KELLY, JOHN John Benedict B3.13.1879 Clifton Heights PA D3.19.1944 Baltimore MD 5-9/165 d4.11

1907	StL N	53	197	12	37	5	0	0	6	13	2		.188	.245	.213	45	-12	7	.968	-3	92		O52(0/16/36)		-2.0

KELLY, JOHN John Francis "Honest John","Father" B3.3.1859 Paterson NJ D4.13.1908 Paterson NJ BR/TR/6-0/185 d6.7

1879	Cle N	1	4	0	1	0	0	0		0			.250	.250	.250	66	0		.571	-1			/C1		-0.1
1882	Cle N	30	104	6	14	2	0	0	5	1			.135	.143	.154	-5	-12		.800	-13			C30		-2.1
1883	Bal AA	48	202	8	46	18	4	0		3			.228	.239	.292	68	-7		.803	-16			C38,O13(0/1/12)		-1.9
	Phi N	1	3	0	0	0	0	0		0			.000	.000	.000	-99	-1		1.000	1	484	0	/OC		0.0
1884	Cin U	38	142	23	40	5	1	1		6			.282	.311	.352	93	-5		.865	-3			C37,O2(0/1/1)		-0.5
	Was U	4	14	1	5	1	0	0		0			.357	.357	.429	142	-1		.967	1			C3/OR		0.1
	Year	42	156	24	45	6	1	1		6			.288	.315	.359	97	-5		.874	-2			C40,O3(0/1/2)		-0.4
Total	4	122	469	46	106	17	3	1	5	10		26	.226	.242	.289	63	-25		.831	-31			C109,O17(0/3/14)/1		-4.5

KELLY, KICK John O. "Diamond John" B10.31.1856 New York NY D3.27.1926 Malba NY 6-0.5/185 d5.1 M2/U4

1879	Syr N	10	36	4	4	0	0	0		2		6	.111	.111	.139	-20	-4		.827	-2			C8,1b2		-0.6
	Tro N	6	22	1	5	0	0	0		0		1	.227	.227	.227	54	-1		.789	-2			C3,O2R/3		-0.3
	Year	16	58	5	9	1	0	0		2		6	.155	.155	.172	9	-5		.817	-4			C11,1b2,O2R/3		-0.9

KELLY, JOE Joseph Henry B9.23.1886 Weir City KS D8.16.1977 St.Joseph MO BR/TR/5-10/175 d4.14 Mil 1918

1914	Pit N	141	508	47	113	19	9	1	48	39	4	59	.222	.283	.301	77	-16	21	.946	-3	100	90	O139C		-3.0
1916	Chi N	54	169	14	43	7	1	2	15	9	1	16	.254	.296	.343	87	-3	10	.953	-1	102	76	O46(16/25/6)		-0.7
1917	Bos N	116	445	41	99	9	8	3	36	26	2	45	.222	.268	.299	78	-13	21	.946	6	112	104	O116(87/29/0)		-1.5
1918	Bos N	47	155	20	36	2	4	0	15	6	1	12	.232	.265	.297	74	-6	12	.933	-1	102	82	O45(22/18/0)		-1.0
1919	Bos N	18	64	3	9	1	0	0	3	0	1	11	.141	.154	.156	-7	-8	2	.943	0	94	146	O16L		-1.0
Total	5	376	1341	129	300	38	22	6	117	80	9	143	.224	.272	.298	75	-46	66	.945	1	104	95	O362(141/211/6)		-7.2

KELLY, JOE Joseph James B4.23.1900 New York NY D11.24.1967 Lynbrook NY BL/TL/6-0/180 d4.13

1926	Chi N	65	176	16	59	15	3	0	32	7	0	15	.335	.361	.455	117	4	0	.953	-3	85	81	O39(25/0/14)		-0.2
1928	Chi N	32	52	3	11	1	0	1	7	1	2	3	.212	.255	.288	42	-5	0	.974	-0	112	101	1b10		-0.5
Total	2	97	228	19	70	16	3	1	39	8	2	14	.307	.336	.417	100	-1	0	.953	-3	85	81	O39(25/0/14),1b10		-0.7

KELLY, KENNY Kenneth Alphonso B1.26.1979 Plant City FL BR/TR/6-3/180* [TBA97 2/82] d9.7 [DL 2002 Sea A 26]

2000	TB A	2	1	0	0	0	0	0	0	0-0	0	0	.000	.000	.000	-99	0	0-0	—	0			/D		0.0
2005	Cin N	7	9	3	3	0	0	0	2	0-0	0	3	.333	.333	.333	78	0	0-1	1.000	0	135		O4(1/2/1)		-0.1
	Was N	17	4	1	1	0	0	0		1-0	0	3	.250	.400	.500	144	0	1-1	—	-0	0		O2R/D	23	-0.1
	Year	24	13	5	4	1	0	0	2	1-0	0	6	.308	.357	.385	100	0	1-2	1.000	0	103		O6(1/2/3)/D		0.0
Total	2	26	14	5	4	1	0	0	2	1-0	0	6	.286	.333	.357	84	0	1-2	1.000	-0	103		O6(1/2/3),D2	49	-0.1

KELLY, KING Michael Joseph B12.31.1857 Troy NY D11.8.1894 Boston MA BR/TR/5-10/170 d5.1 M3 HF1945 OF(2/8/742) ▲

1878	Cin N	60	237	29	67	7	4	0	27	7		7	.283	.303	.321	116	5		.765	8	**199**	118	O47R,C17,3b2		1.3
1879	Cin N	77	345	78	120	20	12	2	47	8		14	.348	.363	.493	**188**	32		.832	10	128	73	3b33,O29(0/2/27),C21/2		**3.9**
1880	Chi N	84	344	72	100	17	9	1	60	12		22	.291	.315	.401	133	11		.779	-1	**203**	41	O64R,C17,3b14/S2P		1.0
1881	Chi N	82	353	84	114	**27**	3	2	55	16		14	.323	.352	.433	139	16		.841	-2	170	79	O72R,C11,3b8		1.7
1882	Chi N	**84**	377	81	115	**37**	4	1	55	10		27	.305	.323	.432	133	14		.810	2	90	87	S42,O38R,C12,3b3/1		1.5
1883	Chi N	**98**	428	92	109	28	10	3	61	16		35	.255	.282	.388	93	-5		.813	5	**218**	174	O82R,C38,2b3,3b2/P		0.1
1884	Chi N	108	452	**120**	160	28	5	13	95	46		24	.354	**.414**	.524	178	**41**		.794	-5	232	45	O63R,C28,S12,3b10,1b2,P2/2		3.3
1885	†Chi N	107	438	**124**	126	24	9	9	75	46		21	.288	.355	.436	136	17		.867	3	208	117	O69(0/1/69),C37,2b6,3b2/1b2		2.3
1886	†Chi N	118	451	**155**	175	32	11	4	79	83		33	**.388**	**.483**	.534	182	48	53	.811	7	210	64	O56(0/1/55),C53,1b9,3b8,2b6,S5		**5.2**
1887	Bos N	116	484	120	156	34	11	8	63	55	1	40	.322	.393	.488	141	29	84	.856	-14	105	100	O61(1/0/61),2b30,C24,P3,S2,3b2,M		1.5
1888	Bos N	107	440	85	140	22	11	9	71	31	4	39	.318	.368	.480	164	31	56	.905	0			2b30,C24		3.7
1889	Bos N	125	507	120	149	**41**	5	9	78	65	2	40	.294	.376	.448	122	15	68	.848	-6	112	109	O113R,C23		0.9
1890	Bos P	89	340	83	111	18	6	4	66	52	2	26	.326	.419	.450	124	10	51	.915	6	**154**	154	C56,S27,O6(0/2/4),1b4,3b2/PM		1.8
1891	Cin AA	82	283	56	84	15	7	1	53	51	2	28	.297	.408	.410	124	10	22	.904	8	88	156	C66,3b8,O7(0/2/5),2b6,1b5,P3/SM		1.9
	Bos AA	4	15	2	4	0	0	1	4	1	0	1	.267	.267	.467	111	0	1	.950	0	**136**	91	C4		0.0
	Year	86	298	58	88	15	7	2	57	52	2	29	.295	.402	.413	123	10	23	.906	8	125	82	C70,3b8,O7(0/2/5),2b6,1b5,P3/S		1.9
	Bos N	16	52	7	12	1	0	0	5	6	1	10	.231	.322	.250	60	-3	6	.844	-2	125	82	C11,O6R		-0.4

YEAR	TM LG	G	AB	R	H	2B	3B	HR	RBI	BB-IB	HP	SO	AVG	OBP	SLG	AOPS	ABR	SB-CS	FA	FR	RNG	THR	GAMES AT POSITION	DL	BFW
1892	†Bos N	78	281	40	53	7	0	2	41	39	0	32	.189	.287	.235	53	-15	24	.912	6	133	107	C72,O2(1/0/1),3b2,1b2/P		-0.2
1893	NY N	20	67	9	18	1	0	0	15	6	0	5	.269	.329	.284	63	-4		.895	-3	98	136	C17/OR		-0.4
Total	16	1455	5894	1357	1813	359	102	69	950	549	12	418	.308	.348	.438	136	254	368	.820	27	179	104	O750R,C583,3b96,S90,2b54,1b25,P12		28.9

KELLY, MIKE Michael Raymond B6.2.1970 Los Angeles CA BR/TR/6-4/195* [AtlN91 1/2] d4.5 Col Arizona St.

YEAR	TM LG	G	AB	R	H	2B	3B	HR	RBI	BB-IB	HP	SO	AVG	OBP	SLG	AOPS	ABR	SB-CS	FA	FR	RNG	THR	GAMES AT POSITION	DL	BFW
1994	Atl N	30	77	14	21	10	1	2	9	2-0	1	17	.273	.300	.506	101	0	0-1	.962	-3	71	0	O25(19/6/1)		-0.4
1995	Atl N	97	137	26	26	6	1	3	17	11-0	2	49	.190	.258	.314	48	-11	7-3	.940	-4	90	0	O83(58/8/17)		-1.6
1996	Cin N	19	49	5	9	4	0	1	7	9-0	2	11	.184	.333	.327	74	-1	4-0	.972	1	110	128	O17(6/10/1)		0.0
1997	Cin N	73	140	27	41	13	2	6	19	10-0	0	30	.293	.338	.543	124	5	6-1	.978	4	138	89	O59(17/11/31)/D		0.8
1998	TB A	106	279	39	67	11	2	10	33	22-1	0	80	.240	.295	.401	77	-11	13-6	1.000	-1	96	84	O93(43/0/51),D6	20	-1.4
1999	Col N	2	2	0	1	0	0	0	1	0-0	0		.500	.500	1.000	212	0	0-0	—	-0	0		/OR		0.0
Total	6	327	684	111	165	45	6	22	86	54-1	5	187	.241	.300	.421	84	-18	30-11	.978	-3	101	61	O278(143/35/102),D7	20	-2.6

KELLY, PAT Patrick Franklin B10.14.1967 Philadelphia PA BR/TR/6-0/182* [NYA88 9/235] d5.20 Col West Chester

YEAR	TM LG	G	AB	R	H	2B	3B	HR	RBI	BB-IB	HP	SO	AVG	OBP	SLG	AOPS	ABR	SB-CS	FA	FR	RNG	THR	GAMES AT POSITION	DL	BFW
1991	NY A	96	298	35	72	12	4	3	23	15-0	5	52	.242	.287	.339	73	-12	12-1	.926	3	102	93	3b80,2b19	16	-0.6
1992	NY A	106	318	38	72	22	4	7	27	25-1	10	72	.226	.301	.374	89	-5	8-5	.978	-4	100	92	2b101/D		-0.6
1993	NY A	127	406	49	111	24	1	7	51	24-1	5	68	.273	.317	.389	93	-5	14-11	.978	11	110	108	2b125		1.0
1994	NY A	93	286	35	80	21	3	3	41	19-1	5	51	.280	.330	.399	91	-5	6-5	.978	5	107	127	2b93	15	-0.2
1995	†NY A	89	270	32	64	12	1	4	29	23-0	5	65	.237	.307	.333	68	-13	8-3	.983	6	105	100	2b87/D	41	-0.2
1996	NY A	13	21	4	3	0	0	0	2	2-0	0	9	.143	.217	.143	-6	-4	0-1	.970	2	137	69	2b10,D3	147	-0.2
1997	NY A	67	120	25	29	6	1	2	10	14-1	1	37	.242	.324	.358	79	-4	8-1	.961	0	100	123	2b48,D16	39	-0.1
1998	StL N	53	153	18	33	5	0	4	14	13-0	2	48	.216	.284	.327	61	-9	5-1	.964	-1	108	77	2b41,O3L,S2		-0.7
1999	Tor A	37	116	17	31	7	0	6	20	10-0	0	23	.267	.318	.483	101	0	0-1	.962	-4	97	76	2b35,D2		-0.2
Total	9	681	1988	253	495	109	11	36	217	145-3	33	425	.249	.307	.369	81	-55	61-29	.977	18	105	105	2b559,3b80,D23,O3L,S2	258	-1.1

KELLY, SPEED Robert Brown B8.19.1884 Bryan OH D5.6.1949 Goshen IN BR/TR/6-2/185 d7.13 Col Chicago

YEAR	TM LG	G	AB	R	H	2B	3B	HR	RBI	BB-IB	HP	SO	AVG	OBP	SLG	AOPS	ABR	SB-CS	FA	FR	RNG	THR	GAMES AT POSITION	DL	BFW
1909	Was A	17	42	3	6	2	1	0	1	3	0		.143	.200	.238	40	-3	1	.852	-1	99	207	3b10,2b3/OC		-0.4

KELLY, ROBERTO Roberto Conrado (Gray) "Bobby" B10.1.1964 Panama City, Pan BR/TR/6-2/192(182-202) d7.29

YEAR	TM LG	G	AB	R	H	2B	3B	HR	RBI	BB-IB	HP	SO	AVG	OBP	SLG	AOPS	ABR	SB-CS	FA	FR	RNG	THR	GAMES AT POSITION	DL	BFW
1987	NY A	23	52	12	14	3	0	1	7	5-0	0	15	.269	.328	.385	90	-1	9-3	.985	0	112	0	O17(0/16/1),D2	64	0.0
1988	NY A	38	77	9	19	4	1	1	7	3-0	0	15	.247	.272	.364	78	-3	5-2	.986	2	114	95	O30(1/28/2),D3	17	-0.1
1989	NY A	137	441	65	133	18	3	9	48	41-3	6	89	.302	.369	.417	122	13	35-12	.984	-0	99	124	O137C		1.6
1990	NY A	162	641	85	183	32	4	15	61	33-0	4	148	.285	.323	.418	105	3	42-17	.988	-2	103	60	O160(11/151/0)/D		0.3
1991	NY A	126	486	68	130	22	2	20	69	45-2	5	77	.267	.333	.444	113	8	32-9	.986	-4	91	121	O125(52/73/0)	38	0.5
1992	NY A★	152	580	81	158	31	2	10	66	41-4	4	96	.272	.322	.384	98	2	28-5	.983	2	103	91	O146(47/99/0)		0.2
1993	Cin N★	78	320	44	102	17	3	9	35	17-0	2	43	.319	.354	.475	120	8	21-5	.995	0	102	77	O77C	82	1.2
1994	Cin N	47	179	29	54	8	0	3	21	11-1	3	35	.302	.351	.397	95	-1	9-2	.992	1	108	83	O47C		0.0
	Atl N	63	255	44	73	15	3	6	24	24-0	0	36	.286	.345	.439	100	0	10-3	.985	-3	96	89	O110C		-0.3
	Year	110	434	73	127	23	3	9	45	35-1	3	71	.293	.347	.420	98	-1	19-11	.988	-3	75	77	O24C		-0.6
1995	Mon N	24	95	11	26	4	0	1	9	7-1	2	14	.274	.337	.347	78	-3	4-3	1.000	-8	88	34	O24C		-1.8
	†LA N	112	409	47	114	19	2	6	48	15-5	4	65	.279	.306	.379	87	-9	15-7	.969	-8	88	34	O110(61/48/2)		-2.4
	Year	136	504	58	140	23	2	7	57	22-6	6	79	.278	.312	.373	85	-12	19-10	.974	-11	86	42	O134(61/72/2)		
1996	Min A	98	322	41	104	17	4	6	47	23-0	7	53	.323	.375	.457	109	4	10-2	.990	-2	101	30	O59(1/1/57),D12	15	-0.6
1997	Min A	75	247	39	71	19	2	5	37	17-0	2	50	.287	.336	.441	100	0	7-4	1.000	-3	94	30	O29(28/1/0)/D		-0.6
	†Sea A	30	121	19	36	7	0	7	22	5-0	1	17	.298	.328	.529	120	3	2-1	1.000	-0	107	60	O27(0/0/26),D13		-0.4
	Year	105	368	58	107	26	2	12	59	22-0	3	67	.291	.333	.470	106	3	9-5	1.000	-3	99	41	O88(29/2/57),D13		1.1
1998	†Tex A	75	257	48	83	7	3	16	46	8-0	3	46	.323	.349	.560	125	8	0-2	.976	6	118	133	O71(14/41/31),D2	40	1.1
1999	†Tex A	87	290	41	87	17	1	8	37	21-0	5	57	.300	.355	.448	98	-1	6-1	.981	-3	94	80	O85(18/37/37)		-0.3
2000	NY A	10	25	4	3	1	0	1	1	1-0	1	6	.120	.185	.280	16	-3	0-0	1.000	-0	112	0	O10(7/3/0)	165	-0.3
Total	14	1337	4797	687	1390	241	30	124	585	317-16	49	862	.290	.337	.430	105	24	235-84	.985	-18	99	82	O1283(246/886/184),D23	436	1.2

KELLY, VAN Van Howard B3.18.1946 Charlotte NC BL/TR/5-11/180* d6.13

YEAR	TM LG	G	AB	R	H	2B	3B	HR	RBI	BB-IB	HP	SO	AVG	OBP	SLG	AOPS	ABR	SB-CS	FA	FR	RNG	THR	GAMES AT POSITION	DL	BFW
1969	SD N	73	209	16	51	7	1	3	15	12-2	0	24	.244	.285	.330	74	-8	0-1	.971	-2	103	117	3b49,2b10		-1.1
1970	SD N	38	89	9	15	3	0	1	9	15-0	0	21	.169	.288	.236	44	-7	0-1	.971	2	104	46	3b27/2		-0.6
Total	2	111	298	25	66	10	1	4	24	27-2	0	45	.221	.286	.302	65	-15	0-2	.971	-0	103	94	3b76,2b11		-1.7

KELLY, BILL William Henry "Big Bill" B12.28.1898 Syracuse NY D4.8.1990 Syracuse NY d9.6 Col Dean (MA) JC

YEAR	TM LG	G	AB	R	H	2B	3B	HR	RBI	BB-IB	HP	SO	AVG	OBP	SLG	AOPS	ABR	SB-CS	FA	FR	RNG	THR	GAMES AT POSITION	DL	BFW
1920	Phi A	9	13	0	3	1	0	0	0		2		.231	.231	.308	41	-1	0	1.000	0	111	0	1b2		-0.1
1928	Phi N	23	71	6	12	1	1	0	5	7	0	20	.169	.244	.211	19	-9	0	.991	1	119	88	1b23		-0.9
Total	2	32	84	6	15	2	1	0	5	7	0	22	.179	.242	.226	22	-10	0-0	.992	1	119	83	1b25		-1.0

KELLY, BILL William J. B New York NY d5.4

YEAR	TM LG	G	AB	R	H	2B	3B	HR	RBI	BB-IB	HP	SO	AVG	OBP	SLG	AOPS	ABR	SB-CS	FA	FR	RNG	THR	GAMES AT POSITION	DL	BFW
1871	Kek NA	18	67	16	15	1	1	0	7	6		1	.224	.288	.269	60	-3	0-0	.833	0	47	241	O18(1/4/14)		-0.1

KELLY, BILLY William Joseph B5.1.1886 Baltimore MD D6.3.1940 Detroit MI BR/TR/6-0.5/183 d5.2

YEAR	TM LG	G	AB	R	H	2B	3B	HR	RBI	BB-IB	HP	SO	AVG	OBP	SLG	AOPS	ABR	SB-CS	FA	FR	RNG	THR	GAMES AT POSITION	DL	BFW
1910	StL N	2	2	1	0	0	0	0	0	0	0		.000	.333	.000	-1	0	0	—	-0	0	0	/C		0.0
1911	Pit N	6	8	0	1	0	0	0	0	0	0		.125	.125	.125	-29	-1	0	1.000	1	173	66	/C		-0.1
1912	Pit N	48	132	20	42	3	2	1	11	2	0	16	.318	.328	.394	99	-1	8	.990	-4	124	66	C39		-0.2
1913	Pit N	48	82	11	22	2	0	0	9	2	2	12	.268	.302	.341	87	-2	1-1	.960	1	98	81	C40		0.1
Total	4	104	224	32	65	5	4	1	20	5	2	30	.290	.312	.362	89	-4	9-1	.977	-3	114	71	C81		-0.2

KELSEY, BILLY George William B8.24.1881 Covington OH D4.25.1968 Springfield OH BR/TR/5-10/150 d10.4

YEAR	TM LG	G	AB	R	H	2B	3B	HR	RBI	BB-IB	HP	SO	AVG	OBP	SLG	AOPS	ABR	SB-CS	FA	FR	RNG	THR	GAMES AT POSITION	DL	BFW
1907	Pit N	2	5	1	2	0	0	0	0	0	0		.400	.400	.400	149	0	0	1.000	-0	142	85	C2		0.0

KELTNER, KEN Kenneth Frederick "Butch" B10.31.1916 Milwaukee WI D12.12.1991 New Berlin WI BR/TR/6-0/190* d10.2 Mil 1945

YEAR	TM LG	G	AB	R	H	2B	3B	HR	RBI	BB-IB	HP	SO	AVG	OBP	SLG	AOPS	ABR	SB-CS	FA	FR	RNG	THR	GAMES AT POSITION	DL	BFW
1937	Cle A	1	1	0	0	0	0	0	0	0	0	0	.000	.000	.000	-99	0	0	1.000	0	144	0	/3		0.0
1938	Cle A	149	576	86	159	31	9	26	113	33	3	75	.276	.319	.497	103	-3	4-3	.956	-10	90	69	3b149		-0.7
1939	Cle A	154	587	84	191	35	11	13	97	51	3	41	.325	.379	.489	125	20	6-6	.974	5	94	138	3b154		2.8
1940	Cle A★	149	543	67	138	24	10	15	77	51	3	56	.254	.322	.418	93	-8	10-5	.953	-6	89	105	3b148		-0.8
1941	Cle A★	149	581	83	156	31	13	23	84	51	2	56	.269	.330	.485	119	11	2-2	.971	20	108	129	3b149		3.5
1942	Cle A★	152	624	72	179	34	4	6	78	20	3	36	.287	.312	.383	101	-3	4-3	.945	11	111	135	3b151		1.1
1943	Cle A★	110	427	47	111	31	3	4	39	36	0	29	.260	.317	.375	109	4	2-2	.969	3	104	120	3b107		0.5
1944	Cle A★	149	573	74	169	41	9	13	91	53	1	29	.295	.355	.466	139	27	4-3	.968	12	109	120	3b149		-0.8
1946	Cle A★	116	398	47	96	17	1	13	45	30	0	38	.241	.294	.387	95	-5	0-3	.965	-2	92	77	3b112		-0.8
1947	Cle A	151	541	49	139	29	3	11	76	59	1	45	.257	.331	.383	101	0	5-4	.972	-5	95	116	3b150		-0.8
1948	†Cle A★	153	558	91	166	24	4	31	119	89	1	52	.297	.395	.522	146	37	2-1	.969	-2	106	105	3b153		-0.8
1949	Cle A	80	246	35	57	9	2	8	30	38	0	26	.232	.335	.382	91	-4	0-1	.980	-1	108	75	3b69		-0.6
1950	Bos A	13	28	2	9	2	0	0	2	3	0	6	.321	.387	.393	91	0	0-0	.947	-1	80	0	3b8/1		-0.6
Total	13	1526	5683	737	1570	308	69	163	852	514	13	480	.276	.338	.441	113	76	39-33	.965	26	100	110	3b1500/1		-0.1

KELTON, DAVID David Wayne B12.17.1979 Dothan AL BR/TR/6-3/200* [ChiN98 2/46] d6.8

YEAR	TM LG	G	AB	R	H	2B	3B	HR	RBI	BB-IB	HP	SO	AVG	OBP	SLG	AOPS	ABR	SB-CS	FA	FR	RNG	THR	GAMES AT POSITION	DL	BFW
2003	Chi N	10	12	1	2	1	0	0	1	0-0	0	5	.167	.167	.250	6	-2	0-0	1.000	0	160	0	O2L		-0.2
2004	Chi N	8	10	1	1	1	0	0	1	0-0	0	3	.100	.100	.200	-24	-2	0-0	1.000	-0	85	0	O3(2/0/1)		-0.2
Total	2	18	22	2	3	2	0	0	2	0-0	0	8	.136	.136	.227	-8	-4	0-0	1.000	0	124	0	O5(4/0/1)		-0.5

KELTY, JOHN John James "Chief" B3.10.1871 Jersey City NJ D4.13.1929 Jersey City NJ 5-10/175 d4.19

YEAR	TM LG	G	AB	R	H	2B	3B	HR	RBI	BB-IB	HP	SO	AVG	OBP	SLG	AOPS	ABR	SB-CS	FA	FR	RNG	THR	GAMES AT POSITION	DL	BFW
1890	Pit N	59	207	24	49	10	2	1	27	22	4	42	.237	.322	.319	98	1	10	.898	-1	65	40	O59L		-0.5

KEMMER, BILL William Edward (b William Edward Kemmerer) B11.15.1873 PA D6.8.1945 Washington DC BR/TR/6-2/195 d6.3

YEAR	TM LG	G	AB	R	H	2B	3B	HR	RBI	BB-IB	HP	SO	AVG	OBP	SLG	AOPS	ABR	SB-CS	FA	FR	RNG	THR	GAMES AT POSITION	DL	BFW
1895	Lou N	11	38	5	7	0	0	1	3	2	0	4	.184	.225	.263	27	-4	0	.809	1	113	189	3b9,1b2		-0.5

KEMMLER, RUDY Rudolph (b Rudolph Kemler) B1860 Chicago IL D6.20.1909 Chicago IL BR/TR/5-11/206 d7.26

YEAR	TM LG	G	AB	R	H	2B	3B	HR	RBI	BB-IB	HP	SO	AVG	OBP	SLG	AOPS	ABR	SB-CS	FA	FR	RNG	THR	GAMES AT POSITION	DL	BFW
1879	Pro N	2	7	0	1	0	0	0	0	0	0		.143	.143	.143	-6	-1		.833	1			C2		0.0
1881	Cle N	1	3	0	0	0	0	0	0	0	1		.000	.000	.000	-99	-1		1.000	1			/C		0.0
1882	Cin AA	3	11	0	1	0	0	0					.091	.091	.182	-10	-1		.909	0			C3/OR		-0.5
	Pit AA	24	99	7	25	4	0	0	1				.253	.260	.293	90	-1		.920	3			C23/OR		0.0
	Year	27	110	7	26	5	0	0	1				.236	.243	.282	79	-2		.919	2			C26,O2R		0.0
1883	Col AA	84	318	27	66	6	2	0	13				.208	.239	.239	59	-13		.872	-8			C82,O2C		0.0

YEAR	TM LG	G	AB	R	H	2B	3B	HR	RBI	BB-IB	HP	SO	AVG	OBP	SLG	AOPS	ABR	SB-CS	FA	FR	RNG	THR	GAMES AT POSITION	DL	BFW
1884	Col AA	61	211	28	42	3	3	0		15	0		.199	.252	.242	67	-6		.906	-12			C58,1b2/OL		-1.3
1885	Pit AA	18	64	2	13	2	1	0	5	2	1		.203	.239	.266	60	-3		.870	-3			C18		-0.4
1886	StL AA	35	123	13	17	2	0	0	6	8	1		.138	.197	.154	10	-13	0	.914	4			C32,1b3		-0.6
1889	Col AA	8	26	2	3	0	0	0	0	3	0	3	.115	.207	.115	-8	-4		.930	1			C8		-0.2
Total	8	236	862	79	168	18	6	0	11	42	2	5	.195	.234	.230	52	-43	0	.894	-15			C227,1b5,O5(1/2/2)		-3.4

KEMP, STEVE   Steven F B8.7.1954 San Angelo TX BL/TL/6-0/195* [DetA76*1/1] d4.7 Col USC

YEAR	TM LG	G	AB	R	H	2B	3B	HR	RBI	BB-IB	HP	SO	AVG	OBP	SLG	AOPS	ABR	SB-CS	FA	FR	RNG	THR	GAMES AT POSITION	DL	BFW
1977	Det A	151	552	75	142	29	4	18	88	71-0	6	93	.257	.343	.422	103	4	3-3	.981	-10	84	89	O148L		-1.3
1978	Det A	159	582	75	161	18	4	15	79	97-3	5	87	.277	.379	.399	116	16	2-3	.977	-2	93	100	O157L		0.7
1979	Det A★	134	490	88	156	26	3	26	105	68-2	2	70	.318	.398	.543	148	35	5-6	.976	-0	92	135	O120(117/0/3),D11		2.7
1980	Det A	135	508	88	149	23	9	21	101	69-3	4	64	.293	.376	.474	130	23	5-1	.995	2	106	61	O85L,D46		2.0
1981	Det A	105	372	52	103	18	4	9	49	70-5	1	48	.277	.389	.419	129	17	9-3	.986	-2	99	60	O92L,D12		1.3
1982	Chi A	160	580	91	166	23	1	19	98	89-8	3	83	.286	.381	.428	122	21	7-7	.976	-12	86	64	O154L,D2		0.2
1983	NY A	109	373	53	90	17	3	12	49	41-3	2	37	.241	.318	.399	100	0	1-0	.987	3	109	69	O101(25/0/86),D2		-0.3
1984	NY A	94	313	37	91	12	1	7	41	40-0	1	54	.291	.369	.403	118	9	4-1	.972	-5	93	40	O75L,D12	18	0.1
1985	Pit N	92	236	19	59	13	2	2	21	25-1	0	54	.250	.317	.347	88	-4	1-0	1.000	5	105	26	O63L	16	-0.6
1986	Pit N	13	16	1	3	0	0	1	1	4-0	0	6	.188	.350	.375	97	0	1-0	1.000	1	183	0	O4L	13	0.1
1986	Tex A	16	36	2	8	0	0	0	2	2-0	0	9	.222	.256	.222	36	-3	1-0	1.000	-0	91	0	O5(5/0/1)/1D		-0.3
Total	11	1168	4058	581	1128	179	25	130	634	576-25	19	605	.278	.367	.431	118	118	39-24	.982	-25	95	78	O1004(925/0/90),D92/1	47	4.6

KENDALL, FRED   Fred Lyn B1.31.1949 Torrance CA BR/TR/6-1/190* [CinN67 4/68] d9.8 C6 s-Jason

YEAR	TM LG	G	AB	R	H	2B	3B	HR	RBI	BB-IB	HP	SO	AVG	OBP	SLG	AOPS	ABR	SB-CS	FA	FR	RNG	THR	GAMES AT POSITION	DL	BFW
1969	SD N	10	26	2	4	0	0	0	0	2-0	1	5	.154	.214	.154	9	-3	0-0	1.000	0	150	103	C9		-0.3
1970	SD N	4	9	0	0	0	0	0	1	0-0	0	0	.000	.000	.000	-99	-3	0-0	1.000	-1	93	0	C2/1OL		-0.4
1971	SD N	49	111	2	*19	1	0	1	7	7-3	0	16	.171	.220	.207	23	-12	1-0	1.000	0	62	91	C39/13		-1.1
1972	SD N	91	273	18	59	3	4	6	18	11-3	1	42	.216	.247	.322	66	-15	0-0	.995	1	85	99	C82/1		-1.1
1973	SD N	145	507	39	143	22	3	10	59	30-4	1	35	.282	.320	.396	107	3	3-1	.984	-10	100	100	C138		0.0
1974	SD N	141	424	32	98	15	2	8	45	49-7	1	33	.231	.308	.333	84	-9	0-1	.983	-19	77	104	C133		-2.4
1975	SD N	103	286	16	57	12	1	0	24	26-5	0	28	.199	.265	.248	46	-21	0-1	.977	-10	74	126	C85		-2.9
1976	SD N	146	456	30	112	17	0	2	39	36-4	3	42	.246	.302	.296	77	-14	0-1	.994	-12	114	90	C102/D		-2.1
1977	Cle A	103	317	18	79	11	1	3	39	16-1	1	27	.249	.283	.325	68	-14	0-1	.991	-22	68	74	C102/D		-3.3
1978	Bos A	20	41	3	8	1	0	0	4	1-0	0	2	.195	.205	.220	20	-4	0-0	1.000	0	134	102	1b13,C5/D		-0.5
1979	SD N	46	102	8	17	2	0	1	6	11-2	0	7	.167	.248	.216	29	-10	0-0	.977	1	92	133	C40,1b2		-0.9
1980	SD N	19	24	2	7	0	0	0	2	2-0	0	3	.292	.292	.292	68	-1	0-0	.938	-1	85	83	C14/1		-0.2
Total	12	877	2576	170	603	86	11	31	244	189-29	6	240	.234	.285	.312	72	-103	5-5	.987	-72	88	99	C795,1b19,D2/3OL		-15.2

KENDALL, JASON   Jason Daniel B6.26.1974 San Diego CA BR/TR/6-0/193(181-195) [PitN92 1/23] d4.1 f-Fred

YEAR	TM LG	G	AB	R	H	2B	3B	HR	RBI	BB-IB	HP	SO	AVG	OBP	SLG	AOPS	ABR	SB-CS	FA	FR	RNG	THR	GAMES AT POSITION	DL	BFW
1996	Pit N★	130	414	54	124	23	5	3	42	35-11	15	30	.300	.372	.401	101	2	5-2	.980	-6	69	110	C129		0.4
1997	Pit N	144	486	71	143	36	4	8	49	49-2	31	53	.294	.391	.434	115	14	18-6	.990	18	110	112	C142		4.2
1998	Pit N★	149	535	95	175	36	3	12	75	51-3	31	51	.327	.411	.473	132	29	26-5	.992	8	103	79	C144		5.0
1999	Pit N★	78	280	61	93	20	3	8	41	38-3	12	32	.332	.428	.511	137	19	22-3	.988	13	142	132	C75		3.7
2000	Pit N★	152	579	112	185	33	6	14	58	79-3	15	79	.320	.412	.470	123	24	22-12	.991	3	102	92	C147		3.5
2001	Pit N	157	606	84	161	22	2	10	53	44-4	20	48	.266	.335	.358	78	-20	13-14	.985	-11	94	85	C133,O27(18/0/10)		-2.4
2002	Pit N	145	545	59	154	25	3	3	44	49-1	9	29	.283	.350	.356	88	-10	15-8	.990	-3	100	109	C143		-0.3
2003	Pit N	150	587	84	191	29	3	6	58	49-3	25	40	.325	.399	.416	112	14	8-7	.989	-14	114	71	C146		0.9
2004	Pit N	147	574	86	183	32	0	3	51	60-2	19	41	.319	.399	.390	106	10	11-8	.991	12	120	126	C146		3.0
2005	Oak A	150	601	70	163	28	1	0	53	50-0	20	39	.271	.345	.321	79	-16	8-3	.993	1	80	65	C147,D3		-0.5
Total	10	1402	5207	776	1572	284	30	67	524	504-32	197	442	.302	.382	.407	105	66	148-68	.989	22	102	96	C1352,O27(18/0/10),D3	91	17.5

KENDERS, AL   Albert Daniel George B4.4.1937 Barrington NJ BR/TR/6-0/185 d8.14

YEAR	TM LG	G	AB	R	H	2B	3B	HR	RBI	BB-IB	HP	SO	AVG	OBP	SLG	AOPS	ABR	SB-CS	FA	FR	RNG	THR	GAMES AT POSITION	DL	BFW
1961	Phi N	10	23	0	4	0	0	0	1	1-0	0	0	.174	.208	.217	13	-3	0-0	1.000	-3	49	65	C10		-0.5

KENNA, EDDIE   Edward Aloysius "Scrap Iron" B9.30.1897 San Francisco CA D8.21.1972 San Francisco CA BR/TR/5-7.5/150 d6.2

YEAR	TM LG	G	AB	R	H	2B	3B	HR	RBI	BB-IB	HP	SO	AVG	OBP	SLG	AOPS	ABR	SB-CS	FA	FR	RNG	THR	GAMES AT POSITION	DL	BFW
1928	Was A	41	118	14	35	4	2	1	20	14	1	8	.297	.376	.390	102	1	1-5	.942	-1	116	108	C33		0.0

KENNEDY, ADAM   Adam Thomas B1.10.1976 Riverside CA BL/TR/6-1/192(180-192) [StLN97 1/20] d8.21 Col Cal St.-Northridge

YEAR	TM LG	G	AB	R	H	2B	3B	HR	RBI	BB-IB	HP	SO	AVG	OBP	SLG	AOPS	ABR	SB-CS	FA	FR	RNG	THR	GAMES AT POSITION	DL	BFW
1999	StL N	33	102	12	26	10	1	1	16	3-0	1	16	.255	.284	.402	71	-5	0-1	.971	-2	91	78	2b29		-0.6
2000	Ana A	156	598	82	159	33	11	9	72	28-5	3	73	.266	.300	.403	74	-26	22-8	.976	-13	96	100	2b155		-2.8
2001	Ana A	137	478	48	129	25	3	6	40	27-3	11	71	.270	.318	.372	81	-13	12-7	.984	2	107	81	2b131,D5	12	-0.5
2002	†Ana A	144	474	65	148	32	6	7	52	19-1	7	80	.312	.345	.449	112	7	17-4	.983	9	101	120	2b139/OCD		2.4
2003	Ana A	143	449	71	121	17	1	13	49	45-4	9	73	.269	.344	.399	100	1	22-9	.990	-3	97	96	2b140/D	15	0.6
2004	Ana A	144	468	70	130	20	5	10	48	41-7	13	92	.278	.351	.406	101	1	15-5	.982	-10	92	83	2b144		-0.1
2005	†LA A	129	416	49	125	23	0	2	37	29-1	9	64	.300	.354	.370	95	-2	19-4	.991	-12	93	91	2b127	29	-0.4
Total	7	886	2985	397	838	160	27	48	314	192-21	52	461	.281	.332	.401	92	-37	107-38	.983	-29	97	95	2b865,D7/OC	56	-1.4

KENNEDY, ED   Edward B4.1.1856 Carbondale PA D5.20.1905 New York NY 5-6/150 d5.1

YEAR	TM LG	G	AB	R	H	2B	3B	HR	RBI	BB-IB	HP	SO	AVG	OBP	SLG	AOPS	ABR	SB-CS	FA	FR	RNG	THR	GAMES AT POSITION	DL	BFW
1883	NY AA	94	356	57	78	6	7	2		72			.219	.255	.292	72	-12		.884	-8	54		O94L		-1.9
1884	†NY AA	103	378	49	72	6	2	1	16		1		.190	.225	.225	49	-21		.915	7	68	165	O100(99/1/0)/S2C		-1.5
1885	NY AA	96	349	35	71	8	4	2	21	12	4		.203	.238	.266	62	-15		.841	2	94	32	O96(95/1/0)		-1.4
1886	Bro AA	6	22	1	4	0	0	0	2	2	0		.182	.250	.182	36	-2	1	.909	-0		0	O6(3/4/0)		-0.2
Total	4	299	1105	142	225	20	13	5	23	47	5		.204	.239	.259	60	-50	1	.878	1	71	66	O296(291/6/0)/C2S		-5.0

KENNEDY, JIM   James Earl B11.1.1946 Tulsa OK BL/TR/5-9/160 d6.14 b-Junior

YEAR	TM LG	G	AB	R	H	2B	3B	HR	RBI	BB-IB	HP	SO	AVG	OBP	SLG	AOPS	ABR	SB-CS	FA	FR	RNG	THR	GAMES AT POSITION	DL	BFW
1970	StL N	12	24	1	3	0	0	0	0	5-0	0	9	.125	.125	.125	-32	-5	0-0	.909	-1	88	80	S7,2b5		-0.5

KENNEDY, JOHN   John Edward B5.29.1941 Chicago IL BR/TR/6-0/185* d9.5 Mil 1968

YEAR	TM LG	G	AB	R	H	2B	3B	HR	RBI	BB-IB	HP	SO	AVG	OBP	SLG	AOPS	ABR	SB-CS	FA	FR	RNG	THR	GAMES AT POSITION	DL	BFW
1962	Was A	14	42	6	11	0	1	1	2	2-0	1	7	.262	.295	.381	81	-1	0-1	.974	-1	96	72	S9,3b2		-0.2
1963	Was A	36	62	3	11	1	0	4	6	6-0	1	22	.177	.261	.226	38	-5	2-0	.954	3	125	110	3b26,S2		-0.2
1964	Was A	148	482	55	111	16	4	7	35	29-2	5	119	.230	.280	.324	68	-22	3-3	.941	5	111	90	3b106,S49,2b2		-1.5
1965	†LA N	104	105	12	18	3	0	1	5	8-1	2	33	.171	.243	.229	36	-9	1-0	.971	-6	78	91	3b95,S5		-1.5
1966	†LA N	125	274	15	55	9	2	3	24	10-1	5	64	.201	.241	.281	49	-20	1-2	.965	-3	104	102	3b87,S28,2b15		-2.2
1967	NY A	78	179	22	35	4	0	1	17	17-0	1	35	.196	.265	.235	52	-11	2-1	.915	-4	103	99	S36,3b34,2b2		-1.3
1969	Sea A	61	128	18	30	3	1	4	14	14-1	1	25	.234	.315	.367	91	-2	4-0	.916	-1	86	90	S33,3b23	65	0.0
1970	Mil A	25	55	8	14	2	0	2	6	5-0	0	9	.255	.317	.400	96	0	0-1	.921	-7	73	70	2b16,3b5,S4/1		-0.7
	Bos A	43	129	15	33	7	1	4	17	6-1	1	14	.256	.292	.419	96	-2	0-0	.960	3	110	66	3b33,2b2		0.1
	Year	68	184	23	47	9	1	6	23	11-1	1	23	.255	.299	.413	91	-3	0-1	.962	-4	111	95	3b38,2b18,S4/1		-0.6
1971	Bos A	74	272	41	75	12	5	.5	22	14-0	4	42	.276	.330	.412	99	-1	1-1	.974	-15	89	73	2b37,S33,3b5		-1.1
1972	Bos A	71	212	22	52	11	1	2	22	18-4	2	45	.245	.311	.335	88	-3	0-1	.962	-7	100	128	2b32,S27,3b11		-0.6
1973	Bos A	67	155	17	28	9	1	1	16	12-0	2	45	.181	.246	.271	44	-12	0-0	.980	-1	93	129	2b31,3b24,D9		-1.1
1974	Bos A	10	15	3	2	0	0	1	1	1-0	0	6	.133	.188	.333	44	-1	0-0	.778	-2	85	139	2b6,3b4		-1.1
Total	12	856	2110	237	475	77	17	32	185	142-10	25	461	.225	.281	.323	70	-89	14-10	.953	-36	102	94	3b455,S226,2b143,D9/1	65	-10.6

KENNEDY, JOHN   John Irvin B10.12.1926 Jacksonville FL D4.27.1998 Jacksonville FL BR/TR/5-10/175 d4.22

YEAR	TM LG	G	AB	R	H	2B	3B	HR	RBI	BB-IB	HP	SO	AVG	OBP	SLG	AOPS	ABR	SB-CS	FA	FR	RNG	THR	GAMES AT POSITION	DL	BFW
1957	Phi N	5	2	1	0	0	0	0	0	0-0	0	0	.000	.000	.000	-99	-1	0-0	.500	0	113	1294	3b2		-0.1

KENNEDY, JUNIOR   Junior Raymond B8.9.1950 Fort Gibson OK BR/TR/6-0/185* [BalA68 1/10] d8.9 b-Jim

YEAR	TM LG	G	AB	R	H	2B	3B	HR	RBI	BB-IB	HP	SO	AVG	OBP	SLG	AOPS	ABR	SB-CS	FA	FR	RNG	THR	GAMES AT POSITION	DL	BFW
1974	Cin N	22	19	2	3	0	0	0	6	6-1	0	4	.158	.360	.158	49	-1	0-0	.909	-4	64	30	2b17,3b5		-0.5
1978	Cin N	89	157	22	40	2	2	0	11	31-2	1	28	.255	.381	.293	90	0	4-1	.979	-2	99	93	2b71,3b4		0.1
1979	Cin N	83	220	29	60	7	0	1	17	28-0	0	31	.273	.355	.318	85	-3	4-3	.980	-4	100	94	2b50,S5,3b4		-0.4
1980	Cin N	104	337	31	88	16	3	1	34	36-6	0	34	.261	.325	.335	88	-4	3-1	.988	1	102	91	2b103		0.2
1981	Cin N	27	44	5	11	1	0	0	5	5-0	0	5	.250	.255	.273	53	-3	0-0	.980	-1	87	142	2b16,3b5		-0.3
1982	Chi N	105	242	22	53	3	1	2	25	21-1	4	34	.219	.278	.264	51	-16	1-4	.978	-2	106	87	2b71,S28,3b7		-1.5
1983	Chi N	17	22	3	5	1	0	0	2	6-0	0	5	.136	.167	.136	-12	-3	1-0	1.000	-0	110	92	2b7,3b4/S		-0.4
Total	7	447	1041	114	258	29	6	4	95	124-10	5	141	.248	.325	.299	75	-30	12-9	.982	-11	101	92	2b344,S34,3b29		-2.8

KENNEDY, DOC   Michael Joseph B8.11.1853 Brooklyn NY D5.23.1920 Grove NY BR/TR/5-9.5/185 d5.1

YEAR	TM LG	G	AB	R	H	2B	3B	HR	RBI	BB-IB	HP	SO	AVG	OBP	SLG	AOPS	ABR	SB-CS	FA	FR	RNG	THR	GAMES AT POSITION	DL	BFW
1879	Cle N	49	193	19	56	8	2	1	18	2		10	.290	.297	.368	119	4		.891	3			C46,1b4		0.7
1880	Cle N	66	250	26	50	10	1	0	18	5		12	.200	.216	.248	58	-10		.899	-2			C65,O2(1/1/0)		-1.0

YEAR	TM LG	G	AB	R	H	2B	3B	HR	RBI	BB-IB	HP	SO	AVG	OBP	SLG	AOPS	ABR	SB-CS	FA	FR	RNG	THR	GAMES AT POSITION	DL	BFW
1881	Cle N	39	150	19	47	7	1	0	15	5		13	.313	.335	.373	129	5		.920	2			C35,O3(2/1/0)/3		0.7
1882	Cle N	1	3	0	1	0	0	0	0	1		0	.333	.333	.333	180	0		.857	2			/C		0.2
1883	Buf N	5	19	3	6	0	0	0	2	2		2	.316	.381	.316	113	0		.583	-2	0		O4(1/3/0)/1		-0.2
Total	5	160	615	67	160	25	4	1	53	15		37	.260	.278	.319	98	-1		.901	4			C147,O9(4/5/0),1b5/3		0.4

KENNEDY, RAY Raymond Lincoln B5.19.1895 Pittsburgh PA D1.18.1969 Casselberry FL BR/TR/5-9/165 d9.8

YEAR	TM LG	G	AB	R	H	2B	3B	HR	RBI	BB-IB	HP	SO	AVG	OBP	SLG	AOPS	ABR	SB-CS	FA	FR	RNG	THR	GAMES AT POSITION	DL	BFW
1916	StL A	1	1	0	0	0	0	0	0	0	0	0	.000	.000	.000	-99	0		—	0			/H		0.0

KENNEDY, BOB Robert Daniel B8.18.1920 Chicago IL D4.7.2005 Mesa AZ BR/TR/6-2/193* d9.14 Mil 1942-45, 1952 M4/C5 s-Terry OF(204/30/601)

YEAR	TM LG	G	AB	R	H	2B	3B	HR	RBI	BB-IB	HP	SO	AVG	OBP	SLG	AOPS	ABR	SB-CS	FA	FR	RNG	THR	GAMES AT POSITION	DL	BFW
1939	Chi A	3	8	0	2	0	0	0	0	0	0	0	.250	.250	.250	27	-1	0-0	.750	-1	90	0	3b2		-0.1
1940	Chi A	154	606	74	153	23	3	3	52	42	0	58	.252	.301	.315	59	-37	3-7	.938	-5	97	94	3b154		-3.7
1941	Chi A	76	257	16	53	9	3	1	29	17	0	23	.206	.255	.276	41	-23	5-3	.934	0	102	100	3b71		-2.0
1942	Chi A	113	412	37	95	18	5	0	38	22	0	41	.231	.270	.299	61	-23	11-7	.956	7	110	101	3b96,O16(13/0/3)		-1.5
1946	Chi A	113	411	43	106	13	5	5	34	24	1	42	.258	.300	.350	85	-11	6-8	.965	4	95	194	O75(59/12/4),3b29		-1.4
1947	Chi A	115	428	47	112	19	5	6	48	18	0	38	.262	.291	.362	84	-12	3-4	.968	-4	93	103	O106(14/1/91)/3		-2.1
1948	Chi A	30	113	4	28	8	1	0	14	4	0	17	.248	.274	.336	64	-6	0-2	.970	0	97	141	O30(25/0/5)		-0.9
	†Cle A	66	73	10	22	3	2	0	5	4	0	6	.301	.338	.397	98	-1	0-0	1.000	2	107	152	O50(2/0/48),2b2/1		0.0
	Year	96	186	14	50	11	3	0	19	8	0	23	.269	.299	.360	77	-7	0-2	.981	2	101	152	O80(27/0/53),2b2/1		-0.9
1949	Cle A	121	424	49	117	23	5	9	57	37	0	40	.276	.334	.417	100	-2	5-5	.990	4	100	131	O98(1/0/98),3b21		-0.2
1950	Cle A	146	540	79	157	27	5	9	54	53	1	31	.291	.355	.409	99	-2	3-4	.987	2	102	108	O144(0/10/138)		-0.5
1951	Cle A	108	321	30	79	15	4	7	29	34	1	33	.246	.320	.383	95	-3	4-2	.968	-3	101	143	O106(1/0/105)		-0.4
1952	Cle A	22	40	6	12	3	1	0	12	9	0	5	.300	.429	.425	148	3	1-0	1.000	2	120	0	O13(1/5/8),3b3		0.5
1953	Cle A	100	161	22	38	5	0	3	22	19	1	11	.236	.320	.323	76	-5	0-2	1.000	0	107	57	O89(42/2/52)		-0.8
1954	Cle A	1	0	0	0	0	0	0	0	0	0	0	—	—	—		0	0-0	—	-0	0	0	/OL		0.0
	Bal A	106	323	37	81	13	2	6	45	28	0	43	.251	.306	.359	90	-6	2-1	.938	-4	95	73	3b71,O21(12/0/9)		-1.1
	Year	107	323	37	81	13	2	6	45	28	0	43	.251	.306	.359	90	-6	2-1	.938	-4	95	73	3b71,O22(13/0/9)		-1.1
1955	Bal A	26	70	10	10	1	0	0	5	10-0	0	10	.143	.250	.157	12	-9	0-1	1.000	0	111	0	O14R,1b6/3		-1.0
	Chi A	83	214	28	65	10	2	9	43	16-0	0	16	.304	.352	.495	122	6	0-2	.938	-6	85	132	3b55,O20(4/0/16),1b3		-0.2
	Year	109	284	38	75	11	2	9	48	26-0	0	26	.264	.326	.412	97	-2	0-3	.938	-7	85	131	3b56,O34(4/0/30),1b9		-1.2
1956	Chi A	8	13	0	1	0	0	0	0	2-0	0	4	.077	.200	.077	-24	-2	0-0	.931	-3	111	113	3b6		-0.3
	Det A	70	177	17	41	5	0	4	22	24-2	2	19	.232	.328	.328	74	-6	2-2	.909	-3	76	92	O30(21/0/9),3b27		-1.0
	Year	78	190	17	42	5	0	4	22	26-2	2	23	.221	.320	.311	67	-9	2-2	.909	-3	76	92	3b33,O30(21/0/9)		-1.3
1957	Chi A	4	0	0	0	0	0	0	0	0-0	0	0	.000	.000	.000	-99	-1	0-0	—	0			/H		-0.1
	Bro N	19	31	5	4	1	0	1	5	4-0	0	5	.129	.156	.258	8	-4	0-0	1.000	-1	79	0	O9(8/0/1),3b3		-0.6
Total	16	1484	4624	514	1176	196	41	63	514	364-2	6	443	.254	.309	.355	80	-145	45-50	.978	-3	100	117	O822R,3b540,1b10,2b2		-17.4

KENNEDY, SNAPPER Sherman Montgomery B11.1.1878 Conneaut OH D8.15.1945 Pasadena TX BB/TR/5-10/165 d5.1

YEAR	TM LG	G	AB	R	H	2B	3B	HR	RBI	BB-IB	HP	SO	AVG	OBP	SLG	AOPS	ABR	SB-CS	FA	FR	RNG	THR	GAMES AT POSITION	DL	BFW
1902	Chi N	1	5	0	0	0	0	0	0	0	0	0	.000	.000	.000	-99	-1	0-0	0	0	0	0	/OC		-0.2

KENNEDY, TERRY Terrence Edward B6.4.1956 Euclid OH BL/TR/6-3/220* [StLN77 1/6] d9.4 f-Bob Col Florida St.

YEAR	TM LG	G	AB	R	H	2B	3B	HR	RBI	BB-IB	HP	SO	AVG	OBP	SLG	AOPS	ABR	SB-CS	FA	FR	RNG	THR	GAMES AT POSITION	DL	BFW
1978	StL N	10	29	0	5	0	0	0	2	4-2	0	3	.172	.273	.172	27	-3	0-0	.980	-0	130	65	C10		-0.3
1979	StL N	33	109	11	31	7	0	2	17	6-2	0	20	.284	.319	.404	95	-1	0-0	.993	-5	85	67	C32		-0.5
1980	StL N	84	248	28	63	12	3	4	34	28-3	0	34	.254	.325	.375	92	-2	0-0	.967	-4	76	78	C41,O28L		-0.6
1981	SD N★	101	382	32	115	24	1	2	41	22-6	2	53	.301	.341	.385	116	7	0-2	.964	-7	96	121	C100		0.4
1982	SD N	153	562	75	166	42	1	21	97	26-9	5	91	.295	.328	.486	134	23	1-0	.990	-11	121	65	C139,1b12		1.9
1983	SD N☆	149	549	47	156	27	2	17	98	51-15	2	89	.284	.342	.434	119	13	1-3	.986	-7	92	101	C143,1b4		1.2
1984	†SD N	148	530	54	127	16	1	14	57	33-8	2	99	.240	.284	.353	78	-17	1-2	.982	-9	119	71	C147		-2.1
1985	SD N★	143	532	54	139	27	1	10	74	31-10	4	102	.261	.301	.372	88	-10	0-0	.986	6	113	110	C140,1b5		0.2
1986	SD N	141	432	46	114	22	1	12	57	37-7	2	74	.264	.324	.403	102	0	0-3	.990	1	104	95	C123		0.6
1987	Bal A★	143	512	51	128	13	1	18	62	35-6	1	112	.250	.299	.385	81	-15	0-0	.993	-10	95	106	C142		-1.9
1988	Bal A	85	265	20	60	10	0	3	16	15-0	1	53	.226	.269	.298	60	-14	0-0	.994	-13	78	112	C79		-2.4
1989	†SF N	125	355	19	85	15	0	5	34	35-7	0	56	.239	.306	.324	83	-8	1-3	.986	-9	128	101	C121,1b2		0.0
1990	SF N	107	303	25	84	22	0	2	26	31-7	0	38	.277	.342	.370	100	1	1-2	.991	-11	122	78	C103		-0.6
1991	SF N	69	171	12	40	9	1	3	13	11-4	1	31	.234	.283	.339	77	-6	0-0	.978	-3	87	190	C58,1b2		-0.6
Total	14	1491	4979	474	1313	244	12	113	628	365-86	16	855	.264	.314	.386	96	-32	6-15	.985	-71	105	97	C1378,O28L,1b25		-4.7

KENNEDY, ED William Edward B4.5.1861 Bellevue KY D12.22.1912 Cheyenne WY BR/TR/5-7/160 d5.17

YEAR	TM LG	G	AB	R	H	2B	3B	HR	RBI	BB-IB	HP	SO	AVG	OBP	SLG	AOPS	ABR	SB-CS	FA	FR	RNG	THR	GAMES AT POSITION	DL	BFW
1884	Cin U	13	48	6	10	1	1	0		1			.208	.224	.271	46	-5		.857	0	97	143	3b8,S4/OR		-0.4

KENNEY, JERRY Gerald T B6.30.1945 St.Louis MO BL/TR/6-1/170* d9.5 Mil 1968

YEAR	TM LG	G	AB	R	H	2B	3B	HR	RBI	BB-IB	HP	SO	AVG	OBP	SLG	AOPS	ABR	SB-CS	FA	FR	RNG	THR	GAMES AT POSITION	DL	BFW
1967	NY A	20	58	4	18	2	0	1	5	10-0	0	8	.310	.412	.397	145	4	2-1	.952	-2	98	51	S18		0.3
1969	NY A	130	447	49	115	14	2	2	34	48-2	1	36	.257	.328	.311	83	-9	25-14	.975	14	122	133	3b83,O31C,S10		0.5
1970	NY A	140	404	46	78	10	7	4	35	52-2	0	44	.193	.284	.282	60	-23	20-6	.960	16	128	80	3b135,2b2		-0.5
1971	NY A	120	325	50	85	10	3	0	20	56-3	1	38	.262	.368	.311	100	3	9-8	.953	10	119	111	3b109,S5/1		1.2
1972	NY A	50	119	16	25	2	0	0	7	16-2	0	13	.210	.304	.227	61	-5	3-0	.969	3	112	136	S45/3		-0.1
1973	Cle A	5	16	0	4	0	1	0	2	2-0	1	5	.250	.316	.375	97	0	0-0	1.000	-1	94	31	2b5		1.7
Total	6	465	1369	165	325	38	13	7	103	184-9	2	139	.237	.326	.299	81	-30	59-29	.962	40	121	104	3b328,S78,O31C,2b7/1		1.7

KENNEY, JOHN John d5.2

YEAR	TM LG	G	AB	R	H	2B	3B	HR	RBI	BB-IB	HP	SO	AVG	OBP	SLG	AOPS	ABR	SB-CS	FA	FR	RNG	THR	GAMES AT POSITION	DL	BFW
1872	Atl NA	5	19	0	0	0	0	0	1	0		1	.000	.000	.000	-85	-4	0-0	.692	-2	76	125	2b3,O3(2/0/1)		-0.5

KENT, JEFF Jeffrey Franklin B3.7.1968 Bellflower CA BR/TR/6-1/190(185-220) [TorA89 20/523] d4.12 Col California-Davis

YEAR	TM LG	G	AB	R	H	2B	3B	HR	RBI	BB-IB	HP	SO	AVG	OBP	SLG	AOPS	ABR	SB-CS	FA	FR	RNG	THR	GAMES AT POSITION	DL	BFW
1992	Tor A	65	192	36	46	13	1	8	35	20-0	6	47	.240	.324	.443	109	3	2-1	.915	-3	87	43	3b49,2b17,1b3		0.0
	NY N	37	113	16	27	8	1	3	15	7-0	1	29	.239	.289	.407	96	-1	0-2	.980	1	95	99	2b34/3S		0.0
1993	NY N	140	496	65	134	24	0	21	80	30-2	8	88	.270	.320	.446	104	2	4-4	.969	-20	90	92	2b127,3b12,S2		-1.2
1994	NY N	107	415	53	121	24	5	14	68	23-3	10	84	.292	.341	.475	112	6	1-4	.976	-6	101	114	2b107		0.5
1995	NY N	125	472	65	131	22	3	20	65	29-3	8	89	.278	.327	.464	110	5	3-3	.984	-8	100	94	2b122		1.3
1996	NY N	89	335	45	97	20	1	9	39	21-1	6	56	.290	.331	.436	106	2	4-3	.992	1	93	116	1b20,2b9,3b6,D5		-0.1
	†Cle A	39	102	16	27	7	0	3	16	10-0	1	22	.265	.328	.422	90	-1	2-1	.992	1	93	116	2b23,S5		2.9
1997	†SF N	155	580	90	145	38	2	29	121	48-6	13	133	.250	.316	.472	107	4	11-3	.979	19	110	116	2b148,1b13	30	4.4
1998	SF N	137	526	94	156	37	3	31	128	48-4	9	110	.297	.359	.555	125	33	9-4	.972	5	108	103	2b134/1	18	1.9
1999	SF N★	138	511	86	148	40	2	23	101	61-3	5	112	.290	.366	.511	128	23	13-6	.984	-9	93	107	2b133/1		6.4
2000	†SF N★	159	587	114	196	41	7	33	125	90-6	9	107	.334	.424	.596	166	63	12-9	.986	8	110	104	2b150,1b30		4.2
2001	†SF N★	159	607	84	181	49	6	22	106	65-4	11	100	.298	.369	.507	133	32	7-6	.987	8	110	104	2b140,1b30	6	4.8
2002	†SF N	152	623	102	195	42	2	37	108	52-3	4	101	.313	.368	.565	150	40	5-1	.978	2	102	125	2b149,1b9	21	1.9
2003	Hou N	130	505	77	150	39	1	22	93	39-2	5	85	.297	.351	.509	115	11	6-2	.983	1	96	100	2b128,D2		2.8
2004	†Hou N★	145	540	96	156	34	8	27	107	49-3	6	96	.289	.348	.531	121	16	7-3	.989	7	95	88	2b139,D2		4.0
2005	LA N★	149	553	100	160	36	0	29	105	72-8	9	85	.289	.377	.512	131	26	6-2	.978	8	104	99	2b140,1b14		4.0
Total	14	1926	7157	1139	2070	474	42	331	1312	664-48	105	1340	.289	.354	.506	125	264	92-54	.980	19	101	103	2b1677,3b157,1b107,D7,S3	90	34.1

KENWORTHY, DICK Richard Lee B4.1.1941 Red Oak IA BR/TR/5-9/170* d9.8 Col Missouri

YEAR	TM LG	G	AB	R	H	2B	3B	HR	RBI	BB-IB	HP	SO	AVG	OBP	SLG	AOPS	ABR	SB-CS	FA	FR	RNG	THR	GAMES AT POSITION	DL	BFW
1962	Chi A	3	4	0	0	0	0	0	0	0-0	0	3	.000	.000	.000	-99	-1	0-0	1.000	1	159	346	2b2		0.0
1964	Chi A	2	2	0	0	0	0	0	0	0-0	0	0	.000	.000	.000	-99	-1	0-0	—	0			/H		-0.1
1965	Chi A	3	1	0	0	0	0	0	0	1-0	1	0	.000	.667	.000	113	0	0-0	—	0			/H		0.0
1966	Chi A	9	25	1	5	0	0	0	0	0-0	0	4	.200	.200	.200	16	-3	0-0	.875	-3	66	0	3b6		-0.6
1967	Chi A	50	97	9	22	4	1	4	11	4-0	1	17	.227	.262	.412	101	2	0-2	.971	-2	100	28	3b35		-0.4
1968	Chi A	58	122	9	27	2	0	2	6	10-0	2	42	.221	.252	.238	48	-5	0-3	.948	-5	103	49	3b79,2b2		-1.1
Total	6	125	251	12	54	6	2	6	18	4	13	10-0	.215	.250	.295	63	-14	0-3	.948	-5	103	49	3b79,2b2		-2.2

KENWORTHY, BILL William Jennings "Duke" B7.4.1886 Cambridge OH D9.21.1950 Eureka CA BR/TR/5-7/165 d8.28

YEAR	TM LG	G	AB	R	H	2B	3B	HR	RBI	BB-IB	HP	SO	AVG	OBP	SLG	AOPS	ABR	SB-CS	FA	FR	RNG	THR	GAMES AT POSITION	DL	BFW
1912	Was A	12	38	6	9	1	0	0	2	2	1		.237	.293	.263	59	-2	3	1.000	1	80	263	O12(7/5/0)		-0.2
1914	KC F	146	545	93	173	40	14	15	91	36	11	44	.317	.356	.525	143	26	37	.952	22	100	143	2b145		5.1
1915	KC F	122	396	59	118	30	7	3	52	28	7	32	.298	.355	.432	126	7	20	.936	-4	97	93	2b108,O7R		0.5
1917	StL A	5	10	1	1	0	0	0	1	1	0	1	.100	.182	.100	-14	-1	1	.889	1	118	226	2b4		-0.1
Total	4	285	989	159	301	71	21	18	146	67	19	77	.304	.360	.473	135	30	61	.945	20	99	123	2b257,O19(7/5/7)		5.3

YEAR	TM LG	G	AB	R	H	2B	3B	HR	RBI	BB-IB	HP	SO	AVG	OBP	SLG	AOPS	ABR	SB-CS	FA	FR	RNG	THR	GAMES AT POSITION	DL	BFW

KEOUGH, JOE Joseph William B1.7.1946 Pomona CA BL/TL/6-0/185* [OakA65 2/21] d8.7 b-Marty Col Mt. San Antonio (CA) JC

1968	Oak A	34	98	7	21	2	1	2	18	8-0	0	11	.214	.274	.316	82	-3	1-0	.962	1	106	127	O29(28/0/1)/1		-0.3
1969	KC A	70	166	17	31	2	0	0	7	13-0	2	13	.187	.254	.199	28	-16	5-2	1.000	-0	104	73	O49(3/26/21)/1		-1.9
1970	KC A	57	183	28	59	6	2	4	21	23-3	0	18	.322	.396	.443	131	8	1-1	.985	0	102	91	O34(18/1/15),1b18	95	0.5
1971	KC A	110	351	34	87	14	2	3	30	35-5	1	26	.248	.318	.325	83	-8	0-6	.982	-6	88	63	O100(1/7/93)		-2.2
1972	KC A	56	64	8	14	2	0	0	5	8-1	0	7	.219	.324	.250	73	-2	0-0	1.000	-8	58	125	O16(9/2/5)		-0.4
1973	Chi A	5	1	1	0	0	0	0	0	0-0	0	0	.000	.000	.000	-97	-0	0-0	—	0			/H		0.0
Total	6	332	863	95	212	26	5	9	81	87-9	5	75	.246	.317	.319	82	-21	9-9	.984	-7	94	81	O228(59/36/135),1b20	95	-4.3

KEOUGH, MARTY Richard Martin B4.14.1934 Oakland CA BL/TL/6-0/180* d4.21 b-Joe s-Matt

1956	Bos A	3	2	1	0	0	0	0	1	1-0	0	1	.000	.333	.000	-5	0	0-0	—	0			/H		0.0
1957	Bos A	9	17	1	1	0	0	0	0	4-0	0	3	.059	.238	.059	-14	-3	0-0	1.000	0	116	0	O7(0/2/5)		-0.3
1958	Bos A	68	118	21	26	3	3	1	9	7-0	0	29	.220	.262	.322	57	-7	1-1	.974	-3	86	0	O25(1/21/3),1b2		-1.2
1959	Bos A	96	251	40	61	13	5	7	27	26-0	3	40	.243	.320	.418	97	-1	3-1	.993	1	100	126	O69C,1b3		-0.3
1960	Bos A	38	105	15	26	6	1	1	9	8-1	0	8	.248	.296	.352	73	-4	2-2	1.000	-1	99	204	O29(1/28/0)		-0.5
	Cle A	65	149	19	37	5	0	3	11	9-0	1	23	.248	.294	.342	74	-6	2-3	.986	-2	91	96	O42(2/25/16)		-0.5
	Year	103	254	34	63	11	1	4	20	17-1	1	31	.248	.295	.346	74	-10	4-5	.992	-1	94	142	O71(3/53/16)		-1.0
1961	Was A	135	390	57	97	18	9	9	34	32-1	2	60	.249	.307	.410	92	-6	12-5	.978	4	109	106	O100(63/25/18),1b10		-1.5
1962	Cin N	111	230	34	64	8	2	7	27	21-4	4	37	.278	.346	.422	102	3	3-1	.992	0	107	65	O71(48/17/10),1b29		-0.7
1963	Cin N	95	172	21	39	8	2	6	21	25-4	4	37	.227	.337	.401	109	3	1-4	.992	0	122	114	O81(1/11/71),1b4		0.2
1964	Cin N	109	276	29	71	9	1	9	28	22-1	1	58	.257	.314	.395	90	-5	2-3	.991	-2	95	91	O81(1/11/71),1b4		-0.1
1965	Cin N	62	43	14	5	0	0	0	3	3-0	1	14	.116	.191	.116	-10	-6	0-0	.988	-0	80	51	O1b32,O4(3/0/1)		-0.9
1966	Atl N	17	17	1	1	0	0	0	1	1-0	0	6	.059	.111	.059	-50	-3	0-0	1.000	-1	0	0	1b4,O3(2/0/1)		-0.5
	Chi N	33	26	3	6	1	0	0	5	5-0	1	9	.231	.375	.269	82	0	1-0	1.000	-0	65	0	O5(2/2/1)		0.0
	Year	50	43	4	7	1	0	0	6	6-0	1	15	.163	.280	.186	32	-4	1-0	.667	-1	51	0	O8(4/2/2),1b4		-0.5
Total	11	841	1796	256	434	71	23	43	176	164-11	17	318	.242	.309	.379	86	-34	26-19	.984	-4			O464(127/203/148),1b130		-6.1

KEPPINGER, JEFF Jeffrey Scott B4.21.1980 Miami FL BR/TR/6-0/180 [PitN01 4/114] d8.20 Col Georgia [DL 2005 NY N 24]

2004	NY N	33	116	9	33	3	0	3	9	6-0	0	7	.284	.317	.379	82	-4	2-1	.987	1	107	104	2b32		-0.1

KERINS, JOHN John Nelson B7.15.1858 Indianapolis IN D9.8.1919 Louisville KY BR/TR/5-10/177 d5.1 M2/U3 OF(13/9/49)

1884	Ind AA	94	364	58	78	10	3	6		6		1	.214	.229	.308	76	-10		.972	6	142	47	1b87,C5,O5(0/2/3)/3		-1.0
1885	Lou AA	112	456	65	111	9	16	3	51	20	4		.243	.281	.353	100	-2		.947	3	111	100	1b96,C19,O3R/3		-0.5
1886	Lou AA	120	487	113	131	19	9	4	50	66	3		.269	.360	.370	122	13	26	.933	28			C65,1b47,O7(2/2/3)/S		3.7
1887	Lou AA	112	476	101	140	18	19	5	57	38	2		.294	.349	.443	118	8	49	.970	14	78	79	1b74,C35,O5(1/1/3)		1.6
1888	Lou AA	83	319	38	75	11	4	2	41	25		1	.235	.297	.313	98	0	16	.844	-4	29	64	O47(10/2/35),C33,1b4,3b2/2M		-0.2
1889	Lou AA	2	9	2	3	1	0	0	3	0		1	.333	.333	.444	123	0	0	.500	-1	0	0	O2R/C		0.0
	Bal AA	16	53	7	15	2	0	0	12	2	1	5	.283	.321	.321	82	-1	2	.981	-1	131	28	1b9,C4,O2C/S		-0.2
	Year	18	62	9	18	3	0	0	15	2	1	5	.290	.323	.339	87	-1	2	.981	-2	131	28	1b9,C5,O4(0/2/2)/S		-0.2
1890	StL AA	18	63	8	8	0	0	0	3	8	0		.127	.225	.159	12	-7	-2	.968	1	148	143	1b17/CM		-0.2
Total	7	557	2227	392	561	72	51	20	217	165		14	5	.252	.308	.357	102	1	95	.963	47			1b334,C163,O71R,3b4,S2/2		2.7

KERLIN, ORIE Orie Milton "Cy" B1.23.1891 Summerfield LA D10.29.1974 Shreveport LA BL/TR/5-7/149 d6.6 Col Louisiana St.

1915	Pit F	3	1	0	0	0	0	0	0	0	0	0	.000	.000	.000	-99	0	0-0	—	-0	0		C3		0.0

KERN, BILL William George B2.28.1933 Coplay PA BR/TR/6-2/185 d9.19 Col Muhlenberg

1962	KC A	8	16	1	4	0	0	1	1	0-0	0	3	.250	.250	.438	77	-1	0-0	1.000	1	53	1257	O3L		0.0

KERNAN, JOE Joseph B Baltimore MD d4.14

1873	Mar NA	2	8	1	3	0	0	0		1	0		.375	.375	.375	161	1		.700	0	126	0	/2OC		0.0

KERNEK, GEORGE George Boyd B1.12.1940 Holdenville OK BL/TL/6-3/170* d9.5 Col Oklahoma

1965	StL N	10	31	6	9	3	1	0	3	2-0	0	4	.290	.333	.452	109	0	0-0	.972	-0	107	165	1b7		0.0
1966	StL N	20	50	5	12	0	1	0	3	4-0	1	9	.240	.309	.280	65	-2	1-0	.984	-0	95	129	1b16		-0.4
Total	2	30	81	11	21	3	2	0	6	6-0	1	13	.259	.318	.346	82	-2	1-0	.980	-1	99	141	1b23		-0.4

KERNS, RUSS Russell Eldon B11.10.1920 Fremont OH D8.21.2000 Placerville CA BL/TR/6-0/188 d8.18

1945	Det A	1	1	0	0	0	0	0	0	0-0	0	0	.000	.000	.000	-94	0	0-0	—	0			/H		0.0

KERR, JOHN John Francis B11.26.1898 San Francisco CA D10.19.1993 Long Beach CA BR/TR (BB 1923-24)/5-8/158 d5.1 C1

1923	Det A	19	42	4	9	1	0	0	4	4	0	5	.214	.283	.238	39	-4	0-0	.877	1	120	81	S15		-0.2
1924	Det A	17	11	3	3	0	0	0	1	0	0	0	.273	.273	.273	42	-1	0-0	0	0	0	0	3b3,O2		-0.1
1929	Chi A	127	419	50	108	20	4	1	39	31	5	24	.258	.310	.332	66	-22	9-8	.971	17	113	110	2b122/S		-0.2
1930	Chi A	70	266	37	77	11	6	3	27	21	4	23	.289	.351	.410	95	-2	4-2	.980	-1	100	100	2b52,S20		0.0
1931	Chi A	128	444	51	119	17	2	2	50	35	2	22	.268	.324	.329	77	-15	9-3	.968	1	102	103	2b117,3b7/S		-0.6
1932	Was A	51	132	14	36	6	1	0	15	13	0	3	.273	.338	.333	75	-5	3-2	.954	-2	96	81	2b17,S14,3b8		-0.5
1933	†Was A	28	40	3	8	0	0	0	3	0	0	2	.200	.256	.200	22	-5	0-0	.966	1	112	84	2b16/3		-0.3
1934	Was A	31	103	8	28	4	0	0	12	8	0	13	.272	.324	.311	67	-5	1-1	.971	4	131	116	3b17,2b13		0.0
Total	8	471	1457	172	388	59	13	6	145	115	7	92	.266	.323	.337	73	-59	26-16	.970	21	105	103	2b337,S51,3b36,O2		-1.9

KERR, DOC John Jonas B1.17.1882 Dellroy OH D6.9.1937 Baltimore MD BB/TR/5-10.5/190 d4.22

1914	Pit F	42	71	3	17	4	2	0	7	10	0	13	.239	.333	.394	99	-1	0	.970	0	105	111	C18		0.0
	Bal F	14	34	4	9	1	0	1	1	1	0	6	.265	.286	.353	71	-2	1	.979	2	137	81	C13/1		0.1
	Year	56	105	7	26	5	3	1	8	11	0	19	.248	.319	.381	90	-3	1	.974	3	118	98	C31/1		0.1
1915	Bal F	3	6	1	2	0	0	0		1	0	0	.333	.429	.333	112	0	0	1.000	-1	83	75	C2/1		-0.1
Total	2	59	111	8	28	5	3	1	8	12	0	19	.252	.325	.378	91	-3	1	.975	2	117	97	C33,1b2		0.0

KERR, BUDDY John Joseph B11.6.1922 Astoria NY BR/TR/6-2/180* d9.8

1943	NY N	27	98	14	28	3	0	2	12	8	2	5	.286	.352	.378	110	1	1	.955	3	103	57	S27		0.6
1944	NY N	150	548	68	146	31	4	9	63	37	3	32	.266	.316	.387	97	-3	14	.954	19	106	90	S149		2.8
1945	NY N	149	546	53	136	20	4	8	40	41	2	34	.249	.304	.319	72	-21	5	.964	30	111	101	S148		2.1
1946	NY N	145	497	50	124	20	3	6	40	53	2	31	.249	.324	.338	87	-8	7	.982	8	101	83	S126,3b18		0.8
1947	NY N	138	547	73	157	23	5	7	49	36	0	49	.287	.331	.386	89	-10	2	.977	12	106	88	S138		1.1
1948	NY N★	144	496	41	119	16	4	0	46	56	0	36	.240	.317	.288	64	-24	0	.967	4	106	88	S143		-1.1
1949	NY N	90	220	16	46	4	0	1	19	21	2	23	.209	.284	.227	39	-19	0	.959	4	103	85	S89		-1.1
1950	Bos N	155	507	45	115	24	6	2	46	50	0	50	.227	.296	.310	64	-27	0	.965	2	100	96	S155		-1.6
1951	Bos N	69	172	18	32	4	0	1	18	22	1	20	.186	.282	.227	41	-14	0-0	.969	7	107	86	S63,2b5		-0.3
Total	9	1067	3631	378	903	145	25	31	333	324	12	280	.249	.312	.328	76	-125	38-0	.967	89	105	90	S1038,3b18,2b5		3.3

KERR, MEL John Melville B5.22.1903 Souris MB, Can. D8.9.1980 Vero Beach FL BL/TL/5-11.5/155 d9.16

1925	Chi N	1	0	1	0	0	0	0	0	0-0	0	0					0	0-0	—	0			/R		0.0

KERWIN, DAN Daniel Patrick (b Daniel Patrick Kervin) B7.9.1879 Philadelphia PA D7.13.1960 Philadelphia PA BL/TL/5-9/164 d9.27

1903	Cin N	2	6	1	4	1	0	0	1		2		.667	.778	.833	323	2	0	.500	-1	0	0	O2L		0.1

KESSINGER, DON Donald Eulon B7.17.1942 Forrest City AR BB/TR (BR 1964-65)/6-1/175* d9.7 M1 s-Keith Col U. of Mississippi

1964	Chi N	4	12	1	2	0	0	0	0	0-0	0	5	.167	.167	.167	-6	-2	0-0	1.000	-0	107	77	S4		-0.2
1965	Chi N	106	309	19	62	4	0	0	14	20-1	2	44	.201	.252	.233	37	-26	1-2	.948	11	113	113	S105		-0.8
1966	Chi N	150	533	50	146	8	2	1	43	26-5	0	46	.274	.306	.302	70	-22	13-7	.951	-17	100	74	S148		-2.8
1967	Chi N	145	580	61	134	10	7	0	42	33-1	4	80	.231	.275	.272	55	-34	6-13	.973	-4	102	97	S143		-3.2
1968	Chi N★	160	655	63	157	14	7	1	32	38-1	0	86	.240	.283	.287	67	-26	9-9	.962	27	112	112	S159		1.5
1969	Chi N★	158	664	109	181	38	6	4	53	61-4	1	70	.273	.332	.366	85	-11	11-8	.976	25	109	112	S157		3.3
1970	Chi N★	154	631	100	168	21	14	6	39	66-6	2	59	.266	.337	.349	75	-22	12-6	.972	12	103	98	S154		0.9
1971	Chi N★	155	617	77	159	18	6	2	38	52-6	3	54	.258	.318	.316	70	-23	15-8	.966	15	103	103	S154		0.7
1972	Chi N	149	577	77	158	20	6	1	39	67-8	4	44	.274	.351	.334	86	-8	8-7	.965	17	110	106	S146		2.7
1973	Chi N	160	577	52	151	22	3	0	43	57-18	4	44	.262	.327	.310	72	-20	6-6	.964	27	110	114	S158		2.5
1974	Chi N★	153	599	83	155	20	7	1	42	62-7	4	54	.259	.332	.321	80	-15	7-7	.958	7	103	91	S150		0.9
1975	Chi N	154	601	77	146	26	10	0	46	68-2	1	47	.243	.319	.319	70	-20	4-7	.967	7	102	112	S140,3b13		0.2

YEAR TM LG	G	AB	R	H	2B	3B	HR	RBI	BB-IB	HP	SO	AVG	OBP	SLG	AOPS	ABR	SB-CS	FA	FR	RNG	THR	GAMES AT POSITION	DL	BFW
1976 StL N	145	502	55	120	22	6	1	40	61-5	1	51	.239	.320	.313	79	-12	3-0	.969	-2	98	120	S113,2b31,3b2		0.1
1977 StL N	59	134	14	32	4	0	0	7	14-1	0	26	.239	.309	.269	57	-8	0-0	.978	4	98	155	S26,2b24,3b4		-0.1
Chi A	39	119	12	28	3	2	0	11	13-2	0	7	.235	.308	.294	66	-6	2-1	.959	-6	69	104	S21,2b13,3b9		-0.9
1978 Chi A	131	431	35	110	18	1	1	31	36-1	0	34	.255	.312	.309	74	-14	2-4	.974	-18	91	85	S123,2b9		-2.2
1979 Chi A	56	110	14	22	6	0	1	7	10-1	0	12	.200	.264	.282	48	-8	1-0	.988	-9	84	65	S54/12M		-1.2
Total 16	2078	7651	899	1931	254	80	14	527	684-69	22	759	.252	.314	.312	72	-277	100-85	.966	92	104	102	S1955,2b78,3b28/1		1.4

KESSINGER, KEITH Robert Keith B2.19.1967 Forrest City AR BB/TR/6-2/185 [BalA89 36/921] d9.15 f-Don Col U. of Mississippi

YEAR TM LG	G	AB	R	H	2B	3B	HR	RBI	BB-IB	HP	SO	AVG	OBP	SLG	AOPS	ABR	SB-CS	FA	FR	RNG	THR	GAMES AT POSITION	DL	BFW
1993 Cin N	11	27	4	7	1	0	1	3	4-0	0	4	.259	.344	.407	103	0	0-0	.935	-2	91	100	S11		-0.1

KESSLER, HENRY Henry "Lucky" B1847 Brooklyn NY D1.9.1900 Franklin PA BR/TR/5-10/144 d8.4

YEAR TM LG	G	AB	R	H	2B	3B	HR	RBI	BB-IB	HP	SO	AVG	OBP	SLG	AOPS	ABR	SB-CS	FA	FR	RNG	THR	GAMES AT POSITION	DL	BFW
1873 Atl NA	1	5	0	1	0	0	0	1	0		0	.200	.200	.200	21	0	0-0	.882	0	355	0	/1		0.0
1874 Atl NA	14	56	8	17	1	0	0	4	0		2	.304	.304	.321	114	1	0-0	.737	-4			C9,2b4,O4(2/2/0)/3		-0.2
1875 Atl NA	25	105	17	26	2	0	0	7	1		2	.248	.255	.267	93	0	0-2	.794	-3	107	29	S18,O7(0/4/3),C3/12		-0.3
1876 Cin N	59	248	26	64	5	0	0	11	7		10	.258	.278	.278	100	2		.788	-8	85	106	S46,O16(0/2/14)		-0.7
1877 Cin N	6	20	0	2	0	0	0	0	2		1	.100	.182	.100	-10	-2		.500	-5			C5/1		-0.5
Total 3 NA	40	166	25	44	3	0	0	12	1		4	.265	.269	.283	98	1	0-2	.794	-7			S18,C12,O11(2/6/3),2b5,1b2/3		-0.5
Total 2	65	268	26	66	5	0	0	11	9		11	.246	.271	.265	91	0		.794	-13			S46,O16(0/2/14),C5/1		-1.0

KETCHUM, FRED Frederick L. B7.27.1875 Elmira NY D3.12.1908 Cortland NY BL/TR/5-8/157 d9.12

YEAR TM LG	G	AB	R	H	2B	3B	HR	RBI	BB-IB	HP	SO	AVG	OBP	SLG	AOPS	ABR	SB-CS	FA	FR	RNG	THR	GAMES AT POSITION	DL	BFW
1899 Lou N	15	61	13	18	1	0	0	5	0	1		.295	.306	.311	70	-3	2	1.000	-2	0	0	O15(4/1/10)		-0.5
1901 Phi A	5	22	5	5	0	0	0	2	0	0		.227	.227	.227	25	-2	0	.875	-1	0	0	O5L		-0.3
Total 2	20	83	18	23	1	0	0	7	0	1		.277	.286	.289	58	-5	2	.960	-3	0		O20(9/1/10)		-0.8

KETTER, PHIL Philip (b Philip Ketterer) B4.13.1884 St.Louis MO D4.9.1965 St.Louis MO TR d5.23

YEAR TM LG	G	AB	R	H	2B	3B	HR	RBI	BB-IB	HP	SO	AVG	OBP	SLG	AOPS	ABR	SB-CS	FA	FR	RNG	THR	GAMES AT POSITION	DL	BFW
1912 StL A	2	6	1	2	0	0	0	0	0	0		.333	.333	.333	94	0	0	1.000	-1	68	121	C2		-0.1

KHALIFA, SAMMY Sam B12.5.1963 Fontana CA BR/TR/5-11/170* [PitN82 1/7] d6.25

YEAR TM LG	G	AB	R	H	2B	3B	HR	RBI	BB-IB	HP	SO	AVG	OBP	SLG	AOPS	ABR	SB-CS	FA	FR	RNG	THR	GAMES AT POSITION	DL	BFW
1985 Pit N	95	320	30	76	14	3	2	31	34-8	0	56	.237	.307	.319	77	-10	5-2	.967	9	106	75	S95		1.0
1986 Pit N	64	151	8	28	6	0	0	4	19-6	0	28	.185	.276	.225	39	-12	0-2	.961	6	112	87	S60,2b6		-0.2
1987 Pit N	5	17	1	3	0	0	0	2	0-0	0	2	.176	.176	.176	-6	-3	0-0	.917	-4	43	37	S5		-0.7
Total 3	164	488	39	107	20	3	2	37	53-14	0	86	.219	.294	.285	62	-25	5-4	.964	11	106	78	S160,2b6		0.1

KIBBIE, HOD Horace Kent B7.18.1903 Ft.Worth TX D10.19.1975 Ft.Worth TX BR/TR/5-10/150 d6.13 Col Texas

YEAR TM LG	G	AB	R	H	2B	3B	HR	RBI	BB-IB	HP	SO	AVG	OBP	SLG	AOPS	ABR	SB-CS	FA	FR	RNG	THR	GAMES AT POSITION	DL	BFW
1925 Bos N	11	41	5	11	2	0	0	5			6	.268	.348	.317	78	-1	0-0	.904	-2	95	38	2b8,S3		-0.2

KIBBLE, JACK John Westly "Happy" B1.2.1892 Seatonville IL D12.13.1969 Roundup MT BB/TR/5-9.5/154 d9.10

YEAR TM LG	G	AB	R	H	2B	3B	HR	RBI	BB-IB	HP	SO	AVG	OBP	SLG	AOPS	ABR	SB-CS	FA	FR	RNG	THR	GAMES AT POSITION	DL	BFW
1912 Cle A	5	8	1	0	0	0	0	0		0	5	.000	.111	.000	-65	-2		1.000	2	171	721	3b4/2		0.1

KIEFER, STEVE Steven George B10.18.1960 Chicago IL BR/TR/6-1/180* [OakA81*1/16] d9.3 b-Mark Col Fullerton (CA) JC

YEAR TM LG	G	AB	R	H	2B	3B	HR	RBI	BB-IB	HP	SO	AVG	OBP	SLG	AOPS	ABR	SB-CS	FA	FR	RNG	THR	GAMES AT POSITION	DL	BFW
1984 Oak A	23	40	7	7	1	0	2	0	2-0	0	10	.175	.209	.300	43	-3	2-1	.904	-4	92	61	S17,3b2,D3		-0.6
1985 Oak A	40	66	8	13	1	1	1	10	1-0	0	18	.197	.203	.288	37	-6	0-0	.881	-4	88	119	3b34,D2		-1.0
1986 Mil A	2	6	0	0	0	0	0	0	0-0	0	4	.000	.000	.000	-97	-2		1.000	2	155	175	S2		0.1
1987 Mil A	28	99	17	20	4	0	5	17	7-0	1	28	.202	.257	.394	68	-5	0-0	.966	-4	84	62	3b26,2b4		0.2
1988 Mil A	7	10	2	3	1	0	1	1	2-0	1	3	.300	.462	.700	218	2	0-0	1.000	0	151	206	2b4,3b4	16	-0.3
1989 NY A	5	8	0	1	0	0	0	0	0-0	0	5	.125	.125	.125	-30	-1	0-0	1.000	-1	24	0	3b5	16	-2.4
Total 6	105	229	34	44	7	3	7	30	12-0	2	68	.192	.234	.341	55	-15	2-1	.920	-10	82	80	3b71,S19,2b8,D5		

KIELTY, BOBBY Robert Michael B8.5.1976 Fontana CA BB/TR/6-1/215* d4.10 Col U. of Mississippi

YEAR TM LG	G	AB	R	H	2B	3B	HR	RBI	BB-IB	HP	SO	AVG	OBP	SLG	AOPS	ABR	SB-CS	FA	FR	RNG	THR	GAMES AT POSITION	DL	BFW
2001 Min A	37	104	8	26	8	0	2	14	8-2	1	25	.250	.297	.385	113	-7	3-0	.956	-1	95	107	O34(11/11/17)/D		-0.4
2002 †Min A	112	289	49	84	14	3	12	46	52-4	5	66	.291	.405	.484	131	15	4-1	1.000	0	102	95	O82(9/34/50),D11,1b5		1.2
2003 Min A	75	238	40	60	13	0	9	32	42-2	4	36	.252	.370	.420	104	3	6-2	.972	-2	94	50	O36(1/2/33),D32		-0.1
Tor A	62	189	31	44	13	1	4	25	29-4	4	56	.233	.342	.376	87	-2	2-1	.989	-3	87	69	O60(3/1/56),1b3		-0.8
Year	137	427	71	104	26	1	13	57	71-6	7	92	.244	.358	.400	97	1	8-3	.981	-5	90	61	O96(4/3/89),D32,1b3		-0.9
2004 Oak A	83	238	29	51	14	1	7	31	35-0	2	47	.214	.321	.370	80	-6	1-0	.990	-4	90	37	O67(51/0/21),D11		-1.3
2005 Oak A	116	377	55	99	20	0	10	57	50-3	2	67	.263	.350	.395	97	0	3-2	.983	-2	95	102	O96(58/0/42),D17		-0.6
Total 5	485	1435	212	364	82	5	44	205	216-15	18	297	.254	.355	.410	100	7	19-6	.985	-11	94	79	O375(133/48/219),D72,1b8		-2.0

KIENZLE, BILL William H. B Philadelphia PA BL/TL d9.15

YEAR TM LG	G	AB	R	H	2B	3B	HR	RBI	BB-IB	HP	SO	AVG	OBP	SLG	AOPS	ABR	SB-CS	FA	FR	RNG	THR	GAMES AT POSITION	DL	BFW
1882 Phi AA	9	33	8	11	3	2	0		9	5		.333	.421	.545	210	4		.842	-1	47	0	O9C		0.2
1884 Phi U	67	299	76	76	13	8	0	21				.254	.303	.351	106	-6		.772	-5	107	62	O67C		-1.2
Total 2	76	332	84	87	16	10	0	9	26			.262	.316	.370	117	-2		.781	-7	100	55	O76C		-1.0

KIESCHNICK, BROOKS Michael Brooks B6.6.1972 Robstown TX BL/TR/6-4/230(220-250) [ChiN93 1/10] d4.3 Col Texas ▲

YEAR TM LG	G	AB	R	H	2B	3B	HR	RBI	BB-IB	HP	SO	AVG	OBP	SLG	AOPS	ABR	SB-CS	FA	FR	RNG	THR	GAMES AT POSITION	DL	BFW
1996 Chi N	25	29	6	10	2	0	1	6	3-0	0	8	.345	.406	.517	137	2	0-0	.833	-1	68	0	O8(4/0/5)		0.1
1997 Chi N	39	90	9	18	2	0	4	12	12-0	1	21	.200	.294	.356	67	-5	1-0	.952	0	104	76	O27(26/0/1)		-0.5
2000 Cin N	14	12	0	0	0	0	0	0	1-0	0	5	.000	.077	.000	-76	-3	0-0	1.000	0	0	0	/1		-0.3
2001 Col N	35	42	5	10	2	1	3	9	3-0	0	13	.238	.289	.548	91	-1	0-0	.818	-1	106	0	O12(8/0/4)/1	15	-0.1
2003 Mil N	70	70	12	21	1	0	7	12	6-0	0	13	.300	.355	.614	147	4	0-0	1.000	0	145	346	P42,O3L,D4	25	0.0
2004 Mil N	77	63	2	17	3	0	1	7	5-1	0	26	.270	.324	.365	77	6	0-0	1.000	-1	33	0	P32	40	0.0
Total 6	260	306	34	76	10	1	16	46	30-1	0	76	.248	.315	.444	91	3	1-0	1.000	-2	95	191	P74,O50(41/0/10),D4,1b2		-0.7

KILDUFF, PETE Peter John B4.4.1893 Weir City KS D2.14.1930 Pittsburg KS BR/TR/5-7/155 d4.18 Mil 1918

YEAR TM LG	G	AB	R	H	2B	3B	HR	RBI	BB-IB	HP	SO	AVG	OBP	SLG	AOPS	ABR	SB-CS	FA	FR	RNG	THR	GAMES AT POSITION	DL	BFW
1917 NY N	31	78	12	16	3	1	0	12	4	1	11	.205	.253	.282	66	-3	2	.954	-1	97	160	2b21,S5/3		-0.5
Chi N	56	202	23	56	9	5	0	15	12	2	19	.277	.324	.371	105	1	11	.920	-14	76	83	S51,2b5		-1.1
Year	87	280	35	72	12	5	1	27	16	3	30	.257	.304	.346	95	-2	13	.917	-15	77	79	S56,2b26/3		-1.6
1918 Chi N	30	93	7	19	2	2	0	13	7	1	7	.204	.267	.269	62	-4	1	.935	-4	82	162	2b30		-0.8
1919 Chi N	31	88	5	24	4	2	0	8	10	2	5	.273	.360	.364	117	2	1	.974	-3	105	129	3b14,2b8,S7		0.1
Bro N	32	73	9	22	3	1	0	8	12	1	11	.301	.407	.370	132	4	5	.862	-4	91	134	3b26/2		0.2
Year	63	161	14	46	7	3	0	16	22	3	16	.286	.382	.366	124	6	6	.903	-7	96	132	3b40,2b9,S7		1.1
1920 †Bro N	141	478	62	130	26	8	0	58	58	3	43	.272	.351	.360	101	3	2-9	.967	7	101	111	2b134,3b5		1.0
1921 Bro N	107	372	45	107	15	10	3	45	31	1	36	.288	.344	.406	94	-3	6-6	.963	12	106	107	2b105/3		-0.1
Total 5	428	1384	163	374	62	28	4	159	134	11	132	.270	.338	.364	98	0	28-15	.963	-7	101	117	2b304,S63,3b47		

KILEY, JOHN John Frederick B7.1.1859 Dedham MA D12.18.1940 Norwood MA BL/TL/5-7/147 d5.1

YEAR TM LG	G	AB	R	H	2B	3B	HR	RBI	BB-IB	HP	SO	AVG	OBP	SLG	AOPS	ABR	SB-CS	FA	FR	RNG	THR	GAMES AT POSITION	DL	BFW
1884 Was AA	14	56	9	12	1	2	0		3	1		.214	.267	.321	103	-3		.571	-3	36	0	O14(13/1/1)		-0.3
1891 Bos N	1	2	0	0	0	0	0	0	1	1		.000	.500	.000	45	0	0	1.000	-3	0	121	0/P		0.0
Total 2	15	58	9	12	1	2	0	3	2	1		.207	.281	.310	102	0	0	.571	-3	36	0	O14(13/1/1)/P		-0.3

KILHULLEN, PAT Joseph Isadore B8.10.1890 Carbondale PA D11.2.1922 Oakland CA BR/TR/5-9/175 d6.10 Col Villanova

YEAR TM LG	G	AB	R	H	2B	3B	HR	RBI	BB-IB	HP	SO	AVG	OBP	SLG	AOPS	ABR	SB-CS	FA	FR	RNG	THR	GAMES AT POSITION	DL	BFW
1914 Pit N	1	1	0	0	0	0	0	0	0	0		.000	.000	.000	-99	0	0	—	-0	0	0	/C		0.0

KILLEBREW, HARMON Harmon Clayton "Killer" B6.29.1936 Payette ID BR/TR/5-11/213(193-214) d6.23 HF1984 OF(470/0/1)

YEAR TM LG	G	AB	R	H	2B	3B	HR	RBI	BB-IB	HP	SO	AVG	OBP	SLG	AOPS	ABR	SB-CS	FA	FR	RNG	THR	GAMES AT POSITION	DL	BFW
1954 Was A	9	13	1	4	1	0	0	3	2	0	3	.308	.400	.385	122	1	0-0	1.000	-1	47	0	2b3		0.0
1955 Was A	38	80	12	16	1	0	4	7	9-0	1	31	.200	.281	.363	76	-3	0-0	.935	2	112	67	3b23,2b3		-0.1
1956 Was A	44	99	10	22	0	0	5	13	10-0	1	39	.222	.291	.394	80	-3	0-0	.951	0	106	72	3b20,2b4		0.1
1957 Was A	9	31	4	9	2	0	2	5	2-0	0	25	.290	.333	.548	139	1	0-0	.947	0	116	141	3b7/2		-0.4
1958 Was A	13	31	2	6	0	0	0	2	0-0	1	12	.194	.212	.194	15	-4	0-0	1.000	-0	92	63	3b9		-0.4
1959 Was A★	153	546	98	132	20	2	42	105	90-1	7	116	.242	.354	.516	137	28	3-2	.938	-3	105	65	3b150,O4L		1.0
1960 Was A★	124	442	84	122	19	1	31	80	71-3	1	106	.276	.375	.534	145	28	1-0	.987	-9	71	106	1b71,3b65		1.6
1961 Min A★	150	541	94	156	20	7	46	122	107-6	3	109	.288	.405	.606	159	47	1-2	.987	-5	86	92	1b119,3b45,O2L		1.3
1962 Min A★	155	552	85	134	21	1	48	126	106-6	1	142	.243	.366	.545	147	37	1-2	.967	-8	86	80	O151L,1b4		2.3
1963 Min A★	142	515	88	133	18	0	45	96	72-4	3	105	.258	.349	.555	147	32	0-0	.987	-1	93	80	O137L		2.8
1964 Min A★	158	577	95	156	11	1	49	111	93-5	8	135	.270	.377	.548	153	43	0-0	.971	-10	89	77	O157(157/0/1)		1.9
1965 †Min A★	113	401	78	108	16	1	25	75	72-12	4	69	.269	.384	.501	144	25	1-0	.972	-9	81	124	1b72,3b44/OL		1.6
1966 Min A★	162	569	89	160	27	1	39	110	103-18	4	98	.281	.391	.538	155	44	0-0	.951	-16	89	66	3b107,1b42,O18L		4.2
1967 Min A★	163	547	105	147	24	1	44	113	131-15	3	111	.269	.408	.558	170	54	1-0	.992	-6	84	93	1b160,3b3		4.1
1968 Min A★	100	295	40	62	7	2	17	40	70-9	2	70	.210	.361	.420	130	14	0-0	.994	5	106	95	1b77,3b11	53	1.1

YEAR	TM LG	G	AB	R	H	2B	3B	HR	RBI	BB-IB	HP	SO	AVG	OBP	SLG	AOPS	ABR	SB-CS	FA	FR	RNG	THR	GAMES AT POSITION	DL	BFW
1969 †Min A★		162	555	106	153	20	2	49	140	145-20	5	84	.276	.427	.584	176	64	8-2	.929	-14	97	67	3b105,1b80		4.6
1970 †Min A★		157	527	96	143	20	1	41	113	128-23	2	84	.271	.411	.546	161	49	0-3	.948	-25	79	59	3b138,1b28		2.2
1971 Min A★		147	500	61	127	19	1	28	119	114-14	0	96	.254	.386	.464	138	30	3-2	.997	-12	109	74	1b90,3b64		1.2
1972 Min A		139	433	53	100	13	2	26	74	94-12	1	91	.231	.367	.450	136	23	0-1	.992	11	140	92	1b130		2.7
1973 Min A		69	248	29	60	9	1	5	32	41-2	1	59	.242	.352	.347	93	-1	0-0	.998	5	130	93	1b57,D9	54	0.0
1974 Min A		122	333	28	74	7	0	13	54	45-6	0	61	.222	.312	.360	91	-4	0-0	.992	-4	131	93	D57,1b33		-0.5
1975 KC A		106	312	25	62	13	0	14	44	54-4	1	70	.199	.317	.375	93	-2	1-2	1.000	-1	0	126	D92,1b6		-0.6
Total 22		2435	8147	1283	2086	290	24	573	1584	1559-160	48	1699	.256	.376	.509	142	496	19-18	.992	-95	97	96	1b969,3b791,O470L,D158,2b11	107	32.0

KILLEFER, RED Wade B4.13.1885 Bloomingdale MI D9.4.1958 Los Angeles CA BR/TR/5-9/175 b-Bill Col Michigan OF(135/135/27)

YEAR	TM LG	G	AB	R	H	2B	3B	HR	RBI	BB-IB	HP	SO	AVG	OBP	SLG	AOPS	ABR	SB-CS	FA	FR	RNG	THR	GAMES AT POSITION	DL	BFW
1907 Det A		1	4	0	0	0	0	0	0	0			.000	.000	.000	-97	-1	0	1.000	0			/OR		-0.1
1908 Det A		28	75	9	16	1	0	0	11	3	1		.213	.253	.227	54	-4	0	.956	-5	90	171	2b16,S7,3b4		-1.0
1909 Det A		23	61	6	17	2	2	1	4	3	3		.279	.343	.426	137	2	2	.912	-1	115	53	2b17/OR		0.1
Was A		40	121	11	21	1	0	0	5	13	2		.174	.265	.182	43	-7	4	.957	-4	36	0	O24(6/17/1),3b6,C3,2b3/S		-1.4
Year		63	182	17	38	3	2	1	9	16	5		.209	.291	.264	76	-5	6	.957	-5	36	0	O25(6/17/2),2b20,3b6,C3/S		-1.3
1910 Was A		106	345	35	79	17	1	0	24	29	16		.229	.318	.284	93	0	17	.940	-4	97	94	2b88,O12(6/0/6)		-0.5
1914 Cin N		42	141	16	39	6	1	0	12	20	5	18	.277	.386	.333	111	3	11	.968	-4	80	103	O37(1/18/18),2b5/3		-0.4
1915 Cin N		155	555	75	151	25	11	1	41	38	19	33	.272	.340	.362	110	8	12-18	.970	1	102	93	O150(79/73/0),1b2		-0.4
1916 Cin N		70	234	29	57	9	1	1	18	21	8		.244	.327	.303	96	0	7	.966	-0	102	83	O68(43/27/0)		-0.4
NY N		2	1	0	1	0	0	0	1	1	0		1.000	1.000	1.000	544	1	0	—	0			/H		0.1
Year		72	235	29	58	9	1	1	19	22	8		.247	.332	.306	99	1	7	.966	-0	102	83	O68(43/27/0)		-0.3
Total 7		467	1537	181	381	61	16	3	116	128	54	59	.248	.328	.314	98	2	57-18	.965	-18	93	88	O293L,2b129,3b11,S8,C3,1b2		-3.9

KILLEFER, BILL William "Reindeer Bill" B10.10.1887 Bloomingdale MI D7.3.1960 Elsmere DE BR/TR/5-10.5/170 d9.13 M9/C6 b-Red Col St. Edwards

YEAR	TM LG	G	AB	R	H	2B	3B	HR	RBI	BB-IB	HP	SO	AVG	OBP	SLG	AOPS	ABR	SB-CS	FA	FR	RNG	THR	GAMES AT POSITION	DL	BFW
1909 StL A		11	29	0	4	0	0	0	0	0			.138	.138	.138	-14	-4	2	.905	0	99	166	C11		-0.3
1910 StL A		74	193	14	24	2	2	0	7	12	2		.124	.184	.155	7	-21	0	.938	3	89	124	C73		-1.3
1911 Phi N		6	16	3	3	0	0	0	2	0			.188	.188	.188	5	-2	0	.975	1	91	137	C6		-0.1
1912 Phi N		85	268	18	60	6	3	1	21	4		14	.224	.241	.280	40	-24	6	.973	11	92	118	C85		-0.6
1913 Phi N		120	360	25	88	14	3	0	24	4	1	17	.244	.255	.300	56	-22	2-4	.988	8	111	117	C118/1		-0.5
1914 Phi N		98	299	27	70	10	1	0	27	8	4	17	.234	.261	.274	56	-17	3-3	.978	4	77	117	C90		-0.5
1915 †Phi N		105	320	26	76	9	2	0	24	18	4	14	.237	.287	.278	70	-12	5-3	.972	10	117	97	C104		0.8
1916 Phi N		97	286	22	62	5	4	3	27	8	3	14	.217	.246	.294	63	-14	2	.985	-1	111	92	C91		-0.8
1917 Phi N		125	409	28	112	12	0	0	31	15	4	21	.274	.306	.303	84	-8	4	.984	11	119	89	C120/OL		1.5
1918 †Chi N		104	331	30	77	10	3	0	22	17	3	10	.233	.276	.281	68	-13	5	.982	7	110	95	C104		0.4
1919 Chi N		103	315	17	90	10	1	0	22	15	2	8	.286	.322	.330	96	-2	5	.987	14	107	95	C100		2.3
1920 Chi N		62	191	16	42	7	1	0	16	8	2	5	.220	.280	.267	56	-10	2-2	.977	12	114	117	C61		0.8
1921 Chi N		45	133	11	43	1	0	0	16	4	3		.323	.357	.331	83	-3	3-3	.964	-1	98	103	C42,M		-0.2
Total 13		1035	3150	237	751	86	21	4	240	113	35	126	.238	.273	.283	63	-152	39-12	.976	79	105	105	C1005/OL1		1.5

KIMBALL, GENE Eugene Boynton B8.31.1850 Rochester NY D8.2.1882 Rochester NY 5-10/160 d5.4

YEAR	TM LG	G	AB	R	H	2B	3B	HR	RBI	BB-IB	HP	SO	AVG	OBP	SLG	AOPS	ABR	SB-CS	FA	FR	RNG	THR	GAMES AT POSITION	DL	BFW
1871 Cle NA		29	131	18	25	1	0	0	9	3		2	.191	.209	.198	19	-13	5-1	.743	-7	83	59	2b17,O9(2/1/7),S6,3b2		-1.3

KIMBLE, DICK Richard Lewis B7.27.1915 Buchtel OH D5.7.2001 Toledo OH BL/TR/5-9/160 d8.20 Col Ohio U.

YEAR	TM LG	G	AB	R	H	2B	3B	HR	RBI	BB-IB	HP	SO	AVG	OBP	SLG	AOPS	ABR	SB-CS	FA	FR	RNG	THR	GAMES AT POSITION	DL	BFW
1945 Was A		20	49	5	12	2	0	0	2	2			.245	.315	.306	88	-1	0-0	.950	-3	96	69	S15		-0.3

KIMM, BRUCE Bruce Edward B6.29.1951 Cedar Rapids IA BR/TR/5-11/175* [ChiA69 7/145] d5.4 M1/C12

YEAR	TM LG	G	AB	R	H	2B	3B	HR	RBI	BB-IB	HP	SO	AVG	OBP	SLG	AOPS	ABR	SB-CS	FA	FR	RNG	THR	GAMES AT POSITION	DL	BFW
1976 Det A		63	152	13	40	8	0	1	6	15-0	0	20	.263	.329	.336	91	-1	4-3	.970	2	113	139	C61,D2		0.3
1977 Det A		14	25	2	2	1	0	0	1	0-0	0	4	.080	.115	.120	-34	-5	0-1	.958	-1	110	85	C12,D2		-0.6
1979 Chi N		9	11	0	1	0	0	0	0	0-0	0	0	.091	.091	.091	-46	-2	0-1	.969	1	69	72	C9		-0.2
1980 Chi A		100	251	20	61	10	1	0	19	17-0	0	26	.243	.290	.291	60	-14	1-3	.985	-3	107	84	C98		-1.4
Total 4		186	439	35	104	19	1	1	26	32-0	1	50	.237	.290	.292	62	-22	5-8	.977	-1	108	104	C180,D4		-1.9

KIMMICK, WALLY Walter Lyons B5.30.1897 Turtle Creek PA D7.24.1989 Boswell PA BR/TR/5-11/174 d9.13

YEAR	TM LG	G	AB	R	H	2B	3B	HR	RBI	BB-IB	HP	SO	AVG	OBP	SLG	AOPS	ABR	SB-CS	FA	FR	RNG	THR	GAMES AT POSITION	DL	BFW
1919 StL N		2	1	1	0	0	0	0	0	1	0		.000	.500	.000	61	0	1	1.000	0	130	0	/S		0.0
1921 Cin N		3	6	0	1	0	0	0	0	1	0	1	.167	.167	.167	-12	-1	0-0	.667	0	94	359	3b2		-0.1
1922 Cin N		39	89	11	22	2	1	0	12	3	0	12	.247	.272	.292	46	-7	0-0	.965	2	109	109	S30,2b3/3		-0.3
1923 Cin N		29	80	11	18	2	1	0	6	5	0	15	.225	.271	.275	45	-7	3-0	.972	6	127	78	2b17,3b4/S		0.1
1925 Phi N		70	141	16	43	3	2	1	10	22	0	26	.305	.399	.376	91	-1	0-3	.904	-3	106	51	S28,3b21,2b13		-0.2
1926 Phi N		20	28	0	6	2	1	0	2	1	0	7	.214	.290	.357	70	-1	0	1.000	-2	0	0	1b5,S4,3b4/2		-0.3
Total 6		163	345	39	90	9	5	1	31	34	0	61	.261	.327	.325	67	-17	4-3	.933	3	107	84	S64,2b34,3b32,1b5		-0.8

KINDALL, JERRY Gerald Donald "Slim" B5.27.1935 St.Paul MN BR/TR (BB 1960p)/6-2.5/175* d7.1 Col Minnesota

YEAR	TM LG	G	AB	R	H	2B	3B	HR	RBI	BB-IB	HP	SO	AVG	OBP	SLG	AOPS	ABR	SB-CS	FA	FR	RNG	THR	GAMES AT POSITION	DL	BFW
1956 Chi N		32	55	7	9	1	0	0		6-1	0	17	.164	.246	.218	27	-6	0-0	.956	0	102	101	S18		-0.4
1957 Chi N		72	181	18	29	3	0	6	12	8-0	0	48	.160	.196	.276	25	-20	1-0	.920	-5	96	46	2b28,3b19,S9		-2.4
1958 Chi N		3	6	0	1	1	0	0		0-0	0	3	.167	.167	.333	29	-1	0-0	1.000	1	104	154	2b3		0.0
1960 Chi N		89	246	17	59	16	2	2	23	5-3	0	52	.240	.253	.346	63	-13	4-3	.966	8	116	101	2b82,S2		0.0
1961 Chi N		96	310	37	75	22	3	9	44	18-0	2	89	.242	.288	.419	84	-8	2-2	.950	2	102	110	2b50,S47		0.1
1962 Cle A		154	530	51	123	21	1	13	55	45-9	0	107	.232	.290	.349	74	-21	4-3	.978	23	113	112	2b154		1.5
1963 Cle A		86	234	27	48	4	1	5	20	18-0	2	71	.205	.266	.295	58	-14	3-1	.958	-6	86	69	S46,2b37,1b4		-1.4
1964 Cle A		23	25	5	9	1	0	2	2	2-0	0	7	.360	.407	.640	188	3	0-0	.989	2	169	85	1b23		0.4
Min A		62	128	8	19	2	0	1	6	7-1	1	44	.148	.199	.188	8	-16	0-0	.969	-1	100	76	2b51,S7/1		-1.5
Year		85	153	13	28	3	0	3	8	9-1	1	51	.183	.233	.261	37	-13	0-0	.969	1	100	76	2b51,1b24,S7		-1.1
1965 Min A		125	342	41	67	12	1	6	36	36-3	3	97	.196	.274	.289	59	-18	2-2	.963	-4	98	105	2b106,3b10,S7		-1.4
Total 9		742	2057	211	439	83	9	44	198	145-17	8	535	.213	.266	.327	62	-114	17-11	.967	20	107	101	2b511,S136,3b29,1b28		-5.1

KINER, RALPH Ralph McPherran B10.27.1922 Santa Rita NM BR/TR/6-2/195* d4.16 HF1975

YEAR	TM LG	G	AB	R	H	2B	3B	HR	RBI	BB-IB	HP	SO	AVG	OBP	SLG	AOPS	ABR	SB-CS	FA	FR	RNG	THR	GAMES AT POSITION	DL	BFW
1946 Pit N		144	502	63	124	17	3	23	81	74	1	109	.247	.345	.430	116	10	3	.969	-5	102	47	O140(64/76/0)		-0.1
1947 Pit N		152	565	118	177	23	4	51	127	98	2	81	.313	.417	.639	172	58	1	.983	8	115	69	O152L		5.3
1948 Pit N★		156	555	104	147	19	5	40	123	112	1	61	.265	.391	.533	145	37	1	.975	3	111	47	O154L		2.7
1949 Pit N★		152	549	116	170	19	5	54	127	117	1	61	.310	.432	.658	183	67	6	.979	-3	94	95	O152L		5.1
1950 Pit N★		150	547	112	149	21	6	47	118	122	3	79	.272	.408	.590	154	45	2	.965	-5	89	115	O150L		2.8
1951 Pit N★		151	531	124	164	31	6	42	109	137	2	57	.309	.452	.627	182	69	2-1	.967	-9	94	82	O94L,1b58		5.0
1952 Pit N☆		149	516	90	126	17	2	37	87	110	7	77	.244	.384	.500	140	31	3-0	.970	-10	85	81	O149L		1.1
1953 Pit N		41	148	27	40	6	1	7	29	25	2	21	.270	.383	.466	121	5	1-0	1.000	1	93	154	O41L		0.4
Chi N★		117	414	73	117	14	2	28	87	75	1	67	.283	.394	.529	135	23	1-1	.964	-5	98	65	O116L		1.1
Year		158	562	100	157	20	3	35	116	100	3	88	.279	.391	.512	131	28	2-1	.973	-4	97	88	O157L		1.5
1954 Chi N		147	557	88	159	36	5	22	73	76	2	90	.285	.371	.487	121	18	2-0	.971	1	105	67	O147L		1.0
1955 Cle A		113	321	56	78	13	0	18	54	65-1	0	46	.243	.367	.452	116	8	0-0	.986	-6	90	32	O87L		-0.2
Total 10		1472	5205	971	1451	216	39	369	1015	1011-1	24	749	.279	.398	.548	148	371	22-2	.974	-30	99	74	O1382(1306/76/0),1b58		24.2

KING, CHICK Charles Gilbert B11.10.1930 Paris TN BR/TR/6-2/190* d8.27 Col Memphis

YEAR	TM LG	G	AB	R	H	2B	3B	HR	RBI	BB-IB	HP	SO	AVG	OBP	SLG	AOPS	ABR	SB-CS	FA	FR	RNG	THR	GAMES AT POSITION	DL	BFW
1954 Det A		11	28	4	6	0	0	0	0			8	.214	.290	.286	59	-2	0-0	.958	1	105	138	O7C		-0.2
1955 Det A		7	21	3	5	0	0	0		1-0	0	2	.238	.273	.238	39	-2	0-0	.923	-1	100	0	O6L		-0.3
1956 Det A		6	9	0	2	0	0	0		1-0	0	4	.222	.300	.222	40	-1	0-0	.800	-0	109	0	O3L		-0.1
1958 Chi N		8	8	1	2	0	0	0		3-1	0	1	.250	.455	.250	95	0	0-0	1.000	-0	95	0	O7C		-0.1
1959 Chi N		7	3	3	0	0	0	0		0-0	0	1	.000	.000	.000	-99	-1	0-0	1.000	0	118	0	/OC		-0.1
StL N		5	7	0	3	1	0	0		0-0	0	2	.429	.375	.429	121	0	0-0	1.000	0	124	0	O4(1/3/0)		0.0
Year		12	10	3	3	1	0	0		0-0	0	3	.300	.273	.300	59	-1	0-0	1.000	0	123	0	O5(1/4/0)		-0.1
Total 5		44	76	11	18	1	0	0	8	8-1	0	8	.237	.306	.263	56	-6	0-0	.947	-0	106	51	O28(10/18/0)		-0.7

KING, LEE Edward Lee B3.28.1894 Waltham MA D9.7.1938 Chelsea MA BR/TR/5-10/160 d6.24 Mil 1918 Col Massachusetts

YEAR	TM LG	G	AB	R	H	2B	3B	HR	RBI	BB-IB	HP	SO	AVG	OBP	SLG	AOPS	ABR	SB-CS	FA	FR	RNG	THR	GAMES AT POSITION	DL	BFW
1916 Phi A		42	144	13	27	1	2	0	8	7	1	15	.188	.230	.230	38	-12	4	1.000	-5	81	53	O22(21/2/1),S11,3b5,2b2		-1.9
1919 Bos N		2	1	0	0	0	0	0	0	0	0		.000	.000	.000	-99	-0	0	—	0			/H		0.0
Total 2		44	145	13	27	1	2	0	8	7	1	15	.186	.229	.221	37	-12	4	1.000	-5	81	53	O22(21/2/1),S11,3b5,2b2		-1.9

YEAR	TM	LG	G	AB	R	H	2B	3B	HR	RBI	BB-IB	HP	SO	AVG	OBP	SLG	AOPS	ABR	SB-CS	FA	FR	RNG	THR	GAMES AT POSITION	DL	BFW

KING, HAL Harold B2.1.1944 Oviedo FL BL/TR/6-1/200* d9.6

																										-0.2
1967	Hou	N	15	44	2	11	1	2	0	6	2-0	0	9	.250	.283	.364	87	-1	0-0	1.000	-2	57	139	C11		-0.8
1968	Hou	N	27	55	4	8	2	1	0	2	7-0	0	16	.145	.242	.218	40	-4	0-0	.968	-3	38	58	C19		-0.1
1970	Atl	N	89	204	29	53	8	0	11	30	32-6	2	41	.260	.364	.461	113	4	1-0	.985	-8	80	73	C62		-0.1
1971	Atl	N	86	198	14	41	9	0	5	19	29-5	4	43	.207	.320	.328	79	-4	0-0	.983	-2	146	90	C60		-0.3
1972	Tex	A	50	122	12	22	5	0	4	12	25-1	3	35	.180	.333	.320	98	1	0-0	.970	-5	106	90	C38		-0.1
1973	†Cin	N	35	43	5	8	0	1	0	4	6-0	0	10	.186	.286	.465	109	0	0-0	1.000	-1	131	6	C9		-0.1
1974	Cin	N	20	17	1	3	1	0	0	3	3-0	0	4	.176	.300	.235	52	-1	0-0	1.000	-0	0	199	C5		-2.0
Total	7		322	683	67	146	26	3	24	82	104-12	9	158	.214	.325	.366	92	-5	1-0	.982	-21	102	83	C204		

KING, JIM James Hubert B8.27.1932 Elkins AR BL/TR/6-0/185* d4.17

																										0.0
1955	Chi	N	113	301	43	77	12	3	11	45	24-1	2	39	.256	.312	.425	95	-3	2-1	.990	7	111	141	O93(17/0/76)		0.8
1956	Chi	N	118	317	32	79	13	2	15	54	30-5	1	40	.249	.313	.445	103	1	1-2	.990	12	123	189	O82(69/0/14)		0.8
1957	StL	N	22	35	1	11	0	0	2	4	2-1	0	2	.314	.385	.314	89	0	0-0	1.000	-1	70	0	O8(1/3/4)		-0.1
1958	SF	N	34	56	8	12	2	1	2	8	10-1	1	8	.214	.343	.393	96	0	0-1	1.000	-1	92	0	O15(9/0/6)		-0.2
1961	Was	A	110	263	43	71	12	1	11	46	38-3	2	45	.270	.363	.449	118	8	4-0	.980	1	97	127	O91(25/0/67)/C		0.2
1962	Was	A	132	333	39	81	15	0	11	35	55-9	3	37	.243	.353	.387	101	2	4-2	.987	2	95	164	O123(2/0/122)		-0.4
1963	Was	A	136	459	61	106	16	5	24	62	45-3	1	43	.231	.300	.444	106	2	3-0	.973	10	**122**	147	O121R		0.8
1964	Was	A	134	415	46	100	15	1	18	55	55-7	5	65	.241	.335	.412	108	5	3-1	.993	4	106	163	O88(1/0/87)		0.7
1965	Was	A	120	258	46	55	10	2	14	49	44-2	5	50	.213	.337	.430	119	7	1-0	.987	-1	105	92	O85R		0.1
1966	Was	A	117	310	41	77	14	2	10	38	38-2	0	41	.248	.330	.403	111	5	4-0	.987	5	94	92	O85R		-0.4
1967	Was	A	47	100	10	21	2	2	1	12	15-0	3	13	.210	.328	.300	91	-1	1-1	.962	-1	111	0	O31R/C		-0.9
	Chi	A	23	50	2	6	1	0	0	2	4-0	0	16	.120	.185	.140	-3	-6	0-0	1.000	-1	83	0	O12(1/0/12)		-0.3
	Cle	A	19	21	2	3	0	0	0	0	1-0	0	2	.143	.182	.143	-3	-3	0-0	1.000	-0	54	0	/OR		-1.6
	Year		89	171	14	30	3	2	1	14	20-0	3	31	.175	.272	.234	53	-10	1-1	.971	-3	101	0	O44(1/0/44)/C		
Total	11		1125	2918	374	699	112	19	77	401	363-35	23	400	.240	.326	.411	104	17	23-8	.984	37	107	140	O851(145/3/707),C2		0.8

KING, JEFF Jeffrey Wayne B12.26.1964 Marion IN BR/TR/6-1/180* [PitN86 1/1] d6.2 Col Arkansas-Monticello

																										-1.1
1989	Pit	N	75	215	31	42	13	3	5	19	20-1	2	34	.195	.266	.353	79	-6	4-2	.995	-1	79	112	1b46,3b13,2b7/S		-1.1
1990	†Pit	N	127	371	46	91	17	1	14	53	21-1	1	50	.245	.283	.410	92	-6	3-3	.938	6	**114**	117	3b115/1		0.0
1991	Pit	N	33	109	16	26	1	1	4	18	14-3	1	15	.239	.328	.376	99	0	3-1	.975	-4	93	0	3b33	131	-0.4
1992	†Pit	N	130	480	56	111	21	2	14	65	27-3	2	56	.231	.272	.371	82	-14	4-6	.953	3	109	137	3b156,2b2,S2		-1.9
1993	Pit	N	158	611	82	180	35	3	9	98	59-4	4	54	.295	.356	.406	105	6	8-6	.964	14	**113**	108	3b156,1b32,2b32,S6/OR		2.0
1994	Pit	N	94	339	36	89	23	0	5	42	30-1	0	38	.263	.316	.375	80	-10	3-2	.955	7	106	**182**	3b91/2	15	-0.2
1995	Pit	N	122	445	61	118	27	2	18	87	55-5	1	63	.265	.342	.456	107	5	7-4	.997	3	89	93	1b92,2b71,3b17	15	0.1
1996	Pit	N	155	591	91	160	36	4	30	111	70-3	2	95	.271	.346	.497	116	13	15-1	.996	21	**155**	110	1b150,D2		1.5
1997	KC	A	155	543	84	129	30	1	28	112	89-4	2	96	.238	.341	.451	103	3	16-5	.995	6	120	110	1b112,D16,3b4	16	1.2
1998	KC	A	131	486	83	128	17	1	24	93	42-1	2	73	.263	.319	.451	95	-5	10-2	.990	-1	127	110	1b20/D	20	-0.8
1999	KC	A	21	72	14	17	2	0	3	11	15-1	1	10	.236	.385	.389	96	0	2-0	.990	1	127	110	1b20/D		0.4
Total	11		1201	4262	600	1091	222	18	154	709	442-27	20	584	.256	.324	.425	99	-14	75-32	.953	48	109	119	3b586,1b488,2b121,D19,S11/OR	197	

KING, LEE Lee B12.26.1892 Hundred WV D9.16.1967 Shinnston WV BR/TR/5-8/160 d9.20

																										-0.4
1916	Pit	N	8	18	0	2	0	0	1	0	0	7	.111	.111	.111	-31	-3	0-0	.714	-1	57	211	O8(2/0/4)		-0.8
1917	Pit	N	111	381	32	95	14	5	1	35	15	2	58	.249	.281	.320	82	-9	8	.968	8	112	121	O102(7/0/95)		-0.9
1918	Pit	N	36	112	9	26	3	2	1	11	11	0	15	.232	.301	.321	87	-2	3	.909	-5	88	0	O36(32/0/4)		-0.4
1919	Pit	N	21	20	5	2	1	0	0	1	1	0	6	.100	.143	.150	-12	-3	0	.667	-1	52	0	O7(2/1/3)		-1.9
1920	NY	N	93	261	32	72	11	4	7	42	21	2	38	.276	.335	.429	120	6	3-7	.951	-16	73	61	O84(0/83/1)		-0.6
1921	NY	N	39	94	17	21	4	2	0	7	13	1	6	.223	.324	.309	68	-4	0-2	.921	-0	86	164	O35(0/24/12)/1		-1.2
	Phi	N	64	216	25	58	19	4	4	32	8	1	37	.269	.298	.449	88	-4	1-4	.911	-2	94	114	O57(55/1/2)		-1.8
	Year		103	310	42	79	23	6	4	39	21	2	43	.255	.306	.406	83	-8	1-6	.914	-2	92	129	O92(55/25/14)/1		-0.2
1922	Phi	N	19	53	8	12	5	1	2	13	8	0	6	.226	.328	.472	95	0	0-0	.946	-1	102	54	O15(11/4/0)		-0.3
	†NY	N	20	34	6	6	3	0	0	2	5	0	2	.176	.282	.265	41	-3	1-0	1.000	-0	77	61	1b5,O5(0/1/4)		-0.5
	Year		39	87	14	18	8	1	2	15	13	0	8	.207	.310	.391	76	-3	1-0	.961	-1	107	40	O20(11/5/4),1b5		-1.1
Total	7		411	1189	134	294	60	18	15	144	82	6	175	.247	.299	.366	87	-22	16-13	.940	-17	93	92	O349(109/114/125),1b6		-6.7

KING, LYNN Lynn Paul "Dig" B11.28.1907 Villisca IA D5.11.1972 Atlantic IA BL/TR/5-9/165 d9.21 Col Drake

																										-0.1
1935	StL	N	8	22	6	4	0	0	0	4	0	1	.182	.308	.182	34	-2	1	1.000	1	130	0	O6C		-0.8
1936	StL	N	78	100	12	19	2	1	0	10	9	0	14	.190	.257	.230	32	-10	2	.984	2	128	55	O34(7/12/15)		-0.2
1939	StL	N	89	85	10	20	2	0	0	11	15	0	3	.235	.350	.259	62	-4	2	.982	2	132	78	O44(14/29/1)		-1.1
Total	3		175	207	28	43	4	1	0	21	28	0	18	.208	.302	.237	45	-16	6	.986	5	130	54	O84(21/47/16)		

KING, MART Marshal Ney B12.1849 Troy NY D10.19.1911 Troy NY TR/5-9.5/176 d5.8

																										-0.6
1871	Chi	NA	20	101	23	21	1	0	2	16	8		1	.208	.266	.277	51	-7	5-0	.786	-2	0	0	O11(1/10/0),C9,S3/3		-0.2
1872	Tro	NA	3	11	0	0	0	0	0	1	0			.000	.000	.000	-99	-3	0-0	.857	-0	0	0	O3C		
Total	2	NA	23	112	23	21	1	0	2	17	8		2	.188	.242	.250	39	-10	5-0	.810	-2	0	0	O14(1/13/0),C9,S3/3		-0.8

KING, SAM Samuel Warren B5.17.1852 Peabody MA D8.11.1922 Peabody MA BL/TL/6-0/? d5.1

| | | | | | | | | | | | | | | | | | | | | | | | | | | -0.4 |
| 1884 | Was | AA | 12 | 45 | 3 | 8 | 2 | 0 | 0 | | 1 | 1 | | .178 | .213 | .222 | 48 | -2 | | .912 | -1 | 96 | 85 | 1b12 | | |

KING, STEVE Stephen F. B1842 Troy NY D7.8.1895 Troy NY 5-9/175 d5.9

																										1.0
1871	Tro	NA	**29**	144	45	57	10	6	0	34	1		1	.396	.400	.549	167	12	3-3	.833	3	182	0	O29L		0.2
1872	Tro	NA	**25**	128	33	39	8	0	0	20	1		2	.305	.310	.367	106	1	1-1	.776	1	183	203	O25L		0.2
Total	2	NA	54	272	78	96	18	6	0	54	2		3	.353	.358	.463	139	13	4-4	.807	4	182	96	O54L		

KINGDON, WES Westcott William B7.4.1900 Los Angeles CA D4.19.1975 San Juan Capistrano CA BR/TR/5-8/148 d6.12

| | | | | | | | | | | | | | | | | | | | | | | | | | | 0.1 |
| 1932 | Was | A | 18 | 34 | 10 | 11 | 3 | 1 | 0 | 3 | 4 | 0 | 3 | .324 | .410 | .471 | 129 | 2 | 0-0 | .929 | -1 | 92 | 122 | 3b8,S4 | | |

KINGERY, MIKE Michael Scott B3.29.1961 St.James MN BL/TL/6-0/180* d7.7

																										-0.8
1986	KC	A	62	209	25	54	8	5	3	14	12-2	0	30	.258	.296	.388	83	-6	7-3	.973	-1	88	166	O59(1/13/51)		0.7
1987	Sea	A	120	354	38	99	25	4	9	52	27-0	2	43	.280	.329	.449	100	0	7-9	.992	14	118	219	O114(0/6/111),D4		-0.3
1988	Sea	A	57	123	21	25	6	0	1	9	19-1	1	25	.203	.313	.276	64	-5	3-1	.989	3	106	174	O44(9/24/13),1b10		0.0
1989	Sea	A	31	76	14	17	3	0	2	6	7-0	0	14	.224	.286	.342	75	-3	1-1	1.000	3	137	0	O23(2/20/1)		0.0
1990	SF	N	105	207	24	61	7	1	0	24	12-0	1	19	.295	.335	.338	89	-3	6-1	.978	4	107	175	O95(15/9/74)		-0.9
1991	SF	N	91	110	13	20	2	2	0	8	15-1	0	21	.182	.280	.236	48	-8	1-0	.975	-0	113	0	O38(14/2/22),1b6		-0.8
1992	Oak	A	12	28	3	3	0	0	0	0	3-0	0	3	.107	.138	.107	-32	-5	0-0	1.000	-1	78	0	O10(2/6/2)		0.8
1994	Col	N	105	301	56	105	27	8	4	41	30-2	2	26	.349	.402	.532	123	11	5-7	.979	-1	96	111	O98(20/77/2)/1		-1.6
1995	†Col	N	119	350	66	94	18	4	8	37	45-1	0	40	.269	.351	.411	78	-10	13-5	.979	-8	86	84	O108C,1b5		-1.6
1996	Pit	N	117	276	32	68	12	2	3	27	23-2	1	29	.246	.304	.337	67	-13	2-1	.985	-3	93	59	O83(5/64/16)		-4.3
Total	10		819	2034	292	546	108	26	30	219	191-9	7	248	.268	.330	.391	86	-42	45-28	.984	9	101	128	O672(68/329/292),1b22,D4		

KINGMAN, DAVE David Arthur "Kong" B12.21.1948 Pendleton OR BR/TR/6-6/210* [SFN70 S1/1] d7.30 Col USC OF(508/0/144)

																										0.3
1971	†SF	N	41	115	17	32	10	4	6	24	9-0	1	35	.278	.328	.557	151	7	5-0	.981	-3	78	67	1b20,O14(7/0/7)		0.3
1972	SF	N	135	472	65	106	17	4	29	83	51-2	4	140	.225	.303	.462	113	6	16-6	.932	4	120	104	3b59,1b56,O22L		0.7
1973	SF	N	112	305	54	62	10	1	24	55	41-3	2	122	.203	.300	.479	108	2	8-5	.910	3	114	64	3b60,1b46,P2		0.2
1974	SF	N	121	350	41	78	18	2	18	55	37-2	1	125	.223	.302	.440	102	-1	8-8	.983	1	128	110	1b91,3b21,O2R		-0.7
1975	NY	N	134	502	65	116	22	1	36	88	34-5	5	153	.231	.284	.494	117	4	7-5	.958	0	108	61	O71(68/0/3),1b58,3b12		0.2
1976	NY	N★	123	474	70	113	14	1	37	86	28-4	5	135	.238	.286	.506	128	12	7-4	.959	1	99	119	O111(5/0/106),1b16	38	-1.4
1977	NY	N	58	211	22	44	7	0	9	28	13-3	1	66	.209	.263	.370	70	-10	3-2	.974	-1	104	0	O45(26/0/20),1b17		0.3
	SD	N	56	168	16	40	9	0	11	39	12-1	0	48	.238	.292	.488	118	3	2-3	.964	3	100	171	O73(54/0/20),1b30,3b2		-1.1
	Year		114	379	38	84	16	0	20	67	25-4	1	114	.222	.276	.422	91	-7	5-5	.970	2	98		1b8,O2L		-0.2
	Cal	A	10	36	4	7	2	0	2	4	1-0	1	6	.194	.237	.417	77	-1	0-0	.974	-1	94	77	1b8,D6,O2L		0.3
	NY	A	8	24	5	6	2	0	4	7	2-0	1	13	.250	.333	.833	207	3	0-1	—	0		77	D6		0.1
	Year		18	60	9	13	4	0	6	11	3-0	2	29	.217	.277	.583	130	2	0-1	.974	-1	94	98	O100L,1b6	25	0.6
1978	Chi	N	119	395	65	105	17	4	28	79	39-8	6	111	.266	.336	.542	128	13	3-4	.978	-3	89	98	O139L		2.3
1979	Chi	N★	145	532	97	153	19	5	**48**	115	45-7	4	131	.288	.343	**.613**	143	28	4-2	.954	-0	93	111	O139L		3.3
1980	Chi	N★	81	255	31	71	8	0	18	57	21-3	0	44	.278	.329	.522	125	7	2-2	.941	2	93	194	O61(63/0/1),1b2	48	0.6

YEAR	TM LG	G	AB	R	H	2B	3B	HR	RBI	BB-IB	HP	SO	AVG	OBP	SLG	AOPS	ABR	SB-CS	FA	FR	RNG	THR	GAMES AT POSITION	DL	BFW
1981	NY N	100	353	40	78	11	3	22	59	55-7	1	105	.221	.326	.456	121	9	6-0	.974	-5	92	100	1b56,O48L		0.0
1982	NY N	149	535	80	109	9	1	**37**	99	59-9	4	156	.204	.285	.432	98	-4	4-0	.986	-14	71	79	1b143		-2.7
1983	NY N	100	248	25	49	7	0	13	29	22-1	1	57	.198	.265	.383	78	-9	2-1	.994	-5	76	109	1b50,O5R		-1.8
1984	Oak A	147	549	68	147	23	1	35	118	44-8	6	119	.268	.321	.505	135	24	2-1	1.000	-2	34	41	D139,1b9		1.8
1985	Oak A	158	592	66	141	16	0	30	91	62-6	2	114	.238	.309	.417	105	2	3-2	1.000	-1	22	55	D149,1b9		-0.4
1986	Oak A	144	561	70	118	19	0	35	94	33-3	3	126	.210	.255	.431	90	-12	3-3	.895	-1	0	129	D140,1b3		-1.8
Total	16	1941	6677	901	1575	240	25	442	1210	608-72	53	1816	.236	.302	.478	114	85	85-49	.957	-18	96	100	O648L,1b603,D434,3b154,P2	111	-1.0

KINGMAN, HARRY Henry Lees B4.3.1892 Tientsin, China D12.27.1982 Oakland CA BL/TL/6-1.5/165 d7.1 Col Springfield

1914	NY A	4	3	0	0	0	0	0	0			2	.000	.250	.000	-24	0	0	1.000	-0	0	0	/1		-0.1

KINGSALE, EUGENE Eugene Humphrey B8.20.1976 Solito, Aruba BB/TR/6-3/194(170-194) d9.3

1996	Bal A	3	0	0	0	0	0	0	0	0-0							0	0-0	1.000	0	226	0	O2C		0.0
1998	Bal A	11	2	1	0	0	0	0	0	0-0	0	1	.000	.000	.000	-99	-1	0-0	1.000	0	99	0	O4C		-0.1
1999	Bal A	28	85	9	21	2	0	0	7	5-0	2	13	.247	.301	.271	50	-6	1-3	.980	-3	80	68	O24C,D2		-1.0
2000	Bal A	26	88	13	21	2	1	0	9	2-0	0	14	.239	.253	.284	38	-9	1-2	.954	1	105	179	O24C/D		-0.8
2001	Bal A	3	4	0	0	0	0	0	0	0-0	0	2	.000	.000	.000	-99	-1	1-1	1.000	-0	38	0	/OC	145	-0.2
	Sea A	10	15	4	5	0	0	0	1	0-0	1	2	.333	.444	.333	116	1	2-0	1.000	0	117	0	O9(5/1/3)		0.1
	Year	13	19	4	5	0	0	0	1	0-0	1	4	.263	.364	.263	73	-1	3-1	1.000	-0	103	0	O10(5/2/3)		-0.1
2002	Sea A	2	3	0	2	0	0	0	0	0-0	0	0	.667	.667	.667	265	1	0-0	1.000	0	129	0	O2(0/1/1)		0.1
	SD N	89	216	27	60	10	3	2	28	20-0	3	47	.278	.346	.380	103	3	9-2	.985	4	116	116	O82(26/17/50)		0.3
2003	Det A	39	120	11	25	3	1	1	8	10-0	1	17	.208	.265	.275	46	-10	1-3	.985	-4	84	0	O30(8/23/0),D4		0.3
Total	7	211	533	65	134	17	5	3	53	39-0	6	95	.251	.307	.319	70	-25	15-11	.979	-3	101	86	O178(39/97/54),D7	165	-3.0

KINKADE, MIKE Michael A. B5.6.1973 Livonia MI BR/TR/6-1/210* [MilA95 9/236] d9.8 Col Washington St.

1998	NY N	3	2	0	0	0	0	0	0	0-0	0	0	.000	.000	.000	-99	-1	0-0	—	-0	0	0	/3		-0.1
1999	NY N	28	46	3	9	2	1	2	6	3-0	2	9	.196	.275	.413	74	-2	1-0	1.000	-0	77	168	O17(12/0/8),3b3/C1		-0.3
2000	NY N	2	2	0	0	0	0	0	0	0-0	0	1	.000	.000	.000	-99	-0	0-0	—	-0	0	0	/OR		-0.1
	Bal A	3	7	0	3	0	0	0	1	0-0	1	0	.429	.500	.571	179	1	0-0	1.000	0	0	0	/1D		0.1
2001	Bal A	61	160	19	44	5	0	4	16	14-0	3	31	.275	.345	.381	96	-1	2-1	.962	-1	95	63	O32(29/0/3),3b10,D10,1b3,C2	30	-0.3
2002	LA N	37	50	7	19	5	0	2	11	4-0	6	14	.380	.483	.600	199	8	1-0	1.000	-1	128	74	1b11,O8L		0.6
2003	LA N	88	162	25	35	7	0	5	14	13-2	16	38	.216	.335	.352	82	-4	1-3	.914	-6	70	48	O36(34/0/2),1b13,3b2/D	30	-1.0
Total	6	222	429	56	110	20	1	13	48	34-2	28	89	.256	.350	.399	100	0	5-4	.953	-6	78	48	O94(83/0/14),1b29,3b16,D13,C3	30	-1.1

KINLOCK, BILLY William Francis B3.31.1874 Providence RI D2.15.1931 New York NY d8.1

1895	StL N	1	3	0	1	0	0	0	0			2	.333	.333	.333	73	0	0	1.000	0	46	608	/3		0.0

KINSELLA, BOB Robert Francis "Red" B1.5.1899 Springfield IL D12.30.1951 Los Angeles CA BL/TR/5-9.5/165 d9.20

1919	NY N	3	9	1	2	0	0	0	0	0		3	.222	.222	.222	34	-1	0	.500	-1	32	0	O3(2/0/1)		-0.2
1920	NY N	1	3	0	1	0	0	0	1	0		0	.333	.333	.333	93	0	0	.500	0	66	0	/OR		-0.1
Total	2	4	12	1	3	0	0	0	1	0		3	.250	.250	.250	49	-1	1-0	.500	-1	43	0	O4(2/0/2)		-0.3

KINSLER, WILLIAM William H. B11.9.1867 New York NY D8.10.1963 Miami Beach FL d6.8

1893	NY N	1	3	1	0	0	0	0	1	0		1	.000	.250	.000	-31	-1	0	1.000	-0	0	0	/OR		-0.1

KINSLOW, TOM Thomas F. B1.12.1866 Washington DC D2.22.1901 Washington DC BR/TR/5-10/160 d6.4

1886	Was N	3	8	1	2	0	0	0	1	0		1	.250	.250	.250	57	0		1.000	-0			C3		0.0
1887	NY AA	2	6	0	0	0	0	0	0		0		.000	.000	.000	-99	-2	0	1.000	0			C2		-0.1
1890	Bro P	64	242	30	64	11	6	4	46	10	2	22	.264	.299	.409	83	-8	2	.909	14	128	93	C64		0.9
1891	Bro N	61	228	22	54	6	0	0	33	9	0	22	.237	.266	.263	55	-14	3	.922	-6	97	82	C61		-1.3
1892	Bro N	66	246	37	75	6	11	2	40	13	1	17	.305	.342	.443	142	10	4	.933	2	104	112	C66		1.7
1893	Bro N	78	312	38	76	8	4	4	45	11	1	13	.244	.272	.333	63	-19	4	.932	-1	94	94	C76,O2R		-1.1
1894	Bro N	62	223	39	68	5	6	2	41	20	1	11	.305	.362	.408	92	-3	4	.907	-10	90	79	C61/1		-0.7
1895	Pit N	19	62	10	14	2	0	0	5	2	0	2	.226	.250	.258	33	-6	1	.962	-3	87	66	C18		-0.6
1896	Lou N	8	25	4	7	0	1	0	7	1	0	5	.280	.308	.360	78	-1	0	.810	-2	76	60	C5/1		-0.2
1898	Was N	3	9	0	1	0	0	0	0	0	0	0	.111	.111	.111	-36	-2	0	.800	-1	72	172	C3/1		-0.2
	StL N	14	53	5	15	2	1	0	4	1	1	5	.283	.309	.358	89	-1	0	.925	-1	74	120	C14		-0.1
	Year	17	62	5	16	2	1	0	4	1	1	5	.258	.281	.323	72	-3	0	.909	-2	74	127	C17/1		-0.3
Total	10	380	1414	186	376	40	29	12	222	67	5	93	.266	.301	.361	81	-46	18	.923	-9	102	93	C373,1b3,O2R		-1.7

KINZIE, WALT Walter Harris B3.1858 KS D11.5.1909 Chicago IL BR/TR/5-10.5/161 d7.17

1882	Det N	13	53	5	5	0	1	0	2	0		8	.094	.094	.132	-28	-8		.852	-2	96	28	S13		-0.9
1884	Chi N	19	82	4	13	3	0	2	8	0		13	.159	.159	.268	29	-7		.831	-2	97	112	S17,3b2		-0.7
	StL AA	2	9	0	1	0	0	0	0	0			.111	.111	.111	-26	-1		.727	-2	62	0	2b2		-0.3
Total	2	34	144	9	19	3	1	2	10	0		21	.132	.132	.208	6	-16		.840	-6	97	75	S30,2b2,3b2		-1.9

KIPPERT, ED Edward August "Kickapoo" B1.3.1880 Detroit MI D6.3.1960 Detroit MI BR/TR/5-10.5/180 d4.14

1914	Cin N	2	2	0	0	0	0	0	0	0			.000	.000	.000	-97	0	0	1.000	-0	71	0	O2(1/1/0)		-0.1

KIRBY, JIM James Herschel B5.5.1923 Nashville TN BR/TR/5-11/175 d5.1

1949	Chi N	3	2	1	1	0	0	0	0	0		0	.500	.500	.500	174	0	0	—	0			/H		0.0

KIRBY, LA RUE La Rue B12.30.1889 Eureka MI D6.10.1961 Lansing MI BB/TR/6-0/185 d8.7 ▲

1912	NY N	3	5	1	1	0	0	0	0	0	0	0	.200	.200	.400	60	0	0	1.000	0	109	0	P3		0.0
1914	StL F	52	195	21	48	6	3	2	18	14	2	30	.246	.303	.338	71	-11	5	.973	2	103	107	O50(0/49/1)		-1.4
1915	StL F	61	178	15	38	7	2	0	16	17	0	31	.213	.282	.275	54	-13	3	.969	-0	93	128	O52(9/40/4)/P		-1.7
Total	3	116	378	37	87	14	5	2	34	31	2	61	.230	.292	.310	63	-24	8	.971	2	98	117	O102(9/89/5),P4		-3.1

KIRBY, WAYNE Wayne Leonard B1.22.1964 Williamsburg VA BL/TR/5-10/185* [LAN83*/13/291] d9.12

1991	Cle A	21	43	4	9	2	0	0	5	2-0	0	6	.209	.239	.256	38	-4	1-2	1.000	2	133	95	O21(5/1/17)		-0.3
1992	Cle A	21	18	9	3	1	0	1	1	3-0	0	3	.167	.286	.389	88	0	0-3	1.000	0	205	0	O2(1/0/1),D4		-0.1
1993	Cle A	131	458	71	123	19	5	6	60	37-2	3	58	.269	.323	.371	87	-9	17-5	.983	14	110	**227**	O123(2/15/113),D5		0.2
1994	Cle A	78	191	33	56	6	0	5	23	13-0	1	30	.293	.341	.403	90	-3	11-4	.959	-4	56	70	O68(8/6/55),D2		-0.7
1995	†Cle A	101	188	29	39	10	2	1	14	13-0	1	32	.207	.260	.298	44	-16	10-3	.990	-1	93	81	O68(1/34/35),D7		-1.6
1996	Cle A	27	16	3	4	1	0	0	1	2-0	0	2	.250	.333	.313	65	-1	0-1	1.000	-1	80	0	O18(2/5/11)		-0.2
	†LA N	65	188	23	51	10	1	1	11	17-1	1	17	.271	.333	.351	86	-3	4-2	.969	-2	91	87	O53(8/47/0)		-0.5
1997	LA N	46	65	6	11	2	0	0	4	10-0	0	12	.169	.280	.262	30	-7	0-0	1.000	-2	121	136	O26(9/16/2)		-0.5
1998	NY N	26	31	5	6	0	0	0	1	1-0	0	9	.194	.219	.258	26	-4	1-1	1.000	1	115	239	O19(3/4/12)		-0.3
Total	8	516	1198	183	302	51	9	14	119	98-3	6	168	.252	.309	.345	74	-47	44-21	.981	11	103	140	O398(39/128/246),D18		-4.0

KIRK, TOM Thomas Daniel B9.27.1927 Philadelphia PA D8.1.1974 Philadelphia PA BL/TL/5-10.5/182 d6.24

1947	Phi A	1	1	0	0	0	0	0	0	0-0	0	0	.000	.000	.000	-98	0	0-0	—	0			/H		0.0

KIRKE, JAY Judson Fabian B6.16.1888 Fleischmanns NY D8.31.1968 New Orleans LA BL/TR/6-0/195 d9.28 OF(102/2/38)

1910	Det A	8	25	3	5	1	0	0	3	1	0		.200	.231	.240	44	-2	1	.917	-2	86	39	2b7/OL		-0.4
1911	Bos N	20	89	9	32	5	0	0	12	2	1	4	**.360**	.380	.528	142	4	3	.929	-1	94	110	O14L,1b3/2S3		0.3
1912	Bos N	103	359	53	115	11	4	4	62	9	1	46	.320	.339	.407	102	-1	7	.903	-0	82	211	O72(62/0/10),3b14,S2/1		0.3
1913	Bos N	18	38	3	9	2	0	0	3	1	2	6	.237	.293	.289	65	-2	0-1	.923	2	93	344	O13(3/2/8)		0.0
1914	Cle A	67	242	18	66	10	2	1	25	7	1	30	.273	.296	.343	89	-5	5-10	.974	1	113	57	O42(22/0/20),1b18		-0.9
1915	Cle A	87	339	35	105	19	2	4	40	14	5	21	.310	.346	.395	120	7	5-6	.986	1	97	79	1b87		0.3
1918	NY N	17	56	1	14	1	0	0	3	3		6	.250	.262	.304	63	-3	0	.978	1	121	86	1b16		-0.3
Total	7	320	1148	122	346	49	13	7	148	35	10	112	.301	.328	.385	103	-2	21-17	.927	0	93	165	O142L,1b125,3b15,2b8,S3		-1.4

KIRKLAND, WILLIE Willie Charles B2.17.1934 Siluria AL BL/TR/6-1/206(195-206) d4.15

1958	SF N	122	418	48	108	25	6	14	56	43-7	5	69	.258	.332	.447	107	4	3-2	.961	-0	95	137	O115(5/0/112)		0.0
1959	SF N	126	463	64	126	22	3	22	68	42-3	5	78	.272	.335	.475	116	5	3-3	.969	-2	98	89	O117(13/0/109)		0.3
1960	SF N	146	515	59	130	21	10	21	65	44-8	4	86	.252	.315	.454	115	8	12-7	.978	2	99	127	O143(5/0/143)		0.5
1961	Cle A	146	525	84	136	22	5	27	95	48-4	1	77	.259	.318	.474	113	7	7-0	.974	6	107	114	O138R		0.5

YEAR	TM LG	G	AB	R	H	2B	3B	HR	RBI	BB-IB	HP	SO	AVG	OBP	SLG	AOPS	ABR	SB-CS	FA	FR	RNG	THR	GAMES AT POSITION	DL	BFW
1962	Cle A	137	419	56	84	9	1	21	72	43-3	0	62	.200	.272	.377	76	-17	9-1	.972	6	109	170	O125(0/12/121)		-1.7
1963	Cle A	127	427	51	98	13	2	15	47	45-5	1	99	.230	.303	.375	90	-6	8-2	.984	3	102	159	O112(5/64/45)		-0.8
1964	Bal A	66	150	14	30	5	0	3	22	17-4	1	26	.200	.281	.293	62	-8	3-2	.989	5	109	266	O58(2/10/48)		-0.5
	Was A	32	102	8	22	6	0	5	13	6-0	1	30	.216	.259	.422	86	-2	0-0	.907	2	84	0	O27(12/1/15)		-0.8
	Year	98	252	22	52	11	0	8	35	23-4	1	56	.206	.272	.345	72	-10	3-2	.964	2	100	166	O85(14/11/63)		-1.3
1965	Was A	123	312	38	72	9	1	14	54	19-1	0	65	.231	.270	.401	91	-5	3-2	.987	2	111	64	O92(32/5/67)		-0.9
1966	Was A	124	163	21	31	2	1	6	17	16-3	0	50	.190	.261	.325	68	-7	2-0	.983	-0	91	141	O68(50/0/19)		-1.0
Total	9	1149	3494	443	837	134	29	148	509	323-38	15	648	.240	.304	.422	99	-17	52-19	.974	18	102	129	O995(122/92/817)		-4.4

KIRKPATRICK, ED Edgar Leon B10.8.1944 Spokane WA BL/TR/5-11.5/195(185-200) d9.13 OF(236/62/291)

YEAR	TM LG	G	AB	R	H	2B	3B	HR	RBI	BB-IB	HP	SO	AVG	OBP	SLG	AOPS	ABR	SB-CS	FA	FR	RNG	THR	GAMES AT POSITION	DL	BFW
1962	LA A	3	6	0	0	0	0	0	0	0-0	0	2	.000	.000	.000	-99	-2	0-0	1.000	1	0	0	/C		-0.1
1963	LA A	34	77	4	15	5	0	2	7	6-0	1	19	.195	.259	.338	71	-3	1-0	.986	1	30	143	C14,O10L		-0.2
1964	LA A	75	219	20	53	13	3	2	22	23-6	2	30	.242	.315	.356	97	-1	2-2	.969	-2	86	102	O63(63/0/1)		-0.7
1965	Cal A	19	73	8	19	5	0	3	8	3-0	0	9	.260	.289	.452	110	1	1-2	.969	0	82	246	O19R		-0.1
1966	Cal A	117	312	31	60	7	4	9	44	51-8	5	67	.192	.313	.327	87	-4	7-4	.994	-3	93	77	O102(17/0/86),1b3		-1.4
1967	Cal A	3	8	0	0	0	0	0	0	0-0	0	2	.000	.000	.000	-99	-2	0-0	1.000	-1	0	0	C2/OL		-0.3
1968	Cal A	89	161	23	37	4	0	1	15	25-2	1	32	.230	.332	.273	89	-1	1-3	.982	-1	92	104	O45(12/1/34),C4,1b2		-0.6
1969	KC A	120	315	40	81	11	4	14	49	43-4	3	42	.257	.348	.451	121	9	3-5	.995	7	119	139	O82(29/24/32),C8,1b2,3b2/2		1.2
1970	KC A	134	424	59	97	17	2	18	62	55-8	1	65	.229	.319	.406	98	-1	4-4	.978	-2	79	163	C89,O19(8/3/8),1b16		-0.2
1971	KC A	120	365	46	80	12	1	9	46	48-8	2	60	.219	.308	.332	83	-4	3-4	.992	6	112	62	O61(30/16/18),C59		-0.2
1972	KC A	113	364	43	100	15	1	9	43	51-9	3	50	.275	.365	.396	128	14	3-5	.991	-3	85	98	C108/1		1.7
1973	KC A	126	429	61	113	24	3	6	45	46-6	1	48	.263	.333	.373	93	-3	3-7	.990	-0	96	43	O108(27/11/72),C14,D8		-1.0
1974	†Pit N	116	271	32	67	9	0	6	38	51-13	2	30	.247	.367	.347	104	4	1-2	.993	-1	99	122	1b59,O14(0/2/12),C6		-0.2
1975	†Pit N	89	144	15	34	5	0	5	16	18-2	0	22	.236	.319	.375	92	-2	1-0	1.000	0	99	82	1b28,O14(8/0/6)		-0.4
1976	Pit N	83	146	14	34	9	0	0	16	14-2	0	15	.233	.294	.295	68	-6	1-0	.990	0	114	90	1b25,O9(3/4/2)/3		-0.8
1977	Pit N	21	28	5	4	2	0	1	4	8-0	0	6	.143	.324	.321	74	-1	1-0	.972	0	107	145	O6(5/0/1),1b3/CD		-0.1
	Tex A	20	48	2	9	1	0	0	3	4-1	0	11	.188	.250	.208	26	-5	2-0	1.000	1	148	0	O22L/3D		-0.3
	Mil A	29	77	8	21	4	0	0	6	10-1	1	8	.273	.364	.325	89	-1	0-1	.973	-1	103	0	O28(27/0/1),D8,1b3/C3		-0.7
	Year	49	125	10	30	5	0	0	9	14-2	1	19	.240	.321	.280	65	-5	2-1	.980	-1	112	0			
Total	16	1311	3467	411	824	143	18	85	424	456-70	22	518	.238	.327	.363	96	-12	34-39	.989	1	100	80	O577R,C306,1b149,D16,3b5/2		-4.1

KIRKPATRICK, ENOS Enos Claire B12.9.1884 Pittsburgh PA D4.14.1964 Pittsburgh PA BR/TR/5-10/175 d8.24 Col Duquesne

YEAR	TM LG	G	AB	R	H	2B	3B	HR	RBI	BB-IB	HP	SO	AVG	OBP	SLG	AOPS	ABR	SB-CS	FA	FR	RNG	THR	GAMES AT POSITION	DL	BFW
1912	Bro N	32	94	13	18	1	1	1	6	9	1	15	.191	.269	.223	37	-8	5	.968	5	129	85	3b29,S3		-0.3
1913	Bro N	48	89	13	22	4	1	1	5	3	2	18	.247	.287	.348	79	-3	5	.897	-2	71	51	S10,1b8,2b6,3b4		-0.4
1914	Bal F	55	174	22	44	7	2	2	16	18	2	30	.253	.330	.351	83	-7	10	.932	-1	80	25	3b36,S11,O3(2/0/1)/1		-0.6
1915	Bal F	68	171	22	41	8	2	0	19	24	1	15	.240	.337	.310	80	-6	12	.911	-3	94	72	3b28,2b21,1b5,S5		-0.9
Total	4	203	528	70	125	20	6	3	46	54	6	78	.237	.315	.314	74	-24	32-1	.936	-1	101	59	3b97,S29,2b27,1b14,O3(2/0/1)		-2.2

KIRRENE, JOE Joseph John B10.4.1931 San Francisco CA BR/TR/6-2/195* d10.1 Mil 1952-53

YEAR	TM LG	G	AB	R	H	2B	3B	HR	RBI	BB-IB	HP	SO	AVG	OBP	SLG	AOPS	ABR	SB-CS	FA	FR	RNG	THR	GAMES AT POSITION	DL	BFW
1950	Chi A	1	4	0	1	0	0	0	0	0	0	0	.250	.250	.250	29	0	0-0	1.000	-0	59	0	/3		-0.1
1954	Chi A	9	23	4	7	1	0	0	4	5	1	2	.304	.448	.348	116	1	1-0	.947	-1	77	173	3b9		0.0
Total	2	10	27	4	8	1	0	0	4	5	1	2	.296	.424	.333	105	1	1-0	.952	-1	75	154	3b10		-0.1

KISH, ERNIE Ernest Alexander B2.6.1918 Washington DC D12.21.1993 Kirtland OH BL/TR/5-9.5/170 d7.29 Col Ohio U.

YEAR	TM LG	G	AB	R	H	2B	3B	HR	RBI	BB-IB	HP	SO	AVG	OBP	SLG	AOPS	ABR	SB-CS	FA	FR	RNG	THR	GAMES AT POSITION	DL	BFW
1945	Phi A	43	110	10	27	5	1	0	9	13	3	9	.245	.320	.309	83	-2	0-3	.932	-2	85	118	O30(13/8/11)		-0.7

KISSINGER, BILL William Francis "Shang" B8.15.1871 Dayton KY D4.20.1929 Cincinnati OH BR/TR/5-11/185 d5.30 ▲

YEAR	TM LG	G	AB	R	H	2B	3B	HR	RBI	BB-IB	HP	SO	AVG	OBP	SLG	AOPS	ABR	SB-CS	FA	FR	RNG	THR	GAMES AT POSITION	DL	BFW
1895	Bal N	2	5	1	1	0	0	0	0	0	0	1	.200	.200	.200	3	0	1	1.000	-0	80	0	P2		0.0
	StL N	33	97	8	24	6	1	0	8	0	0	11	.247	.247	.330	49	-8	1	.975	-3	97	87	P24,S4,O4(1/0/3)/3		-0.4
	Year	35	102	9	25	6	1	0	8	0	0	12	.245	.245	.324	46	-9	1	.976	-3	96	81	P26,S4,O4(1/0/3)/3		-0.4
1896	StL N	23	73	8	22	4	0	0	12	0	1	4	.301	.301	.356	76	-3	0	.906	0	127	155	P20,O3L/3		-0.1
1897	StL N	14	39	7	13	3	2	0	6	3	0	5	.333	.381	.513	138	2	0	.786	-1	0	0	O7(6/1/0),P7		0.0
Total	3	72	214	24	60	13	3	0	26	3	0	16	.280	.290	.369	73	-9	1	.935	-4	111	105	P53,O14(10/1/3),S4,3b2		-0.5

KITSOS, CHRIS Christopher Anestos B2.11.1928 New York NY D6.7.2004 Mobile AL BB/TR/5-9/165 d4.21

YEAR	TM LG	G	AB	R	H	2B	3B	HR	RBI	BB-IB	HP	SO	AVG	OBP	SLG	AOPS	ABR	SB-CS	FA	FR	RNG	THR	GAMES AT POSITION	DL	BFW
1954	Chi N	1	0	0	0	0	0	0	0	0	0	0	—	—	—		0	0-0	1.000	0	191	0	/S		0.0

KITTLE, RON Ronald Dale B1.5.1958 Gary IN BR/TR/6-4/220(200-220) d9.2

YEAR	TM LG	G	AB	R	H	2B	3B	HR	RBI	BB-IB	HP	SO	AVG	OBP	SLG	AOPS	ABR	SB-CS	FA	FR	RNG	THR	GAMES AT POSITION	DL	BFW
1982	Chi A	20	29	3	7	2	0	1	7	3-0	0	12	.241	.313	.414	97	0	0-0	1.000	-1	43	0	O5R,D3		-0.1
1983	†Chi A★	145	520	75	132	19	3	35	100	39-8	8	150	.254	.314	.504	116	9	8-3	.964	-13	83	67	O139L,D2		-0.9
1984	Chi A	139	466	67	100	15	0	32	74	49-5	6	137	.215	.295	.453	99	-2	3-6	.972	-1	87	166	O124L,D7		-1.0
1985	Chi A	116	379	51	87	12	0	26	58	31-1	5	92	.230	.295	.467	101	-1	1-4	.989	-2	92	67	O57L,D57	21	-0.8
1986	Chi A	86	296	34	63	11	0	17	48	28-0	3	87	.213	.282	.422	87	-6	2-1	1.000	1	93	244	D62,O20L		-0.8
	NY A	30	80	8	19	2	0	4	12	7-1	0	23	.237	.292	.412	92	-1	0-0	1.000	0	106	0	D24/OL		-0.2
	Year	116	376	42	82	13	0	21	60	35-1	3	110	.218	.284	.420	88	-8	4-1	.973	1	94	232	D86,O21L		-1.0
1987	NY A	59	159	21	44	5	0	12	28	10-1	1	36	.277	.318	.535	123	4	0-1	1.000	1	198	1409	D49,O2L	40	0.3
1988	Cle A	75	225	31	58	8	0	18	43	16-1	8	65	.258	.323	.533	133	9	0-1	—	0	0	0	D63		0.7
1989	Chi A	51	169	26	51	10	0	11	37	22-1	1	42	.302	.378	.556	165	15	0-1	.982	-2	67	132	1b27,D17,O5L	113	1.1
1990	Chi A	83	277	29	68	14	0	16	43	24-2	3	77	.245	.311	.469	118	6	0-0	.987	-4	38	115	D54,1b25		-0.1
	Bal A	22	61	4	10	2	0	2	3	2-0	1	14	.164	.203	.295	39	-5	0-0	1.000	-1	42	37	D13,1b5		-0.7
	Year	105	338	33	78	16	0	18	46	26-2	4	91	.231	.293	.438	104	0	0-0	.989	-4	39	104	D67,1b30		-0.8
1991	Chi A	17	47	7	9	0	0	2	7	5-0	2	19	.191	.291	.319	72	-2	0-0	.982	-1	75	89	1b15		-0.4
Total	10	843	2708	356	648	100	3	176	460	236-20	38	744	.239	.306	.473	109	26	16-16	.974	-21	87	121	O353(348/0/5),D351,1b72	174	-2.9

KITTRIDGE, MALACHI Malachi Jeddidah "Jeddidah" B10.12.1869 Clinton MA D6.23.1928 Gary IN BR/TR/5-7/170 d4.19 M1

YEAR	TM LG	G	AB	R	H	2B	3B	HR	RBI	BB-IB	HP	SO	AVG	OBP	SLG	AOPS	ABR	SB-CS	FA	FR	RNG	THR	GAMES AT POSITION	DL	BFW
1890	Chi N	96	333	46	67	8	3	3	35	39	1	53	.201	.287	.270	60	-17	7	.944	5	112	95	C96		-0.4
1891	Chi N	79	296	26	62	8	5	2	27	17	0	28	.209	.252	.291	58	-17	4	.940	5	132	91	C79		-0.5
1892	Chi N	69	229	19	41	6	0	0	10	11	0	27	.179	.217	.201	26	-21	2	.945	8	105	100	C69		-0.6
1893	Chi N	70	255	32	59	9	5	2	30	17	0	15	.231	.279	.329	62	-15	3	.939	4	90	116	C70		-0.4
1894	Chi N	51	168	36	53	8	2	0	23	26	0	20	.315	.407	.387	87	-3	2	.925	-0	80	71	C51		-0.3
1895	Chi N	60	212	30	48	6	3	3	29	16	1	9	.226	.284	.325	53	-16	6	.976	0	95	84	C59		-0.9
1896	Chi N	65	215	17	48	4	1	1	19	14	1	14	.223	.274	.265	41	-19	6	.962	-0	93	90	C64/P		-1.2
1897	Chi N	79	262	25	53	5	5	1	30	22	0	9	.202	.264	.271	40	-24	9	.952	-1	87	99	C79		-1.6
1898	Lou N	86	287	27	70	8	5	1	31	15	0	12	.244	.281	.317	72	-12	9	.944	-13	81	103	C86		-1.6
1899	Lou N	46	131	11	26	2	1	0	13	26	1	7	.198	.335	.229	56	-7	3	.975	6	116	110	C44		0.3
	Was N	44	133	14	20	3	0	0	11	10	1	5	.150	.215	.173	7	-17	2	.949	-0	78	118	C43		-1.6
	Year	90	264	25	46	5	1	0	24	36	2	12	.174	.278	.201	32	-24	5	.962	3	98	114	C87		-1.6
1901	Bos N	114	381	46	96	14	0	2	40	32	1	25	.252	.312	.304	72	-13	2	.984	17	130	97	C113		1.5
1902	Bos N	80	255	18	60	7	0	2	30	24	1	20	.235	.304	.286	81	-5	4	.981	6	110	97	C72		0.9
1903	Bos N	32	99	10	21	2	0	0	6	11	0	9	.212	.291	.232	52	-6	1	.981	4	98	85	C30		0.1
	Was A	60	192	8	41	4	1	0	16	10	0	13	.214	.252	.245	49	-12	1	.978	-8	74	118	C60		-1.5
1904	Was A	81	265	11	64	7	0	0	24	8	1	20	.242	.266	.268	70	-9	2	.982	-5	73	118	C79,M		-0.7
1905	Was A	77	238	16	39	8	0	0	14	15	1	17	.164	.213	.197	32	-18	1	.978	7	96	112	C76		-0.5
1906	Was A	22	68	5	13	0	0	0	3	1	0	9	.191	.203	.191	25	-6	1	.946	-3	81	72	C22		-0.8
	Cle A	5	10	0	1	0	0	0	0	0	0	5	.100	.100	.100	-38	-2	0	.938	-1	118	35	C5		-1.0
	Year	27	78	5	14	0	0	0	3	1	0	14	.179	.190	.179	16	-8	1	.945	-4	86	67	C27		-1.6
Total	16	1216	4029	375	882	108	31	17	391	314	8	166	.219	.277	.274	56	-239	64	.961	22	99	100	C1197/P		-10.0

KLASSEN, DANNY Daniel Victor B9.22.1975 Leamington ON, Can. BR/TR/6-0/175(175-190) [MilA93 2/65] d7.4 [DL 2001 Ari N 189]

YEAR	TM LG	G	AB	R	H	2B	3B	HR	RBI	BB-IB	HP	SO	AVG	OBP	SLG	AOPS	ABR	SB-CS	FA	FR	RNG	THR	GAMES AT POSITION	DL	BFW
1998	Ari N	29	108	12	21	2	1	3	8	9-0	1	33	.194	.263	.315	51	-8	1-1	.964	-3	97	95	2b29		-1.0
1999	Ari N	1	1	0	1	0	0	0	0	0-0	0	0	1.000	1.000	1.000	406	0	0-0	—	0	0	0	/H		0.0
2000	Ari N	29	76	13	18	3	0	2	8	8-0	1	24	.237	.318	.355	67	-4	1-1	.962	-2	93	115	3b25,S3	54	-0.5
2002	Ari N	4	3	0	1	0	0	0	0	0-0	1	1	.333	.333	.333	72	-0	0-0	1.000	-0	146	0	3b2/S	24	0.0
2003	Det A	22	73	9	18	2	1	1	7	4-0	0	26	.247	.286	.356	71	-3	0-1	1.000	4	105	131	3b13,2b4,S3		0.1
Total	5	85	261	34	59	8	2	6	23	21-0	2	84	.226	.289	.341	63	-15	2-3	.978	-1	98	120	3b40,2b33,S7	267	-1.4

YEAR	TM LG	G	AB	R	H	2B	3B	HR	RBI	BB-IB	HP	SO	AVG	OBP	SLG	AOPS	ABR	SB-CS	FA	FR	RNG	THR	GAMES AT POSITION	DL	BFW
KLAUS, BOBBY	Robert Francis B12.27.1937 Spring Grove IL BR/TR/5-10/170* d4.21 b-Billy Col Illinois																								
1964	Cin N	40	93	10	17	5	1	2	6	4-0	0	13	.183	.212	.323	48	-7	1-0	.972	-1	83	82	2b18,3b11,S3		-0.6
	NY N	56	209	25	51	8	3	2	11	25-0	0	30	.244	.325	.340	90	-2	3-4	.986	-3	115	71	2b25,3b28,S5		-0.4
	Year	96	302	35	68	13	4	4	17	29-0	0	43	.225	.291	.334	76	-10	4-4	.981	-4	102	75	2b43,3b39,S8		-1.0
1965	NY N	119	288	30	55	12	0	2	12	45-0	1	49	.191	.302	.253	61	-13	1-6	.968	7	110	116	2b72,S28,3b25		-0.3
Total	2	215	590	65	123	25	4	6	29	74-0	1	92	.208	.297	.295	69	-22	5-10	.973	3	107	100	2b115,3b64,S36		-1.3
KLAUS, BILLY	William Joseph B12.9.1928 Spring Grove IL BL/TR/5-10/165* d4.16 b-Bobby																								
1952	Bos N	7	4	3	0	0	0	0	1	0-0	0	1	.000	.200	.000	-42	-1	0-0	.500	-1	0	0	S4		-0.2
1953	Mil N	2	2	1	0	0	0	0	1	0	0	0	.000	.000	.000	-99	-1	0-0	—	0			/H		-0.1
1955	Bos A	135	541	83	153	26	2	7	60	60-0	0	44	.283	.351	.377	89	-7	6-0	.955	-3	104	72	S126,3b8		0.1
1956	Bos A	135	520	91	141	29	5	7	59	90-0	1	43	.271	.378	.387	92	-3	1-0	.945	2	113	79	3b106,S26		0.1
1957	Bos A	127	477	76	120	18	4	10	42	55-0	0	53	.252	.326	.369	85	-9	2-0	.961	19	113	111	S118		2.0
1958	Bos A	61	88	5	14	4	0	1	7	5-0	0	16	.159	.204	.239	20	-10	0-0	.883	-4	94	23	S27		-1.4
1959	Bal A	104	321	33	80	11	0	3	25	51-1	0	38	.249	.350	.312	86	-4	2-4	.970	-8	97	71	S59,3b49/2		-0.9
1960	Bal A	46	43	8	9	2	0	1	6	9-0	0	9	.209	.346	.326	84	-1	0-0	.960	2	104	129	2b30,S12,3b2		0.2
1961	Was A	91	251	26	57	8	2	7	30	30-3	2	34	.227	.311	.359	81	-7	2-2	.961	1	114	31	3b51,S18/2OL		-0.7
1962	Phi N	102	248	30	51	8	2	4	20	29-3	1	43	.206	.290	.302	61	-14	1-1	.983	2	96	53	3b53,S30,2b11		-1.0
1963	Phi N	11	18	1	1	0	0	0	1	1-0	0	4	.056	.105	.056	-53	-4	0-0	1.000	-1	50	0	S5,3b3		-0.5
Total	11	821	2513	357	626	106	15	40	250	331-7	4	285	.249	.335	.351	82	-61	14-7	.955	6	105	84	S425,3b272,2b43/OL		-2.4
KLEE, OLLIE	Ollie Chester "Babe" B5.20.1900 Piqua OH D2.9.1977 Toledo OH BL/TL/5-9.5/160 d8.10 Col Ohio St.																								
1925	Cin N	3	1	0	0	0	0	0	0	0	0	1	.000	.000	.000	-99	0	0-0	—	-0	0	0	/OC		0.0
KLEIN, CHUCK	Charles Herbert B10.7.1904 Indianapolis IN D3.28.1958 Indianapolis IN BL/TR/6-0/185 d7.30 C4 HF1980																								
1928	Phi N	64	253	41	91	14	4	11	34	14	1	22	.360	.396	.577	146	16	0	.978	-0	95	109	O63R		1.0
1929	Phi N	149	616	126	219	45	6	**43**	145	54	1	61	.356	.407	.657	149	45	5	.966	-1	96	117	O149(0/25/123)		3.0
1930	Phi N	156	648	158	250	59	8	40	170	54	4	50	.386	.436	.687	155	58	0	.960	21	102	**217**	O156R		**5.7**
1931	Phi N	148	594	**121**	200	34	10	**31**	**121**	59	1	49	.337	.398	**.584**	149	40	7	.971	-2	94	121	O148(90/17/43)		3.0
1932	Phi N	154	650	**152**	**226**	50	15	**38**	137	60	1	49	.348	.404	**.646**	158	-53	**20**	.960	7	96	179	O154R		4.9
1933	Phi N★	152	606	101	**223**	44	7	28	**120**	56	1	36	**.368**	**.422**	**.602**	168	55	15	.986	8	103	142	O152(0/1/152)		**5.6**
1934	Chi N★	115	435	78	131	27	2	20	80	47	1	38	.301	.372	.510	136	23	3	.962	-3	97	76	O110(97/1/15)		1.3
1935	†Chi N	119	434	71	127	14	4	21	73	41	1	42	.293	.355	.488	123	13	4	.958	-3	94	94	O111R		0.3
1936	Chi N	29	109	19	32	5	0	5	18	16	0	14	.294	.384	.477	128	5	0	.917	-1	104	89	O29R		0.2
	Phi N	117	492	83	152	30	7	20	86	33	0	45	.309	.352	.520	120	12	6	.930	-3	96	105	O117(2/0/115)		0.2
	Year	146	601	102	184	35	7	25	104	49	0	59	.306	.358	.512	122	17	6	.927	-4	98	102	O146(2/0/144)		0.4
1937	Phi N	115	406	74	132	20	2	15	57	39	1	21	.325	.386	.495	127	16	3	.949	-2	94	120	O102(29/0/75)		0.8
1938	Phi N	129	458	53	113	22	2	8	61	38	0	30	.247	.304	.356	83	-11	7	.960	-0	106	81	O119(3/0/118)		-1.8
1939	Phi N	25	47	8	9	2	1	1	9	10	0	4	.191	.333	.340	84	-1	1	1.000	0	100	108	O11R/1		-0.1
	Pit N	85	270	37	81	16	4	11	47	26	0	17	.300	.361	.511	134	12	1	.951	-3	96	75	O66(30/0/37)		0.5
	Year	110	317	45	90	18	5	12	56	36	0	21	.284	.357	.486	127	11	2	.958	-3	97	79	O77(30/0/48)/1		0.4
1940	Phi N	116	354	39	77	16	2	7	37	44	0	30	.218	.304	.333	79	-10	2	.984	-0	106	58	O96(6/0/90)		-1.6
1941	Phi N	50	73	6	9	0	1	3	10	9	1	6	.123	.229	.164	12	-9	0	.958	-0	101	106	O14(2/0/12)		-1.0
1942	Phi N	14	14	0	1	0	0	0	0	0	0	2	.071	.071	.071	-61	-3	0	—	0			/H		-0.3
1943	Phi N	12	20	0	2	0	0	0	0	0	0	3	.100	.100	.100	-44	-1	0	.000	-1	0	0	O2/1		-0.5
1944	Phi N	4	7	1	1	0	0	0	0	0	0	2	.143	.143	.143	-20	-1	0	1.000	0	141	0	/OR		-0.1
Total	17	1753	6486	1168	2076	398	74	300	1201	601	12	521	.320	.379	.543	135	309	79	.962	17	98	122	O1600(261/44/1305)/1		21.1
KLEIN, LOU	Louis Frank B10.22.1918 New Orleans LA D6.20.1976 Metairie LA BR/TR/5-11/170* d4.21 Mil 1944-45 M3/C6																								
1943	†StL N	154	627	91	180	28	14	7	62	50	2	70	.287	.342	.410	112	8	9	.973	-4	98	**141**	2b126,S51		1.4
1945	StL N	19	57	12	13	4	1	1	6	14	1	9	.228	.389	.386	113	2	0	.929	-1	81	110	S7,O7(4/0/3),3b4,2b2		0.1
1946	StL N	23	93	12	18	3	0	1	4	9	0	7	.194	.265	.258	47	-7	1	.975	-1	93	140	2b23		-0.7
1949	StL N	58	114	25	25	6	0	2	12	22	1	20	.219	.355	.325	80	-2	0	.890	-2	111	68	S21,2b9,3b7		-0.3
1951	Cle A	2	2	0	0	0	0	0	0	0	0	1	.000	.000	.000	-99	-1	0-0	—	0			/H		-0.1
	Phi A	49	144	22	33	7	0	5	17	10	0	12	.229	.279	.382	76	-6	0-0	.975	0	106	117	2b42		-0.3
	Year	51	146	22	33	7	0	5	17	10	0	13	.226	.276	.377	74	-6	0-0	.975	0	106	117	2b42		-0.4
Total	5	305	1037	162	269	48	15	16	101	105	5	119	.259	.330	.381	97	-6	10-0	.975	-8	99	135	2b202,S79,3b11,O7(4/0/3)		0.1
KLEINOW, RED	John Peter B7.20.1877 Milwaukee WI D10.9.1929 New York NY BR/TR/5-10/165 d5.3 Col St. Edwards																								
1904	NY A	68	209	12	43	8	4	0	16	15	0		.206	.259	.282	68	-8	4	.966	-4	88	104	C62,3b2/OR		-0.7
1905	NY A	88	253	23	56	6	3	1	24	20	2		.221	.284	.281	71	-8	7	.978	-3	111	99	C83,1b3		-0.5
1906	NY A	96	268	30	59	9	3	0	31	24	1		.220	.287	.276	69	-9	8	.974	1	103	103	C95/1		0.0
1907	NY A	90	269	30	71	6	4	0	26	24	1		.264	.327	.316	97	-1	5	.970	-2	90	100	C86/1		0.6
1908	NY A	96	279	16	47	3	2	1	13	22	3		.168	.237	.204	43	-17	5	.973	-9	78	117	C89,2b2		-2.1
1909	NY A	78	206	24	47	11	4	0	15	25	1		.228	.315	.320	100	1	7	.966	-3	90	95	C77		0.5
1910	NY A	6	12	5	5	0	0	0	2	1	0		.417	.462	.417	166	1	2	1.000	0	108	86	C5		0.2
	Bos A	50	147	9	22	1	0	1	8	20	0		.150	.251	.177	34	-11	3	.968	1	110	84	C49		-0.5
	Year	56	159	11	27	1	0	1	10	21	0		.170	.267	.195	44	-10	5	.970	1	110	84	C54		-0.3
1911	Bos A	8	14	0	3	0	0	0	0	2	0		.214	.313	.214	48	-1	1	1.000	0	98	125	C8		0.0
	Phi A	4	8	0	1	0	0	0	1	0	0		.125	.125	.250	-4	-1	0	1.000	0	95	88	C4		-0.1
Total	8	584	1665	146	354	45	20	3	135	153	8	1	.213	.282	.269	71	-54	42	.972	-19	95	101	C558,1b5,2b2,3b2/OR		-2.6
KLESKO, RYAN	Ryan Anthony B6.12.1971 Westminster CA BL/TL/6-3/235(220-235) [AtlIN89 5/116] d9.12																								
1992	Atl N	13	14	0	0	0	0	0	0	0-0	1	5	.000	.067	.000	-75	-3	0-0	1.000	-1	0	134	1b5		-0.4
1993	Atl N	22	17	3	6	1	0	2	5	3-1	0	4	.353	.450	.765	213	3	0-0	1.000	-0	0	0	1b3,O2L		0.2
1994	Atl N	92	245	42	68	13	3	17	47	26-3	2	48	.278	.344	.563	128	9	1-0	.921	-7	72	96	O74L,1b6		0.0
1995	†Atl N	107	329	48	102	25	2	23	70	47-10	2	72	.310	.396	.608	154	26	5-4	.942	-10	79	40	O102L,1b4		1.2
1996	†Atl N	153	528	90	149	21	4	34	93	68-10	2	129	.282	.364	.530	125	19	6-3	.975	-9	82	78	O144L,1b2		0.4
1997	†Atl N	143	467	67	122	23	6	24	84	48-5	4	130	.261	.334	.490	111	6	4-4	.969	-9	89	40	O130L,1b22		-0.9
1998	†Atl N	129	427	69	117	29	1	18	70	56-5	3	66	.274	.359	.473	118	12	5-3	.994	-3	81	139	O120L,1b7		0.5
1999	†Atl N	133	404	55	120	28	2	21	80	53-8	2	69	.297	.376	.532	129	18	5-2	.989	-8	81	85	1b75,O53L/D		0.4
2000	SD N	145	494	88	140	33	2	26	92	91-9	1	81	.283	.393	.516	136	31	23-7	.992	-1	101	99	1b136,O4(2/0/2)		1.9
2001	SD N★	146	538	105	154	34	6	30	113	88-7	3	89	.286	.384	.539	148	40	23-4	.991	-5	88	93	1b145		2.5
2002	SD N	146	540	90	162	39	1	29	95	76-11	4	86	.300	.388	.537	158	44	6-2	.993	-3	100	93	1b112,O31R/D		3.0
2003	SD N	121	397	47	100	18	0	21	67	65-5	3	83	.252	.354	.456	122	14	2-5	.994	6	119	75	1b111/D		0.9
2004	SD N	127	402	58	117	32	2	9	66	73-6	1	67	.291	.399	.448	125	19	3-2	.986	-2	90	44	O104L,1b18,D3	20	1.2
2005	†SD N	137	443	61	110	19	1	18	58	75-2	1	80	.248	.358	.418	108	6	3-4	.981	3	101	116	O121L/1D		0.4
Total	14	1614	5245	823	1467	315	30	272	941	769-82	28	1009	.280	.371	.507	130	244	86-40	.974	-50	84	76	O885(852/0/33),1b647,D9	63	11.3
KLEVEN, JAY	Jay Allen B12.2.1949 Oakland CA BR/TR/6-2/190 d6.20 Col Cal St.-Hayward																								
1976	NY N	2	5	0	1	0	0	0	1	0-0	0	1	.200	.200	.200	14	-1	0-0	1.000	-0	0	0	C2		0.0
KLIMCHOCK, LOU	Louis Stephen B10.15.1939 Hostetter PA BL/TR/5-11/180* d9.27																								
1958	KC A	2	10	2	2	0	0	1	1	0-0	0	1	.200	.200	.500	84	0	0-0	1.000	-0	114	67	2b2		-0.1
1959	KC A	17	66	10	18	1	0	4	13	1-0	0	6	.273	.284	.470	101	0	0-0	.949	-2	97	98	2b16		-0.1
1960	KC A	10	10	0	3	0	0	0	0	0-0	0	1	.300	.300	.300	62	-1	0-0	—	0	0	0	/2		-0.1
1961	KC A	57	121	8	26	1	1	1	16	5-0	0	13	.215	.244	.289	42	-10	0-0	.976	-5	60	44	1b11,O7(4/0/3),3b6/2		-1.6
1962	Mil N	8	8	0	0	0	0	0	0	0-0	0	2	.000	.000	.000	-99	-2	0-0	—	0			/H		-0.2
1963	Was A	9	14	1	2	0	0	0	0	0-0	1	1	.143	.143	.143	-20	-2	0-0	1.000	0	140	63	2b3		-0.2
	Mil N	24	46	3	9	1	0	0	1	0-0	0	12	.196	.196	.217	19	-5	0-1	.988	0	121	190	1b12		-0.6
1964	Mil N	10	21	3	7	2	0	0	2	2-0	0	4	.333	.364	.429	121	1	0-0	1.000	-0	50	0	3b4,2b2		-0.1
1965	Mil N	34	39	3	3	0	0	1	3	2-0	0	8	.077	.119	.077	-42	-7	0-0	.923	1	256	151	1b4		-0.7
1966	NY N	3	3	0	0	0	0	0	0	0-0	0	3	.000	.000	.000	-99	-1	0-0	—	0			/H		-0.2
1968	Cle A	11	15	0	2	0	0	0	0	1-1	0	6	.133	.176	.133	-2	-2	0-0	.500	-0	2	41	3b4/12		-0.5
1969	Cle A	90	258	26	74	13	2	6	26	18-3	0	14	.287	.331	.422	107	2	0-0	.934	-13	78	67	3b56,2b21/C		-1.1

YEAR	TM LG	G	AB	R	H	2B	3B	HR	RBI	BB-IB	HP	SO	AVG	OBP	SLG	AOPS	ABR	SB-CS	FA	FR	RNG	THR	GAMES AT POSITION	DL	BFW
1970	Cle A	41	56	5	9	0	0	1	2	3-1	1	9	.161	.213	.214	18	-6	0-0	1.000	-2	41	124	1b5,2b5		-0.9
Total	12	318	669	64	155	21	3	13	69	31-5	1	71	.232	.264	.330	63	-33	0-1	.906	-25	73	55	3b70,2b52,1b33,O7(4/0/3)/C		-6.3

KLINE, BOBBY John Robert B1.27.1929 St.Petersburg FL BR/TR/6-0/179 d4.11

1955	Was A	77	140	12	31	5	0	0	9	11-0	2	27	.221	.288	.257	50	-10	0-0	.943	7	107	108	S69,2b4,3b3/P		0.1

KLING, JOHNNY John "Noisy" B2.25.1875 Kansas City MO D1.31.1947 Kansas City MO BR/TR/5-9.5/160 d9.11 M1 b-Bill

1900	Chi N	15	51	8	15	3	1	0	7	2	0		.294	.321	.392	100	0	0	.901	-2	94	85	C15		-0.1
1901	Chi N	74	256	26	70	6	3	0	21	9	1		.273	.301	.320	83	-6	8	.952	-9	87	101	C69/1OR		-0.9
1902	Chi N	115	436	50	126	19	3	0	59	29	0		.289	.333	.346	113	7	25	.974	8	107	107	C113/S		2.7
1903	Chi N	132	491	67	146	29	13	3	68	22	2		.297	.330	.428	118	9	23	.969	8	116	106	C132		2.8
1904	Chi N	123	452	41	110	18	0	2	46	16	1		.243	.271	.296	75	-14	7	.974	-4	120	99	C104,O10(9/0/1),1b6		-0.9
1905	Chi N	111	380	26	83	8	6	1	52	28	0		.218	.272	.279	62	-19	13	.966	6	115	95	C106,O4R/1		-0.2
1906	†Chi N	107	343	45	107	15	8	2	46	23	1		.312	.357	.420	134	12	14	**.982**	14	163	101	C96,O3R		3.9
1907	†Chi N	104	334	44	95	15	8	1	43	27	2		.284	.342	.386	120	7	9	**.987**	9	114	91	C98,1b2		2.9
1908	†Chi N	126	424	51	117	23	5	4	59	21	3		.276	.315	.382	117	7	16	.979	2	108	108	C117,O6(1/1/4),1b2		2.4
1910	†Chi N	91	297	31	80	17	2	2	32	37	2	27	.269	.354	.360	109	5	3	.979	5	**135**	88	C86		1.9
1911	Chi N	27	80	8	14	3	2	1	5	8	0	14	.175	.250	.300	54	-5	1	.969	5	170	93	C25		0.2
	Bos N	75	241	32	54	8	1	2	24	30	0	29	.224	.310	.290	63	-12	0	.951	-12	75	115	C71/3		-1.8
	Year	102	321	40	68	11	3	3	29	38	0	43	.212	.295	.293	61	-17	1	.956	-6	100	109	C96/3		-1.6
1912	Bos N	81	252	26	80	10	3	2	30	15	0	30	.317	.356	.405	106	1	3	.958	-0	94	107	C74,M		0.7
1913	Cin N	80	209	20	57	7	6	0	23	14	0	14	.273	.318	.364	95	-2	2-1	.975	4	108	107	C63		0.8
Total	13	1261	4246	475	1154	181	61	20	515	281	12	114	.272	.319	.357	100	-10	124-1	.971	36	115	101	C1169,O24(10/1/13),1b12/3S		14.4

KLING, RUDY Rudolph A. B3.23.1870 St.Louis MO D3.14.1937 St.Louis MO BR/TR/5-10/178 d9.21

1902	StL N	4	10	1	2	0	0	0	4	0	0		.200	.429	.200	99	0	1	.842	-2	63	151	S4		-0.1

KLINGER, JOE Joseph John B8.2.1902 Canonsburg PA D7.31.1960 Little Rock AR BR/TR/6-0/190 d9.13

1927	NY N	3	5	0	2	0	0	0	0	0	0	2	.400	.400	.400	115	0	0-0	1.000	0	141	0	/OL		0.0
1930	Chi A	4	8	0	3	0	0	0	1	0	0	0	.375	.375	.375	94	0	0-0	1.000	-1	0	0	C2,1b2		-0.1
Total	2	7	13	0	5	0	0	0	1	0	0	2	.385	.385	.385	102	0	0-0	1.000	0	0	178	1b2,C2/OL		-0.1

KLOZA, NAP John Clarence B9.7.1903 , Poland D6.11.1962 Milwaukee WI BR/TR/5-11/180 d8.16

1931	StL A	3	7	1	1	0	0	0	1	0	0	4	.143	.250	.143	5	-1	0-0	1.000	0	33	682	O3R		-0.1
1932	StL A	19	13	4	2	0	1	0	2	4	0	4	.154	.353	.308	69	-1	0-0	1.000	0	115	0	O3(1/2/0)		-0.1
Total	2	22	20	5	3	0	1	0	2	5	0	8	.150	.320	.250	48	-2	0-0	1.000	0	59	467	O6(1/2/3)		-0.2

KLUGMANN, JOE Josie B3.26.1895 St.Louis MO D7.18.1951 Moberly MO BR/TR/5-11/175 d9.23

1921	Chi N	6	21	3	6	0	0	0	1	2	0	2	.286	.348	.286	69	-1	0-1	.969	-0	90	37	2b5		-0.1
1922	Chi N	2	2	0	0	0	0	0	0	0	0	0	.000	.000	.000	-98	-1	0-0	1.000	1	129	274	2b2		0.0
1924	Bro N	31	79	7	13	2	1	0	3	2	0	9	.165	.185	.215	7	-11	0-0	.929	-3	85	107	2b28/S		-1.3
1925	Cle A	38	85	12	28	9	2	0	12	8	0	4	.329	.387	.482	119	2	3-1	.959	-3	100	79	2b29,1b4,3b2		0.0
Total	4	77	187	22	47	11	3	0	17	11	1	15	.251	.296	.342	67	-11	3-2	.947	-5	93	90	2b64,1b4,3b2/S		-1.4

KLUMPP, ELMER Elmer Edward B8.26.1906 St.Louis MO D10.18.1996 Menomonee Falls WI BR/TR/6-0/184 d4.17

1934	Was A	12	15	2	2	0	0	0	2	1	0	1	.133	.188	.133	-17	-3	0-0	.889	-1	194	94	C11		-0.3
1937	Bro N	5	11	0	1	0	0	0	2	1	0	4	.091	.167	.091	-28	-2	0-0	1.000	1	98	0	C3		-0.1
Total	2	17	26	2	3	0	0	0	2	1	0	5	.115	.179	.115	-21	-5	0-0	.943	-1	156	57	C14		-0.4

KLUSMAN, BILLY William F. B3.24.1865 Cincinnati OH D6.24.1907 Cincinnati OH BR/TR/5-10.5/185 d6.21

1888	Bos N	28	107	9	18	4	0	2	11	5	0	13	.168	.205	.262	47	-6	3	.914	-6	89	62	2b28		-1.1
1890	StL AA	15	65	9	18	4	1	1	11	1	0		.277	.288	.415	94	-1	1	.896	-1	116	55	2b15		-0.1
Total	2	43	172	18	36	8	1	3	22	6	0	13	.209	.236	.320	66	-7	4	.908	-6	98	60	2b43		-1.2

KLUSZEWSKI, TED Theodore Bernard "Big Klu" B9.10.1924 Argo IL D3.29.1988 Cincinnati OH BL/TL/6-2/225(225-245) d4.18 C9 Col Indiana

1947	Cin N	9	10	1	1	0	0	0	1	1	0	2	.100	.182	.100	-23	-2	0-0	1.000	-0	0	115	1b2		-0.2
1948	Cin N	113	379	49	104	23	4	12	57	18	0	32	.274	.307	.451	107	1	1	.990	2	106	80	1b98		0.0
1949	Cin N	136	531	63	164	26	2	8	68	19	0	24	.309	.333	.411	97	-4	3	.989	-6	84	97	1b134		-1.4
1950	Cin N	134	538	76	165	37	0	25	111	33	1	28	.307	.348	.515	123	16	3	.987	-12	66	83	1b131		0.0
1951	Cin N	154	607	74	157	35	2	13	77	35	2	33	.259	.301	.387	83	-16	6-2	**.997**	-7	80	81	1b154		-2.8
1952	Cin N	135	497	62	159	24	11	16	86	47	4	28	.320	.383	.509	146	30	3-3	**.993**	-8	76	97	1b133		1.8
1953	Cin N★	149	570	97	180	25	0	40	108	55	4	34	.316	.380	.570	142	35	2-0	**.995**	-15	62	115	1b147		1.2
1954	Cin N★	149	573	104	187	28	3	**49**	**141**	78	3	35	.326	.407	.642	165	54	0-2	**.996**	-2	94	117	1b149		4.2
1955	Cin N★	153	612	116	**192**	25	0	47	113	66-25	4	40	.314	.382	.585	144	39	1-1	**.995**	-8	81	118	1b153		2.1
1956	Cin N★	138	517	91	156	14	1	35	102	49-22	3	31	.302	.362	.536	130	21	1-0	.990	-5	90	101	1b131		0.9
1957	Cin N	69	127	12	34	7	0	6	21	5-3	1	5	.268	.301	.465	95	-1	0-0	.989	-0	101	66	1b23		-0.2
1958	Pit N	100	301	29	88	13	4	4	37	26-6	0	16	.292	.348	.402	101	1	0-0	.994	-5	73	102	1b72		-0.9
1959	Pit N	60	122	11	32	10	1	2	17	5-1	0	14	.262	.291	.410	85	-3	0-0	1.000	0	90	93	1b20		-0.3
	†Chi A	31	101	11	30	2	1	2	10	9-3	0	10	.297	.351	.396	107	1	0-1	1.000	-2	62	64	1b29		0.0
1960	Chi A	81	181	20	53	9	0	5	39	22-5	0	10	.293	.364	.425	116	4	0-1	.997	-2	80	113	1b39		-1.2
1961	LA A	107	263	32	64	12	0	15	39	24-5	0	23	.243	.303	.460	91	-4	0-0	.989	-5	67	99	1b66		2.8
Total	15	1718	5929	848	1766	290	29	279	1028	492-70	23	365	.298	.353	.498	122	172	20-10	.993	-74	80	99	1b1481	32	

KLUTTS, MICKEY Gene Ellis B9.20.1954 Montebello CA BR/TR/5-11/189(170-189) [NYA72 4/86] d7.7 [DL 1978 Oak A 21]

1976	NY A	2	3	0	0	0	0	0	0	0-0	1	1	.000	.000	.000	-99	-1	0-0	.875	-0	83	0	S2		-0.1
1977	NY A	5	15	3	4	1	0	1	4	2-0	1	1	.267	.389	.533	149	1	0-1	1.000	3	168	155	3b4/S	24	0.2
1978	NY A	1	2	1	2	1	0	0	0	0-0	0	0	1.000	1.000	1.500	605	2	0-0	.750	0	92	555	/3	27	0.2
1979	Oak A	24	73	14	21	2	1	1	4	7-0	0	20	.192	.262	.288	51	-5	0-1	.882	-3	105	60	S10,2b8,3b6,D2	130	-0.8
1980	Oak A	75	197	20	53	14	0	4	21	13-1	0	41	.269	.313	.401	100	0	1-4	.947	-7	92	35	3b62,S8,2b7/D	64	-0.8
1981	†Oak A	15	46	9	17	0	0	5	11	2-1	0	9	.370	.396	.696	217	6	0-0	.957	-3	69	51	3b14	141	0.3
1982	Oak A	55	157	10	28	8	0	0	14	9-0	0	18	.178	.222	.229	25	-16	0-0	.946	-3	94	63	3b49	21	-2.0
1983	Tor A	22	43	3	11	0	0	3	5	1-1	1	11	.256	.289	.465	97	0	0-1	1.000	-4	57	94	3b17,D2		-0.5
Total	8	199	536	49	129	26	1	14	59	34-3	3	101	.241	.289	.371	83	-13	1-7	.948	-18	91	57	3b153,S21,2b15,D5	428	-3.5

KLUTTZ, CLYDE Clyde Franklin B12.12.1917 Rockwell NC D5.12.1979 Salisbury NC BR/TR/6-0/198* d4.20 Col Catawba

1942	Bos N	72	210	21	56	10	1	1	31	7	1	13	.267	.294	.338	86	-5	0	.979	-3	75	92	C57		-0.4
1943	Bos N	66	207	13	51	7	0	0	20	15	0	9	.246	.297	.280	68	-9	0	.973	-3	58	158	C55		-0.9
1944	Bos N	81	229	20	64	12	2	2	19	13	0	14	.279	.318	.376	91	-3	0	.980	1	64	155	C58		0.1
1945	Bos N	25	81	9	24	4	1	0	10	2	0	6	.296	.313	.370	89	0	0	.987	0	106	123	C19		0.0
	NY N	73	222	25	62	14	0	4	21	15	2	10	.279	.331	.396	100	0	1	.978	-1	161	115	C57		0.2
	Year	98	303	34	86	18	1	4	31	17	2	16	.284	.326	.389	97	-2	1	.981	-1	146	117	C76		0.2
1946	NY N	5	8	0	3	0	0	0	1	0	0	1	.375	.375	.375	112	0	0	.857	-1	49	0	C2		0.0
	StL N	52	136	8	36	7	0	0	14	10	0		.265	.315	.316	76	-4	0	.980	3	149	105	C49		0.1
	Year	57	144	8	39	7	0	0	15	10	0	11	.271	.318	.319	78	-4	0	.976	2	146	102	C51		0.1
1947	Pit N	73	232	26	70	9	2	6	42	17	2	18	.302	.355	.435	106	1	1	.987	2	91	150	C69		0.7
1948	Pit N	94	271	26	60	12	2	4	20	20	2	19	.221	.275	.325	61	-16	3	.978	2	104	156	C91		-0.9
1951	StL A	4	4	2	2	1	0	0	1	1	0	1	.500	.600	.750	256	1	0-0	1.000	0	0	509	/C		0.1
	Was A	53	159	15	49	9	0	1	22	20	1	8	.308	.389	.384	111	4	0-0	.968	-6	96	65	C46		0.0
	Year	57	163	17	51	10	0	1	23	21	1	9	.313	.395	.393	115	5	0-0	.968	-6	94	73	C47		0.1
1952	Was A	58	144	7	33	5	0	1	11	12	1	11	.229	.293	.285	63	-7	0-0	.979	1	107	88	C52	30	-0.5
Total	9	656	1903	172	510	90	8	19	212	132	7	119	.268	.318	.354	86	-40	5-0	.978	-5	98	126	C556	30	-1.5

KMAK, JOE Joseph Robert B5.3.1963 Napa CA BR/TR/6-0/185* [SFN85 10/238] d4.6 Col California-Santa Barbara

1993	Mil A	51	110	9	24	5	0	0	7	14-0	1	18	.218	.317	.264	59	-6	6-2	1.000	-2	88	114	C50		-0.5
1995	Chi N	19	53	7	13	3	0	1	6	6-0	1	12	.245	.328	.358	83	-1	0-0	1.000	-3	118	91	C18/3	35	-0.3
Total	2	70	163	16	37	8	0	1	13	20-0	3	25	.227	.321	.294	67	-7	6-2	1.000	-5	97	107	C68/3	35	-0.8

YEAR	TM LG	G	AB	R	H	2B	3B	HR	RBI	BB-IB	HP	SO	AVG	OBP	SLG	AOPS	ABR	SB-CS	FA	FR	RNG	THR	GAMES AT POSITION	DL	BFW

KNABE, OTTO Franz Otto "Dutch" B6.12.1884 Carrick PA D5.17.1961 Philadelphia PA BR/TR/5-8/175 d10.3 M2

YEAR	TM LG	G	AB	R	H	2B	3B	HR	RBI	BB-IB	HP	SO	AVG	OBP	SLG	AOPS	ABR	SB-CS	FA	FR	RNG	THR	GAMES AT POSITION	DL	BFW
1905	Pit N	3	10	1	3	1	0	0	2	3	0		.300	.462	.400	154	1		.786	0	130	247	3b3		0.1
1907	Phi N	129	444	67	113	16	9	1	34	52	5		.255	.339	.338	114	8	18	.960	2	95	129	2b121,O5(1/0/3)		1.2
1908	Phi N	151	555	63	121	26	8	0	27	49	7		.218	.290	.294	84	-9	27	.969	10	104	102	2b151		0.2
1909	Phi N	113	402	40	94	13	3	0	34	35	8		.234	.308	.281	82	-8	9	.938	5	101	105	2b110/OL		-0.2
1910	Phi N	137	510	73	133	18	6	1	44	47	3	42	.261	.327	.325	87	-8	15	.954	14	97	119	2b136		0.7
1911	Phi N	142	528	99	125	15	6	1	42	94	0	35	.237	.352	.294	89	-10	23	.950	2	100	88	2b142		-0.6
1912	Phi N	126	426	56	120	11	4	0	46	55	2	20	.282	.366	.326	85	-7	16	.952	2	101	93	2b123		-0.4
1913	Phi N	148	571	70	150	25	7	2	53	45	3	26	.263	.320	.342	85	-11	14-18	.959	6	106	97	2b148		-0.6
1914	Bal F	147	469	45	106	26	2	2	42	53	2	28	.226	.307	.303	65	-29	10	.956	2	99	98	2b144,M		-2.6
1915	Bal F	103	320	38	81	16	2	1	25	37	2	16	.253	.334	.325	83	-10	7	.975	5	98	129	2b94/ORM		-0.4
1916	Pit N	28	89	4	17	3	1	0	9	6	2	5	.191	.258	.247	55	-5	-1	.962	-3	103	27	2b28		-0.9
	Chi N	51	145	17	40	8	0	0	7	9	2	18	.276	.327	.331	92	-1	3	.939	3	113	113	2b42/S3OR		0.4
	Year	79	234	21	57	11	1	0	16	15	4	23	.244	.300	.299	79	-5	4	.948	0	109	77	2b70/S3OR		-0.5
Total	11	1278	4469	572	1103	178	48	8	365	485	36	191	.247	.325	.313	84	-89	143-18	.957	47	101	104	2b1239,O8(2/0/5),3b4/S		-3.1

KNAUPP, COTTON Henry Antone B8.13.1889 San Antonio TX D7.6.1967 New Orleans LA BR/TR/5-9/165 d8.30

YEAR	TM LG	G	AB	R	H	2B	3B	HR	RBI	BB-IB	HP	SO	AVG	OBP	SLG	AOPS	ABR	SB-CS	FA	FR	RNG	THR	GAMES AT POSITION	DL	BFW
1910	Cle A	18	59	3	14	3	1	0	11	8		0	.237	.338	.322	105	-1		.884	-7	91	81	S18		-0.6
1911	Cle A	13	39	2	4	1	0	0	0	3		0	.103	.103	.128	-35	-7	3	.964	2	118	57	S13		-0.5
Total	2	31	98	5	18	4	1	0	11	8	1	0	.184	.252	.245	48	-6	4	.913	-6	100	73	S31		-1.1

KNICELY, ALAN Alan Lee B5.19.1955 Harrisonburg VA BR/TR/6-0.5/194* [HouN74 3/63] d8.12

YEAR	TM LG	G	AB	R	H	2B	3B	HR	RBI	BB-IB	HP	SO	AVG	OBP	SLG	AOPS	ABR	SB-CS	FA	FR	RNG	THR	GAMES AT POSITION	DL	BFW
1979	Hou N	7	6	0	0	0	0	0	2-0	0		3	.000	.250	.000	-27	-1	0-0	1.000	-1	0	0	C3/3		-0.2
1980	Hou N	1	1	0	0	0	0	0	0-0	0		1	.000	.000	.000	-99	0	0-0	—	0			/H		0.0
1981	Hou N	3	7	2	4	0	0	-2	2	0-0	0	0	.571	.571	1.429	482	3	0-0	1.000	1	0	0	C2/OL		0.4
1982	Hou N	59	133	10	25	2	0	2	12	14-3	1	30	.188	.270	.248	50	-9	0-1	.977	0	119	91	C23,O16(1/0/15)/3		-1.0
1983	Cin N	59	98	11	22	3	0	2	10	16-3	0	28	.224	.333	.316	78	-2	0-2	1.000	1	82	113	C31,O8(3/0/5),1b2		-0.3
1984	Cin N	10	29	0	4	0	0	0	5	3-0	0	6	.138	.200	.138	2	-4	0-0	.984	-2	92	76	1b8/C		-0.6
1985	Cin N	48	158	17	40	9	0	5	26	16-2	1	34	.253	.322	.405	98	0	0-0	.968	-9	73	75	C46		-0.8
	Phi N	7	7	0	0	0	0	0	0	0-0	0	4	.000	.000	.000	-98	-2	0-0	1.000	-0	335	1	/1		-0.2
	Year	55	165	17	40	9	0	5	26	16-2	1	38	.242	.310	.388	91	-2	0-0	.968	-10	73	75	C46/1		-1.0
1986	StL N	34	82	8	16	3	0	1	6	17-0	0	21	.195	.330	.268	68	-3	1-1	.995	-0	104	125	1b29,C2		-0.5
Total	8	228	521	48	111	17	0	12	61	68-8	2	128	.213	.303	.315	73	-18	1-4	.979	-10	83	84	C108,1b40,O25(5/0/20),3b2		-3.2

KNICKERBOCKER, AUSTIN Austin Jay B10.15.1918 Bangall NY D2.18.1997 Clinton Corners NY BR/TR/5-11/185 d4.19

YEAR	TM LG	G	AB	R	H	2B	3B	HR	RBI	BB-IB	HP	SO	AVG	OBP	SLG	AOPS	ABR	SB-CS	FA	FR	RNG	THR	GAMES AT POSITION	DL	BFW
1947	Phi A	21	48	8	12	3	2	0	2	3	0	4	.250	.294	.396	89	-1	0-1	.943	1	117	110	O14(2/2/10)		-0.1

KNICKERBOCKER, BILL William Hart B12.29.1911 Los Angeles CA D9.8.1963 Sebastopol CA BR/TR/5-11/170 d4.12

YEAR	TM LG	G	AB	R	H	2B	3B	HR	RBI	BB-IB	HP	SO	AVG	OBP	SLG	AOPS	ABR	SB-CS	FA	FR	RNG	THR	GAMES AT POSITION	DL	BFW
1933	Cle A	80	279	20	63	16	3	2	32	11	0	30	.226	.255	.326	51	-21	1-4	.939	2	104	97	S80		-1.4
1934	Cle A	146	593	82	188	32	5	4	67	25	2	40	.317	.347	.408	93	-8	6-6	.962	-7	96	114	S146		-0.5
1935	Cle A	132	540	77	161	34	5	0	55	27	1	31	.298	.332	.380	82	-15	2-12	.956	9	108	105	S128		-0.1
1936	Cle A	155	618	81	182	35	3	8	73	56	1	30	.294	.354	.400	85	-15	5-14	.952	-1	98	92	S155		-0.7
1937	StL A	121	491	53	128	29	5	4	61	30	0	32	.261	.303	.365	67	-26	3-2	.958	-9	103	73	S115,2b6		-2.5
1938	NY A	46	128	15	32	8	3	1	21	11	0	10	.250	.309	.383	73	-6	0-0	.982	1	96	117	2b34,S3		-0.3
1939	NY A	6	13	2	2	1	0	0	1	0	0	0	.154	.154	.231	-3	-2	0-0	1.000	1	111	97	2b2,S2		-0.1
1940	NY A	45	124	17	30	8	1	1	10	14	3	8	.242	.333	.347	80	-3	1-1	.985	-0	103	147	S19,3b17		-0.2
1941	Chi A	89	343	51	84	23	2	7	29	41	2	27	.245	.329	.385	89	-5	6-5	.970	-13	90	113	2b88		-1.3
1942	Phi A	87	289	25	73	12	0	1	19	29	1	30	.253	.323	.304	79	-3	1-2	.964	-10	93	85	2b81/S		-1.4
Total	10	907	3418	423	943	198	27	28	368	244	9	238	.276	.326	.374	79	-109	25-46	.955	-28	101	98	S649,2b211,3b17		-8.5

KNIGHT, LON Alonzo P. B6.16.1853 Philadelphia PA D4.23.1932 Philadelphia PA BR/TR/5-11.5/165 d9.4 M2/U3 ▲

YEAR	TM LG	G	AB	R	H	2B	3B	HR	RBI	BB-IB	HP	SO	AVG	OBP	SLG	AOPS	ABR	SB-CS	FA	FR	RNG	THR	GAMES AT POSITION	DL	BFW
1875	Ath NA	13	47	5	6	2	0	0	2	0		2	.128	.128	.170	2	-5	2-0	.875	-0	112	113	P13/S		-0.1
1876	Phi N	55	240	32	60	9	3	0	24	2		2	.250	.256	.313	89	-3		.804	-6	92	56	P34,1b13,O9(0/3/6),2b6		-0.6
1880	Wor N	49	201	31	48	11	3	0	21	5		8	.239	.257	.323	88	-3		.863	2	181	49	O49R		0.0
1881	Det N	83	340	67	92	16	3	1	52	23		21	.271	.317	.344	104	2		.890	0	98	184	O82R/21		0.2
1882	Det N	86	347	39	72	12	6	0	24	16		21	.207	.242	.277	66	-13		.867	-1	130	50	O84R,1b2		-1.4
1883	Phi AA	97	429	80	108	23	9	1	53	21			.252	.287	.354	96	-3		.858	-1	120	235	O93R,3b3,2b2,M		-0.4
1884	Phi AA	108	484	94	131	18	12	1		10	1		.271	.287	.364	104	0		.911	11	176	198	O108R,P2/1M		0.9
1885	Phi AA	29	119	8	25	1	0	0	14	9	1		.210	.271	.235	58	-6		.921	4	174	295	O29R/P		-0.2
	Pro N	25	81	8	13	1	0	0	8	11		17	.160	.261	.173	44	-4		.957	3	144	353	O25(0/4/22)/P		-0.2
Total	7	532	2241	386	549	91	37	3	196	97		69	.245	.277	.323	89	-30		.887	11	140	170	O479(0/7/473),P38,1b17,2b9,3b3		-1.7

KNIGHT, RAY Charles Ray B12.28.1952 Albany GA BR/TR/6-2/190(182-195) [CinN70 10/238] d9.10 M3/C5 OF(9/0/1)

YEAR	TM LG	G	AB	R	H	2B	3B	HR	RBI	BB-IB	HP	SO	AVG	OBP	SLG	AOPS	ABR	SB-CS	FA	FR	RNG	THR	GAMES AT POSITION	DL	BFW
1974	Cin N	14	11	1	2	1	0	0	2	1-0	0	2	.182	.250	.273	47	-1	0-0	1.000	-1	78	0	3b14		-0.2
1977	Cin N	80	92	8	24	5	1	1	13	9-1	0	16	.261	.324	.370	84	-2	1-1	.941	-1	96	120	3b37,2b17,O5L,S3		-0.3
1978	Cin N	83	65	7	13	3	0	1	4	3-0	0	13	.200	.235	.292	46	-5	0-0	.868	-0	115	35	3b60,2b4,O3(2/0/1)/1S		-0.6
1979	†Cin N	150	551	64	175	37	4	10	79	38-4	3	57	.318	.360	.454	122	11	4-4	.962	-10	92	101	3b149		0.5
1980	Cin N★	162	618	71	163	39	7	14	78	36-9	4	62	.264	.307	.417	103	0	1-2	.969	-11	89	80	3b162		-1.5
1981	Cin N	106	386	43	100	23	1	6	34	33-3	4	51	.259	.322	.370	97	-1	2-4	.957	-7	88	110	3b105		-1.2
1982	Hou N★	158	609	72	179	36	6	6	70	48-9	4	58	.294	.344	.402	119	16	2-5	.990	-2	78	111	1b96,3b67		1.0
1983	Hou N	145	507	43	154	36	4	9	70	42-9	4	62	.304	.355	.444	129	20	0-3	.993	-11	73	128	1b143		-0.1
1984	Hou N	88	278	15	62	10	0	2	29	14-1	1	30	.223	.259	.281	56	-17	0-3	.946	-6	89	77	3b54,1b24		-2.8
	NY N	27	93	13	26	4	0	1	6	7-1	1	13	.280	.337	.355	96	0	0-0	.962	-5	73	92	3b27,1b3		-0.6
	Year	115	371	28	88	14	0	3	35	21-2	2	43	.237	.279	.299	67	-17	0-3	.951	-11	83	82	3b81,1b27		-3.4
1985	NY N	90	271	22	59	12	0	6	36	13-1	1	32	.218	.252	.328	64	-14	1-1	.958	-9	81	86	3b73,2b2/1		-2.6
1986	†NY N	137	486	51	145	24	2	11	76	40-2	2	63	.298	.351	.424	117	11	2-1	.948	-19	81	86	3b132/1		-1.1
1987	Bal A	150	563	46	144	24	0	14	65	39-3	6	90	.256	.310	.373	82	-15	0-0	.956	12	113	113	3b130,D14,1b6		-0.5
1988	Det A	105	299	34	65	12	2	3	33	20-0	1	30	.217	.271	.301	63	-15	1-1	.991	-4	84	95	1b64,D25,3b11,O2L		-2.4
Total	13	1495	4829	490	1311	266	27	84	595	343-43	36	579	.271	.321	.390	100	-6	14-25	.957	-70	92	96	3b1021,1b339,D39,2b23,O10L,S4	33	-12.4

KNIGHT, JOHN John Wesley "Schoolboy" B10.6.1885 Philadelphia PA D12.19.1965 Walnut Creek CA BR/TR/6-2.5/180 d4.14 Col Penn

YEAR	TM LG	G	AB	R	H	2B	3B	HR	RBI	BB-IB	HP	SO	AVG	OBP	SLG	AOPS	ABR	SB-CS	FA	FR	RNG	THR	GAMES AT POSITION	DL	BFW
1905	Phi A	88	325	28	66	12	1	3	29	9			.203	.227	.274	58	-17	4	.895	-26	79	39	S79,3b4		-4.5
1906	Phi A	74	253	29	49	7	2	3	20	19	0		.194	.250	.273	62	-11	6	.922	2	102	98	3b67,2b7		-0.8
1907	Phi A	40	139	6	29	7	1	0	12	10			.209	.272	.273	72	-4	1	.862	-3	90	115	3b40		-0.6
	Bos N	98	360	31	78	9	3	2	29	19	0		.217	.256	.275	70	-13	8	.924	3	104	136	3b92,2b4		-0.8
	Year	138	499	37	107	16	4	2	41	29	2		.214	.260	.275	71	-17	9	.906	-0	100	130	3b132,2b4		-1.4
1909	NY A	116	360	46	85	8	5	0	40	37	2		.236	.311	.286	88	-4	15	.901	-4	97	81	S76,1b19,2b17,3b3		-0.7
1910	NY A	117	414	58	129	25	4	3	45	34	6		.312	.372	.413	138	19	23	.929	-2	97	143	S79,1b23,2b7,3b4/OR		2.1
1911	NY A	132	470	69	126	16	7	3	62	42	11		.268	.342	.351	88	-8	18	.907	-6	89	99	S82,1b27,2b21/3		-0.8
1912	Was A	32	93	10	15	2	1	0	9	16	0		.161	.284	.204	40	-7	4	.926	-5	71	107	2b27,1b5		-1.2
1913	NY A	70	250	24	59	10	0	0	24	25	2	27	.236	.310	.276	72	-8	7	.980	8	148	95	1b124,2b104/OR		-0.1
Total	8	767	2664	301	636	96	24	14	270	211	24	27	.239	.300	.309	84	-53	86	.909	-33	90	91	S316,3b211,1b124,2b104/OR		-7.4

KNIGHT, JOE Jonah William "Quiet Joe" B9.28.1859 Port Stanley ON, Can. D10.16.1938 Lynhurst ON, Can. BL/TL/5-11/185 d5.16 ▲

YEAR	TM LG	G	AB	R	H	2B	3B	HR	RBI	BB-IB	HP	SO	AVG	OBP	SLG	AOPS	ABR	SB-CS	FA	FR	RNG	THR	GAMES AT POSITION	DL	BFW
1884	Phi N	6	24	7	6	3	0	0	2	0		2	.250	.250	.375	98	1		.789	-0	115	0	P6		0.0
1890	Cin N	127	481	67	150	26	8	4	38		4	31	.312	.367	.422	131	18	17	.925	-6	51	0	O127L		0.8
Total	2	133	505	69	156	29	8	4	69	38	4	33	.309	.362	.422	130	19	17	.925	-7	51	0	O127L,P6		0.8

KNISELY, PETE Peter Cole B8.11.1887 Waynesburg PA D7.1.1948 Brownsville PA BR/TR/5-9/185 d9.4

YEAR	TM LG	G	AB	R	H	2B	3B	HR	RBI	BB-IB	HP	SO	AVG	OBP	SLG	AOPS	ABR	SB-CS	FA	FR	RNG	THR	GAMES AT POSITION	DL	BFW
1912	Cin N	21	67	10	22	7	3	0	7	4		5	.328	.375	.522	148	4	3	.939	-1	92	207	O13C,2b3/S		0.2
1913	Cin N	2	2	0	0	0	0	0	0	0	0	1	.000	.000	.000	-99	-1	0	—	0			/H		-0.1
1914	Chi N	37	69	5	9	0	1	0	5	5		6	.130	.200	.159	7	-8	0	.975	2	116	130	O17(10/1/6)		-0.8
1915	Chi N	64	134	12	33	9	0	0	17	15		18	.246	.331	.313	95	0	1-2	.940	-3	98	109	O33(8/9/16),2b9		-0.5
Total	4	124	272	27	64	16	4	0	29	24		30	.235	.324	.324	86	-5	4-2	.951	-2	102	138	O63(18/23/22),2b12/S		-1.2

YEAR	TM LG	G	AB	R	H	2B	3B	HR	RBI	BB-IB	HP	SO	AVG	OBP	SLG	AOPS	ABR	SB-CS	FA	FR	RNG	THR	GAMES AT POSITION	DL	BFW
KNOBLAUCH, CHUCK			Edward Charles B7.7.1968 Houston TX							BR/TR/5-9/181(169-181)			[MinA89 1/25]		d4.9	Col Texas A&M-Commerce								
1991	†Min A	151	565	78	159	24	6	1	50	59-0	4	40	.281	.351	.350	91	-5	25-5	.975	2	107	104	2b148,S2		0.4
1992	Min A★	155	600	104	178	19	6	2	56	88-1	5	60	.297	.384	.358	107	10	34-13	.992	-8	96	107	2b154/SD		0.9
1993	Min A	153	602	82	167	27	4	2	41	65-1	9	44	.277	.354	.346	89	-7	29-11	.988	-2	100	98	2b148,S6/OC		0.0
1994	Min A★	109	445	85	139	45	3	5	51	41-2	10	56	.312	.381	.461	115	13	35-6	.994	-21	91	84	2b109/S		0.2
1995	Min A	136	538	107	179	34	8	11	63	78-3	10	95	.333	.424	.487	136	33	46-18	.985	-9	98	94	2b136,S2		3.2
1996	Min A★	153	578	140	197	35	14	13	72	98-6	19	74	.341	.448	.517	142	44	45-14	.988	-17	93	94	2b151,D2		3.5
1997	Min A★	156	611	117	178	26	10	9	58	84-6	17	84	.291	.390	.411	108	11	62-10	.985	-7	101	105	2b154/SD		2.0
1998	†NY A	150	603	117	160	25	4	17	64	76-1	18	70	.265	.361	.405	104	6	31-12	.981	1	100	106	2b149/D		1.5
1999	†NY A	150	603	120	176	36	4	18	68	83-0	21	57	.292	.393	.454	118	21	28-9	.963	-20	94	68	2b150		1.0
2000	†NY A	102	400	75	113	22	2	5	26	46-0	8	45	.283	.366	.385	92	-3	15-7	.958	-13	86	82	2b82,D20	28	-1.3
2001	†NY A	137	521	66	130	20	3	9	44	58-1	14	73	.250	.339	.351	82	-12	38-9	.989	-2	89	133	O108,D24		-1.3
2002	KC A	80	300	41	63	9	0	6	22	28-1	4	32	.210	.284	.300	50	-22	19-3	.980	-0	96	115	O74L,D2	44	-2.1
Total	12	1632	6366	1132	1839	322	64	98	615	804-22	139	730	.289	.378	.406	105	89	407-117	.982	-96			2b1381,O183(182/1/0),D51,S13	72	8.1
KNODE, MIKE			Kenneth Thomson B11.8.1895 Westminster MD							D12.20.1980 South Bend IN			BR/TR/5-10/160		d6.28	b-Ray Col Michigan								
1920	StL N	42	65	11	15	1	1	0	12	5	2	6	.231	.306	.277	71	-2	0-1	.824	-1	85	102	O9(2/0/7),2b4,S2,3b2		-0.4
KNODE, RAY			Robert Troxell "Bob" B1.28.1901 Westminster MD							D4.13.1982 Battle Creek MI			BL/TL/5-10/160		d6.30	b-Mike Col Michigan								
1923	Cle A	22	38	7	11	0	0	4	2	0	0	4	.289	.325	.447	102	0	1-0	.992	0	105	100	1b21		-0.1
1924	Cle A	11	37	6	9	1	0	0	4	3	0	4	.243	.300	.270	47	-3	2-1	.992	1	130	141	1b10		-0.3
1925	Cle A	45	108	13	27	5	0	0	11	10	0	4	.250	.314	.296	55	-7	3-3	.990	1	107	120	1b34		-0.8
1926	Cle A	31	24	6	8	1	1	0	2	2	0	3	.333	.385	.458	118	1	0-0	.984	0	148	97	1b11		0.1
Total	4	109	207	32	55	7	1	2	21	17	0	11	.266	.321	.338	69	-9	6-4	.990	2	114	118	1b76		-1.1
KNOEDLER, JUSTIN			Justin Joseph B7.17.1980 Springfield IL							BR/TR/6-2/210*			[SFN01 5/166]		d10.3	Col Miami								
2004	SF N	1	1	0	1	0	0	0	0	0-0	0	1	1.000	1.000	1.000	-97	0	0-0	1.000	0	0	0	/C		0.0
2005	SF N	8	10	0	1	0	0	0	0	0-0	1	1	.100	.182	.100	-22	-2	0-0	1.000	-0	0	0	C4		-0.2
Total	2	9	11	0	2	0	0	0	0	0-0	1	2	.091	.167	.091	-29	-2	0-0	1.000	-0	0	0	C5		-0.2
KNOLL, PUNCH			Charles Elmer B10.7.1881 Evansville IN							D2.8.1960 Evansville IN			BR/TR/5-7.5/170		d4.27									
1905	Was A	79	244	24	52	10	5	0	29	9	2		.213	.247	.295	75	-8	3	.927	-1	75	63	O63(10/0/53),C5,1b2		-1.3
KNOOP, BOBBY			Robert Frank B10.18.1938 Sioux City IA							BR/TR/6-1/170(170-183)			d4.13		M1/C21									
1964	LA A	162	486	42	105	8	1	7	38	46-6	5	109	.216	.289	.280	66	-23	3-2	.978	38	119	123	2b161		2.9
1965	Cal A	142	465	47	125	24	4	7	43	31-5	0	101	.269	.313	.383	99	-1	3-2	.971	23	117	107	2b142		3.5
1966	Cal A★	161	590	54	137	18	11	17	72	43-8	1	144	.232	.282	.386	94	-8	1-5	.981	22	113	129	2b161		2.8
1967	Cal A	159	511	51	125	18	5	9	38	44-13	1	136	.245	.305	.352	98	-2	2-2	.986	9	102	107	2b159		2.1
1968	Cal A	152	494	48	123	20	4	3	39	35-6	3	128	.249	.301	.324	93	-5	3-2	.981	19	110	114	2b151		3.0
1969	Cal A	27	71	5	14	1	0	1	9	6-1	0	16	.197	.318	.254	65	-3	1-3	.977	2	99	95	2b27		0.0
	Chi A	104	345	34	79	14	1	6	41	35-3	2	68	.229	.301	.328	73	-12	2-0	.985	31	123	113	2b104	21	2.6
	Year	131	416	39	93	15	1	7	48	48-4	2	84	.224	.304	.315	72	-15	3-3	.984	33	118	110	2b131		2.6
1970	Chi A	130	402	34	92	13	2	5	36	34-4	2	79	.229	.290	.348	63	-20	0-1	.984	27	123	120	2b126		1.5
1971	KC A	72	161	14	33	8	1	1	11	15-1	0	36	.205	.270	.286	59	-9	0-0	.968	-8	95	103	2b52/3		-1.4
1972	KC A	44	97	8	23	5	0	0	7	9-1	0	16	.237	.299	.289	77	-3	0-0	.972	4	113	145	2b33,3b4		0.3
Total	9	1153	3622	337	856	129	29	56	331	305-48	14	833	.236	.296	.334	83	-86	16-17	.980	167	113	116	2b1116,3b5	21	17.3
KNORR, RANDY			Randy Duane B11.12.1968 San Gabriel CA							BR/TR/6-2/215(205-230)			[TorA86 10/263]		d9.5									
1991	Tor A	3	1	0	0	0	0	0	2	1-0	0	1	1.000	1.000	.000	49	0	0-0	1.000	1	0	0	C3		0.1
1992	Tor A	8	19	1	5	0	0	1	1	1-1	0	5	.263	.300	.421	95	0	0-0	1.000	1	392	147	C8	41	0.1
1993	†Tor A	39	101	11	25	3	2	4	20	9-0	0	29	.248	.309	.436	96	-1	0-0	1.000	-3	67	98	C39		-0.2
1994	Tor A	40	124	20	30	2	0	7	19	10-0	1	35	.242	.301	.427	85	-4	0-0	.993	-2	72	89	C40		-0.3
1995	Tor A	45	132	18	28	8	0	3	16	11-0	0	28	.212	.273	.341	58	-8	0-0	.971	-6	66	83	C45	41	-1.1
1996	Hou N	37	87	7	17	5	0	1	7	5-2	1	18	.195	.245	.287	44	-7	0-1	1.000	5	160	116	C33		-0.1
1997	Hou N	4	8	1	3	0	0	1	1	0-0	0	2	.375	.375	.750	192	1	0-0	1.000	1	85	251	C3,1b2	15	0.2
1998	Fla N	15	49	4	10	4	1	2	11	1-0	0	10	.204	.216	.449	75	-2	0-0	.989	-4	59	79	C15		-0.5
1999	Hou N	13	30	2	5	1	0	0	1	0-0	1	8	.167	.194	.200	-0	-5	0-0	1.000	-1	66	0	C11		-0.1
2000	Tex A	15	34	5	10	2	0	2	2	0-0	1	3	.294	.294	.529	101	0	0-0	.985	-1	90	150	C15		-0.1
2001	Mon N	34	91	13	20	2	0	3	10	8-0	1	22	.220	.287	.341	63	-5	0-0	.989	-7	48	89	C27	97	-1.1
Total	11	253	676	82	153	27	3	24	88	47-3	3	161	.226	.278	.382	71	-31	0-1	.990	-15	87	94	C239,1b2		-3.5
KNOTHE, GEORGE			George Bertram B1.12.1898 Bayonne NJ							D7.3.1981 Toms River NJ			BR/TR/5-10/165		d4.25	b-Fritz Col Penn								
1932	Phi N	6	12	2	1	1	0	0	0	0	0	0	.083	.083	.167	-31	-2	0	.923	-1	98	120	2b5		-0.3
KNOTHE, FRITZ			Wilfred Edgar B5.1.1903 Passaic NJ							D3.27.1963 Passaic NJ			BR/TR/5-10.5/180		d4.12	b-George								
1932	Bos N	89	344	45	82	19	1	1	36	39	1	37	.238	.318	.308	72	-12	5	.947	-6	98	45	3b87		-1.5
1933	Bos N	44	158	15	36	5	2	1	6	13	1	25	.228	.291	.304	76	-5	1	.978	-3	91	148	3b33,S9		-0.7
	Phi N	41	113	10	17	2	0	0	11	6	0	19	.150	.193	.168	3	-14	2	.949	9	127	151	3b32,2b4		-0.4
	Year	85	271	25	53	7	2	1	17	19	1	44	.196	.251	.247	42	-21	3	.961	5	110	150	3b65,S9,2b4		-1.1
Total	2	174	615	70	135	26	3	2	53	58	2	81	.220	.289	.281	59	-31	8	.953	-1	103	88	3b152,S9,2b4		-2.6
KNOTT, JON			Jonathan David B8.4.1978 Manassas VA							BR/TR/6-3/220			d5.30		Col Mississippi St.									
2004	SD N	9	14	1	3	2	0	0	1	1-0	0	5	.214	.267	.357	62	-1	0-0	1.000	-0	81	0	O5L		-0.1
KNOTTS, JOE			Joseph Steven B3.3.1884 Greensboro PA							D9.15.1950 Philadelphia PA			BR/TR/5-9/170		d9.18									
1907	Bos N	3	8	0	0	0	0	0	0	1	0		.000	.111	.000	-65	-2	0	1.000	-0	77	118	C3		-0.2
KNOUFF, ED			Edward "Fred" B6.1868 Philadelphia PA							D9.14.1900 Philadelphia PA			BR/TR/?/160		d7.1 ▲									
1885	Phi AA	14	48	5	9	0	0	0	2	2		1	.188	.220	.188	28	-4		.867	1	126	442	P14/OR		0.0
1886	Bal AA	1	3	0	0	0	0	0	0	0	1		.000	.250	.000	-20	0	0	1.000	1	324	0	/P		0.0
1887	Bal AA	9	31	4	9	0	0	0	3	1	0		.290	.313	.290	73	-1	1	.889	0	109	356	P9,O3(2/0/1)		-0.5
	StL AA	15	56	4	10	1	2	0	6	1	1		.179	.207	.268	29	-6	1	.800	-2	0	96	O9(0/4/5),P6		-0.5
	Year	24	87	8	19	1	2	0	9	2	1		.218	.244	.276	43	-7	2	.897	-2	96	412	P15,O12(2/4/6)		-0.5
1888	StL AA	9	31	1	3	0	0	0	1	3	1		.097	.200	.097	-3	-2	1	1.000	1	62	0	P9		0.0
	Cle AA	2	6	0	1	1	0	0	0	1	0		.167	.286	.333	101	0	0	1.000	1	252	0	P2/2		0.0
	Year	11	37	1	4	1	0	0	1	4	1		.108	.214	.135	12	-4	1	.880	-1	81	0	P11/2		0.0
1889	Phi AA	3	12	3	3	1	0	0	2	1	0	1	.250	.308	.333	84	0	1	1.000	-1	40	0	P3		0.0
Total	5	53	187	16	35	3	2	0	14	9	3	1	.187	.236	.225	35	-13	4	.891	-2	103	272	P44,O13(2/4/7)/2		-0.5
KNOWDELL, JAKE			Jacob Augustus B7.27.1840 Brooklyn NY							5-7.5/148			d5.15											
1874	Atl NA	24	86	8	12	1	1	0	3	1		3	.140	.149	.174	4	-8	1-0	.824	-2			C21,O4L		-0.8
1875	Atl NA	43	163	17	32	2	0	0	9	1		3	.196	.201	.209	49	-7	0-1	.781	-10			C33,S11,O4(0/3/1)/2		-1.5
1878	Mil N	4	14	2	3	1	0	0	2	0		3	.214	.214	.286	59	-1		.875	-2			C2/ORS		-0.3
Total	2 NA	67	249	25	44	3	1	0	12	2		6	.177	.183	.197	32	-15	1-1	.796	-12			C54,S11,O8(4/3/1)/2		-2.3
KNOWLES, JIMMY			James "Darby" B9.5.1856 Toronto ON, Can.							D2.11.1912 Jersey City NJ			BR/5-9/160		d5.2									
1884	Pit AA	46	182	19	42	5	7	0		5	2		.231	.259	.335	94	-2		.961	-0	95	80	1b46		-0.6
	Bro AA	41	153	19	36	5	1	1		3	1		.235	.255	.301	80	-3		.953	1	176	122	1b30,3b11		-0.5
	Year	87	335	38	78	10	8	1		8	3		.233	.257	.319	87	-5		.958	0	127	97	1b76,3b11		-1.1
1886	Was N	115	443	43	94	16	11	3	35	15		73	.212	.238	.318	73	-15	20	.899	21	113	103	2b62,3b53		0.9
1887	NY AA	16	60	12	15	1	1	0	6	1		0	.250	.262	.300	59	-4	6	.934	-2	85	60	2b16/3		-0.4
1890	Roc AA	123	491	83	138	12	8	5	84	59	1		.281	.359	.369	124	16	55	.881	7	111	99	3b123		2.2
1892	NY N	16	59	2	9	1	0	0	2	6	1		.153	.231	.169	22	-5	1	.792	-4	81	92	3b15/S		-0.8
Total	5	357	1388	185	334	40	28	9	132	89	4	81	.241	.288	.329	92	-13	83	.861	23	109	101	3b203,2b78,1b76/S		0.8
KNOX, ANDY			Andrew Jackson "Dasher" B1.6.1864 Philadelphia PA							D9.14.1940 Philadelphia PA			BR/TR		d9.19									
1890	Phi AA	21	75	6	19	3	0	0	8	9	0		.253	.333	.293	85	-1	5	.963	-2	63	65	1b21		-0.4

YEAR TM LG	G	AB	R	H	2B	3B	HR	RBI	BB-IB	HP	SO	AVG	OBP	SLG	AOPS	ABR	SB-CS	FA	FR	RNG	THR	GAMES AT POSITION	DL	BFW

KNOX, CLIFF Clifford Hiram "Bud" B1.7.1902 Coalville IA D9.24.1965 Oskaloosa IA BB/TR/5-11.5/178 d7.1

YEAR TM LG	G	AB	R	H	2B	3B	HR	RBI	BB-IB	HP	SO	AVG	OBP	SLG	AOPS	ABR	SB-CS	FA	FR	RNG	THR	GAMES AT POSITION	BFW
1924 Pit N	6	18	1	4	0	0	0	2	0	0	2	.222	.300	.222	41	-1	0-0	.917	1	191	133	C6	0.0

KNOX, JOHN John Clinton B7.26.1948 Newark NJ BL/TR/6-0/170* [DetA70 8/193] d8.1 Col Bowling Green

YEAR TM LG	G	AB	R	H	2B	3B	HR	RBI	BB-IB	HP	SO	AVG	OBP	SLG	AOPS	ABR	SB-CS	FA	FR	RNG	THR	GAMES AT POSITION	BFW
1972 †Det A	14	13	1	1	1	0	0	0	1-0	0	2	.077	.143	.154	-11	-2	0-0	1.000	3	226	281	2b4	0.1
1973 Det A	12	32	1	9	1	0	0	3	3-0	0	1	.281	.343	.313	80	-1	1-1	1.000	-3	74	52	2b9	-0.4
1974 Det A	55	88	11	27	1	1	0	6	6-0	0	13	.307	.351	.341	96	-1	5-4	.956	-2	92	117	2b33/3D	-0.1
1975 Det A	43	86	8	23	1	0	0	2	10-0	0	9	.267	.344	.279	74	-3	1-2	.980	-3	101	67	2b23,3b3,D3	-0.5
Total 4	124	219	21	60	4	1	0	11	20-0	0	27	.274	.335	.301	79	-7	7-7	.973	-5	97	93	2b69,D5,3b4	-0.9

KOBACK, NICK Nicholas Nicholie B7.19.1935 Hartford CT BR/TR/6-0/187* d7.29

YEAR TM LG	G	AB	R	H	2B	3B	HR	RBI	BB-IB	HP	SO	AVG	OBP	SLG	AOPS	ABR	SB-CS	FA	FR	RNG	THR	GAMES AT POSITION	BFW
1953 Pit N	7	16	1	2	0	1	0	0	0	0	4	.125	.176	.250	10	-2	0-0	1.000	-2	44	192	C6	-0.4
1954 Pit N	4	10	0	0	0	0	0	0	0	0	8	.000	.000	.000	-99	-3	0-0	1.000	0	79	0	C4	-0.3
1955 Pit N	5	7	0	2	0	0	0	0	0-0	0	1	.286	.286	.286	53	0	0-0	1.000	0	0	401	C2	0.0
Total 3	16	33	1	4	0	1	0	0	1-0	0	13	.121	.147	.182	-15	-5	0-0	1.000	-2	51	147	C12	-0.7

KOCH, BARNEY Barnett B3.23.1923 Campbell NE D6.6.1987 Tacoma WA BR/TR/5-8/140 d7.23 Col Oregon

YEAR TM LG	G	AB	R	H	2B	3B	HR	RBI	BB-IB	HP	SO	AVG	OBP	SLG	AOPS	ABR	SB-CS	FA	FR	RNG	THR	GAMES AT POSITION	BFW
1944 Bro N	33	96	11	21	2	0	0	1	3	0	9	.219	.242	.240	37	-8	0	.956	-5	87	59	2b29/S	-1.2

KOCHER, BRAD Bradley Wilson B1.16.1888 White Haven PA D1.13.1965 White Haven PA BR/TR/5-11/188 d4.24

YEAR TM LG	G	AB	R	H	2B	3B	HR	RBI	BB-IB	HP	SO	AVG	OBP	SLG	AOPS	ABR	SB-CS	FA	FR	RNG	THR	GAMES AT POSITION	BFW
1912 Det A	29	63	5	13	1	0	0	9	2	0		.206	.231	.286	49	-5	0	.904	-6	81	107	C24	-0.9
1915 NY N	4	11	3	5	0	1	0	2	0	0	1	.455	.455	.636	243	2	0	1.000	-1	85	140	C3	0.1
1916 NY N	34	65	1	7	2	0	0	1	2	0	10	.108	.134	.138	-17	-9	0	.978	-4	101	48	C30	-1.3
Total 3	67	139	9	25	5	2	0	12	4	0	11	.180	.203	.245	34	-12	0	.943	-10	90	83	C57	-2.2

KOEGEL, PETE Peter John B7.31.1947 Mineola NY BR/TR/6-6.5/230* [OakA65 4/79] d9.1

YEAR TM LG	G	AB	R	H	2B	3B	HR	RBI	BB-IB	HP	SO	AVG	OBP	SLG	AOPS	ABR	SB-CS	FA	FR	RNG	THR	GAMES AT POSITION	BFW
1970 Mil A	7	8	2	2	0	0	1	1	1-0	0	3	.250	.333	.625	158	1	0-0	1.000	-0	60	0	/OL	0.0
1971 Mil A	2	3	0	0	0	0	0	0	1-0	0	2	.000	.400	.000	22	0	0-0	1.000	-0	0		/1	0.0
Phi N	12	26	1	6	1	0	0	2	2-0	0	7	.231	.286	.269	58	-1	0-0	1.000	-1	53	87	C7/OL	-0.3
1972 Phi N	41	49	3	7	2	0	0	1	6-0	0	16	.143	.236	.184	20	-5	0-0	1.000	-1	81	81	1b8,C5,3b4,O2R	-0.7
Total 3	62	86	6	15	3	0	1	5	11-0	0	28	.174	.268	.244	45	-5	0-0	.971	-3	49	68	C12,1b9,3b4,O4(2/0/2)	-1.0

KOEHLER, BEN Benard James B1.26.1877 Schoerndorn, Germany D5.21.1961 South Bend IN BR/TR/5-10.5/175 d4.23

YEAR TM LG	G	AB	R	H	2B	3B	HR	RBI	BB-IB	HP	SO	AVG	OBP	SLG	AOPS	ABR	SB-CS	FA	FR	RNG	THR	GAMES AT POSITION	BFW
1905 StL A	142	536	55	127	14	6	2	47	32	4		.237	.285	.297	89	-8	22	.969	1	170	336	O124C,1b12,2b6	-1.5
1906 StL A	66	186	27	41	1	1	0	15	24	4		.220	.322	.237	79	-3	9	.957	-2	142	363	O52(1/34/17),2b7/S3	-0.7
Total 2	208	722	82	168	15	7	2	62	56	8		.233	.295	.281	87	-11	31	.966	-1	163	343	O176(1/158/17),2b13,1b12/3S	-2.2

KOEHLER, PIP Horace Levering B1.16.1902 Gilbert PA D12.8.1986 Tacoma WA BR/TR/5-10/165 d4.22 Col Penn St.

YEAR TM LG	G	AB	R	H	2B	3B	HR	RBI	BB-IB	HP	SO	AVG	OBP	SLG	AOPS	ABR	SB-CS	FA	FR	RNG	THR	GAMES AT POSITION	BFW
1925 NY N	12	2	1	0	0	0	0	0	0	0	1	.000	.000	.000	-99	-1	0-0	1.000	0	178	0	O3(1/0/2)	0.0

KOELLING, BRIAN Brian Wayne B6.11.1969 Cincinnati OH BR/TR/6-1/185 [CinN91 14/379] d8.21 Col Bowling Green

YEAR TM LG	G	AB	R	H	2B	3B	HR	RBI	BB-IB	HP	SO	AVG	OBP	SLG	AOPS	ABR	SB-CS	FA	FR	RNG	THR	GAMES AT POSITION	BFW
1993 Cin N	7	15	2	1	0	0	0	0	2-0	0	7	.067	.125	.067	-47	-3	0-0	.941	-0	146	58	2b3,S2	-0.3

KOENECKE, LEN Leonard George B1.18.1904 Baraboo WI D9.17.1935 Toronto ON, Can. BL/TR/5-11/180 d4.12

YEAR TM LG	G	AB	R	H	2B	3B	HR	RBI	BB-IB	HP	SO	AVG	OBP	SLG	AOPS	ABR	SB-CS	FA	FR	RNG	THR	GAMES AT POSITION	BFW
1932 NY N	42	137	33	35	5	0	4	14	11	2	13	.255	.320	.380	89	-2	3	.924	-4	87	0	O35L	-0.8
1934 Bro N	123	460	79	147	31	7	14	73	70	1	38	.320	.411	.509	152	37	8	.994	0	102	72	O121C	3.3
1935 Bro N	100	325	43	92	13	2	4	27	43	1	45	.283	.369	.372	102	3	0	.966	-4	101	42	O91(16/68/7)	-0.4
Total 3	265	922	155	274	49	9	22	114	124	4	96	.297	.383	.441	125	38	11	.976	-8	100	51	O247(51/189/7)	2.1

KOENIG, MARK Mark Anthony B7.19.1904 San Francisco CA D4.22.1993 Willows CA BB/TR/6-0/180 d9.8 ▲

YEAR TM LG	G	AB	R	H	2B	3B	HR	RBI	BB-IB	HP	SO	AVG	OBP	SLG	AOPS	ABR	SB-CS	FA	FR	RNG	THR	GAMES AT POSITION	BFW
1925 NY A	28	110	14	23	6	1	0	4	5	0	4	.209	.243	.282	34	-12	0-1	.944	-2	95	99	S28	-1.0
1926 †NY A	147	617	93	167	26	8	5	62	43	1	37	.271	.319	.363	79	-22	4-3	.931	2	101	90	S141	-0.4
1927 †NY A	123	526	99	150	20	11	3	62	25	2	21	.285	.320	.382	84	-15	3-2	.936	12	109	121	S122	1.0
1928 †NY A	132	533	89	170	19	10	4	63	32	2	19	.319	.360	.415	106	3	3-5	.923	-19	89	98	S125	-0.3
1929 NY A	116	373	44	109	27	5	3	41	23	1	17	.292	.335	.416	99	-2	1-1	.911	-9	96	97	S61,3b37/2	-0.2
1930 NY A	21	74	9	17	5	0	0	9	6	1	5	.230	.296	.297	53	-5	0-0	.905	1	105	120	S19	-0.2
Det A	76	267	37	64	9	2	1	16	20	1	15	.240	.295	.300	50	-21	2-0	.922	-8	92	98	S70,P2,3b2/OR	-1.9
Year	97	341	46	81	14	2	1	25	26	2	20	.238	.295	.299	51	-26	2-0	.918	-8	95	103	S89,P2,3b2/OR	-2.1
1931 Det A	106	364	33	92	24	4	1	39	14	1	12	.253	.282	.349	63	-21	8-2	.955	-19	88	83	2b55,S35,P3	-3.1
1932 †Chi N	33	102	15	36	5	1	3	11	3	0	5	.353	.377	.510	137	5	0	.932	3	120	133	S31	1.4
1933 Chi N	80	218	32	62	12	1	3	25	15	0	9	.284	.330	.390	105	2	5	.922	3	100	173	3b37,S26,2b2	0.7
1934 Cin N	151	633	60	172	26	6	1	67	15	0	24	.272	.289	.336	68	-30	5	.930	-3	100	64	3b64,S58,2b26,1b4	-2.4
1935 NY N	107	396	40	112	12	0	3	37	13	0	18	.283	.306	.336	74	-15	0	.968	-4	105	64	2b64,S21,3b15	-1.3
1936 †NY N	42	58	7	16	4	0	1	7	8	1	4	.276	.397	.397	109	1	0	.905	-1	121	97	S10,2b8,3b3	0.1
Total 12	1162	4271	572	1190	195	49	28	443	222	11	190	.279	.316	.367	81	-132	31-14	.927	-39	100	103	S747,3b158,2b156,P5,1b4/OR	-7.6

KOHLER, HENRY Henry C. B5.5.1852 Baltimore MD D8.27.1934 Baltimore MD d7.12

YEAR TM LG	G	AB	R	H	2B	3B	HR	RBI	BB-IB	HP	SO	AVG	OBP	SLG	AOPS	ABR	SB-CS	FA	FR	RNG	THR	GAMES AT POSITION	BFW
1871 Kek NA	3	12	0	2	1	0	0	0	0	0		.167	.167	.250	17	-1	0-0	—	-1			C2,1b2/3	-0.1
1873 Mar NA	6	25	2	3	0	0	0	1	0	0		.120	.120	.120	-37	-4	0-0	.686	-3	48	0	3b6/C1OC	-0.5
1874 Bal NA	2	4	0	0	0	0	0	0	0	0		.000	.000	.000	-99	-1	0-0	.714	-1	426	0	/1	-0.1
Total 3 NA	11	41	2	5	1	0	0	2	0	0	1	.122	.122	.146	-24	-6	0-0	.700	-5			3b7,1b4,C3/OC	-0.7

KOKOS, DICK Richard Jerome (b Richard Jerome Kokoszka) B2.28.1928 Chicago IL D4.9.1986 Chicago IL BL/TL/5-8.5/170* d7.8 Mil 1951-52

YEAR TM LG	G	AB	R	H	2B	3B	HR	RBI	BB-IB	HP	SO	AVG	OBP	SLG	AOPS	ABR	SB-CS	FA	FR	RNG	THR	GAMES AT POSITION	BFW
1948 StL A	71	258	40	77	15	3	4	40	28	3	32	.298	.374	.426	110	4	4-3	.964	0	92	166	O71R	0.2
1949 StL A	143	501	80	131	28	1	23	77	66	3	91	.261	.351	.459	109	5	3-5	.981	7	109	124	O138R	0.6
1950 StL A	143	490	77	128	27	5	18	67	88	1	73	.261	.375	.447	106	5	8-8	.970	3	110	70	O127(81/0/50)	-0.1
1953 StL A	107	299	41	72	12	0	13	38	56	0	53	.241	.361	.411	106	4	0-5	.963	-2	97	82	O83(61/0/22)	-0.4
1954 Bal A	11	10	1	2	0	0	1	4	1	0	3	.200	.429	.500	166	1	0-0	1.000	0	112	0	/OL	0.1
Total 5	475	1558	239	410	82	9	59	223	242	7	252	.263	.365	.441	108	19	15-21	.971	9	104	105	O420(143/0/281)	0.4

KOLB, GARY Gary Alan B3.13.1940 Rock Falls IL BL/TR/6-0/195* d9.7 Col Illinois

YEAR TM LG	G	AB	R	H	2B	3B	HR	RBI	BB-IB	HP	SO	AVG	OBP	SLG	AOPS	ABR	SB-CS	FA	FR	RNG	THR	GAMES AT POSITION	BFW
1960 StL N	9	3	1	0	0	0	0	0	0	0		.000	.000	.000	-92	-1	0-0	1.000	0	196	0	O2(1/1/1)	-0.1
1962 StL N	6	14	1	5	0	0	0	0	1-0	0	3	.357	.400	.357	96	0	0-0	1.000	0	126	0	O6(1/0/5)	0.0
1963 StL N	75	96	23	26	1	5	3	10	22-0	0	26	.271	.403	.479	141	6	2-1	.981	-2	91		O58(25/0/35)/C3	0.2
1964 Mil N	36	64	7	12	1	0	1	6	6-1	0	10	.188	.257	.203	31	-6	3-2	1.000	-4	96	0	O14(5/3/7),3b7,2b6,C2	-1.1
1965 Mil N	24	27	3	7	0	0	0	1	1-0	0	6	.259	.286	.259	54	-2	0-0	1.000	0	121	0	O13(9/3/2)	-0.2
NY N	40	90	8	15	2	0	1	7	3-0	0	28	.167	.191	.222	17	-10	3-0	.976	1	87	298	O29(10/10/9)/13	-1.1
Year	64	117	11	22	2	0	1	8	4-0	0	34	.188	.213	.231	26	-12	3-0	.981	1	93	241	O42(19/13/11)/13	-1.3
1968 Pit N	74	119	16	26	4	1	2	6	11-2	0	17	.218	.285	.319	82	-3	2-1	.900	-1	102	137	O25(6/1/18),C10,3b4/2	-0.5
1969 Pit N	29	37	4	3	1	0	0	2	3-0	0	14	.081	.128	.108	-34	-7	0-0	1.000	-1	100	0	C7	-0.2
Total 7	293	450	63	94	9	6	6	29	46-3	0	104	.209	.281	.296	65	-23	10-4	.965	-7	97	116	O147(57/18/77),C20,3b13,2b7/1	-3.6

KOLLOWAY, DON Donald Martin "Butch","Cab" B8.4.1918 Posen IL D6.30.1994 Blue Island IL BR/TR/6-3/200* d9.16 Mil 1943-45

YEAR TM LG	G	AB	R	H	2B	3B	HR	RBI	BB-IB	HP	SO	AVG	OBP	SLG	AOPS	ABR	SB-CS	FA	FR	RNG	THR	GAMES AT POSITION	BFW
1940 Chi A	10	40	5	9	1	0	0	3	0	0	3	.225	.225	.250	23	-5	1-0	.922	-2	94	115	2b10	-0.6
1941 Chi A	71	280	33	76	8	3	3	24	6	2	12	.271	.292	.354	71	-13	11-4	.955	-8	106	64	2b62,1b4	-1.6
1942 Chi A	147	601	72	164	40	4	3	60	30	3	39	.273	.311	.368	92	-8	16-14	.966	-4	99	108	2b116,1b33	-0.9
1943 Chi A	85	348	29	75	14	4	1	33	9	0	30	.216	.234	.287	53	-23	11-7	.968	1	97	118	2b85	-1.9
1946 Chi A	123	482	45	135	23	4	3	53	9	0	29	.280	.293	.363	86	-12	14-6	.972	5	110	119	2b90,3b31	-0.1
1947 Chi A	124	485	49	135	25	4	2	35	17	0	34	.278	.303	.359	87	-11	11-4	.962	6	109	104	2b99,1b11,3b8	0.1
1948 Chi A	119	417	60	114	14	4	6	38	18	0	18	.273	.303	.369	81	-14	2-4	.966	11	109	94	2b83,3b18	0.1
1949 Chi A	4	4	0	0	0	0	0	0	0	0	1	.000	.000	.000	-99	-1	0-0	—	-0	0	0	3b2	-0.1
Det A	126	483	71	142	19	3	2	47	49	2	25	.294	.361	.368	91	-6	7-7	.956	-16	86	98	2b62,1b57,3b7	-2.1
Year	130	487	71	142	19	3	2	47	49	2	26	.292	.359	.355	89	-8	7-7	.956	-16	86	98	2b62,1b57,3b9	-2.2
1950 Det A	125	467	55	135	20	4	6	62	29	1	28	.289	.331	.388	81	-15	1-3	.989	2	107	120	1b118/2	-1.7
1951 Det A	78	212	28	54	7	0	2	17	15	1	12	.255	.307	.302	65	-11	2-3	.992	6	139	106	1b59	-0.7
1952 Det A	65	173	19	42	7	0	2	21	7	2	19	.243	.280	.329	69	-8	0-2	.979	1	132	51	1b32,2b8	-0.8
1953 Phi A	11	10	1	2	0	0	0	1	0	0	0	.200	.200	.200	-96	-0	0-0	—	-0	0	0	/3	0.0
Total 12	1079	3993	466	1081	180	30	29	393	189	10	251	.271	.305	.353	80	-127	76-54	.964	2	103	103	2b616,1b314,3b67	-10.4

YEAR	TM LG	G	AB	R	H	2B	3B	HR	RBI	BB-IB	HP	SO	AVG	OBP	SLG	AOPS	ABR	SB-CS	FA	FR	RNG	THR	GAMES AT POSITION	DL	BFW

KOLSETH, KARL Karl Dickey "Koley" B12.25.1892 Cambridge MA D5.3.1956 Cumberland MD BL/TR/6-0/182 d9.30
| 1915 | Bal F | 6 | 23 | 1 | 6 | 1 | 1 | 0 | 1 | 1 | 0 | | .261 | .292 | .391 | 89 | -1 | 0 | .915 | -2 | 57 | 132 | 1b6 | | -0.3 |

KOMMERS, FRED Frederick Raymond "Bugs" B3.31.1886 Chicago IL D6.14.1943 Chicago IL BL/TR/6-0/175 d6.25
1913	Pit N	40	155	14	36	5	4	0	22	10	0	29	.232	.279	.316	73	-6	1-6	.979	-3	103	18	O40C		-1.4
1914	StL F	76	244	33	75	9	8	3	41	24	3	33	.307	.376	.447	117	2	7	.908	-1	97	121	O67(3/36/28)		-0.2
	Bal F	16	42	5	9	1	0	1	1	7	1	10	.214	.340	.310	75	-2	0	.938	-2	86	0	O12(11/1/0)		-0.4
	Year	92	286	38	84	10	8	4	42	31	4	43	.294	.371	.427	111	0	7	.911	-2	95	103	O79(14/37/28)		-0.6
Total	2	132	441	52	120	15	12	4	64	41	4	72	.272	.340	.388	99	-6	8-6	.938	-5	98	73	O119(14/77/28)		-2.0

KOMMINSK, BRAD Brad Lynn B4.4.1961 Lima OH BR/TR/6-2/205* [AtlN79 1/4] d8.14
1983	Atl N	19	36	2	8	2	0	0	4	5-0	0	7	.222	.317	.278	62	-2	0-0	.944	-0	90	148	O13(1/0/12)		-0.3
1984	Atl N	90	301	37	61	10	4	8	36	29-0	2	77	.203	.276	.316	62	-15	18-8	.993	-6	87	35	O80(28/2/50)		-2.6
1985	Atl N	106	300	52	68	12	3	4	21	38-1	1	71	.227	.314	.327	75	-9	10-8	.959	-1	107	36	O92(28/1/63)		-1.6
1986	Atl N	5	5	1	2	0	0	0	1	0-0	0	1	.400	.400	.400	116	0	0-1	1.000	-0	95	0	3b2,O2R		-0.1
1987	Mil A	7	15	0	1	0	0	0	0	1-0	0	7	.067	.125	.067	-46	-3	1-0	1.000	0	142	0	O5R/D		-0.3
1989	Cle A	71	198	27	47	8	2	8	33	24-0	1	55	.237	.319	.419	105	1	8-2	.995	4	113	90	O68(2/66/2)	25	0.6
1990	SF N	8	5	2	1	0	0	0	0	1-0	0	2	.200	.333	.200	52	0	0-0	1.000	-1	58	0	O7(2/2/3)		-0.1
	Bal A	46	101	18	24	4	0	3	8	14-1	2	29	.238	.342	.366	101	1	1-1	1.000	-0	100	101	O40(6/12/26),D2		-0.4
1991	Oak A	24	25	1	3	1	0	0	2	2-0	0	9	.120	.185	.160	-4	-4	1-0	1.000	-0	88	178	O22(7/8/8)		-0.4
Total	8	376	986	140	215	37	5	23	105	114-2	6	258	.218	.301	.336	75	-31	39-20	.984	-4	101	63	O329(74/91/171),D3,3b2	25	-4.8

KONERKO, PAUL Paul Henry B3.5.1976 Providence RI BR/TR/6-3/211* [LAN94 1/13] d9.8
1997	LA N	6	7	0	1	0	0	0	1	1-0	0	2	.143	.250	.143	7	-1	0-0	1.000	-1	0	605	/13		-0.2
1998	LA N	49	144	14	31	1	0	4	16	10-0	1	30	.215	.272	.306	55	-10	0-1	.995	1	107	54	1b23,3b11,O11L		-1.2
	Cin N	26	73	7	16	3	0	3	13	6-0	1	10	.219	.284	.384	74	-3	0-0	1.000	1	110	0	3b9,1b7,O7L,D3		-0.3
	Year	75	217	21	47	4	0	7	29	16-0	2	40	.217	.276	.332	62	-13	0-1	.996	1	118	48	1b30,3b20,O18L,D3		-1.5
1999	Chi A	142	513	71	151	31	4	24	81	45-0	3	68	.294	.352	.511	115	10	0-0	.995	3	113	87	1b92,D46/3		0.3
2000	†Chi A	143	524	84	156	31	1	21	97	47-0	10	72	.298	.363	.481	108	7	1-0	.991	-8	99	109	1b122,3b7,D7		-1.0
2001	Chi A	156	582	92	164	35	0	32	99	54-6	9	89	.282	.349	.507	115	13	0-0	.994	-3	95	101	1b144,D11		-0.3
2002	Chi A★	151	570	81	173	30	0	27	104	44-2	9	72	.304	.359	.498	121	17	0-0	.993	-5	85	102	1b140,D7		0.0
2003	Chi A	137	444	49	104	19	0	18	65	43-7	4	50	.234	.305	.399	81	-13	0-0	.998	5	112	120	1b119,D14		-1.7
2004	Chi A	155	563	84	156	22	0	41	117	69-5	6	107	.277	.359	.535	125	21	1-0	.995	-2	93	125	1b139,D16		0.6
2005	†Chi A★	158	575	98	163	24	0	40	100	81-10	5	109	.283	.375	.534	132	28	0-0	.996	-5	87	118	1b146,D11		0.9
Total	9	1123	3995	580	1115	196	5	210	692	400-30	48	609	.279	.349	.488	112	69	4-1	.995	-12	95	108	1b933,D115,3b29,O18L		-2.9

KONETCHY, ED Edward Joseph "Big Ed" B9.3.1885 LaCrosse WI D5.27.1947 Ft.Worth TX BR/TR/6-2.5/195 d6.29 ▲
1907	StL N	91	331	34	83	11	9	2	30	26			.251	.317	.356	115	5	13	.975	4	125	94	1b91		0.8
1908	StL N	154	545	46	135	19	12	5	50	38	10		.248	.309	.354	117	9	16	.986	11	128	85	1b154		2.0
1909	StL N	152	576	88	165	23	14	4	80	65	7		.286	.366	.396	145	31	25	.985	5	117	87	1b152		3.6
1910	StL N	144	520	87	157	23	16	3	78	78	4	59	.302	.397	.425	145	32	18	.991	9	123	90	1b144/P		3.9
1911	StL N	158	571	90	165	38	13	6	88	81	7	63	.289	.384	.433	132	27	27	.991	-6	79	91	1b158		2.6
1912	StL N	143	538	81	169	26	13	8	82	62	4	66	.314	.389	.455	134	25	25	.991	6	114	93	1b142/OL		1.7
1913	StL N	140	504	75	139	18	17	8	68	53	7	41	.276	.353	.427	124	15	27-25	.995	8	119	92	1b140/P		1.7
1914	Pit N	154	563	56	140	23	9	4	51	32	2	48	.249	.291	.343	92	-8	20	.995	0	95	94	1b154		-0.8
1915	Pit F	152	576	79	181	31	18	10	93	41	3	52	.314	.363	.483	138	18	27	.994	9	124	121	1b158		1.8
1916	Bos N	158	566	76	147	29	13	3	70	43	7	46	.260	.320	.373	117	11	13	.994	2	99	82	1b129		1.3
1917	Bos N	130	474	56	129	19	13	2	54	36	5	40	.272	.330	.380	125	13	16	.992	-8	85	102	1b112,O6(1/4/1)/P		-1.4
1918	Bos N	119	437	33	103	15	5	2	56	32	2	35	.236	.291	.307	86	-8	5	.992	-5	87	103	1b132		-1.4
1919	Bro N	132	486	46	145	24	9	1	47	29	3	39	.298	.342	.391	117	10	14	.994	6	114	86	1b132		0.9
1920	†Bro N	131	497	62	153	22	12	5	63	33	1	18	.308	.352	.431	120	12	3-2	.990	0	99	85	1b130		-0.8
1921	Bro N	55	197	25	53	6	5	3	23	19	1	21	.269	.336	.396	90	-3	3-3	.987	-1	93	104	1b54		1.0
	Phi N	72	268	38	86	17	4	8	59	21	4	17	.321	.379	.504	122	9	3-0	.986	5	139	70	1b71		0.2
	Year	127	465	63	139	23	9	11	82	40	5	38	.299	.361	.458	122	6	6-3	.986	4	119	85	1b125		1.2
Total	15	2085	7649	972	2150	344	182	74	992	689	73	545	.281	.346	.403	122	198	255-30	.990	60	110	93	1b2073,O7(2/4/1),P3		21.2

KONNICK, MIKE Michael Aloysius B1.13.1889 Glen Lyon PA D7.9.1971 Wilkes-Barre PA BR/TR/5-9/180 d10.3
1909	Cin N	2	5	0	2	1	0	0	1	0	0		.400	.400	.600	211	-0	0	1.000	-0	82	73	C2		0.0
1910	Cin N	1	3	0	0	0	0	0	0	1	0	0	.000	.250	.000	-27	0	0	1.000	-0	72	0	/S		-0.1
Total	2	3	8	0	2	1	0	0	1	1	0	0	.250	.333	.375	117	1	0	1.000	-1	82	73	C2/S		-0.1

KONOPKA, BRUCE Bruno Bruce B9.16.1919 Hammond IN D9.27.1996 Denver CO BL/TL/6-2/190 d6.7 Mil 1943-45 Col USC
1942	Phi A	5	10	2	3	0	0	0	1	1	0	1	.300	.364	.300	88	-1	0-0	1.000	-0	68	110	1b3		0.0
1943	Phi A	2	2	0	0	0	0	0	0	0	0	1	.000	.000	.000	-99	-1	0-0	—	0			/H		-0.1
1946	Phi A	38	93	7	22	4	1	0	9	4	0	8	.237	.268	.301	59	-5	0-0	.994	2	129	75	1b20/OL		-0.5
Total	3	45	105	9	25	4	1	0	10	5	0	9	.238	.273	.295	59	-6	0-0	.995	2	123	78	1b23/OL		-0.6

KOONCE, GRAY Graham Clinton B5.15.1975 El Cajon CA BL/TL/6-4/220 [DetA93 60/1561] d9.20
| 2003 | Oak A | 6 | 8 | 0 | 1 | 1 | 0 | 0 | 0 | 0-0 | 0 | 6 | .125 | .125 | .250 | -5 | -1 | 0-0 | 1.000 | 1 | 216 | 169 | 1b5 | | -0.1 |

KOONS, HARRY Henry M. B1863 Philadelphia PA BR/TR/5-8/174 d4.17
1884	Alt U	21	78	8	18	2	1	0		2			.231	.250	.282	60	-6		.866	5	126	39	3b21/C		-0.1
	CP U	1	3	0	0	0	0	0		0			.000	.000	.000	-99	-1		—	-0	0	0	0/3		-0.1
	Year	22	81	8	18	2	1	0		2			.222	.241	.272	54	-7		.866	5	125	39	3b22/C		-0.2

KOPACZ, GEORGE George Felix "Sonny" B2.26.1941 Chicago IL BL/TL/6-1/195* d9.18
1966	Atl N	6	9	1	0	0	0	0	0	1-0	0	5	.000	.100	.000	-68	-2	0-0	.909	-1	0	0	1b2		-0.3
1970	Pit N	10	16	1	3	0	0	0	0	0-0	0	5	.188	.188	.188	1	-2	0-0	1.000	-1	99	59	1b3		-0.3
Total	2	16	25	2	3	0	0	0	0	1-0	0	10	.120	.154	.120	-24	-4	0-0	.964	-1	59	15	1b5		-0.6

KOPF, WALLY Walter Henry B7.10.1899 Stonington CT D4.30.1979 Hamilton Co. OH BB/TR/5-11/168 d10.1 b-Larry Col Dartmouth
| 1921 | NY N | 2 | 3 | 0 | 1 | 0 | 0 | 0 | 0 | 1 | 0 | 1 | .333 | .500 | .333 | 125 | 0 | 0-0 | 1.000 | 1 | 222 | 435 | 3b2 | | 0.1 |

KOPF, LARRY William Lorenz (aka Fred Brady in 1913) B11.3.1890 Bristol CT D10.15.1986 Anderson Twp. OH BB/TR/5-9/160 d9.2 Def 1918 b-Wally Col Fordham
1913	Cle A	6	10	2	3	1	0	0	1	0	0	0	.300	.300	.400	102	0	0	.923	1	146	150	2b4/3		0.2
1914	Phi A	37	69	8	13	2	2	0	12	8	1	14	.188	.300	.275	76	-2	6	.899	-3	85	62	S13,3b8,2b5		-0.2
1915	Phi A	118	386	39	87	10	4	1	33	41	9	45	.225	.314	.269	77	-10	5-9	.920	-7	92	71	S74,3b42,2b2		-1.4
1916	Cin N	11	40	2	11	2	0	0	5	1	0	8	.275	.293	.325	92	0	1	.942	-1	103	89	S11		-0.1
1917	Cin N	148	573	81	146	19	8	2	26	28	6	48	.255	.297	.326	95	-5	17	.916	-9	100	88	S145		-0.4
1919	†Cin N	135	503	51	136	18	5	0	58	28	3	27	.270	.313	.326	95	-4	18	.943	-35	86	75	S135		-3.3
1920	Cin N	126	458	56	112	15	6	0	59	35	5	24	.245	.305	.303	76	-14	14-13	.929	-33	85	90	S123,2b2,3b2/OC		-4.3
1921	Cin N	107	367	36	80	8	3	1	25	43	6	20	.218	.310	.264	56	-22	3-14	.947	-17	93	81	S93,2b4,3b3/OL		-3.3
1922	Bos N	126	466	59	124	6	3	1	37	45	1	22	.266	.332	.298	75	-5	0-3	.905	-5	99	110	S37,2b4		-0.7
1923	Bos N	39	138	15	38	3	1	0	13	6	2	6	.275	.338	.312	75	-3	0-0	.905	-1	101	107	S5,2b28,3b6		-0.3
Total	10	853	3010	349	750	84	30	5	266	242	33	214	.249	.312	.302	78	-84	72-48	.928	-120	92	84	S664,2b99,3b69,O2(1/1/0)		-16.3

KOPP, MERLIN Merlin Henry "Manny" B1.2.1892 Toledo OH D5.6.1960 Sacramento CA BB/TR (BR 1915)/5-8/158 d8.2 Mil 1918
1915	Was A	16	32	2	8	0	0	0	5	0	0	7	.250	.351	.250	79	-1	1	.933	-1	109	0	O9(8/0/1)		-0.1
1918	Phi A	96	363	60	85	7	7	0	18	42	4	55	.234	.320	.292	84	-7	22	.972	10	108	149	O96L		-0.2
1919	Phi A	75	235	34	53	2	4	1	12	42	1	43	.226	.348	.281	77	-6	16	.924	-3	95	101	O65(58/7/0)		-1.2
Total	3	187	630	96	146	9	11	1	30	89	5	105	.232	.332	.286	81	-14	39	.953	7	103	125	O170(162/7/1)		-1.5

KOPPE, JOE Joseph (b Joseph Kopchia) B10.19.1930 Detroit MI BR/TR/5-10/165* d8.9
1958	Mil N	16	9	3	4	0	0	0	1	0	0	1	.444	.500	.444	167	1	0-0	.833	2	192	284	S3		0.3
1959	Phi N	126	422	68	110	18	7	7	28	41-0	2	80	.261	.327	.386	88	-7	7-7	.954	8	104	101	S113,2b11		0.9
1960	Phi N	58	170	13	29	6	1	1	13	23-3	1	47	.171	.274	.235	41	-14	3-2	.956	-6	91	76	S55,3b2	39	-1.6
1961	Phi N	6	3	1	0	0	0	0	0	0-0	0	1	.000	.000	.000	-99	-1	0-0	.800	-1	53	118	S5		-0.2

YEAR	TM LG	G	AB	R	H	2B	3B	HR	RBI	BB-IB	HP	SO	AVG	OBP	SLG	AOPS	ABR	SB-CS	FA	FR	RNG	THR	GAMES AT POSITION	DL	BFW
1962	LA A	91	338	46	85	12	2	5	40	45-0	1	77	.251	.339	.343	75	-11	3-3	.947	-3	99	89	S88,2b3/3		-0.6
1963	LA A	128	375	47	85	16	0	4	40	73-3	2	84	.227	.352	.301	81	-6	2-1	.957	-1	108	85	S118,2b5,3b4		0.4
1963	LA A	76	143	11	30	4	1	1	12	9-1	1	30	.210	.258	.273	53	-9	0-0	.962	4	116	66	S19,3b18,2b14,O3R		-0.4
1964	LA A	54	113	10	29	4	1	0	6	14-1	1	16	.257	.339	.310	91	-1	0-0	.945	9	129	115	S31,2b13,3b3		1.1
1965	Cal A	23	33	3	7	1	0	1	2	3-1	0	10	.212	.278	.333	75	-1	0-0	.979	4	158	90	2b10,S4,3b4		0.4
Total	8	578	1606	202	379	61	12	19	141	209-9	7	345	.236	.324	.324	76	-49	16-13	.952	16	105	91	S436,2b56,3b32,O3R	39	0.3

KOPPSHAW, GEORGE George Karl B7.5.1895 Passaic NJ D12.26.1934 Lynchburg VA BR/TR/5-11.5/176 d8.4
| | | | | | | | | | | | | | | | | | | | | | | | | | |
| 1923 | StL N | 2 | 5 | 1 | 1 | 1 | 0 | 0 | 2 | 1-0 | 0 | 1 | .200 | .200 | .400 | 56 | 0 | 0-0 | 1.000 | -1 | 54 | 0 | /C | | -0.1 |

KORCHECK, STEVE Stephen Joseph "Hoss" B8.11.1932 McClellandtown PA BR/TR/6-1/205* d9.6 Mil 1956-57 Col George Washington
1954	Was A	2	7	0	1	0	0	0	0	0-0	0	2	.143	.143	.143	-23	-1	0-0	.857	-1	50	0	C2		-0.2
1955	Was A	13	36	3	10	2	0	0	2	0-0	1	5	.278	.297	.333	73	-1	0-0	1.000	0	86	207	C12		-0.1
1958	Was A	21	51	6	4	2	1	0	1	1-1	0	16	.078	.096	.157	-32	-9	0-0	.975	-1	64	144	C20		-1.0
1959	Was A	22	51	3	8	2	0	0	4	5-0	0	13	.157	.228	.196	19	-6	0-0	.974	2	72	93	C22		-0.3
Total	4	58	145	12	23	6	1	0	7	6-1	1	36	.159	.194	.214	13	-17	0-0	.976	1	72	131	C56		-1.6

KORES, ART Arthur Emil "Dutch" B7.22.1886 Milwaukee WI D3.26.1974 Milwaukee WI BR/TR/5-9/167 d7.24
| | | | | | | | | | | | | | | | | | | | | | | | | | |
| 1915 | StL F | 60 | 201 | 18 | 47 | 9 | 2 | 1 | 22 | 21 | 0 | 13 | .234 | .306 | .313 | 71 | -11 | 6 | .960 | 16 | 127 | 141 | 3b60 | | 0.8 |

KOSCO, ANDY Andrew John B10.5.1941 Youngstown OH BR/TR/6-3/207* d8.13
1965	Min A	23	55	3	13	4	0	1	6	1-0	0	15	.236	.241	.364	69	-2	0-0	1.000	1	90	442	O14R,1b2		-0.2
1966	Min A	57	158	11	35	5	0	2	13	7-1	0	31	.222	.251	.291	53	-10	0-1	.986	0	109	95	O40(31/7/5),1b5		-1.3
1967	Min A	9	28	4	4	1	0	0	4	2-0	0	4	.143	.200	.179	12	-3	0-0	.923	-0	112	0	O7R		-0.4
1968	NY A	131	466	47	112	19	1	15	59	16-2	3	71	.240	.268	.382	99	-1	2-2	.960	-1	97	166	O95(1/0/94),1b28		-1.4
1969	LA N	120	424	51	105	13	2	19	74	21-2	1	66	.248	.282	.422	102	-2	1-1	.981	-4	88	38	O109(38/0/76),1b3		-1.3
1970	LA N	74	224	21	51	12	0	8	27	1-0	0	40	.228	.230	.388	65	-13	1-1	.981	-1	102	55	O58(3/0/55)/1		-1.6
1971	Mil A	98	264	27	60	6	2	10	39	24-5	0	57	.227	.291	.379	90	-5	1-3	.988	-1	118	87	O45(26/0/19),1b29,3b12		-1.1
1972	Cal A	49	142	15	34	4	2	6	15	5-1	1	23	.239	.267	.423	110	0	1-0	.985	1	108	86	O36(24/0/13)		-0.1
	Bos A	17	47	5	10	2	1	3	6	2-0	1	9	.213	.260	.489	113	0	1-0	1.000	-0	90	115	O12L		0.0
	Year	66	189	20	44	6	3	9	19	7-1	2	32	.233	.265	.439	110	1	1-0	.988	1	103	94	O48(36/0/13)		-0.1
1973	†Cin N	47	118	17	33	7	0	9	21	13-6	0	26	.280	.346	.568	157	9	0-0	1.000	4	82	73	O36(1/7/28)/1		0.4
1974	Cin N	33	37	3	7	2	0	0	5	7-1	0	8	.189	.311	.342	59	-2	0-0	.846	-2	65	0	3b8/OR		-0.4
Total	10	658	1963	204	464	75	8	73	267	99-18	6	350	.236	.273	.394	92	-31	5-8	.979	-10	98	107	O453(136/14/312),1b69,3b20	40	-7.4

KOSHOREK, CLEM Clement John "Scooter" B6.20.1925 Royal Oak MI D9.8.1991 Royal Oak MI BR/TR/5-4.5/165* d4.15
1952	Pit N	98	322	27	84	17	0	0	15	26	2	39	.261	.320	.314	74	-10	4-7	.949	4	117	124	S33,2b27,3b26		-0.5
1953	Pit N	1	1	0	0	0	0	0	0	0	0	1	.000	.000	.000	-99	0	0-0	—	0			/H		
Total	2	99	323	27	84	17	0	0	15	26	2	40	.260	.319	.313	74	-10	4-7	.949	4	117	124	S33,2b27,3b26	55	-0.5

KOSKIE, COREY Cordel Leonard B6.28.1973 Anola MB, Can. BL/TR/6-3/217* [MinA94 26/715] d9.9 Col Des Moines Area (IA) CC
1998	Min A	11	29	2	4	0	0	1	2	2-0	0	10	.138	.194	.241	12	-4	0-0	.941	-2	68	82	3b10		-0.6
1999	Min A	117	342	42	106	21	0	11	58	40-4	5	72	.310	.387	.468	112	7	4-4	.962	0	72	79	3b79,O25R,D12		0.6
2000	Min A	146	474	79	142	32	4	9	65	77-7	4	104	.300	.400	.441	106	8	5-4	.966	-5	90	113	3b139/D		0.3
2001	Min A	153	562	100	155	37	2	26	103	68-9	12	118	.276	.362	.488	116	14	27-6	.964	-1	103	79	3b150/D		1.8
2002	†Min A	140	490	71	131	37	3	15	69	72-4	9	127	.267	.368	.447	112	12	10-11	.969	4	101	76	3b138/D	16	1.4
2003	†Min A	131	469	76	137	29	2	14	69	77-5	7	113	.292	.393	.452	120	17	11-5	.973	-6	96	73	3b131	23	1.2
2004	†Min A	118	422	68	106	24	2	25	71	49-10	12	103	.251	.342	.495	113	8	9-3	.963	-3	98	79	3b115/D	15	0.6
2005	Tor A	97	354	49	88	20	4	11	36	44-3	4	90	.249	.337	.398	90	-4	4-1	.968	-2	103	144	3b76,D19	67	-0.2
Total	8	913	3142	487	869	200	13	112	473	429-42	53	737	.277	.369	.455	110	58	70-34	.966	-10	99	89	3b838,D36,O25R	121	5.1

KOSLOFSKI, KEVIN Kevin Craig B9.24.1966 Decatur IL BL/TR/5-8/165* [KCA84 20/512] d6.28
1992	KC A	55	133	20	33	0	2	3	13	12-0	1	23	.248	.313	.346	82	-4	2-1	.991	4	110	190	O52(15/18/23)		0.0
1993	KC A	15	26	4	7	0	0	2	4	2-0	1	5	.269	.387	.385	101	0	0-1	1.000	3	123	459	O13(3/4/7)/D		0.2
1994	KC A	2	4	1	1	0	0	0	0	2-1	0	1	.250	.500	.250	97	0	0-0	.750	0	75	1130	O2(0/1/1)		0.0
1996	Mil A	25	42	5	9	3	2	0	4	4-1	1	12	.214	.298	.381	67	-2	0-0	.972	-0	106	0	O22(6/14/2)/D		-0.2
Total	4	97	205	31	50	3	4	5	21	22-2	3	41	.244	.325	.356	82	-6	2-2	.983	7	110	202	O89(24/37/33),D2		0.0

KOSMAN, MIKE Michael Thomas B11.26.1917 Hamtramck MI D12.10.2002 Lafayette IN BR/TR/5-9/160 d4.20 Col Indiana
| | | | | | | | | | | | | | | | | | | | | | | | | | |
| 1944 | Cin N | 1 | 0 | 0 | 0 | 0 | 0 | 0 | 0 | 0-0 | 0 | 0 | — | — | — | — | 0 | 0-0 | — | 0 | | | /R | | 0.0 |

KOSTER, FRED Frederick Charles "Fritz" B12.21.1905 Louisville KY D4.24.1979 St.Matthews KY BL/TL/5-10.5/165 d4.27 Col Louisville
| | | | | | | | | | | | | | | | | | | | | | | | | | |
| 1931 | Phi N | 76 | 151 | 21 | 34 | 2 | 0 | 2 | 8 | 14 | 0 | 21 | .225 | .291 | .265 | 47 | -11 | 4 | .923 | 0 | 102 | 120 | O41(6/14/22) | | -1.3 |

KOSTRO, FRANK Frank Jerry B8.4.1937 Windber PA BR/TR/6-2/190* d9.2
1962	Det A	16	41	5	11	3	0	0	3	1-0	0	6	.268	.279	.341	66	-2	0-0	.967	0	102	115	3b11		-0.2
1963	Det A	31	52	4	12	1	0	0	0	9-0	0	13	.231	.344	.250	67	-2	0-0	.929	-2	122	0	3b6,1b3,O3(1/0/2)		-0.2
	LA A	43	99	6	22	2	1	2	10	6-0	0	17	.222	.264	.323	68	-5	0-0	.960	-2	85	153	3b19,1b5,O3(1/0/2)		-0.7
	Year	74	151	10	34	3	1	2	10	15-0	0	30	.225	.293	.298	68	-7	0-0	.953	-2	93	120	3b25,1b8,O6(2/0/4)		-0.9
1964	Min A	59	103	10	28	5	0	3	12	4-0	1	21	.272	.303	.408	96	-1	0-0	.912	-4	92	51	3b12,2b7,O2L/1		-0.5
1965	Min A	20	31	4	5	2	0	0	1	4-0	0	5	.161	.250	.226	37	-2	0-0	.923	1	89	128	2b7,3b6,O2(1/0/1)		-0.2
1967	Min A	32	31	4	10	0	0	0	2	3-0	0	2	.323	.382	.323	102	0	0-0	1.000	-1	30	0	O3(2/0/1)/3		-0.1
1968	Min A	63	108	9	26	4	1	0	9	6-1	0	20	.241	.274	.296	71	-4	0-0	1.000	0	101	192	O24(14/0/10),1b5		-0.5
1969	Min A	2	2	0	0	0	0	0	0	0-0	0	1	.000	.000	.000	-97	-1	0-0	—	0			/H		-0.1
Total	7	266	467	40	114	17	2	5	37	33-1	1	85	.244	.291	.321	74	-17	0-0	.926	-5	98	136	3b55,O37(21/0/16),2b14,1b14		-2.5

KOTCHMAN, CASEY Casey John B2.22.1983 St. Petersburg FL BL/TL/6-3/210* [AnaA01 1/13] d5.9
2004	†Ana A	38	116	7	26	6	0	0	15	7-3	4	11	.224	.289	.276	51	-8	3-0	.988	-3	71	70	1b34,D2		-1.2
2005	†LA A	47	126	16	35	5	0	7	22	15-0	0	18	.278	.352	.484	122	4	1-1	1.000	-1	70	84	1b20,D20		0.0
Total	2	85	242	23	61	11	0	7	37	22-3	4	29	.252	.322	.384	88	-4	4-1	.992	-3	71	75	1b54,D22		-1.2

KOTSAY, MARK Mark Steven B12.2.1975 Whittier CA BL/TL/6-0/190(180-201) [FlaN96 1/9] d7.11 Col Cal St.-Fullerton
1997	Fla N	14	52	5	10	1	0	4	4	4-0	0	7	.192	.250	.250	33	-5	3-0	1.000	-1	108	331	O14C		-0.3
1998	Fla N	154	578	72	161	25	7	11	68	34-2	1	61	.279	.318	.403	94	-7	10-5	.984	19	118	211	O145(0/46/107),1b3		0.7
1999	Fla N	148	495	57	134	23	9	8	50	29-5	0	50	.271	.306	.402	83	-15	7-6	.981	13	107	246	O129R,1b19		-1.0
2000	SD N	119	406	67	118	29	1	10	58	42-2	0	46	.298	.347	.443	104	2	19-9	.990	11	111	173	O142(0/9/139),1b2		0.8
2001	SD N	153	578	82	169	27	7	17	61	59-3	8	89	.292	.359	.452	127	18	11-9	.989	5	106	144	O147C	15	1.6
2002	SD N	153	578	82	169	27	7	17	61	59-3	8	89	.292	.359	.452	127	18	11-9	.989	5	106	144	O147C	15	1.6
2003	SD N	128	482	64	128	24	1	7	38	56-3	1	82	.266	.343	.384	98	-1	6-3	.991	-6	116	200	O126C		2.3
2004	Oak A	148	606	78	190	37	3	15	63	55-5	2	70	.314	.370	.459	116	15	8-5	.984	-4	94	151	O145C/D	17	1.4
2005	Oak A	139	582	75	163	35	4	15	82	40-3	1	51	.280	.325	.421	96	-4	5-5	.987	-8	88	107	O137C,D2		-1.1
Total	9	1155	4309	587	1231	236	38	95	481	367-21	10	514	.286	.341	.424	104	15	82-47	.987	56	106	166	O1096(1/730/380),1b24,D3	32	5.8

KOWITZ, BRIAN Brian Mark B8.7.1969 Baltimore MD BL/TL/5-10/182 [AtlN90 9/237] d6.4 Col Clemson
| | | | | | | | | | | | | | | | | | | | | | | | | | |
| 1995 | Atl N | 10 | 24 | 3 | 4 | 1 | 0 | 0 | 2 | 1-0 | 0 | 5 | .167 | .259 | .208 | 24 | -3 | 0-1 | 1.000 | -1 | 53 | 0 | O8(2/1/5) | | -0.5 |

KOY, ERNIE Ernest Anyz "Chief" B9.17.1909 Sealy TX BR/TR/6-0/200 d4.19 Mil 1943-45 Col Texas
1938	Bro N	142	521	78	156	29	13	11	76	38	4	76	.299	.352	.468	121	13	15	.984	-0	104	66	O135(54/64/18)/3		0.8
1939	Bro N	125	425	57	118	37	5	8	67	39	0	64	.278	.338	.445	105	3	11	.962	0	106	56	O114(110/3/3)		-0.3
1940	Bro N	24	48	9	11	2	1	1	8	3	0	3	.229	.275	.375	73	-2	1	1.000	-0	105	0	O19(11/5/2)		-0.3
	StL N	93	348	42	108	19	5	8	52	28	4	59	.310	.368	.463	121	10	12	.970	-3	99	30	O91L		0.2
	Year	117	396	53	119	21	6	9	60	31	4	62	.301	.357	.452	115	8	13	.973	-3	100	27	O110(102/5/2)		-0.1
1941	StL N	13	40	5	8	1	0	0	2	1-0	0	6	.200	.220	.225	61	-2	0	1.000	-0	98	0	O12L		-0.3
	Cin N	67	204	24	51	11	2	2	27	14	1	24	.250	.301	.353	84	-5	1	.990	-2	90	89	O49(42/1/6)		-0.3
	Year	80	244	29	59	12	2	4	31	15	1	30	.242	.288	.357	80	-7	1	.991	-2	91	76	O61(54/1/6)		-1.2
1942	Cin N	3	2	0	0	0	0	0	0	0-0	0	0	.000	.000	.000	-99	0	0	—	0			/H		-0.1
	Phi N	91	258	21	63	9	3	4	26	14	0	50	.244	.283	.349	89	-5	0	.981	-1	100	73	O78(28/52/4)		-1.0

YEAR	TM LG	G	AB	R	H	2B	3B	HR	RBI	BB-IB	HP	SO	AVG	OBP	SLG	AOPS	ABR	SB-CS	FA	FR	RNG	THR	GAMES AT POSITION	DL	BFW
Year		94	260	21	63	9	3	4	26	14	0	52	.242	.281	.346	87	-6	0	.981	-1	100	73	O78(28/52/4)		-1.1
Total	5	558	1846	238	515	108	29	36	260	137	9	284	.279	.332	.427	107	11	40	.977	-7	101	57	O498(348/125/33)/3		-1.9

KOZAR, AL Albert Kenneth B7.5.1921 McKees Rocks PA BR/TR/5-9.5/173* d4.19

YEAR	TM LG	G	AB	R	H	2B	3B	HR	RBI	BB-IB	HP	SO	AVG	OBP	SLG	AOPS	ABR	SB-CS	FA	FR	RNG	THR	GAMES AT POSITION	DL	BFW
1948	Was A	150	577	61	144	25	8	1	58	66	0	52	.250	.327	.326	76	-20	4-2	.967	-21	98	74	2b149		-3.2
1949	Was A	105	350	46	94	15	2	4	31	25	2	23	.269	.321	.357	81	-11	2-1	.977	-8	94	75	2b102		-1.4
1950	Was A	20	55	7	11	1	0	0	3	5	0	8	.200	.267	.218	27	-6	0-0	.962	-0	113	69	2b15		-0.5
	Chi A	10	10	4	3	0	0	1	2	0	0	3	.300	.300	.600	129	0	0-0	1.000	1	154	190	2b4/3		0.2
	Year	30	65	11	14	1	0	1	5	5	0	11	.215	.271	.277	42	-6	0-0	.968	1	118	84	2b19/3		-0.3
Total	3	285	992	118	252	41	10	6	94	96	2	86	.254	.321	.334	76	-37	6-3	.971	-27	98	75	2b270/3		-4.9

KRACHER, JOE Joseph Peter "Jug" B11.4.1915 Philadelphia PA D12.24.1981 San Angelo TX BR/TR/5-11/185 d9.17

YEAR	TM LG	G	AB	R	H	2B	3B	HR	RBI	BB-IB	HP	SO	AVG	OBP	SLG	AOPS	ABR	SB-CS	FA	FR	RNG	THR	GAMES AT POSITION	DL	BFW
1939	Phi N	5	5	1	1	0	0	0	1	0	0	1	.200	.429	.200	76	0	0-0	1.000	-1	0	0	C2		0.0

KRAFT, CLARENCE Clarence Otto "Big Boy" B6.9.1887 Evansville IN D3.26.1958 Fort Worth TX BR/TR/6-0/190 d5.1

YEAR	TM LG	G	AB	R	H	2B	3B	HR	RBI	BB-IB	HP	SO	AVG	OBP	SLG	AOPS	ABR	SB-CS	FA	FR	RNG	THR	GAMES AT POSITION	DL	BFW
1914	Bos N	3	3	0	1	0	0	0	0	0	0	1	.333	.333	.333	99	-0	0-0	1.000	-0	0	0	/1		0.0

KRANEPOOL, ED Edward Emil B11.8.1944 New York NY BL/TL/6-3/215* d9.22

YEAR	TM LG	G	AB	R	H	2B	3B	HR	RBI	BB-IB	HP	SO	AVG	OBP	SLG	AOPS	ABR	SB-CS	FA	FR	RNG	THR	GAMES AT POSITION	DL	BFW
1962	NY N	3	6	0	1	1	0	0	0	0-0	0	1	.167	.167	.333	30	-1	0-0	1.000	1	292	0	1b3		0.0
1963	NY N	86	273	22	57	12	2	2	14	18-0	0	50	.209	.256	.289	56	-15	4-2	.954	-1	89	131	O55(6/0/50),1b20		-2.2
1964	NY N	119	420	47	108	19	4	10	45	32-2	0	50	.257	.310	.393	100	-1	0-1	.991	2	113	91	1b104,O6(0/1/5)		-0.6
1965	NY N☆	153	525	44	133	24	4	10	53	39-7	2	71	.253	.303	.371	94	-5	1-4	.992	1	104	101	1b147		-1.5
1966	NY N	146	464	51	118	15	2	16	57	41-9	1	66	.254	.316	.399	100	0	1-1	.992	4	113	98	1b132,O11L		-0.4
1967	NY N	141	469	37	126	17	1	10	54	37-15	1	51	.269	.321	.373	100	0	0-4	.992	3	107	101	1b139		-0.7
1968	NY N	127	373	29	86	13	1	3	20	19-5	2	39	.231	.271	.295	70	-14	0-3	.994	4	113	105	1b113,O2L		-2.0
1969	†NY N	112	353	36	84	9	2	11	49	37-7	0	32	.238	.307	.368	87	-7	3-2	.993	2	106	110	1b106,O2L		-1.3
1970	NY N	43	47	2	8	0	0	0	3	5-0	0	2	.170	.250	.170	15	-6	0-0	1.000	-0	74	113	1b8		-0.7
1971	NY N	122	421	61	118	20	4	14	58	38-6	1	33	.280	.340	.447	122	11	0-4	.998	-1	88	83	1b108,O11(6/0/5)		0.1
1972	NY N	122	327	28	88	15	1	8	34	34-13	1	35	.269	.336	.394	110	4	1-0	.996	0	96	95	1b108/OR		-0.2
1973	†NY N	100	284	28	68	12	2	1	35	30-4	0	28	.239	.310	.306	72	-10	1-0	.998	-1	104	108	1b51,O32(31/0/1)		-1.5
1974	NY N	94	217	20	65	11	1	4	24	18-0	0	14	.300	.350	.415	115	4	1-0	.977	-4	80	50	O33(32/0/1),1b24		-0.3
1975	NY N	106	325	42	105	16	0	4	43	27-6	0	21	.323	.370	.409	121	10	1-1	.997	0	94	82	1b82,O4L		0.3
1976	NY N	123	415	47	121	17	1	10	49	35-4	0	38	.292	.344	.410	119	10	1-0	.996	-4	70	88	1b86,O31(23/0/8)		-0.2
1977	NY N	108	281	28	79	17	0	10	40	23-7	0	20	.281	.330	.448	112	4	1-4	.984	2	99	0	O42(10/0/32),1b41		0.1
1978	NY N	66	81	7	17	2	0	3	19	8-2	1	12	.210	.280	.346	79	-3	0-0	1.000	-0	68	0	O12(3/0/9),1b3		-0.4
1979	NY N	82	155	7	36	5	0	2	17	13-2	1	18	.232	.287	.303	65	-7	0-1	1.000	1	119	84	1b29,O8(2/0/6)		-0.9
Total	18	1853	5436	536	1418	225	25	118	614	454-89	14	581	.261	.316	.377	97	-26	15-27	.994	10	104	97	1b1304,O250(132/1/118)		-12.4

KRAUSE, CHARLIE Charles B10.2.1873 Detroit MI D3.30.1948 Eloise (now part of Westland) MI TR d7.27

YEAR	TM LG	G	AB	R	H	2B	3B	HR	RBI	BB-IB	HP	SO	AVG	OBP	SLG	AOPS	ABR	SB-CS	FA	FR	RNG	THR	GAMES AT POSITION	DL	BFW
1901	Cin N	1	4	0	1	0	0	0	0	0	0	0	.250	.250	.250	48	0	0	—	-0	0	0	/2		0.0

KRAVITZ, DANNY Daniel "Dusty","Beak" B12.21.1930 Lopez PA BL/TR/5-11/195* d4.17

YEAR	TM LG	G	AB	R	H	2B	3B	HR	RBI	BB-IB	HP	SO	AVG	OBP	SLG	AOPS	ABR	SB-CS	FA	FR	RNG	THR	GAMES AT POSITION	DL	BFW
1956	Pit N	32	68	6	18	2	2	2	10	5-1	0	9	.265	.311	.441	103	0	1-1	.944	-0	116	115	C26,3b2		0.0
1957	Pit N	19	41	2	6	1	0	0	4	2-0	0	10	.146	.186	.171	-3	-6	0-0	1.000	1	112	192	C15		-0.5
1958	Pit N	45	100	9	24	3	2	1	5	11-5	0	10	.240	.313	.340	76	-4	0-0	.967	-2	105	134	C37		-0.5
1959	Pit N	52	162	18	41	9	1	3	21	5-1	0	14	.253	.274	.377	72	-7	0-1	.986	-2	105	102	C45		-0.7
1960	Pit N	8	6	0	0	0	0	0	0	1-0	0	2	.000	.143	.000	-57	-1	0-0	1.000	0	0	0	/C		-0.1
	KC A	59	175	17	41	7	2	4	14	11-1	0	19	.234	.280	.366	73	-7	0-0	.971	-4	70	37	C47		-1.0
Total	5	215	552	52	130	22	7	10	54	35-8	0	64	.236	.280	.355	70	-25	1-2	.973	-8	96	96	C171,3b2		-2.8

KREEVICH, MIKE Michael Andreas B6.10.1908 Mt.Olive IL D4.25.1994 Pana IL BR/TR/5-7.5/168 d9.7

YEAR	TM LG	G	AB	R	H	2B	3B	HR	RBI	BB-IB	HP	SO	AVG	OBP	SLG	AOPS	ABR	SB-CS	FA	FR	RNG	THR	GAMES AT POSITION	DL	BFW
1931	Chi N	5	12	0	2	0	0	0	0	0-0	0	6	.167	.167	.167	-10	-2	1	1.000	0	77	371	O4(1/1/2)		-0.2
1935	Chi N	6	23	3	10	2	0	0	2	1	0	0	.435	.458	.522	149	2	1-1	1.000	-2	44	0	3b6		0.0
1936	Chi A	137	550	99	169	32	11	5	69	61	2	46	.307	.378	.433	96	-3	10-5	.964	-2	92	136	O133(17/65/57)		-0.9
1937	Chi A	144	583	94	176	29	16	12	73	43	0	45	.302	.350	.468	104	1	10-1	.988	4	103	96	O138(6/138/1)		-0.2
1938	Chi A★	129	489	73	145	26	12	6	73	55	2	23	.297	.371	.436	99	-1	13-5	.975	1	105	55	O127(0/127/1)		-0.4
1939	Chi A	145	541	85	175	30	8	5	77	59	0	40	.323	.390	.436	108	8	23-10	.975	9	105	146	O139C,3b4		1.4
1940	Chi A	144	582	86	154	27	10	8	55	34	0	26	.265	.305	.387	77	-22	15-7	.982	7	107	109	O144C		-1.7
1941	Chi A	121	436	44	101	16	8	0	37	35	0	26	.232	.289	.305	58	-28	17-5	.994	-2	98	74	O107C		-3.0
1942	Phi A	116	444	57	113	19	1	1	30	47	0	31	.255	.346	.309	79	-11	7-9	.981	-0	106	49	O107C		-1.6
1943	StL A	60	161	24	41	6	0	0	10	26	0	13	.255	.358	.292	89	-1	4-1	.993	5	112	132	O51(3/47/1)		0.3
1944	†StL A	105	402	55	121	15	6	5	44	27	2	24	.301	.348	.405	108	4	3-3	.986	-3	102	42	O100(0/93/7)		-0.3
1945	StL A	84	295	34	70	11	1	2	21	37	0	27	.237	.322	.302	78	-8	4-1	.991	2	112	46	O81C		-0.8
	Was A	45	158	22	44	8	2	1	23	21	0	9	.278	.363	.373	124	5	7-5	.971	-2	96	62	O40C		-0.6
	Year	129	453	56	114	19	3	3	44	58	0	36	.252	.337	.327	92							O121C		
Total	12	1241	4676	676	1321	221	75	45	514	446	7	339	.283	.346	.391	92	-56	115-53	.982	15	103	90	O1177(27/1095/69),3b10		-6.8

KREHMEYER, CHARLIE Charles L. B7.5.1863 St.Louis MO D2.10.1926 St.Louis MO BL/TL/5-11/179 d7.8

YEAR	TM LG	G	AB	R	H	2B	3B	HR	RBI	BB-IB	HP	SO	AVG	OBP	SLG	AOPS	ABR	SB-CS	FA	FR	RNG	THR	GAMES AT POSITION	DL	BFW
1884	StL AA	21	70	3	16	0	1	0	5	2	0		.229	.250	.257	64	-3		.619	-3	87	0	O15(5/9/1),C7/1		-0.6
1885	Lou AA	7	31	4	7	1	0	0	5	1	0		.226	.250	.323	80	-1		.909	-2			C4,O2(1/0/1)/1		-0.3
	StL N	1	3	0	0	0	0	0	0	0	0		.000	.000	.000	-99	-1		.429	-2			/C		-0.3
Total	2	29	104	7	23	1	2	0	10	3	2		.221	.243	.269	64	-5		.571	-7			O17(6/9/2),C12,1b2		-1.1

KREITNER, MICKEY Albert Joseph B10.9.1922 Nashville TN D3.6.2003 Nashville TN BR/TR/6-3/190 d9.28

YEAR	TM LG	G	AB	R	H	2B	3B	HR	RBI	BB-IB	HP	SO	AVG	OBP	SLG	AOPS	ABR	SB-CS	FA	FR	RNG	THR	GAMES AT POSITION	DL	BFW
1943	Chi N	3	8	0	3	0	0	0	2	1	0	2	.375	.444	.375	140	0	0	1.000	-0	67	0	C3		0.0
1944	Chi N	39	85	3	13	2	0	0	1	8	1	16	.153	.234	.176	17	-9	0	.992	-0	93	109	C39		-0.8
Total	2	42	93	3	16	2	0	0	3	9	1	18	.172	.252	.194	27	-9	0	.992	-0	91	100	C42		-0.8

KREITZ, RALPH Ralph Wesley "Red" B11.13.1885 Plum Creek (now Lexington) NE D7.20.1941 Portland OR BR/TR/5-9.5/175 d8.1

YEAR	TM LG	G	AB	R	H	2B	3B	HR	RBI	BB-IB	HP	SO	AVG	OBP	SLG	AOPS	ABR	SB-CS	FA	FR	RNG	THR	GAMES AT POSITION	DL	BFW
1911	Chi A	7	17	0	4	1	0	0	2	0	0		.235	.316	.294	73	-1	0	1.000	-1	127	58	C7		-0.1

KREMERS, JIMMY James Edward B10.8.1965 Little Rock AR BL/TR/6-3/205 [AtlN88 2/33] d6.5 Col Arkansas-Monticello

YEAR	TM LG	G	AB	R	H	2B	3B	HR	RBI	BB-IB	HP	SO	AVG	OBP	SLG	AOPS	ABR	SB-CS	FA	FR	RNG	THR	GAMES AT POSITION	DL	BFW
1990	Atl N	29	73	7	8	1	1	2		6-1	0	27	.110	.177	.192	1	-10	0-0	.992	-5	77	69	C27		-1.5

KRENCHICKI, WAYNE Wayne Richard B9.17.1954 Trenton NJ BL/TR/6-1/180* [BalA76*S1/7] d6.15 Col Miami

YEAR	TM LG	G	AB	R	H	2B	3B	HR	RBI	BB-IB	HP	SO	AVG	OBP	SLG	AOPS	ABR	SB-CS	FA	FR	RNG	THR	GAMES AT POSITION	DL	BFW
1979	Bal A	16	21	1	4	1	0	0		0-0	0	0	.190	.190	.238	15	-3	0-0	.875	-2	71	0	3b7,2b6		-0.5
1980	Bal A	9	14	1	2	0	0	0		1-0	0	3	.143	.200	.143	-4	-2	0-0	1.000	-0	73	91	S6/2D		-0.2
1981	Bal A	33	56	7	12	4	0	0	6	4-0	0	9	.214	.267	.286	59	-3	0-0	.964	1	119	109	S16,2b7,3b6/D		-0.1
1982	Cin N	94	187	19	53	6	1	2	21	13-1	0	23	.283	.324	.358	92	-2	5-3	.955	4	106	96	3b70,2b9		0.1
1983	Cin N	51	77	6	21	2	0	0	11	8-2	1	4	.273	.345	.299	78	-2	0-0	.980	-1	103	85	3b39/2		-0.3
	Det A	59	133	18	37	7	0	1	16	11-0	1	27	.278	.333	.353	93	-1	0-0	.934	0	87	124	3b48,2b6,S6,1b3		-0.1
1984	Cin N	97	181	18	54	9	2	6	22	19-3	0	23	.298	.358	.470	127	7	0-1	.967	2	111	71	3b62,1b3,2b3		0.4
1985	Cin N	90	173	16	47	9	0	4	25	28-4	0	20	.272	.369	.393	109	3	0-0	.967	1	97	128	3b52,2b3		-1.0
1986	Mon N	101	221	21	53	6	2	2	23	22-3	0	32	.240	.306	.312	72	-9	2-4	.991	3	91	86	1b41,3b24/2OL		-0.9
Total	8	550	1063	107	283	44	5	15	124	106-13	2	141	.266	.330	.359	92	-12	7-8	.955	8	102	102	3b308,1b47,2b37,S28,D2/OL		

KRESS, CHUCK Charles Steven B12.9.1921 Philadelphia PA BL/TL/6-0/190* d4.16

YEAR	TM LG	G	AB	R	H	2B	3B	HR	RBI	BB-IB	HP	SO	AVG	OBP	SLG	AOPS	ABR	SB-CS	FA	FR	RNG	THR	GAMES AT POSITION	DL	BFW
1947	Cin N	11	27	4	4	0	0	0	0	3	0	4	.148	.303	.148	23	-3	0	.983	1	157	85	1b8		-0.2
1949	Cin N	27	29	3	6	3	0	0	3	3	0	5	.207	.281	.310	58	-2	0	.974	-0	100	103	1b16		-0.2
	Chi A	97	353	45	98	17	6	1	44	39	0	44	.278	.349	.368	93	-4	6-7	.994	1	102	105	1b95		-0.7
1950	Chi A	3	6	0	0	0	0	0	0	0	0	2	.000	.000	.000	-99	-2	0-0	1.000	-0	78	94	1b2		-0.3
1954	Det A	24	37	4	7	0	0	0	2	2	0	4	.189	.211	.243	24	-4	0-1	.971	-0	121	74	1b7/OR		-0.5
	Bro N	3	3	0	0	0	0	0	0	0	0	0	.083	.083	.083	-55	-3	0-0	.500	-0	0	505	/1		-0.3
Total	4	175	466	57	116	20	7	1	52	49	0	59	.249	.320	.328	74	-18	6-8	.990	1	106	103	1b129/OR		-2.6

KRESS, RED Ralph B1.2.1905 Columbia CA D11.29.1962 Los Angeles CA BR/TR/5-11.5/165 d9.24 C15 OF(22/0/103) ▲

YEAR	TM LG	G	AB	R	H	2B	3B	HR	RBI	BB-IB	HP	SO	AVG	OBP	SLG	AOPS	ABR	SB-CS	FA	FR	RNG	THR	GAMES AT POSITION	DL	BFW
1927	StL A	7	23	3	7	2	1	1	3	3	0	3	.304	.385	.609	150	2	0-0	.974	1	114	91	S7		0.3
1928	StL A	150	560	78	153	26	10	3	81	48	1	70	.273	.332	.371	82	-15	4-4	.929	-17	91	118	S150		-1.6

YEAR	TM LG	G	AB	R	H	2B	3B	HR	RBI	BB-IB	HP	SO	AVG	OBP	SLG	AOPS	ABR	SB-CS	FA	FR	RNG	THR	GAMES AT POSITION	DL	BFW
1929	StL A	147	557	82	170	38	4	9	107	52	1	54	.305	.366	.436	102	2	5-8	.946	2	100	113	S146		1.7
1930	StL A	**154**	614	94	192	43	8	16	112	50	2	56	.313	.366	.487	110	9	3-12	.938	-11	95	111	S123,3b31		1.0
1931	StL A	150	605	87	188	46	8	16	114	46	1	48	.311	.360	.493	118	14	3-16	.936	-5	94	86	3b84,O40R,S38,1b10		0.4
1932	StL A	14	52	9	9	1	2	9	4	4	0	6	.173	.232	.327	41	-5	1-1	.909	1	95	193	3b14		-0.4
	Chi A	135	515	83	147	42	4	9	57	47	1	36	.285	.346	.435	108	6	6-3	.956	11	94	214	O64(16/0/49),S53,3b19/1		1.6
	Year	149	567	85	156	42	5	11	66	51	1	42	.275	.336	.425	101	0	7-4	.956	12	94	214	O64(16/0/49),S53,3b33/1		1.2
1933	Chi A	129	467	47	116	20	5	10	78	37	0	20	.248	.304	.377	82	-14	4-4	.978	-5	99	96	1b111,O8R		-2.9
1934	Chi A	8	14	3	4	0	0	0	1	3	0	3	.286	.412	.286	80	1	0-0	1.000	-2	28	0	2b3		-0.2
	Was A	56	171	18	39	4	3	4	24	17	0	19	.228	.298	.357	71	-9	3-0	.993	-0	74	64	1b30,O10(6/0/4),2b6/S3		-1.0
	Year	64	185	21	43	4	3	4	25	20	0	22	.232	.307	.351	72	-9	3-0	.993	-3	74	64	1b30,O10(6/0/4),2b9/S3		-1.2
1935	Was A	84	252	32	75	13	4	2	42	25	0	16	.298	.361	.405	101	0	3-3	.964	11	112	137	S53,1b5,P3,O2R/2		1.3
1936	Was A	109	391	51	111	20	6	8	51	39	0	25	.284	.349	.427	96	-4	6-0	.927	4	101	121	S64,2b33,1b5		0.6
1938	StL A	150	566	74	171	33	3	7	79	69	0	47	.302	.378	.408	97	-1	5-4	**.965**	-12	86	90	S150		-0.2
1939	StL A	13	43	5	12	1	0	0	8	6	0	2	.279	.367	.302	72	-2	1-0	.933	-1	84	123	S13		-0.2
	Det A	51	157	19	38	7	0	1	22	17	0	16	.242	.316	.306	55	-10	2-1	.959	1	93	104	S25,2b16,3b4		-0.6
	Year	64	200	24	50	8	0	1	30	23	0	18	.250	.327	.305	59	-12	3-1	.951	-1	90	110	S38,2b16,3b4		-0.8
1940	Det A	33	99	13	22	3	1	1	11	10	0	12	.222	.294	.303	50	-7	0-0	.924	5	109	29	3b17,S12		-0.1
1946	NY N	1	1	0	0	0	0	0	0	1	0	0	.000	.500	.000	48	0	0-0	1.000	1	377	1785	/P		0.0
Total	14	1391	5087	691	1454	298	58	89	799	474	6	453	.286	.347	.420	96	-34	46-56	.944	-19	96	110	S835,3b170,1b162,O124R,2b59,P4		-0.3

KREUTER, CHAD Chadden Michael B8.26.1964 Greenbrae CA BB/TR (BR 1989p, 90)/6-2/195* [TexA85 5/109] d9.14 Col Pepperdine

YEAR	TM LG	G	AB	R	H	2B	3B	HR	RBI	BB-IB	HP	SO	AVG	OBP	SLG	AOPS	ABR	SB-CS	FA	FR	RNG	THR	GAMES AT POSITION	DL	BFW
1988	Tex A	16	51	3	14	2	1	1	5	7-0	0	13	.275	.362	.412	113	1	0-0	.990	1	77	118	C16		0.3
1989	Tex A	87	158	16	24	3	1	5	9	27-0	0	40	.152	.274	.266	52	-10	0-0	.992	-1	65	73	C85		-0.8
1990	Tex A	22	22	2	1	1	0	0	2	8-0	0	9	.045	.290	.091	14	-2	0-0	.977	-4	100	94	C20/D		-0.6
1991	Tex A	3	4	0	0	0	0	0	0	0-0	0	1	.000	.000	.000	-99	-1	0-0	1.000	0	0	0	/C		-0.1
1992	Det A	67	190	22	48	9	0	2	16	20-1	0	38	.253	.321	.332	83	-4	0-1	.983	3	158	112	C62/D		0.2
1993	Det A	119	374	59	107	23	3	15	51	49-4	3	92	.286	.371	.484	128	16	2-1	.988	1	121	116	C112/1D		2.2
1994	Det A	65	170	17	38	8	0	1	19	28-0	0	36	.224	.327	.288	61	-9	0-1	.987	1	143	123	C64/1OL		-0.4
1995	Sea A	26	75	12	17	5	0	1	8	5-0	2	22	.227	.293	.333	62	-4	0-0	.976	2	99	122	C23		-0.1
1996	Chi A	46	114	14	25	8	0	3	18	13-0	2	29	.219	.308	.368	74	-5	0-0	.990	1	78	146	C38,1b2	17	-0.1
1997	Chi A	19	37	6	8	2	1	1	3	8-0	0	9	.216	.356	.405	101	0	0-1	.984	-0	120	69	C13,1b2	72	0.0
	Ana A	70	218	19	51	7	1	4	18	21-0	0	57	.234	.301	.330	64	-12	0-2	.994	6	134	122	C67,D2		-0.2
	Year	89	255	25	59	9	2	5	21	29-0	0	66	.231	.310	.341	70	-12	0-3	.992	5	132	115	C80,1b2,D2		-0.2
1998	Chi A	93	245	26	62	9	1	2	33	32-1	3	45	.253	.345	.322	77	-7	1-0	.985	-5	107	99	C94		-0.2
	Ana A	3	7	1	1	0	0	0	0	1-0	0	4	.143	.250	.286	38	-1	0-0	.882	-2	48	116	C3		-0.7
	Year	96	252	27	63	10	1	2	33	33-1	3	49	.250	.343	.321	76	-8	1-0	.981	-6	105	100	C94		-0.9
1999	KC A	107	324	31	73	15	0	5	35	34-1	6	65	.225	.309	.318	59	-20	0-1	.994	-7	81	130	C101/D		-2.0
2000	LA N	80	212	32	56	13	0	6	28	54-0	2	48	.264	.416	.410	116	9	1-0	.994	5	194	100	C78		1.8
2001	LA N	73	191	21	41	11	1	6	17	41-2	1	52	.215	.355	.377	96	0	0-0	1.000	6	123	97	C70/D		1.0
2002	LA N	41	95	8	25	5	0	2	12	10-4	1	31	.263	.333	.379	98	-1	1-0	.986	-0	95	131	C41	17	0.1
2003	Tex A	7	18	0	2	0	0	0	2	3-0	0	2	.111	.238	.167	9	-2	0-0	1.000	-2	64	0	C7		-0.4
Total	16	944	2505	289	593	123	8	54	274	361-13	20	593	.237	.335	.357	83	-52	5-7	.990	5	117	110	C892,D8,1b6/OL	106	-0.0

KRICHELL, PAUL Paul Bernard B12.19.1882 New York NY D6.4.1957 Bronx NY BR/TR/5-7/150 d5.12

YEAR	TM LG	G	AB	R	H	2B	3B	HR	RBI	BB-IB	HP	SO	AVG	OBP	SLG	AOPS	ABR	SB-CS	FA	FR	RNG	THR	GAMES AT POSITION	DL	BFW
1911	StL A	28	82	6	19	3	0	0	8	4	1		.232	.276	.268	54	-5	2	.943	-3	75	105	C25		-0.7
1912	StL A	59	161	19	35	6	0	0	8	19	1		.217	.304	.255	62	-7	2	.959	-3	88	88	C59		-0.5
Total	2	87	243	25	54	9	0	0	16	23	2		.222	.295	.259	60	-12	4	.955	-6	84	93	C84		-1.2

KRIEG, BILL William Frederick B1.29.1859 Petersburg IL D3.25.1930 Chillicothe IL BR/TR/5-8/180 d4.20

YEAR	TM LG	G	AB	R	H	2B	3B	HR	RBI	BB-IB	HP	SO	AVG	OBP	SLG	AOPS	ABR	SB-CS	FA	FR	RNG	THR	GAMES AT POSITION	DL	BFW
1884	CP U	71	279	35	69	15	4	0		11			.247	.276	.330	84	-14		.932	9			C52,O20(13/6/2)/S1		-0.1
1885	Chi N	1	3	0	0	0	0	0	0	0			.000	.000	.000	-88	-1		.800	1	344	0	/OR		0.0
	Bro AA	17	60	7	9	4	0	1	5	2	0		.150	.177	.267	39	-4		.910	-3			C12,1b5		-0.6
1886	Was N	27	98	11	25	6	3	1	15	3		12	.255	.277	.408	115	2	2	.975	-1	57	55	1b27		-0.1
1887	Was N	25	95	9	24	4	1	2	17	7	1	5	.253	.311	.379	97	0	2	.973	-1	96	62	1b16,O9(7/2/0)/S		-0.2
Total	4	141	535	62	127	29	8	4	37	23	1	19	.237	.270	.344	85	-17	4	.929	5			C64,1b49,O30(20/8/3)/S		-1.0

KROEGER, JOSH Joshua J. B8.31.1982 Davenport IA BL/TL/6-2/200 [AriN00 4/129] d9.2

YEAR	TM LG	G	AB	R	H	2B	3B	HR	RBI	BB-IB	HP	SO	AVG	OBP	SLG	AOPS	ABR	SB-CS	FA	FR	RNG	THR	GAMES AT POSITION	DL	BFW
2004	Ari N	22	54	5	9	3	0	2	1-0		0	21	.167	.182	.222	3	-8	0-1	1.000	1	133	0	O19(11/2/8)		-0.7

KRONER, JOHN John Harold B11.13.1908 St.Louis MO D8.26.1968 St.Louis MO BR/TR/6-0/185 d9.29

YEAR	TM LG	G	AB	R	H	2B	3B	HR	RBI	BB-IB	HP	SO	AVG	OBP	SLG	AOPS	ABR	SB-CS	FA	FR	RNG	THR	GAMES AT POSITION	DL	BFW
1935	Bos A	2	4	1	1	0	0	0	1		0	1	.250	.400	.250	67	0	0-0	1.000	-0	65	0	3b2		0.0
1936	Bos A	84	298	40	87	17	8	4	62	26		24	.292	.349	.443	89	-6	2-3	.964	-4	101	79	2b38,3b28,S18/OR		-0.6
1937	Cle A	86	283	29	67	14	1	2	26	22		25	.237	.292	.314	52	-21	1-1	.969	3	99	105	2b64,3b11		-1.3
1938	Cle A	51	117	13	29	16	0	1	17	19		6	.248	.353	.410	92	-1	0-1	.974	6	102	130	2b31,1b7,3b3/S		0.6
Total	4	223	702	83	184	47	9	7	105	68		56	.262	.327	.385	75	-28	3-5	.968	5	100	103	2b133,3b44,S19,1b7/OR		-1.3

KRSNICH, MIKE Michael B9.24.1931 W.Allis WI BR/TR/6-1/190* d4.23 b-Rocky

YEAR	TM LG	G	AB	R	H	2B	3B	HR	RBI	BB-IB	HP	SO	AVG	OBP	SLG	AOPS	ABR	SB-CS	FA	FR	RNG	THR	GAMES AT POSITION	DL	BFW
1960	Mil N	4	9	0	3	1	0	0	2	0-0	0	3	.333	.333	.444	120	0	0-0	1.000	0	143	0	O3L		0.0
1962	Mil N	11	12	0	1	1	0	0	2	0-0	1	4	.083	.083	.167	-36	-2	0-0	1.000	0	91	0	O3L/13		-0.2
Total	2	15	21	0	4	2	0	0	4	0-0	1	4	.190	.190	.286	28	-2	0-0	1.000	1	122	0	O6L/31		-0.2

KRSNICH, ROCKY Rocco Peter B8.5.1927 W.Allis WI BR/TR/6-1/170* d9.13 b-Mike

YEAR	TM LG	G	AB	R	H	2B	3B	HR	RBI	BB-IB	HP	SO	AVG	OBP	SLG	AOPS	ABR	SB-CS	FA	FR	RNG	THR	GAMES AT POSITION	DL	BFW
1949	Chi A	16	55	7	12	3	1	1	9	6	0	4	.218	.295	.364	76	-2	0-1	.935	2	116	104	3b16		-0.1
1952	Chi A	40	91	11	21	7	2	1	15	12	1	9	.231	.327	.385	97	0	0-0	.959	6	114	92	3b37		0.6
1953	Chi A	64	129	9	26	8	0	1	14	12	0	11	.202	.270	.287	49	-9	0-2	.929	4	122	80	3b57		-0.6
Total	3	120	275	27	59	18	3	3	38	30	1	24	.215	.294	.335	70	-11	0-3	.942	12	118	89	3b110		-0.1

KRUEGER, OTTO Arthur William "Oom Paul" B9.17.1876 Chicago IL D2.20.1961 St.Louis MO BR/TR/5-7/165 d9.16

YEAR	TM LG	G	AB	R	H	2B	3B	HR	RBI	BB-IB	HP	SO	AVG	OBP	SLG	AOPS	ABR	SB-CS	FA	FR	RNG	THR	GAMES AT POSITION	DL	BFW
1899	Cle N	13	44	4	10	1	0	2	8	1			.227	.358	.250	73	-1	1	.763	-2	83	113	3b9,S2,2b2		-0.2
1900	StL N	12	35	8	14	3	2	1	3	10	1		.400	.543	.686	240	8	0	.852	-6	79	45	2b12		0.3
1901	StL N	142	520	77	143	16	12	2	79	50	13		.275	.353	.363	114	11	19	.881	-10	98	73	3b142		0.5
1902	StL N	128	467	55	124	7	8	0	46	29	3		.266	.313	.315	98	-2	14	.897	3	**112**	114	S107,3b18		-0.4
1903	Pit N	80	256	42	63	6	8	1	28	21	8		.246	.323	.344	87	-5	5	.884	-1	97	171	S29,O28L,3b13,2b3		-0.7
1904	Pit N	86	268	34	52	6	2	1	26	29	4		.194	.282	.243	61	-11	8	.905	-3	113	92	O33(23/0/10),S32,3b10		-1.6
1905	Phi N	46	114	10	21	1	1	0	12	13	1		.184	.273	.211	47	-7	1	.905	-3	92	119	S23,O6(0/3/3)/3		-1.3
Total	7	507	1704	230	427	40	33	5	196	160	31		.251	.326	.322	94	-7	48	.902	-24	107	117	S193,3b193,O67(51/3/13),2b17		-2.6

KRUEGER, ERNIE Ernest George B12.27.1890 Chicago IL D4.22.1976 Waukegan IL BR/TR/5-10.5/185 d8.4 Mil 1918 Col Lake Forest

YEAR	TM LG	G	AB	R	H	2B	3B	HR	RBI	BB-IB	HP	SO	AVG	OBP	SLG	AOPS	ABR	SB-CS	FA	FR	RNG	THR	GAMES AT POSITION	DL	BFW
1913	Cle A	5	6	0	0	0	0	0	0		0	2	.000	.000	.000	-97	-2	0	1.000	0	78	159	C4		
1915	NY A	10	29	3	5	1	0	0	0	4	0	5	.172	.200	.207	22	-3	0-1	.905	-3	83	80	C8		-0.2
1917	NY N	8	10	0	0	0	0	0	0		0	4	.000	.000	.000	-99	-2	0	.857	-1	70	0	C5		-0.6
	Bro N	31	81	10	22	2	2	1	6	5	2	7	.272	.330	.383	115	1	1	.979	-1	103	87	C23		-0.4
	Year	39	91	10	22	2	2	1	6	5	2	11	.242	.296	.341	94	-1	1	.973	-1	101	81	C28		0.4
1918	Bro N	30	87	4	25	4	2	0	7	4	0	2	.287	.319	.379	113	1	2	.986	3	92	118	C23		0.0
1919	Bro N	80	226	24	56	7	4	5	36	19		25	.248	.312	.381	105	1	4	.963	0	91	104	C66		0.7
1920	†Bro N	52	146	21	42	4	2	1	17	16	0	13	.288	.358	.363	104	1	2-0	.959	-3	95	103	C46		0.8
1921	Bro N	65	163	18	43	11	4	3	20	14		12	.264	.322	.436	95	-1	2-2	.969	-2	85	73	C52		0.2
1925	Cin N	37	88	7	27	4	0	1	7	6		8	.307	.351	.386	90	-1	1-2	.946	-3	74	69	C30		0.0
Total	8	318	836	87	220	33	14	11	93	64		85	.263	.319	.386	90	-8	1-5	.964	-8	90	94	C257		0.6

KRUG, CHRIS Everett Ben B12.25.1939 Los Angeles CA BR/TR/6-4/200* d5.30 C1 Col Riverside (CA) CC

YEAR	TM LG	G	AB	R	H	2B	3B	HR	RBI	BB-IB	HP	SO	AVG	OBP	SLG	AOPS	ABR	SB-CS	FA	FR	RNG	THR	GAMES AT POSITION	DL	BFW
1965	Chi N	60	169	16	34	5	0	5	24	13-2	1	52	.201	.258	.320	61	-9	0-0	.980	2	107	117	C58		-0.5
1966	Chi N	11	28	1	6	1	0	0	1	1-0	0	8	.214	.241	.250	36	-2	0-0	1.000	1	61	163	C10		-0.1
1969	SD N	8	17	0	1	0	0	0	0	1-0	0	6	.059	.111	.059	-53	-4	0-0	.938	-1	106	145	C7		-0.4
Total	3	79	214	17	41	6	0	5	25	15-2	1	66	.192	.245	.290	50	-15	0-1	.980	2	101	126	C75		-1.0

YEAR	TM	LG	G	AB	R	H	2B	3B	HR	RBI	BB-IB	HP	SO	AVG	OBP	SLG	AOPS	ABR	SB-CS	FA	FR	RNG	THR	GAMES AT POSITION	DL	BFW

KRUG, GENE Gary Eugene B2.12.1955 Garden City KS BL/TL/6-4/225 [ChiN77 29/689] d4.29 Col Oklahoma

| 1981 | Chi | N | 7 | 5 | 0 | 2 | 0 | 0 | 0 | | 1-0 | 0 | 1 | .400 | .500 | .400 | 149 | 0 | 0-0 | — | 0 | | | /H | | 0.0 |

KRUG, HENRY Henry Charles B12.4.1876 San Francisco CA D1.14.1908 San Francisco CA BR/TR d7.26

| 1902 | Phi | N | 53 | 198 | 20 | 45 | 3 | 3 | 0 | 14 | 7 | | 2 | .227 | .261 | .273 | 65 | -9 | 2 | .947 | -4 | 108 | 98 | O28L,2b13,S9,3b6 | | -1.5 |

KRUG, MARTY Martin John B9.10.1888 Koblenz, Germany D6.27.1966 Glendale CA BR/TR/5-9/165 d5.29

1912	Bos	A	20	39	6	12	1	0	7	5	0			.308	.386	.410	122	1	2	.895	-1	83	141	S11,2b4		0.0
1922	Chi	A	127	450	67	124	23	4	4	60	43	3	43	.276	.343	.371	82	-11	7-9	.937	-7	93	111	3b104,2b23/S		-1.1
Total	2		147	489	73	136	25	5	4	67	48	3	43	.278	.346	.374	85	-10	9-9	.937	-8	93	111	3b104,2b27,S12		-1.1

KRUGER, ART Arthur T. B3.16.1881 San Antonio TX D11.28.1949 Hondo (now part of Downey) CA BR/TR/6-0/185 d4.11

1907	Cin	N	100	317	25	74	10	9	0	28	18	5		.233	.285	.322	87	-6	10	.972	2	88	96	O96(26/70/1)		-1.0
1910	Cle	A	47	168	14	26	4	2	0	10	15	3		.155	.237	.202	37	-12	10	.947	2	99	126	O47L		-1.5
	Bos	N	1	1	0	0	0	0	0	0	0	0		.000	.000	.000	-96	0	0	—	0			/H		0.0
	Cle	A	15	55	5	12	2	1	0	4	5	1		.218	.295	.291	82	-1	2	.974	1	99	126.	O15L		-0.1
1914	KC	F	122	441	45	114	24	7	4	47	23		59	.259	.297	.372	85	-19	11	.963	-2	99	83	O120(7/113/0)		-3.1
1915	KC	F	80	240	24	57	9	2	2	26	12	1	29	.237	.277	.317	70	-15	5	.984	1	101	94	O66(33/3/30)		-1.9
Total	4		365	1222	113	283	49	21	6	115	73	11	88	.232	.281	.321	76	-53	38	.968	3	98	95	O344(128/186/31)		-7.6

KRUK, JOHN John Martin B2.9.1961 Charleston WV BL/TL/5-10/204(190-220) [SDN81 S3/62] d4.7 Col Allegany (MD) CC

1986	SD	N	122	278	33	86	16	2	4	38	45-0	0	58	.309	.403	.424	132	15	2-4	.981	-2	90	98	O74(70/0/6),1b9		0.9
1987	SD	N	138	447	72	140	14	2	20	91	73-15	0	93	.313	.406	.488	142	29	18-10	.996	2	107	99	1b101,O29L		2.4
1988	SD	N	120	378	54	91	17	1	9	44	80-12	0	68	.241	.369	.362	114	11	5-3	.995	-2	77	114	1b63,O55(29/0/26)		0.3
1989	SD	N	31	76	7	14	0	0	3	6	17-0	0	14	.184	.333	.303	83	-1	0-0	.962	2	103	231	O27(2/0/25)	16	-0.1
	Phi	N	81	281	46	93	13	6	5	38	27-2	0	39	.331	.386	.473	146	16	3-0	.983	-3	85	136	O72(63/0/12),1b7	25	1.3
	Year		112	357	53	107	13	6	8	44	44-2	0	53	.300	.374	.437	132	15	3-0	.977	-1	90	161	O99(65/0/37),1b7		1.2
1990	Phi	N	142	443	52	129	25	8	7	67	69-16	0	70	.291	.386	.431	125	18	10-5	.986	-2	89	35	O87(68/0/21),1b61		1.1
1991	Phi☆	N	152	538	84	158	27	6	21	92	67-16	1	100	.294	.367	.483	140	29	3-5	.997	-3	74	81	1b102,O52(36/11/6)		2.0
1992	Phi★	N	144	507	86	164	30	4	10	70	92-8	1	88	.323	.423	.458	151	40	3-5	.993	-11	73	93	1b121,O35(6/0/29)		2.1
1993	†Phi★	N	150	535	100	169	33	5	14	85	111-10	0	87	.316	.430	.475	145	42	6-2	.993	-10	70	72	1b144		1.9
1994	Phi	N	75	255	35	77	17	0	5	38	42-4	0	51	.302	.395	.427	114	8	4-1	.995	-0	97	81	1b69	28	0.2
1995	Chi	A	45	159	13	49	7	0	2	23	26-0	1	33	.308	.399	.390	113	4	0-1	.909	-0	0	118	D42/1	16	0.1
Total	10		1200	3897	582	1170	199	34	100	592	649-83	2	701	.300	.397	.446	134	211	58-31	.995	-31	85	88	1b678,O431(303/11/125),D42	85	12.2

KRYHOSKI, DICK Richard David B3.24.1925 Leonia NJ BL/TL/6-2/200* d4.19

1949	NY	A	54	177	18	52	10	3	1	27	9	2	17	.294	.335	.401	94	-2	2-4	.983	-1	96	82	1b51		-0.5
1950	Det	A	53	169	20	37	10	0	4	19	8	1	11	.219	.258	.349	53	-13	0-1	.991	-1	94	110	1b47		-1.5
1951	Det	A	119	421	58	121	19	4	12	57	28	2	29	.287	.335	.437	107	2	1-2	.991	3	110	91	1b112		0.1
1952	StL	A	111	342	38	83	13	1	11	42	23	3	42	.243	.296	.383	86	-8	2-0	.989	-4	85	102	1b86		-1.5
1953	StL	A	104	338	35	94	18	4	16	50	26	2	33	.278	.333	.497	119	7	0-5	.992	5	120	90	1b88		0.6
1954	Bal	A	100	300	32	78	13	2	1	34	19	2	24	.260	.305	.327	80	-9	0-0	.992	2	105	80	1b69		-1.2
1955	KC	A	28	47	2	10	2	0	2	6-0		1	7	.213	.302	.255	50	-3	0-1	.988	0	107	81	1b14		-0.4
Total	7		569	1794	203	475	85	14	45	231	119-0	12	163	.265	.314	.403	93	-26	5-13	.990	5	103	92	1b467		-4.4

KRYNZEL, DAVE David Benjamin B11.7.1981 Dayton OH BL/TL/6-1/180* [MilN00 1/11] d9.1

2004	Mil	N	16	41	6	9	1	0	0	3	3-0	1	15	.220	.319	.244	48	-3	0-0	.968	3	160	187	O10(0/2/8)		-0.1
2005	Mil	N	5	7	0	0	0	0	0	0	3-0		3	.000	.300	.000	-99	-2	0-0	1.000	-0.	95	0	/OC		-0.3
Total	2		21	48	6	9	1	0	0	3	3-0	1	18	.188	.278	.208	28	-5	0-0	.970	3	154	170	O11(0/3/8)		-0.3

KUBEK, TONY Anthony Christopher B10.12.1936 Milwaukee WI BL/TR/6-3/191* d4.20 OF(80/46/31)

1957	†NY	A	127	431	56	128	21	3	3	39	24-3	1	48	.297	.335	.381	98	-2	6-6	.938	-2	81	68	O50(29/23/0),S41,3b38/2		-0.5
1958	†NY	A☆	138	559	66	148	21	1	2	48	25-3	1	57	.265	.295	.317	72	-23	5-4	.961	20	110	112	S134,O3(0/1/2)/12		0.9
1959	†NY	A★	132	512	67	143	25	7	6	51	24-3	2	46	.279	.313	.391	95	-5	3-3	.968	2	102	97	S67,O53(22/15/26),3b17/2		0.1
1960	†NY	A	147	568	77	155	25	3	14	62	31-5	3	42	.273	.312	.401	94	-5	3-0	.968	8	108	101	S136,O29(22/6/1)		1.4
1961	†NY	A★	153	617	84	170	38	6	8	46	27-1	1	60	.276	.306	.395	91	-10	1-3	.959	18	106	132	S145		1.9
1962	NY	A	45	169	28	53	6	4	1	17	12-0	0	17	.314	.357	.432	115	3	2-1	.980	8	103	113	S132/OC		0.3
1963	†NY	A	135	557	72	143	21	3	7	44	28-6	2	68	.257	.294	.343	79	-17	4-2	.978	-7	107	98	S99		-0.3
1964	NY	A	106	415	46	95	16	3	8	31	26-3	1	55	.229	.275	.340	69	-18	4-1	.964	-4	97	112	S93,O3(1/0/2)/1		-1.8
1965	NY	A	109	339	26	74	5	3	5	35	20-0	1	48	.218	.258	.295	58	-20	1-3	.964	-7	66	106	S882,O145L,3b55,2b3,1b2		3.4
Total	9		1092	4167	522	1109	178	30	57	373	217-24	13	441	.266	.303	.364	85	-97	29-23	.967	66	106	112			

KUBEL, JASON Jason James B5.25.1982 Belle Fourche SD BL/TR/5-11/200 [MinA00 12/342] d8.31 [DL 2005 Min A 183]

| 2004 | †Min | A | 23 | 60 | 10 | 18 | 2 | 0 | 2 | 7 | 6-0 | 0 | 9 | .300 | .358 | .433 | 104 | 0 | 1-1 | 1.000 | 1 | 97 | 220 | O10(2/0/8),D9 | | 0.0 |

KUBIAK, TED Theodore Rodger B5.12.1942 New Brunswick NJ BB/TR/6-0/175* d4.14 Mil 1968

1967	KC	A	53	102	6	16	2	1	0	5	12-0	1	20	.157	.243	.196	33	-9	0-0	.984	-3	95	60	S20,2b10,3b5		-1.1
1968	Oak	A	48	120	10	30	5	2	0	8	8-1	2	18	.250	.305	.325	96	-1	1-1	.929	-5	86	81	2b24,S12		-0.4
1969	Oak	A	92	305	38	76	9	1	2	27	25-2	1	35	.249	.304	.305	75	-11	2-0	.976	2	100	103	S42,2b33		-0.1
1970	Mil	A	158	540	63	136	9	6	4	41	72-16	0	51	.252	.340	.313	81	-13	4-9	.989	-12	90	105	2b91,S73		-1.3
1971	Mil	A	89	260	26	59	6	5	3	17	41-3	0	31	.227	.330	.323	87	-4	0-5	.971	-4	88	75	2b48,S39		-0.3
	StL	N	32	72	8	18	3	2	1	10	11-3	0	12	.250	.345	.389	104	1	1-0	.959	-5	82	68	S17,2b14		-0.2
1972	Tex	A	46	116	5	26	3	0	0	12	12-3	1	12	.224	.300	.250	68	-4	0-1	.990	-4	91	84	2b25,S15/3		-0.7
	†Oak	A	51	94	14	17	4	1	0	8	9-0	1	11	.181	.250	.245	51	-6	0-0	.988	1	104	112	2b49/3		-0.3
	Year		97	210	19	43	7	1	0	15	21-3	2	23	.205	.278	.248	60	-10	0-1	.989	-3	99	101	2b74,S15,3b2		-1.0
1973	†Oak	A	106	182	15	40	6	1	3	17	12-1	0	19	.220	.267	.313	66	-9	1-1	.973	3	111	102	2b71,S19,3b14,D2		-2.2
1974	Oak	A	99	220	22	46	3	0	0	18	18-0	0	15	.209	.268	.223	45	-16	1-1	.995	-10	96	101	S7,3b7,2b6		-0.1
1975	Oak	A	20	28	2	7	1	0	0	4	2-0	0	2	.250	.300	.286	68	-1	0-0	1.000	-0	83	106	S7,3b7,2b6		-1.3
	SD	N	87	196	13	44	5	0	0	14	24-5	0	18	.224	.308	.250	60	-10	3-1	.954	-3	105	104	3b64,2b11/1		-1.3
1976	SD	N	96	212	16	50	5	2	0	26	25-2	0	28	.236	.314	.278	76	-6	0-3	.971	-7	99	124	2b490,S276,3b121,1b2,D2		-1.3
Total	10		977	2447	238	565	61	21	13	202	271-36	4	272	.231	.307	.289	72	-89	13-22	.981	-45	94	94			-9.4

KUBISZYN, JACK John Henry B12.19.1936 Buffalo NY BR/TR/5-11/170* d4.23 Col Alabama

1961	Cle	A	25	42	4	9	0	0	0	0	2-0	0	5	.214	.250	.214	26	-5	0-0	1.000	2	111	0	3b8,S7,2b2		-0.2
1962	Cle	A	25	59	3	10	2	0	1	2	5-0	0	7	.169	.231	.254	32	-6	0-0	.964	0	100	133	S18/3		-0.4
Total	2		50	101	7	19	2	0	1	2	7-0	0	12	.188	.239	.238	30	-11	0-0	.969	3	103	145	S25,3b9,2b2		-0.6

KUBSKI, GIL Gilbert Thomas B10.12.1954 Longview TX BL/TR/6-3/185 [AnaA75*S1/12] d9.2 Col Cal St.-Northridge

| 1980 | Cal | A | 22 | 63 | 11 | 16 | 3 | 0 | 0 | 6 | 10 | | | .254 | .319 | .302 | 72 | -2 | 1-1 | 1.000 | 2 | 111 | 164 | O20(1/0/19) | | -0.2 |

KUCZEK, STEVE Stanislaw Leo B12.28.1924 Amsterdam NY BR/TR/6-0/160 d9.29 Col Colgate

| 1949 | Bos | N | 1 | 1 | 0 | 1 | 1 | 0 | 0 | 0 | 0 | | 0 | 1.000 | 1.000 | 2.000 | 723 | 1 | 0 | — | 0 | | | /H | | 0.1 |

KUEHNE, BILL William J. (b William J. Knelme) B10.24.1858 Leipzig, Germany D10.27.1921 Sulphur Springs OH BR/TR/5-8/185 d5.1 OF(33/9/30)

1883	Col	AA	95	374	38	85	8	14	1		2			.227	.231	.332	86	-6		.833	-3	99	139	3b69,2b18,S7,O3(1/2/0)		-0.6
1884	Col	AA	110	415	48	98	13	16	5		5			.236	.254	.381	113	5		.881	11	110	123	3b110		1.7
1885	Pit	AA	104	411	54	93	9	19	0	43	15	2		.226	.257	.341	89	-7		.865	-5	98	107	3b97,S7		-0.9
1886	Pit	AA	117	481	73	98	16	17	1	48	19			.204	.237	.314	72	-18	26	.899	1	126	0	O54(24/5/24),3b47,1b18		-1.7
1887	Pit	N	102	402	68	120	18	15	1	41	14	1	39	.299	.324	.425	115	7	17	.883	-13	101	101	S91,3b4,1b4,O3(0/1/2)		-0.3
1888	Pit	N	138	524	60	123	22	11	6	62	9	2	68	.235	.250	.336	94	-5	34	.910	1	111	98	3b75,S63		-0.1
1889	Pit	N	97	390	43	96	15	5	5	51	16	2	36	.246	.263	.362	82	-12	15	.885	-2	100	109	3b75,O13(8/1/4),2b5,S2,1b2		-1.1
1890	Pit	P	126	528	66	126	21	12	5	73	28		37	.239	.277	.352	74	-22	21	.850	7	111	88	3b126		-1.4
1891	Col	AA	68	261	32	56	9	2	0	22	10		22	.215	.244	.272	50	-18	21	.885	0	101	144	3b68		-0.4
	Lou	AA	39	152	25	41	3	1	1	17	7		13	.270	.306	.322	81	-5	9	.896	-1	99	107	3b39		-1.8
	Year		107	413	57	97	12	3	1	39	17.		35	.235	.267	.291	62	-22	30	.889	-0	100	130	3b107		-2.7
1892	Lou	N	76	287	22	48	4	5	0	36	13		36	.167	.203	.216	29	-26	6	.874	-4	95	143	3b76		-0.2
	StL	N	6	24	1	4	1	0	0	4	0		5	.167	.200	.208	25	-2	1	.895	-0	98	0	3b5/S		-0.2

YEAR	TM LG	G	AB	R	H	2B	3B	HR	RBI	BB-IB	HP	SO	AVG	OBP	SLG	AOPS	ABR	SB-CS	FA	FR	RNG	THR	GAMES AT POSITION	DL	BFW
	Cin N	6	24	3	5	1	0	1	4	1	0	5	.208	.240	.375	87	-1	0	.941	0	107	356	3b4,2b2		0.0
	StL N	1	4	0	0	0	0	0	0	0	0	1	.000	.000	.000	-99	-1	0	1.000	1	98	0	/3		0.0
	Year	89	339	26	57	6	5	1	40	14	1	45	.168	.203	.224	32	-29	7	.880	-3	97	154	3b86,2b2/S		-2.9
Total	10	1085	4277	533	993	145	115	25	403	136	10	260	.232	.258	.337	82	-111	150	.875	-5	104	115	3b796,S171,O73L,2b25,1b24		-8.8

KUENN, HARVEY   Harvey Edward B12.4.1930 W.Allis WI D2.28.1988 Peoria AZ BR/TR/6-2/190(182-197) d9.6 M3/C12 Col Wisconsin-Madison OF(354/163/343)

YEAR	TM LG	G	AB	R	H	2B	3B	HR	RBI	BB-IB	HP	SO	AVG	OBP	SLG	AOPS	ABR	SB-CS	FA	FR	RNG	THR	GAMES AT POSITION	DL	BFW
1952	Det A	19	80	2	26	2	2	0	8	2	1	13	.325	.349	.400	107	0	2-1	.962	1	96	91	S19		0.3
1953	Det A★	155	679	94	209	33	7	2	48	50	1	31	.308	.356	.386	101	7	6-5	.973	-24	89	68	S155		-1.0
1954	Det A☆	155	656	81	201	28	6	5	48	29	1	13	.306	.335	.390	100	-2	9-9	.966	5	104	86	S155		1.5
1955	Det A★	145	620	101	190	38	5	8	62	40-3	1	27	.306	.347	.423	109	7	8-3	.956	-26	88	95	S141		-0.6
1956	Det A★	146	591	96	196	32	7	12	88	55-3	3	34	.332	.387	.470	126	23	9-5	.968	-14	92	90	S141/OL		1.9
1957	Det A★	151	624	74	173	30	6	9	44	47-4	0	28	.277	.327	.388	92	-7	5-8	.955	-46	80	95	S136,3b17/1		-4.6
1958	Det A☆	139	561	73	179	39	3	8	54	51-8	0	34	.319	.373	.442	116	14	5-10	.984	1	106	116	O138C		0.9
1959	Det A★	139	561	99	198	42	7	9	71	48-1	1	37	.353	.402	.501	140	32	7-2	.988	-2	102	82	O137(0/23/116)		2.6
1960	Cle A★	126	474	65	146	24	0	9	54	55-6	1	25	.308	.379	.416	119	14	3-0	.988	-2	104	95	O119(2/2/117),3b5		0.9
1961	SF N	131	471	60	125	22	4	5	46	47-2	1	37	.265	.329	.361	87	-8	5-4	.988	-6	100	124	O93(67/0/31),3b32/S		-1.9
1962	†SF N	130	487	73	148	23	5	10	68	49-3	1	37	.304	.365	.433	116	12	3-6	.970	-3	98	45	O105(99/0/10),3b30		0.2
1963	SF N	120	417	61	121	13	2	6	31	44-3	2	38	.290	.358	.374	113	8	2-1	.975	-16	87	118	O64(45/0/27),3b53		-1.2
1964	SF N	111	351	42	92	16	2	4	22	35-4	1	32	.262	.329	.353	91	-3	0-1	.952	-8	73	39	O88(65/0/36),1b11,3b2		-1.8
1965	SF N	23	59	4	14	0	0	0	6	10-0	1	9	.237	.352	.237	69	-2	3-1	1.000	-0	72	0	O14(12/0/2),1b7		-0.3
	Chi N	54	120	11	26	5	0	0	6	22-1	0	13	.217	.336	.258	69	-4	1-0	.975	-1	80	202	O35(31/0/4)/1		-0.6
	Year	77	179	15	40	5	0	0	12	32-1	1	16	.223	.341	.251	69	-6	4-1	.981	-1	78	139	O49(43/0/6),1b8		-0.9
1966	Chi N	3	3	0	1	0	0	0	0	0-0	0	1	.333	.333	.333	85	0	0-0	—	-0	0	0	/OL		0.0
	Phi N	86	159	15	47	9	0	0	15	10-1	0	16	.296	.333	.352	92	-1	0-0	1.000	-3	85	0	O31L,1b13/3		-0.7
	Year	89	162	15	48	9	0	0	15	10-1	0	17	.296	.333	.352	92	-1	0-0	1.000	-3	84	0	O32L,1b13/3		-0.7
Total	15	1833	6913	951	2092	356	56	87	671	594-39	15	404	.303	.408	108	84	68-56	.978	-143	97	89	O826L,S748,3b140,1b33		-4.4

KUHEL, JOE   Joseph Anthony B6.25.1906 Cleveland OH D2.26.1984 Kansas City KS BL/TL/6-0/180 d7.31 M2

YEAR	TM LG	G	AB	R	H	2B	3B	HR	RBI	BB-IB	HP	SO	AVG	OBP	SLG	AOPS	ABR	SB-CS	FA	FR	RNG	THR	GAMES AT POSITION	DL	BFW
1930	Was A	18	63	9	18	3	0	0	17	5	1	6	.286	.348	.429	95	-1	1-0	.981	-1	87	84	1b16		-0.2
1931	Was A	139	524	70	141	34	8	8	85	47	5	45	.269	.335	.410	94	-5	7-5	.991	-6	77	121	1b139		-2.3
1932	Was A	101	347	52	101	21	5	4	52	32	1	19	.291	.353	.415	99	0	5-2	.994	-2	89	98	1b85		-0.9
1933	†Was A	153	602	89	194	34	10	11	107	59	2	48	.322	.385	.467	126	22	17-8	.996	-6	76	115	1b153		-0.9
1934	Was A	63	263	49	76	12	3	3	25	30	1	14	.289	.364	.392	99	0	2-7	.994	-4	72	116	1b63		0.2
1935	Was A	151	633	99	165	25	9	2	74	78	4	44	.261	.345	.338	80	-18	5-4	.991	1	104	109	1b151		-1.1
1936	Was A	149	588	107	189	42	8	16	118	64	4	30	.321	.392	.502	126	24	15-7	.993	-2	92	110	1b149		-3.0
1937	Was A	136	547	73	155	24	11	6	61	63	0	39	.283	.357	.400	95	-5	6-3	.993	3	109	116	1b136		0.8
1938	Chi A	117	412	67	110	27	4	8	51	72	0	35	.267	.376	.410	95	-2	9-7	.988	0	79	95	1b111		-1.4
1939	Chi A	139	546	107	164	24	9	15	56	64	2	51	.300	.376	.460	110	8	18-5	.992	-4	89	107	1b136		-1.9
1940	Chi A	155	603	111	169	28	8	27	94	87	3	59	.280	.374	.488	120	18	12-5	.988	-5	91	93	1b155		-0.6
1941	Chi A	153	600	99	150	39	5	12	63	70	3	55	.250	.331	.392	92	-7	20-5	.994	0	100	94	1b151		0.0
1942	Chi A	115	413	60	103	14	4	4	52	60	2	22	.249	.347	.332	94	-2	22-9	.991	-3	91	103	1b112		-1.8
1943	Chi A	153	531	55	113	21	5	1	46	76	7	45	.213	.319	.284	77	-13	14-8	.995	2	103	107	1b153		-1.4
1944	Was A	139	518	90	144	26	7	4	51	68	2	40	.278	.364	.378	117	14	11-6	.987	-1	98	94	1b138		-2.0
1945	Was A	142	543	73	152	29	13	2	75	79	1	31	.285	.378	.400	137	28	10-5	.989	-6	87	91	1b141		0.6
1946	Was A	14	20	2	3	0	0	0	2	5	0	2	.150	.320	.150	36	-1	0-0	1.000	0	125	61	1b5		1.5
	Chi A	64	238	24	65	9	3	4	20	21	1	24	.273	.335	.387	105	1	4-4	.994	-1	95	122	1b63		-0.1
	Year	78	258	26	68	9	3	4	22	26	1	26	.264	.333	.368	100	0	4-4	.994	-1	97	119	1b68		-0.3
1947	Chi A	3	3	0	0	0	0	0	0	0	0	3	.000	.000	.000	-99	-1	0-0	—	0			/H		-0.4
Total	18	2104	7984	1236	2212	412	111	131	1049	980	39	612	.277	.359	.406	104	60	178-90	.992	-42	92	105	1b2057		-14.0

KUHN, KENNY   Kenneth Harold B3.20.1937 Louisville KY BL/TR/5-10.5/175* d7.7

YEAR	TM LG	G	AB	R	H	2B	3B	HR	RBI	BB-IB	HP	SO	AVG	OBP	SLG	AOPS	ABR	SB-CS	FA	FR	RNG	THR	GAMES AT POSITION	DL	BFW
1955	Cle A	4	6	0	2	0	0	0	0	1-0	0	0	.333	.429	.333	103	0	1-0	1.000	-1	72	0	S4	41	0.0
1956	Cle A	27	22	7	6	1	0	0	2	0-0	0	4	.273	.273	.318	54	-2	0-1	1.000	1	92	127	S17,2b5		-0.1
1957	Cle A	40	53	5	9	0	0	0	5	4-0	0	9	.170	.228	.170	10	-7	0-0	.974	-3	62	35	2b14,3b2/S		-0.1
Total	3	71	81	12	17	1	0	0	7	5-0	0	13	.210	.256	.222	30	-9	1-1	.963	-3	82	83	S22,2b19,3b2	41	-1.0

KUHN, WALT   Walter Charles "Red" B2.2.1884 Fresno CA D6.14.1935 Fresno CA BR/TR/5-7/162 d4.18

YEAR	TM LG	G	AB	R	H	2B	3B	HR	RBI	BB-IB	HP	SO	AVG	OBP	SLG	AOPS	ABR	SB-CS	FA	FR	RNG	THR	GAMES AT POSITION	DL	BFW
1912	Chi A	76	178	16	36	1	0	0	10	20	1		.202	.286	.242	53	-10	4	.966	5	102	103	C75/2		0.0
1913	Chi A	26	50	5	8	1	0	0	5	13	0		.160	.333	.180	52	-2	1	.980	0	124	89	C24		0.0
1914	Chi A	17	40	4	11	1	0	0	0	8	0	11	.275	.396	.300	111	1	2-3	.987	1	121	85	C16		0.3
Total	3	119	268	25	55	9	0	0	15	41	1	19	.205	.313	.239	62	-11	7-3	.971	7	109	98	C115/2		0.3

KUHNS, CHARLIE   Charles Benton B10.27.1876 Freeport PA D7.15.1922 Pittsburgh PA 5-9/160 d6.4

YEAR	TM LG	G	AB	R	H	2B	3B	HR	RBI	BB-IB	HP	SO	AVG	OBP	SLG	AOPS	ABR	SB-CS	FA	FR	RNG	THR	GAMES AT POSITION	DL	BFW
1897	Pit N	1	3	0	0	0	0	0	0	1	0		.000	.000	.000	-32	-1	0	.667	-0	120	0	/3		-0.1
1899	Bos N	7	18	2	5	0	0	0	3	2	0		.278	.350	.278	67	-1	0	.813	-1	95	214	S3,3b3		-0.2
Total	2	8	21	2	5	0	0	0	3	3	0		.238	.333	.238	53	-2	0	.733	-1	112	0	3b4,S3		-0.2

KUIPER, DUANE   Duane Eugene B6.19.1950 Racine WI BL/TR/6-0/175* [CleA72*S1/21] d9.9 Col Southern Illinois

YEAR	TM LG	G	AB	R	H	2B	3B	HR	RBI	BB-IB	HP	SO	AVG	OBP	SLG	AOPS	ABR	SB-CS	FA	FR	RNG	THR	GAMES AT POSITION	DL	BFW
1974	Cle A	10	22	7	11	2	0	0	4	2-0	0	2	.500	.542	.591	227	4	1-1	1.000	1	115	73	2b8		0.5
1975	Cle A	90	346	42	101	11	6	0	25	30-0	8	26	.292	.362	.329	96	0	19-18	.972	-14	90	107	2b87/D		-1.1
1976	Cle A	135	506	47	133	13	6	0	37	30-2	1	42	.263	.303	.312	82	-13	10-17	.987	17	99	115	2b128,1b5,D2	20	0.9
1977	Cle A	148	610	62	169	15	8	1	50	37-1	7	55	.277	.324	.333	82	-16	11-11	.985	-3	95	105	2b148		-1.2
1978	Cle A	149	547	52	155	18	6	1	40	19-1	4	35	.283	.311	.338	84	-13	4-9	.979	-12	93	89	2b149		-2.1
1979	Cle A	140	479	46	122	9	5	0	39	37-7	4	27	.255	.313	.294	65	-24	4-9	.988	-5	92	88	2b140		-2.3
1980	Cle A	42	149	10	42	5	0	0	13	13-3	0	8	.282	.337	.315	80	-4	0-1	.995	-5	88	90	2b42		-0.6
1981	Cle A	72	206	15	53	6	0	0	14	8-2	0	13	.257	.284	.286	65	-10	1-1	.983	-11	90	53	2b72	126	-1.8
1982	SF N	107	218	26	61	9	1	0	17	32-0	2	24	.280	.375	.330	100	2	2-2	.978	-8	90	85	2b51	22	-0.4
1983	SF N	72	176	14	44	2	2	0	14	27-6	2	13	.250	.353	.284	82	-1	0-0	.988	-13	87	49	2b64	41	-1.5
1984	SF N	83	115	13	23	1	0	0	11	12-5	0	10	.200	.273	.209	39	-9	0-1	.969	4	109	99	2b31/1		-0.5
1985	SF N	9	5	3	0	0	0	0	1	1-0	0	4	.000	.667	.600	269	-1	0	—	0			/H	29	0.1
Total	12	1057	3379	329	917	91	29	1	263	248-27	28	255	.271	.325	.316	81	-85	52-71	.983	-49	93	92	2b920,1b6,D3	238	-10.0

KUNKEL, JEFF   Jeffrey William B3.25.1962 W.Palm Beach FL BR/TR/6-2/180* [TexA83 1/3] d7.23 f-Bill Col Rider OF(14/30/5) [DL 1991 Tex A 182]

YEAR	TM LG	G	AB	R	H	2B	3B	HR	RBI	BB-IB	HP	SO	AVG	OBP	SLG	AOPS	ABR	SB-CS	FA	FR	RNG	THR	GAMES AT POSITION	DL	BFW
1984	Tex A	50	142	13	29	2	3	3	7	2-0	1	35	.204	.218	.324	47	-11	4-3	.922	-1	96	85	S48/D		-0.8
1985	Tex A	2	4	1	1	0	0	0	0	0-0	0	3	.250	.250	.250	37	0	0-0	1.000	1	192	171	S2		0.1
1986	Tex A	8	13	3	3	0	0	1	0	0-0	0	2	.231	.231	.462	80	0	0-0	.769	-4	53	0	S5/D		-0.4
1987	Tex A	15	32	1	7	0	0	1	2	0-0	1	10	.219	.242	.313	45	-3	0-1	.955	1	103	140	2b10,3b3,O3(1/2/0)/1SD	30	-0.2
1988	Tex A	55	154	14	35	8	3	2	15	4-1	1	35	.227	.250	.357	67	-8	0-1	.949	4	111	101	2b28,S19,3b10,O6(4/2/0)/PD		-0.3
1989	Tex A	108	293	39	79	21	2	8	29	20-0	3	75	.270	.323	.437	110	4	3-2	.936	-5	92	60	S59,O30(5/24/3),2b8,3b4/PD		0.2
1990	Tex A	99	200	17	34	11	1	3	17	11-0	2	66	.170	.221	.280	39	-17	2-1	.958	5	103	101	S67,3b15,2b13,O5(1/2/2)/D	32	-0.8
1992	Chi N	20	29	0	4	2	0	0	0	1-0	0	8	.138	.138	.207	-3	-4	0-0	1.000	2	172	90	S6,2b3,O3L		-0.2
Total	8	357	867	88	192	44	9	18	73	37-1	8	234	.221	.259	.355	69	-39	9-8	.940	2	97	80	S207,2b62,O47C,3b32,D12,P2/1	244	-2.4

KUNTZ, RUSTY   Russell Jay B2.4.1955 Orange CA BR/TR/6-3/190* [ChiA77 11/261] d9.1 C11 Col Cal St.-Stanislaus

YEAR	TM LG	G	AB	R	H	2B	3B	HR	RBI	BB-IB	HP	SO	AVG	OBP	SLG	AOPS	ABR	SB-CS	FA	FR	RNG	THR	GAMES AT POSITION	DL	BFW
1979	Chi A	5	11	0	1	0	0	0	0	2-0	0	6	.091	.231	.091	-9	-2	1-0	1.000	2	183	444	O5(1/1/3)		0.0
1980	Chi A	36	62	5	14	4	0	0	5	5-0	0	13	.226	.284	.290	58	-3	1-0	.979	1	106	145	O34(19/9/6)		-0.3
1981	Chi A	67	55	15	14	2	0	0	4	6-0	1	8	.255	.339	.291	84	-1	1-0	1.000	0	111	0	O51(28/13/13),D5		-0.1
1982	Chi A	28	42	6	11	1	0	0	4	6-0	0	8	.262	.354	.286	75	-1	1-0	.976	-1	83	0	O21(1/20/1)		-0.4
1983	Min A	31	100	13	19	3	0	3	14	12-0	1	28	.190	.274	.310	59	-6	0-0	.986	-0	90	172	O30(0/27/3)		-0.2
	Year	59	142	19	30	4	0	3	18	18-0	1	36	.211	.298	.303	64	-7	1-0	.982	-1	95	110	O57(2/52/3)/P		-0.9
1984	†Det A	84	140	32	40	12	0	2	22	25-1	0	41	.286	.393	.414	125	7	2-2	.987	-4	89	80	O67(19/22/37),D10		0.1
1985	Det A	5	5	0	0	0	0	0	0	2-0	0	2	.000	.286	.000	-13	-1	0-1	1.000	-0	0	0	/1D		-0.1
Total	7	277	441	75	104	23	0	5	38	60-1	2	106	.236	.328	.322	69	-9	5-3	.988	-3	97	89	O235(63/117/63),D19/1		-1.7

KUROWSKI, WHITEY George John B4.19.1918 Reading PA D12.9.1999 Sinking Spring PA BR/TR/5-11/193 d9.23 — BFW 0.0

YEAR	TM LG	G	AB	R	H	2B	3B	HR	RBI	BB-IB	HP	SO	AVG	OBP	SLG	AOPS	ABR	SB-CS	FA	FR	RNG	THR	GAMES AT POSITION	DL	BFW
1941	StL N	5	9	1	3	2	0	0	2	1	0	2	.333	.400	.556	157	1	0	1.000	-0	75	0	3b4		0.0
1942	†StL N	115	366	51	93	17	3	9	42	33	6	60	.254	.326	.391	102	0	7	.944	6	101	119	3b104/SOL		1.1
1943	†StL N☆	139	522	69	150	24	8	13	70	31	2	54	.287	.330	.439	116	8	3	.952	-4	89	135	3b137,S2		0.6
1944	†StL N★	149	555	95	150	25	7	20	87	58	2	40	.270	.341	.449	119	13	2	.965	-1	92	95	3b146,2b9/S		1.4
1945	StL N★	133	511	84	165	27	3	21	102	45	5	45	.323	.383	.511	144	29	1	.964	-4	90	130	3b131,S6		2.6
1946	†StL N★	142	519	76	156	32	5	14	89	72	5	47	.301	.391	.462	136	26	2	.966	-3	91	88	3b138		2.4
1947	StL N★	146	513	108	159	27	6	27	104	87	10	56	.310	.420	.544	148	38	4	.954	-7	85	79	3b65		2.2
1948	StL N	77	220	34	47	8	0	2	33	42	5	28	.214	.352	.277	68	-8	0	1.000	-0	57	0	3b2	71	-1.5
1949	StL N	10	14	0	2	0	0	0	0	1		0	.143	.200	.143	-6	-2	0	.957	-0	91	0		71	-0.2
Total	9	916	3229	518	925	162	32	106	529	369	36	332	.286	.366	.455	124	105	19	.957	-29	91	103	3b868,S10,2b9/OL		8.6

KUSICK, CRAIG Craig Robert B9.30.1948 Milwaukee WI BR/TR/6-3/230(210-232) d9.8 Col Wisconsin-La Crosse — -0.3

YEAR	TM LG	G	AB	R	H	2B	3B	HR	RBI	BB-IB	HP	SO	AVG	OBP	SLG	AOPS	ABR	SB-CS	FA	FR	RNG	THR	GAMES AT POSITION	DL	BFW
1973	Min A	15	48	4	12	2	0	0	4	7-0	1	9	.250	.357	.292	81	-1	0-0	.989	-1	75	81	1b11,O2L,D2		0.3
1974	Min A	76	201	36	48	7	1	8	26	35-1	1	36	.239	.353	.403	114	5	0-0	.996	3	112	85	1b75		0.0
1975	Min A	57	156	14	37	8	0	6	27	21-1	5	23	.259	.346	.404	110	3	0-0	.990	1	102	121	1b51		0.5
1976	Min A	109	266	33	69	13	0	11	36	35-0	1	44	.259	.344	.432	125	9	5-1	.977	2	160	127	D79,1b23		-1.0
1977	Min A	115	268	34	68	12	0	12	45	49-5	3	60	.254	.370	.433	121	10	3-1	.987	5	145	76	D35,1b27,O9L		-0.1
1978	Min A	77	191	23	33	3	2	4	20	37-2	1	38	.173	.305	.272	63	-9	3-2	1.000	0	100	151	D12,1b8		-0.2
1979	Min A	24	54	8	13	4	0	3	6	3-0	0	11	.241	.281	.481	97	0	1-0	.978	1	129	88	1b20/PD		-0.3
	Tor A	24	54	3	11	1	0	2	7	7-0	1	7	.204	.302	.333	72	-2	0-0	.983	-1	123	101	1b28,D13/P		-0.3
	Year	48	108	11	24	5	0	5	13	10-0	1	18	.222	.292	.407	85	-3	1-0							0.1
Total	7	497	1238	155	291	50	3	46	171	194-9	13	228	.235	.342	.392	105	15	11-4	.988	6	113	96	1b238,D214,O11L/P		0.1

KUSNYER, ART Arthur William B12.19.1945 Akron OH BR/TR/6-2/198* [ChiA66 37/698] d9.21 C24 Col Kent St. — -0.2

YEAR	TM LG	G	AB	R	H	2B	3B	HR	RBI	BB-IB	HP	SO	AVG	OBP	SLG	AOPS	ABR	SB-CS	FA	FR	RNG	THR	GAMES AT POSITION	DL	BFW
1970	Chi A	4	10	1	1	0	0	0	0	0-0	0	4	.100	.100	.100	-43	-2	0-0	.941	0	20	152	C3		-0.3
1971	Cal A	6	13	0	2	0	0	0	0	0-0	0	3	.154	.154	.154	-14	-2	0-0	.958	-1	93	332	C6		-1.1
1972	Cal A	64	179	13	37	2	1	2	13	16-3	1	33	.207	.276	.263	64	-8	0-0	.975	-4	69	95	C63		-1.3
1973	Cal A	41	64	5	8	2	0	0	3	2-0	1	12	.125	.149	.156	-14	-10	0-1	.979	-4	98	77	C41		-0.7
1976	Mil A	15	34	2	4	1	0	0	2	1-1	1	5	.118	.167	.147	-8	-5	1-0	.938	-2	117	87	C14		0.3
1978	KC A	9	13	1	3	1	0	1	2	2-0	0	4	.231	.333	.538	137	1	0-0	.946	2	56	110	C9		-0.2
Total	6	139	313	21	55	6	1	3	21	21-4	2	61	.176	.231	.230	37	-26	1-1	.970	-9	80	102	C136		-3.3

KUSTUS, JOE Joseph J. "Jul" B9.5.1882 Detroit MI D4.27.1916 Eloise (now part of Westland) MI BR/TR/5-10/? d4.17 — -2.0

YEAR	TM LG	G	AB	R	H	2B	3B	HR	RBI	BB	HP	SO	AVG	OBP	SLG	AOPS	ABR	SB	FA	FR	RNG	THR	GAMES AT POSITION	DL	BFW
1909	Bro N	53	173	12	25	5	0	1	11	11		2	.145	.204	.191	23	-16	9	.951	0	87	61	O50(1/18/31)		-2.0

KUTCHER, RANDY Randy Scott B4.20.1960 Anchorage AK BR/TR/5-11/175* [SFN79 4/96] d6.19 OF(26/78/52) — -0.6

YEAR	TM LG	G	AB	R	H	2B	3B	HR	RBI	BB-IB	HP	SO	AVG	OBP	SLG	AOPS	ABR	SB-CS	FA	FR	RNG	THR	GAMES AT POSITION	DL	BFW
1986	SF N	71	186	28	44	9	1	7	16	11-0	0	41	.237	.279	.409	92	-3	6-5	.990	-2	115	138	O51(7/44/1),S13,3b4,2b3		0.0
1987	SF N	14	16	7	3	1	0	1	0	1-0	0	5	.188	.235	.375	61	-1	1-0	1.000	1	147	0	O6(1/4/1),2b2,3b2/S		-0.1
1988	Bos A	19	12	2	2	1	0	0	0	0-0	0	2	.167	.167	.250	14	-1	0-1	1.000	1	116	0	O57(11/21/25),3b6/CD	15	-0.6
1989	Bos A	77	160	28	36	10	3	2	18	11-0	0	46	.225	.273	.363	73	-6	3-0	.982	1	116	0	O34(2/9/23),3b11,2b5,D5		0.2
1990	†Bos A	63	74	18	17	4	1	1	5	13-0	0	18	.230	.345	.351	90	-1	3-3	1.000	3	114	0	O155C,3b25,D18,S14,2b10/C	15	-1.1
Total	5	244	448	83	102	25	6	10	40	36-0	0	112	.228	.285	.377	82	-12	13-9	.989	4	115	69			-1.1

KUTINA, JOE Joseph Peter B1.16.1885 Chicago IL D4.13.1945 Chicago IL BR/TR/6-2/205 d9.6 — -0.2

YEAR	TM LG	G	AB	R	H	2B	3B	HR	RBI	BB	HP	SO	AVG	OBP	SLG	AOPS	ABR	SB	FA	FR	RNG	THR	GAMES AT POSITION	DL	BFW
1911	StL A	26	101	12	26	6	2	3	15	2	1		.257	.279	.446	100	0	2	.981	-1	92	127	1b26		-1.5
1912	StL A	69	205	18	42	9	3	1	18	13	3		.205	.262	.293	61	-11	0	.985	-2	79	109	1b51/OL		-1.7
Total	2	95	306	30	68	15	5	4	33	15	4		.222	.268	.343	76	-11	2	.984	-3	83	115	1b77/OL		

KVASNAK, AL Alexander B1.11.1921 Sagamore PA D9.26.2002 Arcadia CA BR/TR/6-1/170 d4.15 Mil 1942-45 — -0.1

YEAR	TM LG	G	AB	R	H	2B	3B	HR	RBI	BB	HP	SO	AVG	OBP	SLG	AOPS	ABR	SB-CS	FA	FR	RNG	THR	GAMES AT POSITION	DL	BFW
1942	Was A	5	11	3	2	0	0	0	2	1	0		.182	.308	.182	40	-1	0-0	1.000	0	109	0	O3(1/0/2)		-0.1

KYLE, ANDY Andrew Ewing B10.29.1889 Toronto ON, Can. D9.6.1971 Toronto ON, Can. BL/TL/5-8/160 d9.7 — 0.1

YEAR	TM LG	G	AB	R	H	2B	3B	HR	RBI	BB	HP	SO	AVG	OBP	SLG	AOPS	ABR	SB	FA	FR	RNG	THR	GAMES AT POSITION	DL	BFW
1912	Cin N	9	21	3	7	0	0	4	4	2			.333	.440	.381	129	1		1.000	1	112	112	O7(2/5/0)		0.1

LAABS, CHET Chester Peter B4.30.1912 Milwaukee WI D1.26.1983 Warren MI BR/TR/5-8/175 d5.5 Def 1944 Mil 1945 — -1.3

YEAR	TM LG	G	AB	R	H	2B	3B	HR	RBI	BB	HP	SO	AVG	OBP	SLG	AOPS	ABR	SB-CS	FA	FR	RNG	THR	GAMES AT POSITION	DL	BFW
1937	Det A	72	242	31	58	13	5	8	37	24	0	66	.240	.308	.434	83	-8	6-2	.971	-5	92	39	O62(22/40/0)		-1.3
1938	Det A	64	211	26	50	7	3	7	37	15	0	52	.237	.288	.398	66	-13	3-2	.971	0	102	91	O53(22/32/0)		0.1
1939	Det A	5	16	1	5	1	0	2	2		0		.313	.389	.500	117	0	0-0	.933	1	112	283	O5L		0.3
	StL A	95	317	52	95	20	5	10	62	33	1	62	.300	.368	.489	115	6	4-1	.972	-2	96	107	O79(3/70/6)		0.4
	Year	100	333	53	100	21	6	10	64	35	1	62	.300	.369	.489	115	7	3-3	.969	-1	99	77	O63(25/29/10)		0.3
1940	StL A	105	218	32	59	11	5	10	40	34	1	59	.271	.372	.505	122	7	5-2	.982	-1	102	66	O100(21/15/64)		0.3
1941	StL A	118	392	64	109	23	6	15	59	51	0	88	.278	.361	.482	117	9	0-3	.970	-3	92	124	O139(36/25/80)		1.9
1942	StL A	144	520	90	143	21	7	27	99	88	0	88	.275	.380	.498	144	10	0-0	.976	5	101	136	O150(125/24/6)		0.6
1943	StL A★	151	580	83	145	27	7	17	85	73	4	105	.250	.338	.409	115	11	3-1	1.000	1	101	76	O55(38/0/18)		-0.3
1944	†StL A	66	201	28	47	10	2	5	23	29	0	33	.234	.330	.378	96	-1	3-1	1.000	-0	107	37	O35(34/2/2)		-0.2
1945	StL A	35	109	15	26	4	3	1	8	16	3	17	.239	.352	.358	101	1	0-0	.987	2	111	83	O72(6/0/66)		0.5
1946	StL A	80	264	40	69	13	0	16	52	20	1	50	.261	.316	.492	117	5	3-1	1.000	1	105	199	O7(6/0/1)		-0.1
1947	Phi A	15	32	5	7	1	0	1	5	4			.219	.306	.344	79	-1	0-0							0.8
Total	11	950	3102	467	813	151	44	117	509	389	10	595	.262	.346	.452	113	46	32-22	.977	-3	100	98	O820(343/237/253)		

LABANDEIRA, JOSH John Joshua B2.25.1979 Tulare CA BR/TR/5-7/180 [MonN01 6/172] d9.17 Col Cal St.-Fresno — -0.7

YEAR	TM LG	G	AB	R	H	2B	3B	HR	RBI	BB	HP	SO	AVG	OBP	SLG	AOPS	ABR	SB-CS	FA	FR	RNG	THR	GAMES AT POSITION	DL	BFW
2004	Mon N	7	14	0	0	0	0	0	0	0	0	4	.000	.000	.000	-96	-4	0-0	.833	-3	49	0	S3,2b2		-0.7

LABOY, COCO Jose Alberto B7.3.1939 Ponce, PR BR/TR/5-10/170* d4.8 — 0.3

YEAR	TM LG	G	AB	R	H	2B	3B	HR	RBI	BB-IB	HP	SO	AVG	OBP	SLG	AOPS	ABR	SB-CS	FA	FR	RNG	THR	GAMES AT POSITION	DL	BFW
1969	Mon N	157	562	53	145	29	1	18	83	40-2	2	96	.258	.308	.409	100	-1	0-2	.944	5	104	94	3b156		-4.1
1970	Mon N	137	432	37	86	26	1	6	53	31-5	2	81	.199	.254	.299	48	-32	0-2	.946	-7	90	81	3b132,2b3		-0.9
1971	Mon N	76	151	10	38	4	0	1	14	11-0	0	19	.252	.302	.298	70	-6	0-1	.937	-2	93	54	3b65,2b2	83	-0.2
1972	Mon N	28	69	6	18	2	0	3	14	10-3	1	16	.261	.350	.420	117	2	0-0	.980	-3	90	61	3b20/2		-0.4
1973	Mon N	22	33	2	4	1	0	1	2	5-1	0	8	.121	.237	.242	32	-3	0-0	.889	-1	88	87	3b20/2	83	-0.4
Total	5	420	1247	108	291	62	2	28	166	97-11	6	220	.233	.289	.354	77	-40	0-5	.944	-8	97	83	3b397,2b9,S2		-5.3

LaCHANCE, CANDY George Joseph B2.14.1870 Putnam CT D8.18.1932 Waterville CT BB/TR/6-1/183 d8.15 — -0.7

YEAR	TM LG	G	AB	R	H	2B	3B	HR	RBI	BB	HP	SO	AVG	OBP	SLG	AOPS	ABR	SB	FA	FR	RNG	THR	GAMES AT POSITION	DL	BFW
1893	Bro N	10	35	1	6	1	0	0		1		12	.171	.237	.200	17	-4	0	.654	-4	104	73	C6,O5(4/0/1)		-0.3
1894	Bro N	69	261	48	83	13	8	5	52	16	1	32	.318	.360	.487	110	3	20	.979	-8	52	72	1b56,C11,O3R		0.2
1895	Bro N	128	541	102	170	23	9	8	111	29	1	48	.314	.358	.434	113	9	37	.983	-6	78	98	1b89		-0.1
1896	Bro N	89	348	60	99	10	13	7	58	23	1	32	.284	.331	.448	110	2	17	.978	-4	90	110	1b126		0.0
1897	Bro N	126	520	86	160	28	16	4	90	15	5		.308	.333	.446	111	4	26	.988	-16	56	116	1b74,S48,O13(11/2/0)		-2.5
1898	Bro N	136	526	62	130	23	7	5	65	31	5		.247	.299	.346	85	-12	23	.984	-7	65	102	1b125		-0.7
1899	Bal N	125	472	65	145	23	10	1	75	21	10		.307	.350	.405	101	-1	31	.979	-3	85	89	1b133		-0.9
1901	Cle A	133	548	81	166	22	9	1	75	7	2		.303	.314	.381	94	-5	11	.979	-3	85	89	1b133		-2.9
1902	Bos A	138	541	60	151	13	4	6	56	18	7		.279	.309	.351	80	-16	8	.983	-12	59	106	1b138		-2.5
1903	†Bos A	141	522	60	134	22	6	1	53	28	7		.257	.303	.328	85	-9	12	.984	-11	64	107	1b141		-4.2
1904	Bos A	157	573	55	130	19	5	1	47	23	7		.227	.265	.283	69	-20	7	.992	-14	59	111	1b157		-0.4
1905	Bos A	12	41	1	6	1	0	0	5	1	0		.146	.255	.171	36	-3	0	.988	-1	80	117	1b12		
Total	12	1265	4928	681	1380	198	87	39	693	219	55	124	.280	.318	.379	93	-52	192	.984	-90	69	104	1b1177,S48,O24(15/2/7),C17		-15.9

LACHEMANN, RENE Rene George B5.4.1945 Los Angeles CA BR/TR/6-0/198* d5.4 M8/C17 b-Marcel Col USC — -1.0

YEAR	TM LG	G	AB	R	H	2B	3B	HR	RBI	BB-IB	HP	SO	AVG	OBP	SLG	AOPS	ABR	SB-CS	FA	FR	RNG	THR	GAMES AT POSITION	DL	BFW
1965	KC A	92	216	20	49	7	1	9	29	12-3	0	57	.227	.264	.394	87	-5	0-0	.980	-7	54	66	C75		0.0
1966	KC A	7	5	0	1	0	0	0	1	0-0	0	1	.200	.200	.400	70	0	0-0	1.000	0	0	0	C6		-1.1
1968	Oak A	19	60	3	9	1	0	1	9	3-3	0	11	.150	.167	.167	5	-7	0-0	.967	-7	59	46	C16		-2.1
Total	3	118	281	23	59	9	1	9	33	13-3	0	69	.210	.245	.345	70	-12	0-0	.978	-14	54	60	C97		

LaCOCK, PETE Ralph Pierre B1.17.1952 Burbank CA BL/TL/6-3/210* [ChiN70*1/20] d9.6 — 0.0

YEAR	TM LG	G	AB	R	H	2B	3B	HR	RBI	BB-IB	HP	SO	AVG	OBP	SLG	AOPS	ABR	SB-CS	FA	FR	RNG	THR	GAMES AT POSITION	DL	BFW
1972	Chi N	5	6	3	3	0	0	0	4	0-0	0	2	.500	.429	.500	167	0	1-0	1.000	-0	68	0	O3R		0.0
1973	Chi N	11	16	1	4	0	0		3	1-0	0	3	.250	.294	.313	63	-1	0-0	1.000	1	97	401	O5R		0.0
1974	Chi N	35	110	9	20	4	1	1	8	12-2	1	16	.182	.268	.264	47	-8	0-0	.974	2	114	170	O22R,1b11		

YEAR	TM LG	G	AB	R	H	2B	3B	HR	RBI	BB-IB	HP	SO	AVG	OBP	SLG	AOPS	ABR	SB-CS	FA	FR	RNG	THR	GAMES AT POSITION	DL	BFW
1975	Chi N	106	249	30	57	8	1	6	30	37-7	0	27	.229	.324	.341	82	-5	0-2	.988	3	136	95	1b53,O26(11/0/15)		-0.8
1976	Chi N	106	244	34	54	9	2	8	28	42-6	1	37	.221	.337	.373	93	-1	1-4	.975	-4	85	117	1b54,O19(7/0/12)		-1.2
1977	†KC A	88	218	25	66	12	1	3	29	15-1	1	25	.303	.345	.408	105	2	2-1	.990	2	122	98	1b29,D26,O12(8/1/3)		0.1
1978	KC A	118	322	44	95	21	2	5	48	21-2	0	27	.295	.335	.419	109	4	1-0	.993	-6	74	104	1b106		-0.7
1979	KC A	132	408	54	113	25	4	3	56	37-7	1	26	.277	.334	.380	91	-4	2-1	.997	2	107	95	1b108,D16		-0.8
1980	†KC A	114	156	14	32	6	0	1	18	17-1	1	10	.205	.284	.263	51	-10	1-0	.991	-0	102	100	1b86,O29(26/0/5)		-1.4
Total	9	715	1729	214	444	86	11	27	224	182-26	5	171	.257	.326	.366	89	-23	8-8	.997	-1	117	109	1b447,O116(52/1/65),D42		-5.6

LACY, LEE Leondaus B4.10.1948 Longview TX BR/TR/6-1/175(175-195) [LAN69*2/29] d6.30 Col Laney (CA) JC OF(417/77/594)

YEAR	TM LG	G	AB	R	H	2B	3B	HR	RBI	BB-IB	HP	SO	AVG	OBP	SLG	AOPS	ABR	SB-CS	FA	FR	RNG	THR	GAMES AT POSITION	DL	BFW
1972	LA N	60	243	34	63	7	3	0	12	19-0	0	37	.259	.312	.313	79	-7	5-3	.973	-2	104	113	2b58		
1973	LA N	57	135	14	28	2	0	0	8	15-1	0	34	.207	.287	.222	44	-10	2-3	.965	-5	90	112	2b41		-0.5
1974	†LA N	48	78	13	22	6	0	0	8	2-0	0	14	.282	.293	.359	87	-2	2-0	.968	-2	99	75	2b34/3		-1.5
1975	LA N	101	306	44	96	11	5	7	40	22-1	0	29	.314	.356	.451	129	10	5-9	.935	-7	77	63	2b43,O43(37/3/8)/S		-0.2
1976	Atl N	50	180	25	49	4	3	2	20	6-1	1	12	.272	.299	.367	83	-5	2-2	.969	-11	80	88	2b44,O5(1/4/1)/3		0.1
	LA N	53	158	17	42	7	1	0	14	16-2	0	13	.266	.330	.323	88	-2	1-2	.969	-1	102	38	O37(5/23/10),3b3,2b2		-1.4
	Year	103	338	42	91	11	3	3	34	22-3	1	25	.269	.314	.346	86	-7	3-4	.970	-12	79	85	2b46,O42(6/27/11),3b4		-0.6
1977	†LA N	75	169	28	45	7	0	3	6	21	10-0	0	21	.266	.306	.414	91	-3	4-0	1.000	-2	60	0	O32(18/0/18),2b22,3b12		-2.0
1978	†LA N	103	245	29	64	16	4	13	40	27-4	1	30	.261	.335	.518	136	11	7-4	.971	-4	99	70	O44(17/0/27),2b24,3b9/S		0.7
1979	†Pit N	84	182	17	45	9	3	5	15	22-2	1	36	.247	.327	.412	96	-1	6-1	.973	-3	94	102	O41L,2b5		-0.4
1980	Pit N	109	278	45	93	20	4	6	33	28-3	2	33	.335	.394	.511	147	18	18-9	.984	5	120	130	O88(86/3/0),3b3		2.5
1981	Pit N	78	213	31	57	11	4	2	10	13-2	1	29	.268	.307	.385	91	-3	24-3	.977	5	115	153	O63(34/1/29)/3		0.4
1982	Pit N	121	359	66	112	16	3	5	31	32-4	1	57	.312	.369	.415	114	7	40-15	.965	1	105	106	O113(40/17/71),3b2		0.9
1983	Pit N	108	288	40	87	12	3	4	13	22-2	0	36	.302	.352	.406	106	2	31-13	1.000	4	120	44	O98(59/24/28)		0.6
1984	Pit N	138	474	66	152	26	3	12	70	32-2	0	61	.321	.362	.464	131	19	21-11	**.996**	13	115	171	O127(78/0/88),2b2		2.8
1985	Bal A	121	492	69	144	22	4	9	48	39-0	2	95	.293	.343	.409	108	6	10-3	.984	1	100	117	O115(0/1/115),D5	35	0.2
1986	Bal A	130	491	77	141	18	0	11	47	37-2	0	71	.287	.334	.391	98	-1	6-3	.992	3	104	101	O120R,D3		-0.5
1987	Bal A	87	258	35	63	13	3	7	28	32-0	0	49	.244	.326	.399	94	-2	4-6	.973	5	100	228	O80(1/1/79),D4	20	-0.1
Total	16	1523	4549	650	1303	207	42	91	458	372-26	9	657	.286	.339	.410	107	37	185-86	.983	5	107	124	O1006R,2b275,3b32,D12,S2	80	2.7

LACY, GUY Osceola Guy B6.12.1897 Cleveland TN D11.19.1953 Cleveland TN BR/TR/5-11.5/170 d5.7

| 1926 | Cle A | 13 | 24 | 2 | 4 | 0 | 0 | 1 | 2 | 2 | 1 | 2 | .167 | .259 | .292 | 43 | -2 | 0-0 | .976 | -0 | 104 | 83 | 2b11,3b2 | | -0.2 |

LADD, HI Arthur Clifford B2.9.1870 Willimantic CT D5.7.1948 Cranston RI BL/TR/6-4/180 d7.12

1898	Pit N	1	1	0	0	0	0	0	0	0			.000	.000	.000	-99	-1			0			/H		0.0
	Bos N	1	4	1	1	0	0	0	0	0			.250	.250	.250	41	0	0	1.000	0	0	0	/OL		0.0
	Year	2	5	1	1	0	0	0	0	0			.200	.200	.200	14	-1	0	1.000	0	0	0	/OL		0.0

LADEW, STEVE Stephen F. B St.Louis MO d9.27

| 1889 | KC AA | 2 | 4 | 0 | 0 | 0 | 0 | 0 | 0 | 0 | | 0 | 3 | .000 | .000 | .000 | -94 | -1 | 0 | 1.000 | 0 | 0 | 0 | /OLP | | -0.1 |

LAFATA, JOE Joseph Joseph B8.3.1921 Detroit MI D5.6.2004 Roseville MI BL/TL/6-0/163 d4.17

1947	NY N	62	95	13	21	1	0	2	18	15	1	18	.221	.333	.295	68	-4	1	.974	1	93	241	O19(20/1/0),1b2		-0.5
1948	NY N	1	1	0	0	0	0	0	0	0	0	1	.000	.000	.000	-99	0	0		-0			/H		0.0
1949	NY N	64	140	18	33	2	2	3	16	9	0	23	.236	.282	.343	67	-7	1	.984	-4	51	97	1b47	60	-1.3
Total	3	127	236	31	54	3	2	5	34	24	1	42	.229	.303	.322	67	-11	2	.985	-4	49	101	1b49,O19(20/1/0)	60	-1.8

LAFFERTY, FLIP Frank Bernard B5.4.1854 Scranton PA D2.8.1910 Wilmington DE TR d9.15 ▲

1876	Phi N	3	0	0	0	0	0	0	0	0			.000	.000	.000	-99	-1		.750	0.	141	1747	/P		0.0
1877	Lou N	4	17	2	1	1	0	0	0			4	.059	.059	.118	-39	-3		.750	-1	0	0	O4C		-0.3
Total	2	5	20	2	1	1	0	0	0			4	.050	.050	.100	-46	-4		.750	-1	0	0	O4C/P		-0.3

LaFOREST, TY Byron Joseph (b Biron Joseph La Forest) B4.18.1917 Edmundston NB, Can. D5.5.1947 Arlington MA BR/TR/5-9/165 d8.4

| 1945 | Bos A | 52 | 204 | 25 | 51 | 7 | 4 | 2 | 16 | 9-0 | 0 | 35 | .250 | .285 | .353 | 83 | -6 | 4-4 | .966 | 4 | 111 | 121 | 3b45,O5(3/0/2) | | -0.2 |

LAFOREST, PETE Pierre Luc B1.27.1978 Hull QC, Can. BL/TR/6-2/200* d9.2 Col Fort Scott (KS) CC

2003	TB A	19	48	0	8	2	0	0	6	1-0	1	14	.167	.196	.208	8	-6	0-0	1.000	-1	29	0	D12,C4		-0.8
2005	TB A	25	64	5	11	3	0	1	4	6-0	0	23	.172	.243	.266	36	-6	0-1	1.000	-6	125	121	C21/1D		-1.1
Total	2	44	112	5	19	5	0	1	10	7-1	1	37	.170	.223	.241	24	-12	0-1	1.000	-7	110	103	C25,D14/1		-1.9

LaFRANCOIS, ROGER Roger Victor B8.2.1956 Norwich CT BL/TR/6-2/215 [BosA77 8/195] d5.27 Col Oklahoma

| 1982 | Bos A | 8 | 10 | 1 | 4 | 1 | 0 | 0 | 1 | 0-0 | 1 | 1 | .400 | .400 | .500 | 137 | 1 | 0-0 | 1.000 | 0 | 0 | 0 | C8 | | 0.1 |

LAGA, MIKE Michael Russell B6.14.1960 Ridgewood NJ BL/TL/6-2/210* [DetA80*1/17] d9.1 Col Bergen (NJ) CC

1982	Det A	27	88	6	23	9	0	3	11	4-0	0	23	.261	.293	.466	104	0	1-0	.994	-3	33	127	1b19,D8		-0.4
1983	Det A	12	21	2	4	0	0	0	2	1-0	0	9	.190	.227	.190	17	-2	0-0	1.000	0	97	180	1b5,D6		-0.3
1984	Det A	9	11	1	6	0	0	0	1	1-0	0	2	.545	.583	.545	215	2	0-0	1.000	0	100	101	1b4,D4		0.2
1985	Det A	9	36	3	6	1	0	2	6	0-0	0	9	.167	.167	.361	40	-3	0-0	.974	1	163	123	1b4,D5		-0.3
1986	Det A	15	45	6	9	0	0	3	8	5-1	0	13	.200	.280	.422	88	-1	0-0	1.000	1	80	111	1b12,D2		-0.3
	StL N	18	46	7	10	4	0	3	8	5-1	1	18	.217	.308	.500	119	1	0-0	1.000	2	169	105	1b16	109	-0.2
1987	StL N	17	29	4	4	1	0	1	4	2-1	0	7	.138	.182	.276	22	-3	0-0	.973	1	143	170	1b12		0.3
1988	StL N	41	100	5	13	0	1	4	21	2-0	1	6	.130	.147	.160	-12	-15	0-0	1.000	-0	91	133	1b37	101	-0.3
1989	SF N	17	20	1	4	1	0	1	7	1-0	0	6	.200	.238	.400	82	-1	0-0	1.000	-0	62	0	1b4		-1.9
1990	SF N	23	27	4	5	1	0	2	4	1-0	1	7	.185	.241	.444	87	-1	0-0	.996	-0	98	124	1b4		-0.1
Total	9	188	423	39	84	18	0	16	55	22-3	2	115	.199	.241	.355	63	-23	1-0	.996	1	132	114	1b123,D25	210	-3.1

LAHOUD, JOE Joseph Michael B4.14.1947 Danbury CT BL/TL/6-0/198(188-202) d4.10 Col New Haven

1968	Bos A	29	78	5	15	1	0	1	6	16-0	0	16	.192	.330	.244	71	-2	0-2	.926	-3	61	162	O25(3/1/22)		-0.8
1969	Bos A	101	218	32	41	8	0	9	21	40-0	1	43	.188	.317	.335	79	-6	2-1	.979	-3	89	73	O66(24/12/33)/1		-1.2
1970	Bos A	17	49	6	12	1	0	2	5	7-1	0	6	.245	.339	.388	94	0	1-0	.963	2	109	401	O13(9/0/5)		0.1
1971	Bos A	107	256	39	55	9	3	14	34	40-3	4	45	.215	.330	.438	108	3	2-2	.993	3	109	91	O69(7/0/63)		0.2
1972	Mil A	111	316	35	75	9	3	12	34	45-7	0	54	.237	.331	.399	119	7	3-4	.974	-1	99	30	O97(38/0/63)		0.1
1973	Mil A	96	225	29	46	9	0	5	26	27-1	5	36	.204	.302	.311	74	-7	5-5	1.000	4	130	87	D41,O40(2/0/39)		-0.7
1974	Cal A	127	325	46	88	16	3	13	44	47-3	3	57	.271	.367	.458	144	20	4-5	.976	1	99	105	O106(70/0/39),D10		1.5
1975	Cal A	76	192	21	41	6	2	6	33	48-2	1	33	.214	.372	.359	116	7	2-1	1.000	-1	91	54	D35,O29(7/0/22)	39	0.3
1976	Cal A	42	96	8	17	4	0	0	4	18-2	2	16	.177	.319	.219	63	-3	0-0	.962	-0	114	0	O26(21/1/6),D3		-0.5
	Tex A	38	89	10	20	3	1	1	5	10-1	0	16	.225	.303	.315	79	-2	1-0	1.000	-0	65	0	D22,O5(4/0/1)		-0.3
	Year	80	185	18	37	7	1	1	9	28-3	2	32	.200	.312	.265	71	-6	1-0	.964	-1	110	0	O31(25/1/7),D25		-0.8
1977	†KC A	34	65	8	17	5	0	2	8	11-1	0	16	.262	.364	.431	116	2	1-0	.952	-7	83	247	O15(13/0/2),D4		0.2
1978	KC A	13	16	0	2	0	0	0	0	0-0	0	1	.125	.125	.125	-29	-3	0-0		-0	0	0	/ORD		-0.3
Total	11	791	1925	239	429	68	12	65	218	309-21	16	339	.223	.334	.372	103	16	20-20	.979	1	102	88	O492(198/14/296),D116/1	39	-1.4

LAIRD, GERALD Gerald Lee B11.13.1979 Westminster CA BR/TR/6-2/190(190-220) [OakA98 2/45] d4.30 Col Cal St.-Fullerton

2003	Tex A	19	44	9	12	2	1	1	4	5-0	1	11	.273	.360	.432	101	0	0-0	.986	-2	178	98	C16		-0.1
2004	Tex A	49	147	20	33	6	0	1	16	12-0	1	35	.224	.287	.286	50	-11	0-1	.983	3	138	128	C49	63	-0.5
2005	Tex A	13	40	7	9	2	0	1	4	2-0	0	7	.225	.262	.350	59	-2	0-0	.957	-2	75	113	C13/OR		-0.4
Total	3	81	231	36	54	10	1	3	24	19-0	2	53	.234	.297	.325	61	-13	0-1	.980	-2	135	120	C78/OR	63	-1.0

LAJESKIE, DICK Richard Edward B1.8.1926 Passaic NJ D8.15.1976 Ramsey NJ BR/TR/5-11/175 d9.10

| 1946 | NY N | 6 | 10 | 3 | 2 | 0 | 0 | 0 | 3 | 1 | | 2 | .200 | .429 | .200 | 81 | 0 | 0 | .964 | 3 | 179 | 42 | 2b4 | | 0.3 |

LAJOIE, NAP Napoleon "Larry" B9.5.1874 Woonsocket RI D2.7.1959 Daytona Beach FL BR/TR/6-1/195 d8.12 M5 HF1937 OF(4/5/18)

1896	Phi N	39	175	36	57	12	4	4	42	1	0	11	.326	.330	.543	129	5	7	.995	-3	53	107	1b39		0.2
1897	Phi N	127	545	107	197	40	23	9	127	15	12		.361	.392	**.569**	156	39	20	.984	-6	61	77	1b108,O19(2/0/18),3b2		2.7
1898	Phi N	147	608	113	197	**43**	11	6	**127**	21	7		.324	.354	.461	139	27	25	.949	0	90	101	2b146/1		3.2
1899	Phi N	77	312	70	118	19	9	6	70	12	10		.378	.419	.554	172	29	13	.954	4	103	145	2b67,O5C		4.1
1900	Phi N	102	451	95	152	33	12	7	92	10	8		.337	.362	.510	140	22	22	.954	22	114	152	2b102/3		4.4
1901	Phi A	131	544	**145**	**232**	48	14	**14**	**125**	24		13	**.426**	**.463**	**.643**	196	69	27	.960	22	99	111	2b119,S12		8.1
1902	Phi A	1	1	0	0	0	0	0	0				.250	.250	.250	37	0	1	1.000	-0	98	0	/2		0.0

YEAR	TM LG	G	AB	R	H	2B	3B	HR	RBI	BB-IB	HP	SO	AVG	OBP	SLG	AOPS	ABR	SB-CS	FA	FR	RNG	THR	GAMES AT POSITION	DL	BFW
	Cle A	86	348	81	132	35	5	7	64	19	6		.379	.421	.569	180	38	19	.974	23	105	133	2b86		5.6
	Year	87	352	81	133	35	5	7	65	19	6		.378	.419	.565	178	37	20	.974	23	105	132	2b87		5.6
1903	Cle A	125	485	90	167	41	11	7	93	24	3		.344	.379	.518	170	41	21	.955	39	111	.146	2b122/13		8.1
1904	Cle A	140	553	92	208	49	15	5	102	27	8		.376	.413	.546	204	64	29	.962	2	90	155	2b95,S44,1b2		7.4
1905	Cle A	65	249	29	82	12	2	2	41	17	2		.329	.377	.418	150	14	11	.991	8	105	165	2b59,1b5,M		2.4
1906	Cle A	152	602	88	214	48	9	0	91	30	6		.355	.392	.465	170	48	20	.973	21	108	188	2b130,3b15,S7,M		7.6
1907	Cle A	137	509	53	152	30	6	2	63	30	6		.299	.345	.393	134	19	24	.969	45	120	211	2b128,1b9,M		7.0
1908	Cle A	157	581	77	168	32	6	2	74	47	9		.289	.352	.375	136	24	15	.964	47	114	178	2b156/1M		8.0
1909	Cle A	128	469	56	152	33	7	1	47	35	6		.324	.378	.431	149	27	13	.959	23	110	135	2b120,1b8,M		5.7
1910	Cle A	159	591	94	227	51	7	4	76	60	5		.384	.445	.514	198	69	26	.966	13	102	110	2b149,1b10		8.9
1911	Cle A	90	315	36	115	20	1	2	60	26	4		.365	.420	.454	142	19	13	.990	-5	61	88	1b41,2b37		1.3
1912	Cle A	117	448	66	165	34	4	0	90	28	7		.368	.414	.462	146	27	18	.959	9	97	147	2b97,1b20		3.6
1913	Cle A	137	465	66	156	25	2	1	68	33	15	17	.335	.398	.404	131	20	17	.970	15	102	136	2b126		3.8
1914	Cle A	121	419	37	108	14	3	0	50	32	2	15	.258	.313	.305	83	-9	14-15	.959	8	96	152	2b80,1b31		-0.3
1915	Phi A	129	490	40	137	24	5	1	61	11	4	16	.280	.301	.355	100	-4	10-6	.962	17	104	118	2b110,S10,1b5,3b2		1.7
1916	Phi A	113	426	33	105	14	4	2	35	14	1	26	.246	.272	.312	79	-14	15	.973	27	107	119	2b105,1b5,O2L		1.6
Total	21	2480	9589	1504	3242	657	163	82	1599	516	134	85	.338	.380	.466	150	574	380-21	.963	339	104	144	2b2035,1b286,S73,O26R,3b21		95.1

LAKE, EDDIE Edward Erving "Sparky" B3.18.1916 Antioch CA D6.7.1995 Castro Valley CA BR/TR/5-7/160* d9.26 ▲

YEAR	TM LG	G	AB	R	H	2B	3B	HR	RBI	BB-IB	HP	SO	AVG	OBP	SLG	AOPS	ABR	SB-CS	FA	FR	RNG	THR	GAMES AT POSITION	DL	BFW
1939	StL N	2	4	0	1	0	0	0	0	1	0		.250	.400	.250	74	0	1	.857	-1	66	112	S2		-0.1
1940	StL N	32	66	12	14	3	0	2	7	12	1	17	.212	.342	.348	86	-1	1	.957	-4	87	47	2b17,S6		-0.4
1941	StL N	45	76	9	8	2	0	0	0	15	0	22	.105	.253	.132	10	-9	3	.903	1	79	141	S15,3b15,2b5		-0.7
1943	Bos A	75	216	26	43	10	0	3	16	47	1	35	.199	.345	.287	84	-2	3-6	.961	3	107	103	S63		0.5
1944	Bos A	57	126	21	26	5	0	0	8	23	0	22	.206	.329	.246	66	-4	5-2	.927	-1	97	125	S41,P6,2b3/3		-0.3
1945	Bos A	133	473	81	132	27	1	1	51	106	1	37	.279	.412	.410	136	29	9-7	.948	24	112	128	S130/2		6.5
1946	Det A	155	587	105	149	24	1	8	31	103	4	69	.254	.369	.339	93	-1	15-9	.947	-21	88	99	S155		-1.3
1947	Det A	158	602	96	127	19	6	12	46	120	1	54	.211	.343	.322	83	-10	11-10	.947	-29	90	86	S158		-3.2
1948	Det A	64	198	51	52	6	0	2	18	57	0	20	.263	.427	.323	99	4	3-3	.972	-3	96	95	2b45,3b17		0.3
1949	Det A	94	240	38	47	9	1	1	15	61	0	33	.196	.359	.254	63	-10	2-8	.959	-7	98	103	S38,2b19,3b18		-1.6
1950	Det A	20	7	3	0	0	0	0	1	1	0	3	.000	.125	.000	-64	-2	0-0	—	0	0	0	/S3		-0.2
Total	11	835	2595	442	599	105	9	39	193	546	8	312	.231	.366	.323	91	-6	52-45	.947	-38	97	104	S609,2b90,3b52,P6		-0.5

LAKE, FRED Frederick Lovett B10.16.1866 Cornwallis NS, Can. D11.24.1931 Boston MA BR/TR/5-10/170 d5.7 M3

YEAR	TM LG	G	AB	R	H	2B	3B	HR	RBI	BB-IB	HP	SO	AVG	OBP	SLG	AOPS	ABR	SB-CS	FA	FR	RNG	THR	GAMES AT POSITION	DL	BFW
1891	Bos N	5	7	1	1	0	0	0	0	2	0	4	.143	.333	.143	36	0	0	1.000	1	162	106	C4/OR		0.0
1894	Lou N	16	42	8	12	2	0	1	10	11	4	6	.286	.414	.405	122	3	2	.864	-3	80	226	2b6,S5,C5		0.1
1897	†Bos N	19	62	2	15	4	0	0	5	1	0		.242	.254	.306	45	-5	2	.970	-5	150	93	C18		-0.2
1898	Pit N	5	13	1	1	0	0	0	1	2	0		.077	.200	.077	-20	-2	0	1.000	-0	64	165	1b3		-0.2
1910	Bos N	3	1	0	0	0	0	0	0	1	0		.000	.500	.000	46	0	0	—	0			/HM		0.0
Total	5	48	125	12	29	6	0	1	16	17	4	10	.232	.342	.304	68	-4	4	.930	-1	137	90	C27,2b6,S5,1b3/OR		-0.3

LAKE, STEVE Steven Michael B3.14.1957 Inglewood CA BR/TR/6-1/190(180-202) [BalA75 3/71] d4.9

YEAR	TM LG	G	AB	R	H	2B	3B	HR	RBI	BB-IB	HP	SO	AVG	OBP	SLG	AOPS	ABR	SB-CS	FA	FR	RNG	THR	GAMES AT POSITION	DL	BFW
1983	Chi N	38	85	9	22	4	1	1	7	2-2	1	6	.259	.284	.365	75	-3	0-0	1.000	2	101	164	C32		0.0
1984	†Chi N	25	54	4	12	4	0	2	7	0-0	1	7	.222	.232	.407	72	-2	0-0	.955	-1	151	164	C24	81	-0.2
1985	Chi N	58	119	5	18	2	0	1	11	3-1	1	21	.151	.177	.193	4	-16	1-0	.995	3	179	152	C55		-1.2
1986	Chi N	10	19	4	8	1	0	0	4	1-1	0	2	.421	.450	.474	144	1	0-0	1.000	-1	64	126	C10		0.0
	StL N	26	49	4	12	1	0	2	10	2-0	0	5	.245	.275	.388	81	-2	0-0	.976	2	253	144	C26		0.1
	Year	36	68	8	20	2	0	2	14	3-1	0	7	.294	.324	.412	100	0	0-0	.983	1	201	139	C36		0.1
1987	†StL N	74	179	19	45	7	2	2	19	10-4	0	18	.251	.289	.346	66	-9	0-0	.996	-2	169	101	C59		-0.9
1988	StL N	36	54	5	15	3	0	1	4	3-0	2	15	.278	.339	.389	107	1	0-0	.983	-1	117	126	C19		0.1
1989	Phi N	58	155	9	39	5	1	2	14	12-4	0	12	.252	.304	.335	83	-4	0-0	.990	7	127	162	C55	35	0.7
1990	Phi N	29	80	4	20	2	0	0	6	3-1	1	12	.250	.286	.275	55	-5	0-0	.993	5	294	130	C28	42	0.1
1991	Phi N	58	158	12	36	4	1	1	11	2-1	0	26	.228	.237	.285	47	-12	0-0	.993	-2	116	81	C58	45	-0.5
1992	Phi N	20	53	3	13	2	0	1	2	1-0	0	8	.245	.255	.340	68	-2	0-0	.975	-3	80	72	C17		-0.4
1993	Chi N	44	120	11	27	6	0	5	13	4-3	0	19	.225	.250	.400	71	-6	0-0	.985	-0	260	100	C41		-0.4
Total	11	476	1125	89	267	41	5	18	108	43-17	6	159	.237	.268	.331	64	-59	1-0	.989	9	166	124	C424		203	-3.4

LAKEMAN, AL Albert Wesley "Moose" B12.31.1918 Cincinnati OH D5.25.1976 Spartanburg SC BR/TR/6-2/195* d4.19 C5

YEAR	TM LG	G	AB	R	H	2B	3B	HR	RBI	BB-IB	HP	SO	AVG	OBP	SLG	AOPS	ABR	SB-CS	FA	FR	RNG	THR	GAMES AT POSITION	DL	BFW
1942	Cin N	20	38	6	6	1	0	0	2	3	1	10	.158	.238	.184	24	-4	0	.970	1	99	120	C17		-0.2
1943	Cin N	22	55	5	14	2	1	0	6	3	0	11	.255	.293	.327	80	-2	0	1.000	0	108	88	C21		-0.1
1944	Cin N	1	1	0	0	0	0	0	0	0	0	0	.000	.000	.000	-99	0	0	—	0			/H		0.0
1945	Cin N	76	258	22	66	9	4	8	31	17	1	45	.256	.304	.415	101	-2	0	.963	-8	84	73	C74		-0.5
1946	Cin N	23	30	0	4	0	0	0	4	2	0	7	.133	.188	.133	-9	-4	0	1.000	0	119	110	C6		-0.5
1947	Cin N	2	2	0	0	0	0	0	0	0	0	0	.000	.000	.000	-99	-1	0	—	0			/H		-0.1
	Phi N	55	182	11	29	0	0	6	19	5	1	39	.159	.186	.275	22	-22	0	.995	-3	82	77	1b29,C23		-2.5
	Year	57	184	11	29	0	0	6	19	5	1	40	.158	.184	.272	20	-23	0	.995	-3	82	77	1b29,C23		-2.6
1948	Phi N	32	68	2	11	2	0	1	4	5	0	22	.162	.219	.235	23	-8	0	1.000	-2	61	55	C22/P		-0.8
1949	Bos N	3	6	0	1	0	0	0	0	1	0	0	.167	.286	.167	26	-1	0	1.000	0	180	130	1b2		0.0
1954	Det A	5	6	0	0	0	0	0	0	0	0	0	.000	.000	.000	-99	-2	0-0	1.000	0	0	0	C4		-0.1
Total	9	239	646	40	131	17	5	15	66	36	3	137	.203	.248	.314	55	-46	0-0	.974	-11	84	76	C167,1b31/P		-4.8

LAKER, TIM Timothy John B11.27.1969 Encino CA BR/TR/6-3/200(195-225) [MonN88 6/154] d8.18 Col Oxnard (CA) JC [DL 1996 Mon N 182]

YEAR	TM LG	G	AB	R	H	2B	3B	HR	RBI	BB-IB	HP	SO	AVG	OBP	SLG	AOPS	ABR	SB-CS	FA	FR	RNG	THR	GAMES AT POSITION	DL	BFW
1992	Mon N	28	46	8	10	3	0	0	4	2-0	0	14	.217	.250	.283	51	-3	1-1	.991	2	83	37	C28		-0.1
1993	Mon N	43	86	3	17	2	1	0	7	2-0	1	16	.198	.222	.244	24	-9	2-0	.987	-3	65	67	C43		-1.1
1995	Mon N	64	141	17	33	8	1	3	20	14-4	1	38	.234	.306	.369	75	-5	0-1	.977	-5	81	100	C61		-0.7
1997	Bal A	7	14	0	0	0	0	0	1	2-0	0	9	.000	.118	.000	-66	-4	0-0	.966	-2	51	67	C7		-0.5
1998	TB A	3	5	1	1	0	0	0	0	1-0	0	1	.200	.333	.200	42	0	0-1	1.000	-0	0	0	C2/D		-0.5
	Pit N	14	24	2	9	1	0	1	2	1-0	0	2	.375	.385	.542	144	1	0-0	1.000	-1	42	157	1b4/C		0.0
1999	Pit N	6	9	0	3	0	0	0	0	0-0	0	2	.333	.333	.333	69	-0	0-0	1.000	0	77	0	C2		-0.2
2001	Cle A	16	33	5	6	0	0	1	5	6-0	1	8	.182	.308	.273	53	-2	0-0	.988	-1	47	69	C14/P		-0.5
2003	Cle A	52	162	17	39	11	0	3	21	9-1	1	38	.241	.281	.364	69	-8	2-2	.983	-1	110	106	C50,D2		-0.3
2004	Cle A	44	117	12	25	2	0	3	17	7-1	1	28	.214	.262	.308	50	-9	0-0	.984	-2	79	85	C41/P		-0.3
2005	TB A	1	1	0	0	0	0	0	0	0-0	0	1	.000	.000	.000	-99	0	0-0	1.000	0	0	0	/C		0.0
Total	10	278	638	65	143	27	2	11	77	44-6	3	158	.224	.275	.324	58	-39	5-5	.983	-13	83	85	C250,1b4,D3,P2	182	-3.1

LALLY, DAN Daniel J. B8.12.1867 Jersey City NJ D4.14.1936 Milwaukee WI d8.19

YEAR	TM LG	G	AB	R	H	2B	3B	HR	RBI	BB-IB	HP	SO	AVG	OBP	SLG	AOPS	ABR	SB-CS	FA	FR	RNG	THR	GAMES AT POSITION	DL	BFW
1891	Pit N	41	143	24	32	6	2	1	17	16	4	20	.224	.319	.315	87	-2	0	.839	-4	39	0	O41(0/4/37)		-0.5
1897	StL N	88	359	57	102	16	5	2	42	9	7		.284	.315	.373	83	-10	12	.896	-0	70	68	O85(83/1/1),1b3		-1.1
Total	2	129	502	81	134	22	7	3	59	25	11	20	.267	.316	.357	84	-12	12	.885	-4	62	49	O126(83/5/38),1b3		-2.

LAMANNO, RAY Raymond Simond B11.17.1919 Oakland CA D2.9.1994 Berkeley CA BR/TR/6-0/185 d9.11 Mil 1943-45

YEAR	TM LG	G	AB	R	H	2B	3B	HR	RBI	BB-IB	HP	SO	AVG	OBP	SLG	AOPS	ABR	SB-CS	FA	FR	RNG	THR	GAMES AT POSITION	DL	BFW
1941	Cin N	1	1	1	1	0	0	0	0	0	0	0	—	1.000	—	197	0	0	1.000	-0	0	0	/C		0.0
1942	Cin N	111	371	40	98	12	2	12	43	31	2	54	.264	.324	.404	113	-3	0	.978	-6	97	105	C104		0.5
1946	Cin N★	85	239	18	58	12	0	1	30	11	3	26	.243	.285	.305	70	-10	0	.974	3	121	114	C61		-0.
1947	Cin N	118	413	33	106	21	3	5	50	28	2	39	.257	.307	.358	77	-15	0	.986	6	100	113	C109		-0.
1948	Cin N	127	385	31	93	12	0	2	27	48	2	32	.242	.329	.273	71	-16	2	.978	-13	71	71	C125		-2.
Total	5	442	1408	122	355	57	5	18	150	118	10	151	.252	.314	.338	82	-36	2	.980	-11	94	98	C400		-2.

LAMAR, BILL William Harmong "Good Time Bill" B3.21.1897 Rockville MD D5.24.1970 Rockport MA BL/TR/6-1/185 d9.19 Mil 1918

YEAR	TM LG	G	AB	R	H	2B	3B	HR	RBI	BB-IB	HP	SO	AVG	OBP	SLG	AOPS	ABR	SB-CS	FA	FR	RNG	THR	GAMES AT POSITION	DL	BFW
1917	NY A	11	41	2	10	0	0	0	2	0	1		.244	.244	.244	48	-3	1	1.000	-1	98	55	O11(10/1/0)		-1.
1918	NY A	28	110	12	25	3	0	0	2	6	0		.227	.267	.255	56	-6	2	.884	-3	88	73	O27(8/17/2)		-1.
1919	NY A	11	16	1	3	1	0	0	0	2	0	1	.188	.278	.250	44	-1	1	1.000	-1	79	0	O3(0/1/2)/1		-0.
	Bos A	48	148	18	43	5	1	0	14	5	0		.291	.314	.338	88	-3	3	.922	-2	80	143	O39(6/30/3)/1		-0.
	Year	59	164	19	46	6	1	0	14	7	0	10	.280	.310	.329	83	-4	4	.926	-2	80	143	O42(6/31/5)/2		-0.
1920	†Bro N	24	44	5	12	4	0	0	4	0	0		.273	.273	.364	79	-1	0-0	1.000	-0	81	109	O12(0/6/6)		-0.
1921	Bro N	3	3	2	1	0	0	0	0	0	0		.333	.333	.333	74	0	0-0	—	-0	0	0	/OC		-0.
1924	Phi A	87	367	68	121	22	5	7	48	18	0		.330	.361	.474	113	5	8-8	.971	2	96	136	O87L		-0.

YEAR	TM LG	G	AB	R	H	2B	3B	HR	RBI	BB-IB	HP	SO	AVG	OBP	SLG	AOPS	ABR	SB-CS	FA	FR	RNG	THR	GAMES AT POSITION	DL	BFW
1925	Phi A	138	568	85	202	39	8	3	77	21		17	.356	.379	.468	107	5	2-6	.953	1	98	118	O131L		-0.6
1926	Phi A	116	419	62	119	17	6	5	50	18	1	15	.284	.315	.389	78	-15	4-5	.954	-2	96	102	O107L		-2.6
1927	Phi A	84	324	48	97	23	3	4	47	16	1	10	.299	.334	.426	91	-5	4-8	.952	-5	84	109	O79(76/3/0)		-2.6
Total 9		550	2040	303	633	114	23	19	245	86	2	78	.310	.339	.417	94	-24	25-27	.952	-10	93	114	O494(425/58/11)/1		-8.0

LAMB, DAVID David Christian B6.6.1975 West Hills CA BB/TR/6-2/165* [BalA93 2/61] d4.12

YEAR	TM LG	G	AB	R	H	2B	3B	HR	RBI	BB-IB	HP	SO	AVG	OBP	SLG	AOPS	ABR	SB-CS	FA	FR	RNG	THR	GAMES AT POSITION	DL	BFW
1999	TB A	55	124	18	28	5	1	1	13	10-0	0	18	.226	.284	.306	50	-10	0-1	.945	3	100	142	S35,2b15,D3		-0.4
2000	NY N	7	5	1	1	0	0	0	1-0		0	1	.200	.333	.200	41	0	0-0	1.000	1	140	0	3b3,2b2,S2	18	-0.1
2002	†Min A	7	10	0	1	0	0	0	0	0-0	0	2	.100	.100	.100	-45	-2	0-0	1.000	-1	31	147	S4,2b2/3		-0.2
Total 3		69	139	19	30	5	1	1	13	11-0	0	21	.216	.273	.288	43	-12	0-1	.949	2	95	136	S41,2b19,3b4,D3	18	-0.7

LAMB, LYMAN Laymon Raymond B3.17.1895 Lincoln NE D10.5.1955 Fayetteville AR BR/TR/5-7/150 d9.14

YEAR	TM LG	G	AB	R	H	2B	3B	HR	RBI	BB-IB	HP	SO	AVG	OBP	SLG	AOPS	ABR	SB-CS	FA	FR	RNG	THR	GAMES AT POSITION	DL	BFW
1920	StL A	9	24	4	9	2	0	0	4	0	0	7	.375	.375	.458	116	1	2-0	1.000		-1	97		O7(5/2/0)		0.0
1921	StL A	45	134	18	34	9	2	1	17	4	1	12	.254	.281	.373	62	-8	2-0	.942	-4	94	0	3b25,2b7,O6(2/0/4)		0.0
Total 2		54	158	22	43	11	2	1	21	4	1	19	.272	.294	.386	70	-7	2-0	.942	-4	94	0	3b25,O13(7/2/4),2b7		-1.0

LAMB, MIKE Michael Robert B8.9.1975 West Covina CA BL/TR/6-1/190* [TexA97 7/227] d4.23 Col Cal St.-Fullerton OF(26/0/6)

YEAR	TM LG	G	AB	R	H	2B	3B	HR	RBI	BB-IB	HP	SO	AVG	OBP	SLG	AOPS	ABR	SB-CS	FA	FR	RNG	THR	GAMES AT POSITION	DL	BFW
2000	Tex A	138	493	65	137	25	2	6	47	34-6	4	60	.278	.328	.373	77	-18	0-2	.913	-11	89	91	3b135,D2		-2.7
2001	Tex A	76	284	42	87	18	0	4	35	14-1	5	27	.306	.348	.412	97	-1	2-1	.914	-5	95	102	3b74		-0.5
2002	Tex A	115	314	54	89	13	0	9	33	33-5	3	48	.283	.354	.411	101	1	0-0	.987	-0	115	104	1b52,D21,O16(12/0/5),3b14,C3/2		-0.4
2003	Tex A	28	38	3	5	0	0	0	2	1-0	1	7	.132	.190	.132	-11	-6	0-0	1.000	-0	209	0	1b5,O2L/3D		-0.4
2004	†Hou N	112	278	38	80	14	3	14	58	31-3	0	63	.288	.356	.511	117	7	1-1	.919	5	109	98	3b57,1b10,2b7/D		-0.6
2005	†Hou N	125	322	41	76	13	5	12	53	22-1	1	65	.236	.284	.419	82	-10	1-1	.989	3	92	102	1b68,3b15,O13(12/0/1)/D		1.1
Total 6		594	1729	243	474	83	10	45	228	136-16	14	270	.274	.329	.412	90	-27	5-5	.919	-9	97	87	3b296,1b135,O31L,D31,2b8,C3		-1.2 / -4.3

LAMER, PETE Pierre B12.27.1873 New York NY D10.24.1931 Brooklyn NY TR/5-10/170 d9.10

YEAR	TM LG	G	AB	R	H	2B	3B	HR	RBI	BB-IB	HP	SO	AVG	OBP	SLG	AOPS	ABR	SB-CS	FA	FR	RNG	THR	GAMES AT POSITION	DL	BFW
1902	Chi N	2	9	2	2	0	0	0	0	0	0		.222	.222	.222	38	-1	0	.857	-0	131	95	C2		-0.1
1907	Cin N	1	2	0	0	0	0	0	0	0	0		.000	.000	.000	-96	0	0	1.000	-0	39	309	/C		-0.1
Total 2		3	11	2	2	0	0	0	0	0	0		.182	.182	.182	13	-1	0	.867	-0	119	123	C3		-0.2

LAMONT, GENE Gene William B12.25.1946 Rockford IL BL/TR/6-1/195* [DetA65 1/13] d9.2 M8/C11

YEAR	TM LG	G	AB	R	H	2B	3B	HR	RBI	BB-IB	HP	SO	AVG	OBP	SLG	AOPS	ABR	SB-CS	FA	FR	RNG	THR	GAMES AT POSITION	DL	BFW
1970	Det A	15	44	3	13	3	1	1	4	2-0	1	9	.295	.340	.477	122	1	0-0	1.000	-0	83	135	C15		0.2
1971	Det A	7	15	2	1	0	0	0	1	0-0	0	5	.067	.067	.067	-60	-3	0-0	.952	1	215	76	C7		-0.2
1972	Det A	1	0	0	0	0	0	0	0	0-0	0		—	—	—		0	0-0	1.000	-0	0	0	/C		0.0
1974	Det A	60	92	9	20	4	0	3	8	7-0	0	19	.217	.273	.359	78	-3	0-0	.974	1	95	112	C60		-0.1
1975	Det A	4	8	1	3	1	0	0	1	0-0	0	2	.375	.375	.500	139	0	1-0	.944	1	38	110	C4		0.1
Total 5		87	159	15	37	8	1	4	14	9-0	1	35	.233	.278	.371	80	-5	1-0	.977	2	100	114	C87		0.0

LaMOTTE, BOBBY Robert Eugene B2.15.1898 Savannah GA D11.2.1970 Chatham GA BR/TR/5-11/160 d9.1

YEAR	TM LG	G	AB	R	H	2B	3B	HR	RBI	BB-IB	HP	SO	AVG	OBP	SLG	AOPS	ABR	SB-CS	FA	FR	RNG	THR	GAMES AT POSITION	DL	BFW
1920	Was A	4	3	0	0	0	0	0	1	0	0	1	.000	.250	.000	-31	-1	0-0	.750	0	139	0	/S3		0.0
1921	Was A	16	41	5	8	0	0	0	2	5	0		.195	.283	.195	25	-5	0-0	.940	1	118	19	S12		0.0
1922	Was A	68	214	22	54	10	2	1	23	15	2	21	.252	.307	.332	70	-10	6-1	.954	5	106	87	3b62,S6		-0.3
1925	StL A	97	356	61	97	20	4	2	51	34	1	22	.272	.338	.368	75	-14	5-5	.926	-0	96	114	S93,3b3		-0.4
1926	StL A	36	79	11	16	4	3	0	9	11	0	6	.203	.300	.329	61	-5	0-0	.919	-2	97	110	S30/3		-0.4
Total 5		221	693	99	175	34	9	3	85	66	3	50	.253	.320	.341	69	-35	11-6	.927	3	97	100	S142,3b67		-1.1

LAMPARD, KEITH Christopher Keith B12.20.1945 Warrington, England BL/TR/6-2/197(185-200) [HouN65 2/24] d9.15 Col Oregon

YEAR	TM LG	G	AB	R	H	2B	3B	HR	RBI	BB-IB	HP	SO	AVG	OBP	SLG	AOPS	ABR	SB-CS	FA	FR	RNG	THR	GAMES AT POSITION	DL	BFW
1969	Hou N	9	12	2	3	0	1	0	2	0-0	1	3	.250	.250	.500	107	0	0-0	1.000	1	180	1408	/OL		0.1
1970	Hou N	53	72	8	17	8	1	0	5	5-0	1	24	.236	.295	.375	81	-2	0-0	1.000	3	119	294	O16(13/0/4),1b2		-0.1
Total 2		62	84	10	20	8	1	1	7	5-0	1	27	.238	.289	.393	85	-2	0-0	1.000	3	125	403	O17(14/0/4),1b2		0.0

LAMPKIN, TOM Thomas Michael B3.4.1964 Cincinnati OH BL/TR/5-11/185(183-198) [CleA86 11/265] d9.10 Col Portland

YEAR	TM LG	G	AB	R	H	2B	3B	HR	RBI	BB-IB	HP	SO	AVG	OBP	SLG	AOPS	ABR	SB-CS	FA	FR	RNG	THR	GAMES AT POSITION	DL	BFW
1988	Cle A	4	4	0	0	0	0	0	1-0		0	0	.000	.200	.000	-38	-1	0-0	1.000	-1	0	0	C3		-0.1
1990	SD N	26	63	4	14	0	1	1	4	4-1	0	9	.222	.269	.302	56	-4	0-1	.971	-0	115	149	C20		-0.4
1991	SD N	38	58	4	11	3	1	0	3	3-0	0	9	.190	.230	.276	40	-5	0-0	1.000	-1	76	82	C11		-0.5
1992	SD N	9	17	3	4	0	0	0	0	6-0	0	1	.235	.458	.235	100	1	2-0	1.000	-1	116	93	C7/OL		0.0
1993	Mil N	73	162	22	32	8	0	4	25	20-3	1	26	.198	.280	.321	63	-8	7-3	.978	-0	107	78	C60,O3(2/0/1)/D		-0.5
1995	SF N	65	76	8	21	2	0	1	9	9-1	1	11	.276	.360	.342	89	-1	2-0	1.000	3	332	141	C17,O6L		0.3
1996	SF N	66	177	26	41	8	0	6	29	20-2	5	22	.232	.324	.379	87	-3	1-5	.992	15	222	122	C53		1.3
1997	StL N	108	229	28	56	8	1	7	22	28-5	4	30	.245	.335	.380	87	-4	2-1	.989	-6	85	99	C86	58	-0.6
1998	StL N	93	216	25	50	12	1	6	28	24-5	1	32	.231	.328	.380	86	-4	3-2	.986	-4	111	82	C62,O5(4/0/1),1b2		-0.5
1999	Sea A	76	206	29	60	11	2	9	34	13-1	5	32	.291	.345	.495	113	3	1-3	.985	-4	107	160	C56,O2L,D2		0.2
2000	Sea A	36	103	15	26	6	1	7	23	9-1	3	17	.252	.325	.534	116	2	0-0	.987	-2	81	134	C28,D3	106	0.2
2001	†Sea A	79	204	28	46	10	0	5	22	18-1	7	41	.225	.309	.348	77	-7	1-0	.995	3	153	58	C71/ORD		0.0
2002	SD N	104	281	32	66	11	0	10	37	38-7	3	45	.235	.319	.381	87	-37	23-17	.992	-7	121	84	C94	164	-0.7
Total 13		777	1796	224	422	78	8	56	236	193-27	36	286	.235	.319	.381	87	-37	23-17	.992	-5	126	100	C568,O18(15/0/3),D7,1b2	164	-1.3

LANCELLOTTI, RICK Richard Anthony B7.5.1956 Providence RI BL/TL/6-3/195(195-210) [PitN77 11/278] d8.27 Col Rowan

YEAR	TM LG	G	AB	R	H	2B	3B	HR	RBI	BB-IB	HP	SO	AVG	OBP	SLG	AOPS	ABR	SB-CS	FA	FR	RNG	THR	GAMES AT POSITION	DL	BFW
1982	SD N	17	39	2	7	2	0	0	4	2-0	0	8	.179	.220	.231	28	-4	0-0	1.000	-1	48	156	1b7,O3(2/0/1)		-0.6
1986	SF N	15	18	2	4	0	0	2	6	0-0	0	7	.222	.222	.556	113	0	0-0	1.000	1	0	0	/1OR		0.0
1990	Bos A	4	8	0	0	0	0	0	1	0-0	0	3	.000	.000	.000	-95	-2	0-0	1.000	0	146	186	1b2		-0.1
Total 3		36	65	4	11	2	0	2	11	2-0	0	18	.169	.191	.292	35	-6	0-0	1.000	-0	68	158	1b10,O4(2/0/2)		-0.8

LAND, GROVER Grover Cleveland B9.22.1884 Frankfort KY D7.22.1958 Phoenix AZ BR/TR/6-0/190 d9.2 C7

YEAR	TM LG	G	AB	R	H	2B	3B	HR	RBI	BB-IB	HP	SO	AVG	OBP	SLG	AOPS	ABR	SB-CS	FA	FR	RNG	THR	GAMES AT POSITION	DL	BFW
1908	Cle A	8	16	1	3	0	0	0	1	0	0		.188	.188	.188	22	-1	0	.955	-0	149	54	C8		-0.2
1909	Cle A	1	4	0	2	0	0	0	1	0	0		.500	.500	.500	207	-2	0	1.000	0	142	85	/C		0.1
1910	Cle A	34	111	4	23	0	0	0	7	2	1		.207	.228	.207	36	-9	1	.982	0	91	95	C33		-0.6
1911	Cle A	35	107	5	15	1	2	0	10	3	0		.140	.164	.187	-2	-15	2	.961	-1	87	119	C34/1		-1.4
1913	Cle A	17	47	3	11	1	0	0	4	2	2		.234	.321	.255	67	-2	1	.924	1	122	96	C17		0.1
1914	Bro F	102	335	24	92	6	2	0	29	12	3	23	.275	.306	.304	67	-21	7	.970	-7	86	107	C97		-2.1
1915	Bro F	96	290	25	75	13	2	0	22	6	2	20	.259	.279	.317	68	-18	3	.960	-10	81	112	C81		-2.2
Total 7		293	910	62	221	21	6	0	80	27		44	.243	.271	.279	55	-66	14	.964	-17	89	107	C271/1		-6.3

LAND, DOC William Gilbert (b Doc Burrell Land) B5.14.1903 Binnsville MS D4.14.1986 Livingston AL BL/TL/5-11/165 d10.6 Col Alabama

YEAR	TM LG	G	AB	R	H	2B	3B	HR	RBI	BB-IB	HP	SO	AVG	OBP	SLG	AOPS	ABR	SB-CS	FA	FR	RNG	THR	GAMES AT POSITION	DL	BFW
1929	Was A	1	3	0	0	0	0	0	0	0	0		.000	.000	.000	-30	-1	0	1.000	0	54	0	/OC		-0.1

LANDENBERGER, KEN Kenneth Henry "Red" B7.29.1928 Lyndhurst OH D7.28.1960 Cleveland OH BL/TL/6-3/200 d9.20 Col Ohio U.

YEAR	TM LG	G	AB	R	H	2B	3B	HR	RBI	BB-IB	HP	SO	AVG	OBP	SLG	AOPS	ABR	SB-CS	FA	FR	RNG	THR	GAMES AT POSITION	DL	BFW
1952	Chi A	2	5	0	1	0	0	0	0	0	0	2	.200	.200	.200	11	-1	0-0	1.000	0	135		/1		-0.1

LANDESTOY, RAFAEL Rafael Silvaldo (Santana) B5.28.1953 Bani, D.R. BB/TR (BR 1977)/5-10/165(163-180) d8.27 C3 OF(12/4/7)

YEAR	TM LG	G	AB	R	H	2B	3B	HR	RBI	BB-IB	HP	SO	AVG	OBP	SLG	AOPS	ABR	SB-CS	FA	FR	RNG	THR	GAMES AT POSITION	DL	BFW
1977	†LA N	15	18	6	5	0	0	0	3-0	0	2	.278	.381	.278	80	0	2-0	1.000	-1	129	110	2b8,S3		-0.1
1978	Hou N	59	218	18	58	5	1	0	9	8-0	0	23	.266	.292	.298	70	-10	7-4	.980	-5	92	68	S50,O3(1/2/0),2b2		-1.1
1979	Hou N	129	282	33	76	9	6	0	30	29-5	1	24	.270	.338	.344	92	-3	13-4	.971	-6	95	112	2b114,S3		-0.3
1980	†Hou N	149	393	42	97	13	8	1	27	31-2	3	37	.247	.306	.328	84	-10	23-12	.991	-3	84	111	2b94,S65,3b3		-0.4
1981	Hou N	35	74	6	11	1	0	0	1	16-4	0	9	.149	.300	.189	44	-5	4-1	.966	-6	82	82	2b31		-0.9
	Cin N	12	11	2	2	0	0	0	0	1-0	0	0	.182	.250	.182	24	-1	1-0	1.000	-1	29	0	2b3		-0.2
	Year	47	85	8	13	1	0	0	1	17-4	0	9	.153	.294	.188	41	-6	5-1	.967	-6	80	79	2b34		-1.1
1982	Cin N	73	111	11	21	9	1	0	9	8-1	1	14	.189	.250	.243	38	-9	2-1	1.000	5	120	326	3b21,2b16,O3L,S2		-0.4
1983	Cin N	7	5	0	0	0	0	0	0	0-0	0	0	.000	.000	.000	-97	-1	0-0	1.000	-1	0	272	1b2/3OL		-0.4
	†LA N	64	64	6	11	1	1	0	3	3-0	0	9	.172	.209	.266	31	-6	0-2	1.000	-1	104	142	2b14,3b10,O10(6/1/3)/S		-0.2
	Year	71	69	6	11	1	1	0	3	3-0	0	9	.159	.194	.246	21	-8	0-2	1.000	-1	104	142	2b14,3b11,O11(7/1/3),1b2/S		-0.6
1984	LA N	53	54	10	10	0	0	0	4	3-0	0	8	.185	.200	.241	21	-6	2-1	.886	-2	85	99	2b14,3b11,O5(1/1/4)		-0.8
Total 8		596	1230	134	291	32	17	4	83	100-12	5	123	.237	.296	.300	70	-51	54-24	.976	-16	90	107	2b296,S124,3b46,O22L,1b2		-4.8

LANDIS, JIM James Henry B3.9.1934 Fresno CA BR/TR/6-1/180* d4.16 Col Contra Costa (CA) JC

YEAR	TM LG	G	AB	R	H	2B	3B	HR	RBI	BB-IB	HP	SO	AVG	OBP	SLG	AOPS	ABR	SB-CS	FA	FR	RNG	THR	GAMES AT POSITION	DL	BFW
1957	Chi A	96	274	38	58	11	1	8	45	42-2	3	61	.212	.329	.296	72	-9	14-4	.985	5	109	137	O90(11/38/44)		-0.6
1958	Chi A	142	523	72	145	23	7	15	64	52-1	8	80	.277	.351	.434	117	12	19-7	.986	-3	96	113	O142C		0.4
1959	†Chi A	149	515	78	140	26	7	5	60	78-5	8	68	.272	.370	.379	109	10	20-9	.993	7	109	96	O148C		1.1

YEAR	TM LG	G	AB	R	H	2B	3B	HR	RBI	BB-IB	HP	SO	AVG	OBP	SLG	AOPS	ABR	SB-CS	FA	FR	RNG	THR	GAMES AT POSITION	DL	BFW
1960	Chi A	148	494	89	125	25	6	10		80-4	9	84	.253	.365	.389	106	7	23-6	.985	3	104	146	O147C		0.6
1961	Chi A	140	534	87	151	18	8	22	85	65-0	4	71	.283	.362	.470	123	17	19-5	.988	8	113	120	O139C		2.3
1962	Chi A★	149	534	82	122	21	6	15	61	80-3	9	105	.228	.337	.375	92	-4	19-7	**.993**	-1	108	29	O144C		-0.8
1963	Chi A	133	396	56	89	6	6	13	45	47-4	6	75	.225	.316	.369	93	-4	8-6	.995	1	109	91	O124C		-0.7
1964	Chi A	106	298	30	62	8	4	1	18	36-1	6	64	.208	.305	.272	64	-14	5-0	.995	-1	94	119	O101C		-1.8
1965	KC A	118	364	46	87	15	1	3	36	57-1	3	84	.239	.346	.310	90	-2	8-3	.985	2	115	0	O108(0/108/1)		-0.6
1966	Cle A	85	158	23	35	5	1	3	14	20-1	2	25	.222	.317	.323	84	-3	2-1	1.000	-1	107	0	O61(18/37/17)		-0.1
1967	Det A	25	48	4	10	0	0	2	4	7-0	0	12	.208	.304	.333	87	-1	0-2	.952	1	105	316	O12(6/1/6)		0.0
	Bos A	5	7	1	1	0	0	1	1	1-0	0	3	.143	.250	.571	126	0	0-0	1.000	0	117	0	O5R		-0.1
	Year	30	55	5	11	0	0	3	5	8-0	0	15	.200	.297	.364	92	-1	0-2	.960	1	78	253	O17(6/1/11)		0.1
	Hou N	50	143	19	36	11	4	1	14	20-0	1	35	.252	.341	.364	107	2	2-1	1.000	1	78	253	O44(28/3/14)		-0.4
Total	11	1346	4288	625	1061	169	50	93	467	588-22	59	767	.247	.344	.375	100	11	139-51	.989	20	106	99	O1265(63/1132/87)		

LANDREAUX, KEN Kenneth Francis B12.22.1954 Los Angeles CA BL/TR/5-10/165(164-190) [AnaA76 1/6] d9.11 Col Arizona St.

YEAR	TM LG	G	AB	R	H	2B	3B	HR	RBI	BB-IB	HP	SO	AVG	OBP	SLG	AOPS	ABR	SB-CS	FA	FR	RNG	THR	GAMES AT POSITION	DL	BFW
1977	Cal A	23	76	6	19	5	1	0	5	5-1	0	15	.250	.296	.342	76	-3	1-1	.970	4	114	358	O22C		0.1
1978	Cal A	93	260	37	58	7	5	5	23	20-4	2	20	.223	.284	.346	79	-9	7-3	.986	1	97	137	O83(32/23/35)/D		-1.0
1979	Min A	151	564	81	172	27	5	15	83	37-4	4	57	.305	.347	.450	110	7	10-3	.981	-15	81	99	O147(49/98/0)		-0.9
1980	Min A★	129	484	56	136	23	11	7	62	39-4	1	42	.281	.334	.417	98	-2	8-6	**1.000**	9	86	62	O95C		-1.9
1981	†LA N	99	390	48	98	16	4	7	41	25-3	1	42	.251	.297	.367	92	-6	18-4	.986	-5	100	44	O117(1/116/0)		0.6
1982	LA N	129	461	71	131	23	7	7	50	39-2	1	54	.284	.341	.410	114	8	31-10	.986	-5	100	44	O137(7/131/2)		0.7
1983	†LA N	141	481	63	135	25	3	17	66	34-5	2	52	.281	.328	.451	115	8	30-11	.990	-3	98	68	O137(7/131/2)	15	-2.8
1984	LA N	134	438	39	110	11	5	4	47	29-3	1	35	.251	.295	.374	88	-9	10-9	.986	-15	79	46	O129(9/105/18)		-0.8
1985	†LA N	147	482	70	129	26	2	12	50	33-2	1	37	.268	.311	.405	102	0	15-5	.975	-8	94	55	O140(11/126/4)	37	-0.6
1986	LA N	103	283	34	74	13	2	4	29	22-3	1	39	.261	.313	.364	94	-3	10-5	.955	-2	98	128	O85(20/69/1)		-1.2
1987	LA N	115	182	17	37	4	0	6	23	16-2	1	28	.203	.269	.324	58	-12	5-3	.951	1	96	190	O63(15/6/45)	52	-1.5
Total	11	1264	4101	522	1099	180	45	91	479	299-33	19	421	.268	.317	.400	99	-21	145-60	.981	-63	90	87	O1138(198/859/105),D7		-9.3

LANDRITH, HOBIE Hobert Neal B3.16.1930 Decatur IL BL/TR/5-10/170* d7.30 C1 Col Michigan St.

YEAR	TM LG	G	AB	R	H	2B	3B	HR	RBI	BB-IB	HP	SO	AVG	OBP	SLG	AOPS	ABR	SB-CS	FA	FR	RNG	THR	GAMES AT POSITION	DL	BFW
1950	Cin N	4	14	1	3	0	0	0	1	2-0	0	1	.214	.313	.214	41	-1	0-0	1.000	-1	107	118	C4	100	-0.2
1951	Cin N	4	13	3	5	1	0	0	0	1-0	0	0	.385	.429	.462	137	1	0-0	1.000	1	82	99	C4		0.2
1952	Cin N	15	50	1	13	4	0	0	4	0-1	0	4	.260	.260	.340	65	-2	0-1	1.000	0	101	101	C14		-0.2
1953	Cin N	52	154	15	37	3	1	3	16	12-1	1	8	.240	.299	.331	64	-9	2-0	.986	2	181	116	C42		-0.6
1954	Cin N	48	81	12	16	0	0	5	14	18-1	0	9	.198	.340	.383	86	-1	1-0	1.000	3	117	131	C27	44	0.2
1955	Cin N	43	87	9	22	3	0	4	7	10-1	0	14	.253	.330	.425	93	-1	0-1	.975	-2	75	136	C99		-1.2
1956	Chi N	111	312	22	69	10	3	4	32	39-15	1	38	.221	.307	.311	69	-13	0-2	.975	-2	75	136	C99		-0.3
1957	StL N	75	214	18	52	6	1	3	26	25-1	0	27	.243	.318	.313	70	-8	1-2	.987	3	110	95	C67		-0.4
1958	StL N	70	144	9	31	4	0	3	13	26-4	1	21	.215	.335	.306	68	-6	0-1	.992	-6	67	88	C45		0.5
1959	SF N	109	283	30	71	14	0	3	29	43-7	0	23	.251	.345	.332	85	-4	0-4	.992	6	101	95	C109		-0.9
1960	SF N	71	190	18	46	10	0	1	20	23-2	1	11	.242	.321	.311	79	-5	1-1	.966	-7	72	85	C70		0.1
1961	SF N	43	71	11	17	4	0	2	10	12-3	0	7	.239	.337	.380	97	0	0-0	.985	-2	101	117	C30		0.1
1962	NY N	23	45	6	13	3	0	1	7	8-0	1	9	.289	.389	.422	118	2	0-0	.968	-2	55	91	C21		-0.4
	Bal A	60	167	18	37	4	1	4	17	19-1	0		.222	.302	.329	75	-6	0-0	.982	-1	79	177	C60		0.0
1963	Bal A	2	1	0	0	0	0	0	0	0-0	0	0	.000	.000	.000	-99	-7	0-0	1.000	0	0	0	/C	29	-0.6
	Was A	42	103	6	18	3	0	1	7	15-1	0	12	.175	.280	.233	46	-7	0-0	.978	0	70	185	C38		
	Year	44	104	6	18	3	0	1	7	15-1	0	12	.173	.277	.231	44	-7	0-0	.978	0	70	184	C38		
Total	14	772	1929	179	492	65	5	34	203	253-35	3	188	.233	.320	.327	76	-60	5-12	.983	3	94	113	C677	173	-3.5

LANDRUM, CED Cedric Bernard B9.3.1963 Butler AL BL/TR/5-7/167* d5.28 Col North Alabama

YEAR	TM LG	G	AB	R	H	2B	3B	HR	RBI	BB-IB	HP	SO	AVG	OBP	SLG	AOPS	ABR	SB-CS	FA	FR	RNG	THR	GAMES AT POSITION	DL	BFW
1991	Chi N	56	86	28	20	2	1	0	6	10-0	0	18	.233	.313	.279	65	-4	27-5	.968	-1	104	0	O44(25/18/8)		-0.1
1993	NY N	22	19	2	5	1	0	0	1	10-0	0	5	.263	.263	.316	55	-1	0-0	—	-0	-0	0	O3L		-0.1
Total	2	78	105	30	25	3	1	0	7	10-0	0	23	.238	.304	.286	63	-5	27-5	.968	-1	102	0	O47(28/18/8)		-0.2

LANDRUM, DON Donald Leroy B2.16.1936 Santa Rosa CA D1.9.2003 Pittsburg CA BL/TR/6-0/180* d9.28

YEAR	TM LG	G	AB	R	H	2B	3B	HR	RBI	BB-IB	HP	SO	AVG	OBP	SLG	AOPS	ABR	SB-CS	FA	FR	RNG	THR	GAMES AT POSITION	DL	BFW
1957	Phi N	2	7	1	1	1	0	0	0	2-0	0	1	.143	.333	.286	71	0	0-0	1.000	1	162	0	O2C		0.0
1960	StL N	13	49	7	12	0	1	2	3	4-0	1	6	.245	.315	.408	88	-1	3-0	1.000	1	124	107	O13(2/13/3)		0.1
1961	StL N	28	66	5	11	2	0	1	3	5-0	0	14	.167	.225	.242	22	-7	1-0	1.000	-1	97	0	O26(16/4/7)		-0.6
1962	StL N	32	35	11	11	0	0	1	3	4-1	0	2	.314	.375	.314	82	-3	9-2	.969	-2	98	73	O59(1/41/18)		-0.1
	Chi N	83	238	29	67	5	2	1	15	30-0	3	31	.282	.369	.332	87	-3	9-2	.973	-2	98	61	O85(17/45/25)		-0.6
	Year	115	273	40	78	5	2	1	18	34-1	3	33	.286	.370	.330	85	-6	11-2	.972	-5	82	85	O57(0/55/3)		-0.7
1963	Chi N	84	227	27	55	4	1	1	10	13-1	4	42	.242	.294	.282	82	-10	6-3	1.000	1	42	1462	/OC		-1.9
1964	Chi N	11	11	2	0	0	0	0	0	1-0	0	2	.000	.083	.000	-71	-3	0-0	1.000	1	42	1462	/OC		-0.2
1965	Chi N	131	425	60	96	20	4	6	34	36-3	10	84	.226	.300	.334	77	-12	14-8	.988	-2	102	49	O115(3/111/1)		-1.9
1966	SF N	72	102	9	19	4	0	1	9	18-1	0	18	.186	.299	.255	42	-8	1-1	.982	4	104	313	O54(38/14/3)		-0.6
Total	8	456	1160	151	272	36	8	12	75	104-5	19	200	.234	.307	.310	69	-45	36-14	.982	-1	99	102	O352(66/261/39)/2		-5.8

LANDRUM, JESSE Jesse Glenn B7.31.1912 Crockett TX D6.27.1983 Beaumont TX BR/TR/5-11.5/175 d4.26 Col Texas A&M-Commerce

YEAR	TM LG	G	AB	R	H	2B	3B	HR	RBI	BB-IB	HP	SO	AVG	OBP	SLG	AOPS	ABR	SB-CS	FA	FR	RNG	THR	GAMES AT POSITION	DL	BFW
1938	Chi A	4	6	0	0	0	0	0	0	2-0	0	2	.000	.000	.000	-98	-2	0-0	1.000	-0	109	156	2b3		-0.2

LANDRUM, TITO Terry Lee B10.25.1954 Joplin MO BR/TR/5-11/175* d7.23

YEAR	TM LG	G	AB	R	H	2B	3B	HR	RBI	BB-IB	HP	SO	AVG	OBP	SLG	AOPS	ABR	SB-CS	FA	FR	RNG	THR	GAMES AT POSITION	DL	BFW
1980	StL N	35	77	6	19	2	2	0	7	6-0	1	17	.247	.306	.325	74	-3	3-2	.976	-1	93	65	O29(17/8/6)		-0.5
1981	StL N	81	119	13	31	5	4	0	10	6-0	1	14	.261	.297	.370	86	-3	4-2	1.000	2	94	190	O67(43/6/24)		-0.2
1982	StL N	79	72	12	20	3	0	2	14	8-0	1	18	.278	.358	.403	109	1	0-1	1.000	2	111	124	O56(24/6/29)		0.2
1983	StL N	6	5	0	1	0	1	0	0	1-0	0	2	.200	.333	.600	153	0	1-0	1.000	-0	72	0	O5(4/0/1)		0.0
	†Bal A	26	42	8	13	2	0	1	4	1-0	0	11	.310	.318	.429	107	0	0-2	.979	-3	90	30	O26(11/4/15)		0.1
1984	StL N	105	173	21	47	9	1	3	26	10-1	0	27	.272	.306	.387	97	-1	3-4	1.000	1	108	65	O73(10/0/67)		-0.8
1985	†StL N	85	161	21	45	8	2	4	21	19-1	0	30	.280	.356	.429	119	4	3-1	.993	7	123	135	O78(9/4/70)	21	0.2
1986	StL N	96	205	24	43	7	1	2	17	20-2	1	41	.210	.279	.283	57	-12	3-1	1.000	3	148	114	O23(2/7/17)/1		-0.8
1987	StL N	30	50	5	10	1	0	0	6	7-2	0	16	.200	.282	.328	63	-4	1-1	.971	4	136	110	O31(19/0/14)	34	-0.2
	LA N	51	67	8	16	3	0	1	4	3-0	1	14	.239	.282	.328	52	-8	1-1	.987	4	136	110	O54(21/7/31)/1		-0.3
	Year	81	117	13	26	4	0	1	10	10-2	1	30	.222	.289	.282	52	-2	2-2	1.000	-1	90	0	O12(5/0/8)/D		-0.5
1988	Bal A	13	24	2	5	1	0	0	4	1-0	0	6	.125	.250	.208	30	-2	0-0	1.000	-1	90	0	O12(5/0/8)/D		-0.3
Total	9	607	995	120	248	40	12	13	111	85-6	5	196	.249	.309	.353	84	-24	17-18	.992	13	109	93	O488(199/55/276)/D1	55	-2.6

LANE, CHAPPY George M. B Pittsburgh PA BR/?/165 d5.16

YEAR	TM LG	G	AB	R	H	2B	3B	HR	RBI	BB-IB	HP	SO	AVG	OBP	SLG	AOPS	ABR	SB-CS	FA	FR	RNG	THR	GAMES AT POSITION	DL	BFW
1882	Pit AA	57	214	26	38	8	2	3				5	.178	.196	.276	60	-8		.974	5	111	108	1b43,O13(0/12/1),C2		-0.7
1884	Tol AA	57	215	26	39	9	5	1				7	.228	.242	.330	82	-5		.948	2	125	79	1b46,O9(5/0/4),3b2/C		-0.7
Total	2	114	429	52	87	17	7	4				12	.203	.219	.303	72	-13		.961	7	118	93	1b89,O22(5/12/5),C3,3b2		-1.4

LANE, HUNTER James Hunter "Dodo" B7.20.1900 Pulaski TN D9.12.1994 Memphis TN BR/TR/5-11/165 d5.13 Col Tennessee

YEAR	TM LG	G	AB	R	H	2B	3B	HR	RBI	BB-IB	HP	SO	AVG	OBP	SLG	AOPS	ABR	SB-CS	FA	FR	RNG	THR	GAMES AT POSITION	DL	BFW
1924	Bos N	7	15	1	1	0	0	0	1			1	.067	.125	.067	-49	-3	0-0	.909	-1	62	0	3b4/2		-0.4

LANE, JASON Jason Dean B12.22.1976 Santa Rosa CA BR/TL/6-2/220* [HouN99 6/203] d5.10 Col USC

YEAR	TM LG	G	AB	R	H	2B	3B	HR	RBI	BB-IB	HP	SO	AVG	OBP	SLG	AOPS	ABR	SB-CS	FA	FR	RNG	THR	GAMES AT POSITION	DL	BFW
2002	Hou N	44	69	12	20	3	1	4	10	10-1	0	12	.290	.375	.536	131	3	1-1	.980	3	118	226	O38(11/1/27)		0.5
2003	Hou N	18	27	5	8	2	0	1	10	0-0	0	10	.296	.296	.815	167	2	0-0	1.000	-1	68	0	O10(3/6/2)		0.1
2004	†Hou N	107	136	21	37	10	2	4	19	16-0	1	33	.272	.348	.463	105	1	9-8	.984	-9	98	110	O76(35/17/24),1b3		0.0
2005	†Hou N	145	517	65	138	34	4	26	78	32-1	7	105	.267	.316	.499	110	5	6-2	.976	-4	97	81	O265(53/30/190),1b3		-0.7
Total	4	314	749	103	203	49	7	38	117	58-2	8	152	.271	.327	.507	113	11	8-3	.978	-4	97	81			-0.1

LANE, MARVIN Marvin B1.18.1950 Sandersville GA BR/TR/5-11/180* [DetA68 10/222] d9.4

YEAR	TM LG	G	AB	R	H	2B	3B	HR	RBI	BB-IB	HP	SO	AVG	OBP	SLG	AOPS	ABR	SB-CS	FA	FR	RNG	THR	GAMES AT POSITION	DL	BFW
1971	Det A	8	14	2	0	0	0	0	0	1-0	0	3	.143	.200	.143	-1	-2	0-0	1.000	-0	90	0	O6(3/0/3)		-0.3
1972	Det A	8	6	2	0	0	0	0	0	0-0	0	2	.000	.000	.000	-97	-1	0-0	1.000	-0	96	0	O3(1/1/1)		-0.2
1973	Det A	6	8	2	2	0	0	1	2	2-0	0	2	.250	.400	.625	174	1	0-0	1.000	-0	147	0	O4(3/0/3)		0.0
1974	Det A	50	103	16	24	4	1	2	9	19-1	0	24	.233	.352	.350	99	1	0-0	.986	1	105	127	O46(40/2/6)/D		-0.5
1976	Det A	18	48	3	9	1	0	1	3	5-0	0	11	.188	.273	.208	42	-3	0-0	.960	0	84	116	O15(10/5/0)		-0.9
Total	5	90	179	23	37	5	1	3	17	28-1	0	42	.207	.313	.296	74	-4	2-0	.983	0	101	106	O74(57/8/13)/D		

YEAR	TM LG	G	AB	R	H	2B	3B	HR	RBI	BB-IB	HP	SO	AVG	OBP	SLG	AOPS	ABR	SB-CS	FA	FR	RNG	THR	GAMES AT POSITION	DL	BFW

LANE, DICK Richard Harrison B6.28.1927 Highland Park MI BR/TR/5-11/178 d6.20 Col Detroit Mercy

| 1949 | Chi A | 12 | 42 | 4 | 5 | 0 | 0 | 0 | 4 | 5 | 0 | 3 | .119 | .213 | .119 | -11 | -7 | 0-1 | 1.000 | 1 | 103 | 245 | O11L | | -0.7 |

LANG, DON Donald Charles B3.15.1915 Selma CA BR/TR/6-0/175 d7.4

1938	Cin N	21	50	5	13	3	1	1	11	2	0	7	.260	.288	.420	95	-1	0	.976	1	106	155	3b15/2S		0.1
1948	StL N	117	323	30	87	14	1	4	31	47	1	38	.269	.364	.356	90	-3	2	.964	4	106	97	3b95,2b2		0.1
Total	2	138	373	35	100	17	2	5	42	49	1	45	.268	.355	.365	91	-4	2	.966	5	106	104	3b110,2b3/S		0.2

LANGE, BILL William Alexander "Little Eva" B6.6.1871 San Francisco CA D7.23.1950 San Francisco CA BR/TR/6-1.5/190 d4.27 OF(15/702/2)

1893	Chi N	117	469	92	132	8	7	8	88	52	4	20	.281	.358	.380	98	-2	47	.888	-5	93	70	2b57,O40(14/27/0),3b8,S7,C7		-0.5
1894	Chi N	113	449	86	146	17	9	6	91	56	2	18	.325	.402	.443	98	-2	66	.912	4	136	207	O111(1/108/2),S2/3		-0.3
1895	Chi N	123	478	120	186	27	16	10	98	55	4	24	.389	.456	.575	155	39	67	.924	7	152	140	O123C		3.1
1896	Chi N	122	469	114	153	21	16	4	92	65	5	24	.326	.414	.465	126	19	84	.932	6	105	67	O121C/C		1.5
1897	Chi N	118	479	119	163	24	14	5	83	48	5		.340	.406	.480	129	19	**73**	.946	1	102	116	O118C		1.1
1898	Chi N	113	442	79	141	16	11	5	69	36	5		.319	.377	.439	134	18	22	.970	6	120	113	O111C,1b2		1.6
1899	Chi N	107	416	81	135	21	7	1	58	38	1		.325	.382	.416	122	13	41	.976	7	146	281	O94C,1b14		1.3
Total	7	813	3202	691	1056	134	80	39	579	350	26	86	.330	.400	.458	123	104	400	.942	26	125	144	O718C,2b57,1b16,S9,3b9,C8		7.8

LANGERHANS, RYAN Ryan David B2.20.1980 San Antonio TX BL/TL/6-3/195* [AtlN98 3/101] d4.28

2002	Atl N	1	1	0	0	0	0	0	0	0-0	0	0	.000	.000	.000	-99	-1	0-0	—	-0	0	0	/OL		0.0
2003	Atl N	16	15	2	4	0	0	0	0	0-0	0	6	.267	.267	.267	40	-1	0-0	1.000	1	109	305	O14(3/4/9)		-0.1
2005	†Atl N	128	326	48	87	22	3	8	42	37-3	5	75	.267	.348	.426	100	1	0-2	.995	-1	102	114	O114(54/19/48)		-0.4
Total	3	145	342	50	91	22	3	8	42	37-3	5	81	.266	.344	.418	97	0	0-2	.995	-0	102	68	O129(58/23/57)		-0.5

LANGFORD, SAM Elton B5.21.1900 Briggs TX D7.31.1993 Plainview TX BL/TR/6-0/180 d4.13

1926	Bos A	1	1	0	0	0	0	0	0	0-0	0	0	.000	.000	.000	-99	0	0-0	—	0			/H		0.0
1927	Cle A	20	67	10	18	5	0	1	7	5	3	7	.269	.347	.388	90	-1	0-1	1.000	-1	91	58	O20(1/18/1)		-0.3
1928	Cle A	110	427	50	118	17	8	4	50	21	1	35	.276	.312	.382	81	-14	3-8	.972	-8	93	46	O107(32/76/0)		-2.9
Total	3	131	495	61	136	22	8	5	57	26	4	42	.275	.316	.382	81	-15	3-9	.976	-10	93	46	O127(33/94/1)		-3.2

LANGSFORD, BOB Robert William (b Robert Hugo Lankswert) B8.5.1865 Louisville KY D1.10.1907 Louisville KY BL/TL/5-7/168 d6.18

| 1899 | Lou N | 1 | 4 | 0 | 0 | 0 | 0 | 0 | 0 | 0 | 0 | | .000 | .000 | .000 | -99 | -1 | 0-0 | 1.000 | -1 | 0 | 63 | 0/S | | -0.1 |

LANIER, HAL Harold Clifton B7.4.1942 Denton NC BR/TR (BB 1967p, 68-70)/6-2/180* d6.18 M3/C7 f-Max

1964	SF N	98	383	40	105	16	3	2	28	5-0	0	44	.274	.283	.347	75	-14	2-1	.979	12	108	88	2b98,S3		0.7
1965	SF N	159	522	41	118	15	9	0	39	21-4	1	67	.226	.256	.289	52	-35	2-1	.976	-6	97	86	2b158/S		-2.9
1966	SF N	149	459	37	106	14	2	3	37	16-7	0	49	.231	.256	.290	50	-31	1-0	.991	5	104	111	2b112,S41		-1.5
1967	SF N	151	525	37	112	16	3	0	42	16-2	2	66	.213	.239	.255	42	-41	2-2	.974	20	**109**	107	S137,2b34		-0.8
1968	SF N	151	486	30	100	14	1	0	27	12-0	1	57	.206	.222	.239	39	-37	2-2	**.979**	17	104	94	S150		-0.9
1969	SF N	150	495	37	113	9	1	0	35	25-5	0	68	.228	.263	.251	46	-37	0-1	.969	24	**116**	118	S150		0.4
1970	SF N	134	438	33	101	13	1	2	41	21-4	0	41	.231	.265	.279	46	-34	1-2	.967	8	101	103	S130,2b4,1b2		-1.2
1971	†SF N	109	206	21	48	8	0	1	13	15-3	0	26	.233	.283	.286	63	-10	0-0	.957	-5	83	76	3b83,2b13,S8,1b3		-1.6
1972	NY A	60	103	5	22	3	0	0	6	2-0	1	13	.214	.234	.243	43	-7	1-2	.973	1	107	148	3b47,S9,2b3		-0.7
1973	NY A	35	86	9	18	3	0	0	5	3-0	1	10	.209	.244	.244	39	-7	0-0	.960	-2	99	107	S26,2b8/3		-0.6
Total	10	1196	3703	297	843	111	20	8	273	136-25	4	436	.228	.255	.275	50	-253	11-11	.971	73	107	104	S655,2b430,3b131,1b5		-9.1

LANIER, RIMP Lorenzo B10.19.1948 Tuskegee AL BL/TR/5-8/150 d9.11

| 1971 | Pit N | 6 | 4 | 0 | 0 | 0 | 0 | 0 | 0 | 0-0 | 1 | 1 | .000 | .200 | .000 | -39 | -1 | 0-0 | — | 0 | | | /H | | -0.1 |

LANKFORD, RAY Raymond Lewis B6.5.1967 Los Angeles CA BL/TL/5-11/198(180-200) [StLN87 3/72] d8.21 Col Modesto (CA) JC

1990	StL N	39	126	12	36	10	1	3	12	13-0	0	27	.286	.353	.452	119	3	8-2	.989	1	113	57	O35C		0.5
1991	StL N	151	566	83	142	23	**15**	9	69	41-1	1	114	.251	.301	.392	93	-8	44-20	.984	0	107	89	O149C		-0.6
1992	StL N	153	598	87	175	40	6	20	86	72-6	3	147	.293	.371	.480	143	35	42-24	.996	-4	102	53	O153C		3.3
1993	StL N	127	407	64	97	17	3	7	45	81-7	3	111	.238	.366	.346	93	0	14-14	.978	-4	97	93	O121C		3.0
1994	StL N	109	416	89	111	25	5	19	57	58-3	4	113	.267	.359	.488	119	12	11-10	.978	-2	99	87	O104C		-0.4
1995	StL N	132	483	81	134	35	2	25	82	63-6	2	110	.277	.360	.513	126	9	24-8	.990	-2	98	100	O129C		1.0
1996	†StL N	149	545	100	150	36	8	21	86	79-10	3	133	.275	.366	.486	123	20	35-7	**.997**	4	105	122	O144C		2.0
1997	StL N★	133	465	94	137	36	3	31	98	95-10	0	125	.295	.411	.585	158	43	21-11	.971	-6	99	64	O131C		3.0
1998	StL N	154	533	94	156	37	1	31	105	86-5	3	151	.293	.391	.540	143	36	26-5	.986	-5	98	77	O145C/D		3.8
1999	StL N	122	422	77	129	32	1	15	63	49-3	3	110	.306	.380	.493	117	12	14-4	.987	-5	98	92	O106(105/2/0)/D		3.5
2000	†StL N	128	392	73	99	16	3	26	65	70-1	4	148	.253	.367	.508	117	10	5-6	.973	-4	90	63	O117(116/2/0)/D		1.2
2001	StL N	91	264	38	62	18	3	15	39	44-8	2	105	.235	.345	.496	112	5	4-2	.966	-1	96	98	O85L		0.1
	SD N	40	125	20	36	10	1	4	19	18-1	2	40	.288	.386	.480	132	7	6-0	.985	-2	92	49	O38(21/16/2)		0.2
	Year	131	389	58	98	28	4	19	58	62-9	4	145	.252	.358	.491	118	12	10-2	.971	-3	95	83	O123(106/16/2)		0.5
2002	SD N	81	205	20	46	7	1	6	26	30-3	2	61	.224	.326	.356	91	-4	2-2	.953	-2	105	131	O59(59/3/0)/D		0.7
2004	StL N	92	200	36	51	14	1	6	22	29-4	2	55	.255	.349	.425	99	1	2-2	.956	-2	95	38	O70(66/4/0)/D		-0.4
Total	14	1701	5747	968	1561	356	54	238	874	828-68	36	1550	.272	.364	.477	122	191	258-117	.980	-22	100	83	O1586(452/1138/2),D4	164	17.3

LANNING, RED Lester Alfred B5.13.1895 Harvard IL D6.13.1962 Bristol CT BL/TL/5-9/165 d6.20 Col Wesleyan ▲

| 1916 | Phi A | 19 | 33 | 5 | 6 | 2 | 0 | 0 | 1 | 10 | 0 | 9 | .182 | .372 | .242 | 89 | 0 | 0 | .909 | -1 | 82 | 0 | O9(7/0/6),P6 | | -0.1 |

LANSFORD, CARNEY Carney Ray B2.7.1957 San Jose CA BR/TR/6-2/195* [CalA75 3/49] d4.8 C3 b-Jody

1978	Cal A	121	453	63	133	23	2	8	52	31-2	4	67	.294	.339	.406	114	8	20-9	.942	-21	75	80	3b117,S2/D	26	-1.4
1979	†Cal A	157	654	114	188	30	5	19	79	39-2	3	115	.287	.329	.436	108	5	20-8	**.983**	-15	82	93	3b157		-1.0
1980	Cal A	151	602	87	157	27	3	15	80	50-2	0	93	.261	.312	.390	94	-6	14-5	.955	-20	79	88	3b150		-2.7
1981	Bos A	102	399	61	134	23	4	4	52	34-3	2	28	**.336**	.389	.439	130	17	15-10	.951	-2	97	104	3b86,D16		1.3
1982	Bos A	128	482	65	145	28	4	11	63	46-2	2	48	.301	.359	.444	114	10	9-4	.968	-15	86	77	3b114,D13	27	-0.6
1983	Oak A	80	299	43	92	16	2	10	45	22-4	3	33	.308	.357	.475	135	14	3-8	.957	-6	94	105	3b78/S	19	0.5
1984	Oak A	151	597	70	179	31	5	14	74	40-6	3	62	.300	.342	.439	123	18	9-3	.957	-2	97	90	3b151		1.4
1985	Oak A	98	401	51	111	18	2	13	46	18-1	4	27	.277	.311	.429	109	3	2-3	.976	-27	64	59	3b97	33	-1.4
1986	Oak A	151	591	80	168	16	4	19	72	39-2	5	51	.284	.332	.421	112	7	16-7	.982	-18	85	78	3b100,1b60/2D		-1.4
1987	Oak A★	151	554	89	160	27	4	19	76	60-11	9	44	.289	.366	.455	124	21	27-8	**.980**	3	100	60	3b142,1b17,D4		2.3
1988	†Oak A	150	556	80	155	20	2	7	57	35-4	7	35	.279	.327	.360	96	-4	29-8	**.979**	-12	87	72	3b143,1b9/2D		-1.2
1989	†Oak A	148	551	81	185	28	2	2	52	51-2	9	25	.336	.398	.405	132	26	37-15	.957	-20	77	55	3b136,1b15,D3		0.8
1990	†Oak A	134	507	58	136	15	1	3	50	45-4	6	50	.268	.333	.320	87	-8	16-14	**.970**	-9	89	116	3b126,1b5,D5	15	-1.9
1991	Oak A	5	16	0	1	0	0	0	1	0-0	0	2	.063	.063	.063	-69	-4	0-0	1.000	-2	53	0	3b4/D	176	-0.6
1992	†Oak A	135	496	65	130	30	1	7	75	43-0	7	39	.262	.325	.369	100	1	7-2	.965	-20	79	52	3b119,1b18/SD		-2.0
Total	15	1862	7158	1007	2074	332	40	151	874	553-45	64	719	.290	.343	.411	111	108	224-104	.966	-186	85	80	3b1720,1b124,D49,S4,2b2	296	-9.1

LANSFORD, JODY Joseph Dale B1.15.1961 San Jose CA BR/TR/6-5/225* [SDN79 1/14] d7.31 b-Carney

1982	SD N	13	22	6	4	0	0	0	3	6-0	0	4	.182	.345	.182	58	-1	0-1	.986	-1	74	208	1b9		-0.2
1983	SD N	12	8	1	2	0	0	1	2	0-0	0	3	.250	.250	.625	139	0	0-0	1.000	0	98	88	1b8		0.0
Total	2	25	30	7	6	0	0	1	5	6-0	0	7	.200	.324	.300	82	-1	0-1	.988	-1	79	185	1b17		-0.2

LANSING, MIKE Michael Thomas B4.3.1968 Rawlins WY BR/TR/6-0/185(180-195) [MiaI90 5/155] d4.7 Col Wichita St.

1993	Mon N	141	491	64	141	29	1	3	45	46-2	5	56	.287	.352	.369	90	-5	23-5	.942	10	118	171	3b81,S51,2b25		1.2
1994	Mon N	106	394	44	105	21	3	5	35	30-3	7	37	.266	.328	.368	81	-11	12-8	.983	1	93	111	2b82,3b27,S12		-0.6
1995	Mon N	127	467	47	119	30	2	10	62	28-2	9	65	.255	.299	.392	78	-15	27-4	.991	15	107	97	2b127,S2		1.0
1996	Mon N	159	641	99	183	40	2	11	53	44-1	10	85	.285	.341	.406	94	-5	23-8	.985	-2	93	93	2b159,S2	15	0.3
1997	Mon N	144	572	86	161	45	2	20	70	45-2	5	92	.281	.338	.472	111	9	11-5	.987	-3	96	111	2b144		1.3
1998	Col N	153	584	73	161	39	2	12	66	39-4	5	78	.276	.325	.411	76	-19	10-3	.987	6	100	114	2b153/3		-0.5
1999	Col N	35	145	24	45	9	0	4	15	7-0	1	22	.310	.344	.455	80	-4	2-0	.990	8	103	154	2b35	136	0.5
2000	Col N	90	365	62	94	14	6	11	47	31-1	0	49	.258	.315	.419	68	-19	8-2	.983	-7	94	101	2b88		-2.0
	Bos A	49	139	10	27	4	0	3	13	7-1	0	26	.194	.230	.323	16	-18	0-0	1.000	-6	89	47	2b49/3		-2.1
2001	Bos A	106	352	45	88	23	0	8	34	22-1	1	50	.250	.294	.384	77	-12	3-3	.966	-4	89	84	2b31	28	-1.0
Total	9	1110	4150	554	1124	254	17	84	440	299-17	37	570	.271	.324	.401	83	-99	119-38	.986	17	97	103	2b893,S143,3b110	179	-1.9

YEAR	TM LG	G	AB	R	H	2B	3B	HR	RBI	BB-IB	HP	SO	AVG	OBP	SLG	AOPS	ABR	SB-CS	FA	FR	RNG	THR	GAMES AT POSITION	DL	BFW

LAPAN, PETE   Peter Nelson B6.25.1891 Easthampton MA D1.5.1953 Norwalk CA BR/TR/5-7/165 d9.16

																									0.2
1922	Was A	11	34	7	11	4	0	0	6	3	0	4	.324	.378	.441	119	1	1-0	.958	0	106	119	C11		-0.1
1923	Was A	2	2	0	0	0	0	0	0	0	0	0	.000	.000	.000	-99	-1	0-0	—	0		/H			0.1
Total	2	13	36	7	11	4	0	0	6	3	0	4	.306	.359	.417	107	1	1-0	.958	0	106	119	C11		

LaPOINTE, RALPH   Ralph Robert B1.8.1922 Winooski VT D9.13.1967 Burlington VT BR/TR/5-11/185 d4.15 Col Vermont

																									-0.3
1947	Phi N	56	211	33	65	7	0	1	15	17	1	15	.308	.362	.355	95	-1	8	.956	-5	100	81	S54		-1.0
1948	StL N	87	222	27	50	3	0	0	15	18	0	19	.225	.283	.239	40	-18	1	.965	5	101	107	2b44,S25/3		-1.3
Total	2	143	433	60	115	10	0	1	30	35	1	34	.266	.322	.296	66	-19	9	.955	0	102	96	S79,2b44/3		

LaPORTE, FRANK   Frank Breyfogle "Pot" B2.6.1880 Uhrichsville OH D9.25.1939 Newcomerstown OH BR/TR/5-8/175 d9.29

																									0.1
1905	NY A	11	40	4	16	1	0	1	12	1	0		.400	.415	.500	170	3	1	.918	-2	90	145	2b11		-0.3
1906	NY A	123	454	60	120	23	9	2	54	22	1		.264	.300	.368	99	-2	10	.904	-4	94	106	3b114,2b5/OL		-0.5
1907	NY A	130	470	56	127	20	11	0	48	27	5		.270	.317	.360	107	3	10	.896	-6	95	58	2b27,3b12,O5(0/2/3)		0.4
1908	Bos A	62	156	14	37	1	3	0	15	12	1		.262	.301	.359	113	1	3	.934	-2	99	111	2b26,O11(3/0/8)		-0.1
	NY A	39	145	7	38	3	4	1	15	8	0		.262	.298	.379	98	-1	6	.942	4	112	96	2b53,O16(3/2/11),3b12		0.3
	Year	101	301	21	75	4	7	1	30	20	1		.249	.298	.319				.938	-16	89	99	2b83		-0.7
1909	NY A	89	309	35	92	19	3	0	31	18	2		.298	.340	.379	126	9	5	.959	-4	106	83	2b79,O23(17/1/5),3b15		-0.5
1910	NY A	124	432	43	114	14	6	2	67	33	3		.264	.321	.338	100	0	16	.950	-3	105	120	2b133,3b3		1.8
1911	StL A	136	507	71	159	37	12	2	82	34	4		.314	.361	.446	130	19	4	.944	2	102	154	2b39,O32R		0.8
1912	StL A	80	266	32	83	11	4	1	38	20	3		.312	.367	.395	122	7	7	.939	-0	107	84	2b37		0.3
	Was A	40	136	13	42	9	1	0	17	12	0		.309	.365	.390	115	3	3	.941	1	105	119	2b76,O32R		1.1
	Year	120	402	45	125	20	5	1	55	32	3		.311	.366	.393	120	10	10	.952	4	108	142	3b46,2b13,O12(4/0/8)		-0.3
1913	Was A	79	242	25	61	5	4	0	30	13	3	16	.252	.309	.306	78	-7	10	.956	4	100	124	2b132		0.2
1914	Ind F	133	505	86	157	27	12	4	**107**	36	4	36	.311	.361	.436	105	-3	15	.960	-1	99	**117**	2b146		-1.5
1915	New F	148	550	55	139	28	9	3	56	48	1	33	.253	.314	.353	93	-15	14	.952	-22	101	114	2b731,3b254,O147(39/16/92)/1		-0.3
Total	11	1194	4212	501	1185	198	78	16	560	288	27	85	.281	.331	.377	107	15	101	.952	-22	101	114			

LAPP, JACK   John Walker B9.10.1884 Frazer PA D2.6.1920 Philadelphia PA BL/TR/5-8/160 d9.11

																									-0.5
1908	Phi A	13	35	4	5	0	1	0	1	5	1		.143	.268	.200	49	-2	0	.947	-3	67	109	C13		0.7
1909	Phi A	21	56	8	19	3	1	0	10	3	0		.339	.373	.429	150	3	1	.938	1	130	99	C19		1.1
1910	†Phi A	71	192	18	45	4	3	0	17	20	1		.234	.310	.286	88	-2	0	.980	7	112	89	C57,1b4		1.6
1911	†Phi A	68	167	35	59	10	3	1	26	24	0		.353	.435	.467	154	13	4	.972	-1	112	68	C61		0.7
1912	Phi A	91	281	26	82	15	6	1	35	19	0		.292	.337	.399	114	4	3	.958	-4	127	88	C83		-0.6
1913	†Phi A	82	238	23	54	4	4	1	20	37	2	26	.227	.336	.290	85	-3	1	.968	-8	105	100	C78/1		-0.3
1914	†Phi A	69	199	22	46	7	2	0	19	31	1	14	.231	.338	.286	91	-1	1-4	.977	-6	86	96	C67		-0.1
1915	Phi A	112	312	26	85	16	5	2	31	30	2	29	.272	.340	.375	118	6	5-2	.967	-14	60	116	C89,1b12		-0.2
1916	Chi A	40	101	6	21	0	1	0	7	8	0	10	.208	.266	.228	48	-7	1	.989	3	147	115	C34		2.4
Total	9	567	1581	168	416	56	26	5	166	177	7	79	.263	.340	.343	105	11	16-6	.969	-25	103	96	C503,1b17		

LARKER, NORM   Norman Howard John B12.27.1930 Beaver Meadows PA BL/TL/6-0/200(169-200) d4.15

																									-0.2
1958	LA N	99	253	32	70	16	5	4	29	29-0	3	21	.277	.352	.427	103	2	1-1	.985	-0	96	120	O43(41/0/2),1b35		-0.2
†1959	†LA N	108	311	37	90	14	5	8	49	26-1	2	25	.289	.344	.418	96	-1	0-1	.990	5	114	120	1b55,O30(22/0/8)		0.8
1960	LA N★	133	440	56	142	26	3	5	78	36-2	1	24	.323	.368	.430	112	9	1-0	.993	5	107	103	1b119,O2L		0.9
1961	LA N	97	282	29	76	16	1	9	38	24-7	1	22	.270	.326	.387	82	-7	0-0	.995	2	100	107	1b135,O6L		0.2
1962	Hou N	147	506	58	133	19	5	9	63	70-7	7	47	.263	.358	.374	105	6	1-1	.991	5	109	93	1b135,O6L		-0.6
1963	Mil N	64	147	15	26	6	0	1	14	24-2	2	24	.177	.297	.238	58	-7	0-2	.992	4	148	88	1b42		-0.3
	SF N	19	14	0	1	0	0	0	0	2-0	0	2	.071	.188	.071	-22	-2	0-0	.929	-0	107	143	1b11		-0.9
	Year	83	161	15	27	6	0	1	14	26-2	2	26	.168	.288	.224	51	-9	0-2	.987	4	145	90	1b53		-1.2
Total	6	667	1953	227	538	97	15	32	271	211-19	16	165	.275	.347	.390	97	0	3-5	.991	20	110	101	1b483,O82(71/0/11)		

LARKIN   d5.29

																									-0.8
1884	Was U	17	70	11	17	0	0	0		4			.243	.284	.243	63	-5		.726	-4	52	113	3b17		

LARKIN, BARRY   Barry Louis B4.28.1964 Cincinnati OH BR/TR/6-0/190(180-196) [CinN85 1/4] d8.13 b-Stephen Col Michigan

																									0.6
1986	Cin N	41	159	27	45	4	3	3	19	9-1	0	21	.283	.320	.403	95	-2	8-0	.976	3	113	104	S36,2b3	19	-0.4
1987	Cin N	125	439	64	107	16	2	12	43	36-3	5	52	.244	.306	.371	76	-16	21-6	.965	-2	102	110	S119		4.3
1988	Cin N★	151	588	91	174	32	5	12	56	41-3	8	24	.296	.347	.429	118	14	40-7	.960	9	105	90	S148	52	4.1
1989	Cin N☆	97	325	47	111	14	4	4	36	20-5	2	23	.342	.375	.446	132	13	10-5	.976	20	118	76	S82		4.2
1990	†Cin N★	158	614	85	185	25	6	7	67	49-3	7	49	.301	.358	.396	103	4	30-5	.977	23	107	109	S119	17	**6.2**
1991	Cin N★	123	464	88	140	27	4	20	69	55-1	3	64	.302	.378	.506	141	26	24-6	.976	23	107	109	S119	19	5.5
1992	Cin N	140	533	76	162	32	6	12	78	63-8	1	58	.304	.377	.454	132	24	15-4	.983	15	102	94	S140	60	2.7
1993	Cin N	100	384	57	121	20	3	8	51	51-6	1	33	.315	.394	.445	124	15	14-1	.980	2	95	97	S110		2.0
1994	Cin N	110	427	78	119	23	5	9	52	64-3	0	58	.279	.369	.419	106	6	26-2	.980	-6	97	100	S130		3.0
1995	†Cin N★	131	496	98	158	29	6	15	66	61-2	5	52	.319	.394	.492	131	24	51-5	.975	4	99	89	S151		6.6
1996	Cin N★	152	517	117	154	32	4	33	89	96-3	7	52	.298	.410	.567	143	36-10	.975	3	90	98	S63,D2	74	2.
1997	Cin N★	73	224	34	71	17	3	4	20	47-6	3	24	.317	.440	.473	137	16	14-3	.980	-1	100	98	S145	7	2.
1998	Cin N	145	538	93	166	34	10	17	72	79-5	2	69	.309	.397	.504	134	29	26-3	.979	-4	89	89	S161		0.
1999	Cin N★	161	583	108	171	30	4	12	75	93-5	2	57	.293	.390	.420	103	6	30-8	.973	-16	91	72	S102/D	23	0.
2000	Cin N★	102	396	71	124	26	5	11	41	48-0	1	31	.313	.389	.487	116	11	14-6	.973	-16	91	72	S102/D	130	-0.
2001	Cin N	45	156	29	40	12	0	2	17	27-2	2	25	.256	.373	.372	89	-1	3-2	.951	-4	98	92	S44		-0.
2002	Cin N	145	507	72	124	37	2	7	47	44-9	3	57	.245	.305	.367	77	-18	13-4	.979	2	105	99	S135	84	-0.
2003	Cin N	70	241	39	68	16	1	2	18	22-0	1	32	.282	.345	.382	94	-2	2-0	.962	-4	103	99	S85		-0.
2004	Cin N★	111	346	55	100	15	3	8	41	39-2	1	39	.289	.352	.419	101	0	2-0	.988	-10	97	65	S85	485	41.
Total	19	2180	7937	1329	2340	441	76	198	960	939-66	55	817	.295	.371	.444	115	193	379-77	.975	13	100	95	S2085,D3,2b3		

LARKIN, ED   Edward Francis B7.1.1885 Wyalusing PA D3.28.1934 Wyalusing PA BR/TR/5-8/? d10.2 Col Lehigh

																									-0.
1909	Phi A	2	6	0	1	0	0	0	1	1	0		.167	.286	.167	42	0	0	.769	-1	111	54	C2		

LARKIN, GENE   Eugene Thomas B10.24.1962 Flushing NY BB/TR/6-3/205(195-212) [MinA84 20/504] d5.21 Col Columbia

																									-0.
1987	†Min A	85	233	23	62	11	2	4	28	25-3	2	31	.266	.340	.382	88	-4	1-4	.989	-2	66	72	D40,1b26		-0.
1988	Min A	149	505	56	135	30	2	8	70	68-8	**15**	55	.267	.368	.382	108	9	3-2	.994	-5	69	98	D86,1b60		-0.
1989	Min A	136	446	61	119	25	1	6	46	54-6	9	57	.267	.353	.368	98	1	5-2	.992	-4	76	90	1b67,D41,O32(1/0/31)		-0.
1990	Min A	119	401	46	108	26	4	5	42	42-2	5	55	.269	.343	.392	99	1	5-3	1.000	-2	87	161	O47R,D43,1b28	16	-0.
1991	†Min A	98	255	34	73	14	1	2	19	30-3	1	21	.286	.361	.373	99	1	2-3	.968	-5	79	37	O47(2/0/48),1b39/23D	15	-0.
1992	Min A	115	337	38	83	18	1	6	42	28-6	1	43	.246	.308	.359	84	-7	7-2	.992	-2	91	124	1b55,O43R,D4		-1.
1993	Min A	56	144	17	34	8	1	1	19	21-3	2	26	.236	.357	.347	92	-1	0-1	1.000	-4	74	65	O28(4/0/25),1b18,3b2,D3	99	-0.
Total	7	758	2321	275	618	131	12	32	266	268-31	38	278	.266	.348	.374	97	0	23-17	.992	-23	78	102	1b293,D221,O197(7/0/193),3b3/2	130	-5

LARKIN, TERRY   Frank S. D9.16.1894 Brooklyn NY BR/TR d5.20 ▲

																									0
1876	NY N	1	4	0	0	0	0	0		0			.000	.000	.000	-99	-1		.500	-0	141	0	/P		-0
1877	Har N	58	228	28	52	6	5	1	18	5		23	.228	.245	.311	83	-4		.885	-1	100		P56,3b2/2		-0
1878	Chi N	58	226	33	65	9	4	0	32	**17**		17	.288	.337	.363	122	6		.858	-4	86	0	P56/OL3		-0
1879	Chi N	60	228	26	50	12	2	0	18	8		24	.219	.246	.289	71	-7		.918	-7	74	47	P58,O3(2/1/0)		-0
1880	Tro N	6	20	1	3	1	0	0	4	1			.150	.261	.200	56	-1		1.000	0	105	684	P5,O2(0/1/1)/S		-0
1884	Ric AA	40	139	17	28	1	0	0		3		3	.201	.265	.266	75	-4		.907	4	109	79	2b40		-0
Total	6	223	845	105	198	29	11	1		69	42	68	.234	.273	.308	88	-11		.884	-8	87	32	P176,2b41,O6(3/2/1),3b3/S		-0

LARKIN, HENRY   Henry E. "Ted" B1.12.1860 Reading PA D1.31.1942 Reading PA BR/TR/5-10/175 d5.1 M1

																									0
1884	Phi AA	85	326	59	90	21	9	3	37	15	6		.276	.324	.423	133	11		.856	-6	47	0	O85(30/55/0),2b2		0
1885	Phi AA	108	453	114	149	**37**	14	8	88	26	6		.329	.373	.525	171	36		.882	9	120	**239**	O108(48/61/0)		3
1886	Phi AA	**139**	565	130	180	**36**	16	2	74	59	7		.319	.390	.450	161	41	32	.866	5	91	44	O139L		0
1887	Phi AA	126	497	105	154	22	12	5	88	48	8		.310	.380	.421	123	16	37	.967	-8	80	87	1b122,2b14		0
1888	Phi AA	135	546	92	147	18	12	7	101	33	13		.269	.326	.403	134	20	20	.973	-5	90	118	1b131/32		1
1889	Phi AA	133	516	105	164	23	12	3	74	83	16	41	.318	.428	.426	145	37	11	.978	-5	90	118	1b131/32		1
1890	Cle P	125	506	93	167	32	15	5	112	65	12	18	.330	.419	.482	153	43	5	.978	-8	64	78	1b125/OCM		

YEAR	TM LG	G	AB	R	H	2B	3B	HR	RBI	BB-IB	HP	SO	AVG	OBP	SLG	AOPS	ABR	SB-CS	FA	FR	RNG	THR	GAMES AT POSITION	DL	BFW
1891	Phi AA	133	526	94	147	27	14	10	93	66	15	56	.279	.376	.441	133	23	2	.974	-7	73	92	1b111,O23(5/0/18)		0.5
1892	Was N	119	464	76	130	13	7	8	96	39	8	21	.280	.346	.390	126	14	21	.969	2	116	115	1b117,O2R		1.4
1893	Was N	81	319	54	101	20	3	4	73	50	8	5	.317	.422	.436	132	18	1	.963	-9	64	80	1b81		0.7
Total	10		1184	4718	925	1429	259	114	53	836	484	101	141	.303	.380	.440	142	259	129	.971	-23	80	96	1b710,O451(308/124/20),2b27/3		15.2

LARKIN, STEPHEN Stephen Karari B7.24.1973 Cincinnati OH BL/TL/6-0/190 [TexA94 10/281] d9.27 b-Barry Col Texas

YEAR	TM LG	G	AB	R	H	2B	3B	HR	RBI	BB-IB	HP	SO	AVG	OBP	SLG	AOPS	ABR	SB-CS	FA	FR	RNG	THR	GAMES AT POSITION	DL	BFW
1998	Cin N	1	3	0	1	0	0	0	0	0-0	0	1	.333	.333	.333	75	0	0-0	1.000	-0	.0	0	/1		0.0

LARMORE, BOB Robert McKahan "Red" B12.6.1896 Anderson IN D1.15.1964 St.Louis MO BR/TR/5-10.5/185 d5.14 Col Missouri

YEAR	TM LG	G	AB	R	H	2B	3B	HR	RBI	BB-IB	HP	SO	AVG	OBP	SLG	AOPS	ABR	SB-CS	FA	FR	RNG	THR	GAMES AT POSITION	DL	BFW
1918	StL N	4	7	0	2	0	0	0	1	0	0	2	.286	.286	.286	77	0	0	.778	-1	85	0	S2		-0.1

LaROCCA, GREG Gregory Mark B11.10.1972 Oswego NY BR/TR/5-11/185* [SDN94 10/262] d9.7 Col Massachusetts

YEAR	TM LG	G	AB	R	H	2B	3B	HR	RBI	BB-IB	HP	SO	AVG	OBP	SLG	AOPS	ABR	SB-CS	FA	FR	RNG	THR	GAMES AT POSITION	DL	BFW
2000	SD N	13	27	1	6	2	0	0	2	1-0	0	4	.222	.250	.296	40	-3	0-0	1.000	-4	54	0	3b8,S4,2b2		-0.6
2002	Cle A	21	52	12	14	3	1	0	4	6-0	2	6	.269	.367	.365	94	0	0-0	.800	-4	62	43	3b15,2b3/D		-0.4
2003	Cle A	5	9	3	3	1	0	0	0	1-0	0	1	.333	.400	.444	123	0	0-0	1.000	1	156	0	3b2		0.1
Total	3		39	88	16	23	6	1	0	6	8-0	2	11	.261	.337	.352	81	-3	0-0	.857	-8	71	31	3b25,2b5,S4/D		-0.9

LaROCHE, ADAM David Adam B11.6.1979 Orange Co. CA BL/TL/6-3/180* [AtlN00 29/880] d4.7 f-Dave Col Seminole St. (OK) JC

YEAR	TM LG	G	AB	R	H	2B	3B	HR	RBI	BB-IB	HP	SO	AVG	OBP	SLG	AOPS	ABR	SB-CS	FA	FR	RNG	THR	GAMES AT POSITION	DL	BFW
2004	†Atl N	110	324	45	90	27	1	13	45	27-1	1	78	.278	.333	.488	108	4	0-0	.994	-6	74	130	1b98	34	-1.0
2005	†Atl N	141	451	53	117	28	0	20	78	39-7	4	87	.259	.320	.455	99	-1	0-2	.994	0	104	105	1b125		-1.3
Total	2		251	775	98	207	55	1	33	123	66-8	5	165	.267	.326	.468	103	3	0-2	.994	-6	92	115	1b223	34	-2.3

LaROQUE, SAM Simeon Henry Jean B2.26.1863 St.Mathias QC, Can. D6.5.1933 Highland Park MI BR/TR/5-11/190 d7.30

YEAR	TM LG	G	AB	R	H	2B	3B	HR	RBI	BB-IB	HP	SO	AVG	OBP	SLG	AOPS	ABR	SB-CS	FA	FR	RNG	THR	GAMES AT POSITION	DL	BFW
1888	Det N	2	9	1	4	0	0	0	2	1	0	1	.444	.500	.444	201	1	0	.789	-1	86	300	2b2		0.1
1890	Pit N	111	434	59	105	20	4	1	40	35	12	29	.242	.316	.313	95	-1	27	.925	-9	102	81	2b78,S31,1b2/OL		-0.5
1891	Pit N	1	4	0	0	0	0	0	0	0	0	0	.000	.000	.000	-99	-1	0	.714	-0	97	0	/3		-0.1
	Lou AA	10	35	6	11	2	1	1	8	5	2	8	.314	.429	.514	172	4	1	.875	-3	71	92	2b10/1		0.0
Total	3		124	482	66	120	22	5	2	50	41	14	39	.249	.326	.328	101	3	28	.916	-14	98	89	2b90,S31,1b3/3OL		-0.5

LaROSE, VIC Victor Raymond B12.23.1944 Los Angeles CA BR/TR/5-11/185 d9.13

YEAR	TM LG	G	AB	R	H	2B	3B	HR	RBI	BB-IB	HP	SO	AVG	OBP	SLG	AOPS	ABR	SB-CS	FA	FR	RNG	THR	GAMES AT POSITION	DL	BFW
1968	Chi N	4	2	0	0	0	0	0	0	0-0	0	1	.000	.333	.000	6	0	0-0	1.000	-0	103	0	2b2,S2		0.0

LaROSS, HARRY Harry Raymond "Spike" B1.2.1888 Easton PA D3.22.1954 Chicago IL BR/TR/5-11.5/170 d6.24

YEAR	TM LG	G	AB	R	H	2B	3B	HR	RBI	BB-IB	HP	SO	AVG	OBP	SLG	AOPS	ABR	SB-CS	FA	FR	RNG	THR	GAMES AT POSITION	DL	BFW
1914	StL N	22	48	7	11	1	0	0	2	0	0	10	.229	.260	.250	50	-3	4	.739	-2	63	143	O20(10/10/0)		-0.7

LARSEN, SWEDE Erling Adeli B11.15.1913 Jersey City NJ BR/TR/5-11/170 d6.17 Col Colgate

YEAR	TM LG	G	AB	R	H	2B	3B	HR	RBI	BB-IB	HP	SO	AVG	OBP	SLG	AOPS	ABR	SB-CS	FA	FR	RNG	THR	GAMES AT POSITION	DL	BFW
1936	Bos N	3	1	0	0	0	0	0	0	0	0	0	.000	.000	.000	-99	-0	0	1.000	-0	0	0	2b2		-0.1

LARSON, BRANDON Brandon John B5.24.1976 San Angelo TX BR/TR/6-0/210* [CinN97 1/14] d5.4 Col Louisiana St.

YEAR	TM LG	G	AB	R	H	2B	3B	HR	RBI	BB-IB	HP	SO	AVG	OBP	SLG	AOPS	ABR	SB-CS	FA	FR	RNG	THR	GAMES AT POSITION	DL	BFW
2001	Cin N	14	33	2	4	2	0	0	1	2-0	0	10	.121	.171	.182	-8	-5	0-0	.939	2	131	125	3b9		-0.3
2002	Cin N	23	51	8	14	2	0	4	13	6-1	1	10	.275	.362	.549	134	2	1-0	1.000	0	100	0	O9L,3b5,1b2		0.2
2003	Cin N	32	89	6	9	1	0	1	5	13-0	0	31	.101	.212	.146	-3	-14	2-2	.943	5	117	168	3b24,O3L	41	-1.0
2004	Cin N	40	118	13	25	6	0	3	14	14-0	2	35	.212	.304	.339	68	-6	1-0	.937	-5	85	67	3b35	43	-1.0
Total	4		109	291	29	52	11	0	8	37	35-1	3	86	.179	.271	.299	50	-23	4-2	.943	2	104	125	3b73,O12L,1b2	178	-2.4

LaRUE, JASON Michael Jason B3.19.1974 Houston TX BR/TR/5-11/200* [CinN95 5/139] d6.15 Col Dallas Baptist

YEAR	TM LG	G	AB	R	H	2B	3B	HR	RBI	BB-IB	HP	SO	AVG	OBP	SLG	AOPS	ABR	SB-CS	FA	FR	RNG	THR	GAMES AT POSITION	DL	BFW
1999	Cin N	36	90	12	19	7	0	3	10	11-1	2	32	.211	.311	.389	73	-4	4-1	.990	3	154	120	C35		0.2
2000	Cin N	31	98	12	23	3	0	5	12	5-2	4	19	.235	.299	.418	76	-4	4-1	.991	6	148	60	C31		0.4
2001	Cin N	121	364	39	86	21	2	12	43	27-4	9	106	.236	.303	.404	77	-13	3-3	.991	13	194	161	C107,3b3,O2L/1		0.6
2002	Cin N	113	353	42	88	17	1	12	52	27-6	13	117	.249	.324	.405	91	-6	1-2	.994	2	171	103	C110		0.2
2003	Cin N	118	379	52	87	23	1	16	50	33-4	20	111	.230	.321	.422	97	-2	3-3	.984	-8	115	70	C114/1OL	7	-0.3
2004	Cin N	114	390	46	98	24	2	14	55	26-5	24	108	.251	.334	.431	98	-1	0-2	.989	-9	150	72	C111/ORD	15	-0.3
2005	Cin N	110	361	38	94	27	0	14	60	41-7	13	101	.260	.355	.452	114	9	0-0	.993	-4	106	111	C109/OR		1.1
Total	7		643	2035	241	495	122	6	76	282	170-29	85	594	.243	.326	.421	93	-21	11-11	.990	3	147	101	C617,O5(3/0/2),3b3,1b2/D	22	1.9

LaRUSSA, TONY Anthony B10.4.1944 Tampa FL BR/TR/6-1/190(175-190) d5.10 M27/C1 [DL 1967 KC A 24]

YEAR	TM LG	G	AB	R	H	2B	3B	HR	RBI	BB-IB	HP	SO	AVG	OBP	SLG	AOPS	ABR	SB-CS	FA	FR	RNG	THR	GAMES AT POSITION	DL	BFW
1963	KC A	34	44	4	11	1	1	0	7	7-0	0	12	.250	.346	.318	85	-1	0-0	.957	-5	65	98	S14,2b3		-0.5
1968	Oak A	5	3	0	1	0	0	0	0	0-0	0	0	.333	.333	.333	107	-1	0-0	—	0			/H		0.0
1969	Oak A	8	8	0	0	0	0	0	0	0-0	0	1	.000	.000	.000	-99	-2	0-0	—	0			/H		-0.2
1970	Oak A	52	106	6	21	4	1	0	6	15-1	1	19	.198	.301	.255	57	-6	0-0	.969	-2	100	115	2b44		-0.4
1971	Oak A	23	8	3	0	0	0	0	0	0-0	1	4	.000	.000	.000	-99	-2	0-0	.833	-0	27	122	2b7,S4,3b2		-0.2
	Atl N	9	7	1	2	0	0	0	1	1-0	0	1	.286	.375	.286	84	0	0-0	.933	1	64	138	2b9		-0.1
1973	Chi N	1	0	1	0	0	0	0	0	0-0	0	0	—	—	—	—	0	0-0	—	0			/R		0.0
Total	6		132	176	15	35	5	2	0	23-1	1	37	.199	.292	.250	53	-11	0-0	.963	-7	92	116	2b63,S18,3b2	24	-1.4

LARY, LYN Lynford Hobart "Broadway" B1.28.1906 Armona CA D1.9.1973 Downey CA BR/TR/6-0/165 d5.11

YEAR	TM LG	G	AB	R	H	2B	3B	HR	RBI	BB-IB	HP	SO	AVG	OBP	SLG	AOPS	ABR	SB-CS	FA	FR	RNG	THR	GAMES AT POSITION	DL	BFW
1929	NY A	80	236	48	73	9	2	5	26	24	3	15	.309	.380	.428	115	6	4-1	.943	2	104	115	3b55,S14,2b6		1.2
1930	NY A	117	464	93	134	20	8	3	52	45	3	40	.289	.357	.386	92	-5	14-2	.940	-4	97	84	S113		0.5
1931	NY A	155	610	100	171	35	9	10	107	88	6	54	.280	.376	.416	115	16	13-10	.946	4	98	97	S155		2.9
1932	NY A	91	280	56	65	14	4	3	39	52	3	28	.232	.358	.343	87	-3	9-3	.941	-1	94	86	S80,1b5,2b2,3b2/OL		0.2
1933	NY A	52	127	25	28	3	3	0	13	28	0	17	.220	.361	.291	79	-3	2-1	.938	1	89	106	3b28,S16,1b3/OL		-0.1
1934	NY A	1	0	0	0	0	0	0	0	0	0	0	—	1.000	—	189	0	0-0	.800	-0	0	288	/1		0.0
	Bos A	129	419	58	101	20	4	2	54	66	0	51	.241	.344	.322	68	-19	12-5	.965	-7	95	80	S129		-1.4
	Year	130	419	58	101	20	4	2	54	67	0	51	.241	.346	.322	68	-18	12-5	.965	-7	95	80	S129/1		-1.4
1935	Was A	39	103	8	20	4	0	0	7	12	0	10	.194	.278	.233	35	-10	3-0	.953	-3	91	71	S30		-1.0
	Year	132	474	86	127	29	7	2	42	76	2	53	.288	.396	.410	104	5	25-4	.962	10	100	100	S93		2.4
1936	StL A	155	619	112	179	30	6	2	52	117	2	54	.289	.404	.367	90	-4	37-9	.956	-2	101	77	S155		1.4
1937	Cle A	156	644	110	187	46	7	8	77	88	3	64	.290	.378	.421	100	9	18-8	.963	8	99	95	S156		0.8
1938	Cle A	141	568	94	152	36	4	3	51	88	1	65	.268	.366	.361	84	-11	23-6	.964	-2	93	91	S141		2.1
1939	Cle A	3	2	0	0	0	0	0	0	0	0	1	.000	.000	.000	-99	-1	0-0	.000	-1	0	0	S2		0.0
	Bro N	29	31	7	5	1	1	0	1	12	1	6	.161	.409	.258	80	0	1	.947	-1	84	130	S12,3b7		-0.1
	StL N	34	75	11	14	3	0	0	9	16	0	15	.187	.330	.227	49	-5	1	.961	-4	90	58	S30,3b3		0.0
	Year	63	106	18	19	4	1	0	10	28	1	21	.179	.356	.236	59	-5	2	.958	-5	89	73	S42,3b10		-0.7
1940	StL A	27	54	3	3	2	0	0	3	4	1	7	.056	.136	.111	-35	-11	0-0	.952	0	101	95	S12/2		-0.7
Total	12		1302	4603	805	1239	247	56	38	526	705	25	470	.269	.369	.372	90	-43	162-49	.956	-0	97	88	S1138,3b95,1b9,2b5,O2L		5.8

LASSETTER, DON Donald O'Neal B3.27.1933 Newnan GA BR/TR/6-3/200 d9.21 Col Georgia

YEAR	TM LG	G	AB	R	H	2B	3B	HR	RBI	BB-IB	HP	SO	AVG	OBP	SLG	AOPS	ABR	SB-CS	FA	FR	RNG	THR	GAMES AT POSITION	DL	BFW
1957	StL N	4	13	2	2	0	0	0	0	1-0	0	3	.154	.214	.308	37	-1	0-0	1.000	-0	101	0	O3L		-0.2

LATHAM, CHRIS Christopher Joseph B5.26.1973 Coeur D'Alene ID BB/TR/6-0/198(185-198) [LAN91 11/299] d4.12

YEAR	TM LG	G	AB	R	H	2B	3B	HR	RBI	BB-IB	HP	SO	AVG	OBP	SLG	AOPS	ABR	SB-CS	FA	FR	RNG	THR	GAMES AT POSITION	DL	BFW
1997	Min A	15	22	4	4	1	0	0	1	0-0	0	8	.182	.182	.227	6	-3	0-0	.917	-1	89	0	O10(0/8/3)		-0.4
1998	Min A	34	94	14	15	1	0	1	5	13-0	0	36	.160	.262	.202	22	-11	4-2	.972	0	110	56	O32(13/15/5)		-1.1
1999	Min A	14	22	1	2	0	0	0	3	0-0	0	13	.091	.083	.091	-51	-5	0-0	1.000	-1	80	0	O14(6/5/4)		-0.6
2001	Tor A	43	73	12	20	3	1	2	10	10-1	1	28	.274	.369	.425	106	1	4-1	1.000	3	122	162	O31(15/2/14)		0.3
2003	NY A	4	2	3	2	0	0	0	0	0-0	0	0	1.000	1.000	1.000	436	1	0-0	1.000	0	193	0	O2(0/1/1)		0.1
Total	5		110	213	34	43	5	1	3	19	23-1	1	85	.202	.280	.277	46	-17	9-3	.980	1	109	78	O89(34/31/27)		-1.7

LATHAM, JUICE George Warren "Jumbo" B9.6.1852 Utica NY D5.26.1914 Utica NY BR/TR/5-8/164 d4.19 M2

YEAR	TM LG	G	AB	R	H	2B	3B	HR	RBI	BB-IB	HP	SO	AVG	OBP	SLG	AOPS	ABR	SB-CS	FA	FR	RNG	THR	GAMES AT POSITION	DL	BFW
1875	Bos NA	16	78	23	21	4	0	0	13	0		2	.269	.269	.321	100	0		.927	0	154	206	1b16		0.1
	NH NA	20	76	6	15	1	0	0	5	0		4	.197	.197	.211	48	-3	6-0	.954	2	219	113	1b14,S4,3b3,M		0.0
	Year	36	154	29	36	5	0	0	18	0		6	.234	.234	.266	78	-3	6-0	.941	2	184	163	1b30,S4,3b3		0.1
1877	Lou N	59	278	42	81	10	6	0	22	5		6	.291	.304	.317	94	-4		.950	2	127	113	1b59		-0.4
1882	Phi AA	74	323	47	92	10	2	0	38	10			.285	.306	.328	107	1		.972	-0	64	89	1b74,M		-0.5
1883	Lou AA	88	368	60	92	7	2	0	0				.250	.274	.302	92	-2		.955	-1	110	132	1b67,2b14,S9		-0.8
1884	Lou AA	77	308	31	52	3	0	0	23	8	3		.169	.197	.198	31	-23		.961	3	121	160	1b76/3		-2.5
Total	4		298	1277	180	317	30	17	0	83	35	3	6	.248	.270	.298	83	-28		.960	3	104	124	1b276,2b14,S9/3		-4.2

YEAR	TM LG	G	AB	R	H	2B	3B	HR	RBI	BB-IB	HP	SO	AVG	OBP	SLG	AOPS	ABR	SB-CS	FA	FR	RNG	THR	GAMES AT POSITION	DL	BFW

LATHAM, ARLIE Walter Arlington "The Freshest Man On Earth" B3.15.1860 W.Lebanon NH D11.29.1952 Garden City NY BR/TR/5-8/150 d7.5 M1/C2/U2 OF(2/0/11)   -0.7

											8	.127	.138	.190	10	-7		.887	-0	104	32	S12,O10R/C		-0.7
1880	Buf N	22	79	9	10	3	1	0	3	1			.236	.269	.300	79	-10		.866	21	125	162	3b98/C		1.1
1883	StL AA	98	406	86	96	12	7	0		18	6		.274	.311	.367	116	7		.864	37	148	138	3b110/C		4.1
1884	StL AA	110	474	115	130	17	12	1		18	5		.206	.242	.256	55	-25		.875	0	104	118	3b109,C2		-2.1
1885	†StL AA	110	485	84	100	15	3	1	35	18	5		.301	.368	.374	127	18	60	.827	-0	106	132	3b133/2		1.8
1886	†StL AA	134	578	152	174	23	8	1	47	55	6		.301	.368	.374	127	18	60	.877	0	106	92	3b132,2b5,C2		0.4
1887	†StL AA	136	627	163	198	35	10	2	83	45		5	.316	.366	.413	106	2	129	.882	3	101	123	3b133/S		0.2
1888	†StL AA	133	570	119	151	19	5	2	31	43	8		.265	.325	.326	98	-2	109	.883	0	100	117	3b116,2b3		-1.0
1889	StL AA	118	512	110	126	13	3	4	49	42	11	30	.246	.317	.307	69	-23	69	.880	1	102	105	3b52		-0.8
1890	Chi P	52	214	47	49	7	2	1	20	22	3	22	.229	.310	.294	59	-13	20	.853	3	115	158	3b41/OR		0.2
	Cin N	41	164	35	41	6	2	0	15	23	1	18	.250	.346	.311	92	-1	20	.879	21	122	125	3b135/C		3.4
1891	Cin N	135	533	119	145	20	10	7	53	74	11	35	.272	.372	.386	120	16	87	.883	-6	103	122	3b142,2b9/OL		-1.5
1892	Cin N	152	622	111	148	20	4	0	44	60	5	55	.238	.310	.283	81	-13	66	.892	-13	94	99	3b127		-1.5
1893	Cin N	127	531	101	150	18	6	2	49	62	10	24	.282	.368	.350	89	-7	57	.861	-12	97	93	3b129,2b2		-1.4
1894	Cin N	131	534	132	167	23	6	4	60	61	9	24	.313	.392	.401	88	-9	62	.861	-13	92	85	3b108,1b3/2		-1.4
1895	Cin N	112	460	93	143	14	6	2	69	42	5	25	.311	.375	.380	91	-6	48	.744	-2	80	137	3b8,M		-0.5
1896	StL N	8	35	3	7	0	0	0	5	4	0	3	.200	.282	.200	29	-3	2	1.000	0	0	0	/OL2		-0.1
1899	Was N	6	6	1	1	0	0	0	0	1	0	1	.167	.286	.167	26	-1	0	1.000	-0	217	0	2b2		0.0
1909	NY N	4	2	1	0	0	0	0	0	0	0		.000	.000	.000	-99	-1		1.000	-0	0	0	/2		0.2
Total	17	1629	6832	1481	1836	245	85	27	563	589	85	240	.269	.334	.341	91	-77	742	.870	48	108	118	3b1573,2b24,O13R,S13,C8,1b3	

LATHERS, CHICK Charles Ten Eyck B10.22.1888 Detroit MI D7.26.1971 Petoskey MI BL/TR/6-0/180 d5.1 Col Michigan   0.0

1910	Det A	41	82	4	19	2	0	0	3	8	0		.232	.300	.256	70	-3	0	.926	2	128	162	3b14,2b7,S4		-0.4
1911	Det A	29	45	5	10	1	0	0	4	5	1		.222	.314	.244	54	-3	0	.867	-2	115	101	2b9,3b8,S4,1b3		-0.4
Total	2	70	127	9	29	3	0	0	7	13	1		.228	.305	.252	64	-6	0	.933	0	131	111	3b22,2b16,S8,1b3	

LATIMER, TACKS Clifford Wesley B11.30.1877 Loveland OH D4.24.1936 Loveland OH BR/TR/6-0/160 d10.1   -0.1

1898	NY N	5	17	1	5	1	0	0	1	0	0		.294	.294	.353	88	0	0	.889	-1	89	168	C4,O2R		0.1
1899	Lou N	9	29	3	8	1	0	0	4	2	0		.276	.323	.310	74	-1	1	.980	2	113	84	C8/1		0.0
1900	Pit N	4	12	1	4	0	0	0	2	0	0		.333	.333	.417	106	0	0	1.000	-0	133	0	/C		0.0
1901	Bal A	1	4	0	1	0	0	0	0	0	0		.042	.042	.042	-74	-5	0	.947	-1	81	136	C8		-0.6
1902	Bro N	8	24	0	1	0	0	0	0	2	0		.221	.239	.256	41	-6	1	.949	-0	104	110	C25,O2R/1		-0.6
Total	5	27	86	5	19	3	0	0	7	2	0		.221	.239	.256	41	-6	1	.949	-0	104	110	C25,O2R/1	

LAU, CHARLIE Charles Richard B4.12.1933 Romulus MI D3.18.1984 Key Colony Beach FL BL/TR/6-0/190(175-190) d9.12 C15   -0.1

1956	Det A	3	9	1	2	0	0	0	0-0	0	1	.222	.222	.222	18	-1	0-0	1.000	0	0	0	C3		-0.3
1958	Det A	30	68	8	10	1	2	0	6	12-2	2	15	.147	.293	.221	41	-5	0-0	.985	-1	98	105	C27		0.0
1959	Det A	2	6	0	1	0	0	0	0	0-0	0	1	.167	.167	.167	-8	-1	0-0	1.000	0	0	0	C2		0.1
1960	Mil N	21	53	4	10	2	0	0	2	6-1	0	11	.189	.317	.226	65	-3	1-1	.968	-3	100	89	C25		-0.5
1961	Mil N	28	82	3	17	5	0	0	6	14-3	1	11	.207	.323	.268	65	-3	1-1	.990	2	83	37	C17		-0.3
	Bal A	17	47	5	9	0	0	1	4	1-1	0	3	.170	.188	.234	12	-6	0-0	.996	-4	51	58	C56		0.1
1962	Bal A	81	197	21	58	11	2	6	37	7-1	1	11	.294	.319	.462	115	7	0-0	.964	1	115	85	C8		-0.4
1963	Bal A	29	48	4	9	2	0	0	6	1-0	0	5	.188	.204	.229	22	-5	0-0	.982	-11	59	101	C50		-0.8
	KC A	62	187	15	55	11	0	3	26	14-3	0	17	.294	.340	.401	102	1	0-0	.979	-10	66	99	C58		-1.2
	Year	91	235	19	64	13	0	3	32	15-3	0	22	.272	.313	.366	88	-4	0-0	.990	-7	48	67	C35		0.2
1964	KC A	43	118	11	32	7	1	2	9	10-1	1	18	.271	.326	.398	98	0	0-0	.992	-1	77	54	C47		-0.4
	Bal A	62	158	16	41	15	1	1	14	17-5	1	45	.259	.333	.386	100	1	0-0	.991	-8	65	60	C82		0.2
	Year	105	276	27	73	22	2	3	23	27-6	1	18	.295	.371	.409	120	4	0-0	.989	-21	81	76	C321		-2.3
1965	Bal A	68	132	15	39	5	2	2	18	17-5	0		.500	.588	.833	120	4	0-0	—	0			/H	113	0.4
1966	Bal A	18	12	1	6	2	0	0	3	2-0	0		.125	.273	.250	65	0	0-0	—	0			/H		0.0
1967	Bal A	11	8	0	1	1	0	0	5	4-1	0		.200	.265	.289	59	-2	0-0	—	0			/H	113	-0.3
	Atl N	52	45	3	9	1	0	0	140	109-24	5	150	.255	.318	.365	89	-14	3-1	.988	-21	81	76	C321		-2.3
Total	11	527	1170	105	298	63	9	16	140	109-24	5	150	.255	.318	.365	89	-14	3-1	.988	-21	81	76	C321	

LAUDER, BILLY William B2.23.1874 New York NY D5.20.1933 Norwalk CT BR/TR/5-10/160 d6.25 C1 Col Brown   -2.1

1898	Phi N	97	361	42	95	14	7	2	67	19		0	.263	.300	.357	92	-9	6	.866	-19	82	42	3b97		-2.7
1899	Phi N	151	583	74	156	17	6	3	90	34		2	.268	.310	.333	79	-18	15	.893	-14	91	104	3b151		-0.1
1901	Phi A	2	8	1	1	0	0	0	0	0	0		.125	.125	.125	-29	-1	0	.833	0	111	0	3b2		-1.8
1902	NY N	127	490	42	115	20	1	4	43	10		0	.235	.250	.280	64	-22	19	.908	2	97	106	3b123,O4(2/0/2)		-1.8
1903	NY N	108	395	52	111	13	0	0	53	14		1	.281	.307	.314	74	-14	19	.908	-8	90	99	3b108		-1.5
Total	5	485	1837	211	478	64	14	5	253	77		3	.260	.291	.318	76	-60	59	.894	-38	91	90	3b481,O4(2/0/2)	

LAUDNER, TIM Timothy Jon B6.7.1958 Mason City IA BR/TR/6-3/212(195-218) [MinA79 3/63] d8.28 Col Missouri [DL 1990 Min A 17]   -0.2

1981	Min A	14	43	4	7	0	0	0	3-1	0	1	17	.163	.234	.349	62	-2	0-0	1.000	-0	108	51	C12,D2		-1.1
1982	Min A	93	306	37	78	19	1	7	33	34-2	0	74	.255	.328	.392	94	-2	0-2	.976	-13	74	107	C93		-0.9
1983	Min A	62	168	20	31	9	0	6	18	15-0	0	49	.185	.250	.345	60	-10	0-0	.978	9	137	126	C81,D2		0.2
1984	Min A	87	262	31	54	16	1	10	35	18-0	1	78	.206	.258	.389	73	-10	0-0	.969	-6	110	94	C68/1		-1.8
1985	Min A	72	164	16	39	5	0	7	19	12-0	1	45	.238	.292	.396	82	-5	0-1	.984	-13	115	107	C68		-1.5
1986	Min A	76	193	21	47	10	0	10	29	24-0	3	56	.244	.333	.451	109	3	1-0	.987	-3	92	79	C101,1b7,D2		-0.1
1987	†Min A	113	288	30	55	7	1	16	43	23-0	1	80	.191	.252	.389	64	-16	1-0	.992	5	88	84	C109,1b3,D4		-0.9
1988	Min A★	117	375	38	94	18	1	13	54	36-0	1	65	.251	.316	.408	99	-1	0-0	.991	-2	86	111	C68,D19,1b11		-0.0
1989	Min A	100	239	24	53	11	1	6	27	25-0	0	65	.222	.293	.351	77	-8	1-0	.984	-24	96	95	C657,D33,1b22	17	-4.0
Total	9	734	2038	221	458	97	5	77	263	190-3	8	553	.225	.292	.391	83	-51	3-3	.984	-24	96	95	C657,D33,1b22	

LAUER, CHUCK John Charles B4.5.1865 Pittsburgh PA D5.14.1915 Buffalo NY TR d7.17 ▲   -0.0

													.114	.114	.114	-26	-6		.938	-1	60	0	O10(0/2/8),P3/1		-0.0
1884	Pit AA	13	44	5	5	0	0	0		0	0	5	.188	.188	.188	5	-2	0	.815	0			C3/OL		-0.0
1889	Pit N	4	16	2	4	0	0	0	1	0	0		.250	.250	.375	78	0	0	.833	-1	103	100	C2		0.0
1890	Chi N	2	8	1	2	1	0	0	2	0	0		.250	.250	.375	78	0	0	.944	-1	55	0	O11(1/2/8),C5,P3/1		-0.0
Total	3	19	68	8	10	1	0	0	3	0	0	5	.147	.147	.162	-5	-8	0						

LAUGHLIN, BEN Benjamin d4.28   -0.0

| | | | | | | | | | | | | 1 | .235 | .235 | .235 | 44 | -3 | 0-0 | .698 | -3 | 105 | 108 | 2b12 | | |
| 1873 | Res NA | 12 | 51 | 3 | 12 | 0 | 0 | 0 | 5 | 0 | | | .235 | .235 | .235 | 44 | -3 | 0-0 | .698 | -3 | 105 | 108 | 2b12 | |

LAUTERBORN, BILL William Bernard B6.9.1879 Hornell NY D4.19.1965 Andover NY BR/TR/5-6/140 d9.20 Col Fordham   -0.4

1904	Bos N	20	69	7	19	2	0	0	1	9		2	.275	.286	.304	85	-1	1	.943	-2	99	29	2b20		-0.5
1905	Bos N	67	200	11	37	1	1	0	9	12		2	.185	.238	.200	32	-17	1	.843	-10	91	0	3b29,2b23,S3,O2C		-3.1
Total	2	87	269	18	56	3	1	0	10	21		4	.208	.250	.227	45	-18	2	.929	-11	101	3	2b43,3b29,S3,O2C	

LAVAGETTO, COOKIE Harry Arthur B12.1.1912 Oakland CA D8.10.1990 Orinda CA BR/TR/6-0/170 d4.17 Mil 1942-45 M5/C12   -2.2

1934	Pit N	87	304	41	67	16	3	6	46	32	0	39	.220	.295	.322	64	-16	0	.961	-12	89	83	2b83		-1.7
1935	Pit N	78	231	27	67	9	4	0	19	18	0	15	.290	.341	.364	87	-4	1	.951	-9	92	49	2b42,3b15		-0.0
1936	Pit N	60	197	21	48	15	2	2	26	15	1	13	.244	.300	.371	78	-6	0	.951	-4	94	123	2b37,3b13/S		1.1
1937	Bro N	149	503	64	142	26	6	8	70	74	2	41	.282	.375	.406	110	10	13	.929	-8	91	114	3b132,2b4		1.1
1938	Bro N☆	137	487	68	133	34	6	6	99	68	2	31	.273	.364	.405	109	8	15	.948	-5	96	113	3b149		1.5
1939	Bro N☆	153	587	93	176	28	5	10	87	78	5	30	.300	.387	.416	112	13	14	.932	-18	84	73	3b116		-0.8
1940	Bro N★	118	448	56	115	21	3	4	43	70		32	.257	.361	.344	90	-3	4	.938	-18	87	89	3b120		-0.5
1941	†Bro N★	132	441	75	122	24	7	1	78	80		21	.277	.388	.370	109	9	7	.927	-4	91	118	3b67		-0.0
1946	Bro N	88	242	36	57	9	1	3	33	38		17	.236	.339	.318	86	-3	1	.961	1	100	116	3b18,1b3		-0.8
1947	†Bro N	41	69	6	13	2	0	3	11	12	12		.244	.269	.360	98	8	63	.936	-79	91	0	3b675,2b266,1b3/S		-0.3
Total	10	1043	3509	487	945	183	39	40	486	485	12	244	.269	.360	.377	98	8	63	.936	-79	91	0	3b675,2b266,1b3/S	

LaVALLIERE, MIKE Michael Eugene B8.18.1960 Charlotte NC BL/TR/5-9/190(180-210) d9.9 Col Massachusetts-Lowell   -0.0

1984	Phi N	6	17	0	0	0	0	0	2-0	0	5	.000	.222	.000	-32	-1	0-0	1.000	1	0	90	C6		-0.0
1985	StL N	12	34	2	5	1	0	0	7-0	0	1	.147	.273	.176	34	-3	0-0	1.000	-0	159	54	C12		-0.0
1986	StL N	110	303	18	71	10	2	1	30	36-5	1	37	.234	.318	.310	74	-10	0-1	.988	8	167	84	C108		2.2
1987	Pit N	121	340	33	102	19	0	1	36	43-9	1	32	.300	.377	.365	97	1	0-0	.992	18	136	148	C112		

YEAR	TM LG	G	AB	R	H	2B	3B	HR	RBI	BB-IB	HP	SO	AVG	OBP	SLG	AOPS	ABR	SB-CS	FA	FR	RNG	THR	GAMES AT POSITION	DL	BFW
1988	Pit N	120	352	24	92	18	0	2	47	50-10	2	34	.261	.353	.330	99	2	3-2	.987	7	111	123	C114		1.7
1989	Pit N	68	190	15	60	10	0	2	23	29-7	0	24	.316	.406	.400	136	11	3-2	.991	-10	69	66	C65		0.3
1990	†Pit N	96	279	27	72	15	0	3	31	44-8	2	20	.258	.362	.344	99	2	0-3	.991	5	114	113	C95	78	0.3
1991	†Pit N	108	336	25	97	11	3	3	41	33-4	2	27	.289	.351	.360	103	2	2-1	.990	5	114	113	C105		1.1
1992	†Pit N	95	293	22	75	13	1	2	29	44-14	1	21	.256	.350	.328	95	0	0-3	.998	-3	91	95	C105		0.5
1993	Pit N	1	5	0	1	0	0	0	0	0-0	0	0	.200	.200	.200	7	-1	0-0	.994	-1	98	133	C92/3		0.3
	†Chi A	37	97	6	25	2	0	0	8	4-0	0	14	.258	.282	.278	54	-7	0-1	1.000	1	77	0	/C		0.0
1994	Chi A	59	139	6	39	4	0	1	24	20-0	1	15	.281	.368	.331	85	-2	0-2	1.000	5	250	213	C37		0.0
1995	Chi A	46	98	7	24	6	0	1	19	9-0	0	15	.245	.303	.337	71	-4	0-0	.991	3	77	116	C57	34	0.3
Total 12		879	2473	185	663	109	5	18	294	321-57	10	244	.268	.351	.338	93	-10	5-15	.992	39	119	117	C850/3	112	6.6

LAVAN, DOC John Leonard (b John Leonard Laven) B10.28.1890 Grand Rapids MI D5.29.1952 Detroit MI BR/TR/5-8.5/151 d6.22 Col Michigan

YEAR	TM LG	G	AB	R	H	2B	3B	HR	RBI	BB-IB	HP	SO	AVG	OBP	SLG	AOPS	ABR	SB-CS	FA	FR	RNG	THR	GAMES AT POSITION	DL	BFW
1913	StL A	46	149	8	21	4	0	0	4	10	3	46	.141	.210	.168	11	-17	3	.899	-5	101	132	S46		-2.1
	Phi A	5	14	1	1	0	0	0	0	0			.071	.071	.214	-17	-2		1.000	0	107	0	S5		-0.2
	Year	51	163	9	22	4	0	0	5	10	3	46	.135	.199	.172	9	-19	3	.906	-5	101	122	S51		-2.3
1914	StL A	75	239	21	63	7	4	1	21	17	2	39	.264	.318	.339	101	-1	6-12	.916	-14	89	60	S74		-1.4
1915	StL A	157	514	44	112	17	7	1	48	42	3	83	.218	.281	.284	72	-15	13-19	.913	9	104	139	S157		-0.4
1916	StL A	110	343	32	81	13	1	0	19	32	2	38	.236	.305	.280	80	-8	7	.950	26	121	140	S106		2.7
1917	StL A	118	355	19	85	8	5	0	30	19	3	34	.239	.284	.290	78	-11	5	.923	13	107	135	S110,2b7		1.0
1918	Was A	117	464	44	129	17	2	0	45	14	2	21	.278	.302	.323	90	-8	12	.917	-18	91	96	S117/OC		-2.0
1919	StL N	100	356	25	86	12	2	1	25	11	0	30	.242	.264	.295	72	-13	4	.929	9	105	110	S99		0.3
1920	StL N	142	516	52	149	21	10	1	63	19	3	38	.289	.318	.374	102	-1	11-14	.942	10	103	108	S138		1.8
1921	StL N	150	560	58	145	23	11	2	82	23	2	30	.259	.291	.350	70	-26	7-7	.950	21	104	110	S150		1.0
1922	StL N	89	264	24	60	8	1	0	27	13	1	7	.227	.271	.265	41	-24	3-1	.937	5	102	92	S82,3b5		-1.0
1923	StL N	50	111	10	22	6	0	1	12	9	1	7	.198	.264	.279	44	-9	0-3	.924	-2	99	119	S40,3b4,1b3/2		-0.8
1924	StL N	4	6	0	0	0	0	0	0	0		0	.000	.000	.000	-99	-2	0-0	1.000	1	124	0	2b2,S2		-0.1
Total 12		1163	3891	338	954	134	45	7	377	209	24	376	.245	.288	.308	75	-141	71-56	.930	54	103	114	S1126,2b10,3b9,1b3/OC		-1.2

LAVIGNE, ART Arthur David B1.26.1885 Worcester MA D7.18.1950 Worcester MA BR/TR/5-10/162 d4.24

YEAR	TM LG	G	AB	R	H	2B	3B	HR	RBI	BB-IB	HP	SO	AVG	OBP	SLG	AOPS	ABR	SB-CS	FA	FR	RNG	THR	GAMES AT POSITION	DL	BFW
1914	Buf F	51	90	10	14	2	0	0	4		0	25	.156	.216	.178	8	-13	0	.967	4	125	112	C34,1b3		-0.7

LAVIN, JOHNNY John B Troy NY 5-11/175 d9.10

YEAR	TM LG	G	AB	R	H	2B	3B	HR	RBI	BB-IB	HP	SO	AVG	OBP	SLG	AOPS	ABR	SB-CS	FA	FR	RNG	THR	GAMES AT POSITION	DL	BFW
1884	StL AA	16	52	9	11	2	0	0		3		1	.212	.268	.250	68	-2		.750	-2	41	0	O16(0/15/1)		-0.4

LAW, RUDY Rudy Karl B10.7.1956 Waco TX BL/TL/6-1/165(165-176) d9.12

YEAR	TM LG	G	AB	R	H	2B	3B	HR	RBI	BB-IB	HP	SO	AVG	OBP	SLG	AOPS	ABR	SB-CS	FA	FR	RNG	THR	GAMES AT POSITION	DL	BFW
1978	LA N	11	12	2	3	0	0	0	1	1-0	0	1	.250	.308	.250	57	-1	3-1	1.000	-1	49	0	O6(3/3/0)		-0.1
1980	LA N	128	388	55	101	5	4	1	23	23-1	3	27	.260	.306	.302	72	-15	40-13	.988	-1	98	97	O106(5/102/0)		-1.4
1982	Chi A	121	336	55	107	15	8	3	32	23-0	0	41	.318	.361	.438	118	8	36-10	.973	-2	102	38	O94(4/90/0),D3		0.9
1983	†Chi A	141	501	95	142	20	7	3	34	42-2	2	36	.283	.340	.369	92	-5	77-12	.994	-5	94	69	O132C,D3		0.1
1984	Chi A	136	487	68	122	14	7	6	37	39-6	3	42	.251	.309	.345	77	-16	29-17	.985	-5	97	62	O130(10/122/0)		-2.2
1985	Chi A	125	390	62	101	21	6	4	36	27-0	3	40	.259	.311	.374	83	-9	29-6	.987	5	108	116	O120(104/32/0),D3	15	-0.4
1986	KC A	87	307	42	80	26	5	4	36	29-0	2	22	.261	.327	.388	92	-3	14-6	.987	-4	94	40	O77(54/3/36),D2	56	-0.9
Total 7		749	2421	379	656	101	37	18	199	184-9	13	210	.271	.325	.366	88	-41	228-65	.986	-14	98	72	O665(180/484/36),D11	71	-4.0

LAW, VANCE Vance Aaron B10.1.1956 Boise ID BR/TR/6-2/190* [PitN78 39/758] d6.1 f-Vern Col Brigham Young OF(6/7/2)

YEAR	TM LG	G	AB	R	H	2B	3B	HR	RBI	BB-IB	HP	SO	AVG	OBP	SLG	AOPS	ABR	SB-CS	FA	FR	RNG	THR	GAMES AT POSITION	DL	BFW
1980	Pit N	25	74	11	17	2	2	0	3	3-0	0	7	.230	.260	.311	57	-5	2-0	.964	-2	93	79	2b11,S8/3		
1981	Pit N	30	67	1	9	0	1	0	3	2-0	1	15	.134	.157	.164	-8	-10	1-1	1.000	1	99	99	2b19,S7,3b2		-0.5
1982	Chi A	114	359	40	101	20	1	5	54	26-1	1	46	.281	.327	.384	95	-2	4-2	.953	3	102	96	S85,3b39,2b10/OL		-1.0
1983	†Chi A	145	408	55	99	21	5	4	51	51-1	0	56	.243	.325	.348	83	-9	3-1	.966	9	104	106	3b139,2b3,S2/OCD		0.9
1984	Chi A	151	481	60	121	18	2	17	59	41-2	1	75	.252	.309	.403	91	-6	4-1	.955	-16	87	112	3b137,2b22,O5C,S4		-0.1
1985	Mon N	147	519	75	138	30	6	10	52	86-0	2	96	.266	.369	.405	124	20	6-5	.985	4	100	111	2b126,1b20,3b11/OR		-2.3
1986	Mon N	112	360	37	81	17	2	5	44	37-1	1	66	.225	.298	.325	72	-14	3-5	.993	10	105	97	2b94,1b20,3b13,P3/OR		3.1
1987	Mon N	133	436	52	119	27	1	12	56	51-5	0	62	.273	.347	.422	99	1	8-5	.980	-12	96	83	2b106,3b22,1b17,P3		-0.1
1988	Chi N★	151	556	73	163	29	2	11	88	55-4	3	79	.293	.358	.412	116	13	14-5	.953	-10	92	83	3b150/OL		-0.7
1989	†Chi N	130	408	38	96	22	3	7	42	38-0	0	73	.235	.296	.355	81	-10	2-2	.949	-16	82	74	3b119/OL		0.2
1991	Oak A	74	134	11	28	7	1	0	18	18-0	0	27	.209	.303	.276	65	-6	0-0	.951	-7	78	82	3b67,S3,O3L/1P		-2.8
Total 11		1212	3802	453	972	193	26	71	442	408-14	9	602	.256	.326	.376	93	-28	34-26	.951	-7	78	82	3b700,2b391,S109,1b58,O14C,P7/D	15	-4.6

LAWING, GARLAND Garland Frederick "Knobby" B8.29.1919 Gastonia NC D9.27.1996 Murrells Inlet SC BR/TR/6-1/180 d5.29

YEAR	TM LG	G	AB	R	H	2B	3B	HR	RBI	BB-IB	HP	SO	AVG	OBP	SLG	AOPS	ABR	SB-CS	FA	FR	RNG	THR	GAMES AT POSITION	DL	BFW
1946	Cin N	2	3	0	0	0	0	0	0		0	2	.000	.000	.000	-99	-1	0	—	-0	0	0	/OC		-0.1
	NY N	8	12	2	2	0	0	0	0		0	3	.167	.167	.167	-5	-2	0	1.000	-0	109	0	O4(3/0/1)		-0.2
	Year	10	15	2	2	0	0	0	0		0	5	.133	.133	.133	-24	-3	0	1.000	-0	105	0	O5(3/1/1)		-0.3

LAWLESS, TOM Thomas James B12.19.1956 Erie PA BR/TR/5-11/170* [CinN78 17/433] d7.15 Col Behrend

YEAR	TM LG	G	AB	R	H	2B	3B	HR	RBI	BB-IB	HP	SO	AVG	OBP	SLG	AOPS	ABR	SB-CS	FA	FR	RNG	THR	GAMES AT POSITION	DL	BFW
1982	Cin N	49	165	19	35	6	0	2	4	9-0	1	30	.212	.253	.248	41	-13	16-5	.978	6	104	134	2b47		
1984	Cin N	43	80	10	20	2	0	1	8	8-1	0	12	.250	.318	.313	74	-3	6-3	1.000	-5	75	49	2b23,3b6		-0.3
	Mon N	11	17	1	3	1	0	0	2	0-0	0	4	.176	.176	.235	15	-2	1-0	1.000	-2	80	69	2b9		-0.7
	Year	54	97	11	23	3	0	1	10	8-1	0	16	.237	.295	.299	65	-4	7-3	1.000	-7	76	54	2b32,3b6		-0.3
1985	†StL N	47	58	8	12	3	1	0	5	5-0	0	8	.207	.270	.293	58	-3	2-1	.971	1	137	145	3b13,2b11		-1.0
1986	StL N	46	39	5	11	1	0	0	2	3-0	0	8	.282	.310	.308	73	-1	8-1	.875	-1	86	159	3b12,2b7/OL		-0.2
1987	†StL N	19	25	5	2	1	0	0	3	0-0	0	6	.080	.179	.120	-19	-4	2-0	1.000	0	142	132	2b7,3b3/OR		-0.1
1988	StL N	54	65	9	10	2	1	0	3	7-0	1	9	.154	.236	.262	42	-5	6-0	1.000	1	81	47	3b24,O6(4/0/2),2b5/1	15	-0.4
1989	Tor A	59	70	20	16	1	0	0	3	7-0	1	12	.229	.295	.243	55	-4	12-1	1.000	-1	95	0	O16(7/0/9),3b12,D12,2b7/C		-0.5
1990	Tor A	15	12	1	1	0	0	0	0	0-0	0	3	.083	.083	.083	-52	-2	0-2	.800	1	88	0	3b4,O2L/2D		-0.4
Total 8		343	531	78	110	17	2	2	24	41-1	3	85	.207	.268	.258	46	-37	53-13	.988	-2	98	108	2b117,3b74,O26(14/0/12),D17/C1	15	-3.1

LAWLOR, MIKE Michael H. B3.11.1854 Troy NY D8.3.1918 Troy NY TR/6-0/180 d5.27

YEAR	TM LG	G	AB	R	H	2B	3B	HR	RBI	BB-IB	HP	SO	AVG	OBP	SLG	AOPS	ABR	SB-CS	FA	FR	RNG	THR	GAMES AT POSITION	DL	BFW
1880	Tro N	4	9	1	1	0	0	0		1			.111	.200	.111	8	-1		.867	-0			C4		-0.1
1884	Was U	2	7	0	0	0	0	0		0			.000	.000	.000	-99	-2		1.000	1			C2		-0.1
Total 2		6	16	1	1	0	0	0		1			.063	.118	.063	-39	-3		.920	1			C6		-0.2

LAWRENCE, JIM James Ross B2.12.1939 Hamilton ON, Can. BL/TR/6-1/185 d5.30

YEAR	TM LG	G	AB	R	H	2B	3B	HR	RBI	BB-IB	HP	SO	AVG	OBP	SLG	AOPS	ABR	SB-CS	FA	FR	RNG	THR	GAMES AT POSITION	DL	BFW
1963	Cle A	2	0	0	0	0	0	0									0	0-0	.750	-1	4	0	C2		-0.1

LAWRENCE, JOE Joseph Dudley B2.13.1977 Lake Charles LA BR/TR/6-2/190 [TorA96 1/16] d4.8

YEAR	TM LG	G	AB	R	H	2B	3B	HR	RBI	BB-IB	HP	SO	AVG	OBP	SLG	AOPS	ABR	SB-CS	FA	FR	RNG	THR	GAMES AT POSITION	DL	BFW
2002	Tor A	55	150	16	27	4	0	2	15	16-0	2	38	.180	.262	.247	37	-14	2-1	.967	-7	97	64	2b49/D		-1.8

LAWRENCE, BILL William Henry B3.11.1906 San Mateo CA D6.15.1997 Redwood City CA BR/TR/6-4/194 d4.13 Col Santa Clara

YEAR	TM LG	G	AB	R	H	2B	3B	HR	RBI	BB-IB	HP	SO	AVG	OBP	SLG	AOPS	ABR	SB-CS	FA	FR	RNG	THR	GAMES AT POSITION	DL	BFW
1932	Det A	25	46	10	10	1	0	0	3	5	0	5	.217	.294	.239	38	-4	0-2	1.000	3	124	189	O15(0/8/7)		-0.3

LAWRY, OTIS Otis Carroll "Rabbit" B11.1.1893 Fairfield ME D10.23.1965 China ME BL/TR/5-8/133 d6.28 Mil 1918 Col Maine

YEAR	TM LG	G	AB	R	H	2B	3B	HR	RBI	BB-IB	HP	SO	AVG	OBP	SLG	AOPS	ABR	SB-CS	FA	FR	RNG	THR	GAMES AT POSITION	DL	BFW
1916	Phi A	41	123	10	25	0	0	0	9		1	21	.203	.263	.203	42	-9	4	.905	-4	101	67	2b29,O5(3/2/0)		-1.4
1917	Phi A	30	55	7	9	1	0	0	1	2	0	9	.164	.193	.182	15	-6	1	.921	-2	97	36	2b17/OL		-0.9
Total 2		71	178	17	34	1	0	0	5	11			.191	.242	.197	34	-15	5	.911	-6	100	57	2b46,O6(4/2/0)		-2.3

LAWTON, MARCUS Marcus Dwayne B8.18.1965 Gulfport MS BB/TR/6-1/160 [NYN83 6/136] d8.11 b-Matt

YEAR	TM LG	G	AB	R	H	2B	3B	HR	RBI	BB-IB	HP	SO	AVG	OBP	SLG	AOPS	ABR	SB-CS	FA	FR	RNG	THR	GAMES AT POSITION	DL	BFW
1989	NY A	10	14	1	3	0	0	0	0	0	0	2	.214	.214	.214	21	-2	1-0	.818	-0	116	0	O8(7/0/1)/D		-0.2

LAWTON, MATT Matthew B11.30.1971 Gulfport MS BL/TR/5-10/186(186-200) [MinA91 13/336] d9.5 b-Marcus Col Mississippi Gulf Coast CC

YEAR	TM LG	G	AB	R	H	2B	3B	HR	RBI	BB-IB	HP	SO	AVG	OBP	SLG	AOPS	ABR	SB-CS	FA	FR	RNG	THR	GAMES AT POSITION	DL	BFW
1995	Min A	21	60	11	19	4	1	1	12	7-0	3	11	.317	.414	.467	128	3	1-1	.972	-1	90	112	O19(11/8/1)/D		0.2
1996	Min A	79	252	34	65	7	1	6	42	28-1	4	28	.258	.339	.365	77	-9	4-4	.985	9	133	85	O75(1/18/60)/D		-0.2
1997	Min A	142	460	74	114	29	3	14	60	76-3	10	81	.248	.366	.415	102	4	7-4	.976	1	101	109	O138(58/24/66)		0.0
1998	Min A	152	557	91	155	36	6	21	77	86-6	15	64	.278	.387	.478	121	20	16-8	.990	14	119	112	O151(12/47/100)		-0.2
1999	Min A	118	406	58	105	18	0	7	54	57-7	6	42	.259	.353	.355	79	-12	26-4	.982	-3	102	41	O109(10/6/103),D6	39	-1.4
2000	Min A★	156	561	84	171	44	2	13	88	91-8	7	63	.305	.405	.460	112	15	23-7	.983	-1	106	33	O143(67/3/83),D9		0.7
2001	Min A	103	376	71	110	25	0	10	51	63-6	5	46	.293	.396	.439	114	11	19-6	.980	-1	106	33	O94R,D7		0.7
	NY N	48	183	24	45	11	3	5	30	51-2	3	34	.246	.342	.399	94	-3	8-9	.975	5	114	97	O48R		-0.2
2002	Cle A	114	416	71	98	19	2	15	57	59-0	8	34	.236	.342	.399	94	-1	10-2	.975	5	114	97	O108(23/0/85),D3	41	-0.3

(continued)

YEAR TM LG	G	AB	R	H	2B	3B	HR	RBI	BB-IB	HP	SO	AVG	OBP	SLG	AOPS	ABR	SB-CS	FA	FR	RNG	THR	GAMES AT POSITION	DL	BFW
2003 Cle A	99	374	57	93	19	0	15	53	47-0	7	47	.249	.343	.420	100	1	10-3	.993	-4	89	87	O74(62/0/13),D21	60	-0.6
2004 Cle A★	150	591	109	164	25	0	20	70	74-3	11	84	.277	.366	.421	109	10	23-9	.986	-1	96	112	O142(124/0/19),D3		0.5
2005 Chi N	19	78	8	19	2	0	1	5	4-0	1	8	.244	.289	.308	55	-5	1-0	.971	-1	102		O19(18/0/3)		-0.7
Pit N	101	374	53	102	28	1	10	44	58-0	9	61	.273	.366	.433	114	11	16-9	.995	2	106	71	O98R		0.8
Year	120	452	61	121	30	1	11	49	62-0	10	69	.268	.366	.412	104	5	17-9	.992	2	100		O117(18/0/101)		0.1
NY A	21	48	6	13	2	0	2	4	7-0	2	4	.125	.263	.250	37	-4	1-0	.969	-1	100		O19(8/0/12)		-0.6
Total 11	1323	4736	751	1266	267	17	138	630	679-34	94	611	.267	.368	.418	103	42	165-66	.984	18	106	78	Q1237(384/110/792),D51	140	1.7

LAYDEN, GENE Eugene Francis B3.14.1894 Pittsburgh PA D12.12.1984 Pittsburgh PA BL/TL/5-10/160 d7.29

YEAR TM LG	G	AB	R	H	2B	3B	HR	RBI	BB-IB	HP	SO	AVG	OBP	SLG	AOPS	ABR	SB-CS	FA	FR	RNG	THR	GAMES AT POSITION	DL	BFW
1915 NY A	3	7	2	2	0	0	0	0		0	1	.286	.286	.286	71	0	0-1	.750	-0	94	0	O2C		-0.1

LAYDEN, PETE Peter John B12.30.1919 Dallas TX D7.18.1982 Edna TX BR/TR/5-11/185 d4.20 Col Texas

YEAR TM LG	G	AB	R	H	2B	3B	HR	RBI	BB-IB	HP	SO	AVG	OBP	SLG	AOPS	ABR	SB-CS	FA	FR	RNG	THR	GAMES AT POSITION	DL	BFW
1948 StL A	41	104	11	26	2	1	0	4		1	10	.250	.297	.288	55	-7	4-2	.973	1	99	146	O30(1/24/5)		-0.7

LAYNE, HERMAN Herman B2.13.1901 New Haven WV D8.27.1973 Gallipolis OH BR/TR/5-11/165 d4.16 Col West Virginia

YEAR TM LG	G	AB	R	H	2B	3B	HR	RBI	BB-IB	HP	SO	AVG	OBP	SLG	AOPS	ABR	SB-CS	FA	FR	RNG	THR	GAMES AT POSITION	DL	BFW
1927 Pit N	11	6	3	0	0	0	0	0		0	0	.000	.143	.000	-55	-1	0	.000	-1	0	0	O2(1/1/0)		-0.2

LAYNE, HILLIS Ivoria Hillis "Tony" B2.23.1918 Whitwell TN BL/TR/6-0/170 d9.16 Mil 1942-43

YEAR TM LG	G	AB	R	H	2B	3B	HR	RBI	BB-IB	HP	SO	AVG	OBP	SLG	AOPS	ABR	SB-CS	FA	FR	RNG	THR	GAMES AT POSITION	DL	BFW
1941 Was A	13	50	8	14	2	0	0	6	4	0	5	.280	.333	.320	77	-2	1-1	.953	-0	108	39	3b13		-0.5
1944 Was A	33	87	6	17	2	0	0	8	6	2	10	.195	.263	.218	40	-7	2-0	.949	1	106	32	3b18,2b3		0.2
1945 Was A	61	147	23	44	5	4	1	14	10	2	7	.299	.352	.408	132	5	0-1	.956	-3	88	57	3b33		-0.4
Total 3	107	284	37	75	9	4	1	28	20	4	22	.264	.321	.335	92	-4	3-2	.953	-2	97	46	3b64,2b3		-0.4

LAYTON, LES Lester Lee B11.18.1921 Nardin OK BR/TR/6-0/165 d4.24 Col Oklahoma

YEAR TM LG	G	AB	R	H	2B	3B	HR	RBI	BB-IB	HP	SO	AVG	OBP	SLG	AOPS	ABR	SB-CS	FA	FR	RNG	THR	GAMES AT POSITION	DL	BFW
1948 NY N	63	91	14	21	4	4	2	12	6	1	21	.231	.286	.429	90	-2	1	.951	0	112	84	O20(12/3/3)		-0.2

LAZOR, JOHNNY John Paul B9.9.1912 Taylor WA D12.9.2002 Renton WA BL/TR/5-9.5/180 d4.22

YEAR TM LG	G	AB	R	H	2B	3B	HR	RBI	BB-IB	HP	SO	AVG	OBP	SLG	AOPS	ABR	SB-CS	FA	FR	RNG	THR	GAMES AT POSITION	DL	BFW
1943 Bos A	83	208	21	47	10	2	0	13	21	0	25	.226	.297	.293	72	-7	5-6	.979	3	102	153	O63(51/7/8)		-0.4
1944 Bos A	16	24	0	2	1	0	0	0	1	0	0	.083	.120	.125	-30	-4	0-0	1.000	1	85	694	O6(1/0/5)/C		-0.5
1945 Bos A	101	335	35	104	19	2	5	45	18	0	17	.310	.346	.424	120	7	3-2	.961	-6	88	76	O81(12/0/73)		-0.4
1946 Bos A	23	29	1	4	0	0	1	4	2	0	11	.138	.194	.241	20	-3	0-0	1.000	-0	95	0	O7(3/0/4)		-0.4
Total 4	223	596	57	157	30	4	6	62	42	0	53	.263	.312	.357	92	-7	8-8	.971	-3	94	123	O157(67/7/90)/C		-2.

LAZZERI, TONY Anthony Michael "Poosh 'Em Up Tony" B12.6.1903 San Francisco CA D8.6.1946 San Francisco CA BR/TR/5-11.5/170 d4.13 C1 HF1991

YEAR TM LG	G	AB	R	H	2B	3B	HR	RBI	BB-IB	HP	SO	AVG	OBP	SLG	AOPS	ABR	SB-CS	FA	FR	RNG	THR	GAMES AT POSITION	DL	BFW
1926 †NY A	**155**	589	79	162	28	14	18	114	54	2	96	.275	.338	.462	109	3	16-7	.961	-18	95	90	2b149,S5/3		3.
1927 †NY A	153	570	92	176	29	8	18	102	69	0	82	.309	.383	.482	127	22	22-14	.971	8	**111**	104	2b113,S38,3b9		2.
1928 †NY A	116	404	62	134	30	11	10	82	43	1	50	.332	.397	.535	148	28	15-5	.956	-7	97	92	2b110		5.
1929 NY A	147	545	101	193	37	11	18	106	68	4	45	.354	.429	.561	164	54	9-10	.969	1	97	112	2b147		2.
1930 NY A	143	571	109	173	34	15	9	121	60	3	62	.303	.372	.462	115	13	4-4	.971	2	99	79	2b77,3b60,S8/1OL		1.
1931 NY A	135	484	67	129	27	7	8	83	79	1	60	.267	.371	.401	109	9	18-9	.958	-4	100	96	2b90,3b39		1.
1932 †NY A	142	510	79	153	28	16	15	113	82	2	64	.300	.399	.506	130	14	10-11	.978	4	91	84	2b134,3b5		2.
1933 NY A☆	139	523	94	154	22	12	18	104	73	2	62	.294	.383	.486	137	28	15-7	.968	-12	88	80	2b138		2.
1934 NY A	123	438	59	117	24	6	14	67	71	0	64	.267	.369	.445	117	12	11-1	.976	-15	91	91	2b92,3b30		-0.
1935 NY A	130	477	72	130	18	6	13	83	63	3	75	.273	.361	.417	107	5	11-5	.970	-21	85	103	2b118,S9		-1.
1936 †NY A	150	537	82	154	29	6	14	109	97	1	76	.287	.397	.441	110	12	8-5	.968	-37	84	87	2b148,S2		-1.
1937 †NY A	126	446	56	109	21	3	14	70	71	0	76	.244	.348	.399	87	-9	7-1	.966	-9	101	84	2b125		0.
1938 †Chi N	54	120	21	32	5	0	5	23	22	0	30	.267	.380	.433	120	4	0	.946	-5	88		S25,3b7,2b4/OL		-0.
1939 Bro N	14	39	6	11	2	0	3	6	10	0	6	.295	.392	.564	103	0	0	.914	-2	97	124	2b11,3b2		-0.
NY N	13	44	7	13	0	0	1	8	7	0	7	.295	.392	.455	103	0	0	.889	-2	86	45	3b13		0.
Year	27	83	13	24	2	0	4	14	17	0	13	.289	.422	.458	133	5	1	.897	-4	87		3b15,2b11		0.
Total 14	1740	6297	986	1840	334	115	178	1191	869	21	864	.292	.380	.467	122	217	148-79	.967	-115	94	93	2b1456,3b166,S87,O2L/1		17.

LEACH, FREDDY Frederick B11.23.1897 Springfield MO D12.10.1981 Hagerman ID BL/TR/5-11/183 d5.24

YEAR TM LG	G	AB	R	H	2B	3B	HR	RBI	BB-IB	HP	SO	AVG	OBP	SLG	AOPS	ABR	SB-CS	FA	FR	RNG	THR	GAMES AT POSITION	DL	BFW
1923 Phi N	52	104	5	27	4	0	1	16	3	0	14	.260	.280	.327	54	-7	1-2	.950	-2	97	0	O26(17/9/1)		-1
1924 Phi N	8	28	6	13	2	1	2	7	2	0	1	.464	.552	.821	221	5	0-0	1.000	-0	67	172	O65C		0
1925 Phi N	65	292	47	91	15	4	5	28	5	1	21	.312	.323	.442	86	-7	1-2	.979	6	105	126	O123(48/84/8)		-1
1926 Phi N	129	492	73	162	29	7	11	70	16	1	33	.329	.352	.484	117	10	6	.981	16	107	**182**	O140(18/123/5)		1
1927 Phi N	140	536	69	164	30	4	12	83	21	8	32	.306	.342	.444	108	4	2	.978	7	108	109	O120(93/22/7),1b25		0
1928 Phi N	145	588	83	179	36	11	13	96	30	4	30	.304	.342	.469	107	3	4	.974	-12	78	32	O95(94/0/1)		-2
1929 NY N	113	411	74	119	22	6	8	47	17	4	14	.290	.324	.431	85	-11	10	.978	-5	85	125	O124L		-1
1930 NY N	126	544	90	178	19	13	13	71	22	2	25	.327	.361	.482	104	1	3	.976	-1	100	98	O125L		-0
1931 NY N	129	515	75	159	30	5	6	61	29	2	9	.309	.348	.421	109	5	4	.977	-2	100	43	O50(8/22/21)		-1
1932 Bos N	84	223	21	55	9	2	1	29	18	1	10	.247	.306	.318	71	-9	1							-5
Total 10	991	3733	543	1147	196	53	72	509	163	27	189	.307	.341	.446	101	-6	32-4	.975	3	98	104	O875(534/325/43),1b25		

LEACH, JALAL Jalal Donnell B3.14.1969 San Francisco CA BL/TL/6-2/200 [NYA90 7/192] d9.5 Col Pepperdine

YEAR TM LG	G	AB	R	H	2B	3B	HR	RBI	BB-IB	HP	SO	AVG	OBP	SLG	AOPS	ABR	SB-CS	FA	FR	RNG	THR	GAMES AT POSITION	DL	BFW
2001 SF N	8	10	0	1	0	0	0	1	2-0	0	3	.100	.250	.100	-2	2-0	0-0	1.000	-1	35	0	O3(1/0/2)		-0

LEACH, RICK Richard Max B5.4.1957 Ann Arbor MI BL/TL/6-0/195* [DetA79 1/13] d4.30 Col Michigan

YEAR TM LG	G	AB	R	H	2B	3B	HR	RBI	BB-IB	HP	SO	AVG	OBP	SLG	AOPS	ABR	SB-CS	FA	FR	RNG	THR	GAMES AT POSITION	DL	BFW
1981 Det A	54	83	9	16	3	1	1	11	16-1	1	15	.193	.320	.289	75	-2	0-1	1.000	-1	132	122	1b32,O15R,D2		-0
1982 Det A	82	218	23	52	7	2	3	12	21-2	1	29	.239	.303	.330	74	-8	4-0	.995	-3	88	98	1b56,O14(4/0/10),D4		-0
1983 Det A	99	242	22	60	17	0	3	26	19-1	1	21	.248	.305	.355	83	-5	2-2	.994	2	113	87	1b73,O13(2/0/11),D3		-0
1984 Tor A	65	88	11	23	6	2	0	7	8-0	0	9	.200	.263	.375	42	-3	0-0	.987	0	106	141	1b10,O4(1/0/3)		-0
1985 Tor A	16	35	2	7	0	1	0	1	3-1	0	9	.200	.263	.257		-4	79	.978	-4	79	0	D42,O39(19/0/22),1b7	35	-0
1986 Tor A	110	246	35	76	14	1	5	39	13-3	1	24	.309	.335	.435	107	2	0-1	.981	-2	95	53	O43(21/0/22),D30,1b5		-0
1987 Tor A	98	195	26	55	13	1	3	25	25-2	3	25	.282	.371	.405	104	2	0-1	1.000	2	107	51	O49(14/0/36),D25,1b4		-0
1988 Tor A	87	199	21	55	13	1	0	23	32-7	1	33	.272	.358	.351	99	1	2-1	.951	-1	96	59	D44,O41(37/0/3),1b4		-0
1989 Tex A	110	239	32	65	14	1	3	23	32-7	1	20	.272	.358	.351	99	1	2-1	.989	2	109	109	O52(13/0/40),1b7		-0
1990 SF N	78	174	24	51	13	0	2	16	21-0	1	20	.293	.372	.402	117	5	0-2	.983	-3	95	59	O293(116/1/177),1b213,D156/P	35	-3
Total 10	799	1719	205	460	100	10	18	183	176-20	8	217	.268	.335	.369	94	-11	8-8							

LEACH, TOMMY Thomas William B11.4.1877 French Creek NY D9.29.1969 Haines City FL BR/TR/5-6,5/150 d9.28 OF(74/996/13)

YEAR TM LG	G	AB	R	H	2B	3B	HR	RBI	BB-IB	HP	SO	AVG	OBP	SLG	AOPS	ABR	SB-CS	FA	FR	RNG	THR	GAMES AT POSITION	DL	BFW
1898 Lou N	3	10	0	1	0	0	0	0		0	0	.100	.100	.100	-43	-2	0	.727	-1	116	0	3b3/2		
1899 Lou N	106	406	75	117	10	6	5	57	37	0	0	.288	.349	.399	100	-1	19	.908	-5	105	108	3b80,S25,2b2		
1900 †Pit N	51	160	20	34	1	2	1	16	21	0	0	.213	.304	.262	57	-9	8	.864	0	97	110	3b31,S8,2b7,O4(2/0/2)		
1901 Pit N	98	374	64	114	12	13	2	44	20	4	0	.305	.347	.422	119	7	16	.903	10	112	105	3b92,S4		
1902 †Pit N	135	514	97	143	14	**22**	**6**	85	45	2	0	.278	.341	.426	132	17	25	.926	12	112	66	3b134		
1903 †Pit N	127	507	97	151	16	17	7	87	40	2	0	.298	.352	.438	121	11	22	.879	4	**111**	129	3b127		
1904 Pit N	146	579	92	149	15	12	6	56	45	5	0	.257	.316	.335	98	-2	23	.907	36	**128**	153	3b146		
1905 Pit N	131	499	71	128	10	14	4	53	37	1	0	.257	.309	.345	92	-6	17	.988	9	117	92	O71(16/51/6),3b58,2b2,S2		
1906 Pit N	133	476	66	136	10	7	1	39	33	1	0	.286	.333	.342	106	2	21	.929	-2	103	58	3b65,O60(15/44/1)/S		
1907 Pit N	149	547	102	166	19	12	4	43	40	1	0	.303	.352	.404	135	20	43	.980	5	96	136	O111(2/109/0),3b33,S6/2		
1908 Pit N	152	583	93	151	24	16	5	41	54	2	0	.259	.324	.381	125	15	24	.937	-7	96	109	3b150,O2C		
1909 †Pit N	151	587	**126**	153	29	8	6	43	66	2	0	.261	.337	.368	110	7	18	.966	4	**113**	76	O131C,S2/2		
1910 Pit N	135	529	83	143	24	5	4	52	38	0	62	.270	.319	.357	92	-7	18	.987	4	**111**	126	O89(1/89/0),S13/3		
1911 Pit N	108	386	60	92	12	6	3	43	46	0	50	.238	.323	.324	78	-11	19	.986	2	109	103	O24C		
1912 Pit N	28	97	24	29	4	2	0	19	12	0	9	.299	.376	.381	109	1	6	.975	-0	93	0	O73C,3b4		
Chi N	82	265	50	64	10	3	2	32	55	3	29	.242	.398	.325	93	1	14	.978	1	102	95	O97C,3b4		
Year	110	362	74	93	14	5	2	51	67	3	29	.257	.377	.340	98	2	20	.990	-0	99	93	O121(3/118/0),3b2		
1913 Chi N	131	456	**99**	131	23	10	6	32	77	1	44	.287	.391	.424	132	22	21-10	.968	3	108	103	O136C,3b16		
1914 Chi N	153	577	80	152	19	4	7	46	95	2	38	.263	.353	.373	116	13	16	.959	-2	98	85	O96(17/81/0)		
1915 Cin N	107	335	42	75	7	5	0	17	56	0	29	.224	.338	.275	85	-3	20-14	.952	-1	95	128	O23(3/118/0),S3		
1918 Pit N	30	72	14	14	2	0	0	8	7	0	9	.194	.304	.306	101	1	2	.952	-1	95	91			
Total 19	2156	7564	1355	2143	266	172	63	810	820	32	278	.269	.340	.370	108	76	361-24	.975	68	98	91	O1079C,3b955,S64,2b14		

LEAHY, DAN Daniel C. B8.8.1870 Knoxville TN D12.30.1903 Knoxville TN 5-9/155 d9.2

YEAR TM LG	G	AB	R	H	2B	3B	HR	RBI	BB-IB	HP	SO	AVG	OBP	SLG	AOPS	ABR	SB-CS	FA	FR	RNG	THR	GAMES AT POSITION	DL	BFW
1896 Phi N	2	6	0	2	1	0	0	1	1	0	2	.333	.429	.500	146	0	0	.857	0	121	0	S2		

YEAR	TM LG	G	AB	R	H	2B	3B	HR	RBI	BB-IB	HP	SO	AVG	OBP	SLG	AOPS	ABR	SB-CS	FA	FR	RNG	THR	GAMES AT POSITION	DL	BFW

LEAHY, TOM — Thomas Joseph B6.2.1869 New Haven CT D6.11.1951 New Haven CT BR/TR/5-7.5/168 d5.18 Col Holy Cross

YEAR	TM LG	G	AB	R	H	2B	3B	HR	RBI	BB-IB	HP	SO	AVG	OBP	SLG	AOPS	ABR	SB-CS	FA	FR	RNG	THR	GAMES AT POSITION	BFW
1897	Pit N	24	92	10	24	3	3	0	12	7	1		.261	.320	.359	82	-3	3	.935	-4	52	0	O13(7/4/2),C6,3b6	-0.6
	Was N	19	52	12	20	2	1	0	7	9	7		.385	.529	.462	164	7	6	.727	-1	237	0	O10(2/8/0),3b5,2b3/C	0.5
	Year	43	144	22	44	5	4	0	19	16	8		.306	.405	.396	115	4	9	.881	-5	108	0	O23(9/12/2),3b11,C7,2b3	-0.1
1898	Was N	15	55	10	10	2	0	0	5	8	1		.182	.297	.218	48	-3	6	.913	0	99	51	3b12,2b3	-0.2
1901	Mil A	33	99	18	24	6	2	0	10	11	5		.242	.348	.343	97	0	3	.941	-6	70	106	C28,O2R/2	-0.2
	Phi A	5	15	1	5	1	0	0	1	1	0		.333	.375	.400	110	0		1.000	0	0	0	O2L/CS	0.0
	Year	38	114	19	29	7	2	0	11	12	5		.254	.351	.351	99	1	3	.944	-6	74	109	C29,O4(2/0/2)/2S	-0.2
1905	StL N	35	97	3	22	1	3	0	7	8	0		.227	.286	.299	77	-3	0	.946	-7	79	92	C29	-0.2
Total 4		131	410	54	105	15	9	0	42	44	14		.256	.348	.337	93	-2	18	.942	-17	77	98	C65,O27(11/12/4),3b23,2b7/S	-0.8

LEAR, FRED — Frederick Francis "King" B4.7.1894 New York NY D10.13.1955 E.Orange NJ BR/TR/6-0.5/180 d6.7 Col Villanova

YEAR	TM LG	G	AB	R	H	2B	3B	HR	RBI	BB-IB	HP	SO	AVG	OBP	SLG	AOPS	ABR	SB-CS	FA	FR	RNG	THR	GAMES AT POSITION	BFW
1915	Phi A	2	2	0	0	0	0	0	0	0	0	2	.000	.000	.000	-99	-1	0	.600	-4	52	0	3b2	-0.1
1918	Chi N	2	1	0	0	0	0	0	0	1	0		.000	.500	.000	56	0	0	.600			0	3b2	0.0
1919	Chi N	40	76	8	17	3	1	1	11	8	1	11	.224	.306	.329	90	-1	2	—				/H	-0.4
1920	NY N	31	87	12	22	0	1	0	7	8	1	15	.253	.323	.310	83	-2	0-2	.990	-3	40	94	1b9,2b9,S3	-0.3
Total 4		75	166	20	39	3	2	2	18	17	2	28	.235	.314	.313	84	-4	2-2	.951	-1	101	163	3b24/2	-0.8

LEARD, BILL — William Wallace "Wild Bill" B10.14.1885 Oneida NY D1.15.1970 San Francisco CA BR/TR/5-10/155 d7.21

YEAR	TM LG	G	AB	R	H	2B	3B	HR	RBI	BB-IB	HP	SO	AVG	OBP	SLG	AOPS	ABR	SB-CS	FA	FR	RNG	THR	GAMES AT POSITION	BFW
1917	Bro N	3	3	0	0	0	0	0	0	0	0	1	.000	.000	.000	-97	-1	0	—	0	0	0	/2	-0.1

LEARY, JACK — John J. B7.1857 New Haven CT TL/5-11/186 d8.21 ▲

YEAR	TM LG	G	AB	R	H	2B	3B	HR	RBI	BB-IB	HP	SO	AVG	OBP	SLG	AOPS	ABR	FA	FR	RNG	THR	GAMES AT POSITION	BFW
1880	Bos N	1	3	1	0	0	0	0	0	1		0	.000	.250	.000	-7	0	1.000	1	940	0	/ORP	0.0
1881	Det N	3	11	2	3	1	1	0	1	1		1	.273	.333	.545	165	1	.833	-0	145	0	O2(0/1/1),P2	0.0
1882	Pit AA	60	257	32	75	7	3	1				5	.292	.305	.354	128	7	.759	-9	93	33	3b33,O27(0/8/19),P3/12	-0.2
	Bal AA	4	18	3	4	1	0	0				0	.222	.222	.278	73	0	.900	-5	105	0	P3/OC	
	Year	64	275	35	79	8	3	1				5	.287	.300	.349	124	7	.759	-9	93	33	3b33,O28(0/9/19),P6/12	-0.2
1883	Lou AA	40	165	16	31	1	3	3				2	.188	.198	.285	58	-8	.816	-4	91	121	S40	-0.9
	Bal AA	3	11	1	2	0	2	0				0	.182	.182	.545	122	0	.727	-1	69	228	2b3	-0.1
	Year	43	176	17	33	1	5	3				2	.188	.197	.301	62	-8	.816	-5	91	121	S40,2b3	-1.0
1884	Alt U	8	33	1	3	0	0	0				1	.091	.118	.091	-36	-7	.692	-2	0	0	O6(4/2/0),P3/3	-0.6
	CP U	10	40	0	7	1	0	0				0	.175	.175	.200	13	-5	.840	-2	83	0	2b4,3b3,O3C,P2	-0.6
	Year	18	73	1	10	1	0	0				1	.137	.149	.151	-9	-12	.625	-4	79	0	O9(4/5/0),P5,3b4,2b4	-1.2
Total 5		129	538	56	125	11	9	4	4	10		1	.232	.246	.309	84	-12	.816	-17	91	121	S40,O40(4/15/21),3b37,P14,2b8/1	-2.4

LEARY, JOHN — John Louis "Jack" B5.2.1891 Waltham MA D8.18.1961 Waltham MA BR/TR/5-11.5/180 d4.14

YEAR	TM LG	G	AB	R	H	2B	3B	HR	RBI	BB-IB	HP	SO	AVG	OBP	SLG	AOPS	ABR	SB-CS	FA	FR	RNG	THR	GAMES AT POSITION	BFW
1914	StL A	144	533	35	141	28	7	0	45	10	3	71	.265	.282	.343	91	-9	9-15	.987	-3	94	99	1b130,C15	-2.0
1915	StL A	75	227	19	55	10	0	0	15	5	3	36	.242	.268	.286	69	-10	2-4	.985	-2	118	164	1b53,C11	-1.4
Total 2		219	760	54	196	38	7	0	60	15	6	107	.258	.278	.326	85	-19	11-19	.987	-5	100	116	1b183,C26	-3.4

LEATHERS, HAL — Harold Langford "Chuck" B12.2.1898 Selma CA D4.12.1977 Modesto CA BL/TR/5-8/152 d9.13

YEAR	TM LG	G	AB	R	H	2B	3B	HR	RBI	BB-IB	HP	SO	AVG	OBP	SLG	AOPS	ABR	SB-CS	FA	FR	RNG	THR	GAMES AT POSITION	BFW
1920	Chi A	9	23	3	7	1	0	1	0	1	0	1	.304	.333	.478	129	1	1-0	.825	-2	89	0	S6,2b3	0.0

LEBER, EMIL — Emil Bohmiel B5.15.1881 Cleveland OH D11.6.1924 Cleveland OH BR/TR/5-11/170 d9.2

YEAR	TM LG	G	AB	R	H	2B	3B	HR	RBI	BB-IB	HP	SO	AVG	OBP	SLG	AOPS	ABR	SB-CS	FA	FR	RNG	THR	GAMES AT POSITION	BFW
1905	Cle A	2	6	1	0	0	0	0	0	1	0		.000	.143	.000	-53	-1	0	1.000	0	137	0	3b2	-0.1

LEBOURVEAU, BEVO — De Witt Wiley B8.24.1894 Dana CA D12.10.1947 Nevada City CA BL/TR/5-11/175 d9.9 Col Santa Clara

YEAR	TM LG	G	AB	R	H	2B	3B	HR	RBI	BB-IB	HP	SO	AVG	OBP	SLG	AOPS	ABR	SB-CS	FA	FR	RNG	THR	GAMES AT POSITION	BFW
1919	Phi N	17	63	4	17	0	1	0	10	0			.270	.370	.270	88	0	2	1.000	2	82	275	O15(15/0/2)	0.1
1920	Phi N	84	261	29	67	7	2	3	12	11	3	36	.257	.295	.333	76	-8	9-6	.949	5	91	195	O72(51/17/4)	-1.0
1921	Phi N	93	281	42	83	12	5	6	35	29	0	51	.295	.361	.438	102	1	4-5	.911	-6	89	76	O76(27/1/48)	-1.1
1922	Phi N	74	167	24	45	8	3	2	20	24	2	29	.269	.368	.389	87	-3	0-3	.920	-3	92	81	O42(33/4/5)	-0.9
1929	Phi A	12	16	1	5	0	1	0	2	5	0	1	.313	.476	.438	132	1	0-1	1.000	0	116	0	O3(0/2/1)	0.1
Total 5		280	788	100	217	27	11	11	69	79	5	125	.275	.345	.379	91	-9	15-15	.935	-4	90	134	O208(126/24/60)	-2.8

LECROY, MATTHEW — Matthew Hanks B12.13.1975 Belton SC BR/TR/6-2/225* [MinA97 1/50] d4.3 Col Clemson

YEAR	TM LG	G	AB	R	H	2B	3B	HR	RBI	BB-IB	HP	SO	AVG	OBP	SLG	AOPS	ABR	SB-CS	FA	FR	RNG	THR	GAMES AT POSITION	DL	BFW
2000	Min A	56	167	18	29	10	0	5	17	17-2	2	38	.174	.254	.323	43	-15	0-0	.988	2	124	76	C49,1b3,D3		-0.9
2001	Min A	15	40	6	17	5	0	3	12	4-0	1	8	.425	.429	.775	200	6	0-1	1.000	0	72	338	C3,1b2,D9		0.5
2002	Min A	63	181	19	47	11	1	7	27	13-1	0	38	.260	.306	.448	95	-2	0-2	.976	-1	31	205	D41,1b8,C6		-0.6
2003	Min A	107	345	39	99	19	0	17	64	25-1	4	82	.287	.342	.490	112	6	0-1	.980	-8	71	71	D64,C22,1b17		-0.6
2004	Min A	88	264	25	71	14	0	9	39	16-0	5	60	.269	.321	.424	90	-4	0-0	.967	-7	55	26	D30,C26,1b23		-1.3
2005	Min A	101	304	33	79	5	0	17	50	41-2	6	65	.260	.354	.444	108	4	0-0	.986	-3	61	115	D63,1b23/C	33	-1.3
Total 6		430	1301	140	342	64	1	58	209	112-6	16	311	.263	.327	.447	98	-5	0-4	.983	-16	94	71	D210,C107,1b76	33	-3.3

LEDEE, RICKY — Ricardo Alberto B11.22.1973 Ponce, PR BL/TL/6-1/190(160-215) [NYA90 16/435] d6.14

YEAR	TM LG	G	AB	R	H	2B	3B	HR	RBI	BB-IB	HP	SO	AVG	OBP	SLG	AOPS	ABR	SB-CS	FA	FR	RNG	THR	GAMES AT POSITION	DL	BFW
1998	NY A	42	79	13	19	5	2	1	12	7	0	29	.241	.299	.392	82	-2	3-1	.981	5	163	265	O42(36/3/4)		-0.2
1999	NY A	88	250	45	69	13	5	9	40	28-5	1	71	.276	.346	.476	109	3	4-3	.942	-1	107	71	O77(69/6/3),D5		0.0
2000	NY A	62	191	23	46	11	1	7	31	26-2	1	39	.241	.332	.419	91	-1	7-3	.979	-1	101	37	O49(46/4/1),D10		-0.5
	Cle A	17	63	13	14	2	1	2	8	8-0	0	12	.222	.310	.381	71	-3	0-0	1.000	1	119	99	O17(12/0/6)		-0.2
	Tex A	58	213	23	50	6	3	4	38	25-2	1	50	.235	.317	.347	68	-11	6-3	.977	-1	110	0	O57(20/3/42)		-1.3
	Year	137	467	59	110	19	5	13	77	59-4	2	98	.236	.322	.381	77	-17	13-6	.981	-1	108	28	O123(78/7/49),D10		-2.0
2001	Tex A	78	242	33	56	21	1	2	36	23-0	3	58	.231	.303	.351	71	-10	3-3	.979	-2	102	24	O72(6/10/60)		-1.5
2002	Phi N	96	203	33	46	13	1	8	23	35-0	1	50	.227	.342	.419	110	6	1-2	1.000	0	98	0	O51(10/40/5)	73	-1.5
2003	Phi N	121	255	37	63	15	2	13	46	34-5	0	59	.247	.334	.475	117	6	0-0	1.000	-2	98	156	O71(29/42/1),D2		0.2
2004	SF N	31	53	6	6	2	0	0	4	5-0	1	20	.113	.200	.151	-6	-9	1-0	1.000	3	109	282	O22(9/13/1)	15	0.8
	LA N	102	237	31	66	16	1	7	39	20-1	1	47	.233	.337	.403	88	-3	3-0	.987	2	107	181	O37(10/16/12),D2		-0.9
	Year	104	176	25	41	9	0	7	30	27-2	1	47	.233	.322	.354	104	1	1-0	.960	-1	103	0	O15(1/3/11),D2		-0.1
Total 8		768	1909	276	470	111	17	60	303	233-17	10	469	.246	.328	.416	93	-20	27-15	.978	-12	98	74	O542(295/124/151),D19	121	-4.4

LEDESMA, AARON — Aaron David B6.3.1971 Union City CA BR/TR/6-2/200* [NYN90 2/57] d7.2 Col Chabot (CA) JC

YEAR	TM LG	G	AB	R	H	2B	3B	HR	RBI	BB-IB	HP	SO	AVG	OBP	SLG	AOPS	ABR	SB-CS	FA	FR	RNG	THR	GAMES AT POSITION	DL	BFW
1995	NY N	21	33	4	8	0	3	0	6	6-1	0		.242	.359	.242	65	-1	0-0	.875	-1	113	0	3b10,1b2,S2		-0.2
1997	Bal A	43	88	24	31	5	1	2	11	13-0	1	9	.352	.437	.500	149	7	1-0	.973	-3	87	79	2b22,3b11,1b5,S4		0.5
1998	TB A	95	299	30	97	16	3	0	29	9-1	1	51	.324	.344	.398	91	-4	9-7	.971	16	110	154	S58,2b19,3b7,1b2,D6		1.5
1999	TB A	93	294	30	78	15	0	0	30	14-1	3	35	.265	.305	.316	58	-19	1-1	.978	12	95	99	S5b,3b26,2b17,1b4/D	37	-0.3
2000	Col N	32	40	4	9	2	0	0	3	2-0	0	9	.225	.279	.275	33	-4	0-0	1.000	0	58	0	3b5,1b3		-0.4
Total 5		284	754	94	223	38	4	2	76	44-3	6	111	.296	.338	.365	80	-21	11-8	.974	24	102	126	S114,3b59,2b58,1b16,D7	37	1.1

LEDWITH, MIKE — Michael B Brooklyn NY D1.2.1929 Bronx NY d8.19

YEAR	TM LG	G	AB	R	H	2B	3B	HR	RBI	BB-IB	HP	SO	AVG	OBP	SLG	AOPS	ABR	SB-CS	FA	FR	RNG	THR	GAMES AT POSITION	BFW
1874	Atl NA	1	4	1	1	0	0	0	0	0			.250	.250	.250	69	0	0-0	.600	-1			/C	-0.1

LEE, CARLOS — Carlos (Noriel) B6.20.1976 Aguadulce, Pan BR/TR/6-2/235(220-240) d5.7

YEAR	TM LG	G	AB	R	H	2B	3B	HR	RBI	BB-IB	HP	SO	AVG	OBP	SLG	AOPS	ABR	SB-CS	FA	FR	RNG	THR	GAMES AT POSITION	BFW
1999	Chi A	127	492	66	144	32	2	16	84	13-0	4	72	.293	.312	.463	94	-6	4-2	.981	-2	103	47	O105L,D16,1b5	-1.2
2000	Chi A	152	572	107	172	29	2	24	92	38-1	9	94	.301	.345	.484	104	2	13-4	.990	-4	92	113	O149L,D2	-0.6
2001	Chi A	150	558	75	150	33	3	24	84	38-2	6	85	.269	.321	.468	99	-2	17-7	.969	-1	97	117	O130L,D17	-0.7
2002	Chi A	140	492	82	130	26	2	26	80	75-4	2	73	.264	.359	.498	118	14	14-4	.978	1	93	103	O156L/D	0.6
2003	Chi A	158	623	100	181	35	4	31	113	37-2	4	91	.291	.331	.499	111	9	18-4	.996	-2	93	103	O137L,D2	0.5
2004	Chi A	153	591	103	180	37	0	31	99	54-3	7	86	.305	.366	.525	125	22	11-5	.978	1	98	113	O148L,D5	1.9
2005	Mil N★	162	618	85	164	41	0	32	114	57-7	7	86	.265	.324	.487	110	8	13-4	**1.000**	4	101	137	O162L	0.7
Total 7		1042	3946	618	1121	233	10	184	666	312-19	28	588	.284	.337	.488	109	47	77-30	.985	0	100	101	O987L,D43,1b5	1.2

LEE, CLIFF — Clifford Walker B8.4.1896 Lexington NE D8.25.1980 Denver CO BR/TR/6-1/175 d5.15

YEAR	TM LG	G	AB	R	H	2B	3B	HR	RBI	BB-IB	HP	SO	AVG	OBP	SLG	AOPS	ABR	SB-CS	FA	FR	RNG	THR	GAMES AT POSITION	BFW
1919	Pit N	42	112	5	22	6	1	1	8	8	0	8	.196	.237	.286	55	-7	2	.962	-6	116	54	C28,O6(2/2/2)	-1.2
1920	Pit N	37	76	5	18	2	1	0	8	4	0	14	.237	.275	.316	67	-3	0-1	.974	0	93	134	C19,O2(1/1/0)	-0.3
1921	Phi N	88	286	31	88	14	4	4	29	13	0	34	.308	.338	.427	94	-3	5-2	.987	-5	79	101	1b48,O27(2/1/24),C2	-1.2
1922	Phi N	122	422	65	130	26	2	17	77	32	1	43	.322	.371	.540	121	12	2-3	.967	-4	92	92	O89(83/0/6),1b18/3	-0.1
1923	Phi N	107	355	54	114	20	4	11	47	20	1	39	.321	.357	.493	110	4	3-3	.959	-2	98	58	O83(54/0/32),1b16	-0.5
1924	Phi N	21	56	4	14	3	2	1	7	2	0	5	.250	.276	.429	77	-2	0-1	1.000	1	116	82	O13R,1b4	-0.3

YEAR	TM LG	G	AB	R	H	2B	3B	HR	RBI	BB-IB	HP	SO	AVG	OBP	SLG	AOPS	ABR	SB-CS	FA	FR	RNG	THR	GAMES AT POSITION	DL	BFW
	Cin N	6	6	1	2	1	0	0	2	0-0	0	2	.333	.333	.500	122	0	0-0	—	-0	0	0	/OR		0.0
	Cin N	6	6	1	2	1	0	0	0	0-0	0	7	.258	.281	.435	82	-2	0-1	1.000	0	115	81	O14R,1b4		-0.3
	Year	27	62	5	16	4	2	1	9	2	0							2-1	.951	1	105	113	O70(0/15/56)		-0.4
1925	Cle A	77	230	43	74	15	6	4	42	21	0	33	.322	.378	.491	118	6	2-1	1.000	0	121	0	O9(6/1/2),C3		-0.4
1926	Cle A	21	40	4	7	1	0	1	2	6	0	8	.175	.283	.275	45	-3	0-0	.960	-15	99	80	O52/3		-3.7
Total	8	521	1583	216	475	87	28	38	216	104	1	186	.300	.344	.462	103	4	14-11							

LEE, DEREK   Derek Gerald   B7.28.1966 Chicago IL   BL/TR/6-1/200   [ChiA88 42/1078]   d6.27   Col South Florida   -0.6

1993	Min A	15	33	1	5	1	1	0	4	1-0	0	4	.152	.176	.182	-3	-5	0-0	1.000	-1	83	0	O13(9/0/4)		

LEE, DERREK   Derrek Leon   B9.6.1975 Sacramento CA   BR/TR/6-5/225(205-245)   [SDN93 1/14]   d4.28

1997	SD N	22	54	9	14	3	0	1	4	9-0	0	24	.259	.365	.370	99	0	0-0	1.000	1	119	95	1b21		0.0
1998	Fla N	141	454	62	106	29	1	17	74	47-1	10	120	.233	.318	.414	97	-2	5-2	.993	10	132	103	1b132		-0.3
1999	Fla N	70	218	21	45	9	1	5	20	17-1	0	70	.206	.263	.326	51	-18	2-1	.994	3	119	89	1b66		-1.9
2000	Fla N	158	477	70	134	18	3	28	70	63-6	4	123	.281	.368	.507	125	17	0-3	.993	6	117	96	1b147		1.0
2001	Fla N	158	561	83	158	37	4	21	75	50-1	8	126	.282	.346	.474	114	11	4-2	.994	6	115	**116**	1b156		0.4
2002	Fla N	**162**	581	95	157	35	7	27	86	98-8	5	164	.270	.378	.494	137	30	19-9	.992	5	113	96	1b162		2.1
2003	†Fla N	155	539	91	146	31	2	31	92	88-7	10	131	.271	.379	.508	135	30	21-8	.996	2	101	**104**	1b155		2.0
2004	Chi N	161	605	90	168	39	1	32	98	68-4	8	128	.278	.356	.504	116	15	12-5	.996	11	115	89	1b161		1.1
2005	Chi N★	158	594	120	**199**	**50**	3	46	107	85-23	5	109	**.335**	.418	**.662**	**173**	**65**	15-3	.996	15	116	98	1b1158		**6.3**
Total	9	1185	4083	641	1127	251	22	208	626	525-51	50	995	.276	.363	.501	125	148	78-33							10.7

LEE, DUD   Ernest Dudley (aka Ernest Dudley in 1920-21)   B8.22.1899 Denver CO   D1.7.1971 Denver CO   BL/TR/5-9/150   d10.3

1920	StL A	1	2	2	2	0	0	0	1	0	0	0	1.000	1.000	1.000	418	-1	1-0	.333	-1	47	0	/S		0.0
1921	StL A	72	180	18	30	4	2	0	11	14	2	34	.167	.235	.211	14	-24	1-1	.922	-1	94	63	S31,2b30,3b3		-2.0
1924	Bos A	94	288	36	73	9	4	0	29	40	3	17	.253	.350	.313	72	-11	8-4	.937	6	92	96	S90		-0.7
1925	Bos A	84	255	22	57	7	3	0	19	34	1	19	.224	.315	.275	51	-19	2-3	.924	13	109	127	S84		0.1
1926	Bos A	2	7	2	1	0	0	0	0	0	0	0	.143	.250	.143	4	-1	0-0	1.000	-0	64	112	S2		-0.1
Total	5	253	732	80	163	20	9	0	60	88	6	70	.223	.311	.275	45	50	12-8	.928	4	99	103	S208,2b30,3b3		-2.7

LEE, HAL   Harold Burnham "Sheriff"   B2.15.1905 Ludlow MS   D9.4.1989 Pascagoula MS   BR/TR/5-11/180   d4.19   Col Mississippi College

1930	Bro N	22	37	5	6	0	0	1	4	5	1	5	.162	.244	.243	19	-5	0-0	1.000	0	112	0	O12(10/0/1)		-0.5
1931	Phi N	44	131	13	29	10	0	2	12	10	1	18	.221	.282	.344	62	-7	0	.967	1	110	45	O38(26/11/2)		-0.8
1932	Phi N	149	595	76	180	42	10	18	85	36	1	45	.303	.343	.497	110	8	6	.965	9	114	114	O148(136/12/0)		0.9
1933	Phi N	46	167	25	48	12	2	0	12	18	1	13	.287	.360	.383	100	1	1	.981	1	100	141	O45L		-1.5
	Bos N	88	312	32	69	15	9	1	28	18	1	26	.221	.266	.337	77	-11	1	.977	2	106	84	O87(85/2/0)		-1.5
	Year	134	479	57	117	27	11	1	40	36	2	39	.244	.300	.353	87	-9	2	.978	3	104	103	O132(130/2/0)		0.3
1934	Bos N	139	521	70	152	23	6	8	79	47	2	43	.292	.353	.405	111	8	3	.985	3	114	54	O128L,2b4		-0.2
1935	Bos N	112	422	49	128	18	6	0	39	18	1	35	.303	.333	.374	98	-3	0	.962	6	116	86	O110(98/0/12)		-3.0
1936	Bos N	152	565	46	143	24	7	3	64	52	2	50	.253	.318	.336	82	-15	4	.973	-8	96	43	O150L		-4.8
Total	7	752	2750	316	755	144	40	33	323	203	9	225	.275	.326	.392	95	-24	15	.973	14	108	77	O718(678/25/15),2b4		

LEE, LEONIDAS   Leonidas Pyrrhus (b Leonidas Pyrrhus Funkhouser)   B12.13.1860 St.Louis MO   D6.11.1912 Hendersonville NC   d7.17   Col Princeton   -0.2

1877	StL N	4	18	0	5	1	0	0	0	0	0	1	.278	.278	.333	97	0		.667	-2	0	74	O4(1/2/1)/S		

LEE, LERON   Leron   B3.4.1948 Bakersfield CA   BL/TR/6-0/196*   [StLN66 1/7]   d9.5

1969	StL N	7	23	3	5	1	0	0	3	3-0	0	8	.217	.308	.261	60	-1	0-0	1.000	-0	60	230	O7(4/0/3)		-0.2
1970	StL N	121	264	28	60	13	1	6	23	24-4	1	66	.227	.290	.352	70	-11	5-1	.969	-2	98	68	O77(1/0/76)		-1.6
1971	StL N	25	28	3	5	1	0	1	2	4-0	0	12	.179	.281	.321	67	-1	0-1	.800	-1	55	0	O8(5/0/4)		-0.3
	SD N	79	256	29	70	20	2	4	21	18-4	0	45	.273	.321	.414	114	4	4-5	.914	-6	65	121	O76(73/0/4)		-0.6
	Year	104	284	32	75	21	2	5	23	22-4	0	57	.264	.317	.405	107	2	4-6	.975	3	105	93	O96(96/0/1)		-0.9
1972	SD N	101	370	50	111	23	7	12	47	29-4	1	58	.300	.353	.497	151	23	2-5	.970	2	100	126	O84(72/0/14)		2.0
1973	SD N	118	333	36	79	7	2	3	30	33-3	1	61	.237	.306	.297	74	-12	4-0	.958	4	108	121	O62(60/0/2),D2		-1.4
1974	Cle A	79	232	18	54	13	0	5	25	15-2	1	42	.233	.279	.353	82	-6	3-2	1.000	-0	113	0	O5L,D3		-0.6
1975	Cle A	13	23	3	3	1	0	0	2	3-1	0	9	.130	.231	.174	16	-3	1-0	1.000	-0	40	0	O4L		-0.3
	LA N	48	43	2	11	4	0	0	2	3-1	0	9	.256	.298	.349	84	-1	0-0	1.000	-2	71	0	O10R		-0.1
1976	LA N	23	45	1	6	0	1	0	2	2-1	0	9	.133	.170	.178	-1	-6	0-0	.962	-1	94	104	O421(315/0/110),D5	40	-0.9
Total	8	614	1617	173	404	83	13	31	152	133-19	6	315	.250	.307	.375	94	-14	19-14							-4.0

LEE, MANUEL   Manuel Lora "Manny" (b Manuel Lora (Lee))   B6.17.1965 San Pedro de Macoris, D.R.   BB/TR/5-9/161(150-166)   d4.10

1985	†Tor A	64	40	9	8	0	0	0	0	2-0	0	9	.200	.238	.200	21	-4	1-4	.971	1	98	97	2b38,S8,3b5,D8		-0.4
1986	Tor A	35	78	8	16	0	1	1	7	4-0	0	10	.205	.241	.269	38	-7	0-1	.990	-2	110	71	2b29,S5,3b2		-0.8
1987	Tor A	56	121	14	31	2	3	1	11	6-0	0	13	.256	.289	.347	67	-6	2-0	.966	6	107	130	2b27,S26/D	28	0.3
1988	Tor A	116	381	38	111	16	3	2	38	26-1	0	64	.291	.333	.365	95	-2	3-3	.988	8	102	106	2b98,S23,3b8,D2	37	0.9
1989	†Tor A	99	300	27	78	9	2	3	34	20-1	0	60	.260	.305	.333	81	-8	4-2	.985	-5	85	114	2b40,S28,3b17,D13/OR		-1.0
1990	Tor A	117	391	45	95	12	4	6	41	26-0	2	90	.243	.288	.340	74	-15	3-1	**.993**	-12	89	93	2b112,S9		-2.4
1991	Tor A	138	445	41	104	18	3	0	29	24-0	2	107	.234	.274	.288	54	-28	7-2	.967	-20	91	68	S138		-3.8
1992	†Tor A	128	396	49	104	10	1	3	39	50-0	2	73	.263	.343	.316	82	-8	6-2	.987	-11	89	88	S128	80	-0.8
1993	Tex A	73	205	31	45	3	1	1	12	22-3	2	39	.220	.300	.259	54	-13	2-4	.968	1	104	83	S72/D	15	-0.7
1994	Tex A	95	335	41	93	18	2	2	38	21-0	0	66	.278	.319	.361	74	-13	3-1	.967	-1	105	95	S85,2b13	36	-0.2
1995	StL N	1	1	1	1	0	0	0	0	0-0	0	0	1.000	1.000	1.000	422	0	0-0	.800	0	206	0	/2	196	-9.5
Total	11	922	2693	304	686	88	20	19	249	201-5	4	531	.255	.305	.323	72	-104	31-20	.972	-35	96	85	S522,2b358,3b32,D25/OR		

LEE, TERRY   Terry James   B3.13.1962 San Francisco CA   BR/TR/6-5/215*   d9.3   Col Chemeketa (OR) CC

1990	Cin N	12	19	1	4	1	0	0	3	2-0	0	2	.211	.273	.263	50	-1	0-0	1.000	0	113	40	1b6		-0.1
1991	Cin N	3	6	0	0	0	0	0	0	0-0	0	2	.000	.000	.000	-96	-2	0-0	1.000	1	413	0	1b2		0.0
Total	2	15	25	1	4	1	0	0	3	2-0	0	4	.160	.214	.200	17	-3	0-0	1.000	1	193	29	1b8		-0.1

LEE, TRAVIS   Travis Reynolds   B5.26.1975 San Diego CA   BL/TL/6-3/214(210-225)   d3.31   Col San Diego St.

1998	Ari N	146	562	71	151	20	2	22	72	67-5	0	123	.269	.346	.429	102	2	8-1	.998	-2	96	92	1b146	15	-1.2
1999	Ari N	120	375	57	89	16	2	9	50	58-4	0	50	.237	.337	.363	77	-13	17-3	**.997**	2	105	90	1b114,O2R	26	-1.0
2000	Ari N	72	224	34	52	13	0	8	40	25-1	0	46	.232	.308	.397	74	-9	5-1	.983	5	125	105	O55(0/2/54),1b23	14	-0.8
	Phi N	56	180	19	43	11	1	1	14	40-0	2	33	.239	.381	.328	82	-3	3-0	1.000	2	126	121	1b47,O10L		-0.3
	Year	128	404	53	95	24	1	9	54	65-1	2	79	.235	.342	.366	78	-12	8-1	.996	7	117	128	1b70,O65(10/2/54)		-1.1
2001	Phi N	157	555	75	143	34	2	20	90	71-5	4	109	.258	.341	.434	105	5	3-4	.996	-7	81	101	1b156		-2.2
2002	Phi N	153	536	55	142	26	2	13	70	54-10	0	104	.265	.331	.394	100	-4	5-3	.998	0	99	93	1b142,D2	15	0.2
2003	TB A	145	542	75	149	37	3	19	70	64-4	0	97	.275	.348	.459	114	12	6-2	1.000	0	120	52	1b6	174	-0.1
2004	NY A	7	19	1	2	1	0	0	2	1-1	0	3	.105	.150	.158	-20	-3	0-0	1.000	-1	106	86	1b124	18	-0.2
2005	TB A	129	404	54	110	22	4	12	45	45-34	1	104	.272	.331	.426	102	1	7-4	.997	-3	95	97	1b906,O67(10/2/56),D2	262	-8.2
Total	8	985	3397	441	881	180	14	104	457	415-34	7	631	.259	.339	.412	97	-12	54-18							

LEE, BILLY   William Joseph   B1.9.1892 Bayonne NJ   D1.6.1984 West Hazleton PA   BR/TR/5-9/165   d4.15

1915	StL A	18	59	2	11	1	0	4	6	0	3	.186	.262	.203	41	-4	1-1	1.000	2	121	100	O15(7/6/2)/3		-0.4
1916	StL A	7	11	1	2	0	0	0	1	0	3	.182	.250	.182	31	-1	1-1	1.000	-0	105	0	O4(0/2/2)		-0.3
Total	2	25	70	3	13	1	0	0	4	7	0	6	.186	.260	.200	39	-5	1-1	1.000	2	119	87	O19(7/8/4)/3		-0.3

LEE, WATTY   Wyatt Arnold   B8.12.1879 Lynch Station VA   D3.6.1936 Washington DC   BL/TL/5-10.5/171   d4.30 ▲

1901	Was A	43	129	15	33	6	3	0	12	7	.256	.304	.349	82	-3	0	.948	1	108	120	P36,O7(2/1/4)		0.0
1902	Was A	109	391	61	100	21	5	4	45	33	3	.256	.319	.366	89	-6	8	.916	2	118	40	O96(22/20/54),P13		-0.1
1903	Was A	75	231	17	48	8	4	0	13	18	0	.208	.265	.277	62	-11	5	.930	5	110	136	O47(0/10/37),P22		-0.8
1904	Pit N	8	12	1	4	0	0	0	2	0	.333	.333	.500	152	1	0	.889	-0	111	0	P5		-0.1
Total	4	235	763	94	185	35	13	4	70	58	0	.242	.300	.338	80	-19	13	.917	8	117	72	O150(24/31/95),P76		-1.7

LEEK, GENE   Eugene Harold   B7.15.1936 San Diego CA   BR/TR/6-0/185*   d4.22   Col Arizona

																7	.222	.263	.389	80	-1	0-0	.955	-2	87	0	3b13/S		-0.5
1959	Cle A	13	36	7	8	2	0	1	5	2-0	0	7	.222	.263	.389	80	-1	0-0	.955	-2	87	0	3b13/S		-0.5
1961	LA A	57	199	16	45	9	1	5	20	7-0	2	54	.226	.260	.357	57	-13	0-1	.958	18	126	105	3b49,S7/OL		-0.8
1962	LA A	7	14	0	2	0	0	0	0	0-0	0	6	.143	.143	.143	-24	-2	0-0	1.000	-1	58	152	3b4		-0.2
Total	3	77	249	23	55	11	1	6	25	9-0	2	67	.221	.254	.349	55	-16	0-1	.959	16	117	94	3b66,S8/OL		-1.5

YEAR	TM LG	G	AB	R	H	2B	3B	HR	RBI	BB-IB	HP	SO	AVG	OBP	SLG	AOPS	ABR	SB-CS	FA	FR	RNG	THR	GAMES AT POSITION	DL	BFW

LEEPER, DAVE David Dale B10.30.1959 Santa Ana CA BL/TL/5-11/170* [KCA81 1/23] d9.10 Col USC

1984	KC A	4	6	1	0	0	0	0	4	1-0	0	1	.000	.000	.000	-99	-2	0-0	1.000	0	134	0	O2L/D		
1985	KC A	15	34	1	3	0	0	0	4	1-0	0	3	.088	.114	.088	-43	-7	0-0	.929	-1	86	0	O8(2/0/6)		-0.2
Total	2	19	40	2	3	0	0	0	4	1-0	0	4	.075	.098	.075	-51	-9	0-0	.944	-1	94	0	O10(4/0/6)/D		-0.8
																									-1.0

LEES, GEORGE George Edward B2.2.1895 Bethlehem PA D1.2.1980 Harrisburg PA BR/TR/5-9/150 d5.7 Col Lehigh

| 1921 | Chi A | 20 | 42 | 3 | 9 | 2 | 0 | 0 | 4 | 0 | 0 | 3 | .214 | .214 | .262 | 25 | -5 | 0-1 | .951 | -2 | 84 | 75 | C16 | | -0.6 |

LEFEBVRE, JIM James Kenneth B1.7.1942 Inglewood CA BB/TR/6-0/185* d4.12 M6/C11

1965	†LA N	157	544	57	136	21	4	12	69	71-7	2	92	.250	.337	.369	106	6	3-5	.970	0	100	104	2b156		2.0
1966	†LA N★	152	544	69	149	23	3	24	74	48-6	3	72	.274	.333	.460	120	20	1-1	.980	3	106	90	2b119,3b40		3.4
1967	LA N	136	494	51	129	18	5	8	50	44-11	3	64	.261	.322	.366	106	3	1-5	.955	5	106	78	3b92,2b34,1b5		0.9
1968	LA N	84	286	23	69	12	1	5	31	26-4	1	55	.241	.304	.343	102	1	0-0	.978	-4	92	92	2b62,3b16,O5L,1b3		0.1
1969	LA N	95	275	29	65	15	2	4	44	48-10	1	37	.236	.349	.349	103	2	0-0	.978	-4	92	92	2b62,3b16,O5L,1b3		0.1
1970	LA N	109	314	33	79	15	1	4	44	29-2	1	42	.252	.314	.344	80	-9	1-1	.985	1	116	107	3b44,2b37,1b6		0.6
1971	LA N	119	388	40	95	14	2	12	68	39-6	2	55	.245	.314	.384	103	1	0-2	.988	-9	94	84	2b70,3b21/1		-1.4
1972	LA N	70	169	11	34	8	0	5	24	17-6	0	30	.201	.271	.337	74	-6	0-0	.988	-6	92	109	2b102,3b7		0.1
Total	8	922	3014	313	756	126	18	74	404	322-52	13	447	.251	.323	.378	105	19	8-15	.979	-11	100	99	2b613,3b231,1b15,O5L		-0.5
																									5.2

LEFEBVRE, JOE Joseph Henry B2.22.1956 Concord NH BL/TR/5-10/175* [NYA77 3/75] d5.22 C4 Col Eckerd [DL 1985 Phi N 182]

1980	†NY A	74	150	26	34	1	1	8	21	27-3	0	30	.227	.345	.407	107	2	0-0	.975	-4	81	88	O71(20/3/52)		-0.4
1981	SD N	86	246	31	63	13	4	8	31	35-7	2	33	.256	.352	.439	135	12	6-4	.994	4	111	95	O84(0/2/83)		1.2
1982	SD N	102	239	25	57	9	0	4	21	18-2	1	50	.238	.292	.326	78	-7	0-0	.972	-2	98	115	3b39,O36(18/2/18),C3		-1.2
1983	SD N	18	20	1	5	0	0	0	1	2-0	0	3	.250	.318	.250	61	-1	0-0	1.000	1	23	611	O6R,3b4,C2		-0.1
	†Phi N	101	258	34	80	20	8	8	38	31-6	3	46	.310	.388	.543	157	20	5-3	.990	-4	90	103	O74(22/0/58),3b9,C3		1.4
	Year	119	278	35	85	20	8	8	39	33-6	3	49	.306	.383	.522	151	19	5-3	.990						
1984	Phi N	52	160	22	40	9	0	3	18	23-4	2	37	.250	.348	.363	99	1	0-2	.966	0	101	133	O80(22/0/64),3b13,C5		1.3
1986	Phi N	14	18	1	2	0	0	0	0	3-0	0	5	.111	.238	.111	-1	-2	0-0	1.000	-0	95	102	O3R	105	-0.2
Total	6	447	1091	139	281	52	13	31	139	139-22	8	204	.258	.344	.414	115	25	11-9	.986	-5	95	102	O321(76/7/254),3b53,C8	287	0.4

LEFEBVRE, BILL Wilfred Henry "Lefty" B11.11.1915 Natick RI BL/TL/5-11.5/180 d6.10 Mil 1945 Col Holy Cross ▲

1938	Bos A	1	1	0	1	0	0	0	1	0	0	0	1.000	1.000	1.000	1048	1	0-0	—	-0	0	0	/P		0.0
1939	Bos A	7	10	3	3	0	0	0	1	2	0	2	.300	.417	.300	83	1	0-0	1.000	-1	45	0	P5		0.0
1943	Was A	7	14	0	4	2	0	0	1	1	0	0	.286	.333	.500	148	2	0-0	1.000	-0	92	249	P6		0.0
1944	Was A	60	62	4	16	2	2	0	8	12	0	9	.258	.378	.355	115	2	0-0	.933	-0	99	209	P24,1b2		0.0
Total	4	75	87	8	24	5	2	1	11	15	0	11	.276	.382	.414	129	6	0-0	.960	-1	84	171	P36,1b2		0.0

LEFEVRE, AL Alfred Modesto B9.16.1898 New York NY D1.21.1982 Glen Cove NY BR/TR/5-10.5/160 d6.28 Col Fordham

| 1920 | NY N | 17 | 27 | 5 | 4 | 0 | 0 | 0 | 0 | 0 | 0 | 13 | .148 | .148 | .222 | 5 | -3 | 0-0 | 1.000 | 3 | 142 | 115 | S9,2b6/3 | | -0.1 |

LEFLER, WADE Wade Hampton B6.5.1896 Cooleemee NC D3.6.1981 Hickory NC BL/TR/5-11/162 d4.16 Col Duke

1924	Bos N	1	1	0	0	0	0	0	0	0	0	1	.000	.000	.000	-99	0	0-0	—	0			/H		0.0
	Was A	5	8	0	5	3	0	0	4	0	0	0	.625	.625	1.000	325	3	0-0	1.000	0	121	0	/OR		0.2
Total	1	6	9	0	5	3	0	0	4	0	0	1	.556	.556	.889	279	3	0-0	1.000	0	121	0	/OR		0.2

LeFLORE, RON Ronald B6.16.1948 Detroit MI BR/TR/6-0/200* d8.1

1974	Det A	59	254	37	66	8	1	2	13	13-0	3	58	.260	.301	.323	77	-8	23-9	.935	-2	92	181	O59C		-1.0
1975	Det A	136	550	66	142	13	6	8	37	33-1	2	139	.258	.302	.347	80	-16	28-20	.973	-3	94	144	O134C		-2.5
1976	Det A★	135	544	93	172	23	8	4	39	51-2	2	111	.316	.376	.410	125	18	58-20	.973	5	104	142	O132C/D		2.6
1977	Det A	154	652	100	212	30	10	16	57	37-1	4	121	.325	.363	.475	121	18	39-19	.972	-12	88	107	O152C	19	0.7
1978	Det A	155	666	126	198	30	3	12	62	65-7	4	104	.297	.361	.405	112	12	68-16	.976	-5	98	85	O155C		1.6
1979	Det A	148	600	110	180	22	10	9	57	52-2	0	95	.300	.355	.415	104	3	78-14	.990	0	101	85	O113C,D34		1.3
1980	Mon N	139	521	95	134	21	11	4	39	62-1	1	99	.257	.337	.363	93	-4	97-19	.957	-2	96	153	O130L		0.8
1981	Chi A	82	337	46	83	10	4	0	24	28-0	1	70	.246	.304	.300	76	-10	36-11	.960	-2	96	110	O82(76/7/0)		-1.2
1982	Chi A	91	334	58	96	15	4	4	25	22-1	1	91	.287	.331	.392	97	-2	28-14	.939	-5	88	140	O83(2/81/0),D2		-0.6
Total	9	1099	4458	731	1283	172	57	59	353	363-15	17	888	.288	.342	.392	102	11	455-142	.968	-22	96	123	O1040(208/833/0),D37	19	1.7

LEGETT, LOU Louis Alfred "Doc" B6.1.1901 New Orleans LA D3.6.1988 New Orleans LA BR/TR/5-10/166 d5.8

1929	Bos N	39	81	7	13	2	0	0	6	3	0	18	.160	.190	.185	-7	-14	0-0	.914	-1	108	128	C28		-1.3
1933	Bos A	8	5	1	1	1	0	0	1	0	0	0	.200	.200	.400	56	0	0-0	1.000	0	0	0	C2		0.0
1934	Bos A	19	38	4	11	0	0	0	1	2	0	4	.289	.325	.289	56	-3	0-0	.977	0	91	88	C17		-0.2
1935	Bos A	2	0	1	0	0	0	0	0	0	0	0	—	—	—		0	0-0	—	0			/R		0.0
Total	4	68	124	13	25	3	0	0	8	5	0	22	.202	.233	.226	16	-17	2-0	.938	-1	101	113	C47		-1.5

LEGG, GREG Gregory Lynn B4.21.1960 San Jose CA BR/TR/6-1/185* [PhiN82 22/559] d4.18 Col Southeastern Oklahoma

1986	Phi N	11	20	2	9	1	0	0	1	0-0	0	3	.450	.450	.500	156	1	0-0	.941	1	143	167	2b4/S		0.3
1987	Phi N	3	2	1	0	0	0	0	0	0-0	0	0	.000	.000	.000	-97	-1	0-0	1.000	0	158	674	/2S3		0.0
Total	2	14	22	3	9	1	0	0	1	0-0	0	3	.409	.409	.455	132	0	0-0	.952	1	144	205	2b5,S2/3		0.3

LEHAN, JAMES James Francis B5.14.1856 Hartford CT D7.18.1946 Hartford CT d4.26

| 1884 | Was U | 3 | 12 | 1 | 4 | 2 | 0 | 0 | | | | | .333 | .333 | .500 | 155 | 1 | | .688 | -1 | 104 | 0 | S3/OL3 | | 0.0 |

LEHANE, MIKE Michael Patrick B4.15.1865 New York NY BR/6-1.5/180 d4.17

1890	Col AA	140	512	54	108	19	5	0	56	43	3		.211	.276	.268	65	-22	13	.982	10	131	127	1b140		-2.2
1891	Col AA	137	511	59	110	12	7	1	52	34	3	77	.215	.268	.272	58	-29	16	.981	7	125	128	1b137		-3.0
Total	2	277	1023	113	218	31	12	1	108	77	6	77	.213	.272	.270	61	-51	29	.982	17	128	127	1b277		-5.2

LEHNER, PAUL Paul Eugene "Peanuts","Gulliver" B7.1.1920 Dolomite AL D12.27.1967 Birmingham AL BL/TL/5-9/165* d9.10

1946	StL A	16	45	6	10	1	0	0	2	5	0	5	.222	.239	.333	56	-3	0-0	.941	-1	71	178	O12(0/11/1)		-0.5
1947	StL A	135	483	59	120	25	9	7	48	28	3	29	.248	.294	.381	85	-12	0-0	.980	-8	97	12	O127(2/125/0)		-2.6
1948	StL A	103	333	23	92	15	4	2	46	30	4	19	.276	.336	.363	84	-8	5-5	.974	-5	94	59	O89C,1b2		-1.6
1949	StL A	104	297	25	68	13	0	3	37	16	1	20	.229	.271	.303	50	-23	0-2	.987	1	114	25	O56(12/35/10),1b18		-2.5
1950	Phi A	114	427	48	132	17	5	9	52	32	0	33	.309	.357	.436	104	1	1-1	.981	4	105	119	O101(80/7/15)		-0.2
1951	Phi A	9	28	4	4	1	0	0	1	1	0	4	.143	.172	.179	-5	-4	0-0	1.000	1	103	183	O6L		-0.4
	StL A	23	72	9	15	3	1	0	3	10	0	4	.208	.305	.278	60	-4	0-0	.980	1	97	171	O20(8/13/9)		-0.4
	Cle A	12	13	2	3	0	0	0	2	6	1	5	.134	.205	.254	23	-7	0-1	1.000	-1	105	0	O18(1/17/0)		-0.9
	Year	65	180	14	31	9	1	7	18			12	.231	.286	.231	43	-1	0-0	1.000	-0	78	0	/OL		-0.1
1952	Bos A	3	3	0	2	0	0	0	2	0	0	2	.667	.800	.667	288	1	0-0	1.000	0	131	0	O2R		0.1
Total	7	540	1768	175	455	80	21	22	197	127	4	118	.257	.309	.364	78	-60	6-11	.981	-8	101	63	O432(110/297/37),1b20		-9.1

LEHR, CLARENCE Clarence Emanuel "King" B5.16.1886 Escanaba MI D1.31.1948 Highland Park MI BR/TR/5-11/165 d5.18

| 1911 | Phi N | 23 | 27 | 2 | 4 | 0 | 0 | 0 | 2 | 0 | 0 | 7 | .148 | .148 | .148 | -17 | -4 | 0 | 1.000 | 1 | 85 | 0 | O5(1/1/3),2b4,S4 | | -0.4 |

LEIBER, HANK Henry Edward B1.17.1911 Phoenix AZ D11.8.1993 Tucson AZ BR/TR/6-1.5/205 d4.16 Col Arizona ▲

1933	NY N	6	10	1	2	0	0	0	0	0	0	2	.200	.200	.200	15	-1	0	1.000	1	88	804	/OL		-0.1
1934	NY N	63	187	17	45	5	3	2	25	4	0	29	.241	.257	.332	58	-12	1	.971	-3	86	94	O51(2/49/0)		-1.7
1935	NY N	154	613	110	203	37	4	22	107	48	10	29	.331	.389	.512	143	37	0	.965	-22	83	38	O154C		1.1
1936	†NY N	101	337	44	94	19	7	9	67	32	1	41	.279	.352	.457	118	8	1	.961	-8	77	150	O86(7/78/1)/1		-0.2
1937	†NY N★	51	184	24	54	7	4	4	32	15	0	27	.293	.347	.429	108	2	1	.988	-6	80	30	O46(1/42/3)		-0.5
1938	NY N★	98	360	50	97	18	4	12	65	31	0	45	.269	.327	.442	109	3	0	.974	-9	84	91	O89(2/86/4)		2.5
1939	Chi N	112	365	65	113	16	1	24	88	59	4	33	.310	.411	.556	155	30	1	.977	-2	101	63	O98C		1.1
1940	Chi N★	117	440	68	133	24	2	17	86	45	2	68	.302	.371	.482	136	22	1	.985	-6	85	101	O103(0/53/52),1b12		-0.8
1941	Chi N★	53	162	20	35	6	0	3	23	19	2	25	.216	.291	.377	90	-3	0	.964	-2	94	94	O29(23/2/5),1b15		-0.3
1942	NY N	58	147	11	32	6	0	4	23	19	2	20	.218	.315	.340	91	-1	0	.990	-0	103	58	O41(1/40/0)/P		0.3
Total	10	813	2805	410	808	137	24	101	518	274	21	319	.288	.356	.461	122	85	5	.973	-58	87	77	O698(37/602/65),1b28/P		

LEIBOLD, NEMO   Harry Loran   B2.17.1892 Butler IN   D2.4.1977 Detroit MI   BL/TR/5-6.5/157   d4.12

YEAR	TM LG	G	AB	R	H	2B	3B	HR	RBI	BB-IB	HP	SO	AVG	OBP	SLG	AOPS	ABR	SB-CS	FA	FR	RNG	THR	GAMES AT POSITION	DL	BFW
1913	Cle A	93	286	37	74	11	6	0	12	21	0	43	.259	.309	.339	87	-6	16	.945	-2	93	109	O74(4/66/2)		-1.3
1914	Cle A	115	402	46	106	13	3	0	32	54	2	56	.264	.354	.311	96	0	12-14	.931	4	99	**159**	O107(0/90/17)		-0.5
1915	Cle A	57	207	28	53	5	4	0	4	24	2	16	.256	.339	.319	95	-1	5-3	.969	5	113	124	O52C		0.0
	Chi A	36	74	10	17	1	0	0	11	15	0	11	.230	.360	.243	78	-1	1-3	1.000	3	114	157	O22(10/12/0)		0.0
	Year	93	281	38	70	6	4	0	15	39	2	27	.249	.345	.299	91	-2	6-6	.978	8	113	134	O74(10/64/0)		-0.4
1916	Chi A	45	82	5	20	1	2	0	13	7	0	7	.244	.303	.305	82	-2	7	1.000	-1	95	48	O24(2/16/6)		-0.2
1917	†Chi A	125	428	59	101	12	6	0	29	74	1	34	.236	.350	.292	94	0	27	.961	3	104	117	O122(16/4/102)		
1918	Chi A	116	440	57	110	14	7	0	31	63	0	32	.250	.344	.314	97	0	15	.979	7	111	104	O114(95/7/12)		1.5
1919	†Chi A	122	434	81	131	18	2	0	26	72	2	30	.302	.404	.353	113	12	17	.928	8	103	162	O105(3/4/98)		-2.6
1920	Chi A	108	413	61	91	16	3	0	28	55	3	30	.220	.316	.281	59	-23	7-15	.977	6	102	130	O117(0/107/10)		-0.9
1921	Bos A	123	467	88	143	26	6	0	31	41	1	27	.306	.363	.388	94	-1	13-7	.949	-1	98	100	O71(1/66/4)		-1.1
1922	Bos A	81	271	42	70	8	1	1	18	41	1	14	.258	.360	.306	76	-8	1-6	.966	2	100	126	O10C		-1.1
1923	Bos A	12	18	1	2	0	0	0	0	1	0	2	.111	.158	.111	-28	-3	0-1	.909	0	88	218	O5C		0.4
	Was A	95	315	60	96	13	4	1	22	53	2	16	.305	.408	.381	114	10	7-6	.980	-2	88	137	O84C		0.0
	Year	107	333	69	98	13	4	1	22	54	2	18	.294	.396	.366	106	6	7-7	.994	1	102	144	O70(4/52/14)		-0.1
1924	†Was A	84	246	41	72	6	4	0	20	42	1	10	.293	.398	.350	97	1	7-5	.972	0	97	144	O26(2/22/2)/3		-0.4
1925	†Was A	56	84	14	23	1	1	0	7	8	0	7	.274	.337	.310	66	-4	1-0	.961	35	101	126	O70(4/52/14)		
Total	13	1268	4167	638	1109	145	49	3	284	571	16	335	.266	.357	.327	91	-28	136-60	.961	35	101	126	O1120(144/593/381)/3		-5.8

LEIFER, ELMER   Elmer Edwin   B5.23.1893 Clarington OH   D9.26.1948 Everett WA   BL/TR/5-9.5/170   d9.7

YEAR	TM LG	G	AB	R	H	2B	3B	HR	RBI	BB-IB	HP	SO	AVG	OBP	SLG	AOPS	ABR	SB-CS	FA	FR	RNG	THR	GAMES AT POSITION	DL	BFW
1921	Chi A	9	10	0	3	0	0	0	1	0	0	4	.300	.300	.300	54	-1	0-0	1.000	-0	67	0	/3OL		-0.1

LEIGHTON, JOHN   John Atkinson   B10.4.1861 Peabody MA   D10.31.1956 Lynn MA   BL/TL/5-11/170   d7.12

YEAR	TM LG	G	AB	R	H	2B	3B	HR	RBI	BB-IB	HP	SO	AVG	OBP	SLG	AOPS	ABR	SB-CS	FA	FR	RNG	THR	GAMES AT POSITION	DL	BFW
1890	Syr AA	7	27	6	8	2	0	0	3				.296	.367	.370	131	-1	0	0	.938	-0	0	O7C		0.1

LEINHAUSER, BILL   William Charles   B11.4.1893 Philadelphia PA   D4.14.1978 Elkins Park PA   BR/TR/5-10/150   d5.18

YEAR	TM LG	G	AB	R	H	2B	3B	HR	RBI	BB-IB	HP	SO	AVG	OBP	SLG	AOPS	ABR	SB-CS	FA	FR	RNG	THR	GAMES AT POSITION	DL	BFW
1912	Det A	1	4	0	0	0	0	0	0	0	0	0	.000	.000	.000	-99	-1	0	1.000	1	0	0	/OC		0.0

LEIP, ED   Edgar Ellsworth   B11.29.1910 Trenton NJ   D11.24.1983 Zephyrhills FL   BR/TR/5-9/160   d9.16   Mil 1942-45

YEAR	TM LG	G	AB	R	H	2B	3B	HR	RBI	BB-IB	HP	SO	AVG	OBP	SLG	AOPS	ABR	SB-CS	FA	FR	RNG	THR	GAMES AT POSITION	DL	BFW
1939	Was A	9	32	4	11	1	0	0	2	2	0	4	.344	.382	.375	102	0	0-1	.951	-0	110	102	2b8		-0.1
1940	Pit N	3	5	2	1	0	0	0	0	0	0	0	.200	.200	.200	11	-1	0	1.000	-0	81	183	2b2		-0.1
1941	Pit N	15	25	1	5	0	2	0	3	1	0	2	.200	.231	.360	65	-2	1	.889	0	120	84	2b7/3		0.0
1942	Pit N	3	0	0	0	0	0	0	0	0	0	0	—	—	—					0	0		/R		-0.2
Total	4	30	62	7	17	1	2	0	5	3	0	6	.274	.308	.355	80	-3	1-1	.931	0	111	101	2b17/3		

LEIUS, SCOTT   Scott Thomas   B9.24.1965 Yonkers NY   BR/TR/6-3/195(180-208)   [MinA86 13/325]   d9.3   Col Concordia (NY)

YEAR	TM LG	G	AB	R	H	2B	3B	HR	RBI	BB-IB	HP	SO	AVG	OBP	SLG	AOPS	ABR	SB-CS	FA	FR	RNG	THR	GAMES AT POSITION	DL	BFW
1990	Min A	14	25	6	4	1	0	1	4	2-0	0		.240	.296	.400	87	0	0-0	1.000	2	96	174	S12/3		0.2
1991	†Min A	109	199	35	57	7	2	5	20	30-1	0	35	.286	.378	.417	115	5	5-5	.953	2	101	88	3b79,S19,O2C		0.7
1992	Min A	129	409	50	102	18	2	2	35	34-0	1	61	.249	.309	.318	73	-15	6-5	.955	-0	105	63	3b125,S10		-1.5
1993	Min A	10	18	4	3	0	0	0	2	2-0	0	6	.167	.227	.167	14	-2	0-0	.947	2	126	153	S9	165	0.0
1994	Min A	97	350	57	86	16	1	14	49	37-0	1	58	.246	.318	.417	87	-7	2-4	.969	-1	103	87	3b112,S7,D3		-1.3
1995	Min A	117	372	51	92	16	1	4	45	49-3	2	54	.247	.335	.349	79	-11	2-1	1.000	-1	76	0	3b8,1b7,2b6/D	20	-0.6
1996	Cle A	27	43	3	6	4	0	1	3	2-0	0	8	.140	.178	.302	18	-6	0-0	.867	1	91	118	3b15,S2/D	21	-0.8
1998	KC A	17	46	2	8	0	0	0	4	1-0	0	7	.174	.191	.174	-4	-7	0-0	.971	1	140	188	1b13,3b10,S2/2D	92	-0.7
1999	KC A	37	74	8	15	1	0	1	10	4-0	1	8	.203	.244	.257	29	-8	1-0	.954	1	102	98	2b7,O2C		
Total	9	557	1536	214	375	63	10	28	172	161-4	5	236	.244	.316	.353	77	-51	16-15	.954	1	102	98	3b445,S63,1b20,D11,2b7,O2C	298	-4.8

LEJA, FRANK   Frank John   B2.7.1936 Holyoke MA   D5.3.1991 Boston MA   BL/TL/6-4/205*   d5.1

YEAR	TM LG	G	AB	R	H	2B	3B	HR	RBI	BB-IB	HP	SO	AVG	OBP	SLG	AOPS	ABR	SB-CS	FA	FR	RNG	THR	GAMES AT POSITION	DL	BFW
1954	NY A	12	5	2	1	0	0	0	0	0	0		.200	.200	.200	10	-1	0-0	1.000	-0	0	0	1b6		-0.1
1955	NY A	7	2	1	0	0	0	0	0	0-0	0	1	.000	.000	.000	-99	-1	0-0	1.000	-0	0	507	1b2		-0.1
1962	LA A	7	16	0	0	0	0	0	0	1-0	0	6	.000	.059	.000	-85	-4	0-0	.953	-0	108	120	1b4		-0.1
Total	3	26	23	3	1	0	0	0	0	1-0	0	8	.043	.083	.043	-67	-6	0-0	.958	-1	97	134	1b12		

LeJEUNE, LARRY   Sheldon Aldenbert   B7.22.1885 Chicago IL   D4.21.1952 Eloise (now part of Westland) MI   BR/TR/6-0/185   d5.10

YEAR	TM LG	G	AB	R	H	2B	3B	HR	RBI	BB-IB	HP	SO	AVG	OBP	SLG	AOPS	ABR	SB-CS	FA	FR	RNG	THR	GAMES AT POSITION	DL	BFW
1911	Bro N	6	19	2	3	0	0	0	2	2	0	8	.158	.238	.158	12	-2	2	.818	-3	82	0	O6C		-0.1
1915	Pit N	18	65	4	11	0	1	0	2	2	1	15	.169	.206	.200	23	-6	4-3	.940	2	105	192	O18C		-0.1
Total	2	24	84	6	14	0	1	0	4	4	1	15	.167	.213	.190	21	-8	6-3	.918	1	100	151	O24C		-1.

LeJOHN, DON   Donald Everett   B5.13.1934 Daisytown PA   D2.25.2005 California PA   BR/TR/5-10/175   d6.30

YEAR	TM LG	G	AB	R	H	2B	3B	HR	RBI	BB-IB	HP	SO	AVG	OBP	SLG	AOPS	ABR	SB-CS	FA	FR	RNG	THR	GAMES AT POSITION	DL	BFW
1965	†LA N	34	78	2	20	2	0	0	7	5-0	0	13	.256	.301	.282	70	-3	0-1	.959	-0	101	80	3b26		-0.

LELIVELT, JACK   John Frank   B11.14.1885 Chicago IL   D1.20.1941 Seattle WA   BL/TL/5-11.5/175   d6.24   b-Bill

YEAR	TM LG	G	AB	R	H	2B	3B	HR	RBI	BB-IB	HP	SO	AVG	OBP	SLG	AOPS	ABR	SB-CS	FA	FR	RNG	THR	GAMES AT POSITION	DL	BFW
1909	Was A	91	318	25	93	8	6	0	24	19	1		.292	.334	.355	124	7	8	.970	6	116	104	O91(41/35/15)		0.
1910	Was A	110	347	40	92	10	3	0	33	40	1		.265	.343	.311	110	5	20	.964	6	112	126	O86(80/5/1),1b7		0.
1911	Was A	72	225	29	72	12	4	0	22	22	2		.320	.386	.409	124	8	7	.939	2	93	134	O49(36/0/13),1b7		0.
1912	NY A	36	149	12	54	6	7	2	23	4	1		.362	.383	.537	153	9	7	.963	-2	95	77	O36C		0.
1913	NY A	18	28	2	6	0	0	0	4	2	0	2	.214	.267	.286	61	-2	1	1.000	0	110	128	O5C		0.
	Cle A	23	23	9	9	2	0	0	7	0	0	3	.391	.391	.478	150	1	1	—	-0	0	0	O6C		0.
	Year	41	51	9	15	2	1	0	11	2	0		.294	.321	.373	101	0	2	1.000	0	108	125	O13(0/7/6)/1		0.
1914	Cle A	34	64	6	21	5	1	0	13	2	0	15	.301	.353	.381	124	30	46-3	.962	11	107	110	O281(157/88/35),1b15		2.
Total	6	384	1154	114	347	43	22	2	126	89	5	15	.301	.352	.397										

LeMASTER, JOHNNIE   Johnnie Lee   B6.19.1954 Portsmouth OH   BR/TR/6-2/167(160-180)   [SFN73 1/6]   d9.2

YEAR	TM LG	G	AB	R	H	2B	3B	HR	RBI	BB-IB	HP	SO	AVG	OBP	SLG	AOPS	ABR	SB-CS	FA	FR	RNG	THR	GAMES AT POSITION	DL	BFW
1975	SF N	22	74	4	14	2	0	2	4	4-0	1	15	.189	.241	.324	54	-5	2-1	.967	-3	93	92	S22		-0.
1976	SF N	33	100	9	21	3	2	0	9	2-0	1	21	.210	.223	.280	42	-8	2-0	.937	7	122	95	S31		-0.
1977	SF N	68	134	13	20	5	1	0	8	13-3	1	27	.149	.229	.201	15	-16	2-1	.934	-3	103	66	S54,3b2		-0.
1978	SF N	101	272	23	64	18	3	1	14	21-1	1	45	.235	.293	.335	77	-9	6-6	.966	-7	96	87	S96,2b2		-0.
1979	SF N	108	343	42	87	11	2	3	29	23-1	2	55	.254	.304	.324	77	-12	9-5	.959	-1	96	88	S106		-0.
1980	SF N	135	405	33	87	16	6	3	31	25-5	0	57	.215	.257	.306	60	-23	3-7	.964	-10	94	92	S103		-0.
1981	SF N	104	324	27	82	9	1	0	28	24-7	1	46	.253	.306	.287	71	-12	13-4	.963	-12	95	86	S130	17	-2
1982	SF N	130	436	34	94	14	1	2	30	31-10	0	78	.216	.265	.266	50	-29	13-4	.964	-12	97	71	S139		-1
1983	SF N	141	534	81	128	16	1	6	30	60-3	2	96	.240	.317	.307	76	-16	39-19	.964	5	104	89	S129		-0
1984	SF N	132	451	46	98	13	2	4	32	31-5	1	97	.217	.265	.282	56	-28	17-5	.964	5	100	64	S10	45	-0
1985	SF N	12	16	1	0	0	0	0	0	1-0	1	5	.000	.059	.000	-86	-4	0-0	.955	-3	49	29	S10		-0
	Cle A	11	20	0	3	0	0	0	2	0-0	0	6	.150	.150	.150	-18	-3	0-1	.983	10	129	108	S21	32	-0
	Pit N	22	58	4	9	0	1	0	6	5-2	0	12	.155	.222	.207	-1	-4	1-0	1.000	0	133	445	3b8,S7,2b5/D		-0
1987	Oak A	20	24	3	2	0	0	0	1	1-0	0	4	.083	.120	.083	-48	-5	0-1	.961	-44	98	84	S10		-0
Total	12	1039	3191	320	709	109	19	22	229	241-37	7	564	.222	.277	.289	60	-176	94-51	.961	-44	98	84	S992,3b10,2b7/D	94	-12

LEMBO, STEVE   Stephen Neal   B11.13.1926 Brooklyn NY   D12.4.1989 Flushing NY   BR/TR/6-1/185*   d9.16

YEAR	TM LG	G	AB	R	H	2B	3B	HR	RBI	BB-IB	HP	SO	AVG	OBP	SLG	AOPS	ABR	SB-CS	FA	FR	RNG	THR	GAMES AT POSITION	DL	BFW
1950	Bro N	5	6	0	1	0	0	0	0	1-0	0	0	.167	.286	.167	22	-1	0	1.000	2	0	196	C5		0
1952	Bro N	2	5	0	1	0	0	0	1	0-0	0	1	.200	.200	.200	11	-1	0-0	1.000	0	0	0	C2		0
Total	2	7	11	0	2	0	0	0	1	1	0	1	.182	.250	.182	18	-2	0-0	1.000	2	0	125	C7		

LEMKE, MARK   Mark Alan   B8.13.1965 Utica NY   BB/TR/5-9/167*   [AtlN83 27/677]   d9.17

YEAR	TM LG	G	AB	R	H	2B	3B	HR	RBI	BB-IB	HP	SO	AVG	OBP	SLG	AOPS	ABR	SB-CS	FA	FR	RNG	THR	GAMES AT POSITION	DL	BFW
1988	Atl N	16	58	8	13	4	0	0	2	4-0	0	5	.224	.274	.293	60	-3	0-2	.970	1	100	98	2b16		-0
1989	Atl N	14	55	4	10	2	1	2	10	5-0	0	7	.182	.250	.364	72	-2	0-1	.989	19	120	145	3b45,2b44/S	49	-0
1990	Atl N	102	239	22	54	13	0	0	21	21-3	0	22	.226	.286	.280	54	-14	0-1	.978	9	110	115	2b110,3b15		-0
1991	†Atl N	136	269	36	63	11	2	2	23	29-2	0	27	.234	.305	.312	71	-10	2-1	.984	-13	96	81	2b145,3b13		-0
1992	†Atl N	155	427	38	97	7	4	6	26	50-11	1	39	.227	.307	.304	70	-17	0-3	.984	18	105	123	2b150		-0
1993	†Atl N	151	493	52	124	19	2	7	49	65-13	0	50	.252	.335	.341	81	-12	1-2	**.994**	9	101	95	2b103		-0
1994	Atl N	104	350	35	103	15	0	3	31	38-12	0	37	.294	.363	.363	87	-5	0-3	.990	12	100	94	2b115	23	-0
1995	†Atl N	116	399	42	101	16	5	5	38	44-4	2	40	.253	.325	.356	76	-13	2-2	.977	11	**113**	93	2b133	17	-0
1996	†Atl N	135	498	64	127	17	5	5	37	53-1	1	48	.255	.323	.319	67	-23	5-2	.980	17	104	122	2b104	39	-0
1997	Atl N	109	351	33	86	17	1	2	26	33-2	0	51	.245	.306	.316	64	-18	2-0	.970						

YEAR	TM LG	G	AB	R	H	2B	3B	HR	RBI	BB-IB	HP	SO	AVG	OBP	SLG	AOPS	ABR	SB-CS	FA	FR	RNG	THR	GAMES AT POSITION	DL	BFW
1998	Bos A	31	91	10	17	4	0	0	7	6-0	0	15	.187	.232	.231	22	-11	0-1	1.000	-7	86	91	2b31	125	-1.6
Total	11	1069	3230	349	795	125	15	32	270	348-48	0	341	.246	.317	.324	71	-128	11-19	.984	61	105	102	2b965,3b73/S	253	-4.0

LEMON, CHET Chester Earl B2.12.1955 Jackson MS BR/TR/6-0/195(185-196) [OakA72 1/22] d9.9

YEAR	TM LG	G	AB	R	H	2B	3B	HR	RBI	BB-IB	HP	SO	AVG	OBP	SLG	AOPS	ABR	SB-CS	FA	FR	RNG	THR	GAMES AT POSITION	DL	BFW
1975	Chi A	9	35	2	9	2	0	0	1	2-0	0	6	.257	.297	.314	72	-1	1-0	.923	-3	57	0	3b6/OCD		-0.4
1976	Chi A	132	451	46	111	15	5	4	38	28-0	7	65	.246	.298	.328	83	-10	13-7	.992	8	108	136	O131(1/130/0)		-0.6
1977	Chi A	150	553	99	151	38	4	19	67	52-1	11	88	.273	.343	.459	118	0	8-7	.978	23	132	114	O149C		3.5
1978	Chi A★	105	357	51	107	24	6	13	55	39-2	-8	46	.300	.377	.510	147	23	5-9	.983	11	120	137	O95(0/84/12),D10	15	3.0
1979	Chi A★	148	556	79	177	44	2	17	86	56-6	13	68	.318	.391	.496	138	32	7-11	.977	-0	101	101	O147C/D		2.7
1980	Chi A	147	514	76	150	32	6	11	51	71-6	12	56	.292	.388	.442	128	23	6-6	.981	-5	93	117	O139C/2D		1.6
1981	Chi A	94	328	50	99	23	6	9	50	33-0	13	48	.302	.384	.491	154	24	5-8	.984	-2	103	38	O93C		2.0
1982	Det A	125	436	75	116	20	1	19	52	56-2	15	69	.266	.368	.447	122	15	1-4	.984	-3	93	128	O121(0/29/93)/D		0.6
1983	Det A	145	491	78	125	21	5	24	69	54-1	20	70	.255	.360	.464	125	18	0-7	.988	-1	104	68	O145C		2.0
1984	†Det A★	141	509	77	146	34	4	20	76	51-9	7	83	.287	.357	.495	134	24	5-5	.995	4	110	65	O140C/D		2.6
1985	Det A	145	517	69	137	28	4	18	68	45-3	10	93	.265	.334	.439	110	7	0-2	.990	-0	105	65	O144C		0.5
1986	Det A	126	403	45	101	21	3	12	53	39-3	8	53	.251	.326	.407	99	-1	2-1	.985	-0	101	95	O124C		-0.2
1987	†Det A	146	470	75	130	30	3	20	75	70-1	8	82	.277	.376	.481	131	24	0-0	.992	-1	100	66	O145C		2.0
1988	Det A	144	512	67	135	29	4	17	64	59-6	7	65	.264	.346	.436	122	16	1-2	.974	-1	99	92	O144R		1.0
1989	Det A	127	414	45	98	19	2	7	47	46-3	8	71	.237	.323	.343	90	-4	1-5	.985	-7	86	75	O111R,D13		-1.7
1990	Det A	104	322	39	83	16	4	5	32	48-3	4	61	.258	.359	.379	106	4	3-2	.973	-5	111	107	O96(0/3/94),D6	15	-0.3
Total	16	1988	6868	973	1875	396	61	215	884	749-46	151	1024	.273	.355	.442	120	208	58-76	.984	26	104	93	O1925(1/1473/454),D40,3b6/2	30	18.5

LEMON, JIM James Robert B3.23.1928 Covington VA BR/TR/6-4/200* d8.20 M1/C7

YEAR	TM LG	G	AB	R	H	2B	3B	HR	RBI	BB-IB	HP	SO	AVG	OBP	SLG	AOPS	ABR	SB-CS	FA	FR	RNG	THR	GAMES AT POSITION	DL	BFW
1950	Cle A	12	34	4	6	1	0	1	3	3	0	12	.176	.243	.294	38	-3	0-0	.824	-1	74	168	O10L		-0.5
1953	Cle A	16	46	5	8	1	0	1	5	3	0	15	.174	.224	.261	32	-5	0-0	.913	-1	90	130	O11L,1b2		-0.7
1954	Was A	37	128	12	30	2	3	2	13	9	0	34	.234	.283	.344	76	-5	0-0	.951	-4	88	0	O33(1/0/32)		-1.1
1955	Was A	10	25	3	5	2	0	1	3	3-0	0	4	.200	.286	.400	88	-1	0-0	.923	-1	102	0	O6(1/0/5)		-0.1
1956	Was A	146	538	77	146	21	11	27	96	65-2	2	138	.271	.349	.502	123	15	2-4	.963	4	107	104	O141(12/0/130)		1.3
1957	Was A	137	518	58	147	23	6	17	64	49-3	3	94	.284	.345	.450	118	12	1-7	.971	-6	99	42	O131R,1b3		-0.1
1958	Was A	142	501	65	123	15	9	26	75	50-3	1	120	.246	.314	.467	114	7	2-4	.978	-1	103	72	O137(2/0/135)		0.0
1959	Was A	147	531	72	148	18	3	33	100	46-0	1	99	.279	.334	.510	130	19	5-2	.969	-2	102	46	O142(117/0/25)		1.0
1960	Was A★	148	528	81	142	10	1	38	100	67-8	7	114	.269	.354	.508	133	23	2-0	.960	-4	88	112	O145L		1.2
1961	Min A	129	423	57	109	26	1	14	52	44-2	4	98	.258	.329	.423	95	-2	1-1	.940	-2	95	92	O120(120/0/1)		-1.1
1962	Min A	12	17	1	3	0	0	1	5	3-0	0	4	.176	.286	.353	72	-1	0-0	1.000	-1	23	0	O3(2/0/1)		-0.2
1963	Min A	7	17	0	2	0	0	0	1	1-0	0	5	.118	.167	.118	-18	-3	0-0	.800	-1	60	0	O4L		-0.4
	Phi N	31	59	6	16	2	0	2	6	8-1	0	18	.271	.353	.407	121	2	0-0	.963	0	117	0	O18(16/0/4)		0.1
	Chi A	36	80	4	16	0	1	1	8	12-0	0	26	.200	.304	.262	62	-4	0-0	.979	-2	61	144	1b25		-0.8
Total	12	1010	3445	446	901	121	35	164	529	363-19	18	787	.262	.332	.460	114	54	13-18	.961	-21	98	74	O901(441/0/464),1b30	119	-1.4

LEMON, BOB Robert Granville B9.22.1920 San Bernardino CA D1.11.2000 Long Beach CA BL/TR/6-0/185* d9.9 Mil 1943-45 M8/C6 HF1976 ▲

YEAR	TM LG	G	AB	R	H	2B	3B	HR	RBI	BB-IB	HP	SO	AVG	OBP	SLG	AOPS	ABR	SB-CS	FA	FR	RNG	THR	GAMES AT POSITION	DL	BFW
1941	Cle A	5	4	0	1	0	0	0	0	0	0	1	.250	.250	.250	34	0	0-0	1.000	0	103	0	/3		0.0
1942	Cle A	5	5	0	0	0	0	0	0	0	0	3	.000	.000	.000	-99	-1	0-0	.500	-0	107	0	/3		-0.2
1946	Cle A	55	89	9	16	3	0	1	4	7	0	18	.180	.240	.247	39	-8	0-1	.976	5	173	484	P32,O12C		-0.2
1947	Cle A	47	56	11	18	4	3	2	5	6	0	9	.321	.387	.607	179	5	0-0	.983	4	170	242	P37,O2(0/1/1)		0.2
1948	†Cle A☆	52	119	20	34	9	0	5	21	8	0	23	.286	.331	.487	119	13	0-0	.965	8	166	238	P43		0.0
1949	Cle A☆	46	108	17	29	6	2	7	19	10	0	25	.269	.331	.556	135	15	0-0	.963	6	137	137	P37		0.0
1950	Cle A★	72	136	22	37	9	1	6	26	13	1	25	.272	.340	.485	113	17	0-0	.957	5	131	158	P44		0.0
1951	Cle A★	56	102	11	21	4	1	6	13	9	0	22	.206	.270	.353	72	4	0-0	.976	4	132	138	P42		0.0
1952	Cle A	54	124	14	28	9	2	4	9	4	0	21	.226	.250	.315	60	6	0-0	.982	6	149	186	P42		0.0
1953	Cle A☆	51	112	12	26	9	2	1	17	7	0	20	.232	.277	.384	79	8	2-0	.972	8	159	466	P41		0.0
1954	†Cle A★	40	98	11	21	4	1	2	10	6	0	24	.214	.257	.337	61	5	0-0	.963	4	131	263	P36		0.0
1955	Cle A	49	78	11	19	0	0	1	9	13-0	0	16	.244	.344	.282	69	5	0-0	.983	2	121	144	P35		0.0
1956	Cle A	43	93	8	18	0	0	5	12	9-0	1	21	.194	.272	.355	63	4	0-0	.934	4	148	186	P39		0.0
1957	Cle A	25	46	3	3	0	0	1	1	1-0	0	14	.065	.065	.152	-43	-3	0-0	1.000	3	159	265	P21		0.0
1958	Cle A	15	13	1	3	0	0	0	1	1-0	0	4	.231	.286	.231	45	0	0-0	1.000	1	172	256	P11	31	0.0
Total	15	615	1183	148	274	54	9	37	147	93-0	2	241	.232	.288	.386	82	70	0-0	.969	59	146	228	P460,O14(0/13/1),3b2	31	-0.2

LENHARDT, DON Donald Eugene "Footsie" B10.4.1922 Alton IL BR/TR/6-3/190* d4.18 C4 Col Illinois

YEAR	TM LG	G	AB	R	H	2B	3B	HR	RBI	BB-IB	HP	SO	AVG	OBP	SLG	AOPS	ABR	SB-CS	FA	FR	RNG	THR	GAMES AT POSITION	DL	BFW
1950	StL A	139	480	75	131	22	6	22	81	90	2	94	.273	.390	.481	118	14	3-2	.988	-9	73	87	1b86,O39L,3b10		-0.1
1951	StL A	31	103	9	27	3	0	5	18	6	0	13	.262	.303	.437	95	-1	1-0	.982	-2	97	0	O27L/1		-0.5
	Chi A	64	199	23	53	9	1	10	45	24	2	25	.266	.351	.472	124	6	1-1	.983	-2	98	50	O53L,1b2		0.0
	Year	95	302	32	80	12	1	15	63	30	2	38	.265	.335	.460	114	4	2-1	.983	-3	98	34	O80L,1b3		-0.5
1952	Bos A	30	105	18	31	4	0	7	24	15	0	18	.295	.383	.533	142	6	0-1	.981	-2	94	0	O27L		0.2
	Det A	45	144	18	27	3	1	13	28	0	0	18	.188	.320	.278	67	-6	0-0	.989	3	102	191	O43L		-0.7
	StL A	18	48	5	13	4	1	1	5	4	0	8	.271	.327	.458	114	1	0-0	1.000	1	110	0	O11(10/1/0),1b2		0.0
	Year	93	297	41	71	10	2	11	42	41	0	44	.239	.343	.397	102	1	0-2	.988	2	100	103	O81(80/1/0),1b2		-0.5
1953	StL A	97	303	37	96	15	0	10	35	41	1	41	.317	.400	.465	131	14	1-2	.969	1	96	143	O77(72/0/5),3b6		1.0
1954	Bal A	13	33	2	5	1	0	0	3	1	0	9	.152	.182	.182	12	-4	0-0	1.000	-0	84	0	O7L,1b2		-0.5
	Bos A	44	66	5	18	4	1	3	17	3	1	17	.273	.310	.470	101	0	0-0	1.000	-0	87	0	O13L/3		-0.1
	Year	57	99	7	23	5	0	3	20	4	1	26	.232	.280	.374	74	-4	0-0	1.000	-0	86	0	O20L,1b2/3		-0.6
Total	5	481	1481	192	401	64	9	61	239	214	6	235	.271	.365	.450	114	14	6-7	.980	-11	97	82	O297(291/1/5),1b93,3b17		-0.7

LENNON, PATRICK Patrick Orlando B4.27.1968 Whiteville NC BR/TR/6-2/200(200-240) [SeaA86 1/8] d9.15

YEAR	TM LG	G	AB	R	H	2B	3B	HR	RBI	BB-IB	HP	SO	AVG	OBP	SLG	AOPS	ABR	SB-CS	FA	FR	RNG	THR	GAMES AT POSITION	DL	BFW
1991	Sea A	9	8	2	1	0	0	0	1	3-0	0	1	.125	.364	.250	73	0	0-0	1.000	0	438	0	/OLD		0.0
1992	Sea A	1	2	0	0	0	0	0	0	0-0	0	0	.000	.000	.000	-99	-1	0-0	1.000	-0	314	0	/1		-0.1
1996	KC A	14	30	5	7	3	0	1	7	7-0	0	10	.233	.378	.333	82	0	0-0	.947	-0	105	0	O11L/D		-0.1
1997	Oak A	56	116	14	34	6	1	4	14	15-0	1	35	.293	.374	.388	99	0	0-1	.948	-1	110	0	O36(23/1/12),D17	23	-0.2
1998	Tor A	2	4	1	2	0	0	0	0	0-0	1	1	.500	.500	1.000	276	1	0-0	1.000	0	172	0	O2R		0.1
1999	Tor A	9	29	3	6	2	0	1	6	2-0	1	12	.207	.281	.379	65	-2	0-0	1.000	2	159	204	O8(5/0/4)		0.0
Total	6	91	189	25	50	14	1	9	22	27-0	2	59	.265	.359	.381	92	-2	0-1	.962	2	121	37	O58(40/1/18),D23/1	23	-0.3

LENNON, BOB Robert Albert "Arch" B9.15.1928 Brooklyn NY D6.14.2005 Dix Hills NY BL/TL/6-0/200* d9.9

YEAR	TM LG	G	AB	R	H	2B	3B	HR	RBI	BB-IB	HP	SO	AVG	OBP	SLG	AOPS	ABR	SB-CS	FA	FR	RNG	THR	GAMES AT POSITION	DL	BFW
1954	NY N	3	3	0	0	0	0	0	0	0-0	0	0	.000	.000	.000	-1	-0	0-0	—	0			/H		
1956	NY N	26	55	3	10	1	0	1	4	4-1	0	17	.182	.233	.200	19	-6	0-0	.885	-1	79	174	O21(5/1/18)		-0.1
1957	Chi N	9	21	2	3	1	0	1	3	1-0	0	9	.143	.182	.333	35	-2	0-0	1.000	-1	53	0	O4C		-0.8
Total	3	38	79	5	13	2	0	1	4	5-1	0	26	.165	.212	.228	19	-8	0-0	.900	-1	74	143	O25(5/5/18)		-1.2

LENNON, BILL William H. B1848 Brooklyn NY D8.19.1910 Philadelphia PA 5-7/145 d5.4 M1/U2

YEAR	TM LG	G	AB	R	H	2B	3B	HR	RBI	BB-IB	HP	SO	AVG	OBP	SLG	AOPS	ABR	SB-CS	FA	FR	RNG	THR	GAMES AT POSITION	DL	BFW
1871	Kek NA	12	48	5	11	3	0	0	5	1		0	.229	.245	.292	52	-3	1-0	.887	-2			C12,S2/ORM		-0.3
1872	Nat NA	11	54	11	11	1	0	0	0	0		0	.204	.204	.222	26	-5	0-0	.765	-5			C11/1		-0.7
1873	Mar NA	5	19	2	4	0	0	0	2	0		0	.211	.211	.211	33	-1	0-0	.942	-1	0		1b4/C3		-0.2
Total	3 NA	28	121	18	26	4	0	0	7	1		0	.215	.221	.248	38	-9	1-0	.817	-9			C24,1b5,S2/3OR		-1.2

LENNOX, ED James Edgar "Eggie" B11.3.1885 Camden NJ D10.26.1939 Camden NJ BR/TR/5-10/174 d8.8

YEAR	TM LG	G	AB	R	H	2B	3B	HR	RBI	BB-IB	HP	SO	AVG	OBP	SLG	AOPS	ABR	SB-CS	FA	FR	RNG	THR	GAMES AT POSITION	DL	BFW
1906	Phi A	6	17	1	1	0	0	0	1	1		0	.059	.111	.118	-28	-2	0	.909	3	145	0	3b6		0.1
1909	Bro N	126	435	33	114	18	9	2	44	47		2	.262	.337	.359	120	10	11	.959	-3	88	115	3b121		1.1
1910	Bro N	110	367	19	95	19	4	3	32	36		5	.259	.333	.357	104	2	7	.950	-16	78	97	3b100		-1.2
1912	Chi N	27	81	13	19	4	1	0	16	12		2	.235	.347	.346	90	-1	1	.934	-3	84	38	3b24		-0.3
1914	Pit F	124	430	71	134	25	10	11	84	71		4	.312	.414	.493	148	25	19	.954	-17	87	65	3b123		0.3
1915	Pit F	55	53	1	16	3	1	1	9	7		1	.302	.383	.453	136	2	0	1.000	1	135	0	3b3		0.3
Total	6	448	1383	138	379	70	25	18	185	174		13	.99	.274	.361	.400	122	36	38	.953	-35	86	87	3b377		1.2

LENTINE, JIM James Matthew B7.16.1954 Los Angeles CA BR/TR/6-0/175* [StLN75 12/280] d9.3 Col La Verne

YEAR	TM LG	G	AB	R	H	2B	3B	HR	RBI	BB-IB	HP	SO	AVG	OBP	SLG	AOPS	ABR	SB-CS	FA	FR	RNG	THR	GAMES AT POSITION	DL	BFW
1978	StL N	8	11	2	2	0	0	0	1	0-0	1	0	.182	.250	.182	22	-1	1-0	1.000	-0	72	0	O3(2/0/1)		-0.2
1979	StL N	11	23	2	9	1	0	0	2	1-0	0	2	.391	.462	.435	143	2	0-1	1.000	1	99	221	O8(3/2/3)		0.2
1980	StL N	9	10	1	2	0	0	0	0	0-0	0	2	.100	.100	.100	-2	-0	0-0	1.000	-0	79	0	O6(5/1/0)		-0.2

YEAR	TM LG	G	AB	R	H	2B	3B	HR	RBI	BB-IB	HP	SO	AVG	OBP	SLG	AOPS	ABR	SB-CS	FA	FR	RNG	THR	GAMES AT POSITION	DL	BFW
	Det A	67	161	19	42	8	1	1	17	28-1	2	30	.261	.377	.342	96	1	2-1	.963	2	102	156	O55(40/10/6),D9		0.1
Total 3		95	205	23	54	9	1	1	20	31-1	0	38	.263	.368	.332	91	0	3-2	.969	2	99	148	O72(50/13/10),D9		-0.1

LENZ, DAVID   David B1.1.1851, Germany D5.21.1886 Brooklyn NY   d5.7

YEAR	TM LG	G	AB	R	H	2B	3B	HR	RBI	BB-IB	HP	SO	AVG	OBP	SLG	AOPS	ABR	SB-CS	FA	FR	RNG	THR	GAMES AT POSITION	DL	BFW
1872	Eck NA	4	12	2	1	0	0	0	0	0	0	0	.083	.083	.083	-57	-2	0-0	.733	-3			C4		-0.4

LEON, EDDIE   Eduardo Antonio B8.11.1946 Tucson AZ   BR/TR/6-0/175*   [CleA67 S2/35] d9.9   Col Arizona

YEAR	TM LG	G	AB	R	H	2B	3B	HR	RBI	BB-IB	HP	SO	AVG	OBP	SLG	AOPS	ABR	SB-CS	FA	FR	RNG	THR	GAMES AT POSITION	DL	BFW
1968	Cle A	6	1	0	0	0	0	0	0	0-0	1	1	.000	.000	.000	-99	0	0-0	1.000	1	114	406	S6		0.1
1969	Cle A	64	213	20	51	6	0	3	19	19-3	0	37	.239	.300	.310	69	-9	2-2	.952	-1	94	110	S64		-0.2
1970	Cle A	152	549	58	136	20	4	10	56	47-2	2	89	.248	.308	.353	79	-17	1-2	.982	17	100	111	2b141,S23/3		1.1
1971	Cle A	131	429	35	112	12	2	4	35	34-5	1	69	.261	.317	.326	75	-14	3-5	.983	0	95	93	2b36,S35		-0.6
1972	Cle A	89	225	14	45	2	1	4	16	20-1	1	47	.200	.265	.271	59	-12	0-2	.993	2	108	95	2b36,S35		-0.6
1973	Chi A	127	399	37	91	10	3	3	30	34-0	3	103	.228	.291	.291	63	-20	1-5	.972	-6	95	95	S122,2b3		-1.4
1974	Chi A	31	46	1	5	1	0	0	3	2-0	1	12	.109	.143	.130	-20	-7	0-0	.962	4	101	126	S21,2b7,3b2/D		-0.2
1975	NY A	1	0	0	0	0	0	0	0	0-0	0	0	—	—	—		0	0-0	—	-0	0	0	/S		0.0
Total 8		601	1862	165	440	51	10	24	159	156-11	7	358	.236	.296	.313	69	-79	7-16	.963	17	97	108	S296,2b294,3b3/D		-1.8

LEON, JOSE   Jose Geraldo (Vega) B12.8.1976 Cayey, PR   BR/TR/6-0/175(175-220)   [StLN94 22/614] d6.16

YEAR	TM LG	G	AB	R	H	2B	3B	HR	RBI	BB-IB	HP	SO	AVG	OBP	SLG	AOPS	ABR	SB-CS	FA	FR	RNG	THR	GAMES AT POSITION	DL	BFW
2002	Bal A	36	89	8	22	2	0	3	10	3-0	1	20	.247	.280	.371	75	-4	1-0	1.000	0	92	132	1b17,3b12,O2L,D2		-0.4
2003	Bal A	21	54	6	13	1	0	0	3	3-0	2	18	.241	.305	.259	51	-4	0-0	.963	0	103	196	3b10,1b7,D3		-0.6
2004	Bal A	31	66	4	12	2	0	2	8	2-0	0	19	.182	.203	.303	31	-7	0-0	1.000	2	145	93	1b16,3b6,D5		-1.4
Total 3		88	209	18	47	5	0	5	18	8-0	3	57	.225	.262	.321	54	-15	1-0	.996	2	104	121	1b40,3b28,D10,O2L		-1.4

LEONARD   d9.12

YEAR	TM LG	G	AB	R	H	2B	3B	HR	RBI	BB-IB	HP	SO	AVG	OBP	SLG	AOPS	ABR	SB-CS	FA	FR	RNG	THR	GAMES AT POSITION	DL	BFW
1892	StL N	1	0	0	0	0	0	0	0	1	0		—	1.000	—	219	0	1	—	-0	0	0	/OR		0.0

LEONARD, ANDY   Andrew Jackson B6.1.1846 Co. Cavan, Ireland D8.21.1903 Boston MA   BR/TR/5-7/168   d5.5

YEAR	TM LG	G	AB	R	H	2B	3B	HR	RBI	BB-IB	HP	SO	AVG	OBP	SLG	AOPS	ABR	SB-CS	FA	FR	RNG	THR	GAMES AT POSITION	DL	BFW
1871	Oly NA	31	148	33	43	8	3	0	30	3		1	.291	.305	.385	102	1	14-3	.863	-2	98	105	2b19,O11L/S		0.1
1872	Bos NA	46	241	57	84	7	1	2	42	2		2	.349	.349	.411	126	6	8-5	.828	-4	176		O38L,3b6,2b4/S		0.2
1873	Bos NA	58	300	81	96	13	6	0	60	2		2	.320	.325	.403	106	0	27-9	.750	1	259	84	O45(45/0/1),2b12,1b2/S		0.3
1874	Bos NA	71	339	68	106	18	4	0	50	2		2	.313	.317	.389	119	6	11-3	.807	-2	81	80	O51L,2b11,S11		0.6
1875	Bos NA	80	396	87	127	14	6	1	74	2		6	.321	.324	.394	143	15	14-8	.806	-2	101		O35L,2b30		1.4
1876	Bos N	64	303	53	85	10	2	0	27	4		5	.281	.290	.327	103	1		.925	2	109	157	O35L,S21		0.2
1877	Bos N	58	272	46	78	5	0	0	27	5			.287	.300	.305	88	-4		.875	-3	68	186	O37L,S21		-0.8
1878	Bos N	60	262	41	68	8	5	0	16	3		19	.260	.268	.328	88	-4		.777	-7	51	45	O60L		-1.4
1880	Cin N	33	133	15	28	3	0	1	17	8		11	.211	.255	.256	75	-3		.833	-7	90	69	S23,3b10		-0.8
Total 5 NA		286	1424	326	456	60	20	3	256	9		11	.320	.324	.397	121	28	74-28	.787	-6	149	37	O218(218/0/1),2b48,S17,3b9,1b2		2.6
Total 4		215	970	155	259	26	7	1	87	20		41	.267	.282	.311	91	-10		.856	-14	70	114	O132L,S44,2b30,3b10		-2.8

LEONARD, JEFFREY   Jeffrey B9.22.1955 Philadelphia PA   BR/TR/6-2/200(187-205)   d9.2

YEAR	TM LG	G	AB	R	H	2B	3B	HR	RBI	BB-IB	HP	SO	AVG	OBP	SLG	AOPS	ABR	SB-CS	FA	FR	RNG	THR	GAMES AT POSITION	DL	BFW
1977	LA N	11	10	1	3	0	1	0	2	1-0	0	4	.300	.364	.500	128	0	0-0	1.000	0	123	0	O10(6/0/4)		0.0
1978	Hou N	8	26	2	10	2	0	0	4	1-0	0	6	.385	.407	.462	152	2	0-1	.959	-6	98	65	O8(4/2/2)		0.2
1979	Hou N	134	411	47	119	15	5	0	47	46-7	2	68	.290	.360	.350	102	2	23-10	.979	0	100	161	O123(4/22/100)		-0.8
1980	†Hou N	88	216	29	46	7	5	3	20	19-2	0	46	.213	.274	.324	76	-2	1-0	1.000	-1	63	0	1b2,O2R		-1.1
1981	Hou N	7	18	1	3	1	1	0	3	0-0	0	4	.167	.158	.333	41	10	4-2	1.000	1	114	91	O28(8/19/4),1b5		-0.2
	SF N	37	127	20	39	11	3	4	26	12-3	1	21	.307	.371	.535	160	8	5-2	1.000	1	112	85	O30(8/19/6),1b7		1.1
	Year	44	145	21	42	12	4	4	29	12-3	1	25	.290	.346	.510	146	1	18-5	.958	-7	90	36	O74(56/17/2)/1		0.9
1982	SF N	80	278	32	72	16	1	9	49	19-2	2	65	.259	.306	.421	104	10	26-7	.975	-4	96	171	O136(127/12/2)	57	-0.7
1983	SF N	139	516	74	144	17	7	21	87	35-2	1	116	.279	.323	.461	119	26	17-7	.970	-0	92	135	O131(116/18/4)		1.3
1984	SF N	136	514	76	155	27	2	21	86	47-3	0	123	.302	.357	.484	139	-12	11-6	.977	-3	92	115	O126(125/3/0)		2.2
1985	SF N	133	507	49	122	20	3	17	62	21-5	1	107	.241	.272	.393	88	-1	16-3	.970	-1	95	69	O87L	67	-2.1
1986	SF N	89	341	48	95	11	3	6	42	20-1	3	62	.279	.322	.381	99	3	16-7	.966	-7	84	85	O127(127/1/0)		-0.5
1987	†SF N★	131	503	70	141	29	4	19	63	21-6	2	68	.280	.309	.467	108	-3	7-5	.987	-4	90	0	O43L	9	-0.8
1988	SF N	44	160	12	41	8	1	2	20	9-1	0	24	.256	.292	.356	90	-15	10-4	.985	-2	98	73	O91L,D2		-1.9
	Mil A	94	374	45	88	19	0	8	44	16-1	3	68	.235	.270	.350	72	-2	6-1	.982	1	105	137	D123,O26(25/0/1)		-0.5
1989	Sea A★	150	566	69	144	20	1	24	93	38-2	5	125	.254	.301	.420	100	-11	4-2	.983	-9	80	0	O79(74/0/6),D48		-2.4
1990	Sea A	134	478	39	120	20	0	10	75	37-6	3	97	.251	.305	.356	84	-1	163-61	.974	-31	93	93	O1147(896/103/171),D173,1b19	133	-7.0
Total 14		1415	5045	614	1342	223	37	144	723	342-41	23	1000	.266	.312	.411	102									-7.0

LEONARD, JOE   Joseph Howard B11.15.1894 W.Chicago IL D5.1.1920 Washington DC   BL/TR/5-7.5/156   d4.24   Mil 1918

YEAR	TM LG	G	AB	R	H	2B	3B	HR	RBI	BB-IB	HP	SO	AVG	OBP	SLG	AOPS	ABR	SB-CS	FA	FR	RNG	THR	GAMES AT POSITION	DL	BFW
1914	Pit N	53	126	17	25	2	4	0	12	4	0	21	.198	.268	.246	56	-7	4	.909	-6	88	53	3b38/S		-1.3
1916	Cle A	3	2	1	0	0	0	0	0	0	0	1	.000	.000	.000	-94	0		1.000	0	102	0	/2		0.0
	Was A	42	168	20	46	7	0	0	14	22	0	23	.274	.358	.315	103	2	4	.952	-7	75	78	3b42/2		-0.4
	Year	45	170	21	46	7	0	0	14	22	0	24	.271	.354	.312	101	1	4	.952	-7	75	78	3b42/2		-0.4
1917	Was A	99	297	30	57	6	7	0	23	45	1	40	.192	.302	.272	72	-9	6	.925	-2	89	158	3b68,1b19/SOR		-0.8
1919	Was A	71	198	26	51	8	3	2	20	20	1	28	.258	.329	.359	94	-2	3	.944	-7	80	96	2b28,3b25,1b4/OL/R		0.0
1920	Was A	1	0	0	0	0	0	0	0	0	0	0	—	—	—		0								
Total 5		269	791	94	179	23	12	2	61	99	3	113	.226	.315	.293	82	-16	17-0	.937	-21	85	114	3b173,2b29,1b23,O2(1/0/1),S2		-3.6

LEONARD, MARK   Mark David B8.14.1964 Mountain View CA   BL/TR/6-0/195(195-212)   [SFN86 29/709] d7.21   Col California-Santa Barbara

YEAR	TM LG	G	AB	R	H	2B	3B	HR	RBI	BB-IB	HP	SO	AVG	OBP	SLG	AOPS	ABR	SB-CS	FA	FR	RNG	THR	GAMES AT POSITION	DL	BFW
1990	SF N	11	17	3	3	0	0	1	2	3-0	0	8	.176	.300	.412	97	0	0-0	1.000	0	112	0	O7(2/0/5)	28	0.0
1991	SF N	64	129	14	31	7	1	2	14	12-1	1	25	.240	.306	.357	89	-2	0-1	1.000	-0	74	0	O34(24/0/12)	57	0.1
1992	SF N	55	128	13	30	7	0	4	16	16-0	3	31	.234	.331	.383	108	2	0-1	.984	1	98	132	O37(33/0/4)		-0.2
1993	Bal A	10	15	1	1	1	0	0	3	3-0	0	5	.067	.190	.133	-2	-2	0-0	.833	0	133	0	O4L,D3		0.2
1994	SF N	14	11	2	4	1	0	2	4	3-0	0	2	.364	.500	.636	201	2	0-0	1.000	0	99	0	O6(1/0/5)		0.0
1995	SF N	14	21	4	4	1	0	1	4	5-1	0	5	.190	.346	.381	94	0	0-0	1.000	-0	90	59	O90(66/0/26),D3		0.0
Total 6		168	321	37	73	18	2	8	41	42-2	4	75	.227	.319	.371	97	0	0-2	.985	-3	90	59	O90(66/0/26),D3	85	-0.8

LEONE, JUSTIN   Justin Paul B3.9.1977 Las Vegas NV   BR/TR/6-1/190   [SeaA99 13/395] d7.2   Col St. Martins

YEAR	TM LG	G	AB	R	H	2B	3B	HR	RBI	BB-IB	HP	SO	AVG	OBP	SLG	AOPS	ABR	SB-CS	FA	FR	RNG	THR	GAMES AT POSITION	DL	BFW
2004	Sea A	31	102	15	22	5	0	8	13	9-0	3	32	.216	.298	.441	94	-1	1-0	.901	-3	93	44	3b28,S2/D	47	-0.4

LEOVICH, JOHN   John Joseph B5.5.1918 Portland OR D2.3.2000 Lincoln City OR   BR/TR/6-0.5/200   d5.1   Col Oregon St.

YEAR	TM LG	G	AB	R	H	2B	3B	HR	RBI	BB-IB	HP	SO	AVG	OBP	SLG	AOPS	ABR	SB-CS	FA	FR	RNG	THR	GAMES AT POSITION	DL	BFW
1941	Phi A	1	2	0	1	1	0	0	0	0	0	0	.500	.500	1.000	296	0	1-0	—	-0	0	0	/C		0.6

LEPCIO, TED   Thaddeus Stanley B7.28.1930 Utica NY   BR/TR/5-10/177*   d4.15   Col Seton Hall

YEAR	TM LG	G	AB	R	H	2B	3B	HR	RBI	BB-IB	HP	SO	AVG	OBP	SLG	AOPS	ABR	SB-CS	FA	FR	RNG	THR	GAMES AT POSITION	DL	BFW
1952	Bos A	84	274	34	72	17	2	5	26	24	3	41	.263	.329	.394	93	-2	3-3	.972	8	113	98	2b57,3b25/S		0.8
1953	Bos A	66	161	17	38	4	2	4	11	17	1	24	.236	.313	.360	77	-6	0-0	.981	11	121	126	2b34,S20,3b11		0.8
1954	Bos A	116	398	42	102	19	4	8	45	42	3	62	.256	.328	.384	86	-7	3-4	.971	8	107	94	2b80,3b24,S14		0.3
1955	Bos A	51	134	19	31	9	0	6	15	12-0	4	36	.231	.313	.433	91	-2	1-1	.943	3	107	78	3b45		0.1
1956	Bos A	83	284	34	74	10	0	15	51	30-1	3	77	.261	.335	.454	96	-2	0-0	.966	5	110	122	2b68		-0.1
1957	Bos A	79	232	24	56	10	2	7	37	29-1	1	61	.241	.328	.418	97	-1	0-0	.980	-2	99	90	2b40		-0.6
1958	Bos A	50	136	10	27	3	0	6	14	12-1	1	47	.199	.268	.353	65	-7	0-1	1.000	-2	99	158	/2		-0.3
1959	Bos A	3	3	1	1	1	0	0	0	0-0	0	2	.333	.333	.667	160	-1	2-0	.951	-2	95	92	S35,2b24,3b11		0.0
	Det A	76	215	25	60	8	0	7	24	17-2	2	49	.279	.332	.414	98	-1	0-0	.951	-2	95	33	S35,2b25,3b11		0.0
	Year	79	218	26	61	9	0	7	25	17-2	2	51	.280	.332	.417	99	0	0-3	.942	-8	89	32	3b50,S14,2b5		-1.4
1960	Phi N	69	141	16	32	7	0	2	8	17-1	0	41	.227	.315	.319	75	-4	0-3	.000	-2	0	0	/3		-0.2
1961	Chi A	5	2	0	0	0	0	0	0	0-0	0	0	.000	.000	.000	-2	0	0-0	—	-0	0	0	/3		-0.0
	Min A	47	112	11	19	3	1	7	19	8-0	1	31	.170	.230	.402	62	-7	1-0	.919	-1	73	74	3b35,2b22,S6		-0.1
	Year	52	114	11	19	3	1	7	19	9-1	1	31	.167	.232	.395	62	-7	1-0	.895	-1	72	73	3b36,2b22,S6		-0.1
Total 10		729	2092	233	512	91	11	69	251	209-7	19	471	.245	.318	.398	87	-39	11-15	.972	23	107	107	2b388,3b224,S90		1.1

LePINE, PETE   Louis Joseph B9.5.1876 Montreal QC, Can. D12.3.1949 Woonsocket RI   BL/TL/5-10/142   d7.21

YEAR	TM LG	G	AB	R	H	2B	3B	HR	RBI	BB-IB	HP	SO	AVG	OBP	SLG	AOPS	ABR	SB-CS	FA	FR	RNG	THR	GAMES AT POSITION	DL	BFW
1902	Det A	30	96	8	20	3	1	2	19	8	1		.208	.275	.323	62	-5	1	1.000	1	115	274	O19R,1b8		-0.2

LEPPERT, DON   Don Eugene "Tiger" B11.20.1930 Memphis TN   BL/TR/5-8/175   d4.11

YEAR	TM LG	G	AB	R	H	2B	3B	HR	RBI	BB-IB	HP	SO	AVG	OBP	SLG	AOPS	ABR	SB-CS	FA	FR	RNG	THR	GAMES AT POSITION	DL	BFW
1955	Bal A	40	70	6	8	0	1	0	2	9-0	0	10	.114	.213	.143	-2	-10	1-1	.937	-7	72	72	2b35		-1.3

YEAR	TM	LG	G	AB	R	H	2B	3B	HR	RBI	BB-IB	HP	SO	AVG	OBP	SLG	AOPS	ABR	SB-CS	FA	FR	RNG	THR	GAMES AT POSITION	DL	BFW

LEPPERT, DON Donald George B10.19.1931 Indianapolis IN BR/TR/6-2/220* d6.18 C18 Col Wabash

1961	Pit	N	22	60	6	16	2	1	3	5	1-0	0	11	.267	.279	.483	97	-1	0-0	.968	1	157	81	C21		0.1
1962	Pit	N	45	139	14	37	6	1	3	18	12-2	1	21	.266	.327	.388	92	-2	0-1	.989	1	83	60	C44		0.1
1963	Was	A☆	73	211	20	50	11	0	6	24	20-2	1	29	.237	.305	.374	90	-3	0-0	.984	-5	93	34	C60		-0.5
1964	Was	A	50	122	6	19	3	0	3	12	11-1	0	32	.156	.224	.254	33	-11	0-0	.990	-2	72	103	C43		-1.2
Total	4		190	532	46	122	22	2	15	59	44-5	2	93	.229	.289	.363	78	-17	0-1	.985	-4	92	63	C168		-1.5

LERCHEN, DUTCH Bertram Roe B4.4.1889 Detroit MI D1.7.1962 Detroit MI BR/TR/5-8/160 d8.14 s-George

| 1910 | Bos | A | 6 | 15 | 1 | 0 | 0 | 0 | 0 | 1 | 0 | 0 | | .000 | .063 | .000 | -78 | -3 | | .929 | -2 | 37 | 87 | S6 | | -0.6 |

LERCHEN, GEORGE George Edward B12.1.1922 Detroit MI BB/TR (BL 1953)/5-11/175* d4.15 f-Dutch

1952	Det	A	14	32	5	5	1	0	1	3	7	0	10	.156	.308	.281	64	-1	1-0	1.000	-1	97	0	O7(0/3/4)		-0.2
1953	Cin	N	22	17	2	5	1	0	0	2	5	0	6	.294	.455	.353	113	1	0-0	1.000	0	102	0	/OC		0.1
Total	2		36	49	3	10	2	0	1	5	12	0	16	.204	.361	.306	82	0	1-0	1.000	-1	97	0	O8(0/4/4)		-0.1

LERIAN, WALT Walter Irvin "Peck" B2.10.1903 Baltimore MD D10.22.1929 Baltimore MD BR/TR/5-11/170 d4.16

1928	Phi	N	96	239	28	65	16	2	2	25	41	3	29	.272	.385	.381	97	1	1	.977	-5	75	126	C74		0.1
1929	Phi	N	105	273	28	61	13	2	6	25	53	2	37	.223	.354	.352	71	-12	0	.986	-2	92	119	C103		-0.7
Total	2		201	512	56	126	29	4	8	50	94	5	66	.246	.368	.365	83	-11	1	.982	-8	84	122	C177		-0.6

LESHER, BRIAN Brian Herbert B3.5.1971 Wilrijk, Belgium BR/TL/6-5/216(205-222) [OakA92 25/704] d8.25 Col Delaware

1996	Oak	A	26	82	11	19	3	0	5	16	5-0	1	17	.232	.281	.451	83	-3	0-0	.977	-1	89	129	O25(14/0/14)/1		-0.4
1997	Oak	A	46	131	17	30	4	1	4	16	9-0	0	30	.229	.275	.366	67	-7	4-1	.958	2	106	152	O32(31/0/3),1b3,D3		-0.6
1998	Oak	A	7	7	0	1	1	0	0	1	0-0	0	3	.143	.143	.286	8	-1	0-0	1.000	2	108	1788	O4L/1	41	0.1
2000	Sea	A	5	5	1	4	1	1	0	3	1-0	0	0	.800	.833	1.400	459	3	1-0	1.000	0	154	0	1b4		0.3
2002	Tor	A	24	38	2	5	1	0	0	2	4-0	0	15	.132	.209	.158	1	-5	0-0	1.000	1	122	24	1b12,O5(3/0/2),D3		-0.5
Total	5		108	263	31	59	10	2	9	38	19-0	1	65	.224	.275	.380	68	-13	5-1	.970	4	102	186	O66(52/0/19),1b21,D6	41	-1.1

LESLIE, ROY Roy Reid B8.23.1894 Bailey TX D4.9.1972 Sherman TX BR/TR/6-1/175 d9.6

1917	Chi	N	7	19	1	4	0	0	1	1	0	0	5	.211	.250	.211	39	-1	1	.969	-0	102	90	1b6		-0.2
1919	StL	N	12	24	2	5	1	0	0	4	4	0	3	.208	.321	.250	78	0	1	.957	-0	111	142	1b9		-0.1
1922	Phi	N	141	513	44	139	23	2	6	50	37	0	49	.271	.320	.359	68	-24	3-7	.990	-5	86	102	1b139		-3.8
Total	3		160	556	47	148	24	2	6	55	42	0	57	.266	.318	.349	68	-25	4-7	.988	-5	88	103	1b154		-4.1

LESLIE, SAM Samuel Andrew "Sambo" B7.26.1905 Moss Point MS D1.21.1979 Pascagoula MS BL/TL/6-0/192 d10.6

1929	NY	N	1	1	0	0	0	0	0	0	0	0	0	.000	.000	.000	-99	0		1.000	-0	85	0	/OL		0.0
1930	NY	N	2	2	0	1	0	0	0	0	0	0	1	.500	.500	.500	146	0	0		0			/H		0.0
1931	NY	N	53	53	11	16	4	0	3	5	1	0	2	.302	.315	.547	131	2	3	1.000	-0	110	0	1b6		0.2
1932	NY	N	77	75	5	22	4	0	1	15	2	2	5	.293	.329	.387	94	-1	0	1.000	0	0	0	1b2		-0.1
1933	NY	N	40	137	21	44	12	3	3	27	12	1	9	.321	.380	.518	157	10	0	.990	-0	95	111	1b35		0.7
	Bro	N	96	364	41	104	11	4	5	46	23	7	14	.286	.340	.379	110	4	1	.982	-6	81	57	1b95		-1.1
	Year		136	501	62	148	23	7	8	73	35	8	23	.295	.351	.417	123	15	1	.984	-6	85	72	1b130		-0.4
1934	Bro	N	146	546	75	181	29	6	9	102	69	3	34	.332	.409	.456	138	33	5	.993	5	112	93	1b138		2.4
1935	Bro	N	142	520	72	160	30	4	5	93	55	5	19	.308	.379	.421	117	15	4	.989	0	101	108	1b138		0.3
1936	†NY	N	117	417	49	123	19	5	6	54	23	2	16	.295	.335	.408	100	-1	0	.991	1	104	110	1b99		-1.0
1937	†NY	N	72	191	25	59	7	2	3	30	20	2	12	.309	.380	.414	114	4	1	.990	4	128	142	1b44		0.4
1938	NY	N	76	154	12	39	7	1	1	16	11	1	6	.253	.307	.331	75	-5	0	.988	-2	76	91	1b32		-1.0
Total	10		822	2460	341	749	123	28	36	389	216	23	118	.304	.366	.421	117	61	14	.989	0	101	98	1b589/OL		0.8

LETCHAS, CHARLIE Charlie B10.3.1915 Thomasville GA D3.14.1995 Tampa FL BR/TR/5-10/150 d9.16 Mil 1945-46

1939	Phi	N	12	44	2	10	2	0	1	3	1	0	2	.227	.244	.341	57	-3	0	.933	-1	97	117	2b12		-0.3
1941	Was	A	2	8	0	1	0	0	0	1	1	0	1	.125	.222	.125	-6	-1	0-0	.800	-1	121	74	2b2		-0.2
1944	Phi	N	116	396	29	94	8	0	0	33	32	2	27	.237	.298	.258	59	-21	0-0	.968	4	101	146	2b47,3b32,S29		-1.3
1946	Phi	N	6	13	1	3	0	0	0	0	1	0	1	.231	.286	.231	49	-1	0	1.000	0	89	204	2b4		0.0
Total	4		136	461	32	108	10	0	1	37	35	2	31	.234	.291	.262	58	-26	0-0	.959	3	100	142	2b65,3b32,S29		-1.8

LETCHER, TOM Frederick Thomas B1.1868 Bryan OH BL/6-0/? d9.27

| 1891 | Mil | AA | 6 | 21 | 3 | 4 | 1 | 0 | 0 | 2 | 0 | 0 | | .190 | .190 | .238 | 19 | -2 | 1 | .857 | 1 | 241 | 1241 | O6(1/0/5) | | -0.1 |

LEVAN, JESSE Jesse Roy B7.15.1926 Reading PA D11.30.1998 Reading PA BL/TR/6-0/172* d9.27

1947	Phi	N	2	9	3	4	0	0	0	1	0	0	0	.444	.444	.444	142	0	0	1.000	-0	60	0	O2L		0.0
1954	Was	A	7	10	1	3	0	0	0	1	0	0	0	.300	.300	.300	68	-1	0-0		-0	0	0	3b4/1		-0.1
1955	Was	A	16	16	1	3	0	0	1	4	0-0	0	2	.188	.188	.375	51	-1	0-0		-0	0	0	/H		-0.1
Total	3		25	35	5	10	0	0	1	5	0-0	0	2	.286	.286	.371	80	-2	0-0	.000	-0	0	0	3b4,O2L/1		-0.2

LEVEY, JIM James Julius B9.13.1906 Pittsburgh PA D3.14.1970 Dallas TX BB/TR (BR 1930-31)/5-10.5/154 d9.17

1930	StL	A	8	37	7	9	2	0	0	3	3	0	2	.243	.300	.297	50	-3	0-0	.958	1	102	117	S8		-0.1
1931	StL	A	139	498	53	104	19	2	5	38	35	2	83	.209	.264	.285	43	-43	13-8	.920	-12	96	114	S139		-4.2
1932	StL	A	152	568	59	159	30	8	4	63	21	4	48	.280	.310	.382	74	-24	6-4	.939	-19	94	83	S152		-3.0
1933	StL	A	141	529	43	103	10	4	2	36	26	3	68	.195	.237	.240	25	-59	4-6	.945	-6	97	89	S138		-5.4
Total	4		440	1632	162	375	61	14	11	140	85	9	201	.230	.272	.305	48	-129	23-18	.936	-36	96	95	S437		-12.7

LEVIS, CHARLIE Charles H. B6.21.1860 St.Louis MO D10.16.1926 St.Louis MO BR d4.17

1884	Bal	U	87	373	59	85	11	4	5					.228	.234	.319	60	-30		.955	-0	89	100	1b87		-3.5
	Was	U	1	3	0	0	0	0	0	0				.000	.000	.000	-99	-1		1.000	0	0	0	/1		-0.1
	Ind	AA	3	10	0	2	0	0	0	3				.226	.232	.316	59	-31		.955	-0	128	86	1b88		-3.6
	Year		88	376	59	85	11	4	5					.226	.232	.316	59	-31		.955	-0	128	86	1b89		-3.6
1885	Bal	AA	1	4	2	1	0	0	0	0		0		.250	.400	.250	110	0		.889	-0	0	0	/1		-0.1
Total	2		92	390	61	88	11	4	5	0	3	1		.226	.234	.313	59	-32		.956	-0	88	97	1b92		-3.7

LEVIS, JESSE Jesse B4.14.1968 Philadelphia PA BL/TR/5-9/180(180-200) [CleA89 4/98] d4.24 Col North Carolina-Asheville

1992	Cle	A	28	43	2	12	4	0	1	3	0	0	5	.279	.279	.442	100	0	0-0	.985	0	104	54	C21/D		0.0
1993	Cle	A	31	63	7	11	2	0	0	4	2-0	0	10	.175	.197	.206	9	-8	0-0	.991	0	89	103	C29		-0.6
1994	Cle	A	1	1	0	1	0	0	0	0	0-0	0	0	1.000	1.000	1.000	414	0	0-0		0			/H		0.0
1995	Cle	A	12	18	1	6	2	0	0	3	1-0	0	0	.333	.333	.444	108	0	0-0	1.000	-1	50	168	C12		0.0
1996	Mil	A	104	233	27	55	6	1	1	21	38-0	2	15	.236	.348	.283	60	-13	0-0	.998	9	106	83	C90,D6		0.0
1997	Mil	A	99	200	19	57	7	0	1	19	24-0	1	17	.285	.361	.335	83	-4	1-0	.994	0	90	82	C78,D8		-0.1
1998	Mil	N	22	37	4	13	0	0	0	4	7-2	2	6	.351	.468	.351	121	2	1-0	1.000	1	89	36	C14		0.4
1999	Cle	A	10	26	0	4	0	0	0	3	1-0	1	6	.154	.214	.154	-4	-4	0-0	1.000	-0	93	42	C9		-0.4
2001	Mil	N	12	33	6	8	2	0	0	3	3-0	0	7	.242	.306	.303	59	-2	0-0	.984	-2	87	38	C11		-0.3
Total	6		319	654	66	167	23	1	3	60	76-2	6	66	.255	.336	.307	68	-29	2-0	.995	8	95	79	C264,D15	143	-1.0

LEVY, ED Edward Clarence (b Edward Clarence Whitner) B10.28.1916 Birmingham AL BR/TR/6-5.5/190 d4.16 Col Rollins

1940	Phi	N	1	1	0	0	0	0	0	0	0	0	0	.000	.000	.000	-99	0	0		0			/H		0.0
1942	NY	A	13	41	5	5	0	0	0	3	4	0	5	.122	.200	.122	-9	-6	1-0	.992	1	132	142	1b13		-0.6
1944	NY	A	40	153	12	37	11	2	4	29	6	0	19	.242	.270	.418	92	-3	0-1	.962	-2	96	67	O36L		-0.7
Total	3		54	195	17	42	11	2	4	32	10	0	24	.215	.254	.354	70	-9	2-1	.962	-0	96	67	O36L,1b13		-1.3

LEWIS, ALLAN Allan Sidney "The Panamanian Express" B12.12.1941 Colon, Pan BB/TR/6-0/170* d4.11

1967	KC	A	34	6	7	1	0	0	0	0	0-0	0	3	.167	.167	.167	-1	-1	14-5		0			/H		0.1
1968	Oak	A	26	4	9	1	0	0	0	0	1-0	0	0	.250	.400	.250	105	-0	8-4		-0	0	0	/OL		0.0
1969	Oak	A	12	1	2	0	0	0	0	0	0-0	0	0	.000	.000	.000	-99	-0	9-2		0			/H		0.0
1970	Oak	A	25	8	8	2	0	0	1	1	0-0	0	0	.250	.250	.625	138	0	7-1	1.000	-0	63	0	O2L		0.1
1972	†Oak	A	24	10	5	2	0	0	0	1	1-0	0	1	.200	.200	.300	50	-1	9-4	.900	0	143	0	O6(5/0/1)		0.0
1973	†Oak	A	35	0	16	0	0	0	0	0	0-0	0						0	7-4	1.000	0	456	0	/OLD		0.0
Total	6		156	29	47	6	0	0	1	3	1-0	0	4	.207	.233	.345	69	-2	44-17	.923	0	116	0	O10(9/0/1),D6		0.2

YEAR	TM LG	G	AB	R	H	2B	3B	HR	RBI	BB-IB	HP	SO	AVG	OBP	SLG	AOPS	ABR	SB-CS	FA	FR	RNG	THR	GAMES AT POSITION	DL	BFW

LEWIS, DARREN Darren Joel B8.28.1967 Berkeley CA BR/TR/6-0/189(175-195) [OakA88 18/463] d8.21 Col California-Davis

YEAR	TM LG	G	AB	R	H	2B	3B	HR	RBI	BB-IB	HP	SO	AVG	OBP	SLG	AOPS	ABR	SB-CS	FA	FR	RNG	THR	GAMES AT POSITION	DL	BFW
1990	Oak A	25	35	4	8	0	0	1	7-0	1		4	.229	.372	.229	74	-1	2-0	1.000	0	107	0	O23(3/16/5),D2		0.0
1991	SF N	72	222	41	55	5	3	1	15	36-0	2	30	.248	.358	.311	92	-1	13-7	1.000	2	113	62	O68C		0.1
1992	SF N	100	320	38	74	8	1	1	18	29-0	1	46	.231	.303	.272	65	-15	28-8	1.000	-0	104	63	O94C		-1.3
1993	SF N	136	522	84	132	17	7	2	48	30-0	7	40	.253	.302	.324	70	-24	46-15	1.000	3	106	62	O131C	15	-1.5
1994	SF N	114	451	70	116	15	9	4	29	53-0	4	50	.257	.340	.357	85	-10	30-13	.993	-3	97	79	O113C		-1.0
1995	SF N	74	309	47	78	10	3	1	16	17-0	6	37	.252	.303	.314	65	-16	21-7	.995	2	110	48	O73C		-1.2
†Cin N		58	163	19	40	3	0	0	8	17-0	2	20	.245	.324	.264	57	-10	11-11	.992	3	116	126	O57C		-0.7
Year		132	472	66	118	13	3	1	24	34-0	8	57	.250	.311	.297	62	-26	32-18	.994	5	112	77	O130C		-1.9
1996	Chi A	141	337	55	77	12	2	4	53	45-1	3	40	.228	.321	.312	65	-18	21-5	.990	-6	104	0	O138(1/137/0)		-1.8
1997	Chi A	81	77	15	18	1	0	0	5	11-0	0	14	.234	.330	.247	55	-5	11-4	1.000	4	127	70	O64C,D6		0.0
LA N		26	77	7	23	1	1	1	10	6-0	0	17	.299	.349	.403	103	-0	3-2	.980	2	108	61	O25(23/2/1)		0.1
1998	†Bos A	155	585	95	157	25	3	8	63	70-0	8	94	.268	.352	.362	85	-11	29-12	.994	1	107	50	O152(4/109/55)/D		-0.8
1999	†Bos A	135	470	63	113	14	6	2	40	45-0	5	52	.240	.311	.309	58	-13	16-10	.994	1	107	112	O89(18/41/37),D5	14	-2.9
2000	Bos A	97	270	44	65	12	0	2	17	22-0	3	34	.241	.305	.307	54	-19	10-5	.981	-3	90	112	O69(27/21/29),D6		-2.2
2001	Bos A	82	164	18	46	9	1	1	12	8-0	5	23	.280	.326	.366	82	-4	5-6	1.000	3	106	143	O47(22/18/9)		-0.3
2002	Chi A	58	79	7	19	3	1	0	7	7-0	3	11	.241	.326	.304	70	-4	1-3	1.000	5	119	192	O1273(98/1032/187),D22	29	-13.7
Total	13	1354	4081	607	1021	137	37	27	342	403-1	48	514	.250	.323	.322	72	-169	247-107	.994	11	106	67			

LEWIS, FRED Frederick Miller B10.13.1858 Buffalo NY D6.5.1945 Utica NY BB/TR/5-10.5/194 d7.2

YEAR	TM LG	G	AB	R	H	2B	3B	HR	RBI	BB-IB	HP	SO	AVG	OBP	SLG	AOPS	ABR	SB-CS	FA	FR	RNG	THR	GAMES AT POSITION	DL	BFW
1881	Bos N	27	114	17	25	6	0	0	9	7		5	.219	.264	.272	72	-3		.837	-3	82	90	O27(0/3/24)		-0.6
1883	Phi N	38	160	21	40	7	0	0	18	4		13	.250	.268	.294	78	-4		.814	-1	91	55	O38C		-0.5
StL AA		49	209	37	63	8	4	1	33	1			.301	.305	.392	116	3		.848	-3	61	0	O49C		-0.2
1884	StL AA	73	300	59	97	25	3	0	16	4			.323	.366	.427	152	18		.853	-1	100	46	O73C		1.3
StL U		8	30	6	9	0	0	0	3				.300	.364	.333	108	0		.909	-1	0	0	O8C		-0.2
1885	StL N	45	181	12	53	9	0	1	27	9		10	.293	.326	.359	130	6		.957	7	216	173	O45(9/37/0)		1.1
1886	Cin N	77	324	72	103	14	6	2	32	20	4		.318	.365	.417	140	14	8	.884	-4	88	41	O76C/3		0.6
Total	5	317	1318	224	390	70	13	4	119	60	8	28	.296	.330	.378	124	34	8	.866	-6	102	59	O316(9/284/24)/3		1.5

LEWIS, DUFFY George Edward B4.18.1888 San Francisco CA D6.17.1979 Salem NH BL/TL/5-10.5/165 d4.16 Mil 1918 C5 Col St. Marys (CA)

YEAR	TM LG	G	AB	R	H	2B	3B	HR	RBI	BB-IB	HP	SO	AVG	OBP	SLG	AOPS	ABR	SB-CS	FA	FR	RNG	THR	GAMES AT POSITION	DL	BFW
1910	Bos A	151	541	64	153	29	7	8	68	32	4		.283	.328	.407	127	15	10	.944	12	106	147	O149L		1.9
1911	Bos A	130	469	64	144	32	4	7	86	25	10		.307	.355	.437	122	13	11	.939	5	93	145	O125L		1.2
1912	†Bos A	154	581	85	165	36	9	6	109	52	3		.284	.346	.408	110	7	9	.947	6	103	121	O154L		0.6
1913	Bos A	149	551	54	164	31	12	0	90	30	2	55	.298	.336	.397	112	6	12	.960	11	105	159	O142L/P3		1.1
1914	Bos A	146	510	53	142	37	9	2	79	57	5	41	.278	.357	.398	127	18	22-31	.952	-3	92	105	O142L		0.3
1915	†Bos A	152	557	69	162	31	7	2	76	45	4	63	.291	.348	.382	122	14	14-7	.952	-6	93	80	O152L		0.2
1916	†Bos A	152	563	56	151	29	5	1	56	33	4	46	.268	.313	.343	97	-4	16	.970	-3	98	80	O151(136/15/0)		-1.8
1917	Bos A	150	553	55	167	29	4	7	89	17	5	54	.302	.342	.392	125	14	8	.972	5	108	96	O150L		1.4
1919	NY A	141	559	67	152	23	4	7	89	17	0	42	.272	.293	.365	84	-15	8	.985	-8	86	86	O141L		-3.1
1920	NY A	107	365	34	99	4	1	4	61	24	2	32	.271	.320	.332	70	-16	2-8	.961	-1	93	114	O99(98/0/1)		-2.1
1921	Was A	27	102	11	19	4	1	0	14	8	1	10	.186	.252	.245	29	-11	1-1	.980	-1	88	96	O27(26/0/1)		-1.4
Total	11	1459	5351	612	1518	289	68	38	793	352	40	303	.284	.333	.384	108	41	113-47	.959	16	98	112	O1432(1415/15/2)/3P		-1.7

LEWIS, JACK John David B2.14.1884 Pittsburgh PA D2.25.1956 Steubenville OH BR/TR/5-8/158 d9.16

YEAR	TM LG	G	AB	R	H	2B	3B	HR	RBI	BB-IB	HP	SO	AVG	OBP	SLG	AOPS	ABR	SB-CS	FA	FR	RNG	THR	GAMES AT POSITION	DL	BFW
1911	Bos A	18	59	7	16	0	0	0	6				.271	.368	.271	80	1	2	.931	0	106	88	2b18		-0.1
1914	Pit F	117	394	32	92	14	5	1	48	17	6	46	.234	.276	.302	58	-31	9	.949	3	103	77	2b115/S		-2.8
1915	Pit F	82	231	24	61	6	5	0	26	8	1	31	.264	.292	.333	76	-12	7	.962	-0	102	107	2b45,S11,O6R,1b5/3		-1.2
Total	3	217	684	63	169	20	10	1	80	32	9	77	.247	.290	.310	66	-44	18	.951	2	103	86	2b178,S12,O6R,1b5/3		-4.1

LEWIS, BUDDY John Kelly B8.10.1916 Gastonia NC BL/TR/6-1/175 d9.16 Mil 1942-45

YEAR	TM LG	G	AB	R	H	2B	3B	HR	RBI	BB-IB	HP	SO	AVG	OBP	SLG	AOPS	ABR	SB-CS	FA	FR	RNG	THR	GAMES AT POSITION	DL	BFW
1935	Was A	8	28	3	3	0	0	0	2	0		5	.107	.107	.107	-46	-6	0-0	.941	0	111	129	3b6		-0.1
1936	Was A	143	601	100	175	21	13	6	67	47	4	46	.291	.347	.399	89	-14	6-6	.933	6	108	105	3b139		-0.1
1937	Was A	156	668	107	210	32	6	10	79	52	3	44	.314	.367	.425	104	3	11-5	.938	-20	91	99	3b156		-1.0
1938	Was A★	151	656	122	194	35	9	12	91	58	1	35	.296	.354	.431	103	1	17-9	.912	-5	103	109	3b151		0.8
1939	Was A	140	536	87	171	23	16	10	75	72	2	36	.319	.402	.478	134	28	10-9	.933	11	114	117	3b134		1.5
1940	Was A	148	600	101	190	38	10	6	63	74	1	36	.317	.393	.443	124	24	15-10	.960	1	96	127	O112R,3b36		1.7
1941	Was A	149	569	97	169	29	11	9	72	82	0	30	.297	.386	.434	122	20	10-7	.972	5	116	169	O96R,3b49		1.9
1945	Was A	69	258	42	86	14	7	2	37	37	3	15	.333	.423	.465	172	25	18	.970	2	101	119	O145(8/1/137)		1.6
1946	Was A	150	582	82	170	28	13	7	45	59	2	26	.292	.359	.421	125	18	5-3	.968	0	101	118	O130R		0.7
1947	Was A★	140	506	67	132	15	4	6	48	51	1	27	.261	.330	.342	89	-8	6-6	.979	2	114	69	O67R		-0.4
1949	Was A	95	257	25	63	14	4	3	28	41	3	12	.245	.355	.366	93	-2	2-2	.979	2	104	109	3b671,O619(8/1/611)		8.2
Total	11	1349	5261	830	1563	249	93	71	607	573	20	303	.297	.368	.420	112	-89	83-59	.927	4	102	109			

LEWIS, JOHNNY Johnny Joe B8.10.1939 Greenville AL BL/TR/6-1/189* d4.14 C9

YEAR	TM LG	G	AB	R	H	2B	3B	HR	RBI	BB-IB	HP	SO	AVG	OBP	SLG	AOPS	ABR	SB-CS	FA	FR	RNG	THR	GAMES AT POSITION	DL	BFW
1964	StL N	40	94	10	22	2	2	7	13-1		0	23	.234	.324	.362	86	-2	2-2	.966	1	105	143	O36(2/0/34)		-0.3
1965	NY N	148	477	64	117	15	3	15	45	59-4	3	117	.245	.331	.384	105	4	4-7	.975	4	100	163	O142(0/48/101)		-0.6
1966	NY N	65	166	21	32	6	1	5	20	21-0	0	43	.193	.282	.331	72	-6	2-0	.988	-2	94	94	O49(11/8/31)		-1.0
1967	NY N	13	34	2	4	1	0	0	2	2-0	0	11	.118	.167	.147	-10	-5	0-0	1.000	1	107	180	O10(2/0/9)		-0.2
Total	4	266	771	97	175	24	6	22	74	95-5	3	194	.227	.313	.359	90	-9	8-9	.977	4	100	140	O237(15/56/175)		

LEWIS, MARK Mark David B11.30.1969 Hamilton OH BR/TR/6-1/190* [CleA88 1/2] d4.26

YEAR	TM LG	G	AB	R	H	2B	3B	HR	RBI	BB-IB	HP	SO	AVG	OBP	SLG	AOPS	ABR	SB-CS	FA	FR	RNG	THR	GAMES AT POSITION	DL	BFW
1991	Cle A	84	314	29	83	15	1	0	30	15-0	0	45	.264	.293	.318	70	-13	2-2	.966	-12	95	84	2b50,S36		-2.5
1992	Cle A	122	413	44	109	21	0	5	30	25-1	3	69	.264	.308	.351	86	-8	4-5	.954	-15	93	S121/3		-0.1
1993	Cle A	14	52	6	13	2	0	1	5	0-0	0	7	.250	.250	.346	58	-3	3-0	.964	-3	82	116	S13		-0.5
1994	Cle A	20	73	6	15	5	0	1	8	2-0	0	13	.205	.227	.315	37	-7	1-0	.968	-1	105	56	3b72,2b2,S2		0.0
1995	†Cin N	81	171	25	58	13	1	3	30	21-2	0	33	.339	.407	.480	133	9	0-3	.987	-9	98	81	2b144/D		-1.0
1996	Det A	145	545	69	147	30	3	11	55	42-0	5	109	.270	.326	.396	82	-16	6-1	.945	-15	84	93	3b69,2b29/D		-1.9
1997	†SF N	118	341	50	91	14	6	10	42	23-2	3	62	.267	.318	.431	97	-3	3-2	.978	7	106	83	2b140		-0.4
1998	Phi N	142	518	52	129	21	2	9	54	48-2	3	111	.249	.312	.349	75	-19	3-3	.938	-8	78	129	3b52,2b2		-1.3
1999	Cin N	88	173	18	44	16	0	6	28	7-1	0	24	.254	.280	.451	79	-6	0-0	.909	1	134	0	3b5		-1.0
2000	Cin N	11	19	1	2	1	0	0	3	1-0	0	3	.105	.150	.158	-22	-4	0-0	1.000	0	0	3b29,2b21,S14,D4	15	-0.5
Bal A		71	163	19	44	17	0	2	21	12-0	1	31	.270	.322	.411	89	-3	7-2	.857	-6	91	52	3b24,2b3		-0.3
2001	Cle A	6	13	1	1	0	0	0	0-0		1	4	.077	.077	.077	-57	-3	0-0	.889	0	123	225	3b4,2b3	27	-1.0
Total	11	902	2795	320	736	155	13	48	306	196-8	16	511	.263	.312	.380	82	-76	29-18	.977	-62	100	83	2b392,3b238,S199,D6		

LEWIS, PHIL Philip B10.8.1884 Pittsburgh PA D8.8.1959 Port Wentworth GA BR/TR/6-0/195 d4.14 Col Cornell

YEAR	TM LG	G	AB	R	H	2B	3B	HR	RBI	BB-IB	HP	SO	AVG	OBP	SLG	AOPS	ABR	SB-CS	FA	FR	RNG	THR	GAMES AT POSITION	DL	BFW
1905	Bro N	118	433	32	110	9	2	3	33	16	1		.254	.282	.305	81	-12	16	.904	-3	97	120	S118		-1.7
1906	Bro N	136	452	40	110	8	4	0	37	43	5		.243	.309	.279	90	-5	14	.922	-20	98	80	S135		-3.2
1907	Bro N	136	475	52	118	11	1	0	30	23	2		.248	.286	.276	83	-11	16	.938	-23	90	80	S136		-2.4
1908	Bro N	118	415	22	91	5	6	1	30	13	0		.219	.243	.267	66	-19	9	.943	-2	95	94	S116		-0.8
Total	4	508	1775	146	429	33	13	4	130	95	3		.242	.281	.282	80	-47	55	.926	-48	95	93	S505		-8.1

LEWIS, BILL William Henry "Buddy" B10.15.1904 Ripley TN D10.24.1977 Memphis TN BR/TR/5-9/165 d6.3

YEAR	TM LG	G	AB	R	H	2B	3B	HR	RBI	BB-IB	HP	SO	AVG	OBP	SLG	AOPS	ABR	SB-CS	FA	FR	RNG	THR	GAMES AT POSITION	DL	BFW
1933	StL N	15	35	8	14	1	0	1	8	2	0	3	.400	.432	.514	161	3	0	1.000	0	79	99	C8		0.0
1935	Bos N	6	4	1	0	0	0	0	0	1	0	1	.000	.200	.000	-45	-1	0	—	-0	0	0	/C		-0.1
1936	Bos N	29	62	11	19	4	0	3	12	6	0	7	.306	.419	.339	113	2	0	.967	-2	134	65	C21		-0.1
Total	3	50	101	20	33	3	0	1	15	15	0	11	.327	.414	.386	124	3	0	.981	-2	114	77	C30		-0.2

LEYRITZ, JIM James Joseph B12.27.1963 Lakewood OH BR/TR/6-0/195(190-220) d6.8 Col Kentucky OF(25/0/30)

YEAR	TM LG	G	AB	R	H	2B	3B	HR	RBI	BB-IB	HP	SO	AVG	OBP	SLG	AOPS	ABR	SB-CS	FA	FR	RNG	THR	GAMES AT POSITION	DL	BFW
1990	NY A	92	303	28	78	13	1	5	25	27-1	7	51	.257	.331	.356	92	-3	2-3	.929	-14	76	40	3b69,O14(10/0/4),C11		-1.0
1991	NY A	32	77	8	14	3	0	0	4	13-0	0	15	.182	.300	.221	46	-5	0-1	.909	3	65	64	3b18,C5,1b3/D		-0.4
1992	NY A	63	144	17	37	6	0	7	26	14-1	6	22	.257	.341	.444	121	4	0-1	.993	-2	79	106	1b29,O28(6/0/23),D21,C12		-0.4
1993	NY A	95	259	43	80	14	0	14	53	37-3	8	59	.309	.410	.525	154	20	0-0	1.000	-1	153	47	C37,D25,1b10		1.4
1994	NY A	75	249	47	66	12	0	17	58	35-1	6	61	.265	.365	.518	130	11	0-0	.993	-5	70	77	C46,1b18,D15		1.0
1995	†NY A	77	264	37	71	12	0	7	37	37-2	2	73	.269	.374	.394	101	2	1-1	.995	-5	70	77	C55,3b13,D12,1b5,O3L,2b2		-0.2
1996	†NY A	88	265	23	70	10	0	7	40	30-3	9	68	.264	.355	.381	87	-4	2-0	.995	-2	106	87	C55,3b13,D12,1b5,O3L,2b2		-0.2

YEAR	TM LG	G	AB	R	H	2B	3B	HR	RBI	BB-IB	HP	SO	AVG	OBP	SLG	AOPS	ABR	SB-CS	FA	FR	RNG	THR	GAMES AT POSITION	DL	BFW
1997	Ana A	84	294	47	81	7	0	11	50	37-2	3	56	.276	.357	.412	101		1-1	1.000	4	100	172	C58,1b15,D13		0.7
	Tex A	37	85	11	24	4	0	0	14	23-0	3	22	.282	.446	.329	101	2	1-0	.984	-2	62	184	C11,1b9,D9		0.0
	Year	121	379	58	105	11	0	11	64	60-2	6	78	.277	.379	.393	101	3	2-1	.998	2	94	174	C69,1b24,D22		0.7
1998	Bos A	52	129	17	37	6	0	8	24	21-1	2	34	.287	.385	.519	132	7	0-0	1.000	0	34	0	D39/C1		0.5
	†SD N	62	143	17	38	10	0	4	18	21-0	7	40	.266	.384	.420	120	6	0-0	.987	-1	117	37	C24,1b20/3OL		0.5
1999	SD N	50	134	17	32	5	0	8	21	15-1	4	37	.239	.331	.455	105	0	0-0	.994	1	54	86	C24,1b19/3		0.1
	†NY A	31	66	8	15	4	1	0	5	13-1	0	17	.227	.354	.318	75	-2	0-0	.986	1	191	102	D14,1b9/C3	37	-0.2
2000	NY A	24	55	2	12	0	0	1	4	7-0	1	14	.218	.317	.273	52	-4	0-0	1.000	-1	53	0	D15,C2/1		-0.5
	LA N	41	60	3	12	1	0	1	8	7-0	1	12	.200	.294	.267	45	-5	0-0	1.000	-2	80	108	1b8,O6(5/0/1),C3		-0.7
Total 11		903	2527	325	667	107	2	90	387	337-16	65	581	.264	.362	.415	106	31	7-7	.995	-24	104	101	C308,D195,1b149,3b105,O54R,2b3	37	0.3

LEZCANO, CARLOS   Carlos Manuel (Rubio) B9.30.1955 Arecibo, PR   BR/TR/6-2/185* d4.10   Col Florida St.

1980	Chi N	42	88	15	18	4	1	3	12	11-0	1	29	.205	.294	.375	81	-2	1-2	.948	-1	98	158	O39C		-0.4
1981	Chi N	7	14	1	1	0	0	0	2	0-0	0	4	.071	.071	.071	-56	-2	0-0	1.000	0	118	0	O5(1/0/4)		-0.3
Total 2		49	102	16	19	4	1	3	14	11-0	1	33	.186	.267	.333	63	-5	1-2	.952	-1	100	142	O44(1/39/4)		-0.7

LEZCANO, SIXTO   Sixto Joaquin (Curras) B11.28.1953 Arecibo, PR   BR/TR/5-11/175(165-190) d9.10

1974	Mil A	15	54	5	13	2	0	2	9	4-0	0	9	.241	.283	.389	95	-1	1-1	.972	2	101	245	O15R		0.0
1975	Mil A	134	429	55	106	19	3	11	43	46-1	4	93	.247	.324	.382	99	-1	5-5	.977	-3	98	95	O129(0/2/128),D2		-1.1
1976	Mil A	145	513	53	146	19	5	7	56	51-2	2	112	.285	.348	.382	117	11	14-10	.973	6	**111**	94	O142(64/17/66),D3		1.0
1977	Mil A	109	400	50	109	21	4	21	49	52-1	2	78	.273	.358	.503	132	18	6-5	.988	9	111	142	O108R		2.0
1978	Mil A	132	442	62	129	21	4	15	61	64-6	1	83	.292	.377	.459	135	22	3-3	.979	5	95	184	O127R,D3	24	2.1
1979	Mil A	138	473	84	152	29	3	28	101	77-5	3	74	.321	.414	.573	164	46	4-3	.986	-4	94	93	O135R/D		3.3
1980	Mil A	112	411	51	94	19	3	18	55	39-3	0	75	.229	.298	.421	98	-3	1-1	.983	1	101	94	O108R,D4		-0.8
1981	StL N	72	214	26	57	8	2	5	28	40-2	0	40	.266	.376	.393	115	6	0-1	.973	-6	79	87	O65(32/0/34)		3.8
1982	SD N	138	470	73	136	26	6	16	84	78-10	2	69	.289	.388	.472	150	34	2-1	.990	9	104	101	O134R		3.8
1983	SD N	97	317	41	74	11	2	8	49	47-3	1	66	.233	.331	.356	94	-2	0-0	.968	2	101	128	O134R		3.8
	†Phi N	18	39	8	11	1	0	0	7	5-0	0	9	.282	.364	.308	88	0	1-0	1.000	1	97	300	O91R		-0.5
	Year	115	356	49	85	12	2	8	56	52-3	1	75	.239	.334	.351	93	-2	1-0	.971	3	101	146	O106(2/1/104)		0.0
1984	Phi N	109	256	36	71	6	2	14	40	38-1	0	43	.277	.371	.480	135	12	0-1	.981	3	118	67	O87(4/0/83)		-0.5
1985	Pit N	72	116	16	24	2	0	3	9	35-3	1	27	.207	.392	.302	98	2	0-0	.967	-0	99	92	O40(25/0/16)		1.2
Total 12		1291	4134	560	1122	184	34	148	591	576-37	19	768	.271	.360	.440	124	144	37-31	.980	24	101	120	O1196(127/20/1058),D13	24	10.6

LIBBY, STEVE   Stephen Augustus B12.8.1853 Scarborough ME D3.31.1935 Milford CT   6-1.5/168 d5.10

| 1879 | Buf N | 1 | 2 | 0 | 0 | 0 | 0 | 0 | 0 | | 1 | | .000 | .000 | .000 | -98 | | | 1.000 | 0 | 0 | 0 | /1 | | 0.0 |

LIBKE, AL   Albert Walter B9.12.1918 Tacoma WA D3.7.2003 Wenatchee WA   BL/TR/6-4/215 d4.19 ▲

1945	Cin N	130	449	41	117	23	5	4	53	34	2	62	.261	.336	.383	102	0	6	.963	1	96	131	O108(27/0/82),P4,1b2		-0.6
1946	Cin N	124	431	32	109	22	1	5	42	43	1	50	.253	.322	.343	92	-5	0	.972	-4	86	121	O115R/P		-1.3
Total 2		254	880	73	236	45	6	9	95	77	3	112	.268	.329	.364	97	-5	6	.967	-4	91	126	O223(27/0/197),P5,1b2		-1.9

LIBRAN, FRANKIE   Francisco (Rosas) B5.6.1948 Mayaguez, PR   BR/TR/6-0/175 d9.3

| 1969 | SD N | 10 | 11 | 1 | 1 | 0 | 0 | 0 | 1 | 2-0 | 0 | 1 | .091 | .182 | .182 | .200 | | 7 | -1 | 0-0 | 1.000 | -2 | 85 | 41 | S9 | | -0.2 |

LICKERT, JOHN   John Wilbur B4.4.1960 Pittsburgh PA   BR/TR/5-11/175 [BosA78 13/336] d9.19

| 1981 | Bos A | 1 | 0 | 0 | 0 | 0 | 0 | 0 | 0 | 0-0 | 0 | 0 | — | — | — | — | 0 | 0-0 | 1.000 | 0 | 0 | 0 | /C | | 0.0 |

LIDDELL, DAVE   David Alexander (b Desmond Lane Liddell) B6.15.1966 Los Angeles CA   BR/TR/6-0/190 [ChiN84 4/83] d6.3

| 1990 | NY N | 1 | 1 | 1 | 1 | 0 | 0 | 0 | 1 | 0-0 | 0 | 0 | 1.000 | 1.000 | 1.000 | 451 | 0 | 0-0 | 1.000 | 0 | 0 | 0 | /C | | 0.0 |

LIEBERTHAL, MIKE   Michael Scott B1.18.1972 Glendale CA   BR/TR/6-0/186(170-190) [PhiN90 1/3] d6.30

1994	Phi N	24	79	6	21	3	1	1	5	3-0	1	5	.266	.301	.367	72	-4	0-0	.969	-5	106	29	C22		-0.7
1995	Phi N	16	47	1	12	2	0	0	4	5-0	1	5	.255	.327	.298	66	-2	0-0	.991	0	71	89	C14		-0.1
1996	Phi N	50	166	21	42	8	0	7	23	10-0	2	30	.253	.297	.428	90	-3	0-0	.990	5	154	93	C43		0.4
1997	Phi N	134	455	59	112	27	1	20	77	44-1	4	76	.246	.314	.442	98	-3	3-4	.988	4	126	93	C129/D	39	0.9
1998	Phi N	86	313	39	80	15	3	8	45	17-1	7	44	.256	.304	.399	84	-8	2-1	.988	6	**151**	78	C83	40	0.3
1999	Phi N★	145	510	84	153	33	1	31	96	44-7	11	86	.300	.363	.551	127	20	0-0	**.997**	4	153	73	C143		3.1
2000	Phi N★	108	389	55	108	30	0	15	71	40-3	6	53	.278	.352	.470	106	4	2-0	.993	1	140	98	C106	36	1.2
2001	Phi N	34	121	21	28	8	0	2	11	12-2	3	21	.231	.316	.347	75	-4	2-0	.992	4	189	56	C33	148	0.2
2002	Phi N	130	476	46	133	29	2	15	52	38-2	14	58	.279	.349	.443	118	10	0-1	.993	-8	143	82	C129		1.0
2003	Phi N	131	508	68	159	30	1	13	81	38-2	12	59	.313	.373	.453	124	18	0-0	.990	-12	77	64	C131		1.4
2004	Phi N	131	476	58	129	31	1	17	61	37-2	11	69	.271	.335	.447	98	-2	1-1	.993	-9	90	76	C129		-0.2
2005	Phi N	118	392	48	103	25	0	12	47	35-14	11	35	.263	.336	.418	94	-2	0-0	.993	-8	91	70	C117		-0.3
Total 12		1107	3932	506	1080	241	10	141	573	323-34	82	541	.275	.339	.449	105	24	8-7	.992	-18	123	78	C1079/D	263	7.2

LIEFER, JEFF   Jeffrey David B8.17.1974 Fontana CA   BL/TR/6-3/210(195-210) [ChiA95 1/25] d4.7   Col Cal St.-Long Beach

1999	Chi A	45	113	8	27	7	1	0	14	8-0	0	28	.248	.295	.327	58	-7	2-0	1.000	2	106	114	O17(14/0/3),1b15,D7		-0.6
2000	Chi A	5	11	0	2	0	0	0	0	0-0	0	4	.182	.182	.182	-7	-2	0-0		0	51	0	O5R/1	13	-0.2
2001	Chi A	83	254	36	65	13	0	18	39	20-1	2	69	.256	.313	.520	108	2	0-1	1.000	-7	73	90	O38(35/0/4),1b15,3b15,D10		-0.7
2002	Mon N	35	88	6	17	3	0	3	18	3-0	1	26	.193	.217	.330	40	-8	0-1	.980	-3	56	125	1b21		-1.4
2003	TB A	9	25	4	3	1	0	1	3	3-1	1	13	.120	.214	.280	30	-3	0-0	1.000	-3	94	0	O36(24/0/12),1b31,D6		-1.3
2004	Mil N	16	28	3	6	2	0	1	5	2-0	1	8	.214	.258	.393	67	-1	0-0	.929	-0	89	0	3b6/OLD		-0.3
2005	Cle A	19	56	5	11	2	0	1	8	4-1	0	15	.196	.211	.286	31	-6	0-0	.950	-1	108	88	1b5,O3R,D9		-0.2
Total 7		288	779	89	179	36	1	31	113	56-4	2	223	.230	.281	.398	74	-33	2-2	1.000	-11	87	75	O103(74/0/30),1b88,D37,3b21	13	-5.3

LIESE, FRED   Frederick Richard B10.7.1885 WI D6.30.1967 Los Angeles CA   BL/TL/5-8/150 d4.14   Col Wisconsin-Madison

| 1910 | Bos N | 5 | 4 | 0 | 0 | 0 | 0 | 0 | 0 | | 1 | 2 | .000 | .200 | .000 | -39 | -1 | 0 | | | | | /H | | -0.1 |

LILLARD, GENE   Robert Eugene B11.12.1913 Santa Barbara CA D4.12.1991 Goleta CA   BR/TR/5-10.5/178 d5.8 b-Bill ▲

1936	Chi N	19	34	6	7	1	0	2	3		0	8	.206	.270	.235	36	-3	0	.947	-1	81	98	S4,3b3		-0.4
1939	Chi N	23	10	3	1	0	0	0	0	6	0	3	.100	.438	.100	51	1	0	1.000	0	98	0	P20		0.0
1940	StL N	2	0	0	0	0	0	0	0	0-0	0	0	—	—	—		0	0	1.000	0	99	0	P2		0.0
Total 3		44	44	9	8	1	0	2	3		0	11	.182	.321	.205	43	-2	0	1.000	-1	98	0	P22,S4,3b3		-0.4

LILLARD, BILL   William Beverly B1.10.1918 Goleta CA   BR/TR/5-10/170 d9.11 b-Gene

1939	Phi A	7	19	4	6	1	0	0	1	3		1	.316	.409	.368	102	0	0-0	.974	2	128	70	S7		0.2
1940	Phi A	73	206	26	49	8	2	1	21	28	1	28	.238	.332	.311	69	-9	0-1	.921	-13	90	72	S69/2		-1.7
Total 2		80	225	30	55	9	2	1	22	31	1	29	.244	.339	.316	72	-9	0-1	.927	-12	94	72	S76/2		-1.5

LILLIE, JIM   James J. "Grasshopper" (b James J. Lilly) B7.27.1861 New Haven CT D11.9.1890 Kansas City MO   BR d5.17 ▲

1883	Buf N	50	201	25	47	7	3	1	29	1		31	.234	.238	.313	64	-9		.835	-6	82	132	O47(12/34/1),P3,C2/S32		-1.4
1884	Buf N	114	471	68	105	12	5	3	53	5		71	.223	.231	.289	60	-23		.852	16	**180**	197	O114R,P2		-0.7
1885	Buf N	112	430	49	107	13	3	2	30	6		39	.249	.259	.307	80	-11		.862	2	112	121	O112(21/4/89),S3/1		-1.0
1886	KC N	114	416	37	73	9	0	0	22	11		80	.175	.197	.197	19	-41	13	.884	11	132	75	O114L/P		-3.0
Total 4		390	1518	179	332	41	11	6	134	23		221	.219	.230	.272	54	-84	13	.863	23	135	131	O387(147/38/204),P6,S4,C2/123		-6.1

LILLIS, BOB   Robert Perry B6.2.1930 Altadena CA   BR/TR/5-11/160* d8.30 M4/C22   Col USC

1958	LA N	20	69	10	27	3	1	0	4	0-1	0	4	.391	.421	.507	142	4	1-2	.964	-0	99	81	S19		0.5
1959	LA N	30	48	7	11	2	0	0	5	3-1	0	4	.229	.275	.271	43	-4	0-0	.919	3	113	113	S20		0.1
1960	LA N	48	60	6	16	4	0	0	2	2-1	0	6	.267	.290	.333	66	-3	2-0	.982	6	103	148	S23,3b14/2		0.5
1961	LA N	19	9	0	1	0	0	0	1	1-0	0	1	.111	.200	.111	-13	-1	0-0	.982	6	103	148	S23,3b14/2		0.5
	StL N	86	230	24	50	4	0	0	21	7-2	0	13	.217	.245	.235	26	-24	3-3	1.000	-1	39	0	3b12/2S		-0.2
	Year	105	239	24	51	4	0	0	22	8-2	0	14	.213	.242	.230	25	-26	3-3	.928	-1	102	65	S56,2b24		-2.1
1962	Hou N	129	457	38	114	12	4	1	30	28-1	2	23	.249	.292	.300	64	-24	3-3	.924	-2	101	104	S57,2b25,3b12		-2.3
1963	Hou N	147	469	31	93	13	1	1	19	15-1	4	35	.198	.229	.237	37	-39	3-4	.957	-5	99	79	S124,2b19,3b6		0.2
1964	Hou N	109	332	19	89	11	2	0	17	11-1	0	13	.268	.291	.310	75	-12	4-9	.995	-7	100	87	2b52,S43,3b12		-3.8
1965	Hou N	124	408	34	90	12	1	0	20	20-6	6	10	.221	.267	.255	51	-27	2-2	.968	-15	89	80	S104,3b9,2b6		-3.5

YEAR	TM LG	G	AB	R	H	2B	3B	HR	RBI	BB-IB	HP	SO	AVG	OBP	SLG	AOPS	ABR	SB-CS	FA	FR	RNG	THR	GAMES AT POSITION	DL	BFW
1966	Hou N	68	164	14	38	6	0	0	11	7-0	0	4	.232	.260	.268	52	-11	1-1	.951	-7	78	82	2b35,S18,3b6		-1.5
1967	Hou N	37	82	3	20	1	0	0	5	1-0	0	8	.244	.253	.256	48	-6	0-1	.947	-0	109	70	S23,2b3,3b2		-0.5
Total	10	817	2328	198	549	68	9	3	137	99-13	13	116	.236	.270	.277	54	-147	23-25	.959	3	100	86	S530,2b174,3b70		-10.5

LIMMER, LOU Louis B.3.10.1925 New York NY BL/TL/6-2/190* d4.22

1951	Phi A	94	214	25	34	9	1	5	30	28	0	40	.159	.256	.280	44	-18	1-0	.988	3	124	113	1b58		-1.6
1954	Phi A	115	316	41	73	10	3	14	32	35	0	37	.231	.305	.415	96	-3	2-3	.988	3	115	84	1b79		-0.6
Total	2	209	530	66	107	19	4	19	62	63	0	77	.202	.285	.360	75	-21	3-3	.988	5	119	95	1b137		-2.2

LINARES, RUFINO Rufino (b Rufino De La Cruz (Linares)) B2.28.1951 San Pedro de Macoris, D.R. D5.16.1998 San Pedro de Macoris, D.R. BR/TR/6-0/170(165-190) d4.10 [DL 1983 Atl N 182]

1981	Atl N	78	253	27	67	9	2	5	25	9-2	0	28	.265	.289	.375	87	-5	8-4	.963	3	107	119	O60L		-0.5
1982	Atl N	77	191	28	57	7	1	2	17	7-0	1	29	.298	.325	.377	94	-2	5-2	1.000	3	104	113	O53(51/0/4)		-0.2
1984	Atl N	34	58	4	12	3	0	1	10	6-0	0	12	.207	.273	.310	62	-3	0-0	.958	1	101	241	O13(12/0/1)		-0.2
1985	Cal A	18	43	7	11	2	0	3	11	2-0	0	5	.256	.283	.512	114	1	2-0	1.000	0	140	0	D14,O2R		0.1
Total	4	207	545	66	147	21	3	11	63	24-2	1	74	.270	.299	.380	89	-9	15-6	.977	7	105	128	O128(123/0/7),D14	182	-0.7

LIND, CARL Henry Carl "Hooks" B9.19.1903 New Orleans LA D8.4.1946 New York NY BR/TR/6-0/160 d9.14 Col Tulane

1927	Cle A	12	37	2	5	0	0	0	1	5	1	7	.135	.256	.135	4	-5	1-0	.969	1	120	92	2b11/S		-0.3
1928	Cle A	154	650	102	191	42	4	1	54	36	1	48	.294	.331	.375	84	-15	8-3	.960	5	101	114	2b154		-0.5
1929	Cle A	66	225	19	54	8	1	0	13	13	0	17	.240	.282	.284	44	-19	0-2	.957	10	101	158	2b64/3		-0.7
1930	Cle A	24	69	8	17	3	0	0	6	3	0	7	.246	.278	.290	43	-6	0-1	.940	8	127	142	S22,2b2		0.3
Total	4	256	981	131	267	53	5	1	74	57	1	79	.272	.313	.339	69	-45	9-6	.960	24	102	125	2b231,S23/3		-1.2

LIND, JACK Jackson Hugh B6.8.1946 Denver CO BB/TR/6-0/170* d9.10 C4 Col Arizona St.

1974	Mil A	9	17	4	4	2	0	0	1	3-0	0	2	.235	.350	.353	103	0	0-0	1.000	-2	73	85	S5,2b4		-0.1
1975	Mil A	17	20	1	1	0	0	0	0	2-0	0	12	.050	.136	.050	-45	-4	1-0	.919	1	136	52	S9,3b6/1		-0.2
Total	2	26	37	5	5	2	0	0	1	5-0	0	14	.135	.238	.189	23	-4	1-0	.943	-1	111	65	S14,3b6,2b4/1		-0.3

LIND, JOSE Jose (Salgado) "Chico" B5.1.1964 Toa Baja, PR BR/TR/5-11/175* d8.28

1987	Pit N	35	143	21	46	8	4	0	11	8-1	0	12	.322	.358	.434	107	1	2-1	.995	6	127	55	2b35		0.9
1988	Pit N	154	611	82	160	24	4	2	49	42-0	1	75	.262	.308	.324	83	-14	15-4	.987	1	104	84	2b153		-0.8
1989	Pit N	153	578	52	134	21	3	2	48	39-7	2	64	.232	.280	.289	66	-27	15-1	.976	-10	101	95	2b151		-3.2
1990	†Pit N	152	514	46	134	28	5	1	48	35-19	2	52	.261	.305	.340	81	-14	8-0	.991	20	111	103	2b152		1.2
1991	†Pit N	150	502	53	133	16	6	3	54	30-10	2	56	.265	.306	.339	83	-13	7-4	.989	26	112	111	2b149		1.8
1992	†Pit N	135	468	38	110	14	1	0	39	26-12	1	29	.235	.275	.269	55	-28	3-1	.992	9	109	100	2b134		-1.6
1993	KC A	136	431	33	107	13	2	0	37	13-0	2	36	.248	.271	.288	48	-33	3-2	.994	-10	92	88	2b136		-3.6
1994	KC A	85	290	34	78	16	2	1	31	16-1	0	34	.269	.306	.348	65	-15	9-5	.988	-9	95	86	2b84/D		-1.9
1995	KC A	29	97	4	26	3	0	0	6	3-0	0	8	.268	.290	.299	52	-7	0-0	1.000	1	105	114	2b15		-1.0
	Cal A	15	43	5	7	2	0	0	1	3-0	0	4	.163	.217	.209	12	-6	0-0	.995	-3	96	101	2b44		-0.4
	Year	44	140	9	33	5	0	0	7	6-0	0	12	.236	.267	.271	40	-13	0-1	.998	-1	102	111	2b59		-1.4
Total	9	1044	3677	368	935	145	27	9	324	215-50	8	370	.254	.295	.316	70	-156	62-19	.988	29	105	95	2b1038/D		-8.6

LINDBECK, EM Emerit Desmond B8.27.1935 Kewanee IL BL/TR/6-0/185 d4.22 Col Illinois

1960	Det A	2	1	0	0	0	0	0	0	1-0	0	0	.000	.500	.000	46	0	0-0	—		0		/H		0.0

LINDELL, JOHNNY John Harlan B8.30.1916 Greeley CO D8.27.1985 Newport Beach CA BR/TR/6-4.5/217* d4.18 Mil 1945 ▲

1941	NY A	1	1	0	0	0	0	0	0	0	0	0	.000	.000	.000	-99	0	0-0	.923	-0	66	279	P23		0.0
1942	NY A	27	24	1	6	1	0	0	4	0	0	5	.250	.250	.292	53	1	0-0	.966	-2	96	123	O122(3/55/66)		-0.5
1943	†NY A☆	122	441	53	108	17	12	4	51	51	4	55	.245	.329	.365	102	0	5-4	.986	4	110	61	O149(2/148/0)		2.5
1944	NY A	149	594	91	178	33	16	18	103	44	3	56	.300	.351	.500	137	25	5-4	.982	-1	102	59	O41C		5.2
1945	NY A	41	159	26	45	6	3	1	20	17	1	10	.283	.363	.377	110	2	2-1	.982	-1	98	141	O74(5/31/39),1b14		-0.2
1946	NY A	102	332	41	86	10	5	10	40	32	2	47	.259	.328	.410	104	0	4-1	.982	-1	96	72	O118(102/10/11)		-0.3
1947	†NY A	127	476	66	131	18	7	11	67	35	0	50	.275	.322	.412	104	0	1-2	.994	2	99	125	O79(72/1/7)		1.1
1948	NY A	88	309	58	98	17	2	13	55	35	0	27	.317	.387	.511	139	16	0-0	.983	-1	96	102	O65(63/3/1)		-0.3
1949	†NY A	78	211	33	51	10	0	6	27	35	0	30	.242	.350	.374	92	-2	3-0	.857	-1	70	0	O6L		-0.2
1950	NY A	7	21	2	4	0	0	0	2	4	0	2	.190	.320	.190	34	-2	0-0	.984	-1	96	45	O33(29/4/0)		-0.1
	StL N	36	113	16	21	3	2	5	16	15	1	24	.186	.287	.398	74	-5	0-0	.962	-2	139	74	P27,1b2		-0.1
1953	Pit N	58	91	11	26	6	1	4	15	16	1	15	.286	.404	.505	136	6	0-0	1.000	-1	76	0	P5,O2R		0.1
	Phi N	11	18	3	7	1	0	0	2	6	0	9	.389	.542	.444	162	2	0-0	1.000	-1	132	65	P32,1b2,O2R		0.1
	Year	69	109	14	33	7	1	4	17	22	2	17	.303	.429	.495	141	8	0-0	.964		0		/H		0.1
1954	Phi N	7	5	0	1	0	0	0	0	0	0	3	.200	.429	.200	70	0	0-0	—		0		/H		0.0
Total	12	854	2795	401	762	124	48	72	404	289	16	366	.273	.344	.429	113	43	17-13	.980	6	103	92	O689(282/293/126),P55,1b16		0.1

LINDEMAN, JIM James William B1.10.1962 Evanston IL BR/TR/6-1/200* [StLN83 1/24] d9.3 Col Bradley

1986	StL N	19	55	7	14	1	0	1	6	3-0	0	10	.255	.276	.327	67	-3	1-1	.992	0	116	90	1b17/3OL	47	-0.1
1987	†StL N	75	207	20	43	13	0	8	28	11-0	3	56	.208	.253	.386	66	-11	3-1	.976	2	99	141	O49(1/0/48),1b20	74	-1.2
1988	StL N	17	43	3	9	1	0	2	7	2-0	0	9	.209	.244	.372	73	-2	0-0	.941	-0	95	0	O12(4/0/8),1b3	31	-0.3
1989	StL N	73	45	8	5	1	0	0	8	3-0	1	13	.111	.163	.133	-13	-7	0-0	.989	1	118	141	1b42,O5(3/0/2)		-0.3
1990	Det A	12	32	5	7	1	0	2	8	2-0	0	13	.219	.265	.438	92	-1	0-0	1.000	0		0	D10/1OR		-0.1
1991	Phi N	65	95	13	32	5	0	0	12	13-1	0	14	.337	.413	.389	129	5	0-1	1.000	-2	81	85	O30(14/6/10)/1	95	-0.5
1992	Phi N	29	39	6	10	1	0	1	6	3-0	0	11	.256	.310	.359	89	-1	0-0	1.000	1	131	162	1b9		-0.0
1993	Hou N	9	23	2	8	3	0	0	0	0-0	0	7	.348	.348	.478	122	1	0-0	.948	-2	95	51	O33(21/0/14),1b4		-0.0
1994	NY N	52	137	18	37	8	1	7	20	6-2	1	35	.270	.303	.496	106	0	4-3	.970	-2	93	85	O140(48/6/90),1b97,D10/3	247	-2.2
Total	9	351	676	82	165	34	1	21	89	42-3	4	173	.244	.289	.391	83	-19	4-3	.970	-2	93	85			

LINDEMANN, BOB John Frederick Mann B6.5.1881 Philadelphia PA D12.19.1951 Williamsport PA BB/TR/6-0/175 d8.28

1901	Phi A	3	9	0	1	0	0	0	0	0	0		.111	.111	.111	-37	-2	0	.600	-0	294	0	O3R		-0.0

LINDEN, TODD Todd Anthony B6.30.1980 Edmonds WA BB/TR/6-3/210* [SFN01 1/41] d8.18 Col Louisiana St./Washington

2003	SF N	18	38	2	8	1	0	1	6	1-0	0	8	.211	.231	.316	40	-4	0-0	.929	-1	82	0	O13(9/0/6)		-0.0
2004	SF N	16	32	6	5	1	0	0	1	5-0	1	7	.156	.289	.188	26	-3	0-0	1.000	-2	62	0	O11(7/0/4)		-0.1
2005	SF N	60	171	20	37	8	0	4	13	10-0	5	54	.216	.280	.333	58	-11	3-0	.983	3	126	0	O52(18/0/50)		-0.2
Total	3	94	241	28	50	10	0	5	20	16-0	6	69	.207	.274	.311	51	-18	3-0	.978	-0	112	0	O76(34/0/50)		-0.2

LINDEN, WALT Walter Charles B3.27.1924 Chicago IL BR/TR/6-1/190 d4.30 Col Illinois

1950	Bos N	3	5	0	2	1	0	0	1	0	0	0	.400	.500	.600	201	1	0	1.000	-0	0	0	C3		0.0

LINDSAY, CHRIS Christian Haller "Pinky","The Crab" B7.24.1878 Beaver Co. PA D1.25.1941 Cleveland OH BR/TR/6-0/190 d7.6

1905	Det A	88	329	38	88	14	1	0	31	18	5		.267	.315	.316	100	0	10	.978	0	102	106	1b88		-0.0
1906	Det A	141	499	59	112	16	2	0	33	45	3		.224	.293	.265	73	-14	18	.977	-7	93	101	1b210,2b17/3		-2.9
Total	2	229	828	97	200	30	3	0	64	63	8		.242	.301	.285	83	-14	28	.978	-7	97	101	1b210,2b17/3		-2.9

LINDSAY, BILL William Gibbons B2.24.1881 Madison NC D7.14.1963 Greensboro NC BL/TR/5-10.5/165 d6.21 Col Guilford

1911	Cle A	19	66	6	16	2	0	0	5	8	1		.242	.265	.273	49	-5	2-1	.883	1	123	43	3b15/2		-0.0

LINDSEY, DOUG Michael Douglas B9.22.1967 Austin TX BR/TR/6-2/200* [PhiN87 6/156] d10.6 Col Seminole St. (OK) JC

1991	Phi N	1	3	0	0	0	0	0	0	0-0	0	3	.000	.000	.000	-99	-1	0-0	1.000	0	0	0	/C		-0.0
1993	Phi N	2	2	0	1	0	0	0	0	0-0	0	0	.500	.500	.500	171	0	0-0	1.000	0	0	0	C2		-0.0
	Chi A	2	1	0	0	0	0	0	0	0-0	0	1	.000	.000	.000	-99	-0	0-0	1.000	0	0	0	C2		
Total	3	5	6	0	1	0	0	0	0	0-0	0	4	.167	.167	.167	-8	-1	0-0	1.000	0	0	0	C5		-0.0

LINDSEY, ROD Rodney Lee B1.28.1976 Opelika AL BR/TR/5-8/175 [SDN94 39/1074] d9.2

2000	Det A	11	3	6	1	0	0	0	0	0-0	0	1	.333	.500	.667	194	1	2-1	1.000	-1	48	0	O7(2/4/2)		-0.0

LINDSEY, BILL William Donald B4.12.1960 Staten Island NY BR/TR/6-3/195 d7.18 Col Broward (FL) CC

1987	Chi A	9	16	2	3	0	0	0	1	0-0	0		.188	.176	.188	-0	-1	0-0	1.000	1	226	196	C9		

LINDSTROM, CHUCK Charles William B9.7.1936 Chicago IL BR/TR/5-11/175 d9.28 f-Freddie Col Northwestern

1958	Chi A	1	1	1	1	1	0	0	1	1-0	0	0	1.000	1.000	3.000	975	1	0-0	1.000	-0	0	0	/C		

LINDSTROM, FREDDIE Frederick Charles (b Frederick Anthony Lindstrom) B11.21.1905 Chicago IL D10.4.1981 Chicago IL BR/TR/5-11/170 d4.15 HF1976 s-Chuck

YEAR	TM	LG	G	AB	R	H	2B	3B	HR	RBI	BB-IB	HP	SO	AVG	OBP	SLG	AOPS	ABR	SB-CS	FA	FR	RNG	THR	GAMES AT POSITION	DL	BFW
1924	†NY	N	52	79	19	20	3	1	0	4	6	1	10	.253	.314	.316	71	-3	3-1	.911	3	122	134	2b23,3b11		0.1
1925	NY	N	104	356	43	102	15	12	4	33	22	2	20	.287	.332	.430	97	-4	5-9	.957	-3	88	58	3b96/2S		-0.3
1926	NY	N	140	543	90	164	19	9	9	76	39	2	21	.302	.351	.420	108	5	11	.962	-1	97	103	3b138/OR		1.2
1927	NY	N	138	562	107	172	36	8	7	58	40	2	40	.306	.354	.436	111	8	10	.968	2	107	85	3b87,O51L		1.2
1928	NY	N	153	646	99	231	39	9	14	107	25	2	21	.358	.383	.511	131	27	15	.958	15	112	132	3b153		4.9
1929	NY	N	130	549	99	175	23	6	15	91	30	0	28	.319	.354	.464	101	-1	10	.966	6	104	140	3b128		1.1
1930	NY	N	148	609	127	231	39	7	22	106	48	0	12	.379	.425	.575	142	42	15	.953	4	103	96	3b148		4.7
1931	NY	N	78	303	38	91	12	6	5	36	26	0	12	.300	.356	.429	113	5	5	.953	4	103	96	O73R,2b4		-0.6
1932	NY	N	144	·595	83	161	26	4	15	92	27	1	28	.271	.303	.407	91	-10	6	.975	-7	96	45	O128C,3b15		-1.8
1933	Pit	N	138	538	70	167	39	10	5	55	33	0	22	.310	.350	.448	127	18	6	.982	-5	88	156	O130(20/111/0)		2.1
1934	Pit	N	97	383	59	111	24	4	4	49	23	2	21	.290	.333	.405	94	-3	1	.988	6	112	73	O92L		-0.7
1935	†Chi	N	90	342	49	94	22	4	3	62	10	1	13	.275	.297	.389	82	-9	1	.990	1	97	127	O50C,3b33		-1.4
1936	Bro	N	26	106	12	28	4	0	0	10	5	0	7	.264	.297	.389	82	-6	1	.979	1	95	113	O26(24/2/0)		-0.6
Total	13		1438	5611	895	1747	301	81	103	779	334	13	276	.311	.351	.449	110	69	84-10	.959	17	101	108	3b809,O551(187/291/74),2b28/S		9.9

LINHART, CARL Carl James B12.14.1929 Zborov, Czechoslovakia BL/TR/5-11/184 d8.2

YEAR	TM	LG	G	AB	R	H	2B	3B	HR	RBI	BB-IB	HP	SO	AVG	OBP	SLG	AOPS	ABR	SB-CS	FA	FR	RNG	THR	GAMES AT POSITION	DL	BFW
1952	Det	A	3	2	0	0	0	0	0	0	0	0	0	.000	.000	.000	-99	-1	0-0	—	.	0		/H		-0.1

LINIAK, COLE Cole Edward B8.23.1976 Encinitas CA BR/TR/6-1/190(180-195) [BosA95 7/186] d9.3

YEAR	TM	LG	G	AB	R	H	2B	3B	HR	RBI	BB-IB	HP	SO	AVG	OBP	SLG	AOPS	ABR	SB-CS	FA	FR	RNG	THR	GAMES AT POSITION	DL	BFW
1999	Chi	N	12	29	3	7	2	0	0	2	1-0	0	4	.241	.267	.310	46	-2	0-1	1.000	-3	52	73	3b10		-0.5
2000	Chi	N	3	3	0	0	0	0	0	0	0-0	0	2	.000	.000	.000	-99	-1	0-0	—				/H		-0.1
Total	2		15	32	3	7	2	0	0	2	1-0	0	6	.219	.242	.281	32	-3	0-1	1.000	-3	52	73	3b10		-0.6

LINTON, BOB Claud Clarence B4.18.1903 Emerson AR D4.3.1980 Destin FL BL/TR/6-0/185 d4.26 Col Wyoming

YEAR	TM	LG	G	AB	R	H	2B	3B	HR	RBI	BB-IB	HP	SO	AVG	OBP	SLG	AOPS	ABR	SB-CS	FA	FR	RNG	THR	GAMES AT POSITION	DL	BFW
1929	Pit	N	17	18	0	2	0	0	0	1	0	0	2	.111	.158	.111	-31	-4	0-0	1.000	0	125	220	C8		-0.3

LINTZ, LARRY Larry B10.10.1949 Martinez CA BB/TR/5-9/150* [MonN71 6/125] d7.16 Col San Jose St.

YEAR	TM	LG	G	AB	R	H	2B	3B	HR	RBI	BB-IB	HP	SO	AVG	OBP	SLG	AOPS	ABR	SB-CS	FA	FR	RNG	THR	GAMES AT POSITION	DL	BFW
1973	Mon	N	52	116	20	29	1	0	0	3	17-0	1	18	.250	.351	.259	69	-4	12-4	.945	-2	109	86	2b34,S15		-0.2
1974	Mon	N	113	319	60	76	10	1	0	20	44-0	2	50	.238	.334	.276	68	-12	50-7	.961	-7	98	77	2b67,S31/3		-0.3
1975	Mon	N	46	132	18	26	0	1	0	3	23-0	0	18	.197	.316	.197	43	-10	17-9	.970	-4	95	69	2b39,S2		-1.1
	StL	N	27	18	6	5	1	0	0	1	3-0	0	2	.278	.381	.333	95	4	4-0	.889	2	98	0	2b6,S6		0.3
	Year		73	150	24	31	1	1	0	4	26-0	0	20	.207	.324	.213	49	-9	21-9	.963	-3	95	63	2b45,S8		-0.8
1976	Oak	A	68	1	21	0	0	0	0	0	2-0	0	0	.000	.667	.000	111	0	31-11	1.000	-1	66	0	D19,2b5,O3(1/0/2)		0.2
1977	Oak	A	41	30	11	4	1	0	0	0	8-1	1	13	.133	.333	.167	42	-2	13-5	1.000	-1	94	106	2b28,S2/3D		-0.1
1978	Cle	A	3	0	0	0	0	0	0	0	0-0	0	0	—	—	—	—	—	1-2		0			/R		-0.1
Total	6		350	616	137	140	13	1	0	27	97-1	4	101	.227	.336	.252	63	-28	128-38	.962	-13	99	77	2b179,S56,D24,O3(1/0/2),3b2		-1.3

LINZ, PHIL Philip Francis B6.4.1939 Baltimore MD BR/TR/6-1/180* d4.13

YEAR	TM	LG	G	AB	R	H	2B	3B	HR	RBI	BB-IB	HP	SO	AVG	OBP	SLG	AOPS	ABR	SB-CS	FA	FR	RNG	THR	GAMES AT POSITION	DL	BFW
1962	NY	A	71	129	28	37	8	0	1	14	6-2	0	17	.287	.316	.372	88	-2	6-2	.937	-7	80	69	S21,3b8,2b5,O2R		-0.7
1963	†NY	A	72	186	22	50	9	0	2	12	15-0	2	18	.269	.328	.349	91	-2	1-6	.963	0	113	118	S22,3b13,O12(2/5/5),2b6		-0.2
1964	†NY	A	112	368	63	92	21	3	5	25	43-2	2	61	.250	.332	.364	92	-3	3-4	.952	7	115	123	S55,3b41,2b5,O3(1/2/0)		0.9
1965	NY	A	99	285	37	59	12	1	2	16	30-1	0	33	.207	.281	.277	60	-15	2-1	.954	3	101	74	S71,3b4,O4R/2		-0.6
1966	Phi	N	40	70	4	14	3	0	0	6	2-0	0	14	.200	.222	.243	29	-7	0-0	.971	-4	90	91	3b14,S6,2b3		-1.1
1967	Phi	N	23	18	4	4	2	0	1	5	2-0	0	1	.222	.300	.500	124	1	0-0	.833	-3	29	0	S7/3		-0.2
	NY	N	24	58	8	12	2	0	0	1	4-0	1	10	.207	.270	.241	48	-4	0-0	.964	-2	88	104	2b11,S8/3OL		-0.5
	Year		47	76	12	16	4	0	1	6	6-0	1	11	.211	.277	.303	66	-3	0-0	.963	-4	64	25	S15,2b11,3b2/OL		-0.7
1968	NY	N	78	258	19	54	7	0	0	19	1-0	2	41	.209	.243	.236	45	-18	1-0	.952	-15	102	92	2b71		-2.7
Total	7		519	1372	185	322	64	4	11	96	112-5	7	195	.235	.295	.311	72	-50	13-13	.968	-11	88	98	S190,2b102,3b82,O22(4/7/11)		-5.1

LIPON, JOHNNY John Joseph "Skids" B11.10.1922 Martins Ferry OH D8.17.1998 Houston TX BR/TR/6-0/175* d8.16 Mil 1943-45 M1/C4

YEAR	TM	LG	G	AB	R	H	2B	3B	HR	RBI	BB-IB	HP	SO	AVG	OBP	SLG	AOPS	ABR	SB-CS	FA	FR	RNG	THR	GAMES AT POSITION	DL	BFW
1942	Det	A	34	131	5	25	2	0	0	9	7	0	7	.191	.232	.206	22	-14	1-3	.945	3	98	107	S34		-0.9
1946	Det	A	14	20	4	6	0	0	1	0	5	0	3	.300	.440	.300	103	0	0-0	.933	1	87	160	S8/3		0.1
1948	Det	A	121	458	65	133	18	8	5	52	68	2	22	.290	.384	.397	105	5	4-4	.970	-10	94	76	S117/23		0.1
1949	Det	A	127	439	57	110	14	6	3	59	75	2	24	.251	.362	.330	84	-9	2-4	.965	0	99	107	S120		-0.2
1950	Det	A	147	601	104	176	27	6	2	63	81	1	26	.293	.378	.368	89	-8	9-6	.958	9	106	120	S147		0.9
1951	Det	A	129	487	56	129	15	1	0	38	49	2	27	.265	.335	.300	72	-18	7-6	.949	-11	98	87	S125		-2.1
1952	Det	A	39	136	17	30	4	2	0	12	16	0	6	.221	.303	.279	62	-7	3-1	.978	-2	92	49	S39		-0.7
	Bos	A	79	234	25	48	8	1	0	18	32	0	20	.205	.301	.248	50	-15	1-1	.982	12	113	121	S69,3b7		0.1
	Year		118	370	42	78	12	3	0	30	48	0	26	.211	.301	.259	54	-22	4-2	.981	10	105	95	S108,3b7		-0.6
1953	Bos	A	60	145	18	31	7	0	0	13	14	0	16	.214	.283	.262	46	-11	1-0	.951	2	105	86	S58		-0.5
	StL	A	7	9	0	2	0	0	0	1	0	0	1	.222	.222	.222	20	-1	0-0	1.000	-1	148	0	3b6/2		-0.2
	Year		67	154	18	33	7	0	0	14	14	0	17	.214	.280	.260	44	-12	1-0	.951	1	105	86	S58,3b6/2		-0.7
1954	Cin	N	1	1	0	0	0	0	0	0	0	0	0	.000	.000	.000	-97	0	0-0	—	0			/H		0.0
Total	9		758	2661	351	690	95	24	10	266	347	7	152	.259	.346	.324	77	-78	28-25	.961	2	101	98	S717,3b15,2b2		-3.4

LIPSCOMB, NIG Gerard B2.24.1911 Rutherfordton NC D2.27.1978 Huntersville NC BR/TR/6-0/175 d4.23 ▲

YEAR	TM	LG	G	AB	R	H	2B	3B	HR	RBI	BB-IB	HP	SO	AVG	OBP	SLG	AOPS	ABR	SB-CS	FA	FR	RNG	THR	GAMES AT POSITION	DL	BFW
1937	StL	A	36	96	11	31	9	1	0	8	11	1	10	.323	.398	.438	110	2	0-0	.963	-0	97	130	2b27,P3/3		0.3

LIPSKI, BOB Robert Peter B7.7.1938 Scranton PA BL/TR/6-1/180 d4.28

YEAR	TM	LG	G	AB	R	H	2B	3B	HR	RBI	BB-IB	HP	SO	AVG	OBP	SLG	AOPS	ABR	SB-CS	FA	FR	RNG	THR	GAMES AT POSITION	DL	BFW
1963	Cle	A	2	1	0	0	0	0	0	0	0-0	0	1	.000	.000	.000	-99	0	0-0	1.000	0	0	0	C2		0.0

LIRIANO, NELSON Nelson Arturo (Bonilla) B6.3.1964 Puerto Plata, D.R. BB/TR/5-10/172(165-185) d8.25

YEAR	TM	LG	G	AB	R	H	2B	3B	HR	RBI	BB-IB	HP	SO	AVG	OBP	SLG	AOPS	ABR	SB-CS	FA	FR	RNG	THR	GAMES AT POSITION	DL	BFW
1987	Tor	A	37	158	29	38	6	2	2	10	16-2	0	22	.241	.310	.342	71	-7	13-2	.995	3	99	120	2b37		0.0
1988	Tor	A	99	276	36	73	6	2	3	23	11-0	2	40	.264	.297	.333	76	-10	12-5	.961	-14	90	104	2b80,D11/3		-2.1
1989	†Tor	A	132	418	51	110	26	3	5	53	43-0	2	51	.263	.331	.376	101	2	16-7	.980	-14	95	97	2b128,D5		-0.8
1990	Tor	A	50	170	16	36	7	2	1	15	16-0	1	20	.212	.282	.294	60	-14	3-5	.983	-8	93	84	2b49		-1.7
	Min	A	53	185	30	47	5	7	0	13	22-0	0	24	.254	.332	.357	87	-3	5-2	.968	-9	95	83	2b50/SD		-1.0
	Year		103	355	46	83	12	9	1	28	38-0	1	44	.234	.308	.327	75	-12	8-7	.975	-16	94	84	2b99,D2/S		-2.7
1991	KC	A	10	22	5	9	0	0	0	0	1-0	0	2	.409	.409	.409	126	1	0-1	1.000	1	116	69	2b10		0.1
1993	Col	N	48	151	28	46	6	3	2	15	18-2	0	22	.305	.374	.424	98	0	6-4	.975	-8	87	69	S35,2b16/3		-0.5
1994	Col	N	87	255	39	65	17	5	3	31	42-5	0	44	.255	.357	.396	83	-5	0-2	.973	-8	96	81	2b79,S3,3b2		-1.0
1995	Pit	N	107	259	29	74	12	1	5	38	24-3	2	34	.286	.347	.398	95	-2	2-2	.981	-11	86	84	2b79,S3,3b2		-1.0
1996	Pit	N	112	217	23	58	14	2	3	30	14-2	0	22	.267	.308	.392	81	-6	0-0	.984	-2	105	79	2b67,3b5/S		-0.6
1997	LA	N	76	88	10	20	6	0	1	11	6-1	0	12	.227	.274	.330	62	-5	0-0	.949	-4	76	103	2b17,1b2/3S		-0.8
1998	Col	N	12	17	0	0	0	0	0	0	7-0	0	7	.000	.000	.000	-83	-4	0-0	1.000	-2	43	90	2b3/S	11	-0.6
Total	11		823	2216	296	576	105	27	25	240	212-15	7	300	.260	.324	.366	84	-48	59-30	.976	-73	94	92	2b566,S47,3b19,D18,1b2	11	-10.0

LIS, JOE Joseph Anthony B8.15.1946 Somerville NJ BR/TR/6-0/195* d9.5

YEAR	TM	LG	G	AB	R	H	2B	3B	HR	RBI	BB-IB	HP	SO	AVG	OBP	SLG	AOPS	ABR	SB-CS	FA	FR	RNG	THR	GAMES AT POSITION	DL	BFW
1970	Phi	N	13	37	1	7	2	0	1	4	5-0	0	11	.189	.286	.324	65	-2	0-0	.947	0	121	0	O9L		-0.2
1971	Phi	N	59	123	16	26	6	0	6	16	10-0	2	43	.211	.308	.407	102	0	0-1	.978	-2	77	102	O35L		-0.4
1972	Phi	N	62	140	13	34	6	0	6	18	30-1	1	34	.243	.380	.414	122	6	0-1	.996	2	97	90	1b30,O14(8/0/6)		0.5
1973	Min	A	103	253	37	62	11	1	9	25	28-1	3	66	.245	.325	.403	100	0	0-1	.987	-1	99	93	1b96/D		-0.7
1974	Min	A	24	41	5	8	2	0	1	5	5-0	1	12	.195	.298	.195	43	-3	0-0	.992	-1	78	83	1b18		-0.5
	Cle	A	57	109	15	22	3	0	6	16	14-1	0	30	.202	.293	.394	97	1	1-0	1.000	-2	81	85	1b31,3b9/OLD		-0.4
	Year		81	150	20	30	5	0	6	19	19-1	1	42	.200	.294	.340	82	-2	1-0	.997	-3	80	84	1b49,3b9,D9/OL		-0.9
1975	Cle	A	9	13	4	4	0	0	2	8	3-0	2	8	.308	.444	.923	285	4	0-0	1.000	-0	62	51	1b8/D		0.3
1976	Cle	A	20	51	4	16	2	0	2	7	8-0	2	7	.314	.400	.451	152	4	0-0	1.000	-1	72	79	1b17/D		0.2
1977	Sea	A	9	13	1	3	0	0	0	1	1-0	0	8	.231	.286	.231	43	-4	0-0	1.000	-1	55	136	1b4/C		-0.2
Total	8		356	780	96	182	31	1	32	92	110-3	8	209	.233	.332	.399	105	6	1-3	.992	-5	90	89	1b204,O59(53/0/6),D12,3b9/C		-1.4

LISI, RICK Riccardo Patrick Emilio B3.17.1956 Halifax NS, Can. BR/TR/6-0/175 [TexA74 13/290] d5.9

YEAR	TM	LG	G	AB	R	H	2B	3B	HR	RBI	BB-IB	HP	SO	AVG	OBP	SLG	AOPS	ABR	SB-CS	FA	FR	RNG	THR	GAMES AT POSITION	DL	BFW
1981	Tex	A	9	16	6	5	0	0	0	1	4-0	0	6	.313	.450	.313	129	1	0-1	1.000	-1	79	0	O8(0/2/6)		0.0

LISTACH, PAT Patrick Alan B9.12.1967 Natchitoches LA BB/TR/5-9/170* [MilA88 5/133] d4.8 Col Arizona St. [DL 1996 NY A 38]

YEAR	TM	LG	G	AB	R	H	2B	3B	HR	RBI	BB-IB	HP	SO	AVG	OBP	SLG	AOPS	ABR	SB-CS	FA	FR	RNG	THR	GAMES AT POSITION	DL	BFW
1992	Mil	A	149	579	93	168	19	6	1	47	55-0	1	124	.290	.352	.349	99	-1	54-18	.966	2	104	107	S148/2OC		1.8
1993	Mil	A	98	356	50	87	15	1	3	30	37-0	3	70	.244	.319	.302	73	-13	18-9	.975	-10	100	92	S95,O6C	46	-1.5

YEAR	TM LG	G	AB	R	H	2B	3B	HR	RBI	BB-IB	HP	SO	AVG	OBP	SLG	AOPS	ABR	SB-CS	FA	FR	RNG	THR	GAMES AT POSITION	DL	BFW
1994	Mil A	16	54	8	16	3	0	0	2	3-0		8	.296	.333	.352	73	-2	2-1	.958	2	122	113	S16	110	0.1
1995	Mil A	101	334	35	73	8	2	0	25	25-0	2	61	.219	.276	.254	37	-31	13-3	1.000	11	112	118	2b59,S36,O11(1/10/1),3b2		-1.4
1996	Mil A	87	317	51	76	16	2	1	33	36-0	1	51	.240	.317	.312	58	-20	25-5	.982	-7	97	154	O68(2/66/0),2b12,S7	15	-2.0
1997	Hou N	52	132	13	24	2	2	0	6	11-2		24	.182	.251	.227	27	-15	4-2	.951	-10	85	75	S31,O6(1/4/1)		-2.3
Total	6	503	1772	250	444.	63	13	5	143	167-2	8	338	.251	.316	.309	67	-82	116-38	.967	-13	103	103	O333,O92(4/87/2),2b72,3b2	209	-5.3

LISTER, PETE   Morris Elmer   B7.21.1881 Savanna IL   D3.27.1947 St.Petersburg FL   BR/TR/6-0/190   d9.14

YEAR	TM LG	G	AB	R	H	2B	3B	HR	RBI	BB-IB	HP	SO	AVG	OBP	SLG	AOPS	ABR	SB-CS	FA	FR	RNG	THR	GAMES AT POSITION	DL	BFW
1907	Cle A	22	65	5	18	2	0	0	4	3	1		.277	.319	.308	99	0		.974	-1	83	141	1b22		-0.2

LITTLE, SCOTT   Dennis Scott   B1.19.1963 E.St.Louis IL   BR/TR/6-0/198   [NYN84*7/158]   d7.27 Col Missouri

| 1989 | Pit N | 3 | 4 | 0 | 1 | 0 | 0 | 0 | 0 | | | | .250 | .250 | .250 | 45 | 0 | 0-0 | 1.000 | 1 | 84 | 3020 | /OR | | 0.1 |

LITTLE, HARRY   Henry Alexander   B11.9.1850 Pocahontas MO   D2.17.1927 Bremen Twp. (Cook Co.) IL   TR   d7.16

1877	StL N	3	12	2	2	0	0	0		1		6	.167	.231	.167	29	-1		1.000	-0	0	0	O3C		-0.1
	Lou N	1	3	0	0	0	0	0	0	1		1	.000	.250	.000	-13	-0		.857	0	145	0	/2		0.0
	Year	4	15	2	2	0	0	0	0	2		7	.133	.235	.133	19	-1		1.000	-0	0	0	O3C/2		-0.1

LITTLE, MARK   Mark Travis   B7.11.1972 Edwardsville IL   BR/TR/6-0/195*   [TexA94 8/225]   d9.12 Col Memphis

1998	StL N	7	12	1	1	0	0	0	0	2-0	0	5	.083	.214	.083	-18	-2	1-0	1.000	0	128	0	O7(3/0/4)		-0.2
2001	Col N	51	85	18	29	6	0	3	13	1-1	4	28	.341	.378	.518	107	1	5-2	1.000	3	102	303	O36(16/11/16)	113	0.4
2002	Col N	61	105	20	21	5	2	0	5	13-0	4	28	.200	.311	.286	54	-7	2-1	.970	3	118	130	O36(16/11/16)		-0.5
	NY N	3	3	0	0	0	0	0	0		0	1	.000	.000	.000	-99	-1	0-1	—	-0	0	0	/OR		-0.1
	†Ari N	15	22	8	6	0	1	0	2	2-0	4	5	.273	.429	.364	105	2	0-0	1.000	0	113	0	O12(4/2/7)		0.0
	Year	79	130	28	27	5	3	0	7	15-0	8	34	.208	.327	.292	60	-8	2-2	.975	2	116	101	O49(20/13/24)		-0.6
2004	Cle A	11	20	0	4	0	0	0	2	0-0	2	7	.200	.261	.200	27	-2	0-0	1.000	0	89	284	O11(4/5/4)	113	-0.2
Total	4	148	247	46	61	11	3	3	22	18-1	14	66	.247	.332	.352	72	-11	8-4	.986	6	110	169	O96(40/32/38)		-0.6

LITTLE, BRYAN   Richard Bryan "Twig"   B10.8.1959 Houston TX   BB/TR/5-10/160*   [MonN80 9/229]   d7.29 C3 Col Texas A&M-Commerce

1982	Mon N	29	42	2	9	0	0	0	3	4-0	0	6	.214	.277	.214	39	-3	2-1	1.000	-5	72	23	2b16,S10		-0.8
1983	Mon N	106	350	48	91	15	3	1	36	50-1	2	22	.260	.352	.329	91	-2	4-5	.968	-18	79	83	2b77,S2		-1.4
1984	Mon N	85	266	31	65	11	1	0	9	34-0	1	19	.244	.332	.293	80	-6	2-3	.982	-7	93	109	2b77,S2		-1.0
1985	Chi A	73	188	35	47	9	1	2	27	26-0	3	21	.250	.345	.340	86	-3	0-1	1.000	6	107	92	2b68,3b2/S		0.6
1986	Chi A	20	35	3	6	1	0	0	0	4-0	0	4	.171	.256	.200	25	-4	0-0	1.000	2	102	67	2b12,S7/3		-0.7
	NY A	14	41	3	8	1	0	0	2	2-0	0	7	.195	.233	.220	24	-4	0-0	.975	4	120	114	2b14		0.6
	Year	34	76	6	14	2	0	0	2	6-0	0	11	.184	.244	.211	25	-8	0-0	.983	6	114	91	2b26,S7/3		-2.2
Total	5	327	922	126	226	37	5	3	77	120-1	6	79	.245	.333	.306	79	-22	8-10	.987	-18	99	92	2b238,S86,3b3		0.6

LITTLE, JACK   William Arthur   B3.12.1891 Mart TX   D7.27.1961 Dallas TX   BR/TR/5-11/175   d7.2 Col Baylor

| 1912 | NY A | 3 | 12 | 2 | 3 | 0 | 0 | 0 | 1 | 1 | 1 | | .250 | .357 | .250 | 70 | 0 | 2 | 1.000 | 0 | 85 | 217 | O3C | | 0.6 |

LITTLEJOHN, DENNIS   Dennis Gerald   B10.4.1954 Santa Monica CA   BR/TR/6-2/200*   [SFN76*S1/2]   d7.9 Col USC

1978	SF N	2	0	0	0	0	0	0	0	0	0						-0	0-0	-0	0	0	C2		-1.6
1979	SF N	63	193	15	38	6	1	1	13	21-4	0	46	.197	.272	.254	49	-14	0-0	.986	-2	69	129	C63		0.2
1980	SF N	13	29	2	7	1	0	0	2	7-1	0	7	.241	.368	.276	92	0	0-0	.983	2	108	103	C10		0.7
Total	3	78	222	17	45	7	1	1	15	28-5	0	53	.203	.286	.257	55	-14	0-0	.985	-0	74	125	C75		-1.5

LITTLETON, LARRY   Larry Marvin   B4.3.1954 Charlotte NC   BR/TR/6-1/185   [PitN76*S1/6]   d4.12 Col Georgia

| 1981 | Cle A | 26 | 23 | 2 | 0 | 0 | 0 | 0 | 1 | 3-0 | 0 | 6 | .000 | .111 | .000 | -65 | -5 | 0-0 | 1.000 | -2 | 57 | 0 | O24(19/6/1) | | -0.7 |

LITTON, GREG   Jon Gregory   B7.13.1964 New Orleans LA   BR/TR/6-0/190(175-190)   [SFN84*1/10]   d5.2 Col Pensacola (FL) JC   OF(42/0/50)

1989	†SF N	71	143	12	36	5	3	4	17	7-0	1	29	.252	.291	.413	102	-1	0-2	.953	-2	103	30	3b34,2b15,S9,O6(4/0/2),C2		-0.2
1990	SF N	93	204	17	50	11	1	1	24	11-0	1	45	.245	.284	.314	67	-10	1-0	.985	3	89	257	O56(14/0/42),2b18,S7,3b5	12	-0.2
1991	SF N	59	127	13	23	7	1	1	15	11-0	1	25	.181	.250	.276	50	-9	0-2	.989	3	158	150	1b15,2b15,3b11,S9,O6(2/0/4)/CP	17	-0.5
1992	SF N	68	140	9	32	5	0	4	15	11-0	0	33	.229	.285	.350	83	-4	0-1	.992	-1	98	124	2b31,3b10,1b8,S3/OL		-0.5
1993	Sea A	72	174	25	52	17	0	3	25	18-2	1	30	.299	.366	.448	116	5	0-1	1.000	1	83	327	O22(21/0/2),2b17,1b13,D12,3b7,S5		-0.5
1994	Bos A	11	21	2	2	0	0	1	0	0-0	1	5	.095	.091	.095	-48	-5	0-0	1.000	0	76	0	2b4,1b3,3b2/D		-0.5
Total	6	374	809	78	195	45	5	13	97	58-2	4	167	.241	.293	.355	81	-24	1-6	.997	4	90	118	2b100,091R,3b69,1b39,S33,D13,C3/P29		-2.1

LITTRELL, JACK   Jack Napier   B1.22.1929 Louisville KY   BR/TR/6-0/179*   d4.19

1952	Phi A	4	2	0	0	0	0	0	0	1	0	2	.000	.333	.000	-2	0	0-0	1.000	0	150	345	S2/3		0.0
1954	Phi A	9	30	7	9	2	0	1	3	6	0	3	.300	.417	.467	141	2	1-0	.976	-1	84	123	S9		0.0
1955	KC A	37	70	7	14	0	1	0	1	4-0	0	12	.200	.243	.229	27	-8	0-0	.947	-1	93	77	S22,1b6,2b4		-0.5
1957	Chi N	61	153	8	29	4	2	1	17	9-1	0	43	.190	.233	.261	34	-15	0-0	.944	3	95	75	S47,2b6,3b5		-2.0
Total	4	111	255	22	52	6	3	2	17	20-1	0	60	.204	.261	.275	45	-21	0-0	.949	-5	94	94	S80,2b10,1b6,3b6		0.0

LITWHILER, DANNY   Daniel Webster   B8.31.1916 Ringtown PA   BR/TR/5-10.5/198*   d4.25 Mil 1945-46 C1 Col Bloomsburg

1940	Phi N	36	142	10	49	8	2	5	17	17	1	13	.345	.363	.493	139	6	1	.986	2	103	152	O34(2/3/31)		0.0
1941	Phi N	151	590	72	180	29	6	18	66	39	2	43	.305	.350	.466	134	23	1	.964	13	118	113	O150(148/0/2)		2.2
1942	Phi N★	151	591	59	160	25	9	9	56	27	7	42	.271	.310	.389	109	3	2	1.000	4	113	142	O34L		-0.7
1943	Phi N	36	139	23	36	6	0	5	17	11	0	14	.259	.313	.410	113	2	1	1.000	3	107	115	O70L		0.3
	†StL N	80	258	40	72	14	3	7	31	19	2	31	.279	.333	.438	117	5	1	.996	7	109	125	O104L		-0.4
	Year	116	397	63	108	20	3	12	48	30	2	45	.272	.326	.428	115	6	2	.974	-2	104	60	O136L		-0.1
1944	†StL N	140	492	53	130	25	5	15	82	37	10	56	.264	.328	.427	109	5	2	—	0			/H		-0.8
1946	StL N	6	5	0	0	0	0	0	0	1	0	1	.000	.167	.000	-49	-1	0	.985	-1	105	39	O65L,3b2		-0.1
	Bos N	79	247	29	72	12	2	8	38	19	1	23	.291	.347	.453	125	7	1	.985	-1	105	39	O65L,3b2		1.1
	Year	85	252	29	72	12	2	8	38	20	1	24	.286	.343	.444	121	6	1	.976	-2	101	49	O66(64/0/1)		1.1
1947	Bos N	91	226	38	59	7	2	7	31	25	1	43	.261	.337	.394	96	-2	1	1.000	4	114	128	O8L		0.9
1948	Bos N	13	33	0	9	2	0	0	6	4	2	2	.273	.385	.333	97	0	0	.988	3	105	51	O83(5/1/77),3b15		1.0
	Cin N	106	338	51	93	19	2	14	44	48	0	41	.275	.365	.467	128	14	1	.990	4	106	59	O91(13/1/77),3b15		1.1
	Year	119	371	51	102	21	2	14	50	52	2	43	.275	.367	.456	125	14	1	.987	0	101	94	O82(11/1/71),3b3		1.1
1949	Cin N	102	292	35	85	18	1	11	48	44	0	42	.291	.384	.473	127	12	0	.958	-1	105	0	O29(8/0/21)		0.0
1950	Cin N	54	112	15	29	4	0	6	12	20	0	21	.259	.371	.455	116	3	0	.933	-1	103	0	O7R		0.0
1951	Cin N	12	29	3	8	1	0	2	3	2	0	5	.276	.323	.517	120	1	0	.982	17	105	83	O915(681/5/234),3b20		4.0
Total	11	1057	3494	428	982	162	32	107	451	299	27	377	.281	.342	.438	149	78	11-0							

LIVINGSTON, PADDY   Patrick Joseph   B1.14.1880 Cleveland OH   D9.19.1977 Cleveland OH   BR/TR/5-8/197   d9.2 C1

1901	Cle A	1	2	0	0	0	0	0	0				.000	.333	.000	-2	0	0	1.000	-0	79	159	/C		-0.0
1906	Cin N	50	139	8	22	1	4	0	8	12		7	.158	.259	.223	48	-8	0	.960	2	101	108	C47		-0.4
1909	Phi A	64	175	15	41	6	4	0	15	15	8		.234	.323	.314	99	0	4	.969	10	125	121	C64		-0.6
1910	Phi A	37	120	11	25	4	3	0	9	6	3		.208	.264	.292	75	-4	2	.977	3	111	112	C37		-0.6
1911	Phi A	27	71	9	17	4	1	0	7	3	1		.239	.316	.296	72	-2	1	.976	1	93	91	C14		-0.6
1912	Cle A	20	47	5	11	2	0	0	2	6	0		.234	.280	.319	69	-2	1	1.000	0	120	81	C6		-0.6
1917	StL N	7	20	0	4	0	0	0	2	0		22	1	.209	.287	.280	73	-18	9	.969	19	113	111	C195		-0.6
Total	7	206	574	48	120	17	12	0	45	41															

LIVINGSTON, MICKEY   Thompson Orville   B11.15.1914 Newberry SC   D4.3.1983 Houston TX   BR/TR/6-1.5/185*   d9.17 Mil 1944

1938	Was A	2	4	1	3	0	1	0	1			1	.750	.750	1.250	421	2	0	.667	-1	0	0	C2		-0.0
1941	Phi N	95	207	16	42	6	1	0	18	20		38	.203	.276	.242	49	-14	2	.974	-3	75	94	C71/1		-0.0
1942	Phi N	89	239	20	49	6	1	2	22	25		20	.205	.283	.264	64	-11	0	.987	-7	67	97	C78,1b6		-0.0
1943	Phi N	84	265	25	66	9	2	3	18	19		18	.249	.304	.332	87	-5	1	.988	1	94	109	C84,1b2		-0.0
	Chi N	36	111	11	29	5	1	4	16	12		26	.261	.333	.432	122	3	1	1.000	0	122	59	C31,1b4		-0.0
	Year	120	376	36	95	14	3	7	34	31		44	.253	.313	.362	98	-2	2	.991	0	102	95	C115,1b6		-0.0
1945	†Chi N	71	224	19	57	14	2	2	23	19		22	.254	.324	.317	80	-6	2	.990	3	153	70	C68/1		0.0
1946	Chi N	66	176	14	45	14	0	2	20	20		19	.256	.338	.369	103	1	0	.981	-1	111	78	C56		0.0
1947	Chi N	19	33	2	7	2	0	0	3	1		6	.212	.235	.273	36	-3	0	.800	-0	86	0	C7		-0.0
	NY N	5	6	1	0	0	0	0	1	0		7	.000	.143	.000								/C		-0.0
	NY N	5	6	1	0	0	0	0	0	1		7	.205	.244	.256	34	-4	0	.970	-0	74	0	C8		-0.0
	Year	24	39	3	7	2	0	0	4	2		11	.212	.350	.333	85	-1	0	.980	-0	111	54	C42		-0.0
1948	NY N	45	99	8	21	3	1	2	12	21		9													

YEAR	TM LG	G	AB	R	H	2B	3B	HR	RBI	BB-IB	HP	SO	AVG	OBP	SLG	AOPS	ABR	SB-CS	FA	FR	RNG	THR	GAMES AT POSITION	DL	BFW
1949	NY N	19	57	6	17	2	0	4	12	2	1	8	.298	.333	.544	132	2	0	.985	-1	85	61	C19		0.2
	Bos N	28	64	6	15	2	1	0	6	3	2	5	.234	.290	.297	61	-4	0	.977	0	100	104	C22		-0.3
	Year	47	121	12	32	4	1	4	18	5	3	13	.264	.310	.413	95	-1	0	.980	-1	93	84	C41		
1951	Bro N	2	5	0	2	0	0	0	2	1	0	0	.400	.500	.400	142	0	0	1.000	0	0	364	C2		-0.1
Total	10	561	1490	128	354	56	9	19	153	144	13	141	.238	.310	.326	82	-37	7-0	.984	-10	100	85	C483,1b14		-2.6

LIVINGSTONE, SCOTT   Scott Louis B7.15.1965 Dallas TX BL/TR/6-0/198(185-198) [DetA88 2/56] d7.19 Col Texas A&M-Commerce

YEAR	TM LG	G	AB	R	H	2B	3B	HR	RBI	BB-IB	HP	SO	AVG	OBP	SLG	AOPS	ABR	SB-CS	FA	FR	RNG	THR	GAMES AT POSITION	DL	BFW
1991	Det A	44	127	19	37	5	0	2	11	10-0	0	25	.291	.341	.378	97	0	2-1	.980	-3	89	80	3b43		-0.4
1992	Det A	117	354	43	100	21	0	4	46	21-1	0	36	.282	.319	.376	94	-3	1-3	.962	-4	100	86	3b112		-0.8
1993	Det A	98	304	39	89	10	2	2	39	19-1	0	32	.293	.328	.359	86	-6	1-3	.955	-10	85	58	3b62,D32		-1.8
1994	Det A	15	23	0	5	1	0	0	1	1-0	0	4	.217	.250	.261	32	-2	0-0	1.000	0	0	142	1b5/3D		-0.2
	SD N	57	180	11	49	12	1	2	10	6-0	0	22	.272	.294	.383	78	-6	2-2	.942	0	100	89	3b50		-0.7
1995	SD N	99	196	26	66	15	0	5	32	15-1	0	22	.337	.380	.490	132	9	2-1	.991	-1	67	94	1b43,3b13,2b4		0.5
1996	†SD N	102	172	20	51	4	1	2	20	9-0	0	22	.297	.331	.366	88	-4	0-1	.993	-1	87	130	1b22,3b16		
1997	SD N	23	26	1	4	1	0	0	3	2-0	0	1	.154	.214	.192	9	-4	0-0	.750	-1	154	0	3b3,1b2/2	20	-0.6
	StL N	42	41	3	7	1	0	0	3	1-0	0	10	.171	.182	.195	1	-6	0-0	1.000	-1	47	0	3b2/ORD	27	-0.3
	Year	65	67	4	11	2	0	0	6	3-0	0	11	.164	.194	.194	4	-10	1-0	.778	0	111	0	3b5,1b2/2ORD	21	-0.6
1998	Mon N	76	110	1	23	6	0	0	12	5-2	0	15	.209	.237	.264	34	-11	1-1	.938	0	113	0	3b17,1b3,D5		-0.9
Total	8	673	1533	163	431	76	4	17	177	89-5	0	189	.281	.317	.369	86	-33	10-12	.958	-19	97	74	3b319,1b75,D43,2b5/OR	68	-6.0

LIZOTTE, ABEL   Abel B4.13.1870 Lewiston ME D12.4.1926 Wilkes-Barre PA 5-8/174 d9.17

YEAR	TM LG	G	AB	R	H	2B	3B	HR	RBI	BB-IB	HP	SO	AVG	OBP	SLG	AOPS	ABR	SB-CS	FA	FR	RNG	THR	GAMES AT POSITION	DL	BFW
1896	Pit N	7	29	3	3	0	0	0	2	1			.103	.161	.103	-31	-6	1	.952	1	163	72	1b7		-0.4

LLENAS, WINSTON   Winston Enriquillo (Davila) B9.23.1943 Santiago, D.R. BR/TR/5-10/165* d8.15 C1

YEAR	TM LG	G	AB	R	H	2B	3B	HR	RBI	BB-IB	HP	SO	AVG	OBP	SLG	AOPS	ABR	SB-CS	FA	FR	RNG	THR	GAMES AT POSITION	DL	BFW
1968	Cal A	16	39	5	5	1	0	0	1	2-0	1	5	.128	.190	.154	5	-4	0-0	.800	-2	85	0	3b9		-0.8
1969	Cal A	34	47	4	8	2	0	0	2	2-0	0	10	.170	.204	.213	17	-5	0-0	.929	-1	93	88	3b9		-0.7
1972	Cal A	44	64	3	17	3	0	0	7	3-0	0	8	.266	.290	.313	86	-1	0-0	.950	-1	95	137	3b10,2b2,O2L		-0.2
1973	Cal A	78	130	16	35	1	0	1	25	10-0	1	16	.269	.317	.300	83	-3	0-0	1.000	2	77	38	2b20,3b11,O4L,D4		-0.1
1974	Cal A	72	138	16	36	6	0	2	17	11-1	0	19	.261	.301	.348	81	-1	0-0	1.000	-1	91	82	O32(25/0/7),2b15,D10,3b2	15	-0.3
1975	Cal A	56	113	6	21	4	0	0	11	10-0	0	11	.186	.250	.221	37	-9	0-1	1.000	4	111	94	2b12,O10(9/0/1),1b6,3b3,D6		-0.6
Total	6	300	531	50	122	17	0	3	61	38-1	2	69	.230	.277	.279	65	-23	0-1	1.000	1	89	62	2b49,O48(40/0/8),3b44,D20,1b6	15	-2.7

LOAN, MIKE   William Joseph B9.27.1894 Philadelphia PA D11.21.1966 Springfield PA BR/TR/5-11/185 d9.18 Col Villanova

YEAR	TM LG	G	AB	R	H	2B	3B	HR	RBI	BB-IB	HP	SO	AVG	OBP	SLG	AOPS	ABR	SB-CS	FA	FR	RNG	THR	GAMES AT POSITION	DL	BFW
1912	Phi N	1	2	1	1	0	0	0	0	0-0	0	0	.500	.500	.500	163	0	0	1.000	-0	44	0	/C		0.0

LOANE, BOB   Robert Kenneth B8.5.1914 Berkeley CA D12.11.2002 Monterey CA BR/TR/6-0/190 d7.29

YEAR	TM LG	G	AB	R	H	2B	3B	HR	RBI	BB-IB	HP	SO	AVG	OBP	SLG	AOPS	ABR	SB-CS	FA	FR	RNG	THR	GAMES AT POSITION	DL	BFW
1939	Was A	3	5	2	0	0	0	0		4	0	4	.000	.308	.000	-16	-1	0-0	.909	1	89	715	O3C		0.0
1940	Bos N	13	22	4	5	3	0	0	1	2	0	5	.227	.292	.364	84	-1	2	1.000	2	114	364	O10(2/8/0)		0.1
Total	2	16	31	6	5	3	0	0	1	2	0	9	.161	.297	.258	54	-1	2-0	.969	3	106	478	O13(2/11/0)		0.1

LOBERT, FRANK   Frank John B11.26.1883 Williamsport PA D5.29.1932 Pittsburgh PA BR/TR/6-0/180 d6.6 b-Hans

YEAR	TM LG	G	AB	R	H	2B	3B	HR	RBI	BB-IB	HP	SO	AVG	OBP	SLG	AOPS	ABR	SB-CS	FA	FR	RNG	THR	GAMES AT POSITION	DL	BFW
1914	Bal F	11	30	3	6	0	1	0	2	0	0	4	.200	.200	.267	26	-4	0	.870	-2	31	96	3b7/2		-0.6

LOBERT, HANS   John Bernard "Honus" B10.18.1881 Wilmington DE D9.14.1968 Philadelphia PA BR/TR/5-9/170 d9.21 M2/C11 b-Frank Col Carnegie Mellon

YEAR	TM LG	G	AB	R	H	2B	3B	HR	RBI	BB-IB	HP	SO	AVG	OBP	SLG	AOPS	ABR	SB-CS	FA	FR	RNG	THR	GAMES AT POSITION	DL	BFW
1903	Pit N	5	13	1	1	0	0	0	1	0-0	0		.077	.143	.154	-15	-2	1	.778	-1	86	0	3b3/2S		-0.3
1905	Chi N	14	46	7	9	2	0	0	1	3	1		.196	.260	.239	47	-3	4	.918	-1	90	137	3b13/OC		-0.4
1906	Cin N	79	268	39	83	5	5	0	19	19			.310	.366	.366	123	7	20	.959	-7	99	98	3b35,S31,2b10/OC		0.2
1907	Cin N	148	537	61	132	9	12	1	41	37	4		.246	.299	.313	88	-9	30	.941	-16	89	111	S142,3b5		-2.3
1908	Cin N	155	570	71	167	17	18	4	63	46	2		.293	.348	.407	145	27	47	.921	-21	91	89	3b99,S35,O21L		1.0
1909	Cin N	122	425	50	90	13	5	4	52	48	8		.212	.304	.294	86	-6	30	.921	-13	84	104	3b122		-1.8
1910	Cin N	93	314	43	97	6	6	3	40	30	0	9	.309	.369	.395	128	10	41	.932	1	99	85	3b90		1.4
1911	Phi N	147	541	94	154	20	9	9	72	66	5	31	.285	.368	.405	128	11	40	.954	-8	78	62	3b147		-0.2
1912	Phi N	65	257	37	84	12	5	2	33	19	5	13	.327	.373	.436	113	4	13	.976	-8	76	38	3b64		-0.2
1913	Phi N	150	573	98	172	28	11	7	55	42	5	34	.300	.353	.424	117	12	41-21	.974	-16	83	67	3b145,S3/2		0.2
1914	Phi N	135	505	83	139	24	5	11	52	49	5	32	.275	.343	.349	99	1	31	.943	-23	68	52	3b133,S2		-2.1
1915	NY N	106	386	46	97	18	4	0	38	25	3	32	.251	.304	.319	94	-3	14-15	.950	-4	95	65	3b103		-0.7
1916	NY N	48	76	6	17	3	2	0	11	5	0	8	.224	.272	.316	84	-2	2	.961	2	115	97	3b20		0.0
1917	NY N	50	52	4	10	1	0	1	5	5	1		.192	.276	.269	70	-2	2	.906	1	114	167	3b21		-0.1
Total	14	1317	4563	640	1252	159	82	32	482	395	38	156	.274	.337	.366	109	45	316-36	.944	-123	85	74	3b1000,S214,O23(21/2/0),2b12		-5.3

LOCHHEAD, HARRY   Robert Henry B3.29.1876 Stockton CA D8.22.1909 Stockton CA BR/TR/5-11/172 d4.16

YEAR	TM LG	G	AB	R	H	2B	3B	HR	RBI	BB-IB	HP	SO	AVG	OBP	SLG	AOPS	ABR	SB-CS	FA	FR	RNG	THR	GAMES AT POSITION	DL	BFW
1899	Cle N	148	541	52	129	7	1	1	43	21	10		.238	.280	.261	52	-36	23	.909	12	104	78	S146/2P		-1.5
1901	Det A	1	4	2	0	0	0	0	1		0		.500	.600	.500	198	1	0	.857	-0	108	0	/S		0.0
	Phi A	9	34	3	3	0	0	0	2	3	0		.088	.162	.088	-28	-6	0	.757	-6	71	33	S9		-1.1
	Year	10	38	5	3	0	0	0	2	3	0		.132	.214	.132	-3	-5	0	.773	-6	76	29	S10		-1.1
Total	2	158	579	57	134	7	1	1	45	24	11		.231	.275	.252	48	-41	23	.903	6	102	75	S156/P2		-2.6

LOCK, DON   Don Wilson B7.27.1936 Wichita KS BR/TR/6-2/202* d7.17 Col Wichita St.

YEAR	TM LG	G	AB	R	H	2B	3B	HR	RBI	BB-IB	HP	SO	AVG	OBP	SLG	AOPS	ABR	SB-CS	FA	FR	RNG	THR	GAMES AT POSITION	DL	BFW
1962	Was A	71	225	30	57	6	2	12	37	30-0	0	63	.253	.336	.458	114	4	4-5	.973	3	111	52	O67(67/1/0)		0.2
1963	Was A	149	531	71	134	20	1	27	82	70-3	2	151	.252	.338	.446	119	14	7-3	.980	6	109	144	O146(10/135/9)		1.7
1964	Was A	152	512	73	127	17	4	28	80	79-3	1	137	.248	.346	.461	124	17	4-2	.987	9	105	182	O149(0/135/25)		2.2
1965	Was A	143	418	52	90	15	1	16	39	57-4	5	115	.215	.315	.371	96	-1	1-3	.969	-1	101	115	O136C		-0.7
1966	Was A	138	386	52	90	13	1	16	48	57-5	2	126	.233	.333	.396	110	6	2-6	.977	5	112	115	O129(0/126/4)		0.6
1967	Phi N	112	313	46	79	13	1	14	51	43-4	5	98	.252	.349	.435	123	10	9-5	.977	-0	93	172	O97(1/96/1)		0.9
1968	Phi N	99	248	27	52	7	2	8	34	26-0	1	64	.210	.283	.351	90	-3	3-4	.955	-0	110	45	O78(8/46/27)		-0.8
1969	Phi N	4	4	0	0	0	0	0	0	0-0	0	1	.000	.000	.000	-99	-1	0-0	—	0	0		/OL		-0.1
	Bos A	53	58	8	13	1	0	1	2	11-0	0	21	.224	.348	.293	77	-1	0-1	1.000	-1	89	0	O28(15/9/4),1b4		-0.3
Total	8	921	2695	359	642	92	12	122	373	373-19	16	776	.238	.331	.417	111	45	30-29	.976	21	105	127	O831(102/684/70),1b4		3.7

LOCKE, MARSHALL   Marshall Pinkney Wilder B3.12.1857 Ashland OH D3.6.1940 Ashland OH d7.5

YEAR	TM LG	G	AB	R	H	2B	3B	HR	RBI	BB-IB	HP	SO	AVG	OBP	SLG	AOPS	ABR	SB-CS	FA	FR	RNG	THR	GAMES AT POSITION	DL	BFW
1884	Ind AA	7	29	5	7	0	1	0	5	0	0		.241	.241	.310	81	-1		.800	-1	87	0	O7(0/3/4)		-0.1

LOCKHART, KEITH   Keith Virgil B11.10.1964 Whittier CA BL/TR/5-10/170* [CinN86 11/280] d4.5 Col Oral Roberts

YEAR	TM LG	G	AB	R	H	2B	3B	HR	RBI	BB-IB	HP	SO	AVG	OBP	SLG	AOPS	ABR	SB-CS	FA	FR	RNG	THR	GAMES AT POSITION	DL	BFW
1994	SD N	27	43	4	9	0	0	2	6	4-0	1	10	.209	.286	.349	68	-2	1-0	1.000	1	56	0	3b13,2b5/SOR		-0.1
1995	KC A	94	274	41	88	19	3	6	33	14-2	4	21	.321	.355	.478	114	5	8-1	.974	4	109	134	2b61,3b17,D14		1.2
1996	KC A	138	433	49	118	33	3	7	55	30-4	2	40	.273	.319	.411	83	-11	11-6	.975	-5	106	121	2b84,3b55/D		-1.1
1997	†Atl N	96	147	25	41	5	3	6	32	14-0	1	17	.279	.337	.476	111	2	0-0	.983	-2	100	124	2b20,3b11,D4	16	0.0
1998	Atl N	109	366	50	94	21	0	9	37	29-0	1	37	.257	.311	.388	84	-9	2-2	.984	6	109	117	2b97/3D		0.1
1999	Atl N	108	161	20	42	3	1	1	21	19-0	1	21	.261	.337	.311	67	-8	3-1	1.000	-1	110	97	2b25,3b10/D4		-0.8
2000	†Atl N	113	275	32	73	13	2	3	29	29-7	0	31	.265	.331	.353	75	-11	4-1	.979	-1	111	90	2b74,3b18		-0.4
2001	†Atl N	104	178	17	39	6	0	3	12	16-1	2	22	.219	.289	.303	53	-13	1-2	1.000	-6	89	98	2b47,3b4		-1.7
2002	†Atl N	128	296	34	64	13	3	5	32	27-9	1	50	.216	.282	.331	64	-17	0-1	.979	5	116	101	2b89/3		-0.9
2003	SD N	62	95	18	23	5	1	3	8	13-0	1	19	.242	.339	.411	104	1	0-1	.986	-3	75	78	2b27,3b3	59	-0.2
Total	10	979	2268	290	591	117	17	44	268	195-23	14	268	.261	.319	.385	82	-63	30-15	.981	3	107	109	2b529,3b133,D25/ORS	75	-3.9

LOCKLEAR, GENE   Gene B7.19.1949 Lumberton NC BL/TR/5-10/165* d4.5

YEAR	TM LG	G	AB	R	H	2B	3B	HR	RBI	BB-IB	HP	SO	AVG	OBP	SLG	AOPS	ABR	SB-CS	FA	FR	RNG	THR	GAMES AT POSITION	DL	BFW
1973	Cin N	29	26	6	5	0	0	0	2	0-0	1	5	.192	.276	.192	33	-2	0-0	1.000	-1	71	0	O5(1/0/4)		-0.3
	SD N	67	154	20	37	6	1	3	25	21-1	0	22	.240	.330	.351	97	0	9-4	.952	2	103	78	O37L		-0.3
	Year	96	180	26	42	6	1	3	25	23-1	1	27	.233	.322	.328	87	-3	9-4	.954	1	101	72	O42(38/0/4)		-0.3
1974	SD N	39	74	7	20	3	1	2	11	4-0	0	12	.270	.308	.405	103	-3	0-1	1.000	-0	97	121	O12(8/0/4)		-0.1
1975	SD N	100	237	31	76	11	1	5	27	22-4	1	26	.321	.374	.439	136	11	4-2	.970	-0	97	106	O51(50/0/2)		0.9
1976	SD N	43	67	9	15	3	0	0	8	4-1	0	15	.224	.264	.269	57	-4	0-0	.952	-1	103	0	O11L		0.9
	NY A	13	32	2	7	1	0	0	2	1-0	0	7	.219	.265	.250	51	-2	0-0	1.000	-1	70	0	O3L,D6		-0.5
1977	NY A	1	5	1	3	0	0	0	1	0-0	0		.600	.600	.600	230	1	0-0	.667	-0	111	0	/OL		0.1
Total	5	292	595	76	163	24	4	6	66	55-6	2	87	.274	.364	.373	105	4	13-7	.962	0	98	83	O120(111/0/10),D6		-0.2

YEAR	TM LG	G	AB	R	H	2B	3B	HR	RBI	BB-IB	HP	SO	AVG	OBP	SLG	AOPS	ABR	SB-CS	FA	FR	RNG	THR	GAMES AT POSITION	DL	BFW

LOCKLIN, STU   Stuart Carlton   B7.22.1928 Appleton WI   BL/TL/6-1.5/190*   d6.23 Col Wisconsin-Madison

																									-0.2
1955	Cle A	16	18	4	3	1	0	0	0	3-0	0	4	.167	.286	.222	37	-3	0-0	1.000	-0	65	0	O7(0/4/3)		-0.1
1956	Cle A	9	6	0	1	0	0	0	0	0-0	0	1	.167	.167	.167	-12	-1	0-0	1.000	0	151	0	/OR		-0.1
Total	2	25	24	4	4	1	0	0	0	3-0	0	5	.167	.259	.208	26	-3	0-0	1.000	-0	77	0	O8(0/4/4)		-0.3

LOCKMAN, WHITEY   Carroll Walter   B7.25.1926 Lowell NC   BL/TR/6-1/175*   d7.5 Mil 1945-46 M3/C7

1945	NY N	32	129	16	44	9	0	3	18	13	2	10	.341	.410	.481	145	8	1	.961	-4	87	40	O32C		0.4
1947	NY N	2	2	0	1	0	0	0	1	0	0	0	.500	.500	.500	165	0	0	—	0			/H		0.0
1948	NY N	146	584	117	167	24	10	18	59	68	1	63	.286	.361	.454	119	14	8	.987	-3	102	52	O144(53/91/0)		0.5
1949	NY N	151	617	97	186	32	7	11	65	62	3	31	.301	.368	.429	113	12	12	.973	1	104	78	O128(123/6/0)		0.2
1950	NY N	129	532	72	157	28	5	6	52	42	2	29	.295	.344	.400	96	-3	1	.978	4	103	109	O128(123/6/0)		-0.9
1951	†NY N	153	614	85	173	27	7	12	73	50	3	32	.282	.339	.407	99	-2	4-5	.986	0	104	111	1b119,O34L		-0.9
1952	NY N★	154	606	99	176	17	4	13	58	67	2	52	.290	.363	.396	110	9	2-4	.992	2	105	115	1b154		0.5
1953	NY N	150	607	85	179	22	4	9	61	52	0	36	.295	.351	.389	91	8	3-4	.989	5	114	88	1b120,O30(0/3/28)		-1.1
1954	†NY N	148	570	73	143	17	3	16	60	59	0	31	.251	.318	.375	80	-17	2-2	.987	-7	85	97	1b145,O2(1/1/0)		-3.3
1955	NY N	147	576	76	157	19	0	15	49	39-2	3	34	.273	.320	.384	86	-12	3-3	.983	-4	105	122	O39(38/1/1),1b7		-2.5
1956	NY N	48	169	13	46	7	1	1	10	16-2	0	17	.272	.333	.343	83	-4	0-2	.960	-1	95	122	O57(32/23/8),1b2		-0.8
	StL N	70	193	14	48	0	2	0	10	18-4	0	8	.249	.311	.269	59	-11	2-2	.955	-5	94	85	O96(70/24/9),1b9		-1.9
	Year	118	362	27	94	7	3	1	20	34-6	0	25	.260	.322	.304	70	-15	2-4	.957	-5	94	105	O153(102/47/9),1b11		-2.7
1957	NY N	133	456	51	113	9	4	7	30	39-3	2	19	.248	.308	.331	73	-18	5-5	.991	-4	97	112	1b102,O27(22/3/4)		-3.1
1958	SF N	92	122	15	29	5	0	2	7	13-4	0	18	.238	.311	.328	71	-5	0-0	1.000	-4	105	0	O25(23/0/4),2b15,1b7		-0.9
1959	Bal A	38	69	7	15	1	1	0	3	8-0	0	4	.217	.299	.261	56	-4	0-0	.992	-3	38	128	1b22,2b5/OR		-0.7
	Cin N	52	84	10	22	5	1	0	7	4-0	0	6	.262	.292	.345	68	-4	0-0	.971	-0	131	101	1b20,2b6/3OC		-0.4
1960	Cin N	21	10	2	2	0	0	1	1	2-0	1	3	.200	.385	.500	138	1	0-0	1.000	-0	0	171	1b5		0.0
Total	15	1666	5940	836	1658	222	49	114	563	552-15	19	383	.279	.342	.391	95	-44	43-27	.989	-20	96	104	1b771,O752(556/163/47),2b26/3		-14.9

LOCKWOOD, SKIP   Claude Edward   B8.17.1946 Boston MA   BR/TR/6-0/190(180-200)   d4.23 ▲

1965	KC A	42	33	4	4	0	0	0	0	7-0	1	11	.121	.293	.121	23	-3	0-0	1.000	0	62	147	3b7		-0.3
1969	Sea A	6	7	0	0	0	0	0	0	0-0	0	2	.000	.000	.000	-99	-1	0-0	.970	-2	145	330	P6		0.0
1970	Mil A	27	53	2	12	1	0	1	2	1-0	0	11	.226	.236	.302	49	2	0-0	.970	-2	71	56	P27		0.0
1971	Mil A	36	62	2	5	1	0	1	4	5-0	0	20	.081	.149	.145	-17	-1	0-1	.958	-3	49	50	P29		0.0
1972	Mil A	31	53	3	7	0	0	0	0	3-0	1	12	.132	.193	.132	-2	-1	0-0	.944	-0	98	56	P37		0.0
1973	Mil A	37	0	0	0	0	0	0	0	0-0	0	0	—	—	—	—	0	0-0	1.000	-0	93	116	P37		0.0
1974	Cal A	37	0	0	0	0	0	0	0	0-0	0	0	—	—	—	—	0	0-0	.800	-1	42	0	P24		0.0
1975	NY N	24	6	0	1	0	0	0	0	0-0	0	1	.167	.167	.167	-8	0	0-0	.867	-1	78	139	P56		0.0
1976	NY N	56	18	2	6	1	0	0	2	2-0	0	3	.333	.400	.389	130	3	0-1	.875	-2	38	0	P63		0.0
1977	NY N	63	15	1	3	0	0	0	0	1-0	0	1	.200	.200	.200	8	0	0-0	.900	-2	35	106	P57		0.0
1978	NY N	57	11	0	2	1	0	1	1	0-0	0	5	.182	.182	.545	99	1	0-0	.800	-1	50	220	P27	103	0.0
1979	NY N	28	2	0	0	0	0	0	0	0-0	0	1	.000	.000	.000	-99	0	0-0	1.000	-1	44	0	P24		0.0
1980	Bos A	24	0	0	0	0	0	0	0	0-0	0	0	—	—	—	—	0	0-2	.947	-13	64	78	P420,3b7	103	-0.3
Total	13	468	260	15	40	4	0	3	11	18-0	2	66	.154	.214	.204	19	0	0-2	.947	-13	64	78	P420,3b7		-0.3

LOCKWOOD, MILO   Milo Hathaway   B4.7.1858 Solon OH   D10.9.1897 Economy PA   5-10/160   d4.17 ▲

1884	Was U	20	67	9	14	1	0	0			0		.209	.293	.224	61	-5		.773	1	46	284	O11(1/7/3),P11,3b3		-0.2

LODIGIANI, DARIO   Dario Antonio   B6.6.1916 San Francisco CA   BR/TR/5-8/150   d4.18 Mil 1943-45 C2

																									-0.4
1938	Phi A	93	325	36	91	15	1	6	44	34	7	25	.280	.361	.388	90	-5	3-0	.953	-6	98	77	2b80,3b13		-0.6
1939	Phi A	121	393	46	102	22	4	6	44	42	4	18	.260	.337	.382	85	-9	2-0	.944	-3	104	43	3b89,2b28		-0.7
1940	Phi A	1	0	1	0	0	0	0	0	0	0	0	.000	.000	.000	-99	0	0-0	—	0			/H		-0.5
1941	Chi A	87	322	39	77	19	2	6	40	31	5	19	.239	.316	.348	76	-11	0-4	.962	4	99	146	3b86		0.4
1942	Chi A	59	168	9	47	7	0	0	15	18	1	10	.280	.353	.321	92	-1	3-4	.944	2	117	55	3b43,2b7		-0.7
1946	Chi A	44	155	12	38	8	0	0	13	16	2	14	.245	.324	.297	77	-4	4-0	.935	-3	99	45	3b44		-1.8
Total	6	405	1364	142	355	71	7	16	156	141	19	86	.260	.338	.358	84	-30	12-8	.947	-4	103	82	3b275,2b115		-1.8

LoDUCA, PAUL   Paul Anthony   B4.12.1972 Brooklyn NY   BR/TR/5-10/210(185-210)   [LAN93 25/690]   d6.21 Col Arizona St.

1998	LA N	6	14	2	4	1	0	0	1	0-0	0	1	.286	.286	.357	71	-1	0-0	1.000	0	83	259	C4		0.0
1999	LA N	36	95	11	22	1	0	3	11	10-4	0	9	.232	.312	.337	69	-5	1-2	.990	0	103	119	C34		-0.1
2000	LA N	34	65	6	16	2	0	2	8	6-0	0	9	.246	.301	.369	74	-3	0-2	.992	4	117	206	C20,O8(7/0/2)/3		0.2
2001	LA N	125	460	71	147	28	2	25	90	39-2	6	30	.320	.374	.543	144	30	2-4	.991	-8	105	123	C99,1b33,O5(4/0/1)/D	22	2.4
2002	LA N	149	580	74	163	38	1	10	64	34-2	10	31	.281	.330	.402	101	-3	3-1	.992	1	83	116	C137,1b18,O9L		0.3
2003	LA N★	147	568	64	155	34	2	7	52	44-6	10	54	.273	.335	.377	88	-10	0-2	.987	32	74	207	C123,1b22,O6L		2.8
2004	LA N★	91	349	41	105	18	1	10	49	22-0	6	27	.301	.351	.444	106	3	2-4	.995	-3	77	130	C81,O9L,1b3		-0.1
	Fla N	52	186	27	48	11	1	3	31	14-0	3	22	.258	.314	.376	83	-5	2-1	.997	-1	64	156	C49		-0.4
	Year	143	535	68	153	29	2	13	80	36-0	9	49	.286	.338	.421	98	-2	4-5	.996	-4	72	140	C130,O9L,1b3		-0.4
2005	Fla N★	132	445	45	126	23	1	6	57	34-5	4	31	.283	.334	.380	94	-4	4-3	.991	-8	68	118	C128		0.4
Total	8	772	2762	341	786	156	6	66	363	203-19	41	213	.285	.339	.417	102	-5	14-19	.991	18	81	142	C675,1b76,O37(35/0/3)/D3	22	5.5

LOEPP, GEORGE   George Herbert   B9.11.1901 Detroit MI   D9.4.1967 Los Angeles CA   BR/TR/5-11/170   d8.29

1928	Bos A	15	51	6	9	3	1	0	3	5	0	12	.176	.250	.275	38	-5	0-0	.949	0	103	128	O14(1/10/6)		-0.8
1930	Was A	50	134	23	37	7	1	0	14	20	3	9	.276	.382	.343	85	-2	0-4	.958	-1	97	109	O48(12/34/3)		-1.1
Total	2	65	185	29	46	10	2	0	17	25	3	21	.249	.347	.324	73	-7	0-4	.956	-0	99	114	O62(13/44/9)		-1.9

LOFTON, JAMES   James O'Neal   B3.6.1974 Los Angeles CA   BB/TR/5-10/170   [CinN93 13/372]   d9.19 Col Los Angeles (CA) City

2001	Bos A	28	26	1	5	1	0	0	4		0		.192	.214	.231	20	-3	2-1	.920	-1	84	78	S7		-0.4

LOFTON, KENNY   Kenneth   B5.31.1967 E.Chicago IN   BL/TL/6-0/190*   [HouN88 17/428]   d9.14 Col Arizona

1991	Hou N	20	74	9	15	1	0	0	0	5-0	0	19	.203	.253	.216	35	-7	2-1	.977	-0	101	107	O20C		-0.1
1992	Cle A	148	576	96	164	15	8	5	42	68-3	2	54	.285	.362	.365	105	5	66-12	.982	7	104	170	O143C		2.4
1993	Cle A	148	569	116	185	28	8	1	42	81-6	1	83	.325	.408	.408	120	20	70-14	.979	5	105	138	O146C		3.2
1994	Cle A★	112	459	105	160	32	9	12	57	52-5	2	56	.349	.412	.536	142	30	60-12	.993	9	91	214	O112C		3.6
1995	Cle A★	118	481	93	149	22	13	7	53	40-6	1	49	.310	.362	.453	109	5	54-15	.970	-5	86	197	O114C,D2	15	2.0
1996	Cle A★	154	662	132	210	35	4	14	67	61-3	0	82	.317	.372	.446	106	7	75-17	.975	-5	95	138	O152C		1.5
1997	†Atl N★	122	493	90	164	20	6	5	48	64-5	2	83	.333	.409	.428	119	16	27-20	.983	1	108	88	O122C	39	1.6
1998	†Cle A★	154	600	101	169	31	6	12	64	87-1	2	80	.282	.371	.413	101	3	54-10	.978	-4	86	199	O154C	32	1.0
1999	†Cle A★	120	465	110	140	28	6	7	39	79-2	6	84	.301	.405	.432	109	10	25-6	.989	-3	91	159	O135C/D	14	0.9
2000	Cle A	137	543	107	151	23	5	15	73	79-3	4	72	.278	.369	.422	98	-1	30-7	.981	-2	105	45	O130C	16	-1.0
2001	†Cle A	133	517	91	135	21	4	14	66	47-1	2	69	.261	.322	.398	86	-11	16-8	1.000	0	103	67	O92C		0.0
2002	Chi A	93	352	68	91	20	6	8	42	49-0	0	51	.259	.348	.418	99	-1	22-8	1.000	0	113	126	O44C		0.0
	†SF N	46	180	30	48	10	3	3	9	23-0	1	22	.267	.353	.406	106	1	7-3	1.000	1	101	107	O81C		0.0
2003	Pit N	84	339	58	94	19	4	9	26	28-1	2	29	.277	.333	.437	98	-1	18-5	.974	-1	99	116	O55C		0.0
	†Chi N	56	208	39	68	13	4	3	20	18-2	2	22	.327	.381	.471	119	6	12-4	.991	-0	100	113	O136C		0.0
	Year	140	547	97	162	32	8	12	46	46-3	4	51	.296	.352	.450	106	5	30-9	.989	-0	99	114	O74(0/65/10),D4	30	0.0
2004	†NY A	83	276	51	76	10	7	3	18	31-1	1	27	.275	.346	.395	94	-3	7-3	.989	4	109	117	O97C/D	17	1.0
2005	Phi N	110	367	67	123	15	5	2	36	32-2	2	41	.335	.392	.420	109	6	22-3	.981	3	103	166	O109C/D	163	17.0
Total	15	1838	7161	1363	2142	343	98	120	702	844-41	30	923	.299	.372	.425	107	86	567-148	.984	6	100	135	O1790(0/1781/10),D9	163	17.0

LOFTUS, DICK   Richard Joseph   B3.7.1901 Concord MA   D1.21.1972 Concord MA   BL/TR/6-0/155   d4.20

1924	Bro N	46	81	18	22	6	0	0	8	7	0	2	.272	.330	.346	84	-2	1-0	1.000	1	111	49	O29(6/14/9)/1		-0.1
1925	Bro N	51	131	16	31	4	0	0	13	5	2	5	.237	.275	.282	44	-11	2-0	.985	2	113	71	O38(3/0/35)		-1.0
Total	2	97	212	34	53	10	0	0	21	12	2	7	.250	.296	.307	59	-13	3-0	.985	2	113	71	O67(9/14/44)/1		-1.0

LOFTUS, TOM   Thomas Joseph   B11.15.1856 St.Louis MO   D4.16.1910 Dubuque IA   BR/?/168   d8.17 M9

1877	StL N	3	11	2	2	0	0	0		1			.182	.182	.182	16	-1		.778	1	434	0	O3(1/0/2)		-0.0
1883	StL AA	6	22	1	4	0	0	0		2			.182	.250	.182	39	-1		.882	-1	0	0	O6C		-0.0
Total	2	9	33	3	6	0	0	0	0	2		1	.182	.229	.182	32	-2		.846	1	148	0	O9(1/6/2)		-0.0

YEAR	TM LG	G	AB	R	H	2B	3B	HR	RBI	BB-IB	HP	SO	AVG	OBP	SLG	AOPS	ABR	SB-CS	FA	FR	RNG	THR	GAMES AT POSITION	DL	BFW

LOGAN, NOOK   Exavier Prente B11.28.1979 Natchez MS BB/TR/6-2/180* [DetA00 3/78] d7.21 Col Copiah-Lincoln (MS) CC

YEAR	TM LG	G	AB	R	H	2B	3B	HR	RBI	BB-IB	HP	SO	AVG	OBP	SLG	AOPS	ABR	SB-CS	FA	FR	RNG	THR	GAMES AT POSITION	DL	BFW
2004	Det A	47	133	12	37	5	2	0	10	13-0	1	24	.278	.340	.346	83	-3	8-2	.984	3	112	146	O46C		0.1
2005	Det A	129	322	47	83	12	5	1	17	21-3	1	52	.258	.305	.335	72	-13	23-6	.979	2	109	60	O123C,D3		-0.7
Total 2		176	455	59	120	17	7	1	27	34-3	1	76	.264	.316	.338	76	-16	31-8	.981	5	110	85	O169C,D3		-0.6

LOGAN, JOHNNY   John "Yatcha" B3.23.1927 Endicott NY BR/TR/5-11/175(175-186) d4.17

YEAR	TM LG	G	AB	R	H	2B	3B	HR	RBI	BB-IB	HP	SO	AVG	OBP	SLG	AOPS	ABR	SB-CS	FA	FR	RNG	THR	GAMES AT POSITION	DL	BFW
1951	Bos N	62	169	14	37	7	1	0	18	18	1	13	.219	.298	.272	59	-10	0-0	.958	2	102	91	S58		-0.5
1952	Bos N	117	456	56	129	21	3	4	42	31	4	33	.283	.334	.368	98	-2	1-2	.972	13	107	99	S117		1.8
1953	Mil N	150	611	100	167	27	8	11	73	41	7	33	.273	.326	.398	93	-7	2-2	.975	21	105	115	S150		2.5
1954	Mil N	154	560	66	154	17	7	8	66	51	6	51	.275	.339	.373	92	-7	2-0	.969	13	103	107	S154		1.9
1955	Mil N★	154	595	95	177	37	5	13	83	58-1	4	58	.297	.360	.442	118	17	3-3	.963	13	103	97	S154		3.4
1956	Mil N	148	545	69	153	27	5	15	46	46-2	5	49	.281	.340	.431	113	10	3-0	.968	4	107	106	S148		2.7
1957	†Mil N☆	129	494	59	135	19	7	10	49	31-2	4	49	.273	.319	.401	100	-2	5-0	.960	22	113	112	S129		3.2
1958	†Mil N★	145	530	54	120	20	0	11	53	40-1	5	57	.226	.286	.326	68	-26	1-2	.959	15	109	110	S144		0.0
1959	Mil N☆	138	470	59	137	17	0	13	50	57-9	3	45	.291	.369	.411	118	14	1-3	.975	-2	101	97	S138		2.3
1960	Mil N	136	482	52	118	14	4	7	42	43-6	2	40	.245	.309	.334	82	-13	1-1	.956	-1	103	96	S136		-0.3
1961	Mil N	18	19	0	2	1	0	0	1	0-0	1	3	.105	.150	.158	-19	-3	0-0	1.000	-1	88	142	S2		-0.4
	Pit N	27	52	5	12	4	0	0	5	4-0	0	8	.231	.286	.308	57	-3	0-0	1.000	0	113	212	3b7,S6		-0.3
	Year	45	71	5	14	5	0	0	6	5-0	1	11	.197	.250	.268	38	-6	0-0	.964	-1	95	99	S8,3b7		-0.3
1962	Pit N	44	80	7	24	3	0	1	12	7-0	0	6	.300	.348	.375	96	0	0-0	.980	1	109	164	3b19		-0.7
1963	Pit N	81	181	15	42	2	1	0	9	23-5	2	27	.232	.325	.254	69	-6	0-0	.920	-4	98	110	S44,3b4		0.1
Total 13		1503	5244	651	1407	216	41	93	547	451-26	43	472	.268	.330	.378	95	-38	19-13	.965	86	106	104	S1380,3b30		15.6

LOHMAN, PETE   George F. B10.21.1864 Washington Co. MN D11.21.1928 Los Angeles CA BR/TR d5.11

YEAR	TM LG	G	AB	R	H	2B	3B	HR	RBI	BB-IB	HP	SO	AVG	OBP	SLG	AOPS	ABR	SB-CS	FA	FR	RNG	THR	GAMES AT POSITION	DL	BFW
1891	Was AA	32	109	18	21	1	4	1	11	16	1	17	.193	.302	.303	77	-4	1	.914	-3	87	86	C21,O8(1/1/6),3b4/S2		-0.4

LOHR, HOWARD   Howard Sylvester B6.3.1892 Philadelphia PA D6.9.1977 Philadelphia PA BR/TR/6-0/165 d6.17

YEAR	TM LG	G	AB	R	H	2B	3B	HR	RBI	BB-IB	HP	SO	AVG	OBP	SLG	AOPS	ABR	SB-CS	FA	FR	RNG	THR	GAMES AT POSITION	DL	BFW
1914	Cin N	18	47	6	10	1	1	0	7	0	0	8	.213	.213	.277	44	-4	1	.926	-1	89	68	O17(0/17/1)		-0.6
1916	Cle A	3	7	0	1	0	0	0	1	0	0	1	.143	.143	.143	-13	-1	1	1.000	-0	104	0	O3R		-0.1
Total 2		21	54	6	11	1	1	0	8	0	0	9	.204	.204	.259	36	-5	3	.933	-1	91	59	O20(0/17/4)		-0.7

LOHRKE, JACK   Jack Wayne "Lucky" B2.25.1924 Los Angeles CA BR/TR/6-0/180* d4.18

YEAR	TM LG	G	AB	R	H	2B	3B	HR	RBI	BB-IB	HP	SO	AVG	OBP	SLG	AOPS	ABR	SB-CS	FA	FR	RNG	THR	GAMES AT POSITION	DL	BFW
1947	NY N	112	329	44	79	12	4	11	35	46	2	29	.240	.337	.401	95	-3	3	.939	-2	94	108	3b111		-0.5
1948	NY N	97	280	35	70	15	1	5	31	30	0	30	.250	.323	.364	85	-6	3	.898	-4	94	64	3b50,2b36		-0.8
1949	NY N	55	180	32	48	11	4	5	22	16	2	12	.267	.333	.456	110	2	3	.969	1	135	36	2b23,3b19,S15		0.5
1950	NY N	30	43	4	8	0	0	0	4	4	2	8	.186	.255	.186	18	-5	0	.958	0	101	145	3b16/2		-0.5
1951	†NY N	23	40	3	8	0	1	0	3	10	0	2	.200	.360	.275	73	-1	0-0	.943	-1	103	84	3b17/S		-0.2
1952	Phi N	25	29	4	6	0	0	1	4	4	0	3	.207	.303	.207	44	-2		1.000	0	113	123	S5,3b3/2		-0.1
1953	Phi N	12	13	3	2	0	0	0	1	1	0	2	.154	.214	.154	-2	-2	0-0	.750	0	178	0	2b2,S2/3		-0.2
Total 7		354	914	125	221	38	9	22	96	111	4	86	.242	.327	.375	87	-17	9-0	.928	-5	94	96	3b217,2b63,S23		-1.8

LOIS, ALBERTO   Alberto (b Alberto Louis (Pie)) B5.6.1956 Hato Mayor, D.R. BR/TR/5-9/175(160-175) d9.8 [DL 1980 Pit N 133]

YEAR	TM LG	G	AB	R	H	2B	3B	HR	RBI	BB-IB	HP	SO	AVG	OBP	SLG	AOPS	ABR	SB-CS	FA	FR	RNG	THR	GAMES AT POSITION	DL	BFW
1978	Pit N	3	4	0	1	0	1	0		0-0	0	1	.250	.250	.750	162	0		1.000	0	160		O2(2/1/0)		0.0
1979	Pit N	11	0	6	0	0	0	0		0-0	0	0	—	—	—		0	1-1	—	0			/R		0.0
Total 2		14	4	6	1	0	1	0		0-0	0	1	.250	.250	.750	162	0	1-1	1.000	0	160		O2(2/1/0)	133	0.0

LOLICH, RON   Ronald John B9.19.1946 Portland OR BR/TR/6-1/185* [ChiA65 8/197] d7.18

YEAR	TM LG	G	AB	R	H	2B	3B	HR	RBI	BB-IB	HP	SO	AVG	OBP	SLG	AOPS	ABR	SB-CS	FA	FR	RNG	THR	GAMES AT POSITION	DL	BFW
1971	Chi A	2	8	0	1	1	0	0	0	0	0	2	.125	.125	.250	4	-1	0-0	1.000	-1	29	0	O2R		-0.2
1972	Cle A	24	80	4	15	1	0	2	8	4-1	0	20	.188	.224	.275	47	-6	0-0	1.000	-1	97	64	O22(4/0/19)		-0.8
1973	Cle A	61	140	16	32	7	0	2	15	7-0	0	27	.229	.265	.321	63	-7	0-2	.909	-2	80	121	O32(5/0/27),D12		-1.2
Total 3		87	228	20	48	9	0	4	23	11-1	0	49	.211	.246	.303	56	-14	0-2	.953	-4	86	91	O56(9/0/48),D12		-2.2

LOLLAR, SHERM   John Sherman B8.23.1924 Durham AR D9.24.1977 Springfield MO BR/TR/6-1/185(180-195) d4.20 C5 Col Pittsburg St. (KS)

YEAR	TM LG	G	AB	R	H	2B	3B	HR	RBI	BB-IB	HP	SO	AVG	OBP	SLG	AOPS	ABR	SB-CS	FA	FR	RNG	THR	GAMES AT POSITION	DL	BFW
1946	Cle A	28	62	7	15	6	0	1	9	5	0	9	.242	.299	.387	97	0	0-1	.990	-2	106	114	C24		-0.1
1947	†NY A	11	32	4	7	0	1	1	6	1	0	5	.219	.242	.375	71	-2	0-1	1.000	0	89	44	C9		-0.1
1948	NY A	22	38	0	8	0	0	0	4	1	0	6	.211	.231	.211	18	-5	0-0	.976	1	109	118	C10		-0.4
1949	StL A	109	284	28	74	9	1	8	49	32	2	22	.261	.340	.384	88	-6	0-1	.988	-2	98	107	C93		-0.4
1950	StL A☆	126	396	55	111	22	3	13	65	64	2	25	.280	.391	.449	110	8	2-0	.981	-4	93	152	C109		0.9
1951	StL A	98	310	44	78	21	0	8	44	43	4	26	.252	.350	.397	99	0	1-0	.989	-3	71	80	C120		0.2
1952	Chi A	132	375	35	90	15	0	13	50	54	12	34	.240	.354	.384	104	4	1-0	.995	-3	91	138	C85/3		0.7
1953	Chi A	113	334	46	96	19	0	8	54	47	8	29	.287	.388	.416	114	9	1-0	.994	1	85	106	C107/1		1.5
1954	Chi A☆	107	316	31	77	13	0	7	34	37	7	28	.244	.334	.351	85	-5	0-1	.993	2	113	107	C93		0.0
1955	Chi A☆	138	426	67	111	13	1	16	61	68-12	10	34	.261	.374	.408	108	7	2-2	.995	12	119	84	C136		2.5
1956	Chi A★	136	450	55	132	28	2	11	75	53-4	16	34	.293	.383	.438	116	13	2-0	.993	3	145	67	C132		2.1
1957	Chi A	101	351	33	90	11	2	11	70	35-2	13	24	.256	.342	.393	101	1	2-0	.998	-0	98	87	C96		0.7
1958	Chi A☆	127	421	53	115	11	0	20	84	57-3	8	37	.273	.367	.454	128	18	2-1	.987	2	97	94	C116		2.5
1959	†Chi A★	140	505	63	134	22	3	22	84	55-6	5	49	.265	.345	.451	119	13	4-3	.993	7	80	101	C122,1b24		2.5
1960	Chi A★	129	421	43	106	23	0	7	46	42-3	8	39	.252	.326	.356	87	-7	2-0	.995	4	120	127	C123		0.4
1961	Chi A	116	337	38	95	10	1	7	41	37-10	2	22	.282	.360	.380	100	1	0-0	.995	-7	74	99	C66		-0.1
1962	Chi A	84	220	17	59	12	0	2	26	32-9	3	23	.268	.369	.350	95	0	1-0	.991	-7	113	121	C107		-0.3
1963	Chi A	35	73	4	17	4	0	0	6	8-0	1	7	.233	.317	.288	72	-2	0-0	.981	-2	118	112	C23,1b2	34	-0.3
Total 18		1752	5351	623	1415	244	14	155	808	671-49	115	453	.264	.357	.402	104	47	20-10	.992	3	102	104	C1571,1b27/3	34	12.3

LOMAN, DOUG   Douglas Edward B5.9.1958 Bakersfield CA BL/TL/5-11/185* [MilA78*2/33] d9.3 Col Bakersfield (CA) JC

YEAR	TM LG	G	AB	R	H	2B	3B	HR	RBI	BB-IB	HP	SO	AVG	OBP	SLG	AOPS	ABR	SB-CS	FA	FR	RNG	THR	GAMES AT POSITION	DL	BFW
1984	Mil A	23	76	13	21	4	0	2	12	15-2	1	7	.276	.402	.408	129	4	0-2	.967	3	108	249	O23(21/0/4)		0.5
1985	Mil A	24	66	10	14	3	2	0	7	1-0	1	12	.212	.221	.318	46	-5	0-0	1.000	3	100	344	O20(0/8/15)		-0.3
Total 2		47	142	23	35	7	2	2	19	16-2	1	19	.246	.325	.366	92	-1	0-2	.981	6	105	290	O43(21/8/19)		0.2

LOMASNEY, STEVE   Steven James B8.29.1977 Melrose MA BR/TR/6-0/195 [BosA95 5/130] d10.3

YEAR	TM LG	G	AB	R	H	2B	3B	HR	RBI	BB-IB	HP	SO	AVG	OBP	SLG	AOPS	ABR	SB-CS	FA	FR	RNG	THR	GAMES AT POSITION	DL	BFW
1999	Bos A	1	2	0	0	0	0	0	0	0-0	0	2	.000	.000	.000	-97	-1	0-0	1.000	2	0	1103	/C		0.1

LOMBARD, GEORGE   George Paul B9.14.1975 Atlanta GA BL/TR/6-0/212* [AtlN94 2/61] d9.4 [DL 2001 Atl N 190, 2002 Atl N 80]

YEAR	TM LG	G	AB	R	H	2B	3B	HR	RBI	BB-IB	HP	SO	AVG	OBP	SLG	AOPS	ABR	SB-CS	FA	FR	RNG	THR	GAMES AT POSITION	DL	BFW
1998	Atl N	6	6	2	2	0	0	1	1	0-0	0	4	.333	.333	.833	195	1	1-0	1.000	-0	87	0	O2R		0.1
1999	Atl N	6	6	1	2	0	0	0	0	1-0	0	2	.333	.429	.333	97	0	2-0	1.000	0	129	0	O4(2/0/2)		0.0
2000	Atl N	27	39	8	4	0	0	0	2	1-0	1	14	.103	.146	.103	-36	-8	4-0	1.000	0	93	170	O15(5/0/11)		-0.7
2002	Det A	72	241	34	58	11	3	5	13	20-1	1	78	.241	.300	.373	81	-7	13-2	.982	-2	100	54	O69(29/40/1),D2		-0.7
2003	TB A	13	37	8	8	1	0	1	4	4-3	0	11	.216	.317	.324	47	-3	1-0	.964	1	121	160	O13(3/0/11)		-0.2
Total 5		124	329	53	74	12	3	7	20	22-1	3	101	.225	.279	.343	65	-17	21-2	.981	-0	102	78	O103(39/40/27),D2	270	-1.5

LOMBARDI, ERNIE   Ernesto Natali "Schnozz","Bocci" B4.6.1908 Oakland CA D9.26.1977 Santa Cruz CA BR/TR/6-3/230 d4.15 HF1986

YEAR	TM LG	G	AB	R	H	2B	3B	HR	RBI	BB-IB	HP	SO	AVG	OBP	SLG	AOPS	ABR	SB-CS	FA	FR	RNG	THR	GAMES AT POSITION	DL	BFW
1931	Bro N	73	182	20	54	7	1	4	23	12	0	12	.297	.340	.412	102	0	1	.984	1	105	80	C50		0.4
1932	Cin N	118	413	43	125	22	9	11	68	41	4	19	.303	.371	.479	131	18	0	.963	-9	91	115	C110		1.6
1933	Cin N	107	350	30	99	21	4	4	47	16	4	17	.283	.322	.383	102	1	2	.972	-9	94	95	C95		-0.3
1934	Cin N	132	417	42	127	19	4	9	62	16	3	22	.305	.335	.434	107	2	0	.989	-3	99	105	C111		0.6
1935	Cin N	120	332	36	114	23	3	12	64	16	6	16	.343	.359	.539	144	22	0	.983	-4	88	121	C82		2.2
1936	Cin N☆	121	387	42	129	23	2	12	68	19	7	16	.333	.375	.496	142	22	1	.962	-9	96	94	C105		1.8
1937	Cin N★	120	368	41	123	22	1	9	59	14	2	17	.334	.362	.473	132	15	1	.973	-12	74	109	C90		0.8
1938	Cin N★	129	489	60	167	30	1	19	95	40	3	14	.342	.391	.524	154	35	0	.985	-2	127	102	C123		4.1
1939	†Cin N★	130	450	43	129	26	2	20	85	35	3	19	.287	.342	.487	120	11	0	.984	1	113	60	C120		1.9
1940	†Cin N★	109	376	50	120	22	0	14	74	31	7	14	.319	.382	.489	137	20	0	.989	-1	113	111	C101		2.5
1941	Cin N	117	398	33	105	12	1	10	60	36	1	14	.264	.325	.374	96	-3	1	.983	-4	77	117	C116		0.0
1942	Bos N★	105	309	32	102	14	0	11	46	37	1	12	.330	.403	.482	162	25	1	.980	-12	76	92	C85		1.4
1943	NY N★	104	295	19	90	7	0	10	51	16	5	25	.305	.347	.431	123	7	1	.971	-10	88	73	C73		0.2
1944	NY N★	117	373	37	95	13	0	10	58	33	4	11	.255	.317	.370	93	-4	0	.968	-9	105	90	C100		-0.8
1945	NY N★	115	368	46	113	7	1	19	70	43	5	11	.307	.387	.486	140	19	0	.983	3	160	88	C96		2.8
1946	NY N	88	238	19	69	4	1	12	39	18	1	24	.290	.347	.466	140	-0	0	.978	-0	87	110	C63		1.1

YEAR	TM LG	G	AB	R	H	2B	3B	HR	RBI	BB-IB	HP	SO	AVG	OBP	SLG	AOPS	ABR	SB-CS	FA	FR	RNG	THR	GAMES AT POSITION	DL	BFW
1947	NY N	48	110	8	31	5	0	4	21	7	1	9	.282	.325	.436	100	0	0-0	.980	-1	163	96	C24		-0.1
Total 17		1853	5855	601	1792	277	27	190	990	430	46	262	.306	.358	.460	126	198	8	.979	-79	102	99	C1544		20.6

LOMBARDI, PHIL Phillip Arden B2.20.1963 Abilene TX BR/TR/6-2/200* [NYA81 3/77] d4.26

																									0.2
1986	NY A	20	36	6	10	3	0	2	6	4-0	1	7	.278	.366	.528	140	2	0-0	.867	0	100	255	O8L,C3		-0.1
1987	NY A	5	8	0	1	0	0	0	0	0-0	0	2	.125	.125	.125	-34	-2	0-0	1.000	1	61	367	C3		-0.3
1989	NY N	18	48	4	11	1	0	1	3	5-0	0	8	.229	.302	.313	79	-1	0-0	.980	-2	56	22	C16/1		-0.2
Total 3		43	92	10	22	4	0	3	9	9-0	1	17	.239	.314	.380	95	-1	0-0	.975	-1	56	38	C22,O8L/1		

LOMBARDOZZI, STEVE Stephen Paul B4.26.1960 Malden MA BR/TR/6-0/175* [MinA81 9/218] d7.12 Col Florida

1985	Min A	28	54	10	20	4	1	0	6	6-0	0	6	.370	.426	.481	141	3	3-2	.982	5	130	117	2b26		0.9
1986	Min A	156	453	53	103	20	5	8	33	52-2	1	76	.227	.308	.347	76	-15	3-1	.991	7	102	106	2b155		-1.4
1987	†Min A	136	432	51	103	19	3	8	38	33-1	4	66	.238	.298	.352	69	-20	5-1	.977	-2	97	94	2b133		-1.9
1988	Min A	103	287	34	60	15	2	3	27	35-2	2	48	.209	.295	.307	68	-12	2-5	.986	-9	95	94	2b90,S12,3b5		-0.4
1989	Hou N	21	37	5	8	3	1	1	3	4-1	0	9	.216	.293	.432	108	0	0-0	.983	-4	82	77	2b18/3		0.0
1990	Hou N	2	1	0	0	0	0	0	0	1-0	0	1	.000	.500	.000	51	0	0-0	—		0		/H	43	-2.8
Total 6		446	1264	153	294	61	12	20	107	131-6	7	206	.233	.307	.347	75	-44	13-9	.983	-2	100	99	2b422,S12,3b6	43	

LONERGAN, WALTER Walter E. B9.22.1885 Boston MA D1.23.1958 Lexington MA BR/TR/5-7/156 d8.17

1911	Bos A	10	26	2	7	0	0	0	1	1	0		.269	.296	.269	59	-2	1	.935	-1	80	104	2b7/S3		-0.2

LONG d8.29

1888	Lou AA	1	2	0	0	0	0	0	0	1	0		.000	.333	.000	11	0	0	—	0	0	0	/OR		0.0

LONG, DAN Daniel W. B8.27.1867 Boston MA D4.30.1929 Sausalito CA d8.27

1890	Bal AA	21	77	19	12	0	0	0	14	2			.156	.301	.156	33	-6	16	.939	0	159	0	O21C		-0.6

LONG, HERMAN Herman C. "Germany","Flying Dutchman" B4.13.1866 Chicago IL D9.17.1909 Denver CO BL/TR/5-8.5/160 d4.17

																									3.0
1889	KC AA	136	574	137	158	32	6	3	60	64	10	63	.275	.358	.368	101	1	89	.874	31	108	110	S128,2b8/OL		0.2
1890	Bos N	101	431	95	108	15	3	8	52	40	4	34	.251	.320	.355	90	-7	49	.898	7	100	121	S101		2.6
1891	Bos N	139	577	129	163	21	12	9	75	80	8	51	.282	.377	.407	115	10	60	.902	15	95	143	S139		2.2
1892	†Bos N	151	646	115	181	33	6	6	78	44	8	36	.280	.334	.378	105	-2	57	.889	15	105	145	S141,O12(11/1/0)/3		1.4
1893	Bos N	128	552	149	159	22	6	6	58	73	5	32	.288	.376	.382	94	-5	38	.883	16	110	144	S123,2b5		0.3
1894	Bos N	104	475	136	154	28	11	12	79	35	4	17	.324	.375	.505	103	-1	24	.885	1	105	125	S98,O5L,2b3		-1.0
1895	Bos N	125	540	109	170	23	10	9	75	31	13	13	.315	.355	.444	98	-5	36	.892	-13	94	100	S123,2b2		2.1
1896	Bos N	120	502	106	173	26	6	6	101	26	5	16	.345	.383	.464	116	0	38	.897	9	103	110	S120		0.3
1897	†Bos N	107	450	89	145	32	7	3	69	23	2		.322	.358	.444	105	1	22	.905	-3	97	109	S107/OL		-0.5
1898	Bos N	144	589	99	156	21	10	6	99	39	0		.265	.311	.365	89	-12	20	.923	-1	97	124	S142,2b2		-2.1
1899	Bos N	145	578	91	153	30	6	6	100	45	3		.265	.321	.375	83	-16	20	.929	-15	87	138	S143,1b2		-1.1
1900	Bos N	125	486	80	127	19	4	12	66	44	2		.261	.323	.391	86	-11	26	.937	-8	99	71	S125		-3.6
1901	Bos N	138	518	54	112	14	6	3	68	25	1		.216	.254	.284	51	-34	20	.946	-7	97	112	S107,2b13		0.9
1902	Bos N	120	437	40	101	11	0	2	44	31	1		.231	.284	.270	70	-15	24	.946	20	103	123	S107,2b13		-1.1
1903	NY A	22	80	6	15	3	0	0	8	2	0		.188	.207	.225	28	-7	3	.889	-4	87	83	S22		-1.2
	Det A	69	239	21	53	12	0	0	23	10	1		.222	.256	.272	60	-11	11	.879	-1	88	89	S38,2b31		-2.3
	Year	91	319	27	68	15	0	0	31	12	1		.213	.244	.260	52	-18	14	.883	-5	88	87	S60,2b31		0.0
1904	Phi N	1	4	0	1	0	0	0	0	0	0		.250	.250	.250	56	0	0	.889	0	102	0	/2		2.4
Total 16		1875	7678	1456	2129	342	97	91	1055	612	57	262	.277	.335	.383	93	-100	537	.906	63	99	119	S1795,2b65,O19(18/1/0),1b2/3		

LONG, JIMMIE James Albert B6.29.1898 Ft.Dodge IA D9.14.1970 Ft.Dodge IA BR/TR/5-11/160 d9.12

1922	Chi A	3	3	0	0	0	0	0	1	0	0		.000	.250	.000	-30	-1	0-0	1.000	-0	0	0	C2		-0.1

LONG, JIM James M. B11.15.1862 Louisville KY D12.12.1932 Louisville KY 5-10/160 d8.9

1891	Lou AA	6	25	5	6	0	0	0	4	3	2	6	.240	.367	.240	75	0	1	.857	1	186	435	O6(4/2/0)		0.0
1893	Bal N	55	226	31	48	8	1	2	25	16	4	27	.212	.276	.283	48	-18	23	.893	-1	86	48	O55L		-1.9
Total 2		61	251	36	54	8	1	2	29	19	6	33	.215	.286	.279	51	-18	24	.890	0	96	86	O61(59/2/0)		

LONG, JEOFF Jeoffrey Keith B10.9.1941 Covington KY BR/TR/6-1/200* d7.31

1963	StL N	5	5	0	1	0	0	0	0	0-0	1		.200	.200	.200	14	-1	0-0	—	0			/H		-0.3
1964	StL N	28	43	5	10	1	0	1	4	6-0	0	18	.233	.340	.326	81	-1	0-0	.833	-1	88	0	O4R,1b3		-0.5
	Chi A	23	35	0	5	0	0	0	5	4-0	0	15	.143	.225	.143	7	-4	0-0	1.000	1	207	142	1b5,O5L		-0.9
Total 3		56	83	5	16	1	0	1	9	10-0	1	34	.193	.284	.241	48	-6	0-0	.750	-1	82	0	O9(5/0/4),1b8		

LONG, DALE Richard Dale B2.6.1926 Springfield MO D1.27.1991 Palm Coast FL BL/TL/6-4/210* d4.21 C1

1951	Pit N	10	12	1	2	0	0	1	2	0		3	.167	.167	.417	50	-1	0-0	1.000	-0	0	0	/1		-0.1
	StL N	34	105	11	25	5	1	2	11	10	1	22	.238	.310	.362	79	-3	0-0	.988	-1	96	74	1b28/OL		-0.5
1955	Pit N	131	419	59	122	19	13	16	79	48-6	1	72	.291	.362	.513	132	18	0-1	.988	6	120	105	1b119		1.7
1956	Pit N★	148	517	64	136	20	7	27	91	54-11	0	85	.263	.336	.485	119	12	1-0	.982	-4	94	80	1b138		0.0
1957	Pit N	7	22	0	4	1	0	0	5	4-0	0	10	.182	.296	.227	48	-1	0-0	1.000	0	105	116	1b7		-0.2
	Chi N	123	397	55	121	19	0	21	62	52-4	1	63	.305	.383	.511	141	21	1-1	.995	-2	87	88	1b104		1.6
	Year	130	419	55	125	20	0	21	67	56-4	1	73	.298	.378	.496	136	23	1-1	.995	-2	88	90	1b111		1.4
1958	Chi N	142	480	68	130	26	4	20	75	66-9	2	64	.271	.357	.467	119	14	2-0	.992	-2	92	101	1b137,C2		0.5
1959	Chi N	110	296	34	70	10	3	14	37	31-2	0	53	.236	.306	.432	96	-3	0-0	.985	-4	90	105	1b85		-0.3
1960	SF N	37	54	4	9	0	0	3	6	7-1	0	6	.167	.262	.333	66	-3	0-0	1.000	0	100	73	1b10		-0.5
	†NY A	26	41	6	15	3	1	3	10	5-1	0	6	.366	.435	.707	216	7	0-0	.988	-1	73	41	1b11		-0.9
1961	Was A	123	377	52	94	20	4	17	49	39-5	1	41	.249	.317	.459	107	3	0-0	.983	-6	88	106	1b95		-0.8
1962	Was A	67	191	17	46	8	0	4	24	18-0	1	22	.241	.307	.346	77	-6	5-1	.996	0	100	119	1b51		-0.6
	†NY A	41	94	12	28	4	0	4	17	18-0	1	9	.298	.404	.468	140	6	1-0	.995	1	115	106	1b82		-0.2
	Year	108	285	29	74	12	0	8	41	36-0	2	31	.260	.340	.386	98	0	6-1	.995	1	105	114	1b82		-0.2
1963	NY A	14	15	1	3	0	0	0	0	1-0	0	3	.200	.250	.200	28	-1	0-0	.917	-0	136	62	1b2		-0.1
Total 10		1013	3020	384	805	135	33	132	467	353-39	7	460	.267	.341	.464	116	66	10-3	.988	-12	96	97	1b819,C2/OL		

LONG, RYAN Ryan Marcus B2.3.1973 Houston TX BR/TR/6-2/215 [KCA91 1/45] d7.16

1997	KC A	6	9	2	2	0	0	0	2	0-0	0	3	.222	.300	.222	38	-1	0-0	1.000	1	157	0	O5(1/0/4)/D		-0.1

LONG, TERRENCE Terrence Deon B2.29.1976 Montgomery AL BL/TL/6-1/197* [NYN94 1/20] d4.14

1999	NY N	3	3	0	0	0	0	0	0	0-0	0	2	.000	.000	.000	-99	-1	0-0	—	0			/H		-0.1
2000	†Oak A	138	584	104	168	34	4	18	80	43-1	1	77	.288	.336	.452	99	-2	5-0	.971	-11	94	29	O137C		-1.6
2001	†Oak A	162	629	90	178	37	4	12	85	52-8	0	103	.283	.335	.412	96	-4	9-3	.980	-10	92	51	O162(62/74/28)		-2.8
2002	†Oak A	162	587	71	141	32	4	16	67	48-6	2	96	.240	.298	.390	82	-16	3-6	.980	-13	90	58	O162C		-2.9
2003	†Oak A	140	486	64	119	22	2	14	61	31-4	3	67	.245	.293	.385	77	-17	4-1	.984	-7	94	40	O137(75/0/74)/D		-2.5
2004	SD N	136	288	31	85	19	4	3	28	19-4	1	51	.295	.335	.420	100	0	3-2	.986	2	109	59	O87(61/28/9)/D		-0.5
2005	KC A	137	455	62	127	21	3	6	53	30-0	0	56	.279	.321	.378	91	-6	3-3	.986	2	92	202	O121(103/6/17),D4		-9.2
Total 7		878	3032	422	818	165	21	69	374	223-23	7	452	.270	.319	.406	90	-46	27-15	.980	-37	94	69	O806(301/407/128),D6		

LONG, TOM Thomas Augustus B6.1.1890 Mitcham (now Chilton) AL D6.15.1974 Mobile AL BR/TR/5-10.5/165 d9.11

1911	Was A	14	48	1	11	3	0	0	5	1	0		.229	.245	.292	50	-3	4	.875	-2	78	56	O13(4/0/9)		-0.6
1912	Was A	1	1	0	0	0	0	0	0	0	0		.000	.000	.000	-99	0	0	—	0			/H		0.0
1915	StL N	140	507	61	149	21	25	2	61	31	4	50	.294	.339	.446	137	19	19-15	.927	-3	95	118	O136(2/51/87)		-0.5
1916	StL N	119	403	37	118	11	11	1	33	10	1	43	.293	.312	.377	112	3	21-14	.919	-19	85	108	O119(30/0/109)		-3.9
1917	StL N	144	530	49	123	12	14	3	41	37	2	44	.232	.285	.325	89	-9	21-10	.928	-28	85	91	O392(39/63/299)		-0.8
Total 5		418	1489	148	401	47	49	6	140	79	7	137	.269	.309	.379	110	10	65-29							

LONGMIRE, TONY Anthony Eugene B8.12.1968 Vallejo CA BL/TR/6-1/197* [PitN86 8/186] d9.3 [DL 1992 Phi N 182, 1996 Phi N 182]

1993	†Phi N	11	13	1	3	0	0	0	1	1-0	0	3	.231	.231	.231	24	-1	0-0	1.000	0	166	0	O2L		-1.
1994	Phi N	69	139	10	33	11	0	0	17	10-1	1	27	.237	.289	.317	58	-2	1-1	.941	-1	85	159	O32(13/0/21)		-0.
1995	Phi N	59	104	21	37	7	0	3	19	11-1	1	19	.356	.419	.510	144	7	1-1	1.000	1	103	186	O23(19/2/2)	420	-0.
Total 3		139	256	32	73	18	0	3	37	21-2	2	47	.285	.340	.391	91	-2	3-2	.967	1	94	165	O57(34/2/23)		

YEAR	TM LG	G	AB	R	H	2B	3B	HR	RBI	BB-IB	HP	SO	AVG	OBP	SLG	AOPS	ABR	SB-CS	FA	FR	RNG	THR	GAMES AT POSITION	DL	BFW

LONNETT, JOE Joseph Paul B2.7.1927 Beaver Falls PA BR/TR/5-10/180* d4.22 C14

YEAR	TM LG	G	AB	R	H	2B	3B	HR	RBI	BB-IB	HP	SO	AVG	OBP	SLG	AOPS	ABR	SB-CS	FA	FR	RNG	THR	GAMES AT POSITION	DL	BFW
1956	Phi N	16	22	2	4	0	0	0		2-0	0	7	.182	.250	.182	19	-3	0-0	1.000	-0	64	117	C7		-0.3
1957	Phi N	67	160	12	27	5	0	5	15	22-1	1	39	.169	.272	.294	54	-10	0-0	.997	2	70	71	C65		-0.7
1958	Phi N	17	50	0	7	2	0	0		2-0	0	11	.140	.167	.180	-6	-8	0-0	.988	1	85	117	C15		-0.7
1959	Phi N	43	93	8	16	1	0	1	10	14-2	1	17	.172	.284	.215	36	-8	0-1	.983	-5	73	33	C43		-0.7
Total 4		143	325	22	54	8	0	6	27	40-3	2	74	.166	.259	.246	37	-29	0-1	.992	-3	73	68	C130		-2.9

LOOK, BRUCE Bruce Michael B6.9.1943 Lansing MI BL/TR/5-11/185 d4.17 b-Dean Col Michigan St.

YEAR	TM LG	G	AB	R	H	2B	3B	HR	RBI	BB-IB	HP	SO	AVG	OBP	SLG	AOPS	ABR	SB-CS	FA	FR	RNG	THR	GAMES AT POSITION	DL	BFW
1968	Min A	59	118	7	29	4	0	0	9	20-3	0	24	.246	.353	.280	89	0	0-1	.996	1	81	89	C41		0.2

LOOK, DEAN Dean Zachary B7.23.1937 Lansing MI BR/TR/5-11/185 d9.22 b-Bruce Col Michigan St.

YEAR	TM LG	G	AB	R	H	2B	3B	HR	RBI	BB-IB	HP	SO	AVG	OBP	SLG	AOPS	ABR	SB-CS	FA	FR	RNG	THR	GAMES AT POSITION	DL	BFW
1961	Chi A	3	6	0	0	0	0	0		0-0	0	1	.000	.000	.000	-99	-2	0-0	1.000	-0	57	0	/OL		-0.2

LOPATA, STAN Stanley Edward "Stash" B9.12.1925 Delray MI BR/TR/6-2/210* d9.19

YEAR	TM LG	G	AB	R	H	2B	3B	HR	RBI	BB-IB	HP	SO	AVG	OBP	SLG	AOPS	ABR	SB-CS	FA	FR	RNG	THR	GAMES AT POSITION	DL	BFW
1948	Phi N	6	15	2	2	1	0	0		2	0	4	.133	.133	.200	-11	-2	0	1.000	0	59	126	C4		-0.2
1949	Phi N	83	240	31	65	9	2	8	27	21	0	44	.271	.330	.425	104	0	1	.973	-2	86	75	C58		0.1
1950	†Phi N	58	129	10	27	2	2	1	11	22	0	25	.209	.325	.279	61	-7	1	.974	1	104	66	C51		-0.4
1951	Phi N	3	5	0	0	0	0	0	0	0	0	0	.000	.000	.000	-99	-1	0-0	1.000	0	0	0	/C		-0.1
1952	Phi N	57	179	25	49	9	1	4	27	36	0	33	.274	.395	.432	123	8	1-1	.987	4	101	80	C55		1.4
1953	Phi N	81	234	34	56	12	3	8	31	28	0	39	.239	.321	.419	91	-3	3-1	.987	2	114	71	C80		0.3
1954	Phi N	86	259	42	75	14	5	14	42	33	1	37	.290	.369	.544	136	13	1-3	.989	6	123	74	C75/1		0.3
1955	Phi N★	99	303	49	82	9	3	22	58	58-6	2	62	.271	.388	.538	146	21	4-1	.995	7	109	86	C66,1b24		2.2
1956	Phi N☆	146	535	96	143	33	7	32	95	75-10	1	93	.267	.353	.535	138	30	5-2	.982	-19	74	54	C102,1b39		3.0
1957	Phi N	116	388	50	92	18	2	18	67	56-7	1	81	.237	.331	.433	108	5	2-2	.988	-8	68	72	C108		1.4
1958	Phi N	86	258	36	64	9	0	9	33	60-9	2	63	.248	.391	.388	109	7	0-1	.987	-8	85	69	C80		0.2
1959	Mil N	25	48	0	5	0	0	0	4	3-0	0	13	.104	.157	.104	-31	-9	0-0	1.000	-2	148	0	C11,1b2		0.2
1960	Mil N	7	8	0	1	0	0	0		1-0	0	3	.125	.222	.125	-2	-1	0-0	.944	1	0	0	C4		-1.1
Total 13		853	2601	375	661	116	25	116	397	393-32	7	497	.254	.351	.452	115	61	18-11	.986	-18	93	70	C695,1b66		7.0

LOPES, DAVEY David Earl B5.3.1945 E.Providence RI BR/TR/5-9/170* [LAN68*S2/26] d9.22 M3/C15 Col Washburn Topeka OF(86/98/66)

YEAR	TM LG	G	AB	R	H	2B	3B	HR	RBI	BB-IB	HP	SO	AVG	OBP	SLG	AOPS	ABR	SB-CS	FA	FR	RNG	THR	GAMES AT POSITION	DL	BFW
1972	LA N	11	42	6	9	4	0	0	1	7-0	0	6	.214	.327	.310	83	-1	4-0	.964	-2	91	77	2b11		
1973	LA N	142	535	77	147	13	5	6	37	62-6	5	77	.275	.352	.351	100	1	36-16	.984	-2	101	115	2b135,O5(0/2/3),S2/3		-0.1
1974	†LA N	145	530	95	141	26	3	10	35	66-3	4	71	.266	.350	.383	109	8	59-18	.965	-12	93	93	2b143		1.1
1975	LA N	155	618	108	162	24	6	8	41	91-3	2	93	.262	.358	.359	104	6	77-12	.979	-17	92	78	2b137,O24(0/23/1),S14		1.2
1976	LA N	117	427	72	103	17	7	4	20	56-1	4	49	.241	.333	.342	93	-3	63-10	.964	-17	94	96	2b100,O19C		1.0
1977	†LA N	134	502	85	142	19	5	11	53	73-3	2	69	.283	.372	.406	109	9	47-12	.979	13	108	108	2b130	25	-0.4
1978	†LA N★	151	587	93	163	25	4	17	73	71-3	0	70	.278	.355	.421	116	13	45-4	.974	12	106	111	2b147,O2C		3.5
1979	LA N★	153	582	109	154	20	6	28	73	97-4	8	88	.265	.372	.464	129	26	44-4	.981	-31	84	83	2b152		4.3
1980	LA N	141	553	79	139	15	3	10	49	58-2	1	71	.251	.321	.344	89	-8	23-7	.980	-5	98	106	2b140		1.2
1981	†LA N★	58	214	35	44	2	0	5	17	22-1	3	35	.206	.289	.285	66	-10	20-2	.993	3	99	97	2b55		-0.3
1982	Oak A	128	450	58	109	19	3	11	42	40-1	1	51	.242	.304	.371	88	-8	28-12	.977	-16	92	91	2b125,O6C	15	-0.1
1983	Oak A	147	494	64	137	13	4	17	67	51-7	2	61	.277	.341	.423	117	11	22-4	.983	-25	85	96	2b123,D12,O7(0/2/5),3b5		-1.6
1984	Oak A	72	230	32	59	11	1	9	36	31-1	1	36	.257	.343	.430	121	7	12-0	.965	-4	100	179	O42(3/8/31),2b17,3b5,D9	30	-0.5
	†Chi N	16	17	5	4	1	0	0	0	6-0	0	5	.235	.435	.294	100	1	3-0	1.000	-1	123	0	O9(2/1/6),2b2		0.5
1985	Chi N	99	275	52	78	11	0	11	44	46-1	0	37	.284	.383	.444	120	9	47-4	.991	-6	83	44	O79(46/25/17),3b4/2		0.9
1986	Chi N	59	157	38	47	8	2	6	22	31-0	2	16	.299	.419	.490	140	10	17-6	.902	2	110	66	3b32,O22(21/0/2)		1.3
	†Hou N	37	98	11	23	2	1	1	13	12-0	0	9	.235	.315	.306	75	-3	8-2	1.000	3	121	270	O19(9/10/1),3b5		0.0
	Year	96	255	49	70	10	3	7	35	43-0	2	25	.275	.381	.420	117	7	25-8	.991	-1	114	156	O41(30/10/3),3b37		1.3
1987	Hou N	47	43	4	10	2	0	1	6	13-2	0	8	.233	.411	.349	108	1	2-1	.857	-1	73	0	O5L	68	0.1
Total 16		1812	6354	1023	1671	232	50	155	614	833-38	31	852	.263	.349	.388	106	69	557-114	.977	-107	95	97	2b1418,O239C,3b52,D21,S16	138	12.1

LOPEZ, AL Alfonso Ramon B8.20.1908 Tampa FL D10.30.2005 Tampa FL BR/TR/5-11/165 d9.27 M17 HF1977

YEAR	TM LG	G	AB	R	H	2B	3B	HR	RBI	BB-IB	HP	SO	AVG	OBP	SLG	AOPS	ABR	SB-CS	FA	FR	RNG	THR	GAMES AT POSITION	DL	BFW
1928	Bro N	3	12	0	0	0	0	0	0	0-0	0	2	.000	.000	.000	-99	-4	0	1.000	-1	111	0	C3		-0.4
1930	Bro N	128	421	60	130	20	4	6	57	33	2	35	.309	.362	.418	89	-7	3	.983	9	104	101	C126		0.8
1931	Bro N	111	360	38	97	13	4	0	40	28	1	33	.269	.324	.328	76	-12	1	.977	-5	102	113	C105		-1.1
1932	Bro N	126	404	44	111	18	6	1	43	34	1	35	.275	.331	.356	87	-7	3	.976	-4	95	124	C125		-0.3
1933	Bro N	126	372	39	112	11	4	3	41	21	0	39	.301	.338	.376	108	3	10	.991	14	96	129	C124/2		2.5
1934	Bro N★	140	439	58	120	23	2	7	54	49	2	44	.273	.349	.383	101	2	2	.982	-7	93	109	C137,2b2,3b2		0.2
1935	Bro N	128	379	50	95	12	4	3	39	35	1	36	.251	.316	.327	75	-13	2	.980	6	115	99	C126		0.4
1936	Bos N	128	426	46	103	12	5	7	50	41	2	41	.242	.311	.343	81	-12	1	.975	8	145	108	C127/1		0.4
1937	Bos N	105	334	31	68	11	3	3	38	35	1	57	.204	.281	.269	55	-21	3	.984	11	191	93	C102		0.4
1938	Bos N	71	236	19	63	6	1	1	14	11	2	24	.267	.305	.314	78	-8	5	.989	4	169	98	C71		-0.3
1939	Bos N	131	412	32	104	22	1	8	49	40	5	45	.252	.319	.369	91	-6	1	.986	4	147	107	C129		0.1
1940	Bos N	36	119	20	35	3	1	2	17	6	0	8	.294	.328	.387	102	0	1	.987	2	100	152	C36		0.6
	Pit N	59	174	15	45	6	2	1	24	13	0	13	.259	.310	.333	78	-5	5	.992	1	72	99	C59		0.3
	Year	95	293	35	80	9	3	3	41	19	0	21	.273	.317	.355	87	-6	6	.990	2	83	120	C95		-0.2
1941	Pit N★	114	317	33	84	9	1	5	43	31	0	23	.265	.330	.347	91	-4	0	.980	2	106	91	C114		0.1
1942	Pit N	103	289	17	74	8	2	1	26	34	2	17	.256	.338	.308	88	-4	0	.995	5	88	102	C99		0.7
1943	Pit N	118	372	40	98	9	4	1	39	44	0	25	.263	.341	.317	88	-5	2	.991	11	137	104	C116/3		1.4
1944	Pit N	115	331	27	76	12	1	1	34	34	1	24	.230	.303	.281	62	-16	4	.984	6	100	118	C115		-0.4
1945	Pit N	91	243	22	53	8	0	0	18	35	0	12	.218	.317	.251	57	-13	1	.992	3	82	94	C91		-0.5
1946	Cle A	56	150	13	46	2	0	1	12	23	0	12	.307	.399	.340	108	3	1	.985	-1	68	125	C56		0.5
1947	Cle A	61	126	9	33	1	0	0	14	9	1	10	.262	.311	.270	64	-5	1-1	1.000	2	167	152	C57		-0.3
Total 19		1950	5916	613	1547	206	43	51	652	556	14	538	.261	.326	.337	83	-135	46-1	.985	69	116	109	C1918,3b3,2b3/1		4.3

LOPEZ, ART Arturo (Rodriguez) B5.8.1937 Mayaguez, PR BL/TL/5-9/170 d4.12 Col New Jersey City

YEAR	TM LG	G	AB	R	H	2B	3B	HR	RBI	BB-IB	HP	SO	AVG	OBP	SLG	AOPS	ABR	SB-CS	FA	FR	RNG	THR	GAMES AT POSITION	DL	BFW
1965	NY A	38	49	5	7	0	0	0	0	1-0	0	6	.143	.160	.143	-13	-7	0-0	.958	0	125	0	O16(3/0/14)		-0.9

LOPEZ, CARLOS Carlos Antonio (Morales) B9.27.1948 Mazatlan, Sonora, Mexico BR/TR/6-0/190(162-190) d9.17

YEAR	TM LG	G	AB	R	H	2B	3B	HR	RBI	BB-IB	HP	SO	AVG	OBP	SLG	AOPS	ABR	SB-CS	FA	FR	RNG	THR	GAMES AT POSITION	DL	BFW
1976	Cal A	9	10	1	0	0	0	0	0	2-0	0	3	.000	.167	.000	-52	-2	2-0	1.000	-1	59	0	O4(1/0/4)/D		-0.3
1977	Sea A	99	297	39	84	18	1	8	34	14-1	3	61	.283	.319	.431	103	1	16-4	.972	5	103	198	O90(0/7/87),D2		0.5
1978	Bal A	129	193	21	46	6	0	4	20	9-1	1	34	.238	.273	.332	74	-7	5-7	.988	5	102	166	O114(0/41/91)/D	21	-0.7
Total 3		237	500	61	130	24	1	12	54	25-2	4	98	.260	.298	.384	90	-8	23-11	.979	9	102	180	O208(1/48/182),D4	21	-0.5

LOPEZ, FELIPE Felipe B5.12.1980 Bayamon, PR BB/TR/6-0/175* [TorA98 1/8] d8.3

YEAR	TM LG	G	AB	R	H	2B	3B	HR	RBI	BB-IB	HP	SO	AVG	OBP	SLG	AOPS	ABR	SB-CS	FA	FR	RNG	THR	GAMES AT POSITION	DL	BFW
2001	Tor A	49	177	21	46	4		5	23	12-1	0	39	.260	.304	.418	87	-4	4-3	.940	1	114	74	3b47,S3		-0.3
2002	Tor A	85	282	35	64	15	3	8	34	23-1	1	90	.227	.287	.387	74	-11	5-4	.975	-8	94	98	S79,3b2/D		-1.4
2003	Cin N	59	197	28	42	7	2	2	13	28-1	1	59	.213	.313	.299	64	-10	8-5	.928	-12	101	65	S50,3b8,2b3		-1.9
2004	Cin N	79	264	35	64	18	2	7	31	25-0	3	81	.242	.314	.405	86	-6	1-1	.957	0	108	85	S51,3b24,2b2		-0.1
2005	Cin N★	148	580	97	169	34	5	23	85	57-2	1	111	.291	.352	.486	122	18	15-7	.970	-26	91	77	S140,2b7/3		0.3
Total 5		420	1500	216	385	79	16	45	186	145-5	6	380	.257	.322	.421	95	-13	33-20	.962	-44	96	82	S323,3b82,2b12/D		-3.4

LOPEZ, HECTOR Hector Headley (Swainson) B7.9.1929 Colon, Pan BR/TR/5-11/182(168-182) d5.12 OF(477/21/172)

YEAR	TM LG	G	AB	R	H	2B	3B	HR	RBI	BB-IB	HP	SO	AVG	OBP	SLG	AOPS	ABR	SB-CS	FA	FR	RNG	THR	GAMES AT POSITION	DL	BFW
1955	KC A	128	483	50	140	15	2	15	68	33-1	3	58	.290	.337	.422	103	0	1-4	.936	10	116	122	3b93,2b36		1.1
1956	KC A	151	561	91	153	27	3	18	69	63-3	3	73	.273	.347	.428	104	3	4-5	.940	3	105	89	3b121,O20C,2b8,S4		0.4
1957	KC A	121	391	51	115	19	4	11	35	41-5	0	66	.294	.357	.448	118	10	1-6	.937	3	106	100	3b111,2b4,O3(2/0/1)		1.1
1958	KC A	151	564	84	147	28	4	17	73	49-2	2	61	.261	.317	.415	99	-1	2-2	.974	2	107	105	2b96,3b55/SOL		1.1
1959	KC A	35	135	22	38	10	3	6	24	8-0	1	25	.281	.324	.533	129	5	1-0	.933	-8	83	66	2b33		-0.1
	NY A	112	406	60	115	16	2	16	69	28-1	6	54	.283	.336	.451	119	5	1-0	.926	-5	98	115	3b76,O35L		0.2
	Year	147	541	82	153	26	5	22	93	36-1	7	77	.283	.333	.471	122	14	2-0	.926	-13	98	115	3b76,O35L,2b33		0.1
1960	†NY A	131	408	66	116	14	6	9	42	46-0	4	64	.284	.361	.414	116	9	1-1	.976	2	101	119	O106(93/0/17),2b5/3		0.5
1961	†NY A	93	243	27	54	7	2	3	22	24-1	1	38	.222	.292	.305	64	-13	1-0	.977	3	102	148	O72(65/0/9)		-1.3
1962	†NY A	106	335	45	92	19	1	6	48	35-3	0	71	.275	.353	.391	95	-4	1-2	.984	2	108	63	O84(64/0/21)/23		-0.3
1963	†NY A	130	433	54	108	13	4	14	52	35-5	0	71	.249	.304	.395	95	-4	1-2	.957	-2	86	138	O124(104/0/21)/2		-1.4
1964	†NY A	127	285	34	74	9	3	10	34	24-2	1	54	.260	.317	.418	101	1	1-1	.971	-2	100	50	O103(80/1/31)/3		-0.7
1965	NY A	111	283	25	74	12	2	7	39	26-2	1	61	.261	.322	.392	104	1	0-0	.942	-6	82	74	O75(20/0/55),1b2		-1.0

YEAR	TM LG	G	AB	R	H	2B	3B	HR	RBI	BB-IB	HP	SO	AVG	OBP	SLG	AOPS	ABR	SB-CS	FA	FR	RNG	THR	GAMES AT POSITION	DL	BFW
1966	NY A	54	117	14	25	4	1	4	16	8-0	1	20	.214	.268	.368	84	-3	0-0	.936	-2	91	64	O29(13/0/17)		-0.7
Total	12	1450	4644	623	1251	193	37	136	591	418-24	23	696	.269	.330	.415	104	16	16-23	.967	1	95	100	O652l,3b459,2b184,S5,1b2		-1.5

LOPEZ, JAVY Javier (Torres) B11.5.1970 Ponce, PR BR/TR/6-3/200(185-230) d9.18

YEAR	TM LG	G	AB	R	H	2B	3B	HR	RBI	BB-IB	HP	SO	AVG	OBP	SLG	AOPS	ABR	SB-CS	FA	FR	RNG	THR	GAMES AT POSITION	DL	BFW
1992	†Atl N	9	16	3	6	2	0	0	2	0-0	0	1	.375	.375	.500	137	1	0-0	1.000	-1	46	57	C9		0.0
1993	Atl N	8	16	1	6	1	1	1	2	0-0	0	2	.375	.412	.750	199	2	0-0	.975	2	104	138	C7		0.4
1994	Atl N	80	277	27	68	9	0	13	35	17-0	5	61	.245	.299	.419	82	-8	0-2	.995	-0	80	83	C75		-0.4
1995	Atl N	100	333	37	105	11	4	14	51	14-0	2	57	.315	.344	.498	114	5	0-1	.988	2	113	60	C93		1.2
1996	Atl N	138	489	56	138	19	1	23	69	28-5	3	84	.282	.322	.466	100	-2	1-6	.994	20	104	91	C135		2.4
1997	†Atl N★	123	414	52	122	28	1	23	68	40-10	5	82	.295	.361	.534	130	18	1-1	.993	7	117	85	C117	16	3.1
1998	†Atl N★	133	489	73	139	21	1	34	106	30-1	6	85	.284	.328	.540	126	15	5-3	.995	24	146	76	C128/D		4.6
1999	Atl N	65	246	34	78	18	1	11	45	20-2	3	41	.317	.375	.533	127	10	0-3	.991	2	90	89	C132	95	1.4
2000	Atl N	134	481	60	138	21	0	24	89	35-3	4	80	.287	.337	.484	106	3	0-0	.993	1	105	67	C132		1.1
2001	Atl N	128	438	45	117	16	1	17	66	28-3	10	82	.267	.322	.425	91	-7	1-0	.989	4	101	97	C127		0.5
2002	Atl N	109	347	31	81	15	0	11	52	26-8	1	63	.233	.299	.372	79	-13	0-1	.986	13	100	132	C103	15	0.7
2003	†Atl N★	129	457	89	150	29	3	43	109	33-5	4	90	.328	.378	.687	171	45	0-1	.994	5	109	89	C120,D3		5.5
2004	Bal A	150	579	83	183	33	3	23	86	47-4	6	97	.316	.370	.503	127	23	0-0	.994	-4	93	87	C132,D21	61	2.4
2005	Bal A	103	395	47	110	24	1	15	49	19-2	7	68	.278	.322	.458	104	2	0-1	.994	-0	73	100	C75,D28/1		0.3
Total	14	1409	4977	638	1441	247	18	252	864	337-43	64	893	.290	.340	.498	115	94	8-19	.992	75	105	87	C1313,D57/1	187	23.3

LOPEZ, JOSE Jose Celestino B11.24.1983 Anzoategui, Venez BR/TR/6-2/170(170-200) d7.31

YEAR	TM LG	G	AB	R	H	2B	3B	HR	RBI	BB-IB	HP	SO	AVG	OBP	SLG	AOPS	ABR	SB-CS	FA	FR	RNG	THR	GAMES AT POSITION	DL	BFW
2004	Sea A	57	207	22	48	13	0	5	22	8-0	1	31	.232	.263	.367	65	-11	0-1	.956	-18	77	67	S57/3		-2.4
2005	Sea A	54	190	18	47	19	0	2	25	6-0	4	25	.247	.282	.379	80	-5	4-2	.979	9	109	95	2b51/3		0.6
Total	2	111	397	46	95	32	0	7	47	14-0	5	56	.239	.272	.373	72	-16	4-3	.956	-9	77	67	S57,2b51,3b2		-1.8

LOPEZ, LUIS Luis B10.5.1973 Brooklyn NY BR/TR/6-0/205* d4.29 Col Coastal Carolina

YEAR	TM LG	G	AB	R	H	2B	3B	HR	RBI	BB-IB	HP	SO	AVG	OBP	SLG	AOPS	ABR	SB-CS	FA	FR	RNG	THR	GAMES AT POSITION	DL	BFW
2001	Tor A	41	119	10	29	4	0	3	10	8-1	0	16	.244	.291	.353	67	-6	0-0	.936	1	113	87	3b28,1b5,D4		-0.4
2004	Mon N	11	26	0	4	0	0	0	0	0-0	1	9	.154	.185	.154	-10	-4	0-0	1.000	-1	45	94	1b8		-0.6
Total	2	52	145	10	33	4	0	3	10	8-1	1	25	.228	.273	.317	53	-10	0-0	.936	0	113	87	3b28,1b13,D4		-1.0

LOPEZ, LUIS Luis Antonio B9.1.1964 Brooklyn NY BR/TR/6-1/190* [LAN83 2/48] d9.14

YEAR	TM LG	G	AB	R	H	2B	3B	HR	RBI	BB-IB	HP	SO	AVG	OBP	SLG	AOPS	ABR	SB-CS	FA	FR	RNG	THR	GAMES AT POSITION	DL	BFW
1990	LA N	6	6	0	0	0	0	0	0	0-0	0	2	.000	.000	.000	-99	-2	0-0	1.000	-0	0	333	/1		-0.2
1991	Cle A	35	82	7	18	4	1	0	7	4-1	1	7	.220	.261	.293	53	-5	0-0	1.000	-1	86	138	C12,1b10/3OLD		-0.7
Total	2	41	88	7	18	4	1	0	7	4-1	1	9	.205	.245	.273	43	-7	0-0	1.000	-2	86	138	C12,1b11,D6/OL3		-0.9

LOPEZ, LUIS Luis Manuel (Santos) B9.4.1970 Cidra, PR BB/TR/5-11/166(166-185) d9.7 OF(8/0/1) [DL 1995 SD N 160]

YEAR	TM LG	G	AB	R	H	2B	3B	HR	RBI	BB-IB	HP	SO	AVG	OBP	SLG	AOPS	ABR	SB-CS	FA	FR	RNG	THR	GAMES AT POSITION	DL	BFW
1993	SD N	17	43	1	5	1	0	0	1	0-0	0	8	.116	.114	.140	-32	-8	0-0	.983	-2	90	65	2b15		-1.0
1994	SD N	77	235	29	65	16	1	2	20	15-2	3	39	.277	.325	.379	86	-5	3-2	.941	1	104	89	S43,2b29,3b5		0.0
1996	†SD N	63	139	10	25	3	0	2	11	9-1	1	35	.180	.233	.245	32	-15	0-0	.981	-7	92	76	S35,2b20,3b4	49	-1.9
1997	NY N	78	178	19	48	12	1	1	19	12-2	4	42	.270	.330	.365	86	-4	2-6	.966	9	113	117	S45,2b20,3b4		0.7
1998	NY N	117	266	37	67	13	2	2	22	20-3	4	60	.252	.312	.338	74	-10	2-2	.975	-3	93	81	2b50,S39,3b11,O9(8/0/1)		-1.1
1999	NY N	68	104	11	22	4	0	2	13	12-0	1	33	.212	.308	.308	60	-6	1-1	.971	-1	106	93	S45,2b22,3b6		-0.5
2000	Mil N	78	201	24	53	14	0	6	27	9-1	5	35	.264	.309	.423	84	-5	1-2	.959	-1	100	120	S45,2b22,3b6		-0.3
2001	Mil N	92	222	22	60	8	3	4	18	14-2	5	44	.270	.326	.387	86	-5	0-1	.922	0	93	150	3b46,S17,2b15		-0.4
2002	Mil N	6	8	1	0	0	0	0	0	2-0	0	1	.000	.200	.000	-40	-2	0-0	1.000	-2	22	0	S4	49	-1.3
	Bal A	52	109	10	23	6	0	2	9	3-0	1	20	.211	.232	.321	47	-9	1-0	.967	-6	114	60	S22,2b12/1D		-1.1
2004	Bal A	56	88	7	16	5	0	1	8	3-0	1	20	.182	.211	.273	27	-10	0-0	.944	-2	92	116	S14,3b11,1b6,2b6,D8	105	-1.3
2005	Cin N	17	27	0	6	3	0	0	2	0-0	1	6	.222	.207	.333	53	-2	0-0	.900	-1	60	0	3b6,2b4		-0.3
Total	12	721	1620	171	390	85	7	22	151	100-11	26	343	.241	.293	.343	67	-81	10-12	.959	-14	101	102	S297,2b211,3b100,D9,O9L,1b7	363	-7.5

LOPEZ, MENDY Mendy (Aude) B10.15.1973 Pimentel, D.R. BR/TR/6-2/190* d6.3

YEAR	TM LG	G	AB	R	H	2B	3B	HR	RBI	BB-IB	HP	SO	AVG	OBP	SLG	AOPS	ABR	SB-CS	FA	FR	RNG	THR	GAMES AT POSITION	DL	BFW
1998	KC A	74	206	18	50	10	2	1	15	12-0	1	40	.243	.286	.325	57	-13	5-2	.955	12	115	123	S72,3b2		0.3
1999	KC A	7	20	2	8	0	1	0	3	0-0	1	5	.400	.429	.500	131	1	0-0	1.000	-1	96	120	2b6/S		0.0
2000	Fla N	4	3	0	0	0	0	0	0	1-0	0	1	.000	.250	.000	-31	-1	0-0	—	0			/H		-0.1
2001	Hou N	10	15	3	4	0	0	1	3	2-0	1	4	.267	.389	.467	112	0	0-0	1.000	-1	44	0	2b3,3b2		-0.1
	Pit N	22	43	5	10	3	1	0	4	4-1	0	16	.233	.292	.349	65	-2	0-0	.970	2	101	89	2b9,S6,3b4		0.0
	Year	32	58	8	14	3	1	1	7	6-1	1	20	.241	.318	.379	78	-2	0-0	.975	1	90	72	2b12,3b6,S6		-0.1
2002	Pit N	3	3	0	0	0	0	0	0	0-0	0	3	.000	.000	.000	-98	-1	0-0	—	0			/H		-0.1
2003	KC A	52	94	13	26	5	1	3	11	4-0	1	28	.277	.306	.447	89	-2	2-0	1.000	-2	206	50	1b17,3b13,2b11,S4,O3(1/0/2)	58	-0.3
2004	KC A	18	38	4	4	1	0	1	4	4-0	1	9	.105	.209	.184	4	-6	0-0	.941	-3	61	80	2b6,3b4,S4,O4(2/0/2),1b2		-0.8
Total	7	190	422	45	102	18	5	6	40	27-1	4	106	.242	.292	.351	64	-24	7-2	.957	7	114	126	S87,2b35,3b25,1b19,O7(3/0/4)	58	-1.1

LOPEZ, PEDRO Pedro Michel B4.28.1984 Moca, D.R. BR/TR/6-1/160 d5.1

YEAR	TM LG	G	AB	R	H	2B	3B	HR	RBI	BB-IB	HP	SO	AVG	OBP	SLG	AOPS	ABR	SB-CS	FA	FR	RNG	THR	GAMES AT POSITION	DL	BFW
2005	Chi A	2	7	1	2	0	0	0	0	0-0	0	0	.286	.286	.286	51	-1	0-0	1.000	0	166	319	/2S		0.0

LOPEZ, MICKEY Raymond Michael B11.17.1973 Miami FL BB/TR/5-9/170 [MilA95 13/348] d9.6 Col Florida St.

YEAR	TM LG	G	AB	R	H	2B	3B	HR	RBI	BB-IB	HP	SO	AVG	OBP	SLG	AOPS	ABR	SB-CS	FA	FR	RNG	THR	GAMES AT POSITION	DL	BFW
2004	Sea A	6	4	1	1	0	0	0	0	1-0	1	0	.250	.500	.250	110	0	0-0	1.000	0	139	0	2b3,D3		0.0

LORD, BRIS Bristol Robotham "The Human Eyeball" B9.21.1883 Upland PA D11.13.1964 Prince Frederick MD BR/TR/5-9/185 d4.21

YEAR	TM LG	G	AB	R	H	2B	3B	HR	RBI	BB-IB	HP	SO	AVG	OBP	SLG	AOPS	ABR	SB-CS	FA	FR	RNG	THR	GAMES AT POSITION	DL	BFW
1905	†Phi A	66	238	38	57	14	0	0	13	14	1		.239	.285	.298	83	-4	3	.963	3	142	216	O61(4/38/19)		-0.8
1906	Phi A	118	434	50	101	13	7	1	44	27	2		.233	.281	.302	80	-11	12	.941	-3	91	130	O115(5/103/7)		-2.2
1907	Phi A	57	170	12	31	3	0	1	11	14	1		.182	.249	.218	48	-10	2	.951	-2	88	0	O53(10/40/4)/P		0.0
1909	Cle A	69	249	26	67	7	3	1	25	8	1		.269	.295	.333	94	-3	10	.992	7	154	215	O67(48/3/16)		-0.0
1910	Cle A	58	210	23	46	8	7	0	17	12	2		.219	.268	.324	84	-5	4	.958	4	90	184	O56(24/0/32)		-0.0
	†Phi A	70	279	54	78	13	11	1	20	23	1		.280	.337	.416	137	11	6	.980	1	112	61	O70(64/4/2)		0.0
	Year	128	489	77	124	21	18	1	37	35	3		.254	.307	.376	114	6	10	.972	5	103	112	O126(88/4/34)		0.0
1911	†Phi A	134	574	92	178	37	11	3	55	35	5		.310	.355	.429	120	14	15	.963	-2	99	78	O132(122/1/9)		-1.1
1912	Phi A	97	378	63	90	12	9	2	25	34	5		.238	.309	.317	82	-9	15	.942	-2	90	100	O97(19/0/78)		-1.1
1913	Bos N	73	235	22	59	12	1	6	26	26	0	22	.251	.276	.387	86	-5	7-6	.914	-6	85	59	O62(25/3/35)		-1.1
Total	8	742	2767	380	707	119	49	13	236	175	18	22	.256	.304	.348	95	-22	74-6	.957	2	106	113	O713(321/192/202)/P		-6.1

LORD, HARRY Harry Donald B3.8.1882 Porter ME D8.9.1948 Westbrook ME BL/TR/5-10.5/165 d9.25 M1 Col Bates

YEAR	TM LG	G	AB	R	H	2B	3B	HR	RBI	BB-IB	HP	SO	AVG	OBP	SLG	AOPS	ABR	SB-CS	FA	FR	RNG	THR	GAMES AT POSITION	DL	BFW
1907	Bos A	10	38	4	6	1	0	0	3	1	0		.158	.179	.184	16	-4	1	.919	0	106	0	3b10		-0.
1908	Bos A	145	560	61	145	15	6	2	37	22	8		.259	.297	.318	97	-3	23	.902	-8	94	83	3b144		-0.
1909	Bos A	136	534	89	168	12	7	0	31	20	8		.315	.349	.363	122	12	36	.929	-10	95	59	3b134		-0.
1910	Bos A	77	288	25	72	5	3	0	10	14	0		.250	.294	.313	88	-5	17	.927	-5	92	105	3b70/S		-0.
	Chi A	44	165	26	49	6	3	0	14	14	0		.297	.352	.370	132	6	17	.935	-10	89	94	3b44		0.
	Year	121	453	51	121	11	8	1	42	28	4		.267	.315	.333	103	0	34	.930	-15	90	100	3b114/S		0.
1911	Chi A	141	561	103	180	18	13	3	61	32	6		.321	.364	.433	126	16	43	.941	-19	80	117	3b138		-2
1912	Chi A	151	570	81	152	19	12	5	54	52	5		.267	.333	.368	104	2	30	.895	-25	79	77	3b106,O45(32/4/9)		-3.
1913	Chi A	150	547	62	144	18	12	1	42	45	7	39	.263	.327	.346	98	-3	24	.924	-29	81	70	3b150		-0.
1914	Chi A	21	69	8	13	1	1	1	3	5	0	3	.188	.243	.275	57	-4	2-2	.933	-2	101	0	3b19/OL		-2.
1915	Buf F	97	359	50	97	12	6	1	21	21	0	15	.270	.311	.345	83	-15	15	.946	-8	94	100	3b92/ORM		-9.
Total	9	972	3691	509	1026	107	70	14	294	226	38	57	.278	.326	.356	104	2	208-2	.924	-111	82		3b907,O47(33/4/10)/S		

LORD, CARLTON William Carlton B1.7.1900 Philadelphia PA D8.15.1947 Chester PA BR/TR/5-11/170 d7.12

YEAR	TM LG	G	AB	R	H	2B	3B	HR	RBI	BB-IB	HP	SO	AVG	OBP	SLG	AOPS	ABR	SB-CS	FA	FR	RNG	THR	GAMES AT POSITION	DL	BFW
1923	Phi N	17	47	3	11	2	0	0	2	2	0	3	.234	.265	.277	39	-4	0-1	.833	-2	100	40	3b14		-0.

LORETTA, MARK Mark David B8.14.1971 Santa Monica CA BR/TR/6-0/186(175-190) [MilA93 7/207] d9.4 Col Northwestern

YEAR	TM LG	G	AB	R	H	2B	3B	HR	RBI	BB-IB	HP	SO	AVG	OBP	SLG	AOPS	ABR	SB-CS	FA	FR	RNG	THR	GAMES AT POSITION	DL	BFW
1995	Mil A	19	50	13	13	3	0	1	3	4-0	1	7	.260	.327	.380	79	-2	1-1	.979	-3	100	64	S13,2b4/D		-0.
1996	Mil A	73	154	20	43	3	0	1	13	14-0	0	15	.279	.339	.318	65	-8	2-1	.989	-2	107	91	2b28,3b23,S21		-0.
1997	Mil A	132	418	56	120	17	5	5	47	47-2	2	60	.287	.354	.388	95	-3	5-5	.980	5	105	148	2b63,S44,1b19,3b15/D		1
1998	Mil A	140	434	55	137	29	6	5	54	42-1	7	47	.316	.382	.424	111	7	9-6	.992	6	79	119	1b70,S56,3b22,2b13/OL		-1
1999	Mil N	153	587	93	170	34	6	5	67	52-1	10	59	.290	.354	.390	89	-9	4-3	.986	-4	92	92	S74,1b66,2b17,3b14		-1
2000	Mil N	91	352	49	99	21	1	7	40	37-2	1	38	.281	.350	.406	91	-4	0-3	.995	-1	107	95	S90/2	75	-0.
2001	Mil N	102	384	40	111	14	2	0	28	28-0	1	46	.289	.346	.352	84	-9	1-2	.992	-7	88	67	2b52,3b39,S9/PD	48	-0.
2002	Mil N	86	217	23	58	14	0	2	19	23-1	5	32	.267	.350	.359	92	-3	0-0	.991	-7	88	67	3b47,S12,1b5,2b3		-0.

YEAR	TM LG	G	AB	R	H	2B	3B	HR	RBI	BB-IB	HP	SO	AVG	OBP	SLG	AOPS	ABR	SB-CS	FA	FR	RNG	THR	GAMES AT POSITION	DL	BFW
	Hou N	21	66	10	28	4	0	2	8	9-0	0	5	.424	.481	.576	171	7	1-1	.944	-1	66	58	3b10,S6,2b3/D		0.7
	Year	107	283	33	86	18	0	4	27	32-1	5	37	.304	.381	.410	112	5	1-1	.984	-7	84	65	3b57,S18,2b6,1b5/D		-0.2
2003	SD N	154	589	74	185	28	4	13	72	54-2	3	62	.314	.372	.441	123	19	5-4	.990	-6	97	84	2b150,S3		2.0
2004	SD N★	154	620	108	208	47	2	16	76	58-3	5	45	.335	.391	.495	136	36	5-3	.987	4	102	112	2b154		4.6
2005	†SD N	105	404	54	113	16	1	3	38	45-4	8	34	.280	.360	.347	92	-3	8-4	.987	-17	85	91	2b105/3	60	-1.5
Total	11	1230	4275	595	1285	230	20	63	466	413-16	53	450	.301	.365	.408	103	30	41-31	.987	-22	99	103	2b593,S328,3b171,1b160,D7/POL	183	4.3

LOUCKS, SCOTT Scott Gregory B11.11.1956 Anchorage AK BR/TR/6-0/178* [HouN77 5/118] d9.1 Col Southeastern Oklahoma [DL 1984 Hou N 61]

YEAR	TM LG	G	AB	R	H	2B	3B	HR	RBI	BB-IB	HP	SO	AVG	OBP	SLG	AOPS	ABR	SB-CS	FA	FR	RNG	THR	GAMES AT POSITION	DL	BFW
1980	Hou N	8	3	4	1	0	0	0	0	0-0	0	2	.333	.333	.333	94	0	0-0	1.000	-0	52	0	O4(0/2/2)		0.0
1981	Hou N	10	7	2	4	0	0	0	0	1-0	0	3	.571	.625	.571	256	2	0-0	1.000	-0	91	0	O5C		0.2
1982	Hou N	44	49	6	11	2	0	0	3	3-0	0	17	.224	.269	.265	54	-3	4-1	.978	3	114	343	O37C		0.0
1983	Hou N	7	14	2	3	0	0	0	0	1-0	0	4	.214	.267	.214	37	-1	2-2	1.000	-1	127	533	O6(1/5/0)		0.0
1985	Pit N	4	7	1	2	2	0	0	1	2-0	0	2	.286	.444	.571	184	1	0-0	1.000	-0	63	0	O4(3/0/1)		0.0
Total	5	73	80	15	21	4	0	0	4	7-0	0	28	.262	.322	.313	83	-1	7-3	.985	3	108	304	O56(4/49/3)	61	0.3

LOUDEN, BALDY William P. B8.27.1883 Pittsburgh PA D12.8.1935 Piedmont WV BR/TR/5-11/175 d9.13

YEAR	TM LG	G	AB	R	H	2B	3B	HR	RBI	BB-IB	HP	SO	AVG	OBP	SLG	AOPS	ABR	SB-CS	FA	FR	RNG	THR	GAMES AT POSITION	DL	BFW
1907	NY A	4	9	4	1	0	0	0	2	0			.111	.273	.111	21	-1	0-0	.750	-0	111	0	3b3		-0.1
1912	Det A	122	403	57	97	12	4	1	36	58	11		.241	.352	.298	89	-2	27	.951	18	126	81	2b87,3b26,S5		1.8
1913	Det A	76	191	28	46	4	5	0	23	24	6	22	.241	.344	.314	94	-1	6	.906	1	106	67	2b30,3b26,S6,O5(0/1/4)		0.1
1914	Buf F	126	431	73	135	11	4	6	63	52	3	41	.313	.391	.399	113	3	35	.931	-19	81	83	S115		-0.8
1915	Buf F	141	469	67	132	18	5	4	48	64	4	45	.281	.372	.367	106	0	30	.978	12	104	100	2b88,S27,3b19		1.7
1916	Cin N	134	439	38	96	16	4	1	32	54	6	54	.219	.313	.280	85	-6	12	.968	17	111	107	2b108,S23		1.6
Total	6	603	1942	267	507	61	22	12	202	254	30	162	.261	.355	.334	98	-7	111	.961	28	113	94	2b313,S176,3b74,O5(0/1/4)		4.3

LOUDENSLAGER, CHARLIE Charles Edward B5.21.1881 Baltimore MD D10.31.1933 Baltimore MD TR/5-9/186 d4.15

| 1904 | Bro N | 1 | 2 | 0 | 0 | 0 | 0 | 0 | 0 | 0 | 0 | 0 | .000 | .000 | .000 | -99 | 0 | | 1.000 | -0 | 70 | 0 | /2 | | -0.1 |

LOUGHLIN B Baltimore MD d5.9

| 1883 | Bal AA | 1 | 5 | 0 | 2 | 0 | 0 | 0 | | 0 | | | .400 | .400 | .400 | 154 | 0 | | — | -0 | 0 | 0 | /OR | | 0.0 |

LOUGHRAN, BILL William H. B6.1862 New York NY D8.7.1917 New York NY d6.6 Col Manhattan

| 1884 | NY N | 9 | 29 | 4 | 3 | 1 | 1 | 0 | 3 | 7 | | 11 | .103 | .278 | .207 | 54 | -1 | | .857 | -2 | | | C9/OR | | -0.3 |

LOVELACE, TOM Thomas Rivers B10.19.1897 Wolfe City TX D7.12.1979 Dallas TX BR/TR/5-11/170 d9.23

| 1922 | Pit N | 1 | 1 | 0 | 0 | 0 | 0 | 0 | 0 | 0 | 0 | 0 | .000 | .000 | .000 | -99 | 0 | 0-0 | — | 0 | | | /H | | 0.0 |

LOVETT, LEN Leonard Walker B7.17.1852 Lancaster Co. PA D11.18.1922 Newark DE BR/TR d8.4 ▲

1873	Res NA	1	5	1	2	0	0	0		1	0		.400	.400	.400	150	1	0-0	.500	-0	68	0	/P		0.0
1875	Cen NA	6	21	2	5	1	0	0	2	1		5	.238	.273	.286	103	0	0-0	.700	-0	136	0	O6(1/0/5)		0.0
Total	2 NA	7	26	3	7	1	0	0	3	1		5	.269	.296	.308	113	0	0-0	.700	-1	136	0	O6(1/0/5)/P		0.0

LOVETT, MEM Merritt Marwood B6.15.1912 Chicago IL D9.19.1995 Downers Grove IL BR/TR/5-9.5/165 d9.4

| 1933 | Chi A | 1 | 1 | 0 | 0 | 0 | 0 | 0 | 0 | 0 | 0 | 0 | .000 | .000 | .000 | -99 | 0 | 0-0 | — | 0 | | | /H | | 0.0 |

LOVIGLIO, JAY John Paul B5.30.1956 Freeport NY BR/TR/5-9/160* d9.2 Col Suffolk (NY) CC

1980	Phi N	16	5	7	0	0	0	0		1-0	0	0	.000	.167	.000	-47	-1	1-2	1.000	-1	60	0	/2		-0.2
1981	Chi A	14	15	5	4	0	0	0	2	1-0	0	1	.267	.313	.267	69	-1	2-2	.786	0	100	347	3b4,2b3,D2		-0.1
1982	Chi A	15	31	5	6	0	0	0	2	1-0	0	4	.194	.219	.194	14	-4	2-1	.964	1	107	72	2b13,D2		-0.3
1983	Chi N	1	1	0	1	0	0	0		0-0	0		1.000	1.000	1.000	-95	0	0-0	—	0			/H		0.0
Total	4	46	52	17	10	0	0	0	4	3-0	0	6	.192	.236	.192	21	-6	5-5	.971	0	99	57	2b17,D4,3b4		-0.6

LOVITTO, JOE Joseph B1.6.1951 San Pedro CA D5.19.2001 Arlington TX BB/TR/6-0/185* [TexA69*1/2] d4.15

1972	Tex A	117	330	23	74	9	1	1	19	37-2	2	54	.224	.306	.267	74	-10	13-11	.976	4	109	114	O103(8/77/23)		-1.2
1973	Tex A	26	44	3	6	1	0	0		5-0	0	7	.136	.224	.159	10	-5	1-0	.898	0	80	109	3b20,O3(0/2/1)		-0.5
1974	Tex A	113	283	27	63	9	3	2	26	25-4	0	36	.223	.285	.297	69	-11	6-8	.972	-5	92	119	O107(0/105/2),1b5		-2.2
1975	Tex A	50	106	17	22	3	0	1	8	13-1	0	16	.208	.289	.264	59	-6	2-2	.985	-1	89	150	O38(18/25/0),1b2/CD		-0.8
Total	4	306	763	70	165	22	4	4	53	80-7	2	113	.216	.291	.271	66	-32	22-21	.975	-2	99	120	O251(26/209/26),3b20,1b7,D2/C	40	-4.7

LOVULLO, TOREY Salvatore Anthony B7.25.1965 Santa Monica CA BB/TR/6-0/180* [DetA87 5/131] d9.10 Col UCLA OF(1/0/2)

1988	Det A	12	21	2	8	1	0	2		1-0	0	2	.381	.409	.667	203	3	0-0	1.000	-0	101	53	2b9,3b3		0.3
1989	Det A	29	87	8	10	2	0	1	4	14-0	0	20	.115	.233	.172	18	-9	0-0	1.000	-1	37	81	1b18,3b11		-1.2
1991	NY A	22	51	0	9	2	0	0	2	5-1	0	7	.176	.250	.216	30	-5	0-0	.940	1	106	33	3b22		-0.8
1993	Cal A	116	367	42	92	20	0	6	30	36-1	1	49	.251	.318	.354	78	-11	7-6	.981	-0	98	121	2b91,3b14,S9,O2R/1		-0.8
1994	Sea A	36	72	9	16	5	0	2	7	9-1	0	13	.222	.309	.375	73	-3	1-0	1.000	2	113	87	2b30,3b5,D2		0.0
1996	Oak A	65	82	15	18	4	0	3	9	11-0	2	17	.220	.323	.378	78	-3	1-2	1.000	-1	94	160	1b42,3b11,2b2/SOLD		-0.2
1998	Cle A	6	19	1	4	1	0	0	1	1-0	0	2	.211	.250	.263	33	-2	0-0	.947	0	112	111	2b5/3		-0.5
1999	Phi N	17	38	3	8	0	0	2	5	3-0	0	11	.211	.268	.368	58	-3	0-0	1.000	0			1b6,2b6		-0.3
Total	8	303	737	80	165	35	1	15	60	80-3	3	121	.224	.301	.335	69	-33	9-8	.984	-0	99	109	2b133,1b67,3b67,S10,D6,O3R		-3.1

LOW, FLETCHER Fletcher B4.7.1893 Essex MA D6.6.1973 Hanover NH BR/TR/5-10.5/175 d10.7 Col Dartmouth

| 1915 | Bos N | 1 | 4 | 1 | 1 | 0 | 1 | 0 | 1 | 0 | 0 | 0 | .250 | .250 | .750 | 207 | 0 | 0 | 1.000 | -0 | 50 | 0 | /3 | | 0.0 |

LOWE, CHARLIE Charles B Baltimore MD d9.24

| 1872 | Atl NA | 7 | 31 | 2 | 5 | 0 | 0 | 0 | 3 | 0 | | 2 | .161 | .161 | .161 | -0 | -4 | 0-0 | .827 | -1 | 88 | 30 | 2b7 | | -0.4 |

LOWE, DICK Richard Alvern B1.28.1854 Evansville WI D6.28.1922 Janesville WI d6.26

| 1884 | Det N | 1 | 3 | 0 | 1 | 0 | 0 | 0 | 0 | 0 | | 1 | .333 | .333 | .333 | 117 | 0 | | .125 | -3 | | | /C | | -0.3 |

LOWE, BOBBY Robert Lincoln "Link" B7.10.1865 Pittsburgh PA D12.8.1951 Detroit MI BR/TR/5-10/150 d4.19 M1 OF(173/56/11)

1890	Bos N	52	207	35	58	13	2	2	21	26	2	32	.280	.366	.391	112	-3	15	.951	-7	88	14	S24,O15(3/11/1),3b12		-0.3
1891	Bos N	125	497	92	129	19	5	6	74	53	5	54	.260	.342	.354	92	-6	43	.927	-5	99	82	O107(64/38/5),2b17,S2/3P		-1.2
1892	†Bos N	124	475	75	115	16	7	3	57	37	8	47	.242	.308	.324	83	-11	36	.928	11	120	74	O90(87/3/0),3b14,S13,2b10		-0.6
1893	Bos N	126	526	130	157	19	5	14	89	55	4	29	.298	.369	.433	105	1	22	.936	1	104	111	2b121,S5		0.6
1894	Bos N	133	613	158	212	34	11	17	115	50	6	25	.346	.401	.520	112	9	23	.927	-7	98	106	2b130,S2/3		0.6
1895	Bos N	100	417	102	124	12	7	7	62	40	8	16	.297	.370	.410	94	-5	24	.954	10	106	126	2b100		0.8
1896	Bos N	73	306	59	98	11	4	2	48	20	1	12	.320	.370	.402	98	-2	15	.965	18	117	104	2b73		1.6
1897	†Bos N	123	499	87	154	24	8	5	106	32	4		.309	.355	.419	98	-3	16	.952	-9	101	99	2b123		-0.6
1898	Bos N	147	559	65	152	11	7	4	94	29	3		.272	.311	.338	82	-16	12	.958	12	100	124	2b145,S2		0.3
1899	Bos N	152	559	81	152	5	9	4	88	35	1		.272	.316	.335	72	-24	17	.954	-1	99	129	2b148,S4		-1.7
1900	Bos N	127	474	65	132	11	5	3	71	26	5		.278	.323	.342	74	-18	15	.951	-9	93	78	2b127		-2.0
1901	Bos N	129	491	47	125	11	1	3	47	17	3		.255	.284	.299	63	-24	22	.912	-6	88	110	3b111,2b18		-2.6
1902	Chi N	121	480	44	119	13	3	0	35	12	5		.248	.274	.287	75	-15	17	.956	18	111	136	2b119,3b2		0.3
1903	Chi N	32	105	14	28	5	3	0	15	4			.267	.319	.371	99	-1	5	.948	2	118	125	2b22,1b6/3		0.2
1904	Pit N	1	1	0	0	0	0	0	0	0			.000	.000	.000	-97	-0		—	0			/H		0.0
	Det A	140	506	47	105	14	6	0	40	17	2		.208	.236	.259	58	-25	15	.964	0	98	103	2b140,M		-2.7
1905	Det A	58	181	17	35	7	2	0	9	13	2		.193	.266	.254	61	-8	3	.980	2	196	0	O24(17/3/4),3b22,2b6,S4/1		-0.8
1906	Det A	41	145	11	30	3	0	1	12	4	1		.207	.233	.248	49	-3	3	.915	4	114	14	S19,2b17,3b5		-0.4
1907	Det A	17	37	2	9	0	0	0	5	4	0		.243	.317	.297	93	-0	0	.870	-2	101	0	3b10,O4(2/1/1),S2		-0.2
Total	18	1821	7078	1135	1934	230	85	71	988	474	71	215	.273	.325	.360	86	-154	303	.951	33	102	109	2b1316,O240L,3b179,S77,1b7/P		-8.7

LOWELL, MIKE Michael Averett B2.24.1974 San Juan, PR BR/TR/6-4/205(193-212) [NYA95 20/562] d9.13 Col Florida International

1998	NY A	8	15	1	4	0	0	0		0-0	1	5	.267	.267	.267	40	-1	0-0	1.000	-1	66	162	3b7		-0.2
1999	Fla N	97	308	32	78	15	0	12	47	26-1	5	69	.253	.317	.419	90	-5	0-0	.981	-3	97	82	3b83	54	-0.8
2000	Fla N	140	508	73	137	38	0	22	91	54-4	9	75	.270	.344	.474	111	9	4-0	.968	4	102	74	3b136	15	1.4
2001	Fla N	146	551	65	156	37	0	18	100	43-3	10	79	.283	.340	.448	107	6	1-2	.976	10	103	138	3b144		1.5
2002	Fla N★	160	597	88	165	44	0	24	92	65-5	4	92	.276	.346	.471	122	16	4-3	.969	1	94	109	3b159		1.8
2003	†Fla N★	130	492	76	136	27	1	32	105	56-6	2	78	.276	.350	.530	132	22	3-1	.973	-3	93	119	3b128,D2	28	1.9
2004	Fla N★	158	598	87	175	44	1	27	85	64-8	6	77	.293	.365	.505	129	26	5-1	.982	-3	92	114	3b154,D3		2.5

YEAR	TM LG	G	AB	R	H	2B	3B	HR	RBI	BB-IB	HP	SO	AVG	OBP	SLG	AOPS	ABR	SB-CS	FA	FR	RNG	THR	GAMES AT POSITION	DL	BFW
2005	Fla N	150	500	56	118	36	1	8	58	46-1	2	58	.236	.298	.360	77	-17	4-0	.983	-1	94	134	3b135,2b8		-1.5
Total	8	989	3569	478	969	241	3	143	578	354-28	39	529	.272	.339	.461	111	56	21-7	.976	3	96	112	3b946,2b8,D5	97	6.6

LOWENSTEIN, JOHN John Lee B1.27.1947 Wolf Point MT BL/TR/6-0/175* [CleA68 18/402] d9.2 Col California-Riverside OF(687/49/201)

																									0.4
1970	Cle A	17	43	5	11	3	1	1	6	1-0	0	9	.256	.273	.442	90	-1	1-0	1.000	4	146	96	2b10,3b2,O2L/S		
1971	Cle A	58	140	15	26	5	0	4	9	16-1	0	28	.186	.269	.307	57	-8	1-5	.986	0	87	93	2b29,O18(7/5/8),S3	31	0.0
1972	Cle A	68	151	16	32	8	1	6	21	20-0	0	43	.212	.304	.397	104	1	2-4	1.000	3	91	219	O58(27/3/29),1b2		0.3
1973	Cle A	98	305	42	89	16	1	6	40	23-0	0	41	.292	.338	.410	108	3	5-3	.931	1	70	166	O51(12/4/36),2b25,3b8/1D		-0.8
1974	Cle A	140	508	65	123	14	2	8	48	53-2	2	85	.242	.313	.325	85	-9	36-17	.986	5	99	89	O100(88/8/7),3b28,1b12,2b4		-0.7
1975	Cle A	91	265	37	64	5	1	12	33	28-2	1	28	.242	.313	.404	101	0	15-10	.983	-4	82	77	O36(19/3/17),D31,3b8,2b2		-1.5
1976	Cle A	93	229	33	47	8	2	2	14	25-3	0	35	.205	.283	.284	67	-9	11-8	.972	-4	90	203	O61(13/19/29),D11,1b9		-0.6
1977	Cle A	81	149	24	36	6	1	4	12	21-1	0	29	.242	.335	.376	96	0	1-8	1.000	-1	100	46	O39(18/5/17),D19/1		0.3
1978	Tex A	77	176	28	39	8	3	5	21	37-2	2	29	.222	.363	.386	110	4	16-3	.992	4	116	106	O72(44/1/41)/13D	15	1.1
1979	†Bal A	97	197	33	50	8	2	11	34	30-3	1	37	.254	.351	.482	128	8	16-4	.992	1	106	69	O91(88/0/3),D3	23	0.8
1980	Bal A	104	196	38	61	8	0	4	27	32-1	0	29	.311	.403	.413	128	9	7-3	.992	1	106	69	O73(67/0/10),D4		-0.6
1981	Bal A	83	189	19	47	7	0	6	20	22-1	1	32	.249	.329	.381	105	1	7-6	.990	-4	86	77	O111(110/0/2)		2.9
1982	Bal A	122	322	69	103	15	2	24	66	54-10	1	59	.320	.415	.602	178	36	7-6	1.000	-2	102	35	O107(106/1/0)/2D		1.0
1983	†Bal A	122	310	52	87	13	2	15	60	49-1	1	55	.281	.374	.481	137	17	2-1	.982	-4	86	120	O67L,D22,1b2	18	-0.7
1984	Bal A	105	270	34	64	13	0	8	28	33-3	1	54	.237	.319	.374	94	-2	1-0	.971	-3	85	137	O906L,D125,3b72,2b71,1b28,S4		-0.5
1985	Bal A	12	26	0	2	0	0	0	2	2-0	1	3	.077	.138	.077	-39	-5	0-0	1.000	0	129		O4L,D6	87	0.6
Total	16	1368	3476	510	881	137	18	116	441	446-30	9	596	.253	.337	.403	108	45	128-78	.984	-2	94	108	O906L,D125,3b72,2b71,1b28,S4		

LOWERY, TERRELL Quenton Terrell B10.25.1970 Oakland CA BR/TR/6-3/180(180-195) [TexA91 2/63] d9.13 Col Loyola Marymount

																									0.2
1997	Chi N	9	14	2	4	0	0	0	3-0		0	3	.286	.412	.286	84	0	1-0	1.000	2	106	921	O6(5/2/0)		-0.1
1998	Chi N	24	15	2	3	1	0	0	1	3-0	0	7	.200	.333	.267	58	-1	0-0	.929	-1	101	0	O22(2/20/0)		-0.8
1999	TB A	66	185	25	48	15	1	2	17	19-0	1	53	.259	.330	.384	81	-5	0-2	.971	-2	87	133	O60(29/36/1)		0.5
2000	SF N	24	34	13	15	4	0	1	5	7-0	1	8	.441	.548	.647	214	7	1-0	.917	-1	72	0	O108(49/58/9)/D		-0.2
Total	4	123	248	42	70	20	1	3	23	32-0	2	71	.282	.367	.407	98	1	2-2	.964	-2	87	147	O108(49/58/9)/D		

LOWREY, PEANUTS Harry Lee B8.27.1917 Culver City CA D7.2.1986 Inglewood CA BR/TR/5-8.5/170* d4.14 Mil 1944 C17 OF(548/387/62)

																									-0.4
1942	Chi N	27	58	4	11	0	0	1	4	4	0	4	.190	.242	.241	43	-4	0	.978	2	112	143	O19(7/15/0)		1.2
1943	Chi N	130	480	59	140	25	12	1	63	35	0	24	.292	.340	.400	115	7	13	.982	6	106	121	O113C,S16,2b3		0.0
1945	†Chi N	143	523	72	148	22	7	7	89	48	0	27	.283	.343	.392	106	3	11	.987	4	95	176	O138(125/14/0),S2		-1.2
1946	Chi N★	144	540	75	139	24	5	4	54	56	1	22	.257	.328	.343	92	-6	10	.979	2	100	127	O126(73/60/0),3b20		0.3
1947	Chi N	115	448	56	126	17	5	5	37	38	1	26	.281	.339	.375	93	-5	2	.945	10	117	132	3b91,O25(18/6/1),2b6		-1.0
1948	Chi N	129	435	47	128	12	3	2	54	34	1	31	.294	.347	.349	93	-5	2	.983	-0	98	119	O103(63/43/0),3b9,2b2/S		-0.6
1949	Chi N	38	111	18	30	5	0	2	10	9	0	8	.270	.325	.369	88	-2	3	.995	-5	112	150	O78(77/1/0)		-0.3
	Cin N	89	309	48	85	16	2	2	25	37	1	11	.275	.354	.359	91	-3	1	.989	4	108	88	O109(105/4/1)/3		-0.9
	Year	127	420	66	115	21	2	4	35	46	1	19	.274	.347	.362	90	-5	4	.987	2	107	81	O72(66/2/6)/2		-1.6
1950	Cin N	91	264	34	60	14	0	1	11	36	0	7	.227	.320	.292	62	-14	0	1.000	1	96	85	2b6,3b5,O4(3/1/0)		-0.1
	StL N	17	56	10	15	0	0	1	4	6	1	1	.268	.333	.321	74	-2	0	.982	3	106	78	O76(69/3/6),2b7,3b5		-1.7
	Year	108	320	44	75	14	0	2	15	42	1	8	.234	.325	.297	64	-16	0	.983	-4	92	75	O85(13/74/0),3b11,2b3		-0.5
1951	StL N	114	370	52	112	19	5	5	40	35	2	12	.303	.366	.422	111	6	0-1	.978	-5	96	42	O106(63/35/6),3b6		-1.1
1952	StL N	132	374	48	107	18	2	1	48	34	1	13	.286	.352	.353	96	-1	3-2	1.000	-3	87	56	O38(3/10/25),2b10/3		-0.5
1953	StL N	104	182	26	49	9	2	5	27	15	1	21	.269	.325	.423	93	-2	1-0	1.000	-0	104	0	O12(3/1/9)		-0.5
1954	StL N	74	61	6	7	1	2	0	5	9	0	12	.115	.222	.197	12	-8	0-0	1.000	-0	104	0	O28(6/9/14),2b2/1		-1.3
1955	Phi N	54	106	9	20	4	0	1	8	7-0	0	10	.189	.237	.226	25	-12	2-0	.973	-1	95	73	O28(6/9/14),2b2/1		-7.9
Total	13	1401	4317	564	1177	186	45	37	479	403-0	11	226	.273	.336	.362	92	-48	48-3	.983	13	100	108	O978L,3b144,2b33,S19/1		

LOWRY, DWIGHT Dwight (b Dwight Lowery) B10.23.1957 Lumberton NC D7.10.1997 Jamestown NY BL/TR/6-3/210* [DetA80 11/278] d4.3 Col North Carolina-Asheville

																									0.1
1984	Det A	32	45	8	11	2	0	2	7	3-0	0	11	.244	.292	.422	95	0	0-0	1.000	1	107	83	C31		0.1
1986	Det A	56	150	21	46	4	0	3	18	17-0	4	19	.307	.392	.393	114	4	0-0	.992	-5	97	72	C55/1OR		-0.4
1987	Det A	13	25	0	5	2	0	0	1	0-0	0	6	.200	.200	.280	26	-3	0-0	1.000	-2	63	45	C12/1		-0.2
1988	Min A	7	7	0	0	0	0	0	0	0-0	0	2	.000	.000	.000	-97	-2	0-0	1.000	0	26	214	C5		-0.4
Total	4	108	227	29	62	8	0	5	26	20-0	4	38	.273	.343	.374	95	-1	0-0	.995	-6	94	75	C103,1b2/OR		

LOWRY, JOHN John D. B Baltimore MD d6.26

																									-0.3
1875	Was NA	6	22	2	3	0	0	0		1			.136	.174	.136	10	-2	0-1	.727	-1	0	0	O6C		

LOZADO, WILLIE William B5.12.1959 New York NY BR/TR/6-0/166 d7.16 Col Miami-Dade Wolfson (FL) CC

																									-0.3
1984	Mil A	43	107	15	29	8	2	1	20	12-0	0	23	.271	.339	.411	112	2	0-3	.925	-4	90	121	3b36,S6/2D		

LUBRATICH, STEVE Steven George B5.1.1955 Oakland CA BR/TR/6-0/170* d9.27 Col California-Riverside

																									-0.1
1981	Cal A	7	21	2	3	1	0	0	7	4-0	0	3	.143	.143	.190	-5	-3	1-0	1.000	2	139	185	3b6		-0.2
1983	Cal A	57	156	12	34	9	0	0	7	4-0	0	17	.218	.236	.276	41	-13	0-1	.949	9	105	130	S23,3b22,2b14		-0.3
Total	2	64	177	14	37	10	0	0	14	8-0	0	20	.209	.225	.266	36	-16	1-1	.988	10	134	143	3b28,S23,2b14		

LUBY, HUGH Hugh Max "Hal" B6.13.1913 Blackfoot ID D5.4.1986 Eugene OR BR/TR/5-10/185 d9.10 Mil 1945 Col Creighton

																									-0.8
1936	Phi N	9	38	3	7	1	0	0	3	1	0	7	.184	.205	.211	3	-6	2-0	.880	-3	98	48	2b9		1.5
1944	NY N	111	323	30	82	10	2	2	35	52	4	15	.254	.364	.316	93	0	2	.943	13	107	129	3b65,2b45/1		0.7
Total	2	120	361	33	89	11	2	2	38	52	5	22	.247	.349	.305	83	-6	4-0	.943	9	107	129	3b65,2b54/1		

LUCADELLO, JOHNNY John B2.22.1919 Thurber TX D10.30.2001 San Antonio TX BB/TR/5-11/160 d9.24 Mil 1942-45

																									-0.4
1938	StL A	7	20	1	3	1	0	0	0	0	0	0	.150	.150	.200	-13	-4	0-0	.909	-1	64	0	3b6		-0.5
1939	StL A	9	30	0	7	2	0	0	4	2	0	4	.233	.281	.300	48	-2	0-0	.912	-3	75	58	2b7		0.5
1940	StL A	17	63	15	20	4	2	2	10	6	2	4	.317	.394	.540	137	3	1-0	.968	1	107	116	2b16		-0.9
1941	StL A	107	351	58	98	22	4	2	31	48	0	23	.279	.366	.382	95	-1	5-2	.962	-13	98	87	2b70,S12,3b6/OL		-0.8
1946	StL A	87	210	21	52	7	1	1	15	36	0	20	.248	.358	.305	82	-3	0-1	.942	-5	98	52	3b37,2b19		-0.3
1947	NY A	12	12	0	1	0	0	0	0	1	0	5	.083	.154	.083	-33	-2	0-0	1.000	-1	0	0	2b5		-2.4
Total	6	239	686	95	181	36	7	5	60	93	2	56	.264	.353	.359	88	-9	6-3	.965	-22	97	0	2b117,3b49,S12/OL		

LUCAS, RED Charles Fred "The Nashville Narcissus" B4.28.1902 Columbia TN D7.9.1986 Nashville TN BL/TR/5-9.5/170 d4.19 ▲

																									0.0
1923	NY N	3	2	0	0	0	0	0	0	0	0	0	1.000	1.000	.000	-99	0	0-0	1.000	1	257		P3		0.0
1924	Bos N	33	33	5	11	1	0	0	5	1	0	4	.333	.353	.364	96	0	0-0	1.000	1	107	95	P27,3b2		-0.3
1925	Bos N	6	20	1	3	0	0	0	2	2	0	4	.150	.227	.150	-2	-3	0-0	.968	-0	109	122	2b6		-0.1
1926	Cin N	66	76	15	23	4	4	0	14	10	1	13	.303	.384	.461	130	3	0-0	.983	-4	97	84	P37,2b5,S3/OL		-0.3
1927	Cin N	80	150	14	47	5	4	0	28	12	1	10	.313	.368	.373	102	1	0-0	1.000	-0	95	137	P27		0.0
1928	Cin N	39	73	8	23	2	1	0	7	4	0	6	.315	.351	.370	90	6	0-0	.949	2	105	89	P32		0.0
1929	Cin N	76	140	15	41	6	0	0	13	13	0	15	.293	.353	.336	75	12	1	1.000	-3	70	69	P33		0.0
1930	Cin N	80	113	18	38	4	2	0	19	17	0	4	.336	.423	.442	115	16	0	.984	1	108	88	P29		0.0
1931	Cin N	97	153	15	43	0	0	0	17	12	0	9	.281	.333	.307	78	12	0	.973	1	98	126	P31		0.0
1932	Cin N	76	150	13	43	11	2	0	19	10	1	9	.287	.335	.387	97	15	0	1.000	0	107	98	P29		0.0
1933	Cin N	75	122	14	35	6	1	1	15	12	1	6	.287	.356	.377	111	13	1	.939	-3	67	98	P29		0.0
1934	Pit N	68	105	11	23	5	1	0	10	7	1	16	.219	.261	.286	45	3	1	.968	-1	87	77	P20		0.0
1935	Pit N	47	66	6	21	6	0	0	10	7	1	11	.318	.392	.409	112	4	0-0	.976	1	88	175	P27		0.0
1936	Pit N	69	108	11	26	4	1	0	17	3	0	17	.241	.293	.296	58	4	0-0	1.000	-2	70	76	P20		0.0
1937	Pit N	59	82	8	22	3	0	0	17	7	0	8	.268	.326	.305	72	-5	0	1.000	0	82	98	P13		0.0
1938	Pit N	33	46	3	5	0	0	0	0	2	0	6	.109	.163	.109	-24	-2	0	.981	-14	93	107	P396,2b12,S3,3b2/OL		-0.7
Total	16	907	1439	155	404	61	13	3	190	124	4	133	.281	.340	.347	84	93	2-0	.981	-14	93	107	P396,2b12,S3,3b2/OL		

LUCAS, FRED Frederick Warrington "Fritz" B1.19.1903 Vineland NJ D3.11.1987 Cambridge MD BR/TR/5-10/165 d7.15

																									-0.3
1935	Phi N	20	34	1	9	0	0	0	2	3	0	6	.265	.324	.265	55	-2	0	.944	-0	105	0	O10(4/3/3)		

LUCAS, JOHNNY John Charles "Buster" B2.10.1903 Glen Carbon IL D10.31.1970 Maryville IL BR/TL/5-10/186 d4.15

																									-0.1
1931	Bos A	3	2	0	2	0	0	0	0	0	0	0	1.000	.000	.000	-99	-1	0-0	—	-0	0	0	O2(1/1/0)		0.0
1932	Bos A	1	1	0	0	0	0	0	0	0	0	0	.000	.000	.000	-99	-1	0-0	.000	-0	0	0	/H		-0.1
Total	2	4	3	0	2	0	0	0	0	0	0	0	.000	.000	.000	-99	-1	0-0	.000	-0	0	0	O2(1/1/0)		

YEAR	TM LG	G	AB	R	H	2B	3B	HR	RBI	BB-IB	HP	SO	AVG	OBP	SLG	AOPS	ABR	SB-CS	FA	FR	RNG	THR	GAMES AT POSITION	DL	BFW

LUCE, FRANK Frank Edward B12.6.1896 Spencer OH D2.3.1942 Milwaukee WI BL/TR/5-11/180 d9.17
| 1923 | Pit N | 9 | 12 | 2 | 6 | 0 | 0 | 0 | 3 | 2 | | 0 | 2 | .500 | .571 | .500 | 181 | 2 | 2-1 | 1.000 | -0 | 89 | 0 | O5(3/1/1) | | 0.1 |

LUDERUS, FRED Frederick William B9.12.1885 Milwaukee WI D1.5.1961 Three Lakes WI BL/TR/5-11.5/185 d9.23
1909	Chi N	11	37	8	11	1	1	1	9	3	1		.297	.366	.459	152	2	0	.950	-2	67	88	1b11		0.0
1910	Chi N	24	54	5	11	1	1	0	3	4		0	.204	.259	.259	52	-4	0	.975	-1	88	93	1b17		-0.5
	Phi N	21	68	10	20	5	2	0	14	9	1		.294	.385	.426	132	3	2	.981	-0	111	135	1b19		0.3
	Year	45	122	15	31	6	3	0	17	13	1	8	.254	.331	.352	98	0	2	.981	-0	101	117	1b36		-0.2
1911	Phi N	146	551	69	166	24	11	16	99	40	4	76	.301	.353	.472	128	17	6	.985	-2	92	102	1b146		1.2
1912	Phi N	148	572	77	147	31	5	10	69	44	7	65	.257	.318	.381	85	-13	8	.990	10	128	96	1b146		-0.6
1913	Phi N	155	588	67	154	32	7	18	86	34	2	51	.262	.304	.432	105	1	5-8	.984	1	104	90	1b146		-0.4
1914	Phi N	121	443	55	110	16	5	12	55	33	5	31	.248	.308	.388	100	-1	2	.975	1	114	72	1b121		-0.3
1915	†Phi N	141	499	55	157	36	7	7	62	42	7	36	.315	.376	.457	150	31	9-7	.993	10	129	107	1b141		4.0
1916	Phi N	146	508	52	143	26	3	5	53	41	5	35	.281	.341	.374	115	10	8	.982	-2	99	109	1b146		0.6
1917	Phi N	154	522	57	136	24	4	5	72	65	6	35	.261	.349	.351	110	10	5	.991	4	109	102	1b154		1.1
1918	Phi N	125	468	54	135	23	2	5	67	42	3	33	.288	.351	.378	115	10	4	.988	6	119	95	1b125		1.4
1919	Phi N	138	509	60	149	30	6	5	49	54	4	48	.293	.365	.405	123	16	6	.985	9	131	92	1b138		2.4
1920	Phi N	16	32	1	5	2	0	0	4	3		6	.156	.229	.219	28	-3	0-1	.983	0	114	143	1b7		-0.4
Total	12	1346	4851	570	1344	251	54	84	642	414	45	421	.277	.340	.403	113	79	55-16	.986	37	113	97	1b1326		8.8

LUDWICK, RYAN Ryan Andrew B7.13.1978 Satellite Beach FL BR/TL/6-3/203* [OakA99 2/60] d6.5 b-Eric Col Nevada-Las Vegas
2002	Tex A	23	81	10	19	6	0	1	9	7-0		24	.235	.295	.346	68	-3	2-1	1.000	-3	75	0	O22(2/21/1)		-0.7
2003	Tex A	8	26	3	4	1	0	0	0	4-0	0	9	.154	.267	.192	23	-3	0-0	1.000	-0	98	0	O8(4/0/6)		-0.4
	Cle A	39	136	14	36	7	1	7	26	8-1	0	39	.265	.306	.485	104	0	2-0	1.000	1	108	105	O32(13/0/19),D4	20	0.0
	Year	47	162	17	40	8	1	7	26	12-1	0	48	.247	.299	.438	90	-2	2-0	1.000	1	106	83	O40(17/0/25),D4		-0.4
2004	Cle A	15	50	3	11	2	0	2	4	2-0	2	14	.220	.278	.380	72	-2	0-0	.970	-0	114	0	O15R	92	-0.3
2005	Cle A	19	41	8	9	0	0	4	5	7-0	1	13	.220	.333	.512	125	1	0-1	.957	-0	105	0	O15(9/0/6),D3		0.0
Total	4	104	334	38	79	16	1	14	44	28-1	2	99	.237	.299	.416	86	-8	4-2	.989	-3	99	39	O92(28/21/47),D7	112	-1.4

LUDWIG, BILL William Lawrence B5.27.1882 Louisville KY D9.5.1947 Louisville KY BR/TR d4.16
| 1908 | StL N | 66 | 187 | 15 | 34 | 2 | 2 | 0 | 16 | 8 | 0 | | .182 | .246 | .214 | 50 | -11 | 3 | .952 | -10 | 65 | 127 | C62 | | -1.8 |

LUEBBE, ROY Roy John B9.17.1900 Parkersburg IA D8.21.1985 Papillion NE BB/TR/6-0/175 d8.22
| 1925 | NY A | 8 | 15 | 1 | 0 | 0 | 0 | 0 | 3 | 2 | | 6 | .000 | .118 | .000 | -69 | -4 | 0-0 | 1.000 | 1 | 103 | 81 | C8 | | -0.3 |

LUFF, HENRY Henry T. B9.14.1856 Philadelphia PA D10.11.1916 Philadelphia PA 5-11/175 d4.19 ▲
1875	NH NA	38	166	15	45	10	3	2	18	0		5	.271	.271	.404	150	10	3-3	.689	-5	99	161	3b30,P10,O4(0/1/3)/S		0.2
1882	Det AA	3	11	1	3	2	0	0	1	0		0	.273	.273	.455	129	0		.667	-2	90	231	2b3/OC		-0.1
	Cin AA	28	120	16	28	2	2	0	6	2			.233	.246	.283	74	-4		.922	-2	95	112	1b27/OR		-0.8
1883	Lou AA	6	23	1	4	0	0	0		2			.174	.174	.174	13	-2		.868	-1	0	65	1b4,O2(0/1/1)		-0.3
1884	Phi U	26	111	9	30	4	2	0		4			.270	.296	.342	101	-3		.733	-4	57	0	O12(11/0/1),1b6,3b5,2b3		-0.7
	KC U	5	19	0	1	0	0	0		1			.053	.100	.053	-60	-4		.444	-3	82	0	3b4,O4(3/1/1)		-0.7
	Year	31	130	9	31	4	2	0		5			.238	.267	.300	78	-7		.706	-7	51	0	O16(14/1/2),3b9,1b6,2b3		-1.4
Total	3	68	284	27	66	8	4	0	9	7		0	.232	.251	.289	73	-13		.911	-12	107	108	1b37,O20(14/3/4),3b9,2b6		-2.6

LUGO, JULIO Julio Cesar B11.16.1975 Santa Cruz de Barahona, D.R. BR/TR/6-0/165* [HouN94 43/1193] d4.15 Col Connors St. (OK) JC
2000	Hou N	116	420	78	119	22	5	10	40	37-0	4	93	.283	.346	.431	88	-8	22-9	.951	-9	93	84	S60,2b45,O6(3/1/2)		-0.9
2001	†Hou N	140	513	93	135	20	3	10	37	46-0	5	116	.263	.326	.372	76	-19	12-11	.964	15	106	101	S133,O8(6/0/2),2b2		0.5
2002	Hou N	88	322	45	84	15	1	8	35	28-3	2	74	.261	.322	.388	83	-7	9-3	.976	-10	88	62	S84		-1.3
2003	Hou N	22	65	6	16	3	0	0	2	9-1	0	12	.246	.338	.292	63	-3	2-1	.966	-1	95	83	S22	48	-0.3
	TB A	117	433	58	119	13	4	15	53	35-0	4	88	.275	.333	.427	101	0	10-3	.970	3	104	93	S117		1.2
2004	TB A	157	581	83	160	41	4	7	75	54-0	5	106	.275	.338	.396	94	-4	21-5	.963	2	104	97	S143,2b8,D5		1.1
2005	TB A	158	616	89	182	36	6	6	57	61-0	5	57	.295	.362	.403	107	8	39-11	.968	9	95	85	S156		2.5
Total	6	798	2950	452	815	150	23	56	299	270-4	26	561	.276	.340	.400	91	-35	115-43	.966	1	99	89	S715,2b55,O14(9/1/4),D5	48	2.8

LUKACHYK, ROB Robert James B7.24.1968 Jersey City NJ BL/TR/6-0/185 [ChiA87 10/245] d7.5 Col Brookdale (NJ) CC
| 1996 | Mon N | 2 | 2 | 0 | 0 | 0 | 0 | 0 | 0 | 0-0 | 0 | 1 | .000 | .000 | .000 | -98 | -1 | 0-0 | — | 0 | | | /H | | -0.1 |

LUKE, MATT Matthew Clifford B2.26.1971 Long Beach CA BL/TL/6-5/220* [NYA92 8/214] d4.3 Col California-Davis
1996	NY A	1	0	1	0	0	0	0	0	0-0	0		—	—	—	—	0	0-0	—	0			/R		0.0
1998	LA N	33	77	10	22	7	0	3	11	3-0	0	18	.286	.313	.494	113	0	0-0	.958	-13	23	62	O15(13/0/2),1b12		-1.5
	Cle A	2	2	0	0	0	0	0	0	0-0	0		.000	.000	.000	-96	-1	0-0	—	0			/H		-0.1
	LA N	69	160	24	34	5	1	9	23	14-2	1	42	.213	.278	.425	86	-4	2-1	1.000	-3	23	62	O48(36/0/12),1b6		-1.0
Total	3	123	269	39	65	12	1	15	40	19-2	1	70	.242	.293	.461	98	-3	2-1	.991	-15	55	90	O69(51/0/18),1b22	69	-2.4

LUKON, EDDIE Edward Paul "Mongoose" B8.5.1920 Burgettstown PA D11.7.1996 Canonsburg PA BL/TL/5-10/168 d8.6 Mil 1943-45
1941	Cin N	23	86	6	23	3	0	3	6	3	0	6	.267	.315	.302	74	-3	1	.980	1	110	103	O22R		-0.4
1945	Cin N	2	8	1	1	0	0	0	0	0	0	1	.125	.125	.125	-31	-1	0	1.000	1	126	0	O2C		-0.1
1946	Cin N	102	312	31	78	8	12	8	34	26	1	29	.250	.310	.442	116	3	3	.985	-3	97	59	O83(72/0/11)		-0.6
1947	Cin N	86	200	26	41	6	1	11	33	28	1	36	.205	.306	.410	89	-4	0	1.000	1	99	101	O55(33/0/25)		-0.6
Total	4	213	606	64	143	17	9	23	70	60	2	72	.236	.307	.408	99	-5	4	.989	-2	100	77	O162(105/2/58)		-1.7

LUM, MIKE Michael Ken-Wai B10.27.1945 Honolulu HI BL/TL/6-0/180* d9.12 C3
1967	Atl N	9	26	1	6	0	0	0	1	1-0	0	4	.231	.259	.231	42	-2	0-1	.944	1	114	287	O6C		-0.2
1968	Atl N	122	232	22	52	7	3	3	21	14-2	4	35	.224	.277	.319	79	-6	3-5	.976	3	103	160	O95(74/7/21)		-0.9
1969	†Atl N	121	168	20	45	8	0	1	22	16-4	0	18	.268	.326	.333	86	-3	0-0	.992	7	134	70	O89(56/16/21)		0.2
1970	Atl N	123	291	25	74	17	2	7	28	17-0	5	43	.254	.306	.399	83	-8	3-2	.988	5	120	67	O90(36/33/35)		-0.6
1971	Atl N	145	454	56	122	14	1	13	55	47-5	5	43	.269	.340	.390	101	1	0-3	.990	9	106	106	O125(10/17/104)/1		0.4
1972	Atl N	123	369	40	84	14	2	9	38	50-4	3	52	.228	.323	.350	84	-6	1-4	.976	-8	117	55	O109(30/20/62),1b2		-0.7
1973	Atl N	138	513	74	151	26	6	16	82	41-7	6	89	.294	.351	.462	116	11	2-5	.991	-6	79	95	1b84,O64(48/2/14)		-0.1
1974	Atl N	106	361	50	84	11	2	11	50	45-12	2	49	.233	.319	.366	89	-6	0-2	.994	-6	75	117	1b60,O50(24/9/25)	38	-2.0
1975	Atl N	124	364	32	83	8	2	8	36	39-7	0	38	.228	.302	.327	72	-14	2-4	.992	-9	90	83	1b60,O38(1/32/5)		-2.5
1976	†Cin N	84	136	15	31	5	1	3	20	22-1	1	24	.228	.331	.346	92	-1	0-1	1.000	-4	80	0	O38(33/2/5)		-0.7
1977	Cin N	81	125	14	20	1	0	5	16	9-1	1	33	.160	.221	.288	35	-12	2-0	1.000	-1	108	0	O24(12/1/11),1b8		-1.4
1978	Cin N	86	146	15	39	7	1	6	23	22-4	0	18	.267	.361	.452	126	5	0-0	.987	3	97	305	O43(10/26/9),1b7		0.8
1979	Atl N	111	217	29	54	6	0	6	18-1	0	34	.249	.304	.359	76	-7	0-2	.998	1	106	100	1b51,O3L		-1.0
1980	Atl N	93	83	7	17	3	0	0	5	18-3	0	19	.205	.343	.241	66	-3	0-0	1.000	0	105	0	O19L,1b10		-0.3
1981	Atl N	10	11	1	1	0	0	0	0	2-1	0	2	.091	.231	.091	-6	-2	0-0	1.000	0	157	0	/OL		-0.3
	Chi N	41	58	5	14	1	0	2	7	5-2	1	5	.241	.308	.362	86	-1	0-0	.923	-2	64	0	O14(12/0/3)/1		-0.1
	Year	51	69	6	15	1	0	2	7	7-3	1	7	.217	.295	.319	72	-3	0-0	.938	-2	72	0	O15(13/0/3)/1		-0.4
Total	15	1517	3554	404	877	128	20	90	431	366-54	28	506	.247	.319	.370	89	-54	13-29	.986	19	108	80	O816(369/171/315),1b284	38	-9.5

LUMLEY, HARRY Harry Garfield "Judge" B9.29.1880 Forest City PA D5.22.1938 Binghamton NY BL/TL/5-10/183 d4.14 M1
1904	Bro N	150	577	79	161	23	18	9	78	41		4	.279	.331	.428	137	22	30	.955	4	141	104	O150R		2.1
1905	Bro N	130	505	50	148	19	16	7	47	36		0	.293	.340	.412	134	19	22	.912	-0	128	88	O129R		1.4
1906	Bro N	133	484	72	157	23	12	9	61	48		1	.324	.386	.477	184	45	35	.949	2	81	126	O131R		4.5
1907	Bro N	127	454	47	121	23	11	6	66	31		2	.267	.316	.425	144	19	18	.959	-2	95	178	O118R		1.4
1908	Bro N	127	440	36	95	13	12	4	39	29		1	.216	.266	.327	93	-6	9	.955	-3	93	177	O116R		-1.7
1909	Bro N	55	172	13	43	8	3	0	14	16		0	.250	.314	.331	104	1	3	.948	2	123	57	O52R,M		0.0
1910	Bro N	8	21	3	3	0	0	0	3			1	.143	.280	.143	25	-2	0	.833	-1	80	0	O4R		-0.3
Total	7	730	2653	300	728	109	66	38	305	204		9	.274	.328	.408	135	98	110	.946	-1	110	134	O700R		7.4

LUMPE, JERRY Jerry Dean B6.2.1933 Lincoln MO BL/TR/6-2/185(179-190) d4.17 C1
1956	NY A	20	62	12	16	3	0	0	4	5-2	0	11	.258	.313	.306	66	-3	1-1	.916	1	105	135	S17/3		0.0
1957	†NY A	40	103	15	35	6	2	0	11	9-0	0	13	.340	.389	.437	128	4	2-2	.956	-1	92	142	3b30,S6		0.3
1958	†NY A	81	232	34	59	8	4	3	32	23-2	1	21	.254	.319	.362	92	-3	1-2	.943	4	106	114	3b65,S5		0.1

YEAR	TM LG	G	AB	R	H	2B	3B	HR	RBI	BB-IB	HP	SO	AVG	OBP	SLG	AOPS	ABR	SB-CS	FA	FR	RNG	THR	GAMES AT POSITION	DL	BFW
1959	NY A	18	45	2	10	0	0	0	2	6-5	0	7	.222	.314	.222	52	-3	0-0	1.000	2	126	182	3b12,S4/2		0.0
	KC A	108	403	47	98	11	5	3	28	41-1	0	32	.243	.313	.318	72	-15	2-1	.986	-1	105	102	2b61,S56,3b4		-0.8
	Year	126	448	49	108	11	5	3	30	47-6	0	39	.241	.313	.308	70	-18	2-1	.987	-2	105	104	2b62,S60,3b16		-0.8
1960	KC A	146	574	69	156	19	3	8	53	48-1	0	49	.272	.326	.357	85	-13	1-1	.982	9	100	99	2b134,S15		0.7
1961	KC A	148	569	81	167	29	5	3	54	48-0	2	39	.293	.348	.392	96	-3	1-0	.979	21	111	111	2b147		3.0
1962	KC A	156	641	89	193	34	10	10	83	44-0	0	38	.301	.341	.432	103	2	0-2	.986	-5	98	90	2b156,S2		0.9
1963	KC A	157	595	75	161	26	7	5	59	58-3	0	44	.271	.333	.363	91	-6	3-2	.988	-1	101	92	2b155		0.6
1964	Det A☆	158	624	75	160	21	6	6	46	50-3	2	61	.256	.312	.338	80	-17	2-1	.985	-17	92	94	2b158		-2.1
1965	Det A	145	502	72	129	15	3	4	39	56-1	1	34	.257	.333	.323	87	-7	7-0	.985	-9	92	89	2b139		-0.4
1966	Det A	113	385	30	89	14	3	1	26	24-1	0	44	.231	.275	.291	62	-19	0-3	.991	1	95	94	2b95		-1.3
1967	Det A	81	177	19	41	4	0	4	17	16-2	0	18	.232	.295	.322	80	-4	0-0	.963	1	108	75	2b54,3b6		0.0
Total	12	1371	4912	620	1314	190	52	47	454	428-21	8	411	.268	.325	.356	87	-87	20-15	.984	7	99	93	2b1100,3b118,S105		1.0

LUNA, HECTOR   Hector R.   B2.1.1980 Monte Cristi, D.R.   BR/TR/6-1/170*   d4.8

		G	AB	R	H	2B	3B	HR	RBI	BB-IB	HP	SO	AVG	OBP	SLG	AOPS	ABR	SB-CS	FA	FR	RNG	THR	GAMES AT POSITION	DL	BFW
2004	†StL N	83	173	25	43	7	2	3	22	13-0	2	37	.249	.304	.364	72	-8	6-3	.947	6	123	130	S24,2b19,3b16,O10(8/2/0)		0.0
2005	†StL N	64	137	26	39	10	2	1	18	9-0	4	25	.285	.344	.409	95	-1	10-2	.947	6	113	348	O25(3/1/21),2b2,3b7,S6		0.7
Total	2	147	310	51	82	17	4	4	40	22-0	6	62	.265	.322	.384	82	-9	16-5	.987	12	108	130	2b41,O35(11/3/21),S30,3b23		0.7

LUNAR, FERNANDO   Fernando Jose   B5.25.1977 Cantaura, Venez   BR/TR/6-1/190*   d5.8

		G	AB	R	H	2B	3B	HR	RBI	BB-IB	HP	SO	AVG	OBP	SLG	AOPS	ABR	SB-CS	FA	FR	RNG	THR	GAMES AT POSITION	DL	BFW
2000	Atl N	22	54	5	10	1	0	0	5	3-1	3	15	.185	.267	.204	21	-7	0-2	.993	4	60	109	C22		-0.2
	Bal A	9	16	0	2	0	0	0	1	0-0	1	4	.125	.176	.125	-23	-3	0-0	1.000	3	0	177	C9		0.0
2001	Bal A	64	167	8	41	7	0	0	16	7-0	3	32	.246	.287	.287	55	-11	0-0	.987	-3	97	124	C64		-1.0
2002	Bal A	2	0	0	0	0	0	0	0	0-0	0	0	—	—	—	4	0	0-0	1.000	0	0	0	C2		0.0
Total	3	97	237	13	53	8	0	0	22	10-1	7	51	.224	.275	.257	42	-21	0-2	.990	4	82	124	C97		-1.2

LUND, DON   Donald Andrew   B5.18.1923 Detroit MI   BR/TR/6-0/200*   d7.3   C2   Col Michigan

		G	AB	R	H	2B	3B	HR	RBI	BB-IB	HP	SO	AVG	OBP	SLG	AOPS	ABR	SB-CS	FA	FR	RNG	THR	GAMES AT POSITION	DL	BFW
1945	Bro N	4	3	0	0	0	0	0	1	0	0	1	.000	.250	.000	-27	0	0	—	0			/H		0.0
1947	Bro N	11	20	5	6	2	0	2	5	3	0	7	.300	.391	.700	178	2	0	1.000	0	118	0	O5L		0.2
1948	Bro N	27	69	9	13	4	0	1	5	5	0	16	.188	.243	.290	42	-6	1	.977	1	105	136	O25(17/0/8)		-0.6
	StL A	63	161	21	40	7	4	3	25	10	3	17	.248	.305	.398	84	-5	0-0	1.000	0	95	115	O45(21/0/25)		-0.7
1949	Det A	2	2	0	0	0	0	0	0	0	0	1	.000	.000	.000	-99	-1	0-0	—	0			/H		-0.1
1952	Det A	8	23	1	7	0	0	0	1	3	0	3	.304	.385	.304	93	0	0-1	1.000	0	99	220	O7R		-0.6
1953	Det A	131	421	51	108	21	4	9	47	39	2	65	.257	.323	.390	93	-5	3-3	.980	5	109	118	O123(37/29/69)		-0.8
1954	Det A	35	54	4	7	2	0	0	3	4	0	3	.130	.186	.167	-2	-8	1-0	.971	0	107	99	O31(19/3/11)		-0.6
Total	7	281	753	91	181	36	8	15	86	65	5	113	.240	.305	.369	81	-23	5-4	.983	7	106	118	O236(99/32/120)		-2.6

LUND, GORDY   Gordon Thomas   B2.23.1941 Iron Mountain MI   BR/TR/5-11/170*   d8.1

		G	AB	R	H	2B	3B	HR	RBI	BB-IB	HP	SO	AVG	OBP	SLG	AOPS	ABR	SB-CS	FA	FR	RNG	THR	GAMES AT POSITION	DL	BFW
1967	Cle A	3	8	1	2	1	0	0	0	0-0	0	2	.250	.250	.375	82	0	0-0	.667	-2	51	182	S2		-0.2
1969	Sea A	20	38	4	10	0	0	0	1	5-1	0	7	.263	.349	.263	74	-1	1-1	.927	-2	99	88	S17/23		-0.2
Total	2	23	46	5	12	1	0	0	1	5-1	0	9	.261	.333	.283	76	-1	1-1	.902	-4	92	101	S19/32		-0.4

LUNDSTEDT, TOM   Thomas Robert   B4.10.1949 Davenport IA   BB/TR/6-4/195*   [ChiN70 S1/17]   d8.31   Col Michigan

		G	AB	R	H	2B	3B	HR	RBI	BB-IB	HP	SO	AVG	OBP	SLG	AOPS	ABR	SB-CS	FA	FR	RNG	THR	GAMES AT POSITION	DL	BFW
1973	Chi N	4	5	0	0	0	0	0	0	0-0	0	1	.000	.000	.000	-93	-1	0-0	1.000	-0	45	0	C4		-0.2
1974	Chi N	22	32	1	3	0	0	0	0	5-0	0	7	.094	.216	.094	-11	-5	0-0	.987	-1	81	59	C22		-0.6
1975	Min A	18	28	2	3	0	0	1	1	4-1	0	5	.107	.219	.107	-5	-4	0-0	1.000	-1	51	59	C14,D2		-0.5
Total	3	44	65	3	6	0	0	1	1	9-1	0	13	.092	.203	.092	-15	-10	0-0	.993	-3	67	54	C40,D2		-1.3

LUNSFORD, TREY   James Lewis   B5.25.1979 Odessa TX   BR/TR/6-1/195*   [SFN00 33/991]   d9.12   Col Texas Tech

		G	AB	R	H	2B	3B	HR	RBI	BB-IB	HP	SO	AVG	OBP	SLG	AOPS	ABR	SB-CS	FA	FR	RNG	THR	GAMES AT POSITION	DL	BFW
2002	SF N	3	3	1	2	1	0	0	1	0-0	0	1	.667	.667	1.000	349	1	0-0	.800	-1	46	0	C3		0.0
2003	SF N	1	1	0	0	0	0	0	0	0-0	0	1	.000	.000	.000	-99	-1	0-0	—	-0	0	0	/C		-0.1
Total	2	4	4	1	2	1	0	0	1	0-0	0	1	.500	.500	.750	231	1	0-0	.800	-1	40	0	C4		-0.1

LUNTE, HARRY   Harry August   B9.15.1892 St.Louis MO   D7.27.1965 St.Louis MO   BR/TR/5-11.5/165   d5.19

		G	AB	R	H	2B	3B	HR	RBI	BB-IB	HP	SO	AVG	OBP	SLG	AOPS	ABR	SB-CS	FA	FR	RNG	THR	GAMES AT POSITION	DL	BFW
1919	Cle A	26	77	2	15	2	0	0	2	1	1	7	.195	.215	.221	21	-8	0	.935	-1	105	69	S24		-0.8
1920	†Cle A	23	71	6	14	0	0	0	7	5	0	6	.197	.250	.197	19	-8	0-1	.979	4	121	115	S21,2b2		-0.4
Total	2	49	148	8	29	2	0	0	9	6	1	13	.196	.232	.209	20	-16	0-1	.955	3	112	90	S45,2b2		-1.2

LUPIEN, TONY   Ulysses John   B4.23.1917 Chelmsford MA   D7.9.2004 Norwich VT   BL/TL/5-10.5/185   d9.12   Mil 1945   Col Harvard

		G	AB	R	H	2B	3B	HR	RBI	BB-IB	HP	SO	AVG	OBP	SLG	AOPS	ABR	SB-CS	FA	FR	RNG	THR	GAMES AT POSITION	DL	BFW
1940	Bos A	10	19	5	9	3	2	0	4	1	0	1	.474	.500	.842	232	4	0-0	1.000	-0	79	109	1b8		0.3
1942	Bos A	128	463	63	130	25	7	3	70	50	0	20	.281	.351	.384	103	2	10-12	.992	-7	79	102	1b121		-1.8
1943	Bos A	154	608	65	155	21	9	4	47	54	1	23	.255	.317	.339	90	-9	16-9	.993	3	108	105	1b153		-1.5
1944	Phi N	153	597	82	169	23	9	5	52	56	2	29	.283	.347	.377	107	5	18	1.000	3	163	89	1b15		0.2
1945	Phi N	15	54	1	17	1	0	0	3	6	0	2	.315	.383	.333	103	0	2	1.000	-4	91	99	1b154		-3.2
1948	Chi A	**154**	617	69	152	19	3	6	54	74	0	38	.246	.327	.316	74	-23	11-7	.993	-4	98	100	1b602		-6.1
Total	6	614	2358	285	632	92	30	18	230	241	3	111	.268	.337	.355	94	-21	57-28	.993	-3	98	100	1b602		-1.5

LUPLOW, AL   Alvin David   B3.13.1939 Saginaw MI   BL/TR/5-11/180*   d9.16   Col Michigan St.

		G	AB	R	H	2B	3B	HR	RBI	BB-IB	HP	SO	AVG	OBP	SLG	AOPS	ABR	SB-CS	FA	FR	RNG	THR	GAMES AT POSITION	DL	BFW
1961	Cle A	5	18	0	1	0	0	0	0	2-0	0	6	.056	.150	.056	-44	-4	0-0	1.000	1	89	510	O5(1/0/4)		-0.3
1962	Cle A	97	318	54	88	15	3	14	45	36-0	6	44	.277	.359	.475	127	12	1-0	.960	1	102	86	O86(70/0/24)		0.8
1963	Cle A	100	295	34	69	6	2	7	27	33-2	3	62	.234	.316	.339	85	-6	4-4	.994	5	110	138	O85(14/0/73)		-0.7
1964	Cle A	19	18	1	2	0	0	0	1	1-0	0	6	.111	.158	.111	-24	-3	0-0	1.000	1	223	0	O5(0/1/4)		-0.3
1965	Cle A	53	45	3	6	2	0	1	4	8-0	0	14	.133	.188	.244	22	-5	0-1	1.000	0	214	0	O6(2/1/3)		-0.5
1966	NY N	111	334	31	84	9	1	7	31	38-3	2	46	.251	.331	.347	91	-3	2-6	.987	-5	89	65	O101(16/24/71)		-1.6
1967	NY N	41	112	11	23	1	0	3	9	8-1	1	19	.205	.260	.295	61	-6	0-0	.966	-0	105	59	O33(6/16/16)		-0.8
	Pit N	55	103	13	19	1	0	1	8	6-0	1	14	.184	.232	.223	32	-9	1-0	.961	3	116	280	O25(15/2/8)		-0.8
	Year	96	215	24	42	2	0	4	17	14-1	2	33	.195	.247	.260	47	-15	1-0	.963	3	110	157	O58(21/18/24)		-1.6
Total	7	481	1243	147	292	34	6	33	125	127-6	13	213	.235	.311	.352	85	-24	8-11	.977	5	102	111	O346(124/44/203)		-4.2

LUSADER, SCOTT   Scott Edward   B9.30.1964 Chicago IL   BL/TL/5-10/165*   [DetA85 6/158]   d9.1   Col Florida

		G	AB	R	H	2B	3B	HR	RBI	BB-IB	HP	SO	AVG	OBP	SLG	AOPS	ABR	SB-CS	FA	FR	RNG	THR	GAMES AT POSITION	DL	BFW
1987	Det A	23	47	8	15	1	1	3	8	5-1	0	7	.319	.377	.489	135	1	1-0	.967	-1	98	0	O22(6/3/16)/D		0.1
1988	Det A	16	16	3	1	0	0	0	3	1-0	0	4	.063	.141	.250	-0	-2	0-0	1.000	-0	84	0	O4(2/2/2),D6		-0.3
1989	Det A	40	103	15	26	4	0	1	8	9-0	0	21	.252	.310	.320	80	-3	3-0	.933	-2	99	0	O33(4/8/24)/D		-0.4
1990	Det A	45	87	13	21	2	0	2	16	12-0	0	8	.241	.324	.333	86	-1	0-0	.982	-2	90	51	O42(12/5/27),D2	47	-0.1
1991	NY A	11	7	2	1	0	0	0	1	1-0	0	3	.143	.250	.143	12	-1	0-1	1.000	-0	86	0	O4(1/3/0)/D	79	-1.2
Total	5	135	260	41	64	9	1	5	36	28-1	0	43	.246	.313	.346	86	-5	4-1	.961	-6	95	20	O105(25/21/69),D11		

LUSH, ERNIE   Ernest Benjamin   B10.31.1884 Bridgeport CT   D2.26.1937 Detroit MI   BR/TL   d7.20   b-Billy   Col Niagara

		G	AB	R	H	2B	3B	HR	RBI	BB-IB	HP	SO	AVG	OBP	SLG	AOPS	ABR	SB-CS	FA	FR	RNG	THR	GAMES AT POSITION	DL	BFW
1910	StL N	1	4	0	0	0	0	0	1	0	0	1	.000	.200	.000	-42	-1	0	1.000	-0	55	0	/OC		-0.1

LUSH, JOHNNY   John Charles   B10.8.1885 Williamsport PA   D11.18.1946 Beverly Hills CA   BL/TL/5-9.5/165   d4.22 ▲

		G	AB	R	H	2B	3B	HR	RBI	BB-IB	HP	SO	AVG	OBP	SLG	AOPS	ABR	SB-CS	FA	FR	RNG	THR	GAMES AT POSITION	DL	BFW
1904	Phi N	106	369	39	102	22	3	2	42	27	6		.276	.336	.369	122	10	12	.950	-8	71	94	1b62,O33R,P7		-0.1
1905	Phi N	6	16	3	5	0	0	0					.313	.389	.313	114	0	0	.667	-1	0	0	O3(0/2/1),P2		-0.1
1906	Phi N	76	212	28	56	7	1	0	15	14	0		.264	.310	.307	92	-2	6	.907	4	111	76	P37,O22(0/6/16),1b2		-0.1
1907	Phi N	17	40	5	8	1	1	0	5	1	0		.200	.220	.275	56	-2	1	1.000	0	114	386	P8,O4(0/3/1)		-0.2
	StL N	27	82	6	23	2	3	0	5	5	0		.280	.322	.378	123	2	4	.917	-1	88	141	P20,O7(0/3/4)		-0.1
	Year	44	122	11	31	3	4	0	10	6	0		.254	.289	.344	101	-1	5	.941	-1	95	210	P28,O11(0/6/5)		-0.3
1908	StL N	45	89	7	15	2	0	0	2	7	0		.169	.229	.191	36	1	1	.945	-1	98	0	P38		-0.0
1909	StL N	45	92	5	22	5	0	0	14	6	0		.239	.293	.293	87	-1	2	.928	-2	89	86	P34,O3R		0.0
1910	StL N	47	93	8	21	3	1	0	10	8	0	11	.226	.287	.301	74	4	2	.928	-2	89	86	P36		0.0
Total	7	369	993	107	252	40	11	2	94	69	8	11	.254	.307	.322	98	12	28	.926	-9	101	75	P182,O72(0/14/58),1b64		-0.5

LUSH, BILLY   William Lucas   B11.10.1873 Bridgeport CT   D8.28.1951 Hawthorne NY   BB/TR/5-7/165   d9.3   b-Ernie

		G	AB	R	H	2B	3B	HR	RBI	BB-IB	HP	SO	AVG	OBP	SLG	AOPS	ABR	SB-CS	FA	FR	RNG	THR	GAMES AT POSITION	DL	BFW
1895	Was N	5	18	2	6	0	0	0	2	2	0	1	.333	.400	.333	91	0	0	.692	-2	0	0	O5(4/0/1)		-0.2
1896	Was N	97	352	74	87	9	11	4	45	66	2	49	.247	.369	.369	95	-1	28	.885	-0	155	117	O91(10/14/68),2b3		-0.5
1897	Was N	3	12	1	0	0	0	0	0	0	0		.000	.143	.000	-61	-3	0	1.000	0	208	0	O3R		0.1
1901	Bos N	7	22	5	5	1	0	0	2	6	0		.185	.367	.227	58	-2	0	.960	-3	188	406	O7C		0.2
1902	Bos N	120	413	68	92	8	1	2	19	76	1		.223	.346	.262	87	-1	30	.952	9	152	127	O116(10/104/2)/3		0.2
1903	Det A	119	423	71	116	18	14	1	33	70	1		.274	.379	.390	135	22	14	.968	8	138	125	O101(89/0/12),3b12,2b3,S3		

YEAR	TM LG	G	AB	R	H	2B	3B	HR	RBI	BB-IB	HP	SO	AVG	OBP	SLG	AOPS	ABR	SB-CS	FA	FR	RNG	THR	GAMES AT POSITION	DL	BFW
1904	Cle A	138	477	76	123	13	8	1	50	72	3		.258	.359	.325	118	14	12	.959	2	71	101	O138(125/13/0)		0.9
Total	7	489	1722	294	429	49	35	8	152	291	8	50	.249	.360	.332	107	29	84	.943	19	124	120	O461(238/138/86),3b13,2b6,S3		2.7

LUSKEY, CHARLIE Charles Melton B4.6.1876 Washington DC D12.20.1962 Bethesda MD BR/TR/5-7/165 d9.12

YEAR	TM LG	G	AB	R	H	2B	3B	HR	RBI	BB-IB	HP	SO	AVG	OBP	SLG	AOPS	ABR	SB-CS	FA	FR	RNG	THR	GAMES AT POSITION	DL	BFW
1901	Was A	11	41	8	8	3	1	0	3	2			.195	.233	.317	52			.818	-2	88	0	O8L,C3		-0.4

LUTENBERG, LUKE Charles William B10.4.1864 Quincy IL D12.24.1938 Quincy IL BR/TR/6-2/225 d7.7

1894	Lou N	70	255	43	49	10	4	0	23	23		9	21	.192	.282	.263	34	-28	4	.977	2	104	124	1b68,2b2		-2.0

LUTTRELL, LYLE Lyle Kenneth B2.22.1930 Bloomington IL D7.11.1984 Chattanooga TN BR/TR/6-0/180* d5.15 Col Illinois Wesleyan

1956	Was A	38	122	17	23	5	3	2	9	8-0	3	19	.189	.254	.328	53	-9	5-1	.939	-5	91	71	S37		-1.0
1957	Was A	19	45	4	9	4	0	0	5	3-0	0	8	.200	.250	.289	47	-3	0-0	.927	-3	80	60	S17		-0.6
Total	2	57	167	21	32	9	3	2	14	11-0	3	27	.192	.253	.317	52	-12	5-1	.936	-8	88	68	S54		-1.6

LUTZ, RED Louis William B12.17.1898 Cincinnati OH D2.22.1984 Cincinnati OH BR/TR/5-10/170 d5.31

1922	Cin N	1	1	0	1	0	0	0	0				1.000	1.000	2.000	669	1	0-0	—	0	0	0	/C		0.1

LUTZ, JOE Rollin Joseph B2.18.1925 Keokuk IA BL/TL/6-0/195 d4.17 C3

1951	StL A	14	36	7	6	0	1	0	2	6	0	9	.167	.286	.222	38	-3	0-0	1.000	-1	60	85	1b11		-0.4

LUTZKE, RUBE Walter John B11.17.1897 Milwaukee WI D3.6.1938 Granville WI BR/TR/5-11/175 d4.18

1923	Cle A	143	511	71	131	20	6	3	65	59	4	57	.256	.338	.337	78	-16	9-6	.939	16	**113**	89	3b141,S2		0.9
1924	Cle A	106	341	37	83	18	3	0	42	38	5	46	.243	.328	.314	65	-17	4-0	.947	17	**113**	140	3b103,2b3		0.6
1925	Cle A	81	238	31	52	9	0	1	16	26	0	29	.218	.295	.269	44	-21	2-4	.936	0	108	77	3b69,2b10		-1.7
1926	Cle A	142	475	42	124	28	6	0	59	34	2	35	.261	.313	.345	71	-21	6-3	.960	-3	99	124	3b142		-1.4
1927	Cle A	100	311	35	78	12	3	0	41	22	3	29	.251	.307	.309	60	-19	2-1	.938	4	105	124	3b98		-0.9
Total	5	572	1876	216	468	87	18	4	223	179	14	196	.249	.319	.321	66	-94	23-14	.945	34	107	113	3b553,2b13,S2		-2.5

LUULOA, KEITH Keith H. M. B12.24.1974 Honolulu HI BR/TR/6-0/185 [CalA93 33/915] d5.17 Col Modesto (CA) JC

2000	Ana A	6	18	3	6	0	0	0	0	1-0	0	1	.333	.368	.333	77	-1	0-0	.833	-2	42	60	S4,2b3		-0.2

LUZINSKI, GREG Gregory Michael B11.22.1950 Chicago IL BR/TR/6-1/225(210-256) [PhiN68 1/11] d9.9 C4

1970	Phi N	8	12	0	2	0	0	0	0	3-0	0	5	.167	.333	.167	39	-1	0-1	1.000	1	170	46	1b3		-0.1
1971	Phi N	28	100	13	30	8	0	3	15	12-0	0	32	.300	.386	.470	141	6	2-0	.996	6	189	70	1b28		1.1
1972	Phi N	150	563	66	158	33	5	18	68	42-4	3	114	.281	.331	.453	119	13	0-4	.960	-1	99	93	O145(145/0/1),1b2		-0.1
1973	Phi N	161	610	76	174	26	4	29	97	51-9	7	135	.285	.346	.484	124	19	3-3	.993	-7	87	67	O159L		0.2
1974	Phi N	85	302	29	82	14	1	7	48	29-3	0	76	.272	.330	.394	99	-1	3-0	.981	5	100	189	O82L		0.1
1975	Phi N★	161	596	85	179	35	3	34	**120**	89-17	8	151	.300	.394	.540	151	43	3-6	.966	-12	83	84	O159L	81	0.1
1976	†Phi N★	149	533	74	162	28	1	21	95	50-2	**11**	107	.304	.369	.478	136	26	1-2	.964	-9	84	91	O144L		2.1
1977	†Phi N★	149	554	99	171	35	3	39	130	80-14	3	140	.309	.394	.594	154	44	3-2	.964	-10	78	118	O148L		1.0
1978	†Phi N★	155	540	85	143	32	2	35	101	100-15	11	135	.265	.388	.526	151	41	8-7	.984	-11	85	58	O154L		2.8
1979	Phi N	137	452	47	114	23	1	18	81	56-5	10	103	.252	.343	.427	105	5	3-3	.946	-16	73	35	O125L		2.4
1980	Phi N	106	368	44	84	19	1	19	56	60-5	**6**	100	.228	.342	.440	111	7	3-0	.993	-14	74	28	O105L	47	-1.7
1981	Chi A	104	378	55	100	15	1	21	62	58-1	3	80	.265	.365	.476	143	22	0-0	—	0	0	0	D103		-1.1
1982	Chi A	159	583	87	170	37	1	18	102	89-11	6	120	.292	.386	.451	130	29	1-1	—	0	0	0	D156		2.0
1983	†Chi A	144	502	73	128	26	1	32	95	70-6	11	117	.255	.352	.502	128	21	2-1	1.000	0	122	98	D139,1b2		2.4
1984	Chi A	125	412	47	98	13	0	13	58	56-3	3	80	.238	.329	.364	88	-5	5-1	—	0	0	0	D114		1.6
Total	15	1821	6505	880	1795	344	24	307	1128	845-95	84	1495	.276	.363	.478	128	269	37-31	.972	-66	85	82	O1221(1221/0/1),D512,1b35	128	12.1

LYDEN, MITCH Mitchell Scott B12.14.1964 Portland OR BR/TR/6-3/225 [NYA83 4/93] d6.16

1993	Fla N	6	10	2	3	0	1	0	2				.300	.300	.600	126	0	0-0	1.000	-1	93	0	C2		-0.1

LYDY, SCOTT Donald Scott B10.26.1968 Mesa AZ BR/TR/6-5/195 [OakA89 2/56] d5.18 Col South Mountain (AZ) CC

1993	Oak A	41	102	11	23	5	0	2	7	8-0	1	39	.225	.288	.333	70	-4	2-0	.958	-0	100	101	O38(17/5/16),D2		-0.5

LYNCH, JERRY Gerald Thomas B7.17.1930 Bay City MI BL/TR/6-1/189(180-202) d4.15

1954	Pit N	98	284	27	68	4	5	8	36	20	1	43	.239	.290	.373	73	-13	2-2	.965	3	95	201	O83(46/4/36)		-1.4
1955	Pit N	88	282	43	80	18	6	5	28	22-4	0	33	.284	.331	.443	106	2	2-2	.950	1	85	224	O71(40/0/32),C2		0.0
1956	Pit N	19	19	1	3	0	1	0	0	1-0	0	4	.158	.200	.263	24	-2	0-0	1.000	0	166	0	/OL	103	-0.2
1957	Cin N	67	124	11	32	4	1	4	13	6-1	0	18	.258	.290	.403	79	-4	0-0	1.000	-1	108	0	O24(1/0/22),C2		-0.5
1958	Cin N	122	420	58	131	20	5	16	68	18-1	0	54	.312	.338	.498	112	6	1-4	.970	-5	92	67	O101(1/0/101)		-0.3
1959	Cin N	117	379	49	102	16	3	17	58	29-1	1	50	.269	.320	.462	103	1	2-0	.979	1	103	70	O98(97/0/1)		-0.3
1960	Cin N	102	159	23	46	8	2	6	27	16-3	1	25	.289	.356	.478	124	5	0-0	.913	-2	87	48	O32(31/0/1)		0.2
1961	†Cin N	96	181	33	57	13	2	13	50	27-6	1	25	.315	.407	.624	166	18	2-2	.948	-3	83	71	O44(42/0/2)		1.3
1962	Cin N	114	288	41	81	15	4	12	57	24-4	1	38	.281	.335	.486	115	5	3-3	.970	-6	84	165	O73(70/0/3)		0.1
1963	Cin N	22	32	5	8	3	0	2	9	1-0	1	5	.250	.294	.531	129	1	0-0	1.000	1	72	0	O7(4/0/3)		0.0
	Pit N	88	237	26	63	6	3	10	36	22-2	1	28	.266	.328	.443	105	6	0-1	.960	-6	75	58	O64L		-0.4
	Year	110	269	31	71	9	3	12	45	23-2	2	33	.264	.324	.454	121	7	0-1	.962	-6	75	54	O71(68/0/3)		-0.4
1964	Pit N	114	297	35	81	14	2	16	66	26-3	1	57	.273	.330	.495	130	11	0-1	.983	-11	55	0	O71(77/0/1)		-0.4
1965	Pit N	73	121	7	34	1	0	5	16	8-3	1	26	.281	.328	.413	108	1	0-2	.903	-2	76	85	O26(23/0/3)		-0.3
1966	Pit N	64	56	5	12	1	0	1	4	4-1	0	10	.214	.267	.286	54	-4	0-0	1.000	0	157	0	O4L		-0.3
Total	13	1184	2879	364	798	123	34	115	470	224-29	9	416	.277	.329	.463	110	33	12-17	.964	-25	86	98	O706(501/4/205),C4	103	-2.6

LYNCH, HENRY Henry W. B4.8.1866 Worcester MA D11.23.1925 Worcester MA BB/5-7/143 d9.21

1893	Chi N	4	14	0	3	2	0	0	2	1	0	1	.214	.267	.357	66	-1	0	.833	-1	0	0	O4R		-0.1

LYNCH, DANNY Matt Dan "Dummy" B2.7.1926 Dallas TX D6.30.1978 Plano TX BR/TR/5-11/174 d9.14 Col SMU

1948	Chi N	7	7	3	2	1	0	0	0			0	1	.286	.375	.714	197	1	0	1.000	0	160	0	/2		0.1

LYNCH, MIKE Michael Joseph B9.10.1875 St.Paul MN D4.1.1947 Jennings Lodge OR TR/5-10/155 d4.24

1902	Chi N	7	28	4	4	0	0	0	0			6		.143	.200	.143	6	-3	0	.929	-0	117	0	O7C		-0.4

LYNCH, TOM Thomas James B4.3.1860 Bennington VT D3.28.1955 Cohoes NY BL/TR/5-10.5/170 d8.18 U12 Col Gallaudet

1884	Wil U	16	58	6	16	3	1	0		5				.276	.333	.362	108	-1		.846	-0			C8,O8L/1		-0.1
	Phi N	13	48	7	15	4	2	0	3	4		5		.313	.365	.479	171	4		.860	-0			C7,O7(1/6/0)		0.4
1885	Phi N	13	53	7	10	3	0	0	1	10		3		.189	.317	.245	86	0		.838	2	171	268	O13(9/4/0)		0.1
Total	2	42	159	20	41	10	3	0	4	19		8		.258	.337	.358	119	3		.887	1			O28(18/10/0),C15/1		0.4

LYNCH, WALT Walter Edward "Jabber" B4.15.1897 Buffalo NY D12.21.1976 Daytona Beach FL TR/6-0/176 d7.8 Col Niagara

1922	Bos A	3	2	1	0	0	0	0	0	0-0	0			.500	.500	.500	163	0						C3		0.0

LYNN, BYRD Byrd "Birdie" B3.13.1889 Unionville IL D2.5.1940 Napa CA BR/TR/5-11/165 d4.16

1916	Chi A	31	40	4	9	1	0	0	3	4	1	7	.225	.311	.250	68	-1	2	.952	-4	219	259	C13		0.4
1917	†Chi A	35	72	7	16	2	0	0	5	7	3	11	.222	.300	.250	67	-3	1	.959	1	145	55	C29		0.0
1918	Chi A	5	8	0	2	0	0	0	0	1			.250	.400	.250	95	0		1.000	-1	95	132	C4		0.0
1919	†Chi A	29	66	4	15	4	0	0	4	4	0	9	.227	.271	.288	57	-4	0	.982	1	121	94	C28		-0.1
1920	Chi A	16	25	0	8	2	1	0	3	4	0		.320	.346	.480	117	0	0-0	1.000	-0	133	78	C14		0.1
Total	5	116	211	15	50	9	1	0	15	18	2	31	.237	.303	.289	72	-8	3-0	.969	5	147	107	C88		0.4

LYNN, FRED Fredric Michael B2.3.1952 Chicago IL BL/TL/6-1/190* [BosA73 2/41] d9.5 Col USC

1974	Bos A	15	43	5	18	2	2	2	10	6	1	6	.419	.490	.698	226	7	0-0	1.000	-1	70	238	O12(6/4/2)/D		0.6
1975	†Bos A★	145	528	**103**	175	**47**	7	21	105	62-10	1	90	.331	.401	**.566**	159	42	10-5	.983	2	105	107	O144C		4.1
1976	Bos A★	132	507	76	159	32	8	10	65	48-2	1	67	.314	.367	.467	130	20	14-9	.984	4	102	134	O128(0/127/1),D5		2.1
1977	Bos A★	129	497	81	129	29	5	18	76	51-2	1	63	.260	.327	.447	99	-1	2-3	.994	-2	100	78	O125C/D	30	-0.4
1978	Bos A★	150	541	75	161	33	3	22	82	75-11	1	51	.298	.380	.492	131	24	3-6	.994	-2	100	78	O149C		1.6
1979	Bos A★	147	531	116	177	42	1	39	122	82-4	4	79	**.333**	**.423**	**.637**	173	57	2-2	.987	-0	99	107	O143C/D		5.3
1980	Bos A★	110	415	67	125	32	3	12	61	58-4	3	39	.301	.383	.480	119	19	12-0	.994	-2	99	143	O110C		2.3
1981	Cal A★	76	256	28	56	8	1	5	31	38-4	1	42	.219	.322	.316	85	-4	1-2	.978	-3	99	0	O69C		-0.8
1982	†Cal A★	138	472	89	141	38	1	21	86	58-4	3	72	.299	.374	.517	142	29	7-8	.991	-10	89	68	O133C		1.7

YEAR	TM LG	G	AB	R	H	2B	3B	HR	RBI	BB-IB	HP	SO	AVG	OBP	SLG	AOPS	ABR	SB-CS	FA	FR	RNG	THR	GAMES AT POSITION	DL	BFW
1983	Cal A★	117	437	56	119	20	3	22	74	55-10	2	83	.272	.352	.483	129	17	2-2	.993	-11	82	105	O113C,D2		0.5
1984	Cal A	142	517	84	140	28	4	23	79	77-8	2	97	.271	.366	.474	131	24	2-2	.982	0	96	132	O140(0/62/112)		1.8
1985	Bal A	124	448	59	118	12	1	23	68	53-6	1	100	.263	.339	.449	117	10	7-3	.994	-5	95	77	O123C		0.4
1986	Bal A	112	397	67	114	13	-1	23	67	53-1	2	59	.287	.371	.499	136	21	2-2	.984	-10	88	36	O107C/D	16	0.9
1987	Bal A	111	396	49	100	24	0	23	60	39-6	1	72	.253	.320	.487	113	7	3-7	.991	-7	90	46	O101C,D8	15	-0.3
1988	Bal A	87	301	37	76	13	1	18	37	28-1	0	66	.252	.312	.482	123	8	2-2	.991	-0	105	25	O83(0/64/21),D2	28	0.6
	Det A	27	90	9	20	1	0	7	19	5-0	1	16	.222	.265	.467	106	0	0-0	1.000	1	96	178	O22(19/3/0),D3		0.0
	Year	114	391	46	96	14	1	25	56	33-1	1	82	.246	.302	.478	119	8	2-2	.992	0	103	56	O105(19/67/21),D5		0.6
1989	Det A	117	353	44	85	11	1	11	46	47-1	5	71	.241	.328	.371	100	0	1-1	1.000	-4	89	29	O55(42/6/8)	15	-0.9
1990	SD N	90	196	18	47	3	1	6	23	22-2	1	44	.240	.315	.357	85	-4	2-0	.988	-4	95	95	O1825(135/1584/144),D70	104	19.2
Total	17	1969	6925	1063	1960	388	43	306	1111	857-77	30	1116	.283	.360	.484	128	276	72-54							

LYNN, JERRY   Jerome Edward   B4.14.1916 Scranton PA   D9.25.1972 Scranton PA   BR/TR/5-10/164   d9.19

YEAR	TM LG	G	AB	R	H	2B	3B	HR	RBI	BB-IB	HP	SO	AVG	OBP	SLG	AOPS	ABR	SB-CS	FA	FR	RNG	THR	GAMES AT POSITION	DL	BFW
1937	Was A	1	3	1	2	1	0	0	0	0-0	0	0	.667	.667	1.000	329	1	0-0	1.000	0	93	275	/2		0.1

LYON, RUSS   Russell Mayo   B6.26.1913 Ball Ground GA   D12.24.1975 Charleston SC   BR/TR/6-1/230   d4.21   Col Georgia Tech

| 1944 | Cle A | 7 | 11 | 1 | 2 | 0 | 0 | 0 | 0 | 1-0 | 0 | 1 | .182 | .250 | .182 | 25 | -1 | 0-0 | .909 | 0 | 95 | 175 | C3 | | -0.1 |

LYONS, BARRY   Barry Stephen   B6.3.1960 Biloxi MS   BR/TR/6-1/202*   [NYN82 15/371]   d4.19   Col Delta St.

YEAR	TM LG	G	AB	R	H	2B	3B	HR	RBI	BB-IB	HP	SO	AVG	OBP	SLG	AOPS	ABR	SB-CS	FA	FR	RNG	THR	GAMES AT POSITION	DL	BFW
																									-0.4
1986	NY N	6	9	1	0	0	0	0	2	1-1	0	2	.000	.100	.000	-71	-2	0-0	.941	-2	36	0	C3		-0.8
1987	NY N	53	130	15	33	4	1	4	24	8-1	1	24	.254	.301	.392	87	-3	0-0	.984	-6	85	79	C49		-0.7
1988	NY N	50	91	5	21	7	1	0	11	3-0	0	12	.231	.253	.330	70	-4	0-0	.979	-4	78	108	C32/1		-0.3
1989	NY N	79	235	15	58	13	0	3	27	11-1	2	28	.247	.283	.340	82	-6	0-1	.980	-1	86	87	C76	28	-0.3
1990	NY N	24	80	8	19	0	0	2	7	2-0	1	9	.237	.265	.313	58	-5	0-0	.980	-1	56	84	C23	54	-0.5
	LA N	3	5	1	1	0	0	1	2	0-0	1	0	.200	.400	.800	165	2	0-0	1.000	-0	0	0	C2		0.0
	Year	27	85	9	20	0	0	3	9	2-0	2	10	.235	.261	.341	64	-5	0-0	.980	-1	55	82	C25		-0.5
1991	LA N	9	9	0	0	0	0	0	0	0-0	0	2	.000	.000	.000	-99	-2	0-0	1.000	1	0	0	1b2		-0.2
	Cal A	2	5	0	1	0	0	0	0	0-0	0	0	.200	.200	.200	11	-1	0-0	1.000	0	142	0	C1		-0.1
1995	Chi A	27	64	8	17	2	0	5	16	4-0	0	14	.266	.304	.531	118	1	0-0	.987	1	41	215	C16,1b4,D6	82	0.2
Total	7	253	628	53	150	26	2	15	89	29-3	5	92	.239	.275	.358	77	-22	0-1	.981	-12	77	93	C207,1b7,D6		-2.8

LYONS, DENNY   Dennis Patrick Aloysius   B3.12.1866 Cincinnati OH   D1.2.1929 W.Covington KY   BR/TR/5-10/185   d9.18

YEAR	TM LG	G	AB	R	H	2B	3B	HR	RBI	BB-IB	HP	SO	AVG	OBP	SLG	AOPS	ABR	SB-CS	FA	FR	RNG	THR	GAMES AT POSITION	DL	BFW
1885	Pro N	4	16	3	2	1	0	0	1	0		3	.125	.125	.188	-0	-2		.824	-0	95	0	3b4		-0.2
1886	Phi AA	32	123	22	26	3	1	0	11	8	4		.211	.281	.252	67	-5	7	.807	-5	89	22	3b32		-0.8
1887	Phi AA	137	570	128	209	43	14	6	102	47	6		.367	.421	.523	162	48	73	.866	-5	78	144	3b137		3.6
1888	Phi AA	111	456	93	135	22	5	6	83	41	7		.296	.363	.406	147	25	39	.878	-12	82	76	3b111		1.4
1889	Phi AA	131	510	135	168	36	4	9	82	79	7	44	.329	.426	.469	157	43	10	.860	9	107	125	3b130/1		4.5
1890	Phi AA	88	339	79	120	29	5	7	73	57	10		.354	.461	.531	193	44	21	.909	10	105	93	3b88		4.7
1891	StL AA	120	451	124	142	24	3	11	84	88	18	58	.315	.445	.455	137	25	9	.871	-5	93	87	3b120		1.9
1892	NY N	108	389	71	100	16	7	8	51	59	3	37	.257	.359	.396	130	16	11	.918	-8	99	102	3b131		1.0
1893	Pit N	131	490	103	150	19	16	3	105	97	9	29	.306	.430	.429	131	28	19	.897	4	102	90	3b72		2.7
1894	Pit N	72	257	52	82	14	4	4	51	43	3	13	.319	.424	.451	112	9	14	.889	-5	71	37	3b34		0.9
1895	StL N	34	132	24	39	6	0	2	25	15	3	7	.295	.380	.386	99	1	3	.893	-16	81	86	3b116		-0.3
1896	Pit N	118	436	77	134	25	6	4	71	67	5	25	.307	.406	.420	123	19	13	.989	-1	76	73	1b35,3b2		0.4
1897	Pit N	37	131	22	27	6	4	2	17	22	6		.206	.346	.359	90	-1	5	.882	-30	91	95	3b1085,1b36		-0.2
Total	13	1123	4300	933	1334	244	69	62	756	623	82	216	.310	.407	.442	138	249	224							19.6

LYONS, ED   Edward Hoyte "Mouse"   B5.12.1923 Winston-Salem NC   BR/TR/5-9/165   d9.15   C1

| 1947 | Was A | 7 | 26 | 2 | 4 | 0 | 0 | 0 | 2 | 0-0 | 0 | 2 | .154 | .214 | .154 | 3 | -3 | 0-0 | 1.000 | 3 | 127 | 123 | 2b7 | | 0.0 |

LYONS, HARRY   Harry Pratt   B3.25.1866 Chester PA   D6.29.1912 Mauricetown NJ   BR/TR/5-10.5/157   d8.29

YEAR	TM LG	G	AB	R	H	2B	3B	HR	RBI	BB-IB	HP	SO	AVG	OBP	SLG	AOPS	ABR	SB-CS	FA	FR	RNG	THR	GAMES AT POSITION	DL	BFW
1887	Phi N	1	4	0	0	0	0	0	1	0	0		.000	.000	.000	-38	-1	0	.500	-1	0	0	/OL		-0.1
	†StL AA	2	8	2	1	0	0	0	1	0	0		.125	.125	.125	-27	-1	2	1.000	1	178	280	/2OR		-0.1
1888	†StL AA	123	499	66	97	10	5	4	63	20	3		.194	.230	.259	51	-30	36	.891	5	163	115	O122(0/112/10),3b2/S2		-2.8
1889	NY N	5	20	1	2	0	1	0	2	2	0		.100	.182	.200	7	-3	0	1.000	-1	0	0	O5(0/1/4)		-0.3
1890	Roc AA	133	584	83	152	11	11	3	58	27	1		.260	.294	.332	91	10	47	.921	10	113	79	O132(130/0/2),3b2/CP		-0.2
1892	NY N	96	411	67	98	5	2	0	53	33	1	29	.238	.297	.260	70	-15	25	.910	-1	101	29	O96(10/86/0)		-1.0
1893	NY N	47	187	27	51	5	2	0	21	14	0	6	.273	.323	.321	71	-8	10	.917	-1	104	166	O47(1/46/0)		-1.0
Total	6	407	1713	246	401	31	21	7	198	97	5	35	.234	.277	.289	69	-68	120	.908	13	122	87	O404(142/245/17),3b4,2b2/PCS		-6.6

LYONS, PAT   Patrick Jerry   B3.1860 Belleville ON, Can.   D1.20.1914 Springfield OH   BR/TR/5-7/155   d7.21

| 1890 | Cle N | 11 | 38 | 2 | 2 | 1 | 0 | 0 | 4 | 0 | 0 | | .053 | .143 | .079 | -36 | -7 | 0 | .839 | -5 | 84 | 44 | 2b11 | | -1.0 |

LYONS, STEVE   Stephen John   B6.3.1960 Tacoma WA   BL/TR/6-3/195*   [BosA81 1/19]   d4.15   Col Oregon St.   OF(59/237/43)

YEAR	TM LG	G	AB	R	H	2B	3B	HR	RBI	BB-IB	HP	SO	AVG	OBP	SLG	AOPS	ABR	SB-CS	FA	FR	RNG	THR	GAMES AT POSITION	DL	BFW
																									-1.6
1985	Bos A	133	371	52	98	14	3	5	30	32-0	1	64	.264	.322	.358	83	-9	12-9	.973	-6	96	64	O114(2/111/2)/3SD		-0.2
1986	Bos A	59	124	20	31	7	2	1	14	12-2	2	23	.250	.312	.363	84	-3	2-3	.972	2	106	158	O55C		-1.3
	Chi A	42	123	10	25	2	1	0	6	7-0	1	24	.203	.248	.236	33	-12	2-3	.987	1	105	96	O35(22/6/7),3b3/1D		-1.5
	Year	101	247	30	56	9	3	1	20	19-2	1	47	.227	.280	.300	58	-15	4-6	.978	2	106	129	O90(22/61/7),3b3/1D		0.0
1987	Chi A	76	193	26	54	11	1	1	19	12-0	1	37	.280	.320	.363	79	-6	3-1	.971	7	114	132	3b51,O15(6/8/2)/2D		0.3
1988	Chi A	146	472	59	127	28	3	5	45	32-1	1	59	.269	.313	.373	92	-5	1-2	.982	2	101	109	2b70,1b40,3b28,O20(10/1/9),S3/CD		-0.6
1989	Chi A	140	443	51	117	21	3	2	50	35-3	1	68	.264	.317	.339	87	-7	9-6	.991	0	105	123	1b61,2b15,O7(2/3/3),3b5/SDP		-1.3
1990	Chi A	94	146	22	28	6	1	1	11	10-1	1	41	.192	.245	.247	45	-11	1-0	1.000	0	106	0	O45(8/36/3),2b16,3b12,1b2/SDP		-0.6
1991	Bos A	87	212	15	51	10	1	4	17	11-2	0	35	.241	.277	.354	70	-9	10-3	1.000	2	106	0	O6(2/0/4),2b2		-0.3
1992	Atl N	11	14	0	1	0	1	0	1	0-0	0	4	.071	.071	.214	-21	-2	0-0	1.000	0	76	0	O8(7/1/0)/1		-0.1
	Mon N	16	13	2	3	0	0	0	1	1-0	0	3	.231	.286	.231	48	-1	1-2	1.000	0	138	0	O14(9/1/4),2b2/1		-0.4
	Year	27	27	2	4	0	1	0	2	1-0	0	7	.148	.179	.222	13	-3	1-2	1.000	-0	140	67	1b8,O5(0/2/3)/2D		-0.1
	Bos A	21	28	3	7	0	1	0	2	2-0	0	5	.250	.300	.321	69	-1	0-1	1.000	1	85	0	O10(0/6/4),2b9/C13D		-0.1
1993	Bos A	28	23	4	3	1	1	0	2	2-0	0	5	.130	.200	.174	1	-3	1-2	1.000	1	85	0	O10(0/6/4),2b9/C13D		-0.3
Total	9	853	2162	264	545	100	17	19	196	156-9	5	364	.252	.301	.340	77	-69	42-32	.979	17	102	81	O334C,3b229,2b118,1b115,D24,S6,C4,P2		
-6.1																									

LYONS, TERRY   Terence Hilbert   B12.14.1908 New Holland OH   D9.9.1959 Dayton OH   BR/TR/6-0.5/165   d4.19

| 1929 | Phi N | 1 | 0 | 0 | 0 | | | | | | | | | | | | 0 | 0 | — | 0 | 0 | 0 | /1 | | 0.0 |

LYONS, BILL   William Allen   B4.26.1958 Alton IL   BR/TR/6-1/175*   d7.20   Col Southern Illinois

YEAR	TM LG	G	AB	R	H	2B	3B	HR	RBI	BB-IB	HP	SO	AVG	OBP	SLG	AOPS	ABR	SB-CS	FA	FR	RNG	THR	GAMES AT POSITION	DL	BFW
																									-1.0
1983	StL N	42	60	4	10	1	0	0	3	1-0	0	11	.167	.180	.217	9	-8	3-2	.985	-2	107	90	2b23,3b8,S2		0.4
1984	StL N	46	73	13	16	3	0	0	3	9-1	0	13	.219	.305	.260	61	-3	3-1	.991	6	110	163	2b25,S11,3b3		-0.6
Total	2	88	133	16	26	4	0	0	6	10-1	0	24	.195	.252	.241	38	-11	6-3	.989	4	109	134	2b48,S13,3b11		

LYTLE, DAD   Edward Benson "Pop"   B3.10.1862 Racine WI   D12.21.1950 Long Beach CA   BR/TR/5-11/160   d8.11

YEAR	TM LG	G	AB	R	H	2B	3B	HR	RBI	BB-IB	HP	SO	AVG	OBP	SLG	AOPS	ABR	SB-CS	FA	FR	RNG	THR	GAMES AT POSITION	DL	BFW
1890	Chi N	1	4	1	0	0	0	0	1	0-0	0	1	.000	.000	.000	-96	-1	0	1.000	1	370	0	/OR		0.0
	Pit N	15	55	7	8	1	0	0	8	0	0	9	.145	.254	.164	25	-5	0	.837	-5	89	0	2b8,O7(0/4/3)		-0.8
	Year	16	59	8	8	1	0	0	9			10	.136	.239	.153	16	-6	0	.824	-4	80	0	O8(0/4/4),2b8		-0.8

LYTTLE, JIM   James Lawrence   B5.20.1946 Hamilton OH   BL/TR/6-0/186*   [NYA66 1/10]   d5.17   Col Florida St.

YEAR	TM LG	G	AB	R	H	2B	3B	HR	RBI	BB-IB	HP	SO	AVG	OBP	SLG	AOPS	ABR	SB-CS	FA	FR	RNG	THR	GAMES AT POSITION	DL	BFW
																									-0.9
1969	NY A	28	83	7	15	4	0	0	4	4-0	1	19	.181	.218	.229	26	-8	1-2	.983	1	98	196	O28C		0.2
1970	NY A	87	126	20	39	7	1	3	14	10-1	2	26	.310	.355	.452	128	5	3-6	.989	1	109	72	O70(2/4/64)		-0.7
1971	NY A	49	86	7	17	3	0	0	7	8-2	1	18	.198	.271	.291	63	-4	0-2	1.000	0	100	65	O29(3/6/20)		-0.6
1972	Chi A	44	82	9	19	5	2	0	5	1-0	0	28	.232	.241	.341	70	-3	0-1	.974	4	104	164	O36(29/7/0)		0.1
1973	Mon N	49	116	12	30	5	1	4	19	9-2	0	14	.259	.305	.422	98	-1	0-0	1.000	1	88	433	O18(14/5/0)		0.0
1974	Mon N	25	9	1	3	0	0	0	2	1-1	0	6	.333	.364	.333	101	0	0-0	1.000	-1	106	16(5/8/3)			0.0
1975	Mon N	44	55	7	15	4	0	0	6	13-3	1	15	.273	.406	.345	106	1	0-1	.977	2	101	199	O29(12/0/20)		0.0
1976	Mon N	42	85	6	23	4	1	0	8	7-1	0	10	.271	.326	.376	94	-1	0-0	.977	2	104	441	O18(1/17/1)		0.0
	LA N	23	68	3	15	3	0	0	5	8-4	0	12	.221	.303	.265	63	-3	0-1	1.000	4	104	200	O18(0/17/1)		
	Year	65	153	9	38	7	1	1	13	15-5	0	25	.248	.315	.327	80	-4	0-1	.990	6	102	313	O47(13/17/21)		

YEAR	TM LG	G	AB	R	H	2B	3B	HR	RBI	BB-IB	HP	SO	AVG	OBP	SLG	AOPS	ABR	SB-CS	FA	FR	RNG	THR	GAMES AT POSITION	DL	BFW

MAAS, KEVIN Kevin Christian B1.20.1965 Castro Valley CA BL/TL/6-3/209* [NYA86 22/572] d6.29 Col California-Davis

1990	NY A	79	254	42	64	9	0	21	41	43-10	3	76	.252	.367	.535	148	17	1-2	.983	-2	95	92	1b57,D18		1.0
1991	NY A	148	500	69	110	14	1	23	63	83-3	4	128	.220	.333	.390	99	-1	5-1	.983	-1	92	71	D109,1b36		-0.6
1992	NY A	98	286	35	71	12	0	11	35	25-4	2	63	.248	.305	.406	99	-1	3-1	.986	-3	37	83	D62,1b22		-0.7
1993	NY A	59	151	20	31	4	0	9	25	24-2	1	32	.205	.316	.411	97	-1	1-1	.984	-1	70	144	D31,1b17		-0.5
1995	Min A	22	57	5	11	4	0	1	5	7-2	0	11	.193	.281	.316	55	-4	0-0	.936	-2	25	82	D12,1b8	16	-0.6
Total	5	406	1248	171	287	43	1	65	169	182-21	8	310	.230	.329	.422	107	12	10-5	.982	-9	82	89	D232,1b140	16	-1.4

MABRY, JOHN John Steven B10.17.1970 Wilmington DE BL/TR/6-4/195(195-210) [StLN91 6/155] d4.23 Col West Chester OF(184/11/379)

1994	StL N	6	23	2	7	3	0	0	3	2-0	0	4	.304	.360	.435	106	0	0-0	1.000	1	145	0	O6R		0.1
1995	StL N	129	388	35	119	21	1	5	41	24-5	2	45	.307	.347	.405	97	-2	0-3	.994	5	118	124	1b73,O39(11/0/29)		-0.5
1996	†StL N	151	543	63	161	30	2	13	74	37-11	3	84	.297	.342	.431	103	2	3-2	.994	-10	78	103	1b146,O14(1/0/13)		-2.0
1997	StL N	116	388	40	110	19	0	5	36	39-9	3	77	.284	.352	.371	90	-5	0-1	1.000	-3	86	165	O78(4/6/71),1b49/3	35	-1.5
1998	StL N	142	377	41	94	22	0	9	46	30-6	1	76	.249	.305	.379	79	-12	0-2	.971	-5	98	205	O80(46/0/37),3b38,1b16		-2.0
1999	Sea A	87	262	34	64	14	0	9	33	20-1	1	60	.244	.297	.401	77	-10	2-1	.989	5	113	251	O43(7/2/35),3b24,1b20/D	51	-0.8
2000	Sea A	48	103	18	25	5	0	1	7	10-0	2	31	.243	.322	.320	65	-5	0-1	.862	-5	71	122	3b22,O19(7/0/12),1b3/PD	19	-1.0
	SD N	48	123	17	28	7	0	7	25	5-0	0	38	.228	.256	.463	82	-4	0-0	.980	-1	94	60	O32(2/0/30),1b2		-0.7
2001	StL N	5	7	0	0	0	0	0	0	0-0	0	2	.000	.000	.000	-98	-2	0-0	1.000	-1	94	192	1b2,O2R		-0.3
	Fla N	82	147	14	32	7	0	6	20	13-1	5	44	.218	.299	.388	79	-5	1-0	.958	-2	82	111	O39(3/2/34)/1PD	34	-0.8
	Year	87	154	14	32	7	0	6	20	13-1	5	46	.208	.287	.370	71	-7	1-0	.958	-2	80	109	O41(3/2/36),1b3/PD		-1.1
2002	Phi N	21	21	1	6	0	0	3	1	1-0	0	5	.286	.304	.286	68	-1	0-0	1.000	0	194		/1OR		-0.1
	†Oak A	89	193	27	53	13	1	11	40	14-1	1	37	.275	.322	.523	122	5	1-1	.978	2	106	140	O53(33/0/21),1b50		0.4
2003	Sea A	64	104	12	22	6	0	3	16	15-2	3	21	.212	.328	.356	85	-2	0-0	.957	-1	86	140	O22(8/0/14),D12,1b9	23	-0.2
2004	†StL N	87	240	32	71	11	0	13	40	26-5	1	63	.296	.363	.504	121	7	0-1	.986	0	94		O57(39/1/25),3b20,1b14		0.5
2005	†StL N	112	246	26	59	15	1	8	32	20-1	1	63	.240	.295	.407	80	-8	0-0	.965	-7	65	40	O70(23/0/49),3b18,1b14		-0.6
Total	12	1187	3165	362	851	174	5	90	416	256-43	21	650	.269	.325	.412	92	-42	7-12	.983	-19	93	118	O555R,1b400,3b123,D19,P2	162	-10.6

MacDONALD, HARVEY Harvey Forsyth B5.18.1898 New York NY D10.4.1965 Manoa PA BL/TL/5-11/170 d6.12 Col Albright

1928	Phi N	13	16	4	4	0	0	0	2	2-0	0	3	.250	.333	.250	53	-1	0	1.000	-0	94		O2R		-0.1

MACEY B Columbus OH d10.2

1890	Phi AA	1	1	0	0	0	0	0	0	0-0	0		.000	.000	.000	-99	0	0	1.000	-1	56	0	/C		-0.1

MACFARLANE, MIKE Michael Andrew B4.12.1964 Stockton CA BR/TR/6-1/205* [KCA85 4/97] d7.23 Col Santa Clara

1987	KC A	8	19	0	4	1	0	0	3	2-0	0	2	.211	.286	.263	46	-1	0-0	1.000	-1	120	184	C8		-0.2
1988	KC A	70	211	25	56	15	0	4	26	21-2	1	37	.265	.332	.393	102	1	0-0	.994	-12	90	75	C68		-0.8
1989	KC A	69	157	13	35	6	0	2	19	7-0	2	27	.223	.263	.299	59	-9	0-0	.996	5	153	98	C59,D4		-0.2
1990	KC A	124	400	37	102	24	4	6	58	25-2	7	69	.255	.306	.380	93	-4	1-0	.991	-12	100	40	C112,D5		-1.0
1991	KC A	84	267	34	74	18	2	13	41	17-0	6	52	.277	.330	.506	128	9	1-0	.993	-0	197	80	C69,D4	60	1.3
1992	KC A	129	402	51	94	28	3	17	48	30-2	15	89	.234	.310	.445	106	3	1-5	.993	3	102	78	C104,D13		0.9
1993	KC A	117	388	55	106	27	0	20	67	40-4	16	83	.273	.360	.497	121	12	2-5	.985	12	101	136	C114		2.9
1994	KC A	92	314	53	80	17	3	14	47	35-1	18	71	.255	.359	.462	105	3	1-0	.993	6	80	82	C81,D8		1.3
1995	†Bos A	115	364	45	82	18	1	15	51	38-0	14	78	.225	.319	.404	85	-8	2-1	.993	1	125	91	C111,D3		0.1
1996	KC A	112	379	58	104	24	2	19	54	31-5	7	57	.274	.339	.499	108	4	3-3	.993	-1	144	100	C99,D9		0.8
1997	KC A	82	257	34	61	14	2	8	35	24-3	6	47	.237	.316	.401	83	-7	0-2	.991	-7	192	46	C81	33	-0.9
1998	KC A	3	11	1	1	0	0	0	0	0-0	0	2	.091	.091	.091	-50	-2	0-0	1.000	0	201	214	C3		-0.2
	Oak A	78	207	28	52	12	0	7	34	12-0	4	34	.251	.301	.411	85	-5	1-0	.989	4	119	72	C70		0.2
	Year	81	218	29	53	12	0	7	34	12-0	4	36	.243	.291	.394	78	-8	1-0	.990	4	123	79	C73		0.0
1999	Oak A	81	226	29	55	11	0	4	31	13-0	1	52	.243	.282	.372	68	-11	0-0	.997	2	110	129	C79/D	15	-0.4
Total	13	1164	3602	458	906	221	17	129	514	295-17	97	700	.252	.322	.430	98	-15	12-16	.992	-0	123	87	C1058,D47	108	3.8

MACHA, KEN Kenneth Edward B9.29.1950 Monroeville PA BR/TR/6-2/217(205-217) [PitN72 6/143] d9.14 M3/C12 b-Mike Col Pittsburgh

1974	Pit N	5	5	1	3	1	0	0	1	0-0	0	1	.600	.600	.800	297	1	0-0	1.000	0	0	0	/C		0.2
1977	Pit N	35	95	2	26	4	0	0	11	6-0	0	17	.274	.317	.316	68	-4	1-1	.964	-6	73	0	3b17,1b11,O4(3/0/1)		-1.2
1978	Pit N	29	52	5	11	1	1	0	5	12-1	0	10	.212	.354	.269	74	-1	2-0	.970	-4	65	120	3b21		-0.6
1979	Mon N	25	36	8	10	3	1	0	4	2-1	1	9	.278	.333	.417	103	0	1-0	1.000	1	99	70	3b13,1b2,O2R/C		0.1
1980	Mon N	49	107	10	31	5	1	1	8	11-1	1	17	.290	.361	.383	106	1	1-0	1.000	1	99	73	3b33,1b2/COR		-0.7
1981	Tor A	37	85	4	17	2	0	0	6	8-0	0	15	.200	.266	.224	41	-6	1-1	.892	-1	108	78	3b19,1b16/CD		-0.9
Total	6	180	380	30	98	16	3	1	35	39-3	2	68	.258	.329	.324	79	-9	4-4	.938	-18	82	70	3b103,1b31,O7(3/0/4),C4,D2		-3.1

MACHA, MIKE Michael William B2.17.1954 Victoria TX BR/TR/5-11/180* [AtlN76*S1/10] d4.20 b-Ken Col Rice

1979	Atl N	6	13	2	2	0	0	0	1	1-0	0	5	.154	.214	.154	2	-2	0-0	.769	0	152	0	3b3		-0.1
1980	Tor A	5	8	0	0	0	0	0	0	0-0	0	1	.000	.000	.000	-96	-2	0-0	.778	1	146	265	3b2/C		-0.2
Total	2	11	21	2	2	0	0	0	1	1-0	0	6	.095	.136	.095	-34	-4	0-0	.773	1	150	102	3b5/C		-0.3

MACHADO, ALEJANDRO Alejandro Jose B4.26.1982 Caracas, Venez BB/TR/6-0/185 d9.2

2005	†Bos A	10	5	4	1	1	0	0	0	1-0	0	1	.200	.333	.400	89	0	0-0	1.000	-2	95	0	O6(2/3/1),2b3/SD		-0.1

MACHADO, ANDERSON Anderson Javier B1.25.1981 Caracas, Venez BB/TR/5-11/165* d9.27

2003	Phi N	1	0	0	0	0	0	0	0	0-0	0		—	—	—	—	0	1-0			0		/R		0.0
2004	Cin N	17	56	6	15	5	1	0	4	10-2	0	26	.268	.379	.393	102	1	3-1	.937	-7	74	63	S17		-0.5
2005	Cin N	2	2	0	0	0	0	0	0	0-0	0	1	.000	.000	.000	-99	-1	0-0	—	0			/H		-0.5
	Col N	4	10	1	0	0	0	0	2	2-0	0	5	.000	.154	.000	-45	-2	0-0	.929	-2	53	35	S4	94	-0.1
	Year	6	12	1	0	0	0	0	2	2-0	0	6	.000	.133	.000	-53	-3	0-0	.929	-2	53	35	S4		-0.5
Total	3	24	68	7	15	5	1	0	6	12-2	0	32	.221	.333	.324	72	-2	4-1	.935	-10	70	58	S21	94	-1.1

MACHADO, ROBERT Robert Alexis B6.3.1973 Puerto Cabello, Venez BR/TR/6-1/205(205-220) d7.24

1996	Chi A	4	6	1	4	1	0	0	2	0-0	0	0	.667	.667	.833	288	2	0-0	1.000	-2	65	176	C4		0.0
1997	Chi A	10	15	1	3	0	1	0	2	1-0	0	6	.200	.250	.333	52	-1	0-0	1.000	0	58	237	C10		-0.1
1998	Chi A	34	111	14	23	6	0	3	15	7-0	0	22	.207	.254	.342	54	-8	0-0	.981	-2	95	113	C34		-0.7
1999	Mon N	17	22	3	4	1	0	0	1	2-0	0	6	.182	.250	.227	23	-3	0-0	1.000	-0	0	55	C17		-0.2
2000	Sea A	8	14	2	3	0	0	1	1	0-0	0	4	.214	.267	.429	73	-1	0-0	1.000	-0	0	0	C8		0.2
2001	Chi N	52	135	13	30	10	0	2	13	7-3	1	26	.222	.266	.341	57	-9	0-0	.997	1	77	125	C47		-0.5
2002	Chi N	22	58	5	16	4	0	1	5	5-0	0	11	.276	.333	.397	94	-1	0-0	.985	-2	92	231	C21/1		0.3
	Mil N	51	153	14	39	10	1	2	17	12-4	1	30	.255	.310	.373	83	-4	0-0	.987	-1	78	122	C48,1b2		-0.3
	Year	73	211	19	55	14	1	3	22	17-4	1	41	.261	.316	.379	86	-5	0-0	.987	1	82	151	C69,1b3		0.0
2003	Bal A	18	49	8	13	1	0	1	3	6-0	0	12	.265	.345	.347	84	-1	0-0	.990	0	62	200	C18		0.0
2004	Bal A	37	73	5	11	3	0	1	3	6-0	0	18	.151	.195	.233	11	-10	0-0	.994	6	272	136	C35		-0.2
Total	9	253	636	66	146	36	2	11	61	45-7	2	135	.230	.282	.344	64	-36	0-0	.994	7	104	137	C242,1b3		-1.5

MACHEMER, DAVE David Ritchie B5.24.1951 St.Joseph MO BR/TR/5-11.5/180* [AnaA72 4/82] d6.21 Col Central Michigan

1978	Cal A	10	22	6	6	1	0	1	2	2-0	0	1	.273	.333	.455	123	1	0-1	1.000	-4	76	0	2b5,3b3/S		-0.4
1979	Det A	19	26	8	5	1	0	0	2	3-0	0	7	.192	.276	.231	37	-2	0-3	.972	-1	84	111	2b11/OLD		-0.4
Total	2	29	48	14	11	2	0	1	4	5-0	0	8	.229	.302	.333	74	-1	0-4	.978	-5	82	80	2b16,3b3/DOLS		-0.8

MACIAS, JOSE Jose Prado (Salazar) B1.25.1972 Panama City, Pan BB/TR/5-10/173(173-190) d5.12 OF(57/110/36)

1999	Det A	5	4	2	1	0	0	0	1	0-0	0	1	.250	.250	1.000	196	0	0-0	1.000	1	216	0	/2		0.1
2000	Det A	73	173	25	44	3	5	2	24	18-0	1	24	.254	.328	.364	76	-7	2-0	.976	-2	106	106	2b39,3b26,O3(0/1/2)/SD		-0.6
2001	Det A	137	488	62	131	24	6	8	51	32-0	3	54	.268	.316	.391	87	-10	21-6	.955	12	120	146	3b89,O29(3/22/4),2b18,D2		-0.7
2002	Det A	33	107	10	25	4	0	0	6	8-0	1	13	.234	.291	.271	53	-7	3-2	.964	-1	129	49	2b17,O10(0/9/1),3b8		-0.7
	Mon N	90	231	33	59	17	1	7	33	13-0	1	44	.255	.294	.429	91	-3	5-6	.978	6	111	230	O49C,3b22,2b6,S4	20	0.1
2003	Mon N	111	272	31	65	15	2	4	22	11-1	2	45	.239	.273	.353	60	-17	4-3	.977	-0	97	157	O62(41/15/8),3b25,2b4/D		-1.8
2004	Chi N	98	194	23	52	6	3	3	22	6-0	2	28	.268	.292	.376	69	-10	4-3	1.000	-2	101	231	O28(8/7/13),3b18,2b16	10	-1.1
2005	Chi N	112	177	15	45	8	0	1	13	6-0	0	24	.254	.274	.316	54	-12	4-1	.913	-5	69	49	O28,2b20,O20(5/7/8)		-1.2
Total	7	659	1646	201	422	77	17	26	173	93-1	10	243	.256	.298	.371	74	-69	43-21	.948	14	106	95	3b211,O201C,2b121,S5,D4	30	-4.7

YEAR	TM LG	G	AB	R	H	2B	3B	HR	RBI	BB-IB	HP	SO	AVG	OBP	SLG	AOPS	ABR	SB-CS	FA	FR	RNG	THR	GAMES AT POSITION	DL	BFW

MACK, CONNIE Cornelius Alexander "The Tall Tactician" (b McGillicuddy) B12.22.1862 E.Brookfield MA D2.8.1956 Philadelphia PA BR/TR/6-1/150 d9.11 M53 HF1937 s-Earle

1886	Was N	10	36	4	13	2	1	0	5	0		2	.361	.361	.472	164	3	0	.957	5			C10		0.7
1887	Was N	82	314	35	63	6	1	0	20	8	3	17	.201	.248	.226	28	-30	26	.906	1			C76,O5(2/2/1),2b2		-1.9
1888	Was N	85	300	49	56	5	6	3	29	17	8	18	.187	.249	.273	71	-9	31	.916	10			C79,O4(2/0/2)/S1		0.6
1889	Was N	98	386	51	113	16	1	0	42	15	8	12	.293	.333	.339	94	-4	26	.891	7			C45,O34(1/0/33),1b22		0.4
1890	Buf P	123	503	95	134	15	12	0	53	47	20	13	.266	.353	.344	94	-1	16	.925	-22	81	104	C112,O9(0/1/8),1b5		-1.2
1891	Pit N	75	280	43	60	10	0	0	29	19	9	11	.214	.286	.250	58	-14	4	.926	8	104	97	C72,1b3		0.0
1892	Pit N	97	346	39	84	9	4	1	31	21	6	22	.243	.298	.301	81	-9	11	.951	23	113	134	C92,O3(1/0/2)/1		2.1
1893	Pit N	37	133	22	38	3	1	0	15	10	5	9	.286	.358	.323	83	-3	4	.941	4	98	117	C37		0.4
1894	Pit N	70	231	33	57	7	1	1	21	21	4	14	.247	.320	.299	50	-19	8	.948	2	102	96	C70,M		-0.8
1895	Pit N	14	49	12	15	2	0	0	4	7	1	1	.306	.404	.347	100	1	1	.962	-2	88	93	C12/1M		0.0
1896	Pit N	33	120	9	26	4	1	0	16	5	0	8	.217	.248	.267	37	-11	0	.974	0	112	87	1b28,C5,M		-0.9
Total	11	724	2698	392	659	79	28	5	265	170	64	127	.244	.305	.300	72	-96	127	.927	35	98	109	C610,1b61,O55(6/3/46),2b2/S		-0.6

MACK, DENNY Dennis Joseph (b Dennis Joseph McGee) B1851 Easton PA D4.10.1888 Wilkes-Barre PA BR/TR/5-7/164 d5.6 M1/U2 Col Villanova ▲

1871	Rok NA	25	122	34	30	7	1	0	17	8		7	.246	.292	.320	79	-2	12-0	.936	1	162	104	1b24,P3/SOL		0.1
1872	Ath NA	47	205	68	59	9	1	0	34	23		9	.288	.360	.341	116	6	9-5	.948	-1	349	81	1b26,S21		0.3
1873	Phi NA	48	205	55	60	5	0	0	19	15		9	.293	.341	.317	93	-3	6-2	.938	3	86	109	1b42,O5(1/1/3),S3/2		0.2
1874	Phi NA	56	246	48	51	8	4	0	22	2		5	.207	.214	.272	53	-13	4-0	.900	-4	77	159	1b56		-1.2
1876	StL N	48	180	32	39	5	0	1	7	11		5	.217	.262	.261	79	-3		.886	-5	89	106	S41,2b5,O2(1/1/0)		-0.6
1880	Buf N	17	59	5	12	0	0	0	3	5		7	.203	.266	.203	60	-2		.940	1	99	72	S16/2		-0.1
1882	Lou AA	72	264	41	48	3	1	0		16			.182	.229	.201	49	-13		.898	2	100	85	S49,2b24,O5(1/3/1),M		-0.8
1883	Pit AA	60	224	26	44	5	3	0		13			.196	.241	.246	59	-9	31-7	.844	5	112	83	S38,1b25/2		-0.4
Total	4 NA	176	778	205	200	29	6	0	92	48		28	.257	.300	.313	85	-11	31-7	.927	-2	143	123	1b148,S25,O6(2/1/3),P3/2		-0.6
Total	4	197	727	104	143	13	4	1	10	45		12	.197	.244	.230	60	-27		.886	2	100	84	S144,2b31,1b25,O7(2/4/1)		-1.9

MACK, EARLE Earle Thaddeus (b McGillicuddy) B2.1.1890 Spencer MA D2.4.1967 Upper Darby Twp. PA BL/TR/5-8/140 d10.5 M2/C27 f-Connie Col Niagara

1910	Phi A	1	4	0	2	0	1	0	0	0		0	.500	.500	1.000	372	1	0	1.000	-0	118	105	/C		0.1
1911	Phi A	2	4	0	0	0	0	0	0	0		0	.000	.000	.000	-99	-1	0		-0	0	0	3b2		-0.1
1914	Phi A	2	8	0	0	0	0	0	1	0		0	.000	.000	.000	-99	-2	1	1.000	0	83	0	1b2		-0.2
Total	3	5	16	0	2	0	1	0	1	0		0	.125	.125	.250	11	-2	1	1.000	-0	83	0	1b2,3b2/C		-0.2

MACK, REDDY Joseph (b Joseph McNamara) B5.2.1866 , Ireland D12.30.1916 Newport KY 5-8/182 d9.16

1885	Lou AA	11	41	7	10	1	0	0	5	2	1		.244	.295	.268	79	-1		.885	1	103	193	2b11		0.1
1886	Lou AA	137	483	82	118	23	11	0	56	68	4		.244	.342	.344	109	6	13	.900	6	103	99	2b137		1.5
1887	Lou AA	128	478	117	147	23	8	1	69	83	5		.308	.415	.395	124	21	22	.912	1	99	91	2b128		2.1
1888	Lou AA	112	446	77	97	13	5	3	34	52	15		.217	.320	.289	98	-2	18	.907	5	103	81	2b112		1.1
1889	Bal AA	136	519	84	125	24	7	1	87	60	8	69	.241	.329	.320	84	-10	23	.897	-7	93	112	2b135/OC		-1.0
1890	Bal AA	26	95	14	27	3	5	1	11	10	3		.284	.370	.421	127	3	7	.932	3	109	67	2b26		0.6
Total	6	550	2062	381	524	87	36	6	262	275	36	69	.254	.352	.340	104	21	83	.905	9	100	97	2b549/OC		4.4

MACK, JOE Joseph John (b Joseph John Maciarz) B1.4.1912 Chicago IL D12.19.1998 Atlanta GA BB/TL/5-11.5/185 d4.17

| 1945 | Bos N | 66 | 260 | 30 | 60 | 13 | 1 | 3 | 44 | 34 | 0 | 39 | .231 | .320 | .323 | 79 | -7 | 1 | .991 | -0 | 102 | 92 | 1b65 | | -1.1 |

MACK, QUINN Quinn David B9.11.1965 Los Angeles CA BL/TL/5-10/185 d6.16 b-Shane Col California-Santa Barbara

| 1994 | Sea N | 5 | 21 | 1 | 5 | 3 | 0 | 0 | 2 | 1-0 | 0 | 4 | .238 | .273 | .381 | 65 | -1 | 0-0 | 1.000 | -0 | 84 | 0 | O4(3/1/0)/D | | -0.1 |

MACK, RAY Raymond James (b Raymond James Mlckovsky) B8.31.1916 Cleveland OH D5.7.1969 Bucyrus OH BR/TR/6-0/200 d9.9 Mil 1945 Col Case Western Reserve

1938	Cle A	2	6	2	2	0	1	0	2	0	0	1	.333	.333	.667	147	0	0-0	1.000	1	102	0	2b2		0.1
1939	Cle A	36	112	12	17	4	1	1	6	12	1	19	.152	.240	.232	22	-14	0-2	.976	1	94	131	2b34/3		-1.1
1940	Cle A★	146	530	60	150	21	5	12	69	51	0	77	.283	.346	.409	98	-3	4-2	.965	-5	94	117	2b146		0.2
1941	Cle A	145	500	54	114	22	4	9	44	54	0	69	.228	.303	.342	74	-20	8-4	.970	-2	93	114	2b145		-1.2
1942	Cle A	143	481	43	108	14	6	2	45	41	2	51	.225	.288	.291	67	-23	9-3	.969	-1	104	117	2b143		-1.4
1943	Cle A	153	545	56	120	25	2	7	62	47	2	61	.220	.285	.312	79	-16	8-3	.967	-4	98	116	2b153		-1.2
1944	Cle A	83	284	24	66	15	3	0	29	28	1	45	.232	.301	.306	77	-9	4-1	.951	2	103	117	2b83		-0.1
1946	Cle A	61	171	13	35	6	2	1	9	23	0	27	.205	.299	.281	67	-8	2-2	.970	-3	93	103	2b61		-0.8
1947	NY A	1	0	0	0	0	0	0	0	0	0	0	—	—	—		0	0-0		0			/R		0.0
	Chi N	21	78	9	17	6	0	2	12	5	1	15	.218	.274	.372	73	-3	0	.966	4	118	92	2b21		0.2
Total	9	791	2707	273	629	113	24	34	278	261	6	365	.232	.301	.330	76	-96	35-17	.966	-7	98	115	2b788/3		-5.3

MACK, SHANE Shane Lee B12.7.1963 Los Angeles CA BR/TR/6-0/190* [SDN84 1/11] d5.25 b-Quinn Col UCLA [DL 1989 SD N 31]

1987	SD N	105	238	28	57	11	3	4	25	18-0	3	47	.239	.299	.361	77	-8	4-6	.982	-1	108	28	O91(0/90/2)		-1.1
1988	SD N	56	119	13	29	3	0	0	12	14-0	2	36	.244	.336	.269	78	-3	5-1	.983	4	111	214	O55(9/46/6)		0.2
1990	Min A	125	313	50	102	10	4	8	44	29-1	5	69	.326	.392	.460	129	12	13-4	.988	8	114	145	O140(48/36/81)/D		2.0
1991	†Min A	143	442	79	137	27	8	18	74	34-1	6	79	.310	.363	.529	138	22	13-9	.977	3	110	76	O140(48/36/81)/D		2.1
1992	Min A	156	600	101	189	31	6	16	75	64-1	15	106	.315	.394	.467	135	30	26-14	.988	-1	101	88	O155(150/9/4)		2.6
1993	Min A	128	503	66	139	30	4	10	61	41-1	6	76	.276	.335	.412	99	-1	15-5	.986	9	114	107	O128(64/67/2)		0.7
1994	Min A	81	303	55	101	21	2	15	61	32-1	6	51	.333	.402	.564	146	22	4-1	.990	4	120	39	O75(66/24/0),D4	30	2.2
1997	Bos N	60	130	13	41	7	0	3	17	9-1	3	24	.315	.364	.415	109	2	2-1	1.000	5	83	0	O45(3/43/0),D5	25	-0.1
1998	Oak A	3	2	1	0	0	0	0	0	0	0	2	.000	.000	.000	-99	-1	0-0	—	0			/H		-0.1
	KC A	66	207	30	58	15	1	6	29	15-0	6	36	.280	.345	.449	101	0	8-2	.982	-2	91	54	O32(30/0/3),D21	59	-0.2
	Year	69	209	31	58	15	1	6	29	15-0	6	36	.278	.342	.445	99	-0	8-2	.982	-2	91	54	O32(30/0/3),D21		-0.3
Total	9	923	2857	436	853	155	28	80	398	256-6	51	509	.299	.364	.456	119	75	90-43	.985	19	108	87	O830(393/358/149),D35	160	8.2

MACKANIN, PETE Peter B8.1.1951 Chicago IL BR/TR/6-2/190(180-196) [TexA69 4/71] d7.3 M1/C7 OF(4/0/1)

1973	Tex A	44	90	3	9	2	0	0	2	4-0	1	26	.100	.146	.122	-24	-15	0-0	.947	-5	95	75	S33,3b10		-1.7
1974	Tex A	2	6	0	1	0	1	0	0	0	0	1	.167	.167	.500	88	1	0-0	1.000	2	151	293	S2		0.2
1975	Mon N	130	448	59	101	19	6	12	44	31-4	2	99	.225	.276	.375	76	-17	11-5	.966	14	111	115	2b127/S3		0.6
1976	Mon N	114	380	36	85	15	2	8	33	15-1	2	66	.224	.256	.337	64	-19	6-2	.973	3	105	90	2b100,3b8,S3/OL		-1.0
1977	Mon N	55	85	9	19	2	2	1	6	4-1	0	17	.224	.258	.329	58	-6	3-1	1.000	2	89	96	2b9,S8,3b5,O4(3/0/1)		-0.2
1978	Phi N	5	8	0	2	0	0	0	1	0-0	0	4	.250	.250	.250	39	-1	0-0	1.000	0	190	0	/13		0.0
1979	Phi N	13	9	2	1	0	1	0	2	1-0	0	2	.111	.200	.444	68	-1	0-0	1.000	2	231	0	2b2,S2,3b2	30	0.1
1980	Min A	108	319	31	85	18	0	4	35	14-2	0	34	.266	.296	.361	74	-12	6-2	.968	5	108	111	2b71,S30,1b4,3b3,D5		0.0
1981	Min A	77	225	21	52	7	1	4	18	7-2	1	37	.231	.258	.324	63	-11	1-2	.980	-5	110	88	2b31,S28,1b10,3b4,D6		-1.5
Total	9	548	1570	161	355	63	12	30	141	76-10	6	290	.226	.263	.339	65	-82	27-12	.968	19	108	103	2b340,S107,3b34,1b15,D11,O5L	30	-3.5

MACKENZIE, ERIC Eric Hugh B8.29.1932 Glendon AL, Can. BL/TR/6-0/185 d4.23

| 1955 | KC A | 1 | 1 | 0 | 0 | 0 | 0 | 0 | 0 | 0-0 | 0 | 0 | .000 | .000 | .000 | -99 | 0 | 0-0 | — | 0 | 0 | 0 | /C | | 0.0 |

MACKENZIE, GORDON Henry Gordon B7.9.1937 St.Petersburg FL BR/TR/5-11/175 d8.13 C7

| 1961 | KC A | 11 | 24 | 1 | 3 | 0 | 0 | 1 | 0 | 1-0 | 0 | 6 | .125 | .160 | .125 | -22 | -4 | 0-0 | 1.000 | -0 | 94 | 0 | C7 | | -0.4 |

MACKIEWICZ, FELIX Felix Thaddeus B11.20.1917 Chicago IL D12.20.1993 Olivette MO BR/TR/6-2/195 d9.7 Col Purdue

1941	Phi A	5	14	3	4	0	1	0	0	1	0		.286	.333	.429	103	-0	0-0	1.000	-0	86	0	O3(0/1/2)		-0.1
1942	Phi A	6	14	3	3	2	0	0	2	0	0	4	.214	.214	.357	59	-1	0-0	1.000	1	94	526	O3(0/2/1)		0.0
1943	Phi A	9	16	1	1	0	0	0	0	2	0	8	.063	.167	.063	-32	-3	0-0	1.000	0	123	0	O3(0/2/1)		-0.3
1945	Cle A	120	359	42	98	14	7	2	37	44	2	41	.273	.356	.368	115	7	5-5	.987	7	109	131	O112C		1.2
1946	Cle A	78	258	35	67	15	4	0	16	16	1	32	.260	.305	.349	88	-5	5-1	.983	-0	105	48	O72(0/71/1)		-0.7
1947	Cle A	2	5	0	0	0	0	0	0	0	0	2	.000	.000	.000	-99	-0	0-0	1.000	-0	119	0	O2C		-0.1
	Was A	3	6	1	1	1	0	0	0	0	0	1	.167	.167	.333	38	-1	0-0	1.000	-0	103	0	O5C		-0.1
	Year	5	11	1	1	1	0	0	0	0	0	3	.091	.091	.182	-26	-2	0-0	1.000	-0	103	0	O3C		-0.2
Total	6	223	672	85	174	32	12	2	55	63	3	88	.259	.325	.351	97	-4	10-6	.986	7	107	100	O198(0/193/5)		-0.1

MACKO, STEVE Steven Joseph B9.6.1954 Burlington IA D11.15.1981 Arlington TX BL/TR/5-10/160* [ChiN77 5/116] d8.18 Col Baylor [DL 1981 Chi N 177]

1979	Chi N	19	40	2	9	1	0	0	3	4-0	0	8	.225	.295	.250	46	-3	0-0	1.000	3	93	80	2b10,3b4	38	0.0
1980	Chi N	6	20	2	6	2	0	0	2	0-0	0	3	.300	.300	.400	86	-0	0-0	1.000	1	149	227	S3,3b2/2	215	0.1
Total	2	25	60	4	15	3	0	0	5	4-0	0	11	.250	.297	.300	59	-3	0-0	1.000	4	85	70	2b11,3b6,S3		0.1

YEAR	TM LG	G	AB	R	H	2B	3B	HR	RBI	BB-IB	HP	SO	AVG	OBP	SLG	AOPS	ABR	SB-CS	FA	FR	RNG	THR	GAMES AT POSITION	DL	BFW

MACKOWIAK, ROB Robert William B6.20.1976 Oak Lawn IL BL/TR/5-10/168(168-195) [PitN96 53/1499] d5.19 Col South Suburban (IL) JC OF(46/110/232)

2001	Pit N	83	214	30	57	15	2	4	21	15-5	3	52	.266	.319	.411	86	-5	4-3	.986	2	94	121	O46(10/0/40),2b21,3b2/1	29	-0.3
2002	Pit N	136	385	57	94	22	0	16	48	42-5	7	120	.244	.328	.426	98	-3	9-3	.988	1	86	139	O106(2/42/76),3b26,2b3		-0.3
2003	Pit N	77	174	20	47	4	4	6	19	15-2	4	53	.270	.342	.443	101	0	6-0	1.000	-4	93	0	O30(8/8/14),3b19,2b15		-0.3
2004	Pit N	155	491	65	121	22	6	17	75	50-2	6	114	.246	.319	.420	90	-8	13-4	.974	0	86	188	O118(25/19/79),3b55/1		-0.9
2005	Pit N	142	463	57	126	21	3	9	58	43-4	3	100	.272	.337	.389	90	-7	8-4	.952	4	114	148	3b65,O63(1/41/23),2b20,1b3		-0.1
Total	5	593	1727	229	445	84	15	52	221	165-18	23	439	.258	.328	.414	93	-23	40-14	.983	3	89	147	O363R,3b167,2b59,1b5	29	-1.9

MACLIN, LONNIE Lonnie Lee B2.17.1967 Clayton MO BL/TL/5-11/185 [StLN86 S3/63] d9.7 Col St. Louis-Meramec (MO) CC

| 1993 | StL N | 12 | 13 | 2 | 1 | 0 | 0 | 0 | 1 | 0-0 | 0 | 5 | .077 | .071 | .077 | -59 | -3 | 1-0 | 1.000 | -1 | 64 | 0 | O5L | | -0.3 |

MACON, MAX Max Cullen B10.14.1915 Pensacola FL D8.5.1989 Jupiter FL BL/TL/6-3/175 d4.21 Mil 1945-46 ▲

1938	StL N	46	36	5	11	0	0	0	3	2	0	4	.306	.342	.306	75	-1	0	.946	1	123	120	P38/OR		0.0
1940	Bro N	2	1	0	1	0	0	0	0	0	0	0	1.000	1.000	1.000	427	0	0	—	-0	0	0	P2		0.0
1942	Bro N	26	43	4	12	2	1	0	1	2	0	4	.279	.311	.372	98	3	1	.960	-0	83	0	P14		0.0
1943	Bro N	45	55	7	9	0	0	0	6	0	0	1	.164	.164	.164	-5	-4	1	1.000	0	121	174	P25,1b3		-0.1
1944	Bos N	106	366	38	100	15	3	3	36	12	0	23	.273	.296	.355	79	-11	7	.977	-2	106	115	1b72,O22(21/2/0)/P		-1.8
1947	Bos N	1	1	0	0	0	0	0	0	0	0	0	.000	.000	.000	-99	0	0	1.000	0	267	0	/P		0.0
Total	6	226	502	54	133	17	4	3	46	16	0	32	.265	.288	.333	72	-17	9	.965	-1	112	97	P81,1b75,O23(21/2/1)		-1.9

MacPHEE, WADDY Walter Scott B12.23.1899 Brooklyn NY D1.20.1980 Charlotte NC BR/TR/5-8/140 d9.27 Col Princeton

| 1922 | NY N | 2 | 7 | 2 | 2 | 0 | 1 | 0 | 1 | 0 | 0 | 0 | .286 | .375 | .571 | 140 | 0 | 0 | .889 | 0 | 116 | 0 | 3b2 | | 0.1 |

MACULLAR, JIMMY James F. "Little Mac" B1.16.1855 Boston MA D4.8.1924 Baltimore MD BR/TL/5-6/155 d5.5 M1/U1

1879	Syr N	64	246	24	52	9	0	0	13	3		27	.211	.221	.248	61	-9		.865	-4	93	100	S37,O26C,2b4/3M		-1.2
1882	Cin AA	79	299	44	70	6	6	0	22	14			.234	.268	.294	85	-5		.922	-4	68	122	O79C		-1.1
1883	Cin AA	14	48	4	8	2	0	0	4	4			.167	.231	.208	40	-3		.900	-2	53	0	O14(2/6/7)/S		-0.4
1884	Bal AA	107	360	73	73	16	6	4		36	8		.203	.290	.314	93	-1		.866	-2	93	87	S107		0.0
1885	Bal AA	100	320	52	61	7	6	3	26	49	4		.191	.306	.278	82	-2		.877	-0	90	90	S98,O2R/P		0.0
1886	Bal AA	85	268	49	55	7	1	0	26	49	2		.205	.332	.239	82	-2	23	.852	-8	81	81	S82,O2C/2P		-0.6
Total	6	449	1541	246	319	47	19	7	91	155	14	27	.207	.285	.276	83	-22	23	.865	-19	90	88	S325,O123(2/113/9),2b5,P2/3		-3.3

MADDEN, GENE Eugene B6.5.1890 Elm Grove WV D4.6.1949 Utica NY BL/TR/5-10/155 d4.20

| 1916 | Pit N | 1 | 1 | 0 | 0 | 0 | 0 | 0 | 0 | 0 | 0 | 0 | .000 | .000 | .000 | -99 | 0 | 0 | | | 0 | | /H | | 0.0 |

MADDEN, FRANK Francis A. "Red" B10.17.1892 Pittsburgh PA D4.30.1952 Pittsburgh PA d7.4

| 1914 | Pit F | 2 | 2 | 0 | 1 | 0 | 0 | 0 | 1 | 0 | 0 | 0 | .500 | .500 | .500 | 174 | 0 | 0 | — | -0 | 0 | 0 | /C | | 0.0 |

MADDEN, BUNNY Thomas Francis B9.14.1882 Boston MA D1.20.1954 Cambridge MA BR/TR/5-10/190 d6.3 Col Villanova

1909	Bos A	10	17	0	4	0	0	0	1	0	0		.235	.235	.235	48	-1	0	.941	1	141	86	C7		0.0
1910	Bos A	14	35	4	13	0	0	0	4	3	1		.371	.436	.457	175	3	0	.938	-3	102	65	C12		0.2
1911	Bos A	4	15	2	3	0	0	0	2	2	0		.200	.294	.200	39	-1	0	1.000	-1	82	50	C4		-0.2
	Phi N	28	76	4	21	1	1	0	4	0	0	13	.276	.276	.316	65	-4	0	.924	-1	94	110	C22		-0.3
Total	3	56	143	10	41	4	1	0	11	5	1	13	.287	.315	.329	87	-3	0	.935	-4	101	90	C45		-0.3

MADDEN, TOMMY Thomas Joseph B7.31.1883 Philadelphia PA D7.26.1930 Philadelphia PA BL/TL/5-11/160 d9.10

1906	Bos N	4	15	1	4	0	0	0	1		0		.267	.313	.267	83	0	0	1.000	0	243	0	O4L		-0.1
1910	NY A	1	1	0	0	0	0	0	0		0		.000	.000	.000	-95	0	0		0			/H		0.0
Total	2	5	16	1	4	0	0	0	1		0		.250	.294	.250	71	0	0	1.000	0	243	0	O4L		-0.1

MADDERN, CLARENCE Clarence James B9.26.1921 Lowell AZ D8.9.1986 Tucson AZ BR/TR/6-1/185* d9.19

1946	Chi N	3	3	0	0	0	0	0	0	0	0	0	.000	.250	.000	-27	0	0	1.000	0	149	0	O2L		0.0
1948	Chi N	80	214	16	54	12	1	4	27	10	5	25	.252	.301	.374	85	-5	0	.981	1	95	154	O55(48/0/10)		-0.8
1949	Chi N	10	9	1	3	0	0	1	2	2	0	2	.333	.455	.667	202	1	0	1.000	0	352	0	/1		0.2
1951	Cle N	11	12	0	2	0	0	0	0	1	0	1	.167	.167	.167	-10	-2	0-0	.667	-0	86	0	/OL		-0.2
Total	4	104	238	17	59	12	1	5	29	12	6	28	.248	.301	.370	84	-6	0-0	.973	1	96	147	O58(51/0/10)/1		-0.8

MADDOX, ELLIOTT Elliott B12.21.1947 East Orange NJ BR/TR/5-11/181* [DetA68 S1/20] d4.7 Col Michigan OF(77/472/189)

1970	Det A	109	258	30	64	13	4	3	24	30-1	3	42	.248	.332	.364	91	-3	2-3	.919	3	103	101	3b40,O37(28/1/9),S19/2		-0.1
1971	Was A	128	258	38	56	8	2	1	18	51-3	0	42	.217	.344	.275	82	-4	10-4	.990	8	116	154	O103(12/84/10),3b12		0.2
1972	Tex A	98	294	40	74	7	2	0	10	49-4	2	53	.252	.361	.289	99	2	20-10	.990	3	102	126	O94(11/70/14)		0.3
1973	Tex A	100	172	24	41	1	0	1	17	29-2	3	28	.238	.356	.262	80	-3	5-4	.981	5	107	176	O89(22/58/11),3b7/D	15	0.3
1974	NY A	137	466	75	141	26	2	3	45	69-4	4	48	.303	.395	.386	127	21	6-5	.986	9	103	202	O135(1/112/25),2b2/3		2.7
1975	NY A	55	218	36	67	10	3	1	23	21-0	7	24	.307	.382	.394	122	7	9-3	1.000	4	110	131	O55C/2	107	1.1
1976	†NY A	18	46	4	10	2	0	0	3	4-1	0	3	.217	.275	.261	59	-2	0-1	1.000	0	80	248	O13(0/6/7),D2	138	-0.3
1977	Bal A	49	107	14	28	7	0	2	9	13-0	4	9	.262	.357	.383	110	2	2-2	.990	1	119	0	O45(1/44/0)/3	99	0.3
1978	NY N	119	389	43	100	18	2	2	39	71-1	2	38	.257	.370	.329	101	4	2-11	.988	4	115	152	O70(9/13/72),3b43/1	20	0.2
1979	NY N	86	224	21	60	13	0	1	12	20-0	3	27	.268	.335	.339	87	-3	3-2	.985	4	116	126	O65(2/26/40),3b11	22	-0.1
1980	NY N	130	411	35	101	16	1	4	34	52-5	6	44	.246	.336	.319	86	-6	1-9	.956	3	96	106	3b115,O4(0/3/1),1b2		-0.8
Total	11	1029	2843	360	742	121	16	18	234	409-21	34	358	.261	.358	.334	99	15	60-54	.989	44	109	149	O719C,3b230,S19,2b4,1b3,D3	401	3.5

MADDOX, GARRY Garry Lee B9.1.1949 Cincinnati OH BR/TR/6-3/184(170-195) [SFN68*2/38] d4.25

1972	SF N	125	458	62	122	26	7	12	58	14-3	4	97	.266	.293	.432	102	-1	13-6	.979	-1	101	94	O121(20/96/6)		-0.5
1973	SF N	144	587	81	187	30	10	11	76	24-2	6	73	.319	.350	.460	118	13	24-10	.969	-4	107	44	O140C		0.7
1974	SF N	135	538	74	153	31	3	8	50	29-3	3	64	.284	.322	.398	97	-3	21-9	.986	-3	105	37	O131C		-0.8
1975	SF N	17	52	4	7	1	0	1	4	6-1	1	3	.135	.237	.212	24	-5	1-1	1.000	2	106	346	O13C		-0.4
	Phi N	99	374	50	109	25	8	4	46	36-5	5	54	.291	.359	.433	114	7	24-3	.983	13	121	169	O97C	36	2.2
	Year	116	426	54	116	26	8	5	50	42-6	6	57	.272	.344	.406	103	2	25-4	.985	15	119	192	O110C		1.8
1976	†Phi N	146	531	75	175	37	6	6	68	42-8	4	59	.330	.377	.456	132	23	29-12	.989	14	123	114	O144C		3.7
1977	†Phi N	139	571	85	167	27	10	14	74	24-8	4	58	.292	.323	.448	100	2	22-6	.977	3	111	77	O138C	15	0.2
1978	†Phi N	155	598	62	172	34	3	11	68	39-11	2	89	.288	.332	.410	105	3	33-7	.983	6	112	81	O154C		1.4
1979	†Phi N	148	548	70	154	28	6	13	61	17-5	4	75	.281	.304	.425	94	-7	26-13	.996	17	123	130	O140C		1.1
1980	†Phi N	143	549	59	142	31	3	11	73	18-5	0	52	.259	.278	.386	80	-16	25-5	.976	1	107	71	O143C		-1.4
1981	†Phi N	94	323	37	85	7	1	5	40	17-1	1	42	.263	.295	.337	77	-10	9-4	.977	8	115	139	O94C		-0.3
1982	Phi N	119	412	39	117	27	2	8	61	12-0	0	32	.284	.303	.417	97	-3	7-5	.992	3	104	135	O111C	33	-0.1
1983	†Phi N	97	324	27	89	14	2	4	32	17-5	1	31	.275	.312	.367	88	-6	7-6	.977	-2	105	26	O95C	15	-0.9
1984	Phi N	77	241	29	68	11	0	5	19	13-1	1	29	.282	.316	.390	97	-2	3-2	1.000	3	110	93	O69C	57	-1.0
1985	Phi N	105	218	22	52	8	1	4	23	13-2	1	26	.239	.281	.339	72	-9	4-2	.980	-0	104	88	O69C		-1.0
1986	Phi N	6	7	1	3	0	0	1	4	2-0	1	1	.429	.556	.429	169	1	0-1	1.000	-1	25	0	O3C	14	0.4
Total	15	1749	6331	777	1802	337	62	117	754	323-60	36	781	.285	.320	.413	100	-17	248-92	.983	59	111	93	O1687(20/1660/6)	170	3.9

MADDOX, JERRY Jerry Glenn B7.28.1953 Whittier CA BR/TR/6-2/200 [AtlN75 8/186] d6.3 Col Arizona St.

| 1978 | Atl N | 7 | 14 | 1 | 3 | 0 | 0 | 1 | 1 | 1-0 | 0 | 2 | .214 | .267 | .214 | 32 | -1 | 0-0 | .909 | -1 | 90 | 0 | 3b5 | | -0.2 |

MADISON, ART Arthur M. B1.14.1871 Clarksburg MA D1.27.1933 N.Adams MA BR/TR/5-9/165 d9.9

1895	Phi N	11	34	6	12	3	0	0	8	1	1		.353	.371	.441	109	-1	4	.955	-1	96	0	S6,2b3,3b2		0.0
1899	Pit N	42	118	20	32	2	4	0	19	11	1		.271	.338	.356	91	-2	1	.953	-5	89	71	2b19,S15,3b2		-0.5
Total	2	53	152	26	44	5	4	0	27	12	1	1	.289	.345	.375	95	-2	5	.926	-6	90	82	2b22,S21,3b4		-0.5

MADISON, SCOTTI Charles Scott B9.12.1959 Pensacola FL BB/TR/5-11/195* [MinA80 3/64] d7.6 Col Vanderbilt

1985	Det A	6	11	0	0	0	0	0	0	2-0	0	1	.000	.143	.000	-53	-2	0-0	1.000	0	0	0	/CD		-0.2
1986	Det A	7	2	0	0	0	0	0	0	1-0	0	0	.000	.000	.000	-99	-2	0-0	.667	-0	51	580	/3D	22	-0.2
1987	KC A	7	15	4	4	0	0	1	1	1-0	0	5	.267	.313	.467	100	0	0-0	1.000	1	141	234	1b4,C3		-0.2
1988	KC A	16	35	4	6	2	0	0	4	4-0	1	5	.171	.256	.229	36	-3	1-0	1.000	-2	104	0	C4,O3(2/0/1),1b2,D4		-0.2
1989	Cin N	40	98	13	17	7	0	1	9	8-2	1	10	.173	.241	.276	46	-7	0-1	1.000	1	99	81	3b26		-0.6
Total	5	71	166	21	27	12	0	1	11	15-2	1	22	.163	.240	.253	37	-14	1-1	.985	-1	97	103	3b27,D8,C8,1b6,O3(2/0/1)	22	-1.4

YEAR	TM LG	G	AB	R	H	2B	3B	HR	RBI	BB-IB	HP	SO	AVG	OBP	SLG	AOPS	ABR	SB-CS	FA	FR	RNG	THR	GAMES AT POSITION	DL	BFW

MADJESKI, ED Edward William (b Edward William Majewski) B7.20.1908 Far Rockaway NY D11.11.1994 Montgomery OH BR/TR/5-11/178 d5.2 Col Seton Hall

YEAR	TM LG	G	AB	R	H	2B	3B	HR	RBI	BB-IB	HP	SO	AVG	OBP	SLG	AOPS	ABR	SB-CS	FA	FR	RNG	THR	GAMES AT POSITION	DL	BFW
1932	Phi A	17	35	4	8	0	0	0	3	3	0	6	.229	.289	.229	35	-3	0-0	1.000	1	99	133	C8		-0.2
1933	Phi A	51	142	17	40	4	0	0	17	4	0	21	.282	.301	.310	62	-8	0-0	.958	-4	86	61	C41		-0.9
1934	Phi A	8	8	1	3	1	0	0	2	0	0	1	.375	.375	.500	129	0	0-0	.000	-1	0	0	/C		0.0
	Chi A	85	281	36	62	14	2	5	32	14	1	31	.221	.260	.338	52	-22	2-0	.973	-3	64	123	C79		-1.8
	Year	93	289	37	65	15	2	5	34	14	1	32	.225	.263	.343	54	-21	2-0	.971	-4	64	123	C80		-1.8
1937	NY N	5	15	0	3	0	0	0	2	0	0	2	.200	.200	.200	9	-2	0	1.000	-1	104	111	C5		-0.3
Total 4		166	481	58	116	19	2	5	56	21	1	61	.241	.274	.320	53	-35	2-0	.970	-7	73	107	C134		-3.2

MADLOCK, BILL Bill B1.2.1951 Memphis TN BR/TR/5-11/185(180-210) [TexA70*S5/99] d9.7 C2 Col Southeastern (IA) CC

YEAR	TM LG	G	AB	R	H	2B	3B	HR	RBI	BB-IB	HP	SO	AVG	OBP	SLG	AOPS	ABR	SB-CS	FA	FR	RNG	THR	GAMES AT POSITION	DL	BFW
1973	Tex A	21	77	16	27	5	3	1	5	7-0	1	9	.351	.412	.532	170	7	3-2	.918	-4	79	47	3b21		0.3
1974	Chi N	128	453	65	142	21	5	9	54	42-8	1	39	.313	.374	.442	123	14	11-7	.946	-8	96	55	3b121	31	0.6
1975	Chi N★	130	514	77	182	29	7	7	64	42-5	3	34	.354	.402	.479	138	27	9-7	.943	-3	102	59	3b128		2.4
1976	Chi N	142	514	68	174	36	1	15	84	56-15	11	27	.339	.412	.500	146	34	15-11	.961	-9	93	85	3b136		2.5
1977	SF N	140	533	70	161	28	1	12	46	43-14	2	33	.302	.360	.426	110	8	13-10	.949	-20	86	77	3b126,2b6		-1.5
1978	SF N	122	447	76	138	26	3	15	44	48-11	3	39	.309	.378	.481	144	27	16-5	.974	-8	102	78	2b114,1b3		-0.2
1979	SF N	69	249	37	65	9	2	7	41	18-3	0	19	.261	.309	.398	99	-2	11-3	.976	-9	88	78	2b63,1b5		0.5
	†Pit N	85	311	48	102	17	3	7	44	34-8	1	22	.328	.390	.469	128	13	21-8	.969	-9	89	82	3b85		-0.1
	Year	154	560	85	167	26	5	14	85	52-11	1	41	.298	.355	.438	116	12	32-11	.969	-18	89	82	3b85,2b63,1b5		-1.7
1980	Pit N	137	494	62	137	22	4	10	53	45-12	4	33	.277	.341	.399	103	2	16-10	.955	-16	93	99	3b127,1b12		2.2
1981	Pit N★	82	279	35	95	23	1	6	45	34-7	3	17	.341	.412	.495	150	21	18-6	.956	-0	102	139	3b78		1.9
1982	Pit N	154	568	92	181	33	3	19	95	48-16	4	34	.319	.368	.488	134	26	18-6	.952	-7	93	101	3b146,1b3		0.0
1983	Pit N★	130	473	68	153	21	0	12	68	49-10	2	24	.323	.386	.444	127	18	3-4	.958	-16	82	106	3b126	49	-2.8
1984	Pit N	103	403	38	102	16	0	4	44	26-5	1	29	.253	.297	.323	75	-14	3-1	.942	-11	85	112	3b98/1		-1.4
1985	Pit N	110	399	49	100	23	1	10	41	39-2	5	42	.251	.323	.388	99	0	3-3	.940	-11	92	58	3b98,1b12		1.3
	†LA N	34	114	20	41	4	0	2	15	10-0	3	11	.360	.422	.447	147	8	7-1	.948	4	107	165	3b32		-0.1
	Year	144	513	69	141	27	1	12	56	49-2	8	53	.275	.345	.402	110	8	10-4	.943	-7	95	82	3b130,1b12	35	0.2
1986	LA N	111	379	38	106	17	0	10	60	30-4	5	43	.280	.336	.404	112	6	3-3	.910	-2	97	48	3b101,1b2	23	-0.6
1987	LA N	21	61	5	11	1	0	3	7	6-0	1	5	.180	.265	.344	61	-4	0-0	.912	-2	84	86	3b16/1		-0.6
	†Det A	87	326	56	91	17	0	14	50	28-1	10	45	.279	.351	.460	118	9	4-3	.989	-2	78	94	D64,1b22/3		-0.1
Total 15		1806	6594	920	2008	348	34	163	860	605-121	68	510	.305	.365	.442	122	200	174-90	.948	-132	92	86	3b1440,2b183,D64,1b61	138	6.5

MADRID, SAL Salvador B6.9.1920 El Paso TX D2.24.1977 Ft.Wayne IN BR/TR/5-9/165 d9.17

YEAR	TM LG	G	AB	R	H	2B	3B	HR	RBI	BB-IB	HP	SO	AVG	OBP	SLG	AOPS	ABR	SB-CS	FA	FR	RNG	THR	GAMES AT POSITION	DL	BFW
1947	Chi N	8	24	0	3	1	0	0	1	1	0	6	.125	.160	.167	-14	-4	0	.956	2	118	126	S8		-0.1

MAGADAN, DAVE David Joseph B9.30.1962 Tampa FL BL/TR/6-3/200(190-215) [NYN83 2/32] d9.7 C3 Col Alabama

YEAR	TM LG	G	AB	R	H	2B	3B	HR	RBI	BB-IB	HP	SO	AVG	OBP	SLG	AOPS	ABR	SB-CS	FA	FR	RNG	THR	GAMES AT POSITION	DL	BFW
1986	NY N	10	18	3	8	0	0	0	3	3-0	0	1	.444	.524	.444	173	2	0-0	1.000	1	128	130	1b9		0.2
1987	NY N	85	192	21	61	13	1	3	24	22-2	0	22	.318	.386	.443	124	3	0-0	.981	5	122	86	3b50,1b13	11	1.2
1988	†NY N	112	314	39	87	15	0	1	35	60-4	2	39	.277	.393	.334	116	11	0-1	.988	3	93	95	1b71,3b48	15	1.0
1989	NY N	127	374	47	107	22	3	4	41	49-6	1	37	.286	.367	.393	123	13	1-0	.991	3	117	98	1b87,3b28		1.1
1990	NY N	144	451	74	148	28	6	6	72	74-4	2	55	.328	.417	.457	142	31	2-1	.998	4	98	79	1b113,3b19		2.8
1991	NY N	124	418	58	108	23	0	4	51	83-3	2	50	.258	.378	.342	106	9	1-1	.996	4	105	94	1b122		0.9
1992	NY N	99	321	33	91	9	1	3	28	56-3	1	44	.283	.390	.346	111	8	1-0	.941	-14	81	70	3b93,1b2	57	-0.7
1993	Fla N	66	227	22	65	12	0	4	29	44-4	1	30	.286	.400	.392	108	5	0-1	.961	5	105	115	3b63,1b2		1.0
	Sea A	71	228	27	59	11	0	1	21	36-3	0	33	.259	.356	.320	83	-4	0-2	.991	7	88	106	1b41,3b27,D2	32	-0.7
1994	Fla N	74	211	30	58	7	0	1	17	39-0	1	35	.275	.386	.322	85	-2	0-0	.958	-4	96	73	3b48,1b16		1.2
1995	Hou N	127	348	44	109	24	0	2	51	71-9	0	56	.313	.428	.399	129	20	2-1	.922	-8	92	64	3b100,1b11	60	1.2
1996	Chi N	78	169	23	43	10	0	3	17	29-3	0	23	.254	.360	.367	90	-1	0-2	.963	-4	96	72	3b51,1b10		0.9
1997	Oak A	128	271	38	82	10	1	4	30	50-1	2	40	.303	.414	.391	112	8	1-0	.940	-4	113	134	3b49,1b30,D25		0.9
1998	Oak A	35	109	12	35	8	0	1	13	13-1	0	12	.321	.390	.422	114	3	0-1	.918	-4	126	195	3b30,1b7	135	-0.7
1999	SD N	116	248	26	68	12	1	2	30	45-2	1	36	.274	.377	.355	96	1	1-3	.969	-2	94	79	3b52,1b42		0.5
2000	SD N	95	132	13	36	7	0	2	21	32-1	0	21	.273	.410	.371	107	4	0-0	.952	-2	83	74	3b22,1b9/2SD	18	0.5
2001	SD N	91	128	12	32	7	0	1	12	12-0	1	20	.250	.317	.328	73	-5	0-0	.950	-2	83	74	3b22,1b9/2		-0.7
Total 16		1582	4159	516	1197	218	13	42	495	718-46	12	546	.288	.390	.377	112	111	11-11	.951	0	98	92	3b709,1b593,D31,S3/2	328	7.4

MAGALLANES, EVER Everardo (Espinoza) B11.6.1965 El Sauz, Chihuahua, Mexico BL/TR/5-10/165 [CleA87 10/255] d5.17 Col Texas A&M-Commerce

YEAR	TM LG	G	AB	R	H	2B	3B	HR	RBI	BB-IB	HP	SO	AVG	OBP	SLG	AOPS	ABR	SB-CS	FA	FR	RNG	THR	GAMES AT POSITION	DL	BFW
1991	Cle A	3	2	0	0	0	0	0	0	1-0	0	1	.000	.333	.000	1	0	0-0	1.000	-0	98	0	S2		0.0

MAGEE, LEE Leo Christopher (b Leopold Christopher Hoernschemeyer) B6.4.1889 Cincinnati OH D3.14.1966 Columbus OH BB/TR/5-11/179 d7.4 M1 OF(230/285/8)

YEAR	TM LG	G	AB	R	H	2B	3B	HR	RBI	BB-IB	HP	SO	AVG	OBP	SLG	AOPS	ABR	SB-CS	FA	FR	RNG	THR	GAMES AT POSITION	DL	BFW
1911	StL N	26	69	9	18	1	1	0	8	8	0	8	.261	.338	.304	82	-2	4	.975	-2	83	91	2b18,S3		-0.3
1912	StL N	128	458	60	133	13	8	0	40	39	1	29	.290	.347	.354	94	-4	16	.956	6	104	134	O85L,2b23,1b6/S		-0.2
1913	StL N	137	531	54	142	13	7	2	31	34	2	30	.267	.314	.330	85	-11	23-26	.982	11	104	134	O108(108/3/1),2b22,1b6,S2		-1.0
1914	StL N	142	529	59	150	23	4	2	40	42	1	24	.284	.337	.353	107	4	36	.970	-1	91	115	O102(2/100/0),1b39,2b6		-0.3
1915	Bro F	121	452	87	146	19	10	4	49	22	1	19	.323	.356	.436	123	5	34	.937	-3	100	99	2b115,1b2,M		0.9
1916	NY A	131	510	57	131	18	4	3	45	50	1	31	.257	.324	.325	93	-4	29-25	.975	-1	99	91	O128(21/107/0),2b2		-1.7
1917	NY A	51	173	17	38	4	1	0	8	13	1	18	.220	.278	.254	62	-8	3	.938	-4	84	100	O50(2/48/0)		-1.1
	StL A	36	112	11	19	1	0	0	4	6	1	6	.170	.212	.179	20	-11	3	.971	2	84	99	O51(2/48/1),3b20,2b6,1b5		-2.2
	Year	87	285	28	57	5	1	0	12	19	2	24	.200	.252	.225	46	-19	6	.938	2	84	99	O101(4/96/1),3b20,2b6,1b5		
1918	Cin N	119	459	61	133	22	13	0	28	28	1	19	.290	.331	.394	123	11	19	.956	7	101	**139**	2b114,3b3		2.2
1919	Bro N	45	181	16	43	7	2	0	7	5	1	16	.238	.262	.298	67	-8	5	.938	-3	104	64	2b36,3b9		-1.1
	Chi N	79	267	36	78	12	4	1	17	18	1	8	.292	.339	.378	115	5	14	.978	-8	128	128	O45(12/27/6),S13,3b10,2b7		-1.3
	Year	124	448	52	121	19	6	1	24	23	2	24	.270	.309	.346	95	-3	19	.978	-8	97	99	O45(12/27/6),2b43,3b19,S13		
Total 9		1015	3741	467	1031	133	54	12	277	265	9	208	.276	.325	.350	98	-23	186-51	.970	-9	96	71	O519C,2b349,1b58,3b42,S19		-4.0

MAGEE, SHERRY Sherwood Robert B8.6.1884 Clarendon PA D3.13.1929 Philadelphia PA BR/TR/5-11/179 d6.29 U1 OF(1601/140/125)

YEAR	TM LG	G	AB	R	H	2B	3B	HR	RBI	BB-IB	HP	SO	AVG	OBP	SLG	AOPS	ABR	SB-CS	FA	FR	RNG	THR	GAMES AT POSITION	DL	BFW
1904	Phi N	95	364	51	101	15	12	3	57	14	2		.277	.308	.409	125	8	11	.921	5	165	52	O94(19/1/74)/1		1.0
1905	Phi N	155	603	100	180	24	17	5	98	44	8		.299	.354	.420	135	25	48	.963	10	92	122	O155L		2.6
1906	Phi N	154	563	77	159	36	8	6	67	52	5		.282	.348	.407	135	23	55	.982	12	95	44	O154L		2.9
1907	Phi N	140	503	75	165	28	12	4	**85**	53	4		.328	.396	.455	169	41	46	.978	8	68	154	O139L		4.5
1908	Phi N	143	508	79	144	30	16	2	57	49	11		.283	.359	.417	143	25	40	.970	3	85	124	O142L		2.3
1909	Phi N	143	522	60	141	33	14	2	66	43	11		.270	.339	.398	128	16	38	.970	-7	54	0	O143L		0.1
1910	Phi N	154	519	**110**	172	39	17	6	**123**	94	12	36	.331	.445	.507	172	53	49	.974	-12	92	47	O154(126/23/5)		3.4
1911	Phi N	121	445	79	128	32	5	15	94	69	6	33	.288	.366	.483	135	20	22	.981	1	103	81	O120(120/0/1)		1.6
1912	Phi N	132	464	79	142	25	9	6	66	55	7	54	.306	.388	.438	118	12	30	.963	-11	96	43	O124L,1b6		-0.4
1913	Phi N	138	470	92	144	36	6	11	70	38	1	36	.306	.369	.479	136	22	23-8	.968	-11	92	41	O123(106/8/9),1b4		0.8
1914	Phi N	146	544	96	**171**	39	11	15	**103**	48	3	42	.314	.380	.509	154	35	25	.940	5	115	39	O67L,S39,1b32,2b8		4.2
1915	Bos N	156	571	72	160	34	12	2	87	54	7	39	.280	.350	.392	130	22	15-12	.981	7	109	95	O120(102/3/19),1b2/S		2.0
1916	Bos N	122	419	44	101	17	5	3	54	44	6	52	.241	.322	.327	104	3	10	.978	-4	95	45	O65(63/0/2),1b2		-1.1
1917	Bos N	72	246	24	63	8	4	0	29	13	3	23	.256	.302	.333	100	-1	7	.954	-2	109	89	O41(29/0/12),1b2		-0.2
	Cin N	45	137	17	44	8	4	0	23	16	2	7	.321	.400	.438	164	11	4	.989	4	110	141	O106(92/0/14),1b4		1.5
	Year	117	383	41	107	16	8	0	52	29	5	30	.279	.338	.371	124	11	11	.967	6	109	109	O147(121/0/26),1b6		1.3
1918	Cin N	115	400	46	119	15	13	2	**76**	29	9	18	.298	.370	.415	142	20	14	.981	-3	93	100	1b66,O38(34/2/1),2b6		1.7
1919	†Cin N	56	163	11	35	6	1	0	21	26	4	19	.215	.337	.264	84	-1	4	.990	-3	106	17	O47(44/1/2)/23		-0.7
Total 16		2087	7441	1112	2169	425	166	83	1176	736	109	359	.291	.364	.427	137	334	441-20	.970	5	96	71	O1861L,1b136,S40,2b15/3		26.2

MAGEE, WENDELL Wendell Errol B8.3.1972 Hattiesburg MS BR/TR/6-0/220* [PhiN94 12/338] d8.16 Col Samford

YEAR	TM LG	G	AB	R	H	2B	3B	HR	RBI	BB-IB	HP	SO	AVG	OBP	SLG	AOPS	ABR	SB-CS	FA	FR	RNG	THR	GAMES AT POSITION	DL	BFW
1996	Phi N	38	142	9	29	7	0	2	14	9-0	0	33	.204	.252	.296	44	-12	0-0	.978	3	120	94	O37(6/18/18)		-1.0
1997	Phi N	38	115	7	23	4	0	1	9	9-1	0	20	.200	.254	.261	37	-11	1-4	.960	4	129	129	O38C		-0.8
1998	Phi N	20	75	9	22	6	1	1	11	1-0	0	19	.293	.344	.440	107	2	0-0	.941	-1	86	80	O19L		0.2
1999	Phi N	12	14	4	5	1	0	1	5	1-0	1	5	.357	.400	.857	204	2	0-0	1.000	-0	133	0	O4(1/2/1)		0.2
2000	Det A	91	186	31	51	4	2	7	35	10-0	1	28	.274	.310	.430	86	-5	1-0	1.000	-2	88	95	O74(21/36/19),D11	21	-0.9
2001	Det A	90	207	26	44	11	4	5	21	13-1	0	77	.213	.293	.377	77	-7	3-0	.992	2	97	208	O74(21/36/19),D11	23	-0.6
2002	Det A	97	347	32	94	19	1	6	35	10-0	1	64	.271	.289	.383	81	-11	2-4	.982	8	115	125	O91(5/78/9),D4		-0.4
Total 7		386	1086	120	268	52	8	24	122	69-2	2	204	.247	.291	.376	75	-43	7-8	.981	13	107	129	O339(70/177/103),D21	44	-3.6

YEAR	TM LG	G	AB	R	H	2B	3B	HR	RBI	BB-IB	HP	SO	AVG	OBP	SLG	AOPS	ABR	SB-CS	FA	FR	RNG	THR	GAMES AT POSITION	DL	BFW

MAGGERT, HARL Harl Vestin B2.13.1883 Cromwell IN D1.7.1963 Fresno CA BL/TR/5-8/155 d9.4 s-Harl

	1907 Pit N	3	6	1	0	0	0	0	0	2	0		.000	.250	.000	-21	-1	1	1.000	0	0	0	O2L		-0.1
	1912 Phi A	74	242	39	62	8	6	1	13	36	2		.256	.357	.351	107	3	10	.939	-5	90	65	O61(39/17/5)		-0.5
	Total 2	77	248	40	62	8	6	1	13	38	2		.254	.354	.343	104	2	11	.942	-5	87	63	O63(41/17/5)		-0.6

MAGGERT, HARL Harl Warren B5.4.1914 Los Angeles CA D7.10.1986 Citrus Heights CA BR/TR/6-0/190 d4.19 f-Harl

| | 1938 Bos N | 66 | 89 | 12 | 25 | 3 | 0 | 3 | 19 | 10 | 0 | 20 | .281 | .354 | .416 | 123 | 3 | 0 | .944 | 0 | 94 | 153 | O10(8/0/2),3b8 | | 0.3 |

MAGNER, STUBBY Edmund Burke B2.10.1888 Kalamazoo MI D9.6.1956 Chillicothe OH BR/TR/5-3/135 d7.12 Col Cornell

| | 1911 NY A | 13 | 33 | 3 | 7 | 0 | 0 | 0 | 4 | 4 | 0 | | .212 | .297 | .212 | 40 | -3 | 1 | .970 | 0 | 100 | 137 | S6,2b5 | | -0.2 |

MAGNER, JOHN John T. B1855 St.Louis MO 5-7.5/170 d7.14 U1

| | 1879 Cin N | 1 | 4 | 0 | 0 | 0 | 0 | 0 | | | 0 | | 1.000 | .000 | .000 | -99 | -1 | | .500 | -1 | 0 | 0 | /OC | | -0.1 |

MAGOON, GEORGE George Henry "Maggie","Topsy" B3.27.1875 St.Albans ME D12.6.1943 Rochester NH BR/TR/5-10/160 d6.29

	1898 Bro N	93	343	35	77	7	0	1	39	30	3		.224	.293	.254	57	-19	7	.925	10	113	94	S93		-0.4
	1899 Bal N	62	207	26	53	8	3	0	31	26	5		.256	.353	.324	82	-4	7	.923	0	101	84	S62		-0.1
	Chi N	59	189	24	43	5	1	0	21	24	6		.228	.333	.265	67	-7	5	.896	5	107	154	S59		0.0
	Year	121	396	50	96	13	4	0	52	50	11		.242	.344	.295	75	-11	12	.909	5	104	118	S121		-0.1
	1901 Cin N	127	460	47	116	16	7	1	53	52	2		.252	.331	.324	97	0	15	.919	-18	90	78	S112,2b15		-1.4
	1902 Cin N	45	162	29	44	9	2	0	23	13	5		.272	.344	.352	105	1	7	.930	3	116	102	2b41,S3		0.5
	1903 Cin A	42	139	6	30	6	0	0	9	19	1		.216	.314	.259	58	-7	2	.971	2	97	75	2b32,3b9		-0.5
	Chi A	94	334	32	76	11	3	0	25	30	6		.228	.303	.278	79	-7	4	.936	-25	89	81	2b94		-3.3
	Total 5	522	1834	199	439	62	16	2	201	194	28		.239	.321	.294	78	-43	47	.916	-23	101	99	S329,2b182,3b9		-5.2

MAGRANN, TOM Thomas Joseph B12.9.1963 Hollywood FL BR/TR/6-3/177 d9.7 Col Broward (FL) CC

| | 1989 Cle A | 9 | 10 | 0 | 0 | 0 | 0 | 0 | 0 | 0-0 | 0 | 4 | .000 | .000 | .000 | -98 | -3 | 0-0 | 1.000 | 1 | 34 | 163 | C9 | | -0.2 |

MAGRUDER, CHRIS Christopher James B4.26.1977 Tacoma WA BB/TR/5-11/200* [SFN98 2/72] d9.4 Col Washington

	2001 Tex A	17	29	3	5	0	0	1	1	1-0	1	5	.172	.226	.172	7	-4	0-0	1.000	2	150	225	O12(8/1/3)		-0.2
	2002 Cle A	87	258	34	56	15	1	6	29	15-2	1	55	.217	.261	.353	60	-15	2-0	.987	-1	102	51	O83(45/20/27)		-1.7
	2003 Cle A	9	26	3	9	2	1	1	3	3-0	1	6	.346	.433	.615	173	3	0-1	1.000	-1	76	0	O8(5/0/3)		0.1
	2004 Mil N	56	89	11	21	6	1	2	10	8-2	2	21	.236	.310	.393	80	-3	0-1	1.000	0	102	100	O24(10/0/16)		-0.3
	2005 Mil N	101	138	16	28	9	0	2	13	7-1	5	33	.203	.265	.312	51	-10	3-0	.964	-1	103	0	O45(5/9/31)		-1.1
	Total 5	270	540	67	119	32	3	11	56	34-5	10	120	.220	.277	.352	64	-29	5-2	.985	-1	103	53	O172(73/30/80)		-3.2

MAGUIRE, FREDDIE Frederick Edward B5.10.1899 Roxbury MA D11.3.1961 Boston MA BR/TR/5-11/155 d9.22 Col Holy Cross

	1922 NY N	5	12	4	4	0	0	0	1	0	0	1	.333	.333	.333	72	-1	1-0	.944	1	140	77	2b3		0.1
	1923 †NY N	41	30	11	6	1	0	0	2	2	0	4	.200	.250	.233	29	-3	1-0	.881	5	149	205	2b16/3		0.2
	1928 Chi N	140	574	67	160	24	7	1	41	25	3	38	.279	.312	.350	74	-23	6	.976	49	112	140	2b138		2.9
	1929 Bos N	138	496	54	125	26	8	0	41	19	3	40	.252	.284	.337	55	-37	8	.971	8	102	114	2b138/S		-2.3
	1930 Bos N	146	516	54	138	21	5	0	52	20	2	22	.267	.297	.328	53	-41	4	.969	-2	97	104	2b146		-3.5
	1931 Bos N	148	492	36	112	18	2	0	26	16	5	26	.228	.259	.272	45	-39	3	.976	10	105	103	2b148		-2.0
	Total 6	618	2120	226	545	90	22	1	163	82	13	131	.257	.289	.322	57	-144	23-0	.971	71	105	116	2b589/S3		-4.6

MAGUIRE, JACK Jack B2.5.1925 St.Louis MO D9.28.2001 Kerrville TX BR/TR/5-11/165* d4.18

	1950 NY N	29	40	3	7	2	0	0	3	3	0	13	.175	.233	.225	21	-5	0	1.000	2	114	429	O9(4/0/5),1b2		-0.3
	1951 NY N	16	20	6	8	1	1	1	4	2	0	7	.400	.455	.700	204	3	0-0	1.000	1	133	233	O8R		0.4
	Pit N	8	5	1	0	0	0	0	0	1	0	1	.000	.167	.000	-50	-1	0-0	1.000	1	205	0	/23		-0.1
	Year	24	25	7	8	1	1	1	4	3	0	8	.320	.393	.560	151	2	0-0	1.000	2	98	95	O8R/23		0.3
	StL A	41	127	15	31	2	1	1	14	12	0	21	.244	.309	.299	63	-7	1-0	.969	-1	98	95	O26L,3b5,2b2		-1.0
	Total 2	94	192	25	46	5	2	2	21	18	0	36	.240	.305	.318	66	-10	1-0	.979	3	105	166	O43(30/0/13),3b6,2b3,1b2		-1.0

MAHADY, JIM James Bernard B4.22.1901 Cortland NY D8.9.1936 Cortland NY BR/TR/5-11/170 d10.2

| | 1921 NY N | 1 | 0 | 0 | 0 | 0 | 0 | 0 | 0 | 0 | 0 | 0 | — | — | — | 0 | 0-0 | | 1.000 | 0 | 133 | 0 | /2 | | 0.0 |

MAHAN, ART Arthur Leo B6.8.1913 Somerville MA BL/TL/5-11/178 d4.30 Col Villanova

| | 1940 Phi N | 146 | 544 | 55 | 133 | 24 | 5 | 2 | 39 | 40 | 1 | 37 | .244 | .297 | .318 | 73 | -21 | 4 | .992 | 4 | 109 | 100 | 1b145/P | | -3.1 |

MAHAR, FRANK Frank Edward B12.4.1878 Natick MA D12.5.1961 Somerville MA TR/5-10.5/? d8.29

| | 1902 Phi N | 1 | 1 | 0 | 0 | 0 | 0 | 0 | 0 | 0 | 0 | | .000 | .000 | .000 | -99 | 0 | 0 | — | 0 | | | /H | | 0.0 |

MAHARG, BILLY William Joseph B3.19.1881 Philadelphia PA D11.20.1953 Philadelphia PA BR/TR/5-4.5/155 d5.18

	1912 Det A	1	1	0	0	0	0	0	0	0	0		.000	.000	.000	-99	0	0	1.000	0	215	0	/3		0.0
	1916 Phi N	1	1	0	0	0	0	0	0	0	0		.000	.000	.000	-97	0	0	—	-0	0	0	/OR		0.0
	Total 2	2	2	0	0	0	0	0	0	0	0		.000	.000	.000	-99	0	0	.000	0	0	0	/OR3		0.0

MAHER, TOM Thomas Francis B7.6.1870 Philadelphia PA D8.25.1929 Philadelphia PA d4.24

| | 1902 Phi N | 1 | 0 | 0 | 0 | 0 | 0 | 0 | 0 | 0 | 0 | 0 | — | — | — | 0 | 0 | 0 | — | 0 | | | /R | | 0.0 |

MAHLBERG, GREG Gregory John B8.8.1952 Milwaukee WI BR/TR/5-10/180* d9.24 Col Wisconsin-Madison

	1978 Tex A	1	1	0	0	0	0	0	0	0-0	0	0	.000	.000	.000	-99	0	0-0	1.000	-0	0	584	/C		0.0
	1979 Tex A	7	17	2	2	0	0	1	0	2-0	0	4	.118	.211	.294	35	-2	0-0	1.000	-2	62	0	C7		-0.4
	Total 2	8	18	2	2	0	0	1	0	2-0	0	4	.111	.200	.278	28	-2	0-0	1.000	-2	57	44	C8		-0.4

MAHONEY, DAN Daniel J. B3.20.1864 Springfield MA D1.31.1904 Springfield MA BR/TR/5-9.5/165 d8.20

	1892 Cin N	5	21	4	4	0	1	0	1	1	0	4	.190	.227	.286	56	-1	0	.943	1	124	120	C5		0.0
	1895 Was N	6	12	2	2	0	0	0	1	0	0	0	.167	.167	.167	-14	-2	0	1.000	-1	73	117	C2/1		-0.2
	Total 2	11	33	6	6	0	1	0	2	1	0	4	.182	.206	.242	28	-3	0	.949	1	118	120	C7/1		-0.2

MAHONEY, DANNY Daniel Joseph B9.6.1888 Haverhill MA D9.28.1960 Utica NY BR/TR/5-6.5/145 d5.15 Col Holy Cross

| | 1911 Cin N | 1 | 0 | 0 | 0 | 0 | 0 | 0 | 0 | 0 | 0 | 0 | — | — | — | 0 | 0 | 0 | — | 0 | | | /R | | 0.0 |

MAHONEY, MIKE George W. "Big Mike" B12.5.1873 Boston MA D1.3.1940 Boston MA BR/6-4/220 d5.18 Col Georgetown

	1897 Bos N	2	2	1	1	0	0	0	1	0	0		.500	.500	.500	155	0	0	1.000	0	0	0	/CP		0.0
	1898 StL N	2	7	0	0	0	0	0	0	0	0		.000	.000	.000	-98	-2	0	.920	-0	106	81	1b2		-0.2
	Total 2	4	9	1	1	0	0	0	1	0	0		.111	.111	.111	-36	-2	0	.920	-0	106	81	1b2/PC		-0.2

MAHONEY, JIM James Thomas "Moe" B5.26.1934 Englewood NJ BR/TR/6-0/175* d7.28 C7

	1959 Bos A	31	23	10	3	0	0	1	4	3-0	0	7	.130	.231	.261	33	-2	0-0	.940	4	130	76	S30		0.3
	1961 Was A	43	108	10	26	0	1	0	6	5-0	0	23	.241	.274	.259	44	-9	1-2	.968	6	116	143	S31,2b2		-0.1
	1962 Cle A	41	74	12	18	4	0	3	5	3-2	0	14	.243	.269	.419	86	-2	0-0	.964	1	104	103	S23,2b8/3		-0.1
	1965 Hou N	5	5	0	1	0	0	0	0	0-0	0	3	.200	.200	.200	14	-1	0-0	1.000	-1	34	257	S5		-0.1
	Total 4	120	210	32	48	4	1	4	15	11-2	0	47	.229	.266	.314	57	-14	1-2	.962	10	112	123	S89,2b10/3		0.2

MAHONEY, MIKE Michael John B12.5.1972 Des Moines IA BR/TR/6-1/200* [AtlN95 39/1093] d9.8 Col Creighton

	2000 Chi N	4	7	1	2	1	0	0	1	1-0	0	0	.286	.444	.429	124	0	0-0		-1	104	0	C4		-0.1
	2002 Chi N	16	29	2	6	3	0	0	3	1-0	1	10	.207	.233	.310	44	-2	0-0	1.000	2	0	154	C16		0.0
	2005 StL N	26	64	5	10	1	0	1	6	4-1	1	10	.156	.217	.219	15	-8	0-0	.984	-2	157	0	C25		-0.9
	Total 3	46	100	8	18	5	0	1	10	6-2	2	20	.180	.241	.260	31	-10	0-0	.991	-2	108	45	C45		-1.0

MAIER, BOB Robert Phillip B9.5.1915 Dunellen NJ D8.4.1993 S.Plainfield NJ BR/TR/5-8/180 d4.17

| | 1945 †Det A | 132 | 486 | 58 | 128 | 25 | 7 | 1 | 34 | 38 | | 32 | .263 | .317 | .350 | 88 | -8 | 7-11 | .936 | -15 | 85 | 80 | 3b124,O5L | | -2.6 |

MAILHO, EMIL Emil Pierre "Lefty" B12.16.1909 Berkeley CA BL/TL/5-10/165 d4.14 Col California-Davis

| | 1936 Phi A | 21 | 18 | 5 | 1 | 0 | 0 | 0 | 1 | 8 | 0 | 3 | .056 | .261 | .056 | -18 | -3 | 0-0 | 1.000 | 0 | 123 | 0 | /OL | | -0.3 |

MAISEL, CHARLIE Charles Louis B4.21.1894 Catonsville MD D8.25.1953 Baltimore MD BR/TR/6-0/? d10.2

| | 1915 Bal F | 1 | 4 | 0 | 0 | 0 | 0 | 0 | 0 | 0 | 0 | 0 | .000 | .000 | .000 | -97 | -1 | 0 | 1.000 | 0 | 138 | 90 | /C | | -0.1 |

MAISEL, FRITZ Frederick Charles "Flash" B12.23.1889 Catonsville MD D4.22.1967 Baltimore MD BR/TR/5-7.5/170 d8.11 b-George

YEAR	TM LG	G	AB	R	H	2B	3B	HR	RBI	BB-IB	HP	SO	AVG	OBP	SLG	AOPS	ABR	SB-CS	FA	FR	RNG	THR	GAMES AT POSITION	DL	BFW
1913	NY A	51	187	33	48	4	8	0	12	34	0	20	.257	.371	.310	99	1	25	.950	-2	91	44	3b51		0.1
1914	NY A	150	548	78	131	23	9	2	47	76	2	69	.239	.334	.325	98	1	**74-17**	.928	-17	85	91	3b148		-0.2
1915	NY A	135	530	77	149	16	6	4	46	48	1	35	.281	.342	.357	109	5	51-12	.940	-9	88	96	3b134		0.7
1916	NY A	53	158	18	36	5	0	0	7	20	1	18	.228	.318	.259	72	-5	4	.980	-4	95	33	O26C,3b11,2b4		-1.0
1917	NY A	113	404	46	80	4	4	0	20	36	2	18	.198	.267	.228	51	-24	29	.967	-3	97	92	2b100,3b7		-2.8
1918	StL A	90	284	43	66	4	0	0	16	46	1	17	.232	.341	.261	84	-3	11	.949	-3	94	67	3b79/OR		-0.5
Total	6	592	2111	295	510	56	24	6	148	260	7	177	.242	.327	.299	88	-25	194-**29**	.938	-38	89	83	3b430,2b104,O27(O/26/1)		-3.7

MAISEL, GEORGE George John B3.12.1892 Catonsville MD D11.20.1968 Baltimore MD BR/TR/5-10.5/180 d5.1 b-Fritz

YEAR	TM LG	G	AB	R	H	2B	3B	HR	RBI	BB-IB	HP	SO	AVG	OBP	SLG	AOPS	ABR	SB-CS	FA	FR	RNG	THR	GAMES AT POSITION	DL	BFW
1913	StL A	11	18	2	3	2	0	0	1	1	0	7	.167	.211	.278	44	-1	0	.833	-1	80	0	O5(2/3/0)		-0.2
1916	Det A	8	5	2	0	0	0	0	0	0	0	2	.000	.000	.000	-97	-1	0	.857	1	210	457	3b3		0.0
1921	Chi N	111	393	54	122	7	2	0	43	11	3	13	.310	.334	.338	78	-12	17-7	.978	-1	102	84	O108(0/107/1)		-1.6
1922	Chi N	38	84	9	16	1	1	0	6	8	0	2	.190	.261	.226	26	-9	1-3	1.000	0	103	77	O26(2/13/11)		-1.1
Total	4	168	500	67	141	10	3	0	50	20	3	24	.282	.314	.314	66	-23	18-**10**	.979	-0	102	81	O139(4/123/12),3b3		-2.9

MAJESKI, HANK Henry "Heeney" B12.13.1916 Staten Island NY D8.9.1991 Staten Island NY BR/TR/5-9/180* d5.17 Mil 1943-45

YEAR	TM LG	G	AB	R	H	2B	3B	HR	RBI	BB-IB	HP	SO	AVG	OBP	SLG	AOPS	ABR	SB-CS	FA	FR	RNG	THR	GAMES AT POSITION	DL	BFW
1939	Bos N	106	367	35	100	16	1	7	54	18	2	30	.272	.310	.379	91	-6	2	.945	10	113	118	3b99		0.7
1940	Bos N	3	3	0	0	0	0	0	0	0	0	0	.000	.000	.000	-99	-1	0	—	0			/H		-0.1
1941	Bos N	19	55	5	8	5	0	0	3	1	0	13	.145	.161	.236	11	-7	0	.911	0	104	86	3b11		-0.6
1946	NY A	8	12	1	1	0	1	0	0	0	0	3	.083	.083	.250	-9	-2	0	.750	-1	73	0	3b2		-0.3
	Phi A	78	264	25	66	14	3	1	25	26	1	13	.250	.320	.337	84	-6	3-2	.967	11	114	134	3b72		0.2
	Year	86	276	26	67	14	4	1	25	26	1	16	.243	.310	.333	80	-8	3-2	.964	10	113	131	3b74		0.2
1947	Phi A	141	479	54	134	26	5	8	72	53	5	31	.280	.358	.405	110	7	1-0	**.988**	8	104	119	3b134,S4/2		1.5
1948	Phi A	148	590	88	183	41	4	12	120	48	6	43	.310	.368	.454	118	14	2-1	.975	3	103	72	3b142,S8		1.6
1949	Phi A	114	448	62	124	26	5	9	67	29	4	23	.277	.326	.417	99	-4	0-1	.957	-5	96	138	3b113		-0.9
1950	Chi A	122	414	47	128	18	2	6	46	42	3	34	.309	.377	.406	103	2	1-4	.970	8	106	**132**	3b112		0.8
1951	Phi A	12	35	4	9	4	0	0	6	1	0	7	.257	.278	.371	76	-1	0-0	.950	0	116	156	3b9		-0.1
	Phi A	89	323	41	92	19	4	5	42	35	2	24	.285	.358	.415	106	3	1-2	.974	13	123	95	3b88		1.5
	Year	101	358	45	101	23	4	5	48	36	2	24	.282	.351	.411	104	2	1-2	.972	13	122	99	3b97		1.4
1952	Phi A	34	117	14	30	2	2	2	20	19	1	10	.256	.365	.359	96	0	0-1	.976	3	114	109	3b34		0.0
	Cle A	36	54	7	16	2	0	0	9	7	1	17	.296	.377	.333	106	1	0-0	.913	-1	80	182	3b11,2b3		0.3
	Year	70	171	21	46	4	2	2	29	26	2	17	.269	.369	.351	101	1	0-1	.966	3	108	122	3b45,2b3		0.3
1953	Cle A	50	50	6	15	1	0	2	12	3	1	8	.300	.352	.440	116	1	0-0	1.000	-1	85	84	2b10,3b7/OL		0.0
1954†	Cle A	57	121	10	34	4	0	3	17	7	0	14	.281	.320	.388	92	-2	0-0	.990	1	99	98	2b25,3b10		-0.2
1955	Cle A	36	48	3	9	2	0	2	6	8-0	2	8	.188	.322	.354	80	-1	0-0	1.000	-2	93	81	3b9,2b4		-0.7
	Bal A	16	41	6	7	1	0	0	2	2-1	0	5	.171	.209	.195	10	-5	0-0	1.000	-6	90	0	3b17,2b9		-0.9
	Year	52	89	5	16	3	0	2	8	10-1	2	13	.180	.275	.281	50	-6	0-0	1.000	-8	88	103	3b26,2b13		-1.6
Total	13	1069	3421	404	956	181	27	57	501	299-1	27	260	.279	.342	.398	100	-7	10-**11**	.968	48	107	113	3b861,2b48,S12/OL		4.0

MAJEWSKI, VAL Walter V. B6.19.1981 New Brunswick NJ BL/TL/6-2/200 (BalA02 3/76) d8.20 Col Rutgers [DL 2005 Bal A 183]

YEAR	TM LG	G	AB	R	H	2B	3B	HR	RBI	BB-IB	HP	SO	AVG	OBP	SLG	AOPS	ABR	SB-CS	FA	FR	RNG	THR	GAMES AT POSITION	DL	BFW
2004	Bal A	9	13	2	2	1	0	0	1	0-0	0	2	.154	.154	.231	-2	-2	0-0	1.000	1	158	0	O4(0/3/1),D3		-0.1

MAKSUDIAN, MIKE Michael Bryant B5.28.1966 Belleville IL BL/TR/5-11/220(200-220) d9.2 Col South Alabama

YEAR	TM LG	G	AB	R	H	2B	3B	HR	RBI	BB-IB	HP	SO	AVG	OBP	SLG	AOPS	ABR	SB-CS	FA	FR	RNG	THR	GAMES AT POSITION	DL	BFW
1992	Tor A	3	3	0	0	0	0	0	0	0	0	0	.000	.000	.000	-95	-1	0-0	—	0	0	0	/1	13	0.1
1993	Min A	5	12	2	2	1	0	0	2	4-0	0	3	.167	.353	.250	71	0	0-0	1.000	1	233	93	1b4/3		0.1
1994	Chi N	26	26	8	7	2	0	0	4	10-0	0	6	.269	.412	.346	118	2	0-1	1.000	1	120	170	1b3,C2,3b2	13	0.2
Total	3	34	41	8	9	3	0	0	6	14-0	0	9	.220	.411	.293	91	1	0-1	1.000	2	187	119	1b8,3b3,C2		0.2

MALAVE, JOSE Jose Francisco B5.31.1971 Cumana, Venez BR/TR/6-2/212* d5.23

YEAR	TM LG	G	AB	R	H	2B	3B	HR	RBI	BB-IB	HP	SO	AVG	OBP	SLG	AOPS	ABR	SB-CS	FA	FR	RNG	THR	GAMES AT POSITION	DL	BFW
1996	Bos A	41	102	12	24	3	0	4	17	2-0	1	25	.235	.257	.382	58	-7	0-0	.978	-3	82	55	O38(8/0/30)	19	-1.0
1997	Bos A	4	4	0	0	0	0	0	0	0-0	0	2	.000	.000	.000	-98	-1	0-0	1.000	1	129	0	O4L	19	-0.1
Total	2	45	106	12	24	3	0	4	17	2-0	1	27	.226	.248	.368	52	-8	0-0	.979	-2	84	53	O42(12/0/30)	19	-1.1

MALAY, CHARLIE Charles Francis B6.13.1879 Brooklyn NY D9.18.1949 Brooklyn NY BB/TR/5-11.5/175 d4.24 s-Joe

YEAR	TM LG	G	AB	R	H	2B	3B	HR	RBI	BB-IB	HP	SO	AVG	OBP	SLG	AOPS	ABR	SB-CS	FA	FR	RNG	THR	GAMES AT POSITION	DL	BFW
1905	Bro N	102	349	33	88	7	2	1	31	22	2		.252	.300	.292	83	-8	13	.932	-3	101	66	2b75,O25(1/23/1)/S		-1.2

MALAY, JOE Joseph Charles B10.25.1905 Brooklyn NY D3.19.1989 Bridgeport CT BL/TL/6-0/175 d9.7 f-Charlie

YEAR	TM LG	G	AB	R	H	2B	3B	HR	RBI	BB-IB	HP	SO	AVG	OBP	SLG	AOPS	ABR	SB-CS	FA	FR	RNG	THR	GAMES AT POSITION	DL	BFW
1933	NY N	8	24	0	3	0	0	0	2	0	0	5	.125	.125	.125	-29	-4	0	1.000	2	195	49	1b8		-0.3
1935	NY N	1	1	0	1	0	0	0	0	0	0	0	1.000	1.000	1.000	447	0	0	—	0			/H		0.0
Total	2	9	25	0	4	0	0	0	2	0	0	5	.160	.160	.160	-9	-4	0	1.000	2	195	49	1b8		-0.3

MALDONADO, CANDY Candido (Guadarrama) B9.5.1960 Humacao, PR BR/TR/6-0/190(185-220) d9.7

YEAR	TM LG	G	AB	R	H	2B	3B	HR	RBI	BB-IB	HP	SO	AVG	OBP	SLG	AOPS	ABR	SB-CS	FA	FR	RNG	THR	GAMES AT POSITION	DL	BFW
1981	LA N	11	12	1	1	0	0	0	0	0	0	5	.083	.083	.083	-55	-2	0-0	1.000	0	140	0	O9(4/0/5)		-0.3
1982	LA N	6	4	0	0	0	0	0	0	1-1	0	2	.000	.200	.000	-41	-1	0-0	1.000	1	253	0	O3(3/0/1)		0.0
1983†	LA N	42	62	5	12	1	1	1	6	5-0	0	14	.194	.254	.290	50	-4	0-0	1.000	-2	81	0	O33(12/3/19)		-0.8
1984	LA N	116	254	25	68	14	0	5	28	19-0	1	29	.268	.318	.382	97	-1	0-3	.955	-5	89	96	O102(7/31/67),3b4		-1.0
1985†	LA N	121	213	20	48	7	1	5	19	19-4	0	40	.225	.288	.338	76	-7	1-1	.984	1	92	161	O113(44/57/24)		-0.9
1986	SF N	133	405	49	102	31	3	18	85	20-4	3	77	.252	.289	.477	114	5	4-4	.983	1	93	147	O101(47/6/62)/3		0.3
1987†	SF N	118	442	69	129	28	4	20	85	34-4	6	78	.292	.346	.509	130	18	3-0	.973	-8	82	89	O116(4/0/115)	40	-0.9
1988	SF N	142	499	53	127	23	4	12	68	37-1	7	89	.255	.311	.377	102	1	6-5	.962	-4	96	75	O139R		-0.6
1989†	SF N	129	345	39	75	23	0	9	41	37-4	3	69	.217	.296	.362	91	-4	4-1	.974	1	100	118	O116R		1.1
1990	Cle A	155	590	76	161	32	2	22	95	49-4	5	134	.273	.330	.446	116	12	3-5	.993	5	106	101	O134(104/0/41),D20		1.1
1991	Mil A	34	111	11	23	6	0	5	20	13-0	2	23	.207	.288	.396	90	-2	1-0	.976	-2	88	0	O24(12/0/13)	75	-0.4
	†Tor A	52	177	26	49	9	0	7	28	23-4	6	53	.277	.375	.446	122	6	3-0	.990	-2	95	71	O52(52/0/1),D9		0.6
	Year	86	288	37	72	15	0	12	48	36-4	8	76	.250	.342	.427	111	4	4-0	.986	-4	93	50	O76(64/0/14),D9		1.3
1992†	Tor A	137	489	64	133	25	4	20	66	59-3	7	112	.272	.357	.462	122	15	2-2	.978	1	96	138	O132(129/0/4),D4		-1.4
1993	Chi N	70	140	8	26	5	0	3	15	13-0	1	40	.186	.260	.286	46	-11	0-0	.914	-1	86	134	O41(29/0/14)		-0.2
	Cle A	28	81	11	20	2	0	5	20	11-2	0	18	.247	.333	.457	111	1	0-1	.976	-1	90	65	O26(2/0/25),D2		-0.2
1994	Cle A	42	92	14	18	5	1	5	12	19-1	0	31	.196	.333	.435	95	-1	1-1	1.000	-0	87	0	O58(26/0/38)/D		-0.2
1995	Tor A	61	160	22	43	13	0	7	25	25-0	2	45	.269	.368	.481	120	6	1-1	.988	-3	87	66	O69(35/0/42)/D		0.6
	Tex A	13	30	6	7	3	0	2	5	7-0	0	5	.233	.378	.533	130	2	0-1	1.000	1	111	165	O11(9/0/4)		0.1
	Year	74	190	28	50	16	0	9	30	32-0	2	50	.263	.370	.489	122	7	1-2	.990	-2	91	82	O69(35/0/42)/D		0.6
Total	15	1410	4106	498	1042	227	17	146	618	391-32	41	864	.254	.322	.424	107	33	34-33	.977	-20	94	103	O1215(489/97/688),D61,3b5	115	-3.5

MALER, JIM James Michael B8.16.1958 New York NY BR/TR/6-4/230* [SeaA78*1/5] d9.3 Col Miami

YEAR	TM LG	G	AB	R	H	2B	3B	HR	RBI	BB-IB	HP	SO	AVG	OBP	SLG	AOPS	ABR	SB-CS	FA	FR	RNG	THR	GAMES AT POSITION	DL	BFW
1981	Sea A	12	23	1	8	1	0	0	2	2-0	1		.348	.423	.391	130	1	1-0	1.000	-0	71	126	1b5,D2		0.1
1982	Sea A	64	221	18	50	8	3	4	26	12-3	3	35	.226	.274	.344	66	-11	0-0	.991	2	108	95	1b57,D5		-1.3
1983	Sea A	26	66	5	12	1	0	1	3	5-0	2	11	.182	.260	.242	38	-6	0-3	1.000	0	88	58	1b19,D5		-0.8
Total	3	102	310	24	70	10	3	5	31	19-3	6	47	.226	.283	.326	65	-16	1-3	.994	2	102	90	1b81,D12		-2.0

MALINOSKY, TONY Anthony Francis B10.5.1909 Collinsville IL BR/TR/5-10.5/165 d4.26 Col Whittier

YEAR	TM LG	G	AB	R	H	2B	3B	HR	RBI	BB-IB	HP	SO	AVG	OBP	SLG	AOPS	ABR	SB-CS	FA	FR	RNG	THR	GAMES AT POSITION	DL	BFW
1937	Bro N	35	79	7	18	2	0	0	3	9	0	11	.228	.307	.253	53	-5	0	.833	-6	88	132	3b13,S11		

MALKMUS, BOBBY Robert Edward B7.4.1931 Newark NJ BR/TR/5-9/180(165-180) d6.1

YEAR	TM LG	G	AB	R	H	2B	3B	HR	RBI	BB-IB	HP	SO	AVG	OBP	SLG	AOPS	ABR	SB-CS	FA	FR	RNG	THR	GAMES AT POSITION	DL	BFW
1957	Mil N	13	22	6	2	0	1	0	3	3-0	0	3	.091	.200	.182	4	-3	0-0	.972	2	127	116	2b7		-0.1
1958	Was A	41	70	5	13	2	1	0	3	10-0	0	15	.186	.230	.243	31	-7	0-0	.964	2	104	92	2b26,3b2/S		-0.2
1959	Was A	6	0	0	0	0	0	0	0	0-0	0	0	—	—	—		0	0-0	—	0	0	0	/R		-0.0
1960	Phi N	79	133	16	28	4	1	1	12	11-0	0	28	.211	.267	.278	51	-9	2-2	1.000	1	112	162	S29,2b23,3b12		-0.1
1961	Phi N	121	342	39	79	8	2	7	31	20-1	5	45	.231	.276	.327	61	-20	1-3	.988	24	109	124	2b58,S34,3b25		1.1
1962	Phi N	8	5	3	1	1	0	0	0	2-0	0	4	.200	.200	.400	58	0	0-0	1.000	1	227	265	/S		-0.1
Total	6	268	572	69	123	15	5	8	46	38-1	2	90	.215	.265	.301	53	-39	3-5	.982	30	107	110	2b114,S65,3b39		-0.2

MALLETT, JERRY Gerald Gordon B9.18.1935 Bonne Terre MO BR/TR/6-5/208 d9.19 Col Baylor

YEAR	TM LG	G	AB	R	H	2B	3B	HR	RBI	BB-IB	HP	SO	AVG	OBP	SLG	AOPS	ABR	SB-CS	FA	FR	RNG	THR	GAMES AT POSITION	DL	BFW
1959	Bos A	4	15	1	4	0	0	0	1	1-0	0	3	.267	.313	.267	58	-1	0-0	1.000	2	108	572	O4C		

YEAR	TM LG	G	AB	R	H	2B	3B	HR	RBI	BB-IB	HP	SO	AVG	OBP	SLG	AOPS	ABR	SB-CS	FA	FR	RNG	THR	GAMES AT POSITION	DL	BFW

MALLON, LES Leslie Clyde B11.21.1905 Sweetwater TX D4.17.1991 Granbury TX BR/TR/5-8/160 d4.14

1931	Phi N	122	375	41	116	19	2	1	45	29	0	40	.309	.359	.379	91	-4	0	.956	6	103	88	2b97,1b5,S3,3b3		0.8
1932	Phi N	103	347	44	90	16	2	0	35	28		28	.259	.318	.349	71	-14	1	.955	-24	85	77	2b88,3b5		-3.2
1934	Bos N	42	166	23	49	6	1	0	18	15	0	12	.295	.354	.343	95	-1	0	.967	-5	103	69	2b42		-0.3
1935	Bos N	116	412	48	113	24	2	2	25	28	1	37	.274	.322	.357	89	-6	3	.975	-9	97	74	2b73,3b36/OR		-0.9
Total	4	383	1300	156	368	65	5	8	119	100	3	117	.283	.336	.359	85	-25	4	.962	-32	96	79	2b300,3b44,1b5,S3/OR		-3.6

MALLONEE, BEN Howard Bennett "Lefty" B3.31.1894 Baltimore MD D2.19.1978 Baltimore MD BL/TL/5-6/150 d9.14

1921	Phi A	7	25	2	6	1	0	0	2	4	0	2	.240	.269	.280	40	-1	1-0	1.000	1	96	126	O6C		-0.2

MALLONEE, JULE Julius Norris B4.4.1900 Charlotte NC D12.26.1934 Charlotte NC BL/TR/6-2/180 d8.4

1925	Chi A	2	3	1	0	0	0	0	1	0		0	.000	.250	.000	-34	-1	0-0	1.000	-0	62	0	/OC		-0.1

MALLORY, JIM James Baugh "Sunny Jim" B9.1.1918 Lawrenceville VA D8.6.2001 Greenville NC BR/TR/6-1/170 d9.8 Col North Carolina-Asheville

1940	Was A	4	12	2	2	0	0	0	1		0	1	.167	.231	.167	5	-2	0-0	1.000	0	130	0	O3(1/1/1)		-0.2
1945	StL N	13	43	3	10	2	0	0	5	0	0	2	.233	.233	.279	41	-4	0	.923	-0	99	126	O18(3/8/3)		-0.4
	NY N	37	94	10	28	1	0	0	9	6	0	7	.298	.340	.309	80	-3	1	.979	-0	94	127	O21(8/9/4)		-0.4
	Year	50	137	13	38	3	0	0	14	6	0	9	.277	.308	.299	68	-6	1	.959	-0	96	127	O32(16/12/6)		-0.8
Total	2	54	149	15	40	3	0	0	14	7	0	10	.268	.301	.289	63	-9	1-0	.964	0	99	114	O35(17/13/7)		-1.0

MALLORY, SHELDON Sheldon B7.16.1953 Argo IL BL/TL/6-2/175 d4.10 Col Manatee (FL) CC

1977	Oak A	64	126	19	27	4	1	0	5	11-0	3	18	.214	.291	.262	53	-8	12-5	.977	1	112	127	O45(9/17/21),1b4,D7	29	-0.7

MALLOY, MARTY Marty Thomas B4.6.1972 Gainesville FL BL/TR/5-10/160* d9.6 Col Santa Fe (FL) CC

1998	†Atl N	11	28	3	5	1	0	1	1	2-0		2	.179	.233	.321	44	-2	0-0	1.000	1	106	93	2b10		-0.1
2002	Fla N	24	25	1	3	0	0	0	1	2-0		8	.120	.185	.120	-16	-4	0-0	1.000	-0	72	98	2b3,3b2		-0.5
Total	2	35	53	4	8	1	0	1	2	4-0		10	.151	.211	.226	16	-6	0-0	1.000	1	100	94	2b13,3b2		-0.6

MALMBERG, HARRY Harry William "Swede" B7.31.1925 Fairfield AL D10.29.1976 San Francisco CA BR/TR/6-1/170 d4.12 C2

1955	Det A	67	208	25	45	5	2	0	19	21	0	19	.216	.310	.260	56	-12	0-1	.985	3	109	91	2b65		-0.5

MALONE, EDDIE Edward Russell B6.16.1920 Chicago IL BR/TR/5-10/175* d7.17

1949	Chi A	55	170	17	46	7	2	1	16	29	0	19	.271	.377	.353	97	0	2-1	.990	-2	83	85	C51		0.1
1950	Chi A	31	71	2	16	2	0	0	10	10	0	8	.225	.321	.254	50	-5	0-0	1.000	1	70	119	C21		-0.3
Total	2	86	241	19	62	9	2	1	26	39	0	27	.257	.361	.324	83	-5	2-1	.993	-0	79	94	C72		-0.2

MALONE, FERGY Fergus G. B1842 , Ireland D1.1.1905 Seattle WA BR/TL/5-8/156 d5.20 M3/U1

1871	Ath NA	27	134	33	46	7	1	1	33	9		4	.343	.385	.433	136	7	9-3	.856	9			C27		1.1
1872	Ath NA	41	213	46	60	5	3	0	39	4		5	.282	.295	.333	92	-2	3-0	.884	5			C24,1b17		0.2
1873	Phi NA	53	259	59	75	11	2	0	41	14		7	.290	.326	.347	97	-1	6-1	.898	5			C53/SM		0.3
1874	Chi NA	47	223	33	56	5	0	0	28	4		0	.251	.264	.274	72	-7	2-1	.820	3			C47,M		-0.3
1875	Phi NA	29	123	15	28	2	1	0	10	1		2	.228	.234	.260	69	-4	1-0	.919	-3	25	53	1b22,C6,O2C		-0.5
1876	Phi N	22	96	14	22	0	0	0		1		1	.229	.229	.250	60	-4		.777	-2			C20,O3R/S		-0.5
1884	Phi U	1	4	0	1	0	0	0	0	0			.250	.250	.250	56	0		.818	-1			/CM		-0.1
Total	5 NA	197	952	186	265	30	7	1	151	32		18	.278	.302	.328	93	-7	21-5	.856	19			C157,1b39,O2C/S		0.8
Total	2	23	100	14	23	2	0	0	6	0		1	.230	.230	.250	60	-4		.780	-3			C21,O3R/S		-0.6

MALONE, LEW Lewis Aloysius B3.13.1897 Baltimore MD D2.17.1972 Brooklyn NY BR/TR/5-11/175 d5.31 Mil 1918

1915	Phi A	76	201	17	41	4	4	1	17	21	1	40	.204	.283	.279	70	-8	7-1	.919	-6	87	44	2b43,3b12,O4R,S2		-1.2
1916	Phi A	5	4	1	0	0	0	0	0	1	0	2	.000	.200	.000	-42	-1	0	1.000	1	0	0	/S		-0.1
1917	Bro N	1	0	1	0	0	0	0	0	0		0				0	0		—	0			/R		0.0
1919	Bro N	51	162	9	33	7	3	0	11	6	0	18	.204	.232	.284	54	-10	1	.934	-7	83	66	3b47,2b2,S2		-1.7
Total	4	133	367	28	74	11	7	1	28	28	1	60	.202	.260	.278	62	-19	8-1	.910	-13	84	65	3b59,2b45,S5,O4R		-3.0

MALONE, MARTIN Martin d6.20 ▲

1872	Eck NA	5	16	2	6	0	0	0	3	1		3	.375	.412	.375	169	2	0-1	.333	-3	0	0	O3(0/1/2),P2,2b2		-0.1

MALONEY, JOHN John d9.15

1876	NY N	2	7	1	2	0	1	0	2	0		1	.286	.286	.571	206	1		.800	-0	0	0	O2C		0.0
1877	Har N	1	4	0	1	0	0	0	0	0		0	.250	.250	.250	65	0		.250	-1	0	0	/OC		-0.1
Total	2	3	11	1	3	0	1	0	2	0		1	.273	.273	.455	152	1		.556	-2	0	0	O3C		-0.1

MALONEY, PAT Patrick William B1.19.1888 Grosvenor Dale CT D6.27.1979 Pawtucket RI BR/TR/6-0/150 d6.19

1912	NY A	25	79	9	17	1	0	0	8	7	0	0	.215	.279	.228	43	-6	3	.926	-1	111	56	O20C		-0.8

MALONEY, BILLY William Alphonse B6.5.1878 Lewiston ME D9.2.1960 Breckenridge TX BL/TR/5-10/177 d5.2

1901	Mil A	86	290	42	85	3	4	0	22	7	8		.293	.328	.331	87	-5	11	.952	-4	78	124	C72,O8C		-0.2
1902	StL N	30	112	8	23	3	0	0	11	6	2		.205	.258	.232	37	-9	0	.906	-3	112	194	O23(1/0/22),C7		-1.2
	Cin N	27	89	13	22	4	0	1	7	2	1		.247	.272	.326	77	-3	8	.848	-0	199	0	O18(10/6/2),C7		-0.3
1905	Chi N	145	558	78	145	17	14	2	56	43	11		.260	.325	.351	98	-2	59	.954	-1	90	96	O145(0/12/134)		-1.0
1906	Bro N	151	566	71	126	15	7	0	32	49	3		.221	.286	.272	80	-13	38	.966	9	102	130	O151(0/149/2)		-1.3
1907	Bro N	144	502	51	115	7	10	0	32	31	10		.229	.287	.283	86	-10	25	.967	1	89	99	O144C		-1.8
1908	Bro N	113	359	31	70	5	7	3	17	24	5		.195	.255	.273	71	-13	14	.947	2	87	130	O103(5/95/3),C4		-1.8
Total	6	696	2476	294	585	54	42	6	177	162	40		.236	.294	.299	83	-55	155	.954	5	94	111	O592(16/414/163),C90		-7.6

MALZONE, FRANK Frank James B2.28.1930 Bronx NY BR/TR/5-10/180* d9.17

1955	Bos A	6	20	2	7	1	0	0	1	1-0		3	.350	.381	.400	101	0	0-0	1.000	2	152	103	3b4		0.2
1956	Bos A	27	103	15	17	3	1	2	11	9-0	0	8	.165	.230	.272	29	-11	1-0	.931	2	117	77	3b26		-0.9
1957	Bos A★	153	634	82	185	31	5	15	103	31-1	1	41	.292	.323	.427	98	-3	2-1	.954	21	120	101	3b153		1.8
1958	Bos A★	155	627	76	185	30	2	15	87	33-3	4	53	.295	.333	.421	100	-1	1-3	.950	17	118	106	3b155		1.5
1959	Bos A★	154	604	90	169	34	2	19	92	46-3	1	58	.280	.323	.437	103	2	6-0	.953	10	109	131	3b154		1.2
1960	Bos A★	152	595	60	161	30	2	14	79	36-4	2	42	.271	.313	.398	89	-10	2-3	.948	13	108	103	3b151		0.1
1961	Bos A	151	590	74	157	21	4	14	87	44-3	1	49	.266	.314	.386	85	-14	1-3	.950	1	101	137	3b149		-1.4
1962	Bos A	156	619	74	175	20	3	21	95	35-2	0	43	.283	.319	.426	96	-5	0-1	.967	8	104	106	3b156		0.1
1963	Bos A★	151	580	66	169	25	2	15	71	31-5	2	45	.291	.327	.419	105	3	0-2	.964	3	99	64	3b148		0.5
1964	Bos A☆	148	537	62	142	19	0	13	56	37-1	2	43	.264	.312	.372	86	-10	0-0	.959	6	97	89	3b143		-0.5
1965	Bos A	106	364	40	87	20	0	3	34	28-0	1	38	.239	.293	.319	70	-14	1-1	.969	-1	97	101	3b96		-1.6
1966	Cal A	82	155	6	32	5	0	2	12	10-1	0	11	.206	.253	.277	54	-9	0-0	.925	-0	100	56	3b35		-1.0
Total	12	1441	5428	647	1489	239	21	133	728	337-26	21	434	.274	.315	.399	91	-72	14-14	.955	80	107	103	3b1370		-0.0

MANCUSO, GUS August Rodney "Blackie" B12.5.1905 Galveston TX D10.26.1984 Houston TX BR/TR/5-10/185 d4.30 C1 b-Frank

1928	StL N	11	38	2	7	0	1	0	5		1	5	.184	.184	.237	9	-5	0	.984	2	138	90	C11		-0.2
1930	†StL N	76	227	39	83	17	2	7	59	18	1	16	.366	.415	.551	127	10	1	.969	1	114	100	C61		1.4
1931	†StL N	67	187	13	49	16	1	1	23	18	0	13	.262	.327	.374	85	-3	2	.972	5	100	140	C56		0.5
1932	StL N	103	310	25	88	23	1	5	43	30	0	15	.284	.347	.413	100	1	0	.977	4	74	125	C82		1.0
1933	†NY N	144	481	39	127	17	2	6	56	48	0	21	.264	.331	.345	95	-2	0	.972	-1	105	102	C142		0.6
1934	NY N	122	383	32	94	14	0	7	46	27	0	19	.245	.295	.337	70	-17	0	.977	4	110	118	C122		-0.5
1935	NY N★	128	447	33	133	18	2	5	56	30	0	16	.298	.342	.380	95	-3	1	.972	-4	117	99	C126		0.1
1936	†NY N	139	519	55	156	21	3	6	63	39	1	28	.301	.351	.405	104	3	0	.977	7	134	111	C138		1.8
1937	†NY N★	86	287	30	80	17	1	4	39	17	0	20	.279	.319	.387	90	-4	1	.982	11	159	110	C81		1.2
1938	NY N	52	158	19	55	8	0	2	15	17	0	13	.348	.411	.437	132	4	0	.977	3	127	77	C44		1.3
1939	Chi N	80	251	17	58	10	0	2	23	22	0	19	.231	.294	.287	59	-14	0	.981	2	127	93	C76		-0.8
1940	Bro N	60	144	16	33	8	0	0	16	13	0	7	.229	.293	.285	56	-8	0	.982	5	123	92	C56		-0.1
1941	StL N	106	328	25	75	13	1	2	37	37	1	19	.229	.309	.293	66	-14	0	.989	8	125	101	C105		0.0
1942	StL N	5	13	0	1	0	0	0	0		0	1	.077	.077	.077	-52	-2	0	.917	-1	0	0	C3		-0.3
	NY N	39	109	4	21	1	0	0	8	14	0	5	.193	.285	.220	48	-7	1	.982	2	129	92	C38		-0.3
	Year	44	122	4	22	1	0	0	8	14	0	7	.180	.265	.205	38	-10	1	.977	1	120	86	C41		-0.6
1943	NY N	94	252	11	50	5	0	2	20	28		16	.198	.284	.242	52	-15	0	.974	-4	80	96	C77		-1.6

YEAR	TM LG	G	AB	R	H	2B	3B	HR	RBI	BB-IB	HP	SO	AVG	OBP	SLG	AOPS	ABR	SB-CS	FA	FR	RNG	THR	GAMES AT POSITION	DL	BFW
1944	NY N	78	195	15	49	4	1	1	25	30	0	20	.251	.351	.297	84	-3	0	.976	2	107	111	C72		0.2
1945	Phi N	70	176	11	35	5	0	0	16	28	0	10	.199	.309	.227	52	-10	2	.988	-2	69	123	C70		-0.9
Total	17	1460	4505	386	1194	197	16	53	543	418	5	264	.265	.328	.351	85	-85	8	.977	44	113	106	C1360		3.4

MANCUSO, FRANK Frank Octavius B5.23.1918 Houston TX BR/TR/6-0/195 d4.18 b-Gus

YEAR	TM LG	G	AB	R	H	2B	3B	HR	RBI	BB-IB	HP	SO	AVG	OBP	SLG	AOPS	ABR	SB-CS	FA	FR	RNG	THR	GAMES AT POSITION	DL	BFW
1944	†StL A	88	244		50	11	0	1	24	20	2	32	.205	.271	.262	50	-16	1-0	.953	-6	91	70	C87		-1.8
1945	StL A	119	365	39	98	13	3	1	38	46	2	44	.268	.354	.329	94	-1	0-2	.989	-4	101	74	C115		0.1
1946	StL A	87	262	22	63	8	3	2	23	30	2	31	.240	.323	.328	78	-7	1-0	.973	-14	62	74	C85		-1.9
1947	Was A	43	131	5	30	5	1	0	13	5	0	11	.229	.257	.282	51	-9	0-0	.958	-4	96	92	C35		-1.2
Total	4	337	1002	85	241	37	7	5	98	101	6	118	.241	.314	.306	74	-33	2-2	.972	-28	88	75	C322		-4.8

MANDA, CARL Carl Alan B11.16.1886 Little River KS D3.9.1983 Artesia NM BR/TR/5-10/170 d9.11

YEAR	TM LG	G	AB	R	H	2B	3B	HR	RBI	BB-IB	HP	SO	AVG	OBP	SLG	AOPS	ABR	SB-CS	FA	FR	RNG	THR	GAMES AT POSITION	DL	BFW
1914	Chi A	9	15	2	4	0	0	0	1	3	0	3	.267	.389	.267	99	0	1	.971	3	144	60	2b7		0.3

MANEY, VINCENT S. Vincent B10.14.1887 Batavia NY D3.13.1952 Batavia NY BR/TR/6-0/175 d5.18

YEAR	TM LG	G	AB	R	H	2B	3B	HR	RBI	BB-IB	HP	SO	AVG	OBP	SLG	AOPS	ABR	SB-CS	FA	FR	RNG	THR	GAMES AT POSITION	DL	BFW
1912	Det A	1	2	0	0	0	0	0	0	0	0	0	.000	.500	.000	48	0	0	.833	-0	71	315	/S		0.0

MANGAN, JIM James Daniel B9.24.1929 San Francisco CA BR/TR/5-10/190* d4.16 Mil 1953-54 Col Santa Clara

YEAR	TM LG	G	AB	R	H	2B	3B	HR	RBI	BB-IB	HP	SO	AVG	OBP	SLG	AOPS	ABR	SB-CS	FA	FR	RNG	THR	GAMES AT POSITION	DL	BFW
1952	Pit N	11	13	1	2	0	0	0	2	1	0	3	.154	.214	.154	4	-2	0-0	.833	-1	47	279	C4		-0.2
1954	Pit N	14	26	2	5	0	0	0	2	4	0	9	.192	.300	.192	32	-3	0-0	1.000	-0	53	88	C7		-0.2
1956	NY N	20	20	2	2	0	0	0	1	4-0	0	6	.100	.250	.100	-1	-3	0-0	1.000	-0	153	0	C15		-0.2
Total	3	45	59	5	9	0	0	0	5	9-0	0	18	.153	.265	.153	15	-8	0-0	.985	-0	96	72	C26		-0.6

MANGUAL, ANGEL Angel Luis (Guilbe) B3.19.1947 Juana Diaz, PR BR/TR/5-10/180* d9.15 b-Pepe

YEAR	TM LG	G	AB	R	H	2B	3B	HR	RBI	BB-IB	HP	SO	AVG	OBP	SLG	AOPS	ABR	SB-CS	FA	FR	RNG	THR	GAMES AT POSITION	DL	BFW
1969	Oak A	6	4	1	1	0	0	0	0	0	0	0	.250	.250	.500	108	0	0-0	.000	-0	0	0	O3(2/0/1)		0.0
1971	†Oak A	94	287	32	82	8	1	4	30	17-1	0	27	.286	.324	.362	96	-2	1-4	.988	-2	99	66	O81(17/57/9)	21	-0.8
1972	†Oak A	91	272	19	67	13	2	5	32	14-1	1	48	.246	.285	.364	97	-2	0-1	.971	3	112	81	O74(22/22/52)		-0.4
1973	†Oak A	74	192	20	43	4	1	3	13	8-1	1	34	.224	.257	.302	60	-11	1-1	.947	0	103	72	O50(14/17/21),D14,1b2/2		-1.5
1974	†Oak A	115	365	37	85	14	4	9	43	17-2	0	59	.233	.265	.367	86	-9	3-0	.961	0	104	111	O74(26/28/29),D37/3		-1.2
1975	Oak A	62	109	13	24	3	0	1	6	3-0	0	18	.220	.241	.275	47	-8	0-1	.978	-1	95	60	O39(21/6/14),D15		-1.1
1976	Oak A	8	12	0	2	1	0	0	0	0-0	0	1	.167	.167	.250	22	-1	0-1	1.000	0	61	429	O7R		-0.2
Total	7	450	1241	122	304	44	8	22	125	59-5	2	187	.245	.279	.346	83	-33	5-8	.969	-1	103	85	O328(82/130/133),D66,1b2/32	21	-5.2

MANGUAL, PEPE Jose Manuel (Guilbe) B5.23.1952 Ponce, PR BR/TR/5-10/165* d9.6 b-Angel

YEAR	TM LG	G	AB	R	H	2B	3B	HR	RBI	BB-IB	HP	SO	AVG	OBP	SLG	AOPS	ABR	SB-CS	FA	FR	RNG	THR	GAMES AT POSITION	DL	BFW
1972	Mon N	8	11	2	3	0	0	0	0	1-0	0	5	.273	.333	.273	73	0	0-1	1.000	-1	37	0	O3(2/0/1)		-0.2
1973	Mon N	33	62	9	11	2	1	3	7	6-0	0	18	.177	.246	.387	71	-3	2-4	.966	-1	85	0	O22(20/1/1)		-0.6
1974	Mon N	23	61	10	19	3	0	0	4	5-0	0	15	.311	.353	.361	98	0	5-0	1.000	-2	69	0	O22(18/2/8)		-0.2
1975	Mon N	140	514	84	126	16	2	9	45	74-1	4	115	.245	.340	.337	85	-8	33-11	.972	-11	88	90	O138(1/135/2)		-2.1
1976	Mon N	66	215	34	56	9	1	3	16	50-2	2	49	.260	.403	.353	111	7	17-7	.968	1	106	77	O62(34/36/1)		0.6
	NY N	41	102	15	19	5	2	1	9	10-0	0	32	.186	.259	.304	62	-5	7-3	.985	1	104	116	O40(12/26/2)		0.0
	Year	107	317	49	75	14	3	4	25	60-2	2	81	.237	.361	.338	98	2	24-10	.973	2	105	89	O100(46/58/6)		0.0
1977	NY N	8	7	1	1	0	0	0	2	1-0	0	4	.143	.250	.143	9	-1	0-0	.833	0	241	0	O4(2/2/0)		-0.2
Total	6	319	972	155	235	35	6	16	83	147-3	6	238	.242	.341	.340	88	-10	64-26	.972	-14	92	78	O289(89/198/18)		-3.2

MANGUS, GEORGE George Graham B5.22.1890 Red Creek NY D8.10.1933 Rutland MA BL/TR/5-11.5/165 d8.20

YEAR	TM LG	G	AB	R	H	2B	3B	HR	RBI	BB-IB	HP	SO	AVG	OBP	SLG	AOPS	ABR	SB-CS	FA	FR	RNG	THR	GAMES AT POSITION	DL	BFW
1912	Phi N	10	25	2	5	3	0	1	3	1	0	6	.200	.231	.320	47	-2	0	.750	-2	80	0	O5L		-0.4

MANION, CLYDE Clyde Jennings "Pete" B10.30.1896 Big River MO D9.4.1967 Detroit MI BR/TR/5-11/175 d5.5

YEAR	TM LG	G	AB	R	H	2B	3B	HR	RBI	BB-IB	HP	SO	AVG	OBP	SLG	AOPS	ABR	SB-CS	FA	FR	RNG	THR	GAMES AT POSITION	DL	BFW
1920	Det A	32	80	4	22	4	1	0	7	4	1	7	.275	.318	.350	79	-3	0-0	.940	-3	92	114	C30		-0.3
1921	Det A	12	10	0	2	0	0	0	2	2	1	2	.200	.385	.200	53	-1	0-0	1.000	0	80	312	C3		0.0
1922	Det A	42	69	9	19	4	1	0	12	4	0	6	.275	.315	.362	79	-2	0-1	.932	-3	83	47	C22/1		-0.5
1923	Det A	23	22	0	3	0	0	0	1	2	0	1	.136	.208	.136	-8	-4	0-0	.857	-1	82	147	C3/1		-0.2
1924	Det A	14	13	1	3	0	0	0	1	0	0	1	.231	.286	.231	35	-1	0-0	.750	-1	61	0	C3/1		-0.2
1926	Det A	75	176	15	35	6	0	0	14	24	0	16	.199	.295	.222	36	-16	1-1	.972	-3	87	102	C74		-1.6
1927	Det A	1	0	0	0	0	0	0	0	1	0	0	—	1.000	—	174	-0	0-0	—	0	0	0	/H		-1.0
1928	StL A	76	243	25	55	5	1	2	31	15	1	18	.226	.274	.280	44	-20	3-0	.980	5	100	83	C71		-0.1
1929	StL A	35	111	16	27	2	0	0	11	15	0	3	.243	.333	.261	53	-7	1-0	.976	3	155	80	C34		-0.2
1930	StL A	57	148	12	32	1	0	1	11	24	0	17	.216	.326	.243	45	-12	0-1	.985	7	141	144	C56		-0.8
1932	Cin N	49	135	7	28	4	0	0	12	14	0	16	.207	.282	.237	43	-11	0-0	.970	1	88	92	C47		-0.5
1933	Cin N	36	84	3	14	1	0	0	4	6	0	7	.167	.239	.179	21	-9	0	.981	2	93	114	C34		-0.4
1934	Cin N	25	54	4	10	0	0	0	4	4	0	7	.185	.241	.185	16	-6	0-0	1.000	4	93	148	C24		-0.4
Total	13	477	1145	96	250	25	3	3	112	118	3	102	.218	.293	.253	45	-92	5-3	.973	9	106	103	C401,1b3		-6.0

MANKOWSKI, PHIL Philip Anthony B1.9.1953 Buffalo NY BL/TR/6-0/180* [DetA70 9/218] d8.30

YEAR	TM LG	G	AB	R	H	2B	3B	HR	RBI	BB-IB	HP	SO	AVG	OBP	SLG	AOPS	ABR	SB-CS	FA	FR	RNG	THR	GAMES AT POSITION	DL	BFW
1976	Det A	24	85	9	23	2	1	1	4	4-0	0	8	.271	.300	.353	88	-2	0-0	.971	2	103	211	3b23		0.1
1977	Det A	94	286	21	79	7	3	3	27	16-4	2	41	.276	.318	.353	79	-9	1-2	.964	12	118	103	3b85/2		0.2
1978	Det A	88	222	28	61	8	0	4	20	22-3	2	28	.275	.344	.365	97	0	2-3	.972	2	106	148	3b80/D		-0.5
1979	Det A	42	99	11	22	4	0	0	8	10-4	0	16	.222	.286	.263	50	-7	0-0	.963	-2	104	121	3b36/D	55	-0.2
1980	NY N	8	12	1	2	1	0	0	1	2-0	0	4	.167	.286	.250	51	-1	0-0	.571	-1	93	0	3b3	147	-0.2
1982	NY N	13	35	2	8	1	0	0	4	1-0	0	6	.229	.237	.257	42	-3	0-1	.957	-0	107	123	3b13	202	-0.8
Total	6	269	739	72	195	23	4	8	64	55-11	4	103	.264	.315	.338	79	-22	3-6	.962	17	110	131	3b240,D2/2		-0.8

MANLOVE, CHARLIE Charles Henry Weeks "Chick" B10.8.1862 Philadelphia PA D2.12.1952 Altoona PA BR/TR/5-9/165 d5.31

YEAR	TM LG	G	AB	R	H	2B	3B	HR	RBI	BB-IB	HP	SO	AVG	OBP	SLG	AOPS	ABR	SB-CS	FA	FR	RNG	THR	GAMES AT POSITION	DL	BFW
1884	Alt U	2	7	1	3	0	0	0					.429	.429	.429	159	0		1.000	-1			/COC		0.0
	NY N	3	10	0	0	0	0	0	0	0			.000	.000	.000	-98	-2		.833	-0			C3/OR		-0.2
Total	1	5	17	1	3	0	0	0		0		4	.176	.176	.176	9	-2		.880	-1			C4,O2(0/1/1)		-0.2

MANN, GARTH Ben Garth "Red" B11.16.1915 Brandon TX D9.11.1980 Italy TX BR/TR/6-0/155 d5.14

YEAR	TM LG	G	AB	R	H	2B	3B	HR	RBI	BB-IB	HP	SO	AVG	OBP	SLG	AOPS	ABR	SB-CS	FA	FR	RNG	THR	GAMES AT POSITION	DL	BFW
1944	Chi N	1	0		1	0	0	0	0	0	0	0	—	—	—	—	0	0	—		0		/R		0.0

MANN, FRED Fred J. B4.1.1858 Sutton VT D4.6.1916 Springfield MA BL/TR/5-10.5/178 d5.1 OF(39/444/28)

YEAR	TM LG	G	AB	R	H	2B	3B	HR	RBI	BB-IB	HP	SO	AVG	OBP	SLG	AOPS	ABR	SB-CS	FA	FR	RNG	THR	GAMES AT POSITION	DL	BFW
1882	Wor N	19	77	12	18	5	0	0	7	2		15	.234	.253	.299	74	-2		.703	-5	81	75	3b18/1		-0.6
	Phi AA	29	121	13	28	7	4	0		4			.231	.256	.355	98	-1		.798	-7	68	109	3b29		-0.7
1883	Col AA	96	394	61	98	18	13	1		18			.249	.282	.368	117	9		.854	-4	104	194	O82(2/80/0),1b9,3b6/S		0.1
1884	Col AA	99	366	70	101	12	8	7		25	11		.276	.341	.464	174	31		.857	-8	65	79	O97C,2b2		1.8
1885	Pit AA	99	391	60	99	17	6	0	41	31	6		.253	.318	.327	106	4		.908	-10	59	69	O97C,3b3		-0.8
1886	Pit AA	116	440	85	110	16	14	2	60	45	11	26	.250	.335	.364	119	11	26	.878	-4	71	100	O64(37/0/27)		1.0
1887	Cle AA	64	259	45	80	15	7	2	41	23	9		.309	.385	.444	135	13	25	.879	1	102	142	O55C		-0.3
	Phi AA	55	229	42	63	14	6	0	32	15	6		.275	.336	.389	102	0	16	.917	-2	85	114	O55C		0.7
	Year	119	488	87	143	29	13	2	73	38	15		.293	.362	.418	119	13	41	.896	-2	95	130	O119(37/55/27)		0.7
Total	6	577	2277	388	597	104	68	12	181	163	43	15	.262	.323	.383	122	65	67	.881	-40	78	112	O511C,3b56,1b10,2b2/S		0.7

MANN, JOHNNY John Leo B2.4.1898 Fontane IN D3.31.1977 Terre Haute IN BR/TR/5-11/160 d4.18

YEAR	TM LG	G	AB	R	H	2B	3B	HR	RBI	BB-IB	HP	SO	AVG	OBP	SLG	AOPS	ABR	SB-CS	FA	FR	RNG	THR	GAMES AT POSITION	DL	BFW
1928	Chi A	6	6	0	2	0	0	0	1	1	0	0	.333	.429	.333	104	0	0-0	1.000	0	125	0	3b2		0.0

MANN, KELLY Kelly John B8.17.1967 Santa Monica CA BR/TR/6-3/215* [ChiN85 20/520] d9.4

YEAR	TM LG	G	AB	R	H	2B	3B	HR	RBI	BB-IB	HP	SO	AVG	OBP	SLG	AOPS	ABR	SB-CS	FA	FR	RNG	THR	GAMES AT POSITION	DL	BFW
1989	Atl N	7	24	1	5	2	0	0	1	1-0		6	.208	.240	.292	50	-2	0-0	1.000	2	88	165	C7		0.1
1990	Atl N	11	28	2	4	1	0	0	1	0-0		6	.143	.143	.286	14	-3	0-0	1.000	-2	78	108	C10		-0.6
Total	2	18	52	3	9	3	0	0	1	1-0		12	.173	.189	.288	30	-5	0-0	1.000	-1	83	135	C17		-0.5

MANN, LES Leslie "Major" B11.18.1893 Lincoln NE D1.14.1962 Pasadena CA BR/TR/5-9/172 d4.30

YEAR	TM LG	G	AB	R	H	2B	3B	HR	RBI	BB-IB	HP	SO	AVG	OBP	SLG	AOPS	ABR	SB-CS	FA	FR	RNG	THR	GAMES AT POSITION	DL	BFW
1913	Bos N	120	407	54	103	24	7	3	51	18	4	73	.253	.291	.369	86	-9	7-16	.960	1	103	95	O120(12/103/6)		-2.0
1914	†Bos N	126	389	44	96	16	11	4	40	24	1	50	.247	.292	.375	99	-3	9	.952	10	104	**161**	O123(5/104/14)		-0.1
1915	Chi F	135	470	74	144	12	**19**	4	58	36	1	40	.306	.357	.438	131	9	18	.969	5	110	97	O130(94/7/33)/S		0.8
1916	Chi N	127	415	46	113	13	9	2	29	19	2	31	.272	.307	.361	95	-3	11-7	.972	0	99	77	O116(106/11/2)		-1.3
1917	Chi N	117	444	63	121	19	10	1	44	27	1	46	.273	.316	.367	101	0	14	.953	-1	88	141	O129L		-0.7
1918	†Chi N	129	489	69	141	27	7	2	55	38	1	45	.288	.342	.384	118	11	21	.961	1	88	107	O78L		0.0
1919	Chi N	80	299	31	68	8	8	1	22	11	1	29	.227	.257	.318	72	-12	12	.982	1	101	101	O78L		-0.4

YEAR	TM LG	G	AB	R	H	2B	3B	HR	RBI	BB-IB	HP	SO	AVG	OBP	SLG	AOPS	ABR	SB-CS	FA	FR	RNG	THR	GAMES AT POSITION	DL	BFW
	Bos N	40	145	15	41	6	4	3	20	9	1	14	.283	.329	.441	136	6	7	.929	2	97	165	O40L		0.6
	Year	120	444	46	109	14	12	4	42	20	2	43	.245	.281	.358	92	-6	19	.962	2	100	123	O118L		-1.0
1920	Bos N	115	424	48	117	7	8	3	32	38	4	42	.276	.341	.351	104	-2	7-7	.980	0	99	102	O110(102/0/8)		-0.4
1921	StL N	97	256	57	84	12	7	7	30	23	3	28	.328	.390	.512	140	14	5-5	.969	3	105	114	O79(1/66/12)		1.3
1922	StL N	84	147	42	51	14	1	2	20	16	1	12	.347	.415	.497	141	10	0-1	.978	1	109	78	O57(10/47/0)		0.8
1923	StL N	38	89	20	33	5	2	5	11	9	1	5	.371	.434	.640	184	11	0-0	.979	1	104	135	O26(5/6/16)		1.0
	Cin N	8	1	0	0	0	0	0	0	0	0	0	.000	.000	.000	-99	0	0-0	—	0			/H		0.0
	Year	46	90	21	33	5	2	5	11	9	1	5	.367	.430	.633	181	10	0-0	.979	1	104	135	O26(5/6/16)		1.0
1924	Bos N	32	102	13	28	7	4	0	10	8	1	10	.275	.333	.422	105	1	1-0	1.000	1	104	121	O28(7/0/21)		0.0
1925	Bos N	60	184	27	63	11	4	2	20	5	6	11	.342	.373	.478	127	7	6-1	.992	3	107	110	O57(5/11/41)		0.6
1926	Bos N	50	129	23	39	8	2	1	20	6	0	9	.302	.348	.419	116	3	5	.966	2	108	142	O46(17/17/16)		0.3
1927	Bos N	29	66	8	17	3	1	0	6	8	0	3	.258	.338	.333	87	-1	2	.955	2	101	202	O24(5/3/17)		-0.1
	NY N	29	67	13	22	4	1	2	10	8	0	7	.328	.400	.507	142	4	2	1.000	-0	85	142	O22(15/5/2)		0.3
	Year	58	133	21	39	7	2	2	16	16	0	10	.293	.369	.421	116	3	4	.973	2	94	175	O46(20/8/19)		0.2
1928	NY N	82	193	29	51	7	1	2	25	18	1	9	.264	.330	.342	76	-7	2	.952	-3	91	64	O68(3/14/63)		-1.3
Total	16	1498	4716	677	1332	203	106	44	503	324	28	464	.282	.332	.398	109	43	129-37	.966	18	100	113	O1368(708/414/277)/S		-1.8

MANNING, JIMMY James H. B1.31.1862 Fall River MA D10.22.1929 Edinburg TX BB/TR/5-7/157 d5.16 M1

1884	Bos N	89	345	52	83	8	6	2	35	19		47	.241	.280	.316	88	-5		.878	-3	95	97	O73(1/72/0),S9,2b9,3b3		-0.9
1885	Bos N	84	306	34	63	8	9	2	27	19		36	.206	.252	.310	84	-6		.898	7	130	131	O83(12/63/8)/S		-0.1
	Det N	20	78	15	21	4	0	1	9	4		10	.269	.305	.359	114	1		.802	-6	83	113	S20		-0.4
	Year	104	384	49	84	12	9	3	36	23		46	.219	.263	.320	90	-4		.898	1	130	131	O83(12/63/8),S21		-0.5
1886	Det N	26	97	14	18	2	3	0	7	6		10	.186	.233	.268	50	-6	7	.947	0	85	158	O26L/S		-0.6
1887	Det N	13	52	5	10	1	0	0	3	5	1	4	.192	.276	.212	36	-4	3	.867	-5	0	0	O10L,S3		-0.8
1889	KC AA	132	506	68	103	16	7	3	68	54	13	61	.204	.297	.281	61	-27	58	.927	-8	154	63	O69L,2b63/S3		-2.9
Total	5	364	1384	188	298	39	25	8	149	107	14	168	.215	.278	.297	73	-47	68	.903	-15	118	102	O261(118/135/8),2b72,S35,3b4		-5.7

MANNING, JACK John E. B12.20.1853 Braintree MA D8.15.1929 Boston MA BR/TR/5-8.5/158 d4.23 M1 OF NA(2/2/69) OF(2/16/605) ▲

1873	Bos NA	31	154	28	41	4	1	0	21	1		14	.266	.271	.305	65	-8	5-2	.920	-1	168	132	1b28,O7(2/0/5)		-0.5
1874	Bal NA	42	174	32	61	8	2	0	18	2		2	.351	.358	.420	149	9	0-0	.839	-5	109	0	P22,2b22,S4/13		-0.1
	Har NA	1	5	-1	1	0	0	0	0	0		0	.200	.200	.200	27	0	0-0	.167	-2	38	0	/3		-0.2
	Year	43	179	33	62	8	2	0	18	2		2	.346	.354	.413	146	9	0-0	.793	-7	109	0	P22,2b22,S4,3b2/1		-0.3
1875	Bos NA	77	348	71	94	11	3	1	46	2		9	.270	.274	.328	104	1	5-5	.802	-1	151	117	O65(0/2/64),P27,1b3/3		0.3
1876	Bos N	70	288	52	76	13	6	2	25	7		5	.264	.281	.330	101	1		.777	-4	85	0	O56(0/1/55),P34/S2		-0.3
1877	Cin N	57	252	47	80	16	7	0	36	5		6	.317	.331	.437	157	17		.742	-10	87	30	S26,1b17,O12(1/10/1),P10,2b2,M		0.5
1878	Bos N	60	248	41	63	10	1	0	23	10		16	.254	.283	.302	86	-4		.753	-15	57	45	O59(0/3/56),P3		-1.8
1880	Cin N	48	190	20	41	8	2	3	17	7		15	.216	.244	.311	87	-2		.798	-3	108	45	O47(0/2/47)/1		-0.6
1881	Buf N	1	1	0	0	0	0	0	0	0		0	.000	.000	.000	-99	0		1.000	1	1112	0	/OL		0.0
1883	Phi N	98	420	60	112	31	5	0	37	20		37	.267	.300	.364	110	8		.853	7	167	108	O98R		1.2
1884	Phi N	104	424	71	115	29	4	5	52	40		67	.271	.334	.394	134	20		.847	-6	129	194	O104R		1.7
1885	Phi N	107	445	61	114	24	4	3	40	37		27	.256	.313	.348	116	10		.896	-6	106	119	O107R		0.3
1886	Bal AA	137	556	78	124	18	4	1	45	50	3		.223	.291	.286	83	-10	24	.887	-9	71	72	O137R		-1.8
Total	3 NA	151	681	132	197	23	6	1	85	5		25	.289	.294	.345	105	2	10-7	.781	-8	139	102	O72R,P49,1b32,2b22,S4,3b3		-0.5
Total	9	682	2824	430	725	147	31	13	275	176	3	173	.257	.301	.345	108	40	24	.844	-39	106	94	O621R,P47,S27,1b18,2b3		-0.8

MANNING, RICK Richard Eugene B9.2.1954 Niagara Falls NY [CleA72 1/2] d5.23

1975	Cle A	120	480	69	137	16	5	3	35	44-2	2	62	.285	.347	.358	100	0	19-11	.974	10	115	133	O118(28/69/32)/D		0.6
1976	Cle A	138	552	73	161	24	5	7	43	41-1	0	75	.292	.337	.393	115	10	16-10	.987	-2	99	82	O136C		0.4
1977	Cle A	68	252	33	57	7	3	5	18	21-0	0	35	.226	.282	.337	71	-11	9-5	.990	1	111	43	O68C		0.4
1978	Cle A	148	566	65	149	27	3	5	50	38-1	1	62	.263	.309	.337	83	-13	12-12	.995	-3	98	78	O144C		-2.0
1979	Cle A	144	560	65	145	12	2	3	51	55-3	1	48	.259	.323	.304	71	-22	30-8	.986	7	110	97	O141C/D		-1.2
1980	Cle A	140	471	55	110	17	4	3	52	63-11	2	66	.234	.321	.306	73	-16	12-6	.990	1	104	76	O139C		-1.6
1981	Cle A	103	360	47	88	15	3	4	33	40-2	0	57	.244	.318	.306	90	-4	25-3	.987	8	116	101	O103C		0.8
1982	Cle A	152	562	71	152	18	2	8	44	54-5	0	60	.270	.334	.352	88	-8	12-8	.978	-7	93	98	O152C		-1.7
1983	Cle A	50	194	20	54	6	0	1	10	12-1	0	22	.278	.319	.325	75	-7	7-3	.987	-1	104	31	O50C		-0.8
	Mil A	108	375	40	86	14	4	3	33	26-4	1	40	.229	.279	.312	68	-18	11-2	.991	-1	107	14	O108C		-1.8
	Year	158	569	60	140	20	4	4	43	38-5	1	62	.246	.292	.316	70	-24	18-5	.990	-2	106	20	O158C		-2.6
1984	Mil A	119	341	53	85	10	5	7	31	34-1	1	32	.249	.318	.370	93	-4	5-7	.987	-13	84	31	O74(1/57/17),D2		-1.9
1985	Mil A	79	216	19	47	9	1	2	18	14-0	1	19	.218	.265	.296	54	-14	1-0	.976	-2	101	50	O74(1/57/17),D2	19	-1.7
1986	Mil A	89	205	31	52	7	3	8	27	17-2	1	20	.254	.310	.434	98	-1	5-3	.988	4	115	81	O83(40/29/18),D5		0.0
1987	Mil A	97	114	21	26	7	1	0	13	12-0	1	18	.228	.299	.307	60	-6	4-0	.958	-1	102	45	O78(21/8/51),D2		-0.2
Total	13	1555	5248	664	1349	189	43	56	458	471-33	9	616	.257	.317	.341	84	-114	168-78	.985	-1	104	75	O1508(90/1317/118),D12	91	-12.7

MANNING, TIM Timothy Edward B12.3.1853 Henley-On-Thames, England D6.11.1934 Oak Park IL BR/TR/5-10/170 d5.1

1882	Pro N	21	76	7	8	0	0	0	8	5		13	.105	.160	.105	-13	-9		.787	-9	79	72	S17,C4		-1.7
1883	Bal AA	35	121	23	26	5	0	0		14			.215	.296	.256	77	-2		.913	3	106	53	2b35		0.2
1884	Bal AA	91	341	49	70	14	5	2		26	7		.205	.275	.293	82	-6		.907	-2	96	73	2b91		-0.5
1885	Bal AA	43	157	17	32	8	1	0	16	10	3		.204	.265	.268	70	-5		.919	2	103	99	2b41,3b3		-0.1
	Pro N	10	35	3	2	1	0	0	0	1		11	.057	.083	.086	-47	-6		.854	-3	74	64	S10		-0.8
Total	4	200	730	99	138	28	6	2	24	56		24	.189	.256	.252	63	-28		.911	-10	100	75	2b167,S27,C4,3b3		-2.9

MANNO, DON Donald D. B5.4.1915 Williamsport PA D3.11.1995 Williamsport PA BR/TR/6-1/190 d9.22 Col West Chester

1940	Bos N	3	7	1	2	0	0	1	4	0	0	2	.286	.286	.714	177	1	0	1.000	0	134	0	O2R		0.1
1941	Bos N	22	30	2	5	1	0	0	4	3	0	7	.167	.242	.200	27	-3	0	1.000	-1	94	0	O5L,3b3/1		-0.4
Total	2	25	37	3	7	1	0	1	8	3	0	9	.189	.250	.297	56	-2	0	1.000	-1	109	0	O7(5/0/2),3b3/1		-0.3

MANRIQUE, FRED Fred Eloy (Reyes) B11.5.1961 Edo Bolivar, Venez BR/TR/6-1/175* d8.23

1981	Tor A	14	28	1	4	0	0	0	1	0-0	1	12	.143	.172	.143	-4	-4	0-1	.949	1	124	144	S11,3b2/D		-0.3
1984	Tor A	10	9	0	3	0	0	0	1	0-0	0	1	.333	.333	.333	82	0	0-0	.938	1	136	204	2b9/D		0.1
1985	Mon N	9	13	5	4	1	1	0	1	1-0	0	3	.308	.357	.769	218	2	0-0	1.000	1	115	0	2b2,S2/3		0.3
1986	StL N	13	17	2	3	0	0	1	1	1-0	0	4	.176	.222	.353	56	-1	1-0	1.000	-2	60	0	3b4/2		-0.3
1987	Chi A	115	298	30	77	13	3	4	29	19-1	0	69	.258	.302	.362	74	-12	5-3	.984	-4	105	120	2b92,S23,D5		-0.9
1988	Chi A	140	345	43	81	10	6	5	37	21-1	3	54	.235	.283	.342	75	-13	6-5	.985	5	105	108	2b129,S12/D		-0.6
1989	Chi A	65	187	23	56	13	1	2	30	8-1	3	30	.299	.333	.412	111	3	0-4	.961	-9	90	91	2b57,S2/3D		-0.6
	Tex A	54	191	23	55	12	0	2	22	9-0	0	33	.288	.318	.382	95	-1	4-1	.963	4	87	112	S37,2b17,3b6		-0.2
	Year	119	378	46	111	25	1	4	52	17-1	2	63	.294	.326	.397	103	3	4-5	.952	-12	89	86	2b74,S39,3b7/D		-0.8
1990	Min A	69	228	22	54	10	0	5	29	4-0	2	35	.237	.254	.346	63	-12	2-0	.974	-7	96	103	2b67/D		-1.7
1991	Oak A	9	21	2	3	0	0	0	0	2-0	0	1	.143	.217	.143	2	-3	0-0	.955	-0	83	52	S7,2b2		-0.3
Total	9	498	1337	151	340	59	11	20	151	65-3	9	239	.254	.292	.360	79	-41	18-14	.976	-17	101	106	2b376,S94,3b14,D10		-4.5

MANSELL, JOHN John B1859 Auburn NY D2.20.1925 Romulus NY BL/5-10/168 d5.9 b-Mike b-Tom

| 1882 | Phi AA | 31 | 126 | 17 | 30 | 3 | 1 | 0 | 17 | 4 | | | .238 | .262 | .278 | 77 | -4 | | .791 | -5 | 54 | 0 | O31C | | -0.9 |

MANSELL, MIKE Michael R. B1.15.1858 Auburn NY D12.4.1902 Auburn NY BL/5-11/175 d5.1 b-John b-Tom

1879	Syr N	67	242	24	52	4	2	1	13	5		45	.215	.231	.260	69	-7		.881	15	71	103	O67L		0.3
1880	Cin N	53	187	22	36	6	2	2	12	4		37	.193	.209	.278	64	-7		.865	12	102	196	O53L		0.2
1882	Pit AA	79	347	59	96	18	16	2		7			.277	.291	.438	150	17		.829	3	86	55	O79L		1.6
1883	Pit AA	96	412	90	106	12	13	3		25			.257	.300	.371	120	10		.883	3	59	39	O96L		0.9
1884	Pit AA	27	100	15	14	0	3	1		7	1		.140	.204	.230	42	-6		.796	-1	60	110	O27(24/0/3)		-0.8
	Phi AA	20	70	6	14	1	1	0		5	0		.200	.253	.243	59	-3		.762	-2	48	0	O20(16/4/0)		-0.5
	Ric AA	29	113	21	34	2	5	0		8	3		.301	.363	.407	153	7		.763	-3	106	125	O29(0/2/27)		0.3
	Year	76	283	42	62	3	9	1		20	4		.219	.284	.304	90	-3		.775	-6	72	82	O76(40/6/30)		-1.0
Total	5	371	1471	237	352	43	42	9	25	61	4	82	.239	.284	.344	106	11		.854	26	76	86	O371(335/6/30)		2.0

MANSELL, TOM   Thomas E. "Brick" B1.1.1855 Auburn NY D10.6.1934 Auburn NY   BL/TR/5-8/160   d5.1   b-John b-Mike

YEAR	TM LG	G	AB	R	H	2B	3B	HR	RBI	BB-IB	HP	SO	AVG	OBP	SLG	AOPS	ABR	SB-CS	FA	FR	RNG	THR	GAMES AT POSITION	DL	BFW
1879	Tro N	40	177	29	43	6	0	0	11	3		9	.243	.256	.277	81	-3		.742	-7	31	82	O40(38/2/0)		-1.2
	Syr N	1	4	0	1	0	0	0	0	0		0	.250	.250	.250	74	0		1.000	-0	0	0	/OR		0.0
	Year	41	181	29	44	6	0	0	11	3		9	.243	.255	.276	81	-3		.747	-7	30	80	O41(38/2/1)		-1.2
1883	Det N	34	131	22	29	4	1	0	10	8		13	.221	.266	.267	66	-5		.758	-6	18	0	O28(25/2/1)		0.4
	StL AA	28	112	23	45	8	1	0	24	7			.402	.437	.491	188	11		.786	-6	18	0	O65(41/25/1)		-1.2
1884	Cin AA	65	266	49	66	4	6	0	23	15	5		.248	.301	.308	94	-2		.667	-3	85		O23L		-0.4
	Col AA	23	77	9	15	1	3	0	6	6	1		.195	.262	.286	85	-1		.739	-12	39		O88(64/25/1)		-1.6
	Year	88	343	58	81	5	9	0	29	21	6		.236	.292	.303	93	-3		.739	-12	39				-3.2
Total 3		191	767	132	199	23	11	0	74	39		22	.259	.300	.318	100	0		.751	-29	54	33	O191(127/29/37)/P		-3.2

MANTILLA, FELIX   Felix (Lamela) B7.29.1934 Isabela, PR   BR/TR/6-0/160*   d6.21   OF(74/76/10) [DL 1967 Chi N 81]

YEAR	TM LG	G	AB	R	H	2B	3B	HR	RBI	BB-IB	HP	SO	AVG	OBP	SLG	AOPS	ABR	SB-CS	FA	FR	RNG	THR	GAMES AT POSITION	DL	BFW
1956	Mil N	35	53	9	15	1	0	0	3	1-0		8	.283	.309	.340	79	-2	0-1	1.000	5	144	138	S15,3b3		0.4
1957	†Mil N	71	182	28	43	9	1	4	21	14-2	2	34	.236	.296	.363	82	-5	2-0	.931	5	108	116	S35,2b13,3b7/OC		0.3
1958	†Mil N	85	226	37	50	5	1	7	19	20-2	1	20	.221	.282	.345	72	-10	6-1	.987	-3	90	76	O43(12/33/0),2b21,S5,3b2		-1.3
1959	Mil N	103	251	26	54	5	0	3	19	16-1	2	31	.215	.266	.271	48	-19	6-1	.970	0	105	98	2b60,S23,3b9/O7C		-1.4
1960	Mil N	63	148	21	38	7	0	3	11	7-1	1	16	.257	.291	.365	86	-3	3-1	.956	-9	68	67	2b26,S25,O8(3/5/0)		-1.0
1961	Mil N	45	93	13	20	3	0	1	5	10-0	1	16	.215	.298	.280	58	-6	1-1	.933	-3	91	98	S19,2b10,O10(2/6/2),3b6		-0.8
1962	NY N	141	466	54	128	17	4	11	59	37-0	5	51	.275	.330	.399	94	-4	3-1	.948	-7	107	126	S27,O11C,2b5		0.9
1963	Bos A	66	178	27	56	8	0	6	15	20-1	0	14	.315	.384	.461	131	8	2-1	.965	-1	93	117	3b95,S25,2b14		2.3
1964	Bos A	133	425	69	123	20	1	30	64	41-1	4	46	.289	.357	.553	142	24	0-1	.984	-3	82	93	2b123,O27(20/8/0),1b2		2.3
1965	Bos A★	150	534	60	147	17	2	18	92	79-5	8	84	.275	.374	.416	118	16	7-3	.976	-23	86	78	1b14,3b14,2b9/OL	25	-0.8
1966	Hou N	77	151	16	33	5	0	6	22	11-0	2	32	.219	.279	.371	85	-3	1-0	.990	-4	41	89	2b36,S18,3b16,1b6	106	-2.0
Total 11		969	2707	360	707	97	10	89	330	256-13	26	352	.261	.329	.403	100	0	27-10	.977	-43	90	81	2b326,S180,O156C,3b143,1b16	106	-2.0

MANTLE, MICKEY   Mickey Charles "The Commerce Comet" B10.20.1931 Spavinaw OK D8.13.1995 Dallas TX   BB/TR/5-11/198(175-201)   d4.17   C1 HF1974   OF(129/1745/146)

YEAR	TM LG	G	AB	R	H	2B	3B	HR	RBI	BB-IB	HP	SO	AVG	OBP	SLG	AOPS	ABR	SB-CS	FA	FR	RNG	THR	GAMES AT POSITION	DL	BFW
1951	†NY A	96	341	61	91	11	5	13	65	43	0	74	.267	.349	.443	117	7	8-7	.959	-5	90	74	O86(0/3/85)		-0.1
1952	†NY A☆	142	549	94	171	37	7	23	87	75	0	111	.311	.394	.530	166	48	4-1	.968	-6	90	132	O141(0/121/20)/3		3.9
1953	†NY A★	127	461	105	136	24	3	21	92	79	0	90	.295	.398	.497	145	31	8-4	.982	-3	97	95	O121(0/116/4)/S		2.3
1954	NY A★	146	543	129	163	17	12	27	102	102	0	107	.300	.408	.525	160	47	5-2	.975	-4	88	156	O144(0/143/1),S4/2		3.8
1955	†NY A★	147	517	121	158	25	11	37	99	113-6	3	97	.306	.431	.611	181	62	8-1	.995	-1	97	129	O145C,S2		5.5
1956	†NY A★	150	533	132	188	22	5	52	130	112-6	2	99	.353	.464	.705	213	90	10-1	.990	0	100	105	O144C		8.1
1957	†NY A★	144	474	121	173	28	6	34	94	146-23	0	75	.365	.512	.665	223	94	16-3	.979	-8	95	64	O139C		8.2
1958	†NY A★	150	519	127	158	21	1	42	97	129-13	2	120	.304	.443	.592	189	71	18-3	.977	-8	94	62	O150C		6.0
1959	NY A★	144	541	104	154	23	4	31	75	93-6	2	126	.285	.390	.514	152	41	21-3	.995	-1	101	72	O143C		3.6
1960	†NY A★	153	527	119	145	17	6	40	94	111-6	0	125	.275	.399	.558	166	51	14-3	.991	-11	89	100	O150C		3.6
1961	†NY A★	153	514	132	163	16	6	54	128	126-9	0	112	.317	.448	.687	210	86	12-1	.983	-6	99	77	O150C		7.5
1962	†NY A★	123	377	96	121	15	1	30	89	122-9	1	78	.321	.486	.605	198	63	9-0	.978	-10	87	73	O117(0/94/23)	35	5.0
1963	†NY A★	65	172	40	54	8	0	15	35	40-4	1	32	.314	.441	.622	197	25	2-1	.990	-2	99	74	O52C		2.2
1964	†NY A★	143	465	92	141	25	2	35	111	99-18	0	102	.303	.423	.591	177	53	6-3	.978	-16	80	36	O132(17/102/13)		1.5
1965	NY A★	122	361	44	92	12	1	19	46	73-7	0	76	.255	.379	.452	136	20	4-1	.966	-1	102	54	O108L		2.4
1966	NY A	108	333	40	96	12	1	23	56	57-5	0	76	.288	.389	.538	171	32	1-1	1.000	-7	91	40	O97(4/93/0)		3.3
1967	NY A★	144	440	63	108	17	0	22	55	107-7	1	113	.245	.391	.434	150	34	1-1	.993	-6	115	92	1b131		2.3
1968	NY A★	144	435	57	103	14	1	18	54	106-7	1	97	.237	.385	.398	143	29	6-2	.988	-2	99	102	1b131	35	2.3
Total 18		2401	8102	1677	2415	344	72	536	1509	1733-126	13	1710	.298	.421	.557	173	884	153-38	.982	-86	94	88	O2019C,1b262,S7/23	35	72.5

MANTO, JEFF   Jeffrey Paul B8.23.1964 Bristol PA   BR/TR/6-3/210*   [CalA85 14/355]   d6.7   Col Temple

YEAR	TM LG	G	AB	R	H	2B	3B	HR	RBI	BB-IB	HP	SO	AVG	OBP	SLG	AOPS	ABR	SB-CS	FA	FR	RNG	THR	GAMES AT POSITION	DL	BFW
1990	Cle A	30	76	12	17	5	1	2	14	21-1	0	18	.224	.392	.395	121	3	0-1	.990	1	132	103	1b25,3b5		0.3
1991	Cle A	47	128	15	27	7	0	2	13	14-0	4	22	.211	.306	.313	72	-5	2-0	.929	-1	97	203	3b32,1b14,C5/OL		-0.6
1993	Phi N	8	18	0	1	0	0	0	0	0-0	1	3	.056	.105	.056	-56	-4	0-0	1.000	-0	84	0	3b6/S		-0.5
1995	Bal A	89	254	31	65	9	0	17	38	24-0	1	69	.256	.325	.492	107	1	0-3	.959	-2	91	117	3b69,D13,1b4	17	0.6
1996	Bos A	10	30	5	8	3	1	2	4	3-0	1	6	.267	.353	.633	140	2	0-0	.963	4	134	90	3b16/OLD	32	-0.4
	Sea A	21	54	7	10	3	0	1	4	5-0	0	12	.185	.302	.296	52	-4	0-1	.971	0	104	82	3b10/1		0.0
	Bos A	12	18	3	2	0	0	1	2	5-0	0	6	.111	.304	.111	11	-2	0-0	.960	3	146	77	3b10/1		-0.3
	Year	43	102	15	20	6	1	4	10	13-0	1	24	.196	.317	.363	70	-5	0-1	.967	7	118	80	3b26,2b4,S4,D2/OL1		-0.2
1997	Cle A	16	30	3	8	2	0	2	7	1-0	0	10	.267	.290	.567	112	0	0-1	1.000	-0	72	0	3b7,1b6/OL		-0.9
1998	Cle A	7	14	3	1	0	0	0	1	1-0	0	5	.071	.133	.071	-43	-3	0-0	1.000	-5	0	23	1b4/OLD		-0.2
	Det A	16	30	6	8	2	0	1	3	1-0	0	11	.267	.353	.433	102	1	1-0	.977	-2	0	68	1b10/OLD		-0.3
	Cle A	8	23	5	7	1	0	3	6	1-0	0	5	.304	.333	.609	133	1	0-1	1.000	-3	12	0	3b6,1b3		-1.4
	Year	31	67	14	16	3	0	3	9	5-0	1	21	.239	.301	.418	82	-2	1-1	.979	-10	18	54	1b17,3b8,D6/2OL		0.2
1999	Cle A	12	25	5	6	1	0	1	2	11-0	0	11	.240	.444	.320	95	1	0-0	1.000	1	110	148	3b10/1		-0.1
	NY A	6	8	0	2	0	0	0	0	2-0	0	4	.125	.300	.125	14	-1	0-0	1.000	0	112	80	1b3/3		0.1
	Year	18	33	5	8	1	0	1	2	13-0	0	15	.182	.413	.273	78	0	0-0	1.000	1	108	146	3b11,1b4		0.1
2000	Col N	7	5	2	4	2	0	1	4	1-0	0	1	.800	.857	1.800	444	0	0-0	1.000	0	0	1047	/13		-0.2
Total 9		289	713	97	164	35	2	31	97	97-1	9	182	.230	.329	.415	93	-8	3-6	.960	-6	92	123	3b165,1b72,D21,2b5,S5,C5,O4L	49	-2.0

MANUEL, CHARLIE   Charles Fuqua B1.4.1944 Northfork WV   BL/TR/6-4/200(180-200)   d4.8   M4/C8

YEAR	TM LG	G	AB	R	H	2B	3B	HR	RBI	BB-IB	HP	SO	AVG	OBP	SLG	AOPS	ABR	SB-CS	FA	FR	RNG	THR	GAMES AT POSITION	DL	BFW
1969	†Min A	83	164	14	34	6	0	2	24	28-4	0	33	.207	.320	.280	68	-6	1-0	.967	-3	82	69	O46(41/1/4)		-1.1
1970	†Min A	59	64	4	12	0	0	1	7	6-2	0	17	.188	.260	.234	39	-5	0-0	1.000	-1	66	0	O11(9/0/2)		-0.7
1971	Min A	18	16	1	2	1	0	0	1	1-0	0	8	.125	.176	.188	3	-2	0-0	.977	1	91	233	O28(20/0/9)		-0.9
1972	Min A	63	122	6	25	5	0	1	8	1-0	1	16	.205	.233	.270	48	-8	0-0	—	0			/H		0.0
1974	LA N	3	3	0	1	0	0	0	0	1-0	0	0	.333	.500	.333	141	0	0-0	—	0			/H		-0.3
1975	LA N	15	15	0	2	0	0	0	0	0-0	0	3	.133	.133	.133	-27	-3	0-0	.973	-2	83	120	O86(70/1/16)		-3.2
Total 6		242	384	25	76	12	0	4	40	40-6	2	77	.198	.273	.260	52	-24	1-0	.973	-2	83	120	O86(70/1/16)		

MANUEL, JERRY   Jerry B12.23.1953 Hahira GA   BB/TR (BR 1981-82)/6-0/165*   [DetA72 1/20]   d9.18   M6/C8

YEAR	TM LG	G	AB	R	H	2B	3B	HR	RBI	BB-IB	HP	SO	AVG	OBP	SLG	AOPS	ABR	SB-CS	FA	FR	RNG	THR	GAMES AT POSITION	DL	BFW
1975	Det A	6	18	0	1	0	0	0	0	4-0	0	4	.056	.056	.056	-66	-2	1-0	.944	2	140	99	2b6		-0.1
1976	Det A	54	43	4	6	1	0	0	3	3-0	1	9	.140	.213	.163	-5	-1	1-0	.921	-1	108	64	2b47,S4/D		-0.4
1980	Mon N	7	6	0	0	0	0	0	0	0-0	0	2	.000	.000	.000	-98	-2	0-0	.941	3	142	0	S7		-0.2
1981	†Mon N	27	55	10	11	5	0	3	8	6-1	0	11	.200	.270	.455	102	0	0-0	.987	-3	80	115	2b23,S2	107	-0.1
1982	SD N	2	5	0	1	0	0	0	1	1-0	0	1	.200	.333	.600	166	0	0-0	1.000	-2	0	172	/2S3	107	-0.8
Total 5		96	127	14	19	6	1	3	13	10-1	1	26	.150	.214	.283	41	-11	1-0	.949	-2	99	91	2b77,S14/3D		

MANUSH, FRANK   Frank Benjamin B9.18.1883 Tuscumbia AL D1.5.1965 Laguna Beach CA   BR/TR/5-10.5/175   d8.31   b-Heinie

YEAR	TM LG	G	AB	R	H	2B	3B	HR	RBI	BB-IB	HP	SO	AVG	OBP	SLG	AOPS	ABR	SB-CS	FA	FR	RNG	THR	GAMES AT POSITION	DL	BFW
1908	Phi A	23	77	6	12	2	1	0	0	2			.156	.188	.208	27	-6	2	.933	-4	71	89	3b20,2b2		0.2

MANUSH, HEINIE   Henry Emmett B7.20.1901 Tuscumbia AL D5.12.1971 Sarasota FL   BL/TL/6-1/200   d4.20   C2 HF1964   b-Frank

YEAR	TM LG	G	AB	R	H	2B	3B	HR	RBI	BB-IB	HP	SO	AVG	OBP	SLG	AOPS	ABR	SB-CS	FA	FR	RNG	THR	GAMES AT POSITION	DL	BFW
1923	Det A	109	308	59	103	20	5	4	54	20	17	21	.334	.406	.471	133	15	3-5	.953	-6	93	61	O79(72/0/7)		0.2
1924	Det A	120	422	83	122	24	8	9	68	27	16	30	.289	.355	.448	108	3	14-5	.979	-9	97	35	O106(99/1/6)/1		-1.0
1925	Det A	99	278	46	84	14	5	3	47	24	2	21	.302	.362	.428	110	0	8-3	.967	-6	96	60	O73(13/56/5)		2.6
1926	Det A	136	498	95	188	35	8	14	86	31	6	28	.378	.414	.564	153	37	11-5	.967	-6	96	60	O120(11/104/5)		-1.4
1927	Det A	151	593	102	177	31	18	6	90	47	4	29	.298	.354	.442	104	1	12-8	.971	-9	94	60	O149(3/147/0)		3.3
1928	StL A	154	638	104	241	47	20	13	108	39	1	24	.378	.414	.575	153	46	16-5	.992	-2	104	40	O154L		0.5
1929	StL A	142	574	85	204	45	10	6	81	43	1	23	.355	.401	.500	126	23	9-9	.987	-5	93	77	O141L		-1.2
1930	StL A	49	198	26	65	16	4	2	29	5	0	7	.328	.345	.480	103	3	3-1	.990	3	105	147	O86L		1.2
	Was A	88	356	74	129	33	8	7	65	26	0	24	.362	.406	.559	141	22	4-3	.989	-0	97	102	O134L		1.2
	Year	137	554	100	194	49	12	9	94	31	0	31	.350	.385	.531	128	7	7-4	.977	-12	86	50	O143L		
1931	Was A	146	616	110	189	41	11	6	70	36	2	27	.307	.351	.438	106	4	3-3	.988	-1	101	54	O146L		-0.8
1932	Was A	149	625	121	214	41	14	14	116	36	2	25	.342	.383	.520	133	29	7-2	.984	3	99	64	O150L		2.2
1933	†Was A	153	658	115	221	32	17	5	95	36	2	18	.336	.372	.459	120	17	6-4	.982	-5	93	84	O131(130/1/0)		-0.9
1934	Was A★	137	556	88	194	42	11	11	89	36	4	17	.349	.392	.523	140	31	7-3	.980	-2	105	83	O111L		-1.3
1935	Was A	119	479	68	131	26	9	4	56	35	1	24	.273	.328	.390	88	-10	2-0	.966	-4	90	70	O72L		-0.2
1936	Bos A	82	313	43	91	15	6	0	45	17	1	11	.291	.329	.371	69	-16	1-3	.970	-6	94	64	O123R		1.2
1937	Bro N	132	466	57	155	25	7	4	73	40	3	24	.333	.389	.442	103	16	6	1.000	1	118	88	O12R		0.2
1938	Bro N	17	51	9	12	3	1	0	6	3	0	5	.235	.304	.333	12	-4	1					O12R		

YEAR TM LG	G	AB	R	H	2B	3B	HR	RBI	BB-IB	HP	SO	AVG	OBP	SLG	AOPS	ABR	SB-CS	FA	FR	RNG	THR	GAMES AT POSITION	DL	BFW
Pit N	15	13	2	4	1	1	0	4	2	0	0	.308	.400	.538	155	1	0		—	0		/H		0.1
Year	32	64	11	16	4	2	0	10	7	0	4	.250	.324	.375	90	-1	1	1.000	1	118	88	O12R		-0.1
1939 Pit N	10	12	0	0	0	0	0	1	1	0	1	.000	.077	.000	-79	-3	0	1.000	-0	74	0	/OR		-0.3
Total 17	2008	7654	1287	2524	491	160	110	1183	506	70	345	.330	.377	.449	121	214	113-59	.979	-59	97	62	O1845(1379/309/159)/1		4.5

MANWARING, KIRT Kirt Dean B7.15.1965 Elmira NY BR/TR/5-11/190(185-203) [SFN86 2/31] d9.15 Col Coastal Carolina

YEAR TM LG	G	AB	R	H	2B	3B	HR	RBI	BB-IB	HP	SO	AVG	OBP	SLG	AOPS	ABR	SB-CS	FA	FR	RNG	THR	GAMES AT POSITION	DL	BFW
1987 SF N	6	7	0	1	0	0	0	0	0-0	1		.143	.250	.143	8	-1	0-0	.909	-1	206	0	C6		-0.2
1988 SF N	40	116	12	29	7	0	1	15	2-0	3	21	.250	.279	.336	80	-3	0-1	.979	-3	109	92	C40		-0.5
1989 †SF N	85	200	14	42	4	1	0	18	11-1	4	28	.210	.264	.250	49	-14	2-1	.982	1	148	86	C81		-0.1
1990 SF N	8	13	0	2	0	1	0	1	0-0	3		.154	.154	.308	24	-2	0-0	1.000	0	92	0	C8	15	-1.0
1991 SF N	67	178	16	40	9	0	0	19	9-0	3	22	.225	.271	.275	56	-10	1-1	.988	1	131	90	C67		-0.1
1992 SF N	109	349	24	85	10	5	4	26	29-0	5	42	.244	.311	.335	87	-7	2-1	.994	7	172	108	C108	41	-0.7
1993 SF N	130	432	48	119	15	1	5	49	41-13	6	76	.275	.345	.350	90	-5	1-3	.994	7	127		C130	15	0.7
1994 SF N	97	316	30	79	17	1	1	29	25-3	6	50	.250	.308	.320	67	-15	1-1	.998	7	154	122	C97		0.9
1995 SF N	118	379	21	95	15	2	1	36	27-6	10	72	.251	.314	.332	73	-15	1-0	.993	2	108	102	C118		-0.7
1996 SF N	49	145	9	34	6	0	1	14	16-1	3	24	.234	.319	.297	66	-7	0-1	.990	-12	121	77	C49		-1.9
Hou N	37	82	5	18	3	0	0	4	3-0	2	16	.220	.264	.256	41	-7	0-1	.993	-1	120	161	C37	43	-0.5
Year	86	227	14	52	9	0	1	18	19-1	5	40	.229	.300	.282	58	-14	0-1	.995	2	113	194	C86		-0.4
1997 Col N	104	337	22	76	6	4	1	27	30-0	2	78	.226	.291	.276	41	-29	0-1	.994	1	117	173	C100		-4.0
1998 Col N	110	291	30	72	12	3	2	26	38-3	3	49	.247	.339	.330	64	-14	1-5	.994	-15	87	84	C108		-1.1
1999 Col N	48	137	11	41	7	1	2	14	12-1	5	23	.299	.374	.409	79	-4	1-5	.988	-2	90	116	C44/D	33	-0.7
Total 13	1008	2982	248	733	111	20	21	278	243-28	50	505	.246	.311	.318	68	-133	10-19	.981	-6	72	83	C993/D	147	-10.2

MAPES, CLIFF Clifford Franklin B3.13.1922 Sutherland NE D12.5.1996 Pryor OK BL/TR/6-3/205* d4.20

YEAR TM LG	G	AB	R	H	2B	3B	HR	RBI	BB-IB	HP	SO	AVG	OBP	SLG	AOPS	ABR	SB-CS	FA	FR	RNG	THR	GAMES AT POSITION	DL	BFW
1948 NY A	53	88	19	22	11	1	1	12	6	0	13	.250	.298	.432	94	-1	0-0	.958	3	109	321	O21(9/6/6)		0.1
1949 †NY A	111	304	56	75	13	3	7	38	58	1	50	.247	.369	.378	98	0	6-0	.976	6	103	186	O108(4/58/49)		0.5
1950 †NY A	108	356	60	88	14	6	12	61	47	2	61	.247	.338	.421	96	-1	1-6	.950	-4	93	105	O102(4/21/80)		-1.1
1951 NY A	45	51	6	11	3	1	2	8	4	0	14	.216	.273	.431	92	-1	0-0	1.000	0	115	0	O34(2/3/29)		-0.1
StL A	56	201	32	55	7	2	7	30	26	1	33	.274	.360	.433	110	3	0-1	.983	0	100	100	O53(15/12/31)		-0.1
Year	101	252	38	66	10	3	9	38	30	1	47	.262	.343	.433	109	2	0-1	.986	0	103	82	O87(17/15/60)		0.0
1952 Det A	86	193	26	38	7	0	9	23	27	0	42	.197	.295	.373	84	-5	0-1	.967	-2	94	87	O63(5/18/43)		-0.1
Total 5	459	1193	199	289	55	13	38	172	168	4	213	.242	.338	.406	97	-8	8-9	.969	4	99	135	O381(39/118/238)		-1.5

MAPLE, HOWARD Howard Albert "Mape" B7.20.1903 Adrian MO D11.9.1970 Portland OR BL/TR/5-7/175 d5.19 Col Oregon St.

YEAR TM LG	G	AB	R	H	2B	3B	HR	RBI	BB-IB	HP	SO	AVG	OBP	SLG	AOPS	ABR	SB-CS	FA	FR	RNG	THR	GAMES AT POSITION	DL	BFW
1932 Was A	44	41	6	10	0	1	0	7	7	1	7	.244	.367	.293	74	-1	0-0	1.000	-1	153	86	C41		-0.2

MAPPES, GEORGE George Richard "Dick" B12.25.1865 St.Louis MO D2.20.1934 St.Louis MO d9.23

YEAR TM LG	G	AB	R	H	2B	3B	HR	RBI	BB-IB	HP	SO	AVG	OBP	SLG	AOPS	ABR	SB-CS	FA	FR	RNG	THR	GAMES AT POSITION	DL	BFW
1885 Bal AA	6	19	2	4	0	1	0	0	1			.211	.250	.316	79	-1		.875	-2	76	43	2b6		-0.2
1886 StL N	6	14	1	2	0	0	0	0	1		5	.143	.200	.143	6	-2	0	1.000	-1			C3,3b2/2		-0.2
Total 2	12	33	3	6	0	1	0	0	2		5	.182	.229	.242	48	-3	0	.848	-3			2b7,C3,3b2		-0.4

MARANVILLE, RABBIT Walter James Vincent B11.11.1891 Springfield MA D1.5.1954 New York NY BR/TR/5-5/155 d9.10 Mil 1918 HF1954

YEAR TM LG	G	AB	R	H	2B	3B	HR	RBI	BB-IB	HP	SO	AVG	OBP	SLG	AOPS	ABR	SB-CS	FA	FR	RNG	THR	GAMES AT POSITION	DL	BFW
1912 Bos N	26	86	8	18	2	0	0	8	9	1	14	.209	.292	.233	44	-7	1	.929	1	110	90	S26		-0.4
1913 Bos N	143	571	68	141	13	8	2	48	68	3	62	.247	.330	.308	81	-12	25-19	.949	17	106	93	S143		1.4
1914 †Bos N	156	586	74	144	23	6	4	78	45	6	56	.246	.306	.326	88	-9	28	.938	50	116	168	S156		5.5
1915 Bos N	149	509	51	124	23	6	2	43	45	2	65	.244	.308	.324	96	-3	18-12	.941	20	103	107	S149		3.0
1916 Bos N	155	604	79	142	16	13	4	38	50	2	69	.235	.296	.325	94	-5	32-15	.947	23	101	133	S155		3.4
1917 Bos N	142	561	69	146	19	13	3	43	40	2	47	.260	.312	.357	111	-6	27	.947	14	100	106	S142		3.3
1918 Bos N	11	38	3	12	0	1	0	4	3	0	0	.316	.381	.368	134	2	0	.932	1	89	43	S11		0.2
1919 Bos N	131	480	44	128	18	10	5	43	36	1	23	.267	.319	.377	113	7	12	.941	26	108	126	S131		4.6
1920 Bos N	134	493	48	131	19	15	1	43	28	0	24	.266	.305	.371	98	-4	14-11	.948	15	105	97	S133		2.1
1921 Pit N	153	612	90	180	25	12	1	70	47	3	38	.294	.347	.379	90	-8	25-12	.962	-17	97	94	S153		-0.7
1922 Pit N	155	672	115	198	26	15	0	63	61	2	43	.295	.355	.378	88	-11	24-13	.961	3	95	104	S138,2b18		0.7
1923 Pit N	141	581	78	161	19	9	1	41	42	1	34	.277	.327	.346	76	-21	14-11	.965	11	101	111	S141		0.5
1924 Pit N	152	594	62	158	33	20	2	71	35	0	53	.266	.307	.399	86	-14	18-14	.973	5	103	123	2b152		-0.5
1925 Chi N	75	266	37	62	10	3	0	23	29	0	20	.233	.308	.293	54	-18	6-5	.955	2	102	79	S74,M		-0.8
1926 Bro N	78	234	32	55	8	5	0	24	26	0	24	.235	.312	.312	69	-10	7	.948	7	102	79	S60,2b18		0.4
1927 StL N	9	29	0	7	1	0	0	0	2	0	2	.241	.290	.276	51	-2	0	.962	2	121	125	S9		0.1
1928 †StL N	112	366	40	88	14	10	1	34	36	1	27	.240	.310	.342	69	-18	3	.969	-9	98	87	S112,2b2		-1.4
1929 Bos N	146	560	87	159	26	10	0	55	47	4	33	.284	.344	.366	79	-18	13	.961	21	110	108	S145/2		1.7
1930 Bos N	142	558	85	157	26	8	2	43	48	5	23	.281	.344	.360	75	-23	9	.965	-14	91	96	S138,3b4		-1.9
1931 Bos N	145	562	69	146	22	5	0	33	56	2	34	.260	.329	.317	77	-17	6	.949	-24	93	103	S137,2b11		-3.1
1932 Bos N	149	571	67	134	20	4	0	37	46	3	26	.235	.295	.284	59	-33	4	.975	4	103	104	2b149		-1.9
1933 Bos N	143	478	46	104	15	4	0	38	36	1	34	.218	.274	.266	59	-26	2	.971	-28	87	106	2b142		-4.8
1935 Bos N	23	67	3	10	2	0	0	5	3	0	3	.149	.186	.179	-2	-10		.963	-3	94	110	2b20		-1.1
Total 23	2670	10078	1255	2605	380	177	28	884	839	39	756	.258	.318	.340	82	-254	291-112	.952	126	102	109	S2153,2b513,3b4		10.3

MARION, RED John Wyeth B3.14.1914 Richburg SC D3.13.1975 San Jose CA BR/TR/6-2/175 d9.16 b-Marty

YEAR TM LG	G	AB	R	H	2B	3B	HR	RBI	BB-IB	HP	SO	AVG	OBP	SLG	AOPS	ABR	SB-CS	FA	FR	RNG	THR	GAMES AT POSITION	DL	BFW
1935 Was A	4	11	1	2	0	0	0	1	3	0	2	.182	.182	.545	85	0	0-0	.833	0	67	463	O3(1/1/1)		0.0
1943 Was A	14	17	2	3	0	0	0	0	1	0	1	.176	.300	.176	42	-1	0-0	1.000	0	119	0	O4L		-0.1
Total 2	18	28	3	5	1	0	0	1	3	0	3	.179	.258	.321	63	-1	0-0	.923	0	93	232	O7(5/1/1)		-0.1

MARION, MARTY Martin Whiteford "Slats","The Octopus" B12.1.1917 Richburg SC BR/TR/6-2/170* d4.16 M6/C2 b-Red [DL 1951 StL N 76]

YEAR TM LG	G	AB	R	H	2B	3B	HR	RBI	BB-IB	HP	SO	AVG	OBP	SLG	AOPS	ABR	SB-CS	FA	FR	RNG	THR	GAMES AT POSITION	DL	BFW
1940 StL N	125	435	44	121	18	1	3	46	21	2	34	.278	.311	.345	76	-14	9	.949	-8	95	101	S125		-1.4
1941 StL N	155	547	50	138	22	3	3	58	42	2	48	.252	.308	.320	72	-20	8	.954	2	101	103	S155		-0.7
1942 †StL N	147	485	66	134	38	5	0	54	48	1	50	.276	.343	.375	102	3	8	.960	6	99	113	S147		2.1
1943 †StL N★	129	418	38	117	15	3	1	52	32	2	37	.280	.334	.337	90	-5	1	.970	16	103	138	S128		2.2
1944 †StL N★	144	506	50	135	26	2	6	63	43	0	50	.267	.324	.362	91	-6	1	.972	3	98	126	S144		0.9
1945 StL N★	123	430	63	119	27	5	1	59	39	2	39	.277	.340	.370	95	-3	2	.967	-6	97	114	S122		0.1
1946 †StL N★	146	498	51	116	29	4	3	46	59	3	53	.233	.318	.325	79	-12	1	.973	18	104	125	S145		1.5
1947 StL N★	149	540	57	147	19	6	4	74	49	1	58	.272	.334	.352	79	-16	3	.981	16	99	123	S141		0.8
1948 StL N★	144	567	70	143	26	4	4	43	37	0	54	.252	.298	.333	67	-27	1	.974	10	103	106	S142		-0.8
1949 StL N☆	134	515	61	140	31	2	5	70	37	2	42	.272	.323	.369	81	-13	0	.976	12	106	99	S134		-0.7
1950 StL N	106	372	36	92	10	2	4	40	44	0	55	.247	.327	.317	67	-17	1	.978	2	100	112	S101		-0.9
1952 StL A	67	186	16	46	11	0	2	19	19	1	17	.247	.320	.339	81	-4	0-2	.980	-2	95	118	S63,M		-0.8
1953 StL A	3	0	0	0	0	0	0	0	0	0	0	.000	.000	.000	-98	-2	0-0	1.000	-1	0		3b2,M		-0.3
Total 13	1572	5506	602	1448	272	37	36	624	470	16	537	.263	.323	.345	81	-136	35-2	.969	65	100	115	S1547,3b2	76	3.4

MARIS, ROGER Roger Eugene (b Roger Eugene Maras) B9.10.1934 Hibbing MN D12.14.1985 Houston TX BL/TR/6-0/204(185-204) d4.16

YEAR TM LG	G	AB	R	H	2B	3B	HR	RBI	BB-IB	HP	SO	AVG	OBP	SLG	AOPS	ABR	SB-CS	FA	FR	RNG	THR	GAMES AT POSITION	DL	BFW
1957 Cle A	116	358	61	84	9	5	14	51	60-5	1	79	.235	.344	.405	106	3	8-4	.975	7	110	147	O112(26/87/8)		0.5
1958 Cle A	51	182	26	41	5	1	9	27	17-2	0	33	.225	.287	.412	94	-2	4-2	.967	2	103	173	O47(0/27/23)		-0.2
KC A	99	401	61	99	14	3	19	53	28-1	2	52	.247	.298	.439	99	-3	0-0	.975	-3	91	107	O99(0/21/90)		-1.0
Year	150	583	87	140	19	4	28	80	45-3	2	85	.240	.294	.431	97	-5	4-2	.972	-1	95	127	O146(0/48/113)		-1.2
1959 KC A★	122	433	69	118	21	7	16	72	58-5	3	53	.273	.359	.464	123	14	2-1	.975	3	109	107	O117(0/6/113)	31	1.3
1960 †NY A★	136	499	98	141	18	7	39	112	70-4	7	65	.283	.371	.581	164	42	2-2	.985	-0	106	71	O131(0/7/128)		3.7
1961 †NY A★	161	590	132	159	16	4	61	142	94-0	7	67	.269	.372	.620	170	57	0-1	.968	-14	82	75	O160(0/11/156)		3.1
1962 †NY A★	157	590	92	151	34	1	33	100	87-11	4	78	.256	.356	.485	128	25	1-0	.991	-6	97	103	O154(0/64/103)		1.1
1963 NY A	90	312	53	84	14	1	23	53	35-3	2	40	.269	.342	.542	146	19	1-0	.988	3	107	114	O86(0/1/86)		1.7
1964 †NY A	141	513	86	144	12	2	26	71	62-1	6	78	.281	.364	.464	127	19	3-0	.996	-6	94	107	O137(0/32/105)		0.6
1965 NY A	46	155	22	37	7	0	8	27	29-1	0	29	.239	.357	.439	126	0	0-0	.971	-3	90	38	O43R		0.0
1966 NY A	119	348	37	81	9	2	13	43	36-3	5	60	.233	.307	.382	101	0	0-0	.993	-7	82	60	O95(0/1/94)		-1.4
1967 †StL N	125	410	64	107	18	7	9	55	52-3	4	61	.261	.346	.405	117	10	0-0	.991	2	111	63	O118(0/2/118)		0.5
1968 †StL N	100	310	25	79	18	2	5	45	24-3	5	38	.255	.307	.374	106	-2	0-0	.991	2	104	62	O84R		0.1
Total 12	1463	5101	826	1325	195	42	275	851	652-42	38	733	.260	.345	.476	128	192	21-9	.982	-20	100	84	O1383(26/259/1151)	31	10.0

YEAR	TM LG	G	AB	R	H	2B	3B	HR	RBI	BB-IB	HP	SO	AVG	OBP	SLG	AOPS	ABR	SB-CS	FA	FR	RNG	THR	GAMES AT POSITION	DL	BFW

MARKLAND, GENE Cleneth Eugene "Mousey" B12.26.1919 Detroit MI D6.15.1999 Barefoot Bay FL BR/TR/5-10/160 d4.25
| 1950 | Phi A | 5 | 8 | 2 | 1 | 0 | 0 | 0 | 3 | 0 | 0 | .125 | .364 | .125 | 30 | -1 | 0-0 | 1.000 | -0 | 92 | 31 | 2b5 | | -0.1 |

MARNIE, HARRY Harry Sylvester B7.6.1918 Philadelphia PA D1.7.2002 Philadelphia PA BR/TR/6-1/178 d9.15 Mil 1943-45
1940	Phi N	11	34	4	6	0	0	0	4	4	0	2	.176	.263	.176	24	-3	0	.984	4	132	123	2b11		0.1
1941	Phi N	61	158	12	38	3	3	0	11	13	0	25	.241	.298	.297	71	-7	0	.990	2	93	91	2b39,S16,3b3		-0.2
1942	Phi N	24	30	3	5	0	0	0	0	1	0	2	.167	.194	.167	6	-4	1	.971	5	155	175	2b11,S7/3		0.1
Total	3	96	222	19	49	3	3	0	15	18	0	29	.221	.279	.261	55	-14	1	.987	10	107	105	2b61,S23,3b4		0.0

MAROLEWSKI, FRED Fred Daniel "Fritz" B10.6.1928 Chicago IL BR/TR/6-2.5/205 d9.19
| 1953 | StL N | 1 | 0 | 0 | 0 | 0 | 0 | 0 | 0 | 0 | 0 | 0 | — | — | — | 0 | 0-0 | — | 0 | 0 | 0 | /1 | | 0.0 |

MARQUARDT, OLLIE Albert Ludwig B9.22.1902 Toledo OH D2.7.1968 Port Clinton OH BR/TR/5-9/156 d4.14
| 1931 | Bos A | 17 | 39 | 4 | 7 | 1 | 0 | 0 | 2 | 3 | 0 | 4 | .179 | .238 | .205 | 18 | -5 | 0-1 | .946 | -2 | 105 | 66 | 2b13/S3 | | -0.6 |

MARQUEZ, GONZALO Gonzalo Enrique (Moya) B3.31.1946 Carupano, Venez D12.20.1984 Valencia, Venez BL/TL/5-11/180* d8.11
1972	†Oak A	23	21	2	8	0	0	0	4	3-0	1	4	.381	.462	.381	166	2	1-1	.929	-0	119	90	1b2		0.2
1973	Oak A	23	25	1	6	1	0	0	0	0	0	4	.240	.240	.280	48	-2	0-0	—	0	0	0	2b2/1ORD		-0.2
	Chi N	19	58	5	13	2	0	0	4	3-1	0	2	.224	.270	.310	57	-3	0-0	.994	2	135	103	1b18		-0.3
1974	Chi N	11	11	1	0	0	0	0	0	1-1	0	2	.000	.083	.000	-72	-3	0-0	1.000	0	0	0	/1		-0.3
Total	3	76	115	9	27	3	0	1	10	7-2	1	12	.235	.286	.287	62	-6	1-1	.989	2	132	101	1b22,2b2/DOR		-0.6

MARQUEZ, LUIS Luis Angel (Sanchez) "Canena" B10.28.1925 Aguadilla, PR D3.1.1988 Aguadilla, PR BR/TR/5-10.5/174(174-190) d4.18 Negro Lg 1945-48
1951	Bos N	68	122	19	24	5	1	0	11	10	3	20	.197	.274	.254	46	-9	4-4	1.000	3	123	67	O43(21/23/3)		-0.8
1954	Chi N	17	12	2	1	0	0	0	0	4	0	4	.083	.214	.083	-19	-2	3-0	1.000	1	140	0	O14(4/10/0)		-0.1
	Pit N	14	9	3	1	0	0	0	0	4	0	0	.111	.385	.111	37	-1	0-0	1.000	0	136	0	O4(1/1/2)		0.0
	Year	31	21	5	2	0	0	0	0	8	0	4	.095	.296	.095	7	-3	3-0	1.000	1	139	0	O18(5/11/2)		-0.1
Total	2	99	143	24	26	5	1	0	11	18	3	24	.182	.278	.231	40	-12	7-4	1.000	4	125	57	O61(26/34/5)		0.0

MARQUIS, BOB Robert Rudolph B12.23.1924 Oklahoma City OK BL/TL/6-1/170 d4.17
| 1953 | Cin N | 40 | 44 | 9 | 12 | 1 | 1 | 0 | 3 | 11 | 0 | 11 | .273 | .333 | .477 | 107 | 0 | 0-0 | .905 | -0 | 116 | 0 | O10(2/8/0) | | 0.0 |

MARQUIS, ROGER Roger Julian "Noonie" B4.5.1937 Holyoke MA D7.19.2004 Holyoke MA BL/TL/6-0/190 d9.25
| 1955 | Bal A | 1 | 1 | 0 | 0 | 0 | 0 | 0 | 0 | 0-0 | 0 | 0 | .000 | .000 | .000 | -99 | 0 | 0-0 | — | -0 | 0 | 0 | /OR | | 0.0 |

MARR, LEFTY Charles W. B9.19.1862 Cincinnati OH D1.11.1912 New Britain CT BL/TL/5-9/180 d10.3
1886	Cin AA	8	29	2	8	1	0	0	2	1		1	.276	.323	.379	116	0	1	.696	-2	61	0	O8C		-0.2
1889	Col AA	139	546	110	167	26	15	1	75	87	6	32	.306	.407	.414	141	35	29	.856	7	106	101	3b66,O47(0/1/47),S26,1b2/C		3.6
1890	Cin N	130	527	91	157	17	12	1	73	46	6	29	.298	.361	.381	117	11	44	.930	-7	115	152	O64R,3b63,S3		-1.1
1891	Cin N	72	286	32	74	9	7	0	32	25		15	.259	.323	.339	92	-3	16	.835	-9	58	0	O72R		-0.5
	Cin AA	14	57	9	11	1	0	0	4	7	0	4	.193	.281	.211	38	-5	2	.923	-1	42	0	O14R		2.2
Total	4	363	1445	244	417	54	35	2	186	166	15	80	.289	.368	.379	118	38	92	.853	-11	80	57	O205(0/9/197),3b129,S29,1b2/C		2.2

MARRERO, ELI Elieser B11.17.1973 Havana, Cuba BR/TR/6-1/180* [StLN93 3/88] d9.3
1997	StL N	17	45	4	11	2	0	2	7	2	1	13	.244	.271	.422	80	-2	4-0	.969	1	122	173	C17		0.1
1998	StL N	83	254	28	62	18	1	4	20	28-5	1	42	.244	.318	.370	81	-7	6-2	.991	0	133	95	C73,1b2		-0.1
1999	StL N	114	317	32	61	13	1	6	34	18-4	1	56	.192	.236	.297	34	-34	11-2	.987	0	143	119	C96,1b20		-2.6
2000	†StL N	53	102	21	23	3	1	5	17	9-0	3	16	.225	.302	.422	80	-4	5-0	1.000	5	277	118	C38,1b7	60	0.4
2001	StL N	86	203	37	54	11	3	6	23	15-2	1	36	.266	.312	.438	90	-4	6-3	.984	4	129	66	C65,O15(8/0/7),1b6		0.4
2002	†StL N	131	397	63	104	19	1	18	66	40-11	1	72	.262	.327	.451	105	0	14-2	.985	6	104	166	O106(39/36/46),C44,1b4		0.7
2003	StL N	41	107	10	24	4	2	2	20	7-0	1	18	.224	.267	.355	62	-5	0-1	.980	3	114	73	O31(10/6/21),C6,1b2	112	-0.5
2004	†Atl N	90	250	37	80	18	1	10	40	23-1	1	50	.320	.374	.520	128	11	4-1	.992	2	101	161	O73(47/4/25)	44	1.1
2005	KC A	32	88	11	14	4	0	4	9	7-0	1	18	.159	.222	.341	52	-6	1-0	.967	-1	90	263	O20(8/5/7),1b9,D2	68	-0.1
	Bal A	22	50	8	11	3	2	3	10	4-0	0	20	.220	.268	.540	110	0	0-0	.966	-1	100	0	O16(7/3/6)		-0.9
	Year	54	138	19	25	7	2	7	19	11-0	1	38	.181	.239	.413	74	-6	1-0	.966	-2	95	133	O36(15/8/13),1b9,D2	297	-1.4
Total	9	669	1813	251	444	95	12	60	246	153-24	6	341	.245	.302	.410	84	-52	51-11	.987	20	142	102	C339,O261(119/54/112),1b50,D2	297	-1.4

MARRERO, ORESTE Oreste Vilato (Vazquez) B10.31.1969 Bayamon, PR BL/TL/6-0/195* d8.12
1993	Mon N	32	81	10	17	5	1	1	4	14-0	0	16	.210	.326	.333	74	-3	1-3	.991	-1	93	121	1b32		-0.6
1996	LA N	10	8	2	3	1	0	0	1	1-0	0	3	.375	.444	.500	158	1	0-0	1.000	0	0	0	/1		0.1
Total	2	42	89	12	20	6	1	1	5	15-0	0	19	.225	.337	.348	81	-2	1-3	.991	-1	93	120	1b33		-0.5

MARRIOTT, WILLIAM William Earl B4.18.1893 Pratt KS D8.11.1969 Berkeley CA BL/TR/6-0/170 d9.6 Mil 1918
1917	Chi N	3	6	0	0	0	0	0	0	0	0	0	.000	.000	.000	-93	-1	0	.667	-0	77	0	/OL		-0.2
1920	Chi N	14	43	7	12	0	0	0	5	6	0	5	.279	.367	.465	135	2	1-1	.892	-3	94	31	2b14		-0.1
1921	Chi N	30	38	3	12	1	1	0	7	4	0	1	.316	.381	.395	105	0	3-1	.826	-1	81	53	2b6/S3OL		-0.1
1925	Bos N	103	370	37	99	9	1	0	40	28	2	26	.268	.322	.305	67	-18	3-8	.928	-3	103	74	3b89/OL		-1.2
1926	Bro N	109	360	39	96	13	4	3	42	17	2	20	.267	.303	.378	84	-10	12	.927	-6	97	37	3b104		0.6
1927	Bro N	6	9	0	1	0	1	0	2	2	0	2	.111	.273	.333	61	-1	0	.889	0	105	0	3b2		0.0
Total	6	265	826	86	220	27	14	6	95	57	4	55	.266	.317	.347	78	-28	16-10	.925	-14	100	57	3b196,2b20,O3L/S		-0.9

MARSANS, ARMANDO Armando B10.3.1887 Matanzas, Cuba D9.3.1960 Havana, Cuba BR/TR/5-10/157 d7.4 OF(51/459/71)
1911	Cin N	58	138	17	36	2	0	0	11	15	3	11	.261	.346	.304	86	-2	11	.968	-3	99	0	O34(5/16/13)/13		-0.1
1912	Cin N	110	416	59	132	19	7	1	38	20	3	25	.317	.353	.404	110	4	35	.975	-1	106	77	O98(7/82/13),1b6		-0.1
1913	Cin N	118	435	49	129	7	6	0	38	17	3	25	.297	.327	.340	91	-6	37-11	.963	-2	98	106	O94(3/56/37),1b22,3b2/S		-0.5
1914	Cin N	36	124	16	37	3	0	0	21	14	1	6	.298	.374	.323	105	1	1-3	.916	-1	100	85	O36L		-0.6
	StL F	9	40	5	14	0	2	0	2	3	0	0	.350	.395	.450	123	1	4	.927	-1	88	244	O35C		-1.3
1915	StL F	36	124	16	22	3	0	0	6	14	0	5	.177	.261	.202	29	-13	5	.975	2	94	164	O35C		-1.5
1916	StL A	151	528	51	134	12	1	1	60	57	6	41	.254	.333	.286	91	-5	46-26	.977	-2	115	107	O150C		-1.9
1917	StL A	75	257	31	59	12	0	0	20	20	0	20	.230	.285	.276	74	-8	11	.963	-5	100	33	O67C,3b5/2		-1.4
	NY A	25	88	10	20	4	0	0*	15	8	0	9	.227	.292	.273	72	-3	6	.974	-2	113	107	O25C		-2.2
	Year	100	345	41	79	16	0	0	35	28	0	9	.229	.287	.275	73	-11	17	.967	-3	104	55	O92C,3b5/2		-1.2
1918	NY A	37	123	13	29	5	1	0	9	5	0	9	.236	.266	.293	67	-5	3	.943	-4	91	45	O36(10/28/8)		-1.2
Total	8	655	2273	267	612	67	19	2	221	173	16	117	.269	.325	.318	88	-36	171-37	.967	-13	99	90	O575C,1b29,2b8,3b8,S3		-8.1

MARSH, FRED Fred Francis B1.5.1924 Valley Falls KS BR/TR/5-10/180* d4.19
1949	Cle A	1	0	0	0	0	0	0	0	0	0	0	—	—	—	—	0	0-0	—	0		0	/R		-1.2
1951	StL A	130	445	44	108	21	4	4	43	36	0	56	.243	.299	.335	69	-20	4-4	.928	3	103	113	3b117,S3,2b2		0.1
1952	StL A	11	24	3	5	1	0	0	1	5	0	4	.208	.345	.250	65	-1	0-1	.963	0	109	86	2b9,S3		0.0
	Was A	9	24	1	1	0	0	0	1	1	0	1	.042	.080	.042	-68	-6	0-0	1.000	-2	59	103	2b5,O2L		-1.0
	StL A	76	223	25	64	8	1	2	26	22	0	29	.287	.351	.359	95	-1	3-2	.945	-10	97	216	S60,3b21,2b14,O2L		-1.3
	Year	96	271	29	70	9	1	2	28	28	0	37	.258	.328	.321	79	-7	3-3	.945	-12	89	109	S63,3b21,2b14,O2L		-1.2
1953	Chi A	67	95	22	19	1	0	2	2	13	1	26	.200	.300	.274	55	-6	0-3	.940	-3	101	158	3b32,S17,1b5,2b2		-1.0
1954	Chi A	62	98	21	30	5	2	0	4	9	0	16	.306	.364	.398	105	1	4-2	.975	10	132	158	3b36,S3,1b2/OR		-3.0
1955	Bal A	89	303	30	66	7	4	1	21	35-1	3	33	.218	.300	.267	58	-18	1-0	.983	-17	82	89	2b76,3b18,S16	30	-3.0
1956	Bal A	24	24	3	3	0	0	0	0	4-0	0	2	.125	.250	.125	-2	-3	1-0	.929	-1	99	115	S8,3b8,2b5	30	-0.9
Total	7	465	1236	148	296	43	8	10	96	125-1	2	171	.239	.310	.311	69	-54	13-14	.928	-13	107	121	3b232,S107,2b99,1b7,O3(2/0/1)		-1.1

MARSH, TOM Thomas Owen B12.27.1965 Toledo OH BR/TR/6-2/180* [PhiN88 16/406] d6.5 Col Toledo
1992	Phi N	42	125	7	25	3	2	2	16	2-0	1	23	.200	.215	.304	47	-10	0-1	.971	-1	105	0	O35(25/0/12)	31	-1.4
1994	Phi N	8	18	3	5	1	0	1	3	1-0	1	1	.278	.316	.444	94	0	0-1	.889	-0	95	0	O7(3/0/4)	16	-0.3
1995	Phi N	43	109	13	32	1	1	1	15	4-0	1	25	.294	.316	.422	93	-2	0-2	.939	0	102	141	O29(24/4/1)	47	-1.0
Total	3	93	252	23	62	7	4	5	34	7-0	1	49	.246	.266	.365	71	-12	0-4	.952	-1	103	56	O71(52/4/17)		-1.0

MARSHALL, CHARLIE Charles Anthony (b Charles Anthony Marchlewicz) B8.28.1919 Wilmington DE BR/TR/5-10.5/178 d6.14
| 1941 | StL N | 1 | 0 | 0 | 0 | 0 | 0 | 0 | 0 | 0 | 0 | 0 | — | — | — | 0 | 0 | 0-0 | 1.000 | -0 | 0 | 0 | /C | | 0.0 |

YEAR	TM	LG	G	AB	R	H	2B	3B	HR	RBI	BB-IB	HP	SO	AVG	OBP	SLG	AOPS	ABR	SB-CS	FA	FR	RNG	THR	GAMES AT POSITION	DL	BFW

MARSHALL, DAVE   David Lewis   B1.14.1943 Artesia CA   BL/TR/6-1/190(190-205)   d9.7   Col Long Beach (CA) City

1967	SF	N	1	0	0	0	0	0	0	0	0-0		0	—	—	—		0	0-0	—				/R		0.0
1968	SF	N	76	174	17	46	5	0	4	16	20-2	1	37	.264	.338	.322	101	7	2-1	.924	-4	78	93	O50(24/0/28)		-0.6
1969	SF	N	110	267	32	62	7	1	2	33	40-3	5	68	.232	.340	.288	79	-6	1-8	.956	-5	85	70	O87(79/0/17)		-1.8
1970	NY	N	92	189	21	46	10	1	6	29	17-0	0	43	.243	.304	.402	87	-4	4-1	.973	-0	102	76	O43(12/0/33)		-0.6
1971	NY	N	100	214	28	51	9	1	3	21	26-3	2	54	.238	.322	.332	87	-3	3-1	.989	-1	100	59	O64(25/0/39)		-0.7
1972	NY	N	72	156	21	39	5	0	4	11	22-1	1	28	.250	.346	.359	102	1	3-3	.972	-2	107	0	O42(1/4/38)		-0.3
1973	SD	N	39	49	4	14	5	0	4	8-0	1	9	.286	.390	.388	128	3	0-1	1.000	-1	100	0	O8R		0.1
Total	7		490	1049	123	258	41	4	16	114	133-9	10	239	.246	.333	.338	91	-8	13-15	.966	-11	93	60	O294(141/4/163)		-3.9

MARSHALL, DOC   Edward Harbert "Eddie"   B6.4.1906 New Albany MS   D9.1.1999 Lake San Marcos CA   BR/TR/5-11/150   d9.28   Col U. of Mississippi

1929	NY	N	5	15	6	6	2	0	0	2	1	0	0	.400	.438	.533	140	1	0	1.000		-1	94	0	2b5		0.0
1930	NY	N	78	223	33	69	5	3	0	21	13	1	9	.309	.350	.359	73	-10	1	.947	-1	96	92	S45,2b17,3b5		-0.6
1931	NY	N	68	194	15	39	6	2	0	10	8	0	8	.201	.233	.253	31	-20	1	.956	2	103	102	2b47,S11,3b3		-1.4
1932	NY	N	68	226	18	56	8	1	0	28	6	1	11	.248	.270	.292	52	-16	1	.922	-3	98	100	S63		-1.4
Total	4		219	658	72	170	21	6	0	61	28	2	28	.258	.291	.309	56	-45	2	.931	-3	96	98	S119,2b69,3b8		-3.4

MARSHALL, JOE   Joseph Hanley "Home Run Joe"   B2.19.1876 Audubon MN   D9.11.1931 Santa Monica CA   BR/TR/5-8/170   d9.7

1903	Pit	N	10	23	2	6	1	2	0	2	0	0		.261	.261	.478	106	0	0	1.000	-2	71	115	S3,O3(2/1/0)/2		-0.2
1906	StL	N	33	95	2	15	1	0	0	7	6	1		.158	.216	.211	34	-8	0	.903	1	246		O23R,1b4		-0.9
Total	2		43	118	4	21	2	4	0	9	6	1		.178	.224	.263	50	-8	0	.903	-1	242		O26(2/1/23),1b4,S3/2		-1.1

MARSHALL, KEITH   Keith Alan   B7.2.1951 San Francisco CA   BR/TR/6-2/175   [KCA69 5/117]   d4.7

| 1973 | KC | A | 8 | 9 | 0 | 2 | 1 | 0 | 0 | 3 | 0-0 | | 0 | .222 | .300 | .333 | 73 | 0 | 0-0 | 1.000 | -0 | 94 | 0 | O8(5/2/2) | | -0.1 |

MARSHALL, MIKE   Michael Allen   B1.12.1960 Libertyville IL   BR/TR/6-5/220*   [LAN78 6/151]   d9.7

1981	†LA	N	14	25	2	5	3	0	0	1	1-0	1	1	.200	.259	.320	66	-1	0-0	1.000	-1	0	200	1b3,3b3,O2(1/0/1)		-0.3
1982	LA	N	49	95	10	23	3	0	5	9	13-1	1	23	.242	.336	.432	118	2	2-0	1.000	-2	79	0	O19(3/0/16),1b13		-0.1
1983	†LA	N	140	465	47	132	17	1	17	65	43-4	5	127	.284	.347	.434	116	10	7-3	.976	-6	92	76	O109R,1b33		-0.2
1984	LA	N☆	134	495	68	127	27	0	21	65	40-6	3	93	.257	.315	.438	110	4	4-3	.981	-1	95	102	O118(116/0/4),1b15	21	-0.1
1985	†LA	N	135	518	72	152	27	2	28	95	37-6	3	137	.293	.342	.515	140	26	3-10	.991	-5	86	106	O125(1/0/124),1b7	28	1.1
1986	†LA	N	103	330	47	77	11	0	19	53	27-3	4	90	.233	.298	.439	108	2	4-4	.963	-3	89	112	O97(1/0/97)	15	-0.7
1987	LA	N	104	402	45	118	19	0	16	72	18-2	2	79	.294	.327	.460	109	4	0-5	.987	-9	80	60	O102R	38	-1.2
1988	†LA	N	144	542	63	150	27	2	20	82	24-7	7	93	.277	.314	.445	119	11	4-1	.966	-2	86	98	O90R,1b53		0.3
1989	LA	N	105	377	41	98	21	1	11	42	33-4	5	78	.260	.325	.408	111	5	2-5	.978	-5	95	38	O102R	31	-0.5
1990	NY	N	53	163	24	39	8	1	6	27	7-0	3	40	.239	.278	.411	88	-3	0-2	.993	-0	88	77	1b42/OR	15	-0.7
	†Bos	A	30	112	10	32	6	1	4	12	4-0	1	26	.286	.316	.464	110	1	0-0	1.000	0	157	95	D14,1b8,O8R		0.0
1991	Bos	A	22	62	4	18	4	0	1	7	0-0	0	19	.290	.290	.403	85	-1	0-0	.979	-2	0	114	1b5,O4(1/0/3),D7	16	-0.4
	Cal	A	2	7	0	0	0	0	0	0	0-0	0	1	.000	.000	.000	-99	-2	0-0	1.000	0	157	239	/1D		-0.2
	Year		24	69	4	18	4	0	1	7	0-0	0	20	.261	.261	.362	67	-3	0-0	.984	-2	31	138	D8,1b6,O4(1/0/3)		-0.6
Total	11		1035	3593	433	971	173	8	148	530	247-33	37	810	.270	.321	.446	114	60	26-33	.978	-35	89	78	O777(123/0/657),1b180,D22,3b3	164	-3.0

MARSHALL, MAX   Milo May   B9.18.1913 Randolph IA   D9.16.1993 Salem OR   BL/TR/6-1/180   d5.10   Mil 1944-45

1942	Cin	N	131	530	49	135	17	6	7	43	34		38	.255	.301	.349	90	-9	4	.976	-11	91	27	O129(43/11/79)		-3.0
1943	Cin	N	132	508	55	120	11	8	4	39	34		52	.236	.287	.313	74	-19	8	.981	-5	92	89	O129R		-3.5
1944	Cin	N	66	229	36	56	13	2	4	23	21		10	.245	.308	.371	94	-2	3	.965	1	104	89	O59(1/0/58)		-0.6
Total	3		329	1267	140	311	41	16	15	105	89		100	.245	.297	.339	84	-30	15	.975	-16	94	63	O317(44/11/266)		-7.1

MARSHALL, JIM   Rufus James   B5.25.1931 Danville IL   BL/TL/6-1/190*   d4.15   M4/C1   Col Compton (CA) CC

1958	Bal	A	85	191	17	41	4	3	5	19	18-1		30	.215	.280	.346	76	-7	3-2	1.000	-2	75	99	1b52,O8(3/0/5)		-1.2
	Chi	A	26	81	12	22	2	0	5	11	12-0	1	13	.272	.372	.481	126	3	0-1	.992	-1	73	81	1b15,O11R		0.2
1959	Chi	N	108	294	39	74	10	1	11	40	33-1	0	39	.252	.324	.405	95	-2	0-1	.997	3	110	102	1b72,O8(7/0/3)		-0.4
1960	SF	N	75	118	19	28	2	2	2	13	17-1	2	24	.237	.331	.339	90	-2	0-1	.968	-3	68	86	1b28,O6L		-0.7
1961	SF	N	44	36	5	8	0	0	1	7	3-0	0	8	.222	.275	.306	58	-2	0-0	1.000	0	133	117	1b4,O2(1/0/1)		-0.2
1962	NY	N	17	32	6	11	1	0	3	4	3-0	0	6	.344	.400	.656	175	3	0-0	1.000	-0	123	136	1b5/OR		0.3
	Pit	N	55	100	13	22	5	1	2	12	15-0	1	19	.220	.319	.350	80	-3	1-0	1.000	1	104	116	1b26		-0.3
	Year		72	132	19	33	6	1	5	16	18-0	1	25	.250	.338	.424	103	1	1-0	1.000	1	107	120	1b31/OR		0.0
Total	5		410	852	111	206	24	7	29	106	101-3		139	.242	.320	.388	93	-10	5-4	.994	-2	93	100	1b202,O36(17/0/21)		-2.3

MARSHALL, WILLARD   Willard Warren   B2.8.1921 Richmond VA   D11.5.2000 Norwood NJ   BL/TR/6-1/205(190-205)   d4.14   Mil 1943-45   Col Wake Forest

1942	NY	N★	116	401	41	103	9	2	11	59	26	3	20	.257	.307	.372	98	-3	1	.975	1	94	157	O107(67/46/1)		-0.7
1946	NY	N	131	510	63	144	18	3	13	48	33	1	29	.282	.327	.406	107	2	3	.978	-4	89	125	O125(51/59/15)		-0.9
1947	NY	N★	155	587	102	171	19	6	36	107	67	2	30	.291	.366	.528	134	26	3	.972	9	108	142	O155R		3.0
1948	NY	N	143	537	72	146	21	8	14	86	64	1	34	.272	.350	.419	107	5	2	.983	1	93	148	O142R		0.1
1949	NY	N★	141	499	81	153	19	3	12	70	78	1	20	.307	.401	.429	123	19	4	.974	2	105	100	O138(2/0/136)		1.7
1950	Bos	N	105	298	38	70	10	2	5	40	36	1	5	.235	.319	.332	77	-10	1	.958	4	101	191	O85(14/9/64)		-0.9
1951	Bos	N	136	469	65	132	24	7	11	62	48	2	18	.281	.351	.433	118	11	0-3	1.000	-3	93	99	O136R		0.4
1952	Bos	N	21	66	5	15	4	1	2	11	4	0	4	.227	.271	.409	89	-1	0-0	.938	0	82	186	O16R		-0.2
	Cin	N	107	397	52	106	23	1	8	46	37	2	25	.267	.333	.390	100	0	0-1	.979	-5	145	0121R		-0.4
	Year		128	463	57	121	27	2	10	57	41	2	29	.261	.323	.395	97	-1	0-1	.985	-5	97	138	O105R		-0.5
1953	Cin	N	122	357	51	95	14	6	17	62	41	0	28	.266	.342	.482	111	5	0-0	.995	5	102	157	O95R		0.6
1954	Chi	A	47	71	7	18	2	0	1	11	9	0	9	.254	.349	.324	84	-1	0-0	.960	-1	84	99	O29(7/0/22)		-0.3
1955	Chi	A	22	41	6	7	0	0	1	6	13-1	1	6	.171	.364	.171	48	-2	0-0	.957	-1	105	0	O12(4/0/8)	9	-0.3
Total	11		1246	4233	583	1160	163	39	130	604	458-1	13	219	.274	.347	.423	109	51	14-4	.979	15	98	135	O1145(145/114/895)	9	2.3

MARSHALL, BILL   William Henry   B2.14.1911 Dorchester MA   D5.5.1977 Sacramento CA   BR/TR/5-8.5/156   d6.20

1931	Bos	A	1	0	1	0	0	0	0	0	0			—	—	—		0	0-0			0		/R		0.0
1934	Cin	N	6	8	0	1	0	0	0	0	0		2	.125	.125	.125	-34	-2	0	.875	0	133	0	2b2		-0.1
Total	2		7	8	1	1	0	0	0	0	0		2	.125	.125	.125	-34	-2	0-0	.875	0	133	0	2b2		-0.1

MARSHALL, DOC   William Riddle   B9.22.1875 Butler PA   D12.11.1959 Clinton IL   BR/TR/6-0/185   d4.15   Col Grove City

1904	Phi	N	8	20	1	2	0	0	0	1	0			.100	.100	.100	-40	-3	0	.944	1	87	185	C7		-0.2
	NY	N	1	0	0	0	0	0	0	0	0			—	—	—		0	0		0			/C		0.0
	Bos	N	13	43	3	9	0	1	0	2	2			.209	.244	.256	56	-2	2	.955	-0	87	126	C10/OL		-0.2
	NY	N	10	17	3	6	1	0	0	2	1			.353	.389	.412	141	1	0	.955	1	0		C2,O2(1/0/1)/2		0.2
	Year		32	80	7	17	1	1	0	5	3			.213	.241	.250	52	-5	2	.952	1	98	145	C20,O3(2/0/1)/2		-0.2
1906	NY	N	38	102	8	17	3	2	0	7	7	2		.167	.234	.235	45	-7	1	1.000	1	0		C38		-0.2
	StL	N	39	123	6	34	4	1	0	10	6	1		.276	.315	.325	104	0	1	.961	1	169	0	O16(1/3/13),C13,1b2		-0.6
	Year		77	225	14	51	7	3	0	17	13	3		.227	.278	.284	76	-7	2	.969	2	90	108	C51,O16(1/3/13),1b2		0.5
1907	StL	N	84	268	19	54	8	2	2	18	12	4		.201	.246	.269	64	-12	2	.952	-3	81	123	C83		-0.1
1908	StL	N	6	14	0	1	0	0	0	0	1			.071	.071	.071	-57	-2	0	1.000	1	74	92	C6		-0.8
	Chi	N	12	20	4	6	0	1	0	3	0			.300	.300	.400	118	0	0	1.000	2	120	197	C4,O3(0/1/2)		-0.2
	Year		18	34	4	7	0	1	0	3	1			.206	.206	.265	49	-2	0	1.000	3	83	113	C10,O3(0/1/2)		0.0
1909	Bro	N	50	149	7	30	7	1	0	10	6			.201	.232	.262	55	-8	3	1.000	4	88	96	C49/OR		-0.9
Total	5		261	756	51	159	23	8	2	51	35			.210	.251	.270	64	-33	15	.961	-1	86	115	C213,O23(3/4/17),1b2/2		-2.0

MARTE, ANDY   Andy Manuel   B10.21.1983 Villa Tapia, D.R.   BR/TR/6-1/185   d6.7

| 2005 | Atl | N | 24 | 57 | 3 | 8 | 2 | 1 | 0 | 4 | 7-0 | 1 | 13 | .140 | .227 | .211 | 17 | -7 | 0-1 | .857 | -9 | 48 | 36 | 3b17 | | -1.7 |

MARTEL, DOC   Leon Alphonse "Marty"   B6.29.1883 Weymouth MA   D10.11.1947 Washington DC   BR/TR/6-0/185   d7.6   Col Georgetown

1909	Phi	N	24	41	1	11	3	1	0	7	4	0		.268	.333	.390	123	1	0	.974	3	109	130	C12		0.5
1910	Bos	N	10	31	0	4	0	0	0	1	0	0		.129	.182	.129	-9	-4	0	.980	-0	101	91	1b10		-0.5
Total	2		34	72	1	15	3	1	0	8	6	0	3	.208	.269	.278	64	-3	0	.974	2	109	130	C12,1b10		0.0

MARTIN, AL   Albert De Groot (aka Albert May in 1872)   B8.1847 NY   D3.17.1915 Brooklyn NY   d5.7

| 1872 | Eck | NA | 4 | 18 | 2 | 5 | 0 | 0 | 0 | 1 | 0 | | | .278 | .278 | .278 | 84 | 0 | 0-0 | .700 | -2 | 69 | 59 | 2b4 | | -0.2 |
| 1874 | Atl | NA | 7 | 29 | 1 | 4 | 0 | 0 | 0 | 1 | 0 | 1 | | .138 | .138 | .138 | -13 | -3 | 0-0 | .646 | -3 | 102 | 57 | 2b6/OL | | -0.5 |

YEAR	TM LG	G	AB	R	H	2B	3B	HR	RBI	BB-IB	HP	SO	AVG	OBP	SLG	AOPS	ABR	SB-CS	FA	FR	RNG	THR	GAMES AT POSITION	DL	BFW
1875	Atl NA	6	26	1	3	0	0	0	1	0		0	.115	.115	.115	-22	-3	0-0	.909	-0	0		O6C		-0.3
Total	3 NA	17	73	4	12	0	0	0	3	0		1	.164	.164	.164	9	-6	0-0	.662	-6	89	58	2b10,O7(1/6/0)		-1.0

MARTIN, AL   Albert Lee   B11.24.1967 West Covina CA   BL/TL/6-2/210(207-220)   [AtlN85 8/198]   d7.28

YEAR	TM LG	G	AB	R	H	2B	3B	HR	RBI	BB-IB	HP	SO	AVG	OBP	SLG	AOPS	ABR	SB-CS	FA	FR	RNG	THR	GAMES AT POSITION	DL	BFW
																		0-0	1.000	0	119	0	O7L		-0.1
1992	Pit N	12	12	1	2	0	1	0	2	0		5	.167	.154	.333	39	-1	0-0	.975	-6	94	73	O136(81/63/6)		0.3
1993	Pit N	143	480	85	135	26	8	18	64	42-5		122	.281	.338	.481	117	10	16-9	.979	-1	89	177	O77(67/13/0)	32	0.1
1994	Pit N	82	276	48	79	12	4	9	33	34-3	2	56	.286	.367	.457	112	5	15-6	.977	-0	97	124	O121(95/42/0)		-0.9
1995	Pit N	124	439	70	124	25	3	13	41	44-6	2	92	.282	.351	.442	105	3	20-11	.965	-16	78	58	O152(142/26/0)		-0.9
1996	Pit N	155	630	101	189	40	4	18	72	54-2	2	116	.300	.354	.452	108	8	38-12	.957	-13	63	114	O110L	33	-0.5
1997	Pit N	113	423	64	123	24	7	13	59	45-7	3	83	.291	.359	.473	115	9	23-7	.957	-13	63	114	O114L,D2		-1.8
1998	Pit N	125	440	57	105	15	2	12	47	32-2	5	91	.239	.296	.364	72	-19	20-3	.985	2	99	89	O133L		-0.8
1999	Pit N	143	541	97	150	36	8	24	63	49-5	1	119	.277	.337	.506	109	6	6-8	.950	-7	79	77	O89L		-0.4
2000	SD N	93	346	62	106	13	6	11	27	28-5	2	54	.306	.360	.474	116	7	4-1	.963	3	117	163	O35(20/7/9),D2		-0.4
	†Sea A	42	134	19	31	4	4	4	9	8-0	1	31	.231	.283	.396	71	-7	4-1	.971	2	109	81	O73(72/1/1),D16		-0.3
2001	†Sea A	100	283	41	68	15	2	7	42	37-4	2	59	.240	.330	.382	93	-3	9-3	1.000	0	112	0	D57,O13(8/0/5)/1		-1.2
2003	TB A	100	238	19	60	12	2	3	26	17-4	2	51	.252	.306	.357	76	-8	2-2	1.000	0	112	0	O1060(938/152/21),D77/1	65	-5.7
Total	11	1232	4242	664	1172	220	48	132	485	390-43	24	879	.276	.339	.444	103	10	173-65	.969	-49	87	89			

MARTIN, BILLY   Alfred Manuel   B5.16.1928 Berkeley CA   D12.25.1989 Johnson City NY   BR/TR/5-11.5/165*   d4.18 Mil 1954-55   M16/C4

YEAR	TM LG	G	AB	R	H	2B	3B	HR	RBI	BB-IB	HP	SO	AVG	OBP	SLG	AOPS	ABR	SB-CS	FA	FR	RNG	THR	GAMES AT POSITION	DL	BFW
																		0-0	.976	-2	75	82	2b22/3		-0.3
1950	NY A	34	36	10	9	1	0	1	8	3	0	3	.250	.308	.361	73	-2	0-0	.988	9	137	171	2b23,S6,3b2/OC		0.8
1951	†NY A	51	58	10	15	1	0	0	2	4		2	.259	.328	.345	85	-1	0-1	.984	18	112	130	2b107		1.8
1952	†NY A	109	363	32	97	13	3	3	33	22	8	31	.267	.323	.345	94	-5	3-6	.985	2	100	117	2b146,S18		0.4
1953	†NY A	149	587	72	151	24	6	15	75	43	6	56	.257	.314	.395	94	-8	6-7	.977	2	106	161	2b17,S3		0.3
1955	NY A	20	70	8	21	2	0	1	9	7-1		9	.300	.354	.371	100	1	1-2	.980	-6	98	114	2b105,3b16		-0.7
1956	†NY A★	121	458	76	121	24	5	9	49	30-0	5	56	.264	.310	.397	90	-9	7-3	.980	-6	98	114	2b26,3b13		-0.9
1957	NY A	43	145	12	35	5	2	1	12	3-0	1	14	.241	.257	.324	60	-9	2-1	.947	-2	99	101	2b53,3b20,S2		-1.5
	KC A	73	265	33	68	9	3	9	27	12-0	3	20	.257	.295	.415	91	-5	7-1	.987	-14	82	76	2b52,3b20,S2		-2.4
	Year	116	410	45	103	14	5	10	39	15-0	4	34	.251	.282	.383	80	-13	9-2	.973	-16	88	84	2b78,3b33,S2		-3.1
1958	Det A	131	498	56	127	19	7	7	42	16-0	3	62	.255	.279	.339	65	-24	5-3	.958	-13	86	103	S88,3b41	30	-1.0
1959	Cle A	73	242	37	63	7	0	9	24	8-2	3	18	.260	.290	.401	92	-4	0-2	.997	-10	87	87	2b67,3b4		-1.9
1960	Cin N	103	317	34	78	17	1	3	16	27-5	0	34	.246	.304	.334	74	-11	0-1	.975	-14	87	96	2b97		-0.2
1961	Mil N	6	6	1	0	0	0	0	0	0-0		1	.000	.000	.000	-99	-2	0-0	—	0			/H		-1.9
	Min A	108	374	44	92	16	3	6	36	13-0	3	32	.246	.275	.361	65	-20	3-2	.980	-35	97	108	2b767,S118,3b97/OC	30	-8.2
Total	11	1021	3419	425	877	137	28	64	333	188-8	32	355	.257	.300	.369	81	-100	34-29	.980	-35	97	108			

MARTIN, PHONNEY   Alphonse Case   B8.4.1845 New York NY   D5.24.1933 Hollis NY   5-7/148   d4.26   M1 ▲

YEAR	TM LG	G	AB	R	H	2B	3B	HR	RBI	BB-IB	HP	SO	AVG	OBP	SLG	AOPS	ABR	SB-CS	FA	FR	RNG	THR	GAMES AT POSITION	DL	BFW
1872	Tro NA	25	119	27	36	2	1	0	14	0		1	.303	.303	.336	95	-1	0-0	.780	-2	0	0	O25R,P8		-0.1
	Eck NA	18	78	13	15	1	1	0	9	2		3	.192	.213	.231	43	-4	3-2	.833	1	98	0	P10,O9R,M.		0.0
	Year	43	197	40	51	3	2	0	23	2		4	.259	.266	.294	76	-4	3-2	.776	-1	59	0	O34R,P18		-0.1
1873	Mut NA	31	140	12	31	1	0	0	14	0		4	.221	.221	.229	41	-11	1-1	.680	-6	0	0	O30R,P6		-1.0
Total	2 NA	74	337	52	82	4	2	0	37	2		8	.243	.248	.267	58	-16	4-3	.747	-7	33	0	O64R,P24		-1.1

MARTIN, BABE   Boris Michael (b Boris Michael Martinovich)   B3.28.1920 Seattle WA   BR/TR/5-11.5/194*   d9.25

YEAR	TM LG	G	AB	R	H	2B	3B	HR	RBI	BB-IB	HP	SO	AVG	OBP	SLG	AOPS	ABR	SB-CS	FA	FR	RNG	THR	GAMES AT POSITION	DL	BFW
1944	StL A	2	4	0	3	1	0	0	1	0		0	.750	.750	1.000	376		0-0	1.000	-0	82	0	/OL		0.1
1945	StL A	54	185	13	37	5	2	2	16	11		24	.200	.245	.281	50	-13	0-1	.992	6	117	162	O48(43/0/6),1b6		-1.1
1946	StL A	3	9	0	2	0	0	0	1	1		0	.222	.300	.222	45	-1	0-0	1.000	0	107	0	C2		0.0
1948	Bos A	4	4	0	2	0	0	0	0	0		1	.500	.500	.500	158	-0	0-0	—	0	0	0	/C		-0.1
1949	Bos A	2	2	0	0	0	0	0	0	0		1	.000	.000	.000	-93	-1	0-0	—	0	0	0	/C		0.0
1953	StL A	4	2	0	0	0	0	0	0	1		0	.000	.333	.000	-4	-0	0-0	—	0	0	0	/C		-0.1
Total	6	69	206	13	44	6	2	2	18	13		27	.214	.260	.291	54	-14	0-1	.992	6	117	160	O49(44/0/6),1b6,C5		-1.1

MARTIN, FRANK   Frank   B2.28.1879 Chicago IL   D9.30.1924 Chicago IL   d6.30

YEAR	TM LG	G	AB	R	H	2B	3B	HR	RBI	BB-IB	HP	SO	AVG	OBP	SLG	AOPS	ABR	SB-CS	FA	FR	RNG	THR	GAMES AT POSITION	DL	BFW
1897	Lou N	2	8	1	2	0	0	0	0	0		0	.250	.250	.250	33	-1	0	.813	-1	117	0	2b2		-0.1
1898	Chi N	1	4	0	0	0	0	0	0	0		0	.000	.000	.000	-99	-1	0	1.000	-0	56	0	/2		-0.2
1899	NY N	17	54	5	14	2	0	0	1	2		1	.259	.298	.296	66	-3	0	.824	-0	97	171	3b17		-0.4
Total	3	20	66	6	16	2	0	0	1	2		1	.242	.275	.273	52	-5	0	.824	-1	97	171	3b17,2b3		

MARTIN, HERSH   Hershel Ray   B9.19.1909 Birmingham AL   D11.17.1980 Cuba MO   BB/TR/6-2/190   d4.23

YEAR	TM LG	G	AB	R	H	2B	3B	HR	RBI	BB-IB	HP	SO	AVG	OBP	SLG	AOPS	ABR	SB-CS	FA	FR	RNG	THR	GAMES AT POSITION	DL	BFW
1937	Phi N	141	579	102	164	35	6	8	49	69	2	66	.283	.362	.409	101	3	11	.978	-3	98	76	O139(3/136/0)		-0.4
1938	Phi N☆	120	466	58	139	36	6	3	39	34	1	48	.298	.347	.421	113	9	8	.965	-2	105	73	O116(0/115/2)		0.4
1939	Phi N	111	393	59	111	28	5	1	22	42	2	27	.282	.355	.387	102	2	4	.979	1	92	257	O23(0/19/4)		0.8
1940	Phi N	33	83	10	21	6	1	0	5	9		9	.253	.326	.349	90	-1	1	.964	0	97	114	O80(78/2/0)		0.6
1944	NY A	85	328	49	99	12	4	9	47	34	2	26	.302	.371	.445	128	12	5-2	.984	1	104	86	O102(97/3/2)		0.9
1945	NY A	117	408	53	109	18	6	7	53	65	0	31	.267	.368	.392	115	10	4-1	.984	9	103	86	O555(187/348/21)		1.6
Total	6	607	2257	331	643	135	29	28	215	253	7	207	.285	.359	.408	109	35	33-3	.974	5	103	86	O555(187/348/21)		

MARTIN, JERRY   Jerry Lindsey   B5.11.1949 Columbia SC   BR/TR/6-1/195*   d9.7   f-Barney   Col Furman

YEAR	TM LG	G	AB	R	H	2B	3B	HR	RBI	BB-IB	HP	SO	AVG	OBP	SLG	AOPS	ABR	SB-CS	FA	FR	RNG	THR	GAMES AT POSITION	DL	BFW
1974	Phi N	13	14	2	3	1	0	0	1	1-0	1	5	.214	.267	.286	52	-1	0-0	1.000	-1	59	0	O11(6/3/2)		-0.2
1975	Phi N	57	113	15	24	7	1	2	11	11-4	1	16	.212	.288	.345	71	-4	2-2	.979	2	111	143	O49(8/41/0)		-0.3
1976	†Phi N	130	121	30	30	7	0	2	15	7-0	0	28	.248	.288	.355	79	-3	3-2	.975	-2	100	0	O110(73/23/15)/1		-0.8
1977	†Phi N	116	215	34	56	16	3	6	28	18-2	4	42	.260	.328	.447	100	6	6-4	.984	-1	95	91	O106(45/18/51)/1		-0.3
1978	†Phi N	128	266	40	72	13	4	9	36	28-3	2	65	.271	.339	.451	118	9	9-5	.987	4	105	147	O112(48/22/55)		-1.2
1979	Chi N	150	534	74	145	34	3	19	73	38-8	3	85	.272	.321	.453	100	4	2-4	.981	-9	88	113	O129(5/103/42)		-2.6
1980	Chi N	141	494	57	112	22	6	23	73	38-6	2	107	.227	.281	.419	87	-10	8-3	.993	-5	86	88	O64(10/58/0)		-1.1
1981	SF N	72	241	23	58	5	3	4	25	21-2	3	52	.241	.308	.336	86	-5	6-2	.980	1	110	39	O142(11/3/134),D3		-1.1
1982	KC A	147	519	52	138	22	1	15	65	38-0	2	138	.266	.316	.399	95	-4	1-1	.957	-2	80	0	O13R	156	-0.9
1983	KC A	13	44	4	14	2	0	2	13	1-0	0	7	.318	.313	.500	125	1	1-0	1.000	0	123	169	O30(9/0/21),1b3		-0.8
1984	NY N	51	91	6	14	1	0	3	5	6-0	0	29	.154	.206	.264	32	-9	0-0	1.000	-22	96	87	O910(215/411/337),1b5,D3	156	-7.4
Total	11	1018	2652	337	666	130	17	85	345	207-20	16	574	.251	.307	.409	93	-29	38-23	.982	-22	96	87			

MARTIN, JACK   John Christopher   B4.19.1887 Plainfield NJ   D7.4.1980 Plainfield NJ   BR/TR/5-9/159   d4.25

YEAR	TM LG	G	AB	R	H	2B	3B	HR	RBI	BB-IB	HP	SO	AVG	OBP	SLG	AOPS	ABR	SB-CS	FA	FR	RNG	THR	GAMES AT POSITION	DL	BFW
1912	NY A	71	231	30	52	6	1	0	17	37	6		.225	.347	.260	70	-7	14	.898	-2	104	77	S65,3b4/2		-0.1
1914	Bos N	33	85	10	18	2	0	0	5	6		7	.212	.264	.235	49	-5	0	.949	-0	96	167	3b26/12		-0.1
	Phi N	83	292	26	74	5	3	0	21	27	1	29	.253	.319	.291	77	-8	6	.930	-3	96	73	S83,3b26/12		-1.0
	Year	116	377	36	92	7	3	0	26	33	1	36	.244	.307	.279	71	-13	6	.930	-3	96	73	S83,3b26/12		-1.1
Total	2	187	608	66	144	13	4	0	43	70	7	36	.237	.323	.271	71	-20	20	.915	-5	100	75	S148,3b30,2b2/1		

MARTIN, PEPPER   Johnny Leonard Roosevelt "The Wild Horse of the Osage"   B2.29.1904 Temple OK   D3.5.1965 McAlester OK   BR/TR/5-8/170   d4.16   C1

YEAR	TM LG	G	AB	R	H	2B	3B	HR	RBI	BB-IB	HP	SO	AVG	OBP	SLG	AOPS	ABR	SB-CS	FA	FR	RNG	THR	GAMES AT POSITION	DL	BFW
1928	†StL N	39	13	11	4	0	0	0	1	1		2	.308	.400	.308	86	0	2	1.000	0	157	0	O4R		0.
1930	StL N	6	5	0	0	0	0	0	0	0		0	.000	.000	.000	-97	0	0	—	0			/H		0.
1931	†StL N	123	413	68	124	32	8	7	75	30	2	40	.300	.351	.467	114	8	16	.967	0	99	116	O69(5/64/0),3b15		-1.
1932	StL N	85	323	47	77	19	6	4	34	30	1	31	.238	.305	.372	79	-10	9	.976	-3	86	178	O69(5/64/0),3b15		2.
1933	StL N★	145	599	122	189	36	12	8	57	67	3	41	.316	.387	.456	133	28	26	.936	-5	96	50	3b107/P		0.
1934	†StL N★	110	454	76	131	25	11	5	49	32	1	41	.289	.337	.425	106	5	23	.904	-14	86	108	3b114,O16(1/5/10)		-0.
1935	StL N★	135	539	121	161	41	6	9	54	33	2	58	.299	.342	.447	106	5	23	.976	-7	93	97	O127(0/3/124),3b15/P		-0.
1936	StL N	143	552	121	177	36	11	11	76	58	4	66	.309	.373	.469	126	21	23	.973	1	100	154	O82(0/40/42),3b5		0.
1937	StL N☆	98	339	60	103	27	8	5	38	33	2	34	.304	.366	.475	124	9	9	.986	-2	107	21	O62(1/38/23),3b4		0.
1938	StL N	91	269	34	79	18	2	2	38	18	1	34	.294	.340	.390	97	-1	4	.975	-4	99	105	O51(8/37/8),3b22		0.
1939	StL N	88	281	48	86	17	7	6	37	30		35	.306	.375	.448	113	6	6	.974	4	102	211	O63(16/10/40),3b2		0.
1940	StL N	86	228	28	72	15	4	3	39	22		11	.279	.386	.395	118	7	2	.980	-1	105	46	O29(0/7/22)		0.
1944	StL N	86	86	19	25	6	0	3	9	15		6	.291	.393	.465	115	3	8	.973	-28	99	117	O613(31/314/273),3b429,P2		0.
Total	13	1189	4117	756	1227	270	75	59	501	369	13	438	.298	.358	.443	112	76	146	.973	-28	99	117			

MARTIN, J. C.   Joseph Clifton   B12.13.1936 Axton VA   BL/TR/6-2/200(185-200)   d9.10   C1

YEAR	TM LG	G	AB	R	H	2B	3B	HR	RBI	BB-IB	HP	SO	AVG	OBP	SLG	AOPS	ABR	SB-CS	FA	FR	RNG	THR	GAMES AT POSITION	DL	BFW
1959	Chi A	3	4	0	1	0	0	0	1	0-0		1	.250	.250	.250	38	0	0-0	.667	-0	119	0	3b2		0.
1960	Chi A	7	20	0	2	0	0	0	0	0-0		6	.100	.100	.150	-34	-4	0-0	1.000	-1	74	0	3b5/1		0.
1961	Chi A	110	274	26	63	8	3	5	32	21-2	2	31	.230	.290	.336	68	-14	1-2	.988	7	106	81	1b60,3b36		0.

YEAR	TM	LG	G	AB	R	H	2B	3B	HR	RBI	BB-IB	HP	SO	AVG	OBP	SLG	AOPS	ABR	SB-CS	FA	FR	RNG	THR	GAMES AT POSITION	DL	BFW
1962	Chi	A	18	26	0	2	0	0	0	2	0-0	0	3	.077	.077	.077	-59	-6	0-0	1.000	-2	69	0	C6/13		
1963	Chi	A	105	259	25	53	11	1	5	28	26-6	1	35	.205	.278	.313	67	-11	0-0	.983	14	128	125	C98,1b3/3		-0.7
1964	Chi	A	122	294	23	58	10	1	4	22	16-7	2	30	.197	.241	.279	46	-22	0-0	.986	9	177	107	C120		0.6
1965	Chi	A	119	230	21	60	12	0	4	21	24-10	1	29	.261	.333	.339	98	-5	2-1	.982	-5	96	89	C112,1b4,3b2		-1.0
1966	Chi	A	67	157	13	40	5	3	2	20	14-6	1	24	.255	.316	.363	103	0	2-0	.982	-5	77	63	C63	33	-0.2
1967	Chi	A	101	252	20	59	12	1	4	22	30-4	1	41	.234	.317	.337	97	0	4-4	.987	6	87	77	C96/1		1.0
1968	NY	N	78	244	20	55	9	2	3	31	21-3	5	31	.225	.298	.316	84	-4	0-0	.994	-5	79	125	C53,1b14	21	-0.9
1969	†NY	N	66	177	12	37	5	1	4	21	12-1	0	32	.209	.257	.316	59	-10	0-0	.996	-4	121	33	C48,1b2		-1.3
1970	Chi	N	40	77	11	12	1	0	1	4	20-7	1	11	.156	.333	.208	44	-5	0-0	.983	-0	128	119	C36,1b3		-0.4
1971	Chi	N	47	125	13	33	5	0	2	17	12-6	2	16	.264	.336	.352	83	-2	1-1	.996	2	72	125	C43/OL		0.2
1972	Chi	N	25	50	3	12	3	0	0	7	5-1	0	9	.240	.304	.300	66	-2	1-0	.970	-3	41	29	C17		-0.4
Total	14		908	2189	189	487	82	12	32	230	201-53	17	299	.222	.291	.315	72	-80	9-8	.987	13	110	94	C692,1b89,3b47/OL	95	-4.9

MARTIN, MIKE   Joseph Michael B12.3.1958 Portland OR BL/TR/6-2/193 [SDN78*S1/6] d8.15 Col Linn-Benton (OR) CC

YEAR	TM	LG	G	AB	R	H	2B	3B	HR	RBI	BB-IB	HP	SO	AVG	OBP	SLG	AOPS	ABR	SB-CS	FA	FR	RNG	THR	GAMES AT POSITION	DL	BFW
1986	Chi	N	8	13	1	1	0	0	0	0	2-1	0	4	.077	.200	.154	-1	-2	0-0	1.000	-3	43	101	C8		-0.5

MARTIN, JOE   Joseph Samuel "Silent Joe" B1.1.1876 Hollidaysburg PA D5.25.1964 Altoona PA BL/TR/5-9.5/155 d4.28

YEAR	TM	LG	G	AB	R	H	2B	3B	HR	RBI	BB-IB	HP	SO	AVG	OBP	SLG	AOPS	ABR	SB-CS	FA	FR	RNG	THR	GAMES AT POSITION	DL	BFW
1903	Was	A	35	119	11	27	4	1	0	7	5	0		.227	.258	.345	78	-4	2	.892	-4	106	66	2b15,3b13,O7(1/0/6)		-0.8
	StL	A	44	173	18	37	6	4	0	7	6	2		.214	.249	.295	64	-8	2	.983	-2	138	281	O38(4/0/34),2b6/3		-1.2
Year			79	292	29	64	10	9	0	14	11	2		.219	.252	.315	70	-12	2	.959	-6	119	242	O45(5/0/40),2b21,3b14		-2.0

MARTIN, NORBERTO   Norberto Edonal (McDonald) B12.10.1966 San Pedro de Macoris, D.R. BR/TR/5-10/164(164-182) d9.20

YEAR	TM	LG	G	AB	R	H	2B	3B	HR	RBI	BB-IB	HP	SO	AVG	OBP	SLG	AOPS	ABR	SB-CS	FA	FR	RNG	THR	GAMES AT POSITION	DL	BFW
1993	Chi	A	8	14	3	5	0	0	0	2	1-0	1	5	.357	.400	.357	107	0	0-0	.957	1	88	181	2b5/D		
1994	Chi	A	45	131	19	36	7	1	1	16	9-0	0	16	.275	.317	.366	78	-4	0-0	.982	-6	79	69	2b28,S6,3b5,O2L/D		0.1
1995	Chi	A	72	160	17	43	7	4	2	17	3-0	1	25	.269	.281	.400	79	-6	5-0	.950	2	95	112	2b17,O12(5/0/7),D10,3b9,S7		-0.2
1996	Chi	A	70	140	30	49	7	0	1	14	6-0	1	17	.350	.374	.421	106	1	10-2	.943	7	94	158	S24,D22,2b10,3b3	60	0.9
1997	Chi	A	71	213	24	64	7	1	2	27	6-0	0	31	.300	.320	.371	82	-6	1-4	.960	-12	71	47	S28,3b17,2b9,D6	36	-1.6
1998	Ana	A	79	195	20	42	2	0	1	13	6-0	0	29	.215	.236	.241	25	-22	3-1	.982	4	110	108	2b54,D10,3b5,O5L,S2	15	-1.5
1999	Tor	A	9	27	3	6	2	0	0	1	3-0	0	2	.222	.364	.296	70	-1	0-0	.974	1	126	148	2b8/S		0.1
Total	7		354	880	116	245	32	6	7	89	35-0	3	123	.278	.306	.352	72	-38	23-9	.976	-3	103	101	2b131,S68,D50,3b39,O19(12/0/7)	111	-3.0

MARTIN, STU   Stuart McGuire B11.17.1913 Rich Square NC D1.11.1997 Severn NC BL/TR/6-0/155 d4.14 Col Guilford

YEAR	TM	LG	G	AB	R	H	2B	3B	HR	RBI	BB-IB	HP	SO	AVG	OBP	SLG	AOPS	ABR	SB-CS	FA	FR	RNG	THR	GAMES AT POSITION	DL	BFW
1936	StL	N☆	92	332	63	99	21	4	6	41	29	1	27	.298	.356	.440	114	6	17	.949	-14	92	105	2b83,S3		-0.2
1937	StL	N	90	223	34	58	6	1	1	17	32	1	28	.260	.353	.309	80	-5	3	.946	-6	96	102	2b48,1b9/S		-0.9
1938	StL	N	114	417	54	116	26	2	1	27	30	1	28	.278	.328	.357	84	-9	4	.967	-4	99	95	2b99		-0.6
1939	StL	N	120	425	60	114	26	7	3	30	33	1	40	.268	.325	.384	85	-9	4	.977	-2	97	96	2b107/1		-0.5
1940	StL	N	112	369	45	88	12	6	4	32	33	0	35	.238	.301	.336	71	-15	4	.972	-16	78	22	3b73,2b33		-2.8
1941	Pit	N	88	233	37	71	13	2	0	19	10	3	17	.305	.341	.378	103	1	2	.972	-0	105	87	2b53,3b2/1		0.4
1942	Pit	N	42	120	16	27	2	1	1	12	8	1	10	.225	.273	.317	71	-5	1	.979	-8	84	81	2b30/1S		-1.2
1943	Chi	N	64	118	13	26	4	0	0	5	15	0	10	.220	.308	.254	64	-5	1	.980	3	119	99	2b22,3b8,1b2		-0.2
Total	8		722	2237	322	599	112	24	16	183	190	8	185	.268	.327	.361	86	-41	36	.966	-47	97	95	2b475,3b83,1b14,S5		-6.0

MARTIN, GENE   Thomas Eugene B1.12.1947 Americus GA BL/TR/6-0.5/190 [TexA65 3/43] d7.28

YEAR	TM	LG	G	AB	R	H	2B	3B	HR	RBI	BB-IB	HP	SO	AVG	OBP	SLG	AOPS	ABR	SB-CS	FA	FR	RNG	THR	GAMES AT POSITION	DL	BFW
1968	Was	A	9	11	4	4	1	0	1	1	0-0	1	1	.364	.364	.727	232	2	0-0	—	-1	0	0	O2L		0.1

MARTIN, JOE   William Joseph "Smokey Joe" B8.28.1911 Seymour MO D9.28.1960 Buffalo NY BR/TR/5-11.5/181 d4.27 Col California-Santa Barbara

YEAR	TM	LG	G	AB	R	H	2B	3B	HR	RBI	BB-IB	HP	SO	AVG	OBP	SLG	AOPS	ABR	SB-CS	FA	FR	RNG	THR	GAMES AT POSITION	DL	BFW
1936	NY	N	7	15	0	4	1	0	0	2	0	1	4	.267	.313	.333	75	-1	0	1.000	0	104	193	3b7		0.0
1938	Chi	A	1	0	0	0	0	0	0	0	0	0	0	—	—	—	—	-0	0		0			/R		0.0
Total	2		8	15	0	4	1	0	0	2	0	1	4	.267	.313	.333	75	-1	0-0	1.000	0	104	193	3b7		0.0

MARTIN, BILLY   William Lloyd B2.13.1894 Washington DC D9.14.1949 Arlington VA BR/TR/5-8.5/170 d10.6 Col Georgetown

YEAR	TM	LG	G	AB	R	H	2B	3B	HR	RBI	BB-IB	HP	SO	AVG	OBP	SLG	AOPS	ABR	SB-CS	FA	FR	RNG	THR	GAMES AT POSITION	DL	BFW
1914	Bos	N	1	3	0	0	0	0	0	0	0	0		.000	.000	.000	-99	-1	0	.500	-1	57	0	/S		-0.2

MARTINEZ, SANDY   Angel Sandy (Martinez) B10.3.1970 Villa Mella, D.R. BL/TR/6-2/205(200-215) d6.24

YEAR	TM	LG	G	AB	R	H	2B	3B	HR	RBI	BB-IB	HP	SO	AVG	OBP	SLG	AOPS	ABR	SB-CS	FA	FR	RNG	THR	GAMES AT POSITION	DL	BFW
1995	Tor	A	62	191	12	46	12	0	2	25	7-0	1	45	.241	.270	.335	57	-13	0-0	.986	1	178	80	C61		-0.8
1996	Tor	A	76	229	17	52	9	3	3	18	16-0	4	58	.227	.288	.332	57	-16	0-0	.993	4	131	91	C75	15	-0.7
1997	Tor	A	3	2	1	0	0	0	0	0	1-0	0	1	.000	.333	.000	-3	-0	0-0	.933	0	32	209	C3		0.0
1998	†Chi	N	45	87	7	23	9	1	0	7	13-0	1	21	.264	.363	.391	96	0	1-0	.985	3	116	64	C33		0.4
1999	Chi	N	17	30	1	5	0	0	1	1	0-0	0	11	.167	.167	.267	7	-4	0-0	.959	0	490	0	C12	28	-0.4
2001	Mon	N	1	1	0	0	0	0	0	0	0-0	0	0	.000	.000	.000	-99	0	0-0	1.000	1	161	0	C9		0.0
2004	Cle	A	1	2	0	0	0	0	0	0	0-0	0	0	.000	.000	.000	-99	0	0-0	1.000	0	6	0	/C	188	0.0
	Bos	A	3	4	0	0	0	0	0	0	1-0	0	1	.000	.000	.000	-99	-1	0-0	1.000	0	20	539	/C		0.0
	Year		4	6	0	0	0	0	0	0	1-0	0	2	.000	.000	.000	-94	-1	0-0	1.000	-1	0	0	/C3		-0.2
Total	8		218	564	39	130	32	4	6	51	37-0	6	147	.230	.284	.333	58	-37	1-0	.988	9	158	79	C198	231	-1.7

MARTINEZ, CARLOS   Carlos Alberto Escobar (b Carlos Alberto Escobar (Martinez)) B8.11.1964 LaGuaira, Venez BR/TR/6-5/175(175-215) d9.2

YEAR	TM	LG	G	AB	R	H	2B	3B	HR	RBI	BB-IB	HP	SO	AVG	OBP	SLG	AOPS	ABR	SB-CS	FA	FR	RNG	THR	GAMES AT POSITION	DL	BFW
1988	Chi	A	17	55	5	9	1	0	0	0	0	0	12	.164	.164	.182	-3	-8	1-0	.909	0	118	40	3b15,D2		-0.8
1989	Chi	A	109	350	44	105	22	0	5	32	21-2	1	57	.300	.340	.406	112	5	4-1	.912	-5	98	106	3b68,1b34,O10L/D	21	-0.1
1990	Chi	A	92	272	18	61	6	5	4	24	10-2	0	40	.224	.252	.327	62	-16	0-4	.988	-6	75	84	1b82/OLD		-2.9
1991	Cle	A	72	257	22	73	14	0	5	30	10-2	2	43	.284	.310	.397	95	-2	3-2	.968	-4	63	125	D41,1b31		-1.4
1992	Cle	A	69	228	23	60	9	1	5	35	7-1	1	21	.263	.283	.377	86	-5	1-2	.996	-6	95	152	1b37,3b28,D4	53	-1.4
1993	Cle	A	80	262	26	64	10	4	5	31	20-3	1	29	.244	.295	.340	71	-11	1-1	.934	-7	78	89	3b35,1b22,D19		-2.1
1995	Cal	A	26	61	7	11	1	0	1	9	6-2	1	7	.180	.265	.246	34	-2	0-0	.968	1	112	374	3b16,1b4,D2		-0.5
Total	7		465	1485	145	383	63	6	25	161	74-11	5	209	.258	.293	.359	81	-43	10-10	.986	-26	74	98	1b210,3b162,D72,O11L	74	-8.8

MARTINEZ, CARMELO   Carmelo (Salgado) B7.28.1960 Dorado, PR BR/TR/6-2/220(185-225) d8.22

YEAR	TM	LG	G	AB	R	H	2B	3B	HR	RBI	BB-IB	HP	SO	AVG	OBP	SLG	AOPS	ABR	SB-CS	FA	FR	RNG	THR	GAMES AT POSITION	DL	BFW
1983	Chi	N	29	89	8	23	3	0	6	16	4-0	0	19	.258	.287	.494	108	0	0-0	.992	0	94	104	1b26/3OL		-0.1
1984	†SD	N	149	488	64	122	28	2	13	66	68-4	4	82	.250	.340	.395	107	7	1-3	.976	11	113	128	O142L,1b2		1.1
1985	SD	N	150	514	64	130	28	1	21	72	87-4	2	91	.253	.362	.434	123	19	0-4	.978	5	102	115	O150L,1b3	7	1.7
1986	SD	N	113	244	28	58	10	0	9	25	35-2	1	46	.238	.333	.389	102	1	1-1	.978	1	90	152	O60L,1b26/3		-0.1
1987	SD	N	139	447	59	122	21	2	15	70	70-5	3	82	.273	.372	.430	117	13	5-5	.968	-1	94	137	O78L,1b65		0.5
1988	SD	N	121	365	48	86	12	0	18	65	35-3	0	57	.236	.301	.416	106	2	1-1	.993	8	117	164	O64(55/0/11),1b41		0.6
1989	SD	N	111	267	23	59	12	2	6	39	32-3	0	54	.221	.302	.348	86	-5	0-0	.982	3	96	166	O65L,1b32		-0.5
1990	Phi	N	71	198	23	48	8	0	8	31	29-0	0	37	.242	.339	.404	104	1	2-1	.994	-1	98	120	1b43,O20(20/0/1)	15	-0.2
	†Pit	N	12	19	3	4	1	0	2	4	1-0	0	5	.211	.250	.579	125	2	0-0	1.000	1	216	240	1b5,O2L		0.1
	Year		83	217	26	52	9	0	10	35	30-0	0	42	.240	.332	.419	106	2	2-1	.995	0	106	128	1b48,O22(22/0/1)		-0.1
1991	Pit	N	11	16	1	4	0	0	0	0	2-0	0	4	.250	.294	.250	55	-1	0-0	.945	-1	31	65	1b8		-0.3
	KC	A	44	121	17	25	6	0	4	17	27-3	0	25	.207	.351	.355	95	0	0-1	.991	3	127	95	1b43/D		0.0
	Cin	N	53	138	12	32	5	0	6	19	15-1	1	37	.232	.301	.399	93	-1	0-0	.985	0	72	88	1b25,O16L		-0.3
Total	9		1003	2906	350	713	134	7	108	424	404-25	11	528	.245	.337	.408	108	36	10-16	.980	30	105	134	O598(588/0/12),1b319,3b2/D	22	2.5

MARTINEZ, TINO   Constantino B12.7.1967 Tampa FL BL/TR/6-2/210(205-230) [SeaA88 1/14] d8.20 Col Tampa

YEAR	TM	LG	G	AB	R	H	2B	3B	HR	RBI	BB-IB	HP	SO	AVG	OBP	SLG	AOPS	ABR	SB-CS	FA	FR	RNG	THR	GAMES AT POSITION	DL	BFW
1990	Sea	A	24	68	4	15	4	0	0	5	9-0	0	9	.221	.308	.279	66	-3	0-0	1.000	0	95	157	1b23		-0.4
1991	Sea	A	36	112	11	23	7	0	4	9	11-0	0	24	.205	.272	.330	67	-5	0-0	.993	2	119	103	1b29,D5		-0.6
1992	Sea	A	136	460	53	118	19	2	16	66	42-9	2	77	.257	.316	.411	103	0	2-1	.995	4	116	88	1b78,D47		-0.3
1993	Sea	A	109	408	48	108	25	1	17	60	45-9	5	56	.265	.343	.456	111	6	0-3	.997	-5	85	98	1b103,D6	55	-0.6
1994	Sea	A	97	329	42	86	21	0	20	61	29-2	1	52	.261	.320	.508	107	2	1-2	.997	1	94	88	1b82,D8		-0.4
1995	†Sea	A★	141	519	92	152	35	3	31	111	62-15	4	91	.293	.369	.551	135	26	0-0	.993	-8	104	71	1b139/D		1.7
1996	†NY	A	155	595	82	174	28	0	25	117	68-4	2	75	.292	.364	.466	109	8	2-1	.996	-2	88	91	1b151,D3		-0.6
1997	†NY	A★	158	594	96	176	31	2	44	141	75-14	3	75	.296	.371	.577	146	40	3-1	.994	7	116	102	1b150,D9		3.1
1998	†NY	A	142	531	92	149	33	1	28	123	61-3	6	83	.281	.355	.505	127	22	2-1	.992	1	103	109	1b142		1.0
1999	†NY	A	159	589	69	155	27	2	28	105	69-7	3	86	.263	.341	.458	104	2	3-4	.995	7	115	85	1b158		-0.4
2000	†NY	A	155	569	69	147	37	4	16	91	52-9	8	74	.258	.328	.422	90	-10	4-1	.994	-1	94	86	1b154		-2.2
2001	†NY	A	154	589	89	165	24	2	34	113	42-9	3	71	.280	.329	.501	114	9	1-3	.996	5	105	91	1b149,D3		0.0
2002	†StL	N	150	511	63	134	25	1	21	75	58-9	2	71	.262	.337	.438	105	1	3-2	.996	4	106	113	1b149		-1.4
2003	StL	N	138	476	66	130	25	2	15	69	53-7	9	71	.273	.352	.429	105	4	1-1	.997	-0	101	91	1b126,D5		-0.7

YEAR	TM LG	G	AB	R	H	2B	3B	HR	RBI	BB-IB	HP	SO	AVG	OBP	SLG	AOPS	ABR	SB-CS	FA	FR	RNG	THR	GAMES AT POSITION	DL	BFW
2004	TB A	138	458	63	120	20	1	7	76	66-9	9	72	.262	.362	.461	116	12	3-1	.997	-1	95	90	1b114,D19		0.1
2005	†NY A	131	303	43	73	9	0	17	49	38-3	3	54	.241	.328	.439	102	1	2-0	.991	-3	87	95	1b122/D		-1.0
Total	16	2023	7111	1008	1925	365	21	339	1271	780-102	59	1069	.271	.344	.471	112	115	27-20	.995	20	100	93	1b1869,D107	55	-2.7

MARTINEZ, DAVE   David B9.26.1964 New York NY BL/TL/5-10/175(150-190) [ChiN83*S3/53] d6.15 Col Valencia (FL) CC [DL 2002 Atl N 183]

YEAR	TM LG	G	AB	R	H	2B	3B	HR	RBI	BB-IB	HP	SO	AVG	OBP	SLG	AOPS	ABR	SB-CS	FA	FR	RNG	THR	GAMES AT POSITION	DL	BFW
1986	Chi N	53	108	13	15	1	1	7	6-0		1	22	.139	.190	.194	6	-14	4-2	.988	2	114	117	O46(9/39/1)		-1.3
1987	Chi N	142	459	70	134	18	8	8	36	57-4	2	96	.292	.372	.418	105	4	16-8	.980	2	101	149	O139(14/134/3)		0.5
1988	Chi N	75	256	27	65	10	1	4	34	21-5	2	46	.254	.311	.348	86	-4	7-3	.970	-3	96	66	O72(0/70/2)		-0.8
	Mon N	63	191	24	49	3	5	2	12	17-3	0	48	.257	.316	.356	88	-3	16-6	.992	0	97	86	O60(1/44/22)		-0.3
	Year	138	447	51	114	13	6	6	46	38-8	2	94	.255	.313	.351	87	-8	23-9	.979	-3	96	144	O118(0/104/38)		-1.1
1989	Mon N	126	361	41	99	16	7	3	27	27-2	0	57	.274	.324	.382	100	-1	23-4	.967	-4	86	144	O118(0/104/38)		-0.3
1990	Mon N	118	391	60	109	13	5	11	39	24-2	1	48	.279	.321	.422	107	2	13-11	.989	2	105	110	O108(0/103/22)/P		0.1
1991	Mon N	124	396	47	117	18	5	7	42	20-3	3	54	.295	.332	.419	112	5	16-7	.982	2	98	152	O112(36/34/54)		0.6
1992	Cin N	135	393	47	100	20	5	3	31	42-4	0	54	.254	.323	.354	90	-5	12-8	.991	2	104	145	O111(3/105/6),1b21		-0.5
1993	SF N	91	241	28	58	12	1	5	27	27-3	0	39	.241	.317	.361	84	-6	6-3	.993	1	96	163	O73(3/43/34)	35	-0.5
1994	SF N	97	235	23	58	9	3	4	27	21-1	2	22	.247	.314	.362	79	-8	3-4	1.000	3	110	103	O58(3/3/53),1b25		0.1
1995	Chi A	119	303	49	93	16	4	5	37	32-2	1	41	.307	.371	.436	115	7	8-2	.976	-2	106	65	O121(3/73/73),1b23		0.1
1996	Chi A	146	440	85	140	20	8	10	53	52-1	3	52	.318	.393	.468	122	16	15-7	.988	5	105	103	O105(4/45/75),1b52/D		0.1
1997	Chi A	145	504	78	144	16	6	12	55	55-7	3	69	.286	.356	.413	104	3	12-6	.996	4	105	153	O86(0/2/85)/1D	68	-1.4
1998	TB A	90	309	31	79	11	0	3	20	35-4	2	52	.256	.334	.320	70	-13	8-7	.994	3	100	153	O86(0/2/85)/1D		-1.5
1999	TB A	143	514	79	146	25	5	6	66	60-3	5	76	.284	.361	.387	90	-6	13-6	.985	-7	90	91	O140(2/52/93)		-0.5
2000	TB A	29	104	12	27	4	1	2	12	10-1	0	17	.260	.319	.365	75	-4	1-4	1.000	3	88	274	O28R		-0.8
	Chi N	18	54	5	10	1	1	0	1	2-0	0	8	.185	.214	.241	15	-7	1-0	1.000	-0	104	0	O10(9/1/0),1b9		-0.1
	Tex A	38	119	14	32	4	1	2	12	14-2	1	20	.269	.351	.370	82	-3	2-1	1.000	4	130	93	O35R,1b4		0.4
	Tor A	47	180	29	56	10	1	2	22	24-0	1	28	.311	.393	.411	101	1	4-2	.982	6	108	249	O47R		-0.1
	Year	114	403	55	115	18	4	5	46	48-3	2	65	.285	.362	.387	87	-6	7-7	.992	11	109	209	O110R,1b4		-0.7
2001	†Atl N	120	237	33	68	11	3	2	21-0		1	44	.287	.347	.384	84	-4	9-3	1.000	-0	91	76	O52(27/0/28),1b10/D	286	-6.7
Total	16	1919	5795	795	1599	238	72	91	580	567-47	28	893	.276	.341	.389	95	-40	183-94	.986	15	100	123	O1580(144/857/731),1b192,D8,P2		-6.7

MARTINEZ, DOMINGO   Domingo Emilio (La Fontaine) B8.4.1967 Santo Domingo, D.R. BR/TR/6-2/215* d9.11

YEAR	TM LG	G	AB	R	H	2B	3B	HR	RBI	BB-IB	HP	SO	AVG	OBP	SLG	AOPS	ABR	SB-CS	FA	FR	RNG	THR	GAMES AT POSITION	DL	BFW
1992	Tor A	7	8	2	5	0	0	1	3	1-0	0	1	.625	.625	1.000	332	2	0-0	1.000	-1	0	113	1b7		0.2
1993	Tor A	8	14	2	4	0	0	1	3	1-0	0	7	.286	.333	.500	119	0	0-0	1.000	1	172	75	1b7/3		0.0
Total	2	15	22	4	9	0	0	2	6	1-0	0	8	.409	.435	.682	194	2	0-0	1.000	-0	101	91	1b14/3		0.2

MARTINEZ, EDGAR   Edgar B1.2.1963 New York NY BR/TR/5-11/175(175-210) d9.12

YEAR	TM LG	G	AB	R	H	2B	3B	HR	RBI	BB-IB	HP	SO	AVG	OBP	SLG	AOPS	ABR	SB-CS	FA	FR	RNG	THR	GAMES AT POSITION	DL	BFW
1987	Sea A	13	43	6	16	5	2	0	5	2-0	1	5	.372	.413	.581	152	3	0-0	1.000	0	91	50	3b12/D		0.3
1988	Sea A	14	32	0	9	4	0	0	5	4-0	0	7	.281	.351	.406	109	1	0-0	.929	-4	46	65	3b13		-0.3
1989	Sea A	65	171	20	41	5	0	2	20	17-1	3	26	.240	.314	.304	74	-5	2-1	.949	-6	80	106	3b61		-1.1
1990	Sea A	144	487	71	147	27	2	11	49	74-3	5	62	.302	.397	.433	131	24	1-4	.928	-5	95	65	3b143,D2		1.9
1991	Sea A	150	544	98	167	35	1	14	52	84-9	8	72	.307	.405	.452	137	32	0-3	.962	3	103	91	3b144,D2		3.4
1992	Sea A★	135	528	100	181	46	3	18	73	54-2	4	61	**.343**	.404	.544	162	45	14-4	.943	2	100	129	3b103,D28,1b2		4.9
1993	Sea A	42	135	20	32	7	0	4	13	28-1	0	19	.237	.366	.378	99	1	0-0	.889	-7	41	42	D24,3b16	126	-0.7
1994	Sea A	89	326	47	93	23	1	13	51	53-3	3	42	.285	.387	.482	120	12	6-2	.950	5	100	119	3b64,D23	20	1.5
1995	†Sea A★	145	511	121	182	52	0	29	113	116-19	4	87	**.356**	**.479**	.628	184	73	4-3	.800	-2	47	0	D138,3b4,1b3	22	4.6
1996	Sea A★	139	499	121	163	52	2	26	103	123-12	5	84	.327	.464	.595	165	60	3-3	.967	-1	41	89	D134,1b4,3b2		4.7
1997	†Sea A★	155	542	104	179	35	1	28	108	119-11	11	86	.330	.456	.554	163	60	2-4	.986	0	100	86	D144,1b7/3		4.2
1998	Sea A	154	556	86	179	46	1	29	102	106-4	3	96	.322	**.429**	.565	156	52	1-1	1.000	2	84	47	D134,1b5		3.8
1999	Sea A	142	502	86	169	35	1	24	86	97-6	6	99	.337	**.447**	.554	156	49	7-2	1.000	0	99	215	D146,1b2		3.9
2000	†Sea A★	153	556	100	180	31	0	37	**145**	96-8	9	95	.324	.423	.579	154	50	3-0	1.000	0	0	0	D127/1		4.1
2001	†Sea A★	132	470	80	144	40	1	23	116	93-9	9	90	.306	.423	.543	163	50	4-1	1.000	0	0	0	D91	62	1.8
2002	Sea A	97	328	42	91	23	0	15	59	67-8	6	69	.277	.403	.485	141	24	1-1	—	0	0	0	D140		2.7
2003	Sea A	145	497	72	146	25	0	24	98	92-7	7	95	.294	.406	.489	144	37	0-1	—	0	0	0	D122/3		3.9
2004	Sea A	141	486	45	128	23	0	12	63	58-10	2	107	.263	.342	.385	94	-3	1-0	.946	-13	95	93	D1403,3b564,1b28	248	44.6
Total	18	2055	7213	1219	2247	514	15	309	1261	1283-113	89	1202	.312	.418	.515	147	565	49-30	.946	-13	95	93	D1403,3b564,1b28		44.6

MARTINEZ, FELIX   Felix (Mata) B5.18.1974 Nagua, D.R. BB/TR/6-0/180* d9.3

YEAR	TM LG	G	AB	R	H	2B	3B	HR	RBI	BB-IB	HP	SO	AVG	OBP	SLG	AOPS	ABR	SB-CS	FA	FR	RNG	THR	GAMES AT POSITION	DL	BFW
1997	KC A	16	31	3	7	1	1	0	3	6-0	0	8	.226	.351	.323	75	-1	0-0	.975	-3	73	106	S12,D2		-0.3
1998	KC A	34	85	7	11	1	1	0	5	5-0	1	21	.129	.187	.165	-7	-14	3-1	.956	-1	96	123	S32,2b2		-1.2
1999	KC A	6	7	1	1	0	0	0	0	0-0	0	6	.143	.143	.143	-26	-1	0-0	—	-2	0	0	S2/2		2.0
2000	TB A	106	299	42	64	11	4	2	17	32-0	8	68	.214	.305	.298	55	-21	9-3	.976	34	124	116	S106		-1.2
2001	TB A	77	219	24	54	13	1	1	14	10-0	5	46	.247	.294	.329	65	-11	6-5	.944	-6	92	100	S219,2b13,D2	18	-1.0
Total	5	239	641	77	137	26	7	3	39	53-0	14	143	.214	.287	.290	50	-48	18-9	.964	22	107	111	S219,2b13,D2	18	-1.0

MARTINEZ, TONY   Gabriel Antonio (Diaz) B3.18.1940 Perico, Cuba D8.24.1991 Miami FL BR/TR/5-10/165* d4.9 Mil 1970

YEAR	TM LG	G	AB	R	H	2B	3B	HR	RBI	BB-IB	HP	SO	AVG	OBP	SLG	AOPS	ABR	SB-CS	FA	FR	RNG	THR	GAMES AT POSITION	DL	BFW
1963	Cle A	43	141	10	22	4	0	0	5	8-0	0	18	.156	.184	.184	4	-18	1-1	.961	-12	78	77	S41		-3.0
1964	Cle A	9	14	1	3	1	0	0	2	0-0	0	2	.214	.214	.286	38	-1	0-0	1.000	3	144	261	2b4/S		0.1
1965	Cle A	4	3	0	0	0	0	0	0	0-0	0	0	.000	.000	.000	-99	-1	0-0	—	0			/H		-0.1
1966	Cle A	17	17	2	5	0	0	0	1	0-0	0	6	.294	.333	.294	82	0	1-1	.833	-1	112	0	S5,2b4		-0.1
Total	4	73	175	13	30	5	0	0	8	8-0	0	26	.171	.198	.200	13	-20	2-3	.958	-11	78	81	S47,2b8		-3.1

MARTINEZ, GREG   Gregory Alfred B1.27.1972 Las Vegas NV BB/TR/5-10/168 [MilA93 24/683] d3.31 Col Barstow (CA) CC

YEAR	TM LG	G	AB	R	H	2B	3B	HR	RBI	BB-IB	HP	SO	AVG	OBP	SLG	AOPS	ABR	SB-CS	FA	FR	RNG	THR	GAMES AT POSITION	DL	BFW
1998	Mil N	13	3	2	0	0	0	0	0	2-0	0	2	.000	.250	.000	-26	-1	2-0	—	-1	0	0	O6L		-0.

MARTINEZ, BUCK   John Albert B11.7.1948 Redding CA BR/TR/5-10/190(185-200) [PhiN67*2/32] d6.18 Mil 1970 M2

YEAR	TM LG	G	AB	R	H	2B	3B	HR	RBI	BB-IB	HP	SO	AVG	OBP	SLG	AOPS	ABR	SB-CS	FA	FR	RNG	THR	GAMES AT POSITION	DL	BFW
																					3	125	83	C55/OR		-0.
1969	KC A	72	205	14	47	6	1	4	23	8-2	0	25	.229	.258	.327	62	-11	0-0	.972	3	125	83	C55/OR		-0.
1970	KC A	6	9	1	1	0	0	0	0	2-0	0	1	.111	.273	.111	10	-1	0-0	.958	-0	72	315	C5		-0.
1971	KC A	22	46	3	7	2	0	1	5	5-0	0	9	.152	.231	.196	23	-5	0-1	.968	-1	106	46	C21		0.0
1973	KC A	14	32	2	8	1	0	1	6	4-0	0	5	.250	.333	.375	92	0	0-1	.966	-1	187	57	C14		0.0
1974	KC A	43	107	10	23	3	1	1	8	14-0	2	19	.215	.317	.290	71	-4	0-1	.977	-0	101	58	C38		0.0
1975	KC A	80	226	15	51	9	1	3	23	21-0	1	28	.226	.293	.323	73	-8	1-0	.980	-4	76	107	C79		-0.
1976	†KC A	95	267	24	61	13	5	4	34	16-1	0	45	.228	.269	.356	82	-7	0-0	.991	3	89	108	C94	16	-0.
1977	KC A	29	80	3	18	4	0	1	9	5-0	0	12	.225	.253	.313	53	-5	0-1	.993	1	116	66	C28		-0.
1978	Mil A	89	256	26	56	10	1	4	20	14-1	1	42	.219	.255	.277	51	-17	1-1	.978	-5	133	100	C68/P		-0.
1979	Mil A	69	196	17	53	8	0	4	22	8-0	0	25	.270	.296	.372	80	-6	0-1	.967	-5	133	101	C76		-0.
1980	Mil A	76	219	16	49	9	0	3	17	12-0	1	16	.224	.266	.306	58	-13	1-0	.985	5	115	101	C45		-0.
1981	Tor A	45	128	13	29	8	1	4	21	11-0	1	16	.227	.287	.398	92	-1	1-0	.991	2	105	88	C45		-0.
1982	Tor A	96	260	26	63	17	0	10	34	24-1	0	39	.242	.301	.423	90	-4	1-1	.989	-2	149	67	C85		0.0
1983	Tor A	88	221	27	56	14	0	10	33	29-0	0	39	.253	.337	.452	109	4	0-0	.995	-1	126	68	C98/D		-0.
1984	Tor A	102	232	24	51	13	1	6	37	29-0	0	49	.220	.301	.349	79	-6	0-3	.988	3	112	109	C42	89	-0.
1985	Tor A	42	99	11	16	3	0	4	14	10-0	0	19	.162	.239	.313	50	-7	0-0	.994	-2	112	76	C78/D		-1.
1986	Tor A	81	160	13	29	8	0	2	12	20-0	0	25	.181	.271	.269	47	-12	0-0	.994	9	119	87	C1008,D2/POR	105	-6.
Total	17	1049	2743	245	618	128	10	58	321	230-5	8	419	.225	.284	.343	73	-104	5-10	.984	9	119	87	C1008,D2/POR	105	-6.

MARTINEZ, JOSE   Jose (Azcuiz) B7.26.1942 Cardenas, Cuba BR/TR/5-10/180* d4.12 C15

YEAR	TM LG	G	AB	R	H	2B	3B	HR	RBI	BB-IB	HP	SO	AVG	OBP	SLG	AOPS	ABR	SB-CS	FA	FR	RNG	THR	GAMES AT POSITION	DL	BFW
1969	Pit N	77	168	20	45	6	0	1	16	9-0	1	32	.268	.309	.321	78	-5	1-3	.975	6	113	123	2b42,S20,3b5,O2L		0.
1970	Pit N	19	20	1	1	0	0	0	0	1-0	0	5	.050	.095	.050	-60	-5	0-0	1.000	2	40	0	3b7,2b4/S		0.
Total	2	96	188	21	46	6	0	1	16	10-0	1	37	.245	.286	.293	63	-10	1-3	.966	7	116	126	2b46,S21,3b12,O2L		0.

MARTINEZ, MANNY   Manuel (De Jesus) B10.3.1970 San Pedro de Macoris, D.R. BR/TR/6-2/169(169-185) d6.14

YEAR	TM LG	G	AB	R	H	2B	3B	HR	RBI	BB-IB	HP	SO	AVG	OBP	SLG	AOPS	ABR	SB-CS	FA	FR	RNG	THR	GAMES AT POSITION	DL	BFW
1996	Sea A	9	17	3	4	2	1	0	3	3-0	0	5	.235	.350	.471	105	0	2-0	1.000	1	103	563	O8(2/4/3)		-0.
	Phi N	13	36	2	8	1	0	0	1	1-0	1	11	.222	.263	.333	56	-3	2-1	.955	1	112	168	O11(1/1/10)		-0.
1998	Pit N	73	180	21	45	11	2	6	24	9-0	2	44	.250	.290	.433	87	-4	0-3	.989	-3	95	0	O62(26/37/3)	15	-1.
1999	Mon N	137	331	48	81	12	7	2	33	30-0	3	111	.245	.284	.374	69	-30	23-10	.974	4	104	154	O207(29/168/17)	15	-2.
Total	3	232	564	74	138	25	12	8	53	30-0			.245												

MARTINEZ, MARTY
Orlando (Oliva) B8.23.1941 Havana, Cuba BB/TR (BR 1962)/6-1/175* d5.2 M1/C4

YEAR	TM	LG	G	AB	R	H	2B	3B	HR	RBI	BB-IB	HP	SO	AVG	OBP	SLG	AOPS	ABR	SB-CS	FA	FR	RNG	THR	GAMES AT POSITION	DL	BFW
1962	Min	A	37	18	13	3	0	1	0		3-0			.167	.286	.278	51	-1	0-0	.920	-3	84	50	S11/3		-0.3
1967	Atl	N	44	73	14	21	2	1	0	5	11-1	1	11	.288	.384	.342	112	2	0-1	.920	-0	110	123	S25,2b9,C3,3b2/1		-0.3
1968	Atl	N	113	356	34	82	5	3	0	12	29-4	2	28	.230	.291	.261	67	-14	6-6	.955	-7	97	124	S54,3b37,2b16,C14	34	0.4
1969	Hou	N	78	198	14	61	5	4	0	15	10-1	0	21	.308	.340	.374	102	0	0-1	1.000	-2	79	116	O21L,S17,3b15,C7/P2	21	-1.9
1970	Hou	N	75	150	12	33	3	0	0	12	9-0	0	22	.220	.264	.240	38	-14	0-0	1.000	-2	97	68	S29,3b10,C6,2b4		-0.2
1971	Hou	N	32	62	4	16	3	1	0	4	3-0	0	6	.258	.292	.339	81	-2	1-0	.990	-3	97	68	2b9,S7,1b4,3b3	21	-1.4
1972	StL	N	9	7	0	3	0	0	0	2	0-0	0	1	.429	.429	.429	145	0	0-0	.968	-1	103	80	2b9,S7,1b4,3b3	16	-0.1
	Oak	A	22	40	3	5	0	0	0	1	3-0	0	6	.125	.186	.125	-7	-5	0-0	1.000	-0	57	0	S3,2b2/3		0.0
	Tex	A	26	41	3	6	1	1	0	3	2-0	0	8	.146	.182	.220	21	-4	0-1	1.000	-0	57	38	2b17,S6/3		-0.4
	Year		48	81	6	11	1	1	0	4	5-0	0	14	.136	.184	.173	8	-10	0-1	.944	-2	57	38	S5,3b4/2	22	-0.7
Total	7		436	945	97	230	19	11	0	57	70-6	3	107	.243	.296	.287	69	-38	7-8	.950	-17	99	101	S157,3b74,2b59,C30,O21L,1b5/P	93	-4.6

MARTINEZ, PABLO
Pablo Made (Valera) B6.29.1969 Sabana Grande, D.R. BB/TR/5-10/155 d7.20

YEAR	TM	LG	G	AB	R	H	2B	3B	HR	RBI	BB-IB	HP	SO	AVG	OBP	SLG	AOPS	ABR	SB-CS	FA	FR	RNG	THR	GAMES AT POSITION	DL	BFW
1996	Atl	N	4	2	1	1	0	0	0		0-0	0	0	.500	.500	.500	155	0	0-1	1.000	-1	63	172	/S		-0.1

MARTINEZ, RAMON
Ramon E. B10.10.1972 Philadelphia PA BR/TR/6-1/187(170-190) d6.20 Col Vernon (TX) JC

YEAR	TM	LG	G	AB	R	H	2B	3B	HR	RBI	BB-IB	HP	SO	AVG	OBP	SLG	AOPS	ABR	SB-CS	FA	FR	RNG	THR	GAMES AT POSITION	DL	BFW
1998	SF	N	19	19	4	6	1	0	0		4-0	0	2	.316	.435	.368	120		1-2	1.000	2	113	176	2b14		0.3
1999	SF	N	61	144	21	38	6	0	5	19	14-0	0	17	.264	.327	.410	91	-2	1-2	.992	5	124	114	2b27,S12,3b11/D	15	0.3
2000	†SF	N	88	189	30	57	13	2	6	25	15-1	1	22	.302	.354	.487	118	5	3-2	.991	-6	87	112	S44,2b32,1b2,3b2		0.1
2001	SF	N	128	391	48	99	18	3	5	37	38-6	5	52	.253	.323	.353	81	-11	1-2	.974	2	89	66	3b70,2b42,S24		-0.7
2002	†SF	N	72	181	26	49	10	2	4	25	14-2	4	26	.271	.335	.414	103	0	2-0	.950	-4	93	138	S40,2b17,1b4,O3L,3b2	15	-0.1
2003	†Chi	N	108	293	30	83	16	1	3	34	24-1	2	50	.283	.333	.375	85	-6	0-1	.979	-1	80	111	2b42,3b37,S32,1b2		-0.4
2004	Chi	N	102	260	22	64	15	1	3	30	26-3	1	40	.246	.313	.346	69	-12	0-1	.977	-4	101	96	S73,3b24,2b6	15	-0.4
2005	Det	A	19	56	4	15	1	0	0	5	3-0	0	4	.268	.300	.286	60	-3	0-0	.955	-2	95	60	S12,2b4,1b2/3	20	-0.4
	Phi	N	33	56	7	16	2	0	1	9	3-0	1	7	.286	.317	.375	83	-1	0-0	1.000	-1	108	116	1b10,3b3,S3/2		-0.3
Total	8		630	1589	192	427	82	9	27	184	141-13	14	220	.269	.329	.383	87	-29	8-7	.967	-1	99	112	S240,2b185,3b150,1b20,O3L/D	65	-1.4

MARTINEZ, CHITO
Reynaldo Ignacio B12.19.1965 Belize City, British Honduras (Belize) BL/TL/5-10/180* [KCA84 6/148] d7.5

YEAR	TM	LG	G	AB	R	H	2B	3B	HR	RBI	BB-IB	HP	SO	AVG	OBP	SLG	AOPS	ABR	SB-CS	FA	FR	RNG	THR	GAMES AT POSITION	DL	BFW
1991	Bal	A	67	216	32	58	12	1	13	33	11-0	0	51	.269	.303	.514	126	6	1-1	.982	1	102	106	O54(1/0/53)/1D		0.5
1992	Bal	A	83	198	26	53	10	1	5	25	31-4	2	47	.268	.366	.404	114	1	0-1	.973	0	101	117	O52R,D4		0.3
1993	Bal	A	8	15	0	0	0	0	0	0	4-0	0	4	.000	.211	.000	-36	-3	0-0	1.000	0	37	0	O5R,D2		-0.4
Total	3		158	429	58	111	22	2	18	58	46-6	2	102	.259	.330	.445	114	8	1-2	.978	1	100	109	O111(1/0/110),D10/1		0.4

MARTINEZ, HECTOR
Rodolfo Hector (Santos) B5.11.1939 Las Villas, Cuba D12.1999 , Cuba BR/TR/5-10/160* d9.30

YEAR	TM	LG	G	AB	R	H	2B	3B	HR	RBI	BB-IB	HP	SO	AVG	OBP	SLG	AOPS	ABR	SB-CS	FA	FR	RNG	THR	GAMES AT POSITION	DL	BFW
1962	KC	A	1	1	0	0	0	0	0		0-0	0	1	.000	.000	.000	-96	0	0-0					/H		0.0
1963	KC	A	6	14	2	4	0	0	1	3	1-0	1	3	.286	.375	.500	135	1	0-1	1.000	-0	100	0	O3C		0.0
Total	2		7	15	2	4	0	0	1	3	1-0	1	4	.267	.353	.467	120	1	0-1	1.000	-0	100	0	O3C		0.0

MARTINEZ, TED
Teodoro Noel (Encarnacion) B12.10.1947 Santa Cruz de Barahona, D.R. BR/TR (BB 1973p)/6-0/160* d7.18 [DL 1976 Oak A 29]

YEAR	TM	LG	G	AB	R	H	2B	3B	HR	RBI	BB-IB	HP	SO	AVG	OBP	SLG	AOPS	ABR	SB-CS	FA	FR	RNG	THR	GAMES AT POSITION	DL	BFW
1970	NY	N	4	16	1	1	0	0	0	0	0-0	0	5	.063	.063	.063	-66	-4	0-0	1.000	0	76	153	2b4/S		-0.3
1971	NY	N	38	125	16	36	5	2	1	10	4-2	3	22	.288	.323	.384	100	0	6-0	.976	-7	83	120	S23,2b13,3b3/OL	17	-0.3
1972	NY	N	103	330	22	74	5	1	1	19	12-2	1	49	.224	.254	.279	52	-22	7-4	.994	-12	72	39	2b47,S42,O15(6/4/5),3b2		-3.1
1973	†NY	N	92	263	34	67	11	0	1	14	13-2	1	38	.255	.294	.308	68	-12	3-5	.941	-8	91	58	S44,O21(4/18/0),3b14,2b5		-1.8
1974	NY	N	116	334	32	73	15	7	2	43	14-4	0	40	.219	.247	.323	60	-20	3-2	.952	-1	96	83	S75,3b12,2b11,O10(1/9/0)		-1.3
1975	StL	N	16	21	1	4	2	0	0	3	2-0	0	5	.190	.190	.286	29	-2	0-0	1.000	0	118	0	O7(3/0/4),2b2/S3		-0.2
	†Oak	A	86	87	7	15	0	0	0	3	2-0	1	9	.172	.200	.172	6	-11	1-1	.955	-8	77	74	S45,2b31,3b14		-1.7
1977	LA	N	67	137	21	41	6	1	1	10	2-0	0	20	.299	.309	.380	83	-4	3-4	.992	3	109	192	2b27,S13,3b12	38	0.1
1978	LA	N	54	55	13	14	1	0	1	5	4-1	1	14	.255	.317	.327	80	-2	3-2	.912	0	88	68	S17,3b16,2b10		0.0
1979	LA	N	81	112	19	30	5	1	0	16	4-1	0	16	.268	.293	.330	71	-5	3-2	.769	-14	42	74	3b23,S21,2b18		-1.8
Total	9		657	1480	165	355	50	16	7	108	55-12	8	213	.240	.270	.309	62	-82	29-20	.956	-46	88	82	S282,2b168,3b97,O54(15/31/9)	84	-10.4

MARTINEZ, VICTOR
Victor Jesus B12.23.1978 Ciudad Bolivar, Venez BB/TR/6-2/170(170-195) d9.10

YEAR	TM	LG	G	AB	R	H	2B	3B	HR	RBI	BB-IB	HP	SO	AVG	OBP	SLG	AOPS	ABR	SB-CS	FA	FR	RNG	THR	GAMES AT POSITION	DL	BFW
2002	Cle	A	12	32	2	9	1	0	0	5	3-0	1	2	.281	.333	.406	96	0	0-0	.983	-2	40	100	C9/D		-0.2
2003	Cle	A	49	159	15	46	4	0	1	16	13-0	1	21	.289	.345	.333	81	-4	1-1	.996	3	108	102	C40,D5	24	0.2
2004	Cle	A★	141	520	77	147	38	1	23	108	60-11	5	69	.283	.359	.492	124	20	0-1	.994	-10	72	102	C132,D8		1.7
2005	Cle	A	147	547	73	167	33	0	20	80	63-9	5	78	.305	.378	.475	131	27	0-1	.995	-2	79	92	C142,D2		3.2
Total	4		349	1258	167	369	76	1	45	209	139-20	11	170	.293	.365	.463	121	43	1-3	.994	-11	79	97	C323,D16	24	4.9

MARTY, JOE
Joseph Anton B9.1.1913 Sacramento CA D10.4.1984 Sacramento CA BR/TR/6-0/182 d4.22 Mil 1942-45 Col St. Marys (CA)

YEAR	TM	LG	G	AB	R	H	2B	3B	HR	RBI	BB-IB	HP	SO	AVG	OBP	SLG	AOPS	ABR	SB-CS	FA	FR	RNG	THR	GAMES AT POSITION	DL	BFW
1937	Chi	N	88	290	41	84	17	2	5	44	28	2	30	.290	.356	.414	104	2	3	.976	-3	97	60	O84(1/83/0)		-0.3
1938	†Chi	N	76	235	32	57	8	3	7	35	18	1	26	.243	.305	.391	88	-5	0	.987	-2	93	113	O68(0/64/6)		-0.9
1939	Chi	N	23	76	6	10	1	0	2	10	4	0	13	.132	.175	.224	6	-11	2	.933	-0	73	273	O21(1/1/19)		-1.2
	Phi	N	91	299	32	76	12	6	9	44	24	0	27	.254	.310	.425	98	-3	1	.974	3	103	151	O79(6/56/18)/P		-0.2
	Year		114	375	38	86	13	6	11	54	28	0	40	.229	.283	.384	79	-13	3	.968	3	97	174	O100(7/57/37)/P		-1.4
1940	Phi	N	123	455	52	123	21	8	13	50	17	1	50	.270	.298	.437	105	-1	2	.974	-1	104	74	O118(0/115/3)		-0.5
1941	Phi	N	137	477	60	128	19	3	8	39	51	4	41	.268	.344	.371	105	4	6	.964	-8	93	71	O132(0/131/1)		-0.8
Total	5		538	1832	223	478	78	22	44	222	142	10	187	.261	.318	.400	97	-14	14	.972	-11	97	95	O502(8/450/47)/P		-3.9

MARTYN, BOB
Robert Gordon B8.15.1930 Weiser ID BL/TR/6-0/176* d6.18 Col Linfield

YEAR	TM	LG	G	AB	R	H	2B	3B	HR	RBI	BB-IB	HP	SO	AVG	OBP	SLG	AOPS	ABR	SB-CS	FA	FR	RNG	THR	GAMES AT POSITION	DL	BFW
1957	KC	A	58	131	10	35	2	4	1	12	11-3	0	20	.267	.322	.366	87	-3	1-3	.976	1	103	117	O49(13/9/28)		-0.5
1958	KC	A	95	226	25	59	10	7	2	23	26-5	0	36	.261	.336	.394	99	0	1-4	.967	1	104	95	O63(27/1/45)		-0.3
1959	KC	A	1	1	0	0	0	0	0	0	0-0	0	0	.000	.000	.000	-98	0	0-0	—	0			/R		0.0
Total	3		154	358	35	94	12	11	3	35	37-8	0	56	.263	.330	.383	94	-3	2-7	.970	1	104	104	O112(40/10/73)		-0.8

MARTZ, GARY
Gary Arthur B1.10.1951 Spokane WA BR/TR/6-4/210 [MilA69 5/115] d7.8

YEAR	TM	LG	G	AB	R	H	2B	3B	HR	RBI	BB-IB	HP	SO	AVG	OBP	SLG	AOPS	ABR	SB-CS	FA	FR	RNG	THR	GAMES AT POSITION	DL	BFW
1975	KC	A	1	0	0	0	0	0	0	0	0-0	0	0	.000	.000	.000	-98	0	0-0	1.000	0	411	0	/OL		0.0

MARZANO, JOHN
John Robert B2.14.1963 Philadelphia PA BR/TR/5-11/197(185-197) [BosA84 1/14] d7.31 Col Temple

YEAR	TM	LG	G	AB	R	H	2B	3B	HR	RBI	BB-IB	HP	SO	AVG	OBP	SLG	AOPS	ABR	SB-CS	FA	FR	RNG	THR	GAMES AT POSITION	DL	BFW
1987	Bos	A	52	168	20	41	11	0	5	24	7-0	3	41	.244	.283	.399	77	-6	0-0	.986	4	114	97	C52		0.0
1988	Bos	A	10	29	3	4	1	0	0	1	1-0	0	3	.138	.167	.172	-5	-4	0-0	1.000	3	86	111	C10		0.0
1989	Bos	A	7	18	5	8	3	0	1	3	0-0	1	5	.444	.421	.778	224	3	0-0	1.000	-1	98	113	C7		0.2
1990	Bos	A	32	83	8	20	4	0	0	6	5-0	0	10	.241	.281	.289	58	-5	0-1	1.000	1	84	100	C32		-0.1
1991	Bos	A	49	114	10	30	8	0	0	9	1-0	1	16	.263	.271	.333	64	-6	0-0	.985	-3	130	122	C48		-0.6
1992	Bos	A	19	50	4	4	2	1	0	1	2-0	1	12	.080	.132	.160	-17	-8	0-0	.968	-2	79	58	C18/D		-0.9
1995	Tex	A	2	6	1	2	0	0	0	0	0-0	0	0	.333	.333	.333	72	0	0-0	1.000	-0	27	281	C2	111	-0.9
1996	Sea	A	41	106	8	26	6	0	0	7	7-0	4	15	.245	.316	.302	57	-7	0-1	.986	-2	123	35	C39		-0.6
1997	Sea	A	39	87	7	25	3	0	1	10	7-0	1	15	.287	.340	.356	82	-2	0-0	.976	-2	85	105	C37/D		-0.3
1998	Sea	A	50	133	13	31	7	1	1	9	9-1	5	24	.233	.325	.391	84	-3	0-0	.997	4	92	95	C48/D		0.4
Total	10		301	794	79	191	45	2	11	72	39-1	18	141	.241	.289	.344	67	-38	0-2	.988	4	103	94	C293,D3	111	-1.9

MASHORE, CLYDE
Clyde Wayne B5.29.1945 Concord CA BR/TR/5-11/184* d7.11 s-Damon

YEAR	TM	LG	G	AB	R	H	2B	3B	HR	RBI	BB-IB	HP	SO	AVG	OBP	SLG	AOPS	ABR	SB-CS	FA	FR	RNG	THR	GAMES AT POSITION	DL	BFW
1969	Cin	N	2	6	1	0	0	0	0	0	0-0	0	0	.000	.000	.000	-95	0	0-0	—	0			/H		0.0
1970	Mon	N	13	25	2	4	0	0	1	3	4-2	0	11	.160	.276	.280	49	-2	0-0	1.000	-1	77	0	O10(2/8/0)		-0.3
1971	Mon	N	66	114	20	22	5	0	1	7	10-1	0	22	.193	.258	.263	47	-8	1-0	.967	-2	91	0	O47(19/29/5)/3		-1.2
1972	Mon	N	93	176	23	40	1	0	3	23	14-1	0	41	.227	.278	.330	73	-7	6-1	.988	-2	87	85	O74(23/8/46)	38	-1.1
1973	Mon	N	67	103	12	21	3	0	3	12	6-0	1	28	.204	.300	.320	71	-4	4-3	.958	-2	102	189	O44(43/3/1)/2	20	-0.3
Total	5		241	419	58	87	15	1	8	47	43-4	1	102	.208	.278	.305	64	-21	11-4	.991	-3	91	84	O175(87/48/52)/23	58	-2.9

MASHORE, DAMON
Damon Wayne B10.31.1969 Ponce, PR BR/TR/5-11/195(195-209) [OakA91 9/255] d6.5 f-Clyde Col Arizona

YEAR	TM	LG	G	AB	R	H	2B	3B	HR	RBI	BB-IB	HP	SO	AVG	OBP	SLG	AOPS	ABR	SB-CS	FA	FR	RNG	THR	GAMES AT POSITION	DL	BFW
1996	Oak	A	50	105	20	28	7	1	3	12	16-0	1	31	.267	.366	.438	104	2	4-0	.985	-1	94	45	O48(35/7/15)	48	0.0
1997	Oak	A	92	279	55	69	10	2	3	18	50-1	5	82	.247	.370	.330	85	-4	5-4	.991	9	108	246	O89(28/71/6)	64	0.4
1998	Ana	A	43	98	13	23	6	0	2	11	9-0	3	22	.235	.318	.357	87	-7	1-0	1.000	-1	95	54	O35(1/7/28),D7		-0.5
Total	3		185	482	88	120	23	3	8	41	75-1	9	135	.249	.359	.359	87	-7	10-4	.991	7	102	161	O172(64/85/49),D7	112	-0.1

MASI, PHIL   Philip Samuel B1.6.1916 Chicago IL D3.29.1990 Mt.Prospect IL BR/TR/5-10/180* d4.23   −0.1

YEAR	TM LG	G	AB	R	H	2B	3B	HR	RBI	BB-IB	HP	SO	AVG	OBP	SLG	AOPS	ABR	SB-CS	FA	FR	RNG	THR	GAMES AT POSITION	DL	BFW
1939	Bos N	46	114	14	29	7	2	1	14	9	1	15	.254	.315	.377	92	−2	0	.960	−1	148	93	C42		−0.8
1940	Bos N	63	138	11	27	4	1	1	18	14	0	14	.196	.270	.261	50	−10	0	.966	−1	105	126	C52		−0.7
1941	Bos N	87	180	17	40	8	2	3	18	16	0	13	.222	.286	.339	79	−6	4	.978	−5	95	95	C83		−0.1
1942	Bos N	57	87	14	19	3	1	0	9	12	0	4	.218	.313	.276	74	−3	2	.961	0	75	159	C39,O4(1/0/4)		−0.2
1943	Bos N	80	238	27	65	9	1	2	28	27	0	20	.273	.347	.345	102	1	7	.991	−7	57	128	C73		0.5
1944	Bos N	89	251	33	69	13	5	3	23	31	0	20	.275	.355	.402	108	3	4	.977	−1	65	141	C63,1b12,3b2		1.2
1945	Bos N★	114	371	55	101	25	4	7	46	42	1	32	.272	.348	.418	112	6	9	.980	1	101	114	C95,1b7		0.1
1946	Bos N★	133	397	52	106	17	5	3	62	55	1	41	.267	.358	.358	102	2	5	.981	−8	81	87	C124		1.5
1947	Bos N★	126	411	54	125	22	4	9	50	47	1	27	.304	.377	.443	120	12	7	.989	−3	82	111	C123		−0.5
1948	†Bos N★	113	376	43	95	19	0	5	44	35	1	26	.253	.318	.343	80	−10	2	.988	0	93	76	C109		−0.7
1949	Bos N★	37	105	13	22	2	0	0	6	14	0	10	.210	.303	.229	47	−8	1	.993	−1	100	87	C37		0.2
	Pit N	48	135	16	37	6	1	2	13	17	0	16	.274	.355	.378	94	−1	1	.994	1	118	109	C44,1b2		−0.5
	Year	85	240	29	59	8	1	2	19	31	0	26	.246	.332	.313	74	−8	2	.994	0	110	99	C81,1b2		0.6
1950	Chi A	122	377	38	105	17	2	7	55	49	3	36	.279	.366	.390	96	−1	2-1	.979	0	80	54	C78		0.7
1951	Chi A	84	225	24	61	11	2	4	28	32	2	27	.271	.367	.391	107	3	1-0	.956	−1	72	66	C25		−0.1
1952	Chi A	30	63	9	16	1	1	0	7	10	0	10	.254	.356	.302	84	−1	0-0	.956	−1	72	66	C25		1.6
Total 14		1229	3468	420	917	164	31	47	417	410	10	311	.264	.344	.370	97	−15	45-1	.983	−24	87	102	C1101,1b21,O4(1/0/4),3b2		

MASKREY, HARRY   Harry H. B12.21.1861 Mercer PA D8.17.1930 Mercer PA d9.21 b-Leech

YEAR	TM LG	G	AB	R	H	2B	3B	HR	RBI	BB-IB	HP	SO	AVG	OBP	SLG	AOPS	ABR	SB-CS	FA	FR	RNG	THR	GAMES AT POSITION	DL	BFW
1882	Lou AA	1	4	0	0	0	0	0		0				.000	.000	.000	−99	−1		.000	−1	0	0	/OC		−0.1

MASKREY, LEECH   Samuel Leech B2.11.1854 Mercer PA D4.1.1922 Mercer PA BR/TR/5-8/150 d5.2 b-Harry

YEAR	TM LG	G	AB	R	H	2B	3B	HR	RBI	BB-IB	HP	SO	AVG	OBP	SLG	AOPS	ABR	SB-CS	FA	FR	RNG	THR	GAMES AT POSITION	DL	BFW
1882	Lou AA	76	288	50	65	14	2	0		9				.226	.249	.288	85	−3		.902	−2	60	58	O76(75/0/1)/2		−0.6
1883	Lou AA	96	361	50	73	13	8	1		10				.202	.224	.291	70	−11		.914	10	103	46	O96(45/41/14)/S		−0.3
1884	Lou AA	105	412	48	103	13	4	0	36	17		1		.250	.281	.301	94	−2		.896	−4	88	81	O103(97/0/7),3b3/S		0.0
1885	Lou AA	109	423	54	97	8	11	3	46	19		4		.229	.269	.307	82	−10		.899	−4	48	59	O108L,3b3		−1.5
1886	Lou AA	5	19	1	3	1	0	0	2	1		0		.158	.200	.211	27	−2	0	.800	−1		9	O5(3/0/2)		−0.2
	Cin AA	27	98	7	19	3	1	0	10	5		1		.194	.240	.245	51	−6	4	.926	−1	91	116	O26(0/7/19),3b2		−0.6
	Year	32	117	8	22	4	1	0	12	6		1		.188	.234	.239	47	−7	4	.904	5	75	64	O31(3/7/21),3b2		−0.8
Total 5		418	1601	190	360	52	26	2	94	61		6		.225	.256	.294	80	−34	4	.904	6	75	64	O414(328/48/43),3b8,S2/2		−3.2

MASON, CHARLIE   Charles E. B6.25.1853 New Orleans LA D10.21.1936 Philadelphia PA BR/TR/?/175 d4.26 M1

YEAR	TM LG	G	AB	R	H	2B	3B	HR	RBI	BB-IB	HP	SO	AVG	OBP	SLG	AOPS	ABR	SB-CS	FA	FR	RNG	THR	GAMES AT POSITION	DL	BFW
1875	Cen NA	12	47	5	11	0	0	0	3	0				.234	.234	.234	69	−1	0-0	.719	−0	174	0	O10(3/0/7),1b2/C		−0.1
	Was NA	8	33	2	3	0	0	0	1	0			3	.091	.091	.091	−38	−4	0-0	.909	2	251	0	O8L/P		−0.2
	Year	20	80	7	14	0	0	0	4	0			4	.175	.175	.175	23	−6	0-0	.796	2	205	0	O18(11/0/7),1b2/CP		0.0
1883	Phi A	1	2	0	1	0	0	0	1	0				.500	.500	.500	204	0		—	−0	0	0	/OR		0.0

MASON, DON   Donald Stetson B12.20.1944 Boston MA BL/TR/5-11/160* d4.14

YEAR	TM LG	G	AB	R	H	2B	3B	HR	RBI	BB-IB	HP	SO	AVG	OBP	SLG	AOPS	ABR	SB-CS	FA	FR	RNG	THR	GAMES AT POSITION	DL	BFW
1966	SF N	42	25	8	3	0	0	0	1	0-0	0	2	.120	.120	.240	−3	−4	0-1	.905	0	99	56	2b9		−0.4
1967	SF N	4	3	0	0	0	0	0	0	0-0	0	0	.000	.000	.000	−99	−1	0-0	1.000	−1	106	0	2b2		−0.1
1968	SF N	10	19	3	3	0	0	0	0	1-0	0	4	.158	.200	.158	8	−2	1-1	1.000	−2	63	0	2b5,S4,3b2		−0.5
1969	SF N	104	250	43	57	4	2	0	13	36-0	0	29	.228	.324	.260	67	−10	1-5	.956	2	108	127	2b51,3b21,S7		−0.7
1970	SF N	46	36	4	5	0	0	0	0	5-0	0	7	.139	.244	.139	5	−5	0-0	.950	−3	61	32	2b14		−0.7
1971	SD N	113	344	43	73	12	1	2	11	27-0	0	35	.212	.270	.270	57	−20	6-4	.965	−6	97	80	2b90,3b3		−2.2
1972	SD N	9	11	1	2	0	0	0	0	0-0	0	2	.182	.250	.182	26	−1	0-0	.692	−2	96	0	2b3		−0.3
1973	SD N	8	8	0	0	0	0	0	0	0-0	0	2	.000	.000	.000	−99	−2	0-0	.750	0	199	420	/2		−0.2
Total 8		336	696	102	143	16	3	3	27	70-0	0	80	.205	.278	.250	52	−45	8-11	.955	−10	99	91	2b175,3b26,S11		−5.1

MASON, JIM   James Percy B8.14.1950 Mobile AL BL/TR/6-2/190(170-190) [TexA68 2/28] d9.26

YEAR	TM LG	G	AB	R	H	2B	3B	HR	RBI	BB-IB	HP	SO	AVG	OBP	SLG	AOPS	ABR	SB-CS	FA	FR	RNG	THR	GAMES AT POSITION	DL	BFW
1971	Was A	3	9	0	3	0	0	0	0	1-0	0	3	.333	.400	.333	115	0	0-0	.955	2	144	54	S3		0.2
1972	Tex A	46	147	10	29	3	0	0	10	9-0	1	39	.197	.247	.218	41	−11	0-0	.948	−7	94	66	S32,3b10		−1.7
1973	Tex A	92	238	23	49	7	2	3	19	23-0	0	48	.206	.273	.290	62	−13	0-1	.947	−2	98	91	S74,2b19/3		−0.6
1974	NY A	152	440	41	110	18	6	5	37	35-1	0	87	.250	.302	.352	90	−7	1-2	.964	0	98	103	S152		1.0
1975	NY A	94	223	17	34	3	2	2	16	22-0	1	49	.152	.228	.211	25	−23	0-2	.955	−1	93	110	S93/2		−1.7
1976	†NY A	93	217	17	39	7	1	1	14	9-0	0	37	.180	.210	.235	31	−19	0-0	.966	5	108	123	S93		−0.6
1977	Tor A	22	79	10	13	3	0	0	2	7-0	0	10	.165	.233	.203	20	−9	1-1	.971	−3	82	66	S22		0.1
	Tex A	36	55	9	12	3	0	1	7	6-0	0	10	.218	.290	.327	48	−1	0-0	.976	2	111	115	S32/3D		−0.8
	Year	58	134	19	25	6	0	1	9	13-0	0	20	.187	.257	.254	40	−11	1-1	.938	−4	103	84	S42,3b11/2D		−1.2
1978	Tex A	55	105	10	20	4	0	0	3	5-0	0	17	.190	.227	.229	28	−10	0-2	.966	−4	84	84	S33,3b6		−0.9
1979	Mon N	40	71	3	13	5	1	0	6	6-0	0	16	.183	.256	.282	47	−5	0-2	.959	−11	98	100	S576,3b29,2b21,D2		−6.3
Total 9		633	1584	140	322	53	12	12	114	124-2	1	316	.203	.259	.275	54	−99	2-8							

MASSA, GORDON   Gordon Richard "Moose","Duke" B9.2.1935 Cincinnati OH BL/TR/6-3/210* d9.24 Mil 1959 Col Holy Cross

YEAR	TM LG	G	AB	R	H	2B	3B	HR	RBI	BB-IB	HP	SO	AVG	OBP	SLG	AOPS	ABR	SB-CS	FA	FR	RNG	THR	GAMES AT POSITION	DL	BFW
1957	Chi N	6	15	2	7	1	0	0	3	4-0	0	3	.467	.579	.533	205	3	0-0	1.000	−2	68	0	C6		0.1
1958	Chi N	2	2	0	0	0	0	0	0	0-0	0	0	.000	.000	.000	−99	−1	0-0	—			0	/H		−0.1
Total 2		8	17	2	7	1	0	0	3	4-0	0	5	.412	.524	.471	172	2	0-0	1.000	−2	68	0	C6		0.0

MASSEY, ROY   Roy Hardee "Red" B10.9.1890 Sevierville TN D6.23.1954 Atlanta GA BL/TR/5-11/170 d4.16 Col Tennessee

YEAR	TM LG	G	AB	R	H	2B	3B	HR	RBI	BB-IB	HP	SO	AVG	OBP	SLG	AOPS	ABR	SB-CS	FA	FR	RNG	THR	GAMES AT POSITION	DL	BFW
1918	Bos N	66	203	20	59	6	2	0	18	23	0	20	.291	.363	.340	120	6	1	.954	−2	91	106	O45(21/29/0),3b2/1S		0.1

MASSEY, BILL   William Harry "Big Bill" B1.1871 Philadelphia PA D10.9.1940 Manila, Philippines BR/TR/5-11/168 d9.18

YEAR	TM LG	G	AB	R	H	2B	3B	HR	RBI	BB-IB	HP	SO	AVG	OBP	SLG	AOPS	ABR	SB-CS	FA	FR	RNG	THR	GAMES AT POSITION	DL	BFW
1894	Cin N	13	53	7	15	3	0	0	5	3	0	2	.283	.321	.340	57	−4	0	.991	−2	86	227	1b10,2b2/3		−0.4

MASSEY, MIKE   William Herbert B9.28.1893 Galveston TX D10.17.1971 Shreveport LA BB/TR/6-0/195 d4.12 Col Texas

YEAR	TM LG	G	AB	R	H	2B	3B	HR	RBI	BB-IB	HP	SO	AVG	OBP	SLG	AOPS	ABR	SB-CS	FA	FR	RNG	THR	GAMES AT POSITION	DL	BFW
1917	Bos N	31	91	12	18	0	0	0	2	15	1	15	.198	.318	.198	63	−3	2	.900	−7	91	89	2b25		−1.1

MASTELLER, DAN   Dan Patrick B3.17.1968 Toledo OH BL/TL/6-0/190 [MinA89 11/295] d6.23 Col Michigan St.

YEAR	TM LG	G	AB	R	H	2B	3B	HR	RBI	BB-IB	HP	SO	AVG	OBP	SLG	AOPS	ABR	SB-CS	FA	FR	RNG	THR	GAMES AT POSITION	DL	BFW
1995	Min A	71	198	21	47	12	0	3	21	18-0	1	19	.237	.303	.343	68	−9	1-2	.994	−2	81	112	1b48,O22(6/0/16),D8		−1.5

MATA, VICTOR   Victor Jose (Abreu) B6.17.1961 Santiago, D.R. BR/TR/6-1/165* d7.22

YEAR	TM LG	G	AB	R	H	2B	3B	HR	RBI	BB-IB	HP	SO	AVG	OBP	SLG	AOPS	ABR	SB-CS	FA	FR	RNG	THR	GAMES AT POSITION	DL	BFW
1984	NY A	30	70	8	23	5	0	1	6	0-0	1	12	.329	.333	.443	118	2	1-1	.942	−2	92	0	O28(2/21/8)		−0.2
1985	NY A	6	7	1	1	0	0	0	0	0-0	0	0	.143	.143	.143	−22	−1	0-0	1.000	−1	27	0	O3(1/1/2)		−0.3
Total 2		36	77	9	24	5	0	1	6	0-0	1	12	.312	.316	.416	105	1	1-1	.943	−3	87	0	O31(3/22/10)		

MATCHICK, TOM   John Thomas B9.7.1943 Hazleton PA BL/TR/6-0/175* d9.2

YEAR	TM LG	G	AB	R	H	2B	3B	HR	RBI	BB-IB	HP	SO	AVG	OBP	SLG	AOPS	ABR	SB-CS	FA	FR	RNG	THR	GAMES AT POSITION	DL	BFW
1967	Det A	8	6	1	1	0	0	0	0	0-0	0	2	.167	.167	.167	−1	−1	0-0	1.000	0	0	0	/S		−0.1
1968	†Det A	80	227	18	46	6	2	3	14	10-3	4	46	.203	.248	.286	60	−11	0-2	.950	−2	94	99	S59,2b13,1b6		−1.2
1969	Det A	94	298	25	72	11	2	0	32	15-3	0	51	.242	.276	.292	57	−17	3-0	.972	−7	101	117	2b47,3b27,S6,1b2		−2.2
1970	Det A	10	14	2	1	0	0	0	0	2-0	0	2	.071	.188	.071	−24	−2	0-1	1.000	−0	105	0	3b2/2S		−0.3
	Bos A	55	158	11	31	3	2	0	11	5-2	1	23	.196	.226	.241	28	−16	0-0	.985	11	115	138	S43,2b10/3	21	0.0
	KC A	55	158	11	31	3	2	0	11	5-2	1	23	.186	.222	.227	24	−18	0-1	.985	11	115	138	S44,2b11,3b3		−0.3
	Year	65	172	13	32	3	2	0	11	7-2	1	25	.186	.222	.227				.979	0	98	90			−0.9
1971	Mil A	42	114	6	25	1	0	1	7	7-0	0	23	.219	.264	.254	48	−8	3-2					3b41/2		−0.2
1972	Bal A	3	9	0	2	0	0	0	0	1-0	1	1	.222	.222	.222	31	−1	0-1	.857	−1	78	0	3b3		
Total 6		292	826	63	178	21	6	4	64	39-8	5	148	.215	.254	.270	49	−56	6-6	.967	1	100	113	S110,3b74,2b72,1b8	21	−4.9

MATEO, HENRY   Henry Antonio (Valera) B10.14.1976 Santo Domingo, D.R. BB/TR/5-11/180* [MonN95 2/58] d7.28

YEAR	TM LG	G	AB	R	H	2B	3B	HR	RBI	BB-IB	HP	SO	AVG	OBP	SLG	AOPS	ABR	SB-CS	FA	FR	RNG	THR	GAMES AT POSITION	DL	BFW
2001	Mon N	5	9	1	3	1	0	0	0	0-0	1	1	.333	.333	.444	99	−1	0-0	.818	−1	104	0	2b2		−0.1
2002	Mon N	22	23	1	4	0	1	0	0	2-0	1	6	.174	.240	.261	32	−3	0-0	1.000	2	204	111	2b3,S2		−0.5
2003	Mon N	100	154	29	37	3	1	0	7	11-0	3	38	.240	.304	.273	51	−11	11-1	.970	3	106	137	2b43,O10(2/2/6),S2,D3		−0.6
2004	Mon N	40	44	3	12	2	0	0	7	1-0	0	9	.273	.289	.318	55	−3	2-3	.879	2	138	109	2b9/OL	118	0.0
2005	Was N	1	1	0	0	0	0	0	0	0-0	0	0	.000	.000	.000	50	0	0-1	1.000	−0	97	0	/2	118	0.0
Total 5		168	231	34	56	6	2	0	21	15-1	3	54	.242	.297	.286	52	−17	15-4	.948	5	114	121	2b58,O11(3/2/6),S4,D3		

MATEO, RUBEN   Ruben Amaury B2.10.1978 San Cristobal, D.R. BR/TR/6-0/185(185-210) d6.12

YEAR	TM LG	G	AB	R	H	2B	3B	HR	RBI	BB-IB	HP	SO	AVG	OBP	SLG	AOPS	ABR	SB-CS	FA	FR	RNG	THR	GAMES AT POSITION	DL	BFW
1999	Tex A	32	122	16	29	9	1	5	18	4-0	1	28	.238	.268	.451	74	−5	3-0	1.000	−3	80	156	O31C	76	−0.6
2000	Tex A	52	206	32	60	11		9		10-1	1	34	.291	.339	.447	96	−2	6-0	.980	1	102	150	O52C	120	0.1
2001	Tex A	40	129	18	32	5	2	1	13	9-0	6	28	.248	.322	.341	74	−5	1-0	.986	−3	92	0	O39R		−0.9

YEAR	TM LG	G	AB	R	H	2B	3B	HR	RBI	BB-IB	HP	SO	AVG	OBP	SLG	AOPS	ABR	SB-CS	FA	FR	RNG	THR	GAMES AT POSITION	DL	BFW
2002	Cin N	46	86	11	22	6	0	2	7	6-0	2	20	.256	.319	.395	87	-2	0-0	1.000	-1	93	84	O24(0/2/23)		-0.3
2003	Cin N	74	207	16	50	9	0	3	18	12-1	3	53	.242	.290	.329	65	-11	0-0	.982	-1	101	62	O54(4/14/39)		-1.4
2004	Pit N	19	33	4	8	0	0	3	7	5-1	1	6	.242	.359	.515	122	1	0-0	.933	-0	76	228	O10(2/5/4)/D		0.0
	KC A	32	93	9	18	4	3	0	7	3-0	2	20	.194	.235	.301	38	-9	1-1	1.000	2	101	274	O30(11/5/15)		-0.7
Total	6	295	876	106	219	44	6	21	89	49-3	20	189	.250	.303	.386	77	-33	11-1	.986	-4	95	117	O240(17/109/120)/D	196	-3.8

MATHENY, MIKE Michael Scott B9.22.1970 Columbus OH BR/TR/6-3/205(205-220) [MilA91 8/208] d4.7 Col Michigan

YEAR	TM LG	G	AB	R	H	2B	3B	HR	RBI	BB-IB	HP	SO	AVG	OBP	SLG	AOPS	ABR	SB-CS	FA	FR	RNG	THR	GAMES AT POSITION	DL	BFW
1994	Mil A	28	53	3	12	3	0	1	2	3-0	2	13	.226	.293	.340	59	-3	0-1	.989	-1	83	98	C27		-0.3
1995	Mil A	80	166	13	41	9	1	0	21	12-0	2	28	.247	.306	.313	58	-10	0-1	.986	-2	125	60	C80		-0.8
1996	Mil A	106	313	31	64	15	2	8	46	14-0	3	80	.204	.243	.342	44	-28	3-2	.985	-5	114	97	C104/D		-2.4
1997	Mil A	123	320	29	78	16	1	4	32	17-0	7	68	.244	.294	.338	64	-17	0-1	.993	11	103	109	C121,1b2		0.0
1998	Mil N	108	320	24	76	13	0	6	27	11-0	7	63	.237	.278	.334	59	-20	1-0	.987	-12	84	83	C107		0.0
1999	Tor A	57	163	16	35	6	0	3	17	12-0	1	37	.215	.271	.307	47	-14	0-0	.995	8	80	126	C57	28	-2.6
2000	StL N	128	417	43	109	22	1	6	47	32-8	4	96	.261	.317	.362	70	-19	0-0	.994	16	163	149	C124,1b8		-0.2
2001	†StL N	121	381	40	83	12	0	7	42	28-5	2	76	.218	.276	.304	50	-29	0-1	.995	15	210	88	C121,1b2		0.5
2002	†StL N	110	315	31	77	12	1	3	35	32-6	2	49	.244	.331	.317	71	-15	1-3	.994	3	127	91	C106/1		-0.6
2003	StL N	141	441	43	111	18	2	8	47	44-16	2	81	.252	.320	.356	78	-15	1-1	.994	3	155	53	C138,1b4		-0.9
2004	†StL N	122	385	28	95	22	1	5	50	23-7	3	83	.247	.292	.348	65	-21	0-2	1.000	-3	95	71	C122/1		0.1
2005	SF N	134	443	42	107	34	0	13	59	29-10	6	91	.242	.295	.406	79	-14	0-2	.999	14	154	71	C132	15	0.4
Total	12	1258	3717	343	888	182	9	64	425	257-52	43	765	.239	.293	.344	64	-205	8-14	.994	54	133	99	C1239,1b18/D	43	-7.5

MATHES, JOE Joseph John B7.28.1891 Milwaukee WI D12.21.1978 St.Louis MO BB/TR/6-0.5/180 d9.19

YEAR	TM LG	G	AB	R	H	2B	3B	HR	RBI	BB-IB	HP	SO	AVG	OBP	SLG	AOPS	ABR	SB-CS	FA	FR	RNG	THR	GAMES AT POSITION	DL	BFW
1912	Phi A	4	14	0	2	0	0	0	0	0	1		.143	.200	.143	-2	-2	0	.889	-0	115	0	3b4		-0.2
1914	StL F	26	85	10	25	3	0	0	6	9	0	11	.294	.362	.329	85	-3	1	.938	-4	91	60	2b23		-0.6
1916	Bos N	2	0	0	0	0	0	0	0	0	0	0	.000	—	—	—	0	0	.000	-1	0	0	2b2		-0.1
Total	3	32	99	10	27	3	0	0	6	9	1	11	.273	.339	.303	74	-5	1	.921	-5	90	59	2b25,3b4		-0.9

MATHEWS, EDDIE Edwin Lee B10.13.1931 Texarkana TX D2.18.2001 LaJolla CA BL/TR/6-1/200(185-200) d4.15 M3/C2 HF1978

YEAR	TM LG	G	AB	R	H	2B	3B	HR	RBI	BB-IB	HP	SO	AVG	OBP	SLG	AOPS	ABR	SB-CS	FA	FR	RNG	THR	GAMES AT POSITION	DL	BFW
1952	Bos N	145	528	80	128	23	5	25	58	59	1	115	.242	.320	.447	114	8	6-4	.957	-9	92	88	3b142		-0.1
1953	Mil N★	157	579	110	175	31	8	47	135	99	2	83	.302	.406	.627	175	65	1-3	.939	1	99	105	3b157		6.1
1954	Mil N	138	476	96	138	21	4	40	103	113	2	61	.290	.423	.603	177	58	10-3	.966	-2	99	128	3b157		5.4
1955	Mil N★	141	499	108	144	23	5	41	101	109-20	1	98	.289	.413	.601	175	58	3-4	.952	-7	98	84	3b137		4.9
1956	Mil N☆	151	552	103	150	21	2	37	95	91-17	1	86	.272	.373	.518	146	37	6-0	.944	-14	97	92	3b137		2.5
1957	†Mil N☆	148	572	109	167	28	9	32	94	90-5	0	79	.292	.387	.540	157	48	3-1	.964	-4	102	98	3b147		4.3
1958	†Mil N☆	149	546	97	137	18	1	31	77	85-5	2	85	.251	.349	.458	123	19	5-0	.955	-8	110	89	3b149		2.5
1959	Mil N★	148	594	118	182	16	8	46	114	80-2	3	71	.306	.390	.593	172	60	2-1	.961	2	103	92	3b148		6.0
1960	Mil N★	153	548	108	152	19	7	39	124	111-3	2	113	.277	.397	.551	170	57	7-3	.950	-14	92	85	3b153		4.3
1961	Mil N★	152	572	103	175	23	6	32	91	93-3	2	95	.306	.402	.535	156	49	12-7	.961	-7	96	107	3b151		4.1
1962	Mil N★	152	536	106	142	25	6	29	90	101-7	2	90	.265	.381	.496	138	32	4-2	.964	1	101	92	3b140,1b7		3.1
1963	Mil N	158	547	82	144	27	4	23	84	124-14	1	119	.263	.399	.453	147	41	3-4	.968	13	112	135	3b121,O42L		5.3
1964	Mil N	141	502	83	117	19	1	23	74	85-5	1	100	.233	.344	.412	112	10	2-2	.962	6	99	99	3b128,1b7		1.6
1965	Mil N	156	546	77	137	23	0	32	95	73-7	3	110	.251	.341	.469	125	19	1-0	.956	5	105	79	3b153		2.5
1966	Atl N	134	452	72	113	21	4	16	53	63-6	0	82	.250	.341	.420	109	7	1-1	.946	-0	99	134	3b127		0.6
1967	Hou N	101	328	39	78	13	2	10	38	48-12	1	65	.238	.333	.381	109	5	2-4	.987	-2	97	88	1b79,3b24		-0.3
	Det A	36	108	14	25	3	0	6	19	15-0	2	23	.231	.331	.426	121	3	0-0	.933	-2	76	0	3b21,1b13		0.0
1968	†Det A	31	52	4	11	0	0	3	8	5-1	0	12	.212	.281	.385	97	0	0-0	.974	1	95	151	1b6,3b6		0.0
Total	17	2391	8537	1509	2315	354	72	512	1453	1444-107	26	1487	.271	.376	.509	145	576	68-39	.956	-30	100	98	3b2181,1b112,O52L	85	52.8

MATHEWS, NELSON Nelson Elmer B7.21.1941 Columbia IL BR/TR/6-4/195* d9.9 s-Timothy

YEAR	TM LG	G	AB	R	H	2B	3B	HR	RBI	BB-IB	HP	SO	AVG	OBP	SLG	AOPS	ABR	SB-CS	FA	FR	RNG	THR	GAMES AT POSITION	DL	BFW
1960	Chi N	3	8	1	2	0	0	0	0	0-0	0	2	.250	.250	.250	38	-1	0-0	1.000	0	147	0	O2R		-0.1
1961	Chi N	3	9	0	1	0	0	0	0	0-0	0	2	.111	.111	.111	-40	-2	0-0	1.000	-0	98	0	O2C		-0.1
1962	Chi N	15	49	5	15	2	0	2	13	5-0	2	4	.306	.393	.469	126	2	3-3	.962	-3	76	0	O14C		-0.2
1963	Chi N	61	155	12	24	3	2	4	10	16-2	0	48	.155	.234	.277	44	-11	3-4	.979	-3	93	36	O46C		-1.8
1964	KC A	157	573	58	137	27	5	14	60	43-7	1	143	.239	.293	.377	82	-14	3-4	.968	-1	109	47	O154C		-2.1
1965	KC A	67	184	17	39	7	7	2	15	24-4	0	45	.212	.300	.359	89	-3	0-2	.981	-2	100	37	O57(25/26/8)		-0.8
Total	6	306	978	93	218	39	14	22	98	88-13	3	248	.223	.288	.359	78	-29	8-12	.972	-8	103	40	O275(25/242/10)		-5.1

MATHEWS, BOBBY Robert T. B11.21.1851 Baltimore MD D4.17.1898 Baltimore MD BR/TR/5-5.5/140 d5.4 U3 ▲

YEAR	TM LG	G	AB	R	H	2B	3B	HR	RBI	BB-IB	HP	SO	AVG	OBP	SLG	AOPS	ABR	SB-CS	FA	FR	RNG	THR	GAMES AT POSITION	DL	BFW
1871	Kek NA	19	89	15	24	3	1	0	10	2		0	.270	.286	.326	74	-2	2-1	.840	-1	79	145	P19		0.0
1872	Bal NA	50	222	36	50	2	0	0	22	3		3	.225	.236	.234	43	-16	3-1	.780	-5	75	95	P49,O8R,3b3		-0.3
1873	Mut NA	52	223	40	43	3	3	0	14	10		3	.193	.227	.233	37	-17	1-1	.780	-3	80	47	P52,O5R		-0.2
1874	Mut NA	65	298	46	72	6	1	0	30	3		4	.242	.249	.268	64	-12	2-0	.774	-2	94	108	P65/3OL		-0.1
1875	Mut NA	70	264	23	48	6	2	0	15	2		5	.182	.188	.220	39	-16	1-2	.838	-6	81	72	P70/OL		-0.2
1876	NY N	56	218	19	40	4	1	0	9	3		2	.183	.195	.211	40	-12		.810	-3	96	0	P56/OR		-0.2
1877	Cin N	15	59	5	10	0	0	0	2	1		2	.169	.183	.169	13	-5		.862	-3	79	0	P15/OLS		-0.1
1879	Pro N	43	173	25	35	2	0	1	10	7		12	.202	.233	.231	55	-8		.956	-4	99	0	P27,O21R,3b5		-0.2
1881	Pro N	16	57	6	11	1	0	0	4	0		6	.193	.258	.211	50	-3		.810	-2	82	264	P14,O5R		-0.8
	Bos N	19	71	2	12	2	0	0	4	0		5	.169	.169	.197	15	-7		.818	-2	74	0	O18(1/9/9),P5		-0.2
	Year	35	128	8	23	3	0	0	8	0		11	.180	.211	.203	32	-10		.811	-4	64	0	O23(1/9/14),P19		-1.0
1882	Bos N	45	169	17	38	6	0	0	13	8		18	.225	.260	.260	67	-6		.867	-8	63	67	P34,O13R/S		-0.7
1883	Phi AA	45	167	15	31	2	0	1	8	5	0		.186	.209	.198	29	-14		.874	-1	88	101	P44,O3(1/1/1)		-0.1
1884	Phi AA	49	184	26	34	1	0	0	7		0		.185	.215	.223	40	-12		.775	-3	90	57	P49/OR		-0.1
1885	Phi AA	48	179	22	30	3	0	0	12	10	0		.168	.212	.184	24	-15		.881	-0	96	55	P48/OR		0.0
1886	Phi AA	24	88	16	21	0	0	0	10	3	0		.239	.264	.273	67	-3	1	.843	-0	112	266	P24/OR		0.0
1887	Phi AA	7	25	5	5	0	0	0	0	4	0		.200	.310	.200	44	0		.889	0	118	386	P7		0.0
Total 5 NA		256	1096	160	237	20	7	0	91	20		14	.216	.230	.247	49	-63	9-5	.801	-15	83	86	P255,O15(2/0/13),3b4		-0.8
Total 10		367	1390	158	267	28	2	1	73	53	0	45	.192	.222	.217	42	-85	1	.845	-25	91	76	P323,O65(3/10/53),3b5,S2		-3.0

MATHIS, JEFF Jeffery Stephen B3.31.1983 Marianna FL BR/TR/6-0/180 d8.12

YEAR	TM LG	G	AB	R	H	2B	3B	HR	RBI	BB-IB	HP	SO	AVG	OBP	SLG	AOPS	ABR	SB-CS	FA	FR	RNG	THR	GAMES AT POSITION	DL	BFW
2005	LA A	5	3	1	1	0	0	0	0	0-0	0	1	.333	.333	.333	80	0	0-0	1.000	0	0	0	C3,D2		0.0

MATHISON, JIMMY James Michael Ignatius B11.11.1878 Baltimore MD D7.4.1911 Baltimore MD TR d8.29

YEAR	TM LG	G	AB	R	H	2B	3B	HR	RBI	BB-IB	HP	SO	AVG	OBP	SLG	AOPS	ABR	SB-CS	FA	FR	RNG	THR	GAMES AT POSITION	DL	BFW
1902	Bal A	29	91	12	24	2	1	0	7	9		6	.264	.368	.308	85	-1	2	.889	-4	85	86	3b28/S		-0.4

MATIAS, JOHN John Roy B8.15.1944 Honolulu HI BL/TL/5-11/170 d4.7

YEAR	TM LG	G	AB	R	H	2B	3B	HR	RBI	BB-IB	HP	SO	AVG	OBP	SLG	AOPS	ABR	SB-CS	FA	FR	RNG	THR	GAMES AT POSITION	DL	BFW
1970	Chi A	58	117	7	22	2	0	2	6	3-1	1	22	.188	.215	.256	28	-12	1-0	.941	-0	55	219	O22(5/0/17),1b18		-1.4

MATOS, FRANCISCO Francisco Aguirre (Mancebo) B7.23.1969 Santo Domingo, D.R. BR/TR/6-1/160 d7.17

YEAR	TM LG	G	AB	R	H	2B	3B	HR	RBI	BB-IB	HP	SO	AVG	OBP	SLG	AOPS	ABR	SB-CS	FA	FR	RNG	THR	GAMES AT POSITION	DL	BFW
1994	Oak A	14	28	1	7	1	0	0	2	1-0	0	2	.250	.267	.286	49	-2	1-0	.925	-2	90	71	2b12,D2		-0.3

MATOS, JULIUS Julius B12.12.1974 New York NY BR/TR/5-11/175* [CleA94 16/437] d5.31 Col South Suburban (IL) JC

YEAR	TM LG	G	AB	R	H	2B	3B	HR	RBI	BB-IB	HP	SO	AVG	OBP	SLG	AOPS	ABR	SB-CS	FA	FR	RNG	THR	GAMES AT POSITION	DL	BFW
2002	SD N	76	185	19	44	3	0	2	19	9-0	2	33	.238	.279	.286	57	-13	1-1	.963	3	107	101	2b49,3b17,S4,O3R,1b2/D		-0.9
2003	KC A	28	57	7	15	1	0	2	7	1-0	0	12	.263	.276	.386	57	-3	1-0	1.000	-3	55	0	3b13,2b11,S2/ORD		-0.5
Total	2	104	242	26	59	4	0	4	26	10-0	2	45	.244	.278	.310	60	-16	2-1	.964	-1	110	98	2b60,3b30,S6,O4R,D2,1b2		-1.4

MATOS, LUIS Luis David B10.30.1978 Bayamon, PR BR/TR/6-0/180(179-210) [BalA96 10/291] d6.19

YEAR	TM LG	G	AB	R	H	2B	3B	HR	RBI	BB-IB	HP	SO	AVG	OBP	SLG	AOPS	ABR	SB-CS	FA	FR	RNG	THR	GAMES AT POSITION	DL	BFW
2000	Bal A	72	182	21	41	6	3	1		12-0	3	30	.225	.281	.308	52	-14	13-4	.988	6	121	96	O69(1/44/25),D3		-0.7
2001	Bal A	31	98	16	21	7	0	4	12	11-0	1	30	.214	.300	.408	89	-2	7-0	.985	0	99	119	O31(1/23/10)		0.0
2002	Bal A	17	31	0	4	1	0	0	1	1-0	0	6	.129	.156	.161	-16	-4	1-0	1.000	-1	84	0	O14(2/6/7)/D	145	-0.6
2003	Bal A	109	439	70	133	23	3	13	45	28-0	7	90	.303	.353	.458	113	8	15-7	.987	-4	108	101	O107(0/106/4),D2	67	1.3
2004	Bal A	89	330	36	74	18	0	6	28	19-2	5	60	.224	.275	.333	59	-21	12-4	.996	-2	99	68	O89C	74	-1.9
2005	Bal A	121	349	52	109	20	2	9	53	27-0	10	58	.260	.340	.373	90	-5	17-9	.984	4	107	129	O120C	39	0.1
Total	6	439	1469	196	382	75	8	28	135	98-2	26	274	.260	.316	.379	83	-39	65-24	.988	11	106	100	O430(4/388/46),D6	325	-1.8

MATOS, PASCUAL Pascual (Cuevas) B12.23.1974 Santa Cruz de Barahona, D.R. BR/TR/6-2/180 d5.11

YEAR	TM LG	G	AB	R	H	2B	3B	HR	RBI	BB-IB	HP	SO	AVG	OBP	SLG	AOPS	ABR	SB-CS	FA	FR	RNG	THR	GAMES AT POSITION	DL	BFW
1999	Atl N	6	8	0	1	0	0	0	2	0-0	0	1	.125	.125	.125	-37	-2	0-0	1.000	0	59	0	C5		-0.1

YEAR	TM LG	G	AB	R	H	2B	3B	HR	RBI	BB-IB	HP	SO	AVG	OBP	SLG	AOPS	ABR	SB-CS	FA	FR	RNG	THR	GAMES AT POSITION	DL	BFW

MATRANGA, DAVE David Michael B1.8.1977 Orange CA BR/TR/6-0/170* [HouN98 6/182] d6.27 Col Pepperdine

																							2b2		0.0
2003	Hou N	6	5	1	1	0	0	0	1	0-0		2	.200	.200	.800	137	0	0-0	1.000	-0	0	0	/2		0.0
2005	LA A	1	1	0	0	0	0	0	0	0-0		0	.000	.000	.000	-99	0	0-0	1.000	1	146	707	2b3		0.0
Total	2	7	6	1	1	0	0	0	1	0-0		2	.167	.167	.667	100	0	0-0	1.000	0	58	283	2b3		0.0

MATSUI, HIDEKI Hideki "Godzilla" B6.12.1974 Ishikawa, Japan BL/TR/6-1/210(210-230) d3.31

2003	†NY A★	163	623	82	179	42	1	16	106	63-5	3	86	.287	.353	.435	109	9	2-2	.977	-1	94	147	O159(118/46/0),D4		0.4
2004	†NY A★	162	584	109	174	34	2	31	108	88-2	3	103	.298	.390	.522	136	33	3-0	.978	-1	96	91	O160(160/3/0)		2.5
2005	†NY A	162	629	108	192	45	3	23	116	63-7	3	78	.305	.367	.496	127	26	2-2	.990	-3	96	94	O142(115/28/4),D19		1.7
Total	3	487	1836	299	545	121	6	70	330	214-14	9	267	.297	.370	.484	124	68	7-4	.981	-5	95	111	O461(393/77/4),D23		4.6

MATSUI, KAZUO Kazuo B10.23.1975 Osaka, Japan BB/TR/5-10/185* d4.6

2004	NY N	114	460	65	125	32	2	7	44	40-4	2	97	.272	.331	.396	89	-7	14-3	.956	-2	102	94	S110,2b3	46	0.2
2005	NY N	87	267	31	68	9	4	3	24	14-1	5	43	.255	.300	.352	73	-11	6-1	.970	-6	102	79	2b71	52	-1.3
Total	2	201	727	96	193	41	6	10	68	54-5	7	140	.265	.320	.380	84	-18	20-4	.956	-7	102	94	S110,2b74	98	-1.1

MATTHEWS, GARY Gary Nathaniel Jr. B8.25.1974 San Francisco CA BB/TR/6-3/210(200-225) [SDN01 13/366] d6.4 f-Gary Col Mission (CA) JC

1999	SD N	23	36	4	8	0	0	0	7	9-0	0	9	.222	.378	.222	61	-2	2-0	1.000	-0	109	0	O17(6/2/10)		-0.2
2000	Chi N	80	158	24	30	4	0	4	14	15-1	1	28	.190	.264	.297	42	-15	3-0	.978	3	110	136	O61(46/21/1)		-1.2
2001	Chi N	106	258	41	56	9	1	9	30	38-2	1	55	.217	.320	.364	79	-8	5-3	.976	-2	98	78	O100(20/88/1)		-1.0
	Pit N	46	147	22	36	6	1	5	14	22-0	1	45	.245	.341	.401	89	-2	3-2	.971	-3	99	43	O44C		-0.4
	Year	152	405	63	92	15	2	14	44	60-2	2	100	.227	.328	.378	83	-10	8-5	.974	-5	98	66	O144(20/132/1)		-1.4
2002	NY N	2	1	0	0	0	0	0	0	0-0	0	0	.000	.000	.000	-99	0	0-0	—				/H		0.0
	Bal A	109	344	54	95	25	3	7	38	43-1	1	69	.276	.355	.427	114	8	15-5	.969	-4	92	106	O100(16/16/76),D2	17	0.2
2003	Bal A	41	162	21	33	12	1	2	20	9-0	1	29	.204	.250	.327	51	-12	0-3	1.000	-1	95	110	O40C/D		-1.3
	SD N	103	306	50	83	19	1	4	22	34-0	1	66	.271	.346	.379	98	-1	12-5	.993	-2	99	45	O92(33/35/35)		-0.4
2004	Tex A	87	280	37	77	17	1	11	36	33-5	1	64	.275	.350	.461	106	3	5-1	.990	6	108	158	O85(3/30/66)	24	0.6
2005	Tex A	131	475	72	121	25	1	17	55	45-1	0	90	.255	.320	.436	95	-4	9-2	.982	-1	101	98	O662(129/373/211),D4	41	-3.7
Total	7	728	2167	325	539	114	15	59	236	250-10	6	455	.249	.327	.397	90	-33	54-21	.982	-1	101	98	O662(129/373/211),D4		

MATTHEWS, GARY Gary Nathaniel Sr. B7.5.1950 San Fernando CA BR/TR/6-3/190(188-205) [SFN68 1/17] d9.6 C6 s-Gary

1972	SF N	20	62	11	18	1	4	4	14	7-2	0	13	.290	.357	.532	149	4	0-1	.971	-1	100	110	O19(10/0/9)		0.2
1973	SF N	148	540	74	162	22	10	12	58	58-7	1	83	.300	.367	.444	119	14	17-5	.983	1	93	110	O145(144/0/1)		0.5
1974	SF N	154	561	87	161	27	6	16	82	70-5	3	69	.287	.368	.442	121	17	11-9	.970	-1	95	85	O151(150/0/1)		0.6
1975	SF N	116	425	67	119	22	3	12	58	65-5	2	53	.280	.377	.431	120	13	13-4	.967	3	102	127	O113L	43	1.2
1976	SF N	156	587	79	164	28	4	20	84	75-3	1	94	.279	.359	.443	124	19	12-5	.975	-11	81	71	O145L		-0.1
1977	Atl N	148	555	89	157	25	5	17	64	67-3	2	90	.283	.362	.438	102	3	22-8	.969	-1	101	99	O127(1/0/127)	17	0.8
1978	Atl N	129	474	75	135	20	5	18	62	61-2	2	92	.285	.366	.462	118	13	8-7	.969	-5	96	93	O156R		-0.1
1979	Atl N★	156	631	97	192	34	5	27	90	60-5	9	75	.304	.363	.502	127	23	18-6	.960	-8	95	64	O143(6/0/137)		0.8
1980	Atl N	155	571	79	159	17	3	19	75	42-2	0	93	.278	.325	.419	106	3	11-3	.963	-1	93	132	O100L		1.1
1981	†Phi N	101	359	62	108	21	3	9	67	59-2	3	42	.301	.398	.451	135	19	15-2	.966	-2	91	116	O162L		1.2
1982	Phi N	162	616	89	173	31	1	19	83	66-1	2	87	.281	.349	.427	113	12	21-4	.974	-3	89	68	O122L		-1.0
1983	†Phi N	132	446	66	115	18	2	10	50	69-3	0	81	.258	.352	.374	104	4	13-9	.955	-7	88	68	O145L		-0.1
1984	†Chi N	147	491	101	143	21	2	14	82	103-2	3	97	.291	.410	.428	127	24	17-8	.977	-2	85	130	O85L	39	2.5
1985	Chi N	97	298	45	70	12	0	13	40	59-2	1	64	.235	.362	.406	105	4	2-0	.940	-7	80	82	O105L		-0.5
1986	Chi N	123	370	49	96	16	1	21	46	60-1	0	59	.259	.361	.478	121	11	3-2	1.000	-0	92	0	O2L		0.0
1987	Chi N	44	42	3	11	3	0	0	8	4-1	0	11	.262	.326	.333	72	-2	0-0	—	-0	0	0	D39		-0.1
	Sea A	45	119	10	28	1	0	3	15	15-0	1	22	.235	.319	.319	67	-6	0-1	—	0	0	0	O1876(1446/0/431),D39	99	5.0
Total	16	2033	7147	1083	2011	319	51	234	978	940-46	21	1125	.281	.364	.439	116	175	183-74	.968	-44	92	99	O1876(1446/0/431),D39		

MATTHEWS, BOB Robert B Camden NJ d9.25

| 1891 | Phi AA | 1 | 3 | 1 | 1 | 0 | 0 | 0 | | 0 | 0 | 2 | 1 | .333 | .600 | .333 | 167 | 1 | 0 | — | -0 | 0 | 0 | /OR | | |

MATTHEWS, WID Wid Curry "Matty" B10.20.1896 Raleigh IL D10.5.1965 Hollywood CA BL/TL/5-8.5/155 d4.18

1923	Phi A	129	485	52	133	11	6	1	25	50	1	27	.274	.343	.328	76	-17	16-16	.947	-15	95	20	O127(2/125/0)		-3
1924	Was A	53	169	25	51	10	4	0	13	11	3	4	.302	.355	.408	100	-1	3-8	.985	5	109	177	O44(1/43/0)		0
1925	Was A	10	9	2	4	0	0	0	1	0	0	1	.444	.444	.444	129	0	0-0	1.000	0	106	0	/OC		-3
Total	3	192	663	79	188	21	10	1	39	61	4	32	.284	.348	.350	83	-18	19-24	.957	-10	98	58	O172(3/169/0)		

MATTHIAS, STEVE Stephen J. B1860 Mitchellville MD D7.29.1891 Baltimore MD BR/TR/5-8/160 d4.20

| 1884 | CP U | 37 | 142 | 34 | 39 | 7 | 1 | 1 | | | | | .275 | .299 | .338 | 94 | -5 | | .840 | 1 | 95 | 92 | S36,O2C | | -0 |

MATTICK, BOBBY Robert James B12.5.1915 Sioux City IA D12.16.2004 Scottsdale AZ BR/TR/5-11/178 d5.5 M2 f-Wally

																							/S		0
1938	Chi N	1	1	0	1	0	0	0	0	0-0	1	0	1.000	1.000	1.000	439	0	0	—	-0	0	0	S48		0
1939	Chi N	51	178	16	51	10	1	0	23	6	1	19	.287	.314	.365	80	-5	1	.927	4	110	84	S126/3		-2
1940	Chi N	128	441	30	96	15	0	0	33	19	1	33	.218	.250	.252	39	-37	5	.946	8	108	103	S12,3b5/2		-2
1941	Cin N	20	60	8	11	3	0	0	7	8	1	6	.183	.279	.233	45	-4	1	.982	-1	90	97	S3		-0
1942	Cin N	6	10	0	2	1	0	0	1	0	0	1	.200	.200	.300	45	-1	0	1.000	0	91	85	S190,3b6/2		0
Total	5	206	690	54	161	31	1	0	64	33	4	60	.233	.269	.281	52	-47	7	.943	11	107	97	S190,3b6/2		

MATTICK, WALLY Walter Joseph "Chick" B3.12.1887 St.Louis MO D11.5.1968 Los Altos CA BR/TR/5-10/180 d4.11 s-Bobby

1912	Chi A	90	285	45	74	7	3	1	35	27	5		16	.260	.334	.358	101	0	16	.982	-5	91	70	O79(2/66/10)		-1
1913	Chi A	71	207	15	39	8	1	0	11	18		0	16	.188	.253	.237	44	-15	3	.977	2	91	152	O64(7/56/0)		-1
1918	StL N	8	14	0	2	0	0	0	1	2	2	3	.143	.333	.143	49	-1	0	1.000	0	84	182	O3R		-1
Total	3	169	506	60	115	15	4	1	47	47	7	19	.227	.302	.302	77	-16	19	.980	-3	91	107	O146(9/122/13)		

MATTIMORE, MIKE Michael Joseph B8.1858 North Bend PA D4.28.1931 Butte MT BL/TL/5-8.5/160 d5.3 ▲

1887	NY N	8	32	5	8	1	0	0	4	0	0		.250	.250	.281	50	-2	1	.889	-1	47		P7,O2C		-0
1888	Phi AA	41	142	22	38	6	5	0	12	12	3	16	.268	.333	.380	129	5	16	.915	4	137	338	P26,O16(1/1/15)		-0
1889	Phi AA	23	73	10	17	1	2	1	8	9	2	7	.233	.333	.342	94	-1	6	.944	-2	90		O12(3/5/4),1b7,P5		-0
	KC AA	19	75	6	12	1	1	0	5	3	0	16	.160	.192	.200	11	-9	0	.844	-1	82		O19(19/1/0)/P		-0
	Year	42	148	16	29	2	3	1	13	12	2	23	.196	.265	.270	52	-10	6	.873	-3	56		O31(22/6/4),1b7,P6		-0
1890	Bro AA	33	129	14	17	1	1	0	7	16	2		.132	.238	.155	17	-13	11	.887	-4	106		P19,O14(0/1/13)		-0
Total	4	124	451	57	92	10	9	1	36	40	6	29	.204	.278	.273	64	-20	34	.853	-5	69	105	O63(23/10/32),P58,1b7		

MATTINGLY, DON Donald Arthur "Donnie Baseball" B4.20.1961 Evansville IN BL/TL/6-0/175(175-200) [NYA79 19/493] d9.8 C2

1982	NY A	7	12	0	2	0	0	0	1	0-0	0	1	.167	.154	.167	-8	-2	0-0	1.000	2	200	603	O6(5/0/1)/1		0.0
1983	NY A	91	279	34	79	15	4	4	32	21-5	1	31	.283	.333	.409	107	2	0-0	.974	-5	86	97	O48(13/1/39),1b42/2		-0.1
1984	NY A★	153	603	91	207	44	2	23	110	41-8	1	33	.343	.381	.537	158	47	1-1	.996	16	135	115	1b133,O19(13/1/6)		3.4
1985	NY A★	159	652	107	211	48	3	35	145	56-13	2	41	.324	.371	.567	158	51	2-2	.996	-10	75	117	1b159		3.9
1986	NY A★	162	677	117	238	53	2	31	113	53-11	2	35	.352	.394	.573	162	58	0-0	.996	-1	97	108	1b140/D		6.8
1987	NY A★	141	569	93	186	38	2	30	115	51-13	0	38	.327	.378	.559	146	38	1-4	.996	-1	97	105	1b143/OLD	18	3.6
1988	NY A★	144	599	94	186	37	0	18	88	41-14	3	29	.311	.353	.462	128	22	1-0	.993	-2	98	105	1b145,D17/OR		1.7
1989	NY A★	158	631	79	191	37	2	23	113	51-18	5	30	.303	.351	.477	134	27	3-0	.995	-4	90	102	1b89,D13/OL	47	0.9
1990	NY A	102	394	40	101	16	0	5	42	28-13	2	20	.256	.308	.335	80	-11	1-0	.997	-3	88	124	1b127,D22		-0.9
1991	NY A	152	587	64	169	35	0	9	68	46-11	4	42	.288	.339	.394	103	3	2-0	.997	6	113	103	1b143,D15		0.3
1992	NY A	157	640	89	184	40	4	14	86	39-7	1	43	.287	.327	.416	120	8	3-0	.998	1	100	116	1b130,D5	27	0.9
1993	NY A	134	530	78	154	27	2	17	86	61-9	2	42	.291	.364	.445	120	16	0-0	.998	5	122	123	1b97	15	1.4
1994	NY A	97	372	62	113	20	1	6	51	60-7	0	24	.304	.397	.411	114	11	0-0	.994	0	98	91	1b125/D		1.0
1995	†NY A	128	458	59	132	32	2	7	49	40-7	1	35	.288	.341	.413	97	1	0-0	.996	13	109	104	1b125/D	122	1.1
Total	14	1785	7003	1007	2153	442	20	222	1099	588-136	21	444	.307	.358	.471	127	266	14-9	.996	24	99	107	1b1634,D76,O76(33/2/47),3b3/2		

MATTIS, RALPH Ralph "Matty" B8.24.1890 Philadelphia PA D9.13.1960 Williamsport PA BR/TR/5-11/172 d4.22

| 1914 | Pit F | 36 | 85 | 14 | 21 | 4 | 0 | 8 | 9 | | | 1 | 11 | .247 | .326 | .318 | 77 | -4 | 2 | .938 | 2 | 106 | 167 | O24(12/0/12) | | -0 |

MATTOX, CLOY Cloy Mitchell "Monk" B11.24.1902 Leesville VA D8.3.1985 Danville VA BL/TL/5-8/168 d9.1 b-Jim Col VPI

| 1929 | Phi N | 3 | 6 | 0 | 1 | 0 | 0 | 0 | 1 | | | | 1 | .167 | .286 | .167 | 19 | -1 | 0-0 | .875 | -0 | 85 | 145 | C3 | | |

YEAR	TM LG	G	AB	R	H	2B	3B	HR	RBI	BB-IB	HP	SO	AVG	OBP	SLG	AOPS	ABR	SB-CS	FA	FR	RNG	THR	GAMES AT POSITION	DL	BFW

MATTOX, JIM   James Powell   B12.17.1896 Leesville VA   D10.12.1973 Myrtle Beach SC   BL/TR/5-9.5/168   d4.30   b-Cloy   Col Washington and Lee

1922	Pit N	29	51	11	15	1	0	0	3	1	0	3	.294	.308	.353	69	-3	0-0	.984	0	98	78	C21		-0.1
1923	Pit N	22	32	4	6	1	0	1	0	2		5	.188	.235	.281	35	-3	0-0	.960	0	111	139	C8		-0.2
Total	2	51	83	15	21	2	2	0	4	1	2	8	.253	.279	.325	56	-6	0-0	.978	1	102	97	C29		-0.3

MATUSZEK, LEN   Leonard James   B9.27.1954 Toledo OH   BL/TR/6-2/195(190-205)   [PhiN76 5/113]   d9.3   Col Toledo

1981	Phi N	13	11	1	3	1	0	0	1	3-1	0	1	.273	.429	.364	120	0	0-1	1.000	1	0	538	/13		0.1
1982	Phi N	25	39	1	3	1	0	0	3	1-0	1	10	.077	.119	.103	-35	-7	0-1	.750	-2	83	0	3b8,1b3	16	-1.0
1983	Phi N	28	80	12	22	6	1	4	16	4-1	0	14	.275	.306	.525	128	3	0-1	1.000	-1	72	58	1b21		0.0
1984	Phi N	101	262	40	65	17	1	12	43	39-4	4	54	.248	.350	.458	125	10	4-3	.990	5	136	79	1b81/OL	43	1.1
1985	Tor A	62	151	23	32	6	2	2	15	11-0	0	24	.212	.259	.318	57	-9	2-1	1.000	0	126	63	D54,1b5		-1.1
†LA N	43	63	10	14	2	1	3	13	8-2	1	14	.222	.307	.429	110	4	0-1	1.000	0	120	0	O17L,1b10/3		0.0
1986	LA N	91	199	26	52	7	0	9	28	21-1	1	47	.261	.333	.432	118	4	2-2	1.000	-0	173	0	O37(35/0/2),1b31	47	0.1
1987	LA N	16	15	0	1	0	0	0	1	1-0	0	5	.067	.125	.067	-49	-3	0-0	1.000	0	1b3			157	-0.3
Total	7	379	820	113	192	40	5	30	119	88-9	7	168	.234	.309	.405	99	-0	8-10	.990	4	119	80	1b155,O55(53/0/2),D54,3b10	263	-1.1

MAUCH, GENE   Gene William "Skip"   B11.18.1925 Salina KS   D8.8.2005 Rancho Mirage CA   BR/TR/5-10/165*   d4.18   Mil 1944-45   M26/C1

1944	Bro N	5	15	2	2	1	0	0	2	2	0	3	.133	.235	.200	24	-1	0	1.000	-1	75	120	S5		-0.2
1947	Pit N	16	30	8	9	0	0	1	7		0	6	.300	.432	.300	95	0	0	.963	-3	88	0	2b6,S4		-0.2
1948	Bro N	12	13	1	2	0	0	0	1	1	0	4	.154	.214	.154	1	-2	0	.950	0	82	109	2b7/S		-0.2
Chi N	53	138	18	28	3	2	1	26		0	10	.203	.329	.275	68	-6	1	.925	-3	90	130	2b26,S19		-0.6
Year	65	151	19	30	3	2	1	27		0	14	.199	.320	.265	62	-8	1	.929	-3	89	127	2b33,S20		-0.8
1949	Chi N	72	150	15	37	6	2	1	21		0	15	.247	.339	.333	83	-3	3	.971	-3	124	108	2b25,S19,3b7		0.7
1950	Bos N	48	121	17	28	5	0	1	15	14	1	9	.231	.316	.298	67	-6	1	.968	-3	95	82	2b28,3b7,S5		-0.6
1951	Bos N	19	20	5	2	0	0	0	1	7	0	2	.100	.333	.100	24		0-0	1.000	-1	89	50	S10,3b3,2b2		-0.2
1952	StL N	7	3	0	0	0	0	0	0	1	0	2	.000	.250	.000	-25	-0	0-0	.500	-1	0	0	S2		-0.1
1956	Bos A	7	25	4	8	0	0	0	1	3-0	0	3	.320	.393	.320	80	-1	0-0	.935	-1	100	85	2b6		-0.1
1957	Bos A	65	222	23	60	10	3	2	28	22-0	1	26	.270	.335	.369	88	-3	1-0	.962	-8	95	94	2b58		-0.7
Total	9	304	737	93	176	25	7	5	62	104-0	2	64	.239	.333	.312	75	-24	6-0	.958	-12	98	96	2b158,S65,3b17		-2.2

MAUER, JOE   Joseph Patrick   B4.19.1983 St. Paul MN   BL/TR/6-4/220*   [MinA01 1/1]   d4.5

2004	Min A	35	107	18	33	8	1	6	17	11-0	1	14	.308	.369	.570	139	6	1-0	.991	3	133	101	C32/D		1.1
2005	Min A	131	489	61	144	26	2	9	55	61-12	1	64	.294	.372	.411	106	6	13-1	.993	14	191	91	C116,D13	136	2.8
Total	2	166	596	79	177	34	3	15	72	72-12	2	78	.297	.371	.440	112	12	14-1	.993	17	179	93	C148,D14	136	3.9

MAUL, AL   Albert Joseph "Smiling Al"   B10.9.1865 Philadelphia PA   D5.3.1958 Philadelphia PA   BR/TR/6-0/175   d6.20 ▲

1884	Phi U	1	4	0	0	0	0	0	0				.000	.000	.000	-99	-1		1.000	-0	55	0	/P		0.0
1887	Phi N	16	56	15	17	2	2	1	4	15		10	.304	.451	.464	146	4	5	.818	-2	0	0	O8(7/1/0),P7,1b2		0.0
1888	Pit N	74	259	21	54	9	4	0	31	21	3	45	.208	.276	.274	83	-4	9	.975	-0	59	115	1b38,O34(0/3/31),P3		-0.7
1889	Pit N	68	257	37	71	6	6	4	44	29	3	41	.276	.356	.393	121	7	18	.946	10	134	179	O64(39/0/25),P6		1.3
1890	Pit P	45	162	31	42	6	2	0	21	22	0	12	.259	.348	.321	86	-2	5	.904	5	123	205	P30,O15(11/3/1)/S		0.2
1891	Pit N	47	149	15	28	2	4	0	14	20	1	28	.188	.284	.255	59	-8	4	.878	1	132	223	O40(20/12/8),P8		-0.6
1893	Was N	44	134	10	34	8	4	0	12	33	1	14	.254	.405	.373	110	4	1	.889	-0	105	40	P37,O7(5/0/2)		0.0
1894	Was N	41	124	23	30	3	3	2	20	14	7	11	.242	.363	.363	75	-5	1	.877	2	129	-0	P28,O12(1/0/11)		-0.1
1895	Was N	22	72	9	18	5	2	1	16	8	0	7	.250	.308	.375	76	-3	0	.933	0	104	255	P16,O4(2/0/2)		-0.1
1896	Was N	8	28	6	8	1	1	0	5	3	0	2	.286	.355	.393	97	0	2	.923	-1	65	169	P8		0.0
1897	Was N	1	1	0	0	0	0	0	0				.000	.000	.000	-99	-0		1.000	0	219	0	/P		0.0
Bal N	2	3	1	1	0	0	0	0				.333	.333	.333	76	0	1	1.000	-0	55	0	P2		0.0
Year	3	4	1	1	0	0	0	0				.250	.250	.250	32	0	0	1.000	-0	88	0	P3		0.0
1898	Bal N	29	93	21	19	3	2	0	10	16			.204	.333	.280	75	-2	1	.978	-6	64	0	P28/OC		-0.3
1899	Bro N	4	11	2	3	0	0	0	1				.273	.333	.273	66	0	0	.900	-3	137	0	P4		0.0
1900	Phi N	5	15	2	3	0	0	0	1	2			.200	.294	.200	38	0	0	.917	0	115	0	P5		0.0
1901	NY N	3	8	3	3	0	0	0	1				.375	.375	.375	123	1	0	1.000	0	145	0	P3		0.0
Total	15	410	1376	193	331	45	30	7	179	182	16	170	.241	.336	.332	91	-7	44	.910	9	105	94	P187,O185(85/20/80),1b40/S		-0.3

MAULDIN, MARK   Marshall Reese   B11.5.1914 Atlanta GA   D9.2.1990 Union City GA   BR/TR/5-11/170   d9.10

| 1934 | Chi A | 10 | 38 | 3 | 10 | 2 | 0 | 1 | 3 | 3 | 0 | 3 | .263 | .263 | .395 | 66 | -2 | 0 | .906 | -0 | 95 | 155 | 3b10 | | -0.2 |

MAURER, ROB   Robert John   B1.7.1967 Evansville IN   BL/TL/6-3/210*   [TexA88 6/141]   d9.8   Col Evansville   [DL 1993 Tex A 182]

1991	Tex A	13	16	0	1	0	0	0	1	6	0	5	.063	.211	.125	-5	-2	0-0	1.000	1	366	193	1b4,D2		-0.1
1992	Tex A	8	9	1	2	0	0	0	1	1-0	0	2	.222	.300	.222	50	-1	0-0	1.000	1	98	0	1b3/D		-0.1
Total	2	21	25	1	3	0	0	0	3	3-0	1	8	.120	.241	.160	14	-3	0-0	1.000	1	220	88	1b7,D3	182	-0.2

MAURO, CARMEN   Carmen Louis   B11.10.1926 St.Paul MN   D12.19.2003 Carmichael CA   BL/TR/6-0/167*   d10.1

1948	Chi N	3	5	2	1	0	0	1	2		0	0	.200	.429	.800	235	1	0	1.000	0	117	0	O2(0/1/1)		0.1
1950	Chi N	62	185	19	42	4	3	1	10	13	2	31	.227	.285	.297	54	-13	3	.946	-4	92	56	O49(18/1/30)		-1.9
1951	Chi N	13	29	3	5	1	0	0	3	2	1	6	.172	.250	.207	24	-3	0-0	.900	-0	97	166	O6(0/5/1)		-0.4
1953	Bro N	8	9	1	0	0	0	0	0		0	4	.000	.000	.000	-98	-3	0-0	1.000	1	114	344	O6(3/3/0)		-0.3
Was A	17	23	1	4	0	1	0	2	2	0	3	.174	.208	.261	27	-3	0-0	1.000	1	96	0	/OR		-0.2
Phi A	64	165	14	44	4	0	1	17	19	0	21	.267	.342	.339	81	-4	3-4	.969	2	108	135	O49(4/38/7)/3		-0.5
Year	81	188	15	48	4	1	1	19	20	0	24	.255	.327	.330	76	-7	3-4	.971	3	108	151	O55(7/41/7)/3		-0.7
Total	4	167	416	40	96	9	4	3	33	37	3	65	.231	.298	.305	61	-25	6-4	.958	-1	100	104	O113(25/48/40)/3		-3.2

MAVIS, BOB   Robert Henry   B4.8.1918 Milwaukee WI   D3.1.2005 Little Rock AR   BL/TR/5-7/160   d9.17

| 1949 | Det A | 1 | 0 | 0 | 0 | 0 | 0 | 0 | 0 | | | | | | | | | 0-0 | — | 0 | | | /R | | 0.0 |

MAXVILL, DAL   Charles Dallan   B2.18.1939 Granite City IL   BR/TR/5-11/160*   d6.10   C7   Col Washington-St. Louis

1962	StL N	79	189	20	42	3	1	1	18	17-2	1	39	.222	.287	.265	46	-14	1-2	.962	-6	92	115	S76/3		-1.5
1963	StL N	53	51	12	12	2	0	0	3	6-0	0	11	.235	.316	.275	66	-2	0-0	.974	-5	68	84	S24,2b9,3b3		-0.6
1964	†StL N	37	26	4	6	0	0	0	4	0-0	0	7	.231	.231	.231	28	-3	1-0	.972	-2	91	154	2b15,S13/3OR		-0.3
1965	StL N	68	89	10	12	2	0	2	10	7-3	1	15	.135	.206	.202	14	-10	0-0	.993	0	97	132	2b49,S12		-0.8
1966	StL N	134	394	25	96	14	3	0	24	37-9	2	61	.244	.312	.294	69	-15	3-0	.967	18	109	125	S128,2b5/OL		1.4
1967	†StL N	152	476	37	108	14	4	1	41	48-12	1	66	.227	.297	.279	67	-20	0-2	.974	2	102	93	S148,2b7		-0.6
1968	†StL N	151	459	51	116	8	5	1	24	52-9	1	71	.253	.329	.298	91	-4	0-2	.969	-10	96	107	S151		-0.2
1969	StL N	132	372	27	65	10	2	2	32	44-2	1	52	.175	.263	.228	39	-30	1-1	.969	14	107	113	S131		-0.2
1970	StL N	152	399	35	80	5	0	2	28	51-3	0	56	.201	.287	.223	39	-34	0-0	.982	28	118	110	S136,2b22		0.8
1971	StL N	142	356	31	80	10	1	0	24	43-3	1	45	.225	.307	.258	60	-18	1-2	.979	11	108	89	S140		0.7
1972	StL N	105	276	22	61	6	1	1	23	31-4	0	47	.221	.299	.261	61	-14	0-1	.980	5	99	116	S95,2b11		0.1
†Oak A	27	36	2	9	1	0	0	1	6	0	11	.250	.279	.278	66	-2	0-1	.983	-1	108	123	2b24,S4		-0.2
1973	Oak A	29	19	0	4	0	0	0	1	1-0	0	3	.211	.250	.211	32	-2	0-0	.966	-3	76	118	S18,2b11/3		-0.4
Pit N	74	217	19	41	4	3	0	17	22-2	0	40	.189	.261	.235	40	-18	0-0	.971	7	109	105	S74		-0.3
1974	†Oak A	8	22	3	4	0	0	0	4		0	4	.182	.250	.182	23	-2	0-0	.946	1	106	205	S8		-0.1
1975	Oak A	60	52	3	10	0	0	0	6	8-0	0	10	.192	.300	.192	47	-3	0-0	1.000	-2	95	40	2b30,S29/3	23	-0.2
	Oak A	20	10	1	2	0	0	0	1		0	2	.200	.200	.200	14	-1	0-0	.955	-2	80	35	S20,2b2		-0.3
Total	14	1423	3443	302	748	79	24	6	252	370-49	8	538	.217	.293	.259	57	-192	7-11	.972	57	104	107	S1207,2b185,3b7,O2(1/0/1)	23	-2.7

MAXWELL, CHARLIE   Charles Richard "Smokey"   B4.8.1927 Lawton MI   BL/TL/5-11/185*   d9.20   Col Western Michigan

1950	Bos A	3	8	1	0	0	0	0	0		0	3	.000	.111	.000	-63	-2	0-0	1.000	0	124	0	O2R		-0.2
1951	Bos A	49	80	8	15	1	0	3	12	9	0	3	.188	.270	.313	52	-6	0-1	.926	-1	96	0	O13(5/0/8)		-0.8
1952	Bos A	8	15	0	1	0	0	0	2	3	0	11	.067	.222	.133	0	-2	0-0	.966	1	233	0	1b3,O3(0/1/2)		-0.1
1954	Bos A	74	104	9	26	5	1	5	12	0	21	.250	.328	.308	67	-4	3-0	1.000	-1	85	104	O27(21/3/6)		-0.5
1955	Bal A	4	4	0	0	0	0	0	0		0	0	.000	.000	.000	-99	-1	0-0	—	0			/H		-0.1
Det A	55	109	19	29	7	1	7	18	8-0	1	20	.266	.325	.541	134	4	0-0	.967	1	107	145	O26(22/0/4),1b2		0.4
Year	59	113	19	29	7	1	7	18	8-0	1	20	.257	.315	.522	126	3	0-0	.967	1	107	145	O26(22/0/4),1b2		0.3
1956	Det A☆	141	500	96	163	14	3	28	87	79-1	2	74	.326	.414	.534	150	37	1-1	.987	6	117	121	O136(134/0/2)		3.4
1957	Det A★	138	492	75	136	23	3	24	82	76-7	5	84	.276	.377	.482	150	22	3-2	.997	10	114	80	O137(137/0/3)		2.4

YEAR	TM LG	G	AB	R	H	2B	3B	HR	RBI	BB-IB	HP	SO	AVG	OBP	SLG	AOPS	ABR	SB-CS	FA	FR	RNG	THR	GAMES AT POSITION	DL	BFW
1958	Det A	131	397	56	108	14	4	13	65	64-4	0	54	.272	.369	.426	111	8	6-1	.986	-1	102	65	O114(113/0/3),1b14		0.1
1959	Det A	145	518	81	130	12	4	31	95	81-5	6	91	.251	.357	.461	117	13	0-2	.986	4	107	70	O136L		0.8
1960	Det A	134	482	70	114	16	5	24	81	58-6	6	75	.237	.325	.440	102	0	5-0	.996	-0	98	57	O120L		-0.6
1961	Det A	79	131	11	30	4	2	5	18	20-2	1	24	.229	.333	.405	94	-1	0-0	.965	2	122	119	O25(22/0/4)		0.0
1962	Det A	30	67	5	13	2	0	1	9	8-1	0	10	.194	.273	.269	47	-5	0-0	.966	-0	109	0	O15R/1		-0.7
	Chi A	69	206	30	61	8	3	9	43	34-3	0	32	.296	.394	.495	139	12	0-0	.990	1	106	72	O56(49/0/7),1b6		1.0
	Year	99	273	35	74	10	3	10	52	42-4	0	42	.271	.365	.440	115	7	0-0	.985	1	107	56	O71(49/0/22),1b7		0.3
1963	Chi A	71	130	17	30	4	2	3	17	31-2	0	27	.231	.370	.362	111	3	0-0	1.000	-1	80	150	O24L,1b17		-0.1
1964	Chi A	2	2	0	0	0	0	0	0	0-0	0	1	.000	.000	.000	-99	-1	0-0	—	0			/H		5.0
Total	14	1133	3245	478	856	110	26	148	532	484-31	22	545	.264	.360	.451	116	77	18-7	.988	22	105	83	O834(783/4/55),1b43		

MAXWELL, JASON Jason Ramond B3.26.1972 Lewisburg TN BR/TR/6-0/185* [ChiN93 74/1667] d9.1 Col Middle Tennessee

YEAR	TM LG	G	AB	R	H	2B	3B	HR	RBI	BB-IB	HP	SO	AVG	OBP	SLG	AOPS	ABR	SB-CS	FA	FR	RNG	THR	GAMES AT POSITION	DL	BFW
																									0.1
1998	Chi N	7	3	2	1	0	0	1	2	0-0	0	2	.333	.333	1.333	301	1	0-0	1.000	0	296	0	/2		0.1
2000	Min A	64	111	14	27	6	0	1	11	9-0	1	32	.243	.298	.324	56	-7	2-1	.967	4	133	114	2b30,3b19,S5,O2(0/1/1),D7	16	-0.2
2001	Min A	39	68	4	13	4	0	1	10	9-2	0	23	.191	.286	.294	51	-5	2-0	.893	-4	91	77	S12,3b11,2b9,D6	30	-0.7
Total	3	110	182	20	41	10	0	3	23	18-2	1	57	.225	.294	.330	58	-11	4-1	.974	1	124	82	2b40,3b30,S17,D13,O2(0/1/1)	46	-0.8

MAY, CARLOS Carlos B5.17.1948 Birmingham AL BL/TR/6-0/215* [ChiA66 1/18] d9.6 b-Lee

YEAR	TM LG	G	AB	R	H	2B	3B	HR	RBI	BB-IB	HP	SO	AVG	OBP	SLG	AOPS	ABR	SB-CS	FA	FR	RNG	THR	GAMES AT POSITION	DL	BFW
																									-1.1
1968	Chi A	17	67	4	12	1	0	0	1	3-1	0	15	.179	.214	.194	24	-6	0-0	.960	-2	80	0	O17(15/0/2)		-1.1
1969	Chi A★	100	367	62	103	18	2	18	62	58-7	6	66	.281	.385	.488	137	20	1-4	.982	-4	83	126	O100(80/0/22)		0.9
1970	Chi A	150	555	83	158	28	4	12	68	79-9	3	96	.285	.373	.414	114	13	12-5	.991	-2	81	135	O141L,1b7		0.3
1971	Chi A	141	500	64	147	21	7	7	70	62-5	6	61	.294	.375	.406	119	15	16-7	.986	-2	93	85	1b130,O9L	17	0.3
1972	Chi A☆	148	523	83	161	26	3	12	68	79-14	9	70	.308	.405	.438	148	36	23-14	.983	-6	84	119	O145L,1b5		2.5
1973	Chi A	149	553	62	148	20	0	20	96	53-5	5	73	.268	.334	.412	106	4	8-6	.992	0	91	150	D75,O70L,1b2		-0.2
1974	Chi A	149	551	66	137	19	2	8	58	46-3	1	76	.249	.306	.334	82	-13	8-9	.988	1	98	122	O129L,D13		-2.2
1975	Chi A	128	454	55	123	19	2	8	53	67-13	9	46	.271	.373	.374	111	10	12-7	.988	3	129	98	1b63,O46L,D19		0.5
1976	Chi A	20	63	7	11	2	0	0	3	6-0	1	5	.175	.278	.206	43	-4	4-0	1.000	-1	92	0	D10,O9L		-0.5
	†NY A	87	288	38	80	11	2	3	40	34-2	5	32	.278	.358	.361	113	6	1-1	.950	-1	112	0	D71,O7L/1		0.4
	Year	107	351	45	91	13	2	3	43	43-2	5	37	.259	.344	.333	101	2	5-1	.933	-1	103	0	D53,O4(2/0/2)		-0.1
1977	NY A	65	181	21	41	7	1	2	16	17-4	1	24	.227	.292	.309	66	-3	0-0	1.000	-0	107	43	1b3/D		0.1
	Cal A	11	18	0	6	0	0	0	1	5-0	0	1	.333	.478	.333	130	1	0-0	1.000	0	60	0	D54,O4(2/0/2),1b3		-1.0
	Year	76	199	21	47	7	1	2	17	22-4	1	25	.236	.311	.312	72	-7	0-0	1.000	-0	87	127	O677(653/0/26),D242,1b211	17	-0.1
Total	10	1165	4120	545	1127	172	23	90	536	512-63	45	565	.274	.357	.392	111	85-53		.984	-13	87				

MAY, DAVE David La France B12.23.1943 New Castle DE BL/TR/5-10.5/186(185-210) d7.28 s-Derrick

YEAR	TM LG	G	AB	R	H	2B	3B	HR	RBI	BB-IB	HP	SO	AVG	OBP	SLG	AOPS	ABR	SB-CS	FA	FR	RNG	THR	GAMES AT POSITION	DL	BFW
1967	Bal A	36	85	12	20	1	1	1	7	6-2	0	13	.235	.286	.306	73	-3	0-0	.969	-0	99	87	O19(1/0/18)		-0.5
1968	Bal A	84	152	15	29	6	3	0	7	19-3	1	27	.191	.285	.270	69	-5	3-3	.984	-4	83	43	O61(1/16/47)		-1.4
1969	†Bal A	78	120	8	29	6	0	3	10	9-0	2	23	.242	.305	.367	86	-2	2-1	.940	1	94	204	O40R		-0.3
1970	Bal A	25	31	6	6	0	1	1	6	4-0	0	4	.194	.286	.355	74	-1	0-0	1.000	1	47	0	O9R		-0.7
	Mil A	100	342	36	82	8	1	7	31	44-6	2	56	.240	.329	.330	83	-8	8-6	.989	4	112	98	O99(0/99/1)		-1.0
	Year	125	373	42	88	8	2	8	37	48-6	2	60	.236	.325	.332	82	-9	8-6	.989	2	108	93	O108(0/99/10)		1.3
1971	Mil A	144	501	74	139	20	3	16	65	50-4	5	99	.277	.343	.425	119	12	15-9	.975	5	111	100	O142(2/94/48)		1.3
1972	Mil A	143	500	49	119	20	2	9	45	47-8	3	56	.238	.306	.340	94	-4	11-13	.985	5	111	100	O138C		1.3
1973	Mil A★	156	624	96	189	23	4	25	93	44-6	5	78	.303	.352	.473	133	25	6-7	.989	-7	97	76	O121(5/17/108),D8		0.6
1974	Mil A	135	477	56	108	15	4	10	42	28-4	5	73	.226	.273	.325	72	-19	4-3	.964	-0	101	90	O53(13/17/24)		-0.9
1975	Atl N	82	203	28	56	8	0	12	40	25-3	2	27	.276	.361	.493	131	8	1-1	.972	2	101	141	O60(41/0/19)		-1.3
1976	Atl N	105	214	27	46	5	3	3	23	26-3	1	31	.215	.300	.308	70	-4	5-1	.972	2	101	104	O111(21/2/92),D5		-0.2
1977	Tex A	120	340	46	82	14	1	7	42	32-1	4	43	.241	.311	.350	80	-9	4-3	.944	1	99	212	O16(4/7/5),D8		-0.2
1978	Mil A	39	77	14	15	4	0	2	11	9-1	2	10	.195	.295	.325	74	-3	0-0	—	0			/H		-5.1
	Pit N	5	4	0	0	0	0	0	0	1-0	0	1	.000	.200	.000	-38	-1	0-0					/H		
Total	12	1252	3670	462	920	130	20	96	422	344-41	28	501	.251	.318	.375	97	-18	60-47	.978	6	102	104	O1021(88/542/411),D23		

MAY, DERRICK Derrick Brant B7.14.1968 Rochester NY BL/TR/6-4/225(205-235) [ChiN86 1/9] d9.6 f-Dave

YEAR	TM LG	G	AB	R	H	2B	3B	HR	RBI	BB-IB	HP	SO	AVG	OBP	SLG	AOPS	ABR	SB-CS	FA	FR	RNG	THR	GAMES AT POSITION	DL	BFW
1990	Chi N	17	61	8	15	3	0	1	11	2-0	0	7	.246	.270	.344	63	-3	1-0	.972	0	104	89	O17L		-0.
1991	Chi N	15	22	4	5	2	0	1	3	2-0	0	1	.227	.280	.455	102	0	0-0	1.000	1	111	365	O7L		0.
1992	Chi N	124	351	33	96	11	0	8	45	14-4	3	40	.274	.306	.373	89	-6	5-3	.969	-8	81	65	O108(98/0/14)		-1.
1993	Chi N	128	465	62	137	25	2	10	77	31-6	1	41	.295	.336	.422	103	2	10-3	.970	-3	95	90	O122(121/0/2)		-0.
1994	Chi N	100	345	43	98	19	2	8	51	30-4	0	34	.284	.340	.420	97	-2	0-1	.971	-0	106	48	O32L		-0.
1995	Mil A	32	113	15	28	3	1	1	9	5-0	1	18	.248	.286	.319	54	-8	0-1	.974	-4	91	0	O55(43/0/12)/1		0.
	Hou N	78	206	29	62	15	1	8	41	19-0	1	24	.301	.358	.500	133	10	5-0	.970	5	117	145	O71(70/0/3)	15	0.
1996	Hou N	109	259	24	65	12	3	5	33	30-8	2	33	.251	.330	.378	94	-2	2-2	.961	5	113	167	O56(7/0/49)		-1.
1997	Phi N	83	149	8	34	5	1	1	13	8-3	0	26	.228	.266	.295	48	-12	4-1	.984	-0	87	131	O48L,D2		-1.
1998	Mon N	85	180	13	43	8	0	5	15	11-1	0	24	.239	.281	.367	71	-8	0-0	1.000	1	119	491	O5(2/0/3),D9		0.
1999	Bal A	26	49	5	13	1	0	4	12	4-0	0	6	.265	.315	.510	111	0	0-0	.975	-6	96	0	O613(537/0/83),D11/1	15	-5.
Total	10	797	2200	244	596	103	10	52	310	156-26	8	254	.271	.319	.398	92	-29	30-12	.975	-6	96				

MAY, JERRY Jerry Lee B12.14.1943 Staunton VA D6.30.1996 Swoope VA BR/TR/6-2.5/195(185-200) d9.19

YEAR	TM LG	G	AB	R	H	2B	3B	HR	RBI	BB-IB	HP	SO	AVG	OBP	SLG	AOPS	ABR	SB-CS	FA	FR	RNG	THR	GAMES AT POSITION	DL	BFW
1964	Pit N	11	31	1	8	1	0	0	3	3-0	0	9	.258	.314	.258	66	-1	0-0	.988	2	59	38	C11		0.
1965	Pit N	4	2	0	1	0	0	0	1	0-0	0	1	.500	.500	.500	182	0	0-0	1.000	-1	0	0	C4		-0.
1966	Pit N	42	52	6	13	4	0	1	2	2-1	1	15	.250	.291	.385	86	-1	0-1	.984	4	262	99	C41	21	-0.
1967	Pit N	110	325	23	88	13	2	3	22	36-19	3	55	.271	.348	.351	100	1	0-0	.993	7	119	104	C110		-0.
1968	Pit N	137	416	26	91	15	2	1	33	41-12	3	80	.219	.293	.272	72	-13	0-0	.994	-6	142	95	C52	30	-0.
1969	Pit N	62	190	21	44	8	0	7	23	9-0	2	53	.232	.268	.384	84	-5	1-1	.994	11	110	185	C45		0.
1970	Pit N	51	139	13	29	4	2	1	16	21-6	1	25	.209	.313	.288	63	-7	0-0	.997	0	107	99	C71	34	0.
1971	KC A	71	218	16	55	13	2	1	24	27-8	0	37	.252	.329	.344	93	-1	0-0	.979	-6	78	95	C41		-1
1972	KC A	53	116	10	22	5	1	1	6	14-2	1	16	.190	.277	.276	65	-5	0-0	.940	-3	42	32	C11	31	-0
1973	KC A	11	30	4	4	1	1	0	2	3-0	1	5	.133	.235	.233	30	-3	0-0	1.000	0	0	0	C4	31	-0
	NY N	4	8	0	2	0	0	0	1	1-0	1	1	.250	.333	.250	64	0	0-0	.990	7	117	106	C525	116	-0
Total	10	556	1527	120	357	63	10	15	130	157-48	11	293	.234	.307	.318	81	-35	1-2							

MAY, LEE Lee Andrew B3.23.1943 Birmingham AL BR/TR/6-3/205(195-225) d9.1 C10 b-Carlos

YEAR	TM LG	G	AB	R	H	2B	3B	HR	RBI	BB-IB	HP	SO	AVG	OBP	SLG	AOPS	ABR	SB-CS	FA	FR	RNG	THR	GAMES AT POSITION	DL	BFW
1965	Cin N	5	4	1	0	0	0	0	0	0-0	0	1	.000	.000	.000	-94	-1	0-0	—	0			/H		-0
1966	Cin N	25	75	14	25	5	1	2	10	0-0	0	14	.333	.333	.507	119	2	0-1	.972	-1	88	112	1b16		-1
1967	Cin N	127	438	54	116	29	2	12	57	19-3	0	80	.265	.308	.422	97	-1	4-8	.994	1	91	88	1b81,O48(32/0/16)		-1
1968	Cin N	146	559	78	162	32	1	22	80	34-11	6	100	.290	.337	.469	132	21	4-7	.996	-1	91	91	1b122,O33(11/0/22)		-1
1969	Cin N★	158	607	85	169	32	3	38	110	45-8	6	142	.278	.331	.529	132	23	5-4	.993	0	104	95	1b156,O7(5/0/2)		-1
1970	†Cin N	153	605	78	153	34	2	34	94	38-5	2	125	.253	.297	.484	106	-1	1-1	.993	-1	100	114	1b153		-1
1971	Cin N★	147	553	85	154	17	3	39	98	42-2	4	135	.278	.332	.532	143	28	3-0	.996	-3	86	109	1b146	18	-1
1972	Hou N★	148	592	87	168	31	2	29	98	52-12	2	145	.284	.343	.490	138	28	3-1	.996	-2	91	94	1b144		-0
1973	Hou N	148	545	65	147	24	3	28	105	34-10	2	122	.270	.310	.479	118	10	1-0	.994	2	106	103	1b145		-0
1974	Hou N	152	556	59	149	26	0	24	85	17-2	7	97	.268	.294	.444	111	3	1-2	.993	4	113	134	1b144,D2		-0
1975	Bal A	146	580	67	152	28	3	20	99	36-8	5	91	.262	.308	.424	112	7	1-0	.996	3	114	93	1b94,D52		-0
1976	Bal A	148	530	61	137	18	4	25	109	41-8	3	100	.258	.312	.447	129	16	4-1	.995	-3	88	123	1b110,D39		-1
1977	Bal A	150	585	75	148	16	2	27	99	38-5	1	119	.253	.296	.426	100	-3	5-2	.973	0	83	105	D140,1b4		-C
1978	Bal A	148	556	56	137	16	1	25	80	31-5	1	110	.246	.286	.414	101	-3	0-2	.913	-1	0	125	D117,1b2		-C
1979	†Bal A	124	456	59	116	15	0	19	69	28-4	1	100	.254	.297	.412	93	-7	3-4	1.000	-0	71	70	D58,1b7		-C
1980	Bal A	78	222	20	54	10	2	7	31	15-1	0	53	.243	.289	.401	89	-4	0-1	1.000	0	47	142	1b8,D4		-C
1981	†KC A	26	55	3	16	3	0	0	3	3-0	0	14	.291	.328	.345	94	0	0-0	.989	-1	79	102	1b32,D2		-C
1982	KC A	42	91	12	28	5	0	3	12	14-1	0	18	.308	.393	.505	146	6	0-0	.994	-8	97	106	1b1507,D414,O88(48/0/40)	18	-1
Total	18	2071	7609	959	2031	340	31	354	1244	487-85	49	1607	.267	.313	.459	116	126	39-35	.994	-8	97				

MAY, PINKY Merrill Glend B1.18.1911 Laconia IN D9.4.2000 Corydon IN BR/TR/5-11.5/165 d4.21 Mil 1944-45 s-Milt Col Indiana

YEAR	TM LG	G	AB	R	H	2B	3B	HR	RBI	BB-IB	HP	SO	AVG	OBP	SLG	AOPS	ABR	SB-CS	FA	FR	RNG	THR	GAMES AT POSITION	DL	BFW
1939	Phi N	135	464	49	133	27	3	2	62	41	1	20	.287	.346	.371	95	-2	4	.956	10	106	109	3b132		-0
1940	Phi N★	136	501	59	147	24	2	1	48	58	4	30	.293	.371	.355	105	7	2	.954	16	118	58	3b135/S		-1
1941	Phi N	142	490	46	131	14	0	0	39	55	1	17	.267	.344	.318	91	-5	2	.972	24	111	107	3b140		-C
1942	Phi N	115	345	25	82	15	0	0	18	51	1	17	.238	.338	.281	86	-3	3	.963	19	123	120	3b107		-C

YEAR	TM LG	G	AB	R	H	2B	3B	HR	RBI	BB-IB	HP	SO	AVG	OBP	SLG	AOPS	ABR	SB-CS	FA	FR	RNG	THR	GAMES AT POSITION	DL	BFW
1943	Phi N	137	415	31	117	19	2	1	48	56	1	21	.282	.369	.345	.345	111	8	2	.963	9	108	90	3b132		1.9
Total	5	665	2215	210	610	102	11	4	215	261	9	121	.275	.354	.337		98	5	13	.962	77	113	95	3b646/S		10.2

MAY, MILT   Milton Scott B8.1.1950 Gary IN   BL/TR/6-0/190(175-192)   [PitN68 11/237]   d9.8   C14   f-Pinky

1970	Pit N	5	4	1	2	1	0	0	2	0-0	1	0	.500	.600	.750	260	1	0-0	—	0			/H		0.1
1971	†Pit N	49	126	15	35	1	0	6	25	9-3	0	16	.278	.321	.429	111	1	0-0	1.000	4	330	97	C31		0.7
1972	†Pit N	57	139	12	39	10	0	0	14	10-2	0	13	.281	.325	.353	95	-1	0-0	.985	3	139	121	C33		0.5
1973	Pit N	101	283	29	76	8	1	7	31	34-12	2	26	.269	.349	.378	104	2	0-1	.973	-6	101	93	C79		0.0
1974	Hou N	127	405	47	117	17	4	7	54	39-8	1	33	.289	.349	.402	116	8	0-1	.993	3	97	123	C116		1.7
1975	Hou N	111	386	29	93	15	1	4	52	26-3	0	41	.241	.287	.316	73	-16	1-2	.986	8	87	176	C102		-0.4
1976	Det A	6	25	2	7	1	0	0	0	0-0	0	1	.280	.280	.320	72	-1	0-0	1.000	2	133	147	C6	135	0.1
1977	Det A	115	397	32	99	9	3	12	46	26-2	0	31	.249	.291	.378	78	-13	0-0	.986	6	117	106	C111		-0.2
1978	Det A	105	352	24	88	9	0	10	37	27-3	2	26	.250	.305	.361	85	-8	0-0	.979	2	108	95	C94		-0.2
1979	Det A	6	11	1	3	2	0	0	3	1-1	0	1	.273	.333	.455	107	0	0-0	1.000	0	35	0	C5		0.0
	Chi A	65	202	23	51	13	0	7	28	14-1	2	27	.252	.306	.421	94	-2	0-0	.981	2	106	105	C65		0.2
	Year	71	213	24	54	15	0	7	31	15-2	2	28	.254	.307	.423	94	-2	0-0	.982	2	103	100	C70		0.2
1980	SF N	111	358	27	93	16	2	6	50	25-4	1	40	.260	.305	.366	91	-5	0-1	.986	2	98	108	C103	16	0.9
1981	SF N	97	316	20	98	17	0	2	33	34-10	0	29	.310	.376	.383	120	9	1-4	.989	-3	82	93	C93		0.2
1982	SF N	114	395	29	104	19	0	9	39	28-8	0	38	.263	.311	.380	94	-4	0-1	.987	-4	79	144	C110		-0.4
1983	SF N	66	186	18	46	6	0	6	20	21-6	0	23	.247	.324	.376	96	-1	2-2	.981	-1	90	102	C56		0.0
	Pit N	7	12	0	3	0	0	0	0	1-1	0	1	.250	.308	.250	55	-1	0-0	1.000	1	52	242	C4	7	0.0
	Year	73	198	18	49	6	0	6	20	22-7	0	24	.247	.323	.369	93	-2	2-2	.983	-0	88	110	C60		0.0
1984	Pit N	50	96	4	17	3	0	1	8	10-1	0	15	.177	.255	.240	39	-8	0-1	.993	2	97	83	C26		-0.5
Total	15	1192	3693	313	971	147	11	77	443	305-65	9	361	.263	.318	.371	93	-39	4-13	.986	21	105	116	C1034	158	2.5

MAYBERRY, JOHN   John Claiborn B2.18.1949 Detroit MI   BL/TL/6-3/220(215-239)   [HouN67 1/6]   d9.10   C2

1968	Hou N	4	9	0	0	0	0	0	0	0-0	1	2	.000	.100	.000	-69	-2	0-0	1.000	-0	0	65	1b2		-0.3
1969	Hou N	5	4	0	0	0	0	0	0	1-0	0	1	.000	.200	.000	-40	-1	0-0	—	0			/H		-0.1
1970	Hou N	50	148	23	32	3	2	5	14	21-6	2	33	.216	.318	.365	87	-3	1-1	.995	3	125	85	1b45		-0.3
1971	Hou N	46	137	16	25	0	1	7	14	13-2	1	32	.182	.260	.350	75	-5	0-0	.997	-4	57	68	1b37		-0.3
1972	KC A	149	503	65	150	24	3	25	100	78-13	3	74	.298	.394	.507	168	45	0-2	.995	-1	96	120	1b146		-1.4
1973	KC A★	152	510	87	142	20	2	26	100	**122-17**	5	79	.278	**.417**	.478	142	35	3-0	.994	-6	84	110	1b149/D		3.5
1974	KC A★	126	427	63	100	13	1	22	69	77-11	6	72	.234	.358	.424	118	12	4-2	.990	-3	95	112	1b106,D16		1.8
1975	KC A	156	554	95	161	38	1	34	106	**119-16**	4	73	.291	.416	.547	**167**	55	5-3	.988	1	104	97	1b131,D27		0.1
1976	†KC A	161	594	76	138	22	2	13	95	82-7	2	73	.232	.322	.342	95	-22	3-2	.996	-3	93	105	1b160,D2		4.5
1977	†KC A	153	543	73	125	22	1	23	82	83-9	7	86	.230	.336	.401	100	2	1-3	**.995**	-5	83	103	1b145,D8		-1.8
1978	Tor A	152	515	51	129	15	2	22	70	60-2	4	57	.250	.329	.416	107	5	1-2	.993	-13	60	101	1b139,D7		-1.3
1979	Tor A	137	464	61	127	22	1	21	74	69-7	5	60	.274	.372	.461	122	16	1-1	.995	-7	80	103	1b135		0.1
1980	Tor A	149	501	62	124	19	2	30	82	77-9	3	80	.248	.349	.473	119	13	0-0	.994	-5	86	106	1b136,D8		0.0
1981	Tor A	94	290	34	72	6	1	17	43	44-4	8	45	.248	.360	.452	126	11	1-1	.993	-8	67	97	1b80,D10		-0.2
1982	Tor A	17	33	7	9	0	0	2	3	7-1	1	5	.273	.405	.455	127	2	0-0	1.000	-1	36	94	D13,1b4		-1.0
	NY A	69	215	20	45	7	0	8	27	28-2	5	38	.209	.313	.353	84	-4	0-0	.996	-2	78	104	1b63,D4		-1.0
	Year	86	248	27	54	7	0	10	30	35-3	6	43	.218	.326	.367	90	-3	0-0	.996	-3	75	103	1b67,D17		-1.0
Total	15	1620	5447	733	1379	211	19	255	879	881-106	55	810	.253	.360	.439	122	179	20-17	.994	-53	85	104	1b1478,D96		1.8

MAYE, LEE   Arthur Lee B12.11.1934 Tuscaloosa AL   D7.17.2002 Riverside CA   BL/TR/6-2/190*   d7.17

1959	Mil N	51	140	17	42	5	1	4	16	7-2	1	26	.300	.338	.436	114	2	2-2	.976	2	109	98	O44(24/0/21)		0.1
1960	Mil N	41	83	14	25	6	0	1	4	7-2	1	21	.301	.359	.373	110	2	5-0	.968	-1	89	67	O19(15/0/4)		0.1
1961	Mil N	110	373	68	101	11	5	14	41	36-2	3	50	.271	.337	.440	112	5	10-1	.972	-3	98	71	O96(26/0/72)		-0.2
1962	Mil N	99	349	40	85	10	0	10	41	25-2	1	58	.244	.294	.358	77	-12	9-3	.977	1	110	33	O94(38/60/2)	35	-1.5
1963	Mil N	124	442	67	120	22	7	11	34	36-2	3	52	.271	.329	.428	118	10	14-2	.983	1	108	57	O111(70/73/3)		1.0
1964	Mil N	153	588	96	179	**44**	5	10	74	34-3	4	54	.304	.346	.447	121	17	5-10	.961	-4	103	86	O135(54/92/0),3b5		0.6
1965	Mil N	15	53	8	16	2	0	2	7	2-0	1	6	.302	.339	.453	120	1	0-0	.962	1	93	295	O13(4/9/0)		0.1
	Hou N	108	415	38	104	17	7	3	36	20-3	1	37	.251	.285	.347	83	-11	1-5	.953	-3	101	110	O103(92/11/3)		-1.8
	Year	123	468	46	120	19	7	5	43	22-3	2	43	.256	.291	.359	88	-10	1-5	.954	1	100	131	O116(96/20/3)		-1.7
1966	Hou N	115	358	38	103	12	4	9	36	20-5	2	26	.288	.323	.419	113	5	4-3	.949	-2	95	68	O97L		-0.3
1967	Cle A	115	297	43	77	20	4	9	27	26-4	1	47	.259	.321	.444	123	8	3-3	.981	-4	90	49	O77(23/10/54)/2		0.0
1968	Cle A	109	299	20	84	13	2	4	26	15-0	1	24	.281	.316	.378	112	3	0-0	.984	3	113	104	O80(71/0/10)/1		0.3
1969	Cle A	43	108	9	27	5	0	1	15	8-2	1	15	.250	.305	.324	75	-4	1-0	.982	1	125	0	O28(26/0/2)		-0.4
	Was A	71	238	41	69	9	3	9	26	20-0	0	26	.290	.345	.466	132	5	1-3	.944	-4	99	23	O65(6/4/56)		0.2
	Year	114	346	50	96	14	3	10	41	28-2	1	40	.277	.332	.422	112	5	2-3	.957	-3	107	16	O93(32/4/58)		-0.2
1970	Was A	96	255	28	67	12	1	7	30	21-1	1	32	.263	.321	.400	102	0	4-2	1.000	-5	71	104	O68(6/0/63)/3		-0.8
	Chi A	6	6	1	1	0	0	0	0	0-0	0	1	.167	.167	.167	-8	-1	0-0	—	0			/H		-0.1
	Year	102	261	28	68	12	1	7	31	21-1	1	33	.261	.318	.395	99	-1	4-2	1.000	-5	71	104	O68(6/0/63)/3		-0.9
1971	Chi A	32	44	6	9	2	0	1	7	5-1	0	7	.205	.280	.318	69	-2	0-0	1.000	0	82	217	O10(2/0/8)		-0.2
Total	13	1288	4048	533	1109	190	39	94	419	282-29	19	481	.274	.323	.410	108	32	59-34	.970	-14	101	75	O1040(554/259/298),3b6/12	50	-2.9

MAYER, ED   Edward H. B8.16.1866 Marshall IL   D5.18.1913 Chicago IL   5-8.5/155   d4.19

1890	Phi N	120	484	49	117	25	5	1	70	22	8	36	.242	.286	.320	75	-17	20	.878	-11	90	111	3b117,O4C		-2.3
1891	Phi N	68	268	24	50	2	4	0	31	14	4	29	.187	.238	.224	40	-24	7	.895	-3	103	65	3b31,O29(4/24/1),S7/2		-2.4
Total	2	188	752	73	167	27	9	1	101	36	12	65	.222	.269	.286	60	-41	27	.882	-13	93	102	3b148,O33(4/28/1),S7/2		-4.7

MAYER, SAM   Samuel Frankel (b Samuel Frankel Erskine) B2.28.1893 Atlanta GA   D7.1.1962 Atlanta GA   BR/TL/5-10/164   d9.14   b-Erskine

1915	Was A	11	29	5	7	0	0	1	4	4	0	2	.241	.333	.345	101	0	1-2	1.000	-1	97	96	O9(1/0/8)/P1		-0.1

MAYER, WALLY   Walter A. B7.8.1890 Cincinnati OH   D11.18.1951 Minnetonka MN   BR/TR/5-11/168   d9.28   Mil 1918

1911	Chi A	1	3	0	0	0	0	0	0	0	0		.000	.000	.000	16	0	0	.900	-0	190	64	/C		0.0
1912	Chi A	9	9	0	0	0	0	0	0	1	0		.000	.100	.000	-73	-2	0	1.000	-0	95	44	C6		-0.2
1914	Chi A	40	85	7	14	3	1	0	5	14	1	23	.165	.290	.224	55	-4	1-1	.968	5	133	109	C33/3		0.3
1915	Chi A	22	54	3	12	3	1	0	5	5	0		.222	.288	.315	78	-2	0-2	.990	1	181	61	C20		0.2
1917	Bos A	4	12	2	2	0	0	0	0	5	0	2	.167	.412	.167	78	0	0	.964	1	125	125	C4		0.2
1918	Bos A	26	49	7	11	4	0	0	5	5	0	4	.224	.321	.306	91	0	0	.964	-0	108	89	C23		0.1
1919	StL A	30	62	2	14	4	1	0	5	8	0	11	.226	.314	.323	77	-2	0	.959	3	107	123	C25		0.3
Total	7	132	274	22	53	14	3	0	20	42	1	51	.193	.303	.266	68	-10	1-3	.969	8	131	98	C112/3		0.7

MAYES, PADDY   Adair Bushyhead B3.17.1885 Locust Grove OK   D5.28.1962 Fayetteville AR   BL/TR/5-11/160   d6.11

1911	Phi N	5	5	1	0	0	0	0	0	0-0	0	0	.000	.286	.000	-17	-1	0	1.000	0	0	0	O2		0.0

MAYNARD, BUSTER   James Walter B3.25.1913 Henderson NC   D9.7.1977 Durham NC   BR/TR/5-11/170   d9.17   Mil 1944-45

1940	NY N	7	29	6	8	2	1	2	2	2	0	6	.276	.323	.586	145	1	0	.929	-1	87	0	O7(0/3/4)		0.0
1942	NY N	89	190	17	47	4	1	4	32	19	1	19	.247	.319	.342	93	-2	3	.982	5	105	160	O58(7/48/4),3b10/2		0.2
1943	NY N	121	393	43	81	8	2	9	32	24	0	27	.206	.252	.305	60	-22	3	.965	-2	86	145	O74(25/39/13),3b22		-2.9
1946	NY N	7	4	2	0	0	0	0	0	1	0	1	.000	.200	.000	-41	-1	0	.750	-0	103	0	O3(0/1/2)		-0.1
Total	4	224	616	68	136	14	5	14	66	46	1	53	.221	.276	.328	74	-24	6	.967	2	93	140	O142(32/91/23),3b32/2		-2.8

MAYNARD, CHICK   Le Roy Evans B11.2.1896 Turners Falls MA   D1.31.1957 Bangor ME   BL/TR/5-9/150   d6.27   Col Dartmouth

1922	Bos A	12	24	1	3	0	0	0	3	0-0	0	2	.125	.222	.125	-8	-4	0-1	.872	-3	90	26	S12		-0.6

MAYNE, BRENT   Brent Danem B4.19.1968 Loma Linda CA   BL/TR/6-1/190*   [KCA89 1/13]   d9.18   Col Cal St.-Fullerton

1990	KC A	5	13	2	3	0	0	0	1	3-0	0	3	.231	.375	.231	74	-0	0-0	.970	0	52	74	C5		0.0
1991	KC A	85	231	22	58	8	0	3	31	23-4	1	42	.251	.315	.325	78	-7	2-4	.987	-0	82	104	C80/D		-0.4
1992	KC A	82	213	16	48	10	0	0	18	11-0	1	26	.225	.260	.272	49	-15	0-4	.990	3	146	94	C62,3b8/D		-1.0
1993	KC A	71	205	22	52	9	1	2	22	18-7	1	31	.254	.317	.337	71	-8	3-2	.995	-0	81	84	C68/D		-0.5
1994	KC A	46	144	19	37	5	1	2	20	14-1	1	27	.257	.323	.347	69	-7	1-0	.996	2	94	96	C42,D3		-0.2
1995	KC A	110	307	23	77	18	1	1	27	25-1	3	41	.251	.313	.326	65	-15	0-1	.995	11	108	57	C103		0.1
1996	NY N	70	99	9	26	6	0	1	6	5-2	0	23	.263	.342	.354	88	-1	0-1	1.000	-8	54	21	C21		-0.8
1997	Oak A	85	256	29	74	12	0	6	22	18-1	4	33	.289	.342	.414	95	-2	1-0	.996	-12	88	95	C83		-0.8

YEAR	TM LG	G	AB	R	H	2B	3B	HR	RBI	BB-IB	HP	SO	AVG	OBP	SLG	AOPS	ABR	SB-CS	FA	FR	RNG	THR	GAMES AT POSITION	DL	BFW
1998	SF N	94	275	26	75	15	0	3	32	37-3	1	47	.273	.359	.360	95	-1	2-1	.991	-7	88	70	C88		-0.2
1999	SF N	117	322	39	97	32	0	2	39	43-5	5	65	.301	.389	.419	113	9	2-2	.995	-2	96	116	C105		-0.1
2000	Col N	117	335	36	101	21	0	6	64	47-13	1	48	.301	.381	.418	84	-6	1-3	.990	0	101	79	C105/P		0.8
2001	Col N	49	160	15	53	7	0	0	20	16-3	0	24	.331	.385	.375	83	-3	0-0	.997	8	118	114	C44/1		-1.1
	KC A	51	166	13	40	4	1	2	20	10-2	1	17	.241	.283	.313	53	-12	1-2	.993	-3	101	91	C49		-1.1
2002	KC A	101	326	35	77	8	2	4	30	34-1	0	54	.236	.309	.310	59	-19	4-4	.993	-1	115	100	C99	28	-1.4
2003	KC A	113	372	39	91	17	1	6	36	32-5	3	59	.245	.307	.344	68	-17	0-2	.994	-1	104	102	C112		-1.1
2004	Ari N	36	94	9	24	6	1	0	10	13-4	0	17	.255	.343	.340	73	-3	1-0	.990	-1	105	213	C30/1	39	-0.2
	†LA N	47	96	5	18	0	0	0	5	14-4	0	24	.188	.286	.188	28	-10	0-0	1.000	-0	117	88	C47		-0.8
Year		83	190	14	42	6	1	0	15	27-8	0	41	.221	.314	.263	52	-13	1-0	.995	-1	112	144	C77/1		-1.0
Total	15	1279	3614	359	951	178	8	38	403	370-55	21	580	.263	.332	.348	76	-117	18-27	.993	-11	101	93	C1143,3b8,D6,1b2/P	67	-6.5

MAYO, EDDIE   Edward Joseph "Hotshot" (b Edward Joseph Mayoski) B4.15.1910 Holyoke MA   BL/TR/5-11/178   d5.22 C4

YEAR	TM LG	G	AB	R	H	2B	3B	HR	RBI	BB-IB	HP	SO	AVG	OBP	SLG	AOPS	ABR	SB-CS	FA	FR	RNG	THR	GAMES AT POSITION	DL	BFW
1936	†NY N	46	141	11	28	4	1	1	8	11	0	12	.199	.257	.262	40	-12	0	.981	3	111	191	3b40		-0.8
1937	Bos N	65	172	19	39	6	1	1	18	15	1	20	.227	.293	.291	65	-8	1	.956	-5	90	37	3b50		-1.2
1938	Bos N	8	14	2	3	0	0	1	4	1	0	0	.214	.267	.429	98	-4	0	.923	1	114	332	3b6,S2		0.1
1943	Phi A	128	471	49	103	10	1	0	28	34	5	32	.219	.278	.244	54	-28	2-0	.978	34	114	121	2b143,S11		-2.9
1944	Det A	154	607	76	151	18	3	5	63	57	4	23	.249	.317	.313	76	-18	9-13	.980	20	112	115	2b124		2.2
1945	†Det A*	134	501	71	143	24	3	10	54	47	0	29	.285	.347	.405	111	7	7-7	.965	-6	92	49	2b49		3.5
1946	Det A	51	202	21	51	9	2	0	22	14	0	12	.252	.301	.317	68	-9	6-2	.983	-14	93	83	2b142		-1.2
1947	Det A	142	535	66	149	28	4	6	48	48	0	28	.279	.338	.379	96	-3	3-7	.975	-7	91	83	2b86,3b10		-1.1
1948	Det A	106	370	35	92	20	1	2	42	30	3	19	.249	.310	.324	67	-18	1-9	.978	26	103	102	2b544,3b229,S13		-2.3
Total	9	834	3013	350	759	119	16	26	287	257	13	175	.252	.313	.328	78	-89	29-38							-3.7

MAYO, JACKIE   John Lewis B7.26.1925 Litchfield IL   BL/TR/6-1/190*   d9.19 Col Notre Dame

YEAR	TM LG	G	AB	R	H	2B	3B	HR	RBI	BB-IB	HP	SO	AVG	OBP	SLG	AOPS	ABR	SB-CS	FA	FR	RNG	THR	GAMES AT POSITION	DL	BFW
1948	Phi N	12	35	7	8	2	1	0	3	7	2	7	.229	.386	.343	101	1	1	1.000	1	114	114	O11L		0.1
1949	Phi N	45	39	3	5	0	0	0	2	4	0	5	.128	.209	.128	-8	-6	0	.889	0	123	117	O25(0/1/24)		-0.6
1950	†Phi N	18	36	1	8	3	0	0	3	2	0	5	.222	.263	.306	50	-3	0	.958	-0	113	0	O15L		-0.3
1951	Phi N	9	7	1	1	0	0	0	0	0	0	1	.143	.143	.143	-23	-1	0-0	1.000	0	147	0	O5L		-0.1
1952	Phi N	50	119	13	29	5	0	1	4	12	0	17	.244	.313	.311	74	-4	1-3	1.000	3	111	48	O27(24/1/2),1b6		-0.4
1953	Phi N	5	4	0	0	0	0	0	0	0	0	0	.000	.000	.000	-99	-1	0-0	—	-0	0	0	/OR		-0.1
Total	6	139	240	25	51	10	1	1	12	25	2	35	.213	.292	.275	56	-14	2-3	.972	4	114	62	O84(55/2/27),1b6		-1.4

MAYS, WILLIE   Willie Howard "The Say Hey Kid" B5.6.1931 Westfield AL   BR/TR/5-11/180(170-185)   d5.25 Mil 1952-53 C6 HF1979 Negro Lg 1948-50

YEAR	TM LG	G	AB	R	H	2B	3B	HR	RBI	BB-IB	HP	SO	AVG	OBP	SLG	AOPS	ABR	SB-CS	FA	FR	RNG	THR	GAMES AT POSITION	DL	BFW
1951	†NY N	121	464	59	127	22	5	20	68	57	2	60	.274	.356	.472	120	13	7-4	.976	2	105	110	O121C		0.4
1952	NY N	34	127	17	30	2	4	4	23	16	1	17	.236	.326	.409	102	9	4-1	.991	4	110	161	O34C		6.2
1954	†NY N	151	565	119	195	33	13	41	110	66	2	57	.345	.411	.667	176	61	8-5	.985	10	109	112	O151C		6.8
1955	NY N★	152	580	123	185	18	13	51	127	79-13	4	60	.319	.400	.659	176	62	24-4	.982	12	102	195	O152C		4.1
1956	NY N★	152	578	101	171	27	8	36	84	68-20	1	65	.296	.369	.557	146	37	40-10	.979	6	104	126	O152C		5.6
1957	NY N★	152	585	112	195	26	20	35	97	76-15	1	62	.333	.407	.626	174	61	38-19	.980	1	100	150	O150C		6.3
1958	SF N★	152	600	121	208	33	11	29	96	78-12	1	56	.347	.419	.583	157	47	31-6	.980	7	106	136	O151C		4.1
1959	SF N★	151	575	125	180	43	5	34	104	65-9	2	58	.313	.381	.583	164	51	27-4	.984	-3	101	72	O147(2/146/0)		5.0
1960	SF N★	153	595	107	190	29	12	29	103	61-11	4	70	.319	.381	.555	157	47	25-10	.981	4	105	108	O152C		4.5
1961	SF N★	154	572	129	176	32	3	40	123	81-15	2	77	.308	.393	.584	162	52	18-9	.980	-2	106	64	O153C		6.1
1962	†SF N★	162	621	130	189	36	5	49	141	78-11	4	85	.304	.384	.615	167	58	18-2	.991	7	115	57	O157C/S		6.0
1963	SF N★	157	596	115	187	32	7	38	103	66-5	2	83	.314	.380	.582	156	50	8-3	.981	3	110	68	O157C/1S3		5.8
1964	SF N★	157	578	121	171	21	9	47	111	82-13	1	72	.296	.383	.607	171	54	19-5	.984	4	110	103	O155C/1(1/147/5)		6.9
1965	SF N★	157	558	118	177	21	3	52	112	76-16	0	71	.317	.398	.645	184	62	9-4	.980	3	110	163	O151(1/147/5)		3.9
1966	SF N★	152	552	99	159	29	4	37	103	70-11	2	81	.288	.368	.556	149	37	5-1	.982	5	113	79	O150(1/145/5)		1.1
1967	SF N★	141	486	83	128	22	2	22	70	51-7	2	92	.263	.334	.453	125	16	6-0	.976	-3	101	44	O134C		3.7
1968	SF N★	148	498	84	144	20	5	23	79	67-7	2	81	.289	.372	.488	125	14	6-2	.978	-10	87	63	O108(0/106/2)/1		0.3
1969	SF N★	117	403	64	114	17	3	13	58	49-7	3	90	.283	.362	.437	125	14	5-0	.975	-2	101	89	O129C,1b5		2.5
1970	SF N★	139	478	94	139	15	2	28	83	79-3	3	90	.291	.390	.506	141	29	23-3	.970	-4	104	47	O84C,1b48		3.7
1971	†SF N★	136	417	82	113	24	5	18	61	112-11	3	123	.271	.425	.482	159	41	23-3	1.000	-1	91	0	O14C		-0.1
1972	SF N	19	49	8	9	2	0	0	3	17-1	0	5	.184	.394	.224	78	0	3-0	.974	-1	108	120	O49(1/48/0),1b11		1.
	NY N★	69	195	27	52	9	1	8	19	43-5	1	43	.267	.402	.446	143	13	1-5	.979	-1	104	93	O63(1/62/0),1b11		1.0
Year		88	244	35	61	11	1	8	22	60-6	1	48	.250	.400	.402	129	13	4-5	.991	1	115	85	O45(5/43/9),1b17	21	-0.7
1973	†NY N★	66	209	24	44	10	0	6	25	27-0	1	47	.211	.303	.344	80	-6	1-0	.981	1	105	100	O...	21	
Total	22	2992	10881	2062	3283	523	140	660	1903	1464-192	44	1526	.302	.384	.557	156	855	338-103	.981	50	105	100	O2842(10/2827/21),1b84,S2/3		84.5

MAZEROSKI, BILL   William Stanley "Maz" B9.5.1936 Wheeling WV   BR/TR/5-11.5/183*   d7.7 C3 HF2001

YEAR	TM LG	G	AB	R	H	2B	3B	HR	RBI	BB-IB	HP	SO	AVG	OBP	SLG	AOPS	ABR	SB-CS	FA	FR	RNG	THR	GAMES AT POSITION	DL	BFW
1956	Pit N	81	255	30	62	8	1	3	14	18-1	1	24	.243	.293	.318	66	-13	0-0	.981	9	111	110	2b81		0.
1957	Pit N	148	526	59	149	27	7	8	54	27-2	1	49	.283	.318	.407	96	-4	3-3	.978	3	108	105	2b144		0.
1958	Pit N★	152	567	69	156	24	6	19	68	25-3	3	71	.275	.308	.439	98	-4	1-1	.980	18	113	110	2b152		2.
1959	Pit N	135	493	50	119	15	6	7	59	29-1	1	54	.241	.283	.339	66	-26	1-1	.989	30	109	144	2b133		-2.3
1960	†Pit N★	151	538	58	147	21	5	11	64	40-15	1	55	.273	.320	.392	95	-5	4-0	.975	37	115	129	2b151		3.
1961	Pit N	152	558	71	148	21	2	13	59	26-10	3	55	.265	.298	.380	79	-18	2-1	.985	41	112	135	2b152		3.
1962	Pit N★	159	572	55	155	24	9	14	81	37-16	2	47	.271	.315	.418	95	-9	0-3	.984	56	127	153	2b159		5.
1963	Pit N★	142	534	43	131	22	8	8	52	32-6	0	46	.245	.286	.343	80	-14	2-0	.975	35	118	119	2b138		4.
1964	Pit N☆	162	601	66	161	22	8	10	64	29-11	0	52	.268	.300	.381	81	-9	1-1	.988	26	116	142	2b162		4.
1965	Pit N	130	494	52	134	17	1	6	54	18-5	2	34	.271	.294	.346	81	-13	2-1	.992	41	116	149	2b127		4.
1966	Pit N	162	621	56	163	22	7	16	82	31-9	1	62	.262	.296	.398	91	-9	4-3	.981	21	110	116	2b162		2.
1967	Pit N★	163	639	62	167	25	3	9	77	30-7	0	55	.261	.292	.352	84	-15	1-2	.981	20	114	124	2b163		2.
1968	Pit N	143	506	36	127	18	2	6	42	38-10	2	38	.251	.304	.312	87	-8	3-4	.988	14	113	115	2b142		1.
1969	Pit N	67	227	13	52	7	1	3	25	22-3	1	16	.229	.298	.308	73	-8	1-1	.987	20	114	128	2b65		1.
1970	†Pit N	112	367	29	84	14	0	7	39	27-9	2	40	.229	.283	.324	63	-20	2-0	.986	-4	100	82	2b46,3b7		-1.
1971	†Pit N	70	193	17	49	3	1	1	16	15-1	0	21	.254	.303	.295	71	-7	0-0	.986	-1	106	96	2b15,3b3	19	-0.
1972	†Pit N	34	64	3	12	4	0	0	3	3-1	0	5	.188	.217	.250	35	-5	0-0	.983	361	113	127	2b2094,3b10	19	35.
Total	17	2163	7755	769	2016	294	62	138	853	447-110	20	706	.260	.299	.367	84	-184	27-23							

MAZZERA, MEL   Melvin Leonard "Mike" B1.31.1914 Stockton CA D12.17.1997 Stockton CA   BL/TL/5-11/180   d9.9

YEAR	TM LG	G	AB	R	H	2B	3B	HR	RBI	BB-IB	HP	SO	AVG	OBP	SLG	AOPS	ABR	SB-CS	FA	FR	RNG	THR	GAMES AT POSITION	DL	BFW
1935	StL A	12	30	4	7	2	0	1	2	4	0	9	.233	.324	.400	82	-1	0-0	.950	0	105	161	O10(4/3/3)		-0.
1937	StL A	7	7	1	2	2	0	0	0	0	0	2	.286	.286	.571	110	0	0-0	—	0			/H		-0.
1938	StL A	86	204	33	57	8	2	6	29	12	3	25	.279	.329	.426	88	-5	1-1	.976	2	93	230	O47(25/8/14)		-0.
1939	StL A	33	110	21	33	5	2	3	22	10	1	20	.300	.364	.464	108	1	0-0	.983	0	105	57	O25(18/0/7)		-0.
1940	Phi N	69	156	16	37	5	4	0	13	19	0	15	.237	.320	.321	80	-4	1	.985	1	90	202	O42(26/2/16),1b11		-1
Total	5	207	507	75	136	22	8	10	66	45	4	71	.268	.333	.402	90	-9	2-2	.978	3	96	175	O124(73/13/40),1b11		-1

MAZZILLI, LEE   Lee Louis B3.25.1955 New York NY   BB/TR/6-1/185(180-195)   [NYN73 1/14] d9.7 M2/C4

YEAR	TM LG	G	AB	R	H	2B	3B	HR	RBI	BB-IB	HP	SO	AVG	OBP	SLG	AOPS	ABR	SB-CS	FA	FR	RNG	THR	GAMES AT POSITION	DL	BFW
1976	NY N	24	77	9	15	2	0	2	7	14-0	1	10	.195	.323	.299	82	-1	5-4	.983	2	112	165	O23(2/21/0)		0
1977	NY N	159	537	66	134	24	3	6	46	72-6	1	72	.250	.340	.339	86	-8	22-15	.992	3	108	95	O156C		1
1978	NY N	148	542	78	148	28	5	16	61	69-6	1	82	.273	.353	.432	122	17	20-13	.987	-1	101	96	O144C		2
1979	NY N★	158	597	78	181	34	4	15	79	93-5	1	74	.303	.395	.449	134	32	34-12	.989	-5	94	111	O143C,1b15		-1
1980	NY N	152	578	82	162	31	4	16	76	82-11	3	92	.280	.370	.431	125	22	41-15	.983	-4	83	99	1b92,O66C		-0
1981	NY N	95	324	56	74	14	5	6	34	46-3	2	53	.228	.324	.358	95	-2	17-7	.970	-1	102	75	O89(51/40/0)		-0
1982	Tex A	58	195	23	47	8	0	4	17	28-0	1	15	.241	.339	.344	92	-1	11-6	.945	-2	88	65	O26(11/15/2),D24	40	-0
	NY A	37	128	20	34	2	0	4	16	15-0	1	15	.266	.347	.422	112	2	2-3	.995	-2	54	136	1b23,O2L,D9		-0
Year		95	323	43	81	10	0	8	33	43-0	2	30	.251	.342	.375	100	1	13-9	.949	-4	89	60	D33,O28(13/15/2),1b23		-0
1983	Pit N	109	246	37	59	9	0	5	24	49-1	1	43	.240	.365	.337	100	1	15-5	.985	-1	102	122	O57(5/53/0),1b7		0
1984	Pit N	111	266	37	75	14	2	6	39	40-2	1	42	.282	.388	.414	127	7	8-1	.986	-6	63	129	O74L,1b5	15	-1
1985	Pit N	92	117	20	33	8	0	1	9	26-1	0	25	.282	.425	.376	92	1	3-3	1.000	-1	63	129	O18(16/3/0),1b7		-0
1986	Pit N	61	93	18	21	9	0	2	8	26-1	0	25	.226	.392	.301	92	1	1-1	1.000	-1	120	0	O10(8/0/2),1b8		-0
	†NY N	39	58	10	16	3	0	2	7	12-1	2	14	.276	.401	.431	137	7	4-4	1.000	-2	110		O28(24/3/2),1b15		-0
Year		100	151	28	37	5	1	3	15	38-2	2	36	.245	.401	.351	109	7	5-3	1.000	-1	87	101	O25(12/2/13),1b13		-0
1987	NY N	88	124	26	38	8	1	3	24	21-3	0	14	.306	.399	.460	135	7	5-3							

YEAR	TM LG	G	AB	R	H	2B	3B	HR	RBI	BB-IB	HP	SO	AVG	OBP	SLG	AOPS	ABR	SB-CS	FA	FR	RNG	THR	GAMES AT POSITION	DL	BFW
1988	†NY N	68	116	9	17	2	0	0	12	12-0	1	16	.147	.227	.164	16	-13	4-1	1.000	-1	100	147	O18(13/0/6),1b16		-1.6
1989	NY N	48	60	10	11	2	0	2	7	17-0	0	19	.183	.364	.317	100	1	3-0	.889	-1	93	0	O10(4/1/5),1b8		0.0
	†Tor A	28	66	12	15	3	0	4	11	17-1	2	16	.227	.395	.455	142	5	2-0	.944	-1	96	74	D19,1b2,O2R		0.4
Total 14		1475	4124	571	1068	191	24	93	460	642-41	20	627	.259	.359	.385	108	71	197-90	.986	-24	100	92	O868(201/647/30),1b215,D52	55	3.2

McALEER, JIMMY James Robert "Loafer" B7.10.1864 Youngstown OH D4.29.1931 Youngstown OH BR/TR/6-0/175 d4.24 M11

YEAR	TM LG	G	AB	R	H	2B	3B	HR	RBI	BB-IB	HP	SO	AVG	OBP	SLG	AOPS	ABR	SB-CS	FA	FR	RNG	THR	GAMES AT POSITION	DL	BFW
1889	Cle N	110	447	66	105	6	6	0	35	30	4	49	.235	.289	.275	59	-26	37	.955	8	136	237	O110C		-2.0
1890	Cle P	86	341	58	91	8	7	1	42	37	1	33	.267	.340	.340	89	-4	21	.940	6	90	109	O86C		-0.1
1891	†Cle N	136	565	97	135	16	11	1	61	49	5	47	.239	.305	.312	77	-11	51	.924	5	88	26	O136(124/13/0)		-1.5
1892	†Cle N	149	571	92	136	26	7	4	70	63	4	54	.238	.318	.329	92	-5	40	.948	9	75	135	O149C		-0.6
1893	Cle N	91	350	63	83	5	1	2	41	35	4	21	.237	.314	.274	53	-24	32	.928	-1	98	91	O91(2/89/0)		-2.6
1894	Cle N	64	253	36	73	15	1	2	40	13	4	17	.289	.331	.379	68	-14	14	.953	3	85	126	O64C		-1.2
1895	†Cle N	132	532	85	144	17	3	0	68	38	6	37	.271	.326	.314	62	-31	32	.934	-2	70	25	O132C		-3.4
1896	†Cle N	116	455	70	131	16	4	1	54	47	1	32	.288	.361	.347	82	-11	24	.958	3	108	133	O116C		-1.3
1897	Cle N	24	91	6	20	2	0	0	10	7	1		.220	.283	.242	37	-8	4	.947	-0	94	0	O24(1/23/0)		-0.9
1898	Cle N	106	366	47	87	3	0	0	48	46	5		.238	.331	.246	67	-13	7	.965	1	70	131	O104(1/102/1),2b2		-1.7
1901	Cle A	3	7	0	1	0	0	0	0	0			.143	.143	.143	-22	-1	0	1.000	-0	0	0	O2C/P3M		-0.1
1902	StL A	2	3	0	2	0	0	0	0	0			.667	.667	.667	274	1	0	—	-0	0	0	O2(0/1/1),M		0.1
1907	StL A	2	0	0	0	0	0	0	0	0	0					0	0	0	—	0			/RM		0.0
Total 13		1021	3981	620	1008	114	40	11	469	365	38	290	.253	.322	.310	72	-154	262	.944	31	90	106	O1016(128/887/2),2b2/3P		-15.3

McALEESE, JACK John James B1877 Sharon PA D11.15.1950 New York NY BR/TR/5-8/? d8.10

YEAR	TM LG	G	AB	R	H	2B	3B	HR	RBI	BB-IB	HP	SO	AVG	OBP	SLG	AOPS	ABR	SB-CS	FA	FR	RNG	THR	GAMES AT POSITION	DL	BFW
1901	Chi A	1	1	0	0	0	0	0	0	0	0		.000	.000	.000	-99	0	0	1.000	0	117	0	/P		0.0
1909	StL A	85	267	33	57	7	0	0	12	32	9		.213	.318	.240	82	-3	18	.910	-1	119	93	O79(27/32/20),3b2		-0.8
Total 2		86	268	33	57	7	0	0	12	32	9		.213	.317	.239	82	-3	18	.910	-1	119	93	O79(27/32/20),3b2/P		-0.8

McALLESTER, BILL William Lusk B12.29.1889 Chattanooga TN D3.3.1970 Chattanooga TN BR/TR/6-0/175 d5.2 Col Tennessee

YEAR	TM LG	G	AB	R	H	2B	3B	HR	RBI	BB-IB	HP	SO	AVG	OBP	SLG	AOPS	ABR	SB-CS	FA	FR	RNG	THR	GAMES AT POSITION	DL	BFW
1913	StL A	49	85	3	13	4	0	0	6	11	0	12	.153	.250	.200	33	-7	2	.908	-2	110	84	C39		-0.8

McALLISTER, SPORT Lewis William B7.23.1874 Austin MS D7.17.1962 Wyandotte MI BB/TR/5-11/180 d8.7 OF(17/10/123) ▲

YEAR	TM LG	G	AB	R	H	2B	3B	HR	RBI	BB-IB	HP	SO	AVG	OBP	SLG	AOPS	ABR	SB-CS	FA	FR	RNG	THR	GAMES AT POSITION	DL	BFW
1896	Cle N	8	27	2	6	2	0	0	1	0	1	2	.222	.250	.296	41	-2	1	.500	-1	0	0	O4R,C2/P		-0.3
1897	Cle N	43	137	23	30	5	1	0	11	12	1		.219	.287	.270	45	-11	3	.894	-4	59	0	O28(1/3/24),S4,P4,1b3,C2/2		-1.3
1898	Cle N	17	57	8	13	3	1	0	9	3	0		.228	.290	.316	75	-2	0	.941	0	87	0	P9,O8(0/4/4)		-0.1
1899	Cle N	113	418	29	99	6	8	1	31	19	2		.237	.273	.297	61	-24	5	.943	-11	94	107	O79(9/3/70),C17,3b7,1b6,S3,P3/2		-3.4
1901	Det A	90	306	45	92	9	4	3	57	15	5		.301	.344	.386	97	-2	17	.898	-13	107	92	C35,1b28,O11(5/0/6),3b10,S3		-1.1
1902	Det A	21	67	8	14	1	0	1	8	2	1		.209	.243	.269	41	-6	0	1.000	0	307	93	1b5,S5,2b3,C2,3b2/OL		-0.5
	Bal A	3	11	0	1	0	0	0	0	1	0		.091	.167	.091	-26	-2	0	.923	-0	118	0	2b2/S		-0.2
	Det A	45	162	11	34	4	2	0	24	3	1		.210	.229	.259	34	-15	1	.991	0	307	93	1b21,O11(1/0/10),C7,3b4/S		-1.5
	Year	69	240	19	49	5	2	1	33	6	2		.204	.222	.254	33	-22	1	.992	-1	105	96	1b27,O12(2/0/10),C9,S6,3b6,2b5/D		-2.2
1903	Det A	78	265	31	69	8	2	0	22	10	4		.260	.297	.306	84	-5	5	.888	-6	96	80	S46,C18,O5R,3b4/1		-0.8
Total 7		418	1450	157	358	38	18	5	164	61	15	2	.247	.287	.308	67	-69	32	.914	-35	87	89	O147R,C83,1b65,S62,3b27,P17,2b7		-9.2

McANANY, JIM James B9.4.1936 Los Angeles CA BR/TR/5-10/196* d9.19 Col USC

YEAR	TM LG	G	AB	R	H	2B	3B	HR	RBI	BB-IB	HP	SO	AVG	OBP	SLG	AOPS	ABR	SB-CS	FA	FR	RNG	THR	GAMES AT POSITION	DL	BFW
1958	Chi A	5	13	0	2	0	0	0	0	0	0	5	.000	.000	.000	-99	-4	0-0	1.000	0	126	0	O3R		-0.4
1959	†Chi A	67	210	22	58	9	3	0	27	19-4	1	26	.276	.339	.348	90	-3	2-1	.966	0	94	171	O67(4/2/63)		-0.5
1960	Chi A	3	2	0	0	0	0	0	0	0-0	0	2	.000	.000	.000	-99	-1	0-0	—	0			/H		-0.1
1961	Chi N	11	10	1	3	0	0	0	1	1-0	0	3	.300	.364	.400	101	0	0-0	—	0			/H		0.0
1962	Chi N	7	6	0	0	0	0	0	0	0-0	0	2	.000	.143	.000	-56	-1	0-0	—	0	0	0	/OR		0.0
Total 5		93	241	23	61	10	3	0	27	21-4	1	38	.253	.316	.320	75	-9	2-1	.968	0	96	161	O71(4/2/67)		-1.1

McANULTY, PAUL Paul Michael B2.24.1981 Oxnard CA BL/TR/5-10/220 d6.22 Col Cal St.-Long Beach

YEAR	TM LG	G	AB	R	H	2B	3B	HR	RBI	BB-IB	HP	SO	AVG	OBP	SLG	AOPS	ABR	SB-CS	FA	FR	RNG	THR	GAMES AT POSITION	DL	BFW
2005	SD N	22	24	4	5	0	0	0		3-1	1	7	.208	.321	.208	45	-1	1-0	1.000	-1	79	0	O6L/1		-0.2

McATEE, BUB Michael James "Butch" B3.1845 Troy NY D10.18.1876 Troy NY TR/5-9/160 d5.8

YEAR	TM LG	G	AB	R	H	2B	3B	HR	RBI	BB-IB	HP	SO	AVG	OBP	SLG	AOPS	ABR	SB-CS	FA	FR	RNG	THR	GAMES AT POSITION	DL	BFW
1871	Chi NA	26	135	34	37	8	2	0	10	5		2	.274	.300	.363	81	-5	5-3	.943	1	117	130	1b26		-0.2
1872	Tro NA	25	126	30	28	3	1	0	15	3		2	.222	.240	.262	54	-7	0-2	.948	1	67	70	1b25		-0.4
Total 2 NA		51	261	64	65	11	3	0	25	8		4	.249	.271	.314	69	-12	5-5	.945	2	93	101	1b51		-0.6

McAULEY, IKE James Earl B8.19.1891 Wichita KS D4.6.1928 Des Moines IA BR/TR/5-9.5/150 d9.10

YEAR	TM LG	G	AB	R	H	2B	3B	HR	RBI	BB-IB	HP	SO	AVG	OBP	SLG	AOPS	ABR	SB-CS	FA	FR	RNG	THR	GAMES AT POSITION	DL	BFW
1914	Pit N	15	24	3	3	0	0	0	0	0	0	8	.125	.125	.125	-27	-4	0	.900	0	104	266	S5,3b3,2b2		-0.4
1915	Pit N	5	15	0	2	0	0	0	0	0	0	6	.133	.133	.200	-2	-2	0	.917	-1	90	95	S5		-0.3
1916	Pit N	4	8	1	2	0	0	0	1	0	0	2	.250	.250	.250	53	0	0	.938	0	83	178	S4		0.0
1917	StL N	3	7	0	2	0	0	0	1	0	0	1	.286	.286	.286	78	0	0	.833	0	58	0	S3		-0.2
1925	Chi N	37	125	10	35	7	2	0	11	11	1	12	.280	.343	.368	80	-3	1-0	.949	-7	79	95	S37		-0.2
Total 5		64	179	14	44	8	2	0	13	11	1	28	.246	.293	.313	62	-9	1-0	.940	-9	81	109	S54,3b3,2b2		-1.5

McAULIFFE, GENE Eugene Leo B2.28.1872 Randolph MA D4.29.1953 Randolph MA BR/TR/6-1/180 d8.17

YEAR	TM LG	G	AB	R	H	2B	3B	HR	RBI	BB-IB	HP	SO	AVG	OBP	SLG	AOPS	ABR	SB-CS	FA	FR	RNG	THR	GAMES AT POSITION	DL	BFW
1904	Bos N	1	2	0	1	0	0	0	0	0	0		.500	.500	.500	217	0	0	.667	-1	75	156	/C		0.0

McAULIFFE, DICK Richard John B11.29.1939 Hartford CT BL/TR/5-11/176* d9.17

YEAR	TM LG	G	AB	R	H	2B	3B	HR	RBI	BB-IB	HP	SO	AVG	OBP	SLG	AOPS	ABR	SB-CS	FA	FR	RNG	THR	GAMES AT POSITION	DL	BFW
1960	Det A	8	27	2	7	0	1	0	1	2-0	0	6	.259	.310	.333	72	-1	0-0	.884	2	122	164	S7		0.1
1961	Det A	80	285	36	73	12	4	6	33	24-0	4	39	.256	.322	.389	87	-6	2-3	.933	-18	82	105	S55,3b22		-2.0
1962	Det A	139	471	50	124	20	5	12	63	64-3	0	76	.263	.349	.403	99	0	4-2	.965	-24	78	71	2b70,3b49,S16		-1.7
1963	Det A	150	568	77	149	18	6	13	61	64-1	0	75	.262	.334	.384	98	-1	11-5	.963	-21	91	91	S133,2b15		-0.9
1964	Det A	162	557	85	134	18	7	24	66	77-8	3	96	.241	.334	.427	100	7	8-5	.958	-6	100	89	S160		1.6
1965	Det A★	113	404	61	105	13	6	15	54	49-4	3	62	.260	.342	.433	118	9	6-9	.956	-8	91	98	S112		1.0
1966	Det A★	124	430	83	118	16	8	23	56	66-2	3	80	.274	.373	.509	148	28	5-7	.964	1	100	84	S105,3b15	43	3.8
1967	Det A★	153	557	92	133	16	7	22	65	105-4	7	118	.239	.364	.411	126	22	6-5	.965	-4	97	115	2b145,S43		3.3
1968	†Det A	151	570	95	142	24	10	16	56	82-8	2	99	.249	.344	.411	125	19	8-7	.986	-21	88	105	2b148,S5		1.2
1969	Det A	74	271	49	71	10	5	11	33	47-1	0	41	.262	.369	.458	125	10	2-5	.976	5	102	92	2b72	81	1.9
1970	Det A	146	530	73	124	21	1	12	50	101-7	3	75	.234	.358	.345	99	0	5-6	.975	14	105	91	2b127,S15,3b12		2.2
1971	Det A	128	477	67	99	16	4	18	57	53-4	5	67	.208	.293	.379	86	-10	4-1	.987	11	101	106	2b123,S7		1.0
1972	†Det A	122	408	47	98	16	3	8	30	59-7	2	59	.240	.339	.353	102	3	0-0	.975	-5	90	94	2b116,S3/3		0.6
1973	Det A	106	343	39	94	18	1	12	47	49-5	1	52	.274	.366	.437	118	9	0-4	.986	3	103	96	2b102,S2/D		1.8
1974	Bos A	100	272	32	57	13	1	5	24	39-5	1	40	.210	.310	.320	76	-7	2-0	.971	6	91	99	2b53,3b40,S3,D3		-1.0
1975	Bos A	7	15	0	2	0	0	0	0	2-0	0	2	.133	.188	.133	-7	-2	0-0	.769	-2	73	105	3b7		-0.5
Total 16		1763	6185	888	1530	231	71	197	697	882-59	33	974	.247	.343	.403	108	80	63-59	.977	-78	95	98	2b971,S666,3b146,D4	124	12.4

McAVOY, GEORGE George Robert B3.12.1884 E.Liverpool OH D8.19.1952 Miami FL BL/TR d7.17

YEAR	TM LG	G	AB	R	H	2B	3B	HR	RBI	BB-IB	HP	SO	AVG	OBP	SLG	AOPS	ABR	SB-CS	FA	FR	RNG	THR	GAMES AT POSITION	DL	BFW
1914	Phi N	1	1	0	0	0	0	0	0	0	0	0	.000	.000	.000	-94	0	0	—	0			/H		0.0

McAVOY, WICKEY James Eugene B10.22.1894 Rochester NY D7.6.1973 Rochester NY BR/TR/5-11/172 d9.29

YEAR	TM LG	G	AB	R	H	2B	3B	HR	RBI	BB-IB	HP	SO	AVG	OBP	SLG	AOPS	ABR	SB-CS	FA	FR	RNG	THR	GAMES AT POSITION	DL	BFW
1913	Phi A	4	9	0	1	0	0	0	0	0	1	4	.111	.200	.111	-9	-1	0	1.000	1	132	156	C4		0.0
1914	Phi A	8	16	1	2	0	1	0	0	0	0	4	.125	.125	.250	13	-2	0	.971	9	127		C8		0.0
1915	Phi A	68	184	12	35	7	2	0	6	11	0	32	.190	.236	.250	47	-13	0-2	.931	-7	64	150	C64		-0.1
1917	Phi A	10	24	1	6	1	0	0	1	3	0		.250	.250	.417	105	0	0	.955	1	85	182	C8		-1.7
1918	Phi A	83	271	14	66	5	3	0	32	13	2	23	.244	.283	.284	70	-11	0	.960	4	87	119	C74/P1OR		0.1
1919	Phi A	62	170	10	24	5	2	0	11	14	0	21	.141	.195	.194	13	-20	1	.973	6	76	130	C57		-0.1
Total 6		235	674	38	134	18	8	1	53	38	3	87	.199	.245	.254	47	-47	6-2	.954	-4	79	133	O215/OR1P		-3.9

McBRIDE, ALGIE Algernon Griggs B5.23.1869 Washington DC D1.10.1956 Georgetown OH BL/TL/5-9/152 d5.12

YEAR	TM LG	G	AB	R	H	2B	3B	HR	RBI	BB-IB	HP	SO	AVG	OBP	SLG	AOPS	ABR	SB-CS	FA	FR	RNG	THR	GAMES AT POSITION	DL	BFW
1896	Chi N	9	29	2	7	1	1	0	1	7	0	3	.241	.389	.448	116	-1	0	.917	-0	74	0	O9L		0.0
1898	Cin N	120	486	94	147	14	12	3	43	51	12		.302	.383	.393	114	10	16	.959	3	105	75	O120(4/115/1)		0.4
1899	Cin N	64	251	57	87	12	5	1	23	30	7		.347	.431	.446	138	15	5	.950	-1	87	84	O64(5/45/14)		0.9
1900	Cin N	112	436	59	120	15	8	4	59	25	4		.275	.320	.374	94	-5	12	.915	-5	73	140	O110(14/10/86)		-1.5
1901	Cin N	30	123	19	29	7	0	2	18	7	1		.236	.283	.341	86	-2	9	.968	-2	28	0	O28(11/19/0)		-0.5
	NY N	68	264	27	74	10	0	2	29	12	2		.280	.317	.345	95	-2	3	.948	-3	100	135	O65R		-0.7

YEAR	TM LG	G	AB	R	H	2B	3B	HR	RBI	BB-IB	HP	SO	AVG	OBP	SLG	AOPS	ABR	SB-CS	FA	FR	RNG	THR	GAMES AT POSITION	DL	BFW
	Year	98	387	46	103	18	0	4	47	19	3		.266	.306	.344	92	-4	3	.956	-5	78	93	O93(11/19/65)		-1.2
Total	5	403	1589	258	464	60	26	12	179	132	26	3	.292	.356	.385	108	17	36	.946	-8	86	96	O396(43/189/166)		-1.4

McBRIDE, BAKE Arnold Ray B2.3.1949 Fulton MO BL/TR/6-2/187(175-190) [StLN70 37/811] d7.26 Col Westminster (MO)

YEAR	TM LG	G	AB	R	H	2B	3B	HR	RBI	BB-IB	HP	SO	AVG	OBP	SLG	AOPS	ABR	SB-CS	FA	FR	RNG	THR	GAMES AT POSITION	DL	BFW
																									0.1
1973	StL N	40	63	8	19	3	0	0	5	4-0	2	10	.302	.352	.349	97	0	0-1	.976	2	136	132	O17(1/16/0)		1.1
1974	StL N	150	559	81	173	19	5	6	56	43-9	13	57	.309	.361	.394	114	11	30-11	.990	1	105	97	O144C		1.1
1975	StL N	116	413	70	124	10	9	5	36	34-1	1	52	.300	.354	.404	106	2	26-8	.990	4	113	63	O107C	22	0.6
1976	StL N☆	72	272	40	91	13	4	3	24	18-0	6	28	.335	.386	.445	134	12	10-5	.981	4	116	118	O66C	89	1.6
1977	StL N	43	122	21	32	5	1	4	20	7-2	0	19	.262	.298	.418	92	-2	9-3	1.000	-3	75	118	O33C		-0.5
	†Phi N	85	280	55	95	20	5	11	41	25-2	3	25	.339	.392	.564	147	19	27-4	.986	2	102	150	O73(0/21/54)		2.2
	Year	128	402	.76	127	25	6	15	61	32-4	3	44	.316	.364	.520	132	17	36-7	.990	2	94	123	O106(0/54/54)		1.7
1978	†Phi N	122	472	68	127	20	4	10	49	28-3	5	68	.269	.315	.392	95	-4	28-3	.996	4	108	88	O119(0/1/118)		-0.1
1979	Phi N	151	582	82	163	16	12	12	60	41-3	4	77	.280	.328	.411	97	-4	25-14	.989	13	122	103	O147R		0.2
1980	†Phi N	137	554	68	171	33	10	9	87	26-4	5	58	.309	.342	.453	114	9	13-10	.990	2	112	53	O133(0/1/133)	75	0.4
1981	†Phi N	58	221	26	60	17	1	2	21	11-1	0	25	.271	.303	.385	90	-3	5-0	1.000	-1	103	0	O22R	114	-0.9
1982	Cle A	27	85	8	31	5	0	0	13	2-1	0	12	.365	.375	.471	131	3	2-2	.977	-6	105	137	O46R,D15	52	0.1
1983	Cle A	70	230	21	67	8	1	1	18	9-2	1	26	.291	.318	.348	81	-6	8-2	.977	1	105	137	O963(1/389/576),D15	352	-0.6
Total	11	1071	3853	548	1153	167	.55	63	430	248-28	40	457	.299	.345	.420	108	37	183-63	.989	24	109	88			4.2

McBRIDE, GEORGE George Florian B11.20.1880 Milwaukee WI D7.2.1973 Milwaukee WI BR/TR/5-11/170 d9.12 M1/C3

YEAR	TM LG	G	AB	R	H	2B	3B	HR	RBI	BB-IB	HP	SO	AVG	OBP	SLG	AOPS	ABR	SB-CS	FA	FR	RNG	THR	GAMES AT POSITION	DL	BFW
																									-0.1
1901	Mil A	3	12	0	2	0	0	0	0	1	0		.167	.231	.167	12	-1	0	1.000	0	86	201	S3		-0.6
1905	Pit N	27	87	9	19	4	0	0	7	6	1		.218	.277	.264	60	-16	2	.902	-4	93	171	3b17,S8		-1.7
	StL N	81	281	22	61	1	2	2	34	14	4		.217	.264	.256	57	-16	10	.938	-4	106	90	S80/1		-2.3
	Year	108	368	31	80	5	2	2	41	20	5		.217	.267	.258	58	-20	12	.935	-5	106	90	S88,3b17/1		-2.3
1906	StL N	90	313	24	53	8	2	0	13	17	1		.169	.215	.208	33	-25	5	.944	2	103	101	S90		3.7
1908	Was A	155	518	47	120	10	6	0	34	41	3		.232	.292	.274	92	-5	12	.948	33	106	121	S155		0.9
1909	Was A	156	504	38	118	16	0	0	34	36	7		.234	.294	.266	81	-10	17	.935	13	100	101	S156		4.1
1910	Was A	154	514	54	118	19	4	1	55	61	8		.230	.321	.288	95	0	11	.939	33	107	110	S154		1.2
1911	Was A	154	557	58	131	11	4	0	59	52	10		.235	.312	.269	64	-26	15	.941	28	105	116	S152		1.2
1912	Was A	152	521	56	118	13	7	1	52	38	7		.226	.288	.284	63	-26	17	.960	9	100	109	S150		-0.3
1913	Was A	150	499	52	107	18	7	1	52	43	7.	46	.214	.286	.285	66	-22	12	.958	10	97	129	S156		-1.2
1914	Was A	156	503	49	102	12	4	0	24	43	6	70	.204	.251	.252	50	-32	10-5	.968	7	96	98	S146		-1.5
1915	Was A	146	476	54	97	8	6	1	30	29	1	60	.204	.251	.252	47	-21	8	.957	14	101	104	S139		0.3
1916	Was A	139	466	36	106	15	4	1	36	23	5	58	.227	.271	.283	67	-21	6	.943	0	96	91	S41,3b6,2b2		-0.7
1917	Was A	50	141	6	27	3	0	0	9	10	1	17	.191	.265	.213	46	-9	1	.986	1	106	84	S14,2b2		-0.7
1918	Was A	18	53	2	7	0	0	0	1	0	0	11	.132	.132	.132	-21	-8	1	.986	-0	100	141	S15		-0.2
1919	Was A	15	40	3	8	1	0	0	4	3	0	6	.200	.256	.275	49	-3	0	.932	-0	100	141	S15		-0.6
1920	Was A	13	41	6	9	1	0	0	3	2	0	3	.220	.256	.244	34	-4	0-0	.966	-3	84	62	S13		1.5
Total	16	1659	5526	516	1203	140	47	7	447	419	64	271	.218	.281	.264	65	-241	133-19	.948	168	102	108	S1626,3b23,2b4/1		

McBRIDE, JOHN John F. d10.12

YEAR	TM LG	G	AB	R	H	2B	3B	HR	RBI	BB-IB	HP	SO	AVG	OBP	SLG	AOPS	ABR	SB-CS	FA	FR	RNG	THR	GAMES AT POSITION	DL	BFW
1890	Phi AA	1	2	0	0	0	0	0	0	0	0		.000	.000	.000	-99	-1	0	1.000	1	632	0	/OC		0.00

McBRIDE, TOM Thomas Raymond B11.2.1914 Bonham TX D12.26.2001 Wichita Falls TX BR/TR/6-0/190 d4.23

YEAR	TM LG	G	AB	R	H	2B	3B	HR	RBI	BB-IB	HP	SO	AVG	OBP	SLG	AOPS	ABR	SB-CS	FA	FR	RNG	THR	GAMES AT POSITION	DL	BFW
1943	Bos A	26	96	11	23	3	1	0	7	7	3		.240	.291	.292	70	-4	2-0	.984	-0	96	109	O24(0/21/3)		-0.5
1944	Bos A	71	216	29	53	7	3	0	24	8	1	13	.245	.276	.306	67	-10	4-0	.992	4	103	203	O57(23/14/22),1b5		-0.9
1945	Bos A	100	344	38	105	11	7	1	47	26	0	17	.305	.354	.387	112	4	2-2	.984	1	95	142	O81(15/50/22),1b11		0.2
1946	†Bos A	61	153	21	46	5	2	0	19	9	6	20	.301	.340	.359	90	-2	0-1	1.000	-2	93	37	O43(10/2/32)		-0.6
1947	Bos A	2	5	0	1	0	0	0	0	0	0	0	.200	.200	.200	11	-1	0-0	1.000	1	80	1087	/OR		0.0
	Was A	56	166	19	45	4	2	0	15	15	0	9	.271	.331	.319	84	-4	3-1	.972	-0	104	66	O51(43/4/5)/3		-0.7
	Year	58	171	19	46	4	2	0	15	15	0	9	.269	.328	.316	81	-5	3-1	.973	1	103	95	O52(43/4/6)/3		-0.2
1948	Was A	92	206	22	53	9	1	1	29	28	0	15	.257	.346	.325	81	-5	2-2	.983	5	108	204	O55(25/0/30)		-2.7
Total	6	408	1186	140	326	39	16	2	141	93	1	63	.275	.328	.340	82	-22	13-6	.985	9	100	141	O312(116/91/115),1b16/3		

McCABE, SWAT James Arthur B11.20.1881 Towanda PA D12.9.1944 Bristol CT BL/TR/5-10/187 d9.23

YEAR	TM LG	G	AB	R	H	2B	3B	HR	RBI	BB-IB	HP	SO	AVG	OBP	SLG	AOPS	ABR	SB-CS	FA	FR	RNG	THR	GAMES AT POSITION	DL	BFW
1909	Cin N	3	11	2	6	1	0	0	0	0	0		.545	.545	.636	269	-1	0	.625	-1	0	0	O3C		0.1
1910	Cin N	13	35	3	9	1	0	0	5	1	1	2	.257	.297	.286	73	-1	0	1.000	1	102	172	O9R		-0.1
Total	2	16	46	5	15	2	0	0	5	1	1	2	.326	.354	.370	118	1	1	.875	-0	74	125	O12(0/3/9)		0.0

McCABE, JOE Joseph Robert B8.27.1938 Indianapolis IN BR/TR/6-0/190* d4.18 Col Purdue

YEAR	TM LG	G	AB	R	H	2B	3B	HR	RBI	BB-IB	HP	SO	AVG	OBP	SLG	AOPS	ABR	SB-CS	FA	FR	RNG	THR	GAMES AT POSITION	DL	BFW
																									-0.4
1964	Min A	14	19	1	3	0	0	0	2	0-0	0	8	.158	.150	.158	-12	-3	0-0	1.000	-1	59	94	C12		-0.4
1965	Was A	14	27	1	5	0	0	1	5	4-0	0	13	.185	.281	.296	68	-1	1-0	.972	-3	182	218	C11		-0.8
Total	2	28	46	2	8	0	0	1	7	4-0	0	21	.174	.231	.239	36	-4	1-0	.986	-4	133	169	C23		

McCABE, BILL William Francis B10.28.1892 Chicago IL D9.2.1966 Chicago IL BB/TR (BL 1918)/5-9.5/180 d4.16

YEAR	TM LG	G	AB	R	H	2B	3B	HR	RBI	BB-IB	HP	SO	AVG	OBP	SLG	AOPS	ABR	SB-CS	FA	FR	RNG	THR	GAMES AT POSITION	DL	BFW
																									0.0
1918	†Chi N	29	45	9	8	0	1	0	5	4	0	7	.178	.245	.222	42	-3	2	.939	3	126	24	2b13,O4(1/0/2)		-0.9
1919	Chi N	33	84	8	13	3	1	0	5	9	2	15	.155	.253	.214	41	-6	3	.950	-1	101	72	O20(0/1/19),S4/3		0.0
1920	Chi N	3	2	1	1	0	0	0	0	0	0	0	.500	.500	.500	184	0	0-0	0-0	0	0	0	/H		-1.8
	†Bro N	41	68	10	10	0	0	0	3	2	0	6	.147	.171	.147	-8	-9	1-2	.882	5	111	92	S13,O6L,2b4,3b3		-1.0
	Year	44	70	11	11	0	0	0	3	2	0	6	.157	.181	.157	-2	-9	1-2	.882	5	111	92	S13,O6L,2b4,3b3		-1.0
Total	3	106	199	28	32	3	2	0	13	15	2	28	.161	.227	.196	26	-18	6-2	.943	7	2	103	86	O30(7/1/21),S17,2b17,3b4		-1.9

McCAFFERY, HARRY Harry Charles B11.25.1858 St.Louis MO D4.19.1928 St.Louis MO BR/TR/5-10.5/185 d6.15 U1

YEAR	TM LG	G	AB	R	H	2B	3B	HR	RBI	BB-IB	HP	SO	AVG	OBP	SLG	AOPS	ABR	SB-CS	FA	FR	RNG	THR	GAMES AT POSITION	DL	BFW
1882	Lou AA	1	4	1	1	0	0	0					.250	.250	.250	73	0		1.000	-0	44	0	/2		0.
	StL AA	38	153	23	42	8	6	0		3			.275	.288	.405	127	4		.891	3	196	337	O23(5/0/18),2b8,3b7/1		0.
	Year	39	157	24	43	8	6	0		3			.274	.287	.401	125	3		.891	3	196	337	O23(5/0/18),2b9,3b7/1		-0.
1883	StL AA	5	18	0	1	0	0	1	1				.056	.105	.056	-44	-3		.900	2	332	2340	O5C		-0.
Total	2	44	175	24	44	8	6	0	1	4			.251	.268	.366	107	1		.893	5	218	665	O28(5/5/18),2b9,3b7/1		

McCAFFREY, SPARROW Charles P. B1868 Philadelphia PA D4.29.1894 Philadelphia PA ?/120 d8.13

YEAR	TM LG	G	AB	R	H	2B	3B	HR	RBI	BB-IB	HP	SO	AVG	OBP	SLG	AOPS	ABR	SB-CS	FA	FR	RNG	THR	GAMES AT POSITION	DL	BFW
1889	Col AA	2	1	1	1	0	0	0					1.000	1.000	1.000	495	1		—	-0			C2		0,

McCALL, BRIAN Brian Allen "Bam" B1.25.1943 Kentfield CA BL/TL/5-10/175* d9.18

YEAR	TM LG	G	AB	R	H	2B	3B	HR	RBI	BB-IB	HP	SO	AVG	OBP	SLG	AOPS	ABR	SB-CS	FA	FR	RNG	THR	GAMES AT POSITION	DL	BFW
																									0.
1962	Chi A	4	8	2	3	0	0	2	3	0-0	0	2	.375	.375	1.125	287	2	0-0	1.000	0	163	0	/OC		-0.
1963	Chi A	3	7	1	0	0	0	0	0	1-0	0	2	.000	.125	.000	-62	-2	0-0	1.000	-0	99	0	O2R		0.
Total	2	7	15	3	3	0	0	2	3	1-0	0	4	.200	.250	.600	126	0	0-0	1.000	0	124	0	O3(0/1/2)		

McCANDLESS, JACK Scott Cook B5.5.1891 Pittsburgh PA D8.17.1961 Pittsburgh PA BL/TR/6-0/170 d9.10

YEAR	TM LG	G	AB	R	H	2B	3B	HR	RBI	BB-IB	HP	SO	AVG	OBP	SLG	AOPS	ABR	SB-CS	FA	FR	RNG	THR	GAMES AT POSITION	DL	BFW
																									-0.
1914	Bal F	11	31	5	8	0	1	0	1	3			.258	.343	.323	79	-1	0	1.000	-0	94	91	O8(0/1/7)		-3.
1915	Bal F	117	406	47	87	6	7	5	34	41	6	99	.214	.296	.300	66	-25	9	.945	1	100	111	O105(23/58/25)		-3.
Total	2	128	437	52	95	6	8	5	35	44	7	99	.217	.299	.302	67	-26	9	.948	1	100	110	O113(23/59/32)		

McCANN, BRIAN Brian Michael B2.20.1984 Athens GA BL/TR/6-3/210 d6.10

YEAR	TM LG	G	AB	R	H	2B	3B	HR	RBI	BB-IB	HP	SO	AVG	OBP	SLG	AOPS	ABR	SB-CS	FA	FR	RNG	THR	GAMES AT POSITION	DL	BFW
2005	†Atl N	59	180	20	50	7	0	5	23	18-5	1	26	.278	.345	.400	93	-2	1-1	.991	1	119	46	C57		0

McCANN, EMMETT Robert Emmett B3.4.1902 Philadelphia PA D4.15.1937 Philadelphia PA BR/TR/5-11/150 d4.19

YEAR	TM LG	G	AB	R	H	2B	3B	HR	RBI	BB-IB	HP	SO	AVG	OBP	SLG	AOPS	ABR	SB-CS	FA	FR	RNG	THR	GAMES AT POSITION	DL	BFW
1920	Phi A	13	34	4	9	1	1	0	3	3	1		.265	.342	.353	83	-1	0-1	.907	-0	99	79	S11		-0
1921	Phi A	52	157	15	35	5	0	0	15	4	0	6	.223	.242	.255	27	-18	0-0	.949	-3	101	81	S32,3b9,2b2/1		-1
1926	Bos A	6	3	0	0	0	0	0	0	0	0	1	.000	.250	.000	-32	-1	0-0	1.000	0	0	0	/S3		-1
Total	3	71	194	19	44	6	1	0	18	8	1	7	.227	.261	.268	42	-20	0-2	.939	-4	100	80	S44,3b10,2b2/1		-1

McCARDELL, ROGER Roger Morton B8.29.1932 Gorsuch Mills MD D11.13.1996 Perry Point MD BR/TR/6-0/210 d5.8 Col Boston U.

YEAR	TM LG	G	AB	R	H	2B	3B	HR	RBI	BB-IB	HP	SO	AVG	OBP	SLG	AOPS	ABR	SB-CS	FA	FR	RNG	THR	GAMES AT POSITION	DL	BFW
1959	SF N	4	4	0	0	0	0	0	0	0	0		.000	.000	.000	-99	-1	0-0	1.000	0	0	0	C3		-0

McCARREN, BILL William Joseph B11.4.1895 Fortenia PA D9.11.1983 Denver CO BR/TR/5-11.5/170 d5.4

YEAR	TM LG	G	AB	R	H	2B	3B	HR	RBI	BB-IB	HP	SO	AVG	OBP	SLG	AOPS	ABR	SB-CS	FA	FR	RNG	THR	GAMES AT POSITION	DL	BFW
1923	Bro N	69	216	28	53	10	1	3	27	22	4	39	.245	.326	.343	79	-6	0-1	.927	-2	92	102	3b66/OR		-0

YEAR	TM	LG	G	AB	R	H	2B	3B	HR	RBI	BB-IB	HP	SO	AVG	OBP	SLG	AOPS	ABR	SB-CS	FA	FR	RNG	THR	GAMES AT POSITION	DL	BFW

McCARTHY, ALEX Alexander George B5.12.1888 Chicago IL D3.12.1978 Salisbury MD BR/TR/5-9/150 d10.7 Col Notre Dame

1910	Pit	N	3	12	1	1	0	1	0	0	0		2	.083	.083	.250	-3	-2	0	.875	0	115	187	S3		-0.2
1911	Pit	N	50	150	18	36	5	1	2	31	14	0	24	.240	.305	.327	74	-6	4	.981	3	91	112	2b105,3b4		0.0
1912	Pit	N	111	401	53	111	12	4	1	41	30	1	26	.277	.332	.334	84	-9	8	.962	-9	95	119	2b105,3b4		-1.6
1913	Pit	N	31	74	7	15	5	0	0	10	7	3	7	.203	.298	.270	66	-3	1-2	.902	-1	93	89	S12,3b12,2b6		-0.4
1914	Pit	N	57	173	14	26	0	1	1	14	6	3	17	.150	.192	.179	11	-20	2	.975	6	118	139	3b6,2b10,S6		-1.4
1915	Pit	N	21	49	3	10	1	0	0	3	5	1	10	.204	.291	.245	64	-2	1-2	.950	1	90	67	2b9,S5,3b4/1		-0.2
	Chi	N	23	72	4	19	3	0	1	6	5	2	7	.264	.329	.347	105	1	2-3	.972	7	105	165	2b12,3b12/S		0.8
	Year		44	121	7	29	3	1	1	9	10	3	17	.240	.313	.306	88	-2	3-5	.964	8	99	126	2b21,3b16,S6/1		0.6
1916	Chi	N	37	107	10	26	2	3	0	6	11	5	7	.243	.341	.318	93	0	1	.931	-2	106	76	2b34,S3		-0.2
	Pit	N	50	146	11	29	3	0	0	3	15	2	10	.199	.282	.219	54	-7	3	.955	-4	84	95	S39,2b7,3b5		-1.0
	Year		87	253	21	55	5	3	0	9	26	7	17	.217	.308	.261	72	-7	4	.951	-6	83	92	S42,2b41,3b5		-1.2
1917	Pit	N	49	151	15	33	4	0	0	8	11	1	13	.219	.276	.245	54	-7	1	.964	3	82	229	3b26,2b13,S9		-0.3
Total	8		432	1335	136	306	34	11	5	122	104	20	123	.229	.295	.282	67	-55	23-7	.957	3	100	111	2b207,S111,3b100/1OL		-4.5

McCARTHY, JERRY Jerome Francis B5.23.1923 Brooklyn NY D10.3.1965 Oceanside NY BL/TL/6-1/205 d6.19 Col Penn

| 1948 | StL | A | 2 | 3 | 0 | 1 | 0 | 0 | 0 | 0 | 0 | 0 | 1 | .333 | .333 | .333 | 76 | 0 | 0 | .600 | -1 | 0 | 0 | 1b2 | | -0.1 |

McCARTHY, JACK John Arthur B3.26.1869 Gilbertville MA D9.11.1931 Chicago IL BL/TL/5-9/155 d8.3 Col Holy Cross

1893	Cin	N	49	195	28	55	8	3	0	22	22	0	7	.282	.355	.354	86	-4	6	.887	-1	88	0	O47(10/1/37),1b2		-0.6
1894	Cin	N	40	167	29	45	9	1	0	21	17	3	6	.269	.348	.335	63	-10	3	.895	2	142	0	O25(5/0/20),1b15		-0.7
1898	Pit	N	137	537	75	155	13	12	4	78	34	4		.289	.336	.380	107	3	7	.935	4	98	93	O137L		-0.5
1899	Pit	N	139	565	109	173	22	17	4	69	39	4		.306	.355	.427	114	9	28	.962	-5	87	105	O139(133/6/0)		-0.8
1900	Chi	N	124	503	68	148	16	7	0	48	24	2		.294	.329	.354	92	-7	22	.944	-1	117	90	O123(96/1/26)		-1.6
1901	Cle	A	86	343	60	110	14	7	0	32	30	4		.321	.382	.402	123	12	9	.949	-1	83	183	O86(85/1/0)		0.7
1902	Cle	A	95	359	45	102	31	5	0	41	24	0		.284	.329	.398	105	3	12	.944	-4	50	0	O95L		-0.6
1903	Chi	N	24	101	11	28	5	0	0	14	4	0		.277	.305	.327	82	-3	8	.947	-1	103	154	O108L		-1.2
1904	Chi	N	115	432	36	114	14	2	0	51	23	4		.264	.307	.306	89	-6	14	.961	-7	56	0	O115(25/90/0)		-0.5
1905	Chi	N	59	170	16	47	4	3	0	14	10	1		.276	.320	.335	92	-2	8	.986	2	191	410	O37(18/19/0),1b6		-1.9
1906	Bro	N	91	322	23	98	13	1	0	35	20	1		.304	.347	.351	128	10	9	.924	2	122	38	O86(83/3/0)		-0.2
1907	Bro	N	25	91	4	20	2	0	0	8	2	0		.220	.237	.242	54	-5	4	1.000	-3	0	0	O25L		0.8
Total	12		1092	4200	551	1205	171	66	8	476	268	24	13	.287	.333	.365	101	-2	145	.946	-12	91	91	O1047(844/121/83),1b23		-1.1

McCARTHY, JOHNNY John Joseph B1.7.1910 Chicago IL D9.13.1973 Mundelein IL BL/TL/6-1.5/185 d9.2 Mil 1943-45

1934	Bro	N	17	39	7	7	2	0	1	5	2	0	2	.179	.220	.308	42	-3	0	.961	1	157	170	1b13		-8.2
1935	Bro	N	22	48	9	12	1	0	0	4	2	0	9	.250	.280	.313	60	-3	1	.982	-3	0	135	1b19		-0.4
1936	NY	N	4	16	1	7	0	0	1	2	0	0	1	.438	.438	.625	185	2	1	.981	-3	213	157	1b4		-0.7
1937	†NY	N	114	420	53	117	19	3	10	65	24	1	37	.279	.322	.410	96	-3	2	.987	3	112	113	1b110		0.2
1938	NY	N	134	470	55	128	13	4	8	59	39	1	28	.272	.329	.368	91	-7	3	.993	-3	92	114	1b125		-1.0
1939	NY	N	50	80	12	21	6	1	1	11	3	1	8	.262	.298	.400	85	-2	0	1.000	-2	28	130	1b12,O4(0/1/3)/P		-2.1
1940	NY	N	51	67	6	16	4	0	0	5	2	0	8	.239	.261	.299	54	-4	0	1.000	1	139	131	1b6		-0.5
1941	NY	N	14	40	1	13	3	0	0	12	3	0	0	.325	.372	.400	115	1	0	1.000	1	143	60	1b8/OL		-0.4
1943	Bos	N	78	313	32	95	24	6	2	33	10	1	19	.304	.327	.438	122	7	1	.996	-1	99	79	1b78		0.1
1946	Bos	N	2	7	0	1	0	0	0	1	2	0	0	.143	.333	.143	37	0	0	1.000	-1	209	162	1b2		0.2
1948	NY	N	56	57	6	15	0	1	2	12	3	1	3	.263	.300	.404	88	-1	0	.966	-1	56	99	1b6		-0.1
Total	11		542	1557	182	432	72	16	25	209	90	6	114	.277	.319	.392	95	-13	8	.990	-2	99	109	1b383,O5(1/1/3)/P		-4.9

McCARTHY, JOE Joseph Nicodemus B12.25.1881 Syracuse NY D1.12.1937 Syracuse NY BR/TR Col Niagara

1905	NY	A	1	2	0	0	0	0	0	0	0	0		.000	.000	.000	-90	0	0	1.000	-0	59	210	/C		-0.1
1906	StL	N	15	37	3	9	2	0	0	2	2	0		.243	.282	.297	84	-1	0	.984	-1	77	99	C15		-0.1
Total	2		16	39	3	9	2	0	0	2	2	0		.231	.268	.282	74	-1	0	.985	-1	76	105	C16		-0.2

McCARTHY, TOMMY Thomas Francis Michael B7.24.1863 Boston MA D8.5.1922 Boston MA BR/TR/5-7/170 d7.10 M1 HF1957 OF(514/32/647) ▲

1884	Bos	U	53	209	37	45	2	2	0		6			.215	.237	.244	47	-20		.794	0	104	65	O48(41/2/7),P7		-1.7
1885	Bos	N	40	148	16	27	2	0	0	11	5		25	.182	.209	.196	33	-11		.865	1	96	0	O40(39/0/1)		-1.0
1886	Phi	N	8	27	6	5	2	1	0	3	2		3	.185	.241	.333	73	-1	1	.818	-1	82	0	O8R/P		-0.1
1887	Phi	N	18	70	7	13	4	0	0	6	2	1	5	.186	.219	.243	27	-7	15	.897	-7	95	0	O8(6/2/0),2b5,S3,3b2		-1.2
1888	†StL	AA	131	511	107	140	20	3	1	68	38	3	26	.274	.328	.331	100	-1	93	.931	26	189	306	O131(0/12/119),P2		2.1
1889	StL	AA	140	604	136	176	24	7	2	63	46	6		.291	.348	.364	91	-10	57	.893	12	138	200	O140(1/3/137),2b2/P		0.1
1890	StL	AA	133	548	137	192	28	9	6	69	66	11		.350	.430	.467	144	30	83	.893	6	107	135	O102(2/0/100),3b32/2M		3.0
1891	StL	AA	134	570	124	176	20	6	8	92	49	10	19	.309	.374	.407	107	2	37	.898	1	124	129	O112(7/0/106),2b14,S12,3b2/P		0.2
1892	†Bos	N	152	603	119	146	19	5	4	63	93	4	29	.242	.347	.310	91	-5	53	.883	-1	119	86	O152(0/1/151)		-1.1
1893	Bos	N	116	462	107	160	28	6	5	111	64	3	10	.346	.429	.465	128	20	46	.902	2	149	109	O108(88/3/17),2b7,S3		1.1
1894	Bos	N	127	539	118	188	21	8	13	126	59	6	17	.349	.419	.490	110	8	43	.904	10	128	199	O127(119/9/0),S2/P		0.5
1895	Bos	N	117	452	90	131	13	2	2	73	72	3		.290	.391	.341	83	-9	18	.885	-10	94	57	O109L,2b9		-2.4
1896	Bro	N	104	377	62	94	8	4	3	47	34	3	17	.249	.316	.316	71	-16	22	.920	-1	142	170	O103(102/0/1)		-2.2
Total	13		1273	5120	1066	1493	191	53	44	732	536	50	163	.292	.364	.375	99	-20	468	.897	39	130	146	O1188R,2b39,3b36,S20,P13		-2.7

McCARTHY, BILL William John B2.14.1886 Boston MA D2.4.1928 Washington DC TR d6.5 Col Fordham

1905	Bos	N	1	3	0	0	0	0	0	0	0	0		.000	.000	.000	-99	-1	0	.667	-1	153	80	/C		-0.2
1907	Cin	N	3	8	1	1	0	0	0	0	0	0		.125	.125	.125	-21	-1	0	1.000	-0	110	164	C3		-0.1
Total	2		4	11	1	1	0	0	0	0	0	0		.091	.091	.091	-43	-2	0	.842	-1	126	133	C4		-0.3

McCARTON, FRANK Francis J. B10.6.1854 New York NY D6.17.1907 New York NY d4.26

| 1872 | Man | NA | 19 | 82 | 19 | 25 | 5 | 0 | 0 | 12 | 3 | | | .305 | .329 | .366 | 120 | 3 | 0-0 | .743 | -3 | 52 | 0 | O19(0/18/1) | | 0.0 |

McCARTY, DAVID David Andrew B11.23.1969 Houston TX BR/TL/6-5/215* [MinA91 1/3] d5.17 Col Stanford

1993	Min	A	98	350	36	75	15	2	2	21	19-0	1	80	.214	.257	.286	45	-28	2-6	.959	6	101	187	O67(38/2/34),1b36,D2		-2.9
1994	Min	A	44	131	21	34	8	2	1	12	7-1	5	32	.260	.322	.374	78	-4	2-1	.981	3	157	80	1b32,O14(9/0/5)		-0.3
1995	Min	A	25	55	10	12	3	1	0	4	4-0	1	18	.218	.279	.309	54	-4	2-1	.993	-1	93	101	1b18,O5(2/0/4)		-0.6
	SF	N	12	20	1	5	1	0	0	4	2-0	0		.250	.318	.300	66	-1	1-0	.833	-1	97	0	O4R,1b2		-0.2
1996	SF	N	91	175	16	38	3	0	6	24	18-0	2	43	.217	.294	.337	68	-8	2-1	.990	-1	71	114	1b51,O20(5/0/15)		-1.2
1998	Sea	A	8	18	1	5	0	0	1	2	5-0	0		.278	.435	.444	128	1	0-0	1.000	-1	00	0	1b5,O2	21	0.0
2000	KC	A	103	270	34	75	14	2	12	53	22-1	0	68	.278	.329	.478	96	-2	0-0	.992	10	160	127	1b63,O11(7/0/4),SD		0.2
2001	KC	A	98	200	26	50	10	0	7	26	24-1	1	45	.250	.328	.405	85	-4	0-0	.988	2	128	133	1b68,O9(8/0/1),D7		-0.7
2002	KC	A	13	32	2	3	1	0	0	1	2-0	0	10	.094	.147	.219	-4	-5	0-0	1.000	0	97	73	1b9,D2		-0.2
	TB	A	12	34	2	6	0	0	1	2	4-0	2	9	.176	.300	.265	53	-2	0-0	1.000	1	102	176	O11L		-0.2
	Year		25	66	4	9	1	0	1	3	6-0	2	19	.136	.230	.242	24	-7	0-0	1.000	1	102	176	O11L,1b9,D2		-0.4
2003	Oak	A	8	26	3	7	2	0	0	2	1-0	0	9	.269	.286	.346	68	-1	0-0	1.000	-1	55	0	O5L,1b3		-0.8
	†Bos	A	16	27	4	11	3	0	1	6	2-0	0	10	.407	.448	.630	173	3	0-0	1.000	-1	72	0	O8(7/0/1),1b5/D		-0.3
	Year		24	53	6	18	5	0	1	8	3-0	0	14	.340	.368	.491	122	2	0-0	1.000	-2	64	0	O13(12/0/1),1b8/D		0.2
2004	Bos	A	91	151	24	39	8	1	4	17	14-0	2	40	.258	.327	.404	85	-3	1-0	.991	3	132	89	1b67,O17(10/0/7),P3,D3	19	-0.3
2005	Bos	A	13	4	2	2	0	0	0	2	1-0	0	6	.500	.667	.500	206	1	0-0	1.000	-1	176	128	1b12/OL		0.1
Total	11		632	1493	182	362	68	8	36	175	126-3	14	367	.242	.305	.371	74	-57	9-9	.990	20	128	107	1b368,O177(103/2/80),D22,P3/S	40	-6.8

McCARTY, LEW George Lewis B11.17.1888 Milton PA D6.9.1930 Reading PA BR/TR/5-11.5/192 d8.30

1913	Bro	N	9	26	1	6	0	0	0	2	4	0	2	.231	.286	.231	47	-2	0	1.000	0	96	80	C9		-0.1
1914	Bro	N	90	284	20	72	14	2	1	30	14	2	22	.254	.293	.327	83	-7	1	.970	-2	88	102	C84		-0.2
1915	Bro	N	84	276	19	66	9	4	0	19	7	1	23	.239	.261	.301	68	-12	7-4	.969	-7	85	107	C81		-1.4
1916	Bro	N	55	150	17	47	6	1	0	13	14	3	16	.313	.383	.367	127	6	4	.985	-1	94	99	C27,1b17		0.7
	NY	N	25	68	6	27	3	4	0	9	7	0	9	.397	.453	.559	222	10	0	.993	1	114	78	C24		1.4
	Year		80	218	23	74	9	5	0	22	21	3	25	.339	.405	.427	155	15	4	.989	1	104	89	C51,1b17		2.1
1917	†NY	N	56	162	15	40	3	2	2	19	14	1	24	.247	.311	.321	99	0	1	.979	-2	107	56	C54		0.2
1918	NY	N	86	257	16	69	7	3	0	24	17	1	13	.268	.321	.319	97	-1	3	.975	-6	97	65	C75		0.0
1919	NY	N	85	210	17	59	5	4	2	21	18	1	15	.281	.341	.371	94	4	2	.970	-6	99	74	C59		0.3

YEAR	TM LG	G	AB	R	H	2B	3B	HR	RBI	BB-IB	HP	SO	AVG	OBP	SLG	AOPS	ABR	SB-CS	FA	FR	RNG	THR	GAMES AT POSITION	DL	BFW
1920	NY N	36	38	2	5	0	0	0	4	2-0	0	2	.132	.214	.132	1	-5	2-0	1.000	1	145	116	C5		-0.3
	StL N	5	7	0	2	0	0	0	0	5	0	0	.286	.583	.286	160	1	0-0	1.000	-1	82	138	C3		0.1
	Year	41	45	2	7	0	0	0	0	9	0	2	.156	.296	.156	33	-3	2-0	1.000	1	122	124	C8		-0.2
1921	StL N	1	1	0	0	0	0	0	0	0	0	0	.000	.000	.000	-99	0	0-0	—	0			/H		0.0
Total	9	532	1479	113	393	47	20	5	137	102	11	109	.266	.318	.335	97	-6	20-4	.975	-22	96	85	C421,1b17		0.7

McCARVER, TIM James Timothy B10.16.1941 Memphis TN BL/TR/6-1/195(185-201) d9.10

YEAR	TM LG	G	AB	R	H	2B	3B	HR	RBI	BB-IB	HP	SO	AVG	OBP	SLG	AOPS	ABR	SB-CS	FA	FR	RNG	THR	GAMES AT POSITION	DL	BFW
1959	StL N	8	24	3	4	1	0	0	0	2-0	0	1	.167	.231	.208	17	-3	0-0	.971	-1	98	87	C6		-0.4
1960	StL N	10	10	3	2	0	0	0	0	0	0	5	.200	.200	.200	9	-1	0-0	1.000	-1	25	0	C5		-0.2
1961	StL N	22	67	5	16	2	1	1	6	0-0	0	5	.239	.239	.343	47	-5	0-0	.969	-1	92	150	C20		-0.6
1963	StL N	127	405	39	117	12	7	4	51	27-5	2	43	.289	.333	.383	97	-1	5-2	.994	-4	103	82	C126		0.1
1964	†StL N	143	465	53	134	19	3	9	52	40-15	1	44	.276	.327	.400	101	1	2-0	.987	-3	112	57	C137		0.6
1965	StL N	113	409	48	113	17	2	11	48	31-11	1	26	.276	.319	.424	98	-1	5-1	.995	1	105	69	C111		0.7
1966	StL N★	150	543	50	149	19	13	12	68	36-10	2	30	.274	.319	.424	105	3	9-6	.992	3	112	84	C148		1.2
1967	†StL N★	138	471	68	139	26	3	14	69	54-19	5	32	.295	.369	.452	137	24	8-8	.997	9	172	102	C130		4.1
1968	†StL N	128	434	35	110	15	6	5	48	26-8	1	31	.253	.295	.350	95	-4	4-9	.986	4	116	72	C109		0.6
1969	StL N	138	515	46	134	27	3	7	51	49-9	2	26	.260	.323	.365	93	-4	4-9	.986	6	88	81	C136		0.6
1970	Phi N	44	164	16	47	11	1	4	14	14-4	1	10	.287	.346	.439	111	3	2-2	.991	-1	70	73	C44	122	0.3
1971	Phi N	134	474	51	132	20	5	8	46	43-7	1	26	.278	.337	.392	106	4	5-3	.985	-9	59	125	C125		0.1
1972	Phi N	45	152	14	36	8	0	2	14	17-2	2	15	.237	.318	.329	83	-3	1-2	.989	-0	96	61	C40		-0.2
	Mon N	77	239	19	60	5	1	5	20	19-3	1	14	.251	.309	.343	83	-6	4-4	.990	7	100	126	C45,O14(14/0/1),3b6		0.2
	Year	122	391	33	96	13	1	7	34	36-5	3	29	.246	.313	.338	83	-8	5-6	.990	7	98	95	C85,O14(14/0/1),3b6		0.0
1973	StL N	130	331	30	88	16	4	3	49	38-6	2	31	.266	.339	.366	96	-1	2-0	.986	-7	67	88	1b77,C11		-1.3
1974	StL N	74	106	13	23	0	1	0	11	22-0	3	6	.217	.353	.236	71	-3	0-1	.969	-3	51	139	C21,1b6		-0.6
	Bos A	11	28	3	7	1	0	0	1	4-2	1	0	.250	.344	.286	77	-1	1-0	1.000	1	71	76	C8,D2		0.1
1975	Bos A	12	21	1	8	2	1	0	3	1-1	0	3	.381	.409	.571	161	2	0-0	.957	1	61	70	C7/1		0.2
	Phi N	47	59	6	15	2	0	1	7	14-3	0	7	.254	.397	.339	101	1	0-0	.984	1	61	129	C10/1		0.3
1976	†Phi N	90	155	26	43	11	2	3	29	35-2	1	14	.277	.409	.432	135	9	2-1	.988	1	83	107	C41,1b2		1.8
1977	†Phi N	93	169	28	54	13	2	6	30	28-1	2	11	.320	.410	.527	145	12	3-5	.988	1	83	107	C42,1b3		1.4
1978	†Phi N	90	146	18	36	9	1	1	14	28-6	1	24	.247	.367	.342	100	2	2-2	.995	5	158	150	C34,1b11		0.8
1979	Phi N	79	137	13	33	5	1	1	12	19-5	1	12	.241	.333	.314	75	-4	0-0	.989	6	148	123	C31/OL		0.3
1980	Phi N	6	5	1	1	0	0	0	2	1-0	0	0	.200	.333	.400	97	0	0-0	1.000	0	0	0	1b2		0.0
Total	21	1909	5529	590	1501	242	57	97	645	548-119	30	422	.271	.337	.388	102	23	61-49	.990	20	105	89	C1387,1b103,O15(15/0/1),3b6,D2	122	10.1

McCAULEY, AL Allen A. B3.4.1863 Indianapolis IN D8.24.1917 Wayne Twnshp. IN BL/TL/6-0/180 d6.21 ▲

YEAR	TM LG	G	AB	R	H	2B	3B	HR	RBI	BB-IB	HP	SO	AVG	OBP	SLG	AOPS	ABR	SB-CS	FA	FR	RNG	THR	GAMES AT POSITION	DL	BFW
1884	Ind AA	17	53	7	10	1	0	0	5	12	2		.189	.358	.226	97	1		1.000	1	144	286	P10,1b5,O3R		0.0
1890	Phi N	116	418	63	102	25	7	1	42	57	8	38	.244	.346	.344	99	1	8	.973	-6	63	107	1b116		-1.4
1891	Was AA	59	206	36	58	5	9	1	31	30	2	13	.282	.378	.398	128	9	9	.969	-1	95	71	1b59		0.2
Total	3	192	677	106	170	30	16	2	78	99	12	51	.251	.357	.352	107	10	17	.971	-6	73	97	1b180,P10,O3R		-1.2

McCAULEY, JIM James Adelbert B3.24.1863 Stanley NY D9.14.1930 Canandaigua NY BL/TR/6-0/180 d9.17 Col Union (NY)

YEAR	TM LG	G	AB	R	H	2B	3B	HR	RBI	BB-IB	HP	SO	AVG	OBP	SLG	AOPS	ABR	SB-CS	FA	FR	RNG	THR	GAMES AT POSITION	DL	BFW
1884	StL AA	1	2	0	0	0	0	0		0	0		.000	.000	.000	-97	0		.818				/C		0.0
1885	Buf N	24	84	4	15	2	1	0	7	11		12	.179	.274	.226	61	-3		.936	2			C21,O4C		0.1
	Chi N	3	6	1	1	0	0	0	2			3	.167	.375	.167	70	0		.800	-2			C2,O2R		0.1
	Year	27	90	5	16	2	1	0	7	13		15	.178	.282	.222	62	-3		.927	1			C23,O6(0/4/2)		0.1
1886	Bro AA	11	30	5	7	1	0	0	10	11	0		.233	.439	.267	122	2	2	.846	-2			C11		0.0
Total	3	39	122	10	23	3	1	0	10	24		15	.189	.322	.230	76	-1	2	.893	-1			C35,O6(0/4/2)		0.1

McCAULEY, PAT Patrick F. B6.10.1870 Ware MA D1.17.1917 Hoboken NJ TR/5-10.5/156 d9.5

YEAR	TM LG	G	AB	R	H	2B	3B	HR	RBI	BB-IB	HP	SO	AVG	OBP	SLG	AOPS	ABR	SB-CS	FA	FR	RNG	THR	GAMES AT POSITION	DL	BFW
1893	StL N	5	16	1	1	0	0	0	0	1	0	1	.063	.063	.063	-67	-4	0	.808	-1	83	136	C5		-0.3
1896	Was N	26	84	14	21	3	0	3	11	7	1	8	.250	.315	.393	86	-2	3	.917	-2	87	124	C24/OR		-0.5
1903	NY A	6	19	0	1	0	0	0	1	0	0	0	.053	.053	.053	-64	-4	0	.920	-2	99	51	C6		-0.3
Total	3	37	119	14	23	3	0	3	12	7	1	9	.193	.244	.294	44	-10	3	.900	-4	88	114	C35/OR		-0.9

McCAULEY, BILL William H. B12.20.1869 Washington DC D1.27.1926 Washington DC d8.31

YEAR	TM LG	G	AB	R	H	2B	3B	HR	RBI	BB-IB	HP	SO	AVG	OBP	SLG	AOPS	ABR	SB-CS	FA	FR	RNG	THR	GAMES AT POSITION	DL	BFW
1895	Was N	1	2	0	0	0	0	0	0	0	0	0	.000	.000	.000	-99	-1	0	.714	0	143	0	/S		0.0

McCHESNEY, HARRY Harry Vincent "Pud" B6.1.1880 Pittsburgh PA D8.11.1960 Pittsburgh PA BR/TR/5-9/165 d9.17

YEAR	TM LG	G	AB	R	H	2B	3B	HR	RBI	BB-IB	HP	SO	AVG	OBP	SLG	AOPS	ABR	SB-CS	FA	FR	RNG	THR	GAMES AT POSITION	DL	BFW
1904	Chi N	22	88	9	23	6	2	0	11	4	0		.261	.293	.375	106	0	5	.967	-2	75	142	O22(0/1/21)		-0.5

McCLAIN, SCOTT Scott Michael B5.19.1972 Simi Valley CA BR/TR/6-3/210(209-220) [BalA90 22/604] d5.14

YEAR	TM LG	G	AB	R	H	2B	3B	HR	RBI	BB-IB	HP	SO	AVG	OBP	SLG	AOPS	ABR	SB-CS	FA	FR	RNG	THR	GAMES AT POSITION	DL	BFW
1998	TB A	9	20	2	2	0	0	0	1	2-0	1	6	.100	.217	.100	-13	-3	0-0	.966	-1	192	38	1b5,3b3		-0.5
2005	Chi N	13	14	1	2	1	0	0	1	2-0	0	2	.143	.250	.214	23	-2	0-0	1.000	-1	0	67	1b4,3b3		-0.5
Total	2	22	34	3	4	1	0	0	1	4-0	1	8	.118	.231	.147	2	-5	0-0	.978	-1	121	49	1b9,3b6		-0.8

McCLANAHAN, PETE Robert Hugh B10.24.1906 Coldspring TX D10.28.1987 Mont Belvieu TX BR/TR/5-9/170 d4.24

YEAR	TM LG	G	AB	R	H	2B	3B	HR	RBI	BB-IB	HP	SO	AVG	OBP	SLG	AOPS	ABR	SB-CS	FA	FR	RNG	THR	GAMES AT POSITION	DL	BFW
1931	Pit N	7	4	2	2	0	0	0	2	0	0	0	.500	.667	.500	220	1	0	—	0			/H		0.0

McCLELLAN, HARVEY Harvey McDowell "Little Mac" B12.22.1894 Cynthiana KY D11.6.1925 Cynthiana KY BR/TR/5-9.5/143 d5.31

YEAR	TM LG	G	AB	R	H	2B	3B	HR	RBI	BB-IB	HP	SO	AVG	OBP	SLG	AOPS	ABR	SB-CS	FA	FR	RNG	THR	GAMES AT POSITION	DL	BFW
1919	Chi A	7	12	2	4	0	0	0	1	1	0	1	.333	.385	.333	102	0	0	1.000	-0	141	330	3b3,S2		0.0
1920	Chi A	10	18	4	6	1	1	0	5	4	0	1	.333	.455	.500	153	2	2-0	.917	-2	54	0	S4,3b2		0.0
1921	Chi A	63	196	20	35	4	1	1	14	14	1	18	.179	.237	.224	18	-25	2-3	.968	14	123	40	2b21,S15,O15R,3b5		-1.1
1922	Chi A	91	301	28	68	17	3	2	28	16	3	32	.226	.270	.322	55	-21	3-2	.971	-3	103	111	3b71,S8,2b2/OC		-1.1
1923	Chi A	141	550	67	129	29	3	1	41	27	0	44	.235	.270	.304	52	-41	14-11	.958	-17	95	92	S139,2b2		-0.9
1924	Chi A	32	85	9	15	3	0	0	9	6	1	7	.176	.239	.212	17	-11	2-0	.938	2	120	64	S21,2b7/3OR		-0.7
Total	6	344	1162	130	257	54	8	4	98	68	5	103	.221	.267	.292	46	-96	23-16	.952	-7	99	90	S189,3b82,2b32,O17(0/1/16)		-6.0

McCLELLAN, BILL William Henry B3.22.1856 Chicago IL D7.3.1929 Chicago IL BB/TL/5-5.5/156 d5.20

YEAR	TM LG	G	AB	R	H	2B	3B	HR	RBI	BB-IB	HP	SO	AVG	OBP	SLG	AOPS	ABR	SB-CS	FA	FR	RNG	THR	GAMES AT POSITION	DL	BFW
1878	Chi N	48	205	26	46	8	1	0		29	2		13	.224	.232	.263	59	-9		.866	-8	97	94	2b42,S5/OR		-1.7
1881	Pro N	68	259	30	43	3	1	0	16	15			21	.166	.212	.185	26	-21		.855	-7	91	117	S50,O17(0/1/16)/2		-2.8
1883	Phi N	80	326	42	75	21	4	1	33	19			18	.230	.272	.328	89	-2		.849	5	105	91	S78,O2C/3		-0.6
1884	Phi N	111	450	71	116	13	2	3	33	28			43	.258	.301	.316	99	1		.852	-9	95	81	S111/OC		-0.4
1885	Bro AA	112	464	85	124	22	7	0	46	28	6			.267	.317	.345	108	5	43	.907	-8	98	97	2b141		0.0
1886	Bro AA	141	595	131	152	33	9	1	68	56	6			.255	.322	.346	108	7	70	.879	-21	97	87	2b136		-1.7
1887	Bro AA	136	548	109	144	24	6	1	53	80	6			.263	.363	.334	94	-1	70	.905	-7	89	128	2b56,O18(0/1/17)		-0.5
1888	Bro AA	74	278	33	57	7	3	0	21	40	1			.205	.307	.252	80	-4	13	.875	-1	91	78	O15R,2b5,S2		-0.4
	Cle AA	22	72	6	16	0	0	0	5	6	0			.222	.282	.222	64	-3	6	.897	-8	90	132	2b61,O33(0/1/32),S2		-1.0
	Year	96	350	39	73	7	3	0	26	46	1			.209	.302	.246	77	-7	19	.893	-63	97	97	2b436,S246,3b58,O54(0/5/49)		-6.7
Total	8	792	3197	533	773	129	33	6	304	274	15		95	.242	.305	.308	90	-27	132	.893	-63	97	97	2b436,S246,3b58,O54(0/5/49)		-6.7

McCLENDON, LLOYD Lloyd Glenn B1.11.1959 Gary IN BR/TR/5-11/195(195-212) [NYN80 8/183] d4.6 M5/C4 Col Valparaiso

YEAR	TM LG	G	AB	R	H	2B	3B	HR	RBI	BB-IB	HP	SO	AVG	OBP	SLG	AOPS	ABR	SB-CS	FA	FR	RNG	THR	GAMES AT POSITION	DL	BFW
1987	Cin N	45	72	8	15	5	0	2	13	4-0	0	15	.208	.247	.361	57	-5	1-0	.981	-1	121	65	C12,1b5/3OL		-0.3
1988	Cin N	72	137	9	30	4	0	3	14	15-1	2	22	.219	.301	.314	75	-4	4-0	1.000	3	181	65	O45L,1b28,3b6,C5		-0.3
1989	†Chi N	92	259	47	74	12	6	12	40	37-3	1	31	.286	.368	.479	134	12	6-4	.962	-5	92	90	O23L,C8,1b8		0.9
1990	Chi N	49	107	5	17	3	0	1	10	14-2	0	21	.159	.254	.215	29	-10	0-0	.980	3	117	0	O23L,C8,1b8		-0.9
	Pit N	4	3	1	1	0	0	0	1	0-0	1	1	.333	.333	1.333	347	1	0-0	—	-0	0	0	/OL		0.0
	Year	53	110	6	18	3	0	1	12	14-2	1	22	.164	.256	.245	37	-9	1-0	.980	3	116	0	O24L,C8,1b8		-0.9
1991	†Pit N	85	163	24	47	7	0	7	24	18-0	2	23	.288	.366	.460	132	7	2-1	.966	-2	69	152	O32(14/0/18),1b22,C2		-1.1
1992	†Pit N	84	190	26	48	8	1	3	20	28-0	2	24	.253	.350	.353	101	1	1-3	.967	-1	96	90	O61(21/0/47),1b6		-1.3
1993	Pit N	88	181	21	40	11	1	2	19	23-1	0	17	.221	.306	.326	70	-7	0-3	.967	-1	88	89	O20(12/0/9),1b2		-1.7
1994	Pit N	51	92	9	22	4	0	2	12	4-0	1	11	.239	.278	.413	76	-4	0-1	.967	-7	91	69	O260(138/0/130),1b101,C50,3b9		-2.1
Total	8	570	1204	150	294	54	8	35	154	143-7	8	165	.244	.325	.381	94	-9	15-12	.967	-7	91	69	O260(138/0/130),1b101,C50,3b9		-8.1

McCLESKEY, JEFF Jefferson Lamar B11.6.1891 Americus GA D5.11.1971 Americus GA BL/TR/5-11/160 d9.8 Col Georgia

YEAR	TM LG	G	AB	R	H	2B	3B	HR	RBI	BB-IB	HP	SO	AVG	OBP	SLG	AOPS	ABR	SB-CS	FA	FR	RNG	THR	GAMES AT POSITION	DL	BFW
1913	Bos N	2	3	0	0	0	0	0	1	0	0	0	.000	.250	.000	-25	0	0	.750	-1	47	0	3b2		-0.0

McCLOSKEY B Brooklyn NY d5.25

YEAR	TM LG	G	AB	R	H	2B	3B	HR	RBI	BB-IB	HP	SO	AVG	OBP	SLG	AOPS	ABR	SB-CS	FA	FR	RNG	THR	GAMES AT POSITION	DL	BFW
1875	Was NA	11	40	1	7	0	0	0		4	1		2	.175	.195	.175	31	-3	0-1	.673	-6			C11		

YEAR	TM LG	G	AB	R	H	2B	3B	HR	RBI	BB-IB	HP	SO	AVG	OBP	SLG	AOPS	ABR	SB-CS	FA	FR	RNG	THR	GAMES AT POSITION	DL	BFW

McCLOSKEY, BILL William George B5.1854 PA 5-8/155 d8.18

| 1884 | Wil U | 9 | 30 | 0 | 3 | 0 | 0 | 0 | | 0 | | | .100 | .100 | .100 | -38 | -6 | | .588 | -0 | 262 | 0 | O5(3/3/0),C5 | | -0.6 |

McCLURE, HAL Harold Murray "Mac" B8.8.1859 Lewisburg PA D3.1.1919 Lewisburg PA BR/TR/6-0/165 d5.10 Col Bucknell

| 1882 | Bos N | 2 | 6 | 1 | 2 | 0 | 0 | 0 | 0 | 0 | | | 1 | .333 | .333 | .333 | 114 | 0 | | .750 | -1 | 0 | 0 | O2R | 0.0 |

McCLURE, LARRY Lawrence Ledwith B10.8.1884 Wayne WV D9.1.1949 Huntington WV BR/TR/5-6.5/130 d7.26 Col West Virginia

| 1910 | NY A | 1 | 1 | 0 | 0 | 0 | 0 | 0 | | 0 | | | .000 | .000 | .000 | -95 | 0 | | — | -0 | 0 | 0 | /OL | | 0.0 |

McCONNELL, AMBY Ambrose Moses B4.29.1883 N.Pownal VT D5.20.1942 Utica NY BL/TR/5-7/150 d4.17 Col Beloit

1908	Bos A	140	502	77	140	10	6	2	43	38	11			.279	.343	.335	117	10	31	.939	-16	95	86	2b126,S3	-0.5
1909	Bos A	121	453	61	108	7	8	0	36	34	6			.238	.300	.289	84	-8	26	.954	11	112	101	2b121	0.4
1910	Bos A	11	35	6	6	0	0	0	1	5	2			.171	.310	.171	50	-2	4	.959	-1	108	0	2b10	-0.3
	Chi A	33	120	13	33	2	3	0	5	7	1			.275	.320	.342	112	1	4	.952	-0	97	109	2b32	0.1
	Year	44	155	19	39	2	3	0	6	12	3			.252	.318	.303	97	-1	8	.954	-1	100	81	2b42	-0.2
1911	Chi A	104	396	45	111	11	5	1	34	23	7			.280	.331	.341	90	-6	7	.973	0	102	103	2b103	-0.4
Total 4		409	1506	202	398	30	22	3	119	107	27			.264	.324	.319	98	-5	72	.954	-6	102	94	2b392,S3	-0.7

McCONNELL, GEORGE George Neely "Slats" B9.16.1877 Shelbyville TN D5.10.1964 Chattanooga TN BR/TR/6-3/190 d4.13 ▲

1909	NY A	13	43	4	9	0	1	0	5	1	0			.209	.227	.256	52	-3	1	.964	2	154	116	1b11,P2	-0.2
1912	NY A	42	91	11	27	4	2	0	8	4	1			.297	.333	.385	99	0	0	.913	5	146	193	P23,1b2	0.2
1913	NY A	39	67	4	12	2	0	0	2	0	0		11	.179	.179	.209	13	-8	0	.965	4	140	115	P35/1	0.2
1914	Chi N	1	2	0	0	0	0	0	0	0	0		0	1	.000	.000	.000	-99	0	0	1.000	0	162	0	/P	0.0
1915	Chi F	53	125	14	31	6	2	1	18	0	1		16	.248	.254	.352	74	4	2	.974	3	113	144	P44	0.0
1916	Chi N	28	57	2	9	0	0	0	0	2	0		4	.158	.200	.158	10	-2	0	.952	2	111	218	P28	0.0
Total 6		176	385	35	88	12	5	1	33	7	3		32	.229	.248	.294	57	-9	3	.953	15	126	161	P133,1b14	0.2

McCONNELL, SAM Samuel Faulkner B6.8.1895 Philadelphia PA D6.27.1981 Phoenixville PA BL/TR/5-6.5/150 d4.19

| 1915 | Phi A | 6 | 11 | 1 | 2 | 1 | 0 | 0 | 1 | 0 | 1 | | | .182 | .250 | .273 | 58 | -1 | 0 | .842 | 1 | 134 | 0 | 3b5 | 0.0 |

McCORMACK, DON Donald Ross B9.18.1955 Omak WA BR/TR/6-3/205* [PhiN74 4/75] d9.30

1980	Phi N	2	1	0	1	0	0	0		0-0	0		0	1.000	1.000	1.000	431	0	0-0	1.000	1	0	0	C2	0.1
1981	Phi N	3	4	0	1	0	0	0		0-0	0		1	.250	.250	.250	40	0	0-0	1.000	-0	0	165	C3	-0.1
Total 2		5	5	0	2	0	0	0		0-0	0		1	.400	.400	.400	120	0	0-0	1.000	1	0	126	C5	0.0

McCORMICK, FRANK Frank Andrew "Buck" B6.9.1911 New York NY D11.21.1982 Manhasset NY BR/TR/6-4/205 d9.11 C2

1934	Cin N	12	16	1	5	2	1	0	5	0	0		1	.313	.313	.563	132	1	0	.941	-1	0	76	1b2	0.0
1937	Cin N	24	83	5	27	5	0	0	9	2	0		4	.325	.341	.386	102	0	1	1.000	1	123	123	1b20,2b4/OR	-0.1
1938	Cin N★	151	640	89	209	40	4	5	106	18	3	17	.327	.348	.425	115	11	1	.995	-4	89	103	1b151	-0.7
1939	†Cin N★	156	630	99	209	41	4	18	128	41	2	16	.332	.374	.495	131	26	1	.996	1	97	117	1b156	1.3
1940	†Cin N★	155	618	93	191	44	3	19	127	52	5	26	.309	.367	.482	131	27	2	.995	-1	95	130	1b155	1.1
1941	Cin N★	154	603	77	162	31	5	17	97	40	4	13	.269	.318	.421	107	3	2	.995	-0	94	108	1b154	-1.2
1942	Cin N★	145	564	58	156	24	0	13	89	45	2	18	.277	.332	.388	111	7	1	.993	5	111	124	1b144	-0.2
1943	Cin N*	126	472	56	143	28	0	8	59	29	1	15	.303	.345	.413	120	11	2	.995	4	111	116	1b120	0.9
1944	Cin N☆	153	581	85	177	37	3	20	102	57	4	17	.305	.371	.482	144	34	7	.992	12	133	122	1b153	3.8
1945	Cin N*	152	580	68	160	33	0	10	81	56	5	22	.276	.345	.384	105	4	6	.994	5	109	90	1b151	0.1
1946	Phi N★	135	504	46	143	20	2	11	66	36	1	21	.284	.333	.397	110	4	2	.999	5	108	83	1b134	0.5
1947	Phi N	15	40	7	9	2	0	1	8	3	0	2	.225	.279	.350	69	-2	0	.989	-1	63	115	1b12	-0.3
	Bos N	81	212	24	75	18	2	2	43	11	0	8	.354	.386	.486	133	10	2	.996	-1	90	92	1b46	0.7
	Year	96	252	31	84	20	2	3	51	14	0	10	.333	.368	.464	123	8	2	.995	-2	85	96	1b58	0.4
1948	†Bos N	75	180	14	45	9	2	4	34	10	0	9	.250	.289	.389	84	-5	0	.987	2	126	112	1b50	-0.4
Total 13		1534	5723	722	1711	334	26	128	954	399	27	189	.299	.348	.434	118	131	27	.995	28	105	110	1b1448,2b4/OR	5.5

McCORMICK, MOOSE Harry Elwood B2.28.1881 Philadelphia PA D7.9.1962 Lewisburg PA BL/TL/5-11/180 d4.14 Col Bucknell

1904	NY N	59	203	28	54	9	5	1	26	13	4			.266	.323	.374	110	2	13	.916	-4	47	124	O55(2/52/1)	-0.5
	Pit N	66	238	25	69	10	6	2	23	13	2			.290	.332	.408	124	6	6	.940	-3	94	0	O66(18/0/48)	0.0
	Year	125	441	53	123	19	11	3	49	26	6			.279	.328	.392	118	8	19	.928	-7	72	58	O121(20/52/49)	-0.5
1908	Phi N	11	22	0	2	0	0	0	2	2	0			.091	.167	.091	-17	-3	0	1.000	0	36	113	O5L	-0.4
	NY N	73	252	31	76	16	3	0	32	4	1			.302	.315	.389	119	4	6	.901	-8	33	105	O65(59/0/12)	-0.9
	Year	84	274	31	78	16	3	0	34	6	1			.285	.302	.365	108	1	6	.910	-8	33	105	O70(64/0/12)	-1.3
1909	NY N	110	413	68	120	21	8	3	27	49	5			.291	.373	.402	138	20	4	.924	-10	90	198	O110(87/0/23)	0.5
1912	†NY N	42	39	4	13	4	1	0	4	1	0		9	.333	.422	.487	144	3	1	.667	-1	54	0	O6(1/1/4)/1	0.2
1913	†NY N	57	80	9	22	3	0	1	15	5	0		13	.275	.318	.375	97	-1	0	.909	-0	103	72	O15(0/2/13)	0.2
Total 5		418	1247	165	356	62	26	6	133	92	12	22	.285	.340	.391	122	31	30	.920	-26	70	118	O322(172/55/101)/1	-1.3

McCORMICK, JIM James Ambrose B11.2.1868 Spencer MA D2.1.1948 Saco ME BR/TR/6-1/160 d9.10

| 1892 | StL N | 3 | 11 | 0 | 0 | 0 | 0 | 0 | | 5 | 0 | | | .000 | .083 | .000 | -78 | -2 | 0 | 1.000 | -0 | 102 | 0 | 2b2/3 | -0.2 |

McCORMICK, JERRY John B Philadelphia PA D9.19.1905 Philadelphia PA d5.1

1883	Bal AA	93	389	40	102	16	6	0		2				.262	.266	.334	89	-6		.799	1	101	87	3b93	-0.3
1884	Phi U	67	295	41	84	12	2	0		4				.285	.294	.339	99	-9		.811	11	118	118	3b54,2b5,O5(5/0/1),S3/P	0.3
	Was U	42	157	23	34	8	2	0		1				.217	.222	.293	57	-13		.792	-3	72	149	3b38,S4	-1.4
	Year	109	452	64	118	20	4	0		5				.261	.269	.323	84	-23		.806	9	101	129	3b92,S7,2b5,O5(5/0/1)/P	-1.1
Total 2		202	841	104	220	36	10	0		7				.262	.268	.328	86	-28		.802	9	101	108	3b185,S7,O5(5/0/1),2b5/P	-1.4

McCORMICK, MIKE Michael J. "Kid","Dude" B5.1883 , Scotland D11.18.1953 Jersey City NJ BR/TR/5-3/155 d4.14

| 1904 | Bro N | 105 | 347 | 28 | 64 | 5 | 4 | 0 | 27 | 43 | 2 | | | .184 | .278 | .222 | 56 | -17 | 22 | .914 | -2 | 93 | 181 | 3b104/2 | -1.7 |

McCORMICK, MIKE Myron Winthrop B5.6.1917 Angels Camp CA D4.13.1976 Los Angeles CA BR/TR/6-0/200* d4.16 Mil 1943-45

1940	†Cin N	110	417	48	125	20	0	1	30	13	3	36	.300	.326	.355	87	-8	8	.986	2	102	102	O107(51/50/6)	-1.1
1941	Cin N	110	369	52	106	17	3	4	31	30	0	24	.287	.341	.382	103	1	4	.976	2	101	119	O101(82/19/0)	-0.2
1942	Cin N	40	135	18	32	4	3	1	11	13	0	7	.237	.304	.319	82	-3	0	.990	-0	104	61	O38(13/26/0)	67	-0.5
1943	Cin N	4	15	0	2	0	0	0	2	0	0	2	.133	.235	.133	8	-7	0	.909	-1	83	0	O4C	-0.3
1946	Cin N	23	74	10	16	2	0	0	5	8	0	7	.216	.293	.243	55	-4	0	1.000	-1	96	50	O21C	-0.7
	Bos N	59	164	23	43	6	2	1	16	11	0	7	.262	.309	.341	83	-4	0	.973	-1	110	27	O48(10/33/5)	-0.7
	Year	82	238	33	59	8	2	1	21	19	0	11	.248	.304	.311	75	-8	0	.982	-2	105	35	O69(10/54/5)	-1.4
1947	Bos N	92	284	42	81	13	7	3	36	20	0	21	.285	.332	.412	99	-2	1	.981	-3	94	84	O79(26/62/1)	-0.7
1948	†Bos N	115	343	45	104	22	7	1	39	32	0	34	.303	.363	.417	112	6	1	.975	-1	96	106	O100(56/34/20)	-1.1
1949	†Bro N	55	139	17	29	5	1	2	14	14	0	12	.209	.281	.302	54	-9	1	1.000	0	97	106	O49(38/7/5)	-1.1
1950	NY N	4	4	0	0	0	0	0	0	0	0	2	.000	.000	.000	-99	-1	0	—	0	0	0	/H	-0.1
	Chi A	55	108	16	32	4	3	0	10	16	0	6	.232	.312	.304	60	-9	0-1	.982	2	107	130	O44(2/42/0)	-0.7
1951	Was A	81	243	31	70	9	4	3	23	20	0	20	.288	.364	.362	98	0	1-2	.966	3	106	156	O62(24/12/28)	0.0
Total 10		748	2325	302	640	100	29	14	215	188	3	173	.275	.330	.361	90	-35	16-3	.980	5	101	100	O653(302/310/65)	67	-6.0

McCORMICK, BARRY William J. B12.25.1874 Maysville KY D1.28.1956 Cincinnati OH TR/5-9/? d9.25 U13

1895	Lou N	3	12	2	3	1	0	0		0	0		0	.250	.250	.417	75	-1		1.000	-1	96	141	S2/2	-0.1
1896	Chi N	45	168	22	37	3	1	0	23	14	0	30	.220	.280	.268	43	-14	9	.835	-5	98	93	3b35,S6,2b3/OR	-1.6
1897	Chi N	101	419	87	112	8	10	3	55	33	2			.267	.324	.348	75	-17	44	.851	2	108	137	3b56,S46/2	-1.1
1898	Chi N	137	530	76	131	15	9	2	78	47	5			.247	.314	.321	82	-13	15	.888	3	112	171	3b136/S2	-0.7
1899	Chi N	102	376	48	97	15	4	0	52	25	4			.258	.311	.324	76	-12	14	.941	1	110	124	2b99,S3	-0.6
1900	Chi N	110	379	35	83	13	5	3	48	38	1			.219	.292	.303	67	-17	8	.907	-9	98	94	S84,3b21,2b5	-2.0
1901	Chi N	115	427	45	100	15	1	3	32	11	1			.234	.248	.304	74	-14	12	.911	-4	103	103	S112,3b3	-1.4
1902	StL A	139	504	55	124	14	4	3	51	37	5			.246	.304	.308	71	-20	10	.905	-15	92	142	S7/3b2,S7/OC	-3.0
1903	StL A	61	207	13	45	6	1	1	16	18	1			.217	.283	.271	69	-7	5	.969	-1	95	85	2b28,3b28,S4	-0.7
	Was A	63	219	14	47	10	2	0	23	10	2			.215	.255	.279	59	-11	3	.960	9	124	115	2b63	-0.2
	Year	124	426	27	92	16	3	1	39	28	3			.216	.269	.275	64	-18	8	.962	8	107	106	2b91,3b28,S4	-0.9

YEAR	TM LG	G	AB	R	H	2B	3B	HR	RBI	BB-IB	HP	SO	AVG	OBP	SLG	AOPS	ABR	SB-CS	FA	FR	RNG	THR	GAMES AT POSITION	DL	BFW
1904	Was A	113	404	36	88	11	1	0	39	27	4	45	.218	.274	.250	67	-14	9	.938	4	109	106	2b113		-1.1
Total	10	989	3645	433	867	110	42	15	417	280	25	30	.238	.297	.303	71	-140	130	.885	-18	103	145	3b411,2b314,S265,O2(0/1/1)		-12.5

McCOSKY, BARNEY William Barney B4.11.1917 Coal Run PA D9.6.1996 Venice FL BL/TR/6-1/184* d4.18 Mil 1943-45 [DL 1949 Phi A 129]

YEAR	TM LG	G	AB	R	H	2B	3B	HR	RBI	BB-IB	HP	SO	AVG	OBP	SLG	AOPS	ABR	SB-CS	FA	FR	RNG	THR	GAMES AT POSITION	DL	BFW
																									0.3
1939	Det A	147	611	120	190	33	14	4	58	70	2	45	.311	.384	.430	100	1	20-4	.986	3	108	57	O145C		1.0
1940	†Det A	143	589	123	200	39	19	4	57	67	1	41	.340	.408	.491	120	19	13-9	.983	-5	96	70	O141C		0.4
1941	Det A	127	494	80	160	25	8	3	55	61	3	33	.324	.401	.425	108	8	8-3	.985	-0	104	59	O122(21/101/0)		0.0
1942	Det A	154	600	75	176	28	11	7	50	68	0	37	.293	.365	.412	109	8	11-5	.981	-0	105	58	O154(145/7/2)		-0.6
1946	Det A	25	91	11	18	5	0	1	11	17	0	9	.198	.324	.286	67	-3	0-0	.966	-2	90	63	O24C		1.8
	Phi A	92	308	33	109	17	4	1	34	43	0	13	.354	.433	.445	146	22	2-2	.981	-1	104	39	O85C		1.2
	Year	117	399	44	127	22	4	2	45	60	0	22	.318	.407	.409	127	18	2-2	.978	-4	101	45	O109C		0.5
1947	Phi A	137	546	77	179	22	7	1	52	57	4	29	.328	.395	.399	119	16	1-4	.983	-0	100	80	O136(114/23/0)		-0.2
1948	Phi A	135	515	95	168	21	5	0	46	68	0	22	.326	.405	.386	111	11	1-3	.990	-2	91	94	O134L		-1.4
1950	Phi A	66	179	19	43	10	1	0	11	22	0	12	.240	.323	.307	63	-10	0-0	.987	-2	91	35	O42L		0.0
1951	Phi A	12	27	4	8	2	0	1	1	3	0	4	.296	.367	.481	125	1	0-0	1.000	0	101	0	O7(5/0/2)		0.0
	Cin N	25	50	2	16	2	1	1	11	4	0	2	.320	.370	.460	120	1	0-0	1.000	-1	84	0	O11(4/7/1)		-0.4
	Cle A	31	61	8	13	3	0	0	2	8	0	5	.213	.304	.262	57	-3	1-1	1.000	-0	107	0	O16(1/2/13)		-0.6
1952	Cle A	54	80	14	17	4	1	1	6	8	0	5	.213	.284	.325	74	-3	1-1	.944	-2	80	0	O19(11/0/9)		0.1
1953	Cle A	22	21	3	4	3	0	0	3	1	0	4	.190	.227	.333	51	-1	0-0	—	0			/H		-0.1
Total	11	1170	4172	664	1301	214	71	24	397	497	10	261	.312	.386	.414	109	67	58-31	.984	-13	101	63	O1036(477/535/27)	129	0.7

McCOVEY, WILLIE Willie Lee "Stretch" B1.10.1938 Mobile AL BL/TL/6-4/210(190-230) d7.30 HF1986

YEAR	TM LG	G	AB	R	H	2B	3B	HR	RBI	BB-IB	HP	SO	AVG	OBP	SLG	AOPS	ABR	SB-CS	FA	FR	RNG	THR	GAMES AT POSITION	DL	BFW
																									2.0
1959	SF N	52	192	32	68	9	5	13	38	22-1	4	35	.354	.429	.656	189	24	2-0	.989	-1	89	77	1b51		0.5
1960	SF N	101	260	37	62	15	3	13	51	45-4	0	53	.238	.349	.469	130	12	1-1	.985	-2	88	84	1b71		0.4
1961	SF N	106	328	59	89	12	3	18	50	37-3	5	60	.271	.350	.491	126	12	1-2	.985	-2	93	81	1b84		1.5
1962	†SF N	91	229	41	67	6	1	20	54	29-1	0	53	.293	.368	.590	156	17	3-3	.976	-0	111	66	O57(45/0/12),1b17		3.6
1963	SF N★	152	564	103	158	19	5	44	102	50-5	11	119	.280	.350	.566	161	42	1-1	.942	-0	100	86	O135(134/0/2),1b23		-0.5
1964	SF N	130	364	55	80	14	1	18	54	61-5	5	73	.220	.336	.412	108	6	2-1	.935	-8	80	111	O83(78/0/5),1b26		2.5
1965	SF N	160	564	93	149	17	4	39	92	88-5	6	118	.276	.381	.539	152	40	0-4	.991	-6	83	87	1b156		3.1
1966	SF N★	150	502	85	148	26	6	36	96	76-10	6	100	.295	.391	.586	163	45	2-1	.984	-7	87	89	1b145		3.3
1967	SF N	135	456	73	126	17	4	31	91	71-17	6	110	.276	.378	.535	162	38	3-3	.989	1	108	112	1b127		4.9
1968	SF N★	148	523	81	153	16	4	36	105	72-20	5	71	.293	.378	.545	176	49	4-2	.985	3	115	91	1b146		6.5
1969	SF N★	149	491	101	157	26	2	45	126	.121-45	4	66	.320	.453	.656	211	80	0-0	.992	-5	90	107	1b148		6.5
1970	SF N★	152	495	98	143	39	2	39	126	137-40	3	75	.289	.444	.612	182	67	0-0	.989	12	132	95	1b146	15	1.6
1971	†SF N★	105	329	45	91	13	0	18	70	64-21	4	57	.277	.396	.480	150	25	0-2	.983	-2	100	110	1b95	44	-1.0
1972	SF N	81	263	30	56	8	0	14	35	38-5	2	45	.213	.316	.403	102	1	0-0	.986	-4	79	95	1b74		3.1
1973	SF N	130	383	52	102	14	3	29	75	105-25	1	78	.266	.420	.546	160	36	1-0	.988	2	110	102	1b117		2.3
1974	SD N	128	344	53	87	19	1	22	63	96-9	1	76	.253	.416	.506	136	16	1-0	.987	-6	76	65	1b104		1.0
1975	SD N	122	413	43	104	17	0	23	68	57-8	3	80	.252	.345	.460	131	17	1-0	.986	1	113	107	1b115		-0.2
1976	SD N	71	202	20	41	9	0	7	36	21-7	1	39	.203	.281	.351	85	-5	0-0	—	0			D9		-0.2
	Oak A	11	24	0	5	0	0	0	3-1		0	4	.208	.296	.208	51	-1	0-0	.989	4	78	95	1b136		0.7
1977	SF N	141	478	54	134	21	0	28	86	67-16	0	106	.280	.367	.500	130	21	3-0	.989	-2	92	80	1b97		-1.1
1978	SF N	108	351	32	80	19	2	12	64	36-8	1	57	.228	.298	.396	96	-3	1-0	.987	1	104	87	1b89		-0.5
1979	SF N	117	353	34	88	9	0	15	57	36-2	1	70	.249	.318	.402	103	0	0-2	.987	1	104	75	1b27		-0.8
1980	SF N	48	113	8	23	8	0	1	16	13-2	1	23	.204	.285	.301	68	-5	0-0	.992	2	75	85	1b27		0.0
Total	22	2588	8197	1229	2211	353	46	521	1555	1345-260	69	1550	.270	.374	.515	148	554	26-22	.987	-23	99	94	1b2045,O275(257/0/19),D9	59	39.2

McCOY, ART Arthur Gray B7.15.1864 Danville PA D3.22.1904 Danville PA ?/168 d7.8

YEAR	TM LG	G	AB	R	H	2B	3B	HR	RBI	BB-IB	HP	SO	AVG	OBP	SLG	AOPS	ABR	SB-CS	FA	FR	RNG	THR	GAMES AT POSITION	DL	BFW
1889	Was N	2	6	0	0	0	0	0	2	0	1		.000	.250	.000	-29	-1	0	.889	-1	38	0	2b2		-0.2

McCOY, BENNY Benjamin Jenison B11.9.1915 Jenison MI BL/TR/5-9/170 d9.14 Mil 1942-45

YEAR	TM LG	G	AB	R	H	2B	3B	HR	RBI	BB-IB	HP	SO	AVG	OBP	SLG	AOPS	ABR	SB-CS	FA	FR	RNG	THR	GAMES AT POSITION	DL	BFW
1938	Det A	7	15	2	3	1	0	0	1	1	0	2	.200	.250	.267	28	-2	0-0	.963	1	136	144	2b6/3		-0.1
1939	Det A	55	192	38	58	13	6	1	33	29	0	26	.302	.394	.448	107	3	3-1	.958	-1	101	87	2b34,S16		0.4
1940	Phi A	134	490	56	126	26	5	7	62	65	1	44	.257	.345	.373	88	-8	2-2	.951	-10	102	90	2b130/3		-1.0
1941	Phi A	141	517	86	140	12	7	8	61	95	0	50	.271	.384	.368	102	5	3-3	.963	-11	104	96	2b135		-0.5
Total	4	337	1214	182	327	52	18	16	156	190	1	122	.269	.369	.381	97	-2	8-6	.957	-22	103	93	2b305,S16,3b2		

McCRACKEN, QUINTON Quinton Antoine B3.16.1970 Wilmington NC BB/TR/5-7/173(170-190) [ColN92 25/711] d9.17 Col Duke

YEAR	TM LG	G	AB	R	H	2B	3B	HR	RBI	BB-IB	HP	SO	AVG	OBP	SLG	AOPS	ABR	SB-CS	FA	FR	RNG	THR	GAMES AT POSITION	DL	BFW
1995	Col N	3	1	0	0	0	0	0	0	0	0	1	.000	.000	.000	-78	0	0-0	—	0			/OC		0.0
1996	Col N	124	283	50	82	13	6	3	40	32-4	1	62	.290	.363	.410	84	-6	17-6	.957	-7	82	84	O93(8/85/4)		-1.1
1997	Col N	147	325	69	95	11	1	3	36	42-0	1	62	.292	.374	.360	76	-10	28-11	.980	-4	94	114	O132C		-1.0
1998	TB A	155	614	77	179	38	7	7	59	41-1	3	107	.292	.335	.410	91	-8	19-10	.992	5	95	193	O40(26/20/0)		-1.0
1999	TB A	40	148	20	37	6	1	1	18	14-0	1	23	.250	.317	.324	64	-8	6-5	1.000	-0	104	0	O11(9/3/0)		-0.5
2000	TB A	15	31	5	4	0	0	0	2	6-0	0	4	.129	.270	.129	6	-2	0-1	1.000	0	106	0	O10(6/2/3),D9		-0.6
2001	Min A	24	64	7	14	2	2	0	5	5-0	0	13	.219	.275	.313	52	-5	0-1	1.000	4	110	100	O97(7/31/68)		0.4
2002	†Ari N	123	349	60	108	27	8	3	40	32-0	2	68	.309	.367	.458	109	4	5-4	.995	4	110	100	O55(10/16/34)/D		-2.3
2003	Ari N	115	203	17	46	5	2	0	18	15-2	0	34	.227	.276	.271	41	-18	5-1	1.000	-0	72	287	O8(4/4/0),D6		-0.3
2004	Sea A	19	20	6	3	0	0	0	0	2-0	0	4	.150	.227	.150	1	-3	2-4	.979	-3	76	107	O37(27/3/10)		-0.8
	Ari N	55	156	20	45	11	1	2	13	13-0	0	23	.288	.341	.410	88	-3	2-4	.975	-4	80	95	O59(11/46/2)		-1.6
2005	Ari N	134	215	23	51	4	3	1	13	23-4	1	35	.237	.313	.298	59	-13	4-0	.984	-17	92	117	O696(166/446/121),D16	132	-9.2
Total	11	954	2409	354	664	117	31	20	242	225-11	9	436	.276	.337	.375	79	-74	87-44							

McCRAW, TOM Tommy Lee B11.21.1940 Malvern AR BL/TL/6-0/183* d6.4 C24 Col Santa Monica (CA) City

YEAR	TM LG	G	AB	R	H	2B	3B	HR	RBI	BB-IB	HP	SO	AVG	OBP	SLG	AOPS	ABR	SB-CS	FA	FR	RNG	THR	GAMES AT POSITION	DL	BFW
1963	Chi A	102	280	38	71	11	3	6	33	21-1	3	46	.254	.309	.379	94	-3	15-4	.993	-2	88	112	1b97		-0.8
1964	Chi A	125	368	47	96	11	6	6	36	32-4	4	65	.261	.325	.367	95	-3	15-7	.992	-3	89	125	1b84,O36(32/2/3)		-1.1
1965	Chi A	133	273	38	65	12	1	5	21	25-4	3	48	.238	.309	.344	91	-3	12-7	.993	-2	132	97	1b72,O64(37/31/3)		-0.9
1966	Chi A	151	389	49	89	16	4	5	48	29-7	5	40	.229	.288	.329	83	-9	20-11	.990	3	120	93	1b121,O41(29/0/16)		-1.4
1967	Chi A	125	453	55	107	18	3	11	45	33-2	1	55	.236	.288	.362	95	-4	24-10	.991	11	140	114	1b123,O6(1/4/1)		0.1
1968	Chi A	136	477	51	112	16	12	9	44	36-9	5	58	.235	.293	.375	101	-1	20-5	.986	3	119	107	1b135	42	-0.4
1969	Chi A	93	240	21	62	12	2	2	25	21-6	3	24	.258	.326	.350	85	-5	1-3	.989	-6	91	98	1b59,O49(21/12/16)		-1.6
1970	Chi A	129	332	39	73	11	2	6	31	21-3	4	50	.220	.273	.319	61	-18	12-3	.987	0	135	99	1b59,O49(24/22/24),1b38		-2.2
1971	Was A	122	207	33	44	6	4	7	25	19-2	5	34	.213	.291	.382	95	-3	3-3	.958	-3	102	33	O60(26/1/37),1b30		-0.9
1972	Cle A	129	391	43	101	13	5	7	33	41-5	4	47	.258	.333	.371	106	3	12-10	1.000	-4	91	156	O34(32/1/1),1b25,D8		-0.4
1973	Cal A	99	264	25	70	7	0	3	24	30-1	2	42	.265	.343	.326	96	0	3-2	1.000	4	91	94	1b29,O12(7/0/5),D3		-0.1
1974	Cle A	56	119	21	34	8	0	3	17	12-2	1	11	.286	.348	.429	130	5	2-1	.990	2	130	115	1b38/OC		0.5
	Cle A	45	112	17	34	4	0	3	17	5-0	1	13	.304	.336	.455	128	4	0-0	.994	3	115	91	1b67,O13(7/1/5),D3		0.3
	Year	101	231	38	68	16	0	6	34	17-2	1	24	.294	.343	.442	129	2	2-2	1.000	4	102	96	1b105,O3L		0.8
1975	Cle A	23	51	7	14	1	1	2	5	7-2	0	7	.275	.362	.451	128	2	4-1	1.000	-1	79	96	1b16,O3L		0.0
Total	13	1468	3956	484	972	150	42	75	404	332-48	40	544	.246	.309	.362	94	-35	143-68	.991	16	106	116	1b911,O431(241/90/125),D11	42	-8.9

McCRAY, RODNEY Rodney Duncan B9.13.1963 Detroit MI BR/TR/5-10/175* [SDN84*9/219] d4.30 Col West Los Angeles (CA) CC

YEAR	TM LG	G	AB	R	H	2B	3B	HR	RBI	BB-IB	HP	SO	AVG	OBP	SLG	AOPS	ABR	SB-CS	FA	FR	RNG	THR	GAMES AT POSITION	DL	BFW
1990	Chi A	32	6	8	0	0	0	0	0	1-0	0	4	.000	.143	.000	-58	-1	6-0	1.000	0	135	0	O13(3/7/4),D7		0.0
1991	Chi A	17	7	2	2	0	0	0	0	0-0	0	1	.286	.286	.286	60	0	1-1	1.000	0	162	0	O8(4/2/2),D6		0.1
1992	NY N	18	1	3	1	0	0	0	1	0-0	0	1	1.000	1.000	1.000	472	-0	2-0	1.000	0	153	0	O13(1/1/11)		0.1
Total	3	67	14	13	3	0	0	1	1-0	0	6	.214	.267	.214	36	-1	9-1	1.000	1	150	0	O34(8/10/17),D13		0.1

McCREA, FRANK Francis William B9.6.1896 Jersey City NJ D2.25.1981 Dover NJ BR/TR/5-9/155 d9.26

YEAR	TM LG	G	AB	R	H	2B	3B	HR	RBI	BB-IB	HP	SO	AVG	OBP	SLG	AOPS	ABR	SB-CS	FA	FR	RNG	THR	GAMES AT POSITION	DL	BFW
1925	Cle A	1	5	1	1	0	0	0	0	0	0		.200	.200	.200	2	-1	0-0	1.000	-0	65	0	/C		-0.1

McCREDIE, WALT Walter Henry B11.29.1876 Manchester IA D7.29.1934 Portland OR BL/TR/6-2/195 d4.20

YEAR	TM LG	G	AB	R	H	2B	3B	HR	RBI	BB-IB	HP	SO	AVG	OBP	SLG	AOPS	ABR	SB-CS	FA	FR	RNG	THR	GAMES AT POSITION	DL	BFW
1903	Bro N	56	213	40	69	5	0	0	24	20	24		.324	.397	.347	116	6	10	.925	-4	79	165	O56R		0.6

McCREERY, TOM Thomas Livingston B10.19.1874 Beaver PA D7.3.1941 Beaver PA BB/TR/5-11/180 d6.8 Col Georgetown OF(39/203/390) ▲

YEAR	TM LG	G	AB	R	H	2B	3B	HR	RBI	BB-IB	HP	SO	AVG	OBP	SLG	AOPS	ABR	SB-CS	FA	FR	RNG	THR	GAMES AT POSITION	DL	BFW
																									-0.2
1895	Lou N	31	108	18	35	3	1	0	10	8	1	15	.324	.376	.370	99	0	3	.875	-4	49		O18R,P8,S4/31		2.4
1896	Lou N	115	441	87	155	23	21	7	65	42	1	58	.351	.409	.546	156	34	26	.916	0	128	48	O111(0/2/109)/2P		-1.2
1897	Lou N	91	344	55	96	5	4	1	40	40	1		.279	.354	.363	93	-3	13	.859	-6	100	74	O91(1/1/89)		0.1
	NY N	49	177	36	53	8	5	1	28	18	1		.299	.380	.418	114	4	15	.900	-1	160	85	O45R,2b3		0.1

YEAR	TM LG	G	AB	R	H	2B	3B	HR	RBI	BB-IB	HP	SO	AVG	OBP	SLG	AOPS	ABR	SB-CS	FA	FR	RNG	THR	GAMES AT POSITION	DL	BFW
	Year	140	521	91	149	13	11	5	68	62	1		.286	.363	.382	100	1	28	.871	-6	120	78	O136(1/1/134),2b3		-1.1
1898	NY N	35	121	15	24	4	3	1	17	19	0		.198	.307	.306	78	-3	3	.820	-5	85	0	O35(1/0/35)		-0.9
	Pit N	53	190	33	59	5	7	2	20	26	0		.311	.394	.442	142	10	3	.934	-1	88	66	O51(0/46/5)		0.6
	Year	88	311	48	83	9	10	3	37	45	0		.267	.363	.389	117	7	6	.901	-6	87	39	O86(1/46/40)		-0.3
1899	Pit N	119	460	77	149	21	9	3	65	47	3		.324	.390	.428	125	17	11	.911	-12	102	48	O98(15/50/33),S9,2b7		0.0
1900	Pit N	43	132	20	29	4	3	1	13	16	0		.220	.304	.318	71	-5	2	.887	1	179	169	O35(17/1/17)/P		-0.6
1901	Bro N	91	335	47	97	11	14	3	53	32	2		.290	.355	.433	124	9	13	.947	1	83	70	O82(4/78/0),1b4,S2		0.6
1902	Bro N	112	430	49	105	8	4	4	57	29	2		.244	.295	.309	86	-8	16	.979	-1	94	97	1b108,O4(1/0/3)		-1.2
1903	Bro N	40	141	13	37	5	2	0	10	20	0		.262	.354	.326	97	0	5	.892	-3	72	149	O38(0/2/36)		-0.5
	Bos N	23	83	15	18	2	1	1	10	9	0		.217	.293	.301	72	-3	6	.900	-1	59	115	O23C		-0.5
	Year	63	224	28	55	7	3	1	20	29	0		.246	.332	.317	88	-3	11	.896	-4	67	136	O61(0/25/36)		-1.0
Total	9	802	2962	465	857	99	76	27	388	310	10	73	.289	.359	.401	113	52	116	.906	-30	106	83	O631R,1b113,S15,2b11,P10/3		-1.6

McCUE, FRANK Frank Aloysius B10.4.1898 Chicago IL D7.5.1953 Chicago IL BB/TR/5-9/150 d9.15

| 1922 | Phi A | 2 | 5 | 0 | 0 | 0 | 0 | 0 | 0 | 0 | 0 | | .000 | .000 | .000 | -97 | -1 | 0-0 | — | -0 | 0 | 0 | 3b2 | | -0.2 |

McCULLOUGH, CLYDE Clyde Edward B3.4.1917 Nashville TN D9.18.1982 San Francisco CA BR/TR/5-11.5/180* d4.28 Mil 1944-45 C4

1940	Chi N	9	26	4	4	1	0	0	1	5	0	5	.154	.290	.192	36	-2	0-0	1.000	1	108	76	C7		0.0
1941	Chi N	125	418	41	95	9	2	9	53	34	2	67	.227	.289	.323	75	-16	5	.982	-6	89	93	C119		-1.5
1942	Chi N	109	337	39	95	22	1	5	31	25	1	47	.282	.331	.398	117	7	7	.980	0	110	108	C97		1.3
1943	Chi N	87	266	20	63	5	2	2	23	24	1	33	.237	.302	.293	73	-9	6	.977	-10	126	41	C81		-1.6
1946	Chi N	95	307	38	88	18	5	4	34	22	2	39	.287	.338	.417	116	5	2	.991	-3	111	74	C89		0.7
1947	Chi N	86	234	25	59	12	4	3	30	20	1	20	.252	.314	.376	86	-6	1	.984	4	110	107	C64		0.2
1948	Chi N☆	69	172	10	36	4	2	1	7	15	0	25	.209	.273	.273	46	-13	0	.973	1	93	125	C51		-0.9
1949	Pit N	91	241	30	57	9	3	4	21	24	4	30	.237	.316	.349	76	-8	1	.985	6	122	100	C90		0.2
1950	Pit N	103	279	28	71	16	4	6	34	31	5	35	.254	.340	.405	92	-3	3	.985	-4	126	95	C100	30	-0.2
1951	Pit N	92	259	26	77	9	2	8	39	27	1	31	.297	.366	.440	113	5	2-0	.988	6	108	109	C87		1.6
1952	Pit N	66	172	10	40	5	1	5	15	10	2	18	.233	.283	.291	58	-10	0-1	.981	4	82	143	C61/1		-0.4
1953	Chi N☆	77	229	21	59	3	2	6	23	15	0	23	.258	.303	.367	72	-10	0-0	.987	-2	84	112	C73		-0.9
1954	Chi N	31	81	9	21	7	0	3	17	5	1	15	.259	.310	.457	96	-1	0-0	.981	-2	61	26	C26,3b3	46	-0.2
1955	Chi N	44	81	7	16	0	0	0	10	8-3	1	15	.198	.272	.198	29	-8	0-0	.989	3	77	79	C37		-0.4
1956	Chi N	14	19	0	4	1	0	0	1	0-0	1	5	.211	.200	.263	27	-2	0-0	1.000	-0	60	129	C7		-0.1
Total	15	1098	3121	308	785	121	28	52	339	265-3	20	398	.252	.314	.358	85	-71	27-1	.984	-2	105	95	C989,3b3/1	76	-2.2

McCURDY, HARRY Harry Henry "Hank" B9.15.1899 Stevens Point WI D7.21.1972 Houston TX BL/TR/5-11/187 d7.4 Col Illinois

1922	StL N	13	27	3	8	2	0	0	7	2	0	7	.296	.321	.519	119	0	0-0	.967	-1	95	94	C9,1b2		0.0
1923	StL N	67	185	17	49	11	2	0	15	11	0	11	.265	.306	.346	73	-7	0-0	.969	-6	94	68	C58		-0.9
1926	Chi A	44	86	16	28	7	2	1	11	6	0	10	.326	.370	.488	127	3	0-1	.974	-2	126	73	C25,1b8		0.2
1927	Chi A	86	262	34	75	19	3	1	27	32	1	24	.286	.366	.393	99	1	6-4	.972	-1	115	84	C82		0.5
1928	Chi A	49	103	12	27	10	0	2	13	8	0	15	.262	.315	.417	92	-1	1-3	.964	-1	130	52	C34		-0.2
1930	Phi N	80	148	23	49	6	2	1	25	15	0	12	.331	.393	.419	90	-2	2-0	.966	-6	76	95	C41		-0.5
1931	Phi N	66	150	21	43	9	0	1	25	23	1	16	.287	.382	.367	95	0	2	.968	-3	75	111	C45		0.0
1932	Phi N	62	136	13	32	6	1	1	14	17	1	13	.235	.325	.316	65	-6	0-0	.974	-1	89	76	C42		-0.5
1933	Phi N	73	54	9	15	1	0	2	12	16	1	6	.278	.451	.407	130	3	0	—	0	0	0	C2		0.4
1934	Cin N	3	6	0	0	0	0	0	1	0	0	0	.000	.000	.000	-99	-2	0	1.000	1	293	212	/1		-0.1
Total	10	543	1157	148	326	71	12	9	148	129	3	108	.282	.355	.387	92	-11	12-9	.970	-19	100	82	C338,1b11		-1.1

McDANIEL, TERRY Terrence Keith B12.6.1966 Kansas City MO BR/TR/5-9/205 [NYN86*6/152] d8.30

| 1991 | NY N | 23 | 29 | 3 | 6 | 1 | 0 | 0 | 1-0 | 1 | 0 | 11 | .207 | .233 | .241 | 34 | -3 | 2-0 | 1.000 | 1 | 128 | 0 | O14(7/5/4) | | -0.2 |

McDAVID, RAY Ray Darnell B7.20.1971 San Diego CA BL/TR/6-3/200* [SDN89 9/234] d7.15 Col Arizona Western CC

1994	SD N	9	28	2	7	1	0	0	2-0	1	0	8	.250	.276	.286	48	-2	1-0	1.000	-1	83	0	O7(4/2/1)		-0.3
1995	SD N	11	17	2	3	0	0	0	2-0	0	0	6	.176	.263	.176	19	-2	1-1	1.000	-1	72	0	O7C		-0.3
Total	2	20	45	4	10	1	0	0	3-0	1	0	14	.222	.271	.244	37	-4	2-1	1.000	-1	79	0	O14(4/9/1)		-0.6

McDERMOTT, RED Frank A. B11.11.1888 Philadelphia PA D9.11.1964 Philadelphia PA BR/TR/5-6/150 d8.6

| 1912 | Det A | 5 | 15 | 2 | 4 | 1 | 0 | 0 | 0 | 1 | | | .267 | .313 | .333 | 87 | 0 | 1 | 1.000 | 0 | 86 | 187 | O5L | | 0.0 |

McDERMOTT, MICKEY Maurice Joseph "Maury" B8.29.1929 Poughkeepsie NY D8.7.2003 Phoenix AZ BL/TL/6-2/170(170-190) d4.24 C1 ▲

1948	Bos A	7	8	2	3	1	0	0	0	0	0		.375	.375	.500	125	1	0-0	1.000	1	197	0	P7		0.0
1949	Bos A	12	33	3	7	3	0	0	6	3	0	6	.212	.278	.303	50	1	0-0	.941	-0	94	0	P12		0.0
1950	Bos A	39	44	11	16	5	0	0	12	6	0	3	.364	.472	.477	131	7	0-0	.938	1	110	52	P38		0.0
1951	Bos A	43	66	8	18	1	1	1	6	3	1	14	.273	.314	.364	76	2	0-1	.950	2	114	196	P34		0.0
1952	Bos A	36	62	10	14	1	1	1	7	4	0	11	.226	.273	.323	60	2	0-0	.944	0	86	47	P30		0.0
1953	Bos A	45	93	9	28	8	1	1	13	2	0	13	.301	.316	.419	92	7	0-1	.957	1	120	124	P32		0.0
1954	Was A	54	95	7	19	3	0	4	7	0	0	12	.200	.255	.232	36	-3	0-0	.955	1	118	72	P30		0.0
1955	Was A	70	95	10	25	4	0	1	10	6-0	1	16	.263	.311	.337	79	8	1-0	.943	0	115	54	P31		0.0
1956	†NY A	46	52	4	11	0	0	1	4	8-0	0	11	.212	.317	.269	58	3	0-0	1.000	-0	92	167	P23		0.0
1957	KC A	58	49	6	12	1	0	4	7	9-2	0	16	.245	.362	.510	133	2	0-0	.960	1	147	0	P29,1b2		0.0
1958	Det A	4	3	0	1	0	0	0	0	0	0	2	.333	.333	.333	78	-0	0-0	—	-0	0	0	P2		0.0
1961	StL N	22	14	1	1	0	0	0	3	0-0	0	4	.071	.071	.143	-41	-1	0-0	1.000	-0	63	0	P19		0.0
	KC A	7	5	0	1	0	0	0	1	0-0	0	4	.200	.333	.400	93	1	0-0	.500	-0	0	0	P4		0.0
Total	12	443	619	71	156	29	2	9	74	52-2	2	112	.252	.312	.349	76	36	1-2	.951	5	111	84	P291,1b2		0.0

McDERMOTT, TERRY Terrence Michael B3.20.1951 Rockville Cen. NY BR/TR/6-3/205 [LAN69 1/8] d9.12

| 1972 | LA N | 9 | 23 | 2 | 3 | 0 | 0 | 0 | 2-0 | 1 | 0 | 8 | .130 | .200 | .130 | -4 | -3 | 0-0 | 1.000 | -0 | 68 | 97 | 1b7 | | -0.4 |

McDERMOTT, SANDY Thomas Nathaniel B3.15.1856 Zanesville OH D11.23.1922 Mansfield OH d6.18

| 1885 | Bal AA | 1 | 1 | 0 | 0 | 0 | 0 | 0 | 0 | 0 | | | — | — | — | 0 | | | — | -0 | 0 | 0 | /2 | | 0.0 |

McDONALD d5.18

| 1872 | Eck NA | 1 | 4 | 0 | 0 | 0 | 0 | 0 | 0 | 0 | | | .000 | .000 | .000 | -99 | -1 | 0-0 | .333 | -1 | 59 | 0 | /S | | -0.2 |

McDONALD, TEX Charles E. (b Charles C. Crabtree) B1.31.1891 Farmersville TX D3.31.1943 Houston TX BL/TR/5-10/160 d4.11

1912	Cin N	61	140	16	36	3	4	1	15	13	2	24	.257	.329	.357	90	-2	5	.915	-8	81	49	S42		-0.8
1913	Cin N	11	10	1	3	0	0	0	2	0	0	1	.300	.300	.300	72	0	0	—	-0	0	0	/S		-0.1
	Bos N	62	145	24	52	4	4	0	18	15	1	17	.359	.422	.441	144	9	4-6	.869	-2	104	169	3b31,2b6/OR		0.7
	Year	73	155	25	55	4	4	0	20	15	1	18	.355	.415	.432	140	9	4-6	.869	-2	104	169	3b31,2b6/SOR		0.6
1914	Pit F	67	223	27	71	16	7	3	29	13	2	23	.318	.361	.493	132	6	9	.925	3	82	270	O29R,2b27,S5		0.8
	Buf F	69	250	32	74	13	6	3	32	20	2	26	.296	.353	.432	111	0	11	.953	-2	103	71	O61(2/1/58),2b10		-0.6
	Year	136	473	59	145	29	13	6	61	33	4	49	.307	.357	.461	121	5	20	.943	1	96	135	O90(2/1/87),2b37,S5		0.2
1915	Buf F	87	251	31	68	9	6	3	39	27	2	34	.271	.346	.426	114	1	5	.924	-5	96	53	O65(12/0/53)		-0.8
Total	4	357	1019	131	304	45	27	13	135	88			.298	.359	.429	113	4	34-6	.936	-14	96	101	O156(14/1/141),S48,2b43,3b31		-0.8

McDONALD, JACK Daniel B1844 Brooklyn NY D11.23.1880 Brooklyn NY 5-11/154 d5.2

| 1872 | Atl NA | 15 | 62 | 9 | 16 | 3 | 1 | 0 | 4 | 0 | | 1 | .258 | .258 | .339 | 70 | -3 | 0-0 | .720 | -2 | 0 | 0 | O15(1/0/14) | | -0.3 |

McDONALD, DARNELL Darnell T. B11.17.1978 Fort Collins CO BR/TR/5-11/210 [BalA97 1/26] d4.30 b-Donzell

| 2004 | Bal A | 17 | 32 | 3 | 5 | 1 | 0 | 0 | 2-0 | 0 | 0 | 6 | .156 | .206 | .188 | 4 | -5 | 1-0 | 1.000 | -1 | 99 | 0 | O13(1/4/8)/D | | -0.5 |

McDONALD, DAVE David Bruce B5.20.1943 New Albany IN BL/TR/6-3/215(215-227) d9.15 Col Nebraska

1969	NY A	9	23	0	5	2	0	0	2-0	0	5	.217	.280	.261	54	-1	0-1	.960	-1	84	47	1b7		-0.3
1971	Mon N	24	39	3	4	2	0	1	4	4-0	0	14	.103	.178	.231	17	-4	0-0	.983	-1	81	146	1b8/OL		-0.6
Total	2	33	62	3	9	4	0	1	6	6-0	0	19	.145	.214	.242	30	-5	0-1	.972	-1	82	101	1b15/OL		-0.9

YEAR	TM LG	G	AB	R	H	2B	3B	HR	RBI	BB-IB	HP	SO	AVG	OBP	SLG	AOPS	ABR	SB-CS	FA	FR	RNG	THR	GAMES AT POSITION	DL	BFW
McDONALD, DONZELL			Donzell B2.20.1975 Long Beach CA BB/TR/5-11/180* [NYA95 22/618] d4.19 b-Darnell Col Yavapai (AZ) JC																						0.0
2001	NY A	5	3	0	1	0	0	0	0	0-0	0	1	.333	.333	.333	76	0	0-0	1.000	-0	94	0	O3(1/2/0)		-0.3
2002	KC A	10	22	3	4	2	0	0	1	4-0	0	5	.182	.296	.273	50	-1	1-0	1.000	-2	25	0	O7L		-0.3
Total	2	15	25	3	5	2	0	0	1	4-0	0	7	.200	.300	.280	53	-1	1-0	1.000	-2	35	0	O10(8/2/0)		-0.3
McDONALD, ED			Edward C. B10.28.1886 Albany NY D3.11.1946 Albany NY BR/TR/6-0/180 d8.5																						-0.4
1911	Bos N	54	175	28	36	7	3	1	21	40	2	39	.206	.359	.297	78	-3	11	.955	-2	95	121	3b53/S		0.2
1912	Bos N	121	459	70	119	23	6	2	34	70	5	91	.259	.363	.349	94	-1	22	.940	1	99	109	3b118		0.0
1913	Chi N	1	0	0	0	0	0	0	0	0	0	0	—	—	—		0	0		0			/R		-0.2
Total	3	176	634	98	155	30	9	3	55	110	7	130	.244	.362	.334	89	-4	33	.945	-1	98	113	3b171/S		
McDONALD, JIM			James B Philadelphia PA BR/TR/6-0/180 d6.2																						0.0
1902	NY N	2	9	0	3	0	0	0	0	0	0		.333	.333	.333	107	0	0	1.000	-0	0	0	O2R		
McDONALD, JIM			James Augustus B8.6.1860 San Francisco CA D9.14.1914 San Francisco CA BR/5-9.5/180 d6.20																						-0.2
1884	Was U	2	6	0	1	0	0	0	0	0			.167	.167	.167	1	-1		.700	-1			/COR		-1.7
	Pit AA	38	145	11	23	3	0	0		2	0		.159	.170	.179	14	-13		.795	-5	97	74	3b22,O15(1/12/2)/2		-0.2
1885	Buf N	5	14	0	0	0	0	0	0	0		4	.000	.000	.000	-97	-3		.875	1	135	102	S4/OC		-2.1
Total	2	45	165	11	24	3	0	0		2		4	.145	.156	.164	4	-17		.795	-5			3b22,O17(1/13/3),S4/2C		
McDONALD, JASON			Jason Adam B3.20.1972 Modesto CA BB/TR/5-8/182(175-190) [OakA93 4/125] d6.5 Col Houston																						-0.2
1997	Oak A	78	236	47	62	11	4	4	14	36-0	1	49	.263	.361	.394	98	0	13-8	.961	-2	100	64	O74(17/66/0)	87	0.0
1998	Oak A	70	175	25	44	9	0	1	16	27-0	3	33	.251	.359	.320	80	-4	10-4	.956	4	106	221	O89(31/53/13)/2D		-0.9
1999	Oak A	100	187	26	39	2	1	3	8	25-0	1	48	.209	.310	.310	54	-13	6-3	.993	4	113	85	O32(11/3/26)		0.3
2000	Tex A	38	94	15	22	5	0	3	13	17-0	1	25	.234	.357	.383	86	-2	4-4	.988	7	124	314	O32(11/3/26)	87	-0.8
Total	4	286	692	113	167	27	5	11	51	105-0	8	155	.241	.347	.342	80	-19	33-19	.973	14	109	148	O255(70/155/64),D5/2		
McDONALD, JOHN			John Joseph B9.24.1974 New London CT BR/TR/5-11/175* [CleA96 12/363] d7.4 Col Providence																						0.2
1999	Cle A	18	21	2	7	0	0	0	0	0-0	0	3	.333	.333	.333	67	-1	0-1	1.000	3	149	244	2b7,S6		0.1
2000	Cle A	9	9	0	4	0	0	0	0	0-0	0	1	.444	.444	.444	122	0	0-0	1.000	0	93	66	S7,2b2		-0.4
2001	Cle A	17	22	1	2	1	0	0	0	1-0	1	7	.091	.167	.136	-18	-4	0-0	.955	-1	83	55	S9,2b3,3b3		0.1
2002	Cle A	93	264	35	66	11	3	1	12	10-0	5	50	.250	.288	.326	62	-15	3-0	.986	12	118	107	2b64,S21,3b10/D		-2.1
2003	Cle A	82	214	21	46	9	1	1	14	11-0	2	31	.215	.258	.280	43	-18	3-3	.980	-7	110	134	2b37,S27,3b23	50	0.1
2004	Cle A	66	93	17	19	5	1	2	7	4-0	0	12	.204	.237	.344	51	-7	0-0	.947	9	119	128	S30,2b12,3b9,D8		0.0
2005	Tor A	37	93	8	27	3	0	0	12	6-0	2	12	.290	.340	.323	76	-3	5-0	.977	6	119	120	S32,2b5		0.0
	Det A	31	73	10	19	3	1	0	4	5-0	0	12	.260	.308	.329	71	-3	1-1	.951	6	137	146	S22,2b8/3		1.8
	Year	68	166	18	46	6	1	0	16	11-0	2	24	.277	.326	.325	74	-6	6-1	.966	12	126	130	S54,2b13/3	50	0.0
Total	7	353	789	94	190	32	6	4	49	37-0	10	127	.241	.281	.312	57	-51	12-5	.961	29	110	116	S154,2b138,3b46,D9		
McDONALD, JOE			Malcolm Joseph B4.9.1888 TX D5.30.1963 Baytown TX BR/TR/5-11/175 d9.6																						-0.0
1910	StL A	10	32	4	5	0	0	1		6	-4	0	.156	.182	.156	6	-4	0	.821	-2	77	156	3b10		
McDONALD, KEITH			William Keith B2.8.1973 Yokosuka, Japan BR/TR/6-2/215* [StLN94 24/670] d7.4 Col Pepperdine																						0.0
2000	StL N	6	7	3	3	0	0	3	5	2-0	0	1	.429	.556	1.714	433	4	0-0	1.000	1	83	0	C4		0.0
2001	StL N	2	2	0	0	0	0	0	0	0-0	0	1	.000	.000	.000	-98	-1	0-0	1.000	0	0	0	C2		0.0
Total	2	8	9	3	3	0	0	3	5	2-0	0	2	.333	.455	1.333	323	3	0-0	1.000	1	66	0	C6		
McDONNELL, JIM			James William "Mack" B8.15.1922 Gagetown MI D4.24.1993 Detroit MI BL/TR/5-11/165 d9.23																						0.0
1943	Cle A	2	1	1	1	0	0	0	0	0	0	0	1.000	.667	.000	108	-0	0-0	1.000	-0	0	0	/C		-0.0
1944	Cle A	20	43	5	10	0	0	0	4	4	0	3	.233	.298	.233	55	-3	0-0	.900	-2	91	73	C13		0.0
1945	Cle A	28	51	3	10	2	0	0	8	8	0	4	.196	.226	.235	36	-4	0-0	.980	5	104	123	C23		0.0
Total	3	50	95	9	20	2	0	0	12	8	0	8	.211	.272	.232	48	-7	0-0	.953	2	97	101	C37		
McDONOUGH, ED			Edward Sebastian B9.11.1886 Elgin IL D9.2.1926 Elgin IL BR/TR/6-0/160 d8.3 Col Notre Dame																						0.0
1909	Phi N	1	1	0	0	0	0	0	0	0	0	0	.000	.000	.000	-99	-0	0	1.000	0	0	294	/C		-0.0
1910	Phi N	5	9	1	1	0	0	0	0	0	0	1	.111	.111	.111	-34	-2	0	1.000	-1	82	51	C4		-0.0
Total	2	6	10	1	1	0	0	0	0	0	0	1	.100	.100	.100	-40	-2	0	1.000	-0	70	87	C5		
McDOUGALD, GIL			Gilbert James B5.19.1928 San Francisco CA BR/TR/6-1/180* d4.20 Col San Francisco																						2
1951	†NY A	131	402	72	123	23	4	14	63	56	4	54	.306	.396	.488	143	25	14-5	.949	-8	91	167	3b82,2b55		1
1952	†NY A★	152	555	65	146	16	5	11	78	57	4	73	.263	.336	.369	102	1	6-5	.968	16	113	149	3b117,2b38		1
1953	†NY A	141	541	82	154	27	7	10	83	60	5	65	.285	.361	.416	113	10	3-4	.953	7	105	124	3b136,2b26		2
1954	NY A	126	394	66	102	22	2	12	48	62	1	64	.259	.364	.416	118	12	3-4	.989	10	103	138	2b92,3b35		3
1955	†NY A	141	533	79	152	10	8	13	53	65-2	2	77	.285	.361	.407	109	6	6-4	.985	22	106	127	2b126,3b17		3
1956	†NY A☆	120	438	79	136	13	3	13	56	68-1	3	59	.311	.405	.443	128	20	3-8	.970	9	97	129	S92,2b31,3b5		4
1957	†NY A★	141	539	87	156	25	9	13	62	59-1	4	71	.289	.362	.442	121	16	2-5	.976	17	101	131	2b115,S19		3
1958	†NY A★	138	503	69	126	19	1	14	65	59-1	3	75	.250	.329	.376	98	-1	6-2	.977	1	97	112	2b115,S19		1
1959	NY A★	127	434	44	109	16	8	4	34	35-3	3	40	.251	.309	.353	85	-10	0-3	.989	9	104	115	2b53,S52,3b25		0
1960	†NY A	119	337	54	87	16	4	8	34	38-0	3	45	.258	.337	.401	105	2	2-4	.945	12	108	119	3b84,2b42		1
Total	10	1336	4676	697	1291	187	51	112	576	559-8	36	623	.276	.356	.410	112	81	45-44	.984	95	102	117	2b599,3b508,S284		23
McDOUGALL, MARSHALL			Marshall James B12.19.1978 Jacksonville FL BR/TR/6-1/200 d6.7 Col Florida St.																						-0.0
2005	Tex A	18	18	3	1	1	0	0	4	0	0	10	.167	.167	.222	2	-3	0-0	1.000	-1	69	0	3b5,O3R,2b2/SD		
McDOWELL, ODDIBE			Oddibe B8.25.1962 Hollywood FL BL/TL/5-9/165* [TexA84 1/12] d5.19 Col Arizona St.																						0
1985	Tex A	111	406	63	97	14	5	18	42	36-2	1	85	.239	.304	.431	97	-3	25-7	.993	6	109	147	O103C,D4		0
1986	Tex A	154	572	105	152	24	7	18	49	65-5	1	112	.266	.341	.427	105	4	33-15	.991	-3	89	177	O148C/D		0
1987	Tex A	128	407	65	98	26	4	14	52	51-0	0	99	.241	.324	.428	97	-2	24-2	.989	-2	97	107	O125C		-1
1988	Tex A	120	437	55	108	19	5	6	37	41-2	2	89	.247	.311	.355	85	-9	33-10	.992	1	99	136	O64(63/1/0),D2		-1
1989	Cle A	69	239	33	53	5	2	3	22	25-0	1	36	.222	.296	.297	67	-11	12-5	.992	9	101	58	O68C		-1
	Atl N	76	280	56	85	18	4	7	24	27-3	0	37	.304	.365	.471	135	13	15-10	.978	8	83	53	O72(12/60/1)		-1
1990	Atl N	113	305	47	74	14	0	7	25	21-0	2	53	.243	.306	.357	75	-11	13-2	.983	-1	103	66	O53(0/31/27),D2	30	-0
1994	Tex A	59	183	34	48	6	1	1	15	28-0	2	39	.262	.355	.317	76	-6	14-2	.987	-13	97	107	O746(75/649/28),D12	30	-2
Total	7	830	2829	458	715	125	28	74	266	294-12	9	550	.253	.323	.395	94	-25	169-53	.987	-13	97	107	O746(75/649/28),D12		
McELVEEN, PRYOR			Pryor Mynatt "Humpty" B11.5.1881 Atlanta GA D10.27.1951 Pleasant Hill TN BR/TR/5-10/168 d4.26 Col Carson-Newman																						-1
1909	Bro N	81	258	22	51	3	1	25	14		61	-13	6	.198	.242	.271				.938	-3	93	111	3b37,O13(1/3/7),S10,1b5,2b5		-1
1910	Bro N	74	213	19	48	8	3	1	26	22	3	47	.225	.307	.305	81	-5	6	.943	-7	79	161	3b54,S6,2b3/C		-0
1911	Bro N	16	31	1	6	0	0	0	5	0			.194	.194	.194	9	-4	0	.929	-2	66	177	2b5/S		-1
Total	3	171	502	42	105	16	4	4	56	36	4	50	.209	.268	.281	67	-22	12	.941	-12	85	141	3b91,S17,2b13,O13(1/3/7),1b5/C		
McELWEE, LEE			Leland Stanford B5.23.1894 LaMesa CA D2.8.1957 Union ME BR/TR/5-10.5/160 d7.3 Col Bowdoin																						-0
1916	Phi A	54	155	9	41	8	3	0	18	17		.265	.301	.284	79		4	.883	1	96	114	3b30,O9R,2b3/1S		
McELYEA, FRANK			Frank B8.4.1918 Hawthorne Twp. IL D4.19.1987 Evansville IN BR/TR/6-6/221 d9.10 Mil 1943-45																						-1
1942	Bos N	7	4	2	0	0	0	0	0	0		.000	.000	.000	-99	-1	0	1.000	0	200	0	/OL		
McEWING, JOE			Joseph Earl B10.19.1972 Bristol PA BR/TR/5-10/170(170-210) [StLN92 28/783] d9.2 Col CC of Morris (NJ) OF(161/46/79)																						-1
1998	StL N	10	20	5	4	1	0	0	1	1-0	1	3	.200	.273	.250	39	-2	0-1	1.000	-1	83	106	2b6,O3(1/1/1)		-1
1999	StL N	152	513	65	141	28	4	9	44	41-8	6	87	.275	.333	.398	83	-13	7-4	.980	8	104	88	O52(43/11/6),3b19,2b16,S4		-0
2000	†NY N	87	153	20	34	14	1	2	19	5-0	1	29	.222	.248	.366	56	-11	3-1	1.000	-3	94	74	O62(48/2/25),3b25,S12,2b5,1b3/D		-2
2001	NY N	116	283	41	80	17	3	8	30	17-0	10	57	.283	.342	.449	111	4	8-5	1.000	0	89	71	O35(10/1/24),S21,1b20,2b13,3b10	17	-1
2002	NY N	105	196	22	39	8	1	3	16	9-0	2	50	.199	.242	.296	47	-17	4-4	1.000	1	129	0	2b55,S42,O18(16/1/2),1b5,3b2		-1
2003	NY N	119	278	31	67	11	0	1	16	25-4	2	57	.241	.309	.291	61	-16	3-0	.995	4	89	88	2b55,S42,O18(16/1/2),1b5,3b2		-2
2004	NY N	75	138	17	33	3	1	1	16	9-4	0	32	.254	.297	.312	60	-9	4-1	.981	5	109	83	2b34,O15(8/6/1),S13,1b11/3	45	-1
2005	KC A	83	180	16	43	7	0	1	6	6-0	0	35	.239	.263	.294	51	-13	4-4	.962	7	124	40	3b29,1b20,2b11,S6,O5(3/1/1),D6	62	-1
Total	8	747	1761	217	443	89	10	25	158	113-16	24	350	.252	.303	.356	73	-77	33-20	.997	20	108	66	O256L,2b236,S99,3b92,1b61,D7		

YEAR	TM	LG	G	AB	R	H	2B	3B	HR	RBI	BB-IB	HP	SO	AVG	OBP	SLG	AOPS	ABR	SB-CS	FA	FR	RNG	THR	GAMES AT POSITION	DL	BFW

McFADDEN, GUY Guy G. B9.3.1872 Topeka KS D3.10.1911 Topeka KS d8.24

| 1895 | StL | N | 4 | 14 | 1 | 3 | 0 | 0 | 0 | 2 | 0 | 0 | 2 | .214 | .214 | .214 | 11 | -2 | 0 | .968 | -1 | 0 | 135 | 1b4 | | -0.2 |

McFADDEN, LEON Leon B4.26.1944 Little Rock AR BR/TR/6-2/195* d9.6

1968	Hou	N	16	47	2	13	1	0	0	1	6-2	0	10	.277	.358	.298	101	0	1-0	.968	-3	93	35	S16		-0.1
1969	Hou	N	44	74	3	13	2	0	0	3	4-0	0	9	.176	.218	.203	19	-8	1-2	.944	-2	91		O17(4/0/13),S8		-1.1
1970			2	0	0	0	0	0	0	0	0-0	0	0	—	—	—	—	0	0-0	—	0			/R		0.0
Total 3			62	121	5	26	3	0	0	4	10-2	0	19	.215	.275	.240	50	-8	2-2	.966	-5	92	25	S24,O17(4/0/13)		-1.2

McFARLAN, ALEX Alexander Shepherd B11.11.1866 KY D3.2.1939 Pewee Valley KY 5-9/165 d6.19 b-Dan

| 1892 | Lou | N | 14 | 42 | 2 | 7 | 0 | 0 | 0 | 1 | 0 | 0 | 11 | .167 | .300 | .167 | 46 | -1 | 0 | .773 | -2 | 57 | 0 | O12R,2b2 | | -0.4 |

McFARLAND, CHRIS Christopher B8.17.1861 Fall River MA D5.24.1918 New Bedford MA 5-9/170 d4.19

| 1884 | Bal | U | 3 | 14 | 2 | 3 | 1 | 0 | 0 | | 0 | | | .214 | .214 | .286 | 46 | -1 | | .571 | -1 | 0 | 0 | O3C/P | | -0.2 |

McFARLAND, ED Edward William B8.3.1874 Cleveland OH D11.28.1959 Cleveland OH BR/TR/5-10/180 d7.7

1893	Cle	N	8	22	5	9	2	1	0	6	1	1	2	.409	.458	.591	168	2	0	1.000	-1	0		O5C,3b2/C		0.0
1896	StL	N	83	290	48	70	13	4	3	36	15	1	17	.241	.281	.345	67	-15	7	.961	-9	85	144	C80,O2R		-0.6
1897	StL	N	31	107	14	35	5	2	1	17	8	0		.327	.374	.439	117	2	5	.965	-5	68	124	C23,1b3,O3L/2		-0.3
	Phi	N	38	130	18	29	3	5	1	16	14	2		.223	.308	.346	75	-5	2	.951	-2	104	98	C37		
	Year		69	237	32	64	8	7	2	33	22	2		.270	.337	.388	93	-3	4	.957	-7	89	109	C60,1b3,O3L/2		-0.3
1898	Phi	N	121	429	65	121	21	5	3	71	44	2		.282	.352	.375	113	8	4	.960	2	110	122	C121		2.0
1899	Phi	N	96	324	59	108	22	9	2	57	36	2		.333	.403	.475	146	21	9	.968	11	109	103	C94		3.6
1900	Phi	N	94	344	50	105	14	8	0	38	29	3		.305	.364	.392	110	5	9	.963	-12	78	112	C93/3		0.1
1901	Phi	N	74	295	33	84	14	2	1	32	18	0		.285	.326	.356	96	-2	11	.970	2	99	113	C74		0.8
1902	Chi	A	75	246	29	56	9	2	1	25	19	3		.228	.291	.293	65	-11	8	.967	7	128	90	C69/1		0.2
1903	Chi	A	61	201	15	42	7	2	1	19	14	1		.209	.264	.279	66	-8	3	.968	0	110	101	C56/1		-0.2
1904	Chi	A	50	160	22	44	11	3	0	20	17	1		.275	.348	.381	136	7	2	.975	-4	117	77	C49		0.9
1905	Chi	A	80	250	24	70	13	4	0	31	23	2		.280	.345	.364	130	9	5	.973	8	132	94	C70		2.6
1906	†Chi	A	12	23	0	4	1	0	0	3	3	0		.174	.269	.217	54	-1	0	.973	6	161	46	C7		0.0
1907	Chi	A	52	138	11	39	9	1	0	8	12	0		.283	.340	.362	128	5	3	.972	-1	118	92	C43		0.9
1908	Bos	A	19	48	5	10	2	1	0	4	1	0		.208	.224	.292	66	-2	0	.978	3	100	128	C13		0.3
Total 14			894	3007	398	826	146	49	13	383	254	18	19	.275	.335	.369	104	15	65	.967	10	106	105	C830,O10(3/5/2),1b5,3b3/2		10.3

McFARLAND, HERM Hermas Walter B3.11.1870 Des Moines IA D9.21.1935 Richmond VA BL/TR/5-6/150 d4.21

1896	Lou	N	30	110	11	21	4	1	1	12	9		14	.191	.252	.273	40	-10	4	.833	-3	104	268	O28(3/18/9)/C		-1.3
1898	Cin	N	19	64	10	18	3	1	0	11	7	1		.281	.361	.391	108	0	4	.968	-1	47	0	O17(13/3/1)		-0.2
1901	Chi	A	132	473	83	130	21	9	4	59	75	9		.275	.384	.383	116	15	33	.946	5	82	83	O132L		1.2
1902	Chi	A	7	27	5	5	0	0	0	4	2	0		.185	.241	.185	20	-3	1	1.000	-0	0	0	O7(2/0/5)		-0.3
	Bal	A	61	242	54	78	19	6	3	36	36	4		.322	.418	.488	144	16	10	.965	4	146	52	O61C		1.6
	Year		68	269	59	83	19	6	3	40	38	4		.309	.402	.457	133	14	11	.967	4	132	47	O68(2/61/5)		1.3
1903	NY	A	103	362	41	88	16	9	5	45	46	3		.243	.333	.378	106	4	13	.939	-3	79	72	O103(39/58/7)		-0.5
Total 5			352	1278	204	340	61	28	13	167	175	17	14	.266	.362	.388	110	22	64	.941	2	91	83	O348(189/140/22)/C		0.5

McFARLAND, HOWIE Howard Alexander B3.7.1910 El Reno OK D4.7.1993 Wichita KS BR/TR/6-0/175 d7.16

| 1945 | Was | A | 6 | 11 | 0 | 1 | 0 | 0 | 0 | 3 | 0 | 0 | 3 | .091 | .091 | .091 | -52 | -2 | 0-0 | 1.000 | 0 | 61 | 639 | O3(1/0/2) | | -0.2 |

McFARLANE, ORLANDO Orlando Dejesus (Quesada) B6.28.1938 Oriente, Cuba BR/TR/6-0/180* d4.23

1962	Pit	N	8	23	0	2	0	0	0	1	1-0	0	4	.087	.125	.087	-42	-5	0-0	1.000	-0	46	109	C8		-0.5
1964	Pit	N	37	78	5	19	5	0	1	4-2	0	27		.244	.280	.308	66	-3	0-0	.983	-4	215	72	C35/OR		-0.7
1966	Det	A	49	138	16	35	7	0	5	13	9-1	1	46	.254	.304	.413	102	0	0-0	.991	-2	116	78	C33		0.0
1967	Cal	A	12	22	0	5	0	0	0	3	1-0	0	7	.227	.250	.227	47	-2	0-0	.935	-2	68	144	C6	17	-0.3
1968	Cal	A	18	31	1	9	0	0	0	2	5-1	0	9	.290	.389	.290	112	1	0-0	.977	-0	46	56	C9	39	0.1
Total 5			124	292	22	70	12	0	5	20	20-4	1	93	.240	.290	.332	78	-9	0-0	.985	-9	129	82	C91/OR	94	-1.4

McGAFFIGAN, PATSY Mark Andrew B9.12.1888 Carlyle IL D12.22.1940 Carlyle IL BR/TR/5-8/140 d4.16 Mil 1918

1917	Phi	N	19	60	5	10	1	0	0	6	0	0	7	.167	.167	.183	7	-7	1	.920	1	103	82	S17/OR		-0.5
1918	Phi	N	54	192	17	39	3	2	1	8	16	1	23	.203	.268	.255	56	-10	3	.948	-8	98	84	2b53/S		-1.9
Total 2			73	252	22	49	4	2	1	14	16	1	30	.194	.245	.238	45	-17	4	.948	-7	98	84	2b53,S18/OR		-2.4

McGAH, EDDIE Edward Joseph B9.30.1921 Oakland CA D9.30.2002 Oakland CA BR/TR/6-0/183 d4.26

1946	Bos	A	15	37	2	8	1	1	0	3	6	0	7	.216	.341	.297	75	-1	0-0	.981	-1	116	68	C14		-0.2
1947	Bos	A	9	14	1	0	0	0	0	0	4	0	0	.000	.176	.000	-45	-3	0-0	.964	1	151	79	C7		-0.1
Total 2			24	51	3	8	1	1	0	3	10	0	7	.157	.295	.216	41	-4	0-0	.975	-0	127	71	C21		-0.3

McGAMWELL, ED Edward M. B1.10.1879 Buffalo NY D5.26.1924 Albany NY BL/TL d4.14

| 1905 | Bro | N | 4 | 16 | 0 | 4 | 0 | 0 | 0 | 1 | 0 | | .250 | .294 | .250 | 68 | -1 | 0 | .951 | -1 | 74 | 0 | 1b4 | | -0.1 |

McGANN, AMBROSE Ambrose J. B1868 Baltimore MD D2.2.1941 Baltimore MD ?/170 d5.2

| 1895 | Lou | N | 20 | 73 | 9 | 21 | 5 | 2 | 0 | 6 | | | .288 | .358 | .411 | 105 | 1 | 6 | .852 | -2 | 86 | 25 | S8,3b6,O5R | | -0.1 |

McGANN, DAN Dennis Lawrence "Cap" B7.15.1871 Shelbyville KY D12.13.1910 Louisville KY BB/TR/6-0/190 d8.8

1896	Bos	N	43	171	25	55	6	7	2	30	12	5	10	.322	.383	.474	118	4	2	.905	-11	89	64	2b43		-0.5
1898	Bal	N	145	535	99	161	18	8	5	106	53	39		.301	.404	.393	126	22	33	.983	2	98	102	1b145		2.2
1899	Bro	N	63	214	49	52	11	4	2	32	21	19		.243	.362	.360	96	0	16	.985	1	102	137	1b61		0.1
	Was	N	76	280	65	96	9	4	5	58	14	18		.343	.410	.486	147	18	11	.990	3	101	77	1b76		1.8
	Year		139	494	114	148	20	12	7	90	35	37		.300	.389	.431	124	18	27	.988	4	101	105	1b137		1.9
1900	StL	N	121	444	79	132	10	9	4	58	32	24		.297	.376	.387	112	8	26	.990	-1	85	63	1b121/2		0.6
1901	StL	N	103	423	73	115	15	9	6	56	16	23		.272	.333	.392	116	8	17	.984	-3	85	127	1b103		0.3
1902	Bal	A	68	250	40	79	10	8	0	42	19	6		.316	.378	.420	116	5	17	.987	3	113	117	1b68		0.7
	NY	N	61	227	25	68	5	7	0	21	12	8		.300	.356	.383	130	7	12	.981	1	109	112	1b61		0.8
1903	NY	N	129	482	75	130	21	6	3	50	32	12		.270	.331	.357	93	-5	36	.988	-1	85	97	1b129		-0.8
1904	NY	N	141	517	81	148	22	6	6	71	36	18		.286	.354	.387	123	15	42	.991	3	98	119	1b141		1.6
1905	†NY	N	136	491	88	147	23	14	5	75	55	19		.299	.391	.434	143	28	22	.991	5	102	101	1b136		3.1
1906	NY	N	134	451	62	107	14	8	0	37	60	13		.237	.344	.304	100	3	30	.995	4	99	102	1b133		0.4
1907	NY	N	81	262	29	78	9	1	2	36	29	7		.298	.383	.363	129	11	9	.994	5	113	95	1b81		1.6
1908	Bos	N	135	475	52	114	8	5	2	55	38	19		.240	.321	.291	97	0	9	.988	6	125	124	1b121,2b9		0.5
Total 12			1436	5222	842	1482	181	100	42	727	429	230	10	.284	.364	.381	117	124	282	.989	16	100	105	1b1376,2b53		12.4

McGARR, CHIPPY James B. B5.10.1863 Worcester MA D6.6.1904 Worcester MA BR/TR/5-7/168 d7.11 U1

1884	CP	U	19	70	10	11	2	0	0		4	-10		.157	.157	.186	4	-10		.905	-3	74	56	2b13,O6(5/0/1)		-1.2
1886	Phi	AA	71	267	41	71	9	3	2	31	9	2		.266	.295	.345	99	-1	17	.850	-1	100	110	S71		0.0
1887	Phi	AA	137	536	93	158	23	6	1	63	23	2		.295	.326	.366	93	-7	84	.875	-1	95	123	S137		-0.3
1888	StL	AA	34	132	17	31	1	0	0	13	6	0		.235	.268	.242	58	-7	25	.895	-6	99	109	2b33/S		-1.1
1889	KC	AA	25	108	22	31	3	0	0	16	6	1	11	.287	.330	.315	79	-3	12	.857	-2	78	282	3b11,O6(2/0/4),2b5,S3		-0.4
	Bal	AA	3	7	1	1	0	0	0	0	1	0		.143	.250	.143	13	-1	0	.583	-2	53	0	S3		-0.3
	Year		28	115	23	32	3	0	0	16	7	1	12	.278	.325	.304	75	-4	12	.857	-5	78	282	3b11,O6(2/0/4),S6,2b5		-0.7
1890	Bos	N	121	487	68	115	12	7	1	51	34	4	38	.236	.291	.296	66	-23	39	.933	-3	95	78	3b115,S5/OR		-2.1
1893	Cle	N	63	249	38	77	12	0	0	28	20	1	15	.309	.363	.357	86	-5	24	.886	-3	103	66	3b63		-0.3
1894	Cle	N	128	523	94	144	24	6	2	74	28	1	29	.275	.316	.356	59	-37	31	.902	-6	95	93	3b109,2b4		-3.1
1895	†Cle	N	113	422	86	114	14	2	2	59	35	1	33	.270	.328	.327	65	-23	19	.872	-5	98	93	3b109,2b4		-3.1
1896	†Cle	N	113	455	68	122	16	4	1	52	30	2	30	.268	.302	.327	62	-26	16	.924	-7	96	132	3b113/C		-2.7
Total 10			827	3256	538	875	116	28	9	388	184	14	157	.269	.311	.330	71	-143	267	.903	-35	96	98	3b539,S220,2b55,O13(7/0/6)/C		-13.6

McGARR, JIM James Vincent "Reds" B11.9.1888 Philadelphia PA D7.21.1981 Miami FL BR/TR/5-9.5/170 d5.18

| 1912 | Det | A | 1 | 4 | 0 | 0 | 0 | 0 | 0 | 0 | 0 | 0 | 1 | .000 | .000 | .000 | -99 | -1 | 0 | .800 | -0 | 124 | 0 | /2 | | -0.1 |

YEAR	TM LG	G	AB	R	H	2B	3B	HR	RBI	BB-IB	HP	SO	AVG	OBP	SLG	AOPS	ABR	SB-CS	FA	FR	RNG	THR	GAMES AT POSITION	DL	BFW

McGARVEY, DAN Daniel Francis B12.2.1887 Philadelphia PA D3.7.1947 Philadelphia PA d5.18

																									0.1
1912	Det A	1	3	0	0	0	0	0	0	1	0	1	.000	.400	.000	18	0	0	.667	1	0	0	/OL		

McGEACHY, JACK John Charles B5.23.1864 Clinton MA D4.5.1930 Cambridge MA BR/TR/5-8/165 d6.17 ▲

																									0.0
1886	Det N	6	27	3	9	0	1	0	4	0		3	.333	.333	.407	120	0	2	.875	-1	89	0	O6L		-1.1
	StL N	59	226	31	46	12	3	2	24	1		37	.204	.207	.310	59	-11	8	.880	0	138	173	O55C,2b2,3b2		-1.1
	Year	65	253	34	55	12	4	2	28	1		40	.217	.220	.320	66	-11	10	.880	-0	133	157	O61(6/55/0),2b2,3b2		-1.2
1887	Ind N	99	405	49	109	17	3	1	56	5	1	21	.269	.280	.333	72	-16	27	.894	4	125	85	O98(0/97/2)/3P		-1.9
1888	Ind N	118	452	45	99	15	2	0	30	5	2	21	.219	.231	.261	56	-23	49	.932	5	137	117	O117(2/6/109)/SP		-1.7
1889	Ind N	131	532	83	142	32	1	2	63	9	2	39	.267	.282	.342	73	-22	37	.918	8	144	170	O131R,P3		-2.8
1890	Bro P	104	443	84	108	24	4	1	65	19	2	12	.244	.278	.323	57	-30	21	.906	-3	81	24	O104(22/31/52)		-1.0
1891	Phi AA	50	201	24	46	4	3	2	13	6	1	12	.229	.255	.308	61	-12	9	.910	-4	57	0	O41(38/0/3)		-1.0
	Bos AA	41	178	26	45	2	1	1	21	12	1	8	.253	.304	.292	72	-7	11	.916	-2	89	0	O91(42/12/37)		-2.0
	Year	91	379	50	91	6	4	3	34	18	2	20	.240	.278	.301	66	-19	20							-1.0
Total	6	608	2464	345	604	106	18	9	276	57	9	148	.245	.265	.314	65	-121	164	.909	11	119	94	O602(72/201/331),P5,3b3,2b2/S		-10.4

McGEARY, MIKE Michael Henry B1851 Philadelphia PA BR/TR/5-7/138 d5.9 M3

																									-0.3
1871	Tro NA	29	148	42	39	4	0	0	12	6		0	.264	.292	.291	67	-6	20-4	.897	-1			C26,S3		1.0
1872	Ath NA	47	225	68	81	9	2	0	35	2		1	.360	.366	.418	140	10	13-8	.867	5			C23,S23/OR		-1.0
1873	Ath NA	52	275	63	83	8	1	0	31	1		1	.302	.304	.338	84	-7	4-6	.804	-2	95	105	S43,C14/3		0.9
1874	Ath NA	54	271	61	87	10	2	0	22	1		2	.321	.324	.373	113	2	10-2	.837	8			C28,S26,O4R		0.2
1875	Phi NA	68	310	71	90	6	2	0	37	1		1	.290	.293	.323	109	2	19-4	.743	1	84	71	3b27,2b23,S18,O3(0/1/2),M		0.5
1876	StL N	61	276	48	72	3	0	0	30	2		1	.261	.266	.272	84	-4		.889	8	112	117	2b56,C5/OC3		0.1
1877	StL N	57	258	35	65	3	2	0	20	2		6	.252	.258	.279	73	-8		.883	6	102	82	2b39,3b19		0.3
1879	Pro N	85	374	62	103	7	2	0	35	5		13	.275	.285	.305	96	-2		.884	1	97	80	2b73,3b12		-0.2
1880	Pro N	18	59	5	8	0	0	0	1	0		6	.136	.136	.136	-8	-6		.887	4	147	101	3b17,2b2/SM		-0.5
	Cle N	31	111	14	28	2	1	0	6	4		3	.252	.278	.288	94	-1		.887	-5	81	140	3b29,O2R		-0.7
	Year	49	170	19	36	2	1	0	7	4		9	.212	.230	.235	60	-7		.724	-5	64	69	3b11,M		-0.7
1881	Cle N	11	41	1	9	0	0	0	5	0		20	.220	.220	.220	41	-3		.928	4	102	51	S33,2b3		-0.7
1882	Det N	34	133	14	19	4	1	0	2	2		5	.143	.156	.188	10	-13		.807	9			S113,C91,3b28,2b23,O8(0/1/7)		0.8
Total	5 NA	250	1229	305	380	37	7	0	137	11		5	.309	.315	.351	104	1	66-24	.807				2b173,3b89,S34,C5,O3(0/1/2)		-1.1
Total	6	297	1252	179	304	19	6	0	99	15		55	.243	.252	.268	72	-37		.885	13					

McGEE, DAN Daniel Aloysius B9.29.1911 New York NY D12.4.1991 Lakehurst NJ BR/TR/5-8.5/152 d7.14

																									-0.1
1934	Bos N	7	22	3	3	2	0	0	1	3	0	6	.136	.240	.136	4	-3	0	.951	1	118	79	S7		

McGEE, FRANK Francis De Sales B4.28.1899 Columbus OH D1.30.1934 Columbus OH BR/TR/5-11.5/175 d9.19 Col Ohio St.

																									-0.1
1925	Was A	2	3	0	0	0	0	0	0	0		1	.000	.000	.000	-99	-1	0-0	1.000	0	147	125	1b2		

McGEE, PAT Patrick B Philadelphia PA D6.20.1889 New York NY d9.24

																									-0.
1874	Atl NA	16	65	4	11	1	0	0	6	0		3	.169	.169	.185	15	-5	0-0	.795	-2	46	0	O15(6/9/0),S2/2		-0.
1875	Mut NA	25	95	4	17	2	0	0	9	0		10	.179	.179	.200	30	-7	0-0	.848	-2	53	0	O25C		0.
	Atl NA	18	65	3	10	3	0	0	5	1		4	.154	.167	.231	42	-3	0-0	.912	5	381	229	O13C,2b6/3		-0.
	Year	43	160	7	27	5	1	0	14	1		14	.169	.174	.213	34	-10	0-0	.875	3	161	75	O38C,2b6/3		-0.
Total	2 NA	59	225	11	38	6	1	0	20	1		17	.169	.173	.204	29	-15	0-0	.849	1	125	52	O53(6/47/0),2b7,S2/3		-0.

McGEE, WILLIE Willie Dean B11.2.1958 San Francisco CA BB/TR/6-1/175(160-195) [NYA77*S1/15] d5.10 Col Diablo Valley (CA) JC

																									-1.
1982	†StL N	123	422	43	125	12	8	5	56	12-2	2	58	.296	.318	.391	95	-5	24-12	.958	-11	91	46	O117(1/116/0)	25	-1.
1983	StL N★	147	601	75	172	22	8	5	75	26-2	0	98	.286	.314	.374	90	-10	39-8	.987	-4	97	93	O145C	15	0.
1984	StL N	145	571	82	166	19	11	6	50	29-2	1	80	.291	.325	.394	104	0	43-10	.985	3	103	85	O141C		4.
1985	†StL N★	152	612	114	216	26	18	10	82	34-2	0	86	.353	.384	.503	148	36	56-16	.978	0	102	118	O149(3/146/0)	24	-1.
1986	StL N	124	497	65	127	22	7	7	48	37-7	1	82	.256	.306	.370	86	-11	19-16	.991	-1	102	114	O152C/S		-1.
1987	†StL N★	153	620	76	177	37	11	11	105	24-5	2	90	.285	.312	.434	100	-1	41-6	.975	-3	96	140	O135C		0.
1988	StL N★	137	562	73	164	24	6	3	50	32-5	1	84	.292	.329	.372	100	-1	8-6	.975	-2	97	80	O47C	60	-1.
1989	StL N	58	199	23	47	10	2	3	17	10-0	1	34	.236	.275	.352	76	-7	28-9	.957	4	105	182	O124(0/118/6)		2.
1990	StL N	125	501	76	168	32	5	3	62	38-6	1	86	.335	.382	.437	124	17	28-9	.957	4	105	182	O28C/D		-0.
	†Oak A	29	113	23	31	3	2	0	15	10-0	0	18	.274	.333	.336	91	-2	0	.986	0	103	73	O128(0/89/48)	19	0.
1991	SF N	131	497	67	155	30	3	4	43	34-3	2	74	.312	.357	.408	119	12	17-9	.978	-5	95	80	O119(0/31/90)		0.
1992	SF N	138	474	56	141	20	2	1	36	29-3	1	88	.297	.339	.354	102	0	13-3	.976	1	95	150	O126R	19	-0.
1993	SF N	130	475	53	143	28	1	4	46	38-7	1	67	.301	.353	.389	97	2	10-9	.988	-1	98	64	O42R	65	-0.
1994	SF N	45	156	19	44	3	0	5	23	15-2	0	24	.282	.337	.397	97	-6	5-2	.973	3	94	250	O64(3/27/47)		-0.
1995	†Bos A	67	200	32	57	11	3	2	15	9-0	0	41	.285	.311	.400	82	-6	5-2	.962	1	95	149	O83(35/11/42),1b6		-0.
1996	†StL N	123	309	52	95	15	2	5	41	18-2	2	60	.307	.348	.417	101	0	5-5	.981	-1	87	154	O81(18/18/53),D3	17	-0.
1997	StL N	122	300	29	90	19	4	3	38	22-2	0	59	.300	.347	.420	100	0	8-2	.938	1	92	159	O88(56/6/38)/1D		-1
1998	StL N	120	269	27	68	10	1	3	34	14-5	0	49	.253	.287	.331	63	-15	7-2	.972	-4	89	58	O89(30/19/43),1b3		-2
1999	StL N	132	271	25	68	7	0	0	20	17-3	0	60	.251	.293	.277	45	-23	7-4	.976	-4	89			244	-2
Total	18	2201	7649	1010	2254	350	94	79	856	448-58	15	1238	.295	.333	.396	100	-22	352-121	.976	-31	97	117	O1979(146/1351/535),1b10,D7/S		

McGEEHAN, DAN Daniel De Sales B6.7.1885 Jeddo PA D7.12.1955 Hazleton PA BR/TR/5-6/135 d4.22 b-Conny

																									-0
1911	StL N	3	9	0	2	0	0	0	1	0		1	.222	.222	.222	25	-1	0	.818	-1	80	0	2b3		

McGHEE, ED Warren Edward B9.29.1924 Perry AR D2.13.1986 Memphis TN BR/TR/5-11/170* d9.20 Col Arkansas St.

																									-0
1950	Chi A	3	6	0	1	0	0	0	0	0		1	.167	.167	.500	67	-1	0-0	1.000	-0	71	0	/OR		-1
1953	Phi A	104	358	36	94	11	4	1	29	32		3	.263	.328	.324	74	-13	4-3	.982	5	117	47	O99(1/97/1)		-0
1954	Phi A	21	53	5	11	2	0	2	9	4		0	.208	.259	.358	69	-3	0-1	.933	1	115	0	O13(2/11/0)		-0
	Chi A	42	75	12	17	1	0	0	5	12		8	.227	.333	.240	57	-4	5-0	.982	2	102	227	O34(5/18/11)		-0
	Year	63	128	17	28	3	0	2	14	16		16	.219	.303	.289	62	-7	5-1	.960	3	107	138	O47(7/29/11)		-0
1955	Chi A	26	13	6	1	0	0	0	0	6-0		1	.077	.368	.077	24	-1	2-1	.923	0	131	6	O17(5/12/0)		-2
Total	4	196	505	59	124	14	4	3	43	54-0		3	.246	.321	.311	70	-22	11-5	.975	7	115	69	O164(13/138/13)		

McGHEE, BILL William Mac "Fibber" B9.5.1905 Shawmut AL D3.10.1984 Decatur GA BL/TL/5-10.5/185 d7.5

																									-0
1944	Phi A	77	287	27	83	12	0	1	19	21		20	.289	.338	.341	96	-2	2-1	.989	-1	95	82	1b75		-1
1945	Phi A	93	250	24	63	6	1	0	19	24	1	16	.252	.320	.284	76	-7	3-2	.989	-3	86	47	O48(40/0/9),1b8		-1
Total	2	170	537	51	146	18	1	1	38	45		36	.272	.329	.315	87	-9	5-3	.989	-4	98	85	1b83,O48(40/0/9)		

McGILVRAY, BILL William Alexander "Big Bill" B4.29.1883 Portland OR D5.23.1952 Denver CO BL/TL/6-0/160 d4.17 Col Stanford

																									-0
1908	Cin N	2	2	0	0	0	0	0	0	0		0	.000	.000	.000	-99	0	0	—	0			/H		

McGINLEY, TIM Timothy S. B1854 Philadelphia PA D11.2.1899 Oakland CA 5-9.5/155 d4.21

																									-0
1875	Cen NA	13	52	5	12	0	1	0	5	0		4	.231	.231	.269	80	-1	0-0	.646	-6			C12,O2R		-0
	NH NA	32	131	13	36	3	1	0	10	0		7	.275	.275	.313	119	3	1-1	.807	-7			C32,3b2		-0
	Year	45	183	18	48	3	2	0	15	0		11	.262	.262	.301	107	2	1-1	.762	-13			C44,O2R,3b2		-0
1876	Bos N	9	40	5	6	0	0	0	2	0		1	.150	.150	.150	0	-4		.600	-4	0	0	O6C,C3		-0

McGINN, FRANK Frank J. B1869 Cincinnati OH D11.19.1897 Cincinnati OH d6.9

																									-0
1890	Pit N	1	4	0	0	0	0	0	0	0		2	.000	.000	.000	-99	-1	0	1.000	-0	0	0	/OC		

McGINNIS, RUSS Russell Brent B6.18.1963 Coffeyville KS BR/TR/6-3/225* [MilA85 14/341] d6.3 Col Oklahoma

																									-1
1992	Tex A	14	33	2	8	4	0	3	4	4-0		7	.242	.306	.364	89	-3	0-0	1.000	-3	76	75	C10,1b2,3b2		-1
1995	KC A	3	5	1	0	0	0	0	0	1-0		1	.000	.167	.000	-51	-1	0-0	1.000	-1	0	0	/13OL		-1
Total	2	17	38	3	8	4	0	3	4	5-0		8	.211	.286	.316	68	-4	0-0	1.000	-4	76	75	C10,3b3,1b3/OL		

McGLONE, JOHN John T. B1864 Brooklyn NY D11.22.1927 Brooklyn NY TR/5-10/165 d10.7

																									-0
1886	Was N	4	15	2	1	0	0	0	1	0		3	.067	.067	.067	-64	-3	0	.846	-1	55	0	3b4		-0
1887	Cle AA	21	79	14	20	2	1	0	10	7	3		.253	.337	.304	82	-2	15	.854	1	90	75	3b21		-0
1888	Cle AA	55	203	22	37	1	3	1	22	16	2		.182	.249	.232	56	-10	26	.787	-6	89	65	3b48,O7C		-0
Total	3	80	297	38	58	3	4	1	33	23		5	.195	.265	.242	58	-15	41	.810	-7	88	65	3b73,O7C		

YEAR	TM LG	G	AB	R	H	2B	3B	HR	RBI	BB-IB	HP	SO	AVG	OBP	SLG	AOPS	ABR	SB-CS	FA	FR	RNG	THR	GAMES AT POSITION	DL	BFW

McGOVERN, ART Arthur John B2.27.1882 St.John NB, Can. D11.14.1915 Danvers MA BR/TR/5-10/160 d4.21

| 1905 | Bos A | 15 | 44 | 1 | 5 | 1 | 0 | 0 | 1 | 4 | | 1 | .114 | .204 | .136 | 9 | -4 | 0 | .951 | -2 | 120 | 61 | C15 | | -0.6 |

McGOWAN, BEAUTY Frank Bernard B11.8.1901 Branford CT D5.6.1982 Hamden CT BL/TR/5-11/190 d4.12

1922	Phi A	99	300	36	69	10	5	1	20	40	1	46	.230	.323	.307	63	-16	6-5	.965	6	108	145	O82(0/56/28)		-1.5
1923	Phi A	95	287	41	73	9	1	1	19	36	1	25	.254	.340	.303	69	-12	4-3	.971	2	99	132	O79(26/17/36)		-1.5
1928	StL A	47	168	35	61	13	4	2	19	16	2	15	.363	.425	.524	143	11	2-1	.962	-1	105	61	O47(0/11/37)		0.6
1929	StL A	125	441	62	112	26	6	2	51	61	1	34	.254	.346	.354	78	-13	5-2	.975	2	97	124	O117(0/34/84)		-1.9
1937	Bos N	9	12	0	1	0	0	0	0	1		2	.083	.154	.083	-37	-2	0	1.000	-0	89	0	O2R		-0.3
Total	5	375	1208	174	316	58	16	6	108	154	5	122	.262	.347	.351	80	-32	17-11	.970	9	101	122	O327(26/118/187)		-4.6

McGRAW, JOHN John Joseph "Mugsy", "Little Napoleon" B4.7.1873 Truxton NY D2.25.1934 New Rochelle NY BL/TR/5-7/155 d8.26 M33 HF1937

1891	Bal AA	33	115	17	31	3	5	0	14	12	4	7	.270	.359	.383	111	1	4	.811	-12	70	98	S21,O9R,2b3		-0.8
1892	Bal N	79	286	41	77	13	2	1	26	32	6	21	.269	.355	.339	107	4	15	.897	3	151	86	O34(8/6/20),2b34,S8,3b3		0.6
1893	Bal N	127	480	123	154	9	10	5	64	101	16	11	.321	.454	.412	129	28	38	.894	-17	90	82	S117,O11(10/0/1)		1.3
1894	†Bal N	124	512	156	174	18	14	1	92	91	13	12	.340	.451	.436	110	13	78	.892	1	107	98	3b118,2b6		1.2
1895	†Bal N	96	388	110	143	13	6	3	48	60	5	9	.369	.451	.448	131	22	61	.878	8	119	**148**	3b95/2		2.5
1896	†Bal N	23	77	20	25	2	0	0	14	11	2	4	.325	.422	.403	116	2	13	.833	-2	97	157	3b18/1		0.0
1897	†Bal N	106	391	90	127	15	3	0	48	99	9		.325	**.471**	.379	126	25	44	.886	-12	91	**134**	3b105		1.3
1898	Bal N	143	515	**143**	176	8	10	0	53	**112**	19		.342	**.475**	.396	148	44	43	.900	-8	97	96	3b137,O3C		3.5
1899	Bal N	117	399	**140**	156	13	3	1	33	**124**	14		.391	**.547**	.446	165	53	73	.945	1	102	85	3b117,M		4.9
1900	StL N	99	334	84	115	10	4	0	33	85	23		.344	**.505**	.416	157	38	29	.909	-6	97	58	3b99		3.1
1901	Bal A	73	232	71	81	14	9	0	28	61	**14**		.349	.508	.487	169	29	24	.890	-14	78	56	3b69,M		1.5
1902	Bal A	20	63	14	18	3	2	1	3	17	2		.286	.451	.444	143	5	5	.864	-5	63	202	3b19,M		0.0
	NY N	35	107	13	25	0	0	0	5	26	4		.234	.401	.234	98	3	7	.926	-2	99	96	S34,M		0.2
1903	NY N	12	11	2	3	0	0	0	1	1	3		.273	.467	.273	109	1	1	—	-1	0	0	2b2,O2L/S3M		-0.1
1904	NY N	5	12	0	4	0	0	0	0	3	0		.333	.467	.333	142	1	0	.947	2	129	381	2b2,S2,M		0.3
1905	NY N	3	0	0	0	0	0	0	0	0	0		—	—	—	—	0	1	—	-0	0	0	/OLM		0.0
1906	NY N	4	2	0	0	0	0	0	0	0	0		.000	.333	.000	4	-0	0	—	-0	0	0	/3M		0.0
Total	16	1099	3924	1024	1309	121	70	13	462	836	134	74	.334	.466	.410	135	269	436	.898	-65	99	102	3b782,S183,O60(21/9/30),2b48/1		19.5

McGRIFF, FRED Frederick Stanley "Crime Dog" B10.31.1963 Tampa FL BL/TL/6-3/215(200-225) [NYA81 9/233] d5.17

1986	Tor A	3	5	1	1	0	0	0	0	0-0		2	.200	.200	.200	9	-1	0-0	1.000	-0	0	0	/1D		-0.1
1987	Tor A	107	295	58	73	16	0	20	43	60-4	1	104	.247	.376	.505	128	14	3-2	.983	-1	84	56	D90,1b14		0.9
1988	Tor A	154	536	100	151	35	4	34	82	79-3	4	149	.282	.376	.552	156	41	6-1	**.997**	-3	90	113	1b153		2.9
1989	†Tor A	161	551	98	148	27	3	**36**	92	119-12	4	132	.269	.399	.525	**161**	**50**	7-4	.989	2	109	109	1b159,D2		4.0
1990	Tor A	153	557	91	167	21	1	35	88	94-12	2	108	.300	.400	.530	155	44	5-3	.996	10	124	99	1b147,D6		4.3
1991	SD N	153	528	84	147	19	1	31	106	105-26	2	135	.278	.396	.494	145	36	4-1	.990	-10	79	113	1b153		1.6
1992	SD N★	152	531	79	152	30	4	**35**	104	96-23	1	108	.286	.394	.556	164	47	8-6	.991	-0	100	89	1b153		3.8
1993	SD N	83	302	52	83	11	1	18	46	42-4	1	55	.275	.361	.497	127	12	4-3	.983	-7	75	77	1b83		-0.7
	†Atl N	68	255	59	79	18	1	19	55	34-2	1	51	.310	.392	.612	160	22	1-0	.992	-5	95	114	1b66		1.7
	Year	151	557	111	162	29	2	37	101	76-6	2	106	.291	.375	.549	142	34	5-3	.987	-7	86	94	1b149		1.4
1994	Atl N★	113	424	81	135	25	1	34	94	50-8	2	76	.318	.389	.623	153	33	7-3	.994	-3	86	86	1b112		2.0
1995	†Atl N★	**144**	528	85	148	27	1	27	93	65-6	5	99	.280	.361	.489	117	14	3-6	.996	3	101	100	1b144		0.2
1996	†Atl N★	159	617	81	182	37	1	28	107	68-12	2	116	.295	.365	.494	117	16	7-3	.992	8	115	102	1b158		0.9
1997	Atl N	152	564	77	156	25	1	22	97	68-4	4	112	.277	.356	.441	107	6	5-0	.990	-2	95	111	1b149		-0.8
1998	TB A	151	564	73	160	33	0	19	81	79-9	2	118	.284	.371	.443	109	10	7-2	.995	-4	88	**123**	1b135,D14		-0.6
1999	TB A	144	529	75	164	30	1	32	104	86-11	1	107	.310	.405	.552	139	34	1-0	.989	6	121	**109**	1b125,D18		2.6
2000	TB A★	158	566	82	157	18	0	27	106	91-10	0	120	.277	.373	.452	110	21	2-0	.993	-7	83	108	1b144,D10		-0.9
2001	TB A	97	343	40	109	18	0	19	61	40-9	0	69	.318	.387	.536	143	22	1-1	.986	4	120	85	1b74,D17		1.7
	Chi N	49	170	27	48	7	2	12	41	26-4	3	37	.282	.383	.559	145	12	0-1	.990	-2	77	85	1b49		0.5
2002	Chi N	146	523	67	143	27	2	30	103	63-6	4	99	.273	.353	.505	127	17	1-2	.993	-9	67	76	1b137,D2		-0.4
2003	LA N	86	297	32	74	14	0	13	40	31-4	1	66	.249	.322	.428	96	-2	0-0	.989	-3	85	114	1b79	65	-1.2
2004	TB A	27	72	7	13	3	0	2	7	9-2	0	19	.181	.272	.306	51	-5	0-0	1.000	-0	79	54	D14,1b6	65	-0.7
Total	19	2460	8757	1349	2490	441	24	493	1550	1305-171	39	1882	.284	.377	.509	133	432	72-38	.992	-19	96	102	1b2239,D175	65	22.1

McGRIFF, TERRY Terence Roy B9.23.1963 Fort Pierce FL BR/TR/6-2/195* [CinN81 8/197] d7.11

1987	Cin N	34	89	6	20	3	0	2	11	8-0	0	17	.225	.289	.326	60	-5	0-0	.983	2	98	111	C33		-0.2
1988	Cin N	35	96	9	19	3	0	1	4	12-0	0	31	.198	.284	.260	56	-5	1-0	.990	0	74	141	C32		-0.3
1989	Cin N	6	11	1	3	0	0	0	0	2-1	0	3	.273	.385	.273	88	0	0-0	.929	0	63	86	C6		0.1
1990	Cin N	2	4	0	0	0	0	0	0	0-0	0	1	.000	.000	.000	-96	-1	0-0	1.000	0	23	535	/C		-0.1
	Hou N	4	5	0	0	0	0	0	0	0-0	0	0	.000	.000	.000	-99	-1	0-0	.900	-1	54	0	C4		-0.1
	Year	6	9	0	0	0	0	0	0	0-0	0	1	.000	.000	.000	-99	-2	0-0	.938	-1	43	193	C5		-0.3
1993	Fla N	3	7	0	0	0	0	0	0	1-0	0	2	.000	.125	.000	-60	-2	0-0	1.000	-0	0	0	C3		-0.4
1994	StL N	42	114	10	25	6	0	0	13	13-1	2	11	.219	.308	.272	53	-7	0-0	.991	2	79	131	C39		-0.2
Total	6	126	326	26	67	12	0	3	30	36-2	2	65	.206	.287	.270	51	-21	1-0	.985	3	79	126	C118		-1.3

McGRILLIS, MARK Mark A. B10.22.1872 Philadelphia PA D5.16.1935 Philadelphia PA 6-0/148 d9.17 Col Penn

| 1892 | StL N | 3 | 3 | 0 | 0 | 0 | 0 | 0 | 0 | 0 | 0 | 1 | .000 | .000 | .000 | -99 | -1 | 0 | 1.000 | 0 | 131 | 0 | /3 | | -0.1 |

McGUCKIN, JOE Joseph W. B3.13.1862 Paterson NJ D12.31.1903 Yonkers NY 5-8.5/160 d8.27

| 1890 | Bal AA | 11 | 37 | 2 | 4 | 0 | 0 | 0 | 2 | 6 | 1 | | .108 | .250 | .108 | 6 | -4 | 3 | .962 | 3 | 200 | 230 | O11R | | -0.1 |

McGUINNESS, JOHN John James B1857 , Ireland D12.19.1916 Binghamton NY 5-10.5/150 d5.6

1876	NY N	1	4	0	0	0	0	0	0	0			.000	.000	.000	-99	-1		.500	-2	79	0	/2C		-0.2
1879	Syr N	12	51	7	15	1	1	0	4	0		6	.294	.294	.353	126	1		.928	-1	94	129	1b12		0.0
1884	Phi U	53	220	25	52	8	1	0		5			.236	.253	.282	67	-15		.959	0	81	88	1b48,2b5/S		-1.8
Total	3	66	275	32	67	9	2	0	4	5		6	.244	.257	.291	75	-15		.954	-2	84	96	1b60,2b6/SC		-2.0

McGUIRE, JIM James A. B2.4.1875 Dunkirk NY D1.26.1917 Buffalo NY TR d9.10

| 1901 | Cle A | 18 | 69 | 4 | 16 | 2 | 0 | 0 | 3 | 0 | 0 | | .232 | .232 | .261 | 38 | -6 | 0 | .913 | 0 | 93 | 134 | S18 | | -0.5 |

McGUIRE, DEACON James Thomas B11.18.1863 Youngstown OH D10.31.1936 Duck Lake MI BR/TR/6-1/185 d6.21 M6/C6

1884	Tol AA	45	151	12	28	7	0	1		5	1		.185	.217	.252	50	-8		.906	-6			C41,O4(1/3/0),S3		-1.0
1885	Det N	34	121	11	23	4	2	0	9	5		23	.190	.222	.256	54	-6		.920	9			C31,O3L		0.5
1886	Phi N	50	167	25	33	7	1	2	18	19		25	.198	.280	.287	72	-5	2	.899	-5			C49/OR		-0.6
1887	Phi N	41	150	22	46	6	6	2	23	11	2		.307	.362	.467	121	4	3	.884	-1			C41		0.5
1888	Phi N	12	51	7	17	4	2	0	11	4		9	.333	.382	.490	167	4	0	.800	-5			C10,3b2		0.0
	Det N	3	13	0	0	0	0	0	0	0			.000	.000	.000	-99	-3	0	.810	-2			C3		-0.5
	Year	15	64	7	17	4	2	0	11	4	0	13	.266	.309	.391	116	1	0	.802	-7			C13,3b2		-0.5
	Cle AA	26	94	15	24	1	3	1	13	7		4	.255	.333	.362	126	3	2	.891	-1			C17,1b6,O3R		-0.5
1890	Roc AA	87	331	46	99	16	4	4	53	21	8		.299	.356	.408	135	14	8	.938	11	115	86	C71,1b15,O3(0/1/2)/P		2.6
1891	Was AA	114	413	55	125	22	10	3	66	43	10	34	.303	.382	.426	138	21	10	.911	-13	87	111	C98,O18R,3b3/1		1.3
1892	Was N	97	315	46	73	14	4	4	43	61		9	.232	.360	.340	115	9	7	.936	-15	67	103	C89,1b8/OR		0.2
1893	Was N	63	237	29	61	14	1	1	26	26	3	12	.257	.338	.354	86	-4	3	.889	-9	78	98	C50,1b12		-0.7
1894	Was N	104	425	67	130	18	6	6	78	33	7	19	.306	.366	.419	91	-6	11	.918	-17	71	110	C104		-1.1
1895	Was N	**133**	538	89	181	30	8	10	97	40		8	.336	.388	.478	124	18	17	.937	-1	78	**142**	C133/S		2.3
1896	Was N	108	389	60	125	25	3	2	70	30	6	14	.321	.379	.416	109	6	12	.936	-6	87	92	C98/1		0.8
1897	Was N	93	327	51	112	17	4	1	53	21	2		.343	.384	.474	127	12	9	.947	-1	80	123	C73,1b6		1.5
1898	Was N	131	489	59	131	18	3	1	57	24	6		.268	.310	.323	82	-12	10	.967	-8	65	103	C93,1b37,M		-1.2
1899	Was N	59	199	25	54	3	1	1	12	16	3		.271	.335	.312	79	-5	3	.973	-8	77	110	C56/1		-0.1
	Bro N	46	157	22	50	12	4	0	23	12	5		.318	.385	.446	125	6	4	.971	2	92	107	C46		1.0
	Year	105	356	47	104	15	5	1	35	28			.292	.357	.371	99	0	7	.972	-6	84	109	C102/1		0.9
1900	†Bro N	71	240	20	69	15	2	0	34	19	4		.286	.348	.365	91	-2	2	.952	-5	93	97	C69		-0.1
1901	Bro N	85	301	28	89	16	4	0	40	18	2		.296	.342	.375	105	4	2	.960	-9	79	96	C81,1b3		0.1
1902	Det A	73	229	27	52	14	1	2	23	24	0		.227	.300	.323	71	-8	0	.952	-6	82	88	C70		-0.8

YEAR	TM LG	G	AB	R	H	2B	3B	HR	RBI	BB-IB	HP	SO	AVG	OBP	SLG	AOPS	ABR	SB-CS	FA	FR	RNG	THR	GAMES AT POSITION	DL	BFW
1903	Det A	72	248	15	62	12	1	0	21	19	1		.250	.306	.306	87	-3	3	.960	-8	77	96	C69/1		-0.5
1904	NY A	101	322	17	67	12	2	0	20	27	3		.208	.276	.258	66	-11	2	.970	6	95	108	C97/1		0.5
1905	NY A	72	228	9	50	7	2	0	33	18	5		.219	.291	.268	69	-7	3	.975	-3	114	85	C71		-0.3
1906	NY A	51	144	11	43	5	0	0	14	12	3		.299	.365	.333	108	2	3	.966	0	108	75	C49/1		0.7
1907	NY A	1	1	0	0	0	0	0	0	0	0		.000	.000	.000	-93	0	0	1.000	0			/C		0.0
	Bos A	6	4	1	3	0	0	1	1	0	0		.750	.750	1.500	620	2	0		0			/HM		0.2
	Year	7	5	1	3	0	0	1	1	0	0		.600	.600	1.200	470	2	0	1.000	0	0	255	/C		0.2
													.000	.000	.000	-97	0	0	—	0			/HM		0.0
1908	Bos A	1	1	0	0	0	0	0	0	0	0		.250	.250	.500	142	0	0	1.000	-0	0	0	/1		0.0
	Cle A	1	4	0	1	1	0	0	2	0	0		.200	.200	.400	93	0	0	1.000	-0	0	0	/1		0.0
	Year	2	5	0	1	1	0	0	2	0	0		.333	.500	.333	159	0	0	1.000	-1	53	118	/CM		0.0
1910	Cle A	1	3	0	1	0	0	0	0	0	1		.500	.500	.500	192	0	0	.714	-0	129	194	/C		0.0
1912	Det A	1	2	1	1	0	0	0	0	0	0														
Total	26	1782	6295	770	1750	300	79	45	840	515	84	215	.278	.341	.372	101	22	118	.938	-101	85	104	C1612,1b94,O33(4/4/25),3b5,S4/P		4.8

McGUIRE, MICKEY M C Adolphus B1.18.1941 Dayton OH BR/TR/5-10/170* d9.7

YEAR	TM LG	G	AB	R	H	2B	3B	HR	RBI	BB-IB	HP	SO	AVG	OBP	SLG	AOPS	ABR	SB-CS	FA	FR	RNG	THR	GAMES AT POSITION	DL	BFW
1962	Bal A	6	4	0	0	0	0	0	0	0-0	0	0	.000	.000	.000	-99	-1	0-0	1.000	-1	51	0	S5		-0.2
1967	Bal A	10	17	2	4	0	0	0	2	0-0	0	2	.235	.235	.235	40	-1	0-0	1.000	-3	36	0	2b4		-0.5
Total	2	16	21	2	4	0	0	0	2	0-0	0	2	.190	.190	.190	11	-2	0-0	1.000	-4	51	0	S5,2b4		-0.7

McGUIRE, RYAN Ryan Byron B11.23.1971 Bellflower CA BL/TL/6-2/215(200-215) [BosA93 3/79] d6.5 Col UCLA

YEAR	TM LG	G	AB	R	H	2B	3B	HR	RBI	BB-IB	HP	SO	AVG	OBP	SLG	AOPS	ABR	SB-CS	FA	FR	RNG	THR	GAMES AT POSITION	DL	BFW
1997	Mon N	84	199	22	51	15	2	3	17	19-1	0	34	.256	.320	.397	88	-4	1-4	.960	2	109	126	O44(21/2/22),1b30,D3		-0.6
1998	Mon N	130	210	17	39	9	0	1	10	32-0	0	55	.186	.292	.243	44	-17	0-0	.980	-2	101	66	1b78,O46(33/7/8)		-2.2
1999	Mon N	88	140	17	31	7	2	2	18	27-0	0	33	.221	.347	.343	79	-4	1-1	.997	8	165	71	1b58,O23(16/1/7)		0.1
2000	NY N	1	2	0	0	0	0	0	0	1-0	0	0	.000	.333	.000	-6	0	0-0	1.000	0	215	0	/OR		-0.4
2001	Fla N	48	54	8	10	2	0	1	8	7-0	0	15	.185	.270	.278	46	-4	1-0	1.000	1	139	0	O9R,1b4		-0.5
2002	Bal A	17	26	0	2	1	0	0	2	2-0	0	7	.077	.143	.115	-32	-5	0-0	1.000	0	99	113	1b7/D		-3.6
Total	6	368	631	64	133	34	4	7	55	88-1	0	144	.211	.306	.311	63	-34	3-5	.992	10	124	84	1b177,O123(70/10/47),D4		

McGUIRE, BILL William Patrick B2.14.1964 Omaha NE BR/TR/6-3/205(195-215) [SeaA85 1/27] d8.2 Col Nebraska

YEAR	TM LG	G	AB	R	H	2B	3B	HR	RBI	BB-IB	HP	SO	AVG	OBP	SLG	AOPS	ABR	SB-CS	FA	FR	RNG	THR	GAMES AT POSITION	DL	BFW
1988	Sea A	9	16	1	3	0	0	0	2	3-0	0	2	.188	.316	.188	43	-1	0-0	1.000	-3	69	54	C9		-0.3
1989	Sea A	14	28	2	5	0	0	1	4	2-0	0	6	.179	.233	.286	44	-2	0-0	1.000	2	119	63	C14		0.0
Total	2	23	44	3	8	0	0	1	6	5-0	0	8	.182	.265	.250	44	-3	0-0	1.000	-1	100	60	C23		-0.3

McGUNNIGLE, BILL William Henry "Gunner" B1.1.1855 Boston MA D3.9.1899 Brockton MA BR/TR/5-9/155 d5.2 M5 ▲

YEAR	TM LG	G	AB	R	H	2B	3B	HR	RBI	BB-IB	HP	SO	AVG	OBP	SLG	AOPS	ABR	SB-CS	FA	FR	RNG	THR	GAMES AT POSITION	DL	BFW
1879	Buf N	47	171	22	30	1	0	5	5			24	.175	.199	.187	27	-13		.918	3	87	0	O34R,P14		-0.7
1880	Buf N	7	22	0	4	0	0	1	0			4	.182	.182	.182	23	-2		1.000	-2	54	0	P5,O3(1/1/1)		-0.2
	Wor N	1	4	0	0	0	0	0	0			2	.000	.000	.000	-92	-1		1.000	-0	0	0	/O(1/0/1)		-0.1
	Year	8	26	0	4	0	0	1	0			6	.154	.154	.154	5	-3		1.000	-2	54	0	P5,O4(2/1/2)		-0.3
1882	Cle N	1	5	2	1	0	0	0	1			1	.200	.200	.200	30	0		—	-0	0	0	/OC		0.0
Total	3	56	202	24	35	0	1	0	6	5		31	.173	.193	.183	25	-16		.900	1	77	0	O39(2/2/36),P19		-1.0

McGWIRE, MARK Mark David "Big Mac" B10.1.1963 Pomona CA BR/TR/6-5/225(215-250) [OakA84 1/10] d8.22 Col USC

YEAR	TM LG	G	AB	R	H	2B	3B	HR	RBI	BB-IB	HP	SO	AVG	OBP	SLG	AOPS	ABR	SB-CS	FA	FR	RNG	THR	GAMES AT POSITION	DL	BFW
1986	Oak A	18	53	10	10	1	0	3	9	4-0	1	18	.189	.259	.377	76	-2	0-1	.833	-4	78	40	3b16		-0.6
1987	Oak A★	151	557	97	161	28	4	49	118	71-8	5	131	.289	.370	.618	167	53	1-1	.992	-7	85	80	1b145,3b8,O3R		3.5
1988	†Oak A★	155	550	87	143	22	1	32	99	76-4	4	117	.260	.352	.478	135	26	0-0	.993	-10	78	97	1b154/OR		0.5
1989	†Oak A★	143	490	74	113	17	0	33	95	83-5	3	94	.231	.339	.467	131	21.	1-1	.995	5	110	108	1b141,D2	15	1.6
1990	†Oak A*	156	523	87	123	16	0	39	108	110-9	7	116	.235	.370	.489	145	35	2-1	.997	-8	83	108	1b154,D2		-0.7
1991	Oak A*	154	483	62	97	22	0	22	75	93-3	3	116	.201	.330	.383	103	4	2-1	.997	-1	94	93	1b152	20	2.9
1992	†Oak A*	139	467	87	125	22	0	42	104	90-12	5	105	.268	.385	.585	178	51	0-1	1.000	-2	77	90	1b25	112	1.2
1993	Oak A	27	84	16	28	6	0	9	24	21-5	1	19	.333	.467	.726	229	17	0-1	.988	-3	74	89	1b40,D5	65	0.4
1994	Oak A	47	135	26	34	3	0	9	25	37-3	0	40	.252	.413	.474	139	10	0-0	.986	-3	98	85	1b91,D10	36	3.8
1995	Oak A★	104	317	75	87	13	0	39	90	88-5	11	77	.274	.441	.685	199	51	1-1	.990	-5	87	125	1b109,D18	22	4.9
1996	Oak A★	130	423	104	132	21	0	52	113	116-16	8	112	.312	.467	.730	199	71	0-0	.994	-3	90	94	1b101		2.0
1997	Oak A★	105	366	48	104	24	0	34	81	58-8	4	98	.284	.383	.628	160	33	1-0	.998	-1	88	101	1b50		1.5
	StL N★	51	174	38	44	3	0	24	42	43-8	2	61	.253	.411	.684	181	22	2-0	.992	-9	87	101	1b51		7.1
1998	StL N★	155	509	130	152	21	0	70	147	162-28	6	155	.299	.470	.752	217	96	1-0	.992	-9	87	101	1b151		4.1
1999	StL N★	153	521	118	145	21	1	65	147	133-21	2	141	.278	.424	.697	175	63	0-0	.990	-6	89	97	1b151	62	2.5
2000	†StL N★	89	236	60	72	8	0	32	73	76-12	7	78	.305	.483	.746	201	41	1-0	.994	-8	62	95	1b90	42	-1.5
2001	†StL N	97	299	48	56	4	0	29	64	56-3	7	118	.187	.316	.492	104	0	0-0	.994	-8	85	98	1b90	374	34.8
Total	16	1874	6187	1167	1626	252	6	583	1414	1317-150	75	1596	.263	.394	.588	163	592	12-8	.993	-83	85	98	1b1763,D37,3b24,O4R		

McHALE, JIM James Bernard "J.B." B12.17.1875 Miners Mills PA D6.17.1959 Los Angeles CA BR/TR/5-11/165 d4.14 Col St. Marys (CA)

YEAR	TM LG	G	AB	R	H	2B	3B	HR	RBI	BB-IB	HP	SO	AVG	OBP	SLG	AOPS	ABR	SB-CS	FA	FR	RNG	THR	GAMES AT POSITION	DL	BFW
1908	Bos A	21	67	9	15	2	2	0	7	4	1		.224	.278	.313	90	-1	4	.970	-1	104	0	O19(1/18/0)		-0.3

McHALE, JOHN John Joseph B9.21.1921 Detroit MI BL/TR/6-0/200 d5.28 Mil 1943 Col Notre Dame

YEAR	TM LG	G	AB	R	H	2B	3B	HR	RBI	BB-IB	HP	SO	AVG	OBP	SLG	AOPS	ABR	SB-CS	FA	FR	RNG	THR	GAMES AT POSITION	DL	BFW
1943	Det A	4	3	0	0	0	0	0	1	0	0	1	.000	.250	.000	-23	0	0-0	—	0			/H		0.0
1944	Det A	1	1	0	0	0	0	0	0	0	0	0	.000	.000	.000	-95	0	0-0	—	0			/H		-0.1
1945	†Det A	19	14	0	2	0	0	0	1	1	1	4	.143	.250	.143	14	-1	0-0	1.000	0	302	0	1b3		-0.8
1947	Det A	39	95	10	20	1	0	3	11	7	0	24	.211	.265	.316	59	-6	1-1	.995	-1	82	64	1b25		0.0
1948	Det A	1	1	0	0	0	0	0	0	0	0	0	.000	.000	.000	-97	0	0-0	.995	-0	87	63	/H		-0.9
Total	5	64	114	10	22	1	0	3	12	9	1	29	.193	.258	.281	49	-7	1-1	.995	-0	87	63	1b28		

McHALE, BOB Robert Emmet "Rabbit" B2.25.1872 Michigan Bluff CA D6.9.1952 Sacramento CA TR/5-11/152 d5.9

YEAR	TM LG	G	AB	R	H	2B	3B	HR	RBI	BB-IB	HP	SO	AVG	OBP	SLG	AOPS	ABR	SB-CS	FA	FR	RNG	THR	GAMES AT POSITION	DL	BFW
1898	Was N	11	33	5	6	0	0	0	7	1	3		.182	.270	.242	47	-1	2	.900	-1	0	0	O9C/S1		-0.3

McHENRY, AUSTIN Austin Bush "Mac" B9.22.1895 Wrightsville OH D11.27.1922 Jefferson Twp. OH BR/TR/5-11/152 d6.22

YEAR	TM LG	G	AB	R	H	2B	3B	HR	RBI	BB-IB	HP	SO	AVG	OBP	SLG	AOPS	ABR	SB-CS	FA	FR	RNG	THR	GAMES AT POSITION	DL	BFW
1918	StL N	80	272	32	71	12	6	1	29	21	2	24	.261	.319	.360	111	3	8	.952	1	89	159	O80L		0.0
1919	StL N	110	371	41	106	19	11	1	47	19	1	57	.286	.322	.404	125	10	7	.985	4	93	164	O103(73/26/7)		1.0
1920	StL N	137	504	66	142	19	11	10	65	25		73	.282	.316	.423	115	7	8-11	.952	4	102	129	O133(89/52/0)		2.5
1921	StL N	152	574	92	201	37	8	17	102	38	2	48	.350	.393	.531	145	37	10-20	.965	5	114	70	O152(146/0/6)		0.5
1922	StL N	64	238	31	72	18	3	5	43	14	1	27	.303	.344	.466	112	4	2-2	.935	5	104	171	O61L		4.0
Total	5	543	1959	262	592	105	39	34	286	117	6	229	.302	.343	.448	126	61	35-33	.960	19	102	128	O529(449/78/13)		

McHENRY, VANCE Vance Loren B7.10.1956 Chico CA BR/TR/5-9/165* [SeaA78 11/266] d8.13 Col Nevada-Las Vegas

YEAR	TM LG	G	AB	R	H	2B	3B	HR	RBI	BB-IB	HP	SO	AVG	OBP	SLG	AOPS	ABR	SB-CS	FA	FR	RNG	THR	GAMES AT POSITION	DL	BFW
1981	Sea A	15	18	3	4	0	0	0	2	1-0	0	1	.222	.263	.222	39	-1	0-0	.893	-2	90	137	S13/D		-0.3
1982	Sea A	3	1	0	0	0	0	0	0	0-0	0	0	.000	.000	.000	-97	0	0-0	.500	0	0	0	/SD		0.0
Total	2	18	19	3	4	0	0	0	2	1-0	0	1	.211	.250	.211	32	-1	0-0	.867	-2	88	135	S14,D2		

McILVEEN, IRISH Henry Cooke B7.27.1880 Belfast, Ireland D10.18.1960 Lorain OH BL/TL/5-11.5/180 d7.10 Col Penn St.

YEAR	TM LG	G	AB	R	H	2B	3B	HR	RBI	BB-IB	HP	SO	AVG	OBP	SLG	AOPS	ABR	SB-CS	FA	FR	RNG	THR	GAMES AT POSITION	DL	BFW
1906	Pit N	5	5	1	2	0	0	0	0	0	0		.400	.400	.400	143	0	1.000		0	100	0	P2		0.0
1908	NY A	44	169	17	36	3	3	0	8	14	1		.213	.277	.266	76	-5	6	.949	-1	77	0	O44(13/1/30)		-0.8
1909	NY A	4	3	0	0	0	0	0	0	1	0		.000	.250	.000	-20	0		—	0			/H		-0.8
Total	3	53	177	18	38	3	3	0	8	15	1		.215	.280	.266	76	-5	6	.949	-0	77	0	O44(13/1/30),P2		-0.8

McINNIS, STUFFY John Phalen "Jack" B9.19.1890 Gloucester MA D2.16.1960 Ipswich MA BR/TR/5-9.5/162 d4.12 Mil 1918 M1

YEAR	TM LG	G	AB	R	H	2B	3B	HR	RBI	BB-IB	HP	SO	AVG	OBP	SLG	AOPS	ABR	SB-CS	FA	FR	RNG	THR	GAMES AT POSITION	DL	BFW
1909	Phi A	19	46	4	11	0	0	4		1			.239	.286	.304	85	-1	0	.886	-1	92	111	S14		-0.1
1910	Phi A	38	73	10	22	2	4	0	12	7	0		.301	.363	.438	152	4	3	.927	-4	83	80	S17,2b5,3b4/OL		-0.1
1911	†Phi A	126	468	76	150	20	10	3	77	25	3		.321	.361	.425	121	11	23	.982	-15	85	122	1b97,S24		2.1
1912	Phi A	153	568	83	186	25	11	3	101	49	3		.327	.384	.433	138	28	27	.984	3	110	121	1b153		2.1
1913	†Phi A	148	543	79	176	30	4	4	90	45	4	31	.324	.382	.416	137	26	16	.992	-1	89	110	1b148		2.0
1914	†Phi A	143	576	75	181	18	8	1	95	19	4	27	.314	.341	.368	118	8	25-19	.995	6	90	109	1b149		0.8
1915	Phi A	119	456	44	143	14	4	0	49	14	2	17	.314	.337	.362	113	4	8-8	.989	7	115	93	1b140		1.3
1916	Phi A	140	512	42	151	18	6	1	60	25	3	19	.295	.331	.361	114	6	7	.992	7	114	86	1b150		0.5
1917	Phi A	150	567	50	172	19	4	0	44	33	0	19	.303	.342	.351	113	7	18	.993	2	99	86	1b94,3b23		0.5
1918	†Bos A	117	423	40	115	11	5	0	56	19	2	10	.272	.306	.302	91	-7	10	.992	9	104	133	1b118		0.3
1919	Bos A	120	440	32	134	12	5	1	71	18	2	19	.305	.341	.361	103	-16	6-11	.996	-2	92	118	1b148		-2.0
1920	Bos A	148	559	50	166	21	3	2	71	16			.297	.321	.356	83									

YEAR	TM LG	G	AB	R	H	2B	3B	HR	RBI	BB-IB	HP	SO	AVG	OBP	SLG	AOPS	ABR	SB-CS	FA	FR	RNG	THR	GAMES AT POSITION	DL	BFW
1921	Bos A	152	584	72	179	31	10	0	76	21	4	9	.307	.335	.394	88	-13	2-4	.999	4	103	109	1b152		-1.8
1922	Cle A	142	537	58	164	28	7	1	78	15	1	5	.305	.325	.389	85	-14	1-5	.997	-5	81	94	1b140		-2.8
1923	Bos N	154	607	70	191	23	9	2	95	26	0	12	.315	.343	.392	97	-4	7-8	.991	4	112	107	1b154		-1.1
1924	Bos N	146	581	57	169	23	7	1	59	15	2	6	.291	.314	.360	83	-9	9-3	.994	7	118	101	1b146		-1.8
1925	†Pit N	59	155	19	57	10	4	0	24	17	2	1	.368	.437	.484	126	7	1-1	.993	1	111	127	1b46		0.5
1926	Pit N	47	127	12	38	6	1	0	13	7	0	3	.299	.336	.362	83	-3	1	.988	-1	94	126	1b40		-0.6
1927	Phi N	1	0	0	0	0	0	0	0	0	0	0	—	—	—				1.000	-0	0	0	/1M		0.0
Total	19	2128	7822	872	2405	312	101	20	1062	380	38	189	.307	.343	.381	106	27	172-59	.993	15	102	106	1b1995,S55,3b27,2b5/OL		0.0

McINTOSH, TIM Timothy Allen B3.21.1965 Minneapolis MN BR/TR/5-11/195* [MilA86 3/61] d9.3 Col Minnesota

1990	Mil A	5	5	1	1	0	0	1	1	0-0	0	2	.200	.200	.800	168	0	0-0	.875	-1	107		C4		-0.1
1991	Mil A	7	11	2	4	1	0	1	1	0-0	0	4	.364	.364	.727	198	1	0-0	—	-0			O4L/1D		0.1
1992	Mil A	35	77	7	14	3	0	0	6	3-0	0	9	.182	.229	.221	28	-8	1-3	.983	1	60	65	C14,O10(9/0/1),1b7,D3	15	-0.7
1993	Mil A	1	0	0	0	0	0	0	0	0-0	0	0	—	—	—			0-0	—	-0	0	0	/C		0.0
	Mon N	20	21	2	2	1	0	0	2	0-0	0	7	.095	.095	.143	-36	-4	0-0	1.000	-0	72		O7(2/0/6),C5		-0.4
1996	NY A	3	3	0	0	0	0	0	0	0-0	0	0	.000	.000	.000	-99	-1	0-0	—	-0	0	0	/C13		-0.1
Total	5	71	117	12	21	5	0	2	10	3-0	0	22	.179	.211	.274	34	-12	1-3	.973	-1	60	48	C25,O21(15/0/7),1b9,D5/3	15	-1.2

McINTYRE, MATTY Matthew W. B6.12.1880 Stonington CT D4.2.1920 Detroit MI BL/TL/5-11/175 d7.3

1901	Phi A	82	308	38	85	12	4	0	46	30	3		.276	.346	.341	87	-5	11	.921	-4	72	90	O82L		-1.2
1904	Det A	152	578	74	146	11	10	2	46	44	4		.253	.310	.317	101	1	11	.959	12	94	85	O152(151/0/1)		0.4
1905	Det A	131	495	59	130	21	5	0	30	48	2		.263	.330	.325	107	5	9	.968	18	126	172	O131L		1.7
1906	Det A	133	493	63	128	19	11	0	39	56	2		.260	.338	.343	110	7	29	.982	12	147	198	O133(132/1/0)		1.3
1907	Det A	20	81	6	23	1	1	0	9	7	0		.284	.341	.321	107	1	3	1.000	3	119	170	O20L		1.3
1908	†Det A	151	569	105	168	24	13	0	28	83	1		.295	.392	.383	146	33	20	.977	16	97	81	O151L		4.6
1909	†Det A	125	476	65	116	19	9	1	34	54	3		.244	.325	.326	101	2	13	.975	-1	87	29	O122(119/3/0)		-0.7
1910	Det A	83	305	40	72	15	5	0	25	39	0		.236	.323	.318	94	-1	4	.946	2	103	110	O77(58/17/2)		-0.4
1911	Chi A	146	569	102	184	19	11	1	52	64	5		.323	.397	.401	127	22	17	.948	-3	105	76	O146(0/31/115)		1.1
1912	Chi A	49	84	10	14	0	0	0	10	14	2		.167	.300	.167	34	-6	3	1.000	-0	100	71	O25(14/1/10)		-0.8
Total	10	1072	3958	562	1066	140	69	4	319	439	28		.269	.346	.343	110	59	120	.964	55	105	98	O1039(858/53/128)		6.3

McIVOR, OTTO Edward Otto B7.26.1884 Greenville TX D5.4.1954 Dallas TX BB/TL/5-11.5/175 d4.18

1911	StL N	30	62	11	14	2	1	1	9	9	5		.226	.333	.339	91	-1	0	.926	-1	93	54	O17(3/6/8)		-0.3

McKAY, CODY Cody Dean B1.11.1974 Vancouver BC, Can. BL/TR/6-0/212* [OakA96 9/255] d9.22 f-Dave Col Arizona St.

2002	Oak A	2	3	2	2	0	0	0	2	0-0	1		.667	.500	.667	258	1	0-0	1.000	0	0	0	/C		0.1
2004	StL N	35	74	5	17	2	0	0	6	2-0	2	14	.230	.269	.257	37	-7	0-0	1.000	-2	131	164	C18,3b7/1P		-0.8
Total	2	37	77	7	19	2	0	0	8	2-0	2	15	.247	.280	.273	45	-6	0-0	1.000	-2	124	155	C19,3b7/P1		-0.7

McKAY, DAVE David Lawrence B3.14.1950 Vancouver BC, Can. BB/TR (BR 1975-76, 77p)/6-1/195* d8.22 C22 s-Cody Col Creighton

1975	Min A	33	125	8	32	4	1	2	16	6-0	1	14	.256	.291	.352	81	-4	1-1	.923	1	95	172	3b33		-0.3
1976	Min A	45	138	8	28	2	0	0	8	9-0	4	27	.203	.272	.217	44	-10	1-2	.911	-1	101	186	3b41,S2/D		-1.2
1977	Tor A	95	274	18	54	4	3	3	22	7-0	2	51	.197	.222	.266	32	-27	2-1	.968	-4	97	81	2b40,3b32,S20,D2		-2.8
1978	Tor A	145	504	59	120	20	8	7	45	20-2	1	91	.238	.268	.351	71	-21	4-4	.984	-2	98	96	2b140,S3,3b2/D		-1.7
1979	Tor A	47	156	19	34	9	0	2	12	7-0	1	19	.218	.256	.276	43	-12	1-1	.974	7	109	107	2b46,3b2		-0.3
1980	Oak A	123	295	29	72	16	1	1	29	10-0	6	57	.244	.283	.315	68	-13	1-1	.977	-6	91	72	2b62,3b54,S10		-1.9
1981	†Oak A	79	224	25	59	11	4	1	21	16-0	2	43	.263	.313	.375	103	1	4-1	.926	-4	93	52	3b43,2b38,S7		-0.2
1982	Oak A	78	212	25	42	4	1	4	11	11-0	0	35	.198	.235	.283	44	-17	6-1	.968	-9	88	68	2b59,3b16,S3		-2.3
Total	8	645	1928	191	441	70	15	21	170	86-2	17	337	.229	.266	.313	62	-103	20-12	.976	-20	97	89	2b385,3b223,S45,D4		-10.7

McKEAN, ED Edwin John "Mack" B6.6.1864 Grafton OH D8.16.1919 Cleveland OH BR/TR/5-9/160 d4.16

1887	Cle AA	132	539	97	154	16	13	2	54	60	1		.286	.358	.375	108	7	76	.847	-5	95	87	S123,2b8,O4L		0.4
1888	Cle AA	131	548	94	164	21	15	6	68	28	6		.299	.340	.425	149	28	52	.909	5	100	65	S78,O48(43/4/1),2b9/3		3.1
1889	Cle N	123	500	88	159	22	8	5	75	42		25	.318	.375	.424	126	16	35	.907	9	105	101	S122/2		2.5
1890	Cle N	136	530	95	157	15	14	7	61	87	6	25	.296	.401	.417	141	31	23	.903	-12	97	91	S134,2b3		2.0
1891	Cle N	141	603	115	170	13	12	6	69	64	1	19	.282	.352	.373	107	4	14	.887	-12	99	82	S141		-0.4
1892	†Cle N	129	531	76	139	14	10	0	93	49		19	.262	.325	.326	93	-5	19	.862	-44	85	72	S129		-4.0
1893	Cle N	125	545	103	169	29	24	4	133	50		12	.310	.372	.473	117	9	16	.902	-3	100	112	S125		1.0
1894	Cle N	130	554	116	198	30	15	8	128	49	2	12	.357	.412	.509	116	13	33	.905	-20	91	81	S130		0.0
1895	†Cle N	132	569	131	194	32	17	8	119	46	7		.341	.397	.499	123	17	13	.907	-20	93	86	S132		0.3
1896	†Cle N	133	571	100	193	29	12	7	112	45	2		.338	.388	.468	118	13	13	.915	-34	88	113	S133		-1.2
1897	Cle N	125	523	83	143	21	14	2	78	40	1		.273	.330	.379	82	-16	15	.920	-28	90	82	S125		-3.2
1898	Cle N	151	604	89	172	23	1	9	94	56	1		.285	.346	.371	107	6	11	.932	-31	86	84	S151		-1.6
1899	StL N	67	277	40	72	7	3	3	40	20	1		.260	.310	.339	76	-10	4	.886	-9	94	93	S42,1b15,2b10		-1.5
Total	13	1655	6894	1227	2084	272	158	67	1124	636	39	159	.302	.365	.417	114	113	324	.900	-205	94	89	S1565,O52(47/4/1),2b31,1b15/3		-2.6

McKECHNIE, BILL William Boyd "Deacon" B8.7.1886 Wilkinsburg PA D10.29.1965 Bradenton FL BB/TR/5-10/160 d9.8 M25/C7 HF1962

1907	Pit N	3	8	0	1	0	0	0	0	0			.125	.125	.125	-21	-1	0	1.000	-0	97		3b2/2		-0.1
1910	Pit N	71	212	23	46	1	2	0	12	11	0	23	.217	.256	.241	42	-16	4	.971	4	106	98	2b36,S14,3b8,1b4		-1.2
1911	Pit N	104	321	40	73	8	7	2	37	28	2	18	.227	.293	.315	68	-15	9	.975	-0	98	99	1b57,2b17,S12,3b6		-1.6
1912	Pit N	24	73	8	18	0	1	0	4	4	0	5	.247	.286	.274	54	-5	2	.978	-0	104		3b13,S4,2b3,1b2		-0.4
1913	Bos N	1	4	1	0	0	0	0	0	0	0		1.000	.200	.000	-39	-1	0	1.000	0	94		/OC		-0.1
	NY A	45	112	7	15	0	0	0	8	8	1	17	.134	.198	.134	-2	-15	2	.950	4	114	143	2b28,S7,3b2		-1.1
1914	Ind F	149	570	107	173	24	6	2	38	53	5	36	.304	.368	.377	93	-11	47	.939	23	117	122	3b149		1.6
1915	New F	127	451	49	113	22	5	1	43	41	2	31	.251	.316	.328	86	-16	28	.956	-9	96	98	3b117/ORM		-1.3
1916	NY N	71	260	22	64	9	1	0	17	7	1	20	.246	.269	.288	75	-8	7	.940	-2	98	87	3b71		-1.0
	Cin N	37	130	4	36	3	0	0	10	3	0	12	.277	.293	.300	84	-3	4	.960	-2	90	119	3b35		-0.4
	Year	108	390	26	100	12	1	0	27	10	1	32	.256	.277	.292	78	-11	11	.947	-4	95	97	3b106		-1.4
1917	Cin N	48	134	11	34	3	1	0	15	7	1	7	.254	.296	.291	84	-3	5	.943	-4	88	119	2b26,S13,3b4		-0.7
1918	Pit N	126	435	34	111	13	9	2	43	24	2	22	.255	.297	.340	91	-6	12	.966	-1	95	131	3b126		-0.4
1920	Pit N	40	133	13	29	3	1	1	13	4	0	7	.218	.241	.278	47	-9	7-4	.943	-2	90	78	3b20,S10,2b6/1		-1.1
Total	11	846	2843	319	713	86	33	8	240	190	15	199	.251	.301	.313	76	-109	127-4	.952	19	101	107	3b553,2b117,1b64,S60,O2(0/1/1)		-7.8

McKEE, FRANK Frank B Philadelphia PA d6.11

1884	Was U	4	17	2	3	0	0	0		1			.176	.222	.176	23	-2		.200	-2	142	0	O3R,3b2/C		-0.3

McKEE, RED Raymond Ellis B7.20.1890 Shawnee OH D8.5.1972 Saginaw MI BL/TR/5-11/180 d4.19

1913	Det A	68	187	18	53	3	4	1	20	21	1	21	.283	.359	.358	112	3	7	.950	-10	83	104	C62		-0.2
1914	Det A	34	64	7	12	1	1	0	8	14	1	16	.188	.342	.234	71	-1	1-2	.964	-5	85	71	C27		-0.5
1915	Det A	55	106	10	29	5	0	1	17	13	0	16	.274	.353	.349	105	1	1	.954	-5	93	83	C35		-0.1
1916	Det A	32	76	3	16	1	2	0	4	6	0	11	.211	.268	.276	61	-4	0	.955	-4	84	107	C26		-0.7
Total	4	189	433	38	110	10	7	2	49	54	2	64	.254	.339	.323	95	-1	9-2	.954	-24	86	95	C150		-1.5

McKEEL, WALT Walt Thomas B1.17.1972 Wilson NC BR/TR/6-2/200* [BosA90 3/91] d9.14

1996	Bos A	1	0	0	0	0	0	0	0	0-0	0		—	—	—		0	0-0	—	-0	0	0	/C		0.0
1997	Bos A	5	3	0	0	0	0	0	0	0-0	0	1	.000	.000	.000	-98	-1	0-0	1.000	0	0	0	C4/1		-0.1
2002	Col N	5	13	1	4	0	0	0	0	0-0	0	3	.308	.308	.308	58	-1	0-0	1.000	-2	26	0	C5		-0.1
Total	3	11	16	1	4	0	0	0	0	0-0	0	4	.250	.250	.250	30	-2	0-0	1.000	-2	21	0	C10/1		-0.3

McKEEVER, JIM James B4.19.1861 St.John NB, Can. D8.19.1897 Boston MA BR/5-10/170 d4.17

1884	Bos U	16	66	13	9	0	0	0					.136	.136	.136	-17	-12		.869	-4			C12,O4R		-1.4

McKELVEY, JOHN John Wellington B8.27.1847 Rochester NY D5.31.1944 Rochester NY BR/TR/5-7.5/175 d4.19

1875	NH NA	43	188	26	43	3	1	0	10	5		8	.229	.249	.255	86	-1	3-1	.656	-9	88	68	O39(0/4/35),3b5		-0.6

YEAR	TM LG	G	AB	R	H	2B	3B	HR	RBI	BB-IB	HP	SO	AVG	OBP	SLG	AOPS	ABR	SB-CS	FA	FR	RNG	THR	GAMES AT POSITION	DL	BFW

McKELVY, RUSS   Russell Errett   B9.8.1854 Swissvale PA   D10.19.1915 Omaha NE   BR/TR   d5.1   Col Allegheny ▲

																								-0.1
1878	Ind N	**63**	253	33	57	4	3	2	36	5		38	.225	.240	.289	84	-3		.846	5	113	82	O62C,P4		-0.1
1882	Pit AA	1	4	0	0	0	0	0	0	0			.000	.000	.000	-99	-1		—	-0	0	0	/OR		-0.1
Total	2	64	257	33	57	4	3	2	36	5		38	.222	.237	.284	81	-4		.846	4	113	82	O63(0/62/1),P4		-0.2

McKENNA, ED   Edward J.   B St.Louis MO   d7.29

1874	Phi NA	1	4	0	0	0	0	0	0	0		1	.000	.000	.000	-97	-1	0-0	1.000	0	0	0	/1		-0.1
1877	StL N	1	5	0	1	0	0	0	0	0		1	.200	.200	.200	28	0		1.000	-0	0	0	/OC		-0.1
1884	Was U	32	117	19	22	1	0	0		4			.188	.215	.197	26	-14		.876	-8			C23,O10(0/2/8),3b7		-1.9
Total	2	33	122	19	23	1	0	0	0	4		1	.189	.214	.197	26	-14		1.000	-8			C23,O11(0/3/8),3b7		-2.0

McKEOUGH, DAVE   David J.   B12.1.1863 Utica NY   D7.11.1901 Utica NY   5-7/158   d4.22

1890	Roc AA	62	218	38	49	5	0	0	20	29			.225	.316	.248	72	-6	14	.929	2	114	112	C47,S13,2b2/3		0.0
1891	Phi AA	15	54	4	14	1	1	0	3	8	0	6	.259	.355	.315	92	0	0	.854	-4	109	84	C14/S		-0.3
Total	2	77	272	42	63	6	1	0	23	37		6	.232	.324	.261	76	-6	14	.912	-2	113	105	C61,S14,2b2/3		-0.3

McKINNEY, RICH   Charles Richard   B11.22.1946 Piqua OH   BR/TR/5-11/185*   [ChiA68 1/14]   d6.26   Col Ohio U.   OF(6/0/27)

1970	Chi A	43	119	12	20	5	0	4	17	11-0	1	25	.168	.242	.311	50	-8	3-2	.931	1	95	44	3b23,S11		-0.7
1971	Chi A	114	369	35	100	11	2	8	46	35-1	2	37	.271	.334	.377	99	-0	0-0	.968	-8	93	79	2b67,O25R,3b5		-0.5
1972	NY A	37	121	10	26	2	0	1	7	7-0	0	13	.215	.258	.256	54	-7	0-0	.917	-1	110	86	3b33		-1.0
1973	Oak A	48	65	9	16	3	0	1	7	7-0	0	4	.246	.319	.338	89	-1	0-0	.900	-1	96	84	3b17,2b7,O3L,D6		-0.2
1974	Oak A	5	7	0	1	0	0	0	0	0-0	0	0	.143	.143	.143	-19	-1	0-0	1.000	-1	0	0	2b3		-0.3
1975	Oak A	8	7	0	1	0	0	0	2	1-0	0	2	.143	.200	.143	14	-1	0-0	1.000	-1	0	0	/1D		-0.1
1977	Oak A	86	198	13	35	7	0	6	21	16-0	0	43	.177	.236	.303	47	-15	0-1	.978	-2	101	93	1b32,D18,3b7,O5(3/0/2),2b3		-2.0
Total	7	341	886	79	199	28	2	20	100	77-1	3	124	.225	.286	.328	73	-33	4-3	.911	-12	103	77	3b85,2b80,1b33,O33R,D26,S11		-4.8

McKINNEY, BOB   Robert Francis   B10.4.1875 McSherrystown PA   D8.19.1946 Hanover PA   BR/TR/5-7/165   d7.23

1901	Phi A	2	2	0	0	0	0	0	0				.000	.000	.000	-96	-1	0	—	-1	0	0	/23		-0.1

McKINNON, ALEX   Alexander J.   B8.14.1856 Boston MA   D7.24.1887 Charlestown MA   BR/5-11.5/170   d5.1   M1

1884	NY N	**116**	470	66	128	21	13	3	73	8		62	.272	.285	.391	108	2		.955	-2	93	102	1b116		-0.9
1885	StL N	100	411	42	121	21	6	1	44	8		31	.294	.308	.382	130	13		.978	-2	77	96	1b100,M		0.2
1886	StL N	122	491	75	148	24	7	8	72	21		23	.301	.330	.428	138	22	10	.963	-6	79	105	1b119,O3C		0.5
1887	Pit N	48	200	26	68	16	4	1	30	8		9	.340	.365	.475	142	12	6	.977	3	139	101	1b48		0.9
Total	4	386	1572	209	465	82	30	13	219	45		0	125	.296	.315	.411	127	49	16	.967	-6	90	101	1b383,O3C		0.7

McKNIGHT, JIM   James Arthur   B6.1.1936 Bee Branch AR   D2.24.1994 Van Buren Co. AR   BR/TR/6-1/185*   d9.22   s-Jeff

1960	Chi A	3	6	0	2	0	0	0	1	0-0	0	1	.333	.333	.333	84	0	0-0	.667	-0	159	342	/2OR		-0.1
1962	Chi N	60	85	6	19	0	1	0	5	2-0	0	13	.224	.241	.247	30	-9	0-0	.955	3	161	218	3b9,O5R,2b2		-0.6
Total	2	63	91	6	21	0	1	0	6	2-0	0	14	.231	.247	.253	34	-9	0-0	.955	3	161	218	3b9,O6R,2b3		-0.7

McKNIGHT, JEFF   Jefferson Alan   B2.18.1963 Conway AR   BB/TR/6-0/188(175-188)   [NYN83*S2/29]   d6.6   f-Jim   Col Arkansas-Fort Smith [JC]   OF(10/0/6)

1989	NY N	6	12	2	3	0	0	0	3	0-0	0	1	.250	.357	.250	80	0	0-0	1.000	-1	97	101	2b4/13S		-0.2
1990	Bal A	29	75	11	15	2	0	1	4	5-0	1	17	.200	.259	.267	49	-5	0-0	1.000	-1	115	83	O7(6/0/1),1b2,D4	125	-0.6
1991	Bal A	16	41	2	7	1	0	0	2	2-0	0	7	.171	.209	.195	13	-5	1-0	.980	1	113	89	2b14,1b9,3b3,S3/OR		-0.1
1992	NY N	31	85	10	23	3	1	2	13	2-0	0	9	.271	.287	.400	94	-1	0-1	.980	1	113	89	2b14,1b9,3b3,S3/OR		-0.5
1993	NY N	105	164	19	42	3	1	2	13	13-0	1	31	.256	.311	.323	72	-7	0-0	.943	0	99	109	S29,2b15,1b10,3b9/C		-0.3
1994	NY N	31	27	1	4	1	0	0	2	4-0	1	12	.148	.250	.185	18	-3	0-0	1.000	-0	0	0	1b2	62	-0.3
Total	6	218	404	45	94	10	2	5	34	28-0	2	76	.233	.284	.304	63	-21	1-1	.996	-1	102	81	1b39,2b38,S34,O16L,3b13,D5/C	187	-2.4

McLANE, ED   Edward Cameron   B8.20.1881 Weston MA   D8.21.1975 Baltimore MD   BR/TR/5-10/179   d10.6   Col Fordham

1907	Bro N	1	2	0	0	0	0	0	0	0		1	.000	.333	.000	5	0		.333	-1	0	0	/OR		-0.1

McLARNEY, ART   Arthur James   B12.20.1908 Ft.Worden WA   D12.20.1984 Seattle WA   BB/TR/6-0/168   d8.23   Col Washington St.

1932	NY N	9	23	2	3	1	0	0	3	1		3	.130	.167	.174	-8	-4	0	1.000	-1	87	84	S7		-0.4

McLARRY, POLLY   Howard Zell   B3.25.1891 Leonard TX   D11.4.1971 Bonham TX   BL/TR/6-0/185   d9.2

1912	Chi A	2	2	0	0	0	0	0	0	0			.000	.000	.000	-99	-1	0	—	0			/H		-0.1
1915	Chi N	68	127	16	25	3	0	1	12	14		20	.197	.277	.244	58	-6	2-2	.957	1	105	45	2b21,1b18		-0.6
Total	2	70	129	16	25	3	0	1	12	14		20	.194	.273	.240	56	-7	2-2	.957	1	105	45	2b21,1b18		-0.7

McLAUGHLIN, BARNEY   Bernard   B1857, Ireland   D2.13.1921 Lowell MA   d8.2   b-Frank ▲

1884	KC U	42	162	15	37	7	3	0		9			.228	.269	.309	86	-7		.762	-1	185	360	O24(4/3/17),2b12,P7,S2		-0.7
1887	Phi A	50	205	26	45	8	1	1	26	11	1	27	.220	.263	.302	53	-14	2	.879	-14	90	71	2b50		-2.2
1890	Syr AA	86	329	43	87	8	1	2	40	47	2		.264	.360	.313	110	8	13	.902	-6	96	82	S86		0.3
Total	3	178	696	84	169	23	7	3	66	67	3	27	.243	.312	.309	86	-13	15	.900	-22	97	80	S88,2b62,O24(4/3/17),P7		-2.6

McLAUGHLIN, FRANK   Francis Edward   B6.19.1856 Lowell MA   D4.5.1917 Lowell MA   BR/TR/5-9/160   d8.9   b-Barney ▲

1882	Wor N	15	55	7	12	0	2	1	4	0		11	.218	.218	.345	76	-2		.760	-4	99	44	S14/OC		-0.5
1883	Pit AA	29	114	15	25	2	0	1	6				.219	.258	.263	71	-3		.802	-0	112	64	S25,O4(0/3/1),2b2,P2		-0.2
1884	Cin U	16	67	10	16	4	1	2		2			.239	.261	.418	95	-3		.740	-6	73	139	S16		0.0
	CP U	15	67	16	11	4	1	0		1			.239	.250	.328	75	-4		.888	3	114	179	2b14/SOR		-0.7
	KC U	32	123	17	28	11	0	1		9			.228	.280	.341	101	-3		.847	-6	105	58	2b10,O10(2/6/2),3b9,S5,P2		-1.4
	Year	63	257	38	60	19	2	3		12			.233	.268	.358	92	-10		.873	-9	111	134	2b24,S22,O11(2/6/3),3b9,P2		-2.1
Total	3	107	426	60	97	21	4	5	4	18		11	.228	.259	.331	85	-15		.769	-13	98		S61,2b26,O16(2/10/4),3b9,P4		-2.6

McLAUGHLIN, KID   James Anson "Sunshine"   B4.12.1888 Randolph NY   D11.13.1934 Allegany NY   BL/TR/5-8.5/158   d6.30   Col Colgate

1914	Cin N	3	2	1	0	0	0	0	0	0			.000	.000	.000	-97	-0		1.000	0	130	0	O2C		-0.1

McLAUGHLIN, JIM   James Robert   B1.3.1902 St.Louis MO   D12.18.1968 Mount Vernon IL   BR/TR/5-8.5/168   d4.18

1932	StL A	1	1	0	0	0	0	0	1	0			.000	.000	.000	-95	-0	0-0	—	-0	0	0	/3		0.0

McLAUGHLIN, TOM   Thomas   B3.28.1860 Louisville KY   D7.21.1921 Louisville KY   TR   d7.17

1883	Lou AA	42	146	16	28	1	2	0		5			.192	.219	.226	47	-8		.844	2	118	129	S19,O17(8/9/1),1b5,3b2,2b2		-0.5
1884	Lou AA	98	335	41	67	11	6	0	21	22		6	.200	.262	.269	77	-7		.892	13	109	**171**	S94,3b4/2		0.8
1885	Lou AA	**112**	411	49	87	13	9	2	41	15		3	.212	.245	.302	72	-14		.883	-1	92	112	2b93,S19		-0.9
1886	NY AA	74	250	27	34	3	1	0	16	26		1	.136	.220	.156	20	-21	13	.886	7	102	65	S63,2b10/OL		-1.1
1891	Was AA	14	41	9	11	0	1	0	3	7		2	.268	.400	.317	111	1	3	.871	1	98	128	S14		0.2
Total	5	340	1183	142	227	28	19	2	81	75		6	.192	.247	.253	62	-49	16	.886	22	106	128	S209,2b106,O18(9/9/1),3b6,1b5		-1.5

McLAUGHLIN, BILL   William   B San Francisco CA   d5.3

1884	Was U	10	37	3	7	1	0	0		0			.189	.189	.270	39	-4		.696	-4	75	0	S9/3		-0.2

McLAURIN, RALPH   Ralph Edgar   B5.23.1885 Kissimmee FL   D2.11.1943 McColl SC   d9.5

1908	StL N	8	22	2	5	0	0	0		0			.227	.227	.227	47	-1	0	.875	-1	0	0	O6L		-0.1

McLEAN, LARRY   John Bannerman   B7.18.1881 Fredericton NB, Can.   D3.24.1921 Boston MA   BR/TR/6-5/228   d4.26

1901	Bos A	9	19	4	4	1	0	0	2	1	0		.211	.211	.263	31	-2	1	1.000	0	107	114	1b5		-0.1
1903	Chi N	1	4	0	0	0	0	0	0	1	0		.000	.200	.000	-42	-1	0	.889	0	182	67	/C		-0.1
1904	StL N	27	84	5	14	1	0	0	4	4	0		.167	.205	.214	31	-7	1	.954	-4	88	52	C24		-0.2
1906	Cin N	12	35	3	7	2	0	0	4	2	0		.200	.282	.257	65	-1	0	.954	-1	101	90	C12		-0.1
1907	Cin N	113	374	35	108	19	9	0	54	13		0	.289	.313	.361	107	0	4	.975	-0	100	91	C89,1b13		0.9
1908	Cin N	99	309	24	67	9	1	0	28	15		2	.217	.258	.282	74	-10	2	.963	-3	108	101	C69,1b19		0.0
1909	Cin N	95	324	26	83	12	2	0				3	.256	.307	.324	97	-2	1	.978	-3	89	106	C95		0.2
1910	Cin N	127	423	27	126	14	7	2	71	26	1	23	.298	.340	.378	114	6	4	.983	7	118	104	C119		2.0
1911	Cin N	107	328	24	94	7	2	0	27	22	1	18	.287	.334	.320	85	-7	1	.968	14	132	110	C98		-1.1
1912	Cin N	102	333	17	81	15	1	1	27	18	1	15	.243	.284	.303	63	-18	1	.973	-1	94	109	C98		-1.7
1913	StL N	48	152	7	41	9	0	1	12	6		4	.270	.297	.329	80	-7	1	.981	-7	71	112	C42		0.0
	†NY N	30	75	3	24	4	0	0	9	4		3	.320	.354	.373	107	1	1	.953	-1	114	65	C28		0.4

YEAR	TM LG	G	AB	R	H	2B	3B	HR	RBI	BB-IB	HP	SO	AVG	OBP	SLG	AOPS	ABR	SB-CS	FA	FR	RNG	THR	GAMES AT POSITION	DL	BFW
1914	NY N	78	227	10	65	13	0	0	21	10	0	13	.286	.316	.344	89	-3	1	.970	-8	86	96	C70		-0.6
1915	NY N	79	154	8	40	4	0	0	14	4	1	9	.260	.283	.299	76	-5	4	.973	-0	133	69	C74		-0.2
	NY N	13	33	0	5	0	0	0	4	0	0	1	.152	.152	.152	9	-9	4	.985	1	89	161	C12		-0.4
Total	13	862	2647	183	694	90	26	6	298	136	9	79	.262	.301	.323	86	-54	20	.973	2	106	100	C761,1b37		1.1

McLEMORE, MARK   Mark Tremell B10.4.1964 San Diego CA BB/TR/5-11/195(175-207) [CalA82 9/218] d9.13 OF(250/21/147)

YEAR	TM LG	G	AB	R	H	2B	3B	HR	RBI	BB-IB	HP	SO	AVG	OBP	SLG	AOPS	ABR	SB-CS	FA	FR	RNG	THR	GAMES AT POSITION	DL	BFW
1986	Cal A	5	4	0	0	0	0	0	0	1-0	0	2	.000	.200	.000	-40	-7	0-1	1.000	2	171	86	2b2		0.0
1987	Cal A	138	433	61	102	13	3	3	41	48-0	0	72	.236	.310	.300	65	-21	25-8	.974	-8	93	117	2b132,S6,D3		-1.8
1988	Cal A	77	233	38	56	11	2	2	16	25-0	0	28	.240	.312	.330	83	-5	13-7	.979	4	107	138	2b63,3b5/D	70	0.1
1989	Cal A	32	103	12	25	3	1	0	14	7-0	1	19	.243	.295	.291	68	-5	6-1	.966	4	111	147	2b27/D		0.2
1990	Cal A	20	48	4	7	2	0	0	2	4-0	0	9	.146	.212	.188	13	-6	1-0	1.000	-5	79	62	2b8,S8/D	92	-1.0
	Cle A	8	12	2	2	0	0	0	0	0-0	0	6	.167	.167	.167	-7	-2	0-0	1.000	1	73	395	3b4,2b3/D		-0.1
	Year	28	60	6	9	2	0	0	2	4-0	0	15	.150	.203	.183	9	-7	1-0	1.000	-4	85	94	2b11,S8,3b4,D2		-1.1
1991	Hou N	21	61	6	9	1	0	0	2	6-0	0	13	.148	.221	.164	11	-7	0-1	.975	-1	103	83	2b19	47	-0.9
1992	Bal A	101	228	40	56	7	2	0	27	21-1	0	26	.246	.308	.294	68	-10	11-5	.978	2	103	121	2b70,D17		-0.6
1993	Bal A	148	581	81	165	27	5	4	72	64-4	1	92	.284	.353	.368	91	-6	21-15	.987	12	109	141	O124R,2b25,3b4/D		-0.1
1994	Bal A	104	343	44	88	11	1	3	29	51-3	1	50	.257	.354	.329	72	-13	20-5	.981	2	99	98	2b96,O7R/D		-0.4
1995	Tex A	129	467	73	122	20	5	5	41	59-6	3	71	.261	.346	.358	81	-12	21-11	.986	-2	103	0	O73(69/0/5),2b66,D2		-1.2
1996	†Tex A	147	517	84	150	23	4	5	46	87-5	0	69	.290	.389	.379	91	-4	27-10	.985	24	109	113	2b147/OR		2.6
1997	Tex A	89	349	47	91	17	2	1	25	40-1	2	54	.261	.338	.330	71	-14	7-5	.980	-1	104	106	2b89/OL	70	-1.1
1998	†Tex A	126	461	79	114	15	1	5	53	89-1	2	64	.247	.369	.317	77	-12	12-4	.975	-5	94	90	2b122,D2	15	-0.9
1999	†Tex A	144	566	105	155	20	7	6	45	83-2	0	79	.274	.363	.366	83	-13	16-8	.983	10	106	102	2b135,O11(4/0/7)		0.3
2000	†Sea A	138	481	72	118	23	1	3	46	81-2	1	78	.245	.353	.316	73	-17	30-14	.987	-1	96	103	2b129,O14(14/1/0)		-1.0
2001	†Sea A	125	409	78	117	16	9	5	57	69-0	0	84	.286	.384	.406	116	12	39-7	.988	-5	97	121	O68(63/8/2),3b36,S35,2b9,D2		1.4
2002	Sea A	104	337	54	91	17	2	7	41	61-1	1	63	.270	.380	.395	111	8	18-10	.972	-2	109	45	O88(82/12/1),3b14,2b2/SD		0.4
2003	Sea A	99	309	34	72	15	2	2	37	38-0	0	71	.233	.318	.314	72	-12	5-5	.972	1	98	130	S38,3b29,O16L,D11,2b6		0.4
2004	Oak A	77	250	29	62	14	0	2	21	41-3	1	33	.248	.355	.328	81	-5	0-2	.975	8	107	138	2b47,3b27/OL	36	0.4
Total	19	1832	6192	943	1602	255	47	53	615	875-29	15	983	.259	.349	.341	81	-145	272-119	.981	39	101	110	2b1197,O404L,3b119,S88,D47	330	-4.7

McLEOD, RALPH   Ralph Alton B10.19.1916 N.Quincy MA BL/TL/6-0/170 d9.14

| 1938 | Bos N | 6 | 7 | 1 | 2 | 1 | 0 | 0 | 0 | 1-0 | 0 | 2 | .286 | .286 | .429 | 105 | 0 | 0 | 1.000 | 0 | 98 | 0 | /OL | | 0.0 |

McLEOD, JIM   Soule James B9.12.1908 Jones LA D8.3.1981 Little Rock AR BR/TR/6-0/187 d5.22 Col Arkansas-Little Rock

1930	Was A	18	34	3	9	1	0	0	1	1	0	5	.265	.306	.294	53	-2	1-1	1.000	-1	101	0	3b10,S7		-0.2
1932	Was A	7	0	1	0	0	0	0	0	1	0	0	—	1.000	—	183	-0	0-0	1.000	0	145	0	/S		0.0
1933	Phi N	67	232	20	45	6	1	0	15	12	1	25	.194	.237	.228	30	-21	1	.914	-3	101	85	3b67/S		-2.3
Total	3	92	266	24	54	7	1	0	16	14	1	30	.203	.248	.237	33	-23	2-1	.922	-3	101	76	3b77,S9		-2.5

McLOUTH, NATE   Nathan Richard B10.28.1981 Muskegon MI BL/TR/5-11/185 d6.29

| 2005 | Pit N | 41 | 109 | 20 | 28 | 6 | 0 | 5 | 12 | 3-0 | 5 | 20 | .257 | .305 | .450 | 96 | -1 | 2-0 | .958 | -4 | 78 | 0 | O29(0/21/8) | | -0.5 |

McMAHON, JACK   John Henry B10.15.1869 Waterbury CT D12.30.1894 Bridgeport CT BR/TL/5-10/165 d8.8

1892	NY N	40	147	21	33	5	7	1	24	10	1	9	.224	.278	.374	98	-2	3	.973	-3	74	68	1b36,C5		-0.4
1893	NY N	11	30	5	10	2	1	0	4	2	0	0	.333	.375	.467	122	1	0	.891	-1	101	103	C11		0.0
Total	2	51	177	26	43	7	8	1	28	12	1	9	.243	.295	.390	103	-1	3	.973	-4	74	68	1b36,C16		-0.4

McMANUS, FRANK   Francis E. B9.21.1875 Lawrence MA D9.1.1923 Syracuse NY TR/5-7/150 d9.14

1899	Was N	7	21	3	8	1	0	0	2	2	0		.381	.435	.429	139	1	3	.931	-1	78	162	C7		0.1
1903	Bro N	2	7	0	0	0	0	0	0	0	0		.000	.000	.000	-99	-2	0	.929	-2	90	135	C2		-0.1
1904	Det A	1	0	0	0	0	0	0	0	0	0						0	0	—	0	0	0	/C		
	NY A	4	7	0	0	0	0	0	0	0	0		.000	.000	.000	-96	-2	0	.900	-1	81	0	C4		-0.2
	Year	5	7	0	0	0	0	0	0	0	0		.000	.000	.000	-97	-2	0	.900	-1	76	0	C5		-0.2
Total	3	14	35	3	8	1	0	0	2	2	0		.229	.270	.257	50	-3	3	.925	-1	80	125	C14		-0.2

McMANUS, JIM   James Michael B7.20.1936 Brookline MA BL/TL/6-4/215 d9.21

| 1960 | KC A | 5 | 13 | 3 | 4 | 0 | 1 | 0 | 2 | 1 | 0 | 5 | .308 | .357 | .538 | 138 | 1 | 0-0 | 1.000 | -0 | 48 | 34 | 1b3 | | 0.0 |

McMANUS, MARTY   Martin Joseph B3.14.1900 Chicago IL D2.18.1966 St.Louis MO BR/TR/5-10.5/160 d9.26 M2

1920	StL A	1	3	0	1	0	1	0	1	0		0	.333	.333	1.000	236	0	0-0	.667	-1	95	0	/3		0.0
1921	StL A	121	412	49	107	19	8	3	64	27	2	30	.260	.308	.367	68	-22	5-3	.952	-12	91	87	2b96,3b13,1b9,S2		-2.9
1922	StL A	154	606	88	189	34	11	11	109	38	6	41	.312	.358	.459	108	5	9-6	.964	1	96	130	2b153/1		1.0
1923	StL A	154	582	86	180	35	10	15	94	49	4	50	.309	.367	.481	116	11	14-10	.960	-4	91	112	2b133,1b20		0.9
1924	StL A	123	442	71	147	23	5	5	80	55	2	40	.333	.409	.441	112	10	13-9	.972	8	102	103	2b119		2.0
1925	StL A	154	587	108	169	44	8	13	90	73	5	69	.288	.371	.457	104	4	5-11	.967	2	97	94	2b154/OR		0.6
1926	StL A	149	549	102	156	30	10	9	68	55	1	62	.284	.350	.424	97	-4	5-7	.958	12	104	113	3b84,2b61,1b4		1.3
1927	Det A	108	369	60	99	19	7	9	69	34	1	38	.268	.332	.431	95	-4	4-7	.960	0	95	93	S39,2b35,3b22,1b6		0.1
1928	Det A	139	500	78	144	37	5	8	73	51	1	32	.288	.355	.430	104	3	11-13	.955	2	101	89	3b92,1b45,S2		0.6
1929	Det A	154	599	99	168	32	8	18	90	60	1	52	.280	.347	.451	103	2	16-11	.972	7	101	89	3b150,S8		1.7
1930	Det A	132	484	74	155	40	4	9	89	59	2	28	.320	.396	.475	118	15	23-8	.966	7	100	100	3b79,2b21/1		3.0
1931	Det A	107	362	39	98	17	3	3	53	49	2	22	.271	.361	.359	87	-6	7-3	.950	7	100	120	3b79,2b21/1		0.6
	Bos A	17	62	8	18	4	0	1	9	8	0	1	.290	.371	.403	110	.1	1-1	1.000	6	151	299	3b11,2b7		0.7
	Year	124	424	47	116	21	3	4	62	57	2	23	.274	.362	.366	90	-5	8-4	.956	13	114	142	3b90,2b28/1		1.3
1932	Bos A	93	302	39	71	19	4	5	24	36	3	30	.235	.317	.374	80	-9	1-2	.969	1	107	80	2b49,3b30,S2/1M		-0.4
1933	Bos A	106	366	51	104	30	4	3	36	49	0	21	.284	.369	.413	108	6	3-0	.957	-2	97	73	3b76,2b26,1b4,M		0.8
1934	Bos N	119	435	56	120	18	0	8	47	32	3	42	.276	.330	.372	95	-3	5	.964	-8	103	92	2b73,3b37		-0.3
Total	15	1831	6660	1008	1926	401	88	120	996	675	30	558	.289	.357	.430	101	9	126-91	.965	29	98	104	2b927,3b725,1b92,S56/OR		9.7

McMATH, JIMMY   Jimmy Lee B8.10.1949 Tuscaloosa AL BL/TL/6-1.5/195 [ChiN67 2/22] d9.7

| 1968 | Chi N | 6 | 14 | 0 | 2 | 0 | 0 | 0 | 1 | 0 | 0 | 6 | .143 | .143 | .143 | -13 | -2 | 0-0 | 1.000 | 0 | 135 | 0 | O3L | | -0.2 |

McMILLAN, GEORGE   George A. "Reddy" B9.1.1863 Ontario, Can D4.18.1920 Cleveland OH 5-8/175 d8.11

| 1890 | NY N | 10 | 35 | 4 | 5 | 0 | 0 | 0 | 1 | 7 | 0 | 4 | .143 | .286 | .143 | 26 | -3 | 1 | .800 | -2 | 58 | 0 | O10(1/0/9) | | -0.4 |

McMILLAN, NORM   Norman Alexis "Bub" B10.5.1895 Latta SC D9.28.1969 Marion SC BR/TR/6-0/175 d4.12 Col Clemson OF(0/15/12)

1922	†NY A	33	78	7	20	1	2	0	11	6	0	10	.256	.310	.321	63	-5	4-1	.921	-3	92	0	O26(0/15/12),3b5		-0.8
1923	Bos A	131	459	37	116	24	5	0	42	28	2	44	.253	.299	.327	64	-25	13-5	.942	3	88	93	3b67,2b34,S28		-1.2
1924	StL A	76	201	25	56	12	2	0	27	12	4	17	.279	.332	.358	73	-8	6-4	.966	-3	96	94	2b37,3b19,S7,1b2		-0.8
1928	Chi N	49	121	11	27	2	2	1	12	13	1	19	.223	.299	.289	56	-9	0	.977	2	116	136	2b19,3b18		-0.5
1929	†Chi N	124	495	77	134	35	5	5	55	36	3	43	.271	.324	.392	76	-19	13	.944	6	101	111	3b120		-0.5
Total	5	413	1356	157	353	74	16	6	147	95	10	133	.260	.313	.352	69	-65	36-10	.944	5	95	93	3b229,2b90,S35,O26C,1b2		-3.8

McMILLAN, ROY   Roy David B7.17.1929 Bonham TX D11.2.1997 Bonham TX BR/TR/5-11/170* d4.17 M2/C7

1951	Cin N	85	199	21	42	4	0	1	8	17	0	26	.211	.273	.246	40	-17	0-0	.963	2	101	85	S54,3b12/2		-1.2
1952	Cin N	154	540	60	132	32	2	7	57	45	3	81	.244	.306	.350	82	-13	4-5	.971	10	107	97	S154		0.6
1953	Cin N	155	557	51	130	15	4	5	43	43	1	52	.233	.290	.302	54	-38	2-4	.972	10	109	115	S155		-1.6
1954	Cin N	154	588	86	147	21	4	2	42	47	5	54	.250	.308	.313	61	-33	4-2	.959	7	99	124	S154		-1.3
1955	Cin N	151	470	50	126	21	2	1	37	66-7	5	33	.268	.356	.328	81	-9	4-4	.969	18	110	118	S150		2.0
1956	Cin N★	150	479	51	126	16	7	3	62	76-9	6	54	.263	.366	.344	88	-5	4-3	.975	29	114	108	S150		3.7
1957	Cin N★	151	448	50	122	25	5	1	55	66-8	6	44	.272	.371	.357	91	-2	5-1	.977	-7	98	94	S151		0.4
1958	Cin N	145	393	48	90	14	3	1	25	47-5	1	33	.229	.312	.298	60	-22	5-2	.980	2	100	96	S145		-0.9
1959	Cin N	79	246	38	65	14	2	9	34	27-3	4	27	.264	.345	.447	106	3	0-2	.974	-2	93	112	S73		0.6
1960	Cin N	124	399	42	94	12	2	10	42	35-5	4	40	.236	.301	.351	77	-13	2-2	.964	-9	101	110	S116,2b10	44	-1.2
1961	Mil N	154	505	42	111	16	0	7	48	61-2	4	86	.220	.305	.293	65	-25	2-4	.975	-1	107	115	S154		-1.3
1962	Mil N	137	468	66	116	13	0	12	44	60-0	5	53	.248	.336	.350	87	-7	2-2	.972	13	107	115	S135		1.7
1963	Mil N	100	320	35	80	10	1	4	29	17-2	2	25	.250	.291	.325	78	-9	1-5	.979	5	105	122	S94		0.3
1964	Mil N	8	13	1	4	1	0	0	0	0-0	0	1	.308	.308	.308	73	-1	1-0	.933	-2	56	87	S8		0.1
	NY N	113	379	30	80	8	2	1	25	14-2	4	16	.211	.246	.251	42	-30	3-1	.976	7	109	95	S111		-1.4

YEAR	TM LG	G	AB	R	H	2B	3B	HR	RBI	BB-IB	HP	SO	AVG	OBP	SLG	AOPS	ABR	SB-CS	FA	FR	RNG	THR	GAMES AT POSITION	DL	BFW
	Year	121	392	31	84	8	2	1	27	14-2	4	18	.214	.248	.253	43	-31	4-1	.975	5	107	95	S119		-1.6
1965	NY N	157	528	46	128	19	2	1	42	24-1	1	60	.242	.280	.292	64	-26	1-0	.964	1	108	88	S153		-1.0
1966	NY N	76	220	24	47	9	1	1	12	20-3	2	25	.214	.284	.277	59	-12	1-1	.975	1	104	86	S71	20	-0.6
Total	16	2093	6752	739	1639	253	35	68	594	665-47	57	711	.243	.314	.321	72	-259	41-36	.972	87	105	106	S2028,3b12,2b11	64	-1.6

McMILLAN, TOM   Thomas Erwin   B9.13.1951 Richmond VA   BR/TR/5-9/165   [CleA73 2/29]   d9.17   Col Jacksonville   -0.1

YEAR	TM LG	G	AB	R	H	2B	3B	HR	RBI	BB-IB	HP	SO	AVG	OBP	SLG	AOPS	ABR	SB-CS	FA	FR	RNG	THR	GAMES AT POSITION	DL	BFW
1977	Sea A	2	5	0	0	0	0	0	0	0-0	0	1	.000	.000	.000	-99	-1	0-0	1.000	0	89	141	S2		-0.1

McMILLAN, TOMMY   Thomas Law "Rebel"   B4.18.1888 Pittston PA   D7.15.1966 Orlando FL   BR/TR/5-5/130   d8.19   Col Georgia Tech   -1.1

YEAR	TM LG	G	AB	R	H	2B	3B	HR	RBI	BB-IB	HP	SO	AVG	OBP	SLG	AOPS	ABR	SB-CS	FA	FR	RNG	THR	GAMES AT POSITION	DL	BFW
1908	Bro N	43	147	9	35	3	0	0	3	9	3		.238	.296	.259	80	-3	5	.873	-7	91	111	S29,O14C		-2.9
1909	Bro N	108	373	18	79	15	1	0	24	20	1		.212	.254	.257	61	-18	11	.914	-11	96	81	S105,2b2/3		-0.9
1910	Bro N	23	74	2	13	1	0	0	2	6	0	10	.176	.237	.189	26	-7	4	.898	-2	99	79	S23		-0.7
	Cin N	82	248	20	46	0	3	0	13	31	2	23	.185	.281	.210	46	-17	7	.927	8	111	95	S82		-1.6
	Year	105	322	22	59	1	3	0	15	37	2	33	.183	.271	.205	41	-24	11	.921	6	108	92	S105		-1.0
1912	NY A	41	149	24	34	2	0	0	12	15	1		.228	.303	.242	53	-9	18	.948	-3	92	91	S41		-1.0
Total	4	297	991	73	207	21	4	0	54	81	7	33	.209	.273	.238	56	-54	45	.917	-15	100	91	S280,O14C,2b2/3		-6.6

McMILLON, BILLY   William Edward   B11.17.1971 Almagordo NM   BL/TL/5-11/179(172-195)   [FlaN93 8/239]   d7.26   Col Clemson   -0.6

YEAR	TM LG	G	AB	R	H	2B	3B	HR	RBI	BB-IB	HP	SO	AVG	OBP	SLG	AOPS	ABR	SB-CS	FA	FR	RNG	THR	GAMES AT POSITION	DL	BFW
1996	Fla N	28	51	4	11	0	0	0	4	5-1	0	14	.216	.286	.216	36	-5	0-0	1.000	-1	92	0	O15L		-0.6
1997	Fla N	13	18	0	2	1	0	0	1	0-0	0	7	.111	.111	.167	-30	-3	0-0	1.000	0	110	0	O2L		-0.3
	Phi N	24	72	10	21	4	1	2	13	6-0	0	17	.292	.333	.458	110	1	2-1	.957	2	126	170	O21(19/0/2)		0.3
	Year	37	90	10	23	5	1	2	14	6-0	0	24	.256	.293	.400	84	-2	2-1	.960	3	125	155	O23(21/0/2)		0.0
2000	Det A	46	123	20	37	7	1	4	19	19-0	1	19	.301	.388	.472	120	4	1-0	.964	1	137	0	D24,O15(3/0/13)		-0.5
2001	Det A	20	34	1	3	1	0	0	1	0-0	0	12	.088	.162	.206	-4	-5	0-0	1.000	0	111	0	O7(1/0/6),D3		-0.5
	Oak A	20	58	6	17	7	1	0	10	5-0	1	13	.293	.354	.448	111	1	1-0	.950	-2	60	106	O16(15/0/2)/D	77	-0.2
	Year	40	92	7	20	8	1	1	14	7-0	2	25	.217	.284	.359	69	-4	1-0	.967	-2	72	82	O23(16/0/8),D4		-0.7
2003	†Oak A	66	153	15	41	11	0	6	26	19-1	2	36	.268	.354	.458	112	3	0-0	.979	-2	98	0	O36(35/0/1),1b3,D9	55	-0.9
2004	Oak A	52	92	16	20	4	0	3	11	8-0	1	22	.185	.255	.326	51	-7	1-0	1.000	-2	82	0	O21(20/0/1),1b3,D6	132	-1.9
Total	6	269	601	66	149	35	3	16	93	64-2	6	140	.248	.322	.396	88	-11	4-2	.974	-3	99	48	O133(110/0/25),D43,1b6		-1.9

McMULLEN, HUGH   Hugh Raphael   B12.16.1901 LaCygne KS   D5.23.1986 Whittier CA   BB/TR/6-1/180   d9.19   -0.3

YEAR	TM LG	G	AB	R	H	2B	3B	HR	RBI	BB-IB	HP	SO	AVG	OBP	SLG	AOPS	ABR	SB-CS	FA	FR	RNG	THR	GAMES AT POSITION	DL	BFW
1925	NY N	5	15	1	2	1	0	0	0	0-0	0	3	.133	.133	.200	-17	-3	0-0	1.000	-1	91	0	C5		-0.3
1926	NY N	57	91	5	17	2	0	0	6	2	0	18	.187	.204	.209	11	-12	1	.942	1	86	104	C56		-1.1
1928	Was A	1	1	0	0	0	0	0	0	0-0	0		.000	.000	.000	-99	0	0-0		—	0			/H		0.0
1929	Cin N	1	1	0	0	0	0	0	0	0-0	0		.000	.000	.000	-99	0	0	1.000	0	0	0	/C		0.0
Total	4	64	108	6	19	3	0	0	6	2	0	22	.176	.191	.204	3	-15	1-0	.947	-3	85	92	C62		-1.4

McMULLEN, KEN   Kenneth Lee   B6.1.1942 Oxnard CA   BR/TR/6-3/195*   d9.17   OF(12/0/8)   -0.1

YEAR	TM LG	G	AB	R	H	2B	3B	HR	RBI	BB-IB	HP	SO	AVG	OBP	SLG	AOPS	ABR	SB-CS	FA	FR	RNG	THR	GAMES AT POSITION	DL	BFW
1962	LA N	6	11	0	3	0	0	0	0	0-0	0	1	.273	.273	.273	50	-1	0-0	1.000	-0	35	0	O2L		-0.1
1963	LA N	79	233	16	55	9	0	5	28	20-2	1	46	.236	.297	.339	89	-3	1-2	.933	-3	95	95	3b71/2OL		-0.7
1964	LA N	24	67	3	14	0	0	1	2	3-1	0	7	.209	.243	.254	43	-5	0-1	.991	-2	92	82	1b13,3b4,O3(1/0/2)		-0.9
1965	Was A	150	555	75	146	18	6	18	54	47-4	4	90	.263	.323	.414	110	6	2-0	.954	6	102	98	3b142,O8(3/0/5)/1		1.2
1966	Was A	147	524	48	122	19	4	13	54	44-1	0	89	.233	.289	.359	87	-10	3-1	.951	-1	99	115	3b141,1b8/OR		-1.3
1967	Was A	146	563	73	138	22	2	16	67	46-2	1	84	.245	.301	.377	104	1	5-3	.965	9	108	153	3b145,S11		1.0
1968	Was A	151	557	66	138	11	2	20	62	63-5	3	66	.248	.326	.382	119	12	1-3	.962	8	105	93	3b145		3.9
1969	Was A	158	562	83	153	25	2	19	87	70-6	1	103	.272	.349	.425	123	18	4-5	.976	21	110	109	3b154		3.9
1970	Was A	15	59	5	12	0	0	0	5	5-0	0	10	.203	.266	.237	42	-5	0-0	.971	5	119	207	3b15		0.5
	Cal A	124	422	50	98	9	3	14	61	59-10	3	81	.232	.329	.367	95	-3	1-0	.959	8	102	139	3b122		0.6
	Year	139	481	55	110	11	3	14	66	64-10	3	91	.229	.321	.351	89	-7	1-0	.960	13	104	147	3b137		-0.4
1971	Cal A	160	593	63	148	19	2	21	68	53-10	3	74	.250	.312	.395	107	1	3-1	.966	-6	96	100	3b137		1.0
1972	Cal A	137	472	36	127	18	1	9	34	48-2	0	59	.269	.335	.369	116	9	1-2	.970	1	96	100	3b137		0.6
1973	LA N	42	85	6	21	5	0	3	18	6-1	0	13	.247	.297	.482	116	1	0-0	.922	5	145	71	3b24		-0.1
1974	†LA N	44	60	5	15	1	0	3	12	2-0	0	12	.250	.274	.417	95	-1	0-0	1.000	0	104	0	3b7,2b3		-0.3
1975	LA N	39	46	4	11	1	1	2	14	7-0	0	12	.239	.340	.435	118	1	0-0	1.000	1	86	0	3b11,1b3		-0.1
1976	Oak A	98	186	20	41	6	2	5	23	22-3	1	33	.220	.305	.355	97	-1	1-1	.952	-3	104	44	3b35,1b26,D23,O5L/2		-0.5
1977	Mil A	63	136	15	31	7	1	5	19	15-0	1	33	.228	.305	.404	91	-2	0-0	.978	1	138	109	D29,1b11,3b7		-0.3
Total	16	1583	5131	568	1273	172	26	156	606	510-47	17	815	.248	.316	.383	105	20	20-19	.961	51	104	109	3b1318,1b62,D52,O20L,S11,2b5		6.1

McMULLIN, FRED   Fred Drury   B10.13.1891 Scammon KS   D11.20.1952 Los Angeles CA   BR/TR/5-11/170   d8.27   0.0

YEAR	TM LG	G	AB	R	H	2B	3B	HR	RBI	BB-IB	HP	SO	AVG	OBP	SLG	AOPS	ABR	SB-CS	FA	FR	RNG	THR	GAMES AT POSITION	DL	BFW
1914	Det A	1	1	0	0	0	0	0	0	0-0	0	1	.000	.000	.000	-97	0	0	.667	-0	97	0	/S		0.0
1916	Chi A	68	187	8	48	3	0	0	19	19	2	30	.257	.332	.273	81	-4	9	.950	-3	93	113	3b63,S2/2		-0.5
1917	†Chi A	59	194	35	46	2	1	0	12	27	3	17	.237	.339	.258	81	-3	9	.932	-10	86	58	3b52,S2		-1.3
1918	Chi A	70	235	32	65	7	0	1	16	25	4	26	.277	.356	.319	103	2	8	.941	-3	102	69	3b69/2		0.1
1919	†Chi A	60	170	31	50	8	4	0	19	11	1	5	.294	.355	.388	108	2	4	.931	-2	100	157	3b46,2b5		0.1
1920	Chi A	46	127	14	25	1	4	0	13	9	1	13	.197	.255	.268	39	-12	1-1	.962	-3	94	81	3b29,2b3/S		-1.5
Total	6	304	914	120	234	21	9	1	70	91	15	105	.256	.333	.302	85	-15	31-1	.942	-21	95	94	3b259,2b10,S6		-3.1

McMULLIN, JOHN   John F. "Lefty"   B1848 Philadelphia PA   D4.11.1881 Philadelphia PA   BR/TL/5-9/160   d5.9 ▲   0.0

YEAR	TM LG	G	AB	R	H	2B	3B	HR	RBI	BB-IB	HP	SO	AVG	OBP	SLG	AOPS	ABR	SB-CS	FA	FR	RNG	THR	GAMES AT POSITION	DL	BFW
1871	Tro NA	29	136	38	38	0	5	0	32	8		6	.279	.319	.353	92	-2	11-1	.871	-0	100	44	P29/S		0.0
1872	Mut NA	54	236	47	60	4	1	0	24	11		6	.254	.287	.288	83	-2	8-2	.871	3	46	0	O53(41/1/11),P3		-0.6
1873	Ath NA	52	227	54	62	7	1	0	28	8		6	.273	.298	.313	76	-8	9-1	.822	-4	41	81	O51L/P		-0.7
1874	Ath NA	55	260	61	90	10	2	2	32	8		13	.346	.366	.423	140	10	4-3	.771	-6	62	80	O55(5/51/1)		0.0
1875	Phi NA	54	222	33	57	9	4	2	19	5		12	.257	.273	.360	114	3	6-10	.835	-1	47	132	O54(22/32/0),P4		0.4
Total	5 NA	244	1081	233	307	32	13	4	135	40		41	.284	.310	.349	102	1	38-17	.827	-8	49	71	O213(119/84/12),P37/S		0.0

McNABB, CARL   Carl Mac "Skinny"   B1.25.1917 Stevenson AL   BR/TR/5-9/155   d4.20   0.0

YEAR	TM LG	G	AB	R	H	2B	3B	HR	RBI	BB-IB	HP	SO	AVG	OBP	SLG	AOPS	ABR	SB-CS	FA	FR	RNG	THR	GAMES AT POSITION	DL	BFW
1945	Det A	1	1	0	1	0	0	0	0	0-0	0		1.000	.000	.000	-94	0	0-0	—				/H		0.0

McNAIR, ERIC   Donald Eric "Boob"   B4.12.1909 Meridian MS   D3.11.1949 Meridian MS   BR/TR/5-8.5/160   d9.20   0.0

YEAR	TM LG	G	AB	R	H	2B	3B	HR	RBI	BB-IB	HP	SO	AVG	OBP	SLG	AOPS	ABR	SB-CS	FA	FR	RNG	THR	GAMES AT POSITION	DL	BFW
1929	Phi A	4	8	2	4	1	0	0	3	0	0	0	.500	.500	.625	181	-1	1-0	1.000	-0	75	0	S4		0.0
1930	†Phi A	78	237	27	63	12	2	0	34	9	1	19	.266	.296	.333	57	-16	5-2	.915	-11	78	68	S31,3b29,2b5/OR		-2.4
1931	†Phi A	79	280	41	76	10	1	5	33	11	3	19	.271	.306	.368	72	-12	1-4	.915	-4	98	220	3b47,2b16,S13		-1.4
1932	Phi A	135	554	87	158	47	3	18	95	28	2	29	.285	.323	.478	101	-1	8-4	.953	-12	92	111	S133		-0.8
1933	Phi A	89	310	57	81	15	4	0	48	15	3	32	.261	.302	.403	84	-9	2-1	.966	-2	95	99	S46,2b27		-0.8
1934	Phi A	151	599	80	168	20	4	17	82	35	1	42	.280	.321	.412	91	-12	7-8	.951	8	102	108	S151		-3.3
1935	Phi A	137	526	55	142	22	2	4	57	35	5	33	.270	.319	.342	72	-23	3-7	.955	-17	91	91	S121,3b11,1b2		-3.4
1936	Bos A	128	494	68	141	36	4	2	74	27	5	34	.285	.329	.391	73	-22	3-3	.966	-10	91	96	2b106,S9,3b4/1		-2.5
1937	Bos A	126	455	60	133	29	4	12	76	30	3	33	.292	.340	.453	94	-5	10-7	.969	-6	91	99	2b106,S9,3b4/1		-0.5
1938	Bos A	46	96	9	15	1	1	0	7	3	1		.156	.182	.188	-7	-17	0-0	.870	1	119	58	S15,2b14,3b3		-1.7
1939	Chi A	129	479	62	155	18	5	7	82	38	1	41	.324	.375	.426	102	1	17-9	.958	-16	91	71	2b65/3		-2.1
1940	Chi A	66	251	26	57	13	1	7	31	12	1	26	.227	.265	.371	62	-15	1-7	.953	-3	90	91	3b11,S3		-1.1
1941	Det A	23	59	5	11	4	0	0	3	2	1	5	.186	.250	.203	19	-7	0-0	.970	-1	91	91	3b11,S3		-1.3
1942	Det A	26	68	8	11	2	0	0	4	3	0	5	.162	.197	.235	20	-7	0-1	.881	-5	76	67	S21		-0.3
	Phi A	34	103	8	25	2	0	0	8	11	0	5	.243	.316	.262	64	-5	1-0	.952	-5	92	60	S29/2		-1.0
	Year	60	171	13	36	4	0	1	8	14	0	10	.211	.270	.251	46	-13	1-1	.927	-10	86	63	S50/2		-2.2
Total	14	1251	4519	592	1240	229	29	82	633	261	25	328	.274	.318	.392	80	-149	59-54	.949	-79	91	89	S669,2b288,3b220,1b3,OR		-15.1

McNALLY, MIKE   Michael Joseph "Minooka Mike"   B9.9.1892 Minooka PA   D5.29.1965 Bethlehem PA   BR/TR/5-11/150   d4.21   Mil 1918   -0.0

YEAR	TM LG	G	AB	R	H	2B	3B	HR	RBI	BB-IB	HP	SO	AVG	OBP	SLG	AOPS	ABR	SB-CS	FA	FR	RNG	THR	GAMES AT POSITION	DL	BFW
1915	Bos A	23	53	7	8	0	1	0	3	9	0	7	.151	.196	.189	16	-6	0-2	.891	-1	92	154	3b18,2b5		-0.1
1916	†Bos A	87	135	28	23	0	0	0	9	10	0	19	.170	.228	.170	20	-14	9	.964	2	116	103	2b35,3b14,S7/OC		-1.7
1917	Bos A	42	50	9	15	4	1	0	6	1	0	3	.300	.375	.320	111	1	4	.935	3	118	86	3b14,S9,2b6		-0.2
1919	Bos A	33	42	10	11	4	0	0	6	1	0	2	.262	.279	.357	83	-1	4	.950	5	125	86	S11,3b11,2b3		-0.3
1920	Bos A	93	312	42	80	5	4	0	23	31	0	24	.256	.326	.279	64	-16	13-0	.930	-8	100	115	2b76,S8,1b6		-2.0
1921	†NY A	71	215	36	56	4	2	2	24	14	0	14	.260	.306	.312	56	-15	5-6	.974	14	132	60	3b49,2b16		0.4
1922	†NY A	52	143	20	36	2	0	0	18	16	1	14	.252	.331	.294	63	-3	3-0	.983	-2	94	95	3b34,2b9,S4/1		0.5
1923	NY A	30	38	5	9	1	1	0	2	3	0	3	.237	.268	.211	7	-3	2-0	1.000	1	97	0	S13,3b7,2b5		-0.2
1924	NY A	49	69	11	17	0	0	0	7	8	0	6	.246	.321	.246	46	-6	1-1	.985	5	119	125	2b25,3b13,S6		-0.2

YEAR	TM LG	G	AB	R	H	2B	3B	HR	RBI	BB-IB	HP	SO	AVG	OBP	SLG	AOPS	ABR	SB-CS	FA	FR	RNG	THR	GAMES AT POSITION	DL	BFW
1925	Was A	12	21	1	3	0	0	0	1	0	0	4	.143	.182	.143	-17	-4	0-0	1.000	-1	91	97	3b7,S2/2		-0.4
Total	10	492	1078	169	257	16	6	1	85	92	2	97	.238	.299	.267	54	-73	40-19	.946	18	108	109	2b181,3b167,S60,1b7/OC		-4.6

McNAMARA, GEORGE George Francis B1.11.1901 Chicago IL D6.12.1990 Hinsdale IL BL/TR/6-0/175 d9.28

| 1922 | Was A | 3 | 11 | 3 | 3 | 0 | 0 | 0 | 1 | | 0 | 2 | .273 | .333 | .273 | 63 | -1 | 0-0 | 1.000 | -0 | 74 | 0 | O3R | | -0.1 |

McNAMARA, JIM James Patrick B6.10.1965 Nashua NH BL/TR/6-4/210* [SFN86 5/110] d4.9 Col North Carolina St.

1992	SF N	30	74	6	16	1	0	1	9	6-2	0	25	.216	.275	.270	58	-4	0-0	.993	-1	179	60	C30		-0.5
1993	SF N	4	7	0	1	0	0	0	1	0-0	0	1	.143	.143	.143	-24	-1	0-0	1.000	-0	144	0	C4		-0.2
Total	2	34	81	6	17	1	0	1	10	6-2	0	26	.210	.264	.259	51	-5	0-0	.993	-2	176	55	C34		-0.7

McNAMARA, DINNY John Raymond B9.16.1905 Lexington MA D12.20.1963 Arlington MA BL/TR/5-9/165 d7.2 Col Boston College

1927	Bos N	11	9	3	0	0	0	0	0		0	3	.000	.000	.000	-99	-3	0	1.000	1	180	0	O3C		-0.2
1928	Bos N	9	4	2	1	0	0	0	0		0	1	.250	.250	.250	33	0	0	1.000	1	198	0	O3(0/1/2)		0.0
Total	2	20	13	5	1	0	0	0	0		0	4	.077	.077	.077	-63	-3	0	1.000	1	188	0	O6(0/4/2)		-0.2

McNAMARA, BOB Robert Maxey B9.19.1916 Denver CO BR/TR/5-10/170 d5.27 Col California-Davis

| 1939 | Phi A | 9 | 9 | 0 | 2 | 1 | 0 | 0 | 2 | | 1 | 0 | .222 | .300 | .333 | 63 | 0 | 0 | 1.000 | -0 | 109 | 0 | 3b5,S2/12 | | -0.1 |

McNAMARA, TOM Thomas Henry B11.5.1895 Roxbury MA D5.5.1974 Danvers MA BR/TR/6-2/200 d6.25 Col Princeton

| 1922 | Pit N | 1 | 1 | 0 | 0 | 0 | 0 | 0 | 0 | | 0 | 0 | .000 | .000 | .000 | -99 | -0 | 0 | | | — | 0 | /H | | 0.0 |

McNEALY, RUSTY Robert Lee B8.12.1958 Sacramento CA BL/TL/5-8/160 [SeaA80 17/422] d9.4 Col Florida International

| 1983 | Oak A | 15 | 4 | 5 | 0 | 0 | 0 | 0 | 0 | 0-0 | 0 | 0 | .000 | .000 | .000 | -99 | -1 | 0-1 | 1.000 | 1 | 216 | 0 | O5(1/4/1),D7 | | -0.1 |

McNEELY, EARL George Earl B5.12.1898 Sacramento CA D7.16.1971 Sacramento CA BR/TR/5-9/155 d8.9 C3

1924	†Was A	43	179	31	59	5	6	0	15	5	2	21	.330	.355	.425	104	-1	3-3	.973	-1	101	79	O42(0/42/2)		-0.2
1925	†Was A	122	385	76	110	14	2	3	37	48	9	54	.286	.378	.356	89	-5	15-16	.975	2	99	123	O112(7/103/2)/1		-0.9
1926	Was A	124	442	84	134	20	12	0	48	44	5	28	.303	.373	.403	105	3	18-6	.969	3	108	83	O118(65/52/2)		0.1
1927	Was A	73	185	40	51	10	4	0	16	11	1	13	.276	.320	.373	80	-6	11-4	.977	-1	98	83	O47(3/32/14),1b4		-0.8
1928	StL A	127	496	66	117	27	7	0	44	37	8	39	.236	.299	.319	61	-29	8-6	.984	5	100	150	O120(2/1/118)		-3.3
1929	StL A	69	230	27	56	8	1	1	18	7	2	13	.243	.272	.300	45	-19	2-1	.980	-3	91	74	O62(18/2/42)		-2.5
1930	StL A	76	235	33	64	19	1	0	20	22	2	14	.272	.340	.362	75	-8	8-3	.939	-2	86	94	O38(8/26/4),1b27		-1.2
1931	StL A	49	102	12	23	4	0	0	15	9	0	5	.225	.288	.265	45	-8	4-4	.969	-0	93	137	O37(2/23/12)/1		-0.9
Total	8	683	2254	369	614	107	33	4	213	183	29	187	.272	.335	.354	78	-73	69-41	.974	2	99	109	O576(105/281/196),1b33		-9.7

McNEELY, JEFF Jeffrey Lavern B10.18.1969 Monroe NC BR/TR/6-2/200 [BosA89 2/53] d9.5 Col Spartanburg Methodist (SC) JC

| 1993 | Bos A | 21 | 37 | 10 | 11 | 1 | 1 | 0 | 1 | 7-0 | 0 | 7 | .297 | .409 | .378 | 106 | 1 | 6-0 | .917 | -3 | 73 | 0 | O13C,D3 | | 0.0 |

McNEIL, NORM Norman Francis B10.22.1892 Chicago IL D4.11.1942 Buffalo NY BR/TR/5-11/180 d6.21

| 1919 | Bos A | 5 | 9 | 0 | 3 | 0 | 0 | 0 | 1 | 1 | 0 | 0 | .333 | .400 | .333 | 113 | 0 | 0 | .818 | -1 | 91 | 68 | C5 | | -0.1 |

McNERTNEY, JERRY Gerald Edward B8.7.1936 Boone IA BR/TR/6-1/195* d4.16 C2 Col Iowa St.

1964	Chi A	73	186	16	40	5	0	3	23	19-4	3	24	.215	.290	.290	66	-8	0-0	.987	9	124	77	C69		0.4
1966	Chi A	44	59	3	13	0	0	1	7	7-0	1	6	.220	.303	.220	57	-3	1-1	.969	0	76	209	C37		-0.2
1967	Chi A	56	123	8	28	6	0	3	13	6-3	2	14	.228	.275	.350	87	-2	0-0	.996	4	81	214	C52		0.4
1968	Chi A	74	169	18	37	4	1	3	18	18-3	2	29	.219	.300	.308	84	-3	0-0	.985	6	88	114	C64/1		0.7
1969	Sea A	128	410	39	99	18	1	8	55	29-3	1	63	.241	.291	.349	79	-13	1-0	.988	-5	82	112	C122		-1.3
1970	Mil A	111	296	27	72	11	1	6	22	22-4	4	33	.243	.302	.348	79	-9	1-4	.984	-4	64	131	C94,1b13		-1.2
1971	StL N	56	128	15	37	4	1	2	22	12-1	0	14	.289	.343	.445	118	3	0-0	.985	-3	147	40	C36		0.2
1972	StL N	39	48	3	10	3	1	0	9	6-1	0	16	.208	.291	.313	73	-2	0-0	.982	2	159	205	C10		0.1
1973	Pit N	9	4	0	1	0	0	0	0		0	0	.250	.250	.250	40	-0	0-0	1.000	-0	0	172	C9		0.0
Total	9	590	1423	129	337	51	6	27	163	119-19	11	199	.237	.298	.338	81	-37	3-5	.987	9	92	121	C493,1b14	21	-0.9

McNULTY, PAT Patrick Howard B2.27.1899 Cleveland OH D5.4.1963 Hollywood CA BL/TR/5-11/160 d9.5 Col Ohio St.

1922	Cle A	22	59	10	16	2	1	0	5	9	0	5	.271	.368	.339	85	-1	4-1	.956	-1	103	0	O22(1/19/2)		-0.3
1924	Cle A	101	291	46	78	13	5	0	26	33	2	22	.268	.347	.347	78	-9	10-7	.961	-2	93	106	O75(11/20/44)		-1.5
1925	Cle A	118	373	70	117	18	2	6	43	47	1	23	.314	.392	.421	105	4	7-7	.965	4	100	157	O111(3/29/81)		0.1
1926	Cle A	48	56	3	14	2	1	0	6	5	0	9	.250	.311	.321	65	-3	0-1	.909	4	68	387	O9(2/5/2)		-0.3
1927	Cle A	19	41	3	13	1	0	0	4	8	0	3	.317	.378	.341	87	-1	1-2	.906	-0	103	92	O12(1/11/0)		-0.2
Total	5	308	820	132	238	36	9	6	84	98	3	62	.290	.368	.378	91	-10	22-18	.957	1	97	128	O229(18/84/129)		-2.2

McNULTY, BILL William Francis B8.29.1946 Sacramento CA BR/TR/6-4/205(190-205) d7.9

1969	Oak A	5	17	0	0	0	0	0	0	0-0	0	10	.000	.000	.000	-99	-5	0-0	1.000	2	122	667	O5L		-0.3
1972	Oak A	4	10	0	1	0	0	0	0	2-0	0	1	.100	.250	.100	7	-1	0-0	.800	-2	35	0	3b3		-0.3
Total	2	9	27	0	1	0	0	0	0	2-0	0	11	.037	.103	.037	-61	-6	0-0	1.000	0	122	667	O5L,3b3		-0.6

McPHEE, BID John Alexander B11.1.1859 Massena NY D1.3.1943 San Diego CA BR/TR/5-8/152 d5.2 M2 HF2000

1882	Cin AA	78	311	43	71	8	7	1	31	11				.228	.255	.309	84	-6		.920	-4	90	130	2b78		-0.7
1883	Cin AA	96	367	61	90	10	10	2	42	18				.245	.281	.343	95	-3		.928	4	97	149	2b96		0.4
1884	Cin AA	112	450	107	125	8	7	5	64	27	6			.278	.327	.360	118	8		.924	15	103	154	2b112		2.5
1885	Cin AA	110	431	78	114	12	4	0	46	19	7			.265	.306	.311	94	-3		.936	4	103	116	2b110		0.5
1886	Cin AA	140	560	139	150	23	12	8	70	59	5			.268	.343	.395	127	17	40	.939	27	104	133	2b140		4.2
1887	Cin AA	129	540	137	156	20	19	2	87	55	5			.289	.360	.407	111	7	95	.924	23	109	147	2b129		2.8
1888	Cin AA	111	458	88	110	12	10	4	51	43	5			.240	.312	.336	102	0	54	.940	26	107	164	2b111		2.8
1889	Cin AA	135	540	109	145	25	7	5	57	60	4	29		.269	.346	.369	100	0	63	.946	37	112	133	2b135/3		3.6
1890	Cin N	132	528	125	135	16	22	3	39	82	6	26		.256	.362	.386	119	13	55	.942	26	104	130	2b132		3.9
1891	Cin N	138	562	107	144	14	16	6	38	74	2	35		.256	.345	.370	107	5	33	.954	24	99	123	2b138		3.0
1892	Cin N	144	573	111	157	19	12	4	60	84	7	48		.274	.373	.370	127	22	44	.948	23	105	146	2b144		4.7
1893	Cin N	127	491	101	138	17	11	3	68	94	4	20		.281	.401	.379	105	7	25	.954	31	109	168	2b127		3.6
1894	Cin N	128	483	113	151	21	10	5	93	91	6	23		.313	.428	.429	100	6	33	.945	30	113	115	2b128		3.2
1895	Cin N	115	432	107	129	24	12	1	75	73	8	30		.299	.409	.417	109	9	30	.955	12	101	114	2b115		2.1
1896	Cin N	117	433	81	132	18	7	1	39	51	10	18		.305	.391	.386	98	0	48	.978	8	101	130	2b117		1.2
1897	Cin N	81	282	45	85	13	7	1	39	35	4			.301	.386	.408	103	1	9	.966	3	106	129	2b81		1.5
1898	Cin N	133	486	72	121	26	9	1	60	66	2			.249	.341	.346	91	-5	21	.956	-13	97	145	2b130,O3R		-1.1
1899	Cin N	112	377	60	105	17	7	1	65	40	7			.279	.358	.369	98	0	18	.955	-4	98	109	2b106/OC		0.1
Total	18	2138	8304	1684	2258	303	189	53	1072	982	88	229		.272	.355	.373	106	78	568	.944	283	104	136	2b2129,O4(0/1/3)/3		38.3

McPHERSON, DALLAS Dallas Lyle B7.23.1980 Greensboro NC BL/TR/6-4/230* [AnaA01 2/57] d9.10

2004	†Ana A	16	40	5	9	1	0	3	6	3-0	0	17	.225	.279	.475	95	-1	1-0	1.000	2	122	60	3b14		0.2
2005	LA A	61	205	29	50	14	2	8	26	14-0	1	64	.244	.295	.449	96	-2	3-3	.944	-7	83	154	3b60	87	-0.8
Total	2	77	245	34	59	15	2	11	32	17-0	1	81	.241	.293	.453	96	-3	4-3	.955	-5	89	139	3b74	87	-0.6

McQUAID, MART Mortimer Martin B6.28.1861 Chicago IL D3.5.1928 Chicago IL 5-9/160 d8.15

1891	StL AA	4	11	1	4	2	0	0	1	0		0	1	.364	.364	.545	139	-1	0	1.000	0	88	112	2b3/OL		0.1
1898	Was N	1	4	0	0	0	0	0	0		0	0	.000	.000	.000	-99	-1	0	.333	-1	0	0	/OL		-0.2
Total	2	5	15	1	4	2	0	0	1	0		0	1	.267	.267	.400	82	-1	1	1.000	-1	88	112	2b3,O2L		-0.1

McQUAIG, JERRY Gerald Joseph B1.31.1912 Douglas GA D2.5.2001 Buford GA BR/TR/5-11/183 d8.25 Col Mercer

| 1934 | Phi N | 7 | 16 | 2 | 1 | 0 | 0 | 0 | 1 | | 0 | 4 | .063 | .167 | .063 | -40 | -3 | 0-0 | .889 | -1 | 95 | 0 | O6(5/0/1) | | -0.4 |

McQUERY, MOX William Thomas B6.28.1861 Garrard Co. KY D6.12.1900 Cincinnati OH 6-4/? d8.20

1884	Cin U	35	132	31	37	5	0	2	8				.280	.321	.364	99	-4		.978	1	80	88	1b35		-0.5
1885	Det N	70	278	34	76	15	4	3	30	8			29	.273	.294	.388	119	5		.976	3	117	88	1b70		0.2
1886	KC N	122	449	62	111	27	4	4	38	36			44	.247	.303	.352	93	-4	4	.969	1	108	90	1b122		-1.3
1890	Syr AA	122	461	64	142	17	4	4	55	53	3			.308	.383	.384	141	27	26	.972	-1	94	93	1b122		1.3
1891	Was AA	68	261	40	63	9	4	2	37	18	6	19		.241	.305	.330	86	-5	3	.977	1	107	85	1b68		-0.9
Total	5	417	1581	231	429	73	16	13	160	123	9	92		.271	.327	.365	110	19	33	.973	5	103	90	1b417		-1.2

YEAR	TM LG	G	AB	R	H	2B	3B	HR	RBI	BB-IB	HP	SO	AVG	OBP	SLG	AOPS	ABR	SB-CS	FA	FR	RNG	THR	GAMES AT POSITION	DL	BFW

McQUILLEN, GLENN Glenn Richard "Red" B4.19.1915 Strasburg VA D6.8.1989 Baltimore MD BR/TR/6-0/198 d6.16 Mil 1943-45 Col McDaniel

1938	StL A	43	116	14	33	4	0	0	13	4	0	12	.284	.308	.319	57	-8	0-1	.971	1	122	0	O30L		-0.8
1941	StL A	7	21	4	7	2	1	0	3	1	0	2	.333	.364	.524	128	1	0-1	.933	-0	108	0	O6(3/0/3)		0.0
1942	StL A	100	339	40	96	15	12	3	47	10	1	17	.283	.304	.425	130	-2	1-1	.969	-6	93	32	O77(68/0/9)		-1.3
1946	StL A	59	166	24	40	3	3	1	12	19	0	18	.241	.319	.313	73	-6	0-2	.977	3	94	299	O48(44/0/5)		-0.6
1947	StL A	1	1	0	0	0	0	0	0	0	0	0	.000	.000	.000	-98	0	0-0			0		/H		0.0
Total	5	210	643	82	176	24	16	4	75	34	1	49	.274	.311	.379	87	-15	1-5	.970	-2	99	93	O161(145/0/17)		-2.7

McQUINN, GEORGE George Hartley B5.29.1910 Arlington VA D12.24.1978 Alexandria VA BL/TL/5-11/165 d4.14

1936	Cin N	38	134	5	27	3	4	0	13	10	1	22	.201	.262	.284	50	-10	0	.992	1	111	100	1b38		-1.2
1938	StL A	148	602	100	195	42	7	12	82	58	1	49	.324	.384	.477	125	14	4-5	.992	1	95	92	1b148		0.0
1939	StL A☆	154	617	101	195	37	13	20	94	65	2	42	.316	.383	.515	125	22	6-5	.993	10	123	80	1b154		1.5
1940	StL A	151	594	78	166	39	10	16	84	57	0	58	.279	.343	.460	104	2	3-3	.992	9	126	112	1b150		-0.3
1941	StL A	130	495	93	147	28	4	18	80	74	0	30	.297	.388	.479	124	19	5-4	.995	7	117	102	1b125		1.3
1942	StL A☆	145	554	86	145	32	5	12	78	60	1	77	.262	.335	.403	105	3	1-1	.991	1	103	96	1b144		-0.9
1943	StL A	125	449	53	109	19	2	12	74	56	0	65	.243	.327	.374	103	1	4-3	.992	2	104	84	1b122		-0.3
1944	†StL A★	146	516	63	129	26	3	11	72	85	1	74	.250	.357	.376	103	5	4-3	.994	6	80	93	1b146		-0.9
1945	StL A✱	139	483	69	134	31	3	7	61	65	1	51	.277	.364	.398	115	11	1-1	.991	4	107	81	1b136		0.9
1946	Phi A	136	484	47	109	23	6	3	35	64	1	62	.225	.317	.316	78	-14	4-2	.988	2	106	88	1b134		-1.7
1947	†NY A★	144	517	84	157	24	3	13	80	78	0	66	.304	.395	.437	132	25	0-2	.994	-2	89	98	1b142		1.8
1948	NY A★	94	302	33	75	11	4	11	41	40	0	38	.248	.336	.421	102	-1	0-2	.993	-1	90	106	1b90		-0.5
Total	12	1550	5747	832	1588	315	64	135	794	712	8	634	.276	.357	.424	109	77	32-31	.992	28	104	94	1b1529		-0.3

McRAE, BRIAN Brian Wesley B8.27.1967 Bradenton FL BB/TR/6-0/185(180-195) [KCA85 1/17] d8.7 f-Hal

1990	KC A	46	168	21	48	8	3	2	23	9-0	2	14	.286	.318	.405	103	0	4-3	1.000	1	110	47	O45C		0.1
1991	KC A	152	629	86	164	28	9	8	64	24-1	2	99	.261	.288	.372	81	-19	20-11	.993	-2	106	26	O150C		-2.1
1992	KC A	149	533	63	119	23	5	4	52	42-1	6	88	.223	.285	.308	65	-23	18-5	.993	1	102	95	O148C		-2.4
1993	KC A	153	627	78	177	28	9	12	69	37-1	5	105	.282	.325	.413	91	-10	23-14	.983	-6	98	48	O153C		-1.3
1994	KC A	114	436	71	119	22	6	4	40	54-3	6	67	.273	.359	.378	87	-8	28-8	.988	-12	85	34	O110C,D4		-1.4
1995	Chi N	137	580	92	167	38	7	12	48	47-1	7	92	.288	.348	.440	106	5	27-8	.991	-2	104	53	O137C		0.8
1996	Chi N	157	624	111	172	32	5	17	66	73-6	12	84	.276	.360	.425	103	4	37-9	.986	-12	92	84	O155C		-0.1
1997	Chi N	108	417	63	100	27	5	6	28	52-2	4	62	.240	.329	.372	81	-11	14-6	.996	-2	103	60	O107C		-1.0
	NY N	45	145	23	36	5	2	5	15	13-0	2	22	.248	.317	.414	94	-2	3-4	.957	-6	77	56	O41C		-0.8
	Year	153	562	86	136	32	7	11	43	65-2	6	84	.242	.326	.383	84	-13	17-10	.987	-7	96	59	O148C		-1.8
1998	NY N	159	552	79	146	36	5	21	79	80-3	5	90	.264	.360	.462	119	16	20-11	.987	-13	86	86	O154C		-2.3
1999	NY N	96	298	35	66	12	1	8	36	39-1	5	57	.221	.320	.349	73	-13	2-6	.994	-11	80	24	O87C		-0.1
	Col N	7	23	1	6	0	1	1	1	2-0	2	7	.261	.370	.478	90	0	0-0	1.000	1	90	0	O7C		-2.4
	Year	103	321	36	72	14	1	9	37	41-1	7	64	.224	.323	.358	75	-13	2-6	.994	-12	90	130	O94C		-0.4
	Tor A	31	82	11	16	3	1	3	11	16-1	2	22	.195	.340	.366	79	-2	0-1	1.000	-0	90	130	D15,O13C		-0.1
Total	10	1354	5114	734	1336	264	58	103	532	488-20	57	824	.261	.331	.396	91	-66	196-86	.990	-63	96	52	O1307C,D19		-10.4

McRAE, HAL Harold Abraham B7.10.1945 Avon Park FL BR/TR/5-11/180* [CinN65 6/117] d7.11 M6/C11 s-Brian Col Florida A&M OF(360/33/94)

1968	Cin N	17	51	1	10	1	0	0	2	4-2	0	14	.196	.255	.216	40	-4	1-1	.926	-6	70	64	2b16		-1.1
1970	†Cin N	70	165	18	41	6	1	8	23	15-2	1	23	.248	.313	.442	100	-1	0-2	.981	-3	89	41	O46(46/0/1),3b6/2		-0.7
1971	Cin N	99	337	39	89	24	2	9	34	11-0	2	35	.264	.291	.427	102	0	3-2	.966	-0	94	109	O91(66/28/0)		-0.5
1972	†Cin N	61	97	9	27	4	0	5	26	2-0	2	10	.278	.295	.474	125	2	0-0	.867	-3	101	0	O12(0/3/9),3b11		-0.1
1973	KC A	106	338	36	79	18	3	9	50	34-2	6	38	.234	.312	.385	89	-5	2-2	.963	-1	96	110	O64(3/0/63),D37,3b2		-1.0
1974	KC A	148	539	71	167	36	4	15	88	54-6	5	68	.310	.375	.475	136	27	11-8	.950	2	115	49	D90,O56(40/0/19)/3		2.0
1975	KC A★	126	480	58	147	38	6	5	71	47-7	4	48	.306	.366	.442	126	18	11-8	.986	-4	88	86	O114(112/2/0),D12/3		3.1
1976	†KC A★	149	527	75	175	34	5	8	73	64-7	8	43	.332	.407	.461	154	39	22-12	.970	0	104	95	D115,O47L		3.2
1977	†KC A	162	641	104	191	54	11	21	92	59-5	13	43	.298	.366	.515	136	33	18-14	1.000	0	55	557	D153,O3L		0.7
1978	†KC A	156	623	90	170	39	5	16	72	51-6	6	62	.273	.329	.429	110	8	17-8	1.000	0	0	0	D100	52	0.2
1979	KC A	101	393	55	113	32	4	10	74	38-0	4	46	.288	.351	.466	117	10	5-4		—	0	0	0	D110,O9L	20	1.0
1980	KC A	124	489	73	145	39	5	14	83	29-4	8	56	.297	.342	.483	123	15	10-2	1.000	-1	99	0	D97,O4(2/0/2)		0.7
1981	KC A★	101	389	38	106	23	2	7	36	34-3	2	33	.272	.330	.396	110	5	3-4	.909	0	128	0	D158/OL		3.1
1982	KC A★	159	613	91	189	46	8	27	133	55-7	5	61	.308	.369	.542	145	38	4-4	.500	-1	45	0	D156		1.8
1983	KC A	157	589	84	183	41	6	12	82	50-7	10	68	.311	.372	.462	128	24	2-3		—	0	0	0	D94		0.8
1984	†KC A	106	317	30	96	13	4	3	42	34-3	1	47	.303	.363	.397	112	6	0-3		—	0	0	0	D106		0.1
1985	†KC A	112	320	41	83	19	0	14	70	44-3	1	45	.259	.349	.450	116	8	0-1		—	0	0	0	D75		-1.0
1986	KC A	112	278	22	70	14	0	7	37	18-4	1	39	.252	.298	.378	81	-8	0-0		—	0	0	0	D7		0.1
1987	KC A	18	32	5	10	3	0	1	9	5-1	0	1	.313	.405	.500	134	2	0-0		—	0	0	0	D1427,O478L,3b21,2b17	72	13.1
Total	19	2084	7218	940	2091	484	66	191	1097	648-69	79	779	.290	.351	.454	122	217	109-78	.966	-11	97	103	D1427,O478L,3b21,2b17		13.3

McREMER d6.20

| 1884 | Was U | 1 | 3 | 0 | 0 | 0 | 0 | 0 | 0 | | | | .000 | .000 | .000 | -99 | -1 | | 1.000 | 0 | 0 | 0 | /OR | | -0.1 |

McREYNOLDS, KEVIN Walter Kevin B10.16.1959 Little Rock AR BR/TR/6-1/210(205-225) [SDN81 1/6] d6.2 Col Arkansas-Monticello

1983	SD N	39	140	15	31	3	1	4	14	12-1	0	29	.221	.277	.343	75	-5	2-1	.989	0	92	190	O38(3/32/10)		-0.6
1984	†SD N	147	525	68	146	26	6	20	75	34-8	0	69	.278	.317	.465	118	10	3-6	.991	10	113	122	O143C		1.1
1985	SD N	152	564	61	132	24	4	15	75	43-6	3	81	.234	.290	.371	85	-13	4-0	.993	9	111	125	O150C		0.2
1986	SD N	158	560	89	161	31	6	26	96	66-6	1	83	.287	.358	.504	140	30	8-6	.977	2	102	96	O154(108/109/3)		2.6
1987	NY N	151	590	86	163	32	5	29	95	39-5	1	70	.276	.318	.495	117	11	14-1	.987	-1	101	79	O150L		0.9
1988	†NY N	147	552	82	159	30	2	27	99	38-3	4	56	.288	.336	.496	143	28	21-0	.985	6	93	213	O147(147/1/0)		3.7
1989	NY N	148	545	74	148	25	3	22	85	46-10	1	74	.272	.326	.450	126	16	15-7	.969	8	112	129	O145L		2.1
1990	NY N	147	521	75	140	23	1	24	82	71-11	1	61	.269	.353	.455	122	16	9-2	.988	-2	88	147	O144L		1.4
1991	NY N	143	522	65	135	32	1	16	74	49-7	2	46	.259	.322	.416	107	5	6-6	.993	1	99	116	O141(125/33/2)		0.5
1992	KC A	109	373	45	92	25	0	13	49	67-3	0	48	.247	.357	.418	114	9	7-1	.986	-7	90	115	O106(94/0/12)/D	27	0.8
1993	KC A	110	351	44	86	22	4	11	42	37-6	1	56	.245	.316	.425	92	-5	2-2	.990	0	99	89	O104L/D	23	-0.4
1994	NY N	51	180	23	46	11	2	4	21	20-1	0	34	.256	.328	.406	92	-2	2-0	1.000	-0	100	34	O47L	62	-0.1
Total	12	1502	5423	727	1429	284	35	211	807	522-67	14	707	.265	.324	.447	115	100	93-32	.987	27	101	119	O1469(1067/468/27),D2	112	10.8

McSHANNIC, PETE Peter Robert B3.20.1864 Pittsburgh PA D11.30.1946 Toledo OH BB/TR/5-7/190 d9.15

| 1888 | Pit N | 26 | 98 | 5 | 19 | 1 | 0 | 0 | 5 | 1 | 2 | 9 | .194 | .218 | .204 | 38 | -7 | 3 | .907 | -1 | 95 | 29 | 3b26 | | -0.6 |

McSORLEY, TRICK John Bernard B12.6.1852 St.Louis MO D2.9.1936 St.Louis MO BR/TR/5-4/142 d5.6

1875	RS NA	15	52	4	11	0	0	0	2	0		3	.212	.212	.212	53	-2	3-0	.745	0	121	0	3b9,O7(6/1/0)		-0.1
1884	Tol AA	21	68	12	17	1	0	0	3	0			.250	.282	.265	77	-2		.974	1	150	207	1b16,O5L/3P		-0.1
1885	StL N	2	6	2	3	1	0	0	1	2			.500	.625	.667	340	2		.400	-2	29	0	3b2		-0.0
1886	StL AA	5	20	1	3	3	0	0	0	0			.150	.150	.300	38	-1	0	.765	-3	66	0	S5		-0.0
Total	3	28	94	15	23	5	0	0	1	5	0	1	.245	.283	.298	85	-1	0	.745	-3	150	207	1b16,S5,O5L,3b3/P		-0.1

McSWEENEY, PAUL Paul A. B4.3.1867 St.Louis MO D8.12.1951 St.Louis MO d9.20

| 1891 | StL AA | 3 | 12 | 2 | 3 | 1 | 0 | 0 | 2 | 0 | 1 | 0 | .250 | .308 | .333 | 73 | 0 | 1 | .643 | -3 | 69 | 0 | 2b3/3 | | -0.1 |

McTAMANY, JIM James Edward B7.1.1863 Philadelphia PA D4.16.1916 Lenni PA BR/TR/5-8/190 d8.15

1885	Bro AA	35	131	21	36	7	2	1	13	9	0		.275	.321	.382	121	3		.896	-4	0	0	O35L		-0.1
1886	Bro AA	111	418	86	106	23	10	2	56	54	10		.254	.353	.371	126	15	18	.893	11	150	145	O111(0/107/4)		2.4
1887	Bro AA	134	520	123	134	22	10	1	68	76	12		.258	.365	.344	97	1	66	.918	6	147	162	O134C		0.0
1888	KC AA	130	516	94	127	12	10	4	41	67	11		.246	.345	.331	110	7	55	.913	0	121	87	O130(0/80/50)		0.3
1889	Col AA	139	529	113	146	21	7	4	52	116	1	66	.276	.407	.365	127	28	40	.902	-7	107	128	O139C		2.2
1890	Col AA	125	466	140	120	27	7	1	48	112	4		.258	.405	.352	132	30	43	.940	0	198	0	O125C		2.0
1891	Col AA	81	304	59	76	17	9	3	35	58	2	48	.250	.374	.395	127	13	20	.929	-3	71	137	O81C		0.1
	Phi AA	58	218	57	49	6	3	3	21	43	5	44	.225	.365	.321	96	1	13	.901	-1	97	47	O58(0/57/1)		0.0
	Year	139	522	116	125	23	12	6	56	101	7	92	.239	.370	.364	114	14	33	.917	-4	82	99	O139(0/138/1)		0.1
Total	7	813	3102	693	794	135	58	19	334	535	45	158	.256	.373	.355	117	98	255	.913	3	109	130	O813(35/723/55)		6.0

YEAR	TM LG	G	AB	R	H	2B	3B	HR	RBI	BB-IB	HP	SO	AVG	OBP	SLG	AOPS	ABR	SB-CS	FA	FR	RNG	THR	GAMES AT POSITION	DL	BFW

McVEY, CAL Calvin Alexander B8.30.1850 Montrose IA D8.20.1926 San Francisco CA BR/TR/5-9/170 d5.5 M3 OF NA(4/32/66) ▲

1871	Bos NA	29	153	43	66	9	5	0	43	1		2	.431	.435	.556	177	14	6-0	.873	2			C29,O5R/3		1.1
1872	Bos NA	46	237	56	76	10	2	0	41	1		1	.321	.324	.380	110	1	6-1	.869	6			C39,O11(2/0/9)/3		0.6
1873	Bal NA	38	192	49	73	5	5	2	35	3		2	.380	.390	.490	160	13	2-1	.907	-1			C25,O6(1/4/1),S5,2b4,1b3,3b2,M		0.8
1874	Bos NA	70	343	91	123	21	6	3	71	1		3	.359	.362	.481	159	20	5-0	.710	-2	91	0	O57(0/8/49),C23		1.7
1875	Bos NA	82	389	89	138	36	9	3	87	1		5	.355	.356	.517	193	35	7-0	.949	7	129	155	1b55,O23(1/20/2),C16,P3		3.7
1876	Chi N	63	308	62	107	15	0	1	53	2			.347	.352	.406	186	10		.959	4	110	145	1b55,P11,C6/OL3		0.9
1877	Chi N	60	266	58	98	9	7	0	36	8		11	.368	.387	.455	147	13		.859	-10			C40,3b17,P17/21		0.2
1878	Cin N	61	271	43	83	10	4	2	28	5		10	.306	.319	.395	147	14		.814	-10	82	89	3b61,C3,M		0.6
1879	Cin N	81	354	64	105	18	6	0	55	8		13	.297	.312	.381	134	13		.946	-7	27	101	1b72,O7(0/1/6),P3/3CM		0.2
Total	5 NA	265	1314	328	476	81	27	8	277	7		13	.362	.366	.483	161	83	26-2	.876	12			C132,O102R,1b58,S5,2b4,3b4,P3		7.9
Total	4	265	1199	227	393	52	17	3	172	23		38	.328	.340	.425	148	50		.951	-23			1b128,3b80,C50,P31/O8(1/1/6)/2		1.9

McVEY, GEORGE George W. B9.16.1865 Port Jervis NY D5.3.1896 Quincy NY BR/TR/6-1/185 d9.19

| 1885 | Bro AA | 6 | 21 | 2 | 3 | 0 | 0 | 0 | 2 | 1 | | 3 | .143 | .217 | .143 | 15 | -2 | | .967 | 0 | 0 | 139 | 1b3,C3 | | -0.2 |

McWILLIAMS, BILL William Henry B11.28.1910 Dubuque IA D1.21.1997 Garland TX BR/TR/6-0/185 d7.8 Col Iowa

| 1931 | Bos A | 2 | 2 | 0 | 0 | 0 | 0 | 0 | 0 | 0 | | 1 | .000 | .000 | .000 | -99 | -1 | 0-0 | — | 0 | | | /H | | -0.1 |

MEACHAM, BOB Robert Andrew B8.25.1960 Los Angeles CA BB/TR (BR 1987-88)/6-1/180* [StL N81 1/8] d6.30 Col San Diego St.

1983	NY A	22	51	5	12	2	0	0	4	4-0	1	10	.255	.304	.275	62	-3	8-0	.929	4	124	103	S18,3b4		0.5
1984	NY A	99	360	62	91	13	4	2	25	32-0	3	70	.253	.312	.328	82	-9	9-5	.955	-12	91	87	S96,2b2		-1.1
1985	NY A	156	481	70	105	16	2	1	47	54-1	5	102	.218	.302	.266	59	-26	25-7	.963	-20	87	112	S155		-2.7
1986	NY A	56	161	19	36	7	1	0	10	17-0	3	39	.224	.309	.280	62	-3	3-6	.948	-4	101	100	S56		-0.8
1987	NY A	77	203	28	55	11	1	5	21	19-0	6	33	.271	.349	.409	101	1	6-5	.961	-5	94	93	S56,2b25/D	15	0.1
1988	NY A	47	115	18	25	9	0	0	7	14-0	2	22	.217	.308	.296	72	-4	7-1	.959	-7	81	101	S24,2b21,3b5	81	-0.8
Total	6	457	1371	202	324	58	8	8	114	140-1	20	276	.236	.313	.308	73	-49	58-24	.957	-44	92	101	S405,2b48,3b9/D	96	-4.8

MEAD, CHARLIE Charles Richard B4.9.1921 Vermilion AL, Can. BL/TR/6-1.5/185 d8.28

1943	NY N	37	146	9	40	6	1	1	13	10		0	15	.274	.321	.349	93	-2	3	.976	-0	100	77	O37(0/3/34)		-0.5
1944	NY N	39	78	5	14	1	0	1	8	5		0	7	.179	.229	.231	30	-8	0	.981	4	115	245	O23(13/3/7)		-0.5
1945	NY N	11	37	4	10	1	0	1	6	5		0	2	.270	.357	.378	103	0	0	.962	1	93	285	O11(0/1/11)		0.1
Total	3	87	261	18	64	8	1	3	27	20		0	24	.245	.299	.318	75	-10	3	.975	4	103	158	O71(13/7/52)		-0.9

MEADOWS, LOUIE Michael Ray B4.29.1961 Maysville NC BL/TL/5-11/190* [Hou N82 2/43] d7.3 Col North Carolina St.

1986	Hou N	6	6	1	2	0	0	0	0	0-0	0	0	.333	.333	.333	87	0	1-0	—	-0	0	0	/OR		0.0
1988	Hou N	35	42	5	8	0	1	2	3	6-0	0	8	.190	.292	.381	95	0	4-2	1.000	-1	128	237	O10(7/1/3)		0.1
1989	Hou N	31	51	5	9	0	0	3	10	1-0	0	14	.176	.189	.353	55	-4	1-2	1.000	-2	65	0	O14(12/0/4)/1		-0.6
1990	Hou N	15	14	3	2	0	0	0	0	2-0	0	4	.143	.250	.143	11	-2	0-0	1.000	-0	107	0	O9(7/0/2)		-0.2
	Phi N	15	14	1	1	0	0	0	0	1-0	0	2	.071	.133	.071	-42	-3	0-0	1.000	-1	32	0	O4(3/2/0)		-0.3
	Year	30	28	4	3	0	0	0	0	3-0	0	6	.107	.194	.107	-15	-4	0-0	1.000	-1	84	0	O13(10/2/2)		-0.5
Total	4	102	127	15	22	0	1	5	13	10-0	0	28	.173	.232	.307	54	-9	6-4	1.000	-1	91	82	O38(29/3/10)/1		-1.0

MEARA, CHARLIE Charles Edward "Goggy" B4.16.1891 New York NY D2.8.1962 Bronx NY BL/TR/5-10/160 d6.1 Col Manhattan

| 1914 | NY A | 4 | 7 | 2 | 2 | 0 | 0 | 0 | 1 | 2 | | 2 | .286 | .444 | .286 | 120 | 0 | 0-1 | 1.000 | -0 | 105 | 0 | O3(0/2/2) | | 0.0 |

MEARES, PAT Patrick James B9.6.1968 Salina KS BR/TR/6-0/187* [Min A90 12/329] d5.5 Col Wichita St. [DL 2002 Pit N 183, 2003 Pit N 183]

1993	Min A	111	346	33	87	14	3	0	33	7-0	1	52	.251	.266	.309	54	-23	4-5	.961	-0	101	105	S111		-1.7
1994	Min A	80	229	29	61	12	1	2	24	14-0	2	50	.266	.310	.354	71	-10	5-1	.963	-2	98	98	S79	15	-0.5
1995	Min A	116	390	57	105	19	4	12	49	15-0	11	68	.269	.311	.431	91	-7	10-4	.965	-3	100	93	S114,O3(0/2/1)		-0.1
1996	Min A	152	517	66	138	26	7	8	67	17-1	5	90	.267	.298	.391	72	-24	9-4	.965	-27	83	92	S150/OC		-3.6
1997	Min A	134	439	63	121	23	3	10	60	18-0	16	86	.276	.323	.410	89	-7	7-7	.969	15	112	112	S134	15	1.5
1998	Min A	149	543	56	141	26	3	9	70	24-1	6	86	.260	.296	.386	70	-25	7-4	.966	-9	96	100	S149		-2.2
1999	Pit N	21	91	15	28	4	0	0	7	9-0	2	20	.308	.382	.352	87	-1	0-0	.939	1	110	96	S21	150	0.1
2000	Pit N	132	462	55	111	22	2	13	47	36-6	8	91	.240	.305	.381	72	-21	1-0	.967	22	115	118	S126		0.9
2001	Pit N	87	270	27	57	11	1	4	25	10-3	2	45	.211	.244	.304	40	-25	0-2	.973	3	111	110	2b85	27	-1.9
Total	9	982	3287	401	849	157	24	58	382	150-11	57	588	.258	.298	.374	72	-143	43-27	.965	-1	101	103	S884,2b85,O4(0/3/1)	573	-7.5

MEDEIROS, RAY Ray Antone "Pep" B5.9.1926 Oakland CA D6.6.2003 San Mateo CA BR/TR/5-10/163 d4.25

| 1945 | Cin N | 1 | 0 | 0 | 0 | 0 | 0 | 0 | 0 | 0 | | 0 | — | — | — | — | 0 | 0-0 | — | 0 | | | /R | | 0.0 |

MEDINA, LUIS Luis Main B3.26.1963 Santa Monica CA BR/TL/6-4/195* [Cle A85 9/219] d9.2 Col Arizona St.

1988	Cle A	16	51	10	13	0	0	6	8	2-0	2	18	.255	.309	.608	146	3	0-0	1.000	-0	86	111	1b16		0.1
1989	Cle A	30	83	8	17	1	0	4	8	6-0	0	35	.205	.258	.361	71	-4	0-1	.500	-1	48	0	D25,O3(1/0/2)/1		-0.6
1991	Cle A	5	16	0	1	0	0	0	0	1-0	0	7	.063	.118	.063	-48	-3	0-0	—	0			D5		-0.4
Total	3	51	150	18	31	1	0	10	16	9-0	2	60	.207	.261	.413	84	-4	0-1	1.000	-1	85	110	D30,1b17,O3(1/0/2)		-0.9

MEDWICK, JOE Joseph Michael "Ducky","Muscles" B11.24.1911 Carteret NJ D3.21.1975 St.Petersburg FL BR/TR/5-10/187 d9.2 HF1968

1932	StL N	26	106	13	37	12	1	2	12	2		1	10	.349	.367	.538	136	5	3	.970	-1	95	99	O26(7/19/0)		0.4
1933	StL N	148	595	92	182	40	10	18	98	26		2	56	.306	.337	.497	129	20	5	.980	7	103	150	O147L		2.0
1934	†StL N★	149	620	110	198	40	18	18	106	21		1	83	.319	.343	.529	122	16	3	.960	3	105	97	O149(144/0/5)		1.0
1935	StL N★	154	634	132	224	46	13	23	126	30		4	59	.353	.386	.576	149	42	4	.965	3	108	74	O154L		3.4
1936	StL N★	155	636	115	223	64	13	18	138	34		4	33	.351	.387	.577	157	49	3	.985	14	114	141	O155L		5.2
1937	StL N★	156	633	111	237	56	10	31	154	41		2	50	.374	.414	.641	179	68	4	.988	4	107	81	O156L		6.0
1938	StL N★	146	590	100	190	47	8	21	122	42		2	41	.322	.369	.536	138	30	0	.974	8	109	105	O144L		3.0
1939	StL N★	150	606	98	201	48	8	14	117	45		2	44	.332	.380	.507	128	24	6	.976	5	106	113	O149L		2.1
1940	StL N★	37	158	21	48	12	0	3	20	6		0	8	.304	.329	.437	104	1	0	.988	-1	101	37	O37L		-0.2
	Bro N★	106	423	62	127	18	12	14	66	26		3	28	.300	.345	.499	123	11	2	.980	4	107	92	O103L		0.9
	Year	143	581	83	175	30	12	17	86	32		3	36	.301	.341	.482	118	12	2	.982	3	105	77	O140L		
1941	†Bro N★	133	538	100	171	33	10	18	88	38		1	35	.318	.364	.517	140	26	2	.983	-3	90	116	O131(130/0/1)		1.6
1942	Bro N★	142	553	69	166	37	4	4	96	32		2	25	.300	.338	.403	115	9	2	.990	-3	99	55	O140L		-0.1
1943	Bro N	48	173	13	47	10	0	0	25	10		1	9	.272	.315	.329	86	-3	1	.971	-3	88	60	O42L		-0.9
	NY N	78	324	41	91	20	3	5	45	9		0	14	.281	.300	.407	103	-1	0	.988	3	100	138	O74L,1b3		-0.3
	Year	126	497	54	138	30	3	5	70	19		1	23	.278	.306	.380	97	-4	1	.983	-0	96	113	O116L,1b3		-1.2
1944	NY N★	128	490	64	165	24	3	7	85	38		1	24	.337	.386	.441	133	21	2	.993	7	114	89	O122L		2.1
1945	NY N	26	92	14	28	4	0	3	11	2		1	2	.304	.319	.446	110	1	2	.979	-1	95	63	O23L		-0.2
	Bos N	66	218	21	62	13	0	0	26	12		1	12	.284	.325	.344	85	-4	3	1.000	2	97	261	O38L,1b15		-0.6
	Year	92	310	31	90	17	0	3	37	14		2	14	.290	.323	.374	93	-4	5	.992	1	96	185	O61L,1b15		-0.8
1946	Bro N	41	77	7	24	4	0	2	18	6		1	5	.312	.369	.442	128	3	0	1.000	-1	66	0	O18L/1		0.1
1947	StL N	75	150	19	46	12	0	4	28	16		2	12	.307	.373	.467	117	0	1	1.000	-0	95	122	O43(7/0/36)		0.3
1948	StL N	20	19	0	4	0	0	0	2	1		0	2	.211	.250	.211	24	-2	0	—	-0	0	0	/OR		-0.2
Total	17	1984	7635	1198	2471	540	113	205	1383	437		26	551	.324	.362	.505	133	320	42	.980	47	104	103	O1852(1790/19/43),1b19		25.6

MEE, TOMMY Thomas William "Judge" B3.18.1890 Chicago IL D5.16.1981 Chicago IL BR/TR/5-8/165 d6.14

| 1910 | StL A | 8 | 19 | 1 | 3 | 2 | 0 | 0 | 1 | 1 | | | .158 | .158 | .263 | 34 | -1 | 0 | .828 | -1 | 116 | 0 | S6/23 | | -0.3 |

MEEK, DAD Frank J. B3.14.1867 St.Louis MO D12.22.1922 St.Louis MO 6-0/? d5.10

1889	StL AA	2	2	2	1	0	0	1	0	0		0	.500	.500	.500	164	0	1	.667	0			C2		0.0
1890	StL AA	4	16	3	5	0	0	1	2	1		0	.313	.313	.313	74	-1	1	.913	1	96	129	C4		0.1
Total	2	6	18	5	6	0	0	2	2	1		0	.333	.333	.333	84	-1	2	.898	1	96	129	C6		0.1

MEEKS, SAMMY Samuel Mack B4.23.1923 Anderson SC BR/TR/5-9/160* d4.29

1948	Was A	24	33	4	4	1	0	0	2	1		0	12	.121	.147	.152	-21	-6	0-0	.939	-1	93	120	S10/2		-0.6
1949	Cin N	16	36	10	11	2	0	2	6	2		0	6	.306	.342	.528	128	1	1	1.000	4	119	177	2b8,S3		0.5
1950	Cin N	39	95	7	27	5	0	1	8	6		0	14	.284	.327	.368	82	-1	1	.951	-2	95	89	S29,3b2		-0.3
1951	Cin N	23	35	4	8	1	0	0	2	0		0	4	.229	.229	.229	23	-4	1-0	.929	1	47	215	3b4/S		-0.5
Total	4	102	199	25	50	8	0	3	18	9		0	36	.251	.284	.337	64	-11	3-0	.953	-1	97	104	S43,2b9,3b6		-0.9

YEAR	TM LG	G	AB	R	H	2B	3B	HR	RBI	BB-IB	HP	SO	AVG	OBP	SLG	AOPS	ABR	SB-CS	FA	FR	RNG	THR	GAMES AT POSITION	DL	BFW
MEIER, DUTCH	Arthur Ernst B3.30.1879 St.Louis MO D3.23.1948 Chicago IL BR/TR/5-10/175 d5.12 Col Princeton																								
1906	Pit N	82	273	32	70	11	4	0	16	13	3		.256	.298	.326	90	-4	4	.975	-6	90	164	O52(29/6/18),S17		-1.2
MEIER, DAVE	David Keith B8.8.1959 Helena MT BR/TR/6-0/185* [MinA81 5/114] d4.3 Col Stanford																								
1984	Min A	59	147	18	35	8	1	0	13	6-0	1	9	.238	.271	.306	57	-9	0-1	.978	-1	99	71	O50(41/0/10)/3D		-1.2
1985	Min A	71	104	15	27	6	0	1	8	18-0	1	12	.260	.374	.346	93	0	0-6	.987	-0	102	44	O63(55/3/4),D3		-0.4
1987	Tex A	13	21	4	6	1	0	0	0	0-0	0	4	.286	.286	.333	63	-1	0-0	.917	-1	100	0	O8(6/0/2)		-0.2
1988	Chi N	2	5	0	2	0	0	0	1	0-0	0	1	.400	.400	.400	124	0	0-0	1.000	-1	0	0	/3		-0.1
Total	4	145	277	37	70	15	1	1	22	24-0	2	26	.253	.316	.325	73	-10	0-7	.978	-2	100	54	O121(102/3/16),D7,3b2		-1.9
MEINERT, WALT	Walter Henry B12.11.1890 New York NY D11.9.1958 Decatur IL BL/TL/5-7.5/150 d9.6																								
1913	StL A	4	8	1	3	0	0	0	1			3	.375	.444	.375	144	1	1	1.000	-0	120	0	O2R		0.0
MEINKE, FRANK	Frank Louis B10.18.1863 Chicago IL D11.8.1931 Chicago IL BR/5-10.5/172 d5.1 s-Bob ▲																								
1884	Det N	92	341	28	56	5	7	6	24	6		89	.164	.179	.273	42	-23		.839	-2	100	135	S51,P35,O4(1/0/4),3b3,2b3		-1.3
1885	Det N	1	3	0	0	0	0	0	0	0		1	.000	.000	.000	-99	-1		1.000	0	0	0	/OLP		0.0
Total	2	93	344	28	56	5	7	6	24	6		90	.163	.177	.270	41	-24		.839	-2	100	135	S51,P36,O5(2/0/4),3b3,2b3		-1.3
MEINKE, BOB	Robert Bernard B6.25.1887 Chicago IL D12.29.1952 Chicago IL BR/TR/5-10/135 d8.22 f-Frank																								
1910	Cin N	2	1	0	0	0	0	0	0	0-0	0	0	.000	.000	.000	51	0	1	1.000	1	144	0	S2		0.1
MEISTER, GEORGE	George B. B6.5.1864 Dorzbach, Germany D8.24.1908 Pittsburgh PA ?/160 d8.15																								
1884	Tol AA	34	119	9	23	6	0	0	3	5		33	.193	.244	.244	58	-5		.817	-7	72	91	3b34		-1.1
MEISTER, JOHN	John F. B5.10.1863 Allentown PA D1.17.1923 Philadelphia PA 5-8/175 d8.24																								
1886	NY AA	45	186	35	44	7	3	2	21	4		92	.237	.253	.339	92	-2	1	.906	-5	88	94	2b45		-0.5
1887	NY AA	39	158	24	35	6	2	1	21	16	2		.222	.301	.304	72	-5	9	.930	-5	91	248	O22C,2b14,3b3/S		-0.9
Total	2	84	344	59	79	13	5	3	42	20	2		.230	.276	.323	82	-7	10	.905	-10	89	96	2b59,O22C,3b3/S		-1.4
MEISTER, KARL	Karl Daniel "Dutch" B5.15.1891 Marietta OH D8.15.1967 Marietta OH BR/TR/6-0/178 d8.10																								
1913	Cin N	4	7	0	2	0	1	0	0	0	0	4	.286	.286	.429	103	0	0	.667	-1	59	0	O4(1/3/0)		-0.1
MEIXELL, MOXIE	Merton Merrill B10.18.1887 Lake Crystal MN D8.17.1982 Los Angeles CA BL/TR/5-10/168 d7.7																								
1912	Cle A	3	2	1	1	0	0	0	0	0-0	0	0	.500	.500	.500	181	0	0	—	-0	0	0	/OR		0.0
MEJIA, MIGUEL	Miguel B3.25.1975 San Pedro de Macoris, D.R. BR/TR/6-1/155 d4.4																								
1996	†StL N	45	23	10	2	0	0	0	0	0-0	0	10	.087	.087	.087	-54	-5	6-3	.933	-0	112	0	O21(5/11/6)	30	-0.5
MEJIA, ROBERTO	Roberto Antonio (Diaz) B4.14.1972 Hato Mayor, D.R. BR/TR/5-11/160(160-183) d7.15																								
1993	Col N	65	229	31	53	14	5	5	20	13-1	1	63	.231	.275	.402	67	-1	4-1	.963	-1	102	88	2b65		-0.8
1994	Col N	38	116	11	28	8	1	4	14	15-2	0	33	.241	.326	.431	82	-3	3-1	.959	-5	91	79	2b34		-0.6
1995	Col N	23	52	5	8	1	0	1	6	0-0	1	17	.154	.167	.231	3	-7	0-1	.971	-5	73	42	2b16		-1.2
1997	StL N	7	14	0	1	1	0	0	0	0-0	0	5	.071	.067	.143	-46	-3	0-0	.900	-1	94	224	2b3/O(1/0/1)	170	-0.4
Total	4	133	411	47	90	24	6	10	40	28-3	2	118	.219	.270	.380	60	-24	7-3	.961	-11	95	82	2b118/O(1/0/1)	170	-3.0
MEJIAS, ROMAN	Roman (Gomez) B8.9.1930 Abreus, Cuba BR/TR/6-0/175* d4.13																								
1955	Pit N	71	167	14	36	8	1	3	21	9-0	0	13	.216	.256	.329	55	-11	1-3	.926	2	90	278	O44(30/1/14)		-1.2
1957	Pit N	58	142	12	39	7	4	2	15	6-1	1	13	.275	.309	.423	97	-1	2-2	1.000	3	98	268	O42(7/7/29)		-0.5
1958	Pit N	76	157	17	42	3	2	5	19	2-1	1	27	.268	.280	.408	82	-5	2-0	.973	3	116	90	O57(41/10/8)		-1.3
1959	Pit N	96	276	28	65	6	1	7	28	21-7	5	48	.236	.298	.341	71	-12	1-2	.970	2	102	143	O85(15/21/52)		-0.4
1960	Pit N	3	1	1	0	0	0	0	0	0-0	0	1	.000	.000	.000	-99	0	0-0	—	0			/H		0.0
1961	Pit N	4	1	1	0	0	0	0	0	0-0	0	1	.000	.000	.000	-99	0	0-0	1.000	0	244	0	O2L		-0.7
1962	Hou N	146	566	82	162	12	3	24	76	30-1	6	83	.286	.326	.445	114	8	12-4	.946	-2	94	90	O142(1/1/141)		-1.9
1963	Bos A	111	357	43	81	18	0	11	39	14-2	1	36	.227	.260	.370	72	-14	4-1	.973	-2	99	116	O86(7/65/15)		-0.4
1964	Bos A	62	101	14	24	3	1	2	4	7-1	1	16	.238	.294	.347	74	-4	0-0	.962	1	110	146	O37(14/13/11)		-0.4
Total	9	627	1768	212	449	57	12	54	202	89-13	17	238	.254	.294	.391	86	-39	22-12	.963	3	99	136	O495(117/118/270)		-6.0
MEJIAS, SAM	Samuel Elias B5.9.1952 Santiago, D.R. BR/TR/6-0/170(160-180) d9.6 C7																								
1976	StL N	18	21	1	3	1	0	0	0	2-1	0	2	.143	.217	.190	16	-2	2-0	1.000	1	120	156	O17(3/1/13)		-0.1
1977	Mon N	74	101	14	23	4	1	3	8	2-0	0	17	.228	.243	.376	65	-6	1-0	.966	-0	101	106	O56(4/21/31)		-0.7
1978	Mon N	67	56	9	13	1	0	0	6	2-1	0	5	.232	.259	.250	43	-4	0-0	.949	0	98	142	O52(24/4/25)/P		-0.5
1979	Chi N	31	11	4	2	0	0	0	2	2-0	0	5	.182	.308	.182	34	-1	0-0	.875	-1	71	0	O23(15/5/3)		-0.2
	Cin N	7	2	1	1	0	0	0	0	0-0	0	0	.500	.500	.500	174	0	0-0	1.000	-0	48	0	O5C		-0.0
	Year	38	13	5	3	0	0	0	2	2-0	0	5	.231	.333	.231	53	-1	0-0	.889	-1	68	0	O28(15/10/3)		-0.2
1980	Cin N	71	108	16	30	5	1	1	10	6-0	1	13	.278	.322	.370	94	-1	4-2	.989	3	106	160	O67(8/50/17)		0.1
1981	Cin N	66	49	6	14	2	0	0	7	16-3	0	9	.286	.302	.327	82	-1	1-0	.972	-1	83	73	O58(0/16/42)		-0.7
Total	6	334	348	51	86	13	2	4	31	16-3	1	51	.247	.281	.330	69	-15	8-2	.973	1	99	121	O278(54/102/131)/P		-1.7
MELE, DUTCH	Albert Ernest B1.11.1915 New York NY D2.12.1975 Hollywood FL BL/TL/6-0.5/195 d9.14																								
1937	Cin N	6	14	1	2	1	0	0	1	0-0	0	1	.143	.200	.214	13	-2	0	1.000	-1	28	0	O5(2/0/3)		-0.3
MELE, SAM	Sabath Anthony B1.21.1923 Astoria NY BR/TR/6-1/187* d4.15 M7/C3 Col NYU																								
1947	Bos A	123	453	71	137	14	8	12	73	37	1	35	.302	.356	.448	114	7	0-3	.992	-1	95	126	O116(3/29/87)/1		0.1
1948	Bos A	66	180	25	42	12	1	2	25	13		21	.233	.292	.344	66	-9	1-1	.971	-1	104	60	O55(3/0/52)		-1.1
1949	Bos A	18	46	1	9	1	1	0	7	7		14	.196	.302	.261	46	-4	2-0	.955	-1	91	95	O11R		-1.6
	Was A	78	264	21	64	12	2	3	25	17		34	.242	.288	.337	67	-14	2-1	.966	0	98	119	O63(1/24/44),1b11		-2.0
	Year	96	310	22	73	13	3	3	32	24		48	.235	.290	.326	63	-18	4-1	.964	-0	97	115	O74(1/24/55),1b11		-2.0
1950	Was A	126	435	57	119	21	6	12	86	51		40	.274	.351	.432	105	2	2-0	.990	-0	94	102	O99(6/26/72),1b16		-1.2
1951	Was A	143	558	58	153	36	7	5	94	32	1	31	.274	.315	.391	92	-9	2-3	.993	-8	90	124(2/17/107),1b15		0.4
1952	Was A	9	28	2	12	3	0	2	10	1	0	2	.429	.448	.750	237	5	0-0	.917	-1	94	0	O7(0/1/6)		-1.1
	Chi A	123	423	46	105	18	2	14	59	48	2	40	.248	.328	.400	101	0	1-2	1.000	-6	86	95	O112R,1b3		-0.7
	Year	132	451	48	117	21	2	16	69	49	2	42	.259	.335	.421	109	4	1-2	.994	-7	86	90	O119(0/1/118),1b3		-0.7
1953	Chi A	140	481	64	132	26	8	12	82	58		47	.274	.353	.437	109	6	3-1	.996	-8	83	115	O138(0/4/138),1b2		-1.0
1954	Bal A	72	230	17	55	9	4	5	32	18		26	.239	.290	.378	90	-5	0-1	.962	-2	88	136	O62(40/0/24)		0.2
	Bos A	42	132	22	42	6	0	7	23	12		12	.318	.378	.523	132	4	0-1	.994	-4	87	132	O75(43/0/37),1b22		-0.3
	Year	114	362	39	97	15	4	12	55	30		38	.268	.322	.431	107	2	1-1	.961	-4	87		O... 1b22		-0.3
1955	Bos A	14	31	1	4	2	0	1	0	0-0		7	.129	.125	.194	-13	-2	1-0	1.000	-2	100	534	O7(6/0/1)		-0.5
	Cin N	35	62	4	13	1	0	2	7	5-0	1	13	.210	.279	.323	56	-4	0-0	.960	-0	110	0	O13(12/0/1)/1		-0.2
1956	Cle A	57	114	17	29	7	0	4	20	12-0	0	20	.254	.320	.421	94	-1	0-0	.969	1	96	175	O20(14/0/6),1b8		-0.2
Total	10	1046	3437	406	916	168	39	80	544	311-0	10	342	.267	.328	.408	97	-25	15-14	.985	-16	94	109	O840(90/101/674),1b79		-7.6
MELENDEZ, FRANCISCO	Francisco Javier (Villegas) B1.25.1964 Rio Piedras, PR BL/TL/6-0/190(170-190) d8.26																								
1984	Phi N	21	23	0	3	0	0	0	1	2-0	0	5	.130	.167	.130	-15	-4	0-0	1.000	1	174	35	1b10		-0.3
1986	Phi N	9	8	0	2	0	0	0	0	2-0	0	2	.250	.250	.250	37	-1	0-0	1.000	0	0	0	1b2		-0.1
1987	SF N	12	16	2	5	0	0	1	1	0-0	0	3	.313	.313	.500	116	0	0-0	1.000	-1	0	0	1b5		0.0
1988	SF N	23	26	1	5	0	0	0	3	3-0	0	2	.192	.276	.192	38	-2	0-0	1.000	0	0	0	1b6/OL	39	-0.3
1989	Bal A	9	11	1	3	0	0	0	1	5-0	0	2	.273	.308	.273	75	0	0-0	1.000	0	101	167	1b5	39	-0.1
Total	5	74	84	4	18	0	0	1	5	5-0	0	14	.214	.256	.250	43	-7	0-0	1.000	-1	83	79	1b28/OL		-0.8
MELENDEZ, LUIS	Luis Antonio (Santana) B8.11.1949 Aibonito, PR BR/TR/6-0/165* d9.7																								
1970	StL N	21	70	11	21	1	0	0	8	2-0	0	12	.300	.315	.314	68	-3	3-0	1.000	0	90	179	O18(0/5/13)	22	-0.3
1971	StL N	88	173	25	39	3	1	0	11	24-1	0	29	.225	.320	.254	61	-8	2-0	.959	-1	100	97	O66(4/20/45)		-1.2
1972	StL N	118	332	32	79	11	3	5	28	25-0	1	34	.238	.292	.334	78	-10	5-4	.990	2	103	131	O95(2/65/30)		-1.4
1973	StL N	121	341	35	91	18	1	2	35	27-2	0	50	.267	.319	.343	84	-7	2-7	.990	2	103	0	O105(4/69/40)		-1.1
1974	StL N	83	124	15	27	4	3	0	8	11-0	1	9	.218	.283	.298	64	-6	2-2	.977	1	119	0	O46(23/22/10)/S		-0.7
1975	StL N	110	291	33	77	8	5	2	27	16-3	0	25	.265	.301	.347	75	-10	3-2	.983	-0	102	62	O89(36/49/7)		-1.4
1976	StL N	20	24	3	0	0	0	0	5	0-0	0	5	.125	.125	.125	-28	-4	0-0	1.000	1	163	0	O8(4/4/0)		-0.8
	SD N	72	119	15	29	5	0	0	5	3-1	0	12	.244	.260	.286	60	-7	1-1	.988	1	112	0	O60(24/29/10)		-0.8

YEAR	TM LG	G	AB	R	H	2B	3B	HR	RBI	BB-IB	HP	SO	AVG	OBP	SLG	AOPS	ABR	SB-CS	FA	FR	RNG	THR	GAMES AT POSITION	DL	BFW
	Year	92	143	15	32	5	0	0	5	3-1	0	15	.224	.238	.259	44	-11	1-1	.990	2	117	0	O68(28/33/10)		-1.1
1977	SD N	8	3	1	0	0	0	0	0	1-0	0	1	.000	.250	.000	-29	-1	0-0	1.000	0	172	0	O2C	31	0.0
Total	8	641	1477	167	366	50	13	9	122	109-7	2	175	.248	.299	.318	72	-56	18-16	.977	5	105	84	O489(97/265/155)/S	53	-7.2

MELHUSE, ADAM Adam Michael B3.27.1972 Santa Clara CA BB/TR/6-2/185(185-200) [TorA93 13/378] d6.16 Col UCLA

YEAR	TM LG	G	AB	R	H	2B	3B	HR	RBI	BB-IB	HP	SO	AVG	OBP	SLG	AOPS	ABR	SB-CS	FA	FR	RNG	THR	GAMES AT POSITION	DL	BFW
2000	LA N	1	1	0	0	0	0	0	0	0-0	0	1	.000	.000	.000	-99	0	0-0	—	-0			/H		0.0
	Col N	23	23	3	4	0	1	0	4	0-0	0	5	.174	.269	.261	28	-3	0-0	1.000	-0	94	75	1b3/COR		-0.3
	Year	24	24	3	4	0	1	0	4	0-0	0	6	.167	.259	.250	24	-3	0-0	1.000	-0	94	75	1b3/COR		-0.3
2001	Col N	40	71	5	13	2	0	1	8	6-0	0	18	.183	.241	.254	25	-8	1-0	.991	-4	54	23	C23/1		-1.1
2003	†Oak A	40	77	13	23	7	0	5	14	9-0	0	19	.299	.372	.584	146	5	0-0	.993	-0	93	95	C33,3b2/1		0.7
2004	Oak A	69	214	23	55	11	0	11	31	16-1	0	47	.257	.309	.463	98	-1	0-1	.995	-3	113	91	C64,3b3/1		-0.1
2005	Oak A	39	97	11	24	7	0	2	12	5-0	0	28	.247	.284	.381	74	-4	0-0	1.000	-0	127	71	C24,D8		-0.3
Total	5	212	483	55	119	27	1	19	69	39-1	0	118	.246	.302	.424	84	-11	1-1	.995	-8	103	79	C145,D8,1b6,3b5/OR		-1.1

MELILLO, SKI Oscar Donald "Spinach" B8.4.1899 Chicago IL D11.14.1963 Chicago IL BR/TR/5-8/150 d4.18 M1/C13

YEAR	TM LG	G	AB	R	H	2B	3B	HR	RBI	BB-IB	HP	SO	AVG	OBP	SLG	AOPS	ABR	SB-CS	FA	FR	RNG	THR	GAMES AT POSITION	DL	BFW
1926	StL A	99	385	54	98	18	5	1	30	32	2	31	.255	.315	.335	66	-20	6-7	.965	10	106	120	2b88,3b11		-0.7
1927	StL A	107	356	45	80	18	2	0	26	25	0	28	.225	.276	.287	45	-30	3-6	.935	3	99	122	2b101		-2.5
1928	StL A	51	132	9	25	2	0	0	9	9	0	11	.189	.241	.205	18	-16	2-1	.961	0	97	101	2b28,3b19		-1.4
1929	StL A	141	494	57	146	17	10	5	67	29	2	30	.296	.337	.401	86	-12	11-6	.973	20	110	118	2b141		1.2
1930	StL A	149	574	62	147	30	10	5	59	23	4	44	.256	.287	.369	63	-35	15-9	.979	25	112	110	2b148		-0.5
1931	StL A	151	617	88	189	34	11	2	75	37	0	29	.306	.346	.407	94	-7	7-11	.968	35	113	123	2b151		3.3
1932	StL A	**154**	612	71	148	19	11	3	66	36	2	42	.242	.286	.324	54	-44	6-6	.981	11	104	104	2b153		-2.2
1933	StL A	132	496	50	145	23	6	3	79	29	1	18	.292	.333	.381	83	-13	12-10	**.991**	22	105	133	2b130		1.6
1934	StL A	144	552	54	133	19	3	2	55	28	1	27	.241	.279	.297	45	-47	4-6	**.981**	17	102	110	2b141		-2.1
1935	StL A	19	62	8	13	3	0	0	5	8	0	4	.210	.300	.258	43	-5	0-0	.970	-0	108	73	2b18		-0.4
	Bos A	106	400	45	104	13	2	1	39	38	2	22	.260	.327	.310	61	-23	3-2	.973	17	109	120	2b105		0.1
	Year	125	462	53	117	16	2	1	44	46	2	26	.253	.324	.303	59	-28	3-2	.973	17	109	114	2b123		-0.3
1936	Bos A	98	327	39	74	12	4	0	32	28	0	16	.226	.287	.294	40	-32	3-0	.973	-7	87	107	2b93		-3.0
1937	Bos A	26	56	8	14	2	0	0	6	5	0	4	.250	.311	.286	50	-4	0-1	.939	-3	77	80	2b19,S2,3b2		-0.6
Total	12	1377	5063	590	1316	210	64	22	548	327	12	306	.260	.306	.340	64	-288	69-65	.973	151	105	115	2b1316,3b32,S2		-7.2

MELLANA, JOE Joseph Peter B3.11.1905 Oakland CA D11.1.1969 Larkspur CA BR/TR/5-10/180 d9.21

| 1927 | Phi A | 4 | 7 | 1 | 2 | 0 | 0 | 0 | 2 | 0 | 0 | 1 | .286 | .286 | .286 | 46 | -1 | 0-0 | .889 | 1 | 201 | 273 | 3b2 | | 0.1 |

MELLOR, BILL William Harpin B6.6.1874 Camden NJ D11.5.1940 Bridgeton RI BR/TR/6-0/190 d7.28 Col Virginia

| 1902 | Bal A | 10 | 36 | 4 | 13 | 3 | 0 | 0 | 5 | 3 | 0 | | .361 | .410 | .444 | 131 | 2 | 1 | .978 | -1 | 41 | 17 | 1b10 | | 0.0 |

MELO, JUAN Juan Esteban B11.11.1976 Bani, D.R. BB/TR/6-3/206 d9.2

| 2000 | SF N | 11 | 13 | 0 | 1 | 0 | 0 | 0 | 1 | 0-0 | 0 | 5 | .077 | .077 | .077 | -65 | -3 | 0-0 | 1.000 | -2 | 57 | 0 | 2b6 | | -0.5 |

MELOAN, PAUL Paul B. "Molly" B8.23.1888 Paynesville MO D2.11.1950 Taft CA BR/TL/5-10.5/175 d8.2 Col Washington-St. Louis

1910	Chi A	65	222	23	54	6	0	0	23	17			.243	.314	.324	104	1	4	.948	4	90	192	O65R		0.2
1911	Chi A	1	3	0	1	0	0	0	1	0			.333	.333	.333	89	0	0	.000	-1	0	0	/OR		-0.1
	StL A	64	206	30	54	11	4	2	14	15			.262	.318	.379	98	-1	7	.904	-4	96	70	O54(1/0/53)		-0.7
	Year	65	209	30	55	11	4	2	15	15			.263	.318	.378	98	-1	7	.893	-4	94	69	O55(1/0/54)		-0.8
Total	2	130	431	53	109	17	4	2	38	32	8		.253	.316	.350	101	0	11	.923	-0	92	138	O120(1/0/119)		-0.6

MELTON, DAVE David Olin B10.3.1928 Pampa TX BR/TR/6-0/185* d4.17 Col Stanford

1956	KC A	3	3	0	1	0	0	0	0	0-0	0		.333	.333	.333	76	0	0-0	1.000	-0	139	0	O3L		0.0
1958	KC A	9	6	0	0	0	0	0	0	0-0	0	5	.000	.000	.000	-98	-2	0-0	1.000	-0	210	0	O2L		-0.2
Total	2	12	9	0	1	0	0	0	0	0-0	0	5	.111	.111	.111	-39	-2	0-0	1.000	-0	161	0	O5L	121	-0.2

MELTON, BILL William Edwin B7.7.1945 Gulfport MS BR/TR/6-2/195* d5.4 Col Citrus (CA) JC

1968	Chi A	34	109	5	29	8	0	2	16	10-0	0	32	.266	.322	.394	117	2	1-1	.968	-0	114	89	3b33		0.2
1969	Chi A	157	556	67	142	26	2	23	87	56-7	5	106	.255	.326	.433	107	4	1-2	.952	-0	102	117	3b148,O11(3/0/8)		0.2
1970	Chi A	141	514	74	135	15	1	33	96	56-2	9	107	.263	.340	.488	123	15	2-4	1.000	7	86	171	O71R,3b70		1.8
1971	Chi A☆	150	543	72	146	18	2	**33**	86	61-5	11	87	.269	.352	.492	134	24	3-3	.968	24	115	90	3b148		4.9
1972	Chi A	57	208	22	51	5	0	7	30	23-2	0	31	.245	.319	.370	103	1	1-1	.935	3	104	110	3b56	97	0.4
1973	Chi A	152	560	83	155	29	1	20	87	75-7	2	66	.277	.363	.439	121	17	4-4	.953	10	109	104	3b151/D		2.7
1974	Chi A	136	495	63	120	17	0	21	63	59-3	5	60	.242	.326	.404	107	5	3-2	.939	-8	93	103	3b123,D11		-0.4
1975	Chi A	149	512	62	123	16	0	15	70	78-1	8	106	.240	.346	.359	99	2	5-4	.945	-8	93	78	3b138,D11		-0.8
1976	Cal A	118	341	31	71	17	3	6	42	44-2	2	53	.208	.300	.328	90	-4	2-0	.992	-5	88	102	D51,1b30,3b21		-1.2
1977	Cle A	50	133	17	32	1	0	0	14	17-0	2	21	.241	.331	.323	83	-2	1-3	1.000	-1	89	97	1b15,D14,3b13		-0.5
Total	10	1144	3971	496	1004	162	9	160	591	479-29	44	669	.253	.337	.419	112	64	23-24	.949	22	104	100	3b901,D88,O82(3/0/79),1b45	97	7.3

MELUSKEY, MITCH Mitchell Wade B9.18.1973 Yakima WA BB/TR/6-0/185* d8.30 [CleA92 12/322] d8.30 [DL 2001 Det A 190]

1998	Hou N	8	8	1	2	1	0	0	1	1-0	0	4	.250	.333	.375	88	0	0-0	1.000	0	0	0	C3		0.0
1999	Hou N	10	33	4	7	1	0	1	3	5-1	0	6	.212	.316	.333	65	-2	1-0	1.000	-1	55	151	C10	161	-0.1
2000	Hou N	117	337	47	101	21	0	14	69	55-10	4	74	.300	.401	.487	115	10	1-0	.982	-8	83	81	C103/3		0.8
2002	Det A	8	27	3	6	0	0	1	3	5-0	1	2	.222	.353	.222	63	-1	0-0	1.000	-2	223	148	C8	17	0.8
2003	Hou N	12	9	1	1	1	0	0	2	2-0	0	2	.111	.250	.222	30	-1	0-0	—	0			/H	162	-0.2
Total	5	155	414	56	117	24	0	15	75	68-11	5	89	.283	.386	.449	106	6	2-0	.985	-10	91	91	C124/3	530	0.3

MELVIN, BOB Robert Paul B10.28.1961 Palo Alto CA BR/TR/6-4/205* [DetA81*S1/2] d5.25 M3/C4 Col California-Davis

1985	Det A	41	82	10	18	4	1	0	4	3-0	0	21	.220	.247	.293	47	-6	0-0	.989	3	91	72	C41		-0.2
1986	SF N	89	268	24	60	14	2	5	25	15-1	0	69	.224	.262	.347	71	-12	3-2	.988	6	103	140	C84/3		-0.3
1987	†SF N	84	246	31	49	8	0	11	31	17-3	0	44	.199	.249	.366	64	-14	0-4	.998	7	127	155	C78/1		-0.6
1988	SF N	92	273	23	64	13	1	8	27	13-0	0	46	.234	.268	.377	87	-6	0-2	.984	-4	149	68	C89/1		-0.7
1989	Bal A	85	278	22	67	10	1	1	32	15-3	0	53	.241	.279	.295	64	-14	1-4	.991	-10	99	88	C75,D9	15	-2.2
1990	Bal A	93	301	30	73	14	1	5	37	11-1	0	53	.243	.267	.346	73	-12	0-1	.997	-4	108	77	C76,D10/1		-1.3
1991	Bal A	79	228	11	57	10	0	1	23	11-2	0	46	.250	.279	.307	66	-11	0-0	.998	-1	91	85	C72,D4		-0.8
1992	KC A	32	70	5	22	5	0	0	6	5-0	0	13	.314	.351	.386	105	-1	0-0	1.000	-0	102	106	C21,1b3		0.1
1993	Bos A	77	176	13	39	7	0	3	23	7-0	1	44	.222	.251	.313	49	-13	0-0	.994	-3	116	39	C76/1		-1.3
1994	NY A	9	14	2	4	0	0	1	3	0-0	0	3	.286	.286	.500	101	0	0-0	1.000	-1	64	178	C4,1b4/D	15	-0.1
	Chi A	11	19	3	3	0	0	0	0	1-0	0	4	.158	.200	.158	-6	-3	0-0	1.000	-1	0	53	C11	29	-0.4
	Year	20	33	5	7	0	0	1	4	1-0	0	7	.212	.235	.303	38	-3	0-0	1.000	-1	56	41	C15,1b4/D		
Total	10	692	1955	174	456	85	6	35	212	98-10	1	396	.233	.268	.337	68	-90	4-13	.993	-9	111	93	C627,D24,1b11/3	74	-7.7

MENCH, KEVIN Kevin Ford B1.7.1978 Wilmington DE BR/TR/6-0/225(215-230) [TexA99 4/118] d4.9 Col Delaware

2002	Tex A	110	366	52	95	20	2	15	60	31-0	0	83	.260	.327	.448	102	1	1-1	.990	0	98	117	O106(57/1/62),D2		-0.4
2003	Tex A	38	125	15	40	12	0	2	11	10-0	3	17	.320	.381	.464	115	3	1-1	.984	-2	87	51	O35(34/3/2)	100	0.0
2004	Tex A	125	438	69	122	30	3	26	71	33-2	6	63	.279	.335	.539	119	11	0-0	.995	1	100	93	O109(53/5/62),D14	19	0.6
2005	Tex A	150	557	71	147	33	3	25	73	50-4	5	68	.264	.328	.469	105	4	4-3	.987	-1	97	97	O148(119/1/41)/D		-0.4
Total	4	423	1486	207	404	95	8	68	215	124-6	22	231	.272	.334	.484	109	19	6-5	.990	-3	97	97	O398(263/10/167),D17	119	-0.2

MENDEZ, CARLOS Carlos Alberto (Castillo) B6.18.1974 Caracas, Venez BR/TR/6-0/210 d5.22

| 2003 | Bal A | 26 | 45 | 3 | 10 | 2 | 0 | 0 | 5 | 0-0 | 0 | 12 | .222 | .217 | .267 | 28 | -5 | 0-0 | .939 | -0 | 111 | 29 | 1b9,D8 | | -0.5 |

MENDEZ, DONALDO Donaldo Alfonso B6.7.1978 Barquisimeto, Venez BR/TR/6-1/155* d4.5

2001	SD N	46	118	11	18	2	1	1	5	5-2	3	37	.153	.206	.212	9	-17	1-2	.920	-6	94	72	S46	91	-2.1
2003	SD N	26	84	10	19	6	0	2	9	7-1	2	32	.226	.298	.369	81	-2	1-0	.951	-4	96	60	S26		-0.5
Total	2	72	202	21	37	8	1	3	14	12-3	5	69	.183	.245	.277	39	-19	2-2	.933	-11	95	67	S72	91	-2.6

MENDOZA, CARLOS Carlos Ramon B11.4.1974 Bolivar, Venez BL/TL/5-11/165(160-175) d9.3

1997	NY N	15	12	6	3	0	0	0	1	4-0	2	4	.250	.500	.250	109	1	0-0	1.000	-0	80	0	O3(2/3/0)		0.0
2000	Col N	13	10	0	1	0	0	0	1	1-0	0	2	.100	.182	.100	-21	-2	0-1	1.000	-1	0	0	O3L		-0.3
Total	2	28	22	6	4	0	0	0	2	5-0	2	6	.182	.379	.182	48	-1	0-1	.833	-1	64	0	O6(5/3/0)		-0.3

YEAR	TM LG	G	AB	R	H	2B	3B	HR	RBI	BB-IB	HP	SO	AVG	OBP	SLG	AOPS	ABR	SB-CS	FA	FR	RNG	THR	GAMES AT POSITION	DL	BFW

MENDOZA, MINNIE Cristobal Rigoberto (Carreras) B11.16.1933 Ceiba Del Agua, Cuba BR/TR/6-0/180 d4.9 C1

| 1970 | Min A | 16 | 16 | 2 | 3 | 0 | 0 | 0 | 2 | 0-0 | | 1 | .188 | .188 | .188 | | 4 | -2 | 0-0 | 1.000 | 1 | 168 | 0 | 3b5,2b4 | | -0.2 |

MENDOZA, MARIO Mario (Aizpuru) B12.26.1950 Chihuahua, Chihuahua, Mexico BR/TR/5-11/187(158-187) d4.26

1974	†Pit N	91	163	10	36	1	2	0	15	8-2	1	35	.221	.259	.252		45	-13	1-1	.964	-4	106	66	S87		-1.0
1975	Pit N	56	50	8	9	1	0	0	3	3-0	0	17	.180	.226	.200		19	-6	0-0	.952	-4	95	78	S53/3		-0.7
1976	Pit N	50	92	6	17	5	0	0	12	4-1	0	15	.185	.216	.239		29	-9	0-1	.967	1	107	111	S45,3b2/2		-0.5
1977	Pit N	70	81	5	16	3	0	0	4	3-0	0	10	.198	.226	.235		23	-9	0-0	.928	-5	99	100	S45,3b19/P		-1.2
1978	Pit N	57	55	5	12	1	0	1	3	2-1	3	9	.218	.283	.291		58	-3	3-1	.980	-1	114	53	2b21,3b18,S14		-0.3
1979	Sea A	148	373	26	74	10	3	1	29	9-0	1	62	.198	.216	.249		26	-40	3-0	.968	7	107	102	S148		-1.9
1980	Sea A	114	277	27	68	6	3	2	14	16-0	0	42	.245	.286	.310		63	-15	3-4	.959	-1	101	108	S114		-0.1
1981	Tex A	88	229	18	53	6	1	0	22	7-0	1	25	.231	.254	.266		54	-14	2-1	.970	6	109	97	S88		-0.3
1982	Tex A	12	17	1	2	0	0	0	0	0-0	0	4	.118	.118	.118		-37	-3	0-0	.882	-1	84	157	S12		-0.3
Total	9	686	1337	106	287	33	9	4	101	52-4	6	219	.215	.245	.262		41	-112	12-8	.961	-2	104	96	S606,3b40,2b22/P		-6.7

MENECHINO, FRANK Frank B1.7.1971 Staten Island NY BR/TR/5-8/199(175-200) [ChiA93 45/1261] d9.6 Col Alabama

1999	Oak A	9	9	0	2	0	0	0	0	0-0	0	4	.222	.222	.222		14	-1	0-0	1.000	0	100	139	S5/3		-0.1
2000	†Oak A	66	145	31	37	9	1	6	26	20-0	1	45	.255	.345	.455	103	1	1-4		.973	10	121	114	2b51,S5,3b4/PD		1.0
2001	†Oak A	139	471	82	114	22	2	12	60	79-0	19	97	.242	.369	.374	97	-2	2-3		.978	18	111	119	2b136,S3/3D		2.4
2002	Oak A	38	132	22	27	7	0	3	15	20-0	1	32	.205	.312	.326	71	-5	0-0		.992	-5	103	51	2b32,3b4,S2/D		-0.9
2003	†Oak A	43	83	10	16	0	0	2	9	19-1	4	16	.193	.364	.265	71	-3	0-0		.986	-0	103	120	2b22,3b19,S3/D		-0.2
2004	Oak A	13	33	0	3	0	0	0	1	1-0	1	8	.091	.143	.091	-38	-7	0-0		.978	-1	111	33	2b12	18	-0.7
	Tor A	72	236	40	71	13	4	9	25	36-1	3	44	.301	.400	.504	126	10	0-2		1.000	-5	90	71	2b30,D19,S14,3b7/P		0.6
	Year	85	269	40	74	13	4	9	26	37-1	4	52	.275	.371	.454	108	4	0-2		.994	-5	96	61	2b42,D19,S14,3b7/P		-0.1
2005	Tor A	70	148	22	32	7	0	4	13	25-0	6	33	.216	.352	.345	82	-3	0-1		.991	6	121	137	2b26,D25,3b9/S		0.2
Total	7	450	1257	207	302	58	7	36	149	200-2	35	279	.240	.358	.383	94	-6	3-10		.982	23	110	104	2b309,D51,3b45,S33,P2	18	2.3

MENEFEE, JOCK John B1.15.1868 Rowlesburg WV D3.11.1953 Belle Vernon PA BR/TR/6-0/165 d8.17 ▲

1892	Pit N	2	3	0	0	0	0	0	0	0-0	0	0	.000	.000	.000		-99	-1	0	1.000	0	0	0	/ORP		0.0
1893	Lou N	22	73	10	20	2	1	0	12	13	1	5	.274	.391	.329	100	1	2	.913	2	126	97	P15,O7(1/2/4)		0.1
1894	Lou N	29	79	7	13	1	0	0	4	8	1	7	.165	.250	.177	5	-12	2	.940	2	113	0	P28/2		0.1
	Pit N	13	47	6	12	1	2	0	7	3	0	3	.255	.300	.362	59	0	2	.909	3	142	0	P13		0.0
	Year	42	126	13	25	2	2	0	11	11	1	10	.198	.268	.246	26	-16	4	.928	4	123	0	P41/2		0.1
1895	Pit N	2	0	0	0	0	0	0	0	0	0	0	.——	.——	.——		0	0	.667	0	220	0	P2		0.0
1898	NY N	1	5	0	0	0	0	0	0	0	0	0	.000	.000	.000		-99	-1	0	.750	0	135	0	/P		0.0
1900	Chi N	17	46	5	5	0	0	0	4	2	2		.109	.180	.109	-20	-3	0	.889	-2	71	126	P16		0.0
1901	Chi N	48	152	19	39	5	3	0	13	8	8		.257	.327	.329	94	-1	4	.913	-2	103	132	O24(5/1/18),P21,1b2/2		-0.3
1902	Chi N	65	216	24	50	4	1	0	15	15	7		.231	.303	.259	76	-5	4	.952	-5	62	130	O23(1/0/21),P22,1b18,3b2/2		-1.0
1903	Chi N	22	64	3	13	3	0	0	2	3	0		.203	.239	.250	40	-5	0	.896	3	140	0	P20,1b2		0.1
Total	9	221	685	74	152	16	7	0	57	52	19	15	.222	.295	.266	60	-27	14	.918	0	110	50	P139,O55(7/3/44),1b22,2b3,3b2		-1.0

MENKE, DENIS Denis John B7.21.1940 Bancroft IA BR/TR/6-0/185(178-190) d4.14 C20 OF(3/0/2)

1962	Mil N	50	146	12	28	3	1	2	16	16-0	1	38	.192	.277	.267	49	-11	0-1	.980	2	104	99	2b20,3b15,S9,1b2/OL		-0.7
1963	Mil N	146	518	58	121	16	4	11	50	37-4	6	106	.234	.289	.344	83	-12	6-7	.976	8	112	109	S82,3b51,2b22/1OL		0.4
1964	Mil N	151	505	79	143	29	5	20	65	68-13	1	77	.283	.368	.479	137	27	4-2	.964	12	105	103	S141,2b15,3b6		5.3
1965	Mil N	71	181	16	44	13	1	4	18	18-3	1	28	.243	.313	.392	97	0	1-3	.967	2	108	86	S54,1b8,3b4	35	0.5
1966	Atl N	138	454	55	114	20	4	15	60	71-8	6	87	.251	.355	.412	112	10	0-7	.955	-19	91	83	S106,3b39,1b7		-1.5
1967	Atl N	129	418	37	95	14	3	9	39	65-5	3	62	.227	.333	.325	91	-3	5-7	.965	-21	92	94	S124,3b3		-1.5
1968	Hou N	150	542	56	135	23	6	6	56	64-6	6	81	.249	.334	.347	107	7	5-8	.982	-9	90	65	2b119,S35,1b5,3b4		0.9
1969	Hou N★	154	553	72	149	25	5	10	90	87-12	1	87	.269	.369	.387	115	14	2-7	.956	-11	90	83	S131,2b23,1b9/3		1.8
1970	Hou N★	154	562	82	171	26	6	13	92	82-10	5	80	.304	.392	.441	129	27	6-5	.954	-17	95	80	S133,2b21,1b5,3b5,O3(1/0/2)		2.6
1971	Hou N	146	475	57	117	26	3	1	43	59-4	2	66	.246	.328	.320	88	-5	4-5	.997	-4	89	103	1b101,3b32,S17,2b5		-1.8
1972	†Cin N	140	447	41	104	19	2	9	50	58-2	5	76	.233	.322	.345	96	-1	0-1	.955	-4	103	105	3b130,1b11		-0.8
1973	†Cin N	139	241	38	46	10	0	3	26	69-6	2	53	.191	.368	.270	85	0	1-1	.966	-0	104	123	3b123,S7,2b5/1		-0.1
1974	Hou N	30	29	2	3	1	0	0	0	1-0	0	10	.103	.200	.138	-1	-4	0-0	1.000	1	89	264	1b12,3b7,2b3,S2		-0.3
Total	13	1598	5071	605	1270	225	40	101	606	698-73	46	853	.250	.343	.370	104	49	34-54	.961	-60	97	92	S841,3b420,2b233,1b162,O5L	35	6.0

MENOSKY, MIKE Michael William "Leaping Mike" B10.16.1894 Glen Campbell PA D4.11.1983 Detroit MI BL/TR/5-10/163 d4.18 Mil 1918 Col Indiana (PA)

1914	Pit F	68	140	26	37	4	1	2	9	16	3	30	.264	.352	.350	92	-3	5	.942	0	111	91	O41(6/3/32)		-0.5
1915	Pit F	17	21	3	2	0	0	0	1	2	1	0	.095	.208	.095	-13	-4	2	.917	-0	122	0	O9(6/1/2)		-0.4
1916	Was A	11	37	5	6	1	1	0	3	1	0	10	.162	.184	.243	29	-4	1	.952	2	92	265	O9(1/8/0)		-0.3
1917	Was A	114	322	46	83	12	10	1	34	45	6	55	.258	.359	.366	123	10	-22	.982	11	121	126	O94(93/0/1)		1.8
1918	Was A	116	342	60	98	15	3	6	39	44	7	46	.287	.379	.401	120	11	13	.979	1	108	65	O103(87/15/1)		0.7
1920	Bos A	141	532	80	158	24	9	3	64	65	5	52	.297	.383	.393	110	11	23-19	.961	-5	93	89	O141L		-0.2
1921	Bos A	133	477	77	143	18	5	3	45	60	9	45	.300	.388	.377	99	2	12-6	.970	-4	97	72	O133L		-1.1
1922	Bos A	126	406	61	115	16	5	3	32	40	5	33	.283	.355	.369	90	-6	9-5	.977	6	108	108	O103(74/4/26)		-0.8
1923	Bos A	84	188	22	43	4	4	0	25	22	0	19	.229	.310	.314	64	-10	3-6	.920	3	96	214	O49(28/18/3)		-1.1
Total	9	810	2465	380	685	98	38	18	252	295	40	290	.278	.364	.370	100	7	90-36	.967	13	103	100	O682(569/49/65)		-1.9

MENSOR, ED Edward "The Midget" B11.7.1886 Woodville (now Rogue River) OR D4.20.1970 Salem OR BB/TR/5-6/145 d7.15

1912	Pit N	39	99	19	26	3	0	1	23	0	12	.263	.402	.333	104	2	10	.955	1	104	72	O32(0/20/12)		-0.1
1913	Pit.N	44	56	9	10	1	0	0	1	8	1	13	.179	.292	.196	43	-4	2-4	.971	2	107	236	O18(1/16/1)/2S		-0.4
1914	Pit N	44	89	15	18	2	1	1	6	22	2	13	.202	.372	.281	99	2	2	.969	0	117	54	O25(4/10/11)		0.0
Total	3	127	244	43	54	6	3	1	8	53	3	38	.221	.367	.283	89	0	14-4	.964	1	110	95	O75(5/46/24)/S2		-0.5

MENZE, TED Theodore Charles B11.4.1897 St.Louis MO D12.23.1969 St.Louis MO BR/TR/5-9/172 d4.23

| 1918 | StL N | 1 | 3 | 0 | 0 | 0 | 0 | 0 | 0 | 0 | 0 | .000 | .000 | .000 | | -99 | -1 | 0 | 1.000 | -0 | 73 | 0 | /OL | | -0.1 |

MEOLI, RUDY Rudolph Bartholomew B5.1.1951 Troy NY BL/TR/5-9/165* [AnaA69 4/75] d9.9

1971	Cal A	7	3	0	0	0	0	0	0	0-0	0	1	.000	.000	.000		-99	-1	0-0	—	0			/H		-0.1
1973	Cal A	120	305	36	68	12	1	2	23	31-1	0	38	.223	.290	.289	70	-12	2-4	.933	-11	90	94	S95,3b13,2b8		-1.4
1974	Cal A	36	90	9	22	2	0	0	3	8-0	0	10	.244	.306	.267	69	-3	2-4	.946	2	124	0	3b20,S8/12		-0.2
1975	Cal A	70	126	12	27	2	1	0	6	15-0	0	20	.214	.298	.246	59	-7	3-0	.976	-5	110	73	S28,3b15,2b11,D3		-0.9
1978	Chi N	47	29	10	3	0	1	0	2	6-0	0	4	.103	.257	.172	20	-3	1-0	.900	1	94	0	2b6,3b5		-0.2
1979	Phi N	30	73	2	13	4	1	0	6	9-1	0	15	.178	.268	.260	43	-6	2-0	.984	2	96	74	S16,2b15/3		-0.2
Total	6	310	626	69	133	20	4	2	40	69-2	0	88	.212	.289	.267	60	-32	10-8	.944	-11	94	91	S147,3b54,2b41,D3/1		-3.0

MERCADO, ORLANDO Orlando (Rodriguez) B11.7.1961 Arecibo, PR BR/TR/6-0/195(180-195) d9.13 C3

1982	Sea A	9	17	1	2	0	1	0	6	0-0	0	5	.118	.118	.294		8	-2	0-0	1.000	-2	82	54	C8/D		-0.4
1983	Sea A	66	178	10	35	11	2	1	16	14-0	0	27	.197	.256	.298	51	-12	2-2	.995	1	81	61	C65		-0.9
1984	Sea A	30	78	5	17	3	1	0	5	4-0	1	12	.218	.265	.282	52	-5	1-0	.992	-5	82	101	C29		-1.0
1986	Tex A	46	102	7	24	1	1	1	7	6-0	1	13	.235	.279	.294	56	-6	0-1	.996	7	81	115	C45		0.2
1987	Det A	10	22	3	3	0	0	0	1	1-0	0	4	.136	.208	.136	-6	-3	0-0	.980	1	115	79	C10		-0.2
	LA N	7	5	0	3	0	0	0	0	1-0	0	1	.600	.667	.800	294	-2	0-0	1.000	-1	206	0	C7		0.1
1988	Oak A	16	24	1	3	0	0	0	1	1-0	0	8	.125	.222	.250	33	-2	0-0	.959	-3	97	37	C16		-0.5
1989	Min A	19	38	1	4	0	0	0	4	4-0	0	4	.105	.190	.105	-14	-6	1-0	1.000	3	146	75	C19		-0.2
1990	NY N	42	90	10	19	1	0	2	7	8-3	2	11	.211	.290	.322	68	-4	0-0	.991	-4	75	47	C40		-0.7
	Mon N	8	8	0	2	0	0	0	0	0-0	0	1	.250	.250	.250	39	-1	0-0	1.000	-0	49	84	C8		-0.1
	Year	50	98	10	21	1	0	2	7	8-3	2	12	.214	.287	.316	66	-5	0-0	.992	-4	72	51	C48		-0.8
Total	8	253	562	40	112	17	4	4	45	32-3	2	82	.199	.259	.281	48	-39	4-3	.993	-3	88	74	C247/D		-3.7

MERCED, ORLANDO Orlando Luis (Villanueva) B11.2.1966 Hato Rey, PR BL/TR (BB 1990-92)/5-11/183(170-195) d6.27

1990	Pit N	25	24	3	5	1	0	0	0	9	.208	.240	.250	36	-2	0-0	—	-0	0	0	/COR		-0.2
1991	†Pit N	120	411	83	113	17	2	10	50	64-4	1	81	.275	.373	.399	119	13	8-4	.988	-4	90	100	1b105,O7R		0.2
1992	†Pit N	134	405	50	100	28	5	6	60	52-8	2	63	.247	.332	.385	104	3	5-3	.995	2	107	111	1b114,O17R		-0.3
1993	Pit N	137	447	68	140	26	4	8	70	77-10	1	64	.313	.414	.443	130	24	3-3	.965	8	114	158	O109R,1b42		2.4

YEAR	TM LG	G	AB	R	H	2B	3B	HR	RBI	BB-IB	HP	SO	AVG	OBP	SLG	AOPS	ABR	SB-CS	FA	FR	RNG	THR	GAMES AT POSITION	DL	BFW
1994	Pit N	108	386	48	105	21	3	9	51	42-5	1	58	.272	.343	.412	95	-3	4-1	.981	-5	87	71	O68R,1b55		-1.4
1995	Pit N	132	487	75	146	29	4	15	83	52-9	1	74	.300	.365	.468	116	12	7-2	.976	2	101	109	O107(4/0/104),1b35		0.7
1996	Pit N	120	453	69	130	24	1	17	80	51-5	0	74	.287	.357	.457	109	7	8-4	.988	10	107	179	O115R/1	47	1.1
1997	Tor A	98	368	45	98	23	2	9	40	47-1	1	62	.266	.352	.413	99	1	7-3	.985	5	103	169	O96R/1D	61	0.1
1998	Min A	63	204	22	59	12	0	5	33	17-3	1	29	.289	.345	.422	96	-1	1-4	.982	-0	94	115	1b38,O13R,D8		-0.6
	Bos A	9	9	0	0	0	0	0	2	2-0	0	3	.000	.167	.000	-46	-2	0-0	1.000	0	297	0	/ORD		-0.2
	Year	72	213	22	59	12	0	5	35	19-3	1	32	.277	.336	.404	90	-3	1-4	.982	-0	94	115	1b38,O14R,D9		-0.8
	Chi N	12	10	2	3	0	0	1	5	1-0	0	2	.300	.333	.600	143	1	0-0	1.000	0	201	0	O4L		0.1
1999	Mon N	93	194	25	52	12	1	8	26	26-0	0	27	.268	.353	.464	109	3	2-1	.962	2	108	141	O44L,1b7,D2	27	0.3
2001	†Hou N	94	137	19	36	6	1	6	29	14-1	1	32	.263	.333	.453	94	-1	5-1	.975	-1	98	76	O31(11/0/21),3b2/1	19	-0.2
2002	Hou N	123	251	35	72	13	3	6	30	26-5	0	50	.287	.350	.434	101	0	4-0	.980	5	108	251	O56(20/0/44),1b7/3D		0.3
2003	Hou N	123	212	20	49	17	2	3	26	15-2	1	33	.231	.283	.373	66	-11	3-2	.959	2	106	293	O31(10/0/21),1b12,3b2,D7		-1.0
Total	13	1391	3998	564	1108	229	28	103	585	487-53	12	661	.277	.355	.426	106	44	57-29	.978	26	104	157	O700(93/0/617),1b418,D20,3b5/C	154	1.3

MERCEDES, HENRY Henry Felipe (Perez) B7.23.1969 Santo Domingo, D.R. BR/TR/6-1/210(185-210) d4.22

YEAR	TM LG	G	AB	R	H	2B	3B	HR	RBI	BB-IB	HP	SO	AVG	OBP	SLG	AOPS	ABR	SB-CS	FA	FR	RNG	THR	GAMES AT POSITION	DL	BFW
1992	Oak A	9	5	1	4	0	1	0	1	0-0	0	1	.800	.800	1.200	476	2	0-0	.875	-1	41	0	C9		0.1
1993	Oak A	20	47	5	10	2	0	0	3	2-0	1	15	.213	.260	.255	41	-4	1-1	.987	-1	180	155	C18/D		-0.4
1995	KC A	23	43	7	11	2	0	0	9	8-0	1	13	.256	.370	.302	80	-1	0-0	.986	-4	92	90	C22		-0.4
1996	KC A	4	4	1	1	0	0	0	0	0-0	0	1	.250	.250	.250	27	0	0-0	1.000	-1	67	0	C4		-0.1
1997	Tex A	23	47	4	10	4	0	0	4	6-0	0	25	.213	.302	.298	54	-3	0-0	.988	-3	92	21	C23		-0.5
Total	5	79	146	18	36	8	1	0	17	16-0	2	55	.247	.325	.315	70	-6	1-1	.983	-11	115	82	C76/D		-1.3

MERCEDES, LUIS Luis Roberto (Santana) B2.15.1968 San Pedro de Macoris, D.R. BR/TR/6-0/180(180-193) d9.8

YEAR	TM LG	G	AB	R	H	2B	3B	HR	RBI	BB-IB	HP	SO	AVG	OBP	SLG	AOPS	ABR	SB-CS	FA	FR	RNG	THR	GAMES AT POSITION	DL	BFW
1991	Bal A	19	54	10	11	2	0	0	9	2-0	0	9	.204	.259	.241	40	-4	0-0	.982	-2	74	0	O15(13/0/3)/D		-0.7
1992	Bal A	23	50	7	7	2	0	0	4	8-0	1	9	.140	.267	.180	28	-5	0-1	.956	3	146	219	O16(1/2/13),D7		-0.2
1993	Bal A	10	24	1	7	2	0	0	5	0-0	0	5	.292	.414	.375	108	1	1-1	1.000	-0	68	172	O8R,D2		0.0
	SF N	18	25	1	4	0	1	0	3	1-0	2	3	.160	.250	.240	33	-3	0-1	1.000	-1	52	0	O5(1/3/1)		-0.4
Total	3	70	153	19	29	6	1	0	18	10-0	3	25	.190	.286	.242	47	-11	1-3	.976	-0	96	112	O44(15/5/25),D10		-1.3

MERCER, WIN George Barclay B6.20.1874 Chester WV D1.12.1903 San Francisco CA BR/TR/5-7/140 d4.21 OF(21/25/30) ▲

YEAR	TM LG	G	AB	R	H	2B	3B	HR	RBI	BB-IB	HP	SO	AVG	OBP	SLG	AOPS	ABR	SB-CS	FA	FR	RNG	THR	GAMES AT POSITION	DL	BFW
1894	Was N	53	165	29	48	5	2	2	29	9	0	20	.291	.328	.382	73	-8	9	.944	1	108	40	P50,O4R		0.0
1895	Was N	64	201	26	51	9	1	1	26	12	3	33	.254	.306	.323	63	-11	7	.874	-6	82	74	P44,S7,O6(1/0/5),3b3/2		-0.7
1896	Was N	49	156	23	38	1	1	1	14	9	4	18	.244	.302	.282	54	-11	9	.856	0	98	86	P46/OC		0.0
1897	Was N	50	139	23	44	2	5	0	19	6	2		.317	.354	.403	100	8	7	.858	-2	88	149	P47		0.0
1898	Was N	80	249	38	80	3	5	2	25	18	1		.321	.369	.398	120	6	14	.863	-6	85	96	P33,S23,O19(2/17/0),3b5/2		-0.1
1899	Was N	108	375	73	112	6	7	1	35	32	4		.299	.360	.360	99	-1	16	.846	-10	78	68	3b62,P23,O16(15/0/1)/S1		-1.1
1900	NY N	76	248	32	73	4	0	0	27	26	2		.294	.366	.310	92	-1	15	.931	0	110	159	P33,3b19,O14R,S7,2b3		-0.1
1901	Was N	51	140	26	42	7	2	0	16	23	1		.300	.402	.379	119	5	10	.944	-1	97	58	P24,O16(3/7/6),1b7/S3		0.1
1902	Det A	35	100	8	18	2	0	0	6	6	0		.180	.226	.200	19	-2	1	.935	3	125	66	P35		-0.1
Total	9	566	1773	278	506	39	23	7	197	141	17	71	.285	.344	.345	87	-15	88	.903	-19	101	89	P335,3b90,O76R,S39,1b8,2b5		-1.9

MERCER, JOHN John Locke B6.22.1892 Taylortown LA D12.22.1982 Shreveport LA BL/TL/5-10.5/155 d6.25 Col Louisiana St.

YEAR	TM LG	G	AB	R	H	2B	3B	HR	RBI	BB-IB	HP	SO	AVG	OBP	SLG	AOPS	ABR	SB-CS	FA	FR	RNG	THR	GAMES AT POSITION	DL	BFW
1912	StL N	1	0	0	0	0	0	0	0	0	0	0	.000	.000	.000	-99	0	0	.500	-0	0	0	/1		-0.1

MERCHANT, ANDY James Anderson B8.30.1950 Mobile AL BL/TR/5-11/190* [BosA72 10/232] d9.28 Col Auburn-Montgomery

YEAR	TM LG	G	AB	R	H	2B	3B	HR	RBI	BB-IB	HP	SO	AVG	OBP	SLG	AOPS	ABR	SB-CS	FA	FR	RNG	THR	GAMES AT POSITION	DL	BFW
1975	Bos A	1	4	1	2	0	0	0	0	1-0	0	1	.500	.600	.500	197	1	0-0	1.000	-1	73	232	/C		0.0
1976	Bos A	2	2	0	0	0	0	0	0	0-0	0	2	.000	.000	.000	-90	0	0-0	1.000	0	0	0	/C		0.0
Total	2	3	6	1	2	0	0	0	0	1-0	0	3	.333	.429	.333	110	1	0-0	1.000	-0	66	209	C2		0.0

MEREWETHER, ART Arthur Francis "Merry" B7.7.1902 E.Providence RI D2.2.1997 Bayside NY BR/TR/5-9.5/155 d7.10 Col Brown

YEAR	TM LG	G	AB	R	H	2B	3B	HR	RBI	BB-IB	HP	SO	AVG	OBP	SLG	AOPS	ABR	SB-CS	FA	FR	RNG	THR	GAMES AT POSITION	DL	BFW
1922	Pit N	1	1	0	0	0	0	0	0	0	0	0	.000	.000	.000	-99	0	0-0	—	—			/H		0.0

MERKLE, FRED Frederick Charles (b Carl Frederick Rudolf Merkle) B12.20.1888 Watertown WI D3.2.1956 Daytona Beach FL BR/TR/6-1/190 d9.21 C2

YEAR	TM LG	G	AB	R	H	2B	3B	HR	RBI	BB-IB	HP	SO	AVG	OBP	SLG	AOPS	ABR	SB-CS	FA	FR	RNG	THR	GAMES AT POSITION	DL	BFW
1907	NY N	15	47	0	12	1	0	0	5	1	0		.255	.271	.277	69	-2	0	.949	-1	88	65	1b15		-0.4
1908	NY N	38	41	6	11	2	1	1	7	4	0		.268	.333	.439	140	2	0	1.000	-1	33	106	1b11,O5(2/0/3)/23		0.1
1909	NY N	79	236	15	45	9	1	0	20	16	1		.191	.245	.237	49	-14	8	.976	-3	82	105	1b70/0		-2.1
1910	NY N	144	506	75	148	35	14	4	70	44	3	59	.292	.353	.441	131	18	23	.981	1	103	111	1b144		1.7
1911	†NY N	149	541	80	153	24	10	12	84	43	6	60	.283	.342	.431	112	6	49	.985	16	**143**	101	1b148		1.8
1912	†NY N	129	479	82	148	22	6	11	84	42	8	70	.309	.374	.449	121	13	37	.980	-1	101	122	1b129		0.9
1913	NY N	153	563	78	147	30	12	3	69	41	3	60	.261	.315	.373	95	-5	35-18	.986	-4	88	121	1b153		-1.2
1914	NY N	146	512	71	132	25	7	7	63	52	1	80	.258	.327	.375	112	8	23	.990	4	110	114	1b146		0.8
1915	NY N	140	505	52	151	25	3	4	62	36	2	39	.299	.348	.384	129	17	20-15	.989	-2	88	101	1b110,O30(0/27/5)		1.1
1916	NY N	112	401	45	95	19	3	7	44	33	8	46	.237	.308	.352	108	4	17	.984	0	103	103	1b112		0.2
	†Bro N	23	69	6	16	1	0	0	2	7	1	4	.232	.312	.246	70	-2	2	.992	-1	60	43	1b15,O4(3/1/0)		-0.4
	Year	135	470	51	111	20	3	7	46	40	9	50	.236	.308	.336	102	2	19	.985	-0	98	97	1b127,O4(3/1/0)		-0.2
1917	Bro N	2	8	1	1	0	0	0	0	2	1		.125	.125	.250	13	-1	0	1.000	0	86	76	1b2		-0.1
	Chi N	146	549	65	146	30	9	3	57	57	4	60	.266	.323	.370	104	3	13	.983	-4	86	96	1b140,O6(5/1/0)		-0.5
	Year	148	557	66	147	31	9	3	57	42	4	61	.264	.320	.368	103	2	13	.983	-4	86	96	1b142,O6(5/1/0)		-0.6
1918	†Chi N	129	482	55	143	25	6	3	65	35	4	36	.297	.349	.388	122	13	21	.990	1	100	98	1b129		1.2
1919	Chi N	133	498	52	133	20	6	3	62	33	2	35	.267	.315	.349	99	-1	20	.985	-10	71	98	1b132/2		-1.6
1920	Chi N	92	330	33	94	20	4	3	38	24	1	32	.285	.335	.397	108	3	3-5	.985	1	105	89	1b85/OL		0.1
1925	NY A	7	13	4	5	1	0	0	1	1	0	1	.385	.429	.462	128	1	1-0	1.000	-0	48	124	1b5		0.0
1926	NY A	1	2	0	0	0	0	0	0	0	0	0	.000	.000	.000	-99	-1	0-0	1.000	-0	0	0	/		-0.1
Total	16	1638	5782	720	1580	290	81	61	733	454	44	583	.273	.331	.383	109	62	272-38	.985	-5	98	105	1b1547,O46(11/29/8),2b3/3		1.5

MERLONI, LOU Louis William B4.6.1971 Framingham MA BR/TR/5-10/200* [BosA93 10/275] d5.10 Col Providence OF(9/0/1)

YEAR	TM LG	G	AB	R	H	2B	3B	HR	RBI	BB-IB	HP	SO	AVG	OBP	SLG	AOPS	ABR	SB-CS	FA	FR	RNG	THR	GAMES AT POSITION	DL	BFW
1998	Bos A	39	96	10	27	6	0	1	15	7-1	2	20	.281	.343	.375	85	-2	1-0	.974	-2	94	72	2b32,3b5/S	75	-0.2
1999	†Bos A	43	126	18	32	7	0	1	13	8-0	2	16	.254	.307	.333	62	-7	0-0	.956	2	94	105	S24,3b9,2b8/1OLD		-0.3
2000	Bos A	40	128	10	41	11	2	0	18	4-1	0	22	.320	.341	.438	94	-1	0-0	.928	0	100	53	3b40		-0.1
2001	Bos A	52	146	21	39	10	0	3	13	6-0	3	31	.267	.306	.397	84	-3	2-1	.987	1	97	81	S45,2b5/3	15	0.1
2002	Bos A	84	194	28	48	12	2	4	18	20-0	5	35	.247	.332	.392	90	-2	1-2	.988	4	94	92	2b66,3b8,S5,1b3,O2(1/0/1)		0.4
2003	SD N	65	151	20	41	7	2	1	17	22-2	1	33	.272	.362	.364	101	1	2-3	.925	1	104	66	3b25,S23,2b10,1b2,O2L	26	0.3
	Bos A	15	30	4	7	1	0	0	1	4-0	0	8	.233	.324	.267	56	-2	0-0	1.000	1	53	148	2b7,3b7/OL		0.0
2004	Cle A	71	190	25	55	12	1	4	28	14-1	1	41	.289	.343	.426	104	1	1-2	.997	-1	64	62	1b42,3b10,2b7,O4L,D3	23	-0.3
2005	LA A	5	6	1	0	0	0	0	0	1-0	0	2	.000	.143	.000	-51	-1	0-0	1.000	2	220	0	3b4/1	154	0.0
Total	8	414	1066	137	290	66	7	14	124	86-5	17	208	.272	.332	.386	88	-16	8-8	.977	9	94	90	2b135,3b109,S98,1b49,O10L,D6	293	-0.1

MERRILL, ED Edward Mason B5.22.1860 Maysville KY D1.29.1946 Elmwood Park IL 5-11/176 d5.5

YEAR	TM LG	G	AB	R	H	2B	3B	HR	RBI	BB-IB	HP	SO	AVG	OBP	SLG	AOPS	ABR	SB-CS	FA	FR	RNG	THR	GAMES AT POSITION	DL	BFW
1882	Lou AA	1	0	0	0	0	0	0	0	0	0						-0		—	-0	0	0	/OC		0.0
	Wor N	2	8	0	1	0	0	0	0	0	0		.125	.125	.125	-19	-1		.714	-0	112	0	3b2		-0.1
1884	Ind AA	55	196	14	35	3	1	0		6		1	.179	.207	.204	35	-13		.900	-3	96	60	2b55		-1.4
Total	2	58	204	14	36	3	1	0	0	6		1	.176	.204	.201	33	-14		.900	-4	96	60	2b55,3b2/OC		-1.5

MERRIMAN, LLOYD Lloyd Archer "Citation" B8.2.1924 Clovis CA D1.20.2004 Fresno CA BL/TL/6-0/195* d4.24 Mil 1952-53 Col Stanford

YEAR	TM LG	G	AB	R	H	2B	3B	HR	RBI	BB-IB	HP	SO	AVG	OBP	SLG	AOPS	ABR	SB-CS	FA	FR	RNG	THR	GAMES AT POSITION	DL	BFW
1949	Cin N	103	287	35	66	12	5	4	26	21	1	36	.230	.285	.348	68	-14	2	.969	1	102	128	O86C		-1.5
1950	Cin N	92	298	44	77	15	2	9	31	30	2	23	.258	.330	.349	79	-9	6	.989	-4	93	65	O84(2/81/1)		-1.5
1951	Cin N	114	359	34	87	23	2	5	36	31	0	34	.242	.303	.359	76	-12	8-4	.997	6	117	55	O102(31/76/0)		-1.0
1954	Cin N	73	112	12	30	8	1	0	16	23	3	10	.268	.397	.357	98	1	3-0	.981	-0	112	0	O25(9/0/16)		0.1
1955	Chi A	1	0	0	0	0	0	0	0	0-0	0	0	.000	.000	.000	-97	0	0-0	—	—			/H		0.0
	Chi N	72	145	15	31	6	1	1	8	21-0	0	21	.214	.311	.290	62	-8	1-0	.977	-1	95	73	O47(8/36/3)		-1.0
Total	5	455	1202	140	291	64	12	12	117	126-0	6	124	.242	.316	.345	75	-42	20-4	.985	2	105	73	O344(50/279/20)		-4.9

MERRITT, GEORGE George Washington B4.14.1880 Paterson NJ D2.21.1938 Memphis TN TR/6-0/160 d9.6

YEAR	TM LG	G	AB	R	H	2B	3B	HR	RBI	BB-IB	HP	SO	AVG	OBP	SLG	AOPS	ABR	SB-CS	FA	FR	RNG	THR	GAMES AT POSITION	DL	BFW
1901	Pit N	4	11	2	3	0	1	0	5	2	0	0	.273	.385	.455	139	1	0	1.000	-0	82	0	P3		0.0
1902	Pit N	2	9	2	3	1	0	0	2	0	0		.333	.333	.444	135	0	0	1.000	1	297	0	O2L		0.1
1903	Pit N	9	27	4	4	0	1	0	3	2	1		.148	.233	.222	29	-3	1	.889	-1	93	0	O7(1/0/6)/P		-0.4
Total	3	15	47	8	10	1	2	0	10	5	2	3	.213	.288	.319	74	-2	1	.929	-1	93	0	O9(3/0/6),P4		-0.3

YEAR	TM LG	G	AB	R	H	2B	3B	HR	RBI	BB-IB	HP	SO	AVG	OBP	SLG	AOPS	ABR	SB-CS	FA	FR	RNG	THR	GAMES AT POSITION	DL	BFW

MERRITT, HERM Herman G. B11.12.1900 Independence KS D5.26.1927 Kansas City MO BR/TR d8.24
| 1921 | Det A | 20 | 46 | 3 | 17 | 1 | 2 | 0 | 6 | 1 | | 5 | .370 | .396 | .478 | 123 | 1 | 1-0 | .882 | -5 | 64 | 0 | S17 | | -0.3 |

MERRITT, JOHN John Howard B10.12.1894 Tupelo MS D11.3.1955 Tupelo MS BR/TL/5-11/170 d9.27
| 1913 | NY N | 1 | 0 | 0 | 0 | 0 | 0 | 0 | 0 | 0 | 0 | 0 | — | — | — | | 0 | 0 | — | -0 | 0 | 0 | /OR | | 0.0 |

MERRITT, BILL William Henry B7.30.1870 Lowell MA D11.17.1937 Lowell MA BR/TR/5-7/160 d8.8 Col Holy Cross
1891	Chi N	11	42	4	9	1	0	0	4	2		2	.214	.250	.238	42	-3	0	.955	-1	131	109	C11/1		-0.3
1892	Lou N	46	168	22	33	4	2	1	13	11		15	.196	.246	.262	58	-9	3	.940	-5	89	105	C46		-0.9
1893	Bos N	39	141	30	49	6	3	3	26	13		13	.348	.403	.496	128	5	3	.945	0	131	56	C37,O2L		0.7
1894	Bos N	10	26	3	6	1	0	0	6	8		0	.231	.412	.269	62	-1	0	.881	1	118	89	C8,OC		0.0
	Pit N	36	109	18	30	1	2	1	18	15		7	.275	.363	.349	73	-5	2	.952	0	102	130	C28,1b4,O2L		-0.2
	Cin N	30	117	17	38	6	1	1	22	10		2	.325	.388	.419	91	-2	4	.956	-1	99	115	C25,3b3/1OR		0.0
	Year	76	252	38	74	8	3	2	46	33		10	.294	.380	.373	80	-7	6	.942	0	103	118	C61,1b5,O4(2/1/1),3b3		-0.2
1895	Cin N	22	79	9	14	2	0	0	12	6		5	.177	.235	.203	13	-11	2	.955	0	103	100	C20/2		-0.7
	Pit N	67	239	32	68	5	1	0	27	18		16	.285	.340	.314	73	-9	2	.935	-7	88	93	C63,1b2		-0.8
	Year	89	318	41	82	7	1	0	39	24		21	.258	.314	.286	57	-20	4	.939	-6	92	95	C83,1b2/2		-1.5
1896	Pit N	77	282	26	82	8	2	1	42	18	1	10	.291	.336	.344	83	-7	3	.941	-6	84	121	C62,3b5,2b3,1b3,S2		-0.6
1897	Pit N	62	209	21	55	6	1	1	26	9	1		.263	.297	.316	64	-11	2	.946	-8	83	79	C53,1b7		-1.3
1899	Bos N	1	2	0	0	0	0	0	0	0	1		.000	.333	.000	-5	0	0	1.000	0	120	211	/C		0.0
Total	8	401	1414	182	384	40	13	8	196	110	7	71	.272	.327	.334	75	-53	21	.942	-25	96	99	C354,1b18,3b8,O6(4/1/1),2b4,S2		-4.1

MERSON, JACK John Warren B1.17.1922 Elkridge MD D4.28.2000 Elkridge MD BR/TR/5-11/175* d9.14
1951	Pit N	13	50	6	18	2	1	1	14	1		7	.360	.373	.540	138	2	0-0	.987	2	122	64	2b13		0.5
1952	Pit N	111	398	41	98	20	2	5	38	22	1	38	.246	.287	.344	72	-15	1-1	.978	-0	99	107	2b81,3b27		-1.2
1953	Bos A	1	4	0	0	0	0	0	0	0		0	.000	.000	.000	-95	-1	0-0	.875	0	127	0	/2		-0.1
Total	3	125	452	47	116	22	4	6	52	23	1	45	.257	.294	.363	78	-14	1-1	.978	2	103	99	2b95,3b27		-0.8

MERTES, SAM Samuel Blair "Sandow" B8.6.1872 San Francisco CA D3.11.1945 San Francisco CA BR/TR/6-0/225 d6.30 OF(687/182/110)
1896	Phi N	37	143	20	34	4	4	0	14	8	2	10	.238	.288	.322	61	-9	19	.907	-1	64	0	O35(1/33/1)/S2		-1.0
1898	Chi N	83	269	45	80	4	8	1	47	34	6		.297	.388	.383	121	8	27	.880	0	149	308	O60(4/5/53),S14,2b4,1b2		0.6
1899	Chi N	117	426	83	127	13	16	9	81	33			.298	.349	.467	126	12	45	.923	-2	121	93	O108(16/47/46),1b3/S		0.3
1900	Chi N	127	481	72	142	25	4	7	60	42	3		.295	.356	.407	114	10	38	.923	-4	112	133	O88(10/78/0),1b33,S7		0.0
1901	Chi A	137	545	94	151	16	17	5	98	52	6		.277	.347	.396	108	6	46	.940	-10	94	101	2b132,O5L		-0.3
1902	Chi A	129	497	60	140	23	7	1	79	37	2		.282	.334	.362	97	-2	46	.922	3	**160**	158	O120(111/0/9),S5,C2/P123		-0.5
1903	NY N	138	517	100	145	**32**	14	7	**104**	61	3		.280	.360	.437	122	15	45	**.973**	8	126	117	O137L/C1		1.4
1904	NY N	148	532	83	147	28	11	4	78	54	3		.276	.346	.393	123	15	47	.956	-2	90	21	O147(130/17/0)/S		0.5
1905	†NY N	150	551	81	154	27	17	5	108	56	5		.279	.351	.417	126	17	52	.960	-9	51	73	O150(149/2/0)		-0.1
1906	NY N	71	253	37	60	9	6	1	33	29	3		.237	.323	.332	102	1	21	.970	0	107	0	O71(71/0/1)		-0.4
	StL N	53	191	20	47	7	4	0	19	16			.246	.304	.325	100	0	10	.890	-5	63	0	O53L		-0.9
	Year	124	444	57	107	16	10	1	52	45	3		.241	.315	.329	101	0	31	.938	-5	89	0	O124(124/0/1)		-1.3
Total	10	1190	4405	695	1227	188	108	40	721	422	33	10	.279	.346	.398	114	73	396	.938	-22	105	92	O974L,2b138,1b40,S29,C3/3P		-0.4

MERULLO, LENNIE Leonard Richard B5.5.1917 Boston MA BR/TR/5-11/168 d9.12 gs-Matt Col Villanova
1941	Chi N	7	17	3	6	1	0	0	1	2	0	0	.353	.421	.412	140	1	1	.968	1	107	156	S7		0.3
1942	Chi N	143	515	53	132	23	3	2	37	35	5	45	.256	.310	.324	89	-8	14	.946	-1	102	93	S143		0.2
1943	Chi N	129	453	37	115	18	5	1	25	26	2	42	.254	.297	.313	78	-14	7	.940	-6	100	97	S125		-1.1
1944	Chi N	66	193	20	41	8	1	1	16	16	1	18	.212	.276	.280	57	-11	3	.937	1	101	86	S56/1		-0.6
1945	†Chi N	121	394	40	94	18	0	2	37	31	2	30	.239	.297	.299	68	-17	7	.948	1	99	96	S118		-0.8
1946	Chi N	65	126	14	19	8	0	0	7	11		13	.151	.219	.214	24	-13	2	.946	8	117	106	S116		-0.2
1947	Chi N	108	373	24	90	16	1	0	29	15	2	26	.241	.274	.290	52	-27	4	.949	6	101	116	S108		-1.4
Total	7	639	2071	191	497	92	8	6	152	136	12	174	.240	.291	.301	69	-89	38	.945	12	102	99	S601/1		-3.6

MERULLO, MATT Matthew Bates B8.4.1965 Winchester MA BL/TR/6-2/200* [ChiA86 7/179] d4.12 gf-Lennie Col North Carolina-Asheville
1989	Chi A	31	81	5	18	1	0	1	8	6-0	0	14	.222	.273	.272	56	-5	0-1	.973	-4	78	45	C27/D		-0.9
1991	Chi A	80	140	8	32	1	0	5	21	9-1	0	18	.229	.268	.343	71	-6	0-0	.989	-3	64	163	C27,1b16,D6		-0.9
1992	Chi A	24	50	3	9	1	0	0	3	1-0	1	8	.180	.208	.240	26	-5	0-0	.971	-2	88	66	C16/D		-0.7
1993	Chi A	8	20	1	1	0	0	0	0	0-0	0	1	.050	.050	.050	-74	-5	0-0	—	0			D6		-0.5
1994	Cle A	4	10	1	1	0	0	0	0	2-0	0	1	.100	.250	.100	-5	-2	0-0	.957	-2	35	0	C4		-0.3
1995	Min A	76	195	19	55	14	1	1	27	14-0	3	27	.282	.335	.379	86	-4	0-1	.987	-10	67	47	C46,D13,1b2		-1.1
Total	6	223	496	37	116	17	2	7	59	32-1	4	69	.234	.281	.319	64	-27	0-2	.981	-21	71	67	C120,D27,1b18		-4.4

MESNER, STEVE Stephan Mathias B1.13.1918 Los Angeles CA D4.6.1981 San Diego CA BR/TR/5-9/178 d9.23
1938	Chi N	2	4	2	1	0	0	0	1				.250	.400	.250	80	0	1-0	.667	-1	80	0	/S		-0.1
1939	Chi N	17	43	7	12	4	0	0	6	3	1	4	.279	.340	.372	90	0	0-0	.927	1	124	109	S12/23		0.2
1941	StL N	24	69	8	10	1	0	0	10	5	0	6	.145	.203	.159	3	-9	0-0	.958	3	108	246	3b22		-0.6
1943	Cin N	137	504	53	137	26	1	0	52	26		20	.272	.309	.327	85	-10	6	.944	-1	102	130	3b130		-1.0
1944	Cin N	121	414	31	100	17	4	1	47	34	1	20	.242	.301	.309	75	-14	1	.951	-8	**99**	**120**	3b120		-2.2
1945	Cin N	150	540	52	137	19	1	1	52	52	2	18	.254	.322	.298	74	-18	4	.971	15	**113**	127	3b148,2b3		-0.1
Total	6	451	1574	153	397	67	6	2	167	121	5	69	.252	.308	.306	75	-51	11	.956	10	105	131	3b421,S13,2b4		-3.8

MESSENGER, BOBBY Charles Walter B3.19.1884 Bangor ME D7.10.1951 Bath ME BB/TR/5-10.5/165 d8.30
1909	Chi A	31	112	18	19	1	1	0	13		2		.170	.268	.196	49	-6	7	.950	-2	102	126	O31R		-1.0
1910	Chi A	9	26	7	6	0	1	0	4	4	2		.231	.375	.308	119	1	3	.846	-0	66	190	O8L		0.0
1911	Chi A	13	17	4	2	0	1	0	0	3			.118	.250	.235	37	-2	0	.875	-1	97	0	O4L		-0.2
1914	StL A	1	2	0	0	0	0	0	0	0			.000	.000	.000	-99	-1	0	—	0	0	0	/OR		-0.1
Total	4	54	157	29	27	1	3	0	4	20	4	0	.172	.282	.217	57	-8	10	.918	-3	94	126	O44(12/0/32)		-1.3

MESSITT, JACK Thomas John B7.27.1874 Philadelphia PA D9.22.1934 Chicago IL 5-9/177 d9.14
| 1899 | Lou N | 3 | 11 | 0 | 1 | 0 | 0 | 0 | 0 | 0 | 0 | | .091 | .091 | .091 | -50 | -2 | 0 | 1.000 | 1 | 134 | 219 | C3 | | -0.1 |

METCALFE, AL Alfred Tristram B12.31.1852 Brooklyn NY D9.2.1914 Brooklyn NY d5.27
| 1875 | Mut NA | 8 | 32 | 2 | 7 | 0 | 0 | 0 | | | | | .219 | .219 | .219 | 50 | -2 | 2-0 | .667 | -1 | 113 | | 3b5,O2R/S | | -0.2 |

METCALFE, MIKE Michael Henry B1.2.1973 Quantico VA BR/TR/5-10/175* [LAN94 3/76] d9.18 Col Miami
1998	LA N	4	1	0	0	0	0	0	0	0-0	0	1	.000	.000	.000	-99	-0	2-0	—	-0	0	0	/2		0.0
2000	LA N	4	12	1	1	0	0	0	0	1-0	0	2	.083	.154	.083	-44	-3	0-0	1.000	-1	115	0	O4(3/1/0),2		-0.3
Total	2	8	13	1	1	0	0	0	0	1-0	0	3	.077	.143	.077	-44	-3	2-0	1.000	-1	115	0	O4(3/1/0),2b2		-0.3

METHA, SCAT Frank Joseph B12.13.1913 Los Angeles CA D3.2.1975 Fountain Valley CA BR/TR/5-11/165 d4.22
| 1940 | Det A | 26 | 37 | 6 | 9 | 0 | 1 | 0 | 3 | 2 | | 8 | .243 | .282 | .297 | 46 | -3 | 0-1 | .960 | 2 | 113 | 101 | 2b10,3b6 | | -0.1 |

METHENY, BUD Arthur Beauregard B6.1.1915 St.Louis MO D1.2.2003 Virginia Beach VA BL/TL/5-11/190 d4.27 Col William and Mary
1943	†NY A	103	360	51	94	18	2	9	36	39	0	34	.261	.333	.397	113	5	2-3	.963	-9	88	16	O91R		-1.1
1944	NY A	137	518	72	124	16	1	14	67	56		89	.239	.316	.355	89	-8	5-5	.956	-7	90	90	O132(11/0/121)		-2.5
1945	NY A	133	509	64	126	18	2	8	53	54	4	31	.248	.325	.338	88	-7	5-2	.984	-6	90	94	O128R		-2.2
1946	NY A	3	3	0	0	0	0	0	0	0		0	.000	.000	.000	-99	-1	0-0	—	0			/H		-0.1
Total	4	376	1390	187	344	52	5	31	156	149	6	122	.247	.323	.359	94	-11	12-10	.968	-22	89	72	O351(11/0/340)		-5.9

METKOVICH, CATFISH George Michael B10.8.1920 Angels Camp CA D5.17.1995 Costa Mesa CA BL/TL/6-1/185* d7.16
1943	Bos A	78	321	34	79	14	4	5	27	19	3	38	.246	.294	.361	90	-6	1-3	.955	-3	92	100	O76(0/54/25),1b2		-1.4
1944	Bos A	134	549	94	152	28	8	9	59	31	3	57	.277	.319	.406	108	3	13-4	.962	0	102	97	O82(0/81/3),1b50		-0.1
1945	Bos A	138	539	65	140	26	3	6	62	51	6	70	.260	.331	.347	94	-3	19-6	.985	-3	101	108	1b97,O42(0/29/14)		-1.2
1946	†Bos A	86	281	42	69	15	2	4	25	36	1	39	.246	.331	.356	88	-4	8-3	.948	-7	88	14	O81(6/2/73)		-1.3
1947	Cle A	126	473	68	120	22	7	5	40	37	1	51	.254	.302	.362	86	-11	5-3	.989	-3	101	24	O119(0/119/2)/1		-1.8
1949	Chi A	93	338	50	80	9	4	5	45	41	1	24	.237	.321	.331	75	-13	5-4	.968	-8	94	17	O87(9/79/1)		-2.4
1951	Pit N	120	423	51	124	21	3	6	40	28	1	23	.293	.338	.378	90	-6	3-2	.994	-5	95	68	O69(3/66/0),1b37		-1.1
1952	Pit N	125	373	41	101	18	3	7	41	32		29	.271	.338	.391	98	-6	79	102	1b72,O33(5/25/8)		-1.0

YEAR	TM LG	G	AB	R	H	2B	3B	HR	RBI	BB-IB	HP	SO	AVG	OBP	SLG	AOPS	ABR	SB-CS	FA	FR	RNG	THR	GAMES AT POSITION	DL	BFW
1953	Pit N	26	41	6	6	0	1	1	7	6	0	3	.146	.255	.268	37	-4	0-0	1.000	-1	0	44	1b5,O4(0/3/1)		-0.5
	Chi N	61	124	19	29	9	0	2	12	16	1	10	.234	.326	.355	76	-4	2-1	1.000	-1	111	44	O38(10/11/18),1b7		-0.6
	Year	87	165	24	35	9	1	3	19	22	1	13	.212	.309	.333	66	-8	2-1	1.000	-1	110	77	O42(10/14/19),1b12		-1.1
1954	Mil N	68	123	7	34	5	1	1	15	15	1	15	.276	.352	.358	94	-1	0-0	1.000	2	129	118	1b18,O13R		0.0
Total	10	1055	3585	476	934	167	36	47	373	307	22	359	.261	.322	.367	91	-50	61-28	.976	-31	97	59	O644(33/465/158),1b289		-11.4

METRO, CHARLIE   Charles (b Charles Moreskonich)   B4.28.1919 Nanty Glo PA   BR/TR/5-11.5/178   d5.4   M2/C3

1943	Det A	44	40	12	8	0	0	0	2	3	0	6	.200	.256	.200	32	-3	1-1	.966	1	139	0	O14(1/11/2)		-0.3
1944	Det A	38	78	8	15	0	1	0	5	3	0	10	.192	.222	.218	25	-8	1-1	1.000	0	106	66	O20(9/10/2)		-0.9
	Phi A	24	40	4	4	0	0	0	1	7	0	6	.100	.234	.100	-3	-5	0-0	1.000	1	117	195	O11(9/0/2),3b5,2b2		-0.5
	Year	62	118	12	19	0	1	0	6	10	0	16	.161	.227	.178	16	-13	1-1	1.000	1	109	101	O31(18/10/4),3b5,2b2		-1.4
1945	Phi A	65	200	18	42	10	1	3	15	23	0	33	.210	.291	.315	76	-6	1-1	.972	-2	90	106	O57(53/1/4)		-1.2
Total	3	171	358	42	69	10	2	3	23	36	0	55	.193	.266	.257	51	-22	3-2	.980	0	100	94	O102(72/22/10),3b5,2b2		-2.9

METZ, LENNY   Leonard Ray   B7.6.1899 Superior CO   D2.24.1953 Denver CO   BR/TR/5-10.5/170   d9.11

1923	Phi N	12	37	4	8	0	0	0	3	4	1	3	.216	.310	.216	37	-3	0-0	.969	0	75	83	2b6,S6		-0.2
1924	Phi N	7	7	1	2	0	0	0	1	1	0	0	.286	.375	.286	71	0	0-0	.846	-0	121	71	S6		0.0
1925	Phi N	11	14	1	0	0	0	0	0	0	0	0	.000	.000	.000	-92	-4	0-0	1.000	1	113	0	S9,2b2		-0.3
Total	3	30	58	6	10	0	0	0	4	5	1	3	.172	.250	.172	11	-7	0-0	.951	1	114	74	S21,2b8		-0.5

METZGER, ROGER   Roger Henry   B10.10.1947 Fredericksburg TX   BB/TR (BL 1970, 80)/6-0/165*   [ChiN69 1/16]   d6.16   Col St. Edwards

1970	Chi N	1	2	0	0	0	0	0	0	0-0	0	0	.000	.000	.000	-89	-2	0-0	.833	1	157	217	/S		0.0
1971	Hou N	150	562	64	132	14	**11**	0	26	44-4	4	50	.235	.294	.299	71	-23	15-6	.977	-4	96	100	S148		-0.9
1972	Hou N	**153**	641	84	142	12	3	2	38	60-1	1	71	.222	.288	.259	58	-35	23-9	.971	5	100	105	S153		-1.1
1973	Hou N	154	580	67	145	11	**14**	1	35	59-0	3	70	.250	.299	.322	73	-23	10-4	**.982**	-18	90	90	S149		-2.4
1974	Hou N	143	572	66	145	18	10	0	30	37-1	0	73	.253	.297	.320	76	-20	9-7	.976	-7	98	99	S143	18	-1.2
1975	Hou N	127	450	54	102	7	9	2	26	41-10	0	39	.227	.289	.296	68	-22	4-5	.977	16	**110**	104	S126		0.8
1976	Hou N	152	481	37	101	13	8	0	29	52-10	0	63	.210	.286	.270	64	-24	1-1	**.986**	0	98	97	S150,2b2		-0.6
1977	Hou N	97	269	24	50	9	6	0	16	32-3	0	24	.186	.272	.264	48	-20	2-0	.973	-9	96	93	S96/2	50	-2.0
1978	Hou N	45	123	11	27	4	1	0	6	12-3	0	9	.220	.287	.268	60	-11	0-0	.964	-4	88	97	S42/2		-0.7
	SF N	75	235	17	61	6	1	0	17	12-0	0	17	.260	.294	.294	67	-11	8-1	.974	-13	85	82	S74		-1.7
	Year	120	358	28	88	10	2	0	23	24-3	0	26	.246	.292	.285	65	-18	8-1	.970	-17	86	87	S116/2		-2.4
1979	SF N	94	259	24	65	7	8	0	31	23-2	0	31	.251	.311	.340	84	-7	11-3	.956	-1	98	80	S78,2b10/3		0.1
1980	SF N	28	27	5	2	0	0	0	0	3-0	0	2	.074	.167	.074	-32	-5	0-0	.971	-3	73	84	S13/2		-0.7
Total	11	1219	4201	453	972	101	71	5	254	355-34	8	449	.231	.291	.293	67	-198	83-36	.976	-38	97	96	S1173,2b15/3	68	-10.4

METZIG, WILLIAM   William Andrew   B12.4.1918 Ft.Dodge IA   BR/TR/6-1/180   d9.19   Mil 1945

1944	Chi A	5	16	1	2	0	0	0	1	1-0	0	4	.125	.176	.125	-13	-2	0-0	1.000	1	118	65	2b5		-0.1

METZLER, ALEX   Alexander   B1.4.1903 Fresno CA   D11.30.1973 Fresno CA   BL/TR/5-9/167   d9.16

1925	Chi A	9	38	2	7	2	0	0	2	3	0	7	.184	.244	.237	23	-4	0-0	1.000	2	96	351	O9C		-0.3
1926	Phi A	20	67	8	16	3	0	0	12	7	0	5	.239	.311	.284	53	-5	1-0	1.000	1	97	180	O17(15/1/1)		-0.4
1927	Chi A	134	543	87	173	29	11	3	61	61	9	39	.319	.396	.429	117	15	15-11	.965	7	109	111	O134(0/133/4)		1.5
1928	Chi A	139	464	71	141	18	14	3	55	77	6	30	.304	.410	.422	121	17	15-8	.968	-1	102	84	O134(50/43/46)		0.8
1929	Chi A	146	568	80	156	23	13	2	49	80	3	45	.275	.367	.371	92	-5	9-5	.960	-5	92	103	O142(132/10/0)		-2.0
1930	Chi A	56	79	12	14	4	0	0	5	11	0	6	.177	.278	.228	31	-8	0-2	.969	-0	99	85	O27(21/1/5)		-0.9
	StL A	56	209	30	54	6	3	1	23	21	0	12	.258	.326	.330	65	-11	5-1	.951	-6	85	46	O56(1/36/19)		-1.8
	Year	112	288	42	68	10	3	1	28	32	0	18	.236	.313	.302	57	-19	5-3	.955	-7	88	54	O83(22/37/24)		-2.7
Total	6	560	1968	290	561	85	41	9	207	260	18	144	.285	.374	.384	97	-1	45-27	.965	-2	99	99	O519(219/233/75)		-3.1

MEULENS, HENSLEY   Hensley Filemon Acasio "Bam-Bam"   B6.23.1967 Willemstad, Curacao   BR/TR/6-3/212(190-217)   d8.23

1989	NY A	8	28	3	5	0	0	0	1	2-0	0	8	.179	.233	.179	18	-3	0-1	.875	2	141	68	3b8		-0.2
1990	NY A	23	83	12	20	7	0	3	10	9-0	3	25	.241	.337	.434	113	2	1-0	.963	2	106	205	O23L		0.3
1991	NY A	96	288	37	64	8	1	6	29	18-1	4	97	.222	.276	.319	64	-15	3-0	.967	2	110	106	O73(61/0/13),D13,1b7		-1.5
1992	NY A	2	5	1	3	0	0	1	1	1-0	0	1	.600	.667	1.200	414	2	0-0	1.000	0	113	814	3b2		0.2
1993	NY A	30	53	8	9	1	0	2	5	8-0	0	19	.170	.279	.340	67	-3	0-1	1.000	-2	93	0	O24(22/0/1),1b3/3		-0.5
1997	Mon N	16	24	6	7	1	0	2	6	4-0	0	10	.292	.379	.583	153	2	0-1	1.000	-1	65	0	O8L,1b3		0.0
1998	Ari N	7	15	1	1	0	0	1	1	0-0	0	6	.067	.067	.267	-18	-3	0-0	1.000	1	105	499	O4R		-0.2
Total	7	182	496	67	109	17	2	15	53	42-1	7	165	.220	.288	.353	76	-18	4-3	.972	4	105	118	O132(114/0/18),1b13,D13,3b11		-1.9

MEUSEL, IRISH   Emil Frederick   B6.9.1893 Oakland CA   D3.1.1963 Long Beach CA   BR/TR/5-11.5/178   d10.1   C1   b-Bob

1914	Was A	1	2	0	0	0	0	0	0	0	0	0	.000	.000	.000	-96	0	0-0	1.000	-0	97	0	/OL		-0.1
1918	Phi N	124	473	48	132	25	6	4	62	30	1	21	.279	.323	.383	108	4	18	.972	2	106	94	O120(71/45/0),2b4		-0.1
1919	Phi N	135	521	65	159	26	7	5	59	15	2	13	.305	.327	.411	113	7	24	.968	-3	99	79	O128(59/15/54)		-0.3
1920	Phi N	138	518	75	160	27	8	14	69	32	0	27	.309	.349	.473	129	18	17-11	.929	-5	94	99	O129(99/0/43),1b3		0.6
1921	Phi N	84	343	59	121	21	7	12	51	18	0	17	.353	.385	.560	136	17	8-4	.929	0	87	160	O84(38/1/46)		1.0
	†NY N	62	243	37	80	12	6	2	36	15	2	12	.329	.373	.453	117	6	5-9	.971	0	93	133	O62(62/0/1)		-0.1
	Year	146	586	96	201	33	13	14	87	33	2	29	.343	.380	.515	129	23	13-13	.947	0	89	149	O146(100/1/47)		0.9
1922	†NY N	154	617	100	204	28	17	16	132	35	2	33	.331	.369	.509	123	8	12-10	.980	-10	88	79	O154L		-0.5
1923	†NY N	146	595	102	177	22	14	19	**125**	38	1	16	.297	.341	.477	115	9	8-8	.949	-9	90	75	O145L		-1.2
1924	†NY N	139	549	75	170	26	9	6	102	33	1	18	.310	.351	.423	109	6	11-7	.967	-8	100	28	O138L		-1.2
1925	NY N	135	516	82	169	35	8	21	111	26	3	19	.328	.363	.548	135	24	5-4	.959	-6	86	125	O126(118/0/8)		0.8
1926	NY N	129	449	51	131	25	10	6	65	16	4	23	.292	.322	.432	103	-1	5	.958	-4	92	100	O112L		-1.3
1927	Bro N	42	74	7	18	3	1	1	7	11	0	5	.243	.341	.351	85	-1	0	1.000	0	93	134	O17(11/0/6)		-0.2
Total	11	1289	4900	701	1521	250	93	106	819	269	17	199	.310	.348	.464	118	107	113-53	.959	-43	94	92	O1216(1008/61/158),2b4,1b3		-2.6

MEUSEL, BOB   Robert William "Long Bob"   B7.19.1896 San Jose CA   D11.28.1977 Downey CA   BR/TR/6-3/190   d4.14   b-Irish

1920	NY A	119	460	75	151	40	7	11	83	20	2	72	.328	.359	.517	126	15	4-4	.947	-8	94	112	O64(16/0/48),3b45,1b2		0.4
1921	†NY A	149	598	104	190	40	16	24	135	34	2	88	.318	.356	.559	128	20	17-6	.934	4	97	143	O147(10/0/137)		1.3
1922	†NY A	121	473	61	151	26	11	16	84	40	3	58	.319	.376	.522	129	18	13-8	.950	2	88	**174**	O121(47/1/74)		1.1
1923	†NY A	132	460	59	144	29	10	9	91	31	2	52	.313	.359	.478	117	9	13-15	.953	-1	92	126	O121(78/0/43)		-0.3
1924	NY A	143	579	93	188	40	11	12	120	32	5	43	.325	.365	.494	120	14	26-14	.951	-4	92	110	O143(93/2/49),3b2		0.1
1925	NY A	**156**	624	101	181	34	12	**33**	**138**	54	1	55	.290	.348	.542	125	18	13-14	.985	-6	95	65	O131(86/0/46),3b27		0.1
1926	†NY A	108	413	52	130	22	3	12	81	37	1	32	.315	.373	.470	121	11	16-17	.960	-6	100	37	O107(68/1/38)		-0.5
1927	NY A	135	516	75	174	47	9	8	103	45	2	58	.337	.393	.510	137	28	24-10	.950	-4	92	110	O131(83/0/48)		1.5
1928	†NY A	131	518	77	154	45	5	11	113	39	2	56	.297	.349	.467	116	12	6-9	.975	2	96	124	O131(87/0/44)		0.1
1929	NY A	100	391	46	102	15	3	10	57	17	0	42	.261	.292	.391	79	-15	2-5	.968	-3	109	96	O96(56/0/40)		-2.0
1930	Cin N	113	443	62	128	30	8	10	62	26	1	63	.289	.330	.460	93	-7	9	.962	-3	95	100	O112(70/39/4)		-1.4
Total	11	1407	5475	826	1693	368	95	156	1067	375	21	619	.309	.356	.497	119	123	143-102	.958	-20	95	110	O1304(694/43/571),3b74,1b2		0.4

MEYER, BENNY   Bernhard "Earache"   B1.21.1885 Hematite MO   D2.6.1974 Festus MO   BR/TR/5-9/170   d4.9   C6

1913	Bro N	38	87	12	17	0	1	1	10	10	0	14	.195	.278	.253	51	-6	8-3	.943	-1	97	98	O26(2/17/7),C		-0.8
1914	Bal F	143	500	76	152	18	10	5	40	71	4	53	.304	.395	.410	116	6	23	.916	-9	94	71	O132(12/2/118),S4		-0.9
1915	Bal F	35	120	20	29	2	0	0	5	37	1	13	.242	.424	.258	91	0	6	.931	-4	96	22	O34R		-0.6
	Buf F	93	333	37	77	8	6	1	29	40	1	37	.231	.316	.300	72	-17	9	.947	-5	88	83	O88(73/0/15)		-2.9
	Year	128	453	57	106	10	6	1	34	77	2	50	.234	.348	.289	78	-17	15	.943	-9	90	65	O122(73/0/49)		-3.5
1925	Phi N	1	1	1	1	0	0	0	0	0	0	0	1.000	1.000	2.000	594	1	0-0	—	-0	0	0	/2		0.1
Total	4	310	1041	146	276	29	17	7	84	158	6	117	.265	.365	.346	95	-16	46-3	.931	-19	93	71	O280(87/19/174),S4/2C		-5.1

MEYER, DAN   Daniel Thomas   B8.3.1952 Hamilton OH   BL/TR/5-11/180*   [DetA72 4/92]   d9.14   Col Arizona

1974	Det A	13	50	5	10	1	1	2	7	1-1	1	2	.200	.231	.440	86	-1	1-0	.967	0	122	0	O12L		-0.2
1975	Det A	122	470	56	111	17	3	8	47	26-1	2	25	.236	.277	.336	70	-20	8-3	.950	-2	88	77	O74L,1b46	17	-3.0
1976	Det A	105	294	37	74	8	4	2	16	17-0	2	22	.252	.292	.337	78	-9	10-0	.988	-4	82	122	O47L,1b19/D		-1.6
1977	Sea A	159	582	75	159	24	4	22	90	43-4	1	51	.273	.320	.442	107	4	11-8	.992	-1	97	98	1b159		-0.7
1978	Sea A	123	444	38	101	18	1	8	56	24-6	0	39	.227	.264	.327	66	-21	7-3	.989	-2	98	115	1b121,O2L/D	15	-3.1
1979	Sea A	144	525	72	146	21	7	20	74	29-10	3	35	.278	.317	.459	105	1	11-7	.936	-9	96	111	3b101,O31L,1b15		-1.0
1980	Sea A	146	531	56	146	25	6	11	71	31-4	1	42	.275	.314	.407	95	-5	8-4	.961	-11	76	112	O123L,3b5,1b4,D7		-2.1

YEAR	TM LG	G	AB	R	H	2B	3B	HR	RBI	BB-IB	HP	SO	AVG	OBP	SLG	AOPS	ABR	SB-CS	FA	FR	RNG	THR	GAMES AT POSITION	DL	BFW
1981	Sea A	83	252	26	66	10	1	3	22	10-1	1	16	.262	.291	.345	79	-7	4-3	.961	-4	91	137	3b49,O14(13/1/0),1b3,D3	13	-1.4
1982	Oak A	120	383	28	92	17	3	8	59	18-3	0	33	.240	.271	.363	76	-14	1-1	.990	-1	91	84	1b58,D38,O11(4/0/8)		-2.0
1983	Oak A	69	169	15	32	9	0	1	13	19-2	0	11	.189	.268	.260	50	-11	0-0	.987	-3	70	86	1b41,D12,O11(9/0/2)/3	39	-1.7
1984	Oak A	20	22	1	7	3	1	0	4	0-0	0	2	.318	.318	.545	142	1	0-0	.944	0	233	93	1b3/D		0.1
1985	Oak A	14	12	2	0	0	0	0	0	1-0	0	1	.000	.077	.000	-82	-3	0-0	—	0	0	0	/3ORD		-0.3
Total	12	1118	3734	411	944	153	31	86	459	219-32	10	277	.253	.293	.379	85	-85	61-29	.991	-35	94	100	1b469,O326(315/1/11),3b157,D64	84	-17.0

MEYER, GEORGE   George Francis   B8.3.1909 Chicago IL   D1.3.1992 Hoffman Estates IL   BR/TR/5-9/160   d9.3

1938	Chi A	24	81	10	24	2	2	0	17	4-1	1	17	.296	.387	.370	89	-1	3-1	.967	2	116	69	2b24		0.2

MEYER, DUTCH   Lambert Dalton   B10.6.1915 Waco TX   D1.19.2003 Fort Worth TX   BR/TR/5-10.5/181   d6.23   Mil 1943-44   Col TCU

1937	Chi N	1	0	0	0	0	0	0	0	0-0	0		—	—	—		0	0	—	0			/R		0.0
1940	Det A	23	58	12	15	3	0	0	6	4	1	10	.259	.317	.310	58	-3	2-0	.960	-1	98	60	2b21		-0.3
1941	Det A	46	153	12	29	9	1	1	14	8	0	13	.190	.230	.281	31	-15	1-1	.972	2	92	77	2b40		-1.1
1942	Det A	14	52	5	17	3	0	2	9	4	1	7	.327	.386	.500	137	3	0-1	.989	5	124	146	2b14		0.8
1945	Cle A	130	524	71	153	29	8	7	48	40	0	32	.292	.342	.418	125	15	2-4	.978	-28	84	79	2b130		-0.8
1946	Cle A	72	207	13	48	5	3	0	16	26	1	16	.232	.321	.285	75	-7	0-1	.977	-10	91	67	2b64		-1.5
Total	6	286	994	113	262	49	12	10	93	82	3	75	.264	.322	.367	94	-7	5-7	.977	-32	90	79	2b269		-2.9

MEYER, LEO   Leo   B3.29.1888 Iowa City IA   D9.2.1968 Smyrna DE   TR   d9.27

1909	Bro N	7	23	1	3	0	0	0	2	2	0		.130	.200	.130	3	-3	0	.882	-1	89	63	S7		-0.4

MEYER, SCOTT   Scott William   B8.19.1957 Evergreen Park IL   BR/TR/6-1/195   [OakA78 5/108]   d9.10   Col Western Michigan

1978	Oak A	8	9	1	1	1	0	0	0	0-0	0	4	.111	.111	.222	-9	-1	0-0	1.000	-0	120	0	C7		-0.1

MEYER, JOEY   Tanner Joe   B5.10.1962 Honolulu HI   BR/TR/6-3/260*   [MilA83 5/132]   d4.4   Col Hawaii-Manoa

1988	Mil A	103	327	22	86	18	0	11	45	23-2	1	88	.263	.313	.419	102	0	0-1	.986	-0	101	99	D66,1b33		-0.4
1989	Mil A	53	147	13	33	6	0	7	29	12-1	0	36	.224	.274	.408	93	-2	1-0	.982	-1	87	143	D31,1b18		-0.4
Total	2	156	474	35	119	24	0	18	74	35-3	1	124	.251	.300	.416	99	-2	1-1	.984	-1	97	113	D97,1b51		-0.8

MEYER, BILLY   William Adam   B1.14.1892 Knoxville TN   D3.31.1957 Knoxville TN   BR/TR/5-9.5/170   d9.6   M5

1913	Chi A	1	1	1	1	0	0	0	0	0	0	0	1.000	1.000	1.000	490	0	0	.857	0	0	130	/C		0.1
1916	Phi A	50	138	6	32	2	2	1	12	8	0	11	.232	.274	.297	75	-5	3	.961	-2	63	145	C48		-0.4
1917	Phi A	62	162	9	38	5	1	0	9	7	1	14	.235	.271	.278	68	-7	0	.962	1	84	110	C55		-0.1
Total	3	113	301	15	71	7	3	1	21	15	1	25	.236	.274	.289	73	-12	3	.960	-0	74	126	C104		-0.4

MEYERLE, LEVI   Levi Samuel "Long Levi"   B7.1845 Philadelphia PA   D11.4.1921 Philadelphia PA   BR/TR/6-1/177   d5.20   OF NA(2/0/29) ▲

1871	Ath NA	26	130	45	64	9	4	4	40	2		1	.492	.500	.700	243	23	4-0	.646	-9	67	32	3b26/P		0.9
1872	Ath NA	27	146	31	48	10	5	1	31	0		1	.329	.329	.486	147	7	0-0	.773	3	165	0	O26R/3		0.9
1873	Phi NA	48	238	53	83	14	4	3	59	2		1	.349	.354	.479	140	10	5-0	.746	-7	89	106	3b48/S		0.2
1874	Chi NA	53	254	65	100	19	1	1	45	3		4	.394	.401	.488	182	23	3-1	.833	-12	79	113	2b31,3b14,S5,O5(2/0/3)		0.7
1875	Phi NA	68	301	55	95	14	8	1	54	0		2	.316	.316	.425	149	13	7-2	.859	-6	98	99	2b36,3b20,1b16		0.5
1876	Phi N	55	256	46	87	12	8	0	34	3		1	.340	.347	.449	165	17		.791	-4	101	75	3b49,O3R,2b3,P2		1.3
1877	Cin N	27	107	11	35	7	2	0	15	0		4	.327	.327	.430	154	7		.822	0	99	88	S18,2b12/OC		0.7
1884	Phi U	3	11	0	1	3	0	0	0	0			.091	.091	.182	-21	-2		.789	-1	77	0	1b2/OR		-0.3
Total	5 NA	222	1069	249	390	66	21	10	229	7		8	.365	.369	.494	166	76	19-3	.705	-30	76	99	3b109,2b67,O31R,1b16,S6/P		3.2
Total	3	85	374	57	123	20	10	0	49	3		6	.329	.334	.436	156	22		.705	-4	101	75	3b49,S18,2b15,O5(0/1/4),1b2,P2		1.7

MEYERS, CHAD   Chad William   B8.8.1975 Omaha NE   BR/TR/6-0/190*   [ChiN96 5/142]   d8.6   Col Creighton

1999	Chi N	43	142	17	33	9	0	0	4	9-1	3	27	.232	.292	.296	49	-11	4-2	.983	-7	89	71	2b32,O14(4/10/0)		-1.6
2000	Chi N	36	52	8	9	2	0	0	5	3-0	1	15	.173	.228	.212	13	-7	1-0	1.000	-1	94	115	2b8,3b8		-0.8
2001	Chi N	18	17	1	2	0	0	0	0	2-0	4	5	.118	.348	.118	29	-2	0-1	1.000	2	172	82	2b4,O4(2/2/0)/3		0.0
2003	Sea A	9	1	1	0	0	0	0	0	0-0	0	1	.000	.000	.000	-99	0	1-0	—	0	0	0	O3L,D6		0.0
Total	4	106	212	27	44	11	0	0	9	14-1	8	43	.208	.281	.259	39	-20	6-3	.987	-6	95	78	2b44,O21(9/12/0),3b9,D6		-2.4

MEYERS, HENRY   Henry L.   B1860 Philadelphia PA   D6.28.1898 Harrisburg PA   d8.30

1890	Phi AA	5	19	2	3	0	0	0	1	1	1		.158	.238	.158	17	-2	2	.684	-2	67	0	3b5		-0.4

MEYERS, CHIEF   John Tortes   B7.29.1880 Riverside CA   D7.25.1971 San Bernardino CA   BR/TR/5-11/194   d4.16

1909	NY N	90	220	15	61	10	5	1	30	22	6		.277	.359	.382	128	8	3	.963	2	117	87	C64		1.7
1910	NY N	127	365	25	104	18	0	1	62	40	4	18	.285	.362	.342	106	4	4	.969	2	99	101	C117		1.9
1911	†NY N	133	391	48	130	18	9	1	61	25	13	33	.332	.392	.432	126	14	7	.979	10	130	76	C128		3.3
1912	†NY N	126	371	60	133	16	5	6	54	47	8	20	.358	.441	.477	147	26	8	.973	5	124	84	C122		4.0
1913	†NY N	120	378	37	118	18	5	3	47	37	9	22	.312	.387	.410	127	15	7-9	.967	6	117	97	C116		3.0
1914	NY N	134	381	33	109	13	5	1	55	34	8	25	.286	.357	.354	116	8	4	.970	-2	130	96	C126		1.7
1915	NY N	110	289	24	67	10	5	1	26	26	7	18	.232	.311	.311	94	-2	4-4	.986	-6	89	97	C96		-0.1
1916	†Bro N	80	239	21	59	10	3	0	21	26	6	15	.247	.336	.314	97	1	2	.984	5	104	104	C74		1.4
1917	Bro N	47	132	8	28	3	0	0	3	13	0	7	.212	.283	.235	58	-6	4	.974	-4	97	77	C44		-0.8
	Bos N	25	68	5	17	4	4	0	4	4	2	4	.250	.311	.426	133	2	0	1.000	5	124	123	C24		1.1
	Year	72	200	13	45	7	4	0	7	17	2	11	.225	.292	.300	82	-4	4	.984	1	107	94	C68		0.3
Total	9	992	2834	276	826	120	41	14	363	274	63	162	.291	.367	.378	117	70	44-13	.974	24	114	91	C911		17.2

MEYERS, LOU   Lewis Henry "Crazy Horse"   B12.9.1859 Cincinnati OH   D11.30.1920 Cincinnati OH   BR/TR/5-11/165   d5.10

1884	Cin U	2	3	1	0	0	0	0	1				.000	.250	.000	-17	-1		.667	-1			C2/OR		-0.1

MICELOTTA, MICKEY   Robert Peter   B10.20.1928 Corona NY   BR/TR/5-11/170(170-185)   d4.20

1954	Phi N	13	3	2	0	0	0	0	0	1	0	1	.000	.250	.000	-28	-1	0-0	1.000	0	145	0	/S		-0.1
1955	Phi N	4	4	0	0	0	0	0	0	0-0	0	0	.000	.000	.000	-99	-1	0-0	1.000	-0	74	184	S2		-0.1
Total	2	17	7	2	0	0	0	0	0	1-0	0	1	.000	.125	.000	-64	-2	0-0	1.000	-0	88	147	S3		-0.2

MICHAEL, GENE   Eugene Richard "Stick"   B6.2.1938 Kent OH   BB/TR/6-2/183*   d7.15   M4/C8   Col Kent St.

1966	Pit N	30	33	9	5	2	1	0	2	0-0	0	7	.152	.152	.273	15	-4	0-0	.903	1	115	220	S8,2b2/3		-0.3
1967	LA N	98	223	20	45	9	1	0	7	11-0	2	30	.202	.246	.224	39	-18	1-3	.950	-10	93	75	S83		-2.5
1968	NY A	61	116	8	23	3	0	1	8	2	1	23	.198	.218	.250	43	-8	3-2	.939	-5	95	79	S43/P		-1.2
1969	NY A	119	412	41	112	24	4	2	31	43-1	1	56	.272	.341	.364	101	1	7-4	.968	0	102	103	S118		1.6
1970	NY A	134	435	42	93	10	1	2	38	50-5	0	93	.214	.292	.255	55	-26	3-1	.957	-1	102	113	S123,3b4,2b3		-1.3
1971	NY A	139	456	36	102	15	0	3	35	48-8	3	64	.224	.299	.276	68	-19	3-3	.973	25	117	119	S136		2.2
1972	NY A	126	391	29	91	7	4	1	32	32-4	1	45	.233	.290	.279	72	-14	4-2	.969	24	117	126	S121		2.7
1973	NY A	129	418	30	94	11	1	3	47	26-0	0	51	.225	.270	.278	56	-25	1-3	.965	11	107	110	S129		-0.1
1974	NY A	81	177	19	46	9	0	0	13	14-0	0	24	.260	.313	.311	81	-4	0-0	.970	2	102	104	2b45,S39,3b2		0.3
1975	Det A	56	145	15	31	6	0	3	13	8-0	0	28	.214	.253	.290	51	-10	0-0	.938	0	98	109	S44,2b7,3b4		-0.5
Total	10	973	2806	249	642	86	12	15	226	234-18	8	421	.229	.288	.284	66	-127	22-18	.962	48	106	109	S844,2b57,3b11/P		0.9

MICHAELS, CASS   Casimir Eugene (Played in 1943 Under Real Name of Casimir Eugene Kwietniewski)   B3.4.1926 Detroit MI   D11.12.1982 Grosse Pointe MI   BR/TR/5-11/175*   d8.19

1943	Chi A	2	7	0	0	0	0	0	0	0-0	0	0	.000	.000	.000	-99	-2	0-0	1.000	1	87	0	3b2		-0.3
1944	Chi A	27	68	4	12	4	1	0	5	2	0	5	.176	.200	.265	33	-6	0-0	.930	2	111	97	S21,3b3		-0.3
1945	Chi A	129	445	47	109	8	5	2	54	37	3	28	.245	.307	.299	78	-13	8-7	.936	8	105	93	S123,3b2		0.4
1946	Chi A	91	291	37	75	8	1	22	29		6	36	.258	.333	.296	80	-7	9-3	.957	1	104	112	2b66,3b13,S6		-0.1
1947	Chi A	110	355	31	97	15	4	3	34	39	3	28	.273	.350	.363	102	1	10-5	.982	11	111	126	2b60,3b44,S2		1.4
1948	Chi A	145	484	47	120	12	6	5	56	69	2	42	.248	.344	.329	82	-12	8-4	.957	16	111	100	S85,2b55/OC		1.3
1949	Chi A★	154	561	73	173	27	6	6	83	101	3	50	.308	.417	.421	126	25	5-7	.976	15	111	109	2b154		4.5
1950	Chi A	36	138	21	43	6	3	4	19	13	1	9	.312	.373	.486	122	4	0-0	.964	-3	80	122	2b35		0.2
	Was A★	106	388	48	97	8	4	4	47	55	1	39	.250	.345	.322	75	-14	2-3	.975	7	107	100	2b104		-0.2
	Year	142	526	69	140	14	7	8	66	68	2	47	.266	.352	.365	88	-10	2-3	.972	3	100	105	2b139		0.0
1951	Was A	138	485	59	125	20	4	4	45	61	1	41	.258	.342	.340	86	-8	1-1	.964	-22	100	84	2b128		-2.3
1952	Was A	22	86	10	20	4	1	1	7	7	1	15	.233	.290	.337	77	-3	0-0	.977	-2	106	92	2b22		-0.3
	StL A	55	166	21	44	8	2	3	25	23	1	16	.265	.354	.392	104	1	1-0	.916	-0	105	129	3b42,2b8		0.1
	Phi A	55	200	22	50	4	5	1	18	23	0	11	.250	.330	.335	80	-5	3-0	.993	-9	86	74	2b55		-1.2

YEAR	TM LG	G	AB	R	H	2B	3B	HR	RBI	BB-IB	HP	SO	AVG	OBP	SLG	AOPS	ABR	SB-CS	FA	FR	RNG	THR	GAMES AT POSITION	DL	BFW
	Year	132	452	53	114	16	8	5	50	53	1	42	.252	.332	.356	89	-7	4-0	.989	-11	92	81	2b85,3b42		-1.4
1953	Phi A	117	411	53	103	10	0	12	42	51		56	.251	.335	.363	85	-9	7-0	.970	-12	96	87	2b110		-1.1
1954	Chi A	101	282	35	74	13	2	7	44	56	4	31	.262	.392	.397	113	8	10-4	.958	-2	96	66	3b91,2b2		0.6
Total	12	1288	4367	508	1142	147	46	53	501	566	24	406	.262	.349	.353	92	-40	64-32	.973	6	103	101	2b800,S240,3b195/OC		2.7

MICHAELS, JASON Jason Drew B5.4.1976 Tampa FL BR/TR/6-0/204* [PhiN98 4/104] d4.6 gf-John Col Miami

YEAR	TM LG	G	AB	R	H	2B	3B	HR	RBI	BB-IB	HP	SO	AVG	OBP	SLG	AOPS	ABR	SB-CS	FA	FR	RNG	THR	GAMES AT POSITION	DL	BFW
2001	Phi N	6	6	0	1	0	0	0	1	0-0	1	.167	.167	.167		-14	-1	0-0	—	-0	0	0	/OL		-0.1
2002	Phi N	81	105	16	28	10	3	2	11	13-1	1	33	.267	.347	.476	127	4	1-1	1.000	-1	76	254	O26(6/14/7)/3D		0.3
2003	Phi N	76	109	20	36	11	0	5	17	15-1	1	22	.330	.416	.569	166	11	0-0	.976	1	92	237	O38(23/5/13)	15	1.1
2004	Phi N	115	299	44	82	12	0	10	40	42-1	2	80	.274	.364	.415	99	0	2-2	.983	4	109	131	O78(39/44/12)/D		0.3
2005	Phi N	105	289	54	88	16	2	4	31	44-1	4	45	.304	.399	.415	112	7	3-3	.990	9	114	218	O91(22/75/13)		1.6
Total	5	383	808	134	235	49	5	21	100	114-4	8	182	.291	.380	.442	114	21	6-6	.986	13	107	188	O234(91/138/45),D3/3	15	3.2

MICHAELS, RALPH Ralph Joseph B5.3.1902 Etna PA D8.5.1988 Monroeville PA BR/TR/5-10.5/178 d4.16

YEAR	TM LG	G	AB	R	H	2B	3B	HR	RBI	BB-IB	HP	SO	AVG	OBP	SLG	AOPS	ABR	SB-CS	FA	FR	RNG	THR	GAMES AT POSITION	DL	BFW
1924	Chi N	8	11	0	4	0	0	0	2	0	0	.364	.364	.364	95	0	0-0	.929	-0	95	73	S4		0.0
1925	Chi N	22	50	10	14	1	0	0	6	6	0	9	.280	.357	.300	69	-2	1-0	.975	2	121	190	3b15/12S		0.1
1926	Chi N	2	0	1	0	0	0	0	0	0	0	0	—	—	—	—	0	0-0	—	0			/H		0.0
Total	3	32	61	11	18	1	0	0	8	6	0	10	.295	.358	.311	73	-2	1-0	.975	2	121	190	3b15,S5/21		0.1

MICKELSON, ED Edward Allen B9.9.1926 Ottawa IL BR/TR/6-3/205* d9.18 Col Oklahoma St.

YEAR	TM LG	G	AB	R	H	2B	3B	HR	RBI	BB-IB	HP	SO	AVG	OBP	SLG	AOPS	ABR	SB-CS	FA	FR	RNG	THR	GAMES AT POSITION	DL	BFW
1950	StL N	5	10	1	1	0	0	0	2	0	3	.100	.250	.100	-4	-2	0-0	1.000	1	182	32	1b4		-0.1
1953	StL A	7	15	1	2	1	0	0	2	2	0	6	.133	.235	.200	18	-2	0-0	1.000	0	111	71	1b3		-0.2
1957	Chi N	6	12	0	0	0	0	0	1	0-0	0	4	.000	.000	.000	-99	-7	0-0	1.000	0	169	151	1b2		-0.3
Total	3	18	37	2	3	1	0	0	4-0	0	13	.081	.171	.108	-23	-7	0-0	1.000	1	155	77	1b9		-0.6

MIDKIFF, EZRA Ezra Millington "Salt Rock" B11.13.1882 Salt Rock WV D3.20.1957 Huntington WV BL/TR/5-10/180 d10.5

YEAR	TM LG	G	AB	R	H	2B	3B	HR	RBI	BB-IB	HP	SO	AVG	OBP	SLG	AOPS	ABR	SB-CS	FA	FR	RNG	THR	GAMES AT POSITION	DL	BFW
1909	Cin N	1	2	0	0	0	0	0	0	0	.000	.000	.000	-99	0	0	.000	-1	0	0	/3		-0.1
1912	NY A	21	86	9	21	1	0	0	9	7	0	.244	.301	.256	56	-5	4	.901	2	120	32	3b21		-0.3
1913	NY A	83	284	22	56	9	1	0	14	12	1	33	.197	.232	.236	37	-23	9	.957	14	121	105	3b76,S4,2b2		-0.8
Total	3	105	372	31	77	10	1	0	23	19	1	33	.207	.247	.239	41	-28	13	.942	15	120	90	3b98,S4,2b2		-1.2

MIENTKIEWICZ, DOUG Douglas Andrew B6.19.1974 Toledo OH BL/TR/6-2/200(193-205) [MinA95 5/128] d9.18 Col Florida St.

YEAR	TM LG	G	AB	R	H	2B	3B	HR	RBI	BB-IB	HP	SO	AVG	OBP	SLG	AOPS	ABR	SB-CS	FA	FR	RNG	THR	GAMES AT POSITION	DL	BFW
1998	Min A	8	25	1	5	1	0	0	2	4-0	0	3	.200	.310	.240	45	-2	1-1	1.000	-1	61	50	1b8		-0.3
1999	Min A	118	327	34	75	21	3	2	32	43-3	4	51	.229	.324	.330	65	-17	1-1	.997	-2	89	91	1b110		-2.6
2000	Min A	3	14	0	6	0	0	0	4	0-0	0	0	.429	.400	.429	111	0	0-0	1.000	-1	0	109	1b3		-0.1
2001	Min A	151	543	77	166	39	1	15	74	67-6	9	32	.306	.387	.464	118	17	2-6	.997	-9	74	83	1b148,D2		-0.7
2002	†Min A	143	467	60	122	29	1	10	64	74-8	6	69	.261	.365	.392	99	3	1-2	.996	-6	81	90	1b143		-1.5
2003	†Min A	142	487	67	146	38	1	11	65	74-4	5	55	.300	.393	.450	119	17	4-1	.997	-8	78	83	1b139,O3R/23D		-0.2
2004	Min A	78	284	34	70	18	0	5	25	38-2	3	38	.246	.340	.363	82	-7	2-2	.994	-4	77	102	1b77	16	-1.7
	†Bos A	49	107	13	23	6	1	1	10	10-0	1	18	.215	.286	.318	54	-7	0-1	.997	2	116	58	1b47/2		-0.8
	Year	127	391	47	93	24	1	6	35	48-2	4	56	.238	.326	.350	74	-14	2-3	.995	-3	88	89	1b124/2		-2.5
2005	NY N	87	275	36	66	13	0	11	29	32-7	3	39	.240	.322	.407	92	-3	0-1	.995	-3	86	93	1b83	49	-1.3
Total	8	779	2529	322	679	165	7	55	305	342-30	30	365	.268	.359	.405	97	1	11-15	.996	-32	81	87	1b758,O3R,D3,2b2/3	65	-9.2

MIERKOWICZ, ED Edward Frank "Butch","Mouse" B3.6.1924 Wyandotte MI BR/TR/6-4/205* d8.31

YEAR	TM LG	G	AB	R	H	2B	3B	HR	RBI	BB-IB	HP	SO	AVG	OBP	SLG	AOPS	ABR	SB-CS	FA	FR	RNG	THR	GAMES AT POSITION	DL	BFW
1945	†Det A	10	15	0	2	2	0	0	2	1	0	3	.133	.188	.267	29	-1	0-0	1.000	-0	109	0	O6L		-0.2
1947	Det A	21	42	6	8	1	0	1	1	1	0	12	.190	.209	.286	36	-4	1-0	.947	-0	104	0	O10L		-0.5
1948	Det A	3	5	0	1	0	0	0	1	2	0	2	.200	.429	.200	69	0	0-0	1.000	-0	128	0	/OL		0.0
1950	StL N	1	1	0	0	0	0	0	0	0	0	1	.000	.000	.000	-95	0	0	—	0			/H		0.0
Total	4	35	63	6	11	3	0	1	4	4	0	18	.175	.224	.270	36	-5	1-0	.968	-0	108	0	O17L		-0.7

MIESKE, MATT Matthew Todd B2.13.1968 Midland MI BR/TR/6-0/192* [SDN90 17/471] d5.3 Col Western Michigan

YEAR	TM LG	G	AB	R	H	2B	3B	HR	RBI	BB-IB	HP	SO	AVG	OBP	SLG	AOPS	ABR	SB-CS	FA	FR	RNG	THR	GAMES AT POSITION	DL	BFW
1993	Mil A	23	58	9	14	0	0	3	7	4-0	0	14	.241	.290	.397	83	-2	0-2	.936	-1	96	78	O22(1/9/12)		-0.4
1994	Mil A	84	259	39	67	13	1	10	38	21-0	3	62	.259	.320	.432	88	-5	3-5	.976	0	99	122	O80(6/0/80)/D		-0.9
1995	Mil A	117	267	42	67	13	1	12	48	27-0	4	45	.251	.323	.442	93	-3	2-4	.979	5	112	130	O108R,D2		-0.3
1996	Mil A	127	374	46	104	24	3	14	64	26-2	2	76	.278	.324	.471	95	-4	1-5	.996	7	**114**	95	O122(9/10/108)		-0.2
1997	Mil A	84	253	39	63	15	3	5	21	19-2	0	50	.249	.300	.391	78	-9	1-0	.962	-1	93	146	O74(26/0/52),D5	25	-1.2
1998	Chi N	77	97	16	29	7	0	1	12	11-1	1	17	.299	.373	.402	101	-2	0-0	.974	-2	83	67	O62(50/3/12)		-0.2
1999	Sea A	24	41	11	15	0	0	4	7	2-1	0	9	.366	.395	.659	164	4	0-0	1.000	5	133	162	O20(6/3/13)/D		0.4
	†Hou N	54	109	13	31	5	0	5	22	6-1	0	22	.284	.316	.468	98	-1	0-0	1.000	3	120	69	O37(30/0/7)		0.0
2000	Hou N	62	81	7	14	1	2	1	5	7-0	1	17	.173	.247	.272	29	-9	0-0	.933	-1	75	0	O18(14/0/4)	9	-1.1
	Ari N	11	8	3	2	0	0	1	2	1-0	0	1	.250	.300	.625	130	0	0-0	1.000	0	886	0	/OR		0.1
	Year	73	89	10	16	1	2	2	7	8-0	1	18	.180	.253	.303	38	-9	0-0	.941	-1	85	0	O19(14/0/5)		-1.0
Total	8	663	1547	225	406	78	10	56	226	124-7	11	333	.262	.316	.422	89	-28	7-16	.979	12	105	110	O544(142/25/397),D9	34	-3.9

MIGGINS, LARRY Lawrence Edward "Irish" B8.20.1925 Bronx NY BR/TR/6-4/195* d10.3 Col St. Thomas (MN)

YEAR	TM LG	G	AB	R	H	2B	3B	HR	RBI	BB-IB	HP	SO	AVG	OBP	SLG	AOPS	ABR	SB-CS	FA	FR	RNG	THR	GAMES AT POSITION	DL	BFW
1948	StL N	1	1	0	0	0	0	0	0	0	0	0	.000	.000	.000	-95	0	0	—	0			/H		0.0
1952	StL N	42	96	7	22	5	1	2	10	3	0	19	.229	.253	.365	69	-5	0-1	.967	-2	87	0	O25(23/0/2)/1		-0.8
Total	2	43	97	8	22	5	1	2	10	3	0	19	.227	.250	.361	67	-5	0-1	.967	-2	87	0	O25(23/0/2)/1		-0.8

MIHALIC, JOHN John Michael B11.13.1911 Cleveland OH D4.24.1987 Ft.Oglethorpe GA BR/TR/5-11/172 d9.18

YEAR	TM LG	G	AB	R	H	2B	3B	HR	RBI	BB-IB	HP	SO	AVG	OBP	SLG	AOPS	ABR	SB-CS	FA	FR	RNG	THR	GAMES AT POSITION	DL	BFW
1935	Was A	6	22	4	5	3	0	0	6	2	0	3	.227	.292	.364	71	-1	1-0	.966	-0	96	133	S6		0.0
1936	Was A	25	88	15	21	2	1	0	8	14	0	14	.239	.343	.284	60	-5	2-1	.972	1	101	147	2b25		-0.2
1937	Was A	38	107	13	27	5	2	0	8	17	0	9	.252	.355	.336	79	-3	2-1	.981	1	98	126	2b28,S3		-0.2
Total	3	69	217	32	53	10	3	0	22	33	0	26	.244	.344	.318	70	-9	5-2	.977	2	99	136	2b53,S9		-0.2

MIKSIS, EDDIE Edward Thomas B9.11.1926 Burlington NJ D4.8.2005 Huntingdon Valley PA BR/TR/6-0.5/185* d6.17 Mil 1945 OF(34/106/88)*

YEAR	TM LG	G	AB	R	H	2B	3B	HR	RBI	BB-IB	HP	SO	AVG	OBP	SLG	AOPS	ABR	SB-CS	FA	FR	RNG	THR	GAMES AT POSITION	DL	BFW
1944	Bro N	26	91	12	20	2	0	0	11	6	0	11	.220	.268	.242	45	-7	4	.896	-4	78	275	3b15,S10		-1.1
1946	Bro N	23	48	3	7	0	0	0	5	3	1	3	.146	.212	.146	2	-6	0	.970	-0	96	0	3b13/2		0.0
1947	†Bro N	45	86	18	23	1	0	4	10	9	0	8	.267	.337	.419	96	-1	0	1.000	2	113	82	2b13,O11L,3b5,S2		0.0
1948	Bro N	86	221	28	47	7	1	2	16	19	1	27	.213	.278	.281	50	-16	5	.967	-1	96	66	2b54,3b22,S5		-1.4
1949	†Bro N	50	113	17	25	5	0	1	6	7	0	8	.221	.267	.292	48	-8	3	.978	4	111	79	3b29,S4,2b3/1		-0.5
1950	Bro N	51	76	13	19	2	1	2	10	5	0	10	.250	.296	.382	75	-3	3	.964	1	80	61	2b15,S15,3b7		-0.1
1951	Bro N	19	10	6	2	1	0	0	0	1	1	2	.200	.333	.300	70	0	0-0	1.000	1	150	699	3b6/2		0.1
	Chi N	102	421	48	112	13	3	4	35	33	0	36	.266	.319	.340	76	-15	11-5	.969	1	106	85	2b102		-0.7
	Year	121	431	54	114	14	3	4	35	34	1	38	.265	.320	.339	76	-15	11-5	.969	2	106	85	2b103,3b6		-0.6
1952	Chi N	93	383	44	89	20	1	2	19	20	1	32	.232	.272	.305	59	-22	4-4	.950	-14	91	63	2b54,S40		-3.2
1953	Chi N	142	577	61	145	17	6	8	39	33	1	59	.251	.293	.343	64	-32	13-4	.954	-15	96	91	2b92,S53		-3.4
1954	Chi N	38	99	9	20	3	0	2	3	3	0	9	.202	.225	.293	33	-10	1-0	.961	2	104	101	2b21,3b2/OL		-0.6
1955	Chi N	131	481	52	113	14	2	9	41	32-3	1	55	.235	.282	.328	62	-27	3-6	.989	-1	100	66	O111(0/76/41),3b18		-3.5
1956	Chi N	114	356	54	85	10	3	9	27	32-2	1	40	.239	.303	.360	79	-11	4-2	.975	1	99	55	3b48,O33(6/25/2),2b19,S2		-1.0
1957	StL N	49	38	3	8	0	0	1	2	7-1	0	7	.211	.333	.289	68	-2	0-0	1.000	0	97	0	O31(11/3/18)		-0.2
	Bal A	1	1	0	0	0	0	0	0	0	0	0	.000	.000	.000	-99	0	0-0	—	0			/H		0.0
1958	Bal A	3	2	0	0	0	0	0	0	1	0	1	.000	.000	.000	-99	-1	0-0	—	-0	0	0	/S		0.0
	Cin N	69	50	15	7	0	0	0	4	5-0	0	5	.140	.218	.140	-2	-7	1-1	1.000	3	142	0	O32(5/2/27),3b14,2b7,S5/1		-0.5
Total	14	1042	3053	383	722	95	17	44	228	215-6	6	313	.236	.288	.322	62	-168	52-22	.962	-22	100	81	2b382,O219C,3b179,S137,1b2		-16.9

MILAN, HORACE Horace Robert B4.7.1894 Linden TN D6.29.1955 Texarkana AR BR/TR/5-9/175 d8.29 Mil 1918 b-Clyde

YEAR	TM LG	G	AB	R	H	2B	3B	HR	RBI	BB-IB	HP	SO	AVG	OBP	SLG	AOPS	ABR	SB-CS	FA	FR	RNG	THR	GAMES AT POSITION	DL	BFW
1915	Was A	11	27	6	11	1	1	0	7	8	0	7	.407	.543	.519	214	5	2	1.000	-1	79	0	O10(2/4/4)		0.4
1917	Was A	31	73	8	21	1	0	0	9	4	2	9	.288	.342	.356	114	1	4	.932	-1	120	0	O23L		-0.1
Total	2	42	100	14	32	2	1	0	16	12	2	16	.320	.404	.400	144	6	6	.944	-2	108	0	O33(25/4/4)		0.3

MILAN, CLYDE Jesse Clyde "Deerfoot" B3.25.1887 Linden TN D3.3.1953 Orlando FL BL/TR/5-9/168 d8.19 M1/C17 b-Horace

YEAR	TM LG	G	AB	R	H	2B	3B	HR	RBI	BB-IB	HP	SO	AVG	OBP	SLG	AOPS	ABR	SB-CS	FA	FR	RNG	THR	GAMES AT POSITION	DL	BFW
1907	Was A	48	183	22	51	3	3	0	9	8	3	.279	.323	.328	117	3	8	.929	4	203	68	O47(0/30/17)		0.5
1908	Was A	130	485	55	116	10	12	1	32	38	7	.239	.304	.315	110	5	29	.959	5	126	156	O122C		0.4
1909	Was A	130	400	36	80	12	4	1	15	31	6	.200	.268	.257	69	-14	10	.972	5	130	86	O120(29/89/2)		-1.7
1910	Was A	142	531	89	148	17	6	0	16	71	15	.279	.379	.333	129	23	44	.946	8	99	154	O142C		2.6

YEAR	TM LG	G	AB	R	H	2B	3B	HR	RBI	BB-IB	HP	SO	AVG	OBP	SLG	AOPS	ABR	SB-CS	FA	FR	RNG	THR	GAMES AT POSITION	DL	BFW
1911	Was A	154	616	109	194	24	8	3	35	74	7		.315	.395	.394	123	22	58	.957	7	102	131	O154C		1.8
1912	Was A	154	601	105	184	19	11	1	79	63	5		.306	.377	.379	116	13	88	.935	7	102	148	O154C		1.0
1913	Was A	154	579	92	174	18	9	3	54	58	3	25	.301	.367	.378	116	12	75	.932	-12	88	83	O154C		-1.2
1914	Was A	115	437	63	129	19	11	1	39	32	2	26	.295	.344	.396	118	8	38-21	.949	-6	96	71	O113(1/112/0)		-0.5
1915	Was A	153	573	83	165	13	7	2	66	53	5	32	.288	.353	.346	107	5	40-19	.946	-6	102	61	O151C		-1.0
1916	Was A	150	565	58	154	14	3	1	45	56	5	31	.273	.343	.313	98	0	34-21	.961	14	114	136	O149C		0.4
1917	Was A	155	579	60	170	15	4	0	48	58	6	26	.294	.364	.333	114	11	20	.962	-6	96	86	O153C		-0.6
1918	Was A	128	503	56	146	18	5	0	56	36	5	14	.290	.344	.346	110	5	26	.972	-4	95	90	O124C		-0.9
1919	Was A	88	321	43	92	12	6	0	37	40	3	16	.287	.371	.361	107	4	11	.953	-1	103	83	O86C		-0.2
1920	Was A	126	506	70	163	22	5	3	41	28	5	12	.322	.364	.403	106	4	10-12	.971	4	109	88	O123(115/0/8)		0.0
1921	Was A	113	406	55	117	19	11	1	40	37	2	13	.288	.351	.397	95	-4	4-5	.931	3	98	147	O99(34/15/52)		-0.9
1922	Was A	42	74	8	17	5	0	0	5	2	0	2	.230	.250	.297	44	-6	0-0	1.000	1	91	249	O12(3/0/9),M		-0.6
Total 16		1982	7359	1004	2100	240	105	17	617	685	80	197	.285	.353	.353	109	91	495-78	.953	21	106	109	O1903(182/1635/88)		-0.9

MILBOURNE, LARRY Lawrence William B2.14.1951 Port Norris NJ BB/TR/6-0/165(153-165) d4.6 [DL 1985 Sea A 106]

YEAR	TM LG	G	AB	R	H	2B	3B	HR	RBI	BB-IB	HP	SO	AVG	OBP	SLG	AOPS	ABR	SB-CS	FA	FR	RNG	THR	GAMES AT POSITION	DL	BFW
1974	Hou N	112	136	31	38	2	1	0	9	10-0	0	14	.279	.329	.309	83	-3	6-2	.974	2	112	86	2b87,S8,O4L		0.2
1975	Hou N	73	151	17	32	1	2	1	9	6-1	1	14	.212	.245	.265	45	-12	1-2	.968	-2	95	130	2b43,S22		-1.1
1976	Hou N	59	145	22	36	4	0	0	7	14-0	1	10	.248	.319	.276	76	-4	6-1	.965	-3	98	84	2b32		-0.4
1977	Sea A	86	242	24	53	10	0	2	21	6-0	2	20	.219	.239	.285	44	-19	3-1	.982	4	112	108	2b41,S40/3D		-1.0
1978	Sea A	93	234	31	53	6	2	2	20	9-1	0	6	.226	.254	.295	54	-15	5-7	.989	4	96	65	3b32,S23,2b15,D10		-1.1
1979	Sea A	123	356	40	99	13	4	2	26	19-2	0	20	.278	.313	.354	78	-11	5-3	.981	4	113	92	S65,2b49,3b11		-0.3
1980	Sea A	106	258	31	68	6	6	0	26	19-4	1	13	.264	.313	.333	77	-9	7-6	.976	3	113	114	2b38,S34,3b6,D8		-0.2
1981	†NY A	61	163	24	51	7	2	1	12	9-2	1	14	.313	.351	.399	117	3	2-0	.955	-2	89	84	S39,2b14,3b3,D3		-0.5
1982	NY A	14	27	2	4	1	0	0	0	1-0	0	4	.148	.179	.185	0	-4	0-1	.917	-2	62	0	S9,2b3,3b3		-0.5
	Min A	29	98	9	23	1	1	0	1	7-0	0	8	.235	.283	.265	51	-7	1-1	.981	-7	76	82	2b26		-1.3
	Cle A	82	291	29	80	11	4	2	25	12-0	2	20	.275	.301	.361	83	-8	2-5	.981	-3	99	83	2b63,S21,3b9/D		-0.8
	Year	125	416	40	107	13	5	2	26	20-0	2	32	.257	.293	.327	70	-18	3-7	.979	-12	93	87	2b92,S30,3b12/D		-2.6
1983	Phi N	41	66	3	16	0	1	0	4	4-0	0	7	.242	.282	.273	56	-4	2-1	.963	-3	83	39	2b27,S8,3b3		-0.6
	NY A	31	70	5	14	4	0	0	2	5-0	1	10	.200	.263	.257	45	-5	1-1	1.000	4	104	85	2b19,S6,3b4		-0.2
1984	Sea A	79	211	22	56	5	1	1	22	12-0	1	16	.265	.304	.313	72	-8	0-2	.900	-7	74	87	3b40,2b14,S5,D6	15	-1.6
Total 11		989	2448	290	623	71	24	11	184	133-10	9	176	.254	.293	.302	70	-106	41-33	.974	-10	102	98	2b471,S280,3b112,D29,O4L	121	-8.3

MILES, AARON Aaron Wade B12.15.1976 Pittsburg CA BB/TR/5-8/170* [HouN95 19/529] d9.11

YEAR	TM LG	G	AB	R	H	2B	3B	HR	RBI	BB-IB	HP	SO	AVG	OBP	SLG	AOPS	ABR	SB-CS	FA	FR	RNG	THR	GAMES AT POSITION	DL	BFW
2003	Chi A	8	12	3	4	3	0	0	2	0-0	0	0	.333	.333	.583	130	1	0-0	1.000	0	130	0	2b3,D2		0.1
2004	Col N	134	522	75	153	15	3	6	47	29-0	1	53	.293	.329	.368	72	-22	12-7	.984	10	112	81	2b128		-0.5
2005	Col N	99	324	37	91	12	3	2	28	8-1	4	38	.281	.306	.355	63	-17	4-2	.984	7	106	93	2b79/S	33	-0.7
Total 3		241	858	115	248	30	6	8	77	37-1	5	91	.289	.320	.366	69	-38	16-9	.984	17	110	85	2b210,D2/S	33	-1.1

MILES, DON Donald Ray B3.13.1936 Indianapolis IN BL/TR/6-1/210 d9.9 Col Indianapolis

YEAR	TM LG	G	AB	R	H	2B	3B	HR	RBI	BB-IB	HP	SO	AVG	OBP	SLG	AOPS	ABR	SB-CS	FA	FR	RNG	THR	GAMES AT POSITION	DL	BFW
1958	LA N	8	22	2	4	0	0	0	0	0-0	1	6	.182	.217	.182	7	-3	0-0	1.000	1	140	0	O5L		-0.3

MILES, DEE Wilson Daniel B2.15.1909 Kellerman AL D11.2.1976 Birmingham AL BL/TR/6-0/175 d7.7

YEAR	TM LG	G	AB	R	H	2B	3B	HR	RBI	BB-IB	HP	SO	AVG	OBP	SLG	AOPS	ABR	SB-CS	FA	FR	RNG	THR	GAMES AT POSITION	DL	BFW
1935	Was A	60	215	28	57	5	2	0	29	7	1	13	.265	.291	.307	57	-15	6-4	.970	1	102	129	O45R		-1.6
1936	Was A	25	59	8	14	1	2	0	7	1	0	5	.237	.250	.322	43	-6	0-1	.958	0	103	102	O10(1/0/9)		-0.6
1939	Phi A	106	320	49	96	17	6	1	37	15	0	17	.300	.331	.400	88	-7	3-4	.968	-3	96	72	O77(1/20/57)		-1.3
1940	Phi A	88	236	26	71	9	6	1	23	8	1	18	.301	.327	.403	90	-5	1-1	.945	0	106	82	O50(15/18/18)		-0.7
1941	Phi A	80	170	14	53	7	1	0	15	4	1	8	.312	.331	.365	86	-4	0-1	1.000	2	115	73	O35(25/2/8)		-0.4
1942	Phi A	99	346	41	94	12	5	0	22	12	2	10	.272	.300	.335	79	-11	5-3	.984	0	99	109	O81(9/46/28)		-1.5
1943	Bos A	45	121	9	26	2	2	0	10	3	0	3	.215	.234	.264	45	-9	0-2	.968	-1	89	159	O25(1/24/0)		-1.2
Total 7		503	1467	175	411	53	24	2	143	50	5	74	.280	.306	.353	76	-57	15-16	.971	1	101	100	O323(52/110/165)		-7.3

MILEY, MIKE Michael Wilfred B3.30.1953 Yazoo City MS D1.6.1977 Baton Rouge LA BB/TR (BR 1975p)/6-1/185* [AnaA74 1/10] d7.6 Col Louisiana St.

YEAR	TM LG	G	AB	R	H	2B	3B	HR	RBI	BB-IB	HP	SO	AVG	OBP	SLG	AOPS	ABR	SB-CS	FA	FR	RNG	THR	GAMES AT POSITION	DL	BFW
1975	Cal A	70	224	17	39	3	2	4	26	16-0	1	54	.174	.230	.259	41	-19	0-1	.939	-9	86	123	S70		-2.0
1976	Cal A	14	38	4	7	2	0	0	4	4-1	0	8	.184	.256	.237	50	-2	1-0	.981	-3	74	122	S14		-0.3
Total 2		84	262	21	46	5	2	4	30	20-1	1	62	.176	.234	.256	43	-21	1-1	.945	-11	84	123	S84		-2.3

MILLAN, FELIX Felix Bernardo (Martinez) B8.21.1943 Yabucoa, PR BR/TR/5-11/172* d6.2

YEAR	TM LG	G	AB	R	H	2B	3B	HR	RBI	BB-IB	HP	SO	AVG	OBP	SLG	AOPS	ABR	SB-CS	FA	FR	RNG	THR	GAMES AT POSITION	DL	BFW
1966	Atl N	37	91	20	25	6	0	0	5	2-2	0	6	.275	.290	.341	74	-3	3-1	.973	-6	86	82	2b25/S3		-0.7
1967	Atl N	41	136	13	32	3	3	2	4	10-1	2	10	.235	.266	.346	75	-5	0-3	.972	6	118	102	2b41		0.3
1968	Atl N	149	570	49	165	22	2	1	33	22-7	6	26	.289	.321	.340	99	-1	6-6	.980	1	102	111	2b145		1.3
1969	†Atl N★	162	652	82	174	23	5	6	57	34-5	8	35	.267	.310	.345	83	-16	14-3	**.980**	8	94	76	2b162		-2.2
1970	Atl N★	142	590	100	183	25	5	2	37	35-2	5	23	.310	.352	.380	91	-7	16-5	.979	-11	89	95	2b142		-0.6
1971	Atl N★	143	577	65	167	20	8	2	45	37-7	3	22	.289	.332	.362	91	-6	11-7	.982	6	101	119	2b141		0.9
1972	Atl N	125	498	46	128	19	3	1	38	23-1	3	28	.257	.292	.313	67	-22	6-4	.987	-11	96	84	2b120		-2.7
1973	†NY N	153	638	82	185	23	4	3	37	35-3	6	22	.290	.332	.353	91	-9	2-2	.989	5	102	153	2b153		0.6
1974	NY N	136	518	50	139	15	2	1	33	31-2	8	14	.268	.317	.311	77	-16	5-1	.979	-10	87	96	2b134		-1.7
1975	NY N	162	676	81	191	37	2	1	56	36-2	**12**	28	.283	.329	.348	91	-8	1-6	.972	-23	86	89	2b162		-2.4
1976	NY N	139	531	55	150	25	2	1	35	41-5	7	19	.282	.341	.343	99	0	2-4	.977	-15	84	90	2b136		-2.2
1977	NY N	91	314	40	78	11	2	2	21	18-3	3	9	.248	.294	.315	66	-16	1-1	.977	-9	83	92	2b89	24	-2.1
Total 12		1480	5791	699	1617	229	38	22	403	318-40	63	242	.279	.322	.343	86	-109	67-43	.980	-85	93	95	2b1450/3S	24	-10.0

MILLAR, KEVIN Kevin Charles B9.24.1971 Los Angeles CA BR/TR/6-1/195(185-210) d4.11 Col Lamar

YEAR	TM LG	G	AB	R	H	2B	3B	HR	RBI	BB-IB	HP	SO	AVG	OBP	SLG	AOPS	ABR	SB-CS	FA	FR	RNG	THR	GAMES AT POSITION	DL	BFW
1998	Fla N	2	2	1	1	0	0	0	0	1-0	0	0	.500	.667	.500	227	1	0-0	.833	1	221	704	3b2	161	0.1
1999	Fla N	105	351	48	100	17	4	9	67	40-2	7	64	.285	.362	.433	108	5	1-0	.995	-4	87	105	1b94/3OL		-0.6
2000	Fla N	123	259	36	67	14	3	14	42	36-0	8	47	.259	.364	.498	122	9	0-0	.989	6	159	-79	1b34,O18(17/0/1),3b13,D6		1.1
2001	Fla N	144	449	62	141	39	5	20	85	39-2	5	70	.314	.374	.557	141	27	0-0	.986	-7	92	38	O86(27/0/66),1b15,3b10,D6		1.5
2002	Fla N	126	438	58	134	41	0	16	57	40-0	5	74	.306	.366	.509	137	22	0-2	.985	0	97	92	O108(89/0/22),1b2,3b2,D6	29	1.7
2003	†Bos A	148	544	83	150	30	1	25	96	60-5	5	108	.276	.348	.472	110	9	3-2	.996	6	115	98	1b101,O31(19/0/12),D19		0.4
2004	†Bos A	150	508	74	151	36	0	18	74	57-0	**17**	91	.297	.383	.474	116	14	1-1	.976	4	99	25	O74(20/0/55),1b69,D8		0.9
2005	†Bos A	134	449	57	122	28	1	9	50	54-0	8	74	.272	.355	.399	96	0	0-1	.992	9	144	82	1b110,O34(20/0/14)		-0.1
Total 8		932	3000	419	866	205	14	111	471	327-9	55	528	.289	.365	.477	118	87	5-6	.993	16	122	94	1b425,O352(193/0/170),D45,3b28	190	5.0

MILLARD, FRANK Frank E. B7.4.1865 E.St.Louis IL D7.4.1892 Dallas TX d5.4

YEAR	TM LG	G	AB	R	H	2B	3B	HR	RBI	BB-IB	HP	SO	AVG	OBP	SLG	AOPS	ABR	SB-CS	FA	FR	RNG	THR	GAMES AT POSITION	DL	BFW
1890	StL AA	1	1	0	0	0	0	0	0	1	0		.000	.500	.000	42	0	0	.625	-0	153	0	/2		0.0

MILLER, CORKY Abraham Philip B3.18.1976 Yucaipa CA BR/TR/6-1/225(225-245) d9.4 Col Nevada-Reno

YEAR	TM LG	G	AB	R	H	2B	3B	HR	RBI	BB-IB	HP	SO	AVG	OBP	SLG	AOPS	ABR	SB-CS	FA	FR	RNG	THR	GAMES AT POSITION	DL	BFW
2001	Cin N	17	49	5	9	2	0	3	7	4-0	2	16	.184	.263	.408	69	-3	1-0	.991	3	108	186	C17		0.2
2002	Cin N	39	114	9	29	10	0	3	15	9-2	1	20	.254	.328	.421	96	-1	0-0	.992	5	138	78	C38		0.6
2003	Cin N	14	30	4	8	0	0	1	1	5-0	2	7	.267	.395	.267	84	0	0-0	1.000	-0	45	99	C11		0.0
2004	Cin N	13	39	2	1	0	0	0	3	6-0	3	12	.026	.204	.026	-34	-8	0-0	.989	1	318	40	C12		-0.6
2005	Min A	5	12	0	0	0	0	0	0	0-0	1	2	.000	.000	.000	-97	-3	0-0	1.000	2	160	294	C4/D		-0.1
Total 5		88	244	20	47	12	0	6	26	24-2	11	57	.193	.289	.316	60	-15	1-0	.993	11	150	107	C82/D		0.1

MILLER, DUSTY Charles Bradley B9.10.1868 Oil City PA D9.3.1945 Memphis TN BL/TR/5-11.5/170 d9.23 Col Niagara

YEAR	TM LG	G	AB	R	H	2B	3B	HR	RBI	BB-IB	HP	SO	AVG	OBP	SLG	AOPS	ABR	SB-CS	FA	FR	RNG	THR	GAMES AT POSITION	DL	BFW
1889	Bal AA	11	40	4	6	1	1	0	6	2	1	11	.150	.209	.225	23	-4	3	.636	-8	69	0	S8,O3(2/1/0)		-1.0
1890	StL AA	26	96	17	21	5	3	1	10	8			.219	.279	.365	78	-4	4	.872	3	195	351	O24(9/15/0),S3		-0.2
1895	Cin N	132	529	103	177	31	16	10	112	33	4	34	.335	.378	.510	123	15	43	.937	10	129	183	O132(0/11/121)		1.5
1896	Cin N	125	504	90	162	38	12	4	93	33	4	30	.321	.368	.468	112	7	76	.902	-2	122	176	O125(1/0/124)		-0.1
1897	Cin N	119	440	83	139	27	4	4	70	48	8		.316	.393	.409	105	5	29	.929	2	108	64	O119R		0.1
1898	Cin N	152	586	99	175	24	12	3	90	38	9		.299	.351	.396	106	3	32	.929	5	106	79	O152R		0.0
1899	Cin N	81	327	45	83	12	6	0	37	9	3		.254	.280	.327	65	-17	18	.927	6	144	123	O81(1/2/79)		-1.4
	StL N	10	39	3	8	1	0	0	3	3	1		.205	.279	.231	40	-3	1	.875	-1	64	249	O10C		-0.5
	Year	91	366	48	91	13	6	0	40	12	4		.249	.280	.317	62	-20	19	.921	4	135	137	O91(1/12/79)		-1.9
Total 7		656	2561	445	771	139	51	22	421	174	30	75	.301	.353	.421	103	2	206	.923	15	121	134	O646(13/39/595),S11		-1.6

YEAR	TM	LG	G	AB	R	H	2B	3B	HR	RBI	BB-IB	HP	SO	AVG	OBP	SLG	AOPS	ABR	SB-CS	FA	FR	RNG	THR	GAMES AT POSITION	DL	BFW

MILLER, BRUCE Charles Bruce B3.4.1947 Fort Wayne IN BR/TR/6-1/185* [ChiA70 20/469] d8.4 Col Indiana

YEAR	TM LG	G	AB	R	H	2B	3B	HR	RBI	BB-IB	HP	SO	AVG	OBP	SLG	AOPS	ABR	SB-CS	FA	FR	RNG	THR	GAMES AT POSITION	DL	BFW
1973	SF N	12	21	1	3	0	0	0	2	2-1	0	3	.143	.217	.143	2	-3	0-0	.900	0	124	0	3b4,2b3/S		-0.3
1974	SF N	73	198	19	55	7	1	0	16	11-2	1	15	.278	.324	.323	77	-6	1-1	.938	8	138	46	3b41,S13,2b9		0.4
1975	SF N	99	309	22	74	6	3	1	31	15-0	1	26	.239	.275	.288	55	-20	0-1	.949	5	97	101	3b68,2b21,S6		-1.4
1976	SF N	12	25	1	4	1	0	0	2	2-1	0	5	.160	.222	.200	20	-3	0-0	.920	-3	93	83	2b8,3b2		-0.5
Total 4		196	553	43	136	14	4	1	51	30-4	2	49	.246	.285	.291	59	-32	1-2	.944	11	111	78	3b115,2b41,S20		-1.8

MILLER, CHARLIE Charles Elmer B1.4.1892 Warrensburg MO D4.23.1972 Warrensburg MO TR d9.18

YEAR	TM LG	G	AB	R	H	2B	3B	HR	RBI	BB-IB	HP	SO	AVG	OBP	SLG	AOPS	ABR	SB-CS	FA	FR	RNG	THR	GAMES AT POSITION	DL	BFW
1912	StL A	1	2	0	0	0	0	0	0		0		.000	.000	.000	-99	-1	0	1.000	0	142	0	/S		0.0

MILLER, CHARLIE Charles Hess B12.30.1877 Conestoga PA D1.13.1951 Millersville PA BR/TR/6-0/190 d10.2

YEAR	TM LG	G	AB	R	H	2B	3B	HR	RBI	BB-IB	HP	SO	AVG	OBP	SLG	AOPS	ABR	SB-CS	FA	FR	RNG	THR	GAMES AT POSITION	DL	BFW
1915	Bal F	1	1	0	0	0	0	0	0		0		.000	.000	.000	-97	-1	0	—	0			/H		0.0

MILLER, CHUCK Charles Marion B9.18.1889 Woodville OH D6.16.1961 Houston TX BL/TL/5-8.5/155 d9.19

YEAR	TM LG	G	AB	R	H	2B	3B	HR	RBI	BB-IB	HP	SO	AVG	OBP	SLG	AOPS	ABR	SB-CS	FA	FR	RNG	THR	GAMES AT POSITION	DL	BFW
1913	StL N	4	12	0	2	0	0	0	1		0	2	.167	.167	.167	-5	-2	0	1.000	-0	85	0	O3(2/0/1)		-0.2
1914	StL N	36	36	4	7	1	0	0	2	3	0	9	.194	.256	.222	43	-3	2	1.000	1	107	153	O14(6/5/2)		-0.2
Total 2		40	48	4	9	1	0	0	3	3	0	11	.188	.235	.208	31	-5	2	1.000	0	100	103	O17(8/5/3)		-0.4

MILLER, DUSTY Dakin Evans B9.3.1876 Malvern IA D4.19.1950 Stockton CA BL/TR/5-10/175 d4.17

YEAR	TM LG	G	AB	R	H	2B	3B	HR	RBI	BB-IB	HP	SO	AVG	OBP	SLG	AOPS	ABR	SB-CS	FA	FR	RNG	THR	GAMES AT POSITION	DL	BFW
1902	Chi N	51	187	17	46	4	1	0	13	7	7		.246	.299	.278	80	-4	10	.955	2	132	0	O51(46/1/4)		-0.6

MILLER, DAMIAN Damian Donald B10.13.1969 LaCrosse WI BR/TR/6-2/212(190-220) [MinA90 20/544] d8.10 Col Viterbo

YEAR	TM LG	G	AB	R	H	2B	3B	HR	RBI	BB-IB	HP	SO	AVG	OBP	SLG	AOPS	ABR	SB-CS	FA	FR	RNG	THR	GAMES AT POSITION	DL	BFW
1997	Min A	25	66	5	18	1	0	2	13	0-0	0	12	.273	.282	.379	73	-3	0-0	1.000	-2	249	61	C20,D3		-0.3
1998	Ari N	57	168	17	48	14	2	3	14	11-2	0	25	.286	.337	.446	104	1	1-0	.986	1	121	94	C46,O2R/1D		0.5
1999	Ari N	86	296	35	80	19	0	11	47	19-3	2	78	.270	.316	.446	90	-5	0-0	.991	16	90	143	C86		1.5
2000	Ari N	100	324	43	89	24	0	10	44	36-4	1	74	.275	.347	.441	94	-2	2-2	.992	0	111	127	C97,1b2/S		0.4
2001	†Ari N	123	380	45	103	19	0	13	47	35-9	4	80	.271	.337	.424	89	-6	0-1	.993	29	92	126	C121		2.9
2002	†Ari N★	101	297	40	74	22	0	11	42	38-5	3	88	.249	.340	.434	96	-2	0-0	.997	11	122	108	C100	21	1.5
2003	†Chi N	114	352	34	82	19	1	9	36	39-6	1	91	.233	.310	.369	75	-13	1-0	.997	21	126	113	C114		1.5
2004	Oak A	110	397	39	108	25	1	9	58	39-0	2	87	.272	.339	.403	93	-3	0-1	.999	5	127	128	C109		0.8
2005	Mil N	114	385	50	105	25	1	9	43	37-6	4	94	.273	.340	.413	97	-1	0-1	.996	-3	104	109	C111		0.2
Total 9		830	2665	308	707	168	4	77	344	256-35	19	647	.265	.332	.418	91	-34	4-5	.995	79	114	119	C804,D5,1b3,O2R/S	21	9.0

MILLER, DARRELL Darrell Keith B2.26.1958 Washington DC BR/TR/6-2/200* [CalA79 9/223] d8.14 Col Cal Poly-Pomona

YEAR	TM LG	G	AB	R	H	2B	3B	HR	RBI	BB-IB	HP	SO	AVG	OBP	SLG	AOPS	ABR	SB-CS	FA	FR	RNG	THR	GAMES AT POSITION	DL	BFW
1984	Cal A	17	41	5	7	0	0	0	1	4-0	0	9	.171	.244	.171	17	-5	0-0	.990	-1	76	114	1b16/OL		-0.7
1985	Cal A	51	48	8	18	2	1	2	7	1-0	1	10	.375	.400	.583	165	4	0-1	.952	2	126	205	O45(1/3/41)/C3D	22	0.5
1986	Cal A	33	57	6	13	2	1	0	4	4-0	0	8	.228	.274	.298	58	-3	0-0	1.000	-5	41	0	O23(11/3/9),C10,D2		-0.9
1987	Cal A	53	108	14	26	5	0	4	16	9-0	2	13	.241	.303	.398	89	-2	1-0	.984	0	171	144	C33,O18(14/0/4)/3D	47	-0.1
1988	Cal A	70	140	21	31	4	1	2	7	9-0	5	29	.221	.292	.307	70	-6	2-1	.987	1	99	113	C53,O8(7/2/0)/D	15	-0.3
Total 5		224	394	54	95	13	3	8	35	27-0	8	69	.241	.300	.350	80	-12	3-2	.987	-3	118	120	C97,O95(34/8/54),1b16,D8,3b2	84	-1.5

MILLER, BING Edmund John B8.30.1894 Vinton IA D5.7.1966 Philadelphia PA BR/TR/6-0/185 d4.16 C17 b-Ralph

YEAR	TM LG	G	AB	R	H	2B	3B	HR	RBI	BB-IB	HP	SO	AVG	OBP	SLG	AOPS	ABR	SB-CS	FA	FR	RNG	THR	GAMES AT POSITION	DL	BFW
1921	Was A	114	420	57	121	28	8	9	71	25	4	50	.288	.334	.457	105	1	3-4	.945	-0	102	89	O109(92/3/14)		-0.8
1922	Phi A	143	535	90	179	29	12	21	90	24	7	42	.335	.371	.551	134	23	10-10	.977	5	102	132	O139(15/90/36)		1.9
1923	Phi A	123	458	68	137	25	4	12	64	27	4	34	.299	.344	.450	106	2	9-3	.978	-2	103	67	O119(104/0/15)		-0.8
1924	Phi A	113	398	62	136	22	4	6	62	12	10	24	.342	.376	.462	114	7	11-5	.975	-3	94	89	O94(10/9/75),1b7		-0.2
1925	Phi A	124	474	78	151	29	10	10	81	19	8	14	.319	.355	.485	105	1	11-6	.975	-8	89	60	O115(22/0/96),1b12		-1.6
1926	Phi A	38	110	13	32	6	2	2	13	11	0	6	.291	.355	.436	100	0	4-1	1.000	-2	99	34	O34(10/0/26)/1		-0.3
	StL A	94	353	60	117	27	5	4	50	22	7	12	.331	.382	.470	116	8	7-9	.939	3	108	116	O94(26/16/54)		0.2
	Year	132	463	73	149	33	7	6	63	33	7	18	.322	.376	.462	112	8	11-10	.950	2	106	97	O128(36/16/80)/1		-0.1
1927	StL A	143	492	83	160	32	7	5	75	30	9	26	.325	.375	.449	109	6	8-7	.970	3	111	72	O126(37/61/29)		0.1
1928	Phi A	139	510	76	168	34	7	8	85	27	8	24	.329	.372	.471	117	12	10-6	.968	-1	107	60	O133(28/43/66)		0.2
1929	†Phi A	147	556	84	184	32	16	8	93	40	4	25	.331	.380	.489	118	13	24-10	.970	-1	107	64	O145(9/4/133)		0.2
1930	†Phi A	154	585	89	177	38	7	9	100	44	3	22	.303	.357	.438	96	-3	13-13	.976	4	111	78	O154(0/13/142)		-1.2
1931	†Phi A	137	534	75	150	43	5	8	77	36	10	16	.281	.338	.425	94	-5	5-3	.987	5	115	55	O137R		-0.8
1932	Phi A	95	305	40	90	17	4	7	58	20	2	11	.295	.343	.446	99	-1	7-3	.979	4	118	52	O84(5/0/79)		-0.2
1933	Phi A	67	120	22	33	7	1	2	17	12	1	7	.275	.340	.400	96	-1	4-2	1.000	-1	99	57	O30(10/3/18),1b6		-0.2
1934	Phi A	81	177	22	43	10	2	1	22	16	1	14	.243	.309	.339	70	-8	1-0	1.000	0	101	70	O46(4/0/42)		-1.0
1935	Bos A	78	138	18	42	8	1	3	26	10	1	8	.304	.356	.442	99	-1	0-1	.962	-0	101	99	O29(1/0/28)		-0.2
1936	Bos A	30	47	9	14	2	1	1	6	5	1	5	.298	.377	.447	97	0	0-0	1.000	8	141	153	O13(7/0/7)		-0.1
Total 16		1820	6212	946	1934	389	96	116	990	383	80	340	.311	.359	.461	108	54	127-83	.971	6	105	77	O1601(380/242/997),1b26		-4.8

MILLER, EDDIE Edward Lee B6.29.1957 San Pablo CA BB/TR/5-9/175(160-175) [TexA75 2/41] d9.5

YEAR	TM LG	G	AB	R	H	2B	3B	HR	RBI	BB-IB	HP	SO	AVG	OBP	SLG	AOPS	ABR	SB-CS	FA	FR	RNG	THR	GAMES AT POSITION	DL	BFW
1977	Tex A	17	6	7	2	0	0	0	1	1-0	0	1	.333	.429	.333	110	0	3-1	1.000	-0	88	0	O2C,D3		0.0
1978	Atl N	6	21	5	3	1	0	0	2	2-0	1	4	.143	.250	.190	22	-2	3-0	1.000	-2	53	0	O5(2/3/0)		-0.3
1979	Atl N	27	113	12	35	1	0	0	5	5-1	2	24	.310	.350	.319	79	-3	15-2	.988	1	114	50	O27(1/27/0)		0.0
1980	Atl N	11	19	3	3	0	0	0	0	0-0	0	5	.158	.158	.158	-12	-3	1-2	1.000	-2	46	0	O9(1/8/0)		-0.6
1981	Atl N	50	134	29	31	3	1	0	7	7-1	3	29	.231	.285	.269	57	-8	23-5	.985	-0	101	72	O36(28/2/7)	23	-0.6
1982	Det A	14	25	3	1	0	0	0	0	4-0	1	4	.040	.250	.040	-14	-4	0-3	1.000	-0	80	195	O8(0/3/5)/D	23	-0.6
1984	SD N	13	14	4	4	0	1	1	2	0-0	1	6	.286	.286	.643	153	1	4-0	1.000	1	62	828	O8(0/4/4)		-0.2
Total 7		138	332	63	79	5	2	1	17	19-2	9	71	.238	.297	.274	58	-19	49-13	.989	-3	95	98	O95(32/49/16),D4	46	-1.9

MILLER, EDDIE Edward Robert "Eppie" B11.26.1916 Pittsburgh PA D7.31.1997 Lake Worth FL BR/TR/5-9/180* d9.9

YEAR	TM LG	G	AB	R	H	2B	3B	HR	RBI	BB-IB	HP	SO	AVG	OBP	SLG	AOPS	ABR	SB-CS	FA	FR	RNG	THR	GAMES AT POSITION	DL	BFW
1936	Cin N	5	10	1	1	0	0	0	0	0-1	0	1	.100	.182	.100	-24	-2	0	.938	-1	112	54	S4/2		-0.2
1937	Bos N	36	60	3	9	3	1	0	5	3	0	8	.150	.190	.233	15	-7	0	.926	3	107	126	S30,3b4		-0.3
1939	Bos N	77	296	32	79	12	2	4	31	16	5	21	.267	.315	.361	88	-6	4	.970	10	106	141	S77		1.0
1940	Bos N★	151	569	78	157	33	3	14	79	41	5	43	.276	.330	.418	111	8	8	.970	15	99	118	S151		3.4
1941	Bos N★	154	585	54	140	27	6	16	68	35	4	72	.239	.288	.326	76	-20	8	.966	13	104	120	S154		0.4
1942	Bos N★	142	534	47	130	28	2	6	47	22	4	42	.243	.279	.337	81	-15	11	.983	6	105	93	S142		0.2
1943	Cin N★	154	576	49	129	26	4	2	71	33	4	43	.224	.271	.293	64	-28	8	.979	24	105	130	S154		0.9
1944	Cin N★	155	536	48	112	21	5	4	55	41	3	41	.209	.269	.302	59	-30	9	.971	12	106	125	S155		-0.6
1945	Cin N★	115	421	46	100	27	2	13	49	18	4	38	.238	.275	.404	89	-9	4	.975	6	105	95	S115		0.7
1946	Cin N★	91	299	30	58	10	0	6	36	25	1	25	.194	.258	.288	57	-18	5	.970	16	111	163	S88		0.3
1947	Cin N★	151	545	69	146	**38**	4	19	87	49	4	40	.268	.333	.457	109	5	5	.972	-6	94	91	S151		0.8
1948	Phi N	130	468	45	115	20	1	14	61	19	4	40	.246	.281	.382	79	-16	1	.966	-12	93	89	S122		-2.1
1949	Phi N	85	266	21	55	10	1	6	29	29	4	21	.207	.294	.320	66	-13	1	.986	-11	86	104	S82		-2.0
1950	StL N	64	172	17	39	8	0	3	22	19	1	21	.227	.307	.326	64	-9	0	.980	10	120	96	S51/2		0.3
Total 14		1510	5337	539	1270	263	28	97	640	351	44	465	.238	.290	.349	85	-160	64	.972	85	103	114	S1395,2b84,3b4		2.8

MILLER, ED Edwin Collins "Big Ed" B11.24.1888 Annville PA D4.17.1980 S.Lebanon Twp. PA BR/TR/6-0/180 d6.29

YEAR	TM LG	G	AB	R	H	2B	3B	HR	RBI	BB-IB	HP	SO	AVG	OBP	SLG	AOPS	ABR	SB-CS	FA	FR	RNG	THR	GAMES AT POSITION	DL	BFW
1912	StL A	13	46	4	9	1	0	0	5	4	0		.196	.245	.217	34	-4	1	.951	-4	43	75	1b8,S5		-0.8
1914	StL A	41	58	8	8	0	1	0	4	2		13	.138	.219	.172	18	-6	1-3	.981	-2	66	162	1b8,2b5,O5R,3b2		-1.0
1918	Cle A	32	96	9	22	4	3	0	3	12	1	10	.229	.321	.333	89	-1	0-3	.977	2	126	118	1b22,O4(1/0/3)		0.0
Total 3		86	200	21	39	5	4	0	12	18	4	23	.195	.275	.260	58	-11	4-3	.972	-4	99	114	1b38,O9(1/0/8),2b5,S5,3b2		-1.8

MILLER, ELMER Elmer B7.28.1890 Sandusky OH D11.28.1944 Beloit WI BR/TR/6-0/175 d4.26

YEAR	TM LG	G	AB	R	H	2B	3B	HR	RBI	BB-IB	HP	SO	AVG	OBP	SLG	AOPS	ABR	SB-CS	FA	FR	RNG	THR	GAMES AT POSITION	DL	BFW
1912	StL N	12	37	5	7	1	0	0	3	4	0	9	.189	.268	.216	34	-3	1	1.000	1	118	66	O11(4/3/4)		-0.3
1915	NY A	26	83	4	12	1	0	0	3	4	1	14	.145	.193	.157	5	-10	0	.955	-2	92	34	O26(0/20/6)		-1.5
1916	NY A	43	152	12	34	3	2	1	18	11	1	18	.224	.280	.289	70	-6	8	.969	4	101	161	O42(18/9/15)		-0.5
1917	NY A	114	379	43	95	11	3	3	35	40	**9**	44	.251	.336	.319	99	1	11	.961	-4	91	108	O112(33/53/26)		-1.0
1918	NY A	67	202	18	49	9	2	1	22	19	2	17	.243	.317	.322	91	-2	4	.947	-3	99	141	O62(3/53/6)		-0.6
1921	†NY A	56	242	41	72	9	8	4	36	19	3	16	.298	.356	.450	102	0	2-2	.947	-1	91	133	O56C		-0.4
1922	NY A	51	172	31	46	7	3	2	18	11	0	12	.267	.311	.384	79	-6	2-3	.982	1	95	150	O51(7/41/3)		-0.8
	Bos A	44	147	16	28	2	3	4	16	5	1	10	.190	.222	.327	42	-14	3-1	.957	-0	97	82	O25(2/33/0)		-1.6
	Year	95	319	47	74	9	5	7	34	16	1	22	.232	.271	.357	62	-20	5-4	.970	-0	96	120	O86(9/74/3)		-2.4
Total 7		413	1414	170	343	43	20	16	151	113	18	140	.243	.300	.335	80	-40	31-6	.960	-2	95	121	O395(67/268/60)		-6.7

YEAR	TM LG	G	AB	R	H	2B	3B	HR	RBI	BB-IB	HP	SO	AVG	OBP	SLG	AOPS	ABR	SB-CS	FA	FR	RNG	THR	GAMES AT POSITION	DL	BFW

MILLER, ELMER Elmer Joseph "Lefty" B4.17.1903 Detroit MI D1.8.1987 Corona CA BL/TL/5-11/189 d6.21 ▲

| 1929 | Phi N | 31 | 38 | 3 | 9 | 1 | 0 | 1 | 4 | 1 | 0 | 5 | .237 | .256 | .342 | 44 | -4 | 0 | .750 | 2 | 82 | 0 | P8,O4R | | -0.1 |

MILLER, KOHLY Frank A. B1.1874 Cumru Twp. PA D3.29.1951 Reading PA d9.16

1892	Was N	1	3	0	0	0	0	0	0	0	0	1	.000	.000	.000	-99	-1	0	.400	-1	74	0	/S		-0.2
	StL N	1	4	0	0	0	0	0	0	0	0	0	.000	.000	.000	-99	-1	0	.500	-1	0	0	/3		-0.2
	Year	2	7	0	0	0	0	0	0	0	0	1	.000	.000	.000	-99	-2	0	.400	-2	74	0	/S3		-0.4
1897	Phi N	3	11	2	2	0	0	0	1	2	0		.182	.308	.182	32	-1	0	.857	-2	45	104	2b3		-0.3
Total	2	5	18	2	2	0	0	0	1	2	0	1	.111	.200	.111	-13	-3	0	.857	-4	45	104	2b3/3S		-0.7

MILLER, GEORGE George C. B2.19.1853 Newport KY D7.24.1929 Norwood OH BR/TR/5-5/160 d9.6

1877	Cin N	11	37	4	6	1	0	0	3	5		2	.162	.262	.189	50	-1		.918	-0			C11		-0.1
1884	Cin AA	6	20	6	5	1	0	0	3	1	1		.250	.318	.400	127	1		.975	2			C6		0.3
Total	2	17	57	10	11	2	0	0	6	6	1	2	.193	.281	.263	79	0		.938	2			C17		0.2

MILLER, DOGGIE George Frederick "Foghorn", "Calliope" B8.15.1864 Brooklyn NY D4.6.1909 Ridgewood NY BR/TR/5-6/145 d5.1 M1 OF(146/68/96)

1884	Pit AA	89	347	46	78	10	2	0		13		2	.225	.257	.265	71	-10		.798	-2	131	56	O49(48/0/1),C36,3b3/2		-1.0
1885	Pit AA	42	166	19	27	3	1	0	13	4			.163	.182	.193	19	-15		.893	-6			C33,O6(3/3/0),S2,3b2		-1.6
1886	Pit AA	83	317	70	80	15	1	2	36	43	1		.252	.343	.325	110	6	35	.918	-14			C61,O22(12/10/1)/2		-0.3
1887	Pit N	87	342	58	83	17	4	1	34	35	2	13	.243	.317	.325	85	-5	33	.928	-20			C73,O14(2/11/1)/3		-1.7
1888	Pit N	103	404	50	112	17	5	0	36	18	7	16	.277	.319	.344	122	11	27	.908	-12			C76,O27(6/5/16),3b3		0.3
1889	Pit N	104	422	77	113	25	4	6	56	31	2	11	.268	.321	.384	107	3	16	.889	-7			C40,O25(1/2/22),S13,C10,2b6		0.2
1890	Pit N	138	549	85	150	24	3	4	66	68	4	11	.273	.357	.350	120	19	32	.850	-4	121	100	3b88,O25(1/2/22),S13,C10,2b6		2.3
1891	Pit N	135	548	80	156	19	6	4	57	59	3	26	.285	.357	.363	113	10	35	.938	-9	105	110	C41,S37,3b34,O24(22/0/2)/1		0.5
1892	Pit N	149	623	103	158	15	12	2	59	69	7	14	.254	.335	.326	99	0	28	.906	1	99	92	O76(24/30/23),C63,S19,3b2		0.4
1893	Pit N	41	154	23	28	6	1	0	17	17	5	8	.182	.284	.234	39	-13	3	.916	-1	98	100	C40		-0.9
1894	StL N	127	481	93	163	9	11	8	86	58	4	9	.339	.414	.453	109	8	17	.832	-11	90	73	3b52,C41,2b18,1b12,O4(2/0/2)/SM		0.1
1895	StL N	122	494	81	144	15	4	5	74	25	6	12	.291	.333	.368	82	-14	18	.829	-21	81	74	3b46,C47,O21R,S9,1b6		-2.6
1896	Lou N	98	324	54	89	17	4	1	33	27	2	9	.275	.334	.361	86	-6	16	.922	-11	78	118	C48,2b25,O8(1/2/5),3b8,1b3,S2		-1.1
Total	13	1318	5171	839	1381	192	57	33	567	467	45	129	.267	.333	.345	97	-6	260	.918	-108	96	107	C637,O308L,3b243,S83,2b51,1b22		-5.4

MILLER, HUGHIE Hugh Stanley "Cotton" B12.22.1886 St.Louis MO D12.24.1945 Jefferson Barracks MO BR/TR/6-1.5/175 d6.18

1911	Phi N	1	0	0	0	0	0	0	0	0	0	0	—	—	—	0	0			0			/R		0.0
1914	StL F	132	490	51	109	20	5	0	46	27	1	57	.222	.264	.284	47	-44	4	.990	-1	95	68	1b130		-5.1
1915	StL F	7	6	0	3	0	0	0	3	0	0	0	.500	.500	.667	216	1	0	1.000	-0	0		1b6		0.1
Total	3	140	496	51	112	21	5	0	49	27	1	57	.226	.267	.288	49	-43	4	.990	-0	94	67	1b136		-5.0

MILLER, JAKE Jacob George (b Jacob George Muenzing) B12.1.1895 Baltimore MD D8.24.1974 Towson MD BR/TR/5-10/170 d7.15

| 1922 | Pit N | 3 | 11 | 0 | 1 | 0 | 0 | 0 | 0 | 2 | 0 | 0 | .091 | .231 | .091 | -14 | -2 | 1-0 | .889 | -0 | 114 | 0 | O3R | | -0.2 |

MILLER, HACK James Eldridge B2.13.1913 Celeste TX D11.21.1966 Dallas TX BR/TR/5-11.5/215 d4.18 Col Southeastern Oklahoma

1944	Det A	5	5	1	1	0	0	0	3	1	0	1	.200	.333	.800	207	0	0-0	1.000	0	0	269	C5		0.1
1945	Det A	2	4	0	3	0	0	0	1	0	0	0	.750	.750	.750	315	1	0-0	1.000	0	0	0	C2		0.1
Total	2	7	9	1	4	0	0	0	4	1	0	1	.444	.500	.778	250	2	0-0	1.000	1	0	152	C7		0.2

MILLER, JIM James McCurdy "Rabbit" B10.2.1880 Pittsburgh PA D2.7.1937 Pittsburgh PA BR/TR/5-8/165 d9.9

| 1901 | NY N | 18 | 58 | 3 | 8 | 0 | 0 | 0 | 3 | 6 | 0 | | .138 | .219 | .138 | 5 | -7 | 1 | .936 | -2 | 99 | 98 | 2b18 | | -0.9 |

MILLER, JOHN John Allen B3.14.1944 Alhambra CA BR/TR/5-11/195(175-195) d9.11

1966	NY N	6	23	1	2	0	0	1	2	0-0	0	9	.087	.087	.217	-16	-4	0-0	1.000	-1	0	49	1b3,O3L		-0.6
1969	LA N	26	38	3	8	1	0	1	1	2-0	0	9	.211	.250	.316	61	-2	0-0	1.000	-2	18	0	O6L,1b5,3b2/2		-0.5
Total	2	32	61	4	10	1	0	2	3	2-0	0	18	.164	.190	.279	33	-6	0-0	1.000	-3	44	0	O9L,1b8,3b2/2		-1.1

MILLER, DOTS John Barney B9.9.1886 Kearny NJ D9.5.1923 Saranac Lake NY BR/TR/5-11.5/170 d4.16 Mil 1918

1909	†Pit N	151	556	71	156	31	13	3	87	39	3		.279	.329	.396	115	8	14	.953	-12	102	113	2b150		-0.3
1910	Pit N	120	444	45	101	13	10	1	48	33		41	.227	.284	.309	69	-19	11	.946	-15	95	93	2b119/1S		-3.5
1911	Pit N	137	470	82	126	17	8	6	78	51	7	48	.268	.348	.377	99	-1	17	.943	-3	98	137	2b129		-0.1
1912	Pit N	148	567	74	156	33	12	4	87	37	4	45	.275	.324	.397	98	-4	18	.985	-0	102	124	1b147		-0.8
1913	Pit N	154	580	75	158	24	20	7	90	37	1	52	.272	.317	.419	114	7	20-13	.985	-4	92	86	1b150,S3		-0.2
1914	StL N	155	573	67	166	27	10	4	88	34	9	52	.290	.339	.393	119	12	16	.993	-6	107	97	1b91,S60,2b5		0.9
1915	StL N	150	553	73	146	17	10	2	72	43	3	46	.264	.324	.342	101	0	27-19	.991	3	99	102	1b94,2b55,3b9,S3		0.2
1916	StL N	143	505	47	120	22	7	1	46	40	5	49	.238	.300	.315	89	-6	18	.993	7	98	110	1b93,2b38,S21/3		1.3
1917	StL N	148	544	61	135	15	9	2	45	33	5	52	.248	.295	.320	91	-7	14	.960	17	112	135	2b92,1b46,S11		1.6
1919	StL N	101	346	38	80	10	4	1	24	13	3	23	.231	.265	.292	72	-13	6	.981	3	107	93	1b68,2b28		-1.3
1920	Phi N	98	343	41	87	12	2	1	27	16	1	17	.254	.289	.309	68	-14	13-6	.948	-7	87	115	2b59,3b17,S12,1b9/OC		-2.0
1921	Phi N	84	320	37	95	11	3	0	23	15	1	27	.297	.330	.350	74	-11	3-5	.940	-3	110	132	3b41,1b38,2b6		-0.9
Total	12	1589	5805	711	1526	232	108	32	715	391	45	454	.263	.314	.357	95	-48	177-43	.988	-14	101	104	1b737,2b681,S111,3b68/OC		-6.7

MILLER, JOE Joseph A. B2.17.1861 Baltimore MD D4.23.1928 Wheeling WV BR/5-9.5/165 d5.1

1884	Tol AA	105	423	46	101	12	8	1		26	1		.239	.284	.312	91	-4		.864	2	98	102	S105		0.0
1885	Lou AA	98	339	44	62	9	5	0	24	28	2		.183	.249	.239	55	-17		.891	2	102	104	S79,3b11,2b8		-1.1
Total	2	203	762	90	163	21	13	1	24	54	3		.214	.269	.280	75	-21		.876	4	100	103	S184,3b11,2b8		-1.1

MILLER, JOE Joseph Wick B7.24.1850 , Germany D8.28.1891 White Bear Lake MN 5-10.5/169 d6.26

1872	Nat NA	1	4	0	1	0	0	0	0	0	0		.250	.250	.250	46	0	0-0	.923	-0	0	0	/1		0.0
1875	Wes NA	13	50	4	6	0	0	0	0	0		3	.120	.120	.140	-9	-5	0-0	.870	5	107	109	2b13		-0.1
	Chi NA	15	54	1	8	0	0	0	1	0		7	.148	.148	.148	3	-5	0-0	.788	-3	100	54	2b14/O(1/0/1)		-0.8
	Year	28	104	5	14	1	0	0	1	0		10	.135	.135	.144	-3	-11	0-0	.832	2	104	82	2b27/O(1/0/1)		-0.9
Total	2 NA	29	108	5	15	1	0	0	1	0		10	.139	.139	.148	-1	-10	0-0	.870	2	104	82	2b27/O(1/0/1)1		-0.9

MILLER, KEITH Keith Alan B6.12.1963 Midland MI BR/TR/5-11/185* d6.16 Col Oral Roberts OF(49/65/28)

1987	NY N	25	51	14	19	2	2	0	1	2-0	1	6	.373	.407	.490	142	3	8-1	.967	-2	97	74	2b16	64	0.3
1988	NY N	40	70	9	15	1	1	1	5	6-0	0	10	.214	.276	.300	68	-3	0-5	.946	-9	59	43	2b16,S8,3b6/OR		-1.4
1989	NY N	57	143	15	33	7	0	1	7	5-0	0	27	.231	.262	.301	63	-7	6-0	.967	-1	81	78	2b23,O14(0/10/4),S8,3b2		-0.7
1990	NY N	88	233	42	60	8	1	1	12	23-1	2	46	.258	.327	.305	76	-7	16-3	.980	3	133	40	O61(7/53/5),2b11,S4	39	0.3
1991	NY N	98	275	41	77	22	1	4	23	23-0	5	44	.280	.345	.411	113	5	14-4	.972	12	106	113	2b60,O28(14/2/17),3b2,S2	20	2.1
1992	KC A	106	416	57	118	24	4	4	38	31-0	14	80	.284	.352	.389	104	3	16-6	.971	-9	93	99	2b93,O16L/D	49	-0.2
1993	KC A	37	108	12	18	3	0	0	3	8-0	1	19	.167	.229	.194	15	-13	3-1	.889	-3	87	64	3b21,O4L,2b3,D6	94	-1.6
1994	KC A	5	15	1	2	0	0	0	0	0-0	0	3	.133	.133	.133	-29	-3	0-0	1.000	0	105	440	O4L,3b2	102	0.3
1995	KC A	9	15	2	5	0	0	1	3	2-0	0	4	.333	.412	.533	141	1	0-0	1.000	1	156	938	O4(4/0/1),D4		0.2
Total	9	465	1326	190	347	67	8	12	92	100-1	24	205	.262	.323	.351	87	-21	63-20	.969	-3	94	98	2b222,O132C,3b33,S22,D11	368	-1.3

MILLER, ED L. Edward B Tecumseh MI d7.18

| 1884 | Tol AA | 8 | 24 | 2 | 6 | 0 | 0 | 1 | 1 | 0 | | | .250 | .280 | .250 | 72 | -1 | | .615 | -0 | 210 | 0 | O8(6/1/2) | | -0.1 |

MILLER, HACK Laurence H. B1.1.1894 New York NY D9.16.1971 Oakland CA BR/TR/5-9/195 d9.22

1916	Bro N	3	3	0	1	0	0	1	1	0		1	.333	.500	1.000	345	1	0	1.000	-0	58	0	O3(0/2/1)	*	0.1
1918	†Bos A	12	29	2	8	2	0	0	4	0		4	.276	.276	.345	89	-1	0	1.000	-1	86	0	O10(9/1/0)		0.1
1922	Chi N	122	466	61	164	28	5	12	78	26	2	39	.352	.389	.511	128	19	3-3	.959	-3	92	105	O116(115/0/2)		0.6
1923	Chi N	135	485	74	146	24	2	20	88	27	4	39	.301	.343	.482	116	9	6-5	.978	3	96	143	O129L		0.1
1924	Chi N	53	131	17	44	8	1	4	25	8	1	11	.336	.379	.504	133	6	1-0	.948	-3	92	35	O32L		-0.7
1925	Chi N	24	86	10	24	3	2	1	9	3	1	9	.279	.303	.430	84	-3	0-1	.878	-3	83	59	O21L		-0.1
Total	6	349	1200	164	387	65	11	38	205	64	8	103	.322	.361	.490	120	31	10-9	.962	-6	93	109	O311(306/3/3)		0.1

MILLER, LEMMIE Lemmie Earl B6.2.1960 Dallas TX BR/TR/6-1/190 [LAN81 2/50] d5.22 Col Arizona St.

| 1984 | LA N | 8 | 12 | 1 | 2 | 0 | 0 | 0 | 0 | 1-0 | 0 | 2 | .167 | .231 | .167 | 13 | -1 | 0-0 | 1.000 | -0 | 75 | 0 | O5(4/0/1) | | -0.2 |

YEAR	TM LG	G	AB	R	H	2B	3B	HR	RBI	BB-IB	HP	SO	AVG	OBP	SLG	AOPS	ABR	SB-CS	FA	FR	RNG	THR	GAMES AT POSITION	DL	BFW

MILLER, OTTO Lowell Otto "Moonie" B6.1.1889 Minden NE D3.29.1962 Brooklyn NY BR/TR/6-0/196 d7.16 C11

1910	Bro N	31	66	5	11	3	0	0	2	2	1	19	.167	.203	.212	22	-7	1	.987	6	106	104	C28		0.1
1911	Bro N	25	62	7	13	2	2	0	8	0	0	4	.210	.210	.306	46	-5	2	.927	-4	79	124	C22		-0.8
1912	Bro N	98	316	35	88	18	1	1	31	18	4	50	.278	.325	.351	88	-5	11	.975	8	94	112	C94		1.1
1913	Bro N	104	320	26	87	11	7	0	26	10	1	31	.272	.294	.350	81	-9	7-12	.971	9	103	103	C103/1		0.6
1914	Bro N	54	169	17	39	6	1	0	9	7	0	20	.231	.261	.278	59	-9	0	.964	-2	89	98	C50/1		-0.7
1915	Bro N	84	254	20	57	4	6	0	25	6	1	28	.224	.245	.287	60	-14	3	.981	2	91	95	C83		-0.4
1916	†Bro N	73	216	16	55	9	2	1	17	7	1	29	.255	.281	.329	85	-4	6	.968	4	103	80	C69		0.6
1917	Bro N	92	274	19	63	5	4	1	17	14	2	29	.230	.272	.288	70	-10	5	.979	0	102	94	C91		-0.3
1918	Bro N	75	228	8	44	6	1	0	8	9	2	20	.193	.230	.228	40	-17	1	.972	2	90	99	C62/1		-1.1
1919	Bro N	51	164	18	37	5	0	0	5	7	0	14	.226	.257	.256	53	-9	2	.966	-0	89	94	C51		-0.6
1920	†Bro N	90	301	16	87	9	2	0	33	9	1	18	.289	.312	.332	82	-7	0-5	.986	-2	99	66	C89		-0.4
1921	Bro N	91	286	22	67	8	6	1	27	5	1	26	.234	.260	.315	50	-22	2-1	.972	4	87	104	C91		-1.2
1922	Bro N	59	180	20	47	11	1	1	23	6	0	13	.261	.285	.350	63	-10	0	.964	-1	76	114	C57		-0.7
Total	13	927	2836	229	695	97	33	5	231	104	13	301	.245	.275	.308	67	-128	40-18	.973	25	94	97	C890,1b3		-3.8

MILLER, KEITH Neal Keith B3.7.1963 Dallas TX BB/TR/5-11/175* [PhiN84 16/413] d4.23 Col Lubbock Christian

1988	Phi N	47	48	4	8	3	0	0	6	5-0	0	13	.167	.245	.229	36	-4	0-0	1.000	-0	57	0	O4(2/1/1),3b3/S		-0.5
1989	Phi N	8	10	0	3	1	0	0	0	0-0	0	3	.300	.300	.400	98	-0	0-0	1.000	-0	69	0	O2C		0.0
Total	2	55	58	4	11	4	0	0	6	5-0	0	16	.190	.254	.259	46	-4	0-0	1.000	-1	62	0	O6(2/3/1),3b3/S		-0.5

MILLER, NORM Norman Calvin B2.5.1946 Los Angeles CA BL/TR/5-11/195(175-195) d9.11 Mil 1967 Col Los Angeles Valley (CA) JC

1965	Hou N	11	15	2	3	0	1	0	1	1-0	0	7	.200	.250	.333	67	-1	0-0	1.000	-0	59	0	O2L		-0.1
1966	Hou N	11	34	1	5	0	0	1	3	2-1	0	4	.147	.194	.235	20	-4	0-0	1.000	1	100	0	O8(5/0/3),3b2		-1.0
1967	Hou N	64	190	15	39	9	3	1	14	19-2	0	42	.205	.278	.300	68	-8	2-0	.967	2	109	105	O53L		-0.3
1968	Hou N	79	257	35	61	18	2	6	28	22-1	5	48	.237	.304	.393	112	4	6-5	.971	-2	107	19	O74(2/7/65)		-0.4
1969	Hou N	119	409	58	108	21	4	4	50	47-3	7	77	.264	.348	.364	102	3	4-4	.984	-1	97	99	O114(8/14/97)		-0.5
1970	Hou N	90	226	29	54	9	0	4	29	41-7	1	33	.239	.357	.332	90	-2	3-1	.947	-1	90	147	O72(4/3/68)/C		-0.1
1971	Hou N	45	74	5	19	5	0	2	10	5-0	1	13	.257	.313	.405	105	0	0-0	1.000	-1	93	0	O20(0/6/15)/C		-0.1
1972	Hou N	67	107	18	26	4	0	4	13	13-0	1	23	.243	.331	.393	108	1	1-0	1.000	-2	82	72	O29(6/10/13)		-0.1
1973	Hou N	3	3	0	0	0	0	0	0	0-0	0	2	.000	.000	.000	-99	-1	0-0	—	-0	0	0	/OR		-0.1
	Atl N	9	8	2	3	1	0	1	6	3-0	0	3	.375	.500	.875	267	2	0-0	.667	-0	39	0	/OL		0.2
	Year	12	11	2	3	1	0	1	6	3-0	0	5	.273	.400	.636	182	1	0-0	.667	-0	34	0	O2(1/0/1)	131	0.1
1974	Atl N	42	41	1	7	1	0	1	5	7-1	0	9	.171	.292	.268	55	-2	0-0	1.000	0	55	484	O4(1/0/4)	16	-0.3
Total	10	540	1364	166	325	68	10	24	159	160-15	15	265	.238	.323	.356	94	-8	16-10	.972	-5	98	87	O378(82/40/266),C2,3b2	180	-3.2

MILLER, ORLANDO Orlando (Salmon) B1.13.1969 Changuinola, Pan BR/TR/6-1/180* d7.8

1994	Hou N	16	40	3	13	0	1	2	9	2-2	0	12	.325	.386	.525	142	2	1-0	1.000	-1	99	68	S11,2b3		0.2
1995	Hou N	92	324	36	85	20	1	5	36	22-8	5	71	.262	.319	.377	88	-6	3-4	.964	4	102	99	S89	15	0.4
1996	Hou N	139	468	43	120	26	2	15	58	14-4	10	116	.256	.291	.417	91	-8	3-7	.958	-13	95	85	S117,3b29		-1.5
1997	Det A	50	111	13	26	7	1	2	10	5-0	4	24	.234	.289	.369	71	-5	1-0	.979	-0	102	132	S31,D11,3b4,1b3	70	-0.4
Total	4	297	943	95	244	53	5	24	113	43-14	21	223	.259	.305	.402	90	-17	8-11	.964	-11	99	94	S248,3b33,D11,1b3,2b3	85	-1.3

MILLER, OTTO Otis Louis B2.2.1901 Belleville IL D7.26.1959 Belleville IL BR/TR/5-10.5/168 d4.17

1927	StL A	51	76	8	17	5	0	0	8	8	1	5	.224	.306	.289	53	-5	0-1	.938	-1	100	88	S35,3b11		-0.5
1930	Bos A	112	370	49	106	22	5	0	40	26	0	21	.286	.333	.373	82	-10	2-4	.948	-1	110	95	3b83,2b15		-0.7
1931	Bos A	107	389	38	106	12	1	0	43	15	1	20	.272	.301	.308	64	-21	1-1	.953	2	112	97	3b75,2b25		-1.4
1932	Bos A	2	2	0	0	0	0	0	0	0	0	0	.000	.000	.000	-99	-1	0-0	—	-0	0	0	/H		-0.1
Total	4	272	837	95	229	39	6	0	91	49	2	46	.274	.315	.335	71	-37	3-6	.949	-0	111	98	3b169,2b40,S35		-2.7

MILLER, RALPH Ralph Joseph B2.29.1896 Ft.Wayne IN D3.18.1939 Ft.Wayne IN BR/TR/6-0/190 d4.14

1920	Phi N	97	338	28	74	14	1	0	28	11	1	32	.219	.246	.266	45	-24	3-4	.940	5	110	97	3b91,1b3,S2/OL		-1.9
1921	Phi N	57	204	19	62	10	1	3	26	6	1	10	.304	.327	.397	84	-5	3-5	.910	-1	99	88	S46,3b10		-0.1
1924	†Was N	9	15	1	2	0	0	0	0	1	0	1	.133	.188	.133	-17	-3	0-0	.941	0	120	67	2b3		-0.2
Total	3	163	557	48	138	24	1	3	54	18	2	43	.248	.274	.311	59	-32	6-9	.927	4	112	105	3b101,S48,2b3,1b3/OL		-2.2

MILLER, RAY Raymond Peter B2.12.1888 Pittsburgh PA D4.7.1927 Pittsburgh PA BL/TL/5-10/168 d4.14 Mil 1918

1917	Cle A	19	21	1	4	1	0	0	2	8	0	3	.190	.414	.238	92	1	0	1.000	1	226	0	1b4		0.2
	Pit N	6	27	1	4	1	0	0	2	2	0	3	.148	.207	.185	20	-3	0	1.000	0	117	124	1b6		-0.3
Total	1	25	48	2	8	2	0	0	2	10	0	6	.167	.310	.208	56	-2	0	1.000	2	156	80	1b10		-0.1

MILLER, RICK Richard Alan B4.19.1948 Grand Rapids MI BL/TL/6-0/185* [BosA69 2/37] d9.4 Col Michigan St.

1971	Bos A	15	33	9	11	5	0	1	7	8-0	0	8	.333	.452	.576	180	4	0-2	.969	2	140	145	O14(4/4/6)		0.5
1972	Bos A	89	98	13	21	4	1	3	15	11-0	0	27	.214	.291	.367	90	-1	0-2	.967	5	114	312	O75(24/47/4)		0.2
1973	Bos A	143	441	65	115	17	7	6	43	51-2	1	59	.261	.339	.372	95	-2	12-7	.978	-0	107	46	O137(15/71/61)		-0.8
1974	Bos A	114	280	41	73	8	1	5	22	37-2	0	47	.261	.347	.350	94	-1	13-2	.989	9	115	116	O105(21/77/7)		0.8
1975	†Bos A	77	108	21	21	2	1	0	15	21-6	0	20	.194	.326	.231	55	-6	3-2	.981	5	136	78	O65(25/15/26)		-0.2
1976	Bos A	105	269	40	76	15	3	0	27	34-2	0	47	.283	.359	.361	101	2	11-10	.991	9	126	75	O82(17/37/32),D4		0.7
1977	Bos A	86	189	34	48	9	3	0	24	22-1	3	30	.254	.341	.333	76	-6	11-5	.992	-2	87	114	O79(2/29/48)/D	27	-0.9
1978	Cal A	132	475	66	125	25	4	1	37	54-1	4	70	.263	.341	.339	95	-1	3-13	.989	8	112	108	O129(0/93/36)		0.1
1979	†Cal A	120	427	60	125	15	5	2	28	50-1	1	69	.293	.367	.365	102	2	5-4	.989	8	120	42	O117C,D2	37	0.9
1980	Cal A	129	412	52	113	14	3	2	38	48-4	1	71	.274	.349	.337	91	-4	7-3	.984	7	108	147	O118(0/98/24)		0.2
1981	Bos A	97	316	38	92	17	2	2	33	28-1	1	36	.291	.349	.377	103	2	3-5	.987	-6	87	88	O95C		-0.9
1982	Bos A	135	409	50	104	13	2	4	38	40-2	2	41	.254	.323	.325	74	-14	5-6	.983	-10	87	76	O127C		-2.6
1983	Bos A	104	262	41	75	10	2	2	21	28-1	1	30	.286	.356	.363	92	-2	3-3	.993	9	102	91	O66(6/22/40),1b2,D2		-0.5
1984	Bos A	95	123	17	32	5	1	0	12	17-0	0	22	.260	.348	.317	82	-2	1-1	.974	-1	82	93	O31(0/21/10),1b8		-0.4
1985	Bos A	41	45	5	15	2	0	0	5	5-0	0	6	.333	.392	.378	110	1	1-0	1.000	0	127	0	O8(4/1/3),D4	29	0.1
Total	15	1482	3887	552	1046	161	35	28	369	454-23	16	583	.269	.346	.350	92	-28	78-65	.986	31	107	95	O1248(118/854/297),D13,1b10	93	-2.8

MILLER, ROD Rodney Carter B1.16.1940 Portland OR BL/TR/5-10/160 d9.28

| 1957 | Bro N | 1 | 1 | 0 | 0 | 0 | 0 | 0 | 0 | 0-0 | 0 | 1 | .000 | .000 | .000 | -91 | 0 | 0-0 | — | 0 | | | /H | | 0.0 |

MILLER, DOC Roy Oscar B2.4.1883 Chatham ON, Can. D7.31.1938 Jersey City NJ BL/TL/5-10.5/170 d5.4

1910	Chi N	1	1	0	0	0	0	0	0	0	0	0	.000	.000	.000	-99	0	0	—		0		/H		0.0
	Bos N	130	482	48	138	27	4	3	55	33	1	52	.286	.333	.378	103	1	17	.951	-8	98	52	O130(6/0/127)		-1.4
	Year	131	483	48	138	27	4	3	55	33	1	52	.286	.333	.377	102	0	17	.951	-8	98	52	O130(6/0/127)		-1.4
1911	Bos N	146	577	69	192	36	3	7	91	43	0	43	.333	.379	.442	120	15	32	.961	3	99	129	O146(0/3/143)		1.0
1912	Bos N	51	201	26	47	8	1	2	24	14	1	17	.234	.287	.313	63	-11	6	.948	2	91	156	O50R		-1.1
	Phi N	67	177	24	51	12	5	0	21	9	1	13	.288	.323	.412	94	-2	3	.986	2	96	160	O40R		-0.2
	Year	118	378	50	98	20	6	2	45	23	2	30	.259	.303	.360	78	-13	9	.964	4	93	158	O90R		-1.3
1913	Phi N	69	87	9	30	6	0	0	11	6	2	6	.345	.400	.414	127	4	2-1	.800	-2	61	0	O12R		0.1
1914	Cin N	93	192	9	49	7	2	0	33	16	0	18	.255	.313	.313	83	-4	4	.976	-2	105	34	O47(23/3/23)		-0.9
Total	5	557	1717	184	507	96	15	12	235	121	4	149	.295	.343	.390	102	3	64-1	.958	-5	97	100	O425(29/6/395)		-2.5

MILLER, RUDY Rudel Charles B7.12.1900 Kalamazoo MI D1.22.1994 Kalamazoo MI BR/TR/6-1/180 d9.19 Col Western Michigan

| 1929 | Phi A | 2 | 4 | 1 | 1 | 0 | 0 | 0 | 1 | 3 | 0 | 0 | .250 | .571 | .250 | 115 | 1 | 0-0 | .750 | -1 | 72 | 0 | 3b2 | | 0.0 |

MILLER, TOM Thomas P. "Reddy" B1850 Philadelphia PA D5.29.1876 Philadelphia PA d10.24

1874	Ath NA	4	16	1	8	0	0	0	5		0		.500	.500	.500	204	2	0-0	.793	0			C4/O(0/1/1)		0.1
1875	StL NA	56	214	18	35	2	0	0	12	1		8	.164	.167	.173	20	-15	2-0	.827	-4			C53,3b2		-1.7
Total	2 NA	60	230	19	43	2	0	0	17	1		8	.187	.190	.196	37	-13	2-0	.824	-4			C57,3b2/O(0/1/1)		-1.6

MILLER, TOM Thomas Royall B7.5.1897 Powhatan Court House VA D8.13.1980 Richmond VA BL/TR/5-11/180 d7.29 Col Richmond

1918	Bos N	2	2	0	0	0	0	0	0	0	0	0	.000	.000	.000	-99	0	1	—	0			/H		-0.1
1919	Bos N	7	6	2	2	0	0	0	0	0	0	1	.333	.333	.333	105	0	1	—	0			/H		0.0
Total	2	9	8	2	2	0	0	0	0	0	0	1	.250	.250	.250	53	0	1	—	0			/H		-0.1

YEAR	TM	LG	G	AB	R	H	2B	3B	HR	RBI	BB-IB	HP	SO	AVG	OBP	SLG	AOPS	ABR	SB-CS	FA	FR	RNG	THR	GAMES AT POSITION	DL	BFW

MILLER, WARD   Ward Taylor "Windy","Grump"   B7.5.1884 Mt.Carroll IL   D9.4.1958 Dixon IL   BL/TR/5-11/177   d4.14   Col Northern Illinois

																										-0.9
1909	Pit	N	15	56	2	8	0	0	0	4	4	1		.143	.213	.179	20	-5	2	.967	-2	50	0	O14C		0.0
	Cin	N	43	113	17	35	3	1	0	4	6	0		.310	.345	.354	118	2	9	.981	-0	61	0	O26(17/16/3)		-0.9
	Year		58	169	19	43	3	1	0	8	10	1		.254	.300	.296	84	-4	11	.976	-2	57	0	O40(17/30/3)		0.1
1910	Cin	N	81	126	21	30	6	0	0	10	22	1	13	.238	.356	.286	92	0	10	.944	2	94	207	O64(13/38/14)		-0.4
1912	Chi	N	86	241	45	74	11	4	0	22	26	1	33	.307	.377	.386	109	4	11	.943	-5	90	70	O63(47/11/5)		-0.1
1913	Chi	N	80	203	23	48	5	7	1	16	34	1	33	.236	.349	.345	98	0	13-15	.980	4	107	110	O111(74/31/6)		0.3
1914	StL	F	121	402	49	118	17	7	4	50	59	10	36	.294	.397	.400	112	4	18	.953	5	115	86	O136(3/0/133)		0.5
1915	StL	F	154	536	80	164	19	9	1	63	79	5	39	.306	.400	.381	114	7	33	.963	4	111	85	O154L		-0.5
1916	StL	A	146	485	72	129	17	5	1	50	72	9	76	.266	.371	.328	116	13	25-21	.943	-9	96	69	O25(12/4/9)		-0.1
1917	StL	A	43	82	13	17	1	1	1	2	16	2	15	.207	.350	.280	96	1	7	.966	-1	71	166			-1.1
Total	8		769	2244	322	623	79	35	8	221	318	30	230	.278	.375	.355	108	26	128-36	.957	-1	101	84	O619(320/125/185)		

MILLER, WARREN   Warren Lemuel "Gitz"   B7.14.1885 Philadelphia PA   D8.12.1956 Philadelphia PA   BL/TL/5-10/160   d7.29

1909	Was	A	26	51	5	11	0	0	1	4	0		.216	.273	.216	57	-2	0	1.000	1	152	0	O15(1/10/4)		-0.3
1911	Was	A	21	34	3	5	0	0	0	0	0		.147	.147	.147	-18	-6	0	.778	1	72	104	O9(1/0/8)		-0.6
Total	2		47	85	8	16	0	0	1	4	0		.188	.225	.188	25	-8	0	.931	-0	123	38	O24(2/10/12)		-0.9

MILLER, BILL   William Alexander   B5.23.1879 Bad Schwalbach, Germany   D9.8.1957 Ashtabula OH   BL/TL/6-2/170   d8.23

1902	Pit	N	1	5	0	1	0	0	0	2	0	0	.200	.200	.200	23	0	0	—	0	0	0	/OR		-0.1

MILLETTE, JOE   Joseph Anthony   B8.12.1966 Walnut Creek CA   BR/TR/6-1/180*   d7.16   Col St. Marys (CA)

1992	Phi	N	33	78	5	16	0	0	0	2	5-2	2	10	.205	.271	.205	37	-7	1-0	.974	4	120	106	S26,3b3/2		-0.1
1993	Phi	N	10	10	3	2	0	0	0	2	1-0	1	2	.200	.273	.200	29	-1	0-0	1.000	1	130	47	S7,3b3		0.1
Total	2		43	88	8	18	0	0	0	4	6-2	2	12	.205	.271	.205	36	-8	1-0	.978	5	121	98	S33,3b6/2		0.0

MILLIARD, RALPH   Ralph Gregory   B12.30.1973 Willemstad, Curacao   BR/TR/5-11/170*   d5.12   [DL 1999 Cin N 42]

1996	Fla	N	24	62	7	10	2	0	0	1	14-1	0	16	.161	.312	.194	39	-5	2-0	.955	5	123	116	2b24		0.1
1997	Fla	N	8	30	2	6	0	0	0	2	3-0	2		.200	.314	.200	40	-3	1-1	1.000	4	138	176	2b8		0.2
1998	NY	N	10	1	3	0	0	0	0	0	0-0	0		1.000	1.000	.000	-99	0	0-0	.833	1	77	0	2b5/S		-0.1
Total	3		42	93	12	16	2	0	0	3	17-1	2	20	.172	.310	.194	38	-8	3-1	.963	9	126	130	2b37/S	42	0.2

MILLIES, WALLY   Walter Louis   B10.18.1906 Chicago IL   D2.28.1995 Oak Lawn IL   BR/TR/5-10.5/170   d9.23

1934	Bro	N	2	7	0	0	0	0	0	0	0	0	0	.000	.000	.000	-99	-2	0	1.000	0	55	0	C2		-0.2
1936	Was	A	74	215	26	67	10	2	0	25	11	0	8	.312	.345	.377	83	-6	1-0	.968	-0	87	141	C72		-0.2
1937	Was	A	59	179	21	40	7	1	0	28	9	0	15	.223	.261	.274	36	-18	1-0	.971	0	101	126	C56		-1.4
1939	Phi	N	84	205	12	48	3	0	0	12	9	1	5	.234	.270	.249	41	-17	0	.964	-10	54	127	C84		-2.4
1940	Phi	N	26	43	1	3	0	0	0	0	4	0	4	.070	.149	.070	-39	-8	0	.958	0	89	93	C24		-0.7
1941	Phi	N	1	2	0	0	0	0	0	0	0	0	0	.000	.000	.000	-99	-1	0	.800	0	0	469	/C		-0.1
Total	6		246	651	60	158	20	3	0	65	33	1	32	.243	.280	.283	47	-52	2-0	.966	-10	79	129	C239		-5.0

MILLIGAN, JOCKO   John   B8.8.1861 Philadelphia PA   D8.29.1923 Philadelphia PA   BR/TR/6-0/192   d5.1

1884	Phi	AA	66	268	39	77	20	3	3		8	0		.287	.308	.418	126	7		.939	10			C65/OC		2.1
1885	Phi	AA	67	265	35	71	15	4	2	39	7	1		.268	.289	.377	103	0		.935	9			C61,1b6,O2R		1.2
1886	Phi	AA	75	301	52	76	17	3	5	45	21	0		.252	.301	.379	111	3	18	.919	1			C40,1b29,O5(0/4/1),3b2		0.4
1887	Phi	AA	95	377	54	114	27	4	2	50	21	3		.302	.344	.411	110	5	8	.966	1	83	90	C58,1b5		0.4
1888	†StL	AA	63	219	19	55	6	2	5	37	17	2	19	.251	.311	.365	105	0	3	.941	9			C66,1b9		3.4
1889	StL	AA	72	273	53	100	30	2	12	76	16	3	19	.366	.408	.623	170	22	2	.933	9			C59,1b3		0.6
1890	Phi	P	62	234	38	69	9	3	3	57	19	6	19	.295	.363	.397	101	0	2	.893	2	98	92	C59,1b3		1.2
1891	Phi	AA	118	455	75	138	35	12	11	106	56	15	51	.303	.397	.505	158	34	2	.939	-1	108	77	C87,1b32		1.2
1892	Was	N	88	323	40	89	20	9	4	43	26	3	24	.276	.335	.430	135	13	2	.947	-4	67	134	C59,1b28		-0.2
1893	Bal	N	24	102	19	25	5	2	1	19	5	2	7	.245	.294	.363	73	-5	2	.981	2	149	74	1b22/C		0.8
	NY	N	42	147	16	34	5	6	1	25	14	1	14	.231	.302	.367	77	-6	2	.934	8	99	152	C42		0.3
	Year		66	249	35	59	10	8	2	44	19	3	21	.237	.299	.365	75	-11	4	.932	9	99	148	C43,1b22		1.1
Total	10		772	2964	440	848	189	50	49	497	210	36	134	.286	.341	.433	123	73	41	.930	44	95	106	C585,1b184,O9(0/6/3),3b2		13.4

MILLIGAN, RANDY   Randy Andre   B11.27.1961 San Diego CA   BR/TR/6-1/228(215-235)   [NYN81*1/3]   d9.12   Col San Diego Mesa (CA) JC

1987	NY	N	3	1	0	0	0	0	0	0	0-0	0	1	1.000	1.000	.500	49	0	0	—	0	0	0	/H		0.1
1988	Pit	N	40	82	10	18	5	0	3	8	20-0	0	24	.220	.379	.390	122	4	1-2	.987	-1	98	128	1b25,O2L		0.5
1989	Bal	A	124	365	56	98	23	5	12	45	74-2	3	75	.268	.394	.458	144	25	9-5	.995	1	109	100	1b117/D		3.0
1990	Bal	A	109	362	64	96	20	1	20	60	88-3	2	68	.265	.408	.492	156	32	6-3	.990	5	121	115	1b98,D9		3.0
1991	Bal	A	141	483	57	127	17	2	16	70	84-4	4	108	.263	.373	.406	120	16	0-5	.990	2	111	105	1b106,D25,O9L		-0.5
1992	Bal	A	137	462	71	111	21	1	11	53	106-0	4	81	.240	.383	.361	107	10	0-1	.994	-6	84	110	1b129,D6		0.5
1993	Cin	N	83	234	30	64	11	1	6	29	46-0	1	49	.274	.394	.406	114	7	0-2	.994	6	132	104	1b61,O9L		0.5
	Cle	A	19	47	7	20	7	0	0	7	14-0	0	4	.426	.557	.574	204	9	0-0	1.000	-1	81	145	1b18/D		-0.1
1994	Mon	N	47	82	10	19	2	0	2	12	14-1	0	21	.232	.337	.329	76	-3	0-0	.978	2	140	116	1b33		-0.5
Total	8		703	2118	305	553	106	10	70	284	447-10	13	431	.261	.391	.420	127	100	16-18	.992	8	108	109	1b587,D42,O20L	50	6.6

MILLS, JACK   Abbott Paige   B10.23.1889 S.Williamstown MA   D6.3.1973 Washington DC   BL/TR/6-0/165   d7.1   Col Williams

1911	Cle	A	13	17	5	5	0	0	0	1	1	1		.294	.368	.294	85	0	1	1.000	1	147	185	3b7		0.0

MILLS, CHARLIE   Charles F.   B9.1.1844 Brooklyn NY   D4.9.1874 Brooklyn NY   6-0/?   d5.18   U2

1871	Mut	NA	32	146	27	36	4	3	0	22	1		0	.247	.252	.315	68	-5	2-0	.866	-1			C29,O4R/3		-0.5
1872	Mut	NA	6	31	6	4	0	0	0	2	0		0	.129	.129	.129	-22	-4	0-0	.667	-1	0	0	O4R,C3		-0.5
Total	2 NA		38	177	33	40	4	3	0	24	1		0	.226	.230	.282	53	-9	2-0	.854	-2			C32,O8R/3		-0.5

MILLS, BUSTER   Colonel Buster "Bus"   B9.16.1908 Ranger TX   D12.1.1991 Arlington TX   BR/TR/5-11.5/195   d4.18   Mil 1943-45   M1/C7   Col Oklahoma

1934	StL	N	29	72	7	17	4	1	1	8	4	2	11	.236	.295	.361	70	-3	0	1.000	-1	104	0	O18(0/17/1)		-0.5
1935	Bro	N	17	56	12	12	2	1	1	7	5	0	11	.214	.323	.339	80	-1	0	.971	-1	96	69	O17(11/6/0)		-0.1
1937	Bos	A	123	505	69	144	25	8	7	58	46	6	41	.285	.361	.418	92	-6	11-8	.946	-5	94	84	O120(107/10/5)		-1.1
1938	StL	A	123	466	66	133	24	4	3	46	43	3	46	.285	.350	.373	81	-13	7-8	.964	2	104	113	O113(106/6/1)		-1.1
1940	NY	A	34	63	10	25	3	1	0	15	7	0	5	.397	.457	.587	176	7	0-0	1.000	-4	93	0	O14(12/0/2)		0.6
1942	Cle	A	80	195	19	54	4	2	1	26	23	0	18	.277	.353	.333	99	0	5-4	.973	-4	113	107	O53(13/37/3)		0.5
1946	Cle	A	9	22	1	6	0	0	0	3	3	0	5	.273	.360	.273	84	0	0-1	1.000	-0	96	0	O6L		0.0
Total	7		415	1379	200	396	62	19	14	163	131	15	137	.287	.355	.390	91	-16	23-21	.964	-2	101	85	O341(255/76/12)		-3.1

MILLS, EVERETT   Everett   B1.20.1845 Newark NJ   D6.22.1908 Newark NJ   6-1/174   d5.5   M1

1871	Oly	NA	32	157	38	43	6	4	1	24	3		1	.274	.287	.382	95	0	2-3	.967	3	98	120	1b32		0.4
1872	Bal	NA	55	266	55	79	14	2	0	34	3		2	.297	.305	.365	100	-1	0-2	.931	1	91	87	1b55,M		0.0
1873	Bal	NA	54	262	64	87	20	9	0	56	2		1	.332	.337	.477	140	12	1-0	.949	2	65	101	1b53/OC		-0.1
1874	Har	NA	53	244	39	69	6	1	0	19	4		2	.283	.294	.316	91	-3	1-1	.920	-2	88	58	1b53		-0.0
1875	Har	NA	80	342	59	89	8	4	1	48	0		3	.260	.260	.316	94	-3	6-4	.945	2	78	166	1b80		-0.0
1876	Har	N	63	254	28	66	8	1	0	23	1		5	.260	.263	.299	80	-6		.939	-2	63	78	1b63		1.1
Total	5 NA		274	1271	255	367	54	20	2	181	12		9	.289	.295	.367	105	5	10-10	.941	6	82	111	1b273/OC		

MILLS, FRANK   Frank Le Moyne   B5.13.1895 Knoxville OH   D8.31.1983 Youngstown OH   BL/TR/6-0/180   d9.22

1914	Cle	A	4	8	0	1	0	0	0	1	0		2	.125	.222	.125	4	-1	0	.900	-1	75	162	C2		-0.0

MILLS, BRAD   James Bradley   B1.19.1957 Exeter CA   BL/TR/6-0/195*   [MonN79 17/426]   d6.8   C7   Col Arizona

1980	Mon	N	21	60	1	18	1	0	0	8	5-1	0	6	.300	.348	.317	87	-1	0-1	.977	-1	78	131	3b18		-0.0
1981	†Mon	N	17	21	0	5	1	0	0	2	2-1	1	1	.238	.304	.286	66	-1	0-0	.867	-3	60	84	3b13		-0.0
1982	Mon	N	54	67	6	15	3	0	1	2	5-0	0	11	.224	.278	.313	63	-3	0-0	1.000	-0	102	0	3b3/1	16	-0.1
1983	Mon	N	14	20	1	5	0	0	0	0	2-0	0	3	.250	.318	.250	59	-1	0-0	1.000	0	102	0	3b41,2b2/1	16	-0.1
Total	4		106	168	11	43	5	0	1	12	14-2	1	21	.256	.311	.304	71	-6	0-1	.959	-5	74	92	3b41,2b2/1		

MILLS, RUPERT   Rupert Frank   B10.12.1892 Newark NJ   D7.20.1929 Lake Hopatcong NJ   BR/TR/6-2/185   d6.23   Col Notre Dame

1915	New	F	41	134	12	27	5	1	0	16	6		1	21	.201	.241	.254	42	-13	6	.976	-0	108	110	1b37		-0.1

MILLS, BILL William Henry B11.2.1920 Boston MA BR/TR/5-10/175 d5.19 Col Holy Cross

YEAR	TM LG	G	AB	R	H	2B	3B	HR	RBI	BB-IB	HP	SO	AVG	OBP	SLG	AOPS	ABR	SB-CS	FA	FR	RNG	THR	GAMES AT POSITION	DL	BFW
1944	Phi A	5	4	0	1	0	0	0	0	0-1	0	1	.250	.400	.250	89	0	0-0	—	0	0	0	/C		0.0

MILNE, PETE William James B4.10.1925 Mobile AL D4.11.1999 Mobile AL BL/TR/6-1/180* d9.15

YEAR	TM LG	G	AB	R	H	2B	3B	HR	RBI	BB-IB	HP	SO	AVG	OBP	SLG	AOPS	ABR	SB-CS	FA	FR	RNG	THR	GAMES AT POSITION	DL	BFW
1948	NY N	12	27	6	6	0	1	0	2	1	0	6	.222	.250	.296	47	-2	0	.867	-1	90	0	O9(2/5/2)		-0.4
1949	NY N	31	29	5	7	1	0	1	6	3	0	6	.241	.379	.379	85	-1	0	1.000	0	130	0	/OL		-0.1
1950	NY N	4	4	1	1	0	0	1	0	1	0	1	.250	.250	.750	151	0	0	—	0			/H		0.0
Total 3		47	60	6	14	1	2	1	9	4	0	13	.233	.281	.367	73	-3	0	.882	-1	94	0	O10(3/5/2)		-0.5

MILNER, BRIAN Brian Tate B11.17.1959 Fort Worth TX BR/TR/6-2/200 [TorA78 7/158] d6.23

YEAR	TM LG	G	AB	R	H	2B	3B	HR	RBI	BB-IB	HP	SO	AVG	OBP	SLG	AOPS	ABR	SB-CS	FA	FR	RNG	THR	GAMES AT POSITION	DL	BFW
1978	Tor A	2	9	3	4	0	1	0	2	0-0	0	1	.444	.444	.667	204	1	0-0	.800	-2	58	0	C2		-0.1

MILNER, EDDIE Eddie James B5.21.1955 Columbus OH BL/TL/5-11/173* [CinN76 21/503] d9.2 Col Central St.

YEAR	TM LG	G	AB	R	H	2B	3B	HR	RBI	BB-IB	HP	SO	AVG	OBP	SLG	AOPS	ABR	SB-CS	FA	FR	RNG	THR	GAMES AT POSITION	DL	BFW
1980	Cin N	6	3	1	0	0	0	0	0	0-0	0	0	.000	.000	.000	-99	-1	0-0	—	0			/H		-0.1
1981	Cin N	8	5	0	1	1	0	0	1	1-0	0	1	.200	.333	.400	108	0	0-0	1.000	-0	105	0	O4(2/0/2)		0.0
1982	Cin N	113	407	61	109	23	5	4	31	41-1	2	40	.268	.338	.378	100	0	18-12	.987	4	107	113	O107(65/30/37)	27	0.1
1983	Cin N	146	502	77	131	23	6	9	33	68-2	1	60	.261	.350	.384	100	1	41-12	.990	13	118	142	O139(0/138/1)		1.9
1984	Cin N	117	336	44	78	8	9	7	29	51-3	2	50	.232	.333	.342	87	-5	21-13	.983	14	127	162	O108C	37	0.9
1985	Cin N	145	453	82	115	19	7	3	33	61-3	1	31	.254	.342	.347	89	-5	35-13	.983	14	122	173	O135C		1.2
1986	Cin N	145	424	70	110	22	6	15	47	36-2	0	56	.259	.317	.446	104	1	18-11	.990	3	112	93	O127C		0.4
1987	†SF N	101	214	38	54	14	0	4	19	24-3	0	33	.252	.328	.374	90	-3	10-9	.993	-2	107	0	O84C	52	-0.6
1988	Cin N	23	51	3	9	1	0	2	4	4-0	0	9	.176	.236	.196	25	-5	2-2	.968	0	101	178	O15(2/11/2)	21	-0.6
Total 9		804	2395	376	607	111	28	42	195	286-14	6	280	.253	.333	.376	94	-17	145-72	.987	47	116	125	O719(69/633/42)	137	3.2

MILNER, JOHN John David "The Hammer" B12.28.1949 Atlanta GA D1.4.2000 East Point GA BL/TL/6-0/185* [NYN68 14/301] d9.15

YEAR	TM LG	G	AB	R	H	2B	3B	HR	RBI	BB-IB	HP	SO	AVG	OBP	SLG	AOPS	ABR	SB-CS	FA	FR	RNG	THR	GAMES AT POSITION	DL	BFW
1971	NY N	9	18	1	3	1	0	0		0-0	0	3	.167	.167	.222	9	-2	0-0	1.000	0	179	624	O3L		-0.1
1972	NY N	117	362	52	86	12	2	17	38	51-1	5	74	.238	.340	.423	117	9	2-1	.965	3	106	125	O91(88/0/3),1b10		0.7
1973	†NY N	129	451	69	108	12	3	23	72	62-6	1	84	.239	.329	.432	111	6	1-1	.989	1	89	89	1b95,O29L	15	-0.8
1974	NY N	137	507	70	128	19	0	20	63	66-9	0	77	.252	.337	.408	109	6	10-2	.994	1	100	96	1b133		-0.2
1975	NY N	91	220	24	42	11	0	7	29	33-4	2	22	.191	.302	.336	79	-6	1-1	.985	6	113	92	O31(29/2/0),1b29		-0.4
1976	NY N	127	443	56	120	25	4	15	78	65-1	0	53	.271	.362	.447	135	22	0-7	.985	2	103	102	O112L,1b12		1.5
1977	NY N	131	388	43	99	20	3	12	57	61-7	0	55	.255	.353	.415	110	7	6-2	.994	1	99	107	1b87,O22(21/0/1)		0.3
1978	Pit N	108	295	39	80	17	0	6	38	34-6	0	25	.271	.342	.390	100	1	5-0	1.000	1	113	22	O69(68/0/1),1b28		0.0
1979	†Pit N	128	326	52	90	9	4	16	60	53-6	1	37	.276	.373	.475	124	12	3-5	.958	-4	85	111	1b70,O11(10/0/1)		0.7
1980	Pit N	114	238	31	58	6	0	8	34	52-2	0	29	.244	.378	.370	106	4	2-2	.991	4	85	111	1b70,O11(10/0/1)		-0.4
1981	Pit N	34	59	6	14	1	0	2	9	5-0	0	3	.237	.292	.356	80	-2	0-0	.980	-2	25	44	1b8,O8L		-0.5
	†Mon N	31	76	6	18	5	0	3	9	12-2	0	6	.237	.341	.421	112	1	0-1	.978	-2	96	109	1b29,O8L		-0.5
	Year	65	135	12	32	6	0	5	18	17-2	0	9	.237	.320	.393	98	0	0-1	.979	-2	96	89	1b29,O8L		-0.5
1982	Mon N	26	28	1	3	0	0	0	2	4-0	0	2	.107	.212	.107	-6	-4	0-0	1.000	0	88	193	1b5	18	-0.4
	Pit N	33	25	5	6	2	0	2	8	6-1	1	3	.240	.406	.560	160	2	1-0	1.000	0	0	1163	/1		0.3
	Year	59	53	6	9	2	0	2	10	10-1	1	5	.170	.308	.321	74	-2	1-0	1.000	0	85	229	1b6		-0.1
Total 12		1215	3436	455	855	140	16	131	498	504-45	10	473	.249	.344	.413	111	56	31-22	.991	6	99	102	1b547,O440(432/2/6)	33	0.7

MILOSEVICH, MIKE Michael "Mollie" B1.13.1915 Zeigler IL D2.3.1966 E.Chicago IN BR/TR/5-10.5/172 d4.30

YEAR	TM LG	G	AB	R	H	2B	3B	HR	RBI	BB-IB	HP	SO	AVG	OBP	SLG	AOPS	ABR	SB-CS	FA	FR	RNG	THR	GAMES AT POSITION	DL	BFW
1944	NY A	94	312	27	77	11	4	0	32	30	0	37	.247	.313	.308	75	-10	1-2	.954	5	100	121	S91		0.1
1945	NY A	30	69	5	15	2	0	0	7	6	1	6	.217	.289	.246	54	-4	0-0	.957	0	98	110	S22/2		-0.3
Total 2		124	381	32	92	13	4	0	39	36	1	43	.241	.309	.297	71	-14	1-2	.954	5	100	119	S113/2		-0.2

MINCHER, DON Donald Ray B6.24.1938 Huntsville AL BL/TR/6-3/213* d4.18

YEAR	TM LG	G	AB	R	H	2B	3B	HR	RBI	BB-IB	HP	SO	AVG	OBP	SLG	AOPS	ABR	SB-CS	FA	FR	RNG	THR	GAMES AT POSITION	DL	BFW
1960	Was A	27	79	10	19	4	1	2	5	11-0	0	11	.241	.330	.392	96	0	0-1	.977	-4	37	72	1b20		-0.6
1961	Min A	35	101	18	19	5	1	5	11	22-0	0	11	.188	.333	.406	91	-1	0-1	.969	-1	97	119	1b29		-0.4
1962	Min A	86	121	20	29	1	1	9	29	34-3	0	24	.240	.406	.488	134	7	0-0	.978	-1	89	99	1b25		0.5
1963	Min A	82	225	41	58	8	0	17	42	30-0	3	51	.258	.351	.520	138	12	0-0	.983	-4	76	85	1b60		0.5
1964	Min A	120	287	45	68	12	4	23	56	27-2	0	51	.237	.300	.547	130	10	0-0	.992	1	102	93	1b76		0.6
1965	†Min A	128	346	43	87	17	3	22	65	49-15	2	73	.251	.344	.509	134	16	1-3	.992	-5	79	94	1b99/OL		0.4
1966	Min A	139	431	53	108	30	0	14	62	58-9	2	68	.251	.340	.418	110	8	3-2	.992	3	106	73	1b130		0.4
1967	Cal A★	147	487	81	133	23	3	25	76	69-9	4	69	.273	.367	.487	157	36	0-3	.994	-1	97	96	1b142/OR		2.8
1968	Cal A	120	399	35	94	12	1	13	48	43-6	4	65	.236	.312	.368	110	5	0-2	.991	-2	92	116	1b113		-0.5
1969	Sea A★	140	427	53	105	14	0	25	78	78-13	5	69	.246	.366	.454	130	19	10-11	.995	6	113	91	1b122		1.4
1970	Oak A	140	463	62	114	18	0	27	74	56-11	3	71	.246	.327	.460	120	11	5-4	.990	-2	97	106	1b137		-0.1
1971	Oak A	28	92	9	22	6	1	2	8	20-3	0	14	.239	.375	.391	119	3	1-1	.996	3	134	55	1b27		0.4
	Was A	100	323	35	94	15	1	10	45	53-4	2	52	.291	.389	.437	142	20	2-1	.990	1	108	109	1b88		1.5
	Year	128	415	44	116	21	2	12	53	73-7	2	66	.280	.386	.427	136	23	3-2	.991	4	114	96	1b115		1.9
1972	Tex A	61	191	23	45	10	0	6	39	46-1	2	23	.236	.384	.382	135	11	2-1	.994	5	136	91	1b59		-0.7
	†Oak A	47	54	2	8	1	0	0	5	10-0	0	16	.148	.281	.167	37	-4	0-2	.988	-1	68	69	1b11		1.4
	Year	108	245	25	53	11	0	6	44	56-1	2	39	.216	.363	.335	114	8	2-2	.993	4	127	88	1b70		0.7
Total 13		1400	4026	530	1003	176	16	200	643	606-76	27	668	.249	.348	.450	127	153	24-32	.990	-3	99	99	1b1138,O2(1/0/1)		7.6

MINCHER, ED Edward M. B6.17.1850 Baltimore MD D12.8.1918 Brooklyn NY d5.4

YEAR	TM LG	G	AB	R	H	2B	3B	HR	RBI	BB-IB	HP	SO	AVG	OBP	SLG	AOPS	ABR	SB-CS	FA	FR	RNG	THR	GAMES AT POSITION	DL	BFW
1871	Kek NA	9	36	4	8	0	0	0	5	0			.222	.222	.222	28	-3	1-0	.852	0	0		O9L		-0.2
1872	Nat NA	11	53	5	5	0	0	0	4	0		1	.094	.094	.094	-36	-9	0-0	.837	2	83	0	O11L		-0.5
Total 2 NA		20	89	9	13	0	0	0	9	0		1	.146	.146	.146	-11	-12	1-0	.842	2	47	0	O20L		-0.7

MINNEHAN, DAN Daniel Joseph B11.28.1865 Troy NY D8.8.1929 Troy NY BR/TR/5-10/145 d9.20

YEAR	TM LG	G	AB	R	H	2B	3B	HR	RBI	BB-IB	HP	SO	AVG	OBP	SLG	AOPS	ABR	SB-CS	FA	FR	RNG	THR	GAMES AT POSITION	DL	BFW
1895	Lou N	8	34	6	13	0	0	0	6	1		1	.382	.400	.382	109	1	0	.920	0	92	284	3b7,O2C		0.1

MINOR, DAMON Damon Reed B1.5.1974 Canton OH BL/TL/6-7/230* [SFN96 12/342] d9.2 b-Ryan Col Oklahoma

YEAR	TM LG	G	AB	R	H	2B	3B	HR	RBI	BB-IB	HP	SO	AVG	OBP	SLG	AOPS	ABR	SB-CS	FA	FR	RNG	THR	GAMES AT POSITION	DL	BFW
2000	SF N	10	9	3	4	0	0	3	6	2-0	0	5	.444	.545	1.444	405	4	0-0	1.000	-0	0	0	1b4		0.3
2001	SF N	19	45	3	7	1	0	3	3	3-1	0	8	.156	.208	.178	1	-7	0-0	.989	-1	64	49	1b11		-0.9
2002	SF N	83	173	21	41	6	0	10	24	24-6	2	34	.237	.333	.445	111	2	0-0	.997	-1	89	105	1b44,D3	17	-0.2
2004	SF N	24	58	8	14	2	0	0	6	12-0	0	18	.241	.405	.276	78	-1	0-0	1.000	-0	94	100	1b17/D		-0.2
Total 4		136	285	35	66	9	0	13	39	41-7	6	61	.232	.338	.400	97	-2	0-0	.996	-2	84	92	1b76,D4	26	-1.0

MINOR, RYAN Ryan Dale B1.5.1974 Canton OH BR/TR/6-7/225(225-245) [BalA96 33/981] d9.13 b-Damon Col Oklahoma

YEAR	TM LG	G	AB	R	H	2B	3B	HR	RBI	BB-IB	HP	SO	AVG	OBP	SLG	AOPS	ABR	SB-CS	FA	FR	RNG	THR	GAMES AT POSITION	DL	BFW
1998	Bal A	9	14	3	6	1	0	0		0-0	0	5	.429	.429	.500	143	1	0-0	.833	-0	87	0	3b6,1b3/D		0.0
1999	Bal A	46	124	13	24	7	0	3	10	8-0	0	43	.194	.241	.323	44	-11	1-0	.963	6	120	132	3b45/1		-0.5
2000	Bal A	32	84	4	11	1	0	0	3	3-0	0	20	.131	.170	.143	-20	-16	0-0	.927	-1	84	126	3b26,1b5	22	-1.6
2001	Mon N	55	95	10	15	2	0	2	13	9-0	1	31	.158	.234	.242	25	-11	0-0	.970	-6	64	97	3b24,O2L/1D		-1.7
Total 4		142	317	30	56	11	0	5	27	20-0	1	97	.177	.228	.259	26	-37	1-1	.951	-1	97	97	3b101,1b10,D4,O2L	22	-3.8

MINOSO, MINNIE Saturnino Orestes Armas (Arrieta) (b Saturnino Orestes Arrieta (Armas)) B11.29.1922 Havana, Cuba BR/TR/5-10/175* d4.19 C4 Negro Lg 1945-48 OF(1512/83/87)

YEAR	TM LG	G	AB	R	H	2B	3B	HR	RBI	BB-IB	HP	SO	AVG	OBP	SLG	AOPS	ABR	SB-CS	FA	FR	RNG	THR	GAMES AT POSITION	DL	BFW
1949	Cle A	9	16	2	3	0	0	1	2	2	2	2	.188	.350	.375	94	0	0-1	1.000	-0	115	0	O7R		-0.1
1951	Cle A	8	14	3	6	0	0	0	2	1	2	1	.429	.529	.571	209	3	0	.952	-0	97		1b7		-0.1
	Chi A★	138	516	109	167	32	14	10	74	71	14	41	.324	.419	.498	150	39	31-10	.961	-9	88	69	O82(44/2/41),3b68/S		2.8
	Year	146	530	112	173	34	14	10	76	72	16	42	.326	.422	.500	152	42	31-10	.961	-9	88	69	O82(44/2/41),3b68,1b7/S		3.0
1952	Chi A★	147	569	96	160	24	9	13	61	71	14	46	.281	.375	.424	121	37	22-16	.979	-4	92	107	O143(70/63/10),3b9/S		0.5
1953	Chi A★	151	556	104	174	24	8	15	104	74	14	43	.313	.410	.466	132	28	25-16	.967	2	96	146	O147(145/0/2),3b10		2.1
1954	Chi A★	153	568	119	182	29	18	19	116	77	16	46	.320	.411	.535	154	44	18-11	.978	6	103	133	O146(120/16/13),3b9		4.1
1955	Chi A	139	517	79	149	26	7	10	70	76-3	10	43	.288	.387	.424	115	19	19-8	.971	6	99	162	O138(135/2/7),3b2		1.3
1956	Chi A	151	545	106	172	29	11	21	88	86-4	23	40	.316	.425	.525	149	42	12-6	.974	-4	96	148	O148(147/0/1),3b8/1		2.9
1957	Chi A	153	568	96	176	36	5	12	103	79-5	21	54	.310	.408	.454	136	34	18-15	.984	-2	92	105	O152L/3		2.2
1958	Cle A	149	556	94	168	25	2	24	80	59-3	15	53	.302	.383	.484	141	32	14-14	.975	6	104	144	O147L/3		2.8
1959	Cle A★	148	570	92	172	32	0	21	92	54-2	17	55	.302	.377	.468	136	31	8-10	.985	9	105	145	O147L/3		2.8
1960	Chi A★	154	591	89	184	32	4	20	105	52-2	13	63	.311	.374	.481	132	27	17-13	.980	-0	89	128	O154(152/0/5)		1.7
1961	Chi A	152	540	91	151	28	3	14	82	67-2	16	63	.280	.369	.420	114	14	9-4	.956	-19	77	147	O147L		0.5
1962	StL N	39	97	14	19	5	0	1	10	7-0	3	17	.196	.271	.278	44	-8	4-0	.972	-1	81	123	O27L		-0.9
1963	Was A	109	315	38	72	12	2	4	30	33-1	8	38	.229	.315	.317	79	-8	8-6	.955	-3	76	80	O74L,3b8	99	-1.6

YEAR	TM	LG	G	AB	R	H	2B	3B	HR	RBI	BB-IB	HP	SO	AVG	OBP	SLG	AOPS	ABR	SB-CS	FA	FR	RNG	THR	GAMES AT POSITION	DL	BFW
1964	Chi	A	30	31	4	7	0	0	1	5	5-1	1	3	.226	.351	.323	91	0	0-0	1.000	1	174		O5(4/0/1)		0.0
1976	Chi	A	3	8	0	1	0	0	0	0	0-0	0	2	.125	.125	.125	-27	-1	0-0	—	0			D3		-0.1
1980	Chi	A	2	2	0	0	0	0	0	0	0-0	0	0	.000	.000	.000	-99	-1	0-0	—	0			/H		-0.1
Total	17		1835	6579	1136	1963	336	83	186	1023	814-23	192	584	.298	.389	.459	130	306	205-130	.974	5	96	119	O1665L,3b116,1b8,D3,S2	99	21.1

MIRABELLI, DOUG Douglas Anthony B10.18.1970 Kingman AZ BR/TR/6-1/218(210-228) [SFN92 5/131] d8.27 Col Wichita St.

YEAR	TM	LG	G	AB	R	H	2B	3B	HR	RBI	BB-IB	HP	SO	AVG	OBP	SLG	AOPS	ABR	SB-CS	FA	FR	RNG	THR	GAMES AT POSITION	DL	BFW
1996	SF	N	9	18	2	4	1	0	0	1	3-0	0	4	.222	.333	.333	65	-1	0-0	1.000	-2	104	0	C8		-0.2
1997	SF	N	6	7	0	1	0	0	0	0	1-0	0	3	.143	.250	.143	6	-1	0-0	1.000	0	158	0	C6		-0.1
1998	SF	N	10	17	2	4	2	0	1	4	2-0	0	6	.235	.316	.529	123	1	0-0	.974	-0	115	253	C10		0.1
1999	SF	N	33	87	10	22	6	0	1	10	9-1	1	25	.253	.327	.356	79	-3	0-0	1.000	-3	125	132	C30		-0.4
2000	†SF	N	82	230	23	53	10	2	6	28	36-2	2	57	.230	.337	.370	84	-5	1-0	.985	-11	98	107	C80		-0.4
2001	Tex	A	23	49	4	5	2	0	2	3	10-0	0	21	.102	.254	.265	36	-5	0-0	.990	-0	157	246	C23/D		0.8
	Bos	A	54	141	16	38	8	0	9	26	17-2	4	36	.270	.360	.518	129	6	0-0	.995	-1	65	141	C52/D		0.4
	Year		77	190	20	43	10	0	11	29	27-2	4	57	.226	.332	.453	104	1	0-0	.994	-1	91	171	C75,D2		0.0
2002	Bos	A	57	151	17	34	7	0	7	25	17-0	3	33	.225	.312	.411	90	-2	0-0	1.000	-1	63	170	C50,D4		-0.2
2003	†Bos	A	62	163	23	42	13	0	6	18	11-0	1	36	.258	.307	.448	92	-2	0-0	.988	-8	62	114	C53,D4		0.1
2004	†Bos	A	59	160	27	45	12	0	9	32	19-0	3	46	.281	.368	.525	122	5	0-0	.993	-8	49	76	C53,D5		-0.1
2005	†Bos	A	50	136	16	31	7	0	6	18	14-0	2	48	.228	.309	.412	85	-3	2-0	.988	1	96	96	C43,D5	24	0.1
Total	10		445	1159	140	279	68	2	47	165	139-5	16	315	.241	.328	.425	94	-10	3-0	.992	-27	84	124	C410,D19,1b2	24	-1.3

MIRANDA, WILLY Guillermo (Perez) B5.24.1926 Velasco, Cuba D9.7.1996 Baltimore MD BB/TR/5-9.5/150* d5.6

YEAR	TM	LG	G	AB	R	H	2B	3B	HR	RBI	BB-IB	HP	SO	AVG	OBP	SLG	AOPS	ABR	SB-CS	FA	FR	RNG	THR	GAMES AT POSITION	DL	BFW
1951	Was	A	7	9	2	4	0	0	0	0	0-0	0	0	.444	.444	.444	143	0	0-0	.818	-1	40	0	S2/1		-0.1
1952	Chi	A	12	8	1	2	1	0	0	3	0-0	0	1	.250	.455	.375	131	1	0-0	1.000	3	144	156	S4,3b4/2		0.4
	StL	A	7	11	2	1	0	1	0	1	0-0	0	1	.091	.286	.273	54	-1	0-0	.900	-1	100	37	S7		-0.2
	Chi	A	58	142	13	31	3	1	0	7	10	1-0	0	14	.218	.275	.254	47	-10	1-0	.975	6	144	156	S50/23		-0.2
	Year		77	161	16	34	4	2	0	8	16	1	15	.211	.287	.261	52	-10	1-0	.970	7	111	105	S61,3b5,2b2		0.0
1953	StL	A	17	6	2	1	0	0	0	0	1	0	0	.167	.286	.167	24	-1	1-1	.933	1	106	77	S8,3b6		0.1
	NY	A	48	58	12	13	0	1	0	5	5	0	10	.224	.286	.276	54	-4	1-1	.984	5	118	154	S45		0.6
	Year		65	64	14	14	0	1	0	5	6	0	11	.219	.286	.266	51	-5	2-2	.979	10	117	148	S53,3b6		0.7
1954	NY	A	92	116	12	29	4	2	1	12	10	0	10	.250	.300	.345	82	-3	0-3	.948	9	107	146	S88,2b4/3		0.8
1955	Bal	A	153	487	42	124	12	4	1	38	42-4	1	58	.255	.313	.310	74	-19	4-3	.958	20	110	105	S153/2		1.3
1956	Bal	A	148	461	38	100	16	4	2	34	46-3	0	73	.217	.287	.282	55	-31	5-3	.962	4	103	99	S147		-1.6
1957	Bal	A	115	314	29	61	3	0	0	20	24-2	0	42	.194	.249	.204	28	-32	2-1	.966	-3	101	91	S115		-2.8
1958	Bal	A	102	214	15	43	6	0	1	8	14-2	1	25	.201	.250	.243	38	-19	1-1	.962	-7	91	112	S102		-2.0
1959	Bal	A	65	88	8	14	5	0	0	7	7-0	0	16	.159	.221	.216	21	-10	0-0	.974	11	124	150	S47,3b11,2b5		0.3
Total	9		824	1914	176	423	50	14	6	132	165-11	2	250	.221	.282	.271	54	-129	13-16	.962	51	105	108	S768,3b23,2b12/1		-3.4

MISSE, JOHN John Beverly B5.30.1885 Highland KS D3.18.1970 St.Joseph MO BR/TR/5-8/150 d5.26

YEAR	TM	LG	G	AB	R	H	2B	3B	HR	RBI	BB-IB	HP	SO	AVG	OBP	SLG	AOPS	ABR	SB-CS	FA	FR	RNG	THR	GAMES AT POSITION	DL	BFW
1914	StL	F	99	306	28	60	8	1	0	22	36	0	52	.196	.281	.229	38	-31	3	.948	1	105	76	2b50,S48,3b2		-2.7

MITCHELL, CLARENCE Clarence Elmer B2.22.1891 Franklin NE D11.6.1963 Grand Island NE BL/TL/5-11.5/190 d6.2 Mil 1918 C2 ▲

YEAR	TM	LG	G	AB	R	H	2B	3B	HR	RBI	BB-IB	HP	SO	AVG	OBP	SLG	AOPS	ABR	SB-CS	FA	FR	RNG	THR	GAMES AT POSITION	DL	BFW
1911	Det	A	5	4	2	2	0	0	0	1	1	0		.500	.600	.500	198	1	0	1.000	-1	52	0	P5		0.0
1916	Cin	N	56	117	11	28	1	0	0	11	4	0	5	.239	.264	.274	67	-5	1	.985	-0	107	290	P29,1b9,O3L		-0.2
1917	Cin	N	47	90	13	25	3	0	0	5	5	0	5	.278	.316	.311	97	0	0	.982	0	100	128	P32,1b6,O5L		0.0
1918	Bro	N	10	24	2	6	1	0	0	2	0	0	3	.250	.250	.375	90	-1	0	.750	-1	51	0	O6R,1b2/P		-0.2
1919	Bro	N	34	49	7	18	1	0	0	2	4	0	0	.367	.415	.449	156	6	0	.976	1	115	112	P23		-0.4
1920	†Bro	N	55	107	9	25	2	2	0	11	8	0	9	.234	.287	.290	64	-5	1-0	1.000	1	139		P19,1b11,O4(2/0/2)		-0.4
1921	Bro	N	46	91	11	24	5	0	0	12	5	2	7	.264	.316	.319	66	-4	3-1	.945	3	127	326	P37,1b4		0.1
1922	Bro	N	56	155	21	45	6	3	3	28	19	1	11	.290	.371	.426	106	2	0-0	.992	-3	98	129	P29		0.0
1923	Phi	N	53	78	10	21	3	2	1	9	4	0	11	.269	.305	.397	75	3	0	1.000	3	126	135	P30		0.0
1924	Phi	N	69	102	7	26	3	0	0	13	2	1	7	.255	.276	.284	45	0	1-0	1.000	4	132	289	P32,1b2		0.2
1925	Phi	N	52	92	7	18	2	0	0	13	5	0	9	.196	.237	.217	16	-12	2-0	.986	-5	140	107	P28,1b4		0.2
1926	Phi	N	39	78	8	19	4	0	0	6	5	0	5	.244	.289	.295	55	-5	0	.963	0	120	88	P13		0.0
1927	Phi	N	18	42	5	10	2	0	1	6	2	0	7	.238	.273	.357	67	2	0	1.000	-1	215	0	P3		0.0
1928	Phi	N	5	4	0	1	0	0	0	0	0	0	0	.250	.250	.250	30	0	0	1.000	0	0	0	/P		0.0
	†StL	N	19	56	0	7	1	0	0	1	0	0	3	.125	.125	.143	-30	-4	0	.982	2	137	164	P19		0.0
	Year		24	60	0	8	1	0	0	1	0	0	3	.133	.133	.150	-26	-4	0	.983	2	140	158	P22		0.0
1929	StL	N	26	66	9	18	3	1	0	9	4	0	6	.273	.314	.348	63	4	1	.974	-1	96	132	P25		0.0
1930	StL	N	1	2	0	1	0	0	0	0	0	0	0	.500	.500	.500	138	0	0	—	-0	0	0	P24		0.0
	NY	N	24	47	9	12	1	0	0	1	1	0	5	.255	.277	.277	33	0	0	1.000	2	134	60	P24		0.0
	Year		25	49	9	13	1	0	0	1	1	0	5	.265	.280	.286	38	1	0	1.000	2	131	59	P25		0.0
1931	NY	N	27	73	5	16	2	0	1	4	2	0	9	.219	.240	.288	42	2	0	.885	-2	83	87	P27		0.0
1932	NY	N	8	10	2	2	0	0	0	1	1	0	2	.200	.273	.200	30	0	0	.833	-1	48	0	P8		-0.1
Total	18		650	1287	138	324	41	10	7	133	72	4	92	.252	.293	.315	64	-16	9-1	.972	15	114	155	P390,1b80,O18(12/0/8)		-0.1

MITCHELL, FRED Frederick Francis (b Frederick Francis Yapp) B6.5.1878 Cambridge MA D10.13.1970 Newton MA BR/TR/5-9.5/185 d4.27 M7/C3 OF(1/2/0) ▲

YEAR	TM	LG	G	AB	R	H	2B	3B	HR	RBI	BB-IB	HP	SO	AVG	OBP	SLG	AOPS	ABR	SB-CS	FA	FR	RNG	THR	GAMES AT POSITION	DL	BFW
1901	Bos	A	20	44	5	7	0	2	0	4	2	0		.159	.196	.250	23	-5	0	.875	-1	106	223	P17,2b2/S		-0.1
1902	Bos	A	1	1	0	0	0	0	0	0	0	0		.000	.000	.000	-97	0	0	.667	0	171	2645	/P		0.0
	Phi	A	20	48	7	9	1	1	0	3	1	0		.188	.204	.250	24	-5	1	.942	2	136	267	P18/OC		0.1
	Year		21	49	7	9	1	1	0	3	1	0		.184	.200	.245	22	-5	1	.927	2	137	352	P19/OC		0.0
1903	Phi	N	29	95	11	19	4	0	0	10	0	0		.200	.200	.242	27	-1	0	.981	3	154	0	P13,1b9,3b2/OC		0.0
1904	Phi	N	25	82	9	17	3	1	0	3	5	0		.207	.253	.268	63	-4	1	.906	3	128	341	P8		0.8
	Bro	N	8	24	3	7	1	1	0	6	1	1		.292	.346	.417	139	3	0	.952	4	144	129	P21,1b9,3b2/OC		0.8
	Year		33	106	12	24	4	2	0	9	6	1		.226	.274	.302	80	-3	1	.881	-1	123	113	P12,1b7,3b4/SOL		0.0
1905	Bro	N	27	79	4	15	0	0	0	8	4	1		.190	.238	.190	30	-7	6	.968	-9	96	90	C62		-1.2
1910	NY	A	68	196	16	45	7	2	0	18	9	3		.230	.274	.286	71	-7	6	—	0			/H		0.0
1913	Bos	N	4	3	0	1	0	0	0	0	0	0	2	.333	.333	.333	89	0	0	—	0			/H		0.0
Total	7		202	572	55	120	16	7	0	52	22	5	2	.210	.245	.262	52	-26	8	.904	-8	115	182	P97,C62,1b16,3b6,O3C,S2,2b2		-0.3

MITCHELL, JOHNNY John Franklin B8.9.1894 Detroit MI D11.4.1965 Birmingham MI BB/TR/5-8/155 d5.21

YEAR	TM	LG	G	AB	R	H	2B	3B	HR	RBI	BB-IB	HP	SO	AVG	OBP	SLG	AOPS	ABR	SB-CS	FA	FR	RNG	THR	GAMES AT POSITION	DL	BFW
1921	NY	A	13	42	4	11	1	0	0	2	4	0	4	.262	.326	.286	56	-3	110	.958	-4	110	44	S7,2b5		-0.6
1922	NY	A	4	4	1	0	0	0	0	0	0	0	1	.000	.000	.000	-98	-1	0-0	1.000	-0	79	0	S4		-0.5
	Bos	A	59	203	20	51	4	1	1	8	16	4	17	.251	.318	.296	61	-12	1-2	.962	-3	101	105	S58		-0.5
	Year		63	207	21	51	4	1	1	8	16	4	18	.246	.313	.290	58	-13	1-2	.963	-4	102	102	S62		-1.1
1923	Bos	A	92	347	40	78	15	4	0	19	34	1	18	.225	.296	.291	55	-23	7-11	.961	4	102	87	S87,2b5		-1.2
1924	Bro	N	64	243	42	64	10	0	1	16	37	0	22	.263	.361	.317	86	-3	3-1	.951	-3	97	74	S64		0.1
1925	Bro	N	97	336	45	84	8	3	0	18	28	0	19	.250	.308	.292	55	-23	2-0	.947	-2	95	89	S90		-1.6
Total	5		329	1175	152	288	38	12	2	63	119	5	81	.245	.317	.296	62	-65	14-14	.955	-5	99	87	S310,2b10		-3.4

MITCHELL, KEITH Keith Alexander B8.6.1969 San Diego CA BR/TR/5-10/180(180-195) [AtlN87 4/90] d7.23

YEAR	TM	LG	G	AB	R	H	2B	3B	HR	RBI	BB-IB	HP	SO	AVG	OBP	SLG	AOPS	ABR	SB-CS	FA	FR	RNG	THR	GAMES AT POSITION	DL	BFW
1991	†Atl	N	48	66	11	21	0	0	2	5	8-0	0	12	.318	.392	.409	114	2	3-1	.970	-1	91	89	O34(24/1/10)		0.3
1994	Sea	A	46	128	21	29	2	0	5	15	18-0	1	22	.227	.324	.359	75	-5	0-0	.980	-4	84	0	O38(27/3/11),D6	41	-0.5
1996	Cin	N	11	15	2	4	1	0	1	3	1-0	0	5	.267	.313	.533	116	0	0-0	.875	-0	109	0	O5(2/1/2)		-0.2
1998	Bos	A	23	33	4	9	2	0	0	6	7-1	0	5	.273	.400	.333	92	0	1-0	1.000	-1	60	0	D12,O10(4/0/6)		-0.1
Total	4		128	242	38	63	5	0	8	29	34-1	1	42	.260	.353	.380	91	-3	4-1	.969	-6	85	27	O87(57/5/29),D18	41	-0.5

MITCHELL, KEVIN Kevin Darnell B1.13.1962 San Diego CA BR/TR/5-11/210(210-244) d9.4 OF(756/6/53) [DL 1993 SF N 24]

YEAR	TM	LG	G	AB	R	H	2B	3B	HR	RBI	BB-IB	HP	SO	AVG	OBP	SLG	AOPS	ABR	SB-CS	FA	FR	RNG	THR	GAMES AT POSITION	DL	BFW
1984	NY	N	7	14	0	3	0	0	0	1	0	0	3	.214	.214	.214	21	-2	0-1	.833	-0	81	457	3b5		-0.1
1986	†NY	N	108	328	51	91	22	2	12	43	33-0	1	61	.277	.344	.466	124	11	3-3	.983	4	105	73	O68(40/6/29),S24,3b7,1b2		1.1
1987	SD	N	62	196	19	48	7	1	7	26	20-3	2	38	.245	.313	.398	91	-3	0-0	.945	3	113	106	3b51,O3L		1.0
	†SF	N	69	268	49	82	13	1	15	44	28-1	1	50	.306	.376	.530	143	16	9-6	.962	-4	100	99	3b68,O3(2/0/1)/S		1.1
	Year		131	464	68	130	20	2	22	70	48-4	3	88	.280	.350	.474	121	13	9-6	.954	-2	106	99	3b102,O40L		1.1
1988	SF	N	148	505	60	127	25	7	19	80	48-7	2	85	.251	.319	.442	112	3	5-3	.943	-0	96	122	3b102,O40L		6.0
1989	†SF	N★	154	543	100	158	34	6	47	125	87-32	3	115	.291	.387	.635	194	67	3-4	.978	-2	96	87	O147L,3b2		2.1
1990	SF	N★	140	524	90	152	24	2	35	93	58-9	2	87	.290	.360	.544	151	35	4-7	.971	-0	97	87	O138L		2.2
1991	SF	N	113	371	52	95	13	1	27	69	43-8	5	57	.256	.338	.515	119	19	2-3	.970	-1	97	108	O100L/1	22	1.4

YEAR	TM LG	G	AB	R	H	2B	3B	HR	RBI	BB-IB	HP	SO	AVG	OBP	SLG	AOPS	ABR	SB-CS	FA	FR	RNG	THR	GAMES AT POSITION	DL	BFW
1992	Sea A	99	360	48	103	24	0	9	67	35-4	3	46	.286	.351	.428	117	9	0-2	1.000	-1	98	91	O69L,D26	48	0.4
1993	Cin N	93	323	56	110	21	3	19	64	25-4	1	48	.341	.385	.601	160	26	1-0	.957	2	100	124	O87(85/0/2)	15	2.5
1994	Cin N	95	310	57	101	18	1	30	77	59-15	3	62	.326	.429	.681	186	41	2-0	.972	1	89	184	O89L/1		3.8
1996	Bos A	27	92	9	28	4	0	2	13	11-0	1	14	.304	.385	.413	100	0	0-0	.935	-3	78		O21(1/0/21),D4	63	-0.3
	Cin N	37	114	18	37	11	0	6	26	26-2	0	16	.325	.447	.579	166	13	0-0	.978	-1	102		O31L,1b3		1.0
1997	Cle A	20	59	7	9	1	0	4	11	9-2	1	11	.153	.275	.373	65	-3	1-0	.000	-0	0		D16/OL		-0.4
1998	Oak A	51	127	14	29	7	1	2	21	9-0	0	26	.228	.279	.346	62	-7	0-0	1.000	-1	88		D23,O10L,1b2	31	-0.9
Total	13	1223	4134	630	1173	224	25	234	760	491-87	27	719	.284	.360	.520	142	235	30-31	.971	-2	96	99	O807L,3b235,D69,S25,1b9	203	20.3

MITCHELL, DALE Loren Dale B8.23.1921 Colony OK D1.5.1987 Tulsa OK BL/TL/6-1/195* d9.15 Col Oklahoma

YEAR	TM LG	G	AB	R	H	2B	3B	HR	RBI	BB-IB	HP	SO	AVG	OBP	SLG	AOPS	ABR	SB-CS	FA	FR	RNG	THR	GAMES AT POSITION	DL	BFW
1946	Cle A	11	44	7	19	3	0	0	5	1-0	0	2	.432	.444	.500	175	4	1-0	1.000	-0	105	0	O11C		0.4
1947	Cle A	123	493	69	156	16	10	1	34	23	0	14	.316	.347	.396	109	3	2-5	.977	-6	88	101	O115(83/42/1)		-1.2
1948	†Cle A	141	608	82	204	30	8	4	56	45	2	17	.336	.383	.431	119	15	13-18	.991	-8	90	113	O140(140/1/0)		0.1
1949	Cle A★	149	640	81	203	16	23	3	56	43	0	11	.317	.360	.428	110	4	10-3	.994	-3	95	87	O149L		-0.9
1950	Cle A	130	506	81	156	27	5	3	49	67	1	21	.308	.390	.399	106	4	7-7	.972	-11	87	33	O127L		-1.4
1951	Cle A	134	510	83	148	21	7	11	62	53	˙1	16	.290	.358	.424	117	11	7-7	.992	-9	89	32	O124L		-0.9
1952	Cle A★	134	511	61	165	26	3	5	58	52	1	9	.323	.387	.415	132	22	6-6	.992	-7	93	25	O128L		0.6
1953	Cle A	134	500	76	150	26	4	13	60	42	0	20	.300	.354	.446	118	11	3-1	.970	-10	90	23	O125L		-0.5
1954	†Cle A	53	60	6	17	1	0	1	6	9	0	1	.283	.377	.350	98	0	3-1	.889	-0	69	327	O6L/1		0.0
1955	Cle A	61	58	4	15	2	1	0	10	4-2	0	3	.259	.302	.328	68	-3	0-0	1.000	-0	107	208	1b8,O3L		-0.3
1956	Cle A	38	30	2	4	0	0	0	6	7-1	0	3	.133	.297	.133	17	-3	0-0	—	-0	0		O2L		-0.3
	†Bro N	19	24	3	7	1	0	0	1	9-0	0	3	.292	.292	.333	63	-1	0-0	1.000	-0	90	0	/OL		-0.2
Total	11	1127	3984	555	1244	169	61	41	403	346-3	3	119	.312	.368	.416	114	70	45-47	.985	-46	91	62	O931(888/54/1),1b9		-4.6

MITCHELL, MIKE Michael Francis B12.12.1879 Springfield OH D7.16.1961 Phoenix AZ BR/TR/6-1/185 d4.11

YEAR	TM LG	G	AB	R	H	2B	3B	HR	RBI	BB-IB	HP	SO	AVG	OBP	SLG	AOPS	ABR	SB-CS	FA	FR	RNG	THR	GAMES AT POSITION	DL	BFW
1907	Cin N	148	558	64	163	17	12	3	47	37			.292	.339	.382	121	12	17	.962	24	200	186	O146(3/0/144),1b2		3.3
1908	Cin N	119	406	41	90	9	6	3	37	46		2	.222	.304	.281	89	-4	18	.959	2	110	56	O118(3/0/115)/1		-0.9
1909	Cin N	145	523	83	162	17	17	4	86	57		0	.310	.378	.430	152	30	37	.962	5	100	64	O145R/1		3.2
1910	Cin N	156	583	79	167	16	18	5	88	59	4	56	.286	.356	.401	126	17	35	.958	-2	99	92	O149(0/22/127),1b7		0.9
1911	Cin N	142	529	74	154	22	22	2	84	44	2	34	.291	.348	.427	121	11	35	.971	9	114	113	O140(1/0/139)		1.2
1912	Cin N	147	552	60	156	14	13	4	78	41	1	43	.283	.333	.377	97	-5	23	.947	-1	106	85	O144R		-1.3
1913	Chi N	82	279	37	73	11	6	4	35	32	1	33	.262	.340	.387	107	3	15-8	.941	1	100	119	O82(72/0/10)		0.0
	Pit N	54	199	25	54	8	2	1	16	14	0	15	.271	.319	.347	94	-2	8-10	.946	3	110	112	O54C		-0.5
	Year	136	478	62	127	19	8	5	51	46	1	48	.266	.331	.370	102	1	23-18	.943	4	104	116	O136(72/54/10)		-0.5
1914	Pit N	76	273	31	64	11	5	2	23	16	1	16	.234	.279	.333	86	-6	5	.984	6	124	81	O76R		-0.5
	Was A	55	193	20	55	5	3	1	20	22	1	19	.285	.358	.358	112	3	9-7	.957	2	98	142	O53(47/0/6)		0.2
Total	8	1124	4095	514	1138	130	104	27	514	368	15	216	.278	.340	.380	114	59	202-25	.959	49	118	103	O1107(126/76/905),1b11		5.6

MITCHELL, BOBBY Robert Van B4.7.1955 Salt Lake City UT BL/TL/5-10/170* [LAN77 7/176] d9.1 Col USC

YEAR	TM LG	G	AB	R	H	2B	3B	HR	RBI	BB-IB	HP	SO	AVG	OBP	SLG	AOPS	ABR	SB-CS	FA	FR	RNG	THR	GAMES AT POSITION	DL	BFW
1980	LA N	9	3	1	1	0	0	0	0	1-0	0	0	.333	.500	.333	141	0	0-0	1.000	0	139	0	O8(0/7/1)		0.0
1981	LA N	10	8	0	1	0	0	0	0	1-0	0	1	.125	.222	.125	1	-1	0-0	1.000	0	122	0	O7(1/6/1)		-0.1
1982	Min A	124	454	48	113	11	6	2	28	54-4	2	53	.249	.331	.313	76	-14	8-9	.997	11	116	105	O121(5/115/6)		-0.7
1983	Min A	59	152	26	35	4	2	1	15	28-2	1	21	.230	.344	.303	79	-3	1-1	.990	-2	89	84	O44(1/43/0)		-0.6
Total	4	202	617	75	150	15	8	3	43	84-6	3	78	.243	.336	.308	76	-18	9-10	.996	8	110	98	O180(7/171/8)		-1.4

MITCHELL, BOBBY Robert Vance B10.22.1943 Norristown PA BR/TR/6-4/190* d7.5

YEAR	TM LG	G	AB	R	H	2B	3B	HR	RBI	BB-IB	HP	SO	AVG	OBP	SLG	AOPS	ABR	SB-CS	FA	FR	RNG	THR	GAMES AT POSITION	DL	BFW
1970	NY A	10	22	1	5	2	0	0	4	2-0	1	3	.227	.320	.318	80	0	0-2	1.000	2	177	0	O7(0/2/5)		0.0
1971	Mil A	35	55	7	10	1		2	6	6-1	0	18	.182	.262	.345	72	-2	0-2	.974	2	121	228	O19(2/7/10)		-0.2
1973	Mil A	47	130	12	29	6	0	5	20	5-1	0	32	.223	.250	.385	78	-5	4-1	.960	-2	77	0	O20(10/0/10),D19		-0.8
1974	Mil A	88	173	27	42	6	2	5	20	18-1	1	46	.243	.314	.382	102	0	7-6	.969	-1	96	88	D53,O26(10/2/14)		-0.3
1975	Mil A	93	229	39	57	14	3	9	41	25-1	0	69	.249	.320	.454	117	5	3-4	.992	3	108	49	O72L,D11		0.2
Total	5	273	609	86	143	29	6	21	91	56-4	2	168	.235	.299	.406	99	-2	14-15	.984	3	107		O144(94/11/39),D83		-1.1

MITTERLING, RALPH Ralph "Sarge" B4.19.1890 Freeburg PA D1.22.1956 Pittsburgh PA BR/TR/5-10/165 d7.7 Col Springfield

YEAR	TM LG	G	AB	R	H	2B	3B	HR	RBI	BB-IB	HP	SO	AVG	OBP	SLG	AOPS	ABR	SB-CS	FA	FR	RNG	THR	GAMES AT POSITION	DL	BFW
1916	Phi A	13	39	1	6	0	0	0	2	3		6	.154	.214	.154	11	-4	0	.944	-1	85	86	O12(1/11/0)		-0.6

MITTERWALD, GEORGE George Eugene B6.7.1945 Berkeley CA BR/TR/6-2/206(195-206) d9.15 C5 Col Chabot (CA) JC

YEAR	TM LG	G	AB	R	H	2B	3B	HR	RBI	BB-IB	HP	SO	AVG	OBP	SLG	AOPS	ABR	SB-CS	FA	FR	RNG	THR	GAMES AT POSITION	DL	BFW
1966	Min A	3	5	1	1	0	0	0	0				.200	.200	.200	14	-1	0-0	1.000	1	0	0	C3		0.0
1968	Min A	11	34	1	7	1	0	0	1	3-0	0	8	.206	.270	.235	51	-2	0-0	.961	-1	67	36	C10		-0.2
1969	†Min A	69	187	18	48	8	0	5	13	17-1	3	47	.257	.327	.380	95	-1	0-1	.987	9	135	74	C63/OL		1.1
1970	†Min A	117	369	36	82	12	0	15	46	34-6	2	84	.222	.291	.388	84	-9	3-5	.996	26	141	128	C117		2.2
1971	Min A	125	388	38	97	13	1	13	44	39-9	0	104	.250	.316	.389	97	-2	3-3	.986	-2	102	97	C120		0.0
1972	Min A	64	163	12	30	4	1	1	8	9-2	0	37	.184	.225	.239	37	-13	0-1	.984	5	75	152	C61		-0.7
1973	Min A	125	432	50	112	15	0	16	64	39-0	5	111	.259	.326	.405	101	-1	3-1	.992	4	97	99	C122,D3		1.0
1974	Chi N	78	215	17	54	7	0	7	28	18-4	2	42	.251	.310	.381	90	-3	1-3	.974	-6	65	142	C68		-0.8
1975	Chi N	84	200	19	44	4	3	5	26	19-7	0	42	.220	.285	.345	72	-9	0-0	.976	3	118	188	C59,1b10		-0.4
1976	Chi N	101	303	19	65	7	0	5	28	16-2	0	63	.215	.249	.287	49	-21	1-2	.981	-2	93	113	C64,1b25		-2.4
1977	Chi N	110	349	40	83	22	0	9	43	28-7	1	69	.238	.295	.378	72	-14	3-1	.989	10	108	130	C109/1		0.1
Total	11	887	2645	251	623	93	6	76	301	222-38	13	607	.236	.296	.362	80	-75	14-17	.987	47	105	118	C796,1b36,D3/OL		-0.1

MIZE, JOHNNY John Robert "The Big Cat" B1.7.1913 Demorest GA D6.2.1993 Demorest GA BL/TR/6-2/215(205-223) d4.16 Mil 1943-45 C1 HF1981 Col Piedmont

YEAR	TM LG	G	AB	R	H	2B	3B	HR	RBI	BB-IB	HP	SO	AVG	OBP	SLG	AOPS	ABR	SB-CS	FA	FR	RNG	THR	GAMES AT POSITION	DL	BFW
1936	StL N	126	414	76	136	30	8	19	93	50	1	32	.329	.402	.577	162	36	1	.994	0	96	78	1b97,O8R		2.5
1937	StL N	145	560	103	204	40	7	25	113	56	5	57	.364	.427	.595	171	56	2	.988	-14	67	91	1b144		2.9
1938	StL N	149	531	85	179	34	16	27	102	74	4	47	.337	.422	.614	172	53	0	.989	-0	100	96	1b140		3.9
1939	StL N★	153	564	104	197	44	14	28	108	92	4	49	.349	.444	.626	174	62	0	.987	-3	91	94	1b152		4.3
1940	StL N★	155	579	111	182	31	13	43	137	82	5	49	.314	.404	.636	173	57	7	.990	-6	82	83	1b153		3.6
1941	StL N	126	473	67	150	39	8	16	100	70	1	45	.317	.406	.535	153	35	4	.994	4	107	110	1b122		2.7
1942	NY N	142	541	97	165	25	7	26	110	60	5	45	.305	.380	.521	141	41	3	.995	-2	90	98	1b138		2.7
1946	NY N★	101	377	70	127	18	2	22	70	62	5	26	.337	.437	.576	185	44	3	.989	6	121	97	1b101		4.8
1947	NY N★	154	586	137	177	26	2	51	138	74	4	42	.302	.384	.614	160	48	2	.996	9	119	93	1b154		5.0
1948	NY N★	152	560	110	162	26	4	40	125	94	4	37	.289	.395	.564	156	45	4	.991	3	108	97	1b152		4.2
1949	†NY A	106	388	59	102	15	0	18	62	50	3	19	.263	.351	.441	111	6	1	.994	2	106	95	1b101		0.5
1950	†NY A	13	23	4	6	1	0	1	2	4	1	2	.261	.393	.435	119	1	0-0	.980	-0	77	87	1b6		0.0
1951	†NY A	90	274	43	76	12	0	25	72	29	4	24	.277	.351	.595	144	14	0-1	.996	-2	78	117	1b72		0.9
1952	†NY A	113	332	37	86	14	1	10	49	36	4	24	.259	.339	.398	102	1	1-0	.994	-3	81	119	1b93		-0.4
1953	†NY A	78	137	9	36	9	0	4	29	11	2	15	.263	.327	.416	112	2	0-0	.987	0	106	155	1b27		0.2
	†NY A★	81	104	6	26	3	0	4	27	12	2	17	.250	.339	.394	101	0	0-0	1.000	0	89	171	1b15		0.2
Total	15	1884	6443	1118	2011	367	83	359	1337	856	52	524	.312	.397	.562	157	501	28-1	.992	-7	96	97	1b1667,O8R		37.7

MIZEROCK, JOHN John Joseph B12.8.1960 Punxsutawney PA BL/TR/5-11/190* d4.12 M1/C3 [DL 1984 Hou N 79]

YEAR	TM LG	G	AB	R	H	2B	3B	HR	RBI	BB-IB	HP	SO	AVG	OBP	SLG	AOPS	ABR	SB-CS	FA	FR	RNG	THR	GAMES AT POSITION	DL	BFW
1983	Hou N	33	85	8	13	4	1	1	10	12-2	1	15	.153	.263	.259	48	-6	0-0	.967	-2	101	112	C33	23	-0.7
1985	Hou N	15	38	6	9	4	0	0	6	2-0	1	8	.237	.293	.342	79	-1	0-0	.966	2	74	121	C15		0.1
1986	Hou N	44	81	9	15	1	1	1	6	24-2	1	16	.185	.374	.259	81	-1	0-0	.987	-1	106	54	C42		0.0
1989	Atl N	11	27	1	6	0	0	0	2	0-0	0	3	.222	.222	.222	27	-1	0-0	1.000	1	301	73	C11		-0.1
Total	4	103	231	24	43	9	2	2	24	38-4	3	42	.186	.307	.268	64	-11	0-0	.979	0	118	87	C101	102	-0.7

MIZEUR, BILL William Francis "Bad Bill" B6.22.1897 Nokomis IL D8.27.1976 Decatur IL BL/TR/6-0/180 d9.30

YEAR	TM LG	G	AB	R	H	2B	3B	HR	RBI	BB-IB	HP	SO	AVG	OBP	SLG	AOPS	ABR	SB-CS	FA	FR	RNG	THR	GAMES AT POSITION	DL	BFW
1923	StL A	1	1	0	0	0	0	0	0	0-0	0	0	.000	.000	.000	-95	0	0-0	—		0		/H		0.0
1924	StL A	1	1	0	0	0	0	0	0	0-0	0	0	.000	.000	.000	-94	0	0-0	—		0		/H		0.0
Total	2	2	2	0	0	0	0	0	0	0-0	0	0	.000	.000	.000	-94	0	0-0	—		0				0.0

MOATES, DAVE David Allan B1.30.1948 Great Lakes IL BL/TL/5-9/165* [TexA69 S4/87] d9.21 Col Florida St.

YEAR	TM LG	G	AB	R	H	2B	3B	HR	RBI	BB-IB	HP	SO	AVG	OBP	SLG	AOPS	ABR	SB-CS	FA	FR	RNG	THR	GAMES AT POSITION	DL	BFW
1974	Tex A	1	0	0	0	0	0	0	0	0-0	0	0	—	—	—		0	0-0	—		0		/R		0.0
1975	Tex A	54	175	21	48	9	0	3	14	13-0	0	15	.274	.321	.377	99	0	9-2	.984	0	93	184	O51(1/49/1)/D		0.0
1976	Tex A	85	137	21	33	7	1	0	13	11-2	0	18	.241	.293	.307	75	-4	6-3	.991	3	102	137	O66(8/37/25),D7		-0.2
Total	3	140	312	42	81	16	1	3	27	24-2	0	33	.260	.309	.346	89	-4	15-5	.987	4	97	162	O117(9/86/26),D8		-0.2

YEAR	TM LG	G	AB	R	H	2B	3B	HR	RBI	BB-IB	HP	SO	AVG	OBP	SLG	AOPS	ABR	SB-CS	FA	FR	RNG	THR	GAMES AT POSITION	DL	BFW

MOELLER, CHAD Chad Edward B2.18.1975 Upland CA BR/TR/6-3/210* [MinA96 7/187] d6.20 Col USC

YEAR	TM LG	G	AB	R	H	2B	3B	HR	RBI	BB-IB	HP	SO	AVG	OBP	SLG	ABR	SB-CS	FA	FR	RNG	THR	GAMES AT POSITION	DL	BFW
2000	Min A	48	128	13	27	3	1	1	9	9-0	0	33	.211	.261	.273	34	-13	1-0	.979	2	175	51	C48	16	-0.
2001	Ari N	25	56	8	13	0	1	1	2	6-1	0	12	.232	.302	.321	59	-4	0-0	1.000	-4	82	112	C25		-0.
2002	†Ari N	37	105	10	30	11	1	2	16	17-3	0	23	.286	.385	.467	115	3	0-1	.997	9	101	95	C35		-0.
2003	Ari N	78	239	29	64	17	1	7	29	23-11	2	59	.268	.335	.435	92	-3	1-2	.987	-5	84	.93	C76		-0.
2004	Mil N	101	317	25	66	13	1	5	27	21-1	4	74	.208	.265	.303	46	-26	0-1	.999	14	93	88	C100		-0.
2005	Mil N	66	199	23	41	9	1	7	23	13-1	1	48	.206	.257	.367	61	-12	0-0	.994	7	90	80	C65		-0.
Total	6	355	1044	108	241	53	6	23	106	89-17	7	249	.231	.294	.359	66	-55	2-4	.993	22	101	85	C349	16	-1.2

MOELLER, DANNY Daniel Edward B3.23.1885 DeWitt IA D4.14.1951 Florence AL BB/TR/5-11/165 d9.24 Col Millikin

YEAR	TM LG	G	AB	R	H	2B	3B	HR	RBI	BB-IB	HP	SO	AVG	OBP	SLG	ABR	SB-CS	FA	FR	RNG	THR	GAMES AT POSITION	BFW
1907	Pit N	11	42	4	12	1	1	0	3	4	0		.286	.348	.357	119	1	2	.800	-1	76	327	O11R	-0.
1908	Pit N	36	109	14	21	3	1	0	9	9	0		.193	.254	.239	57	-5	4	.950	-3	0	0	O27(3/1/23)	-1.
1912	Was A	132	519	90	143	26	10	6	46	52	4		.276	.346	.399	112	8	30	.944	3	98	124	O132(31/0/101)	0.
1913	Was A	153	589	88	139	15	10	5	42	72	3	103	.236	.322	.321	86	-10	62	.926	3	104	116	O153(16/0/137)	-1.
1914	Was A	151	571	83	143	19	10	1	45	71	7	89	.250	.341	.324	96	-1	26-25	.930	-1	101	104	O150(1/1/149)	-1.
1915	Was A	118	438	65	99	11	9	2	23	59	1	63	.226	.319	.311	87	-7	32-10	.952	-5	89	90	O116(21/0/95)	-1.
1916	Was A	78	240	30	59	8	1	1	23	30	2	35	.246	.335	.300	92	-2	13	.963	4	101	165	O63(23/0/40)	-0.
	Cle A	25	30	5	2	0	0	0	1	5	0	6	.067	.200	.067	-19	-4	2	1.000	-0	108	0	O8(3/2/3)/2	-0.
	Year	103	270	35	61	8	1	1	24	35	2	41	.226	.319	.274	78	-6	15	.966	4	101	154	O71(26/2/43)/2	-0.
Total	7	704	2538	379	618	83	43	15	192	302	17	296	.243	.328	.328	89	-20	171-35	.938	-2	95	113	O660(98/4/559)/2	-6

MOFFETT, JOE Joseph Willliam B6.1859 Wheeling WV D2.24.1935 San Bernardino CA 6-0/179 d5.6 b-Sam

| 1884 | Tol AA | 56 | 204 | 17 | 41 | 5 | 3 | 0 | | | | | .201 | .209 | .255 | 49 | -12 | | .957 | -5 | 46 | 115 | 1b38,3b11,2b4,O3(1/3/0) | -1. |

MOFFETT, SAM Samuel R. B3.14.1857 Wheeling WV D5.5.1907 Butte MT BR/TR/6-0/175 d5.15 b-Joe ▲

1884	Cle N	67	256	26	47	12	2	0	15	8		56	.184	.208	.246	41	-17		.827	6	186	0	O42(13/1/28),P24,1b2/32	-0.
1887	Ind N	11	41	6	5	1	0	0	1	0	0	6	.122	.143	.146	-20	-7	2	.857	-1	75	0	P6,O5(1/2/3)	-0.
1888	Ind N	10	35	6	4	0	0	0	0	5	0	4	.114	.225	.114	11	-3	0	.750	-2	41	342	P7,O3C	-0.
Total	3	88	332	38	56	13	2	0	16	14		66	.169	.202	.220	30	-27	2	.821	2	169	0	O50(14/6/31),P37,1b2/23	-1.

MOHARDT, JOHN John Henry B1.21.1898 Pittsburgh PA D11.24.1961 LaJolla CA BR/TR/5-10/165 d4.15 Col Notre Dame

| 1922 | Det A | 5 | 1 | 2 | 1 | 0 | 0 | 0 | 0 | 1 | 0 | 0 | 1.000 | 1.000 | 1.000 | 436 | 1 | 0-1 | 1.000 | 0 | 407 | 0 | O3(1/1/1) | 0. |

MOHLER, KID Ernest Follette B12.13.1870 Oneida IL D11.4.1961 San Francisco CA BR/TL/5-4.5/145 d9.29

| 1894 | Was N | 3 | 9 | 1 | 0 | 0 | 0 | 0 | 0 | 4 | | | .111 | .273 | .111 | -5 | -2 | 0 | .952 | 1 | 106 | 65 | 2b3 | -0. |

MOHR, DUSTAN Dustan Kyle B6.19.1976 Hattiesburg MS BR/TR/6-0/210* [CleA97 9/291] d8.29 Col Alabama

2001	Min A	20	51	6	12	2	0	0	4	5-0	0	17	.235	.298	.275	51	-4	1-1	1.000	2	139	0	O19(6/0/15)/D	-0
2002	†Min A	120	383	55	103	23	2	12	45	31-3	1	86	.269	.325	.433	96	-2	6-3	.992	5	115	62	O113(28/1/94),D3	-0
2003	Min A	121	348	50	87	22	0	10	36	33-0	1	106	.250	.314	.399	84	-8	5-2	.976	3	117	35	O110(30/11/77),D6	-0
2004	SF N	117	263	52	72	20	1	7	28	46-3	8	64	.274	.394	.437	112	7	0-3	.981	4	108	136	O95(43/6/55),D2	0
2005	Col N	98	266	34	57	10	3	17	38	23-2	2	94	.214	.280	.466	80	-9	1-2	.987	4	114	108	O76(17/10/55)	23	-1
Total	5	476	1311	197	331	77	6	46	151	138-8	12	367	.252	.327	.426	91	-16	13-11	.985	18	115	75	O413(124/28/296),D12	23	-1

MOKAN, JOHNNIE John Leo B9.23.1895 Buffalo NY D2.10.1985 Buffalo NY BR/TR/5-7/165 d4.15

1921	Pit N	19	52	7	14	3	2	0	9	5	0	3	.269	.333	.404	92	-1	0-0	.946	-0	122	0	O15(6/0/7)	-0
1922	Pit N	31	89	9	23	3	1	0	8	9	0	3	.258	.327	.315	65	-4	0-1	.903	-2	72	134	O23(3/0/20)	-0
	Phi N	47	151	20	38	7	1	3	27	16	1	25	.252	.327	.371	73	-6	1-0	.905	-3	83	113	O37(36/2/3),3b2	-1
	Year	78	240	29	61	10	2	3	35	25	1	28	.254	.327	.350	70	-10	1-1	.905	-5	79	120	O60(39/2/23),3b2	-1
1923	Phi N	113	400	76	125	23	3	10	48	53	6	31	.313	.401	.460	113	10	6-11	.969	5	101	150	O105(84/21/2)/3	0
1924	Phi N	96	366	50	95	15	4	7	44	30	3	27	.260	.321	.363	74	-13	7-5	.986	-2	95	90	O94(93/2/0)	-2
1925	Phi N	75	209	30	69	11	2	6	42	27	4	9	.330	.417	.488	120	7	3-5	.984	-4	97	21	O68(36/32/2)	-0
1926	Phi N	127	456	68	138	23	5	6	62	41	4	31	.303	.365	.414	104	3	4	.967	-1	92	117	O123(67/0/67)	-0
1927	Phi N	74	213	22	61	13	2	0	33	25	1	21	.286	.361	.366	94	-1	5	.962	-2	91	95	O63(27/9/28)	-0
Total	7	582	2296	282	563	98	17	32	273	206	18	150	.291	.364	.409	97	-5	26-22	.966	-9	94	104	O528(352/66/129),3b3	-5

MOLE, FENTON Fenton Le Roy "Muscles" B6.14.1925 San Leandro CA BL/TL/6-1.5/200 d9.1

| 1949 | NY A | 10 | 27 | 5 | 5 | 2 | 1 | 0 | 3 | 0 | 0 | 5 | .185 | .267 | .333 | 58 | -2 | 0-0 | 1.000 | 1 | 117 | 160 | 1b8 | -0 |

MOLINA, BENGIE Benjamin Jose B7.20.1974 Rio Piedras, PR BR/TR/5-11/207(200-220) d9.21 b-Jose b-Yadier Col Arizona Western CC

1998	Ana A	2	1	0	0	0	0	0	0	0-0	0	0	.000	.000	.000	-98	-0	0-0	1.000	-0	-0	0	C2	0
1999	Ana A	31	101	8	26	5	0	1	10	6-0	2	6	.257	.312	.337	66	-5	0-1	.991	8	127	109	C30	0
2000	Ana A	130	473	59	133	20	2	14	71	23-0	6	33	.281	.318	.421	84	-13	1-0	.991	9	105	129	C127,D2	0
2001	Ana A	96	325	31	85	11	0	6	40	16-3	8	51	.262	.309	.351	73	-13	0-1	.991	0	107	106	C94/D	53	-0
2002	†Ana A	122	428	34	105	18	0	5	47	15-3	4	34	.245	.274	.322	60	-26	0-1	.999	13	142	122	C121	15	-0
2003	Ana A	119	409	37	115	24	0	14	71	13-2	2	31	.281	.304	.443	98	-3	1-1	.993	13	128	147	C117	25	1
2004	†Ana A	97	337	36	93	13	0	10	54	18-1	2	35	.276	.313	.404	90	-6	0-1	.995	1	83	88	C89,D5	31	0
2005	†LA A	119	410	45	121	17	0	15	69	27-2	1	41	.295	.336	.446	109	4	0-2	.996	-3	111	93	C105,D11	149	1
Total	8	716	2484	250	678	108	2	65	362	118-11	25	231	.273	.309	.397	85	-62	2-6	.994	40	115	116	C685,D19		

MOLINA, IZZY Islay B6.3.1971 New York NY BR/TR/6-0/200(200-224) [OakA90 22/610] d8.15

1996	Oak A	14	25	0	5	2	0	0	1	1-0	0	3	.200	.231	.280	29	-3	0-0	1.000	-3	46	0	C12/D	-0
1997	Oak A	48	111	6	22	3	1	3	7	3-0	0	17	.198	.219	.324	40	-11	0-0	.992	-4	73	87	C48	-1
1998	Oak A	6	2	1	1	0	0	0	0	0-0	0	0	.500	.500	.500	163	0	0-0	1.000	0	32	0	C5	-1
2002	Bal A	1	3	1	1	0	0	0	0	0-0	0	0	.333	.333	.333	82	0	0-0	1.000	0	54	390	/C	-1
Total	4	69	141	8	29	5	1	3	8	4-0	0	20	.206	.228	.319	40	-14	0-0	.993	-6	68	80	C66/D	-1

MOLINA, JOSE Jose Benjamin (Matta) B6.3.1975 Bayamon, PR BR/TR/6-1/195(195-220) [ChiN93 14/390] d9.6 b-Bengie b-Yadier

1999	Chi N	10	19	3	5	1	0	0	1	2-1	0	4	.263	.333	.316	66	-1	0-0	1.000	1	100	150	C10	42	
2001	Ana A	15	37	8	10	3	0	2	4	3-0	0	8	.270	.325	.514	114	1	0-0	1.000	4	77	230	C15	
2002	†Ana A	29	70	2	19	3	0	0	5	5-0	0	15	.271	.312	.314	71	-3	0-2	.983	4	84	151	C29	
2003	Ana A	53	114	12	21	4	0	0	6	1-0	1	26	.184	.210	.219	15	-14	0-0	.996	-2	112	82	C53	
2004	†Ana A	73	203	26	53	10	2	3	25	10-0	0	52	.261	.296	.374	76	-8	4-1	.994	9	126	156	C70,1b2	
2005	†LA A	75	184	14	42	4	0	6	25	13-0	2	41	.228	.286	.348	69	-9	2-0	.993	18	142	170	C65,1b4,D5	42	
Total	6	255	627	68	150	25	2	11	66	34-1	5	146	.239	.283	.358	64	-34	6-3	.993	33	119	149	C242,1b6,D5	

MOLINA, YADIER Yadier B. B7.13.1982 Bayamon, PR BR/TR/5-11/225* [StLN00 4/113] d6.3 b-Bengie b-Jose

2004	†StL N	51	135	12	36	6	0	2	15	13-3	0	20	.267	.329	.356	77	-5	0-1	.993	3	228	101	C51	40	
2005	†StL N	114	385	36	97	15	1	8	49	23-3	2	30	.252	.295	.358	70	-18	2-3	.991	24	403	109	C114/1	40	
Total	2	165	520	48	133	21	1	10	64	36-6	2	50	.256	.304	.358	71	-23	2-4	.991	27	357	107	C165/1	

MOLINARO, BOB Robert Joseph B5.21.1950 Newark NJ BL/TR/6-0/180(175-190) [DetA68 2/38] d9.18

1975	Det A	6	19	2	5	0	1	0	1	1-0	0	3	.263	.300	.368	84	-1	0-0	1.000	0	83	243	O6R	-0
1977	Det A	4	4	0	1	1	0	0	0	0-0	0	2	.250	.250	.500	94	0	0-0		0			/H	-1
	Chi A	1	2	0	1	0	0	0	0	0-0	0	1	.500	.500	.500	174	0	1-0	1.000	-0	90	0	/OR	-0
	Year	5	6	0	2	1	0	0	0	0-0	0	3	.333	.333	.500	119	0	1-0	1.000	-0	90	0	/OR	-1
1978	Chi A	105	286	39	75	5	5	6	27	19-2	3	12	.262	.314	.378	93	-4	22-6	1.000	-3	88	58	O62(12/1/50),D32	0
1979	Bal A	8	6	0	0	0	0	0	0	0-0	0	2	.000	.143	.000	-60	-1	1-0	1.000	0	164	0	O5L	-0
1980	Chi A	119	344	48	100	16	4	5	36	26-7	7	29	.291	.348	.404	107	4	18-7	.957	-2	97	93	O49L,D47	-0
1981	Chi A	47	42	11	7	1	1	1	5	1-0	1	6	.262	.377	.405	132	2	1-1	1.000	0	114	0	O2(1/0/1),D4	-0
1982	Chi A	65	66	6	13	4	0	0	4	1-0	0	12	.197	.264	.258	45	-5	1-1	1.000	-1	27	0	O4L	-0
	Phi N	19	14	0	4	0	0	0	2	3-1	0	4	.286	.412	.286	95	0	1-0		0			/H	-0
	Year	84	80	6	17	4	0	0	6	4-1	0	16	.213	.292	.262	54	-5	2-1	1.000	-1	27	0	O4L	-0
1983	Phi N	19	18	1	2	0	0	0	1	3-0	0	2	.111	.105	.333	19	-2	0-0		0			/H	-0
	Det A	8	2	0	0	0	0	0	0	1-0	0	1	.000	.333	.000	1	0	1-1		0			/D	-0
Total	8	401	803	106	212	25	11	14	90	65-12	11	57	.264	.324	.375	94	-7	46-15	.980	-6	91	77	O129(71/1/58),D84	

YEAR	TM LG	G	AB	R	H	2B	3B	HR	RBI	BB-IB	HP	SO	AVG	OBP	SLG	AOPS	ABR	SB-CS	FA	FR	RNG	THR	GAMES AT POSITION	DL	BFW

MOLITOR, PAUL　Paul Leo　B8.22.1956 St.Paul MN　BR/TR/6-0/185(175-195)　[MilA77 1/3]　d4.7　C4　HF2004　Col Minnesota　OF(4/43/4)

1978	Mil A	125	521	73	142	26	4	6	45	19-2	4	54	.273	.301	.372	88	-9	30-12	.976	5	108	100	2b91,S31/3D		0.7
1979	Mil A	140	584	88	188	27	16	9	62	48-5	2	48	.322	.372	.469	126	20	33-13	.979	6	113	97	2b122,S10,D8		3.5
1980	Mil A*	111	450	81	137	29	2	9	37	48-4	3	48	.304	.372	.438	125	17	34-7	.971	6	104	123	2b91,S12/3D		3.3
1981	†Mil A	64	251	45	67	11	0	2	19	25-1	2	29	.267	.341	.335	99	1	10-6	.976	-2	90	129	O46(0/43/4),D16	24	3.3
1982	†Mil A	160	666	136	201	26	8	19	71	69-1	1	93	.302	.366	.450	130	27	41-9	.942	-3	99	150	3b150,S4,D6	101	-0.3
1983	Mil A	152	608	95	164	28	6	15	47	59-4	2	74	.270	.333	.410	112	9	41-8	.966	2	105	112	3b146,D2		2.8
1984	Mil A	13	46	3	10	1	0	0	6	2-0	0	8	.217	.245	.239	37	-4	1-0	.933	3	156	219	3b7,D4		1.5
1985	Mil A★	140	576	93	171	28	3	10	48	54-6	1	80	.297	.356	.408	109	8	21-7	.953	3	101	115	3b135,D4	152	-0.1
1986	Mil A	105	437	62	123	24	6	9	55	40-0	0	81	.281	.340	.426	104	2	20-5	.944	1	94	155	3b91,D10,O4L	15	0.3
1987	Mil A	118	465	114	164	41	5	16	75	69-2	1	67	.353	.438	.566	159	43	45-10	.947	-6	85	109	D58,3b41,2b19	54	3.9
1988	Mil A★	154	609	115	190	34	6	13	60	71-8	2	54	.312	.384	.452	132	28	41-10	.941	-5	96	96	3b105,D49/2	45	2.8
1989	Mil A	155	615	84	194	35	4	11	56	64-4	4	67	.315	.379	.439	132	28	27-11	.950	11	115	97	3b112,D28,2b16		4.1
1990	Mil A	103	418	64	119	27	6	12	45	37-4	1	51	.285	.343	.464	125	13	18-3	.988	7	112	87	D2b60,1b37,3b2,D4	11	2.1
1991	Mil A★	158	665	133	216	32	13	17	75	77-16	6	62	.325	.399	.489	147	44	19-8	.986	-5	94	130	D112,1b46	55	3.6
1992	Mil A★	158	609	89	195	36	7	12	89	73-12	3	66	.320	.389	.461	141	36	31-6	.996	-5	70	117	D108,1b48		2.9
1993	†Tor A★	160	636	121	211	37	5	22	111	77-3	3	71	.332	.402	.509	142	39	22-4	.985	-2	79	78	D137,1b23		3.1
1994	Tor A★	115	454	86	155	30	4	14	75	55-4	1	48	.341	.410	.518	137	27	20-0	1.000	0	88	139	D110,1b5		2.3
1995	Tor A	130	525	63	142	31	2	15	60	61-1	5	57	.270	.350	.423	100	1	12-0	—	0	0	0	D129		-0.3
1996	Min A	161	660	99	225	41	8	9	113	56-10	3	72	.341	.390	.468	115	17	18-6	.993	1	117	91	D143,1b17		0.9
1997	Min A	135	538	63	164	32	4	10	89	45-8	0	73	.305	.351	.435	104	3	11-4	.991	-0	97	64	D122,1b12	18	-0.3
1998	Min A	126	502	75	141	29	5	4	69	45-5	1	41	.281	.335	.382	86	-10	9-2	1.000	1	124	57	D115,1b9		-0.3
Total	21	2683	10835	1782	3319	605	114	234	1307	1094-100	47	1244	.306	.369	.448	122	340	504-131	.950	20	102	122	D1174,3b791,2b400,1b197,S57,050C499	24	-1.4
																									36.6

MOLLENKAMP, FRED　Frederick Henry　B3.15.1890 Cincinnati OH　D11.1.1948 Cincinnati OH　6-2/195　d8.29

| 1914 | Phi N | 3 | 8 | 0 | 1 | 0 | 0 | 0 | 2 | 0 | 0 | | .125 | .300 | .125 | 26 | -1 | 0 | 1.000 | 2 | 328 | 129 | 1b3 | | 0.1 |

MOLLWITZ, FRITZ　Frederick August　B6.16.1890 Coburg, Germany　D10.3.1967 Bradenton FL　BR/TR/6-2/170　d9.26

1913	Chi N	2	7	1	3	0	0	0	0	0	0		.429	.429	.429	145	0	0	1.000	-0	0	0	1b2		0.0
1914	Chi N	13	20	0	3	0	0	0	1	0	0	3	.150	.150	.150	-11	-3	0	.962	-0	66	0	1b4/OR		-0.4
	Cin N	32	111	12	18	2	0	0	5	3	2	9	.162	.198	.180	12	-12	2	.991	1	112	105	1b32		-1.3
	Year	45	131	12	21	2	0	0	6	3	2	12	.160	.191	.176	9	-15	3	.989	1	108	97	1b36/OR		-1.7
1915	Cin N	153	525	36	136	21	3	1	51	15	1	49	.259	.281	.316	79	-15	19-11	.996	-0	95	122	1b153		-2.1
1916	Cin N	65	183	12	41	4	4	0	16	5	0	12	.224	.245	.290	65	-9	6	.981	-1	100	104	1b54		-1.2
	Chi N	33	71	1	19	2	0	0	11	7	0	6	.268	.333	.296	85	-1	4	.976	-1	123	95	1b19,O6(4/0/2)		-0.2
	Year	98	254	13	60	6	4	0	27	12	0	18	.236	.271	.291	71	-9	10	.980	-1	105	102	1b73,O6(4/0/2)		-1.4
1917	Pit N	36	140	15	36	4	1	0	12	8	0	8	.257	.297	.300	81	-3	4	.994	-1	87	69	1b36/2		-0.6
1918	Pit N	119	432	43	116	12	7	0	45	23	0	24	.269	.305	.329	90	-6	23	.990	-1	95	101	1b119		-1.1
1919	Pit N	56	168	11	29	2	1	0	12	15	2	18	.173	.249	.232	43	-12	9	.994	-3	69	91	1b53/OR		-1.8
	StL N	25	83	7	19	3	0	0	5	7	0	3	.229	.289	.265	71	-3	2	.994	1	102	139	1b25		-0.3
	Year	81	251	18	48	5	1	0	17	22	2	21	.191	.262	.243	52	-15	11	.994	-2	80	108	1b78/OR		-2.1
Total	7	534	1740	138	420	50	19	1	158	83		5	132	.241	.278	.294	72	-64	70-11	.991	-5	94	106	1b497,O8(4/0/4)/2		-9.0

MONACO, BLAS　Blas　B11.16.1915 San Antonio TX　D2.10.2000 San Antonio TX　BB/TR/5-11/170　d8.18

1937	Cle A	5	7	0	2	0	1	0	2	1	0	1	2	.286	.375	.571	134	0	0-0	1.000	0	107	0	2b3		0.0
1946	Cle A	12	6	2	0	0	0	0	0	1	0	1	.143	.143	.000	-62	-1	0-0	—	0		/H		-0.1
Total	2	17	13	2	2	0	1	0	2	1		1	3	.154	.267	.308	53	-1	0-0	1.000	0	107	0	2b3		-0.1

MONAHAN, SHANE　Shane Hartland　B8.12.1974 Syosset NY　BL/TR/6-0/195*　[SeaA95 2/33]　d7.9　Col Clemson

1998	Sea A	62	211	17	51	8	1	4	28	8-0	0	53	.242	.269	.346	58	-14	1-2	.992	2	111	91	O62(61/3/2)		-1.4
1999	Sea A	16	15	3	2	0	0	0	0	0-0	0	6	.133	.133	.133	-32	-3	0-0	1.000	-0	105	0	O9(7/0/3),D3		-0.3
Total	2	78	226	20	53	8	1	4	28	8-0	0	59	.235	.261	.332	52	-17	1-2	.992	1	111	86	O71(68/3/5),D3		-1.7

MONCEWICZ, FREDDIE　Frederick Alfred　B9.1.1903 Brockton MA　D4.23.1969 Brockton MA　BR/TR/5-8.5/175　d6.19　Col Boston College

| 1928 | Bos N | 3 | 1 | 0 | 0 | 0 | 0 | 0 | 0 | 0 | 0 | 0 | 1.000 | .000 | .000 | -99 | 0 | 0-0 | 1.000 | 0 | 101 | 0 | S2 | | 0.0 |

MONCHAK, ALEX　Alex　B12.22.1919 Bayonne NJ　BR/TR/6-0/180　d6.22　C17

| 1940 | Phi N | 19 | 14 | 1 | 2 | 0 | 0 | 0 | 0 | 6 | 0 | | .143 | .143 | .143 | -22 | -2 | 1 | .833 | -1 | 91 | 92 | S9/2 | | -0.3 |

MONDAY, RICK　Robert James　B11.20.1945 Batesville AR　BL/TL/6-3/200*　[OakA65 1/1]　d9.3　Col Arizona St.

1966	KC A	17	41	4	4	1	0	0	2	6-0	0	16	.098	.213	.171	12	-5	1-1	.964	-1	88	130	O15C		-0.7
1967	KC A	124	406	52	102	14	6	14	58	42-2	2	107	.251	.322	.419	122	10	3-6	.972	8	109	220	O113(3/110/0)		1.5
1968	Oak A★	148	482	56	132	24	7	8	49	72-7	4	143	.274	.371	.402	141	27	14-6	.978	-3	94	121	O144C		2.3
1969	Oak A	122	399	57	108	17	4	12	54	72-11	5	100	.271	.388	.424	132	20	12-3	.964	9	96	40	O119C		1.0
1970	Oak A	112	376	63	109	19	7	10	37	58-0	2	99	.290	.387	.457	136	20	17-11	.981	-3	103	45	O109C	29	1.5
1971	†Oak A	116	355	53	87	19	3	18	56	49-5	0	93	.245	.335	.439	121	9	6-9	.984	-5	94	93	O111C		-0.1
1972	Chi N	138	434	68	108	22	5	11	42	78-8	1	102	.249	.362	.399	105	6	12-9	.996	-10	87	78	O134(0/132/2)		-0.8
1973	Chi N	149	554	93	148	24	5	26	56	92-7	1	124	.267	.372	.469	122	19	5-12	.973	-9	93	101	O148C		0.4
1974	Chi N	142	538	84	158	19	7	20	58	70-6	2	94	.294	.375	.467	129	21	7-9	.984	-9	87	118	O139C		0.7
1975	Chi N	136	491	89	131	29	4	17	60	83-12	1	95	.267	.373	.446	121	16	8-3	.973	-7	96	74	O131C		0.7
1976	Chi N	137	534	107	145	20	5	32	77	60-8	2	125	.272	.346	.507	129	19	5-9	.993	-2	105	61	O103(5/99/0),1b32		1.0
1977	†LA N	118	392	47	90	13	1	15	48	60-6	0	109	.230	.330	.383	91	-5	1-4	.991	-16	78	43	O115(0/114/1),1b3		-2.3
1978	†LA N★	119	342	54	87	14	1	19	57	49-11	1	100	.254	.348	.468	126	12	2-4	.995	-6	92	50	O103(11/80/30)/1		0.3
1979	LA N	12	33	2	10	0	0	2	5	5-0	0	6	.303	.395	.303	95	0	0-0	.964	0	123	0	O10(0/8/3)	146	0.0
1980	LA N	96	194	35	52	7	1	10	25	28-3	1	49	.268	.363	.469	134	9	2-2	.969	-4	93	30	O50(1/31/25)		0.4
1981	†LA N	66	130	24	41	1	2	11	25	24-3	1	42	.315	.423	.608	199	17	1-2	.962	-3	85	40	O41(6/0/37)		1.3
1982	LA N	104	210	37	54	6	4	11	42	39-6	1	51	.257	.372	.481	142	13	2-1	.943	-5	70	116	O57(18/0/40),1b4		0.6
1983	†LA N	99	178	21	44	7	1	6	20	29-9	0	42	.247	.351	.399	108	3	0-0	.969	-2	97	41	O44(14/0/31),1b4		-0.1
1984	LA N	31	47	4	9	2	0	1	7	8-3	0	16	.191	.309	.298	71	-2	0-0	.987	-1	79	48	1b10,O2(2/0/1)		-0.3
Total	19	1986	6136	950	1619	248	64	241	775	924-107	24	1513	.264	.361	.443	124	209	98-91	.979	-85	93	86	O1688(60/1490/170),1b54	175	7.4

MONDESI, RAUL　Raul Ramon (Avelino)　B3.12.1971 San Cristobal, D.R.　BR/TR/5-11/215(200-230)　d7.19

1993	LA N	42	86	13	25	3	1	4	10	4-0	0	16	.291	.322	.488	120	2	4-0	.951	2	110	174	O40(20/6/17)		0.3
1994	LA N★	112	434	63	133	27	8	16	56	16-5	2	78	.306	.333	.516	124	12	11-8	.965	9	94	194	O112(0/15/109)		0.8
1995	†LA N	139	536	91	153	23	6	26	88	33-4	4	96	.285	.328	.496	123	14	27-4	.980	9	106	174	O138(0/24/114)		2.2
1996	†LA N	157	634	98	188	40	7	24	88	32-4	5	122	.297	.334	.495	123	18	14-7	.967	7	113	103	O157R		1.6
1997	LA N	159	616	95	191	42	5	30	87	44-7	6	105	.310	.360	.541	141	35	32-15	.989	9	118	87	O159R		3.6
1998	LA N	148	580	85	162	26	5	30	90	30-4	3	112	.279	.316	.490	116	9	16-10	.980	-9	92	67	O148(0/94/54)		-0.2
1999	LA N	159	601	98	152	29	5	33	99	71-6	3	134	.253	.332	.483	109	6	36-9	.982	-3	101	66	O158(0/1/158)		0.0
2000	Tor A	96	388	78	105	24	2	24	67	32-0	3	73	.271	.329	.523	108	3	22-6	.967	1	105	75	O96R	59	0.1
2001	Tor A	149	572	88	144	29	5	27	84	73-3	6	128	.252	.342	.453	105	4	30-11	.972	-1	89	179	O149R		-0.2
2002	Tor A	75	299	51	67	16	1	15	45	31-1	3	57	.224	.301	.435	90	-5	9-2	.984	-2	96	76	O62R,D13		-0.9
	†NY A	71	270	65	65	18	0	11	43	28-2	2	46	.241	.315	.430	97	-1	6-4	.969	-6	81	93	O70(0/11/59)/D		-1.0
	Year	146	569	90	132	34	1	26	88	59-3	5	103	.232	.308	.432	93	-6	15-6	.976	-8	85	85	O132(0/11/121),D14		-1.9
2003	NY A	98	361	56	93	23	3	16	49	38-6	2	66	.258	.330	.471	110	5	17-7	.986	3	103	129	O97R/D		0.4
	Ari N	45	162	27	49	8	1	2	18	18-0	1	31	.302	.372	.512	119	5	5-4	.964	-1	103	38	O43(0/2/42)		0.1
2004	Pit N	26	99	8	28	8	0	2	14	11-0	0	27	.283	.355	.424	100	0	0-2	.939	-1	94	135	O26(14/0/12)		-0.2
	Ana N	8	34	2	4	1	0	1	1	2-0	1	9	.118	.189	.235	10	-5	0-1	1.000	1	101	256	O7C/D	49	-0.4
2005	Atl N	41	142	17	30	7	1	4	17	3-0	2	35	.211	.271	.359	62	-8	0-1	.986	-3	86	87	O40R		-1.3
Total	13	1525	5814	909	1589	319	49	271	860	475-50	41	1130	.273	.331	.485	113	94	229-92	.976	7	101	114	O1502(34/160/1325),D16	108	4.9

MONEY, DON　Donald Wayne "Brooks"　B6.7.1947 Washington DC　BR/TR/6-1/190(170-190)　d4.10　OFL

1968	Phi N	4	13	3	3	2	0	0	2	2-1	0	4	.231	.333	.385	115	-1	0-1	1.000	-1	65	137	S4		-0.1
1969	Phi N	127	450	41	103	22	2	6	42	48-5	1	83	.229	.296	.367	77	-14	1-3	.969	18	111	101	S126		1.8
1970	Phi N	120	447	66	132	25	4	14	66	43-6	7	68	.295	.361	.463	123	15	4-7	.961	5	96	119	3b119,S2		1.8
1971	Phi N	121	439	40	98	22	8	7	38	31-10	3	80	.223	.276	.358	79	-14	4-1	.953	7	110	132	3b68,O40L,2b20		-0.8

YEAR	TM LG	G	AB	R	H	2B	3B	HR	RBI	BB-IB	HP	SO	AVG	OBP	SLG	AOPS	ABR	SB-CS	FA	FR	RNG	THR	GAMES AT POSITION	DL	BFW
1972	Phi N	152	536	54	119	16	2	15	52	41-5	2	92	.222	.278	.343	74	-19	5-7	.978	15	102	128	3b151,S2		-0.8
1973	Mil A	145	556	75	158	28	2	11	61	53-3	3	53	.284	.347	.401	112	10	22-5	.971	-11	93	94	3b124,S21		0.3
1974	Mil A☆	159	629	85	178	32	3	15	65	62-5	2	80	.283	.346	.415	120	16	19-6	.989	-7	98	123	3b157/2D		1.2
1975	Mil A	109	405	58	112	16	1	15	43	31-1	0	51	.277	.331	.432	114	6	7-9	.951	-6	91	108	3b99,S7	27	-0.1
1976	Mil A★	117	439	51	117	18	4	12	62	47-2	0	50	.267	.333	.408	120	11	6-5	.958	-2	95	116	3b103,D10/S		0.8
1977	Mil A✶	152	570	86	159	28	3	25	83	57-2	7	70	.279	.348	.470	121	17	8-5	.981	18	111	112	2b116,O23L,3b15,D7		3.9
1978	Mil A★	137	518	88	152	30	2	14	54	48-2	7	70	.293	.361	.440	123	17	3-0	.994	6	100	105	1b61,2b36,3b25,D15,S2		2.2
1979	Mil A	92	350	52	83	20	1	6	38	40-0	2	47	.237	.316	.351	80	-9	1-0	1.000	-3	124	140	D33,3b26,1b19,2b16	45	-1.3
1980	Mil A	86	289	39	74	17	1	17	46	40-0	1	36	.256	.348	.498	132	13	0-0	.940	1	104	169	3b55,1b14,D14,2b2		1.1
1981	†Mil A	60	185	17	40	7	0	2	14	19-0	1	27	.216	.288	.286	70	-7	0-0	.977	-7	92	83	3b56/1D		-1.6
1982	†Mil A	96	275	40	78	14	3	16	55	32-2	1	38	.284	.360	.531	116	9	0-0	.923	3	117	66	D66,3b16,1b11/2		1.7
1983	Mil A	43	114	5	17	5	0	1	8	11-1	0	17	.149	.220	.219	24	-12	0-0	.980	4	142		D28,3b11,1b2	27	-0.4
Total	16	1720	6215	798	1623	302	36	176	729	600-45	40	866	.261	.328	.406	106	48	80-51	.968	39	99	118	3b1025,2b192,D176,S165,1b108,O63L99		9.2

MONROE, CRAIG Craig Keystone B2.27.1977 Texarkana TX BR/TR/6-1/195(195-220) [TexA95 8/206] d7.28

YEAR	TM LG	G	AB	R	H	2B	3B	HR	RBI	BB-IB	HP	SO	AVG	OBP	SLG	AOPS	ABR	SB-CS	FA	FR	RNG	THR	GAMES AT POSITION	DL	BFW
2001	Tex A	27	52	8	11	1	0	2	5	6-0	0	18	.212	.293	.346	66	-3	0-2	1.000	4	135	292	O24(6/0/21)/D		0.1
2002	Det A	13	25	3	3	1	0	1	1	0-0	1	5	.120	.154	.280	12	-3	0-2	.950	1	133	245	O9(4/0/5),D3		-0.3
2003	Det A	128	425	51	102	18	1	23	70	27-2	2	89	.240	.287	.449	95	-5	4-2	.970	1	99	122	O108(75/2/38),D13		0.4
2004	Det A	128	447	65	131	27	3	18	72	29-1	2	79	.293	.337	.488	116	9	1-3	.960	0	106	72	O125(65/27/51),D2	17	-0.7
2005	Det A	157	567	69	157	30	3	20	89	40-4	3	95	.277	.322	.446	106	4	8-3	.981	-7	89	113	O156(69/33/85)/D	17	-1.4
Total	5	453	1516	196	404	77	7	64	237	102-7	8	286	.266	.313	.453	103	2	17-11	.972	-0	99	112	O422(219/62/200),D20	17	-1.4

MONROE, FRANK Frank W. B Hamilton OH d7.18

1884	Ind AA	2	8	1	0	0	0	0	0		0	0	.000	.000	.000	-99	-2		1.000	-1	0	0	/ORC		-0.3

MONROE, JOHN John Allen B8.24.1898 Farmersville TX D6.19.1956 Conroe TX BL/TR/5-10/160 d4.16

1921	NY N	19	21	4	3	0	0	1	3	3	1	9	.143	.280	.286	50	-2	0-0	.846	-1	98	44	2b8/S		-0.2
	Phi N	41	133	13	38	1	1	1	8	11	1	9	.286	.345	.368	82	-3	2-2	.938	4	122	85	2b28,3b9		0.2
	Year	60	154	17	41	1	1	2	11	14	2	15	.266	.335	.357	79	-4	2-2	.920	3	118	78	2b36,3b9/S		0.0

MONTAGUE, ED Edward Francis B7.24.1905 San Francisco CA D6.17.1988 Daly City CA BR/TR/5-10/165 d5.14

1928	Cle A	32	51	12	12	0	1	0	3	6	2	7	.235	.339	.275	62	-3	0-0	.914	2	117	123	S15,3b9		0.0
1930	Cle A	58	179	37	47	7	2	1	16	37	1	38	.263	.392	.330	82	-3	1-5	.917	-7	91	76	S46,3b13		-0.6
1931	Cle A	64	193	27	55	8	3	1	26	21	1	22	.285	.358	.373	87	-3	3-4	.924	13	118	86	S64		1.2
1932	Cle A	66	192	29	47	5	1	0	24	21	2	24	.245	.326	.281	55	-13	3-3	.891	-14	88	75	S57,3b11		-2.2
Total	4	220	615	105	161	18	7	2	69	85	6	91	.262	.357	.324	74	-22	7-12	.912	-6	102	82	S182,3b33		-1.6

MONTANEZ, WILLIE Guillermo (Naranjo) B4.1.1948 Catano, PR BL/TL/6-1/193* d4.12

1966	Cal A	8	2	2	0	0	0	0	0	0-0	0	2	.000	.000	.000	-99	-1	1-0	1.000	0	0	1092	.1b2		0.0
1970	Phi N	18	25	3	6	0	0	0	3	1-1	0	4	.240	.269	.240	38	-2	0-0	1.000	1	89	306	O10(1/0/9),1b5		-0.2
1971	Phi N	158	599	78	153	27	6	30	99	67-14	3	105	.255	.327	.471	125	19	4-7	.972	-6	93	114	O158(0/137/24),1b9		0.6
1972	Phi N	147	531	60	131	39	3	13	64	58-13	1	108	.247	.320	.405	103	3	1-3	.985	8	106	201	O130C,1b14		0.6
1973	Phi N	146	552	69	145	16	5	11	65	46-7	0	80	.263	.324	.370	90	-8	2-6	.994	-2	91	103	1b99,O51R		-2.3
1974	Phi N	143	527	55	160	33	1	7	79	32-6	3	57	.304	.343	.410	106	4	3-6	.992	-2	92	108	1b137/OR		-1.0
1975	Phi N	21	84	9	24	8	0	2	16	4-0	0	12	.286	.315	.452	107	1	0-1	.990	2	134	122	1b21		0.1
	SF N	135	518	52	158	26	2	8	85	45-8	4	62	.305	.359	.409	111	8	5-3	.994	-1	93	99	1b134		-0.3
	Year	156	602	61	182	34	2	10	101	49-8	4	62	.302	.353	.415	110	9	6-3	.993	1	99	102	1b155		-0.2
1976	SF N	60	230	22	71	15	2	2	20	15-5	1	15	.309	.351	.417	115	4	2-1	.989	3	125	108	1b58		0.3
	Atl N	103	420	52	135	14	0	9	64	21-6	0	32	.321	.353	.419	112	6	0-4	.986	-8	76	96	1b103		-1.2
	Year	163	650	74	206	29	2	11	84	36-11	1	47	.317	.352	.418	113	10	2-5	.987	-4	94	100	1b161		-0.9
1977	Atl N★	136	544	70	156	31	1	20	68	35-3	0	60	.287	.328	.458	98	-2	1-1	.992	-6	80	74	1b134	24	-1.0
1978	NY N	159	609	66	156	32	0	17	96	60-19	1	92	.256	.320	.392	102	1	9-4	.995	2	103	108	1b158		-0.7
1979	NY N	109	410	36	96	19	0	5	47	25-7	1	48	.234	.277	.317	64	-21	0-1	.989	3	115	107	1b108		-2.6
	Tex A	38	144	19	46	6	0	8	24	8-1	0	14	.319	.357	.528	137	7	0-1	.995	1	112	84	1b19,D17		0.5
1980	SD N	128	481	39	132	12	4	6	63	36-9	3	52	.274	.325	.353	97	-3	3-4	.994	4	114	107	1b4		-0.2
	Mon N	14	19	1	4	0	0	0	1	3-0	0	3	.211	.318	.211	49	-1	0-1	1.000	-0	86	0	1b16		-1.0
	Year	142	500	40	136	12	4	6	64	39-10	3	55	.272	.325	.348	94	-5	3-5	.994	4	113	104	1b128		-0.7
1981	Mon N	26	62	6	11	0	1	0	5	4-0	0	9	.177	.227	.210	24	-6	0-0	.992	-1	128	86	1b11		-0.3
	Pit N	29	38	2	10	0	0	1	1	1-0	0	3	.263	.282	.342	73	-2	0-0	1.000	1	23	81	1b27		-1.0
	Year	55	100	8	21	0	1	1	6	5-0	0	11	.210	.248	.260	42	-8	0-0	.995	-0	95	84	1b27		-0.1
1982	Pit N	36	32	4	9	1	0	0	1	3-3	0	3	.281	.343	.313	81	-1	0-0	1.000	1	178	166	1b2,O2L		-0.1
	Phi N	18	16	0	1	0	0	1	1	1-0	0	3	.063	.118	.063	-47	-3	0-0	1.000	0	190		1b6		-0.3
	Year	54	48	4	10	1	0	1	2	4-3	0	6	.208	.269	.229	39	-4	0-0	1.000	1	186	58	1b8,O2L		-0.1
Total	14	1632	5843	645	1604	279	25	139	802	465-103	24	751	.275	.327	.402	101	3	32-42	.992	-0	99	101	1b1164,O352(2/267/85),D17	24	-10.1

MONTEAGUDO, RENE Rene (Miranda) B3.12.1916 Havana, Cuba D9.14.1973 Hialeah FL BL/TL/5-7/165 d9.6 s-Aurelio ▲

1938	Was A	5	6	0	3	0	0	0	1	0	0	0	.500	.500	.500	162	1	0-0	1.000	1	24	0	P5		0.0
1940	Was A	27	33	4	6	1	1	0	1	1	0	4	.182	.206	.273	24	0	0-0	.941	-1	60	83	P27		-0.2
1944	Was A	10	38	2	11	2	0	0	4	0	1	5	.289	.289	.342	84	-1	0-0	.929	-2	82	201	O9R		-0.2
1945	Phi N	114	193	26	58	6	0	0	15	28	0	7	.301	.389	.332	104	3	2	.918	-2	82	196	O35(12/0/23),P14		-0.3
Total	4	156	270	32	78	9	1	0	21	29	1	12	.289	.358	.330	94	3	2-0	.889	-4	57	98	P46,O44(12/0/32)		-0.3

MONTEMAYOR, FELIPE Felipe Angel "Monty" B2.7.1930 Monterrey, Nuevo Leon, Mexico BL/TL/6-2/185* d4.14

1953	Pit N	28	55	5	6	4	0	2	4	3	3	13	.109	.210	.182	3	-8	0-0	1.000	1	100	205	O12(1/11/0)		-0.2
1955	Pit N	36	95	10	20	1	3	2	8	18-2	1	24	.211	.342	.347	85	-2	1-0	.957	-3	89	0	O28(6/14/9)		-0.3
Total	2	64	150	15	26	5	3	2	10	22-2	4	37	.173	.295	.287	55	-10	1-0	.974	-2	93	67	O40(7/25/9)		-1.3

MONTGOMERY, AL Alvin Atlas B7.3.1920 Loving NM D4.26.1942 Waverly VA BR/TR/5-10.5/185 d6.20

1941	Bos N	42	52	4	10	1	0	0	4	9	1	8	.192	.323	.212	55	-3	0	.976	-3	95	92	C30		-0.3

MONTGOMERY, RAY Raymond James B8.8.1969 Bronxville NY BR/TR/6-3/195* [HouN90 13/359] d7.3 Col Fordham

1996	Hou N	12	14	4	3	1	0	1	4	1-0	0	5	.214	.267	.500	104	0	0-0	1.000	0	121	0	O6(5/1/2)	103	-0.2
1997	Hou N	29	68	8	16	4	1	0	4	5-0	0	18	.235	.276	.324	62	-4	0-0	1.000	1	94	195	O18(2/2/15)	6	-0.1
1998	Hou N	6	5	2	2	0	0	0	0	0-0	0	0	.400	.400	.400	114	0	0-0	1.000	0	155	0	O2(1/0/1)	109	-0.2
Total	3	47	87	14	21	5	1	1	8	6-0	0	23	.241	.281	.356	71	-4	0-0	1.000	1	100	160	O26(8/3/18)		-0.5

MONTGOMERY, BOB Robert Edward B4.16.1944 Nashville TN BR/TR/6-1/203(195-210) d9.6

1970	Bos A	22	78	8	14	2	0	1	6	6-0	1	20	.179	.244	.244	34	-7	0-0	.981	0	99	143	C22		-0.2
1971	Bos A	67	205	19	49	11	2	2	24	16-4	3	43	.239	.300	.341	77	-6	1-0	.989	-6	93	68	C66		-0.5
1972	Bos A	24	77	7	22	1	0	2	7	3-0	0	17	.286	.309	.377	99	0	0-0	.985	-3	106	49	C22		-0.1
1973	Bos A	34	128	18	41	6	2	7	25	7-0	0	36	.320	.353	.563	146	7	0-0	.974	-0	80	118	C33		-0.1
1974	Bos A	88	254	26	64	10	0	4	38	13-1	1	50	.252	.287	.339	75	-8	3-0	.977	-3	98	101	C79,D5		-1.1
1975	†Bos A	62	195	16	44	10	1	2	26	4-0	1	37	.226	.241	.318	54	-12	1-1	.987	-7	104	86	C53,1b6,D3		-0.9
1976	Bos A	31	93	10	23	3	1	3	13	5-1	0	20	.247	.283	.398	88	-2	0-1	.983	-3	102	99	C30/D		-0.6
1977	Bos A	17	40	6	12	2	0	2	7	4-0	1	9	.300	.370	.500	123	1	0-0	.982	-3	89	78	C15		-0.3
1978	Bos A	10	29	2	7	1	1	0	2	2-0	0	12	.241	.290	.345	71	-1	0-0	.976	-0	299	83	C10	62	-0.2
1979	Bos A	32	86	13	30	4	1	0	7	4-1	0	24	.349	.374	.419	109	1	6-2	.983	-29	100	85	C31	62	-0.4
Total	10	387	1185	125	306	50	8	23	155	64-7	7	268	.258	.296	.372	83	-27	11-5	.983	-10	100	86	C361,D9,1b6		-4.5

MONTOYO, CHARLIE Jose Carlos (Diaz) B10.17.1965 Florida, PR BR/TR/5-10/170 [MilA87 6/149] d9.7 Col Louisiana Tech

1993	Mon N	4	5	1	2	0	0	0	1	1-0	0	0	.400	.400	.600	156	0	0-0	—	-1	0	0	2b3		-0.0

MONTREUIL, AL Allan Arthur B8.23.1943 New Orleans LA BR/TR/5-5/158 d9.1 Col Loyola-New Orleans

1972	Chi N	5	11	0	1	0	0	0	0	1-0	0	4	.091	.167	.091	-23	-2	0-0	1.000	-1	75	46	2b5		-0.0

YEAR	TM LG	G	AB	R	H	2B	3B	HR	RBI	BB-IB	HP	SO	AVG	OBP	SLG	AOPS	ABR	SB-CS	FA	FR	RNG	THR	GAMES AT POSITION	DL	BFW

MONZON, DAN   Daniel Francisco B5.17.1946 Bronx NY D1.21.1996 Santo Domingo, D.R. BR/TR/5-10/182* [MinA67 S2/23] d4.25 Col Buena Vista

YEAR	TM LG	G	AB	R	H	2B	3B	HR	RBI	BB-IB	HP	SO	AVG	OBP	SLG	AOPS	ABR	SB-CS	FA	FR	RNG	THR	GAMES AT POSITION	DL	BFW
1972	Min A	55	55	13	15	1	0	0	5	8-0	0	12	.273	.365	.291	92	0	1-0	.977	1	102	37	2b13,3b5,S3/OL		0.2
1973	Min A	39	76	10	17	1	1	0	4	11-0	1	9	.224	.326	.263	66	-3	1-0	.968	1	81	93	2b17,3b14/OL		-0.1
Total	2	94	131	23	32	2	1	0	9	19-0	1	21	.244	.342	.275	77	-3	2-0	.971	2	90	69	2b30,3b19,S3,O2L		0.1

MOOCK, JOE   Joseph Geoffrey B3.12.1944 Plaquemine LA BL/TR/6-1/180 [NYN65 3/42] d9.1 Col Louisiana St.

YEAR	TM LG	G	AB	R	H	2B	3B	HR	RBI	BB-IB	HP	SO	AVG	OBP	SLG	AOPS	ABR	SB-CS	FA	FR	RNG	THR	GAMES AT POSITION	DL	BFW
1967	NY N	13	40	2	9	2	0	0	5	0-0	0	7	.225	.225	.275	43	-3	0-0	.917	1	114	166	3b12		-0.2

MOOLIC, GEORGE   George Henry "Prunes" B3.12.1865 Lawrence MA D2.19.1915 Methuen MA BR/TR/5-7/145 d5.1

YEAR	TM LG	G	AB	R	H	2B	3B	HR	RBI	BB-IB	HP	SO	AVG	OBP	SLG	AOPS	ABR	SB-CS	FA	FR	RNG	THR	GAMES AT POSITION	DL	BFW
1886	Chi N	16	56	9	8	3	0	0	2			17	.143	.172	.196	10	-6	0	.945	3			C15,O2R		-0.2

MOON, WALLY   Wallace Wade B4.3.1930 Bay AR BL/TR/6-0/175* d4.13 C1 Col Texas A&M-Commerce

YEAR	TM LG	G	AB	R	H	2B	3B	HR	RBI	BB-IB	HP	SO	AVG	OBP	SLG	AOPS	ABR	SB-CS	FA	FR	RNG	THR	GAMES AT POSITION	DL	BFW
1954	StL N	151	635	106	193	29	9	12	76	71		73	.304	.371	.435	109		18-10	.978	-7	93	93	O148(10/139/0)		-0.4
1955	StL N	152	593	86	175	24	8	19	76	47-4	3	65	.295	.349	.459	113	10	11-11	.975	-5	93	70	O100(34/44/28),1b51		-0.5
1956	StL N	149	540	86	161	22	11	16	68	80-7	1	50	.298	.390	.469	129	25	12-9	.988	-0	92	97	O97(0/1/96),1b52		1.8
1957	StL N★	142	516	86	152	28	5	24	73	62-12	1	57	.295	.367	.508	131	23	5-6	.966	-10	86	80	O133(89/13/48)		0.5
1958	StL N	108	290	66	69	10	3	7	38	47-5	0	30	.238	.342	.366	85	-5	2-3	.984	-3	90	90	O82(31/8/54)		-1.2
1959	†LA N★	145	543	93	164	26	**11**	19	74	81-1	3	64	.302	.394	.495	126	23	15-6	.983	-6	83	116	O143(128/4/29)/1		0.9
1960	LA N	138	469	74	140	21	6	13	69	67-4	1	53	.299	.383	.452	121	16	6-10	.986	1	90	154	O127(115/0/18)		0.8
1961	LA N	134	463	79	152	25	3	17	88	89-9	1	79	.328	**.434**	.505	137	30	7-5	.970	-7	89	53	O133(126/0/19)		1.6
1962	LA N	95	244	36	59	14	1	4	31	30-3	1	33	.242	.326	.336	84	-5	5-2	.981	-1	119	109	O36(24/0/12),1b32		-0.7
1963	LA N	122	343	41	90	13	2	8	48	45-5	1	43	.262	.345	.382	119	9	5-5	.962	-8	85	33	O96(48/3/60)		-0.5
1964	LA N	68	118	8	26	2	1	2	9	12-3	0	22	.220	.292	.305	74	-4	1-1	1.000	-2	89	0	O23(6/0/17)		-0.8
1965	†LA N	53	89	6	18	3	0	1	11	13-3	0	22	.202	.304	.270	67	-3	2-0	1.000	-1	82	91	O23(10/0/13)		-0.5
Total	12	1457	4843	737	1399	212	60	142		644-56	13	591	.289	.371	.445	117	129	89-68	.978	-47	89	89	O1141(621/212/394),1b136		1.0

MOORE, AL   Albert James B8.4.1902 Brooklyn NY D11.29.1974 , At Sea N.Y.to P.R. BR/TR/5-10/174 d9.27 Col St. Johns

YEAR	TM LG	G	AB	R	H	2B	3B	HR	RBI	BB-IB	HP	SO	AVG	OBP	SLG	AOPS	ABR	SB-CS	FA	FR	RNG	THR	GAMES AT POSITION	DL	BFW
1925	NY N	2	8	0	1	0	0	0	1	0		2	.125	.222	.125	-9	-1	0-1	1.000	-0	91	0	O2L		-0.2
1926	NY N	28	81	12	18	4	0	0	10	5	0	7	.222	.267	.272	46	-6	2	.966	-2	97	199	O20(5/16/0)		-0.5
Total	2	30	89	12	19	4	0	0	10	6	0	9	.213	.263	.258	41	-7	2-1	.968	-2	96	181	O22(7/16/0)		-0.7

MOORE, JUNIOR   Alvin Earl B1.25.1953 Waskom TX BR/TR/5-11/185* [AtlN71 11/255] d8.2

YEAR	TM LG	G	AB	R	H	2B	3B	HR	RBI	BB-IB	HP	SO	AVG	OBP	SLG	AOPS	ABR	SB-CS	FA	FR	RNG	THR	GAMES AT POSITION	DL	BFW
1976	Atl N	20	26	1	7	1	0	0	2	4-0	1	4	.269	.387	.308	93	0	0-0	.929	1	118	146	3b6/2OL		0.1
1977	Atl N	112	361	41	94	9	3	5	34	33-0	1	29	.260	.323	.343	71	-14	4-5	.942	4	103	58	3b104/2		-1.3
1978	Chi A	24	65	8	19	0	1	0	4	6-0	0	7	.292	.352	.323	90	-1	1-1	.857	0	87	0	D12,3b6,O5L		-0.1
1979	Chi A	88	201	24	53	6	2	1	23	12-0	1	20	.264	.300	.328	71	-9	0-2	.966	-2	95	91	O61(52/0/12),D10,2b2		-1.3
1980	Chi A	45	121	9	31	4	1	1	10	7-0	1	11	.256	.295	.331	72	-5	0-2	.929	-1	93	92	3b34,O3L/1D		-1.3
Total	5	289	774	83	204	20	7	7	73	62-0	2	71	.264	.318	.335	73	-29	5-10	.936	3	101	66	3b150,O70(61/0/12),D24,2b4/1		-0.7

MOORE, ANSE   Anselm Winn B9.22.1917 Delhi LA D10.29.1993 Pearl MS BL/TR/6-1/190 d4.17

YEAR	TM LG	G	AB	R	H	2B	3B	HR	RBI	BB-IB	HP	SO	AVG	OBP	SLG	AOPS	ABR	SB-CS	FA	FR	RNG	THR	GAMES AT POSITION	DL	BFW
1946	Det A	51	134	16	28	4	0	1	8	12	1	9	.209	.279	.261	48	-9	1-1	.971	-0	100	81	O32(17/0/15)		-1.2

MOORE, ARCHIE   Archie Francis B8.30.1941 Upper Darby PA BL/TL/6-2/190* d4.20 Col Springfield

YEAR	TM LG	G	AB	R	H	2B	3B	HR	RBI	BB-IB	HP	SO	AVG	OBP	SLG	AOPS	ABR	SB-CS	FA	FR	RNG	THR	GAMES AT POSITION	DL	BFW
1964	NY A	31	23	4	4	2	0	0	1	2-0	0	9	.174	.240	.261	39	-2	0-0	1.000	0	75	0	O8(0/5/3),1b7		-0.2
1965	NY A	9	17	1	7	2	0	1	4	4-1	0	4	.412	.524	.706	248	4	0-0	.889	0	97	390	O5(1/0/5)		0.4
Total	2	40	40	5	11	4	0	1	5	6-1	0	13	.275	.370	.450	128	2	0-0	.929	0	88	223	O13(1/5/8),1b7		0.2

MOORE, CHARLEY   Charles Wesley B12.1.1884 Jackson Co. IN D7.29.1970 Portland OR BR/TR/5-10/160 d4.16

YEAR	TM LG	G	AB	R	H	2B	3B	HR	RBI	BB-IB	HP	SO	AVG	OBP	SLG	AOPS	ABR	SB-CS	FA	FR	RNG	THR	GAMES AT POSITION	DL	BFW
1912	Chi N	5	9	2	2	0	0	0	3	0-0	0	0	.222	.222	.444	80	0	0	.800	0	81	0	S2/23		0.0

MOORE, CHARLIE   Charles William B6.21.1953 Birmingham AL BR/TR/5-11/180* [MilA71 5/99] d9.8

YEAR	TM LG	G	AB	R	H	2B	3B	HR	RBI	BB-IB	HP	SO	AVG	OBP	SLG	AOPS	ABR	SB-CS	FA	FR	RNG	THR	GAMES AT POSITION	DL	BFW
1973	Mil A	8	27	0	5	0	0	0	3	2-1	0	4	.185	.241	.259	42	-1	0-0	.981	2	67	197	C8		0.0
1974	Mil A	72	204	17	50	10	4	0	19	21-0	0	34	.245	.316	.333	87	-3	3-4	.985	0	78	62	C61,D6		-0.1
1975	Mil A	73	241	26	70	20	1	0	29	17-0	1	31	.290	.336	.394	105	2	1-5	.960	-2	105	87	C47,O22(16/0/6)/D		0.0
1976	Mil A	87	241	33	46	7	4	3	16	43-0	1	45	.191	.314	.290	80	-5	1-2	.969	1	89	149	C49,O28L/3D		-0.4
1977	Mil A	138	375	42	93	15	6	5	45	31-0	1	39	.248	.306	.360	81	-10	1-7	.980	-1	94	91	C137		-0.8
1978	Mil A	96	268	30	72	7	1	5	31	12-0	1	24	.269	.300	.358	84	-7	4-2	.983	4	**140**	68	C95		0.1
1979	Mil A	111	345	45	101	16	2	5	38	29-1	1	32	.293	.355	.404	104	2	8-5	.979	-2	98	101	C106		1.8
1980	Mil A	111	320	42	93	13	2	2	30	24-2	0	28	.291	.336	.363	95	-2	10-5	.989	-2	139	68	C105		0.0
1981	†Mil A	48	156	16	47	8	3	1	9	12-0	1	13	.301	.351	.410	124	5	1-4	.970	-1	106	79	C34,O8(3/0/5),D6		0.0
1982	†Mil A	133	456	53	116	22	4	6	45	29-2	4	49	.254	.299	.360	95	-11	2-10	.988	8	101	163	O115R,C20/2		0.6
1983	Mil A	151	529	65	150	27	6	2	49	55-5	1	42	.284	.354	.369	107	7	2-10	.988	8	101	163	O143R,C7/D		-1.0
1984	Mil A	70	188	13	44	7	1	2	17	10-0	1	26	.234	.275	.314	65	-9	0-4	.978	-7	95	76	O61(0/7/56),C7/D		-1.4
1985	Mil A	105	349	35	81	13	4	0	31	27-0	1	53	.232	.288	.292	60	-20	4-0	.977	5	114	123	C102,O3R	17	-1.0
1986	Mil A	80	235	24	61	12	3	3	39	21-1	0	38	.260	.317	.374	85	-5	5-5	.992	14	133	140	C72,O4(0/1/3)/2D		1.3
1987	Tor A	51	107	15	23	10	1	1	7	13-0	1	12	.215	.306	.355	73	-4	0-0	.984	2	82	64	C44,O5(2/0/3)		-0.1
Total	15	1334	4033	456	1052	187	43	36	408	346-12	11	470	.261	.319	.355	88	-62	51-57	.980	40	110	96	C894,O396(49/8/341),D18,2b2/3	17	-1.7

MOORE, DEE   D C B4.6.1914 Hedley TX D7.2.1997 Williston ND BR/TR/5-11/190 d9.12 Mil 1944-45

YEAR	TM LG	G	AB	R	H	2B	3B	HR	RBI	BB-IB	HP	SO	AVG	OBP	SLG	AOPS	ABR	SB-CS	FA	FR	RNG	THR	GAMES AT POSITION	DL	BFW
1936	Cin N	6	10	4	4	2	1	0	1	0	0	3	.400	.400	.800	230	2	0	1.000	-0	202	0	P2/C		0.1
1937	Cin N	7	13	2	1	0	0	0	0	1	1	2	.077	.200	.077	-23	-2	0	.931	1	80	143	C6		-0.1
1943	Bro N	37	79	8	20	3	0	0	12	11	0	8	.253	.344	.291	84	-1	1	.982	-4	94	100	C15,3b9		-0.5
1943	Phi N	37	79	13	27	4	1	1	8	15	0	8	.239	.328	.319	91	-1	1	.960	-1	98	111	C21,O6L,3b5/1		-0.1
Year		74	192	21	47	7	1	1	20	26	0	16	.245	.335	.307	88	-2	1	.968	-5	97	107	C36,3b14,O6L/1		-0.6
1946	Phi N	11	13	2	1	0	0	0	1	7	0	3	.077	.400	.077	41	0	0	1.000	-0	74	88	C6,1b2		0.0
Total	4	98	228	29	60	11	2	1	22	34	1	24	.232	.335	.303	85	-2	1	.962	-4	90	105	C49,3b14,O6L,1b3,P2		-0.6

MOORE, GENE   Eugene Jr. "Rowdy" B8.26.1909 Lancaster TX D3.12.1978 Jackson MS BL/TL/5-11/175 d9.19 f-Gene

YEAR	TM LG	G	AB	R	H	2B	3B	HR	RBI	BB-IB	HP	SO	AVG	OBP	SLG	AOPS	ABR	SB-CS	FA	FR	RNG	THR	GAMES AT POSITION	DL	BFW
1931	Cin N	4	14	2	2	1	0	0	0	0	0	1	.143	.143	.214	-6	-2	0	1.000	0	111	0	O3L		-0.2
1933	StL N	11	38	6	15	3	0	0	8	4	0	10	.395	.452	.579	183	4	1	.967	-0	109	0	O10C		0.4
1934	StL N	9	18	2	5	1	0	0	1	2	0	2	.278	.350	.333	79	0	0	.923	-0	112	0	O3C		-0.1
1935	StL N	3	9	0	0	0	0	0	0	0	0	1	.000	.000	.000	-96	-1	0	—	0	0	0	/H		-0.1
1936	Bos N	151	637	91	185	38	12	13	67	40	3	80	.290	.335	.449	117	12	6	.977	13	102	186	O151R		1.6
1937	Bos N☆	148	561	88	159	29	10	16	70	61	4	73	.283	.358	.456	132	24	11	.978	11	**113**	128	O148R		2.6
1938	Bos N	54	180	27	49	8	3	3	19	16	2	20	.272	.338	.400	114	3	1	.981	1	107	95	O47R		0.1
1939	Bro N	107	306	45	69	13	6	3	39	40	0	50	.225	.315	.337	73	-12	4	.961	-4	88	110	O86(2/1/83)/1		-2.0
1940	Bro N	10	26	4	7	2	0	0	2	1	0	0	.269	.296	.346	72	-1	0	1.000	-1	89	0	O6R		-0.2
	Bos N	103	363	46	106	24	1	5	39	25	0	32	.292	.338	.405	110	5	2	.986	6	108	147	O94(0/1/94)		0.5
Year		113	389	49	113	26	1	5	41	26	0	35	.290	.335	.407	107	3	2	.986	5	107	140	O100(0/1/100)		0.3
1941	Bos N	129	397	42	108	17	4	5	43	45	2	37	.272	.349	.393	114	7	5	.968	5	106	147	O100(1/28/84)		0.7
1942	Was A	1	2	0	0	0	0	0	0	0	0	0	.000	.000	.000	-99	-1	0-0	—	-0	0	0	/OC		-0.1
1943	Was A	92	254	41	68	14	3	2	39	19	1	29	.268	.321	.370	106	1	0-2	.985	2	105	119	O57(24/1/32)/1		-0.1
1944	†StL A	110	390	56	93	13	4	6	58	24	1	37	.238	.284	.349	76	-14	0-5	.968	2	110	77	O98R/1		-2.1
1945	StL A	110	354	48	92	16	2	5	50	40	1	26	.260	.333	.400	105	-3	1-3	.973	-4	93	110	O100(1/0/99)		-0.8
Total	14	1042	3543	497	958	179	53	58	436	317	14	401	.270	.333	.400	105	24	31-10	.970	36	105	128	O914(31/45/842),1b3		0.2

MOORE, FERDIE   Ferdinand De Paige B2.22.1896 Camden NJ D5.6.1947 Atlantic City NJ 6-0/212 d10.2

YEAR	TM LG	G	AB	R	H	2B	3B	HR	RBI	BB-IB	HP	SO	AVG	OBP	SLG	AOPS	ABR	SB-CS	FA	FR	RNG	THR	GAMES AT POSITION	DL	BFW
1914	Phi A	2	4	1	2	0	0	0	1	0	0	0	.500	.500	.500	209	0	0	.895	-1	0	0	1b2		0.0

MOORE, GARY   Gary Douglas B2.24.1945 Tulsa OK BR/TL/5-10/175 [LAN65 14/537] d5.3 Col Texas

YEAR	TM LG	G	AB	R	H	2B	3B	HR	RBI	BB-IB	HP	SO	AVG	OBP	SLG	AOPS	ABR	SB-CS	FA	FR	RNG	THR	GAMES AT POSITION	DL	BFW
1970	LA N	7	16	2	3	0	0	0	0	0-0	0	1	.188	.188	.438	64	-1	1-0	1.000	-1	70	0	O5R/1		-0.2

MOORE, EDDIE   Graham Edward B1.18.1899 Barlow KY D2.10.1976 Ft.Myers FL BR/TR/5-7/165 d9.25

YEAR	TM LG	G	AB	R	H	2B	3B	HR	RBI	BB-IB	HP	SO	AVG	OBP	SLG	AOPS	ABR	SB-CS	FA	FR	RNG	THR	GAMES AT POSITION	DL	BFW
1923	Pit N	6	26	6	6	0	0	0	3	1	0	2	.231	.296	.231	65	-1	1-0	.923	-3	63	63	S6		-0.3
1924	Pit N	72	209	47	75	8	4	2	13	27	2	12	.359	.437	.464	139	13	6-7	.988	3	105	134	O35(1/0/34),3b13,2b4		1.2
1925	†Pit N	142	547	106	163	29	8	6	77	73	2	26	.298	.383	.413	97	0	19-7	.952	-6	95	119	2b122,O15R,3b3		-0.2
1926	Bos N	54	184	17	49	3	2	0	15	16	0	12	.266	.325	.304	77	-6	6	.911	-6	84	119	2b24,3b9/S		-0.8

YEAR	TM LG	G	AB	R	H	2B	3B	HR	RBI	BB-IB	HP	SO	AVG	OBP	SLG	AOPS	ABR	SB-CS	FA	FR	RNG	THR	GAMES AT POSITION	DL	BFV
	Year	97	316	36	79	11	3	0	34	28	0	18	.250	.311	.304	68	-14	9	.950	-11	90	115	2b63,S15,3b10	-2.	
1927	Bos N	112	411	53	124	14	4	1	32	39	1	17	.302	.364	.363	103	3	5	.947	8	93	65	3b52,2b39,O16(1/11/4)/S	-0.	
1928	Bos N	68	215	27	51	9	0	2	18	19	0	12	.237	.299	.307	62	-12	7	.958	5	112	161	O54L/2	-1.	
1929	Bro N	111	402	48	119	18	6	0	48	44	3	16	.296	.370	.371	86	-8	3	.955	-14	93	67	2b74,S36,O2R/3	-1.	
1930	Bro N	76	196	24	55	13	1	1	20	21	2	7	.281	.356	.372	77	-6	1	.991	9	111	111	2b23,O23(13/7/3),S17/3	0.	
1932	NY N	37	87	9	23	3	0	1	6	9	1	6	.264	.340	.333	84	-2	1	.930	1	96	92	S21,3b6,2b5	0.	
1934	Cle A	27	65	4	10	2	0	0	8	10	1	4	.154	.267	.185	18	-8	0-0	.932	0	95	107	2b18,3b3,S2	-0.	
Total	10	748	2474	360	706	108	26	13	257	272	11	121	.285	.359	.366	89	-35	52-14	.956	-31	95	104	2b349,O145(69/18/58),S98,3b89	-5.	

MOORE, HARRY Henry S. d4.17

YEAR	TM LG	G	AB	R	H	2B	3B	HR	RBI	BB-IB	HP	SO	AVG	OBP	SLG	AOPS	ABR	SB-CS	FA	FR	RNG	THR	GAMES AT POSITION	DL	BFV
1884	Was U	111	461	77	155	23	5	.1		19			.336	.363	.414	140	10		.820	-7	64	98	O105(102/2/1),S8	0.	

MOORE, JACKIE Jackie Spencer B2.19.1939 Jay FL BR/TR/6-0/180 d4.18 M3/C26

YEAR	TM LG	G	AB	R	H	2B	3B	HR	RBI	BB-IB	HP	SO	AVG	OBP	SLG	AOPS	ABR	SB-CS	FA	FR	RNG	THR	GAMES AT POSITION	DL	BFV
1965	Det A	21	53	2	5	0	0	0	2	6-2	0	12	.094	.183	.094	-17	-8	0-0	.985	2	119	114	C20	-0.	

MOORE, JIMMY James William B4.24.1903 Paris TN D3.7.1986 Memphis TN BR/TR/6-0.5/187 d4.17 Col Union (TN)

YEAR	TM LG	G	AB	R	H	2B	3B	HR	RBI	BB-IB	HP	SO	AVG	OBP	SLG	AOPS	ABR	SB-CS	FA	FR	RNG	THR	GAMES AT POSITION	DL	BFV
1930	Chi A	16	39	4	8	2	0	0	2	6	1	3	.205	.326	.256	52	-3	0-0	.900	1	94	311	O11L	-0.	
	†Phi A	15	50	10	19	3	0	2	12	2	0	4	.380	.404	.560	136	3	1-1	.958	-0	98	113	O13(8/1/4)	0.	
	Year	31	89	14	27	5	0	2	14	8	1	7	.303	.367	.427	100	0	1-1	.932	1	96	197	O24(19/1/4)	-0.	
1931	†Phi A	49	143	18	32	5	1	2	21	11	1	13	.224	.284	.315	54	-10	0-1	.973	2	105	118	O36(24/2/10)	-1.	
Total	2	80	232	32	59	10	1	4	35	19	2	20	.254	.316	.358	71	-10	1-2	.958	2	102	148	O60(43/3/14)	-1.	

MOORE, JERRIE Jeremiah S. B1855 Windsor ON, Can. D9.26.1890 Wayne MI BL/5-11/170 d4.17

YEAR	TM LG	G	AB	R	H	2B	3B	HR	RBI	BB-IB	HP	SO	AVG	OBP	SLG	AOPS	ABR	SB-CS	FA	FR	RNG	THR	GAMES AT POSITION	DL	BFV
1884	Alt U	20	80	10	25	3	1	1					.313	.313	.412	117	-1		.800	-8			C12,O9(1/2/6)	-0.	
	Cle N	9	30	1	6	0	0	0	10	0		5	.200	.200	.200	25	-3		.887	-2			C9	-0.	
1885	Det N	6	23	2	4	1	0	0	1			3	.174	.208	.217	38	-2		.800	-2			C6	-0.	
Total	2	35	133	13	35	4	1	1	10	1		8	.263	.269	.331	83	-6		.830	-12			C27,O9(1/2/6)	-1.	

MOORE, JOHNNY John Francis B3.23.1902 Waterville CT D4.4.1991 Bradenton FL BL/TR/5-10.5/175 d9.15

YEAR	TM LG	G	AB	R	H	2B	3B	HR	RBI	BB-IB	HP	SO	AVG	OBP	SLG	AOPS	ABR	SB-CS	FA	FR	RNG	THR	GAMES AT POSITION	DL	BFV
1928	Chi N	4	4	0	0	0	0	0	0	0	0	0	.000	.000	.000	-99	-1	0	—	0			/H	-0.	
1929	Chi N	37	63	13	18	1	0	2	8	4	1	6	.286	.338	.397	81	-2	0	.971	1	110	100	O15(10/4/1)	-0.	
1931	Chi N	39	104	19	25	3	1	2	16	7	.0	5	.240	.288	.346	69	-5	1	.964	0	95	193	O22(12/9/1)	0.	
1932	†Chi N	119	443	59	135	24	5	13	64	22	3	38	.305	.342	.470	117	9	4	.983	-4	91	119	O109(4/91/14)	-1.	
1933	Cin N	135	514	60	135	19	5	.1	44	29	3	16	.263	.306	.325	81	-13	4	.974	3	102	118	O132(75/57/0)	0.	
1934	Cin N	16	42	5	8	1	0	0	5	3	0	2	.190	.244	.262	36	-4	0	1.000	-0	109	0	O10R	1	
	Phi N	116	458	68	157	34	6	11	93	40	1	18	.343	.397	.515	125	18	7	.981	8	104	175	O115(10/0/108)	1	
	Year	132	500	73	165	35	7	11	98	43	1	20	.330	.384	.494	120	15	7	.983	8	104	161	O125(10/0/118)	1	
1935	Phi N	153	600	84	194	33	3	19	93	45	5	50	.323	.375	.483	117	15	4	.973	-10	78	117	O150(2/0/148)	-0	
1936	Phi N	124	472	85	155	24	3	16	88	26	1	22	.328	.365	.494	117	11	1	.948	-6	96	54	O112(78/0/35)	-0	
1937	Phi N	96	307	46	98	16	2	9	59	18	1	18	.319	.357	.472	114	6	0	.943	-0	93	147	O72(30/2/42)	-0	
1945	Chi N	7	6	0	1	0	0	0	2	1	0	1	.167	.286	.167	28	-1	0	—	0			/H	-1	
Total	10	846	3013	439	926	155	26	73	452	195	14	176	.307	.352	.449	109	33	23	.970	-9	94	120	O737(221/163/359)	-1	

MOORE, JO-JO Joseph Gregg "The Gause Ghost" B12.25.1908 Gause TX D4.1.2001 Bryan TX BL/TR/5-11/155 d9.17

YEAR	TM LG	G	AB	R	H	2B	3B	HR	RBI	BB-IB	HP	SO	AVG	OBP	SLG	AOPS	ABR	SB-CS	FA	FR	RNG	THR	GAMES AT POSITION	DL	BFV
1930	NY N	3	5	1	1	0	0	0	0	0	0	1	.200	.200	.200	-3	-1	0	1.000	-0	75	0	/OC	-0	
1931	NY N	4	8	0	2	1	0	0	3	0	0	0	.250	.250	.375	68	0	1	1.000	-0	96	0	/OL	-1	
1932	NY N	86	361	53	110	15	2	2	27	20	0	18	.305	.341	.374	94	-3	4	.982	-3	88	115	O86(85/1/0)	-1	
1933	†NY N	132	524	56	153	16	5	0	42	21	3	27	.292	.323	.342	91	-7	4	.966	2	90	**185**	O132(111/21/0)	0	
1934	NY N*	139	580	106	192	37	4	15	61	31	5	23	.331	.370	.486	130	24	5	.954	-13	81	83	O131(112/20/0)	0	
1935	NY N★	155	681	108	201	28	9	15	71	53	8	24	.295	.353	.429	111	10	6	.972	-1	98	96	O155L	C	
1936	†NY N☆	152	649	110	205	29	9	7	63	37	6	27	.316	.358	.421	110	8	2	.981	8	94	**224**	O149L	-0	
1937	†NY N★	142	580	89	180	37	10	6	57	46	3	37	.310	.364	.440	116	13	7	.975	-8	83	120	O140L	-0	
1938	NY N☆	125	506	76	153	23	6	11	56	22	3	27	.302	.335	.437	110	5	2	.978	-5	88	88	O114L	-1	
1939	NY N	138	562	80	151	23	2	10	47	45	1	17	.269	.324	.370	85	-12	7	.986	3	95	159	O136L	-1	
1940	NY N★	138	543	83	150	33	4	6	46	43	7	30	.276	.337	.385	98	-1	7	.982	-2	93	95	O133L	-1	
1941	NY N	121	428	47	117	16	2	7	40	30	1	15	.273	.322	.369	93	-5	0	.972	-2	100	66	O116(112/4/0)	-6	
Total	12	1335	5427	809	1615	258	53	79	513	348	37	247	.298	.344	.408	105	31	46	.975	-21	91	125	O1294(1248/47/0)		

MOORE, KELVIN Kelvin Orlando B9.26.1957 Leroy AL BR/TL/6-1/195* [OakA78 6/134] d8.28 Col Jackson St.

YEAR	TM LG	G	AB	R	H	2B	3B	HR	RBI	BB-IB	HP	SO	AVG	OBP	SLG	AOPS	ABR	SB-CS	FA	FR	RNG	THR	GAMES AT POSITION	DL	BFV
1981	†Oak A	14	47	5	12	0	1	1	3	5-0	0	15	.255	.327	.362	102	0	1-0	1.000	-1	72	81	1b13	-C	
1982	Oak A	21	67	6	15	1	1	2	6	3-0	0	23	.224	.250	.358	69	-3	0-1	.971	-2	75	57	1b20	-C	
1983	Oak A	41	124	12	26	4	0	5	16	10-0	1	39	.210	.272	.363	78	-4	2-4	.994	-3	70	115	1b40	-1	
Total	3	76	238	23	53	5	2	8	25	18-0	1	77	.223	.277	.361	80	-7	3-5	.989	-6	72	93	1b73	-C	

MOORE, KERWIN Kerwin Lamar B10.29.1970 Detroit MI BB/TR/6-1/190 [KCA88 16/413] d8.30

YEAR	TM LG	G	AB	R	H	2B	3B	HR	RBI	BB-IB	HP	SO	AVG	OBP	SLG	AOPS	ABR	SB-CS	FA	FR	RNG	THR	GAMES AT POSITION	DL	BFV
1996	KC A	22	16	4	1	0	0	0		2-0	0	6	.063	.167	.125	-25	-3	1-0	1.000	-0	103	0	O18C,D2	-C	

MOORE, MOLLY Maurice TR d6.30

YEAR	TM LG	G	AB	R	H	2B	3B	HR	RBI	BB-IB	HP	SO	AVG	OBP	SLG	AOPS	ABR	SB-CS	FA	FR	RNG	THR	GAMES AT POSITION	DL	BFV
1875	Atl NA	21	86	5	19	4	0	0	5	0		4	.221	.221	.267	79	-1	0-1	.747	-4	111		S14,1b8,O2R/C23		

MOORE, RANDY Randolph Edward B6.21.1906 Naples TX D6.12.1992 Mt.Pleasant TX BL/TR/6-0/185 d4.12 OF(66/13/339)

YEAR	TM LG	G	AB	R	H	2B	3B	HR	RBI	BB-IB	HP	SO	AVG	OBP	SLG	AOPS	ABR	SB-CS	FA	FR	RNG	THR	GAMES AT POSITION	DL	BFV
1927	Chi A	6	15	0	0	0	0	0	0	0	0	2	.000	.000	.000	-99	-5	0-0	1.000	1	119	257	O4R	-C	
1928	Chi A	24	61	6	13	4	1	0	5	3	0	5	.213	.250	.311	47	-5	0-2	.946	9	117	63	O16(2/0/14)	-C	
1930	Bos N	83	191	24	55	9	0	2	34	10	0	13	.288	.323	.366	69	-10	3	.986	1	113	121	O34(11/12/11),3b13	-1	
1931	Bos N	83	192	19	50	8	1	3	34	13	1	3	.260	.311	.359	83	-5	1	.952	1	93	180	O29(17/1/11),3b22/2	-C	
1932	Bos N	107	351	40	103	21	2	3	43	15	0	11	.293	.322	.390	94	-3	1	.987	-2	94	54	O41R,3b31,1b22/C	-C	
1933	Bos N	135	497	64	150	23	7	8	70	40	2	16	.302	.356	.425	133	21	3	.979	-1	101	92	O122(12/0/110),1b10	-C	
1934	Bos N	123	422	55	120	21	2	7	64	40	0	16	.284	.343	.393	105	4	2	.965	-0	108	114	O72(16/0/56),3b37	-C	
1935	Bos N	125	407	42	112	20	4	4	42	26	2	16	.275	.319	.373	93	-5	1	.950	1	104	130	O78(7/0/71),1b21	-C	
1936	Bro N	42	88	4	21	3	0	0	14	8	0	1	.239	.302	.273	55	-5	0	.964	-2	91	0	O21R	-C	
1937	Bro N	13	22	3	3	1	0	0	2	3	0	2	.136	.240	.182	16	-3	0	.889	-4	106	109	C10	-C	
	StL N	8	7	0	0	0	0	0	0	0	0	0	.000	.000	.000	-98	-2	0	—	-0	0	0	/OL	-C	
	Year	21	29	3	3	1	0	0	2	3	0	2	.103	.188	.138	-10	-4	0	.889	-1	106	109	C10/OL	-C	
Total	10	749	2253	258	627	110	17	27	308	158	3	85	.278	.326	.378	95	-18	11-2	.969	-2	103	104	O418R,1b90,3b66,C11/2		

MOORE, BOBBY Robert Vincent B10.27.1965 Cincinnati OH BR/TR/5-9/165 [KCA87 16/405] d9.5 Col Eastern Kentucky

YEAR	TM LG	G	AB	R	H	2B	3B	HR	RBI	BB-IB	HP	SO	AVG	OBP	SLG	AOPS	ABR	SB-CS	FA	FR	RNG	THR	GAMES AT POSITION	DL	BFV
1991	KC A	18	14	3	5	1	0	0		1-0	0	2	.357	.400	.429	128	1	3-2	1.000	0	102	0	O13(9/5/0)		

MOORE, TERRY Terry Bluford B5.27.1912 Vernon AL D3.29.1995 Collinsville IL BR/TR/5-11/195 d4.16 Mil 1943-45 M1/C7

YEAR	TM LG	G	AB	R	H	2B	3B	HR	RBI	BB-IB	HP	SO	AVG	OBP	SLG	AOPS	ABR	SB-CS	FA	FR	RNG	THR	GAMES AT POSITION	DL	BFV
1935	StL N	119	456	63	131	34	3	6	53	15	3	40	.287	.314	.414	90	-6	13	.984	7	109	109	O117C		
1936	StL N	143	590	85	156	39	4	5	47	37	1	52	.264	.309	.369	82	-15	9	.977	13	112	139	O133C		
1937	StL N	115	461	76	123	17	5	3	43	32	2	41	.267	.317	.349	79	-14	13	.988	8	112	100	O106C		
1938	StL N	94	312	49	85	21	3	4	21	46	0	19	.272	.366	.397	104	3	9	.987	4	114	.77	O75C,3b6		
1939	StL N★	120	417	65	123	25	2	17	77	43	1	38	.295	.362	.487	119	11	6	**.994**	8	102	175	O121C/P		
1940	StL N	136	537	92	163	33	4	17	64	42	2	44	.304	.356	.475	121	15	18	.987	13	**120**	104	O133C		
1941	StL N★	122	493	86	145	26	4	6	68	52	2	31	.294	.364	.400	108	6	3	.984	0	95	140	O121(0/121/1)		
1942	†StL N	130	489	80	141	26	3	6	49	56	2	26	.288	.364	.391	112	9	10	.986	-8	92	80	O126C/3		
1946	†StL N	91	278	32	73	14	1	3	28	18	2	26	.263	.312	.353	85	-6	0	.982	-2	97	89	O120C		
1947	StL N	127	460	61	130	17	1	7	45	38	1	39	.283	.339	.370	84	-10	1	.983	-7	92	71	O120C		
1948	StL N	91	207	30	48	11	0	4	18	27	1	12	.232	.321	.343	75	-7	0	.993	-3	94	53	O71C		
Total	11	1298	4700	719	1318	263	28	80	513	406	16	368	.280	.340	.399	98	-14	82	.985	33	104	108	O1189(0/1189/1),3b7/P		

MOORE, SCRAPPY William Allen B12.16.1892 St.Louis MO D10.13.1964 Little Rock AR BR/TR/5-8/153 d6.21 Col Vanderbilt

YEAR	TM LG	G	AB	R	H	2B	3B	HR	RBI	BB-IB	HP	SO	AVG	OBP	SLG	AOPS	ABR	SB-CS	FA	FR	RNG	THR	GAMES AT POSITION	DL	BFV
1917	StL A	4	8	1	1	0	0	0	0	1	0	0	.125	.222	.125	6	-1	0	.750	-0	100	651	3b2		

YEAR	TM LG	G	AB	R	H	2B	3B	HR	RBI	BB-IB	HP	SO	AVG	OBP	SLG	AOPS	ABR	SB-CS	FA	FR	RNG	THR	GAMES AT POSITION	DL	BFW

MOORE, BILL William Henry "Willie" B12.12.1903 Kansas City MO D5.24.1972 Kansas City MO BL/TR/5-11/170 d9.7

1926	Bos A	5	18	2	3	0	0	0	0	0-0	0	2	.167	.167	.167	-13	-3	0-0	1.000	0	66	155	C5		-0.3
1927	Bos A	44	69	7	15	2	0	0	4	13	0	8	.217	.341	.246	56	-4	0-0	.938	-2	68	112	C42		-0.4
Total	2	49	87	9	18	2	0	0	4	13	0	10	.207	.310	.230	43	-7	0-0	.946	-2	68	119	C47		-0.7

MOORE, BILL William Ross B10.10.1960 Los Angeles CA BR/TL/6-1/185 [Mon83 6/146] d7.19 Col Cal St.-Fullerton

| 1986 | Mon N | 6 | 12 | 0 | 2 | 0 | 0 | 0 | 0 | 4-0 | 0 | 4 | .167 | .167 | .167 | -8 | -2 | 0-0 | 1.000 | -0 | 59 | 61 | 1b3/OR | | -0.2 |

MORA, ANDRES Andres (Ibarra) B5.25.1955 Rio Bravo, Coahuila, Mexico BR/TR/6-0/180(162-205) d4.13

1976	Bal A	73	220	18	48	11	0	6	25	13-0	0	49	.218	.258	.350	83	-6	1-0	.951	0	99	152	D34,O31(30/0/2)		-0.8
1977	Bal A	77	233	32	57	8	2	13	44	5-1	1	53	.245	.261	.464	99	-2	0-0	1.000	-7	70	55	O57L/3D		-1.2
1978	Bal A	76	229	21	49	8	0	8	14	13-1	1	47	.214	.258	.354	75	-9	0-1	.978	1	105	100	O69L/D		-1.1
1980	Cle A	9	18	0	2	0	0	0	0	0-0	0	0	.111	.111	.111	-38	-3	0-0	1.000	-0	99	0	O3(2/0/1)		-0.4
Total	4	235	700	71	156	27	2	27	83	31-2	2	149	.223	.256	.383	83	-20	1-1	.978	-6	91	92	O160(158/0/3),D40/3		-3.5

MORA, MELVIN Melvin B2.2.1972 Agua Negra, Venez BR/TR/5-10/180(180-200) d5.30 OF(170/158/29)

1999	†NY N	66	31	6	5	0	0	1	4-0		1	7	.161	.278	.161	16	-4	2-1	1.000	-1	98		O45(28/11/8),2b4,3b3/S		-0.4
2000	NY N	79	215	35	56	13	2	6	30	18-3	2	48	.260	.317	.423	91	-3	7-3	.958	-6	89	68	S44,O28(12/16/3),2b4,3b4	16	-0.5
	Bal A	53	199	25	58	9	3	2	17	17-0	4	32	.291	.359	.397	96	-1	5-8	.952	2	107	88	S52/2		0.3
2001	Bal A	128	436	49	109	28	0	7	48	41-2	14	91	.250	.329	.362	88	-6	11-4	.987	7	105	86	O88C,S43/2		0.6
2002	Bal A	149	557	86	130	30	4	19	64	70-2	20	108	.233	.338	.404	102	3	16-10	.989	16	109	152	O104(74/31/5),S41,2b12,D3		1.9
2003	Bal A★	96	344	68	109	17	1	15	48	49-0	12	71	.317	.418	.503	143	24	6-3	.994	5	102	205	O79(56/12/13),S11,2b6/1	32	2.7
2004	Bal A★	140	550	111	187	41	0	27	104	66-0	11	95	.340	**.419**	.562	155	48	11-6	.948	6	102	86	3b137/SD	15	5.1
2005	Bal A★	149	593	86	168	30	1	27	88	50-0	10	112	.283	.348	.474	115	13	7-4	.957	5	103	84	3b148/D		1.8
Total	7	860	2925	466	822	168	11	103	400	315-7	74	564	.281	.363	.452	116	74	65-39	.989	35	105	135	O344L,3b292,S193,2b28,D5/1	63	11.5

MORALES, JOSE Jose Manuel (Hernandez) B12.30.1944 Frederiksted, V.I. BR/TR/6-0/195(187-210) d8.13 C9

1973	Oak A	6	14	4	4	1	0	0	1	5	0	.286	.313	.357	99	0	0-1	—	0			D3		0.0
	Mon N	5	5	0	2	0	0	0	0	0-0	0	0	.400	.400	.400	118	0	0-0	—	0			/H		0.0
1974	Mon N	25	26	3	7	4	0	1	5	1-0	0	7	.269	.296	.538	123	1	0-0	.800	-1	0	0	C2		0.0
1975	Mon N	93	163	18	49	6	1	2	24	14-9	0	21	.301	.354	.387	101	0	0-2	.983	5	191	103	1b27,O6L,C5		0.3
1976	Mon N	104	158	12	50	11	0	4	37	3-3	2	20	.316	.333	.462	119	4	0-0	.977	-0	208	73	1b21,C12		0.3
1977	Mon N	65	74	3	15	4	1	1	9	5-3	0	12	.203	.247	.324	55	-5	0-0	1.000	-2	51	104	C8,1b8		-0.8
1978	Min A	101	242	22	76	13	1	2	38	20-3	1	35	.314	.363	.401	113	5	0-1	—	0			D77/C1OL		0.3
1979	Min A	92	191	21	51	5	1	2	27	14-5	2	27	.267	.319	.335	75	-7	0-0	1.000	-0	0		D77/1		-0.9
1980	Min A	97	241	36	73	17	2	8	36	22-4	1	19	.303	.361	.490	123	8	0-0	1.000	-0	0		D86,C2,1b2		-0.3
1981	Bal A	38	86	6	21	3	0	2	14	3-0	0	13	.244	.270	.349	77	-3	0-0	1.000	-0	66		D22,1b3	6	0.5
1982	Bal A	3	3	0	0	0	0	0	0	0-0	0	0	.000	.000	.000	-99	-1	0-0	—	0			/H		-0.4
	LA N	35	30	1	9	1	0	1	8	4-0	0	8	.300	.382	.433	132	1	0-0	—	0			/H		-0.1
1983	†LA N	47	53	4	15	3	0	3	8	1-0	0	11	.283	.296	.509	119	1	0-0	.951	-1	84	77	1b4		0.0
1984	LA N	22	19	0	3	0	0	0	0	1-1	0	2	.158	.190	.158	2	-3	0-0	—	0			/H		-0.3
Total	12	733	1305	126	375	68	6	26	207	89-28	6	182	.287	.332	.408	102	1	0-4	.981	1	166	96	D265,1b67,C30,O7L	6	-1.1

MORALES, JERRY Julio Ruben (Torres) B2.18.1949 Yabucoa, PR BR/TR/5-10/175(155-175) d9.5 C3

1969	SD N	19	41	5	8	2	0	1	6	5-0	0	7	.195	.283	.317	70	-2	0-2	1.000	2	105	259	O19(10/9/1)		-0.1
1970	SD N	28	58	6	9	0	1	1	4	3-0	1	15	.155	.197	.241	17	-7	0-0	.926	-2	86	9	O26(23/0/4)		-1.0
1971	SD N	12	17	1	2	0	0	0	1	2-0	0	2	.118	.211	.118	-5	-2	1-0	1.000	-0	89	0	O7(4/1/2)		-0.3
1972	SD N	115	347	38	83	15	7	4	18	35-3	0	54	.239	.307	.357	96	-3	4-6	.987	5	108	139	O96(34/56/12),3b4		-0.3
1973	SD N	122	388	47	109	23	2	9	34	27-3	0	55	.281	.325	.420	115	7	6-5	.991	2	107	77	O100(31/50/27)		0.4
1974	Chi N	151	534	70	146	21	7	15	82	46-3	2	63	.273	.330	.423	106	3	2-12	.975	-5	95	54	O143(83/32/41)		-1.4
1975	Chi N	153	578	62	156	21	4	12	91	50-9	5	65	.270	.328	.369	90	-7	3-7	.979	-3	95	111	O151(0/20/136)		-2.0
1976	Chi N	140	537	66	147	17	0	16	67	41-7	0	49	.274	.323	.395	95	-4	3-8	.983	-0	100	104	O136(3/8/131)		-1.4
1977	Chi N★	136	490	56	142	34	5	11	69	43-4	2	75	.290	.348	.447	101	1	0-3	.985	-1	81	98	O128(6/125/3)		-1.4
1978	StL N	130	457	44	109	19	4	4	46	33-1	1	44	.239	.288	.341	77	-16	4-4	.977	-4	102	56	O126(0/34/94)		-2.7
1979	Det A	129	440	50	93	23	1	14	56	30-0	2	56	.211	.260	.364	65	-23	10-4	.986	-7	88	75	O119(18/20/88),D7		-3.4
1980	NY N	94	193	19	49	7	1	3	30	13-2	1	31	.254	.293	.347	83	-5	2-3	.973	-2	94	97	O63(3/55/6)		-0.8
1981	Chi N	84	245	27	70	6	2	1	25	22-0	1	29	.286	.343	.339	90	-3	1-1	.986	-3	94	94	O72(17/49/8)		-0.8
1982	Chi N	65	116	14	33	2	2	4	30	9-1	0	7	.284	.333	.440	111	1	1-2	1.000	5	110	299	O41(12/36/4)		0.5
1983	Chi N	63	87	11	17	9	0	0	11	7-0	0	19	.195	.253	.299	51	-6	0-0	1.000	-0	89	109	O29(17/10/3)	41	
Total	15	1441	4528	516	1173	199	36	95	570	366-33	14	567	.259	.313	.382	91	-66	37-57	.983	-26	96	92	O1256(261/505/560),D7,3b4	56	-15.4

MORALES, RICH Richard Angelo B9.20.1943 San Francisco CA BR/TR/5-11/170* d8.8 C2 Col San Mateo (CA) [JC]

1967	Chi A	8	10	0	0	0	0	0	0	0-0	0	2	.000	.000	.000	-99	-3	0-0	.944	-1	97	51	S7		-0.3
1968	Chi A	10	29	2	5	0	0	0	0	2-0	0	5	.172	.226	.172	22	-3	0-0	.966	9	186	260	S7,2b5		-0.2
1969	Chi A	55	121	12	26	0	1	0	6	7-0	2	18	.215	.269	.231	39	-10	1-0	.976	5	123	90	2b38,S13/3		-0.2
1970	Chi A	62	112	6	18	2	0	1	9	9-0	1	16	.161	.208	.205	20	-12	1-0	.967	-1	108	88	S24,3b20,2b12	21	-1.2
1971	Chi A	84	185	19	45	8	0	2	14	22-4	4	26	.243	.336	.319	84	-3	2-3	.976	-6	95	74	S57,3b18,2b3/OR		-0.5
1972	Chi A	110	287	24	59	7	1	2	20	19-2	3	49	.206	.261	.258	54	-17	2-3	.968	-5	94	76	S86,2b16,3b14		-1.5
1973	Chi A	7	4	1	1	0	0	0	1	1-0	0	1	.000	.200	.000	-38	-1	0-0	1.000	0	123	0	3b5,2b2		-0.1
	SD N	90	244	9	40	6	1	0	16	27-6	0	36	.164	.245	.197	27	-25	0-1	.988	15	113	90	2b79,S10		-0.5
1974	SD N	54	61	8	12	3	0	1	5	8-1	0	14	.197	.290	.295	67	-3	1-0	.933	0	99	71	S29,2b18,3b6/1		-0.1
Total	8	480	1053	81	205	26	3	6	64	95-13	10	159	.195	.267	.242	46	-77	7-7	.970	7	99	74	S233,2b173,3b64/1OR	21	-4.6

MORALES, WILLIE William Anthony B9.7.1972 Tucson AZ BR/TR/5-10/182 [Oak93 14/405] d4.9

| 2000 | Bal A | 3 | 11 | 1 | 3 | 0 | 0 | 0 | 3 | .273 | .273 | .364 | 62 | -1 | 0-0 | 1.000 | 2 | 0 | 278 | C3 | | 25 | 0.1 |

MORAN, CHARLIE Charles Barthell "Uncle Charlie" B2.22.1878 Nashville TN D6.14.1949 Horse Cave KY BR/TR/5-8/180 d9.9 U22 Col Vanderbilt ▲

1903	StL N	4	14	2	6	0	0	0	0		0		.429	.429	.429	149	-1	1	1.000	-1	46	0	P3/S		0.0
1908	StL N	21	63	2	11	1	2	0	2	0		0	.175	.175	.254	38	-5	0	.903	-5	65	133	C16		-1.0
Total	2	25	77	4	17	1	2	0	2	0		0	.221	.221	.286	61	-4	1	.903	-6	65	133	C16,P3/S		-1.0

MORAN, CHARLES Charles Vincent B3.26.1879 Washington DC D4.11.1934 Washington DC TR d4.29 Col Georgetown

1903	Was A	98	373	41	84	14	5	1	24	33	5		.225	.297	.298	77	-9	8	**.943**	6	100	106	S96,2b2		0.0
1904	Was A	62	243	27	54	10	0	0	7	23	0		.222	.289	.263	77	-5	7	.919	-8	94	85	S61/3		-1.1
	StL A	82	272	15	47	3	1	0	14	25	0		.173	.242	.191	40	-18	2	.937	-3	109	27	3b82,S61/OR		-2.1
	Year	144	515	42	101	13	1	0	21	48	0		.196	.265	.225	58	-23	9	.938	-9	109	27			
1905	StL A	27	82	6	16	1	0	0	5	10	1		.195	.290	.207	62	-3	4	.954	-3	98	132	2b20,3b5		-3.2
Total	3	269	970	89	201	28	6	1	50	91	6		.207	.279	.252	66	-35	20	.935	-6	98	98	S157,3b87,2b22/OR		-3.9

MORAN, HERBIE John Herbert B2.16.1884 Costello PA D9.21.1954 Clarkson NY BL/TR/5-5/150 d4.16

1908	Phi A	19	59	4	9	0	0	0	4	6	1		.153	.242	.153	27	-5	1	.952	0	47	0	O19(0/10/9)		-0.6
	Bos N	8	8	3	0	0	0	0	2	2			.276	.364	.276	106	0	1	1.000	2	168	1021	O8L		0.2
1909	Bos N	8	31	8	7	1	0	0	0	5	0		.226	.333	.258	80	0	0	1.000	0	98	0	O8L		-0.4
1910	Bro N	20	67	11	8	0	0	0	3	13			.119	.280	.119	17	-6	6	.958	4	98	245	O20(11/0/9)		-0.4
1912	Bro N	130	508	77	140	18	10	1	40	69	58		.276	.368	.356	102	4	28	.961	2	98	118	O129(2/73/55)		-0.3
1913	Bro N	132	515	71	137	15	5	1	26	45	7		.266	.333	.315	83	-10	21-16	.950	-1	104	70	O129(3/6/121)		-1.9
1914	Cin N	107	395	43	93	10	5	1	35	41	3		.235	.312	.294	78	-10	26	.954	-7	93	70	O107(1/24/82)		-2.5
	†Bos N	41	154	24	41	3	0	1	4	17	2		.266	.347	.299	93	-1	4	.940	-5	90	70	O41(0/17/30)		-0.8
	Year	148	549	67	134	13	5	1	39	58	5		.244	.322	.295	82	-11	30	.950	-11	90	70	O148(1/41/112)		-3.3
1915	Bos N	130	419	59	84	13	6	0	16	66	8		.200	.320	.255	79	-7	16-10	.964	1	92	140	O123(15/12/101)		-1.3
Total	7	595	2177	300	527	60	26	4	135	264		30	162	.242	.332	.296	83	-35	103-26	.957	-4	96	118	O584(48/142/407)		-7.7

MORAN, PAT Patrick Joseph B2.7.1876 Fitchburg MA D3.7.1924 Orlando FL BR/TR/5-10/180 d5.15 M9

1901	Bos N	52	180	12	38	5	1	2	18	3	1		.211	.228	.283	44	-14	9	.973	-2	130	55	C28,1b13,3b4,S3,O3R/2		-1.3
1902	Bos N	80	251	22	60	5	5	1	24	17	6		.239	.303	.311	89	-4	6	**.982**	3	107	99	C71,1b3/OR		0.7
1903	Bos N	109	389	40	102	25	5	7	54	29	11		.262	.331	.406	114	7	8	.967	13	97	**121**	C107/1		2.9
1904	Bos N	113	398	26	90	11	3	4	34	18	4		.226	.267	.299	77	-12	10	.957	1	86	107	C72,3b39,1b2		-0.3

YEAR	TM LG	G	AB	R	H	2B	3B	HR	RBI	BB-IB	HP	SO	AVG	OBP	SLG	AOPS	ABR	SB-CS	FA	FR	RNG	THR	GAMES AT POSITION	DL	BFW
1905	Bos N	85	267	22	64	11	5	2	22	8	3		.240	.270	.341	83	-7	3	**.986**	0	79	99	C78		0.1
1906	†Chi N	70	226	22	57	13	1	0	35	7	2		.252	.281	.319	82	-5	6	.979	8	161	97	C61		1.0
1907	†Chi N	65	198	8	45	5	1	1	19	10	2		.227	.271	.278	68	-8	5	.973	2	112	106	C59		0.0
1908	Chi N	50	150	12	39	5	1	0	12	13	1		.260	.323	.307	97	0	6	.968	-0	110	103	C45		0.5
1909	Chi N	77	246	18	54	11	1	1	23	16	4		.220	.278	.285	73	-8	2	.984	5	128	96	C74		0.5
1910	Phi N	68	199	13	47	7	1	0	11	17	3	16	.236	.306	.281	69	-8	6	.989	-0	94	104	C56		-0.3
1911	Phi N	34	103	2	19	3	0	0	8	3	0	13	.184	.208	.214	18	-12	0	.984	-2	86	104	C32		-1.1
1912	Phi N	13	26	1	3	1	0	0	1	1	0	7	.115	.148	.154	-16	-4	0	.955	-1	89	71	C13		-0.5
1913	Phi N	1	1	0	0	0	0	0	0	0	0	0	.000	.000	.000	-96	0	0	—	0			/H		0.0
1914	Phi N	1	0	0	0	0	0	0	0	0	0	0	—	—	—	—	0	0	—	-0	0	0	/C		0.0
Total	14	818	2634	198	618	102	24	18	262	142	37	36	.235	.283	.312	78	-75	55	.976	27	107	102	C697,3b43,1b19,O4R,S3/2		2.2

MORAN, AL   Richard Alan   B12.5.1938 Detroit MI   BR/TR/6-1.5/190*   d4.9

YEAR	TM LG	G	AB	R	H	2B	3B	HR	RBI	BB-IB	HP	SO	AVG	OBP	SLG	AOPS	ABR	SB-CS	FA	FR	RNG	THR	GAMES AT POSITION	DL	BFW
1963	NY N	119	331	26	64	5	2	1	23	36-1	1	60	.193	.274	.230	46	-23	3-7	.951	-1	105	82	S116/3		-1.8
1964	NY N	16	22	2	5	0	0	0	4	2-0	0	2	.227	.280	.227	50	-1	0-0	.957	1	118	92	S15/3		0.0
Total	2	135	353	28	69	5	2	1	27	38-1	1	62	.195	.274	.229	46	-24	3-7	.951	-0	106	83	S131,3b2		-1.8

MORAN, ROY   Roy Ellis "Deedle"   B9.17.1884 Vincennes IN   D7.18.1966 Atlanta GA   BR/TR/5-8/155   d9.3

YEAR	TM LG	G	AB	R	H	2B	3B	HR	RBI	BB-IB	HP	SO	AVG	OBP	SLG	AOPS	ABR	SB-CS	FA	FR	RNG	THR	GAMES AT POSITION	DL	BFW
1912	Was A	7	13	1	2	0	0	0	0	8	0		.154	.476	.154	82	1	3	.889	-0	73	158	O6(5/1/0)		0.0

MORAN, BILL   William L.   B10.10.1869 Joliet IL   D4.8.1916 Joliet IL   5-10.5/175   d5.7

YEAR	TM LG	G	AB	R	H	2B	3B	HR	RBI	BB-IB	HP	SO	AVG	OBP	SLG	AOPS	ABR	SB-CS	FA	FR	RNG	THR	GAMES AT POSITION	DL	BFW
1892	StL N	24	81	2	11	1	0	0	5	2	0	12	.136	.157	.148	-8	-11	0	.898	-5	96	91	C22,O2L		-1.3
1895	Chi N	15	55	8	9	2	1	1	9	3	1		.164	.220	.291	29	-6	2	.827	-3	94	109	C15		-0.7
Total	2	39	136	10	20	3	1	1	14	5	1	14	.147	.183	.206	10	-17	2	.871	-8	95	99	C37,O2L		-2.0

MORAN, BILLY   William Nelson   B11.27.1933 Montgomery AL   BR/TR/5-11/185*   d4.15

YEAR	TM LG	G	AB	R	H	2B	3B	HR	RBI	BB-IB	HP	SO	AVG	OBP	SLG	AOPS	ABR	SB-CS	FA	FR	RNG	THR	GAMES AT POSITION	DL	BFW
1958	Cle A	115	257	26	58	11	0	1	18	13-1	0	23	.226	.262	.280	51	-18	3-2	.960	3	110	89	2b74,S38		-1.0
1959	Cle A	11	17	1	5	0	0	0	2	0-0	0	1	.294	.294	.294	64	-1	0-0	1.000	-4	103	52	2b6,S5		-0.2
1961	LA A	54	150	17	45	7	1	2	22	17-1	1	16	.260	.328	.347	73	-6	0-0	.966	-4	92	91	2b51,S2		-0.6
1962	LA A★	160	659	90	186	25	3	17	74	39-2	4	80	.282	.324	.407	99	-3	5-1	.986	18	108	92	2b160		2.9
1963	LA A	153	597	67	164	29	5	7	65	31-2	3	57	.275	.310	.375	98	-3	1-1	.973	9	**105**	100	2b151		1.9
1964	LA A	50	198	26	53	10	1	0	11	13-1	1	20	.268	.315	.328	88	-3	1-3	.929	-6	91	59	3b47,2b3/S		-1.1
	Cle A	69	151	14	31	6	0	1	10	18-3	1	16	.205	.291	.265	57	-8	0-1	.972	-1	94	60	3b42,2b15,1b2		-0.9
	Year	119	349	40	84	16	1	1	21	31-4	2	36	.241	.304	.301	73	-12	1-4	.947	-7	92	59	3b89,2b18,1b2/S		-2.0
1965	Cle A	22	24	1	3	0	0	0	0	2-0	1	5	.125	.222	.125	1	-3	0-0	1.000	-0	73	111	2b7/S		-0.3
Total	7	634	2076	242	545	88	10	28	202	133-10	11	218	.263	.308	.355	85	-45	10-8	.976	16	105	93	2b467,3b89,S47,1b2		0.7

MORANDINI, MICKEY   Michael Robert   B4.22.1966 Kittanning PA   BL/TR/5-11/171(167-182)   [PhiN88 5/120]   d9.1   Col Indiana

YEAR	TM LG	G	AB	R	H	2B	3B	HR	RBI	BB-IB	HP	SO	AVG	OBP	SLG	AOPS	ABR	SB-CS	FA	FR	RNG	THR	GAMES AT POSITION	DL	BFW
1990	Phi N	25	79	9	19	4	0	1	3	6-0	0	19	.241	.294	.329	71	-3	3-0	.990	-4	98	78	2b25		-0.6
1991	Phi N	98	325	38	81	11	4	1	20	29-0	2	45	.249	.313	.317	79	-9	13-2	.986	-0	101	91	2b97		-0.5
1992	Phi N	127	422	47	112	8	8	3	30	25-2	0	64	.265	.305	.344	84	-11	8-3	.991	9	106	96	2b124,S3		0.2
1993	†Phi N	120	425	57	105	19	9	3	33	34-2	5	73	.247	.309	.355	79	-14	13-2	.990	-7	96	74	2b111		-1.3
1994	Phi N	87	274	40	80	16	5	2	26	34-5	4	33	.292	.378	.409	103	3	10-5	.985	1	100	85	2b79		0.7
1995	Phi N★	127	494	65	140	34	7	6	49	42-3	9	80	.283	.350	.417	101	1	9-8	.989	2	98	98	2b122		0.9
1996	Phi N	140	539	64	135	24	6	3	32	49-0	9	87	.250	.321	.334	73	-20	26-5	.982	-2	97	105	2b137	15	-1.2
1997	Phi N	150	553	83	163	40	2	1	39	62-0	8	91	.295	.371	.380	99	3	16-13	.990	-16	85	96	2b146/S		-1.0
1998	†Chi N	154	582	93	172	20	4	8	53	72-4	5	84	.296	.380	.385	99	2	13-1	**.993**	-22	92	72	2b152		-2.0
1999	Chi N	144	456	60	110	18	5	4	37	48-2	6	61	.241	.319	.329	65	-24	6-6	.991	-1	101	97	2b132		-2.0
2000	Phi N	91	302	31	76	13	3	0	22	29-1	4	54	.252	.324	.315	63	-17	5-2	.987	-8	88	85	2b85		-0.5
	Tor A	35	107	10	29	2	1	0	7	7-0	0	23	.271	.316	.308	57	-7	1-0	.993	-0	99	123	2b35		-0.3
Total	11	1298	4558	597	1222	209	54	32	351	437-19	56	714	.268	.338	.359	85	-96	123-45	.989	-47	96	91	2b1245,S4	15	-8.1

MORBAN, JOSE   Jose   B10.2.1979 Santiago, D.R.   BR/TR/6-1/170   d4.6

YEAR	TM LG	G	AB	R	H	2B	3B	HR	RBI	BB-IB	HP	SO	AVG	OBP	SLG	AOPS	ABR	SB-CS	FA	FR	RNG	THR	GAMES AT POSITION	DL	BFW
2003	Bal A	61	71	14	10	0	0	2	5	3-0	1	21	.141	.187	.225	8	-10	8-0	1.000	-3	51	121	S14,D13,2b12/3		-1.1

MORDECAI, MIKE   Michael Howard   B12.13.1967 Birmingham AL   BR/TR/5-11/175*   [AtlN89 6/142]   d5.8   Col South Alabama   OF(1/1/2)

YEAR	TM LG	G	AB	R	H	2B	3B	HR	RBI	BB-IB	HP	SO	AVG	OBP	SLG	AOPS	ABR	SB-CS	FA	FR	RNG	THR	GAMES AT POSITION	DL	BFW
1994	Atl N	4	4	1	1	0	0	1	3	1-0	0	0	.250	.400	1.000	240	1	0-0	1.000	-0	105	0	S4		0.0
1995	†Atl N	69	75	10	21	6	0	3	11	9-0	0	16	.280	.353	.480	113	2	0-0	.985	-2	84	165	2b21,1b9,3b6,S6/OC	22	0.0
1996	Atl N	66	108	12	26	5	0	2	8	9-1	0	24	.241	.297	.343	65	-6	1-0	1.000	-2	54	129	3b19,2b4,S4,1b3/ORD		-1.2
1997	Atl N	61	81	8	14	2	1	0	3	6-0	0	16	.173	.227	.222	19	-10	0-1	1.000	-1	93	136	2b20,3b10,S6/1	30	-1.2
1998	Mon N	73	119	12	24	4	2	3	10	9-0	0	20	.202	.258	.345	44	-8	1-0	.953	-6	108	68	S30,2b21,3b11/1		-0.7
1999	Mon N	109	226	29	53	10	2	5	25	20-0	1	31	.235	.297	.363	69	-12	2-5	.962	-1	93	136	2b38,S38,3b32/1		-0.5
2000	Mon N	86	169	20	48	16	0	4	16	12-0	1	34	.284	.335	.450	95	-1	2-2	.937	-1	102	126	3b58,S10,2b9,1b3		-0.8
2001	Mon N	96	254	28	71	17	2	3	32	19-1	5	53	.280	.330	.398	88	-4	2-2	.974	-8	86	33	3b28,2b4,1b3,S3/OL		-0.7
2002	Mon N	55	74	9	15	4	0	0	4	8-3	1	14	.203	.289	.257	46	-6	1-1	.931	-0	98	133	3b28,2b4,1b3,S3/OL		-0.7
	Fla N	38	77	10	22	4	0	0	7	5-1	1	13	.286	.337	.338	85	-2	1-1	.988	-1	105	0	S24,3b7/1		-0.1
	Year	93	151	19	37	8	0	0	11	13-4	2	27	.245	.313	.298	64	-8	2-2	.976	-7	82	171	S14,2b12,3b12/1		-1.1
2003	†Fla N	65	89	11	19	4	0	2	8	8-3	0	21	.213	.276	.326	59	-6	3-0	.929	2	107	226	3b19,2b4,S3/C		-0.3
2004	Fla N	69	84	7	19	3	0	1	5	6-0	0	18	.226	.278	.298	51	-6	0-1	1.000	-0	104	0	/2S		-0.0
2005	Fla N	2	2	0	0	0	0	0	0	0-0	0	1	.000	.000	.000	-99	-1	0-0	1.000	-0	104	0	0		-0.0
Total	12	793	1362	157	333	75	7	24	132	112-9	5	261	.244	.303	.363	72	-59	13-13	.956	-23	91	93	3b244,2b166,S147,1b24,O4R,C2,D2	52	-7.7

MOREHART, RAY   Raymond Anderson   B12.2.1899 Terrell TX   D1.13.1989 Dallas TX   BL/TR/5-9/157   d8.9   Col Austin

YEAR	TM LG	G	AB	R	H	2B	3B	HR	RBI	BB-IB	HP	SO	AVG	OBP	SLG	AOPS	ABR	SB-CS	FA	FR	RNG	THR	GAMES AT POSITION	DL	BFW
1924	Chi A	31	100	10	20	4	2	0	8	17	0	7	.200	.316	.280	56	-6	3-1	.873	-9	92	94	S27,2b2		-1.1
1926	Chi A	73	192	27	61	10	3	0	21	11	1	15	.318	.358	.401	101	0	3-11	.950	-5	103	61	2b48		-0.5
1927	NY A	73	195	45	50	7	2	1	20	29	0	18	.256	.353	.328	80	-5	4-4	.945	1	109	104	2b53		-0.5
Total	3	177	487	82	131	21	7	1	49	57	1	40	.269	.347	.347	83	-11	10-16	.946	-12	105	83	2b103,S27		-2.1

MOREJON, DANNY   Daniel (Torres)   B7.21.1930 Havana, Cuba   BR/TR/6-1/175   d7.11

YEAR	TM LG	G	AB	R	H	2B	3B	HR	RBI	BB-IB	HP	SO	AVG	OBP	SLG	AOPS	ABR	SB-CS	FA	FR	RNG	THR	GAMES AT POSITION	DL	BFW
1958	Cin N	12	26	4	5	0	0	1	1	9-1	0	2	.192	.400	.192	60	-1	1-0	1.000	-1	87		O11(2/6/3)		-0.1

MORELAND, KEITH   Bobby Keith   B5.2.1954 Dallas TX   BR/TR/6-0/200(186-200)   [PhiN75 7/156]   d10.1   Col Texas   OF(119/0/560)

YEAR	TM LG	G	AB	R	H	2B	3B	HR	RBI	BB-IB	HP	SO	AVG	OBP	SLG	AOPS	ABR	SB-CS	FA	FR	RNG	THR	GAMES AT POSITION	DL	BFW
1978	Phi N	1	2	0	0	0	0	0	0	0-0	0	0	.000	.000	.000	-98	-1	0-0	1.000	-1	7	0	/C		-0.0
1979	Phi N	14	48	3	18	3	0	0	8	3-0	0	5	.375	.412	.521	146	3	0-0	1.000	-1	78	105	C13		0.0
1980	†Phi N	62	159	13	50	8	0	4	29	8-2	0	14	.314	.341	.440	111	2	3-1	.967	-1	80	128	C39,3b4,O2R		0.3
1981	†Phi N	61	196	16	50	7	0	6	37	15-1	1	13	.255	.307	.383	91	-3	1-2	.982	-3	72	112	C50,3b7,1b2,O2R		0.2
1982	Chi N	138	476	50	124	17	2	15	68	46-8	3	71	.261	.326	.399	99	-4	0-3	.976	-10	88	69	O151R,C3		-0.6
1983	Chi N	154	533	76	161	30	3	16	70	68-8	3	73	.302	.378	.460	127	0	1-4	.976	-8	89	97	O103(1/0/102),1b29,3b8,C3		-1.1
1984	†Chi N	140	495	59	138	17	3	16	80	34-5	3	71	.279	.326	.422	101	0	1-0	.976	-8	87	103	O148R,1b12,3b11,C2		-1.0
1985	Chi N	161	587	74	180	30	3	14	106	68-7	1	58	.307	.374	.440	117	15	12-3	.976	-8	87	139	O121R,3b24,C13,1b12		2.8
1986	Chi N	156	586	72	159	30	0	12	79	53-10	0	48	.271	.326	.384	90	-7	3-6	.980	-8	84	139	O121R,3b24,C13,1b12		-2.0
1987	Chi N	153	563	63	150	29	1	27	88	39-4	2	66	.266	.309	.465	99	-2	3-3	.934	7	106	102	3b150/1		-2.3
1988	SD N	143	511	40	131	23	0	5	64	40-6	1	51	.256	.305	.331	86	-9	2-3	.994	-2	60	115	1b73,O64L,3b2		-0.3
1989	Det A	90	318	34	95	16	0	5	35	27-5	2	33	.299	.357	.396	114	7	3-2	1.000	-2	60	76	D51,1b31,3b12/C		-0.0
	Bal A	33	107	11	23	4	0	1	10	4-0	0	12	.215	.243	.280	48	-8	0-0	—	0	0	0	D29		-0.0
	Year	123	425	45	118	20	0	6	45	31-5	2	45	.278	.330	.367	98	-1	3-2	1.000	-2	60	76	D80,1b31,3b12/C		-0.6
Total	12	1306	4581	511	1279	214	14	121	674	405-56	13	515	.279	.335	.411	103	17	28-33	.979	-34	89	103	O677R,3b220,C169,1b160,D80		-6.0

MORELOCK, HARRY   A. Harry   B11.1869 Philadelphia PA   d8.21

YEAR	TM LG	G	AB	R	H	2B	3B	HR	RBI	BB-IB	HP	SO	AVG	OBP	SLG	AOPS	ABR	SB-CS	FA	FR	RNG	THR	GAMES AT POSITION	DL	BFW
1891	Phi N	4	14	1	1	0	0	0	0	3		3	.071	.235	.071	-9	-2	0	.824	-2	77		S4		-0.0
1892	Phi N	1	3	0	0	0	0	0	0	1		0	.000	.250	.000	-23	0	0	.600	-1	44		0 /3		-0.0
Total	2	5	17	1	1	0	0	0	0	4		3	.059	.238	.059	-11	-2	0	.824	-3	77		S4/3		-0.0

MORENO, JOSE   Jose De Los Santos (b Jose De Los Santos Mauricio (Moreno))   B11.1.1957 Santo Domingo, D.R.   BB/TR/6-0/175*   d5.24

YEAR	TM LG	G	AB	R	H	2B	3B	HR	RBI	BB-IB	HP	SO	AVG	OBP	SLG	AOPS	ABR	SB-CS	FA	FR	RNG	THR	GAMES AT POSITION	DL	BFW
1980	NY N	37	46	6	9	2	1	2	9	3-2	0	12	.196	.240	.413	82	-2	1-0	.917	2	120	393	2b4,3b4		-0.0
1981	SD N	34	48	5	11	2	0	0	6	1-1	0	8	.229	.245	.271	50	-3	4-1	1.000	1	101	176	O9(4/0/5)/2		-0.0

YEAR	TM LG	G	AB	R	H	2B	3B	HR	RBI	BB-IB	HP	SO	AVG	OBP	SLG	AOPS	ABR	SB-CS	FA	FR	RNG	THR	GAMES AT POSITION	DL	BFW
1982	Cal A	11	3	0	0	0	0	0	0	2-0	0	0	.000	.400	.000		21	0	0-2	1.000	-1	65	0	2b2/D		-0.1
Total	3	82	97	14	20	4	1	2	15	6-3	0	20	.206	.250	.330		66	-5	5-3	1.000	3	101	176	O9(4/0/5),2b7,3b4/D		-0.3

MORENO, OMAR   Omar Renan (Quintero)   B10.24.1952 Puerto Armuelles, Pan   BL/TL/6-2/180(170-188)   d9.6

YEAR	TM LG	G	AB	R	H	2B	3B	HR	RBI	BB-IB	HP	SO	AVG	OBP	SLG	AOPS	ABR	SB-CS	FA	FR	RNG	THR	GAMES AT POSITION	DL	BFW
1975	Pit N	6	6	1	1	0	0	0	0	1-0	0	1	.167	.286	.167		28	-1	1-0	.000	-1	0	0	/OL		
1976	Pit N	48	122	24	33	4	1	2	12	16-0	1	24	.270	.357	.369		105	1	15-5	.960	1	111	146	O42C		-0.1
1977	Pit N	150	492	69	118	19	9	7	34	38-5	1	102	.240	.295	.358		72	-21	53-16	.977	5	109	113	O147C		0.4
1978	Pit N	155	515	95	121	15	7	2	33	81-4	3	104	.235	.339	.303		78	-13	71-22	.984	5	108	110	O152C		-1.2
1979	†Pit N	162	695	110	196	21	12	8	69	51-9	3	104	.282	.333	.381		89	-11	77-21	.975	5	111	88	O162C		-0.1
1980	Pit N	**162**	676	87	168	20	**13**	2	36	57-11	2	101	.249	.306	.325		75	-24	96-33	.990	11	110	133	O162C		0.2
1981	Pit N	103	434	62	120	18	8	1	35	26-4	3	76	.276	.319	.362		89	-7	39-14	.997	2	107	81	O103C		-0.4
1982	Pit N	158	645	82	158	18	9	3	44	44-2	1	121	.245	.292	.315		67	-29	60-26	.983	1	104	108	O157C		-0.2
1983	Hou N	97	405	48	98	12	11	0	25	22-3	1	72	.242	.282	.326		72	-18	30-13	.977	3	102	171	O97C		-2.7
	NY A	48	152	17	38	9	1	1	17	8-0	0	31	.250	.287	.342		75	-5	7-3	.992	-1	100	37	O48C		-1.5
1984	NY A	117	355	37	92	12	6	4	38	18-1	1	48	.259	.294	.361		84	-9	20-11	.985	-1	96	138	O108C/D		-1.1
1985	NY A	34	66	12	13	4	1	1	4	1-0	0	16	.197	.209	.333		46	-5	1-1	1.000	3	132	184	O26(3/19/4)/D		-0.2
	KC A	24	70	9	17	1	3	2	12	3-0	1	8	.243	.280	.429		91	-1	0-1	1.000	-3	67	83	O21(0/13/8)		-0.5
	Year	58	136	21	30	5	4	3	16	4-0	1	24	.221	.246	.382		70	-7	1-2	1.000	0	99	132	O47(3/32/12)/D		-0.7
1986	Atl N	118	359	46	84	18	6	4	27	21-2	0	77	.234	.276	.351		69	-16	17-16	.970	0	95	127	O97(18/12/71)		-2.3
Total	12	1382	4992	699	1257	171	87	37	386	387-41	17	885	.252	.306	.343		78	-159	487-182	.982	30	105	114	O1323(22/1221/83),D2		-10.4

MORGAN, CHET   Chester Collins "Chick"   B6.6.1910 Cleveland MS   D9.20.1991 Pasadena TX   BL/TR/5-9/160   d4.19

1935	Det A	14	23	2	4	0	0	0	1	5	0	0	.174	.321	.217		43	-2	0-0	.909	-0	110	0	O4L		-0.2
1938	Det A	74	306	50	87	6	1	0	27	20	1	12	.284	.330	.310		58	-20	5-6	.980	-2	96	85	O74(6/68/0)		-2.3
Total	2	88	329	52	91	7	1	0	28	25	1	12	.277	.330	.304		57	-22	5-6	.977	-2	97	80	O78(10/68/0)		-2.5

MORGAN, DAN   Daniel   B5.1853 MO   D1.30.1910 St.Louis MO   d5.4 ▲

| 1875 | RS NA | **19** | 69 | 11 | 18 | 4 | 0 | 0 | | 5 | | 4 | .261 | .311 | .319 | | 132 | 3 | 2-1 | .824 | -4 | 79 | 0 | O10(3/7/0),P7,3b7 | | -0.1 |
| 1878 | Mil N | 14 | 56 | 2 | 11 | 0 | 0 | 0 | | 3 | | 9 | .196 | .237 | .196 | | 41 | -4 | | .769 | -4 | 47 | 0 | O13(0/1/12),3b3/2 | | -0.7 |

MORGAN, ED   Edward Carre   B5.22.1904 Cairo IL   D4.9.1980 New Orleans LA   BR/TR/6-0.5/180   d4.11   Col Tulane

1928	Cle A	76	265	42	83	24	6	4	54	21	1	17	.313	.366	.494		123	8	5-5	.968	2	124	122	1b36,O21(0/18/3),3b14		0.8
1929	Cle A	93	318	60	101	19	10	3	37	37	2	24	.318	.392	.469		116	8	4-3	.908	-8	74	108	O80R		-0.6
1930	Cle A	150	584	122	204	47	11	26	136	62	1	66	.349	.413	.601		148	42	8-4	.987	-1	107	103	1b129,O19R		2.9
1931	Cle A	131	462	87	162	33	4	11	86	83	1	46	.351	.451	.511		144	35	4-5	.984	2	112	107	1b117,3b3		2.3
1932	Cle A	144	532	96	156	32	7	4	68	94	3	44	.293	.402	.402		102	6	7-6	.985	-10	81	81	1b142/3		-1.6
1933	Cle A	39	121	10	32	3	3	1	13	7	0	9	.264	.305	.364		73	-5	1-1	.997	2	128	65	1b32/OL		-0.6
1934	Bos A	138	528	95	141	28	4	3	79	81	2	46	.267	.367	.352		80	-13	7-1	.988	-6	80	94	1b137		-2.9
Total	7	771	2810	512	879	186	45	52	473	385	10	252	.313	.398	.467		117	81	36-25	.986	-18	97	97	1b593,O121(1/18/102),3b18		0.3

MORGAN, EDDIE   Edwin Willis "Pepper"   B11.19.1914 Brady Lake OH   D6.27.1982 Lakewood OH   BL/TL/5-10/160   d4.14   Col Miami-Ohio

1936	StL N	8	18	4	5	0	1	1	8	4	0	4	.278	.350	.444		113	0	0	.889	-1	102	0	O4R		0.0
1937	Bro N	31	48	4	9	3	0	1	5	9	0	7	.188	.316	.250		55	-3	0	.984	-2	24	83	1b7,O7(1/1/5)		-0.5
Total	2	39	66	8	14	3	1	2	13	13	0	11	.212	.325	.303		70	-3	0	.842	-2	90	123	O11(1/1/9),1b7		-0.5

MORGAN, BILL   Henry William   B10.1857 Washington DC   d8.17

1882	Pit AA	17	66	10	17	2	1	0		4			.258	.300	.318		114	1		.688	-6	0	418	O11R,C7		-0.4
1884	Ric AA	6	20	0	2	0	0	0		1	0		.100	.143	.100		-20	-3		.850	-2			C3,O2R/2		-0.4
	Bal U	2	9	1	2	0	0	0		1			.222	.300	.222		55	-1		.909	-1			/C2OR		-0.1
Total	2	25	95	11	21	2	1	0		6			.221	.267	.263		78	-3		.727	-9			O14R,C11,2b2		-0.9

MORGAN, RED   James Edward   B10.6.1883 Neola IA   D3.25.1981 New York NY   BR/TR   d6.20   Col Georgetown

| 1906 | Bos A | 88 | 307 | 20 | 66 | 6 | 3 | 1 | 21 | 16 | 7 | | .215 | .270 | .264 | | 67 | -12 | 7 | .866 | -11 | 82 | 98 | 3b88 | | -2.3 |

MORGAN, JOE   Joe Leonard   B9.19.1943 Bonham TX   BL/TR/5-7/160(148-165)   d9.21   HF1990

1963	Hou N	8	25	5	6	0	1	0	3	5-0	0	5	.240	.367	.320		106	0	1-0	.909	-2	83	57	2b7		-0.1
1964	Hou N	10	37	4	7	0	0	0	0	6-0	0	7	.189	.302	.189		44	-3	0-1	.949	-2	77	64	2b10		-0.5
1965	Hou N	157	601	100	163	22	12	14	40	**97**-1	3	77	.271	.373	.418		132	29	20-9	.969	-7	99	81	2b157		3.8
1966	Hou N*	122	425	60	121	14	8	5	42	89-3	2	43	.285	.410	.391		134	25	11-8	.965	-17	91	79	2b117	40	1.9
1967	Hou N	133	494	73	136	27	11	6	42	81-5	2	51	.275	.378	.411		131	23	29-5	.979	1	97	77	2b130/OL		4.2
1968	Hou N	10	20	6	5	1	0	0	0	7-0	0	4	.250	.444	.350		142	2	3-0	.882	-4	44	64	2b5/OL	119	-0.1
1969	Hou N*	147	535	94	126	18	5	15	43	110-1	1	74	.236	.365	.372		109	11	49-14	.972	3	90	95	2b132,O14(12/2/0)		2.9
1970	Hou N*	144	548	102	147	28	9	8	52	102-3	1	55	.268	.383	.396		114	15	42-13	.979	11	106	101	2b142		3.9
1971	Hou N	160	583	87	149	27	**11**	13	56	88-2	1	52	.256	.351	.407		118	16	40-8	.986	-7	100	89	2b157		2.7
1972	†Cin N*	149	552	**122**	161	23	4	16	73	**115**-1	6	44	.292	**.417**	.435		150	49	58-17	**.990**	-6	100	103	2b149		5.8
1973	†Cin N*	157	576	116	167	35	2	26	82	111-3	4	61	.290	.406	.493		155	49	67-15	.990	5	102	109	2b154		7.4
1974	†Cin N*	149	512	107	150	31	3	22	67	120-8	3	69	.293	**.427**	.494		160	49	58-12	.982	2	97	110	2b142		7.0
1975	†Cin N*	146	498	107	163	27	6	17	94	**132**-3	3	52	.327	**.466**	.508		**169**	**57**	67-10	**.986**	2	103	112	2b142		8.1
1976	†Cin N*	141	472	113	151	30	5	27	111	114-8	1	41	.320	**.444**	**.576**		**186**	**60**	60-9	.981	-4	87	104	2b133		6.7
1977	Cin N*	153	521	113	150	21	6	22	78	117-2	5	58	.288	.417	.478		137	34	49-10	**.993**	-3	89	117	2b151		4.6
1978	Cin N*	132	441	68	104	27	0	13	75	79-3	2	40	.236	.347	.385		106	7	19-5	.980	-23	85	69	2b124		-0.7
1979	†Cin N*	127	436	70	109	26	1	9	32	93-11	2	45	.250	.379	.376		108	10	28-6	.980	-12	93	101	2b121		0.9
1980	†Hou N	141	461	66	112	17	5	11	49	**93**-6	0	47	.243	.367	.373		118	15	24-6	.988	-11	92	96	2b130		-1.4
1981	SF N	90	308	47	74	16	1	8	31	66-7	3	37	.240	.371	.377		117	10	14-5	.991	-4	97	112	2b87		1.4
1982	SF N	134	463	68	134	19	4	14	61	85-4	2	60	.289	.400	.438		136	27	24-4	.989	-3	102	94	2b120,3b3		3.5
1983	†Phi N	123	404	72	93	20	1	16	59	89-1	4	54	.230	.370	.403		116	13	18-2	.971	17	107	96	2b117		4.1
1984	Oak A	116	365	50	89	21	0	6	43	66-4	1	39	.244	.356	.351		104	6	8-3	.977	-16	85	98	2b100,D5	15	-0.4
Total	22	2649	9277	1650	2517	449	96	268	1133	1865-76	40	1015	.271	.392	.427		133	499	689-162	.981	-89	96	97	2b2527,O16(14/2/0),D5,3b3	174	68.5

MORGAN, JOE   Joseph Michael   B11.19.1930 Walpole MA   BL/TR/5-10/170*   d4.14   M4/C5   Col Boston College

1959	Mil N	13	23	2	5	1	0	0	3	2-0	0	4	.217	.280	.261		49	-2	0-0	.913	-2	91	34	2b7		-0.3
	KC A	20	21	2	4	0	0	0	3	3-0	0	4	.190	.292	.286		58	-1	0-0	1.000	-0	82	0	3b2		-0.2
1960	Phi N	26	83	5	11	2	0	2	6	6-1	0	11	.133	.191	.205		8	-11	0-0	.971	1	106	79	3b24		-1.0
	Cle A	22	47	6	14	2	0	2	4	6-0	0	4	.298	.377	.468		131	2	0-0	.889	-0	109	47	3b12,O2R		0.2
1961	Cle A	4	10	0	2	0	0	0	0	1-0	0	3	.200	.273	.200		29	-1	0-0	1.000	-0	106	0	O2C		-0.1
1964	StL N	3	3	0	0	0	0	0	0	0-0	0	2	.000	.000	.000		-92	-1	0-0	—	0			/H		-0.1
Total	4	88	187	15	36	5	3	2	10	18-1	0	21	.193	.263	.283		49	-14	0-0	.944	-1	106	66	3b38,2b7,O4(0/2/2)		-1.5

MORGAN, KEVIN   Kevin Lee   B3.3.1970 Lafayette LA   BR/TR/6-1/170   [DetA91 30/790]   d6.15   Col Southeastern Louisiana

| 1997 | NY N | 1 | 1 | 0 | 0 | 0 | 0 | 0 | 0 | 0-0 | 0 | 0 | .000 | .000 | .000 | | -99 | -0 | 0-0 | 1.000 | 0 | 235 | 0 | /3 | | 0.0 |

MORGAN, RAY   Raymond Caryll   B6.14.1889 Baltimore MD   D2.15.1940 Baltimore MD   BR/TR/5-8.5/155   d8.7

1911	Was A	25	89	11	19	2	0	0	5	4	0		.213	.247	.236		36	-8	2	.900	-2	95	31	3b25		-0.9
1912	Was A	81	273	40	65	10	4	0	30	29	3		.238	.318	.337		87	-5	12	.939	-9	87	90	2b76,S4/3		-1.3
1913	Was A	138	481	58	131	19	8	0	57	68	6	63	.272	.369	.345		107	7	19	.950	-8	93	**141**	2b134,S4		0.2
1914	Was A	147	491	50	126	22	8	1	49	62	4	34	.257	.352	.340		104	5	24-17	.948	-13	90	**128**	2b146		-0.7
1915	Was A	62	193	21	45	5	4	0	21	30	2	15	.233	.342	.301		91	-1	6-5	.965	-3	100	114	2b57,S2,3b2		-0.4
1916	Was A	99	315	41	84	12	4	1	29	59	10	29	.267	.398	.340		123	14	14	.957	-11	94	104	2b82,S9,1b3/3		0.4
1917	Was A	101	338	32	90	9	1	1	33	40	1	26	.266	.346	.308		101	2	7	.961	-8	88	113	2b95,3b3		-0.5
1918	Was A	88	300	25	70	11	4	0	30	28	6	14	.233	.311	.277		79	-7	4	.959	-8	88	92	2b80,O2R		-0.5
Total	8	741	2480	278	630	90	33	4	254	320	38	184	.254	.348	.322		98	7	88-22	.953	-61	92	115	2b670,3b32,S19,1b3,O2R		-4.8

MORGAN, BOBBY   Robert Morris   B6.29.1926 Oklahoma City OK   BR/TR/5-9/175*   d4.18

1950	Bro N	67	199	38	45	10	3	7	21	32	3	43	.226	.342	.412		95	-1	0	.969	8	122	154	3b52,S10		0.7
1952	†Bro N	67	191	36	45	8	0	7	16	46	3	35	.236	.392	.387		115	7	2-2	.968	1	108	121	3b60,2b5,S4		0.7
1953	†Bro N	69	196	35	51	6	2	7	33	33	1	47	.260	.370	.418		103	2	2-2	.920	-2	98	99	3b36,S21		0.0
1954	Phi N	135	455	58	119	25	2	14	50	70	0	68	.262	.357	.418		104	2	3-1	.954	-19	93	91	S129,3b8,2b5		-0.5

YEAR	TM LG	G	AB	R	H	2B	3B	HR	RBI	BB-IB	HP	SO	AVG	OBP	SLG	AOPS	ABR	SB-CS	FA	FR	RNG	THR	GAMES AT POSITION	DL	BFW
1955	Phi N	136	483	61	112	20	2	10	49	73-0	0	72	.232	.331	.344	81	-11	6-4	.980	-17	87	87	2b88,S41,3b6/1		-1.9
1956	Phi N	8	25	1	5	0	0	0	1	6-0	0	4	.200	.355	.200	56	-1	0-0	.857	-1	94	101	3b5,2b3		-0.6
	StL N	61	113	14	22	7	0	3	20	15-0	0	24	.195	.287	.336	67	-5	0-2	.980	-1	101	52	2b13,3b11,S6		-0.8
	Year	69	138	15	27	7	0	3	21	21-0	0	28	.196	.300	.312	65	-6	0-2	.877	-1	102	70	3b16,2b16,S6		
1957	Phi N	2	0	0	0	0	0	0	0	0-0	0	0	—	—	—	—	0	0-0	1.000	-0	0	0	/2		-0.5
	Chi N	125	425	43	88	20	2	5	27	52-1	1	87	.207	.294	.299	61	-23	5-0	.976	8	110	80	2b116,3b12		-0.5
	Year	127	425	43	88	20	2	5	27	52-1	1	87	.207	.294	.299	61	-23	5-0	.976	8	**110**	80	2b117,3b12		0.0
1958	Chi N	1	0	0	0	0	0	0	0	0-0	1	0	.000	.000	.000	-99	0	0-0	—	0			/H		0.0
Total	8	671	2088	286	487	96	11	53	217	327-1	8	381	.233	.338	.366	88	-29	18-11	.978	-24	100	80	2b231,S211,3b190/1		-2.3

MORGAN, VERN Vernon Thomas B8.8.1928 Emporia VA D11.8.1975 Minneapolis MN BL/TR/6-1/190* d8.10 C7 Col Richmond

1954	Chi N	24	64	3	15	2	0	0	2	1-0	0	10	.234	.242	.266	33	-6	0-0	.895	-3	91	38	3b15		-0.9
1955	Chi N	7	7	1	1	0	0	0	1	3-0	0	4	.143	.400	.143	52	0	0-0	.667	-1	62	0	3b2		-0.1
Total	2	31	71	4	16	2	0	0	3	4-0	0	14	.225	.263	.254	36	-6	0-0	.864	-4	88	34	3b17		-1.0

MORGAN, BILL William B1856 Brooklyn NY D9.7.1908 New York NY d8.6

1883	Pit AA	32	114	12	18	2	1	0		7			.158	.207	.193	31	-8		.825	-2	93	58	S21,O6(1/4/1),C5,2b2		-0.8
1884	Was AA	45	162	8	28	1	1	0		8	1		.173	.216	.191	39	-10		.781	-4	70	92	O31(17/2/13),C12,2b2,S2		-1.2
Total	2	77	276	20	46	3	2	0		15	1		.167	.212	.192	35	-18		.771	-6	64	84	O37(18/6/14),S23,C17,2b4		

MORHARDT, MOE Meredith Goodwin B1.16.1937 Manchester CT BL/TL/6-1/185* d9.7 Col Connecticut

1961	Chi N	7	18	3	5	0	0	0	1	3-0	0	5	.278	.381	.278	78	0	0-0	.962	-1	65	157	1b7		-0.2
1962	Chi N	18	16	1	2	0	0	0	2	2-0	0	8	.125	.222	.125	-4	-2	0-0	—	0			/H		-0.2
Total	2	25	34	4	7	0	0	0	3	5-0	0	13	.206	.308	.206	39	-2	0-0	.962	-1	65	157	1b7		-0.4

MORIARITY, GENE Eugene John B7.5.1855 Holyoke MA BL/TL/5-8/130 d6.18 ▲

1884	Bos N	4	16	1	1	0	0	0	0	0	0	8	.063	.063	.063	-61	-3		.714	-0	131	0	O4(1/3/0)		-0.3
	Ind AA	10	37	4	8	0	2	0	4	0	0		.216	.216	.324	54	-1		.769	-1	76	0	O7R,P2/3		-0.2
1885	Det N	11	39	1	1	0	0	0	0	0	0	10	.026	.026	.051	-75	-7		.905	-0	59	0	O6(1/0/5),3b4/SP		-0.7
1892	StL N	47	177	20	31	4	1	3	19	4	3	37	.175	.207	.260	43	-13	7	.820	1	114	0	O47L		-1.6
Total	3	72	269	26	41	5	3	3	23	4	55	.152	.174	.227	24	-24	7	.822	-1	104	0	O64(49/3/12),3b5,P3/S		-2.8

MORIARTY, ED Edward Jerome B10.12.1912 Holyoke MA D9.29.1991 Holyoke MA BR/TR/5-10.5/180 d6.21 Col Holy Cross

1935	Bos N	8	34	4	11	2	1	1	0	0	6	.324	.324	.529	136	-1	0	.923	-3	103	0	2b8		-0.1
1936	Bos N	6	6	1	1	0	0	0	0	0	1	.167	.167	.167	-11	-1	0	—	0			/H		-0.1
Total	2	14	40	5	12	2	1	1	0	0	7	.300	.300	.475	114	0	0	.923	-3	103	0	2b8		-0.2

MORIARTY, GEORGE George Joseph B6.7.1884 Chicago IL D4.8.1964 Miami FL BR/TR/6-0/185 d9.27 M2/U22 b-Bill

1903	Chi N	1	5	1	0	0	0	0	0	0	0	.000	.000	.000	-99	-1	0	1.000	-0	39	0	/3		-0.2
1904	Chi N	4	13	0	0	0	0	0	0	1	0	.000	.071	.000	-77	-3	0	.778	-1	66	0	3b2,O2C		-0.2
1906	NY A	65	197	22	46	7	0	0	23	17	1	.234	.298	.340	90	-3	8	.912	-0	98	82	3b39,O15(14/2/0),1b5/2		-0.2
1907	NY A	126	437	51	121	16	5	0	43	25	3	.277	.320	.336	101	0	28	.899	-9	93	81	3b91,1b22,O9(1/4/3),2b8/S		0.0
1908	NY A	101	348	25	82	12	1	0	27	11	5	.236	.269	.276	76	-9	22	.976	7	85	108	1b52,3b28,O10(8/0/2),2b4		0.1
1909	†Det A	133	473	43	129	20	4	1	39	24	7	.273	.309	.338	100	-1	34	**.939**	-1	**111**	84	3b106,1b24		0.5
1910	Det A	136	490	53	123	24	3	2	60	33	7	.251	.308	.324	92	-4	33	.927	1	**107**	80	3b134		-2.0
1911	Det A	130	478	51	116	20	4	1	60	27	3	.243	.287	.308	63	-25	28	.929	-5	104	57	3b129/1		-1.9
1912	Det A	105	375	38	93	23	1	0	54	26	11	.248	.316	.315	83	-7	30	.987	-1	65	52	1b71,3b33		-1.4
1913	Det A	104	347	29	83	5	2	0	30	24	7	25	.239	.302	.265	67	-14	33	.956	16	**125**	91	3b126,1b3		1.3
1914	Det A	132	465	56	118	19	5	1	40	39	5	27	.254	.318	.323	90	-6	34-15	.875	-0	115	101	3b12/12OC		-0.7
1915	Det A	31	34	2	8	0	0	0	4	0	1	.200	.429	.200	88	-1	1-1	1.000	0	740	0	/13		0.0
1916	Chi A	7	5	1	0	0	0	0	0	1	0	.000	.167	.000	-46	-1	0-0	.931	-0	108	79	3b796,1b180,O44(30/9/5),2b14/S		-5.2
Total	13	1075	3671	372	920	147	32	5	376	234	44	59	.251	.303	.312	84	-74	251-16	.931	-0	108	79	3b796,1b180,O44(30/9/5),2b14/S		

MORIARTY, MIKE Michael Thomas B3.8.1974 Camden NJ BR/TR/6-0/195 [MinA95 7/184] d4.11 Col Seton Hall

2002	Bal A	8	16	0	3	1	0	0	3	0-0	1	2	.188	.188	.250	16	-2	0-1	1.000	3	146	0	S4,2b2/3		-0.2

MORIARTY, BILL William Joseph B8.1883 Chicago IL D12.25.1916 Elgin IL BR/TR/6-2/180 d4.29 b-George

1909	Cin N	6	20	1	4	0	0	1	0	0	0	.200	.200	.250	40	-1	0	.944	-0	84	89	S6		-0.1

MORLEY, BILL William M. (b William Morley Jennings) B1.23.1890 Holland MI D5.14.1985 Lubbock TX BR/TR/5-11/170 d9.8

1913	Was A	2	3	0	0	0	0	0	0	0	0	.000	.000	.000	-98	-0	0	—	-0	0	0	/2		-0.1

MORMAN, RUSS Russell Lee B4.28.1962 Independence MO BR/TR/6-4/220* [ChiA83 1/28] d8.3 Col Wichita St.

1986	Chi A	49	159	18	40	5	0	4	17	16-0	2	36	.252	.324	.358	84	-4	1-0	.989	-4	72	85	1b47		-1.2
1988	Chi A	40	75	8	18	2	0	3	9	3-0	0	17	.240	.269	.267	51	-5	0-0	.981	-3	65	83	1b22,O10L,D3		-0.7
1989	Chi A	37	58	5	13	2	0	0	6	6-1	0	16	.224	.292	.259	59	-3	1-0	.988	-1	94	116	1b35/D		-0.5
1990	KC A	12	37	5	10	4	2	1	3	3-0	0	5	.270	.317	.568	147	2	0-0	1.000	0	57	238	O8L,1b3/D		0.2
1991	KC A	12	23	1	6	0	0	1	1	1-1	0	5	.261	.292	.261	54	-2	0-0	1.000	0	81	47	1b8,O2L/D		0.1
1994	Fla N	13	33	2	7	0	1	1	2	2-0	1	12	.212	.278	.364	63	-2	0-0	.955	-1	83	0	O18(6/0/12),1b3	21	-0.3
1995	Fla N	34	72	9	20	2	0	3	8	2-0	1	9	.278	.316	.458	94	1	0-0	1.000	0	535	0	1b2		0.3
1996	Fla N	6	6	0	1	0	0	0	0	1-0	0	3	.167	.286	.333	64	0	0-0	1.000	0	1726	0	O2R/1		0.0
1997	Fla N	4	7	3	2	1	0	1	2	0-0	0	1	.286	.286	.857	193	2	1-0	.989	-8	87	95	1b129,O40(26/0/14),D6	21	-0.2
Total	9	207	470	51	117	17	4	10	43	35-2	4	102	.249	.304	.366	81	-13	3-1	.989	-8	87	95	1b129,O40(26/0/14),D6		

MORNEAU, JUSTIN Justin Ernest George B5.15.1981 New Westminster BC, Can. BL/TR/6-4/200(200-230) [MinA99 3/89] d6.10

2003	Min A	40	106	14	24	4	0	4	9-1		0	20	.226	.287	.377	71	-5	0-0	.971	0	152	32	D23,1b7		-0.5
2004	†Min A	74	280	39	76	17	0	19	58	28-8	2	54	.271	.340	.536	120	8	0-2	.995	1	106	113	1b61,D11	15	-1.3
2005	Min A	141	490	62	117	23	4	22	79	44-8	4	94	.239	.304	.437	92	-7	0-2	.994	3	106	120	1b138/D	15	-0.8
Total	3	255	876	115	217	44	4	45	153	81-17	6	178	.248	.313	.461	99	-4	0-2	.994	3	107	116	1b206,D35		

MORONKO, JEFF Jeffrey Robert B8.17.1959 Houston TX BR/TR/6-2/190* [CleA80 6/140] d9.1 Col Texas Wesleyan

1984	Cle A	7	19	1	3	0	0	0	3	3-0	0	5	.158	.273	.211	35	-2	0-0	.895	-0	69	190	3b6/D		-0.1
1987	NY A	7	11	0	1	0	0	0	0	0-0	1	2	.091	.167	.091	-2	-2	0-0	1.000	-0	141	0	3b3,S2,O2(1/0/1)		-0.1
Total	2	14	30	1	4	0	0	0	3	3-0	1	7	.133	.235	.167	12	-4	0-0	.926	-0	91	132	3b9,O2(1/0/1),S2/D		-0.2

MORRILL, JOHN John Francis "Honest John" B2.19.1855 Boston MA D4.2.1932 Brookline MA BR/TR/5-10.5/155 d4.24 M8 OF(2/12/12) ▲

1876	Bos N	66	278	38	73	5	2	0	26	3		5	.263	.270	.295	87	-4		.857	5	110	133	2b37,C23,O5(1/3/1),1b3		0.1
1877	Bos N	**61**	242	47	73	5	1	0	28	6		15	.302	.319	.331	101	0		.864	-9	76	36	3b30,1b18,O11R,2b3		-0.1
1878	Bos N	60	233	26	56	5	1	0	23	5		16	.240	.256	.270	68	-9		.957	2	130	**139**	1b59/OC3		0.8
1879	Bos N	**84**	348	56	98	18	5	0	49	14		32	.282	.309	.362	118	7		.878	1	87	34	3b51,1b33		1.0
1880	Bos N	**86**	342	51	81	16	8	2	44	11		37	.237	.261	.348	108	3		.966	-7	138	76	1b74,2b4,P3,3b2		-0.1
1881	Bos N	81	311	47	90	19	3	1	39	12		30	.289	.316	.379	123	9		.964	-2	76	73	1b76,S3,2b2/OC3		-0.1
1882	Bos N	83	349	73	101	19	11	2	54	18		29	.289	.324	.424	137	14		**.974**	-1	76	93	1b81,O7C,3b6,S2,2b2,P2,M		0.7
1883	Bos N	97	404	83	129	33	16	6	68	15		68	.319	.344	.525	155	26		.971	2	125	96	1b91,2b17,P7,3b2/OLM		1.2
1884	Bos N	111	438	80	114	19	7	3	61	30		78	.226	.334	.343	124	15		.969	-0	103	108	1b92,2b17,3b2,M		-0.1
1885	Bos N	111	394	74	89	20	7	4	44	64		81	.247	.333	.381	120	13	9	.895	-8	87	78	S55,1b42,2b20/PM		-1.0
1886	Bos N	117	430	86	106	25	6	7	69	56		81	.247	.333	.381	120	13	9	.895	-8	87	78	1b127,M		-0.1
1887	Bos N	**127**	504	79	141	32	6	12	81	37	1	86	.280	.332	.438	110	7	19	.984	9	**147**	104	1b133,2b2,M		1.7
1888	Bos N	135	486	60	96	18	4	4	39	55	2	68	.198	.282	.288	80	-9	21	.980	-1	104	60	1b40,3b3/2PM		-0.5
1889	Was N	44	146	20	27	4	0	2	16	30	1	23	.185	.328	.260	70	-1	0	.750	-1	88	0	/S1		-0.4
1890	Bos P	7	1	1	0	0	0	0	2	1			.143	.333	.143	28	-1	0	1.000	0	80	0	/1		0.0
Total	15	1265	4912	821	1275	239	80	43	643	358	4	656	.260	.310	.367	111	72	61	.971	11	124	101	1b916,3b138,2b105,S61,O26C,C23,P18		

MORRIS, DOYT Doyt Theodore B7.15.1916 Stanley NC D7.4.1984 Gastonia NC BR/TR/6-4/195 d6.6 Col Wake Forest

1937	Phi A	6	13	2	2	0	0	0	0	0-0	0	3	.154	.154	.154	-23	-3	0-0	1.000	0	111	0	O3(2/1/0)		-0.2

MORRIS, E. E. B Trenton NJ d9.11

1884	Bal U	1	3	0	0	0	0	0	0	0			.000	.000	.000	-91	-1		—	-0	0	0	/OCP		

YEAR	TM LG	G	AB	R	H	2B	3B	HR	RBI	BB-IB	HP	SO	AVG	OBP	SLG	AOPS	ABR	SB-CS	FA	FR	RNG	THR	GAMES AT POSITION	DL	BFW

MORRIS, JOHN John Daniel B2.23.1961 N.Bellmore NY BL/TL/6-1/185* [KCA82 1/10] d8.5 Col Seton Hall

1986	StL N	39	100	8	24	0	1	1	14	7-2	0	15	.240	.287	.290	60	-6	6-2	.986	2	130	0	O31(5/4/26)		-0.5
1987	†StL N	101	157	22	41	6	4	3	23	11-4	1	22	.261	.314	.408	87	-4	5-2	.989	0	113	0	O74(2/8/68)		-0.5
1988	StL N	20	38	3	11	2	1	0	3	1-0	0	7	.289	.308	.395	99	0	0-0	.857	-2	65	0	O16(11/3/2)		
1989	StL N	96	117	8	28	4	1	2	14	4-0	0	22	.239	.264	.342	70	-5	1-0	1.000	-2	94	0	O51(10/11/32)	151	-0.3
1990	StL N	18	18	0	2	0	0	0	0	3-0	0	6	.111	.238	.111	-1	-2	0-0	1.000	-0	87	0	O6(0/1/5)		-0.8
1991	Phi N	85	127	15	28	2	1	1	6	12-4	1	25	.220	.293	.276	61	-7	2-0	1.000	-1	104	51	O57(11/27/24)	121	-0.3
1992	Cal A	43	57	4	11	1	0	1	3	4-1	1	11	.193	.258	.263	46	-4	1-0	1.000	-1	94	0	O14(5/0/9),D6	18	-0.8
Total	7	402	614	60	145	15	8	8	63	42-11	3	108	.236	.288	.326	69	-28	15-4	.981	-3	106	12	O249(44/54/166),D6	290	-3.7

MORRIS, WALTER John Walter B1.31.1880 Rockwall TX D8.2.1961 Dallas TX BR/TR/5-11/? d8.31 Col Texas

1908	StL N	23	73	1	13	1	1	0	2	0		0	.178	.178	.219	28	-6	1	.938	2	103	109	S23		-0.4

MORRIS, P. P. B Rockford IL d5.14

1884	Was U	1	3	0	0	0	0	0	0				.000	.000	.000	-99	-1		.750	-0	113	0	/S		-0.1

MORRIS, WARREN Warren Randall B1.11.1974 Alexandria LA BL/TR/5-11/180* [TexA96 5/143] d4.5 Col Louisiana St.

1999	Pit N	147	511	65	147	20	3	15	73	59-3	2	88	.288	.360	.427	99	-1	3-7	.979	3	104	111	2b144		0.7
2000	Pit N	144	528	68	137	31	2	3	43	65-3	2	78	.259	.341	.343	74	-20	7-10	.979	19	114	97	2b134		0.4
2001	Pit N	48	103	6	21	6	0	2	11	3-0	2	9	.204	.239	.320	42	-9	2-3	.965	2	122	105	2b29/3	19	-0.7
2002	Min A	4	7	0	0	0	0	0	0	0-0	0	1	.000	.000	.000	-97	-2	0-0	1.000	0	117	91	2b4		
2003	Det A	97	346	37	94	13	2	6	33	23-1	1	42	.272	.316	.373	85	-8	4-2	.987	12	111	138	2b89		-0.2
Total	5	440	1495	176	399	70	7	26	164	150-7	7	218	.267	.334	.375	82	-40	16-22	.980	36	110	112	2b400/3	19	1.0

MORRIS, HAL William Harold B4.9.1965 Fort Rucker AL BL/TL/6-4/215(195-215) [NYA86 8/210] d7.29 Col Michigan

1988	NY A	15	20	1	2	0	0	0	0	0	0	9	.100	.100	.100	-44	-4	0-0	1.000	0	125	0	O4(3/0/2)/D		-0.4
1989	NY A	15	18	2	5	0	0	0	4	1-0	0	4	.278	.316	.278	69	-1	0-0	1.000	-0	109	0	O5(2/0/3),1b2/D		-0.1
1990	†Cin N	107	309	50	105	22	3	7	36	21-4	1	32	.340	.381	.498	135	15	9-3	.995	1	104	104	1b80,O6L		1.2
1991	Cin N	136	478	72	152	33	1	14	59	46-7	1	61	.318	.374	.479	134	23	10-4	.992	6	116	103	1b128/OL		2.1
1992	Cin N	115	395	41	107	21	3	6	53	45-8	2	53	.271	.347	.385	105	4	6-6	.999	7	116	91	1b109		0.2
1993	Cin N	101	379	48	120	18	0	7	49	34-4	2	51	.317	.371	.420	112	7	2-2	.994	3	106	81	1b98	45	1.1
1994	Cin N	112	436	60	146	30	4	10	78	34-8	5	62	.335	.385	.491	128	19	6-2	.994	2	102	94	1b112	63	
1995	†Cin N	101	359	53	100	25	2	11	51	29-7	1	58	.279	.333	.451	104	2	1-1	.994	5	119	116	1b99		-0.2
1997	Cin N	96	333	42	92	20	1	1	33	23-2	3	43	.276	.328	.351	77	-11	3-1	.990	-3	86	101	1b89	15	-0.4
1998	KC A	127	472	50	146	27	2	1	40	32-6	1	52	.309	.350	.381	88	-8	1-0	.990	-2	127	98	1b46,O39L,D39	44	-2.1
1999	Cin N	80	102	10	29	9	0	0	16	0-0	0	21	.284	.348	.373	80	-3	0-0	.991	-1	78	112	1b25,O4L/D	28	-1.5
2000	Cin N	59	63	9	14	2	1	2	6	12-3	1	10	.222	.351	.381	84	-1	0-0	1.000	3	239	100	1b16/ORD		-0.5
	Det A	40	106	15	33	7	0	1	8	19-1	0	16	.311	.416	.406	110	3	0-0	.990	1	109	101	1b36/OL	26	0.1
Total	13	1246	3998	535	1216	246	21	76	513	356-55	22	548	.304	.361	.433	110	63	45-24	.994	19	107	107	1b982,O61(56/0/6),D43	261	0.5

MORRISON, JIM James Forrest B9.23.1952 Pensacola FL BR/TR/5-11/182(175-186) [PhiN74 5/99] d9.18 Col Georgia Southern OF(9/0/3)

1977	Phi N	5	7	3	3	0	0	1	1	1-0	0	1	.429	.500	.429	144	1	0-0	.875	-0	119	0	3b5		0.0
1978	†Phi N	53	108	12	17	1	1	3	10	10-1	1	21	.157	.235	.269	40	-9	1-1	.968	11	122	144	2b31,3b3/OL		0.3
1979	Chi A	67	240	38	66	14	0	14	35	15-0	4	48	.275	.324	.508	121	6	11-3	.982	5	100	102	2b48,3b29		1.4
1980	Chi A	162	604	66	171	40	0	15	57	36-2	8	74	.283	.329	.424	106	5	9-6	.969	9	101	96	2b161/SD		2.2
1981	Chi A	90	290	27	68	8	1	10	34	10-0	2	29	.234	.261	.372	83	-8	3-2	.956	9	108	92	3b87/2D		-0.1
1982	Pit N	44	86	10	24	4	1	4	15	5-0	0	14	.279	.309	.488	117	2	2-0	.914	-10	85	101	3b50/D		-1.5
1983	Pit N	66	158	16	48	7	2	6	25	9-1	2	14	.304	.347	.487	126	5	2-0	.964	1	100	65	3b26,O2L/2S		0.3
1984	Pit N	100	304	38	87	14	2	11	45	20-1	1	52	.286	.328	.454	119	6	2-6	.973	1	104	119	2b28,3b26,S7		0.6
1985	Pit N	92	244	17	62	10	0	4	22	8-1	1	44	.254	.277	.344	74	-9	0-1	.938	-4	98	89	3b61,2b26,S2/1		0.2
1986	Pit N	154	537	58	147	35	4	23	88	47-5	4	88	.274	.334	.482	120	14	9-8	.961	1	90	106	3b59,2b15/OL		-0.8
1987	Pit N	96	348	41	92	22	1	9	46	27-3	1	57	.264	.315	.411	91	-5	8-5	.975	4	105	89	3b82,S17,2b9		-0.2
	†Det A	34	117	15	24	1	1	4	19	2-0	1	26	.205	.221	.333	47	-10	2-1	.962	4	152	37	3b16,2b3,S3,O3(1/0/2)/1D		-0.5
1988	Det A	24	74	7	16	5	0	0	6	0-0	0	14	.216	.216	.284	40	-6	0-2	1.000	0	130	0	D14,1b4,3b4,O2(1/0/1)/S		-0.8
	Atl N	51	92	6	14	2	0	2	13	10-1	0	15	.152	.229	.239	35	-8	0-1	.933	-2	84	34	3b20,O4L,P3		-1.0
Total	12	1089	3375	371	876	170	16	112	435	213-15	25	521	.260	.305	.419	98	-19	50-37	.949	16	100	79	3b619,2b324,S33,D25,O13L,1b6,P3		0.0

MORRISON, JON Jonathan W. B1859 London ON, Can. 5-9.5/167 d8.1

1884	Ind AA	44	182	26	48	6	8	1		7		4	.264	.306	.401	132	6		.784	2	107	282	O44C		0.6
1887	NY AA	9	34	7	4	0	0	0	3	6		1	.118	.268	.118	10	-4	0	.600	-4	0	0	O9C		-0.7
Total	2	53	216	33	52	6	8	1	3	13		5	.241	.299	.356	110	2	0	.756	-2	89	235	O53C		-0.1

MORRISON, TOM Thomas J. B8.1870 St.Louis MO D3.27.1902 St.Louis MO 5-3/145 d9.18

1895	Lou N	6	22	3	6	0	2	0	4	1	0	1	.273	.304	.455	100	0	0	1.000	-1	59	108	S3,3b3		-0.1
1896	Lou N	8	27	3	4	1	0	0	4	0	0	4	.148	.258	.185	19	-3	0	.864	1	131	0	3b5,O2R/S		-0.2
Total	2	14	49	6	10	1	2	0	4	5	0	5	.204	.278	.306	55	-3	0	.839	-1	117	0	3b8,S4,O2R		-0.3

MORRISSEY, JACK John Albert "King" B5.2.1876 Lansing MI D10.30.1936 Lansing MI BB/TR/5-10/160 d9.18

1902	Cin N	12	39	5	11	1	1	0	3	4	0		.282	.349	.359	108	0	0	.941	-1	96	87	2b11/OL		0.0
1903	Cin N	29	89	14	22	1	0	0	9	14	0		.247	.350	.258	69	-3	3	.922	-9	82	0	2b17,O8(6/2/0),S2		-1.3
Total	2	41	128	19	33	2	1	0	12	18	0		.258	.349	.289	78	-3	3	.930	-10	87	32	2b28,O9(7/2/0),S2		-1.3

MORRISSEY, JOHN John J. B12.30.1856 Janesville WI D4.29.1884 Janesville WI d5.2 b-Tom

1881	Buf N	12	47	3	10	2	0	0	3	0		3	.213	.213	.255	47	-3		.865	-1	103	0	3b12		-0.4
1882	Det N	2	7	1	2	0	0	0	0	0			.286	.286	.286	84	0		.714	-1	23	0	3b2		-0.1
Total	2	14	54	4	12	2	0	0	3	0		5	.222	.222	.259	52	-3		.841	-3	90	0	3b14		-0.5

MORRISSEY, JO-JO Joseph Anselm B1.16.1904 Warren RI D5.2.1950 Worcester MA BR/TR/6-1.5/178 d4.12 Col Holy Cross

1932	Cin N	89	269	15	65	10	1	0	13	14	1	15	.242	.282	.286	53	-17	2	.967	4	102	78	S45,2b42,3b12/OL		-0.9
1933	Cin N	148	534	43	123	20	0	0	26	20	2	22	.230	.261	.268	52	-34	6	.964	-6	113	98	2b88,S63,3b15		-3.3
1936	Chi A	17	38	3	7	1	0	0	6	2	0	3	.184	.225	.211	8	-6	0-0	.895	-1	97	103	3b9,S4/2		-0.5
Total	3	254	841	61	195	31	1	0	45	36	3	40	.232	.266	.271	51	-57	7-0	.971	-3	112	102	2b131,S112,3b36/OL		-4.7

MORRISSEY, TOM Thomas J. B5.1860 Janesville WI D9.23.1941 Janesville WI 5-11/180 d9.27 b-John

1884	Mil U	12	47	3	8	2	0	0		0			.170	.170	.213	28	-6		.710	-1	71	147	3b12		-0.6

MORSE, MIKE Michael John B3.22.1981 Fort Lauderdale FL BR/TR/6-4/220 d5.31

2005	Sea A	72	230	27	64	10	1	3	23	18-0	8	50	.278	.349	.370	99	0	3-1	.946	-11	81	103	S55,O8L,D9		-0.7

MORSE, BUD Newell Obediah B9.4.1904 Berkeley CA D4.6.1987 Sparks NV BL/TR/5-9/150 d9.14 Col Michigan

1929	Phi A	8	27	1	2	0	0	0	0	2	0		.074	.074	.074	-60	-7	0-0	.975	1	103	78	2b8		-0.6

MORSE, HAP Peter Raymond "Pete" B12.6.1886 St.Paul MN D6.19.1974 St.Paul MN BR/TR/5-8/160 d4.18

1911	StL N	4	8	0	0	0	0	0	1	0		2	.000	.111	.000	-70	-2		.750	-1	89	0	S2/OL		-0.3

MORTON, CHARLIE Charles Hazen B10.12.1854 Kingsville OH D12.9.1921 Massillon OH BR/TR/?/150 d5.2 M3/U1 ▲

1882	Pit AA	25	103	12	29	0	3	0		5			.282	.315	.340	127	3		.816	1	159	0	O25C,3b3/S		0.2
	StL AA	9	32	2	2	0	1	0		4	-4		.063	.118	.125	-17	-4		.708	-4	79	48	2b7,O3(1/2/0)		-0.7
	Year	34	135	14	31	0	4	0		7			.230	.268	.289	90	-2		.821	-3	155	0	O28(1/27/0),2b7,3b3/S		-0.5
1884	Tol AA	32	111	11	18	6	2	0		4		10	.162	.212	.252	49	-6		.861	-0	79	78	3b16,O15(14/0/1),P3/2M		-0.5
1885	Det N	22	79	9	14	1	2	0	3	5		10	.177	.226	.265	51	-4		.750	-1	103	85	3b18,S4,M		-0.4
Total	3	88	325	34	63	7	8	0	3	19		10	.194	.238	.265	66	-11		.841	-4	144	0	O43(15/27/1),3b37,2b8,S5,P3		-1.4

MORTON, GUY Guy Jr. "Moose" B11.4.1930 Tuscaloosa AL BR/TR/6-2/200 d9.17 f-Guy Col Alabama

1954	Bos A	1	1	0	0	0	0	0	0	0	0	1	.000	.000	.000	-90	0	0-0	—	0			/H		0.0

YEAR	TM LG	G	AB	R	H	2B	3B	HR	RBI	BB-IB	HP	SO	AVG	OBP	SLG	AOPS	ABR	SB-CS	FA	FR	RNG	THR	GAMES AT POSITION	DL	BFW

MORTON, BUBBA Wycliffe Nathaniel B12.13.1931 Washington DC BR/TR/5-10.5/180* d4.19 Col Howard

																								-0.1
1961	Det A	77	108	26	31	5	1	2	19	9-1	1	25	.287	.342	.407	98	0	3-1	.952	0	107	73	O30(8/2/20)		0.0
1962	Det A	90	195	30	51	6	3	4	17	32-0	0	32	.262	.366	.385	99	0	1-1	.991	3	111	159	O62(1/30/33),1b3		-0.2
1963	Det A	6	11	2	1	0	0	0	2	2-0	0	1	.091	.231	.091	-5	-2	0-0	.875	-0	120	0	O3C		-0.3
	Mil N	15	28	1	5	0	0	0	4	2-1	1	3	.179	.258	.179	28	-3	0-0	1.000	0	99	126	O14R		-0.5
1966	Cal A	15	50	4	11	1	0	0	4	2-0	0	6	.220	.250	.240	43	-4	1-1	1.000	-0	99	126	O61(9/0/55)		0.3
1967	Cal A	80	201	23	63	9	3	0	32	22-1	1	29	.313	.387	.388	135	9	0-3	.985	-1	102	48	O50(3/0/47)/3		-0.2
1968	Cal A	81	163	13	44	6	0	1	18	14-0	1	18	.270	.341	.325	106	2	2-1	1.000	2	101	166	O49(6/0/43)/1		0.7
1969	Cal A	87	172	18	42	10	1	7	32	28-1	3	29	.244	.356	.436	127	7	0-0	1.000	2	101	96	O278(33/38/212),1b4/3		-0.3
Total	7	451	928	117	248	37	8	14	128	111-4	11	143	.267	.351	.370	106	9	7-7	.988	2	104	96			

MORYN, WALT Walter Joseph "Moose" B4.12.1926 St.Paul MN D7.21.1996 Winfield IL BL/TR/6-2/205* d6.29

																								-0.2
1954	Bro N	48	91	16	25	4	2	2	14	7	1	11	.275	.330	.429	94	-1	0-0	.881	0	95	199	O20(6/0/15)		0.0
1955	Bro N	11	19	3	5	1	0	1	3	5-1	0	4	.263	.417	.474	132	1	0-0	.833	-1	67	0	O7(1/0/6)		1.8
1956	Chi N	147	529	69	151	27	3	23	67	50-2	3	67	.285	.348	.478	123	16	4-2	.983	6	104	144	O141(1/0/140)		1.4
1957	Chi N	149	568	76	164	33	9	19	88	50-6	3	90	.289	.348	.447	114	-12	0-2	.960	7	113	131	O147R		0.8
1958	Chi N☆	143	512	77	135	26	7	26	77	62-7	8	83	.264	.350	.494	123	17	1-2	.978	-1	105	42	O141L		-1.2
1959	Chi N	117	381	41	89	14	1	14	48	44-2	3	66	.234	.316	.386	87	-7	0-0	.989	0	94	119	O104(97/1/9)		0.0
1960	Chi N	38	109	12	32	4	0	2	11	13-0	0	19	.294	.366	.385	108	2	2-1	.964	0	103	89	O30(25/0/5)		-0.3
	StL N	75	200	24	49	4	3	11	35	17-4	0	38	.245	.299	.460	97	-2	0-0	.990	1	107	90	O62(29/0/39)		-0.3
	Year	113	309	36	81	8	3	13	46	30-4	0	57	.262	.323	.434	101	0	2-1	.981	1	106	90	O92(54/0/44)		-0.6
1961	StL N	17	32	0	4	2	0	0	2	1-0	1	5	.125	.152	.188	-10	-5	0-0	.889	-1	83	0	O7(3/0/4)		-0.4
	Pit N	40	65	6	13	1	0	3	9	2-0	1	10	.200	.235	.354	53	-5	0-0	.950	1	105	261	O11(6/0/5)		-1.0
	Year	57	97	6	17	3	0	3	11	3-0	1	15	.175	.208	.299	31	-10	0-0	.931	0	97	163	O18(9/0/9)		1.3
Total	8	785	2506	324	667	116	16	101	354	251-22	19	393	.266	.335	.446	108	28	7-7	.972	15	104	110	O670(309/1/370)		

MOSCHITTO, ROSS Rosaire Allen B2.15.1945 Fresno CA BR/TR/6-2/175* d4.15 Mil 1966 Col Fresno (CA) City

																								-0.4
1965	NY A	96	27	12	5	0	0	1	3	0-0	1	12	.185	.179	.296	35	-2	0-0	.941	-1	111	0	O89(10/55/24)		-0.1
1967	NY A	14	9	1	1	0	0	0	0	1-0	0	2	.111	.200	.111	-6	-1	0-0	1.000	0	46	736	O8(2/4/2)		-0.5
Total	2	110	36	13	6	0	0	1	3	1-0	1	14	.167	.184	.250	25	-3	0-0	.944	-0	105	65	O97(12/59/26)		

MOSEBY, LLOYD Lloyd Anthony B11.5.1959 Portland AR BL/TR/6-3/200* [TorA78 1/2] d5.24 C1

																								-1.9
1980	Tor A	114	389	44	89	24	1	9	46	25-4	4	85	.229	.281	.365	73	-15	4-6	.982	2	96	152	O104(12/6/86),D6		-1.8
1981	Tor A	100	378	36	88	16	2	9	43	24-3	1	86	.233	.278	.357	78	-12	11-8	.989	-3	99	62	O100(0/80/21)		-2.3
1982	Tor A	147	487	51	115	20	9	9	52	33-3	2	106	.236	.294	.370	75	-18	11-7	.992	-4	100	45	O145C		2.8
1983	Tor A	151	539	104	170	31	7	18	81	51-4	5	85	.315	.376	.499	131	23	27-8	.983	4	104	116	O147C		3.0
1984	Tor A	158	592	97	166	28	15	18	92	78-9	3	122	.280	.368	.470	126	22	39-9	.990	4	108	77	O156C		-0.1
1985	†Tor A	152	584	92	151	30	4	18	70	76-4	3	91	.259	.345	.426	108	7	37-15	.980	-10	93	70	O147C,D3		-0.6
1986	Tor A★	152	589	89	149	24	5	21	86	64-3	6	122	.253	.329	.418	100	0	32-11	.984	-8	93	75	O147C,D2		0.1
1987	Tor A	155	592	106	167	27	4	26	96	70-4	7	124	.282	.358	.473	116	14	39-7	.980	-17	78	107	O153C,D2		-0.6
1988	Tor A	128	472	77	113	17	7	10	42	70-6	6	93	.239	.343	.369	85	-9	24-7	.986	-12	88	45	O120C,D14	16	-2.0
1989	†Tor A	135	502	72	111	25	3	11	43	56-1	6	101	.221	.306	.349	85	-9	17-5	.983	3	101	153	O116(14/104/0),D4	17	-0.6
1990	Det A	122	431	64	107	16	5	14	51	48-3	5	77	.248	.329	.406	104	2	8-1	.955	-4	98	28	O64L,D7	48	-0.5
1991	Det A	74	260	37	68	15	1	6	35	21-2	6	53	.262	.321	.396	96	-1	8-1	.984	-55	96	82	O1529(101/1327/113),D37	81	-3.3
Total	12	1588	5815	869	1494	273	66	169	737	616-46	58	1135	.257	.332	.414	102	14	280-92	.984						

MOSER, ARNIE Arnold Robert B8.9.1915 Houston TX D8.15.2002 Houston TX BR/TR/5-11/165 d6.20

| | | | | | | | | | | | | | | | | | | | | | | | | -0.1 |
| 1937 | Cin N | 5 | 5 | 0 | 0 | 0 | 0 | 0 | 0 | 0-0 | 0 | 2 | .000 | .000 | .000 | -99 | -1 | 0 | — | 0 | | | /H | | |

MOSES, JERRY Gerald Braheen B8.9.1946 Yazoo City MS BR/TR/6-3/210* d5.9

																								0.1
1965	Bos A	4	4	1	1	0	0	1	1	0-0	0	2	.250	.250	1.000	224	1	0-0	—	0			/H		0.0
1968	Bos A	6	18	2	6	0	0	2	4	1-0	0	4	.333	.368	.667	196	2	0-1	.963	-2	246	0	C6		-0.3
1969	Bos A	53	135	13	41	9	1	4	17	5-1	1	23	.304	.326	.474	118	0	0-1	.981	-7	90	94	C36		0.4
1970	Bos A☆	92	315	26	83	18	1	6	35	21-9	2	45	.263	.313	.384	86	-6	1-1	.990	6	103	71	C88/OL		-0.2
1971	Cal A	69	181	12	41	8	2	4	15	10-4	0	34	.227	.266	.359	82	-6	0-0	.982	-1	130	118	C39,1b3		-0.3
1972	Cle A	52	141	9	31	8	1	4	14	11-3	3	29	.220	.290	.326	80	-4	0-0	1.000	5	112	73	C17/D		0.2
1973	NY A	21	59	5	15	2	0	3	2-0	0	6	.254	.270	.288	61	-2	0-0	.985	-1	109	88	C74	23	-0.4
1974	Det A	74	198	19	47	6	4	3	19	11-2	2	38	.237	.282	.359	81	-6	0-1	.900	-1	51	0	C5		-0.3
1975	SD N	13	19	1	3	2	0	0	1	2-0	0	3	.158	.238	.263	42	-1	0-0	1.000	0	51	0	/1D		0.1
	Chi A	2	2	1	1	0	0	1	0-0	0	0	.500	.500	1.500	442	1	0-0	1.000	-0	-0	-0	/H		-0.7
Total	9	386	1072	89	269	48	8	25	109	63-19	8	184	.251	.295	.381	89	-19	1-4	.984	-0	104	95	C328,1b4,D2,O2(1/0/1)	23	

MOSES, JOHN John William B8.9.1957 Los Angeles CA BB/TL/5-10/170* [SeaA80 16/396] d8.23 C5 Col Arizona

																								0.2
1982	Sea A	22	44	7	14	5	1	1	3	4-0	0	5	.318	.375	.545	144	3	5-1	.947	-1	69	279	O19(8/3/9)		-0.8
1983	Sea A	93	130	19	27	4	1	0	6	12-0	1	20	.208	.280	.254	46	-10	11-5	.979	3	87	297	O71(34/31/7),D10		0.1
1984	Sea A	19	35	3	12	1	1	0	2	2-0	1	5	.343	.395	.429	128	1	1-0	1.000	-3	71	65	O29(1/28/0)		-1.0
1985	Sea A	33	62	4	12	0	0	0	3	2-0	0	8	.194	.219	.194	14	-8	5-2	1.000	-3	88	185	O93(2/91/0),1b7,D4		-1.9
1986	Sea A	103	399	56	102	16	3	3	34	34-3	0	65	.256	.311	.333	75	-14	25-18	.987	-4	88	120	O100(0/97/4),1b16,D5		0.5
1987	Sea A	116	390	58	96	16	4	3	38	29-2	3	49	.246	.301	.331	65	-20	23-15	.987	-3	94	120	O82(29/20/43),D2		0.5
1988	Min A	105	206	33	65	10	3	2	12	15-2	1	21	.316	.366	.422	117	5	11-6	1.000	1	113	35	O108(39/26/63),1b2/PD		-1.1
1989	Min A	129	242	33	68	12	3	1	31	19-1	1	19	.281	.333	.368	92	-2	14-7	.988	3	117	73	O85(16/23/52),D10,1b6,P2		-1.7
1990	Min A	115	172	26	38	3	1	1	14	19-1	2	19	.221	.303	.267	58	-9	2-3	1.000	0	108	68	O85(16/23/52),D10,1b6,P2		-0.4
1991	Det A	13	21	5	1	1	0	0	1	2-0	0	7	.048	.130	.095	-36	-4	4-0	1.000	-1	91	0	O12(11/0/1)		-0.3
1992	Sea A	21	22	3	3	1	0	0	1	5-0	0	4	.136	.296	.182	36	-2	0-0	1.000	-1	95	127	O18(17/1/1)/D		-7.2
Total	11	769	1723	247	438	69	17	11	145	143-9	10	226	.254	.313	.333	75	-60	101-57	.990	-5	97	127	O636(164/334/180),D36,1b31,P3		

MOSES, WALLY Wallace B10.8.1910 Uvalda GA D10.10.1990 Vidalia GA BL/TL/5-10/160* d4.17 C16

																								0.0
1935	Phi A	85	345	60	112	21	3	5	35	25	3	18	.325	.375	.446	113	6	3-4	.943	-1	101	103	O80R		0.0
1936	Phi A	146	585	98	202	35	11	7	66	62	2	32	.345	.410	.479	121	20	12-6	.974	0	101	93	O144(0/136/9)		2.2
1937	Phi A☆	154	649	113	208	48	13	25	86	54	2	38	.320	.374	.550	132	29	9-7	.958	5	108	111	O154R		-0.3
1938	Phi A	142	589	86	181	29	8	8	49	58	0	31	.307	.369	.424	101	4	15-5	.966	4	112	87	O139R		-0.0
1939	Phi A	115	437	68	134	28	7	3	33	44	0	23	.307	.370	.423	105	3	7-4	.965	-1	96	119	O103(0/5/100)		1.9
1940	Phi A	142	537	91	166	41	9	9	50	75	0	44	.309	.396	.469	126	23	6-4	.974	5	110	92	O133(0/2/131)		1.0
1941	Phi A	116	438	78	132	31	4	4	35	62	0	27	.301	.388	.418	116	13	3-3	.975	4	106	129	O145(3/14/130)		0.2
1942	Chi A	146	577	73	156	28	4	9	48	74	0	27	.270	.353	.369	106	6	16-10	.980	6	106	129	O148(0/23/125)		-0.3
1943	Chi A	150	599	82	147	22	12	3	48	55	1	47	.245	.310	.337	89	-10	56-14	.979	7	110	106	O148(0/23/125)		-0.2
1944	Chi A	136	535	82	150	26	9	3	34	52	1	22	.280	.345	.379	108	6	21-7	.975	-2	100	77	O134R		2.0
1945	Chi A★	140	569	79	168	35	15	2	50	69	2	33	.295	.373	.420	134	25	11-5	.977	6	115	85	O139R		0.4
1946	Chi A	56	168	20	46	9	1	4	16	17	1	15	.274	.344	.411	115	3	2-2	1.000	-2	96	63	O36(2/14/22)		-1.1
	†Bos A	48	175	23	36	11	4	2	17	14	1	15	.206	.268	.347	65	-9	2-4	.979	-1	99	72	O44(0/2/43)		-1.0
	Year	104	343	43	82	20	4	6	33	31	2	35	.239	.306	.373	88	-6	4-6	.989	-3	98	68	O80(2/16/65)		-0.6
1947	Bos A	90	255	32	70	18	2	2	27	27	0	16	.275	.344	.384	99	-1	3-0	.974	-4	93	47	O58R		-0.5
1948	Bos A	78	189	26	49	12	1	2	29	21	2	19	.259	.340	.365	83	-4	5-0	.981	1	108	61	O45R		-0.2
1949	Phi A	110	308	49	85	19	3	1	25	51	1	29	.276	.381	.367	102	3	1-3	.983	3	107	128	O62(4/7/51)		-1.3
1950	Phi A	88	265	47	70	16	5	2	21	40	2	17	.264	.365	.385	94	-2	0-1	.984	1	112	59	O27R		-1.0
1951	Phi A	70	136	17	26	6	0	0	9	21	1	17	.191	.304	.235	46	-10	0-2	.973	1	106	51	O29R		4.5
Total	17	2012	7356	1124	2138	435	110	89	679	821	21	457	.291	.364	.416	109	101	174-81	.973	35	106	96	O1792(10/204/1587)		

MOSKIMAN, DOC William Bankhead B12.20.1879 Oakland CA D1.11.1953 San Leandro CA BR/TR/6-0/170 d8.23

| | | | | | | | | | | | | | | | | | | | | | | | | -0.0 |
| 1910 | Bos A | 5 | 9 | 1 | 1 | 0 | 0 | 0 | 2 | 0 | 0 | 2 | .111 | .273 | .111 | 20 | -1 | 0 | 1.000 | 0 | 143 | 185 | 1b2/OR | | |

MOSOLF, JIM James Frederick B8.21.1905 Puyallup WA D12.28.1979 Dallas OR BL/TR/5-10/186 d9.9

																								0.0
1929	Pit N	8	13	3	6	1	0	1	2	1	0	1	.462	.500	.692	188	2	0	1.000	0	128	0	O3L		-0.0
1930	Pit N	40	51	16	17	2	1	0	9	8	0	7	.333	.424	.412	103	2	0	.765	-1	76	120	O12(1/1/9)/P		-0.0
1931	Pit N	39	44	7	11	1	0	1	8	8	0	5	.250	.365	.341	92	0	0	1.000	-1	73	0	O4(3/0/1)		-0.0

YEAR	TM LG	G	AB	R	H	2B	3B	HR	RBI	BB-IB	HP	SO	AVG	OBP	SLG	AOPS	ABR	SB-CS	FA	FR	RNG	THR	GAMES AT POSITION	DL	BFW
1933	Chi N	31	82	13	22	5	1	1	9	5	2	8	.268	.326	.390	104	0	0	.964	1	107	122	O22(19/3/0)		0.0
Total	4	118	190	39	56	9	3	2	28	22	2	21	.295	.374	.405	107	3	0	.929	-1	99	101	O41(26/4/10)/P		0.0

MOSQUERA, JULIO Julio Alberto (Cervantes) B1.29.1972 Panama City, Pan BR/TR/6-0/190(165-192) d8.17

1996	Tor A	8	22	2	5	2	0	0	2	0-0	1	3	.227	.261	.318	46	-2	0-1	1.000	1	203	0	C8		-0.1
1997	Tor A	3	8	0	2	1	0	0	0	0-0	0	0	.250	.250	.375	60	0	0-0	1.000	-0	135	151	C3		-0.1
2005	Mil N	1	1	0	0	0	0	0	0	0-0	0	0	.000	.000	.000	-99	0	0-0	—	0			/H		0.0
Total	3	12	31	2	7	3	0	0	2	0-0	1	5	.226	.250	.323	45	-2	0-1	1.000	0	187	36	C11		-0.2

MOSS, CHARLIE Charles Crosby B3.20.1911 Meridian MS D10.9.1991 Meridian MS BR/TR/5-10/160 d5.19 Col U. of Mississippi

1934	Phi A	10	10	3	2	0	0	0	1	0	0	0	.200	.200	.200	4	-1	0-0	1.000	-1	56	0	C6		-0.2
1935	Phi A	4	3	1	1	0	0	0	1	1	0	0	.333	.500	.333	120	0	0-0		0	0	0	/C		0.0
1936	Phi A	33	44	2	11	1	1	0	10	6	0	5	.250	.340	.318	65	-2	1-0	.929	-2	73	82	C19		-0.4
Total	3	47	57	6	14	1	1	0	12	7	0	5	.246	.328	.298	58	-3	1-0	.935	-3	70	72	C26		-0.6

MOSS, HOWIE Howard Glenn B10.17.1919 Gastonia NC D5.7.1989 Baltimore MD BR/TR/5-11.5/185 d4.14 Mil 1945

1942	NY N	7	14	0	0	0	0	0	0	0	0	4	.000	.000	.000	-99	-4	0-0	1.000	-0	105	0	O3(2/1/0)		-0.4
1946	Cin N	7	26	1	5	0	0	0	1	0	1	5	.192	.222	.192	19	-3	0-0	1.000	0	89	155	O6R		-0.3
	Cle A	8	32	2	2	0	0	0	3	0	0	9	.063	.143	.063	-44	-6	0-1	.857	-1	89	0	3b8		-0.9
Total	3	22	72	3	7	0	0	0	4	0	1	17	.097	.145	.097	-32	-13	0-1	1.000	-1	94	105	O9(2/1/6),3b8		-1.6

MOSS, LES John Lester B5.14.1925 Tulsa OK BR/TR/5-11/205(188-205) d9.10 M2/C13

1946	StL A	12	35	4	13	3	0	0	5	3	1	6	.371	.436	.457	142	2	1-0	.968	-0	66	64	C12		0.3
1947	StL A	96	274	17	43	5	2	6	27	35	1	48	.157	.255	.255	41	-23	0-0	.983	-7	73	106	C96		-2.6
1948	StL A	107	335	35	86	12	1	14	46	39	0	50	.257	.334	.424	98	-2	0-0	.988	-8	62	104	C103		-0.6
1949	StL A	97	278	28	81	11	0	10	39	49	1	32	.291	.399	.439	117	8	0-1	.970	-3	98	103	C83		0.8
1950	StL A	84	222	24	59	6	0	8	34	26	0	32	.266	.343	.401	87	-5	0-1	.957	-3	97	119	C60		-0.5
1951	StL A	16	47	5	8	2	0	1	7	6	0	8	.170	.264	.277	45	-4	0-0	.967	-1	101	171	C12		-0.4
	Bos A	71	202	18	40	6	0	3	26	25	1	34	.198	.289	.272	48	-15	0-0	.984	-1	119	63	C69		-1.3
	Year	87	249	23	48	8	0	4	33	31	1	42	.193	.285	.273	47	-18	0-0	.981	-2	116	81	C81		-1.7
1952	StL A	52	118	11	29	3	0	3	12	15	0	13	.246	.331	.347	86	-2	0-1	.957	-3	99	108	C39		-0.4
1953	StL A	78	239	21	66	14	1	2	28	18	1	31	.276	.329	.368	86	-5	0-1	.978	-7	87	86	C71		-0.8
1954	Bal A	50	126	7	31	3	0	0	5	14	0	16	.246	.321	.270	68	-5	0-0	.972	-3	81	120	C38		-0.7
1955	Bal A	29	56	5	19	1	0	2	6	7-1	1	4	.339	.413	.464	146	4	0-1	1.000	1	85	82	C17		0.5
	Chi A	32	59	5	15	2	0	2	7	6-1	1	10	.254	.333	.390	91	-1	0-0	.990	1	126	64	C32		0.1
	Year	61	115	10	34	3	0	4	13	13-2	2	14	.296	.372	.426	116	3	0-1	.994	2	108	72	C49		0.6
1956	Chi A	56	127	20	31	4	0	10	22	18-0	0	15	.244	.338	.512	120	3	0-1	.994	-3	130	65	C49		0.1
1957	Chi A	42	115	10	31	3	0	2	12	20-1	1	18	.270	.375	.348	99	1	0-0	.980	-4	89	43	C39		-0.2
1958	Chi A	2	1	0	0	0	0	0	0	1-0	0	0	.000	.500	.000	51	0	0-0	—	0			/H		0.0
Total	13	824	2234	210	552	75	4	63	276	282-3	6	316	.247	.333	.369	86	-44	1-5	.978	-41	90	94	C720		-5.7

MOSTIL, JOHNNY John Anthony "Bananas" B6.1.1896 Chicago IL D12.10.1970 Midlothian IL BR/TR/5-8.5/168 d6.20

1918	Chi A	10	33	4	9	2	2	0	4	1	0	6	.273	.294	.455	125	1	1	.923	-2	88	123	2b9		-0.1
1921	Chi A	100	326	43	98	21	3	7	42	28	13	35	.301	.379	.436	109	5	10-12	.946	-3	94	103	O91(1/90/0)/2		-0.4
1922	Chi A	132	458	74	139	28	14	7	70	38	14	39	.303	.375	.472	120	13	14-10	.966	0	107	67	O123(18/105/0)		0.6
1923	Chi A	153	546	91	159	37	15	3	64	62	12	51	.291	.376	.463	113	11	41-16	.974	15	116	126	O143(0/135/8),3b5/S		2.3
1924	Chi A	118	385	75	125	22	5	4	49	45	4	41	.325	.401	.439	120	13	7-11	.974	7	109	130	O102(1/90/12)		1.2
1925	Chi A	153	605	135	181	36	16	2	50	90	12	52	.299	.400	.421	115	17	43-20	.985	-2	102	64	O153C		1.1
1926	Chi A	148	600	120	197	41	15	4	42	79	10	55	.328	.415	.467	135	33	35-14	.968	7	109	96	O147C		3.5
1927	Chi A	13	16	3	2	0	0	0	1	0	1	1	.125	.176	.125	-21	-3	1-0	.857	0	84	427	O6C		-0.4
1928	Chi A	133	503	69	136	19	8	0	51	66	4	54	.270	.360	.340	86	-8	23-20	.976	12	115	123	O131(0/120/11)		-0.4
1929	Chi A	12	35	4	8	3	0	0	3	6	0	2	.229	.341	.314	71	-1	1-1	.963	0	97	99	O11(0/10/1)		-0.2
Total	10	972	3507	618	1054	209	82	23	376	415	70	336	.301	.386	.427	113	81	176-104	.971	34	108	101	O907(20/856/32),2b10,3b5/S		7.4

MOTA, ANDY Andres Alberto (Matos) B3.4.1966 Santo Domingo, D.R. BR/TR/5-10/180 [HouN87 12/314] d8.31 b-Jose f-Manny Col Cal St.-Fullerton

1991	Hou N	27	90	4	17	2	0	1	6	1-0	1	17	.189	.198	.244	25	-9	2-0	.970	-8	86	78	2b27		-1.8

MOTA, JOSE Jose Manuel (Matos) B3.16.1965 Santo Domingo, D.R. BB/TR/5-9/155* [ChiA85 2/33] d5.24 b-Andy f-Manny Col Cal St.-Fullerton

1991	SD N	17	36	4	8	0	0	0	2	2-0	1	7	.222	.282	.222	42	-3	0-0	.962	-2	91	97	2b13,S3		-0.4
1995	KC A	2	2	0	0	0	0	0	0	0-0	0	0	.000	.000	.000	-98	-1	0-0	1.000	0	174	0	2b2	94	0.0
Total	2	19	38	4	8	0	0	0	2	2-0	1	7	.211	.268	.211	35	-4	0-0	.965	-1	95	92	2b15,S3	94	-0.4

MOTA, MANNY Manuel Rafael (Geronimo) B2.18.1938 Santo Domingo, D.R. BR/TR/5-11/168* d4.16 C11 s-Andy s-Jose

1962	SF N	47	74	9	13	1	0	0	9	7-0	1	8	.176	.253	.189	22	-8	3-2	1.000	3	112	348	O27(22/2/4),3b7,2b3		-0.6
1963	Pit N	59	126	20	34	2	3	0	7	7-0	1	18	.270	.313	.333	86	-3	3-2	.953	-2	83	57	O37(35/2/2)/2		-0.8
1964	Pit N	115	271	43	75	8	3	5	32	10-0	3	31	.277	.309	.384	94	-3	4-1	.961	-0	99	99	O93(57/50/7)/C2		-0.6
1965	Pit N	121	294	47	82	7	6	4	29	22-0	2	32	.279	.330	.384	101	-3	2-2	.985	-2	90	122	O95(35/60/15)		-0.6
1966	Pit N	116	322	54	107	16	7	5	46	25-1	4	28	.332	.383	.472	137	17	7-7	.994	-3	99	57	O96(45/52/12),3b4		1.0
1967	Pit N	120	349	53	112	14	8	4	56	14-2	2	46	.321	.343	.441	125	10	3-2	.988	4	96	181	O99(48/48/13),3b2		1.0
1968	Pit N	111	331	35	93	10	2	1	33	20-4	1	19	.281	.320	.332	99	-1	4-2	.981	-2	93	86	O92(50/31/22)/23		-0.8
1969	Mon N	31	89	6	28	1	1	0	6	6-0	0	11	.315	.358	.348	98	0	1-3	.907	-3	94	0	O22(1/17/5)		-0.5
	LA N	85	294	35	95	6	4	3	30	26-1	1	25	.323	.377	.401	127	10	5-4	.969	-1	90	186	O90(75/4/10)		0.7
	Year	116	383	41	123	7	5	3	30	32-1	1	36	.321	.372	.389	120	10	6-7	.954	-1	91	146	O102(76/21/15)		0.2
1970	LA N	124	417	63	127	12	6	3	37	47-4	3	37	.305	.377	.384	109	6	11-6	.973	-0	95	106	O111(109/1/4)/3		0.0
1971	LA N	91	269	24	84	13	5	0	34	20-5	1	20	.312	.361	.398	121	7	4-3	.965	-4	88	67	O80(62/0/24)		-0.1
1972	LA N	118	371	57	120	16	5	5	48	27-6	6	15	.323	.375	.434	132	15	4-4	.993	-7	86	48	O99(96/3/0)		0.3
1973	LA N★	89	293	33	92	11	2	0	23	25-9	1	12	.314	.368	.365	108	4	1-3	1.000	-7	72	84	O74L		-0.9
1974	†LA N	66	57	5	16	2	0	0	16	5-4	1	4	.281	.328	.316	90	-1	0-0	1.000	0	35	0	O3L		-0.1
1975	LA N	52	49	3	6	1	0	0	10	5-0	0	2	.265	.357	.286	83	-1	0-0	1.000	1	165	0	O5L		0.0
1976	LA N	50	52	1	15	3	0	0	13	7-3	0	5	.288	.367	.346	106	-1	0-0	1.000	2	189	485	O6L		0.3
1977	†LA N	49	38	5	15	4	0	0	9	10-3	0	4	.395	.521	.500	174	5	1-1	1.000	0	116	0	/OL		0.5
1978	†LA N	37	33	2	10	1	0	0	6	3-1	0	4	.303	.361	.333	95	0	0-0	—	0			/OL		0.0
1979	LA N	47	42	1	15	1	0	0	3	3-0	0	4	.357	.400	.357	110	1	0-0	—	0			/H		-0.1
1980	LA N	7	7	0	3	0	0	0	2	0-0	0	0	.429	.429	.429	144	0	0-0	—	0	0	0	/OL		0.1
1982	LA N	1	1	0	0	0	0	0	0	0-0	0	1	.000	.000	.000	-99	0	0-0	—	0			/H		0.0
Total	20	1536	3779	496	1149	125	52	31	438	289-43	28	320	.304	.355	.389	112	59	50-42	.979	-21	92	104	O1021(725/270/118),3b15,2b6/C		-1.2

MOTLEY, DARRYL Darryl De Wayne B1.21.1960 Muskogee OK BR/TR/5-9/196* [KCA78 2/51] d8.10

1981	KC A	42	125	15	29	4	0	2	8	7-0	1	15	.232	.276	.312	70	-5	1-3	.968	3	114	112	O39(2/0/38)		-0.6
1983	KC A	19	68	9	16	4	0	2	11	2-0	1	8	.235	.264	.441	90	-2	2-1	.978	1	108	148	O18(3/2/15)/D		-0.1
1984	†KC A	146	522	64	148	25	6	15	70	28-2	1	73	.284	.319	.441	107	3	10-12	.984	2	106	76	O138(105/3/45)		-0.3
1985	†KC A	123	383	45	85	20	1	17	49	18-2	2	57	.222	.257	.413	80	-12	6-4	.967	-5	94	59	O114(44/0/76),D7		-2.2
1986	KC A	72	217	22	44	9	1	7	20	11-1	0	31	.203	.241	.350	57	-14	0-2	.979	-6	70	50	O66(3/1/62),D2		-2.4
	Atl N	5	10	1	2	1	0	0	1	1-1	0	1	.200	.273	.300	55	-1	0-0	1.000	0	104	0	O3R		-0.1
1987	Atl N	6	8	0	0	0	0	0	1	0-0	0	2	.000	.000	.000	-96	-2	0-0	1.000	0	97	0	O2L		-0.2
Total	6	413	1333	156	324	60	10	44	159	67-6	5	186	.243	.280	.402	85	-33	19-22	.976	-6	99	73	O380(159/6/239),D10		-5.9

MOTT, BITSY Elisha Matthew B6.12.1918 Arcadia FL D2.25.2001 Brandon FL BR/TR/5-8/155 d4.17

1945	Phi N	90	289	21	64	8	0	0	7	21	1	25	.221	.290	.249	52	-18	2	.944	12	110	119	S63,2b27,3b7		-0.1

MOTTOLA, CHAD Charles Edward B10.15.1971 Augusta GA BR/TR/6-3/220* [CinN92 1/5] d4.23 Col Central Florida

1996	Cin N	35	79	10	17	3	0	3	6	6-1	0	16	.215	.271	.367	65	-4	2-2	1.000	0	98	134	O31(0/1/30)		-0.5
2000	Tor A	3	9	1	2	0	0	0	2	0-0	1	4	.222	.300	.222	34	-1	0-0	1.000	-0	103	0	O3R		-0.1
2001	Fla N	5	7	1	0	0	0	0	0	1-0	0	2	.000	.200	.000	-36	-1	0-0	1.000	1	142	575	O5(2/1/4)		0.0
2004	Bal A	6	14	2	2	1	0	1	4	3-0	0	3	.143	.250	.429	73	-1	0-0	1.000	1	81	0	O5(3/0/2)		-0.1
Total	4	49	109	14	21	4	0	4	12	10-1	1	25	.193	.264	.339	57	-7	2-2	1.000	1	100	144	O44(5/2/39)		-0.7

YEAR	TM LG	G	AB	R	H	2B	3B	HR	RBI	BB-IB	HP	SO	AVG	OBP	SLG	AOPS	ABR	SB-CS	FA	FR	RNG	THR	GAMES AT POSITION	DL	BFW
MOTTON, CURT	Curtell Howard	B9.24.1940 Darnell LA								BR/TR/5-7.5/175(164-175)			d7.5	C1		Col California-Davis								
1967	Bal A	27	65	5	13	2	0	2	9	5-0	2	14	.200	.267	.323	78	-2	0-1	.973	1	125	0	O18(18/0/1)		-0.3
1968	Bal A	83	217	27	43	7	0	8	25	31-0	1	43	.198	.298	.341	94	-1	1-3	.989	0	101	62	O54L	21	-0.5
1969	†Bal A	56	89	15	27	6	0	6	21	13-0	1	10	.303	.398	.573	167	8	3-1	1.000	-2	87	0	O20(16/0/4)		0.6
1970	Bal A	52	84	16	19	3	1	3	19	18-0	1	20	.226	.369	.393	108	2	1-2	1.000	0	104	90	O21(20/0/2)		0.1
1971	†Bal A	38	53	13	10	1	0	4	8	10-0	1	12	.189	.317	.434	110	1	0-0	1.000	0	94	138	O16(12/0/5)		0.1
1972	Mil A	6	6	1	1	0	0	0	1	2-0	0	2	.167	.286	.667	180	1	0-0	—	-0	0	0	O3L	20	-0.4
	Cal A	42	39	6	6	1	0	0	1	5-0	0	12	.154	.250	.179	31	-3	0-0	1.000	0	130	0	O9L		-0.4
	Year	48	45	7	7	1	0	1	3	6-0	0	14	.156	.255	.244	51	-3	0-0	1.000	0	0	0	/OLD		0.1
1973	Bal A	5	6	2	2	0	0	1	4	1-0	0	1	.333	.429	.833	247	1	0-0	—	0	162	0	O2R/D		-0.1
1974	†Bal A	7	8	0	0	0	0	0	2-0	0	2	.000	.200	.000	-39	-1	0-0	1.000	0	104	52	O144(133/0/14),D2	41	-0.5
Total	8	316	567	85	121	20	1	25	89	86-0	5	116	.213	.319	.384	105	6	5-7	.991	0	104	52	O144(133/0/14),D2	41	-0.5

YEAR	TM LG	G	AB	R	H	2B	3B	HR	RBI	BB-IB	HP	SO	AVG	OBP	SLG	AOPS	ABR	SB-CS	FA	FR	RNG	THR	GAMES AT POSITION	DL	BFW
MOTZ, FRANK	Frank H.	B10.1.1868 Freeburg PA					D3.18.1944 Akron OH			6-0/160		d8.27													
1890	Phi N	1	2	1	0	0	0	0					.000	.333	.000		-1	0	1	1.000	0	315	411	/1		0.0
1893	Cin N	43	156	16	40	7	1	2	25	19	4	10	.256	.352	.353	85	-3	3	.981	6	162	102	1b43		0.2
1894	Cin N	18	69	8	14	4	0	0	12	9	1	1	.203	.304	.261	36	-7	2	.995	4	174	80	1b18		-0.3
Total	3	62	227	25	54	11	1	2	37	29	5	12	.238	.337	.322	68	-10	6	.985	10	168	100	1b62		-0.1

YEAR	TM LG	G	AB	R	H	2B	3B	HR	RBI	BB-IB	HP	SO	AVG	OBP	SLG	AOPS	ABR	SB-CS	FA	FR	RNG	THR	GAMES AT POSITION	DL	BFW
MOULTON, ALLIE	Albert Theodore	B1.16.1886 Medway MA					D7.10.1968 Peabody MA			BR/TR/5-6/155		d9.25													
1911	StL A	4	15	4	1	0	0	0	1	4	0		.067	.263	.067		-6	-2	0	.938	-0	133	0	2b4		-0.2

YEAR	TM LG	G	AB	R	H	2B	3B	HR	RBI	BB-IB	HP	SO	AVG	OBP	SLG	AOPS	ABR	SB-CS	FA	FR	RNG	THR	GAMES AT POSITION	DL	BFW
MOUNTAIN, FRANK	Frank Henry	B5.17.1860 Ft.Edward NY					D11.19.1939 Schenectady NY			BR/TR/5-11/185		d7.19	Col Union (NY) ▲												
1880	Tro N	2	9	1	2	0	0	0			4	.222	.222	.222	49	-1	1.000	0	118	0	P2		0.0
1881	Det N	7	25	0	4	1	1	0	4	2	8	.160	.222	.280	55	0	.923	-1	52	0	P7		0.0
1882	Wor N	5	16	1	1	0	0	0	1	0	5	.063	.063	.063	-58	-2	.889	-1	75	0	P5		0.1
	Phi AA	9	36	5	12	3	0	0		2		.333	.368	.417	154	2	.917	1	136	0	P8/OR		-0.1
	Wor N	20	70	8	19	2	2	2	5	3	18	.271	.301	.443	132	2	.870	-2	75	0	P13,O6(1/5/0),1b2/S		0.0
1883	Col AA	70	276	36	60	14	5	3		9		.217	.242	.337	92	-1	.919	3	121	0	P42,O17(9/7/1)		0.2
1884	Col AA	58	210	26	50	7	3	4		9	4	.238	.283	.357	117	5	.846	1	131	0	P5		0.0
1885	Pit AA	5	20	1	2	0	1	0	1	1	0	.100	.143	.200	8	-1	.959	-0	100	87	1b16,P2		-0.3
1886	Pit AA	18	55	6	8	1	1	0	2	13	1	.145	.319	.200	64	-1	3	.880	2	106	52	P143,O36(18/16/2),1b18/S		-0.1
Total	7	194	717	84	158	28	13	9	13	39	5	35	.220	.265	.333	96	4	3	.880	2	106	52	P143,O36(18/16/2),1b18/S		-0.1

YEAR	TM LG	G	AB	R	H	2B	3B	HR	RBI	BB-IB	HP	SO	AVG	OBP	SLG	AOPS	ABR	SB-CS	FA	FR	RNG	THR	GAMES AT POSITION	DL	BFW
MOUTON, JAMES	James Raleigh	B12.29.1968 Denver CO								BR/TR/5-9/175*	[HouN91 7/183]		d4.4	Col St. Marys (CA)											
1994	Hou N	99	310	43	76	11	0	2	16	27-0	5	69	.245	.315	.300	65	-1	24-5	.982	0	102	92	O96(1/19/80)		-1.5
1995	Hou N	104	298	42	78	18	2	4	27	25-1	2	59	.262	.326	.376	91	-4	25-8	1.000	-1	95	88	O94(38/22/38)	18	-0.5
1996	Hou N	122	300	40	79	15	1	3	34	38-2	0	55	.263	.343	.350	91	-3	21-9	.971	3	103	157	O108(79/29/5)		-0.1
1997	Hou N	86	180	24	38	9	1	3	23	18-0	2	30	.211	.287	.322	62	-10	9-7	1.000	-3	91	40	O61(9/39/14)	16	-1.4
1998	SD N	55	63	8	12	2	1	0	7	7-1	0	11	.190	.268	.254	42	-5	4-3	.969	-0	96	97	O33(16/4/14)/D		-0.6
1999	Mon N	95	122	18	32	5	1	2	13	18-1	3	31	.262	.364	.369	90	-1	6-2	.981	-0	92	127	O56(32/16/11)/D		-0.2
2000	Mil N	87	159	28	37	7	1	2	17	30-0	3	43	.233	.363	.327	77	-1	13-4	.989	1	99	127	O45(19/23/7)	15	-0.3
2001	Mil N	75	138	20	34	8	0	2	10	11-0	6	40	.246	.329	.348	77	-4	7-0	.965	2	111	102	O53(21/28/7)	49	-4.9
Total	8	723	1570	223	386	75	7	18	147	174-5	22	338	.246	.328	.337	78	-47	109-41	.983	1	99	106	O546(215/180/176),D2	49	-4.9

YEAR	TM LG	G	AB	R	H	2B	3B	HR	RBI	BB-IB	HP	SO	AVG	OBP	SLG	AOPS	ABR	SB-CS	FA	FR	RNG	THR	GAMES AT POSITION	DL	BFW
MOUTON, LYLE	Lyle Joseph	B5.13.1969 Lafayette LA								BR/TR/6-4/240*	[NYA91 5/126]		d6.7	Col Louisiana St.											
1995	Chi A	58	179	23	54	16	0	5	27	19-0	2	46	.302	.373	.475	124	7	1-0	.990	3	105	166	O53(29/0/30),D2		0.8
1996	Chi A	87	214	25	63	8	1	7	39	22-4	2	50	.294	.361	.439	107	2	3-0	.970	-2	95	43	O47(21/0/29),D28		-0.2
1997	Chi A	88	242	26	65	9	0	5	23	14-1	1	66	.269	.308	.368	79	-8	4-4	.969	1	113	28	O67(16/0/55),D11	16	-1.1
1998	Bal A	18	39	5	12	2	0	2	7	4-0	0	8	.308	.372	.513	129	2	0-0	1.000	-0	89	135	O16(6/0/12),D2		0.1
1999	Mil N	14	17	2	3	1	0	1	3	2-0	0	5	.176	.263	.412	67	-1	0-0	1.000	-1	26	0	O3(2/0/1)		-0.2
2000	Mil N	42	97	14	27	7	1	2	16	10-0	1	29	.278	.349	.433	98	0	1-0	.978	3	98	301	O27(22/1/4)	19	0.1
2001	Fla N	21	17	1	1	0	0	0	1	0-0	0	7	.059	.059	.059	-72	-4	0-0	1.000	-1	54	0	O11(6/0/5)	35	-1.0
Total	7	328	805	96	225	43	2	22	116	71-5	6	209	.280	.339	.420	98	-2	9-4	.978	3	102	107	O224(102/1/136),D43	35	-1.0

YEAR	TM LG	G	AB	R	H	2B	3B	HR	RBI	BB-IB	HP	SO	AVG	OBP	SLG	AOPS	ABR	SB-CS	FA	FR	RNG	THR	GAMES AT POSITION	DL	BFW
MOWE, RAY	Raymond Benjamin	B7.12.1889 Rochester IN					D8.14.1968 Sarasota FL			BL/TR/5-7.5/160		d9.25													
1913	Bro N	5	9	1	0	0	0	0		1		2	.111	.200	.111	-10	-1	0	.941	0	102	98	S2		-0.1

YEAR	TM LG	G	AB	R	H	2B	3B	HR	RBI	BB-IB	HP	SO	AVG	OBP	SLG	AOPS	ABR	SB-CS	FA	FR	RNG	THR	GAMES AT POSITION	DL	BFW
MOWREY, MIKE	Harry Harlan	B4.20.1884 Browns Mill PA					D3.20.1947 Chambersburg PA			BR/TR/5-10/180		d9.24													
1905	Cin N	7	30	4	8	1	0	0	6	1	0	.267	.290	.300	69	-1	0	.759	-1	116	110	3b7		-0.2
1906	Cin N	21	53	3	17	3	0	0	6	5	0	.321	.379	.377	130	2	2	.930	2	114	58	3b15/2S		0.4
1907	Cin N	138	448	43	113	16	6	1	44	35	1	.252	.308	.321	93	-4	10	.929	-16	84	87	3b127,S11		-1.8
1908	Cin N	77	227	17	50	9	1	0	23	12	2	.220	.266	.269	73	-7	5	.936	-5	102	90	3b56,S3,O3L/2		-1.3
1909	Cin N	38	115	10	22	5	0	0	5	20	0	.191	.311	.235	70	-3	2	.947	0	111	137	3b22,S13		-0.2
	StL N	12	29	3	7	1	0	0	4	4	0	.241	.333	.276	95	0	1	.921	-1	85	0	2b7,3b2		-0.1
	Year	50	144	13	29	6	0	0	9	24	0	.201	.315	.243	75	-3	3	.948	-1	112	135	3b24,S13,2b7		-0.3
1910	StL N	143	489	69	138	24	6	2	70	67	6	38	.282	.375	.368	121	16	21	.927	14	114	139	3b141		3.6
1911	StL N	137	471	59	126	29	7	0	61	59	5	46	.268	.355	.359	103	4	15	.944	7	107	96	3b134/S		1.5
1912	StL N	114	408	59	104	13	8	2	50	46	3	29	.255	.335	.341	87	-7	19	.944	-2	105	139	3b108		-0.2
1913	StL N	132	450	61	117	18	4	0	53	53	3	40	.260	.342	.318	90	-4	21-15	.953	18	121	129	3b131		1.7
1914	Pit N	79	284	24	72	7	5	1	25	22	4	20	.254	.316	.324	94	-2	8	.960	-1	103	82	3b78		-0.1
1915	Pit F	151	521	56	146	26	6	1	49	66	5	39	.280	.367	.359	105	-1	40	**.959**	-17	90	72	3b151		-1.5
1916	†Bro N	144	495	57	121	22	6	0	60	50	5	60	.244	.320	.313	92	-3	16	**.965**	-2	99	87	3b144		0.0
1917	Bro N	83	271	24	58	9	5	0	29	25	1	25	.214	.292	.284	75	-7	7	.952	-1	103	102	3b80,2b2		-0.7
Total	13	1276	4291	485	1099	183	54	7	461	469	35	297	.256	.334	.329	96	-17	167-15	.944	-0	103	103	3b1196,2b11,S29,O3L		1.1

YEAR	TM LG	G	AB	R	H	2B	3B	HR	RBI	BB-IB	HP	SO	AVG	OBP	SLG	AOPS	ABR	SB-CS	FA	FR	RNG	THR	GAMES AT POSITION	DL	BFW
MOWRY, JOE	Joseph Aloysius	B4.6.1908 St.Louis MO					D2.9.1994 St.Louis MO			BB/TR/6-0/198		d5.13	Col Iowa											
1933	Bos N	86	249	25	55	8	5	0	20	15	3	22	.221	.273	.293	67	-11	3	.994	1	108	37	O64(48/5/11)		-1.5
1934	Bos N	25	79	9	17	3	0	1	4	3	0	13	.215	.244	.291	46	-6	0	.976	1	112	66	O20(4/0/16)/2		-0.6
1935	Bos N	81	136	17	36	8	1	1	13	11	1	13	.265	.324	.360	91	-2	0	.970	1	107	137	O45(30/2/13)		-0.2
Total	3	192	464	51	108	19	6	2	37	29	4	48	.233	.284	.313	71	-19	3	.985	3	108	66	O129(82/7/40)/2		-2.3

YEAR	TM LG	G	AB	R	H	2B	3B	HR	RBI	BB-IB	HP	SO	AVG	OBP	SLG	AOPS	ABR	SB-CS	FA	FR	RNG	THR	GAMES AT POSITION	DL	BFW
MOYNAHAN, MIKE	Michael	B1856 Chicago IL					D4.9.1899 Chicago IL			BL/TR		d8.20													
1880	Buf N	27	100	12	33	5	1	0	14	6	9	.330	.368	.400	157	6	.862	-3	91	99	S27		0.4
1881	Cle N	33	135	12	31	5	1	0	8	3	14	.230	.246	.281	69	-5	.883	-2	35	166	O32L/3		-0.9
	Det N	1	4	1	1	0	0	0	0	0	1	.250	.250	.250	55	0	.857	0	111	0	/3		0.0
	Year	34	139	13	32	5	1	0	8	3	15	.230	.246	.281	69	-5	.883	-2	35	166	O32L,3b2		-0.9
1883	Phi AA	95	400	90	124	18	10	1	67	31		.310	.360	.412	135	15	.833	-0	101	69	S95		1.5
1884	Phi AA	1	1	0	0	0	0	0		0	0	.000	.000	.000	-94	-1	.500	-1	0	0	/OC		-0.1
	Cle N	12	45	9	13	2	1	0	6	7	11	.289	.385	.378	136	2	.852	-1	107	0	2b6,S3,O3(1/0/2)		0.2
Total	4	169	688	124	202	30	13	1	95	47	35	.294	.339	.379	125	17	.837	-7	100	77	S125,O36(33/1/2),2b6,3b2		1.1

YEAR	TM LG	G	AB	R	H	2B	3B	HR	RBI	BB-IB	HP	SO	AVG	OBP	SLG	AOPS	ABR	SB-CS	FA	FR	RNG	THR	GAMES AT POSITION	DL	BFW
MUELLER, HEINIE	Clarence Francis	B9.16.1899 Creve Coeur MO					D1.23.1975 DeSoto MO			BL/TL/5-8/158		d9.25													
1920	StL N	4	22	0	7	1	0	0	1	2	0	4	.318	.375	.364	117	1	1-0	1.000	-0	110	0	O4(1/0/4)		0.0
1921	StL N	55	176	25	62	10	6	1	34	11	2	22	.352	.397	.494	137	9	2-4	.976	-1	102	76	O54(0/51/3)		0.5
1922	StL N	61	159	20	43	7	2	3	26	14	1	18	.270	.329	.396	91	-3	2-1	.947	1	96	143	O74(0/71/3)		1.8
1923	StL N	78	265	39	91	16	9	5	41	18	3	16	.343	.392	.528	144	16	4-3	.963	3	108	100	O74(0/73/1)		-1.3
1924	StL N	92	296	39	78	12	6	2	37	19	2	11	.264	.312	.365	82	-8	8-7	.962	-0	106	81	O72(2/57/13)		-0.4
1925	StL N	78	243	33	76	18	4	1	26	17	3	11	.313	.365	.424	99	-2	0-3	.950	0	95	139	O51(0/21/30)		-0.5
1926	StL N	52	191	36	51	7	6	2	4	21	1	17	.249	.300	.321	68	-14	7	.950	1	97	135	O82(10/38/35)		-1.9
	NY N	85	305	36	76	6	4	2	29	11	7	17	.249	.300	.353	78	-17	15	.950	1	97	**131**	O133(10/59/65)		-0.5
	Year	137	496	72	127	13	7	4	57	32	8	23	.256	.312	.353	78	-17	15	.944	-4	100	22	O56(49/5/2)/1		-0.
1927	NY N	84	190	33	55	6	1	3	19	25	4	12	.289	.384	.379	105	3	1	.985	3	107	152	O41(4/37/0)		0.2
1928	Bos N	42	151	24	34	3	1	0	19	17	3	9	.225	.316	.258	54	-10	1	1.000	-0	100	56	O24(4/11/10)		
1929	Bos N	46	93	10	19	2	1	0	11	12	1		.204	.302	.247	39	-9	2							

YEAR	TM LG	G	AB	R	H	2B	3B	HR	RBI	BB-IB	HP	SO	AVG	OBP	SLG	AOPS	ABR	SB-CS	FA	FR	RNG	THR	GAMES AT POSITION	DL	BFW
1935	StL A	16	27	0	5	1	0	0	1	1	0	4	.185	.214	.222	12	-4	0-0	.955	0	204	127	1b3,O2(1/1/0)		-0.4
Total 11		693	2118	296	597	87	37	22	272	168	26	147	.282	.342	.389	94	-21	37-18	.960	3	102	101	O557(83/368/109),1b31		-5.0

MUELLER, DON   Donald Frederick "Mandrake the Magician" B4.14.1927 St.Louis MO   BL/TR/6-0/185(170-185)   d8.2 f-Walter

YEAR	TM LG	G	AB	R	H	2B	3B	HR	RBI	BB-IB	HP	SO	AVG	OBP	SLG	AOPS	ABR	SB-CS	FA	FR	RNG	THR	GAMES AT POSITION	DL	BFW
1948	NY N	36	81	12	29	4	1	1	9	0	0	3	.358	.358	.469	121	2	0	.973	1	92	229	O22(18/1/1)		0.2
1949	NY N	51	56	5	13	4	0	1	5	0	0	6	.232	.295	.304	61	-3	0	1.000	0	108	0	O6(2/0/4)		-0.3
1950	NY N	132	525	60	153	15	6	7	84	10	3	26	.291	.309	.383	80	-18	1	.986	-2	99	82	O125(3/0/122)		-2.3
1951	NY N	122	469	58	130	10	7	16	69	19	1	13	.277	.307	.431	95	-6	1-1	.983	-2	107	48	O115R		-1.2
1952	NY N	126	456	61	128	14	7	12	49	34	1	24	.281	.333	.421	107	3	2-1	.987	-3	99	73	O120R		-0.4
1953	NY N	131	480	56	160	12	2	6	60	19	1	13	.333	.360	.404	97	-3	2-0	.972	-4	94	82	O122(11/0/111)		-1.0
1954	†NY N★	153	619	90	212	35	8	4	71	22	2	17	.342	.363	.444	110	8	2-3	.979	-5	90	102	O153R		-0.3
1955	NY N★	147	605	67	185	21	4	8	83	19-4	3	12	.306	.326	.393	91	-9	1-2	.976	-14	86	41	O146R		-2.9
1956	NY N	138	453	38	122	12	1	5	41	15-2	0	7	.269	.290	.333	68	-21	0-1	.989	-9	89	41	O117R		-3.6
1957	NY N	135	450	45	116	7	1	6	37	13-3	1	16	.258	.280	.318	60	-26	2-0	.989	1	89	167	O115R		-3.0
1958	Chi A	70	166	7	42	5	0	0	16	11-3	0	9	.253	.298	.283	62	-9	0-0	.968	-2	86	101	O43R		-1.2
1959	Chi A	4	4	0	2	0	0	0	0	0-0	0	0	.500	.500	.500	178	0	0-0	—	0			/H		0.0
Total 12		1245	4364	499	1292	139	37	65	520	167-12	13	146	.296	.322	.390	89	-82	11-8	.982	-38	94	81	O1084(34/1/1047)		-16.0

MUELLER, HEINIE   Emmett Jerome B7.20.1912 St.Louis MO D10.3.1986 Orlando FL   BB/TR/5-6/167   d4.19 Mil 1942-45

YEAR	TM LG	G	AB	R	H	2B	3B	HR	RBI	BB-IB	HP	SO	AVG	OBP	SLG	AOPS	ABR	SB-CS	FA	FR	RNG	THR	GAMES AT POSITION	DL	BFW
1938	Phi N	136	444	53	111	12	4	4	34	64	1	43	.250	.346	.322	87	-6	2	.967	-21	87	64	2b111,3b21		-2.0
1939	Phi N	115	341	46	95	19	4	9	43	33	0	34	.279	.342	.437	111	5	4	.964	-6	87	101	2b51,3b17,O17(4/0/13)/S		0.1
1940	Phi N	97	263	24	65	13	2	3	28	37	2	23	.247	.344	.346	95	-1	2	.966	-5	87	68	2b34,O31(29/0/2),3b13,1b2		-0.5
1941	Phi N	93	233	21	53	11	1	1	22	22	3	24	.227	.302	.296	72	-9	2	.980	2	94	106	2b29,O21(0/1/20),3b19		-0.5
Total 4		441	1281	144	324	55	11	17	127	156	6	124	.253	.337	.353	93	-11	10	.968	-30	88	79	2b225,3b70,O69(33/1/35),1b2/S		-2.9

MUELLER, RAY   Ray Coleman "Iron Man" B3.8.1912 Pittsburg KS D6.29.1994 Lower Paxton Twp. PA   BR/TR/5-9/175*   d5.11 Mil 1945-46 C2

YEAR	TM LG	G	AB	R	H	2B	3B	HR	RBI	BB-IB	HP	SO	AVG	OBP	SLG	AOPS	ABR	SB-CS	FA	FR	RNG	THR	GAMES AT POSITION	DL	BFW
1935	Bos N	42	97	10	22	5	0	3	11	3	0	11	.227	.250	.371	70	-5	0	.978	-1	87	174	C40		-0.4
1936	Bos N	24	71	5	14	4	0	0	5	5	0	17	.197	.250	.254	38	-6	0	.986	-2	158	55	C23		-0.6
1937	Bos N	64	187	21	47	9	2	2	26	16	1	36	.251	.317	.353	90	-3	1	.995	6	198	93	C57		0.6
1938	Bos N	83	274	23	65	8	6	4	35	16	1	28	.237	.282	.354	82	-9	3	.993	2	165	105	C75		-0.2
1939	Pit N	86	180	14	42	8	1	1	18	14	0	22	.233	.289	.322	65	-9	0	.971	-1	114	96	C81		-0.7
1940	Pit N	4	3	1	1	0	0	0	1	2	0	0	.333	.600	.333	165	1	0	1.000	0	59	211	C4		0.1
1943	Cin N	141	427	50	111	19	4	8	52	56	1	42	.260	.347	.379	111	7	1	.988	20	118	129	C140		3.8
1944	Cin N★	155	555	54	159	24	4	10	73	53	4	47	.286	.353	.398	115	11	4	.983	1	154	55	C155		2.3
1946	Cin N	114	378	35	96	18	4	8	48	27	3	37	.254	.309	.386	100	-2	0	.994	10	124	116	C100		1.4
1947	Cin N	71	192	17	48	11	0	6	33	16	1	25	.250	.311	.401	88	-4	1	.984	0	101	124	C55		-0.1
1948	Cin N	14	34	2	7	0	2	0	2	4	0	3	.206	.289	.235	45	-3	0	.982	-0	73	82	C10		-0.1
1949	Cin N	32	106	7	29	4	0	1	13	5	2	13	.274	.319	.340	76	-4	1	1.000	-1	121	107	C31	126	-0.2
	NY N	56	170	17	38	2	2	5	23	13	0	14	.224	.279	.347	67	-9	1	.982	1	92	85	C56		-0.3
	Year	88	276	24	67	6	2	6	36	18	2	27	.243	.294	.344	70	-13	2	.988	-1	103	93	C87		-0.6
1950	NY N	4	11	0	1	0	0	0	0	0	0	2	.091	.091	.182	-30	-2	0	1.000	1	113	0	C4		-0.9
	Pit N	67	156	17	42	7	0	6	24	11	1	14	.269	.321	.429	92	-2	2	.996	2	125	110	C63		0.2
	Year	71	167	17	43	8	0	6	24	11	1	16	.257	.307	.413	85	-4	2	.996	3	124	102	C67		0.1
1951	Bos N	28	70	8	11	2	0	1	9	7	0	11	.157	.234	.229	27	-7	0-0	1.000	2	78	163	C23		-0.5
Total 14		985	2911	281	733	123	23	56	373	250	13	322	.252	.314	.368	91	-46	14-0	.988	40	131	101	C917	126	4.7

MUELLER, WALTER   Walter John B12.6.1894 Central MO D8.16.1971 St.Louis MO   BR/TR/5-8/160   d5.7 s-Don

YEAR	TM LG	G	AB	R	H	2B	3B	HR	RBI	BB-IB	HP	SO	AVG	OBP	SLG	AOPS	ABR	SB-CS	FA	FR	RNG	THR	GAMES AT POSITION	DL	BFW
1922	Pit N	32	122	21	33	5	1	2	18	5	1	7	.270	.305	.377	74	-5	1-0	.976	4	108	179	O31R		-0.3
1923	Pit N	40	111	11	34	4	0	0	20	4	1	6	.306	.336	.414	95	-1	2-2	.941	0	113	76	O26(19/0/7)		-0.3
1924	Pit N	30	50	6	13	1	1	0	8	4	1	4	.260	.327	.320	73	-2	1	1.000	2	96	409	O15(8/5/2)		0.0
1926	Pit N	19	62	8	15	0	1	0	3	0	0	2	.242	.242	.274	37	-6	0	.969	1	102	145	O15(14/0/1)		-0.6
Total 4		121	345	46	95	10	7	2	49	13	3	19	.275	.307	.362	74	-14	4-2	.966	8	107	165	O87(41/5/41)		-1.2

MUELLER, BILL   William Lawrence "Hawk" B11.9.1920 Bay City MI D10.24.2001 Glenview IL   BR/TR/6-1.5/180   d8.29 Mil 1943-45

YEAR	TM LG	G	AB	R	H	2B	3B	HR	RBI	BB-IB	HP	SO	AVG	OBP	SLG	AOPS	ABR	SB-CS	FA	FR	RNG	THR	GAMES AT POSITION	DL	BFW
1942	Chi A	26	85	5	14	1	0	0	5	12	1	14	.165	.276	.176	29	-7	2-1	.978	6	114	351	O26(0/23/3)		-0.2
1945	Chi A	13	9	3	0	0	0	0	0	2	0	1	.000	.182	.000	-47	-2	1-0	.778	-0	124	0	O7(0/5/2)		-0.2
Total 2		39	94	8	14	1	0	0	5	14	1	10	.149	.266	.160	22	-10	3-1	.960	6	115	323	O33(0/28/5)		-0.4

MUELLER, BILL   William Richard B3.17.1971 Maryland Heights MO   BB/TR/5-10/180*   [SFN93 15/414]   d4.18 Col Missouri St.

YEAR	TM LG	G	AB	R	H	2B	3B	HR	RBI	BB-IB	HP	SO	AVG	OBP	SLG	AOPS	ABR	SB-CS	FA	FR	RNG	THR	GAMES AT POSITION	DL	BFW
1996	SF N	55	200	31	66	15	1	0	19	24-0	1	26	.330	.401	.415	119	7	0-0	.966	-2	95	141	3b45,2b8		0.6
1997	†SF N	128	390	51	114	26	3	7	44	48-1	3	71	.292	.369	.428	112	8	4-3	.956	4	103	97	3b122	17	1.3
1998	SF N	145	534	93	157	27	0	9	59	79-1	1	83	.294	.383	.395	112	13	3-3	.952	2	106	141	3b137,2b10		1.5
1999	SF N	116	414	61	120	24	0	2	36	65-1	3	52	.290	.388	.362	98	3	4-2	.958	-4	95	96	3b108,2b3		1.1
2000	†SF N	153	560	97	150	29	4	10	55	52-0	6	62	.268	.333	.387	102	3	4-2	.974	-3	95	99	3b145,2b2	41	-1.2
2001	Chi N	70	210	38	62	12	1	6	23	37-3	2	19	.295	.403	.448	125	10	1-1	.942	-0	96	64	3b64/2	91	1.0
2002	Chi N	103	353	51	94	19	4	7	37	51-2	6	41	.266	.355	.402	104	1	0-0	.973	1	92	103	3b101	36	0.2
	SF N	8	13	0	2	0	0	0	1	1-0	0	1	.154	.214	.154	1	-2	0-0	1.000	-0	76	0	3b3		-0.2
	Year	111	366	51	96	19	4	7	38	52-2	6	42	.262	.350	.393	100	-1	0-0	.974	-0	92	101	3b104		0.0
2003	†Bos A	146	524	85	171	45	5	19	85	59-2	7	77	.326	.398	.540	139	32	1-4	.951	1	105	101	3b135,2b10/SD		3.1
2004	†Bos A	110	399	75	113	27	1	12	57	51-1	4	56	.283	.365	.446	105	5	2-2	.943	-2	101	102	3b96,2b14	43	0.3
2005	Bos A	150	519	69	153	34	3	10	62	59-3	2	74	.295	.369	.430	107	7	0-0	.972	-4	99	78	3b142,2b5		0.5
Total 10		1184	4116	651	1202	258	22	82	478	526-14	34	562	.292	.372	.425	110	73	19-17	.960	-7	99	101	3b1098,2b53,D3/S	228	7.1

MULDOON, MIKE   Michael D. B4.9.1858 Co. Westmeath, Ireland   5-8/165   d5.1

YEAR	TM LG	G	AB	R	H	2B	3B	HR	RBI	BB-IB	HP	SO	AVG	OBP	SLG	AOPS	ABR	SB-CS	FA	FR	RNG	THR	GAMES AT POSITION	DL	BFW
1882	Cle N	84	341	50	84	17	5	6	45	10		28	.246	.268	.378	108	3		.880	3	103	158	3b61,O23(21/2/0)		0.6
1883	Cle N	98	378	54	86	22	3	0	29	10		39	.228	.247	.302	67	-14		.825	-9	88	77	3b98,O2R		-1.9
1884	Cle N	110	422	46	101	16	6	2	38	18		67	.239	.270	.320	82	-9		.833	-7	98	106	3b109/OR2		-1.3
1885	Bal AA	102	410	47	103	20	6	2	52	20	4		.251	.293	.344	102	1		.870	-2	98	106	3b101/2		0.1
1886	Bal AA	101	381	57	76	13	8	0	23	34	2		.199	.269	.276	72	-12	12	.912	3	105	81	3b57,3b44		-0.5
Total 5		495	1932	254	450	88	28	10	187	92	6	134	.233	.270	.323	86	-31	12	.846	-12	97	103	3b413,2b59,O26(21/2/3)		-3.0

MULLANE, TONY   Anthony John "Count","The Apollo of the Box" B1.20.1859 Cork, Ireland D4.25.1944 Chicago IL   BB/TR (BL 1882, TB 1882p, 1893p)/5-10.5/165   d8.27 OF(57/59/39) ▲

YEAR	TM LG	G	AB	R	H	2B	3B	HR	RBI	BB-IB	HP	SO	AVG	OBP	SLG	AOPS	ABR	SB-CS	FA	FR	RNG	THR	GAMES AT POSITION	DL	BFW
1881	Det N	5	19	0	5	0	0	1	0	0		0	.263	.263	.263	63	0		.882	0	83	0	P5		0.0
1882	Lou AA	77	303	46	78	13	1	0		13			.257	.288	.307	107	3		.959	10	117	299	P55,1b13,O12(1/12/1),2b2		0.5
1883	StL AA	83	307	38	69	11	6	0	33	13			.225	.256	.300	74	-9		.851	2	103	204	P53,O30(13/10/7),2b3,1b2		-0.2
1884	Tol AA	95	352	49	97	19	3	3		33			.276	.339	.372	127	12		.889	5	126	296	P67,O19(14/0/4),1b7,3b6/S2		0.4
1886	Cin AA	91	324	59	73	12	5	0	39	25	1		.225	.283	.293	78	-9	20	.899	-1	102	235	P63,O27(2/23/2),1b4,3b2/S2		-0.5
1887	Cin AA	56	199	35	44	4	3	3	16	8	4		.221	.292	.327	71	-8	20	.944	-1	85	282	P48,O9(7/2/0)		-0.1
1888	Cin AA	51	175	27	44	4	4	1	16	8	3		.251	.296	.337	97	-1	12	.888	-1	97	48	P44,1b4,O3R,2b2		-0.1
1889	Cin AA	63	196	53	58	16	4	0	29	27	2	21	.296	.387	.418	125	7	24	.920	-3	83	0	P33,3b18,O12(4/5/3),1b4		-0.1
1890	Cin N	81	286	41	79	9	0	0	34	39	6	30	.276	.375	.364	116	7	19	.941	-7	78	0	O28(8/2/18),P25,3b21,S10/1		0.2
1891	Cin N	64	209	16	31	1	2	0	9	18	3	33	.148	.229	.172	17	-22	4	.958	-0	106	66	P51,O12(6/5/1),3b4		-0.3
1892	Cin N	39	118	14	20	3	1	0	9	9	3	13	.169	.246	.212	39	-9	4	.926	5	132	183	P37,1b2		-0.2
1893	Cin N	16	52	11	15	0	0	1	5	5	3	3	.288	.383	.346	92	-0	1	.939	0	107	113	P15/3		0.0
	Bal N	38	114	15	26	2	1	0	14	5	0	14	.228	.261	.263	39	-11	5	.943	-2	110	107	P34,O2L/1		0.0
	Year	54	166	26	41	2	1	1	20	10	3	17	.247	.302	.289	56	-11	6	.942	-2	109	109	P49,O2L/31		0.0
1894	Bal N	21	53	3	21	5	0	0	9	4	2	2	.396	.475	.453	119	5	2	.889	-1	73	128	P21		0.0
	Cle N	4	13	0	1	0	0	0	0	4	0	2	.077	.294	.077	-6	-1	1	.944	2	225	485	P4		0.0
	Year	25	66	3	22	3	0	0	9	8	2	5	.333	.436	.379	94	4	3	.911	1	105	204	P25		0.0
Total 13		784	2720	407	661	99	38	8	223	221	29	114	.243	.307	.316	87	-36	112	.913	13	106	180	P555,O154C,3b52,1b38,S12,2b9		-0.2

MULLEAVY, GREG   Gregory Thomas "Moe" B9.25.1905 Detroit MI D2.1.1980 Arcadia CA   BR/TR/5-9/167   d7.4 C7

YEAR	TM LG	G	AB	R	H	2B	3B	HR	RBI	BB-IB	HP	SO	AVG	OBP	SLG	AOPS	ABR	SB-CS	FA	FR	RNG	THR	GAMES AT POSITION	DL	BFW
1930	Chi A	77	289	27	76	14	0	0	28	20	0	23	.263	.311	.346	69	-14	5-2	.918	-8	99	91	S73		-1.2
1932	Chi A	1	3	0	0	0	0	0	0	0	0	0	.000	.000	.000	-99	-1	0-0	1.000	0	87	207	/2		-0.1
1933	Bos A	1	0	1	0	0	0	0	0	0	0	0							—	0			/R		0.0
Total 3		79	292	28	76	14	0	0	28	20	0	23	.260	.308	.342	67	-15	5-2	.918	-8	99	91	S73/2		-1.3

YEAR	TM LG	G	AB	R	H	2B	3B	HR	RBI	BB-IB	HP	SO	AVG	OBP	SLG	AOPS	ABR	SB-CS	FA	FR	RNG	THR	GAMES AT POSITION	DL	BFW
MULLEN d8.17																									-0.1
1872	Cle NA	1	4	1	0	0	0	0	0	0			0	.000	.000	.000	-99	-1	0-0	.400	-1	0	0	/OR		

MULLEN, CHARLIE Charles George B3.15.1889 Seattle WA D6.6.1963 Seattle WA BR/TR/5-10.5/155 d5.18

YEAR	TM LG	G	AB	R	H	2B	3B	HR	RBI	BB-IB	HP	SO	AVG	OBP	SLG	AOPS	ABR	SB-CS	FA	FR	RNG	THR	GAMES AT POSITION	DL	BFW
1910	Chi A	41	123	15	24	2	1	0	13	4	0		.195	.220	.228	42	-9	4	.982	1	115	145	1b37,O2R		-0.9
1911	Chi A	20	59	7	12	2	1	0	5	5	0		.203	.266	.271	51	-4	4	.969	0	107	27	1b20		-0.4
1914	NY A	93	323	33	84	8	0	0	44	33	2	55	.260	.332	.285	86	-4	11-17	.994	3	106	130	1b93		-0.1
1915	NY A	40	90	11	24	1	0	0	7	10	0	12	.267	.340	.278	85	-1	5-2	.982	1	120	0	1b27		-0.7
1916	NY A	59	146	11	39	9	1	0	18	9	0	13	.267	.310	.342	94	-1	7	.943	-5	73	72	2b20,1b17,O6(1/2/3)		-0.1
Total	5	253	741	77	183	22	3	0	87	61	2	80	.247	.306	.285	78	-19	28-19	.988	-0	109	100	1b194,2b20,O8(1/2/5)		-3.0

MULLEN, MOON Ford Parker B2.9.1917 Olympia WA BL/TR/5-9/165 d4.18 Mil 1945 Col Oregon

YEAR	TM LG	G	AB	R	H	2B	3B	HR	RBI	BB-IB	HP	SO	AVG	OBP	SLG	AOPS	ABR	SB-CS	FA	FR	RNG	THR	GAMES AT POSITION	DL	BFW
1944	Phi N	118	464	51	124	9	4	0	31	28	4	32	.267	.315	.304	77	-15	4	.963	-6	98	81	2b114/3		-1.5

MULLEN, JOHN John B Philadelphia PA BL/TL d9.9

YEAR	TM LG	G	AB	R	H	2B	3B	HR	RBI	BB-IB	HP	SO	AVG	OBP	SLG	AOPS	ABR	SB-CS	FA	FR	RNG	THR	GAMES AT POSITION	DL	BFW
1876	Phi N	1	3	0	0	0	0	0	0	0			.000	.000	.000	-99	-1		.714	-0			/C		-0.1

MULLEN, BILLY William John B1.23.1896 St.Louis MO D5.4.1971 St.Louis MO BR/TR/5-8/160 d10.2

YEAR	TM LG	G	AB	R	H	2B	3B	HR	RBI	BB-IB	HP	SO	AVG	OBP	SLG	AOPS	ABR	SB-CS	FA	FR	RNG	THR	GAMES AT POSITION	DL	BFW
1920	StL A	2	4	0	0	0	0	0	0	0	0	0	.000	.000	.000	-97	-1	0-0	1.000	-0	71	0	/2		-0.2
1921	StL A	4	4	0	0	0	0	0	0	2	0		.000	.333	.000	-8	-1	0-0	1.000	-0	90	0	3b2		0.0
1923	Bro N	4	11	1	3	0	0	0	0	0	0		.273	.273	.273	46	-1	0-0	.875	-0	115	0	3b4		-0.1
1926	Det A	11	13	2	1	0	0	0	0	5	0	1	.077	.333	.077	11	-1	1-0	.875	-1	87	0	3b9		-0.2
1928	StL A	15	18	2	7	1	0	0	2	3	0	4	.389	.476	.444	139	1	1-0	.867	-1	111	141	3b6		0.1
Total	5	36	50	5	11	1	0	0	2	10	0	6	.220	.350	.240	56	-3	1-0	.884	-1	102	47	3b21/2		-0.4

MULLER, FREDDIE Frederick William B12.21.1907 Newark CA D10.20.1976 Davis CA BR/TR/5-10/170 d7.8

YEAR	TM LG	G	AB	R	H	2B	3B	HR	RBI	BB-IB	HP	SO	AVG	OBP	SLG	AOPS	ABR	SB-CS	FA	FR	RNG	THR	GAMES AT POSITION	DL	BFW
1933	Bos A	15	48	6	9	1	1	0	3	5	0	5	.188	.264	.250	37	-5	1-0	.923	-3	94	82	2b14		-0.6
1934	Bos A	2	1	1	0	0	0	0	0	1	0	0	.000	.500	.000	36	0	0-0	.800	-1	47	0	/23		-0.1
Total	2	17	49	7	9	1	1	0	3	6	0	5	.184	.273	.245	38	-5	1-0	.914	-3	91	77	2b15/3		-0.7

MULLIGAN, EDDIE Edward Joseph B8.27.1894 St.Louis MO D3.15.1982 San Rafael CA BR/TR/5-9/152 d9.23 Col St. Louis

YEAR	TM LG	G	AB	R	H	2B	3B	HR	RBI	BB-IB	HP	SO	AVG	OBP	SLG	AOPS	ABR	SB-CS	FA	FR	RNG	THR	GAMES AT POSITION	DL	BFW
1915	Chi N	11	22	5	8	1	0	0	2	5		0	.364	.481	.409	170	2	2-2	.907	0	91	233	S10/3		0.3
1916	Chi N	58	189	13	29	3	4	0	9	8	3	30	.153	.200	.212	24	-17	1-7	.888	-3	103	109	S58		-1.9
1921	Chi A	151	609	82	153	21	12	1	45	32	4	53	.251	.293	.330	59	-40	13-18	.955	-12	94	95	3b151/S		-4.4
1922	Chi A	103	372	39	87	14	8	0	31	22	1	32	.234	.278	.315	55	-26	7-7	.971	3	108	84	3b84,S7		-1.8
1928	Pit N	27	43	4	10	2	0	0	1	3	0	4	.233	.283	.279	45	-3	0	.929	0	92	253	3b6,2b4		-0.3
Total	5	350	1235	143	287	41	24	1	88	70	8	120	.232	.278	.307	54	-84	23-27	.961	-12	99	94	3b242,S76,2b4		-8.1

MULLIGAN, JOHN John d6.14

YEAR	TM LG	G	AB	R	H	2B	3B	HR	RBI	BB-IB	HP	SO	AVG	OBP	SLG	AOPS	ABR	SB-CS	FA	FR	RNG	THR	GAMES AT POSITION	DL	BFW
1884	Was U	1	4	2	1	0	0	0		0			.250	.250	.250	54	0		1.000	1	113	0	/3		0.0

MULLIGAN, SEAN Sean Patrick B4.25.1970 Lynwood CA BR/TR/6-2/210 [SDN91 4/107] d9.1 Col Illinois

YEAR	TM LG	G	AB	R	H	2B	3B	HR	RBI	BB-IB	HP	SO	AVG	OBP	SLG	AOPS	ABR	SB-CS	FA	FR	RNG	THR	GAMES AT POSITION	DL	BFW
1996	SD N	2	1	0	0	0	0	0	.0	0-0	0	0	.000	.000	.000	-99	0	0-0	—	0			/H		0.0

MULLIN, HENRY Henry J. B4.17.1862 St.John NB, Can. D11.8.1927 Beverly MA BR/5-9/160 d6.4

YEAR	TM LG	G	AB	R	H	2B	3B	HR	RBI	BB-IB	HP	SO	AVG	OBP	SLG	AOPS	ABR	SB-CS	FA	FR	RNG	THR	GAMES AT POSITION	DL	BFW
1884	Was AA	34	120	13	17	3	1	0		8			.142	.195	.183	27	-9		.869	1	107	0	O34(4/29/1)/3		-0.8
	Bos U	2	8	1	0	0	0	0		0			.000	.000	.000	-99	-2		1.000	2	506	1163	O2C		-0.0
Total	1	36	128	14	17	3	1	0		8			.133	.184	.172	18	-11		.882	3	137	88	O36(4/31/1)/3		-0.8

MULLIN, JIM James Henry B10.16.1883 New York NY D1.24.1925 Philadelphia PA BR/TR/5-10/173 d6.1 Col Manhattan

YEAR	TM LG	G	AB	R	H	2B	3B	HR	RBI	BB-IB	HP	SO	AVG	OBP	SLG	AOPS	ABR	SB-CS	FA	FR	RNG	THR	GAMES AT POSITION	DL	BFW
1904	Phi A	22	52	5	14	1	0	1	5	3	1		.269	.321	.346	106	0	2	.985	-3	66	68	1b7,2b5,S2/OL		-0.3
	Was A	27	102	10	19	2	1	0	4	4	1		.186	.224	.245	49	-6	3	.981	5	111	98	2b27		-0.1
	Phi A	19	58	4	10	0	0	0	4	2	3		.172	.238	.172	29	-5	2	.984	-1	66	68	1b19		-0.6
	Year	68	212	19	43	3	2	1	13	9	5		.203	.252	.250	58	-10	7	.965	1	109	97	2b32,1b26,S2/OL		-1.0
1905	Was A	50	163	18	31	7	6	0	13	5	0		.190	.214	.307	67	-7	5	.928	-2	100	85	2b40,1b6		-1.0
Total	2	118	375	37	74	10	8	1	26	14	5		.197	.236	.275	62	-18	12	.946	-1	104	91	2b72,1b32,S2/OL		-2.0

MULLIN, PAT Patrick Joseph B11.1.1917 Trotter PA D8.14.1999 Brownsville PA BL/TR/6-2/190* d9.18 Mil 1942-45 C8

YEAR	TM LG	G	AB	R	H	2B	3B	HR	RBI	BB-IB	HP	SO	AVG	OBP	SLG	AOPS	ABR	SB-CS	FA	FR	RNG	THR	GAMES AT POSITION	DL	BFW
1940	Det A	4	4	0	0	0	0	0	0	0	0	0	.000	.000	.000	-91	-0	0-0	—	-0	0	0	/OC		-0.1
1941	Det A	54	220	42	76	11	5	5	23	18	2	18	.345	.400	.509	126	8	5-1	.944	-4	93	52	O51C	53	0.3
1946	Det A	93	276	34	68	13	4	3	35	25	1	36	.246	.311	.355	81	-7	3-5	.949	-2	91	133	O75(0/1/75)		-1.3
1947	Det A	116	398	62	102	28	6	15	62	63	1	66	.256	.359	.470	126	14	3-8	.988	4	107	128	O106R		1.3
1948	Det A☆	138	496	91	143	16	11	23	80	77	1	57	.288	.385	.504	132	21	1-2	.972	-2	101	75	O131(0/10/123)		1.4
1949	Det A★	104	310	55	83	8	6	12	59	42	1	39	.268	.357	.448	112	4	0-0	.989	-2	97	73	O79(61/18/3)		-0.3
1950	Det A	69	142	16	31	5	0	6	23	20	0	23	.218	.315	.380	75	-6	1-4	1.000	1	94	164	O32(21/0/13)		-0.7
1951	Det A	110	295	41	83	11	6	12	51	40	0	38	.281	.367	.481	128	10	2-2	.939	-5	91	69	O83(76/4/6)		0.0
1952	Det A	97	255	29	64	13	5	7	35	31	0	30	.251	.332	.424	108	2	4-2	.979	3	102	151	O65(60/2/5)		0.0
1953	Det A	79	97	11	26	1	0	4	17	14	0	15	.268	.360	.402	107	1	0-1	.944	-1	83	101	O14(10/0/4)	53	0.7
Total	10	864	2493	381	676	106	43	87	385	330	6	312	.271	.358	.453	115	46	20-27	.970	-8	98	101	O637(228/87/335)		

MULLINIKS, RANCE Steven Rance B1.15.1956 Tulare CA BL/TR/6-0/170(160-175) [CalA74 3/58] d6.18

YEAR	TM LG	G	AB	R	H	2B	3B	HR	RBI	BB-IB	HP	SO	AVG	OBP	SLG	AOPS	ABR	SB-CS	FA	FR	RNG	THR	GAMES AT POSITION	DL	BFW
1977	Cal A	78	271	36	73	13	2	3	21	23-2	1	36	.269	.329	.365	92	-3	1-1	.963	3	101	83	S77		0.8
1978	Cal A	50	119	6	22	3	1	1	6	8-0	1	23	.185	.238	.252	40	-10	2-0	.953	-6	81	97	S47,D2		-1.2
1979	Cal A	22	68	7	10	0	0	1	8	4-0	1	14	.147	.192	.191	8	-9	0-0	.957	-5	68	92	S22		-1.
1980	KC A	36	54	8	14	3	0	0	6	7-0	0	10	.259	.339	.315	81	-1	0-0	.981	-3	86	61	S18,2b14		-0.
1981	KC A	24	44	6	10	3	0	0	5	2-0	0	7	.227	.261	.295	60	-2	0-1	.900	-1	94	129	2b10,S7,3b5		-1.2
1982	Tor A	112	311	32	76	25	4	4	35	37-1	1	49	.244	.326	.363	82	-6	3-2	.971	-4	87	59	3b116,S15,2b2		0.
1983	Tor A	129	364	54	100	34	3	10	49	57-5	1	43	.275	.373	.467	122	13	0-2	.971	-4	84	59	3b116,S15,2b2		0.
1984	Tor A	125	343	41	111	21	5	3	42	33-3	1	44	.324	.383	.440	123	12	2-3	.968	-6	91	77	3b119		0.
1985	†Tor A	129	366	55	108	26	1	10	57	55-2	0	54	.295	.383	.454	126	15	2-0	.975	-8	108	90	3b110/2D	26	0.
1986	Tor A	117	348	50	90	22	0	11	45	43-1	1	60	.259	.340	.417	102	2	1-1	.927	-5	98	113	3b96,D22/S		0.
1987	Tor A	124	332	37	103	28	1	11	44	34-1	0	55	.310	.371	.500	126	13	1-0	1.000	-1	63	0	D108,3b7	20	0.
1988	Tor A	119	337	49	101	21	1	12	48	56-3	0	57	.300	.395	.475	142	22	1-0	.985	2	106	236	D73,3b29		-0.
1989	†Tor A	103	273	25	65	11	2	3	29	34-6	0	40	.238	.320	.326	84	-5	0-0	.949	-3	79	150	3b22,D10,1b3		-0.
1990	Tor A	57	97	11	28	4	0	2	16	22-2	0	19	.289	.417	.392	126	5	2-1	1.000	1	63	0	D81,3b5	31	-0.
1991	†Tor A	97	240	27	60	12	1	2	24	44-2	0	44	.250	.364	.333	91	-1	0-0	1.000	-2	44	0	D2	148	0.
1992	Tor A	3	2	1	1	0	0	0		1-0	0	0	.500	.667	.500	220	-0	0-0	—	0			D2	225	0.
Total	16	1325	3569	445	972	226	17	73	435	460-28	7	555	.272	.354	.407	107	45	15-12	.961	-41	93	93	3b730,D303,S206,2b28,1b3		

MULLINS, FRAN Francis Joseph B5.14.1957 Oakland CA BR/TR/6-0/180* [ChiA79 3/61] d9.1 Col Santa Clara

YEAR	TM LG	G	AB	R	H	2B	3B	HR	RBI	BB-IB	HP	SO	AVG	OBP	SLG	AOPS	ABR	SB-CS	FA	FR	RNG	THR	GAMES AT POSITION	DL	BFW
1980	Chi A	21	62	9	12	4	0	0	9-0	0	8	.194	.292	.258	53	-4	0-1	.981	-1	85	173	3b21		55	-0.
1984	SF N	57	110	8	24	8	0	2	10	9-0	0	29	.218	.277	.345	76	-4	3-1	.969	4	119	108	2b13,S11/1D	32	0.
1986	Cle A	28	40	3	7	4	0	0	5	2-0	0	11	.175	.209	.275	32	-4	0-0	.953	2	129	78	2b11,S11/1D	87	-0.
Total	3	106	212	20	43	16	0	2	24	20-0	0	48	.203	.269	.307	61	-12	3-2	.968	5	96	127	3b49,S39,2b17/D1		-0.

MULVEY, JOE Joseph H. B10.27.1858 Providence RI D8.21.1928 Philadelphia PA BR/TR/5-11.5/178 d5.31

YEAR	TM LG	G	AB	R	H	2B	3B	HR	RBI	BB-IB	HP	SO	AVG	OBP	SLG	AOPS	ABR	SB-CS	FA	FR	RNG	THR	GAMES AT POSITION	DL	BFW
1883	Pro N	4	16	1	2	0	0	0		0		1	.125	.125	.188	-6	-2		.692	-2	77	0	S4		-0.
	Phi N	3	12	2	6	1	0	0	3	0		2	.500	.500	.583	250	2		.750	-1	44	171	3b3		-0.
	Year	7	28	3	8	1	0	0		0		2	.286	.286	.357	96	0		.692	-3	77	0	S4,3b3		-0.
1884	Phi N	100	401	47	92	11	2	2	32	4		49	.229	.237	.282	66	-16		.834	13	115	151	3b100		0
1885	Phi N	107	443	74	119	25	6	6	64	3		18	.269	.274	.393	116	6		.848	-5	96	93	3b107		0
1886	Phi N	107	430	71	115	16	10	2	53	15		31	.267	.292	.365	98	-3	27	.879	-19	87	18	3b107/OR		-0
1887	Phi N	111	474	93	136	21	6	2	78	21	3	14	.287	.321	.369	86	-10	43	.865	-17	86	106	3b111		-2
1888	Phi N	100	398	37	86	12	3	0	36	8	1	25	.216	.235	.261	55	-21	18	.891	-13	99	72	3b100		-3
1889	Phi N	129	544	77	157	21	9	6	77	23	1	25	.289	.319	.393	91	-12	23	.893	1	104	83	3b129		-1
1890	Phi P	120	519	96	149	26	16	5	87	27		36	.287	.326	.428	98	-6	20	.857	-17	87	72	3b113		-0
1891	Phi AA	113	453	62	115	9	13	5	66	17		19	.254	.287	.364	86	-13	11	.894	1	96	98	3b113		-0
1892	Phi N	25	98	9	14	1	1	0	4	6		9	.143	.200	.173	13	-11	2	.883	2	105	139	3b25		-0

YEAR	TM LG	G	AB	R	H	2B	3B	HR	RBI	BB-IB	HP	SO	AVG	OBP	SLG	AOPS	ABR	SB-CS	FA	FR	RNG	THR	GAMES AT POSITION	DL	BFW
1893	Was N	55	226	21	53	9	4	0	19	7	2	8	.235	.264	.310	54	-16	2	.874	5	112	88	3b55		-0.9
1895	Bro N	13	49	8	15	4	1	0	8	2	0	0	.306	.333	.429	104	0	1	.917	1	99	50	3b13		0.1
Total	12	987	4063	598	1059	157	71	28	532	134	15	257	.261	.287	.355	84	-102	147	.871	-53	96	88	3b983,S4/OR		-12.2

MUMPHREY, JERRY   Jerry Wayne   B9.9.1952 Tyler TX   BB/TR/6-2/185(175-200)   [StLN71 4/79]   d9.10

YEAR	TM LG	G	AB	R	H	2B	3B	HR	RBI	BB-IB	HP	SO	AVG	OBP	SLG	AOPS	ABR	SB-CS	FA	FR	RNG	THR	GAMES AT POSITION	DL	BFW
1974	StL N	5	2	2	0	0	0	0	0	0-0	0	0	.000	.000	.000	-99	-1	0-0	—	-0	0	0	/OL		-0.1
1975	StL N	11	16	2	6	2	0	0	1	4-0	0	3	.375	.500	.500	170	2	0-0	1.000	1	174	0	O3R		0.3
1976	StL N	112	384	51	99	15	5	1	26	37-0	1	53	.258	.322	.331	85	-7	22-6	.993	5	113	98	O94(15/77/12)		-0.3
1977	StL N	145	463	73	133	20	10	2	38	47-6	1	70	.287	.354	.387	99	0	22-15	.971	6	111	100	O133(49/67/34)		0.2
1978	StL N	125	367	41	96	13	4	2	37	30-0	1	40	.262	.317	.335	83	-9	14-10	.995	-1	89	141	O116(48/30/48)		-1.4
1979	StL N	124	339	53	100	10	3	3	32	26-2	0	39	.295	.341	.369	93	-3	8-11	.984	-3	96	44	O114(83/19/20)	16	-1.3
1980	SD N	160	564	61	168	24	3	4	59	49-4	0	90	.298	.352	.372	110	8	52-5	.974	-3	100	97	O153C		1.4
1981 †NY A	80	319	44	98	11	5	6	32	24-1	0	27	.307	.354	.429	127	10	14-9	.966	3	112	113	O79C			1.3
1982	NY A	123	477	76	143	24	10	9	68	50-4	0	66	.300	.364	.449	124	16	11-3	.986	0	104	63	O123C		1.3
1983	NY A	83	267	41	70	11	4	7	36	28-2	0	33	.262	.327	.412	107	2	2-3	.983	7	113	154	O83C	42	1.6
	Hou N	44	143	17	48	10	2	1	17	22-3	1	23	.336	.425	.455	153	12	5-0	.990	-2	97	50	O43C		0.7
1984	Hou N★	151	524	66	152	30	3	9	83	56-7	1	79	.290	.355	.391	118	13	15-7	.988	-8	93	67	O137C		1.1
1985	Hou N	130	444	52	123	25	2	8	61	37-8	0	57	.277	.329	.396	105	3	6-7	.969	-2	100	81	O126(0/58/68)		0.5
1986	Chi N	111	309	37	94	11	2	5	32	26-4	0	45	.304	.355	.401	101	1	2-3	.982	-0	102	64	O92(39/65/21)		-0.4
1987	Chi N	118	309	41	103	19	2	13	44	35-6	0	47	.333	.400	.534	139	18	1-1	.992	-1	94	105	O85(78/1/6)		-0.2
1988	Chi N	63	66	3	9	2	0	0	9	7-2	0	16	.136	.219	.167	12	-7	0-0	1.000	-1	69	0	O4L		1.4
Total	15	1585	4993	660	1442	217	55	70	575	478-49	4	688	.289	.349	.396	108	58	174-80	.981	2	102	90	O1386(317/935/212)	58	3.9

MUNCE, JOHN   John Lewis "Big John"   B11.18.1857 Philadelphia PA   D3.15.1917 Philadelphia PA   5-8.5/160   d8.19

| 1884 | Wil U | 7 | 21 | 1 | 4 | 0 | 0 | 0 | | 1 | | | .190 | .227 | .190 | 27 | -3 | | .667 | -0 | 136 | 0 | O7(0/2/6) | | -0.3 |

MUNCH, JAKE   Jacob Ferdinand   B11.16.1890 Morton PA   D6.8.1966 Lansdowne PA   BL/TL/6-2.5/170   d5.27

| 1918 | Phi A | 22 | 30 | 3 | 8 | 0 | 1 | 0 | 0 | 2-0 | 0 | | .267 | .267 | .333 | 80 | -1 | 0 | .667 | -1 | 67 | 0 | O3(0/1/2),1b2 | | -0.2 |

MUNDINGER, GEORGE   George   B11.20.1854 New Orleans LA   D10.12.1910 Covington LA   BR/TR/6-2/200   d5.9

| 1884 | Ind AA | 3 | 8 | 1 | 2 | 0 | 0 | 0 | | 3 | 0 | | .250 | .250 | .250 | 65 | 0 | | .750 | -2 | | | C3 | | -0.2 |

MUNDY, BILL   William Edward   B6.28.1889 Salineville OH   D9.23.1958 Kalamazoo MI   BL/TL/5-10/154   d8.17

| 1913 | Bos A | 16 | 47 | 4 | 12 | 0 | 0 | 0 | 4 | 4 | 0 | 12 | .255 | .314 | .255 | 65 | -2 | 0 | .952 | -3 | 47 | 53 | 1b14 | | -0.5 |

MUNN, HORATIO   Horatio Brinsmade   B7.26.1851 Newark NJ   D2.17.1910 Brooklyn NY   d9.4

| 1875 | Atl NA | 1 | 4 | 0 | 0 | 0 | 0 | 0 | | 0 | 0 | | .000 | .000 | .000 | -99 | -1 | 0-0 | .833 | -0 | 111 | 0 | /2 | | -0.1 |

MUNOZ, JOSE   Jose Luis   B11.11.1967 Chicago IL   BB/TR/5-11/165   [LAN87 20/508]   d4.7   Col Florida JC

| 1996 | Chi A | 17 | 27 | 7 | 7 | 0 | 0 | 0 | 1 | 4-0 | 0 | 1 | .259 | .355 | .259 | 61 | -1 | 0-0 | .923 | -3 | 72 | 51 | 2b7,S2/3OLD | | -0.3 |

MUNOZ, NOE   Noe   B11.11.1967 San Cristobal, Estado de Mexico, Mexico   BR/TR/6-2/180   d4.30

| 1995 | LA N | 2 | 1 | 0 | 0 | 0 | 0 | 0 | 0 | 0-0 | 0 | | .000 | .000 | .000 | -99 | 0 | 0-0 | 1.000 | 1 | 0 | 0 | C2 | | 0.0 |

MUNOZ, PEDRO   Pedro Javier (Gonzalez)   B9.19.1968 Ponce, PR   BR/TR/5-10/207(170-208)   d9.1

1990	Min A	22	85	13	23	4	1	0	5	2-0	0	16	.271	.281	.341	71	-4	3-0	.972	-2	81	69	O21(3/0/19)/D		-0.6
1991	Min A	51	138	15	39	7	1	7	26	9-0	1	31	.283	.327	.500	121	3	3-0	.989	3	116	114	O44(10/0/39),D2	15	0.6
1992	Min A	127	418	44	113	16	3	12	71	17-1	1	90	.270	.298	.409	93	-6	4-5	.987	-0	95	106	O122(7/0/117),D3		-1.1
1993	Min A	104	326	34	76	11	1	13	38	25-2	3	97	.233	.294	.393	82	-10	5-2	.983	-5	89	80	O102(64/0/41)	25	-1.9
1994	Min A	75	244	35	72	15	2	11	36	19-0	2	67	.295	.348	.508	117	6	0-0	.965	-3	102	26	O58(42/0/19),D12		0.0
1995	Min A	104	376	45	113	17	0	18	58	19-0	3	86	.301	.338	.489	112	5	0-3	.926	-3	57	225	D77,O25(1/0/24),1b3		-0.4
1996	Oak A	34	121	17	31	5	0	6	18	9-1	0	31	.256	.308	.446	89	-3	0-0	1.000	-3	56	0	D18,O14R	120	-0.7
Total	7	517	1708	203	467	75	8	67	252	100-4	10	418	.273	.315	.444	99	-9	11-10	.980	-12	92	89	O386(127/0/273),D113,1b3	160	-4.1

MUNSON, RED   Clarence Hanford   B7.31.1883 Cincinnati OH   D2.19.1957 Mishawaka IN   TR/5-11/?   d8.28

| 1905 | Phi N | 9 | 26 | 1 | 3 | 1 | 0 | 0 | | 2 | 0 | | .115 | .115 | .154 | -21 | -4 | 0-0 | .857 | -1 | 120 | 89 | C8 | | -0.4 |

MUNSON, ERIC   Eric Walter   B10.3.1977 San Diego CA   BL/TR/6-3/220*   [DetA99 1/3]   d7.18   Col USC

2000	Det A	3	5	0	0	0	0	0	0	0-0	0	1	.000	.000	.000	-99	-2	0-0	.941	-1	0	167	1b3		-0.2
2001	Det A	17	66	4	10	3	1	1	6	3-0	0	21	.152	.188	.273	20	-8	0-1	.994	1	121	92	1b17		-0.9
2002	Det A	18	59	3	11	0	0	2	5	6-0	1	11	.186	.269	.288	51	-4	0-0	.970	0	121	88	D14,1b4		-0.5
2003	Det A	99	313	28	75	9	0	18	50	35-1	1	61	.240	.312	.441	102	0	3-0	.920	-13	90	79	3b91,D3	48	-1.1
2004	Det A	109	321	36	68	14	2	19	49	29-3	6	90	.212	.289	.445	91	-6	1-1	.934	4	111	119	3b94/1CD		-0.1
2005	TB A	11	18	2	3	1	0	0	2	4-0	1	3	.167	.333	.222	58	-1	0-0	1.000	-1	33	0	1OLD		-0.2
Total	6	257	782	73	167	27	3	40	113	77-4	9	187	.214	.288	.409	84	-21	4-2	.928	-10	100	98	3b187,D27,1b25/OLC	82	-3.0

MUNSON, JOE   Joseph Martin Napoleon (b Joseph Martin Napoleon Carlson)   B11.6.1899 Renovo PA   D2.24.1991 Drexel Hill PA   BL/TR/5-9/184   d9.18   Col Lehigh

1925	Chi N	9	35	5	13	3	1	0	3	3	1	1	.371	.436	.514	140	2	1-1	1.000	-0	95	80	O9R		0.1
1926	Chi N	33	101	17	26	2	2	3	15	8	1	4	.257	.318	.406	93	-2	0	.898	-2	95	67	O28(16/0/12)		-0.6
Total	2	42	136	22	39	5	3	3	18	11	2	5	.287	.349	.434	105	0	1-1	.922	-2	95	70	O37(16/0/21)		-0.5

MUNSON, THURMAN   Thurman Lee   B6.7.1947 Akron OH   D8.2.1979 Canton OH   BR/TR/5-11/191*   [NYA68 1/4]   d8.8   Col Kent St.

1969	NY A	26	86	6	22	1	0	1	9	10-1	0	10	.256	.330	.349	94	-1	0-1	.986	1	207	103	C25		0.1
1970	NY A	132	453	59	137	25	4	6	53	57-6	7	56	.302	.386	.415	127	19	5-7	.989	13	167	96	C125		3.8
1971	NY A★	125	451	71	113	15	4	10	42	52-1	7	65	.251	.335	.368	105	3	6-5	.998	8	221	113	C117/OR		1.7
1972	NY A★	140	511	54	143	16	3	7	46	47-5	2	58	.280	.343	.364	113	8	6-7	.977	4	185	77	C132		2.0
1973	NY A★	147	519	80	156	29	4	20	74	48-4	4	64	.301	.362	.487	141	28	4-6	.984	15	158	98	C142/D		4.9
1974	NY A	144	517	64	135	19	2	13	60	44-12	1	66	.261	.316	.381	102	1	2-0	.974	6	123	70	C137/D4		1.4
1975	NY A★	157	597	83	190	24	3	12	102	45-8	6	52	.318	.366	.429	127	21	3-2	.972	3	151	111	C130,D22,1b2,O2(1/0/1)/3		4.4
1976 †NY A★	152	616	79	186	27	1	17	105	29-6	9	38	.302	.337	.432	126	18	14-11	.981	1	111	94	C121,D21,O11(2/0/9)		2.5
1977 †NY A★	149	595	85	183	28	5	18	100	39-8	2	55	.308	.351	.462	121	16	5-6	.984	3	111	92	C136,D10		2.3
1978 †NY A★	154	617	73	183	27	1	6	71	35-6	3	70	.297	.332	.373	101	1	2-3	.986	9	128	103	C125,D14,O13R		2.3
1979	NY A	97	382	42	110	18	3	3	39	32-2	1	37	.288	.340	.374	95	-2	1-2	.978	5	181	85	C88,1b3,D5		0.4
Total	11	1423	5344	696	1558	229	32	113	701	438-59	42	571	.292	.346	.410	116	112	48-50	.982	81	153	94	C1278,D77,O27(3/0/24),1b5/3		24.8

MUNYAN, JOHN   John Baird   B11.14.1860 Chester PA   D2.18.1945 Endicott NY   d7.12

1887	Cle AA	16	58	9	14	1	1	0	6	3			.241	.279	.293	61	-3	4	.762	-1	64	0	O12(3/3/6),C3,3b2		-0.3
1890	Col AA	2	7	1	1	0	0	0	0	1			.143	.250	.143	17	-1	0	.667	0	281	0	O2C		-0.1
	StL AA	96	342	61	91	15	7	4	42	32	7		.266	.341	.386	100	-2	11	.939	-1	100	99	C83,O7L,2b5,3b3/S		0.3
	Year	98	349	62	92	15	7	4	42	32	8		.264	.339	.381	99	-3	11	.939	-1	100	99	C83,O9(7/2/0),2b5,3b3/S		0.2
1891	StL AA	60	176	41	41	4	3	0	19	41	4	39	.233	.389	.290	82	-3	13	.940	-4	115	82	C43,O12(4/0/8),S5,3b3		-0.3
Total	3	174	583	112	147	20	11	4	67	76	12	39	.252	.350	.345	90	-9	28	.937	-6	105	94	C129,O33(14/5/14),3b8,S6,2b5		-0.4

MURCER, BOBBY   Bobby Ray   B5.20.1946 Oklahoma City OK   BL/TR/5-11/180(165-185)   d9.8   Mil 1967-68   OF(56/789/839)

1965	NY A	11	37	2	9	0	1	1	4	5-0	0	12	.243	.333	.378	102	0	0-0	.932	7	130	229	S11		0.8
1966	NY A	21	69	3	12	1	1	0	5	4-0	0	15	.174	.219	.217	27	-7	2-2	.931	-2	97	40	S18		-0.9
1969	NY A	152	564	82	146	24	4	26	82	50-2	3	103	.259	.319	.454	119	12	7-5	.964	-6	94	45	O118(0/27/99),3b31		0.0
1970	NY A	159	581	95	146	23	3	23	78	87-5	2	100	.251	.348	.420	117	14	15-10	.992	-4	93	139	O155C		0.6
1971	NY A★	146	529	94	175	25	6	25	94	91-13	0	60	.331	.427	.543	182	61	14-8	.985	-14	83	103	O143C		4.5
1972	NY A★	153	585	102	171	30	7	33	96	63-7	2	67	.292	.361	.537	169	48	11-9	.992	-9	97	105	O151C		4.3
1973	NY A★	160	616	83	187	29	2	22	95	50-4	3	67	.304	.357	.464	133	26	6-7	.985	-7	92	119	O160C		1.5
1974	NY A★	156	606	69	166	25	4	10	88	57-10	2	59	.274	.332	.378	107	-1	14-5	.978	-5	85	178	O156(0/59/101)		-0.5
1975	SF N	147	526	90	157	29	4	11	91	91-6	2	45	.298	.396	.432	127	24	9-5	.981	-11	77	108	O144(0/2/143)		0.7
1976	SF N	147	533	73	138	20	2	23	90	84-10	1	78	.259	.362	.433	122	17	12-7	.961	-6	96	88	O146R		0.5
1977	Chi N	154	554	90	147	18	3	27	89	80-13	6	77	.265	.355	.455	106	5	16-7	.980	-12	82	94	O150R/2S		-1.4
1978	Chi N	146	499	66	140	22	6	9	64	80-15	0	57	.281	.376	.400	106	-1	14-5	.979	-16	79	74	O138(0/33/121)		-1.4
1979	Chi N	58	190	22	49	4	1	7	22	36-2	1	20	.258	.374	.400	102	2	2-3	1.000	9	2	111	O54R		0.0
	NY A	74	264	42	72	12	0	8	33	25-2	2	32	.273	.339	.409	96	1	1-1	.983	2	98	87	O70(12/59/7)		-0.2

YEAR	TM	LG	G	AB	R	H	2B	3B	HR	RBI	BB-IB	HP	SO	AVG	OBP	SLG	AOPS	ABR	SB-CS	FA	FR	RNG	THR	GAMES AT POSITION	DL	BF
1980	†NY	A	100	297	41	80	9	1	13	57	34-2	2	28	.269	.339	.438	116	6	2-0	.955	-4	90	59	O59(44/0/18),D33		0
1981	†NY	A	50	117	14	31	6	0	6	24	12-1	0	15	.265	.331	.470	131	4	0-0	—	0	0	0	D47		0
1982	NY	A	65	141	12	32	6	0	7	30	12-2	1	15	.227	.288	.418	94	-2	2-1	—	0	0	0	D5		8
1983	NY	A	9	22	2	4	2	0	1	6	1-0	1	9	.182	.217	.409	70	-1	0-0	.981	0		0			0
Total	17		1908	6730	972	1862	285	45	252	1043	862-96	27	841	.277	.357	.445	124	223	127-75	.981	-83	89	105	O1644R,D118,3b31,S30/2		

MURCH, SIMMY   Simeon Augustus   B11.21.1880 Castine ME   D6.6.1939 Exeter NH   BR/TR/6-2/220   d9.20

YEAR	TM	LG	G	AB	R	H	2B	3B	HR	RBI	BB-IB	HP	SO	AVG	OBP	SLG	AOPS	ABR	SB-CS	FA	FR	RNG	THR	GAMES AT POSITION	DL	BF
1904	StL	N	13	51	3	7	1	0	0	1	1	0		.137	.154	.157	-4	-6	0	.905	-1	101	166	2b6,3b6/S		-0
1905	StL	N	4	9	1	0	0	0	0	0	1	0		.111	.111	.111	-35	-2	0	.750	-2	0	0	2b2/S		-0
1908	Bro	N	6	11	1	2	1	0	0	1	0	0		.182	.250	.273	70	0	0	.964	-1	99	162	1b2		-0
Total	3		23	71	4	10	2	0	0	1	2	0		.141	.164	.169	3	-8	0	.880	-4	83	136	2b8,3b6,1b2,S2		-1

MURDOCH, WILBUR   Wilbur Edwin   B3.14.1875 Avon NY   D10.29.1941 Los Angeles CA   TR   d8.29

YEAR	TM	LG	G	AB	R	H	2B	3B	HR	RBI	BB-IB	HP	SO	AVG	OBP	SLG	AOPS	ABR	SB-CS	FA	FR	RNG	THR	GAMES AT POSITION	DL	BF
1908	StL	N	27	62	5	16	3	0	0	5	3	0		.258	.292	.306	96	0	4	.913	-2	0	0	O16(13/5/0)		-0

MURNANE, TIM   Timothy Hayes   B6.4.1852 Naugatuck CT   D2.7.1917 Boston MA   BL/TR/5-9.5/172   d4.26   M1   Col Holy Cross

YEAR	TM	LG	G	AB	R	H	2B	3B	HR	RBI	BB-IB	HP	SO	AVG	OBP	SLG	AOPS	ABR	SB-CS	FA	FR	RNG	THR	GAMES AT POSITION	DL	BF
1872	Man	NA	23	114	28	41	1	1	0	16	0			.360	.360	.386	137	5	1-2	.905	-4	0	62	1b23		-1
1873	Ath	NA	41	176	53	39	2	1	0	10	1		13	.222	.255	.261	50	-12	8-2	.785	-3	55	0	O30(0/24/6),1b10,2b6		-1
1874	Ath	NA	21	82	11	17	2	0	0	11	1		3	.207	.217	.232	40	-6	0-1	.857	-3	132	0	O14(0/1/13),2b6,1b3		-0
1875	Phi	NA	69	313	71	85	5	0	1	30	7		1	.272	.287	.297	100	-1	30-9	.918	-1	86	74	1b31,O26(1/24/1),2b15		-0
1876	Bos	N	69	308	60	87	4	3	2	34	8		12	.282	.301	.334	109	3		.815	-4	102	180	O30(0/25/5),1b5		-0
1877	Bos	N	35	140	23	39	7	1	1	15	6		7	.279	.308	.364	107	1		.940	1	168	111	1b48/OC		-C
1878	Pro	N	49	188	35	45	6	1	0	14	6		12	.239	.270	.282	82	-3		.950	-2	44	39	1b63,O16(1/0/15),M		-C
1884	Bos	U	76	311	55	73	5	2	0		22			.235	.285	.264	68	-21		.824	-9	47	0	O70(1/49/20),1b67,2b27		-1
Total	4	NA	154	685	163	182	10	2	2	67	16		23	.266	.282	.295	84	-14	39-14	.938	-8	81	92	1b181,O50(3/27/20)/2		-3
Total	4		229	947	173	244	22	7	3	63	44		31	.258	.291	.305	90	-20								

MURPHY   d8.16

YEAR	TM	LG	G	AB	R	H	2B	3B	HR	RBI	BB-IB	HP	SO	AVG	OBP	SLG	AOPS	ABR	SB-CS	FA	FR	RNG	THR	GAMES AT POSITION	DL	BF
1884	Bos	U	1	3	0	0	0	0	0		1			.000	.250	.000	-18	0		.333	-2			/COL		-4

MURPHY, CLARENCE   Clarence   d6.17

YEAR	TM	LG	G	AB	R	H	2B	3B	HR	RBI	BB-IB	HP	SO	AVG	OBP	SLG	AOPS	ABR	SB-CS	FA	FR	RNG	THR	GAMES AT POSITION	DL	BF
1886	Lou	AA	1	3	0	0	0	0	0	0	0	0		.000	.000	.000	-95	-1	0	1.000	0	0	0	/OL		-4

MURPHY, CONNIE   Cornelius David "Stone Face"   B11.1.1870 Northfield MA   D12.14.1945 New Bedford MA   BL/TR/5-8/155   d9.17

YEAR	TM	LG	G	AB	R	H	2B	3B	HR	RBI	BB-IB	HP	SO	AVG	OBP	SLG	AOPS	ABR	SB-CS	FA	FR	RNG	THR	GAMES AT POSITION	DL	BF
1893	Cin	N	6	17	3	3	1	0	0	1	1	0	2	.176	.222	.235	21	-2	0	.917	-1	115	30	C4		-0
1894	Cin	N	1	4	0	0	0	0	0	0	1	0	1	.000	.200	.000	-47	-1	0	.500	-1	81	106	/C		-C
Total	2		7	21	3	3	1	0	0	1	2	0	3	.143	.217	.190	6	-3	0	.857	-2	108	45	C5		-C

MURPHY, DALE   Dale Bryan   B3.12.1956 Portland OR   BR/TR/6-5/215(185-227)   [AtlN74 1/5]   d9.13

YEAR	TM	LG	G	AB	R	H	2B	3B	HR	RBI	BB-IB	HP	SO	AVG	OBP	SLG	AOPS	ABR	SB-CS	FA	FR	RNG	THR	GAMES AT POSITION	DL	BF
1976	Atl	N	19	65	3	17	6	0	0	9	7-0	0	9	.262	.333	.354	90	0	0-0	.974	-1	59	151	C19		-0
1977	Atl	N	18	76	5	24	8	1	2	14	0-0	0	8	.316	.316	.526	109	1	0-1	.954	-3	56	66	C18		-0
1978	Atl	N	151	530	66	120	14	3	23	79	42-3	3	145	.226	.284	.394	80	-16	11-7	.984	2	116	81	1b76,C27		-0
1979	Atl	N	104	384	53	106	7	2	21	57	38-5	2	67	.276	.340	.469	113	6	6-1	.980	-12	85	97	1b76,C27		55
1980	Atl	N★	156	569	98	160	27	2	33	89	59-9	1	133	.281	.349	.510	136	26	9-6	.985	-1	96	127	O154(4/129/21)/1		
1981	Atl	N	104	369	43	91	12	1	13	50	44-8	0	72	.247	.325	.390	102	1	14-5	.981	-2	92	151	O103(0/102/1),1b3		
1982	†Atl	N★	**162**	598	113	168	23	2	36	**109**	93-9	3	134	.281	.378	.507	143	36	23-11	.979	-3	96	119	O160(28/136/2)		
1983	Atl	N★	**162**	589	131	178	24	4	36	**121**	90-12	2	110	.302	.393	**.540**	147	39	30-4	.987	-11	88	108	O160C		
1984	Atl	N★	**162**	607	94	176	32	8	**36**	100	79-20	2	134	.290	.372	**.547**	145	36	19-7	.980	-20	81	78	O161C		
1985	Atl	N★	**162**	616	**118**	185	32	2	**37**	111	90-15	1	141	.300	.388	.539	149	42	10-3	.981	-20	82	64	O159(0/155/6)		
1986	Atl	N★	160	614	89	163	29	7	29	83	75-5	2	141	.265	.347	.477	120	16	7-7	.977	5	105	123	O159R		
1987	Atl	N★	159	566	115	167	27	1	44	105	115-**29**	7	136	.295	.417	.580	155	50	16-6	.992	11	95	183	O156R		
1988	Atl	N	156	592	77	134	35	4	24	77	74-16	2	125	.226	.313	.421	105	4	3-5	.985	-7	95	61	O151(0/82/70)		
1989	Atl	N	154	574	60	131	16	0	20	84	65-10	2	142	.228	.306	.361	89	-8	3-2	.981	1	108	45	O97R		
1990	Atl	N	97	349	38	81	14	0	17	55	41-11	1	84	.232	.312	.418	95	-3	9-2	.992	-0	95	99	O55(1/1/53)		
	Phi	N	57	214	22	57	9	1	7	28	20-3	0	46	.266	.328	.416	104	1	0-1	.985	1	103	65	O152(1/1/150)		
	Year		154	563	60	138	23	1	24	83	61-14	1	130	.245	.318	.417	100	-2	9-3	.989	1	103	56	O147R		
1991	Phi	N	153	544	66	137	33	1	18	81	48-3	0	93	.252	.309	.415	104	2	1-0	.983	-6	68	0	O16(1/0/16)		156
1992	Phi	N	18	62	5	10	1	0	2	7	1-0	0	13	.161	.175	.274	25	-6	0-0	1.000	-0	91	148	O13(2/0/11)		
1993	Col	N	26	42	1	6	1	0	0	5	5-1	0	15	.143	.224	.167	8	-5	0-0	.983	-66	96	98	O1853(101/1044/747),1b209,C85		211
Total	18		2180	7960	1197	2111	350	39	398	1266	986-159	28	1748	.265	.346	.469	120	222	161-68	.983	-66	96	98	O1853(101/1044/747),1b209,C85		1

MURPHY, DANNY   Daniel Francis   B8.11.1876 Philadelphia PA   D11.22.1955 Jersey City NJ   BR/TR/5-9/175   d9.17   C6

YEAR	TM	LG	G	AB	R	H	2B	3B	HR	RBI	BB-IB	HP	SO	AVG	OBP	SLG	AOPS	ABR	SB-CS	FA	FR	RNG	THR	GAMES AT POSITION	DL	BF
1900	NY	N	22	74	11	20	1	0	0	6	8	0		.270	.341	.284	77	-2	4	.888	-4	89	102	2b22		
1901	NY	N	5	20	0	4	0	0	0	1	0	0		.200	.238	.200	29	-2	0	.895	-2	85	0	2b5		
1902	Phi	A	76	291	48	91	11	8	1	48	13	4		.313	.351	.416	107	2	12	.963	-13	86	69	2b76		
1903	Phi	A	133	513	66	140	31	11	1	60	13	3		.273	.295	.382	97	-3	17	.941	14	103	84	2b150		
1904	Phi	A	150	557	78	160	30	17	7	77	22	5		.287	.320	.440	132	18	22	.955	-12	92	76	2b151		
1905	†Phi	A	151	537	71	149	34	4	6	71	42	8		.277	.339	.389	129	14	17	.955	-11	90	95	2b119		
1906	Phi	A	119	448	48	135	28	6	2	60	21	6		.301	.341	.404	129	14	17	.965	7	101	73	2b122		
1907	Phi	A	124	469	51	127	23	3	2	57	30	2		.271	.317	.345	109	5	11	.963	7	110	146	O84(2/12/70),2b56,1b2		
1908	Phi	A	142	525	51	139	28	7	0	66	32	2		.265	.309	.368	112	-6	16	**.977**	-4	87	126	O149R		
1909	Phi	A	149	541	61	152	28	14	5	69	35	6		.281	.332	.412	132	18	19	.974	-3	102	74	O151R		
1910	†Phi	A	151	560	70	168	28	18	4	64	31	1		.300	.338	.436	143	24	18	.961	7	87	**153**	O136R,2b4		
1911	†Phi	A	141	508	104	167	27	11	6	66	50	2		.323	.401	.461	147	8	8	.891	-4	81	44	O36R		
1912	Phi	A	36	130	27	42	6	2	2	16	6	0	8	.322	.365	.441	139	2	1	1.000	-1	62	0	O9R		
1913	Phi	A	40	59	3	19	5	1	0	6	4	0	1	.304	.374	.435	121	3	4	.986	2	102	115	O46(1/0/45)		
1914	Bro	F	52	161	16	49	9	0	4	32	17	1	16	.304	.374	.435	121	3	4	1.000	-0	77	0	/2OR		
1915	Bro	F	5	6	0	1	0	0	0	0	0	0	0	.167	.167	.167	-6	-1	0	1.000	-0			1b2		
Total	16		1496	5399	705	1563	289	102	44	702	335	47	24	.289	.336	.405	124	140	193	.953	-32	94	79	2b839,O612(3/12/597),1b2		

MURPHY, DANNY   Daniel Francis   B8.23.1942 Beverly MA   BL/TR/5-11/185*   d6.18 ▲

YEAR	TM	LG	G	AB	R	H	2B	3B	HR	RBI	BB-IB	HP	SO	AVG	OBP	SLG	AOPS	ABR	SB-CS	FA	FR	RNG	THR	GAMES AT POSITION	DL	BF
1960	Chi	N	31	75	7	9	2	0	1	6	4-0	1	13	.120	.175	.187	-1	-11	0-0	.976	0	105	77	O21(0/16/5)		
1961	Chi	N	4	13	3	5	0	0	1	3	1-0	0	5	.385	.429	.846	225	2	0-0	1.000	0	87	345	O4R		
1962	Chi	N	14	35	5	7	3	1	0	2	2-0	0	9	.200	.243	.343	53	-2	0-0	1.000	-2	39	0	O5(2/1/6)		
1969	Chi	A	17	1	0	0	0	0	0	0	0-0	0	0	.000	.667	.000	95	1	0-0	.933	-1	84	112	P51		
1970	Chi	A	51	6	3	2	0	1	0	2	1-0	0	2	.333	.500	.833	252	2	0-0	.947	-3	85	81	P68,O30(2/17/15)		
Total	5		117	130	18	23	5	1	4	13	11-0	1	29	.177	.246	.323	53	-8	0-0							

MURPHY, DANNY   Daniel Joseph "Handsome Dan"   B9.10.1864 Brooklyn NY   D12.14.1915 Brooklyn NY   ?/156   d4.26

YEAR	TM	LG	G	AB	R	H	2B	3B	HR	RBI	BB-IB	HP	SO	AVG	OBP	SLG	AOPS	ABR	SB-CS	FA	FR	RNG	THR	GAMES AT POSITION	DL	BF
1892	NY	N	8	26	2	3	0	0	0	5	4			.115	.258	.115	14	-2	0	.900	-2	69	72	C8		

MURPHY, DAVE   David Francis "Dirty Dave"   B5.4.1876 Adams MA   D4.8.1940 Adams MA   TR   d8.28

YEAR	TM	LG	G	AB	R	H	2B	3B	HR	RBI	BB-IB	HP	SO	AVG	OBP	SLG	AOPS	ABR	SB-CS	FA	FR	RNG	THR	GAMES AT POSITION	DL	BF
1905	Bos	N	3	11	0	2	0	0	0	1	0			.182	.182	.182	9	-1	0	1.000	-1	97	0	S2/3		

MURPHY, DONNIE   Donald Rex   B3.10.1983 Lakewood CA   BR/TR/5-10/180(180-200)   [KCA02 5/138]   d9.18   Col Orange Coast (CA) JC

YEAR	TM	LG	G	AB	R	H	2B	3B	HR	RBI	BB-IB	HP	SO	AVG	OBP	SLG	AOPS	ABR	SB-CS	FA	FR	RNG	THR	GAMES AT POSITION	DL	BF
2004	KC	A	7	27	1	5	3	0	0	3	0-0	0	7	.185	.185	.296	23	-3	1-0	1.000	-1	91	167	2b7		15
2005	KC	A	32	77	4	12	5	0	1	8	9-0	0	23	.156	.241	.260	37	-7	0-1	.972	-5	88	77	2b29,S2/D		15
Total	2		39	104	5	17	8	0	1	11	9-0	0	30	.163	.228	.269	33	-10	1-1	.978	-6	89	98	2b36,S2/D		

MURPHY, DWAYNE   Dwayne Keith   B3.18.1955 Merced CA   BL/TR/6-1/185*   [OakA73 15/359]   d4.8   C6

YEAR	TM	LG	G	AB	R	H	2B	3B	HR	RBI	BB-IB	HP	SO	AVG	OBP	SLG	AOPS	ABR	SB-CS	FA	FR	RNG	THR	GAMES AT POSITION	DL	BF
1978	Oak	A	60	52	15	10	2	0	0	5	7-0	0	14	.192	.279	.231	50	-3	0-1	1.000	2	121	88	O45(21/12/14),D5		23
1979	Oak	A	121	388	57	99	10	4	11	40	84-6	1	80	.255	.387	.387	116	13	15-11	.988	4	103	131	O118(2/115/3)		
1980	Oak	A	159	573	86	157	18	2	13	68	102-7	1	91	.274	.384	.380	118	19	26-15	.990	12	113	115	O158C		
1981	Oak	A	107	390	58	98	10	1	15	60	73-6	0	79	.251	.369	.408	129	10	10-4	.985	3	109	89	O106C/D		
1982	Oak	A	151	543	84	129	15	1	27	94	94-2	3	122	.238	.349	.418	114	13	26-8	.983	10	109	137	O147C/SD		17
1983	Oak	A	130	471	55	107	17	2	17	75	62-4	0	105	.227	.314	.380	96	-2	7-5	.979	-2	103	91	O124C,D7		
1984	Oak	A	153	559	93	143	18	2	33	88	74-1	3	111	.256	.342	.472	132	24	4-5	.988	11	111	138	O153C		
1985	Oak	A	152	523	77	122	21	3	20	59	84-3	3	123	.233	.340	.400	110	4	4-5	.989	-2	104	61	O150C		

YEAR	TM LG	G	AB	R	H	2B	3B	HR	RBI	BB-IB	HP	SO	AVG	OBP	SLG	AOPS	ABR	SB-CS	FA	FR	RNG	THR	GAMES AT POSITION	DL	BFW
1986	Oak A	98	329	50	83	11	3	9	39	56-4	4	80	.252	.364	.386	113	8	3-1	.993	6	111	119	O97C/D	54	1.4
1987	Oak A	82	219	39	51	7	0	8	35	58-2	0	61	.233	.388	.374	112	7	4-4	.984	0	106	33	O79C/12	77	0.6
1988	Det A	49	144	14	36	5	0	4	19	24-2	1	26	.250	.361	.368	108	3	1-1	1.000	3	116	51	O43(4/35/10),D3		0.5
1989	Phi N	98	156	20	34	5	0	9	27	29-2	0	44	.218	.341	.423	117	4	0-1	.986	-1	99	52	O52(30/5/19)		0.2
Total	12	1360	4347	648	1069	139	20	166	609	747-39	19	953	.246	.356	.402	115	112	100-61	.987	53	109	102	O1272(57/1181/46),D18/21S	171	15.1

MURPHY, ED   Edward Joseph   B8.23.1918 Joliet IL   D12.10.1991 Joliet IL   BR/TR/5-11/190   d9.10   Mil 1943-45

| 1942 | Phi N | 13 | 28 | 2 | 7 | 2 | 0 | 0 | 4 | 2 | 0 | 4 | .250 | .300 | .321 | 86 | 0 | 0 | 1.000 | -0 | 72 | 126 | 1b8 | | -0.2 |

MURPHY, TONY   Francis J.   B7.1859 New York NY   D12.15.1915 New York NY   5-6/145   d10.15

| 1884 | NY AA | 1 | 3 | 1 | 1 | 0 | 0 | 0 | | 0 | | 0 | .333 | .333 | .333 | 121 | 0 | | 1.000 | -0 | | | /C | | 0.0 |

MURPHY, FRANK   Francis Patrick   B4.16.1875 N.Tarrytown NY   D11.4.1912 Central Islip NY   BR/TR/d7.2   Col Fordham

1901	Bos N	45	176	13	46	5	3	1	18	4	1		.261	.282	.341	73	-7	6	.939	3	164	71	O45L		-0.6
	NY N	35	130	10	21	3	0	0	8	6	0		.162	.199	.185	12	-15	2	.847	-9	90	34	2b23,O12L		-2.4
	Year	80	306	23	67	8	3	1	26	10	1		.219	.246	.275	49	-21	8	.940	-6	149	59	O57L,2b23		-3.0

MURPHY, DUMMY   Herbert Courtland   B12.18.1886 Olney IL   D8.10.1962 Tallahassee FL   BR/TR/5-10/165   d4.14

| 1914 | Phi N | 9 | 26 | 1 | 4 | 1 | 0 | 0 | 3 | 0 | | 4 | .154 | .185 | .192 | 12 | -3 | 0 | .864 | 0 | 102 | 58 | S9 | | -0.2 |

MURPHY, HOWARD   Howard   B1.1.1882 Birmingham AL   D10.5.1926 Fort Worth TX   BL/TR/5-8.5/150   d8.4

| 1909 | StL N | 25 | 60 | 3 | 12 | 0 | 0 | 0 | 3 | 4 | | | .200 | .250 | .200 | 42 | -4 | 1 | .925 | -1 | 86 | 0 | O19C | | -0.7 |

MURPHY, EDDIE   John Edward   B10.2.1891 Hancock NY   D2.21.1969 Dunmore PA   BL/TR/5-9/155   d8.26   Col Villanova

1912	Phi A	33	142	24	45	4	1	0	6	11	1		.317	.370	.359	113	3	7	.947	-0	90	118	O33R		0.0
1913	†Phi A	137	508	105	150	14	7	1	30	70	10	44	.295	.391	.356	122	18	21	.942	-11	85	72	O135R		0.0
1914	†Phi A	148	573	101	156	12	9	3	43	87	12	46	.272	.379	.340	121	19	36-32	.941	-7	92	80	O148R		0.1
1915	Phi A	68	260	37	60	3	4	0	17	29	3	15	.231	.315	.273	79	-7	13-3	.899	-2	78	125	O58R,3b6		-1.0
	Chi A	70	273	51	86	11	5	0	26	39	5	12	.315	.410	.392	138	14	20-12	.952	-2	104	81	O70(3/0/67)		1.0
	Year	138	533	88	146	14	9	0	43	68	8	27	.274	.365	.334	109	8	33-15	.933	-4	94	99	O128(3/0/125),3b6		0.0
1916	Chi A	51	105	14	22	5	1	0	4	9	2	5	.210	.284	.276	68	-4	3	1.000	-1	98	99	O24R/3		-0.7
1917	Chi A	53	51	9	16	2	1	0	16	5	1		.314	.386	.392	135	2	4	1.000	-1	48	0	O9(1/0/8)		0.2
1918	†Chi A	91	286	36	85	9	3	0	23	22	1	18	.297	.350	.350	110	3	6	.958	-7	101	36	O63(1/0/62),2b8		-0.7
1919	†Chi A	30	35	8	17	4	0	0	5	7	0	0	.486	.571	.600	228	7	0	.917	0	111	163	O6(2/0/4)		0.7
1920	Chi A	58	118	22	40	2	1	0	19	12	1	4	.339	.405	.373	107	2	1-3	.886	2	75	340	O19R,3b3		0.2
1921	Chi A	6	5	1	1	0	0	0	0	0	0	0	.200	.200	.200	2	-1	0-0	—	0			/H		-0.1
1926	Pit N	16	17	3	2	0	0	0	6	3	0	0	.118	.250	.118	2	-2	0	1.000	0	114	0	O3L		-0.3
Total	11	761	2373	411	680	66	32	4	195	294	36	145	.287	.374	.346	114	54	111-50	.942	-28	91	88	O568(10/0/558),3b10,2b8		-0.6

MURPHY, JOHN   John Patrick   B1879 New Haven CT   D4.20.1949 Andover MA   5-7.5/160   d9.10

1902	StL N	1	3	1	2	1	0	0	1	1	0		.667	.750	1.000	458	1	0	1.000	-1	0	0	/3		0.1
1903	Det A	5	22	1	4	1	0	0	1	0	0		.182	.182	.227	23	-2	0	.852	-1	103	58	S5		-0.3
Total	2	6	25	2	6	2	0	0	2	1	0		.240	.269	.320	79	-1	0	.852	-1	103	58	S5/3		-0.2

MURPHY, LEO   Leo Joseph "Red"   B1.7.1889 Terre Haute IN   D8.12.1960 Racine WI   BR/TR/6-1/179   d5.2

| 1915 | Pit N | 31 | 41 | 4 | 4 | 0 | 0 | 0 | 4 | 4 | 0 | 12 | .098 | .178 | .098 | -16 | -6 | 0 | .932 | -2 | 77 | 118 | C20 | | -0.8 |

MURPHY, MIKE   Michael Jerome   B8.19.1888 Forestville PA   D10.26.1952 Johnson City NY   BR/TR/5-9/170   d5.17   Col Villanova

1912	StL N	1	1	0	0	0	0	0	0	0	0	0	.000	.000	.000	-99	-0	0	—	0	0	0	/C		0.0
1916	Phi A	14	27	0	3	0	0	0	1	1	0	3	.111	.143	.111	-25	-4	0	.973	-3	51	75	C12		-0.7
Total	2	15	28	0	3	0	0	0	1	1	0	3	.107	.138	.107	-28	-4	0	.973	-3	50	74	C13		-0.7

MURPHY, MORGAN   Morgan Edward   B2.14.1867 E.Providence RI   D10.3.1938 Providence RI   BR/TR/5-8/160   d4.22

1890	Bos P	68	246	38	56	10	2	2	32	24		31	.228	.301	.309	59	-15	16	.903	14	154	83	C67,S2/OC3		0.3
1891	Bos AA	106	402	60	87	11	4	4	54	36	5	58	.216	.289	.294	68	-18	17	.954	27	140	99	C104,O4(1/2/1)		1.5
1892	Cin N	74	234	29	46	8	2	2	24	25	1	57	.197	.277	.274	67	-9	4	.955	2	118	69	C74		0.0
1893	Cin N	57	200	25	47	5	1	1	19	14	3	35	.235	.295	.285	53	-14	1	.932	-3	110	77	C56/1		-1.0
1894	Cin N	76	261	42	70	9	0	1	37	26	1	36	.268	.337	.314	56	-19	6	.901	-6	99	101	C75/S3		-1.5
1895	Cin N	25	82	15	22	2	0	0	16	11	0	8	.268	.355	.293	66	-4	6	.907	-1	104	85	C25		-0.3
1896	StL N	49	175	12	45	5	2	0	11	8	1	14	.257	.290	.309	60	-11	1	.926	-6	85	99	C48		-1.1
1897	StL N	63	211	13	36	2	1	0	12	6	1		.171	.197	.180	-0	-31	1	.946	-12	68	125	C54,1b8		-3.4
1898	Pit N	5	16	0	2	0	0	0	2	1	0		.125	.176	.125	-14	-2	0	.957	1	110	136	C5		-0.1
	Phi N	25	86	6	17	3	0	0	11	6	1		.198	.258	.233	43	-6	0	.964	1	111	118	C25		-0.3
	Year	30	102	6	19	3	0	0	13	7	1		.186	.245	.216	34	-9	0	.963	2	111	121	C30		-0.4
1900	Phi N	11	36	2	10	1	0	0	3	0	0		.278	.278	.333	69	-2	0	.980	-0	78	116	C11		-0.1
1901	Phi A	9	28	5	6	1	0	0	1	0	0		.214	.214	.250	27	-3	1	.929	-0	107	79	C8/1		-0.2
Total	11	568	1977	247	444	56	12	10	227	157	14	239	.225	.286	.280	53	-134	53	.936	16	114	94	C552,1b10,O5(1/3/1),S3,3b2		-6.2

MURPHY, PAT   Patrick J.   B1.2.1857 Auburn MA   D5.16.1927 Worcester MA   TR/5-10/160   d9.2

1887	NY N	17	56	4	12	2	0	0		4	0	4	.214	.241	.250	38	-5	1	.847	-1			C17		-0.3
1888	†NY N	28	106	11	18	1	0	0	4	6	0	11	.170	.214	.179	27	-9	3	.913	2			C28		-0.4
1889	NY N	9	28	5	10	1	1	0	3	0	0		.357	.400	.571	170	2	0	.872	-1			C9		0.1
1890	NY N	32	119	14	28	5	1	0	9	14	1	13	.235	.321	.294	79	-3	3	.905	-4	99	100	C29,O3(1/1/1)/S		-0.4
Total	4	86	309	34	68	9	2	1	21	24	1	28	.220	.278	.272	64	-15	7	.895	-4	99	100	C83,O3(1/1/1)/S		-1.0

MURPHY, LARRY   Patrick Lawrence   B3.17.1857 Toronto ON, Can.   D10.6.1911 Indianapolis IN   BL/5-8/170   d5.30

| 1891 | Was AA | 101 | 400 | 73 | 106 | 15 | 3 | 1 | 35 | 63 | 5 | 27 | .265 | .372 | .325 | 104 | 7 | 29 | .874 | -6 | 56 | 67 | O101(69/3/30) | | -0.1 |

MURPHY, DICK   Richard Lee   B10.25.1931 Cincinnati OH   BL/TL/5-11/170   d6.13   Mil 1955-57   Col Ohio U.

| 1954 | Cin N | 6 | 1 | 1 | 0 | 0 | 0 | 0 | 0 | 0 | 0 | | 1.000 | .000 | .000 | -97 | -0 | 0-0 | — | 0 | | | /H | | 0.0 |

MURPHY, BUZZ   Robert Sylvester   B4.26.1895 Denver CO   D5.11.1938 Denver CO   BL/TL/5-8.5/155   d7.14

1918	Bos A	9	32	6	12	2	1	1	9	3	0	5	.375	.429	.719	259	6	0	1.000	-1	89	0	O9L		0.5
1919	Was A	79	252	19	66	7	4	0	28	19	5	32	.262	.326	.321	83	-6	5	.959	3	112	91	O73(19/54/0)		-0.8
Total	2	88	284	25	78	9	7	1	37	22	5	37	.275	.338	.366	101	0	5	.961	2	110	82	O82(28/54/0)		-0.3

MURPHY, BILLY   William Eugene   B5.7.1944 Pineville LA   BR/TR/6-1/191   d4.15

| 1966 | NY N | 84 | 135 | 15 | 31 | 4 | 1 | 3 | 13 | 7-0 | 1 | 45 | .230 | .271 | .341 | 71 | -6 | 1-2 | .955 | -1 | 76 | 255 | O57(8/48/1) | | -0.9 |

MURPHY, WILLIE   William H. "Gentle Willie"   B3.23.1864 Springfield MA   BL/5-11/198   d5.1

1884	Cle N	42	168	18	38	3	1	9	1			23	.226	.231	.298	63	-8		.720	-7	72	0	O42(34/3/5)		-1.5
	Was AA	5	21	3	10	0	0	0	1	2	•2		.476	.542	.476	266	4		.700	0	0	0	O4L/3		0.4
Total	1	47	189	21	48	3	1	9	2	2	2	23	.254	.269	.317	83	-4		.718	-7	66	0	O46(38/3/5)/3		-1.1

MURPHY, YALE   William Henry "Tot", "Midget"   B10.11.1869 Southborough MA   D2.14.1906 Westborough MA   BL/TR/5-3/125   d4.19   Col Yale

1894	†NY N	75	283	65	77	9	0	0	28	52	0	23	.272	.385	.307	69	-12	28	.898	-10	87	63	S49,O21(1/0/20),3b3/21		-1.5
1895	NY N	51	184	35	37	6	2	0	16	27	0	13	.201	.303	.255	46	-14	7	.944	-4	78	175	O33(29/2/2),S8,3b8/2		-1.7
1897	NY N	5	8	1	0	0	0	0	1	2	0		.000	.200	.000	-46	-2	0	.800	-2	46	0	S3,2b2		-0.3
Total	3	131	475	101	114	12	4	0	45	81	0	36	.240	.351	.282	59	-28	35	.890	-15	87	64	S60,O54(30/2/22),3b11,2b4/1		-3.5

MURRAY, TONY   Anthony Joseph   B4.30.1904 Chicago IL   D3.19.1974 Chicago IL   BR/TR/5-10.5/154   d10.6   Col DePaul

| 1923 | Chi N | 2 | 4 | 0 | 1 | 0 | 0 | 0 | | | 0 | | .250 | .400 | .250 | 75 | 0 | 0-0 | 1.000 | -0 | 82 | 0 | O2(1/2/1) | | 0.0 |

MURRAY, CALVIN   Calvin Duane   B7.30.1971 Dallas TX   BR/TR/5-11/190*   [SFN92 1/7]   d6.22   Col Texas

1999	SF N	15	19	1	5	0	0	0	5	2-0	0	5	.263	.333	.368	83	0	1-0	1.000	-1	66	0	O9(3/6/0)		-0.1
2000	†SF N	108	194	35	47	12	1	2	22	29-0	3	33	.242	.348	.345	82	-5	9-3	.980	0	108	61	O106(2/104/0)		-0.3
2001	SF N	106	326	60	80	14	2	6	25	32-0	3	57	.245	.319	.356	79	-11	8-8	.979	3	116	87	O104C		-0.7
2002	Tex A	37	77	16	13	5	1	0	6	6-0	1	15	.169	.238	.260	31	-4	0-0	1.000	2	105	150	O34(0/33/1),D2		-0.5
	SF N	11	12	0	0	0	0	0	0	1-0	0	2	.000	.077	.000	-79	-3	0-0	.917	1	122	458	O10(5/4/3)		-0.3

YEAR	TM LG	G	AB	R	H	2B	3B	HR	RBI	BB-IB	HP	SO	AVG	OBP	SLG	AOPS	ABR	SB-CS	FA	FR	RNG	THR	GAMES AT POSITION	DL	BFW
2004	Chi N	11	5	2	1	0	0	0	1	1-0	0	0	.200	.333	.200	41	0	0-0	1.000	1	246	0	O8(1/5/2)		0.0
Total	5	288	633	108	146	33	4	8	54	71-0	7	111	.231	.315	.333		-27	22-11	.981	6	112	94	O271(11/256/6),D2		-1.9

MURRAY, EDDIE   Eddie Clarence   B2.24.1956 Los Angeles CA   BB/TR/6-2/200(180-225)   [BalA73 3/63]   d4.7   C8   HF2003   b-Rich   0.9

YEAR	TM LG	G	AB	R	H	2B	3B	HR	RBI	BB-IB	HP	SO	AVG	OBP	SLG	AOPS	ABR	SB-CS	FA	FR	RNG	THR	GAMES AT POSITION	DL	BFW
1977	Bal A	160	611	81	173	29	2	27	88	48-6	1	104	.283	.333	.470	124	19	0-1	.992	-3	70	108	D111,1b42,O3L		2.7
1978	Bal A☆	161	610	85	174	32	3	27	95	70-7	1	97	.285	.356	.480	142	34	6-5	.997	3	101	115	1b157,3b3/D		1.8
1979	†Bal A	159	606	90	179	30	2	25	99	72-9	2	78	.295	.369	.475	131	28	10-2	.994	-1	96	109	1b157,D2		1.4
1980	Bal A	158	621	100	186	36	2	32	116	54-10	1	43	.300	.354	.519	139	32	7-2	.994	-9	76	115	1b154/D		3.2
1981	Bal A★	99	378	57	111	21	2	22	78	40-10	1	43	.294	.360	.534	156	27	2-3	.999	11	136	116	1b99		3.9
1982	Bal A★	151	550	87	174	30	1	32	110	70-18	1	82	.316	.391	.549	157	44	7-2	.997	3	106	90	1b149,D2		4.2
1983	†Bal A★	156	582	115	178	30	3	33	111	86-13	3	90	.306	.393	.538	157	50	5-1	.993	4	109	104	1b153,D3		5.1
1984	Bal A★	162	588	97	180	26	3	29	110	107-25	2	87	.306	.410	.509	157	50	10-2	.987	12	128	110	1b154,D2		4.4
1985	Bal A★	156	583	111	173	37	1	31	124	84-12	1	68	.297	.383	.523	150	43	5-2	.989	-2	96	101	1b119,D16	28	1.8
1986	Bal A☆	137	495	61	151	25	1	17	84	78-7	0	49	.305	.396	.463	135	28	3-0	.993	12	127	112	1b156,D4		1.8
1987	Bal A	160	618	89	171	28	3	30	91	73-6	0	80	.277	.352	.477	120	18	1-2	.993	10	137	111	1b103,D58		3.0
1988	Bal A	161	603	75	171	27	2	28	84	75-8	0	78	.284	.361	.474	136	29	5-2	.996	10	118	116	1b159,3b2		1.3
1989	LA N	160	594	66	147	29	1	20	88	87-24	2	85	.247	.342	.401	114	13	7-2	.992	2	99	91	1b150		3.9
1990	LA N	155	558	96	184	22	3	26	95	82-21	1	64	.330	.414	.520	160	48	8-5	.995	6	110	100	1b149/3		0.0
1991	LA N★	153	576	69	150	23	1	19	96	55-17	0	74	.260	.321	.403	105	3	10-3	.991	-5	87	101	1b154		-0.3
1992	NY N	156	551	64	144	37	2	16	93	66-8	0	74	.261	.336	.423	116	13	4-2	.988	2	108	101	1b154		-0.4
1993	NY N	154	610	77	174	28	1	27	100	40-4	0	61	.285	.325	.467	112	9	2-2	.988	-2	76	111	D82,1b26		-1.9
1994	Cle A	108	433	57	110	21	1	17	76	31-6	0	53	.254	.302	.425	84	-12	8-4	.984	3	162	85	D95,1b18	29	1.3
1995	†Cle A	113	436	68	141	21	0	21	82	39-5	0	65	.323	.375	.516	128	17	5-1	1.000	0	137	0	D87/1		-1.2
1996	Cle A	88	336	33	88	9	1	12	45	34-2	0	45	.262	.326	.402	84	-9	3-0	—	0	0	0	D62		-0.5
	†Bal A	64	230	36	59	12	0	10	34	27-4	0	42	.257	.327	.439	94	-2	1-0	1.000	0	137	0	D149/1		-1.7
	Year	152	566	69	147	21	1	22	79	61-6	0	87	.260	.327	.417	88	-12	4-0	—	0	0	0	D45	53	-1.3
1997	Ana A	46	160	13	35	7	0	3	15	13-0	0	24	.219	.273	.319	55	-11	0-0	—	0		0	/H		0.0
	LA N	2	7	0	2	0	0	0	2	2-0	0	2	.286	.444	.286	103	0	0-0	—	0		0	/H		
Total	21	3026	11336	1627	3255	560	35	504	1917	1333-222	18	1516	.287	.359	.476	129	468	110-43	.993	66	108	106	1b2413,D573,3b6,O3L	110	35.1

MURRAY, ED   Edward Francis   B5.8.1895 Mystic CT   D11.8.1970 Cheyenne WY   BR/TR/5-6/145   d6.24   Col Trinity (CT)   0.0

YEAR	TM LG	G	AB	R	H	2B	3B	HR	RBI	BB-IB	HP	SO	AVG	OBP	SLG	AOPS	ABR	SB-CS	FA	FR	RNG	THR	GAMES AT POSITION	DL	BFW
1917	StL A	1	1	0	0	0	0	0	0	0-0	0	1	.000	.000	.000	-99	0	0	—	-0	0	0	/S		0.0

MURRAY, GLENN   Glenn Everett   B11.23.1970 Manning SC   BR/TR/6-2/225   [MonN89 2/40]   d5.10

YEAR	TM LG	G	AB	R	H	2B	3B	HR	RBI	BB-IB	HP	SO	AVG	OBP	SLG	AOPS	ABR	SB-CS	FA	FR	RNG	THR	GAMES AT POSITION	DL	BFW
1996	Phi N	38	97	8	19	3	0	2	6	7-0	0	36	.196	.250	.289	41	-9	1-1	1.000	1	117	66	O27(1/2/24)	76	-0.8

MURRAY, JIM   James Oscar   B1.16.1878 Galveston TX   D4.25.1945 Galveston TX   BR/TL/5-10/180   d9.2

YEAR	TM LG	G	AB	R	H	2B	3B	HR	RBI	BB-IB	HP	SO	AVG	OBP	SLG	AOPS	ABR	SB-CS	FA	FR	RNG	THR	GAMES AT POSITION	DL	BFW
1902	Chi N	12	47	3	8	0	0	0			0		.170	.204	.170	16	-5	0	1.000	-1	64	0	O12R		-0.8
1911	StL A	31	102	8	19	5	0	3	11	5	0		.186	.224	.324	54	-7	0	.935	0	106	93	O25(0/1/24)		-1.0
1914	Bos N	39	112	10	26	4	2	0	12	6	1	24	.232	.277	.304	73	-4	2	.941	-4	75	32	O32(18/1/13)		
Total	3	82	261	21	53	9	2	3	24	13	1	24	.203	.244	.287	56	-16	2	.949	-5	86	51	O69(18/2/49)		-2.4

MURRAY, MIAH   Jeremiah J.   B1.1.1865 Boston MA   D1.11.1922 Boston MA   BR/TR/5-11.5/170   d5.17   U1

YEAR	TM LG	G	AB	R	H	2B	3B	HR	RBI	BB-IB	HP	SO	AVG	OBP	SLG	AOPS	ABR	SB-CS	FA	FR	RNG	THR	GAMES AT POSITION	DL	BFW
1884	Pro N	8	27	1	5	0	0	0	1	1		8	.185	.214	.185	27	-2		.836	-4			C7/OC1		-0.2
1885	Lou AA	12	43	4	8	0	0	0	3	2	1		.186	.239	.186	36	-3		.863	-1			C12,1b2		-0.5
1888	Was N	12	42	1	4	1	0	0	3	1	0	7	.095	.116	.119	-27	-6	0	.912	0			C10,1b2		-0.1
1891	Was AA	2	8	0	0	0	0	0	0	0	0		.000	.000	.000	-99	-2	0	1.000	1	87	63	C2		-1.3
Total	4	34	120	6	17	1	0	0	7	4	1	16	.142	.176	.150	3	-13	0	.884	-3	87	63	C31,1b5/OC		

MURRAY, RED   John Joseph   B3.4.1884 Arnot PA   D12.4.1958 Sayre PA   BR/TR/5-10.5/190   d6.16   Col Notre Dame   0.4

YEAR	TM LG	G	AB	R	H	2B	3B	HR	RBI	BB-IB	HP	SO	AVG	OBP	SLG	AOPS	ABR	SB-CS	FA	FR	RNG	THR	GAMES AT POSITION	DL	BFW
1906	StL N	46	144	18	37	9	7	1	16	9	1		.257	.305	.438	137	5	5	.962	-1	194	0	O34(4/11/20),C7		-0.2
1907	StL N	132	485	46	127	10	10	7	46	24	3		.262	.301	.367	113	4	23	.935	3	132	82	O131(124/1/6)		1.7
1908	StL N	154	593	64	167	19	15	7	62	37	8		.282	.332	.400	140	24	48	.914	-3	118	84	O154(0/89/67)		0.1
1909	NY N	149	570	74	150	15	12	7	91	45	2		.263	.319	.368	112	5	48	.947	2	142	22	O149(29/0/120)		0.7
1910	NY N	149	553	78	153	27	8	4	87	52	6	51	.277	.345	.376	110	7	57	.948	6	103	135	O148(24/0/124)		-0.4
1911	†NY N	140	488	57	142	27	15	3	78	43	5	37	.291	.354	.426	114	8	48	.954	-6	95	75	O131(50/2/83)		-0.8
1912	†NY N	143	549	83	152	26	20	3	92	27	8	45	.277	.320	.413	97	-6	38	.968	5	109	101	O143(27/0/117)		-1.0
1913	†NY N	147	520	70	139	21	3	0	59	34	6	28	.267	.320	.331	85	-10	35-25	.965	9	110	127	O147(32/1/116)		-0.7
1914	NY N	86	139	19	31	6	3	0	23	9	0	7	.223	.270	.309	75	-5	11	1.000	0	114	48	O49(16/0/34)		-0.7
1915	NY N	45	127	12	28	1	2	3	11	7	1	15	.220	.261	.331	83	-4	2-3	.959	0	96	111	O34(1/30/3)		0.2
	Chi N	51	144	20	43	6	1	0	11	8	1		.299	.340	.354	110	2	6-5	.966	2	116	91	O40(7/11/25)/2		-0.5
	Year	96	271	32	71	7	3	3	22	15	2	23	.262	.303	.343	98	-2	8-8	.963	2	107	100	O88(8/41/28)/2		-0.3
1917	NY N	22	22	1	1	1	0	0	3	4	0		.045	.192	.091	-12	-3	0	1.000	-0	117	0	O11(4/4/3)/C		-1.0
Total	11	1264	4334	555	1170	168	96	37	579	299	40	194	.270	.323	.379	108	27	321-33	.950	18	118	86	O1171(318/149/718),C8/2		

MURRAY, LARRY   Larry   B4.1.1953 Chicago IL   BB/TR/5-11/179*   [NYA71 5/115]   d9.7

YEAR	TM LG	G	AB	R	H	2B	3B	HR	RBI	BB-IB	HP	SO	AVG	OBP	SLG	AOPS	ABR	SB-CS	FA	FR	RNG	THR	GAMES AT POSITION	DL	BFW
1974	NY A	6	1	1	0	0	0	0	0	0-0	0	0	.000	.000	.000	-99	0	0-1	—	-0	0	0	O3(1/1/2)		0.0
1975	NY A	6	1	1	0	0	0	0	0	0-0	0	0	.000	.000	.000	-99	-0	0-0	1.000	-0	66	0	O4(2/1/1)		-0.1
1976	NY A	8	10	2	1	0	0	0	2	1-0	0	2	.100	.182	.100	-16	-1	2-0	1.000	0	84	340	O7(0/6/1)		-1.3
1977	Oak A	90	162	19	29	5	2	1	9	17-2	0	36	.179	.257	.253	40	-14	12-3	.992	0	101	83	O78(27/36/22)/SD		-0.2
1978	Oak A	11	12	1	1	0	0	0	0	3-0	0	2	.083	.267	.083	3	-1	0-0	.963	7	122	142	O6(5/0/1)		-1.2
1979	Oak A	105	226	25	42	11	2	2	20	28-1	0	34	.186	.275	.279	53	-15	6-6	.975	7	111	119	O90(24/12/57),2b3,D3/S		-2.9
Total	6	226	412	49	73	16	4	3	31	49-3	0	74	.177	.264	.257	44	-31	20-10					O188(59/56/84),2b3,D3/S		

MURRAY, RAY   Raymond Lee "Deacon"   B10.12.1917 Spring Hope NC   D4.9.2003 Fort Worth TX   BR/TR/6-3/204*   d4.25

YEAR	TM LG	G	AB	R	H	2B	3B	HR	RBI	BB-IB	HP	SO	AVG	OBP	SLG	AOPS	ABR	SB-CS	FA	FR	RNG	THR	GAMES AT POSITION	DL	BFW
1948	Cle A	4	4	0	0	0	0	0	0	0-0	0	3	.000	.000	.000	-99	-1	0-0	—	-0	0	0	/H		-0.3
1950	Cle A	55	139	16	38	8	2	1	13	12	0	13	.273	.331	.381	85	-4	1-0	.972	-1	122	116	C45		-0.6
1951	Cle A	1	0	1	0	1	0	0	0	1	0		1.000	1.000	1.000	468	1	0-0	1.000	1	0	0	/C		
	Phi A	40	122	9	26	4	0	0	13	14	0	8	.213	.294	.262	50	-8	0-0	.985	1	136	147	C39		
	Year	41	123	10	27	6	0	0	14	14	0	8	.220	.299	.268	53	-8	0-0	.986	1	134	145	C40		
1952	Phi A	44	136	14	28	5	0	1	10	9	1	13	.206	.255	.265	42	-11	0-0	.995	0	148	127	C78		
1953	Phi A	84	268	25	76	14	3	6	41	18	1	25	.284	.330	.425	99	-1	0-0	.989	0	81	132	C21		
1954	Bal A	22	61	4	15	2	1	0	9	6	1	5	.246	.270	.344	73	-3	1-0	.987	8	132	141	C226		
Total	6	250	731	69	184	37	6	8	80	55	1	67	.252	.305	.352	75	-27	1-0							

MURRAY, RICH   Richard Dale   B7.6.1957 Los Angeles CA   BR/TR/6-4/195*   [SFN75 6/128]   d6.7   b-Eddie

YEAR	TM LG	G	AB	R	H	2B	3B	HR	RBI	BB-IB	HP	SO	AVG	OBP	SLG	AOPS	ABR	SB-CS	FA	FR	RNG	THR	GAMES AT POSITION	DL	BFW
1980	SF N	53	194	19	42	8	2	4	24	11-1	0	48	.216	.259	.340	68	-9	2-1	.987	1	113	78	1b53	60	
1983	SF N	4	10	0	2	0	0	0	1	0-0	0	3	.200	.200	.200	11	-1	0-0	1.000	-0	63	57	1b3		
Total	2	57	204	19	44	8	2	4	25	11-1	0	51	.216	.256	.333	65	-10	2-1	.988	1	111	77	1b56	60	

MURRAY, BOBBY   Robert Hayes   B7.4.1894 St.Albans VT   D1.4.1979 Nashua NH   BL/TR/5-7/155   d9.24   Col Norwich

YEAR	TM LG	G	AB	R	H	2B	3B	HR	RBI	BB-IB	HP	SO	AVG	OBP	SLG	AOPS	ABR	SB-CS	FA	FR	RNG	THR	GAMES AT POSITION	DL	BFW
1923	Was A	10	37	2	7	1	0	0	4	2	0	4	.189	.211	.216	13	-5	1-0	1.000	2	121	0	3b10		

MURRAY, TOM   Thomas W.   B1866 Paterson NJ   BR/5-7/150   d6.20

YEAR	TM LG	G	AB	R	H	2B	3B	HR	RBI	BB-IB	HP	SO	AVG	OBP	SLG	AOPS	ABR	SB-CS	FA	FR	RNG	THR	GAMES AT POSITION	DL	BFW
1894	Phi N	1	2	0	0	0	0	0	0	0	0	2	.000	.000	.000	-99	-1	0	.833	-1	36	0	/S		

MURRAY, BILL   William Allenwood "Dasher"   B9.6.1893 Vinalhaven ME   D9.14.1943 Boston MA   BB/TR/5-11/165   d6.27   Col Brown

YEAR	TM LG	G	AB	R	H	2B	3B	HR	RBI	BB-IB	HP	SO	AVG	OBP	SLG	AOPS	ABR	SB-CS	FA	FR	RNG	THR	GAMES AT POSITION	DL	BFW
1917	Was A	8	21	2	3	0	1	0	4	2	0	2	.143	.217	.238	39	-2	1	.889	-2	79	85	2b6/S		

MURRELL, IVAN   Ivan Augustus (Peters)   B4.24.1943 Almirante, Pan   BR/TR/6-2/196*   d9.28

YEAR	TM LG	G	AB	R	H	2B	3B	HR	RBI	BB-IB	HP	SO	AVG	OBP	SLG	AOPS	ABR	SB-CS	FA	FR	RNG	THR	GAMES AT POSITION	DL	BFW
1963	Hou N	2	5	1	1	0	0	0	0	0-0	0	2	.200	.200	.200	17	-1	0-0	1.000	0	106	0	O2C		
1964	Hou N	10	14	1	2	0	0	0	0	0-0	0	6	.143	.133	.214	-1	-2	0-0	1.000	-1	32	0	O5(4/0/1)		
1967	Hou N	10	29	5	9	0	0	1	1	1-0	0	9	.310	.333	.310	88	-1	0-0	.846	-1	102	0	O6(5/0/1)		
1968	Hou N	32	59	3	6	1	1	0	3	1-0	0	17	.102	.117	.153	-20	-9	0-0	.931	3	118	358	O15(4/2/9)		
1969	SD N	111	247	19	63	10	6	3	25	11-1	2	65	.255	.291	.380	90	-5	3-4	.959	3	114	82	O72(23/41/14),1b2		
1970	SD N	125	347	43	85	9	3	12	33	17-5	4	93	.245	.287	.392	83	-11	9-7	.970	5	109	133	O101(61/24/20)/1		
1971	SD N	103	255	20	60	6	3	7	24	7-1	0	60	.235	.263	.365	82	-8	5-2	.978	2	100	47	O72(55/16/2)		
1972	SD N	5	7	0	1	0	0	0	1	0-0	0	3	.143	.143	.143	-20	-1	0-0	1.000	0	106	0	/OR	34	

YEAR	TM	LG	G	AB	R	H	2B	3B	HR	RBI	BB-IB	HP	SO	AVG	OBP	SLG	AOPS	ABR	SB-CS	FA	FR	RNG	THR	GAMES AT POSITION	DL	BFW
1973	SD	N	93	210	23	48	13	1	9	21	2-0	0	52	.229	.236	.429	87	-6	2-0	.959	2	101	95	O37(10/18/12),1b24		-0.6
1974	Atl	N	73	133	11	33	1	1	2	12	5-1	0	35	.248	.273	.316	63	-7	0-0	.983	3	130	149	O32(13/9/13),1b13		-0.6
Total	10		564	1306	126	308	41	15	33	123	44-9	9	342	.236	.265	.366	77	-51	20-13	.965	16	108	149	O343(175/112/73),1b40		-0.6

MURTAUGH, DANNY Daniel Edward B10.8.1917 Chester PA D12.2.1976 Chester PA BR/TR/5-9/165* d7.6 Mil 1943-45 M15/C2 — 34 -5.2

YEAR	TM	LG	G	AB	R	H	2B	3B	HR	RBI	BB-IB	HP	SO	AVG	OBP	SLG	AOPS	ABR	SB-CS	FA	FR	RNG	THR	GAMES AT POSITION	DL	BFW
1941	Phi	N	85	347	34	76	8	1	0	11	26	1	31	.219	.275	.248	50	-24	18	.978	3	98	86	2b85/S		
1942	Phi	N	144	506	48	122	16	4	0	27	49	2	39	.241	.311	.289	80	-13	13	.939	8	101	87	S60,3b53,2b32		-1.6
1943	Phi	N	113	451	65	123	17	4	1	35	57	2	23	.273	.357	.335	104	4	4	.974	4	99	104	2b113		0.3
1946	Phi	N	6	19	1	4	1	0	1	3	2	0	2	.211	.286	.421	102	0	0	.958	-2	72	0	2b6		1.5
1947	Bos	N	3	8	0	1	0	0	0	0	1	0	2	.125	.222	.125	-6	-1	0	1.000	-0	91	71	2b2,3b2		-0.2
1948	Pit	N	146	514	56	149	21	5	1	71	60	1	40	.290	.365	.356	94	-2	10	.979	3	101	111	2b146		-0.1
1949	Pit	N	75	236	16	48	7	2	2	24	29	0	17	.203	.291	.275	51	-16	2	.975	2	95	120	2b74		0.9
1950	Pit	N	118	367	34	108	20	5	2	37	47	1	42	.294	.376	.392	99	1	2	.976	3	104	103	2b108		-1.0
1951	Pit	N	77	151	9	30	7	0	1	11	16	2	19	.199	.284	.265	40	-11	0-0	.970	-0	98	105	2b65,3b3		0.9
Total	9		767	2599	263	661	97	21	8	219	287	9	215	.254	.331	.317	81	-62	49-0	.975	19	100	102	2b631,S61,3b58		-0.9

MURTON, MATT Matthew Henry B10.3.1981 Fort Lauderdale FL BR/TR/6-1/215 d7.8 Col Georgia Tech — -0.2

YEAR	TM	LG	G	AB	R	H	2B	3B	HR	RBI	BB-IB	HP	SO	AVG	OBP	SLG	AOPS	ABR	SB-CS	FA	FR	RNG	THR	GAMES AT POSITION	DL	BFW
2005	Chi	N	51	140	19	45	3	2	7	14	16-4	0	22	.321	.386	.521	132	6	2-1	.969	-2	92	49	O43L		0.3

MUSER, TONY Anthony Joseph B8.1.1947 Van Nuys CA BL/TL/6-2/190(175-200) d9.14 M6/C13 Col San Diego Mesa (CA) JC

YEAR	TM	LG	G	AB	R	H	2B	3B	HR	RBI	BB-IB	HP	SO	AVG	OBP	SLG	AOPS	ABR	SB-CS	FA	FR	RNG	THR	GAMES AT POSITION	DL	BFW
1969	Bos	A	2	9	0	1	0	0	0	1	1-0	0	1	.111	.200	.111	-11	-1	0-0	1.000	1	226	174	1b2		-0.1
1971	Chi	A	11	16	2	5	0	1	0	0	1-0	0	1	.313	.353	.438	120	0	0-0	.963	0	182	44	1b4		0.0
1972	Chi	A	44	61	6	17	2	2	1	9	2-0	0	6	.279	.302	.426	112	0	1-1	.986	-1	83	97	1b29/OR		-0.2
1973	Chi	A	109	309	38	88	14	3	4	30	33-0	0	36	.285	.352	.388	105	3	8-4	.992	-3	86	106	1b89,D13,O2L		-0.6
1974	Chi	A	103	206	16	60	5	1	1	16	6-0	1	22	.291	.313	.340	86	-4	1-4	.998	-4	51	108	1b80,D13		-1.5
1975	Chi	A	43	111	11	27	3	0	0	6	7-1	0	8	.243	.286	.270	58	-6	2-1	.993	2	121	125	1b41		-0.7
	Bal	A	80	82	11	26	3	0	0	17	8-0	0	9	.317	.374	.354	114	2	0-0	.996	-0	93	129	1b62		-0.1
	Year		123	193	22	53	6	0	0	17	15-1	0	17	.275	.324	.306	82	-4	2-1	.994	1	109	127	1b103		-0.8
1976	Bal	A	136	326	25	74	7	1	1	30	21-4	0	34	.227	.270	.264	61	-17	1-1	.991	3	121	106	1b109,O12(8/4/0),D10		-2.2
1977	Bal	A	120	118	14	27	6	0	0	7	13-5	0	16	.229	.301	.280	64	-5	1-2	.992	1	136	199	1b77,O11(5/6/0)/D		-0.6
1978	Mil	A	15	30	0	4	1	0	0	5	3-0	0	5	.133	.212	.233	25	-3	0-0	.988	-0	95	61	1b12		-0.4
Total	9		663	1268	123	329	41	9	7	117	95-10	1	138	.259	.309	.323	82	-31	14-13	.992	-2	99	115	1b505,D37,O26(15/10/1)		-6.4

MUSIAL, STAN Stanley Frank "Stan the Man" B11.21.1920 Donora PA BL/TL/6-0/175* d9.17 Mil 1945 HF1969 — 76.0

YEAR	TM	LG	G	AB	R	H	2B	3B	HR	RBI	BB-IB	HP	SO	AVG	OBP	SLG	AOPS	ABR	SB-CS	FA	FR	RNG	THR	GAMES AT POSITION	DL	BFW
1941	StL	N	12	47	8	20	4	0	1	7	2	0	1	.426	.449	.574	175	5	1	1.000	-0	93	113	O11(3/0/8)		0.4
1942	†StL	N	140	467	87	147	32	10	10	72	62	2	25	.315	.397	.490	148	30	6	.984	7	**117**	74	O135(133/2/2)		3.2
1943	†StL	N★	**157**	617	108	**220**	48	20	13	81	72	2	18	.357	.425	.562	176	61	9	.982	5	108	88	O155(34/10/117)		5.7
1944	†StL	N★	146	568	112	**197**	51	14	12	94	90	5	28	.347	.440	.549	174	61	7	.987	3	105	99	O146(1/38/124)		5.5
1946	†StL	N★	**156**	624	**124**	**228**	50	20	16	103	73	3	31	.365	.434	.587	180	66	7	.989	-3	83	135	1b114,O42L		5.8
1947	StL	N★	149	587	113	183	30	13	19	95	80	4	24	.312	.398	.504	132	28	4	.994	-6	81	118	1b149		1.6
1948	StL	N★	155	611	135	**230**	46	18	**39**	**131**	79	3	34	.376	.450	.702	196	82	7	.981	-2	98	85	O155(41/64/76),1b2		7.2
1949	StL	N★	**157**	612	128	**207**	41	13	36	123	107	2	38	.338	.438	.624	174	67	3	.991	-10	89	74	O156(3/72/117)/1		5.1
1950	StL	N★	146	555	105	192	41	7	28	109	87	3	36	.346	.437	.596	161	53	5	.964	7	91	39	O91(84/10/1),1b60		3.8
1951	StL	N★	152	578	**124**	205	30	12	32	108	98	1	40	.355	.449	.614	182	70	4-5	.974	2	102	150	O157(141/9/26),1b25/P		6.1
1952	StL	N★	154	578	**105**	**194**	42	6	21	91	96	2	29	.336	.432	.538	167	58	7-7	.987	-10	94	49	O152(8/0/147),1b10		4.2
1953	StL	N★	**157**	593	127	**200**	53	9	30	113	**105**	0	32	.337	.437	.609	169	66	3-4	.984	-9	92	66	O157(141/9/26)		4.4
1954	StL	N★	**153**	591	**120**	**195**	41	9	35	126	103	4	39	.330	.428	.607	166	61	1-7	.990	-5	92	96	1b105,O51(21/0/33)		4.7
1955	StL	N★	154	562	97	179	30	5	33	108	80-19	8	39	.319	.408	.566	156	48	5-4	.992	7	**127**	99	1b103,O53(3/0/51)		4.5
1956	StL	N★	**156**	594	87	**184**	33	6	27	109	75-15	3	39	.310	.386	.522	142	37	2-0	.993	6	124	119	1b130		3.6
1957	StL	N★	134	502	82	176	38	3	29	102	66-19	2	34	.351	.422	.612	172	54	1-1	.992	0	101	125	1b130		4.6
1958	StL	N★	135	472	64	159	35	2	17	62	72-26	1	26	.337	.423	.528	145	35	0-0	.989	7	**122**	111	1b124		3.5
1959	StL	N★	115	341	37	87	13	2	14	44	60-11	0	25	.255	.364	.428	104	4	0-2	.990	4	116	106	1b90,O3L		0.2
1960	StL	N★	116	331	49	91	17	1	17	63	41-7	2	34	.275	.354	.486	118	9	1-1	.990	-1	98	45	O59(53/0/6),1b29		0.3
1961	StL	N★	123	372	46	107	22	4	15	70	52-17	1	35	.288	.371	.489	116	10	0-0	.994	2	95	130	O103L		0.7
1962	StL	N★	135	433	57	143	18	1	19	82	64-4	3	46	.330	.416	.508	135	24	3-0	.977	-3	91	80	O119(97/0/23)		1.5
1963	StL	N★	124	337	34	86	10	2	12	58	35-9	2	43	.255	.325	.404	100	1	2-0	.968	-3	99	22	O96L		-0.6
Total	22		3026	10972	1949	3630	725	177	475	1951	1599-127	53	696	.331	.417	.559	157	930	78-31	.984	-16	98	82	O1890(943/325/750),1b1016/P		

MUSSER, DANNY William Daniel B9.5.1905 Zion PA D3.2.2000 Upper Sandusky OH BL/TR/5-9.5/160 d9.18 Col Penn St.

YEAR	TM	LG	G	AB	R	H	2B	3B	HR	RBI	BB-IB	HP	SO	AVG	OBP	SLG	AOPS	ABR	SB-CS	FA	FR	RNG	THR	GAMES AT POSITION	DL	BFW
1932	Was	A	1	2	0	1	0	0	0	0	0	0		.500	.500	.500	162	0	0		-0	0	0	/3		0.0

MYATT, GEORGE George Edward "Mercury","Stud","Foghorn" B6.14.1914 Denver CO D9.14.2000 Orlando FL BL/TR/5-11/167 d8.16 M2/C23

YEAR	TM	LG	G	AB	R	H	2B	3B	HR	RBI	BB-IB	HP	SO	AVG	OBP	SLG	AOPS	ABR	SB-CS	FA	FR	RNG	THR	GAMES AT POSITION	DL	BFW
1938	NY	N	43	170	27	52	2	1	3	10	14	1	13	.306	.362	.382	104	1	10	.919	5	108	130	S24,3b19		0.9
1939	NY	N	22	53	7	10	2	0	0	3	6	0	6	.189	.271	.226	35	-5	2	.907	0	108	124	3b14		-0.4
1943	Was	A	42	53	11	13	3	0	0	3	13	0	7	.245	.394	.302	109	2	3-0	.930	-1	113	59	2b11,S2,3b2		0.2
1944	Was	A	140	538	86	153	19	6	0	40	54	7	44	.284	.357	.342	105	5	26-10	.957	-20	87	93	2b121,S15,O3R		-0.6
1945	Was	A	133	490	81	145	17	7	1	39	63	2	43	.296	.378	.365	127	19	30-11	.972	-15	88	88	2b94,O32(1/0/31),3b6/S		1.0
1946	Was	A	15	34	7	8	1	0	0	4	2	1	3	.235	.297	.265	61	-2	1-1	1.000	-2	85	68	3b7,2b2		-0.4
1947	Was	A	12	7	1	0	0	0	0	0	0	0	4	.000	.364	.000	6	-1	0-0	1.000	0	152	0	/2		-0.1
Total	7		407	1345	220	381	44	14	4	99	156	11	120	.283	.362	.346	100	19	72-22	.962	-32	89	89	2b229,3b48,S42,O35(1/0/34)		0.6

MYATT, GLENN Glenn Calvin B7.9.1897 Argenta (now N.Little Rock) AR D8.9.1969 Houston TX BL/TR/5-11/165 d4.15 — -6.4

YEAR	TM	LG	G	AB	R	H	2B	3B	HR	RBI	BB-IB	HP	SO	AVG	OBP	SLG	AOPS	ABR	SB-CS	FA	FR	RNG	THR	GAMES AT POSITION	DL	BFW
1920	Phi	A	70	196	14	49	8	3	0	18	12	0	22	.250	.293	.321	62	-11	1-3	.900	-3	77	151	O37(1/0/36),C22		-1.5
1921	Phi	A	44	69	6	14	2	0	0	5	6	0	7	.203	.267	.232	28	-8	1-0	.939	-3	97	139	C27		-0.6
1923	Cle	A	92	220	36	63	7	6	3	40	16	1	18	.286	.338	.414	97	-2	0-2	.934	-5	122	53	C69		-0.4
1924	Cle	A	105	342	55	117	22	7	8	73	33	2	24	.342	.402	.518	134	17	6-1	.978	-9	89	76	C95		1.4
1925	Cle	A	106	358	51	97	15	9	11	54	29	2	24	.271	.329	.455	97	-5	3-1	.973	-9	120	66	C98/OL		-0.7
1926	Cle	A	56	117	14	29	5	2	0	13	13	0	13	.248	.323	.325	69	-5	1-0	1.000	1	162	61	C35		-0.2
1927	Cle	A	55	94	15	23	6	0	2	8	12	1	7	.245	.336	.372	83	-2	1-1	.978	2	118	153	C26		0.1
1928	Cle	A	58	125	9	36	7	2	1	15	13	0	13	.288	.355	.400	97	0	0-2	.967	-5	88	82	C30		-0.4
1929	Cle	A	59	129	14	30	4	1	1	17	7	1	13	.233	.277	.302	47	-11	0-0	.976	-1	87	129	C41		-0.9
1930	Cle	A	86	256	30	78	23	2	2	37	18	1	17	.294	.342	.419	88	-4	2-3	.977	-5	81	97	C71		-0.5
1931	Cle	A	65	195	21	48	14	2	1	29	21	3	21	.246	.319	.354	73	-8	2-1	.991	-2	103	127	C53		-0.6
1932	Cle	A	82	252	45	62	12	1	8	46	27	3	21	.246	.326	.397	81	-7	2-2	.988	-3	116	75	C65		-0.7
1933	Cle	A	40	77	10	18	4	0	0	7	15	2	8	.234	.372	.286	73	-2	0-1	.965	0	129	162	C27		-0.1
1934	†Cle	A	36	107	18	34	6	1	0	12	13	0	9	.318	.392	.393	101	1	0-0	.980	-1	114	64	C34		0.2
1935	Cle	A	10	36	1	3	1	0	0	2	4	0	3	.083	.175	.111	-24	-7	0-0	.980	-1	114	64	C34		-0.7
	NY	N	13	18	2	4	0	1	0	5	0	0	3	.222	.222	.500	90	-1	0-0	1.000	-1	101	75	C10		-0.1
1936	Det	A	27	78	5	17	1	0	0	5	9	0	3	.218	.299	.231	32	-8	0-0	1.000	-1	114	119	C4		-0.1
Total	16		1004	2678	346	722	137	37	38	387	248	12	195	.270	.334	.391	85	-63	20-18	.974	-41	107	90	C734,O38(2/0/36)		-6.4

MYER, BUDDY Charles Solomon B3.16.1904 Ellisville MS D10.31.1974 Baton Rouge LA BL/TR/5-10.5/163 d9.26 Col Mississippi St.

YEAR	TM	LG	G	AB	R	H	2B	3B	HR	RBI	BB-IB	HP	SO	AVG	OBP	SLG	AOPS	ABR	SB-CS	FA	FR	RNG	THR	GAMES AT POSITION	DL	BFW
1925	†Was	A	4	8	1	2	0	0	0	0	0	0	1	.250	.250	.250	28	-1	0-0	1.000	-1	66	0	S4		
1926	Was	A	132	434	66	132	18	6	1	62	45	0	19	.304	.370	.380	98	-1	10-11	.928	-17	93	76	S118,3b8		-0.2
1927	Was	A	15	51	7	11	1	0	0	7	8	0	6	.216	.322	.235	47	-4	3-1	.933	-2	90	115	S15		-0.7
	Bos	A	133	469	59	135	22	11	2	47	48	4	15	.288	.359	.394	97	-2	9-5	.940	6	102	105	S101,3b14,O10L/2		-0.4
	Year		148	520	66	146	23	11	2	54	56	4	18	.281	.355	.379	92	-6	12-6	.939	4	100	106	S116,3b14,O10L/2		1.4
1928	Bos	A	147	536	78	168	26	6	1	44	53	2	26	.313	.379	.390	104	5	30-16	.967	6	108	**133**	3b144		1.0
1929	Was	A	141	563	80	169	29	10	3	82	63	2	33	.300	.373	.403	99	0	19-7	.958	-12	93	92	2b88,3b53		-0.4
1930	Was	A	138	541	97	164	29	6	3	52	69	2	33	.303	.373	.377	90	-7	14-11	.965	-14	92	109	2b137		-0.6
1931	Was	A	139	591	114	173	33	11	3	56	58	4	42	.293	.360	.406	100	1	11-14	.984	-13	90	**114**	2b137		-1.6
1932	Was	A	143	577	120	161	38	16	7	52	69	1	44	.279	.360	.426	104	12	12-7	.975	-17	92	**112**	2b139		-0.4
1933	†Was	A	131	530	95	160	29	10	3	60	58	4	33	.302	.379	.426	104	4	12-7	.975	-17	92	**112**	2b139		-0.4
1934	Was	A	139	524	103	160	33	4	3	57	102	1	32	.305	.419	.416	121	23	6-6	.978	1	99	127	2b129		1.8
1935	Was	A☆	151	616	115	215	36	11	5	100	96	4	40	**.349**	.440	.468	139	42	7-6	.979	-8	100	**123**	2b151		2.1
1936	Was	A	51	156	31	44	7	0	0	15	42	1	11	.269	.427	.327	94	7	7-2	.985	3	100	108	2b43		5.3
																										0.7

YEAR	TM LG	G	AB	R	H	2B	3B	HR	RBI	BB-IB	HP	SO	AVG	OBP	SLG	AOPS	ABR	SB-CS	FA	FR	RNG	THR	GAMES AT POSITION	DL	BFW
1937	Was A☆	125	430	54	126	16	10	1	65	78	5	41	.293	.407	.384	105	7	2-6	.966	-16	90	107	2b119/OL		-0.2
1938	Buf N	127	437	79	147	22	8	6	71	93	1	32	.336	.454	.465	140	34	9-5	.982	-3	100	105	2b121		3.5
1939	Was A	83	258	33	78	10	3	1	32	40	0	18	.302	.396	.376	106	4	4-1	.968	3	100	113	2b65		1.1
1940	Was A	71	210	28	61	14	4	0	29	34	0	10	.290	.389	.395	111	5	6-3	.967	6	110	86	2b54		1.3
1941	Was A	53	107	14	27	3	1	0	9	18	0	10	.252	.360	.299	80	-2	2-0	.982	-3	87	83	2b24		-0.4
Total	17	1923	7038	1174	2131	353	130	38	850	965	33	428	.303	.389	.406	108	122	157-109	.974	-74	96	110	2b1340,S238,3b219,O13(12/0/1)		14.3

MYERS, GEORGE George D. B11.13.1860 Buffalo NY D12.14.1926 Buffalo NY BR/TR/5-8/170 d5.2

YEAR	TM LG	G	AB	R	H	2B	3B	HR	RBI	BB-IB	HP	SO	AVG	OBP	SLG	AOPS	ABR	SB-CS	FA	FR	RNG	THR	GAMES AT POSITION	DL	BFW
												33	.182	.213	.240	41	-22		.837	-14			C49,O34(16/18/0)		-3.0
1884	Buf N	78	325	34	59	9	2	2	32	13		40	.206	.258	.239	60	-14		.899	-4			C69,O23(0/21/1)		-1.3
1885	Buf N	89	326	40	67	7	2	0	19	23		42	.190	.236	.234	46	-18	6	.928	-5			C72,O6(0/5/1)/3		-1.6
1886	StL N	79	295	26	56	7	3	0	27	18	5	7	.217	.298	.272	61	-11	26	.929	-8			C50,O15(3/7/5),1b6/3		-1.3
1887	Ind N	69	235	25	51	8	1	1	20	22	3	14	.238	.292	.298	87	-3	28	.929	-4			C47,3b14,O10(2/1/7)/1		-0.3
1888	Ind N	66	248	36	59	9	0	2	16	15	4	13	.195	.294	.215	42	-11	12	.909	0	158	106	O23(6/17/0),C18/1		-0.9
1889	Ind N	43	149	22	29	3	0	0	12	17	1		.203	.260	.250	56	-79	72	.901	-34			C305,O111(27/69/14),3b16,1b8		-8.4
Total	6	424	1578	183	321	43	8	5	126	109	12	149													

MYERS, GREG Gregory Richard B4.14.1966 Riverside CA BL/TR/6-2/205(202-225) [TorA84 3/74] d9.12

YEAR	TM LG	G	AB	R	H	2B	3B	HR	RBI	BB-IB	HP	SO	AVG	OBP	SLG	AOPS	ABR	SB-CS	FA	FR	RNG	THR	GAMES AT POSITION	DL	BFW
1987	Tor A	7	9	1	1	0	0	0	0	0	0	3	.111	.111	.111	-40	-2	0-0	1.000	2	0	0	C7		0.0
1989	Tor A	17	44	0	5	2	0	0	1	2-0	0	9	.114	.152	.159	-12	-7	0-1	1.000	2	103	84	C11,D6	63	-0.4
1990	Tor A	87	250	33	59	7	1	5	22	22-0	0	33	.236	.293	.332	74	-9	0-1	.993	1	118	105	C87	20	-0.4
1991	Tor A	107	309	25	81	22	0	8	36	21-4	0	45	.262	.306	.411	94	-3	0-0	.979	-8	61	110	C18/D		-0.2
1992	Tor A	22	61	4	14	6	0	1	13	5-0	0	5	.230	.279	.377	81	-2	0-0	.991	-1	61	110	C8	39	-0.1
	Cal A	8	17	0	4	1	0	0	0	0-0	0	6	.235	.235	.294	47	-1	0-0	1.000	0	51	57	C26/D		-0.3
	Year	30	78	4	18	7	0	1	13	5-0	0	11	.231	.271	.359	74	-3	0-0	.993	-1	71	102	C97,D2		-1.3
1993	Cal A	108	290	27	74	10	0	7	40	17-2	2	47	.255	.298	.362	75	-11	3-3	.991	1	123	161	C41/D	58	-0.4
1994	Cal A	45	126	10	31	6	0	2	8	10-3	1	27	.246	.299	.341	64	-7	0-2	.989	3	131	86	C61,D16	33	-0.3
1995	Cal A	85	273	36	71	12	2	9	38	17-3	1	49	.260	.304	.418	87	-7	0-1	.989	1	121	100	C90	19	-0.4
1996	Min A	97	329	37	94	22	3	6	47	19-3	0	52	.286	.320	.426	86	-8	0-0	.985	-2	103	111	C38,D10	15	-0.3
1997	Min A	62	165	24	44	11	1	6	28	16-2	0	29	.267	.328	.436	97	-1	0-0	.986	-2	103	111	C8,D10		
	Atl N	9	9	0	1	0	0	0	1	1-0	0	3	.111	.200	.111	-16	-2	0-0	1.000	1	40	273	C2	50	-0.2
1998	†SD N	69	171	19	42	10	0	4	20	17-1	0	36	.246	.312	.374	86	-4	0-0	.987	-1	107	110	C52	27	0.0
1999	SD N	50	149	17	37	4	0	3	15	13-2	0	14	.289	.355	.391	95	-1	0-0	.986	-6	89	73	C41		0.4
	†Atl N	34	72	10	16	2	0	2	9	13-2	0	16	.222	.337	.333	72	-3	0-0	.994	6	196	110	C31		-0.1
	Year	84	200	19	53	6	0	5	24	26-4	0	30	.265	.348	.370	86	-4	0-0	1.000	-3	59	110	C28,D8	13	-0.9
2000	Bal A	43	125	9	28	6	0	3	12	8-0	0	29	.224	.271	.344	57	-9	0-0	1.000	0	51	175	D11,C8		0.0
2001	Bal A	25	74	11	20	2	0	4	8	8-0	0	17	.270	.341	.459	114	1	0-0	1.000	1	114	120	C28,D2		0.0
	†Oak A	33	87	13	16	1	0	7	13	13-1	0	21	.184	.290	.437	87	-2	0-0	1.000	1	101	133	C36,D13		0.0
	Year	58	161	24	36	3	0	11	21	21-1	0	38	.224	.313	.447	99	-1	0-0	.997	6	95	156	C53/D		0.7
2002	†Oak A	65	144	15	32	5	0	6	21	26-3	0	57	.307	.374	.502	124	12	0-3	.982	-9	77	74	C81,D22		0.0
2003	Tor A	121	329	51	101	19	0	15	52	37-2	5		.307	.374	.502	124	12	0-3	1.000	1	64	113	C4/D	160	0.0
2004	Tor A	8	18	0	4	2	0	0	1	2-0	1	5	.222	.300	.333	61	-1	0-0	1.000	0	51	156	C4		-0.2
2005	Tor A	6	12	0	1	0	0	0	1	1-0	1	5	.083	.154	.083	-32	-2	0-0	.989	-16	99	104	C894,D81	497	-4.1
Total	18	1108	3042	333	776	150	7	87	396	268-28	3	539	.255	.313	.395	86	-70	3-12							

MYERS, HENRY Henry C. B5.1858 Philadelphia PA D4.18.1895 Philadelphia PA BR/TR/5-9/159 d8.20 M1 ▲

YEAR	TM LG	G	AB	R	H	2B	3B	HR	RBI	BB-IB	HP	SO	AVG	OBP	SLG	AOPS	ABR	SB-CS	FA	FR	RNG	THR	GAMES AT POSITION	DL	BFW
1881	Pro N	1	4	0	0	0	0	0	0			2	.000	.000	.000	-99	-1		1.000	-0	76	0	/S		-0.1
1882	Bal AA	69	294	43	53	3	0	0		12			.180	.212	.190	40	-17		.822	-6	107	76	S68,P6,M		-1.9
1884	Wil U	6	24	3	3	0	0	0	0				.125	.125	.125	-23	-4		.875	4	108	0	S5/2		-0.1
Total	3	76	322	46	56	3	0	0	0	12		2	.174	.204	.183	32	-22		.826	-3	107	70	S74,P6/2		-2.1

MYERS, HY Henry Harrison B4.27.1889 E.Liverpool OH D5.1.1965 Minerva OH BR/TR/5-9.5/175 d8.30 OF(5/1150/28)

YEAR	TM LG	G	AB	R	H	2B	3B	HR	RBI	BB-IB	HP	SO	AVG	OBP	SLG	AOPS	ABR	SB-CS	FA	FR	RNG	THR	GAMES AT POSITION	DL	BFW
1909	Bro N	6	22	1	5	0	0	0	6	2	0		.227	.292	.273	78	-1	1	1.000	-1	0	0	O6R		-0.1
1911	Bro N	13	43	2	7	1	0	0	0	2	0		.163	.200	.186	9	-5	1	.889	-1	88	124	O13(0/12/1)		-0.7
1914	Bro N	70	227	35	65	3	9	0	17	7	3	24	.286	.316	.379	104	-1	2	.964	-5	90	59	O60(4/45/12)		-1.0
1915	Bro N	153	605	69	150	21	7	2	46	17	6	51	.248	.275	.316	77	-19	19-22	.969	-5	93	82	O153C		-3.9
1916	†Bro N	113	412	54	108	12	14	3	36	21	0	35	.262	.308	.381	108	-3	4-17	.982	-6	104	67	O66(0/62/4),1b22,2b19,3b15		-1.2
1917	Bro N	120	471	37	126	15	10	1	41	18	0	26	.268	.294	.348	95	-4	17	.975	3	108	119	O107C		-1.7
1918	Bro N	107	407	36	104	9	8	4	40	8	1	26	.256	.292	.346	95	-4	17	.979	4	109	76	O131C		-0.5
1919	Bro N	133	512	62	157	23	14	5	73	23	2	34	.307	.339	.436	129	16	13	.978	-1	101	70	O152C,3b2		1.1
1920	†Bro N	154	582	83	177	36	22	4	80	35	1	54	.304	.345	.462	126	18	9-13	.968	-4	85	136	O124C,2b21/3		0.4
1921	Bro N	144	549	51	158	14	4	4	68	22	2	51	.288	.318	.350	74	-21	8-6	.974	-1	101	88	O152C/2		-3.0
1922	Bro N	153	618	82	196	20	9	6	89	13	0	26	.317	.331	.408	90	-12	9-10	.977	7	108	138	O87C		-0.2
1923	StL N	96	330	29	99	18	2	2	48	12	3	19	.300	.330	.385	90	-5	5-3	.945	-2	107	100	O22(1/17/4),3b12,2b3		-1.4
1924	StL N	43	124	12	26	5	1	1	13	3	0	10	.210	.228	.290	39	-11	1-2	.945	-2	107	100	/H		-0.6
1925	StL N	1	1	0	0	0	0	0	0	0	0		.000	.000	.000	-98	0	0-0		-0			/H		0.0
	Cin N	3	6	1	1	0	0	0	0	0	0		.167	.167	.333	25	-1	0-0	1.000	0	110	0	O3C		-0.1
	StL N	1	1	0	1	0	0	0	0	0	0		1.000	1.000	1.000	403	0	0-0		-0			/H		0.0
	Year	5	8	2	2	1	0	0	0	0	0		.250	.250	.375	58	-1	0-0	1.000	0	110	0	O3C		-0.1
Total	14	1310	4910	555	1380	179	100	32	559	195	24	358	.281	.312	.378	95	-49	107-56	.972	-7	99	98	O1182C,2b44,3b30,1b22		-14.2

MYERS, AL James Albert "Cod" B10.22.1863 Danville IL D12.24.1927 Marshall IL BR/TR/5-8.5/165 d9.27

YEAR	TM LG	G	AB	R	H	2B	3B	HR	RBI	BB-IB	HP	SO	AVG	OBP	SLG	AOPS	ABR	SB-CS	FA	FR	RNG	THR	GAMES AT POSITION	DL	BFW
1884	Mil U	12	46	6	15	6	0	0					.326	.326	.457	247	7		.848	3	93	48	2b12		-2.9
1885	Phi N	93	357	25	73	13	2	1	28	11		41	.204	.228	.261	59	-16		.884	-16	98	85	2b93		-2.1
1886	KC N	118	473	69	131	22	9	4	51	22		42	.277	.309	.387	104	0	3	.913	2	108	88	2b78,S27		0.4
1887	Was N	105	362	45	84	9	5	2	36	40	2	26	.232	.312	.301	76	-10	18	.909	-9	95	71	2b132		-2.2
1888	Was N	132	502	46	104	12	7	2	46	37	4	46	.207	.270	.271	78	-11	20	.918	-22	95	71	2b46		-0.7
1889	Was N	46	176	24	46	3	0	0	20	22	1	7	.261	.347	.278	81	-3	10	.853	-14	101	88	2b75		-1.1
	Phi N	75	305	52	82	14	2	4	28	36	4	9	.269	.354	.328	84	-7	8	.886	-14	98	94	2b121		-1.1
	Year	121	481	76	128	17	2	4	48	58	5	16	.266	.351	.310	83	-10	18	.948	6	94	129	2b117		-1.1
1890	Phi N	117	487	95	135	29	7	2	81	57	10	46	.277	.365	.378	114	10	44	.937	-12	99	111	2b135		-1.3
1891	Phi N	135	514	67	118	27	3	2	69	69	4	46	.230	.331	.302	83	-9	8	.914	-61	98	93	2b806,S27		-6.2
Total	8	833	3222	429	788	135	34	13	359	294	32	263	.245	.314	.320	88	-39	111							

MYERS, BERT James Albert B4.8.1874 Frederick MD D10.12.1915 Washington DC BR/TR/5-10/? d4.25

YEAR	TM LG	G	AB	R	H	2B	3B	HR	RBI	BB-IB	HP	SO	AVG	OBP	SLG	AOPS	ABR	SB-CS	FA	FR	RNG	THR	GAMES AT POSITION	DL	BFW
1896	StL N	122	454	47	116	12	8	0	37	40	3	32	.256	.320	.317	71	-19	8	.867	-6	96	82	3b121/S		-2.2
1898	Was N	31	110	14	29	1	4	0	13	13	0		.264	.341	.345	97	-1	2	.835	-3	94	123	3b31		-0.5
1900	Phi N	7	28	5	5	1	0	0	2	3	0		.179	.258	.214	31	-3	1	.909	1	128	260	3b7		-0.2
Total	3	160	592	66	150	14	12	0	52	56	3	32	.253	.321	.318	71	-23	11	.863	-8	97	99	3b159/S		-2.8

MYERS, LYNN Lynnwood Lincoln B2.23.1914 Enola PA D1.19.2000 Harrisburg PA BR/TR/5-6.5/145 d7.13 b-Billy

YEAR	TM LG	G	AB	R	H	2B	3B	HR	RBI	BB-IB	HP	SO	AVG	OBP	SLG	AOPS	ABR	SB-CS	FA	FR	RNG	THR	GAMES AT POSITION	DL	BFW
1938	StL N	70	227	18	55	10	2	1	19	9	0	25	.242	.271	.317	58	-13	9	.944	-1	101	94	S69		-1.1
1939	StL N	74	117	24	28	6	1	0	10	12	0	23	.239	.310	.308	63	-6	1	.897	-0	95	133	S36,3b13,2b5		-0.7
Total	2	144	344	42	83	16	3	1	29	21	0	48	.241	.285	.314	60	-19	10	.930	-2	99	108	S105,3b13,2b5		-1.5

MYERS, HAP Ralph Edward B4.8.1888 San Francisco CA D6.30.1967 San Francisco CA BR/TR/6-3/175 d4.16 Col California-Davis

YEAR	TM LG	G	AB	R	H	2B	3B	HR	RBI	BB-IB	HP	SO	AVG	OBP	SLG	AOPS	ABR	SB-CS	FA	FR	RNG	THR	GAMES AT POSITION	DL	BFW
1910	Bos A	3	6	0	2	0	0	0	0	0	0		.333	.333	.333	106	0	0	1.000	1	64	648	O2R		0.0
1911	StL A	11	37	4	11	1	0	0	1	1	0		.297	.316	.324	82	-1	0	.976	-2	43	93	1b13		-0.1
	Bos A	13	38	3	14	2	0	0	4	0	0		.368	.429	.421	139	1	4	.947	-1	87	103	1b23		0.0
	Year	24	75	7	25	3	0	0	5	1	0		.333	.375	.373	111	0	4	.963	-3	65	98	1b35		0.0
1913	Bos N	140	524	74	143	20	7	2	50	38	9	48	.273	.324	.326	69	-17	43	.989	1	102	101	1b88		-1.1
1914	Bro F	92	305	61	90	12	6	1	31	48	2		.295	.393	.385	87	-8	57-18	.990	1	105	93	1b107		0.6
1915	Bro F	118	341	61	98	9	1	3	36	32	2	39	.287	.352	.328	93	-7	28	.987	5	106	90	1b353,O2R		-0.3
Total	5	377	1251	203	335	42	14	6	116	119	13	130	.268	.338	.322	85	-31	132-18							

MYERS, RICHIE Richard B4.7.1930 Sacramento CA BR/TR/5-6/150 d4.21

YEAR	TM LG	G	AB	R	H	2B	3B	HR	RBI	BB-IB	HP	SO	AVG	OBP	SLG	AOPS	ABR	SB-CS	FA	FR	RNG	THR	GAMES AT POSITION	DL	BFW
1956	Chi N	4	1	1	0	0	0	0	0	0-0	0		.000	.000	.000	-99	0	0-0	—	0			/H		

YEAR	TM LG	G	AB	R	H	2B	3B	HR	RBI	BB-IB	HP	SO	AVG	OBP	SLG	AOPS	ABR	SB-CS	FA	FR	RNG	THR	GAMES AT POSITION	DL	BFW

MYERS, ROD Roderick Demond B1.14.1973 Conroe TX BL/TL/6-0/190* [KCA91 13/340] d6.21 [DL 1998 KC A 82]

YEAR	TM LG	G	AB	R	H	2B	3B	HR	RBI	BB-IB	HP	SO	AVG	OBP	SLG	AOPS	ABR	SB-CS	FA	FR	RNG	THR	GAMES AT POSITION	DL	BFW
1996	KC A	22	63	9	18	7	0	1	11	7-0		16	.286	.357	.444	101	0	3-2	1.000	-2	80	0	O19(4/15/1)		-0.2
1997	KC A	31	101	14	26	7	0	2	9	17-0	1	22	.257	.370	.386	95	0	4-0	.982	-1	95	61	O26(12/9/10)		-0.1
Total	2	53	164	23	44	14	0	3	20	24-0	1	38	.268	.365	.409	97	0	7-2	.989	-4	89	38	O45(16/24/11)	182	-0.3

MYERS, BILLY William Harrison B8.14.1910 Enola PA D4.10.1995 Carlisle PA BR/TR/5-8/168 d4.16 b-Lynn

YEAR	TM LG	G	AB	R	H	2B	3B	HR	RBI	BB-IB	HP	SO	AVG	OBP	SLG	AOPS	ABR	SB-CS	FA	FR	RNG	THR	GAMES AT POSITION	DL	BFW
1935	Cin N	117	445	60	119	15	10	5	36	29	2	81	.267	.315	.380	89	-9	10	.939	2	101	125	S112		
1936	Cin N	98	323	45	87	9	6	6	27	28	0	56	.269	.328	.390	99	-2	6	.938	4	101	118	S98		0.1
1937	Cin N	124	335	35	84	13	3	7	43	44	1	57	.251	.339	.370	97	-1	2	.948	7	107	99	S121,2b6		0.9
1938	Cin N	134	442	57	112	18	6	12	47	41	0	80	.253	.317	.403	99	-2	2	.939	-2	100	105	S123,2b11		1.4
1939	†Cin N	151	509	79	143	18	6	9	56	71	0	90	.281	.369	.393	104	5	4	.951	3	100	113	S151		0.6
1940	†Cin N	90	282	33	57	14	2	5	30	30	2	56	.202	.283	.319	65	-13	2	.961	-3	99	135	S88		1.9
1941	Chi N	24	63	10	14	1	0	1	4	7	1	25	.222	.310	.286	71	-2	1	.939	2	108	113	S19/2		-1.1
Total	7	738	2399	319	616	88	33	45	243	250	6	445	.257	.328	.377	93	-24	23	.946	13	101	113	S712,2b18		0.2
																									4.0

MYROW, BRIAN Brian Shawn B9.4.1976 Fort Worth TX BL/TR/5-11/190 d9.6 Col Louisiana Tech

YEAR	TM LG	G	AB	R	H	2B	3B	HR	RBI	BB-IB	HP	SO	AVG	OBP	SLG	AOPS	ABR	SB-CS	FA	FR	RNG	THR	GAMES AT POSITION	DL	BFW
2005	LA N	19	20	2	4	1	0	0	5-0		0	8	.200	.360	.250	64	-1	0-0	1.000	-1	0	79	1b5		-0.2

NADY, XAVIER Xavier Clifford B11.14.1978 Salinas CA BR/TR/6-4/220(180-220) [SDN00 2/49] d9.30 Col California-Davis

YEAR	TM LG	G	AB	R	H	2B	3B	HR	RBI	BB-IB	HP	SO	AVG	OBP	SLG	AOPS	ABR	SB-CS	FA	FR	RNG	THR	GAMES AT POSITION	DL	BFW
2000	SD N	1	1	1	1	0	0	0	0-0		0	0	1.000	1.000	1.000	435	1	0-0	—	0			/H		0.0
2003	SD N	110	371	50	99	17	1	9	39	24-0	6	74	.267	.321	.391	93	-5	6-2	.968	1	93	193	O105R		-0.8
2004	SD N	34	77	7	19	4	0	3	9	5-0	1	13	.247	.301	.416	87	-2	0-0	.923	-2	71	108	O22(18/4/2),D2		-0.4
2005	†SD N	124	326	40	85	15	2	13	43	22-1	7	67	.261	.321	.439	102	-1	2-1	.976	-4	79		O68(26/30/13),1b44,3b3/D		-0.9
Total	4	269	775	98	204	36	3	25	91	51-1	14	154	.263	.320	.414	96	-7	8-3	.967	-5	87	126	O195(44/34/120),1b44,3b3,D3		-2.1

NAEHRING, TIM Timothy James B2.1.1967 Cincinnati OH BR/TR/6-2/205(190-205) [BosA88 8/199] d7.15 Col Miami-Ohio [DL 1998 Bos A 181]

YEAR	TM LG	G	AB	R	H	2B	3B	HR	RBI	BB-IB	HP	SO	AVG	OBP	SLG	AOPS	ABR	SB-CS	FA	FR	RNG	THR	GAMES AT POSITION	DL	BFW
1990	Bos A	24	85	10	23	6	0	2	12	8-1	0	15	.271	.333	.412	102	0	0-0	.918	2	105	96	S19,3b5/2	49	0.3
1991	Bos A	20	55	1	6	1	0	0	3	6-0	0	15	.109	.197	.127	-8	-8	0-0	.956	-0	107	86	S17,3b2/2	142	-0.7
1992	Bos A	72	186	12	43	8	0	3	14	18-0	1	31	.231	.308	.323	72	-7	0-0	.992	11	116	116	S30,2b23,3b10/OLD	40	0.7
1993	Bos A	39	127	14	42	10	0	1	17	10-0	0	26	.331	.377	.433	111	2	1-0	.973	-3	91	122	3b48,S4	88	0.0
1994	Bos A	80	297	41	82	18	1	7	42	30-1	4	56	.276	.344	.414	92	-3	1-3	.981	5	108	106	2b49,3b11,1b8,S8,D7	29	0.3
1995	†Bos A	126	433	61	133	27	2	10	57	77-5	4	66	.307	.415	.448	121	18	0-2	.954	7	108	109	3b124/D		2.3
1996	Bos A	116	430	77	124	16	0	17	65	49-4	4	63	.288	.363	.444	102	1	0-2	.963	8	106	78	3b116/2	18	0.9
1997	Bos A	70	259	38	74	18	1	9	40	38-0	1	40	.286	.375	.467	117	8	1-1	.981	-9	88	87	3b68/D	97	-0.1
Total	8	547	1872	254	527	104	4	49	250	236-11	16	312	.282	.365	.420	102	11	5-7	.962	21	101	92	3b345,2b90,S78,D23,1b8/OL	644	3.7

NAGEL, BILL William Taylor B8.19.1915 Memphis TN D10.8.1981 Freehold NJ BR/TR/6-1/190 d4.20

YEAR	TM LG	G	AB	R	H	2B	3B	HR	RBI	BB-IB	HP	SO	AVG	OBP	SLG	AOPS	ABR	SB-CS	FA	FR	RNG	THR	GAMES AT POSITION	DL	BFW
1939	Phi A	105	341	39	86	19	4	12	39	25	2	86	.252	.307	.437	90	-7	2-1	.944	-12	96	82	2b56,3b43/P		-1.4
1941	Phi N	17	56	2	8	1	0	0	6	3	0	14	.143	.186	.196	8	-7	0-0	.935	2	123	100	2b12,O2L/3		-0.5
1945	Chi N	67	220	21	46	10	3	3	27	15	1	41	.209	.263	.323	71	-9	3-1	.984	-2	89	90	1b57/3		-1.5
Total	3	189	617	62	140	30	8	15	72	43	3	141	.227	.281	.374	77	-23	5-2	.942	-13	101	85	2b68,1b57,3b45,O2L/P		-3.4

NAGELSEN, LOU Louis Marcellus (b Louis Marcellus Nageleisen) B6.29.1887 Piqua OH D10.21.1965 Fort Wayne IN BR/TR/6-2/180 d9.10 Col Notre Dame

YEAR	TM LG	G	AB	R	H	2B	3B	HR	RBI	BB-IB	HP	SO	AVG	OBP	SLG	AOPS	ABR	SB-CS	FA	FR	RNG	THR	GAMES AT POSITION	DL	BFW
1912	Cle A	2	3	0	0	0	0	0		0	0	.000	.000	.000	-97	-1	0	1.000	-0	84	0	C2		-0.1

NAGELSON, RUSS Russell Charles B9.19.1944 Cincinnati OH BL/TR/6-0/205* [CleA66 14/272] d9.11 Col Ohio St.

YEAR	TM LG	G	AB	R	H	2B	3B	HR	RBI	BB-IB	HP	SO	AVG	OBP	SLG	AOPS	ABR	SB-CS	FA	FR	RNG	THR	GAMES AT POSITION	DL	BFW
1968	Cle A	5	3	0	1	0	0	0		2-0		2	.333	.600	.333	192	1	0-0		0			/H		
1969	Cle A	12	17	1	6	0	0	0		3-1	1	5	.353	.450	.353	123	1	0-0	1.000	-0	72	0	O3(1/0/2)/1		0.1
1970	Cle A	17	24	3	3	1	0	1	2	3-0	1	9	.125	.222	.292	39	-2	0-0	1.000	-0	84	0	O4(1/0/3)		0.1
	Det A	28	32	5	6	0	0	2	5-0		0	6	.188	.297	.188	36	-3	0-0	1.000	-0	84	0	O4(3/0/2)/1		-0.3
	Year	45	56	8	9	1	0	1	4	8-0	1	15	.161	.266	.232	38	-5	0-0	1.000	-0	84	0	O8(4/0/5)/1		-0.3
Total	3	62	76	9	16	1	0	1	4	13-1	2	20	.211	.326	.263	64	-3	0-0	1.000	-1	83	0	O11(5/0/7),1b2		-0.6
																									-0.4

NAGLE, TOM Thomas Edward B10.30.1865 Milwaukee WI D3.9.1946 Milwaukee WI BR/TR/5-10/150 d4.22

YEAR	TM LG	G	AB	R	H	2B	3B	HR	RBI	BB-IB	HP	SO	AVG	OBP	SLG	AOPS	ABR	SB-CS	FA	FR	RNG	THR	GAMES AT POSITION	DL	BFW
1890	Chi N	38	144	21	39	5	1	1	11	7	3	24	.271	.318	.340	88	-3	4	.939	-4	111	62	C33,O6R		-0.3
1891	Chi N	8	25	3	3	0	0	1	1	1	0	3	.120	.154	.120	-20	-4	0	.906	-2	137	62	C7/OL		-0.5
Total	2	46	169	24	42	5	1	1	12	8	3	27	.249	.294	.308	73	-7	4	.935	-5	115	62	C40,O7(1/0/6)		-0.8

NAHORODNY, BILL William Gerard B8.31.1953 Hamtramck MI BR/TR/6-2/200* [PhiN72 6/123] d9.27 Col St. Clair Co. (MI) CC

YEAR	TM LG	G	AB	R	H	2B	3B	HR	RBI	BB-IB	HP	SO	AVG	OBP	SLG	AOPS	ABR	SB-CS	FA	FR	RNG	THR	GAMES AT POSITION	DL	BFW
1976	Phi N	3	5	0	1	0	0	0		0		0	.200	.200	.400	65	0	0-0	1.000	-0	31	0	C2		
1977	Chi A	7	23	3	6	1	0	1	4	2-0	0	3	.261	.308	.435	103	0	0-0	1.000	-1	79	67	C7		0.0
1978	Chi A	107	347	29	82	11	2	8	35	23-0	2	52	.236	.285	.349	71	-11	1-0	.980	-8	81	82	C104,1b4/D		-0.1
1979	Chi A	65	179	20	46	10	0	6	29	18-1	0	23	.257	.322	.413	97	-1	0-1	.973	-1	63	115	C60,D3		-1.2
1980	Atl N	59	157	14	38	12	0	5	18	8-1	2	21	.242	.287	.414	93	-1	0-2	.990	-6	83	99	C54/1	23	-0.7
1981	Atl N	14	13	0	3	1	0	0	1	1-1	0	3	.231	.286	.308	68	-1	0-0	1.000	-0	0		C3/1	14	-0.1
1982	Cle A	39	94	6	21	5	1	4	18	2-0	0	9	.223	.237	.426	78	-3	0-0	1.000	-5	92	62	C35		-0.7
1983	Det A	2	1	0	0	0	0	0		1-0	0	0	.000	.500	.000	53	0	0-0		0			/H		0.0
1984	Sea A	12	25	2	6	0	0	1	3	1-0	2	7	.240	.310	.360	89	0	0-1	.976	-2	132	44	C10/1		-0.3
Total	9	308	844	74	203	41	3	25	109	56-3	6	118	.241	.290	.385	86	-18	1-4	.983	-19	80	87	C275,1b7,D4	37	-3.1

NAKAMURA, NORIHIRO Norihiro B7.24.1973 Osaka, Japan BR/TR/5-10/200 d4.10

YEAR	TM LG	G	AB	R	H	2B	3B	HR	RBI	BB-IB	HP	SO	AVG	OBP	SLG	AOPS	ABR	SB-CS	FA	FR	RNG	THR	GAMES AT POSITION	DL	BFW
2005	LA N	17	39	1	5	2	0	0	2-0		1	7	.128	.171	.179	-8	-6	0-0	1.000	1	131	170	3b10,1b4,S2/2		-0.6

NALEWAY, FRANK Frank "Chick" B7.5.1902 Chicago IL D1.28.1949 Chicago IL BR/TR/5-9.5/165 d9.16

YEAR	TM LG	G	AB	R	H	2B	3B	HR	RBI	BB-IB	HP	SO	AVG	OBP	SLG	AOPS	ABR	SB-CS	FA	FR	RNG	THR	GAMES AT POSITION	DL	BFW
1924	Chi A	1	2	0	0	0	0	0	1		0	0	.000	.333	.000	-1	0	0-0	.750	-1	73	0	/S		-0.1

NANCE, DOC William G. "Kid" (b Willie G. Cooper) B8.2.1876 Ft.Worth TX D5.28.1958 Fort Worth TX BR/TR/5-7/165 d8.19

YEAR	TM LG	G	AB	R	H	2B	3B	HR	RBI	BB-IB	HP	SO	AVG	OBP	SLG	AOPS	ABR	SB-CS	FA	FR	RNG	THR	GAMES AT POSITION	DL	BFW
1897	Lou N	35	120	25	29	3	3	1	17	20	1		.242	.355	.408	105	1	3	.986	3	161	386	O35(0/7/28)		0.2
1898	Lou N	22	76	13	24	5	0	1	16	12	1		.316	.416	.421	142	5	2	.946	2	235	274	O22R		0.6
1901	Det A	132	461	72	129	24	5	5	66	51	3		.280	.355	.373	98	0	9	.932	2	118	155	O132(130/0/2)		-0.5
Total	3	189	657	110	182	34	8	7	99	83	5		.277	.362	.385	104	6	14	.943	8	139	211	O189(130/7/52)		0.3

NAPLES, AL Aloysius Francis B8.29.1927 St.George NY BR/TR/5-9/168 d6.25 Col Georgetown

YEAR	TM LG	G	AB	R	H	2B	3B	HR	RBI	BB-IB	HP	SO	AVG	OBP	SLG	AOPS	ABR	SB-CS	FA	FR	RNG	THR	GAMES AT POSITION	DL	BFW
1949	StL A	2	7	0	1	1	0	0	0	0	0	1	.143	.143	.286	12	-1	0-0	.875	-1	116	0	S2		-0.1

NAPOLEON, DANNY Daniel B1.11.1942 Claysburg PA D4.26.2003 Trenton NJ BR/TR/5-11/190* d4.14 Col Rider

YEAR	TM LG	G	AB	R	H	2B	3B	HR	RBI	BB-IB	HP	SO	AVG	OBP	SLG	AOPS	ABR	SB-CS	FA	FR	RNG	THR	GAMES AT POSITION	DL	BFW
1965	NY N	68	97	5	14	1	1	0	7	8-1	2	23	.144	.222	.175	15	-11	0-0	.941	-1	142	0	O15(14/0/1),3b7		-1.4
1966	NY N	12	33	2	7	2	0	0	2	1-0	0	10	.212	.235	.273	42	-3	0-1	.929	-0	79	168	O10L		-0.4
Total	2	80	130	7	21	3	1	0	9	9-1	2	33	.162	.225	.200	22	-14	0-1	.938	-1	117	66	O25(24/0/1),3b7		-1.8

NARAGON, HAL Harold Richard B10.1.1928 Zanesville OH BL/TR/6-0/175* d9.23 Mil 1952-53 C7

YEAR	TM LG	G	AB	R	H	2B	3B	HR	RBI	BB-IB	HP	SO	AVG	OBP	SLG	AOPS	ABR	SB-CS	FA	FR	RNG	THR	GAMES AT POSITION	DL	BFW
1951	Cle A	3	8	2	2	0	0	0		1	0	.250	.400	.250	83	0	0-0	.929	-0	82	0	C2		
1954	†Cle A	46	101	10	24	2	0	2	12	9	1	0	12	.238	.300	.297	63	-5	0-0	1.000	0	108	124	C45		0.0
1955	Cle A	57	127	12	41	9	2	1	14	15-0	1	8	.323	.394	.449	122	4	1-0	.991	-1	112	86	C52		-0.4
1956	Cle A	53	122	11	35	3	1	3	18	13-1	1	9	.287	.355	.402	99	0	0-0	.988	-6	78	49	C48		-0.5
1957	Cle A	57	121	12	31	1	0	0	12	12-1	1	9	.256	.326	.281	69	-5	0-0	.990	-7	75	85	C39		-0.6
1958	Cle A	9	9	2	3	0	0	0	0		0	3	.333	.333	.556	144	0	0-0	—	0			/H		
	Was A	71	195	12	47	3	0	1	11	8-0	1	9	.241	.272	.277	52	-13	0-1	1.000	-1	81	59	C10		0.0
	Year	85	231	18	57	7	3	1	16	11-0	2	11	.247	.283	.303	63	-12	0-1	.993	-5	62	56	C54		-1.6
1960	Was A	33	92	7	19	2	0	0	5	8-2	1	4	.207	.275	.228	39	-4	0-0	.978	-4	86	71	C29		-1.0
1961	Min A	57	139	10	42	1	2	11	4-0		1	8	.302	.326	.374	82	-4	0-0	.994	-8	57	83	C36		-1.0
1962	Min A	14	36	6	10	4	1	0	3-1		1	6	.278	.341	.444	114	0	0-0	1.000	-1	81	59	C10		0.0
Total	10	424	985	92	262	27	11	6	87	76-6	7	62	.266	.321	.334	77	-33	1-1	.991	-25	81	74	C324		-4.7

YEAR	TM LG	G	AB	R	H	2B	3B	HR	RBI	BB-IB	HP	SO	AVG	OBP	SLG	AOPS	ABR	SB-CS	FA	FR	RNG	THR	GAMES AT POSITION	DL	BFW
NARLESKI, BILL	William Edward "Cap" B3.9.1900 Perth Amboy NJ D6.20.1964 Laurel Springs NJ BR/TR/5-9/160 d4.18 s-Ray																								-1.2
1929	Bos A	96	260	30	72	16	1	0	25	21	1	22	.277	.333	.346	77	-8	4-4	.957	-9	97	98	S51,2b29,3b7		-0.8
1930	Bos A	39	98	11	23	9	0	0	7	7	3	5	.235	.306	.327	63	-5	0-0	.915	-6	84	121	S19,3b14,2b5		-2.0
Total	2	135	358	41	95	25	1	0	32	28	4	27	.265	.326	.341	73	-13	4-4	.949	-15	95	102	S70,2b34,3b21		
NARRON, JERRY	Jerry Austin B1.15.1956 Goldsboro NC BL/TR/6-3/205(190-205) [NYA74 6/132] d4.13 M3/C12																								-1.2
1979	NY A	61	123	17	21	3	1	4	18	9-0	0	26	.171	.226	.309	44	-10	0-0	.973	-4	108	66	C56/D		-1.0
1980	Sea A	48	107	7	21	3	0	4	18	13-2	0	18	.196	.279	.336	68	-5	0-0	.992	-6	96	82	C39/D		-2.1
1981	Sea A	76	203	13	45	5	0	3	17	16-3	2	35	.222	.285	.291	63	-10	0-0	.996	-13	70	70	C65		-0.3
1983	Cal A	10	22	1	3	0	0	1	4	1-0	0	3	.136	.174	.273	21	-3	0-0	.895	-1	90	156	C6/D		-0.9
1984	Cal A	69	150	9	37	5	0	3	17	8-1	1	12	.247	.286	.340	73	-6	0-0	.994	-5	95	89	C46,1b7		-0.1
1985	Cal A	67	132	12	29	4	0	5	14	11-2	0	17	.220	.280	.364	75	-5	0-0	1.000	3	78	130	C45/1D		-0.4
1986	†Cal A	57	95	5	21	3	1	1	8	9-0	1	14	.221	.292	.305	64	-5	0-0	.988	0	114	132	C51,D2		-0.3
1987	Sea A	4	8	0	0	0	0	0	0	0-0	0	2	.000	.000	.000	-95	-2	0-0	1.000	-1	44	92	C3		-6.3
Total	8	392	840	64	177	23	2	21	96	67-8	4	127	.211	.270	.318	62	-46	0-0	.989	-26	91	92	C311,D12,1b8		
NARRON, SAM	Samuel Woody B8.25.1913 Middlesex NC D12.31.1996 Raleigh NC BR/TR/5-10/180 d9.15 C13 gs-Sam																								0.0
1935	StL N	4	7	0	3	0	0	0	0	0	0	0	.429	.429	.429	126	0	0	1.000	-0	0	0	/C		0.0
1942	StL N	10	10	0	4	0	0	0	1	0	0	0	.400	.400	.400	125	0	0	1.000	1	0	0	C2		-0.1
1943	†StL N	10	11	0	1	0	0	0	0	1	0	2	.091	.167	.091	-24	-2	0	1.000	0	0	0	C3		-0.1
Total	3	24	28	0	8	0	0	0	1	1	0	2	.286	.310	.286	67	-2	0	1.000	0	0	0	C6		
NASH, COTTON	Charles Francis B7.24.1942 Jersey City NJ BR/TR/6-6/220* d9.1 Col Kentucky [DL 1965 Phi N 160]																								-0.1
1967	Chi A	3	3	1	0	0	0	0	0	1-0	0	1	.000	.250	.000	-21	-1	0-0	.833	-1	0	393	1b3		0.0
1969	Min A	6	9	0	2	0	0	0	0	1-0	0	2	.222	.300	.222	47	-1	0-0	1.000	1	272	0	1b6/OL		-0.1
1970	Min A	4	4	1	1	0	0	0	2	1-0	0	1	.250	.400	.250	82	-1	0-1	1.000	0	0	251	1b2		
Total	3	13	16	2	3	0	0	0	2	3-0	0	3	.188	.316	.188	44	-1	0-1	.965	0	155	141	1b11/OL	160	-0.2
NASH, KEN	Kenneth Leland (Played One Game in 1912 Under Name of Costello) B7.14.1888 Weymouth MA D2.16.1977 Epsom NH BB/TR/5-8/140 d7.4 Col Brown																								-0.4
1912	Cle A	11	23	4	4	0	0	0	3	3	0		.174	.269	.174	27	-2	0	.826	-2	86	61	S8		-0.4
1914	StL N	24	51	4	14	3	1	0	6	6	0	10	.275	.351	.373	116	1	0	.875	-5	73	0	3b10,2b6,S3		-0.4
Total	2	35	74	6	18	3	1	0	6	9	0	10	.243	.325	.311	87	-1	0	.760	-7	79	56	S11,3b10,2b6		-0.8
NASH, BILLY	William Mitchell B6.24.1865 Richmond VA D11.15.1929 E.Orange NJ BR/TR/5-8.5/167 d8.5 M1/U1																								1.1
1884	Ric AA	**45**	166	31	33	8	8	1		12	7		.199	.281	.361	109	2		.828	9	114	158	3b45		-0.3
1885	Bos N	26	94	9	24	4	0	0	11	2		9	.255	.271	.298	87	-1		.864	-2	83	139	3b19,2b8		2.1
1886	Bos N	109	417	61	117	11	8	1	45	24		28	.281	.320	.353	107	3	16	.863	-6	96	84	3b90,S17,O2(1/1/0)		4.1
1887	Bos N	121	475	100	144	24	12	6	94	60	2	30	.295	.376	.434	123	16	43	**.913**	18	**119**	**141**	3b105,2b31		1.2
1888	Bos N	135	526	71	149	18	15	4	75	50	4	46	.283	.350	.397	134	21	20	.905	11	102	117	3b128/P		1.6
1889	Bos N	128	481	84	132	20	2	3	76	79	2	43	.274	.379	.343	97	0	26	.866	19	**111**	**171**	3b129/P		-0.5
1890	Bos P	129	488	103	130	28	6	5	90	88	4	46	.266	.383	.379	97	0	26	.900	-12	83	111	3b140		2.4
1891	Bos N	**140**	537	92	148	24	5	4	95	74	5	50	.276	.369	.382	106	-1	31	.898	25	117	**125**	3b135/OL		1.1
1892	†Bos N	135	526	94	137	25	5	4	95	59	3	42	.260	.338	.350	99	-1	30	**.923**	2	100	107	3b128		-0.2
1893	Bos N	128	485	115	141	27	6	10	123	85	2	29	.291	.399	.433	112	9	20	**.933**	4	98	116	3b132		-0.8
1894	Bos N	132	512	132	148	23	6	8	87	91	3	23	.289	.399	.404	87	-1	18	.881	-11	87	145	3b133		0.4
1895	Bos N	**133**	513	97	149	24	6	10	110	74	3	19	.290	.383	.419	99	-1	18	.911	8	112	117	3b65,M		-0.7
1896	Phi N	65	227	29	56	9	4	3	30	34	4	21	.247	.355	.335	83	-4	3	.919	-9	94	101	3b79,S19,2b4		-0.1
1897	Phi N	104	337	45	87	20	2	0	39	60	2		.258	.373	.329	89	-1	4	.958	-1	77	203	3b20		11.3
1898	Phi N	20	70	9	17	2	1	0	9	11	0		.243	.346	.300	89	0	0	.897	62	101	123	3b1465,2b43,S36,O8(6/1/1),P2		
Total	15	1550	5854	1072	1608	267	87	60	979	803	41	384	.275	.366	.381	103	38	265	.897	62	101	123			
NATAL, BOB	Robert Marcel B11.13.1965 Long Beach CA BR/TR/5-11/190* [MonN87 13/330] d7.18 C4 Col California-San Diego																								-0.2
1992	Mon N	5	6	0	0	0	0	0	0	1-0	0	1	.000	.143	.000	-57	-1	0-0	.909	-1	40	0	C4		-0.5
1993	Fla N	41	117	3	25	4	1	1	6	6-0	4	22	.214	.273	.291	49	-9	1-0	1.000	2	104	100	C38	21	0.2
1994	Fla N	10	29	2	8	2	0	0	2	5-0	0	9	.276	.382	.345	88	0	1-0	.988	0	167	86	C13		-0.1
1995	Fla N	16	43	3	10	2	1	2	6	1-0	0	9	.233	.244	.465	82	-2	0-0	.976	-3	88	111	C43		-1.2
1996	Fla N	44	90	4	12	1	1	1	9	15-5	3	31	.133	.257	.167	15	-11	0-1	.976	1	0	0	C4		0.3
1997	Fla N	4	4	1	2	1	0	0	1	2-0	0	5	.500	.571	1.500	468	2	0-0	1.000	1	0	0	C110	21	-1.5
Total	6	120	289	13	57	10	4	5	19	30-5	4	68	.197	.279	.294	52	-21	2-1	.986	1	100	103	C110		
NATON, PETE	Peter Alphonsus B9.9.1931 Flushing NY BR/TR/6-1/200 d6.16 Mil 1953-54 Col Holy Cross																								-0.2
1953	Pit N	6	12	2	2	0	0	0	0	0	0	2	.167	.286	.167	22	-1	0-0	1.000	-1	75	0	C4		
NAVA, SANDY	Vincent Irwin (b Vincent Irwin) B4.12.1850 San Francisco CA D6.15.1906 Baltimore MD 5-6/155 d5.5																								-0.9
1882	Pro N	28	97	15	20	2	0	0	7	1		13	.206	.214	.227	42	-6		.867	-6			C27/OR		-0.4
1883	Pro N	29	100	18	24	4	2	0	16	3		17	.240	.262	.320	74	-3		.813	-3			C27,O2(1/0/1)		-1.7
1884	Pro N	34	116	10	11	0	0	0	6	11		35	.095	.173	.095	-13	-15		.887	-0			C8		-0.4
1885	Bal AA	8	27	1	5	1	0	0	4	1	0		.185	.214	.222	39	-2		.825	-4			C8		-0.2
1886	Bal AA	2	5	0	1	0	0	0	0	0			.200	.200	.200	26	0	1	.500	-1	54	0	/SC		-3.0
Total	5	101	345	45	61	7	2	0	33	16	0	65	.177	.213	.209	33	-26	1	.857	-14			C90,S7,O3(1/0/2)/2		
NAVARRO, DIONER	Dioner Faviau B2.9.1984 Caracas, Venez BB/TR/5-10/190* d9.7																								0.0
2004	NY A	5	7	2	3	0	0	1	1	0-0	0	0	.429	.429	.429	125	0	0-0	1.000	-0	0	0	C4		0.0
2005	LA N	50	176	21	48	9	0	3	14	20-1	2	21	.273	.354	.375	91	-2	0-0	.995	3	79	86	C50		0.0
Total	2	55	183	23	51	9	0	3	15	20-1	2	21	.279	.356	.377	92	-2	0-0	.995	3	77	84	C54		
NAVARRO, TITO	Norberto (Rodriguez) B9.12.1970 Rio Piedras, PR BB/TR/5-10/165 d9.6																								-0.0
1993	NY N	12	17	1	1	0	0	0	1	0	0	5	.059	.059	.059	-69	-4	0-0	1.000	1	118	0	S2		
NAYLOR, EARL	Earl Eugene B5.19.1919 Kansas City MO D1.16.1990 Winter Haven FL BR/TR/6-0/190 d4.15 Mil 1944-45 ▲																								-1.0
1942	Phi N	76	168	9	33	4	1	0	11	4-0	0	18	.196	.246	.232	42	-13	1	.984	-4	87	37	O34(2/22/11),P20		-0.0
1943	Phi N	33	120	12	21	2	0	1	3	14-2	1	16	.175	.256	.267	53	-8	1	.964	3	107	176	O33C		-0.0
1946	Bro N	3	2	1	0	0	0	0	0	0	0	1	.000	.000	.000	-99	-1	0	—	0			/H		-2.0
Total	3	112	290	22	54	6	1	3	28	23	1	35	.186	.248	.245	46	-22	2	.971	-0	98	113	O67(2/55/11),P20		
NEAGLE, JACK	John Henry B1.2.1858 Syracuse NY D9.20.1904 Syracuse NY BR/TR/5-6/155 d7.8 ▲																								0.0
1879	Cin N	3	12	1	2	0	0	0		0			.167	.167	.167	11	-1		—	-0	0	0	O2(0/1/1),P2		-0.0
1883	Phi N	18	73	6	12	1	0	0	4	1		9	.164	.176	.178	9	-8		.840	-2	39	0	O12(11/1/0),P8		-0.0
	Bal AA	9	35	3	10	4	0	0		2			.286	.324	.400	128	1		.769	-1	97	0	P6,O5(1/0/4)		-0.0
	Pit AA	27	101	14	19	0	1	0		5			.188	.226	.208	43	-6		.839	-2	87	0	P16,O15(0/8/7)		-0.0
	Year	36	136	17	29	4	1	0		6			.213	.252	.257	66	-5		.818	-3	90		P22,O20(1/8/11)		-0.0
1884	Pit AA	43	148	13	22	6	0	0	6	14	1		.149	.187	.189	23	-12		.785	-11	85	36	P70,O40(14/12/14)		-1.0
Total	3	100	369	37	65	11	1	0	6	14	1	9	.176	.208	.211	36	-26								
NEAL, CHARLIE	Charles Lenard B1.30.1931 Longview TX D11.18.1996 Dallas TX BR/TR/5-10/165* d4.17 Negro Lg 1955																								0
1956	†Bro N	62	136	22	39	5	1	2	14	14-1	0	19	.287	.353	.382	91	-1	2-2	.972	2	105	120	2b51/S		0
1957	Bro N	128	448	62	121	13	7	12	62	53-0	8	83	.270	.356	.411	96	-1	11-4	.949	-1	100	123	S100,3b23,2b3		2
1958	LA N	140	473	87	120	9	6	22	65	61-4	5	91	.254	.341	.438	102	1	7-6	.976	13	99	**123**	2b132,S9		3
1959	†LA N★	151	616	103	177	30	**11**	19	83	43-2	4	86	.287	.337	.464	103	2	17-6	**.989**	18	98	112	2b151/S		-2
1960	LA N★	139	477	60	122	23	2	6	40	48-2	5	75	.256	.321	.363	83	-10	5-5	.977	-20	82	103	2b136,S3		-1
1961	LA N	108	341	40	80	6	4	8	30	30-6	1	49	.235	.297	.346	65	-18	3-2	.976	-2	90	92	2b104		-0
1962	NY N	136	508	59	132	14	9	11	58	56-1	0	90	.260	.330	.388	91	-7	10-9	.961	6	109	96	3b66,S8		-0
1963	NY N	72	253	26	57	12	1	3	18	27-3	1	49	.225	.302	.316	77	-7	1-2	.961	1	98	84	3b19/2S		-1
	Cin N	34	64	2	10	1	0	0	3	5-0	0	15	.156	.217	.172	13	-7	0-1	.927	-4	55	0	3b19/2S		-1
	Year	106	317	28	67	13	1	3	21	32-3	1	64	.211	.286	.287	64	-14	1-3	.955	2	98	77	3b85,S9/2		1
Total	8	970	3316	461	858	113	38	87	391	337-19	20	557	.259	.329	.394	90	-48	48-36	.978	6	95	107	2b663,S162,3b120		

YEAR TM LG	G	AB	R	H	2B	3B	HR	RBI	BB-IB	HP	SO	AVG	OBP	SLG	AOPS	ABR	SB-CS	FA	FR	RNG	THR	GAMES AT POSITION	DL	BFW

NEAL, OFFA Theophilus Fountain B6.5.1876 Benton IL D4.11.1950 Mt.Vernon IL BL/TR/6-0/185 d9.30

YEAR TM LG	G	AB	R	H	2B	3B	HR	RBI	BB-IB	HP	SO	AVG	OBP	SLG	AOPS	ABR	SB-CS	FA	FR	RNG	THR	GAMES AT POSITION	DL	BFW
1905 NY N	4	13	0	0	0	0	0	0	0	0		.000	.000	.000	-98	-3	0	1.000	0	63	791	3b3/2		-0.3

NEALE, GREASY Alfred Earle B11.5.1891 Parkersburg WV D11.2.1973 Lake Worth FL BL/TR (BB 1916-18p)/6-0/170 d4.12 C1 Col West Virginia Wesleyan

YEAR TM LG	G	AB	R	H	2B	3B	HR	RBI	BB-IB	HP	SO	AVG	OBP	SLG	AOPS	ABR	SB-CS	FA	FR	RNG	THR	GAMES AT POSITION	DL	BFW
1916 Cin N	138	530	53	139	13	5	0	20	19	6	79	.262	.295	.306	87	-10	17	.973	7	104	127	O133(79/55/2)		-1.2
1917 Cin N	121	385	40	113	14	9	3	33	24	5	36	.294	.343	.400	133	14	25	.979	2	103	100	O119(79/27/13)		1.2
1918 Cin N	107	371	57	100	11	11	1	32	24	6	38	.270	.324	.367	112	4	23	.981	7	117	90	O102(78/12/12)		0.7
1919 †Cin N	139	500	57	121	10	12	1	54	47	5	51	.242	.316	.316	93	-4	28	.981	-1	104	77	O138(24/5/109)		-1.5
1920 Cin N	150	530	55	135	10	7	3	46	45	8	48	.255	.322	.317	85	-9	29-12	.987	12	119	97	O150(0/3/148)		-0.4
1921 Phi N	22	57	7	12	1	0	0	1	14		9	.211	.366	.228	56	-3	3-4	.842	-3	68	0	O16R		-0.8
Cin N	63	241	39	58	10	5	0	12	22	1	16	.241	.307	.324	70	-10	9-6	.964	-1	101	81	O60(1/8/53)		-1.6
Year	85	298	46	70	11	5	0	13	36	1	25	.235	.319	.305	67	-13	12-10	.950	-1	96	68	O76(1/8/69)		-2.4
1922 Cin N	25	43	11	10	2	1	0	2	6	2	3	.233	.353	.326	77	-1	5-2	.864	-1	87	76	O16(5/0/11)		-0.3
1924 Cin N	3	4	0	0	0	0	0	0	0	0	1	.000	.000	.000	-99	-1	0	1.000	0	116	0	O2L		-0.1
Total 8	768	2661	319	688	71	50	8	200	201	35	281	.259	.319	.332	94	-20	139-24	.972	20	108	95	O736(268/110/364)		-4.0

NEALON, JIM James Joseph B12.15.1884 Sacramento CA D4.2.1910 San Francisco CA BR/TR/6-1.5/? d4.12

YEAR TM LG	G	AB	R	H	2B	3B	HR	RBI	BB-IB	HP	SO	AVG	OBP	SLG	AOPS	ABR	SB-CS	FA	FR	RNG	THR	GAMES AT POSITION	DL	BFW
1906 Pit N	154	556	82	142	21	12	3	83	53	6		.255	.327	.353	107	4	15	.987	1	102	132	1b154		0.3
1907 Pit N	105	381	29	98	10	8	0	47	23	1		.257	.301	.325	95	-4	11	.978	0	106	69	1b104		-0.6
Total 2	259	937	111	240	31	20	3	130	76	7		.256	.317	.342	102	0	26	.983	1	104	107	1b258		-0.3

NEEDHAM, TOM Thomas Joseph "Deerfoot" B4.17.1879 Steubenville OH D12.14.1926 Steubenville OH BR/TR/5-10/180 d5.12

YEAR TM LG	G	AB	R	H	2B	3B	HR	RBI	BB-IB	HP	SO	AVG	OBP	SLG	AOPS	ABR	SB-CS	FA	FR	RNG	THR	GAMES AT POSITION	DL	BFW
1904 Bos N	84	269	18	70	12	3	4	19	11	1		.260	.292	.372	108	1	3	.945	-3	88	124	C77/OC		0.6
1905 Bos N	83	271	21	59	6	1	2	17	24	5		.218	.293	.269	70	-10	3	.949	-14	73	121	C77,O3C,1b2		-1.7
1906 Bos N	83	285	11	54	8	2	1	12	13	2		.189	.230	.242	49	-18	3	.962	-9	81	115	C76,2b5,1b2/3OC		-2.3
1907 Bos N	86	260	19	51	6	2	1	19	18	6		.196	.264	.246	60	-12	4	.967	-16	73	107	C78/1		-2.4
1908 NY N	54	91	8	19	3	0	0	11	12	6		.209	.339	.242	82	-1	0	.975	4	147	84	C47		0.7
1909 Chi N	13	28	3	4	0	0	0	0	0	0		.143	.143	.143	-11	-4	0	.980	1	137	59	C7		-0.3
1910 †Chi N	31	76	9	14	3	1	0	10	10	1	10	.184	.287	.250	57	-4	1	.982	4	146	82	C27/1		0.2
1911 Chi N	27	62	4	12	2	0	0	5	9	2	14	.194	.315	.226	52	-4	2	.984	5	170	113	C23		0.4
1912 Chi N	33	90	12	16	5	0	0	10	7	3	13	.178	.260	.233	36	-8	3	.994	2	125	104	C32		-0.4
1913 Chi N	20	42	5	10	4	0	0	11	4	0	8	.238	.304	.381	95	0	0	.962	3	123	158	C14/1		0.3
1914 Chi N	9	17	3	2	1	0	0	3	1	0	4	.118	.167	.176	2	-2	1	.943	0	109	160	C7		-0.1
Total 11	523	1491	113	311	50	10	8	117	109	26	49	.209	.274	.272	66	-62	20	.963	-24	97	112	C465,1b7,2b5,O5C/3		-5.0

NEEL, TROY Troy Lee B9.14.1965 Freeport TX BL/TR/6-4/210* [CleA86*/9/208] d5.30 Col Texas A&M-Commerce

YEAR TM LG	G	AB	R	H	2B	3B	HR	RBI	BB-IB	HP	SO	AVG	OBP	SLG	AOPS	ABR	SB-CS	FA	FR	RNG	THR	GAMES AT POSITION	DL	BFW
1992 Oak A	24	53	8	14	3	0	3	9	9	1	15	.264	.339	.491	136	2	0-1	.846	-0	97	311	O9L,1b2,D9		0.2
1993 Oak A	123	427	59	124	21	0	19	63	49-5	4	101	.290	.367	.473	131	19	3-5	.981	-1	100	92	D85,1b34		1.0
1994 Oak A	83	278	43	74	13	0	15	48	38-5	2	61	.266	.357	.475	122	9	2-3	.994	-1	85	105	1b45,D35	21	0.2
Total 3	230	758	110	212	37	0	37	120	92-10	7	177	.280	.362	.475	128	30	5-9	.986	-2	90	98	D129,1b81,O9L	21	1.4

NEEMAN, CAL Calvin Amandus B2.18.1929 Valmeyer IL BR/TR/6-1/192* d4.16 Col Illinois Wesleyan

YEAR TM LG	G	AB	R	H	2B	3B	HR	RBI	BB-IB	HP	SO	AVG	OBP	SLG	AOPS	ABR	SB-CS	FA	FR	RNG	THR	GAMES AT POSITION	DL	BFW
1957 Chi N	122	415	37	107	17	1	10	39	22-5	3	87	.258	.298	.376	81	-12	0-0	.990	-0	85	146	C118		-0.6
1958 Chi N	76	201	30	52	7	0	12	29	21-2	3	41	.259	.336	.473	113	4	0-0	.992	-1	81	96	C71		0.6
1959 Chi N	44	105	7	17	2	0	3	9	11-2	0	23	.162	.241	.267	36	-10	0-0	.994	-4	57	60	C38		-1.3
1960 Chi N	9	13	0	2	1	0	0	0	0-0	0	5	.154	.154	.231	4	-2	0-0	1.000	2	35	169	C9		0.0
Phi N	59	160	13	29	6	2	4	13	16-2	2	42	.181	.264	.319	59	-9	0-0	.979	0	73	152	C52		-0.7
Year	68	173	13	31	7	2	4	13	16-2	2	47	.179	.257	.312	55	-11	0-0	.982	2	70	153	C61		-0.7
1961 Phi N	19	31	0	7	1	0	0	2	4-1	0	8	.226	.306	.258	55	-2	1-0	.986	-1	52	114	C19		-0.2
1962 Pit N	24	50	5	9	1	1	1	5	2	0	10	.180	.226	.300	40	-5	0-0	.983	4	119	95	C24		0.0
1963 Cle A	9	9	0	0	0	0	0	0	1-0	0	5	.000	.100	.000	-70	-2	0-0	1.000	1	143	297	C9		-0.1
Was A	14	18	1	1	0	0	0	0	1-0	0	5	.056	.105	.056	-54	-4	0-0	.970	-1	167	121	C12		-0.2
Year	23	27	1	1	0	0	0	0	2-0	0	5	.037	.103	.037	-59	-6	0-0	.985	2	156	202	C21		-0.3
Total 7	376	1002	93	224	35	4	30	97	79-12	8	221	.224	.284	.356	72	-42	1-0	.988	2	82	126	C352		-2.5

NEFF, DOUG Douglas Williams B10.8.1891 Harrisonburg VA D5.23.1932 Cape Charles VA BR/TR/5-9/141 d6.26 Col Virginia

YEAR TM LG	G	AB	R	H	2B	3B	HR	RBI	BB-IB	HP	SO	AVG	OBP	SLG	AOPS	ABR	SB-CS	FA	FR	RNG	THR	GAMES AT POSITION	DL	BFW
1914 Was A	3	2	0	0	0	0	0	0	0	0		.000	.000	.000	-96	-0	0	.889	1	146	0	S3		0.0
1915 Was A	30	60	1	10	1	0	0	4	4	0	6	.167	.219	.183	20	-6	1-2	.867	-4	91	81	3b12,2b10,S7		-1.1
Total 2	33	62	1	10	1	0	0	4	4	0	6	.161	.212	.177	16	-6	1-2	.867	-4	91	81	3b12,2b10,S10		-1.1

NEIGHBORS, CY Cecil Fleming B9.23.1880 Fayetteville MO D5.20.1964 Tacoma WA BR/5-10/178 d4.29

YEAR TM LG	G	AB	R	H	2B	3B	HR	RBI	BB-IB	HP	SO	AVG	OBP	SLG	AOPS	ABR	SB-CS	FA	FR	RNG	THR	GAMES AT POSITION	DL	BFW
1908 Pit N	1	0	0	0	0	0	0	0	0	0		—	—	—	0	0	0	—	-0	0	0	/OL		0.0

NEIGHBORS, BOB Robert Otis B11.9.1917 Talihina OK D8.8.1952 , North Korea (MIA) BR/TR/5-11/165 d9.16

YEAR TM LG	G	AB	R	H	2B	3B	HR	RBI	BB-IB	HP	SO	AVG	OBP	SLG	AOPS	ABR	SB-CS	FA	FR	RNG	THR	GAMES AT POSITION	DL	BFW
1939 StL A	7	11	3	2	0	0	1	1	0	0		.182	.182	.455	56	-1	0-0	.917	-0	90	64	S5		-0.1

NEILL, MIKE Michael Robert B4.27.1970 Martinsville VA BL/TL/6-2/190 [OakA91 2/60] d7.27 Col Villanova

YEAR TM LG	G	AB	R	H	2B	3B	HR	RBI	BB-IB	HP	SO	AVG	OBP	SLG	AOPS	ABR	SB-CS	FA	FR	RNG	THR	GAMES AT POSITION	DL	BFW
1998 Oak A	6	15	2	4	1	0	0	0	2-0	0	4	.267	.353	.333	81	0	0-0	1.000	1	157	0	O6(4/2/0)	24	0.0

NEILL, TOMMY Thomas White B11.7.1919 Hartselle AL D9.22.1980 Houston TX BL/TR/6-2/200 d9.10

YEAR TM LG	G	AB	R	H	2B	3B	HR	RBI	BB-IB	HP	SO	AVG	OBP	SLG	AOPS	ABR	SB-CS	FA	FR	RNG	THR	GAMES AT POSITION	DL	BFW
1946 Bos N	13	45	8	12	2	0	0	7	2	0	1	.267	.298	.311	72	-2	0	1.000	-0	91	115	O13L		-0.3
1947 Bos N	7	10	1	2	0	1	0	0	1	1	2	.200	.333	.400	96	0	0	1.000	-0	73	0	O2(1/0/1)		0.0
Total 2	20	55	9	14	2	1	0	7	3	1	3	.255	.305	.327	77	-2	0	1.000	-0	89	102	O15(14/0/1)		-0.3

NEIS, BERNIE Bernard Edmund B9.26.1895 Bloomington IL D11.29.1972 Inverness FL BB/TR (BR 1920-21)/5-7/160 d4.14

YEAR TM LG	G	AB	R	H	2B	3B	HR	RBI	BB-IB	HP	SO	AVG	OBP	SLG	AOPS	ABR	SB-CS	FA	FR	RNG	THR	GAMES AT POSITION	DL	BFW
1920 †Bro N	95	249	38	63	11	2	2	22	26	2	35	.253	.329	.337	89	-3	9-9	.957	1	100	118	O83(11/7/65)		-0.7
1921 Bro N	102	230	34	59	5	4	4	34	25	1	41	.257	.332	.365	81	-6	9-7	.946	1	93	151	O77(11/24/45)/2		-1.0
1922 Bro N	61	70	15	16	4	1	1	9	13	0	8	.229	.349	.357	83	-1	3-2	.897	1	106	163	O27(7/3/17)		-0.2
1923 Bro N	126	445	78	122	17	4	5	37	36	1	38	.274	.330	.364	88	-10	8-8	.941	2	96	146	O111(13/87/11)		-1.4
1924 Bro N	80	211	43	64	8	3	4	26	27	1	17	.303	.385	.427	121	7	4-2	.937	-2	97	93	O62(19/22/22)		0.1
1925 Bos N	106	355	47	101	20	2	5	45	38	0	19	.285	.354	.394	100	1	8-10	.970	7	117	93	O87(9/76/2)		0.2
1926 Bos N	30	93	16	20	5	2	0	8	8	0	10	.215	.277	.312	64	-5	4	.925	0	110	87	O23(15/8/0)		-0.6
1927 Cle A	32	96	17	29	9	0	4	18	18	1	9	.302	.412	.521	140	6	0-1	.978	2	106	159	O29(5/24/0)		0.7
Chi A	45	76	9	22	5	0	0	11	10	0	9	.289	.372	.355	92	0	1-0	.927	1	107	129	O21(6/9/7)		0.0
Year	77	172	26	51	14	0	4	29	28	0	18	.297	.395	.448	120	6	1-1	.962	3	106	149	O50(11/33/7)		0.7
Total 8	677	1825	297	496	84	18	25	210	201	5	186	.272	.346	.379	94	-11	46-39	.950	13	102	124	O520(96/260/169)/2		-2.9

NEITZKE, ERNIE Ernest Fredrich B11.13.1894 Toledo OH D4.27.1977 Sylvania OH BR/TR/5-10/180 d6.2

YEAR TM LG	G	AB	R	H	2B	3B	HR	RBI	BB-IB	HP	SO	AVG	OBP	SLG	AOPS	ABR	SB-CS	FA	FR	RNG	THR	GAMES AT POSITION	DL	BFW
1921 Bos A	11	25	3	6	0	0	0	2	4	0	4	.240	.345	.240	53	-2	0-0	.875	-0	89	109	O8(4/1/3),P2		-0.2

NELSON, BRY Bryant Lawrence B1.27.1974 Crossett AR BB/TR/5-10/205 [HouN93 44/1230] d5.14 Col Texarkana (TX) JC

YEAR TM LG	G	AB	R	H	2B	3B	HR	RBI	BB-IB	HP	SO	AVG	OBP	SLG	AOPS	ABR	SB-CS	FA	FR	RNG	THR	GAMES AT POSITION	DL	BFW
2002 Bos A	25	34	6	9	0	0	0	1	0	0		.265	.342	.353	84	-1	1-1	.964	0	86	53	2b11,O11(7/2/2)/D		0.0

NELSON, DAVE David Earl B6.20.1944 Fort Sill OK BR/TR (BB 1968p)/5-10/160* d4.11 C13 Col Cal St.-Los Angeles OF(6/10/1)

YEAR TM LG	G	AB	R	H	2B	3B	HR	RBI	BB-IB	HP	SO	AVG	OBP	SLG	AOPS	ABR	SB-CS	FA	FR	RNG	THR	GAMES AT POSITION	DL	BFW
1968 Cle A	88	189	26	44	4	5	0	19	17-0	1	35	.233	.295	.307	85	-4	23-7	.987	-5	81	95	2b59,S14		-0.1
1969 Cle A	52	123	11	25	0	0	0	6	9-1	1	26	.203	.259	.203	31	-11	4-3	.966	7	111	129	2b33,O2(1/0/1)	50	-0.2
1970 Was A	47	107	5	17	1	0	0	4	7-0	0	24	.159	.207	.168	6	-14	2-1	.986	4	113	117	2b33		-0.8
1971 Was A	85	329	47	92	11	3	5	33	23-2	1	29	.280	.328	.377	104	1	17-8	.938	-12	89	86	3b84/2		-1.2
1972 Tex A	145	499	68	113	16	3	2	28	67-3	5	81	.226	.324	.283	84	-7	51-17	.945	-5	95	99	3b119,O15(5/10/0)		-1.0
1973 Tex A★	142	576	71	165	24	4	7	43	34-3	0	72	.286	.325	.378	102	0	43-16	.984	-5	94	91	2b140		0.7
1974 Tex A	121	474	71	112	13	1	3	42	34-0	4	72	.236	.291	.287	69	-19	25-13	.969	-2	97	86	2b120/D	63	-0.9
1975 Tex A	28	80	9	17	1	0	2	10	8-1	1	10	.213	.289	.300	68	-3	6-0	.959	0	97	113	2b23/D	29	-0.4
1976 †KC A	78	153	24	36	4	2	1	17	14-0	2	35	.235	.298	.307	77	-5	15-5	.975	-2	98	74	2b46,D22,1b3	110	-0.5
1977 KC A	27	48	8	9	3	0	0	7	7-0	0	11	.188	.291	.292	59	-3	1-3	.926	-2	81	82	2b11,D7	20	-0.4
Total 10	813	2578	340	630	77	19	20	211	220-10	13	392	.244	.305	.312	80	-65	187-73	.976	-18	96	94	2b466,3b203,D31,O17C,S14,1b3	272	-4.4

YEAR	TM LG	G	AB	R	H	2B	3B	HR	RBI	BB-IB	HP	SO	AVG	OBP	SLG	AOPS	ABR	SB-CS	FA	FR	RNG	THR	GAMES AT POSITION	DL	BFW

NELSON, ROCKY   Glenn Richard B11.18.1924 Portsmouth OH   BL/TL/5-11/178(170-191)   d4.27   -2.2

1949	StL N	82	244	28	54	8	4	4	32	11	1	12	.221	.258	.336	55	-17	1	1.000	-3	70	101	1b70		-2.2
1950	StL N	76	235	27	58	10	4	1	20	26	1	9	.247	.324	.336	71	-10	4	.992	4	123	112	1b70		-0.2
1951	StL N	9	18	3	4	1	0	0	1	1	0	2	.222	.263	.278	45	-1	0-0	1.000	-1	47	167	1b4/OL		-0.9
	Pit N	71	195	29	52	7	4	1	14	10	0	7	.267	.302	.359	75	-8	1-1	.990	1	115	105	1b32,O12L		-1.1
	Year	80	213	32	56	8	4	1	15	11	0	7	.263	.299	.352	73	-9	1-1	.991	1	109	111	1b36,O13L		-0.1
	Chi A	6	5	0	0	0	0	0	0	1	0	4	.000	.167	.000	-53	-1	0-0	—	0			/H		-0.1
1952	†Bro N	37	39	6	10	1	0	0	3	7	0	4	.256	.370	.282	82	-1	0-0	1.000	-1	0	89	1b5		-0.1
1954	Cle A	4	4	0	0	0	0	0	0	0	0	1	.000	.000	.000	-98	-1	0-0	1.000	-0	0	230	1b2		-0.7
1956	Bro N	31	96	7	20	2	0	4	15	4-1	0	10	.208	.235	.354	53	-7	0-0	.991	1	118	124	1b25		0.1
	StL N	38	56	6	13	5	0	3	8	6-1	0	6	.232	.306	.482	108	1	0-0	1.000	1	165	150	1b39,O8L		-0.8
	Year	69	152	13	33	7	0	7	23	10-2	0	16	.217	.262	.401	73	-6	0-0	.993	3	128	125	1b56,O2(1/0/1)		0.1
1959	Pit N	98	175	31	51	11	0	6	32	23-4	3	19	.291	.379	.457	124	7	0-0	.994	-4	68	150	1b73		0.7
1960	†Pit N	93	200	34	60	11	1	7	35	24-5	5	15	.300	.382	.470	133	10	1-2	.996	0	98	120	1b35		-0.7
1961	Pit N	75	127	15	25	5	1	5	13	17-2	2	11	.197	.301	.370	77	-4	0-0	.995	-2	96	117	1b386,O23(22/0/1)		-4.9
Total	9	620	1394	186	347	61	14	31	173	130-13	12	94	.249	.317	.379	84	-32	7-4	.995	-2	96	117	1b386,O23(22/0/1)		

NELSON, JAMIE   James Victor B9.5.1959 Clinton OK   BR/TR/5-11/180   [NYN78*8/166]   d7.21   Col Orange Coast (CA) JC   -0.2

| 1983 | Sea A | 40 | 96 | 9 | 21 | 3 | 1 | 1 | 5 | 13-1 | 0 | 12 | .219 | .309 | .281 | 62 | -5 | 4-2 | .978 | 1 | 71 | 156 | C39 | | -0.2 |

NELSON, CANDY   John W B3.14.1849 Brooklyn NY D9.4.1910 Brooklyn NY   BL/TR/5-6/145   d6.11   0.0

1872	Tro NA	4	20	7	7	0	0	0		4		2	.350	.350	.350	114	0	0-0	1.000	-1	0		O3C/S		0.0
	Eck NA	18	76	12	19	5	1	0	9	2		5	.250	.269	.342	102	2	1-0	.837	-0	120	93	2b8,O8C,3b4		0.1
	Year	22	96	14	26	5	1	0	13	2		2	.271	.286	.344	105	2	1-0	.813	-1	0		O11C,2b8,3b4/S		0.1
1873	Mut NA	36	168	28	55	4	1	0	22	1		2	.327	.331	.363	107	1	2-0	.867	-9	74	41	2b27,3b6,O6R/C1		-0.7
1874	Mut NA	65	297	55	73	7	5	0	31	9		5	.246	.268	.303	80	-7	6-0	.824	-18	57	57	2b51,S14/OC		-2.1
1875	Mut NA	70	276	28	55	7	1	0	23	9		0	.199	.225	.232	56	-12	4-2	.855	-1	97	93	2b49,3b23,S2/OL		-1.4
1878	Ind N	19	84	12	11	1	0	0	5	5		11	.131	.180	.143	8	-7		.841	-7	81	22	S19		0.6
1879	Tro N	28	106	17	28	7	1	0	10	8		4	.264	.316	.349	127	4		.834	2	105	123	S24,O4L		0.2
1881	Wor N	24	103	13	29	1	0	1	15	5		6	.282	.315	.320	95	-1		.898	2	115	70	S24		0.2
1883	NY AA	97	417	75	127	19	6	0		31			.305	.353	.379	130	14		.875	-7	85	105	S97		0.8
1884	†NY AA	111	432	114	110	15	3	1		74	9		.255	.375	.310	129	21		.879	-16	84	71	S110/2		2.9
1885	NY AA	107	420	98	107	12	4	1	30	61	3		.255	.353	.310	115	13		.892	17	106	103	S107/3		-0.1
1886	NY AA	109	413	89	93	7	2	0	23	64	2		.225	.332	.252	91	2	14	.855	-5	95	83	S73,O36(0/28/8)		0.9
1887	NY AA	68	257	61	63	5	1	0	24	48		1	.245	.380	.272	88	1	29	.895	10	165	365	O37(0/1/36),S32/2		-0.1
	NY N	1	2	0	0	0	0	0	0	0	0		1.000	.000	.000	-99	-1	0	—	-0	0		/3		-0.1
1890	Bro AA	60	223	44	56	3	2	0	12	35		5	.251	.365	.283	94	1	12	.866	-6	113	69	2b135,3b33,O19(1/12/6),S17/1C		-4.1
Total	4 NA	193	837	125	209	23	8	0	89	21		12	.250	.268	.296	81	-16	13-2	.845	-28	86	69	S543,O81(4/29/48),3b2,b2		4.5
Total	9	624	2457	523	624	70	19	3	119	331	27	22	.254	.349	.302	108	47	55	.875	-9					

NELSON, RAY   Raymond "Kell" (b Raymond Nelson Kellogg) B8.4.1875 Holyoke MA D1.8.1961 Mt.Vernon NY   BR/TR/5-9/150   d5.6   Col Amherst   -1.3

| 1901 | NY N | 39 | 130 | 12 | 26 | 2 | 0 | 0 | | 5 | | 1 | .200 | .262 | .215 | 41 | -10 | 3 | .885 | -4 | 113 | 70 | 2b39 | | -1.3 |

NELSON, RICKY   Ricky Lee B5.8.1959 Eloy AZ   BL/TR/6-0/200*   [SeaA81 4/78]   d5.17   Col Arizona St.   -1.5

1983	Sea A	98	291	32	74	13	3	5	36	17-3	0	50	.254	.294	.371	79	-9	7-4	.971	-3	81	179	O91(46/1/50)/D		0.0
1984	Sea A	9	15	2	3	0	0	1	2	2-0	0	4	.200	.294	.400	90	-0	0-0	1.000	-0	147	0	O2R,D3		-0.1
1985	Sea A	6	2	0	0	0	0	0	0	0-0	0	4	.000	.000	.000	-99	-1	0-0	.667	-0	164	0	/OCD		-0.2
1986	Sea A	10	12	2	2	0	0	0	1	0-0	0	1	.167	.167	.167	-9	-2	1-0	.965	-3	82	175	O97(46/2/55),D9		-1.8
Total	4	123	320	38	79	13	3	6	39	19-3	0	59	.247	.288	.363	75	-12	8-4	.965	-3	82	175	O97(46/2/55),D9		

NELSON, ROB   Robert Augustus B5.17.1964 Pasadena CA   BL/TL/6-4/215*   [OakA83 S1/7]   d9.9   Col Mt. San Antonio (CA) JC   0.0

1986	Oak A	5	9	1	2	1	0	0	1-0		0	4	.222	.300	.333	78	-0	0-0	.800	-0	135	129	1b2/D		0.0
1987	Oak A	7	24	1	4	1	0	0	0-0		0	12	.167	.167	.208	-2	-4	0-0	.968	2	221	113	1b7		-0.2
	SD N	10	11	0	1	0	0	0	1-0		0	8	.091	.167	.091	-31	-2	0-0	1.000	-0	122	112	1b2		-0.3
1988	SD N	7	21	4	4	0	0	1	3	2-0	0	9	.190	.261	.333	71	-1	0-0	.981	3	151	110	1b31		0.1
1989	SD N	42	82	6	16	0	1	3	7	20-1	0	29	.195	.353	.329	96	0	1-3	.991	-1	151	110	1b47/D		-0.2
1990	SD N	5	5	0	0	0	0	0	0	0-0	0	4	.000	.000	.000	-99	-1	0-0	—	0			/H		-0.7
Total	5	76	152	12	27	2	1	4	11	24-1	0	66	.178	.290	.283	62	-8	1-3	.983	5	156	116	1b47/D		

NELSON, TEX   Robert Sydney "Babe" B8.7.1936 Dallas TX   BL/TL/6-3/220(205-220)   d6.22   -0.2

1955	Bal A	25	31	4	6	0	0	0	1	7-0	0	13	.194	.342	.194	50	-2	0-0	.889	1	70	582	O6L,1b2		-0.5
1956	Bal A	39	68	5	14	5	1	0	5	7-0	0	22	.206	.276	.235	40	-6	0-0	.939	1	98	277	O24(9/0/16)		-0.1
1957	Bal A	15	23	2	5	0	2	0	5	1-0	1	5	.217	.281	.391	87	-1	0-0	1.000	-1	81	0	O8(2/0/6)		-0.8
Total	3	79	122	11	25	5	2	0	11	15-0	1	40	.205	.295	.254	52	-9	0-0	.938	1	90	280	O38(17/0/22),1b2		

NELSON, TOMMY   Thomas Cousineau B5.1.1917 Chicago IL D9.24.1973 San Diego CA   BR/TR/5-11.5/180   d4.17   -2.0

| 1945 | Bos N | 40 | 121 | 6 | 20 | 2 | 0 | 0 | 6 | 4 | 0 | 13 | .165 | .192 | .182 | 4 | -16 | 1 | .910 | -4 | 106 | 185 | 3b20,2b12 | | -2.0 |

NEN, DICK   Richard Le Roy B9.24.1939 South Gate CA   BL/TL/6-2/205*   d9.18   s-Robb   Col Cal St.-Long Beach   0.0

1963	LA N	7	8	2	1	0	0	1	1	1	0	3	.125	.364	.500	157	1	0-0	1.000	-0	0	0	1b5		0.2
1965	Was A	69	246	18	64	7	1	6	31	19-1	0	47	.260	.312	.370	96	-2	1-2	.993	8	151	89	1b76		-1.3
1966	Was A	94	235	20	50	8	0	6	30	28-2	0	46	.213	.294	.323	79	-6	0-2	.990	-1	95	93	1b65/OL		-0.9
1967	Was A	110	238	21	52	7	1	6	29	21-4	0	39	.218	.280	.332	84	-5	0-1	.995	1	109	117	1b65/OL		-1.0
1968	Chi N	81	94	8	17	1	1	2	16	6-2	0	17	.181	.225	.277	48	-6	0-0	.987	-2	78	75	1b52		-1.0
1970	Was A	6	5	1	1	0	0	0	0	0-0	1	0	.200	.200	.200	-1	-1	0-0	1.000	0	653	0	/1		-3.0
Total	6	367	826	70	185	23	3	21	107	77-10	1	152	.224	.288	.335	82	-19	1-5	.992	7	114	96	1b264/OL		

NESS, JACK   John Charles B11.11.1884 Chicago IL D12.4.1957 DeLand FL   BR/TR/6-2/165   d5.9   -0.5

1911	Det A	12	39	6	6	0	0	2					.154	.195	.154	-2	-5		.977	1	122	72	1b12		-1.0
1916	Chi A	75	258	32	69	7	5	1	34	9	7	32	.267	.310	.345	96	-3	4	.979	-5	77	133	1b69		-1.5
Total	2	87	297	38	75	7	5	1	36	11	7	32	.253	.295	.320	82	-8	4	.978	-4	84	124	1b81		

NETTLES, GRAIG   Graig B8.20.1944 San Diego CA   BL/TR/6-0/186*   [MinA65 4/74]   d9.6   C2   b-Jim   Col San Diego St.   OF(58/2/13)   0.0

1967	Min A	3	3	1	1	0	0	0	0-0		1	.333	.333	.667	175	0	0-0	—	0			/H		0.1
1968	Min A	22	76	13	17	2	1	5	8	7-1	1	20	.224	.298	.474	124	2	0-0	.968	1	112	245	O16(2/1/13),3b5,1b3		-0.4
1969	†Min A	96	225	27	50	9	2	7	26	32-1	1	47	.222	.319	.373	91	0	3-1	.967	26	112	126	3b154,O3L		2.6
1970	Cle A	157	549	81	129	13	1	26	62	81-3	3	77	.235	.336	.404	99	0	3-1	.973	46	125	148	3b158		5.9
1971	Cle A	158	598	78	156	18	1	28	86	82-6	4	50	.261	.350	.435	111	10	7-4	.956	8	111	90	3b150		1.6
1972	Cle A	150	557	65	141	28	0	17	70	57-5	4	55	.253	.325	.395	110	5	0-0	.953	33	128	135	3b157,D2		3.7
1973	NY A	160	552	65	129	18	0	22	81	78-3	7	76	.234	.334	.386	105	5	1-0	.961	20	112	85	3b154/S		2.6
1974	NY A	155	566	74	139	21	1	22	75	59-8	3	75	.246	.316	.403	108	5	1-3	.964	13	106	104	3b157		2.0
1975	NY A★	157	581	71	155	24	4	21	91	51-3	2	88	.267	.322	.430	114	9	11-6	.965	17	115	122	3b158/S		4.2
1976	†NY A★	158	583	88	148	29	2	32	93	62-6	4	94	.254	.327	.475	134	24	11-6	.974	-4	96	112	3b156/D		1.0
1977	†NY A★	158	589	99	150	23	4	37	107	68-8	3	79	.255	.333	.496	124	18	2-5	.975	-5	96	106	3b159,S2		1.4
1978	†NY A★	159	587	81	162	23	2	27	93	59-6	6	69	.276	.343	.460	128	21	1-1	.966	7	105	114	3b144		0.2
1979	NY A★	145	521	71	132	15	1	20	73	59-6	1	42	.253	.325	.401	97	-2	1-2	.960	-7	91	104	3b88/S	67	0.0
1980	†NY A	89	324	52	79	14	0	16	45	42-5	1	35	.244	.333	.435	110	5	0-0	.972	4	98	93	3b97,D4		-0.1
1981	†NY A	103	349	46	85	7	1	15	46	47-4	1	49	.244	.333	.398	112	5	1-5	.934	-2	97	101	3b113,D3	21	-0.6
1982	NY A	122	405	47	94	11	2	18	55	51-4	3	65	.232	.317	.402	98	-1	0-1	.956	-9	93	69	3b126/D		-0.8
1983	NY A	129	462	56	123	17	3	20	75	51-2	3	65	.266	.341	.446	119	12	0-1	.936	-11	90	79	3b119		0.4
1984	†SD N	124	395	42	90	11	1	20	65	58-4	5	59	.261	.363	.420	120	14	0-0	.959	-9	90	79	3b130		-0.2
1985	SD N	137	440	66	115	23	1	15	61	72-5	0	62	.218	.300	.379	88	-7	0-1	.941	-3	93	86	3b114		-1.2
1986	SD N	126	354	36	77	9	0	16	55	41-8	2	62	.218	.294	.350	68	-6	0-0	.951	-1	92	130	3b40,1b6		-0.6
1987	Atl N	112	177	19	38	2	0	1	33	25-4	5	25	.209	.294	.350	68	-4	0-0	.818	-1	95	177	3b12,1b5		-1.0
1988	Mon N	80	93	5	16	4	0	1	14	9-2	1	19	.172	.240	.247	40	-7	0-0	.961	124	105	106	3b2412,O73L,1b14,D11,S5	88	21.2
Total	22	2700	8986	1193	2225	328	28	390	1314	1088-94	50	1209	.248	.329	.421	110	116	32-36	.961	124	105	106	3b2412,O73L,1b14,D11,S5		

YEAR	TM LG	G	AB	R	H	2B	3B	HR	RBI	BB-IB	HP	SO	AVG	OBP	SLG	AOPS	ABR	SB-CS	FA	FR	RNG	THR	GAMES AT POSITION	DL	BFW

NETTLES, JIM James William B3.2.1947 San Diego CA BL/TL/6-0/186(180-194) [MinA68 4/76] d9.7 b-Graig Col San Diego St.

1970	Min A	13	20	3	5	0	0	0	0	1-0	1	5	.250	.286	.250	48	-1	0-1	1.000	-1	83	0	O11(5/1/5)		-0.3
1971	Min A	70	168	17	42	5	1	6	24	19-2	0	24	.250	.321	.399	101	0	3-2	.986	5	120	101	O62(2/57/3)		0.3
1972	Min A	102	235	28	48	5	4	4	33	32-3	1	52	.204	.300	.294	74	-7	4-3	.982	-0	99	111	O78(12/58/8)/1		-1.1
1974	Det A	43	141	20	32	5	1	6	17	15-1	1	26	.227	.306	.404	99	-7	3-4	1.000	2	96	33	O41(8/4/30)		-0.5
1979	KC A	11	23	0	2	0	0	0	1	3-0	0	2	.087	.192	.087	-21	-4	0-0	1.000	1	139	0	O8(7/0/1)/1		-0.4
1981	Oak A	1	0	0	0	0	0	0	0	0-0	0	0	—	—	—	—	0	0-0	—	-0	0	0	/OR		0.0
Total	6	240	587	68	129	15	4	16	57	70-6	2	109	.220	.304	.341	83	-12	10-10	.988	3	105	81	O201(34/120/48),1b2		-2.0

NETTLES, MORRIS Morris B1.26.1952 Los Angeles CA BL/TL/6-1/168* [AnaA70*2/33] d4.26

1974	Cal A	56	175	27	48	4	0	0	16-0	0	38	.274	.335	.297	88	-2	20-11	.990	-5	90	0	O54(3/37/14)		-0.9
1975	Cal A	112	294	50	68	11	0	0	23	26-2	1	57	.231	.295	.269	65	-13	22-15	.974	3	113	76	O90(39/38/17),D9		
Total	2	168	469	77	116	15	0	0	31	42-2	1	95	.247	.310	.279	73	-15	42-26	.980	-2	104	47	O144(42/75/31),D9		-2.3

NETZEL, MILO Miles A. B5.12.1886 Eldred PA D3.18.1938 Oxnard CA BL/TL d9.16

| 1909 | Cle A | 10 | 37 | 2 | 7 | 1 | 0 | 0 | 3 | | | | .189 | .200 | .216 | 46 | -2 | 1 | .800 | -2 | 82 | 156 | 3b6,O2L | | -0.5 |

NEU, OTTO Otto Adam B9.24.1894 Springfield OH D9.19.1932 Kenton OH BR/TR/5-11/170 d7.10

| 1917 | StL A | 1 | 0 | 0 | 0 | 0 | 0 | 0 | 0 | 0-0 | 0 | 0 | — | — | — | — | 0 | 0 | — | -0 | 0 | 0 | /S | | 0.0 |

NEUN, JOHNNY John Henry B10.28.1900 Baltimore MD D3.28.1990 Baltimore MD BB/TL/5-10.5/175 d4.14 M3/C3

1925	Det A	60	75	15	20	3	3	0	4	9	0	12	.267	.345	.387	87	-2	2-3	.990	-1	66	67	1b13		-0.4
1926	Det A	97	242	47	72	14	4	0	15	27	1	26	.298	.370	.388	97	-1	4-7	.993	-2	78	95	1b49		-0.7
1927	Det A	79	204	38	66	9	4	0	27	35	2	13	.324	.427	.407	116	7	22-7	.980	-3	85	107	1b53		0.2
1928	Det A	36	108	15	23	3	1	0	5	7	0	10	.213	.261	.259	36	-10	0	.975	0	115	90	1b25		-1.1
1930	Bos N	81	212	39	69	12	2	2	23	21	1	18	.325	.389	.429	101	9	9	.991	0	101	101	1b55		-0.2
1931	Bos N	79	104	17	23	1	3	0	11	11	1	14	.221	.302	.288	62	-6	2	.994	0	99	106	1b36		-0.7
Total	6	432	945	171	273	42	17	2	85	110	5	93	.289	.366	.376	91	-11	41-19	.987	-6	91	99	1b231		-2.9

NEVIN, ALEXANDER Alexander Brown B10.3.1850 Allegheny City (now part of Pittsburgh) PA D10.10.1921 Pensacola FL d5.6

| 1873 | Res NA | 13 | 55 | 7 | 11 | 1 | 2 | 0 | 1 | | | 4 | .200 | .214 | .291 | 63 | -3 | 0-0 | .561 | -6 | 79 | 0 | 3b12/2OR | | -0.7 |

NEVIN, PHIL Phillip Joseph B1.19.1971 Fullerton CA BR/TR/6-2/231(180-231) [HouN92 1/1] d6.11 Col Cal St.-Fullerton OF(81/0/38)

1995	Hou N	18	60	4	7	1	0	0	1	7-1	1	13	.117	.221	.133	-4	-9	1-0	.933	-1	95	146	3b16		-1.0
	Det A	29	96	9	21	3	1	2	12	11-0	3	27	.219	.318	.333	70	-4	0-0	.963	-1	90	108	O27L,D2		-0.6
1996	Det A	38	120	15	35	5	0	8	19	8-0	1	39	.292	.338	.533	116	2	1-0	.943	3	121	124	3b24,O9L,C4/D		0.5
1997	Det A	93	251	32	59	16	1	9	35	25-1	1	68	.235	.306	.414	86	-5	0-1	.986	-2	91	175	O40L,D30,3b17,1b7/C		-1.0
1998	Ana A	75	237	27	54	8	1	8	27	17-0	5	67	.228	.291	.371	70	-11	0-0	.989	-8	85	100	C69,1b2,D3	15	-1.5
1999	SD N	128	383	52	103	27	0	24	85	51-1	1	82	.269	.352	.527	129	17	1-0	.982	11	116	124	3b67,C31,O13(5/0/9),1b11/D	11	2.7
2000	SD N	143	538	87	167	34	1	31	107	59-9	4	121	.310	.374	.543	137	30	2-0	.929	-8	97	86	3b142		2.2
2001	SD N★	149	546	97	167	31	0	41	126	71-7	4	147	.306	.388	.588	160	49	4-4	.930	5	108	109	3b145/D		5.2
2002	SD N	107	407	53	116	16	0	12	57	38-4	1	87	.285	.344	.413	112	4	0-0	.928	2	103	119	3b71,1b36	58	0.4
2003	SD N	59	226	30	63	8	0	13	46	21-1	0	44	.279	.339	.487	123	7	2-0	.996	-1	104	101	1b31,O29R	115	0.2
2004	SD N	147	547	78	158	31	1	26	105	66-5	5	121	.289	.368	.492	127	22	0-0	.989	-2	97	103	1b144/CD	16	0.8
2005	SD N	73	281	31	72	11	1	9	47	19-0	1	67	.256	.301	.399	87	-7	1-0	.994	-3	82	87	1b71,C2	27	-1.6
	Tex A	29	99	15	18	5	0	3	8	8-0	1	30	.182	.250	.323	49	-7	2-0	1.000	0	151	104	D25,1b3/3		-0.8
Total	11	1088	3791	530	1036	196	6	186	675	401-29	28	913	.273	.345	.475	116	88	18-5	.938	-4	104	107	3b483,1b305,O118L,C108,D65	242	5.5

NEWELL, JOHN John A. B1.14.1868 Wilmington DE D1.28.1919 Wilmington DE BR/TL/5-9/170 d7.22

| 1891 | Pit N | 5 | 18 | 1 | 2 | 0 | 0 | 0 | 2 | 0 | | 1 | 0 | .111 | .158 | .111 | -22 | -3 | 0 | .846 | -1 | 114 | 0 | 3b5 | | -0.3 |

NEWELL, T. E. T. E. B St.Louis MO d8.8

| 1877 | StL N | 1 | 3 | 0 | 0 | 0 | 0 | 0 | 0 | 0 | | | 0 | .000 | .000 | .000 | -99 | -1 | | .833 | 0 | 96 | 0 | /S | | -0.1 |

NEWFIELD, MARC Marc Alexander B10.19.1972 Sacramento CA BR/TR/6-4/205(205-226) [SeaA90 1/6] d7.6

1993	Sea A	22	66	5	15	3	0	1	7	2-0	1	8	.227	.257	.318	54	-5	0-1	—	-1	0	0	D15,O5L		-0.7
1994	Sea A	12	38	3	7	1	0	1	4	2-0	0	4	.184	.225	.289	31	-4	0-0	1.000	-1	53	0	O3L,D9		-0.4
1995	Sea A	24	85	7	16	3	0	3	14	3-1	1	16	.188	.225	.329	41	-8	0-0	1.000	-0	110	0	O24(23/0/1)		-0.8
	SD N	21	55	6	17	5	1	1	7	2-0	0	8	.309	.333	.491	117	1	0-0	1.000	1	110	134	O19L		0.1
1996	SD N	84	191	27	48	11	0	5	26	16-1	2	44	.251	.311	.387	88	-3	1-1	.970	-4	89	0	O51(30/0/23),1b2		-0.9
1997	Mil A	50	157	14	36	8	0	1	18	14-0	2	27	.229	.295	.299	57	-10	0-0	.977	-2	93	0	O49L		-0.1
1998	Mil N	93	186	15	44	7	0	3	25	19-1	1	29	.237	.306	.323	69	-9	0-1	.962	-1	94	108	O55L/D	105	-1.3
Total	6	355	957	98	238	53	1	22	132	69-4	11	162	.249	.303	.375	76	-35	1-4	.981	-8	93	54	O234(212/0/24),D43,1b2	105	-5.3

NEWHAN, DAVID David Matthew B9.7.1973 Fullerton CA BL/TR/5-10/180* [OakA95 17/456] d6.4 Col Pepperdine OF(39/32/59)

1999	SD N	32	43	7	6	1	0	2	6	1-0	0	11	.140	.159	.302	14	-6	2-1	.970	4	117	149	2b19/13		-0.2
2000	SD N	14	20	5	3	1	0	1	2	6-1	0	7	.150	.346	.350	82	0	0-0	1.000	-1	132	0	2b3,O5R,3b2		-0.1
	Phi N	10	17	3	3	0	0	0	2	2-0	0	5	.176	.263	.176	14	-2	0-0	1.000	3	158	221	2b5		0.1
	Year	24	37	8	6	1	0	1	4	8-1	0	12	.162	.311	.270	51	-3	0-0	1.000	2	153	180	2b8,O5R,3b2		0.0
2001	Phi N	7	6	2	2	1	0	0	1	1-0	0	1	.333	.375	.500	146	1.	0-0	1.000	-1	0	0	/2		0.0
2004	Bal A	95	373	66	116	15	7	8	54	27-0	4	72	.311	.361	.453	112	6	11-1	1.000	-4	92	122	O42(19/0/24),D32,3b17,1b2	177	0.1
2005	Bal A	96	218	31	44	9	0	5	21	22-1	2	35	.202	.279	.312	57	-13	9-2	.990	-8	82	35	O73(20/32/30),3b8,D7		-1.9
Total	5	254	677	114	174	27	7	16	84	59-2	6	141	.257	.320	.388	86	-14	22-4	.995	-5	85	68	O120R,D39,3b28,2b28,1b3	177	-2.0

NEWMAN, AL Albert Dwayne B6.30.1960 Kansas City MO BB/TR/5-9/183(175-198) [MonN81 S1/12] d6.14 C4 Col San Diego St. OF(11/1/0)

1985	Mon N	25	29	7	5	1	0	0	1	3-0	0	4	.172	.250	.207	3	-2	2-1	1.000	2	125	108	2b15,S2		0.0
1986	Mon N	95	185	23	37	3	0	1	8	21-2	0	20	.200	.279	.232	31	-3	2-1	.967	1	105	109	2b59,S22		-1.2
1987	†Min A	110	307	44	68	15	5	0	29	34-0	0	27	.221	.298	.303	58	-14	15-11	.982	-0	92	103	S55,2b47,3b12,O2L,D5		-1.3
1988	Min A	105	260	35	58	7	0	0	19	29-0	0	34	.223	.301	.250	54	-11	15-11	.982	-9	92	103	S55,2b47,3b12,O2L,D5		-1.3
1989	Min A	141	446	62	113	18	2	0	38	59-0	2	46	.253	.341	.303	78	-11	25-12	.980	-13	91	83	2b84,3b37,S31,O4(4/1/0),D2		-1.9
1990	Min A	144	388	43	94	14	0	0	30	33-0	2	34	.242	.304	.278	60	-20	13-6	.993	1	99	115	2b89,S48,3b28,O3L		-1.5
1991	†Min A	118	246	25	47	5	0	0	19	23-0	1	26	.191	.260	.211	31	-23	4-5	.987	-2	88	112	S55,2b35,3b35/1OLD		-2.3
1992	Tex A	116	246	25	54	5	0	1	12	34-0	1	26	.220	.317	.240	60	-12	9-6	.983	4	105	96	2b424,S261,3b200,O13,O11L/1		-0.6
Total		854	2107	264	476	68	7	1	156	236-2	6	212	.226	.304	.266	58	-116	91-55	.984	-15	101	96	2b424,S261,3b200,D13,O11L/1		-10.8

NEWMAN, CHARLIE Charles "Decker" B11.5.1868 Juda WI D11.23.1947 San Diego CA BR/TR d7.11

1892	NY N	3	12	1	4	0	0	0	2	1	0	0	.333	.429	.333	133	1	3	.750	-0	219	0	O3L		0.0
	Chi N	16	61	4	10	0	0	0	2	1	0	6	.164	.177	.164	3	-7	2	.950	-1	47	231	O16L		-0.9
	Year	19	73	5	14	0	0	0	4	2	0	6	.192	.224	.192	26	-7	5	.917	-2	77	190	O19L		-0.9

NEWMAN, JEFF Jeffrey Lynn B9.11.1948 Fort Worth TX BR/TR/6-2/218* [CleA70 26/608] d6.30 M1/C11 Col TCU

1976	Oak A	43	77	5	15	4	0	0	4	2-0	1	12	.195	.235	.247	43	-6	0-0	.981	5	169	135	C43		0.1
1977	Oak A	94	162	17	36	9	0	4	15	4-1	1	24	.222	.244	.352	61	-9	2-0	.970	-3	118	**138**	C94/P		-0.9
1978	Oak A	105	268	25	64	7	1	9	32	18-2	1	40	.239	.288	.373	89	-5	0-3	.969	-2	95	84	C61,1b36,D2	15	-0.8
1979	Oak A☆	143	516	53	119	17	2	22	71	27-2	1	88	.231	.267	.399	82	-16	2-1	.977	2	124	**129**	C81,1b46,3b7,D7		-1.4
1980	Oak A	127	438	37	102	19	1	15	56	25-8	1	81	.233	.273	.384	84	-12	3-4	.982	-15	86	59	1b60,C55,3b2/2D		-2.9
1981	†Oak A	68	216	17	50	10	0	3	15	9-1	0	28	.231	.260	.329	72	-8	0-2	.995	0	136	102	C37,1b30		-0.9
1982	Oak A	72	251	19	50	11	0	6	30	14-1	0	49	.199	.240	.315	53	-17	0-1	.989	-4	73	84	C67,1b3/3D		-1.9
1983	Bos A	59	132	11	25	4	0	3	7	10-1	2	31	.189	.255	.288	46	-10	0-1	.990	0	88	135	C51,D6		-0.9
1984	Bos A	24	63	5	14	2	0	1	3	5-0	0	16	.222	.275	.302	58	-4	0-0	.990	0	92	80	C24		-0.2
Total	9	735	2123	189	475	85	4	63	233	116-16	6	369	.224	.264	.357	73	-87	7-12	.981	-16	108	108	C513,1b175,D25,3b10/2P	15	-9.8

NEWNAM, PATRICK Patrick Henry B12.10.1880 Hempstead TX D6.20.1938 San Antonio TX BL/TR/6-0/180 d5.29

1910	StL A	103	384	45	83	9	3	2	26	29		2	.216	.275	.281	79	-11	16	.972	-3	97	100	1b103		-1.8
1911	StL A	20	62	11	12	4	0	0	5	12		3	.194	.351	.258	74	-1	4	.986	1	110	112	1b20		-0.1
Total	2	123	446	56	95	13	3	2	31	41		5	.213	.287	.278	78	-12	20	.974	-3	99	102	1b123		-1.9

YEAR	TM LG	G	AB	R	H	2B	3B	HR	RBI	BB-IB	HP	SO	AVG	OBP	SLG	AOPS	ABR	SB-CS	FA	FR	RNG	THR	GAMES AT POSITION	DL	BFW
NEWSOME, SKEETER								Lamar Ashby B10.18.1910 Phenix City AL D8.31.1989 Columbus GA BR/TR/5-9/170 d4.19																	-1.0
1935	Phi A	59	145	18	30	7	1	1	10	5	0	9	.207	.233	.290		35	-15	2-1	.956	2	97	120	S24,2b13,3b4/OR		-2.8
1936	Phi A	127	471	41	106	15	2	0	46	25	0	27	.225	.266	.265		32	-52	13-4	.957	10	**108**	99	S123,2b2/3OL		-0.8
1937	Phi A	122	438	53	111	22	1	1	30	37	0	22	.253	.312	.315		59	-28	11-5	.954	10	106	97	S122		-0.1
1938	Phi A	17	48	7	13	4	0	0	7	1	0	4	.271	.286	.354		61	-3	1-1	.971	1	109	75	S15		-1.7
1939	Phi A	99	248	22	55	9	1	0	17	19	0	12	.222	.277	.266		40	-23	5-7	.950	9	100	91	S93,2b2		-0.8
1941	Bos A	93	227	28	51	6	0	2	17	22	1	11	.225	.296	.278		51	-16	10-4	.958	9	109	99	S69,2b23		-0.1
1942	Bos A	29	95	7	26	6	0	0	9	9	0	5	.274	.337	.337		87	-1	2-1	.925	1	118	194	3b12,2b10,S7		0.1
1943	Bos A	114	449	48	119	21	2	1	22	21	2	21	.265	.301	.327		82	-11	5-6	.962	9	105	103	S98,3b15		0.5
1944	Bos A	136	472	41	114	26	3	0	41	33	0	21	.242	.291	.309		72	-17	4-3	.963	9	104	90	S126,2b8/3		0.2
1945	Bos A	125	438	45	127	30	1	1	48	20	1	15	.290	.322	.370		98	-2	6-3	.963	16	103	100	2b82,S33,3b11		2.3
1946	Phi N	112	375	35	87	10	2	1	23	30	0	23	.232	.289	.277		63	-19	4	.955	-10	98	81	S107,2b3,3b2		-2.4
1947	Phi N	95	310	36	71	8	2	2	24	24	0	24	.229	.284	.287		54	-21	4	.969	3	105	130	S85,2b6,3b3		-1.3
Total	12	1128	3716	381	910	164	15	9	292	246	5	194	.245	.293	.304		62	-208	67-35	.959	59	105	99	S902,2b149,3b49,O2(1/0/1)		-7.2
NEWSON, WARREN								Warren Dale B7.3.1964 Newnan GA BL/TR/5-7/202(190-202) [SDN86*4/90] d5.29 Col Middle Georgia JC																	0.4
1991	Chi A	71	132	20	39	6	0	4	25	28-1	0	34	.295	.424	.424	137	8	2-2	.962	-3	74	142	O50(16/1/34),D3		0.0
1992	Chi A	63	136	19	30	3	0	1	11	37-2	0	38	.221	.387	.265	86	0	3-0	1.000	1	87	199	O50(17/0/33),D4		0.2
1993	†Chi A	26	40	9	12	0	0	2	6	9-1	0	12	.300	.429	.450	139	3	0-0	1.000	-0	96	0	O34(9/0/26),D3		-0.2
1994	Chi A	63	102	16	26	5	0	2	7	14-1	0	23	.255	.345	.363	84	-2	1-0	.979	1	115	68	O24(12/0/14),D7		0.3
1995	Chi A	51	85	19	20	0	2	3	9	23-0	1	27	.235	.404	.388	112	2	1-1	.978	2	128	86	O23(18/2/4)		0.2
	†Sea A	33	72	15	21	2	0	2	6	16-0	0	18	.292	.404	.403	114	2	1-0	.975	1	115	89	O47(30/2/18),D7		0.5
	Year	84	157	34	41	2	2	5	15	39-0	1	45	.261	.411	.395	113	5	2-1	.975	2	120	91	O66(8/0/58),D9		0.1
1996	†Tex A	91	235	34	60	14	1	10	31	37-1	0	82	.255	.355	.451	96	4	3-0	.992	4	111	130	O58(20/0/44),D9	50	-0.2
1997	Tex A	81	169	23	36	10	1	10	23	31-2	0	53	.213	.333	.462	98	0	3-0	.949	-0	110	37	O6L,D3		-0.2
1998	Tex A	10	21	1	4	1	0	0	2	1-1	0	5	.190	.227	.238	20	-2	0-0	1.000	1	125	0		50	0.6
Total	8	489	992	156	248	40	4	34	120	196-9	1	292	.250	.374	.401	102	10	14-3	.978	5	103	111	O316(108/3/216),D48		
NIARHOS, GUS								Constantine Gregory B12.6.1920 Birmingham AL D12.29.2004 Harrisonburg VA BR/TR/6-0/165* d6.9 C3																	0.5
1946	NY A	37	40	11	9	1	1	0	2	11	0	2	.225	.392	.300	94	0	1-0	.989	4	143	137	C29		1.2
1948	NY A	83	228	41	61	12	2	0	19	52	0	15	.268	.404	.338	99	1	1-3	.990	6	105	99	C82		0.6
1949	†NY A	32	43	7	12	2	1	0	6	13	1	8	.279	.456	.372	120	2	0-0	1.000	3	83	83	C30		0.0
1950	NY A	1	0	0	0	0	0	0	0	0	0	0	—	—	—	—	0	0-0	—	0			/R		0.7
	Chi A	41	105	17	34	4	0	0	16	14	1	6	.324	.408	.362	101	1	0-0	.978	4	86	97	C36		0.7
	Year	42	105	17	34	4	0	0	16	14	1	6	.324	.408	.362	101	1	0-0	.978	4	86	97	C36		1.0
1951	Chi A	66	168	27	43	6	0	1	10	47	0	9	.256	.419	.310	101	4	4-3	.985	3	79	82	C59	42	-0.2
1952	Bos A	29	58	4	6	0	0	0	4	12	1	9	.103	.268	.103	6	-7	0-0	.992	4	142	102	C25		0.0
1953	Bos A	16	35	6	7	1	1	0	2	4	1	4	.200	.300	.286	56	-2	0-1	.985	2	100	76	C16		0.0
1954	Phi N	3	5	0	1	0	0	0	0	0	0	1	.200	.200	.200	5	-1	0-0	1.000	1	0	0	C3		-0.1
1955	Phi N	7	9	1	1	0	0	0	1	0-0	0	2	.111	.111	.111	-42	-2	0-0	1.000	1	72	179	C7	42	-0.1
Total	9	315	691	114	174	26	5	1	59	153-0	4	56	.252	.390	.308	89	-1	6-7	.988	27	99	95	C287		3.7
NICHOLAS, DON								Donald Leigh B10.30.1930 Phoenix AZ BL/TR/5-7/150* d4.16																	-0.1
1952	Chi A	3	2	0	0	0	0	0	0	0	0	0	.000	.000	.000	-99	-1	0-0	—	0			/H		0.0
1954	Chi A	7	0	3	0	0	0	0	0	1	0	0	—	1.000	—	185	0	0-1	—	0			/H		-0.1
Total	2	10	2	3	0	0	0	0	1	0	0	.000	.333	.000	-2	-1	0-1	—	0					
NICHOLL, SAM								Samuel Anderson B4.20.1869 Co. Antrim, Ireland D4.19.1937 Steubenville OH BR/TR/5-10/178 d10.5																	-0.3
1888	Pit N	8	22	3	1	0	0	0	2	0	0	2	.045	.125	.045	-48	-4	0-0	.952	1	90	0	O8C		-0.5
1890	Col AA	14	56	7	9	0	0	0	4	2	0	0	.161	.190	.161	4	-7	3	.903	2	178	375	O14L		-0.8
Total	2	22	78	10	10	0	0	0	4	4	0	2	.128	.171	.128	-10	-11	3	.923	2	152	266	O22(14/8/0)		
NICHOLLS, SIMON								Simon Burdette B7.18.1882 Germantown MD D3.12.1911 Baltimore MD BL/TR/5-11.5/165 d9.18 Col Maryland-Baltimore Co.																	-0.2
1903	Det A	2	8	0	3	0	0	0	0	0	0		.375	.375	.375	129	0	0-0	.600	-2	49	0	S2		-0.4
1906	Phi A	12	44	1	8	1	0	0	1	3	0		.182	.234	.205	36	-3	0	.965	-0	89	112	S12		-0.4
1907	Phi A	124	460	75	139	12	2	0	23	24	1		.302	.338	.337	113	6	13	.930	-13	93	50	S82,2b28,3b13		-3.8
1908	Phi A	150	550	58	119	17	3	4	31	35	1		.216	.265	.280	72	-17	14	.913	-20	89	69	S120,2b23,3b7		-0.6
1909	Phi A	21	71	10	15	2	1	0	3	3	0		.211	.243	.268	60	-3	0	.889	-2	81	80	S14,3b5/1		-0.1
1910	Cle A	3	0	0	0	0	0	0	0	0	0		—	—	—	—	0	0	.000	-1	0	0	S3		-0.1
Total	6	312	1133	144	284	32	6	4	58	65	2		.251	.292	.300	86	-17	27	.917	-38	90	64	S233,2b51,3b25/1		-5.5
NICHOLS, AL								Albert H. B Brooklyn NY 5-11/180 d4.24																	-0.3
1875	Atl NA	32	131	4	20	2	0	0	9	0		6	.153	.153	.168	13	-10	0-0	.785	8	122	194	3b32		-0.7
1876	NY N	**57**	212	20	38	4	0	0	9	2		3	.179	.187	.198	33	-13		.779	4	114	16	3b57		0.1
1877	Lou N	6	19	1	4	0	1	0	0	0		2	.211	.214	.316	54	-1		.706	2	147	0	2b3/S31		-0.6
Total	2	63	231	21	42	4	1	0	9	2		5	.182	.189	.208	35	-14		.785	6	115	16	3b58,2b3/1S		
NICHOLS, ART								Arthur Francis (b Arthur Francis Meikle) B7.14.1871 Manchester NH D8.9.1945 Willimantic CT BR/TR/5-10/175 d9.16																	0.3
1898	Chi N	14	42	7	12	1	0	0	6	4	3		.286	.388	.310	101	1	6	.968	2	146	94	C14		-0.1
1899	Chi N	17	47	5	12	2	0	1	11	0	2		.255	.286	.362	79	-2	3	.931	-1	106	70	C15		-0.2
1900	Chi N	8	25	1	5	0	0	0	0	3	0		.200	.286	.200	36	-2	1	.938	-1	99	101	C7		-0.2
1901	StL N	93	308	50	75	11	3	1	33	10	10		.244	.290	.308	77	-9	14	.960	-0	94	93	C47,O40(0/29/11)		-0.7
1902	StL N	73	251	36	67	12	0	1	31	21	4		.267	.333	.327	108	3	18	.984	-6	76	79	1b56,C11,O4(0/1/3)		-0.3
1903	StL N	36	120	13	23	2	0	0	9	12	3		.192	.281	.208	42	-9	9	.972	-5	21	82	1b25,O7L,C2		-1.4
Total	6	241	793	112	194	28	3	3	90	50	22		.245	.308	.299	81	-18	51	.952	-11	103	92	C96,1b81,O51(7/30/14)		-2.4
NICHOLS, CARL								Carl Edward B10.14.1962 Los Angeles CA BR/TR/6-0/208(184-208) [BalA80 4/104] d9.14																	-0.2
1986	Bal A	5	5	0	0	0	0	0	0	1-1	0	4	.000	.167	.000	-50	-1	0-0	1.000	-1	71	0	C5		0.0
1987	Bal A	13	21	4	8	1	0	0	3	1-0	0	4	.381	.409	.429	126	1	0-0	1.000	1	81	121	C13		0.0
1988	Bal A	18	47	2	9	1	0	1	3	3-0	0	10	.191	.235	.213	29	-5	0-0	.987	6	98	228	C13,O3R		0.0
1989	Hou N	8	13	0	1	0	0	0	2	0-0	0	3	.077	.077	.077	-58	-3	0-0	1.000	0	190	0	C6		0.0
1990	Hou N	32	49	7	10	1	0	0	11	8-1	1	11	.204	.317	.265	67	-2	0-0	.986	3	114	110	C15,1b3/OL		0.0
1991	Hou N	20	51	3	10	3	0	0	1	5-1	0	17	.196	.268	.255	50	-3	0-0	.971	1	151	154	C17	22	-0.2
Total	6	96	186	16	38	6	0	2	18	18-3	1	49	.204	.274	.247	49	-13	0-0	.985	8	118	143	C69,O4(1/0/3),1b3	22	-0.2
NICHOLS, ROY								Roy B3.3.1921 Little Rock AR D4.3.2002 Hot Springs AR BR/TR/5-11/155 d5.6																	0.0
1944	NY N	11	9	3	2	1	0	0	2	0	0	2	.222	.364	.333	97	0	0	1.000	1	177	0	/23		
NICHOLS, REID								Thomas Reid B8.5.1958 Ocala FL BR/TR/5-11/165* [BosA76 12/286] d9.16 C1																	-0.0
1980	Bos A	12	36	5	8	0	1	0	3	3-0	0	7	.222	.282	.278	51	-3	0-1	.962	-1	85	141	O9C/D		-0.0
1981	Bos A	39	48	13	9	1	0	1	3	2-0	0	6	.188	.216	.229	28	-5	0-1	1.000	-0	84	315	O27(1/25/1)/3D		0.4
1982	Bos A	92	245	35	74	16	1	7	33	14-1	1	28	.302	.341	.461	111	4	5-3	.989	3	97	199	O82(30/57/2),D4	16	0.4
1983	Bos A	100	274	35	78	22	1	6	22	26-2	3	36	.285	.352	.438	108	4	7-5	.994	1	102	84	O72(11/32/30),D18/S		-0.0
1984	Bos A	74	124	14	28	5	1	1	14	12-1	3	18	.226	.307	.306	68	-5	2-1	.988	0	93	138	O48(17/26/4)/D		-0.0
1985	Bos A	21	32	3	6	1	0	1	3	2-0	1	6	.188	.250	.313	53	-2	1-0	.933	-1	75	0	O10(2/7/1),2b3,D4		-0.0
	Chi A	51	118	20	35	7	1	1	15	15-1	0	13	.297	.373	.398	107	2	5-5	1.000	1	97	52	O48(25/27/8)/D		-0.0
	Year	72	150	23	41	8	1	2	18	17-1	1	17	.273	.347	.380	96	0	6-5	.988	-2	93	42	O58(27/34/9),D5,2b3	22	-0.0
1986	Chi A	74	136	9	31	4	0	2	18	11-0	0	23	.228	.282	.301	58	-8	5-4	.989	3	112	188	O59(7/50/5),3b3		-0.0
1987	Mon N	77	147	22	39	8	2	4	20	14-1	1	13	.265	.329	.429	96	-1	2-1	.990	7	99	142	O408(124/247/62),D39,2b5,3b4/S	38	-1.0
Total	8	540	1160	160	308	63	8	22	131	89-6	9	149	.266	.324	.400	91	-14	27-21	.990	7	99	142	O408(124/247/62),D39,2b5,3b4/S		
NICHOLSON, DAVE								David Lawrence B8.29.1939 St.Louis MO BR/TR/6-2/215* d5.24																	-0.0
1960	Bal A	54	113	17	21	3	1	5	11	20-0	0	55	.186	.308	.345	77	-4	0-2	.982	-1	80	140	O44(34/0/11)		-0.0
1962	Bal A	97	173	25	30	4	1	9	15	27-0	1	76	.173	.289	.364	79	-6	3-4	.983	1	101	134	O80(34/20/27)		-0.0
1963	Chi A	126	449	53	103	11	4	22	70	63-0	2	175	.229	.319	.419	108	5	2-1	.970	0	92	117	O123L		-0.0
1964	Chi A	97	294	40	60	6	1	13	39	52-0	3	126	.204	.329	.364	95	-1	0-2	.972	-1	94	94	O92(91/0/1)		-1.0
1965	Chi A	54	85	11	13	2	1	2	12	9-0	0	40	.153	.234	.271	46	-6	0-0	1.000	-4	65	0	O36(25/12/1)		

YEAR	TM LG	G	AB	R	H	2B	3B	HR	RBI	BB-IB	HP	SO	AVG	OBP	SLG	AOPS	ABR	SB-CS	FA	FR	RNG	THR	GAMES AT POSITION	DL	BFW
1966	Hou N	100	280	36	69	8	4	10	31	46-6	3	92	.246	.356	.411	122	9	1-1	.968	5	104	210	O90(13/5/73)		1.0
1967	Atl N	10	25	2	5	0	0	0	1	2-1	0	9	.200	.250	.200	34	-2	0-0	1.000	0	75	215	O7(7/1/0)		-0.3
Total	7	538	1419	184	301	32	12	61	179	219-7	7	573	.212	.318	.381	97	-5	6-10	.974	-0	93	129	O472(327/38/113)		-3.1

NICHOLSON, FRED Fred "Shoemaker" B9.1.1894 Honey Grove TX D1.23.1972 Kilgore TX BR/TR/5-10.5/173 d4.11 Mil 1918

YEAR	TM LG	G	AB	R	H	2B	3B	HR	RBI	BB-IB	HP	SO	AVG	OBP	SLG	AOPS	ABR	SB-CS	FA	FR	RNG	THR	GAMES AT POSITION	DL	BFW
1917	Det A	13	14	4	4	1	0	0	1	1	0	2	.286	.333	.357	111	0		1.000	-0	104		O3(1/0/2)		0.0
1919	Pit N	30	66	8	18	2	2	1	6	6	0	11	.273	.333	.409	118	1	2	.939	1	108	113	O17(13/1/3)/1		0.1
1920	Pit N	99	247	33	89	16	7	4	30	18	0	31	.360	.404	.530	162	19	9-6	.957	3	104	129	O58(28/18/13)		2.0
1921	Bos N	83	245	36	80	11	7	5	41	17	0	29	.327	.370	.490	133	11	5-4	.983	-1	105	65	O59(57/0/3),1b4,2b2		0.5
1922	Bos N	78	222	31	56	4	5	2	29	23	5	24	.252	.336	.342	79	-7	5-7	.915	-1	109	69	O63(20/0/44)		-1.4
Total	5	303	794	112	247	34	21	12	107	65	5	97	.311	.367	.452	124	24	21-17	.950	1	106	90	O200(119/19/65),1b5,2b2		1.2

NICHOLSON, KEVIN Kevin Ronald B3.29.1976 Vancouver BC, Can. BB/TR/5-10/190 [SDN97 1/27] d6.23 Col Stetson

YEAR	TM LG	G	AB	R	H	2B	3B	HR	RBI	BB-IB	HP	SO	AVG	OBP	SLG	AOPS	ABR	SB-CS	FA	FR	RNG	THR	GAMES AT POSITION	DL	BFW
2000	SD N	37	97	7	21	6	1	1	8	4-0	1	31	.216	.255	.330	49	-8	1-0	.983	1	111	69	S30,2b4	26	-0.4

NICHOLSON, OVID Ovid Edward B12.30.1888 Salem IN D3.24.1968 Salem IN BL/TR/5-9.5/155 d9.17

YEAR	TM LG	G	AB	R	H	2B	3B	HR	RBI	BB-IB	HP	SO	AVG	OBP	SLG	AOPS	ABR	SB-CS	FA	FR	RNG	THR	GAMES AT POSITION	DL	BFW
1912	Pit N	6	11	2	5	0	0	0	1	0	0	2	.455	.500	.455	164	1	0	1.000	0	125		O4L		0.1

NICHOLSON, PARSON Thomas Clark "Deacon" B4.14.1863 Blaine OH D2.28.1917 Bellaire OH 5-9/148 d9.14

YEAR	TM LG	G	AB	R	H	2B	3B	HR	RBI	BB-IB	HP	SO	AVG	OBP	SLG	AOPS	ABR	SB-CS	FA	FR	RNG	THR	GAMES AT POSITION	DL	BFW
1888	Det N	24	85	11	22	3	1	1	9	2	1	7	.259	.284	.388	111	1	6	.935	-0	105	68	2b24		0.1
1890	Tol AA	134	523	78	140	16	11	4	72	42	9		.268	.333	.363	102	-1	46	.929	-7	102	83	2b134/C		-0.3
1895	Was N	10	38	7	7	2	1	0	5	7	0	4	.184	.311	.289	56	-2	6	.797	-2	101	88	S10		-0.3
Total	3	168	646	96	169	20	15	5	86	51	10	11	.262	.325	.362	100	-2	58	.930	-9	102	81	2b158,S10/C		-0.5

NICHOLSON, BILL William Beck "Swish" B12.11.1914 Chestertown MD D3.8.1996 Chestertown MD BL/TR/6-0/205* d6.13 Col Washington College

YEAR	TM LG	G	AB	R	H	2B	3B	HR	RBI	BB-IB	HP	SO	AVG	OBP	SLG	AOPS	ABR	SB-CS	FA	FR	RNG	THR	GAMES AT POSITION	DL	BFW
1936	Phi A	11	12	2	0	0	0	0	0	0	0	5	.000	.000	.000	-99	-4	0-0	1.000	0	106	0	/OR		-0.4
1939	Chi N	58	220	37	65	12	5	5	38	20	0	29	.295	.354	.464	116	4	0	.955	-1	100	89	O58R		0.0
1940	Chi N★	135	491	78	146	27	7	25	98	50	3	67	.297	.366	.534	148	31	2	.950	-6	91	101	O123(43/0/81)		1.8
1941	Chi N★	147	532	74	135	26	1	26	98	82	3	91	.254	.357	.453	132	23	1	.971	4	111	85	O143(3/0/140)		1.8
1942	Chi N★	152	588	83	173	22	11	21	78	76	8	80	.294	.382	.476	156	42	8	.986	7	107	127	O151R		4.1
1943	Chi N★	154	608	95	188	30	9	29	128	71	5	86	.309	.386	.531	166	50	4	.978	3	107	96	O154R		4.5
1944	Chi N★	156	582	116	167	35	8	33	122	93	6	71	.287	.391	.545	162	49	3	.979	-2	96	105	O156R		3.8
1945	†Chi N★	151	559	82	136	28	4	13	88	92	6	73	.243	.356	.377	106	4	1	.990	-2	99	86	O151R		-0.4
1946	Chi N	105	296	36	65	13	2	8	41	44	2	44	.220	.325	.358	95	-1	1	.973	2	120	51	O80R		-0.2
1947	Chi N	148	487	69	119	28	1	26	75	87	5	83	.244	.364	.466	124	18	1	.990	-5	99	57	O140R		0.9
1948	Chi N	143	494	68	129	24	5	19	67	81	5	60	.261	.371	.445	125	19	2	.980	-5	95	72	O136R		1.0
1949	Phi N	98	299	42	70	8	3	11	40	45	5	53	.234	.344	.391	99	0	1	.995	3	102	118	O91R		0.0
1950	Phi N	41	58	3	13	2	1	3	10	8	0	16	.224	.318	.448	101	0	0	.952	-1	109	0	O15R	30	-0.1
1951	Phi N	85	170	23	41	9	2	8	30	25	1	24	.241	.342	.459	115	4	0-1	.987	-1	105	29	O41R		0.1
1952	Phi N	55	88	17	24	3	0	6	19	14	3	26	.273	.390	.511	150	6	0-0	1.000	-1	109	45	O19R		0.5
1953	Phi N	38	62	12	13	5	1	2	16	12	0	20	.210	.338	.419	97	0	0-0	1.000	-1	77	0	O12R		-0.2
Total	16	1677	5546	837	1484	272	60	235	948	800	52	828	.268	.365	.465	133	249	27-1	.979	-4	102	87	O1471(46/0/1427)	30	17.2

NICOL, GEORGE George Edward B10.17.1870 Barry IL D8.4.1924 Milwaukee WI BR/TL/5-7/155 d9.23 ▲

YEAR	TM LG	G	AB	R	H	2B	3B	HR	RBI	BB-IB	HP	SO	AVG	OBP	SLG	AOPS	ABR	SB-CS	FA	FR	RNG	THR	GAMES AT POSITION	DL	BFW
1890	StL AA	3	7	4	2	1	0	0	1	4	0		.286	.545	.429	164	1	0	1.000	-0	0	0	P3		0.0
1891	Chi N	3	6	0	2	0	1	0	3	0	0	1	.333	.333	.667	159	1	0	.000	-1	0	0	P3		0.0
1894	Pit N	9	22	8	9	1	0	0	3	0	0	1	.409	.409	.455	109	2	0	.800	-1	48	0	P9		0.0
	Lou N	28	112	12	38	6	4	0	19	2	2	4	.339	.362	.464	105	0	4	.791	-4	52	102	O26R,P2		-0.4
	Year	37	134	20	47	7	4	0	22	2	2	5	.351	.370	.463	105	1	4	.791	-5	52	102	O26R,P11		-0.4
Total	3	43	147	24	51	8	5	0	26	6	2	6	.347	.381	.469	112	4	4	.791	-6	52	102	O26R,P17		-0.4

NICOL, HUGH Hugh B1.1.1858 Campsie, Scotland D6.27.1921 Lafayette IN BR/TR/5-4/145 d5.3 M1

YEAR	TM LG	G	AB	R	H	2B	3B	HR	RBI	BB-IB	HP	SO	AVG	OBP	SLG	AOPS	ABR	SB-CS	FA	FR	RNG	THR	GAMES AT POSITION	DL	BFW
1881	Chi N	26	108	13	22	2	0	0	7	4		12	.204	.232	.222	42	-7		.932	4	168	110	O26(2/12/12)/S		-0.4
1882	Chi N	47	186	19	37	9	1	1	16	7		29	.199	.228	.274	57	-9		.887	11	275	55	O47R,S8		0.1
1883	StL AA	94	368	73	105	13	3	0	39	18			.285	.319	.337	105	2		.916	10	181	247	O84(1/1/84),2b11		1.0
1884	StL AA	110	442	79	116	14	5	0		22	3		.262	.302	.317	99	-1		.873	17	264	113	O87R,2b23/S3		1.4
1885	†StL AA	112	425	59	88	11	1	0	45	34	3		.207	.271	.238	59	-19		.888	12	173	64	O111R/3		-0.8
1886	StL AA	67	253	44	52	6	3	0	19	26	0		.206	.280	.253	64	-11	38	.942	-4	116	0	O57(0/1/56),S8,2b4		-1.3
1887	Cin AA	125	475	122	102	18	2	1	34	86	5		.215	.341	.267	69	-16	138	.918	-3	98	24	O125(0/6/119)		-1.6
1888	Cin AA	135	548	112	131	10	2	1	35	67	7		.239	.330	.270	88	-5	103	.957	-3	71	69	O125R,2b12/S		-0.8
1889	Cin AA	122	474	82	121	7	8	2	58	54	5	35	.255	.338	.316	84	-10	80	.918	2	101	85	O115R,2b7,3b3		-0.7
1890	Cin N	50	186	28	39	1	4	0	19	19	0	12	.210	.283	.258	58	-10	24	.921	-6	95	188	O46R,S3/2		-1.5
Total	10	888	3465	631	813	91	29	5	272	337	23	88	.235	.307	.282	78	-86	383	.912	38	144	91	O823(3/20/802),2b58,S22,3b5		-4.6

NICOSIA, STEVE Steven Richard B8.6.1955 Paterson NJ BR/TR/5-10/185* [PitN73 1/24] d7.8

YEAR	TM LG	G	AB	R	H	2B	3B	HR	RBI	BB-IB	HP	SO	AVG	OBP	SLG	AOPS	ABR	SB-CS	FA	FR	RNG	THR	GAMES AT POSITION	DL	BFW
1978	Pit N	3	5	0	0	0	0	0	0	1-0	0	0	.000	.167	.000	-47	-1	0-0	1.000	0	37	278	/C		-0.1
1979	†Pit N	70	191	22	55	16	0	4	13	23-7	0	17	.288	.364	.435	111	4	0-2	.991	1	130	74	C65		0.7
1980	Pit N	60	176	16	38	8	0	1	22	19-5	0	16	.216	.291	.278	59	-9	0-1	.984	-1	128	61	C58		-0.9
1981	Pit N	54	169	21	39	10	1	2	18	13-2	0	10	.231	.286	.337	73	-6	3-1	.982	-1	106	70	C52		-0.5
1982	Pit N	39	100	6	28	3	0	1	7	11-4	0	13	.280	.348	.340	90	-1	0-1	.990	2	104	112	C35,O3L		0.2
1983	Pit N	21	46	4	6	2	0	1	1	1-0	0	7	.130	.149	.239	6	-6	0-0	.988	-3	71	59	C15		-0.5
	SF N	15	33	4	11	0	0	0	6	3-1	0	2	.333	.389	.333	105	0	0-0	.984	-3	107	28	C9	26	-0.9
	Year	36	79	8	17	2	0	1	7	4-1	0	9	.215	.253	.278	47	-6	0-0	.986	-6	86	46	C24		-0.2
1984	SF N	48	132	9	40	11	2	2	19	8-0	0	14	.303	.336	.462	128	5	1-1	.985	-11	74	52	C41		-0.7
1985	Mon N	42	71	4	12	2	0	1	7	7-0	0	11	.169	.244	.197	26	-7	1-0	.988	-3	125	0	C23,1b2	15	-1.0
	Tor A	6	15	0	4	0	0	0	1	0-0	0	0	.267	.267	.267	45	-1	0-0	1.000	2	246	168	C6	26	-1.0
Total	8	358	938	86	233	52	3	11	88	86-19	1	90	.248	.310	.345	81	-22	5-6	.987	-13	112	68	C305,O3L,1b2	67	-2.8

NIEBERGALL, CHARLIE Charles Arthur "Nig" B5.23.1899 New York NY D8.29.1982 Holiday FL BR/TR/5-10/160 d6.17

YEAR	TM LG	G	AB	R	H	2B	3B	HR	RBI	BB-IB	HP	SO	AVG	OBP	SLG	AOPS	ABR	SB-CS	FA	FR	RNG	THR	GAMES AT POSITION	DL	BFW
1921	StL N	5	6	1	1	0	0	0	0	0	0	0	.167	.167	.167	-12	-1	0-0	1.000	-0	52	203	C3		-0.1
1923	StL N	9	28	2	3	1	0	0	1	2	0	0	.107	.167	.143	-18	-5	0-0	1.000	-0	99	75	C7		-0.5
1924	StL N	40	58	6	17	6	0	0	7	3	1	9	.293	.339	.397	98	0	0-0	.951	0	111	117	C34		0.1
Total	3	54	92	9	21	7	0	0	8	5	1	11	.228	.276	.304	55	-6	0-0	.966	-1	105	107	C44		-0.5

NIEHAUS, AL Albert Bernard B6.1.1899 Cincinnati OH D10.14.1931 Cincinnati OH BR/TR/5-11/175 d4.22

YEAR	TM LG	G	AB	R	H	2B	3B	HR	RBI	BB-IB	HP	SO	AVG	OBP	SLG	AOPS	ABR	SB-CS	FA	FR	RNG	THR	GAMES AT POSITION	DL	BFW
1925	Pit N	17	64	7	14	8	0	0	7	1		5	.219	.242	.344	45	-5	0-0	.962	-2	82	89	1b15		-0.7
	Cin N	51	147	16	44	10	2	0	14	13	1	10	.299	.360	.395	95	-1	1-4	.988	2	123	134	1b45		-0.2
	Year	68	211	23	58	18	2	0	21	14	2	15	.275	.326	.379	80	-6	1-4	.981	0	111	121	1b60		-0.9

NIEHOFF, BERT John Albert B5.13.1884 Louisville CO D12.8.1974 Inglewood CA BR/TR/5-10.5/170 d10.4 C1

YEAR	TM LG	G	AB	R	H	2B	3B	HR	RBI	BB-IB	HP	SO	AVG	OBP	SLG	AOPS	ABR	SB-CS	FA	FR	RNG	THR	GAMES AT POSITION	DL	BFW
1913	Cin N	2	8	0	0	0	0	0	0	0	0	0	.000	.000	.000	-99	-2	0	.917	1	177	0	3b2		-0.1
1914	Cin N	142	484	46	117	16	9	4	49	38	1	77	.242	.298	.337	86	-10	20	.924	8	106	83	3b134,2b3		0.2
1915	†Phi N	148	529	61	126	27	2	4	49	30	1	63	.238	.280	.308	77	-15	21-11	.946	-5	97	103	2b148		-1.9
1916	Phi N	146	548	65	133	42	4	4	61	37	1	57	.243	.292	.356	95	-3	20-14	.936	1	102	120	2b144,3b2		0.0
1917	Phi N	114	361	30	92	17	4	2	42	23	2	29	.255	.303	.341	93	-3	20-14	.945	13	112	89	2b96,1b7,3b6		1.3
1918	StL N	22	84	5	15	2	0	0	5	3	0		.179	.207	.202	26	-8	2	.975	2	102	120	2b22		-0.6
	NY N	7	23	3	6	0	0	0	1	0	0	4	.261	.261	.261	60	-1	0	.871	-3	71	89	2b7		-0.4
	Year	29	107	8	21	2	0	0	6	3	0		.196	.218	.215	33	-9	2	.954	-1	95	113	2b29		-1.0
Total	6	581	2037	210	489	104	19	12	207	131	5	242	.240	.288	.327	84	-42	71-25	.943	16	102	106	2b420,3b144,1b7		-1.5

NIEKRO, LANCE Lance Joseph B1.29.1979 Winter Haven FL BR/TR/6-3/210* [SFN00 2/61] d9.5 f-Joe Col Florida Southern [DL 2004 SF N 6]

YEAR	TM LG	G	AB	R	H	2B	3B	HR	RBI	BB-IB	HP	SO	AVG	OBP	SLG	AOPS	ABR	SB-CS	FA	FR	RNG	THR	GAMES AT POSITION	DL	BFW
2003	SF N	5	5	2	1	0	0	1	2	0-0	1	1	.200	.200	.400	-51	0	0-0	1.000	0	156	150	1b3		-0.1
2005	SF N	113	278	32	70	16	3	12	46	17-0	2	53	.252	.295	.460	92	-4	0-2	.991	0	105	106	1b74/D		-1.1
Total	2	118	283	34	71	17	3	12	48	17-0	2	54	.251	.293	.459	94	-4	0-2	.992	-0	104	107	1b77/D	6	-1.2

YEAR	TM LG	G	AB	R	H	2B	3B	HR	RBI	BB-IB	HP	SO	AVG	OBP	SLG	AOPS	ABR	SB-CS	FA	FR	RNG	THR	GAMES AT POSITION	DL	BFW

NIELSEN, MILT Milton Robert B2.8.1925 Tyler MN BL/TL/5-11/190* d9.27

1949	Cle A	3	9	1	1	0	0	0	2	0	0	4	.111	.273	.111		4	-1	0-0	1.000	-0	87	0	O3C		-0.2
1951	Cle A	16	6	1	0	0	0	0	1	0	0	1	.000	.143	.000		-63	-1	0-0	—	0			/H		-0.1
Total	2	19	15	2	1	0	0	0	3	0	0	5	.067	.222	.067		-22	-2	0-0	1.000	-0	87	0	O3C		-0.3

NIEMAN, BUTCH Elmer Le Roy B2.8.1918 Herkimer KS D11.2.1993 Topeka KS BL/TL/6-2/195 d5.2 Col Kansas St.

1943	Bos N	101	335	39	84	15	8	7	46	39	1	39	.251	.331	.466		114	5	4	.963	-1	99	131	O93(76/1/16)		0.1
1944	Bos N	134	468	65	124	16	6	16	65	47		47	.265	.332	.427		108	4	5	.975	-1	96	116	O126(86/0/46)		-0.5
1945	Bos N	97	247	43	61	15	0	14	56	43	1	33	.247	.361	.478		131	11	11	.932	-2	100	84	O57(43/0/14)		0.6
Total	3	332	1050	147	269	46	14	37	167	129	2	119	.256	.339	.432		116	20	20	.961	-1	98	114	O276(205/1/76)		0.2

NIEMAN, BOB Robert Charles B1.26.1927 Cincinnati OH D3.10.1985 Corona CA BR/TR/5-11/195(185-205) d9.14 Col Kent St.

1951	StL A	12	43	6	16	3	1	2	8	3	0	5	.372	.413	.628		174	4	0-0	.962	-0	94	115	O11L		0.3
1952	StL A	131	478	66	138	22	2	18	74	46	1	73	.289	.352	.456		120	12	0-4	.976	1	101	107	O125(32/0/94)		0.7
1953	Det A	142	508	72	143	32	5	15	69	57	0	57	.281	.354	.453		118	12	0-3	.979	-1	103	93	O135(74/0/64)		0.6
1954	Det A	91	251	24	66	14	4	8	35	22	0	32	.263	.319	.422		105	1	0-2	.984	-1	100	55	O62L		-0.4
1955	Chi A	99	272	36	77	11	2	11	53	36-1	2	37	.283	.366	.460		119	7	1-0	.976	-2	94	78	O78(29/0/52)		0.2
1956	Chi A	14	40	3	12	1	0	2	4	4-2	0	4	.300	.364	.475		118	1	0-1	1.000	3	119		O10R		0.0
	Bal A	114	388	60	125	20	6	12	64	86-3	0	59	.322	.442	.497		161	40	1-5	.980	3	112	49	O114L		3.3
	Year	128	428	63	137	21	6	14	68	90-5	0	63	.320	.436	.495		156	40	1-6	.982	4	113	45	O124(114/0/10)		3.3
1957	Bal A	129	445	61	123	17	6	13	70	63-3	2	86	.276	.363	.429		125	16	4-4	.980	4	105	98	O120(116/0/4)		1.3
1958	Bal A	105	366	56	119	20	2	16	60	44-5	0	57	.325	.395	.522		159	30	2-8	.961	-3	96	63	O100L		2.1
1959	Bal A	118	360	49	105	18	2	21	60	42-3	2	55	.292	.367	.528		146	23	1-2	.973	3	105	115	O97L		2.0
1960	StL N	81	188	19	54	13	5	4	31	24-1	2	31	.287	.372	.473		120	6	0-1	.940	-5	88	0	O55(53/0/2)		-0.2
1961	StL N	6	17	0	8	1	0	0	2	0-0	0	4	.471	.471	.529		150	1	0-0	1.000	-1	35	0	O4L		-0.6
	Cle A	39	65	2	23	6	0	2	10	7-0	0	7	.354	.417	.538		157	6	1-0	.960	1	121	136	O12(7/0/5)		0.0
1962	Cle A	2	1	0	0	0	0	0	0	0-0	0	1	.000	.000	.000		-99	0	0-0	—	0			/H		0.0
	†SF N	30	30	1	9	2	0	1	3	1-0	0	9	.300	.323	.467		111	0	0-0	1.000	0	127	0	O3L		0.0
Total	12	1113	3452	455	1018	180	32	125	544	435-18	9	512	.295	.373	.474		132	159	10-30	.975	1	102	80	O926(702/0/231)		10.5

NIEMIEC, AL Alfred Joseph B5.18.1911 Meriden CT D10.29.1995 Kirkland WA BR/TR/5-11/158 d9.19 Col Holy Cross

1934	Bos A	9	32	2	7	0	0	0	3	3	0	4	.219	.286	.219		30	-3	0-0	1.000	3	121	131	2b9		0.0
1936	Phi A	69	203	22	40	3	2	1	20	26	1	16	.197	.291	.246		35	-22	2-2	.972	5	109	89	2b52,S5		-1.2
Total	2	78	235	24	47	3	2	1	23	29	1	20	.200	.291	.243		34	-25	2-2	.976	8	111	95	2b61,S5		-1.2

NIETO, TOM Thomas Andrew B10.27.1960 Downey CA BR/TR/6-1/205(193-210) [StLN81 3/60] d5.10 Col Oral Roberts

1984	StL N	33	86	7	24	4	0	3	12	5-2	0	18	.279	.312	.430		111	1	0-0	.994	0	120	94	C32		0.3
1985	†StL N	95	253	15	57	10	2	0	34	26-8	3	37	.225	.305	.281		65	-11	0-2	.990	-6	115	45	C95		-1.6
1986	Mon N	30	65	5	13	3	1	1	9	6-1	1	21	.200	.278	.323		65	-3	0-1	.978	-9	48	46	C30	21	-1.2
1987	Min A	41	105	7	21	7	1	1	12	8-0	1	24	.200	.276	.314		54	-7	0-0	.996	-3	67	79	C40/D	65	-0.8
1988	Min A	24	60	1	4	0	0	0	0	1-0	1	17	.067	.097	.067		-52	-12	0-0	.991	0	123	55	C24		-1.2
1989	Phi N	11	20	1	3	0	0	0	0	6-0	1	7	.150	.370	.150		54	-1	0-0	1.000	1	85	31	C11	60	0.1
1990	Phi N	17	30	1	5	0	0	0	4	3-0	1	11	.167	.265	.167		21	-3	0-0	.984	-0	94	78	C17	11	-0.3
Total	7	251	619	37	127	24	4	5	69	55-11	10	135	.205	.280	.281		56	-36	0-3	.991	-17	99	60	C249/D	157	-4.7

NIEVES, JOSE Jose Miguel (Pinto) B6.16.1975 Guacara, Venez BR/TR/6-1/180* d8.7

1998	Chi N	2	1	0	0	0	0	0	0	0-0	0	0	.000	.000	.000		-97	0	0-0	—	-0	0	0	/S		-0.1
1999	Chi N	54	181	16	45	9	1	2	18	8-0	4	25	.249	.291	.343		61	-11	0-2	.935	1	112	91	S52		-0.6
2000	Chi N	82	198	17	42	6	3	5	24	11-1	0	43	.212	.251	.348		51	-16	1-1	.949	-2	108	38	3b39,S24,2b7	17	-1.6
2001	Ana A	29	53	5	13	3	1	2	3	2-0	1	20	.245	.298	.453		92	-1	0-1	1.000	5	127	184	2b11,S10,3b2/1D	19	0.4
2002	Ana A	45	97	17	28	2	0	6	2-0		0	14	.289	.303	.309		64	-5	1-1	.938	-7	74	92	2b18,S13,3b5,1b3,O2(0/1/1)		-1.1
Total	5	212	530	55	128	20	5	9	51	23-1	6	102	.242	.278	.349		60	-33	2-5	.945	-3	101	91	S100,3b46,2b36,D4,1b4,O2(0/1/1)	36	-3.0

NIEVES, MELVIN Melvin Ramos B12.28.1971 San Juan, PR BB/TR/6-2/210(186-220) d9.1 b-Wilbert

1992	Atl N	12	19	0	4	1	0	0	1	2-0	0	7	.211	.286	.263		53	-1	0-0	.727	-1	99		O6(3/0/3)		-0.2
1993	SD N	19	47	4	9	0	0	2	3	3-0	1	21	.191	.255	.319		52	-3	0-0	.931	-0	116		O15R		-0.5
1994	SD N	10	19	2	5	1	0	1	4	3-0	0	10	.263	.364	.474		120	1	0-0	1.000	1	145	365	O6(2/0/4)		0.2
1995	SD N	98	234	32	48	6	1	14	38	19-0	5	88	.205	.276	.419		83	-7	2-3	.990	0	96	149	O79(62/6/15),1b2	32	-0.7
1996	Det A	120	431	71	106	23	4	24	60	44-2	6	158	.246	.322	.485		101	-1	1-2	.943	-1	98	122	O105(21/0/84),D11	15	-0.9
1997	Det A	116	359	46	82	18	1	20	64	39-6	5	157	.228	.311	.451		97	-3	1-7	.979	0	103	70	O99(0/2/99),D10	44	-0.2
1998	Cin N	83	119	8	30	4	0	2	17	26-1	0	42	.252	.381	.336		91	0	0-0	1.000	-1	89	82	O25(3/0/22),D3	91	-0.2
Total	7	458	1228	163	284	53	6	63	187	136-9	17	483	.231	.314	.438		93	-14	4-12	.962	-1	100	106	O335(91/8/242),D24,1b2	91	-3.3

NIEVES, WILBERT Wilbert B9.25.1977 San Juan, PR BR/TR/5-11/190* [SDN95 47/1286] d7.21 b-Melvin

2002	SD N	28	72	2	13	3	1	0	3	4-4	0	15	.181	.224	.250		29	-8	1-0	.971	-0	121	54	C27		-0.7
2005	NY A	3	4	0	0	0	0	0	0	0-0	0	1	.000	.000	.000		-99	-1	0-0	1.000	1	0	0	C3		0.0
Total	2	31	76	2	13	3	1	0	3	4-4	0	16	.171	.213	.237		22	-9	1-0	.973	1	115	51	C30		-0.7

NILAND, TOM Thomas James "Honest Tom" B4.14.1870 Brookfield MA D4.30.1950 Lynn MA BR/TR/5-11/160 d4.19

1896	StL N	18	68	3	12	0	1	0	3	5	1	4	.176	.243	.206		20	-8	0	.913	-2	117	210	O13(6/0/7),S5		-1.0

NILES, HARRY Herbert Clyde B9.10.1880 Buchanan MI D4.18.1953 Sturgis MI BR/TR/5-8/175 d4.24

1906	StL A	142	541	71	124	14	4	2	31	46	6		.229	.297	.281		85	11	256	193	O108(0/6/102),3b34	-0.2
1907	StL A	120	492	65	142	9	5	2	35	28	3		.289	.331	.339		114	7	19	.949	-3	102	112	2b116/OR	0.6
1908	NY A	95	361	43	90	14	6	4	24	25	4		.249	.305	.355		113	5	18	.928	-17	89	52	2b85,O7(1/1/5)	-1.4
	Bos A	18	33	4	8	0	1	0	3	6	1		.242	.375	.333		127	1	3	1.000	-1	89	88	2b8,S2	0.1
	Year	113	394	47	98	14	6	5	27	31	5		.249	.312	.353		114	6	21	.934	-18	89	55	2b93,O7(1/1/5),S2	-1.3
1909	Bos A	145	546	65	134	12	5	1	38	39	13		.245	.311	.291		88	-7	27	.952	-2	127	85	O117(77/12/28),3b13,S9,2b5	-1.7
1910	Bos A	18	57	6	12	3	0	1	3	4	0		.211	.262	.316		79	-1	1	.920	0	105	108	O15(4/0/11)	-0.2
	Cle A	70	240	25	51	6	4	1	18	15	3		.213	.267	.283		72	-9	9	.975	-5	97	105	O50(13/0/37),S7,3b5	-1.9
	Year	88	297	31	63	9	4	2	21	19	3		.212	.266	.290		73	-10	10	.962	-5	99	106	O65(17/0/48),S7,3b5	-2.0
Total	5	608	2270	279	561	58	24	12	152	163	30		.247	.306	.310		95	-13	107	.960	-16	165	125	O298(95/19/184),2b214,3b52,S18	-4.5

NILES, BILL William E. B1.11.1867 Covington KY D7.3.1936 Springfield OH ?/160 d5.13

1895	Pit N	11	37	2	8	0	0	0	5		0	2	.216	.310	.216		39	-3	2	.930	0	94	68	3b10/2		-0.2

NILL, RABBIT George Charles B7.14.1881 Ft.Wayne IN D5.24.1962 Fort Wayne IN BR/TR/5-7/160 d9.27

1904	Was A	15	48	4	8	0	1	0	3	5	2		.167	.273	.208		54	-2	0	.878	-3	89	66	2b15		-0.6
1905	Was A	103	319	46	58	7	3	3	31	33	5		.182	.269	.251		68	-11	12	.897	-1	98	135	3b52,2b33,S6		-1.1
1906	Was A	89	315	37	74	8	2	0	15	47	3		.235	.340	.273		97	2	16	.882	2	97	112	S31,2b25,3b15,O15C		0.5
1907	Was A	66	215	21	47	7	3	0	25	15	4		.219	.282	.279		86	0	6	.962	0	99	74	2b39,O18(17/0/1)/3		-0.4
	Cle A	12	43	5	12	1	0	0	2	3	0		.279	.326	.302		100	0	2	.815	-2	107	134	3b7,S4		-0.2
	Year	78	258	26	59	8	3	0	27	18	4		.229	.289	.283		88	-3	8	.962	-2	99	74	2b39,O18(17/0/1),3b8,S4		-0.6
1908	Cle A	11	23	3	5	0	0	0	1	0	0		.217	.217	.217		41	-2	0	.833	-1	109	120	S6,O3(2/0/2)/2		-0.2
Total	5	296	963	116	204	23	9	3	77	103	14		.212	.297	.264		82	-16	36	.943	-5	104	83	2b113,3b75,S47,O36(19/15/3)		-2.0

NILSSON, DAVE David Wayne B12.14.1969 Brisbane, Queensland, Australia BL/TR/6-3/215(185-240) d5.18

1992	Mil A	51	164	15	38	8	0	4	25	17-1	0	18	.232	.304	.354		85	-3	2-2	.992	1	142	78	C46,1b3,D2	18	0.0
1993	Mil A	100	296	35	76	10	2	7	40	37-5	3	36	.257	.336	.375		93	-3	3-6	.981	-8	90	74	C91,1b4,D4	44	-0.7
1994	Mil A	109	397	51	109	28	3	12	69	34-9	6	61	.275	.326	.451		94	-4	1-0	.994	-5	72	58	C60,D43,1b5	60	-0.2
1995	Mil A	81	263	41	73	12	1	12	53	24-4	2	41	.278	.337	.468		102	0	2-0	.981	-1	97	143	O58(15/0/47),D14,1b7,C2	60	-0.2
1996	Mil A	123	453	81	150	33	2	17	84	57-6	3	68	.331	.407	.525		129	22	2-3	.965	-1	88	121	O61(6/0/55),D40,1b24,C2	34	1.2
1997	Mil A	156	554	71	154	33	0	20	81	65-8	2	88	.278	.352	.464		106	6	2-3	.991	-3	84	129	1b74,D59,O22L		-0.7
1998	Mil N	102	309	39	83	14	1	12	56	33-1	1	48	.269	.339	.437		101	0	2-2	.984	-6	77	134	C101/D	43	-1.1
1999	Mil N★	115	343	56	106	19	1	21	62	53-6	2	64	.309	.400	.554		139	21	1-2	.991	-16	63	100	C309,O178(80/0/105),1b166,D163	22	1.0
Total	8	837	2779	389	789	157	10	105	470	320-40	10	424	.284	.356	.462		109	39	15-18	.988	-39	86	78	C309,O178(80/0/105),1b166,D163	221	-1.2

YEAR	TM LG	G	AB	R	H	2B	3B	HR	RBI	BB-IB	HP	SO	AVG	OBP	SLG	AOPS	ABR	SB-CS	FA	FR	RNG	THR	GAMES AT POSITION	DL	BFW

NIVAR, RAMON   Ramon A.   B2.22.1980 San Cristobal, D.R.   BR/TR/5-10/170(170-185)   d7.30

2003	Tex A	28	90	9	19	1	2	0	7	4-0	1	10	.211	.253	.267	35	-9	4-2	.961	2	108	267	O26C/D		-0.6
2004	Tex A	7	18	3	4	0	0	0	4	0-0	0	7	.222	.211	.222	16	-2	1-1	1.000	0	82	349	O6C		-0.2
2005	Bal A	7	13	1	4	0	0	0	1	0-0	1	2	.308	.357	.308	79	0	0-1	1.000	1	142	0	O4C		0.0
Total	3	42	121	13	27	1	2	0	12	4-0	2	19	.223	.258	.264	37	-11	5-4	.970	3	106	258	O36C/D		-0.8

NIX, LAYNCE   Laynce Michael   B10.30.1980 Houston TX   BL/TL/6-0/190*   [TexA00 4/124]   d7.10

2003	Tex A	53	184	25	47	10	0	8	30	9-0	1	53	.255	.289	.440	83	-5	3-0	.963	3	123	39	O52(5/21/37)		-0.3
2004	Tex A	115	371	58	92	20	4	14	46	23-4	2	113	.248	.293	.437	84	-10	1-1	.996	-8	87	78	O114(0/111/3)	26	-1.6
2005	Tex A	63	229	28	55	12	3	6	32	9-3	1	45	.240	.267	.397	71	-10	2-0	.988	0	103	99	O61C	80	-0.8
Total	3	231	784	111	194	42	7	28	108	41-7	2	211	.247	.285	.426	80	-25	6-1	.985	-4	100	75	O227(5/193/40)	106	-2.7

NIXON, AL   Albert Richard "Humpty Dumpty"   B4.11.1886 Atlantic City NJ   D11.9.1960 Opelousas LA   BR/TL/5-7.5/164   d9.4

1915	Bro N	14	26	3	6	1	0	0	2	2	0	4	.231	.286	.269	67	-1	1-1	1.000	0	85	130	O14(8/1/1)		-0.1
1916	Bro N	1	2	0	0	0	0	0	0	0	0	0	1.000	1.000	1.000	501	1	0	—	-0	0	0	/OL		0.1
1918	Bro N	6	11	1	5	0	0	0	0	0	0	0	.455	.455	.455	178	0	0	1.000	1	123	0	O4(2/0/1)		0.1
1921	Bos N	55	138	25	33	6	3	1	9	7	1	11	.239	.281	.348	69	-7	3-2	.980	2	115	83	O43(22/10/13)		-0.7
1922	Bos N	86	318	35	84	14	4	2	22	9	0	19	.264	.284	.352	66	-17	6-6	.975	2	115	65	O79(48/22/11)		-2.0
1923	Bos N	88	321	53	88	12	4	0	19	24	5	14	.274	.334	.336	81	-9	2-3	.987	7	105	141	O80(14/62/4)		-0.6
1926	Phi N	93	311	38	91	18	2	4	41	13	1	20	.293	.323	.402	90	-5	5	.977	2	104	100	O88C		-0.6
1927	Phi N	54	154	18	48	7	0	0	18	5	0	5	.312	.333	.357	84	-4	1	.969	2	116	74	O44(0/43/1)		-0.3
1928	Phi N	25	64	7	15	2	0	0	7	6	0	4	.234	.300	.266	47	-5	1	1.000	1	113	66	O20(10/0/10)		-0.5
Total	9	422	1345	180	372	60	13	7	118	66	7	77	.277	.314	.356	78	-46	19-12	.980	16	110	95	O373(105/226/41)		-4.6

NIXON, TROT   Christopher Trotman   B4.11.1974 Durham NC   BL/TL/6-2/200(196-210)   [BosA93 1/7]   d9.21

1996	Bos A	2	4	2	2	1	0	0	0-0		1	.500	.500	.750	207	1	1-0	1.000	0	134	0	O2R		0.1
1998	†Bos A	13	27	3	7	1	0	0	0	1-0	0	3	.259	.286	.296	51	-2	0-0	1.000	1	148	0	O7(1/0/6),D2		-0.1
1999	†Bos A	124	381	67	103	22	5	15	52	53-1	3	75	.270	.357	.472	108	5	3-1	.968	-7	95	38	O121R		-0.2
2000	Bos A	123	427	66	118	27	8	12	60	63-2	2	85	.276	.368	.461	106	5	8-1	.991	1	100	109	O118(0/6/115)/D	30	0.2
2001	Bos A	148	535	100	150	31	4	27	88	79-1	7	113	.280	.376	.505	130	25	7-4	.973	-5	95	85	O145(0/70/83)/D		1.6
2002	Bos A	152	532	81	136	36	4	24	94	65-2	5	109	.256	.338	.470	111	4	4-2	.984	-1	102	79	O152(0/13/145)		0.1
2003	†Bos A	134	441	81	135	24	6	28	87	65-4	3	96	.306	.396	.578	147	31	4-2	.983	-4	97	58	O130(0/1/129)		2.0
2004	†Bos A	48	149	24	47	9	1	6	23	15-1	1	24	.315	.377	.510	122	5	0-0	.985	-3	91	43	O40R,D3	117	0.1
2005	†Bos A	124	408	64	112	29	1	13	67	53-3	2	59	.275	.357	.446	107	6	2-1	.996	8	112	127	O118R,D2	27	0.8
Total	9	868	2904	488	810	180	28	125	471	394-14	24	565	.279	.366	.489	118	85	29-11	.983	-11	100	79	O833(1/90/759),D9	174	4.1

NIXON, OTIS   Otis Junior   B1.9.1959 Columbus Co. NC   BB/TR/6-2/180*   [NYA79 S1/3]   d9.9   b-Donell   Col Louisburg (NC) JC

1983	NY A	13	14	2	2	0	0	0	0	1-0	0	5	.143	.200	.143	-4	-2	2-0	.938	1	129	303	O9(0/4/5)		-0.1
1984	Cle A	49	91	16	14	0	0	0	1	8-0	0	11	.154	.220	.154	6	-12	12-6	1.000	2	105	124	O46(43/4/0)		-1.1
1985	Cle A	104	162	34	38	4	0	3	9	8-0	0	27	.235	.271	.315	60	-9	20-11	.971	6	122	170	O80(53/26/0),D11		-0.4
1986	Cle A	105	95	33	25	4	1	0	8	13-0	0	12	.263	.352	.326	87	-1	23-6	.969	3	110	132	O95(84/14/0),D5		0.3
1987	Cle A	19	17	2	1	0	0	0	1	3-0	0	4	.059	.200	.059	-26	-3	2-3	1.000	1	121	0	O17(11/7/0),D2		-0.3
1988	Mon N	90	271	47	66	8	2	0	15	28-0	1	42	.244	.312	.288	70	-10	46-13	.994	-1	101	55	O82(25/61/0)		-0.6
1989	Mon N	126	258	41	56	7	2	0	21	33-1	0	36	.217	.306	.260	62	-12	37-12	.988	-1	102	61	O98(13/92/1)		-1.0
1990	Mon N	119	231	46	58	6	2	1	20	28-0	0	33	.251	.331	.307	80	-6	50-13	.994	2	102	145	O88(21/71/0)/S		0.2
1991	Atl N	124	401	81	119	10	1	0	26	47-3	2	40	.297	.371	.327	93	-2	72-21	.987	3	107	92	O115(55/17/48)		0.7
1992	†Atl N	120	456	79	134	14	2	2	22	39-0	0	54	.294	.348	.346	92	-4	41-18	.991	10	119	93	O111(2/102/16)		0.7
1993	†Atl N	134	461	77	124	12	3	1	24	61-2	0	63	.269	.351	.315	79	-12	47-13	.990	1	105	68	O116(0/115/2)		-0.4
1994	Bos A	103	398	60	109	15	1	0	25	55-1	0	65	.274	.360	.317	74	-14	42-10	.989	-2	98	76	O103C		-0.9
1995	Tex A	139	589	87	174	21	2	0	45	58-1	0	85	.295	.357	.338	80	-16	50-21	.989	-5	98	56	O138C		-1.5
1996	Tor A	125	496	87	142	15	1	1	29	71-1	1	68	.286	.377	.327	81	-12	54-13	.994	1	108	66	O125C		-0.2
1997	Tor A	103	401	54	105	12	1	1	16	52-0	0	54	.262	.343	.304	72	-15	47-10	.996	-3	102	20	O102C/D	15	-1.0
	LA N	42	175	30	48	6	2	1	18	13-0	0	24	.274	.323	.349	81	-5	12-2	.990	-1	103	51	O42C		-0.4
1998	Min A	110	448	71	133	6	6	1	20	44-0	2	56	.297	.361	.344	83	-11	37-7	.989	-3	100	59	O108C	30	-0.7
1999	†Atl N	84	151	31	31	2	1	0	8	23-1	0	15	.205	.309	.232	40	-14	26-7	.981	-5	77	0	O52(50/5/0)	34	-1.6
Total	17	1709	5115	878	1379	142	27	11	368	585-10	9	694	.270	.343	.314	76	-160	620-186	.989	8	104	74	O1527(357/1136/72),D19/S	79	-8.3

NIXON, DONELL   Robert Donell   B12.31.1961 Evergreen NC   BR/TR/6-1/185*   [SeaA80 10/240]   d4.7   b-Otis   Col Louisburg (NC) JC   [DL 1985 Sea A 182]

1987	Sea A	46	132	17	33	4	0	3	12	13-0	2	28	.250	.327	.348	75	-5	21-7	1.000	0	101	77	O32(1/32/0),D6		-0.2
1988	SF N	59	78	15	27	3	0	0	6	10-0	1	12	.346	.420	.385	138	4	11-8	.983	1	117	0	O46(32/15/0)		0.5
1989	†SF N	95	166	23	44	2	0	1	15	11-1	0	30	.265	.311	.295	76	-5	10-3	.967	-3	96	0	O64(15/29/26)		-0.9
1990	Bal A	8	20	1	5	2	0	0	2	1-0	0	7	.250	.286	.350	79	-1	5-0	1.000	1	68	0	O4L,D3		0.0
Total	4	208	396	56	109	11	0	4	35	35-1	2	77	.275	.337	.333	88	-7	47-18	.983	-3	102	24	O146(52/76/26),D9	182	-0.6

NIXON, RUSS   Russell Eugene   B2.19.1935 Cleves OH   BL/TR/6-1/200*   d4.20   M5/C12

1957	Cle A	62	185	15	52	11	2	18	12-7	0	12	.281	.323	.362	88	-3	0-1	.984	-5	72	124	C57		-0.6
1958	Cle A	113	376	42	113	17	1	9	46	13-4	0	38	.301	.322	.439	111	3	0-3	.991	-8	84	83	C101		-0.1
1959	Cle A	82	258	23	62	10	3	1	29	15-1	0	28	.240	.277	.314	66	-13	0-1	.985	-6	89	88	C74		-1.6
1960	Cle A	25	82	6	20	5	0	1	6	6-2	0	6	.244	.308	.341	79	-2	0-1	.993	2	123	115	C25		0.0
	Bos A	80	272	24	81	17	3	5	33	13-3	0	23	.298	.329	.438	102	0	0-1	.987	-9	96	63	C74		-0.6
	Year	105	354	30	101	22	3	6	39	19-5	2	29	.285	.324	.415	97	-2	0-2	.989	-8	103	76	C99		-0.6
1961	Bos A	87	242	24	70	12	2	1	19	13-1	2	19	.289	.327	.368	84	-5	0-1	.975	-4	74	61	C66		-0.7
1962	Bos A	65	151	11	42	7	2	1	19	8-3	0	14	.278	.313	.371	81	-4	0-0	1.000	-4	76	69	C38		-0.1
1963	Bos A	98	287	27	77	18	1	5	30	22-5	4	32	.268	.327	.390	98	0	0-0	.992	-5	136	73	C76	31	-0.6
1964	Bos A	81	163	10	38	7	0	1	20	14-3	2	29	.233	.297	.294	64	-8	0-0	.990	-4	103	65	C45		-0.1
1965	Bos A	59	137	11	37	5	1	0	11	6-2	0	23	.270	.295	.321	72	-5	0-0	.981	-8	45	86	C38		-1.0
1966	Min A	51	96	5	25	2	1	0	7	7-3	1	13	.260	.314	.302	74	-3	0-0	.986	-4	75	85	C32		-1.2
1967	Min A	74	170	16	40	4	1	1	22	18-3	0	29	.235	.304	.300	74	-5	0-0	.994	-3	104	80	C69	30	-0.6
1968	Bos A	29	85	1	13	2	0	0	6	7-1	0	13	.153	.217	.176	19	-8	0-0	.994	-4	83	108	C27		-1.3
Total	12	906	2504	215	670	115	19	27	266	154-38	11	279	.268	.310	.361	84	-53	0-7	.988	-63	91	78	C722	31	-9.1

NOBLE, RAY   Rafael Miguel (Magee)   B3.15.1919 Central Hatillo, Cuba   D5.9.1998 Brooklyn NY   BR/TR/5-11/210(185-210)   d4.18   Negro Lg 1945-50

1951	†NY N	55	141	16	33	6	0	5	26	26	0	26	.234	.265	.383	72	-6	0-0	.974	-2	142	54	C41		-0.7
1952	NY N	6	5	0	0	0	0	0	0	1	0	0	1.000	.000	.000	-99	-1	0-0	1.000	0	0	0	C5		-0.1
1953	NY N	46	97	15	20	0	1	4	14	19	3	14	.206	.353	.351	83	-2	1-0	.982	0	146	90	C41		-0.1
Total	3	107	243	31	53	6	1	9	40	25	3	41	.218	.299	.362	74	-9	1-0	.979	-2	142	71	C87		-0.9

NOBOA, JUNIOR   Milciades Arturo (Diaz)   B11.10.1964 Azua, D.R.   BR/TR/5-10/160(155-170)   d8.22   OF(3/0/13)

1984	Cle A	23	11	3	4	0	0	0	0-0		2	.364	.364	.364	100	0	1-0	1.000	-3	74	103	2b19/D		-0.2
1987	Cle A	39	80	7	18	2	1	0	7	3-1	0	6	.225	.253	.275	40	-7	1-0	.983	-3	94	59	2b21,S8,3b5/D		-0.8
1988	Cal A	21	16	4	1	0	0	0	0-0		1	.063	.063	.063	-66	-4	0-0	.967	2	139	154	2b9,S3,3b2		-0.2
1989	Mon N	21	44	3	10	0	0	0	1	1-0	0	9	.227	.244	.227	35	-4	0-0	1.000	4	143	118	2b13,S4/3		0.1
1990	Mon N	81	158	15	42	7	2	0	14	7-2	1	14	.266	.294	.335	78	-5	4-1	1.000	-15	63	73	2b31,O9(2/0/7),3b8,S7/P		-2.0
1991	Mon N	67	95	5	23	3	0	1	2	1-1	0	5	.242	.250	.305	56	-6	2-3	1.000	-1	71	0	O7(1/0/6),2b6,3b2,S2/1		-0.8
1992	NY N	46	47	7	7	0	0	0	3	3-0	1	5	.149	.212	.149	5	-6	0-0	.977	3	133	139	2b16,3b3,S2		-0.3
1994	Oak N	17	40	3	13	1	1	0	2	0-0	0	5	.325	.357	.400	103	0	1-0	.943	-1	92	98	2b14/S		0.0
	Pit N	2	2	0	0	0	0	0	0	0-0	0	0	.000	.000	.000	-98	-1	0-0	1.000	0	286	0	/S		0.0
Total	8	317	493	47	118	13	4	1	33	17-4	2	47	.239	.266	.288	54	-33	9-4	.981	-14	95	95	2b129,S28,3b21,O16R,D2/1P		-4.2

NOCE, PAUL   Paul David   B12.16.1959 San Francisco CA   BR/TR/5-10/175*   [SDN81 14/343]   d6.1   Col Washington St.

1987	Chi N	70	180	17	41	9	2	3	14	6-1	2	49	.228	.261	.350	58	-12	5-3	.983	11	112	116	2b36,S35,3b2		0.3
1990	Cin N	1	1	0	1	0	0	0	0-0		0	1.000	1.000	1.000	434	0	0-0	—	0	0	0	/H		0.0
Total	2	71	181	17	42	9	2	3	14	6-1	2	49	.232	.265	.354	60	-12	5-3	.983	11	112	116	2b36,S35,3b2		0.3

NOFTSKER, GEORGE   George Washington   B8.24.1859 Shippensburg PA   D5.8.1931 Shippensburg PA   BR/TR/5-8/135   d4.17

| 1884 | Alt U | 7 | 25 | 1 | 1 | 0 | 0 | 0 | 0 | | | | .040 | .040 | .040 | -75 | -6 | | .818 | 0 | 0 | 0 | O5(0/1/4),C3 | | -0.5 |

YEAR	TM LG	G	AB	R	H	2B	3B	HR	RBI	BB-IB	HP	SO	AVG	OBP	SLG	AOPS	ABR	SB-CS	FA	FR	RNG	THR	GAMES AT POSITION	DL	BFW

NOKES, MATT Matthew Dodge B10.31.1963 San Diego CA BL/TR/6-1/185(185-210) [SFN81 20/503] d9.3

																									-0.4
1985	SF N	19	53	3	11	2	0	2	5	1-0	1	9	.208	.236	.358	67	-3	0-0	.977	-2	67	23	C14		0.2
1986	Det A	7	24	2	8	1	0	1	2	1-1	0	1	.333	.360	.500	131	1	0-0	1.000	1	147	43	C7		1.7
1987	†Det A★	135	461	69	133	14	2	32	87	35-2	6	70	.289	.345	.536	134	21	2-1	.992	-6	103	55	C109,D19,O3(3/0/1),3b2		1.4
1988	Det A	122	382	53	96	18	0	16	53	34-3	1	58	.251	.313	.424	108	3	0-1	.989	5	135	101	C110,D4		-0.5
1989	Det A	87	268	15	67	10	0	9	39	17-1	2	14	.250	.298	.388	94	-3	1-0	.978	-4	81	135	C51,D33	45	-0.5
1990	Det A	44	111	12	30	5	1	3	8	4-3	0	14	.270	.305	.414	99	-1	0-0	.984	-5	90	195	D24,C19		-0.9
	NY A	92	240	21	57	4	0	8	32	20-3	4	33	.237	.307	.354	84	-6	2-2	.995	-4	75	177	C46,D30,O2R		-1.4
	Year	136	351	33	87	9	1	11	40	24-6	4	47	.248	.306	.373	88	-6	2-2	.993	-9	79	182	C65,D54,O2R		0.3
1991	NY A	135	456	52	122	20	0	24	77	25-5	5	49	.268	.308	.469	112	5	3-2	.992	-10	73	97	C130,D3		-1.0
1992	NY A	121	384	42	86	9	1	22	59	37-11	3	62	.224	.293	.424	100	-2	0-1	.993	-14	72	84	C111	16	-0.9
1993	NY A	76	217	25	54	8	0	10	35	16-2	1	31	.249	.303	.424	97	-2	0-0	.992	-10	70	95	C56,D11	64	0.3
1994	NY A	28	79	11	23	3	0	7	19	5-0	0	16	.291	.329	.595	138	4	0-0	.975	-2	116	50	C17,1b4,D5		-0.5
1995	Bal A	26	49	4	6	1	0	2	6	4-0	0	11	.122	.185	.265	16	-6	0-0	.989	1	56	94	C16,D2	35	-0.1
	Col N	10	11	1	2	1	0	0	1	1-1	0	4	.182	.250	.273	29	-1	0-0	.909	0	0	0	C3		-0.3
Total	11	902	2735	310	695	96	4	136	422	200-32	26	395	.254	.308	.441	106	10	8-7	.990	-49	90	95	C689,D131,O5(3/0/3),1b4,3b2	160	-0.9

NOLAN, JOE Joseph William B5.12.1951 St.Louis MO BL/TR/6-0/190(175-203) [NYN69 2/28] d9.21

1972	NY N	4	10	0	0	0	0	0	0	1-0	0	3	.000	.091	.000	-73	-2	0-0	.938	-1	130	133	C3		-0.3
1975	Atl N	4	4	0	1	0	0	0	0	1-0	0	1	.250	.400	.250	81	0	0-0	1.000	0	0	/C		0.0
1977	Atl N	62	82	13	23	3	0	3	9	13-1	0	12	.280	.375	.427	104	1	1-0	1.000	-3	55	68	C19	15	-0.2
1978	Atl N	95	213	22	49	7	3	4	22	34-5	1	28	.230	.339	.347	83	-4	3-2	.979	-9	78	46	C61		-1.1
1979	Atl N	89	230	28	57	9	3	4	21	27-3	3	28	.248	.333	.365	86	-4	1-3	.983	-9	62	71	C74		-1.1
1980	Atl N	17	22	2	6	1	0	0	2	2-0	0	4	.273	.333	.318	82	0	0-0	1.000	1	66	137	C6		0.2
	Cin N	53	154	14	48	7	0	3	24	13-0	0	8	.312	.353	.416	120	4	0-0	.982	-4	63	96	C51		0.3
	Year	70	176	16	54	8	0	3	26	15-0	0	12	.307	.350	.403	114	4	0-0	.983	-3	63	99	C57		0.4
1981	Cin N	81	236	25	73	18	1	3	26	24-6	1	19	.309	.371	.407	122	8	1-2	.995	-7	81	45	C81		-0.9
1982	Bal A	77	219	24	51	7	1	6	35	16-1	0	35	.233	.278	.356	75	-8	1-1	.978	-3	72	116	C72	22	0.2
1983	†Bal A	73	184	25	51	11	1	5	24	16-1	2	31	.277	.342	.429	112	3	0-0	.962	-0	95	312	D11,C6	90	0.2
1984	Bal A	35	62	2	18	1	1	1	12	12-4	1	10	.290	.400	.387	123	3	0-0	1.000	1	59	0	C5,D4	97	-0.4
1985	Bal A	31	38	1	5	2	0	0	6	5-1	0	5	.132	.227	.184	16	-4	0-0	1.000	1	99	0	C5,D4	224	-3.2
Total	11	621	1454	156	382	66	10	27	178	164-22	7	183	.263	.336	.378	96	-3	7-8	.984	-41	75	74	C444,D15	224	-3.2

NONNENKAMP, RED Leo William B7.7.1910 St.Louis MO D12.3.2000 Little Rock AR BL/TL/5-11/165 d9.6

1933	Pit N	1	1	0	0	0	0	0	0	1-0	0	1	.000	.000	.000	-99	0	0-0	—		0		/H		0.0
1938	Bos A	87	180	37	51	4	1	0	18	21	0	13	.283	.358	.317	67	-9	6-1	.968	3	111	150	O39(5/5/29),1b5		-0.7
1939	Bos A	58	75	12	18	2	1	0	5	12	0	6	.240	.345	.293	62	-4	0-1	.962	-1	99	0	O15(7/4/4)		-0.3
1940	Bos A	9	7	0	0	0	0	0	0	1-0	1	4	.000	.125	.000	-62	-2	0-0	—		0		/H		-0.2
Total	4	155	263	49	69	6	2	0	24	33	1	24	.262	.347	.300	62	-15	6-2	.966	2	108	117	O54(12/9/33),1b5		-1.4

NOONAN, PETE Peter John B11.24.1881 W.Stockbridge MA D2.11.1965 Great Barrington MA BR/TR/6-0/180 d6.20 Col Holy Cross

1904	Phi A	39	114	13	23	3	1	2	13	1	0		.202	.209	.298	56	-6	1	.969	-2	100	110	C22,1b10		-0.7
1906	Chi N	5	3	0	1	0	0	0	0	0	0		.333	.333	.333	102	0	0	1.000	0	2150	/1		-0.8
	StL N	44	125	8	21	1	3	1	9	11	0		.168	.235	.248	53	-7	1	.957	-2	82	111	C23,1b16		-0.8
	Year	49	128	8	22	1	3	1	9	11	0		.172	.237	.250	54	-8	1	.957	-2	82	111	C23,1b17		-0.8
1907	StL N	74	237	19	53	7	3	1	16	9	0		.224	.252	.291	73	-9	3	.951	-3	83	95	C70		-2.1
Total	3	162	479	40	98	11	7	4	38	21	0		.205	.238	.282	64	-22	5	.955	-7	85	101	C115,1b27		-2.1

NORDBROOK, TIM Timothy Charles B7.7.1949 Baltimore MD BR/TR/6-1/170* [BalA70 9/222] d9.13 Col Loyola-Maryland

1974	Bal A	6	15	4	4	0	0	0	2	2-0	0	2	.267	.353	.267	82	1	1-0	1.000	0	100	133	S5/2		0.1
1975	Bal A	40	34	6	4	1	0	0	0	7-0	0	7	.118	.268	.147	21	-3	0-0	.970	-2	110	90	S37,2b3		-0.3
1976	Bal A	27	22	4	5	0	0	0	0	3-0	0	5	.227	.320	.227	66	-1	0-0	1.000	-3	52	58	2b14,S12/D		-0.2
	Cal A	5	8	1	0	0	0	0	0	1-0	0	3	.000	.111	.000	-70	-2	0-0	.941	-1	89	0	S4/2		-0.5
	Year	32	30	5	5	0	0	0	0	4-0	0	8	.167	.265	.167	30	-3	0-0	.978	-4	94	90	S16,2b15/D		-0.2
1977	Chi A	15	20	2	5	0	0	0	1	7-0	0	4	.250	.429	.250	95	0	1-0	.850	-4	70	59	S11/3D		0.1
	Tor A	24	63	9	11	1	0	1	4	4-0	0	11	.175	.224	.206	18	-7	1-0	.989	-3	89	71	S24		-1.0
	Year	39	83	11	16	1	0	1	5	11-0	0	15	.193	.284	.217	39	-7	2-0	.947	-7	84	68	S35,D2/3		0.1
1978	Tor A	7	0	1	0	0	0	0	0	0-0	0			1.000			200		0-0	1.000	0	119	112	S7		0.0
	Mil A	2	5	0	1	0	0	0	0	1-0	0		.200	.167	.200	-49	-1	0-0	.909	0	158	0	S2		0.0
	Year	9	5	1	1	0	0	0	0	1-0	0	1	.200	.286	.000	-13	-1	0-0	.941	1	141	48	S9		-0.1
1979	Mil A	2	2	0	1	0	0	0	0	0-0	0	1	.500	.500	.500	170	0	0-0	1.000	-1	0	0	S2	152	-1.8
Total	6	128	169	27	30	1	1	0	7	33	0	33	.178	.286	.195	38	-14	4-0	.961	-13	95	79	S104,2b19,D3/3	152	-1.8

NORDHAGEN, WAYNE Wayne Oren B7.4.1948 Thief River Falls MN BR/TR/6-2/205(195-210) [NYA68 7/136] d7.16 Col Treasure Valley (OR) CC

1976	Chi A	22	53	6	10	2	0	0	4	4-0	0	12	.189	.233	.226	39	-4	1-0	1.000	1	118	167	O10R,C5,D6		-0.4
1977	Chi A	52	124	16	39	7	3	4	22	2-0	0	12	.315	.323	.516	125	3	1-0	.944	-4	83	45	O46(12/2/34),C3,D2		-0.2
1978	Chi A	68	206	28	62	16	0	5	35	5-0	0	18	.301	.310	.451	113	3	0-1	.941	-6	79	100	O36(19/0/18),D16,C12	44	-0.5
1979	Chi A	78	193	20	54	15	0	7	25	13-2	0	22	.280	.324	.466	110	3	0-0	1.000	1	98	562	D47,O12(6/0/7),C5,P2		0.1
1980	Chi A	123	415	45	115	22	4	15	59	10-3	1	45	.277	.294	.466	103	-1	0-1	.969	-3	88	120	O74(45/0/33),D32		-0.8
1981	Chi A	65	208	19	64	8	1	6	33	10-0	1	25	.308	.338	.442	127	3	0-1	.947	-4	81	111	O60(25/1/36)		-0.1
1982	Tor A	44	115	8	32	3	0	1	14	9-1	0	13	.278	.328	.330	76	-4	0-2	1.000	-0	73	175	D32,O10(10/0/1)	51	-0.6
	Pit N	1	4	2	0	0	0	0	2	0-0	0	1	.500	.500	.500	173	0	0-0	1.000	-0	100		/OL		0.0
	Tor A	28	70	6	18	3	0	0	6	1-0	0	9	.257	.264	.300	51	-5	0-0	—	-0	0		D28		-0.6
1983	Chi N	21	35	1	5	1	0	1	4	0-0	0	5	.143	.162	.257	15	-4	0-0	1.000	-1	65	0	O7L		-0.6
Total	8	502	1423	144	401	77	8	39	206	54-6	3	162	.282	.306	.429	101	-3	1-5	.962	-17	85	124	O256(125/3/139),D163,C25,P2	95	-3.7

NORDYKE, LOU Louis Ellis B8.7.1876 Brighton IA D9.27.1945 Los Angeles CA BL/TR/6-0/185 d4.18

1906	StL A	25	53	4	13	1	0	0	7	10	0		.245	.365	.264	102	1	3	.942	-3	53	261	1b12		-0.2

NOREN, IRV Irving Arnold B11.29.1924 Jamestown NY BL/TL/6-0/190* d4.18 C5 Col Pasadena (CA) City

1950	Was A	138	542	80	160	27	10	14	98	67	2	77	.295	.375	.459	108	14	5-2	.984	9	102	184	O121C,1b17		1.8
1951	Was A	129	509	82	142	33	5	8	86	51	0	35	.279	.345	.411	105	3	10-7	.978	12	117	113	O126C		1.2
1952	Was A	12	49	4	12	3	1	0	2	6	0	3	.245	.327	.347	91	-1	1-0	1.000	2	115	196	O12C		0.1
	†NY A	93	272	36	64	13	2	5	21	26	6	34	.235	.316	.353	91	-4	4-2	1.000	-3	91	83	O60(18/18/25),1b19		-0.9
	Year	105	321	40	76	16	3	5	23	32	6	37	.237	.318	.352	91	-4	5-2	1.000	-1	96	107	O72(18/30/25),1b19		-0.8
1953	†NY A	109	345	55	92	12	6	6	46	42	2	39	.267	.350	.388	103	1	3-3	.991	3	100	143	O96(21/44/38)		1.7
1954	NY A★	125	426	70	136	21	6	12	66	43	1	39	.319	.377	.481	140	23	4-6	.980	1	99	107	O116(55/23/49)/1		-0.6
1955	†NY A	132	371	49	94	19	1	8	59	43-5	3	33	.253	.331	.375	92	-4	3-3	.980	4	108	104	O126(117/10/3)		0.7
1956	NY A	29	37	4	8	1	0	0	6	12-2	0	7	.216	.408	.243	78	1	0-0	.875	-0	58	253	O10(4/0/6)/1	77	-0.1
1957	KC A	81	160	8	34	8	0	2	16	11-2	1	19	.213	.267	.300	54	-10	0-0	.990	-1	86	117	1b25,O6R		-1.3
	StL N	17	30	1	11	4	1	0	4	4-2	0	6	.367	.429	.667	189	4	0-1	1.000	-1	66	0	O8(1/0/7)		0.3
1958	StL N	117	178	24	47	9	1	4	22	13-2	4	21	.264	.327	.393	87	-3	0-0	.974	-2	96	0	O77(59/14/10)		-0.8
1959	StL N	8	8	0	1	0	0	0	1	0-0	0	3	.125	.125	.250	-3	-1	0-0	—	0	0	0	O2L/1		-0.1
	Chi N	65	156	27	50	6	2	4	19	13-1	3	24	.321	.384	.462	125	6	2-0	1.000	2	106	137	O40(16/6/18)/1		0.7
	Year	73	164	27	51	6	2	4	19	13-1	3	27	.311	.372	.451	118	4	2-0	1.000	2	105	136	O42(18/6/18),1b2		0.6
1960	Chi N	12	11	0	1	0	0	0	0	3-0	0	4	.091	.286	.091	9	-0	0-0	.833	0	0	133	/1OR		-0.2
	LA N	26	25	1	5	0	0	1	1-0	1	0	8	.200	.231	.320	46	-2	0-0	1.000	-0	0	0	/H		-0.4
	Year	38	36	1	6	0	0	1	1	4-0	0	12	.167	.250	.250	36	-3	0-0	1.000	-0	0	133	/1OR		-0.7
Total	11	1093	3119	443	857	157	35	65	453	335-14	22	350	.275	.348	.410	106	25	34-24	.984	27	104	124	O801(293/374/163),1b66	77	1.6

NORMAN, DAN Daniel Edmund B1.11.1955 Los Angeles CA BR/TR (BB 1908p)/6-2/195* [CinN74 15/359] d9.27 Col Barstow (CA) CC

1977	NY N	7	16	2	4	1	0	0	4	4-0	0	5	.250	.400	.313	97	-0	0-0	1.000	-1	88	0	O6(0/1/6)		-0.1
1978	NY N	19	64	7	17	1	4	1	10	2-0	0	14	.266	.284	.484	115	0	1-0	1.000	-0	99	70	O18(1/0/18)		-0.1
1979	NY N	44	110	9	27	3	1	3	11	10-2	1	26	.245	.311	.373	89	-2	2-0	.967	1	95	169	O33(8/0/25)		-0.5
1980	NY N	69	92	5	17	1	1	2	9	6-0	0	14	.185	.235	.283	44	-7	5-0	1.000	-1	78	99	O19(9/0/10)		-1.0

YEAR	TM LG	G	AB	R	H	2B	3B	HR	RBI	BB-IB	HP	SO	AVG	OBP	SLG	AOPS	ABR	SB-CS	FA	FR	RNG	THR	GAMES AT POSITION	DL	BFW
1982	Mon N	53	66	6	14	3	0	2	7	7-0	0	20	.212	.288	.348	74	-2	0-1	.969	-1	91	87	O31(17/6/8)		-0.4
Total	5	192	348	29	79	8	3	11	37	29-2	1	76	.227	.287	.362	80	-11	8-1	.981	-2	92	109	O107(35/7/67)		-1.6

NORMAN, BILL   Henry Willis Patrick B7.16.1910 St.Louis MO   D4.21.1962 Milwaukee WI   BR/TR/6-2/190   d8.8   M2/C2   Col St.Louis

YEAR	TM LG	G	AB	R	H	2B	3B	HR	RBI	BB-IB	HP	SO	AVG	OBP	SLG	AOPS	ABR	SB-CS	FA	FR	RNG	THR	GAMES AT POSITION	DL	BFW
1931	Chi A	24	55	7	10	2	0	0	6	4	0	10	.182	.237	.218	22	-6	0-1	.933	1	117	96	O17(3/14/0)		-0.6
1932	Chi A	13	48	6	11	3	1	0	2	2	0	3	.229	.260	.333	56	-3	0-0	.917	-1	72	233	O13(1/11/1)		-0.4
Total	2	37	103	13	21	5	1	0	8	6	0	13	.204	.248	.272	38	-9	0-1	.928	-0	97	156	O30(4/25/1)		-1.0

NORMAN, LES   Leslie Eugene B2.25.1969 Warren MI   BR/TR/6-1/185*   [KCA91 25/652]   d5.29   Col St.Francis (IL)

YEAR	TM LG	G	AB	R	H	2B	3B	HR	RBI	BB-IB	HP	SO	AVG	OBP	SLG	AOPS	ABR	SB-CS	FA	FR	RNG	THR	GAMES AT POSITION	DL	BFW
1995	KC A	24	40	6	9	0	1	0	4	6-0	0	6	.225	.326	.275	57	-3	0-1	.958	-1	88	131	O17(4/5/8),D5		-0.4
1996	KC A	54	49	9	6	0	0	0	0	6-0	1	14	.122	.232	.122	-7	-8	1-1	1.000	2	129	89	O38(15/3/20),D7		-0.6
Total	2	78	89	15	15	0	1	0	4	12-0	1	20	.169	.275	.191	22	-11	1-2	.986	1	112	107	O55(19/8/28),D12	57	-1.0

NORMAN, NELSON   Nelson Augusto B5.23.1958 San Pedro de Macoris, D.R.   BB/TR (BR 1978, 1979p)/6-2/160*   d5.20   C1

YEAR	TM LG	G	AB	R	H	2B	3B	HR	RBI	BB-IB	HP	SO	AVG	OBP	SLG	AOPS	ABR	SB-CS	FA	FR	RNG	THR	GAMES AT POSITION	DL	BFW
1978	Tex A	23	34	1	9	2	0	0	1	0-0	0	5	.265	.265	.324	64	-2	0-0	.984	5	146	118	S18,3b6		0.4
1979	Tex A	147	343	36	76	9	3	0	21	19-0	0	41	.222	.260	.265	43	-28	4-1	.952	-29	83	86	S142/2		-4.4
1980	Tex A	17	32	4	7	0	0	0	1	1-0	0	1	.219	.242	.219	28	-3	0-1	.943	5	124	145	S17		0.3
1981	Tex A	7	13	1	3	1	0	0	2	1-0	0	2	.231	.267	.308	74	0	0-0	.963	3	153	186	S5		0.3
1982	Pit N	3	3	0	0	0	0	0	0	0-0	0	0	.000	.000	.000	-96	-1	0-0	.667	-1	37	0	2b2/S		-0.2
1987	Mon N	1	4	0	0	0	0	0	0	0-0	0	1	.000	.000	.000	-96	-1	0-0	—	-1	0	0	/S		-0.2
Total	6	198	429	42	95	12	3	0	25	21-0	0	50	.221	.256	.263	42	-35	4-2	.954	-18	93	95	S184,3b6,2b3		-3.8

NORRIS, JIM   James Francis B12.20.1948 Brooklyn NY   BL/TL/5-10/175(175-190)   [CleA71*A5/109]   d4.7   Col Maryland-Baltimore Co.

YEAR	TM LG	G	AB	R	H	2B	3B	HR	RBI	BB-IB	HP	SO	AVG	OBP	SLG	AOPS	ABR	SB-CS	FA	FR	RNG	THR	GAMES AT POSITION	DL	BFW
1977	Cle A	133	440	59	119	23	6	2	37	64-4	0	57	.270	.360	.364	102	4	26-17	.982	8	116	108	O124(3/74/49),1b3		0.8
1978	Cle A	113	315	41	89	14	5	2	27	42-4	0	20	.283	.364	.378	111	6	12-7	.982	4	109	126	O78(26/5/51),D15,1b6		0.6
1979	Cle A	124	353	50	87	15	6	3	30	44-1	0	35	.246	.327	.348	83	-8	15-10	.982	3	117	34	O93(47/23/28),D13		-0.8
1980	Tex A	119	174	23	43	5	0	0	16	23-2	0	16	.247	.327	.276	71	-6	6-3	1.000	-3	84	101	O82(7/19/57),1b10/D		-1.1
Total	4	489	1282	173	338	57	17	7	110	173-11	0	128	.264	.348	.351	94	-4	59-37	.985	12	110	91	O377(83/121/185),D29,1b19		-0.5

NORRIS, LEO   Leo John B5.17.1908 Bay St.Louis MS   D2.13.1987 Zachary LA   BR/TR/5-11/165   d4.14

YEAR	TM LG	G	AB	R	H	2B	3B	HR	RBI	BB-IB	HP	SO	AVG	OBP	SLG	AOPS	ABR	SB-CS	FA	FR	RNG	THR	GAMES AT POSITION	DL	BFW
1936	Phi N	154	581	64	154	27	4	11	76	39	3	79	.265	.315	.382	79	-18	4	.936	-3	93	84	S121,2b38		-1.0
1937	Phi N	116	381	45	98	24	3	9	36	21	0	53	.257	.296	.407	82	-10	3	.949	-8	94	83	2b74,3b24,S20		-1.2
Total	2	270	962	109	252	51	7	20	112	60	3	132	.262	.307	.392	80	-28	7	.940	-11	94	84	S141,2b112,3b24		-2.2

NORTH, BILLY   William Alex B5.15.1948 Seattle WA   BB/TR (BR 1971)/5-11/185*   [ChiN69 12/278]   d9.3   Col Central Washington

YEAR	TM LG	G	AB	R	H	2B	3B	HR	RBI	BB-IB	HP	SO	AVG	OBP	SLG	AOPS	ABR	SB-CS	FA	FR	RNG	THR	GAMES AT POSITION	DL	BFW
1971	Chi N	8	16	3	6	0	0	0	0	4-1	1	6	.375	.524	.375	138	1	1-1	1.000	-1	42	0	O6(1/0/5)		-0.1
1972	Chi N	66	127	22	23	2	3	0	4	13-1	1	31	.181	.262	.244	40	-10	6-0	.955	-1	89	146	O48(9/26/15)		-1.2
1973	Oak A	146	554	98	158	10	5	5	34	78-5	3	89	.285	.376	.348	110	-3	53-20	.980	15	**120**	136	O138(0/136/2),D6		2.7
1974	†Oak A	149	543	79	141	20	5	4	33	69-1	5	86	.260	.347	.337	104	1	**54**-26	.991	11	119	92	O138C,D8		1.6
1975	†Oak A	140	524	74	143	17	5	1	43	81-3	4	80	.273	.373	.330	102	6	30-12	.975	11	120	106	O138(4/134/0)/D		1.6
1976	Oak A	154	590	91	163	20	5	2	31	73-3	2	95	.276	.356	.337	108	9	**75**-29	.978	-4	99	74	O144(0/137/7),D8		0.8
1977	Oak A	56	184	32	48	3	1	9	32-2	2	25	.261	.376	.326	95	0	17-13	.983	-4	93	31	O52C/D		-0.5
1978	Oak A	24	52	5	11	4	0	0	5	9-2	2	13	.212	.344	.288	85	0	3-2	1.000	-1	88	120	O17C		-0.1
	†LA N	110	304	54	71	10	0	0	10	65-2	2	48	.234	.371	.266	81	-4	27-8	.975	-3	101	40	O103(1/102/0)		-0.5
1979	SF N	142	460	87	119	15	4	5	30	96-3	1	84	.259	.386	.341	108	11	58-24	.987	4	105	98	O130C		1.6
1980	SF N	128	415	73	104	12	1	1	19	81-5	1	78	.251	.373	.292	91	0	45-19	.982	4	111	82	O115(1/114/0)		0.7
1981	SF N	46	131	22	29	7	0	1	12	26-0	1	39	.221	.354	.298	89	0	26-8	.966	-3	93	42	O37C		-0.1
Total	11	1169	3900	640	1016	120	31	20	230	627-28	25	665	.261	.365	.323	99	28	395-162	.981	26	108	90	O1066(16/1023/29),D24	81	6.5

NORTHEN, HUB   Hubbard Elwin B8.16.1885 Atlanta TX   D10.1.1947 Shreveport LA   BL/TL/5-8/175   d9.10

YEAR	TM LG	G	AB	R	H	2B	3B	HR	RBI	BB-IB	HP	SO	AVG	OBP	SLG	AOPS	ABR	SB-CS	FA	FR	RNG	THR	GAMES AT POSITION	DL	BFW
1910	StL A	26	96	8	19	4	0	0	16	5	0		.198	.238	.208	42	-7	2	.926	-3	94	54	O26C		-1.2
1911	Cin N	1	0	0	0	0	0	0	0	0	0		—	—	—	0	0		—	0			/H		0.0
	Bro N	19	76	16	24	2	2	0	1	14	1	9	.316	.429	.395	137	5	4	.911	0	96	164	O19C		0.4
	Year	20	76	16	24	2	2	0	1	14	1	9	.316	.429	.395	137	5	4	.911	0	96	164	O19C		0.4
1912	Bro N	118	412	54	116	26	6	3	46	41	4	46	.282	.332	.396	109	5	8	.950	-6	92	76	O102(10/43/49)		-0.7
Total	3	164	584	76	159	29	8	3	63	60	5	55	.272	.345	.365	103	3	14	.939	-8	93	85	O147(10/88/49)		-1.5

NORTHEY, RON   Ronald James B4.26.1920 Mahanoy City PA   D4.16.1971 Pittsburgh PA   BL/TR/5-10/195(195-215)   d4.14   Mil 1945   C3   s-Scott   [DL 1951 Chi N 88]

YEAR	TM LG	G	AB	R	H	2B	3B	HR	RBI	BB-IB	HP	SO	AVG	OBP	SLG	AOPS	ABR	SB-CS	FA	FR	RNG	THR	GAMES AT POSITION	DL	BFW
1942	Phi N	127	402	31	101	13	2	5	31	28	0	33	.251	.300	.331	89	-7	2	.952	2	104	130	O109R		-1.2
1943	Phi N	147	586	72	163	31	5	16	68	51	3	52	.278	.339	.430	127	18	2	.978	1	97	122	O145R		1.0
1944	Phi N	152	570	72	164	35	9	22	104	67	4	51	.288	.367	.496	146	34	1	.981	1	90	141	O151R		2.5
1946	Phi N	128	438	55	109	24	6	16	62	39	2	59	.249	.313	.441	116	6	1	.971	-4	97	68	O111R		-0.1
1947	Phi N	13	47	7	12	3	0	0	3	6	0	12	.255	.340	.319	79	-1	1	1.000	-0	87	106	O13R		-0.2
	StL N	110	311	52	91	19	3	15	63	48	2	29	.293	.391	.518	133	16	0	.949	-3	87	137	O94(15/0/79),3b2		1.0
	Year	123	358	59	103	22	3	15	66	54	2	32	.288	.384	.492	127	15	1	.955	-3	87	133	O107(15/0/92),3b2		0.8
1948	StL N	96	246	40	79	10	1	13	64	38	4	25	.321	.420	.528	147	17	0	.989	-4	86	54	O67R		1.2
1949	StL N	90	265	28	69	18	2	7	50	31	0	15	.260	.340	.423	98	0	0	.980	-8	73	68	O73R		-1.1
1950	Cin N	27	77	11	20	5	0	5	9	15	0	6	.260	.380	.519	134	4	0	.955	-2	79	0	O24R		0.1
	Chi N	53	114	11	32	9	0	4	20	10	0	9	.281	.339	.465	110	2	0	.976	0	88	168	O27R		0.1
	Year	80	191	22	52	14	0	9	29	25	0	15	.272	.356	.487	120	6	0	.969	-2	84	102	O51R		0.2
1952	Chi N	1	1	0	0	0	0	0	0	0	0	0	.000	.000	.000	-99	0	0-0	—	0			/H		0.0
1955	Chi A	14	14	1	5	2	0	1	4	3-0	0	3	.357	.471	.714	209	2	0-0	1.000	0	66	0	O2R		0.2
1956	Chi A	53	48	4	17	2	0	3	23	8-2	5	1	.354	.417	.583	168	5	0-0	1.000	0	75	490	O4(3/0/3)		0.5
1957	Chi A	40	27	0	5	1	0	0	7	11-1	0	1	.185	.410	.222	80	0	0-0	—	0			/H		0.0
	Phi N	33	26	1	7	0	0	1	5	6-1	0	4	.269	.406	.385	118	1	0-0	—	0			/H		0.1
Total	12	1084	3172	385	874	172	28	108	513	361-4	15	297	.276	.352	.450	124	97	7-0	.972	-17	92	112	O820(18/0/804),3b2	88	4.1

NORTHEY, SCOTT   Scott Richard B10.15.1946 Philadelphia PA   BR/TR/6-0/175   d9.2   f-Ron

YEAR	TM LG	G	AB	R	H	2B	3B	HR	RBI	BB-IB	HP	SO	AVG	OBP	SLG	AOPS	ABR	SB-CS	FA	FR	RNG	THR	GAMES AT POSITION	DL	BFW
1969	KC A	20	61	11	16	2	2	1	7	7-0	0	19	.262	.338	.410	107	0	6-3	.973	-0	99	104	O18C		

NORTHRUP, JIM   James Thomas B11.24.1939 Breckenridge MI   BL/TR/6-3/190(190-205)   d9.30   Col Alma

YEAR	TM LG	G	AB	R	H	2B	3B	HR	RBI	BB-IB	HP	SO	AVG	OBP	SLG	AOPS	ABR	SB-CS	FA	FR	RNG	THR	GAMES AT POSITION	DL	BFW
1964	Det A	5	12	1	1	1	0	0	0	0	0	3	.083	.083	.167	-32	-2	1-0	1.000	-0	93	0	O2(0/2/1)		-0.2
1965	Det A	80	219	20	45	12	3	4	16	12-1	2	50	.205	.253	.315	60	-12	1-1	.976	-5	90	0	O54(10/6/38)		-2.1
1966	Det A	123	419	53	111	24	6	16	58	33-4	4	52	.265	.322	.465	121	11	4-7	.980	10	**123**	132	O113(3/11/106)		1.3
1967	Det A	144	495	53	134	18	6	10	61	43-6	3	83	.271	.332	.392	110	6	7-1	.972	-2	106	37	O143(65/94/39)		-0.1
1968	†Det A	154	580	76	153	29	7	21	90	50-4	4	87	.264	.324	.447	129	19	4-5	.979	4	**113**	78	O151(12/47/103)		1.6
1969	Det A	148	543	79	160	31	5	25	66	52-1	3	83	.295	.358	.508	135	24	4-2	.985	5	111	83	O143(29/89/49)		2.4
1970	Det A	139	504	71	132	21	3	24	80	58-6	7	68	.262	.343	.458	119	13	3-6	.993	2	110	47	O136(34/39/78)		0.7
1971	Det A	136	459	72	124	27	2	16	71	60-9	2	43	.270	.355	.442	120	13	7-4	.981	-3	94	64	O127(50/42/72),1b32		0.5
1972	†Det A	134	426	40	111	15	2	8	42	38-6	2	47	.261	.324	.362	100	0	4-7	.978	-2	95	103	O127(50/42/72),1b2		-1.0
1973	Det A	119	404	55	124	14	7	12	44	38-6	1	41	.307	.366	.465	125	13	4-4	.982	2	105	90	O116(51/10/78)		0.9
1974	Det A	97	376	41	89	12	1	11	42	36-4	0	46	.237	.300	.362	84	-6	0-0	.973	-1	104	66	O97(0/2/97)		-1.3
	Mon N	21	54	3	13	1	0	2	8	5-1	0	9	.241	.305	.370	84	-1	0-0	1.000	-3	57	0	O13(7/0/6)		-0.5
	Bal A	8	7	2	4	0	0	1	3	2-1	0	1	.571	.667	1.000	383	3	0-0	1.000	1	95	644	O6(4/0/2)/D		0.3
1975	Bal A	84	194	27	53	6	5	5	29	22-1	1	22	.273	.348	.418	124	7	0-1	.979	-6	80	65	O58(3/56/0),D3		-0.1
Total	12	1392	4692	603	1254	218	42	153	610	449-50	30	635	.267	.333	.429	115	88	39-38	.981	3	105	73	O1267(310/466/708),1b34,D4		2.4

NORTON, FRANK   Frank Prescott B7.9.1845 Port Jefferson NY.   D8.1.1920 Greenwich CT   d5.5

YEAR	TM LG	G	AB	R	H	2B	3B	HR	RBI	BB-IB	HP	SO	AVG	OBP	SLG	AOPS	ABR	SB-CS	FA	FR	RNG	THR	GAMES AT POSITION	DL	BFW
1871	Oly NA	1	1	0	0	0	0	0		0	0		1.000	.000	.000	-99	0	0-0	.000	-1	0	0	/3OR		0.0

NORTON, GREG   Gregory Blakemoor B7.6.1972 San Leandro CA   BB/TR/6-1/205(190-205)   [ChiA93 2/59]   d8.18   Col Oklahoma   OF(30/0/7)

YEAR	TM LG	G	AB	R	H	2B	3B	HR	RBI	BB-IB	HP	SO	AVG	OBP	SLG	AOPS	ABR	SB-CS	FA	FR	RNG	THR	GAMES AT POSITION	DL	BFW
1996	Chi A	11	23	4	5	0	0	3	4-0	0	6	.217	.333	.478	106	0	0-0	.778	-3	35	0	S6,3b2,D2		-0.3
1997	Chi A	18	34	5	9	2	0	1	2-0	0	5	.265	.306	.441	95	-1	0-0	.864	1	105	0	3b11,D2		-0.1
1998	Chi A	105	299	38	71	17	2	9	36	26-1	2	77	.237	.301	.398	82	-9	3-3	.994	-5	65	92	1b79,3b11/2D		-1.9
1999	Chi A	132	436	62	111	26	0	16	50	69-3	4	93	.255	.358	.424	97	0	4-4	.922	-6	95	88	3b47,1b17,D3		-0.7
2000	Chi A	71	201	25	49	6	1	6	28	26-0	2	47	.244	.333	.373	77	-7	1-0	1.000	-10	68	66	3b47,1b17,D3		-1.1
2001	Col N	117	225	30	60	13	2	13	40	19-2	0	65	.267	.321	.516	93	-3	1-0	1.000	-8	65	109	O25(22/0/4),3b24,1b13/D		-1.1

YEAR	TM LG	G	AB	R	H	2B	3B	HR	RBI	BB-IB	HP	SO	AVG	OBP	SLG	AOPS	ABR	SB-CS	FA	FR	RNG	THR	GAMES AT POSITION	DL	BFW
2002	Col N	113	168	19	37	8	1	7	37	24-0	0	52	.220	.314	.405	81	-5	2-3	.896	-4	77	108	3b22,1b15,O2L/D	18	-1.1
2003	Col N	114	179	19	47	15	0	6	31	16-0	1	47	.263	.325	.447	87	-3	2-1	.924	-2	94	56	3b34,1b9,O3R		-0.5
2004	Det A	41	86	9	15	1	0	2	12	12-1	0	21	.174	.276	.256	41	-8	0-0	.963	-4	75	0	3b18,1b7,O6L,D7	37	-1.2
Total	9	722	1651	211	404	88	8	61	228	198-7	7	416	.245	.326	.419	86	-36	13-12	.919	-43	86	72	3b289,1b166,O36L,D19,S6/2	55	-8.5

NORWOOD, WILLIE   Willie B11.7.1950 Greene Co. AL   BR/TR/6-0/185*   [MinA72 3/56]   d4.21 Col La Verne

1977	Min A	39	83	15	19	3	0	3	9	6-0	0	17	.229	.281	.373	77	-3	6-1	.952	-0	113	0	O28(3/20/8),D5		-0.3
1978	Min A	125	428	56	109	22	3	8	46	28-0	1	64	.255	.301	.376	88	-7	25-10	.944	-4	94	94	O115(101/14/4),D6		-1.4
1979	Min A	96	270	32	67	13	3	6	30	20-2	0	51	.248	.299	.385	80	-8	9-5	.974	-3	91	90	O71(0/44/28),D14		-1.3
1980	Min A	34	73	6	12	2	0	1	8	3-0	0	13	.164	.197	.233	16	-9	1-1	1.000	1	129	0	O17(0/5/17),D9		-0.8
Total	4	294	854	109	207	40	6	18	93	57-2	3	145	.242	.290	.367	78	-27	41-17	.959	-6	97	77	O231(104/83/57),D34		-3.8

NOSSEK, JOE   Joseph Rudolph B11.8.1940 Cleveland OH   BR/TR/6-0/178*   d4.18   C27 Col Ohio U.

1964	Min A	7	1	1	0	0	0	0	0	0-0	0	0	.000	.000	.000	-99	-1	0-0	—	-0	0	0	O2(1/1/0)		0.0
1965	†Min A	87	170	19	37	9	0	2	16	7-1	1	22	.218	.250	.306	55	-10	2-0	.970	1	93	73	O48(2/46/2),3b9		-1.1
1966	Min A	4	0	0	0	0	0	0	0	0-0	0	0	—	—	—	—	-0	0-0	—	-0	0	0	O2C		-0.2
	KC A	87	230	13	60	10	3	1	27	8-1	0	21	.261	.285	.343	83	-6	4-2	.983	7	115	209	O78(12/65/3)/3		-0.2
	Year	91	230	13	60	10	3	1	27	8-1	0	21	.261	.285	.343	82	-6	4-2	.983	6	115	208	O80(12/67/3)/3		-0.4
1967	KC A	87	166	12	34	6	1	0	10	4-1	0	26	.205	.221	.253	42	-13	2-0	.982	4	126	76	O63(35/32/0)		-0.2
1969	Oak A	13	6	0	0	0	0	0	0	0-0	0	3	.000	.000	.000	-99	-2	0-0	1.000	-0	98	0	O12(9/3/0)		0.0
	StL N	9	5	2	1	0	0	0	0	0-0	0	0	.200	.200	.200	12	-1	0-0	1.000	0	262	0	/OC		0.0
1970	StL N	1	1	0	0	0	0	0	0	0-0	0	0	.000	.000	.000	-97	-0	0-0	—	0			/H		0.0
Total	6	295	579	47	132	25	4	3	53	19-3	1	72	.228	.252	.301	60	-32	8-2	.980	11	113	132	O206(59/150/5),3b10		-2.6

NOVIKOFF, LOU   Louis Alexander "The Mad Russian" B10.12.1915 Glendale AZ   D9.30.1970 South Gate CA   BR/TR/5-10/185   d4.15   Mil 1945

1941	Chi N	62	203	22	49	8	0	5	24	11	1	15	.241	.284	.355	82	-6	0	1.000	-1	91	91	O54(51/0/3)		-1.0
1942	Chi N	128	483	48	145	25	5	7	64	24	3	28	.300	.337	.416	125	12	3	.964	-6	85	136	O120L		0.4
1943	Chi N	78	233	22	65	7	5	0	28	18	1	15	.279	.333	.335	95	-2	0	.980	-6	85	39	O61(60/1/0)		-1.1
1944	Chi N	71	139	15	39	4	2	3	19	10	1	11	.281	.329	.403	106	0	1	.976	-3	77	57	O29(28/1/0)		-0.4
1946	Phi N	17	23	0	7	1	0	0	3	1	0	2	.304	.333	.348	96	0	0	1.000	0	142	0	O3L		0.0
Total	5	356	1081	107	305	45	10	15	138	64	5	71	.282	.325	.384	107	-12	4	.976	-12	89	97	O267(262/2/3)		-2.1

NOVOTNEY, RUBE   Ralph Joseph B8.5.1924 Streator IL   D7.16.1987 Redondo Beach CA   BR/TR/6-0/187   d4.29 Col Illinois

1949	Chi N	22	67	4	18	2	1	0	6	3	0	11	.269	.300	.328	70	-3	0	.958	-2	64	101	C20		-0.4

NUNAMAKER, LES   Leslie Grant B1.25.1889 Aurora NE   D11.14.1938 Hastings NE   BR/TR/6-2/190   d4.28

1911	Bos A	62	183	18	47	4	3	0	19	12	0		.257	.303	.311	72	-7	1	.972	4	100	101	C59		0.1
1912	Bos A	35	103	15	26	5	2	0	6	6	3		.252	.313	.340	82	-3	2	.971	-1	113	74	C35		-0.1
1913	Bos A	29	65	9	14	5	2	0	9	8	1	8	.215	.311	.354	92	-1	2	.977	1	100	66	C27		0.3
1914	Bos A	5	5	0	1	0	0	0	1	1	0		.200	.333	.200	61	0	0	1.000	0	120	306	C3/1		0.0
	NY A	87	257	19	68	10	3	2	29	22	2	34	.265	.327	.350	104	1	11-9	.971	3	92	116	C70,1b5		1.0
	Year	92	262	19	69	10	3	2	29	23	2	34	.263	.328	.347	103	1	11-9	.971	3	92	118	C73,1b6		1.0
1915	NY A	87	249	24	56	6	3	0	17	23	1	24	.225	.293	.273	70	-10	3-2	.964	-4	93	100	C77,1b2		-0.8
1916	NY A	91	260	25	77	14	7	0	28	34	1	21	.296	.380	.404	133	11	4	.983	2	126	99	C79		2.1
1917	NY A	104	310	22	81	9	2	0	33	21	1	25	.261	.310	.303	86	-5	5	.976	3	125	102	C91		0.5
1918	StL A	85	274	22	71	9	2	0	22	28	3	16	.259	.339	.307	98	0	6	.979	-3	81	111	C81/1OR		0.4
1919	Cle A	26	56	6	14	1	1	0	7	2	0	5	.250	.276	.304	59	-3	0	.927	-3	132	80	C16		-0.5
1920	†Cle A	34	54	10	18	3	3	0	14	4	0	5	.333	.379	.500	128	2	1-0	.963	-2	124	89	C17,1b6		0.7
1921	Cle A	46	131	16	47	7	2	0	25	11	0	3	.359	.408	.443	115	3	1-1	.970	2	101	60	C46		-0.3
1922	Cle A	25	43	8	13	2	0	0	7	4	0	3	.302	.362	.349	85	-1	0-0	.936	-3	88	48	C13		0.1
Total	12	716	1990	194	533	75	30	2	216	176	14	150	.268	.332	.339	95	-14	36-12	.972	3	104	97	C614,1b15/OR		3.8

NUNEZ, ABRAHAM   Abraham B2.5.1977 Haina, D.R.   BB/TR/6-3/210*   d9.3   [DL 2003 Fla N 94]

2002	Fla N	19	17	2	2	0	0	1	1	0-0	0	5	.118	.118	.118	-38	-4	0-1	1.000	-0	101	0	O15(2/12/1)		-0.4
2004	Fla N	58	64	9	11	1	1	5	9-0	0	21	.172	.274	.266	43	-6	1-2	1.000	0	113	0	O48(28/0/20),D2		-0.7
	KC A	59	221	31	50	9	0	5	29	25-1	0	48	.226	.304	.335	67	-11	0-1	.993	3	111	79	O57(0/4/54),D2		-1.1
Total	2	136	302	42	63	10	1	6	35	34-1	0	74	.209	.288	.308	56	-21	1-4	.995	3	111	54	O120(30/16/75),D2	94	-2.2

NUNEZ, ABRAHAM   Abraham Orlando (Adames) B3.16.1976 Santo Domingo, D.R.   BB/TR/5-11/185(170-190)   d8.27

1997	Pit N	19	40	3	9	2	0	1	3	6-0	1	10	.225	.289	.375	1.000	1	103	97	S12,2b9		0.0
1998	Pit N	24	52	6	10	2	0	1	2	12-0	0	14	.192	.344	.288	68	-2	4-2	.930	3	110	108	S23		0.2
1999	Pit N	90	259	25	57	8	0	0	17	28-0	1	54	.220	.299	.251	41	-23	9-1	.953	11	108	104	S65,2b14		-0.6
2000	Pit N	40	91	10	20	1	0	1	8	8-1	0	14	.220	.283	.264	39	-9	0-0	.978	4	118	86	S21,2b6		-0.3
2001	Pit N	115	301	30	79	11	4	1	21	28-1	1	44	.262	.326	.336	70	-13	8-2	.990	17	114	119	2b48,S48/3OL		0.9
2002	Pit N	112	253	28	59	14	1	2	15	27-1	2	44	.233	.311	.357	68	-12	3-4	.991	15	127	133	2b46,S24/D		0.5
2003	Pit N	118	311	30	77	8	7	4	35	26-1	2	53	.248	.310	.357	73	-13	1-3	.985	6	113	162	2b32,S13,3b6/PD		-0.6
2004	Pit N	112	182	17	43	9	0	2	13	10-0	0	36	.236	.275	.319	53	-13	0-1	.963	12	127	132	3b98,2b22,S21		0.3
2005	†StL N	139	421	64	120	13	2	5	44	37-4	0	63	.285	.343	.361	83	-10	0-1	.963	12	127	132	S250,2b248,3b106,D2/POL		-0.4
Total	9	769	1910	220	474	68	16	16	161	179-8	8	341	.248	.314	.326	66	-97	35-16	.971	66	110	130	S250,2b248,3b106,D2/POL		-0.4

NUNNALLY, JON   Jonathan Keith B11.9.1971 Pelham NC   BL/TR/5-10/190*   [CleA92 3/70]   d4.26 Col Miami-Dade Kendall (FL) CC

1995	KC A	119	303	51	74	15	6	14	42	51-5	2	86	.244	.357	.472	111	5	6-4	.971	1	108	81	O107(16/7/92),D4		0.1
1996	KC A	35	90	16	19	5	1	5	17	13-2	1	25	.211	.308	.456	90	0	0-0	.968	-0	112	0	O29(7/0/24),D4		-0.3
1997	KC A	13	29	8	7	0	1	4	5	5-0	0	7	.241	.353	.414	96	0	0-0	1.000	-1	74	0	O9(1/0/8)		0.2
	Cin N	65	201	38	64	12	3	13	35	26-0	2	51	.318	.400	.602	156	8	7-3	.984	5	109	108	O60(14/46/11)		1.8
1998	Cin N	74	174	29	36	9	0	7	20	34-3	1	38	.207	.335	.379	88	-2	3-4	.956	5	122	151	O70(6/24/53)		0.0
1999	Bos A	10	14	4	4	1	0	0	1	6-1	0	6	.286	.286	.357	61	-1	0-0	—	0			O2(1/0/1),D3		-0.1
2000	NY N	48	74	16	14	5	1	2	6	17-0	1	26	.189	.337	.365	83	-1	2-1	.977	4	115	403	O34(25/11/4),D11		0.2
Total	6	364	885	162	218	47	12	42	125	146-10	5	239	.246	.354	.469	111	14	19-12	.971	14	111	112	O311(70/88/193),D11		1.5

NUNNARI, TALMADGE   Talmadge Raphael B4.9.1975 Pensacola FL   BL/TL/6-1/205   [MonN97 9/286]   d9.7 Col Jacksonville

2000	Mon N	18	5	2	1	0	0	0	1	2-0	0	2	.200	.583	.200	124	1	0-0	1.000	-0	89	36	1b14		0.1

NUSZ, EMORY   Emory Moberly B4.2.1866 Frederick MD   D8.3.1893 Point Of Rocks MD   d4.26

1884	Was U	1	4	1	0	0	0	0	0				.000	.000	.000	-99	-1		.500	-1	0	0	/OL		-0.2

NUTTER, DIZZY   Everett Clarence B8.27.1893 Roseville OH   D7.25.1958 Battle Creek MI   BL/TR/5-9/160   d9.7

1919	Bos N	18	52	4	11	0	0	0	3	4	0	5	.212	.268	.212	47	-3	1	1.000	1	97	191	O12C		-0.3

NYCE, CHARLIE   Charles Reiff (b Charles Reiff Nice) B7.1.1870 Philadelphia PA   D5.9.1908 Philadelphia PA   5-8/160   d5.28

1895	Bos N	9	35	7	8	3	6	2	6	1	0		.229	.325	.543	113	0	0	.889	-1	99	120	S9		0.0

NYMAN, CHRIS   Christopher Curtis B6.6.1955 Pomona CA   BR/TR/6-4/200*   d7.28   b-Nyls Col Arizona St.

1982	Chi A	28	65	16	16	1	0	0	2	3-0	0	9	.246	.279	.262	49	-5	3-2	.994	1	111	108	1b24,O2(1/0/1)		-0.5
1983	Chi A	21	28	2	8	0	0	2	4	4-0	1	7	.286	.394	.500	138	2	2-2	1.000	-0	88	113	1b10,D10		0.0
Total	2	49	93	18	24	1	0	2	6	7-0	1	16	.258	.317	.333	78	-3	5-4	.996	1	103	110	1b34,D10,O2(1/0/1)		-0.5

NYMAN, NYLS   Nyls Wallace Rex B3.7.1954 Detroit MI   BL/TR/6-0/170*   [ChiA72 16/372]   d9.6   b-Chris

1974	Chi A	5	14	5	9	2	0	0	4	0-0	1	1	.643	.667	.929	346	4	1-0	1.000	1	128	588	O3L		-2.9
1975	Chi A	106	327	36	74	8	3	2	28	11-0	2	34	.226	.255	.281	51	-22	10-4	.958	-3	98	97	O94(62/26/8),D4		-0.2
1976	Chi A	8	15	2	2	1	0	0	1	0-0	0	5	.133	.133	.200	-2	-2	1-0	1.000	0	135	0	O7(6/1/0)		-0.2
1977	Chi A	1	1	0	0	0	0	0	0	0-0	0	0	.000	.000	.000	-99	-0	0-0	—	0			/H		-0.2
Total	4	120	357	43	85	11	3	2	33	11-0	3	40	.238	.266	.303	60	-20	12-4	.962	-1	101	105	O104(71/27/8),D4		-2.5

OAKES, REBEL   Ennis Telfair B12.17.1883 Arizona LA   D3.1.1948 Lisbon LA   BL/TR/5-8/170   d4.14   M2 Col Louisiana Tech

1909	Cin N	120	415	55	112	10	5	3	31	40	5		.270	.341	.340	112	6	23	.979	-1	101	87	O113(4/99/10)		-0.3
1910	StL N	131	468	50	118	14	6	0	43	38	5	38	.252	.315	.308	85	-10	18	.939	-7	97	72	O127(3/118/6)		-2.
1911	StL N	154	551	69	145	13	2	6	59	41	5	35	.263	.320	.319	81	-15	25	.961	6	104	117	O151(1/150/0)		-1.

YEAR	TM LG	G	AB	R	H	2B	3B	HR	RBI	BB-IB	HP	SO	AVG	OBP	SLG	AOPS	ABR	SB-CS	FA	FR	RNG	THR	GAMES AT POSITION	DL	BFW
1912	StL N	136	495	57	139	19	5	3	58	31	4	24	.281	.328	.358	90	-8	26	.947	-5	102	72	O136C		-2.2
1913	StL N	147	539	60	158	14	5	0	49	43	4	32	.293	.350	.338	98	-1	22-26	.968	-9	91	77	O145C		-2.5
1914	Pit F	145	571	82	178	18	10	7	75	35	7	22	.312	.359	.415	111	-1	28	.960	1	98	108	O145C,M		-1.1
1915	Pit F	153	580	55	161	24	5	0	82	37	2	19	.278	.323	.336	95	-20	31	.973	-6	104	55	O153(0/152/1),M		-1.1
Total 7		986	3619	428	1011	112	42	15	397	265	32	170	.279	.334	.346	95	-49	163-26	.961	-21	100	84	O970(8/945/17)		-14.0

OANA, PRINCE   Henry Kawaihoa   B1.22.1908 Waipahu HI   D6.19.1976 Austin TX   BR/TR/6-2/193   d4.22 ▲

YEAR	TM LG	G	AB	R	H	2B	3B	HR	RBI	BB-IB	HP	SO	AVG	OBP	SLG	AOPS	ABR	SB-CS	FA	FR	RNG	THR	GAMES AT POSITION	DL	BFW
1934	Phi N	6	21	3	5	0	0	0	3	0	0	1	.238	.238	.286	35	-2	0	1.000	0	129	0	O4L		-0.2
1943	Det A	20	26	5	10	2	1	1	7	1	0	2	.385	.407	.654	193	4	0-0	.750	-0	87	493	P10		0.0
1945	Det A	4	5	0	1	0	0	0	0	0	0	0	.200	.200	.200	15	0	0-0	1.000	-0	47	0	P3		0.0
Total 3		30	52	8	16	3	1	1	10	1	0	3	.308	.321	.462	108	2	0-0	.778	-0	77	372	P13,O4L		-0.2

OATES, JOHNNY   Johnny Lane   B1.21.1946 Sylva NC   D12.24.2004 Richmond VA   BL/TR/5-11/188*   [BalA67*S1/10]   d9.17   M11/C7   Col VPI

YEAR	TM LG	G	AB	R	H	2B	3B	HR	RBI	BB-IB	HP	SO	AVG	OBP	SLG	AOPS	ABR	SB-CS	FA	FR	RNG	THR	GAMES AT POSITION	DL	BFW
1970	Bal A	5	18	2	5	0	1	0	2	2-0	0	0	.278	.333	.389	102	0	0-0	.939	-1	229	65	C4		-0.1
1972	Bal A	85	253	20	66	12	1	4	21	28-8	0	31	.261	.332	.364	103	3	5-7	.995	4	133	87	C82		0.9
1973	Atl N	93	322	27	80	6	0	4	27	22-4	1	31	.248	.299	.304	63	-16	1-4	.981	-2	92	128	C86	47	-1.6
1974	Atl N	100	291	22	65	10	0	1	21	23-10	1	24	.223	.278	.268	52	-19	2-3	.992	12	107	102	C91		-0.3
1975	Atl N	8	18	0	4	1	0	0	0	1-0	0	4	.222	.263	.278	49	-1	0-0	1.000	-1	98	73	C6		-0.2
	Phi N	90	269	28	77	14	0	1	25	33-10	0	29	.286	.359	.349	94	-1	1-0	.990	9	163	109	C82		1.2
	Year	98	287	28	81	15	0	1	25	34-10	0	33	.282	.354	.345	91	-2	1-0	.990	8	159	107	C88		1.0
1976	†Phi N	37	99	10	25	2	0	0	8	8-0	0	12	.253	.308	.273	63	-5	0-1	.994	2	122	100	C33	48	0.0
1977	†LA N	60	156	13	42	4	0	3	11	11-4	0	11	.269	.314	.353	79	-5	1-0	.987	3	87	106	C56		-0.3
1978	†LA N	40	75	5	23	1	0	0	6	5-1	0	3	.307	.350	.320	88	-1	0-1	.956	-2	100	96	C24		0.0
1979	LA N	26	46	4	6	2	0	0	2	4-1	0	1	.130	.200	.174	3	-6	0-1	.975	-2	126	160	C20		-0.6
1980	NY A	39	64	6	12	3	0	1	3	2-0	1	3	.188	.224	.281	38	-6	1-2	.991	-3	126	160	C39		-0.8
1981	NY A	10	26	4	5	1	0	0	0	2-0	0	5	.192	.250	.231	40	-2	0-0	.963	-2	53	63	C10		-0.4
Total 11		593	1637	146	410	56	2	14	126	141-38	2	149	.250	.309	.313	72	-60	11-19	.987	20	117	108	C533	95	-2.4

OBANDO, SHERMAN   Sherman Omar (Gainor)   B1.23.1970 Bocas Del Toro, Pan   BR/TR/6-4/215*   d4.10

YEAR	TM LG	G	AB	R	H	2B	3B	HR	RBI	BB-IB	HP	SO	AVG	OBP	SLG	AOPS	ABR	SB-CS	FA	FR	RNG	THR	GAMES AT POSITION	DL	BFW
1993	Bal A	31	92	8	25	2	0	3	15	4-0	1	26	.272	.309	.391	83	-3	0-0	.929	0	125	0	D21,O8(1/0/7)	45	-0.4
1995	Bal A	16	38	0	10	1	0	0	3	2-0	1	12	.263	.293	.289	53	-3	1-0	.923	0	143	0	O7R,D7		-0.2
1996	Mon N	89	178	30	44	9	0	8	22	22-1	1	48	.247	.332	.433	98	-1	2-0	.962	1	110	85	O47R	19	-0.1
1997	Mon N	41	47	3	6	1	0	2	9	6-0	1	14	.128	.241	.277	35	-5	0-0	1.000	-0	98	0	O15(1/0/14),D2		-0.1
Total 4		177	355	41	85	13	0	13	49	34-1	3	100	.239	.310	.386	81	-12	3-0	.957	1	113	60	O77(2/0/75),D30	128	-1.2

OBERBECK, HENRY   Henry A.   B5.17.1858 MO   D8.26.1921 St.Louis MO   d5.7 ▲

YEAR	TM LG	G	AB	R	H	2B	3B	HR	RBI	BB-IB	HP	SO	AVG	OBP	SLG	AOPS	ABR	SB-CS	FA	FR	RNG	THR	GAMES AT POSITION	DL	BFW
1883	Pit AA	2	9	1	2	1	0	0		0			.222	.222	.333	80	0		1.000	0	0	173	1b2		0.0
	StL AA	4	14	0	0	0	0	0		0			.000	.000	.000	-95	-3		.833	1	259	1371	O4(3/1/0)		-0.2
	Year	6	23	1	2	1	0	0		0			.087	.087	.130	-30	-3		.833	1	259	1371	O4(3/1/0),1b2		-0.2
1884	Bal U	33	125	19	23	4	0	0		3			.184	.203	.216	25	-15		.878	1	141	86	O28(1/0/27),3b8,P2		-1.2
	KC U	27	90	7	17	3	0	0		7			.189	.247	.222	50	-1		.823	1	149	115	3b15,O7(3/3/1),P6,1b3		-0.1
	Year	60	215	26	40	7	0	0		10			.186	.222	.219	34	-24		.908	7	115	70	O35(4/3/28),3b23,P8,1b3		-1.3
Total 2		66	238	27	42	8	0	0		10			.176	.210	.210	28	-26		.901	8	130	203	O39(7/4/28),3b23,P8,1b5		-1.5

OBERKFELL, KEN   Kenneth Ray   B5.4.1956 Highland IL   BL/TR/6-0/210(175-210)   d8.22   Col Southwestern Illinois CC

YEAR	TM LG	G	AB	R	H	2B	3B	HR	RBI	BB-IB	HP	SO	AVG	OBP	SLG	AOPS	ABR	SB-CS	FA	FR	RNG	THR	GAMES AT POSITION	DL	BFW
1977	StL N	9	9	0	1	0	0	0	1	0-0	0	1	.111	.111	.111	-40	-2	0-0	1.000	-0	94	114	2b6		-0.2
1978	StL N	24	50	7	6	1	0	0	3	3-0	0	1	.120	.170	.140	-13	-8	0-0	.987	2	116	97	2b17,3b4		-0.5
1979	StL N	135	369	53	111	19	5	1	35	57-9	4	35	.301	.396	.388	114	10	4-1	.985	0	105	105	2b17,3b17,S2		1.7
1980	StL N	116	422	58	128	27	6	3	46	51-8	1	23	.303	.377	.417	117	12	4-4	.989	-2	104	98	2b101,3b16		1.7
1981	StL N	102	376	43	110	12	4	2	45	37-6	0	28	.293	.353	.372	102	1	13-5	.956	9	116	146	3b102/S	40	1.0
1982	†StL N	137	470	55	136	22	5	2	34	40-6	1	31	.289	.345	.370	98	-1	11-9	.972	14	121	112	3b135/2	18	1.1
1983	StL N	151	488	62	143	26	5	3	38	61-5	1	27	.293	.371	.385	110	9	12-6	.960	6	112	152	3b127,2b32/S		1.5
1984	StL N	50	152	17	47	11	1	0	16	16-2	1	10	.309	.379	.395	120	5	1-2	.967	4	116	109	3b46,2b2/S		0.8
	Atl N	50	172	21	40	8	1	1	10	15-1	1	17	.233	.289	.308	65	-8	1-3	.964	-4	95	113	3b45,2b4	35	-1.4
	Year	100	324	38	87	19	2	1	21	31-3	1	27	.269	.331	.349	90	-3	2-5	.966	0	105	111	3b91,2b6/S		-0.6
1985	Atl N	134	412	30	112	19	4	3	35	51-6	2	38	.272	.359	.359	96	0	1-2	.963	1	108	93	3b117,2b16		0.0
1986	Atl N	151	503	62	136	24	3	5	48	83-6	2	40	.270	.373	.360	96	3	7-4	.976	18	120	118	3b130,2b41		2.2
1987	Atl N	135	508	59	142	29	2	3	48	48-5	2	29	.280	.342	.362	84	-10	3-3	.979	-2	105	92	3b126,2b11	15	-1.4
1988	Atl N	120	422	42	117	20	4	3	40	32-6	2	28	.277	.325	.365	96	-2	4-5	.951	-1	94	107	3b113/2		-1.0
	Pit N	20	54	7	12	2	0	0	2	5-1	0	6	.222	.288	.259	59	-3	0-0	1.000	-3	89	58	2b11,S3,3b2/1		-0.6
	Year	140	476	49	129	22	4	3	42	37-7	2	34	.271	.321	.353	92	-5	4-5	.952	-10	95	105	3b115,2b12,S3/1		-1.6
1989	†SF N	83	116	17	37	5	1	2	15	8-4	3	9	.319	.367	.431	133	5	0-1	.971	-2	102	51	3b38,1b7,2b7		-0.7
	Year	97	156	19	42	6	1	2	17	10-0	2	10	.269	.316	.359	97	1	0-1	.971	-1	102	51	3b38,1b16,2b10		0.3
1990	Hou N	77	150	10	31	6	1	1	12	15-1	1	17	.207	.281	.280	57	-9	0-0	.971	-1	104	129	3b24,1b11,2b11	15	-1.3
1991	Hou N	53	70	7	16	4	0	0	6	14-4	1	8	.229	.357	.286	88	0	0-0	1.000	-0	130	107	1b13,3b4		-0.1
1992	Cal A	41	91	6	24	1	0	0	10	8-2	0	5	.264	.317	.275	68	-4	0-1	.986	-7	74	35	2b21,1b2,D5		-0.1
Total 16		1602	4874	558	1354	237	44	29	446	546-68	23	356	.278	.351	.362	96	-8	62-47	.965	24	110	114	3b1046,2b402,1b43,S8,D5	123	1.8

O'BERRY, MIKE   Preston Michael   B4.20.1954 Birmingham AL   BR/TR/6-2/195*   [BosA75 22/516]   d4.8   Col South Alabama

YEAR	TM LG	G	AB	R	H	2B	3B	HR	RBI	BB-IB	HP	SO	AVG	OBP	SLG	AOPS	ABR	SB-CS	FA	FR	RNG	THR	GAMES AT POSITION	DL	BFW
1979	Bos A	43	59	8	10	1	0	1	4*	5-0	1	16	.169	.242	.237	29	-6	0-0	.957	-3	120	58	C43		-0.8
1980	Chi N	19	48	7	10	1	0	0	1	5-0	0	13	.208	.273	.229	41	-4	0-0	.982	2	98	173	C19		-0.1
1981	Cin N	55	111	6	20	3	1	1	5	14-0	0	19	.180	.272	.252	50	-7	0-0	.983	-3	113	116	C55		-0.9
1982	Cin N	21	45	5	10	2	0	0	1	10-0	0	13	.222	.364	.267	79	-1	0-0	.990	-0	127	144	C21		0.0
1983	Cal A	26	60	7	10	1	0	1	5	3-0	0	11	.167	.206	.233	21	-7	0-0	1.000	-2	154	91	C26		-0.4
1984	NY A	13	32	3	8	2	0	0	5	2-0	0	5	.250	.294	.313	70	-1	0-0	1.000	-0	548	227	C12/3		-0.1
1985	Mon N	20	21	2	4	0	0	0	6	4-0	0	3	.190	.320	.190	49	-1	1-0	1.000	-1	57	202	C20		-0.1
Total 7		197	376	38	72	10	1	3	27	43-0	1	77	.191	.274	.247	46	-27	1-0	.984	-8	147	126	C196/3		-2.8

OBRADOVICH, JIM   James Thomas   B9.13.1949 Fort Campbell KY   BL/TL/6-2/200   [MinA67 24/472]   d9.12

YEAR	TM LG	G	AB	R	H	2B	3B	HR	RBI	BB-IB	HP	SO	AVG	OBP	SLG	AOPS	ABR	SB-CS	FA	FR	RNG	THR	GAMES AT POSITION	DL	BFW
1978	Hou N	10	17	3	3	0	1	0	2	1-1	0	3	.176	.222	.294	46	-1	0-0	1.000	-0	52	43	1b3		-0.2

O'BRIEN   d8.2

YEAR	TM LG	G	AB	R	H	2B	3B	HR	RBI	BB-IB	HP	SO	AVG	OBP	SLG	AOPS	ABR	SB-CS	FA	FR	RNG	THR	GAMES AT POSITION	DL	BFW
1887	Was N	1	4	0	0	0	0	0	0	0	0	2	.000	.000	.000	-99	-1	0	.714	-0	131	0	/2		-0.1

O'BRIEN, CHARLIE   Charles Hugh   B5.1.1960 Tulsa OK   BR/TR/6-2/190(190-215)   [OakA82 5/132]   d6.2   Col Wichita St.

YEAR	TM LG	G	AB	R	H	2B	3B	HR	RBI	BB-IB	HP	SO	AVG	OBP	SLG	AOPS	ABR	SB-CS	FA	FR	RNG	THR	GAMES AT POSITION	DL	BFW
1985	Oak A	16	11	3	3	1	0	0	1	3-0	0	1	.273	.429	.364	128	2	0-0	.958	-1	0	71	C16		0.0
1987	Mil A	10	35	2	7	3	1	0	4	4-0	0	4	.200	.282	.343	63	-2	0-1	1.000	5	151	265	C10		0.3
1988	Mil A	40	118	12	26	6	0	2	9	5-0	0	16	.220	.252	.322	59	-7	0-1	.991	8	122	101	C40		0.3
1989	Mil A	62	188	22	44	10	0	6	35	21-1	9	11	.234	.339	.383	104	2	0-0	.986	5	125	96	C62		1.1
1990	Mil A	46	145	11	27	7	0	0	11	11-1	2	26	.186	.253	.262	44	-11	0-0	.992	2	130	97	C46		-0.6
	NY N	28	68	6	11	3	0	0	9	10-2	1	8	.162	.272	.206	35	-6	0-0	.986	6	117	174	C28		0.2
1991	NY N	69	168	16	31	6	0	2	14	17-1	4	25	.185	.272	.256	50	-11	0-2	.991	8	83	115	C67		0.0
1992	NY N	68	156	15	33	12	0	2	13	16-1	1	18	.212	.289	.327	75	-5	0-1	.979	1	106	164	C64		-0.1
1993	NY N	67	188	15	48	11	0	4	23	14-1	2	14	.255	.312	.378	85	-4	1-1	.986	6	102	119	C65		0.6
1994	Atl N	51	152	24	37	11	0	8	28	15-2	3	24	.243	.322	.474	101	0	0-0	.991	1	131	84	C48		0.4
1995	†Atl N	67	198	18	45	7	0	9	23	29-2	6	40	.227	.343	.399	91	-2	0-1	.992	-3	66	105	C64		-0.1
1996	Tor A	109	324	33	77	17	0	13	44	29-1	17	68	.238	.331	.410	87	-6	0-1	.995	13	142	95	C105		1.1
1997	Tor A	69	225	22	49	15	1	4	27	22-1	11	45	.218	.311	.347	73	-8	0-2	.995	27	177	142	C69		2.1
1998	Chi A	57	164	12	43	9	0	4	18	9-0	2	31	.262	.303	.390	82	-5	0-0	.988	-5	78	123	C57		1.1
	Ana A	5	11	1	2	1	0	0	0	1-0	0	2	.182	.250	.182	15	-1	0-0	1.000	-0	128	172	C5	11	-0.6
	Year	62	175	13	45	9	0	4	18	10-0	2	33	.257	.300	.377	77	-6	0-0	.989	-6	81	126	C62	43	-0.1
1999	Ana A	27	62	3	6	0	0	4	18	1-0	2	12	.097	.136	.145	-28	-12	0-0	.993	8	159	114	C27	50	-0.7
2000	Mon N	9	19	1	4	1	0	0	2	2-1	0	5	.211	.286	.421	75	-1	0-0	1.000	-3	44	0	C9		-0.3
Total 15		800	2232	216	493	119	4	56	261	209-14	60	354	.221	.303	.353	78	-78	1-10	.990	79	117	117	C782	104	4.0

YEAR	TM LG	G	AB	R	H	2B	3B	HR	RBI	BB-IB	HP	SO	AVG	OBP	SLG	AOPS	ABR	SB-CS	FA	FR	RNG	THR	GAMES AT POSITION	DL	BFW

O'BRIEN, EDDIE Edward Joseph B12.11.1930 S.Amboy NJ BR/TR/5-9/165* d4.25 Mil 1954-55 C1 twb-Johnny Col Seattle ▲   -2.4

YEAR	TM LG	G	AB	R	H	2B	3B	HR	RBI	BB-IB	HP	SO	AVG	OBP	SLG	AOPS	ABR	SB-CS	FA	FR	RNG	THR	GAMES AT POSITION	BFW
1953	Pit N	89	261	21	62	5	3	0	14	17	2	30	.238	.289	.280	50	-20	6-1	.935	-12	96	78	S81	-2.1
1955	Pit N	75	236	26	55	3	1	0	8	18-0	1	13	.233	.290	.254	47	-18	4-5	.993	1	99	201	O56(1/56/0),3b7,S4	0.6
1956	Pit N	63	53	17	14	2	0	0	3	2-0	0	2	.264	.291	.302	61	-3	1-1	.978	5	129	151	S23,O6(5/1/0),3b4,2b2/P	0.0
1957	Pit N	3	4	0	0	0	0	0	0	0-0	0	0	.000	.000	.000	-99	-1	0-0	1.000	0	103	695	P3	0.0
1958	Pit N	1	0	0	0	0	0	0	0	0-0	0	0	—	—	—	—	-	0-0	—	-0	0	0	/P	0.0
Total 5		231	554	64	131	10	4	0	25	37-0	3	45	.236	.288	.269	48	-42	11-7	.942	-4	101	88	S108,O62(6/57/0),3b11,P5,2b2	-3.9

O'BRIEN, DINK Frank Aloysius B9.13.1894 San Francisco CA D11.4.1971 Monterey Park CA BR/TR/5-8/160 d4.26   0.0

YEAR	TM LG	G	AB	R	H	2B	3B	HR	RBI	BB-IB	HP	SO	AVG	OBP	SLG	AOPS	ABR	SB-CS	FA	FR	RNG	THR	GAMES AT POSITION	BFW
1923	Phi N	15	21	3	7	2	0	0	2		0	1	.333	.391	.429	104	0	0-0	.909	-1	80	162	C9	0.0

O'BRIEN, GEORGE George Joseph B11.4.1889 Cleveland OH D3.24.1966 Columbus OH BR/TR/6-0/185 d8.16 Col Mount Union   -0.1

YEAR	TM LG	G	AB	R	H	2B	3B	HR	RBI	BB-IB	HP	SO	AVG	OBP	SLG	AOPS	ABR	SB-CS	FA	FR	RNG	THR	GAMES AT POSITION	BFW
1915	StL A	3	9	1	2	0	0	0	0	1*	0	2	.222	.300	.222	59	0	0	.933	-1	98	93	C3	-0.1

O'BRIEN, JOHN John E. B10.22.1851 Columbus OH D12.31.1914 Fall River MA TR/5-11.5/187 d4.19   -0.7

YEAR	TM LG	G	AB	R	H	2B	3B	HR	RBI	BB-IB	HP	SO	AVG	OBP	SLG	AOPS	ABR	SB-CS	FA	FR	RNG	THR	GAMES AT POSITION	BFW
1884	Bal U	18	77	7	19	1	1	0		0			.247	.266	.286	61	-6		.865	-1	63	257	O18(3/14/1)	-0.7

O'BRIEN, JOHN John Joseph "Chewing Gum" B7.13.1866 St.John NB, Can. D5.13.1913 Lewiston ME BL/TR/5-9/175 d4.22   -2.0

YEAR	TM LG	G	AB	R	H	2B	3B	HR	RBI	BB-IB	HP	SO	AVG	OBP	SLG	AOPS	ABR	SB-CS	FA	FR	RNG	THR	GAMES AT POSITION	BFW
1891	Bro N	43	167	22	41	4	2	0	26	12	3	17	.246	.308	.293	76	-5	4	.854	-18	80	76	2b43	0.0
1893	Chi N	4	14	3	5	0	1	0	1	2	1	2	.357	.471	.500	160	1	0	.900	-2	68	55	2b4	-1.2
1895	Lou N	128	539	82	138	10	4	1	50	45	10	20	.256	.325	.295	65	-27	15	.938	7	105	95	2b125,1b3	0.4
1896	Lou N	49	186	24	63	9	1	2	24	13	1	7	.339	.385	.430	119	5	4	.919	-3	96	81	2b49	0.2
	Was N	73	270	38	72	6	3	4	33	27	5	12	.267	.344	.356	85	-6	4	.952	6	104	103	2b73	0.6
	Year	122	456	62	135	15	4	6	57	40	6	19	.296	.361	.386	98	-1	8	.938	3	101	94	2b122	-0.6
1897	Was N	86	320	37	78	12	3	3	45	19	11		.244	.309	.322	67	-16	6	.942	4	96	139	2b86	-0.3
1899	Bal N	39	135	14	26	4	0	1	17	15	2		.193	.283	.244	43	-10	4	.966	6	107	145	2b39	-1.6
	Pit N	79	279	26	63	2	4	1	33	21	2		.226	.285	.272	53	-19	8	.946	-2	98	106	2b79	-1.9
	Year	118	414	40	89	6	4	2	50	36	4		.215	.284	.263	50	-29	12	.953	4	101	119	2b118	
Total 6		501	1910	246	486	47	17	12	229	154	35	58	.254	.322	.316	72	-77	45	.936	-3	99	106	2b498,1b3	-5.1

O'BRIEN, JACK John Joseph B2.5.1873 Watervliet NY D6.10.1933 Watervliet NY BL/TR/6-1/165 d4.14   -1.0

YEAR	TM LG	G	AB	R	H	2B	3B	HR	RBI	BB-IB	HP	SO	AVG	OBP	SLG	AOPS	ABR	SB-CS	FA	FR	RNG	THR	GAMES AT POSITION	BFW
1899	Was N	127	468	68	132	11	5	6	51	31	3		.282	.331	.365	92	-6	17	.926	6	115	91	O121L,3b4	-0.5
1901	Was A	11	45	5	8	0	0	0	5	3	1		.178	.245	.178	19	-5	2	.929	-0	0	0	O11L	-0.8
	Cle A	92	375	54	106	14	5	0	39	22	4		.283	.329	.347	91	-4	13	.941	-0	81	143	O92(31/0/61)/3	-1.3
	Year	103	420	59	114	14	5	0	44	25	5		.271	.320	.329	83	-9	15	.939	-1	71	126	O103(42/0/61)/3	-2.5
1903	†Bos A	96	338	44	71	14	4	3	38	21	3		.210	.262	.302	65	-14	10	.958	-7	115	111	O71(2/68/1),3b11,2b4/S	-4.8
Total 3		326	1226	171	317	39	14	9	133	77	11		.259	.308	.335	82	-29	42	.937	-2	100	108	O295(165/68/62),3b16,2b4/S	

O'BRIEN, JACK John K. (b John K. Bryne) B6.12.1860 Philadelphia PA D11.20.1910 Philadelphia PA BR/TR/5-10/184 d5.2 OF(5/36/31)   2.2

YEAR	TM LG	G	AB	R	H	2B	3B	HR	RBI	BB-IB	HP	SO	AVG	OBP	SLG	AOPS	ABR	SB-CS	FA	FR	RNG	THR	GAMES AT POSITION	BFW
1882	Phi AA	62	241	44	73	13	3	3	37	13			.303	.339	.419	145	11		.925	10			C45,O18(0/6/12)/31	0.7
1883	Phi AA	94	390	74	113	14	10	0	70	25			.290	.333	.377	117	6		.876	-1			C58,O25C,3b19/S	0.6
1884	Phi AA	36	138	25	39	6	1		9		3		.283	.340	.362	121	3		.930	-1			C43,S9,1b7,O3R,3b2	0.2
1885	Phi AA	62	225	35	60	9	1	2	30	20	5		.267	.340	.342	109	3		.903	-4			C36,3b27,1b24,S10,2b7,O3R	-0.4
1886	Phi AA	105	423	65	107	25	4	0	56	38	7		.253	.325	.345	109	5	23	.918	-12			C25,O4(1/0/3)/2	-0.4
1887	Bro AA	30	123	18	28	4	1	1	17	6	0		.228	.264	.301	57	-8	8	.839	-5			C37,O13(4/0/9),1b7	-0.4
1888	Bal AA	57	196	25	44	11	5	0	18	17	4		.224	.300	.332	105	2	14	.925	-11			C37,O13(4/0/9),1b7	0.8
1890	Phi AA	109	433	80	113	24	14	4	80	52	12		.261	.356	.409	126	14	31	.976	4	122	92	1b109/ORC	0.8
Total 8		555	2169	366	577	106	42	11	308	180	31		.266	.331	.369	115	36	76	.903	-17			C275,1b149,O72C,3b49,S20,2b8	

O'BRIEN, JOHNNY John Thomas B12.11.1930 S.Amboy NJ BR/TR/5-9/170* d4.19 Mil 1954-55 twb-Eddie Col Seattle ▲   -0.8

YEAR	TM LG	G	AB	R	H	2B	3B	HR	RBI	BB-IB	HP	SO	AVG	OBP	SLG	AOPS	ABR	SB-CS	FA	FR	RNG	THR	GAMES AT POSITION	BFW
1953	Pit N	89	279	28	69	13	2	2	22	21	4	36	.247	.309	.330	67	-13	1-1	.982	0	102	90	2b77/S	-0.8
1955	Pit N	84	278	22	83	15	2	1	25	20-1	1	19	.299	.346	.378	94	-2	1-1	.969	3	105	94	2b78	-0.7
1956	Pit N	73	104	13	18	1	0	0	3	5-0	0	7	.173	.209	.183	7	-14	0-0	.959	1	112	84	2b53,P8/S	
1957	Pit N	34	35	7	11	2	1	0	1	1-0	0	1	.314	.368	.429	117	1	0-0	.857	-2	62	0	P16,S8,2b2	
1958	Pit N	3	1	1	0	0	0	0	0	0-0	0	0	.000	.000	.000	-99	-0	0-0	—	-	0		/H	
	StL N	12	2	3	0	0	0	0	0	1-0	0	0	.000	.333	.000	-2	0	0-0	1.000	-0	97	0	S5/P2	
	Year	15	3	4	0	0	0	0	0	1-0	0	0	.000	.250	.000	-26	-1	0-0	1.000	-0	97	0	S5/P2	
1959	Mil N	44	116	16	23	4	1		8	11-1	8	15	.198	.271	.259	47	-9	0-0	.987	-2	96	126	2b37	
Total 6		339	815	90	204	35	5	4	59	59-2	8	82	.250	.306	.320	68	-37	2-2	.974	1	103	96	2b248,P25,S15	-2.1

O'BRIEN, PETE Peter J. B6.17.1877 Binghamton NY D1.31.1917 Jersey City NJ BL/TR/5-7/170 d9.21

YEAR	TM LG	G	AB	R	H	2B	3B	HR	RBI	BB-IB	HP	SO	AVG	OBP	SLG	AOPS	ABR	SB-CS	FA	FR	RNG	THR	GAMES AT POSITION	BFW
1901	Cin N	16	54	1	11	1	0	1	3	0			.204	.232	.278	51	-4	0	.889	-2	89	111	2b15	-5.
1906	StL A	151	524	44	122	9	4	2	57	42	3		.233	.293	.277	82	-10	25	.933	-36	81	86	2b120,3b20,S11	-0.
1907	Cle A	43	145	9	33	5	2	0	6	7			.228	.263	.290	76	-4	1	.949	-4	115	92	2b15,3b12,S12	-0.
	Was A	39	134	6	25	3	1	0	12	12	1		.187	.259	.224	59	-6	4	.912	3	111	111	3b38,S25,2b16	-1.
	Year	82	279	15	58	8	3	0	18	19	1		.208	.261	.258	68	-10	5	.911	-1	111	101	3b26,S13/2	-6.
Total 3		249	857	60	191	18	7	3	78	63	4		.223	.279	.271	76	-24	30	.930	-39	85	89	2b151,3b58,S36	

O'BRIEN, PETE Peter James B6.16.1867 Chicago IL D6.30.1937 York Twp. (Du Page Co.) IL BR/TR/5-9.5/165 d4.29

YEAR	TM LG	G	AB	R	H	2B	3B	HR	RBI	BB-IB	HP	SO	AVG	OBP	SLG	AOPS	ABR	SB-CS	FA	FR	RNG	THR	GAMES AT POSITION	BFW
1890	Chi N	27	106	15	30	7	0	3	16	5	0	10	.283	.315	.434	113	1	4	.929	-2	94	111	2b27	

O'BRIEN, PETE Peter Michael B2.9.1958 Santa Monica CA BL/TL/6-1/198(185-205) [TexA79 15/381] d9.3 Col Nebraska

YEAR	TM LG	G	AB	R	H	2B	3B	HR	RBI	BB-IB	HP	SO	AVG	OBP	SLG	AOPS	ABR	SB-CS	FA	FR	RNG	THR	GAMES AT POSITION	DL	BFW
1982	Tex A	20	67	13	16	4	1	4	13	6	1	8	.239	.297	.507	123	2	1-0	1.000	-0	76	155	O11L,1b3,D4		
1983	Tex A	154	524	53	124	24	5	8	53	58-2	1	62	.237	.313	.347	83	-12	5-4	.993	13	141	100	1b133,O27(9/0/18)/D		
1984	Tex A	142	520	57	149	26	2	18	80	53-8	0	50	.287	.348	.448	115	11	3-5	.992	1	101	86	1b141/OR		
1985	Tex A	159	573	69	153	34	3	22	92	69-4	1	53	.267	.342	.452	114	12	5-10	.995	-6	83	93	1b159		
1986	Tex A	156	551	86	160	23	4	23	90	87-11	0	66	.290	.385	.468	128	24	4-4	.992	1	98	95	1b155		
1987	Tex A	159	569	83	163	26	1	23	88	59-6	0	61	.286	.348	.457	112	10	0-4	.992	15	129	90	1b158,O2R/D		
1988	Tex A	156	547	57	149	24	1	16	71	72-9	0	73	.272	.352	.408	111	10	1-4	.995	-2	131	88	1b154/D		
1989	Cle A	155	554	75	144	24	1	12	55	83-17	2	48	.260	.356	.372	104	6	3-1	.994	5	137	87	1b97,O6L,D6	45	-1
1990	Sea A	108	366	32	82	18	0	5	27	44-1	2	33	.224	.308	.314	74	-12	0-0	.995	5	122	87	1b132,D18,O13L		-1
1991	Sea A	152	560	58	139	29	3	17	88	44-7	1	61	.248	.300	.402	93	-7	0-1	.997	2	103	118	1b81,D36		-1
1992	Sea A	134	396	40	88	15	1	14	52	40-8	0	27	.222	.289	.371	84	-9	2-1	.996	3	115	109	1b81,D36		-0
1993	Sea A	72	210	30	54	7	0	7	27	26-4	0	21	.257	.330	.390	93	-2	0-0	.988	2	202	197	D52,1b9/OL		-0
Total 12		1567	5437	654	1421	254	21	169	736	641-77	7	563	.261	.336	.409	104	33	24-34	.994	54	113	96	1b1377,D120,O61(40/0/21)	45	-1

O'BRIEN, RAY Raymond Joseph B10.31.1892 St.Louis MO D3.31.1942 St.Louis MO BL/TL/5-9/175 d6.27

YEAR	TM LG	G	AB	R	H	2B	3B	HR	RBI	BB-IB	HP	SO	AVG	OBP	SLG	AOPS	ABR	SB-CS	FA	FR	RNG	THR	GAMES AT POSITION	BFW
1916	Pit N	16	57	5	12	3	2	0	3	1	0	14	.211	.224	.333	69	-2	0-0	.864	-0	70	204	O14(7/0/7)	-0

O'BRIEN, SYD Sydney Lloyd B2.18.1944 Compton CA BR/TR/6-1/185* d4.15 Col Long Beach (CA) City

YEAR	TM LG	G	AB	R	H	2B	3B	HR	RBI	BB-IB	HP	SO	AVG	OBP	SLG	AOPS	ABR	SB-CS	FA	FR	RNG	THR	GAMES AT POSITION	BFW
1969	Bos A	100	263	47	64	10	5	9	29	15-0	1	37	.243	.287	.422	99	-5	2-3	.939	-0	111	115	3b53,S15,2b12	-1
1970	Chi A	121	441	48	109	13	2	8	44	22-1	1	62	.247	.285	.340	69	-20	3-3	.938	6	102	125	3b68,2b43,S5	-2
1971	Cal A	90	251	25	50	8	1	5	21	15-4	1	33	.199	.247	.299	58	-15	0-2	.961	-10	85	110	S52,2b7,3b6/1OR	-0
1972	Cal A	36	39	10	7	2	0	1	8	6-0	1	10	.179	.289	.308	82	-1	0-1	.889	-2	103	139	3b9,2b7	-0
	Mil A	31	58	5	12	2	0	1	9	0	0	13	.207	.230	.293	57	-3	0-1	.852	-4	108	196	3b8,2b7	-1
	Year	67	97	15	19	4	0	2	9	6-0	1	23	.196	.255	.299	67	-4	0-1	.861	-5	108	170	3b17,2b10,S4/1	-1
Total 4		378	1052	135	242	35	8	24	100	60-5	4	155	.230	.273	.347	73	-44	5-9	.934	-8	106	121	3b144,S76,2b72,1b2/OR	-4

O'BRIEN, TOMMY Thomas Edward "Obie" B12.19.1918 Anniston AL D11.5.1978 Anniston AL BR/TR/5-11/195* d4.24

YEAR	TM LG	G	AB	R	H	2B	3B	HR	RBI	BB-IB	HP	SO	AVG	OBP	SLG	AOPS	ABR	SB-CS	FA	FR	RNG	THR	GAMES AT POSITION	BFW
1943	Pit N	89	232	35	72	12	7	2	26	15	0	24	.310	.352	.448	126	7	0	.964	-2	94	99	O48(17/0/31),3b9	0
1944	Pit N	85	156	27	39	6	2	3	20	21	1	12	.250	.343	.372	97	0	1	.965	-0	84	176	O48(15/0/33)/3	-0
1945	Pit N	58	161	23	54	6	5	0	18	9	1	13	.335	.374	.435	120	4	0	.961	-2	97	63	O45(12/0/33)	-0
1949	Bos A	49	125	24	39	10	3	0	21	10	1	12	.312	.336	.336	73	-5	0-0	1.000	-0	98	175	O32(0/8/25)	-0
1950	Bos A	9	31	4	4	0	0	0	3	1	0	5	.129	.206	.161	-5	-5	0-0	1.000	0	110	425	O3(2/0/1)	-0
	Was A	3	9	1	1	0	0	0	0	1	0	1	.111	.200	.111	-20	-2	0	1.000	-0	92	248	O12(5/4/3)	-0
	Year	12	40	5	5	0	0	0	3	2	0	6	.125	.205	.150	-8	-7	0-0	1.000	0	92	281	O15(7/4/4)	
Total 5		293	714	110	198	30	14	8	78	70	2	66	.277	.344	.392	100	-1	2-0	.970	-5	92	111	O185(49/12/125),3b10	-1

YEAR	TM LG	G	AB	R	H	2B	3B	HR	RBI	BB-IB	HP	SO	AVG	OBP	SLG	AOPS	ABR	SB-CS	FA	FR	RNG	THR	GAMES AT POSITION	DL	BFW
O'BRIEN, TOM	Thomas H. B6.22.1860 Salem MA D4.21.1921 Worcester MA BR/TR/6-1/185 d6.14																								
1882	Wor N	22	89	9	18	1	1	0	7	1		10	.202	.211	.236	42	-6		.789	-3	81	0	O20(16/4/0),2b2/3		-0.9
1883	Bal AA	33	138	16	37	6	4	0	5				.268	.294	.370	109	1		.825	-4	105	60	2b29,O4C		-0.2
1884	Bos U	103	449	80	118	31	8	4	12				.263	.287	.394	104	-11		.853	0	100	82	2b99,O3(3/1/1),1b2/C		-0.7
1885	Bal AA	8	33	4	7	3	0	0	5	2	0		.212	.257	.303	78	-1		.932	1	235	38	1b6,2b2		0.0
1887	NY AA	31	129	13	25	3	2	0	18	2	1		.194	.212	.248	29	-13	10	.963	-3	87	90	1b20,O8(2/4/2),3b2,2b2/P		-1.4
1890	Roc AA	73	273	36	52	6	5	0	31	30	1		.190	.273	.249	58	-14	6	.971	-4	74	113	1b68,2b8		-2.1
Total 6		270	1111	158	257	50	20	4	61	52	2	10	.231	.267	.323	79	-44	16	.846	-13	102	79	2b142,1b96,O35(19/13/3),3b3/PC		-5.3
O'BRIEN, TOM	Thomas J. B2.20.1873 Verona PA D2.3.1901 Phoenix AZ 5-11/170 d5.10 OF(169/61/32)																								
1897	†Bal N	50	147	25	37	6	0	0	32	20	2		.252	.349	.293	70	-5	7	.968	1	81	70	1b25,O24(13/1/10)		-0.5
1898	Bal N	18	60	9	13	0	0	0	14	10	1		.217	.338	.217	59	-3	0	.833	-0	130	831	O16R		-0.3
	Pit N	107	413	53	107	10	8	1	45	25	11		.259	.318	.329	87	-7	13	.924	-6	155	186	O69(10/59/0),1b21,3b8,2b7,S4		-1.6
	Year	125	473	62	120	10	8	1	59	35	12		.254	.321	.315	84	-10	13	.911	-6	150	310	O85(10/59/16),1b21,3b8,2b7,S4		-1.9
1899	NY N	151	577	101	171	22	10	6	77	44	4		.296	.350	.400	109	7	23	.933	-4	104	110	O128(125/0/3),3b21,S2/21		-0.7
1900	†Pit N	102	376	61	109	22	6	3	61	21	13		.290	.349	.402	107	3	12	.961	-10	69	111	1b65,O25(21/1/3),2b4,S2		-0.8
Total 4		428	1573	249	437	60	24	10	229	120	31		.278	.341	.366	97	-5	55	.928	-18	120	187	O262L,1b112,3b29,2b12,S8		-3.9
O'BRIEN, DARBY	William D. B9.1.1863 Peoria IL D6.15.1893 Peoria IL BR/TR/6-1/186 d4.16																								
1887	NY AA	127	522	97	157	30	13	5	73	40	4		.301	.355	.437	126	18	49	.913	7	102	83	O121(121/1/0),1b10,S2/3P		1.8
1888	Bro AA	136	532	105	149	27	6	2	65	30	7		.280	.327	.365	122	13	55	.932	1	66	23	O136L		0.9
1889	†Bro AA	136	567	146	170	30	11	5	80	61	16	76	.300	.384	.418	128	22	91	.906	-8	53	92	O136L		0.9
1890	†Bro N	85	350	78	110	28	6	2	63	32	4	43	.314	.378	.446	139	18	38	.960	0	90	67	O85(44/42/0)		1.3
1891	Bro N	103	395	79	100	18	6	5	57	39	7	53	.253	.331	.367	104	2	31	.951	2	67	35	O103L		0.1
1892	Bro N	122	490	72	119	14	5	1	56	29	3	52	.243	.289	.298	81	-12	57	.956	1	78	71	O122(115/3/4)		-2.1
Total 6		709	2856	577	805	147	47	20	394	231	41	224	.282	.344	.387	117	61	321	.934	3	75	62	O703(655/46/4),1b10,S2/P3		2.9
O'BRIEN, BILLY	William Smith B3.14.1860 Albany NY D5.26.1911 Kansas City MO BR/TR/6-0/185 d9.27 ▲																								
1884	StP U	8	30	1	7	3	0	0		0			.233	.233	.333	128	0		.840	2	138	0	3b8,P2		0.2
	KC U	4	17	2	4	0	0	0		0			.235	.235	.235	49	-2		.714	1	177	0	3b3/1		-0.1
	Year	12	47	3	11	3	0	0		0			.234	.234	.298	92	-2		.795	3	151	0	3b11,P2/1		0.1
1887	Was N	113	453	71	126	16	12	19	73	21	5	17	.278	.317	.492	130	16	11	.974	-4	69	91	1b104,O4(1/3/0),3b4,2b2		0.2
1888	Was N	133	528	42	119	15	2	9	66	9	0	70	.225	.238	.313	80	-13	10	.975	-4	81	82	1b132/3		-2.8
1889	Was N	2	8	1	0	0	0	0	0	0		1	.000	.111	.000	-72	-2	0	1.000	0	0	0	1b2		-0.2
1890	Bro AA	96	388	47	108	25	8	4	67	28	3		.278	.332	.415	124	10	5	.973	-3	90	111	1b96		-0.1
Total 5		356	1424	164	364	59	22	32	206	59	8	88	.256	.289	.395	109	9	26	.974	-8	80	92	1b335,3b16,O4(1/3/0),2b2,P2		-2.8
OCHOA, ALEX	Alex B3.29.1972 Miami Lakes FL BR/TR/6-0/195(175-200) [BalA91 3/82] d9.18																								
1995	NY N	11	37	7	11	1	0	0	2-0	0		10	.297	.333	.324	77	-1	1-0	1.000	1	120	160	O10R		0.0
1996	NY N	82	282	37	83	19	3	4	33	17-0	2	32	.294	.336	.426	105	2	4-3	.966	1	97	160	O76R		-0.1
1997	NY N	113	338	31	58	14	1	3	22	18-0	2	32	.244	.301	.349	73	-10	3-4	.982	-2	86	149	O88(0/4/84),D		-1.5
1998	Min A	94	249	35	64	14	2	2	25	10-0	1	35	.257	.288	.353	64	-14	6-3	.969	-0	91	179	O74(21/4/52),D3		-1.6
1999	Mil N	119	277	47	83	16	3	8	40	45-2	5	43	.300	.404	.466	120	10	6-4	.979	2	93	110	O85(50/9/31),D		0.5
2000	Cin N	118	244	50	77	21	3	13	58	24-3	3	27	.316	.378	.586	136	13	9-4	.977	2	107	107	O95(74/3/37)		1.3
2001	Cin N	90	349	48	101	20	4	7	35	24-0	2	23	.289	.337	.430	92	-4	12-9	.989	1	100	102	O52(33/2/21)		-0.8
	Col N	58	187	25	47	10	3	1	17	21-0	4	23	.251	.330	.353	65	-9	5-4	.990	2	97	184	O52(33/2/21)		-0.9
	Year	148	536	73	148	30	7	8	52	45-0	4	76	.276	.334	.403	81	-15	17-13	.989	3	99	132	O137(36/2/106)/D		-1.7
2002	Mil N	85	215	32	55	9	0	6	21	32-2	2	30	.256	.357	.381	99	-1	8-5	.993	6	119	130	O72(18/2/61)		0.2
	†Ana A	37	65	8	18	7	0	2	10	10-0		5	.277	.373	.477	126	3	2-2	.975	-1	87	152	O36(7/0/31)		0.1
Total 8		807	2143	320	597	131	19	46	261	203-7	19	288	.279	.344	.422	96	-11	56-38	.981	10	98	139	O673(206/24/488),D6	15	-2.8
CK, WHITEY	Harold David B3.17.1912 Brooklyn NY D3.18.1975 Mt.Kisco NY BR/TR/5-11/180 d9.29 Col Lehigh																								
1935	Bro N	1	3	0	0	0	0	0	0	1	0	2	.000	.250	.000	-27	-1	0	1.000	-0	0	0	/C		-0.1
O'CONNELL, DANNY	Daniel Francis B1.21.1927 Paterson NJ D10.2.1969 Clifton NJ BR/TR/6-0/180* d7.14 Mil 1951-52 C2																								
1950	Pit N	79	315	39	92	16	1	8	32	24	0	33	.292	.342	.425	97	-1	7	.977	7	103	95	S65,3b12		0.9
1953	Pit N	149	588	88	173	26	1	8	55	57	4		.294	.361	.401	99	0	3-4	.958	7	110	66	3b104,2b47		0.9
1954	Mil N	146	541	61	151	28	4	2	37	38	2	46	.279	.326	.357	84	-13	2-2	.979	6	106	114	2b103,3b35,1b8/S		0.9
1955	Mil N	124	453	47	102	15	4	6	40	28-2	5	42	.225	.276	.316	60	-27	2-2	.981	14	111	92	2b114,3b7/S		-0.5
1956	Mil N	139	498	71	119	17	9	4	42	76-0	4	42	.239	.342	.321	86	-8	3-3	.985	-4	104	119	2b138,3b4/S		-0.2
1957	Mil N	48	183	29	43	9	1	1	8	19-0	2	20	.235	.312	.311	74	-6	1-0	.982	6	108	137	2b48		0.4
	NY N	95	364	57	97	18	3	7	28	33-0	2	30	.266	.330	.390	93	-3	8-3	.980	5	105	115	2b68,3b30		0.8
	Year	143	547	86	140	27	4	8	36	52-0	4	50	.256	.324	.364	87	-9	9-3	.981	12	106	124	2b116,3b30		1.2
1958	SF N	107	306	44	71	12	2	3	23	51-0	0	35	.232	.340	.314	77	-9	2-1	.986	2	104	100	2b104,3b3		0.0
1959	SF N	34	58	6	11	3	0	0	6	9	0	15	.190	.254	.241	34	-5	0-1	.927	3	118	131	3b26,2b8		-0.3
1961	Was A	138	493	61	128	30	1	1	37	77-0	3	62	.260	.361	.331	88	-4	15-5	.939	8	116	90	3b73,2b61		1.0
1962	Was A	84	236	24	62	17	2	2	18	23-1	0	28	.263	.327	.335	80	-1	5-1	.961	2	117	194	3b41,2b22		-0.3
Total 10		1143	4035	527	1049	181	35	39	320	431-3	22	396	.260	.333	.351	84	-83	48-22	.980	56	106	108	2b215,3b335,S68,1b8		2.7
O'CONNELL, JIMMY	James Joseph B2.11.1901 Sacramento CA D11.11.1976 Bakersfield CA BL/TR/5-10.5/175 d4.17 Col Santa Clara																								
1923	†NY N	87	252	42	63	9	2	6	39	34	5	32	.250	.351	.373	92	-2	7-3	.980	-10	87	25	O64C,1b8		-1.4
1924	NY N	52	104	24	33	4	2	2	18	11	1	16	.317	.388	.452	128	4	2-1	.952	-2	88	95	O29(1/15/14)/2		0.2
Total 2		139	356	66	96	13	4	8	57	45	6	48	.270	.361	.396	102	2	9-4	.974	-11	87	41	O93(1/79/14),1b8/2		-1.2
O'CONNELL, JOHN	John Charles B6.13.1904 Verona PA D10.17.1992 Canton OH BR/TR/6-0/170 d8.16 Col Duquesne																								
1928	Pit N	1	1	0	0	0	0	0	0	0	0	0	.000	.000	.000	-96	0	0	1.000	1	0	594	/C		0.0
1929	Pit N	2	7	1	1	1	0	0	0			1	.143	.250	.286	32	-1	0	1.000	-0	100	0	C2		-0.1
Total 2		3	8	1	1	1	0	0	0			1	.125	.222	.250	17	-1	0	1.000	0	80	119	C3		-0.1
O'CONNELL, JOHN	John Joseph D5.14.1908 Derry NH 5-9.5/170 d8.22																								
1901	Bal AA	8	29	2	5	1	0	0	7	3	0	6	.172	.250	.207	31	-3	2	.938	-2	99	0	S3,2b3,O2R		-0.4
1902	Det A	8	22	1	4	0	0	0		3	0		.182	.280	.182	29	-2	0	.919	0	113	79	2b6,1b2		-0.2
Total 2		16	51	3	9	1	0	0	7	6	0	6	.176	.263	.196	30	-5	2	.885	-2	99	85	2b9,S3,1b2,O2R		-0.6
O'CONNELL, PAT	Patrick H. B6.10.1861 Bangor ME D1.24.1943 Lewiston ME BL/TR/5-10/175 d7.22																								
1886	Bal AA	42	166	20	30	3	2	0					.181	.236	.223	45	-10	10	.782	-6	58	0	O41C/1P		-1.6
O'CONNOR, DAN	Daniel Cornelius B8.11.1868 Guelph ON, Can. D3.3.1942 Guelph ON, Can. BL/TR/6-2/185 d6.3																								
1890	Lou AA	6	26	3	12	1	1	0	5	1	0		.462	.481	.577	217	4	5	1.000	-1	0	117	1b6		0.2
O'CONNOR, JOHNNY	John Charles "Bucky" B12.1.1891 Cahirciveen, Ireland D5.30.1982 Bonner Springs KS BR/TR/5-9/? d9.16 Col Illinois																								
1916	Chi N	1	0	0	0	0	0	0	0	0	0	0	—	—	—	0	0	0	—	0	0	0	/C		0.0
O'CONNOR, JACK	John Joseph "Rowdy Jack","Peach Pie" B6.2.1869 St.Louis MO D11.14.1937 St.Louis MO BR/TR/5-10/170 d4.20 M1 OF(42/113/217)																								
1887	Cin N	12	40	4	4	0	0	0	1	2	0		.100	.143	.100	-31	-7	3	.947	2	166	414	O7L,C5		-0.4
1888	Cin AA	36	137	14	28	3	1	0	17	6	1		.204	.243	.263	59	-7	12	.795	-2	141	0	O34(11/21/2),C2		-0.9
1889	Col AA	107	398	69	107	17	7	4	60	33	4	37	.269	.331	.377	107	3	26	.955	-1	0	0	C84,O19(3/0/16),2b4,1b3		0.7
1890	Col AA	121	457	89	148	14	10	2	66	38	1		.324	.377	.411	142	23	29	.962	11	105	99	C106,O9(3/4/2),S8,2b2/3		3.7
1891	Col AA	56	229	28	61	12	3	0	37	11	0	14	.266	.300	.345	90	-4	10	.878	0	113	205	O40(7/0/33),C21		-0.2
1892	†Cle N	140	572	71	142	22	5	1	58	25	2	48	.248	.286	.309	76	-19	17	.935	12	125	129	O106(6/0/100),C34		-0.9
1893	Cle N	96	384	72	110	23	1	4	75	29	1		.286	.341	.383	87	-8	29	.949	5	112	104	C56,O44(2/27/15)		0.0
1894	Cle N	86	330	67	104	23	7	2	51	15	0	7	.315	.345	.445	86	-9	15	.942	0	160	77	C45,O33(1/27/5),1b7		-0.3
1895	Cle N	90	343	52	100	23	2	6	51	15	1		.292	.355	.391	87	-8	11	.927	0	119	96	C48,1b41/3		-0.6
1896	†Cle N	68	256	41	76	11	1	1	43	15	3	12	.297	.343	.359	81	-7	15	.966	2	149	95	C48,1b17,O12(0/3/9)		-1.7
1897	Cle N	103	397	49	115	21	4	2	69	26	3		.290	.338	.378	84	-10	20	.941	-8	46	0	O52(0/30/22),1b36,C13		-0.6
1898	Cle N	131	478	50	119	19	4	1	56	26	2		.249	.291	.308	72	-18	4	.983	9	125	99	C57,1b26		-0.6
1899	StL N	84	289	33	73	5	6	0	43	15	4		.253	.299	.311	66	-15	7	.943	6	125	87	C57,1b26		-0.4

YEAR TM LG	G	AB	R	H	2B	3B	HR	RBI	BB-IB	HP	SO	AVG	OBP	SLG	AOPS	ABR	SB-CS	FA	FR	RNG	THR	GAMES AT POSITION	DL	BFW
1900 StL N	10	32	4	7	0	0	0	6	2	2		.219	.306	.219	46	-2	0	.957	-0	92	87	C10		-0.2
†Pit N	43	147	15	35	4	1	0	19	3	2		.238	.263	.279	49	-11	5	.944	-4	130	96	C40,1b2		-1.0
Year	53	179	19	42	4	1	0	25	5	4		.235	.271	.268	49	-13	5	.947	-4	122	96	C50,1b2		-1.2
1901 Pit N	61	202	16	39	7	3	0	22	10	2		.193	.238	.257	42	-15	2	.978	3	131	90	C59		-0.7
1902 Pit N	49	170	13	50	1	2	1	28	3	0		.294	.306	.341	96	-2	2	.979	0	140	100	C42,1b6/OR		0.2
1903 NY A	64	212	13	43	4	1	0	12	8	1		.203	.235	.231	55	-16	4	.988	2	110	80	C63/1		-0.9
1904 StL A	14	47	4	10	1	0	0	2	2	0		.213	.245	.234	55	-2	0	.943	-4	87	72	C14		-0.5
1906 StL A	55	174	8	33	0	0	0	11	2	0		.190	.199	.190	23	-16	4	.990	6	94	109	C51		-0.6
1907 StL A	25	89	2	14	2	0	0	4	0	0		.157	.176	.180	13	-9	0	.991	-2	87	97	C25		-0.9
1910 StL A	1	0	0	0	0	0	0	0	0	0		—	—	—	0	0	0	1.000	-0	30	0	/CM		0.0
Total 21	1452	5383	714	1418	201	66	19	738	302	35	152	.263	.307	.336	79	-159	219	.962	46	118	94	C861,O372R,1b208,S8,2b6,3b2		-5.6

O'CONNOR, PADDY
Patrick Francis B8.4.1879 Co. Kerry, Ireland D8.17.1950 Springfield MA BR/TR/5-8/168 d4.17 C4

YEAR TM LG	G	AB	R	H	2B	3B	HR	RBI	BB-IB	HP	SO	AVG	OBP	SLG	AOPS	ABR	SB-CS	FA	FR	RNG	THR	GAMES AT POSITION	DL	BFW
1908 Pit N	12	16	1	3	0	0	0	2	0	0		.188	.188	.188	20	-2	0	.889	-1	117	51	C4		-0.3
1909 †Pit N	9	16	1	5	0	0	0	3	0	0		.313	.313	.375	104	0	0	.700	-1	116	52	C3/3		-0.1
1910 Pit N	6	4	0	1	0	0	0	0	1	0	1	.250	.400	.250	85	0	0	1.000	-0	0	0	/C		0.0
1914 StL N	10	9	0	0	0	0	0	0	2	1		.000	.250	.000	-24	-1	0	1.000	-0	84	99	C7		-0.2
1915 Pit F	70	219	15	50	10	1	0	16	14	1	30	.228	.278	.283	58	-16	4	.987	7	118	108	C66		-0.3
1918 NY A	1	3	0	1	0	0	0	0	0	0		.333	.333	.333	99	0	0	1.000	-0	66	191	/C		0.0
Total 6	108	267	17	60	11	1	0	21	17	2	34	.225	.276	.273	57	-19	4	.979	4	116	105	C82/3		-0.9

O'DEA, KEN
James Kenneth B3.16.1913 Lima NY D12.17.1985 Lima NY BL/TR/6-0/180 d4.21

YEAR TM LG	G	AB	R	H	2B	3B	HR	RBI	BB-IB	HP	SO	AVG	OBP	SLG	AOPS	ABR	SB-CS	FA	FR	RNG	THR	GAMES AT POSITION	DL	BFW
1935 †Chi N	76	202	30	52	13	2	6	38	26	1	18	.257	.345	.431	106	2	0	.964	-1	107	101	C63		0.5
1936 Chi N	80	189	36	58	10	3	2	38	38	0	18	.307	.423	.423	126	9	0	.979	-1	117	90	C55		1.1
1937 Chi N	83	219	31	66	7	4	5	32	24	0	26	.301	.370	.434	113	4	1	.985	-4	117	80	C64		0.3
1938 †Chi N	86	247	22	65	12	1	3	33	12	0	18	.263	.297	.356	77	-8	1	.970	-1	110	83	C71		-0.3
1939 NY N	52	97	7	17	1	0	3	11	10	0	16	.175	.252	.278	42	-8	0	.992	-3	143	172	C31		-0.5
1940 NY N	48	96	9	23	4	1	0	12	16	0	15	.240	.348	.302	80	-2	0	1.000	-1	110	106	C14		0.0
1941 NY N	59	89	13	19	5	1	3	17	8	0	20	.213	.278	.393	85	-2	0	.979	9	159	134	C49		0.3
1942 †StL N	58	192	22	45	7	1	3	32	17	1	25	.234	.297	.359	85	-4	0	.989	6	176	104	C56		1.2
1943 †StL N	71	203	15	57	11	2	3	25	19	1	25	.281	.345	.399	110	3	0	.994	7	141	89	C69		1.2
1944 †StL N	85	265	35	66	11	2	6	37	37	1	29	.249	.343	.374	100	1	1	**.995**	4	99	**128**	C91		1.1
1945 StL N*	100	307	36	78	18	2	4	43	50	0	31	.254	.359	.365	99	1	0	.991	3	152	120	C22		-0.1
1946 NY N	22	57	2	7	2	0	1	3	8	0	8	.123	.231	.211	25	-6	0	1.000	-1	72	108	C12		-0.2
Bos N	12	32	4	7	0	0	0	2	8	0	12	.219	.375	.219	70	-1	0	.994	3	126	116	C34		-0.2
Year	34	89	6	14	2	0	1	5	16	0	20	.157	.286	.213	41	-7	0	.983		125	106	C627		
Total	832	2195	262	560	101	20	40	323	273	3	251	.255	.338	.374	95	-11	3	.983	27	125	106	C627		5.2

O'DEA, PAUL
Paul "Lefty" B7.3.1920 Cleveland OH D12.11.1978 Cleveland OH BL/TL/6-0/200 d4.19 Col Case Western Reserve

YEAR TM LG	G	AB	R	H	2B	3B	HR	RBI	BB-IB	HP	SO	AVG	OBP	SLG	AOPS	ABR	SB-CS	FA	FR	RNG	THR	GAMES AT POSITION	DL	BFW
1944 Cle A	76	173	25	55	9	0	0	13	23	1	21	.318	.401	.370	126	7	2-2	.949	-2	93	68	O41(36/0/5),P3,1b3		-0.3
1945 Cle A	87	221	21	52	2	2	1	21	20	0	26	.235	.299	.276	70	-9	3-0	.992	3	115	77	O53R/P		-1.0
Total 2	163	394	46	107	11	2	1	34	43	1	47	.272	.345	.317			5-2	.975	0	106	73	O94(36/0/58),P4,1b3		-0.7

ODOM, HEINIE
Herman Boyd B10.13.1900 Rusk TX D8.31.1970 Rusk TX BB/TR/6-0/170 d4.22 Col Texas

YEAR TM LG	G	AB	R	H	2B	3B	HR	RBI	BB-IB	HP	SO	AVG	OBP	SLG	AOPS	ABR	SB-CS	FA	FR	RNG	THR	GAMES AT POSITION	DL	BFW
1925 NY A	1	1	0	1	0	0	0	0	0	0	0	1.000	1.000	1.000	416	0	0-0	1.000	0	148	0	/3		0.

O'DONNELL, HARRY
Harry Herman "Butch" B4.2.1894 Philadelphia PA D1.31.1958 Philadelphia PA BR/TR/5-8/175 d4.30

YEAR TM LG	G	AB	R	H	2B	3B	HR	RBI	BB-IB	HP	SO	AVG	OBP	SLG	AOPS	ABR	SB-CS	FA	FR	RNG	THR	GAMES AT POSITION	DL	BFW
1927 Phi N	16	16	1	1	0	0	0	2	2	0	2	.063	.167	.063	-36	-3	0	1.000	-0	72	72	C12		-0.

O'DONNELL, JOHN
John B Littlestown PA d7.16

YEAR TM LG	G	AB	R	H	2B	3B	HR	RBI	BB-IB	HP	SO	AVG	OBP	SLG	AOPS	ABR	SB-CS	FA	FR	RNG	THR	GAMES AT POSITION	DL	BFW
1884 Phi U	1	4	0	1	0	0	0		0			.250	.250	.250	56	0		.545	-2			/C		-0.

O'DOUL, LEFTY
Francis Joseph B3.4.1897 San Francisco CA D12.7.1969 San Francisco CA BL/TL/6-0/180 d4.29 ▲

YEAR TM LG	G	AB	R	H	2B	3B	HR	RBI	BB-IB	HP	SO	AVG	OBP	SLG	AOPS	ABR	SB-CS	FA	FR	RNG	THR	GAMES AT POSITION	DL	BFW
1919 NY A	19	16	2	4	0	0	0	1	1	0	2	.250	.294	.250	53	-1	1	.500	-0	75	0	P3/OR		-0.
1920 NY A	13	12	2	2	1	0	0	0	1	0	0	.167	.231	.250	26	-1	0-0	—	-0	0	0	P2/OC		-0.
1922 NY A	8	9	0	3	1	0	0	4	0	0	2	.333	.333	.444	99	1	0-0	1.000	0	102	0	P6		-0.
1923 Bos A	36	35	2	5	0	0	0	4	2	0	3	.143	.189	.143	-12	-6	0-0	.958	1	153	0	P23/OR		-0.
1928 NY N	114	354	67	113	19	4	8	46	30	0	19	.319	.372	.463	117	-8	9	.962	-7	86	62	O94L		4.
1929 Phi N	**154**	638	152	**254**	35	6	32	122	76	4	19	**.398**	**.465**	.622	157	59	2	.971	3	100	128	O154(139/0/15)		4.
1930 Phi N	140	528	122	202	37	7	22	97	63	5	21	.383	.453	.604	142	37	3	.953	-5	102	33	O131L		2.
1931 Bro N	134	512	85	172	32	11	7	75	48	3	16	.336	.396	.482	136	27	5	.954	-2	104	35	O132L		1.
1932 Bro N	148	595	120	219	32	8	21	90	50	7	20	**.368**	.423	.555	164	54	11	.979	-5	99	44	O148L		4.
1933 Bro N	43	159	14	40	5	1	5	21	15	1	6	.252	.320	.390	106	1	2	.947	-2	101	32	O41L		-0.
†NY N★	78	229	31	70	9	1	9	35	29	3	17	.306	.388	.472	147	15	1	.974	-3	91	82	O63(32/0/31)		0
Year	121	388	45	110	14	2	14	56	44	4	23	.284	.361	.438	130	16	3	.962	-5	95	61	O104(73/0/31)		0
1934 NY N	83	177	22	56	4	3	9	46	18	1	7	.316	.383	.525	144	10	2	.968	-4	84	38	O38(27/0/11),P34		
Total 11	970	3264	624	1140	175	41	113	542	333	23	122	.349	.413	.532	142	206	36-0	.964	-24	98	65	O804(744/1/59),P34		12

ODWELL, FRED
Frederick William "Fritz" B9.25.1872 Downsville NY D8.19.1948 Downsville NY BL/TR/5-9.5/160 d4.16

YEAR TM LG	G	AB	R	H	2B	3B	HR	RBI	BB-IB	HP	SO	AVG	OBP	SLG	AOPS	ABR	SB-CS	FA	FR	RNG	THR	GAMES AT POSITION	DL	BFW
1904 Cin N	129	468	75	133	22	10	1	58	26	8		.284	.333	.380	110	5	30	.956	12	109	133	O126(107/14/5)/2		1
1905 Cin N	130	468	79	113	10	9	**9**	65	26	8		.241	.293	.359	85	-11	21	.967	2	106	114	O126(56/4/66)		-1
1906 Cin N	58	202	20	45	5	4	0	21	15	3		.223	.286	.287	76	-6	11	.963	2	134	0	O57R		0
1907 Cin N	94	274	24	74	5	7	0	24	22	5		.270	.336	.339	107	2	10	.975	6	77	94	O84(77/0/8)/2		-1
Total 4	411	1412	198	365	42	30	10	168	89	24		.258	.313	.352	96	-10	72	.964	22	105	94	O393(240/18/136),2b2		-1

OERTEL, CHUCK
Charles Frank "Ducky","Snuffy" B3.12.1931 Coffeyville KS D10.4.2000 Royal Oak MI BL/TR/5-8/165 d9.1

YEAR TM LG	G	AB	R	H	2B	3B	HR	RBI	BB-IB	HP	SO	AVG	OBP	SLG	AOPS	ABR	SB-CS	FA	FR	RNG	THR	GAMES AT POSITION	DL	BFW
1958 Bal A	14	12	4	2	1	1	1	1	1-1	0	1	.167	.231	.417	78	0	0-0	1.000	0	111	0	O2(2/0/1)		-0

OESTER, RON
Ronald John B5.5.1956 Cincinnati OH BB/TR/6-2/190(175-195) [CinN74 9/215] d9.10 C7

YEAR TM LG	G	AB	R	H	2B	3B	HR	RBI	BB-IB	HP	SO	AVG	OBP	SLG	AOPS	ABR	SB-CS	FA	FR	RNG	THR	GAMES AT POSITION	DL	BFW
1978 Cin N	6	8	1	3	0	0	0	1	0-0	0	2	.375	.375	.375	110	0	1	1.000	1	117	138	S6		0
1979 Cin N	6	3	0	0	0	0	0	0	0-0	0	1	.000	.000	.000	-99	-1	0-0	1.000	0	112	0	S2		-1
1980 Cin N	100	303	40	84	16	2	2	30	26-7	1	44	.277	.336	.363	97	-1	6-2	.980	-15	89	98	2b79,S17,3b3		1
1981 Cin N	105	354	45	96	16	7	5	42	42-8	0	49	.271	.342	.398	112	6	2-5	.972	3	97	107	2b118,S29,3b13		1
1982 Cin N	151	549	63	143	19	4	9	47	35-8	0	82	.260	.303	.359	85	-13	5-6	.980	-2	80	78	2b154		-2
1983 Cin N	157	549	63	145	23	5	11	58	49-14	1	106	.264	.322	.384	93	-6	2-2	.980	10	100	103	2b147/S		-3
1984 Cin N	150	553	54	134	26	3	3	38	41-7	1	97	.242	.295	.316	69	-23	7-2	.989	10	100	103	2b149		1
1985 Cin N	152	526	59	155	26	3	1	34	51-17	2	65	.295	.354	.360	95	-10	9-2	.978	15	106	108	2b151		1
1986 Cin N	153	523	52	135	23	2	8	44	52-16	1	84	.258	.325	.356	85	-10	2-3	.974	1	96	88	2b69	91	-0
1987 Cin N	69	237	28	60	9	2	2	23	22-4	0	51	.253	.317	.367	77	-8	2-3	.995	-0	93	105	2b49,S5		-0
1988 Cin N	54	150	20	42	7	0	0	10	9-3	1	24	.280	.319	.327	83	-3	0-2	.985	3	97	82	2b102,S2	40	-0
1989 Cin N	109	305	23	75	15	0	1	14	32-8	0	47	.246	.318	.305	76	-8	1-0	.982	-8	82	70	2b50,3b3		-0
1990 †Cin N	64	154	10	46	10	1	0	13	10-1	1	29	.299	.339	.377	92	-1	1-2	.980	-27	95	94		131	-3
Total 13	1276	4214	458	1118	190	33	42	344	369-93	4	681	.265	.323	.356	87	-69	40-26	.980	-27	95	94	2b1171,S71,3b19		

O'FARRELL, BOB
Robert Arthur B10.19.1896 Waukegan IL D2.20.1988 Waukegan IL BR/TR/5-9.5/180 d9.5 M2

YEAR TM LG	G	AB	R	H	2B	3B	HR	RBI	BB-IB	HP	SO	AVG	OBP	SLG	AOPS	ABR	SB-CS	FA	FR	RNG	THR	GAMES AT POSITION	DL	BFW
1915 Chi N	2	3	0	1	0	0	0	0	0	0	0	.333	.333	.333	102	0	1	.667	-1	63	184	C2		-0
1916 Chi N	1	0	0	0	0	0	0	0	0	0	0	—	—	—	0	0	0		0	0		/C		-0
1917 Chi N	3	8	1	3	2	0	0	1	1	0	0	.375	.444	.625	209	1	1	1.000	-1	88	73	C3		-0
1918 †Chi N	52	113	9	32	7	3	1	14	10	1	15	.283	.347	.425	132	4	0	.974	-3	98	108	C45		-0
1919 Chi N	49	125	11	27	4	2	0	9	7	0	10	.216	.258	.280	61	-6	2	.965	-1	96	112	C38		-0
1920 Chi N	94	270	29	67	11	4	3	19	34	0	23	.248	.332	.352	95	-1	1-0	.956	-2	100	117	C86		-0
1921 Chi N	96	260	32	65	12	7	4	32	18	0	14	.250	.299	.396	82	-8	2-0	.967	-4	95	112	C90		-0
1922 Chi N	128	392	68	127	18	4	7	60	79	1	34	.324	.439	.441	125	20	5-3	.977	15	121	**143**	C125		-0
1923 Chi N	131	452	73	144	25	4	12	84	67	4	38	.319	.408	.471	131	23	10-3	.976	9	111	102	C124		-0
1924 Chi N	71	183	25	44	6	2	3	28	30	2	13	.240	.347	.344	85	-3	2-0	.984	-1	115	94	C57		-0
1925 Chi N	17	22	2	4	1	0	1	3	2	0	2	.182	.250	.273	33	-1	0-0	1.000	-1	104	0	C3		-0
StL N	94	317	37	88	13	4	3	32	46	2	26	.278	.373	.360	86	-5	0-1	.975	1	114	81	C92		

YEAR	TM LG	G	AB	R	H	2B	3B	HR	RBI	BB-IB	HP	SO	AVG	OBP	SLG	AOPS	ABR	SB-CS	FA	FR	RNG	THR	GAMES AT POSITION	DL	BFW
	Year	111	339	39	92	13	3	3	35	48	2	31	.271	.365	.354	.83	-7	0-1	.975	0	114	79	C95		-0.1
1926	†StL N	147	492	63	144	30	9	7	68	61	0	44	.293	.371	.433	111	9	1	.983	13	127	101	C146		3.2
1927	StL N	61	178	19	47	10	1	0	18	23	0	22	.264	.348	.331	60	-4	3	.979	1	91	146	C53,M		0.0
1928	StL N	16	52	6	11	1	0	0	4	13	0	9	.212	.369	.231	59	-2	2	.985	0	135	37	C14		-0.1
	NY N	75	133	23	26	6	0	2	20	34	0	16	.195	.359	.286	70	-4	2	.988	1	136	72	C63		-0.1
	Year	91	185	29	37	7	0	2	24	47	0	25	.200	.362	.270	67	-7	4	.987	1	136	63	C77		-0.2
1929	NY N	91	248	35	76	14	3	4	42	28	3	30	.306	.384	.424	103	2	3	.979	-2	138	28	C84		0.4
1930	NY N	94	249	37	75	16	4	4	54	31	1	21	.301	.381	.446	101	1	1	.973	-1	101	101	C69		0.4
1931	NY N	85	174	11	39	8	3	1	19	21	1	23	.224	.311	.322	72	-7	0	.980	2	142	90	C80		-0.2
1932	NY N	50	67	7	16	3	0	0	8	11	1	10	.239	.354	.284	76	-2	0	.969	0	101	88	C41		0.0
1933	StL N	55	163	16	39	4	2	2	20	15	0	25	.239	.303	.325	76	-5	0	.970	-4	89	94	C50		-0.7
1934	Cin N	44	123	10	30	8	3	1	9	11	0	19	.244	.306	.382	85	-3	0	.993	-0	96	131	C42,M		-0.1
	Chi N	22	67	3	15	3	0	0	5	3	0	11	.224	.257	.269	42	-6	0	1.000	2	128	108	C22		-0.3
	Year	66	190	13	45	11	3	1	14	14	0	30	.237	.289	.342	70	-8	0	.996	1	107	123	C64		-0.4
1935	StL N	14	10	0	0	0	0	0	0	2	0	0	.000	.167	.000	-9	-2	0	1.000	0	59	0	C8		-0.2
Total 21		1492	4101	517	1120	201	58	51	549	547	11	408	.273	.360	.388	97	-33	35-7	.976	26	113	101	C1338		10.2

OFFERMAN, JOSE Jose Antonio (Dono) B11.8.1968 San Pedro de Macoris, D.R. BB/TR/6-0/190(160-200) d8.19 OF(5/1/3)

YEAR	TM LG	G	AB	R	H	2B	3B	HR	RBI	BB-IB	HP	SO	AVG	OBP	SLG	AOPS	ABR	SB-CS	FA	FR	RNG	THR	GAMES AT POSITION	DL	BFW
1990	LA N	29	58	7	9	0	0	1	7	4-1	0	14	.155	.210	.207	15	-7	1-0	.946	-3	85	59	S27		-0.9
1991	LA N	52	113	10	22	1	0	0	3	25-2	1	32	.195	.345	.212	61	-4	3-2	.945	-1	106	89	S50		-0.2
1992	LA N	149	534	67	139	20	8	1	30	57-4	0	98	.260	.331	.333	90	-7	23-16	.935	-13	96	87	S149		-0.9
1993	LA N	158	590	77	159	21	6	1	62	71-7	2	75	.269	.346	.331	88	-8	30-13	.950	-7	98	99	S158		-0.1
1994	LA N	72	243	27	51	4	1	1	25	38-4	0	38	.210	.314	.288	63	-13	2-1	.967	4	98	104	S72		-0.4
1995	†LA N★	119	429	69	123	14	6	4	33	69-0	3	67	.287	.389	.375	111	10	2-7	.932	-4	95	99	S115		1.2
1996	KC A	151	561	85	170	33	8	5	47	74-3	1	98	.303	.384	.417	102	5	24-10	.994	4	121	116	1b96,2b38,S36/OC		0.6
1997	KC A	106	424	59	126	23	6	2	39	41-3	0	64	.297	.359	.394	93	-3	9-10	.981	-12	92	102	2b101/D		-1.2
1998	KC A	158	607	102	191	28	13	7	66	89-1	5	96	.315	.403	.438	115	17	45-12	.974	6	105	114	2b152,D6	61	3.3
1999	†Bos A★	149	586	107	172	37	11	8	69	96-5	2	79	.294	.391	.435	108	11	18-12	.975	-22	82	91	2b128,D17,1b8		-0.7
2000	Bos A	116	451	73	115	14	3	9	41	70-0	1	70	.255	.354	.359	80	-13	0-8	.981	6	97	96	2b80,1b38,D9	32	-0.8
2001	Bos A	128	524	76	140	23	3	9	49	61-2	1	97	.267	.342	.374	89	-7	5-2	.974	3	93	77	2b91,1b43		-0.3
2002	Bos A	72	237	39	55	10	0	4	27	33-0	1	29	.232	.325	.325	73	-8	8-5	.994	1	114	124	1b41,D24,O2R		-1.2
	Sea A	29	47	9	11	2	1	1	4	4-0	0	9	.234	.294	.383	81	-1	1-1	1.000	2	174	55	1b11,O6(5/0/1)/2D		0.0
	Year	101	284	48	66	12	1	5	31	37-0	1	38	.232	.320	.335	75	-10	9-6	.995	4	124	113	1b52,D28,O8(5/0/3)/2		-1.2
2004	†Min A	77	172	22	44	14	2	2	22	29-2	0	31	.256	.363	.395	95	0	1-1	.983	0	163	242	D39,1b7,2b3		-0.2
2005	Phi N	33	33	6	6	1	1	1	3	5-0	0	6	.182	.289	.364	68	-2	0-0	.938	-1	0	69	1b4		-0.3
	NY N	53	72	5	18	2	0	1	10	6-0	1	11	.250	.316	.319	69	-3	0-0	.988	-1	72	124	1b11/2		-0.5
	Year	86	105	11	24	3	1	2	13	11-0	1	17	.229	.308	.333	68	-5	0-0	.980	-2	60	115	1b15/2		-0.8
Total 15		1651	5681	840	1551	252	72	57	537	772-34	18	914	.273	.360	.373	93	-33	172-100	.943	-36	97	98	S607,2b595,1b259,D100,O9L	93	-2.6

OFFICE, ROWLAND Rowland Johnie B10.25.1952 Sacramento CA BL/TL/6-0/170* [AtlN70 4/94] d8.5

YEAR	TM LG	G	AB	R	H	2B	3B	HR	RBI	BB-IB	HP	SO	AVG	OBP	SLG	AOPS	ABR	SB-CS	FA	FR	RNG	THR	GAMES AT POSITION	DL	BFW
1972	Atl N	2	5	1	2	0	0	0	1	1-0	0	2	.400	.500	.400	146	0	0-0	1.000	0	106	0	/OC		0.0
1974	Atl N	131	248	20	61	16	1	3	31	16-2	0	30	.246	.288	.355	77	-8	5-3	.994	7	93	0	O119(1/118/0)		-1.8
1975	Atl N	126	355	30	103	14	1	3	30	23-4	3	41	.290	.337	.361	91	-4	2-2	.967	-5	93	98	O107(1/106/0)		-1.3
1976	Atl N	99	359	51	101	17	1	4	34	37-3	2	49	.281	.348	.368	99	0	2-8	.986	-8	91	55	O92C		-1.3
1977	Atl N	124	428	42	103	13	1	5	39	23-1	7	58	.241	.282	.311	53	-28	2-4	.988	2	104	126	O104(1/103/0)/1	16	-1.3
1978	Atl N	146	404	40	101	13	1	9	40	22-2	6	52	.250	.297	.354	74	-14	8-6	.990	2	108	68	O136C	18	-2.9
1979	Atl N	124	277	35	69	14	2	2	37	27-2	2	33	.249	.320	.336	75	-9	5-4	.988	-5	92	79	O97C		-1.5
1980	Mon N	116	292	36	78	13	4	6	30	36-1	0	39	.267	.343	.401	106	3	3-3	.987	-7	92	31	O97(3/27/68)		-1.5
1981	Mon N	26	40	4	7	0	0	0	4	4-0	0	6	.175	.250	.175	22	-4	0-0	.938	-1	84	0	O15(0/3/12)	111	-0.8
1982	Mon N	3	3	0	1	1	0	0	0	0-0	0	1	.333	.333	.667	167	0	0-0	1.000	0	436	0	/OL		-0.6
1983	NY A	2	2	0	0	0	0	0	0	0-0	0	0	.000	.000	.000	-99	-1	0-0	1.000	0	92	0	O2C		-0.1
Total 11		899	2413	259	626	101	11	32	242	189-15	16	311	.259	.315	.350	80	-65	27-30	.985	-29	97	67	O771(7/687/80)/1	145	-11.7

OGLESBY, JIM James Dorn B8.10.1905 Schofield MO D9.1.1955 Tulsa OK BL/TL/6-0/190 d4.14

YEAR	TM LG	G	AB	R	H	2B	3B	HR	RBI	BB-IB	HP	SO	AVG	OBP	SLG	AOPS	ABR	SB-CS	FA	FR	RNG	THR	GAMES AT POSITION	DL	BFW
1936	Phi A	3	11	0	2	0	0	0	2	0-0	0	2	.182	.308	.182	24	-1	0-0	1.000	0	143	83	1b3		-0.1

OGLIVIE, BEN Benjamin Ambrosio (Palmer) B2.11.1949 Colon, Pan BL/TL/6-2/170* [BosA68 11/248] d9.4 C1

YEAR	TM LG	G	AB	R	H	2B	3B	HR	RBI	BB-IB	HP	SO	AVG	OBP	SLG	AOPS	ABR	SB-CS	FA	FR	RNG	THR	GAMES AT POSITION	DL	BFW
1971	Bos A	14	38	2	10	3	0	0	4	0-0	0	5	.263	.263	.342	65	-2	0-0	.958	2	130	176	O11(10/0/1)		-0.1
1972	Bos A	94	253	27	61	10	2	8	30	18-2	1	61	.241	.293	.391	97	-2	1-1	.981	-2	87	113	O65(32/0/33)		-0.8
1973	Bos A	58	147	16	32	9	1	2	9	9-2	2	32	.218	.269	.333	66	-7	1-1	.983	-0	96	101	O32(4/0/28),D13		-0.9
1974	Det A	92	252	28	68	11	3	4	29	34-6	0	38	.270	.353	.385	109	4	12-3	.947	-3	85	82	O63(61/0/2),1b10,D4		-0.1
1975	Det A	100	332	45	95	14	1	9	36	16-0	2	62	.286	.319	.416	103	0	11-8	.975	-1	104	65	O86(76/0/10),1b5,D2		-0.2
1976	Det A	115	305	36	87	12	5	15	47	11-3	0	44	.285	.313	.492	129	9	9-4	.986	1	104	160	O64(16/12/36),1b9/D		0.7
1977	Det A	132	450	63	118	24	2	21	61	40-2	3	80	.262	.325	.464	107	4	9-9	.976	2	100	118	O118R,D2		-0.1
1978	Mil A	128	469	71	142	29	4	18	72	52-10	0	69	.303	.370	.497	141	16	11-7	.980	-2	103	82	O89(65/0/25),D27,1b11		2.0
1979	Mil A	139	514	88	145	30	4	29	81	48-12	2	56	.282	.343	.525	131	21	12-5	.985	-2	101	76	O120(102/0/23),D13,1b9		1.3
1980	Mil A★	156	592	94	180	26	2	41	118	54-19	5	71	.304	.362	.563	155	42	11-9	.978	13	112	147	O152(150/1/2),D4		4.7
1981	†Mil A	107	400	53	97	15	2	14	72	37-10	6	49	.243	.310	.395	108	4	2-2	.982	-8	91	39	O101(99/2/0),D6		-1.0
1982	†Mil A★	159	602	92	147	22	1	34	102	70-13	4	81	.244	.326	.453	118	14	3-5	.982	6	102	147	O159L		1.1
1983	Mil A	125	411	49	115	19	3	13	66	60-12	4	64	.280	.371	.438	132	20	4-6	.985	2	103	87	O113L,D8		1.6
1984	Mil A	131	461	49	121	16	2	12	60	44-5	1	56	.262	.327	.384	100	0	0-6	.970	-3	96	71	O125(113/0/23)/D		-1.1
1985	Mil A	101	341	40	99	17	2	10	61	37-3	2	51	.290	.354	.440	107	10	0-2	.965	-5	100	66	O91(48/0/54),D4		0.3
1986	Mil A	103	346	36	87	16	2	5	53	30-6	0	52	.251	.313	.361	88	-2	1-2	.991	4	118	141	O50(50/0/2),D42		-0.1
Total 16		1754	5913	784	1615	277	33	235	901	560-105	35	852	.273	.336	.450	118	141	87-70	.978	12	101	101	O1439(1098/15/357),D127,1b44		7.3

OGRODOWSKI, BRUCE Ambrose Francis "Brusie" B2.17.1912 Hoytville PA D3.5.1956 San Francisco CA BR/TR/5-11/175 d4.14

YEAR	TM LG	G	AB	R	H	2B	3B	HR	RBI	BB-IB	HP	SO	AVG	OBP	SLG	AOPS	ABR	SB-CS	FA	FR	RNG	THR	GAMES AT POSITION	DL	BFW
1936	StL N	94	237	28	54	15	1	1	20	10	0	20	.228	.259	.312	53	-16	0	.989	1	120	78	C85		-1.1
1937	StL N	90	279	37	65	10	3	3	31	11	2	17	.233	.267	.323	58	-17	2	.984	0	90	88	C87		-1.2
Total 2		184	516	65	119	25	4	4	51	21	2	37	.231	.263	.318	56	-33	2	.986	1	103	84	C172		-2.3

O'HAGEN, HAL Patrick Henry B9.30.1869 Washington DC D1.14.1913 Newark NJ 6-0/173 d9.24

YEAR	TM LG	G	AB	R	H	2B	3B	HR	RBI	BB-IB	HP	SO	AVG	OBP	SLG	AOPS	ABR	SB-CS	FA	FR	RNG	THR	GAMES AT POSITION	DL	BFW
1892	Was N	1	4	1	1	0	0	0	0	0	0	2	.250	.250	.250	53	0	0	1.000	0	79	323	/C		0.0
1902	Chi N	33	115	11	22	3	0	1	10	11	0		.191	.262	.252	60	-6	9	.983	3	147	128	1b33		-0.3
	NY N	4	11	0	1	0	0	0	0	0	0		.091	.091	.091	-44	-2	0	1.000	0	0	0	O4(0/3/1)		-0.2
	Cle A	3	13	2	5	2	0	0	1	0	0		.385	.385	.538	160	1	2	1.000	1	170	0	1b3		0.2
	NY N	22	73	5	11	2	1	0	8	2	0		.151	.195	.205	24	-7	3	.973	-0	109	115	1b18,O4R		-0.8
	Year	59	199	16	34	3	4	0	18	13	2		.171	.229	.226	52	-14	12	.980	3	133	123	1b51,O8(0/3/5)		-1.3
Total 2		63	216	19	40	5	4	0	19	13	2		.185	.238	.245	49	-14	14	.981	4	136	116	1b54,O8(0/3/5)/C		-1.1

O'HALLORAN, GREG Gregory Joseph B5.21.1968 Toronto ON, Can. BL/TR/6-2/205 [TorA88 32/836] d5.16 Col Orange Coast (CA) JC

YEAR	TM LG	G	AB	R	H	2B	3B	HR	RBI	BB-IB	HP	SO	AVG	OBP	SLG	AOPS	ABR	SB-CS	FA	FR	RNG	THR	GAMES AT POSITION	DL	BFW
1994	Fla N	12	11	1	2	0	0	0	1	0-0	0	2	.182	.167	.182	-5	-2	0-0	1.000	0	0	0	/C		-0.2

O'HARA, KID James Francis B12.19.1875 Wilkes-Barre PA D12.1.1954 Canton OH BB/TR/5-7.5/152 d9.15 Col Georgetown

YEAR	TM LG	G	AB	R	H	2B	3B	HR	RBI	BB-IB	HP	SO	AVG	OBP	SLG	AOPS	ABR	SB-CS	FA	FR	RNG	THR	GAMES AT POSITION	DL	BFW
1904	Bos N	8	29	3	6	0	0	0	4		0		.207	.303	.207	60	-1	1	.923	0	196		O8R		-0.2

O'HARA, TOM Thomas F. B7.13.1880 Waverly NY D6.8.1954 Denver CO d9.19 Col Manhattan

YEAR	TM LG	G	AB	R	H	2B	3B	HR	RBI	BB-IB	HP	SO	AVG	OBP	SLG	AOPS	ABR	SB-CS	FA	FR	RNG	THR	GAMES AT POSITION	DL	BFW
1906	StL N	14	53	8	16	1	0	0	3		0		.302	.339	.321	110	1	3	.889	-2	0	0	O14L		-0.2
1907	StL N	48	173	11	41	2	1	0	12	5	0		.237	.286	.260	74	-6	1	.943	-2	73	113	O47(24/0/23)		-1.2
Total 2		62	226	19	57	3	1	0	15		0		.252	.299	.274	82	-5	4	.930	-4	57	88	O61(38/0/23)		-1.4

O'HARA, BILL William Alexander B8.14.1883 Toronto ON, Can. D6.13.1931 Jersey City NJ BL/TR/5-10/165 d4.15

YEAR	TM LG	G	AB	R	H	2B	3B	HR	RBI	BB-IB	HP	SO	AVG	OBP	SLG	AOPS	ABR	SB-CS	FA	FR	RNG	THR	GAMES AT POSITION	DL	BFW
1909	NY N	115	360	48	85	9	3	1	30	41	2		.236	.318	.286	86	-5	31	.978	4	132	132	O111(11/89/11)		-0.6
1910	StL N	9	20	1	3	0	0	0	2	1	0		.150	.190	.150	-0	-3	0	1.000	0	86	208	O4C/P1		-0.3
Total 2		124	380	49	88	9	3	1	32	42	2		.232	.311	.279	82	-8	31	.979	4	130	135	O115(11/93/11)/1P		-0.9

OJEDA, MIGUEL Miguel Arturo B1.29.1975 Guaymas, Sonora, Mexico BR/TR/6-2/190(190-230) d5.17

YEAR	TM LG	G	AB	R	H	2B	3B	HR	RBI	BB-IB	HP	SO	AVG	OBP	SLG	AOPS	ABR	SB-CS	FA	FR	RNG	THR	GAMES AT POSITION	DL	BFW
2003	SD N	61	141	13	33	6	0	4	22		3	26	.234	.331	.362	89	-2	1-1	.981	-1	91	59	C48,1b2		0.0
2004	SD N	62	156	23	40	3	0	8	26	15-1	1	34	.256	.322	.429	98	-1	0-0	.996	-3	265	37	C50	16	-0.1
2005	SD N	43	73	6	10	3	1	0	6	9-2	0	21	.137	.232	.205	17	-9	0-1	1.000	-1	80	0	C25,O5(3/0/2)/D		-0.9
	Sea A	16	29	2	5	0	0	1	3	6-0	0	3	.172	.314	.276	63	-1	0-1	.986	-1	94	210	C16		0.0
Total 3		182	399	44	88	12	1	13	57	48-5	4	84	.221	.308	.353	78	-13	2-3	.989	-3	156	58	C139,O5(3/0/2),1b2/D	16	-1.0

OJEDA, AUGIE Octavio Augie B12.20.1974 Los Angeles CA BB/TR/5-9/165* [BalA96 13/381] d6.4 Col Tennessee

YEAR	TM LG	G	AB	R	H	2B	3B	HR	RBI	BB-IB	HP	SO	AVG	OBP	SLG	AOPS	ABR	SB-CS	FA	FR	RNG	THR	GAMES AT POSITION	DL	BFW
2000	Chi N	28	77	10	17	3	1	2	8	10-1	0	9	.221	.307	.364	70	-4	0-0	.989	-1	106	83	S25,2b4		-0.3
2001	Chi N	78	144	19	29	5	1	1	12	12-1	2	20	.201	.269	.271	42	-13	1-0	.913	3	125	157	3b35,S31,2b10		-0.7
2002	Chi N	30	70	4	13	4	0	0	4	5-0	1	5	.186	.247	.243	33	-7	1-0	.966	0	106	45	S16,2b10,3b5		-0.5
2003	Chi N	12	25	2	3	0	0	0	0	1-1	1	5	.120	.185	.120	-18	-4	0-0	1.000	-1	91	95	S7,2b5/3		-0.4
2004	Min A	30	59	16	20	1	0	2	7	10-0	0	3	.339	.429	.458	130	3	1-1	.969	3	121	105	2b20,S7,3b4		0.6
Total 5		178	375	48	82	13	2	5	31	38-3	4	42	.219	.294	.304	57	-25	3-2	.982	4	97	76	S86,2b49,3b45		-1.3

OKRIE, LEN Leonard Joseph B7.16.1923 Detroit MI BR/TR/6-0/185* d6.16 C5 f-Frank

YEAR	TM LG	G	AB	R	H	2B	3B	HR	RBI	BB-IB	HP	SO	AVG	OBP	SLG	AOPS	ABR	SB-CS	FA	FR	RNG	THR	GAMES AT POSITION	DL	BFW
1948	Was A	19	42	1	10	1	1	0	1	1	0	7	.238	.256	.286	45	-4	0-0	.981	1	154	235	C17		-0.2
1950	Was A	17	27	1	6	0	0	0	2	6	1	7	.222	.382	.222	61	-1	0-0	1.000	1	66	176	C17		0.0
1951	Was A	5	8	1	1	0	0	0	2	2	0	1	.125	.300	.250	51	0	0-0	.850	-0	125	216	C5		0.0
1952	Bos A	1	1	0	0	0	0	0	0	0	0	1	.000	.000	.000	-93	0	0-0	1.000	-0	0	0	/C		0.0
Total 4		42	78	3	17	1	1	0	3	9	1	16	.218	.307	.256	51	-5	0-0	.965	1	116	208	C40		-0.2

OLANDER, JIM James Bentley B2.21.1963 Tucson AZ BR/TR/6-1/185 [PhiN81 7/175] d9.20

YEAR	TM LG	G	AB	R	H	2B	3B	HR	RBI	BB-IB	HP	SO	AVG	OBP	SLG	AOPS	ABR	SB-CS	FA	FR	RNG	THR	GAMES AT POSITION	DL	BFW
1991	Mil A	12	9	2	0	0	0	0	0	2-0	0	5	.000	.182	.000	-46	-2	0-0	1.000	0	115	0	O9(2/5/1),D2		-0.2

OLDFIELD, DAVE David B12.18.1864 Philadelphia PA D8.28.1939 Philadelphia PA BB/TL/5-7/175 d6.28

YEAR	TM LG	G	AB	R	H	2B	3B	HR	RBI	BB-IB	HP	SO	AVG	OBP	SLG	AOPS	ABR	SB-CS	FA	FR	RNG	THR	GAMES AT POSITION	DL	BFW
1883	Bal AA	1	4	0	0	0	0	0	0				.000	.000	.000	-97	-1		.667	-1			/C		-0.2
1885	Bro AA	10	25	2	8	1	0	0	2	3	1		.320	.414	.360	145	2		.873	-1			C9,O2(0/1/1)		0.1
1886	Bro AA	14	55	7	13	1	0	0	5	2	0		.236	.263	.255	62	-3	1	.833	-3			C13/SOR		-0.4
	Was N	21	71	2	10	2	0	0	2	5		15	.141	.197	.169	13	-7	0	.899	-3			C12,O9(0/3/6)/S		-0.8
Total 3		46	155	11	31	4	0	0	9	10		15	.200	.253	.226	50	-9	1	.857	-7			C35,O12(0/4/8)/S		-1.3

OLDHAM, JOHN John Hardin B11.6.1932 Salinas CA BR/TL/6-3/198 d9.2 Col San Jose St.

YEAR	TM LG	G	AB	R	H	2B	3B	HR	RBI	BB-IB	HP	SO	AVG	OBP	SLG	AOPS	ABR	SB-CS	FA	FR	RNG	THR	GAMES AT POSITION	DL	BFW
1956	Cin N	1	0	0	0	0	0	0	0	0-0							0	0-0	—	0			/R		0.0

OLDIS, BOB Robert Carl B1.5.1928 Preston IA BR/TR/6-1/185* d4.28 C5

YEAR	TM LG	G	AB	R	H	2B	3B	HR	RBI	BB-IB	HP	SO	AVG	OBP	SLG	AOPS	ABR	SB-CS	FA	FR	RNG	THR	GAMES AT POSITION	DL	BFW
1953	Was A	7	16	1	4	0	0	0	3	1	0	2	.250	.294	.250	49	-1	0-0	1.000	1	119	82	C7		0.0
1954	Was A	11	24	1	8	1	0	0	0	1	0	3	.333	.360	.375	107	0	0-0	.941	-1	99	61	C8,3b2		-0.1
1955	Was A	6	6	1	0	0	0	0	0	1-0	0	1	.000	.143	.000	-62	-1	0-0	1.000	-0	60	222	C6		-0.1
1960	†Pit N	22	20	1	4	1	0	0	1	1-0	0	2	.200	.238	.250	34	-2	0-0	1.000	0	148	100	C22		0.0
1961	Pit N	4	5	0	0	0	0	0	0	0	0	0	.000	.000	.000	-99	-1	0-0	1.000	1	21	796	C4		-0.1
1962	Phi N	38	80	9	21	1	0	1	10	13-0	0	10	.262	.366	.313	87	-1	0-1	.987	-1	94	154	C30		-0.1
1963	Phi N	47	85	8	19	3	0	0	8	3-1	0	5	.224	.250	.259	47	-6	0-0	.979	1	52	70	C43		-0.5
Total 7		135	236	20	56	6	0	1	22	20-1	0	22	.237	.297	.275	60	-12	0-1	.983	1	85	123	C120,3b2		-0.9

OLDRING, RUBE Reuben Henry B5.30.1884 New York NY D9.9.1961 Bridgeton NJ BR/TR/5-10/186 d10.2 OF(455/627/48)

YEAR	TM LG	G	AB	R	H	2B	3B	HR	RBI	BB-IB	HP	SO	AVG	OBP	SLG	AOPS	ABR	SB-CS	FA	FR	RNG	THR	GAMES AT POSITION	DL	BFW
1905	NY A	8	30	2	9	0	1	1	6	2	0		.300	.344	.467	140	1	4	.967	4	120	136	S8		0.5
1906	Phi A	59	174	15	42	10	1	0	19	2	3		.241	.263	.310	77	-5	7	.897	1	99	119	3b49,S3,2b2/1		-0.3
1907	Phi A	117	441	48	126	27	8	1	40	7	5		.286	.305	.390	118	7	29	.974	-10	69	0	O117(0/116/1)		-0.9
1908	Phi A	116	434	38	96	14	2	1	39	18	9		.221	.267	.270	70	-14	13	.941	-2	65	79	O116(21/95/0)		-0.9
1909	Phi A	90	326	39	75	13	8	1	28	20	6		.230	.287	.328	92	-4	17	.963	-0	65	46	O89(32/56/1)/1		-0.9
1910	Phi A	134	546	79	168	27	14	4	57	23	4		.308	.340	.430	143	23	17	**.978**	-5	96	74	O134(1/130/3)		1.3
1911	†Phi A	121	495	84	147	11	14	3	59	21	5		.297	.332	.394	104	-1	21	**.979**	-8	92	71	O119C		-1.6
1912	Phi A	99	395	61	119	14	5	1	24	10	3		.301	.324	.370	102	-1	17	.974	-3	103	58	O98(11/87/0)		-1.1
1913	†Phi A	137	538	101	152	27	9	5	71	34	2	37	.283	.328	.394	113	7	40	.968	-3	109	57	O131L,S5		-0.1
1914	†Phi A	119	466	68	129	21	7	3	49	18	3	35	.277	.308	.371	108	1	14-16	.965	-3	104	46	O117(105/11/1)		-1.1
1915	Phi A	107	408	49	101	23	3	6	42	22	4	21	.248	.293	.363	100	-3	11-6	.982	4	114	74	O96(88/8/0),3b8		-0.3
1916	Phi A	40	146	10	36	8	3	0	14	9	0	9	.247	.290	.342	95	-2	1	.897	-3	80	118	O40L		-0.7
	NY A	43	158	17	37	8	0	1	12	12	0	13	.234	.288	.304	76	-5	6	.957	-3	102	20	O43(0/2/41)		-1.1
	Year	83	304	27	73	16	3	1	26	21	0	22	.240	.289	.322	85	-7	7	.926	-6	91	70	O83(40/2/41)		-1.8
1918	Phi A	49	183	19	42	9	0	1	11	8	1	10	.230	.282	.263	64	-6	0	.949	-4	75	66	O30(26/3/1),2b2,3b2		-1.2
Total 13		1239	4690	616	1268	205	76	27	471	206	45	125	.270	.307	.364	103	-2	197-22	.966	-35	91	58	O1130C,3b59,S16,2b4,1b2		-10.1

O'LEARY, CHARLEY Charles Timothy B10.15.1882 Chicago IL D1.6.1941 Chicago IL BR/TR/5-7/165 d4.14 C19

YEAR	TM LG	G	AB	R	H	2B	3B	HR	RBI	BB-IB	HP	SO	AVG	OBP	SLG	AOPS	ABR	SB-CS	FA	FR	RNG	THR	GAMES AT POSITION	DL	BFW
1904	Det A	135	456	39	97	10	3	1	16	21	4		.213	.254	.254	63	-20	9	.933	4	102	110	S135		-1.3
1905	Det A	148	512	47	109	13	1	0	33	29	3		.213	.259	.242	59	-24	13	.933	-4	94	83	S148		-2.6
1906	Det A	128	443	34	97	13	2	2	34	17	3		.219	.253	.271	62	-20	8	.926	-7	95	83	S127		-2.5
1907	†Det A	139	465	61	112	19	1	0	34	32	6		.241	.298	.286	83	-8	11	.943	-6	95	83	S138		-1.1
1908	†Det A	65	211	21	53	9	3	0	17	9	4		.251	.295	.322	96	-1	4	.920	-9	90	80	S64/2		-1.0
1909	†Det A	76	261	29	53	10	0	0	13	6	1		.203	.224	.241	45	-17	9	.922	-4	106	63	3b54,2b15,S4,O2(1/0/1)		-2.3
1910	Det A	65	211	23	51	7	1	0	9	9	1		.242	.276	.284	71	-8	7	.935	-0	94	78	2b38,S18,3b6		-0.7
1911	Det A	74	256	29	68	8	2	0	25	21	6		.266	.336	.313	77	-7	10	.966	3	105	78	2b67,3b6		-0.3
1912	Det A	3	10	1	2	0	0	0	1	0	0		.200	.200	.200	15	-1	0	1.000	1	158	0	2b3		0.0
1913	StL N	121	406	32	88	15	5	0	31	20	0	34	.217	.260	.278	55	-25	3-12	.951	-6	99	58	S103,2b15		-2.9
1934	StL N	1	1	1	1	0	0	0	0	0	0	0	1.000	1.000	1.000	385	0	0-0	—	0			/H		0.0
Total 11		955	3232	317	731	104	18	3	213	164	32	34	.226	.270	.272	67	-131	74-12	.935	-29	97	83	S737,2b139,3b66,O2(1/0/1)		-14.7

O'LEARY, DAN Daniel "Hustling Dan" B10.22.1856 Detroit MI D6.24.1922 Chicago IL BL/5-10/165 d9.3 M1

YEAR	TM LG	G	AB	R	H	2B	3B	HR	RBI	BB-IB	HP	SO	AVG	OBP	SLG	AOPS	ABR	SB-CS	FA	FR	RNG	THR	GAMES AT POSITION	DL	BFW
1879	Pro N	2	7	1	3	0	0	0		2	0		.429	.429	.429	187	1		—	-0	0	0	O2R		0.?
1880	Bos N	3	12	1	3	0	0	0		1	0	3	.250	.250	.417	126	0		1.000	-1	0	0	O3R		0.?
1881	Det N	2	8	0	0	0	0	0		0	0	2	.000	.000	.000	-96	-2		.714	-1	0	0	O2C		-0.?
1882	Wor N	6	22	2	4	1	0	0		2	0	5	.182	.333	.227	82	0		.800	-2	0	0	O6C		-0.?
1884	Cin U	32	132	14	34	0	2	1	5			10	.258	.285	.311	74	-9		.862	1	99	0	O32(22/10/0),M		-0.?
Total 5		45	181	18	44	3	2	1	5	10		10	.243	.283	.298	75	-9		.843	-2	76	0	O45(22/18/5)		-1.?

O'LEARY, TROY Troy Franklin B8.4.1969 Compton CA BL/TL/6-0/198(175-200) [MilA87 13/331] d5.9

YEAR	TM LG	G	AB	R	H	2B	3B	HR	RBI	BB-IB	HP	SO	AVG	OBP	SLG	AOPS	ABR	SB-CS	FA	FR	RNG	THR	GAMES AT POSITION	DL	BFW
1993	Mil A	19	41	3	12	3	0	0	3	5-0	0	9	.293	.370	.366	99	0	0-0	1.000	1	111	112	O19(15/0/5)		-0.?
1994	Mil A	27	66	9	18	1	1	2	7	5-0	1	12	.273	.329	.409	86	-2	1-1	1.000	1	101	153	O21(13/0/10)/D		-0.?
1995	Bos A	112	399	60	123	31	6	10	49	29-4	1	64	.308	.355	.491	114	8	5-3	.976	-1	98	91	O105(16/13/91),D3		-2.?
1996	Bos A	149	497	68	129	28	5	15	81	47-3	4	80	.260	.327	.427	87	-11	3-2	.971	-8	87	91	O146(66/17/110)/D		0.?
1997	Bos A	146	499	65	154	34	4	15	80	39-7	2	70	.309	.358	.479	114	10	0-5	.979	-2	97	92	O142(24/0/119)/D		-0.?
1998	†Bos A	156	611	95	165	36	8	23	83	36-2	5	108	.270	.314	.468	98	-4	2-2	.990	1	99	99	O155L		-0.?
1999	†Bos A	157	596	84	167	36	4	28	103	56-5	4	91	.280	.343	.495	108	6	1-2	.993	1	99	99	O157(157/0/2)		-0.?
2000	Bos A	138	513	68	134	30	4	13	70	44-2	5	76	.261	.320	.411	82	-15	0-2	.988	-5	88	112	O89(52/0/41),D4		-1.?
2001	Bos A	104	341	50	82	16	6	13	50	25-2	5	73	.240	.298	.437	91	-6	1-3	.994	-1	100	58	O70(69/0/1),D3		-0.?
2002	Mon N	97	273	27	78	12	2	3	37	34-5	3	47	.286	.371	.377	96	-2	1-2	.977	-1	104	25	O70(40/0/30),D3		-1.?
2003	†Chi N	93	174	18	38	9	0	3	28	14-1	1	31	.218	.275	.356	63	-10	3-0	1.000	-0	90	139	O51(28/0/24)		-1.?
Total 11		1198	4010	547	1100	234	40	127	591	334-31	28	661	.274	.332	.448	97	-26	17-22	.985	-14	96	92	O1092(732/30/403),D12	14	-8.?

OLERUD, JOHN John Garrett B8.5.1968 Seattle WA BL/TL/6-5/218(205-225) [TorA89 3/79] d9.3 Col Washington St.

YEAR	TM LG	G	AB	R	H	2B	3B	HR	RBI	BB-IB	HP	SO	AVG	OBP	SLG	AOPS	ABR	SB-CS	FA	FR	RNG	THR	GAMES AT POSITION	DL	BFW
1989	Tor A	6	8	2	3	0	0	0	0	1	0		.375	.375	.375	114	0	0-0	1.000	0	168	0	1b5/D		0.?
1990	Tor A	111	358	43	95	15	1	14	48	57-6	1	75	.265	.364	.430	120	11	0-2	.986	-1	89	75	D90,1b18		0.?
1991	†Tor A	139	454	64	116	30	1	17	68	68-9	1	84	.256	.353	.438	115	11	0-2	.996	8	88	76	1b135/D		0.?
1992	†Tor A	138	458	68	130	28	0	16	66	70-11	1	61	.284	.375	.450	125	18	1-0	.994	-2	91	91	1b133/D		0.?
1993	†Tor A★	158	551	109	200	**54**	2	24	107	114-33	7	65	**.363**	**.473**	.599	**184**	75	0-2	.992	-2	94	90	1b137,D20		5.?
1994	Tor A	108	384	47	114	29	2	12	67	61-12	3	53	.297	.393	.477	123	16	1-2	.993	1	98	94	1b104,D3		-0.?
1995	Tor A	135	492	72	143	32	0	8	54	84-10	4	54	.291	.398	.424	109	12	0-0	.997	-3	90	82	1b133		-0.?

YEAR	TM LG	G	AB	R	H	2B	3B	HR	RBI	BB-IB	HP	SO	AVG	OBP	SLG	AOPS	ABR	SB-CS	FA	FR	RNG	THR	GAMES AT POSITION	DL	BFW
1996	Tor A	125	398	59	109	25	0	18	61	60-6	10	37	.274	.382	.472	115	11	1-0	.998	-3	85	134	1b101,D15		-0.1
1997	NY N	154	524	90	154	34	1	22	102	85-5	13	67	.294	.400	.489	139	35	0-0	.995	4	112	117	1b146		2.5
1998	NY N	160	557	91	197	36	4	22	93	96-11	4	73	.354	.447	.551	167	61	0-0	.996	3	104	101	1b157		4.8
1999	†NY N	162	581	107	173	39	0	19	96	125-5	11	66	.298	.427	.463	132	38	3-0	.994	3	105	107	1b160		2.6
2000	†Sea A	159	565	84	161	45	0	14	103	102-11	4	96	.285	.392	.439	114	17	0-2	.996	15	134	114	1b158		1.6
2001	†Sea A★	159	572	91	173	32	1	21	95	94-19	5	70	.302	.401	.472	138	36	3-1	.993	8	119	106	1b158		2.9
2002	Sea A	154	553	85	166	39	0	22	102	98-6	5	66	.300	.403	.490	143	40	0-0	.996	4	105	107	1b152,D2		2.8
2003	Sea A	152	539	64	145	35	0	10	83	84-7	6	67	.269	.372	.390	107	10	0-1	.998	10	121	115	1b152		0.7
2004	Sea A	78	261	29	64	13	1	5	22	40-3	6	41	.245	.354	.360	93	-1	0-0	.998	3	114	95	1b77		-0.5
	†NY A	49	164	16	46	7	0	4	26	21-1	2	20	.280	.367	.396	100	1	0-0	.997	-2	79	93	1b47		-0.5
	Year	127	425	45	110	20	1	9	48	61-4	8	61	.259	.359	.374	95	-1	0-0	.998	1	101	94	1b124		-1.0
2005	†Bos A	87	173	18	50	7	0	7	37	16-2	0	20	.289	.344	.451	105	1	0-0	.998	4	125	93	1b80		0.0
Total	17	2234	7592	1139	2239	500	13	255	1230	1275-157	88	1016	.295	.398	.465	129	392	11-14	.995	39	105	100	1b2053,D133	16	24.1

OLIN, FRANK Franklin Walter B1.9.1860 Woodford VT D5.21.1951 St.Louis MO BL d7.4 Col Cornell

YEAR	TM LG	G	AB	R	H	2B	3B	HR	RBI	BB-IB	HP	SO	AVG	OBP	SLG	AOPS	ABR	SB-CS	FA	FR	RNG	THR	GAMES AT POSITION	DL	BFW
1884	Was AA	21	83	12	32	4	1	0	7	0			.386	.433	.458	216	11		.775	-6	77	37	2b12,O11(1/7/3)		0.5
	Was U	1	4	0	0	0	0	0	0	0			.000	.000	.000	-99	-1		—	0	0	0	/OL		-0.1
	Tol AA	26	86	16	22	0	1	1	5		1		.256	.304	.314	99	0		.875	2	141	0	O26L		0.1
1885	Det N	1	4	1	2	0	0	0	0	0			.500	.500	.500	224	1		.667	-0	80	0	/3		0.0
Total	2	49	177	29	56	4	2	1	12		0		.316	.363	.379	148	11		.849	-5	126	83	O38(28/7/3),2b12/3		0.5

OLIVA, JOSE Jose (Galvez) B3.3.1971 San Pedro de Macoris, D.R. D12.22.1997 San Cristobal, D.R. BR/TR/6-3/215* d7.1

YEAR	TM LG	G	AB	R	H	2B	3B	HR	RBI	BB-IB	HP	SO	AVG	OBP	SLG	AOPS	ABR	SB-CS	FA	FR	RNG	THR	GAMES AT POSITION	DL	BFW
1994	Atl N	19	59	9	17	5	0	6	11	7-0	0	10	.288	.364	.678	158	5	0-1	.932	0	99	84	3b16		0.5
1995	Atl N	48	109	7	17	4	0	5	12	7-0	0	22	.156	.207	.330	37	-11	0-0	.902	-3	84	88	3b25/1		-1.3
	StL N	22	74	8	9	1	0	2	8	5-0	2	24	.122	.195	.216	9	-10	0-0	.977	-2	86	142	3b18,1b2		-1.2
	Year	70	183	15	26	5	0	7	20	12-0	2	46	.142	.202	.284	26	-21	0-0	.933	-5	85	111	3b43,1b3		-2.5
Total	2	89	242	24	43	10	0	13	31	19-0	2	56	.178	.242	.380	59	-16	0-1	.932	-5	89	103	3b59,1b3		-2.0

OLIVA, TONY Tony Pedro (b Antonio Oliva) B7.20.1938 Pinar Del Rio, Cuba BL/TR/6-2/190* d9.9 C10

YEAR	TM LG	G	AB	R	H	2B	3B	HR	RBI	BB-IB	HP	SO	AVG	OBP	SLG	AOPS	ABR	SB-CS	FA	FR	RNG	THR	GAMES AT POSITION	DL	BFW
1962	Min A	9	9	3	4	0	0	0	3	3-0	0	2	.444	.583	.556	201	2	0-0	1.000	0	143	0	O2R		0.2
1963	Min A	7	7	0	3	0	0	0	1	0-0	0	2	.429	.429	.429	138	0	0-0	—	0			/H		0.0
1964	Min A★	161	672	109	217	43	9	32	94	34-8	6	68	.323	.359	.557	150	43	12-6	.981	0	109	51	O159(2/9/154)		3.3
1965	†Min A★	149	576	107	185	40	5	16	98	55-12	4	64	.321	.378	.491	141	32	19-9	.964	3	107	109	O147(0/8/143)		2.8
1966	Min A★	159	622	99	191	32	7	25	87	42-10	5	72	.307	.353	.502	135	27	13-7	.972	9	111	103	O159(0/19/140)		2.8
1967	Min A★	146	557	76	161	34	6	17	83	44-12	8	61	.289	.347	.463	128	20	11-3	.987	8	119	89	O146R		2.0
1968	Min A★	128	470	54	136	24	5	18	68	45-16	7	61	.289	.357	.477	144	25	10-9	.983	2	108	102	O126R		2.0
1969	†Min A★	153	637	97	197	39	4	24	101	45-12	3	66	.309	.355	.496	133	26	10-13	.982	6	107	112	O152R		2.2
1970	†Min A★	157	628	96	204	36	7	23	107	38-12	5	67	.325	.364	.514	138	30	5-4	.968	13	122	116	O157(0/3/154)		3.6
1971	†Min A★	126	487	73	164	30	3	22	81	25-8	2	44	.337	.369	.546	153	32	4-1	.969	-2	98	78	O121R		2.6
1972	Min A	10	28	1	9	1	0	0	1	2-0	0	5	.321	.367	.357	110	0	0-0	.857	-2	50	0	O9(8/0/1)	147	-0.2
1973	Min A	146	571	63	166	20	0	16	92	45-14	4	44	.291	.345	.410	108	6	2-1	—	0	0	0	D142		0.2
1974	Min A	127	459	43	131	16	2	13	57	27-11	2	31	.285	.325	.414	109	4	0-1	—	0	0	0	D112		0.1
1975	Min A	131	455	46	123	10	0	13	58	41-15	13	45	.270	.344	.378	104	3	0-1	—	0	0	0	D120		0.1
1976	Min A	67	123	3	26	3	0	1	16	2-1	2	13	.211	.234	.260	44	-9	0-0	—	0	0	0	D32		-1.0
Total	15	1676	6301	870	1917	329	48	220	947	448-131	59	645	.304	.353	.476	130	241	86-55	.975	37	111	94	O1178(10/39/1139),D406	147	20.5

OLIVARES, ED Edward (Balzac) B11.5.1938 Mayaguez, PR BR/TR/5-11/165(160-180) d9.16 s-Omar [DL 1962 Hou N 154]

YEAR	TM LG	G	AB	R	H	2B	3B	HR	RBI	BB-IB	HP	SO	AVG	OBP	SLG	AOPS	ABR	SB-CS	FA	FR	RNG	THR	GAMES AT POSITION	DL	BFW
1960	StL N	3	5	0	0	0	0	0	0	0-0	0	3	.000	.000	.000	-92	-1	0-0	.500	-1	57	0	/3		-0.2
1961	StL N	21	30	2	5	0	0	0	1	0-0	0	4	.167	.161	.167	-10	-5	1-0	1.000	-1	78	0	O10(5/0/5)		-0.6
Total	2	24	35	2	5	0	0	0	1	0-0	0	7	.143	.139	.143	-21	-6	1-0	1.000	-1	78	0	O10(5/0/5)/3	154	-0.8

OLIVER, AL Albert B10.14.1946 Portsmouth OH BL/TL/6-0/195(185-203) d9.23

YEAR	TM LG	G	AB	R	H	2B	3B	HR	RBI	BB-IB	HP	SO	AVG	OBP	SLG	AOPS	ABR	SB-CS	FA	FR	RNG	THR	GAMES AT POSITION	DL	BFW
1968	Pit N	4	8	1	1	0	0	0	0	0-0	0	4	.125	.125	.125	-25	-1	0-0	1.000	0	140	0	/OR		-0.1
1969	Pit N	129	463	55	132	19	2	17	70	21-11	13	38	.285	.333	.445	119	10	8-5	.991	-1	82	110	1b106,O21(13/0/8)		0.0
1970	†Pit N	151	551	63	149	33	5	12	83	35-8	14	35	.270	.326	.414	98	-2	1-1	.986	-1	96	74	O80(28/0/54),1b77		-1.2
1971	†Pit N	143	529	69	149	31	7	14	64	27-2	5	72	.282	.317	.446	115	9	4-3	.981	-1	107	61	O116C,1b25		0.3
1972	†Pit N★	140	565	88	176	27	4	12	89	34-4	5	44	.312	.352	.437	126	18	2-4	.985	-9	96	47	O138C,1b3		0.5
1973	Pit N	158	654	90	191	38	7	20	99	22-1	5	52	.292	.316	.463	117	11	6-0	.964	-11	90	72	O109C,1b50		-0.5
1974	†Pit N	147	617	96	198	38	12	11	85	33-1	5	58	.321	.358	.475	136	26	10-1	.986	-3	107	46	O98C,1b49		2.0
1975	†Pit N★	155	628	90	176	39	8	18	84	25-3	5	73	.280	.309	.454	110	5	4-2	.987	-6	98	52	O153C,1b4		-0.6
1976	Pit N★	121	443	62	143	22	5	12	61	26-7	5	29	.323	.363	.476	136	19	6-2	.984	-3	106	58	O106C,1b3		1.5
1977	Pit N	154	568	75	175	29	6	19	82	40-9	4	38	.308	.353	.481	118	14	13-16	.981	-1	105	62	O148(128/36/0)		0.5
1978	Tex A	133	525	65	170	35	5	14	89	31-6	2	41	.324	.358	.490	137	25	8-9	.987	0	96	112	O107(100/8/0),D26	28	1.8
1979	Tex A	136	492	69	159	28	4	12	76	34-8	4	34	.323	.367	.470	126	18	4-5	.975	-3	93	114	O119(49/71/0),D10		1.1
1980	Tex A★	163	656	96	209	43	3	19	117	39-9	5	47	.319	.357	.480	132	28	5-7	.973	-2	99	80	O157(141/0/16)/1D		1.8
1981	Tex A★	102	421	53	130	29	1	4	55	24-10	2	28	.309	.348	.411	124	13	3-0	1.000	-0	0	0	D101/1		1.1
1982	Mon N	160	617	90	204	43	2	22	109	61-15	4	59	.331	.392	.514	147	40	5-2	.986	-12	76	87	1b159		2.0
1983	Mon N★	157	614	70	184	38	3	8	84	44-17	2	44	.300	.347	.410	110	8	1-3	.990	-0	101	83	1b153/OR		-0.2
1984	SF N	91	339	27	101	19	2	0	34	20-4	1	27	.298	.339	.366	101	0	2-2	.985	1	110	75	1b82		-0.5
	Phi N	28	93	9	29	7	0	0	14	7-2	0	9	.312	.360	.387	108	1	1-2	.987	-2	50	65	1b19,O5L	15	-0.3
	Year	119	432	36	130	26	2	0	48	27-6	1	36	.301	.343	.370	102	2	3-4	.985	-2	99	73	1b101,O5L		-0.8
1985	LA N	35	79	1	20	5	0	0	8	5-0	0	11	.253	.294	.316	73	-3	1-0	.882	-2	52	200	O17L	20	-0.5
	†Tor A	61	187	20	47	6	1	5	23	7-2	1	13	.251	.282	.374	76	-7	0-0	1.000	-0	0	0	D59/1		-0.9
Total	18	2368	9049	1189	2743	529	77	219	1326	535-119	82	756	.303	.344	.451	121	232	84-64	.980	-55	99	72	O1376(481/835/80),1b733,D200	63	7.8

OLIVER, DAVE David Jacob B4.7.1951 Stockton CA BL/TR/5-11/175 [CleA73 3/53] d9.25 C10 Col Cal Poly-San Luis Obispo

YEAR	TM LG	G	AB	R	H	2B	3B	HR	RBI	BB-IB	HP	SO	AVG	OBP	SLG	AOPS	ABR	SB-CS	FA	FR	RNG	THR	GAMES AT POSITION	DL	BFW
1977	Cle A	7	22	2	7	0	1	0	3	4-0	1	0	.318	.444	.409	138	1	0-0	.949	0	84	165	2b7		0.2

OLIVER, GENE Eugene George B3.22.1935 Moline IL BR/TR/6-2/225(210-225) d6.6 Col Northwestern

YEAR	TM LG	G	AB	R	H	2B	3B	HR	RBI	BB-IB	HP	SO	AVG	OBP	SLG	AOPS	ABR	SB-CS	FA	FR	RNG	THR	GAMES AT POSITION	DL	BFW
1959	StL N	68	172	14	42	9	0	6	28	7-0	0	41	.244	.271	.401	72	-7	3-2	.955	-1	110	43	O42(41/0/3),C9,1b5		-1.0
1961	StL N	22	52	8	14	2	0	4	9	6-1	0	10	.269	.367	.538	124	7	0-0	1.000	3	74	36	C15/OL		0.5
1962	StL N	122	345	42	89	19	1	14	45	50-4	1	59	.258	.352	.441	102	2	5-2	.991	5	108	108	C98,O8(6/0/2),1b3		1.1
1963	StL N	39	102	10	23	4	0	6	18	13-3	0	19	.225	.308	.441	105	1	0-0	.981	0	60	107	C35		0.3
	Mil N	95	296	34	74	12	2	11	47	27-1	5	59	.250	.320	.416	112	5	4-4	.985	-10	63	110	1b55,O35L,C2		-1.1
	Year	134	398	44	97	16	2	17	65	40-4	5	78	.244	.317	.422	110	5	4-4	.985	-10	63	110	1b55,C37,O35L		-0.8
1964	Mil N	93	279	45	77	15	1	13	49	17-0	1	41	.276	.319	.477	120	7	3-7	.982	-5	80	98	1b76/C		-0.4
1965	Mil N	122	392	56	106	20	0	21	58	36-5	3	61	.270	.336	.482	127	14	5-4	.976	3	93	162	C64,1b52/OL		1.7
1966	Atl N	76	191	19	37	9	1	8	24	16-3	1	43	.194	.255	.377	72	-8	2-0	.990	6	84	149	C48,1b5,O2L		0.1
1967	Atl N	17	51	8	10	2	0	3	6	6-0	0	8	.196	.281	.412	97	0	0-0	.962	1	61	92	C13/1		0.1
	Phi N	85	263	29	59	16	0	7	34	29-3	1	56	.224	.300	.365	90	-3	2-2	.987	-6	91	46	C79,1b2		-0.7
	Year	102	314	37	69	18	0	10	40	35-3	1	64	.220	.297	.373	91	-3	2-2	.983	-5	87	52	C92,1b3		-0.6
1968	Bos A	16	35	2	5	0	0	0	1	4-1	1	12	.143	.250	.143	20	-3	0-0	.984	-1	51	88	C10/OR		-0.4
	Chi N	8	11	1	4	0	0	1	3	0-0	1	3	.364	.500	.364	152	1	0-0	1.000	1	0	0	1b2/COL	63	0.2
1969	Chi N	23	27	0	6	0	0	0	1	1-1	0	9	.222	.276	.333	62	-1	0-0	1.000	2	153	0	C6		0.1
Total	10	786	2216	268	546	111	5	93	320	215-22	15	420	.246	.315	.427	103	10	24-21	.985	-3	89	105	C381,1b201,O91(87/0/6)	63	0.5

OLIVER, JOE Joseph Melton B7.24.1965 Memphis TN BR/TR/6-3/210* [CinN83 2/41] d7.15

YEAR	TM LG	G	AB	R	H	2B	3B	HR	RBI	BB-IB	HP	SO	AVG	OBP	SLG	AOPS	ABR	SB-CS	FA	FR	RNG	THR	GAMES AT POSITION	DL	BFW
1989	Cin N	49	151	13	41	8	0	3	23	6-1	1	28	.272	.300	.384	92	-2	0-0	.986	4	121	79	C47		0.4
1990	†Cin N	121	364	34	84	23	0	8	52	37-15	2	75	.231	.304	.360	79	-10	1-1	.992	12	150	110	C118		0.9
1991	Cin N	94	269	21	58	11	0	11	41	18-5	0	53	.216	.265	.379	76	-10	0-0	.980	-1	92	88	C90		-0.6
1992	Cin N	143	485	42	131	25	1	10	57	35-19	1	75	.270	.316	.388	97	-2	2-3	.992	7	122	93	C141/1		1.3
1993	Cin N	139	482	40	115	28	0	14	75	27-2	1	91	.239	.276	.384	75	-18	0-0	.992	-6	92	117	C133,1b12/OR		-1.6
1994	Cin N	6	19	1	4	0	0	1	5	3-1	1	8	.211	.286	.526	69	-1	0-0	.980	1	171	C6		122	0.1
1995	Mil A	97	337	43	92	20	0	12	51	27-1	3	66	.273	.332	.439	93	-4	2-4	.982	-6	74	72	C91,1b2,D6	32	-0.4
1996	Cin N	106	289	31	70	12	1	11	46	28-6	2	54	.242	.311	.405	86	-6	2-0	.992	5	107	93	C97,1b3,O3(2/0/1)		0.4
1997	Cin N	111	349	26	90	13	0	14	43	25-1	5	58	.258	.313	.415	90	-7	1-3	.990	-3	108	92	C106,1b4		-0.4

YEAR	TM LG	G	AB	R	H	2B	3B	HR	RBI	BB-IB	HP	SO	AVG	OBP	SLG	AOPS	ABR	SB-CS	FA	FR	RNG	THR	GAMES AT POSITION	DL	BFW
1998	Det A	50	155	8	35	8	0	4	22	7-0	0	33	.226	.253	.355	57	-10	0-1	.982	-2	128	101	C48,1b2		-0.9
	Sea A	29	85	12	19	3	0	2	10	10-0	0	15	.224	.305	.329	65	-4	1-0	.984	-5	85	84	C29		-0.7
	Year	79	240	20	54	11	0	6	32	17-0	0	48	.225	.272	.346	60	-15	1-1	.983	-6	112	95	C77,1b2		-1.6
1999	Pit N	45	134	10	27	8	0	1	13	10-0	0	33	.201	.253	.284	36	-13	2-0	.993	-10	113	48	C44		-1.0
2000	†Sea A	69	200	33	53	13	1	10	35	14-1	0	38	.265	.313	.490	101	-1	2-1	.995	-3	98	71	C66/1D		0.0
2001	NY A	12	36	3	9	1	0	1	2	1-0	0	12	.250	.263	.361	64	-2	0-0	.991	-1	65	61	C12		0.0
	Bos A	5	12	1	3	1	0	0	1	1-0	0	3	.250	.308	.333	69	-1	0-0	.971	-2	60	69	C5		-0.2
	Year	17	48	4	12	2	0	1	3	2-0	0	15	.250	.275	.354	65	-3	0-0	.986	-1	64	63	C17		-0.2
Total	13	1076	3367	320	831	174	3	102	476	248-52	15	637	.247	.299	.391	82	-91	13-13	.989	2	108	96	C1033,1b25,D7,O4(2/0/2)	154	-2.7

OLIVER, NATE Nathaniel "Peewee" B12.13.1940 St.Petersburg FL BR/TR/5-10/160* d4.9

YEAR	TM LG	G	AB	R	H	2B	3B	HR	RBI	BB-IB	HP	SO	AVG	OBP	SLG	AOPS	ABR	SB-CS	FA	FR	RNG	THR	GAMES AT POSITION	DL	BFW
1963	LA N	65	163	23	39	2	3	1	9	13-0	1	25	.239	.298	.307	80	-5	3-4	.961	2	97	105	2b57,S2		0.0
1964	LA N	99	321	28	78	9	0	0	21	31-6	0	57	.243	.309	.271	70	-12	7-4	.967	-12	93	82	2b98/S		-1.6
1965	LA N	8	1	3	1	0	0	0	0	0-0	0	0	1.000	1.000	1.000	498	-1	1-0	1.000	-0	65	0	2b2		0.1
1966	†LA N	80	119	17	23	2	0	0	3	13-2	1	17	.193	.276	.210	41	-9	3-3	.977	-1	101	93	2b68,S2/3	21	-0.5
1967	LA N	77	232	18	55	6	2	0	7	13-0	2	50	.237	.283	.280	67	-10	3-2	.973	-3	94	75	2b39,S32/OL		-1.0
1968	SF N	36	73	3	13	2	0	0	1	1-0	0	13	.178	.189	.205	18	-7	0-1	.950	-1	131	169	2b14,S13/3	56	-0.8
1969	NY A	1	1	0	0	0	0	0	0	0-0	0	0	.000	.000	.000	-99	0	0-0	—	0			/H		0.0
	Chi N	44	44	15	7	4	0	1	4	1-0	1	10	.159	.196	.295	32	-4	0-1	1.000	1	105	140	2b13		-0.3
Total	7	410	954	107	216	24	5	2	45	72-8	5	172	.226	.283	.268	62	-46	17-15	.969	-12	98	94	2b291,S50,3b2/OL	77	-4.1

OLIVER, BOB Robert Lee B2.8.1943 Shreveport LA BR/TR/6-2/215* d9.10 s-Darren Col American River (CA) CC OF(15/48/165)

YEAR	TM LG	G	AB	R	H	2B	3B	HR	RBI	BB-IB	HP	SO	AVG	OBP	SLG	AOPS	ABR	SB-CS	FA	FR	RNG	THR	GAMES AT POSITION	DL	BFW
1965	Pit N	3	2	0	0	0	0	0	0	0-0	0	0	.000	.000	.000	-99	-1	0-0	1.000	0	305	0	O3L		0.0
1969	KC A	118	394	43	100	8	4	13	43	21-2	2	74	.254	.294	.393	90	-8	5-5	.977	4	107	170	O98(9/48/45),1b12,3b8		-1.0
1970	KC A	160	612	83	159	24	6	27	99	42-4	3	126	.260	.309	.451	107	3	3-3	.993	-8	85	105	1b115,3b46		-1.6
1971	KC A	128	373	35	91	12	2	8	52	14-3	5	88	.244	.277	.351	79	-12	0-0	.988	1	96	129	1b68,O48(1/0/47),3b2		-1.9
1972	KC A	16	63	7	17	2	1	1	6	2-0	0	12	.270	.292	.381	100	0	1-0	.979	2	141	83	O16R		0.1
	Cal A	134	509	47	137	20	4	19	70	27-8	3	97	.269	.307	.436	127	13	4-3	.994	-6	74	88	1b127,O8(1/0/7)		-0.4
	Year	150	572	54	154	22	5	20	76	29-8	3	109	.269	.305	.430	124	13	5-3	.994	-4	74	88	1b127,O24(1/0/23)		-0.3
1973	Cal A	151	544	51	144	24	1	18	89	33-7	5	100	.265	.311	.412	110	5	1-1	.952	0	99	53	3b49,O47R,1b32,D12		0.0
1974	Cal A	110	359	22	89	9	1	8	55	16-2	1	51	.248	.277	.345	84	-9	2-1	.985	-12	66	96	1b57,3b46,O4(1/0/3)/D		-2.6
	Bal A	9	20	1	3	2	0	0	4	0-0	0	5	.150	.150	.250	14	-2	1-1	.974	1	258	33	1b4/D		-0.2
	Year	119	379	23	92	11	1	8	59	16-2	1	56	.243	.271	.340	80	-12	3-2	.984	-11	80	91	1b61,3b46,O4(1/0/3),D2		-2.8
1975	NY A	18	38	3	5	1	0	1	1-0		0	9	.132	.154	.158	-12	-6	0-0	1.000	-1	59	228	1b8/3D		-0.7
Total	8	847	2914	293	745	102	19	94	419	156-26	19	562	.256	.295	.400	100	-17	17-14	.991	-18	81	99	1b423,O224R,3b152,D17		-8.3

OLIVER, TOM Thomas Noble "Rebel" B1.15.1903 Montgomery AL D2.26.1988 Montgomery AL BR/TR/6-0/168 d4.14 C4

YEAR	TM LG	G	AB	R	H	2B	3B	HR	RBI	BB-IB	HP	SO	AVG	OBP	SLG	AOPS	ABR	SB-CS	FA	FR	RNG	THR	GAMES AT POSITION	DL	BFW
1930	Bos A	154	646	86	189	34	2	0	46	42		3	25	.293	.339	.351	78	-20	6-6	.982	6	107	75	O154C		-2.0
1931	Bos A	148	586	52	162	35	5	0	70	25		1	17	.276	.307	.353	77	-21	4-6	.993	6	102	122	O148C		-1.9
1932	Bos A	122	455	39	120	23	3	0	37	25		2	12	.264	.305	.327	66	-24	1-6	.983	3	101	121	O116C		-2.4
1933	Bos A	90	244	25	63	9	1	0	23	13		0	7	.258	.296	.303	60	-15	1-1	.985	8	113	196	O86C		-0.8
Total	4	514	1931	202	534	101	11	0	176	105		6	61	.277	.316	.340	73	-80	12-19	.986	22	105	117	O504C		-7.1

OLIVO, MIGUEL Miguel Eduardo (Pena) B7.15.1978 Villa Vasquez, D.R. BR/TR/6-1/215* d9.15

YEAR	TM LG	G	AB	R	H	2B	3B	HR	RBI	BB-IB	HP	SO	AVG	OBP	SLG	AOPS	ABR	SB-CS	FA	FR	RNG	THR	GAMES AT POSITION	DL	BFW
2002	Chi A	6	19	2	4	1	0	1	5	2-0	0	5	.211	.286	.421	81	-1	0-0	1.000	-1	299	71	C6		-0.1
2003	Chi A	114	317	37	75	19	1	6	27	19-0	4	80	.237	.287	.360	67	-15	6-4	.988	15	158	82	C113		0.6
2004	Chi A	46	141	21	38	7	2	7	26	10-1	0	29	.270	.316	.496	104	0	5-4	.984	-9	108	102	C46		-0.6
	Sea A	50	160	25	32	8	2	6	14	10-1	3	55	.200	.260	.387	69	-8	2-2	.997	-4	189	65	C49	15	-0.9
	Year	96	301	46	70	15	4	13	40	20-2	3	84	.233	.286	.439	86	-8	7-6	.991	-13	149	83	C95		-1.4
2005	Sea A	54	152	14	23	4	0	5	18	4-0	0	49	.151	.172	.276	18	-19	1-1	.987	1	113	99	C54		0.3
	†SD N	37	115	16	35	7	1	4	16	4-2	3	31	.304	.341	.487	121	3	6-1	.979	-3	152	59	C37	15	-0.2
Total	4	307	904	115	207	46	6	29	106	49-4	10	249	.229	.275	.389	73	-40	20-12	.988	-0	150	82	C305		-2.1

OLMEDO, RAY Rainer Gustavo B5.31.1981 Maracay, Venez BB/TR/5-11/150* d5.25

YEAR	TM LG	G	AB	R	H	2B	3B	HR	RBI	BB-IB	HP	SO	AVG	OBP	SLG	AOPS	ABR	SB-CS	FA	FR	RNG	THR	GAMES AT POSITION	DL	BFW
2003	Cin N	79	230	24	55	6	1	0	17	13-0	0	46	.239	.280	.274	48	-18	1-1	.929	-10	97	71	S51,2b18		-2.5
2004	Cin N	8	1	0	0	0	0	0	0	1-0	0	0	.000	.500	.000	46	0	0-0	1.000	1	136	149	S7		0.1
2005	Cin N	54	77	10	17	4	1	1	4	6-0	1	22	.221	.282	.338	65	-4	4-0	.975	-1	92	81	2b31,S5	75	-0.3
Total	3	141	308	34	72	10	2	1	21	20-0	1	68	.234	.282	.289	52	-22	5-1	.935	-10	98	76	S63,2b49	75	-2.7

OLMO, LUIS Luis Francisco (Rodriguez) (b Luis Francisco Rodriguez (Olmo)) B8.11.1919 Arecibo, PR BR/TR/5-11.5/190* d7.23

YEAR	TM LG	G	AB	R	H	2B	3B	HR	RBI	BB-IB	HP	SO	AVG	OBP	SLG	AOPS	ABR	SB-CS	FA	FR	RNG	THR	GAMES AT POSITION	DL	BFW
1943	Bro N	57	238	39	72	6	4	4	37	8		0	20	.303	.325	.412	112	2	3	.957	-1	96	122	O57(1/54/2)		-0.1
1944	Bro N	136	520	65	134	20	5	9	85	17		2	37	.258	.284	.367	84	-14	10	.971	-13	119	91	O64(3/61/1),2b42,3b31		-2.8
1945	Bro N	141	556	62	174	27	13	10	110	36		1	33	.313	.356	.462	127	17	15	.971	-8	98	105	O106(100/6/0),3b31/2		0.4
1949	†Bro N	38	105	15	32	4	1	1	14	5		0	11	.305	.336	.390	91	-2	2	.950	-1	91	157	O34(17/16/1)		-0.3
1950	Bos N	69	154	23	35	7	1	5	22	18		0	23	.227	.308	.383	86	-4	3	.974	-2	99	37	O55(18/11/24)/3		-0.7
1951	Bos N	21	56	4	11	1	1	0	4	4		0	4	.196	.250	.250	38	-5	0-1	1.000	0	83	187	O16(10/6/2)		-0.6
Total	6	462	1629	208	458	65	25	29	272	88		3	128	.281	.319	.405	102	-6	33-1	.968	-25	101	105	O332(149/154/30),3b63,2b43		-4.1

OLSEN, BARNEY Bernard Charles B9.11.1919 Everett MA D3.30.1977 Everett MA BR/TR/5-11/179 d8.23

YEAR	TM LG	G	AB	R	H	2B	3B	HR	RBI	BB-IB	HP	SO	AVG	OBP	SLG	AOPS	ABR	SB-CS	FA	FR	RNG	THR	GAMES AT POSITION	DL	BFW
1941	Chi N	24	73	-1	21	6	1	1	11			1	11	.288	.325	.438	118	1	0-0	.947	1	103	188	O23C		0.2

OLSON, GREG Gregory William B9.6.1960 Marshall MN BR/TR/6-0/200* [NYN82 7/163] d6.27 Col Minnesota

YEAR	TM LG	G	AB	R	H	2B	3B	HR	RBI	BB-IB	HP	SO	AVG	OBP	SLG	AOPS	ABR	SB-CS	FA	FR	RNG	THR	GAMES AT POSITION	DL	BFW
1989	Min A	3	2	0	1	0	0	0	0	0-0	1	0	.500	.500	.500	171	-0	0-0	1.000	-0	39	0	C3		0.0
1990	Atl N★	100	298	36	78	12	1	7	36	30-4	2	51	.262	.332	.379	91	-3	1-1	.987	-4	102	76	C97/3		-0.3
1991	†Atl N	133	411	46	99	25	0	6	44	44-3	1	48	.241	.316	.345	82	-9	1-1	.995	9	99	80	C127	16	0.2
1992	Atl N	95	302	27	72	14	2	3	27	34-4	1	31	.238	.316	.328	78	-8	2-1	.998	5	96	140	C94	23	-1.1
1993	†Atl N	83	262	23	59	10	0	4	24	29-0	1	24	.225	.304	.309	63	-13	1-0	.988	-3	97	91	C81	39	-1.3
Total	5	414	1275	132	309	61	3	20	131	137-11	7	157	.242	.317	.342	79	-33	5-3	.992	-2	98	96	C402/3		-1.3

OLSON, IVY Ivan Massie B10.14.1885 Kansas City MO D9.1.1965 Inglewood CA BR/TR/5-10.5/175 d4.12 C4 OF(8/0/2)

YEAR	TM LG	G	AB	R	H	2B	3B	HR	RBI	BB-IB	HP	SO	AVG	OBP	SLG	AOPS	ABR	SB-CS	FA	FR	RNG	THR	GAMES AT POSITION	DL	BFW
1911	Cle A	140	545	89	142	20	8	1	50	34		6		.261	.311	.332	79	-17	20	.909	-16	95	98	S139/3		-2.3
1912	Cle A	125	467	68	118	13	1	0	33	21		4		.253	.291	.285	63	-23	16	.917	2	101	52	S56,3b36,2b21,O3L		-1.6
1913	Cle A	104	370	47	92	13	3	0	32	22		3	28	.249	.296	.300	72	-14	7	.953	2	102	69	3b73,1b21/2		-1.1
1914	Cle A	89	310	22	75	6	2	1	20	13		1	24	.242	.275	.284	65	-14	15-9	.942	7	104	114	S31,2b23,3b19,O6(5/0/1),1b3		-0.5
1915	Cin N	63	207	18	48	5	4	0	14	12		0	13	.232	.274	.295	71	-7	112	.938	7	112	106	2b39,3b15,1b7		0.0
	Bro N	18	26	2	2	0	1	0	3	1		0	0	.077	.111	.154	-20	-4	0	.909	-2	80	85	S7/23OR		-0.6
	Year	81	233	20	50	5	5	0	17	13		0	13	.215	.256	.279	61	-12	10-6	.938	5	111	105	2b40,3b16,1b7,S7/OR		-1.4
1916	†Bro N	108	351	29	89	13	4	1	38	21		1	27	.254	.298	.322	88	-5	14	.941	-6	97	89	S133,3b6		-0.8
1917	Bro N	139	580	64	156	18	5	2	38	14		4	34	.269	.291	.328	87	-10	6	.941	-6	97	89	S133,2b21		-3.2
1918	Bro N	126	506	63	121	16	4	1	17	27		6	18	.239	.286	.292	77	-14	21	.918	-23	88	81	S126		0.2
1919	Bro N	140	590	73	164	14	9	1	38	30		3	12	.278	.316	.337	94	-5	26	.947	-4	92	95	S140		-3.3
1920	†Bro N	143	637	71	162	13	11	1	46	20		1	19	.254	.276	.314	68	-29	4-7	.935	-9	93	87	S125,2b21		-1.1
1921	Bro N	151	652	88	174	22	10	3	58	28		4	26	.267	.301	.345	68	-31	4-9	.943	7	100	97	S133,2b20		-2.1
1922	Bro N	136	551	63	150	26	6	1	47	25		2	10	.272	.306	.347	69	-27	8-5	.960	6	104	85	2b85,S51		-0.7
1923	Bro N	82	292	33	76	11	1	1	35	14		1	10	.260	.296	.315	63	-16	5-0	.974	6	101	93	2b72,3b4,1b2,S2		-0.2
1924	Bro N	10	27	0	6	1	0	0	3			0	1	.222	.300	.259	53	-2	0-0	.941	-1	76	148	S8,2b2		-0.2
Total	14	1574	6111	730	1575	191	69	13	446	285		36	222	.258	.295	.318	74	-219	156-36	.932	-48	94	90	S1054,2b288,3b155,1b34,O10L		-18.7

OLSON, KARL Karl Arthur "Ole" B7.6.1930 Kentfield CA BR/TR/6-3/205* d6.30 Mil 1952-54

YEAR	TM LG	G	AB	R	H	2B	3B	HR	RBI	BB-IB	HP	SO	AVG	OBP	SLG	AOPS	ABR	SB-CS	FA	FR	RNG	THR	GAMES AT POSITION	DL	BFW
1951	Bos A	5	10	1	1	0	0	0	0	0-0	0	3	.100	.100	.100	-42	-2	0-0	1.000	0	122	0	O5(2/0/3)		-0.2
1953	Bos A	25	57	5	7	2	0	1	6	1-0	0	9	.123	.138	.211	-7	-9	0-0	.970	-1	103	93	O24(23/2/0)		-1.0
1954	Bos A	101	227	25	59	12	4	1	20	12		0	10	.260	.293	.344	68	-10	2-1	.957	2	93	225	O78(29/36/16)		-1.1
1955	Bos A	26	48	4	12	0	0	1	7	5-0	0	10	.250	.265	.354	60	-3	0-0	1.000	0	101	113	O21(11/8/5)		-0.3
1956	Was A	106	313	34	77	10	2	4	22	28-1	1	41	.246	.305	.329	69	-15	1-1	.990	-4	94	71	O101(16/84/3)		-2.3
1957	Was A	8	12	2	2	0	0	0	0	0-0	0	2	.167	.231	.167	10	-1	0-0	1.000	0	124		O5(2/4/0)		-0.3
	Det A	8	14	1	2	0	0	0	0	0-0	0	5	.143	.143	.143	-21	-2	0-0	1.000	0	98	0	O5(4/1/0)		-0.3

YEAR	TM LG	G	AB	R	H	2B	3B	HR	RBI	BB-IB	HP	SO	AVG	OBP	SLG	AOPS	ABR	SB-CS	FA	FR	RNG	THR	GAMES AT POSITION	DL	BFW
	Year	16	26	3	4	0	0	0	1	1-0	0	8	.154	.185	.154	-6	-4	0-0	1.000	0	112	0	O11(6/5/0)		-0.5
Total	6	279	681	74	160	25	6	6	50	43-1	1	94	.235	.278	.316	57	-43	3-2	.979	-1	96	121	O240(87/135/27)		-5.4

OLSON, MARV Marvin Clement "Sparky" B5.28.1907 Gayville SD D2.5.1998 Tyndall SD BR/TR/5-7/160 d9.13 Col Luther

1931	Bos A	15	53	8	10	1	0	0	5	9	0	3	.189	.306	.208	40	-4	0-0	.963	1	103	87	2b15		-0.3
1932	Bos A	115	403	58	100	14	6	0	25	61	0	26	.248	.347	.313	74	-14	1-5	.955	-10	96	94	2b106/3		-1.8
1933	Bos A	3	1	1	0	0	0	0	0	0	0	1	.000	.000	.000	-99	0	0-0	—	-0	0	0	/2		0.0
Total	3	133	457	67	110	15	6	0	30	70	0	30	.241	.342	.300	70	-18	1-5	.956	-10	97	93	2b122/3		-2.1

OLSON, TIM Timothy Lane B8.1.1978 Grand Forks ND BR/TR/6-2/200* [AriN00 7/219] d5.30 Col Florida

2004	Ari N	48	97	8	18	7	0	2	5	16-0	0	18	.186	.301	.320	57	-6	1-0	.963	6	151	89	3b19,S17,O4(1/2/1)		0.1
2005	Col N	3	2	0	0	0	0	0	0	0-0	0	2	.000	.333	.000	-2	0	0-0	—	0			/D		0.0
Total	2	51	99	8	18	7	0	2	5	16-0	0	20	.182	.302	.313	56	-6	1-0	.963	6	151	89	3b19,S17,O4(1/2/1)/D		0.1

O'MALLEY, TOM Thomas Patrick B12.25.1960 Orange NJ BL/TR/6-0/190(180-195) [SFN79 16/408] d5.8

1982	SF N	92	291	26	80	12	4	2	27	33-9	1	39	.275	.350	.364	101	7	0-3	.965	-1	100	70	3b83/2S	21	-0.2
1983	SF N	135	410	40	106	16	1	5	45	52-4	4	47	.259	.345	.339	94	-2	2-4	.940	-2	101	67	3b117		-0.7
1984	SF N	13	25	2	3	0	0	0	2	2-0	0	2	.120	.185	.120	-13	-4	0-0	1.000	-1	77	105	3b7		-0.5
	Chi A	12	16	0	2	0	0	0	3	0-0	0	5	.125	.125	.125	-29	-3	0-0	1.000	-1	22	0	3b6		-0.4
1985	Bal A	8	14	1	1	0	0	1	2	0-0	0	2	.071	.071	.286	-8	-2	0-0	.833	-1	56	0	3b3		-0.4
1986	Bal A	56	181	19	46	9	1	18		17-1	0	21	.254	.317	.320	75	-6	0-1	.938	2	105	95	3b55		-0.5
1987	Tex A	45	117	10	32	8	0	1	12	15-1	0	9	.274	.351	.368	92	-1	0-0	.962	-1	97	47	3b40/2		-0.2
1988	Mon N	14	27	3	7	0	0	0	2	3-1	0	4	.259	.323	.259	69	-1	0-0	.905	1	130	0	3b7		0.0
1989	NY N	9	11	2	6	2	0	0	8	0-0	0	2	.545	.545	.727	272	2	0-0	1.000	-0	40	0	3b3		0.2
1990	NY N	82	121	14	27	7	1	1	14	11-1	0	20	.223	.286	.355	76	-4	0-0	.983	-0	76	134	3b38,1b3		-0.4
Total	9	466	1213	117	310	54	5	13	131	133-17	5	151	.256	.329	.340	87	-20	2-8	.951	-5	98	73	3b359,1b3,2b2/S	21	-3.1

O'MARA, OLLIE Oliver Edward B3.8.1891 St.Louis MO D10.24.1989 Reno NV BR/TR/5-9/155 d9.8

1912	Det A	1	4	0	0	0	0	0	0		0		.000	.000	.000	-99	-1	0	.857	0	127	0	/S		-0.1
1914	Bro N	67	247	41	65	10	2	1	7	16	3	26	.263	.316	.332	91	-3	14	.918	-10	94	76	S63		-0.9
1915	Bro N	149	577	77	141	26	3	0	31	51	2	40	.244	.308	.300	83	-11	11-12	.906	-36	91	69	S149		-4.3
1916	†Bro N	72	193	18	39	5	2	0	15	12	1	20	.202	.249	.249	52	-11	10	.898	-7	89	149	S51		-1.6
1918	Bro N	121	450	29	96	8	1	1	24	7	10	18	.213	.242	.242	48	-29	11	.951	-1	100	76	3b121		-2.9
1919	Bro N	2	7	1	0	0	0	0	0	0	0	0	.000	.000	.000	-98	-2	0	.875	1	62	0	3b2		-0.3
Total	6	412	1478	166	341	49	8	2	77	86	15	104	.231	.280	.279	69	-57	46-12	.907	-53	91	86	S264,3b123		-10.1

O'MEARA, ED Thomas Edward B12.12.1872 Chicago IL D2.16.1902 Fort Wayne IN BR d9.29

1895	Cle N	1	1	0	0	0	0	0	1		0		.000	.500	.000	34	0	0	.500	-0	86	200	/C		0.0
1896	Cle N	12	33	5	5	0	0	0	5		0	7	.152	.263	.152	10	-4	0	.914	-0	144	75	C9/1		-0.3
Total	2	13	34	6	5	0	0	0	6		0	7	.147	.275	.147	12	-4	0	.892	-0	141	82	C10/1		-0.3

O'NEAL d10.23

| 1874 | Har NA | 1 | 3 | 0 | 0 | 0 | 0 | 0 | 0 | | | 1 | .000 | .000 | .000 | -95 | -1 | 0-0 | .667 | 1 | 1254 | 0 | /OR | | 0.0 |

O'NEIL, MICKEY George Michael B4.12.1900 St.Louis MO D4.8.1964 St.Louis MO BR/TR/5-10/185 d9.12 C1

1919	Bos N	11	28	3	6	0	0	0	1	1	0	7	.214	.241	.214	39	-2	0-0	.981	2	107	144	C11		0.1
1920	Bos N	112	304	19	86	5	4	0	28	21	5	20	.283	.339	.326	96	-2	4-4	.962	7	112	135	C105/2		1.4
1921	Bos N	98	277	26	69	9	4	2	29	23	0	21	.249	.307	.332	73	-11	2-2	.968	4	114	138	C95		-0.1
1922	Bos N	83	251	18	56	5	2	0	26	14	1	11	.223	.267	.259	38	-24	1-0	.978	-0	101	126	C79		-1.8
1923	Bos N	96	306	29	65	7	4	0	20	17	2	14	.212	.258	.261	39	-28	3-2	.973	6	92	137	C95		-1.5
1924	Bos N	106	362	32	89	4	1	0	22	14	1	27	.246	.276	.252	47	-28	4-3	.985	-2	81	110	C106		-2.3
1925	Bos N	70	222	29	57	6	5	2	30	21	2	16	.257	.327	.356	81	-7	1-2	.972	-6	109	59	C69		-0.8
1926	Bro N	75	201	19	42	5	3	0	20	23	1	8	.209	.293	.264	52	-14	1-3	.965	-3	76	113	C74		-1.2
1927	Was A	5	6	0	0	0	0	0	0	0	1	0	.000	.000	.000	-99	-2	0-0	1.000	-0	75	0	C4		-0.2
	NY N	16	38	2	5	0	0	0	1	6	2	3	.132	.233	.132	-0	-5	0-0	.969	2	114	138	C16		-0.3
Total	9	672	1995	177	475	41	23	4	179	139	12	127	.238	.292	.288	58	-123	18-13	.972	11	98	120	C654/2		-6.7

O'NEIL, JOHN John Francis B4.19.1920 Shelbiana KY BR/TR/5-9/155 d4.16

| 1946 | Phi N | 46 | 94 | 12 | 25 | 3 | 0 | 0 | 9 | 5 | 0 | 12 | .266 | .303 | .298 | 73 | -4 | 0 | .940 | 0 | 100 | 97 | S32 | | -0.2 |

O'NEILL, DENNY Dennis B11.22.1866 Holyoke MA D11.15.1922 Rushville IN BL/TL/6-2.5/200 d6.18 Col Yale

| 1893 | StL N | 7 | 25 | 3 | 3 | 0 | 0 | 0 | 2 | 4 | 0 | 0 | .120 | .241 | .120 | -3 | -4 | 3 | .986 | -1 | 0 | 75 | 1b7 | | -0.4 |

O'NEILL, FRED Frederick James "Tip" B1865 London ON, Can. D3.7.1892 London ON, Can. BR/5-7/142 d5.3

| 1887 | NY AA | 6 | 26 | 4 | 8 | 1 | 0 | 3 | 1 | 1 | 0 | | .308 | .357 | .423 | 123 | 1 | 3 | .800 | -1 | 142 | 0 | O6(0/1/5) | | 0.0 |

O'NEILL, HARRY Harry Mink B5.8.1917 Philadelphia PA D3.6.1945 Iwo Jima, Marianas Islands BR/TR/6-3/205 d7.23 Col Gettysburg

| 1939 | Phi A | 1 | 0 | 0 | 0 | 0 | 0 | 0 | 0 | 0 | 0 | 0 | — | — | — | 0 | 0-0 | | — | 0 | 0 | 0 | /C | | 0.0 |

O'NEILL, TIP James Edward B5.25.1858 Springfield ON, Can. D12.31.1915 Montreal QC, Can. BR/TR/6-1.5/167 d5.5 ▲

1883	NY N	23	76	8	15	3	0	0	5	3		15	.197	.228	.237	42	-5		.917	-2	79	0	P19,O7(0/1/6)		-0.2
1884	StL AA	78	297	49	82	13	11	3	54	12	2		.276	.309	.424	132	9		.811	-5	51	59	O64(59/5/0),P17/1		0.0
1885	†StL AA	52	206	44	72	7	4	3	38	13	4		.350	.399	.466	165	15		.881	-2	66	67	O52L		1.1
1886	†StL AA	138	579	106	190	28	14	3	107	47	7		.328	.385	.440	151	33	9	.927	8	61	107	O138L		3.2
1887	†StL AA	124	517	167	225	52	19	14	123	50	5		**.435**	**.490**	**.691**	205	71	30	.895	-7	39	49	O124L		4.8
1888	†StL AA	130	529	96	177	24	10	5	98	44	4		.335	.390	.446	151	28	26	.937	-1	37	26	O130L		2.2
1889	StL AA	134	534	123	179	33	8	9	110	72	5	37	.335	.419	.478	137	25	28	.936	-4	46	57	O134L		1.5
1890	Chi P	137	577	112	174	20	16	3	75	65	5	36	.302	.377	.407	105	3	29	.926	-13	31	21	O137L		-1.0
1891	StL AA	127	514	111	166	28	4	10	95	61	9	33	.323	.404	.451	126	16	25	.935	-12	23	0	O127L		0.1
1892	Cin N	109	419	63	105	14	6	2	52	53	3	25	.251	.339	.327	103	3	14	.922	-4	73	82	O109L		-1.0
Total	10	1052	4248	879	1385	222	92	52	757	420	44	146	.326	.392	.458	140	198	161	.917	-41	46	50	O1022(1010/6/6),P36/1		10.7

O'NEILL, JIM James Leo B2.23.1893 Minooka PA D9.5.1976 Chambersburg PA BR/TR/5-10.5/165 d4.15 b-Jack b-Mike b-Steve

1920	Was A	86	294	27	85	17	7	1	40	13	2	30	.289	.324	.405	95	-4	7-3	.943	-9	100	68	S80,2b2		-0.6
1923	Was A	23	33	6	9	1	0	0	3	1	0	3	.273	.294	.303	60	-2	0-0	.946	2	110	115	2b8,3b4/SOR		0.0
Total	2	109	327	33	94	18	7	1	43	14	2	33	.287	.321	.394	91	-6	7-3	.943	-7	100	68	S81,2b10,3b4/OR		-0.6

O'NEILL, JOHN John J. B New York NY TR d9.6

1899	NY N	2	7	0	0	0	0	0	0	0	0		.000	.000	.000	-99	-2	0	.929	0	79	159	C2		-0.1
1902	NY N	2	8	0	0	0	0	0	0	0	0		.000	.000	.000	-99	-2	0	.933	0	128	145	C2		-0.2
Total	2	4	15	0	0	0	0	0	0	0	0		.000	.000	.000	-99	-4	0	.931	0	104	152	C4		-0.3

O'NEILL, JACK John Joseph B1.10.1873 Maam, Ireland D6.29.1935 Minooka PA BR/TR/5-10/165 d4.21 b-Jim b-Mike b-Steve

1902	StL N	63	192	13	27	1	1	0	12	13	5		.141	.214	.156	15	-19	2	.973	-2	93	104	C59		-1.6
1903	StL N	75	246	23	58	9	1	0	27	13	5		.236	.288	.280	64	-11	11	.972	9	95	110	C74		0.4
1904	Chi N	51	168	8	36	6	1	0	19	6	4		.214	.258	.262	61	-8	1	.981	5	127	96	C49		0.2
1905	Chi N	53	172	16	34	4	2	0	12	8	11		.198	.277	.244	54	-10	6	.974	7	120	90	C50		0.3
1906	Bos N	61	167	14	30	5	1	0	4	12	2		.180	.243	.222	46	-11	0	.971	4	92	108	C48,1b2/OR		-0.2
Total	5	303	945	74	185	24	5	1	74	52	27		.196	.258	.235	49	-59	20	.974	23	104	102	C280,1b2/OR		-0.9

O'NEILL, PAUL Paul Andrew B2.25.1963 Columbus OH BL/TL/6-4/215(200-215) [CinN81 4/93] d9.3

1985	Cin N	5	12	1	4	1	0	0	1	0-0	0	2	.333	.333	.417	103		0-0	1.000	1	89	767	O2L		0.1
1986	Cin N	3	2	0	0	0	0	0	0	1-0	0	1	.000	.333	.000	-0	-0	0-0	—	0			/H		0.0
1987	Cin N	84	160	24	41	14	1	7	28	18-1	2	29	.256	.331	.488	109	2	2-1	.949	0	112	93	O42(14/10/22),1b2/P		0.1
1988	Cin N	145	485	58	122	25	3	16	73	38-6	1	65	.252	.306	.414	102	4	8-6	.984	1	103	90	O118(0/8/114),1b21		-0.4
1989	Cin N	117	428	49	118	24	2	15	74	46-8	2	64	.276	.346	.446	122	4	20-5	.983	-0	97	111	O115(0/0/115)		0.9
1990	†Cin N★	145	503	59	136	28	0	16	78	53-13	2	103	.270	.339	.421	105	4	13-11	.993	5	99	128	O141(0/1/141)	42	1.2
1991	Cin N★	152	532	71	136	36	0	28	91	73-14	1	107	.256	.346	.481	125	19	12-7	.994	9	108	123	O150R		2.4
1992	Cin N	148	496	59	122	19	1	14	66	77-15	2	85	.246	.346	.373	102	4	6-3	**.997**	9	108	131	O143R		0.9

YEAR TM LG	G	AB	R	H	2B	3B	HR	RBI	BB-IB	HP	SO	AVG	OBP	SLG	AOPS	ABR	SB-CS	FA	FR	RNG	THR	GAMES AT POSITION	DL	BFW
1993 NY A	141	498	71	155	34	1	20	75	44-5	2	69	.311	.367	.504	136	25	2-4	.992	-8	86	78	O138(46/0/103),D2		0.9
1994 NY A★	103	368	68	132	25	1	21	83	72-13	0	56	.359	.460	.603	179	48	5-4	.995	1	100	96	O99(12/0/90),D4		3.9
1995 †NY A★	127	460	82	138	30	4	22	96	71-8	1	76	.300	.387	.526	138	28	1-2	.987	-5	96	38	O121(25/0/107),D4	16	1.5
1996 †NY A	150	546	89	165	35	4	19	91	102-8	4	76	.302	.411	.474	124	26	0-1	1.000	3	104	72	O146R/1D		1.9
1997 †NY A★	149	553	89	179	42	0	21	117	75-8	0	92	.324	.399	.514	139	35	10-7	.984	-1	98	76	O146R,1b2,D2		2.4
1998 †NY A★	152	602	95	191	40	2	24	116	57-2	2	103	.317	.372	.510	134	30	15-1	.987	1	99	102	O150R/D		2.5
1999 †NY A	153	597	70	170	39	4	19	110	66-1	2	89	.285	.353	.459	108	8	11-9	.974	4	102	99	O151R		0.0
2000 †NY A	142	566	79	160	26	0	18	100	51-2	0	90	.283	.336	.424	94	-6	14-9	.993	4	112	56	O140R,D2		-0.8
2001 †NY A	137	510	77	136	33	1	21	70	48-4	2	59	.267	.330	.459	104	3	22-3	.981	-10	91	13	O130R,D6		-0.9
Total 17	2053	7318	1041	2105	451	21	281	1269	892-107	22	1166	.288	.363	.470	121	240	141-73	.988	5	101	88	O1932(99/23/1848),1b26,D24/P	58	15.9

O'NEILL, PEACHES Philip Bernard B8.30.1879 Anderson IN D8.2.1955 Anderson IN BR/TR/5-11/165 d4.16 Col Notre Dame

1904 Cin N	8	15	0	4	0	0	0	1	0	0		.267	.313	.267	73	0	0	.900	2	73	64	C5/1		-0.3

O'NEILL, STEVE Stephen Francis B7.6.1891 Minooka PA D1.26.1962 Cleveland OH BR/TR/5-10/165 d9.18 M14/C4 b-Jim b-Jack b-Mike

1911 Cle A	9	27	1	4	1	0	0	1	4	1		.148	.281	.185	31	-2	2	.986	2	100	123	C9		0.0
1912 Cle A	69	215	17	49	4	0	0	14	12	1	24	.228	.272	.247	47	-15	2	.961	7	97	108	C68		-0.3
1913 Cle A	80	234	19	69	13	3	0	29	10	2	24	.295	.329	.376	103	0	5	.973	9	119	100	C80		1.6
1914 Cle A	87	269	28	68	12	2	0	20	15	0	35	.253	.292	.312	79	-8	1-3	.956	-2	88	113	C82/1		-0.4
1915 Cle A	121	386	32	91	14	2	2	34	26	5	41	.236	.293	.298	75	-13	2-3	.968	9	107	103	C115		0.4
1916 Cle A	130	378	30	89	23	0	0	29	24	4	33	.235	.288	.296	71	-13	6	.971	6	110	88	C128		0.4
1917 Cle A	129	370	21	68	10	2	0	29	41	4	55	.184	.262	.227	47	-22	2	.980	5	105	103	C127		-0.3
1918 Cle A	114	359	34	87	8	7	1	35	48	7	22	.242	.343	.312	89	-3	5	.983	9	123	104	C113		1.7
1919 Cle A	125	398	46	115	35	7	2	47	48	5	21	.289	.373	.427	117	11	4	.977	0	139	84	C123		2.2
1920 †Cle A	149	489	63	157	39	5	3	55	69	3	39	.321	.408	.440	121	19	3-5	.976	2	114	79	C148		3.1
1921 Cle A	106	335	39	108	22	1	1	50	57	2	22	.322	.424	.403	110	9	0-1	.982	4	93	68	C105		1.9
1922 Cle A	133	392	33	122	27	4	2	65	73	3	25	.311	.423	.416	118	16	2-2	.974	-15	81	75	C130		0.8
1923 Cle A	113	330	31	82	12	0	0	50	64	2	34	.248	.374	.285	75	-8	0-4	.968	-6	118	56	C111		-0.9
1924 Bos A	106	307	29	73	15	1	0	38	63	2	23	.238	.371	.293	73	-9	0-2	.970	-1	99	98	C92		-0.4
1925 NY A	35	91	7	26	6	0	1	13	10	1	3	.286	.363	.374	89	-1	0-0	.946	1	101	108	C31		0.2
1927 StL A	74	191	14	44	7	0	1	22	20	0	6	.230	.303	.283	51	-14	0-3	.983	1	106	149	C60		-1.0
1928 StL A	10	24	4	7	1	0	0	6	8	1		.292	.485	.333	115	1	0-0	.958	-3	67	67	C10		-0.1
Total 17	1590	4795	448	1259	248	34	13	537	592	43	<u>383</u>	.263	.349	.337	88	-52	30-<u>23</u>	.972	28	108	92	C1532/1		8.6

O'NEILL, BILL William John B1.22.1880 St.John NB, Can. D7.20.1920 Woodhaven NY BB/TR/5-11/175 d5.7

1904 Bos A	17	51	7	10	1	0	0	5	2	0		.196	.226	.216	38	-1	0	.933	-3	0	0	O9(8/1/0),S2		-0.7
Was A	95	365	33	89	10	1	1	16	22	4		.244	.294	.285	85	-6	22	.893	-9	98	36	O93(14/79/0),2b3		-2.2
Year	112	416	40	99	11	1	1	21	24	4		.238	.286	.276	79	-10	22	.896	-12	90	33	O102(22/80/0),2b3,S2		-2.9
1906 †Chi A	94	330	37	82	4	1	1	21	22	3		.248	.301	.276	83	-6	19	.949	-2	112	49	O93(0/7/87)		-1.4
Total 2	206	746	77	181	15	2	2	42	46	7		.243	.293	.276	81	-16	41	.919	-14	100	41	O195(22/87/87),2b3,S2		-4.3

ONIS, RALPH Manuel Dominguez "Curly" B10.24.1908 Tampa FL D1.4.1995 Tampa FL BR/TR/5-9/180 d4.27

1935 Bro N	1	1	0	1	0	0	0	0	0	0		0 1.000	1.000	1.000	449	0	0	.500	-0	0	0	/C		0.0

ONSLOW, EDDIE Edward Joseph B2.17.1893 Meadville PA D5.8.1981 Dennison OH BL/TL/6-0/170 d8.7 b-Jack

1912 Det A	36	128	11	29	1	4	1	13	3	1		.227	.250	.289	56	-8	3	.972	-4	75	108	1b35		-1.3
1913 Det A	17	55	7	14	1	0	0	8	5	1	9	.255	.328	.273	77	-1	1	.990	-1	70	95	1b17		-0.3
1918 Cle A	2	6	0	1	0	0	0	0	0	0	1	.167	.167	.167	1	-1	0	.000	-1	0	0	/OL		-0.2
1927 Was A	9	18	1	4	1	0	0	1	1	0		.222	.263	.278	41	-2	0-0	1.000	0	90	125	1b5		-0.2
Total 4	64	207	19	48	3	2	1	22	9	2	<u>10</u>	.232	.271	.280	59	-12	4-<u>0</u>	.979	-5	74	105	1b57/OL		-2.0

ONSLOW, JACK John James B10.13.1888 Scottdale PA D12.22.1960 Concord MA BR/TR/5-11/180 d5.2 M2/C7 b-Eddie

1912 Det A	36	69	7	11	1	0	0	4	10	1		.159	.284	.174	33	-6	0	.948	-4	84	110	C35/OC		-0.7
1917 NY N	9	8	1	2	1	0	0	0	0	1	1	.250	.333	.375	121	0	0	.929	-1	110	59	C9		0.0
Total 2	45	77	8	13	2	0	0	4	10	2		.169	.289	.195	41	-6	1	.947	-4	86	105	C44/OC		-0.7

ONTIVEROS, STEVE Steven Robert B10.26.1951 Bakersfield CA BB/TR/6-0/185* [SFN69 6/136] d8.5

1973 SF N	24	33	3	8	0	1	0	5	4-0	0	7	.242	.324	.333	79	-1	0-0	1.000	1	200	53	1b5/OR		0.0
1974 SF N	120	343	45	91	15	1	4	33	57-4	3	41	.265	.375	.350	99	3	0-0	.929	-4	93	111	3b75,1b19,O2(1/0/1)		-0.3
1975 SF N	108	325	21	94	16	0	3	31	55-4	2	44	.289	.391	.366	109	7	2-0	.923	3	106	90	3b89,O8(2/0/7),1b4		1.0
1976 SF N	59	74	8	13	3	0	0	6	6-0	1	11	.176	.244	.216	31	-7	0-0	1.000	-1	113	192	3b7,O7(4/3/2),1b4		-0.8
1977 Chi N	156	546	54	163	32	3	10	68	81-4	0	69	.299	.390	.423	107	9	3-3	.955	3	106	97	3b155		1.0
1978 Chi N	82	276	34	67	14	4	1	22	34-3	0	35	.243	.321	.333	75	-3	0-2	.965	12	123	118	3b77/1		-0.3
1979 Chi N	152	519	58	148	28	2	4	57	58-7	7	68	.285	.362	.370	92	-3	0-1	.941	2	101	104	3b142/1		-0.3
1980 Chi N	31	97	7	16	3	0	1	3	14-1	0	15	.165	.330	.286	67	-3	0-0	.929	-0	104	32	3b24	68	0.5
Total 8	732	2193	230	600	111	10	24	224	309-23	16	290	.274	.365	.366	94	-3	5-6	.944	17	105	101	3b569,1b34,O18(7/3/11)	68	0.5

OQUENDO, JOSE Jose Manuel (Contreras) B7.4.1963 Rio Piedras, PR BB/TR (BR 1983p)/5-10/160(156-171) d5.2 C7 OF(11/7/47)

1983 NY N	120	328	29	70	7	0	1	17	19-2	2	60	.213	.260	.244	41	-27	8-9	.960	0	106	103	S116		-1.8
1984 NY N	81	189	23	42	5	0	0	10	15-2	2	26	.222	.284	.249	52	-12	10-1	.972	9	92	102	S67		-0.4
1986 StL N	76	138	20	41	4	1	0	13	15-4	0	20	.297	.359	.341	96	0	2-3	.956	-9	90	109	S29,2b21/3OL		-0.7
1987 †StL N	116	248	43	71	9	4	1	24	54-6	0	29	.286	.408	.335	99	3	4-4	1.000	9	118	210	2b69,3b47,S17,1b16,O15(2/4/9)/PC		1.1
1988 StL N	148	451	36	125	10	1	7	46	52-4	0	40	.277	.350	.350	100	1	4-6	.997	8	106	116	2b69,3b47,S17,1b16,O15(2/4/9)/PC		1.1
1989 StL N	163	556	59	162	28	7	1	48	79-7	0	59	.291	.375	.372	112	12	3-5	.994	25	110	124	2b156,S7/1		4.3
1990 StL N	156	469	38	118	17	5	1	37	74-8	0	46	.252	.350	.316	85	-7	1-1	.996	-2	102	88	2b150,S4		-0.5
1991 StL N	127	366	37	88	11	4	1	26	67-13	1	48	.240	.357	.301	86	-4	1-2	.988	9	109	112	2b118,S22,1b3/P		0.9
1992 StL N	14	35	3	9	3	0	0	5	5-1	0	3	.257	.350	.400	115	1	0-0	1.000	1	121	147	2b9,S5	131	0.2
1993 StL N	46	73	7	15	0	0	0	4	12-1	0	14	.205	.314	.205	44	-6	0-0	.988	5	122	100	S22,2b16	56	-0.9
1994 StL N	55	129	13	34	2	2	0	9	21-4	0	16	.264	.364	.310	79	-3	1-1	.945	-8	77	56	S28,2b16		-0.1
1995 StL N	88	220	31	46	8	2	1	17	35-3	0	21	.209	.316	.300	63	-11	1-1	.981	7	110	122	2b62,S24,3b2/OR		-0.1
Total 12	1190	3202	339	821	104	24	14	254	448-58	5	376	.256	.346	.317	85	-53	35-33	.992	46	107	114	2b649,S364,O63R,3b58,1b23,P3/C	187	3.5

ORAN, TOM Thomas B1847 CA D9.22.1886 St.Louis MO d5.4

1875 RS NA	19	81	7	15	3	1	0	10	1			.185	.195	.247	58	-3	3-2	.633	-4	102	0	O19(0/2/17)/S		-0.5

ORAVETZ, ERNIE Ernest Eugene B1.24.1932 Johnstown PA BB/TL/5-4/145* d4.11

1955 Was A	100	263	24	71	5	1	0	25	26-0	1	19	.270	.336	.297	76	-9	1-2	.967	-5	94	24	O57(0/17/42)		-1.6
1956 Was A	88	137	20	34	3	2	0	11	27-0	0	20	.248	.370	.299	79	-3	1-0	.946	-1	97	103	O31(20/3/9)		-0.5
Total 2	188	400	44	105	8	3	0	36	53-0	1	39	.262	.348	.298	77	-12	2-2	.961	-5	95	48	O88(20/20/51)		-2.1

ORDAZ, LUIS Luis Javier B8.12.1975 Maracaibo, Venez BR/TR/5-11/170* d9.3

1997 StL N	12	22	3	6	1	0	0	1	0-0	0	2	.273	.304	.318	63	-1	3-0	.964	-1	93	102	S11		-0.1
1998 StL N	57	153	9	31	5	0	0	8	12-1	0	18	.203	.261	.235	32	-15	2-0	.945	6	118	121	S54,3b2/2		-0.5
1999 StL N	10	9	1	1	0	0	0	2	1-0	0	2	.111	.200	.111	-18	-2	1-0	.786	-1	77	192	S8/23		-0.2
2000 KC A	65	104	17	23	2	0	0	11	5-0	1	10	.221	.257	.240	27	-12	4-2	.986	-10	72	117	S38,2b22		-1.8
2001 KC A	28	56	8	14	3	0	0	4	3-0	0	5	.250	.295	.304	54	-4	0-0	.987	5	129	177	2b19,S8/3D	44	0.2
2002 KC A	33	94	11	21	2	0	0	4	12-0	1	13	.223	.308	.245	45	-7	2-3	.982	-6	91	118	S121,2b71,3b10/D	44	-1.2
Total 6	205	438	51	96	13	0	0	30	34-1	2	53	.219	.276	.249	37	-41	12-5	.947	-7	104	118	S121,2b71,3b10/D	44	-3.6

ORDENANA, TONY Antonio (Rodriguez) "Mosquito" B10.30.1918 Guanabacoa, Cuba D9.29.1988 Miami FL BR/TR/5-9/158 d10.3

1943 Pit N	1	4	2	2	0	0	0	3	0	0	0	.500	.500	.500	183	0	0	1.000	1	136	150	/S		0.1

ORDONEZ, MAGGLIO Magglio (Delgado) B1.28.1974 Caracas, Venez BR/TR/6-0/200(170-215) d8.29

1997 Chi A	21	69	12	22	6	0	4	11	2-0	0	8	.319	.338	.580	138	3	1-2	1.000	1	118	87	O19R		0.3
1998 Chi A	145	535	70	151	25	2	14	65	28-1	9	53	.282	.326	.415	93	-6	9-7	.985	5	108	97	O145(0/22/136)		-0.8
1999 Chi A★	157	624	100	188	34	3	30	117	47-4	1	64	.301	.349	.510	114	11	13-6	.991	7	107	111	O153R,D2		1.1
2000 †Chi A★	153	588	102	185	34	3	32	126	60-3	2	64	.315	.371	.546	126	23	18-4	.983	-3	91	114	O152R		1.1

YEAR	TM LG	G	AB	R	H	2B	3B	HR	RBI	BB-IB	HP	SO	AVG	OBP	SLG	AOPS	ABR	SB-CS	FA	FR	RNG	THR	GAMES AT POSITION	DL	BFW
2001	Chi A★	160	593	97	181	40	1	31	113	70-7	5	70	.305	.382	.533	130	27	25-7	.983	-3	94	108	O155(0/1/155),D3		1.8
2002	Chi A	153	590	116	189	47	1	38	135	53-2	7	77	.320	.381	.597	149	42	7-5	.986	-4	96	87	O150R/D		2.9
2003	Chi A★	160	606	95	192	46	3	29	99	57-1	7	73	.317	.380	.546	135	32	9-5	.994	1	111	82	O157(0/4/154),D2		2.7
2004	Chi A	52	202	32	59	8	2	9	37	16-2	3	22	.292	.351	.485	112	3	0-2	.990	1	111	36	O43R,D7	117	0.1
2005	Det A	82	305	38	92	17	0	8	46	30-1	1	35	.302	.359	.436	115	7	0-0	.993	-3	87	108	O81R/D	79	0.0
Total	9	1083	4112	662	1259	257	15	195	749	363-21	35	466	.306	.364	.518	124	142	82-38	.988	5	100	98	O1055(0/27/1043),D16	196	9.4

ORDONEZ, REY Reynaldo B1.11.1971 Havana, Cuba BR/TR/5-9/159* d4.1

YEAR	TM LG	G	AB	R	H	2B	3B	HR	RBI	BB-IB	HP	SO	AVG	OBP	SLG	AOPS	ABR	SB-CS	FA	FR	RNG	THR	GAMES AT POSITION	DL	BFW
1996	NY N	151	502	51	129	12	4	1	30	22-12	1	53	.257	.289	.303	59	-31	1-3	.962	10	106	109	S150		-1.2
1997	NY N	120	356	35	77	5	3	1	33	18-3	1	36	.216	.255	.256	36	-35	11-5	.983	10	112	113	S118	39	-1.6
1998	NY N	153	505	46	124	20	2	1	42	23-7	1	60	.246	.278	.299	54	-35	3-6	.975	-1	93	96	S151		-2.7
1999	†NY N	154	520	49	134	24	2	1	60	49-12	1	59	.258	.319	.317	66	-27	8-4	.994	6	98	106	S154		-0.9
2000	NY N	45	133	10	25	5	0	0	9	17-2	0	16	.188	.274	.226	32	-14	0-0	.965	-5	90	83	S44	124	-1.5
2001	NY N	149	461	31	114	24	4	3	44	34-17	1	43	.247	.299	.336	69	-22	3-2	.980	-3	93	100	S148		-1.5
2002	NY N	144	460	53	117	25	2	1	42	24-11	2	46	.254	.292	.324	69	-24	2-2	.969	1	99	96	S142		-1.3
2003	TB A	34	117	14	37	11	0	3	22	2-0	1	12	.316	.328	.487	115	2	0-2	.970	5	110	134	S34	143	0.9
2004	Chi N	23	61	2	10	3	0	1	5	2-0	0	14	.164	.190	.262	15	-8	0-0	.959	-2	78	88	S22		-0.8
Total	9	973	3115	291	767	129	17	12	287	191-64	8	339	.246	.289	.310	60	-194	28-24	.976	20	99	103	S963	306	-10.6

ORENGO, JOE Joseph Charles B11.29.1914 San Francisco CA D7.24.1988 San Francisco CA BR/TR/6-0/185 d4.18

YEAR	TM LG	G	AB	R	H	2B	3B	HR	RBI	BB-IB	HP	SO	AVG	OBP	SLG	AOPS	ABR	SB-CS	FA	FR	RNG	THR	GAMES AT POSITION	DL	BFW
1939	StL N	7	3	0	0	0	0	0	0	0	0	1	.000	.000	.000	-94	-1	0-0	.667	-1	72	0	S7		-0.2
1940	StL N	129	415	58	119	23	4	7	56	65	0	90	.287	.383	.412	113	10	9	.952	-5	95	96	2b77,3b34,S19		1.2
1941	NY N	77	252	23	54	11	2	4	25	28	2	49	.214	.298	.321	73	-9	1	.958	10	105	108	3b59,S9,2b6		0.4
1943	NY N	83	266	28	58	8	2	6	29	36	0	46	.218	.311	.331	85	-5	1	.992	5	121	67	1b82		-0.5
	Bro N	7	15	1	3	2	0	0	1	4	0	2	.200	.368	.333	103	0	0	1.000	0	100	0	3b6		0.0
	Year	90	281	29	61	10	2	6	30	40	0	48	.217	.315	.331	86	-5	1	.992	5	121	67	1b82,3b6		-0.5
1944	Det A	46	154	14	31	10	4	0	10	20	1	29	.201	.297	.266	58	-8	1-1	.903	3	104	123	S29,3b11,1b5,2b2		-0.5
1945	Chi A	15	15	5	1	0	0	0	1	3	0	7	.067	.222	.067	-15	-2	0-0	.923	-0	100	0	3b7/2		-0.3
Total	6	366	1120	129	266	54	18	17	122	156	3	219	.237	.332	.346	88	-15	12-1	.957	11	97	93	3b117,1b87,2b86,S64		0.3

ORIE, KEVIN Kevin Leonard B9.1.1972 West Chester PA BR/TR/6-4/210* [ChiN93 S1/29] d4.1 Col Indiana

YEAR	TM LG	G	AB	R	H	2B	3B	HR	RBI	BB-IB	HP	SO	AVG	OBP	SLG	AOPS	ABR	SB-CS	FA	FR	RNG	THR	GAMES AT POSITION	DL	BFW
1997	Chi N	114	364	40	100	23	5	8	44	39-3	5	57	.275	.350	.431	101	7	2-2	.971	13	110	84	3b112,S3	30	1.4
1998	Chi N	64	204	24	37	14	0	2	21	18-0	3	35	.181	.253	.279	40	-18	1-1	.966	1	100	72	3b57		-1.7
	Fla N	48	175	23	46	8	1	6	17	14-2	1	24	.263	.335	.423	104	1	1-0	.939	5	113	51	3b48		0.6
	Year	112	379	47	83	22	1	8	38	32-2	4	59	.219	.291	.346	68	-18	2-1	.952	6	106	62	3b105		-1.1
1999	Fla N	77	240	26	61	16	0	6	29	22-1	5	43	.254	.322	.396	86	-5	1-0	.961	4	111	74	3b64/1	83	-0.1
2002	Chi N	13	32	4	9	3	0	0	5	1-0	1	4	.281	.306	.375	86	-1	0-0	.895	-2	77	55	3b12		-0.2
Total	4	316	1015	117	253	64	6	22	116	94-6	17	163	.249	.320	.389	85	-22	5-3	.960	21	108	73	3b293,S3/1	113	-0.0

ORME, GEORGE George William B9.16.1891 Lebanon IN D3.16.1962 Indianapolis IN BR/TR/5-10/160 d9.14

YEAR	TM LG	G	AB	R	H	2B	3B	HR	RBI	BB-IB	HP	SO	AVG	OBP	SLG	AOPS	ABR	SB-CS	FA	FR	RNG	THR	GAMES AT POSITION	DL	BFW
1920	Bos A	4	6	4	2	0	0	0	1	3	0	0	.333	.556	.333	146	1	0-0	1.000	0	146	0	O3(0/1/2)		0.1

ORNDORFF, JESS Jesse Walworth Thayer B1.15.1881 Chicago IL D9.28.1960 Cardiff-By-The- Sea CA BB/TR/6-0/168 d4.18

YEAR	TM LG	G	AB	R	H	2B	3B	HR	RBI	BB-IB	HP	SO	AVG	OBP	SLG	AOPS	ABR	SB-CS	FA	FR	RNG	THR	GAMES AT POSITION	DL	BFW
1907	Bos N	5	17	0	2	0	0	0	0	0	0		.118	.118	.118	-26	-3	0	.900	-2	69	125	C5		-0.5

O'ROURKE, FRANK James Francis "Blackie" B11.28.1894 Hamilton ON, Can. D5.14.1986 Chatham NJ BR/TR/5-10.5/165 d6.12

YEAR	TM LG	G	AB	R	H	2B	3B	HR	RBI	BB-IB	HP	SO	AVG	OBP	SLG	AOPS	ABR	SB-CS	FA	FR	RNG	THR	GAMES AT POSITION	DL	BFW
1912	Bos N	61	196	11	24	3	1	0	16	11	2	50	.122	.177	.148	-10	-31	1	.915	-10	97	67	S59/3		-3.7
1917	Bro N	64	198	18	47	7	1	0	15	14	2	25	.237	.294	.283	75	-5	11	.954	3	106	59	3b58		-0.1
1918	Bro N	4	12	0	2	0	0	0	2	1	0	3	.167	.231	.167	22	-1	0	.857	1	138	103	2b2/O		0.0
1920	Was A	14	54	8	16	1	0	0	5	2	0	5	.296	.321	.315	71	-2	2-1	.952	1	94	195	S13/3		0.0
1921	Was A	123	444	51	104	17	8	3	54	26	3	56	.234	.287	.329	60	-29	6-7	.922	-11	96	90	S122		-2.6
1922	Bos A	67	216	28	57	14	3	1	17	20	3	28	.264	.335	.370	84	-5	6-6	.909	-11	90	70	S49,3b20		-1.0
1924	Det A	47	181	28	50	11	2	0	19	12	3	19	.276	.332	.359	79	-6	7-4	.970	6	109	116	2b40,S7		0.2
1925	Det A	124	482	88	141	40	7	5	57	32	11	37	.293	.350	.436	100	-1	5-8	.971	15	107	98	2b118,3b6		1.4
1926	Det A	111	363	43	88	16	1	1	41	35	7	33	.242	.321	.300	62	-20	8-6	.936	4	95	176	3b60,2b41,S10		-1.1
1927	StL A	140	538	85	144	25	3	1	39	64	12	44	.268	.338	.331	77	-16	18-8	.955	11	99	101	3b121,2b16,1b3		0.4
1928	StL A	99	391	54	103	24	3	1	62	21	1	19	.263	.303	.348	68	-18	10-2	.954	-11	81	74	3b96,S2		-2.1
1929	StL A	154	585	81	147	23	9	2	62	41	5	28	.251	.306	.332	62	-35	14-7	.943	-17	87	113	3b151,2b3,S2		-3.9
1930	StL A	115	400	52	107	15	4	1	41	35	0	30	.268	.326	.333	65	-21	11-9	.950	6	97	111	3b84,S23,1b3		-0.8
1931	StL A	8	9	0	2	0	0	0	0	0	0	1	.222	.222	.222	17	-1	1-1	1.000	1	144	0	S2/1		0.1
Total	14	1131	4069	547	1032	196	42	15	430	314	53	377	.254	.315	.333	68	-191	100-59	.949	-11	93	101	3b598,S289,2b220,1b7/O		-13.4

O'ROURKE, JIM James Henry "Orator Jim" B9.1.1850 Bridgeport CT D1.8.1919 Bridgeport CT BR/TR/5-8/185 d4.26 M5/U1 HF1945 b-John s-Queenie OF NA(0/44/22) OF(770/419/195) ▲

YEAR	TM LG	G	AB	R	H	2B	3B	HR	RBI	BB-IB	HP	SO	AVG	OBP	SLG	AOPS	ABR	SB-CS	FA	FR	RNG	THR	GAMES AT POSITION	DL	BFW
1872	Man NA	23	99	25	27	0	0	0	16	4			.273	.301	.323	98	1	1-0	.735	-2	118	27	S15,C9,3b2/1		-0.1
1873	Bos NA	57	280	79	98	21	2	1	49	15		3	.350	.383	.450	135	11	9-5	.912	1	139	157	1b34,O21R,C12		1.0
1874	Bos NA	70	331	82	104	15	8	5	61	4		5	.314	.322	.453	138	12	11-2	.943	1	90	177	1b70		1.2
1875	Bos NA	75	358	97	106	13	7	6	72	9		6	.296	.313	.422	148	16	17-5	.800	-5	109	79	O68(9/60/0),3b27,1b6/C		1.0
1876	Bos N	70	312	61	102	17	3	2	43	15		17	.327	.358	.420	156	19		.856	-2	74	0	O60(23/35/3)/1		1.1
1877	Bos N	61	265	68	96	14	4	0	23	20		21	.362	.407	.445	162	20		.846	-2	74	0	O60(23/35/3)/1		1.2
1878	Bos N	60	255	44	71	17	7	1	29	5		21	.278	.292	.412	120	5		.860	1	100	189	O57C,1b2,C2		0.3
1879	Pro N	81	362	69	126	19	9	1	46	13		10	.348	.371	.459	174	29		.785	-10	85	149	O56(2/0/56),1b20,C5,3b3		1.7
1880	Bos N	86	363	71	100	20	11	6	45	21		8	.275	.315	.441	158	22		.907	-3	127	58	O37(15/4/19),S19,17,3b10,C9		1.9
1881	Buf N	83	348	71	105	21	3	0	30	27		18	.302	.352	.402	139	17		.821	-19	72	86	3b56,O18L,C8,S3/1M		-0.1
1882	Buf N	84	370	62	104	15	6	2	37	13		13	.281	.305	.370	114	5		.866	-1	87	83	O81(5/77/0),S2,C2/3M		0.1
1883	Buf N	94	436	102	143	29	8	1	38	15		13	.328	.350	.438	135	18		.866	-9	60	0	O61(60/1/0),C33,3b8,S3,P2,M		0.8
1884	Buf N	108	467	119	162	33	7	5	63	35		17	.347	.392	.480	167	36		.894	-9	36	77	O86L,1b18,C10,P4/3M		2.3
1885	NY N	112	477	119	143	21	16	5	42	40		21	.300	.354	.442	158	31		.940	-16	49	0	O112C,C8		1.0
1886	NY N	105	440	106	136	26	6	1	34	39		21	.309	.365	.402	132	18	14	.926	5	91	58	O63(1/62/0),C47,1b2		2.2
1887	NY N	103	397	73	113	15	13	3	88	36	5	11	.285	.352	.411	116	10	46	.890	-7			C40,3b38,O28(19/6/3),2b2		0.5
1888	†NY N	107	409	50	112	16	6	4	50	24	3	30	.274	.319	.372	121	10	25	.960	1	89	39	O87(75/3/9),C15,1b4,3b2		0.9
1889	†NY N	128	502	89	161	36	7	3	81	40	1	34	.321	.372	.438	126	16	33	.893	-7	75	47	O128L/C		0.6
1890	NY P	111	478	112	172	37	5	9	115	33		20	.360	.410	.515	146	22	23	.930	2	117	72	O111(10/1/100)		1.7
1891	NY N	136	555	92	164	28	7	5	95	26		29	.295	.334	.398	118	11	19	.906	-1	92	30	O126(126/1/0),C14		0.7
1892	NY N	115	448	62	136	28	5	0	56	30		30	.304	.354	.388	126	14	14	.913	-8	65	27	O111(106/0/5),C4/1		-0.2
1893	Was N	129	547	75	157	22	5	2	95	49		8	.287	.354	.356	102	-6	15	.927	5	110	56	O87L,1b33,C9,M		-0.6
1904	NY N	1	4	1	1	0	0	0	0	0			.250	.250	.250	52	0	0	.800	-1	109	0	/C		-0.1
Total 4 NA		225	1068	283	335	54	17	12	198	32		14	.314	.334	.430	137	40	38-12	.931	-6	100	167	1b111,O66C,3b29,C22,S15		3.1
Total 19		1774	7435	1446	2304	414	132	50	1010	481	36	348	.310	.355	.421	133	297	191-0	.898	-79	82	53	O1377L,C209,3b119,1b103,S25,P6,2b2		16.0

O'ROURKE, CHARLIE James Patrick B6.22.1937 Walla Walla WA BR/TR/6-2/195 d6.16 Col Santa Clara

YEAR	TM LG	G	AB	R	H	2B	3B	HR	RBI	BB-IB	HP	SO	AVG	OBP	SLG	AOPS	ABR	SB-CS	FA	FR	RNG	THR	GAMES AT POSITION	DL	BFW
1959	StL N	2	2	0	0	0	0	0	0	0	0	0	.000	.000	.000	-94	-1	0	—	0			/H		-0.1

O'ROURKE, QUEENIE James Stephen B12.26.1883 Bridgeport CT D12.22.1955 Sparrows Point MD BR/TR/5-7/150 d8.15 f-Jim Col Holy Cross

YEAR	TM LG	G	AB	R	H	2B	3B	HR	RBI	BB-IB	HP	SO	AVG	OBP	SLG	AOPS	ABR	SB-CS	FA	FR	RNG	THR	GAMES AT POSITION	DL	BFW
1908	NY A	34	108	5	25	1	0	0	3	4	0		.231	.259	.241	62	-5	4	1.000	-2	71	0	O14L,S11,2b4,3b3		-0.9

O'ROURKE, JOHN John W. B8.23.1849 Bridgeport CT D6.23.1911 Boston MA BL/TL/6-0/190 d5.1 b-Jim

YEAR	TM LG	G	AB	R	H	2B	3B	HR	RBI	BB-IB	HP	SO	AVG	OBP	SLG	AOPS	ABR	SB-CS	FA	FR	RNG	THR	GAMES AT POSITION	DL	BFW
1879	Bos N	72	317	69	108	17	11	6	62	8		32	.341	.357	.521	181	26		.882	0	62	122	O71(0/70/1)		2.1
1880	Bos N	81	313	30	86	22	8	3	36	18		32	.275	.314	.425	153	18		.871	4	103	0	O81(3/78/1)		1.8
1883	NY AA	77	315	49	85	19	5	2		21			.270	.315	.381	118	7		.856	-7	79	139	O76C/1		-0.3
Total	3	230	945	148	279	58	24	11	98	47		64	.295	.329	.442	150	51		.871	-3	82	86	O228(3/224/2)/1		3.6

O'ROURKE, JOE Joseph Leo Jr. B10.28.1904 Philadelphia PA D6.27.1990 Philadelphia PA BL/TR/5-7/145 d4.19 f-Patsy

YEAR	TM LG	G	AB	R	H	2B	3B	HR	RBI	BB-IB	HP	SO	AVG	OBP	SLG	AOPS	ABR	SB-CS	FA	FR	RNG	THR	GAMES AT POSITION	DL	BFW
1929	Phi N	3	3	0	0	0	0	0	0	0	0	1	.000	.000	.000	-94	-1		—	0			/H		-0.1

O'ROURKE, PATSY Joseph Leo Sr. B4.13.1881 Philadelphia PA D4.18.1956 Philadelphia PA BR/TR/5-7/160 d4.16 s-Joe

YEAR	TM LG	G	AB	R	H	2B	3B	HR	RBI	BB-IB	HP	SO	AVG	OBP	SLG	AOPS	ABR	SB-CS	FA	FR	RNG	THR	GAMES AT POSITION	DL	BFW
1908	StL N	53	164	8	32	4	2	0	16	14	1		.195	.263	.244	65	-6	2	.860	-8	101	59	S53		-1.5

YEAR	TM LG	G	AB	R	H	2B	3B	HR	RBI	BB-IB	HP	SO	AVG	OBP	SLG	AOPS	ABR	SB-CS	FA	FR	RNG	THR	GAMES AT POSITION	DL	BFW

O'ROURKE, TOM   Thomas Joseph B10.1865 New York NY D7.19.1929 New York NY TR/5-9/158 d5.11

																							C21/OR3		-1.2
1887	Bos N	22	78	12	12	3	0	0	10	1	1	6	.154	.233	.192	19	-8	4	.777	-7			C20/OR		-0.5
1888	Bos N	20	74	3	13	0	0	0	4	1	0	9	.176	.187	.176	16	-7	2	.881	1			C2		-0.1
1890	NY N	2	7	1	0	0	0	0	0	1	0	0	.000	.125	.000	-63	-1	0	.864	-5	95	180	C40/1		-1.6
	Syr AA	41	153	16	33	8	0	0	12	12	1	15	.216	.277	.268	68	-6	2	.907	-15	79	77	C83,O2R/13		-3.4
Total	3	85	312	32	58	11	0	0	26	21		15	.186	.242	.221	39	-22	8	.867	-21	80	83			

O'ROURKE, TIM   Timothy Patrick "Voiceless Tim" B5.18.1864 Chicago IL D4.20.1938 Seattle WA BL/TR/5-10/170 d5.27 OF(32/1/40)

1890	Syr AA	87	332	48	94	13	6	1	46	36	4		.283	.360	.367	128	13	22	.866	-8	92	65	3b87		0.6
1891	Col AA	34	136	22	38	1	3	0	12	15	2	7	.279	.359	.331	104	1	9	.879	0	101	39	3b34		0.2
1892	Bal N	63	239	40	74	8	4	0	35	24	0	19	.310	.373	.377	123	7	12	.869	-8	95	72	S58,O4(2/1/1)/3		0.1
1893	Bal N	31	135	22	49	4	1	0	19	12	2	4	.363	.423	.407	119	4	5	.980	-2	26	0	O25L,3b5/S		0.0
	Lou N	92	352	80	99	8	4	0	53	77	8	15	.281	.421	.327	108	13	22	.865	-11	90	101	S60,O26(4/0/22),3b6		0.3
	Year	123	487	102	148	12	5	0	72	89	10	19	.304	.422	.349	112	17	27	.861	-13	89	99	S61,O51(29/0/22),3b11		0.3
1894	Lou N	55	220	46	61	3	3	0	27	23	2	9	.277	.351	.318	67	-11	9	.977	-1	145	144	1b30,O18(1/0/17),S3,3b3/2		-1.0
	StL N	18	71	10	20	4	1	0	10	8	0	3	.282	.354	.366	74	-3	2	.861	-2	85	99	3b18		-0.4
	Was N	7	25	4	5	2	1	0	2	2	0	1	.200	.259	.360	49	-2	0	.909	0	105		2b4,S3		-1.6
	Year	80	316	60	86	9	5	0	39	33	2	13	.272	.345	.332	67	-16	11	.977	-3	145	144	1b30,3b21,O18(1/0/17),S6,2b5		-0.4
Total	5	387	1510	272	440	43	23	1	204	197	18	58	.291	.380	.347	105	22	81	.861	-31	93	85	3b154,S125,O73R,1b30,2b5		

ORR, DAVE   David L. B9.29.1859 New York NY D6.2.1915 Richmond Hill NY BR/TR/5-11/250 d5.17 M1 ▲

1883	NY AA	1	4	1	1	0	0	0		0			.250	.250	.500	130	0		1.000	0	0	0	/1		0.0
	NY N	1	3	0	0	0	0	0		1			.000	.000	.000	-99	-1		1.000	0	0	0	/OL		-0.1
	NY N	12	46	5	15	3	3	2	11	0			.326	.326	.652	198	5		.938	-2	0	0	1b12		0.2
1884	†NY AA	110	458	82	**162**	32	13	9	112	5		1	**.354**	.362	.539	**195**	**46**		.960	-5	64	69	1b110,O3R		2.8
1885	NY AA	107	444	76	152	29	**21**	6	77	8		3	.342	.358	**.543**	189	42		.966	-3	73	86	1b107,P3		2.6
1886	NY AA	136	571	93	**193**	25	**31**	7	91	17		5	.338	.363	**.527**	193	56	16	**.981**	0	79	95	1b136		3.8
1887	NY AA	84	345	63	127	25	10	4	66	22			.368	.408	.516	164	29	17	.969	-1	107	90	1b81,O3C,M		1.7
1888	Bro AA	99	394	57	120	20	5	1	59	7		8	.305	.330	.388	130	12	11	.979	4	121	106	1b99		0.6
1889	Col AA	134	560	70	183	31	12	4	87	9		2	38	.327	.340	.446	129	18	12	.983	9	130	81	1b134		1.3
1890	Bro P	107	464	89	172	32	13	6	124	30		4	11	.371	.414	.534	144	26	10	.972	-5	78	100	1b107		0.9
Total	8	791	3289	536	1125	198	108	37	**627**	98		24	50	.342	.366	.502	163	233	66	.973	-1	92	89	1b787,O7(1/3/3),P3		13.8

ORR, PETE   Peterson Thomas Gordon B6.8.1979 Richmond Hill ON, Can. BL/TR/6-1/175 d4.5 Col Galveston (TX) JC

| 2005 | †Atl N | 112 | 150 | 32 | 45 | 8 | 1 | 1 | 23 | .300 | .331 | .387 | 85 | -3 | 7-1 | .948 | 0 | 108 | 91 | 2b25,3b12,O3L/SD | | -0.1 |

ORR, BILLY   William John B4.22.1891 San Francisco CA D3.10.1967 St.Helena CA BR/TR/5-11/168 d5.3

1913	Phi A	30	67	6	13	1	0	0	7	4	0	10	.194	.239	.239	41	-5	1	.967	-2	98	22	S16,1b3,3b3,2b2		-0.7
1914	Phi A	10	24	3	4	1	1	0	1	2	0	5	.167	.231	.292	59	-1	1-1	.810	-3	93	0	S6/3		-0.5
Total	2	40	91	9	17	2	2	0	8	6	0	15	.187	.237	.253	46	-6	2-1	.927	-5	97	16	S22,3b4,1b3,2b2		-1.2

ORSATTI, ERNIE   Ernest Ralph B9.8.1902 Los Angeles CA D9.4.1968 Canoga Park CA BL/TL/5-7.5/154 d9.4

1927	StL N	27	92	15	29	7	3	0	12	11		12	.315	.388	.457	122	3	2	.922	-1	97	98	O26(0/6/20)		
1928	†StL N	27	69	10	21	6	0	3	15	10	1	11	.304	.400	.522	137	4	0	1.000	-1	92	136	O17(2/0/15),1b5		
1929	StL N	113	346	64	115	21	7	3	39	33	2	43	.332	.394	.460	110	6	7	.974	6	108	159	O77(9/2/67),1b10		-0.2
1930	†StL N	48	131	24	42	8	4	1	15	12	1	18	.321	.382	.466	100	1	0	.985	5	120	93	1b22,O11R		-0.2
1931	StL N	70	158	27	46	16	6	0	19	14		29	.291	.349	.468	113	3	1	.988	-1	104	0	O45(30/6/9)/1		-0.2
1932	StL N	101	375	44	126	27	6	2	44	18	1	29	.336	.368	.454	117	9	5	.976	-7	92	45	O107(6/96/5),1b3		-0.4
1933	StL N	120	436	55	130	21	4	0	38	33		33	.298	.348	.374	101	1	14	.986	-2	103	68	O90C		-1.6
1934	†StL N	105	337	39	101	14	4	0	31	27	1	31	.300	.353	.365	87	-5	6	.986	-3	96	44	O90C		-1.1
1935	StL N	90	221	28	53	9	3	1	24	18		25	.240	.297	.321	64	-11	10	.975	-1	100	66	O60(6/26/28)		-1.4
Total	9	701	2165	306	663	129	39	10	237	176	6	218	.306	.360	.416	102	10	46	.979	-7	99	84	O529(93/281/156),1b42		

ORSINO, JOHN   John Joseph "Horse" B4.22.1938 Teaneck NJ BR/TR/6-3/215* d7.14

1961	SF N	25	83	5	23	3	2	4	12	3-0	1	13	.277	.310	.506	116	1	0-0	.959	-3	111	85	C25		0.
1962	†SF N	18	48	4	13	2	0	4	5	0-0	0	9	.271	.333	.313	78	-1	0-0	.963	-2	78	96	C16		-0.
1963	Bal A	116	379	53	103	18	1	19	56	38-6	9	53	.272	.349	.475	134	18	2-3	.990	-2	101	97	C109,1b3		2.
1964	Bal A	81	248	21	55	10	0	8	23	23-3	2	55	.222	.290	.359	81	-7	0-0	.976	2	67	87	C66,1b5		-0.
1965	Bal A	77	232	30	54	10	2	9	28	23-2	5	51	.233	.313	.409	102	1	1-0	.987	-4	86	94	C62,1b5		-0.
1966	Was A	14	23	1	4	1	0	0	0	0-0	0	7	.174	.174	.217	12	-3	0-0	1.000	0	90	114	1b5,C2	81	-0.
1967	Was A	1	1	0	0	0	0	0	0	0-0	0	1	.000	.000	.000	-99	0	0-0	—	0			/H	81	0.
Total	7	332	1014	114	252	44	5	40	123	92-11	17	191	.249	.319	.420	106	9	3-3	.982	-9	89	93	C280,1b18		

ORSULAK, JOE   Joseph Michael B5.31.1962 Glen Ridge NJ BL/TL/6-1/196(185-210) [PitN80 6/153] d9.1 [DL 1987 Pit N 46]

1983	Pit N	7	11	2	2	0	0	0	1	0-0	0	2	.182	.167	.182	1	-2	0-1	1.000	1	37	1952	O4C		-0.
1984	Pit N	32	67	12	17	1	2	0	3	1-0	1	7	.254	.271	.328	69	-3	3-1	1.000	1	112	98	O25(7/12/5)	15	-0.
1985	Pit N	121	397	54	119	14	6	0	21	26-3	1	27	.300	.342	.365	99	-1	24-11	.976	4	103	157	O115(41/72/16)		-1
1986	Pit N	138	401	60	100	19	6	2	19	28-2	1	38	.249	.299	.342	75	-15	24-11	.981	2	97	**159**	O120(9/46/73)		-0.
1988	Bal A	125	379	48	109	21	3	8	27	23-2	3	30	.288	.331	.422	113	6	9-8	.979	4	108	105	O117(36/14/76)		0
1989	Bal A	123	390	59	111	22	5	7	55	41-6	2	35	.285	.351	.421	121	11	5-3	.985	9	**124**	124	O109(20/0/91),D5		0
1990	Bal A	124	413	49	111	14	3	11	57	46-9	1	48	.269	.343	.397	109	5	6-8	.989	7	108	286	O109(30/0/80),D5		0
1991	Bal A	143	486	57	135	22	1	5	43	28-1	4	45	.278	.321	.358	91	-6	6-2	.997	17	108	286	O132(85/1/68),D2	16	-0
1992	Bal A	117	391	45	113	19	3	4	39	28-5	4	34	.289	.342	.381	99	0	5-4	.983	2	102	122	O110(14/0/98)/D		-0
1993	NY N	134	409	59	116	15	4	8	35	28-1	2	25	.284	.331	.399	96	-3	5-4	.978	1	99	132	O114(66/40/23),1b4		-0
1994	NY N	96	292	39	76	3	0	8	42	16-2	3	21	.260	.299	.353	72	-13	4-2	.979	-4	81	146	O90(18/13/63),1b6		-0
1995	NY N	108	290	41	82	19	2	1	37	19-2	1	35	.283	.323	.372	87	-5	1-3	.965	-4	99	255	O59(30/14/19),1b2		-1
1996	Fla N	120	217	28	48	6	1	2	19	16-1	1	38	.221	.274	.286	49	-16	1-1	1.000	-1	80	156	O63(37/0/26),1b15/D		-0
1997	Mon N	106	150	13	34	12	1	1	7	18-0	0	17	.227	.310	.340	71	-9	0-1	.982	-1	102	150	O1253(449/216/669),1b28,D14	77	-4
Total	14	1494	4293	559	1173	186	37	57	405	318-34	23	402	.273	.324	.374	93	-43	93-60							

ORTA, JORGE   Jorge (Nunez) B11.26.1950 Mazatlan, Sinaloa, Mexico BL/TR/5-10/175* d4.15 OF(96/3/246)

1972	Chi A	51	124	20	25	3	1	3	11	6-0	1	37	.202	.244	.315	64	-6	3-3	.958	0	86	147	S18,2b14,3b9		-0
1973	Chi A	128	425	46	113	9	10	6	40	37-3	1	87	.266	.323	.376	94	-5	8-8	.969	-23	91	85	2b122/S		-2
1974	Chi A	139	525	71	166	31	2	10	67	40-1	3	88	.316	.365	.440	128	20	9-5	.971	-4	100	99	2b123,D10,S3		2
1975	Chi A*	140	542	64	165	26	10	11	83	48-7	4	67	.304	.363	.450	122	19	16-9	.978	-3	99	94	O77(76/0/2),3b49,D31		-3
1976	Chi A	158	636	74	174	29	8	14	72	38-2	5	77	.274	.316	.410	112	7	24-8	.970	-40	88	96	2b139		-3
1977	Chi A	144	564	71	159	27	8	11	84	46-3	2	49	.282	.334	.417	104	3	1-1	.984	-12	87	81	2b114,D2		-0
1978	Chi A	117	420	45	115	19	2	13	53	42-3	4	39	.274	.340	.421	110	8	1-2	.978	-11	85	72	D62,2b41		-0
1979	Chi A	113	325	49	85	19	3	6	46	44-2	1	33	.262	.348	.437	111	6	1-5	.978	-11	85	72	O120(0/2/118),D7		1
1980	Cle A☆	129	481	78	140	18	3	10	64	71-2	2	44	.291	.379	.403	115	13	6-5	.982	9	118	159	O86(0/1/86)		-1
1981	Cle A	88	338	50	92	14	3	5	34	21-3	1	43	.272	.312	.376	99	-1	4-3	.994	1	88	181	O17(1/0/16)		-0
1982	LA N	86	115	13	25	4	0	2	8	12-3	1	13	.217	.295	.313	73	-4	0-1	.947	2	135	102	O17(7/0/10)		-0
1983	Tor A	103	245	30	58	6	3	9	38	19-0	0	29	.237	.287	.408	85	-6	1-2	1.000	0	88	148	D70,O17(5/0/12)		-0
1984	†KC A	122	403	50	120	23	7	9	50	28-8	2	39	.298	.343	.457	119	10	0-0	.980	-3	91	0	D83,O26(14/0/12)/2		-0
1985	†KC A	110	300	32	80	21	1	4	45	22-5	2	28	.267	.317	.383	91	-3	2-1	—	0	0	0	D85		-0
1986	KC A	106	336	35	93	14	2	9	46	23-3	2	34	.277	.321	.411	96	-3	0-3	—	0	0	0	D87	14	-0
1987	KC A	21	50	3	9	2	1	0	4	3-1	0	8	.180	.226	.380	55	-3	0-0	—	0	0	0	D12	14	-0
Total	16	1755	5829	733	1619	267	63	130	745	500-46	29	715	.278	.334	.412	107	-84	79-60	.974	-84	91	85	2b689,D451,O343R,3b58,S22		

ORTEGA, BILL   William (Bobadilla) B7.24.1975 Havana, Cuba BR/TR/6-4/205 d9.7

| 2001 | StL N | 5 | 5 | 0 | 1 | 0 | 0 | 0 | 1 | .200 | .200 | .200 | 4 | -1 | 0-0 | — | 0 | | | /H | | |

ORTENZIO, FRANK   Frank Joseph B2.24.1951 Fresno CA BR/TR/6-2/215 [KCA69 47/956] d9.9

| 1973 | KC A | 9 | 25 | 1 | 7 | 2 | 0 | 1 | 6 | 2-0 | 1 | 6 | .280 | .333 | .480 | 118 | 1 | 0-0 | .983 | 1 | 161 | 73 | 1b7/D | | |

YEAR	TM LG	G	AB	R	H	2B	3B	HR	RBI	BB-IB	HP	SO	AVG	OBP	SLG	AOPS	ABR	SB-CS	FA	FR	RNG	THR	GAMES AT POSITION	DL	BFW

ORTH, AL Albert Lewis "Smiling Al","The Curveless Wonder" B9.5.1872 Tipton IN D10.8.1948 Lynchburg VA BL/TR/6-0/200 d8.15 U6 Col DePauw ▲

YEAR	TM LG	G	AB	R	H	2B	3B	HR	RBI	BB-IB	HP	SO	AVG	OBP	SLG	AOPS	ABR	SB-CS	FA	FR	RNG	THR	GAMES AT POSITION	DL	BFW
1895	Phi N	11	45	8	16	4	0	1	13	1	0	6	.356	.370	.511	125	4	0	.842	-2	70	0	P11		0.0
1896	Phi N	25	82	12	21	3	3	1	13	3	0	11	.256	.282	.402	80	3	2	.901	1	111	109	P25		0.0
1897	Phi N	53	152	26	50	7	4	1	17	3	0		.329	.342	.447	110	1	5	.929	0	107	46	P36,O6(3/3/0)		0.0
1898	Phi N	39	123	17	36	6	4	1	14	3	0		.293	.310	.431	117	1	1	.959	0	100	49	P32,OR		0.0
1899	Phi N	22	62	5	13	3	1	1	5	1	0		.210	.222	.339	55	-4	2	.793	-4	52	0	P21,OL		-0.2
1900	Phi N	39	129	6	40	4	1	1	21	2	1		.310	.326	.380	95	-1	2	.943	-3	103	156	P33,O3C		0.0
1901	Phi N	41	128	14	36	6	0	1	15	3	1		.281	.303	.352	88	-2	3	.945	2	116	102	P35,O4C		0.0
1902	Was A	56	175	20	38	3	2	2	10	9	0		.217	.255	.291	51	-12	2	.923	0	100	86	P38,O13(1/4/8)/1S		0.1
1903	Was A	55	162	19	49	9	7	0	11	4	1		.302	.323	.444	126	4	3	.920	-2	102	0	P36,S7,O4(2/0/2),1b2		-0.3
1904	Was A	31	102	7	22	3	1	0	11	1	2		.216	.238	.265	60	-5	2	.816	-2	50	0	O18(12/6/0),P10		-0.1
	NY A	24	64	6	19	1	1	0	7	0	1		.297	.308	.344	101	0	2	.968	0	107	82	P20,O2(0/1/1)		-0.8
	Year	55	166	13	41	4	2	0	18	1	3		.247	.265	.295	76	-5	4	.969	-2	106	53	P30,O20(12/7/1)		-0.8
1905	NY A	55	131	13	24	3	1	1	8	4	1		.183	.213	.244	40	-9	2	.940	-1	103	38	P40/1OR		-0.1
1906	NY A	47	135	12	37	2	1	1	17	6	0		.274	.305	.341	93	-2	2	.934	-1	99	38	P45/OR		0.0
1907	NY A	44	105	11	34	6	0	1	13	4	1		.324	.355	.410	133	4	1	.920	-2	122	41	P36/OL		0.1
1908	NY A	38	69	4	20	1	2	0	4	2	0		.290	.310	.362	117	5	0	.980	-2	99	154	P21		0.0
1909	NY A	22	34	3	9	0	1	0	5	5	0		.265	.359	.324	115	1	1	1.000	-1	92	0	2b6/P		-0.1
Total	15	602	1698	183	464	61	30	12	184	51	8	17	.273	.298	.366	91	-12	30	.932	-8	102	63	P440,O55(20/21/14),S8,2b6,1b4		-1.4

ORTIZ, JUNIOR Adalberto Colon B10.24.1959 Humacao, PR BR/TR/5-11/176(174-185) d9.20

YEAR	TM LG	G	AB	R	H	2B	3B	HR	RBI	BB-IB	HP	SO	AVG	OBP	SLG	AOPS	ABR	SB-CS	FA	FR	RNG	THR	GAMES AT POSITION	DL	BFW
1982	Pit N	7	15	1	3	1	0	0	0	1-0	0	3	.200	.250	.267	43	-1	0-0	1.000	-0	227	48	C7		-0.1
1983	Pit N	5	8	1	1	0	0	0	0	1-0	0	0	.125	.222	.125	-1	-1	0-0	1.000	1	0	0	C4		0.0
	NY N	68	185	10	47	5	0	0	12	3-0	1	34	.254	.270	.281	53	-12	1-0	.965	-6	70	95	C67		-1.6
	Year	73	193	11	48	5	0	0	12	4-0	1	34	.249	.268	.275	51	-13	1-0	.967	-5	67	91	C71		-1.6
1984	NY N	40	91	6	18	3	0	0	11	5-0	0	15	.198	.235	.231	33	-8	1-0	.980	-5	97	93	C32		-1.3
1985	Pit N	23	72	4	21	2	0	1	5	3-1	0	17	.292	.320	.361	91	-1	1-0	.985	-1	94	137	C23		-0.1
1986	Pit N	49	110	11	37	6	0	0	14	9-0	0	13	.336	.380	.391	112	2	0-1	.983	-3	99	81	C36		0.0
1987	Pit N	75	192	16	52	8	1	1	22	15-1	0	23	.271	.322	.339	75	-7	0-2	.975	-2	93	121	C72		-0.7
1988	Pit N	49	118	8	33	6	0	2	18	9-0	2	9	.280	.336	.381	108	1	1-4	.983	-3	92	41	C40		-0.7
1989	Pit N	91	230	16	50	6	1	1	22	20-4	2	20	.217	.282	.265	60	-12	2-2	.995	-12	69	96	C84	39	-0.1
1990	Min A	71	170	18	57	7	1	0	18	12-0	2	16	.335	.384	.388	110	3	0-4	1.000	-1	154	89	C68,D3		-2.2
1991	†Min A	61	134	9	28	5	1	0	15	15-0	1	12	.209	.293	.261	52	-9	0-1	.995	-2	177	96	C60		0.3
1992	Cle A	86	244	20	61	7	0	0	24	12-0	4	23	.250	.296	.279	63	-12	1-3	.989	-7	92	98	C86	15	-0.8
1993	Cle A	95	249	19	55	13	0	0	20	11-1	5	26	.221	.267	.273	46	-19	1-0	.990	3	112	127	C95		-1.7
1994	Tex A	29	76	3	21	2	0	0	9	1-0	1	11	.276	.329	.303	64	-4	0-1	.992	-2	145	153	C28		-1.0
Total	13	749	1894	142	484	71	4	5	186	121-7	18	222	.256	.305	.305	69	-80	8-18	.986	-40	105	101	C702,D3	54	-9.7

ORTIZ, DAVID David Americo (Arias) "Big Papi" B11.18.1975 Santo Domingo, D.R. BL/TL/6-4/230(190-230) d9.2

YEAR	TM LG	G	AB	R	H	2B	3B	HR	RBI	BB-IB	HP	SO	AVG	OBP	SLG	AOPS	ABR	SB-CS	FA	FR	RNG	THR	GAMES AT POSITION	DL	BFW
1997	Min A	15	49	10	16	1	0	1	6	2-0	0	19	.327	.353	.449	106	-0	1-0	.989	1	155	119	1b11/D		0.1
1998	Min A	86	278	47	77	20	0	9	46	39-3	5	72	.277	.371	.446	110	6	1-0	.989	-0	102	92	1b70,D10	60	-0.1
1999	Min A	10	20	1	0	0	0	0	0	5-0	0	12	.000	.200	.000	-41	-4	0-0	1.000	-0	204	0	/1D		-0.4
2000	Min A	130	415	59	117	36	1	10	63	57-2	0	81	.282	.364	.446	98	1	1-0	.996	-1	82	78	D88,1b27		-0.6
2001	Min A	89	303	46	71	17	1	18	48	40-8	1	68	.234	.324	.475	102	1	1-0	1.000	-1	49	40	D80,1b8	77	-0.5
2002	†Min A	125	412	52	112	32	1	20	75	43-0	3	87	.272	.339	.500	117	10	1-2	.990	-1	80	89	D95,1b15	23	0.3
2003	†Bos A	128	448	79	129	39	2	31	101	58-8	4	83	.288	.369	.592	142	28	0-2	.992	-0	96	55	D74,1b45		1.9
2004	†Bos A★	150	582	94	175	47	3	41	139	75-8	4	133	.301	.380	.603	143	38	0-0	.986	-0	102	99	D115,1b34		2.7
2005	†Bos A★	159	601	119	180	40	1	47	148	102-9	1	124	.300	.397	.604	154	49	1-0	.976	2	190	100	D148,1b10		4.0
Total	9	892	3108	507	877	234	9	177	626	421-38	15	679	.282	.366	.534	127	129	5-2	.990	0	102	84	D616,1b221	160	7.4

ORTIZ, HECTOR Hector (Montanez) B10.14.1969 Rio Piedras, PR BR/TR/6-0/205* [LAN88 35/894] d9.14 Col Ranger (TX) JC

YEAR	TM LG	G	AB	R	H	2B	3B	HR	RBI	BB-IB	HP	SO	AVG	OBP	SLG	AOPS	ABR	SB-CS	FA	FR	RNG	THR	GAMES AT POSITION	DL	BFW
1998	KC A	4	4	1	0	0	0	0	0	0-0	0	0	.000	.000	.000	-96	-1	0-0	1.000	-1	0	0	C3/1		-0.2
2000	KC A	26	88	15	34	6	0	0	5	8-1	1	8	.386	.443	.455	121	4	0-0	.993	-2	85	107	C26		0.3
2001	KC A	56	154	12	38	6	1	0	11	9-0	1	24	.247	.293	.299	51	-11	1-3	.990	6	126	121	C55/D		-0.2
2002	Tex A	7	14	1	3	1	0	1	2	1-0	0	1	.214	.267	.500	95	-0	0-0	.957	-2	0	0	C7		-0.2
Total	4	93	260	29	75	13	1	1	18	18-1	2	33	.288	.339	.358	75	-8	1-3	.990	1	103	108	C91/D1		-0.3

ORTIZ, JAVIER Javier Victor B1.22.1963 Boston MA BR/TR/6-4/220* [TexA83*1/4] d6.15 Col Florida

YEAR	TM LG	G	AB	R	H	2B	3B	HR	RBI	BB-IB	HP	SO	AVG	OBP	SLG	AOPS	ABR	SB-CS	FA	FR	RNG	THR	GAMES AT POSITION	DL	BFW
1990	Hou N	30	77	7	21	5	1	1	10	12-0	1	10	.273	.367	.403	116	2	1-1	.978	-1	98	65	O25(20/1/9)	69	0.1
1991	Hou N	47	83	7	23	4	1	1	5	14-0	1	14	.277	.381	.386	123	3	0-0	1.000	-0	77	177	O24(15/0/11)		0.2
Total	2	77	160	14	44	9	2	2	15	26-0	2	25	.275	.374	.394	119	5	1-1	.987	-1	88	116	O49(35/1/20)	69	0.3

ORTIZ, JOSE Jose Daniel (Santos) B6.13.1977 Santo Domingo, D.R. BR/TR/5-9/177(160-182) d9.15

YEAR	TM LG	G	AB	R	H	2B	3B	HR	RBI	BB-IB	HP	SO	AVG	OBP	SLG	AOPS	ABR	SB-CS	FA	FR	RNG	THR	GAMES AT POSITION	DL	BFW
2000	Oak A	7	11	4	2	0	0	0	1	2-0	0	3	.182	.308	.182	29	-1	0-0	.857	-1	70	71	2b3,D4		-0.2
2001	Oak A	11	42	4	7	0	0	3	3	3-0	0	5	.167	.217	.167	5	-6	1-0	.951	-2	84	124	2b10/D	31	-0.7
	Col N	53	204	38	52	8	1	13	35	14-0	4	36	.255	.314	.495	87	-4	3-1	.965	1	111	97	2b51		-0.1
2002	Col N	65	192	22	48	7	1	1	12	16-0	3	30	.250	.315	.313	61	-11	2-0	.987	-5	100	70	2b53/3	77	-1.3
Total	3	136	449	68	109	15	2	14	51	35-0	7	74	.243	.305	.379	69	-22	6-1	.973	-7	103	87	2b117,D5/3	108	-2.3

ORTIZ, JOSE Jose Luis (Irizarry) B6.25.1947 Ponce, PR BR/TR/5-9.5/155* d9.4

YEAR	TM LG	G	AB	R	H	2B	3B	HR	RBI	BB-IB	HP	SO	AVG	OBP	SLG	AOPS	ABR	SB-CS	FA	FR	RNG	THR	GAMES AT POSITION	DL	BFW
1969	Chi A	16	11	0	3	1	0	0	2	1-1	0	2	.273	.333	.364	90	0	0-0	1.000	0	58	420	O8(2/5/2)		0.0
1970	Chi A	15	24	4	8	1	0	0	1	2-0	1	2	.333	.407	.375	113	1	1-0	1.000	1	66	706	O8(1/5/2)		0.2
1971	Chi N	36	88	10	26	7	1	0	3	4-0	3	10	.295	.347	.398	96	0	2-2	1.000	-2	88	72	O30(0/29/1)		-0.3
Total	3	67	123	14	37	9	1	0	6	7-1	4	12	.301	.358	.390	99	1	3-2	1.000	-0	81	222	O46(3/39/5)		-0.1

ORTIZ, LUIS Luis Alberto (Galarza) B5.25.1970 Santo Domingo, D.R. BR/TR/6-0/195* [BosA91 8/226] d8.31 Col Union (TN)

YEAR	TM LG	G	AB	R	H	2B	3B	HR	RBI	BB-IB	HP	SO	AVG	OBP	SLG	AOPS	ABR	SB-CS	FA	FR	RNG	THR	GAMES AT POSITION	DL	BFW
1993	Bos A	9	12	3	3	0	0	0	4	0-0	0	2	.250	.250	.250	33	-1	0-0	1.000	-1	50	272	3b5,D3		-0.2
1994	Bos A	7	18	3	3	2	0	0	6	1-0	0	5	.167	.182	.278	23	-2	0-0	—	0		D6		-0.2
1995	Tex A	41	108	10	25	5	2	1	18	6-0	0	18	.231	.270	.343	57	-7	0-1	.867	-8	83	40	3b35,D3		-1.4
1996	Tex A	3	7	1	2	0	1	1	1	0-0	1	1	.286	.286	1.000	194	1	0-0	—	0		/D		0.1
Total	4	60	145	14	33	7	3	2	26	7-0	0	26	.228	.256	.359	58	-9	0-1	.875	-8	81	57	3b40,D13		-1.7

ORTIZ, ROBERTO Roberto Gonzalo (Nunez) B6.30.1915 Camaguey, Cuba D9.15.1971 Miami FL BR/TR/6-4/200* d9.6 b-Baby

YEAR	TM LG	G	AB	R	H	2B	3B	HR	RBI	BB-IB	HP	SO	AVG	OBP	SLG	AOPS	ABR	SB-CS	FA	FR	RNG	THR	GAMES AT POSITION	DL	BFW
1941	Was A	22	79	10	26	4	2	1	17	3	0	10	.329	.354	.430	112	-1	0-1	.860	-0	97	178	O21R		-0.1
1942	Was A	20	42	4	7	1	3	1	4	5	1	11	.167	.271	.405	89	-1	0-0	.941	0	97	174	O9(1/0/8)		-0.2
1943	Was A	1	4	0	1	0	0	0	0	0	0		.250	.250	.250	48	-0	0-1	1.000	0	126	0	/OR		-0.1
1944	Was A	85	316	36	80	11	4	5	35	19	8	47	.253	.312	.361	96	-3	4-1	.949	-2	106	37	O80(10/0/71)		-1.0
1949	Was A	40	129	12	36	3	0	1	9	6	0	12	.279	.326	.326	74	-5	0-0	.946	1	90	204	O32(4/0/28)		-0.5
1950	Was A	39	75	4	17	2	1	0	8	7	1	3	.227	.301	.280	52	-6	0-0	1.000	-0	86	170	O19R		-0.6
	Phi A	6	14	1	1	0	0	0	3	0	0	3	.071	.071	.071	-65	-4	0-0	1.000	-0	98	0	O3(1/0/3)		-0.4
	Year	45	89	5	18	2	1	0	11	7	1	6	.202	.268	.247	34	-9	0-0	1.000	-0	88	144	O22(1/0/22)		-1.0
Total	6	213	659	67	168	18	10	8	78	43	10	95	.255	.310	.349	84	-18	4-3	.942	-2	100	103	O165(16/0/151)		-2.9

ORTMEIER, DAN Daniel D. B5.11.1981 Chattanooga TN BB/TL/6-4/220 d9.5 Col Texas-Arlington

YEAR	TM LG	G	AB	R	H	2B	3B	HR	RBI	BB-IB	HP	SO	AVG	OBP	SLG	AOPS	ABR	SB-CS	FA	FR	RNG	THR	GAMES AT POSITION	DL	BFW
2005	SF N	15	22	1	3	0	0	0	1	3-0	1	6	.136	.269	.136	10	-3	1-0	1.000	0	120	0	O7R		-0.3

ORTON, JOHN John Andrew B12.8.1965 Santa Cruz CA BR/TR/6-1/192* [CalA87 1/25] d8.20 Col Cal Poly-San Luis Obispo

YEAR	TM LG	G	AB	R	H	2B	3B	HR	RBI	BB-IB	HP	SO	AVG	OBP	SLG	AOPS	ABR	SB-CS	FA	FR	RNG	THR	GAMES AT POSITION	DL	BFW
1989	Cal A	16	39	4	7	1	0	0	4	2-0	1	17	.179	.200	.205	21	-4	0-0	.988	2	135	116	C16		-0.2
1990	Cal A	31	84	8	16	5	0	1	6	5-0	1	31	.190	.244	.286	49	-6	0-1	.987	-1	113	91	C31		-0.6
1991	Cal A	29	69	7	14	4	0	0	3	10-0	1	17	.203	.313	.261	60	-3	0-1	.994	6	93	144	C28/D		0.3
1992	Cal A	43	114	11	25	3	0	2	12	7-0	2	32	.219	.276	.298	60	-6	1-1	.981	7	128	130	C43	93	0.3
1993	Cal A	37	95	5	18	5	0	1	4	7-0	1	24	.189	.252	.274	40	-8	1-2	.985	5	112	102	C35/OL	84	-0.1
Total	5	156	401	35	80	18	0	4	29	31-0	5	121	.200	.265	.274	49	-27	2-5	.985	19	117	112	C153/OLD	177	-0.3

YEAR	TM LG	G	AB	R	H	2B	3B	HR	RBI	BB-IB	HP	SO	AVG	OBP	SLG	AOPS	ABR	SB-CS	FA	FR	RNG	THR	GAMES AT POSITION	DL	BFW

ORWOLL, OSSIE Oswald Christian B11.17.1900 Portland OR D5.8.1967 Decorah IA BL/TL/6-0/174 d4.13 Col Luther ▲

																									-0.2
1928	Phi A	64	170	28	52	13	2	0	22	16	0	24	.306	.366	.406	100	0	3-1	.983	-1	96	131	1b34,P27		-0.3
1929	Phi A	30	51	6	13	2	1	0	6	2	0	11	.255	.333	.333	56	-4	0-0	1.000	-1	93	328	P12,O9(1/8/0)		-0.5
Total	2	94	221	34	65	15	3	0	28	18	0	35	.294	.347	.389	90	-4	3-1	.970	-2	85	72	P39,1b34,O9(1/8/0)		

OSBORN, FRED Wilferd Pearl "Ossie" B11.28.1883 Nevada OH D9.2.1954 Upper Sandusky OH BL/TL/5-9/178 d6.8

																									-0.6
1907	Phi N	56	163	22	45	9	3	0	9	3	2		.276	.298	.325	97	-2	4	1.000	-2	48	0	O36(8/26/1)/1		-1.1
1908	Phi N	152	555	62	148	19	12	2	44	30	1		.267	.305	.355	107	2	16	.969	-5	71	67	O152(0/146/6)		-1.0
1909	Phi N	58	189	14	35	4	1	0	19	12	1		.185	.238	.217	41	-13	6	.979	7	175	172	O54C		-2.7
Total	3	266	907	98	228	25	16	2	72	45	4		.251	.290	.321	91	-13	26	.975	1	93	84	O242(8/226/7)/1		

OSBORNE, FRED Frederick W. B Alberta, Can BL/TL d7.14 ▲

| | | | | | | | | | | | | | | | | | | | | | | | | | -0.4 |
| 1890 | Pit N | 41 | 168 | 24 | 40 | 8 | 3 | 1 | 14 | 6 | 1 | 18 | .238 | .269 | .339 | 87 | -4 | 0 | .828 | -1 | 125 | 0 | O35(28/1/6),P8 | | |

OSBORNE, BOBO Lawrence Sidney B10.12.1935 Chattahoochee GA BL/TR/6-1/205* d6.27 f-Tiny

																									-0.4
1957	Det A	11	27	4	4	1	0	0	1	3-0	0	7	.148	.233	.185	15	-3	0-0	1.000	-0	110	0	O5R,1b4		-0.1
1958	Det A	2	0	0	0	0	0	0	0	0-0	0		.000	.000	.000	-93	-1	0-0	—	0			/H		-2.0
1959	Det A	86	209	27	40	7	1	3	21	16-0	2	41	.191	.254	.278	44	-16	1-0	.983	-1	96	101	1b56/OR		-0.3
1961	Det A	71	93	8	20	7	0	2	13	20-0	0	15	.215	.354	.355	88	-1	1-0	.957	-2	79	145	3b8,1b11		-0.5
1962	Det A	64	74	12	17	1	0	0	7	16-0	0	25	.230	.374	.243	68	-2	0-0	.857	-3	83	0	3b13,1b7/C		-1.6
1963	Was A	125	358	42	76	14	1	12	44	49-7	6	171	.212	.308	.358	87	-5	0-0	.988	-5	103	102	1b81,3b16		-4.9
Total	6	359	763	93	157	30	2	17	86	104-7	4		.206	.304	.317	71	-28	2-0	.987	-11	98	97	1b159,3b37,O6R/C		

OSIK, KEITH Keith Richard B10.22.1968 Port Jefferson NY BR/TR/6-0/198(185-215) [PitN90 24/641] d4.5 Col Louisiana St. OF(3/0/1)

																								28	-0.1
1996	Pit N	48	140	18	41	14	1	1	14	14-1	1	22	.293	.361	.429	104	-5	1-0	.977	-5	69	127	C41,3b2,O2L		-0.3
1997	Pit N	49	105	10	27	9	1	0	7	9-1	1	21	.257	.322	.362	77	-3	0-1	.989	-1	133	112	C32,2b4/13		-0.2
1998	Pit N	39	98	8	21	4	0	0	7	13-2	1	16	.214	.316	.255	53	-6	1-2	1.000	3	109	113	C26,3b7	22	-1.5
1999	Pit N	66	167	12	31	3	1	2	13	11-0	1	30	.186	.239	.251	24	-20	1-0	.997	2	121	89	C50/P		-0.1
2000	Pit N	46	123	11	36	6	1	4	22	14-0	5	31	.293	.387	.455	112	3	3-0	.992	-5	83	73	C26,3b12,1b5/PD		-0.6
2001	Pit N	56	120	9	25	4	0	2	13	13-0	3	24	.208	.299	.292	53	-8	1-0	.995	-0	83	101	C39,1b5,3b3,2b2/OR	15	-0.5
2002	Pit N	55	100	6	16	3	0	2	11	6-0	1	25	.160	.211	.250	23	-12	0-0	.993	5	77	113	C27,3b4,1b3/2OL		-0.3
2003	Mil N	80	241	22	60	12	0	2	21	31-0	3	44	.249	.342	.324	75	-8	0-1	.991	1	90	113	C78		-0.6
2004	Bal A	11	25	0	2	0	0	0	0	0-0	0	7	.080	.080	.080	-59	-6	0-0	1.000	-0	113	62	C11		-0.2
2005	Was N	6	4	0	0	0	0	0	0	0-0	0	2	.000	.000	.000	-99	-1	0-0	1.000	-0	16	0	C5	65	-4.4
Total	10	456	1123	96	259	55	4	13	108	111-4	17	202	.231	.308	.321	63	-60	6-4	.991	-1	95	103	C335,3b29,1b14,2b7,O4L,P2/D		

OSTDIEK, HARRY Henry Girard B4.12.1881 Ottumwa IA D5.6.1956 Minneapolis MN BR/TR/5-11/185 d9.10

																									0.0
1904	Cle A	7	18	1	3	0	0	0	3	3	1		.167	.318	.278	90	0	1	.946	-0	110	91	C7		-0.1
1908	Bos A	1	3	0	0	0	0	0	0	0	0		.000	.000	.000	-97	-1	0	.889	-0	123	98	/C		-0.1
Total	2	8	21	1	3	0	0	0	3	3	1		.143	.280	.238	65	-1	1	.935	-0	112	92	C8		

OSTEEN, CHAMP James Champlin B2.24.1877 Hendersonville NC D12.14.1962 Greenville SC BL/TR/5-8/150 d9.18 Col Erskine

																									-0.1
1903	Was A	10	40	4	8	0	4	2		1	1		.200	.256	.300	65	-2	0	.938	1	96	102	S10		-0.5
1904	NY A	28	107	15	21	1	4	2	9	1	2		.196	.218	.336	71	-4	0	.930	-0	114	71	3b17,S8,1b4		-0.1
1908	StL N	29	112	2	22	4	0	0	11	0	1		.196	.204	.232	41	-8	0	.847	-4	80	114	S17,3b12		-0.6
1909	StL N	16	45	6	9	1	0	0	7	7	0		.200	.308	.222	69	-1	1	.879	-4	101	0	S16		-2.6
Total	4	83	304	27	60	6	6	2	31	10	4		.197	.233	.276	60	-15	1	.890	-8	91	72	S51,3b29,1b4		

OSTERGARD, RED Roy Lund B5.16.1896 Denmark WI D1.13.1977 Hemet CA BR/TR/5-10.5/175 d6.14 Col Southwestern (TX)

| | | | | | | | | | | | | | | | | | | | | | | | | | 0.0 |
| 1921 | Chi A | 12 | 11 | 2 | 4 | 0 | 0 | 0 | 2 | | 2 | .364 | .364 | .364 | 87 | -0 | 0-0 | — | 0 | | | /H | | |

OSTERHOUT, CHARLIE Charles H. B6.1856 Syracuse NY D5.21.1933 Syracuse NY TR d6.23

| | | | | | | | | | | | | | | | | | | | | | | | | | -0.2 |
| 1879 | Syr N | 2 | 8 | 0 | 0 | 0 | 0 | 0 | 0 | 0 | | | .000 | .000 | .000 | -99 | -2 | | 1.000 | -0 | 0 | 0 | /OCC | | |

OSTROSSER, BRIAN Brian Leonard B6.17.1949 Hamilton ON, Can. BL/TR/6-0/180 d8.5

| | | | | | | | | | | | | | | | | | | | | | | | | | -0.2 |
| 1973 | NY N | 4 | 5 | 0 | 0 | 0 | 0 | 0 | 0 | 2 | | | .000 | .000 | .000 | -99 | -1 | 0-0 | 1.000 | -1 | 71 | 0 | S4 | | |

OSTROWSKI, JOHNNY John Thaddeus B10.17.1917 Chicago IL D11.13.1992 Chicago IL BR/TR/5-10.5/170* d9.24

																									-0.3
1943	Chi N	10	29	2	6	0	1	0	3	3	1	8	.207	.303	.276	69	-1	0	1.000	-1	89	0	O5L,3b4		-0.1
1944	Chi N	8	13	2	2	1	0	0	2	1	0	4	.154	.214	.231	25	-1	0	.500	-1	31	0	O2L		-0.0
1945	Chi N	7	10	4	3	2	0	0	1	0	0		.300	.300	.500	123	-1	0	.750	-0	63	0	3b4		-0.0
1946	Chi N	64	160	20	34	4	2	3	12	20	0	31	.213	.300	.319	77	-5	1	.934	0	111	89	3b50/2		-0.0
1948	Bos A	1	0	0	0	0	0	0	0	0	0		.000	.000	.000	-95	0		—	0			/H		-0.2
1949	Chi A	49	158	19	42	9	4	5	31	15	1	41	.266	.333	.468	115	2	4-3	.944	-1	100	106	O41(40/0/3),3b8		-0.2
1950	Chi A	21	45	9	10	1	1	2	9	4	1	8	.222	.364	.422	104	0	0	1.000	0	106	106	O14(6/1/8)		-0.0
	Was A	55	141	16	32	2	1	4	23	20	1	31	.227	.327	.340	75	-6	2-0	.947	1	111	92	O45(34/7/4)		-0.0
	Chi A	1	4	1	2	1	0	0	0	0	0	1	.500	.500	.750	223	1	0	.958	2	109	0	/OC		-0.0
	Year	77	190	26	44	4	2	6	32	24	2	40	.232	.339	.368	85	-5	2-0	.950	-2	103	93	O60(40/9/12)		-1.
Total	7	216	561	73	131	20	9	14	74	68	4	125	.234	.321	.376	89	-10	7-3	.950	-2	103	93	O108(87/9/15),3b66/2		

OTANEZ, WILLIS Willis Alexander B4.19.1973 Las Vega Baja, D.R. BR/TR/6-1/200(200-213) d8.25

																								31	-0.
1998	Bal A	3	5	0	1	0	0	0	0	0-0	0	2	.200	.200	.200	5	-1	0-0	1.000	-0	56	0	O2R		-0.
1999	Bal A	29	80	7	17	3	0	2	11	6-0	1	16	.213	.273	.325	54	-6	0-0	.917	-3	80	62	3b22,1b5,D3	21	-0.
	Tor A	42	127	21	32	8	0	5	13	9-0	1	30	.252	.307	.433	84	-3	0-0	.953	-3	71	191	3b24,1b13,D2		-1
	Year	71	207	28	49	11	0	7	24	15-0	2	46	.237	.293	.391	73	-9	0-0	.934	-6	76	125	3b46,1b18,D5	52	-1
Total	2	74	212	28	50	11	0	7	24	15-0	2	48	.236	.291	.387	72	-10	0-0	.917	-6	76	125	3b46,1b18,D5,O2R		

OTERO, REGGIE Regino Jose (Gomez) B9.7.1915 Havana, Cuba D10.21.1988 Hialeah FL BL/TR/6-0/165 d9.2 C8

| | | | | | | | | | | | | | | | | | | | | | | | | | 0 |
| 1945 | Chi N | 14 | 23 | 1 | 9 | 0 | 0 | 0 | 5 | 2 | 0 | 2 | .391 | .440 | .391 | 135 | 1 | 0 | .967 | -0 | 110 | 116 | 1b8 | | |

OTERO, RICKY Ricardo (Figueroa) B4.15.1972 Vega Baja, PR BB/TR/5-7/150* [NYN90 45/1173] d4.26

																									-0
1995	NY N	35	51	5	7	2	0	0	1	3-0	0	10	.137	.185	.176	-4	-8	2-1	1.000	2	130	145	O23(15/9/0)		-0
1996	Phi N	104	411	54	112	11	7	2	32	34-0	1	30	.273	.330	.348	79	-13	16-10	.985	7	111	165	O100C		-0
1997	Phi N	50	151	20	38	6	2	0	3	19-0	1	15	.252	.339	.318	74	-5	0-3	1.000	6	124	247	O42(1/40/1)		-1
Total	3	189	613	79	157	19	9	2	36	56-0	2	55	.256	.320	.326	71	-26	18-14	.990	14	116	184	O165(16/149/1)		

OTIS, AMOS Amos Joseph B4.26.1947 Mobile AL BR/TR/5-11/166(165-186) [BosA65 5/95] d9.6 C4

																									-0
1967	NY N	19	59	6	13	2	0	0	4	5-0	0	13	.220	.292	.254	59	-3	0-4	1.000	-1	66	214	O16(2/14/3)/3		-0
1969	NY N	48	93	6	14	3	1	0	4	6-1	0	27	.151	.202	.204	14	-11	1-0	1.000	1	104	233	O35(16/18/1),3b3		-1
1970	KC A★	159	620	91	176	36	9	11	58	68-3	1	67	.284	.353	.424	114	12	33-2	.990	0	98	141	O159C		3
1971	KC A★	147	555	80	167	26	4	15	79	40-2	2	74	.301	.345	.443	124	16	52-8	.990	8	112	109	O144C		1
1972	KC A★	143	540	75	158	28	2	11	54	50-3	5	59	.293	.352	.413	129	22	28-12	.992	-2	103	66	O137C		1
1973	KC A★	148	583	89	175	21	4	26	93	63-5	1	47	.300	.368	.484	129	22	13-9	.986	-2	104	73	O143C,D2		1
1974	KC A	146	552	87	157	31	9	12	73	58-4	2	67	.284	.348	.438	120	15	39-11	.988	-5	94	102	O130C	19	0
1975	KC A	132	470	87	116	26	9	9	46	66-1	4	48	.247	.342	.385	103	4	39-11	.992	-17	87	43	O152C		0
1976	†KC A★	153	592	93	165	40	2	18	86	55-7	5	100	.279	.341	.444	129	22	26-7	.992	-7	91	103	O140C		0
1977	†KC A	142	478	85	120	20	8	17	78	71-5	2	88	.251	.342	.433	110	7	23-7	.995	2	103	103	O136C/D		3
1978	KC A	141	486	74	145	30	7	22	96	66-7	4	58	.298	.380	.525	149	33	32-8	.992	-4	93	110	O146C,D4		2
1979	KC A	151	577	100	170	28	4	18	90	68-8	3	92	.295	.369	.444	120	15	30-5	.988	-0	103	79	O105C	43	-0
1980	†KC A	107	394	56	99	16	3	10	53	39-0	5	70	.251	.316	.383	91	-5	16-1	.988	0	109	94	O97(13/86/1)/D		1
1981	KC A	99	372	49	100	22	5	9	57	31-1	0	59	.269	.321	.417	114	4	9-5	.997	-8	92	61	O125C		1
1982	KC A	125	475	73	136	25	3	11	88	37-3	2	65	.286	.331	.421	107	1	8-5	.996	1	97	90	O96(0/55/41)/D		0
1983	KC A	98	356	35	93	16	4	4	41	27-3	0	63	.261	.313	.357	83	-8	5-2	.964	3	103	248	O32L	48	-0
1984	Pit N	40	97	6	16	4	0	0	10	7-0	0	15	.165	.213	.206	21	-10	0-0	.991	-1	98	97	O108(87/9/15),3b66/2	110	1
Total	17	1998	7299	1092	2020	374	66	193	1007	757-53	33	1008	.277	.343	.425	114	139	341-93	.991	-31	98	97	O1928(63/1825/46),D23,3b4		11

OTIS, BILL Paul Franklin B12.24.1889 Scituate MA D12.15.1990 Duluth MN BL/TR/5-10.5/150 d7.4 Col Williams

| | | | | | | | | | | | | | | | | | | | | | | | | | -0 |
| 1912 | NY A | 4 | 17 | 1 | 1 | 0 | 0 | 0 | 0 | 2 | 3 | | .059 | .200 | .059 | -24 | -3 | 0 | .917 | 0 | 97 | 148 | O4C | | |

YEAR	TM LG	G	AB	R	H	2B	3B	HR	RBI	BB-IB	HP	SO	AVG	OBP	SLG	AOPS	ABR	SB-CS	FA	FR	RNG	THR	GAMES AT POSITION	DL	BFW
OTT, MEL	Melvin Thomas "Master Melvin" B3.2.1909 Gretna LA D11.21.1958 New Orleans LA BL/TR/5-9/170 d4.27 M7 HF1951																								
1926	NY N	35	60	7	23	2	0	0	4	1	0	9	.383	.393	.417	120	2	1	.913	1	92	329	O10L		0.2
1927	NY N	82	163	23	46	7	3	1	19	13	0	9	.282	.335	.380	91	-2	2	.982	-3	79	75	O32(13/21/0)		-0.7
1928	NY N	124	435	69	140	26	4	18	77	52	2	36	.322	.397	.524	138	25	3	.970	-1	92	127	O115(5/1/108),2b5/3		1.5
1929	NY N	150	545	138	179	37	2	42	151	113	6	38	.328	.449	.635	166	61	6	.973	7	97	156	O149R/2		5.0
1930	NY N	148	521	122	182	34	5	25	119	103	2	35	.349	.458	.578	152	50	9	.969	4	99	126	O146R		3.7
1931	NY N	138	497	104	145	23	8	29	115	80	2	44	.292	.392	.545	153	38	10	.981	3	96	140	O137(0/71/66)		3.4
1932	NY N	154	566	119	180	30	8	38	123	100	4	39	.318	.424	.601	175	64	6	.984	-1	103	70	O154R		5.2
1933	†NY N	152	580	98	164	36	1	23	103	75	2	48	.283	.367	.467	139	32	1	.983	-8	89	89	O152(0/19/143)		1.6
1934	NY N★	153	582	119	190	29	10	35	135	85	3	43	.326	.415	.591	170	59	0	.974	-13	84	84	O153(0/16/137)		3.6
1935	NY N★	152	593	113	191	33	6	31	114	82	3	58	.322	.407	.555	159	51	7	**.990**	-5	98	113	O137R,3b15		4.2
1936	NY N★	150	534	120	175	28	6	33	135	111	5	41	.328	.448	**.588**	179	65	6	.985	-5	85	122	O148R		4.8
1937	†NY N★	151	545	99	160	28	2	31	95	102	3	69	.294	.408	.523	149	41	7	.939	-2	105	75	3b60,O91R		3.5
1938	NY N★	150	527	116	164	23	6	36	116	118	5	47	.311	**.442**	.583	178	62	2	.957	-2	106	78	3b113,O37R		**6.4**
1939	NY N★	125	396	85	122	23	2	27	80	100	1	50	.308	**.449**	.581	173	47	2	.973	-7	91	68	O96R,3b20		3.4
1940	NY N★	151	536	89	155	27	3	19	79	100	6	50	.289	.407	.457	137	32	6	.982	-0	99	104	O111R,3b42		2.6
1941	NY N★	148	525	89	150	29	0	27	90	100	3	68	.286	.403	.495	149	38	5	.968	-3	93	153	O145(1/0/144)		3.0
1942	NY N★	152	549	118	162	21	0	30	93	109	3	61	.295	.415	.497	**165**	50	6	.990	-4	91	110	O152R,M		3.9
1943	NY N★	125	380	65	89	12	2	18	47	95	4	48	.234	.391	.418	133	21	7	.975	-2	98	103	O111R/3M		1.3
1944	NY N★	120	399	91	115	16	4	26	82	90	1	47	.288	.423	.544	171	42	2	.986	-3	102	57	O103R,3b4,M		3.3
1945	NY N★	135	451	73	139	23	0	21	79	71	8	41	.308	.411	.499	150	33	1	.983	-4	92	100	O118R,M		2.1
1946	NY N	31	68	2	5	1	0	1	4	8	0	15	.074	.171	.132	-13	-10	0	1.000	6	88	149	O16R,M		-1.2
1947	NY N	4	4	0	0	0	0	0	0	1	0	0	.000	.000	.000	-99	-1	0	—	0			/HM		-0.1
Total	22	2730	9456	1859	2876	488	72	511	1860	1708	64	896	.304	.414	.533	155	800	89	.980	-34	94	111	O2313(29/128/2167),3b256,2b6		60.7
OTT, ED	Nathan Edward B7.11.1951 Muncy PA BL/TR/5-10/196* [PitN70 23/548] d6.10 C7 [DL 1982 Cal A 182, 1983 Cal A 182]																								
1974	Pit N	7	5	1	0	0	0	0	0	0-0	0	1	.000	.000	.000	-99	-1	0-0	1.000	0	216	0	O2R		-0.1
1975	Pit N	5	5	0	1	0	0	0	0	0-0	0	0	.200	.200	.200	11	-1	0-0	1.000	-0	0	0	C2		-0.1
1976	Pit N	27	39	2	12	2	0	0	5	3-1	0	5	.308	.349	.359	102	0	0-0	1.000	-0	139	187	C8		-0.1
1977	Pit N	104	311	40	82	14	3	7	38	32-6	2	41	.264	.334	.395	92	-3	7-7	.982	4	144	90	C90	22	0.0
1978	Pit N	112	379	49	102	18	4	9	38	27-6	0	56	.269	.315	.409	97	-2	4-1	.975	-4	104	78	C97,O4L		0.3
1979	†Pit N	117	403	49	110	20	2	7	51	26-8	0	62	.273	.314	.385	86	-8	0-1	.994	-1	109	78	C116		-0.2
1980	Pit N	120	392	35	102	14	0	8	41	33-8	0	47	.260	.317	.357	85	-8	1-6	.983	6	117	114	C117,O3L		-0.4
1981	Cal A	75	258	20	56	8	1	2	22	17-1	1	41	.217	.266	.279	57	-14	2-1	.979	-2	93	123	C72		0.1
Total	8	567	1792	196	465	76	10	33	195	138-30	3	254	.259	.311	.368	85	-37	14-16	.983	3	114	96	C502,O9(7/0/2)	386	-1.8
OTT, BILLY	William Joseph B11.23.1940 New York NY BB/TR/6-1/190* d9.4 Col St. Johns																								
1962	Chi N	12	28	3	4	0	0	1	2	2-0	0	10	.143	.200	.250	19	-3	0-0	1.000	0	87	200	O7R		-0.4
1964	Chi N	20	39	4	7	3	0	0	1	3-0	0	10	.179	.238	.256	38	-3	0-1	1.000	-1	85	0	O10R		-0.5
Total	2	32	67	7	11	3	0	1	3	5-0	0	20	.164	.222	.254	30	-6	0-1	1.000	-1	86	86	O17R		-0.9
OTTEN, JOHN	John G. B8.1870 , Netherlands D10.17.1905 Chicago IL TR/?/175 d7.5																								
1895	StL N	26	87	8	21	0	0	0	8	5	0	8	.241	.283	.241	36	-8	2	.947	-5	77	75	C24,O2(1/1/0)		-0.9
OTTERSON, BILLY	William John B5.4.1862 Pittsburgh PA D9.21.1940 Pittsburgh PA BR/TR/5-7/124 d9.4																								
1887	Bro AA	30	100	16	20	4	1	2	15	8	0		.200	.259	.320	60	-6	8	.859	3	108	147	S30		-0.1
OUELLETTE, PHIL	Philip Roland B11.10.1961 Salem OR BB/TR/6-0/190 d9.10 Col Citrus (CA) JC [DL 1987 SF N 96]																								
1986	SF N	10	23	1	4	0	0	0	3	3-0	1	3	.174	.269	.174	26	-2	0-0	1.000	-0	85	75	C9		-0.2
OULLIBER, JOHNNY	John Andrew B2.24.1911 New Orleans LA D12.26.1980 New Orleans LA BR/TR/5-11/165 d7.25																								
1933	Cle A	22	75	9	20	1	0	0	3	4	1	5	.267	.313	.280	55	-5	0-0	1.000	-2	80	0	O18(12/0/6)		-0.8
OUTEN, CHINK	William Austin B6.17.1905 Mt.Holly NC D9.11.1961 Durham NC BL/TR/6-0/200 d4.16 Col North Carolina St.																								
1933	Bro N	93	153	20	38	10	0	4	17	20	0	15	.248	.335	.392	112	3	1	.982	-6	92	64	C56		-0.1
OUTLAW, JIMMY	James Paulus B1.20.1913 Orme TN BR/TR/5-8/168 d4.20 Col Auburn-Montgomery																								
1937	Cin N	49	165	18	45	7	3	0	11	3	1	31	.273	.290	.352	77	-6	2	.914	4	117	74	3b41		-0.1
1938	Cin N	4	0	1	0	0	0	0	0	0	0		—	—	—		0	0	—	0			/R		0.0
1939	Bos N	65	133	15	35	2	0	0	5	10	0	14	.263	.315	.278	65	-7	1	.964	0	111	43	O39(15/22/2),3b2		-0.8
1943	Det A	20	67	8	18	1	0	1	6	8	0	4	.269	.347	.328	91	-1	0-0	1.000	-0	87	162	O16(4/3/9)		-0.2
1944	Det A	139	535	69	146	20	6	3	57	41	2	40	.273	.327	.350	88	-8	7-8	.964	-4	89	133	O137(71/6/60)		-2.3
1945	†Det A	132	446	56	121	16	5	0	34	45	0	33	.271	.338	.330	88	-6	6-7	.967	-2	87	143	O105(82/17/8),3b21		-1.6
1946	Det A	92	299	36	78	14	2	2	31	29	1	24	.261	.328	.341	82	-7	5-4	1.000	-5	87	189	O43(26/10/9),3b38		-1.5
1947	Det A	70	127	20	29	7	1	0	15	21	1	14	.228	.338	.299	76	-3	3-1	.983	-2	107	0	O37(21/3/13),3b9		-0.6
1948	Det A	74	198	33	56	12	0	0	25	31	1	15	.283	.383	.343	91	-1	0-1	.920	-2	101	101	O37,O13(10/0/3),3b9		-0.2
1949	Det A	5	4	1	1	0	0	0	0	0	0	1	.250	.250	.250	32	0	0-0	—	0			/H		0.0
Total	10	650	1974	257	529	79	17	6	184	188	5	176	.268	.333	.334	85	-39	24-21	.972	-9	92	127	O390(229/61/104),3b158		-7.3
OVERBAY, LYLE	Lyle Stefan B1.28.1977 Centralia WA BL/TL/6-2/215* [AriN99 18/538] d9.19 Col Nevada-Reno																								
2001	Ari N	2	2	1	1	0	0	0	1	0-0	0	1	.500	.500	.500	150	0	0-0	—	0			/H		0.0
2002	Ari N	10	10	0	1	0	0	0	1	0-0	0	5	.100	.100	.100	-42	-2	0-0	—	0			/H		-0.3
2003	Ari N	86	254	23	70	20	0	4	28	35-7	2	67	.276	.365	.402	93	-1	1-0	.997	6	125	86	1b75		-0.1
2004	Mil N	159	579	83	174	**53**	1	16	87	81-9	2	128	.301	.385	.478	121	22	2-1	.992	3	108	90	1b158		1.1
2005	Mil N	158	537	80	148	34	1	19	72	78-8	2	98	.276	.367	.449	113	12	1-0	.992	5	111	86	1b154		0.4
Total	5	415	1382	186	394	107	2	39	188	194-24	6	299	.285	.373	.450	111	31	4-1	.993	14	112	88	1b387		1.1
OWEN, MICKEY	Arnold Malcolm B4.4.1916 Nixa MO D7.13.2005 Mount Vernon MO BR/TR/5-10/190* d5.2 Mil 1945 C2																								
1937	StL N	80	234	17	54	4	2	0	20	15	0	13	.231	.277	.265	47	-18	1	.974	-2	89	109	C78		-1.5
1938	StL N	122	397	45	106	25	2	4	38	36	2	14	.267	.325	.370	86	-7	2	.980	1	91	113	C116		0.1
1939	StL N	131	344	32	89	18	2	3	35	43	2	13	.259	.344	.349	82	-8	6	.982	6	120	91	C126		0.4
1940	StL N	117	307	27	81	16	2	0	27	34	2	13	.264	.341	.329	81	-7	4	.980	1	86	118	C113		0.4
1941	†Bro N★	128	386	32	89	15	2	1	44	34	2	17	.231	.296	.288	62	-19	1	.995	9	160	87	C128		-0.3
1942	Bro N★	133	421	53	109	16	3	0	44	44	1	17	.259	.330	.311	87	-6	10	.987	8	144	94	C133		1.1
1943	Bro N	106	365	31	95	11	2	0	54	25	1	15	.260	.309	.301	77	-11	4	.987	-5	97	96	C100,3b3/S		-1.1
1944	Bro N	130	461	43	126	20	3	4	42	36	0	17	.273	.326	.336	88	-7	4	.979	-8	87	98	C125/2		-0.8
1945	Bro N	24	84	5	24	9	0	0	11	10	1	2	.286	.368	.393	113	2	0	.963	-2	105	96	C24		0.2
1949	Chi N	62	198	15	54	9	3	2	18	12	1	13	.273	.318	.379	88	-4	1	.969	-3	65	148	C59		-0.4
1950	Chi N	86	259	22	63	11	0	2	21	13	1	16	.243	.282	.309	56	-17	2	.978	-1	66	119	C86		-1.4
1951	Chi N	58	125	10	23	6	0	1	15	19	0	13	.184	.292	.232	42	-10	1-0	.969	-1	66	133	C57		-0.6
1954	Bos A	32	68	6	16	3	0	1	11	9	0	6	.235	.309	.324	70	-3		.989	-1	70	73	C30		-0.3
Total	13	1209	3649	338	929	163	21	14	378	326	13	181	.255	.318	.322	76	-115	36-1	.982	4	103	105	C1175,3b3/2S		-4.6
OWEN, DAVE	Dave B4.25.1958 Cleburne TX BB/TR/6-2/170* [ChiN79 10/246] d9.6 b-Spike Col Texas-Arlington																								
1983	Chi N	16	22	1	2	0	1	0	2	2-0	0	7	.091	.160	.182	-3	-3	1-0.	1.000	1	119	105	S14,3b3		-0.1
1984	Chi N	47	93	8	18	2	1	2	10	8-1	2	15	.194	.269	.290	54	-6	1-2	.969	1	111	127	S35,3b6,2b4		-0.3
1985	Chi N	22	19	6	7	0	0	0	4	1-0	2	6	.368	.400	.368	106	0	1-1	.917	-2	132	166	S7,3b7,2b4		-0.1
1988	KC A	7	5	0	0	0	0	0	0	0-0	0	2	.000	.000	.000	-99	-1	0-0	.941	2	110	343	S7		0.0
Total	4	92	139	15	27	2	3	1	16	11-1	2	30	.194	.260	.273	47	-10	3-3	.969	3	114	140	S63,3b16,2b8		-0.5
OWEN, LARRY	Lawrence Thomas B5.31.1955 Cleveland OH BR/TR/5-11/185* [AtlN77 17/420] d8.14 Col Bowling Green																								
1981	Atl N	13	16	0	0	0	0	0	0	1-0	0	4	.000	.059	.000	-82	-4	0-0	.964	1	57	50	C10		-0.4
1982	Atl N	2	3	1	1	0	0	0	0	0-0	0	1	.333	.333	.667	170	0	0-0	1.000	0	61	360	C2		0.0
1983	Atl N	17	17	0	2	0	0	0	1	0-0	0	2	.118	.118	.118	-32	-3	0-1	.970	-1	120	0	C16		-0.4
1985	Atl N	26	71	7	17	3	0	2	12	8-3	0	17	.239	.313	.366	85	-1	0-0	.966	1	78	75	C25		0.0
1987	KC A	76	164	17	31	6	0	5	14	16-0	0	51	.189	.260	.317	72	-12	0-0	.983	17	122	136	C75		0.7

YEAR	TM LG	G	AB	R	H	2B	3B	HR	RBI	BB-IB	HP	SO	AVG	OBP	SLG	AOPS	ABR	SB-CS	FA	FR	RNG	THR	GAMES AT POSITION	DL	BFW
1988	KC A	37	81	5	17	1	0	1	3	9-0	2	23	.210	.304	.259	59	-4	0-0	.989	2	127	91	C37		0.0
Total	6	171	352	30	68	11	0	4	34-3		2	98	.193	.267	.293	51	-24	0-1	.980	19	112	106	C165		-0.1

OWEN, MARV Marvin James "Freck" B3.22.1906 Agnew CA D6.22.1991 Mountain View CA BR/TR/6-1/175 d4.16 Col Santa Clara

YEAR	TM LG	G	AB	R	H	2B	3B	HR	RBI	BB-IB	HP	SO	AVG	OBP	SLG	AOPS	ABR	SB-CS	FA	FR	RNG	THR	GAMES AT POSITION	DL	BFW
1931	Det A	105	377	35	84	11	6	3	39	29		2	38	.223	.282	.308	53	-27	2-2	.937	-1	95	94	S37,3b37,1b27,2b4		-2.4
1933	Det A	138	550	77	144	24	9	2	65	44	4	56	.262	.321	.349	76	-20	2-2	.944	-9	83	3b136		0.0
1934	†Det A	154	565	79	179	34	9	8	96	59	4	37	.317	.385	.451	115	13	3-3	.956	-6	84	118	3b154		1.1
1935	†Det A	134	483	52	127	24	5	2	71	43	2	37	.263	.326	.346	76	-17	1-4	.958	-9	87	112	3b131		-2.1
1936	Det A	154	583	72	172	20	4	9	105	59	7	41	.295	.361	.389	85	-14	9-6	.952	-2	93	112	3b153,1b2		-1.0
1937	Det A	107	396	48	114	22	5	1	45	41		2	24	.288	.358	.376	83	-10	3-4	.970	-2	102	78	3b106		-0.8
1938	Chi A	141	577	84	162	23	6	6	55	45	4	31	.281	.337	.373	76	-23	6-4	.948	-1	106	112	3b140		-1.7
1939	Chi A	58	194	22	46	9	0	0	15	16		2	15	.237	.302	.284	49	-15	4-5	.953	-3	90	116	3b55		-1.6
1940	Bos A	20	57	4	12	0	0	0	6	8	0	4	.211	.308	.211	36	-5	0-0	.962	0	99	191	3b9,1b8		-0.4
Total	9	1011	3782	473	1040	167	44	31	497	338	27	283	.275	.339	.367	80	-118	30-30	.953	-32	94	106	3b921,1b37,S37,2b4		-11.3

OWEN, SPIKE Spike Dee B4.19.1961 Cleburne TX BB/TR/5-10/170* [SeaA82 1/6] d6.25 b-Dave Col Texas

YEAR	TM LG	G	AB	R	H	2B	3B	HR	RBI	BB-IB	HP	SO	AVG	OBP	SLG	AOPS	ABR	SB-CS	FA	FR	RNG	THR	GAMES AT POSITION	DL	BFW
1983	Sea A	80	306	36	60	11	3	2	21	24-0		1	44	.196	.257	.271	44	-24	10-6	.970	6	99	92	S80		-1.0
1984	Sea A	152	530	67	130	18	8	3	43	46-0		3	63	.245	.308	.326	76	-17	16-8	.977	16	102	86	S151		1.5
1985	Sea A	118	352	41	91	10	6	6	37	34-0		0	27	.259	.322	.372	89	-6	11-5	.975	25	113	102	S117		3.0
1986	Sea A	112	402	46	99	22	6	0	35	34-1		1	42	.246	.305	.331	73	-15	1-3	.972	36	121	128	S112		3.1
†Bos A	42	126	21	23	2	1	1	10	17-0		1	9	.183	.283	.238	44	-10	3-1	.976	-0	87	139	S42		-0.6
Year	154	528	67	122	24	7	1	45	51-1		2	51	.231	.300	.309	66	-25	4-4	.973	36	112	131	S154		2.5
1987	Bos A	132	437	50	113	17	7	2	48	53-2		1	43	.259	.337	.343	80	-12	11-8	.975	-12	92	88	S130		-1.1
1988	†Bos A	89	257	40	64	14	1	5	18	27-0		2	27	.249	.324	.370	90	-3	0-1	.967	-2	94	76	S76,D7		0.0
1989	Mon N	142	437	52	102	17	4	6	41	76-25	3	44	.233	.349	.332	94	1	3-2	.979	10	101	96	S142	15	2.1
1990	Mon N	149	453	55	106	24	5	5	35	70-12	5	60	.234	.333	.342	90	-4	8-6	.989	-19	89	77	S148		-1.3
1991	Mon N	139	424	39	108	22	8	3	26	42-11	1	61	.255	.321	.366	94	-3	2-6	.986	7	105	105	S133		1.2
1992	Mon N	122	386	52	104	16	3	7	40	50-3		5	30	.269	.348	.381	108	5	9-4	.982	-4	95	76	S116	15	1.1
1993	NY A	103	334	41	78	16	2	2	20	29-2		0	30	.234	.294	.311	65	-17	3-2	.956	-6	93	140	3b70,S5,1b4/2D		0.2
1994	Cal A	82	268	30	83	17	2	3	37	49-0		1	17	.310	.418	.422	115	9	2-8	.956	-6	93	140	3b29,S25,2b16	26	-1.9
1995	Cal A	82	218	17	50	9	3	1	28	18-1		0	22	.229	.288	.312	57	-15	3-2	.977	55	101	93	S1373,3b99,2b17,D11,1b4	73	5.9
Total	13	1544	4930	587	1211	215	59	46	439	569-57	15	519	.246	.324	.341	83	-112	82-62	.977	55	101	93	S1373,3b99,2b17,D11,1b4	73	5.9

OWENS, JAYHAWK Claude Jayhawk B2.10.1969 Cincinnati OH BR/TR/6-1/200(200-213) [MinA90 2/52] d6.6 Col Middle Tennessee

YEAR	TM LG	G	AB	R	H	2B	3B	HR	RBI	BB-IB	HP	SO	AVG	OBP	SLG	AOPS	ABR	SB-CS	FA	FR	RNG	THR	GAMES AT POSITION	DL	BFW
1993	Col N	33	86	12	18	5	0	3	6	6-1	2	30	.209	.277	.372	61	-5	1-0	.957	-2	103	134	C32		-0.5
1994	Col N	6	12	4	3	0	0	1	1	3-0	0	1	.250	.400	.417	97	0	0-0	1.000	0	150	221	C6		0.0
1995	†Col N	18	45	7	11	2	0	4	12	2-0	1	15	.244	.286	.556	91	-1	0-0	.988	3	103	C16		0.3
1996	Col N	73	180	31	43	9	1	4	17	27-0	1	56	.239	.338	.367	70	-7	4-1	.974	-2	97	134	C68	24	-0.5
Total	4	130	323	54	75	16	2	11	36	38-1	4	104	.232	.318	.396	72	-13	5-1	.973	-1	127	138	C122	24	-0.7

OWENS, ERIC Eric Blake B2.3.1971 Danville VA BR/TR/6-0/198(185-198) [CinN92 4/101] d6.6 Col Ferrum OF(291/201/251)

YEAR	TM LG	G	AB	R	H	2B	3B	HR	RBI	BB-IB	HP	SO	AVG	OBP	SLG	AOPS	ABR	SB-CS	FA	FR	RNG	THR	GAMES AT POSITION	DL	BFW
1995	Cin N	2	2	0	2	0	0	0	1	0-0	0	0	1.000	1.000	1.000	425	-1	0-0	-	-1	0	0	3b2	1	0.0
1996	Cin N	88	205	26	41	6	0	0	9	23-1	1	38	.200	.281	.229	37	-19	16-2	.986	-1	95	137	O52L,2b6,3b5		-1.8
1997	Cin N	27	57	8	15	0	0	0	5	4-0	0	11	.263	.311	.263	51	-4	3-2	.938	-5	69	0	O18(9/8/1),2b2		-0.9
1998	Mil N	34	40	5	5	2	0	1	4	2-0	0	6	.125	.167	.250	8	-6	0-0	1.000	-1	73	369	O116(69/47/27),1b12,3b4/2		-0.8
1999	SD N	149	440	55	117	22	3	9	61	38-2	3	50	.266	.327	.391	87	-9	33-7	.990	-1	104	74	O144(65/34/68)/2		-1.0
2000	SD N	145	583	87	171	19	7	6	51	45-4	4	63	.293	.346	.381	90	-11	29-14	1.000	3	105	67	O106(1/37/72)/D	19	-2.8
2001	Fla N	119	400	51	101	16	1	5	28	29-2	0	59	.253	.302	.335	67	-20	8-6	.984	-5	89	100	O121(75/22/39)		-0.2
2002	Fla N	131	385	44	104	15	5	4	37	31-1	0	33	.270	.324	.366	88	-10	26-9	.975	9	114	163	O97(10/48/42),D3		-1.3
2003	Ana A	111	241	29	65	6	0	1	20	10-0	1	24	.270	.300	.307	64	-13	11-8	.971	2	108	89	O670L,2b14,1b12,3b11,D4	20	-9.5
Total	9	806	2353	305	621	86	16	26	214	182-10	9	284	.264	.318	.347	75	-91	126-48	.985	-1	102	102	O670L,2b14,1b12,3b11,D4	20	-9.5

OWENS, FRANK Frank Walter "Yip" B1.26.1886 Toronto ON, Can. D7.2.1958 Minneapolis MN BR/TR/6-0/170 d9.11

YEAR	TM LG	G	AB	R	H	2B	3B	HR	RBI	BB-IB	HP	SO	AVG	OBP	SLG	AOPS	ABR	SB-CS	FA	FR	RNG	THR	GAMES AT POSITION	DL	BFW
1905	Bos A	1	2	0	0	0	0	0	0	0	0		.000	.000	.000	-99	-1		1.000	-0	0	198	/C		-0.1
1909	Chi A	64	174	12	35	4	1	0	17	8		2		.201	.245	.236	54	-9	3	.959	-6	94	85	C57		-1.2
1914	Bro F	58	184	15	51	7	3	2	20	9		1	16	.277	.314	.380	89	-6	2	.967	-11	78	96	C58		-1.4
1915	Bal F	99	334	32	84	14	7	3	28	17		1	34	.251	.290	.362	80	-15	4	.976	-2	107	105	C99		-3.6
Total	4	222	694	59	170	25	11	5	65	34		4	50	.245	.284	.334	77	-30	9	.969	-20	96	98	C215		

OWENS, JACK Furman Lee B5.6.1908 Converse SC D11.14.1958 Greenville SC BR/TR/6-1/186 d9.21

YEAR	TM LG	G	AB	R	H	2B	3B	HR	RBI	BB-IB	HP	SO	AVG	OBP	SLG	AOPS	ABR	SB-CS	FA	FR	RNG	THR	GAMES AT POSITION	DL	BFW
1935	Phi N	2	8	0	2	0	0	0	0	0	0	1	.250	.250	.250	30	-1	0-0	.900	-0	82	180	C2		-0.1

OWENS, RED Thomas Llewellyn B11.1.1874 Pottsville PA D8.20.1952 Harrisburg PA BR/TR d7.28

YEAR	TM LG	G	AB	R	H	2B	3B	HR	RBI	BB-IB	HP	SO	AVG	OBP	SLG	AOPS	ABR	SB-CS	FA	FR	RNG	THR	GAMES AT POSITION	DL	BFW
1899	Phi N	8	21	0	1	0	0	0	1	2	0		.048	.130	.048	-52	-4	0	.914	-0	104	91	2b8		-0.4
1905	Bro N	43	168	14	36	6	2	1	20	6	0		.214	.241	.292	63	-8	1	.929	2	98	118	2b43		-0.8
Total	2	51	189	14	37	6	2	1	21	8	0		.196	.228	.265	49	-12	1	.927	2	99	115	2b51		-1.6

OXLEY, HENRY Henry Havelock B1.4.1858 Covehead PE, Can. D10.12.1945 Somerville MA BR/5-11/163 d7.30

YEAR	TM LG	G	AB	R	H	2B	3B	HR	RBI	BB-IB	HP	SO	AVG	OBP	SLG	AOPS	ABR	SB-CS	FA	FR	RNG	THR	GAMES AT POSITION	DL	BFW
1884	NY N	2	4	0	0	0	0	0	0	1		2	.000	.200	.000	-31	-1		.900	0			C2		0.0
	NY AA	1	3	0	0	0	0	0	0	0		0	.000	.000	.000	-99	-1		.889	-0			/C		-0.1
Total	1	3	7	0	0	0	0	0	0	1		2	.000	.125	.000	-56	-2		.895	0			C3		-0.1

OYLER, ANDY Andrew Paul "Pepper" B5.5.1880 Newville PA D10.24.1970 E.Pennsboro Twp. PA BR/TR/5-6.5/138 d5.8 Col Washington & Jefferson

YEAR	TM LG	G	AB	R	H	2B	3B	HR	RBI	BB-IB	HP	SO	AVG	OBP	SLG	AOPS	ABR	SB-CS	FA	FR	RNG	THR	GAMES AT POSITION	DL	BFW
1902	Bal A	27	77	9	17	1	0	1	6	8	3		.221	.318	.273	62	-4	3	.947	-4	67	36	3b20,O3(0/2/1),S2/2		-0.1

OYLER, RAY Raymond Francis B8.4.1938 Indianapolis IN D1.26.1981 Seattle WA BR/TR/5-11/165* d4.18

YEAR	TM LG	G	AB	R	H	2B	3B	HR	RBI	BB-IB	HP	SO	AVG	OBP	SLG	AOPS	ABR	SB-CS	FA	FR	RNG	THR	GAMES AT POSITION	DL	BFW
1965	Det A	82	194	22	36	6	0	5	13	21-3		0	61	.186	.265	.294	58	-11	1-0	.955	-4	102	59	S57,2b11/13		-1.1
1966	Det A	71	210	16	36	8	3	1	9	23-4		3	62	.171	.263	.252	48	-14	0-0	.965	5	103	111	S69		-0.7
1967	Det A	148	367	33	76	14	2	1	29	37-3		2	91	.207	.281	.264	61	-17	0-2	.964	14	107	99	S146		-2.2
1968	†Det A	111	215	13	29	6	1	1	12	20-0		2	59	.135	.213	.186	22	-20	0-2	.965	-3	104	87	S106		-0.6
1969	Sea A	106	255	24	42	5	0	7	22	31-0		2	80	.165	.260	.267	48	-18	1-2	1.000	-4	60	33	S13,3b2		-0.7
1970	Cal A	24	24	2	2	0	0	0	1	3-0		1	6	.083	.185	.083	-24	-4	0-0	.966	7	101	89	S502,2b11,3b3/1		-0.3
Total	6	542	1265	110	221	39	6	15	86	135-10	9	359	.175	.258	.251	48	-84	2-6	.966	7	101	89	S502,2b11,3b3/1		-6.4

OZUNA, PABLO Pablo Jose B8.25.1974 Santo Domingo, D.R. BR/TR/6-0/160(160-185) d4.23 [DL 2001 Fla N 190]

YEAR	TM LG	G	AB	R	H	2B	3B	HR	RBI	BB-IB	HP	SO	AVG	OBP	SLG	AOPS	ABR	SB-CS	FA	FR	RNG	THR	GAMES AT POSITION	DL	BFW
2000	Fla N	14	24	2	8	1	0	0	0	0-0		2	.333	.333	.375	83	-1	0-0	.967	-1	96	70	2b7		-0.2
2002	Fla N	34	47	4	13	2	2	0	3	1-0	1	3	.277	.300	.404	91	-1	1-1	.967	-2	85	65	2b10/OC		-0.3
2003	Col N	17	40	5	8	1	0	0	2	2-0	2	6	.200	.273	.225	28	-4	3-0	.981	4	140	155	2b8,O5C,S3	68	-0.2
2005	†Chi A	70	203	27	56	7	2	1	11	7-0	2	26	.276	.313	.330	68	-9	14-7	.941	4	116	83	3b32,S15,O10(9/0/1),2b6,1b2,D4	258	-0.1
Total	4	135	314	38	85	11	4	0	16	10-0	7	37	.271	.307	.331	67	-15	19-8	.941	4	116	83	3b32,2b31,S18,O16(9/6/1),D4,1b2	258	-0.8

PABOR, CHARLIE Charles Henry B9.24.1846 New York NY D4.23.1913 New Haven CT BL/TL/5-8/155 d5.4 M2 ▲

YEAR	TM LG	G	AB	R	H	2B	3B	HR	RBI	BB-IB	HP	SO	AVG	OBP	SLG	AOPS	ABR	SB-CS	FA	FR	RNG	THR	GAMES AT POSITION	DL	BFW
1871	Cle NA	29	142	24	42	2	4	0	18	1		3	.296	.301	.366	96	0	1-0	.773	-4	103	0	O28L,P7,M		-0.2
1872	Cle NA	21	92	12	19	0	0	0		1		0	.207	.207	.207	29	-7	0-0	.863	-0	47	209	O19L,P2		-0.3
1873	Atl NA	55	228	36	82	9	3	0	41	6		3	.360	.376	.425	154	17	2-0	.811	-3	51	62	O55L		-0.1
1874	Phi NA	17	77	11	17	0	1	0	4	1		0	.221	.221	.247	48	-5	0-1	.553	-2	196	210	O17(2/3/13)		-0.6
1875	Atl NA	42	153	14	36	2	2	0	11	1		1	.235	.240	.275	90	0	0-0	.803	1	71	60	O42L/PM		-0.1
	NH NA	6	23	4	8	2	0	0	2	0		0	.348	.348	.522	227	3	0-0	.818	-1	0	0	O6L,M		0.0
Year	48	176	18	44	2	4	0	13	1		1	.250	.254	.307	108	2	0-0	.804	0	63	53	O48L/P		-0.1
Total	5 NA	170	715	101	204	13	12	0	80	8		8	.285	.293	.337	103	8	3-1	.789	-10	77	83	O167(152/3/13),P10		-0.9

PABST, ED Edward D. A. B1868 St.Louis MO D6.19.1940 St.Louis MO 5-11/170 d9.26

YEAR	TM LG	G	AB	R	H	2B	3B	HR	RBI	BB-IB	HP	SO	AVG	OBP	SLG	AOPS	ABR	SB-CS	FA	FR	RNG	THR	GAMES AT POSITION	DL	BFW
1890	Phi AA	8	25	7	10	2	0	0	3	5			.400	.500	.480	190	3	3	.963	3	232	0	O8L		0.0
	StL AA	4	14	1	2	0	1	0	2	0			.143	.143	.286	23	-2	0	1.000	1	259	0	O4L		0.0
	Year	12	39	8	12	2	1	0	5	5			.308	.386	.410	129	1	3	.972	4	240	0	O12L		0.0

PACIOREK, JIM James Joseph B6.7.1960 Detroit MI BR/TR/6-3/205 [MilA82 8/209] d4.9 b-John b-Tom Col Michigan

YEAR	TM LG	G	AB	R	H	2B	3B	HR	RBI	BB-IB	HP	SO	AVG	OBP	SLG	AOPS	ABR	SB-CS	FA	FR	RNG	THR	GAMES AT POSITION	DL	BFW
1987	Mil A	48	101	16	23	5	0	2	10	12-0	0	20	.228	.302	.337	69	-4	1-0	.980	-3	75	84	1b21,3b15,O5(4/0/1),D2		-0.1

PACIOREK, JOHN John Francis B2.11.1945 Detroit MI BR/TR/6-2/200 d9.29 b-Jim b-Tom

YEAR	TM LG	G	AB	R	H	2B	3B	HR	RBI	BB-IB	HP	SO	AVG	OBP	SLG	AOPS	ABR	SB-CS	FA	FR	RNG	THR	GAMES AT POSITION	DL	BFW
1963	Hou N	1	3	4	3	0	0	0	3	2-0	0	0	1.000	1.000	1.000	509	2	0-0	1.000	0	116	0	/OR		0.2

PACIOREK, TOM Thomas Marian B11.2.1946 Detroit MI BR/TR/6-4/215(204-215) [LAN68 5/89] d9.12 b-Jim b-John Col Houston OF(476/73/281)

YEAR	TM LG	G	AB	R	H	2B	3B	HR	RBI	BB-IB	HP	SO	AVG	OBP	SLG	AOPS	ABR	SB-CS	FA	FR	RNG	THR	GAMES AT POSITION	DL	BFW
1970	LA N	8	9	2	2	1	0	0	1	0-0	0	3	.222	.300	.333	72	0	0-0	1.000	-0	45	0	O3(1/0/2)		-0.1
1971	LA N	2	2	0	1	0	0	0	1	0-0	0	0	.500	.500	.500	194	0	0-0	1.000	0	243	0	/OL		0.0
1972	LA N	11	47	4	12	4	0	1	6	1-0	0	7	.255	.271	.404	91	-1	0-0	.979	1	97	92	1b6,O6(1/0/5)		0.0
1973	LA N	96	195	26	51	8	0	5	18	11-2	1	35	.262	.304	.379	91	-3	3-3	.979	-3	90	54	O77(36/22/25),1b4		0.0
1974	†LA N	85	175	23	42	8	6	1	24	10-1	1	32	.240	.282	.371	86	-5	1-3	.944	-4	92	33	O77(44/23/15)/1		-1.0
1975	LA N	62	145	14	28	8	0	1	5	11-1	0	29	.193	.250	.269	46	-11	4-3	.972	-3	93	0	O54(30/2/25)		-1.2
1976	Atl N	111	324	39	94	10	4	4	36	19-2	3	57	.290	.333	.383	98	-2	2-3	.983	-7	82	56	O84(38/7/44),1b12/3		-1.7
1977	Atl N	72	155	20	37	8	0	3	15	6-2	0	46	.239	.282	.348	57	-9	1-0	.984	-1	88	82	1b32,O9(4/2/3)/3		-1.5
1978	Atl N	5	9	2	3	0	0	0	0	0-0	0	1	.333	.333	.333	78	0	0-0	1.000	-0	82		1b2		-1.2
	Sea A	70	251	32	75	20	3	4	30	15-0	0	39	.299	.336	.450	120	6	0-0	.980	-2	88	88	O54(53/4/0),D12,1b3		-0.1
1979	Sea A	103	310	38	89	23	4	6	42	28-1	5	62	.287	.353	.445	112	6	2-2	.980	-2	88	88	O75(47/0/29),1b15		0.1
1980	Sea A	126	418	44	114	19	1	15	59	17-1	5	67	.273	.301	.431	97	6	6-4	1.000	-1	101	40	O60(19/1/41),1b36,D23		0.1
1981	Sea A★	104	405	50	132	28	2	14	66	35-3	4	50	.326	.379	.509	149	26	13-10	.974	3	104	128	O103(84/12/14)		-1.0
1982	Chi A	104	382	49	119	27	4	11	55	24-3	5	53	.312	.361	.490	132	17	3-3	.993	3	116	109	1b100,O6L		2.5
1983	†Chi A	115	420	65	129	32	3	9	63	25-4	1	58	.307	.347	.462	116	10	6-1	1.000	3	97	91	1b67,O55(30/0/27),D2	35	1.4
1984	Chi A	111	363	35	93	21	2	4	29	25-4	4	69	.256	.308	.358	81	-9	6-0	.993	-9	57	115	1b67,O41(25/0/17)		0.2
1985	Chi A	46	122	14	30	2	0	0	9	8-0	1	22	.246	.293	.262	53	-8	2-0	.970	0	94	97	O23(21/0/2),D12,1b6	28	-2.2
	NY N	46	116	14	33	3	1	1	11	6-1	1	14	.284	.325	.353	92	-2	1-0	1.000	-2	89	0	O29(6/0/24),1b8		-0.9
1986	Tex A	88	213	17	61	7	0	4	22	3-0	3	41	.286	.305	.376	82	-6	1-3	.967	3	74	271	O25(22/0/3),1b23,3b21/SD		-0.5
1987	Tex A	27	60	6	17	0	0	3	12	1-0	1	19	.283	.302	.483	104	0	0-1	1.000	1	139	155	1b12,O12(8/0/5),D3		-0.5
Total	18	1392	4121	494	1162	232	30	86	503	245-25	38	704	.282	.325	.415	102	6	55-38	.979	-26	93	75	O794L,1b396,D61,3b23/S	118 181	-7.6

PACK, FRANKIE Frank B4.10.1928 Morristown TN D1.26.2000 Hendersonville NC BL/TR/6-0/190 d6.5

YEAR	TM LG	G	AB	R	H	2B	3B	HR	RBI	BB-IB	HP	SO	AVG	OBP	SLG	AOPS	ABR	SB-CS	FA	FR	RNG	THR	GAMES AT POSITION	DL	BFW
1949	StL A	1	1	0	0	0	0	0	0	0-0	0	0	.000	.000	.000	-96	0			0			/H		0.0

PADDEN, DICK Richard Joseph "Brains" B9.17.1870 Martins Ferry OH D10.31.1922 Martins Ferry OH BR/TR/5-10/165 d7.15

YEAR	TM LG	G	AB	R	H	2B	3B	HR	RBI	BB-IB	HP	SO	AVG	OBP	SLG	AOPS	ABR	SB-CS	FA	FR	RNG	THR	GAMES AT POSITION	DL	BFW
1896	Pit N	61	219	33	53	4	8	2	24	14	2	9	.242	.294	.361	75	-10	8	.931	-14	78	56	2b61		-1.8
1897	Pit N	134	517	84	146	16	10	2	58	38	16		.282	.350	.364	92	-5	18	.941	4	95	78	2b134		0.4
1898	Pit N	128	463	61	119	7	6	2	43	35	19		.257	.337	.311	87	-7	11	.947	-1	103	97	2b128		-0.2
1899	Was N	134	451	66	125	20	7	2	61	24	17		.277	.337	.366	94	-4	27	.913	5	103	96	S85,2b48		0.7
1901	StL N	123	489	71	125	17	7	2	62	31	11		.256	.315	.331	92	-5	26	.950	-1	105	121	2b115,S8		-0.4
1902	StL A	117	413	54	109	26	3	1	40	30	9		.264	.327	.349	89	-5	11	.967	12	105	141	2b117		0.8
1903	StL A	29	94	7	19	3	0	0	6	9	5		.202	.306	.234	65	-3	5	.955	2	104	164	2b29		-0.1
1904	StL A	132	453	42	108	19	4	0	36	40	18		.238	.325	.298	104	5	23	.959	-16	95	132	2b132		-1.1
1905	StL A	16	58	5	10	1	1	0	4	3	0		.172	.213	.224	41	-4	3	.950	-0	104	50	2b16		-0.5
Total	9	874	3157	423	814	113	46	11	334	224	97	9	.258	.326	.333	90	-38	132	.950	-8	97	97	2b780,S93		-2.2

PADDEN, TOM Thomas Francis B10.6.1908 Manchester NH D6.10.1973 Manchester NH BR/TR/5-11.5/170 d5.29 Col Holy Cross

YEAR	TM LG	G	AB	R	H	2B	3B	HR	RBI	BB-IB	HP	SO	AVG	OBP	SLG	AOPS	ABR	SB-CS	FA	FR	RNG	THR	GAMES AT POSITION	DL	BFW
1932	Pit N	47	118	13	31	6	1	0	10	9	0	7	.263	.315	.331	75	-4	0	.985	-1	81	88	C43		-0.3
1933	Pit N	30	90	5	19	2	0	0	8	2	1	6	.211	.237	.233	35	-8	0	.984	3	76	129	C27		-0.3
1934	Pit N	82	237	27	76	12	2	0	22	30	1	23	.321	.399	.388	109	5	3	.978	-6	69	65	C76		0.3
1935	Pit N	97	302	35	82	9	1	1	30	48	0	26	.272	.371	.318	84	-4	1	.966	8	83	124	C94		0.9
1936	Pit N	88	281	22	70	9	2	1	31	22	0	41	.249	.304	.306	63	-15	1	.976	1	77	127	C87		-0.9
1937	Pit N	35	98	14	28	2	0	0	8	13	0	11	.286	.369	.306	85	-1	1	.983	2	62	145	C34		0.2
1943	Phi N	17	41	5	12	0	0	0	1	2	1	6	.293	.341	.293	87	-1	0	1.000	0	84	60	C16		0.2
	Was A	3	3	1	0	0	0	0	0	1	0	1	.000	.250	.000	-25	0	0-0	1.000	0	0	0	C2		0.0
Total	7	399	1170	122	318	40	6	2	110	127	3	121	.272	.345	.321	80	-28	5-0	.977	9	76	109	C379		0.1

PADDOCK, DEL Delmar Harold B6.8.1887 Volga SD D2.6.1952 Remer MN BL/TR/5-9/165 d4.14

YEAR	TM LG	G	AB	R	H	2B	3B	HR	RBI	BB-IB	HP	SO	AVG	OBP	SLG	AOPS	ABR	SB-CS	FA	FR	RNG	THR	GAMES AT POSITION	DL	BFW
1912	Chi A	1	1	0	0	0	0	0	0	0-0	0	0	.000	.000	.000	-99	0	0	—	0			/H		0.0
	NY A	46	156	26	45	5	3	1	14	23	4		.288	.393	.378	114	4	9	.894	-5	90	71	3b41,2b2/OR		0.0
	Year	47	157	26	45	5	3	1	14	23	4		.287	.391	.376	113	4	9	.894	-5	90	71	3b41,2b2/OR		0.0

PADGETT, DON Don Wilson B12.5.1911 Caroleen NC D12.9.1980 High Point NC BL/TR/6-0/190 d4.23 Mil 1942-45 Col Lenoir-Rhyne

YEAR	TM LG	G	AB	R	H	2B	3B	HR	RBI	BB-IB	HP	SO	AVG	OBP	SLG	AOPS	ABR	SB-CS	FA	FR	RNG	THR	GAMES AT POSITION	DL	BFW
1937	StL N	123	446	62	140	22	6	10	74	30	0	43	.314	.357	.457	117	10	4	.955	1	108	81	O109(0/6/102)		0.4
1938	StL N	110	388	59	105	26	5	8	65	18	0	28	.271	.303	.425	93	-5	0	.962	6	102	231	O71(3/5/63),1b16,C6		-0.4
1939	StL N	92	233	38	93	15	3	5	53	18	1	11	.399	.444	.554	157	19	1	.978	-1	120	61	C61,1b6		2.1
1940	StL N	93	240	24	58	15	1	6	41	26	2	14	.242	.321	.387	89	-3	1	.962	-6	86	107	C72,1b2		-0.5
1941	StL N	107	324	39	80	18	0	5	44	21	0	16	.247	.293	.349	75	-11	0	.959	-6	96	95	O62(59/0/3),C18,1b2		-2.0
1946	Bro N	19	30	2	5	1	0	1	9	4	0	4	.167	.265	.300	59	-2	0	1.000	0	195	67	C10		-0.1
	Bos N	44	98	6	25	3	0	2	21	5	0	7	.255	.291	.347	80	-3	0	.939	-5	80	109	C26		-0.7
	Year	63	128	8	30	4	0	3	30	9	0	11	.234	.285	.336	75	-5	0	.954	-5	106	99	C36		-0.8
1947	Phi N	75	158	14	50	8	1	0	24	16	1	5	.316	.383	.380	107	2	0	.962	-5	71	117	C39		-0.1
1948	Phi N	36	74	3	17	3	0	0	7	2	0	2	.230	.260	.270	44	-6	0	.957	-3	63	30	C19		-0.8
Total	8	699	1991	247	573	111	16	37	338	141	4	130	.288	.336	.415	101	7	6	.962	-18	96	86	C251,O242(62/11/168),1b26		-2.1

PADGETT, ERNIE Ernest Kitchen "Red" B3.1.1899 Philadelphia PA D4.15.1957 E.Orange NJ BR/TR/5-8/155 d10.3

YEAR	TM LG	G	AB	R	H	2B	3B	HR	RBI	BB-IB	HP	SO	AVG	OBP	SLG	AOPS	ABR	SB-CS	FA	FR	RNG	THR	GAMES AT POSITION	DL	BFW
1923	Bos N	4	11	3	2	0	0	0	0	0-0	0	0	.182	.308	.182	33	-1	0-0	.947	1	92	190	S2/2		0.0
1924	Bos N	138	502	42	128	25	9	1	46	37	3	56	.255	.310	.347	79	-15	4-9	.967	-9	102	108	3b113,2b29		-1.9
1925	Bos N	86	256	31	78	9	4	0	29	14	0	14	.305	.341	.395	96	-3	3-5	.964	-15	85	76	2b47,S18,3b7		-1.6
1926	Cle A	36	62	7	13	0	1	0	6	8	0	3	.210	.300	.242	42	-5	1-0	.930	1	116	158	3b29,S2		-0.3
1927	Cle A	7	7	1	2	0	0	0	0	1	0	2	.286	.286	.286	48	-1	0-0	1.000	-0	60	0	2b4		-0.1
Total	5	271	838	84	223	34	17	1	81	61	3	75	.266	.318	.351	80	-25	8-14	.957	-23	102	113	3b149,2b81,S22		-3.9

PAEPKE, DENNIS Dennis Ray B4.17.1945 Long Beach CA BR/TR/6-0/202* d6.2 Col Fullerton (CA) JC/Orange Coast (CA) JC

YEAR	TM LG	G	AB	R	H	2B	3B	HR	RBI	BB-IB	HP	SO	AVG	OBP	SLG	AOPS	ABR	SB-CS	FA	FR	RNG	THR	GAMES AT POSITION	DL	BFW
1969	KC A	12	27	2	3	1	0	0	0	2-0	0	3	.111	.172	.148	-10	-4	0-0	1.000	2	72	99	C8		-0.2
1971	KC A	60	152	11	31	6	0	2	14	8-1	0	29	.204	.242	.283	49	-11	0-0	.994	-0	83	82	C32,O17(1/0/16)		-1.1
1972	KC A	2	6	0	0	0	0	0	0	1-1	0	2	.000	.143	.000	-55	-1	0-0	.842	-0	30	172	C2		-0.1
1974	KC A	6	12	0	2	0	0	0	0	1-0	0	2	.167	.231	.167	15	-1	0-1	1.000	-1	45	352	C4/OR		-0.2
Total	4	80	197	13	36	7	0	2	14	12-2	0	36	.183	.229	.249	36	-17	0-1	.984	-1	76	106	C46,O18(1/0/17)		-1.6

PAFKO, ANDY Andrew "Handy Andy","Pruschka" B2.25.1921 Boyceville WI BR/TR/6-0/190* d9.24 C3

YEAR	TM LG	G	AB	R	H	2B	3B	HR	RBI	BB-IB	HP	SO	AVG	OBP	SLG	AOPS	ABR	SB-CS	FA	FR	RNG	THR	GAMES AT POSITION	DL	BFW
1943	Chi N	13	58	7	22	3	0	0	10	2	0	5	.379	.400	.431	142	3	1	1.000	-2	87	0	O13C		0.1
1944	Chi N	128	469	47	126	16	3	6	62	28	0	23	.269	.315	.350	87	-9	2	.983	10	100	215	O123(0/123/1)		-0.2
1945	†Chi N★	144	534	64	159	24	12	12	110	45	8	36	.298	.361	.455	129	19	5	.995	-0	100	98	O140C		1.4
1946	Chi N	65	234	18	66	6	4	3	29	27	4	15	.282	.366	.380	114	5	4	.978	3	93	211	O64C		0.6
1947	Chi N★	129	513	68	155	25	7	13	66	31	4	39	.302	.346	.454	115	9	4	.985	-1	99	102	O127C		0.5
1948	Chi N★	142	548	82	171	30	2	26	101	50	5	50	.312	.375	.516	145	33	3	.938	10	109	121	3b139		4.2
1949	Chi N★	144	519	79	146	29	2	18	69	63	9	33	.281	.369	.449	121	17	4	.987	-6	90	120	O98(1/89/9),3b49		0.8
1950	Chi N	146	514	95	156	24	8	36	92	69	11	32	.304	.397	.591	158	43	4	.978	-4	94	110	O144(0/138/6)		3.4
1951	Chi N	49	178	26	47	5	3	12	35	17	4	10	.264	.342	.528	128	6	1-1	.992	-5	91	142	O48C		0.4
	Bro N	84	277	42	69	11	0	18	58	35	8	27	.249	.342	.484	120	8	0	.993	-0	92	076(70/9/0)			0.1
	Year	133	455	68	116	16	3	30	93	52	12	37	.255	.347	.501	123	14	2-5	.993	-1	92	134	O124(70/57/0)		0.5
1952	†Bro N	150	551	76	158	17	5	19	85	64	5	48	.287	.366	.439	121	16	4-3	.988	9	90	175	O139(105/12/38),3b13		0.9
1953	Mil N	140	516	70	153	23	4	17	72	37	3	33	.297	.347	.455	114	10	1-2	.976	-8	92	49	O139R		-0.4
1954	Mil N	138	510	46	146	22	4	14	69	37	4	36	.286	.335	.427	105	2	1-2	.969	-6	93	42	O138(0/7/131)		-0.9
1955	Mil N	86	252	29	67	3	5	7	36	7-1	4	25	.266	.292	.377	81	-9	1-2	.980	-3	101	25	O58(1/7/52),3b12		-1.4
1956	Mil N	45	93	15	24	5	0	2	9	10-0	3	9	.258	.330	.376	95	0	0-0	.978	-0	94	25	O37(33/0/5)		-0.2
1957	†Mil N	83	220	31	61	6	1	8	20	10-2	1	21	.277	.308	.423	102	-1	1-0	.982	-2	101	25	O69(32/1/36)		-0.5
1958	†Mil N	95	164	17	39	7	1	3	23	15-3	2	21	.238	.306	.482	80	-5	0-0	1.000	2	115	49	O93(80/3/17)		-0.5
1959	Mil N	71	142	17	31	8	2	0	15	14-1	1	15	.218	.293	.324	70	-6	0-0	.978	-2	108	35	O64(40/22/9)		-0.9
Total	17	1852	6292	844	1796	264	62	213	976	561-7	76	477	.285	.350	.449	118	141	38-13	.984	-6	96	110	O1570(362/803/443),3b213		7.4

YEAR	TM LG	G	AB	R	H	2B	3B	HR	RBI	BB-IB	HP	SO	AVG	OBP	SLG	AOPS	ABR	SB-CS	FA	FR	RNG	THR	GAMES AT POSITION	DL	BFW
PAGAN, JOSE		Jose Antonio (Rodriguez) B5.5.1935 Barceloneta, PR BR/TR/5-9/165* d8.4 C5 OF(83/0/10)										8	.174	.208	.196	9	-6	1-0	.900	1	103	118	3b18,S5,2b3		-0.5
1959	SF N	31	46	7	8	1	0	0	1	2-0	0	8	.174	.208	.196	9	-6	1-0	.900	1	103	118	3b18,S5,2b3		-0.6
1960	SF N	18	49	8	14	2	2	0	1	1-0	0	6	.286	.300	.408	97	-1	2-2	.917	-6	58	36	S11/3		-2.3
1961	SF N	134	434	38	110	15	2	5	46	31-7	2	45	.253	.306	.332	72	-18	8-5	.964	-16	89	72	S132,O4(3/0/2)		-2.4
1962	†SF N	164	580	73	150	25	6	7	47	47-4	1	77	.259	.312	.359	82	-15	13-9	.973	-22	90	86	S164		-2.1
1963	SF N	148	483	46	113	12	1	6	39	26-5	4	67	.234	.289	.264	57	-20	5-4	.970	-10	94	87	S143/2OL		-3.3
1964	SF N	134	367	33	82	10	1	1	28	35-10	5	66	.223	.289	.264	57	-21	87	.958	-21	80	S132,O8(6/0/2)		3b15,S7	-1.0
1965	SF N	26	83	10	17	4	0	0	5	8-2	0	9	.205	.272	.253	48	-5	1-0	.941	-6	92	52	S26		-0.1
	Pit N	42	38	6	9	1	0	0	1	1-0	1	7	.237	.275	.263	52	-2	1-0	.923	1	112	150	3b15,S7		-1.1
	Year	68	121	16	26	5	0	0	6	9-2	1	16	.215	.273	.256	50	-8	2-0	.923	-5	96	64	S33,3b15		-0.5
1966	Pit N	109	368	44	97	15	6	4	54	13-3	4	38	.264	.292	.370	84	-9	0-2	.949	-4	111	128	3b83,S18,2b3,O3L		0.4
1967	Pit N	81	211	17	61	6	2	1	19	10-3	3	28	.289	.323	.351	95	-2	1-1	.938	6	119	84	3b25,O23L,S16,2b2/C		-0.9
1968	Pit N	80	163	24	36	7	1	4	20	11-3	3	32	.221	.278	.350	90	-2	2-3	.924	-4	99	70	3b30,O19L,S8,2b2/1		0.3
1969	Pit N	108	274	29	78	11	4	9	42	17-2	1	46	.285	.325	.453	119	6	1-0	.954	-2	92	99	3b44,O23(21/0/2)/2		0.0
1970	†Pit N	95	230	21	61	14	1	7	29	20-1	0	24	.265	.321	.426	99	-1	1-1	.957	1	98	154	3b53,O4(1/0/3)/12	39	-0.5
1971	†Pit N	57	158	16	38	1	0	5	15	16-2	1	25	.241	.311	.342	85	-3	0-0	.980	-1	94	135	3b41,O3L,1b2		-1.0
1972	Pit N	53	127	11	32	9	0	3	8	5-0	1	17	.252	.284	.394	93	-2	0-0	.899	-8	69	67	3b32,O2L		-0.9
1973	Phi N	46	78	4	16	5	0	0	5	1-0	1	15	.205	.213	.269	33	-7	0-1	.958	-1	76	48	3b16,1b5,O2(1/0/1)/2	39	-15.4
Total	15	1326	3689	387	922	138	26	52	372	244-43	22	510	.250	.298	.344	79	-108	46-35	.963	-84	91	81	S662,3b358,O92L,2b14,1b9/C		

PAGE, MIKE		Michael Randy B7.12.1940 Woodruff SC BL/TR/6-2.5/210 d6.30																	1.000	-1	69	0	O6(1/0/5)		-0.5
1968	Atl N	20	28	1	5	0	0	0	1	1-0	0	9	.179	.207	.179	16	-3	0-0	1.000	-1	69	0	O6(1/0/5)		-0.5

PAGE, MITCHELL		Mitchell Otis B10.15.1951 Los Angeles CA BL/TR/6-2/205* [PitN73 3/72] d4.9 C7 Col Cal Poly-Pomona										95	.307	.405	.521	153	40	42-5	.954	5	111	116	O133(131/0/5),D8		4.5
1977	Oak A	145	501	85	154	28	8	21	75	78-6	6	95	.307	.405	.521	153	40	42-5	.954	5	111	116	O133(131/0/5),D8	16	1.6
1978	Oak A	147	516	62	147	25	7	17	70	53-6	5	95	.285	.355	.459	134	23	23-19	.973	-0	102	61	O114(112/0/2),D33		-1.8
1979	Oak A	133	478	51	118	11	2	9	42	52-5	3	93	.247	.323	.335	82	-12	17-16	1.000	-1	59	0	D126,O4L		0.2
1980	Oak A	110	348	58	85	10	4	17	51	35-3	1	87	.244	.311	.443	112	4	14-7	—	0	0	0	D101		-0.9
1981	Oak A	34	92	9	13	1	0	4	10	7-0	0	29	.141	.200	.283	40	-8	2-1	—	0	0	0	D29		0.1
1982	Oak A	31	78	14	20	5	0	4	7	7-1	2	24	.256	.333	.474	123	2	3-4	—	0	0	0	D24		-0.3
1983	Oak A	57	79	16	19	3	0	0	6	10-0	2	22	.241	.341	.278	77	-2	3-3	1.000	0	128	0	D34,O10(7/0/3)		0.1
1984	Pit N	16	12	2	4	1	0	0	3	3-0	0	4	.333	.467	.417	150	1	0-0	—	0			/H	16	3.5
Total	8	673	2104	297	560	84	21	72	259	245-21	18	449	.266	.346	.429	117	48	104-55	.963	4	106	89	D355,O261(254/0/10)		

PAGEL, KARL		Karl Douglas B3.29.1955 Madison WI BL/TL/6-2/190* [ChiN76 S1/20] d9.21 Col Texas										1	.000	.000	.000	-89	-1	0-0	—	0			/H	18	-0.1
1978	Chi N	2	2	0	0	0	0	0	0	0-0	0	1	.000	.000	.000	-89	-1	0-0	—	0			/H	18	-0.1
1979	Chi N	1	1	0	0	0	0	0	0	0-0	0	1	.000	.000	.000	-91	0	0-0	—	0			/H		0.4
1981	Cle A	14	15	3	4	0	2	1	4	4-1	0	4	.267	.421	.733	228	2	0-0	1.000	1	225	142	1b6/D		-0.1
1982	Cle A	23	18	3	3	0	0	1	2	7-1	0	11	.167	.400	.167	62	0	0-0	.970	-0	81	66	1b10/D		-0.1
1983	Cle A	8	20	1	6	1	0	0	1	0-0	0	5	.300	.300	.300	63	-1	0-0	.000	-0	0		/OLD	18	0.1
Total	5	48	56	7	13	0	2	1	7	11-2	0	20	.232	.358	.357	98	0	0-0	.985	1	155	105	1b16,D7/OL		

PAGLIARONI, JIM		James Vincent "Pag" B12.8.1937 Dearborn MI BR/TR/6-4/210* d8.13 Mil 1956-57												.000	—	0	0-0	—	0	0	0	/C		0.0
1955	Bos A	1	0	0	0	0	0	0	0	0-0	0			.000	—	0	0-0	—	0	0	0	/C		0.7
1960	Bos A	28	62	7	19	5	2	2	9	13-0	1	11	.306	.434	.548	158	6	0-0	.990	0	106	58	C18		0.4
1961	Bos A	120	376	50	91	17	0	16	58	55-0	4	74	.242	.342	.415	100	1	1-1	.984	-2	98	80	C108		0.7
1962	Bos A	90	260	39	67	14	0	11	37	36-0	5	55	.258	.359	.438	110	5	2-1	.987	-1	88	92	C73		0.5
1963	Pit N	92	252	27	58	5	0	11	26	36-8	2	56	.230	.330	.381	104	2	1-0	.992	-1	102	97	C96		2.0
1964	Pit N	97	302	33	89	12	3	10	36	41-4	2	56	.295	.383	.454	135	15	1-0	.994	3	127	63	C131		1.8
1965	Pit N	134	403	42	108	15	1	17	65	41-11	3	84	.268	.337	.432	115	8	0-5	.997	-9	100	55	C118		-0.5
1966	Pit N	123	374	37	88	20	0	11	49	50-9	4	71	.235	.329	.377	96	0	0-0	.984	2	134	70	C38	27	-0.2
1967	Pit N	44	100	4	20	1	1	0	9	16-5	1	26	.200	.314	.230	59	-5	0-0	.997	-7	82	76	C63	50	-0.2
1968	Oak A	66	199	19	49	4	0	6	20	24-1	2	42	.246	.330	.357	114	4	0-0	.981	3	64	217	C7	22	-0.3
1969	Oak A	14	27	1	4	1	0	1	2	5-0	1	16	.148	.303	.296	71	-1	0-0	.988	-7	45	96	C29,1b2/OR		-0.1
	Sea A	40	110	10	29	4	1	5	14	13-1	1	18	.264	.333	.455	122	3	0-0	.987	-5	49	120	C36,1b2/OR		-0.1
	Year	54	137	11	33	5	1	6	16	18-1	1	18	.241	.327	.423	112	2	0-0	.991	-19	100	81	C767,1b2/OR	99	5.2
Total	11	849	2465	269	622	98	7	90	326	330-39	25	494	.252	.344	.407	109	38	4-7	.991	-19	100	81	C767,1b2/OR		

PAGLIARULO, MIKE		Michael Timothy B3.15.1960 Medford MA BL/TR/6-2/195* [NYA81 6/155] d7.7 Col Miami										46	.239	.288	.448	105	1	0-0	.955	-2	90	147	3b67		-0.2
1984	NY A	67	201	24	48	15	3	7	34	15-0	0	46	.239	.288	.448	105	1	0-0	.955	-2	90	147	3b67		-1.4
1985	NY A	138	380	55	91	16	2	19	62	45-4	4	86	.239	.324	.442	110	5	0-0	.951	-17	84	76	3b134		-0.3
1986	NY A	149	504	71	120	24	3	28	71	54-10	4	120	.238	.316	.464	110	6	1-3	.959	-2	101	130	3b147/1		-1.8
1987	NY A	150	522	76	122	26	3	32	87	53-9	2	111	.234	.305	.479	105	2	1-0	.943	-5	100	79	3b124	17	-1.0
1988	NY A	125	444	46	96	20	1	15	67	37-9	2	104	.216	.276	.367	80	-13	1-0	.936	-2	106	58	3b69/D		-1.6
1989	NY A	74	223	19	44	10	0	4	16	19-0	2	43	.197	.266	.296	59	-12	1-1	.936	-5	96	44	3b49		-1.6
	SD N	50	148	12	29	7	0	3	14	18-4	1	39	.196	.287	.304	69	-6	2-0	.955	-5	95	113	3b116		-1.3
1990	SD N	128	398	29	101	23	2	7	38	39-3	3	66	.254	.322	.374	91	-4	1-2	.965	15	120	158	3b118/2		0.9
1991	†Min A	121	365	38	102	20	6	6	36	21-3	3	55	.279	.322	.384	91	-5	1-2	.962	2	116	70	3b37/D	100	-0.2
1992	Min A	42	105	10	21	4	0	0	9	1-0	1	17	.200	.213	.238	26	-11	0-0	.984	-0	102	85	3b79		0.1
1993	Min A	83	253	31	74	16	4	3	23	18-2	5	34	.292	.350	.423	106	2	6-6	.937	-1	88	126	3b28,1b4		0.1
	Bal A	33	117	24	38	9	0	6	21	8-0	1	15	.325	.373	.556	139	6	0-0	.969	7	98	96	3b107,1b4	16	-0.2
	Year	116	370	55	112	25	4	9	44	26-2	6	49	.303	.357	.465	117	9	6-6	.963	6	111	124	3b68,1b11		0.2
1995	Tex A	86	241	27	56	16	0	4	15-2	1	49	.232	.277	.349	60	-14	0-0	.955	-18	100	104	3b1179,1b16,D2,S2/2	133	-7.1
Total	11	1246	3901	442	942	206	18	134	505	343-46	29	785	.241	.306	.407	93	-43	18-16	.955	-18	100	104	3b1179,1b16,D2,S2/2		

PAGNOZZI, TOM		Thomas Alan B7.30.1962 Tucson AZ BR/TR/6-1/190* [StLN83 8/208] d4.12 Col Arkansas-Monticello										13	.188	.250	.333	52	-4	1-0	1.000	-2	353	66	C25/1		-0.4
1987	†StL N	27	48	8	9	2	0	2	9	4-2	0	13	.188	.250	.333	52	-4	1-0	1.000	-2	353	66	C25/1		-0.4
1988	StL N	81	195	17	55	9	0	0	15	11-1	0	32	.282	.319	.328	85	-4	0-0	.971	-1	85	157	C28,1b28,3b5		-1.0
1989	StL N	52	80	3	12	2	0	0	3	6-2	1	19	.150	.216	.175	13	-9	0-0	.982	-6	61	91	C38,1b2/3		-1.1
1990	StL N	69	220	20	61	15	0	2	23	14-1	1	37	.277	.321	.373	88	-7	9-13	.991	9	122	138	C139,1b3		0.2
1991	StL N	140	459	38	121	24	5	2	57	36-6	4	63	.264	.319	.361	85	-11	2-5	.999	-10	115	78	C138	40	-1.7
1992	StL N★	139	485	33	121	26	3	7	44	28-9	1	64	.249	.290	.359	85	-11	1-0	.991	-6	112	100	C92	32	0.4
1993	StL N	92	330	31	85	15	1	7	41	19-6	3	39	.272	.327	.416	93	-3	0-0	.998	1	189	116	C70/1	39	-1.1
1994	StL N	70	243	21	66	12	1	7	40	21-5	0	31	.215	.254	.315	49	-17	0-1	.995	2	98	145	C61	14	0.0
1995	StL N	62	219	17	47	14	1	2	15	11-0	1	31	.270	.311	.423	92	-6	4-1	.990	-1	126	104	C116/1	128	-1.7
1996	†StL N	119	407	48	110	23	0	13	55	24-2	2	78	.270	.311	.423	92	-6	4-1	1.000	-3	142	59	C13,1b2/3	24	-1.8
1997	StL N	25	50	4	11	3	0	1	9	1-0	0	7	.220	.235	.340	48	-4	0-0	.982	-3	86	98	C44	277	-5.4
1998	StL N	51	160	7	35	9	1	0	10	14-0	1	37	.219	.280	.294	52	-11	0-0	.992	-7	124	113	C827,1b40,3b7		
Total	12	927	2896	247	733	153	11	44	320	189-34	11	450	.253	.299	.359	79	-89	18-21	.992	-7	124	113	C827,1b40,3b7		

PALACIOS, REY		Robert Rey B11.8.1962 Brooklyn NY BR/TR/5-10/190* d9.8 Col Kingsborough (NY) CC										4	.091	.091	.091	-48	-2	0-0	1.000	1	77	0	C3/3D		-0.4
1988	KC A	5	11	2	1	0	0	0	0	0-0	0	4	.091	.091	.091	-48	-2	0-0	1.000	1	77	0	C3/3D		-0.4
1989	KC A	55	47	12	8	0	1	3	8	2-0	1	14	.170	.216	.277	39	-4	0-1	.958	-1	68	0	3b21,1b18,C13/ORD	48	-0.2
1990	KC A	41	56	8	13	3	0	2	9	5-0	0	24	.232	.295	.393	92	-1	2-2	.992	1	104	56	C27,1b7,3b3/OR	48	-0.2
Total	3	101	114	22	22	5	0	3	17	7-0	1	42	.193	.244	.316	57	-7	2-3	.994	1	103	55	C43,1b25,3b25,D3,O2R		

PALMEIRO, ORLANDO		Orlando B1.19.1969 Hoboken NJ BL/TL/5-11/175(155-180) [CalA91 33/870] d7.1 Col Miami										0	.350	.381	.350	93	0	0-0	1.000	-0	93	0	O7(3/4/0)/D		0.2
1995	Cal A	15	20	3	7	0	0	0	1	1-0	0	0	.350	.381	.350	93	0	0-0	1.000	-0	93	0	O7(3/4/0)/D		0.2
1996	Cal A	50	87	6	25	6	0	1	8	8-1	2	13	.287	.361	.379	86	-2	0-1	.975	-1	100	60	O52(4/45/4),D11	15	-0.7
1997	Ana A	74	134	19	29	2	2	0	8	17-1	1	11	.216	.307	.261	51	-10	2-2	1.000	1	118	0	O54(46/6/4),D3		-1.7
1998	Ana A	75	165	28	53	7	2	0	21	20-1	0	11	.321	.395	.388	103	3	5-4	1.000	1	101	118	O92(60/1/35),D10		-1.1
1999	Ana A	109	317	46	88	12	1	1	23	39-1	6	30	.278	.364	.331	80	-8	4-1	.984	3	103	167	O72(40/2/31),D19		-1.9
2000	Ana A	108	243	38	73	20	2	0	25	38-0	2	24	.300	.395	.399	100	2	4-1	.989	-0	102	74	O59(26/7/28),D30		-1.8
2001	Ana A	104	230	29	56	10	1	2	24	23-0	0	22	.243	.319	.322	70	-9	6-6	.993	1	104	74	O86(33/11/47),D6		-1.1
2002	†Ana A	110	263	24	79	12	1	0	31	30-1	0	22	.300	.368	.354	96	0	7-2	1.000	5	112	129	O112(42/17/62)		-0.1
2003	StL N	141	317	37	86	13	1	3	33	32-3	3	31	.271	.336	.347	81	-8	3-3	1.000	5	112	129	O112(42/17/62)		

YEAR	TM LG	G	AB	R	H	2B	3B	HR	RBI	BB-IB	HP	SO	AVG	OBP	SLG	AOPS	ABR	SB-CS	FA	FR	RNG	THR	GAMES AT POSITION	DL	BFW
2004	†Hou N	102	133	19	32	5	0	3	12	18-1	3	19	.241	.344	.346	77	-4	2-1	1.000	-0	105	0	O37(20/4/13)		-0.5
2005	†Hou N	114	204	22	58	17	2	3	20	15-1	4	23	.284	.341	.431	102	1	3-1	.986	-2	87	87	O71(47/5/26)		-0.2
Total	11	1002	2113	282	586	104	13	12	203	243-12	23	205	.277	.355	.356	86	-37	37-26	.992	5	103	88	O673(328/119/258),D84	15	-5.0

PALMEIRO, RAFAEL Rafael (Corrales) B9.24.1964 Havana, Cuba BL/TL/6-0/188(180-215) [ChiN85 1/22] d9.8 Col Mississippi St.

YEAR	TM LG	G	AB	R	H	2B	3B	HR	RBI	BB-IB	HP	SO	AVG	OBP	SLG	AOPS	ABR	SB-CS	FA	FR	RNG	THR	GAMES AT POSITION	DL	BFW
1986	Chi N	22	73	9	18	4	0	3	12	4-0	1	6	.247	.295	.425	89	-1	1-1	.900	1	102	166	O20(19/0/3)		
1987	Chi N	84	221	32	61	15	1	14	30	20-1	1	26	.276	.336	.543	124	7	2-2	1.000	-2	95	41	O45(44/0/2),1b18		-0.2
1988	Chi N★	152	580	75	178	41	5	8	53	38-6	1	34	.307	.349	.436	120	15	12-2	.983	-0	100	67	O147(145/2/3),1b5		0.3
1989	Tex A	156	559	76	154	23	4	8	64	63-3	6	48	.275	.354	.374	104	4	4-3	.991	9	117	85	1b147,D6		1.3
1990	Tex A	154	598	72	191	35	6	14	89	40-6	3	59	.319	.361	.468	131	24	3-3	.995	-3	89	98	1b146,D6		0.3
1991	Tex A★	159	631	115	203	49	3	26	88	68-10	6	72	.322	.389	.532	156	49	4-3	.992	-6	86	84	1b157,D2		1.0
1992	Tex A	159	608	84	163	27	4	22	85	72-8	10	83	.268	.352	.434	124	20	2-3	.995	13	122	92	1b156,D2		3.2
1993	Tex A	160	597	124	176	40	2	37	105	73-22	5	85	.295	.371	.554	151	43	22-3	.997	18	138	96	1b160		2.1
1994	Bal A	111	436	82	139	32	0	23	76	54-1	2	63	.319	.392	.550	133	23	7-3	.996	-1	93	102	1b111		4.8
1995	Bal A	143	554	89	172	30	2	39	104	62-5	3	65	.310	.380	.583	144	35	3-1	.997	10	118	108	1b142		1.1
1996	†Bal A	162	626	110	181	40	2	39	142	95-12	3	96	.289	.381	.546	133	33	3-1	.995	6	113	111	1b159,D3		3.0
1997	†Bal A	158	614	95	156	24	2	38	110	67-7	5	109	.254	.329	.485	113	10	8-0	.995	6	113	111	1b155,D3		2.4
1998	Bal A★	162	619	98	183	36	1	43	121	79-8	7	91	.296	.379	.565	144	41	11-7	.994	8	114	98	1b159,D3		0.2
1999	†Tex A★	158	565	96	183	30	1	47	148	97-14	9	69	.324	.420	.630	155	49	2-4	.996	2	74	91	D128,1b28		3.2
2000	Tex A	158	565	102	163	29	3	39	120	103-17	3	77	.288	.397	.558	137	34	2-1	.995	-3	88	82	1b108,D46		3.4
2001	Tex A	160	600	98	164	33	0	47	123	101-8	7	90	.273	.381	.563	141	38	1-1	.992	4	116	107	1b113,D46		1.8
2002	Tex A	155	546	99	149	34	0	43	105	104-16	6	94	.273	.391	.571	148	41	2-0	.994	10	138	96	1b97,D55		2.8
2003	Tex A	154	561	92	146	21	2	38	112	84-9	5	77	.260	.359	.508	118	15	2-0	.996	5	133	108	D97,1b55		3.8
2004	Bal A	154	550	68	142	29	0	23	88	86-15	6	61	.258	.359	.436	109	2	2-1	.993	5	115		1b130,D20		1.0
2005	Bal A	110	369	47	98	13	0	18	60	43-4	2	43	.266	.339	.447	108	4	2-0	.993	3	109	89	1b93,D15		0.2
Total	20	2831	10472	1663	3020	585	38	569	1835	1353-172	87	1348	.288	.371	.515	132	493	97-40	.994	80	111	97	1b2139,D432,O212(208/2/8)		35.6

PALMER, DEAN Dean William B12.27.1968 Tallahassee FL BR/TR/6-1/210(175-210) [TexA86 3/59] d9.1

YEAR	TM LG	G	AB	R	H	2B	3B	HR	RBI	BB-IB	HP	SO	AVG	OBP	SLG	AOPS	ABR	SB-CS	FA	FR	RNG	THR	GAMES AT POSITION	DL	BFW
1989	Tex A	16	19	0	2	2	0	0	1	0-0	0	12	.105	.100	.211	-13	-3	0-0	.667	-0	82	0	3b6/SOLD		-0.3
1991	Tex A	81	268	38	50	9	2	15	37	32-0	3	98	.187	.281	.403	88	-6	0-2	.944	-9	82	53	3b50,O29L,D5		-1.5
1992	Tex A	152	541	74	124	25	0	26	72	62-2	4	154	.229	.311	.420	107	4	0-4	.945	-1	92	90	3b150		0.4
1993	Tex A	148	519	88	127	31	2	33	96	53-4	8	154	.245	.321	.503	123	14	11-10	.922	-14	91	82	3b148/S		0.0
1994	Tex A	93	342	50	84	14	2	19	59	26-0	2	89	.246	.302	.465	93	-6	3-4	.912	-3	105	54	3b91		-0.8
1995	Tex A	36	119	30	40	6	0	9	24	21-1	4	21	.336	.448	.613	168	13	1-1	.948	2	113	148	3b36	15	1.4
1996	†Tex A	154	582	98	163	26	2	38	107	59-4	5	145	.280	.348	.527	111	8	2-0	.953	-19	84	63	3b154/D	110	-0.9
1997	Tex A	94	355	47	87	21	0	14	55	26-2	1	84	.245	.296	.423	80	-11	1-0	.959	-4	97	61	3b93		-1.3
	KC A	49	187	23	52	10	1	9	31	15-0	2	50	.278	.335	.487	109	2	1-2	.924	-8	87	97	3b48/D		-0.6
	Year	143	542	70	139	31	1	23	86	41-2	3	134	.256	.310	.445	97	-10	2-2	.948	-12	94	74	3b141/D		-1.9
1998	KC A★	152	572	84	159	27	2	34	119	48-3	6	134	.278	.341	.510	113	9	8-2	.921	-24	81	80	3b129,D22		-1.3
1999	Det A	150	560	92	147	25	2	38	100	57-3	10	153	.262	.338	.518	113	9	3-3	.945	-5	96	105	3b141,D9		0.5
2000	Det A	145	524	73	134	22	2	29	102	66-2	4	146	.256	.338	.471	104	2	4-2	.914	-15	92	72	3b115,1b20,D14		-1.2
2001	Det A	57	216	34	48	11	0	11	40	27-0	1	59	.222	.317	.426	96	-1	4-1	—		0		D57	119	-0.4
2002	Det A	4	12	0	0	0	0	0	0	1-0	0	5	.000	.077	.000	-80	-3	0-0	—		0		D4	176	-0.3
2003	Det A	26	86	3	12	2	0	0	6	9-0	1	28	.140	.235	.163	9	-11	0-0	1.000	1	162	0	D22/13	142	-0.3
Total	14	1357	4902	734	1229	231	15	275	849	502-21	54	1332	.251	.324	.472	105	20	48-31	.935	-98	92	80	3b1162,D141,O30L,1b21,S2	562	-7.5

PALMER, EDDIE Edwin Henry "Baldy" B6.1.1893 Petty TX D1.9.1983 Marlow OK BR/TR/5-9.5/175 d9.6

YEAR	TM LG	G	AB	R	H	2B	3B	HR	RBI	BB-IB	HP	SO	AVG	OBP	SLG	AOPS	ABR	SB-CS	FA	FR	RNG	THR	GAMES AT POSITION	DL	BFW
1917	Phi A	16	52	7	11	0	1	0	5	7			.212	.305	.231	65	-2	1	.898	0	106	49	3b13/S		-0.1

PALMISANO, JOE Joseph B11.19.1902 West Point GA D11.5.1971 Albuquerque NM BR/TR/5-8/160 d5.31 Col Georgia Tech

YEAR	TM LG	G	AB	R	H	2B	3B	HR	RBI	BB-IB	HP	SO	AVG	OBP	SLG	AOPS	ABR	SB-CS	FA	FR	RNG	THR	GAMES AT POSITION	DL	BFW
1931	Phi A	19	44	5	10	2	0	0	4	6	0	2	.227	.320	.273	54	-3	0-0	.960	-1	109	77	C16/2		-0.3

PALYS, STAN Stanley Francis B5.1.1930 Blakely PA BR/TR/6-2/190* d9.20

YEAR	TM LG	G	AB	R	H	2B	3B	HR	RBI	BB-IB	HP	SO	AVG	OBP	SLG	AOPS	ABR	SB-CS	FA	FR	RNG	THR	GAMES AT POSITION	DL	BFW
1953	Phi N	2	2	0	0	0	0	0	0	1	0		.000	.333	.000	-4	0	0-0	—	-0	0	0	/OR		0.0
1954	Phi N	2	4	0	1	0	0	0	0	1	0		.250	.400	.250	74	0	0-0	—	-0	0	0	/OR		0.0
1955	Phi N	15	52	8	15	3	0	1	8	6-0	0	5	.288	.362	.404	105	1	1-0	1.000	0	103	93	O15(3/4/8)		0.0
	Cin N	79	222	29	51	14	0	7	30	12-0	1	35	.230	.271	.387	69	-10	1-1	.992	2	113	78	O55L/1		-1.1
1956	Cin N	40	53	5	12	0	0	2	5	6-0	1	40	.241	.289	.391	75	-10	2-1	.993	3	111	81	O70(58/4/8)/1		-1.1
	Year	94	274	37	66	17	0	8	38	18-0	1	40	.226	.300	.340	69	-2	1-0	.929	-1	97	0	O10(7/0/4)		-0.3
Total	4	138	333	42	79	17	0	10	43	26-0	1	54	.237	.293	.378	74	-11	2-1	.988	2	109	72	O82(65/4/14)/1		-1.4

PANKOVITS, JIM James Franklin B8.6.1955 Pennington Gap VA BR/TR/5-10/175(174-195) [HouN76 4/73] d5.27 Col South Carolina-Aiken OF(28/0/20)

YEAR	TM LG	G	AB	R	H	2B	3B	HR	RBI	BB-IB	HP	SO	AVG	OBP	SLG	AOPS	ABR	SB-CS	FA	FR	RNG	THR	GAMES AT POSITION	DL	BFW
1984	Hou N	53	81	6	23	7	0	1	14	2-0	0	20	.284	.298	.407	104	0	1-2	.925	-3	80	138	2b15,S4,O3L		-0.2
1985	Hou N	75	172	24	42	3	0	4	14	17-1	1	20	.244	.316	.331	83	-4	1-0	.983	2	112	108	O33(14/0/20),2b21/S3		-0.2
1986	†Hou N	70	113	12	32	6	1	1	7	11-1	0	25	.283	.347	.381	103	1	1-1	.969	2	102	99	2b26,O5L/C		0.4
1987	Hou N	50	61	7	14	2	0	1	8	6-1	0	13	.230	.299	.311	64	-3	2-0	1.000	3	95	140	2b9,O6L,3b4		-1.0
1988	Hou N	68	140	13	31	7	1	2	12	8-0	2	28	.221	.272	.329	75	-5	2-1	.939	-5	93	128	2b31,3b11,1b2		-1.0
1990	Bos A	2	0	0	0	0	0	0	0	0-0	0	0	—	—	—		0	0-0	—	-1	0	0	2b2		-0.1
Total	6	318	567	62	142	25	2	9	55	44-3	3	115	.250	.307	.349	86	-11	8-3	.961	-1	96	116	2b104,O47L,3b16,S5,1b2/C		-1.1

PAPE, KEN Kenneth Wayne B10.1.1951 San Antonio TX BR/TR/5-11/195 [TexA73 5/97] d5.17 Col Texas

YEAR	TM LG	G	AB	R	H	2B	3B	HR	RBI	BB-IB	HP	SO	AVG	OBP	SLG	AOPS	ABR	SB-CS	FA	FR	RNG	THR	GAMES AT POSITION	DL	BFW
1976	Tex A	21	23	7	5	1	0	0	3	3-1	2	2	.217	.357	.391	117	1	0-1	.968	3	167	161	S6,3b4/2D	44	0.4

PAPI, STAN Stanley Gerard B2.4.1951 Fresno CA BR/TR/6-0/178(165-180) [HouN69 2/26] d4.11

YEAR	TM LG	G	AB	R	H	2B	3B	HR	RBI	BB-IB	HP	SO	AVG	OBP	SLG	AOPS	ABR	SB-CS	FA	FR	RNG	THR	GAMES AT POSITION	DL	BFW
1974	StL N	8	4	1	1	0	0	0	0	0-0	0	0	.250	.250	.250	40	0	0-0	1.000	1	83	443	S7/2		0.0
1977	Mon N	13	43	5	10	2	1	0	4	0-0	0	9	.233	.250	.326	54	-3	1-0	.952	-4	66	0	3b10,S2/2		-0.7
1978	Mon N	67	152	15	35	11	0	0	11	10-1	2	28	.230	.285	.303	65	-7	0-0	.976	-2	93	84	S22,3b15,2b5		-0.8
1979	Bos A	50	117	9	22	8	0	1	6	5-0	0	20	.188	.221	.282	33	-11	0-0	.982	7	118	119	2b26,S21/D	47	-0.2
1980	Bos A	1	0	0	0	0	0	0	0	0-0	0	0	—	—	—		0	0-0	—	-0	0	0	/3		0.0
	Det A	46	114	12	27	3	4	3	17	5-0	0	24	.237	.267	.412	82	-4	0-0	.973	-6	80	88	2b31,3b11,S5/1		-0.8
	Year	47	114	12	27	3	4	3	17	5-0	0	24	.237	.267	.412	82	-4	0-0	.973	-6	80	88	2b31,3b11,S5/1		-0.8
1981	Det A	40	93	8	19	2	1	3	12	3-0	0	18	.204	.224	.344	61	-5	1-0	.941	-0	106	74	3b32/12OLD		-0.6
Total	6	225	523	49	114	26	6	7	51	24-1	2	99	.218	.253	.331	59	-30	2-0	.931	-4	93	74	3b69,2b65,S57,D4,1b2/OL	47	-3.1

PAPPAS, ERIK Erik Daniel B4.25.1966 Chicago IL BR/TR/6-0/190* [CalA84 1/6] d4.19

YEAR	TM LG	G	AB	R	H	2B	3B	HR	RBI	BB-IB	HP	SO	AVG	OBP	SLG	AOPS	ABR	SB-CS	FA	FR	RNG	THR	GAMES AT POSITION	DL	BFW
1991	Chi N	7	17	1	3	0	0	0	2	1-0	0	5	.176	.222	.176	13	-2	0-0	1.000	1	89	116	C6		-0.1
1993	StL N	82	228	25	63	12	0	1	28	35-2	0	55	.276	.368	.342	93	0	0-0	.982	6	110	102	C63,O16(1/0/15),1b2		0.8
1994	StL N	15	44	8	4	1	0	0	5	10-0	1	13	.091	.259	.114	6	-6	1-3	.955	-5	69	21	C15		-1.0
Total	3	104	289	34	70	13	0	1	35	46-2	1	53	.242	.342	.298	75	-8	1-3	.978	3	101	87	C84,O16(1/0/15),1b2		-0.3

PAQUETTE, CRAIG Craig Harold B3.28.1969 Long Beach CA BR/TR/6-0/190* [OakA89 8/218] d6.1 Col Golden West (CA) JC OF(131/0/75)

YEAR	TM LG	G	AB	R	H	2B	3B	HR	RBI	BB-IB	HP	SO	AVG	OBP	SLG	AOPS	ABR	SB-CS	FA	FR	RNG	THR	GAMES AT POSITION	DL	BFW
1993	Oak A	105	393	35	86	20	4	12	46	14-2	0	108	.219	.245	.382	69	-20	4-2	.950	-8	91	87	3b104/OLD		-2.6
1994	Oak A	14	49	0	7	2	0	0	4	0-0	0	14	.143	.143	.184	-18	-9	0-0	1.000	1	95	139	3b14		-0.7
1995	Oak A	105	283	42	64	13	1	13	49	12-0	1	88	.226	.256	.417	76	-12	5-2	.935	-11	73	103	3b75,O20(18/0/2),S8,1b3		-2.2
1996	KC A	118	429	61	111	15	1	22	67	23-2	2	101	.259	.296	.452	86	-12	5-3	.891	-8	99	60	3b51,O47L,1b19,S11,D6		-2.0
1997	KC A	77	252	26	58	15	1	8	33	10-0	1	57	.230	.263	.393	67	-13	2-2	.935	-0	100	133	3b72,O4L		-1.3
1998	NY N	7	19	3	5	2	0	0	2	0-0	0	6	.263	.263	.368	66	-1	1-0	1.000	-2	34	198	3b4,1b2/OL		-0.3
1999	StL N	48	157	21	45	6	0	10	37	6-0	0	38	.287	.309	.516	103	0	1-0	.955	3	90		O27(3/0/25),3b10,2b7,1b6	144	0.1
2000	†StL N	134	384	47	94	24	2	15	61	27-1	2	83	.245	.294	.435	80	-13	4-3	.942	-7	84	88	3b86,O31(18/0/16),1b28,2b13		-2.1
2001	†StL N	123	340	47	96	17	0	15	64	18-1	5	67	.282	.326	.465	99	-1	3-1	1.000	-5	80	66	O56(32/0/26),3b33,1b23,2b4		-0.8
2002	Det A	72	252	20	49	14	1	4	20	10-0	1	53	.194	.223	.306	41	-22	0-0	.936	-2	99	60	1b49,3b33,1b23,2b4		-2.4
2003	Det A	11	33	2	5	0	0	0	2	0-0	0	5	.152	.152	.152	-21	-6	0-0	1.000	1	38	113	1b5,O5(3/0/2)		-0.7
Total	11	814	2591	304	620	128	10	99	377	120-6	12	620	.239	.274	.411	75	-109	27-13	.941	-39	91	95	3b498,O200L,1b100,2b24,S19,D12	144	-15.0

PARDO, AL Alberto Judas B9.8.1962 Oviedo, Spain BB/TR/6-2/187* [BalA80 2/52] d7.3

YEAR	TM LG	G	AB	R	H	2B	3B	HR	RBI	BB-IB	HP	SO	AVG	OBP	SLG	AOPS	ABR	SB-CS	FA	FR	RNG	THR	GAMES AT POSITION	DL	BFW
1985	Bal A	34	75	3	10	1	0	0	3	1-0	0	15	.133	.167	.147	-14	-12	0-0	.979	-3	50	43	C29		-1.4
1986	Bal A	16	51	4	7	1	0	0	3	0-0	0	14	.137	.137	.216	-6	-8	0-0	.987	-2	103	94	C14/D		-0.9

YEAR	TM LG	G	AB	R	H	2B	3B	HR	RBI	BB-IB	HP	SO	AVG	OBP	SLG	AOPS	ABR	SB-CS	FA	FR	RNG	THR	GAMES AT POSITION	DL	BFW
1988	Phi N	2	2	0	0	0	0	0	0	0-0	0	2	.000	.000	.000	-98	-1	0-0	1.000	-0	0	0	C2		-0.1
1989	Phi N	1	1	0	0	0	0	0	0	0-0	0	0	.000	.000	.000	-99	0	0-0	1.000	0	0	0	/C		
Total	4	53	129	6	17	2	0	1	4	3-0	0	31	.132	.152	.171	-12	-21	0-0	.982	-5	68	60	C46/D		-2.4

PAREDES, JOHNNY Johnny Alfonso (Isambert) B9.2.1962 Maracaibo, Venez BR/TR/5-11/165* d4.29 [DL 1989 Mon N 178]

1988	Mon N	35	91	6	17	2	0	1	10	9-0	3	17	.187	.282	.242	49	-6	5-2	.976	-1	100	131	2b28/OR		-0.6
1990	Mon N	6	8	2	1	0	0	0	0	1-0	0	0	.125	.222	.125	-0	-1	0-0	.917	-0	98	115	2b4		-0.1
	Det A	3	6	0	2	1	0	0	1	1-1	0	1	.333	.429	.500	160	1	0-0	.889	1	116	192	2b2		0.0
	Mon N	3	6	0	2	1	0	0	1	0-0	0	1	.333	.333	.333	83	0	1-0	.958	-1	91	150	2b7/3SD		-0.1
1991	Det A	16	18	4	6	0	0	0	0	0-0	0	5	.333	.292	.260	58	-6	6-3	.965	-2	100	136	2b41,D2/S3OR	178	-0.8
Total	3	60	123	12	26	3	0	1	11	11-1	3	18	.211	.292	.260										

PARENT, FREDDY Frederick Alfred B11.25.1875 Biddeford ME D11.2.1972 Sanford ME BR/TR/5-7/154 d7.14

1899	StL N	2	8	0	1	0	0	0	1	0	0		.125	.125	.125	-31	-1		.889	-0	93	157	2b2		-0.2
1901	Bos A	138	517	87	158	23	9	4	59	41	9		.306	.367	.408	117	13	16	.918	-2	100	115	S138		1.4
1902	Bos A	138	567	91	156	31	8	3	62	24	4		.275	.309	.374	86	-12	16	.932	5	102	108	S138		-0.7
1903	†Bos A	139	560	83	170	31	17	4	80	13	6		.304	.326	.441	122	13	24	.930	8	103	82	S139		2.6
1904	Bos A	155	591	85	172	22	9	6	77	26	6		.291	.330	.389	120	12	20	.929	-10	98	107	S155		0.9
1905	Bos A	153	602	55	141	16	5	0	33	47	6		.234	.296	.277	81	-12	25	.920	-11	99	109	S153		-2.0
1906	Bos A	149	600	67	141	14	10	5	49	31	4		.235	.277	.297	80	-16	16	.933	-4	99	104	S143,2b6		-1.7
1907	Bos A	114	409	51	113	19	5	1	26	22	5		.276	.321	.355	116	7	12	.978	-1	186	73	O47(26/13/9),S43,3b7,2b5		0.6
1908	Chi A	119	391	28	81	7	5	0	35	50	7		.207	.300	.251	81	-6	9	.930	2	107	100	S118		-0.1
1909	Chi A	136	472	61	123	10	5	0	30	46	3		.261	.335	.303	106	5	32	.929	14	114	115	S98,O38(7/30/1)/2		2.3
1910	Chi A	81	258	23	46	6	1	1	16	29	2		.178	.266	.221	55	-13	14	.970	-3	87	65	O62(1/59/2),2b11,S4/3		-2.0
1911	Chi A	3	9	2	4	1	0	0	3	2	0		.444	.545	.556	214	2	0	1.000	1	123	0	2b3		0.2
Total	12	1327	4984	633	1306	180	74	20	471	333	51		.262	.315	.340	99	-8	184	.927	-7	102	106	S1129,O147(34/102/12),2b28,3b8		1.3

PARENT, MARK Mark Alan B9.16.1961 Ashland OR BR/TR/6-5/225(215-245) [SDN79 4/92] d9.20

1986	SD N	8	14	1	2	0	0	0	0	1-0	0	5	.143	.200	.143	-4	-2	0-0	.889	-2	38	0	C3		-0.4
1987	SD N	12	25	0	2	0	0	0	2	0-0	0	9	.080	.080	.080	-60	-6	0-0	1.000	-0	190	0	C10		-0.6
1988	SD N	41	118	9	23	3	0	6	15	6-0	0	23	.195	.232	.373	73	-5	0-0	.986	6	172	84	C36		0.3
1989	SD N	52	141	12	27	4	0	7	21	8-2	1	34	.191	.229	.369	70	-6	1-0	1.000	6	143	90	C41/1		-0.3
1990	SD N	65	189	13	42	11	0	3	16	16-3	0	29	.222	.283	.328	67	-9	1-0	.992	2	94	90	C60	151	-0.3
1991	Tex A	3	1	0	0	0	0	0	0	0-0	0	1	.000	.000	.000	-99	0	0-0	1.000	0	0	0	C3		0.4
1992	Bal A	17	34	4	8	1	0	2	4	3-0	1	9	.235	.316	.441	107	0	0-0	.988	3	122	93	C16		-0.1
1993	Bal A	22	54	7	14	2	0	4	12	3-0	0	14	.259	.293	.519	110	0	0-0	.989	-3	161	16	C21/D		0.0
1994	Chi N	44	99	8	26	4	0	3	16	13-1	1	24	.263	.348	.394	95	-1	0-1	.976	-1	88	170	C37		-0.2
1995	Pit N	69	233	25	54	9	0	15	33	23-2	0	62	.232	.301	.464	96	-3	0-0	.990	-4	101	151	C10		0.8
	Chi N	12	32	5	8	2	0	3	5	3-0	0	7	.250	.314	.594	133	1	0-0	1.000	3	165	143	C12		0.3
	Year	81	265	30	62	11	0	18	38	26-2	0	69	.234	.302	.479	100	-1	0-0	.992	-1	108	150	C77		
1996	Det A	38	104	13	25	6	0	7	17	3-0	0	27	.240	.259	.500	86	-3	0-0	.987	0	172	67	C18		-0.2
	†Bal A	18	33	4	6	1	0	2	6	2-0	0	10	.182	.229	.394	54	-3	0-0	.992	-4	135	122	C51/1		-2.6
	Year	56	137	17	31	7	0	9	23	5-0	0	37	.226	.252	.474	78	-6	0-0	.996	-5	89	136	C38		
1997	Phi N	39	113	4	17	3	0	0	8	7-0	0	39	.150	.198	.177	-0	-17	0-1	.987	-6	119	86	C34		-1.2
1998	Phi N	34	113	7	25	4	0	1	13	10-0	0	30	.221	.278	.283	50	-8	1-1	.990	-4	119	110	C427,1b2/D	151	-4.
Total	13	474	1303	112	279	50	0	53	168	98-8	2	319	.214	.268	.375	71	-62	3-3	.990	-4	119	110			

PARIS, KELLY Kelly Jay B10.17.1957 Encino CA BR/TR/6-0/180* [StLN75 2/40] d9.1

1982	StL N	12	29	1	3	0	0	0	1	0-0	0	7	.103	.100	.103	-41	-6	0-0	.867	2	125	382	3b5,S4		-0.
1983	Cin N	56	120	13	30	6	0	0	7	15-1	1	22	.250	.336	.300	75	-3	8-2	1.000	-4	116	0	3b16,2b10,S7,1b3		-0.
1985	Bal A	5	9	0	0	0	0	0	0	0-0	0	1	.000	.000	.000	-99	-3	0-0	.857	-1	61	0	2b2,D2		-0.
1986	Bal A	5	10	0	2	0	0	0	0	0-0	0	3	.200	.200	.200	9	-1	0-1	.857	-0	130	240	3b3,D2		-0.
1988	Chi A	14	44	6	11	0	0	3	6	0-0	0	6	.250	.250	.455	93	-1	0-0	1.000	-0	75	136	1b9,3b4/D	45	-0
Total	5	92	212	20	46	6	0	3	14	15-1	1	39	.217	.270	.288	54	-14	8-3	.944	-4	121	85	3b28,1b12,2b12,S11,D5	45	-1.

PARISSE, TONY Louis Peter B6.25.1911 Philadelphia PA D6.2.1956 Philadelphia PA BR/TR/5-10/165 d9.22

1943	Phi A	6	17	0	3	0	0	0	1	2	0	2	.176	.263	.176	30	-1	0-0	1.000	0	81	173	C5		-0.
1944	Phi A	4	4	0	0	0	0	0	0	0	0	1	.000	.000	.000	-99	-1	0-0	.500	-1	0	0	C2		-0.
Total	2	10	21	0	3	0	0	0	1	2	0	3	.143	.217	.143	6	-2	0-0	.960	-0	74	158	C7		-0.

PARKER, ACE Clarence McKay B5.17.1912 Portsmouth VA BR/TR/6-0/180 d4.24 Col Duke

1937	Phi A	38	94	8	11	0	1	2	13	4	0	17	.117	.153	.202	-11	-17	0-0	.905	-3	93	91	S19,2b9,O5(2/3/0)		-1
1938	Phi A	56	113	12	26	5	0	0	12	10	0	16	.230	.293	.274	44	-10	1-2	.972	-3	91	57	S26,2b9,3b9		-1
Total	2	94	207	20	37	5	1	2	25	14	0	33	.179	.231	.242	19	-27	1-2	.934	-4	92	75	S45,2b18,3b9,O5(2/3/0)		-2

PARKER, PAT Clarence Perkins B5.22.1893 Somerville MA D3.21.1967 Claremont NH BR/TR/5-7/160 d8.10 Col Dubuque

1915	StL A	3	6	0	1	0	0	0	0	0	0		.167	.167	.167	-0	-1	0-0	1.000	0	0	133	O2R		-0

PARKER, DAVE David Gene B6.9.1951 Grenada MS BL/TR/6-5/230(220-250) [PitN70 14/332] d7.12 C2

1973	Pit N	54	139	17	40	9	1	4	14	2-1	0	27	.288	.308	.453	110	1	1-1	.964	3	122	130	O39(4/16/19)		0
1974	†Pit N	73	220	27	62	10	3	4	29	10-1	3	53	.282	.322	.409	106	1	3-3	.964	2	104	158	O49(11/14/27),1b6	47	-0
1975	†Pit N	148	558	75	172	35	10	25	101	38-4	5	89	.308	.357	.541	146	31	8-6	.972	5	110	71	O141R		2
1976	Pit N	138	537	82	168	28	10	13	90	30-6	2	80	.313	.349	.475	131	19	19-7	.956	1	104	102	O134R		1
1977	Pit N★	159	637	107	**215**	**44**	8	21	88	58-13	7	107	**.338**	.397	.531	146	39	17-19	.965	23	**118**	**203**	O158R/2	15	**4**
1978	Pit N★	148	581	102	194	32	12	30	117	57-**23**	2	92	**.334**	.394	**.585**	162	**47**	20-7	.960	0	104	108	O158R		2
1979	†Pit N★	158	622	109	193	45	7	25	94	67-14	9	101	.310	.380	.526	138	34	20-4	.960	0	100	130	O130R		2
1980	Pit N★	139	518	71	153	31	1	17	79	25-5	2	69	.295	.327	.458	114	8	10-7	.965	-3	100	130	O60R	15	-0
1981	Pit N★	67	240	29	62	14	3	9	48	9-3	2	25	.258	.287	.454	104	4	4-5	.957	-3	97	47	O63R	66	-0
1982	Pit N	73	244	41	66	19	3	6	29	28-6	0	89	.279	.311	.411	96	-4	12-9	.973	0	111	32	O142R		-1
1983	Pit N	144	552	68	154	29	4	12	69	28-6	0	89	.279	.311	.410	102	1	11-10	.974	-2	104	60	O151R		-1
1984	Cin N	156	607	73	173	28	0	16	94	41-10	1	89	.285	.328	.410	102	1	11-10	.972	6	109	110	O159R		3
1985	Cin N★	160	635	88	198	**42**	4	34	**125**	52-**24**	3	80	.312	.365	.551	146	38	5-13	.970	-9	91	68	O159R		3
1986	Cin N★	**162**	637	89	174	31	3	31	116	56-16	1	126	.273	.330	.477	116	12	1-6	.967	-4	103	134	O142R,1b9		-1
1987	Cin N	153	589	77	149	28	0	26	97	44-13	1	104	.253	.311	.433	92	-8	7-3	.967	-0	88	164	D61,O34L/1	47	-0
1988	†Oak A	101	377	43	97	18	1	12	55	32-2	0	70	.257	.314	.406	104	1	0-1	1.000	0	104	0	D140/OR		0
1989	†Oak A	144	553	56	146	27	0	22	97	38-13	1	91	.264	.308	.432	111	6	0-0	.960	-1	0	168	D153,1b3		0
1990	Mil A☆	157	610	71	176	30	3	21	92	41-11	4	102	.289	.330	.451	119	14	4-7	—	0	0	0	D119		0
1991	Cal A	119	466	45	108	22	1	11	56	29-3	5	91	.232	.279	.358	76	-17	3-2	—	0	0	11	D11		0
	Tor A	13	36	2	12	4	0	0	3	4-0	1	7	.333	.400	.444	128	2	0-1	—	0	0	130	D130		0
	Year	132	502	47	120	26	1	11	59	33-3	3	98	.239	.288	.365	79	-15	3-3	.965	27	105	101	O1867(49/30/1791),D484,1b19/2	190	1-
Total	19	2466	9358	1272	2712	526	75	339	1493	683-170	56	1537	.290	.339	.471	120	229	154-113							

PARKER, DIXIE Douglas Woolley B4.24.1895 Forest Home AL D5.15.1972 Tuscaloosa AL BL/TR/5-11/160 d7.28

1923	Phi N	4	5	0	1	0	0	0	1	0	0	1	.200	.200	.200	5	-1	0-0	.500	-1	47	0	C2		

PARKER, SALTY Francis James B7.8.1912 E.St.Louis IL D7.27.1992 Houston TX BR/TR/6-0/173 d8.13 M2/C16

1936	Det A	11	25	6	7	2	0	0	4	2	0	3	.280	.333	.360	71	-1	0-2	.906	2	111	151	S7,1b2		

PARKER, WES Maurice Wesley B11.13.1939 Evanston IL BB/TL/6-1/180* d4.19 Col Claremont McKenna

1964	LA N	124	214	29	55	7	1	3	10	14-3	1	45	.257	.303	.341	88	-4	5-4	.971	4	116	92	O69(9/15/49),1b31		
1965	†LA N	154	542	80	129	24	7	8	51	75-1	5	95	.238	.334	.352	101	3	13-7	**.997**	4	104	105	1b154/OC		
1966	†LA N	156	475	67	120	15	5	12	51	69-9	5	83	.253	.351	.385	114	11	7-3	.992	2	95	83	1b140,O14(2/7/5)		
1967	LA N	139	413	56	102	16	5	5	31	65-10	2	83	.247	.358	.346	112	9	10-5	**.996**	5	114	94	1b112,O18C		
1968	LA N	135	468	42	112	22	2	3	27	49-6	2	46	.239	.314	.314	96	-1	4-1	**.999**	3	105	96	1b114,O28(22/6/1)	22	
1969	LA N	132	471	76	131	23	4	13	68	56-6	2	46	.278	.353	.427	127	17	4-1	.995	4	100	95	1b128,O2(0/1/1)		
1970	LA N	**161**	614	84	196	**47**	4	10	111	79-18	0	70	.319	.392	.458	133	32	8-2	**.996**	4	109	92	1b161		
1971	LA N	157	533	69	146	24	1	6	62	63-5	1	63	.274	.347	.356	106	6	6-1	.996	5	116	**111**	1b148,O18(1/0/18)		

YEAR	TM LG	G	AB	R	H	2B	3B	HR	RBI	BB-IB	HP	SO	AVG	OBP	SLG	AOPS	ABR	SB-CS	FA	FR	RNG	THR	GAMES AT POSITION	DL	BFW
1972	LA N	130	427	45	119	14	3	4	59	62-5	1	43	.279	.367	.354	109	7	3-5	.997	4	113	108	1b120,O5(0/3/2)		0.1
Total 9		1288	4157	548	1110	194	32	64	470	532-63	24	615	.267	.351	.375	112	80	60-34	.996	32	108	98	1b1108,O155(34/51/76)	22	3.6

PARKER, RICK Richard Alan B3.20.1963 Kansas City MO BR/TR/6-0/185* [PhiN85 16/408] d5.4 Col Texas

YEAR	TM LG	G	AB	R	H	2B	3B	HR	RBI	BB-IB	HP	SO	AVG	OBP	SLG	AOPS	ABR	SB-CS	FA	FR	RNG	THR	GAMES AT POSITION	DL	BFW
1990	SF N	54	107	19	26	5	0	2	14	10-0	1	15	.243	.314	.346	84	-2	6-1	.978	-2	90	63	O35(13/5/23),2b2/3S		-0.4
1991	SF N	13	14	0	1	0	0	0	1	1-0	0	5	.071	.133	.071	-42	-3	6-1	1.000	0	140	0	O4(4/1/0)		-0.1
1993	Hou N	45	45	11	15	3	0	0	4	3-0	0	8	.333	.375	.400	111	1	1-2	1.000	-1	89	0	O16(3/13/1)/2S	38	-0.1
1994	NY N	8	16	1	1	0	0	0	0	2-0	0	2	.063	.063	.063	-68	-4	0-0	1.000	1	139	282	O6(4/1/3)		-0.1
1995	LA N	27	29	3	8	0	0	0	4	2-0	0	4	.276	.323	.276	64	-2	1-1	1.000	1	130	201	O21(19/1/1),3b2,S2	26	-0.3
1996	LA N	16	14	2	4	1	0	0	1	0-0	1	0	.286	.333	.357	87	0	1-0	1.000	-1	30	0	O4(1/3/0)		-0.1
Total 6		163	225	36	55	9	0	2	24	16-0	2	36	.244	.300	.311	68	-10	9-4	.990	-0	102	96	O86(44/24/28),S4,3b3,2b3	64	-1.3

PARKER, BILLY William David B1.14.1947 Hayneville AL D2.9.2003 Sun City West AZ BR/TR/5-8/168* d9.9

YEAR	TM LG	G	AB	R	H	2B	3B	HR	RBI	BB-IB	HP	SO	AVG	OBP	SLG	AOPS	ABR	SB-CS	FA	FR	RNG	THR	GAMES AT POSITION	DL	BFW
1971	Cal A	20	70	4	16	1	0	0	6	2-0	0	20	.229	.250	.300	59	-4	1-1	.958	-4	97	100	2b20		-0.8
1972	Cal A	36	80	11	17	2	0	2	8	9-0	0	17	.213	.286	.313	84	-2	0-2	.951	-0	77	108	3b21,2b9,O5L/S		-0.3
1973	Cal A	38	102	14	23	2	1	0	7	8-1	1	23	.225	.286	.265	61	-5	0-1	.959	-8	71	72	2b32,S3/D		-0.3
Total 3		94	252	29	56	4	2	3	21	19-1	1	60	.222	.276	.290	68	-11	1-4	.963	-12	85	89	2b61,3b21,O5L,S4/D		-1.2
																									-2.3

PARKINSON, FRANK Frank Joseph "Parky" B3.23.1895 Dickson City PA D7.4.1960 Trenton NJ BR/TR/5-11/175 d4.13

YEAR	TM LG	G	AB	R	H	2B	3B	HR	RBI	BB-IB	HP	SO	AVG	OBP	SLG	AOPS	ABR	SB-CS	FA	FR	RNG	THR	GAMES AT POSITION	DL	BFW
1921	Phi N	108	391	36	99	20	2	5	32	13	0	81	.253	.277	.353	61	-22	3-4	.931	9	111	89	S105/3		-0.2
1922	Phi N	141	545	86	150	18	6	15	70	55	0	93	.275	.344	.413	86	-12	3-4	.963	28	117	98	2b139		1.8
1923	Phi N	67	219	21	53	12	0	3	28	13	1	31	.242	.288	.338	58	-13	0-4	.950	2	105	99	2b37,S15,3b11		-1.0
1924	Phi N	62	156	14	33	7	0	1	19	14	1	28	.212	.281	.276	44	-12	3-1	.952	6	109	128	3b28,S21,2b10		-0.3
Total 4		378	1311	157	335	57	8	24	149	95	4	233	.256	.308	.366	69	-59	9-13	.952	44	115	99	2b186,S141,3b40		0.3

PARKS, ART Artie William B11.1.1911 Paris AR D12.6.1989 Little Rock AR BL/TR/5-9/170 d9.25

YEAR	TM LG	G	AB	R	H	2B	3B	HR	RBI	BB-IB	HP	SO	AVG	OBP	SLG	AOPS	ABR	SB-CS	FA	FR	RNG	THR	GAMES AT POSITION	DL	BFW
1937	Bro N	7	16	2	5	2	0	0	0	2	0	2	.313	.389	.438	122	1	0	1.000	1	67	469	O4L		0.1
1939	Bro N	71	239	27	65	13	2	1	19	28	0	14	.272	.348	.356	86	-4	2	.977	-3	97	41	O65(32/0/34)		-1.1
Total 2		78	255	29	70	15	2	1	19	30	0	16	.275	.351	.361	89	-3	2	.978	-3	96	61	O69(36/0/34)		-1.0

PARKS, DEREK Derek Gavin B9.29.1968 Covina CA BR/TR/6-0/205(205-217) [MinA86 1/10] d9.11

YEAR	TM LG	G	AB	R	H	2B	3B	HR	RBI	BB-IB	HP	SO	AVG	OBP	SLG	AOPS	ABR	SB-CS	FA	FR	RNG	THR	GAMES AT POSITION	DL	BFW
1992	Min A	7	6	1	2	0	0	0	0	1-0	1	1	.333	.500	.333	133	0	0-0	1.000	-0	40	100	C7		0.0
1993	Min A	7	20	3	4	0	0	1	1	1-0	0	2	.200	.238	.200	19	-2	0-0	.970	-1	98	0	C7		-0.3
1994	Min A	31	89	6	17	6	0	1	9	4-0	2	20	.191	.242	.292	37	-9	0-1	.993	-4	84	141	C31		-1.0
Total 3		45	115	10	23	6	0	1	10	6-0	3	23	.200	.258	.278	40	-11	0-1	.989	-5	83	113	C45		-1.3

PARKS, BILL William Robert B6.4.1849 Easton PA D10.10.1911 Easton PA BR/TR/5-8/150 d4.26 M1 ▲

YEAR	TM LG	G	AB	R	H	2B	3B	HR	RBI	BB-IB	HP	SO	AVG	OBP	SLG	AOPS	ABR	SB-CS	FA	FR	RNG	THR	GAMES AT POSITION	DL	BFW
1875	Was NA	27	111	13	20	0	0	0	6	1			.180	.188	.180	29	-7	1-1	.836	3	137	0	O17(16/1/0),P14,M		-0.1
	Phi NA	2	6	0	1	0	0	0	0			1	.167	.167	.167	16	-1	0-0	.500	-0	0	0	P2,O2L		0.0
	Year	29	117	13	21	0	0	0	6	1			.179	.186	.179	29	-8	1-1	.833	2	125	0	O19(18/1/0),P16		-0.1
1876	Bos N	1	4	0	0	0	0	0	0				.000	.000	.000	-98	-1		.750	-0	0	0	/OL		-0.1

PARRILLA, SAM Samuel (Monge) B6.12.1943 Santurce, PR D2.9.1994 Brooklyn NY BR/TR/5-11/185 d4.11

YEAR	TM LG	G	AB	R	H	2B	3B	HR	RBI	BB-IB	HP	SO	AVG	OBP	SLG	AOPS	ABR	SB-CS	FA	FR	RNG	THR	GAMES AT POSITION	DL	BFW
1970	Phi N	11	16	0	2	1	0	0	0	1-0	0	4	.125	.176	.188	-2	-2	0-0	1.000	0	125	0	O3L		-0.2

PARRISH, LANCE Lance Michael B6.15.1956 Clairton PA BR/TR/6-3/220(195-224) [DetA74 1/16] d9.5 C6

YEAR	TM LG	G	AB	R	H	2B	3B	HR	RBI	BB-IB	HP	SO	AVG	OBP	SLG	AOPS	ABR	SB-CS	FA	FR	RNG	THR	GAMES AT POSITION	DL	BFW
1977	Det A	12	46	10	9	2	0	3	7	5-0	0	12	.196	.275	.435	85	-1	0-0	1.000	4	388	101	C12		0.3
1978	Det A	85	288	37	63	11	3	14	41	11-0	3	71	.219	.254	.424	85	-8	0-0	.987	7	161	81	C79		0.3
1979	Det A	143	493	65	136	26	3	19	65	49-2	2	105	.276	.343	.456	110	7	6-7	.989	7	121	121	C142		1.8
1980	Det A★	144	553	79	158	34	6	24	82	31-3	3	109	.286	.325	.499	120	13	6-4	.990	5	128	95	C121,D16,1b5,O5(1/0/4)		2.1
1981	Det A	96	348	39	85	18	2	10	46	34-6	0	52	.244	.311	.394	98	-1	2-3	.993	4	124	104	C90,D5		0.6
1982	Det A	133	486	75	138	19	2	32	87	40-5	1	99	.284	.338	.529	133	20	3-4	.989	17	142	107	C132/OL		4.1
1983	Det A★	155	605	80	163	42	3	27	114	44-7	1	106	.269	.314	.483	120	15	1-3	.995	11	150	131	C131,D27		2.9
1984	†Det A★	147	578	75	137	16	2	33	98	41-6	2	120	.237	.287	.443	100	-3	2-3	.991	16	156	99	C127,D22		1.6
1985	Det A	140	549	64	150	27	1	28	98	41-5	2	90	.273	.323	.479	117	12	2-6	.993	2	128	99	C120,D22		1.6
1986	Det A★	91	327	53	84	6	1	22	62	38-3	5	83	.257	.340	.483	122	9	0-0	.989	11	131	115	C85,D6		2.3
1987	Phi N★	130	466	42	114	21	0	17	67	47-2	1	104	.245	.313	.399	85	-11	0-1	.989	-2	85	110	C127	60	-0.8
1988	Phi N★	123	424	44	91	17	2	15	60	47-7	2	93	.215	.293	.370	88	-7	0-1	.989	-2	85	127	C127		-0.8
1989	Cal A	124	433	48	103	12	1	17	50	42-6	2	104	.238	.306	.388	97	-3	1-1	.988	0	83	119	C117/1	15	0.0
1990	Cal A★	133	470	54	126	14	0	24	70	46-4	5	107	.268	.338	.451	121	12	2-2	.993	19	136	127	C131,1b4/D		3.8
1991	Cal A	119	402	38	87	12	0	19	51	35-2	5	117	.216	.285	.388	85	-10	0-1	.997	12	125	115	C111,1b3,D5	15	0.4
1992	Cal A	24	83	7	19	2	0	4	11	5-1	2	21	.229	.270	.398	85	-2	0-0	.975	-4	66	141	C22,D2	38	-0.5
	Sea A	69	192	19	45	11	1	8	21	19-2	1	48	.234	.304	.427	102	0	1-1	.995	-1	55	110	C34,1b16,D14		-0.1
	Year	93	275	26	64	13	1	12	32	24-3	1	70	.233	.294	.407	97	-2	1-1	.995	-5	60	134	C56,D16,1b16		-0.6
1993	Cle A	10	20	2	4	1	0	1	2	4-0	1	5	.200	.333	.400	96	0	1-0	.950	1	38	222	C10		0.2
1994	Pit N	40	126	10	34	5	0	3	16	18-1	1	28	.270	.363	.381	93	-1	1-1	.988	1	118	92	C38/1		0.2
1995	Tor A	70	178	15	36	9	0	4	15	15-0	1	28	.202	.265	.320	52	-13	2-2	1.000	10	93	169	C67/D		0.1
Total 19		1988	7067	856	1782	305	27	324	1070	612-62	37	1527	.252	.313	.440	105	28	28-37	.991	118	125	110	C1818,D123,1b30,O6(2/0/4)	128	21.7

PARRISH, LARRY Larry Alton B11.10.1953 Winter Haven FL BR/TR/6-3/215(190-215) d9.6 M2/C2 Col Seminole (FL) CC OF(3/0/405)

YEAR	TM LG	G	AB	R	H	2B	3B	HR	RBI	BB-IB	HP	SO	AVG	OBP	SLG	AOPS	ABR	SB-CS	FA	FR	RNG	THR	GAMES AT POSITION	DL	BFW
1974	Mon N	25	69	9	14	5	0	0	4	6-2	2	19	.203	.286	.275	54	-4	0-0	.986	5	125	74	3b24		0.1
1975	Mon N	145	532	50	146	32	5	10	65	28-5	4	74	.274	.314	.410	95	-5	4-5	.919	-8	98	126	3b143/2S		-1.5
1976	Mon N	154	543	65	126	28	5	11	61	41-2	4	91	.232	.285	.363	80	-15	2-4	.945	7	105	116	3b153		-1.2
1977	Mon N	123	402	50	99	19	2	11	46	37-9	4	71	.246	.314	.386	89	-7	2-4	.936	-5	103	63	3b115		-1.5
1978	Mon N	144	520	68	144	39	4	15	70	32-9	2	103	.277	.321	.454	115	9	2-3	.947	-12	92	86	3b139		-0.6
1979	Mon N★	153	544	83	167	39	4	30	82	41-11	2	101	.307	.357	.551	144	31	5-1	.947	-16	89	98	3b153		1.4
1980	Mon N	126	452	55	115	27	3	15	72	36-6	4	80	.254	.310	.427	103	1	2-6	.949	-6	92	80	3b124	28	-0.8
1981	†Mon N	97	349	41	85	19	3	8	44	28-2	0	73	.244	.297	.384	90	-5	0-0	.935	-17	75	51	3b95		-2.6
1982	Tex A	128	440	59	116	15	0	17	62	30-0	4	84	.264	.314	.414	103	1	5-2	.962	-9	78	142	O124R,3b3,D2		-1.4
1983	Tex A	145	555	76	151	24	4	26	88	46-8	3	91	.272	.326	.474	104	14	0-0	.982	-0	90	156	O81(2/0/80),D63,3b12		0.5
1984	Tex A	94	346	44	86	11	1	22	51	33-2	1	77	.249	.314	.434	101	-1	0-2	.991	-4	84	90	O69R,D22,3b2	57	-1.0
1985	Tex A	129	464	67	128	22	1	28	94	52-7	2	114	.276	.347	.509	127	17	3-1	.935	-6	69	39	D98,3b30		0.8
1986	Tex A★	152	557	79	149	22	1	32	100	49-7	5	154	.268	.328	.483	111	7	3-1	.918	-7	57	119	D122,3b28/OL	29	-0.3
1988	Tex A	68	248	22	47	9	1	7	26	20-2	2	79	.190	.253	.319	58	-14	0-0	—	0			D67		-1.7
	†Bos A	52	158	10	41	5	0	7	26	8-0	1	28	.259	.298	.424	94	-2	0-1	.988	3	129	86	1b36,D14		-0.2
	Year	120	406	32	88	14	1	14	52	28-2	3	111	.217	.270	.360	73	-16	0-1	.988	3	129	86	D81,1b36		-1.9
Total 15		1891	6792	850	1789	360	33	256	992	529-79	42	1359	.263	.318	.439	106	40	30-36	.941	-88	93	91	3b1021,O407R,D401,1b36/S2	114	-10.7

PARROTT, TOM Thomas William "Tacky Tom" B4.10.1868 Portland OR D1.1.1932 Dundee OR BR/TR/5-10.5/170 d6.18 b-Jiggs OF(15/88/28) ▲

YEAR	TM LG	G	AB	R	H	2B	3B	HR	RBI	BB-IB	HP	SO	AVG	OBP	SLG	AOPS	ABR	SB-CS	FA	FR	RNG	THR	GAMES AT POSITION	DL	BFW
1893	Chi N	7	27	4	7	1	0	0	3	1	0	2	.259	.286	.296	56	-2	0	.800	-1	17	0	P4,3b2/2		-0.1
	Cin N	24	68	5	13	1	1		9	1	0	11	.191	.203	.279	27	-8	0	.915	1	117	90	P22/OL		-0.1
	Year	31	95	9	20	2	1	1	12	2	0	11	.211	.227	.284	35	-10	0	.906	0	102	77	P26,3b2/2OL		0.0
1894	Cin N	68	229	51	74	12	6	4	40	17	1	10	.323	.372	.480	101	-1	4	.929	2	113	92	P41,O13(9/2/2),1b12/S32		0.0
1895	Cin N	64	201	35	69	13	7	6	41	11	0	9	.343	.377	.522	126	6	10	.922	1	107	100	P41,1b14,O9(1/8/0)		0.1
1896	StL N	118	474	62	138	13	12	7	70	11	1	24	.291	.307	.414	93	-9	12	.951	7	99	156	O108(4/78/26),P7,1b6		-0.7
Total 4		281	999	157	301	40	26	15	163	41	1	53	.301	.329	.438	96	-10	26	.940	11	109	147	O131C,P115,1b32,3b3,2b2/S		-0.7

PARROTT, JIGGS Walter Edward B7.14.1871 Portland OR D4.14.1898 Phoenix AZ 5-11/160 d7.11 b-Tom

YEAR	TM LG	G	AB	R	H	2B	3B	HR	RBI	BB-IB	HP	SO	AVG	OBP	SLG	AOPS	ABR	SB-CS	FA	FR	RNG	THR	GAMES AT POSITION	DL	BFW
1892	Chi N	78	333	38	67	8	2	2	28	8	1	30	.201	.222	.273	49	-23	7	.891	-1	96	63	3b78		-2.1
1893	Chi N	110	455	54	111	10	9	1	65	13	1	25	.244	.267	.312	54	-33	25	.904	10	108	109	3b99,2b7,O4R		-1.8
1894	Chi N	126	525	82	130	17	9	3	65	15	3	35	.248	.291	.331	43	-53	30	.932	-3	100	91	2b125/3		-3.9
1895	Chi N	3	4	0	1	0	0	0	0	0	0	0	.250	.250	.250	27	-0	0	—	-1	0	0	/OLS1		-0.1
Total 4		317	1317	174	309	35	23	6	152	37	5	90	.235	.258	.310	48	-109	62	.899	6	103	89	3b178,2b132,O5(1/0/4)/1S		-7.9

YEAR	TM LG	G	AB	R	H	2B	3B	HR	RBI	BB-IB	HP	SO	AVG	OBP	SLG	AOPS	ABR	SB-CS	FA	FR	RNG	THR	GAMES AT POSITION	DL	BFW

PARSONS, CASEY Casey Robert B4.14.1954 Wenatchee WA BL/TR/6-1/180* d5.31 Col Gonzaga

1981	Sea A	36	22	6	5	1	0	1	5	1-0	2	4	.227	.308	.409	104		0-0	1.000	2	134	387	O24(3/2/19)/1		0.2
1983	Chi A	8	5	1	1	0	0	0	0	2-1	0		.200	.429	.200	76		0-0	1.000	0	194		O3(0/1/2),D2		0.0
1984	Chi A	1	1	0	0	0	0	0	0	0-0	0	1	.000	.000	.000	-95		0-0		0			/H		0.0
1987	Cle A	18	25	2	4	0	0	1	5	0-0	0	5	.160	.160	.280	13	-3	0-0	1.000	0	189		O2(0/1/1)/1D		-0.3
Total 4		63	53	9	10	1	0	2	10	3-1	2	11	.189	.254	.321	57	-3	0-0	1.000	3	141	341	O29(3/4/22),D7,1b2		-0.1

PARSONS, DIXIE Edward Dixon B5.12.1916 Talladega AL D10.31.1991 Longview TX BR/TR/6-2/180 d8.16

1939	Det A	5	1	0	0	0	0	0	0	1	0	1	.000	.500	.000	36	0		1.000	0	0	0	C4		-0.5
1942	Det A	63	188	8	37	4	0	2	11	13	0	22	.197	.249	.250	37	-16	1-0	.981	8	106	112	C62		-0.8
1943	Det A	40	106	2	15	3	0	0	4	6	0	16	.142	.188	.170	4	-13	1-0	.975	4	99	154	C40		-1.3
Total 3		108	295	10	52	7	0	2	15	20	0	39	.176	.229	.220	26	-29	1-0	.979	11	103	127	C106		

PARTEE, ROY Roy Robert B9.7.1917 Los Angeles CA D12.26.2000 Eureka CA BR/TR/5-10/180 d4.23 Mil 1945

1943	Bos A	96	299	30	84	14	2	0	31	39	2	33	.281	.368	.341	106	4	0-0	.983	-5	95	100	C91		0.5
1944	Bos A	89	280	18	68	12	0	2	41	37	1	29	.243	.333	.307	85	-4	0-1	.989	-3	95	93	C85		-0.3
1946	†Bos A	40	111	13	35	5	2	0	9	13	0	14	.315	.387	.396	113	2	0-0	.974	-4	126	71	C38		0.0
1947	Bos A	60	169	14	39	2	0	0	16	18	0	23	.231	.305	.243	50	-11	0-0	.975	-0	90	62	C54		-0.9
1948	StL A	82	231	14	47	8	1	0	17	25	1	21	.203	.284	.247	41	-20	2-2	.982	-4	67	82	C76		-2.0
Total 5		367	1090	89	273	41	5	2	114	132	4	120	.250	.334	.303	78	-29	2-3	.982	-17	91	82	C344		-2.7

PARTENHEIMER, STEVE Harold Philip B8.30.1891 Greenfield MA D6.16.1971 Mansfield OH BR/TR/5-8.5/145 d6.28 s-Stan Col Amherst

| 1913 | Det A | 1 | 2 | 0 | 0 | 0 | 0 | 0 | 0 | 0 | 1 | 0 | .000 | .333 | .000 | -1 | 0 | | .750 | -0 | 156 | 0 | /3 | | 0.0 |

PARTRIDGE, JAY James Bugg B11.15.1902 Mountville GA D1.14.1974 Nashville TN BL/TR/5-11/160 d4.12 Col Oglethorpe

1927	Bro N	146	572	72	149	17	6	7	40	20	3	36	.260	.289	.348	70	-27	9	.938	-13	93	80	2b140		-3.6
1928	Bro N	37	73	18	18	0	1	0	12	13	1	6	.247	.368	.274	71	-3	2	.908	-4	86	76	2b18,3b2		-0.6
Total 2		183	645	90	167	17	7	7	52	33	4	42	.259	.299	.340	70	-30	11	.935	-17	92	80	2b158,3b2		-4.2

PASCHAL, BEN Benjamin Edwin B10.13.1895 Enterprise AL D11.10.1974 Charlotte NC BR/TR/5-11/185 d8.16

1915	Cle A	9	9	0	1	0	0	0	0	0	0	3	.111	.111	.111	-33	-2		—	0			/H		-0.2
1920	Bos A	9	28	5	10	0	0	0	5	5	0	2	.357	.455	.357	122	1	1-0	1.000	0	94	123	O7R		0.1
1924	NY A	4	12	2	3	1	0	0	3	1	0	0	.250	.308	.333	65	-1	0-0	1.000	0	66	470	O4C		0.0
1925	NY A	89	247	49	89	16	5	12	56	22	2	29	.360	.417	.611	161	22	14-9	.953	-1	98	100	O74(12/17/47)		0.2
1926	†NY A	96	258	46	74	12	3	7	32	26	1	35	.287	.354	.438	108	2	7-6	.935	1	101	147	O27(11/4/12)		0.2
1927	NY A	50	82	16	26	9	2	2	16	4	0	10	.317	.349	.549	134	4	1-0	1.000	0	103	84	O25(16/1/8)		-0.8
1928	†NY A	65	79	12	25	6	1	1	15	8	1	11	.316	.379	.456	122	3	1-0	.951	1	113	134	O20(12/4/4)		1.1
1929	NY A	42	72	13	15	3	0	2	9	8	1	9	.208	.269	.333	58	-5	1-2	.953	3	102	121	O223(67/44/114)		
Total 8		364	787	143	243	47	11	24	138	72	3	93	.309	.369	.488	123	24	24-19	.953	3	102	121	O223(67/44/114)		

PASCUCCI, VAL Valentino Martin B11.17.1978 Bellflower CA BR/TR/6-6/235 [MonN99 15/450] d4.26 Col Oklahoma

| 2004 | Mon N | 32 | 62 | 6 | 11 | 1 | 0 | 2 | 6 | 10-1 | 1 | 22 | .177 | .297 | .290 | 52 | -4 | 1-0 | 1.000 | -1 | 111 | 0 | O17(4/0/13),1b5 | | |

PASEK, JOHNNY John Paul B6.25.1905 Niagara Falls NY D3.13.1976 Niagara Falls NY BR/TR/5-10/175 d7.28

1933	Det A	28	61	6	15	4	0	0	4	7	0	7	.246	.324	.311	68	-3	2-0	.989	-1	58	129	C28		
1934	Chi A	4	9	1	3	0	0	0	1	1	0	1	.333	.400	.333	88	0	0-0	1.000	-0	61	144	C4		
Total 2		32	70	7	18	4	0	0	4	8	0	8	.257	.333	.314	70	-3	2-0	.990	-2	58	131	C32		

PASKERT, DODE George Henry B8.28.1881 Cleveland OH D2.12.1959 Cleveland OH BR/TR/5-11/165 d9.21 OF(146/1461/35)

1907	Cin N	16	50	10	14	4	0	1	8	2	2		.280	.333	.420	130	2	2	.973	4	149	0	O16C		0
1908	Cin N	118	395	40	96	14	4	1	36	27	4		.243	.298	.306	96	-2	25	.953	5	103	84	O116(77/34/5)		-0.
1909	Cin N	104	322	49	81	7	4	0	33	34	2		.252	.327	.298	95	-1	23	.968	9	98	115	O82(36/46/1),1b6		2.
1910	Cin N	144	506	63	152	21	5	2	47	70	3	60	.300	.389	.374	128	21	51	.957	9	110	88	O139(6/126/8),1b2		-1.
1911	Phi N	153	560	96	153	18	5	4	47	70	7	67	.273	.358	.345	96	-1	28	.967	-0	103	89	O141C,2b2/3		1.
1912	Phi N	145	540	102	170	37	9	4	42	91	3	69	.262	.358	.374	105	5	12-17	.972	11	114	111	O120(1/119/0)		0.
1913	Phi N	124	454	83	119	21	9	4	29	65	3	68	.264	.349	.366	106	5	23	.958	8	112	133	O128C,S4		0.
1914	Phi N	132	451	59	119	25	6	3	44	56	3	68	.264	.349	.348	106	5	9-6	.970	-3	91	95	O92(19/74/1),1b5		-0.
1915	†Phi N	109	328	51	80	17	4	3	39	35	1	38	.244	.319	.348	100	1	22-21	.983	-5	96	78	O146(2/145/0)/S		0.
1916	Phi N	149	555	82	155	30	7	8	46	54	3	76	.279	.346	.402	125	18	22-21	.984	-11	83	98	O138C		-1.
1917	Phi N	141	546	78	137	27	11	4	43	62	3	63	.251	.331	.363	108	7	19	.980	-8	92	74	O121C,3b6		-0.
1918	†Phi N	127	461	69	132	24	3	3	59	53	2	49	.286	.362	.371	121	14	20	.969	-5	82	126	O80(3/76/3)		-0.
1919	Chi N	88	270	21	53	11	3	2	29	28	1	33	.196	.274	.281	67	-10	7	.956	-2	92	122	O137(0/136/1)		-2.
1920	Chi N	139	487	57	136	22	10	5	71	64	3	58	.279	.366	.396	117	13	16-14	.984	1	112	61	O24(0/15/9)		-1.
1921	Cin N	27	92	8	16	1	0	0	4	4	1	8	.174	.208	.207	11	-12	0-2	.984	1	100	100			-3.
Total 15		1716	6017	868	1613	279	77	42	577	715	41	659	.268	.350	.361	108	81	293-60	.969	2	100	100	O1633C,1b13,3b7,S5,2b2		

PASLEY, KEVIN Kevin Patrick B7.22.1953 Bronx NY BR/TR/6-0/185* [LAN71 29/657] d10.2

1974	LA N	1	0	0	0	0	0	0	0	0-0			—					0	0-0	1.000	0	0	0	/C		0
1976	LA N	23	52	4	12	2	0	0	3	3-1	0	7	.231	.273	.269	55	-3	0-0	.971	1	81	112	C23		-0
1977	LA N	2	3	0	1	0	0	0	0	0-0	0		.333	.333	.333	79	0	0-0	1.000	-1	30	0	C2		-0
	Sea A	4	13	1	5	0	0	0	2	1-0	0	2	.385	.429	.385	124	0	0-0	1.000	-1	108	0	C25		-0
1978	Sea A	25	54	3	13	5	0	1	9	2-0	0	4	.241	.268	.389	83	-1	0-0	.986	-2	107	50	C55		-0
Total 4		55	122	8	31	7	0	1	9	6-1	0	13	.254	.289	.336	76	-4	0-0	.986	-2	107	50	C55		

PASQUA, DAN Daniel Anthony B10.17.1961 Yonkers NY BL/TL/6-0/203(203-218) [NYA82 3/76] d5.30 Col William Paterson

1985	NY A	60	148	17	31	3	1	9	25	16-4	1	38	.209	.294	.426	95	-2	0-0	1.000	4	129	114	O37(31/0/6),D14		
1986	NY A	102	280	44	82	17	0	16	45	47-3	3	78	.293	.399	.525	150	22	2-0	.987	-1	102	84	O81(71/0/12),1b5,D3		
1987	NY A	113	318	42	74	7	1	17	42	40-3	1	99	.233	.319	.421	95	-3	0-2	.985	0		46	O74(61/0/14),D20,1b12		
1988	Chi A	129	422	48	96	16	2	20	50	46-5	3	100	.227	.307	.417	101	4	1-0	.993	3	110	72	O66(52/0/20),D5	80	
1989	Chi A	73	246	26	61	9	1	11	47	25-1	1	58	.248	.315	.427	111	3	1-1	.962	3	108	228	D57,O43(21/0/22)		
1990	Chi A	112	325	43	89	27	3	13	58	37-7	2	86	.274	.347	.495	137	16	0-2	.991	-3	99	92	1b83,O59(9/0/51),D8		
1991	Chi A	134	417	71	108	22	5	18	66	62-4	3	86	.259	.358	.465	129	17	0-1	.963	-2	100	79	O81R,1b5/D	36	
1992	Chi A	93	265	26	56	16	1	6	33	36-1	1	57	.211	.305	.347	84	-5	2-2	.984	-2	89	137	O37(11/0/26),1b32,D6		
1993	†Chi A	78	176	22	36	10	1	5	26	26-1	0	51	.205	.302	.358	79	-5	0-0	.867	-0	148	0	O5(1/0/5),1b3	102	
1994	Chi A	11	23	2	5	2	0	2	4	0-0	1	12	.217	.217	.565	94	0	7-10	.984	8	105	92	O595(322/0/289),1b147,D116	218	
Total 10		905	2620	341	638	129	15	117	390	335-29	15	642	.244	.330	.438	112	43	7-10	.984	8	105	92	O595(322/0/289),1b147,D116		

PASQUELLA, MIKE Michael John "Toney" (b Michael John Pasquariello) B11.7.1898 Philadelphia PA D4.5.1965 Bridgeport CT BR/TR/5-11/167 d7.9 Col Villanova

1919	Phi N	1	1	1	1	0	0	0	0	0-0	0	0	1.000	1.000	1.000	469	0	0-0	—	0	0	0	/1		
	StL N	1	1	0	0	0	0	0	0	0-0	0	0	.000	.000	.000	-99	0	0-0	—	0	0	0	/H		
	Year	2	2	1	1	0	0	0	0	0-0	0	0	.500	.500	.500	200	0	0-0	—	0	0	0	/1		

PASTORNICKY, CLIFF Clifford Scott B11.18.1958 Seattle WA BR/TR/5-10/170 [KCA80 8/198] d6.14 Col Brigham Young

| 1983 | KC A | 10 | 32 | 4 | 4 | 0 | 0 | 2 | 5 | 0-0 | 0 | 3 | .125 | .125 | .313 | 16 | -4 | 0-0 | .929 | -0 | 111 | 0 | 3b10 | | |

PATE, BOB Robert Wayne B12.3.1953 Los Angeles CA BR/TR/6-3.5/200* [MonN76 4/81] d6.2 Col Arizona St.

1980	Mon N	23	39	3	10	2	0	0	5	3-0	0	6	.256	.295	.308	71	-1	0-1	1.000	-1	86	0	O18(2/0/16)		
1981	Mon N	8	6	0	2	0	0	0	0	1-0	0	0	.333	.429	.333	115	0	0-0	1.000	-0	97	0	O5(1/2/2)		
Total 2		31	45	3	12	2	0	0	5	4-0	0	6	.267	.314	.311	77	-1	0-1	1.000	-1	87	0	O23(3/2/18)		

PATEK, FREDDIE Frederick Joseph "The Flea" B10.9.1944 Seguin TX BR/TR/5-5/148(140-165) [PitN65 12/434] d6.3

1968	Pit N	61	208	31	53	4	2		18	12-0	2	37	.255	.298	.322	89	-3	18-7	.976	-0	104	83	S52,O5(2/0/3)/3	27	
1969	Pit N	147	460	48	110	9	5		32	53-15	1	86	.239	.318	.296	75	-15	15-8	.954	-10	90	96	S146		
1970	†Pit N	84	237	42	58	10	5	1	19	29-1	0	46	.245	.322	.342	80	-7	8-2	.968	22	105	126	S147		
1971	KC A	147	591	86	158	21	11	6	36	44-3	3	64	.267	.323	.371	97	-4	49-14	.971	38	120	140	S136	10	
1972	KC A*	136	518	59	110	25	4	0	32	47-4	1	63	.212	.280	.276	67	-21	33-7	.966	40	119	125	S135	15	
1973	KC A	135	501	82	117	19	5	5	45	54-0	3	63	.234	.311	.321	73	-17	36-14	.967	8	106	119	S149		
1974	KC A	149	537	72	121	18	6	3	38	77-1	0	69	.225	.324	.298	76	-14	33-15	.967	8	106	119	S149		

The Batter Register

YEAR	TM LG	G	AB	R	H	2B	3B	HR	RBI	BB-IB	HP	SO	AVG	OBP	SLG	AOPS	ABR	SB-CS	FA	FR	RNG	THR	GAMES AT POSITION	DL	BFW
1975	KC A	136	483	58	110	14	5	5	45	42-0	2	65	.228	.291	.308	68	-21	32-7	.959	4	102	101	S136/D		0.3
1976	†KC A★	144	432	58	104	19	3	1	43	50-5	2	63	.241	.318	.306	84	-7	51-15	.962	-7	98	111	S143/D		0.8
1977	KC A	154	497	72	130	26	6	5	60	41-2	5	84	.262	.320	.368	87	-8	**53-13**	.958	-17	92	84	S154		0.8
1978	†KC A★	138	440	54	109	23	1	2	46	42-1	1	56	.248	.312	.318	76	-13	38-11	.949	-21	87	113	S137		-0.3
1979	KC A	106	306	30	77	17	0	1	37	16-0	1	42	.252	.293	.317	64	-15	11-12	.955	-24	85	88	S104		-1.6
1980	Cal A	86	273	30	72	10	5	5	34	15-1	1	26	.264	.302	.392	91	-5	7-6	.953	-18	84	78	S81	15	-3.2
1981	Cal A	27	47	3	11	1	1	0	5	1-0	1	6	.234	.250	.298	57	-3	1-0	.983	-2	84	96	2b16,3b7,S3		-1.5
Total	14	1650	5530	736	1340	216	55	41	490	523-33	31	787	.242	.309	.324	78	-153	385-131	.962	24	100	108	S1588,2b16,3b8,O5(2/0/3),D2	67	8.9

PATEK, BOB   Robert Lee B10.27.1917 Ft.Smith AR D10.6.1999 Ft.Smith AR BR/TR/6-2/190 d9.20 Mil 1943-45

YEAR	TM LG	G	AB	R	H	2B	3B	HR	RBI	BB-IB	HP	SO	AVG	OBP	SLG	AOPS	ABR	SB-CS	FA	FR	RNG	THR	GAMES AT POSITION	DL	BFW
1941	Det A	5	7	2	2	0	0	0	0	0	0	1	.286	.286	.286	47	-1	0-0	.750	-0	90	0	O3L		-0.1
1942	Det A	4	8	1	2	1	0	1	3	1	0	0	.250	.333	.750	185	1	0-0	1.000	0	116	0	O3R		0.1
Total	2	9	15	3	4	1	0	1	3	1	0	1	.267	.313	.533	118	0	0-0	.889	-0	105	0	O6(3/0/3)		0.0

PATTEE, HARRY   Harry Ernest B1.17.1882 Charlestown MA D7.17.1971 Lynchburg VA BL/TR/5-8/149 d4.14 Col Brown

YEAR	TM LG	G	AB	R	H	2B	3B	HR	RBI	BB-IB	HP	SO	AVG	OBP	SLG	AOPS	ABR	SB-CS	FA	FR	RNG	THR	GAMES AT POSITION	DL	BFW
1908	Bro N	80	264	19	57	5	2	0	9	25	1		.216	.286	.250	74	-7	24	.964	11	111	70	2b74		0.5

PATTERSON, COREY   Donald Corey B8.13.1979 Atlanta GA BL/TR/5-10/180* [ChiN98 1/3] d9.18

YEAR	TM LG	G	AB	R	H	2B	3B	HR	RBI	BB-IB	HP	SO	AVG	OBP	SLG	AOPS	ABR	SB-CS	FA	FR	RNG	THR	GAMES AT POSITION	DL	BFW
2000	Chi N	11	42	9	7	1	0	2		3-0	1	14	.167	.239	.333	42	-4	1-1	.963	-0	109	0	O11C		-0.4
2001	Chi N	59	131	26	29	8	0	4	14	6-0	3	33	.221	.266	.336	58	-9	4-0	.976	1	117	0	O54(13/45/1)		-0.7
2002	Chi N	153	592	71	150	30	5	14	54	19-1	8	142	.253	.284	.392	79	-23	18-3	.990	-4	99	71	O147C		-2.3
2003	Chi N	83	329	49	98	17	7	13	55	15-2	1	77	.298	.329	.511	112	4	16-5	.975	-6	87	74	O82C	84	0.1
2004	Chi N	157	631	91	168	33	6	24	72	45-7	5	168	.266	.320	.452	94	-8	32-9	**.997**	-4	93	110	O157C		-0.6
2005	Chi N	126	451	47	97	15	3	13	34	23-3	1	118	.215	.254	.348	54	-32	15-5	.980	-3	95	110	O122C		-3.3
Total	6	589	2176	293	549	99	21	70	231	111-13	19	552	.252	.293	.414	81	-72	86-23	.986	-18	96	86	O573(13/564/1)	84	-7.2

PATTERSON, GEORGE   George d4.24

YEAR	TM LG	G	AB	R	H	2B	3B	HR	RBI	BB-IB	HP	SO	AVG	OBP	SLG	AOPS	ABR	SB-CS	FA	FR	RNG	THR	GAMES AT POSITION	DL	BFW
1884	Phi U	2	7	0	1	0	0	0		0			.143	.143	.143	-14	-1		.500	-0	221	0	O2(1/0/1)		-0.1

PATTERSON, HAM   Hamilton B10.13.1877 Belleville IL D11.25.1945 E.St.Louis IL BR/TR/6-2/185 d5.18 b-Pat

YEAR	TM LG	G	AB	R	H	2B	3B	HR	RBI	BB-IB	HP	SO	AVG	OBP	SLG	AOPS	ABR	SB-CS	FA	FR	RNG	THR	GAMES AT POSITION	DL	BFW
1909	StL A	17	49	2	10	1	0	0	5	0	0		.204	.204	.224	38	-4	1	1.000	-1	54	66	1b6,O6L		-0.6
	Chi A	1	3	2	0	0	0	0	0	1	0		.000	.250	.000	-21	-4	1	1.000	1	416	0	/1		0.0
	Year	18	52	4	10	1	0	0	5	1	0		.192	.208	.212	35	-4	1	1.000	0	96	58	1b7,O6L		-0.6

PATTERSON, HANK   Henry Joseph Colquit B7.17.1907 San Francisco CA D9.30.1970 Los Angeles CA BR/TR/5-11.5/170 d9.5 C1

YEAR	TM LG	G	AB	R	H	2B	3B	HR	RBI	BB-IB	HP	SO	AVG	OBP	SLG	AOPS	ABR	SB-CS	FA	FR	RNG	THR	GAMES AT POSITION	DL	BFW
1932	Bos A	1	1	0	0	0	0	0	0	0-0	0	0	.000	.000	.000	-99	0						/C		0.0

PATTERSON, JARROD   Jarrod Lane B9.7.1973 Montgomery AL BL/TR/6-1/195* [NYN93 20/556] d6.16 Col Jefferson Davis (AL) CC

YEAR	TM LG	G	AB	R	H	2B	3B	HR	RBI	BB-IB	HP	SO	AVG	OBP	SLG	AOPS	ABR	SB-CS	FA	FR	RNG	THR	GAMES AT POSITION	DL	BFW
2001	Det A	13	41	6	11	1	1	2	4	0-0	2	14	.268	.302	.488	106	-3	0-1	.923	-4	69	0	3b13		-0.4
2003	KC A	13	22	3	4	0	0	0		3-1	0	6	.182	.280	.182	24	-2	0-0	.000	-1	0	0	3b4,1b2,D4		-0.3
Total	2	26	63	9	15	1	1	2	4	3-1	2	10	.238	.294	.381	75	-2	0-1	.889	-5	63	0	3b17,D4,1b2		-0.7

PATTERSON, JOHN   John Allen B2.11.1967 Key West FL BB/TR/5-9/160* [SFN88 23/594] d4.6 Col Grand Canyon

YEAR	TM LG	G	AB	R	H	2B	3B	HR	RBI	BB-IB	HP	SO	AVG	OBP	SLG	AOPS	ABR	SB-CS	FA	FR	RNG	THR	GAMES AT POSITION	DL	BFW
1992	SF N	32	103	10	19	1	1	0	4	5-0	1	24	.184	.229	.214	27	-1	5-1	.960	2	98	144	2b22,O5C	16	-0.8
1993	SF N	16	16	1	3	0	0	1	2	0-0	0	5	.188	.188	.375	48	-1	0-1	—	0			/H	149	-0.3
1994	SF N	85	240	36	57	10	1	3	32	16-0	11	43	.237	.315	.325	70	-11	13-3	.979	-6	94	93	2b63		-1.2
1995	SF N	95	205	27	42	5	3	1	14	14-1	12	41	.205	.294	.273	52	-14	4-2	.983	-5	89	117	2b53		-1.7
Total	4	228	564	74	121	16	5	5	52	35-1	24	113	.215	.289	.287	56	-36	22-7	.977	-10	93	110	2b138,O5C	165	-4.0

PATTERSON, CLARE   Lorenzo Clare B10.5.1887 Arkansas City KS D3.28.1913 Mojave CA BL/TR/6-0/180 d9.5

YEAR	TM LG	G	AB	R	H	2B	3B	HR	RBI	BB-IB	HP	SO	AVG	OBP	SLG	AOPS	ABR	SB-CS	FA	FR	RNG	THR	GAMES AT POSITION	DL	BFW
1909	Cin N	4	8	0	1	0	0	0	0	1	0		.125	.125	.125	-23	-1	0	1.000	0	0	0	O2L		-0.1

PATTERSON, MIKE   Michael Lee B1.26.1958 Santa Monica CA BL/TR/5-10/170(170-190) d4.15

YEAR	TM LG	G	AB	R	H	2B	3B	HR	RBI	BB-IB	HP	SO	AVG	OBP	SLG	AOPS	ABR	SB-CS	FA	FR	RNG	THR	GAMES AT POSITION	DL	BFW
1981	Oak A	12	23	4	8	1	1	0	1	2-1	0	5	.348	.400	.478	158	2	0-1	1.000	-0	94	0	O5(2/0/3),D2		0.1
	NY A	4	9	2	2	0	0	0	0	0-0	0	0	.222	.222	.667	149	0	0-0	1.000	0	120	0	O4(3/0/1)		0.0
	Year	16	32	6	10	1	1	0	1	2-1	0	5	.313	.353	.531	156	2	0-1	1.000	-0	105	0	O9(5/0/4),D2		0.1
1982	NY A	11	16	3	3	1	0	1	2	2-0	0	5	.188	.278	.438	94	0	1-0	1.000	-2	42	0	O9(2/7/0)/D		-0.2
Total	2	27	48	9	13	2	1	1	2	4-1	0	11	.271	.327	.500	134	2	1-1	1.000	-2	77	0	O18(7/7/4),D3		-0.1

PATTERSON, DAN   Thomas W. B1846 New York NY TL/5-9/143 d5.18

YEAR	TM LG	G	AB	R	H	2B	3B	HR	RBI	BB-IB	HP	SO	AVG	OBP	SLG	AOPS	ABR	SB-CS	FA	FR	RNG	THR	GAMES AT POSITION	DL	BFW
1871	Mut NA	32	151	31	31	2	0	0	13	1			.205	.211	.219	26	-13	2-1	.824	-2	58	0	O31(9/0/22),2b2		-0.8
1872	Eck NA	12	47	6	10	1	0	0	3	0			.213	.213	.234	44	-2	0-3	.861	3	272	321	O11(2/9/0)/1		0.0
1874	Mut NA	1	5	1	2	0	0	0	2	0			.400	.400	.400	153	0	0-0	1.000	0			/1OL		0.0
1875	Atl NA	12	45	4	9	0	0	0	4	0			.200	.200	.200	45	-2	1-0	.636	-5	67	0	2b7,O7R		-0.6
Total	4 NA	57	248	42	52	3	0	0	22	1			.210	.213	.222	35	-17	3-4	.827	-4	99	72	O50(12/9/29),2b9,1b2		-1.4

PATTERSON, PAT   William Jennings Bryan B1.29.1901 Belleville IL D10.1.1977 St.Louis MO BR/TR/6-0/175 d4.14 b-Ham

YEAR	TM LG	G	AB	R	H	2B	3B	HR	RBI	BB-IB	HP	SO	AVG	OBP	SLG	AOPS	ABR	SB-CS	FA	FR	RNG	THR	GAMES AT POSITION	DL	BFW
1921	NY N	23	35	5	14	0	0	1	5	2	0	5	.400	.432	.486	142	2	0-1	.970	2	156	0	3b14,S7		0.5

PATTON, GENE   Gene Tunney B7.8.1926 Coatesville PA BL/TR/5-10/165 d6.17 Mil 1945

YEAR	TM LG	G	AB	R	H	2B	3B	HR	RBI	BB-IB	HP	SO	AVG	OBP	SLG	AOPS	ABR	SB-CS	FA	FR	RNG	THR	GAMES AT POSITION	DL	BFW
1944	Bos N	1	0	0	0	0	0	0	0	0	0	0	—	—	—		0	0		0			/R		0.0

PATTON, BILL   George William B10.12.1912 Cornwall PA D3.15.1986 Philadelphia PA BR/TR/6-2/180 d6.29 Col Temple

YEAR	TM LG	G	AB	R	H	2B	3B	HR	RBI	BB-IB	HP	SO	AVG	OBP	SLG	AOPS	ABR	SB-CS	FA	FR	RNG	THR	GAMES AT POSITION	DL	BFW
1935	Phi A	9	10	1	3	1	0	0	2	2	0	3	.300	.417	.400	113	0	0-0	1.000	0	*59*	*499*	C3		0.1

PATTON, TOM   Tommy Allen B9.5.1935 Honey Brook PA BR/TR/5-9.5/185 d4.30

YEAR	TM LG	G	AB	R	H	2B	3B	HR	RBI	BB-IB	HP	SO	AVG	OBP	SLG	AOPS	ABR	SB-CS	FA	FR	RNG	THR	GAMES AT POSITION	DL	BFW
1957	Bal A	1	2	0	0	0	0	0	0	0-0	0	0	.000	.000	.000	-99	-1	0-0	1.000	1	0	*520*	/C		0.0

PAUL, JOSH   Joshua William B5.19.1975 Evanston IL BR/TR/6-1/200(185-200) [ChiA96 2/47] d9.7 Col Vanderbilt

YEAR	TM LG	G	AB	R	H	2B	3B	HR	RBI	BB-IB	HP	SO	AVG	OBP	SLG	AOPS	ABR	SB-CS	FA	FR	RNG	THR	GAMES AT POSITION	DL	BFW
1999	Chi A	6	18	2	4	1	0	0		0-0	0	0	.222	.222	.278	26	-2	0-0	1.000	1	67	0	C6		-0.1
2000	†Chi A	36	71	15	20	3	2	1	8	5-0	1	17	.282	.338	.423	88	-2	1-0	.974	2	114	179	C34/OL		0.2
2001	Chi A	57	139	20	37	11	0	3	18	13-0	0	25	.266	.327	.410	88	-2	6-2	.980	-2	73	69	C56		0.0
2002	Chi A	33	104	11	25	4	0	0	11	9-0	1	22	.240	.302	.279	55	-7	2-0	.990	0	82	39	C32/OL		-0.4
2003	Chi A	13	17	5	6	0	0	0	4	3-0	0	3	.353	.450	.353	111	0	0-0	1.000	-2	171	270	C11/D		-0.1
	Chi A	3	6	0	0	0	0	0	0	0-0	0	3	.000	.000	.000	-98	-2	0-0	1.000	1	108	410	C3		-0.1
2004	Ana A	46	70	11	17	3	0	2	10	7-0	0	17	.243	.308	.371	80	-2	2-1	.993	-1	72	88	C37,O4L,D2		-0.2
2005	†LA A	34	37	4	7	1	0	2	4	2-0	0	9	.189	.231	.378	59	-2	0-0	.989	0	119	77	C29,O2L		-0.2
Total	7	228	462	69	116	23	2	8	56	39-0	2	100	.251	.310	.361	74	-19	11-3	.986	-1	90	94	C208,O8L,D3	24	-0.8

PAUL, LOU   Louis BR/TR d9.5

YEAR	TM LG	G	AB	R	H	2B	3B	HR	RBI	BB-IB	HP	SO	AVG	OBP	SLG	AOPS	ABR	SB-CS	FA	FR	RNG	THR	GAMES AT POSITION	DL	BFW
1876	Phi N	3	12	2	2	1	0	0	0	0			.167	.167	.250	37	-1		.643	-2			C3		-0.2

PAULA, CARLOS   Carlos (Conill) B11.28.1927 Havana, Cuba D4.25.1983 Miami FL BR/TR/6-3/195* d9.6

YEAR	TM LG	G	AB	R	H	2B	3B	HR	RBI	BB-IB	HP	SO	AVG	OBP	SLG	AOPS	ABR	SB-CS	FA	FR	RNG	THR	GAMES AT POSITION	DL	BFW
1954	Was A	9	24	2	4	1	0	0	2	2	0	4	.167	.231	.208	22	-3	0-0	1.000	1	118	266	O6L		-0.2
1955	Was A	115	351	34	105	20	7	6	45	17-3	2	43	.299	.332	.447	115	5	2-3	.941	-4	96	77	O85(6/0/80)		-0.2
1956	Was A	33	82	8	15	2	1	3	13	8-0	0	15	.183	.250	.341	56	-6	0-2	.974	-1	104	0	O20(9/0/11)		-0.8
Total	3	157	457	44	124	23	8	9	60	27-3	2	62	.271	.311	.416	99	-4	2-5	.950	-4	99	74	O111(21/0/91)		-1.2

PAULETTE, GENE   Eugene Edward B5.26.1891 Centralia IL D2.8.1966 Little Rock AR BR/TR/6-0/150 d6.16 OF(1/3/10)

YEAR	TM LG	G	AB	R	H	2B	3B	HR	RBI	BB-IB	HP	SO	AVG	OBP	SLG	AOPS	ABR	SB-CS	FA	FR	RNG	THR	GAMES AT POSITION	DL	BFW
1911	NY N	10	12	1	2	0	0	0	1	0			.167	.167	.167	-6	-2	0	.938	-1	63	0	1b7/S3		-0.3
1916	StL A	5	4	1	2	0	0	0	0	1	0		.500	.600	.500	242	1	0					/H		0.1
1917	StL A	12	22	3	4	0	0	0		3	0		.182	.280	.182	43	-1	0	.982	-0	108	36	1b5,2b3/3		-0.2
	StL N	95	332	32	88	21	7	0	34	16	0	3	.265	.303	.370	109	3	9	.993	-2	88	142	1b93		-0.2
1918	StL N	125	461	33	126	15	3	0	52	27	0	16	.273	.316	.319	97	-2	11	.983	1	97	**108**	1b97,S12,2b7,O6(1/1/3),3b2/P		-0.5
1919	StL N	43	144	11	31	6	0	0	15	6	0		.215	.261	.257	60	-7	4	.990	2	95	100	2b58,O10(0/2/7)/1		-0.6
	Phi N	67	243	20	63	8	3	1	31	19	1		.259	.316	.329	88	-10	4	.957	-2	95	100	1b35,S3		-0.5
	Year	110	387	31	94	14	3	1	46	25	1		.243	.296	.302	78	-10		.957	0	95	100	2b58,1b36,O10(0/2/7),S3		-1.1
1920	Phi N	143	562	59	162	16	9	2	63	33	1		.243	.296	.302	90	-7	9-8	.988	6	**120**	95	1b139,S2		-0.5
Total	6	500	1780	160	478	66	19	2	165	108	9	69	.269	.314	.326	92	-18	43-8	.988	4	105	111	1b377,2b68,S18,O16R,3b4/P		-2.6

YEAR	TM LG	G	AB	R	H	2B	3B	HR	RBI	BB-IB	HP	SO	AVG	OBP	SLG	AOPS	ABR	SB-CS	FA	FR	RNG	THR	GAMES AT POSITION	DL	BFW

PAULINO, RONNY Ronny Leonel B4.21.1981 Santo Domingo, D.R. BR/TR/6-3/235 d9.25

| 2005 | Pit N | 2 | 4 | 1 | 2 | 0 | 0 | 0 | 1-0 | 0 | | | .500 | .600 | .500 | 194 | 1 | 0-0 | 1.000 | 0 | 65 | 0 | C2 | | 0.1 |

PAUXTIS, SI Simon Francis B7.20.1885 Pittston PA D3.13.1961 Philadelphia PA BR/TR/6-0/175 d9.18 Col Penn

| 1909 | Cin N | 4 | 8 | 2 | 1 | 0 | 0 | 0 | | 1 | | | .125 | .222 | .125 | 8 | -1 | 0 | 1.000 | -1 | 85 | 47 | C4 | | -0.1 |

PAVLETICH, DON Donald Stephen B7.13.1938 Milwaukee WI BR/TR/5-11/209(190-214) d4.20 Mil 1957-58

1957	Cin N	1	1	0	0	0	0	0	0-0	0	0	0	.000	.000	.000	-93	0	0-0	—	0			/H		0.0
1959	Cin N	1	0	1	0	0	0	0	0-0	0	0	0	—	—	—		0	0-0	1.000	0	90	82	/R		0.0
1962	Cin N	34	63	7	14	3	0	1	7	8-1	0	18	.222	.310	.317	67	-3	0-0	.991	-1	61	68	1b25,C2		-0.4
1963	Cin N	71	183	18	38	11	0	5	11	17-3	0	12	.208	.274	.350	76	-5	0-0	.983	-3	71	34	C27/1		-0.9
1964	Cin N	34	91	12	22	4	0	5	11	10-1	0	17	.242	.314	.451	109	1	0-0	.986	-7	66	67	C54,1b9		-0.1
1965	Cin N	68	191	25	61	11	1	8	32	23-5	1	27	.319	.394	.513	144	12	1-1	.975	-7	63	116	C55,1b10		0.7
1966	Cin N	83	235	29	69	13	2	12	38	18-3	1	37	.294	.344	.519	126	8	1-0	.975	-7	59	95	C56,1b6/3		0.3
1967	Cin N	74	231	25	55	14	0	6	34	21-7	0	38	.238	.310	.403	93	-2	2-1	.986	-3	59	93	1b22,C5		-0.2
1968	Cin N	46	98	11	28	3	1	2	11	8-2	2	23	.286	.352	.398	117	2	0-0	1.000	-1	88	93	C51,1b13		0.1
1969	Chi A	78	188	26	46	12	0	6	33	28-4	0	45	.245	.338	.404	103	2	1-0	.974	-4	49	124	C51,1b16,C10	31	-0.2
1970	Bos A	32	65	4	9	1	1	0	6	10-0	0	15	.138	.250	.185	21	-7	1-0	1.000	-3	125	123	1b16,C10		-1.1
1971	Bos A	14	27	5	7	1	0	1	3	5-0	0	5	.259	.375	.407	113	1	0-0	.973	-1	43	62	C8	31	0.0
Total	12	536	1373	163	349	73	6	46	193	148-26	8	237	.254	.328	.420	103	9	5-2	.983	-29	60	85	C291,1b159/3		-1.8

PAWELEK, TED Theodore John "Porky" B8.15.1919 Chicago Heights IL D2.12.1964 Chicago Heights IL BL/TR/5-10.5/202 d9.13

| 1946 | Chi N | 4 | 4 | 0 | 1 | 0 | 0 | 0 | 0 | 0 | 0 | 0 | .250 | .250 | .500 | 112 | 0 | 0 | — | -0 | 0 | 0 | /C | | 0.0 |

PAWLOSKI, STAN Stanley Walter B9.6.1931 Wanamie PA BR/TR/6-1/175 d9.24 Col Temple

| 1955 | Cle A | 2 | 8 | 0 | 1 | 0 | 0 | 0 | 0-0 | 0 | 2 | .125 | .125 | .125 | -31 | -2 | 0-0 | 1.000 | 1 | 154 | 0 | 2b2 | | -0.1 |

PAYNE, FRED Frederick Thomas B9.2.1880 Camden NY D1.16.1954 Camden NY BR/TR/5-10/162 d4.21

1906	Det A	72	222	23	60	5	5	0	20	13	2		.270	.316	.338	102	0	4	.966	2	106	81	C47,O17(1/12/4)		0.6
1907	†Det A	53	169	17	28	2	2	0	14	7	5		.166	.221	.201	34	-13	4	.981	5	106	98	C46,O5(3/1/1)		-0.4
1908	Det A	20	45	3	3	0	0	0	2	3	3		.067	.176	.067	-20	-6	1	.954	2	86	70	C17/OR		-0.8
1909	Chi A	32	82	8	20	2	0	0	12	5	1		.244	.295	.268	82	-2	0	.974	2	118	87	C78,O2R		-0.1
1910	Chi A	91	252	17	56	5	4	0	19	11	2		.222	.260	.274	70	-10	6	.963	0	144	81	C56		-0.7
1911	Chi A	66	133	14	27	2	1	1	19	8	2		.203	.259	.256	45	-10	6	.972	7	113	89	C271,O28(4/13/11)		-1.4
Total	6	334	903	82	194	16	12	1	86	47	15		.215	.265	.262	64	-41	21	.972						

PAYNTER, GEORGE George Washington (b George Washington Paner) B7.6.1871 Cincinnati OH D10.1.1950 Cincinnati OH BR/TR/5-9/125 d8.12

| 1894 | StL N | 1 | 4 | 0 | 0 | 0 | 0 | 0 | 0 | 0 | 0 | | .000 | .200 | .000 | -48 | -1 | 1 | 1.000 | 1 | 854 | 0 | /OC | | 0.0 |

PAYTON, JAY Jason Lee B11.22.1972 Zanesville OH BR/TR/5-10/185* [NYN94 S1/29] d9.1 Col Georgia Tech

1998	NY N	15	22	2	7	1	0	0	1	1-0	1	2	.318	.348	.364	90	0	0-0	1.000	0	75	354	O10(8/0/1)		0.0
1999	NY N	13	8	1	2	1	0	0	1	0-0	1	2	.250	.333	.375	83	0	1-2	1.000	0	106	93	O6(5/2/0)	64	-0.1
2000	†NY N	149	488	63	142	23	1	17	62	30-0	5	60	.291	.331	.447	101	-1	5-11	.981	-1	103	93	O146(4/143/0)	49	-0.4
2001	NY N	104	361	44	92	16	1	8	34	18-1	5	52	.255	.298	.371	77	-14	4-3	.994	-1	96	152	O82C		0.0
2002	NY N	87	275	33	78	6	3	8	31	21-0	1	34	.284	.336	.415	106	-1	3-3	1.000	2	106	122	O44(32/16/2)		0.9
	Col N	47	170	36	57	14	4	8	28	8-0	3	20	.335	.376	.606	138	8	3-3	.996	1	100	141	O126(32/98/2)		0.9
	Year	134	445	69	135	20	7	16	59	29-0	4	54	.303	.351	.488	120	6	6-4	.987	3	109	64	O151(149/8/3)		0.4
2003	Col N	157	600	93	181	32	5	28	89	43-3	7	77	.302	.354	.512	108	6	2-0	.989	14	118	179	O137(9/128/0)/D		0.4
2004	SD N	143	458	57	119	17	4	8	55	43-2	2	56	.260	.326	.367	84	-12	2-0	1.000	2	107	151	O53(13/16/31)		-0.1
2005	Bos A	55	133	24	35	7	0	5	21	10-0	0	14	.263	.313	.429	96	-3	0-1	1.000	-1	100	54	O69(47/25/0)		-0.6
	Oak A	69	275	38	74	9	1	13	42	14-2	0	33	.269	.302	.451	96	-2	0-1	1.000	1	102	86	O122(60/41/31)		-0.7
	Year	124	408	62	109	16	1	18	63	24-2	0	47	.267	.306	.444	93	-5	0-1	1.000	0	107	113	O801(267/523/37)/D	113	-0.6
Total	8	839	2790	391	787	126	19	95	363	188-8	24	352	.282	.330	.443	99	-19	25-25	.989	20	107				

PEACOCK, JOHNNY John Gaston B1.10.1910 Fremont NC D10.17.1981 Wilson NC BL/TR/5-11/165 d9.23 Col North Carolina-Asheville

1937	Bos A	9	32	3	10	2	1	0	6	1	0	0	.313	.333	.438	89	-1	0-0	.980	1	126	138	C9		0.1
1938	Bos A	72	195	29	59	7	1	1	39	17	0	4	.303	.358	.364	78	-7	4-1	.984	-5	101	52	C57/1OL		-0.8
1939	Bos A	92	274	33	76	11	4	0	36	29	0	11	.277	.347	.347	75	-10	1-1	.972	-6	87	77	C84		-1.0
1940	Bos A	63	131	20	37	4	1	0	13	23	0	10	.282	.390	.328	85	-2	1-1	.994	-6	90	77	C48		-0.6
1941	Bos A	79	261	28	74	20	1	0	27	21	1	3	.284	.339	.368	85	-5	2-1	.988	-2	102	112	C82		-0.2
1942	Bos A	88	286	17	76	7	3	0	25	21	0	11	.266	.316	.311	74	-10	1-1	.988	-2	103	97	C32		-0.8
1943	Bos A	48	114	7	23	3	1	0	7	10	0	7	.202	.266	.246	49	-7	1-1	.972	-1	102	97	C2		-0.1
1944	Bos A	4	4	0	0	0	0	0	0	0	0	0	.000	.000	.000	-99	-1	0-0	1.000	0	0	0	C73/2		-0.5
	Phi N	83	253	21	57	9	3	0	21	31	0	15	.225	.310	.285	70	-10	1	.990	1	103	106	C23		-0.7
1945	Phi N	33	74	6	15	6	0	0	6	6	0	0	.203	.262	.284	53	-5	1	.975	0	107	71	C38		0.3
	Bro N	48	110	11	28	5	1	0	14	24	0	10	.255	.388	.318	98	1	2	.973	-3	94	76	C61		-0.4
	Year	81	184	17	43	11	1	0	20	30	0	10	.234	.341	.304	82	-3	3	.973	-3	98	89	C518/2OL1		-5.1
Total	9	619	1734	175	455	74	16	1	194	183	1	73	.262	.333	.325	76	-57	14-6	.983	-24	98	89	C518/2OL1		

PEAK, ELIAS Elias B5.23.1859 Philadelphia PA D12.17.1916 Philadelphia PA d4.19

1884	Bos U	1	3	2	2	0	0	0		1			.667	.750	.667	338	1		1.000	-0	0	0	/OR		0.1
	Phi U	54	215	35	42	6	4	0		7			.195	.221	.260	49	-20		.825	-8	106	78	2b47,O5(4/0/1),S2		-2.
	Year	55	218	37	44	6	4	0		8			.202	.230	.266	54	-19		.825	-8	106	78	2b47,O6(4/0/2),S2		-2.

PEARCE, HARRY Harry James B7.12.1889 Philadelphia PA D1.8.1942 Philadelphia PA BR/TR/5-9/158 d10.2

1917	Phi N	7	16	2	4	3	0	0	2	0	1	4	.250	.294	.438	118	0	1	.967	3	166	59	S4		-0.
1918	Phi N	60	164	16	40	3	2	0	18	9	3	31	.244	.295	.287	73	-5	5	.944	-0	110	89	2b46,S2/13		-2.
1919	Phi N	68	244	24	44	3	3	0	9	8	1	27	.180	.209	.217	26	-22	6	.948	-0	101	107	2b43,S23,3b2		-2.
Total	3	135	424	42	88	9	5	0	29	17	5	62	.208	.247	.252	48	-27	11	.946	3	106	97	2b89,S29,3b3/1		

PEARCE, DICKEY Richard J. B2.29.1836 Brooklyn NY D9.18.1908 Wareham MA BR/TR/5-3.5/161 d5.18 M2/U2

1871	Mut NA	33	163	31	44	5	0	0	20	4		1	.270	.287	.301	76	-3	0-0	.793	-7	92	114	S33		-0.
1872	Mut NA	44	206	32	39	2	1	0	22	4		2	.189	.205	.223	34	-14	1-1	.844	2	103	162	S42,O2(1/0/1),M		-1.
1873	Atl NA	55	262	42	72	6	0	0	23	8		2	.275	.296	.309	90	0	3-0	.777	2	116	96	S55/12		0.
1874	Atl NA	56	255	48	75	1	0	0	26	6		1	.294	.310	.298	109	5	1-0	.845	8	109	69	S56,3b2/2		0.
1875	StL NA	70	311	51	77	6	3	0	29	7		7	.248	.264	.286	100	2	8-3	.830	11	113	150	S70,P2,M		1.
1876	StL N	25	102	12	21	1	0	0	10	3		5	.206	.229	.216	51	-5		.950	3	126	169	S8		-0.
1877	StL N	8	29	1	5	0	0	0	4	0		1	.172	.200	.172	19	-3		.818	17	108	118	S256,P2,3b2,2b2,O2(1/0/1)/1		0.
Total	5 NA	258	1197	204	307	20	4	2	120	29		12	.256	.274	.285	84	-10	13-4	.818						
Total	2	33	131	13	26	1	0	0	14	4		9	.198	.222	.206	44	-8		.914	6	113	170	S31/2OL		0

PEARCE, DUCKY William C. B3.17.1885 Corning OH D5.22.1933 Brownstown IN BR/TR/6-1/185 d7.1

1908	Cin N	2	2	0	0	0	0	0	0	0	0		.000	.000	.000	-99	0	0	1.000	1	121	195	C2		0
1909	Cin N	2	2	0	0	0	0	0	0	0	0		.000	.000	.000	-99	0	0	1.000	-0	63	0	C2		-0
Total	2	4	4	0	0	0	0	0	0	0	0		.000	.000	.000	-99	0	0	1.000	1	102	130	C4		-0

PEARSON, ALBIE Albert Gregory B9.12.1934 Alhambra CA BL/TL/5-5/141(141-160) d4.14

1958	Was A	146	530	63	146	25	5	3	33	64-1	2	31	.275	.354	.358	99	1	7-8	.980	-3	101	75	O141(0/136/6)		-0
1959	Was A	25	80	9	15	1	0	0	2	14-0	0	3	.188	.309	.200	43	-6	1-1	.974	-3	84	0	O21(0/11/10)		-1
	Bal A	80	138	22	32	4	2	0	6	13-0	1	5	.232	.296	.290	64	-7	4-0	.987	1	109	97	O50(22/16/16)		-1
	Year	105	218	31	47	5	2	0	8	27-0	1	8	.216	.301	.257	56	-13	5-1	.983	-2	99	60	O71(22/27/26)		-1
1960	Bal A	48	82	17	20	2	0	1	6	17-0	1	5	.244	.370	.305	87	-1	4-0	.975	-1	96	79	O32(11/7/15)		-1
1961	LA A	144	427	92	123	18	4	7	41	96-1	3	40	.288	.420	.400	109	11	11-3	.956	-0	103	98	O113(1/46/76)		-0
1962	LA A	160	614	115	160	29	6	5	47	95-3	1	36	.261	.360	.352	96	-3	15-6	.989	-3	100	102	O160(0/143/17)		-0
1963	LA A★	154	578	92	176	26	5	6	47	92-5	3	37	.304	.402	.398	133	31	17-10	.983	-5	98	103	O148(2/135/15)		-1
1964	LA A	107	265	34	59	5	1	2	16	35-2	1	22	.223	.326	.272	72	-9	4-2	.978	-2	102	25	O66(10/52/7)		-1
1965	Cal A	122	360	41	100	17	2	4	21	51-0	5	17	.278	.365	.428	114	9	2-1	.988	-1	98	88	O101(7/12/87)		-0

YEAR	TM LG	G	AB	R	H	2B	3B	HR	RBI	BB-IB	HP	SO	AVG	OBP	SLG	AOPS	ABR	SB-CS		FA	FR	RNG	THR	GAMES AT POSITION	DL	BFW
1966	Cal A	2	3	0	0	0	0	0	0	0-0	0	1	.000	.000	.000	-99	-1	0-0	—	-0	0	0	/OL	95	-0.1
Total	9	988	3077	485	831	130	24	28	214	477-12	12	195	.270	.369	.355	102	28	77-33	.980	-0	100	86	O833(54/558/249)	95	-1.8

PECHOUS, CHARLIE Charles Edward B10.5.1896 Chicago IL D9.13.1980 Kenosha WI BR/TR/6-0/170 d9.14 Col Loyola-Chicago

1915	Chi F	18	51	4	9	3	0	0	4	4	0	15	.176	.236	.235	35	-5		.938	-0	113	0	3b18		-0.6
1916	Chi N	22	69	5	10	1	1	0	4	3	0	21	.145	.181	.188	12	-7	1	.940	6	137	70	3b22		-0.1
1917	Chi N	13	41	2	10	0	0	0	1	2	1	9	.244	.295	.244	61	-2	1	1.000	-2	67	0	3b7,S5		-0.4
Total	3	53	161	11	29	4	1	0	9	9	1	45	.180	.228	.217	32	-14	3	.947	3	118	35	3b47,S5		-1.1

PECK, HAL Harold Arthur B4.20.1917 Big Bend WI D4.13.1995 Milwaukee WI BL/TL/5-11/175 d5.13

1943	Bro N	1	1	0	0	0	0	0	0	0	0	0	.000	.000	.000	-99	-0			0			/H		0.0
1944	Phi A	2	8	0	2	0	0	0	1	0	0	2	.250	.250	.250	44	-1	0-2	1.000	-0	89	0	O2R		-0.2
1945	Phi A	112	449	51	124	22	9	5	39	37	0	28	.276	.331	.399	112	5	5-3	.943	-10	85	80	O110R		-1.3
1946	Phi A	48	150	14	37	8	2	2	11	16	0	14	.247	.319	.367	92	-2	1-2	.981	-0	85	158	O35R		-0.4
1947	Cle A	114	392	58	115	18	2	8	44	27	2	31	.293	.342	.411	112	5	5-3	.983	-2	97	80	O97(3/0/95)		-0.1
1948	†Cle A	45	63	12	18	3	0	0	8	4	0	8	.286	.328	.333	78	-2	1-0	1.000	-1	93	0	O9(1/0/9)		-0.3
1949	Cle A	33	29	1	9	1	0	0	9	3	0	3	.310	.375	.345	93	0	0-0	1.000	-0	147	0	O2R		0.0
Total	7	355	1092	136	305	52	13	15	112	87	2	86	.279	.334	.392	106	5	10-10	.965	-13	90	87	O255(4/0/253)		-2.3

PECKINPAUGH, ROGER Roger Thorpe B2.5.1891 Wooster OH D11.17.1977 Cleveland OH BR/TR/5-10.5/165 d9.15 M8

1910	Cle A	15	45	1	9	0	0	0	6	1	1		.200	.234	.200	36	-3	3	.906	-5	89	60	S14		-0.9
1912	Cle A	70	236	18	50	4	1	0	22	16	0		.212	.262	.250	45	-17	11	.924	-1	98	77	S68		-1.5
1913	Cle A	1	0	1	0	0	0	0	0	0	0		—	—	—	0	0			0			/H		0.0
	NY A	95	340	35	91	10	7	1	32	24	0	47	.268	.316	.347	94	-4	19	.931	-3	103	79	S93		-0.1
	Year	96	340	36	91	10	7	1	32	24	0	47	.268	.316	.347	94	-4	19	.931	-3	103	79	S93		-0.1
1914	NY A	**157**	570	55	127	14	6	3	51	51	1	73	.223	.288	.284	72	-20	38-17	.956	5	105	82	S157,M		-0.2
1915	NY A	142	540	67	119	18	7	5	44	49	3	72	.220	.289	.307	79	-16	19-12	.942	5	**106**	114	S142		0.0
1916	NY A	145	552	65	141	22	8	4	58	62	1	50	.255	.332	.346	101	1	18	.946	-0	102	96	S145		1.2
1917	NY A	148	543	63	141	24	7	0	41	64	2	46	.260	.340	.330	103	4	17	.934	7	102	133	S148		2.3
1918	NY A	122	446	59	103	15	3	0	43	43	3	41	.231	.303	.278	74	-14	12	.961	**22**	**113**	**148**	S122		1.9
1919	NY A	122	453	89	138	20	2	7	33	59	4	37	.305	.390	.404	122	16	10	.943	**26**	**116**	**139**	S121		5.1
1920	NY A	139	534	109	144	26	6	8	54	72	0	47	.270	.356	.386	93	-4	8-12	.962	8	102	113	S137		1.1
1921	†NY A	149	577	128	166	25	7	8	71	84	2	44	.288	.380	.397	96	-1	2-2	.948	-3	96	111	S149		1.1
1922	Was A	147	520	62	132	14	4	2	48	55	3	36	.254	.329	.308	70	-22	11-6	.951	18	**109**	120	S147		1.2
1924	†Was A	155	523	72	142	20	5	2	73	72	0	45	.272	.360	.340	84	-11	9-6	.963	11	105	**119**	S155		2.0
1925	†Was A	126	422	67	124	16	4	4	64	49	0	23	.294	.367	.379	91	-5	13-4	.952	-14	92	102	S124/1		1.5
1926	Was A	57	147	19	35	4	1	1	14	28	0	12	.238	.360	.299	75	-4	3-0	.960	-1	96	96	S46/1		-0.4
1927	Chi A	68	217	23	64	6	3	0	23	21	1	6	.295	.360	.350	87	-4	0-0	.964	0	104	106	S60		-0.1
Total	17	2012	7233	1006	1876	256	75	48	739	814	22	609	.259	.336	.335	87	-121	205-70	.949	97	104	112	S1982,1b2		14.3

PECOTA, BILL William Joseph B2.16.1960 Redwood City CA BR/TR/6-2/190* [KCA81*10/234] d9.19 Col De Anza (CA) JC OF(13/2/19)

1986	KC A	12	29	3	6	2	0	0	2	3-0	1	5	.207	.294	.276	49	-1	3-0	.974	4	163	62	3b12,S2,D4		0.2
1987	KC A	66	156	22	43	5	1	3	14	15-0	1	25	.276	.343	.378	89	-2	5-0	.977	9	113	129	S36,3b17,2b15/D		1.0
1988	KC A	90	178	25	37	5	3	1	15	18-0	2	34	.208	.286	.275	58	-10	7-2	.976	7	110	96	S41,3b21,1b11,O9(3/0/6),D4,2b3/C		0.0
1989	KC A	65	83	21	17	4	2	3	5	7-1	1	9	.205	.275	.410	91	-2	5-0	.988	1	104	75	S29,O15(4/2/9),2b12,3b7,1b4/D		0.2
1990	KC A	87	240	43	58	15	2	5	20	33-0	1	39	.242	.336	.383	102	1	8-5	.986	10	97	71	2b50,S21,3b11,O6(4/0/3),1b4,D2		1.4
1991	KC A	125	398	53	114	23	2	6	45	41-6	2	45	.286	.356	.399	108	5	16-7	.983	-3	97	82	3b102,2b34,S9,1b8,D2/OLP		0.4
1992	NY N	117	269	28	61	13	0	2	26	25-3	1	40	.227	.293	.297	69	-11	9-3	.926	8	102	140	3b48,S39,2b38/P1	15	0.1
1993	†Atl N	72	62	17	20	2	1	0	5	2-0	0	5	.323	.344	.387	93	-1	1-1	1.000	-1	86	0	3b23,2b4/OR		-0.2
1994	Atl N	64	112	11	24	5	0	2	16	16-1	0	16	.214	.310	.313	61	-6	1-0	.974	6	122	112	3b31/2OL		0.2
Total	9	698	1527	223	380	72	11	22	148	160-11	9	216	.249	.323	.354	86	-28	52-20	.968	43	109	99	3b272,S177,2b157,O33R,1b28,D14,P2/C15		3.2

PEDEN, LES Leslie Earl "Gooch" B9.17.1923 Azle TX D2.11.2002 Jacksonville FL BR/TR/6-1.5/212 d4.17 C1 Col Texas A&M-Commerce

| 1953 | Was A | 9 | 28 | 4 | 7 | 1 | 0 | 1 | 4 | 1-0 | 0 | 3 | .250 | .344 | .393 | 101 | 0 | 0-0 | 1.000 | 0 | 89 | 110 | C8 | | 0.0 |

PEDERSON, STU Stuart Russell B1.28.1960 Palo Alto CA BL/TL/6-0/185 [LAN81 9/229] d9.8 Col USC

| 1985 | LA N | 8 | 4 | 1 | 0 | 0 | 0 | 0 | 1 | 0-0 | 0 | 2 | .000 | .000 | .000 | -99 | -1 | 0-0 | 1.000 | 0 | 120 | 0 | O5(3/0/2) | | -0.1 |

PEDRE, JORGE Jorge Enrique B10.12.1966 Culver City CA BR/TR/5-11/210* [KCA87 33/846] d9.7 Col Los Angeles Harbor (CA) JC

1991	KC A	10	19	2	5	1	1	0	3	3-0	0	5	.263	.364	.421	115	0	0-0	.971	-2	51	110	C9/1		-0.1
1992	Chi N	4	4	0	0	0	0	0	0	0-0	1	1	.000	.000	.000	-97	-1	0-0	1.000	-1	0	0	C4		-0.2
Total	2	14	23	2	5	1	1	0	3	3-0	1	6	.217	.308	.348	81	-1	0-0	.973	-2	44	95	C13/1		-0.3

PEDRIQUE, AL Alfredo Jose (Garcia) B8.11.1960 Valencia, Venez BR/TR/6-0/155* d4.14 M1/C1

1987	NY N	5	6	1	0	0	0	0	0	1-0	0	2	.000	.143	.000	-61	-1	0-0	1.000	1	147	0	S4/2		0.0
	Pit N	88	246	23	74	10	1	1	27	18-4	3	29	.301	.354	.362	90	-3	5-4	.968	-5	93	114	S76,3b3,2b2		-0.1
	Year	93	252	24	74	10	1	1	27	19-4	3	29	.294	.349	.353	86	-5	5-4	.969	-3	94	111	S80,2b3,3b3		-0.1
1988	Pit N	50	128	7	23	5	0	0	4	8-2	1	17	.180	.234	.219	31	-11	0-0	.974	5	112	115	S46,3b5		-0.4
1989	Det A	31	69	1	14	3	0	0	5	2-0	0	15	.203	.225	.246	34	-6	0-0	.960	4	104	63	3b12,S12,2b8		-0.1
Total	3	174	449	32	111	18	1	1	36	29-6	4	61	.247	.298	.298	64	-21	5-4	.971	6	100	112	S138,3b20,2b11		-0.6

PEDROES, CHICK Charles P. (b Charles F. Pedro) B10.27.1869 Havana, Cuba D8.6.1927 Chicago IL d8.21

| 1902 | Chi N | 2 | 6 | 0 | 0 | 0 | 0 | 0 | 0 | 0-0 | 0 | | .000 | .000 | .000 | -99 | -1 | 0-0 | 1.000 | -0 | 0 | 0 | O2R | | -0.2 |

PEEL, HOMER Homer Hefner B10.10.1902 Port Sullivan TX D4.8.1997 Shreveport LA BR/TR/5-9.5/170 d9.13

1927	StL N	2	2	0	0	0	0	0	0	0-0	0	1	.000	.000	.000	-97	-1	0-0	—	-0	0	0	/OR		-0.1
1929	Phi N	53	156	16	42	12	1	0	19	12	2	7	.269	.329	.359	66	-8	1	.990	0	103	61	O39(1/36/2)/1		-0.8
1930	StL N	26	73	9	12	2	0	0	10	3	0	5	.164	.197	.192	-5	-13	0	.968	-2	92	0	O21(6/0/15)		-1.4
1933	†NY N	84	148	16	38	1	1	1	12	14	1	10	.257	.325	.297	80	-4	0	.962	-3	81	48	O45(35/9/1)		-0.9
1934	NY N	21	41	7	8	0	0	1	3	1	0	2	.195	.214	.268	29	-4	0	.929	-1	76	0	O10(0/8/2)		-0.6
Total	5	186	420	48	100	15	2	2	44	30	3	24	.238	.294	.298	53	-30	1	.974	-6	91	40	O116(42/53/21)/1		-3.8

PEERSON, JACK Jack Chiles B8.28.1910 Brunswick GA D10.23.1966 Ft.Walton Beach FL BR/TR/5-11/175 d9.7

1935	Phi A	10	19	3	6	1	0	0	1	1	0	1	.316	.350	.368	87	0	0-0	.952	-1	105	0	S4		-0.1
1936	Phi A	8	34	7	11	1	1	0	5	0	0	3	.324	.324	.412	82	-1	0-1	.942	2	127	59	S7/2		0.1
Total	2	18	53	10	17	2	1	0	6	1	0	4	.321	.333	.396	84	-1	0-1	.945	2	120	59	S11/2		0.0

PEETE, CHARLIE Charles "Mule" B2.22.1929 Franklin VA D11.27.1956 Caracas, Venez BL/TR/5-9.5/190 d7.17 Negro Lg 1950

| 1956 | StL N | 23 | 52 | 3 | 10 | 2 | 0 | 0 | 6 | 6-0 | 0 | 14 | .192 | .288 | .308 | 60 | -3 | 0-2 | 1.000 | 1 | 88 | 256 | O21C | | -0.4 |

PEFFER, MONTE Monte (b Montague Pfeiffer) B10.8.1891 New York NY D9.27.1941 New York NY BR/TR/5-4.5/147 d9.29

| 1913 | Phi A | 1 | 3 | 0 | 0 | 0 | 0 | 0 | 0 | 1 | 0 | 1 | .000 | .250 | .000 | -26 | 0 | 0 | .800 | -0 | 123 | 0 | /S | | -0.1 |

PEGUERO, JULIO Julio Cesar B9.7.1968 San Isidro, D.R. BB/TR/6-0/160 d4.8

| 1992 | Phi N | 14 | 9 | 3 | 2 | 0 | 0 | 0 | 0 | 3-0 | 0 | 3 | .222 | .417 | .222 | 86 | 0 | 0-0 | 1.000 | 0 | 104 | 0 | O14(0/9/5) | | 0.0 |

PEGUES, STEVE Steven Antone B5.21.1968 Pontotoc MS BR/TR/6-2/190* [DetA87 1/21] d7.6

1994	Cin N	11	10	1	3	0	0	0	0	0-0	0	3	.300	.364	.300	76	0	0-0	.833	0	195	0	O4(3/0/1)		0.0
	Pit N	7	26	1	10	2	0	0	4	1-0	0	5	.385	.407	.462	124	1	1-0	1.000	-2	57	0	O7(5/2/0)		0.0
	Year	18	36	2	13	2	0	0	4	1-0	0	8	.361	.395	.417	111	1	1-0	.929	-1	80	0	O11(8/2/1)		0.0
1995	Pit N	82	171	17	42	6	0	6	16	4-0	1	36	.246	.263	.398	70	-7	0-1	.954	1	113	80	O53(31/4/25)		-0.9
Total	2	100	207	19	55	10	0	6	18	6-0	1	41	.266	.286	.401	78	-7	2-2	.950	-0	107	66	O48(39/6/26)		-0.9

PEITZ, HEINIE Henry Clement B11.28.1870 St.Louis MO D10.23.1943 Cincinnati OH BR/TR/5-11/165 d10.15 C3 b-Joe OF(4/0/7) ▲

1892	StL N	3	6	0	0	0	0	0	0	0-0	0		.000	.000	.000	-99	-1	0	1.000	-0	101	0	/C		-0.1
1893	StL N	96	362	53	92	12	9	1	45	54	1	20	.254	.353	.345	86	-1	12	.948	3	87	110	C74,S11,O10(4/0/6),1b5		0.2
1894	StL N	99	338	52	89	19	9	3	49	43	1	21	.263	.348	.399	80	-12	14	.897	3	86	61	3b47,C39,1b14/P		-0.3
1895	StL N	90	334	44	95	12	7	2	65	29	2	20	.284	.345	.416	78	-7	9	.937	-10	77	111	C71,1b11,3b10		-0.5

YEAR	TM LG	G	AB	R	H	2B	3B	HR	RBI	BB-IB	HP	SO	AVG	OBP	SLG	AOPS	ABR	SB-CS	FA	FR	RNG	THR	GAMES AT POSITION	DL	BFW
1896	Cin N	68	211	33	63	12	5	2	34	30	0	15	.299	.386	.431	108	3	7	.968	11	142	68	C67		1.6
1897	Cin N	77	266	35	78	11	7	1	44	18	1		.293	.340	.398	89	-6	3	.979	16	156	85	C71,P2		1.4
1898	Cin N	105	330	49	90	15	5	1	43	35	3		.273	.348	.358	96	-2	9	.945	10	166	78	C101		1.6
1899	Cin N	94	293	45	79	13	2	1	43	46	2		.270	.372	.338	94	0	11	.977	7	130	84	C92/P		1.3
1900	Cin N	91	294	34	75	14	1	2	34	20	7		.255	.318	.330	81	-7	5	.958	7	116	99	C80,1b8		0.7
1901	Cin N	82	269	24	82	13	5	1	24	23	2		.305	.364	.401	130	11	3	.982	3	112	90	C49,2b21,3b6,1b2		1.9
1902	Cin N	112	387	54	122	22	5	1	60	24	9		.315	.369	.406	127	13	7	.919	3	90	129	2b48,C47,1b6,3b6		2.1
1903	Cin N	105	358	45	93	15	3	0	42	37	1		.260	.331	.318	77	-10	7	.970	3	122	82	C78,1b11,3b9,2b4		0.0
1904	Cin N	84	272	32	66	13	2	1	30	14	1		.243	.282	.316	78	-7	1	.975	5	104	104	C64,1b18/3		0.4
1905	Pit N	88	278	18	62	10	0	0	27	24	2		.223	.289	.259	62	-12	2	.965	-2	118	93	C87/2		-0.6
1906	Pit N	40	125	13	30	8	0	0	20	13	2		.240	.321	.304	91	-1	1	.979	1	122	87	C38		0.5
1913	StL N	3	4	1	1	0	1	0	0	0	0	0	.250	.250	.750	182	0		.625	-1	86	77	C2/OR		-0.1
Total 16		1235	4124	532	1117	191	66	16	560	410	34	76	.271	.342	.361	92	-41	91	.963	58	122	93	C961,3b79,1b75,2b74,O11R,S11,P4		10.1

PEITZ, JOE Joseph B.11.8.1869 St.Louis MO D12.4.1919 St.Louis MO d6.28 b-Heinie

1894	StL N	7	26	10	11	2	3	0	3	6	0		.423	.531	.731	202	5	2	.818	-1	67	283	O7R		0.3

PELAEZ, ALEX Alejandro B.4.6.1976 San Diego CA BR/TR/5-9/190 [SDN98 42/1252] d5.16 Col San Diego St.

2002	SD N	3	8	0	2	0	0	0	0	0-0	0	0	.250	.250	.250	38	-1	0-0	1.000	-0	148	325	/123		-0.1

PELLAGRINI, EDDIE Edward Charles B.3.13.1918 Boston MA BR/TR/5-9/165* d4.22 Col Boston College

1946	Bos A	22	71	7	15	3	1	2	.4	3	1	18	.211	.253	.366	68	-3	0-0	.891	-2	88	140	3b14,S9		-0.6
1947	Bos A	74	231	29	47	8	1	4	19	23	2	35	.203	.281	.299	57	-14	2-2	.926	-7	93	107	3b42,S26		-2.0
1948	StL A	105	290	31	69	8	3	2	27	34	1	40	.238	.320	.307	65	-15	1-2	.964	18	110	123	S98		0.8
1949	StL A	79	235	26	56	8	1	2	15	14	1.	24	.238	.284	.306	54	-17	2-1	.961	3	104	64	S76		-0.9
1951	Phi N	86	197	31	46	4	5	5	30	23	4	25	.234	.326	.381	91	-3	5-1	.990	-12	95	64	2b53,S8,3b6		-1.2
1952	Cin N	46	100	15	17	2	0	1	3	8	0	18	.170	.231	.220	26	-10	1-0	.983	4	116	106	2b22,1b8/S3		-0.5
1953	Pit N	78	174	16	44	3	.2	4	19	14	2	20	.253	.309	.362	75	-7	1-1	.972	-2	93	60	2b31,3b12,S3		-0.7
1954	Pit N	73	125	12	27	6	0	0	16	9	4	21	.216	.288	.264	46	-10	1-0	.968	2	113	129	3b31,2b7/S		-0.8
Total 8		563	1423	167	321	42	13	20	133	128	13	201	.226	.295	.316	62	-79	13-7	.956	4	104	99	S222,2b113,3b106,1b8		-5.9

PELLOW, KIT Kit Donovan B.8.28.1973 Kansas City MO BR/TR/6-1/205* [KCA96 22/649] d8.14 Col Arkansas-Monticello

2002	KC A	29	63	6	15	1	0	1	5	9-0	1	21	.238	.342	.302	65	-3	1-1	.844	1	135	185	3b12,1b10,D5		-0.2
2003	Col N	11	18	6	8	3	1	1	4	0-0	2	4	.444	.476	.889	222	3	0-0	1.000	-1	69	0	C7/1OL		0.2
2004	Col N	59	121	15	29	5	1	2	10	8-1	4	43	.240	.308	.347	61	-7	1-0	1.000	-2	67	145	O36(11/0/27),1b5,C4,3b4		-0.9
Total 3		99	202	27	52	9	2	4	19	17-1	7	68	.257	.335	.381	77	-7	2-1	1.000	-2	68	141	O37(12/0/27),1b16,3b16,C11,D5		-0.9

PELOUZE, LOUIS Louis Henri B.9.10.1863 Fort Monroe VA D.1.9.1939 New York NY BL/TL/6-0/175 d7.24

1886	StL N	1	3	0	0	0	0	0	0	0	0		.000	.000	.000	-99	-1	0	1.000	0	0	0	/OC		-0.1

PELTIER, DAN Daniel Edward B.6.30.1968 Clifton Park NY BL/TL/6-1/200* [TexA89 3/65] d6.26 Col Notre Dame

1992	Tex A	12	24	1	4	0	0	0	3	2-0	0	3	.167	.167	.167	-7	-4	0-0	.857	-2	53	0	O10(1/0/9)		-0.5
1993	Tex A	65	160	23	43	7	1	1	17	20-0	1	27	.269	.352	.344	91	-1	0-4	.950	-2	83	130	O55(2/0/54),1b5		-0.7
1996	SF N	31	59	3	15	2	0	0	9	7-1	0	9	.254	.328	.288	67	-3	0-0	1.000	-1	72	113	1b13/OL		-0.5
Total 3		108	243	27	62	9	1	1	28	27-1	1	39	.255	.330	.313	77	-8	0-4	.943	-5	79	113	O66(4/0/63),1b18		-1.7

PELTZ, JOHN John B.4.23.1861 New Orleans LA D.2.27.1906 New Orleans LA BR/TR/5-8/175 d5.1

1884	Ind AA	106	393	40	86	13	17	3		7	2		.219	.236	.361	95	-4		.818	5	81	30	O106L		-0.1
1888	Bal AA	1	4	1	1	0	0	0	0	0	2		.250	.250	.250	62	0	1	.500	-0	0	0	/OL		-0.1
1890	Bro AA	98	384	55	87	9	6	1	33	32	2		.227	.289	.289	73	-14	10	.904	1	107	137	O98C		-1.4
	Syr AA	5	17	2	3	1	1	0	2	3	0		.176	.300	.353	103	0	0	.857	1	316	665	O5C		0.1
	Tol AA	20	73	8	18	2	2	0	13	3	1		.247	.286	.329	79	-3	7	.886	-0	108	171	O20C		-0.3
	Year	123	474	65	108	12	9	1	48	38	3		.228	.289	.297	75	-16	17	.900	1	114	158	O123C		-1.6
Total 3		230	871	106	195	25	26	4	48	45	5		.224	.266	.326	84	-21	18	.865	4	98	98	O230(107/123/0)		-1.8

PEMBERTON, BROCK Brock B.11.5.1953 Tulsa OK BB/TL/6-3/190* [NYN72 6/133] d9.10

1974	NY N	11	22	0	4	0	0	0	1	0-0	0	3	.182	.182	.182	2	-3	0-1	1.000	1	193	138	1b4		-0.3
1975	NY N	2	2	0	0	0	0	0	0	0-0	0	1	.000	.000	.000	-99	-1	0-0	—	0			/H		-0.1
Total 2		13	24	0	4	0	0	0	1	0-0	0	4	.167	.167	.167	-7	-4	0-1	1.000	1	193	138	1b4		-0.4

PEMBERTON, RUDY Rudy Hector (Perez) B.12.17.1969 San Pedro de Macoris, D.R. BR/TR/6-1/185* d4.26

1995	Det A	12	30	3	9	3	1	0	2	1-0	1	5	.300	.344	.467	108	0	0-0	1.000	-1	95	0	O8(6/0/2),D3		0.0
1996	Bos A	13	41	11	21	8	0	1	10	2-0	2	4	.512	.556	.780	229	9	3-1	1.000	-3	42	0	O13(1/0/12)		0.5
1997	Bos A	27	63	8	15	2	0	2	10	4-0	3	13	.238	.314	.365	75	-2	0-0	.949	0	94	170	O23R		-0.3
Total 3		52	134	22	45	13	1	3	23	7-0	6	22	.336	.395	.515	130	7	3-1	.968	-3	79	84	O44(7/0/37),D3		0.2

PENA, BERT Adalberto (Rivera) B.7.11.1959 Santurce, PR BR/TR/5-11/165* d9.14

1981	Hou N	4	2	0	1	0	0	0	0	0-0	0	0	.500	.500	.500	195	0	0-0	1.000	-0	55	325	S3		0.0
1983	Hou N	4	8	0	1	0	0	0	0	2-0	0	1	.125	.300	.125	23	-1	0-0	1.000	-2	72	110	S4		-0.2
1984	Hou N	24	39	3	8	1	0	1	4	3-1	0	8	.205	.262	.308	63	-2	0-0	1.000	-2	98	0	3b7,S6,2b2	15	-0.2
1985	Hou N	20	29	7	6	0	0	0	4	1-0	0	6	.276	.290	.345	82	-1	0-0	.907	1	96	51	S10,3b2/2	83	-0.1
1986	Hou N	15	29	3	6	1	0	0	4	5-2	0	5	.207	.324	.241	60	-1	1-0	.982	-4	81	37	S19/3		-0.2
1987	Hou N	21	46	5	7	0	0	0	1	2-0	1	7	.152	.204	.152	-4	-7	0-0	.953	-6	88	64	S63,3b10,2b3	98	-1.1
Total 6		88	153	18	31	4	0	1	16	13-3	1	28	.203	.268	.248	45	-12	1-0	.953	-6	88	64	S63,3b10,2b3		-0.3

PENA, ANGEL Angel Maria B.2.16.1975 San Pedro de Macoris, D.R. BR/TR/5-10/228* d9.8

1998	LA N	6	13	1	3	0	0	0	0	0-0	0	6	.231	.231	.231	23	-2	0-0	1.000	1	200	107	C4		-0.1
1999	LA N	43	120	14	25	6	0	4	21	12-0	1	24	.208	.276	.358	63	-7	0-1	.989	-1	92	128	C43		0.2
2001	LA N	22	54	3	11	1	0	1	2	1-0	0	17	.204	.214	.278	29	-6	0-0	1.000	6	107	117	C15		0.0
Total 3		71	187	18	39	7	0	5	23	13-0	1	47	.209	.256	.326	51	-15	0-1	.993	6	102	121	C62		0.1

PENA, TONY Antonio Francisco (Padilla) B.6.4.1957 Monte Cristi, D.R. BR/TR/6-0/181(175-190) d9.1 M4/C1 b-Ramon

1980	Pit N	8	21	1	9	1	0	0	0	0-0	0	4	.429	.429	.571	171	2	0-1	.952	7		78	95	C6		0.0
1981	Pit N	66	210	16	63	9	1	2	17	8-2	1	23	.300	.326	.381	96	-1	1-2	.985	8	173	86	C64		0.3
1982	Pit N★	138	497	53	147	28	4	11	63	17-3	1	57	.296	.323	.435	106	2	2-5	.982	7	145	106	C137		1.9
1983	Pit N	151	542	51	163	22	3	15	70	31-8	0	73	.301	.338	.435	110	6	6-7	.992	6	128	90	C149		3.3
1984	Pit N★	147	546	77	156	27	2	15	78	36-5	4	79	.286	.333	.425	112	8	12-8	.991	22	137	111	C146		2.7
1985	Pit N★	147	546	53	136	27	2	10	59	29-4	1	67	.249	.284	.361	84	-16	12-8	.988	16	115	122	C139,1b4		2.1
1986	Pit N★	144	510	56	147	26	2	10	52	53-6	1	69	.288	.356	.406	107	6	9-10	.981	16	131	68	C112,1b4,O2R	41	-1.1
1987	†StL N	116	384	40	82	13	4	5	44	36-9	1	54	.214	.281	.307	55	-26	6-1	.994	10	130	91	C142,1b3		1.1
1988	StL N	149	505	55	133	23	1	10	51	33-11	2	60	.263	.308	.372	85	-8	5-3	.997	13	103	103	C134/OR		1.3
1989	StL N★	141	424	36	110	17	2	4	37	35-19	2	33	.259	.318	.337	85	-11	8-6	.995	10	93	100	C142/1		-0.7
1990	†Bos A	143	491	62	129	19	1	7	56	43-3	1	71	.263	.322	.348	84	-11	8-3	.995	12	107	91	C140		0.6
1991	Bos A	141	464	45	107	23	2	5	48	37-1	1	45	.231	.291	.321	66	-22	3-2	.993	19	121	84	C132		0.3
1992	Bos A	133	410	39	99	21	1	1	38	24-0	1	61	.241	.284	.305	61	-22	3-2	.995	20	138	76	C125/D		0.2
1993	Bos A	126	304	20	55	11	0	4	19	25-0	2	46	.181	.246	.257	34	-29	0-1	.996	2	90	106	C40		-0.6
1994	Cle A	40	112	18	33	4	0	2	10	9-0	0	11	.295	.341	.438	100	0	0-1	.987	-1	74	80	C91		0.6
1995	†Cle A	91	263	25	69	15	0	5	28	14-1	1	34	.262	.302	.376	74	-11	1-0	.992	6	112	120	C67		0.1
1996	†Cle A	67	174	14	34	4	0	1	27	15-0	0	25	.195	.255	.236	26	-20	0-1	1.000	-5	58	43	C30/3	17	-0.1
1997	Chi A	31	67	4	15	4	0	0	8	2-0	1	9	.224	.250	.284	45	-8	0-0	1.000	-2	55	48	C8		-0.7
	†Hou N												.3	.211	.273	.368	72	-1	0-0	1.000	-2	55	48	C8	58	1.2
Total 18		1988	6489	667	1687	298	27	107	708	455-72	23	846	.260	.309	.364	83	-155	80-63	.991	178	121	97	C1950,1b13,O3R/3D		12.0

PENA, BRAYAN Brayan Eduardo B.1.7.1982 Havana, Cuba BB/TR/5-11/210 d5.23

2005	Atl N	18	39	2	7	2	0	0	4	1-1	0	7	.179	.200	.231	12	-5	0-0	1.000	-2	59	102	C15		-0.0

YEAR	TM	LG	G	AB	R	H	2B	3B	HR	RBI	BB-IB	HP	SO	AVG	OBP	SLG	AOPS	ABR	SB-CS	FA	FR	RNG	THR	GAMES AT POSITION	DL	BFW

PENA, CARLOS Carlos Felipe B5.17.1978 Santo Domingo, D.R. BL/TL/6-2/210* [TexA98 1/10] d9.5 Col Northeastern

YEAR	TM	LG	G	AB	R	H	2B	3B	HR	RBI	BB-IB	HP	SO	AVG	OBP	SLG	AOPS	ABR	SB-CS	FA	FR	RNG	THR	GAMES AT POSITION	DL	BFW
2001	Tex	A	22	62	6	16	4	1	3	12	10-0	0	17	.258	.361	.500	120	2	0-0	.987	2	147	87	1b16/D		
2002	Oak	A	40	124	12	27	4	0	6	16	15-0	1	38	.218	.305	.419	91	-2	0-0	.997	8	177	83	1b40		0.2
	Det	A	75	273	31	69	13	4	12	36	26-0	2	73	.253	.321	.462	109	3	2-2	.996	-7	62	110	1b73,D2		0.2
	Year		115	397	43	96	17	4	19	52	41-0	3	111	.242	.316	.448	103	1	2-2	.996	0	102	101	1b113,D2		-1.1
2003	Det	A	131	452	51	112	21	6	18	50	53-1	6	123	.248	.332	.440	107	4	4-5	.990	-0	108	114	1b128/D		-0.9
2004	Det	A	142	481	89	116	22	4	27	82	70-2	3	146	.241	.338	.472	113	9	7-1	.995	-2	94	114	1b135,D5	25	-0.8
2005	Det	A	79	260	37	61	9	0	18	44	31-2	4	95	.235	.325	.477	113	4	0-1	.993	2	117	111	1b51,D24		-0.3
Total	5		489	1652	226	401	73	15	85	240	205-5	16	492	.243	.330	.459	109	20	13-9	.993	2	105	109	1b443,D33	25	-1.8

PENA, ELVIS Elvis (Mendez) B9.15.1976 San Pedro de Macoris, D.R. BB/TR/5-11/164* d9.2

YEAR	TM	LG	G	AB	R	H	2B	3B	HR	RBI	BB-IB	HP	SO	AVG	OBP	SLG	AOPS	ABR	SB-CS	FA	FR	RNG	THR	GAMES AT POSITION	DL	BFW
2000	Col	N	10	9	1	3	1	0	0	1	1-0	0	1	.333	.400	.444	92	0	1-0	1.000	-0	103	228	S3/2		0.0
2001	Mil	N	15	40	5	9	2	0	0	6	6-0	1	6	.225	.333	.275	63	-2	2-0	.980	3	136	116	2b11		0.2
Total	2		25	49	6	12	3	0	0	7	7-0	1	7	.245	.345	.306	70	-2	3-0	.980	3	134	115	2b12,S3		0.2

PENA, GERONIMO Geronimo (Martinez) B3.29.1967 Distrito Nacional, D.R. BB/TR/6-1/195(170-195) d9.5 [DL 1989 StL N 63]

YEAR	TM	LG	G	AB	R	H	2B	3B	HR	RBI	BB-IB	HP	SO	AVG	OBP	SLG	AOPS	ABR	SB-CS	FA	FR	RNG	THR	GAMES AT POSITION	DL	BFW
1990	StL	N	18	45	5	11	2	0	0	2	4-0	1	14	.244	.314	.289	68	-2	1-1	.982	2	111	135	2b11		0.0
1991	StL	N	104	185	38	45	8	3	5	17	18-1	5	45	.243	.322	.400	102	0	15-5	.976	-7	94	107	2b83,O4L		-0.4
1992	StL	N	62	203	31	62	12	1	7	31	24-0	5	37	.305	.386	.478	149	14	13-8	.984	11	116	136	2b57		2.7
1993	StL	N	74	254	34	65	19	2	5	30	25-0	4	71	.256	.330	.406	97	-1	13-5	.966	3	112	121	2b64	100	0.6
1994	StL	N	83	213	33	54	13	1	11	34	24-1	6	54	.254	.344	.479	112	4	9-1	.990	5	105	124	2b59/3	59	1.1
1995	StL	N	32	101	20	27	6	1	1	8	16-1	1	30	.267	.367	.376	96	0	3-2	.976	-1	102	112	2b25	9	0.1
1996	Cle	A	5	9	1	1	0	0	1	2	1-0	0	4	.111	.200	.444	57	-1	0-0	—	-1	0	0	3b3/2	101	-0.1
Total	7		378	1010	162	265	60	8	30	124	112-3	22	255	.262	.345	.427	109	14	54-22	.978	9	107	122	2b300,3b4,O4L	332	3.9

PENA, ROBERTO Roberto Cesar "Baby" (b Roberto Cesar Zapata (Pena)) B4.17.1937 Santo Domingo, D.R. D7.23.1982 Santiago, D.R. BR/TR/5-8/175(163-175) d4.12

YEAR	TM	LG	G	AB	R	H	2B	3B	HR	RBI	BB-IB	HP	SO	AVG	OBP	SLG	AOPS	ABR	SB-CS	FA	FR	RNG	THR	GAMES AT POSITION	DL	BFW
1965	Chi	N	51	170	17	37	5	1	2	12	16-4	2	19	.218	.291	.294	64	-8	1-2	.930	-5	102	97	S50		-1.0
1966	Chi	N	6	17	0	3	0	0	0	0	0-0	0	4	.176	.176	.294	28	-2	0-0	.957	1	99	86	S5		-0.1
1968	Phi	N	138	500	56	130	13	2	1	38	34-2	2	63	.260	.307	.300	84	-10	0-0	.954	9	101	121	S133		1.1
1969	SD	N	139	472	44	118	16	3	4	30	21-0	3	63	.250	.286	.322	72	-19	0-3	.977	-2	104	89	S65,2b33,3b27,1b12		-1.6
1970	Oak	A	19	58	4	15	1	0	0	3	3-0	0	4	.259	.295	.276	60	-3	1-1	.961	-3	89	48	S12,3b5		-0.5
	Mil	A	121	416	36	99	19	1	3	42	25-4	2	45	.238	.282	.310	64	-21	3-5	.981	-13	94	95	S99,2b15,1b7		-2.4
	Year		140	474	40	114	20	1	3	45	28-4	2	49	.241	.283	.306	63	-24	4-6	.979	-16	93	90	S111,2b15,1b7,3b5		-2.9
1971	Mil	A	113	274	17	65	9	3	3	28	15-3	1	37	.237	.279	.325	71	-11	0-0	.996	1	88	87	1b50,3b37,S23/2		-1.2
Total	6		587	1907	174	467	65	10	13	154	114-13	10	235	.245	.290	.310	72	-74	10-17	.962	-13	100	103	S387,1b69,3b69,2b49		-5.7

PENA, WILY MO Wily Modesto B1.23.1982 Laguna Salada, D.R. BR/TR/6-3/215(215-245) d9.10 [DL 2000 NY A 80]

YEAR	TM	LG	G	AB	R	H	2B	3B	HR	RBI	BB-IB	HP	SO	AVG	OBP	SLG	AOPS	ABR	SB-CS	FA	FR	RNG	THR	GAMES AT POSITION	DL	BFW
2002	Cin	N	13	18	1	4	0	0	1	1	0-0	0	11	.222	.222	.389	57	-1	0-0	1.000	-1	68	0	O4(3/0/1)		-0.2
2003	Cin	N	80	165	20	36	6	1	5	16	12-2	3	53	.218	.283	.358	69	-8	3-2	.977	-2	95	41	O47(8/26/14)/3		-1.1
2004	Cin	N	110	336	45	87	10	1	26	66	22-1	6	108	.259	.316	.527	115	5	5-2	.969	6	116	127	O91(1/46/51)	25	0.9
2005	Cin	N	99	311	42	79	17	0	19	51	20-0	3	116	.254	.304	.492	108	2	2-1	.976	-2	100	46	O83(10/25/50)	35	-0.3
Total	4		302	830	108	206	33	2	51	134	54-3	12	288	.248	.303	.477	102	-2	10-5	.973	1	105	77	O225(22/97/116)/3	140	-0.7

PENCE, ELMER Elmer Clair B8.17.1900 Valley Springs CA D9.17.1968 San Francisco CA BR/TR/6-0/185 d8.23

YEAR	TM	LG	G	AB	R	H	2B	3B	HR	RBI	BB-IB	HP	SO	AVG	OBP	SLG	AOPS	ABR	SB-CS	FA	FR	RNG	THR	GAMES AT POSITION	DL	BFW
1922	Chi	A	1	0	0	0	0	0	0	0	0-0	0	—	—	—	—	—	—	0-0	1.000	0	164	0	/OR		0.0

PENDLETON, JIM James Edward B1.7.1924 St.Charles MO D3.20.1996 Houston TX BR/TR/6-0/185* d4.17 Negro Lg 1948

YEAR	TM	LG	G	AB	R	H	2B	3B	HR	RBI	BB-IB	HP	SO	AVG	OBP	SLG	AOPS	ABR	SB-CS	FA	FR	RNG	THR	GAMES AT POSITION	DL	BFW
1953	Mil	N	120	251	48	75	12	4	7	27	7	2	36	.299	.323	.462	108	2	6-5	.961	7	114	138	O105(75/15/25),S7		0.5
1954	Mil	N	71	173	20	38	3	1	1	16	4	1	21	.220	.236	.266	33	-18	2-1	.950	1	98	167	O50(23/18/11)		-1.9
1955	Mil	N	8	10	0	0	0	0	0	0	0-0	0	2	.000	.000	.000	-99	-3	0-0	1.000	-1	0	0	/S3OC		-0.4
1956	Mil	N	14	11	0	0	0	0	0	0	1-0	0	3	.000	.083	.000	-80	-3	0-0	1.000	-0	99	0	S3,3b2/12		-0.3
1957	Pit	N	46	59	9	18	1	1	0	9	9-1	1	14	.305	.394	.356	110	1	0-0	.917	-2	80	217	O9(2/1/6),3b2/S		-0.3
1958	Pit	N	3	3	0	1	0	0	0	0	0-0	0	0	.333	.333	.333	79	0	0-0	—	0			/H		0.0
1959	Cin	N	65	113	13	29	2	0	3	9	8-2	1	18	.257	.309	.354	75	-4	3-0	.971	3	115	181	O24L,3b16,S3		-0.2
1962	Hou	N	117	321	30	79	12	2	8	36	14-2	2	57	.246	.279	.371	79	-11	0-0	.963	-3	100	79	O90(65/7/21),1b8,3b3,S2		-1.9
Total	8		444	941	120	240	30	8	19	97	43-5	6	151	.255	.290	.365	76	-36	11-6	.959	4	104	127	O279(189/42/63),3b24,S17,1b9/2		-4.2

PENDLETON, TERRY Terry Lee B7.16.1960 Los Angeles CA BB/TR/5-9/180(180-195) [StLN82 7/179] d7.18 C4 Col Cal St.-Fresno

YEAR	TM	LG	G	AB	R	H	2B	3B	HR	RBI	BB-IB	HP	SO	AVG	OBP	SLG	AOPS	ABR	SB-CS	FA	FR	RNG	THR	GAMES AT POSITION	DL	BFW
1984	StL	N	67	262	37	85	16	3	1	33	16-3	0	32	.324	.357	.420	122	7	20-5	.943	9	117	91	3b66		1.9
1985	†StL	N	149	559	56	134	16	3	5	69	37-4	0	75	.240	.285	.306	66	-26	17-12	.965	26	121	111	3b149	15	-0.4
1986	StL	N	159	578	56	138	26	5	1	59	34-10	1	59	.239	.279	.306	62	-31	24-6	.962	19	118	150	3b156/OR		-1.2
1987	†StL	N	159	583	82	167	29	4	12	96	70-6	2	74	.286	.360	.412	103	4	19-12	.949	5	108	100	3b158		0.6
1988	StL	N	110	391	44	99	20	2	6	53	21-4	2	51	.253	.293	.361	86	-8	3-3	.963	14	118	81	3b101	27	0.6
1989	StL	N	162	613	83	162	28	5	13	74	44-3	0	81	.264	.313	.390	97	-4	9-5	.971	35	129	101	3b161		3.3
1990	StL	N	121	447	46	103	20	2	6	58	30-8	1	58	.230	.277	.324	65	-22	7-5	.947	8	111	106	3b110	15	-1.4
1991	†Atl	N	153	586	94	187	34	8	22	86	43-8	1	70	.319	.363	.517	138	28	10-2	.950	20	114	139	3b148		5.1
1992	†Atl	N★	160	640	98	199	39	1	21	105	37-8	0	67	.311	.345	.473	123	18	5-2	.960	7	101	109	3b158		2.8
1993	†Atl	N	161	633	81	172	33	1	17	84	36-5	3	97	.272	.311	.408	89	-11	5-1	.959	11	102	138	3b161		0.2
1994	Atl	N	77	309	25	78	18	3	7	30	12-3	0	57	.252	.280	.398	72	-14	2-0	.950	3	96	113	3b77	33	-1.0
1995	Fla	N	133	513	70	149	32	1	14	78	38-7	2	84	.290	.339	.439	102	2	1-2	.952	3	97	129	3b129		0.5
1996	Fla	N	111	406	30	102	20	1	7	58	26-5	3	75	.251	.298	.357	75	-16	0-2	.961	6	103	126	3b108		-1.0
	†Atl	N	42	162	21	33	6	0	4	17	15-1	0	36	.204	.271	.315	51	-12	2-1	.939	1	99	88	3b41		-1.0
	Year		153	568	51	135	26	1	11	75	41-6	3	111	.238	.290	.345	68	-28	2-3	.955	6	102	116	3b149		-2.1
1997	Cin	N	50	113	11	28	9	0	1	17	12-1	0	14	.248	.320	.354	75	-4	2-3	.942	-7	70	24	3b32	44	-1.0
1998	KC	A	79	237	17	61	10	0	3	29	15-1	0	49	.257	.299	.338	63	-13	1-0	.957	1	105	74	D40,3b23	40	-1.4
Total	15		1893	7032	851	1897	356	39	140	946	486-77	15	979	.270	.316	.391	91	-102	127-59	.957	159	110	113	3b1785,D40/OR	174	6.5

PENN, SHANNON Shannon Dion B9.11.1969 Cincinnati OH BB/TR/5-10/163* [TexA88 58/1350] d4.28 Col Lakeland (OH) CC

YEAR	TM	LG	G	AB	R	H	2B	3B	HR	RBI	BB-IB	HP	SO	AVG	OBP	SLG	AOPS	ABR	SB-CS	FA	FR	RNG	THR	GAMES AT POSITION	DL	BFW
1995	Det	A	3	9	0	3	0	0	0	0	1-0	0	2	.333	.400	.333	93	-1	0-0	.864	2	138	248	2b3		0.2
1996	Det	A	6	14	0	1	0	0	0	0	0-0	0	3	.071	.071	.071	-64	-4	0-0	—	-0	0	0	/OLD		-0.3
Total	2		9	23	0	4	0	0	0	0	1-0	0	5	.174	.208	.174	-1	-4	0-0	.864	2	138	248	D4,2b3/OL		-0.1

PENNYFEATHER, WILL William Nathaniel B5.25.1968 Perth Amboy NJ BR/TR/6-2/195(195-215) d6.27

YEAR	TM	LG	G	AB	R	H	2B	3B	HR	RBI	BB-IB	HP	SO	AVG	OBP	SLG	AOPS	ABR	SB-CS	FA	FR	RNG	THR	GAMES AT POSITION	DL	BFW
1992	Pit	N	15	9	2	2	0	0	0	0	0-0	0	0	.222	.222	.222	26	-1	0-0	1.000	0	113	0	O10(1/6/5)		-0.1
1993	Pit	N	21	34	4	7	1	0	0	2	0-0	0	6	.206	.206	.235	18	-4	0-1	1.000	-1	94	0	O17(1/15/2)		-0.5
1994	Pit	N	4	3	0	0	0	0	0	0	0-0	0	0	.000	.000	.000	-98	-1	0-0	—	-0	0	0	/OL		-0.1
Total	3		40	46	6	9	1	0	0	2	0-0	0	6	.196	.196	.217	11	-6	0-1	1.000	-1	98	0	O28(3/21/7)		-0.7

PEOPLES, JIMMY James Elsworth B10.8.1863 Big Beaver MI D8.29.1920 Detroit MI TR/5-8/200 d5.29 U1 OF(5/6/24) ▲

YEAR	TM	LG	G	AB	R	H	2B	3B	HR	RBI	BB-IB	HP	SO	AVG	OBP	SLG	AOPS	ABR	SB-CS	FA	FR	RNG	THR	GAMES AT POSITION	DL	BFW
1884	Cin	AA	69	267	28	45	2	1	1	16	6		0	.169	.187	.202	26	-22		.829	-2	93	160	S47,C14,O10(0/4/6)/31		-2.1
1885	Cin	AA	7	22	1	4	0	0	0	1	1		0	.182	.217	.182	27	-2		.826	-1			C5,P2/OR		-0.2
	Bro	AA	41	151	21	30	4	1	1	15	5		1	.199	.229	.258	53	-8		.902	-0			C37,S2/13OC		-0.5
	Year		48	173	22	34	4	1	1	16	6		1	.197	.228	.249	50	-10		.896	-1			C42,P2,O2(0/1/1),S2/13		-0.7
1886	Bro	AA	93	340	43	74	7	3	3	38	20		0	.218	.261	.282	70	-13	20	.879	14			C76,S14,O8(4/1/3)/3		0.6
1887	Bro	AA	73	268	36	68	14	2	1	38	16		4	.254	.306	.332	77	-9	22	.853	-4			C57,O8(1/0/7),S4,1b4/2		-0.6
1888	Bro	AA	32	103	15	20	5	3	0	17	8		1	.194	.259	.301	79	-2	10	.904	4			C25,S5,O2R		0.4
1889	Col	AA	29	100	13	23	6	2	1	16	6		0	.230	.274	.360	84	-2	3	.922	-4			C22,O5R,2b2/S		-0.4
Total	6		344	1251	157	264	38	13	7	141	62		6	.211	.252	.279	62	-58	55	.887	2			C236,S73,O35R,1b6,2b3,3b3,P2		-2.8

PEPITONE, JOE Joseph Anthony "Pepi" B10.9.1940 Brooklyn NY BL/TL/6-2/200(170-200) d4.10 C1

YEAR	TM	LG	G	AB	R	H	2B	3B	HR	RBI	BB-IB	HP	SO	AVG	OBP	SLG	AOPS	ABR	SB-CS	FA	FR	RNG	THR	GAMES AT POSITION	DL	BFW
1962	NY	A	63	138	14	33	3	2	7	17	3-0	0	21	.239	.255	.442	86	-4	1-1	1.000	-3	66	0	O32(14/7/13),1b16		-0.9
1963	†NY	A★	157	580	79	157	16	3	27	89	23-2	7	63	.271	.304	.448	109	-4	3-5	.995	5	113	114	1b143,O16(0/7/9)		-0.1
1964	†NY	A★	160	613	71	154	12	3	28	100	24-7	3	63	.251	.281	.418	90	-11	2-3	.988	8	124	112	1b155,O30(0/28/3)		-1.6
1965	NY	A	143	531	51	131	18	3	18	62	59-6	2	59	.247	.305	.394	98	-3	4-2	.997	1	100	119	1b115,O41(2/3/36)		-1.1
1966	NY	A	152	585	85	149	21	4	31	83	29-6	2	58	.255	.290	.463	118	10	4-3	.995	10	129	106	1b119,O55(0/49/9)		1.2
1967	NY	A	133	501	45	126	18	3	13	64	34-4	3	62	.251	.301	.377	104	-1	1-3	.976	-7	94	90	O123C,1b6		-1.2
1968	NY	A	108	380	41	93	14	3	15	56	37-9	1	45	.245	.311	.403	120	8	8-2	.980	-10	85	62	O92(4/88/0),1b12	22	-0.6

YEAR	TM LG	G	AB	R	H	2B	3B	HR	RBI	BB-IB	HP	SO	AVG	OBP	SLG	AOPS	ABR	SB-CS	FA	FR	RNG	THR	GAMES AT POSITION	DL	BFW
1969	NY A	135	513	49	124	16	3	27	70	30-11	1	42	.242	.284	.442	104	-1	8-6	**.995**	-4	88	118	1b132		-1.7
1970	Hou N	75	279	44	70	9	5	14	35	18-9	1	28	.251	.298	.470	107	0	5-2	.995	-1	90	116	O28(15/3/13)		-0.5
	Chi N	56	213	38	57	9	2	12	44	15-2	0	15	.268	.328	.498	102	0	0-2	.992	-1	107	35	O56C,1b13		-0.3
	Year	131	492	82	127	18	7	26	79	33-11	1	43	.258	.304	.482	104	0	5-4	.989	-1	109	42	O84(15/59/13),1b63		-0.8
1971	Chi N	115	427	50	131	19	4	16	61	24-8	3	41	.307	.347	.482	116	9	1-2	.990	-4	104	102	1b95,O23(1/22/0)	15	-0.3
1972	Chi N	66	214	23	56	19	0	8	21	13-4	1	22	.262	.309	.397	91	-3	1-2	.997	-1	89	120	1b66		-1.0
1973	Chi N	31	112	16	30	3	0	3	18	8-0	1	6	.268	.320	.375	86	-2	3-1	.985	-0	100	122	1b28		-0.5
	Atl N	3	11	0	4	0	0	0	1	1-0	0	1	.364	.417	.364	110	0	0-0	.963	-1	192	163	1b3		-0.1
	Year	34	123	16	34	3	0	3	19	9-0	1	7	.276	.328	.374	88	-2	3-1	.983	-1	90	129	1b31		-0.1
Total	12	1397	5097	606	1315	158	35	219	721	302-73	28	526	.258	.301	.432	105	8	41-32	.993	-9	107	113	1b953,O496(36/386/83)	37	-8.7

PEPLOSKI, HENRY   Henry Stephen "Pep" B9.15.1905 Garlin, Poland D1.28.1982 Dover NJ BL/TR/5-9/155 d9.19 b-Pepper   -0.1

YEAR	TM LG	G	AB	R	H	2B	3B	HR	RBI	BB-IB	HP	SO	AVG	OBP	SLG	AOPS	ABR	SB-CS	FA	FR	RNG	THR	GAMES AT POSITION	DL	BFW
1929	Bos N	6	10	1	2	0	0	1	1	0-0	0	3	.200	.273	.200	20	-1	0	1.000	-0	82	0	3b2		

PEPLOSKI, PEPPER   Joseph Aloysius B9.12.1891 Brooklyn NY D7.13.1972 New York NY BR/TR/5-8/155 d6.24 b-Henry Col Seton Hall   0.0

1913	Det A	2	4	1	2	0	0	0	0	0-0	0	0	.500	.500	.500	196	0	0	1.000	-0	78	0	3b2		

PEPPER, DON   Donald Hoyte B10.8.1943 Saratoga Sprgs. NY BL/TR/6-4.5/215 d9.10   -0.1

1966	Det A	4	3	0	0	0	0	0	0	0-0	0	1	.000	.000	.000	-98	-1	0-0	1.000	0	0	0	/1		

PEPPER, RAY   Raymond Watson B8.5.1905 Decatur AL D3.24.1996 Belle Mina AL BR/TR/6-2/195 d4.15 Col Alabama   -0.3

YEAR	TM LG	G	AB	R	H	2B	3B	HR	RBI	BB-IB	HP	SO	AVG	OBP	SLG	AOPS	ABR	SB-CS	FA	FR	RNG	THR	GAMES AT POSITION	DL	BFW
1932	StL N	21	57	3	14	2	1	0	7	5-0	0	13	.246	.306	.316	66	-3	1	.971	0	104	108	O17(16/0/1)		0.0
1933	StL N	3	9	2	2	0	0	1	2	0-0	0	1	.222	.222	.556	110	0	0	1.000	-0	86	0	O2L		-2.
1934	StL N	148	564	71	168	24	6	7	101	29-0	0	67	.298	.333	.399	81	-17	1-4	.963	3	100	133	O136(101/37/1)		-1.5
1935	StL A	92	261	20	66	15	4	3	37	20-0	0	32	.253	.306	.379	73	-11	0-2	.982	-1	92	113	O57(27/4/26)		-0.5
1936	StL N	75	124	13	35	5	0	2	23	5-0	1	36	.282	.310	.371	66	-7	0-2	.941	1	93	121	O18(2/5/11)		-4.8
Total	5	339	1015	109	285	46	10	14	170	59	1	136	.281	.321	.387	77	-38	2-8	.967	1	98	121	O230(148/46/39)		

PERALTA, JHONNY   Jhonny Antonio B5.28.1982 Santiago, D.R. BR/TR/6-1/180* d6.12   -0.

YEAR	TM LG	G	AB	R	H	2B	3B	HR	RBI	BB-IB	HP	SO	AVG	OBP	SLG	AOPS	ABR	SB-CS	FA	FR	RNG	THR	GAMES AT POSITION	DL	BFW
2003	Cle A	77	242	24	55	10	1	4	21	20-0	4	65	.227	.295	.326	65	-13	1-3	.976	1	108	94	S72,3b6		-0.
2004	Cle A	8	25	2	6	1	0	0	2	3-0	0	6	.240	.321	.280	61	-1	0-1	.889	-2	94	49	S7,3b2		4.
2005	Cle A	141	504	82	147	35	4	24	78	58-3	3	128	.292	.366	.520	138	28	0-2	.970	5	101	**129**	S141		3.
Total	3	226	771	108	208	46	5	28	101	81-3	7	199	.270	.342	.451	112	14	1-6	.970	5	103	115	S220,3b8		

PERCONTE, JACK   John Patrick B8.31.1954 Joliet IL BL/TR/5-10/160* [LAN76 16/379] d9.13 Col Murray St.   0.

YEAR	TM LG	G	AB	R	H	2B	3B	HR	RBI	BB-IB	HP	SO	AVG	OBP	SLG	AOPS	ABR	SB-CS	FA	FR	RNG	THR	GAMES AT POSITION	DL	BFW
1980	LA N	14	17	2	4	0	0	0	2	2-0	0	1	.235	.316	.235	57	-1	3-1	1.000	2	122	107	2b9		0.
1981	LA N	8	9	2	2	0	1	0	1	2-0	0	2	.222	.364	.444	134	0	1-1	1.000	4	291	355	2b2		-1.
1982	Cle A	93	219	27	52	4	4	0	15	22-1	0	25	.237	.303	.292	65	-11	9-3	.950	7	161	215	2b13		0.
1983	Cle A	14	26	1	7	1	0	0	0	5-0	0	2	.269	.387	.308	90	0	3-1	.981	5	100	85	2b150		1.
1984	Sea A	155	612	93	180	24	4	0	31	57-1	5	47	.294	.357	.346	97	-1	29-6	.986	16	108	105	2b125		1.
1985	Sea A	125	485	60	128	17	7	2	23	50-0	3	36	.264	.335	.340	85	-9	31-2	.990	-8	76	79	2b24		1.
1986	Chi A	24	73	6	16	1	0	0	4	11-1	0	10	.219	.321	.233	52	-5	2-0	.982	21	103	89	2b24		2
Total	7	433	1441	191	389	47	16	2	76	149-3	8	123	.270	.340	.329	85	-27	78-13	.982	21	103	89	2b405,D2		

PEREZ, ANTONIO   Antonio Miguel B1.26.1980 Bani, D.R. BR/TR/5-11/170* d5.14   -1

YEAR	TM LG	G	AB	R	H	2B	3B	HR	RBI	BB-IB	HP	SO	AVG	OBP	SLG	AOPS	ABR	SB-CS	FA	FR	RNG	THR	GAMES AT POSITION	DL	BFW
2003	TB A	48	125	19	31	6	1	2	12	18-0	1	34	.248	.345	.360	89	-1	4-1	.990	-13	77	56	2b31,3b6,S6,D3		0
2004	LA N	13	13	5	3	1	0	0	0	0-0	1	5	.231	.286	.308	54	-1	1-0	.750	-0	40	185	2b2/S		0
2005	LA N	98	259	28	77	13	2	3	23	21-1	5	61	.297	.360	.398	99	0	11-4	.946	2	120	89	3b35,2b29,S9/OLD	39	0
Total	3	159	397	52	111	20	3	5	35	39-1	7	100	.280	.353	.383	94	-2	16-5	.976	-12	83	66	2b62,3b41,S16,D4/OL	39	-0

PEREZ, TONY   Atanasio (Rigal) B5.14.1942 Ciego de Avila, Cuba BR/TR/6-2/205(175-215) d7.26 M2/C6 HF2000 s-Eduardo   -0

YEAR	TM LG	G	AB	R	H	2B	3B	HR	RBI	BB-IB	HP	SO	AVG	OBP	SLG	AOPS	ABR	SB-CS	FA	FR	RNG	THR	GAMES AT POSITION	DL	BFW
1964	Cin N	12	25	1	2	1	0	0	4	3-0	0	9	.080	.179	.120	-14	-4	0-0	.981	-1	0	59	1b6		-0
1965	Cin N	104	281	40	73	14	4	12	47	21-5	2	67	.260	.315	.466	110	3	0-2	.989	-2	96	95	1b93		-1
1966	Cin N	99	257	25	68	10	4	4	39	14-2	2	44	.265	.304	.381	83	-6	1-0	.989	-5	63	96	1b75		-0
1967	Cin N★	156	600	78	174	28	7	26	102	33-10	4	102	.290	.328	.490	119	13	3-2	.952	6	106	100	3b160		2
1968	Cin N★	160	625	93	176	25	7	18	92	51-13	6	92	.282	.338	.430	123	17	3-2	.937	-3	105	114	3b160		4
1969	Cin N★	160	629	103	185	31	2	37	122	63-7	2	131	.294	.357	.526	138	31	4-2	.923	-5	99	122	3b153,1b8		4
1970	†Cin N★	158	587	107	186	28	6	40	129	83-13	4	134	.317	.401	.589	162	52	8-3	.959	5	108	117	3b148,1b44		1
1971	Cin N	158	609	72	164	22	3	25	91	51-5	1	120	.269	.325	.438	116	11	3-0	.993	-5	86	**110**	1b136		1
1972	†Cin N	136	515	64	146	33	7	21	90	55-15	0	117	.283	.349	.497	146	30	4-2	.991	-2	99	110	1b151		3
1973	†Cin N★	151	564	73	177	33	3	27	101	74-10	3	117	.314	.393	.527	160	47	3-1	**.996**	-5	83	99	1b157		-0
1974	Cin N★	158	596	81	158	28	2	28	101	61-7	2	112	.265	.331	.460	124	16	1-2	.993	-6	86	113	1b132		0
1975	†Cin N★	137	511	74	144	28	3	20	109	54-6	3	101	.282	.350	.466	124	11	10-5	.996	-6	82	104	1b136		-0
1976	†Cin N★	139	527	77	137	32	6	19	91	50-9	5	88	.260	.328	.452	117	11	4-3	.992	5	115	79	1b148		-0
1977	Mon N	154	559	71	158	32	6	19	91	63-15	2	111	.283	.352	.463	121	16	2-0	.991	-4	88	114	1b145		0
1978	Mon N	148	544	63	158	38	3	14	78	38-9	2	104	.290	.336	.449	119	13	2-1	.991	-4	88	87	1b129		-0
1979	Mon N	132	489	58	132	29	4	13	73	38-4	4	93	.270	.322	.425	103	1	5-0	.993	-4	90	115	1b137,D13		-0
1980	Bos A	151	585	73	161	31	3	25	105	41-11	1	93	.275	.320	.467	108	5	0-0	.993	-1	94	119	1b56,D23		-0
1981	Bos A	84	306	35	77	11	3	9	39	27-0	0	66	.252	.310	.395	96	-2	0-0	.857	0	169	0	D46,1b2		-0
1982	Bos A	69	196	18	51	14	2	6	31	19-3	0	48	.260	.326	.444	103	1	0-1	.998	1	98	81	1b69		-0
1983	†Phi N	91	253	18	61	11	2	15	43	28-1	1	57	.241	.316	.372	91	-3	1-0	.990	-2	73	85	1b31		-0
1984	Cin N	71	137	9	33	6	1	2	15	11-2	0	21	.241	.295	.343	76	-4	0-0	.995	-3	76	102	1b50		-0
1985	Cin N	72	183	25	60	8	0	6	33	22-1	0	22	.328	.396	.470	136	9	0-2	.984	-3	87	127	1b55		-0
1986	Cin N	77	200	14	51	12	1	2	29	25-2	0	25	.255	.333	.355	88	-3	0-0	.992						1.0
Total	23	2777	9778	1272	2732	505	79	379	1652	925-150	43	1867	.279	.341	.463	121	270	49-33	.992	-53	90	103	1b1778,3b760,D82/2		

PEREZ, DANNY   Daniel B2.26.1971 El Paso TX BR/TR/5-10/188 [MilA92 21/584] d6.30 Col Oklahoma St.

1996	Mil A	4	4	0	0	0	0	0	0	0-0	0	0	.000	.000	.000	-96	-1	0-0	1.000	0	155	0	O3(2/1/0)		

PEREZ, EDUARDO   Eduardo Atanasio B9.11.1969 Cincinnati OH BR/TR/6-4/215(215-240) [CalA91 1/17] d7.27 f-Tony Col Florida St.

YEAR	TM LG	G	AB	R	H	2B	3B	HR	RBI	BB-IB	HP	SO	AVG	OBP	SLG	AOPS	ABR	SB-CS	FA	FR	RNG	THR	GAMES AT POSITION	DL	BFW
1993	Cal A	52	180	16	45	6	2	4	30	9-0	2	39	.250	.292	.372	75	-7	5-4	.962	2	110	88	3b45,D3		
1994	Cal A	38	129	10	27	7	0	5	16	12-1	2	29	.209	.275	.380	66	-7	3-0	.997	-2	74	97	1b38		
1995	Cal A	29	71	9	12	4	1	1	7	12-0	1	9	.169	.302	.296	58	-4	0-2	.883	-2	88	85	3b23/D		
1996	Cin N	18	36	8	8	0	0	3	5	5-1	0	6	.222	.317	.472	103	0	1	1.000	1	147	111	1b8,3b3		
1997	Cin N	106	297	44	75	18	0	16	52	29-1	2	76	.253	.321	.475	104	1	5-1	.996	-2	83	80	1b51/3OL		
1998	Cin N	84	172	20	41	4	0	4	30	21-2	2	45	.238	.325	.331	73	-6	0-1	.985	7	157	113	O6L,1b5		
1999	StL N	21	32	6	11	2	0	1	9	7-0	0	6	.344	.462	.500	141	3	1-0	1.000	1	100	122	1b24,O4L,3b2	35	
2000	StL N	35	91	9	27	4	0	3	10	5-0	1	19	.297	.350	.440	97	-1	1-0	.982	2	125	294	O35(7/0/29),1b10,3b6/D		
2002	†StL N	96	154	22	31	9	0	10	26	17-0	3	36	.201	.290	.455	95	-2	0-0	.966	2	114	30	O71(10/0/64),3b12,1b5/D		
2003	StL N	105	253	47	72	16	0	11	41	29-1	4	53	.285	.365	.478	120	8	5-2	1.000	-1	62	139	1b5,O3(2/0/1)/3D	147	
2004	TB A	13	38	2	8	2	0	1	7	4-0	0	3	.211	.286	.342		8	0-2	.993	-2	82	62	1b49,O4(3/0/1),3b3,D7		
2005	TB A	77	161	23	41	6	0	11	28	26-0	0	30	.255	.368	.497	131	8	0-2	.994	3	98	93		182	
Total	12	674	1614	216	398	78	3	70	261	176-6	21	360	.247	.326	.429	96	-9	19-12	.994	3	98	93	1b262,O136(44/0/96),3b104,D17		

PEREZ, EDDIE   Eduardo Rafael B5.4.1968 Ciudad Ojeda, Venez BR/TR/6-1/185(175-220) d9.10

YEAR	TM LG	G	AB	R	H	2B	3B	HR	RBI	BB-IB	HP	SO	AVG	OBP	SLG	AOPS	ABR	SB-CS	FA	FR	RNG	THR	GAMES AT POSITION	DL	BFW
1995	Atl N	7	13	1	4	1	0	1	4	0-0	0	2	.308	.308	.615	130	0	0-0	1.000	3	0	0	C5/1	15	
1996	†Atl N	68	156	19	40	9	1	4	17	8-0	1	19	.256	.293	.404	78	-5	0-0	.993	-4	160	67	C54,1b7		
1997	†Atl N	73	191	20	41	5	0	6	18	10-0	2	35	.215	.259	.335	54	-14	1-1	.988	-2	87	84	C64,1b6		
1998	†Atl N	61	149	18	50	12	0	6	32	15-0	6	40	.336	.404	.537	146	10	1-1	.997	0	76	115	C45,1b8/D		
1999	†Atl N	104	309	30	77	17	0	7	30	17-4	6	40	.249	.299	.372	70	-15	0-1	.993	6	129	89	C98,1b2	150	
2000	Atl N	7	22	0	4	1	0	0	0	0-0	0	3	.182	.182	.227	2	-3	0-0	.976	-1	71	60	C7	153	
2001	Atl N	5	10	0	3	0	0	0	4	0-0	0	1	.300	.300	.300	55	-1	0-0	.988	-1	83	154	C42		
2002	Cle A	42	117	6	25	7	0	4	17	5-0	1	25	.214	.252	.291	43	-10	0-0	.991	-14	75	91	C102		
2003	Mil N	107	350	26	95	17	1	11	45	17-3	3	29	.271	.304	.420	87	-9	0-0	.990	1	118	134	C66/1		
2004	Atl N	74	170	19	39	8	2	0	13	11-1	3	29	.229	.286	.353	64	-9	0-0	1.000	-3	509	143	C13	112	
2005	Atl N	16	38	5	8	3	2	0	1	1-0	0	5	.211	.231	.421	64	-4	0-0	.991					430	
Total	11	564	1525	137	386	85	2	40	172	84-8	15	234	.253	.297	.390	77	-57	1-4	.991	-16	110	140	C501,1b25/D		

YEAR	TM LG	G	AB	R	H	2B	3B	HR	RBI	BB-IB	HP	SO	AVG	OBP	SLG	AOPS	ABR	SB-CS	FA	FR	RNG	THR	GAMES AT POSITION	DL	BFW

PEREZ, MARTY   Martin Roman B2.28.1946 Visalia CA BR/TR/5-11/160* d9.9

YEAR	TM LG	G	AB	R	H	2B	3B	HR	RBI	BB-IB	HP	SO	AVG	OBP	SLG	AOPS	ABR	SB-CS	FA	FR	RNG	THR	GAMES AT POSITION	DL	BFW
1969	Cal A	13	13	3	3	0	0	0	0	2-0	0	1	.231	.333	.231	63	-1	0-0	1.000	4	145	278	S7,2b2,3b2		0.4
1970	Cal A	3	3	0	0	0	0	0	1	0-0	0	0	.000	.000	.000	-99	-1	0-0	.833	-1	57	155	S2		
1971	Atl N	130	410	28	93	15	3	4	32	25-5	0	44	.227	.272	.307	60	-22	1-2	.955	-13	97	115	S126/2		-0.1
1972	Atl N	141	479	33	109	13	1	1	28	30-1	3	55	.228	.276	.265	50	-31	0-3	.957	-34	87	84	S141		-2.3
1973	Atl N	141	501	66	125	15	5	8	57	49-1	2	66	.250	.316	.347	79	-14	2-3	.962	-6	102	91	S139		-5.4
1974	Atl N	127	447	51	116	20	5	2	34	35-1	1	51	.260	.314	.340	80	-12	2-0	.985	-4	100	108	2b102,S14,3b6		-0.6
1975	Atl N	120	461	50	127	14	2	2	34	37-2	0	44	.275	.327	.328	80	-12	2-2	.985	-4	100	94	2b116,S7		-0.9
1976		31	96	12	24	4	0	1	6	8-0	0	9	.250	.305	.323	75	-3	0-0	.976	0	98	99	S17,3b2	32	-0.9
	SF N	93	332	37	86	13	1	2	26	30-0	0	28	.259	.318	.322	80	-8	3-4	.979	1	107	89	2b89,S5		-0.1
	Year	124	428	49	110	17	1	3	32	38-0	0	37	.257	.315	.322	79	-11	3-4	.978	1	106	90	2b107,S22,3b2		-0.2
1977	NY A	1	4	0	0	0	0	0	0	0-0	0	1	.000	.000	.000	-99	-1	0-0	.978	1	106	90	/3		-0.3
	Oak A	115	373	32	86	14	5	2	23	29-0	3	65	.231	.290	.311	65	-18	0-0	1.000	1	207	621	2b105,3b12,S4		0.1
	Year	116	377	32	88	14	5	2	23	29-0	3	66	.233	.292	.313	66	-18	1-3	.974	4	109	80	2b105,3b13,S4		-1.0
1978	Oak A	16	12	1	0	0	0	0	0	0-0	0	5	.000	.000	.000	-99	-3	1-3	.974	5	109	80			-0.9
Total	10	931	3131	313	771	108	22	22	241	245-10	10	369	.246	.301	.316	70	-125	11-17	.958	-51	96	98	S465,2b434,3b34	32	-11.3

PEREZ, MIGUEL   Miguel Antonio B9.25.1983 Caracas, Venez BR/TR/6-3/190 d9.7

YEAR	TM LG	G	AB	R	H	2B	3B	HR	RBI	BB-IB	HP	SO	AVG	OBP	SLG	AOPS	ABR	SB-CS	FA	FR	RNG	THR	GAMES AT POSITION	DL	BFW
2005	Cin N	2	3	0	0	0	0	0	0	0-0	0	0	.000	.000	.000	-99	-1	0-0	1.000	0	0	0	/C		-0.1

PEREZ, NEIFI   Neifi Neftali (Diaz) B6.2.1973 Villa Mella, D.R. BB/TR/6-0/175(173-195) d8.31

YEAR	TM LG	G	AB	R	H	2B	3B	HR	RBI	BB-IB	HP	SO	AVG	OBP	SLG	AOPS	ABR	SB-CS	FA	FR	RNG	THR	GAMES AT POSITION	DL	BFW
1996	Col N	17	45	4	7	2	0	0	3	0-0	0	8	.156	.156	.200	-6	-7	2-2	.972	-1	86	146	S14,2b4		-0.7
1997	Col N	83	313	46	91	13	10	5	31	21-4	1	43	.291	.333	.444	84	-8	4-3	.975	26	131	123	S45,2b41,3b2		2.2
1998	Col N	162	647	80	177	25	9	9	59	38-0	1	70	.274	.313	.382	68	-30	4-3	.975	26	131	123	S162/C		1.0
1999	Col N	157	690	108	193	27	11	12	70	28-0	1	54	.280	.307	.403	62	-40	5-6	.975	29	113	123	S157		-0.1
2000	Col N	162	651	92	187	39	11	10	71	30-6	1	63	.287	.314	.427	62	-40	13-5	.981	27	109	112	S162		1.6
2001	Col N	87	382	65	114	19	8	7	47	16-1	0	49	.298	.326	.445	80	-11	6-2	.978	37	115	117	S87	15	0.3
	KC A	49	199	18	48	7	1	2	10	10-0	1	19	.241	.277	.302	49	-15	3-4	.976	7	102	114	S46,2b4		-0.4
2002	KC A	145	554	65	131	20	4	3	37	20-2	1	53	.236	.260	.303	44	-45	8-9	.972	6	102	113	S139,2b5		-2.8
2003	†SF N	120	328	27	84	19	4	1	31	14-3	0	23	.256	.285	.348	63	-18	3-2	.987	22	109	103	2b57,S45,3b2		0.8
2004	SF N	103	319	28	74	12	1	2	33	21-3	0	35	.232	.276	.295	47	-25	0-1	.978	11	108	93	S57,2b39,3b2		-0.9
	Chi N	23	62	12	23	5	0	2	6	3-0	0	6	.371	.400	.548	138	3	0-1	.968	4	105	125	S19,2b2		0.8
	Year	126	381	40	97	17	1	4	39	24-3	0	41	.255	.296	.336	62	-22	1-1	.976	15	107	100	S76,2b41,3b2		-0.1
2005	Chi N	154	572	59	157	33	1	9	54	18-3	3	47	.274	.298	.383	65	-22	8-4	.982	25	111	108	S130,2b26,3b4		1.4
Total	10	1262	4762	604	1286	221	60	61	454	219-22	7	470	.270	.301	.380	65	-248	56-44	.978	202	110	117	S1063,2b178,3b10/C	15	3.2

PEREZ, ROBERT   Robert Alexander (Jimenez) B6.4.1969 Bolivar, Venez BR/TR/6-3/215(190-230) d7.20

YEAR	TM LG	G	AB	R	H	2B	3B	HR	RBI	BB-IB	HP	SO	AVG	OBP	SLG	AOPS	ABR	SB-CS	FA	FR	RNG	THR	GAMES AT POSITION	DL	BFW
1994	Tor A	4	8	0	1	0	0	0	0	0-0	0	1	.125	.125	.125	-35	-2	0-0	1.000	0	60	555	O4(2/0/2)		
1995	Tor A	17	48	2	9	2	0	1	3	0-0	0	5	.188	.188	.292	22	-6	0-0	1.000	0	119	0	O15(5/0/11)		-0.1
1996	Tor A	86	202	30	66	10	0	2	21	8-0	1	17	.327	.354	.406	93	-2	3-0	.983	1	102	80	O79(59/0/25),D2		-0.6
1997	Tor A	37	78	4	15	4	1	2	6	2-0	0	16	.192	.192	.346	37	-8	0-0	1.000	-1	102	0	O25(17/0/9),D7		-0.3
1998	Sea A	17	35	3	6	1	0	1	2	6-0	0	5	.171	.171	.371	36	-8	0-0	1.000	-1	112	158	O17(2/0/15)		-0.9
	Mon N	52	106	9	25	1	0	1	8	2-0	1	23	.236	.255	.274	41	-10	0-0	.852	-2	56	239	O29L		-0.3
2001	NY A	6	15	1	4	1	0	0	1	0-0	0	7	.267	.313	.333	70	-1	0-1	1.000	0	94	94	O5(0/3/2)/D	22	-1.2
	Mil N	2	5	0	0	0	0	0	0	0-0	0	5	.000	.000	.000	-99	-2	0-0	1.000	0	146	0	/OR		-0.1
Total	6	221	497	49	126	19	1	8	44	11-0	2	74	.254	.271	.344	58	-35	3-1	.976	-1	96	99	O175(114/3/65),D10	22	-0.1

PEREZ, SANTIAGO   Santiago Alberto B12.30.1975 Santo Domingo, D.R. BB/TR/6-2/150(150-185) d6.3

YEAR	TM LG	G	AB	R	H	2B	3B	HR	RBI	BB-IB	HP	SO	AVG	OBP	SLG	AOPS	ABR	SB-CS	FA	FR	RNG	THR	GAMES AT POSITION	DL	BFW
2000	Mil N	24	52	8	9	2	0	0	8	8-2	1	31	.173	.290	.212	31	-5	4-0	.917	-2	105	108	S20		-0.5
2001	SD N	43	81	13	16	1	0	0	4	15-0	0	29	.198	.320	.210	46	-6	5-1	.947	-3	110	108	O26(9/10/8),S8,2b2	18	-0.8
Total	2	67	133	21	25	3	0	0	6	23-2	1	38	.188	.308	.211	40	-11	9-1	.913	-5	93	87	S28,O26(9/10/8),2b2	18	-1.3

PEREZ, TIMO   Timoniel B4.8.1975 Bani, D.R. BL/TL/5-9/167(165-180) d9.1

YEAR	TM LG	G	AB	R	H	2B	3B	HR	RBI	BB-IB	HP	SO	AVG	OBP	SLG	AOPS	ABR	SB-CS	FA	FR	RNG	THR	GAMES AT POSITION	DL	BFW
2000	†NY N	24	49	11	14	4	1	3	10	1-0	0	25	.286	.333	.469	107	0	1-1	.970	2	120	272	O19(8/7/8)		0.2
2001	NY N	85	239	26	59	9	1	5	22	12-0	2	45	.247	.287	.356	70	-12	1-6	1.000	4	108	133	O73(6/8/62)		-1.2
2002	NY N	136	444	52	131	27	4	8	47	23-2	2	36	.295	.334	.437	110	-2	10-6	.979	7	111	148	O122(24/93/17)		0.9
2003	NY N	127	346	32	93	21	0	4	42	18-1	2	29	.269	.301	.364	78	-2	5-6	.989	1	100	117	O104(58/49/14)	15	-1.3
2004	Chi A	103	293	38	72	12	0	5	40	15-0	2	29	.246	.285	.338	60	-18	3-1	.986	0	88	186	O80(12/25/49),D6	15	-1.8
2005	†Chi A	76	179	13	39	8	0	2	15	12-1	0	25	.218	.266	.296	47	-14	2-2	.964	1	92	223	O50(27/2/21),D11,1b2		-1.5
Total	6	551	1550	172	408	81	8	25	169	83-4	9	149	.263	.302	.374	79	-54	22-22	.984	14	102	158	O448(135/184/171),D17,1b2	33	-4.7

PEREZ, TOMAS   Tomas Orlando B12.29.1973 Barquisimeto, Venez BB/TR/5-11/177(165-190) d5.3

YEAR	TM LG	G	AB	R	H	2B	3B	HR	RBI	BB-IB	HP	SO	AVG	OBP	SLG	AOPS	ABR	SB-CS	FA	FR	RNG	THR	GAMES AT POSITION	DL	BFW
1995	Tor A	41	98	12	24	3	1	1	8	7-0	0	18	.245	.292	.327	61	-6	0-1	.954	-2	99	88	S31,2b7/3		-0.6
1996	Tor A	91	295	24	74	13	4	1	19	25-0	1	29	.251	.311	.332	63	-17	1-2	.970	6	105	133	2b75,3b11,S5		-0.7
1997	Tor A	40	123	9	24	3	2	0	9	11-0	1	28	.195	.267	.252	36	-12	1-1	.993	8	105	119	S32,2b8		-0.1
1998	Tor A	6	9	1	1	0	0	0	0	1-0	0	3	.111	.200	.111	-16	-2	0-0	1.000	-1	56	52	S4/2	28	-0.2
2000	Phi N	45	140	11	31	7	1	1	13	11-2	1	30	.221	.278	.307	48	-12	1-1	.976	-6	79	84	S44		-1.4
2001	Phi N	62	135	11	41	7	1	3	19	7-1	2	22	.304	.347	.437	106	1	0-1	1.000	7	110	108	2b29,3b9,S8/OR		0.8
2002	Phi N	92	212	22	53	13	1	5	20	21-6	1	40	.250	.319	.392	95	-3	1-0	.994	9	113	119	2b50,3b14,S13,1b3/P		0.8
2003	Phi N	125	298	39	79	18	1	5	33	23-11	0	54	.265	.316	.383	88	-6	0-1	.953	-3	99	150	3b58,2b26,1b9,S4	16	-0.4
2004	Phi N	86	176	22	38	13	2	6	21	9-2	1	44	.216	.257	.415	68	-9	0-0	.944	-3	98	51	3b22,2b17,1b10,S10		-1.1
2005	Phi N	94	159	17	37	7	0	0	22	11-2	2	27	.233	.289	.277	48	-12	1-0	1.000	-2	94	108	2b38,3b15,S14		-1.4
Total	10	682	1645	174	402	84	13	22	164	126-24	8	295	.244	.300	.351	70	-78	5-7	.981	17	107	115	2b213,S165,3b130,1b46/POR	44	-4.3

PEREZCHICA, TONY   Antonio Llamas (Gonzales) B4.20.1966 Mexicali, Baja California, Mexico BR/TR/5-11/165* [SFN84 3/63] d9.7

YEAR	TM LG	G	AB	R	H	2B	3B	HR	RBI	BB-IB	HP	SO	AVG	OBP	SLG	AOPS	ABR	SB-CS	FA	FR	RNG	THR	GAMES AT POSITION	DL	BFW
1988	SF N	7	8	1	1	0	0	0	0	2-0	0	1	.125	.273	.125	27	-1	0-0	1.000	-2	59	0	2b7		
1990	SF N	4	3	1	1	0	0	0	0	1-0	0	2	.333	.500	.333	139	-1	0-0	1.000	-1	0	0	2b2,S2		-0.3
1991	SF N	23	48	2	11	4	1	0	3	2-0	0	12	.229	.260	.354	73	-2	0-1	.947	-3	90	72	S13,2b6		-0.1
1992	Cle A	17	22	4	8	2	0	0	0	3-0	0	5	.364	.440	.455	147	2	0-0	1.000	-3	43	50	S6,3b3,2b2/D		-0.4
	Cle A	18	20	2	2	0	0	0	5	2-0	0	7	.100	.182	.150	-6	-3	0-0	.875	-3	131	0	3b9,2b4,S4/D		-0.1
Total	4	69	101	10	23	7	1	0	5	10-0	0	26	.228	.295	.317	74	-4	0-1	.944	-11	73	53	S25,2b20,3b12,D2		-1.5

PERKINS, BRODERICK   Broderick Phillip B11.23.1954 Pittsburg CA BL/TL/5-10/180* [SDN76 15/341] d7.7 Col St. Marys (CA)

YEAR	TM LG	G	AB	R	H	2B	3B	HR	RBI	BB-IB	HP	SO	AVG	OBP	SLG	AOPS	ABR	SB-CS	FA	FR	RNG	THR	GAMES AT POSITION	DL	BFW
1978	SD N	62	217	14	52	14	1	6	33	5-2	0	29	.240	.253	.341	71	-10	4-0	.993	4	135	138	1b59		
1979	SD N	57	87	8	23	0	0	0	8	8-2	0	12	.264	.323	.264	67	-4	0-0	.982	0	105	124	1b28		-0.8
1980	SD N	43	100	18	37	9	0	2	14	11-1	0	10	.370	.432	.520	176	11	2-1	.988	-2	94	110	1b20,O10R		-0.5
1981	SD N	92	254	27	71	18	3	2	40	14-4	0	16	.280	.314	.398	111	3	0-4	.997	-1	94	104	1b80,O3(1/0/2)		0.8
1982	SD N	125	347	32	94	10	4	2	34	26-10	3	20	.271	.325	.340	92	-4	2-1	.994	2	110	99	1b98,O11(4/0/7)		-0.5
1983	Cle A	79	184	23	50	10	1	0	24	9-3	1	19	.272	.299	.326	71	-7	1-5	.991	-1	33	101	1b19,O17(5/0/12),D16	17	-0.9
1984	Cle A	58	66	5	13	1	0	0	7	7-1	0	10	.197	.276	.212	39	-5	0-0	1.000	-0	0	220	D10,1b2		-1.2
Total	7	516	1255	127	340	62	8	8	157	80-23	4	116	.271	.313	.352	91	-16	9-11	.993	1	106	111	1b306,O41(10/0/31),D26	17	-0.6

PERKINS, CY   Ralph Foster B2.27.1896 Gloucester MA D10.2.1963 Philadelphia PA BR/TR/5-10.5/158 d9.25 M1/C17

YEAR	TM LG	G	AB	R	H	2B	3B	HR	RBI	BB-IB	HP	SO	AVG	OBP	SLG	AOPS	ABR	SB-CS	FA	FR	RNG	THR	GAMES AT POSITION	DL	BFW
1915	Phi A	7	20	2	4	1	0	0	0	0-0	0	1	.200	.304	.250	68	-1	0	.920	-1	69	89	C6		
1917	Phi A	6	18	1	3	0	0	0	2	2-0	0	1	.167	.250	.167	28	-2	0	.978	-1	97	164	C6		-0.1
1918	Phi A	68	218	4	41	4	1	1	14	8-0	0	15	.188	.217	.229	34	-18	1	.990	9	89	126	C60		0.1
1919	Phi A	101	305	22	77	12	7	2	29	27-0	0	22	.252	.313	.357	87	-6	0	.971	9	79	135	C87,S8		-0.5
1920	Phi A	148	492	40	128	24	6	5	52	28-0	2	35	.260	.303	.366	75	-19	5-6	.979	15	98	145	C146/2		0.2
1921	Phi A	141	538	58	155	31	4	12	73	32-0	1	32	.288	.329	.428	91	-9	5-9	.971	0	88	118	C141		0.6
1922	Phi A	148	505	58	135	20	6	6	69	40-0	1	30	.267	.322	.366	77	-18	1-7	.984	0	107	115	C141		-0.1
1923	Phi A	143	500	53	135	34	5	2	65	65-0	3	20	.270	.356	.370	90	-5	1-3	.971	-5	104	93	C137		-1.1
1924	Phi A	128	392	31	95	19	4	0	32	31-0	1	20	.242	.304	.311	58	-25	3-4	.971	-5	104	93	C128		-0.2
1925	Phi A	65	140	21	43	10	0	1	26	18-0	3	6	.307	.426	.400	104	3	0-0	.980	6	115	84	C58/3		-1.7
1926	Phi A	63	148	14	43	6	0	0	19	16-0	1	7	.291	.371	.331	80	-4	0-2	.984	1	113	102	C55		1.1
1927	Phi A	59	137	11	35	7	2	1	15	12-0	0	8	.255	.315	.358	70	-6	0-2	.979	1	118	83	C54/1		0.6
1928	Phi A			0	0	0	0	0	1	1-0	0	8	.172	.200	.172		-4	0-1	.982	2	122	88	C19		-0.3
																									-0.2

YEAR	TM LG	G	AB	R	H	2B	3B	HR	RBI	BB-IB	HP	SO	AVG	OBP	SLG	AOPS	ABR	SB-CS	FA	FR	RNG	THR	GAMES AT POSITION	DL	BFW
1929	Phi A	38	76	4	16	4	0	0	9	5	0	4	.211	.259	.263	34	-8	0-0	.990	1	89	88	C38		-0.5
1930	Phi A	20	38	1	6	2	0	0	4	2	0	3	.158	.200	.211	4	-6	0-0	.964	-0	114	31	C19/1		-0.5
1931	NY A	16	47	3	12	1	0	0	7	1	0	4	.255	.286	.277	51	-3	0-0	1.000	-3	90	0	C16		-0.5
1934	Det A	1	1	0	0	0	0	0	0	0	0	0	.000	.000	.000	-99	0	0-0	—	0			/H		0.0
Total	17		1171	3604	329	933	175	35	30	409	301	15	221	.259	.319	.352	75	-131	18-34	.978	35	99	110	C1111,S8,1b2/32		-3.1

PERLOZZO, SAM   Samuel Benedict   B3.4.1951 Cumberland MD   BR/TR/5-9/170*   d9.13   M1/C19   Col George Washington

																									-0.2
1977	Min A	10	24	6	7	0	2	0	2-0	0		3	.292	.346	.458	118	0	0-0	1.000	-3	76	43	2b10/3		-0.1
1979	SD N	2	2	0	0	0	0	0	1-0	0		0	.000	.333	.000	-1	0	0-0	.500	-1	0	0	2b2		-0.3
Total	2		12	26	6	7	0	2	0	2	0	0	3	.269	.345	.423	110	0	0-0	.967	-4	70	40	2b12/3		

PERRIN, JOHN   John Stephenson   B2.4.1898 Escanaba MI   D6.24.1969 Detroit MI   BL/TR/5-9/160   d7.11   Col Michigan

1921	Bos A	4	13	3	3	0	0	0	1	0		3	.231	.231	.231	19	-2	0-0	1.000	-1	33	0	O4R		-0.2

PERRINE, NIG   John Grover   B1.14.1885 Clinton WI   D8.13.1948 Kansas City MO   BR/TR/5-9/160   d4.11

1907	Was A	44	146	13	25	4	1	0	15	13	3		.171	.253	.212	53	-7	10	.946	-4	86	152	2b24,S18,3b2		-1.1

PERRING, GEORGE   George Wilson   B8.13.1884 Sharon WI   D8.20.1960 Beloit WI   BR/TR/6-0/190   d4.25   Col Beloit

1908	Cle A	89	310	33	67	8	5	0	19	16	0		.216	.255	.274	72	-11	8	.928	-11	100	114	S48,3b41		-2.2
1909	Cle A	88	283	26	63	10	9	0	20	19	5		.223	.283	.322	87	-5	6	.932	2	105	71	3b67,S11,2b4		-0.1
1910	Cle A	39	122	14	27	6	1	0	8	3	0		.221	.240	.320	74	-4	3	.931	1	106	96	3b33,1b4		-0.4
1914	KC F	144	496	68	138	28	10	2	69	59	0	39	.278	.355	.387	106	-3	11	.958	8	108	98	3b102,1b31,2b31/S		0.8
1915	KC F	153	553	67	143	23	7	7	67	55	1	30	.259	.327	.363	98	-11	10	.939	11	108	92	3b344,1b76,S61,2b35/P		0.3
Total	5		513	1764	198	438	75	34	9	183	152	6	69	.248	.310	.345	93	-34	34							-1.6

PERRY, BOYD   Boyd Glenn   B3.21.1914 Snow Camp NC   D6.29.1990 Burlington NC   BR/TR/5-10/158   d5.23   Col Guilford

1941	Det A	36	83	9	15	5	0	0	11	10	0	9	.181	.269	.241	32	-8	1-0	.974	0	103	95	S25,2b11		-0.6

PERRY, CHAN   Chan Everett   B9.13.1972 Live Oak FL   BR/TR/6-2/200*   [CleA94 44/1212]   d8.5   Col Florida

																									-0.3
2000	Cle A	13	14	1	1	0	0	0	0-0			5	.071	.071	.071	-61	-3	0-0	1.000	0	110	0	O7(1/0/6)/1D		-0.3
2002	KC A	5	11	0	1	0	0	0	3	0-0		1	.091	.091	.091	-46	-2	0-0	1.000	0	98	74	1b5		-0.3
Total	2		18	25	1	2	0	0	0	3	0-0		6	.080	.080	.080	-54	-5	0-0	1.000	0	110	0	O7(1/0/6),1b6,D4		

PERRY, CLAY   Clayton Shields   B12.18.1881 Clayton WI   D1.13.1954 Rice Lake WI   BR/TR/5-10.5/175   d9.2   Col Wisconsin-Madison

1908	Det A	7	17	0	2	0	0	0	0	1			.118	.167	.118	-7	-2	0	.850	-1	91	160	3b7		-0.3

PERRY, GERALD   Gerald June   B10.30.1960 Savannah GA   BL/TR/6-0/190(172-201)   [AtlN78 11/261]   d8.11   C6

																									0.0
1983	Atl N	27	39	5	14	2	0	1	6	5-0	0	4	.359	.422	.487	144	5	0-1	.982	-2	0	102	1b7/OL		-1.0
1984	Atl N	122	347	52	92	12	2	7	47	61-5	2	38	.265	.372	.372	104	5	15-12	.988	-8	78	112	1b64,O53L		-2.1
1985	Atl N	110	238	22	51	5	0	3	13	23-1	0	28	.214	.282	.273	73	-15	9-5	.985	-2	101	104	1b55/OL		-0.5
1986	Atl N	29	70	6	19	2	0	2	11	8-1	0	4	.271	.342	.386	97	0	0-1	.889	1	53	0	O21(21/0/1)/1		-2.2
1987	Atl N	142	533	77	144	35	2	12	74	48-1	1	63	.270	.329	.411	92	-6	42-16	.988	1	106	91	1b141		-0.2
1988	Atl N★	141	547	61	164	29	1	8	74	36-9	1	49	.300	.338	.400	109	9	29-14	.988	1	108	103	1b72	99	-0.6
1989	Atl N	72	266	24	67	11	0	4	21	32-5	3	28	.252	.337	.338	92	-2	10-6	.987	1	109	94	D68,1b51		-0.9
1990	KC A	133	465	57	118	22	2	8	57	39-4	3	56	.254	.313	.361	90	-7	17-4	.986	1	99	93	1b61,O5(3/0/1)		-1.3
1991	StL N	109	242	29	58	8	4	6	36	22-1	0	34	.240	.300	.380	90	-4	15-8	.989	-5	72	93	1b29		-1.1
1992	StL N	87	143	13	34	8	1	1	18	15-4	1	23	.238	.311	.315	81	-3	3-6	.976	-1	56	82	1b15/OR		0.7
1993	StL N	96	98	21	33	5	0	4	16	18-2	0	23	.337	.440	.510	154	7	1-1	.990	-2	54	99	1b13		-1.1
1994	StL N	60	77	12	25	7	0	3	15	8-1	0	12	.325	.435	.532	150	7	1-1	.990	-1	54	63	1b11		-0.2
1995	StL N	65	79	4	13	4	0	0	5	6-0	0	12	.165	.224	.215	16	-17	142-75	.988	-35	90	102	1b656,O89(87/0/3),D68	114	-9.9
Total	13		1193	3144	383	832	150	11	59	396	328-34	11	374	.265	.333	.376	90	-17	142-75							

PERRY, HERBERT   Herbert Edward   B9.15.1969 Live Oak FL   BR/TR/6-2/220(210-235)   [CleA91 2/57]   d5.3   Col Florida   [DL 1998 TB A 181]

																									0.0
1994	Cle A	4	9	1	1	0	0	0	1	3-1	1		.111	.357	.111	36	1	0-0	1.000	1	176	48	1b2,3b2		-0.1
1995	†Cle A	52	162	23	51	13	1	3	23	13-0	4	28	.315	.376	.463	116	4	1-3	1.000	-1	91	87	1b45/3D	19	-0.2
1996	Cle A	7	12	1	1	0	0	0	1	1-0	0	2	.083	.154	.167	-19	-2	0-0	1.000	0	85	109	1b5/3	41	-0.1
1999	TB A	66	209	29	53	10	1	6	32	16-1	10	42	.254	.331	.397	85	-5	0-0	.955	5	111	162	3b42,1b14,D10,O6L		-0.3
2000	TB A	7	28	2	6	1	0	0	1	2-0	0	7	.214	.267	.250	32	-3	0-0	.938	-1	86	85	3b7/1		1.0
	†Chi A	109	383	69	118	29	1	12	61	22-1	9	68	.308	.356	.483	107	4	4-1	.969	6	103	95	3b104,1b3,D3		-1.2
	Year	116	411	71	124	30	1	12	62	24-1	9	75	.302	.350	.467	102	1	4-1	.940	-6	93	48	3b68,1b12,D10	15	-0.3
2001	Chi A	92	285	38	73	21	1	7	32	23-1	7	55	.256	.326	.411	87	-5	2-2	.951	-1	96	87	3b112,1b12/OLD		0.0
2002	Tex A	132	450	64	124	24	1	22	77	34-1	6	66	.276	.333	.480	110	6	4-2	1.000	0	145	73	1b5,3b2	164	-0.3
2003	Tex A	11	24	1	4	1	0	0	2	0-0	0	3	.167	.167	.208	-2	-4	0-0	1.000	0	38	114	D21,1b15,3b6	60	-0.9
2004	Tex A	49	134	13	30	2	1	5	17	14-0	3	19	.224	.307	.366	73	-6	0-0	.953	1	99	90	3b345,1b114,D56,O7L	480	-0.1
Total	10		529	1696	241	461	102	6	55	246	128-5	40	291	.272	.335	.436	96	-12	12-8							

PERRY, BOB   Melvin Gray   B9.14.1934 New Bern NC   BR/TR/6-2/180*   d5.17

1963	LA A	61	166	16	42	9	0	3	14	9-2	3	31	.253	.300	.361	91	-2	1-1	.946	-5	90	33	O55(7/23/26)		-1.1
1964	LA A	70	221	19	61	8	1	3	16	14-0	0	52	.276	.318	.362	99	-1	1-1	.975	-6	87	50	O62(0/62/1)		-1.2
Total	2		131	387	35	103	17	1	6	30	23-2	3	83	.266	.310	.362	95	-3	2-2	.962	-11	88	42	O117(7/85/27)		

PERRY, HANK   William Henry "Socks"   B7.28.1886 Howell MI   D7.18.1956 Pontiac MI   BL/TR/5-11/190   d4.12

1912	Det A	13	36	3	6	1	0	0	3	0			.167	.231	.194	23	-4	0	1.000	1	108	164	O7C		-0.

PESKY, JOHNNY   John Michael (b John Michael Paveskovich)   B9.27.1919 Portland OR   BL/TR/5-9/168*   d4.14   Mil 1943-45   M3/C13

																									4.
1942	Bos A	147	620	105	205	29	9	2	51	42	2	36	.331	.375	.416	118	14	12-7	.955	20	110	109	S147		0
1946	†Bos A★	153	621	115	208	43	4	2	55	65	3	29	.335	.401	.427	124	23	9-8	.969	12	106	104	S153		0
1947	Bos A	155	638	106	207	27	8	0	39	72	0	22	.324	.393	.392	110	11	12-9	.976	-10	95	95	S133,3b22		2
1948	Bos A	143	565	124	159	26	6	3	55	99	6	32	.281	.394	.365	98	3	3-5	.951	7	113	136	3b141		2
1949	Bos A	148	604	111	185	27	7	2	69	100	4	19	.306	.408	.384	103	7	4-9	.970	19	108	139	3b148		3
1950	Bos A	127	490	112	153	22	6	1	49	104	5	31	.312	.437	.388	103	9	2-1	.974	16	105	112	3b116,S8		2
1951	Bos A	131	480	93	150	20	6	3	41	84	2	15	.313	.417	.398	110	4	2-2	.961	-2	105	95	S106,3b11,2b5		-1
1952	Bos A	25	67	10	10	2	0	0	2	15	1	5	.149	.313	.179	36	-5	0-3	.917	-4	82	0	3b19,S2		0
	Det A	69	177	26	45	4	0	1	9	41	0	11	.254	.394	.294	93	1	1-2	.953	-6	88	101	S43,3b22,2b2		-0
	Year	94	244	36	55	6	0	1	11	56	1	16	.225	.372	.262	77	-4	1-5	.953	-8	89	100	S41,2b22,3b3		-0
1953	Det A	103	308	43	90	22	1	2	24	27	2	10	.292	.353	.390	102	1	3-7	.991	-7	96	83	2b73		-1
1954	Det A	20	17	5	3	0	0	1	9	10		1	.176	.300	.353	80	-1	0-0	—	0			/H		-0
	Was A	49	158	17	40	4	1	0	9	10	1	7	.253	.296	.316	72	-7	1-1	.979	-4	101	81	2b37/S		-0
	Year	69	175	22	43	4	1	1	10	13	1	8	.246	.296	.320	72	-8	1-1	.979	-4	101	81	2b37/S		15
Total	10		1270	4745	867	1455	226	50	17	404	662	25	218	.307	.394	.386	106	67	53-49	.964	50	103	101	S591,3b460,2b137		

PETAGINE, ROBERTO   Roberto Antonio (Guerra)   B6.7.1971 Nueva Esparta, Venez   BL/TL/6-1/170*   d4.4

																									-0
1994	Hou N	8	7	0	0	0	0	0	0	1-0	0	3	.000	.125	.000	-67	-2	0-0	1.000	-0	0	0	1b2		-0
1995	SD N	89	124	15	29	8	0	3	17	26-2	3	41	.234	.367	.371	98	1	0-2	.996	1	113	91	1b40		-0
1996	NY N	50	99	10	23	3	0	4	17	9-1	3	27	.232	.313	.384	88	-2	0-2	.996	1	113	91	1b6/OL		-0
1997	NY N	12	15	2	1	0	0	0	2	3-0	0	6	.067	.222	.067	-21	-3	0-0	1.000	0	193	0	1b6/OL		-0
1998	Cin N	34	62	14	16	2	1	3	7	16-0	0	11	.258	.405	.468	129	3	1-0	.983	0	50	72	1b10,O2L,D3		-0
2005	Bos A	18	32	4	9	4	0	2	5	5-0	1	11	.281	.361	.438	105	0	0-0	.995	4	111	86	1b124,O20(5/0/16),D3		-0
Total	6		211	339	45	78	15	1	11	52	59-3	5	93	.230	.347	.378	93	-3	1-2							-0

PETERMAN, BILL   William David   B3.20.1921 Philadelphia PA   D3.13.1999 Philadelphia PA   BR/TR/6-2/185   d4.26   Mil 1943-45

1942	Phi N	1	1	0	1	0	0	0	0	0		0	1.000	1.000	1.000	512	1	0	—	0	0	0	0 /C		-0

PETERS, JOHN   John Paul   B4.8.1850 New Orleans LA   D1.4.1924 St.Louis MO   BR/TR/5-7/180   d5.23

1874	Chi NA	55	239	39	69	10	0	1	25	2		11	.289	.295	.343	103	1	2-2	.799	2	104	75	S36,2b19		
1875	Chi NA	69	297	40	85	16	2	0	34	0		2	.286	.286	.354	120	6	12-6	.871	9	109	158	S65,2b6		
1876	Chi N	66	316	70	111	14	2	1	47	3		2	.351	.357	.418	141	12		.932	1	91	146	S66/P		
1877	Chi N	60	265	45	84	10	3	0	41	1		7	.317	.320	.377	106	1		.883	20	116	164	S60		

YEAR	TM	LG	G	AB	R	H	2B	3B	HR	RBI	BB-IB	HP	SO	AVG	OBP	SLG	AOPS	ABR	SB-CS	FA	FR	RNG	THR	GAMES AT POSITION	DL	BFW
1878	Mil	N	55	246	33	76	6	1	0	22	5			8	.309	.323	.341	111	2		.853	2	114	96	2b34,S22		0.6
1879	Chi	N	83	379	45	93	13	2	1	31	1			19	.245	.247	.298	74	-11		.837	-7	99	79	S83		-1.4
1880	Pro	N	86	359	30	82	5	0	0	24	5			15	.228	.239	.242	66	-13		.900	-4	94	139	S86		-1.2
1881	Buf	N	54	229	21	49	8	1	0	25	3			12	.214	.224	.258	52	-13		.869	2	100	88	S53/OR		-0.7
1882	Pit	AA	78	333	46	96	10	1	0	4					.288	.297	.324	115	5		.883	6	103	114	S77/2		1.2
1883	Pit	AA	8	28	3	3	0	0	0	0					.107	.107	.107	-32	-4		.818	2	151	150	S8		-0.2
1884	Pit	AA	1	4	0	0	0	0	0	0		0			.000	.000	.000	-99	-1		.667	-1	40	0	/S		-0.2
Total 2	NA		124	536	79	154	26	2	1	59	2			14	.287	.290	.349	112	7	14-8	.846	11	107	129	S101,2b25		1.1
Total 9			491	2159	293	594	66	10	2	190	22	0		63	.275	.282	.318	94	-22		.881	20	100	119	S456,2b35/ORP		1.4

PETERS, JOHN John William "Big Pete","Shotgun" B7.14.1893 Kansas City KS D2.21.1932 Kansas City MO BR/TR/6-0/192 d5.1

YEAR	TM	LG	G	AB	R	H	2B	3B	HR	RBI	BB-IB	HP	SO	AVG	OBP	SLG	AOPS	ABR	SB-CS	FA	FR	RNG	THR	GAMES AT POSITION	DL	BFW
1915	Det	A	1	3	0	0	0	0	0	0	0		1		.000	.000	.000	-95	-1		1.000	1	136	191	/C		
1918	Cle	A	1	1	0	0	0	0	0	1	0		1		.000	.500	.000	46	0		.500	0		140	/C		0.0
1921	Phi	N	55	155	7	45	4	0	3	23	6	3	13		.290	.329	.374	79	-5	1-0	.933	-11	65	69	C44		-0.1
1922	Phi	N	55	143	15	35	9	1	4	24	9	4	18		.245	.308	.406	75	-5	0-1	.953	-5	81	73	C39		-1.3
Total 4			112	302	22	80	13	1	7	47	16	7	33		.265	.317	.384	76	-11	1-1	.934	-16	73	74	C85		-0.8
																										-2.2

PETERS, RICK Richard Devin B11.21.1955 Lynwood CA BB/TR/5-9/170* [DetA77 7/161] d9.8 Col Arizona St. [DL 1982 Det A 182]

YEAR	TM	LG	G	AB	R	H	2B	3B	HR	RBI	BB-IB	HP	SO	AVG	OBP	SLG	AOPS	ABR	SB-CS	FA	FR	RNG	THR	GAMES AT POSITION	DL	BFW
1979	Det	A	12	19	3	5	0	0	0	2	5-0	0	3		.263	.417	.263	85	0	0-0	.000	0	0	0	3b3,2b2/OLD		
1980	Det	A	133	477	79	139	19	7	2	42	54-2	6	48		.291	.369	.373	102	3	13-7	.977	-4	103	13	O109(8/97/5),D11		-0.2
1981	Det	A	63	207	26	53	7	3	0	15	29-2	2	28		.256	.351	.319	91	-1	1-6	.991	3	114	141	O38(5/33/0),D19		-0.2
1983	Oak	A	55	178	20	51	7	0	0	20	12-0	1	21		.287	.337	.326	87	-3	4-9	.986	7	131	100	O47(6/30/16),D8		-0.1
1986	Oak	A	44	38	7	7	1	0	0	1	7-1	0	7		.184	.311	.211	49	-2	2-2	1.000	1	120	0	O27(19/7/1)/2		0.0
Total 5			307	919	135	255	34	10	2	80	107-5	9	107		.277	.356	.343	94	-3	20-24	.983	4	112	54	O222(39/167/22),D41,2b3,3b3	22	-0.2
																										204	-0.7

PETERS, RUSTY Russell Dixon B12.14.1914 Roanoke VA D2.21.2003 Harrisonburg VA BR/TR/5-11/170 d4.14 Mil 1945-46 Col Washington and Lee

YEAR	TM	LG	G	AB	R	H	2B	3B	HR	RBI	BB-IB	HP	SO	AVG	OBP	SLG	AOPS	ABR	SB-CS	FA	FR	RNG	THR	GAMES AT POSITION	DL	BFW
1936	Phi	A	45	119	12	26	3	2	3	16	4	0	28		.218	.244	.353	47	-11	1-1	.898	-1	96	95	S25,3b10,O2L/2		-1.0
1937	Phi	A	116	339	39	88	17	6	3	43	41	0	59		.260	.339	.372	80	-10	4-4	.966	-9	96	84	2b70,3b31,S13		-1.3
1938	Phi	A	2	7	0	0	0	0	0	0	0	0	1		.000	.000	.000	-99	-2	0-0	.714	2	41	0	S2		-1.3
1940	Cle	A	30	71	5	17	3	2	0	7	4	0	14		.239	.280	.338	61	-4	1-0	.922	-2	82	119	2b9,S6,3b6/1		-0.5
1941	Cle	A	29	63	6	13	2	0	0	2	7	0	10		.206	.286	.238	42	-5	0-1	.891	0	115	92	S11,3b9,2b3		-0.5
1942	Cle	A	34	58	6	13	5	1	0	2	8	0	14		.224	.320	.345	70	-3	0-0	.944	0	119	101	S24/23		-0.1
1943	Cle	A	79	215	22	47	6	2	1	19	18	1	29		.219	.282	.279	69	-9	1-1	.913	-5	92	119	3b46,S14,2b6,O2L		-1.4
1944	Cle	A	88	282	23	63	14	0	1	24	15	2	35		.223	.268	.301	65	-14	2-1	.976	2	103	97	2b63,S13,3b8		-1.2
1946	Cle	A	9	21	0	6	0	0	0	2	0	0	8		.286	.318	.286	74	-1	0-1	1.000	1	94	99	S7		0.0
1947	StL	A	39	47	10	16	4	0	0	2	6	0	8		.340	.415	.426	131	2	0-0	.955	3	108	118	2b13,S2		0.6
Total 10			471	1222	123	289	53	16	8	117	98	3	199		.236	.295	.326	69	-57	9-9	.966	-15	98	95	2b166,S117,3b111,O4L/1		-5.8

PETERSEN, CHRIS Christopher Ronald B11.6.1970 Boston MA BR/TR/5-11/180 [ChiN92 9/247] d5.25 Col Georgia Southern

YEAR	TM	LG	G	AB	R	H	2B	3B	HR	RBI	BB-IB	HP	SO	AVG	OBP	SLG	AOPS	ABR	SB-CS	FA	FR	RNG	THR	GAMES AT POSITION	DL	BFW
1999	Col	N	7	13	1	2	0	0	0	3					.154	.267	.154	8	-2	0-0	.955	3	136	208	2b6/S		0.1

PETERSON, BUDDY Carl Francis B4.23.1925 Portland OR BR/TR/5-9.5/170* d9.14

YEAR	TM	LG	G	AB	R	H	2B	3B	HR	RBI	BB-IB	HP	SO	AVG	OBP	SLG	AOPS	ABR	SB-CS	FA	FR	RNG	THR	GAMES AT POSITION	DL	BFW
1955	Chi	A	6	21	4	6	2	0	0	2	3-0		2		.286	.400	.333	96	0	0-0	.962	-1	88	124	S6		-0.2
1957	Bal	A	7	17	1	3	2	0	0	0	2-0		2		.176	.263	.294	55	-1	0-0	.963	-1	82	87	S7		-0.2
Total 2			13	38	5	9	3	0	0	2	5-0		4		.237	.341	.316	80	-1	0-0	.962	-1	85	106	S13		-0.2

PETERSON, CAP Charles Andrew B8.15.1942 Tacoma WA D5.16.1980 Tacoma WA BR/TR/6-2/195* d9.12 OF(142/0/139)

YEAR	TM	LG	G	AB	R	H	2B	3B	HR	RBI	BB-IB	HP	SO	AVG	OBP	SLG	AOPS	ABR	SB-CS	FA	FR	RNG	THR	GAMES AT POSITION	DL	BFW
1962	SF	N	4	6	1	1	0	0	0	1	1-0		4		.167	.286	.167	25	-1	0-0	1.000	-1	51	134	S2		
1963	SF	N	22	54	7	14	2	0	1	2	2-0		13		.259	.286	.352	83	-1	0-0	.917	-2	110	0	2b8,3b5,O3(2/0/1)/S		-0.1
1964	SF	N	66	74	8	15	1	1	1	8	3-1		20		.203	.234	.284	44	-6	0-0	1.000	-1	101	0	O10(10/0/1),1b2/23		-0.4
1965	SF	N	63	105	14	26	7	0	3	15	10-2		32		.248	.310	.400	97	0	0-0	1.000	-2	66	91	O27(23/0/4)		-0.7
1966	SF	N	89	190	13	45	6	1	2	11	11-1		32		.237	.279	.311	63	-10	2-0	1.000	-1	89	74	O51(50/0/1),1b2		-0.4
1967	Was	A	122	405	35	97	17	2	8	46	32-1		61		.240	.299	.351	95	-3	0-3	.970	-1	103	72	O101(18/0/88)		-1.3
1968	Was	A	94	226	20	46	8	1	3	18	18-3		31		.204	.262	.288	70	-9	2-1	1.000	-2	95	68	O53(14/0/39)		-1.5
1969	Cle	A	76	110	8	25	3	0	1	14	24-3		18		.227	.365	.282	82	-1	1-0	.977	-2	106	125	O30(25/0/5),3b4		-0.3
Total 8			536	1170	106	269	44	5	19	122	101-11	6	195		.230	.292	.325	80	-31	4-4	.983	-10	96	76	O275L,3b10,2b9,1b4,S3		-6.0

PETERSON, HARDY Harding William B10.17.1929 Perth Amboy NJ BR/TR/6-0/205(183-205) d5.5 Col Rutgers [DL 1956 Pit N 144]

YEAR	TM	LG	G	AB	R	H	2B	3B	HR	RBI	BB-IB	HP	SO	AVG	OBP	SLG	AOPS	ABR	SB-CS	FA	FR	RNG	THR	GAMES AT POSITION	DL	BFW
1955	Pit	N	32	81	7	20	6	0	1	10	7-1	1	7		.247	.311	.358	79	-2	0-0	.965	3	87	220	C31		0.1
1957	Pit	N	30	73	10	22	2	1	2	11	9-2	0	10		.301	.378	.438	122	2	0-1	.985	1	110	126	C30		0.5
1958	Pit	N	2	6	0	2	0	0	0	0	1-0	0	1		.333	.429	.333	108	1	0-1	1.000	-0	56	0	C2		0.0
1959	Pit	N	2	1	0	0	0	0	0	0	0	0	0		.000	.000	.000	-99	0	0-0	1.000	0	0		C2		0.0
Total 4			66	161	17	44	8	1	3	21	17-3	1	17		.273	.344	.391	99	0	0-1	.976	4	96	166	C65	144	0.6

PETERSON, BOB Robert Andrew B6.16.1884 Philadelphia PA D11.27.1962 Evesham Twp. NJ BR/TR/6-1/160 d4.18

YEAR	TM	LG	G	AB	R	H	2B	3B	HR	RBI	BB-IB	HP	SO	AVG	OBP	SLG	AOPS	ABR	SB-CS	FA	FR	RNG	THR	GAMES AT POSITION	DL	BFW
1906	Bos	A	39	118	10	24	1	1	0	9	11	1			.203	.277	.254	67	-4	1	.899	-9	81	101	C30,2b3,1b2/OL		-1.2
1907	Bos	A	4	13	1	1	0	0	0	0	0				.077	.077	.077	-51	-2	1	1.000	0	113	84	C4		-0.2
Total 2			43	131	11	25	1	1	0	9	11	1			.191	.259	.237	56	-6	1	.910	-8	85	99	C34,2b3,1b2/OL		-1.4

PETOSKEY, TED Frederick Lee B1.5.1911 St.Charles MI D11.30.1996 Elgin SC BR/TR/5-11.5/183 d9.9 Col Michigan

YEAR	TM	LG	G	AB	R	H	2B	3B	HR	RBI	BB-IB	HP	SO	AVG	OBP	SLG	AOPS	ABR	SB-CS	FA	FR	RNG	THR	GAMES AT POSITION	DL	BFW
1934	Cin	N	6	7	0	0	0	0	0	1	0		5		.000	.000	.000	-99	-2	1	1.000	1	164	992	O2C		-0.1
1935	Cin	N	4	5	0	2	0	0	0	0	0		1		.400	.400	.400	119	0	1	1.000	-0	52	0	O2(1/1/0)		0.0
Total 2			10	12	0	2	0	0	0	1	0		6		.167	.167	.167	-11	-2	1	1.000	1	123	627	O4(1/3/0)		-0.1

PETRALLI, GENO Eugene James B9.25.1959 Sacramento CA BL/TR (BB 1982-86, 87p)/6-2/185(180-200) [TorA78*3/53] d9.4 Col Sacramento (CA) City OF(1/0/2)

YEAR	TM	LG	G	AB	R	H	2B	3B	HR	RBI	BB-IB	HP	SO	AVG	OBP	SLG	AOPS	ABR	SB-CS	FA	FR	RNG	THR	GAMES AT POSITION	DL	BFW
1982	Tor	A	16	44	3	16	2	0	0	1	4-0		6		.364	.417	.409	117	1	0-0	.981	-1	77	66	C12,3b3		0.0
1983	Tor	A	6	4	0	0	0	0	0	0	1-0		1		.000	.000	.000	-37	-1	0-0	1.000	-0	0	0	C5/D		-0.1
1984	Tor	A	3	3	0	0	0	0	0	0	0		0		.000	.000	.000	-96	-1	0-0	1.000	-0	0	0	/CD		
1985	Tex	A	42	100	7	27	2	0	0	8	8-0		12		.270	.319	.290	70	-4	1-0	.990	-2	64	105	C41		-0.4
1986	Tex	A	69	137	17	35	9	3	2	18	5-0		14		.255	.282	.409	83	-4	3-0	.988	-7	87	39	C41,3b15,2b2,D2		-0.9
1987	Tex	A	101	202	28	61	11	2	7	31	27-2		29		.302	.388	.436	128	9	0-2	.995	-4	59	144	C63,3b17,1b5,2b4,O3(1/0/2),D2		0.6
1988	Tex	A	129	351	35	99	14	2	7	36	41-5		52		.282	.356	.393	108	5	0-1	.981	1	79	142	C85,D23,3b9,1b2,2b2		0.9
1989	Tex	A	70	184	16	56	7	0	4	23	17-1		24		.304	.368	.408	117	4	0-0	.989	-1	74	116	C49,D16	68	0.6
1990	Tex	A	133	325	28	83	13	1	0	21	50-2		49		.255	.357	.302	86	-3	0-2	.991	-2	106	108	C118,3b7,2b3	40	0.6
1991	Tex	A	87	199	21	54	8	1	2	20	21-1		25		.271	.339	.352	93	-1	2-1	.972	-7	81	113	C66,3b7,D5		-0.6
1992	Tex	A	94	192	11	38	12	0	1	18	20-2		34		.198	.274	.276	56	-11	0-0	.990	-1	143	126	C54,D14,3b4,2b2		-1.0
1993	Tex	A	59	133	16	32	5	0	1	13	22-3		29		.241	.348	.301	79	-3	2-0	.990	-1	87	116	C39/23D	39	-0.9
Total 12			809	1874	184	501	83	9	24	192	216-17	10	263		.267	.344	.360	93	-9	8-6	.987	-33	87	116	C574,D66,3b63,2b14,1b7,O3R	147	-1.8

PETRICK, BEN Benjamin Wayne B4.7.1977 Salem OR BR/TR/6-0/205* [ColN95 2/38] d9.1

YEAR	TM	LG	G	AB	R	H	2B	3B	HR	RBI	BB-IB	HP	SO	AVG	OBP	SLG	AOPS	ABR	SB-CS	FA	FR	RNG	THR	GAMES AT POSITION	DL	BFW
1999	Col	N	19	62	13	20	3	0	4	12	10-0		13		.323	.417	.565	116	2	1-0	.982	-7	65	36	C19		-0.4
2000	Col	N	52	146	32	47	10	1	3	20	20-2		34		.322	.401	.466	98	0	1-2	.985	-3	96	60	C48		0.0
2001	Col	N	85	244	41	58	15	2	11	39	31-3		67		.238	.327	.459	84	-6	3-3	.984	-6	81	74	C77,1b2		-0.8
2002	Col	N	38	95	10	20	3	1	5	11	9-0		23		.211	.283	.421	76	-4	0-1	.952	-1	88	0	O16(15/2/0),C14	30	-0.5
2003	Det	A	43	160	12	36	4	0	4	12	8-0		40		.225	.273	.375	72	-5	0-0	1.000	2	201	3625	O2(1/1/0)/C		0.0
Total 5			240	669	114	172	37	5	27	94	78-5	6	177		.257	.336	.448	87	-14	5-6	.984	-18	85	62	C165,O50(34/17/3),1b4	30	-0.6
																											-2.3

PETROCELLI, RICO Americo Peter B6.27.1943 Brooklyn NY BR/TR/6-0/185* d9.21

YEAR	TM	LG	G	AB	R	H	2B	3B	HR	RBI	BB-IB	HP	SO	AVG	OBP	SLG	AOPS	ABR	SB-CS	FA	FR	RNG	THR	GAMES AT POSITION	DL	BFW
1963	Bos	A	1	4	0	1	1	0	0	0			1		.250	.250	.500	101	0	0-0	.833	-0	69	0	/S		0.0
1965	Bos	A	103	323	38	75	15	2	13	33	36-4	1	71		.232	.309	.412	98	-1	0-2	.958	9	110	83	S93		1.6
1966	Bos	A	139	522	58	124	20	1	18	59	41-2	3	99		.238	.295	.463	85	-10	1-1	.954	5	107	88	S127,3b5		0.6
1967	†Bos	A★	142	491	53	127	24	2	17	66	49-9	3	93		.259	.330	.420	112	4	0-1	.970	5	103	98	S141,3b5	18	0.6
1968	Bos	A	123	406	41	95	11	2	12	46	31-2	5	73		.234	.292	.374	96	-2	0-1	.978	11	109	106	S117/1		2.6
1969	Bos	A★	154	535	92	159	32	2	40	97	98-13	1	68		.297	.403	.589	168	51	3-5	.981	6	102	107	S153/3		2.1
1970	Bos	A	157	583	82	152	31	3	29	103	67-6	2	82		.261	.334	.473	114	11	1-1	.970	-0	94	89	S141,3b18		7.6
1971	Bos	A	158	553	82	150	24	4	28	89	91-5	2	108		.251	.354	.461	122	18	2-0	.976	-1	99	111	3b156		2.7
																											1.7

YEAR	TM LG	G	AB	R	H	2B	3B	HR	RBI	BB-IB	HP	SO	AVG	OBP	SLG	AOPS	ABR	SB-CS	FA	FR	RNG	THR	GAMES AT POSITION	DL	BFW
1972	Bos A	147	521	62	125	15	2	15	75	78-9	2	91	.240	.339	.363	103	4	0-1	.970	5	94	126	3b146		1.0
1973	Bos A	100	356	44	87	13	1	13	45	47-3	1	64	.244	.333	.396	99	0	0-0	.980	6	105	125	3b99	29	0.6
1974	Bos A	129	454	53	121	23	1	15	76	48-4	2	74	.267	.336	.421	110	6	1-0	.962	-13	90	96	3b116,D9		-0.7
1975	†Bos A	115	402	31	96	15	1	7	59	41-1	3	66	.239	.310	.333	77	-12	0-2	.960	-15	92	60	3b113/D	15	-2.7
1976	Bos A	85	240	17	51	7	1	3	24	34-3	0	36	.213	.307	.287	68	-9	0-5	.967	-3	95	104	3b73,2b5/1SD		-1.5
Total	13	1553	5390	653	1352	237	22	210	773	661-61	26	926	.251	.332	.420	108	64	10-22	.969	17	104	96	S774,3b727,D14,2b5,1b2	62	15.6

PETTEE, PAT Patrick E. B1.10.1863 Natick MA D10.9.1934 Natick MA BR/TR/5-10/170 d4.8

YEAR	TM LG	G	AB	R	H	2B	3B	HR	RBI	BB-IB	HP	SO	AVG	OBP	SLG	AOPS	ABR	SB-CS	FA	FR	RNG	THR	GAMES AT POSITION	DL	BFW
1891	Lou AA	2	5	1	0	0	0	0	0	3	0	1	.000	.375	.000	9	0	1	.818	-1	98	116	2b2		-0.1

PETTIGREW, NED Jim Ned B8.25.1881 Honey Grove TX D8.20.1952 Duncan OK BR/TR/5-11/175 d4.23

YEAR	TM LG	G	AB	R	H	2B	3B	HR	RBI	BB-IB	HP	SO	AVG	OBP	SLG	AOPS	ABR	SB-CS	FA	FR	RNG	THR	GAMES AT POSITION	DL	BFW
1914	Buf F	2	2	0	0	0	0	0	0	0	0	0	.000	.000	.000	-98	-1	0	—		0		/H		-0.1

PETTINI, JOE Joseph Paul B1.26.1955 Wheeling WV BR/TR/5-9/165* d7.10 C4 Col Mercer

YEAR	TM LG	G	AB	R	H	2B	3B	HR	RBI	BB-IB	HP	SO	AVG	OBP	SLG	AOPS	ABR	SB-CS	FA	FR	RNG	THR	GAMES AT POSITION	DL	BFW
1980	SF N	63	190	19	44	3	1	1	9	17-1	0	33	.232	.295	.274	62	-10	5-2	.955	-13	81	72	S42,3b18,2b8		-2.0
1981	SF N	35	29	3	2	1	0	0	2	4-0	0	5	.069	.182	.103	-18	-5	1-0	.920	-2	102	31	2b12,S12,3b9		-0.4
1982	SF N	29	39	5	8	1	0	0	2	3-0	0	4	.205	.262	.231	39	-3	0-1	.934	-3	87	72	S26/3		-0.3
1983	SF N	61	86	11	16	0	1	0	7	9-1	0	11	.186	.260	.209	33	-8	4-1	.949	-1	89	119	S26,2b14,3b12		-0.
Total	4	188	344	38	70	5	2	1	20	33-2	0.	53	.203	.272	.238	45	-26	10-4	.943	-16	84	85	S106,3b40,2b34		-3.

PETTIS, GARY Gary George B4.3.1958 Oakland CA BB/TR/6-1/165* [CalA79*6/141] d9.13 C4 Col Laney (CA) JC

YEAR	TM LG	G	AB	R	H	2B	3B	HR	RBI	BB-IB	HP	SO	AVG	OBP	SLG	AOPS	ABR	SB-CS	FA	FR	RNG	THR	GAMES AT POSITION	DL	BFW
1982	Cal A	10	5	5	1	0	0	1	1	0-0	0	2	.200	.200	.800	158	0	0-0	1.000	1	99	798	O8(1/6/1)		0.
1983	Cal A	22	85	19	25	2	3	3	6	7-0	0	15	.294	.348	.494	129	3	8-3	.982	1	82	362	O21(0/20/1)		0.
1984	Cal A	140	397	63	90	11	6	2	29	60-1	3	115	.227	.332	.300	77	-11	48-17	.983	6	106	145	O134C	26	-0.
1985	Cal A	125	443	67	114	10	8	1	32	62-0	0	125	.257	.347	.323	85	-8	56-9	.990	9	108	162	O122C		0.
1986	†Cal A	154	539	93	139	23	4	5	58	69-2	0	132	.258	.339	.343	88	-7	50-13	.985	11	113	109	O153C/D		-1.
1987	Cal A	133	394	49	82	13	2	1	17	52-0	1	124	.208	.302	.259	52	-26	24-5	.980	6	105	90	O131C		0.
1988	Det A	129	458	65	96	14	4	3	36	47-0	0	106	.210	.285	.277	80	-25	44-10	.987	6	110	90	O126C,D2	16	-1.
1989	Det A	119	444	77	114	8	6	1	18	84-0	0	106	.257	.375	.309	97	2	43-15	.988	-2	105	16	O119C	42	-0.
1990	Tex A	136	423	66	101	16	8	3	31	57-0	4	118	.239	.333	.336	88	-6	38-15	.993	1	105	170	O128C,D2		-0
1991	Tex A	137	282	37	61	7	5	0	19	54-0	0	91	.216	.341	.277	74	-8	29-13	.977	1	107	87	O126C,D3		-0
1992	SD N	30	30	0	6	1	0	0	2	2-0	0	11	.200	.250	.233	37	-2	1-0	.952	0	134	0	O14(0/13/1)		0.
	Det A	48	129	27	26	4	3	1	12	23-0	0	34	.202	.338	.302	80	-3	13-4	.993	3	113	76	O46C		0.
Total	11	1183	3629	568	855	109	49	21	259	521-3	9	958	.236	.332	.310	80	-91	354-104	.986	41	107	108	O1128(1/1125/3),D8	84	-1

PETTIT, BOB Robert Henry B7.19.1861 Williamstown MA D11.1.1910 Derby CT BL/TR/5-9/160 d9.3

YEAR	TM LG	G	AB	R	H	2B	3B	HR	RBI	BB-IB	HP	SO	AVG	OBP	SLG	AOPS	ABR	SB-CS	FA	FR	RNG	THR	GAMES AT POSITION	DL	BFW
1887	Chi N	32	138	29	36	3	3	2	12	8	—	0	15	.261	.301	.370	76	-6	16	.894	-1	145	0	O32R/CP	-0
1888	Chi N	43	169	23	43	1	4	4	23	7	1	9	.254	.288	.379	104	0	7	.931	-0	133	246	O43(0/2/42)	-0
1891	Mil AA	21	80	10	14	4	0	1	5	7	3	7	.175	.267	.262	43	-6	2	.932	-3	116	32	2b9,O7(3/2/2),3b6	-0
Total	3	96	387	62	93	8	7	7	40	22	4	31	.240	.288	.351	79	-12	25	.919	-4	131	126	O82(3/4/76),2b9,3b6/PC	-0

PEVEY, MARTY Marty Ashley B12.25.1962 Savannah GA BL/TR/6-1/185 [MinA82 19/474] d5.16 C2 Col Georgia Southern

YEAR	TM LG	G	AB	R	H	2B	3B	HR	RBI	BB-IB	HP	SO	AVG	OBP	SLG	AOPS	ABR	SB-CS	FA	FR	RNG	THR	GAMES AT POSITION	DL	BFW
1989	Mon N	13	41	2	9	1	1	0	3	0-0	0	8	.220	.220	.293	44	-3	0-0	.985	4	50	107	C11/OR		-0

PEZOLD, LARRY Lorenz Johannes B6.22.1893 New Orleans LA D10.22.1957 Baton Rouge LA BR/TR/5-9.5/175 d7.27

YEAR	TM LG	G	AB	R	H	2B	3B	HR	RBI	BB-IB	HP	SO	AVG	OBP	SLG	AOPS	ABR	SB-CS	FA	FR	RNG	THR	GAMES AT POSITION	DL	BFW
1914	Cle A	23	71	4	16	0	1	0	5	9	0	6	.225	.313	.254	68	-3	2-3	.827	-1	105	63	3b20/OR		-0

PFEFFER, FRED Nathaniel Frederick "Fritz","Dandelion" B3.17.1860 Louisville KY D4.10.1932 Chicago IL BR/TR/5-10.5/184 d5.1 M1 ▲

YEAR	TM LG	G	AB	R	H	2B	3B	HR	RBI	BB-IB	HP	SO	AVG	OBP	SLG	AOPS	ABR	SB-CS	FA	FR	RNG	THR	GAMES AT POSITION	BFW
1882	Tro N	85	330	26	72	7	4	1	43	1	—	0	24	.218	.221	.273	60	-15		.857	10	105	133	S83,2b2	
1883	Chi N	96	371	41	87	22	7	1	45	8		0	50	.235	.251	.340	71	-14		.887	16	108	141	2b79,S18/31	
1884	Chi N	112	467	105	135	10	10	25	101	25		0	47	.289	.325	.514	148	22		.903	43	117	185	2b112/P	
1885	†Chi N	112	469	90	113	12	7	5	73	26		0	47	.241	.281	.328	85	-10		.893	22	112	159	2b109,P5/OR	
1886	†Chi N	118	474	88	125	17	8	7	95	36		0	46	.264	.316	.378	96	-5	30	.917	23	98	133	2b123,O2C	
1887	Chi N	123	479	95	133	21	6	16	89	34	1		20	.278	.327	.447	100	-3	57	.931	38	104	151	2b135	
1888	Chi N	135	517	90	129	22	10	8	57	32	3		38	.250	.297	.377	106	2	64	.943	10	104	113	2b134	
1889	Chi N	134	531	85	128	15	7	7	77	53	2		51	.241	.313	.335	77	-19	45	.916	20	98	129	2b124	
1890	Chi P	124	499	86	128	21	8	5	80	44	2		23	.257	.319	.361	78	-18	27	.921	24	105	137	2b137	
1891	Chi N	137	498	93	123	12	9	7	77	79	3		60	.247	.353	.349	105	5	40	.932	8	104	149	2b116,1b10/PM	
1892	Lou N	124	470	78	121	14	9	2	76	67	2		36	.257	.353	.338	119	14	27	.939	12	101	118	2b125	
1893	Lou N	125	508	85	129	29	12	3	75	51	0		18	.254	.322	.376	93	-6	32	.939	15	103	134	2b91,S15/P	
1894	Lou N	105	414	70	128	12	15	5	61	30	1		14	.309	.357	.447	100	-2	32	.742	-3	67	122	S5,2b3,1b3	
1895	Lou N	11	45	8	13	1	0	0	5	5	1		3	.289	.360	.311	79	-1	2	.760	-2	82	0	2b4	
1896	NY N	4	14	1	2	0	0	0	4	1	1		1	.143	.250	.143	5	-2	0						
	Chi N	94	360	45	88	16	7	2	52	23	2		20	.244	.294	.344	65	-20	22	.947	7	105	107	2b94	
	Year	98	374	46	90	16	7	2	56	24	3		21	.241	.292	.337	63	-22	22	.939	5	104	103	2b98	
1897	Chi N	32	114	10	26	0	1	0	11	12	3			.228	.318	.246	48	-8	5	.883	-4	94	104	2b32	
Total	16	1671	6560	1096	1680	231	120	94	1021	527	21		498	.256	.313	.371	93	-80	383	.920	246	104	137	2b1538,S121,1b15,P8,O3(0/2/1)/3	2

PFEIL, BOBBY Robert Raymond B11.13.1943 Passaic NJ BR/TR/6-1/180* d6.26 Col Los Angeles Pierce (CA) JC

YEAR	TM LG	G	AB	R	H	2B	3B	HR	RBI	BB-IB	HP	SO	AVG	OBP	SLG	AOPS	ABR	SB-CS	FA	FR	RNG	THR	GAMES AT POSITION	DL	BFW
1969	NY N	62	211	20	49	9	0	0	10	7-0	1	27	.232	.260	.275	49	-15	0-1	.976	-3	101	120	3b49,2b11,O2L		
1971	Phi N	44	70	5	19	3	0	2	9	6-1	0	9	.271	.329	.400	105	0	1-1	1.000	-2	101	292	3b15,C4,O3(2/0/1)/12S		
Total	2	106	281	25	68	12	0	2	19	13-1	1	36	.242	.278	.306	63	-15	1-2	.980	-4	101	158	3b64,2b12,O5(4/0/1),C4/S1		

PFISTER, GEORGE George Edward B9.4.1918 Bound Brook NJ D8.14.1997 Somerset NJ BR/TR/6-0/200 d9.27 C1

YEAR	TM LG	G	AB	R	H	2B	3B	HR	RBI	BB-IB	HP	SO	AVG	OBP	SLG	AOPS	ABR	SB-CS	FA	FR	RNG	THR	GAMES AT POSITION
1941	Bro N	1	2	0	0	0	0	0	0	0-0	0	0	.000	.000	.000	-96	-1	0	—	0	0	0	/C

PFYL, MONTE Meinhard Charles B5.11.1884 St.Louis MO D10.18.1945 San Francisco CA BL/TL/6-3/190 d7.30

YEAR	TM LG	G	AB	R	H	2B	3B	HR	RBI	BB-IB	HP	SO	AVG	OBP	SLG	AOPS	ABR	SB-CS	FA	FR	RNG	THR	GAMES AT POSITION
1907	NY N	1	0	0	0	0	0	0	0	0		0	—	—	—	—	0		0	0	0		/1

PHELAN, ART Arthur Thomas "Dugan" B8.14.1887 Niantic IL D12.12.1964 Ft.Worth TX BR/TR/5-8/160 d6.25

YEAR	TM LG	G	AB	R	H	2B	3B	HR	RBI	BB-IB	HP	SO	AVG	OBP	SLG	AOPS	ABR	SB-CS	FA	FR	RNG	THR	GAMES AT POSITION
1910	Cin N	23	42	7	9	0	0	0	4	7	0	6	.214	.327	.214	61	-2	5	1.000	-0	112	0	3b8,2b5,O3L/S
1912	Cin N	130	461	56	112	9	11	3	54	46	2	37	.243	.314	.330	79	-15	25	.924	-1	102	103	3b127,2b3
1913	Chi N	91	261	41	65	11	6	2	35	29	3	26	.249	.331	.360	97	-1	8-8	.931	-2	100	82	2b46,3b38/S
1914	Chi N	25	46	5	13	2	1	0	3	4	0	3	.283	.340	.370	111	1	0	.905	-2	94	92	3b7,2b3,S2
1915	Chi N	133	448	41	98	16	7	3	35	55	2	42	.219	.307	.306	86	-7	12-9	.939	-2	94	92	3b110,2b81,S4,O3L
Total	5	402	1258	150	297	38	25	8	131	141	7	114	.236	.317	.325	86	-24	50-17	.931	-6	99	89	3b290,2b81,S4,O3L

PHELAN, DAN Daniel T. B7.23.1864 Thomaston CT D12.7.1945 West Haven CT BL/5-10/175 d4.18

YEAR	TM LG	G	AB	R	H	2B	3B	HR	RBI	BB-IB	HP	SO	AVG	OBP	SLG	AOPS	ABR	SB-CS	FA	FR	RNG	THR	GAMES AT POSITION
1890	Lou AA	8	32	4	8	1	1	0	4	0			.250	.250	.344	77	-1	1	.975	0	99	0	1b8

PHELAN, DICK James Dickson B12.10.1854 Towanda PA D2.13.1931 San Antonio TX BR d4.17

YEAR	TM LG	G	AB	R	H	2B	3B	HR	RBI	BB-IB	HP	SO	AVG	OBP	SLG	AOPS	ABR	SB-CS	FA	FR	RNG	THR	GAMES AT POSITION
1884	Bal U	101	402	63	99	13	3	3		12			.246	.268	.316	69	-28		.872	-12	94	104	2b100,3b5/OC
1885	Buf N	4	16	2	2	0	0	1	3			3	.125	.125	.313	37	-1		.808	-1	120	102	2b4
	StL N	2	4	1	1	0	1	0	1			2	.250	.250	.500	147	0		1.000	-0	0	0	3b2
	Year	6	20	3	3	0	1	1	4			5	.150	.150	.350	58	-1		.808	-1	120	102	2b4,3b2
Total	2	107	422	66	102	14	3	4		12		7	.242	.263	.318	69	-29		.869	-13	95	104	2b104,3b7/OC

PHELPS, NEALY Cornelius Carman B11.19.1840 New York NY D2.12.1885 New York NY d7.1

YEAR	TM LG	G	AB	R	H	2B	3B	HR	RBI	BB-IB	HP	SO	AVG	OBP	SLG	AOPS	ABR	SB-CS	FA	FR	RNG	THR	GAMES AT POSITION
1871	Kek NA	1	3	0	0	0	0	0	0	2		1	.000	.250	.000	-20	0	0-0	.889	-0	0	205	/1
1873	Mut NA	1	6	0	0	0	0	0	0	0		0	.000	.000	.000	-99	-1	0-0	1.000	0	0	0	/1OR
1874	Mut NA	6	24	5	3	0	0	0	2	0		0	.125	.125	.125	-19	-3	0-0	.818	1	196	610	O6R
1875	Mut NA	2	6	1	2	0	0	0	0	1		0	.333	.333	.500	176	0	0-0	1.000	0	389	0	O2R
1876	NY N	1	3	0	0	0	0	0	0	0		1	.000	.000	.000	-99	-1		.667	-0	0		/OC
	Phi N	1	4	0	0	0	0	0	0	2		1	.000	.000	.000	-99	-1		.571	-1			/C
	Year	2	7	0	0	0	0	0	0	2		1	.000	.000	.000	-99	-1		.667	-2	0		/OCC
Total	4 NA	10	39	6	5	1	0	0	2			1	.128	.150	.154	-3	-4	0-0	.857	1			O9R,1b2

YEAR	TM LG	G	AB	R	H	2B	3B	HR	RBI	BB-IB	HP	SO	AVG	OBP	SLG	AOPS	ABR	SB-CS	FA	FR	RNG	THR	GAMES AT POSITION	DL	BFW

PHELPS, ED Edward Jaykill "Yaller" B3.3.1879 Albany NY D1.31.1942 E.Greenbush NY BR/TR/5-11/185 d9.3

YEAR	TM LG	G	AB	R	H	2B	3B	HR	RBI	BB-IB	HP	SO	AVG	OBP	SLG	AOPS	ABR	SB-CS	FA	FR	RNG	THR	GAMES AT POSITION	DL	BFW
1902	Pit N	18	61	5	13	1	0	0	6	4	2		.213	.284	.230	57	-3	2	.968	-3	120	66	C13,1b5		-0.5
1903	†Pit N	81	273	32	77	7	3	2	31	17	6		.282	.338	.352	94	-3	2	.980	0	133	81	C76,1b3		0.4
1904	Pit N	94	302	29	73	5	3	0	28	15	5		.242	.289	.278	73	-10	2	.964	-6	106	84	C91/1		-0.7
1905	Cin N	44	156	18	36	5	3	0	18	12	5		.231	.306	.301	73	-5	4	.949	-3	94	85	C44		-0.4
1906	Cin N	12	40	3	11	0	2	1	5	3	0		.275	.326	.450	136	1	2	.987	-0	95	85	C12		0.3
	Pit N	43	118	9	28	3	1	0	12	9	2		.237	.302	.280	78	-3	1	.971	-1	121	66	C40		0.0
	Year	55	158	12	39	3	3	1	17	12	2		.247	.308	.323	93	-2	3	.975	-1	114	71	C52		0.3
1907	Pit N	43	113	-11	24	1	0	0	12	9	2		.212	.282	.221	57	-5	1	.979	1	126	92	C35/1		-0.1
1908	Pit N	34	64	3	15	2	2	0	11	2	1		.234	.269	.328	90	-1	0	.977	1	127	71	C20		0.1
1909	StL N	104	306	43	76	13	1	0	22	39	9		.248	.350	.297	108	6	7	.954	-14	75	92	C83		-0.1
1910	StL N	93	270	25	71	4	2	0	37	36		29	.263	.356	.293	93	-1	9	.976	-18	73	81	C80		-1.2
1912	Bro N	52	111	8	32	4	3	0	23	16	2	15	.288	.388	.378	114	3	1	.976	-2	86	93	C32		0.3
1913	Bro N	15	18	0	4	0	0	0	1	0	0	2	.222	.263	.222	38	-1	0	.875	1	71	60	C4		0.3
Total	11	633	1832	186	460	45	20	3	205	163	37	46	.251	.325	.302	88	-22	31	.968	-46	101	83	C530,1b10		-2.2

PHELPS, BABE Ernest Gordon "Blimp" B4.19.1908 Odenton MD D12.10.1992 Odenton MD BL/TR/6-2/225 d9.17

YEAR	TM LG	G	AB	R	H	2B	3B	HR	RBI	BB-IB	HP	SO	AVG	OBP	SLG	AOPS	ABR	SB-CS	FA	FR	RNG	THR	GAMES AT POSITION	DL	BFW
1931	Was A	3	3	0	1	0	0	0	0	0	0		.333	.333	.333	75	0	0-0			0		/H		0.0
1933	Chi N	3	7	0	2	0	0	0	2	0	0	1	.286	.286	.286	64	0	0-0	1.000	0	1	0	228 C2		0.0
1934	Chi N	44	70	7	20	5	2	2	12	1	0	8	.286	.296	.500	111	1	0	.981	-1	145	143	C18		0.0
1935	Bro N	47	121	17	44	7	2	5	22	9	0	10	.364	.408	.579	165	11	0	.957	-0	114	97	C34		0.0
1936	Bro N	115	319	36	117	23	2	5	57	27	3	18	.367	.421	.498	145	22	1	.977	-10	65	112	C98/OR		1.2
1937	Bro N	121	409	42	128	37	3	7	58	25	3	28	.313	.357	.469	121	12	2	.971	-3	85	104	C111		1.6
1938	Bro N*	66	208	33	64	12	2	6	46	23	1	15	.308	.379	.457	126	8	2	.980	-2	82	87	C55		1.5
1939	Bro N★	98	323	33	92	21	2	6	42	24	1	24	.285	.336	.418	98	-1	0	.980	3	110	93	C92		0.9
1940	Bro N★	118	370	47	109	24	5	13	61	30	1	27	.295	.349	.492	122	11	2	.977	-4	121	55	C99/1		0.7
1941	Bro N	16	30	3	7	3	0	0	1	0		2	.233	.258	.533	114	0	0	.971	-0	227	0	C11		1.2
1942	Pit N	95	257	21	73	11	1	9	41	20	4	24	.284	.345	.440	126	8	2	.959	-3	87	99	C72		0.1
Total	11	726	2117	239	657	143	19	54	345	160	13	157	.310	.362	.472	124	72	9-0	.974	-19	97	92	C592/1OR		8.2

PHELPS, JOSH Joshua Lee B5.12.1978 Anchorage AK BR/TR/6-3/215* [TorA96 10/279] d6.13

YEAR	TM LG	G	AB	R	H	2B	3B	HR	RBI	BB-IB	HP	SO	AVG	OBP	SLG	AOPS	ABR	SB-CS	FA	FR	RNG	THR	GAMES AT POSITION	DL	BFW
2000	Tor A	1	1	0	0	0	0	0	0	0-0			.000	.000	.000	-97	0	0-0	1.000	-0	0	0	/C		
2001	Tor A	8	12	3	0	0	0	0	1	0-0	0	5	.000	.143	.000	-56	-3	1-0	1.000	0			/C		0.0
2002	Tor A	74	265	41	82	20	1	15	58	19-0	3	82	.309	.362	.562	136	13	1-0	1.000	0	74	161	C7		-0.2
2003	Tor A	119	396	57	106	18	1	20	66	39-3	17	115	.268	.358	.470	112	7	1-2	.967	-1	83	33	D71,1b2		0.9
2004	Tor A	79	295	38	70	13	2	12	51	18-2	7	73	.237	.296	.417	79	-10	0-0	.981	-3	26	70	D65,1b12	18	-1.6
	Cle A	24	76	13	23	6	0	5	10	4-0	0	20	.303	.338	.579	138	4	0-0	.978	-1	49	18	D16,1b8		0.1
	Year	103	371	51	93	19	2	17	61	22-2	7	93	.251	.304	.450	90	-7	0-0	.980	-4	34	51	D81,1b20		-1.5
2005	TB A	47	158	21	42	10	0	5	26	12-1	4	46	.266	.328	.424	102	1	0-0	1.000	-0	0	302	D42/1		-0.2
Total	6	352	1203	173	323	67	4	57	212	94-6	31	344	.268	.336	.473	107	12	2-2	.978	-5	45	55	D300,1b31,C8	18	-1.0

PHELPS, KEN Kenneth Allen B8.6.1954 Seattle WA BL/TL/6-1/209* [KCA76 15/354] d9.20 Col Arizona St.

YEAR	TM LG	G	AB	R	H	2B	3B	HR	RBI	BB-IB	HP	SO	AVG	OBP	SLG	AOPS	ABR	SB-CS	FA	FR	RNG	THR	GAMES AT POSITION	DL	BFW
1980	KC A	3	4	0	0	0	0	0	0	0	0	2	.000	.000	.000	-99	-1	0-0	1.000	-0	0	243	1b2		-0.1
1981	KC A	21	22	1	3	0	1	0	1	1-0	0	3	.136	.174	.227	15	-3	0-0	1.000	-0	0	451	1b2,D4		-0.2
1982	Mon N	10	8	0	2	0	0	0	0	0-0	1	3	.250	.333	.250	63	0	0-0					/H		-0.1
1983	Sea A	50	127	10	30	4	1	7	16	13-0	0	25	.236	.301	.449	101	0	0-0	1.000	2	116	60	1b22,D19		-0.1
1984	Sea A	101	290	52	70	9	4	24	51	61-5	5	73	.241	.378	.521	148	21	3-3	.987	-1	62	84	D84,1b9	41	1.7
1985	Sea A	61	116	18	24	3	0	9	24	24-2	0	33	.207	.343	.466	118	3	2-0	1.000	-1	58	116	D25,1b8		0.2
1986	Sea A	125	344	69	85	16	4	24	64	88-6	6	75	.247	.406	.526	150	28	2-3	.983	-4	82	118	1b55,D52		1.9
1987	Sea A	120	332	68	86	13	1	27	68	80-5	8	75	.259	.410	.548	145	25	1-1	1.000	-0		114	/1		2.0
1988	Sea A	72	190	37	54	8	0	14	32	51-2	1	35	.284	.434	.547	146	20	1-0	.952	-0	105	89	D68,1b3		1.8
	NY A	45	107	17	24	5	0	10	22	19-3	0	26	.224	.339	.551	146	7	0-0		0	0		D24/1		0.6
	Year	117	297	54	78	13	0	24	54	70-5	1	61	.263	.402	.549	160	27	1-0	.952	-0	101	85	D92,1b4		2.4
1989	NY A	86	185	26	46	3	0	7	29	27-2	1	47	.249	.340	.378	104	1	0-0	.980	-1	35	99	D55,1b8		-0.2
	†Oak A	11	9	0	1	1	0	0	0	4-0	0	2	.111	.385	.222	78	0	0-0		-0	0	0	/1D		0.0
	Year	97	194	26	47	4	0	7	29	31-2	1	47	.242	.342	.371	103	2	0-0	.980	-1	28	80	D56,1b9		-0.2
1990	Oak A	32	59	6	11	2	0	1	6	12-1	0	16	.186	.319	.271	71	-2	0-0	.964	0	176	171	D15,1b5		-0.2
	Cle A	24	61	4	7	0	0	0	10	10-2	0	11	.115	.239	.115	2	-8	1-0	1.000	-0	92	41	1b14,D6		-0.9
	Year	56	120	10	18	2	0	1	16	22-3	0	27	.150	.280	.192	36	-10	1-0	.992	0	106	63	D21,1b19		-1.1
Total	11	761	1854	308	443	64	7	123	313	390-28	21	449	.239	.374	.480	131	91	10-7	.987	-5	86	95	D467,1b131	41	6.4

PHILLEY, DAVE David Earl B5.16.1920 Paris TX BB/TR/6-0/188* d9.6 Mil 1943-45

YEAR	TM LG	G	AB	R	H	2B	3B	HR	RBI	BB-IB	HP	SO	AVG	OBP	SLG	AOPS	ABR	SB-CS	FA	FR	RNG	THR	GAMES AT POSITION	DL	BFW
1941	Chi A	7	9	4	2	1	0	0	0	3	0	3	.222	.417	.333	102	0	0-0		-0	0	0	O2L		0.0
1946	Chi A	17	68	10	24	2	3	0	17	4	0	4	.353	.389	.471	145	4	5-0	.983	3	113	197	O17(16/1/0)		0.6
1947	Chi A	143	551	55	142	25	11	2	45	35	1	39	.258	.303	.354	85	-14	21-16	.986	-1	97	97	O133(39/95/0),3b4		-2.2
1948	Chi A	137	488	51	140	28	3	5	42	50	0	33	.287	.353	.387	100	0	8-10	.978	10	100	200	O128(6/123/0)		0.4
1949	Chi A	146	598	84	171	20	8	0	44	54	2	55	.286	.347	.346	86	-13	13-4	.977	-2	95	115	O145(0/3/143)		-1.7
1950	Chi A	156	619	69	150	21	5	14	80	52	1	57	.242	.302	.360	71	-31	6-3	.980	5	100	141	O154(0/78/103)		-2.9
1951	Chi A	7	25	0	6	2	0	0	2	2	0	3	.240	.296	.320	68	-1	0-0	.938	-1	100	0	O6L		-0.2
	Phi A	125	468	71	123	18	7	7	59	63	3	38	.263	.354	.376	95	-2	9-6	.978	-3	92	125	O120(2/116/2),3b2		-0.9
	Year	132	493	71	129	20	7	7	61	65	3	41	.262	.351	.373	94	-4	9-6	.976	-4	92	118	O126(8/116/2),3b2		-1.1
1952	Phi A	151	586	80	154	25	4	7	71	59	4	35	.263	.334	.355	94	-10	11-4	.991	7	106	112	O149C,3b2		-0.7
1953	Phi A	157	620	80	188	30	9	9	59	51	2	35	.303	.358	.424	106	3	13-5	.981	-4	92	118	O157(0/31/129),3b2		-0.4
1954	†Cle A	133	452	48	102	13	3	12	60	57	0	48	.226	.308	.347	79	-14	2-4	.984	-4	99	64	O129(1/0/129)		-2.4
1955	Cle A	43	104	15	31	4	2	2	9	12-2	1	10	.298	.368	.433	111	2	0-2	1.000	0	98	108	O34(2/0/32)		0.0
	Bal A	83	311	50	93	13	3	6	41	34-2	5	38	.299	.367	.418	119	8	1-2	.970	-3	95	92	O82(46/2/48),3b2		0.1
	Year	126	415	65	124	17	5	8	50	46-4	6	48	.299	.367	.422	116	9	1-4	.976	-4	96	96	O116(48/2/80),3b5		0.1
1956	Bal A	32	117	13	24	4	1	1	17	18-3	0	13	.205	.309	.299	67	-6	3-1	.935	-1	101	95	O31(23/0/16),3b5		-0.7
	Chi A	86	279	44	74	14	2	4	47	28-0	1	27	.265	.328	.373	85	-6	1-3	.978	-4	69	88	1b51,O30(17/0/19)		-1.4
	Year	118	396	57	98	18	4	5	64	46-3	1	40	.247	.322	.351	80	-12	4-4	.965	-5	99	98	O61(40/0/35),1b51,3b5		-2.1
1957	Chi A	22	71	9	23	4	0	0	9	4-0	0	10	.324	.360	.380	102	0	1-1	.975	-0	121	0	O17R,1b2		-0.1
	Det A	65	173	16	49	8	1	2	16	7-0	1	16	.283	.309	.376	85	-4	3-1	.996	3	147	80	1b27,O12(4/0/8)/3		-0.3
	Year	87	244	24	72	12	1	2	25	11-0	1	26	.295	.324	.377	90	-4	4-2	.965	2	115		O29(4/0/25),1b29/3		-0.4
1958	Phi N	91	207	30	64	11	4	3	31	15-3	1	20	.309	.357	.444	113	4	1-1	1.000	2	98		O24R,1b18		0.0
1959	Phi N	99	254	32	74	18	2	7	37	18-3	1	27	.291	.339	.461	109	3	0-0	1.000	0	106	156	O34R,1b24		0.1
1960	Phi N	14	15	2	5	2	0	0	4	3-1	0	2	.333	.444	.467	149	1	0-0		-1	0	0	O3(0/2/0/1),1b2		0.1
	SF N	39	61	5	10	0	0	1	7	6-0	0	7	.164	.239	.213	26	-6	0-0	.941	-1	105	0	O10L,3b3		-0.8
	Year	53	76	7	15	2	0	1	11	9-1	0	16	.197	.282	.263	53	-5	0-0	.941	-2	113		O13(12/0/1),3b3,1b2		-0.7
1961	Bal A	14	34	6	9	2	1	1	5	4-0	0	5	.265	.342	.471	119	1	1-0	1.000	0	113		O8(6/0/2)/3		0.1
1962	Bos A	38	42	3	6	2	0	0	4	5-0	1	3	.143	.250	.190	20	-5	0-0	1.000	-3	65		O25(22/0/3)/1		-0.8
Total	18	1904	6296	789	1700	276	72	84	729	594-14	17	551	.270	.334	.377	91	-89	101-63	.981	-1	98	115	O1454(204/590/714),1b125,3b21		-14.6

PHILLIPS, ADOLFO Adolfo Emilio (Lopez) B12.16.1941 Bethania, Pan BR/TR/6-0/177* d9.2

YEAR	TM LG	G	AB	R	H	2B	3B	HR	RBI	BB-IB	HP	SO	AVG	OBP	SLG	AOPS	ABR	SB-CS	FA	FR	RNG	THR	GAMES AT POSITION	DL	BFW
1964	Phi N	13	13	4	3	0	0	0	0	3-0	0	3	.231	.375	.231	76	0	0-0	1.000	1	92	528	O4(3/2/1)		0.0
1965	Phi N	41	87	14	20	4	0	3	5	5-0	1	34	.230	.272	.379	83	-2	3-3	1.000	-1	98	0	O32(2/30/0)		-0.5
1966	Phi N	2	3	1	0	0	0	0	0	0-0	0	1	.000	.000	.000	-99	-1	0-0	1.000	0		0	/OC		-0.1
	Chi N	116	416	68	109	29	1	16	36	43-3	12	135	.262	.348	.452	119	12	32-15	.978	7	106	189	O111C		-0.1
	Year	118	419	69	109	29	1	16	36	43-3	12	135	.260	.346	.449	118	12	32-15	.979	7	106	188	O112C		1.9
1967	Chi N	144	448	66	120	20	7	17	70	80-29	6	93	.268	.384	.458	134	23	24-10	.981	7	106	163	O141C		1.8
1968	Chi N	143	439	49	106	20	5	13	33	47-20	5	90	.241	.320	.399	108	5	9-7	.979	4	103	141	O141C		3.0
1969	Chi N	28	49	5	11	3	1	0	1	16-3	1	15	.224	.424	.327	100	1	1-3	.956	-0	112	0	O25(1/24/0)		0.6
	Mon N	58	199	25	43	4	4	4	19	19-1	1	62	.216	.286	.357	74	-8	6-5	.981	-1	97	106	O53C		-1.1
	Year	86	248	30	54	7	5	4	20	35-4	2	77	.218	.318	.335	80	-6	7-8	.973	-2	99	106	O78(1/77/0)		-1.2
1970	Mon N	92	214	36	51	3	6		21	36-1	2	51	.238	.352	.379		-1	7-1	.985	-1	106	32	O75(6/71/0)		-0.1

YEAR	TM LG	G	AB	R	H	2B	3B	HR	RBI	BB-IB	HP	SO	AVG	OBP	SLG	AOPS	ABR	SB-CS	FA	FR	RNG	THR	GAMES AT POSITION	DL	BFW
1972	Cle A	12	7	2	0	0	0	0		2-0	0	2	.000	.222	.000	-29	-1	0-0	1.000	0	129	0	O10(6/2/2)		-0.1
Total 8		649	1875	270	463	86	21	59	173	251-57	27	485	.247	.343	.410	110	28	82-44	.980	16	104	131	O593(18/576/3)		3.5

PHILLIPS, BRANDON   Brandon Emil B6.28.1981 Raleigh NC   BR/TR/5-11/185*   [MonN99 2/57]   d9.13

YEAR	TM LG	G	AB	R	H	2B	3B	HR	RBI	BB-IB	HP	SO	AVG	OBP	SLG	AOPS	ABR	SB-CS	FA	FR	RNG	THR	GAMES AT POSITION	DL	BFW
2002	Cle A	11	31	5	8	3	0	0	4	3-0	1	6	.258	.343	.419	99	0	0-0	.957	0	108	61	2b11		0.1
2003	Cle A	112	370	36	77	18	1	6	33	14-0	3	77	.208	.242	.311	45	-31	4-5	.981	16	112	112	2b109		-1.0
2004	Cle A	6	22	1	4	2	0	0	1	2-0	0	4	.182	.250	.273	38	-2	0-2	1.000	0	68	163	2b6		-0.1
2005	Cle A	6	9	1	0	0	0	0	0	0-0	0	4	.000	.000	.000	-99	-3	0-0	.973	1	102	94	2b2/SD		-0.2
Total 4		135	432	43	89	23	2	6	38	19-0	4	91	.206	.246	.310	46	-36	4-7	.979	17	110	108	2b128/DS		-1.2

PHILLIPS, J. R.   Charles Gene B4.29.1970 West Covina CA   BL/TL/6-1/185(185-205)   [CalA88 4/91]   d9.3

YEAR	TM LG	G	AB	R	H	2B	3B	HR	RBI	BB-IB	HP	SO	AVG	OBP	SLG	AOPS	ABR	SB-CS	FA	FR	RNG	THR	GAMES AT POSITION	DL	BFW
1993	SF N	11	16	1	5	1	1	1	4	0-0	0	5	.313	.313	.688	164	1	0-0	.971	-0	88	45	1b5		0.1
1994	SF N	15	38	1	5	0	0	1	3	1-0	0	13	.132	.150	.211	-7	-6	1-0	.989	1	154	103	1b10		-0.6
1995	SF N	92	231	27	45	9	0	9	28	19-2	0	69	.195	.256	.351	59	-15	1-1	.993	-3	85	95	1b79/OL		-2.4
1996	SF N	15	25	3	5	0	0	2	5	1-0	0	13	.200	.231	.440	73	-1	0-0	.981	-1	51	87	1b10		-0.3
	Phi N	35	79	9	12	5	0	5	10	10-1	1	38	.152	.250	.405	70	-4	0-0	.957	3	178	119	O15R,1b11		-0.2
	Year	50	104	12	17	5	0	7	15	11-1	1	51	.163	.250	.413	71	-5	0-0	.992	-0	54	102	1b21,O15R		-0.5
1997	Hou N	13	15	2	2	0	1	0	4	0-0	0	7	.133	.125	.333	18	-2	0-0	1.000	-0	0	106	1b3,O3R		-0.6
1998	Hou N	36	58	4	11	0	0	2	4	7-1	0	22	.190	.277	.293	51	-4	0-0	.962	-1	101	107	1b12,O6L		0.0
1999	Col N	25	39	5	9	4	0	2	4	0-0	0	13	.231	.250	.487	64	-2	0-0	.933	2	103	848	O7(1/0/6),1b4		-4.2
Total 7		242	501	52	94	19	1	23	67	38-4	2	180	.188	.247	.367	59	-33	2-1	.989	1	87	97	1b134,O32(8/0/24)		

PHILLIPS, DAMON   Damon Roswell "Dee" B6.8.1919 Corsicana TX   D11.4.2004 Fort Worth TX   BR/TR/6-0/176   Mil 1945

YEAR	TM LG	G	AB	R	H	2B	3B	HR	RBI	BB-IB	HP	SO	AVG	OBP	SLG	AOPS	ABR	SB-CS	FA	FR	RNG	THR	GAMES AT POSITION	DL	BFW
1942	Cin N	28	84	4	17	2	0	0	6	7	0	5	.202	.264	.226	44	-6	0	.964	3	110	124	S27		-0.1
1944	Bos N	140	489	35	126	30	1	1	53	28	2	34	.258	.301	.329	74	-17	1	.932	2	109	155	3b90,S60		-1.0
1946	Bos N	2	2	0	1	0	0	0	0	0-0	0	0	.500	.500	.500	182	0	0		—	0		/H		0.0
Total 3		170	575	39	144	32	1	1	59	35	2	39	.250	.296	.315	70	-23	1	.932	5	109	155	3b90,S87		-1.1

PHILLIPS, EDDIE   Edward David B2.17.1901 Worcester MA   D1.26.1968 Buffalo NY   BR/TR/6-0/178   d5.4   Col Boston College

YEAR	TM LG	G	AB	R	H	2B	3B	HR	RBI	BB-IB	HP	SO	AVG	OBP	SLG	AOPS	ABR	SB-CS	FA	FR	RNG	THR	GAMES AT POSITION	DL	BFW
1924	Bos N	3	3	0	0	0	0	0	0	0-0	0	0	.000	.000	.000	-99	-1	0-0	1.000	-0	0	817	/C		-0.1
1929	Det A	68	221	24	52	13	1	2	21	20	1	16	.235	.302	.330	62	-13	0-1	.967	-8	74	87	C63		-1.6
1931	Pit N	106	353	30	82	18	3	7	44	41	3	49	.232	.317	.360	82	-8	1-0	.986	-5	99	74	C103		-0.7
1932	NY A	9	31	4	9	1	0	2	4	2	0	3	.290	.333	.516	123	1	1-0	1.000	1	113	122	C9		0.2
1934	Was A	56	169	6	33	6	1	2	16	26	1	24	.195	.306	.278	54	-12	0-0	.984	-5	148	98	C53		-1.2
1935	Cle A	70	220	18	60	16	1	1	41	15	0	21	.273	.319	.368	76	-7	0-0	.980	-7	111	71	C69		-1.0
Total 6		312	997	82	236	54	6	14	126	104	5	115	.237	.312	.345	72	-41	2-1	.980	-24	105	82	C298		-4.4

PHILLIPS, ANDY   George Andrew B4.6.1977 Tuscaloosa AL   BR/TR/6-0/205*   [NYA99 7/231]   d9.14   Col Alabama

YEAR	TM LG	G	AB	R	H	2B	3B	HR	RBI	BB-IB	HP	SO	AVG	OBP	SLG	AOPS	ABR	SB-CS	FA	FR	RNG	THR	GAMES AT POSITION	DL	BFW
2004	NY A	5	8	1	2	0	0	1	2	0-0	0	1	.250	.250	.625	117	0	0-0	1.000	0	118	0	3b4		-0.0
2005	NY A	27	40	7	6	4	0	1	4	1-0	0	13	.150	.171	.325	27	-4	0-0	.987	-2	41	105	1b19/3OLD		-0.6
Total 2		32	48	8	8	4	0	2	6	1-0	0	14	.167	.184	.375	42	-4	0-0	.987	-1	41	105	1b19,D6,3b5/OL		-0.6

PHILLIPS, EDDIE   Howard Edward B7.8.1931 St.Louis MO   BB/TR/6-1/180   d9.10

YEAR	TM LG	G	AB	R	H	2B	3B	HR	RBI	BB-IB	HP	SO	AVG	OBP	SLG	AOPS	ABR	SB-CS	FA	FR	RNG	THR	GAMES AT POSITION	DL	BFW
1953	StL N	9	4	0	0	0	0	0	0	—	0	0	—	—	—	0	0	0-0	—	0			/R		

PHILLIPS, JACK   Jack Dorn "Stretch" B9.6.1921 Clarence NY   BR/TR/6-4/193*   d8.22   Col Clarkson

YEAR	TM LG	G	AB	R	H	2B	3B	HR	RBI	BB-IB	HP	SO	AVG	OBP	SLG	AOPS	ABR	SB-CS	FA	FR	RNG	THR	GAMES AT POSITION	DL	BFW
1947 †	NY A	16	36	5	10	1	1	2	3	0	0	5	.278	.333	.417	109	-1	0-0	.986	-2	17	118	1b10		
1948	NY A	1	2	0	2	0	0	0	0	0	0	0	1.000	1.000	1.000	-99	0	0-0	.889	-0	0	0	/1		
1949	NY A	45	91	16	28	4	1	1	10	12	0	9	.308	.388	.407	110	2	1-0	.977	-2	73	110	1b38		
	Pit N	18	56	6	13	3	1	0	3	4	0	6	.232	.283	.321	60	-3	1	1.000	-0	94	91	1b16/3		
1950	Pit N	69	208	25	61	7	6	5	34	20	0	17	.293	.355	.457	108	2	1	.986	1	119	96	1b54,3b3/P		-1.
1951	Pit N	70	156	12	37	7	3	0	12	15	0	17	.237	.304	.321	66	-7	1-2	.991	-1	88	107	1b53,3b4		
1952	Pit N	1	1	0	0	0	0	0	0	0-0	0	0	.000	.000	.000	-97	0	0-0	1.000	0	451	1	/1		
1955	Det A	55	117	15	37	8	2	1	20	10-0	0	12	.316	.364	.444	121	3	0-0	.992	-2	77	71	1b35,3b3		
1956	Det A	67	224	31	66	13	2	1	20	21-0	0	19	.295	.354	.384	95	-1	1-1	.981	-2	97	99	1b56/2OL		
1957	Det A	1	1	0	0	0	0	0	0	0-0	0	0	.000	.000	.000	-97	0	0-0		—	0		/H		-2
Total 9		343	892	111	252	42	16	9	101	85-0	0	86	.283	.344	.396	95	-5	5-3	.986	-8	92	98	1b264,3b11/OL2P		

PHILLIPS, JASON   Jason Lloyd B9.27.1976 LaMesa CA   BR/TR/6-1/177(177-210)   [NYN97 24/720]   d9.19   Col San Diego St.

YEAR	TM LG	G	AB	R	H	2B	3B	HR	RBI	BB-IB	HP	SO	AVG	OBP	SLG	AOPS	ABR	SB-CS	FA	FR	RNG	THR	GAMES AT POSITION	DL	BFW
2001	NY N	6	7	1	1	0	0	0	0	0-0	0	1	.143	.143	.286	7	-1	0-0	1.000	0	96		C5		0
2002	NY N	11	19	4	7	0	1	3	4	1-0	0	1	.368	.400	.526	163	2	0-0	1.000	0	89		C7		0
2003	NY N	119	403	45	120	25	0	11	58	39-3	10	50	.298	.373	.442	116	11	0-1	.998	7	93	87	C87,1b38		-1
2004	NY N	128	362	34	79	18	0	7	34	35-4	8	42	.218	.298	.326	64	-20	0-1	.992	-11	60	102	C93,1b21		-2
2005	LA N	121	399	38	95	20	0	10	55	25-4	5	50	.238	.287	.363	70	-18	0-1	.995	-9	85	103	C29,1b84		-2
Total 5		385	1190	123	302	64	0	29	150	100-11	23	144	.254	.321	.381	85	-26	0-3	.995		85	103	C221,1b143		

PHILLIPS, BUBBA   John Melvin B2.24.1928 West Point MS   D6.22.1993 Hattiesburg MS   BR/TR/5-9/180*   d4.30   Col Southern Mississippi

YEAR	TM LG	G	AB	R	H	2B	3B	HR	RBI	BB-IB	HP	SO	AVG	OBP	SLG	AOPS	ABR	SB-CS	FA	FR	RNG	THR	GAMES AT POSITION	DL	BFW
1955	Det A	95	184	18	43	4	0	3	23	14-1	2	20	.234	.289	.304	63	-10	2-1	.992	3	120	47	O65(61/2/4),3b4		-1
1956	Chi A	67	99	16	27	6	0	2	11	6-0	1	12	.273	.321	.394	87	-2	5-3	.958	11	115	111	3b97,O20(1/13/8)		-0
1957	Chi A	121	393	38	106	13	3	7	42	28-3	3	32	.270	.322	.372	89	-7	3-0	.954	1	103	149	3b47,O37(19/15/4)	37	-0
1958	Chi A	84	260	26	71	10	0	5	30	15-1	1	14	.273	.310	.369	89	-4	3-0	.951	3	109	85	3b100,O23(8/14/1)		-3
1959 †	Chi A	117	379	43	100	27	1	5	40	27-7	4	28	.264	.319	.380	92	-4	1-0	.953	-8	104	87	3b85,O25(15/3/7)/S		-3
1960	Cle A	113	304	34	63	14	1	4	33	14-3	4	37	.207	.249	.299	50	-22	1-0	.958	-15	83	73	3b143		-2
1961	Cle A	143	546	64	144	23	1	18	72	29-4	7	55	.264	.305	.408	92	-9	4-0	.977	-10	88	60	3b145,O3C/2		-2
1962	Cle A	148	562	53	145	26	0	10	54	20-0	5	55	.258	.289	.358	76	-20	6-2	.961	1	97	117	3b117,O5C		-2
1963	Det A	128	464	42	114	11	2	5	45	19-1	2	42	.246	.276	.310	63	-23	1-2	.983	0	100	142	3b22/OL		-2
1964	Det A	46	87	14	22	1	0	3	8	10-2	1	13	.253	.327	.368	92	-1	0-0	.978	-8	96	97	3b2,O?	37	-12
Total 10		1062	3278	348	835	135	8	62	356	182-24	31	314	.255	.297	.358			25-11					3b762,O214(111/62/46)/2S		

PHILLIPS, TONY   Keith Anthony B4.25.1959 Atlanta GA   BB/TR/5-10/175(160-175)   [MonN78*S1/10]   d5.10   Col New Mexico Mil. Inst.   [JC]   OF(566/97/169)

YEAR	TM LG	G	AB	R	H	2B	3B	HR	RBI	BB-IB	HP	SO	AVG	OBP	SLG	AOPS	ABR	SB-CS	FA	FR	RNG	THR	GAMES AT POSITION	DL	BFW
1982	Oak A	40	81	11	17	2	2	0	8	12-0	2	26	.210	.326	.284	72	-3	2-3	.953	-0	107	90	S39		-0
1983	Oak A	148	412	54	102	12	3	4	35	48-1	2	70	.248	.327	.320	84	-8	16-5	.941	-20	101	110	S101,2b63,3b4/D		-0
1984	Oak A	154	451	62	120	24	3	4	37	42-1	0	86	.266	.325	.359	96	-2	10-6	.941	-8	106	107	S91,2b90/OL		
1985	Oak A	42	161	23	45	12	2	4	17	13-0	1	34	.280	.331	.453	121	5	3-2	.980	3	108	108	3b31,2b24	136	
1986	Oak A	118	441	76	113	14	5	5	52	76-0	3	82	.256	.367	.345	103	5	15-10	.976	7	115	71	2b88,3b30,O4C/SD	50	
1987	Oak A	111	379	48	91	20	0	10	46	57-1	0	76	.240	.337	.372	95	-1	7-6	.974	1	103	73	2b87,3b11,S9,O2(1/0/1)/D	47	
1988 †	Oak A	79	212	32	43	8	4	2	17	36-0	1	50	.203	.320	.307	79	-5	0-2	.985	-8	104	96	2b84,3b49,S17,O16(13/0/4)/1	51	
1989 †	Oak A	143	451	48	118	15	6	4	47	58-2	5	66	.262	.345	.348	100	2	3-8	.931	15	112	92	3b104,2b47,S11,O8(4/1/4),D4		
1990	Det A	152	573	97	144	23	5	8	55	99-0	4	85	.251	.364	.351	101	2	19-9	.931	23	123	111	O56(25/9/23),3b46,2b36,D18,S13		
1991	Det A	146	564	87	160	28	4	17	72	79-5	3	95	.284	.371	.438	117	20	10-5	.977	11	122	72	O69(14/24/35),2b57,D34,3b20/S		
1992	Det A	159	606	**114**	167	32	3	10	64	114-2	4	102	.313	.443	.398	128	34	16-11	.969	10	106	83	O108(70/9/34),2b51/3D		
1993	Det A	151	566	113	177	27	0	7	57	**132-5**	2	105	.313	.443	.398	124	22	13-10	.980	8	112	83	O104L,2b12,D6		
1994	Det A	114	438	91	123	19	3	19	45	95-3	2	105	.281	.409	.468	133	26	13-10	.924	7	107	122	3b88,O48(47/8/0),D2		
1995	Cal A	139	525	119	137	21	1	27	61	113-8	3	135	.261	.394	.459	122	17	13-8	.981	10	110	102	O150(150/2/0),2b2/1		
1996	Chi A	153	581	119	161	29	3	12	63	**125-9**	4	132	.277	.404	.399	126	17	4-1	.972	3	129	183	O28R,3b9		
1997	Chi A	36	129	23	40	6	0	2	9	29-0	1	29	.310	.440	.403	128	4	1-1	.973	-1	94	95	O35(31/2/3),D26/3		
	Ana A	105	405	73	107	28	2	6	48	73-5	2	89	.264	.376	.388	100	7	12-9	.968	-12	108	107	O63(31/2/31),2b43,D26,3b10		
	Year	141	534	96	147	34	2	8	57	102-5	3	118	.275	.392	.391	104	11	13-10	.970	-9	108	107	O13(11/0/4)		
1998	Tor A	13	48	9	17	5	0	1	4	9-1	2	14	.354	.457	.521	158	5	0-0	.967	-2	95	62	O51(43/0/15),3b2/SD	49	
	NY N	52	188	25	42	11	0	3	14	38-0	0	44	.223	.351	.330	84	-3	1-1	.974	-7	107	107	2b66,O62(28/32/15),3b2/SD		
1999	Oak A	106	406	76	99	24	4	15	49	71-3	2	94	.244	.362	.433	105	9	11-3	.973	25	108	92	O92,1b5/D		
Total 18		2161	7617	1300	2023	360	45	160	819	1319-44	42	1499	.266	.374	.389			177-114					O786L,2b777,3b428,S294,D101,1b5	333	

PHILLIPS, MARR   Marr B. B6.16.1857 Pittsburgh PA   D4.1.1928 Pittsburgh PA   BR/5-6.5/164   d5.1

YEAR	TM LG	G	AB	R	H	2B	3B	HR	RBI	BB-IB	HP	SO	AVG	OBP	SLG	AOPS	ABR	SB-CS	FA	FR	RNG	THR	GAMES AT POSITION	DL	BFW
1884	Ind AA	97	413	41	111	18	8	0				107	3	.269	.279	.351	107	3		.862	16	**112**	62	S97		
1885	Det N	33	139	13	29	5	0	0		17	0		13	.209	.209	.245	46	-8		.881	0	105	54	S33		
	Pit AA	4	15	4	4	0	0	0	2	2	0			.267	.353	.267	99	0		.875	-1	94	193	S4		

YEAR	TM LG	G	AB	R	H	2B	3B	HR	RBI	BB-IB	HP	SO	AVG	OBP	SLG	AOPS	ABR	SB-CS	FA	FR	RNG	THR	GAMES AT POSITION	DL	BFW
1890	Roc AA	64	257	18	53	8	0	0	34	16	3		.206	.261	.237	51	-16	10	.918	5	106	123	S64		-0.8
Total 3		198	824	73	197	31	8	0	53	23	4	13	.239	.263	.296	79	-21	10	.884	20	108	83	S198		0.4

PHILLIPS, MIKE Michael Dwaine B8.19.1950 Beaumont TX BL/TR/6-1/185(168-185) [SFN69 1/18] d4.15

YEAR	TM LG	G	AB	R	H	2B	3B	HR	RBI	BB-IB	HP	SO	AVG	OBP	SLG	AOPS	ABR	SB-CS	FA	FR	RNG	THR	GAMES AT POSITION	DL	BFW
1973	SF N	63	104	18	25	3	4	1	9	6-0	1	17	.240	.288	.375	79	-4	0-3	.931	-7	83	50	3b28,S20,2b7		-1.0
1974	SF N	100	283	19	62	6	1	2	20	14-0	1	37	.219	.258	.269	46	-21	4-5	.909	3	116	95	3b34,2b30,S23		-1.7
1975	SF N	10	31	3	6	0	0	0	1	6-0	0	4	.194	.324	.194	45	-2	1-0	.969	3	106	108	2b6,3b6		0.1
	NY N	116	383	31	98	10	7	1	28	25-5	1	47	.256	.300	.326	77	-14	3-0	.944	-4	95	82	S115/2		0.1
	Year	126	414	34	104	10	7	1	29	31-5	1	51	.251	.302	.316	75	-16	4-0	.944	-1	95	82	S115,2b7,3b6		-0.4
1976	SF N	87	262	30	67	4	6	4	29	25-8	2	29	.256	.315	.363	98	-2	2-2	.955	-1	88	71	S53,2b19,3b10		-0.3
1977	NY N	38	86	5	18	2	1	1	3	2-0	2	15	.209	.244	.291	44	-7	0-1	1.000	-2	84	64	S24,3b9,2b4		0.3
	StL N	48	87	17	21	3	2	0	9	9-1	1	13	.241	.320	.322	73	-3	1-0	.971	3	105	134	2b31,S5,3b5		-0.8
	Year	86	173	22	39	5	3	1	12	11-1	3	28	.225	.283	.306	59	-11	1-1	.973	1	98	116	2b35,S29,3b14		0.1
1978	StL N	76	164	14	44	8	1	1	28	13-2	2	25	.268	.317	.348	90	-2	0-0	.971	4	98	107	2b55,S10/3		-0.7
1979	StL N	44	97	10	22	3	1	1	6	10-0	1	9	.227	.306	.309	67	-4	0-0	.973	4	126	101	S25,2b16/3		0.4
1980	StL N	63	128	13	30	5	0	0	9	9-3	0	17	.234	.283	.273	54	-8	0-0	.971	7	126	153	S37,2b9,3b8		0.2
1981	SD N	14	29	1	6	0	1	0	0	0-0	0	3	.207	.207	.276	39	-3	1-0	.979	2	105	122	2b9/S		0.2
	†Mon N	34	55	5	12	2	1	0	4	5-0	0	15	.218	.279	.255	52	-3	0-1	.974	-3	89	82	S26,2b6		0.0
	Year	48	84	6	18	2	1	0	4	5-0	0	18	.214	.256	.262	48	-6	1-1	.974	-1	89	101	S27,2b15		-0.5
1982	Mon N	14	8	0	1	0	0	0	0	0-0	0	3	.125	.111	.125	-29	-1	0-0	1.000	-0	88	55	2b10,S2		-0.5
1983	Mon N	5	2	0	0	0	0	0	0	0-0	0	0	.000	.000	.000	-99	-1	0-0	.000	-2	0		S3,3b2		-0.2
Total 11		712	1719	166	412	46	24	11	145	124-19	9	234	.240	.291	.314	69	-75	12-12	.956	5	100	94	S344,2b203,3b104		-3.5

PHILLIPS, PAUL Paul Anthony B4.15.1977 Demopolis AL BR/TR/6-1/210* [KCA98 9/257] d9.9 Col Alabama

YEAR	TM LG	G	AB	R	H	2B	3B	HR	RBI	BB-IB	HP	SO	AVG	OBP	SLG	AOPS	ABR	SB-CS	FA	FR	RNG	THR	GAMES AT POSITION	DL	BFW
2004	KC A	4	5	2	1	0	0	0	1				.200	.333	.200	44	0		1.000	1	0	0	C4		0.0
2005	KC A	23	67	6	18	4	1	1	9	0-0	0	5	.269	.269	.403	80	-2	0-0	.990	-3	247	170	C20,D2		-0.4
Total 2		27	72	8	19	4	1	1	9	0-0	0	6	.264	.274	.389	78	-2	0-0	.990	-2	226	155	C24,D2		-0.4

PHILLIPS, DICK Richard Eugene B11.24.1931 Racine WI D3.29.1998 Burnaby BC, Can. BL/TR/6-0/180* d4.15 C1 Col Valparaiso

YEAR	TM LG	G	AB	R	H	2B	3B	HR	RBI	BB-IB	HP	SO	AVG	OBP	SLG	AOPS	ABR	SB-CS	FA	FR	RNG	THR	GAMES AT POSITION	DL	BFW
1962	SF N	5	3	1	0	0	0	0	1			1	.000	.250	.000	-27	-1	0-0	1.000	1	0		/1		-0.1
1963	Was A	124	321	33	76	8	0	10	32	29-0	2	35	.237	.300	.355	84	-7	1-0	.994	3	129	128	1b68,2b5,3b4		-0.8
1964	Was A	109	234	17	54	6	1	2	23	27-0	1	22	.231	.307	.291	70	-9	1-2	.994	1	111	115	1b61,3b4		-1.3
1966	Was A	25	37	3	6	0	0	0	4	2-1	1	5	.162	.225	.162	13	-4	0-0	1.000	-0	62	52	1b5		-0.5
Total 4		263	595	54	136	14	1	12	60	59-1	4	63	.229	.298	.316	74	-21	2-2	.995	3	119	119	1b135,3b8,2b5		-2.7

PHILLIPS, BILL William B. B4.1857 St.John NB, Can. D10.7.1900 Chicago IL BR/TR/6-0/202 d5.1

YEAR	TM LG	G	AB	R	H	2B	3B	HR	RBI	BB-IB	HP	SO	AVG	OBP	SLG	AOPS	ABR	SB-CS	FA	FR	RNG	THR	GAMES AT POSITION	DL	BFW
1879	Cle N	81	365	58	99	15	4	0	29	2		20	.271	.275	.334	101			.954	-4	120	66	1b75,C11,O2(0/1/1)		-0.6
1880	Cle N	85	334	41	85	14	10	1	36	6		29	.254	.268	.365	115	4		.963	2	110	101	1b85		0.3
1881	Cle N	85	357	51	97	18	10	1	44	5		19	.272	.282	.387	114	5		.966	-1	78	113	1b85		0.0
1882	Cle N	78	335	40	87	17	7	4	47	7		18	.260	.275	.388	114	5		.971	3	112	142	1b78/C		0.1
1883	Cle N	97	382	42	94	29	8	2	46	8		49	.246	.262	.380	93	-3		.967	-2	68	116	1b97		-1.2
1884	Cle N	111	464	58	128	25	12	3	46	18		80	.276	.303	.401	115	7		.959	-2	93	110	1b111		-0.4
1885	Bro AA	99	391	65	118	16	11	3	63	27	11		.302	.364	.422	147	21		.973	0	91	82	1b99		1.1
1886	Bro AA	141	585	68	160	26	15	0	72	33		1	.274	.313	.369	113	6	13	.978	-2	73	90	1b141		1.1
1887	Bro AA	132	533	82	142	34	11	2	101	45	6		.266	.330	.383	97	-2	16	.982	4	107	91	1b132		-0.8
1888	KC AA	129	509	57	120	20	10	1	56	27		7	.236	.284	.320	88	-9	10	.980	3	117	97	1b129		-0.8
Total 10		1038	4255	562	1130	214	98	17	534	178	25	215	.266	.299	.374	109	34	39	.971	2	96	100	1b1032,C12,O2(0/1/1)		-1.6

PHYLE, BILL William Joseph B6.25.1875 Duluth MN D8.6.1953 Los Angeles CA TR d9.17 ▲

YEAR	TM LG	G	AB	R	H	2B	3B	HR	RBI	BB-IB	HP	SO	AVG	OBP	SLG	AOPS	ABR	SB-CS	FA	FR	RNG	THR	GAMES AT POSITION	DL	BFW
1898	Chi N	4	9	1	1	0	0	0	0	2		0	.111	.273	.111	11	0	0	.800	-1	70	0	P3		0.0
1899	Chi N	10	34	2	6	0	0	0	1	0		0	.176	.176	.176	-3	-2	0	.935	0	108	167	P10		0.0
1901	NY N	25	66	8	12	3	0	1	3	2		0	.182	.206	.212	22	-7	0	.903	1	112	0	P24/S		0.0
1906	StL N	22	73	6	13	1	0	4	5	0		0	.178	.231	.247	51	-4	2	.935	-4	102	84	3b21		-0.3
Total 4		61	182	17	32	5	1	0	8	9		0	.178	.215	.214	28	-13	2	.907	2	107	51	P37,3b21/S		-0.3

PIATT, ADAM Adam David B2.8.1976 Chicago IL BR/TR/6-2/195(195-218) [OakA97 8/245] d4.24 Col Mississippi St.

YEAR	TM LG	G	AB	R	H	2B	3B	HR	RBI	BB-IB	HP	SO	AVG	OBP	SLG	AOPS	ABR	SB-CS	FA	FR	RNG	THR	GAMES AT POSITION	DL	BFW
2000	†Oak A	60	157	24	47	5	5	2	23	23-0	1	44	.299	.392	.490	123	6	0-1	.950	-6	79	65	O29(8/0/22),3b13,D13,1b3		-0.2
2001	Oak A	36	95	9	20	5	1	0	6	13-0	0	26	.211	.300	.284	57	-6	0-0	.962	0	92	172	O32R/D		-0.7
2002	†Oak A	55	137	18	32	8	0	4	18	12-0	2	33	.234	.303	.401	86	-3	0-1	1.000	-4	84	43	O50(40/0/12)/1		-0.8
2003	Oak A	47	100	6	24	10	0	4	15	6-0	2	33	.240	.280	.460	91	-1	1-2	.978	-2	79	119	O38(32/0/7)/1D		-0.5
	TB A	14	32	5	6	3	0	2	3	3-0	0	16	.188	.250	.469	88	-1	0-0	1.000	-1	55	0	O7(1/0/6),D4		-0.2
	Year	61	132	11	30	13	0	6	18	9-0	2	49	.227	.273	.462	90	-1	1-2	.981	-4	75	98	O45(33/0/13),D6/1		-0.7
Total		212	521	62	123	29	1	16	65	57-0	3	149	.248	.323	.422	94	-5	3-4	.977	-13	82	91	O156(81/0/79),D20,3b13,1b5	87	-2.4

PIAZZA, MIKE Michael Joseph B9.4.1968 Norristown PA BR/TR/6-3/215(197-223) [LAN88 62/1390] d9.1 Col Miami-Dade North (FL) CC

YEAR	TM LG	G	AB	R	H	2B	3B	HR	RBI	BB-IB	HP	SO	AVG	OBP	SLG	AOPS	ABR	SB-CS	FA	FR	RNG	THR	GAMES AT POSITION	DL	BFW
1992	LA N	21	69	5	16	3	0	1	7	4-0	1	12	.232	.284	.319	71	-3	0-0	.990	-1	123	70	C16		-0.3
1993	LA N★	149	547	81	174	24	2	35	112	46-6	3	86	.318	.370	.561	155	40	3-4	.989	5	97	123	C146/1		5.3
1994	LA N★	107	405	64	129	18	0	24	92	33-10	1	65	.319	.370	.541	144	23	1-3	.985	-10	91	82	C104		1.9
1995	†LA N★	112	434	82	150	17	0	32	93	39-10	1	80	.346	.400	.606	173	44	1-0	.990	-2	94	83	C112	24	4.8
1996	†LA N★	148	547	87	184	16	0	36	105	81-21	1	93	.336	.422	.563	167	55	0-3	.992	-13	72	76	C146		4.9
1997	LA N★	152	556	104	201	32	1	40	124	69-11	3	77	.362	.431	.638	189	73	5-1	.986	-3	93	89	C139,D7		7.7
1998	LA N	37	149	20	42	6	0	9	30	11-4	0	27	.282	.329	.497	120	7	0-0	.993	4	56	120	C37		0.9
	Fla N	5	18	1	5	1	0	0	5	0-0	0	3	.278	.263	.389	78	-1	0-0	.968	0	82	89	C4		0.0
	NY N★	109	394	67	137	33	0	23	76	47-10	2	53	.348	.417	.607	171	42	1-0	.989	4	83	102	C99,D4		5.1
	Year	151	561	88	184	38	1	32	111	58-14	2	80	.328	.390	.570	155	45	1-0	.990	8	76	106	C140,D4		6.0
1999	†NY N★	141	534	100	162	25	0	40	124	51-11	1	70	.303	.361	.575	139	29	2-2	.989	-13	84	93	C137/D	15	2.3
2000	†NY N★	136	482	90	156	26	0	38	113	58-10	3	69	.324	.398	.614	160	44	4-2	.989	-10	66	97	C124,D5		3.9
2001	NY N★	141	503	81	159	29	0	36	94	67-19	2	87	.300	.384	.573	153	40	0-2	.991	-12	61	97	C131,D5		3.4
2002	NY N	135	478	69	134	23	2	33	98	57-9	3	82	.280	.359	.544	146	27	0-3	.986	-18	53	169	C121,D6		1.6
2003	NY N	68	234	37	67	13	0	11	34	35-3	1	40	.286	.377	.483	129	11	0-0	.982	-7	51	169	C64/1		0.8
2004	NY N★	129	455	47	121	21	0	20	54	68-14	2	58	.266	.362	.444	110	8	0-0	.985	-10	93	88	1b68,C50,D8	88	-0.5
2005	NY N★	113	398	41	100	23	0	19	62	41-6	3	67	.251	.326	.452	104	1	0-0	.997	-0	55	101	C101,D5	23	0.7
Total 14		1703	6203	976	1929	308	6	397	1223	707-144	27	986	.311	.382	.555	149	436	17-20	.990	-86	76	95	C1531,1b70,D41	174	42.5

PICCIOLO, ROB Robert Michael B2.4.1953 Santa Monica CA BR/TR/6-2/185* [OakA75*S1/4] d4.9 C16 Col Pepperdine OF(2/0/1)

YEAR	TM LG	G	AB	R	H	2B	3B	HR	RBI	BB-IB	HP	SO	AVG	OBP	SLG	AOPS	ABR	SB-CS	FA	FR	RNG	THR	GAMES AT POSITION	DL	BFW
1977	Oak A	148	419	35	84	12	3	2	22	9-0	1	55	.200	.218	.258	30	-42	1-4	.966	-8	97	88	S148		-3.8
1978	Oak A	78	93	16	21	1	0	2	7	2-0	1	13	.226	.242	.301	54	-6	1-1	.958	-5	83	108	S41,2b19,3b13		-0.9
1979	Oak A	115	348	37	88	16	2	2	27	3-1	1	45	.253	.261	.328	61	-21	2-1	.964	-14	88	68	S105,2b6,3b4/OL		-2.4
1980	Oak A	95	271	32	65	9	2	5	18	2-0	0	63	.240	.245	.343	63	-15	1-1	.977	-25	75	79	S49,2b47/OL		-3.4
1981	†Oak A	82	179	23	48	5	3	4	13	5-0	1	22	.268	.290	.397	100	-1	0-1	.981	-16	84	78	S82		-1.1
1982	Oak A	18	49	3	11	1	0	0	3	0-0	0	10	.224	.240	.245		-5		1.000	-2	44	60	S18		0.2
	Mil A	22	21	7	6	1	0	1	4	1-0	0	4	.286	.318	.333	83	0	0-0	1.000	-2	44	60	S6/1		0.0
	Year	40	70	10	17	2	0	1	4	1-0	0	14	.243	.264	.271	49	-5	0-0	.973	2	113	102	S24,2b11/D		-0.2
1983	Mil A	14	27	2	6	3	0	0	1	0-0	0	4	.222	.214	.333	54	-2	0-0	1.000	1	106	227	S7,2b2,3b2/1D		0.0
1984	Cal A	87	119	18	24	6	0	1	9	0-0	0	21	.202	.200	.277	31	-11	0-1	.974	0	101	83	S66,3b13,2b9/OR		-0.8
1985	Oak A	71	102	19	28	2	0	1	6	0-0	0	17	.275	.288	.324	72	-4	3-2	.889	-3	100	111	3b19,2b17,1b13,D10,S9	22	-0.7
Total 9		730	1628	192	381	56	10	17	109	25-1	3	254	.234	.246	.312	55	-107	9-11	.970	-66	91	84	S531,2b111,3b51,1b14,D12,O3L	22	-13.1

PICCIUTO, NICK Nicholas Thomas B8.27.1921 Newark NJ D1.10.1997 Winchester VA BR/TR/5-8/165 d5.11 Col Michigan St.

YEAR	TM LG	G	AB	R	H	2B	3B	HR	RBI	BB-IB	HP	SO	AVG	OBP	SLG	AOPS	ABR	SB-CS	FA	FR	RNG	THR	GAMES AT POSITION	DL	BFW
1945	Phi N	36	89	7	12	6	0	0	6	6		17	.135	.189	.202	9	-11	0	.967	-5	89	55	3b30,2b4		-1.6

PICINICH, VAL Valentine John B9.8.1896 New York NY D12.5.1942 Nobleboro ME BR/TR/5-9/165 d7.25 Mil 1918 C1

YEAR	TM LG	G	AB	R	H	2B	3B	HR	RBI	BB-IB	HP	SO	AVG	OBP	SLG	AOPS	ABR	SB-CS	FA	FR	RNG	THR	GAMES AT POSITION	DL	BFW
1916	Phi A	40	118	8	23	3	1	0	5	6		33	.195	.234	.237	44	-9	1	.967	-5	60	102	C37		-1.2
1917	Phi A	2	6	0	2	0	0	0	0	0		2	.333	.429	.333	135	0	0	.786	1	78	53	C2		-0.1
1918	Was A	47	148	13	34	3	0	1	12	9		25	.230	.274	.291	72	-6	0	.960	-3	103	79	C46		-0.5
1919	Was A	80	212	18	58	12	3	3	22	17	1	43	.274	.330	.401	106	1	6	.978	10	96	123	C69		1.7
1920	Was A	48	133	14	27	6	2	1	14	9	1	33	.203	.259	.346	68	-4	3	.978	6	103	96	C45		0.1

YEAR	TM LG	G	AB	R	H	2B	3B	HR	RBI	BB-IB	HP	SO	AVG	OBP	SLG	AOPS	ABR	SB-CS	FA	FR	RNG	THR	GAMES AT POSITION	DL	BFW
1921	Was A	45	141	10	39	9	0	0	12	16	1	21	.277	.354	.340	82	-3	0-3	.966	2	154	70	C45		0.1
1922	Was A	76	210	16	48	12	2	0	19	23	2	33	.229	.311	.305	64	-11	1-0	.976	5	102	92	C76		0.5
1923	Bos A	87	268	33	74	21	1	2	31	46	2	32	.276	.386	.384	103	4	3-5	.957	-2	80	128	C81		0.1
1924	Bos A	69	161	25	44	6	3	1	24	29	3	19	.273	.394	.366	97	0	5-1	.951	-9	70	75	C52		-1.1
1925	Bos A	90	251	31	64	21	0	1	25	33	1	21	.255	.344	.351	77	-8	2-0	.968	-9	70	75	C74,1b2		0.0
1926	Cin N	89	240	33	63	16	1	2	31	29	0	22	.262	.342	.363	92	-2	4	.967	-3	108	78	C86		0.1
1927	Cin N	65	173	16	44	8	3	0	12	24	0	15	.254	.345	.335	85	-3	3	.980	0	83	51	C61		0.5
1928	Cin N	96	324	29	98	15	1	0	35	20	0	24	.302	.343	.420	100	-1	1	.983	-1	103	108	C93		-0.9
1929	Bro N	93	273	28	71	16	6	4	31	34	0	24	.260	.342	.407	86	-6	3	.979	-8	59	137	C85		-0.4
1930	Bro N	23	46	4	10	3	0	0	3	5	0	6	.217	.294	.283	41	-4	1	.944	-5	94	109	C22		0.1
1931	Bro N	24	45	5	12	4	0	1	4	4	0	9	.267	.327	.422	100	0	1	.967	-1	107	55	C15		-0.2
1932	Bro N	41	70	8	18	6	0	1	11	4	0	8	.257	.297	.386	84	-2	0	.985	-1	99	75	C24		-0.1
1933	Bro N	6	6	1	1	1	0	0	0	0	0	1	.167	.167	.333	42	0	0	.889	-0	54	217	C6		-0.1
	Pit N	16	52	6	13	4	0	1	7	5	0	10	.250	.316	.385	99	0	0	.982	-2	81	72	C16		-0.1
	Year	22	58	7	14	5	0	1	7	5	0	11	.241	.302	.379	95	0	0	.969	-2	78	88	C22		-0.2
Total	18	1037	2877	298	743	166	26	26	298	314	11	382	.258	.334	.361	86	-58	31-9	.970	-15	92	96	C935,1b2		-1.5

PICK, CHARLIE Charles Thomas B4.10.1888 Brookneal VA D6.26.1954 Lynchburg VA BL/TR/5-10/160 d9.20

1914	Was A	10	23	0	9	0	0	0	1	4	0	4	.391	.481	.391	157	2	1-2	.833	0	73	237	O7(6/0/1)		0.1
1915	Was A	3	2	0	0	0	0	0	0	0	0	0	.000	.000	.000	-98	-0		—	0			/H		-0.1
1916	Phi A	121	398	29	96	10	3	0	20	40	1	24	.241	.315	.281	83	-8	25-16	.899	5	102	103	3b108,O8(5/3/0)		0.7
1918	†Chi N	29	89	13	29	4	1	0	12	14	0	4	.326	.417	.393	144	6	7	.964	-0	104	74	2b20,3b8		0.0
1919	Chi N	75	269	27	65	8	6	1	14	14	5	12	.242	.292	.316	82	-6	17	.946	-5	109	104	2b21,3b5,O3(2/1/0),1b2		-0.6
	Bos N	34	114	12	29	1	1	1	7	7	5	5	.254	.325	.307	94	-1	4	.924	-5	86	130	2b92,3b8,O3(2/1/0),1b2		-0.6
	Year	109	383	39	94	9	7	1	25	21	10	17	.245	.302	.313	86	-7	21	.942	-10	113	92	2b94		-0.2
1920	Bos N	95	383	34	105	16	6	2	28	23	1	11	.274	.320	.363	100	0	10-16	.952	5	105	92	2b206,3b124,O18(13/4/1),1b2		-0.2
Total	6	367	1278	115	333	39	17	3	86	102	16	60	.261	.323	.325	95	-7	64-34	.949	5	105	100	2b206,3b124,O18(13/4/1),1b2		-0.2

PICK, EDDIE Edgar Everett B5.7.1899 Attleboro MA D5.13.1967 Santa Monica CA BB/TR/6-0/185 d9.13

1923	Cin N	9	8	2	3	0	0	0	2	3	0	3	.375	.545	.375	150	1	0-0	1.000	-0	71	0	O4L		0.1
1924	Cin N	3	2	0	0	0	0	0	0	0	0	1	.000	.000	.000	-99	-1	0-0	1.000	0	142	0	/OL		-0.1
1927	Chi N	54	181	23	31	5	2	2	15	20	0	26	.171	.254	.254	36	-17	0	.910	-5	83	124	3b49/2OR		-1.9
Total	3	66	191	25	34	5	2	2	17	23	0	30	.178	.266	.257	40	-17	0-0	.910	-5	83	124	3b49,O6(5/0/1)/2		-1.9

PICKERING, CALVIN Calvin Elroy B9.29.1976 St.Thomas, V.I. BL/TL/6-5/283(260-295) [BalA95 35/976] d9.12 [DL 2002 Bos A 183]

1998	Bal A	9	21	4	5	0	0	3	3-0	0	1	5	.238	.333	.524	120	0	1-0	.969	-1	0	114	150,D3		-0.4
1999	Bal A	23	40	4	5	1	0	1	5	11-0	0	16	.125	.314	.225	42	-3	0-0	.960	-1	59	166	1b8,D7		-0.1
2001	Cin N	4	4	0	1	0	0	0	1	0-0	0	2	.250	.250	.250	28	0	0-0	—	0			/H		0.0
	Bos A	17	50	8	14	1	0	3	7	8-0	0	13	.280	.379	.480	124	2	0-0	1.000	-1	71	92	1b12,D2		0.0
2004	KC A	35	122	21	30	8	1	7	26	18-1	0	42	.246	.338	.500	116	3	0-0	1.000	-0	75	97	D27,1b8		-0.3
2005	KC A	7	27	4	4	0	0	1	3	3-0	0	14	.148	.226	.259	33	-3	0-0	.988	-3	61	106	D46,1b33	183	-0.9
Total	5	95	264	37	59	10	1	14	45	43-1	0	91	.223	.329	.428	97	-1	1-0	.988	-3	61	106	D46,1b33		

PICKERING, OLLIE Oliver Daniel B4.9.1870 Olney IL D1.20.1952 Vincennes IN BL/TR/5-10/175 d8.9

1896	Lou N	45	165	28	50	6	4	1	22	12	0	11	.303	.350	.406	103	0	13	.901	3	190	217	O45(3/44/0)		0.0
1897	Lou N	64	249	34	62	5	2	1	21	26	2		.249	.325	.325	67	-11	20	.938	4	170	109	O63(0/62/1)		-1.0
	Cle N	46	182	33	64	5	2	1	22	11	1		.352	.392	.418	108	2	18	.950	-1	76	86	O46(1/45/1)/2		-0.1
	Year	110	431	67	126	10	4	2	43	37	3		.292	.352	.348	85	-9	38	.943	3	130	99	O109(1/107/2)/2		-1.1
1901	Cle A	137	547	102	169	25	6	0	40	58	8		.309	.383	.377	116	16	36	.949	13	125	204	O137(2/110/25)		2.0
1902	Cle A	69	293	46	75	5	2	3	26	19	2		.256	.306	.317	76	-10	22	.979	-3	62	61	O64(3/57/4),1b2		-1.5
1903	Phi A	137	512	93	144	18	6	1	36	53	4		.281	.353	.346	105	5	40	.970	6	84	71	O135(0/134/1)		0.2
1904	Phi A	124	455	56	103	10	3	0	30	45	2		.226	.299	.262	74	-12	17	.939	-1	99	61	O121(10/111/0)		-2.1
1907	StL A	151	576	63	159	15	10	0	60	35	3		.276	.321	.337	110	5	15	.949	-6	75	120	O151(0/22/128)		-1.1
1908	Was A	113	373	45	84	7	4	2	30	28	3		.225	.285	.282	92	-4	13	.940	-6	57	35	O98(0/27/71)		-1.6
Total	8	886	3352	500	910	96	39	9	287	287	25	11	.271	.334	.331	97	-9	194	.949	3	103	116	O860(19/612/231),1b2/2		-5.2

PICKERING, URBANE Urbane Henry "Pick" B6.3.1899 Hoxie KS D5.13.1970 Modesto CA BR/TR/5-10/180 d4.18

1931	Bos A	103	341	48	86	13	4	9	52	33	0	53	.252	.318	.393	91	-6	3-4	.967	-1	108	64	3b74,2b16		-0.4
1932	Bos A	132	457	47	119	28	5	2	40	39	1	71	.260	.320	.357	77	-16	3-4	.941	-5	101	103	3b126/C		-1.6
Total	2	235	798	95	205	41	9	11	92	72	1	124	.257	.319	.372	83	-22	6-8	.951	-6	104	88	3b200,2b16/C		-2.0

PICKETT, DAVE David T. B5.26.1874 Brookline MA D4.22.1950 Easton MA d7.21

1898	Bos N	14	43	3	12	1	0	0	3	1	0		.279	.380	.302	91	0	2	.955	-1	67	0	O14L		-0.1

PICKETT, JOHN John Thomas B2.20.1866 Chicago IL D7.4.1922 Chicago IL BR/TR/5-10.5/186 d6.6

1889	KC AA	53	201	20	45	7	4	0	12	11	2	21	.224	.271	.259	48	-14	7	.900	-11	43	89	O28(23/4/1),3b14,2b11		-2.2
1890	Phi P	100	407	82	114	7	9	4	64	40	2	17	.280	.347	.371	90	-7	12	.893	-23	91	94	2b100		-2.1
1892	Bal N	36	141	13	30	2	3	1	12	7	2	10	.213	.260	.291	65	-7	2	.915	-1	103	53	2b36		-0.5
Total	3	189	749	115	189	16	12	5	88	58	6	48	.252	.311	.326	74	-28	21	.900	-34	93	81	2b147,O28(23/4/1),3b14		-4.8

PICKUP, TY Clarence William B10.29.1897 Philadelphia PA D8.2.1974 Philadelphia PA BR/TR/6-0/180 d4.30

1918	Phi N	1	1	0	1	0	0	0	0	0	0	0	1.000	1.000	1.000	478	0	0	1.000	0	125	0	/OR		0.0

PIEDRA, JORGE Jorge Moises B4.19.1979 Sun Valley CA BL/TL/6-0/190* d8.7

2004	Col N	38	91	15	27	8	0	3	10	5-0	1	19	.297	.340	.484	97	0	0-1	1.000	-0	96	77	O34(14/18/7)		-0.1
2005	Col N	61	112	19	35	8	1	6	16	10-0	1	15	.313	.371	.563	123	4	2-1	1.000	-2	72	90	O26(9/0/17)/D		0.6
Total	2	99	203	34	62	16	1	9	26	15-0	2	34	.305	.357	.527	112	4	2-2	1.000	-2	85	83	O60(23/18/24)/D		0.4

PIERCE, GRACIE Grayson S. B New York NY D8.28.1894 New York NY BR/TR d5.2 U3

1882	Lou AA	9	33	3	10	1	0	0					.303	.324	.333	129	1		.864	1	113	131	2b9		0.3
	Bal AA	41	151	8	30	2	1	0		3			.199	.214	.225	52	-7		.796	-10	92	95	2b38,O3R/S		-1.1
	Year	50	184	11	40	3	1	0		4			.217	.234	.245	66	-6		.808	-9	96	101	2b47,O3R/S		-0.7
1883	Col AA	11	41	5	7	0	0	0				9	.171	.171	.171	11	-4		.850	-1	30	183	O18(0/17/1)/2		-0.5
	NY N	18	62	3	5	0	1	0	2	1			.081	.095	.113	-37	-10		1.000	-4	0	0	O3(0/2/1),2b3		-2.0
1884	NY AA	5	20	2	5	1	0	0		0	0		.250	.250	.300	81	0		1.000	-0	0	0	1b1,2b2		-0.1
Total	3	84	307	21	57	4	2	0	2	5	0		.186	.199	.212	36	-20		.795	-15	88	98	2b57,O29(0/23/6)/S		-3.3

PIERCE, JACK Lavern Jack B6.2.1948 Laurel MS BL/TR/6-0/210* [AtlN69*S3/63] d4.27 Col San Jose (CA) City

1973	Atl N	11	20	0	1	0	0	0	0	1-0	0	8	.050	.095	.050	-55	-4	0-0	1.000	0	133	26	1b6		-0.7
1974	Atl N	6	9	1	1	0	0	0	0	1-0	0	1	.111	.200	.111	-11	-1	0-0	.958	0	160	74	1b2		-0.3
1975	Det A	53	170	19	40	6	1	8	22	20-1	2	40	.235	.320	.424	105	1	0-0	.971	-4	80	92	1b49		-1.2
Total	3	70	199	20	42	6	1	8	22	22-1	2	48	.211	.293	.372	83	-4	0-0	.973	-4	87	86	1b57		-2.2

PIERCE, MAURY Preston Maurice B1859 MD d4.23

1884	Was U	2	7	0	1	0	0	0		0	0		.143	.143	.143	-14	-1		.778	-0	52	0	3b2		-0.1

PIERCY, ANDY Andrew J. B8.1856 San Jose CA D12.27.1932 San Jose CA TR d5.12

1881	Chi N	2	8	1	2	0	0	0	0	0		1	.250	.250	.250	55	0		.750	-1	0	0	/32		-0.1

PIERRE, JUAN Juan D'Vaughn B8.14.1977 Mobile AL BL/TL/6-0/170* [ColN98 13/390] d8.7 Col South Alabama

2000	Col N	51	200	26	62	2	0	0	13	13-0	1	15	.310	.353	.320	89	-12	7-6	.975	-2	100	70	O50C		-1.6
2001	Col N	156	617	108	202	26	11	2	55	41-1	10	29	.327	.378	.415	87	-10	46-17	.979	-5	104	38	O154C		-2.3
2002	Col N	152	592	90	170	20	5	1	35	31-0	1	35	.287	.332	.343	72	-26	47-12	.995	-2	108	26	O149C		-2.4
2003	†Fla N	162	668	100	204	28	7	1	41	55-1	9	35	.305	.361	.373	96	-3	65-20	.993	2	106	46	O162C		-0.5
2004	Fla N	162	678	100	221	22	12	3	49	45-1	9	35	.326	.374	.407	107	7	45-24	.995	-9	94	37	O160C		-2.0
2005	Fla N	162	656	96	181	19	13	2	47	41-1	9	45	.276	.326	.354	83	-19	57-17	.988	9	100	33	O836C		-2.8
Total	6	845	3411	520	1040	117	48	9	247	226-4	42	211	.305	.355	.373	87	-63	267-96	.989	-25	100	38	O836C		

YEAR	TM LG	G	AB	R	H	2B	3B	HR	RBI	BB-IB	HP	SO	AVG	OBP	SLG	AOPS	ABR	SB-CS	FA	FR	RNG	THR	GAMES AT POSITION	DL	BFW

PIERSALL, JIM   James Anthony   B11.14.1929 Waterbury CT   BR/TR/6-0/175(175-190)   d9.7   C1

1950	Bos A	6	7	4	2	0	0	0		0			.286	.545	.286	107	1	0-0	1.000	1	152	0	O2C		0.1
1952	Bos A	56	161	28	43	8	0	1	16	28	1	26	.267	.379	.335	93	0	3-3	.928	-2	100	77	S30,O22(0/1/21)/3		-0.2
1953	Bos A	151	585	76	159	21	9	3	52	41	9	52	.272	.329	.354	80	-17	11-10	.987	11	117	106	O151(1/2/150)		-1.3
1954	Bos A★	133	474	77	135	24	2	8	38	36	3	42	.285	.338	.395	90	-6	5-1	.985	-2	96	102	O126(0/30/96)		-1.3
1955	Bos A	149	515	68	146	25	5	13	62	67-7	2	52	.283	.364	.427	104	4	6-1	.993	1	103	76	O147C		-0.2
1956	Bos A★	155	601	91	176	40	6	14	87	58-2	1	48	.293	.350	.449	99	-1	7-7	**.991**	7	111	94	O155C		-0.2
1957	Bos A	151	609	103	159	27	5	19	63	62-1	8	54	.261	.331	.415	98	-2	14-6	.990	1	102	112	O151C		-0.7
1958	Bos A	130	417	55	99	13	5	8	48	42-2	0	43	.237	.303	.350	75	-14	12-2	.985	-1	99	110	O125C		-2.0
1959	Cle A	100	317	42	78	13	2	4	30	25-1	2	31	.246	.303	.338	79	-9	6-3	.982	-1	104	54	O91C/3		-1.4
1960	Cle A	138	486	70	137	12	4	18	66	24-3	0	38	.282	.313	.434	104	-1	18-5	.992	9	122	68	O134(8/127/2)		0.4
1961	Cle A	121	484	81	156	26	7	6	40	43-1	2	46	.322	.378	.442	122	16	8-2	**.991**	8	112	142	O120C		2.0
1962	Was A	135	471	38	115	20	4	4	31	39-3	0	53	.244	.301	.329	70	-20	12-7	**.997**	-1	104	83	O132C		-2.4
1963	Was A	29	94	9	23	1	0	1	5	6-0	0	11	.245	.284	.287	63	-5	4-0	1.000	0	118	0	O25C		-0.5
	NY N	40	124	13	24	4	1	1	10	10-1	0	14	.194	.250	.266	49	-8	1-2	1.000	-2	55	139	O38C		-1.2
	LA A	20	52	4	16	1	0	0	4	5-0	0	5	.308	.368	.327	103	0	0-1	1.000	0	81	0	O18(1/12/5)		-0.3
1964	LA A	87	255	28	80	11	0	2	13	16-1	0	32	.314	.353	.380	116	5	5-3	1.000	-2	93	55	O72(48/32/0)		0.0
1965	Cal A	53	112	10	30	5	2	2	12	5-1	1	15	.268	.305	.402	101	0	2-2	.984	1	120	0	O41(29/10/4)		-0.1
1966	Cal A	75	123	14	26	5	0	0	14	13-0	0	19	.211	.283	.252	58	-6	1-2	.973	0	93	129	O63(25/14/22)	55	-1.0
1967	Cal A	5	3	0	0	0	0	0	0		0	2	.000	.000	.000	-99	-1	0-0	1.000	0	474	0	/OL		-0.1
Total	17	1734	5890	811	1604	256	52	104	591	524-23	25	583	.272	.332	.386	92	-64	115-57	.990	26	106	93	O1614(113/1214/305),S30,3b2	55	-10.4

PIERSON, DAVE   David P.   B8.20.1855 Wilkes-Barre PA   D11.11.1922 Newark NJ   BR/TR/5-7/142   d4.25   b-Dick

| | | | | | | | | | | | | | | | | | | | | | | | | | |
|1876|Cin N|57|233|33|55|4|1|0|13|1| |9|.236|.239|.262|78|-4| |.760|-1| | |C31,O30(1/0/29)/S32P| |-0.3|

PIERSON, DICK   Edmund Dana   B10.24.1857 Wilkes-Barre PA   D7.20.1922 Newark NJ   TR   d6.23   b-Dave

| | | | | | | | | | | | | | | | | | | | | | | | | | |
|1885|NY AA|3|9|1|1|0|0|0|0| | |1|.111|.273|.111|26|-1| |.682|-3|61|70|2b3| |-0.3|

PIERZYNSKI, A.J.   Anthony John   B12.30.1976 Bridgehampton NY   BL/TR/6-3/220(218-245)   [MinA94 3/71]   d9.9

1998	Min A	7	10	1	3	0	0	0	1	1-0		2	.300	.385	.300	89	0	0-0	1.000	2	76	73	C6		0.2
1999	Min A	9	22	3	6	2	0	0	3	1-0	1	4	.273	.333	.364	74	-1	0-0	1.000	1	417	49	C9		-0.1
2000	Min A	33	88	12	27	5	1	2	11	5-0	2	14	.307	.354	.455	97	0	1-0	1.000	-2	157	88	C32		0.3
2001	Min A	114	381	51	110	33	2	7	55	16-4	4	57	.289	.322	.441	94	-3	1-7	.985	2	165	71	C110/D		0.3
2002	†Min A★	130	440	54	132	31	6	6	49	13-1	11	61	.300	.334	.439	100	0	1-2	.996	3	143	66	C124		1.0
2003	†Min A	137	487	63	152	35	3	11	74	24-12	15	55	.312	.360	.464	112	9	3-1	.993	4	159	64	C135		2.1
2004	SF N	131	471	45	128	28	2	11	77	19-4	15	27	.272	.319	.410	84	-11	0-1	.999	-8	126	61	C118		-1.2
2005	†Chi A	128	460	61	118	21	0	18	56	23-5	12	68	.257	.308	.420	87	-9	0-2	**.999**	1	81	86	C128		0.0
Total	8	689	2359	290	676	155	14	55	326	102-26	61	288	.287	.330	.434	95	-15	6-13	.995	2	137	70	C662/D		2.3

PIET, TONY   Anthony Francis (b Anthony Francis Pietruszka)   B12.7.1906 Berwick PA   D12.1.1981 Hinsdale IL   BR/TR/6-0/175   d8.15

1931	Pit N	44	167	22	50	12	4	0	24	13	1	24	.299	.354	.419	108	2	10	.987	-5	99	62	2b44/S		0.0
1932	Pit N	154	574	66	162	25	8	7	85	46	7	56	.282	.343	.390	98	-1	19	.970	-26	92	90	2b154		-1.7
1933	Pit N	107	362	45	117	21	5	1	42	19	6	28	.323	.367	.417	124	11	12	.955	-8	98	109	2b97		1.0
1934	Cin N	106	421	58	109	20	5	1	38	23	6	44	.259	.307	.337	74	-16	6	.934	-9	98	92	3b51,2b49		-2.0
1935	Cin N	6	5	2	1	1	0	0	2	0		0	.200	.200	.400	59	0		1.000	0	145	0	/OR		0.0
	Chi A	77	292	47	87	17	5	3	27	33	3	27	.298	.375	.421	103	2	2-1	.975	2	111	85	2b59,3b17		0.8
1936	Chi A	109	352	69	96	15	2	7	42	66	9	48	.273	.400	.386	92	-2	15-5	.966	5	120	108	2b68,3b32		0.9
1937	Chi A	100	332	34	78	15	1	4	38	32	6	36	.235	.314	.322	61	-20	14-6	.939	1	98	77	3b86,2b13		-0.4
1938	Det A	41	80	9	17	6	1	0	14	15	2	11	.213	.351	.287	58	-5	2-4	.919	1	125	90	3b18/2		-0.4
Total	8	744	2585	352	717	132	30	23	312	247	40	274	.277	.350	.378	80	-16	80-16	.952	-39	101	95	2b485,3b204/ORS		-2.8

PIEZ, SANDY   Charles William   B10.13.1888 New York NY   D12.29.1930 Atlantic City NJ   BR/TR/5-10/170   d4.17   Col Bucknell

| | | | | | | | | | | | | | | | | | | | | | | | | | |
|1914|NY N|37|8|9|3|0|1|0|3|0| |1|.375|.375|.625|202|1|4|1.000|1|217|0|O5(2/2/1)| |0.2|

PIGNATANO, JOE   Joseph Benjamin   B8.4.1929 Brooklyn NY   BR/TR/5-10/180*   d4.28   C20

1957	Bro N	8	14	0	3	1	0	0	1	1-0	0	5	.214	.214	.286	30	-1	0-0	1.000	2	135	0	C6		0.1
1958	LA N	63	142	18	31	4	0	9	17	16-1	2	26	.218	.306	.437	91	-2	4-1	1.000	6	154	120	C57		0.6
1959	†LA N	52	139	17	33	4	1	1	11	21-2	2	15	.237	.346	.302	69	-5	1-0	.997	6	230	93	C49		0.3
1960	LA N	58	90	11	21	4	0	2	9	15-2	0	17	.233	.343	.344	83	-1	1-1	.984	5	158	155	C40		0.5
1961	KC A	92	243	31	59	10	3	4	22	36-2	4	42	.243	.347	.358	88	-3	2-2	.979	4	115	89	C83,3b2		0.4
1962	SF N	7	5	2	1	0	0	0	0	4-0	0	2	.200	.556	.200	114	1	0-0	1.000	-1	33	202	C7		0.4
	NY N	27	56	2	13	2	0	0	2	2-0	1	11	.232	.259	.268	41	-5	0-0	.991	0	63	99	C25		-0.3
	Year	34	61	4	14	2	0	0	2	6-0	1	13	.230	.299	.262	51	-4	0-0	.992	-0	60	110	C32		-0.3
Total	6	307	689	81	161	25	4	16	62	94-7	8	116	.234	.332	.351	80	-16	8-4	.990	22	148	106	C267,3b2		1.6

PIKE, JAY   Jacob Emanuel   B Brooklyn NY   d8.27   b-Lip

| | | | | | | | | | | | | | | | | | | | | | | | | | |
|1877|Har N|1|4|0|1|0|0|0|0|0| |0|.250|.250|.250|65|0| |.000|-1|0|0|/OR| |-0.1|

PIKE, JESS   Jess Willard   B7.31.1915 Dustin OK   D3.28.1984 San Diego CA   BL/TL/6-3/175   d4.18

| | | | | | | | | | | | | | | | | | | | | | | | | | |
|1946|NY N|16|41|4|7|1|1|6|9|8-0| |9|.171|.277|.317|68|-2|0|.929|-2|71|0|O10(0/6/4)| |-0.4|

PIKE, LIP   Lipman Emanuel   B5.25.1845 New York NY   D10.10.1893 Brooklyn NY   BL/TL/5-8/158   d5.9   M3   b-Jay   OF NA(7/98/88)

1871	Tro NA	28	130	43	49	10	7	4	39	5		7	.377	.400	.654	194	15	3-2	.850	2	161	0	O18R,2b7,1b4,M		1.1
1872	Bal NA	56	285	68	85	15	8	7	60	5		6	.298	.308	.460	127	7	10-1	.875	-10	0	0	O25(6/5/16),2b24,3b9		-0.1
1873	Bal NA	56	285	71	90	15	8	4	51	8		4	.316	.334	.467	136	12	8-1	.747	-3	114	291	O56(0/2/54),2b2		1.0
1874	Har NA	52	234	58	83	22	5	1	50	5		5	.355	.368	.504	164	17	4-1	.856	7	166	118	O27C,S20,2b7/3M		1.8
1875	StL NA	70	312	61	108	12	12	0	44	3		9	.346	.352	.494	210	35	25-10	.885	-3	51	120	O64(1/64/0),2b10,3b2/S		2.8
1876	StL N	63	282	55	91	19	10	1	50	8		9	.323	.341	.472	178	24		.896	-5	125	312	O62C,2b2		1.4
1877	Cin N	58	262	45	78	12	4	4	23	9		7	.298	.321	.420	148	16		.802	-4	141	67	O38C,2b22,S2,M		0.9
1878	Cin N	31	145	28	47	5	1	0	11	4		9	.324	.342	.372	149	8		.824	3	56	100	O31C		0.3
	Pro N	5	22	4	5	0	1	0	4	4		1	.227	.347	.318	90	0		.788	-3	78	0	2b5		-0.3
	Year	36	167	32	52	5	2	0	15	8		10	.311	.331	.365	140	8		.824	-6	56	100	O31C,2b5		0.0
1881	Wor N	5	18	1	2	0	0	0	0	0		1	.111	.273	.111	24	-1		.647	-2	65	394	O5C		-0.3
1887	NY AA	1	4	1	0	0	0	0	0		0	.000	.000	.000	-99	-1	0	1.000	0	0	0	/OC		-0.3
Total	5 NA	262	1246	301	415	84	37	16	244	25		26	.333	.346	.498	162	86	50-15	.846	-7	91	146	O190C,2b50,S21,3b12,1b4		6.6
Total	5	163	733	133	223	36	16	5	88	26		29	.304	.328	.417	152	46	0	.833	-17	112	231	O137C,2b29,S2		1.9

PILARCIK, AL   Alfred James   B7.3.1930 Whiting IN   BL/TL/5-10/180*   d7.13

1956	KC A	69	239	28	60	10	1	4	22	30-1		32	.251	.333	.351	81	-6	9-2	.976	-4	83	185	O67(0/64/3)		-1.2
1957	Bal A	142	407	52	113	16	3	9	49	53-6	3	28	.278	.359	.398	116	10	14-7	.996	3	96	**177**	O126(2/54/79)		0.9
1958	Bal A	141	379	40	92	21	0	1	24	42-1	2	37	.243	.320	.306	78	-10	7-3	.986	-2	103	63	O119(4/32/104)		-1.6
1959	Bal A	130	273	37	77	12	1	3	16	30-1	1	30	.282	.355	.366	101	1	9-3	.978	-4	92	68	O106(3/8/102)		-0.5
1960	Bal A	104	194	30	48	5	1	4	17	15-2	4	16	.247	.313	.345	79	-6	0-2	1.000	-2	88	135	O75(0/2/74)		-1.0
1961	KC A	35	26	9	12	1	1	0	6	6-0	0	7	.200	.269	.250	40	-5	1-0	1.000	2	116	204	O21(0/2/19)		-0.4
	Chi A	47	62	9	11	1	0	1	6	9-0	0	5	.177	.282	.242	42	-5	1-1	.944	1	100	257	O17(2/14/1)		-0.5
	Year	82	122	18	23	2	1	1	15	15-0	0	12	.189	.275	.246	41	-10	2-1	.971	3	108	231	O38(2/16/20)		-0.9
Total	6	668	1614	205	413	66	7	22	143	185-11	11	150	.256	.334	.346	89	-21	41-18	.986	-6	95	132	O531(11/176/382)		-4.3

PILNEY, ANDY   Antone James   B1.19.1913 Frontenac KS   D9.15.1996 Kenner LA   BR/TL/5-11/174   d6.12   Col Notre Dame

| | | | | | | | | | | | | | | | | | | | | | | | | | |
|1936|Bos N|3|2|0|0|0|0|0|0|0| |1|.000|.000|.000|-99| | |0| | | |/H| |-0.1|

PINELLI, BABE   Ralph Arthur (b Rinaldo Angelo Paolinelli)   B10.18.1895 San Francisco CA   D10.22.1984 Daly City CA   BR/TR/5-9/165   d8.3   U22

1918	Chi A	24	78	17	18	1	1	7	1	2		8	.231	.302	.308	83	-2	3	.847	-7	72	99	3b24		-0.9
1920	Det A	102	284	33	65	9	3	0	21	25		8	.229	.296	.282	74	-5	19-6	.954	12	112	167	3b74,S18/2		-0.5
1922	Cin N	156	547	77	167	19	7	1	72	48		6	.305	.368	.371	93	-4	17-22	.945	22	**117**	83	3b156		2.2
1923	Cin N	117	423	44	117	14	5	0	51	27		6	.277	.320	.333	74	-16	10-14	.938	7	**109**	88	3b116		-0.5
1924	Cin N	144	510	61	156	14	7	0	70	32		5	.306	.353	.365	94	-4	23-17	.956	24	**119**	94	3b143		2.8

YEAR	TM LG	G	AB	R	H	2B	3B	HR	RBI	BB-IB	HP	SO	AVG	OBP	SLG	AOPS	ABR	SB-CS	FA	FR	RNG	THR	GAMES AT POSITION	DL	BFW
1925	Cin N	130	492	68	139	33	6	2	49	22	2	28	.283	.316	.386	80	-15	8-19	.945	17	124	113	3b109,S17		0.5
1926	Cin N	71	207	26	46	7	4	0	24	15	3	5	.222	.284	.295	58	-13	2	.978	2	127	82	3b40,S27,2b3		-0.7
1927	Cin N	30	76	11	15	2	0	1	4	6	1	7	.197	.265	.263	43	-6	2	.968	-1	107	73	3b15,S9,2b5		-0.5
Total	8	774	2617	327	723	101	33	5	298	182	20	162	.276	.328	.346	79	-79	71-80	.947	77	116	100	3b677,S71,2b9		2.4

PINIELLA, LOU Louis Victor B8.28.1943 Tampa FL BR/TR/6-2/198(182-200) d9.4 M19/C2 Col Tampa

YEAR	TM LG	G	AB	R	H	2B	3B	HR	RBI	BB-IB	HP	SO	AVG	OBP	SLG	AOPS	ABR	SB-CS	FA	FR	RNG	THR	GAMES AT POSITION	DL	BFW
1964	Bal A	4	1	0	0	0	0	0	0	0-0	0	0	.000	.000	.000	-99	0	0-0	—	0			/H		0.0
1968	Cle A	6	5	1	0	0	0	0	1	0-0	0	1	.000	.000	.000	-99	-1	0-0	1.000	-0	85	0	O2L		-0.2
1969	KC A	135	493	43	139	21	6	11	68	33-2	3	56	.282	.325	.416	106	3	2-4	.977	10	112	128	O129(126/3/0)		0.4
1970	KC A	144	542	54	163	24	5	11	88	35-6	2	42	.301	.342	.424	111	7	3-6	.984	-1	98	68	O139L/1		-0.4
1971	KC A	126	448	43	125	21	5	3	51	21-4	2	43	.279	.311	.368	93	-5	5-3	.986	-2	99	69	O150L	34	1.8
1972	KC A★	151	574	65	179	33	4	11	72	34-9	8	59	.312	.356	.441	138	26	7-2	.976	-2	99	69	O150L		-3.2
1973	KC A	144	513	53	128	28	1	9	69	30-7	2	65	.250	.291	.361	77	-16	5-7	.986	-7	80	104	O128L,D9		1.1
1974	NY A	140	518	71	158	26	4	9	70	32-7	2	58	.305	.341	.407	118	11	1-8	.989	9	104	176	O130(99/0/34)/1D	19	-2.0
1975	NY A	74	199	7	39	4	1	0	22	16-3	3	22	.196	.262	.226	41	-16	0-0	.986	-1	84	162	O46(15/0/31),D12		0.1
1976	†NY A	100	327	36	92	16	6	3	38	18-8	1	34	.281	.322	.394	110	3	0-1	.982	2	106	113	O49(10/0/39),D38		0.9
1977	†NY A	103	339	47	112	19	3	12	45	20-3	1	31	.330	.365	.510	138	17	2-2	.975	-4	82	58	O51(24/0/27),D43/1		1.1
1978	†NY A	130	472	67	148	34	5	6	69	34-8	2	36	.314	.361	.445	128	18	3-1	.969	-2	103	58	O103(78/2/25),D23		-0.5
1979	NY A	130	461	49	137	22	2	11	69	17-6	2	31	.297	.320	.425	102	0	3-2	.982	1	93	161	O104(102/1/1),D7		-0.6
1980	†NY A	116	321	39	92	18	0	2	27	29-5	0	20	.287	.343	.361	95	-1	0-1	.971	-1	97	134	O112(84/0/29),D16	15	0.4
1981	†NY A	60	159	16	44	9	0	5	18	13-4	0	9	.277	.331	.428	119	4	0-1	.986	2	118	99	O36(11/0/25),D19		0.4
1982	NY A	102	261	33	80	17	1	6	37	18-6	1	18	.307	.352	.448	120	7	0-1	1.000	-0	98	87	D55,O40(13/0/27)	18	-0.1
1983	NY A	53	148	19	43	9	1	2	16	11-3	1	12	.291	.344	.405	109	2	1-1	.959	-1	87	139	O43(15/0/28)/D		0.1
1984	NY A	29	86	8	26	4	1	1	6	7-1	0	5	.302	.355	.407	114	2	0-0	1.000	1	90	210	O24(15/0/9),D2		0.1
Total	18	1747	5867	651	1705	305	41	102	766	368-82	31	541	.291	.333	.409	108	61	32-41	.981	4	97	109	O1401(1126/6/275),D231,1b3	86	-2.2

PINKHAM, ED Edward B1849 Brooklyn NY BL/TL/5-7/142 d5.8 ▲

YEAR	TM LG	G	AB	R	H	2B	3B	HR	RBI	BB-IB	HP	SO	AVG	OBP	SLG	AOPS	ABR	SB-CS	FA	FR	RNG	THR	GAMES AT POSITION	DL	BFW
1871	Chi NA	24	95	27	25	5	5	1	17	18		3	.263	.381	.453	125	2	5-2	.754	9	159	57	3b18,O8R,P3		0.7

PINKNEY, GEORGE George Burton B1.11.1859 Orange Prairie IL D11.10.1926 Peoria IL BR/TR/5-7/160 d8.16

YEAR	TM LG	G	AB	R	H	2B	3B	HR	RBI	BB-IB	HP	SO	AVG	OBP	SLG	AOPS	ABR	SB-CS	FA	FR	RNG	THR	GAMES AT POSITION	DL	BFW
1884	Cle N	36	144	18	45	9	0	0	16	10		7	.313	.357	.375	126	5		.848	-6	83	93	2b25,S11		0.0
1885	Bro AA	110	447	77	124	16	5	0	42	27	7		.277	.328	.336	109	6		.904	-6	101	66	2b57,3b51,S3		0.2
1886	Bro AA	141	597	119	156	22	7	0	37	70	0		.261	.339	.322	106	7	32	.858	-16	84	83	3b141/P		-0.6
1887	Bro AA	138	580	133	155	26	8	4	69	61	6		.267	.343	.348	92	-5	59	.890	15	107	122	3b136,S2		1.0
1888	Bro AA	143	575	134	156	18	8	4	52	66	12		.271	.348	.351	128	21	51	.898	-27	76	78	3b143		-0.3
1889	†Bro AA	138	545	103	134	25	7	4	82	59	7	43	.246	.327	.339	90	-7	47	.897	-9	95	83	3b138		-1.1
1890	†Bro N	126	485	115	150	20	9	7	83	80	4	19	.309	.411	.431	145	31	47	.933	-16	84	78	3b126		1.5
1891	Bro N	135	501	80	137	19	6	2	71	67	7	32	.273	.367	.347	109	9	44	.904	-18	89	52	3b130,S5		-0.6
1892	StL N	78	290	31	50	3	2	0	25	36	2	26	.172	.268	.197	43	-19	4	.888	-8	92	93	3b78		-2.4
1893	Lou N	118	446	64	105	12	6	1	62	50	8	8	.235	.323	.296	71	-17	12	.923	2	105	114	3b118		-1.1
Total	10	1163	4610	874	1212	170	56	21	539	526	53	135	.263	.345	.338	103	31	296	.897	-90	91	86	3b1061,2b82,S21/P		-3.4

PINSON, VADA Vada Edward B8.11.1938 Memphis TN D10.21.1995 Oakland CA BL/TL/5-11/181(170-187) d4.15 C16

YEAR	TM LG	G	AB	R	H	2B	3B	HR	RBI	BB-IB	HP	SO	AVG	OBP	SLG	AOPS	ABR	SB-CS	FA	FR	RNG	THR	GAMES AT POSITION	DL	BFW
1958	Cin N	27	96	20	26	7	0	1	8	11-0	1	18	.271	.352	.375	88	-1	2-1	1.000	2	98	194	O27(4/5/18)		0.0
1959	Cin N★	154	648	131	205	47	9	20	84	55-3	1	98	.316	.371	.509	128	26	21-6	.984	9	112	122	O154C		3.0
1960	Cin N★	154	652	107	187	37	12	20	61	47-3	5	96	.287	.339	.472	117	14	32-12	.981	-2	100	91	O154C		0.8
1961	†Cin N	154	607	101	208	34	8	16	87	39-1	1	63	.343	.379	.504	131	27	23-10	.976	-2	96	129	O152C		0.8
1962	Cin N	155	619	107	181	31	7	23	100	45-7	4	68	.292	.341	.477	114	11	26-8	.989	-2	96	129	O152C		3.2
1963	Cin N	162	652	96	204	37	14	22	106	36-3	1	95	.313	.347	.514	141	32	27-8	.979	-6	91	148	O156C		-0.4
1964	Cin N	156	625	99	166	23	11	23	84	42-2	5	99	.266	.316	.448	109	6	8-2	.972	-6	91	114	O156C		2.2
1965	Cin N	159	669	97	204	34	10	22	94	43-3	7	81	.305	.352	.484	125	21	21-8	.992	2	105	103	O159C		-0.2
1966	Cin N	156	618	70	178	35	6	16	76	33-6	3	83	.288	.326	.442	103	3	18-10	.964	0	106	88	O154(0/139/24)		-0.7
1967	Cin N	158	650	90	187	28	13	18	66	26-1	3	86	.288	.318	.454	106	4	26-8	.978	-5	98	46	O157C		-0.5
1968	Cin N	130	499	60	135	29	6	5	48	32-8	0	59	.271	.311	.383	102	1	17-11	.996	-3	99	64	O124(0/1/124)		-1.0
1969	StL N	132	495	58	126	22	6	10	70	35-2	3	63	.255	.303	.384	92	-7	4-4	.982	4	109	94	O141(15/14/120),1b7		0.6
1970	Cle A	148	574	74	164	28	6	24	82	28-7	3	69	.286	.319	.481	113	8	7-6	.982	4	109	141	O141(9/100/39),1b3		-1.1
1971	Cle A	146	566	60	149	23	4	11	35	21-0	6	54	.263	.295	.376	82	-15	25-6	.978	1	99	130	O134(104/15/29)/1		0.6
1972	Cal A	136	484	56	133	24	2	7	49	30-12	1	54	.275	.321	.376	114	7	5-5	.991	-2	92	144	O120(75/32/25)		-1.1
1973	Cal A	124	466	56	121	14	6	8	57	20-3	0	55	.260	.286	.367	90	-9	5-5	.965	-1	92	94	O110(14/6/91)/1D		-1.1
1974	KC A	115	406	46	112	18	6	4	41	21-4	2	45	.276	.312	.374	92	-5	21-5	.980	-3	91	115	O82(12/12/59),1b4,D5		-2.4
1975	KC A	103	319	38	71	14	5	4	22	21-3	6	33	.223	.248	.335	63	-17	5-6	.993	-1	96	109	O2403(234/1676/549),1b16,D7		3.0
Total	18	2469	9645	1366	2757	485	127	256	1170	574-69	54	1196	.286	.327	.442	110	106	305-122	.981	-4	100	109	O2403(234/1676/549),1b16,D7		3.0

PIPP, WALLY Walter Clement B2.17.1893 Chicago IL D1.11.1965 Grand Rapids MI BL/TL/6-1/180 d6.29 Mil 1918 Col Catholic America

YEAR	TM LG	G	AB	R	H	2B	3B	HR	RBI	BB-IB	HP	SO	AVG	OBP	SLG	AOPS	ABR	SB-CS	FA	FR	RNG	THR	GAMES AT POSITION	DL	BFW
1913	Det A	12	31	3	5	0	0	0	1	6	1	6	.161	.235	.355	73	-2	0	.977	-1	85	136	1b10		-0.1
1915	NY A	136	479	59	118	20	13	4	60	66	1	81	.246	.339	.367	112	7	18-7	.992	2	104	125	1b134		1.0
1916	NY A	151	545	70	143	20	14	12	93	54	2	82	.262	.331	.417	122	12	16	.992	5	111	112	1b148		0.6
1917	NY A	155	587	82	143	29	12	9	70	60	6	66	.244	.320	.380	112	7	11	.990	4	109	110	1b155		0.6
1918	NY A	91	349	48	106	15	9	2	44	22	0	34	.304	.345	.415	127	9	11	.988	1	101	130	1b91		0.8
1919	NY A	138	523	74	144	23	10	7	50	39	4	42	.275	.330	.398	103	0	9	.991	0	99	112	1b138		0.6
1920	NY A	153	610	109	171	30	14	11	76	48	6	54	.280	.339	.430	99	-6	17-10	.991	-5	88	114	1b153		-2.3
1921	†NY A	153	588	96	174	35	9	8	97	45	4	32	.296	.347	.427	94	-6	17-10	.993	-6	85	107	1b152		-2.0
1922	†NY A	152	577	96	190	32	10	9	90	56	6	28	.304	.352	.397	95	-6	6-13	.992	-4	87	99	1b144		-2.2
1923	†NY A	144	569	79	173	19	8	6	108	36	2	36	.304	.347	.457	108	3	12-5	.994	1	98	96	1b153		-0.3
1924	NY A	153	589	88	174	30	19	9	114	51	1	30	.295	.352	.457	108	3	12-5	.994	4	131	119	1b47		-0.1
1925	NY A	62	178	19	41	6	3	3	24	13	1	12	.230	.286	.348	61	-12	3-3	.991	4	131	119	1b47		-0.9
1926	Cin N	155	574	72	167	22	15	6	99	49	5	26	.291	.352	.413	108	5	9	.992	1	104	123	1b155		-2.2
1927	Cin N	122	443	49	115	19	6	2	41	32	0	11	.260	.309	.343	77	-15	2	.996	1	97	104	1b114		-2.0
1928	Cin N	95	272	30	77	11	3	2	26	23	1	1	.283	.341	.368	87	-5	1	.989	1	109	124	1b72		-6.0
Total	15	1872	6914	974	1941	311	148	90	997	596	38	551	.281	.341	.408	104	12	125-60	.992	6	100	114	1b1819		-6.0

PIRIE, JIM James Moir B3.31.1853 Ontario, Can D6.2.1934 Dundas ON, Can. BB/5-8/169 d9.25

YEAR	TM LG	G	AB	R	H	2B	3B	HR	RBI	BB-IB	HP	SO	AVG	OBP	SLG	AOPS	ABR	SB-CS	FA	FR	RNG	THR	GAMES AT POSITION	DL	BFW
1883	Phi N	5	19	1	3	0	0	0	0	0		2	.158	.158	.158	-4	-2		.577	-4	66	65	S5		0.0

PIRKL, GREG Gregory Daniel B8.7.1970 Long Beach CA BR/TR/6-5/225(225-240) [SeaA88 2/44] d8.13

YEAR	TM LG	G	AB	R	H	2B	3B	HR	RBI	BB-IB	HP	SO	AVG	OBP	SLG	AOPS	ABR	SB-CS	FA	FR	RNG	THR	GAMES AT POSITION	DL	BFW
1993	Sea A	7	23	1	4	0	0	1	4	0-0	0	4	.174	.174	.304	25	-3	0-0	1.000	1	149	186	1b5,D2		-0.1
1994	Sea A	19	53	9	14	3	0	6	11	1-1	1	12	.264	.286	.660	133	2	0-0	.983	-1	24	48	D10,1b7	71	-0.0
1995	Sea A	10	17	2	4	0	0	0	0	0-0	0	7	.235	.278	.235	35	-2	0-0	1.000	0	109	28	1b6/D		-0.0
1996	Sea A	7	21	2	4	1	0	1	1	0-0	0	3	.190	.190	.381	39	-2	0-0	1.000	0	160	115	1b2,D3		-0.0
	Bos A	2	2	0	0	0	0	0	0	0-0	0	1	.000	.000	.000	-98	-1	0-0	—	0			/H		-0.0
	Year	9	23	2	4	1	0	1	1	0-0	0	4	.174	.174	.348	27	-3	0-0	1.000	0	160	115	1b20,D16	71	-0.0
Total	4	45	116	14	26	4	0	8	16	2-1	1	27	.224	.242	.466	77	-2	0-0	.994	0	93	90	1b20,D16	71	-0.0

PISONI, JIM James Pete B8.14.1929 St.Louis MO BR/TR/5-10/169* d9.25

YEAR	TM LG	G	AB	R	H	2B	3B	HR	RBI	BB-IB	HP	SO	AVG	OBP	SLG	AOPS	ABR	SB-CS	FA	FR	RNG	THR	GAMES AT POSITION	DL	BFW
1953	StL A	3	12	1	1	0	1	0	0	0-0	0	5	.083	.083	.333	8	-2	0-0	1.000	-0	106		O3(0/2/1)		-0.0
1956	KC A	10	30	4	8	0	0	2	5	2-0	0	6	.267	.303	.467	103	-0	0-0	.966	3	117	517	O9L		-0.0
1957	KC A	44	97	14	23	2	2	3	12	10-1	0	17	.237	.318	.392	92	-1	0-0	.989	3	113	138	O44(0/44/1)		-0.0
1959	Mil N	9	24	4	4	1	0	0	2	2-0	0	6	.167	.231	.208	20	-3	0-0	1.000	0	130		O15(9/3/3)		-0.0
	NY A	17	17	2	3	0	0	1	0	1-0	0	9	.176	.222	.294	42	-2	0-0	1.000	1	124		O18(12/6/0)		-0.0
1960	NY A	20	9	1	1	0	0	0	1	1-0	0	2	.111	.200	.111	-14	-1	0-0	.938	0	124		O6(2/3/0)		-0.0
Total	5	103	189	26	40	3	3	6	20	16-1	0	47	.212	.278	.354	71	-9	0-0	.978	7	114	177	O98(32/63/5)		-0.0

PITKO, ALEX Alexander "Spunk" B11.22.1914 Burlington NJ BR/TR/5-10/180 d9.11

YEAR	TM LG	G	AB	R	H	2B	3B	HR	RBI	BB-IB	HP	SO	AVG	OBP	SLG	AOPS	ABR	SB-CS	FA	FR	RNG	THR	GAMES AT POSITION	DL	BFW
1938	Phi N	7	19	2	6	1	1	0	3	3	0	3	.316	.409	.368	118	1	1	.889	-1	86		O7R		-0.0
1939	Was A	4	8	0	1	0	0	0	1	1	0	3	.125	.222	.125	-10	-1	0-0	1.000	-0	87		O3(2/0/1)		-0.0
Total	2	11	27	2	7	1	1	0	4	4	0	6	.259	.355	.296	80	0	1-0	.917	-1	86		O10(2/0/8)		-0.0

YEAR	TM	LG	G	AB	R	H	2B	3B	HR	RBI	BB-IB	HP	SO	AVG	OBP	SLG	AOPS	ABR	SB-CS	FA	FR	RNG	THR	GAMES AT POSITION	DL	BFW

PITLER, JAKE   Jacob Albert B4.22.1894 New York NY D2.3.1968 Binghamton NY BR/TR/5-8/150 d5.30 C11

1917	Pit	N	109	382	39	89	8	5	0	23	30		5	24	.233	.297	.280	75	-11	6	**.966**	-15	85	90	2b106,O3(1/0/1)		-2.8
1918	Pit	N	2	1	1	0	0	0	0	0	1		0	0	.000	.500	.000	55	0	2	.667	-0	97	0	/2		0.0
Total	2		111	383	40	89	8	5	0	23	31		5	24	.232	.298	.279	75	-11	8	.962	-16	85	89	2b107,O3(1/0/1)		-2.8

PITTARO, CHRIS   Christopher Francis B9.16.1961 Trenton NJ BB/TR/5-11/170* [DetA82 6/152] d4.8 Col North Carolina-Asheville

1985	Det	A	28	62	10	15	3	1	0	7	5-0		0	13	.242	.299	.323	70	-3	1-1	.881	-2	92	37	3b22,2b4/D	18	-0.5
1986	Min	A	11	21	0	2	0	0	0	0	0-0		0	8	.095	.095	.095	-47	-4	0-0	.969	0	92	180	2b8,S4		-0.4
1987	Min	A	14	12	6	4	0	0	0	0	1-0		0	0	.333	.385	.333	89	0	1-0	1.000	-2	48	108	2b8,D2		-0.2
Total	3		53	95	16	21	3	1	0	7	6-0		0	21	.221	.267	.274	47	-7	2-1	.881	-4	92	37	3b22,2b20,S4,D3	18	-1.1

PITTINGER, PINKY   Clarke Alonzo B2.24.1899 Hudson MI D11.4.1977 Ft.Lauderdale FL BR/TR/5-10/160 d4.15 Col Ohio St.

1921	Bos	A	40	91	6	18	1	0	0	5	4		0	13	.198	.232	.209	13	-12	3-2	.985	3	117	132	O27(19/4/4),3b3,S2/2		-1.0
1922	Bos	A	66	186	16	48	3	0	0	7	9		2	10	.258	.299	.274	51	-14	3-2	.920	-2	97	136	3b33,S29		-1.2
1923	Bos	A	60	177	15	38	5	0	0	15	5		0	10	.215	.236	.243	26	-20	3-1	.959	-8	87	61	2b42,S10,3b3		-2.5
1925	Chi	N	59	173	21	54	7	2	0	15	12		2	7	.312	.364	.376	88	-3	5-4	.940	2	100	69	S24,3b24		0.2
1927	Cin	N	31	84	17	23	5	0	1	10	2		0	5	.274	.291	.369	78	-3	4	.963	1	111	158	2b20,S9,3b2		-0.1
1928	Cin	N	40	38	12	9	0	1	0	4	0		1	1	.237	.237	.289	37	-4	2	.892	4	145	221	S12,2b4,3b4		0.1
1929	Cin	N	77	210	31	62	11	0	0	27	5		2	4	.295	.318	.348	68	-11	8	.956	1	99	130	S50,3b8,2b4		-0.3
Total	7		373	959	118	252	32	3	1	83	37		6	50	.263	.294	.306	55	-67	27-12	.938	1	102	103	S136,3b77,2b71,O27(19/4/4)		-4.8

PITTMAN, JOE   Joseph Wayne B1.1.1954 Houston TX BR/TR/6-1/180* [HouN75 5/110] d4.25 Col Southern A&M

1981	†Hou	N	52	135	11	38	4	2	0	7	11-3		0	16	.281	.333	.341	98	-1	4-4	.980	-6	90	82	2b35,3b4		-0.6
1982	Hou	N	15	10	0	2	1	0	0	0	0-0		0	2	.200	.200	.300	41	-1	0-0	1.000	0	76	0	3b3/OR		-0.1
	SD	N	55	118	16	30	2	0	0	7	9-2		0	13	.254	.307	.271	67	-5	8-3	.964	-6	101	106	2b30,S13		-0.9
	Year		70	128	16	32	3	0	0	7	9-2		0	15	.250	.299	.273	65	-6	8-3	.964	-6	101	106	2b30,S13,3b3/OR		-1.0
1984	SF	N	17	22	2	5	0	0	0	2	0-0		0	6	.227	.217	.227	29	-2	1-1	.900	-4	89	0	S6,2b5,3b2		-0.6
Total	3		139	285	29	75	7	2	0	16	20-5		0	37	.263	.309	.302	78	-9	13-8	.974	-16	94	91	2b70,S19,3b9/OR		-2.2

PITTS, GAYLEN   Gaylen Richard B6.6.1946 Wichita KS BR/TR/6-1/175* d5.12 C5

1974	Oak	A	18	41	4	10	3	0	0	3	5-0		0	4	.244	.326	.317	91	0	0-0	.909	-1	96	57	3b11,2b6/1		-0.1
1975	Oak	A	10	3	1	1	1	0	0	1	0-0		0	0	.333	.333	.667	180	0	0-0	.800	1	124	0	3b6,S2/2		0.1
Total	2		28	44	5	11	4	0	0	4	5-0		0	4	.250	.327	.341	97	0	0-0	.895	-0	99	51	3b17,2b7,S2/1		0.0

PITZ, HERMAN   Herman B7.18.1865 Brooklyn NY D9.3.1924 Far Rockaway NY 5-6/140 d4.18

1890	Bro	AA	61	189	26	26	0	0	0	6	45		3		.138	.312	.138	34	-12	25	.885	-11	82	96	C34,3b16,O9(5/0/4),S2/2		-1.8
	Syr	AA	29	95	17	21	0	0	0	3	13		1		.221	.321	.221	67	-3	14	.929	-7	79	108	C27/SOC		-0.7
	Year		90	284	43	47	0	0	0	9	58		4		.165	.315	.165	44	-15	39	.906	-17	81	101	C61,3b16,O10(5/1/4),S3/2		-2.5

PLANTIER, PHIL   Phillip Alan B1.27.1969 Manchester NH BL/TR/5-11/195(175-205) [BosA87 11/292] d8.21

1990	Bos	A	14	15	1	2	1	0	0	3	4-0		1	6	.133	.333	.200	55	-1	0-0	—	-0	0	0	/OLD		-0.1
1991	Bos	A	53	148	27	49	7	1	11	35	23-2		1	38	.331	.420	.615	174	15	1-0	.976	2	120	46	O40(16/0/27),D5		1.6
1992	Bos	A	108	349	46	86	19	0	7	30	44-8		2	83	.246	.332	.361	88	-4	2-3	.975	1	100	125	O76(13/0/63),D23		-0.7
1993	SD	N	138	462	67	111	20	1	34	100	61-7		7	124	.240	.335	.509	122	14	4-5	.990	10	106	147	O134L	15	1.8
1994	SD	N	96	341	44	75	21	0	18	41	36-6		5	91	.220	.302	.440	94	-4	3-1	.988	1	97	97	O91L		-0.6
1995	Hou	N	22	68	12	17	2	0	4	15	11-1		5	19	.250	.349	.456	122	2	0-0	.962	-2	80	0	O20(8/0/12)	51	-0.1
	SD	N	54	148	21	38	4	0	5	19	17-2		1	29	.257	.333	.385	91	-2	1-1	.958	3	104	238	O39L		-0.1
	Year		76	216	33	55	6	0	9	34	28-3		1	48	.255	.339	.407	101	-1	1-1	.959	1	96	162	O59(47/0/12)		-0.2
1996	Oak	A	73	231	29	49	8	1	7	31	28-0		3	56	.212	.304	.346	65	-13	2-2	.973	4	102	175	O68(67/1/1/)/D		-1.1
1997	SD	N	10	8	0	1	0	0	0	0	2-0		0	3	.125	.300	.125	17	-1	0-0	1.000	0	125	0	O3L		-0.1
	StL	N	42	113	13	29	8	0	5	18	11-1		3	27	.257	.333	.460	106	1	0-3	.981	-1	96	48	O32(10/0/23)	36	-0.1
	Year		52	121	13	30	8	0	5	18	13-1		3	30	.248	.331	.438	102	0	0-3	.982	-1	97	46	O35(13/0/23)	51	-0.2
Total	8		610	1883	260	457	90	3	91	292	237-27		23	476	.243	.332	.439	103	7	13-15	.980	17	102	126	O504(382/1/126),D33	153	0.4

PLARSKI, DON   Donald Joseph B11.9.1929 Chicago IL D12.29.1981 St.Louis MO BR/TR/5-6/160 d7.20

1955	KC	A	8	11	0	1	0	0	0	0	0-0		0	2	.091	.091	.091	-50	-2	1-0	1.000	-0	105	0	O6C		-0.2

PLASKETT, ELMO   Elmo Alexander B6.27.1938 Frederiksted, V.I. D11.2.1998 Christiansted, V.I. BR/TR/5-10/190* d9.8

1962	Pit	N	7	14	2	4	0	0	1	3	1-0		0	3	.286	.333	.500	120	0	0-0	1.000	-1	76	0	C4		-0.1
1963	Pit	N	10	21	1	3	0	0	0	2	0-0		0	5	.143	.143	.143	-17	-3	0-0	1.000	-1	0	0	C5/3		-0.5
Total	2		17	35	3	7	0	0	1	5	1-0		0	8	.200	.222	.286	41	-3	0-0	1.000	-3	34	0	C9/3		-0.6

PLATT, WHITEY   Mizell George B8.21.1920 W.Palm Beach FL D7.27.1970 W.Palm Beach FL BR/TR/6-2/195 d9.16 Mil 1944-45

1942	Chi	N	4	16	1	1	0	0	0	2	0		0	3	.063	.063	.063	-66	-4	0	1.000	0	87	352	O4(2/2/0)		-0.4
1943	Chi	N	20	41	2	7	3	0	0	2	1		0	7	.171	.190	.244	25	-4	0	.952	-1	98	0	O14(7/7/0)		-0.6
1946	Chi	A	84	247	28	62	8	5	3	32	17		3	34	.251	.307	.360	89	-5	1-7	.971	-4	96	93	O61(25/23/14)		-1.2
1948	StL	A	123	454	57	123	22	10	7	82	39		2	51	.271	.331	.410	94	-6	1-4	.948	-7	92	60	O114L		-2.3
1949	StL	A	102	244	29	63	8	2	3	29	24		2	27	.258	.325	.344	74	-10	0-1	.986	1	108	73	O59L,1b2		-1.3
Total	5		333	1002	117	256	41	17	13	147	81		5	122	.255	.314	.369	83	-28	2-12	.964	-8	97	73	O252(207/32/14),1b2		-5.8

PLATTE, AL   Alfred Frederick Joseph B4.13.1890 Grand Rapids MI D8.29.1976 Grand Rapids MI BL/TL/5-7/160 d9.1

1913	Det	A	9	18	1	2	1	0	0	4	1		0		.111	.158	.167	-5	-2	0	.800	-1	96	0	O5L		-0.4

PLESS, RANCE   Rance B12.6.1925 Greeneville TN BR/TR/6-0/195 d4.21

1956	KC	A	48	85	4	23	3	1	0	9	10-0		1	13	.271	.354	.329	81	-2	0-1	1.000	2	83	141	1b15,3b5		-0.2

PLEWS, HERB   Herbert Eugene B6.14.1928 Helena MT BL/TR/5-11/160* d4.18 Col Illinois

1956	Was	A	91	256	24	69	10	7	1	25	26-3		1	40	.270	.337	.375	88	-5	1-2	.947	-2	110	77	2b66,S5,3b2		-0.3
1957	Was	A	104	329	51	89	19	4	1	26	28-1		1	39	.271	.326	.362	90	-4	0-3	.979	-9	90	73	2b79,3b11,S4		-1.0
1958	Was	A	111	380	46	98	12	6	2	29	17-1		1	45	.258	.291	.337	74	-15	2-3	.976	-13	93	83	2b64,3b36		-2.6
1959	Was	A	27	40	4	9	0	2	0	2	3-0		0	5	.225	.279	.225	40	-3	0-1	.971	0	96	44	2b6		-0.3
	Bos	A	13	12	0	1	0	0	0	0	0-0		1	4	.083	.083	.167	-32	-2	0-0	.833	-1	106	200	2b2		-0.2
	Year		40	52	4	10	0	2	0	2	3-0		1	9	.192	.236	.212	24	-6	0-1	.951	-0	97	65	2b8		-0.5
Total	4		346	1017	125	266	42	17	4	82	74-5		4	133	.262	.312	.348	80	-29	3-9	.967	-24	97	77	2b217,3b49,S9		-4.4

PLOCK, WALTER   Walter S. B7.2.1869 Philadelphia PA D4.28.1900 Richmond VA 6-3/180 d8.21

1891	Phi	N	2	5	2	2	0	0	0	0	1		1		.400	.500	.400	159	0	0	.000	-1	0	0	O2C		0.0

PLUMMER, BILL   William Francis B3.21.1947 Oakland CA BR/TR/6-1/200(190-210) d4.19 M1/C7

1968	Chi	N	2	2	0	0	0	0	0	0	0-0		0	1	.000	.000	.000	-94	0	0-0	1.000	0	0	0	/C		0.0
1970	Cin	N	4	8	0	1	0	0	0	0	0-0		1	2	.125	.222	.125	-4	-1	0-0	.857	-2	35	0	C4		-0.3
1971	Cin	N	10	19	0	0	0	0	0	0	0-0		0	5	.000	.000	.000	-99	-5	0-0	1.000	-1	0	172	C4,3b2		-0.6
1972	Cin	N	38	102	8	19	4	0	2	9	4-2		0	20	.186	.211	.284	43	-8	0-0	.994	-4	224	84	C36/13	20	-1.1
1974	Cin	N	50	120	7	27	7	0	2	10	6-0		0	21	.225	.258	.333	67	-6	1-0	.974	-2	116	44	C42,3b5		-1.4
1975	Cin	N	65	159	17	29	7	0	1	19	24-2		2	35	.182	.291	.245	51	-10	1-0	.990	-8	117	14	C49/3		-0.6
1976	Cin	N	56	153	16	38	6	0	4	19	14-0		1	36	.248	.311	.379	93	-2	0-2	.977	-2	79	60	C54		-1.6
1977	Cin	N	51	111	10	16	5	0	1	9	17-1		0	26	.144	.244	.205	22	-13	1-1	.986	-6	158	66	C50		-0.2
1978	Sea	A	41	93	6	20	1	0	2	7	12-0		1	19	.215	.305	.333	79	-2	0-0	.986	-3	160	66	C40		-1.5
Total	10		367	892	72	168	37	1	14	82	95-10		4	191	.188	.267	.279	53	-57	4-3	.984	-36	120	50	C343,3b9/1	20	-8.5

POCOROBA, BIFF   Biff B7.25.1953 Burbank CA BB/TR (BL 1975p, 77p, 80p, 81-84)/5-10/180(170-184) [AtlN71 17/399] d4.25

1975	Atl	N	67	188	15	48	7	1	2	22	20-2		0	15	.255	.325	.319	77	-5	0-0	.970	-11	55	79	C62		-1.4
1976	Atl	N	54	174	16	42	7	0	1	14	19-2		0	12	.241	.313	.282	67	-7	1-0	.978	5	114	95	C54		0.1
1977	Atl	N	113	321	46	93	24	1	8	44	57-15		1	27	.290	.394	.445	113	9	3-4	.989	-3	71	133	C100	90	0.9
1978	Atl	N★	92	289	21	70	8	0	2	29	29-6		2	14	.242	.312	.332	73	-10	0-3	.990	-3	66	88	C79	48	-1.1
1979	Atl	N	28	38	6	12	4	0	0	4	7-1		0	2	.316	.422	.421	123	2	1-1	.933	0	55	132	C7	106	0.2
1980	Atl	N	70	83	7	22	4	0	2	8	11-0		0	11	.265	.347	.386	104	1	1-0	.934	-1	51	27	C10	51	0.0

YEAR	TM LG	G	AB	R	H	2B	3B	HR	RBI	BB-IB	HP	SO	AVG	OBP	SLG	AOPS	ABR	SB-CS	FA	FR	RNG	THR	GAMES AT POSITION	DL	BFW
1981	Atl N	57	122	4	22	4	0	0	8	12-1	2	15	.180	.265	.213	37	-10	0-0	.938	-2	80	130	3b21,C9	23	-1.3
1982	†Atl N	56	120	5	33	7	0	2	22	13-2	1	12	.275	.351	.383	103	1	0-0	.988	-7	58	112	C36,3b2	15	-0.5
1983	Atl N	55	120	11	32	6	0	2	16	12-4	0	7	.267	.342	.367	87	-2	0-0	.983	-5	65	74	C34		-0.5
1984	Atl N	4	2	1	0	0	0	0	0	2-0	0	0	.000	.500	.000	48	0	0-0	—	0			/H		0.0
Total	10	596	1457	132	374	71	2	21	172	182-33	6	109	.257	.339	.351	87	-21	6-8	.982	-26	74	100	C391,3b23	333	-3.6

PODSEDNIK, SCOTT   Scott Eric   B3.18.1976 West TX   BL/TL/6-0/170(170-190)   [TexA94 3/85]   d7.6

YEAR	TM LG	G	AB	R	H	2B	3B	HR	RBI	BB-IB	HP	SO	AVG	OBP	SLG	AOPS	ABR	SB-CS	FA	FR	RNG	THR	GAMES AT POSITION	DL	BFW
2001	Sea A	5	6	1	1	0	1	0	3	0-0	0	1	.167	.167	.500	70	0	0-0	1.000	-0	63	0	O5(3/1/1)		-0.1
2002	Sea A	14	20	2	4	0	0	1	5	4-0	0	6	.200	.320	.350	85	0	0-0	.938	0	127	0	O11(9/1/2),D2		0.0
2003	Mil N	154	558	100	.175	29	8	9	58	56-2	4	91	.314	.379	.443	114	13	43-10	.992	2	107	65	O153C		2.0
2004	Mil N	154	640	85	156	27	7	12	39	58-2	7	105	.244	.313	.364	74	-26	70-13	.990	1	106	65	O127(124/7/0)		-1.2
2005	†Chi A★	129	507	80	147	28	1	0	25	47-0	3	75	.290	.351	.349	84	-11	59-23	.989	-0	105	57	O435(139/285/16),D2	16	-0.2
Total	5	456	1731	268	484	84	17	22	130	165-4	14	278	.279	.345	.385	90	-23	172-46	.990	-0	106	57		16	

POEPPING, MIKE   Michael Harold   B8.7.1950 Little Falls MN   BR/TR/6-6/230   d9.6   Col St. Cloud St.

YEAR	TM LG	G	AB	R	H	2B	3B	HR	RBI	BB-IB	HP	SO	AVG	OBP	SLG	AOPS	ABR	SB-CS	FA	FR	RNG	THR	GAMES AT POSITION	DL	BFW
1975	Min A	14	37	0	5	1	0	0	1	5-0	0	7	.135	.238	.162	15	-4	0-0	.950	-1	82	107	O13R		-0.6

POFAHL, JIMMY   James Willard   B6.18.1917 Faribault MN   D9.14.1984 Owatonna MN   BR/TR/5-11/185   d4.16

YEAR	TM LG	G	AB	R	H	2B	3B	HR	RBI	BB-IB	HP	SO	AVG	OBP	SLG	AOPS	ABR	SB-CS	FA	FR	RNG	THR	GAMES AT POSITION	DL	BFW
1940	Was A	119	406	34	95	23	5	2	36	37	0	55	.234	.298	.330	67	-21	2-0	.952	-3	96	98	S112,2b4		-1.4
1941	Was A	22	75	9	14	3	2	0	6	10	0	11	.187	.282	.280	52	-5	1-0	.934	-3	101	61	S21		-0.6
1942	Was A	84	283	22	59	7	2	0	28	29	0	30	.208	.282	.247	50	-19	4-3	.956	-1	96	108	S49,2b15,3b14		-1.6
Total	3	225	764	65	168	33	9	2	70	76	0	96	.220	.290	.295	59	-45	7-3	.951	-7	97	97	S182,2b19,3b14		-3.6

POFF, JOHN   John William   B10.23.1952 Chillicothe OH   BL/TL/6-2/200*   d9.8   Col Duke

YEAR	TM LG	G	AB	R	H	2B	3B	HR	RBI	BB-IB	HP	SO	AVG	OBP	SLG	AOPS	ABR	SB-CS	FA	FR	RNG	THR	GAMES AT POSITION	DL	BFW
1979	Phi N	12	19	2	2	1	0	0	1	1-0	0	4	.105	.150	.158		-15	-3	0-0	.875	-0	107	0	O4L/1		-0.4
1980	Mil A	19	68	7	17	1	2	1	7	3-2	0	7	.250	.282	.368	78	-3	0-0	1.000	-1	104	0	O7R,1b3,D7		-0.4
Total	2	31	87	9	19	2	2	1	8	4-2	0	11	.218	.253	.322	57	-6	0-0	.957	-2	105		O11(4/0/7),D7,1b4		-0.8

POINTER, AARON   Aaron Elton "Hawk"   B4.19.1942 Little Rock AR   BR/TR/6-2/185*   d9.22   Col San Francisco

YEAR	TM LG	G	AB	R	H	2B	3B	HR	RBI	BB-IB	HP	SO	AVG	OBP	SLG	AOPS	ABR	SB-CS	FA	FR	RNG	THR	GAMES AT POSITION	DL	BFW
1963	Hou N	2	5	0	1	0	0	0	1	0-0	0	1	.200	.200	.200	17	0	0-0	1.000	-0	58	0	/OR		-0.1
1966	Hou N	11	26	5	9	1	0	1	5	5-0	1	6	.346	.469	.500	132	3	1-1	1.000	2	95	564	O11L		0.5
1967	Hou N	27	70	6	11	4	0	1	10	13-1	1	26	.157	.291	.257	62	-3	1-0	.951	1	109	158	O22L		-0.3
Total	3	40	101	11	21	5	0	2	15	18-1	2	33	.208	.333	.317	91	-1	2-1	.966	3	104	258	O34(33/0/1)		0.1

POLANCO, PLACIDO   Placido Enrique   B10.10.1975 Santo Domingo, D.R.   BR/TR/5-10/168(168-190)   [StLN94 19/530]   d7.3   Col Miami-Dade Wolfson (FL) CC

YEAR	TM LG	G	AB	R	H	2B	3B	HR	RBI	BB-IB	HP	SO	AVG	OBP	SLG	AOPS	ABR	SB-CS	FA	FR	RNG	THR	GAMES AT POSITION	DL	BFW
1998	StL N	45	114	10	29	3	2	1	11	5-0	1	9	.254	.292	.342	66	-6	2-0	.952	5	124	129	S28,2b14		0.2
1999	StL N	88	220	24	61	9	1	1	19	15-1	0	24	.277	.321	.359	71	-10	1-3	.979	0	99	102	2b66,3b9,S9		-0.7
2000	†StL N	118	323	50	102	12	3	5	39	16-0	1	26	.316	.347	.418	91	-5	4-4	.984	4	95	72	2b51,3b35,S29/1		0.2
2001	†StL N	144	564	87	173	26	4	3	38	25-0	6	31	.307	.342	.383	85	-12	12-3	.985	24	117	104	3b103,S42,2b15/D		1.7
2002	Phi N	94	342	47	97	19	4	5	27	12-1	4	27	.284	.316	.389	87	-9	3-1	.974	6	110	141	3b78,S13,2b6		-0.1
	Phi N	53	206	28	61	13	1	4	22	14-0	4	14	.296	.353	.427	115	3	2-2	.978	12	126	141	3b53		1.5
	Year	147	548	75	158	32	2	9	49	26-1	8	41	.288	.330	.403	97	-6	5-3	.992	18	117	141	3b131,S13,2b6		1.4
2003	Phi N	122	492	87	142	30	3	14	63	42-1	8	38	.289	.352	.447	116	11	14-2	.992	5	103	116	2b99,3b21	15	2.3
2004	Phi N	126	503	74	150	21	0	17	55	27-0	12	39	.298	.345	.441	99	-1	7-4	.995	14	102	116	2b109,3b13	30	1.8
2005	Phi N	43	158	26	50	7	0	3	20	12-0	3	9	.316	.376	.418	104	1	0-0	1.000	7	102	161	2b29,3b8,O5L/S	15	3.
	Det A	86	343	58	116	20	2	6	35	12-0	6	16	.338	.366	.461	128	15	4-3	.993	14	108	128	2b84/3	74	11.0
Total	8	919	3265	491	981	160	19	59	330	189-3	47	245	.300	.346	.415	98	-13	49-22	.991	93	102	115	2b473,3b321,S122,O5L/D1		

POLAND, HUGH   Hugh Reid   B1.19.1913 Tompkinsville KY   D3.30.1984 Guthrie KY   BL/TR/5-11.5/185   d4.22   Mil 1945   Col Western Kentucky

YEAR	TM LG	G	AB	R	H	2B	3B	HR	RBI	BB-IB	HP	SO	AVG	OBP	SLG	AOPS	ABR	SB-CS	FA	FR	RNG	THR	GAMES AT POSITION	DL	BFW
1943	NY N	4	12	1	1	0	0	0	2	1	0	0	.083	.154	.250	16	-1	0	.889	-1	78	162	C4		-0.3
	Bos N	44	141	5	27	7	0	0	13	4	0	11	.191	.214	.241	32	-13	0	.973	-5	58	46	C38		-1.7
	Year	48	153	6	28	7	1	0	15	5	0	11	.183	.209	.242	30	-14	0	.969	-6	59	53	C42		-2.0
1944	Bos N	8	23	1	3	1	0	0	2	0	0	1	.130	.130	.174	-14	-4	0	.939	-0	67	0	C6		-0.4
1946	Bos N	4	6	0	1	0	0	0	0	0	0	0	.167	.167	.333	40	0	0	1.000	-0	47	267	C2		-0.1
1947	Phi N	4	8	0	0	0	0	0	0	0	0	0	.000	.000	.000	-99	-2	0	1.000	-0	40		C3		-0.1
	Cin N	16	18	1	6	1	0	0	2	1	0	4	.333	.368	.389	102	0	0	.667	-1	27	154	C5		-0.3
	Year	20	26	1	6	1	0	0	2	1	0	4	.231	.259	.269	41	-2	0	.867	-1	27	154	C5		-0.4
1948	Cin N	3	3	0	1	0	0	0	0	0	0	0	.333	.333	.333	84	0	0	—	0			/H		-0.0
Total	5	83	211	8	39	10	1	0	19	6	0	16	.185	.207	.242	28	-20	0	.958	-7	58	51	C55		-2.8

POLCOVICH, KEVIN   Kevin Michael   B6.28.1970 Auburn NY   BR/TR/5-9/170(168-182)   [PitN92 30/847]   d5.17   Col Florida

YEAR	TM LG	G	AB	R	H	2B	3B	HR	RBI	BB-IB	HP	SO	AVG	OBP	SLG	AOPS	ABR	SB-CS	FA	FR	RNG	THR	GAMES AT POSITION	DL	BFW
1997	Pit N	84	245	37	67	16	1	4	21	21-4	5	45	.273	.350	.396	94	-1	2-2	.969	13	116	83	S80,2b2/3	16	1.
1998	Pit N	81	212	18	.40	12	0	0	14	15-2	5	33	.189	.255	.245	33	-21	4-3	.916	14	115	113	S54,2b15,3b8	16	1.
Total	2	165	457	55	107	28	1	4	35	36-6	14	78	.234	.307	.326	66	-22	6-5	.948	27	116	95	S134,2b17,3b9		

POLHEMUS, MARK   Mark S. "Humpty Dumpty"   B10.4.1860 Brooklyn NY   D11.12.1923 Lynn MA   5-6.5/185   d7.13

YEAR	TM LG	G	AB	R	H	2B	3B	HR	RBI	BB-IB	HP	SO	AVG	OBP	SLG	AOPS	ABR	SB-CS	FA	FR	RNG	THR	GAMES AT POSITION	DL	BFW
1887	Ind N	20	75	6	18	1	0	0		9			.240	.260	.253	45	-6	4	.744	0	236		O20R		-0.

POLIDOR, GUS   Gustavo Adolfo (Gonzalez)   B10.26.1961 Caracas, Venez   D4.28.1995 Caracas, Venez   BR/TR/6-0/170*   d9.7

YEAR	TM LG	G	AB	R	H	2B	3B	HR	RBI	BB-IB	HP	SO	AVG	OBP	SLG	AOPS	ABR	SB-CS	FA	FR	RNG	THR	GAMES AT POSITION	DL	BFW
1985	Cal A	2	1	1	1	0	0	0	0	0-0	0	0	1.000	1.000	1.000	450	0	0-0	1.000	-0	207	0	/SOR		-0.
1986	Cal A	6	19	1	5	1	0	0	1	1-0	0	3	.263	.300	.316	68	-1	0-0	1.000	-2	71	89	2b4/S3		-0.
1987	Cal A	63	137	12	36	3	0	2	15	2-0	1	15	.263	.277	.328	62	-8	0-0	.984	-2	109	64	S25,3b22,2b3/D	17	-1
1988	Cal A	54	81	4	12	3	0	0	4	3-0	0	11	.148	.179	.185	2	-11	0-0	.984	-5	105	105	3b30,2b29,S21,D2		-2
1989	Mil A	79	175	15	34	7	0	0	14	6-0	2	18	.194	.230	.234	31	-16	0-0	1.000	-1	105		3b14,2b2,S2		-0
1990	Mil A	18	15	0	1	0	0	0	0	0-0	0	1	.067	.067	.067	-63	-3	0-0	1.000	-0	0	0	/23		-0.
1993	Fla N	7	6	0	1	0	0	0	1	0-0	0	2	.167	.167	.333	28	-1	0-0	.970	-0	93	75	S96,3b79,2b42,D3/OR	17	-5
Total	7	229	434	33	90	15	0	2	35	12-0	3	47	.207	.233	.256	35	-40	0-0	.970	-22	93	75	S96,3b79,2b42,D3/OR	17	-5

POLLY, NICK   Nicholas (b Nicholas Joseph Polachanin)   B4.18.1917 Chicago IL   D1.17.1993 Chicago IL   BR/TR/5-11/190   d9.11

YEAR	TM LG	G	AB	R	H	2B	3B	HR	RBI	BB-IB	HP	SO	AVG	OBP	SLG	AOPS	ABR	SB-CS	FA	FR	RNG	THR	GAMES AT POSITION	DL	BFW
1937	Bro N	10	18	2	4	0	0	0	2	0	0	0	1	.222	.222	.222	21	-2	0	.850	1	142	0	3b7		-0
1945	Bos A	4	7	0	1	0	0	0	1	0	0	2	.143	.143	.143	-17	-1	0-0	1.000	1	99	0	3b2		-0
Total	2	14	25	2	5	0	0	0	3	0	0	2	.200	.200	.200	11	-3	0-0	.870	1	135	0	3b9		-0

POLONIA, LUIS   Luis Andrew (Almonte)   B10.12.1963 Santiago, D.R.   BL/TL/5-8/152*   d4.24

YEAR	TM LG	G	AB	R	H	2B	3B	HR	RBI	BB-IB	HP	SO	AVG	OBP	SLG	AOPS	ABR	SB-CS	FA	FR	RNG	THR	GAMES AT POSITION	DL	BFW
1987	Oak A	125	435	78	125	16	10	4	49	32-1	0	64	.287	.335	.398	100	-1	29-7	.979	0	105	40	O104(35/69/8),D18		0
1988	†Oak A	84	288	51	84	11	4	2	27	21-0	0	40	.292	.338	.378	104	1	24-9	.988	1	104	73	O76(76/0/1),D2		0
1989	Oak A	59	206	31	59	6	4	1	17	9-0	0	15	.286	.315	.369	96	-2	13-4	.985	6	123	104	O55L		0
	NY A	66	227	39	71	11	2	2	29	16-1	2	29	.313	.359	.405	117	5	9-4	.982	3	105	203	O53L,D9		0
	Year	125	433	70	130	17	6	3	46	25-1	2	44	.300	.338	.388	107	3	22-8	.984	9	114	154	O108L,D9		-0
1990	NY A	11	22	2	7	0	0	0	3	0-0	1	3	.318	.304	.318	78	-1	1-0	—	0			D4		0
	Cal A	109	381	50	128	7	9	2	32	25-1	1	42	.336	.376	.417	124	11	20-14	.980	-6	86	61	O85(73/13/0),D11		0
	Year	120	403	52	135	7	9	2	35	25-1	2	45	.335	.372	.412	122	10	21-14	.980	-6	86	61	O85(73/13/0),D15		0
1991	Cal A	150	604	92	179	28	8	2	50	52-4	1	74	.296	.352	.379	102	2	48-23	.981	-0	91	116	O143(143/1/0),D4		-0
1992	Cal A	149	577	83	165	17	4	0	35	45-6	1	64	.286	.337	.329	87	-10	51-21	.983	-1	100	123	O99L,D47		-0
1993	Cal A	152	576	75	156	17	4	1	32	48-7	2	53	.271	.328	.326	74	-21	55-24	.983	4	105	143	O141L,D4		-0
1994	NY A	95	350	62	109	21	6	1	36	37-1	4	36	.311	.383	.414	110	6	20-12	.976	-1	94	149	O84L/D		-0
1995	NY A	67	238	37	62	9	3	2	15	25-1	0	29	.261	.326	.349	78	-8	10-4	1.000	6	118	132	O64L/D		-0
	†Atl N	28	53	6	14	7	0	0	2	3-0	0	5	.264	.304	.396	79	-1	3-0	1.000	-2	51	0	O15(11/4/1)		-0
1996	Bal A	58	175	25	42	4	1	2	14	10-0	1	24	.240	.285	.309	50	-14	8-6	.983	-2	94	49	O34(32/0/2),D18		-1
	†Atl N	22	31	3	13	0	0	1	0	1-0	1	5	.419	.424	.419	120	1	1-1	.800	-1	50	0	O7L		-0
1999	Det A	87	333	46	108	21	8	10	32	16-0	2	32	.324	.357	.526	120	9	17-9	.986	2	101	181	D43,O40(31/0/10)		-0
2000	Det A	80	267	37	73	10	5	6	25	22-1	5	25	.273	.325	.416	88	-6	8-5	1.000	2	119	156	D44,O27(1/0/26)		-0
	†NY A	37	77	11	22	1	0	0	7	7-0	1	7	.286	.341	.377	84	-3	4-2	.970	-2	91	80	O28(22/0/6),D7		-0
	Year	117	344	48	95	11	5	6	32	29-1	6	32	.276	.329	.407	87	-8	12-7	.987	0	105	110	O55(23/0/32),D51		-0
Total	12	1379	4840	728	1417	189	70	36	405	369-23	15	543	.293	.342	.383	96	-31	321-145	.983	3	100	110	O1055(927/87/54),D214		

PONCE, CARLOS   Carlos Antonio (Diaz)   B2.7.1959 Rio Piedras, PR   BR/TR/5-10/170   d8.14   Col Abraham Baldwin (GA) JC

YEAR	TM LG	G	AB	R	H	2B	3B	HR	RBI	BB-IB	HP	SO	AVG	OBP	SLG	AOPS	ABR	SB-CS	FA	FR	RNG	THR	GAMES AT POSITION	DL	BFW
1985	Mil A	21	62	4	10	2	0	1	5	1-0	0	9	.161	.169	.242	13	-8	0-0	1.000	-1	60	121	1b10,O6(5/0/1),D3		-4

YEAR	TM LG	G	AB	R	H	2B	3B	HR	RBI	BB-IB	HP	SO	AVG	OBP	SLG	AOPS	ABR	SB-CS		FA	FR	RNG	THR	GAMES AT POSITION		DL	BFW

POND, RALPH Ralph Benjamin B5.4.1890 Eau Claire WI D9.8.1947 Cleveland OH TR/5-9/? d6.8 Col Maine
| 1910 | Bos A | 1 | 4 | 0 | 1 | 0 | 0 | 0 | 0 | 0 | | 0 | .250 | .250 | .250 | 55 | 0 | 1 | | .000 | -1 | 0 | 0 | /OC | | | -0.1 |

POND, SIMON Simon Emilio B10.27.1976 North Vancouver BC, Can. BL/TR/6-1/205 [MonN94 8/224] d4.7
| 2004 | Tor A | 16 | 49 | 4 | 8 | 2 | 0 | 1 | 6 | 5-0 | 1 | 12 | .163 | .250 | .265 | 34 | -5 | 0 | | 1.000 | -0 | 101 | 0 | O9(6/0/3),D6 | | | -0.5 |

POOL, HARLIN Harlin Welty "Samson" B3.13.1908 Lakeport CA D2.15.1963 Rodeo CA BL/TR/5-10/195 d5.30
1934	Cin N	99	358	38	117	22	5	2	50	17	7	18	.327	.369	.433	117	9	3		.953	0	99	115	O94(76/0/18)			0.3
1935	Cin N	28	68	8	12	6	2	0	11	2	0	2	.176	.200	.324	39	-6	0		.962	-1	89	103	O18(15/0/3)			-0.7
Total 2		127	426	46	129	28	7	2	61	19	7	20	.303	.343	.415	105	3	3		.954	-1	98	114	O112(91/0/21)			-0.4

POOLE, JIM James Robert "Easy" B5.12.1895 Taylorsville NC D1.2.1975 Hickory NC BL/TR/6-0/175 d4.14
1925	Phi A	133	480	65	143	29	8	5	67	27	2	37	.298	.338	.423	86	-12	5-4		.982	-8	80	106	1b123			-2.6
1926	Phi A	112	361	49	106	23	5	8	63	23	2	25	.294	.339	.452	99	-2	4-3		.992	1	99	113	1b101/OR			-0.7
1927	Phi A	38	99	4	22	2	0	0	10	9	0	6	.222	.287	.242	36	-9	0-0		.993	0	99	75	1b31			-1.0
Total 3		283	940	118	271	54	13	13	140	59	4	68	.288	.333	.415	86	-23	9-7		.987	-7	89	105	1b255/OR			-4.3

POOLE, RAY Raymond Herman B1.16.1920 Salisbury NC BL/TR/6-0/180 d9.9 Mil 1942-45 Col Catawba
1941	Phi A	2	2	0	0	0	0	0	0	0	0	1	.000	.000	.000	-99	-1	0-0		—	0			/H			-0.1
1947	Phi A	13	13	1	3	0	0	0	1	1	0	4	.231	.286	.231	44	-1	0-0		—	0			/H			-0.1
Total 2		15	15	1	3	0	0	0	1	1	0	5	.200	.250	.200	25	-2	0-0		—	0						-0.2

POORMAN, TOM Thomas Iverson B10.14.1857 Lock Haven PA D2.18.1905 Lock Haven PA BL/TR/5-7/135 d5.5 ▲
1880	Buf N	19	70	5	11	0	0	0		1	0	13	.157	.157	.171	11	-6			.879	-0	141	0	P11,O10C			-0.3
	Chi N	7	25	3	5	1	2	0		0	0	2	.200	.200	.400	92	0			.778	-2	77	0	O7R,P2			-0.1
	Year	26	95	8	16	2	2	0		1	0	15	.168	.168	.232	33	-7			.750	-2	40	0	O17(0/10/7),P13			-0.4
1884	Tol AA	94	382	56	89	8	7	0			10	1	.233	.254	.291	75	-12			.845	3	162	183	O93R/P			-0.8
1885	Bos N	56	227	44	54	5	3	3	25	7		32	.238	.261	.326	92	-2			.867	-3	83	65	O56R			-0.6
1886	Bos N	88	371	72	97	16	6	3	41	19		52	.261	.297	.361	102	1	31		.902	3	115	211	O88R			0.3
1887	Phi AA	135	585	140	155	18	19	4	61	35	10		.265	.317	.381	94	-7	88		.911	2	130	130	O135R,2b2/P			-0.5
1888	Phi AA	97	383	76	87	16	6	2	44	31	5		.227	.294	.316	96	-1	46		.898	-10	52	32	O97R			-1.1
Total 6		496	2043	396	498	65	43	12	172	102	16	99	.244	.285	.335	90	-27	165		.885	-6	97	125	O486(0/10/476),P15,2b2			-3.1

POPE, DAVE David B6.17.1921 Talladega AL D8.28.1999 Cleveland OH BL/TR/5-10.5/170* d7.1 Negro Lg 1946 Col Pittsburgh
1952	Cle A	12	34	9	10	1	1	4	1	0		7	.294	.314	.471	124	4	0-0		1.000	-1	100	0	O10R			0.0
1954	†Cle A	60	102	21	30	2	1	4	13	10	0	22	.294	.354	.451	118	2	2-1		1.000	-0	101	69	O29(18/6/5)			0.1
1955	Cle A	35	104	17	31	5	0	6	22	12-0	1	31	.298	.373	.519	134	5	0-0		.954	-2	100	0	O31(12/14/7)			0.1
	Bal A	86	222	21	55	8	4	1	30	16-3	2	34	.248	.302	.333	77	-8	5-2		1.000	2	110	70	O73(19/37/31)			-0.9
	Year	121	326	38	86	13	4	7	52	28-3	3	65	.264	.325	.393	97	-3	5-2		.986	0	107	47	O104(31/51/38)			-0.8
1956	Bal A	12	19	1	3	0	0	0	1	0-0	1	7	.158	.200	.158	-5	-3	0-0		1.000	-0	69	0	O4(2/0/3)			-0.3
	Cle A	25	70	6	17	3	1	0	3	1-0	0	12	.243	.250	.314	48	-6	0-0		1.000	0	103	104	O18(4/12/2)			-0.6
	Year	37	89	7	20	3	1	0	4	1-0	1	19	.225	.239	.281	38	-8	0-0		1.000	0	99	90	O22(6/12/5)			-0.9
Total 4		230	551	75	146	19	7	12	73	40-3	4	113	.265	.317	.390	92	-9	7-3		.990	-0	104	53	O165(55/69/58)			-1.6

POPOVICH, PAUL Paul Edward B8.18.1940 Flemington WV BB/TR (BR 1964, 66-67)/6-0/175* d4.19 Col West Virginia
1964	Chi N	1	1	0	1	0	0	0	0-0	0		0	1.000	1.000	1.000	447	-0			—	0			/H			0.0
1966	Chi N	2	6	0	0	0	0	0	0-0	0		2	.000	.000	.000	-99	-1	0-0		.889	0	75	101	2b2			-0.2
1967	Chi N	49	159	18	34	4	0	0	2	9-0	2	12	.214	.265	.239	43	-12	0-1		.967	1	95	84	S31,2b17,3b2			-0.9
1968	LA N	134	418	35	97	8	1	2	25	29-2	1	37	.232	.280	.270	72	-15	1-3		.983	4	102	101	2b89,S45,3b7			-0.1
1969	LA N	28	50	5	10	0	0	1	4	1-0	0	4	.200	.212	.200	18	-6	0-0		.985	-4	93	107	2b23,S3			-0.9
	Chi N	60	154	26	48	6	0	1	14	18-0	1	14	.312	.387	.370	100	1	0-1		.974	1	97	91	2b25,S7,3b6/OC			0.4
	Year	88	204	31	58	6	0	1	18	19-0	1	18	.284	.347	.328	85	-4	0-1		.978	-2	95	97	2b48,S10,3b6/OC			-0.5
1970	Chi N	78	186	22	47	5	1	4	20	18-4	2	18	.253	.324	.355	73	-7	0-1		.990	-2	105	151	2b22,S17,3b16			-0.7
1971	Chi N	89	226	24	49	7	1	4	28	14-0	0	17	.217	.260	.310	54	-14	0-1		.985	3	111	108	2b40,3b16/S			-0.9
1972	Chi N	58	129	8	25	3	2	1	11	12-2	0	13	.194	.261	.271	47	-9	0-1		.981	12	126	141	2b36,S8/3		15	0.6
1973	Chi N	99	280	24	66	6	3	2	24	18-5	1	27	.236	.280	.300	58	-16	3-2		.981	16	113	115	2b84,S9/3			0.5
1974	†Pit N	59	83	9	18	2	1	0	5	5-1	0	10	.217	.256	.265	49	-6	0-0		.962	-0	109	76	2b12,S10			-0.6
1975	Pit N	25	40	5	8	1	0	0	1	3-0	1	9	.200	.273	.225	39	-3	0-0		1.000	2	76	48	2b8,S8			-0.4
Total 11		682	1732	176	403	42	9	14	134	127-14	8	151	.233	.286	.292	62	-89	4-10		.982	31	108	112	2b358,S139,3b49/OC		15	-3.2

POPPLEIN, GEORGE George J. B8.1840 Baltimore MD D3.31.1901 Baltimore MD d7.11
| 1873 | Mar NA | 1 | 4 | 0 | 0 | 0 | 0 | 0 | | 0 | | 0 | .000 | .000 | .000 | -99 | -1 | 0-0 | | .500 | -0 | 118 | 0 | /3OC | | | -0.1 |

POQUETTE, TOM Thomas Arthur B10.30.1951 Eau Claire WI BL/TR/5-10/175* [KCA70 4/81] d9.1 C2 [DL 1980 Bos A 180]
1973	KC A	21	28	4	6	1	0	0	3	1-0	1	4	.214	.258	.250	43	-2	1-1		.870	-0	100	155	O20(0/2/18)			-0.3
1976	†KC A	104	344	43	104	18	10	2	34	29-3	4	31	.302	.361	.430	131	13	6-5		.979	-5	100	15	O98(84/0/17),D2		22	0.3
1977	†KC A	106	342	43	100	23	6	2	33	19-2	5	21	.292	.337	.412	102	1	1-4		1.000	1	106	65	O96(72/1/28)		13	-0.3
1978	†KC A	80	204	16	44	9	2	4	30	14-1	0	10	.216	.259	.338	67	-10	0-0		.955	9	142	147	O64(48/1/17)/D			-0.3
1979	KC A	21	26	1	5	0	0	0	3	1-0	1	4	.192	.214	.192	13	-3	0-0		1.000	-0	60	237	O10(2/0/8)			-0.3
	Bos A	63	154	14	51	9	0	2	23	8-1	3	7	.331	.365	.429	110	3	2-2		.949	-4	81	043(3/30/11),D4				-0.4
	Year	84	180	15	56	9	0	2	26	9-1	3	11	.311	.343	.394	97	-1	2-2		.954	-4	80	102	O53(5/30/19),D4			-0.3
1981	Bos A	3	2	0	0	0	0	0	0	0-0	0	0	.000	.000	.000	-94	-0	0-0		—	-0	0	0	O2L			-0.7
	Tex A	30	64	2	10	1	0	0	7	5-0	1	1	.156	.225	.172	18	-7	0-1		.963	-3	73	0	O18(10/5/3)			-1.1
	Year	33	66	2	10	1	0	0	7	5-0	1	1	.152	.219	.167	14	-7	0-1		.963	-3	71	0	O20(12/5/3)			-1.2
1982	KC A	24	62	4	9	1	0	0	3	4-0	1	5	.145	.206	.161	3	-9	0-0		.957	1	125	95	O23(20/0/3)			-0.8
Total 7		452	1226	127	329	62	18	10	136	81-7	15	82	.268	.317	.373	92	-13	13-13		.971	-1	106	70	O373(241/39/105),D7		215	-3.3

PORTER, COLIN Colin Frederick B11.23.1975 Tucson AZ BL/TL/6-2/200* [HouN98 17/512] d5.30 Col Arizona
2003	Hou N	24	32	5	6	0	0	0	1	1-0	0	17	.188	.212	.188	5	-5	1-0		1.000	-0	100	0	O14(1/7/6)			-0.5
2004	StL N	23	35	3	11	1	0	1	2	0-0	0	13	.314	.314	.429	48	-1	0-0		1.000	-0	94	0	O14(6/2/8)			-0.1
Total 2		47	67	8	17	1	0	1	3	1-0	0	30	.254	.265	.313	48	-6	1-0		1.000	-1	97	0	O28(7/9/14)			-0.6

PORTER, DAN Daniel Edward B10.17.1931 Decatur IL BL/TL/6-0/164 d8.16 Mil 1952-53
| 1951 | Was A | 13 | 19 | 2 | 4 | 0 | 0 | 0 | 2 | | 0 | 4 | .211 | .286 | .211 | 36 | -2 | 0-0 | | 1.000 | -0 | 94 | 0 | O3R | | | -0.2 |

PORTER, DARRELL Darrell Ray B1.17.1952 Joplin MO D2.27.2002 Sugar Creek MO BL/TR/6-0/193(190-202) [MilA70 1/4] d9.2
1971	Mil A	22	70	4	15	2	0	2	9		0	20	.214	.300	.329	80	-2	2-2		.977	2	81	229	C22			
1972	Mil A	18	56	2	7	0	1	2	9	5-0	1	21	.125	.210	.196	22	-6	0-0		.976	3	167	78	C18			0.1
1973	Mil A	117	350	50	89	19	2	16	67	57-6	4	85	.254	.363	.457	132	16	5-2		.977	0	101	125	C90,D19			-0.2
1974	Mil A☆	131	432	59	104	15	4	12	56	50-7	5	88	.241	.326	.377	102	2	8-7		.978	1	114	103	C117,D9			2.1
1975	Mil A	130	409	66	95	12	5	18	60	89-10	5	77	.232	.371	.418	123	16	2-5		.979	-3	96	114	C124,D2			0.7
1976	Mil A	119	389	43	81	14	1	5	32	51-3	1	70	.208	.298	.288	74	-11	2-0		.975	-5	106	74	C111,D2			1.7
1977	†KC A	130	425	61	117	21	3	16	60	53-6	1	70	.275	.353	.452	117	11	1-0		.982	6	127	88	C125/D			-1.2
1978	†KC A	150	520	77	138	27	6	18	78	75-14	2	75	.265	.358	.444	121	16	0-5		.988	2	111	83	C145,D4			2.2
1979	KC A★	157	533	101	155	23	10	20	112	121-8	8	65	.291	.421	.484	142	39	3-4		.982	9	133	114	C141,D15			2.3
1980	†KC A	118	418	51	104	14	2	7	51	69-5	2	50	.249	.354	.342	91	-1	1-1		.978	1	125	106	C81,D34			5.0
1981	StL N	61	174	22	39	6	2	6	31	39-7	1	32	.224	.364	.408	115	5	1-2		.979	-3	108	107	C52		23	0.8
1982	†StL N	120	373	46	86	18	5	12	48	66-6	2	66	.231	.347	.402	107	5	1-1		.983	2	99	118	C111		93	1.2
1983	StL N	145	443	57	116	24	3	15	66	68-12	3	94	.262	.363	.431	119	14	1-3		.989	8	167	92	C133		21	2.7
1984	StL N	127	422	56	98	16	3	11	68	60-12	5	79	.232	.331	.363	98	0	5-3		.984	-0	105	102	C122			0.5
1985	†StL N	84	240	30	53	12	1	10	36	41-6	1	48	.221	.335	.412	109	4	6-1		.990	5	111	96	C82			1.3
1986	Tex A	68	155	21	41	6	0	12	29	22-0	1	5	.265	.360	.535	136	8	1-1		.994	-2	46	111	C25,D19		58	0.6
1987	Tex A	85	130	19	31	3	0	7	21	30-4	1	53	.238	.387	.423	115	4	0-0		1.000	-1	69	167	D35,C7,1b5		42	0.6
Total 17		1782	5539	765	1369	237	48	188	826	905-106	45	1025	.247	.354	.409	113	119	39-37		.982	30	116	102	C1506,D140,1b5		237	20.1

PORTER, IRV Irving Marble B5.17.1888 Lynn MA D2.20.1971 Lynn MA BB/TR/5-9/155 d8.20
| 1914 | Chi A | 1 | 4 | 1 | 1 | 0 | 0 | 0 | 0 | 0 | | 0 | .250 | .250 | .250 | 51 | 0 | 0 | | 1.000 | -0 | 88 | 0 | /OR | | | 0.0 |

YEAR	TM LG	G	AB	R	H	2B	3B	HR	RBI	BB-IB	HP	SO	AVG	OBP	SLG	AOPS	ABR	SB-CS	FA	FR	RNG	THR	GAMES AT POSITION	DL	BFW

PORTER, JAY J W "J W" B1.17.1933 Shawnee OK BR/TR/6-2/180* d7.30 Mil 1953

1952	StL A	33	104	12	26	4	1	0	7	10	0	10	.250	.308	.308	72	-4	4-0	.973	0	105	160	O29(3/26/0),3b2		-0.4
1955	Det A	24	55	6	13	2	0	0	3	8-0	0	15	.236	.333	.273	66	-2	0-0	1.000	-2	25	94	1b6,C4,O4L		-0.5
1956	Det A	14	21	0	2	0	0	0	3	0-0	1	8	.095	.091	.095	-49	-5	0-0	1.000	-1	0	0	C2,O2L		-0.5
1957	Det A	58	140	14	35	8	0	2	18	14-1	1	20	.250	.323	.350	82	-3	0-0	.953	0	107	69	O27(5/0/22),C12,1b3		-0.4
1958	Cle A	40	85	13	17	1	0	4	19	9-0	1	23	.200	.284	.353	76	-3	0-0	1.000	-2	89	119	C20,1b4/3		-0.4
1959	Was A	37	106	8	24	4	0	1	10	11-1	1	16	.226	.300	.292	65	-5	0-0	.993	-2	57	119	C34,1b2		-0.5
	StL N	23	33	5	7	3	0	1	2	1-0	1	4	.212	.257	.394	66	-2	0-0	1.000	0	96	119	C19/1		-0.1
Total	6	229	544	58	124	22	1	8	62	53-2	4	96	.228	.300	.316	68	-24	4-0	.990	-5	85	112	C91,O62(14/26/22),1b16,3b3		-2.8

PORTER, BO Marquis Donnell B7.5.1972 Newark NJ BR/TR/6-2/195* [ChiN93 40/1118] d5.9 Col Iowa

1999	Chi N	24	26	2	5	1	0	0	2	2-0	0	13	.192	.250	.231	23	-3	0-0	.941	-0	96	0	O21(16/5/3)		-0.4
2000	†Oak A	17	13	3	2	0	0	1	2	2-0	0	5	.154	.267	.385	63	-1	0-0	1.000	0	115	0	O16(1/2/14)		-0.1
2001	Tex A	48	87	18	20	4	2	1	6	9-0	0	34	.230	.296	.356	71	-4	3-2	.969	0	109	63	O40(18/10/12),D2		-0.4
Total	3	89	126	23	27	5	2	2	13-0	0	52	.214	.284	.333	60	-8	3-2	.968	0	107	42	O77(35/17/29),D2		-0.9

PORTER, MATTHEW Matthew Sheldon B Kansas City MO d6.27 M1

| 1884 | KC U | 3 | 12 | 1 | 1 | 1 | 0 | 0 | | | 0 | | .083 | .083 | .167 | -30 | -2 | | .750 | 1 | 272 | 731 | O3C,M | | -0.1 |

PORTER, DICK Richard Twilley "Wiggles","Twitches" B12.30.1901 Princess Anne MD D9.24.1974 Philadelphia PA BL/TR/5-10/170 d4.16

1929	Cle A	71	192	26	63	16	5	1	24	17	1	14	.328	.386	.479	117	5	3-5	.941	-2	86	146	O28(4/0/24),2b20		0.1
1930	Cle A	119	480	100	168	43	8	4	57	55	3	31	.350	.420	.498	127	22	3-3	.962	-6	85	110	O118R		0.6
1931	Cle A	114	414	82	129	24	3	1	38	56	1	36	.312	.395	.391	102	4	6-9	.970	-5	93	72	O109R/2		-0.8
1932	Cle A	146	621	106	191	42	8	4	60	64	1	43	.308	.373	.420	99	0	2-4	.982	-13	90	17	O124(7/0/119)		-2.2
1933	Cle A	132	499	73	133	19	6	0	41	51	0	42	.267	.335	.329	73	-19	4-4	.996	-2	96	78	O124(7/0/119)		-2.8
1934	Cle A	13	44	9	10	2	1	1	6	4	1	5	.227	.292	.386	73	-2	0-0	1.000	-1	84	0	O10R		-0.3
	Bos A	80	265	30	80	13	6	0	56	21	1	15	.302	.355	.396	87	-5	5-2	.940	-5	91	18	O65(1/0/64)		-1.3
	Year	93	309	39	90	15	7	1	62	25	1	20	.291	.346	.395	85	-7	5-2	.947	-6	91	18	O75(1/0/74)		-1.6
Total	6	675	2515	426	774	159	37	11	282	268	7	186	.308	.376	.414	99	5	23-27	.973	-34	91	64	O599(12/0/589),2b21		-6.7

PORTER, BOB Robert Lee B7.22.1959 Yuma AZ BL/TL/5-10/180* [AtlN77 3/56] d5.13

1981	Atl N	17	14	2	4	1	0	0	4	2-0	0	1	.286	.375	.357	108	0	0-0			0		/H		-0.6
1982	Atl N	24	27	1	3	0	0	0	0	1-0	0	9	.111	.143	.111	-28	-5	0-0	1.000	-1	62	0	O4L/1		-0.6
Total	2	41	41	3	7	1	0	0	4	3-0	0	10	.171	.227	.195	19	-5	0-0	1.000	-1	62	0	O4L/1		-0.6

POSADA, JORGE Jorge Rafael (Villeta) B8.17.1971 Santurce, PR BB/TR/6-2/205* [NYA90 24/646] d9.4 Col Calhoun (AL) CC

1995	†NY A	1	0	0	0	0	0	0	0	0-0	0	0	—	—	—		0	0-0	1.000	0	0	0	/C		0.0
1996	NY A	8	14	1	1	0	0	0	0	1-0	0	6	.071	.133	.071	-46	-3	0-0	1.000	0	0	0	C4,D3		-0.3
1997	†NY A	60	188	29	47	12	0	6	25	30-2	3	33	.250	.359	.410	102	2	1-2	.992	-6	92	57	C60		-0.1
1998	†NY A	111	358	56	96	23	0	17	63	47-7	6	92	.268	.350	.475	118	10	0-1	.994	5	131	110	C99/1D		1.9
1999	†NY A	112	379	50	93	19	2	12	57	52-3	5	91	.245	.341	.401	90	-5	1-0	.993	1	86	93	C109/1D		0.2
2000	†NY A★	151	505	92	145	35	1	28	86	107-10	8	151	.287	.417	.527	139	36	2-2	.993	4	111	101	C142,1b12,D4		4.4
2001	†NY A★	138	484	59	134	28	1	22	95	62-10	6	132	.277	.363	.475	118	14	2-6	.990	-2	94	99	C131,1b2,D6		1.8
2002	†NY A★	143	511	79	137	40	1	20	99	81-9	10	143	.268	.370	.468	122	19	1-0	.988	5	96	90	C138,D5		3.2
2003	†NY A★	142	481	83	135	24	0	30	101	93-6	10	110	.281	.405	.518	144	35	2-4	.994	11	101	82	C137,D2		5.1
2004	†NY A★	137	449	72	122	31	0	21	81	88-5	9	92	.272	.400	.481	129	24	1-3	.990	-3	96	82	C134		2.6
2005	†NY A★	142	474	67	124	23	0	19	71	66-5	2	94	.262	.352	.430	107	6	1-0	.996	-5	72	**139**	C133,D3		0.9
Total	11	1145	3843	588	1034	235	5	175	678	628-56	44	944	.269	.375	.469	120	138	11-18	.992	10	97	97	C1088,D30,1b16		19.7

POSADA, LEO Leopoldo Jesus (Hernandez) B4.15.1936 Havana, Cuba BR/TR/5-11/175* d9.21

1960	KC A	10	36	8	13	0	2	1	2	3-0	0	7	.361	.410	.556	158	3	1-0	1.000	-1	62	165	O9(4/0/8)		0.1
1961	KC A	116	344	37	87	10	4	7	53	36-1	4	84	.253	.321	.366	85	-8	0-0	.973	4	108	119	O102(69/20/29)		-0.9
1962	KC A	29	46	6	9	1	1	0	3	7-1	0	14	.196	.302	.261	51	-3	0-0	1.000	0	85	199	O11(10/0/1)		-0.3
Total	3	155	426	51	109	11	7	8	58	46-2	4	105	.256	.326	.371	87	-8	1-0	.976	4	102	129	O122(83/20/38)		-1.1

POSE, SCOTT Scott Vernon B2.11.1967 Davenport IA BL/TR/5-11/165(165-190) [CinN89 34/888] d4.5 Col Arkansas-Monticello

1993	Fla N	15	41	0	8	2	0	0	3	2-0	0	4	.195	.233	.244	26	-4	0-2	1.000	-2	66	0	O10(6/8/0)		-0.7
1997	†NY A	54	87	19	19	2	1	0	5	9-0	0	11	.218	.292	.264	47	-7	3-1	1.000	-1	88	126	O45(28/3/17),D5		-0.8
1999	KC A	86	137	27	39	3	0	0	12	21-1	0	25	.285	.377	.307	75	-4	6-2	.970	2	96	307	O25(18/1/6),D18		-0.2
2000	KC A	47	48	6	9	0	0	0	1	6-0	0	13	.188	.278	.188	20	-6	0-1	1.000	-1	55	0	O11(3/2/7),D4		-0.2
Total	4	202	313	52	75	7	1	0	21	38-1	0	50	.240	.321	.268	53	-21	9-6	.990	-2	84	143	O91(55/14/30),D27		-2.8

POST, LEW Lewis G. B4.12.1875 Woodland MI D8.21.1944 Chicago IL d9.21

| 1902 | Det A | 3 | 12 | 2 | 1 | 0 | 0 | 0 | 2 | 0-0 | 0 | | .083 | .083 | .083 | -53 | -2 | 0 | .800 | -1 | 0 | 0 | O3R | | -0.1 |

POST, SAM Samuel Gilbert B11.17.1896 Richmond VA D3.31.1971 Portsmouth VA BL/TL/6-1.5/170 d4.22

| 1922 | Bro N | 9 | 25 | 3 | 7 | 0 | 0 | 0 | 4 | 1 | 0 | 4 | .280 | .308 | .280 | 53 | -2 | 1-0 | .982 | -1 | 32 | 22 | 1b8 | | -0.3 |

POST, WALLY Walter Charles B7.9.1929 St.Wendelin OH D1.6.1982 St.Henry OH BR/TR/6-1/203(190-205) d9.18

1949	Cin N	6	8	1	2	0	0	0	1	0	0	3	.250	.250	.250	34	-1	0	.750	-0	91	0	O3(1/1/1)		-0.1
1951	Cin N	15	41	6	9	3	0	1	7	3	0	4	.220	.273	.366	69	-2	1-0	.963	0	102	126	O9C		-0.1
1952	Cin N	19	58	5	9	1	0	2	7	4	1	20	.155	.222	.276	37	-5	0-0	1.000	2	126	86	O16(15/1/0)		0.4
1953	Cin N	11	33	3	8	1	0	1	4	4	0	6	.242	.324	.364	78	-1	1-0	.960	1	98	249	O11(0/4/7)		-1.4
1954	Cin N	130	451	46	115	21	3	18	83	26	3	70	.255	.297	.435	86	-11	2-2	.957	2	102	123	O116(0/1/115)		0.5
1955	Cin N	**154**	601	116	186	33	3	40	109	60-5	2	102	.309	.372	.574	139	33	7-4	.978	-1	100	98	O154R		0.9
1956	Cin N	143	539	94	134	28	1	36	83	37-2	4	124	.249	.301	.506	105	2	6-0	.969	9	114	137	O124(1/0/123)		0.5
1957	Cin N	134	467	68	114	26	2	20	74	33-5	0	84	.244	.291	.437	87	-9	2-2	.952	1	100	100	O91(2/0/90)		0.5
1958	Phi N	110	379	51	107	21	3	12	62	32-5	3	74	.282	.340	.449	109	5	0-2	.951	1	107	134	O120(2/0/118)		0.5
1959	Phi N	132	468	62	119	17	6	22	94	36-4	3	101	.254	.310	.457	100	-2	0-0	.992	7	107	134	O22(18/0/5)		0.6
1960	Phi N	34	84	11	24	6	1	2	12	9-1	0	24	.286	.351	.452	119	2	0-0	1.000	2	130	68	O67(44/0/23)		1.3
	Cin N	77	249	36	70	14	0	17	38	28-3	0	51	.281	.350	.542	139	13	0-2	.985	2	98	136	O89(62/0/28)		0.2
	Year	111	333	47	94	20	1	19	50	37-4	0	75	.282	.350	.520	134	16	0-2	.989	3	105	122	O81(41/0/40)		1.6
1961	†Cin N	99	282	44	83	16	3	20	57	22-1	1	61	.294	.346	.585	140	15	0-1	.959	3	106	118	O90(88/0/2)		-0.4
1962	Cin N	109	285	43	75	10	3	17	62	32-2	2	67	.263	.341	.498	118	7	0-3	.935	-4	86	97	O90(88/0/2)		-0.8
1963	Cin N	5	7	1	0	0	0	0	0	0-0	1	1	.000	.125	.000	-59	-1	0-0	1.000	0	201	0	/OL		-0.0
	Min A	21	47	6	9	0	0	2	6	2-0	0	17	.191	.224	.362	60	-3	0-0	1.000	-1	86	0	O12(2/0/10)		-0.1
1964	Cle A	5	8	1	0	0	0	0	0	3-0	0	4	.000	.273	.000	-16	-1	0-0	.667	-0	75	0	O2R		-0.0
Total	15	1204	4007	594	1064	194	28	210	699	331-28	20	813	.266	.323	.485	109	41	19-13	.970	28	104	121	O1055(215/16/826)		2.0

POTTER, MIKE Michael Gary B5.16.1951 Montebello CA BR/TR/6-1/195* [StLN71*A6/116] d9.6 Col Mt. San Antonio (CA) JC

1976	StL N	9	16	0	0	0	0	0	0	1-0	0	6	.000	.059	.000	-81	-4	0-0	1.000	1	150	0	O4L		-0.0
1977	StL N	5	7	0	0	0	0	0	0	0-0	0	2	.000	.000	.000	-99	-2	0-0	—	-0	0	0	/OR		-0.0
Total	2	14	23	0	0	0	0	0	0	1-0	0	8	.000	.042	.000	-87	-6	0-0	1.000	0	130	0	O5(4/0/1)		-0.0

POTTS, JOHN John Frederick "Fred" B2.6.1887 Tipp City OH D9.5.1962 Cleveland OH BL/TR/5-7/165 d4.18 Col Case Western Reserve

| 1914 | KC F | 41 | 102 | 14 | 27 | 4 | 1 | 0 | 9 | 25 | 1 | 13 | .265 | .414 | .333 | 110 | 2 | 7 | .933 | -3 | 91 | 45 | O31(1/5/25) | | -0.0 |

POTTS, DAN Vivian B1.1869 Bristol PA D8.17.1934 Bristol PA d10.3

| 1892 | Was N | 1 | 4 | 0 | 1 | 0 | 0 | 0 | 0 | 1 | 0 | 1 | .250 | .250 | .250 | 53 | 0 | 0 | 1.000 | 0 | 59 | 287 | /C | | 0.0 |

POULSEN, KEN Ken Sterling B8.4.1947 Van Nuys CA BL/TR/6-1/190 [BosA65 3/45] d7.3

| 1967 | Bos A | 5 | 5 | 0 | 1 | 1 | 0 | 0 | 0 | 0-0 | 0 | 2 | .200 | .200 | .400 | 68 | 0 | 0-0 | .667 | -0 | 175 | 0 | 3b2/S | | 0.0 |

POWELL, ALONZO Alonzo Sidney B12.12.1964 San Francisco CA BR/TR/6-2/190* d4.6

1987	Mon N	14	41	3	8	3	0	0	3	5-0	0	17	.195	.283	.268	45	-3	0-0	1.000	-1	70	0	O11(10/0/1)		-0.6
1991	Sea A	57	111	16	24	6	1	3	12	11-0	1	24	.216	.288	.369	82	-3	0-2	.960	-4	82	0	O40(24/6/15),1b7,D7		-0.6
Total	2	71	152	19	32	9	1	3	16	16-0	1	41	.211	.287	.342	71	-6	0-2	.968	-5	79	0	O51(34/6/16),D7,1b7		-1.2

YEAR	TM LG	G	AB	R	H	2B	3B	HR	RBI	BB-IB	HP	SO	AVG	OBP	SLG	AOPS	ABR	SB-CS	FA	FR	RNG	THR	GAMES AT POSITION	DL	BFW

POWELL, JAKE Alvin Jacob B7.15.1908 Silver Spring MD D11.4.1948 Washington DC BR/TR/5-11.5/180 d8.3

YEAR	TM LG	G	AB	R	H	2B	3B	HR	RBI	BB-IB	HP	SO	AVG	OBP	SLG	AOPS	ABR	SB-CS	FA	FR	RNG	THR	GAMES AT POSITION	DL	BFW
1930	Was A	3	4	1	0	0	0	0	0	0	0	1	.000	.000	.000	-99	-1	0-0	1.000	0	113	0	O2(1/0/1)		-0.1
1934	Was A	9	35	6	10	2	0	0	1	4	0	2	.286	.359	.343	85	-1	1-1	.955	1	81	434	O9C		0.0
1935	Was A	139	551	88	172	26	10	6	98	37	4	37	.312	.360	.428	107	4	15-7	.976	-2	97	94	O136(0/136/1),2b2		-0.1
1936	Was A	53	210	40	62	11	5	1	30	18	2	21	.295	.357	.410	94	-3	10-4	.951	-5	89	48	O53C		-0.7
	†NY A	87	328	62	99	13	3	7	48	33	2	30	.302	.366	.424	98	-2	16-7	.976	1	104	87	O84(42/42/0)		-0.3
	Year	140	538	102	161	24	8	8	78	51	2	51	.299	.362	.418	96	-4	26-11	.967	-4	99	73	O137(42/95/0)		-1.0
1937	†NY A	97	365	54	96	22	3	3	45	25	2	36	.263	.314	.364	70	-18	7-5	.981	-1	99	67	O94L		-2.3
1938	†NY A	45	164	27	42	12	1	2	20	15	2	20	.256	.326	.378	76	-6	3-1	.978	-2	97	31	O43(37/1/6)		-1.0
1939	NY A	31	86	12	21	4	1	1	9	3	0	8	.244	.270	.349	58	-6	1-2	.983	1	112	64	O23(19/2/3)		-0.6
1940	NY A	12	27	3	5	0	0	0	2	1	0	4	.185	.214	.185	5	-4	0-0	1.000	1	109	219	O7(3/2/2)		-0.3
1943	Was A	37	132	14	35	10	2	0	20	5	1	13	.265	.297	.371	99	-1	3-5	.978	1	105	150	O33(25/8/0)		-0.2
1944	Was A	96	367	29	88	9	1	1	37	16	0	26	.240	.272	.278	60	-21	7-2	.980	0	105	72	O90(58/0/32)/3		-2.7
1945	Was A	31	98	4	19	2	0	0	3	8	0	8	.194	.255	.214	40	-8	1-1	.950	-1	108	44	O27(21/0/6)		-1.1
	Phi N	48	173	13	40	5	1	0	14	8	0	13	.231	.265	.249	57	-12	1-1	.986	-0	87	152	O44(4/5/35)		-1.4
Total 11		688	2540	353	689	116	26	22	327	173	11	219	.271	.320	.363	81	-79	65-35	.975	-5	100	87	O645(304/258/86),2b2/3		-10.8

POWELL, ABNER Charles Abner "Ab" B12.15.1860 Shenandoah PA D8.7.1953 New Orleans LA BL/TR/5-7/160 d8.4 ▲

YEAR	TM LG	G	AB	R	H	2B	3B	HR	RBI	BB-IB	HP	SO	AVG	OBP	SLG	AOPS	ABR	SB-CS	FA	FR	RNG	THR	GAMES AT POSITION	DL	BFW
1884	Was U	48	191	36	54	10	5	0		3			.283	.294	.387	109	-4		.875	-0	51	0	O30(0/12/18),P18,3b2/S2		-0.3
1886	Bal AA	11	39	4	7	2	1	0	7	1	0		.179	.200	.282	52	-2	4	.917	1	175	628	P7,O4(3/0/1)		-0.1
	Cin AA	19	74	13	17	1	1	0	8	4	0		.230	.269	.270	67	-3	0	.760	-0	144	0	O13(5/6/2),S6,P4		-0.3
	Year	30	113	17	24	3	2	0	15	5	0		.212	.246	.274	62	-5	4	.735	-2	106	0	O17(8/6/3),P11,S6		-0.3
Total 2		78	304	53	78	13	7	0	15	8	0		.257	.276	.345	91	-9	4	.817	-2	74	0	O47(8/18/21),P29,S7,3b2/2		-0.7

POWELL, HOSKEN Hosken B5.14.1955 Selma AL BL/TL/6-1/185* [MinA75 S1/3] d4.5 Col Chipola (FL) JC

YEAR	TM LG	G	AB	R	H	2B	3B	HR	RBI	BB-IB	HP	SO	AVG	OBP	SLG	AOPS	ABR	SB-CS	FA	FR	RNG	THR	GAMES AT POSITION	DL	BFW
1978	Min A	121	381	55	94	20	2	3	31	45-1		31	.247	.323	.333	84	-7	11-5	.983	0	99	113	O117R		-1.2
1979	Min A	104	338	49	99	17	3	2	36	33-1		25	.293	.360	.379	96	-1	5-1	.977	-2	95	95	O93(8/0/85),D5		-0.6
1980	Min A	137	485	58	127	17	5	6	35	32-2		46	.262	.312	.355	77	-16	14-3	.968	3	104	115	O129R	33	-1.8
1981	Min A	80	264	30	63	11	3	2	25	17-0	1	31	.239	.286	.326	72	-10	7-4	.970	2	102	143	O64(12/0/52),D8		-1.2
1982	Tor A	112	265	43	73	13	4	3	26	12-2		23	.275	.304	.389	82	-7	4-4	.974	-3	99	51	O75(8/0/68),D19		-1.4
1983	Tor A	40	83	6	14	0	0	1	7	5-0		8	.169	.213	.205	15	-10	2-0	.981	1	127	0	O33(5/0/29)/1D		-1.0
Total 6		594	1816	241	470	78	17	17	160	144-6	7	164	.259	.314	.349	79	-51	43-17	.975	1	101	101	O511(33/0/480),D33/1	33	-7.2

POWELL, JIM James Edwin B8.30.1859 Richmond VA D11.20.1929 Butte MT 5-10/170 d8.5

YEAR	TM LG	G	AB	R	H	2B	3B	HR	RBI	BB-IB	HP	SO	AVG	OBP	SLG	AOPS	ABR	SB-CS	FA	FR	RNG	THR	GAMES AT POSITION	DL	BFW
1884	Ric AA	41	151	23	37	8	4	0	7	4	4		.245	.296	.351	112	2		.943	1	136	76	1b41		0.0
1885	Phi AA	19	75	5	12	0	3	0	5	1	2		.160	.192	.240	34	-6		.973	-0	64	63	1b19		-0.7
Total 2		60	226	28	49	8	7	0	5	8	6		.217	.262	.314	84	-4		.952	1	113	72	1b60		-0.7

POWELL, BOOG John Wesley B8.17.1941 Lakeland FL BL/TR/6-4/240(230-250) d9.26

YEAR	TM LG	G	AB	R	H	2B	3B	HR	RBI	BB-IB	HP	SO	AVG	OBP	SLG	AOPS	ABR	SB-CS	FA	FR	RNG	THR	GAMES AT POSITION	DL	BFW
1961	Bal A	4	13	0	1	0	0	0	0	1-0		2	.077	.077	.077	-61	-3	0-0	1.000	-1	53	0	O3L		-0.4
1962	Bal A	124	400	44	97	13	2	15	53	38-5	2	79	.243	.311	.398	95	-4	1-1	.969	-6	91	17	O112L/1		-1.6
1963	Bal A	140	491	67	130	22	2	25	82	49-8	0	87	.265	.328	.470	126	16	1-2	.969	-4	87	77	O121(121/0/1),1b23		0.5
1964	Bal A	134	424	74	123	17	0	39	99	76-6	2	91	.290	.399	.606	176	45	0-0	.974	6	93	235	O124L,1b5		4.6
1965	Bal A	144	472	54	117	20	2	17	72	71-13	4	93	.248	.347	.407	112	10	1-1	.992	3	127	106	1b78,O71L		0.5
1966	†Bal A	140	491	78	141	18	0	34	109	67-9	1	125	.287	.372	.532	159	39	0-4	.989	-8	77	97	1b136		2.3
1967	Bal A	125	415	53	97	14	1	13	55	55-5	2	94	.234	.324	.366	105	4	1-3	.986	-6	83	104	O114		-1.1
1968	†Bal A★	154	550	60	137	21	1	22	85	73-12	3	97	.249	.338	.411	127	19	7-1	.990	-5	83	100	1b149		0.7
1969	†Bal A★	152	533	83	162	25	0	37	121	72-10	1	76	.304	.383	.559	160	43	1-1	.995	-1	97	107	1b144		3.2
1970	†Bal A★	154	526	82	156	28	0	35	114	104-18	5	80	.297	.412	.549	162	49	1-1	.992	-1	98	100	1b145		3.7
1971	†Bal A★	128	418	59	107	19	0	22	92	82-11	4	64	.256	.379	.459	137	24	1-0	.995	-2	94	110	1b124		1.4
1972	Bal A	140	465	53	117	20	1	21	81	65-14	2	92	.252	.346	.434	127	17	4-0	.988	-2	97	120	1b133		0.6
1973	†Bal A	114	370	52	98	13	1	11	54	85-10	0	64	.265	.398	.395	124	17	0-2	.989	4	121	118	1b111		1.2
1974	†Bal A	110	344	37	91	13	1	12	45	52-10	0	58	.265	.358	.413	125	13	0-1	.996	4	121	129	1b102/D		0.9
1975	Cle A	134	435	64	129	18	0	27	86	59-5	1	72	.297	.377	.524	153	31	1-3	.997	-2	89	96	1b121,D5		1.9
1976	Cle A	95	293	29	63	9	0	9	33	41-3	0	43	.215	.305	.338	91	-3	1-1	.987	1	102	111	1b89		-1.0
1977	LA N	50	41	0	10	0	0	0	5	12-1	0	9	.244	.415	.244	81	0	0-0	.938	-1	0	84	1b4		-0.1
Total 17		2042	6681	889	1776	270	11	339	1187	1001-140	29	1226	.266	.361	.462	134	317	20-21	.991	-20	97	107	1b1479,O431(431/0/1),D6	41	17.3

POWELL, DANTE Le Jon Dante B8.25.1973 Long Beach CA BR/TR/6-2/185* [SFN94 1/22] d4.15 Col Cal St.-Fullerton

YEAR	TM LG	G	AB	R	H	2B	3B	HR	RBI	BB-IB	HP	SO	AVG	OBP	SLG	AOPS	ABR	SB-CS	FA	FR	RNG	THR	GAMES AT POSITION	DL	BFW
1997	†SF N	27	39	8	12	1	0	1	3	4-0		11	.308	.372	.410	107	0	1-1	1.000	-0	107	0	O22(0/20/2)		0.0
1998	SF N	8	4	2	2	0	0	0	1	3-0		0	.500	.714	1.250	425	2	0-0	1.000	1	49	0	O8C		0.0
1999	Ari N	22	25	4	4	3	0	0	1	2-0		6	.160	.222	.280	26	-3	2-1	.929	-1	80	0	O15(0/8/7)		-0.4
2001	SF N	13	6	5	2	0	0	0	0	0-0		5	.333	.333	.333	78	0	0-0	1.000	1	172	0	O9(5/1/3)		0.0
Total 4		70	74	19	20	4	0	2	5	9-0		17	.270	.349	.405	96	-1	3-2	.980	-1	100	0	O54(5/37/12)		-0.2

POWELL, MARTIN Martin J. B3.25.1856 Fitchburg MA D2.5.1888 Fitchburg MA BL/TL/6-0/170 d6.18

YEAR	TM LG	G	AB	R	H	2B	3B	HR	RBI	BB-IB	HP	SO	AVG	OBP	SLG	AOPS	ABR	SB-CS	FA	FR	RNG	THR	GAMES AT POSITION	DL	BFW
1881	Det N	55	219	47	74	9	4	1	38	15		9	.338	.380	.429	148	12		.947	-3	85	150	1b55/C		0.6
1882	Det N	80	338	44	81	13	0	0	29	19		27	.240	.280	.278	80	-7		.940	-5	62	64	1b80		-1.7
1883	Det N	101	421	76	115	17	5	1	48	28		23	.273	.318	.344	106	5		.950	-3	97	115	1b101		-0.6
1884	Cin U	43	185	46	59	4	2	1		13			.319	.364	.378	116	-2		.940	-2	81	136	1b43		-0.7
Total 4		279	1163	213	329	43	11	3	115	75		59	.283	.326	.347	109	8		.945	-12	82	110	1b279/C		-2.4

POWELL, PAUL Paul Ray B3.19.1948 San Angelo TX BR/TR/5-11/185* [MinA69 1/7] d4.7 Col Arizona St.

YEAR	TM LG	G	AB	R	H	2B	3B	HR	RBI	BB-IB	HP	SO	AVG	OBP	SLG	AOPS	ABR	SB-CS	FA	FR	RNG	THR	GAMES AT POSITION	DL	BFW
1971	Min A	20	31	7	5	0	0	1	2	3-0		12	.161	.235	.258	38	-3	0-0	1.000	0	117	0	O15C		-0.3
1973	LA N	2	1	0	0	0	0	0	0	0-0		0	1.000	.000	.000	-99	0	0-0	—	-0	0	0	/OL		0.0
1975	LA N	8	10	2	2	1	0	0	0	1-0		2	.200	.273	.300	61	-1	0-0	.955	0	39	395	C7/OL		0.0
Total 3		30	42	9	7	1	0	1	2	4-0		15	.167	.239	.262	41	-4	0-0	1.000	0	107	0	O17(2/15/0),C7		-0.3

POWELL, RAY Raymond Reath "Rabbit" B11.20.1888 Siloam Springs AR D10.16.1962 Chillicothe MO BL/TR/5-9/160 d4.16 Mil 1918

YEAR	TM LG	G	AB	R	H	2B	3B	HR	RBI	BB-IB	HP	SO	AVG	OBP	SLG	AOPS	ABR	SB-CS	FA	FR	RNG	THR	GAMES AT POSITION	DL	BFW
1913	Det A	2	0	0	0	0	0	0	0	0			—	—	—		0	0		—	0	0	0	/OC		0.0
1917	Bos N	88	357	42	97	10	4	4	30	24	0	54	.272	.318	.356	113	4	12	.976	3	104	112	O88C		0.1
1918	Bos N	53	188	31	40	7	5	0	20	29	1	30	.213	.321	.303	95	0	2	.949	-1	94	118	O53C		-0.5
1919	Bos N	123	470	51	111	12	12	2	33	41	4	79	.236	.303	.326	93	-5	16	.951	1	98	118	O122(0/1/120)		-1.4
1920	Bos N	147	609	69	137	12	12	6	29	44	4	83	.225	.282	.314	74	-22	10-18	.956	3	100	118	O147(0/147/1)		-3.6
1921	Bos N	149	624	114	191	25	18	12	74	58	4	89	.306	.369	.462	122	22	6-17	.954	-9	93	91	O149C		0.2
1922	Bos N	142	550	82	163	22	11	6	37	59	4	66	.296	.369	.409	105	3	3-12	.980	6	106	110	O136C		0.1
1923	Bos N	97	338	57	102	20	4	4	38	45	1	36	.302	.385	.420	117	10	1-6	.941	-5	97	74	O84(1/83/0)		0.1
1924	Bos N	74	188	21	49	9	1	1	15	21	1	28	.261	.335	.335	85	-3	1-3	.947	4	104	191	O46(7/36/3)		-0.2
Total 9		875	3324	467	890	117	67	35	276	321	19	461	.268	.336	.375	102	11	51-56	.959	0	98	110	O826(8/694/124)		-5.3

POWELL, LEROY Robert Leroy B10.17.1933 Flint MI BR/TR/6-1/190* d9.16 Mil 1956 Col Michigan St.

YEAR	TM LG	G	AB	R	H	2B	3B	HR	RBI	BB-IB	HP	SO	AVG	OBP	SLG	AOPS	ABR	SB-CS	FA	FR	RNG	THR	GAMES AT POSITION	DL	BFW
1955	Chi A	1	0	0	0	0	0	0	0	0-0			—	—	—		0	0-0	—	0			/R		0.0
1957	Chi A	1	0	1	0	0	0	0	0	0-0			—	—	—		0	0-0	—	0			/R	38	0.0
Total 2		2	0	1	0	0	0	0	0	0-0			—	—	—		0	0-0	—	0					0.0

POWER, TOM Thomas E. B San Francisco CA D2.25.1898 San Francisco CA 5-11/164 d8.27

YEAR	TM LG	G	AB	R	H	2B	3B	HR	RBI	BB-IB	HP	SO	AVG	OBP	SLG	AOPS	ABR	SB-CS	FA	FR	RNG	THR	GAMES AT POSITION	DL	BFW
1890	Bal AA	38	125	11	26	3	1	0	8				.208	.293	.248	57	-7	6	.960	-3	68	60	1b26,2b12		-1.0

POWER, VIC Victor Pellot (b Victor Felipe Pellot (Pove)) B11.1.1927 Arecibo, PR D11.29.2005 Bayamon PR BR/TR/5-11/195(170-195) d4.13 OF(41/56/18)

YEAR	TM LG	G	AB	R	H	2B	3B	HR	RBI	BB-IB	HP	SO	AVG	OBP	SLG	AOPS	ABR	SB-CS	FA	FR	RNG	THR	GAMES AT POSITION	DL	BFW
1954	Phi A	127	462	36	118	17	5	8	38	19	2	19	.255	.287	.366	78	-17	2-1	.985	8	107	141	O101(33/56/12),1b21/S3		-1.5
1955	KC A★	147	596	91	190	34	10	19	76	35-6		27	.319	.354	.505	128	20	0-2	.993	14	140	97	1b144		2.5
1956	KC A★	127	530	77	164	21	5	14	63	24-2		15	.309	.340	.447	106	2	0-2	.993	8	130	101	1b76,2b47,O7L		0.8
1957	KC A	129	467	48	121	14	1	14	42	19-3	3	21	.259	.291	.385	82	-13	3-2	.998	11	148	96	1b113,O6R,2b4		-0.9
1958	KC A	52	205	35	62	13	4	4	27	7-0	1	3	.302	.325	.463	112	1	1-1	.992	6	147	120	1b50/2		0.5
	Cle A	93	385	63	122	24	6	12	53	13-2	1	11	.317	.336	.504	133	15	1-3	.977	5	139	139	3b42,1b41,2b27,S2/OL		2.0
	Year	145	590	98	184	37	10	16	80	20-2	2	14	.312	.332	.490	125	17	3-2	.992	11	149	120	1b91,3b42,2b28,S2/OL		2.5
1959	Cle A★	147	595	102	172	31	6	10	60	40-2	2	22	.289	.334	.412	108	5	9-13	.995	10	147	98	1b121,2b21,3b7		0.7

YEAR	TM LG	G	AB	R	H	2B	3B	HR	RBI	BB-IB	HP	SO	AVG	OBP	SLG	AOPS	ABR	SB-CS	FA	FR	RNG	THR	GAMES AT POSITION	DL	BFW
1960	Cle A★	147	580	69	167	26	3	10	84	24-5	0	20	.288	.313	.395	94	-7	9-5	.996	21	146	106	1b147,S5,3b4		0.6
1961	Cle A	147	563	64	151	34	4	5	63	38-5	1	16	.268	.309	.369	85	-13	4-3	.994	17	133	83	1b141,2b7		-0.5
1962	Min A	144	611	80	177	28	2	16	63	22-0	3	35	.290	.316	.421	93	-7	7-1	.993	17	143	122	1b142,2b2		0.2
1963	Min A	138	541	65	146	28	2	10	52	22-0	0	24	.270	.297	.384	88	-10	3-1	.992	5	110	112	1b124,2b18,3b5		-1.0
1964	Min A	19	45	6	10	2	0	0	1	1-0	0	3	.222	.240	.267	40	-4	0-0	.990	2	162	113	1b12/2		-0.3
	LA A	68	221	17	55	6	0	3	13	8-0	1	14	.249	.275	.317	72	-9	1-1	1.000	3	133	84	1b48,3b28,2b5		-0.9
	Year	87	266	23	65	8	0	3	14	9-0	1	17	.244	.269	.308	66	-13	1-1	.998	5	139	89	1b60,3b28,2b6		-1.2
	Phi N	18	48	1	10	4	0	0	3	2-0	0	3	.208	.240	.292	50	-3	0-0	.993	1	125		1b17		-0.3
1965	Cal A	124	197	11	51	7	1	1	20	5-1	1	13	.259	.281	.320	72	-8	2-2	.996	4	135	92	1b107,2b6,3b2		-0.8
Total	12	1627	6046	765	1716	290	49	126	658	279-26	15	247	.284	.315	.411	97	-46	45-35	.994	130	138	102	1b1304,2b139,O115C,3b89,S8		1.1

POWERS, MIKE Ellis Foree B3.2.1906 Toddspoint KY D12.2.1983 Louisville KY BL/TL/6-1/185 d8.19

YEAR	TM LG	G	AB	R	H	2B	3B	HR	RBI	BB-IB	HP	SO	AVG	OBP	SLG	AOPS	ABR	SB-CS	FA	FR	RNG	THR	GAMES AT POSITION	DL	BFW
1932	Cle A	14	33	4	6	4	0	0	5	2-0	0	2	.182	.229	.303	34	-3	0-0	.917	-1	81	0	O8R		-0.4
1933	Cle A	24	47	6	13	2	1	0	2	6	0	6	.277	.358	.362	87	-1	2-1	.952	-1	102	1	O11(4/0/8)		-0.2
Total	2	38	80	10	19	6	1	0	7	8	0	8	.237	.307	.338	65	-4	2-1	.939	-2	93	1	O19(4/0/16)		-0.6

POWERS, JOHN John Calvin B7.8.1929 Birmingham AL D9.25.2001 Birmingham AL BL/TR/6-0/190* d9.24

YEAR	TM LG	G	AB	R	H	2B	3B	HR	RBI	BB-IB	HP	SO	AVG	OBP	SLG	AOPS	ABR	SB-CS	FA	FR	RNG	THR	GAMES AT POSITION	DL	BFW
1955	Pit N	2	4	0	1	0	0	0	0	0	0	0	.250	.250	.250	34	0	0-0	1.000	0	155	0	O2R		0.0
1956	Pit N	11	21	0	1	0	0	0	0	1-0	0	4	.048	.091	.048	-63	-5	0-0	1.000	0	115	0	O5(4/0/1)		-0.5
1957	Pit N	20	35	7	10	3	0	2	8	5-0	3	9	.286	.409	.543	161	4	0-0	1.000	1	96	185	O9(4/0/4)		0.4
1958	Pit N	57	82	6	15	1	0	2	2	8-0	0	19	.183	.256	.268	40	-7	0-0	1.000	1	116	98	O14(3/0/12)		-0.7
1959	Cin N	43	43	8	11	2	1	2	4	3-0	1	13	.256	.319	.488	108	0	0-0	1.000	-0	103	0	O5(4/0/1)		0.0
1960	Bal A	10	18	3	2	0	0	0	0	3-0	0	1	.111	.238	.111	-2	-3	0-0	.833	-1	88	0	O4R		-0.3
	Cle A	8	12	2	2	1	1	0	0	2-0	0	2	.167	.286	.417	90	0	0-0	1.000	1	180	0	O5(3/0/3)		0.0
	Year	18	30	5	4	1	1	0	0	5-0	0	3	.133	.257	.233	34	-3	0-0	.929	-1	126	0	O9(3/0/7)		-0.3
Total	6	151	215	26	42	7	2	6	14	22-0	4	48	.195	.281	.330	64	-11	0-0	.986	1	114	79	O44(18/0/27)		-1.1

POWERS, LES Leslie Edwin B11.5.1909 Seattle WA D11.13.1978 Santa Monica CA BL/TL/6-0/175 d9.17 Col Loyola Marymount

YEAR	TM LG	G	AB	R	H	2B	3B	HR	RBI	BB-IB	HP	SO	AVG	OBP	SLG	AOPS	ABR	SB-CS	FA	FR	RNG	THR	GAMES AT POSITION	DL	BFW
1938	NY N	2	3	0	0	0	0	0	0	0	0	1	.000	.000	.000	-99	-1	0	—	0			/H		-0.1
1939	Phi N	19	52	7	18	1	1	0	2	4	0	6	.346	.393	.404	118	1	0	.983	-2	48	82	1b13		-0.2
Total	2	21	55	7	18	1	1	0	2	4	0	7	.327	.373	.382	106	0	0	.983	-2	48	82	1b13		-0.3

POWERS, DOC Michael Riley B9.22.1870 Pittsfield MA D4.26.1909 Philadelphia PA BR/TR d6.12 Col Notre Dame

YEAR	TM LG	G	AB	R	H	2B	3B	HR	RBI	BB-IB	HP	SO	AVG	OBP	SLG	AOPS	ABR	SB-CS	FA	FR	RNG	THR	GAMES AT POSITION	DL	BFW
1898	Lou N	34	99	13	27	4	3	1	19	5	0		.273	.308	.404	105	0	1	.962	-3	81	93	C22,1b6/OL		-0.1
1899	Lou N	49	169	15	35	8	2	0	22	6	1		.207	.239	.278	42	-14	1	.942	-2	115	59	C38,1b7		-1.2
	Was N	14	38	3	10	2	0	0	3	1	0		.263	.282	.316	65	-2	0	.942	-2	76	97	C12/1		-0.3
	Year	63	207	18	45	10	2	0	25	7	1		.217	.247	.285	46	-16	1	.942	-4	107	67	C50,1b8		-1.5
1901	Phi A	116	431	53	108	26	5	1	47	18	7		.251	.292	.341	72	-17	10	.952	-6	98	98	C111,1b3		-1.1
1902	Phi A	71	246	35	65	7	1	2	39	14	3		.264	.312	.325	74	-9	3	.950	7	95	132	C68,1b3		0.3
1903	Phi A	75	247	19	56	11	0	0	23	5	0		.227	.242	.279	54	-14	1	.982	1	97	111	C66,1b7		-0.7
1904	Phi A	57	184	11	35	3	0	0	11	6	1		.190	.220	.207	33	-14	3	.965	-3	104	89	C56/OR		-1.3
1905	†Phi A	21	60	6	10	0	0	0	5	0	1		.167	.180	.167	10	-6	2	.928	1	126	126	C21		-0.4
	NY A	11	33	3	6	1	0	0	2	1	0		.182	.206	.212	29	-3	0	.975	-0	110	68	1b7,C4		-0.3
	†Phi A	19	61	2	8	0	0	0	5	3	0		.131	.172	.131	-3	-7	2	.991	-2	126	126	C19		-0.9
	Year	51	154	11	24	1	0	0	12	4	1		.156	.182	.162	9	-16	4	.957	-2	114	111	C44,1b7		-1.6
1906	Phi A	58	185	5	29	1	0	0	7	1	2		.157	.170	.162	4	-21	2	.974	7	99	112	C57/1		-1.0
1907	Phi A	59	159	9	29	3	0	0	9	7	0		.182	.217	.201	33	-12	1	.983	9	99	116	C59		0.2
1908	Phi A	62	172	8	31	6	1	0	7	5	3		.180	.217	.227	41	-11	1	.967	0	75	106	C60,1b2		-0.7
1909	Phi A	1	4	1	1	0	0	0	0	0	0		.250	.250	.250	57	0	0	1.000	0	153	79	/C		0.0
Total	11	647	2088	183	450	72	13	4	199	72	18		.216	.248	.268	51	-130	27	.965	7	97	104	C594,1b37,O2(1/0/1)		-7.5

POWERS, PHIL Phillip J. "Grandmother" B7.26.1854 New York NY D12.22.1914 New York NY BR/TR/5-7/166 d8.31 U8

YEAR	TM LG	G	AB	R	H	2B	3B	HR	RBI	BB-IB	HP	SO	AVG	OBP	SLG	AOPS	ABR	SB-CS	FA	FR	RNG	THR	GAMES AT POSITION	DL	BFW
1878	Chi N	8	31	2	5	1	0	2	1			5	.161	.188	.258	42	-2		.930	3			C8		0.1
1880	Bos N	37	126	11	18	5	0	0	10	5		15	.143	.176	.183	22	-10		.851	-2			C37,O2(1/1/1)		-1.1
1881	Cle N	5	15	1	1	0	0	0	0	1		2	.067	.125	.067	-40	-2		.955	-0			C4/3		-0.2
1882	Cin AA	16	60	4	13	1	1	0	5	3			.217	.254	.267	72	-2		.921	3			C10,1b5/OR		-0.1
1883	Cin AA	30	114	16	28	1	4	0	8	3			.246	.265	.325	84	-3		.893	1			C17,O13(0/2/11)		-0.5
1884	Cin AA	35	133	10	18	1	0	0	8	5	0		.135	.167	.143	2	-14		.891	6			C31,O3R,1b2		-0.3
1885	Cin AA	15	60	6	16	1	0	0	7	0	0		.267	.267	.300	77	-2		.833	-3			C15		-0.6
	Bal AA	9	34	6	4	1	0	0	1	1	0		.118	.143	.147	-8	-4		.844	-3			C8/OR		-0.9
	Year	24	94	12	20	2	0	0	9	1	0		.213	.221	.245	47	-6		.837	-6			C23/OR		-0.9
Total	7	155	573	56	103	12	6	0	42	19	0	22	.180	.206	.222	39	-39		.877	4			C130,O20(1/3/17),1b7/3		-2.6

POWIS, CARL Carl Edgar "Jug" B1.11.1928 Philadelphia PA D5.10.1999 Houston TX BR/TR/6-0/185 d4.15 Col Murray St.

YEAR	TM LG	G	AB	R	H	2B	3B	HR	RBI	BB-IB	HP	SO	AVG	OBP	SLG	AOPS	ABR	SB-CS	FA	FR	RNG	THR	GAMES AT POSITION	DL	BFW
1957	Bal A	15	41	4	8	3	1	0	2	4-1	0	9	.195	.314	.317	82	-1	2-0	.909	-1	89	112	O13R		-0.2

POZO, ARQUIMEDEZ Arquimedez (Ortiz) B8.24.1973 Santo Domingo, D.R. BR/TR/5-10/160* d9.12

YEAR	TM LG	G	AB	R	H	2B	3B	HR	RBI	BB-IB	HP	SO	AVG	OBP	SLG	AOPS	ABR	SB-CS	FA	FR	RNG	THR	GAMES AT POSITION	DL	BFW
1995	Sea A	1	1	0	0	0	0	0	0	0	0	0	.000	.000	.000	-99	0	0-0	1.000	0	148	0	/2		0.0
1996	Bos A	21	58	4	10	3	1	2	11	2-0	1	10	.172	.210	.310	30	-7	1-0	.930	0	95	51	2b10,3b10		-0.5
1997	Bos A	4	15	0	4	1	0	0	3	0-0	0	5	.267	.250	.333	54	-1	0-0	.947	3	191	136	3b4		0.2
Total	3	26	74	4	14	4	1	1	14	2-0	1	15	.189	.215	.311	33	-8	1-0	.952	3	139	84	3b14,2b11		-0.3

PRAMESA, JOHNNY John Steven B8.28.1925 Barton OH D9.9.1996 Los Angeles CA BR/TR/6-2/210(210-225) d4.24

YEAR	TM LG	G	AB	R	H	2B	3B	HR	RBI	BB-IB	HP	SO	AVG	OBP	SLG	AOPS	ABR	SB-CS	FA	FR	RNG	THR	GAMES AT POSITION	DL	BFW
1949	Cin N	17	25	2	6	1	0	1	2	3	0	5	.240	.321	.400	91	0	0	.966	-1	92	0	C13		-0.1
1950	Cin N	74	228	14	70	10	1	5	30	19	1	15	.307	.363	.425	106	2	0	.981	-3	72	116	C73		0.2
1951	Cin N	72	227	12	52	5	2	6	22	5	0	17	.229	.246	.348	57	-15	0-0	.968	-6	74	83	C63		-1.5
1952	Chi N	22	46	1	13	1	0	1	5	4	0	4	.283	.340	.370	96	0	0-0	.958	0	63	68	C17		0.1
Total	4	185	526	29	141	17	3	13	59	31	1	41	.268	.310	.386	84	-13	0-0	.973	-10	73	93	C166		-1.2

PRATT, DEL Derrill Burnham B1.10.1888 Walhalla SC D9.30.1977 Texas City TX BR/TR/5-11/175 d4.11 Col Alabama OF(3/3/8)

YEAR	TM LG	G	AB	R	H	2B	3B	HR	RBI	BB-IB	HP	SO	AVG	OBP	SLG	AOPS	ABR	SB-CS	FA	FR	RNG	THR	GAMES AT POSITION	DL	BFW
1912	StL A	152	570	76	172	26	15	5	69	36	4		.302	.348	.426	125	16	24	.943	13	106	122	2b122,S21,O8(0/3/5)/3		3.0
1913	StL A	155	592	60	175	31	13	2	87	40	1		.296	.341	.402	121	13	37	.951	3	101	104	2b146,1b9		1.4
1914	StL A	158	584	85	165	34	13	5	65	50	2		.283	.341	.411	131	20	37-28	.944	-1	100	95	2b152,O5(2/0/3)/S		2.4
1915	StL A	159	602	61	175	31	11	3	78	26	3		.291	.323	.394	119	10	32-23	.965	16	96	130	2b158		4.4
1916	StL A	158	596	64	159	35	12	5	103	54	3		.267	.331	.391	123	14	26-17	.966	20	105	114	2b158		5.0
1917	StL A	123	450	40	111	22	8	1	53	33	2		.247	.301	.338	98	-2	18	.959	18	103	103	2b119,1b2		1.6
1918	NY A	126	477	65	131	19	7	2	55	35	1		.275	.327	.356	104	1	12	.969	10	100	143	2b126		3.1
1919	NY A	140	527	69	154	27	7	4	56	36	3		.292	.342	.393	105	3	22	.969	25	115	122	2b140		3.0
1920	NY A	154	574	84	180	37	8	4	97	50	2		.314	.372	.427	107	7	12-10	.971	13	101	137	2b134		1.8
1921	Bos A	135	521	80	169	36	10	5	102	44	1		.324	.378	.461	116	12	8-10	.961	0	101		2b154		1.1
1922	Bos A	154	607	73	183	44	7	6	86	53	4		.301	.361	.427	106	6	7-10	.947	-7	96	77	2b60,1b17,3b12		-0.3
1923	Det A	101	297	43	92	18	3	0	40	25	6		.310	.375	.391	104	2	6-9	.948	-2	108	118	2b65,1b51,3b4/OL		-0.2
1924	Det A	121	429	56	130	32	3	1	77	31	2		.303	.353	.399	95	-3	6-9	.960	-4	103	116	2b17,O14R		-0.0
Total	13	1836	6826	856	1996	392	117	43	968	513	37	360	.292	.345	.403	112	99	247-108	.960	94	103	116	2b1688,1b79,S22,3b17,O14R		22.8

PRATT, FRANK Francis Bruce "Truckhorse" B8.24.1897 Blocton AL D3.8.1974 Centreville AL BL/TR/5-9.5/155 d5.13 Col Alabama

YEAR	TM LG	G	AB	R	H	2B	3B	HR	RBI	BB-IB	HP	SO	AVG	OBP	SLG	AOPS	ABR	SB-CS	FA	FR	RNG	THR	GAMES AT POSITION	DL	BFW
1921	Chi A	1	1	0	0	0	0	0	0	0	0	0	.000	.000	.000	-99	0	0-0	—	0			/H		0

PRATT, LARRY Lester John B10.8.1887 Gibson City IL D1.8.1969 Peoria IL BR/TR/6-0/183 d9.19

YEAR	TM LG	G	AB	R	H	2B	3B	HR	RBI	BB-IB	HP	SO	AVG	OBP	SLG	AOPS	ABR	SB-CS	FA	FR	RNG	THR	GAMES AT POSITION	DL	BFW
1914	Bos A	5	4	0	0	0	0	0	0	0	0	4	.000	.000	.000	-99	-1	0	.923	1	210	233	C5		-0
1915	Bro F	20	49	5	9	1	0	1	2	2	0	18	.184	.216	.265	35	-5	2	.949	-2	82	117	C17		-0
	New F	5	4	2	2	2	0	0	0	3	0	1	.500	.714	1.000	403	3	2	1.000	-0	133	93	C3		-0
	Year	25	53	7	11	3	0	1	2	5	0	19	.208	.276	.321	69	-3	4	.953	-2	86	115	C20		-0
Total	2	30	57	7	11	3	0	1	2	5	0	23	.193	.258	.298	58	-4	4	.949	-1	98	127	C25		-0

PRATT, TOM Thomas Jefferson B1.26.1844 Chelsea MA D9.28.1908 Philadelphia PA TL/5-7.5/150 d10.18 U1

YEAR	TM LG	G	AB	R	H	2B	3B	HR	RBI	BB-IB	HP	SO	AVG	OBP	SLG	AOPS	ABR	SB-CS	FA	FR	RNG	THR	GAMES AT POSITION	DL	BFW
1871	Ath NA	1	6	2	2	0	0	0	1	0		0	.333	.333	.333	93	0	0-0	.786	-1	0	0	/1		0

PRATT, TODD Todd Alan B2.9.1967 Bellevue NE BR/TR/6-3/220(195-235) [BosA85 6/153] d7.29

YEAR	TM LG	G	AB	R	H	2B	3B	HR	RBI	BB-IB	HP	SO	AVG	OBP	SLG	AOPS	ABR	SB-CS	FA	FR	RNG	THR	GAMES AT POSITION	DL	BFW
1992	Phi N	16	46	6	13	1	0	2	10	4-0	0	12	.283	.340	.435	118	1	0-0	.972	-1	97	0	C11		0.1
1993	†Phi N	33	87	8	25	6	0	5	13	5-0	1	19	.287	.340	.529	128	3	0-0	.989	2	138	52	C26		0.7
1994	Phi N	28	102	10	20	6	1	2	9	12-0	0	29	.196	.281	.333	58	-6	0-1	1.000	0	168	63	C28	29	
1995	Chi N	25	60	3	8	2	0	0	4	6-1	0	21	.133	.209	.167	2	-9	0-0	.981	0	81	73	C25		-0.5
1997	NY N	39	106	12	30	6	0	2	19	13-0	2	32	.283	.372	.396	106	2	0-1	.990	3	142	148	C36/D		-0.7
1998	NY N	41	69	9	19	9	1	2	18	2-0	0	25	.275	.296	.522	113	1	0-0	.973	-2	132	135	C16,1b3		0.6
1999	†NY N	71	140	18	41	8	0	3	21	15-0	3	32	.293	.369	.386	97	0	2-0	.996	2	131	69	C52/1OL	47	0.4
2000	†NY N	80	160	33	44	6	0	8	25	22-1	5	31	.275	.378	.463	118	5	0-0	.997	-2	131	106	C71/D		0.6
2001	NY N	45	80	6	13	5	0	2	4	15-1	2	36	.162	.306	.300	63	-4	1-0	.994	-7	116	16	C31		-0.9
	Phi N	35	93	12	19	3	0	2	7	19-2	1	25	.204	.345	.301	73	-3	0-0	.985	-3	190	50	C34/1		0.6
	Year	80	173	18	32	8	0	4	11	34-3	3	61	.185	.327	.301	68	-7	1-0	.989	-10	157	35	C65/1		-0.4
2002	Phi N	39	106	14	33	11	0	3	16	24-6	4	38	.311	.449	.500	166	12	2-0	1.000	1	102	70	C34,1b2		1.5
2003	Phi N	43	125	16	34	10	1	4	20	22-0	6	38	.272	.400	.464	136	8	0-0	.996	-4	60	66	C35,1b6		0.6
2004	Phi N	45	128	16	33	5	0	3	16	18-0	1	38	.258	.351	.367	84	-3	0-0	1.000	-6	72	50	C43		-0.6
2005	Phi N	60	175	17	44	4	0	7	23	19-5	2	50	.251	.332	.394	87	-4	0-0	.997	3	132	85	C57		0.3
Total 13		600	1477	180	376	78	3	45	205	196-16	27	411	.255	.350	.403	99	3	5-2	.994	-11	121	74	C499,1b13,D2/OL	76	1.7

PREIBISCH, MEL Melvin Adolphus "Primo" B11.23.1914 Sealy TX D4.12.1980 Sealy TX BR/TR/5-11/185 d9.17 Col Texas

YEAR	TM LG	G	AB	R	H	2B	3B	HR	RBI	BB-IB	HP	SO	AVG	OBP	SLG	AOPS	ABR	SB-CS	FA	FR	RNG	THR	GAMES AT POSITION	DL	BFW
1940	Bos N	11	40	3	9	2	0	0	5	2-0	0	4	.225	.262	.275	51	-3	0	1.000	0	107	111	O11C		-0.3
1941	Bos N	5	4	0	0	0	0	0	0	1-0	0	2	.000	.200	.000	-42	-1	0	1.000	0	392	0	O2(1/1/1)		-0.1
Total 2		16	44	3	9	2	0	0	5	3-0	0	6	.205	.255	.250	42	-4	0	1.000	1	110	110	O13(1/12/1)		-0.4

PRESCOTT, BOBBY George Bertrand B3.27.1931 Colon, Pan BR/TR/5-11/180 d6.17

YEAR	TM LG	G	AB	R	H	2B	3B	HR	RBI	BB-IB	HP	SO	AVG	OBP	SLG	AOPS	ABR	SB-CS	FA	FR	RNG	THR	GAMES AT POSITION	DL	BFW
1961	KC A	10	12	0	1	0	0	0	0	2-0	0	5	.083	.214	.083	-17	-2	0-0	—	-1	0	0	O2L		-0.3

PRESLEY, JIM James Arthur B10.23.1961 Pensacola FL BR/TR/6-1/200(180-200) [SeaA79 4/79] d6.24 C3

YEAR	TM LG	G	AB	R	H	2B	3B	HR	RBI	BB-IB	HP	SO	AVG	OBP	SLG	AOPS	ABR	SB-CS	FA	FR	RNG	THR	GAMES AT POSITION	DL	BFW
1984	Sea A	70	251	27	57	12	1	10	36	6-1	1	63	.227	.247	.402	79	-9	1-1	.958	-5	85	88	3b69/D		-1.6
1985	Sea A	155	570	71	157	33	1	28	84	44-9	1	100	.275	.324	.484	118	13	2-2	.961	5	109	76	3b154		1.5
1986	Sea A☆	155	616	83	163	33	4	27	107	32-3	4	172	.265	.303	.463	104	1	0-4	.965	6	105	103	3b155		0.3
1987	Sea A	152	575	78	142	23	6	24	88	38-1	4	157	.247	.296	.433	86	-14	2-0	.953	11	110	103	3b148,S4/D		-0.4
1988	Sea A	150	544	50	125	26	0	14	62	36-1	4	114	.230	.280	.355	74	-20	3-5	.940	-12	85	102	3b146,D4		-3.3
1989	Sea A	117	390	42	92	20	1	12	41	21-2	1	107	.236	.275	.385	82	-11	0-0	.924	-3	99	89	3b90,1b30/D		-1.5
1990	Atl N	140	541	59	131	34	1	19	72	29-0	3	130	.242	.282	.414	85	-12	1-1	.930	-2	93	94	3b133,1b17		-1.6
1991	SD N	20	59	3	8	0	0	1	5	4-1	1	16	.136	.200	.186	10	-7	0-1	.923	-4	73	0	3b16		-1.6
Total 8		959	3546	413	875	181	14	135	495	210-18	19	859	.247	.290	.420	90	-59	9-14	.949	-3	99	93	3b911,1b47,D7,S4		-7.8

PRESTON, WALT Walter B. B4.6.1868 Richmond VA D12.23.1937 New Orleans LA BL/TR/6-0/175 d4.18

YEAR	TM LG	G	AB	R	H	2B	3B	HR	RBI	BB-IB	HP	SO	AVG	OBP	SLG	AOPS	ABR	SB-CS	FA	FR	RNG	THR	GAMES AT POSITION	DL	BFW
1895	Lou N	50	197	42	55	6	4	1	24	17	10	17	.279	.366	.365	95	0	11	.893	-5	142	221	O26(0/19/7),3b25		-0.5

PRICE, JIM Jimmie William B10.13.1941 Harrisburg PA d4.11

YEAR	TM LG	G	AB	R	H	2B	3B	HR	RBI	BB-IB	HP	SO	AVG	OBP	SLG	AOPS	ABR	SB-CS	FA	FR	RNG	THR	GAMES AT POSITION	DL	BFW
1967	Det A	44	92	9	24	4	0	0	8	4-1	0	10	.261	.292	.304	74	-3	0-0	.974	-2	67	82	C24		-0.5
1968	†Det A	64	132	12	23	4	0	3	13	13-1	1	14	.174	.253	.273	58	-7	0-0	.996	-5	132	19	C42		-1.2
1969	Det A	72	192	21	45	8	0	9	28	18-1	0	20	.234	.294	.417	95	-2	0-0	.989	-2	67	82	C51		-0.2
1970	Det A	52	132	12	24	4	0	5	15	21-0	0	23	.182	.290	.326	70	-5	0-0	.979	-4	89	65	C38		-0.8
1971	Det A	29	54	4	13	2	0	1	7	6-1	1	3	.241	.323	.333	84	-1	0-0	.981	-2	60	113	C25		-0.2
Total 5		261	602	58	129	22	0	18	71	62-4	2	70	.214	.287	.341	78	-18	0-0	.985	-15	86	67	C180	21	-2.9

PRICE, JACKIE John Thomas Reid "Johnny" B11.13.1912 Winborn MS D10.2.1967 San Francisco CA BL/TR/5-10.5/150 d8.18

YEAR	TM LG	G	AB	R	H	2B	3B	HR	RBI	BB-IB	HP	SO	AVG	OBP	SLG	AOPS	ABR	SB-CS	FA	FR	RNG	THR	GAMES AT POSITION	DL	BFW
1946	Cle A	7	13	1	3	0	0	0	0		0		.231	.231	.231	31	-1	0-0	.947	1	119	50	S4		0.0

PRICE, JOE Joseph Preston "Lumber" B4.10.1897 Milligan College TN D1.15.1961 Washington DC BR/TR/6-1.5/187 d9.5 Col Milligan

YEAR	TM LG	G	AB	R	H	2B	3B	HR	RBI	BB-IB	HP	SO	AVG	OBP	SLG	AOPS	ABR	SB-CS	FA	FR	RNG	THR	GAMES AT POSITION	DL	BFW
1928	NY N	1	1	0	0	0	0	0	0		0	1	.000	.000	.000	-99	0	0	—	-0	0	0	/OC		0.0

PRICHARD, BOB Robert Alexander B10.21.1917 Paris TX D9.25.1991 Abilene TX BL/TL/6-1/195 d6.14

YEAR	TM LG	G	AB	R	H	2B	3B	HR	RBI	BB-IB	HP	SO	AVG	OBP	SLG	AOPS	ABR	SB-CS	FA	FR	RNG	THR	GAMES AT POSITION	DL	BFW
1939	Was A	26	85	8	19	3	0	0	8	8-1	0	16	.235	.375	.294	79	-1	0-2	.992	-1	84	135	1b26		-0.5

PRIDDY, JERRY Gerald Edward B11.9.1919 Los Angeles CA D3.3.1980 N.Hollywood CA BR/TR/5-11.5/180* d4.17 Mil 1944-45

YEAR	TM LG	G	AB	R	H	2B	3B	HR	RBI	BB-IB	HP	SO	AVG	OBP	SLG	AOPS	ABR	SB-CS	FA	FR	RNG	THR	GAMES AT POSITION	DL	BFW
1941	NY A	56	174	18	37	7	0	1	26	18	1	16	.213	.290	.270	50	-13	4-2	.968	6	102	160	2b31,3b14,1b10		-0.5
1942	†NY A	59	189	23	53	9	2	2	28	31	1	27	.280	.385	.381	118	6	0-1	.944	3	101	37	3b35,1b11,2b8,S3		0.9
1943	Was A	149	560	68	152	31	3	4	62	67	1	76	.271	.350	.359	112	10	5-5	.971	3	103	111	2b134,S15/3		2.4
1946	Was A	138	511	54	130	22	8	6	58	57	2	73	.254	.332	.364	110	-1	9-3	.962	-1	104	101	2b138		0.7
1947	Was A	147	505	42	108	20	3	3	49	62	1	79	.214	.301	.283	65	-24	7-6	.980	-1	98	84	2b146		-1.8
1948	StL A	151	560	96	166	40	4	8	79	86	1	71	.296	.391	.443	118	17	6-5	.968	-2	99	75	2b145		4.5
1949	StL A	145	544	83	158	26	4	11	63	80	1	81	.290	.382	.414	106	6	5-3	.968	**23**	**108**	111	2b146		1.2
1950	Det A	**157**	618	104	171	26	6	13	75	95	2	77	.277	.376	.401	96	-2	2-7	.981	**28**	**114**	**120**	2b157		3.0
1951	Det A	**154**	584	73	152	22	6	8	57	69	1	73	.260	.338	.360	88	-10	4-3	.980	11	102	99	2b154/S		1.0
1952	Det A	75	279	37	79	23	3	4	20	42	1	29	.283	.379	.430	124	11	1-8	.968	-2	96	80	2b75		1.0
1953	Det A	65	196	14	46	6	2	1	24	17	1	19	.235	.299	.301	63	-10	1-1	.977	1	97	83	2b45,1b11,3b2	74	-0.8
Total 11		1296	4720	612	1252	232	46	61	541	624	13	639	.265	.353	.373	97	-10	44-44	.973	70	104	100	2b1179,3b52,1b32,S19	74	11.7

PRIDE, CURTIS Curtis John B12.17.1968 Washington DC BL/TR/6-0/200(195-210) [NYN86 10/258] d9.14

YEAR	TM LG	G	AB	R	H	2B	3B	HR	RBI	BB-IB	HP	SO	AVG	OBP	SLG	AOPS	ABR	SB-CS	FA	FR	RNG	THR	GAMES AT POSITION	DL	BFW
1993	Mon N	10	9	3	4	1	1	1	5	0-0	0	3	.444	.444	1.111	288	2	1-0	1.000	0	439	0	O2L		0.3
1995	Mon N	48	63	10	11	1	0	2	5	5-0	0	16	.175	.235	.190	13	-8	3-2	.920	-1	100	0	O24(24/1/0)		-1.0
1996	Det A	95	267	52	80	17	5	10	31	31-1	0	63	.300	.372	.513	121	8	11-6	.967	1	116	0	O48(45/0/5),D31	27	0.5
1997	Det A	79	162	21	34	4	4	2	19	24-1	1	45	.210	.314	.321	67	-8	6-4	.980	-2	96	0	O35(34/0/3),D23		-1.2
	Bos A	2	2	1	1	0	0	0	1	0-0	0	1	.500	.500	2.000	501	1	0-0	—	0			/H		-1.2
	Year	81	164	22	35	4	4	2	20	24-1	1	46	.213	.316	.341	72	-7	6-4	.980	-2	96	0	O35(34/0/3),D23		0.1
1998	Atl N	70	107	19	27	6	1	3	14	9-0	3	29	.252	.325	.411	93	-1	4-0	1.000	2	140	0	O22(8/0/14),D2	16	0.1
2000	Bos A	9	20	4	5	1	0	0	0	1-0	0	7	.250	.286	.300	47	-2	0-0	1.000	0	121	0	O9(7/2/0)/D		-0.1
2001	Mon N	36	76	8	19	3	1	1	9	9-0	2	22	.250	.345	.355	82	-2	3-2	1.000	1	107	94	O23(19/1/3),D2	64	-0.2
2003	NY A	4	12	1	1	0	0	0	0	1-0	0	2	.083	.083	.333	-2	-2	0-0	1.000	0	86	0	O3(1/0/2)		-0.2
2004	†Ana A	35	40	5	10	3	0	0	0	1-0	1	11	.250	.268	.325	56	-3	1-0	1.000	2	155	0	O24(15/2/7),D2		-0.2
2005	LA A	11	11	2	1	0	0	0	1	0-0	0	4	.091	.091	.182	-30	-2	0-0	1.000	0	177	0	O4L,D3	24	-0.1
Total 10		399	769	126	193	37	12	19	80	79-2	7	203	.251	.326	.404	87	-17	29-14	.979	2	115	12	O194(159/6/34),D64	131	-2.0

PRIEST, JOHNNY John Gooding B6.23.1886 St.Joseph MO D11.4.1979 Washington DC BR/TR/5-11/170 d5.30

YEAR	TM LG	G	AB	R	H	2B	3B	HR	RBI	BB-IB	HP	SO	AVG	OBP	SLG	AOPS	ABR	SB-CS	FA	FR	RNG	THR	GAMES AT POSITION	DL	BFW
1911	NY A	8	21	2	3	0	0	0	2	2	1		.143	.250	.143	10	-3	3	.824	-2	65	0	2b5,3b2		-0.5
1912	NY A	2	2	1	1	0	0	0	1	0	0		.500	.500	.500	176	0		—	0			/H		0.0
Total 2		10	23	3	4	0	0	0	3	2	1		.174	.269	.174	23	-3	3	.824	-2	65	0	2b5,3b2		-0.5

PRIETO, ALEX Alejandro Antonio B6.19.1976 Caracas, Venez BR/TR/5-10/200* d7.26

YEAR	TM LG	G	AB	R	H	2B	3B	HR	RBI	BB-IB	HP	SO	AVG	OBP	SLG	AOPS	ABR	SB-CS	FA	FR	RNG	THR	GAMES AT POSITION	DL	BFW
2003	Min A	8	11	1	1	0	0	0	0	0-0	0	4	.091	.091	.091	-50	-2	0-0	1.000	-0	97	75	2b5/S		-0.2
2004	Min A	16	32	4	8	1	0	1	4	3-0	0	9	.250	.306	.375	77	-1	0-1	1.000	1	118	158	2b8,3b5,S3/D		0.0
Total 2		24	43	5	9	1	0	1	4	3-0	0	13	.209	.255	.302	45	-3	0-1	1.000	1	113	137	2b13,3b5,S4/D		-0.2

PRIETO, CHRIS Christian Michael B8.24.1972 Carmel CA BL/TL/5-11/180 d5.14 Col Nevada-Reno

YEAR	TM LG	G	AB	R	H	2B	3B	HR	RBI	BB-IB	HP	SO	AVG	OBP	SLG	AOPS	ABR	SB-CS	FA	FR	RNG	THR	GAMES AT POSITION	DL	BFW
2005	LA A	2	1	0	0	0	0	0	0	0-0	0		.000	.000	.000		0	0-0	1.000	0	195	0	O2C		0.0

PRINCE, TOM Thomas Albert B8.13.1964 Kankakee IL BR/TR/5-11/185(185-206) [PitN84*S4/64] d9.22 Col Kankakee (IL) CC

YEAR	TM LG	G	AB	R	H	2B	3B	HR	RBI	BB-IB	HP	SO	AVG	OBP	SLG	AOPS	ABR	SB-CS	FA	FR	RNG	THR	GAMES AT POSITION	DL	BFW
1987	Pit N	4	9	1	2	0	0	0	2	0-0	0	2	.222	.222	.667	123	0	0-0	1.000	1	70	88	C4		0.0
1988	Pit N	29	74	3	13	2	0	1	6	4-0	0	15	.176	.218	.203	22	-8	0-0	.983	-4	98	61	C28		-1.1
1989	Pit N	21	52	1	7	3	0	0	5	6-1	0	12	.135	.220	.212	26	-5	1-1	.960	-2	49	122	C21		-0.7
1990	Pit N	4	10	1	1	0	0	0	1	1-0	0	1	.100	.182	.100	-21	-2	0-0	1.000	0	79	0	C3		-0.2
1991	Pit N	26	34	4	9	3	0	1	7	7-0	1	3	.265	.405	.441	139	2	0-0	.984	0	105	190	C19/1		-0.2
1992	Pit N	27	44	1	4	0	0	0	5	6-0	0	9	.091	.192	.136	-3	-6	1-1	.977	2	128	82	C19/3		-0.4
1993	Pit N	66	179	14	35	14	0	2	24	13-2	7	38	.196	.272	.307	56	-11	1-1	.984	-7	73	96	C59	19	-1.4
1994	LA N	3	3	0	1	0	0	0	1	1-0	0		.333	.429	.333	108	0	0-0	1.000	1	0	0	C3		0.1

YEAR	TM LG	G	AB	R	H	2B	3B	HR	RBI	BB-IB	HP	SO	AVG	OBP	SLG	AOPS	ABR	SB-CS	FA	FR	RNG	THR	GAMES AT POSITION	DL	BFW
1995	LA N	18	40	3	8	2	1	1	4	4-0	0	10	.200	.273	.375	74	-2	0-0	.988	-3	119	99	C17	36	-0.4
1996	LA N	40	64	6	19	6	0	1	11	6-2	2	15	.297	.365	.438	121	2	0-0	.994	2	105	63	C35		0.6
1997	LA N	47	100	17	22	5	0	3	14	5-0	3	15	.220	.360	.360	70	-5	0-0	.996	8	377	143	C45		0.5
1998	LA N	37	81	7	15	5	1	0	5	7-1	2	24	.185	.267	.272	44	-7	0-0	1.000	2	113	174	C32		-0.3
1999	Phi N	4	6	1	1	0	0	0	0	1-0	0	1	.167	.286	.167	18	-1	0-0	1.000	-0	135	0	C4	151	0.0
2000	Phi N	46	122	14	29	9	0	2	16	13-0	1	31	.238	.321	.361	72	-5	1-0	.996	-0	124	84	C46		-0.2
2001	Min A	64	196	19	43	4	1	7	23	12-0	6	39	.219	.284	.357	64	-11	3-1	1.000	14	152	120	C64		0.7
2002	†Min A	51	125	14	28	7	1	4	16	14-0	4	26	.224	.317	.392	86	-2	1-3	.997	2	192	78	C50		0.2
2003	Min A	24	40	5	8	2	0	2	5	5-0	2	7	.200	.319	.400	85	-1	1-0	1.000	1	360	98	C22,D2		0.1
	KC A	8	8	0	2	0	0	0	1	0-0	0	0	.250	.250	.250	30	-1	0-0	1.000	-1	64	0	C7/D		-0.2
	Year	32	48	5	10	2	0	2	6	5-0	2	7	.208	.309	.375	76	-2	1-0	1.000	-0	314	83	C29,D3		-0.1
Total	17	519	1190	113	248	66	4	24	140	105-6	29	252	.208	.286	.331	65	-63	9-8	.992	14	149	103	C478,D3/31	206	-2.4

PRINCE, WALTER   Walter Farr   B5.9.1861 Amherst NH   D3.2.1938 Bristol NH   BL/TR/5-9/150   d8.7

YEAR	TM LG	G	AB	R	H	2B	3B	HR	RBI	BB-IB	HP	SO	AVG	OBP	SLG	AOPS	ABR	SB-CS	FA	FR	RNG	THR	GAMES AT POSITION	DL	BFW
1883	Lou AA	4	11	1	2	0	0	0	0				.182	.182	.182	19	-1		.500	-2	0	0	O2R,1b2/S		-0.3
1884	Det N	7	21	0	3	0	0	0	1	3		4	.143	.250	.143	29	-2		.375	-3	0	0	O7R		-0.4
	Was AA	43	166	22	36	3	2	1	13		3		.217	.286	.277	95	1		.940	-5	28	78	1b43		-0.8
	Was U	1	4	0	1	0	0	0	0				.250	.250	.250	54	0		.818	-0	0	0	/1		-0.1
Total	2	55	202	23	42	3	2	1	14	16		4	.208	.276	.257	83	-2		.935	-11	34	74	1b46,O9R/S		-1.6

PRITCHARD, BUDDY   Harold William   B1.25.1936 South Gate CA   BR/TR/6-1/195   d4.21   Col USC

YEAR	TM LG	G	AB	R	H	2B	3B	HR	RBI	BB-IB	HP	SO	AVG	OBP	SLG	AOPS	ABR	SB-CS	FA	FR	RNG	THR	GAMES AT POSITION	DL	BFW
1957	Pit N	23	11	1	1	0	0	0	0	0-0	0	4	.091	.091	.091	-53	-2	0-0	.947	2	112	219	S10,2b3		0.0

PRITCHETT, CHRIS   Christopher Davis   B1.31.1970 Merced CA   BL/TR/6-4/185(185-212)   [CalA91 2/61]   d9.6   Col UCLA

YEAR	TM LG	G	AB	R	H	2B	3B	HR	RBI	BB-IB	HP	SO	AVG	OBP	SLG	AOPS	ABR	SB-CS	FA	FR	RNG	THR	GAMES AT POSITION	DL	BFW
1996	Cal A	5	13	1	2	0	0	0	1	0-0	0	3	.154	.154	.154	-22	-2	0-0	1.000	-0	53	110	1b5		-0.3
1998	Ana A	31	80	12	23	2	1	2	8	4-0	0	16	.287	.321	.412	88	-2	2-0	.995	2	139	65	1b29/D	16	-0.1
1999	Ana A	20	45	3	7	1	0	1	2	2-0	0	9	.156	.188	.244	10	-6	1-1	.990	1	129	85	1b15,D5		-0.6
2000	Phi N	5	11	0	1	0	0	0	0	1-0	0	3	.091	.167	.091	-33	-2	0-0	1.000	1	217	43	1b3		-0.2
Total	4	61	149	16	33	3	1	3	11	7-0	0	31	.221	.255	.315	46	-12	3-1	.995	4	135	72	1b52,D6	16	-1.2

PROESER, GEORGE   George "Yatz"   B5.30.1864 Cincinnati OH   D10.13.1941 New Burlington OH   BL/TL/5-10/190   d9.15 ▲

YEAR	TM LG	G	AB	R	H	2B	3B	HR	RBI	BB-IB	HP	SO	AVG	OBP	SLG	AOPS	ABR	SB-CS	FA	FR	RNG	THR	GAMES AT POSITION	DL	BFW
1888	Cle AA	7	23	5	7	2	0	0	1	1	0		.304	.333	.391	136	2	0	.846	-1	84	0	P7		0.0
1890	Syr AA	13	53	11	13	1	1	1	6	10	0		.245	.365	.358	126	2	1	.895	-2	47	0	O13R		0.1
Total	2	20	76	16	20	3	1	1	7	11	0		.263	.356	.368	129	4	1	.895	-2	47	0	O13R,P7		0.1

PROPST, JAKE   William Jacob   B3.10.1895 Kennedy AL   D2.24.1967 Columbus MS   BL/TR/5-10/165   d8.7

YEAR	TM LG	G	AB	R	H	2B	3B	HR	RBI	BB-IB	HP	SO	AVG	OBP	SLG	AOPS	ABR	SB-CS	FA	FR	RNG	THR	GAMES AT POSITION	DL	BFW
1923	Was A	1	1	0	0	0	0	0	0	0-0	0	0	.000	.000	.000	-99	0	0-0	—		0		/H		0.0

PROTHRO, DOC   James Thompson   B7.16.1893 Memphis TN   D10.14.1971 Memphis TN   BR/TR/5-10.5/170   d9.26   M3

YEAR	TM LG	G	AB	R	H	2B	3B	HR	RBI	BB-IB	HP	SO	AVG	OBP	SLG	AOPS	ABR	SB-CS	FA	FR	RNG	THR	GAMES AT POSITION	DL	BFW
1920	Was A	6	13	2	5	0	0	0	2	0	0	4	.385	.385	.385	107	-1	0-0	1.000	0	56	290	S2,3b2		0.0
1923	Was A	6	8	2	2	0	1	0	3	1	0	3	.250	.333	.500	124	0	0-0	1.000	2	148	0	3b6		0.2
1924	Was A	46	159	14	53	11	5	0	24	15	1	11	.333	.394	.465	125	6	4-4	.915	-9	80	96	3b45		-0.1
1925	Bos A	119	415	44	130	23	4	0	51	52	3	21	.313	.390	.383	97	-9	9-11	.945	-2	103	73	3b108,S3		0.3
1926	Cin N	3	5	1	1	0	1	0	1	1	0	0	.200	.333	.600	151	0	0-0	1.000	-0	114	0	3b2		0.0
Total	5	180	600	66	191	34	10	0	81	69	1	40	.318	.390	.408	105	6	13-15	.940	-9	98	85	3b163,S5		0.4

PRUESS, EARL   Earl Henry "Gibby"   B4.2.1895 Chicago IL   D8.28.1979 Branson MO   BR/TR/5-10.5/170   d9.15

YEAR	TM LG	G	AB	R	H	2B	3B	HR	RBI	BB-IB	HP	SO	AVG	OBP	SLG	AOPS	ABR	SB-CS	FA	FR	RNG	THR	GAMES AT POSITION	DL	BFW
1920	StL A	1	0	0	0	0	0	0	0	1	0	0	—	1.000	—	176	0	1-0	1.000	0	197	0	/OR		0.1

PRUETT, JIM   James Calvin   B12.16.1917 Nashville TN   D7.29.2003 Waukesha WI   BR/TR/5-10/178   d9.26

YEAR	TM LG	G	AB	R	H	2B	3B	HR	RBI	BB-IB	HP	SO	AVG	OBP	SLG	AOPS	ABR	SB-CS	FA	FR	RNG	THR	GAMES AT POSITION	DL	BFW
1944	Phi A	3	4	1	1	0	0	0	1	1	0	0	.250	.400	.250	119	0	0-0	1.000	0	61	269	C2		0.1
1945	Phi A	6	9	1	2	0	0	0	1	1	0	2	.222	.300	.222	53	-1	0-1	1.000	1	94	0	C4		-0.1
Total	2	9	13	2	3	0	0	0	2		1	2	.231	.375	.231	77	-1	0-1	1.000	1	82	98	C6		0.0

PRUITT, RON   Ronald Ralph   B10.21.1951 Flint MI   BR/TR/6-0/185*   [TexA72 2/28]   d6.25   Col Michigan St.

YEAR	TM LG	G	AB	R	H	2B	3B	HR	RBI	BB-IB	HP	SO	AVG	OBP	SLG	AOPS	ABR	SB-CS	FA	FR	RNG	THR	GAMES AT POSITION	DL	BFW
1975	Tex A	14	17	2	3	0	0	0	0	1-0	0	3	.176	.222	.176	14	-2	0-0	1.000	-1	71	93	C13/OL		-0.3
1976	Cle A	47	86	7	23	1	1	0	5	16-1	0	9	.267	.375	.302	103	1	2-3	1.000	3	119	251	O26(12/1/13),C6,3b6/1D		0.3
1977	Cle A	78	219	29	63	10	2	2	32	28-0	2	22	.288	.369	.379	109	4	2-3	.972	-4	88	47	O69(27/3/42),C4/3D		-0.4
1978	Cle A	71	187	17	44	6	1	6	17	16-3	0	20	.235	.296	.374	88	-4	2-1	.984	-11	55	69	C48,O16(12/0/4),3b2,D5		-1.4
1979	Cle A	64	166	23	47	7	0	2	21	19-1	0	21	.283	.355	.361	94	-1	0-0	.957	-4	80	51	O29(19/0/11),D14,C11,3b3		-0.6
1980	Cle A	23	36	1	11	1	0	0	4	4-0	0	6	.306	.366	.333	95	0	0-0	1.000	0	87	267	O6(0/1/5),3b2,D2		0.0
	Chi A	33	70	8	21	2	0	2	11	8-1	0	7	.300	.372	.414	115	2	0-0	1.000	-2	111	0	O11(10/1/0),C5,3b3/1D		-0.1
	Year	56	106	9	32	3	0	2	15	12-1	0	13	.302	.370	.387	108	2	0-0	1.000	-2	102	102	O17(10/2/5),D9,3b5,C5/1		-0.1
1981	Cle A	5	9	0	0	0	0	0	0	1-0	0	2	.000	.100	.000	-99	-2	0-0	1.000	-1	69	0	O3(2/0/1)/CD		-0.3
1982	SF N	5	4	1	2	1	0	0	2	1-1	0	1	.500	.600	.750	278	1	0-0	1.000	1	0	0	/H		0.2
1983	SF N	1	1	0	0	0	0	0	0	0-0	0	0	.000	.000	.000	-99	0	0-0	—	0	0		/H		0.0
Total	9	341	795	88	214	28	4	12	92	94-7	2	90	.269	.345	.360	97	-1	8-7	.977	-19	94	75	O162(83/6/77),C89,D37,3b17,1b2		-2.6

PRYOR, GREG   Gregory Russell   B10.2.1949 Marietta OH   BR/TR/6-0/186(175-186)   [TexA71 6/128]   d6.4   Col Florida Southern

YEAR	TM LG	G	AB	R	H	2B	3B	HR	RBI	BB-IB	HP	SO	AVG	OBP	SLG	AOPS	ABR	SB-CS	FA	FR	RNG	THR	GAMES AT POSITION	DL	BFW
1976	Tex A	5	8	2	3	0	0	0	1	0-0	1	0	.375	.375	.375	118	0	0-0	1.000	0	92	72	2b3/S3		0.0
1978	Chi A	82	222	27	58	11	6	2	15	11-0	1	18	.261	.298	.338	78	-7	3-1	.966	5	94	74	2b35,S28,3b20		-0.1
1979	Chi A	143	476	60	131	23	3	3	34	35-1	2	41	.275	.324	.355	84	-11	3-4	.961	-2	103	72	S119,2b25,3b22		0.3
1980	Chi A	122	338	32	81	18	4	1	29	12-0	2	35	.240	.265	.325	62	-18	2-2	.975	15	115	99	S76,3b41,2b5/D		-0.4
1981	Chi A	47	76	4	17	1	0	0	6	6-0	2	8	.224	.298	.237	56	-4	0-0	.931	-0	101	29	3b27,S13,2b5		-0.4
1982	KC A	73	152	23	41	10	1	2	12	10-0	0	20	.270	.315	.388	91	-2	2-0	.951	-3	97	109	3b40,2b15,1b14,S7		-0.8
1983	KC A	68	115	9	25	4	1	0	14	7-0	0	8	.217	.260	.313	48	-8	0-0	.958	1	109	96	3b60,1b6,2b3		-0.7
1984	†KC A	123	270	32	71	11	4	4	25	12-0	3	28	.263	.301	.356	80	-8	0-3	.970	2	100	110	3b105,2b22,S2/1D		-1.0
1985	†KC A	63	114	8	25	7	0	1	3	8-0	0	12	.219	.270	.272	49	-8	0-1	.946	-3	111	84	3b26,2b20,S13/1D		-1.3
1986	KC A	63	112	7	19	4	0	0	7	3-0	0	14	.170	.191	.205	22	-14	1-1	.935	1	118	188	3b35,S17,2b12/1		-1.3
Total	10	789	1883	204	471	85	9	14	146	104-1	15	194	.250	.291	.327	70	-80	11-12	.952	12	107	108	3b377,S276,2b145,1b23,D3		-4.5

PUCCINELLI, GEORGE   George Lawrence "Pooch","Count"   B6.22.1907 San Francisco CA   D4.16.1956 San Francisco CA   BR/TR/6-0.5/190   d7.17

YEAR	TM LG	G	AB	R	H	2B	3B	HR	RBI	BB-IB	HP	SO	AVG	OBP	SLG	AOPS	ABR	SB-CS	FA	FR	RNG	THR	GAMES AT POSITION	DL	BFW
1930	†StL N	11	16	5	9	1	0	3	8	0	0	0	.563	.563	1.188	298	5	0	1.000	-0	59	0	O3(3/0/1)		0.4
1932	StL N	31	108	17	30	8	0	3	11	12	0	13	.278	.350	.435	107	1	1	.942	2	94	298	O30(24/0/6)		0.2
1934	StL N	10	26	4	6	1	0	2	5	1	0	5	.231	.286	.500	92	-1	0-0	.941	0	108	176	O6L		0.0
1936	Phi A	135	457	83	127	30	6	3	11	78	65	1	.278	.369	.429	98	0	2-3	.948	1	104	101	O117(1/0/116)		-0.7
Total	4	187	607	109	172	40	6	3	19	102	78	2	.283	.367	.453	105	5	3-3	.948	2	102	143	O156(34/0/123)		-0.1

PUCKETT, KIRBY   Kirby   B3.14.1961 Chicago IL   BR/TR/5-8/210(175-223)   [MinA82*1/3]   d5.8   HF2001   Col Bradley   OF(10/1432/276)   [DL 1996 Min A 182, 1997 Min A 181]

YEAR	TM LG	G	AB	R	H	2B	3B	HR	RBI	BB-IB	HP	SO	AVG	OBP	SLG	AOPS	ABR	SB-CS	FA	FR	RNG	THR	GAMES AT POSITION	DL	BFW
1984	Min A	128	557	63	165	12	5	0	31	16-1	4	69	.296	.320	.336	78	-18	14-7	.993	18	117	179	O128C		0.0
1985	Min A	161	691	80	199	29	13	4	74	41-0	4	87	.288	.330	.385	90	-10	21-12	.984	10	105	182	O161C		-0.2
1986	Min A★	161	680	119	223	37	6	31	96	34-4	7	99	.328	.366	.537	138	33	20-12	.986	1	102	94	O160C		3.2
1987	†Min A★	157	624	96	207	32	6	28	99	32-7	6	91	.332	.367	.534	131	26	12-7	.986	-4	93	126	O147C,D8		2.8
1988	Min A★	158	657	109	234	42	5	24	121	23-4	2	83	.356	.375	.545	151	42	6-7	.994	9	106	166	O158C		4.9
1989	Min A★	159	635	75	215	45	4	9	85	41-9	3	59	.339	.379	.465	129	25	11-4	.991	11	109	159	O157C,D2		3.8
1990	Min A★	146	551	82	164	40	3	12	80	57-11	3	73	.298	.365	.446	119	15	5-4	.989	2	102	123	O152(0/144/19)		1.8
1991	†Min A★	152	611	92	195	29	6	15	89	31-4	4	78	.319	.352	.460	118	13	11-5	.985	1	96	161	O152(0/147/19)		2.7
1992	Min A★	160	639	104	210	38	4	19	110	44-13	7	97	.329	.374	.490	136	30	17-7	.993	-1	99	110	O149C,2b2,3b2/SD		2.5
1993	Min A★	156	622	89	184	39	3	22	89	47-7	7	93	.296	.349	.474	119	16	8-6	.994	-3	90	149	O139(1/95/47),D17		1.5
1994	Min A★	108	439	79	139	32	3	20	112	28-7	7	47	.317	.362	.540	129	18	6-3	.981	6	103	181	O95(0/3/95),D13		1.5
1995	Min A★	137	538	83	169	39	0	23	99	56-18	2	89	.314	.379	.515	130	24	3-2	.981	-2	92	125	O109(0/5/106),D28/23S		1.5
Total	12	1783	7244	1071	2304	414	57	207	1085	450-85	56	965	.318	.360	.477	122	213	134-76	.989	46	101	146	O1696C,D81,3b4,2b4,S3	363	23.8

PUHL, JOHN   John G.   B1.10.1876 Brooklyn NY   D8.24.1900 Bayonne NJ   d10.13

YEAR	TM LG	G	AB	R	H	2B	3B	HR	RBI	BB-IB	HP	SO	AVG	OBP	SLG	AOPS	ABR	SB-CS	FA	FR	RNG	THR	GAMES AT POSITION	DL	BFW
1898	NY N	2	9	1	2	0	0	0	0	0	1		.222	.222	.222	28	-1	0	.667	-1	102	288	3b2		-0.0
1899	NY N	1	2	0	0	0	0	0	0	0	0	1	.000	.333	.000	-6	0	0	.667	-0	110	0	/3		0.0
Total	3	11	1	2	0	0	0	0	0	1	1	.182	.250	.182	24	-1	0	.667	-1	104	213	3b3		-0.0

YEAR	TM LG	G	AB	R	H	2B	3B	HR	RBI	BB-IB	HP	SO	AVG	OBP	SLG	AOPS	ABR	SB-CS	FA	FR	RNG	THR	GAMES AT POSITION	DL	BFW
PUHL, TERRY									Terry Stephen B7.8.1956 Melville SK, Can. BL/TR/6-2/200* d7.12															
1977	Hou N	60	229	40	69	13	5	0	10	30-0	1	31	.301	.385	.402	121	8	10-1	.992	0	98	77	O59(48/11/1)		0.7
1978	Hou N☆	149	585	87	169	25	6	3	35	48-5	4	46	.289	.343	.368	107	5	32-14	.992	7	112	66	O148(43/109/4)		1.1
1979	Hou N	157	600	87	172	22	4	8	49	58-8	4	46	.287	.352	.377	105	5	30-22	**1.000**	-6	97	61	O152(6/109/40)		-0.6
1980	Hou N	141	535	75	151	24	5	13	55	60-3	4	52	.282	.357	.419	127	20	27-11	.991	10	114	126	O135(4/30/107)		2.6
1981	†Hou N	96	350	43	88	19	4	3	28	31-5	4	49	.251	.315	.354	96	-2	22-4	**1.000**	0	103	72	O88(0/20/71)		-0.2
1982	Hou N	145	507	64	133	17	9	8	50	51-2	2	49	.262	.331	.379	107	3	17-9	.989	-4	101	45	O138(0/32/122)		0.4
1983	Hou N	137	465	66	136	25	7	8	44	36-2	2	48	.292	.343	.428	120	11	24-11	.991	-4	100	51	O124(0/13/118)		0.4
1984	Hou N	132	449	66	135	19	7	9	55	59-12	1	45	.301	.384	.434	138	24	13-8	.986	-6	91	73	O126(8/0/123)	17	1.2
1985	Hou N	57	194	34	55	14	3	2	23	18-4	1	23	.284	.343	.418	116	4	6-2	**1.000**	0	100	90	O53(1/0/53)	99	0.3
1986	†Hou N	81	172	17	42	10	0	3	14	15-1	0	24	.244	.302	.355	84	-4	3-2	**1.000**	-2	97	0	O47(5/0/42)	29	-0.9
1987	Hou N	90	122	9	28	5	0	2	15	11-0	0	16	.230	.293	.320	65	-6	1-1	.980	1	128	0	O40(28/5/9)		-0.6
1988	Hou N	113	234	25	71	7	2	3	19	35-3	1	30	.303	.395	.389	131	11	22-4	.983	-0	103	61	O78(48/1/33)		1.3
1989	Hou N	121	354	41	96	25	4	0	27	45-3	1	39	.271	.353	.364	110	6	9-8	**1.000**	-1	100	55	O103(37/11/64),1b3		0.1
1990	Hou N	37	41	5	12	1	0	0	8	5-0	1	7	.293	.375	.317	97	0	1-2	**1.000**	-1	62	0	O12(6/2/0)/1	107	-0.2
1991	KC A	15	18	0	4	0	0	0	3	3-1	0	2	.222	.333	.222	56	-1	0-0	—	-0	0	0	/OLD		-0.1
Total	15	1531	4855	676	1361	226	56	62	435	505-49	26	507	.280	.349	.388	112	84	217-99	.993	-7	102	66	O1300(235/343/787),1b4,D2	252	4.5
PUIG, RICH									Richard Gerald B3.16.1953 Tampa FL BL/TR/5-10/170 d9.13															
1974	NY N	4	10	0	0	0	0	0	0	1-0	0	2	.000	.091	.000	-73	-2	0-0	.923	-0	97	139	2b3/3		-0.2
PUJOLS, ALBERT									Jose Alberto B1.16.1980 Santo Domingo, D.R. BR/TR/6-3/210(210-225) [StLN99 13/402] d4.2 Col Maple Woods (MO) CC															
2001	†StL N★	161	590	112	194	47	4	37	130	69-6	9	93	.329	.403	.610	155	50	1-3	.964	9	95	128	O78(39/0/39),3b55,1b42,D2		5.0
2002	†StL N★	157	590	118	185	40	2	34	127	72-13	9	69	.314	.394	.561	151	42	2-4	.978	-4	91	63	O118(117/0/1),3b41,1b21/SD		3.2
2003	StL N★	157	591	137	212	51	1	43	124	79-12	10	65	**.359**	.439	.667	186	78	5-1	.986	2	98	106	O113L,1b62/D		7.1
2004	StL N★	154	592	133	196	51	2	46	123	84-12	7	52	.331	.415	.657	171	65	5-5	.994	2	106	**120**	1b150,D3		5.0
2005	†StL N★	161	591	129	195	38	2	41	117	97-27	9	65	.330	.430	.609	166	61	16-2	.992	-3	98	**142**	1b157		4.6
Total	5	790	2954	629	982	227	11	201	621	401-70	44	344	.332	.416	.621	166	296	29-15	.992	6	103	128	1b432,O309(269/0/40),3b96,D8/S		24.9
PUJOLS, LUIS									Luis Bienvenido (Toribio) B11.18.1955 Santiago Rodriguez, D.R. BR/TR/6-1/195(175-205) d9.22 M1/C12															
1977	Hou N	6	15	0	1	0	0	0	0	0-0	0	5	.067	.067	.067	-70	-4	0-0	1.000	-1	79	225	C6		-0.5
1978	Hou N	56	153	11	20	8	1	0	11	12-1	1	45	.131	.198	.216	17	-18	0-0	.981	-6	67	76	C55/1		-2.4
1979	Hou N	26	75	7	17	2	1	0	8	2-0	0	14	.227	.247	.280	46	-6	0-0	.993	-0	77	13	C26		-0.5
1980	†Hou N	78	221	15	44	6	1	0	20	13-3	1	29	.199	.245	.235	38	-19	0-0	.990	-5	89	78	C75/3		-2.3
1981	†Hou N	40	117	5	28	3	1	1	14	10-3	0	17	.239	.297	.308	77	-4	1-0	.995	-1	122	77	C39		-0.3
1982	Hou N	65	176	8	35	6	2	4	15	10-2	0	40	.199	.242	.324	62	-10	0-3	.991	-5	91	104	C64		-1.5
1983	Hou N	40	87	4	17	2	0	0	12	5-2	0	14	.195	.234	.218	29	-9	0-0	.971	-4	61	24	C39		-1.2
1984	KC A	4	5	0	1	0	0	0	1	0-0	0	0	.200	.200	.200	11	-1	0-0	1.000	0	0	0	C4		0.0
1985	Tex A	1	1	0	1	0	0	0	0	0-0	0	0	1.000	1.000	1.000	441	0	0-0	1.000	-1	7	0	/C		0.0
Total	9	316	850	50	164	27	6	6	81	52-11	2	164	.193	.240	.260	43	-71	1-3	.987	-23	85	73	C309/31	158	-8.7
PULLIAM, HARVEY									Harvey Jerome B10.20.1967 San Francisco CA BR/TR/6-0/205(205-218) [KCA86 3/79] d8.10															
1991	KC A	18	33	4	9	1	0	1	4	3-1	0	9	.273	.333	.576	145	2	0-0	.917	0	100	155	O15(11/0/5)		0.1
1992	KC A	4	5	2	1	1	0	0	1	1-0	0	3	.200	.333	.400	101	0	0-0	1.000	0	305	0	/OLD		0.0
1993	KC A	27	62	9	16	5	0	1	6	2-0	1	14	.258	.292	.387	76	-2	0-0	.971	-1	100	0	O26(12/0/16)		-0.4
1995	Col N	5	5	1	2	1	0	1	3	0-0	0	2	.400	.400	1.200	235	1	0-0	—	-0	0	0	/OL		0.1
1996	Col N	10	15	2	2	0	0	0	2	2-0	0	6	.133	.235	.133	-0	-2	0-0	1.000	-0	100	0	O3L		-0.2
1997	Col N	59	67	15	19	3	0	3	9	5-0	0	15	.284	.333	.463	86	-1	0-1	.962	0	87	208	O33(24/1/10),D2		-0.2
Total	6	123	187	31	49	11	0	8	22	13-1	1	49	.262	.313	.449	89	-2	0-1	.956	-1	98	103	O79(52/1/31),D2	43	-0.6
PUNTO, NICK									Nicholas Paul B11.8.1977 San Diego CA BB/TR/5-9/170(170-190) [PhiN98 21/614] d9.9 Col Saddleback (CA) CC															
2001	Phi N	4	5	0	2	0	0	0	0	0-0	0	0	.400	.400	.400	113	0	0-0	1.000	-1	67	0	/S		0.0
2002	Phi N	9	6	0	1	0	0	0	0	0-0	0	3	.167	.167	.167	-11	-1	0-0	1.000	0	314	1350	/2S		0.0
2003	Phi N	64	92	14	20	2	0	1	4	7-1	0	22	.217	.273	.272	46	-8	2-1	.985	2	101	95	2b16,3b9,S7		-0.4
2004	Min A	38	91	17	23	0	0	2	12	12-0	0	19	.253	.340	.319	71	-4	6-0	.982	1	94	131	2b19,S11,3b2,O2C,D3	121	0.0
2005	Min A	112	394	45	94	18	4	4	26	36-0	0	86	.239	.301	.335	68	-18	13-8	.979	2	103	114	2b73,S34,3b12,O3(0/2/1),D4	30	-1.0
Total	5	227	588	76	140	20	4	7	42	55-1	0	130	.238	.302	.321	65	-31	21-9	.980	5	102	116	2b109,S54,3b23,D7,O5(0/4/1)	151	-1.5
PURCELL, BLONDIE									William Aloysius B Paterson NJ BR/TR/5-9.5/159 M1 OF(480/92/430) ▲															
1879	Syr N	63	277	32	72	6	3	0	25	3		13	.260	.268	.303	99	0		.773	-11	44	0	O47(0/10/37),P22/C		-0.9
	Cin N	12	50	10	11	0	0	0	4	0		3	.220	.220	.220	48	-3		.750	0	128	0	O10(0/7/3),P2		-0.2
	Year	75	327	42	83	6	3	0	29	3		16	.254	.261	.291	91	-3		.767	-10	61	0	O57(0/17/40),P24/C		-1.1
1880	Cin N	77	325	48	95	13	6	1	24	5		13	.292	.303	.378	131	10		.814	-2	117	42	O55(0/54/2),P25/S		0.3
1881	Cle N	20	80	3	14	2	1	0	4	5		8	.175	.224	.225	44	-5		.786	-3	73	0	O20(7/13/0)		-0.8
	Buf N	30	113	15	33	7	2	0	17	8		8	.292	.339	.389	130	4		.706	-5	65	0	O25L,P9		-0.3
	Year	50	193	18	47	9	3	0	21	13		16	.244	.291	.321	95	0		.748	-7	69	0	O45(32/13/0),P9		-1.1
1882	Buf N	**84**	380	79	105	18	6	2	40	14		27	.276	.302	.371	113	5		.820	-4	60	0	O82(78/5/0),P6		-0.2
1883	Phi N	97	425	70	114	20	5	1	32	13		26	.268	.290	.346	101	2		.777	3	114	83	3b46,O44L,P11,M		0.4
1884	Phi N	103	428	67	108	11	7	1	31	29		30	.252	.300	.318	99	1		.874	1	58	27	O103L/P		-0.1
1885	Phi AA	66	304	71	90	15	5	0	22	16	3		.296	.337	.378	119	6		.858	0	122	48	O66(66/1/0)/P		0.4
	Bos N	21	87	9	19	1	1	0	3	3		15	.218	.244	.253	63	-4		.840	-2	61	0	O21L		-0.6
1886	Bal AA	26	85	17	19	0	1	0	8	17	2		.224	.365	.247	96	1	13	.867	-0	96	0	O26(25/1/0)/SP		0.0
1887	Bal AA	140	567	101	142	25	8	4	96	46	10		.250	.318	.344	90	-6	88	.932	-5	74	130	O140R/P		-1.0
1888	Bal AA	101	406	53	96	9	4	2	39	27	3		.236	.289	.293	89	-5	16	.906	-6	54	78	O100(7/1/95),S2/1		-1.1
	Phi AA	18	66	10	11	3	1	0	6	5	1		.167	.236	.242	54	-3	10	.903	-3	96	160	O17R/3		-0.4
	Year	119	472	63	107	12	5	2	45	32	4		.227	.281	.286	84	-8	26	.905	-7	61	91	O117(7/1/112),S2/13		-1.5
1889	Phi AA	129	507	72	160	19	7	0	85	50	5	27	.316	.383	.381	119	14	22	.903	-11	60	54	O129R		0.2
1890	Phi AA	110	463	110	128	28	3	2	59	43	4		.276	.343	.363	109	5	48	.949	0	93	42	O110(104/0/7)		0.3
Total	12	1097	4563	767	1217	177	60	13	495	284	28	170	.267	.314	.340	103	22	197	.870	-45	78	50	O995L,P79,3b47,S4/1C		-4.0
PURDY, PID									Everett Virgil B6.15.1904 Beatrice NE D1.16.1951 Beatrice NE BL/TR/5-6/150 d9.7 Col Beloit															
1926	Chi A	11	33	5	6	2	1	0	1	0		1	.182	.229	.303	39	-3	0-1	1.000	0	105	104	O9R		-0.4
1927	Cin N	18	62	15	22	2	4	1	12	4	2	3	.355	.412	.565	164	5	0	.946	-3	81	0	O16C		0.1
1928	Cin N	70	223	32	69	11	4	0	25	23	1	13	.309	.377	.368	97	1	1	.966	-0	106	62	O56(1/4)		-0.5
1929	Cin N	82	181	22	49	7	4	1	16	19	3	8	.271	.350	.381	85	-4	2	.978	1	103	103	O42(34/0/8)		-0.6
Total	4	181	499	74	146	22	11	2	54	48	6	25	.293	.362	.393	97	-2	3-1	.969	-3	102	70	O128(90/17/21)		-1.4
PURNELL, JESSE									Jesse Rhoades B5.11.1881 Glenside PA D7.4.1966 Philadelphia PA BL/TR/5-5.5/140 d10.1															
1904	Phi N	7	19	2	2	0	0	0	1	4	1		.105	.292	.105	25	-1	1	.864	-1	93	0	3b7		-0.2
PURTELL, BILLY									William Patrick B1.6.1886 Columbus OH D3.17.1962 Bradenton FL BR/TR/5-9/170 d4.16															
1908	Chi A	26	69	3	9	2	0	0	3	2		7	.130	.155	.159	2	-7	2	.940	5	138	241	3b25		-0.2
1909	Chi A	103	361	34	93	9	3	0	40	19	4		.258	.302	.299	94	-3	14	.929	-1	100	130	3b71,2b32		-0.2
1910	Chi A	102	368	21	82	5	3	1	36	21			.223	.272	.261	70	-14	5	.907	-1	102	117	3b102		-1.3
	Bos A	49	168	15	35	1	2	1	15	18	1		.208	.289	.256	69	-6	2	.908	-4	102	37	3b41,S8		-1.0
	Year	151	536	36	117	6	5	2	51	39	5		.218	.278	.259	70	-19	7	.907	-4	102	95	3b143,S8		-2.3
1911	Bos A	27	82	5	23	5	3	0	1	6			.280	.298	.415	99	-1	1	.867	-1	96	47	3b15,2b3,S3/OC		-0.1
1914	Det A	28	76	4	13	4	0	0	7	1		7	.171	.203	.224	27	-7	0-2	.946	-2	104	113	3b16,S2/2		-0.9
Total	5	335	1124	82	255	26	11	2	104	63	11	7	.227	.271	.275	73	-38	24-2	.915	-2	104	113	3b270,2b36,S13,OC		-3.7
PUTMAN, ED									Eddy William B9.25.1953 Los Angeles CA BR/TR/6-1/190* [ChiN75*S1/3] d9.7 Col USC															
1976	Chi N	5	7	1	3	0	0	0	0	0-0	0	1	.429	.429	.429	132	0	0-0	1.000	0	0	0	C3/1		0.0
1978	Chi N	17	25	2	5	0	0	0	4	4-0	0	6	.200	.310	.200	40	-2	0-0	.950	0	124	111	3b8,1b3,C2		-0.2
1979	Det A	21	39	4	9	3	0	2	4	4-0	0	11	.231	.302	.462	99	0	0-1	1.000	-0	102	69	C16,1b5		-0.1
Total	3	43	71	6	17	3	0	2	7	8-0	0	18	.239	.316	.366	81	-2	0-1	.971	-0	92	62	C21,1b9,3b8		-0.3

YEAR	TM LG	G	AB	R	H	2B	3B	HR	RBI	BB-IB	HP	SO	AVG	OBP	SLG	AOPS	ABR	SB-CS	FA	FR	RNG	THR	GAMES AT POSITION	DL	BFW
PUTNAM, PAT	Patrick Edward B12.3.1953 Bethel VT BL/TR/6-1/214(195-214) [TexA75 S1/22] d9.2 Col South Alabama																								-0.1
1977	Tex A	11	26	3	8	-4	0	0	3	1-1	0	4	.308	.333	.462	113	1	0-1	1.000	-1	33	94	1b7,D3		-0.6
1978	Tex A	20	46	4	7	1	0	1	2	2-1	0	5	.152	.188	.239	19	-5	0-0	1.000	0	107	94	D12,1b4		-0.5
1979	Tex A	139	426	57	118	19	2	18	64	23-6	6	50	.277	.319	.458	109	4	1-6	.994	-0	96	86	1b96,D32		-0.4
1980	Tex A	147	410	42	108	16	2	13	55	36-6	0	49	.263	.319	.407	101	0	0-2	.992	4	108	101	1b94,O3(3/0/1)		0.1
1981	Tex A	95	297	33	79	17	2	8	35	17-3	0	38	.266	.304	.418	112	4	4-2	.993	3	116	99	1b94,O3(3/0/1)		-0.5
1982	Tex A	43	122	14	28	8	0	2	9	10-1	1	18	.230	.293	.344	78	-4	0-2	.990	2	119	91	1b39/3OL		0.1
1983	Sea A	144	469	58	126	23	2	19	67	39-8	3	57	.269	.326	.448	107	4	2-1	.994	4	107	99	1b125,D11		-1.2
1984	Sea A	64	155	11	31	6	0	2	16	12-1	0	27	.200	.254	.277	48	-11	3-0	1.000	1	97	0	D30,O13L,1b6		-0.7
	Min A	14	38	1	3	1	0	0	4	4-0	0	12	.079	.163	.105	-22	-6	0-0	—	0	0	0	D11		-1.9
	Year	78	193	12	34	7	0	2	20	16-1	0	39	.176	.236	.244	34	-17	3-0	1.000	1	97	0	D41,O13L,1b6		-1.9
Total	8	677	1989	223	508	95	8	63	255	144-27	10	260	.255	.309	.406	96	-14	10-14	.993	12	108	97	1b508,D100,O17(17/0/1),3b2		-3.8
PYBURN, JIM	James Edward B11.1.1932 Fairfield AL BR/TR/6-0/190* d4.17 Col Auburn-Montgomery																							62	-1.1
1955	Bal A	39	98	5	20	2	2	0	7	8-0	1	24	.204	.271	.265	48	-8	1-1	1.000	-3	83	22	3b33/OR		-1.3
1956	Bal A	84	156	23	27	3	3	2	11	17-0	0	26	.173	.251	.269	41	-14	4-1	.975	3	106	169	O77(11/64/3)		0.2
1957	Bal A	35	40	8	9	0	0	1	2	9-0	0	6	.225	.367	.300	90	0	1-0	1.000	3	125	296	O28(7/13/9)/C		-1.1
Total	3	158	294	36	56	5	5	3	20	34-0	1	56	.190	.275	.272	51	-22	6-2	.982	4	111	200	O106(18/77/13),3b33/C	62	-2.2
PYE, EDDIE	Robert Edward B2.13.1967 Columbia TN BR/TR/5-10/175* [LAN88 10/244] d6.3 Col Middle Tennessee																								0.0
1994	LA N	7	10	2	1	0	0	0	0	1-0	0	4	.100	.182	.100	-25	-2	0-0	1.000	2	181	227	2b3,S3		-0.3
1995	LA N	7	8	0	0	0	0	0	0	0-0	0	4	.000	.000	.000	-99	-2	0-0	—	-1	0	0	3b2		-0.3
Total	2	14	18	2	1	0	0	0	0	1-0	0	8	.056	.105	.056	-60	-4	0-0	1.000	1	131	201	S3,2b3,3b2		-0.3
PYTLAK, FRANKIE	Frank Anthony B7.30.1908 Buffalo NY D5.8.1977 Buffalo NY BR/TR/5-7.5/160 d4.22 Mil 1942-45																								0.1
1932	Cle A	12	29	5	7	1	1	0	4	3	1	2	.241	.333	.345	71	-1	0-0	1.000	2	149	94	C12		1.2
1933	Cle A	80	248	36	77	10	6	2	33	17	0	10	.310	.355	.423	101	-1	3-4	1.000	10	136	155	C69		-0.8
1934	Cle A	91	289	46	75	12	4	0	35	36	5	11	.260	.352	.329	75	-10	11-2	.989	-6	105	73	C88		-0.2
1935	Cle A	55	149	14	44	6	1	1	12	11	1	4	.295	.348	.369	84	-4	3-2	.984	-1	117	110	C48		0.3
1936	Cle A	75	224	35	72	15	4	0	31	24	3	11	.321	.394	.424	101	1	5-2	.996	-2	88	133	C58		1.7
1937	Cle A	125	397	60	125	15	6	1	44	52	7	15	.315	.404	.390	100	3	16-5	.986	6	87	132	C115		-0.2
1938	Cle A	113	364	46	112	14	7	1	43	36	4	15	.308	.376	.393	95	-3	9-5	.987	-6	76	112	C99		0.0
1939	Cle A	63	183	20	49	2	5	0	14	20	1	5	.268	.343	.333	76	-7	4-1	1.000	4	111	93	C51		-1.1
1940	Cle A	62	149	16	21	2	1	0	16	17	1	5	.141	.234	.168	6	-21	0-1	.996	7	143	124	C58/OR		-0.4
1941	Bos A	106	336	36	91	23	1	2	39	28	1	19	.271	.329	.363	81	-9	5-7	.991	1	109	86	C91		-0.1
1945	Bos A	9	17	1	2	0	0	0	3	0	0	0	.118	.250	.118	8	-2	0-0	1.000	1	150	0	C4		-0.1
1946	Bos A	4	14	1	2	0	0	0	1	0	0	0	.143	.143	.143	-19	-2	0-0	1.000	1	150	0	C4		0.4
Total	12	795	2399	316	677	100	36	7	272	247	24	97	.282	.355	.363	84	-56	56-29	.991	17	105	112	C699/OR		0.4
PYZNARSKI, TIM	Timothy Matthew B2.4.1960 Chicago IL BR/TR/6-2/195 [OakA81 1/15] d9.14 Col Eastern Illinois																								-0.3
1986	SD N	15	42	3	10	1	0	0	6	4-3	0	11	.238	.319	.262	63	-2	2-0	.977	-1	93	117	1b13		
QUALLS, JIM	James Robert B10.9.1946 Exeter CA BB/TR/5-10/158* d4.10																							20	-1.1
1969	Chi N	43	120	12	30	5	3	0	9	2-0	1	14	.250	.266	.342	62	-6	2-1	1.000	-3	87	57	O35C,2b4		-0.2
1970	Mon N	9	9	1	1	0	0	0	1	0-0	0	0	.111	.111	.111	-40	-2	0-0	1.000	-0	120	0	2b2,O2L		-0.3
1972	Chi A	11	10	0	0	0	0	0	0	0-0	0	2	.000	.000	.000	-98	-2	0-0	1.000	0	121	0	/OC		-1.6
Total	3	63	139	13	31	5	3	0	10	2-0	1	16	.223	.238	.302	46	-10	2-1	1.000	-3	86	54	O38(2/36/0),2b6	20	-1.6
QUEEN, MEL	Melvin Douglas B3.26.1942 Johnson City NY BL/TR/6-1/197* d4.13 M1/C5 s-Mel ▲																								-0.1
1964	Cin N	48	95	7	19	2	0	2	12	4-0	0	19	.200	.232	.284	43	-7	0-1	.977	1	139	0	O20R		-0.1
1965	Cin N	5	3	0	0	0	0	0	0	0-0	0	1	.000	.000	.000	-94	-1	0-0	1.000	0	507	0	/OR		-0.1
1966	Cin N	56	55	4	7	1	0	0	5	10-1	0	12	.127	.250	.145	16	-6	0-0	.941	-3	52	106	P31	28	-0.1
1967	Cin N	49	81	6	17	4	0	0	5	4-0	0	10	.210	.244	.259	40	3	2-0	1.000	-1	136	0	P5	84	-0.1
1968	Cin N	10	8	2	1	0	0	0	0	1-0	0	5	.125	.222	.125	6	0	0-0	1.000	-0	52	0	P2		-0.1
1969	Cin N	2	6	0	1	0	0	0	1	0-0	0	2	.167	.167	.167	-6	0	0-0	1.000	0	57	0	P34	21	-0.1
1970	Cal A	37	16	1	4	0	0	0	1	0-0	0	2	.250	.250	.250	39	1	0-0	.900	-1	76	0	P44		-0.1
1971	Cal A	45	4	0	0	0	0	0	0	1-0	0	1	.000	.100	.000	-71	-1	0-0	1.000	-0	83	0	P17		-0.1
1972	Cal A	17	6	0	1	0	0	0	1	0-0	1	0	.167	.333	.167	5	0	0-0	1.000	-0	64	53	P5	133	-0.1
Total	9	269	274	20	49	7	0	2	25	21-1	1	50	.179	.233	.226	30	-11	2-1	.951	-1	64	53	P140,O53(2/0/52)		-0.1
QUEEN, BILLY	William Eddleman "Doc" B11.28.1928 Gastonia NC BR/TR/6-1/190 d4.13																								-0.1
1954	Mil N	3	2	0	0	0	0	0	0	0-0	0	2	.000	.000	.000	-99	-1	0-0	1.000	0	115	0	/OR		
QUELLICH, GEORGE	George William B2.10.1906 Johnsville CA D8.31.1958 Johnsville CA BR/TR/6-1/180 d8.1																								-0.1
1931	Det A	13	54	6	12	5	0	1	11	3	0	4	.222	.263	.370	63	-3	1-0	1.000	1	107	227	O13L		
QUEST, JOE	Joseph L. B11.16.1852 New Castle PA D11.14.1924 San Diego CA BR/TR/5-6/150 d8.30 U2																								-0.1
1871	Cle NA	3	13	1	3	1	0	0	2	1		0	.231	.286	.308	75	0	0-0	.571	-2	114	0	2b2/S		-0.1
1878	Ind N	62	278	45	57	3	2	0	13	12		24	.205	.238	.230	63	-9		.876	-0	92	106	2b62		0.0
1879	Chi N	**83**	334	38	69	16	1	0	22	9		33	.207	.227	.260	57	-15		.925	16	112	97	2b83		-0.1
1880	Chi N	82	300	37	71	12	1	0	27	8		16	.237	.256	.283	78	-7		.895	-3	101	89	2b77/S		-0.2
1881	Chi N	78	293	35	72	6	0	1	26	2		29	.246	.251	.276	63	-13		.879	-5	96	106	2b41/S		-0.1
1882	Chi N	42	159	24	32	5	2	0	15	8		16	.201	.240	.258	57	-8		.897	-3	92	140	2b37		-0.0
1883	Det N	37	137	22	32	8	2	0	15	10		18	.234	.286	.321	88	-1		.890	-3	92	71	2b19		-0.0
	StL AA	19	78	12	20	3	1	0	10	1			.256	.266	.321	83	-2		.893	-11	93	117	2b81		-0.1
1884	StL AA	81	310	46	64	9	5	0		19	2		.206	.257	.268	69	-11		.938	1	110	111	2b7,S5		0.0
	Pit AA	12	43	2	9	3	0	0		0	1		.209	.227	.279	65	-1		.897	-10	94	117	2b88,S5		-0.1
	Year	93	353	48	73	12	5	0		19	3		.207	.253	.269	69	-12		.898	-4	96	72	2b39,S15/OL		-0.0
1885	Det N	55	200	24	39	8	2	0	21	14		25	.195	.248	.255	63	-8		.847	0	104	115	S41,2b2		-0.0
1886	Phi AA	42	150	14	31	4	1	0	10	20	0		.207	.300	.247	71	-4	5	.901	-1	99	97	2b528,S65/OL3		-0.5
Total	9	593	2282	299	496	77	17	1	159	103	3	161	.217	.252	.267	67	-79	5	.901	-1	99	97	2b528,S65/OL3		-0.5
QUICK, HAL	James Harold "Blondie" B10.4.1917 Rome GA D3.9.1974 Swansea IL BR/TR/5-10.5/163 d9.7																								-0.0
1939	Was A	12	41	3	10	1	0	0	1	1		8	.244	.279	.268	44	-4	1-0	.927	-0	106	98	S10		
QUILICI, FRANK	Francis Ralph "Guido" B5.11.1939 Chicago IL BR/TR/6-0/175* d7.18 M4/C2 Col Western Michigan																								-0.0
1965	†Min A	56	149	16	31	5	1	0	7	15-0	0	33	.208	.280	.255	51	-9	1-1	.990	2	105	133	2b52,S4		-0.0
1967	Min A	23	19	2	2	1	0	0	3	3-0	0	4	.105	.227	.158	14	-2	0-0	1.000	-2	82	169	2b13,3b8/S		1
1968	Min A	97	229	22	56	11	4	1	22	21-0	1	45	.245	.305	.341	92	-2	0-0	.935	7	104	39	3b84,2b36/S		-0.0
1969	Min A	118	144	19	25	3	1	2	12	12-0	1	22	.174	.236	.250	35	-13	2-0	.987	-4	93	108	2b73,3b27/S		-0.0
1970	†Min A	111	141	19	32	3	0	2	12	15-3	0	16	.227	.297	.291	63	-9	0-2	.993	14	104	108	2b222,3b159,S13/1		-0.0
Total	5	405	682	78	146	23	6	5	53	66-3	2	120	.214	.281	.287	62	-33	3-3	.993	14	104	108	2b222,3b159,S13/1		-0.0
QUILLEN, LEE	Leon Abner B5.5.1882 North Branch MN D5.14.1965 St.Paul MN BR/TR/5-10/165 d9.30																								-0.0
1906	Chi A	4	9	1	3	0	0	0	0	0		0	.333	.333	.333	112	-0	0	.600	-2	66	155	S3		-0.0
1907	Chi A	49	151	17	29	5	0	0	14	10	3		.192	.256	.225	56	-7	8	.871	-4	105	87	3b48		-0.0
Total	2	53	160	18	32	5	0	0	14	10	3		.200	.260	.231	59	-7	9	.871	-4	105	87	3b48,S3		-0.0
QUINLAN	d9.7																								-0.0
1874	Phi NA	1	4	0	1	0	0	0	1	0		0	.250	.250	.250	59	0	0-0	1.000	0	132	0	/S		
QUINLAN, FRANK	Francis Patrick B3.9.1869 Marlborough MA D5.4.1904 Brockton MA 5-9/180 d10.5																								-0.0
1891	Bos AA	2	5	0	0	0	0	0	0	1		0	.000	.000	.000	-99	-1	0	1.000	0	181	91	/COL		
QUINLAN, ROBB	Robb William B3.17.1977 St.Paul MN BR/TR/6-1/200* [AnaA99 10/311] d7.28 b-Tom Col Minnesota																								-0.0
2003	Ana A	38	94	13	27	4	2	0	4	6-0	1	16	.287	.330	.372	88	-2	1-2	.988	-0	87	87	1b33/OLD		
2004	Ana A	56	160	23	55	14	0	5	23	14-0	2	26	.344	.401	.525	145	11	3-1	.983	-0	104	26	3b32,1b13,O9(6/0/3),D4	49	

YEAR	TM LG	G	AB	R	H	2B	3B	HR	RBI	BB-IB	HP	SO	AVG	OBP	SLG	AOPS	ABR	SB-CS	FA	FR	RNG	THR	GAMES AT POSITION	DL	BFW
2005	†LA A	54	134	17	31	8	0	5	14	7-0	1	26	.231	.273	.403	78	-5	0-1	.913	-2	98	87	3b33,1b9,O6L	53	-0.7
Total	3	148	388	53	113	26	2	10	41	27-0	3	68	.291	.340	.446	109	4	4-4	.942	-2	101	58	3b65,1b55,O16(13/0/3),D7	102	-0.2

QUINLAN, FINNERS Thomas Finners B10.21.1887 Scranton PA D2.17.1966 Scranton PA BL/TL/5-8/154 d9.6

YEAR	TM LG	G	AB	R	H	2B	3B	HR	RBI	BB-IB	HP	SO	AVG	OBP	SLG	AOPS	ABR	SB-CS	FA	FR	RNG	THR	GAMES AT POSITION	DL	BFW
1913	StL N	13	50	1	8	0	0	0	1			9	.160	.176	.160	-4	-7	0	.897	1	99	169	O12(1/0/11)		-0.7
1915	Chi A	42	114	11	22	3	0	0	7	4		11	.193	.270	.219	45	-8	3-4	1.000	1	90	151	O32(9/10/13)		-0.9
Total	2	55	164	12	30	3	0	0	8	5		20	.183	.243	.201	31	-15	3-4	.961	2	93	157	O44(10/10/24)		-1.6

QUINLAN, TOM Thomas Raymond B3.27.1968 St.Paul MN BR/TR/6-3/200(200-214) [TorA86 27/686] d9.4 b-Robb

YEAR	TM LG	G	AB	R	H	2B	3B	HR	RBI	BB-IB	HP	SO	AVG	OBP	SLG	AOPS	ABR	SB-CS	FA	FR	RNG	THR	GAMES AT POSITION	DL	BFW
1990	Tor A	1	2	0	1	0	0	0	0	0-0		1	.500	.667	.500	226		0-0	1.000	-1	55	0	/3		0.0
1992	Tor A	13	15	2	1	1	0	0	2	2-0		9	.067	.176	.133	-12	-2	0-0	.909	-1	64	0	3b13		-0.4
1994	Phi N	24	35	6	7	2	0	1	3	3-1		13	.200	.263	.343	55	-2	0-0	.966	-1	89	.57	3b20		-0.3
1996	Min A	4	6	0	0	0	0	0	0	0-0		3	.000	.000	.000	-98	-2	0-0	.667	-1	51	0	3b4		-0.3
Total	4	42	58	8	9	3	0	1	5	5-1	1	26	.155	.234	.259	30	-5	0-0	.932	-4	77	34	3b38		-1.0

QUINN d5.4

YEAR	TM LG	G	AB	R	H	2B	3B	HR	RBI	BB-IB	HP	SO	AVG	OBP	SLG	AOPS	ABR	SB-CS	FA	FR	RNG	THR	GAMES AT POSITION	DL	BFW
1875	Atl NA	2	8	2	1	0	0	0	0			0	.125	.125	.125	-15	-1	0-0	.800	-1	0	0	O2(0/1/1)/S		-0.3

QUINN, FRANK Frank J. B1876 Grand Rapids MI D2.17.1920 Camden IN 5-8/157 d8.9

YEAR	TM LG	G	AB	R	H	2B	3B	HR	RBI	BB-IB	HP	SO	AVG	OBP	SLG	AOPS	ABR	SB-CS	FA	FR	RNG	THR	GAMES AT POSITION	DL	BFW
1899	Chi N	12	34	6	6	0	1	0	6	0			.176	.300	.235	49	-2	1	.909	-2	0	0	O10(4/6/0)/2		-0.5

QUINN, JOHN John Edward "Pick" B9.12.1885 Framingham MA D4.9.1956 Marlboro MA BR/TR/5-11/150 d10.9

YEAR	TM LG	G	AB	R	H	2B	3B	HR	RBI	BB-IB	HP	SO	AVG	OBP	SLG	AOPS	ABR	SB-CS	FA	FR	RNG	THR	GAMES AT POSITION	DL	BFW
1911	Phi N	1	2	0	0	0	0	0	0	0			.000	.000	.000	-99	-1	0	1.000	-0	79	158	/C		-0.1

QUINN, JOE Joseph B Boston MA D3.1893 5-8/162 d9.7

YEAR	TM LG	G	AB	R	H	2B	3B	HR	RBI	BB-IB	HP	SO	AVG	OBP	SLG	AOPS	ABR	SB-CS	FA	FR	RNG	THR	GAMES AT POSITION	DL	BFW
1881	Bos N	1	4	0	0	0	0	0	0			0	.000	.000	.000	-99	-1		1.000	-0	0	0	/1		-0.1
	Wor N	2	7	0	1	0	0	0	1	1		2	.143	.250	.143	25	-1		.714	-2			C2		-0.3
	Year	3	11	0	1	0	0	0	1	1		2	.091	.167	.091	-16	-1		.714	-2			C2/1		-0.4

QUINN, JOE Joseph J. B12.25.1864 Sydney, New South Wales, Australia D11.12.1940 St.Louis MO BR/TR/5-7/158 d4.26 M2 OF(31/66/27)

YEAR	TM LG	G	AB	R	H	2B	3B	HR	RBI	BB-IB	HP	SO	AVG	OBP	SLG	AOPS	ABR	SB-CS	FA	FR	RNG	THR	GAMES AT POSITION	DL	BFW
1884	StL U	103	429	74	116	21	1	0		9			.270	.285	.324	81	-22		.945	-1	109	186	1b100,O3(1/0/2)/S		-2.9
1885	StL N	97	343	27	73	8	2	0	15	9		38	.213	.233	.248	59	-15		.875	-3	86	0	O57(27/13/17),3b31,1b11		-1.9
1886	StL N	75	271	33	63	11	3	1	21	8		31	.232	.254	.306	75	-8	12	.895	-3	131	64	O48(0/47/1),2b15,1b7,3b4,S2		-1.2
1888	Bos N	38	156	19	47	8	3	4	29	2	0	5	.301	.310	.468	142	6	12	.914	-5	93	78	2b38		0.3
1889	Bos N	112	444	57	116	13	5	2	69	25	5	21	.261	.308	.327	73	-19	24	.860	-17	89	97	S63,2b47,3b2		-2.8
1890	Bos P	130	509	87	153	19	8	7	82	44		24	.301	.359	.411	99	-4	29	.942	16	98	113	2b130		1.3
1891	Bos N	124	508	70	122	8	10	3	63	28	6	28	.240	.288	.313	67	-25	24	.938	-24	89	93	2b124		-4.0
1892	†Bos N	143	532	63	116	14	1	1	59	35	7	40	.218	.275	.254	55	-30	17	.951	5	98	143	2b143		-1.8
1893	StL N	135	547	68	126	18	6	0	71	33	4	7	.230	.279	.285	50	-41	24	.942	-33	83	101	2b135		-5.7
1894	StL N	106	405	59	116	18	1	4	61	24	1	8	.286	.328	.365	67	-23	25	.952	18	99	148	2b106		0.0
1895	StL N	135	547	86	172	19	3	5	76	37	2	7	.314	.360	.399	97	-3	22	.945	1	96	104	2b135,M		0.3
1896	StL N	48	191	19	40	6	1	1	17	9		2	.209	.252	.267	39	-17	8	.956	2	114	33	2b48		-1.2
	†Bal N	24	82	22	27	1	1	0	5	6	0	1	.329	.375	.366	94	-1	6	.951	-2	84	99	2b8,O8(1/1/6),3b5/S		-0.2
	Year	72	273	41	67	7	2	1	22	15		3	.245	.290	.297	56	-18	14	.955	-0	110	43	2b56,O8(1/1/6),3b5/S		-1.4
1897	Bal N	75	285	33	74	11	4	1	45	13	3		.260	.299	.337	68	-14	12	.946	2	114	142	3b37,S21,2b11,O6(1/5/0),1b2		-0.4
1898	Bal N	12	32	5	8	1	0	0	5	1	0	2	.250	.273	.281	58	-2	0	.893	-0	88	114	3b8/2OL		-0.2
	StL N	103	375	35	94	10	5	0	36	24	3		.251	.301	.304	72	-15	13	.962	-1	105	78	2b62,S41/OR		-1.0
	Year	115	407	40	102	11	5	0	41	25	3		.251	.299	.302	71	-16	13	.960	-1	105	77	2b63,S41,3b8,O2(1/0/1)		-1.2
1899	Cle N	147	615	73	176	24	6	0	72	21	2		.286	.312	.345	86	-13	22	.962	11	101	86	2b147,M		0.3
1900	StL N	22	80	12	21	2	0	1	11	10	0		.262	.344	.325	86	-1	4	.933	-6	81	60	2b14,S6/3		-0.6
	Cin N	74	266	18	73	5	2	0	25	16	0		.274	.316	.308	74	-10	7	.950	-10	89	90	2b74		-1.5
	Year	96	346	30	94	7	2	1	36	26	0		.272	.323	.312	77	-11	11	.947	-15	88	85	2b88,S6/3		-2.1
1901	Was A	66	266	33	67	11	2	2	34	11	2		.252	.287	.331	72	-11	7	.954	-6	92	64	2b66		-1.5
Total	17	1769	6883	893	1800	228	70	30	796	365	39	215	.262	.302	.328	74	-268	268	.946	-52	95	101	2b1304,S135,O124C,1b120,3b88		-24.7

QUINN, MARK Mark David B5.21.1974 LaMirada CA BR/TR/6-1/175(175-195) [KCA95 11/302] d9.14 Col Rice

YEAR	TM LG	G	AB	R	H	2B	3B	HR	RBI	BB-IB	HP	SO	AVG	OBP	SLG	AOPS	ABR	SB-CS	FA	FR	RNG	THR	GAMES AT POSITION	DL	BFW
1999	KC A	17	60	11	20	4	1	6	18	4-0	1	11	.333	.385	.733	170	-0	1-0	.964	-1	81	200	O15(15/0/1)/D		0.5
2000	KC A	135	500	76	147	33	2	20	78	35-1	3	91	.294	.342	.488	102	0	5-2	.988	1	90	180	O81(78/1/4),D48		-0.3
2001	KC A	118	453	57	122	31	2	17	60	12-1	7	69	.269	.298	.459	87	-9	9-5	.976	1	97	124	O99(49/0/50),D18		-1.4
2002	KC A	23	76	9	18	4	0	2	11	5-0	2	15	.237	.301	.368	68	-3	2-1	1.000	-1	88	0	O15R,D7	156	-0.3
Total	4	293	1089	153	307	72	5	45	167	56-2	13	186	.282	.324	.481	97	-6	17-8	.981	0	93	143	O210(142/1/70),D74	183	-1.7

QUINN, PADDY Patrick J. B8.1849 Chicago IL D1.2.1909 Chicago IL 5-8.5/148 d7.26

YEAR	TM LG	G	AB	R	H	2B	3B	HR	RBI	BB-IB	HP	SO	AVG	OBP	SLG	AOPS	ABR	SB-CS	FA	FR	RNG	THR	GAMES AT POSITION	DL	BFW
1871	Kek NA	5	17	8	4	0	0	0	4	2		0	.235	.381	.235	81	0	3-1	.964	2			C5		0.1
1875	Wes NA	11	43	4	14	1	0	0	5	0		1	.326	.326	.349	127	1	0-1	.861	1			C10/OC		0.1
	Har NA	5	13	1	3	0	0	0	1	0		0	.231	.286	.231	78	0	0-1	.833	-1			C3,O3(0/1/2)		-0.1
	Chi NA	17	61	12	14	0	0	0	1	0		2	.230	.230	.230	59	-3	1-1	.778	-4			C11,O10(0/9/1)		-0.6
	Year	33	117	17	31	1	0	0	7	1		6	.265	.271	.274	87	-2	1-3	.826	-4			C24,O14(0/11/3)		-0.6
1877	Chi N	4	14	1	1	0	0	0	0	0		0	.071	.133	.071	-30	-2		.667	-0	114	0	O4R		-0.2
Total	2 NA	38	134	25	35	1	0	0	9	5		6	.261	.288	.269	87	-2	4-4	.849	-2			C29,O14(0/11/3)		-0.5

QUINN, TOM Thomas Oscar B4.25.1864 Annapolis MD D7.24.1932 Pittsburgh PA BR/TR/5-8/180 d9.2

YEAR	TM LG	G	AB	R	H	2B	3B	HR	RBI	BB-IB	HP	SO	AVG	OBP	SLG	AOPS	ABR	SB-CS	FA	FR	RNG	THR	GAMES AT POSITION	DL	BFW
1886	Pit AA	3	11	1	0	0	0	0	0	0			.000	.000	.000	-99	-3	1	.929	-1			C3		-0.3
1889	Bal AA	55	194	18	34	2	1	0	15	19		22	.175	.252	.211	32	-18	6	.925	7			C55		-0.5
1890	Pit P	55	207	23	44	4	3	1	15	17	3	8	.213	.282	.275	54	-14	1	.888	-3	103	84	C55		-1.0
Total	3	113	412	42	78	6	4	2	30	36	4	30	.189	.261	.238	40	-35	8	.910	3	103	84	C113		-1.8

QUINONES, LUIS Luis Raul B4.28.1962 Ponce, PR BB/TR/5-11/175(155-185) d5.27

YEAR	TM LG	G	AB	R	H	2B	3B	HR	RBI	BB-IB	HP	SO	AVG	OBP	SLG	AOPS	ABR	SB-CS	FA	FR	RNG	THR	GAMES AT POSITION	DL	BFW
1983	Oak A	19	42	5	8	2	1	0	4	1-0		4	.190	.205	.286	37	-4	1-1	1.000	2	129	99	2b6,3b4,O4R,S3,D4		-0.2
1986	SF N	71	106	13	19	1	3	0	11	3-1	1	17	.179	.207	.245	26	-12	3-1	.922	-6	100	101	S33,3b31,2b8		-1.7
1987	Chi N	49	101	12	22	6	0	0	8	10-0	0	16	.218	.288	.277	49	-7	0-0	.965	-1	89	74	S28,2b4/3		-0.6
1988	Cin N	97	340	43	83	13	4	12	30	25-0	3	46	.244	.300	.412	99	-2	2-4	.979	-2	94	85	S10,2b4,3b4		-0.1
1990	†Cin N	83	145	10	35	7	0	2	17	13-3	1	29	.241	.301	.331	73	-5	1-0	.981	6	122	0	3b22,2b13,S9/1		-0.4
1991	Cin N	97	212	15	47	4	3	4	20	21-3	2	31	.222	.297	.325	72	-8	1-2	.975	-7	101	115	2b33,3b19,S5		0.2
1992	Min A	3	5	0	1	0	0	0	0	1-0	0	2	.200	.167	.200	12	-1	0-0	.714	0	120	0	/3SD		-1.6
Total	8	442	1003	102	227	36	11	19	106	75-8	7	154	.226	.282	.341	72	-41	9-9	.937	-8	94	55	3b132,2b121,S94,D5,O4R/1		-4.5

QUINONES, REY Rey Francisco (Santiago) B11.11.1963 Rio Piedras, PR BR/TR/5-11/185(160-185) d5.17

YEAR	TM LG	G	AB	R	H	2B	3B	HR	RBI	BB-IB	HP	SO	AVG	OBP	SLG	AOPS	ABR	SB-CS	FA	FR	RNG	THR	GAMES AT POSITION	DL	BFW
1986	Bos A	62	190	26	45	12	1	2	15	19-0	3	26	.237	.315	.342	79	-5	3-2	.940	-8	92	71	S62		-0.7
	Sea A	36	122	6	23	4	0	0	7	5-0	0	31	.189	.219	.221	20	-14	1-1	.945	0	99	115	S36		-1.0
	Year	98	312	32	68	16	1	2	22	24-0	3	57	.218	.279	.295	56	-19	4-3	.942	-8	95	87	S98		-1.7
1987	Sea A	135	478	55	132	18	2	12	56	26-0	4	71	.276	.317	.397	84	-12	1-3	.959	-4	100	98	S135		-0.2
1988	Sea A	140	499	63	124	30	3	12	52	23-1	5	71	.248	.284	.393	84	-12	0-3	.963	8	100	119	S135,D4		0.5
1989	Sea A	7	19	2	2	0	0	0	0	1-0	0	1	.105	.150	.105	-26	-3	0-0	.889	-1	98	70	S7		-0.5
	Pit N	71	225	21	47	11	0	3	29	15-2	1	40	.209	.253	.298	61	-12	0-2	.934	-14	95	73	S69		-2.3
Total	4	451	1533	173	373	75	6	29	159	89-3	11	240	.243	.287	.357	74	-58	5-11	.952	-19	98	98	S444,D4	9	-4.2

QUINTANA, CARLOS Carlos Narcis (Hernandez) B8.26.1965 Estado Miranda, Venez BR/TR/6-2/195(195-220) d9.16 [DL 1992 Bos A 182]

YEAR	TM LG	G	AB	R	H	2B	3B	HR	RBI	BB-IB	HP	SO	AVG	OBP	SLG	AOPS	ABR	SB-CS	FA	FR	RNG	THR	GAMES AT POSITION	DL	BFW
1988	Bos A	5	6	1	2	0	0	0	2	2-0	0	3	.333	.500	.333	132	0	0-0	1.000	0	106	0	O3R/D		0.0
1989	Bos A	34	77	6	16	5	0	0	6	7-0	0	12	.208	.274	.273	51	-5	0-0	.926	-2	90	0	O21(4/1/17)/1D	15	-0.7
1990	†Bos A	149	512	56	147	28	0	7	67	52-0	2	74	.287	.354	.383	101	2	1-2	.987	13	133	96	1b148,O3R		0.5
1991	Bos A	149	478	69	141	21	1	11	71	61-2	5	66	.295	.375	.412	112	10	1-0	.993	9	124	102	1b138,O13(1/0/12)/D		0.9
1993	Bos A	101	303	31	74	5	0	1	19	31-2	2	52	.244	.317	.271	66	-18	1-0	.991	-1	80	102	1b53,O51(1/0/50)		-2.4
Total	5	438	1376	163	380	59	1	19	165	153-4	6	207	.276	.350	.362	92	-11	3-2	.990	19	123	99	1b340,O91(6/1/85),D9	197	-1.7

QUINTANILLA, OMAR Omar B10.24.1981 El Paso TX BL/TR/5-9/190 d7.31 Col Texas

YEAR	TM LG	G	AB	R	H	2B	3B	HR	RBI	BB-IB	HP	SO	AVG	OBP	SLG	AOPS	ABR	SB-CS	FA	FR	RNG	THR	GAMES AT POSITION	DL	BFW
2005	Col N	39	128	16	28	1	0	1	10	7	9-0	0	15	.219	.270	.242	31	-13	2-1	.992	-1	100	71	S31,2b6	-1.1

YEAR	TM LG	G	AB	R	H	2B	3B	HR	RBI	BB-IB	HP	SO	AVG	OBP	SLG	AOPS	ABR	SB-CS	FA	FR	RNG	THR	GAMES AT POSITION	DL	BFW

QUINTERO, HUMBERTO Humberto B8.2.1979 Maracaibo, Venez BR/TR/5-9/200(190-215) d9.3

YEAR	TM LG	G	AB	R	H	2B	3B	HR	RBI	BB-IB	HP	SO	AVG	OBP	SLG	AOPS	ABR	SB-CS	FA	FR	RNG	THR	GAMES AT POSITION	DL	BFW
2003	SD N	12	23	1	5	0	0	0	2	1-1	0	6	.217	.250	.217	26	-3	0-0	.982	0	164	68	C11		-0.2
2004	SD N	23	72	7	18	3	0	2	10	5-0	0	16	.250	.295	.375	76	-3	0-2	1.000	-0	134	24	C21		-0.2
2005	Hou N	18	54	6	10	1	0	1	8	1-1	0	10	.185	.200	.259	19	-7	0-0	.989	-3	102	68	C16/1	27	-0.9
Total	3	53	149	14	33	4	0	3	20	7-2	0	32	.221	.255	.309	48	-13	0-2	.993	-3	128	47	C48/1	27	-1.3

QUINTON, MARSHALL Marshall J. B Philadelphia PA 5-11/190 d8.7

YEAR	TM LG	G	AB	R	H	2B	3B	HR	RBI	BB-IB	HP	SO	AVG	OBP	SLG	AOPS	ABR	SB-CS	FA	FR	RNG	THR	GAMES AT POSITION	DL	BFW
1884	Ric AA	26	94	12	22	5	0	0		0	1	1	.234	.242	.287	73	-3		.878	-4			C14,O10R,S2		-0.5
1885	Phi AA	7	29	6	6	1	0	0		4	1	1	.207	.258	.241	55	-1		.869	-2			C7		-0.3
Total	2	33	123	18	28	6	0	0		4	1	2	.228	.246	.276	68	-4		.874	-6			C21,O10R,S2		-0.8

QUIRK, JAMIE James Patrick B10.22.1954 Whittier CA BL/TR/6-4/200(185-200) [KCA72 1/18] d9.4 C13 OF(24/0/8)

YEAR	TM LG	G	AB	R	H	2B	3B	HR	RBI	BB-IB	HP	SO	AVG	OBP	SLG	AOPS	ABR	SB-CS	FA	FR	RNG	THR	GAMES AT POSITION	DL	BFW
1975	KC A	14	39	2	10	0	0	1	5	2-1	0	7	.256	.293	.333	75	-1	0-0	.909	0	106	161	O10L,3b2/D		-0.2
1976	†KC A	64	114	11	28	6	0	1	15	2-0	0	22	.246	.252	.325	69	-5	0-0	1.000	-2	56	77	D19,S12,3b11,1b2		-0.7
1977	Mil A	93	221	16	48	14	1	3	13	8-2	2	47	.217	.251	.330	57	-14	0-1	.950	1	147	218	D53,O10L,3b8		-1.4
1978	KC A	17	29	3	6	2	0	0	2	5-0	0	4	.207	.324	.276	68	-1	0-0	.926	0	96	77	3b10,S2/D	22	-0.1
1979	KC A	51	79	8	24	6	1	1	11	5-0	1	13	.304	.353	.443	111	1	0-0	.944	-1	277	0	C9,S5,3b3,D9		0.1
1980	KC A	62	163	13	45	5	0	5	21	7-2	1	24	.276	.305	.399	91	-2	3-2	.929	-1	111	41	3b28,C15,O7(2/0/5)/1D		-0.3
1981	KC A	46	100	8	25	7	0	0	10	6-1	1	17	.250	.299	.320	78	-3	0-2	.985	-3	67	74	C22,3b8/2OR		-0.7
1982	KC A	36	78	8	18	3	0	1	5	3-0	0	15	.231	.256	.308	55	-5	0-0	1.000	1	91	84	C29,1b6/3OL	22	-1.1
1983	StL N	48	86	3	18	2	1	2	11	6-0	1	27	.209	.269	.326	64	-5	0-0	.929	-7	66	106	C22,3b7/S		-1.0
1984	Chi N	3	2	0	0	0	0	0	1	0-0	0	2	.000	.000	.000	-95	-1	0-0	1.000	0	0	0	/3		0.0
	Cle A	1	1	1	1	0	0	0	0	0-0	0	0	1.000	1.000	4.000	1186	1	0-0	—	-0	6	0	/C		0.1
	Year	4	3	1	1	0	0	0	2	0-0	0	2	.333	.250	1.333	323	1	0-0	1.000	-0	0	0	/3C		0.1
1985	†KC A	19	57	3	16	3	1	0	4	2-0	0	9	.281	.305	.368	83	-1	0-0	.986	-2	83	196	C17/1		-0.3
1986	KC A	80	219	24	47	10	0	8	26	17-3	1	41	.215	.273	.370	72	-9	0-1	.989	18	148	186	C41,3b24,1b6/OL		-0.3
1987	KC A	109	296	24	70	17	0	5	33	28-1	4	41	.236	.307	.345	72	-12	1-0	.986	4	89	107	C108/S	15	-0.3
1988	KC A	84	196	22	47	7	1	8	25	28-2	.1	41	.240	.333	.408	106	2	1-5	.982	14	75	109	C79/13		1.8
1989	NY A	13	24	0	2	0	0	0	0	3-0	0	5	.083	.185	.083	-22	-0	0-1	1.000	0	51	123	C6/SD		-0.4
	Oak A	9	10	1	2	0	0	1	1	0-0	0	0	.200	.200	.500	94	0	0-1	1.000	4	154	160	C24		
	Bal A	25	51	5	11	2	0	1	9	9-0	0	11	.216	.328	.255	70	-2	0-1	1.000	5	129	150	C32,3b3/SD1OR		
	Year	47	85	6	15	2	0	1	10	12-0	0	20	.176	.276	.235	47	-6	0-2	1.000	5	129	150	C37,1b8,3b8/ORD		
1990	†Oak A	56	121	12	34	5	1	3	26	14-1	1	34	.281	.353	.413	120	3	0-0	.977	2	183	112	C37,1b8,3b8/ORD		
1991	Oak A	76	203	16	53	4	0	3	17	16-1	2	28	.261	.321	.296	76	-7	0-3	.982	0	80	150	C54,1b8/3D		
1992	†Oak A	78	177	13	39	7	1	2	11	16-3	3	28	.220	.294	.305	72	-7	0-0	.973	0	78	122	C59,1b9,3b2/D		
Total	18	984	2266	193	544	100	7	43	247	177-17	18	435	.240	.298	.347	78	-72	5-16	.982	32	98	125	C525,3b118,D88,1b43,O32L,S22/2	59	-2.?

QUIROZ, GUILLERMO Guillermo Antonio B11.29.1981 Maracaibo, Venez BR/TR/6-1/200* d9.4

YEAR	TM LG	G	AB	R	H	2B	3B	HR	RBI	BB-IB	HP	SO	AVG	OBP	SLG	AOPS	ABR	SB-CS	FA	FR	RNG	THR	GAMES AT POSITION	DL	BFW
2004	Tor A	17	52	2	11	2	0	0	6	2-0	2	8	.212	.263	.250	34	-5	1-0	.976	-0	138	63	C15,D2		
2005	Tor A	12	36	3	7	2	0	0	4	2-0	1	13	.194	.256	.250	34	-3	1-0	1.000	-0	47	137	C10,D2		
Total	2	29	88	5	18	4	0	0	10	4-0	3	21	.205	.260	.250	34	-8	1-0	.986	-0	99	94	C25,D4		

RAABE, BRIAN Brian Charles B11.5.1967 New Ulm MN BR/TR/5-9/177* [MinA90 41/1081] d9.17 Col Minnesota

YEAR	TM LG	G	AB	R	H	2B	3B	HR	RBI	BB-IB	HP	SO	AVG	OBP	SLG	AOPS	ABR	SB-CS	FA	FR	RNG	THR	GAMES AT POSITION	DL	BFW
1995	Min A	6	14	4	3	0	0	0	1	1-0	0	0	.214	.267	.214	27	-2	0-0	1.000	-0	114	187	2b4,3b2		
1996	Min A	7	9	0	2	0	0	0	1	1-0	0	2	.222	.200	.222	13	-1	0-0	.857	-0	97	253	3b6/2		
1997	Sea A	2	3	0	0	0	0	0	0	1-0	0	2	.000	.250	.000	-27	-1	0-0	1.000	-1	72	0	3b2/2		
	Col N	2	3	0	1	0	0	0	0	0-0	0	0	.333	.333	.333	61	-0	0-0	1.000	-0	144	0	/2		
Total	3	17	29	4	6	0	0	0	2	2-0	0	4	.207	.250	.207	21	-4	0-0	.889	-1	66	141	3b10,2b7		

RABB, JOHN John Andrew B6.23.1960 Los Angeles CA BR/TR/6-1/180* [SFN78 11/267] d9.4

YEAR	TM LG	G	AB	R	H	2B	3B	HR	RBI	BB-IB	HP	SO	AVG	OBP	SLG	AOPS	ABR	SB-CS	FA	FR	RNG	THR	GAMES AT POSITION	DL	BFW
1982	SF N	2	2	0	1	0	0	0	0	0-0	0	1	.500	.500	1.500	444	1	0-0	1.000	0	217	0	/OL		
1983	SF N	40	104	10	24	9	0	1	14	9-1	0	17	.231	.292	.346	78	-3	1-0	.973	-2	73	58	C31,O2R		
1984	SF N	54	82	10	16	1	0	3	9	10-0	0	33	.195	.283	.317	70	-3	1-1	.988	-2	98	37	1b13,O8(3/0/6),C6		
1985	Atl N	3	3	0	0	0	0	0	0	0-0	0	1	.000	.000	.000	-94	-1	0-0	—	-0	0	0	/OL		
1988	Sea A	9	14	2	5	2	0	0	4	0-0	0	1	.357	.357	.500	131	0	0-0	1.000	8	194	0	O2R/1D		
Total	5	108	204	22	46	12	1	4	27	19-1	0	53	.225	.291	.353	81	-5	2-1	.966	-4	72	59	C37,1b14,O14(5/0/10),D5		

RABBITT, JOE Joseph Patrick B1.16.1900 Frontenac KS D12.5.1969 Norwalk CT BL/TR/5-10/165 d9.15

YEAR	TM LG	G	AB	R	H	2B	3B	HR	RBI	BB-IB	HP	SO	AVG	OBP	SLG	AOPS	ABR	SB-CS	FA	FR	RNG	THR	GAMES AT POSITION	DL	BFW
1922	Cle A	2	3	1	1	0	0	0	0	0-0	0	0	.333	.333	.333	74	0	0-0	—	-0	0	0	/OL		

RABURN, RYAN Ryan N. B4.17.1981 Tampa FL BR/TR/6-0/185 [DetA01 5/147] d9.12 Col South Florida JC

YEAR	TM LG	G	AB	R	H	2B	3B	HR	RBI	BB-IB	HP	SO	AVG	OBP	SLG	AOPS	ABR	SB-CS	FA	FR	RNG	THR	GAMES AT POSITION	DL	BFW
2004	Det A	12	29	4	4	1	0	0	1	0-0	0	9	.138	.194	.172	-4	-5	1-0	.969	-1	106	102	2b11		

RACKLEY, MARV Marvin Eugene B7.25.1921 Seneca SC BL/TL/5-10/170* d4.15

YEAR	TM LG	G	AB	R	H	2B	3B	HR	RBI	BB-IB	HP	SO	AVG	OBP	SLG	AOPS	ABR	SB-CS	FA	FR	RNG	THR	GAMES AT POSITION	DL	BFW
1947	Bro N	18	9	2	2	0	0	0	2	1	0	0	.222	.300	.222	39	-1	0	1.000	0	153	0	O2(0/1/1)		
1948	Bro N	88	281	55	92	13	5	0	15	19	0	25	.327	.370	.409	107	3	8	.949	-2	91	137	O74(43/33/1)		
1949	†Bro N	9	9	2	4	1	0	0	1	1	0	0	.444	.500	.556	175	1	0	1.000	-0	90	0	O3L		
	Pit N	11	35	5	11	2	0	0	2	2	0	3	.314	.351	.371	92	0	1	.986	-2	90	0	O44(41/3/0)		
	†Bro N	54	141	23	41	4	1	1	14	13	0	8	.291	.351	.355	86	-3	1	.986	-3	99	0	O55(44/11/0)		
	Year	74	185	30	56	7	1	1	17	16	0	11	.303	.363	.368	91	-2	2	.990	-3	99	0	/H		
1950	Cin N	5	2	0	1	0	0	0	1	0	0	0	.500	.500	.500	163	0	0	—	0			/H		
Total	4	185	477	87	151	20	6	1	35	36	0	36	.317	.365	.390	100	0	10	.966	-4	95	82	O131(87/45/2)		

RADCLIFF, JOHN John Y. B6.29.1846 Philadelphia PA D7.26.1911 Ocean City NJ 5-6/140 d5.20

YEAR	TM LG	G	AB	R	H	2B	3B	HR	RBI	BB-IB	HP	SO	AVG	OBP	SLG	AOPS	ABR	SB-CS	FA	FR	RNG	THR	GAMES AT POSITION	DL	BFW
1871	Ath NA	28	145	47	44	7	5	0	22	6		1	3	.303	.331	.421	116	3	5-1	.804	3	110	79	S28		0
1872	Bal NA	56	297	70	86	13	4	1	44	0		2	.290	.290	.370	97	-3	3-3	.771	-5	92	96	S50,3b6/2		
1873	Bal NA	45	244	59	70	5	0	0	33	4		2	.287	.298	.307	81	-6	0-0	.772	-1	125	60	3b24,S23/2		
1874	Phi NA	23	103	20	25	7	0	1	14	2		1	.243	.257	.340	87	-1	1-1	.800	-1	57	0	O15(0/1/14),2b4,S3,3b3,1b2		
1875	Cen NA	5	23	2	4	0	0	0	1	0-0			.174	.208	.174	37	-1	0-0	.651	-1	97	85	S5		
Total	5 NA	157	812	198	229	32	9	2	113	13		5	.282	.293	.351	93	-8	9-5	.765	-4	97	85	S109,3b33,O15(0/1/14),2b6,1b2		

RADCLIFF, RIP Raymond Allen B1.19.1906 Kiowa OK D5.23.1962 Enid OK BL/TL/5-10/170 d9.17 Mil 1944-46

YEAR	TM LG	G	AB	R	H	2B	3B	HR	RBI	BB-IB	HP	SO	AVG	OBP	SLG	AOPS	ABR	SB-CS	FA	FR	RNG	THR	GAMES AT POSITION	DL	BFW
1934	Chi A	14	56	7	15	2	1	0	5	0	0	2	.268	.268	.339	54	-4	1-0	.946	-0	118	0	O14R		
1935	Chi A	146	623	95	178	28	8	10	68	53	4	21	.286	.346	.404	91	-1	4-4	.968	-17	75	68	O142L		
1936	Chi A★	138	618	120	207	31	7	8	82	44	2	12	.335	.381	.447	100	-1	6-3	.936	-17	79	52	O132L		
1937	Chi A	144	584	105	190	38	10	4	79	53	2	25	.325	.383	.445	108	8	6-1	.966	-3	87	0	O139L		
1938	Chi A	129	503	64	166	23	6	5	81	36	1	17	.330	.376	.429	99	-1	5-7	.979	-3	104	65	O99L,1b23		
1939	Chi A	113	397	49	105	25	5	2	53	26	2	21	.264	.313	.353	68	-19	6-4	.970	-8	88	18	O78(10/0/69),1b20		
1940	StL A	150	584	83	**200**	33	9	7	81	47	1	20	.342	.392	.466	119	17	6-4	.973	-5	93	77	O139(116/0/23),1b44		
1941	StL A	19	71	12	20	2	2	2	14	10	1	1	.282	.370	.451	112	1	1-1	1.000	-2	87	0	O14L,1b3		
	Det A	96	379	47	120	14	5	3	40	19	1	13	.317	.351	.404	94	-6	4-4	.970	-5	88	87	O87(85/0/2)		
	Year	115	450	59	140	16	7	5	54	29	1	14	.311	.354	.411	94	-5	5-5	.974	-7	88	75	O101(99/0/2),1b3		
1942	Det A	62	144	13	36	5	0	1	20	9	0	6	.250	.294	.306	64	-7	0-1	.978	-4	95	60	O24(6/0/18),1b4		
1943	Det A	70	115	3	30	4	0	0	10	13	1	7	.261	.341	.296	81	-2	1-1	1.000	1	97	75	O19(2/0/17)/1		
Total	10	1081	4074	598	1267	205	50	42	533	310	14	141	.311	.362	.417	96	-23	40-30	.967	-59	89	65	O887(745/0/143),1b55		

RADER, DAVE David Martin B12.26.1948 Claremore OK BL/TR/5-11/165(160-176) [SFN67 1/18] d9.5

YEAR	TM LG	G	AB	R	H	2B	3B	HR	RBI	BB-IB	HP	SO	AVG	OBP	SLG	AOPS	ABR	SB-CS	FA	FR	RNG	THR	GAMES AT POSITION	DL	BFW
1971	SF N	3	3	0	0	0	0	0	0	0-0	0	0	.000	.000	.000	-99	-1	0-0	1.000	0	0	0	/C		
1972	SF N	133	459	44	119	14	1	6	41	29-4	3	31	.259	.306	.333	81	-12	1-2	.985	-8	85	99	C127		
1973	SF N	148	462	59	106	15	4	9	41	63-23	6	22	.229	.326	.338	82	-10	0-1	.991	-13	75	77	C148		
1974	SF N	113	323	26	94	16	2	1	26	31-9	0	21	.291	.351	.362	96	-1	1-0	.984	-5	97	76	C109		
1975	SF N	98	292	39	85	15	0	5	31	32-12	1	30	.291	.360	.394	106	3	1-0	.984	-3	85	96	C94		
1976	SF N	88	255	25	67	15	0	2	27	27-8	0	21	.263	.332	.333	87	-3	2-0	.976	-3	96	81	C38		
1977	StL N	66	114	15	30	7	1	1	16	9-0	0	10	.263	.310	.368	84	-3	1-1	.977	-6	116	126	C114		
1978	Chi N	116	305	29	62	13	3	1	36	34-7	1	45	.203	.281	.295	60	-18	1-0	.932	-5	70	151	C25		
1979	Phi N	31	54	3	11	1	1	1	5	6-0	0	7	.204	.283	.315	60	-3	0-0							

YEAR	TM LG	G	AB	R	H	2B	3B	HR	RBI	BB-IB	HP	SO	AVG	OBP	SLG	AOPS	ABR	SB-CS	FA	FR	RNG	THR	GAMES AT POSITION	DL	BFW
1980	Bos A	50	137	14	45	11	0	3	17	14-1	1	0	.328	.388	.474	129	6	1-1	.981	1	93	112	C34,D9		0.8
Total	10	846	2405	254	619	107	12	30	235	245-64	11	180	.257	.326	.349	86	-42	8-4	.983	-41	90	93	C771,D9		-5.4

RADER, DON   Donald Russell B9.5.1893 Wolcott IN D6.26.1983 Walla Walla WA   BL/TR/5-10/164   d7.25   Col Oregon

1913	Chi A	4	3	1	1	1	0	0	0	0	0	0	.333	.333	.667	193	0	0	.000	-1	0	0	/3OL		0.0
1921	Phi N	9	32	4	9	2	0	0	3	3	0	5	.281	.343	.344	76	-1	0-0	1.000	-2	84	67	S9		-0.2
Total	2	13	35	5	10	3	0	0	3	3	0	5	.286	.342	.371	84	-1	0-0	1.000	-3	84	67	S9/OL3		-0.2

RADER, DOUG   Douglas Lee "Rojo","The Red Rooster" B7.30.1944 Chicago IL   BR/TR/6-3/210*   d7.31   M7/C8   Col Illinois Wesleyan

1967	Hou N	47	162	24	54	10	4	2	26	7-2	2	31	.333	.360	.481	146	9	0-3	.972	-1	91	96	1b36,3b7		0.5
1968	Hou N	98	333	42	89	16	4	6	41	31-3	1	51	.267	.328	.393	119	8	2-2	.930	-0	96	83	3b86,1b5		0.8
1969	Hou N	155	569	62	140	25	3	11	83	62-7	6	103	.246	.325	.359	93	-5	1-5	.945	13	100	126	3b154,1b4		0.7
1970	Hou N	156	576	60	145	25	3	25	87	57-7	4	102	.252	.322	.436	106	3	3-2	.966	25	118	128	3b154/1		2.7
1971	Hou N	135	484	51	118	21	4	12	56	40-2	3	112	.244	.303	.378	95	-4	5-1	.946	7	110	129	3b135		0.4
1972	Hou N	152	553	70	131	24	7	22	90	57-8	5	120	.237	.309	.425	111	7	5-5	.958	18	110	119	3b152		2.4
1973	Hou N	154	574	79	146	26	0	21	89	46-6	3	97	.254	.310	.409	99	-2	4-3	.945	-9	91	80	3b152		-1.2
1974	Hou N	152	533	61	137	27	3	17	78	60-7	4	131	.257	.334	.415	114	10	7-2	.965	3	104	91	3b152		1.3
1975	Hou N	129	448	41	100	23	2	12	48	42-3	5	101	.223	.296	.364	89	-8	5-4	.955	6	108	88	3b137		-0.2
1976	SD N	139	471	45	121	22	4	9	55	55-3	3	102	.257	.335	.378	112	8	3-4	.971	7	102	106	3b124,S2		1.3
1977	SD N	52	170	19	46	8	3	5	27	33-1	1	40	.271	.392	.441	136	10	0-1	.961	-1	97	104	3b51		0.8
	Tor A	96	313	47	75	18	2	13	40	38-2	3	65	.240	.323	.435	104	2	2-1	.966	4	114	22	3b45,D34,1b7/OR		0.4
Total	11	1465	5186	631	1302	245	39	155	722	528-51	40	1055	.251	.322	.403	106	38	37-33	.956	73	105	104	3b1349,1b53,D34,S2/OR		9.9

RADFORD, PAUL   Paul Revere "Shorty" B10.14.1861 Roxbury MA D2.21.1945 Boston MA   BR/TR/5-6/148   d5.1   OF(33/153/724) ▲

1883	Bos N	72	258	46	53	6	3	0	14	9		26	.205	.232	.252	46	-17		.836	-3	105	93	O72(1/24/50)		-1.9
1884	†Pro N	97	355	56	70	11	2	1	29	25		43	.197	.250	.248	58	-16		.882	2	125	155	O96R,P2		-1.4
1885	Pro N	105	371	55	90	12	5	0	32	33		43	.243	.304	.302	99	1		.852	3	155	306	O88(2/8/80),S16,P3/2		0.3
1886	KC N	122	493	78	113	17	5	0	58			48	.229	.310	.284	77	-13	39	.890	6	155	151	O92R,S30/2		-0.6
1887	NY AA	128	486	127	129	15	5	4	45	106	6		.265	.403	.342	114	19	73	.833	0	98	127	S76,O37(1/1/36),2b18,P2		1.7
1888	Bro AA	90	308	48	67	9	3	2	29	35	4		.218	.305	.286	99	-2	33	.944	6	151	72	O88(0/83/5),2b2		0.1
1889	Cle N	136	487	94	116	21	5	1	46	91	6	37	.238	.365	.308	91	-1	30	.942	-1	92	129	O136(0/2/136)/3		-0.3
1890	Cle P	122	466	98	136	24	12	2	62	82	8	28	.292	.406	.408	128	6	25	.895	10	113	160	O80(6/35/39),S36,3b7,2b4/P		2.7
1891	Bos AA	133	456	102	118	11	5	0	65	96	5	36	.259	.393	.305	102	8	55	.906	19	111	153	S131,O4L/P		2.6
1892	Was N	137	510	93	130	19	4	1	37	86	8	47	.255	.366	.314	109	11	35	.933	-2	136	352	O62(2/0/60),3b54,S20,2b2		0.8
1893	Was N	124	464	87	106	18	3	2	34	104	8	42	.228	.378	.293	82	-5	32	.901	7	142	79	O123(7/0/116)/2P		-0.3
1894	Was N	95	325	61	78	13	5	0	49	65	1	23	.240	.378	.311	70	-13	24	.852	1	109	65	O47,2b25,O24(10/0/14)		-0.8
Total	12	1361	4979	945	1206	176	57	13	462	790	47	373	.242	.351	.308	92	-2	346	.901	46	132	151	O902R,S356,3b62,2b54,P10		2.9

RADMANOVICH, RYAN   Ryan Ashley B8.9.1971 Calgary AL, Can.   BL/TR/6-2/200   [MinA93 14/401]   d4.13   Col Pepperdine

1998	Sea A	25	69	5	15	4	0	2	10	4-1	0	26	.217	.260	.362	59	-4	1-1	1.000	-0	87	148	O24R/1		-0.6

RADTKE, JACK   Jack William B4.14.1913 Denver CO   BB/TR/5-7/160   d8.1

1936	Bro N	33	31	8	3	0	0	0	2	4	0	9	.097	.200	.097	-18	-5	3	1.000	2	150	0	2b14,3b5,S4		-0.3

RAFTER, JACK   John Cornelius B2.20.1875 Troy NY D1.5.1943 Troy NY   BR/TR/5-8/165   d9.24   Col Fordham

1904	Pit N	1	3	0	0	0	0	0	0	0	0		.000	.000	.000	-97	-1	0	1.000	0	103	114	/C		-0.1

RAFTERY, TOM   Thomas Francis B10.5.1881 Boston MA D12.31.1954 Boston MA   BR/TR/5-10.5/175   d4.18

1909	Cle A	8	32	6	7	2	1	0	4	0			.219	.306	.344	101	0	1	1.000	-1	0	0	O8(1/1/6)		-0.1

RAGLAND, TOM   Thomas B6.16.1946 Talladega AL   BR/TR/5-10/155*   [TexA65 11/358]   d4.5

1971	Was A	10	23	1	4	0	0	0	0	0-0	1	5	.174	.208	.174	10	-3	0-0	1.000	-2	80	64	2b10		-0.4
1972	Tex A	25	58	3	10	2	0	0	2	5-0	0	11	.172	.238	.207	34	-5	0-1	.982	-3	104	68	2b13,3b5,S3		-0.8
1973	Cle A	67	183	16	47	7	1	0	12	8-0	1	31	.257	.292	.306	67	-8	2-3	.984	3	101	104	2b65,S2		-0.3
Total	3	102	264	20	61	9	1	0	14	13-0	2	47	.231	.272	.273	56	-16	2-4	.985	-2	99	95	2b88,S5,3b5		-1.5

RAINES, LARRY   Lawrence Glenn Hope B3.9.1930 St.Albans WV D1.28.1978 Lansing MI   BR/TR/5-10/165*   d4.16

1957	Cle A	96	244	39	64	14	0	2	16	19-1	0	40	.262	.318	.344	82	-6	5-2	.922	-5	96	112	3b27,S25,2b10,O8L		-1.0
1958	Cle A	7	9	1	0	0	0	0	0	0	0	5	.000	.000	.000	-99	-3	0-1	.933	2	157	257	2b2		-0.1
Total	2	103	253	40	64	14	0	2	16	19-1	0	45	.253	.308	.332	76	-9	5-3	.922	-3	96	112	3b27,S25,2b12,O8L		-1.1

RAINES, TIM   Timothy Jr. B8.31.1979 Memphis TN   BB/TR/5-10/183*   [BalA98 6/189]   d10.1   f-Tim

2001	Bal A	7	23	6	4	2	0	0	3	3-0	0	8	.174	.269	.261	43	-2	3-0	1.000	-1	73	0	O7C		-0.2
2003	Bal A	20	43	4	6	1	1	0	2	2-0	1	12	.140	.196	.209	7	-6	0-0	.974	2	125	185	O18(1/17/0),D		-0.4
2004	Bal A	48	94	14	24	6	0	0	5	4-0	1	16	.255	.293	.319	60	-5	7-3	1.000	1	103	148	O38(1/27/10),D4		-0.4
Total	3	75	160	24	34	9	1	0	7	9-0	2	36	.213	.263	.281	43	-13	10-3	.991	1	104	136	O63(2/51/10),D5		-1.0

RAINES, TIM   Timothy Sr. "Rock" B9.16.1959 Sanford FL   BB/TR/5-8/178(165-195)   [MonN77 5/106]   d9.11   C2   s-Tim

1979	Mon N	6	0	3	0	0	0	0	0	0-0	0			—	—		0	2-0	—	0			/R		0.0
1980	Mon N	15	20	5	1	0	0	0	0	6-0	0	3	.050	.269	.050	-6	-3	5-0	1.000	-1	87	54	2b7/OL		0.0
1981	†Mon N★	88	313	61	95	13	7	5	37	45-5	2	31	.304	.391	.438	132	14	71-11	.976	-1	98	83	O81L/2		-0.3
1982	Mon N★	156	647	90	179	32	8	4	43	75-9	2	83	.277	.353	.369	99	1	78-16	.992	-6	95	72	O120L,2b36		2.3
1983	Mon N★	156	615	133	183	32	8	11	71	97-9	2	70	.298	.393	.429	128	28	90-14	.988	9	97	94	O154(153/2/0),2b7		0.4
1984	Mon N★	160	622	106	192	38	9	8	60	87-7	2	69	.309	.393	.437	139	36	75-10	.988	-1	102	88	O160C,2b2		4.6
1985	Mon N★	150	575	115	184	30	13	11	41	81-13	7	60	.320	.405	.475	154	44	70-9	.993	2	101	74	O146L		4.8
1986	Mon N★	151	580	91	194	35	10	9	62	78-9	2	60	.334	.413	.476	146	39	70-9	.979	7	108	93	O139L		5.3
1987	Mon N★	139	530	123	175	34	8	18	68	90-26	4	52	.330	.429	.526	147	40	50-5	.987	7	108	93	O139L		4.9
1988	Mon N	109	429	66	116	19	7	12	48	53-14	2	44	.270	.350	.431	118	11	33-7	.988	2	102	72	O108L		4.8
1989	Mon N	145	517	76	148	29	6	9	60	93-18	3	48	.286	.395	.418	131	26	41-9	.996	-5	89	90	O139L		1.5
1990	Mon N	130	457	65	131	11	5	9	62	70-8	3	43	.287	.379	.392	118	14	49-16	.996	-8	91	33	O139L		2.4
1991	Chi A	155	609	102	163	20	6	5	50	83-9	5	68	.268	.359	.345	98	1	51-15	.990	3	97	157	O133(134/1/0),D19		0.8
1992	Chi A	144	551	102	162	22	9	7	54	81-4	0	48	.294	.380	.405	122	19	45-6	.994	10	112	134	O129(129/1/0),D14		3.2
1993	†Chi A	115	415	75	127	16	4	16	54	64-4	1	35	.306	.401	.480	138	24	21-7	1.000	-3	91	78	O112L		1.8
1994	Chi A	101	384	80	102	15	5	10	52	61-3	1	43	.266	.365	.409	101	7	13-0	.981	1	107	45	O96L		0.1
1995	Chi A	133	502	81	143	25	4	12	67	70-3	3	52	.285	.374	.422	112	11	13-2	.980	-2	96	102	O107(107/0/1),D22		0.5
1996	†NY A	59	201	45	57	10	5	9	33	34-1	1	29	.284	.383	.468	116	6	10-1	.988	-2	87	96	O50L,D2	96	0.3
1997	†NY A	74	271	56	87	20	2	4	38	41-0	2	34	.321	.403	.454	126	13	8-5	.988	-6	82	31	O57L,D13	81	0.4
1998	†NY A	109	321	53	93	13	1	5	47	55-1	3	49	.290	.395	.383	109	7	8-3	.985	-3	78	125	D56,O47L		0.1
1999	Oak A	58	135	20	29	5	0	4	17	26-1	0	17	.215	.337	.341	77	-4	4-1	1.000	-1	101	0	O38(38/1/0),D3	77	-0.5
2001	Mon N	47	78	13	24	8	1	0	4	18-0	0	6	.308	.433	.436	128	8	1-0	1.000	-2	79	0	O20L	110	-0.3
	Bal A	4	11	1	3	0	1	0	5	0-0	0	3	.273	.250	.545	114	0	0-0	1.000	0	151	0	O2L/D		0.0
2002	Fla N	98	89	9	17	3	0	1	7	22-4	1	19	.191	.351	.258	72	-3	0-0	.917	1	107	319	O14L/D		-0.3
Total	23	2502	8872	1571	2605	430	113	170	980	1330-149	42	966	.294	.385	.425	123	331	808-146	.988	-4	98	95	O2123(1965/165/1),D131,2b53	436	37.9

RAINEY, JOHN   John Paul B7.26.1864 Birmingham MI D11.11.1912 Detroit MI   BL/TR/5-10/164   d8.25

1887	NY N	17	58	6	17	3	0	0	12	5	0		.293	.349	.345	98	0		.818	-2	84	128	3b17		-0.2
1890	Buf P	42	166	29	39	5	1	1	20	24	5	15	.235	.349	.295	79	-3	12	.870	3	123	87	O28R,S7,3b6,2b2		-0.2
Total	2	59	224	35	56	8	1	1	32	29	5	15	.250	.349	.308	84	-3	12	.870	2	123	87	O28R,3b23,S7,2b2		-0.4

RAJSICH, GARY   Gary Louis B10.28.1954 Youngstown OH   BL/TL/6-2/206*   [HouN76 11/241]   d4.9   b-Dave   Col Arizona St.

1982	NY N	80	162	17	42	8	3	2	12	17-3	1	40	.259	.333	.432	99	-3	1-3	1.000	-2	95	0	O35(10/0/26),1b2		-0.5
1983	NY N	11	36	5	12	3	0	0	3	3-1	1	5	.333	.400	.500	149	3	0-0	1.000	-1	79	111	1b10		0.1
1984	StL N	7	7	1	1	0	0	0	2	2-0	0	1	.143	.300	.143	39	0	0-0	1.000	-0	171	13	1b3		-0.1
1985	SF N	51	91	5	15	4	0	2	10	14-4	0	22	.165	.296	.231	52	-5	0-1	.990	-1	86	105	1b23		-0.8
Total	4	149	296	28	70	17	3	6	27	39-8	2	64	.236	.328	.345	90	-2	1-4	.994	-4	82	111	1b38,O35(10/0/26)		-1.3

RALSTON, DOC   Samuel Beryl B8.3.1885 Pierpont OH D8.29.1950 Lancaster PA   BR/TR/6-0/185   d9.8   Col Pittsburgh

1910	Was A	21	73	4	15	1	0	0	3	3	2		.205	.256	.219	52	-4	2	.976	2	119	122	O21L		-0.4

YEAR	TM LG	G	AB	R	H	2B	3B	HR	RBI	BB-IB	HP	SO	AVG	OBP	SLG	AOPS	ABR	SB-CS	FA	FR	RNG	THR	GAMES AT POSITION	DL	BFW
RAMAZZOTTI, BOB Robert Louis B1.16.1917 Eleanora PA D2.15.2000 Altoona PA BR/TR/5-8.5/175* d4.20																									
1946	Bro N	62	120	10	25	4	0	0	7	9	0	13	.208	.264	.242	43	-9	0	.939	2	97	99	3b30,2b16		-0.7
1948	Bro N	4	3	0	0	0	0	0	0	0	0	1	.000	.000	.000	-97	-1	0	1.000	-0	0	0	3b2/2		-0.1
1949	Bro N	5	13	1	2	0	0	0	1	3	0	3	.154	.154	.385	38	-1	0	.833	-1	63	0	3b3		-0.2
	Chi N	65	190	14	34	3	1	0	6	5	0	33	.179	.200	.205	9	-25	9	.972	6	111	106	3b36,S12,2b4		-1.8
	Year	70	203	15	36	3	1	1	9	5	0	36	.177	.197	.217	11	-27	9	.965	5	108	99	3b39,S12,2b4		-2.0
1950	Chi N	61	145	19	38	3	3	1	6	4	1	16	.262	.287	.345	66	-8	9	.961	-3	108	79	2b31,3b10,S3		-0.9
1951	Chi N	73	158	13	39	5	2	1	15	10	1	23	.247	.292	.323	64	-8	0-0	.950	6	111	115	S51,2b6/3		0.1
1952	Chi N	50	183	26	52	5	3	0	12	14	1	14	.284	.338	.361	93	-2	3-1	.979	-1	108	93	2b50	50	0.0
1953	Chi N	26	39	3	6	2	0	0	4	3	0	4	.154	.214	.205	10	-5	0-0	.911	-2	81	81	2b18	82	-0.7
Total 7		346	851	86	196	22	9	4	53	45	2	107	.230	.271	.291	52	-59	15-1	.966	8	107	91	2b126,3b82,S66	132	-4.3
RAMIREZ, ALEX Alexander Ramon B10.3.1974 Caracas, Venez BR/TR/5-11/176* d9.19 [DL 1997 Cle A 27]																									
1998	Cle A	3	8	1	1	0	0	0	0	0-0	0	3	.125	.125	.125	-33	-2	0-0	.833	-0	127	0	O3(2/0/1)		-0.2
1999	Cle A	48	97	11	29	6	1	3	18	3-0	1	26	.299	.327	.474	96	-1	1-1	.920	-1	92	122	O29(5/1/23),D14		-0.3
2000	Cle A	41	112	13	32	5	1	5	12	5-0	0	17	.286	.316	.482	95	-1	1-0	.978	-1	95	69	O31(15/1/16),D6		-0.3
	Pit N	43	115	13	24	6	1	4	18	7-2	0	32	.209	.254	.383	58	-8	1-0	.949	-1	101	58	O31R/1		-1.0
Total 3		135	332	38	86	17	3	12	48	15-2	1	78	.259	.293	.437	80	-12	3-1	.949	-2	98	73	O94(22/2/71),D20/1	27	-1.8
RAMIREZ, ARAMIS Aramis (Nin) B6.25.1978 Santo Domingo, D.R. BR/TR/6-1/219(190-219) d5.26																									
1998	Pit N	72	251	23	59	9	1	6	24	18-0	4	72	.235	.296	.351	69	-12	0-1	.941	-11	85	107	3b71	25	-2.3
1999	Pit N	18	56	2	10	2	1	0	7	6-0	0	9	.179	.254	.250	29	-6	0-0	.930	0	103	79	3b17		-0.6
2000	Pit N	73	254	19	65	15	2	6	35	10-0	5	36	.256	.293	.402	74	-11	0-0	.917	-6	101	52	3b72	33	-1.6
2001	Pit N	158	603	83	181	40	0	34	112	40-4	8	100	.300	.350	.536	121	18	5-4	.945	7	112	117	3b157		2.5
2002	Pit N	142	522	51	122	26	0	18	71	29-3	8	95	.234	.279	.387	76	-22	2-0	.946	2	106	128	3b131,D3		-1.9
2003	Pit N	96	375	44	105	25	1	12	67	25-3	7	68	.280	.330	.448	101	0	1-1	.924	5	119	55	3b96		0.6
	†Chi N	63	232	31	60	7	1	15	39	17-0	3	31	.259	.314	.491	104	0	1-1	.939	3	98	124	3b63		0.3
	Year	159	607	75	165	32	2	27	106	42-3	10	99	.272	.324	.465	102	1	2-2	.929	8	**111**	82	3b159		1.6
2004	Chi N	145	547	99	174	32	1	36	103	49-6	3	62	.318	.373	.578	138	30	0-2	.969	-14	82	61	3b144	39	2.1
2005	Chi N★	123	463	72	140	30	0	31	92	35-4	6	60	.302	.358	.568	134	22	0-1	.947	-1	97	67	3b119	97	0.7
Total 8		890	3303	424	916	186	7	158	550	229-20	44	533	.277	.329	.481	106	19	9-10	.943	-15	101	89	3b870,D3		
RAMIREZ, HANLEY Hanley B12.23.1983 Samana, D.R. BR/TR/6-3/195 d9.20																									
2005	Bos A	2	2	0	0	0	0	0	0	0-0	0	2	.000	.000	.000	-95	-1	0-0	1.000	-1	51	0	S2		-0.1
RAMIREZ, JULIO Julio Cesar (Figueroa) B8.10.1977 San Juan de la Maguana, D.R. BR/TR/5-11/170(170-195) d9.10																									
1999	Fla N	15	21	3	3	1	0	0	2	1-0	0	6	.143	.182	.190	-6	-4	0-1	.950	0	131	0	O11C		-0.3
2001	Chi A	22	37	2	3	0	0	0	2	2-0	0	15	.081	.128	.081	-41	-8	2-0	.978	3	123	255	O21(1/21/0)	77	-0.4
2002	Ana A	29	32	6	9	0	1	1	7	2-0	1	14	.281	.343	.438	107	0	0-2	1.000	0	105	161	O23(0/15/9)		0.0
2003	Ana A	6	2	1	0	0	0	0	0	0-0	0	0	.000	.000	.000	-99	-1	0-0	.750	0	161	0	O5(0/3/2)/D		-0.1
2005	SF N	12	4	3	1	0	0	0	1	0-0	0	1	.250	.250	.250	30	0	0-0	1.000	0	117	0	O6(0/2/4)		0.0
Total 5		84	96	15	16	1	1	1	11	5-0	1	36	.167	.216	.229	17	-13	2-3	.970	3	119	162	O66(1/52/15)/D	77	-0.8
RAMIREZ, MANNY Manuel Aristides (Onelcida) B5.30.1972 Santo Domingo, D.R. BR/TR/6-0/190(190-215) [CleA91 1/13] d9.2																									
1993	Cle A	22	53	5	9	1	0	2	5	2-0	0	8	.170	.200	.302	33	-5	0	1.000	0	155	0	D20/OR		-0.6
1994	Cle A	91	290	51	78	22	0	17	60	42-4	0	72	.269	.357	.521	123	10	4-2	.994	-1	96	119	O84R,D5		0.5
1995	†Cle A★	137	484	85	149	26	1	31	107	75-6	3	112	.308	.402	.558	145	34	6-6	.978	-11	88	35	O131R,D5		1.4
1996	†Cle A	152	550	94	170	45	3	33	112	85-8	3	104	.309	.399	.582	152	41	8-5	.970	1	90	178	O149R,D3		3.0
1997	†Cle A	150	561	99	184	40	0	26	88	79-5	7	115	.328	.415	.538	142	38	2-3	.975	-5	90	109	O146R,D4		2.3
1998	†Cle A★	150	571	108	168	35	2	45	145	76-6	6	121	.294	.377	.599	145	38	5-3	.977	-4	97	90	O148R,D2		2.4
1999	†Cle A★	147	522	131	174	34	3	44	**165**	96-9	13	131	.333	.442	**.663**	**170**	**59**	2-4	.975	-2	100	74	O146R,D2		4.4
2000	†Cle A	118	439	92	154	34	2	38	122	86-9	3	117	.351	.457	**.697**	181	55	1-1	.986	-7	78	118	O93R,D25	43	4.1
2001	Bos A★	142	529	93	162	33	2	41	125	81-**25**	8	147	.306	.405	.609	162	50	0-1	1.000	-3	90	31	D87,O55L		3.8
2002	Bos A★	120	436	84	152	31	0	33	107	73-14	8	85	**.349**	**.450**	.647	184	57	0-0	.959	-3	83	157	O68(64/0/7),D51	42	4.6
2003	†Bos A★	154	569	117	185	36	1	37	104	97-**28**	6	94	.325	.427	.587	158	53	3-1	.982	-4	83	150	O128L,D26		4.1
2004	†Bos A★	152	568	108	175	44	0	**43**	130	82-15	6	124	.308	.397	**.613**	150	44	2-4	.967	-10	81	60	O132L,D19		2.5
2005	†Bos A★	152	554	112	162	30	1	45	144	80-9	10	119	.292	.388	.594	148	40	1-0	.977	0	87	**225**	O149L,D2	85	3.3
Total 13		1687	6126	1179	1922	411	15	435	1414	954-138	77	1349	.314	.409	.599	154	517	34-30	.977	-48	89	115	O1430(528/0/904),D251		35.8
RAMIREZ, MARIO Mario (Torres) B9.12.1957 Yauco, PR BR/TR/5-9/159(153-173) d4.25																									
1980	NY N	18	24	2	5	0	0	0	1	1-0	0	7	.208	.240	.208	27	-2	0-0	1.000	-1	82	128	S7,2b4,3b3		-0.3
1981	SD N	13	13	1	1	0	0	0	1	2-1	0	5	.077	.200	.077	-21	-2	0-0	1.000	1	146	0	S2,3b2		-0.1
1982	SD N	13	23	1	4	1	0	0	1	2-0	0	4	.174	.240	.217	31	-2	0-0	.963	1	106	115	S8/23		-0.1
1983	SD N	55	107	11	21	6	3	0	12	20-1	1	23	.196	.326	.308	80	-2	0-0	.985	-10	81	74	S38/3		-1.2
1984	†SD N	48	59	12	7	1	0	2	9	13-1	0	14	.119	.278	.242	46	-4	0-0	.971	-9	69	111	S33,3b6,2b2		-0.9
1985	SD N	37	60	6	17	0	0	2	5	3-0	0	11	.283	.317	.383	96	-1	0-0	.918	-9	72	105	S27,2b7		-0.9
Total 6		184	286	33	55	8	3	4	28	41-3	1	64	.192	.295	.283	64	-13	0-0	.970	-27	79	94	S115,2b14,3b13		-3.5
RAMIREZ, MILT Milton (Barboza) B4.2.1950 Mayaguez, PR BR/TR/5-9/150* d4.11																									
1970	StL N	62	79	8	15	2	1	0	3	8-1	0	9	.190	.264	.241	35	-7	0-1	.923	3	104	141	S59/3		-0.1
1971	StL N	4	11	2	3	0	0	0	0	2-0	0	1	.273	.385	.273	85	0	0-0	.947	-0	68	47	S4		0.0
1979	Oak A	28	62	4	10	1	1	0	3	3-0	0	8	.161	.200	.210	11	-8	0-0	.923	-8	72	0	3b12,2b11,S8		-1.5
Total 3		94	152	14	28	3	2	0	6	13-1	0	18	.184	.248	.230	30	-15	0-1	.920	-5	102	114	S71,3b13,2b11		-1.6
RAMIREZ, ORLANDO Orlando (Leal) B12.18.1951 Cartagena, Colombia BR/TR/5-10/175* d7.6																									
1974	Cal A	31	86	4	14	0	0	0	0	6-0	0	23	.163	.215	.163	11	-10	2-1	.956	2	98	109	S31		-0.5
1975	Cal A	44	100	10	24	4	1	0	4	11-0	0	22	.240	.315	.300	80	-2	9-6	.905	-2	88	134	S40		-0.5
1976	Cal A	30	70	3	14	1	0	0	5	6-0	0	11	.200	.263	.214	44	-5	3-2	.966	-3	97	72	S30		-0.5
1977	Cal A	25	13	1	1	0	0	0	0	0-1	0	3	.077	.077	.077	-60	-3	1-0	1.000	0	98	49	2b5,S3/D	56	-0.2
1979	Cal A	13	12	1	0	0	0	0	0	1-0	1	6	.000	.143	.000	-59	-3	1-0	.844	-2	99	66	S10/D		-0.3
Total 5		143	281	24	53	5	1	0	16	24-0	1	65	.189	.254	.214	37	-23	16-9	.931	-4	95	104	S114,2b5,D2	56	-1.5
RAMIREZ, RAFAEL Rafael Emilio (Peguero) B2.18.1958 San Pedro de Macoris, D.R. BR/TR/6-0/185(168-190) d8.4																									
1980	Atl N	50	165	17	44	6	1	2	11	2-0	4	33	.267	.292	.352	78	-5	2-1	.949	1	107	106	S46		0.0
1981	Atl N	95	307	30	67	16	2	2	20	24-3	1	47	.218	.276	.303	64	-15	7-3	.942	2	105	98	S95		-0.3
1982	†Atl N	157	609	74	169	24	4	10	52	36-7	3	49	.278	.319	.379	93	-7	27-14	.956	18	106	**140**	S157		3.0
1983	Atl N	152	622	82	185	13	5	7	58	36-4	2	48	.297	.337	.368	89	-10	16-12	.949	12	106	**128**	S152		1.8
1984	Atl N☆	145	591	51	157	22	4	2	48	26-1	1	70	.266	.295	.327	70	-24	14-17	.959	5	102	113	S145		-0.8
1985	Atl N	138	568	54	141	25	4	5	58	20-1	0	63	.248	.272	.333	65	-28	2-6	.954	15	**112**	**130**	S133		0.7
1986	Atl N	134	496	57	119	21	1	8	33	21-1	3	60	.240	.273	.335	64	-25	19-8	.952	23	118	125	S86,3b57,O3(2/0/1)	85	-0.4
1987	Atl N	56	179	22	47	12	0	1	21	8-0	2	16	.263	.300	.346	68	-8	6-3	.946	1	106	153	S38,3b12		-1.0
1988	Hou N	155	566	51	156	30	5	6	59	18-6	3	61	.276	.298	.378	98	-4	3-2	.965	-17	90	85	S154		-5.3
1989	Hou N	151	537	46	132	20	2	6	54	29-3	1	64	.246	.283	.324	76	-18	3-1	.945	-41	82	84	S149	15	-2.2
1990	Hou N	132	445	44	116	19	3	2	37	24-9	1	46	.261	.299	.330	75	-16	10-5	.953	-15	95	91	S129		-1.8
1991	Hou N	101	233	17	55	10	0	1	20	13-1	1	40	.236	.274	.292	63	-12	3-3	.953	-8	81	81	S45,2b27,3b2	23	-0.8
1992	Hou N	73	176	17	44	11	0	1	13	7-1	1	24	.250	.283	.301	68	-8	0-0	.961	-3	98	77	S57/3		-0.9
Total 13		1539	5494	562	1432	224	31	53	484	264-37	21	621	.261	.295	.342	77	-180	112-75	.953	-7	101	110	S1386,3b72,2b27,O3(2/0/1)	123	-7.7
RAMOS, DOMINGO Domingo Antonio (De Ramos) B3.29.1958 Santiago, D.R. BR/TR/5-10/155(154-170) d9.8																									
1978	NY A	1	0	0	0	0	0	0	0	0-0	0	0	—	—	—	-0	0	0-0	—	-0	0	0	/S		0.0
1980	Tor A	5	16	0	2	0	0	0	0	0-0	0	5	.125	.222	.125	-2	-2	0-0	1.000	-0	124	86	2b2,S2/D		0.0
1982	Sea A	8	26	3	4	2	0	0	1	3-0	0	2	.154	.241	.231	29	-2	0-0	.920	-5	57	0	S8		0.0
1983	Sea A	53	127	14	36	4	0	2	10	7-0	1	12	.283	.326	.362	86	-3	3-1	.948	7	112	137	S28,2b8,3b8,D2		-1.0
1984	Sea A	59	81	6	15	2	0	0	2	5-0	0	12	.185	.233	.210	24	-8	2-2	.911	-2	74	126	3b38,S13,1b5,2b3		-1.1
1985	Sea A	75	168	19	33	6	1	5	17-0		0	13	.196	.267	.250	43	-13	0-1	.951	-5	86	75	S36,2b20,1b14,3b7		-1.1
1986	Sea A	49	99	8	18	2	0	0	5	8-0	1	13	.182	.250	.250	26	-6	0-1	.966	8	125	75	S21,2b16,3b8,D2		-0.8

YEAR	TM LG	G	AB	R	H	2B	3B	HR	RBI	BB-IB	HP	SO	AVG	OBP	SLG	AOPS	ABR	SB-CS	FA	FR	RNG	THR	GAMES AT POSITION	DL	BFW
1987	Sea A	42	103	9	32	6	0	2	11	3-0	1	12	.311	.336	.427	96	-1	0-1	.953	4	109	131	S25,3b7,2b6,D2		0.5
1988	Cle A	22	46	7	12	1	0	0	5	3-0	1	7	.261	.308	.283	68	-2	0-0	1.000	1	120	139	2b11,1b5,S4,3b2		0.0
	Cal A	10	15	3	2	0	0	0	0	0-0	0	0	.133	.133	.133	-26	-3	0-0	1.000	0	117	0	3b8/OL		-0.3
	Year	32	61	10	14	1	0	0	5	3-0	1	7	.230	.269	.246	47	-4	0-0	1.000	1	120	139	2b13,3b10,1b5,S4/OL		-0.3
1989	†Chi N	85	179	18	47	6	2	1	19	17-4	2	23	.263	.333	.335	86	-3	1-1	.959	3	129	120	S42,3b30		-0.3
1990	Chi N	98	226	22	60	5	0	2	17	27-1	1	29	.265	.342	.314	78	-6	0-2	.932	-12	55	27	3b66,S21/2		-1.8
Total	11	507	1086	109	261	34	2	8	85	92-5	7	138	.240	.302	.297	64	-53	1-8	.955	-1	108	109	S201,3b174,2b67,1b24,D7/OL		-4.0

RAMOS, CHUCHO Jesus Manuel (Garcia) B4.12.1918 Maturin, Venez D9.2.1977 Caracas, Venez BR/TL/5-10.5/167 d5.7

YEAR	TM LG	G	AB	R	H	2B	3B	HR	RBI	BB-IB	HP	SO	AVG	OBP	SLG	AOPS	ABR	SB-CS	FA	FR	RNG	THR	GAMES AT POSITION	DL	BFW
1944	Cin N	4	10	1	5	1	0	0	0	0-0	0	0	.500	.500	.600	217	1	0	1.000	-0	106	0	O3(1/0/3)		0.1

RAMOS, JOHN John Joseph B8.6.1965 Tampa FL BR/TR/6-0/190 [NYA86 5/132] d9.18 Col Stanford [DL 1992 NY A 90]

| 1991 | NY A | 10 | 26 | 4 | 8 | 1 | 0 | 0 | 3 | 0-0 | 0 | 3 | .308 | .310 | .346 | 88 | 0 | 0-0 | 1.000 | -2 | 98 | 0 | C5,D4 | | -0.2 |

RAMOS, KEN Kenneth Cecil B6.6.1967 Sidney NE BL/TL/6-1/185 d5.16 Col Nebraska

| 1997 | Hou N | 14 | 12 | 0 | 0 | 0 | 0 | 0 | 1 | 2-0 | 0 | 5 | .000 | .133 | .000 | -61 | -3 | 0-0 | — | -0 | 0 | 0 | O2(1/0/1) | | -0.3 |

RAMOS, BOBBY Roberto B11.5.1955 Havana, Cuba BR/TR/5-11/208(190-208) [MonN74 7/153] d9.26 C3

1978	Mon N	2	4	0	0	0	0	0	0	0-0	0	1	.000	.000	.000	-99	-0				73	0	/C		-0.1
1980	Mon N	13	32	5	5	2	0	0	2	5-0	0	5	.156	.270	.219	37	-3	0-0	.964	-1	113	141	C12		-0.3
1981	Mon N	26	41	4	8	1	0	1	3	3-0	0	5	.195	.250	.293	52	-3	0-0	.974	0	84	76	C23		-0.3
1982	NY A	4	11	1	1	0	0	1	2	0-0	0	3	.091	.091	.364	18	-1	0-0	1.000	1	190	93	C4		-0.2
1983	Mon N	27	61	2	14	3	1	0	5	8-1	1	11	.230	.329	.311	78	-2	0-0	.984	0	93	125	C25		-0.1
1984	Mon N	31	83	8	16	1	0	2	5	6-1	0	13	.193	.244	.277	49	-6	0-0	.982	2	74	167	C31		-0.3
Total	6	103	232	20	44	7	1	4	17	22-2	1	38	.190	.262	.280	52	-16	0-0	.980	2	92	131	C96		-1.1

RAMSEY, FERNANDO Fernando David (Ramsey) B12.20.1965 Rainbow, Pan BR/TR/6-1/175 [ChiN87 33/841] d9.7

| 1992 | Chi N | 18 | 25 | 0 | 3 | 0 | 0 | 0 | 1 | 0-0 | 0 | 6 | .120 | .120 | .120 | -31 | -4 | 0-0 | 1.000 | -1 | 91 | 0 | O15C | | -0.6 |

RAMSEY, MIKE Michael James B7.8.1960 Thomson GA BB/TL/6-0/173 d4.6 Col Gulf Coast (FL) CC

| 1987 | LA N | 48 | 125 | 18 | 29 | 4 | 2 | 0 | 12 | 10-0 | 1 | 32 | .232 | .287 | .296 | 57 | -8 | 2-4 | .973 | -4 | 85 | 51 | O43(4/38/1) | | -1.3 |

RAMSEY, MIKE Michael Jeffrey B3.29.1954 Roanoke VA BB/TR/6-1/170* [StLN75 3/64] d9.4 Col Appalachian St.

1978	StL N	12	5	4	1	0	0	0	0	0-0	0	1	.200	.200	.200	12	-1	0-0	.909	1	108	291	S4		0.0
1980	StL N	59	126	11	33	8	1	0	8	3-2	0	17	.262	.279	.341	69	-5	0-0	.960	-3	114	118	2b24,S20,3b8		-0.6
1981	StL N	47	124	19	32	3	0	0	9	8-1	0	16	.258	.303	.282	64	-6	4-0	.966	5	119	111	S35,3b5/2OL		-0.3
1982	†StL N	112	256	18	59	8	2	1	21	22-3	1	34	.230	.294	.289	62	-13	6-5	.963	4	96	109	2b43,3b28,S22,O2L		-1.1
1983	StL N	97	175	25	46	4	1	1	16	12-2	1	23	.263	.309	.337	80	-5	4-2	.968	-10	88	110	2b66,S20,3b8/OL		-1.3
1984	StL N	21	15	1	1	1	0	0	0	1-0	0	3	.067	.125	.133	-28	-3	0-0	1.000	1	119	47	2b7,S7/3		-0.2
	Mon N	37	70	2	15	1	0	0	3	1-0	0	13	.214	.214	.229	25	-7	0-0	.975	-4	102	132	S26,2b12		-0.9
	Year	58	85	3	16	2	0	0	3	1-0	0	16	.188	.198	.212	16	-10	0-0	.978	-3	103	148	S33,2b19/3		-1.1
1985	LA N	9	15	1	2	1	0	0	0	1-0	0	4	.133	.235	.200	23	-2	0-0	.923	-1	121	89	S4,2b2		-0.2
Total	7	394	786	81	189	26	6	2	57	48-8	2	111	.240	.285	.296	62	-42	14-7	.964	-12	94	106	2b155,S138,3b50,O4L		-4.0

RAMSEY, BILL William Thrace "Square Jaw" B10.20.1920 Osceola AR BR/TR/6-0/175 d4.19 Col Florida

| 1945 | Bos N | 78 | 137 | 16 | 40 | 8 | 0 | 1 | 12 | 4- | 3 | 22 | .292 | .326 | .372 | 93 | -1 | 1 | .963 | 1 | 116 | 46 | O43(30/13/0) | | -0.2 |

RAND, DICK Richard Hilton B3.7.1931 South Gate CA D1.22.1996 Moreno Valley CA BR/TR/6-2/185* d9.16

1953	StL N	9	31	3	9	1	0	0	1	2	0	6	.290	.333	.323	72	-1	0-0	.984	1	99	111	C9		0.0
1955	StL N	3	10	1	3	0	0	1	3	1-0	0	1	.300	.364	.600	150	-1	0-1	1.000	-1	65	209	C3		-0.1
1957	Pit N	60	105	7	23	2	1	1	9	11-1	0	24	.219	.288	.286	58	-6	0-0	.973	0	120	74	C57		-0.4
Total	3	72	146	11	35	3	1	2	13	14-1	0	31	.240	.302	.315	68	-6	0-0	.977	1	113	89	C69		-0.5

RANDA, JOE Joseph Gregory B12.18.1969 Milwaukee WI BR/TR/5-11/190* [KCA91 11/288] d4.30 Col Tennessee

1995	KC A	34	70	6	12	2	0	1	5	6-0	0	17	.171	.237	.243	25	-8	0-1	.949	-4	104	38	3b22,2b9,D2		-1.1
1996	KC A	110	337	36	102	24	1	6	47	26-4	1	47	.303	.351	.433	97	-1	13-4	.951	-9	91	81	3b92,2b15,1b7/D	22	-0.7
1997	Pit N	126	443	58	134	27	9	7	60	41-1	6	64	.303	.366	.451	112	8	4-2	.937	19	117	119	3b120,2b13	29	2.7
1998	Det A	138	460	56	117	21	2	9	50	41-1	7	70	.254	.323	.367	79	-14	8-7	.976	8	**112**	107	3b118,2b20/1D		-0.5
1999	KC A	156	628	92	197	36	8	16	84	50-4	3	80	.314	.363	.473	108	7	5-4	.952	9	**110**	102	3b156/D		1.5
2000	KC A	158	612	88	186	29	4	15	106	36-3	6	66	.304	.343	.438	92	-8	6-3	.957	9	108	102	3b156/D		0.2
2001	KC A	151	581	59	147	34	2	13	83	42-2	6	80	.253	.307	.386	74	-22	3-2	.966	4	104	**129**	3b137,D14/2		-1.7
2002	KC A	151	549	63	155	36	5	11	80	46-1	9	69	.282	.341	.426	93	-5	2-1	.972	0	102	53	3b129,D19		-0.5
2003	KC A	131	502	80	146	31	1	16	72	41-0	7	61	.291	.348	.452	103	3	1-0	**.980**	0	101	54	3b129,D2	15	-0.5
2004	KC A	128	485	65	139	31	2	8	56	40-1	6	77	.287	.343	.408	96	-2	0-1	.967	4	105	107	3b119,1b3,D6	26	0.4
2005	Cin N	92	332	44	96	26	1	13	48	33-2	2	52	.289	.356	.491	123	11	0-0	.974	5	89	79	3b84		0.7
	†SD N	58	223	27	57	17	1	4	20	14-1	2	29	.256	.303	.395	86	-5	0-1	.955	-10	73	77	3b58,D2		-1.5
	Year	150	555	71	153	43	2	17	68	47-3	4	81	.276	.335	.452	109	7	0-1	.967	-5	82	78	3b142,D2		-0.8
Total	11	1433	5222	674	1488	314	36	119	711	416-20	55	712	.285	.340	.427	95	-36	42-26	.962	25	103	93	3b1320,2b58,D48,1b11	92	-0.3

RANDALL, SAP James Odell B8.19.1960 Mobile AL BB/TR/5-11/195 [CalA81 10/236] d8.2 Col Grambling St.

| 1988 | Chi A | 4 | 12 | 1 | 0 | 0 | 0 | 0 | 1 | 2-0 | 0 | 3 | .000 | .133 | .000 | -56 | -3 | 0-0 | 1.000 | 0 | 155 | 124 | 1b2/ORD | | -0.3 |

RANDALL, NEWT Newton J. B2.3.1880 New Lowell ON, Can. D5.3.1955 Duluth MN BR/TR/5-10/181 d4.18

1907	Chi N	22	78	6	16	4	2	0	4	8	0		.205	.279	.308	79	-2	2	.904	-0	85	134	O21(1/1/21)		-0.4
	Bos N	75	258	16	55	6	3	0	15	19	7		.213	.285	.260	71	-8	4	.920	-6	92	38	O73(59/3/12)		-2.1
	Year	97	336	22	71	10	5	0	19	27	7		.211	.284	.271	73	-10	6	.915	-6	90	63	O94(60/4/33)		-2.5

RANDALL, BOB Robert Lee B6.10.1948 Norton KS BR/TR/6-3/180* d4.13 C1 Col Kansas St.

1976	Min A	153	475	55	127	18	4	1	34	28-0	8	38	.267	.317	.328	88	-7	3-5	.969	-4	96	**123**	2b153		-0.2
1977	Min A	103	306	36	73	13	2	0	22	15-0	1	25	.239	.289	.294	60	-17	1-4	.985	12	107	120	2b101/13D		-0.1
1978	Min A	119	330	36	89	11	3	0	21	24-0	6	22	.270	.329	.321	82	-8	5-3	.983	17	**113**	122	2b116,3b2/D	16	1.5
1979	Min A	80	199	25	49	7	0	0	14	15-0	1	17	.246	.299	.281	55	-12	2-2	.983	10	110	131	2b71,3b7/SOL		0.1
1980	Min A	5	15	2	1	0	0	0	1	1-0	0	1	.200	.250	.267	39	-1	0-0	.909	-0	116	138	3b4/2		-0.1
Total	5	460	1325	154	341	50	9	1	92	83-0	21	102	.257	.310	.311	74	-45	11-14	.979	36	105	123	2b442,3b14,D2/OLS1	16	1.2

RANDLE, LEN Leonard Shenoff B2.12.1949 Long Beach CA BB/TR (BR 1971)/5-10/169* [TexA70.S1/10] d6.16 Col Arizona St. OF(62/85/6)

1971	Was A	75	215	27	47	11	6	2	13	24-2	1	56	.219	.298	.298	73	-7	1-1	.967	8	106	118	2b66		0.5
1972	Tex A	74	249	23	48	13	0	2	21	13-2	1	51	.193	.235	.269	52	-15	4-5	.952	-0	99	86	2b65,S4,O2C		-1.4
1973	Tex A	10	29	3	6	1	1	1	0	0-0	0	2	.207	.207	.414	74	-1	0-2	.964	-3	58	69	2b5,O2C		-0.5
1974	Tex A	151	520	65	157	17	4	1	49	29-2	2	43	.302	.338	.356	103	1	26-17	.935	11	96	125	3b89,2b40,O21(13/5/3)/SD		1.4
1975	Tex A	156	601	85	166	24	7	5	57	57-3	4	80	.276	.341	.359	100	0	16-19	.973	11	104	120	2b79,O66(7/61/0),3b17,CSD		1.2
1976	Tex A	142	539	53	121	11	6	1	51	46-2	2	63	.224	.286	.273	63	-25	30-15	.971	0	95	89	2b113,O30(28/1/1),3b2/D		-1.9
1977	NY N	136	513	78	156	22	7	5	27	65-3	2	70	.304	.383	.404	116	13	33-21	.961	2	96	**152**	3b110,2b20,O6(4/4/0)/S		1.4
1978	NY N	132	437	53	102	16	8	2	35	64-7	1	57	.233	.330	.320	85	-7	14-11	.967	-7	91	108	3b124,2b5		-1.8
1979	NY A	20	39	2	7	0	0	0	3	3-0	0	2	.179	.238	.179	15	-5	0-0	1.000	4		377	O11(4/7/0),D2		-0.4
1980	Chi N	130	489	67	135	16	4	5	39	50-2	1	55	.276	.343	.370	92	-4	19-13	.929	6	109	40	3b111,2b17,O6(4/2/0)		0.0
1981	Sea A	82	273	22	61	10	1	4	25	17-4	1	22	.223	.276	.315	67	-12	11-6	.986	7	111	92	3b59,2b21,O5(2/1/2),S3		-0.4
1982	Sea A	30	46	10	8	2	0	0	1	4-0	0	4	.174	.240	.217	26	-5	2-2	.964	0	112	59	D13,3b9,2b6		-0.4
Total	12	1138	3950	488	1016	145	40	27	322	372-27	15	505	.257	.321	.335	86	-67	156-112	.953	36	99	103	3b521,2b437,O149C,D21,S10/C		-2.4

RANDOLPH, WILLIE Willie Larry B7.6.1954 Holly Hill SC BR/TR/5-11/166* [PitN72 7/167] d7.29 M1/C11

1975	†Pit N	30	61	9	10	1	1	0	6	5-0	0	14	.164	.246	.180	21	-7	1-0	.962	2	115	97	2b14/3		-0.4
1976	†NY A★	125	430	59	115	15	4	1	40	58-5	3	39	.267	.356	.328	102	4	37-12	.974	11	110	99	2b124		2.9
1977	†NY A★	147	551	91	151	28	11	4	40	64-1	1	53	.274	.347	.387	101	2	13-6	.980	14	106	**121**	2b147		2.4
1978	NY A	134	499	87	139	18	6	3	42	82-1	1	51	.279	.381	.357	112	12	36-7	.978	2	99	102	2b134		2.4
1979	NY A	153	574	98	155	15	13	5	61	95-5	3	39	.270	.374	.368	103	6	33-12	.985	17	108	123	2b153	21	2.8
1980	†NY A★	138	513	99	151	23	7	7	46	119-4	2	45	.294	.427	.407	132	32	30-5	.976	7	99	100	2b138		3.3
1981	†NY A★	93	357	59	83	14	3	2	24	57-0	0	24	.232	.336	.305	89	-4	14-5	.977	9	100	**127**	2b93		1.2

YEAR	TM LG	G	AB	R	H	2B	3B	HR	RBI	BB-IB	HP	SO	AVG	OBP	SLG	AOPS	ABR	SB-CS	FA	FR	RNG	THR	GAMES AT POSITION	DL	BFW
1982	NY A	144	553	85	155	21	4	3	36	75-3	3	35	.280	.368	.349	100	3	16-9	.981	11	100	103	2b142/D		2.2
1983	NY A	104	420	73	117	21	1	2	38	53-0	1	32	.279	.361	.348	99	2	12-4	.979	15	106	109	2b104	38	2.3
1984	NY A	142	564	86	162	24	2	2	31	86-4	0	42	.287	.377	.348	107	10	10-6	.983	22	103	119	2b142		3.9
1985	NY A	143	497	75	137	21	2	5	40	85-3	4	39	.276	.382	.356	107	9	16-9	.985	5	100	110	2b143		2.2
1986	NY A	141	492	76	136	15	2	5	50	94-0	3	49	.276	.393	.346	104	9	15-2	.972	3	103	107	2b139/D		2.1
1987	NY A★	120	449	96	137	24	2	7	67	82-1	2	25	.305	.411	.414	122	19	11-1	.981	9	104	115	2b119/D	30	3.4
1988	NY A	110	404	43	93	20	1	2	34	55-2	4	39	.230	.322	.300	76	-11	8-4	.988	14	109	**111**	2b110	40	0.7
1989	LA N★	145	549	62	155	18	0	2	36	71-2	4	51	.282	.366	.326	101	4	7-6	.987	-5	96	112	2b140		0.3
1990	LA N	26	96	15	26	4	0	1	9	13-0	1	9	.271	.364	.344	98	0	1-0	.969	-1	96	77	2b26		0.1
	†Oak A	93	292	37	75	9	3	1	21	32-1	1	25	.257	.331	.318	86	-5	6-1	.982	-8	97	128	2b84,D6	17	-1.0
1991	Mil A	124	431	60	141	14	3	0	54	75-3	0	38	.327	.424	.374	126	20	4-2	.969	9	**108**	**123**	2b121,D2		3.2
1992	NY N	90	286	29	72	11	1	2	15	40-1	4	34	.252	.352	.318	92	-1	1-3	.977	-5	90	118	2b79	50	-0.6
Total	18	2202	8018	1239	2210	316	65	54	687	1243-37	38	675	.276	.373	.351	104	104	271-94	.980	132	103	113	2b2152,D11/3	196	36.0

RANEW, MERRITT Merritt Thomas B5.10.1938 Albany GA BL/TR/5-10/180* d4.13

YEAR	TM LG	G	AB	R	H	2B	3B	HR	RBI	BB-IB	HP	SO	AVG	OBP	SLG	AOPS	ABR	SB-CS	FA	FR	RNG	THR	GAMES AT POSITION	DL	BFW
1962	Hou N	71	218	26	51	6	8	4	24	14-5	3	43	.234	.287	.390	87	-6	2-2	.980	-7	63	87	C58		-1.0
1963	Chi N	78	154	18	52	8	1	3	15	9-1	2	32	.338	.380	.461	134	7	1-0	.980	-1	97	67	C37,1b9		0.7
1964	Chi N	16	33	0	3	0	0	0	1	2-0	1	6	.091	.167	.091	-24	-5	0-0	1.000	1	37	155	C9		-0.5
	Mil N	9	17	1	2	0	0	0	0	0-0	0	3	.118	.118	.118	-33	-3	0-1	1.000	-1	0	303	C3		-0.4
	Year	25	50	1	5	0	0	0	1	2-0	1	9	.100	.151	.100	-27	-8	0-1	1.000	0	28	192	C12		-0.9
1965	Cal A	41	91	12	19	4	0	1	10	7-0	0	22	.209	.260	.286	58	-5	0-0	.988	-5	189	131	C24		-1.0
1969	Sea A	54	81	11	20	2	0	0	4	10-3	0	14	.247	.330	.272	70	-3	0-0	.969	-4	78	0	C13,O3L/3		-0.7
Total	5	269	594	68	147	20	9	8	54	42-9	6	120	.247	.301	.352	83	-15	3-3	.982	-17	89	92	C144,1b9,O3L/3		-2.9

RANSOM, CODY Bryan Cody B2.17.1976 Mesa AZ BR/TR/6-2/190(190-210) [SFN98 9/278] d9.5 Col Grand Canyon

YEAR	TM LG	G	AB	R	H	2B	3B	HR	RBI	BB-IB	HP	SO	AVG	OBP	SLG	AOPS	ABR	SB-CS	FA	FR	RNG	THR	GAMES AT POSITION	DL	BFW
2001	SF N	9	7	1	0	0	0	0	0	0-0	0	5	.000	.000	.000	-99	-2	0-0	1.000	-0	134	0	S6		-0.2
2002	SF N	7	3	2	2	0	0	1	1	1-1	0	1	.667	.750	.667	294	-2	0-0	1.000	-0	76	0	S3		0.1
2003	SF N	20	27	7	6	1	0	1	1	1-0	0	11	.222	.250	.370	58	-2	0-0	.963	-2	82	164	S12		-0.3
2004	SF N	78	68	13	17	6	0	1	11	6-0	1	20	.250	.320	.382	78	-2	2-2	.948	1	109	160	S45,2b16/3OL		0.0
Total	4	114	105	23	25	7	0	2	13	8-1	1	37	.238	.298	.362	69	-5	2-2	.958	-1	99	143	S66,2b16/OL3		-0.4

RANSOM, JEFF Jeffrey Dean B11.11.1960 Fresno CA BR/TR/5-11/185* [SFN78 5/111] d9.5

YEAR	TM LG	G	AB	R	H	2B	3B	HR	RBI	BB-IB	HP	SO	AVG	OBP	SLG	AOPS	ABR	SB-CS	FA	FR	RNG	THR	GAMES AT POSITION	DL	BFW
1981	SF N	5	15	2	4	1	0	0	1	1-1	0	1	.267	.313	.333	86	0	0-0	1.000	2	65	63	C5		0.2
1982	SF N	15	44	5	7	0	0	0	3	6-0	0	7	.159	.255	.159	20	-5	0-0	.988	-0	79	72	C14		-0.5
1983	SF N	6	20	3	4	0	0	1	3	4-0	0	7	.200	.333	.350	92	0	0-0	.946	-4	33	39	C6		-0.4
Total	3	26	79	10	15	1	0	1	6	11-1	0	15	.190	.286	.241	50	-5	0-0	.980	-2	65	62	C25		-0.7

RAPP, EARL Earl Wellington B5.20.1921 Corunna MI D2.13.1992 Swedesboro NJ BL/TR/6-2/185* d4.28

YEAR	TM LG	G	AB	R	H	2B	3B	HR	RBI	BB-IB	HP	SO	AVG	OBP	SLG	AOPS	ABR	SB-CS	FA	FR	RNG	THR	GAMES AT POSITION	DL	BFW
1949	Det A	1	0	0	0	0	0	0	0	1	0	—	1.000	—	175		0			0		/H		0.0
	Chi A	19	54	3	14	1	1	0	11	5	0	6	.259	.322	.315	71	-2	1-1	.974	2	114	178	O13(11/0/2)		-0.2
	Year	20	54	3	14	1	1	0	11	6	0	6	.259	.333	.315	74	-2	1-1	.974	2	114	178	O13(11/0/2)		-0.2
1951	NY N	13	11	0	1	0	0	0	1	2	0	3	.091	.231	.091	-10	-2	0-0	—	0		/H		-0.2
	StL A	26	98	14	32	5	3	2	14	11	0	11	.327	.394	.500	137	5	1-0	.979	-0	97	119	O25R		0.4
1952	StL A	30	49	3	7	4	0	0	4	0	0	8	.143	.143	.224	1	-7	0-0	1.000	-0	112	0	O7R		-0.7
	Was A	46	67	7	19	6	0	0	9	6	1	13	.284	.351	.373	105	1	0-0	.917	-1	82	0	O10R		-0.1
	Year	76	116	10	26	10	0	0	13	6	1	21	.224	.268	.310	61	-6	0-0	.958	-1	95	0	O17R		-0.8
Total	3	135	279	27	73	16	4	2	39	25	1	41	.262	.325	.369	89	-5	2-1	.973	-0	101	105	O55(11/0/44)		-0.8

RAPP, GOLDIE Joseph Aloysius B2.6.1894 Cincinnati OH D7.1.1966 LaMesa CA BB/TR/5-10/165 d4.13

YEAR	TM LG	G	AB	R	H	2B	3B	HR	RBI	BB-IB	HP	SO	AVG	OBP	SLG	AOPS	ABR	SB-CS	FA	FR	RNG	THR	GAMES AT POSITION	DL	BFW
1921	NY N	58	181	21	39	9	1	0	15	15	0	13	.215	.276	.276	46	-14	3-11	.941	9	124	130	3b56		-0.4
	Phi N	52	202	28	56	7	1	1	10	14	0	8	.277	.324	.337	70	-8	6-7	.950	1	97	73	3b50/2		-0.5
	Year	110	383	49	95	16	2	1	25	29	0	21	.248	.301	.308	59	-22	9-18	.945	10	**112**	104	3b106/2		-0.9
1922	Phi N	119	502	58	127	26	3	0	38	32	1	29	.253	.299	.317	54	-34	6-12	.948	3	110	97	3b117,S2		-2.5
1923	Phi N	47	179	27	47	5	0	1	10	14	1	14	.263	.320	.307	59	-10	1-1	.947	-0	96	95	3b45		-0.8
Total	3	276	1064	134	269	47	5	2	73	75	2	64	.253	.303	.312	57	-66	16-31	.947	13	108	99	3b268,S2/2		-4.2

RARIDEN, BILL William Angel "Bedford Bill" B2.4.1888 Bedford IN D8.28.1942 Bedford IN BR/TR/5-10/168 d8.12

YEAR	TM LG	G	AB	R	H	2B	3B	HR	RBI	BB-IB	HP	SO	AVG	OBP	SLG	AOPS	ABR	SB-CS	FA	FR	RNG	THR	GAMES AT POSITION	DL	BFW
1909	Bos N	13	42	1	6	1	0	0	1	4	0		.143	.217	.167	18	-4	1	.912	-3	80	95	C13		-0.6
1910	Bos N	49	137	15	31	5	1	1	14	12	1	22	.226	.293	.299	70	-5	1	.962	-2	87	119	C49		-0.3
1911	Bos N	70	246	22	56	9	0	0	21	21	0	18	.228	.288	.264	51	-16	3	.952	-8	77	124	C65,3b3/2		-1.8
1912	Bos N	79	247	27	55	3	1	1	14	18	2	35	.223	.281	.255	46	-19	3	.964	-6	91	105	C73		-1.9
1913	Bos N	95	246	31	58	9	2	3	30	30	2	21	.236	.324	.325	84	-4	5-1	.976	-0	102	99	C87		0.3
1914	Ind F	131	396	44	93	15	5	0	47	61	0	43	.235	.337	.298	67	-22	12	.981	15	89	**112**	C130		0.4
1915	New F	142	444	49	120	30	7	0	40	60	3	29	.270	.361	.369	112	3	8	.978	25	**123**	103	C142		4.3
1916	NY N	120	351	23	78	9	3	1	29	55	3	32	.222	.333	.274	92	-4	4	.972	-4	113	85	C119		0.7
1917	†NY N	101	266	20	72	10	1	0	25	42	1	17	.271	.372	.316	116	8	3	.971	-10	102	57	C100		0.6
1918	NY N	69	183	15	41	5	1	0	17	15	0	15	.224	.283	.262	68	-7	1	**.984**	-6	93	63	C63		-0.9
1919	†Cin N	74	218	16	47	6	3	1	24	17	1	19	.216	.275	.284	70	-8	4	.983	6	113	80	C70		0.4
1920	Cin N	39	101	9	25	3	0	0	10	5	0		.248	.283	.277	62	-5	2	.973	0	104	106	C37		-0.2
Total	12	982	2877	272	682	105	24	7	272	340	13	251	.237	.320	.298	78	-79	47-1	.973	7	102	96	C948,3b3/2		1.0

RATH, MORRIE Morris Charles B12.25.1886 Mobeetie TX D11.18.1945 Upper Darby PA BL/TR/5-8.5/160 d9.28 Mil 1918

YEAR	TM LG	G	AB	R	H	2B	3B	HR	RBI	BB-IB	HP	SO	AVG	OBP	SLG	AOPS	ABR	SB-CS	FA	FR	RNG	THR	GAMES AT POSITION	DL	BFW
1909	Phi A	7	26	4	7	1	0	0	3	2	3		.269	.387	.308	117	1	1	.846	-1	77	108	S4,3b2		0.0
1910	Phi A	18	26	3	4	0	0	0	1	5	0		.154	.290	.154	40	-2	0	.950	-1	87	0	3b11,2b3		-0.3
	Cle A	24	67	5	13	3	0	0	10	0		.194	.299	.239	68	-2	2	.950	1	104	127	3b22/S		-0.1
	Year	42	93	8	17	3	0	0	1	15	0		.183	.296	.215	60	-3	2	.950	-0	100	97	3b33,2b3/S		-0.4
1912	Chi A	157	591	104	161	10	2	1	19	95	7		.272	.380	.301	98	5	31	**.963**	16	**108**	91	2b157		2.4
1913	Chi A	92	295	37	59	2	0	0	12	46	1	22	.200	.310	.207	52	-16	22	.962	-0	102	114	2b86		-1.6
1919	†Cin N	138	537	77	142	13	1	1	29	64	0	24	.264	.343	.298	96	1	17	.974	13	103	114	2b138		1.7
1920	Cin N	129	506	61	135	7	4	2	28	36	3	24	.267	.319	.308	82	-12	10-11	**.977**	-2	95	101	2b126/3OR		-1.4
Total	6	565	2048	291	521	36	7	4	92	258	14	70	.254	.342	.285	86	-25	83-11	.970	25	102	104	2b510,3b36,S5/OR		0.7

RATLIFF, GENE Kelly Eugene B9.28.1945 Macon GA BR/TR/6-5/185 d5.15

YEAR	TM LG	G	AB	R	H	2B	3B	HR	RBI	BB-IB	HP	SO	AVG	OBP	SLG	AOPS	ABR	SB-CS	FA	FR	RNG	THR	GAMES AT POSITION	DL	BFW
1965	Hou N	4	4	0	0	0	0	0	0	0-0	0	4	.000	.000	.000	-99	-1	0-0	—	0		/H		-0.1

RATLIFF, PAUL Paul Hawthorne B1.23.1944 San Diego CA BL/TR/6-2/190(190-210) d4.14

YEAR	TM LG	G	AB	R	H	2B	3B	HR	RBI	BB-IB	HP	SO	AVG	OBP	SLG	AOPS	ABR	SB-CS	FA	FR	RNG	THR	GAMES AT POSITION	DL	BFW
1963	Min A	10	21	2	4	0	0	0	3	2-0	1	7	.190	.292	.381	85	0	0-0	.976	2	87	235	C7		0.2
1970	†Min A	69	149	19	40	7	2	5	22	15-2	7	51	.268	.363	.443	119	4	0-0	.980	-10	129	28	C53		-0.4
1971	Min A	21	44	3	7	1	0	2	6	4-1	0	17	.159	.224	.318	52	-3	0-0	1.000	1	126	63	C15		-0.1
	Mil A	23	41	3	7	1	0	3	7	5-1	1	21	.171	.277	.415	94	-1	0-0	.966	-0	48	123	C13		0.0
	Year	44	85	6	14	2	0	5	13	9-2	1	38	.165	.250	.365	72	-4	0-0	.985	1	92	89	C28		-0.1
1972	Mil A	22	42	1	3	0	0	1	4	2-1	0	23	.071	.114	.143	-24	-7	0-0	1.000	4	66	106	C13		-1.2
Total	4	145	297	28	61	10	2	12	42	28-5	9	119	.205	.293	.374	85	-7	0-0	.983	-11	107	70	C101		-1.5

RAUB, TOMMY Thomas Jefferson B12.1.1870 Raubsville PA D2.15.1949 Phillipsburg NJ BR/TR/5-10/155 d5.3

YEAR	TM LG	G	AB	R	H	2B	3B	HR	RBI	BB-IB	HP	SO	AVG	OBP	SLG	AOPS	ABR	SB-CS	FA	FR	RNG	THR	GAMES AT POSITION	DL	BFW
1903	Chi N	36	84	6	19	3	2	0	7	5	1		.226	.278	.310	69	-4	3	.900	-3	122	67	C12,1b6,O5R,3b4		-0.6
1906	StL N	24	78	9	22	2	4	0	2	4	1		.282	.325	.410	135	2	2	.957	-4	73	111	C22		0.0
Total	2	60	162	15	41	5	6	0	9	9	2		.253	.301	.358	99	-2	5	.940	-7	88	98	C34,1b6,O5R,3b4		-0.6

RAUDMAN, BOB Robert Joyce "Shorty" B3.14.1942 Erie PA BL/TL/5-9.5/185* d9.13

YEAR	TM LG	G	AB	R	H	2B	3B	HR	RBI	BB-IB	HP	SO	AVG	OBP	SLG	AOPS	ABR	SB-CS	FA	FR	RNG	THR	GAMES AT POSITION	DL	BFW
1966	Chi N	8	29	1	7	2	0	0	2	1-0	0	4	.241	.267	.310	59	-2	0-0	.909	0	61	372	O8L		-0.2
1967	Chi N	8	26	0	4	0	0	1	1	1-1	0	4	.154	.185	.154	-2	-3	0-0	.875	0	101	196	O8R		-0.4
Total	2	16	55	1	11	2	0	1	3	2-1	0	8	.200	.228	.236	30	-5	0-0	.889	1	80	290	O16(8/0/8)		-0.6

RAWLINGS, JOHNNY John William "Red" B8.17.1892 Bloomfield IA D10.16.1972 Inglewood CA BR/TR/5-8/158 d4.14

YEAR	TM LG	G	AB	R	H	2B	3B	HR	RBI	BB-IB	HP	SO	AVG	OBP	SLG	AOPS	ABR	SB-CS	FA	FR	RNG	THR	GAMES AT POSITION	DL	BFW
1914	Cin N	33	60	9	13	1	0	0	8	6	0	8	.217	.288	.233	54	-3	3	.885	-1	115	96	3b10,2b7,S5		-0.3
	KC F	61	193	19	41	3	0	1	15	22	1	25	.212	.296	.228	46	-17	6	.937	10	118	106	S61		-0.3

YEAR	TM LG	G	AB	R	H	2B	3B	HR	RBI	BB-IB	HP	SO	AVG	OBP	SLG	AOPS	ABR	SB-CS	FA	FR	RNG	THR	GAMES AT POSITION	DL	BFW
1915	KC F	120	399	40	86	9	2	2	24	27	2	40	.216	.269	.263	52	-33	17	.926	-5	104	86	S120		-3.2
1917	Bos N	122	371	37	95	9	4	2	31	38	7	32	.256	.337	.318	107	5	12	.977	3	104	95	2b96,S17/3OL		1.2
1918	Bos N	111	410	32	85	7	3	0	21	30	2	31	.207	.265	.239	86	-21	10	.956	8	106	91	S71,2b20,O18R		-1.1
1919	Bos N	77	275	30	70	8	2	1	16	16	1	20	.255	.298	.309	86	-5	10	.961	-9	95	82	2b58,O10(7/1/5),S5		-1.5
1920	Bos N	5	3	0	0	0	0	0	0	2	0	1	.000	.000	.000	-99	-1	0-0	1.000	-0	67	0	/2		-0.1
	Phi N	98	384	39	90	19	2	3	30	22	1	25	.234	.278	.348	67	-16	9-6	.970	-2	98	101	2b97		-1.8
	Year	103	387	39	90	19	2	3	32	22	1	26	.233	.276	.315	67	-17	9-6	.970	-3	98	101	2b98		-1.9
1921	Phi N	60	254	20	74	14	2	1	16	8	2	12	.291	.318	.374	76	-8	4-5	.954	7	109	103	2b60		0.0
	†NY N	86	307	40	82	8	1	1	30	18	4	19	.267	.316	.309	66	-15	4-4	.970	3	99	163	2b86/S		-1.0
	Year	146	561	60	156	22	3	2	46	26	6	31	.278	.317	.339	71	-23	8-9	.963	10	103	138	2b146/S		-1.0
1922	NY N	88	308	46	87	13	8	1	30	23	5	15	.282	.342	.386	87	-6	7-6	.984	-1	99	126	2b77,3b5		-0.5
1923	Pit N	119	461	53	131	18	4	1	45	25	1	29	.284	.322	.347	75	-17	9-0	.958	-8	95	97	2b119		-1.9
1924	Pit N	3	3	0	1	0	0	0	2	0	0	0	.333	.333	.333	78	0	0-0	—	0			/H		0.0
1925	Pit N	36	110	17	31	7	0	2	13	8	1	8	.282	.336	.400	82	-3	0-1	.981	2	106	96	2b29		-0.1
1926	Pit N	61	181	27	42	6	0	0	20	14	0	10	.232	.287	.265	47	-13	3	.970	-1	96	87	2b59		-0.9
Total	12	1080	3719	409	928	122	28	14	303	257	27	275	.250	.303	.309	71	-153	92-22	.968	7	100	106	2b709,S280,O29(8/1/23),3b16		-11.9

RAY, IRV Irving Burton "Stubby" B1.22.1864 Harrington ME D2.21.1948 Harrington ME BL/TR/5-6/165 d7.7 Col Maine

YEAR	TM LG	G	AB	R	H	2B	3B	HR	RBI	BB-IB	HP	SO	AVG	OBP	SLG	AOPS	ABR	SB-CS	FA	FR	RNG	THR	GAMES AT POSITION	DL	BFW
1888	Bos N	50	206	26	51	2	3	2	26	6	1	11	.248	.272	.316	85	-4	7	.879	-7	99	49	S48,2b3		-1.0
1889	Bos N	9	33	8	10	1	0	0	2	4	0	0	.303	.378	.333	94	0	1	.875	-3	83	72	S5,3b4		-0.2
	Bal AA	26	106	20	36	4	1	0	17	7	3	6	.340	.397	.396	124	3	12	.784	-8	79	110	S20,O6R		-0.4
1890	Bal AA	38	139	28	50	6	2	1	20	15	3		.360	.433	.453	154	10	11	.894	-7	88	65	S38		0.3
1891	Bal AA	103	418	72	116	17	5	0	58	54	4	18	.278	.366	.342	102	2	28	.885	-14	99	43	O64R,S40		-0.9
Total	4	226	902	154	263	30	11	3	123	86	11	35	.292	.360	.359	109	11	59	.863	-39	89	68	S151,O70R,3b4,2b3		-2.2

RAY, JOHNNY John Cornelius B3.1.1957 Chouteau OK BB/TR/5-11/185(170-189) [HouN79 12/294] d9.2 Col Arkansas-Monticello

YEAR	TM LG	G	AB	R	H	2B	3B	HR	RBI	BB-IB	HP	SO	AVG	OBP	SLG	AOPS	ABR	SB-CS	FA	FR	RNG	THR	GAMES AT POSITION	DL	BFW
1981	Pit N	31	102	10	25	11	0	0	6	6-2	0	9	.245	.284	.353	77	-3	0-0	.987	2	109	126	2b31		0.1
1982	Pit N	162	647	79	182	30	7	7	63	36-1	1	34	.281	.318	.382	91	-8	16-7	.977	9	102	88	2b162		1.1
1983	Pit N	151	576	68	163	38	7	5	53	35-3	0	26	.283	.323	.399	96	-3	18-9	.983	21	105	111	2b151		2.8
1984	Pit N	155	555	75	173	38	6	6	67	37-2	3	31	.312	.354	.434	121	16	11-6	.984	-3	96	105	2b149		2.2
1985	Pit N	154	594	67	163	33	3	7	70	46-10	1	24	.274	.325	.375	97	-3	13-9	.976	-19	92	85	2b151		-1.4
1986	Pit N	155	579	67	174	33	0	7	78	56-3	3	47	.301	.363	.394	107	8	6-9	.993	8	107	98	2b151		2.3
1987	Pit N	123	472	48	129	19	2	5	54	41-4	1	36	.273	.328	.358	82	-12	4-2	.981	2	100	117	2b119		-0.4
1988	Cal A★	30	127	16	44	11	0	0	15	3-0	1	10	.346	.359	.433	113	2	0-0	.986	0	106	106	2b29/D		0.4
1988	Cal A	153	602	75	184	42	7	6	83	36-2	4	38	.306	.345	.429	119	15	4-1	.972	-5	107	89	2b104,O40L,D6		1.2
1989	Cal A	134	530	52	153	16	3	5	62	36-3	0	30	.289	.327	.358	97	-3	6-3	.984	5	101	120	2b130	15	0.6
1990	Cal A	105	404	47	112	23	0	5	43	19-2	0	44	.277	.308	.371	91	-6	2-3	.987	15	106	117	2b100/D	21	1.2
Total	10	1353	5188	604	1502	294	36	53	594	353-39	12	329	.290	.333	.391	100	3	80-49	.982	36	102	103	2b1277,O40L,D8	36	10.1

RAY, LARRY Larry Dale B3.11.1958 Madison IN BL/TR/6-1/195 [HouN79 4/86] d9.10 Col Kentucky Wesleyan

YEAR	TM LG	G	AB	R	H	2B	3B	HR	RBI	BB-IB	HP	SO	AVG	OBP	SLG	AOPS	ABR	SB-CS	FA	FR	RNG	THR	GAMES AT POSITION	DL	BFW
1982	Hou N	5	6	0	1	0	0	0	1	0-0	0	4	.167	.143	.167	-7	-1	0-0	1.000	-0	81	0	/OL		-0.1

RAYFORD, FLOYD Floyd Kinnard B7.27.1957 Memphis TN BR/TR/5-10/195(195-220) [AnaA75 4/73] d4.17

YEAR	TM LG	G	AB	R	H	2B	3B	HR	RBI	BB-IB	HP	SO	AVG	OBP	SLG	AOPS	ABR	SB-CS	FA	FR	RNG	THR	GAMES AT POSITION	DL	BFW
1980	Bal A	8	18	1	4	0	0	0	0	0-0	0	5	.222	.222	.222	23	-2	0-0	.900	-0	106	0	3b4/2D		-0.2
1982	Bal A	34	53	7	7	0	0	3	5	6-0	0	14	.132	.220	.302	42	-5	0-1	.898	1	114	61	3b27,C2,D2		-0.5
1983	StL N	56	104	5	22	4	0	3	14	10-1	0	27	.212	.278	.337	70	-4	1-0	.883	-3	96	83	3b33		-0.8
1984	Bal A	86	250	24	64	14	0	4	27	12-0	3	51	.256	.296	.360	83	-6	0-3	.991	12	87	108	C66,3b22/1		0.7
1985	Bal A	105	359	55	110	21	4	18	48	10-0	0	69	.306	.324	.521	130	13	3-1	.972	2	107	93	3b78,C29/D		1.5
1986	Bal A	81	210	15	37	4	0	8	19	15-0	0	50	.176	.231	.310	46	-17	0-0	.912	-1	101	146	3b72,C10/D	14	-1.8
1987	Bal A	20	50	5	11	0	0	2	3	2-0	0	9	.220	.250	.340	56	-4	0-0	.980	2	67	107	C17/3D		-0.1
Total	7	390	1044	112	255	43	1	38	117	55-1	3	225	.244	.283	.397	85	-25	4-5	.931	12	105	105	3b237,C124,D6/12	14	-1.2

RAYMER, FRED Frederick Charles B11.12.1875 Leavenworth KS D6.11.1957 Los Angeles CA BR/TR/5-11/185 d4.24

YEAR	TM LG	G	AB	R	H	2B	3B	HR	RBI	BB-IB	HP	SO	AVG	OBP	SLG	AOPS	ABR	SB-CS	FA	FR	RNG	THR	GAMES AT POSITION	DL	BFW
1901	Chi N	120	463	41	108	14	2	0	43	11	4		.233	.257	.272	56	-27	18	.881	-11	94	59	3b82,S29,1b5,2b3		-3.5
1904	Bos N	114	419	28	88	12	3	1	27	13	1		.210	.236	.260	55	-23	17	.958	5	98	94	2b114		-1.9
1905	Bos N	137	498	26	105	14	2	0	31	8	6		.211	.232	.247	44	-36	15	.949	-16	94	80	2b134/1OL		-5.4
Total	3	371	1380	95	301	40	7	1	101	32	11		.218	.242	.259	51	-86	50	.954	-22	96	85	2b251,3b82,S29,1b6/OL		-10.8

RAYMOND, HARRY Harry H. "Jack" B2.20.1862 Utica NY D3.21.1925 San Diego CA 5-9/179 d9.9 ▲

YEAR	TM LG	G	AB	R	H	2B	3B	HR	RBI	BB-IB	HP	SO	AVG	OBP	SLG	AOPS	ABR	SB-CS	FA	FR	RNG	THR	GAMES AT POSITION	DL	BFW
1888	Lou AA	32	123	8	26	2	0	0	13	1	0		.211	.218	.228	44	-8	7	.884	-2	81	21	3b31/OR		-0.9
1889	Lou AA	130	515	58	123	12	9	0	47	19	3	45	.239	.270	.297	63	-28	19	.886	-3	96	87	3b129/OLP		-2.4
1890	†Lou AA	123	521	91	135	7	4	2	51	22	3		.259	.293	.299	76	-18	18	.874	-9	88	113	3b119,S4		-2.2
1891	Lou AA	14	59	4	12	2	0	0	2	5	2	6	.203	.288	.237	51	-4	3	.898	4	110	179	S14		0.1
1892	Pit N	12	49	4	4	0	1	0	2	4	0	8	.082	.151	.122	-17	-7	1	.867	0	95	55	3b12		-0.8
	Was N	4	15	2	1	0	0	0	0	3	0	2	.067	.222	.067	-12	-2	1	.783	0	125	0	3b4		-0.2
	Year	16	64	6	5	0	1	0	2	7	0	10	.078	.169	.109	-16	-9	2	.838	1	104	39	3b16		-1.0
Total	5	315	1282	167	301	23	14	2	115	54	8	61	.235	.270	.279	62	-67	49	.878	-11	92	88	3b295,S18,O2(1/0/1)/P		-6.4

RAYMOND, LOU Louis Anthony (b Louis Anthony Raymondjack) B12.11.1894 Buffalo NY D5.2.1979 Rochester NY BR/TR/5-10.5/187 d5.2

YEAR	TM LG	G	AB	R	H	2B	3B	HR	RBI	BB-IB	HP	SO	AVG	OBP	SLG	AOPS	ABR	SB-CS	FA	FR	RNG	THR	GAMES AT POSITION	DL	BFW
1919	Phi N	1	2	0	1	0	0	0	0	0	0	0	.500	.500	.500	188	0	0	—	-0	0	0	/2		0.0

REACH, AL Alfred James B5.25.1840 London, England D1.14.1928 Atlantic City NJ BL/TL/5-6/155 d5.20 M1 b-Bob

YEAR	TM LG	G	AB	R	H	2B	3B	HR	RBI	BB-IB	HP	SO	AVG	OBP	SLG	AOPS	ABR	SB-CS	FA	FR	RNG	THR	GAMES AT POSITION	DL	BFW
1871	Ath NA	26	133	43	47	7	6	0	34	5		6	.353	.377	.496	150	8	2-0	.644	-1	93	119	2b26		0.4
1872	Ath NA	24	118	21	23	0	0	0		0			.195	.221	.195	29	-10	1-1	.943	4	207	567	O20R,1b4		-0.3
1873	Ath NA	16	73	13	16	5	1	0	9	0			.219	.219	.315	53	-5	2-0	.875	4	140	85	2b8,O8(0/5/3)		0.0
1874	Ath NA	14	55	8	7	2	0	0	2	0		4	.127	.127	.164	-7	-7	2-0	.732	4	277	296	O14R		-0.2
1875	Ath NA	3	14	4	4	1	0	0	1	0			.286	.286	.357	110	0	2-1	1.000	-1	0	0	O2R/2		-0.1
Total	5 NA	83	393	89	97	15	7	0	56	9			.247	.264	.321	73	-14	7-2	.860	10	235	342	O44(0/5/39),2b35,1b4		-0.2

REACH, BOB Robert B8.28.1843 Williamsburg NY D5.19.1922 Springfield MA 5-5/155 d4.18 b-Al

YEAR	TM LG	G	AB	R	H	2B	3B	HR	RBI	BB-IB	HP	SO	AVG	OBP	SLG	AOPS	ABR	SB-CS	FA	FR	RNG	THR	GAMES AT POSITION	DL	BFW
1872	Oly NA	2	8	1	2	0	0	0		0			.250	.250	.250	57	0	0-0	.727	-1	93	0	S2		-0.1
1873	Was NA	1	5	1	1	0	0	0		0			.200	.200	.200	20	0	0-0	.500	-1	67	0	/S		-0.1
Total	2 NA	3	13	2	3	0	0	0		0			.231	.231	.231	42	0	0-0	.632	-2	83	0	S3		-0.2

READY, RANDY Randy Max B1.8.1960 Fremont CA BR/TR/5-11/180* [MilA80 6/155] d9.4 Col Mesa St. OF(167/0/6)

YEAR	TM LG	G	AB	R	H	2B	3B	HR	RBI	BB-IB	HP	SO	AVG	OBP	SLG	AOPS	ABR	SB-CS	FA	FR	RNG	THR	GAMES AT POSITION	DL	BFW
1983	Mil A	12	37	8	15	3	2	1	6	6-1	0	6	.405	.488	.676	232	7	0-1	1.000	0	91	112	3b4,D6		0.6
1984	Mil A	37	123	13	23	6	1	3	13	14-0	0	18	.187	.270	.325	66	-6	0-0	.946	5	121	63	3b36		-0.1
1985	Mil A	48	181	29	48	9	5	1	21	14-0	1	23	.265	.318	.387	93	-2	0-0	.989	-1	107	205	O37(36/0/3),3b7,2b3,D2	50	-0.5
1986	Mil A	23	79	8	15	4	0	1	9	9-0	0	9	.190	.273	.278	49	-6	2-0	.950	-1	92	0	O11L,2b7,3b3/D		-0.6
	SD N	1	3	0	0	0	0	0	0	0-0	0	1	.000	.000	.000	-99	-1	0-0	.667	-0	129	0	/3	18	-0.1
1987	SD N	124	350	69	108	26	6	12	54	67-2	3	44	.309	.423	.520	154	31	7-3	.912	9	117	153	3b52,2b51,O16L		4.0
1988	SD N	114	331	43	88	16	2	7	39	39-1	3	38	.266	.346	.390	114	7	6-2	.952	-2	99	150	3b57,2b26,O16(15/0/1)		0.6
1989	SD N	28	67	4	17	2	1	0	5	11-0	0	6	.254	.354	.313	94	0	0-0	.963	3	121	172	3b18,2b2/OL		0.4
	Phi N	72	187	33	50	11	1	8	21	31-0	2	31	.267	.372	.465	140	11	4-3	.962	-3	81	244	O36L,3b14,2b7		0.8
	Year	100	254	37	67	13	2	8	26	42-0	2	37	.264	.368	.425	127	11	4-3	.962	1	81	243	O37L,3b32,2b9		1.2
1990	Phi N	101	217	26	53	9	1	1	26	29-0	1	35	.244	.332	.309	79	-5	3-2	1.000	1	67	117	O30L,2b28		-0.1
1991	Phi N	76	205	32	51	10	1	1	20	47-3	1	25	.249	.385	.322	104	4	2-1	.989	-3	93	72	2b66	34	0.3
1992	†Oak A	61	125	17	25	2	0	3	17	25-1	0	23	.200	.329	.288	79	-3	1-0	1.000	2	102	96	O24(22/0/2),D24,3b7,1b4,2b4	37	-0.2
1993	Mon N	40	134	22	34	8	1	1	10	23-0	1	18	.254	.362	.351	104	2	2-1	.968	-0	103	113	2b28,1b13,3b3		-0.1
1994	Mon N	17	42	5	16	1	0	3	8	8-0	0	6	.381	.480	.476	148	4	0-1	1.000	-4	83	43	2b11/3		0.0
1995	Phi N	23	29	9	4	0	0	0	3	2-0	0	7	.138	.219	.138	-3	-4	0-1	.967	-2	52	143	1b3/2		-0.7
Total	13	777	2110	312	547	107	21	40	239	326-8	12	276	.259	.359	.387	108	36	27-15	.979	8	100	92	2b234,3b203,O171L,D33,1b20	139	4.3

REAMS, LEROY Leroy B8.11.1943 Pine Bluff AR BL/TR/6-2/175 d5.7

YEAR	TM LG	G	AB	R	H	2B	3B	HR	RBI	BB-IB	HP	SO	AVG	OBP	SLG	AOPS	ABR	SB-CS	FA	FR	RNG	THR	GAMES AT POSITION	DL	BFW
1969	Phi N	1	1	0	0	0	0	0	0	0	0	1	.000	.000	.000	-99	0	0-0	—	0			/H		0.0

YEAR	TM LG	G	AB	R	H	2B	3B	HR	RBI	BB-IB	HP	SO	AVG	OBP	SLG	AOPS	ABR	SB-CS	FA	FR	RNG	THR	GAMES AT POSITION	DL	BFW
REARDON, PHIL	Philip Michael B10.3.1883 Brooklyn NY D9.28.1920 Brooklyn NY BR/TR/5-9/160 d9.19																								-0.2
1906	Bro N	5	14	0	1	0	0	0	0	1-0	1		.071	.133	.071	-39	-2	0	.917	1	176	713	O4(0/1/3)		
REBEL, ART	Arthur Anthony B3.4.1914 Cincinnati OH D7.10.2004 Tampa FL BL/TL/5-8/180 d4.19																								-0.1
1938	Phi N	7	9	2	2	0	0	0	1	1-0	0	4	.222	.300	.222	47	-1	0	1.000	-0	103	0	O3(0/1/2)		0.4
1945	StL N	26	72	12	25	4	0	0	5	6-0	0	5	.347	.397	.403	120	2	1	.976	3	110	259	O18R		0.3
Total	2	33	81	14	27	4	0	0	6	7-0	0	5	.333	.386	.383	112	1	1	.978	2	109	239	O21(0/1/20)		
REBOULET, JEFF	Jeffrey Allen B4.30.1964 Dayton OH BR/TR/6-0/175(165-190) [MinA86 10/247] d5.12 Col Louisiana St. OF(7/3/15)																								1.2
1992	Min A	73	137	15	26	7	1	1	16	23-0	1	26	.190	.311	.277	63	-6	3-2	.971	16	126	131	S36,3b22,2b13,O7(1/1/5)/D		0.7
1993	Min A	109	240	33	62	8	0	1	15	35-0	2	37	.258	.356	.304	79	-6	5-5	.982	10	99	91	S62,3b35,2b11,O3(1/2/0)/D		-0.7
1994	Min A	74	189	28	49	11	4	3	23	18-0	1	23	.259	.327	.376	80	-6	0-0	.963	-4	101	53	S42,2b14,1b10,3b6,O4(1/0/3)/D		1.0
1995	Min A	87	216	39	63	11	0	4	23	27-0	1	34	.292	.373	.398	100	1	1-2	.993	9	101	113	S39,3b22,1b17,2b15/C		-2.7
1996	Min A	107	234	20	52	9	0	0	23	25-1	1	34	.222	.298	.261	43	-20	4-2	.987	-11	72	102	S37,3b36,2b22,1b13,O7(2/0/6),D3		-1.3
1997	†Bal A	99	228	26	54	9	0	4	27	23-0	1	44	.237	.307	.329	69	-10	3-0	.977	-7	98	99	2b63,S22,3b12/ORD		-1.5
1998	Bal A	79	126	20	31	6	0	1	8	19-0	2	34	.246	.351	.317	78	-3	0-1	.974	0	95	117	2b28,S28,3b23		-0.1
1999	Bal A	99	154	25	25	4	0	0	4	33-0	2	29	.162	.317	.188	35	-14	1-0	.987	11	136	106	3b56,2b36,S10		-0.1
2000	KC A	66	182	29	44	7	0	0	14	23-0	0	32	.242	.325	.280	53	-13	3-1	.982	5	114	122	2b50,3b11,S5/D		0.4
2001	LA N	94	214	35	57	15	2	3	22	33-1	1	48	.266	.367	.397	104	3	0-1	.961	-6	83	135	S56,2b22,3b7,O2L		-0.4
2002	LA N	38	48	3	10	3	0	0	2	6-0	0	13	.208	.291	.271	57	-3	0-0	.933	-1	148	59	2b11,S5,3b3/D	42	-0.2
2003	Pit N	93	261	37	63	10	2	3	25	27-3	4	47	.241	.321	.330	70	-12	2-1	.989	6	110	114	2b76,3b7		-0.4
Total	12	1018	2229	310	536	100	6	20	202	292-5	16	401	.240	.332	.318	71	-89	22-15	.984	29	105	110	2b361,S342,3b240,1b40,O24R,D9/C	42	-3.
RECCIUS, JOHN	John B10.29.1859 Louisville KY D9.1.1930 Louisville KY 5-6.5/? d5.2 b-Phil ▲																								0.
1882	Lou AA	74	266	46	63	12	3	1		23			.237	.298	.316	113	6		.857	-3	104	222	O65(0/55/11),P13		-0.
1883	Lou AA	18	63	10	9	2	0	0		3	7		.143	.229	.175	34	-4		.833	-1	31	264	O18(0/15/4)/P		-0.
Total	2	92	329	56	72	14	3	1	3	30			.219	.284	.289	98	2		.851	-3	88	231	O83(0/70/15),P14		-0.
RECCIUS, PHIL	Phillip B6.7.1862 Louisville KY D2.15.1903 Louisville KY 5-9/163 d9.25 b-John ▲																								-0.
1882	Lou AA	4	15	0	2	0	0	0		0			.133	.133	.133	-10	-2		.778	-0	104	0	O4C		-0.
1883	Lou AA	1	3	1	1	0	0	0		0			.333	.333	.667	231	0		1.000	-0	0	0	/OR		-0.
1884	Lou AA	73	263	23	63	9	2	3	21	5	5		.240	.267	.323	96	-1		.845	-3	102	91	3b51,P18,S10		-0.
1885	Lou AA	102	402	57	97	8	10	1	38	13	1		.241	.267	.318	84	-8		.829	-1	99	130	3b97,P7		0.
1886	Lou AA	5	13	4	4	1	0	0	2	3	1		.308	.471	.538	204	2	0	.889	1	278	0	O5(2/0/3)/P		0.
1887	Lou AA	11	37	9	9	2	0	0	4	8	1		.243	.391	.297	92	0	3	.926	1	102	0	O10(2/0/8)/S		0.
	Cle AA	62	229	23	47	6	3	0	29	24	5		.205	.295	.258	56	-13	9	.877	10	113	165	3b62/P		-0.
	Year	73	266	32	56	8	3	0	33	32	6		.211	.309	.263	62	-12	12	.877	11	113	165	3b62,O10(2/0/8)/SP		
1888	Lou AA	2	9	0	2	1	0	0	4	1	0		.222	.300	.333	105	-0	0	.750	-1	78	0	3b2		-0.
1890	Roc AA	1	4	0	0	0	0	0	1	0	0		.000	.000	.000	-99	-1	0	—	-0	0	0	/OR		-0.
Total	8	261	975	117	225	28	16	4	99	54	13		.231	.280	.305	81	-23	12	.848	6	104	130	3b212,P27,O21(4/4/13),S11		-1.
REDER, JOHNNY	John Anthony B9.24.1909 Lublin, Poland D4.12.1990 Fall River MA BR/TR/6-0/184 d4.16																								-0.
1932	Bos A	17	37	4	5	1	0	0	6	.135				.256	.162	11	-5	0-0	.990	0	152	141	1b10/3		-0.
REDFERN, BUCK	George Howard B4.7.1902 Asheville NC D9.8.1964 Asheville NC BR/TR/5-11/165 d4.11 Col North Carolina St.																								-1.
1928	Chi A	86	261	22	61	6	3	0	35	12	0	19	.234	.267	.280	44	-22	8-4	.953	-2	108	83	2b45,S33/3		-1.
1929	Chi A	21	46	0	6	0	0	0	3	3	0	3	.130	.184	.130	-18	-8	1-1	.967	3	82	29	2b11,3b5,S4		-1.
Total	2	107	307	22	67	6	3	0	38	15	0	22	.218	.255	.257	35	-30	9-5	.955	-5	105	77	2b56,S37,3b6		-2.
REDFIELD, JOE	Joseph Randall B1.14.1961 Doylestown PA BR/TR/6-2/185* [NYN82 9/215] d6.4 Col California-Santa Barbara																								-0.
1988	Cal A	1	2	0	0	0	0	0		0-0	0		.000	.000	.000	-99	-1	0-0	1.000	-0	61	614	/3		-0.
1991	Pit N	11	18	1	2	0	0	0		4-0	0		.111	.273	.111	12	-2	0-1	.917	-1	64	373	3b9		-0.
Total	2	12	20	1	2	0	0	0		4-0	0		.100	.250	.100	2	-3	0-1	.923	-1	64	409	3b10		-0.
REDMAN, TIKE	Julian Jawonn B3.10.1977 Tuscaloosa AL BL/TL/5-11/166(166-180) [PitN96 5/126] d6.30 b-Prentice																								0.
2000	Pit N	9	18	2	6	1	0	1	1	1-0	0	7	.333	.368	.556	129	1	1-0	1.000	2	169	442	O6(2/0/4)		-0.
2001	Pit N	37	125	8	28	4	1	1	4	4-0	0	25	.224	.246	.296	39	-12	3-5	.980	6	126	135	O35(0/28/7)		0
2003	Pit N	56	230	36	76	16	5	3	19	14-0	2	41	.330	.374	.483	120	7	7-3	.985	-2	100	34	O54C		-1
2004	Pit N	155	546	65	153	19	4	8	51	23-2	3	52	.280	.310	.374	77	-21	18-6	.986	-2	104	44	O147C		-1
2005	Pit N	135	319	33	80	12	4	2	26	19-0	1	52	.251	.292	.332	65	-17	4-1	.962	2	109	144	O85(2/75/8)		-3.
Total	5	392	1238	144	343	52	14	15	101	61-2	6	129	.277	.312	.378	79	-42	33-15	.979	6	107	95	O327(4/304/19)		
REDMAN, PRENTICE	Prentice Montezz B8.23.1979 Tuscaloosa AL BR/TR/6-3/180 [NYN99 10/316] d8.24 b-Tike Col Bevill St. (AL) JC																								-0.
2003	NY N	15	24	3	3	1	0	1	2	1-0	1	9	.125	.192	.292	25	-3	2-0	1.000	-0	97	0	O10(0/9/2)		
REDMON, GLENN	Glenn Vincent B1.11.1948 Detroit MI BR/TR/5-11/180 d9.8 Col Michigan																								
1974	SF N	7	17	0	4	3	0	0	4	1-0	0	3	.235	.278	.412	87	0	0-0	.955	-1	79	79	2b4		
REDMON, BILLY	William T. B Brooklyn NY BL/TL d5.4																								0
1875	RS NA	19	82	12	16	2	0	0	1	2		7	.195	.214	.220	56	-3	3-0	.837	5	130	0	S19,C2		0.
1877	Cin N	3	12	1	3	1	0	0	3	1			.250	.308	.333	115	0		.833	1	122	0	S3		-1.
1878	Mil N	48	187	16	43	8	0	0	21	8		13	.230	.262	.273	71	-6		.785	-16	83	57	S39,O7(0/4/3),3b3/C		-1
Total	2	51	199	17	46	9	0	0	24	9		14	.231	.264	.276	73	-6		.791	-16	87	52	S42,O7(0/4/3),3b3/C		
REDMOND, HARRY	Harry John B9.13.1887 Cleveland OH D7.10.1960 Cleveland OH BR/TR/5-8/170 d9.7																								-0.
1909	Bro N	6	19	3	0	0	0	0	1	0	0		.000	.000	.000	-99	-5	0	.892	2	134	99	2b5		-0.
REDMOND, WAYNE	Howard Wayne B11.25.1945 Athens AL BR/TR/5-10/165* d9.7																								-0
1965	Det A	4	4	1	0	0	0	0	0	1-0	0	1	.000	.200	.000	-38	-1	0-0	1.000	0	168	0	O2(1/1/0)		-0
1969	Det A	5	3	0	0	0	0	0	0	1-0	0	2	.000	.000	.000	-96	-1	0-0	—	0			/H		-0
Total	2	9	7	1	0	0	0	0	0	2-0	0	3	.000	.125	.000	-62	-2	0-0	1.000	0	168	0	O2(1/1/0)		-0
REDMOND, JACK	John McKittrick "Red" (b Jackson Mc Kittrick Redmond) B9.3.1910 Florence AZ D7.27.1968 Garland TX BL/TR/5-11/185 d4.22 Col Arizona																								-0
1935	Was A	22	34	8	6	1	0	1	7	3	0	1	.176	.243	.294	40	-3	0-0	.978	0	88	82	C15		-0
REDMOND, MIKE	Michael Patrick B5.5.1971 Seattle WA BR/TR/6-1/185(185-200) d5.31 Col Gonzaga																								15	0
1998	Fla N	37	118	10	39	9	0	2	12	5-2	2	16	.331	.368	.458	123	4	0-0	.992	-3	95	171	C37		0
1999	Fla N	84	242	22	73	9	0	1	27	26-2	5	34	.302	.381	.351	92	-2	0-0	.992	2	122	123	C82		-0
2000	Fla N	87	210	17	53	8	1	0	15	13-3	2	19	.252	.316	.300	61	-13	0-0	.996	2	88	124	C85		-0
2001	Fla N	48	141	19	44	4	0	4	14	13-4	2	13	.312	.376	.440	111	2	0-0	.994	1	104	123	C47		-0
2002	Fla N	89	256	19	78	15	0	2	28	21-8	8	34	.305	.372	.387	109	3	0-2	.993	5	95	162	C80,1b2		1
2003	†Fla N	59	125	12	30	7	1	0	11	7-0	5	16	.240	.302	.312	64	-7	0-0	.995	-5	47	85	C37/13		-0
2004	Fla N	81	246	19	63	15	0	2	25	14-0	8	28	.256	.315	.341	74	-9	1-0	1.000	0	71	100	C79		-0
2005	Min A	45	148	17	46	9	0	1	26	6-0	3	14	.311	.350	.392	95	-1	0-0	1.000	-2	247	105	C45		0
Total	8	530	1486	135	426	76	2	12	158	105-19	41	174	.287	.348	.365	90	-23	1-2	.994	1	108	126	C492,1b3/3	15	0
REDUS, GARY	Gary Eugene B11.1.1956 Athens AL BR/TR/6-1/185(180-195) [CinN78 15/381] d9.7 Col Athens St.																								-0
1982	Cin N	20	83	12	18	3	2	1	9	5-0	0	21	.217	.258	.337	66	-4	11-2	.970	-1	75	190	O20L		1
1983	Cin N	125	453	90	112	20	9	17	51	71-4	3	111	.247	.352	.444	115	10	39-14	.972	4	102	123	O120L		1
1984	Cin N	123	394	69	100	21	3	7	22	52-3	1	71	.254	.338	.376	97	0	48-11	.967	-1	97	80	O114(93/24/1)		1
1985	Cin N	101	246	51	62	14	4	6	28	44-2	1	52	.252	.366	.415	113	6	48-12	.986	1	106	71	O85(63/37/0)		64	1
1986	Phi N	90	340	62	84	22	4	11	33	47-4	3	78	.247	.343	.432	109	5	25-7	.980	6	110	132	O89L		1
1987	Chi A	130	475	78	112	26	6	12	48	69-0	0	90	.236	.328	.392	89	-7	52-11	.979	3	98	152	O123(97/19/20),D4		1
1988	Chi A	77	262	42	69	16	4	6	34	33-1	2	52	.263	.342	.401	110	4	26-2	.987	4	92	99	O68(54/16/2),D2		1
	Pit N	30	71	12	14	2	0	2	4	15-0	1	19	.197	.341	.310	90	0	5-2	.957	2	124	206	O19(11/1/7)		1
1989	Pit N	98	279	42	79	18	7	6	33	40-3	1	51	.283	.372	.423	143	16	25-6	.987	2	123	93	1b79,O16(2/1/12)	23	1
1990	†Pit N	96	227	32	56	15	3	6	23	33-0	2	38	.247	.341	.419	113	5	11-5	.988	0	102	79	1b72,O7(4/1/2)		0
1991	†Pit N	98	252	45	62	12	2	7	24	28-2	3	39	.246	.324	.393	103	1	17-3	.990	-3	89	130	1b47,O33(11/12/11)		-0

YEAR	TM LG	G	AB	R	H	2B	3B	HR	RBI	BB-IB	HP	SO	AVG	OBP	SLG	AOPS	ABR	SB-CS	FA	FR	RNG	THR	GAMES AT POSITION	DL	BFW
1992	†Pit N	76	176	26	45	7	3	3	12	17-0	0	25	.256	.321	.381	98	-1	11-4	1.000	-3	79	72	1b36,O15(2/1/12)	33	-0.5
1993	Tex A	77	222	28	64	12	4	6	31	23-1	0	35	.288	.351	.459	121	6	4-4	.981	-2	96	87	O61(5/17/46),1b5/2D	17	0.1
1994	Tex A	18	33	2	9	1	0	0	2	4-1	0	6	.273	.351	.303	70	-1	0-0	1.000	0	108	93	O7(0/3/4),1b5	80	-0.2
Total	13	1159	3513	591	886	183	51	90	352	481-21	17	688	.252	.342	.410	107	40	322-83	.974	9	100	124	O777(571/132/117),1b237,D7/2	217	5.2

REECE, BOB Robert Scott B1.5.1951 Sacramento CA BR/TR/6-1/190 d4.22 Col Stanford

YEAR	TM LG	G	AB	R	H	2B	3B	HR	RBI	BB-IB	HP	SO	AVG	OBP	SLG	AOPS	ABR	SB-CS	FA	FR	RNG	THR	GAMES AT POSITION	DL	BFW
1978	Mon N	9	11	2	2	1	0	0	3	0-0	0	4	.182	.182	.273	26	-1	0-0	.947	-1	94	0	C9		-0.2

REED, DARREN Darren A. Douglas B10.16.1965 Ojai CA BR/TR/6-1/190(190-205) [NYA84 S3/63] d5.1 Col Ventura (CA) JC [DL 1991 Mon N 182, 1993 NY N 157]

YEAR	TM LG	G	AB	R	H	2B	3B	HR	RBI	BB-IB	HP	SO	AVG	OBP	SLG	AOPS	ABR	SB-CS	FA	FR	RNG	THR	GAMES AT POSITION	DL	BFW
1990	NY N	26	39	5	8	4	1	1	2	3-0	0	11	.205	.262	.436	88	-1	1-0	.955	0	100	188	O14(2/7/6)		-0.1
1992	Mon N	42	81	10	14	2	0	5	10	6-2	1	23	.173	.239	.383	74	-3	1-0	1.000	-0	95	81	O29(8/0/21)	36	-0.5
	Min A	14	33	2	6	2	0	0	4	2-0	0	11	.182	.216	.242	31	-3	0-0	1.000	-0	81	175	O13(10/0/4)/D		-0.4
Total	2	82	153	17	28	8	1	6	16	11-2	1	45	.183	.240	.366	68	-7	1-0	.987	-0	93	129	O56(20/7/31)/D	375	-1.0

REED, JEFF Jeffrey Scott B11.12.1962 Joliet IL BL/TR/6-2/190(185-204) [MinA80 1/12] d4.5

YEAR	TM LG	G	AB	R	H	2B	3B	HR	RBI	BB-IB	HP	SO	AVG	OBP	SLG	AOPS	ABR	SB-CS	FA	FR	RNG	THR	GAMES AT POSITION	DL	BFW
1984	Min A	18	21	3	3	0	0	0	1	2-0	0	6	.143	.217	.286	36	-2	0-0	.977	-1	61	73	C18		-0.2
1985	Min A	7	10	2	2	0	0	0	0	0-0	0	3	.200	.200	.200	9	-1	0-0	1.000	-0	89	116	C7		-0.1
1986	Min A	68	165	13	39	6	1	2	9	16-0	1	19	.236	.308	.321	69	-7	1-0	.994	2	83	67	C64		-0.3
1987	Mon N	75	207	15	44	11	0	1	21	12-1	0	20	.213	.254	.280	41	-18	0-1	.970	-10	85	85	C74	35	-2.5
1988	Mon N	43	123	10	27	3	2	0	9	13-1	0	22	.220	.292	.276	61	-6	1-0	.995	-1	72	106	C39		-0.5
	Cin N	49	142	10	33	6	0	1	7	15-0	0	19	.232	.306	.296	71	-5	0-0	.993	4	112	101	C49		0.1
	Year	92	265	20	60	9	2	1	16	28-1	0	41	.226	.299	.287	66	-11	1-0	.994	3	94	103	C88		-0.4
1989	Cin N	102	287	16	64	11	0	3	23	34-5	2	46	.223	.306	.293	71	-10	0-0	.988	-9	81	149	C99		-1.5
1990	†Cin N	72	175	12	44	8	1	3	16	24-5	0	26	.251	.340	.360	90	-2	0-0	.987	-4	74	74	C70		-0.3
1991	Cin N	91	270	20	72	15	2	3	31	23-3	1	38	.267	.321	.370	92	-3	0-1	.991	3	116	86	C89	18	0.5
1992	Cin N	15	25	2	4	0	0	0	2	1-1	0	4	.160	.192	.160	1	-3	0-0	1.000	-0	85	62	C6	127	-0.4
1993	SF N	66	119	10	31	3	0	6	12	16-4	0	22	.261	.346	.437	112	2	0-1	1.000	4	127	130	C37	34	0.7
1994	SF N	50	103	11	18	3	0	1	7	11-4	0	21	.175	.254	.233	29	-11	0-0	.993	0	89	56	C33		-0.9
1995	SF N	66	113	12	30	2	0	0	9	20-3	0	17	.265	.376	.283	79	-2	0-0	.995	5	134	142	C42		0.4
1996	Col N	116	341	48	97	20	1	8	37	43-8	2	65	.284	.365	.419	87	-5	2-2	.982	-10	95	107	C111		-0.9
1997	Col N	90	256	43	76	10	0	17	47	35-1	2	55	.297	.386	.535	113	5	2-1	.987	10	111	107	C78		1.9
1998	Col N	113	259	43	75	17	1	9	39	37-4	1	57	.290	.377	.467	100	1	0-0	.986	3	105	108	C99		0.9
1999	Col N	46	106	11	27	5	0	2	11	17-1	1	24	.255	.360	.358	66	-5	0-1	.983	-7	50	146	C36		-1.0
	Chi N	57	150	18	39	11	2	1	17	28-0	2	34	.260	.381	.380	94	-1	1-1	.987	-2	86	92	C49/3D		0.0
	Year	103	256	29	66	16	2	3	28	45-1	3	58	.258	.373	.371	81	-6	1-2	.985	-9	72	113	C85/3D		-1.0
2000	Chi N	90	229	26	49	10	0	4	25	44-2	1	60	.214	.342	.310	68	-10	0-1	.990	-6	131	87	C71		-1.2
Total	17	1234	3101	311	774	144	10	61	323	391-43	14	566	.250	.334	.361	80	-82	7-9	.988	-20	97	102	C1071/D3	214	-5.3

REED, JEREMY Jeremy Thomas B6.15.1981 San Dimas CA BL/TL/6-0/180* [ChiA02 2/59] d9.8 Col Cal St.-Long Beach

YEAR	TM LG	G	AB	R	H	2B	3B	HR	RBI	BB-IB	HP	SO	AVG	OBP	SLG	AOPS	ABR	SB-CS	FA	FR	RNG	THR	GAMES AT POSITION	DL	BFW
2004	Sea A	18	58	11	23	4	0	0	5	7-1	1	4	.397	.470	.466	152	5	3-1	.981	2	139	0	O16(1/16/0)		0.7
2005	Sea A	141	488	61	124	33	3	3	45	48-1	2	74	.254	.322	.352	85	-9	12-11	.992	8	112	106	O137C		-0.1
Total	2	159	546	72	147	37	3	3	50	55-2	3	78	.269	.338	.364	93	-4	15-12	.991	10	115	95	O153(1/153/0)		0.6

REED, JODY Jody Eric B7.26.1962 Tampa FL BR/TR/5-9/165* [BosA84 8/198] d9.12 Col Florida St.

YEAR	TM LG	G	AB	R	H	2B	3B	HR	RBI	BB-IB	HP	SO	AVG	OBP	SLG	AOPS	ABR	SB-CS	FA	FR	RNG	THR	GAMES AT POSITION	DL	BFW
1987	Bos A	9	30	4	9	1	1	0	8	4-0	0	0	.300	.382	.400	105	0	1-1	1.000	3	97	195	S4,2b2/3		0.3
1988	†Bos A	109	338	60	99	23	1	1	28	45-1	4	21	.293	.380	.376	108	6	1-3	.971	8	98	92	S94,2b11,3b4/D		2.0
1989	Bos A	146	524	76	151	42	2	3	40	73-0	4	44	.288	.376	.393	111	12	4-5	.967	3	94	85	S77,2b70,3b4/ORD		2.1
1990	†Bos A	155	598	70	173	45	0	5	51	75-4	4	65	.289	.371	.390	108	10	4-4	.990	7	106	103	2b119,S50/D		2.3
1991	Bos A	153	618	87	175	42	4	5	60	60-2	4	53	.283	.349	.382	97	-0	6-5	.982	11	100	114	2b152,S6		1.0
1992	Bos A	143	550	64	136	27	1	3	40	62-2	0	44	.247	.321	.316	74	-17	7-8	.982	30	115	116	2b142/D		1.6
1993	LA N	132	445	48	123	21	2	2	31	38-10	1	40	.276	.333	.346	87	-8	1-3	.993	10	102	96	2b132	29	0.8
1994	Mil A	108	399	48	108	22	0	2	37	57-1	2	34	.271	.362	.341	79	-10	5-4	.995	7	109	106	2b106		0.2
1995	SD N	131	445	58	114	18	1	4	40	59-1	5	38	.256	.348	.328	82	-9	6-4	.994	18	100	102	2b130,S5		1.4
1996	†SD N	146	495	45	121	20	0	2	49	59-8	3	53	.244	.325	.297	69	-20	2-5	.987	-5	99	103	2b145		-1.9
1997	Det A	52	112	6	22	2	0	0	8	10-0	3	15	.196	.278	.214	32	-11	3-2	.987	8	131	102	2b41,D5		-0.2
Total	11	1284	4554	566	1231	263	10	27	392	542-29	30	407	.270	.349	.350	90	-47	40-44	.988	100	105	105	2b1050,S236,D9,3b9/OR	29	10.0

REED, JACK John Burwell B2.2.1933 Silver City MS BR/TR/6-0/185* d4.23 Col U. of Mississippi

YEAR	TM LG	G	AB	R	H	2B	3B	HR	RBI	BB-IB	HP	SO	AVG	OBP	SLG	AOPS	ABR	SB-CS	FA	FR	RNG	THR	GAMES AT POSITION	DL	BFW
1961	†NY A	28	13	4	2	0	0	0	1	1-0	0	1	.154	.214	.154	0	-2	0-0	.933	-1	93	0	O27(12/14/1)		-0.3
1962	NY A	88	43	17	13	2	1	1	4	4-1	0	7	.302	.362	.465	125	1	2-1	.941	-1	106	0	O75(20/39/16)		0.0
1963	NY A	106	73	18	15	3	1	0	1	9-0	0	14	.205	.293	.274	60	-4	5-1	1.000	2	119	101	O89(14/30/46)		-0.3
Total	3	222	129	39	30	5	2	1	6	14-1	0	22	.233	.308	.326	76	-5	7-2	.972	1	111	53	O191(46/83/63)		-0.6

REED, KEITH Keith A. B10.8.1978 Yarmouthport MA BR/TR/6-4/205 d5.11 Col Providence

YEAR	TM LG	G	AB	R	H	2B	3B	HR	RBI	BB-IB	HP	SO	AVG	OBP	SLG	AOPS	ABR	SB-CS	FA	FR	RNG	THR	GAMES AT POSITION	DL	BFW
2005	Bal A	6	5	1	1	0	0	0	1	1-0	0	2	.200	.333	.200	47	0	0-0	1.000	-0	63	0	O6(0/1/5)		-0.1

REED, MILT Milton D. B7.4.1890 Atlanta GA D7.27.1938 Atlanta GA BL/TR/5-9.5/150 d9.9

YEAR	TM LG	G	AB	R	H	2B	3B	HR	RBI	BB-IB	HP	SO	AVG	OBP	SLG	AOPS	ABR	SB-CS	FA	FR	RNG	THR	GAMES AT POSITION	DL	BFW
1911	StL N	1	1	0	0	0	0	0	0	0-0	0	0	.000	.000	.000	-99	-0	0	—	0			/H		0.0
1913	Phi N	13	24	4	6	1	0	0	1	0-0	0	5	.250	.280	.292	61	-1	1	.900	-3	85	0	S9,2b3		-0.3
1914	Phi N	44	107	10	22	2	1	0	2	10-	1	13	.206	.280	.243	52	-6	4	.887	-10	76	32	S22,2b11/3		-1.7
1915	Bro F	10	31	2	9	1	0	0	8	2-1	1	0	.290	.353	.387	109	0	2	.864	-4	76	56	S10		-0.4
Total	4	68	163	16	37	4	2	0	10	13	2	18	.227	.292	.276	63	-7	7	.880	-17	77	37	S41,2b14/3		-2.4

REED, TED Ralph Edwin B10.18.1890 Beaver PA D2.16.1959 Beaver PA BR/TR/5-11/190 d9.10 Col Princeton

YEAR	TM LG	G	AB	R	H	2B	3B	HR	RBI	BB-IB	HP	SO	AVG	OBP	SLG	AOPS	ABR	SB-CS	FA	FR	RNG	THR	GAMES AT POSITION	DL	BFW
1915	New F	20	77	5	20	1	2	0	4	2-1	1	7	.260	.287	.325	76	-4	1	.863	-4	77	127	3b20		-0.8

REED, BILLY William Joseph B11.12.1922 Shawano WI BL/TR/5-10.5/175 d4.15 Col Notre Dame

YEAR	TM LG	G	AB	R	H	2B	3B	HR	RBI	BB-IB	HP	SO	AVG	OBP	SLG	AOPS	ABR	SB-CS	FA	FR	RNG	THR	GAMES AT POSITION	DL	BFW
1952	Bos N	15	52	4	13	0	0	0	5	1-0	0	5	.250	.264	.250	45	-4	0-0	.931	-4	70	70	2b14		-0.8

REEDER, ICICLE Julius Edward B1858 Cincinnati OH D1.15.1913 Cincinnati OH BR/6-0/? d6.24

YEAR	TM LG	G	AB	R	H	2B	3B	HR	RBI	BB-IB	HP	SO	AVG	OBP	SLG	AOPS	ABR	SB-CS	FA	FR	RNG	THR	GAMES AT POSITION	DL	BFW
1884	Cin AA	3	14	0	2	0	0	0			0		.143	.143	.143	-6	-2		1.000	-0	0	0	O3L		-0.2
	Was U	3	12	0	2	0	0	0			0		.167	.167	.167	1	-2		.500	-1	0	0	O3(0/1/2)		-0.3
Total	1	6	26	0	4	0	0	0			0		.154	.154	.154	-3	-4		.714	-1	0	0	O6(3/1/2)		-0.5

REEDER, NICK Nicholas (b Nicholas Herchenroeder) B3.22.1867 Louisville KY D9.26.1894 Louisville KY BR/TR/5-9/189 d4.11

YEAR	TM LG	G	AB	R	H	2B	3B	HR	RBI	BB-IB	HP	SO	AVG	OBP	SLG	AOPS	ABR	SB-CS	FA	FR	RNG	THR	GAMES AT POSITION	DL	BFW
1891	Lou AA	1	2	0	0	0	0	0	0	0	0	1	.000	.000	.000	-99	-1	0	1.000	0	131	0	/3		0.0

REESE, RANDY Andrew Jackson B2.7.1904 Tupelo MS D1.10.1966 Tupelo MS BR/TR/5-11/180 d4.15 Col Vanderbilt OF(81/26/15)

YEAR	TM LG	G	AB	R	H	2B	3B	HR	RBI	BB-IB	HP	SO	AVG	OBP	SLG	AOPS	ABR	SB-CS	FA	FR	RNG	THR	GAMES AT POSITION	DL	BFW
1927	NY N	97	355	49	94	14	2	4	21	13	4	52	.265	.298	.349	73	-14	5	.912	-1	107	141	3b64,O16(7/0/9)/1		-1.3
1928	NY N	109	406	61	125	18	4	6	44	13	1	26	.308	.331	.416	94	-5	7	.941	-8	89	65	O64(59/2/4),2b26,1b6,S6,3b6		-1.2
1929	NY N	58	209	36	55	11	3	0	15	1	1	19	.263	.316	.344	64	-12	8	.960	2	110	96	2b44,O8(7/1/0),3b4		-0.8
1930	NY N	67	172	26	47	4	2	4	25	10	0	12	.273	.313	.390	70	-9	1	.957	-4	86	39	O32(8/23/2),3b10/1		-1.3
Total	4	331	1142	166	321	47	11	14	111	51	6	107	.281	.315	.378	78	-40	21	.954	-7	88	92	O120L,3b84,2b70,1b8,S6		-4.6

REESE, POKEY Calvin B6.10.1973 Columbia SC BR/TR/5-11/180* [CinN91 1/20] d4.1 [DL 1996 Cin N 13, 2005 Sea A 183]

YEAR	TM LG	G	AB	R	H	2B	3B	HR	RBI	BB-IB	HP	SO	AVG	OBP	SLG	AOPS	ABR	SB-CS	FA	FR	RNG	THR	GAMES AT POSITION	DL	BFW
1997	Cin N	128	397	48	87	15	0	4	26	31-2	5	82	.219	.284	.287	49	-30	25-7	.966	-6	90	99	S110,2b8,3b8		-2.5
1998	Cin N	59	133	20	34	2	2	1	16	14-1	0	28	.256	.322	.323	71	-6	3-2	.985	-3	96	165	3b32,S18,2b3	59	-0.7
1999	Cin N	149	585	85	167	37	5	10	52	35-3	6	81	.285	.330	.417	85	-14	38-7	.991	17	107	111	2b146,S16		1.5
2000	Cin N	135	518	76	132	20	9	6	40	45-5	6	86	.255	.319	.386	75	-21	29-3	.980	14	110	107	2b133		0.4
2001	Cin N	133	428	50	96	20	2	9	40	34-4	3	81	.224	.284	.343	58	-27	25-4	.972	5	111	111	S78,2b51		-1.0
2002	Pit N	119	421	46	111	25	0	4	50	41-4	3	81	.264	.330	.352	82	-12	12-1	.988	28	117	108	2b117	15	2.3
2003	Pit N	37	107	9	23	2	0	1	12	9-1	1	25	.215	.277	.262	41	-10	6-0	.969	11	133	117	2b33	138	0.4
2004	†Bos A	96	244	32	54	7	2	3	29	17-1	0	60	.221	.271	.303	47	-20	6-2	.979	22	117	106	S71,2b30	49	0.8
Total	8	856	2833	366	704	128	17	44	271	226-21	23	531	.248	.307	.352	68	-140	144-26	.985	88	113	109	2b521,S293,3b40	457	1.2

REESE, PEE WEE Harold Henry B7.23.1918 Ekron KY D8.14.1999 Louisville KY BR/TR/5-9/175* d4.23 Mil 1943-45 C1 HF1984

YEAR	TM LG	G	AB	R	H	2B	3B	HR	RBI	BB-IB	HP	SO	AVG	OBP	SLG	AOPS	ABR	SB-CS	FA	FR	RNG	THR	GAMES AT POSITION	DL	BFW
1940	Bro N	84	312	58	85	8	4	5	28	45-0	1	42	.272	.366	.372	98	15		.960	-13	87	87	S83		-0.6
1941	†Bro N	152	595	76	136	23	5	2	46	68	3	56	.229	.311	.294	68	-24	10	.946	8	102	97	S151		-0.5

YEAR	TM LG	G	AB	R	H	2B	3B	HR	RBI	BB-IB	HP	SO	AVG	OBP	SLG	AOPS	ABR	SB-CS	FA	FR	RNG	THR	GAMES AT POSITION	DL	BFW
1942	Bro N★	151	564	87	144	24	5	3	53	82	0	55	.255	.350	.332	98	2	15	.959	18	103	122	S151		3.3
1946	Bro N★	152	542	79	154	16	10	5	60	87	1	71	.284	.384	.378	116	14	10	.966	-4	97	109	S152		2.0
1947	†Bro N★	142	476	81	135	24	4	12	73	104	2	67	.284	.284	.426	119	19	7	.966	-0	99	115	S142		2.7
1948	Bro N★	151	566	96	155	31	4	9	75	79	0	63	.274	.363	.390	100	3	25	.962	6	97	108	S149		1.8
1949	†Bro N★	155	617	132	172	27	3	16	73	116	4	59	.279	.396	.410	112	16	26	.977	1	92	105	S155		2.6
1950	Bro N★	141	531	97	138	21	5	11	52	91	1	62	.260	.369	.380	96	-1	17	.963	2	94	105	S134,3b7		0.9
1951	Bro N★	154	616	94	176	20	8	10	84	81	2	59	.286	.371	.393	103	5	20-14	.953	-7	92	113	S154		0.7
1952	†Bro N★	149	559	94	152	18	6	6	58	86	5	59	.272	.369	.365	103	4	30-5	.969	-12	90	99	S145		0.7
1953	†Bro N★	140	524	108	142	25	7	13	61	82	4	61	.271	.374	.420	104	6	22-6	.966	1	94	105	S135		2.0
1954	Bro N☆	141	554	98	171	35	8	10	69	90	3	62	.309	.404	.455	121	21	8-5	.965	-3	98	81	S140		2.9
1955	†Bro N★	145	553	99	156	29	4	10	61	78-1	1	60	.282	.371	.403	103	6	8-7	.965	-11	94	101	S142		0.6
1956	†Bro N	147	572	85	147	19	2	9	46	56-1	1	69	.257	.322	.344	94	-20	13-4	.965	-2	94	103	S136,3b12		-0.9
1957	Bro N	103	330	33	74	3	1	1	29	39-1	1	32	.224	.306	.248	47	-24	5-2	.943	7	120	42	3b75,S23		-1.5
1958	LA N	59	147	21	33	7	2	4	17	26-0	0	15	.224	.337	.381	88	-2	1-2	.929	-3	95	109	S22,3b21		-0.4
Total 16		2166	8058	1338	2170	330	80	126	885	1210-3	26	890	.269	.366	.377	98	26	232-45	.962	98	26	232-45	S2014,3b115		16.3

REESE, JIMMIE James Herman (b James Herman Soloman) B10.1.1901 New York NY D7.13.1994 Santa Ana CA BL/TR/5-11.5/165 d4.19 C22

YEAR	TM LG	G	AB	R	H	2B	3B	HR	RBI	BB-IB	HP	SO	AVG	OBP	SLG	AOPS	ABR	SB-CS	FA	FR	RNG	THR	GAMES AT POSITION	DL	BFW
1930	NY A	77	188	44	65	14	2	3	18	11	0	8	.346	.382	.489	125	7	1-1	.974	-5	86	115	2b48,3b5		0.3
1931	NY A	65	245	41	59	10	2	3	26	17	1	10	.241	.293	.335	68	-12	2-3	.972	2	90	125	2b61		-0.7
1932	StL A	90	309	38	82	15	0	2	26	20	2	19	.265	.314	.333	72	-12	4	.979	11	96	107	2b77		0.4
Total 3		232	742	123	206	39	4	8	70	48	3	37	.278	.324	.373	84	-17	7-4	.975	8	92	115	2b186,3b5		0.0

REESE, KEVIN Kevin Patrick B3.11.1978 San Diego CA BL/TL/5-11/195 d6.26 Col San Diego

YEAR	TM LG	G	AB	R	H	2B	3B	HR	RBI	BB-IB	HP	SO	AVG	OBP	SLG	AOPS	ABR	SB-CS	FA	FR	RNG	THR	GAMES AT POSITION	DL	BFW
2005	NY A	2	1	0	0	0	0	0	0	1-0	0	1	.000	.500	.000	50	0	0-0	1.000	-0	93	0	O2(1/1/0)		0.0

REESE, RICH Richard Benjamin B9.29.1941 Leipsic OH BL/TL/6-3/200(185-200) d9.4

YEAR	TM LG	G	AB	R	H	2B	3B	HR	RBI	BB-IB	HP	SO	AVG	OBP	SLG	AOPS	ABR	SB-CS	FA	FR	RNG	THR	GAMES AT POSITION	DL	BFW
1964	Min A	10	7	0	0	0	0	0	0	0-0	0	0	.000	.000	.000	-99	-2	0-0	1.000	0	0	0	/1		-0.2
1965	Min A	14	7	0	2	1	0	0	0	2-1	0	2	.286	.444	.429	143	1	0-0	1.000	0	118	0	1b6/OL		0.1
1966	Min A	3	2	0	0	0	0	0	0	1-0	0	2	.000	.333	.000	5	0	0-0	—	0			/H		0.0
1967	Min A	95	101	13	25	5	0	4	20	8-2	0	17	.248	.300	.416	102	0	0-0	.990	-1	44	69	1b36,O10L		-0.2
1968	Min A	126	332	40	86	15	2	4	28	18-4	3	36	.259	.301	.352	93	-3	3-1	.991	-0	97	76	1b87,O15L		-0.9
1969	†Min A	132	419	52	135	24	4	16	69	23-3	5	57	.322	.362	.513	139	21	1-5	.993	-4	87	122	1b117,O5L		-1.5
1970	†Min A	153	501	63	131	15	5	10	56	48-5	7	70	.261	.332	.371	93	-5	5-4	.992	-2	92	90	1b146		-1.5
1971	Min A	120	329	40	72	8	3	10	39	20-2	5	35	.219	.270	.353	74	-13	7-4	.994	-3	85	103	1b95,O9(8/0/1)		-2.4
1972	Min A	132	197	23	43	3	2	5	26	25-4	0	27	.218	.305	.330	85	-4	0-1	.988	1	109	100	1b98,O13L		-0.8
1973	Det A	59	102	10	14	1	0	2	4	7-1	0	17	.137	.193	.206	12	-12	0-0	1.000	-1	93	66	1b37,O21(21/0/1)		-1.6
	Min A	22	23	7	4	1	1		3	6-0	0	6	.174	.345	.435	113	0	0-0	1.000	1	133	136	1b17		0.1
	Year	81	125	17	18	2	1	3	7	13-1	0	23	.144	.225	.248	31	-12	0-0	1.000	-1	107	90	1b54,O21(21/0/1)		-1.5
Total 10		866	2020	248	512	73	17	52	245	158-22	20	270	.253	.312	.384	95	-17	16-15	.992	-10	92	97	1b640,O74(73/0/2)		-7.1

REEVES, BOBBY Robert Edwin "Gunner" B6.24.1904 Hill City TN D6.4.1993 Chattanooga TN BR/TR/5-11/170 d6.9 Col Georgia Tech

YEAR	TM LG	G	AB	R	H	2B	3B	HR	RBI	BB-IB	HP	SO	AVG	OBP	SLG	AOPS	ABR	SB-CS	FA	FR	RNG	THR	GAMES AT POSITION	DL	BFW
1926	Was A	20	49	4	11	0	1	0	7	6	1	9	.224	.321	.265	56	-3	1-1	.940	-1	87	122	3b16/2S		-0.3
1927	Was A	112	380	37	97	11	5	1	39	21	1	53	.255	.296	.318	60	-24	3-1	.923	-10	98	69	S96,3b12,2b2		-2.
1928	Was A	102	353	44	107	16	8	3	42	24	2	47	.303	.351	.419	102	0	4-8	.908	-6	98	85	S66,2b22,3b8/OR		0.0
1929	Bos A	140	460	66	114	19	2	2	28	60	7	57	.248	.343	.311	71	-18	7-8	.912	5	108	115	3b131,2b2,S2/1		-0.8
1930	Bos A	92	272	41	59	7	4	2	18	50	3	36	.217	.345	.294	66	-13	6-2	.895	0	111	198	3b62,S15,2b11		-0.8
1931	Bos A	36	84	11	14	2	2	0	1	14	1	16	.167	.293	.238	43	-7	0-1	.912	-7	84	77	2b29/P		-4.
Total 6		502	1598	203	402	55	22	8	135	175	15	218	.252	.331	.329	73	-65	21-21	.906	-20	107	136	3b229,S180,2b67/P1OR		-4.5

REGALADO, RUDY Rudolph Valentino B5.21.1930 Los Angeles CA BR/TR/6-1/185* d4.13 Col USC

YEAR	TM LG	G	AB	R	H	2B	3B	HR	RBI	BB-IB	HP	SO	AVG	OBP	SLG	AOPS	ABR	SB-CS	FA	FR	RNG	THR	GAMES AT POSITION	DL	BFW
1954	†Cle A	65	180	21	45	5	0	2	24	19	4	16	.250	.333	.311	76	-5	0-2	.967	-6	83	86	3b50,2b2		-1.
1955	Cle A	10	26	2	7	2	0	0	5	2-0	1	4	.269	.321	.346	77	-1	0-0	.955	1	101	158	3b8/2		0.
1956	Cle A	16	47	4	11	1	0	0	2	4-0	1	1	.234	.308	.255	49	-3	0-0	.783	-5	44	161	3b14/1		-0.
Total 3		91	253	27	63	8	0	2	31	25-0	5	21	.249	.327	.304	71	-9	0-2	.944	-10	79	105	3b72,2b3/1		-1.

REGAN, JOE Joseph Charles B7.12.1872 Seymour CT D11.18.1948 Hartford CT BR/TR/6-1/? d9.21

YEAR	TM LG	G	AB	R	H	2B	3B	HR	RBI	BB-IB	HP	SO	AVG	OBP	SLG	AOPS	ABR	SB-CS	FA	FR	RNG	THR	GAMES AT POSITION	DL	BFW
1898	NY N	2	5	1	1	0	0	0	0	0	0	1	.200	.200	.200	15	-1	0	1.000	-0	0	0	O2R		-0.

REGAN, BILL William Wright B1.23.1899 Pittsburgh PA D6.11.1968 Pittsburgh PA BR/TR/5-10/155 d6.2

YEAR	TM LG	G	AB	R	H	2B	3B	HR	RBI	BB-IB	HP	SO	AVG	OBP	SLG	AOPS	ABR	SB-CS	FA	FR	RNG	THR	GAMES AT POSITION	DL	BFW
1926	Bos A	108	403	40	106	21	3	4	34	23	4	37	.263	.309	.360	77	-15	6-3	.965	16	112	105	2b106		0.
1927	Bos A	129	468	43	128	37	10	2	66	26	2	51	.274	.315	.408	88	-10	10-10	.960	2	101	99	2b121		0.
1928	Bos A	138	511	53	135	30	-6	7	75	21	2	40	.264	.296	.387	90	-17	9-6	.963	15	109	110	2b137/OR		0.
1929	Bos A	104	371	38	107	27	7	1	54	22	0	38	.288	.328	.407	90	-6	7-5	.962	-13	92	112	2b91,3b10/1		-1.
1930	Bos A	134	507	54	135	35	10	3	53	25	2	60	.266	.303	.393	78	-19	4-2	.963	-10	100	113	2b127,3b2		-2.
1931	Pit N	28	104	8	21	8	0	1	10	5	0	19	.202	.239	.308	46	-8	2	.944	-3	103	79	2b28		-1
Total 6		641	2364	236	632	158	36	18	292	122	10	245	.267	.306	.387	81	-75	38-26	.962	5	103	106	2b610,3b12/1OR		-5.

REGO, TONY Antone (b Antone De Rego) B10.31.1897 Wailuku HI D1.6.1978 Tulsa OK BR/TR/5-4/165 d6.21

YEAR	TM LG	G	AB	R	H	2B	3B	HR	RBI	BB-IB	HP	SO	AVG	OBP	SLG	AOPS	ABR	SB-CS	FA	FR	RNG	THR	GAMES AT POSITION	DL	BFW
1924	StL A	24	59	5	13	1	0	0	5	1	0	3	.220	.233	.237	20	-7	0-0	.972	-1	95	110	C23		0.
1925	StL A	20	32	5	13	2	1	0	3	3	1	2	.406	.472	.531	147	2	0-0	.979	1	90	183	C19		0.
Total 2		44	91	10	26	3	1	0	8	4	1	5	.286	.323	.341	66	-5	0-0	.975	0	93	137	C42		0.

REHG, WALLY Walter Phillip B8.31.1888 Summerfield IL D4.5.1946 Burbank CA BR/TR/5-8/160 d4.14 Mil 1918

YEAR	TM LG	G	AB	R	H	2B	3B	HR	RBI	BB-IB	HP	SO	AVG	OBP	SLG	AOPS	ABR	SB-CS	FA	FR	RNG	THR	GAMES AT POSITION	DL	BFW
1912	Pit N	8	9	1	0	0	0	0	0	0	0	0	.000	.000	.000	-99	-3	0	1.000	0	125	0	O2(0/1/1)		-0.
1913	Bos A	30	101	13	28	3	2	0	9	2	0	7	.277	.291	.347	84	-3	4	.943	-1	91	105	O26(8/3/15)		-0.
1914	Bos A	88	151	14	33	4	2	0	11	18	1	11	.219	.306	.272	74	-5	5-8	.980	1	99	106	O43(16/0/28)		-0.
1915	Bos A	5	5	2	1	0	0	0	0	0	0	0	.200	.200	.200	20	-1	1	1.000	0	144	0	/OR		0
1917	Bos N	87	341	48	92	12	6	1	31	24	1	32	.270	.320	.349	111	4	13	.956	-5	87	84	O86R		-0
1918	Bos N	40	133	6	32	5	1	1	12	5	0	14	.241	.268	.316	81	-4	3	.988	3	108	143	O38(30/1/7)		-0
1919	Cin N	5	12	1	2	0	0	0	3	1	0	0	.167	.231	.167	21	-1	0	.875	-1	69	384	O5(0/1/3)		-0
Total 7		263	752	85	188	24	11	2	66	50	2	66	.250	.299	.319	90	-13	26-8	.965	-1	94	108	O201(54/6/141)		-2

REIBER, FRANK Frank Bernard "Tubby" B9.19.1909 Huntington WV D12.26.2002 Bradenton FL BR/TR/5-8.5/169 d4.13

YEAR	TM LG	G	AB	R	H	2B	3B	HR	RBI	BB-IB	HP	SO	AVG	OBP	SLG	AOPS	ABR	SB-CS	FA	FR	RNG	THR	GAMES AT POSITION	DL	BFW
1933	Det A	13	18	3	5	0	1	1	3	2	0	3	.278	.350	.556	134	1	0-0	.929	-1	57	0	C6		0
1934	Det A	3	1	0	0	0	0	0	0	2	0	0	.000	.667	.000	84	0	0-0	—	0			/H		0
1935	Det A	8	11	3	3	0	0	0	1	3	0	0	.273	.429	.273	88	0	0-0	1.000	-0	82	0	C5		-0
1936	Det A	20	55	7	15	2	0	1	5	5	0	7	.273	.333	.364	72	-3	0-1	.982	-2	116	93	C17/OR		-0
Total 4		44	85	13	23	2	1	2	9	12	0	13	.271	.361	.388	89	-2	0-1	.975	-4	102	66	C28/OR		0

REICH, HERMAN Herman Charles B11.23.1917 Bell CA BR/TL/6-2/200 d5.3 Col Loyola Marymount

YEAR	TM LG	G	AB	R	H	2B	3B	HR	RBI	BB-IB	HP	SO	AVG	OBP	SLG	AOPS	ABR	SB-CS	FA	FR	RNG	THR	GAMES AT POSITION	DL	BFW
1949	Was A	2	2	0	0	0	0	0	0	0	0	0	1.000	1.000	1.000	-99	-0	0-0	—	0			/H		-0
	Cle A	1	2	0	1	0	0	0	0	1	0	0	.500	.667	.500	215	1	0-0	—	-0	0	0	/OR		-0
	Year	3	4	0	1	0	0	0	0	1	0	0	.250	.400	.250	75	0	0-0	—	0	83	262	/OR		-0
	Chi N	108	386	43	108	18	2	3	34	13	1	32	.280	.305	.360	80	-12	4-0	.989	13	160	75	1b85,O16R		-0
Total 1		111	390	43	109	18	2	3	34	14	1	33	.279	.306	.359	80	-12	4-0	.989	13	160	75	1b85,O17R		-0

REICHARDT, RICK Frederic Carl B3.16.1943 Madison WI BR/TR/6-3/215* d9.1 Col Wisconsin-Madison

YEAR	TM LG	G	AB	R	H	2B	3B	HR	RBI	BB-IB	HP	SO	AVG	OBP	SLG	AOPS	ABR	SB-CS	FA	FR	RNG	THR	GAMES AT POSITION	DL	BFW
1964	LA A	11	37	0	6	0	0	0	0	1-1	0	12	.162	.184	.162	-3	-5	1-0	1.000	-1	103	0	O11C		-C
1965	Cal A	20	75	8	20	4	0	1	5	12	0	12	.267	.321	.360	95	0	4-1	.975	0	103	88	O20(17/4/0)		-C
1966	Cal A	89	319	48	92	5	4	16	44	27-3	13	61	.288	.367	.480	145	18	8-4	.976	-1	89	142	O87(77/20/0)	51	1
1967	Cal A	146	498	56	132	14	2	17	69	35-4	7	90	.265	.320	.404	118	9	5-3	.974	7	106	108	O138L		1
1968	Cal A	151	534	62	136	20	3	21	73	43-5	18	118	.255	.328	.421	130	19	8-7	.989	6	103	95	O148L		1
1969	Cal A	137	493	60	125	11	4	13	68	43-5	9	100	.254	.319	.371	98	-3	3-6	.981	6	99	128	O136L,1b3		C
1970	Cal A	9	6	1	1	0	0	0	0	3-1	0	6	.167	.400	.167	78	0	0-0	1.000	0	107	0	/OR		C
	Was A	107	277	42	70	14	2	15	46	23-2	9	69	.253	.328	.480	126	9	2-4	.985	-2	103	0	O79(38/18/31)/3		C
	Year	116	283	43	71	14	2	15	47	26-3	9	69	.251	.330	.473	125	9	2-4	.985	-2	103	0	O80(38/18/32)/3		-1
1971	Chi A	138	496	53	138	14	2	19	62	37-0	6	90	.278	.335	.429	116	7	5-10	.981	-8	91	55	O128(117/15/0),1b9		

YEAR TM LG	G	AB	R	H	2B	3B	HR	RBI	BB-IB	HP	SO	AVG	OBP	SLG	AOPS	ABR	SB-CS	FA	FR	RNG	THR	GAMES AT POSITION	DL	BFW
1972 Chi A	101	291	31	73	14	4	8	43	28-1	3	63	.251	.321	.409	114	5	2-2	.981	-7	90	41	O90(11/84/0)		-0.5
1973 Chi A	46	153	15	42	8	1	3	16	8-0	1	29	.275	.315	.399	96	-1	2-3	1.000	-2	90	42	O37(30/6/1),D6		-0.6
KC A	41	127	15	28	5	2	3	17	11-1	0	28	.220	.279	.362	75	-5	0-1	1.000	0	79	326	D31,O7(1/0/6)		-0.6
Year	87	280	30	70	13	3	6	33	19-1	1	57	.250	.298	.382	86	-6	2-4	1.000	-2	89	76	O44(31/6/7),D37		-1.2
1974 KC A	1	1	0	1	0	0	0	0	0-0	0	0	1.000	1.000	1.000	451	0	0-0	—	0			/H		0.0
Total 11	997	3307	391	864	109	24	116	445	263-20	66	672	.261	.326	.414	114	53	40-41	.982	-4	98	87	O882(713/158/39),D37,1b12/3	51	-0.1

REICHLE, DICK Richard Wendell B11.23.1896 Lincoln IL D6.13.1967 Richmond Heights MO BL/TR/6-0/185 d9.19 Col Illinois

YEAR TM LG	G	AB	R	H	2B	3B	HR	RBI	BB-IB	HP	SO	AVG	OBP	SLG	AOPS	ABR	SB-CS	FA	FR	RNG	THR	GAMES AT POSITION	DL	BFW
1922 Bos A	6	24	3	6	1	0	0	0	0	1	2	.250	.280	.292	50	-2	0-0	1.000	-0	100	0	O6C		-0.2
1923 Bos A	122	361	40	93	17	3	1	39	22	8	34	.258	.315	.330	69	-17	3-6	.976	-2	94	108	O93(3/87/4),1b2		-2.3
Total 2	128	385	43	99	18	3	1	39	22	9	36	.257	.313	.327	68	-19	3-6	.977	-2	94	101	O99(3/93/4),1b2		-2.5

REID, HUGH Hugh A. B5.10.1852 Cleveland OH D12.22.1928 Chicago IL d8.26

YEAR TM LG	G	AB	R	H	2B	3B	HR	RBI	BB-IB	HP	SO	AVG	OBP	SLG	AOPS	ABR	SB-CS	FA	FR	RNG	THR	GAMES AT POSITION	DL	BFW
1874 Bal NA	1	4	0	0	0	0	0	0	0-0			.000	.000	.000	-99	-1	0-0	1.000	-0	0		/OR		-0.1

REID, JESSIE Jessie Thomas B6.1.1962 Honolulu HI BL/TL/6-1/200* [SFN80 1/7] d9.9

YEAR TM LG	G	AB	R	H	2B	3B	HR	RBI	BB-IB	HP	SO	AVG	OBP	SLG	AOPS	ABR	SB-CS	FA	FR	RNG	THR	GAMES AT POSITION	DL	BFW
1987 SF N	6	8	1	1	0	0	1	1	1-0	0	5	.125	.222	.500	89	0	0-0	1.000	0	116	0	O3(1/0/2)		0.0
1988 SF N	2	2	0	0	0	0	0	0	0-0	0	1	.000	.000	.000	-99	-1	0-0	—	0			/H		-0.1
Total 2	8	10	1	1	0	0	1	1	1-0	0	6	.100	.182	.400	54	-1	0-0	1.000	0	116	0	O3(1/0/2)		-0.1

REID, SCOTT Scott Donald B1.7.1947 Chicago IL BL/TR/6-1/195* [PhiN67 S2/38] d9.10 Col Arizona St.

YEAR TM LG	G	AB	R	H	2B	3B	HR	RBI	BB-IB	HP	SO	AVG	OBP	SLG	AOPS	ABR	SB-CS	FA	FR	RNG	THR	GAMES AT POSITION	DL	BFW
1969 Phi N	13	19	5	4	0	0	0	0	7-1	0	5	.211	.423	.211	84	0	0-1	1.000	-0	83	0	O5(2/4/0)		-0.1
1970 Phi N	25	49	5	6	1	0	0	1	11-0	0	22	.122	.283	.143	18	-5	0-0	1.000	5	98	759	O18(3/12/5)		-0.1
Total 2	38	68	10	10	1	0	0	1	18-1	0	27	.147	.326	.162	37	-5	0-1	1.000	4	95	588	O23(5/16/5)		-0.2

REID, BILLY William Alexander B5.17.1857 London ON, Can. D6.26.1940 London ON, Can. BL/TR/6-0/170 d5.1

YEAR TM LG	G	AB	R	H	2B	3B	HR	RBI	BB-IB	HP	SO	AVG	OBP	SLG	AOPS	ABR	SB-CS	FA	FR	RNG	THR	GAMES AT POSITION	DL	BFW
1883 Bal AA	24	97	14	27	3	0	0	4				.278	.307	.309	96	-1		.842	-5	92	69	2b23/S		-0.4
1884 Pit AA	19	70	11	17	2	0	0	4		1		.243	.293	.271	86	-1		.724	-4	0		O17L/32		-0.5
Total 2	43	167	25	44	5	0	0	8		1		.263	.301	.293	92	-1		.839	-9	91	67	2b24,O17L/3S		-0.9

REILLEY, DUKE Alexander Aloysius "Midget" B8.25.1884 Chicago IL D3.4.1968 Indianapolis IN BB/TR/5-4.5/148 d8.28

YEAR TM LG	G	AB	R	H	2B	3B	HR	RBI	BB-IB	HP	SO	AVG	OBP	SLG	AOPS	ABR	SB-CS	FA	FR	RNG	THR	GAMES AT POSITION	DL	BFW
1909 Cle A	20	62	10	13	0	0	0	4	4	0		.210	.258	.210	46	-4	5	.979	1	39	178	O18(13/5/0)		-0.4

REILLEY, CHARLIE Charles Augustine (b Charles Augustine O'Reilly) B1856 Providence RI D11.4.1904 Providence RI BR/TR/5-10/165 d5.1

YEAR TM LG	G	AB	R	H	2B	3B	HR	RBI	BB-IB	HP	SO	AVG	OBP	SLG	AOPS	ABR	SB-CS	FA	FR	RNG	THR	GAMES AT POSITION	DL	BFW
1879 Tro N	62	236	17	54	5	1	0	19	1		20	.229	.232	.258	66	-8		.867	-16			C49,1b11,O2(1/0/1)		-2.2
1880 Cin N	30	103	8	21	1	0	0	9	0		5	.204	.204	.214	42	-6		.759	-2	132	0	O16(1/14/1),C13,3b4		-0.8
1881 Det N	19	70	8	12	2	0	0	3	0		10	.171	.171	.200	16	-7		.889	-3			C10,O4(1/1/2),S3,3b3/1		-0.9
Wor N	2	8	2	3	0	0	0	1	0			.375	.375	.375	129	0		1.000	-1			C2		-0.1
Year	21	78	10	15	2	0	0	4	0		11	.192	.192	.218	28	-6		.897	-4			C12,O4(1/1/2),S3,3b3/1		-1.0
1882 Pro N	3	11	0	2	0	0	0	1			2	.182	.250	.182	41	-1		.714	-2			C3		-0.3
1884 Bos U	3	11	1	0	0	0	0		1			.000	.083	.000	-74	-3		1.000	-1	0		O2R/3		-0.3
Total 5	119	439	36	92	8	1	0	34			38	.210	.215	.232	48	-25		.867	-25			C77,O24(3/15/6),1b12,3b8,S3		-4.6

REILLY, ARCH Archer Edwin B8.17.1891 Alton IL D11.29.1963 Columbus OH BR/TR/5-10/163 d6.1 Col Ohio St.

YEAR TM LG	G	AB	R	H	2B	3B	HR	RBI	BB-IB	HP	SO	AVG	OBP	SLG	AOPS	ABR	SB-CS	FA	FR	RNG	THR	GAMES AT POSITION	DL	BFW
1917 Pit N	1	0	0	0	0	0	0	0	—		—	—	—	—	—	-1	—	1.000	-0	0	0	/3		0.0

REILLY, BARNEY Bernard Eugene B2.7.1885 Brockton MA D11.15.1934 St.Joseph MO BR/TR/6-0/175 d7.2 Col Yale

YEAR TM LG	G	AB	R	H	2B	3B	HR	RBI	BB-IB	HP	SO	AVG	OBP	SLG	AOPS	ABR	SB-CS	FA	FR	RNG	THR	GAMES AT POSITION	DL	BFW
1909 Chi A	12	25	3	5	0	0	0	3	3	0		.200	.286	.200	56	-1	2	.962	2	124	0	2b11/OR		0.0

REILLY, CHARLIE Charles Thomas "Princeton Charlie" (b Charles Thomas O'Reilly) B2.15.1867 Princeton NJ D12.16.1937 Los Angeles CA BB/TR/5-11/190 d10.9

YEAR TM LG	G	AB	R	H	2B	3B	HR	RBI	BB-IB	HP	SO	AVG	OBP	SLG	AOPS	ABR	SB-CS	FA	FR	RNG	THR	GAMES AT POSITION	DL	BFW
1889 Col AA	6	23	5	11	1	0	3	6	2	1	2	.478	.538	.913	326	7	9	.923	2	135	0	3b6		0.7
1890 Col AA	137	530	75	141	23	3	4	77	35	6		.266	.319	.343	102	1	43	.893	29	117	143	3b137		2.8
1891 Pit N	114	415	43	91	8	5	3	44	29	4	58	.219	.277	.284	65	-19	20	.857	0	104	57	3b99,S11,O4(1/3/0)		-1.6
1892 Phi N	91	331	42	65	7	3	1	24	18	2	43	.196	.242	.245	47	-22	13	.905	9	111	132	3b70,O15(5/8/2),2b4		-1.2
1893 Phi N	104	416	64	102	16	7	4	56	33	4	36	.245	.314	.346	76	-16	13	.895	1	99	114	3b104		-1.1
1894 Phi N	40	136	21	40	1	2	0	19	16	3	10	.294	.381	.331	74	-5	9	.874	3	121	81	3b28,O6(5/0/1),2b4/S1		-0.1
1895 Phi N	49	179	28	48	6	1	0	25	13	5	12	.268	.335	.313	67	-8	7	.900	-2	100	92	S34,3b11,2b3/OR		-0.7
1897 Was N	101	351	64	97	18	3	2	60	34	11		.276	.359	.362	91	-3	18	.905	16	114	129	3b101		1.3
Total 8	642	2381	342	595	80	24	17	311	180	41	161	.250	.314	.325	80	-65	132	.890	58	110	113	3b556,S46,O26(11/11/4),2b11/1		0.1

REILLY, HAL Harold John B4.1.1894 Oshkosh WI D12.24.1957 Chicago IL BR/TR/6-0/180 d6.19

YEAR TM LG	G	AB	R	H	2B	3B	HR	RBI	BB-IB	HP	SO	AVG	OBP	SLG	AOPS	ABR	SB-CS	FA	FR	RNG	THR	GAMES AT POSITION	DL	BFW
1919 Chi N	1	3	0	0	0	0	0	0				.000	.000	.000	-99	-1	0	—	-0	0	0	/OL		-0.1

REILLY, JOHN John Good "Long John" B10.5.1858 Cincinnati OH D5.31.1937 Cincinnati OH BR/TR/6-3/178 d5.18

YEAR TM LG	G	AB	R	H	2B	3B	HR	RBI	BB-IB	HP	SO	AVG	OBP	SLG	AOPS	ABR	SB-CS	FA	FR	RNG	THR	GAMES AT POSITION	DL	BFW
1880 Cin N	73	272	21	56	4	0	0	16	3		36	.206	.215	.265	62	-11		.947	-3	70	100	1b72,O3R		-1.7
1883 Cin AA	98	437	103	136	21	14	9	79	9			.311	.325	.485	149	21		.961	-1	67	131	1b98/OR		1.0
1884 Cin AA	105	448	114	152	24	19	11	91	5	14		.339	.366	.551	186	39		.971	-1	74	125	1b103,O3R/S		2.6
1885 Cin AA	111	482	92	143	18	11	5	60	11	7		.297	.322	.411	128	13		.963	-3	78	105	1b107,O7(0/2/5)		0.0
1886 Cin AA	115	441	92	117	12	11	6	79	31	5		.265	.321	.383	116	6	19	.967	-0	104	136	1b110,O6(0/5/1)		-0.4
1887 Cin AA	134	551	106	170	35	14	10	96	22	15		.309	.352	.477	127	17	50	.980	-1	79	142	1b127,O9(1/6/2)		0.4
1888 Cin AA	127	527	112	169	28	14	13	103	17	18		.321	.363	.501	167	36	82	.977	0	95	144	1b117,O10(0/2/8)		2.3
1889 Cin AA	111	427	84	111	24	13	5	66	34	18	37	.260	.340	.412	110	5	43	.984	-1	75	124	1b109,O2(1/1/0)		-0.6
1890 Cin N	133	553	114	166	25	26	6	86	16	7	41	.300	.328	.472	133	16	29	.977	-3	82	122	1b132/OC		0.1
1891 Cin N	135	546	60	132	20	9	4	64	9	10	42	.242	.267	.348	78	-19	22	.982	-7	59	116	1b100,O36(25/10/1)		-3.3
Total 10	1142	4684	898	1352	215	139	69	740	157	94	156	.289	.325	.438	128	123	245	.972	-22	79	126	1b1075,O78(27/27/24)/S		0.4

REILLY, JOE Joseph J. B1861 New York NY 5-10/140 d6.8

YEAR TM LG	G	AB	R	H	2B	3B	HR	RBI	BB-IB	HP	SO	AVG	OBP	SLG	AOPS	ABR	SB-CS	FA	FR	RNG	THR	GAMES AT POSITION	DL	BFW
1885 NY AA	10	40	6	7	3	0	0		3	2	0	.175	.214	.250	48	-2		.848	-1	85	73	2b8,3b2		-0.2

REILLY, TOM Thomas Henry B8.3.1884 St.Louis MO D10.18.1918 New Orleans LA BR/TR/5-10/? d7.27

YEAR TM LG	G	AB	R	H	2B	3B	HR	RBI	BB-IB	HP	SO	AVG	OBP	SLG	AOPS	ABR	SB-CS	FA	FR	RNG	THR	GAMES AT POSITION	DL	BFW
1908 StL N	29	81	5	14	1	0	1	3	2	0		.173	.193	.222	34	-6	4	.866	-4	94	136	S29		-1.1
1909 StL N	5	7	0	2	0	1	0	2	0	0		.286	.286	.571	176	0		1.000	0	125	0	S5		0.1
1914 Cle A	1	1	0	0	0	0	0	0	0	0		.000	.000	.000	-96	0	0	—	0			/H		0.0
Total 3	35	89	5	16	1	1	1	5	2	0		.180	.198	.247	44	-6	4	.875	-4	96	126	S34		-1.0

REILLY, JOSH William Henry B5.9.1868 San Francisco CA D6.12.1938 San Francisco CA BR/TR/5-8/160 d5.2

YEAR TM LG	G	AB	R	H	2B	3B	HR	RBI	BB-IB	HP	SO	AVG	OBP	SLG	AOPS	ABR	SB-CS	FA	FR	RNG	THR	GAMES AT POSITION	DL	BFW
1896 Chi N	9	42	6	9	1	0	0	2	1	0	1	.214	.233	.238	23	-5	2	.857	-2	103	27	2b8/S		-0.6

REIMER, KEVIN Kevin Michael B6.28.1964 Macon GA BL/TR/6-2/225(215-230) [TexA85 11/265] d9.13 Col Cal St.-Fullerton

YEAR TM LG	G	AB	R	H	2B	3B	HR	RBI	BB-IB	HP	SO	AVG	OBP	SLG	AOPS	ABR	SB-CS	FA	FR	RNG	THR	GAMES AT POSITION	DL	BFW
1988 Tex A	12	25	2	3	0	0	1	2	0-0	0	6	.120	.115	.240	-2	-4	0-0		-0	0	0	/OLD		-0.4
1989 Tex A	3	5	0	0	0	0	0	0	0-0	0	1	.000	.000	.000	-99	-1	0-0	—	0			/D		-0.1
1990 Tex A	64	100	5	26	9	1	2	15	10-0	1	22	.260	.333	.430	111	2	0-1	.857	-1	97	0	D21,O9(5/0/5)		0.0
1991 Tex A	136	394	46	106	22	0	20	69	33-6	7	93	.269	.332	.477	124	12	0-3	.948	-3	101	0	O66(61/0/6),D56		0.5
1992 Tex A	148	494	56	132	32	2	16	58	42-5	10	103	.267	.336	.437	119	12	2-4	.949	-0	99	111	O110L,D32		0.7
1993 Mil A	125	437	53	109	22	1	13	60	30-4	5	72	.249	.303	.394	87	-9	5-4	.962	1	115	50	D83,O37(28/0/10)		-1.4
Total 6	488	1455	162	376	85	4	52	204	115-15	23	297	.258	.320	.430	f07	12	7-12	.948	-3	102	66	O223(205/0/21),D200		-0.7

REINBACH, MIKE Michael Wayne B8.6.1949 San Diego CA D5.20.1989 Palm Desert CA BL/TR/6-2/195 d4.7 Col UCLA

YEAR TM LG	G	AB	R	H	2B	3B	HR	RBI	BB-IB	HP	SO	AVG	OBP	SLG	AOPS	ABR	SB-CS	FA	FR	RNG	THR	GAMES AT POSITION	DL	BFW
1974 Bal A	12	20	2	5	1	0		2	2-1	0	5	.250	.304	.300	80	0	0-0	1.000	0	123	0	O3(1/0/2),D3		0.0

REINECKER, WALLY Walter (b Walter Joseph Smith) B4.21.1890 Pittsburgh PA D4.18.1957 Pittsburgh PA BR/TR/5-6/150 d9.17

YEAR TM LG	G	AB	R	H	2B	3B	HR	RBI	BB-IB	HP	SO	AVG	OBP	SLG	AOPS	ABR	SB-CS	FA	FR	RNG	THR	GAMES AT POSITION	DL	BFW
1915 Bal F	3	8	0	1	0	0	0	0	1	0		.125	.222	.125	-1	-1	0	.571	-2	24	0	3b3		-0.3

REINHOLZ, ART Arthur August B1.27.1903 Detroit MI D12.29.1980 New Port Richey FL BR/TR/5-10.5/175 d9.27

YEAR TM LG	G	AB	R	H	2B	3B	HR	RBI	BB-IB	HP	SO	AVG	OBP	SLG	AOPS	ABR	SB-CS	FA	FR	RNG	THR	GAMES AT POSITION	DL	BFW
1928 Cle A	2	3	0	1	0	0	0	0	0-0	0		.333	.500	.333	122	0	0-0	.833	0	153	0	3b2		0.0

REIPSCHLAGER, CHARLIE Charles W. B2.1854 D3.16.1910 Atlantic City NJ BR/TR/5-6.5/160 d5.2

YEAR TM LG	G	AB	R	H	2B	3B	HR	RBI	BB-IB	HP	SO	AVG	OBP	SLG	AOPS	ABR	SB-CS	FA	FR	RNG	THR	GAMES AT POSITION	DL	BFW
1883 NY AA	37	145	8	27	4	2	0	4				.186	.208	.241	42	-9		.936	7			C29,O8(0/7/1)		-0.1
1884 †NY AA	59	233	21	56	13	2	0		1	2		.240	.250	.313	85	-4		.925	16			C51,O8(5/2/1)		1.5
1885 NY AA	72	268	29	65	11	1	0	21	9	1		.243	.270	.291	80	-5		.879	1			C59,O6(2/3/1),3b6/S2		0.0

YEAR	TM LG	G	AB	R	H	2B	3B	HR	RBI	BB-IB	HP	SO	AVG	OBP	SLG	AOPS	ABR	SB-CS	FA	FR	RNG	THR	GAMES AT POSITION	DL	BFW
1886	NY AA	65	232	21	49	4	6	0	25	9	1		.211	.244	.280	70	-9	2	.884	-2			C57,O9(1/6/2)		-0.5
1887	Cle AA	63	231	20	49	8	3	0	17	11	1		.212	.251	.273	47	-17	7	.888	5			C48,1b16		-0.7
Total	5	296	1109	99	246	40	14	0	63	34	5		.222	.248	.283	66	-44	9	.901	26			C244,O31(8/18/5),1b16,3b6/2S		0.2

REIS, BOBBY Robert Joseph Thomas B1.2.1909 Woodside NY D5.1.1973 St.Paul MN BR/TR/6-1/175 d9.19 OF(19/17/15) ▲

YEAR	TM LG	G	AB	R	H	2B	3B	HR	RBI	BB-IB	HP	SO	AVG	OBP	SLG	AOPS	ABR	SB-CS	FA	FR	RNG	THR	GAMES AT POSITION	DL	BFW
1931	Bro N	6	17	3	5	0	0	0	2	2	0	0	.294	.368	.294	81	0	0	.933	-1	74	0	3b6		-0.1
1932	Bro N	1	4	0	1	0	0	0	0	0	0	0	.250	.250	.250	36	0	0	.500	-1	67	0	/3		-0.1
1935	Bro N	52	85	10	21	3	0	0	4	6	0	13	.247	.297	.329	70	-4	2	.950	5	103	274	O21(4/3/14),P14,2b4/13		0.0
1936	Bos N	37	60	3	13	2	0	0	5	3	0	6	.217	.254	.250	39	-5	0	1.000	4	160	103	P35,O2C		0.1
1937	Bos N	45	86	10	21	5	0	0	6	13	0	12	.244	.343	.302	84	-1	2	1.000	-2	101	0	O18(6/12/0),P4,1b4		-0.4
1938	Bos N	34	49	6	9	0	0	0	4	1	0	3	.184	.200	.184	7	-6	1	1.000	-3	128	0	P16,O10(9/0/1),S3/C2		-0.5
Total	6	175	301	32	70	10	2	0	21	25	0	35	.233	.291	.279	59	-16	5	.979	-1	128	0	P69,O51L,3b8,1b5,2b5,S3/C		-1.0

REISER, PETE Harold Patrick B3.17.1919 St.Louis MO D10.25.1981 Palm Springs CA BL/TR (BB 1940p,1948-52p)/5-10.5/185* d7.23 Mil 1943-45 C14

YEAR	TM LG	G	AB	R	H	2B	3B	HR	RBI	BB-IB	HP	SO	AVG	OBP	SLG	AOPS	ABR	SB-CS	FA	FR	RNG	THR	GAMES AT POSITION	DL	BFW
1940	Bro N	58	225	34	66	11	4	3	20	15	0	33	.293	.338	.418	101	0	2	.960	-3	95	160	3b30,O17(5/1/9),S5		-0.2
1941	†Bro N★	137	536	117	184	39	17	14	76	46	11	71	.343	.406	.558	163	44	4	.981	4	104	127	O133(0/133/2)		4.5
1942	Bro N★	125	480	89	149	33	5	10	64	48	2	45	.310	.375	.463	142	26	20	.969	8	92	78	O125C		1.5
1946	Bro N☆	122	423	75	117	21	5	11	73	55	1	58	.277	.361	.428	122	13	34	.978	5	98	168	O97(69/28/0),3b15		1.2
1947	†Bro N	110	388	68	120	23	2	5	46	68	2	41	.309	.415	.418	117	14	14	.988	-5	97	41	O108(51/62/0)		0.4
1948	Bro N	64	127	17	30	8	2	1	19	29	1	21	.236	.382	.354	97	1	4	.981	-2	94	54	O30(17/10/5),3b4		-0.2
1949	Bos N	84	221	32	60	8	3	8	40	33	1	42	.271	.369	.443	123	8	3	.980	0	98	115	O63(27/36/0),3b4		0.5
1950	Bos N	53	78	12	16	2	0	1	10	18	2	22	.205	.367	.269	75	-2	1	.979	0	116	0	O24(16/6/0)/3		-0.3
1951	Pit N	74	140	22	38	9	3	2	13	27	0	20	.271	.389	.421	115	4	4-2	.982	-2	91	44	O27(20/6/1),3b5		0.1
1952	Cle A	34	44	7	6	1	0	3	7	4	0	16	.136	.208	.364	61	-3	1-1	1.000	0	110	0	O10(4/6/0)		-0.3
Total	10	861	2662	473	786	151	41	58	368	343	20	369	.295	.380	.450	127	105	87-3	.979	-10	98	93	O634(209/413/17),3b59,S5		7.2

REISING, CHARLIE Charles "Pop" B8.28.1861 Lanesville IN D7.26.1915 Louisville KY d7.19

YEAR	TM LG	G	AB	R	H	2B	3B	HR	RBI	BB-IB	HP	SO	AVG	OBP	SLG	AOPS	ABR	SB-CS	FA	FR	RNG	THR	GAMES AT POSITION	DL	BFW
1884	Ind AA	2	8	0	0	0	0	0		1	0		.000	.111	.000	-62	-1		.400	-1	0	0	O2(1/1/1)		-0.3

REISS, AL Albert Allen B1.8.1909 Elizabeth NJ D5.13.1989 Red Bank NJ BB/TR/5-10.5/165 d6.22

YEAR	TM LG	G	AB	R	H	2B	3B	HR	RBI	BB-IB	HP	SO	AVG	OBP	SLG	AOPS	ABR	SB-CS	FA	FR	RNG	THR	GAMES AT POSITION	DL	BFW
1932	Phi A	9	5	0	1	0	0	0	1	1	0		.200	.333	.200	40	0	0-0	1.000	0	107	0	S6		0.0

REITZ, HEINIE Henry P. B6.29.1867 Chicago IL D11.10.1914 Sacramento CA BL/TR/5-7/158 d4.27

YEAR	TM LG	G	AB	R	H	2B	3B	HR	RBI	BB-IB	HP	SO	AVG	OBP	SLG	AOPS	ABR	SB-CS	FA	FR	RNG	THR	GAMES AT POSITION	DL	BFW
1893	Bal N	130	490	90	140	17	13	1	76	65	7	32	.286	.377	.380	100	1	24	.939	4	102	99	2b130		0.8
1894	†Bal N	108	446	86	135	22	31	3	105	42		15	.303	.372	.504	105	-1	18	.968	21	109	114	2b97,3b12		1.8
1895	Bal N	71	245	45	72	15	5	0	29	18	3	11	.294	.350	.396	89	-4	15	.938	-3	95	140	2b48,3b18/S		-0.4
1896	†Bal N	120	464	76	133	15	6	4	106	49	2	32	.287	.357	.371	91	-6	28	.952	-22	90	120	2b118,S3		-1.9
1897	†Bal N	128	477	76	138	15	4	2	84	50	11		.289	.370	.358	93	-3	23	.962	19	111	151	2b128		1.8
1898	Was N	132	489	62	148	20	2	2	47	32	9		.303	.357	.364	107	5	11	.959	11	101	99	2b132		2.0
1899	Pit N	35	133	12	35	4	2	0	16	10	0		.263	.315	.323	75	-5	3	.976	0	104	59	2b35		-0.3
Total	7	724	2744	447	801	108	65	11	463	266	39	99	.292	.363	.391	97	-13	122	.955	30	102	115	2b688,3b30,S4		3.8

REITZ, KEN Kenneth John B6.24.1951 San Francisco CA BR/TR/6-0/185* [StLN69 31/730] d9.5

YEAR	TM LG	G	AB	R	H	2B	3B	HR	RBI	BB-IB	HP	SO	AVG	OBP	SLG	AOPS	ABR	SB-CS	FA	FR	RNG	THR	GAMES AT POSITION	DL	BFW
1972	StL N	21	78	5	28	4	0	0	10	2-0	0	4	.359	.370	.410	124	2	0-1	.956	-4	71	90	3b20		-0.2
1973	StL N	147	426	40	100	20	2	6	42	9-2	4		.235	.256	.333	62	-23	0-1	.974	-1	99	90	3b135/S		-2.7
1974	StL N	154	579	48	157	28	2	7	54	23-7	2	63	.271	.299	.363	85	-14	0-0	.974	-20	86	96	3b151,S2/2		-3.6
1975	StL N	161	592	43	159	25	1	5	63	22-9	5	54	.269	.298	.340	74	-22	1-1	.946	-15	89	75	3b160		-4.0
1976	SF N	155	577	40	154	21	1	5	66	24-5	1	48	.267	.293	.333	76	-19	5-4	.959	2	101	109	3b155/S		-1.7
1977	StL N	157	587	58	153	36	1	17	79	19-4	7	74	.261	.291	.412	87	-13	2-6	.980	-9	99	143	3b157		-1.1
1978	StL N	150	540	41	133	26	2	10	75	23-5	5	61	.246	.280	.357	83	-17	1-0	.973	10	108	72	3b158		-2.8
1979	StL N	159	605	42	162	41	2	8	73	25-7	4	85	.268	.299	.382	83	-14	1-0	.972	-11	95	93	3b150		-2.1
1980	StL N★	151	523	39	141	33	0	8	53	22-5	3	44	.270	.300	.379	85	-11	0-1	.979	-7	99	113	3b150		-1.5
1981	Chi N	82	260	10	56	9	1	2	28	15-3	3	56	.215	.261	.281	52	-16	0-0	.977	4	105	83	3b81		-1.5
1982	Pit N	7	10	0	0	0	0	0	0	0	0	1	.000	.091	.000	-69	-2	0-0	1.000	0	130	0	3b4		
Total	11	1344	4777	366	1243	243	12	68	548	184-47	35	518	.260	.290	.359	78	-149	10-14	.970	-41	97	98	3b1321,S4/2		-21.9

RELAFORD, DESI Desmond Lamont B9.16.1973 Valdosta GA BB/TR (BL 2003p)/5-9/175(155-180) [SeaA91 4/110] d8.1 OF(48/9/37)

YEAR	TM LG	G	AB	R	H	2B	3B	HR	RBI	BB-IB	HP	SO	AVG	OBP	SLG	AOPS	ABR	SB-CS	FA	FR	RNG	THR	GAMES AT POSITION	DL	BFW
1996	Phi N	15	40	2	7	2	0	0		3-0	0	9	.175	.233	.225	21	-5	1-0	.933	1	80	52	S9,2b4		-0.3
1997	Phi N	15	38	3	7	1	2	0		5-0	0	6	.184	.279	.316	56	-3	3-0	.977	-1	100	46	S12		-0.2
1998	Phi N	142	494	45	121	25	3	5	41	33-4	3	87	.245	.293	.338	66	-25	9-5	.960	-7	98	137	S63		-2.1
1999	Phi N	65	211	31	51	11	2	1	26	19-2	6	34	.242	.322	.327	64	-11	4-3	.952	8	111	119	S63	88	-1.1
2000	Phi N	83	253	29	56	12	3	3	30	48-7	9	45	.221	.363	.328	77	-7	5-0	.930	-12	89	94	S81		-0.6
	SD N	45	157	26	32	2	0	2	16	27-0	3	26	.204	.330	.255	54	-11	8-0	.965	-1	98	120	S45		-0.5
	Year	128	410	55	88	14	3	5	46	75-7	12	71	.215	.351	.300	69	-17	13-0	.943	-13	92	103	S126		0.7
2001	NY N	120	301	43	91	27	0	8	36	27-1	5	65	.302	.364	.472	124	12	13-5	.969	-9	84	112	2b54,S25,3b20/P		-0.4
2002	Sea A	112	329	55	88	13	2	6	43	33-2	6	51	.267	.339	.374	94	-2	10-3	.964	-5	88	118	2b89,3b33,O20(1/5/15),S6,D5		-0.3
2003	KC A	141	500	70	127	27	5	8	59	40-1	6	70	.254	.315	.376	77	-17	20-4	.981	1	99	113	3b42,2b36,O32(22/3/9),S12	23	-1.8
2004	KC A	114	380	45	84	14	0	6	34	34-3	8	56	.221	.296	.305	58	-24	5-4	.927	3	110	79	3b21,2b11,O4(0/1/3)	9	-1.2
2005	Col N	73	210	24	47	13	2	1	16	22-2	4	42	.224	.308	.319	57	-13	3-1	.960	-2	108	68	S37,3b21,2b11,O91L,D9/P	120	-1.2
Total	10	925	2913	373	711	147	19	40	308	291-29	49	491	.244	.321	.349	74	-106	81-27	.955	-22	98	96	S467,2b205,3b154,O91L,D9/P		-7.8

REMENTER, BUTCH Willis J. H. B3.14.1878 Philadelphia PA D9.23.1922 Philadelphia PA BR/TR/5-6.5/180 d10.8

YEAR	TM LG	G	AB	R	H	2B	3B	HR	RBI	BB-IB	HP	SO	AVG	OBP	SLG	AOPS	ABR	SB-CS	FA	FR	RNG	THR	GAMES AT POSITION	DL	BFW
1904	Phi N	1	2	0	0	0	0	0	0	0			.000	.000	.000	-99	0		1.000	-0	74	0	/C		-0.1

REMSEN, JACK John Jay B4.1850 Brooklyn NY BR/TR/5-11/189 d5.2

YEAR	TM LG	G	AB	R	H	2B	3B	HR	RBI	BB-IB	HP	SO	AVG	OBP	SLG	AOPS	ABR	SB-CS	FA	FR	RNG	THR	GAMES AT POSITION	DL	BFW
1872	Atl NA	37	165	25	39	3	5	1	14	2		6	.236	.246	.333	65	-10	1-2	.797	2	123	192	O37C		-0.6
1873	Atl NA	50	224	29	61	5	6	1	29	2		2	.295	.301	.391	117	5	1-2	.793	-2	70	136	O50C		0.2
1874	Mut NA	64	284	52	65	9	3	2	38	0		5	.229	.229	.303	67	-11	6-0	.864	4	134	139	O63(8/57/0),1b3		-0.4
1875	Har NA	86	358	70	96	10	4	0	34	5		4	.268	.278	.318	102	-1	6-3	.887	2	71	48	O60(0/81/5)		0.2
1876	Har N	69	324	62	89	12	5	1	30	1		15	.275	.277	.352	100	-2		.887	7	102	250	O69(3/66/0)		0.2
1877	StL N	33	123	14	32	3	4	0	13	4		3	.260	.284	.350	104	1		.906	0	61	0	O33C		-0.1
1878	Chi N	56	224	32	52	11	1	1	19	17		33	.232	.286	.304	88	-2		.944	4	95	237	O56C		-0.9
1879	Chi N	42	152	14	33	4	2	0	23	7			.217	.227	.270	60	-7		.862	-1	64	149	O31(5/26/0),1b11		-1.4
1881	Cle N	48	172	14	30	4	1	0	13	9		31	.174	.215	.233	43	-11		.873	-2	54	55	O48C		-1.4
1884	Phi N	12	43	9	9	2	0	0	3	6		9	.209	.306	.256	83	0		.952	1	160	0	O12C		0.0
	Bro AA	81	301	45	67	6	6	3		23	0		.223	.278	.312	91	-3		.914	3	45	79	O81(32/49/0)		-0.7
Total	4 NA	237	1014	176	261	27	18	4	115	9		17	.257	.264	.331	88	-1	14-7	.842	5	96	114	O236(8/225/5),1b3		0.0
Total	6	341	1339	190	312	42	21	5	86	62	0	114	.233	.267	.307	84	-24		.900	12	74	135	O330(40/290/0),1b11		-2.4

REMY, JERRY Gerald Peter B11.8.1952 Fall River MA BL/TR/5-9/165* [AnaA71*A8/130] d4.7 [DL 1985 Bos A 182]

YEAR	TM LG	G	AB	R	H	2B	3B	HR	RBI	BB-IB	HP	SO	AVG	OBP	SLG	AOPS	ABR	SB-CS	FA	FR	RNG	THR	GAMES AT POSITION	DL	BFW
1975	Cal A	147	569	82	147	17	5	1	46	45-1	0	55	.258	.311	.311	82	-14	34-21	.982	16	103	109	2b147		1.2
1976	Cal A	143	502	64	132	14	3	0	28	38-1	0	43	.263	.313	.303	87	-9	35-16	.977	19	109	96	2b133,D5		2.2
1977	Cal A	154	575	74	145	19	10	4	44	59-2	2	59	.252	.322	.341	94	-12	41-17	.975	-3	95	92	2b152/3		-0.4
1978	Bos A☆	148	583	87	162	24	6	2	44	40-0	0	55	.278	.321	.350	81	-15	30-13	.983	1	99	123	2b140/SD		-1.9
1979	Bos A	80	306	49	91	11	2	0	29	26-1	0	25	.297	.350	.346	85	-6	14-9	.970	-18	87	83	2b76	52	-0.2
1980	Bos A	63	230	24	72	7	2	0	9	10-0	0	14	.313	.339	.361	88	-4	14-6	.977	-2	106	73	2b60/OR	83	-0.2
1981	Bos A	88	358	55	110	9	1	0	31	36-2	0	30	.307	.368	.338	99	1	9-2	.984	-1	99	91	2b87		-2.5
1982	Bos A	155	636	89	178	22	3	0	47	55-1	2	77	.280	.337	.324	78	-17	16-9	.982	-16	97	96	2b154		-3.1
1983	Bos A	146	592	73	163	16	5	0	43	40-2	1	35	.275	.320	.319	72	-23	11-3	.990	-17	93	100	2b24	11	-3.1
1984	Bos A	30	104	8	26	1	0	0	7	7-0	0	11	.250	.297	.279	58	-6	4-3	.973	-1	101	82	2b24	135	-6.1
Total	10	1154	4455	605	1226	140	38	7	329	356-10	4	404	.275	.327	.328	82	-105	208-99	.981	-31	99	98	2b1117,D9/ORS3	463	-6.1

RENICK, RICK Warren Richard B3.16.1944 London OH BR/TR/6-0/190* d7.11 C13 Col Ohio St.

YEAR	TM LG	G	AB	R	H	2B	3B	HR	RBI	BB-IB	HP	SO	AVG	OBP	SLG	AOPS	ABR	SB-CS	FA	FR	RNG	THR	GAMES AT POSITION	DL	BFW
1968	Min A	42	97	16	21	5	2	3	13	9-1	1	42	.216	.283	.402	100	0	0-0	.946	0	100	84	S40		0.3
1969	†Min A	71	139	21	34	3	0	5	17	12-1	1	32	.245	.307	.374	88	-3	0-1	.913	-6	82	104	3b30,O10(8/0/2),S6	21	-0.9
1970	†Min A	81	179	20	41	8	0	7	25	22-0	1	29	.229	.317	.391	93	-2	0-2	.987	1	95	99	3b30,O25(25/1/0)/S		-0.2
1971	Min A	27	45	4	10	1	0	1	8	5-2	1	14	.222	.308	.333	81	-1	0-0	.846	-2	0	3	3b7,O7L	65	

YEAR	TM LG	G	AB	R	H	2B	3B	HR	RBI	BB-IB	HP	SO	AVG	OBP	SLG	AOPS	ABR	SB-CS		FA	FR	RNG	THR	GAMES AT POSITION		DL	BFW
1972	Min A	55	93	10	16	2	0	4	8	15-0	0	25	.172	.282	.323	77	-2	0-1		1.000	-2	87	0	O21(19/0/2),1b6,3b4/S			-0.6
Total	5	276	553	71	122	20	2	20	71	63-4	3	142	.221	.302	.373	89	-8	0-4		.940	-8	90	86	3b71,O63(59/1/4),S48,1b6		86	-1.7

RENNA, BILL William Beneditto "Big Bill" B10.14.1924 Hanford CA BR/TR/6-3/218(218-230) d4.14 Col Santa Clara

1953	NY A	61	121	19	38	6	2	13	13		1	31	.314	.385	.463	133	5			.983	-1	101	0	O40(32/5/3)			0.2
1954	Phi A	123	422	52	98	15	4	13	53	41	3	60	.232	.302	.379	86	-10	1-3		.972	6	106	156	O115(1/1/114)			-0.9
1955	KC A	100	249	33	53	7	3	7	28	31-0	2	42	.213	.305	.349	75	-10	0-3		.992	0	99	102	O79(8/0/72)			-1.3
1956	KC A	33	48	12	13	3	0	2	5	3-0	0	10	.271	.314	.458	101	0	1-0		.950	-0	93	138	O25(22/0/3)			-0.1
1958	Bos A	39	56	5	15	5	0	4	18	6-1	0	14	.268	.339	.571	136	3	0-0		1.000	-0	103	0	O11L			0.2
1959	Bos A	14	22	2	2	0	0	0	2	5-0	0	9	.091	.259	.091	-0	-3	0-0		.972	0	105	158	O7L			-0.4
Total	6	370	918	123	219	36	10	28	119	99-1	6	166	.239	.315	.391	91	-15	2-7		.979	4	102	113	O277(81/6/192)			-2.3

RENSA, TONY George Anthony "Pug" B9.29.1901 Parsons PA D1.4.1987 Wilkes-Barre PA BR/TR/5-10/180 d5.5

1930	Det A	20	37	6	10	2	1	1	3	6	1	7	.270	.386	.459	141	1	1-0		.964	-1	63	141	C18			0.0
	Phi N	54	172	31	49	11	2	3	31	10	1	18	.285	.328	.424	75	-7	1-0		.932	-11	74	91	C49			-1.3
1931	Phi N	19	29	2	3	1	0	0	2	6	0	2	.103	.257	.138	8	-4	0		.958	1	69	206	C17			-0.2
1933	NY A	8	29	4	9	2	1	0	3	1	0	3	.310	.333	.448	112	0	0-1		.977	-1	125	96	C8			0.0
1937	Chi A	26	57	10	17	5	1	0	5	8	0	6	.298	.385	.421	103	1	3-0		.975	1	119	90	C23			0.3
1938	Chi A	59	165	15	41	5	0	3	19	25	1	16	.248	.351	.333	71	-7	1-1		.982	6	125	105	C57			0.1
1939	Chi A	14	25	3	5	0	0	0	2	1	0	2	.200	.231	.200	11	-3	0-0		.972	0	105	158	C13			-0.2
Total	6	200	514	71	134	26	5	7	65	57	3	54	.261	.338	.372	74	-19	5-2		.965	-5	100	111	C185			-1.3

RENTERIA, EDGAR Edgar Enrique B8.7.1976 Barranquilla, Colombia BR/TR/6-1/180(172-200) d5.10

1996	Fla N	106	431	68	133	18	3	5	31	33-0	2	68	.309	.358	.399	103	3	16-2		.979	14	108	115	S106		17	2.6
1997	†Fla N	154	617	90	171	21	3	4	52	45-1	4	108	.277	.327	.340	80	-19	32-15		.975	-4	92	104	S153			-1.0
1998	Fla N★	133	517	79	146	18	2	3	31	48-1	4	78	.282	.347	.342	88	-9	41-22		.966	-7	98	102	S129		15	-0.4
1999	StL N	154	585	92	161	36	2	11	63	53-0	2	82	.275	.334	.400	84	-14	37-8		.959	-11	96	94	S151			-0.8
2000	†StL N★	150	562	94	156	32	4	16	76	63-3	1	77	.278	.346	.423	93	-6	21-13		.958	-8	94	92	S149			-0.2
2001	†StL N	141	493	54	128	19	3	10	57	39-4	3	73	.260	.314	.371	76	-18	17-4		.961	7	104	109	S137/1D			0.1
2002	†StL N	152	544	77	166	36	2	11	83	49-7	4	57	.305	.364	.439	114	9	22-7		.970	-18	97	79	S149			0.5
2003	StL N★	157	587	96	194	47	1	13	100	65-12	3	54	.330	.394	.480	129	24	34-7		.975	-26	98	85	S156			1.9
2004	†StL N★	149	586	84	168	37	0	10	72	39-5	1	78	.287	.327	.401	87	-11	17-11		.983	-2	99	110	S149			-0.1
2005	†Bos A	153	623	100	172	36	4	8	70	55-0	3	100	.276	.335	.385	87	-11	9-4		.954	-15	94	91	S153			-1.3
Total	10	1449	5545	834	1595	300	21	91	635	489-33	25	775	.288	.345	.399	94	-49	246-93		.968	-69	98	97	S1432/D1		32	1.3

RENTERIA, RICH Richard Avina B12.25.1961 Harbor City CA BR/TR/5-9/172* [PitN80 1/20] d9.14 [DL 1989 Sea A 88]

1986	Pit N	10	12	2	3	1	0	0	1	0-0	0	4	.250	.250	.333	58	-1	0-0		.600	-0	134	0	/3			-0.1
1987	Sea A	12	10	1	1	1	0	0	1	0-0	0	1	.100	.182	.200	1	-1	1-0		.833	1	91	0	2b4/SD		12	-0.1
1988	Sea A	31	88	6	18	9	0	0	6	2-0	0	8	.205	.222	.307	44	-6	1-3		.958	1	90	103	D12,S11,3b5,2b4			-0.6
1993	Fla N	103	263	27	67	7	4	2	30	21-1	2	31	.255	.314	.327	68	-12	0-2		.989	-3	99	65	2b45,3b25/OL			-1.3
1994	Fla N	28	49	5	11	0	0	2	4	1-0	2	4	.224	.269	.347	57	-3	0-1		.929	2	115	285	3b14,2b6,O2L		74	-0.3
Total	5	184	422	42	100	20	4	4	41	25-1	4	49	.237	.285	.322	60	-23	2-6		.986	0	99	73	2b59,3b45,D16,S12,O3L		174	-2.3

REPASS, BOB Robert Willis B11.6.1917 W.Pittston PA BR/TR/6-1/185 d9.18

1939	StL N	3	6	0	2	1	0	0	0	2	0	0	.333	.333	.500	114	0	0		1.000	0	142	137	2b2			0.1
1942	Was A	81	259	30	62	11	1	2	23	33	1	30	.239	.328	.313	81	-6	6-1		.973	-4	89	70	2b33,3b29,S11			-0.5
Total	2	84	265	30	64	12	1	2	24	33	1	32	.242	.328	.317	82	-6	6-1		.973	-4	91	72	2b35,3b29,S11			-0.4

REPKO, JASON Jason Edward B12.27.1980 East Chicago IN BR/TR/5-11/175 d4.6

2005	LA N	129	276	43	61	15	3	8	30	16-1	7	80	.221	.281	.384	72	-12	5-0		.968	2	99	159	O118(24/58/42)			-1.1

REPOZ, ROGER Roger Allen B8.3.1940 Bellingham WA BL/TL/6-3/195(175-195) d9.11 Col Western Washington

1964	NY A	11	1	1	0	0	0	0	0	1-0	0	1	.000	.500	.000	52	0	0-0		1.000	-1	35	0	O9R			-0.1
1965	NY A	79	218	34	48	7	4	12	28	25-4	0	57	.220	.298	.454	112	2	1-1		.993	-3	97	36	O69(0/65/7)			-0.3
1966	NY A	37	43	4	15	4	1	0	9	4-0	0	8	.349	.396	.488	161	4	0-0		1.000	-3	69	0	O30(10/28/5)			0.0
	KC A	101	319	40	69	10	3	11	34	44-4	2	80	.216	.314	.370	99	0	3-3		.991	-5	104	35	O52(8/41/3),1b45			-1.0
	Year	138	362	44	84	14	4	11	43	48-4	2	88	.232	.324	.384	106	4	3-3		.992	-8	96	27	O82(8/69/8),1b45			-1.0
1967	KC A	40	87	9	21	6	1	2	8	12-1	1	20	.241	.340	.402	122	4	4-2		1.000	3	119	203	O31(16/9/6)			0.5
	Cal A	74	176	25	44	9	1	5	20	19-1	0	37	.250	.318	.398	116	4	2-2		.959	0	109	102	O63(6/54/4)			0.2
	Year	114	263	34	65	15	2	7	28	31-2	1	57	.247	.326	.399	118	6	6-4		.972	4	112	135	O94(22/63/10)			0.7
1968	Cal A	133	375	30	90	8	1	13	54	38-3	3	83	.240	.309	.371	111	4	8-7		.987	1	107	63	O114(0/71/52)			-0.1
1969	Cal A	103	219	25	36	1	1	8	19	32-2	0	52	.164	.270	.288	59	-13	1-3		.985	2	98	144	O48(13/22/16),1b31			-1.6
1970	Cal A	137	407	50	97	17	6	18	47	45-6	3	90	.238	.317	.442	111	-1	4-2		.995	-1	103	95	O110(6/42/68),1b18			-0.2
1971	Cal A	113	297	39	59	11	1	13	41	60-6	1	69	.199	.333	.374	108	5	3-5		1.000	-1	96	104	O97(5/25/72),1b13			-0.2
1972	Cal A	3	3	0	1	0	0	0	0		0	2	.333	.333	.333	104	0	0-0		—	0			/H			0.0
Total	9	831	2145	257	480	73	19	82	260	280-27	10	499	.224	.314	.390	105	14	26-25		.989	-7	102	83	O623(54/357/242),1b107			-2.8

REPULSKI, RIP Eldon John B10.4.1927 Sauk Rapids MN D2.10.1993 Waite Park MN BR/TR/6-0/195* d4.14 Col St. Cloud St.

1953	StL N	153	567	75	156	25	4	15	66	33	9	71	.275	.325	.413	91	-9	3-6		.987	-10	92	54	O153C			-2.6
1954	StL N	152	619	99	175	39	5	19	79	43	4	75	.283	.329	.454	102	1	8-10		.975	-9	94	40	O152(137/12/3)			-1.9
1955	StL N	147	512	64	138	28	2	23	73	49-3	4	66	.270	.333	.467	111	8	5-7		.974	-8	100	50	O141(110/1/32)			-0.5
1956	StL N★	112	376	44	104	18	3	11	55	24-3	7	46	.277	.330	.428	102	1	2-2		.974	-3	99	48	O100(99/1/1)			-0.8
1957	Phi N	134	516	65	134	23	4	20	68	19-0	5	74	.260	.290	.436	95	-6	7-1		.968	0	107	64	O130(54/0/84)			-0.1
1958	Phi N	85	238	33	58	9	4	13	40	15-1	4	47	.244	.296	.479	103	0	0-0		.949	-3	89	73	O56(35/0/21)			-0.7
1959	†LA N	53	94	11	24	4	0	2	14	13-2	0	23	.255	.343	.362	83	-2	0-1		1.000	-2	86	0	O31(16/2/13)			-0.5
1960	LA N	4	5	0	1	0	0	0	0	0-0	0	1	.200	.200	.200	9	-1	0-0		1.000	-0	51	0	O2R			-0.1
	Bos A	73	136	14	33	6	1	3	20	10-0	0	25	.243	.289	.368	75	-5	0-0		1.000	-3	106	0	O33L			-0.7
1961	Bos A	15	25	2	7	1	0	0	1	1-0	0	5	.280	.308	.320	66	-1	0-2		1.000	-1	61	0	O4L			-0.3
Total	9	928	3088	407	830	153	23	106	416	207-9	33	433	.269	.319	.436	98	-14	25-29		.976	-31	97	49	O802(488/169/156)			-9.2

RESSLER, LARRY Lawrence P. B8.10.1848 , France D6.12.1918 Reading PA d4.26

1875	Was NA	27	108	17	21	1	0	0	5	0		4	.194	.194	.204	40	-6	4-0		.831	3	281	210	O20(0/3/17),2b7			-0.2

RESTELLI, DINO Dino Paul "Dingo" B9.23.1924 St.Louis MO BR/TR/6-1.5/191* d6.14 Col Santa Clara

1949	Pit N	72	232	41	58	11	0	12	40	35	4	26	.250	.358	.453	113	5	3		.961	-0	103	83	O61(0/47/14)/1			0.3
1951	Pit N	21	38	1	7	1	0	1	3	2	0	4	.184	.225	.289	36	-4	0-0		.920	0	104	124	O11(8/4/0)			-0.4
Total	2	93	270	42	65	12	0	13	43	37	4	30	.241	.341	.430	103	1	3-0		.956	0	103	88	O72(8/51/14)/1			-0.1

RESTOVICH, MICHAEL Michael Jerome B1.3.1979 Rochester MN BR/TR/6-4/233(233-250) [MinA97 2/61] d9.18

2002	Min A	8	13	3	4	0	0	1	1	1-0	0	4	.308	.357	.538	129	0	1-0		1.000	0	111	0	O5(4/0/1),D2			0.1
2003	Min A	24	53	10	15	3	2	0	4	10-0	1	12	.283	.406	.415	113	2	0-0		1.000	-0	95	113	O17(3/0/14),D7			0.1
2004	Min A	29	47	9	12	3	0	2	6	4-0	0	10	.255	.314	.447	92	-1	0-0		1.000	-1	91	0	O19(12/0/7),D5			-0.2
2005	Col N	14	31	5	9	2	0	1	3	3-0	0	5	.290	.353	.452	95	-0	0-0		1.000	1	131	0	O8(1/0/7)			0.0
	Pit N	52	84	10	18	3	1	2	5	8-0	0	24	.214	.283	.345	64	-5	0-0		.976	0	107	91	O31(14/0/20)			-0.5
	Year	66	115	15	27	5	1	3	8	11-0	0	29	.235	.302	.374	74	-5	0-0		.983	1	114	66	O39(15/0/27)			-0.5
Total	4	127	228	37	58	11	3	6	19	26-0	1	55	.254	.333	.408	90	-4	1-0		.991	0	104	62	O80(34/0/49),D14			-0.5

RETTENMUND, MERV Mervin Weldon B6.6.1943 Flint MI BR/TR/5-10/195* d4.14 C20 Col Ball St.

1968	Bal A	31	64	10	19	5	0	2	7	18-0	1	20	.297	.452	.469	181	8	1-1		1.000	-2	78	87	O23(4/13/13)			0.6
1969	†Bal A	95	190	27	47	10	3	4	25	28-1	0	28	.247	.338	.395	105	-2	6-1		.991	-0	100	74	O78(45/18/21)			0.2
1970	†Bal A	106	338	60	109	17	2	18	58	38-1	3	59	.322	.394	.544	154	25	13-7		.976	5	111	107	O93(30/44/36)			2.7
1971	†Bal A	141	491	81	156	23	4	11	75	87-2	4	60	.318	.422	.448	146	35	15-6		.977	1	104	79	O134(46/40/72)			3.3
1972	Bal A	102	301	40	70	10	2	6	21	41-0	0	37	.233	.325	.339	94	-1	6-4		.989	2	104	102	O98(6/23/79)		15	-0.3
1973	†Bal A	95	321	59	84	17	2	9	44	57-4	4	38	.262	.378	.411	122	12	11-2		.985	5	116	70	O90(11/2/81)			1.4
1974	Cin N	80	208	30	45	6	0	8	28	37-1	2	39	.216	.337	.332	90	-2	5-1		1.000	-3	92	77	O69(0/9/60)			-0.7
1975	†Cin N	93	188	24	45	6	1	2	19	35-3	2	22	.239	.356	.314	87	-2	5-0		.972	-1	101	28	O61(20/4/38)/3			-0.5
1976	SD N	86	140	22	32	7	2	11	29	29-0	1	23	.229	.361	.321	103	2	4-1		.977	6	127	261	O43(34/1/11)			0.8

YEAR	TM LG	G	AB	R	H	2B	3B	HR	RBI	BB-IB	HP	SO	AVG	OBP	SLG	AOPS	ABR	SB-CS	FA	FR	RNG	THR	GAMES AT POSITION	DL	BFW
1977	SD N	107	126	23	36	6	1	4	17	33-2	1	28	.286	.432	.444	152	12	1-2	1.000	-2	81	0	O27(23/1/3)/3		0.8
1978	Cal A	50	108	16	29	5	1	1	14	30-0	2	13	.269	.433	.361	130	7	0-3	.968	-2	89	0	O22(5/0/17),D18		0.3
1979	†Cal A	35	76	7	20	2	0	1	10	11-1	1	14	.263	.360	.329	91	0	1-0	1.000	-2	46	0	D17,O9(4/0/5)		-0.3
1980	Cal A	2	4	0	1	0	0	0	0	1-0	0	1	.250	.400	.250	84	0	0-0	—	0			/D		0.0
Total	13	1023	2555	393	693	114	16	66	329	445-15	18	382	.271	.381	.406	123	98	68-28	.985	6	104	84	O747(228/155/436),D36,3b2	15	8.0

RETZER, KEN Kenneth Leo B4.30.1934 Wood River IL BL/TR/6-0/185* d9.9 Col Jefferson City (MO) JC

YEAR	TM LG	G	AB	R	H	2B	3B	HR	RBI	BB-IB	HP	SO	AVG	OBP	SLG	AOPS	ABR	SB-CS	FA	FR	RNG	THR	GAMES AT POSITION	DL	BFW
1961	Was A	16	53	7	18	4	0	1	3	33-2	0	5	.340	.386	.472	130	2	1-0	.988	0	73	211	C16		0.3
1962	Was A	109	340	36	97	11	2	8	37	26-4	0	21	.285	.334	.400	98	-2	2-0	.985	5	97	117	C99		0.9
1963	Was A	95	265	21	64	10	0	5	31	17-2	2	20	.242	.290	.336	76	-9	2-0	.981	-15	61	131	C81		-2.1
1964	Was A	17	32	1	3	0	0	0	1	5-1	1	4	.094	.237	.094	-4	-4	0-0	.971	2	84	407	C13		-0.2
Total	4	237	690	65	182	25	2	14	72	52-7	3	50	.264	.316	.367	87	-13	5-0	.983	-7	81	146	C209		-1.1

REVERING, DAVE David Alvin B2.12.1953 Roseville CA BL/TR/6-4/205* [CinN71 7/170] d4.8

YEAR	TM LG	G	AB	R	H	2B	3B	HR	RBI	BB-IB	HP	SO	AVG	OBP	SLG	AOPS	ABR	SB-CS	FA	FR	RNG	THR	GAMES AT POSITION	DL	BFW
1978	Oak A	152	521	49	141	21	3	16	46	26-5	0	55	.271	.303	.415	106	1	0-1	.989	7	120	88	1b138,D3		0.0
1979	Oak A	125	472	63	136	25	5	19	77	34-5	1	65	.288	.334	.483	124	14	1-4	.986	1	106	72	1b104,D18	15	0.7
1980	Oak A	106	376	48	109	21	5	15	62	32-6	0	37	.290	.344	.492	135	17	1-0	.989	0	102	74	1b95,D5		1.1
1981	Oak A	31	87	12	20	1	1	2	10	11-2	1	12	.230	.320	.333	93	-1	0-1	.995	-2	74	60	1b29,D2		-0.5
	†NY A	45	119	8	28	4	1	2	7	11-5	0	20	.235	.300	.336	84	-3	0-1	.994	-3	120	80	1b73,D2		-0.5
	Year	76	206	20	48	5	2	4	17	22-7	1	32	.233	.309	.335	88	-3	0-2	.994	-3	120	72	1b13/D		-0.7
1982	NY A	14	40	2	6	2	0	0	3	3-2	0	4	.150	.205	.200	13	-5	0-0	1.000	-2	30	72	1b1/3		-0.6
	Tor A	55	135	15	29	6	0	5	18	22-1	0	30	.215	.321	.370	83	-3	0-3	1.000	-0	67	118	D49,1b4		-0.6
	Sea A	29	82	8	17	3	1	3	12	9-0	0	17	.207	.283	.378	78	-3	0-0	.986	-2	71	114	1b27		-1.9
	Year	98	257	25	52	11	1	8	32	34-3	0	51	.202	.292	.346	71	-10	0-3	.992	-5	59	102	D50,1b44		-0.6
Total	5	557	1832	205	486	83	16	62	234	148-26	2	240	.265	.318	.430	109	17	2-10	.989	8	107	81	1b454,D78	15	-0.6

REVILLE, HENRY Henry B Baltimore MD d10.14

YEAR	TM LG	G	AB	R	H	2B	3B	HR	RBI	BB-IB	HP	SO	AVG	OBP	SLG	AOPS	ABR	SB-CS	FA	FR	RNG	THR	GAMES AT POSITION	DL	BFW
1874	Bal NA	1	4	0	0	0	0	0	0	0-0		0	.000	.000	.000	-99	-1	0-0	1.000	1	627	0	/OR		0.0

REXTER, WILLIAM William H. B1850 Brooklyn NY D6.23.1898 Staten Island NY d9.25

YEAR	TM LG	G	AB	R	H	2B	3B	HR	RBI	BB-IB	HP	SO	AVG	OBP	SLG	AOPS	ABR	SB-CS	FA	FR	RNG	THR	GAMES AT POSITION	DL	BFW
1875	Atl NA	1	4	0	0	0	0	0	0	0-0		0	.000	.000	.000	-99	-1	0-0	1.000	0	0	0	/OR		-0.1

REYES, GIL Gilberto Rolando (Polanco) B12.10.1963 Santo Domingo, D.R. BR/TR/6-2/203(175-205) d6.11 [DL 1992 Mon N 28]

YEAR	TM LG	G	AB	R	H	2B	3B	HR	RBI	BB-IB	HP	SO	AVG	OBP	SLG	AOPS	ABR	SB-CS	FA	FR	RNG	THR	GAMES AT POSITION	DL	BFW
1983	LA N	19	31	1	5	2	0	0	0	1	5	.161	.188	.226	14	-4	0-0	.944	0	111	137	C19		-0.3
1984	LA N	4	5	0	0	0	0	0	0	3	.000	.000	.000	-99	-1	0-0	1.000	-0	0	0	C2		-0.2
1985	LA N	6	1	0	0	0	0	0	1-0	1	.000	.667	.000	104	0	0-0	1.000	1	0	203	C6		0.2
1987	LA N	1	0	0	0	0	0	0	0	0-0	0					0	0-0		0	0	/C		0.0
1988	LA N	5	9	1	1	0	0	0	1	0-0	3	.111	.111	.111	-37	-2	0-0	1.000	0	207	0	C5		-0.1
1989	Mon N	4	5	0	1	0	0	0	1	0-0	1	.200	.200	.200	14	-1	0-0	1.000	0	102	0	C4		0.4
1991	Mon N	83	207	11	45	9	0	0	13	19-2	1	51	.217	.285	.261	56	-12	2-4	.975	13	134	171	C80	28	0.0
Total	7	122	258	13	52	11	0	0	14	20-2	1	64	.202	.266	.244	45	-20	2-4	.973	15	129	157	C117	28	0.0

REYES, JOSE Jose Bernabe B6.11.1983 Villa Gonzalez, D.R. BB/TR/6-0/160(160-175) d6.10

YEAR	TM LG	G	AB	R	H	2B	3B	HR	RBI	BB-IB	HP	SO	AVG	OBP	SLG	AOPS	ABR	SB-CS	FA	FR	RNG	THR	GAMES AT POSITION	DL	BFW
2003	NY N	69	274	47	84	12	4	5	32	13-0	0	36	.307	.334	.434	104	0	13-3	.973	3	106	92	S69		1.0
2004	NY N	53	220	33	56	16	2	2	14	5-0	0	31	.255	.271	.373	66	-12	19-2	.980	-0	107	99	2b43,S10	119	-0.6
2005	NY N	161	696	99	190	24	17	7	58	27-0	2	78	.273	.300	.386	81	-24	60-15	.974	-15	93	106	S161	147	-1.9
Total	3	283	1190	179	330	52	23	14	104	45-0	2	145	.277	.303	.395	83	-36	92-20	.973	-12	97	102	S240,2b43	147	-1.5

REYES, NAP Napoleon Aguilera B11.24.1919 Santiago de Cuba, Cuba D9.15.1995 Miami FL BR/TR/6-1/205* d5.19

YEAR	TM LG	G	AB	R	H	2B	3B	HR	RBI	BB-IB	HP	SO	AVG	OBP	SLG	AOPS	ABR	SB-CS	FA	FR	RNG	THR	GAMES AT POSITION	DL	BFW
1943	NY N	40	125	13	32	4	0	0	13	4	2	12	.256	.290	.320	76	-4	2	.994	-5	41	78	1b38/3		-1.2
1944	NY N	116	374	38	108	16	5	8	53	15	5	24	.289	.325	.422	109	3	2	.990	-2	67	93	1b63,3b37,O3L		0.3
1945	NY N	122	431	39	124	15	4	5	44	25	8	26	.288	.338	.376	97	-3	1	.961	1	105	59	3b115,1b5		-0.1
1950	NY N	1	1	0	0	0	0	0	0	0-0	0	0	.000	.000	.000	-99	0	0	.667	-0	0	0	/1		-0.1
Total	4	279	931	90	264	35	11	13	110	44	15	62	.284	.326	.387	99	-4	5	.960	-2	110	67	3b153,1b107,O3L		-1.1

REYES, RENE Rene B2.21.1978 Margarita, Venez BB/TR/5-11/210* d7.22

YEAR	TM LG	G	AB	R	H	2B	3B	HR	RBI	BB-IB	HP	SO	AVG	OBP	SLG	AOPS	ABR	SB-CS	FA	FR	RNG	THR	GAMES AT POSITION	DL	BFW
2003	Col N	53	116	13	30	7	1	2	7	5-0	0	19	.259	.287	.388	65	-6	2-1	.964	0	95	176	O36(11/5/24)		-0.7
2004	Col N	28	61	5	9	2	0	0	1	5-2	0	17	.148	.212	.180	3	-9	0-0	1.000	-1	88	120	O21(1/16/4)		-0.9
Total	2	81	177	18	39	9	1	2	8	10-2	0	36	.220	.261	.316	44	-15	2-1	.977	-0	92	155	O57(12/21/28)		-1.6

REYNOLDS, CARL Carl Nettles B2.1.1903 Larue TX D5.29.1978 Houston TX BR/TR/6-0/194 d9.1 Col Southwestern (TX)

YEAR	TM LG	G	AB	R	H	2B	3B	HR	RBI	BB-IB	HP	SO	AVG	OBP	SLG	AOPS	ABR	SB-CS	FA	FR	RNG	THR	GAMES AT POSITION	DL	BFW
1927	Chi A	14	42	5	9	3	0	1	7	1	7	.214	.313	.357	75	-2	1-2	1.000	2	134	75	O13(11/0/2)		-0.1
1928	Chi A	84	291	51	94	21	11	2	36	17	5	13	.323	.371	.491	126	10	15-3	.979	-0	102	85	O74(15/1/58)		0.6
1929	Chi A	131	517	81	164	24	12	11	67	20	4	37	.317	.348	.474	111	5	19-9	.949	-2	100	96	O130(13/21/98)		-0.5
1930	Chi A	138	563	103	202	25	18	22	104	20	7	39	.359	.388	.584	148	36	16-4	.975	-4	105	97	O109(11/18/90)		2.9
1931	Chi A	118	462	71	134	24	14	6	77	24	6	26	.290	.333	.442	108	3	17-6	.949	-4	95	93	O132(35/54/47)		-0.1
1932	Was A	102	406	53	124	28	7	9	63	13	3	19	.305	.332	.475	108	3	8-4	.983	-2	101	38	O95R		-0.6
1933	StL A	135	475	81	136	26	14	8	71	49	3	25	.286	.357	.451	106	3	5-0	.965	-2	101	74	O100(2/66/33)		-0.8
1934	Bos A	113	413	61	125	26	9	4	86	27	3	28	.303	.350	.438	95	-4	5-3	.977	-4	113	127	O64(3/1/60)		-0.3
1935	Bos A	78	244	33	66	13	4	6	35	24	1	20	.270	.336	.430	91	-4	4-1	.975	-4	100	124	O72(0/4/69)		-1.1
1936	Was A	89	293	41	81	18	2	4	41	21	2	22	.276	.329	.392	82	-9	8-4	.968	-1	99	0	O2L		0.0
1937	Chi N	7	11	0	3	1	0	0	1	2	0	2	.273	.385	.364	100	0	0	.800	-0	99	0	O2L		-0.3
1938	†Chi N	125	497	59	150	28	10	3	67	22	3	32	.302	.335	.416	103	1	9	.983	2	104	90	O125(63/83/4)		-1.4
1939	Chi N	88	281	33	69	10	6	4	44	16	5	38	.246	.298	.367	76	-11	5	.972	-1	100	85	O72(3/51/18)		-2.2
Total	13	1222	4495	672	1357	247	107	80	699	260	42	308	.302	.346	.458	107	30	112-40	.970	-5	103	86	O1112(281/301/574)		

REYNOLDS, CHARLIE Charles Lawrence B5.1.1865 Williamsburg IN D7.3.1944 Denver CO BR/5-9/175 d5.8

YEAR	TM LG	G	AB	R	H	2B	3B	HR	RBI	BB-IB	HP	SO	AVG	OBP	SLG	AOPS	ABR	SB-CS	FA	FR	RNG	THR	GAMES AT POSITION	DL	BFW
1889	KC AA	1	4	1	1	0	0	0	0	1	.250	.250	.250	40	0	0	1.000	-1			/C		-0.1
	Bro AA	12	42	5	9	1	1	0	3	1	0	6	.214	.233	.286	47	-3	2	.892	0			C12		-0.2
	Year	13	46	6	10	1	1	0	4	1	0	7	.217	.234	.283	46	-4	2	.893	-1			C13		-0.3

REYNOLDS, DANNY Daniel Vance "Squirrel" B11.27.1919 Stony Point NC BR/TR/5-11/158 d5.26

YEAR	TM LG	G	AB	R	H	2B	3B	HR	RBI	BB-IB	HP	SO	AVG	OBP	SLG	AOPS	ABR	SB-CS	FA	FR	RNG	THR	GAMES AT POSITION	DL	BFW
1945	Chi A	29	72	6	12	1	0	4	3	0	8	.167	.200	.222	23	-7	1-2	.947	2	109	94	S14,2b11		-0.5

REYNOLDS, DON Donald Edward B4.16.1953 Arkadelphia AR BR/TR/5-8/180* [SDN75 18/410] d4.7 b-Harold Col Oregon

YEAR	TM LG	G	AB	R	H	2B	3B	HR	RBI	BB-IB	HP	SO	AVG	OBP	SLG	AOPS	ABR	SB-CS	FA	FR	RNG	THR	GAMES AT POSITION	DL	BFW
1978	SD N	57	87	8	22	2	0	0	10	15-2	0	14	.253	.363	.276	87	-1	1-0	.923	-1	77	159	O25(22/0/3)	16	-0.2
1979	SD N	30	45	6	10	1	2	0	6	7-1	0	6	.222	.321	.333	86	-1	0-1	.950	1	86	283	O14(7/5/2)		-0.1
Total	2	87	132	14	32	3	2	0	16	22-3	0	20	.242	.348	.295	87	-2	1-1	.935	-0	80	206	O39(29/5/5)	16	-0.3

REYNOLDS, CRAIG Gordon Craig B12.27.1952 Houston TX BL/TR/6-1/175* [PitN71 1/22] d8.1 OF(3/0/1)

YEAR	TM LG	G	AB	R	H	2B	3B	HR	RBI	BB-IB	HP	SO	AVG	OBP	SLG	AOPS	ABR	SB-CS	FA	FR	RNG	THR	GAMES AT POSITION	DL	BFW
1975	†Pit N	31	76	8	17	3	0	0	4	3-1	0	5	.224	.253	.263	43	-6	0-1	.969	3	107	90	S30		-0.1
1976	Pit N	7	4	1	1	0	0	1	0-0	0	0	.250	.250	1.000	238	1	0-0	.889	-0	106	100	S4/2		0.0
1977	Sea A	135	420	41	104	12	3	4	28	15-1	3	23	.248	.277	.319	63	-23	6-6	.955	8	107	110	S134		-0.2
1978	Sea A☆	148	548	57	160	16	7	5	44	36-1	4	41	.292	.334	.374	100	-1	9-6	.960	8	108	110	S146		2.3
1979	Hou N★	146	555	63	147	20	9	0	39	21-0	2	49	.265	.292	.333	75	-21	12-6	.965	-5	98	115	S143		-1.1
1980	†Hou N	137	381	34	86	9	3	3	28	20-1	0	39	.226	.262	.304	64	-21	2-1	.969	5	104	96	S135		-0.5
1981	†Hou N	87	323	43	84	10	12	1	31	12-2	0	31	.260	.286	.402	99	-4	3-3	.973	1	98	80	S85		0.6
1982	Hou N	54	118	16	30	2	1	1	7	11-3	1	9	.254	.321	.347	95	-1	3-1	.958	-4	95	86	S35,3b7	24	-0.2
1983	Hou N	65	98	10	21	3	1	0	6	6-1	0	10	.214	.260	.276	51	-7	0-1	.956	-9	91	79	2b26,3b15,S8/OL		-1.4
1984	Hou N	146	527	61	137	15	11	6	60	22-2	0	53	.260	.286	.364	88	-12	7-1	.965	24	112	118	S143/3		2.9
1985	Hou N	107	379	43	103	18	4	3	32	12-2	0	30	.272	.293	.393	93	-6	4-4	.978	-8	88	87	S98,1b5,3b4,O2(1/0/1)/P		-1.3
1986	†Hou N	114	313	32	78	7	3	6	41	16-3	1	31	.249	.274	.364	77	-13	5-1	.970	-9	90	71	S129,3b2		-1.0
1987	Hou N	135	374	35	95	17	3	4	28	30-8	1	44	.254	.303	.348	77	-13	5-1	.970	-3	100	122	S22,3b19,2b11,1b10		-0.2
1988	Hou N	78	161	16	40	7	0	1	14	8-2	2	21	.255	.290	.317	79	-3	1-0	.970	-3	98	122	2b29,S26,3b10,1b5/POL		-0.2
1989	Hou N	101	189	10	38	7	1	0	12	19-5	0	18	.201	.274	.254	54	-12	1-0	.979	7	119	110	2b29,S26,3b10,1b5/POL		-0.2
Total	15	1491	4466	480	1142	143	65	42	377	227-34	9	406	.256	.291	.345	80	-144	58-32	.966	36	102	102	S1240,2b68,3b58,1b20,O4L,P2	24	1.1

YEAR	TM LG	G	AB	R	H	2B	3B	HR	RBI	BB-IB	HP	SO	AVG	OBP	SLG	AOPS	ABR	SB-CS	FA	FR	RNG	THR	GAMES AT POSITION	DL	BFW

REYNOLDS, HAROLD Harold Craig B11.26.1960 Eugene OR BB/TR/5-11/165* [SeaA80 S1/2] d9.2 b-Don Col Canada (CA) JC

1983	Sea A	20	59	8	12	4	1	0	1	2-0		9	.203	.226	.305	44	-5	0-2	.975	-1	94	112	2b18		-0.5
1984	Sea A	10	10	3	3	0	0	0	0	1-0	1	1	.300	.364	.300	86	0	1-1	1.000	2	127	132	2b6		0.2
1985	Sea A	67	104	15	15	3	1	0	6	17-0		14	.144	.264	.192	27	-10	3-2	.960	5	116	84	2b61		-0.3
1986	Sea A	126	445	46	99	19	4	1	24	29-0	3	42	.222	.275	.290	53	-29	30-12	.977	30	115	122	2b126		1.0
1987	Sea A★	160	530	73	146	31	8	1	35	39-0	2	34	.275	.325	.370	80	-15	60-20	.977	24	111	108	2b160		2.3
1988	Sea A★	158	598	61	169	26	11	4	41	51-1	2	51	.283	.340	.383	98	-2	35-29	.977	8	102	104	2b158		0.8
1989	Sea A	153	613	87	184	24	9	0	43	55-1	3	45	.300	.359	.369	103	3	25-18	.980	25	111	107	2b151/D		3.1
1990	Sea A	160	642	100	162	36	5	5	52	81-3	3	52	.252	.336	.347	91	-5	31-16	.978	20	106	100	2b160		2.1
1991	Sea A	161	631	95	160	34	6	3	57	72-2	5	63	.254	.332	.341	87	-9	28-8	.978	8	98	121	2b159/D		0.7
1992	Sea A	140	458	55	113	23	3	3	33	45-1	4	41	.247	.316	.330	81	-11	15-12	.982	8	102	94	2b134/OLD		-0.1
1993	Bal A	145	485	64	122	20	4	4	47	66-3	1	47	.252	.343	.334	80	-12	12-11	.986	3	99	121	2b141/D		-0.4
1994	Cal A	74	207	33	48	10	1	0	11	23-0		18	.232	.310	.290	55	-13	10-7	.996	-11	85	69	2b65,D3		-2.1
Total	12	1374	4782	640	1233	230	53	21	353	480-11	27	417	.258	.327	.341	82	-108	250-138	.979	122	105	107	2b1339,D7/OL		6.8

REYNOLDS, R. J. Robert James B4.19.1959 Sacramento CA BB/TR/6-0/190(175-190) [LAN80*2/36] d9.1 Col Sacramento (CA) City

1983	LA N	24	55	5	13	0	0	2	11	3-1		11	.236	.267	.345	71	-2	5-0	.931	0	87	222	O18(9/5/7)		-0.2
1984	LA N	73	240	24	62	12	2	2	24	14-0	1	38	.258	.300	.350	83	-6	7-5	.973	-2	90	104	O63(25/19/34)	15	-1.1
1985	LA N	73	207	22	55	10	4	0	25	13-0	1	31	.266	.308	.353	87	-4	6-3	.970	-1	99	87	O54(31/5/24)	30	-0.7
	Pit N	31	130	22	40	5	3	3	17	9-1	1	18	.308	.357	.462	128	4	12-2	.958	1	105	137	O31(29/8/0)		0.6
	Year	104	337	44	95	15	7	3	42	22-1	2	49	.282	.327	.395	104	1	18-5	.965	0	101	106	O85(60/13/24)		-0.1
1986	Pit N	118	402	63	108	30	2	9	48	40-4	1	78	.269	.335	.420	105	3	16-9	.955	-7	94	27	O112(84/12/44)		-0.8
1987	Pit N	117	335	47	87	24	1	7	51	34-8	0	80	.260	.323	.400	91	-4	14-1	.993	-4	83	118	O99(29/0/72)		-0.9
1988	Pit N	130	323	35	80	14	2	6	51	20-3	0	62	.248	.286	.359	87	-6	15-2	.974	1	94	177	O95(19/1/79)		-0.6
1989	Pit N	125	363	45	98	16	2	6	48	34-8	1	66	.270	.331	.375	106	3	22-5	.990	2	100	119	O98(5/30/72)		0.6
1990	†Pit N	95	215	25	62	10	1	0	19	23-1	0	35	.288	.354	.344	97	0	12-2	.972	-3	88	93	O59(13/24/26)		-0.2
Total	8	786	2270	288	605	121	17	35	294	190-26	5	419	.267	.321	.381	96	-12	109-24	.973	-13	93	106	O629(244/104/358)	60	-3.3

REYNOLDS, RONN Ronn Dwayne B9.28.1958 Wichita KS BR/TR/6-0/200* [NYN80 5/105] d9.29 Col Arkansas-Monticello

1982	NY N	2	4	0	0	0	0	0	0	1-0		1	.000	.200	.000	-39	-1	0-0	1.000	-2	153	0	C2		-0.2
1983	NY N	24	66	4	13	1	0	2	8	8-1	0	12	.197	.280	.212	40	-5	0-0	.942	-5	76	109	C24		-0.9
1985	NY N	28	43	4	9	2	0	0	1	0-0	1	18	.209	.227	.256	36	-4	0-0	.990	1	116	178	C25		-0.3
1986	Phi N	43	126	8	27	4	0	3	10	5-0	0	30	.214	.242	.317	52	-9	0-0	.991	-5	71	84	C42		-1.3
1987	Hou N	38	102	5	17	4	0	1	7	3-0	0	29	.167	.189	.235	12	-13	0-1	.975	-2	77	103	C38		-1.4
1990	SD N	8	15	1	1	1	0	0	1	1-0	0	6	.067	.125	.133	-29	-3	0-0	1.000	1	73	113	C8		-0.4
Total	6	143	356	22	67	12	0	4	21	18-1	1	96	.188	.228	.256	32	-35	0-1	.977	-13	81	106	C139		-4.5

REYNOLDS, TOMMIE Tommie D B8.15.1941 Arizona LA BR/TR (BB 1967p)/6-2/190* d9.5 C8 Col San Diego (CA) City

1963	KC A	8	19	1	1	0	0	0	1	1-0	1	7	.053	.143	.105	-28	-3	0-0	.800	-1	83	0	O5L		-0.5
1964	KC A	31	94	11	19	1	0	2	9	10-0	2	22	.202	.292	.277	58	-5	0-0	.976	-0	95	171	O25L,3b3		-0.7
1965	KC A	90	270	34	64	11	3	1	22	36-1	0	41	.237	.327	.311	83	-5	9-2	.982	6	108	168	O83(77/0/6)/3		-0.3
1967	NY N	101	136	16	28	1	0	2	9	11-3	3	26	.206	.278	.257	56	-8	1-1	.971	1	108	142	O72(42/13/21),3b5/C		-1.0
1969	Oak A	107	315	51	81	10	4	0	20	34-1	8	29	.257	.343	.308	87	-4	1-3	.979	5	112	75	O89(81/0/8)	26	-0.5
1970	Cal A	59	120	11	30	3	1	1	6	6-0	1	10	.250	.291	.317	70	-5	1-0	.969	-1	123	56	O32(4/1/28)/3		-0.6
1971	Cal A	45	86	4	16	3	0	2	8	9-1	3	6	.186	.286	.291	68	-4	0-1	.978	2	106	143	O26(6/0/23)/3		-0.4
1972	Mil A	72	130	13	26	5	1	2	13	10-0	1	25	.200	.262	.300	68	-5	0-0	.961	3	134	91	O41(36/0/6)/13		-0.4
Total	8	513	1170	141	265	35	5	12	87	117-6	19	166	.226	.306	.296	73	-39	12-8	.973	16	111	118	O373(276/14/92),3b12/1C	26	-4.4

REYNOLDS, BILL William Dee B8.14.1884 Eastland TX D6.5.1924 Carnegie OK BR/TR/6-0/185 d9.15

1913	NY A	5	5	0	0	0	0	0	0	0-0	0	1	.000	.000	.000	-99	-1	0	.917	-0	72	57	C5		-0.1
1914	NY A	4	5	0	2	0	0	0	0	0-0	0	3	.400	.400	.400	141	0	0	1.000	0	85	138	/C		0.1
Total	2	9	10	0	2	0	0	0	0	0-0	0	4	.200	.200	.200	19	-1	0	.941	0	76	81	C6		0.0

RHAWN, BOBBY Robert John "Rocky" B2.13.1919 Catawissa PA D6.9.1984 Danville PA BR/TR/5-8/180 d9.17

1947	NY N	13	45	7	14	3	1	3	8	1-0	0	3	.311	.415	.444	128	2	0	.913	1	119	76	2b8,3b5		0.3
1948	NY N	36	44	11	12	2	1	1	8	8-0	0	6	.273	.385	.432	120	1	3	.872	-1	104	75	S14,3b7		0.1
1949	NY N	14	29	8	5	0	0	0	2	7-0	0	2	.172	.333	.172	40	-2	1	.959	2	127	134	2b8		0.0
	Pit N	3	7	0	1	0	0	0	0	0-0	0	0	.143	.143	.143	-23	-1	0	.889	0	108	0	3b2		-0.1
	Year	17	36	8	6	0	0	0	2	7-0	0	2	.167	.302	.167	29	-3	1	.959	2	127	134	2b8,3b2		-0.1
	Chi A	24	73	12	15	4	1	0	5	12	0	8	.205	.318	.288	63	-4	0-1	.959	1	101	84	3b19,S3		-0.3
Total	3	90	198	38	47	9	2	4	18	35	0	17	.237	.352	.333	84	-4	4-1	.963	3	103	111	3b33,S17,2b16		0.0

RHEAM, CY Kenneth Johnston B9.28.1893 Pittsburgh PA D10.23.1947 Pittsburgh PA BR/TR/6-0/175 d5.20 Col Indiana (PA)

1914	Pit F	73	214	15	45	5	3	0	20	9	0	33	.210	.242	.262	38	-23	6	.976	-6	59	53	1b43,3b13,2b11/OL		-3.1
1915	Pit F	34	69	10	12	0	0	1	5	1	0	7	.174	.186	.217	13	-9	4	.959	1	129	81	O22(12/4/6)/1		-1.0
Total	2	107	283	25	57	5	3	1	25	10	0	40	.201	.229	.251	32	-32	10	.976	-4	58	52	1b44,O23(13/4/6),3b13,2b11		-4.1

RHIEL, BILLY William Joseph B8.16.1900 Youngstown OH D8.16.1946 Youngstown OH BR/TR/5-11/175 d4.20 Col Newberry

1929	Bro N	76	205	27	57	9	4	4	25	19	0	25	.278	.339	.420	89	-4	0	.979	-2	95	59	2b47,3b7,S2		-0.4
1930	Bos N	20	47	3	8	4	0	0	4	2	0	5	.170	.204	.255	11	-7	0	.947	-2	70	67	3b13,2b2		-0.8
1932	Det A	85	250	30	70	13	3	3	38	17	1	23	.280	.328	.392	82	-7	2-0	.956	-2	85	147	3b37,1b12,O8L/2		-0.8
1933	Det A	19	17	1	3	0	1	0	1	5	0	4	.176	.364	.294	75	-1	0-0	1.000	0	137	0	/OL		0.0
Total	4	200	519	61	138	26	8	7	68	43	1	57	.266	.323	.387	78	-19	2-0	.949	-6	88	136	3b57,2b50,1b12,O9L,S2		-2.0

RHODES, DUSTY James Lamar B5.13.1927 Mathews AL BL/TR/6-0/180* d7.15

1952	NY N	67	176	34	44	8	1	10	36	23	3	33	.250	.340	.477	123	5	1-0	.917	-2	98	79	O56(55/2/0)		0.0
1953	NY N	76	163	18	38	7	0	11	30	10	0	28	.233	.277	.479	91	-3	0-1	.965	2	95	182	O47(25/0/22)		-0.4
1954	†NY N	82	164	31	56	7	3	15	50	18	1	25	.341	.416	.695	181	19	1-0	.984	-1	96	49	O37(33/2/1)		1.5
1955	NY N	94	187	22	57	5	2	6	32	27-2	0	26	.305	.389	.449	122	7	1-1	.986	-1	94	74	O45L		0.3
1956	NY N	111	244	20	53	10	3	8	33	30-2	0	41	.217	.301	.381	83	-6	0-0	.958	-0	87	178	O68(64/0/5)		-1.0
1957	NY N	92	190	20	39	5	1	4	19	18-3	1	34	.205	.276	.332	57	-12	0-0	1.000	-3	90	0	O44(22/0/23)		-1.7
1959	SF N	54	48	1	9	2	0	0	7	5-3	0	9	.188	.259	.229	34	-5	0-0	—	0			/H		-1.7
Total	7	576	1172	146	296	44	10	54	207	131-10	3	196	.253	.328	.445	104	5	3-2	.963	-6	93	101	O297(244/4/51)		-1.8

RHODES, KARL Karl Derrick "Tuffy" B8.21.1968 Cincinnati OH BL/TL/5-11/170(170-195) [HouN86 3/68] d8.7

1990	Hou N	38	86	12	21	6	1	1	3	13-3	0	12	.244	.340	.372	99	0	4-1	.955	1	107	119	O30(19/9/5)		0.1
1991	Hou N	44	136	7	29	1	1	1	12	14-3	1	26	.213	.289	.272	63	-7	2-2	.958	3	115	135	O44R		-0.6
1992	Hou N	5	4	0	0	0	0	0	0	0-0	0	2	.000	.000	.000	-99	-1	0-0	—	-0	0	0	/O(1/0/1)		-0.1
1993	Hou N	5	2	0	0	0	0	0	0	0-0	0	1	.000	.000	.000	-99	-1	0-0	1.000	0	110	0	O4(1/2/1)		-0.1
	Chi N	15	52	12	15	2	1	8	19	11-0	0	9	.288	.413	.538	153	4	2-0	.970	-0	93	140	O14(6/14/1)		0.4
	Year	20	54	12	15	2	1	8	19	11-0	0	9	.278	.400	.519	146	4	2-0	.971	-0	94	132	O18(7/16/2)		0.3
1994	Chi N	95	269	39	63	17	0	8	19	33-1	1	64	.234	.318	.387	83	-6	6-4	.967	-3	90	113	O76(15/67/1)		-0.9
1995	Chi N	13	16	2	2	0	0	0	2	0-0	0	4	.125	.118	.125	-34	-3	0-0	.889	-0	118	0	O11L		-0.3
	Bos A	10	25	2	2	1	0	0	1	3-0	0	4	.080	.179	.120	-20	-5	0-0	.947	-1	101	0	O9C		-0.5
Total	6	225	590	74	132	29	3	13	44	74-7	2	121	.224	.310	.349	78	-19	14-7	.960	-0	101	114	O189(53/101/53)		-2.0

RHOMBERG, KEVIN Kevin Jay B11.22.1955 Dubuque IA BR/TR/6-0/175* [CleA77 14/349] d9.1 Col St. Francis (IL)

1982	Cle A	16	18	3	6	0	0	1	1	2-0	0	4	.333	.400	.500	145	1	0-2	.900	1	113	508	O7L/3D		0.1
1983	Cle A	12	21	2	10	0	0	0	2	2-0	1	5	.476	.500	.476	170	2	1-1	1.000	-1	82	0	O9(8/1/0)/D		0.1
1984	Cle A	13	8	0	2	0	0	0	0	0-0	0	3	.250	.250	.250	38	-1	0-0	1.000	1	129	0	O7L/12D		0.0
Total	3	41	47	5	18	0	0	1	3	4-0	1	18	.383	.442	.447	139	2	1-3	.963	1	101	148	O23(22/1/0),D6/213		0.2

RHYNE, HAL Harold J. B3.30.1899 Paso Robles CA D1.7.1971 Orangevale CA BR/TR/5-8.5/163 d4.18

1926	Pit N	109	366	46	92	14	3	2	39	35	6	21	.251	.327	.322	71	-14	1	.967	5	99	123	2b66,S44/3		-0.3
1927	†Pit N	62	168	21	46	5	0	0	17	14		9	.274	.330	.304	66	-8	0	.963	-8	79	95	2b45,3b10,S7		-1.3
1929	Bos A	120	346	41	87	24	5	0	28	25	4	16	.251	.309	.350	71	-15	4-1	.935	-2	97	112	S113/3OR		-0.5
1930	Bos A	107	296	34	60	8	5	0	23	25	2	19	.203	.269	.264	37	-29	1-4	.944	3	107	117	S107		-1.6

YEAR	TM LG	G	AB	R	H	2B	3B	HR	RBI	BB-IB	HP	SO	AVG	OBP	SLG	AOPS	ABR	SB-CS	FA	FR	RNG	THR	GAMES AT POSITION	DL	BFW
1931	Bos A	147	565	75	154	34	3	0	51	57	2	41	.273	.341	.343	85	-11	3-3	.963	18	115	88	S147		1.6
1932	Bos A	71	207	26	47	12	5	0	14	23	2	14	.227	.310	.333	69	-10	3-2	.966	5	113	96	S55,3b4/2		-0.1
1933	Chi A	39	83	9	22	1	1	0	10	5	1	9	.265	.318	.301	67	-4	1-1	.955	2	108	125	2b19,3b13,S2		-0.2
Total	7	655	2031	252	508	98	22	2	192	184	17	127	.250	.318	.323		-91	13-11	.950	23	107	104	S475,2b131,3b29/OR		-2.4

RICE, DEL
Delbert B10.27.1922 Portsmouth OH D1.26.1983 Buena Park CA BR/TR/6-2/190* d5.2 M1/C7

YEAR	TM LG	G	AB	R	H	2B	3B	HR	RBI	BB-IB	HP	SO	AVG	OBP	SLG	AOPS	ABR	SB-CS	FA	FR	RNG	THR	GAMES AT POSITION	DL	BFW
1945	StL N	83	253	27	66	17	3	1	28	16	3	33	.261	.313	.364	86	-5	0	.994	5	97	120	C77		0.4
1946	†StL N	55	139	10	38	8	1	1	12	8	0	16	.273	.313	.367	89	-2	0	.977	1	152	51	C53		0.1
1947	StL N	97	261	28	57	7	3	12	44	36	1	40	.218	.315	.406	87	-6	1	.981	3	126	74	C94		0.1
1948	StL N	100	290	24	57	10	1	4	34	37	5	46	.197	.298	.279	54	-18	0	.996	11	292	73	C99		-0.2
1949	StL N	92	284	25	67	16	1	4	29	30	5	40	.236	.320	.342	74	-10	0	.992	1	127	66	C92		-0.5
1950	StL N	130	414	39	101	20	3	9	54	43	5	65	.244	.323	.372	78	-13	0	.984	7	134	91	C130		0.1
1951	StL N	122	374	34	94	13	1	9	47	34	3	26	.251	.319	.364	83	-9	0-0	.985	4	124	90	C120		0.1
1952	StL N	147	495	43	128	27	2	11	65	35	6	38	.259	.313	.388	93	-5	0-1	.992	2	139	95	C135		0.4
1953	StL N*	135	419	32	99	22	1	6	37	48	5	49	.236	.323	.337	72	-16	0-0	.988	-5	87	91	C135		-1.4
1954	StL N	56	147	13	37	10	1	2	16	16	0	21	.252	.321	.374	81	-4	0-1	.985	1	165	87	C52		-0.1
1955	StL N	20	59	6	12	3	0	1	7	7-0	0	6	.203	.284	.305	58	-4	0-0	.964	-4	89	92	C18		-0.4
	Mil N	27	71	5	14	0	1	2	7	6-2	0	12	.197	.260	.310	53	-5	0-0	.981	0	117	152	C40		-0.5
	Year	47	130	11	26	3	1	3	14	13-2	0	18	.200	.271	.308	55	-9	0-0	.973	-4	104	125	C65		
1956	Mil N	71	188	15	40	9	1	3	18	18-7	0	37	.213	.282	.319	65	-9	0-0	.992	3	101	65	C48		0.5
1957	†Mil N	54	144	15	33	1	1	9	20	17-7	0	37	.229	.309	.438	106	-8	0-0	.995	1	117	89	C38		-0.6
1958	Mil N	43	121	10	27	7	0	1	8	8-1	0	30	.223	.271	.306	57	-8	0-0	.956	-1	132	0	C9	57	-0.3
1959	Mil N	13	29	3	6	0	0	0	4	2-0	0	3	.207	.250	.207	28	-3	0-0	.968	-5	55	134	C18		-0.8
1960	Chi N	18	52	2	12	3	0	0	4	2-1	0	7	.231	.255	.288	50	-4	0-0	1.000	-0	0	0	/C		-0.1
	StL N	1	2	0	0	0	0	0	0	1-0	0	0	.000	.333	.000	1	0	0-0	.970	-5	0	0	C19		-0.9
	Year	19	54	2	12	3	0	0	4	3-1	0	7	.222	.259	.278	49	-4	0-0	1.000	-0	0	0	/C		
	Bal A	1	1	0	0	0	0	0	0	0-0	0	0	.000	.000	.000	-99	0	0-0	.994	-1	80	208	C30		0.2
1961	LA A	44	83	11	20	4	0	4	11	20-5	0	19	.241	.385	.434	107	2	0-1	.987	25	136	89	C1249		
Total	17	1309	3826	342	908	177	20	79	441	382-23	34	522	.237	.312	.356		-119	2-3	.987	25	136	89	C1249	57	-3.7

RICE, SAM
Edgar Charles B2.20.1890 Morocco IN D10.13.1974 Rossmoor MD BL/TR/5-9/150 d8.7 Mil 1918 HF1963 ▲

YEAR	TM LG	G	AB	R	H	2B	3B	HR	RBI	BB-IB	HP	SO	AVG	OBP	SLG	AOPS	ABR	SB-CS	FA	FR	RNG	THR	GAMES AT POSITION	DL	BFW
1915	Was A	4	8	0	3	0	0	0	0	0	0	1	.375	.375	.375	122	1	0	.889	0	131	592	P4		0.0
1916	Was A	58	197	26	59	8	3	1	17	15	1	13	.299	.352	.386	123	5	4	.957	2	117	94	O46(4/0/42),P5		0.4
1917	Was A	155	586	77	177	25	7	0	69	50	3	41	.302	.360	.369	124	17	35	.960	5	103	124	O155R		1.5
1918	Was A	7	23	3	8	1	0	0	3	2	0	0	.348	.400	.391	141	1	1	1.000	3	94	446	O6R		0.4
1919	Was A	141	557	80	179	23	9	3	71	42	7	26	.321	.376	.411	122	16	26	.962	4	113	92	O141R		1.4
1920	Was A	153	624	83	211	29	9	3	80	39	4	23	.338	.384	.417	117	15	63-30	.960	17	121	124	O153C		2.3
1921	Was A	143	561	83	185	39	13	4	79	38	9	13	.330	.382	.467	121	7	26-12	.964	6	109	101	O141(0/137/4)		1.7
1922	Was A	154	633	91	187	37	13	6	69	48	2	13	.295	.347	.423	105	3	20-9	.951	2	98	143	O154C		0.0
1923	Was A	148	595	117	188	35	18	3	75	57	6	24	.316	.381	.450	125	20	20-8	.967	7	107	108	O147R		0.4
1924	†Was A	154	646	106	216	39	14	1	76	46	4	10	.334	.382	.443	116	14	24-13	.967	7	106	122	O152(0/29/133)		1.0
1925	†Was A	152	649	111	227	31	13	1	87	37	3	10	.350	.388	.442	113	11	26-11	.961	9	106	148	O152(0/44/120)		1.0
1926	Was A	152	641	98	216	32	14	3	76	42	2	11	.337	.380	.445	117	14	24-23	.961	9	106	148	O139(1/0/138)		-1.8
1927	Was A	142	603	89	179	33	14	2	65	36	0	11	.328	.379	.438	115	13	19-6	.975	-2	100	81	O147(1/0/147)		-0.6
1928	Was A	148	616	95	202	32	15	2	55	49	2	15	.328	.382	.424	106	7	16-8	.970	3	99	132	O147R		-0.1
1929	Was A	150	616	119	199	39	10	1	62	55	4	9	.323	.382	.424	106	7	16-8	.963	3	106	101	O145(0/15/133)		0.9
1930	Was A	147	593	121	207	35	13	1	73	55	3	14	.349	.407	.457	108	18	13-8	.970	2	107	76	O105(10/11/85)		-0.4
1931	Was A	120	413	81	128	21	8	0	42	35	1	6	.310	.365	.400	100	0	6-5	.972	2	98	143	O69(10/14/48)		0.8
1932	Was A	106	288	58	93	16	7	1	34	32	2	7	.323	.391	.438	104	0	7-4	1.000	4	120	285	O39(8/10/23)		0.5
1933	†Was A	73	85	19	25	4	3	1	12	2	2	7	.294	.326	.447	104	-1	5-1	.963	-6	90	35	O78(13/0/65)		-1.7
1934	Cle A	97	335	48	98	19	1	1	33	38	2	9	.293	.351	.364	83	-8	5-1	.965						
Total	20	2404	9269	1514	2987	498	184	34	1078	708	56	275	.322	.374	.427	113	163	351-143	.965	58	105	110	O2270(47/601/1657),P9		8.4

RICE, HAL
Harold Housten "Hoot" B2.11.1924 Morganette WV D12.22.1997 Bloomington IN BL/TR/6-1/195* d9.25

YEAR	TM LG	G	AB	R	H	2B	3B	HR	RBI	BB-IB	HP	SO	AVG	OBP	SLG	AOPS	ABR	SB-CS	FA	FR	RNG	THR	GAMES AT POSITION	DL	BFW
1948	StL N	8	31	3	10	1	0	2	3	2	0	4	.323	.364	.484	121	1	0	1.000	-0	105	0	O8L		0.0
1949	StL N	40	46	3	9	2	1	1	9	3	0	7	.196	.245	.348	55	-3	0	1.000	0	89	286	O10L		-0.3
1950	StL N	44	128	12	27	3	1	2	11	10	0	10	.211	.268	.297	46	-10	0-1	.972	1	100	124	O37(33/0/4)		-1.2
1951	StL N	69	236	20	60	12	1	4	38	24	0	26	.254	.323	.364	84	-5	1-3	.953	-0	98	118	O63(48/0/16)		-0.5
1952	StL N	98	295	37	85	14	5	7	45	16	0	26	.288	.325	.441	110	3	1-3	.972	-2	96	92	O81(77/4/5)		-0.5
1953	StL N	8	8	0	0	0	0	0	0	0	0	3	.250	.250	.250	31	-1	0-0	—		0		/H		-0.3
	Pit N	78	286	39	89	16	1	4	42	17	0	22	.311	.350	.416	99	0	0-1	.973	8	109	213	O70(68/0/2)		-0.3
	Year	86	294	39	91	16	1	4	42	17	0	25	.310	.347	.412	97	-1	0-1	.973	8	109	213	O70(68/0/2)		
1954	Pit N	28	81	10	14	4	1	2	9	14	0	24	.173	.295	.284	52	-6	0-2	1.000	3	112	190	O24(24/0/2)		
	Chi N	51	72	5	11	0	0	0	5	8	0	9	.153	.235	.153	4	-10	0-2	.897	-0	94	176	O24(3/0/21)		
	Year	79	153	15	25	4	1	1	14	22	0	39	.163	.267	.222	29	-16	0-2	.966	3	106	185	O48(27/0/23)		
Total	7	424	1183	129	307	52	12	19	162	94	0	133	.260	.314	.372	82	-31	1-7	.969	10	102	145	O317(271/4/50)		

RICE, HARRY
Harry Francis B11.22.1901 Ware Station IL D1.1.1971 Portland OR BL/TR/5-9/185 d4.18 OF(28/465/421)

YEAR	TM LG	G	AB	R	H	2B	3B	HR	RBI	BB-IB	HP	SO	AVG	OBP	SLG	AOPS	ABR	SB-CS	FA	FR	RNG	THR	GAMES AT POSITION	DL	BFW
1923	StL A	4	3	0	0	0	0	0	0	0	0	0	.000	.000	.000	-95	-1	0	.917	-1	94	125	/H		
1924	StL A	54	93	19	26	7	0	0	15	7	3	3	.280	.350	.355	77	-3	1-3	.984	3	102	142	O85(3/6/76),1b3/C23		
1925	StL A	103	354	87	127	25	8	11	47	54	5	15	.359	.450	.568	144	28	8-7	.970	5	102	149	O133(0/47/87),3b8,2b4,S2		
1926	StL A	148	578	86	181	27	11	9	59	63	4	40	.313	.384	.441	110	9	10-11	.938	11	104	196	O130(0/44/87),3b7		
1927	StL A	137	520	90	149	26	9	7	68	50	2	21	.287	.351	.412	94	-5	5-4	.960	1	98	119	O129C,3b2		
1928	Det A	131	510	87	154	21	12	6	81	44	2	22	.302	.360	.425	104	7	6-11	.960	1	98	119	O127C,3b3		
1929	Det A	130	536	97	163	33	7	6	69	61	4	23	.304	.379	.425	106	7	6-11	.944	-1	101	72	O35(19/0/16)		
1930	Det A	37	128	16	39	6	0	2	24	19	2	8	.305	.403	.398	102	1	0-3	.944	-1	101	72	O35(19/0/16)		
	NY A	100	346	62	103	17	5	7	74	31	3	21	.298	.361	.436	106	3	3-3	.969	2	103	109	O87(4/83/0),1b6/3		
	Year	137	474	78	142	23	5	9	98	50	5	29	.300	.372	.426	105	4	3-6	.964	1	102	90	O42(1/19/23)		
1931	Was A	47	162	32	43	5	6	0	15	12	1	10	.265	.320	.370	81	-5	2-1	.968	4	104	106	O141(0/10/131)/3		
1933	Cin N	143	510	44	133	19	6	0	54	35	6	21	.261	.316	.322	84	-11	4	.991	4	104	106	O141(0/10/131)/3		
Total	10	1034	3740	620	1118	186	63	48	506	376	32	194	.299	.368	.421	104	25	59-55	.966	19	102	124	O911C,3b38,1b11,2b9,S4/C		

RICE, JIM
James Edward B3.8.1953 Anderson SC BR/TR/6-2/205(200-217) [BosA71 1/15] d8.19 C7

YEAR	TM LG	G	AB	R	H	2B	3B	HR	RBI	BB-IB	HP	SO	AVG	OBP	SLG	AOPS	ABR	SB-CS	FA	FR	RNG	THR	GAMES AT POSITION	DL	BFW
1974	Bos A	24	67	6	18	2	1	1	13	4-0	1	12	.269	.307	.373	92	-1	0-0	.800	-0	85	0	D16,O3L		
1975	Bos A	144	564	92	174	29	4	22	102	36-7	4	122	.309	.350	.491	126	18	10-5	1.000	-4	87	91	O90L,D54		
1976	Bos A	153	581	75	164	25	8	25	85	28-2	4	123	.282	.315	.482	119	11	8-5	.967	-2	93	109	O98L,D54		
1977	Bos A★	160	644	104	206	29	15	39	114	53-10	8	120	.320	.376	.593	144	37	5-4	.956	-1	94	124	D116,O44(19/0/27)		
1978	Bos A★	163	677	121	213	25	15	46	139	58-7	5	126	.315	.370	.600	153	45	7-5	.989	4	95	158	O114(101/1/15),D49		
1979	Bos A★	158	619	117	201	39	6	39	130	57-4	4	97	.325	.381	.596	152	44	9-4	.984	-6	87	83	O125(124/0/1),D33		
1980	Bos A*	124	504	81	148	22	6	24	86	30-5	3	87	.294	.336	.504	121	12	8-3	.988	-2	95	110	O108L	35	
1981	Bos A	108	451	51	128	18	1	17	62	34-3	3	76	.284	.333	.441	115	8	2-2	.969	-6	88	112	O145L		
1982	Bos A	145	573	86	177	24	5	24	97	55-6	6	98	.309	.375	.494	129	23	0-1	.984	10	103	170	O151L,D4		
1983	Bos A★	155	626	90	191	34	1	39	126	52-10	6	102	.305	.361	.550	137	31	0-2	.989	4	101	110	O157L,D2		
1984	Bos A	159	657	98	184	25	7	28	122	44-8	2	102	.280	.323	.467	111	8	4-0	.989	-8	86	95	O130L,D7		
1985	Bos A★	140	546	85	159	20	3	27	103	51-5	4	75	.291	.349	.487	122	16	2-0	.964	-8	85	89	O156L/D		
1986	†Bos A★	157	618	98	200	39	2	20	110	62-5	4	78	.324	.384	.490	137	33	0-1	.977	8	103	162	O154L,D2		
1987	Bos A	108	404	66	112	14	0	13	62	45-3	7	77	.277	.357	.408	102	1	1-1	.977	1	85	197	O94L,D12		
1988	Bos A	135	485	57	120	13	1	15	72	48-2	3	89	.264	.330	.406	102	1	0-0	—	0	0	0	D55	82	
1989	Bos A	56	209	22	49	10	2	3	28	13-0	1	39	.234	.276	.344	71	-8	1-0	.980	-4	94	125	O1543(1504/1/43),D530	117	
Total	16	2089	8225	1249	2452	373	79	382	1451	670-77	66	1423	.298	.352	.502	128	279	58-34	.980	-4	94	125	O1543(1504/1/43),D530		

RICE, LEN
Leonard Oliver B9.2.1918 Lead SD D6.13.1992 Sonora CA BR/TR/6-0/175 d4.26

YEAR	TM LG	G	AB	R	H	2B	3B	HR	RBI	BB-IB	HP	SO	AVG	OBP	SLG	AOPS	ABR	SB-CS	FA	FR	RNG	THR	GAMES AT POSITION	DL	BFW
1944	Cin N	10	4	1	0	0	0	0	0	0	0	0	.000	.000	.000	-99	-1	0	1.000	0	0	0	C5		
1945	Chi N	32	99	10	23	3	0	0	7	5	0	8	.232	.269	.263	49	-7	2	.976	1	157	55	C29		
Total	2	42	103	11	23	3	0	0	7	5	0	8	.223	.259	.263	44	-8	2	.977	1	153	54	C34		

YEAR	TM LG	G	AB	R	H	2B	3B	HR	RBI	BB-IB	HP	SO	AVG	OBP	SLG	AOPS	ABR	SB-CS	FA	FR	RNG	THR	GAMES AT POSITION	DL	BFW

RICE, BOB Robert Turnbull B5.28.1899 Philadelphia PA D2.20.1986 Elizabethtown PA BR/TR/5-10/170 d9.1

YEAR	TM LG	G	AB	R	H	2B	3B	HR	RBI	BB-IB	HP	SO	AVG	OBP	SLG	AOPS	ABR	SB-CS	FA	FR	RNG	THR	GAMES AT POSITION	DL	BFW
1926	Phi N	19	54	3	8	0	1	0	10	3	0	4	.148	.193	.185	2	-8	0	.864	0	100	242	3b15,2b2,S2		-0.7

RICHARD, CHRIS Christopher Robert B6.7.1974 San Diego CA BL/TL/6-2/185* [StLN95 19/519] d7.17 Col Oklahoma St.

YEAR	TM LG	G	AB	R	H	2B	3B	HR	RBI	BB-IB	HP	SO	AVG	OBP	SLG	AOPS	ABR	SB-CS	FA	FR	RNG	THR	GAMES AT POSITION	DL	BFW
2000	StL N	6	16	1	2	0	0	1		2-0	0	2	.125	.222	.313	32	-2	0-0	1.000	0	121	0	O3(1/0/2),1b2		-0.2
	Bal A	56	199	38	55	14	2	13	36	15-3	4	38	.276	.335	.563	129	8	7-5	.989	-7	50	106	1b53/ORD		-0.4
2001	Bal A	136	483	74	128	31	3	15	61	45-4	8	100	.265	.335	.435	107	5	11-9	1.000	5	115	102	O96(0/36/69),D20,1b18	15	0.4
2002	Bal A	50	155	15	36	11	0	4	21	12-0	2	30	.232	.292	.381	82	-4	0-3	1.000	-1	63	0	D36,1b9	122	0.4
2003	Col N	19	27	3	6	1	1	1	3	3-0	0	6	.222	.300	.444	80	-1	0-1	1.000	0	110	0	O3L/1	151	-0.1
Total 4		267	880	131	227	57	6	34	122	77-7	14	176	.258	.324	.452	106	6	18-18	1.000	6	103	0	O103(4/36/72),1b83,D57	288	-1.1

RICHARD, LEE Lee Edward "Bee Bee" B9.18.1948 Lafayette LA BR/TR (BB 1975)/5-11/165* [ChiA70 1/6] d4.7 Col Southern A&M

YEAR	TM LG	G	AB	R	H	2B	3B	HR	RBI	BB-IB	HP	SO	AVG	OBP	SLG	AOPS	ABR	SB-CS	FA	FR	RNG	THR	GAMES AT POSITION	DL	BFW
1971	Chi A	87	260	38	60	7	3	2	17	20-0	1	46	.231	.286	.304	66	-12	8-9	.920	13	119	92	S68,O16C		0.6
1972	Chi A	11	29	5	7	0	0	0	1	0-0	0	7	.241	.241	.241	43	-2	1-0	1.000	-0	57	268	O6C/S		-0.3
1974	Chi A	32	67	5	11	1	0	0	1	5-1	0	8	.164	.222	.179	16	-7	0-0	.821	-2	95	104	3b12,S6,2b3/ORD		-0.9
1975	Chi A	43	45	11	9	0	1	0	5	4-0	0	7	.200	.265	.244	44	-3	2-3	1.000	-1	97	0	3b12,S9,2b5,D5		-0.4
1976	StL N	66	91	12	16	4	2	0	5	4-1	0	9	.176	.211	.264	33	-8	1-0	.975	-3	100	101	2b26,S12/3		-1.0
Total 5		239	492	71	103	12	6	2	29	33-2	1	77	.209	.259	.270	50	-32	12-12	.923	6	113	102	S96,2b34,3b25,O23(0/22/1),D10		-2.0

RICHARDS, GENE Eugene B9.29.1953 Monticello SC BL/TL/6-0/175* [SDN75*1/1] d4.6 Col South Carolina St.

YEAR	TM LG	G	AB	R	H	2B	3B	HR	RBI	BB-IB	HP	SO	AVG	OBP	SLG	AOPS	ABR	SB-CS	FA	FR	RNG	THR	GAMES AT POSITION	DL	BFW
1977	SD N	146	525	79	152	16	11	5	32	60-12	2	80	.290	.363	.390	114	10	56-12	.963	3	93	200	O109(72/41/1),1b32		1.7
1978	SD N	154	555	90	171	26	12	4	41	64-7	4	80	.308	.381	.420	134	26	37-17	.965	-8	91	88	O124(113/26/0),1b26		1.6
1979	SD N	150	545	77	152	17	9	4	41	47-6	8	62	.279	.343	.365	100	0	24-8	.973	-4	97	73	O132(20/102/10)		-0.4
1980	SD N	158	642	91	193	26	8	4	41	61-7	2	73	.301	.363	.385	117	15	61-16	.979	7	100	174	O156(156/0/1)		2.3
1981	SD N	104	393	47	113	14	**12**	3	42	53-3	1	44	.288	.373	.407	132	17	20-8	.975	-2	88	148	O102L		1.3
1982	SD N	132	521	63	149	13	8	3	28	36-1	2	52	.286	.333	.359	100	-2	30-20	.977	-1	104	98	O103L,1b25		1.3
1983	SD N	95	233	37	64	11	3	3	22	17-1	1	17	.275	.325	.386	100	-1	14-5	.980	1	110	57	O54L	27	-0.9
1984	SF N	87	135	18	34	4	0	0	8	18-2	0	28	.252	.340	.281	78	-3	5-3	.940	-1	103	59	O26(15/1/11)		-0.1
Total 8		1026	3549	502	1028	127	63	26	255	356-39	20	436	.290	.357	.383	113	62	247-89	.972	-5	97	124	O806(634/170/23),1b83	27	5.0

RICHARDS, FRED Fred Charles "Fuzzy" B11.3.1927 Warren OH BL/TL/6-1.5/185 d9.15

YEAR	TM LG	G	AB	R	H	2B	3B	HR	RBI	BB-IB	HP	SO	AVG	OBP	SLG	AOPS	ABR	SB-CS	FA	FR	RNG	THR	GAMES AT POSITION	DL	BFW
1951	Chi N	10	27	1	8	0	0	0	2	2-0	0	3	.296	.345	.370	91	0	0-0	1.000	1	162	44	1b9		0.1

RICHARDS, PAUL Paul Rapier B11.21.1908 Waxahachie TX D5.4.1986 Waxahachie TX BR/TR/6-1.5/180 d4.17 M12

YEAR	TM LG	G	AB	R	H	2B	3B	HR	RBI	BB-IB	HP	SO	AVG	OBP	SLG	AOPS	ABR	SB-CS	FA	FR	RNG	THR	GAMES AT POSITION	DL	BFW
1932	Bro N	3	8	0	0	0	0	0	0	0-2	0	2	.000	.000	.000	-99	-2	0	1.000	2	122	102	C3		0.0
1933	NY N	51	87	4	17	3	0	0	10	3	0	12	.195	.222	.230	30	-8	0	.989	1	112	157	C36		-0.6
1934	NY N	42	75	10	12	1	0	0	3	13	0	8	.160	.284	.173	26	-8	0	1.000	2	118	137	C37		-0.4
1935	NY N	7	4	0	1	0	0	0	0	2	0	1	.250	.500	.250	110	0	0	1.000	1	0	272	C4		-0.4
	Phi A	85	257	31	63	10	1	4	29	24	0	12	.245	.310	.339	68	-13	0-0	.977	-6	72	105	C79		0.1
1943	Det A	100	313	32	69	7	1	5	33	38	1	35	.220	.307	.297	71	-11	1-0	.986	16	102	**139**	C100		-1.3
1944	Det A	95	300	24	71	13	0	3	37	35	1	30	.237	.318	.310	76	-9	8-3	.979	17	**191**	147	C90		1.3
1945	†Det A	83	234	26	60	12	1	3	32	19	1	31	.256	.315	.355	88	-4	4-0	**.995**	9	122	102	C83		1.5
1946	Det A	57	139	13	28	5	2	0	11	23	0	18	.201	.315	.266	60	-7	2-0	.997	10	112	102	C54		1.2
Total 8		523	1417	140	321	51	5	15	155	157	3	149	.227	.305	.301	68	-62	15-3	.987	52	121	125	C486		2.4

RICHARDSON B Boston MA 5-4/136 d7.10

YEAR	TM LG	G	AB	R	H	2B	3B	HR	RBI	BB-IB	HP	SO	AVG	OBP	SLG	AOPS	ABR	SB-CS	FA	FR	RNG	THR	GAMES AT POSITION	DL	BFW
1884	CP U	1	4	0	0	0	0	0	0				.000	.000	.000	-99	-1		.667	-1	46	0	/2		-0.2

RICHARDSON, HARDY Abram Harding "Old True Blue" B4.21.1855 Clarksboro NJ D1.14.1931 Utica NY BR/TR/5-9.5/170 d5.1 OF(375/158/11) ▲

YEAR	TM LG	G	AB	R	H	2B	3B	HR	RBI	BB-IB	HP	SO	AVG	OBP	SLG	AOPS	ABR	SB-CS	FA	FR	RNG	THR	GAMES AT POSITION	DL	BFW
1879	Buf N	**79**	336	54	95	18	10	0	37	16			30	.283	.315	.396	130	11	.843	-7	93	150	3b78/C		0.6
1880	Buf N	83	343	48	89	18	8	0	17	14			37	.259	.289	.359	116	5	.848	-5	98	64	3b81,C5		0.3
1881	Buf N	**83**	344	62	100	18	9	2	53	12			27	.291	.315	.413	129	11	.914	23	**217**	88	O79C,2b5/S3		2.8
1882	Buf N	83	354	61	96	20	8	2	57	11			33	.271	.293	.390	115	5	.898	19	109	75	2b83		2.5
1883	Buf N	92	399	73	124	34	7	1	56	22			20	.311	.347	.439	134	17	.903	16	113	80	2b92		3.1
1884	Buf N	102	439	85	132	27	9	6	60	22			41	.301	.334	.444	138	18	.897	6	106	65	2b71,O24C,3b5,1b3		2.3
1885	Buf N	96	426	90	136	19	11	4	44	20			22	.319	.350	.458	154	24	.905	9	107	69	2b50,O48(1/47/0)/SP		3.0
1886	Det N	125	538	125	**189**	27	11	**11**	61	46			27	.351	.402	.504	168	43	42	.899	61	123	43	O80L,2b42,P4,S3,3b2		4.5
1887	†Det N	120	543	131	178	25	18	8	94	31	2	40	.328	.366	.484	129	19	29	.941	20	104	105	2b64,O59(58/1/0)		3.3
1888	Det N	58	266	60	77	18	2	8	32	17	1	23	.289	.335	.440	144	13	13	.925	-0	94	99	2b58		1.5
1889	Bos N	132	536	122	163	33	10	6	79	44	5	44	.304	.367	.437	117	10	47	.924	10	105	115	2b86,O46L		1.9
1890	Bos P	**130**	555	126	181	26	14	13	**146**	52	0	46	.326	.384	.494	125	16	42	.950	2	56	66	O124L,S6/1		1.2
1891	Bos AA	74	278	45	71	9	4	7	52	40	1	26	.255	.351	.392	114	5	16	.955	-1	48	98	O60(57/1/2),3b9,S4,1b3		0.3
1892	Was N	10	37	2	4	0	0	0	5		0	3	.108	.214	.108	-2	-4	2	.941	0			7L,3b2/2		-0.5
	NY N	64	248	36	53	11	5	2	34	21	1	26	.214	.278	.323	83	-6	14	.931	3	105	77	2b33,O17(2/6/9),1b9,S6		-0.1
	Year	74	285	38	57	11	5	2	34	26	1	29	.200	.266	.295	72	-10	16	.933	3	104	75	2b34,O24(9/6/9),1b9,S6,3b2		-0.1
Total 14		1331	5642	1120	1688	303	126	70	822	377	10	445	.299	.344	.435	129	187	205	.915	102	106	86	2b585,O544L,3b178,S21,1b16,C6,P5		26.7

RICHARDSON, NOLEN Clifford Nolen B1.18.1903 Chattanooga TN D9.25.1951 Athens GA BR/TR/6-1.5/170 d4.16 Col Georgia

YEAR	TM LG	G	AB	R	H	2B	3B	HR	RBI	BB-IB	HP	SO	AVG	OBP	SLG	AOPS	ABR	SB-CS	FA	FR	RNG	THR	GAMES AT POSITION	DL	BFW
1929	Det A	13	21	2	4	0	0	0	2	2	0	1	.190	.261	.190	18	-3	1-1	.839	-4	58	46	S13		-0.6
1931	Det A	38	148	13	40	9	2	0	16	6	0	7	.270	.299	.358	70	-7	2-1	.946	-1	109	30	3b38		-0.5
1932	Det A	69	155	13	34	5	2	0	12	9	0	13	.219	.262	.277	38	-15	5-2	.986	7	111	110	3b65,S4		-0.5
1935	NY A	12	46	3	10	1	1	0	5	3	0	1	.217	.265	.283	44	-4	0-0	.922	-5	67	65	S12		-0.8
1938	Cin N	35	100	8	29	4	0	0	10	3	0	4	.290	.311	.330	78	-3	0	.966	0	101	81	S35		-0.1
1939	Cin N	1	3	0	0	0	0	0	0		0	0	.000	.000	.000	-99	-1		1.000	0	89	155	/S		0.0
Total 6		168	473	39	117	19	5	0	45	23	0	22	.247	.282	.309	55	-33	8-4	.969	-2	110	74	3b103,S65		-2.6

RICHARDSON, DANNY Daniel B1.25.1863 Elmira NY D9.12.1926 New York NY BR/TR/5-8/165 d5.22 M1 OF(41/51/51)

YEAR	TM LG	G	AB	R	H	2B	3B	HR	RBI	BB-IB	HP	SO	AVG	OBP	SLG	AOPS	ABR	SB-CS	FA	FR	RNG	THR	GAMES AT POSITION	DL	BFW
1884	NY N	74	277	36	70	16	1	1	27	16			17	.253	.294	.300	85	-5	.907	2	176	153	O55(11/7/37),S19		-0.3
1885	NY N	49	198	26	52	9	3	0	25	10			14	.263	.298	.338	107	2	.950	0	69	0	O22(10/2/12),3b21,P9		0.2
1886	NY N	68	237	43	55	9	1	1	27	17			21	.232	.283	.291	74	-7	12	.953	1	64	0	O64(28/20/42/2),P5/S32		-0.7
1887	NY N	122	450	79	125	19	10	3	62	36	4	25	.278	.337	.384	105	4	41	.928	18	109	106	2b108,3b14/P		2.1
1888	†NY N	135	561	82	127	16	7	8	61	15	1	37	.226	.248	.323	82	-13	35	**.942**	9	96	97	2b135		0.1
1889	†NY N	125	497	88	139	22	8	7	100	46	1	37	.280	.342	.398	106	2	32	.934	15	102	108	2b125		1.9
1890	NY P	123	520	102	135	12	9	4	80	37	2	19	.256	.307	.335	66	-30	37	.900	14	107	112	S68,2b56		-1.0
1891	NY N	123	516	85	139	18	9	5	51	33	0	27	.269	.313	.347	96	-4	33	.952	**45**	**114**	126	2b114,S9		4.0
1892	Was N	142	551	48	132	13	4	3	58	25	1	45	.240	.274	.294	74	-19	25	.931	45	111	126	S93,2b49/3M		3.0
1893	Bro N	54	206	36	46	6	2	0	21	13	3	18	.223	.279	.272	49	-15	7	.949	-12	77	90	2b46,3b5,S3		-2.1
1894	Lou N	116	430	51	109	17	2	1	40	35	5	31	.253	.317	.309	55	-31	8	.916	5	98	107	S107,2b10		-1.5
Total 11		1131	4451	676	1129	149	52	32	558	283	17	289	.254	.301	.332	82	-116	225	.940	142	103	104	2b644,S300,O141C,3b42,P15		5.7

RICHARDSON, JEFF Jeffrey Scott B8.26.1965 Grand Island NE BR/TR/6-2/175* [CinN86 7/176] d7.14 Col Louisiana Tech

YEAR	TM LG	G	AB	R	H	2B	3B	HR	RBI	BB-IB	HP	SO	AVG	OBP	SLG	AOPS	ABR	SB-CS	FA	FR	RNG	THR	GAMES AT POSITION	DL	BFW
1989	Cin N	53	125	10	21	4	0	2	11	10-0	1	23	.168	.234	.248	37	-10	1-0	.969	-1	76	83	S39,3b8		-2.0
1991	Pit N	6	4	0	1	0	0	0		0-0	0	3	.250	.250	.250	41	0	1-0	—	-1	0	0	3b3,S2		-0.1
1993	Bos A	15	24	3	5	2	0	0	2	1-0	0	3	.208	.240	.292	40	-2	0-0	1.000	4	164	96	2b8,S5/3D		0.2
Total 3		74	153	13	27	6	0	2	13	11-0	1	29	.176	.235	.255	38	-12	1-0	.971	-8	77	86	S46,3b12,2b8,D2	127	-1.9

RICHARDSON, KEN Kenneth Franklin B5.2.1915 Orleans IN D12.7.1987 Woodland Hills CA BR/TR/5-10.5/187 d4.14

YEAR	TM LG	G	AB	R	H	2B	3B	HR	RBI	BB-IB	HP	SO	AVG	OBP	SLG	AOPS	ABR	SB-CS	FA	FR	RNG	THR	GAMES AT POSITION	DL	BFW
1942	Phi A	6	15	1	1	0	0	0	2	0	0	0	.067	.176	.067	-30	-3	0	1.000	0	88	596	O3(1/0/2)/13		-0.3
1946	Phi N	6	20	1	4	1	0	0	0	2	0	2	.150	.150	.200	-3	-3	0	.939	-1	95	29	2b6		-0.4
Total 2		12	35	2	4	1	0	0	2	2	0	2	.114	.162	.143	-14	-6	0	.939	-1	95	29	2b6,O3(1/0/2)/31		-0.7

RICHARDSON, BOBBY Robert Clinton B8.19.1935 Sumter SC BR/TR/5-9/170(160-173) d8.5

YEAR	TM LG	G	AB	R	H	2B	3B	HR	RBI	BB-IB	HP	SO	AVG	OBP	SLG	AOPS	ABR	SB-CS	FA	FR	RNG	THR	GAMES AT POSITION	DL	BFW
1955	NY A	11	26	2	4	0	0	0	3	2-0	0	5	.154	.214	.154	8	-4	1-1	.864	-3	59	30	2b6,S4		-0.7
1956	NY A	5	7	1	1	0	0	0	0	0-0	0	1	.143	.143	.143	-25	-4	1-0	1.000	1	57	102	2b5		-0.1
1957	†NY A☆	97	305	36	78	11	4	0	19	9-3	0	26	.256	.274	.298	58	-18	1-3	.979	4	103	105	2b93		-0.9
1958	†NY A☆	73	182	18	45	6	2	0	14	8-0	5	24	.247	.276	.302	62	-10	1-3	.973	4	99	112	2b51,3b13,S2		-0.4
1959	NY A☆	134	469	53	141	18	6	2	33	26-3		20	.301	.338	.377	99	-2	5-5	.970	1	98	116	2b109,S14,3b12		0.8

YEAR	TM LG	G	AB	R	H	2B	3B	HR	RBI	BB-IB	HP	SO	AVG	OBP	SLG	AOPS	ABR	SB-CS	FA	FR	RNG	THR	GAMES AT POSITION	DL	BFW
1960	†NY A	150	460	45	116	12	3	1	26	35-6	0	19	.252	.303	.298	68	-22	6-6	.973	-13	94	111	2b141,3b11		-2.7
1961	†NY A	162	662	80	173	17	5	3	49	30-1	2	23	.261	.295	.316	67	-34	9-7	.978	-4	91	**135**	2b161		-2.4
1962	†NY A★	161	692	99	**209**	38	5	8	59	37-1	1	24	.302	.337	.406	103	1	11-9	.982	-3	101	116	2b161		1.2
1963	†NY A★	151	630	72	167	20	6	3	48	25-0	2	22	.265	.294	.330	76	-22	15-1	.984	13	105	123	2b150		0.7
1964	†NY A★	159	679	90	181	25	4	4	50	28-1	0	36	.267	.294	.333	73	-25	11-2	.982	-13	94	110	2b157/S		-2.4
1965	NY A★	160	664	76	164	28	2	6	47	37-4	1	39	.247	.287	.322	74	-24	7-5	.981	7	108	101	2b147,3b2		-1.0
1966	NY A★	149	610	71	153	21	3	7	42	25-1	1	28	.251	.280	.330	78	-19	6-6	.980	-5	99	116	2b148		-0.1
Total	12	1412	5386	643	1432	196	37	34	390	262-20	7	243	.266	.299	.335	77	-180	73-48	.979	-5	99	116	2b1339,3b38,S21		-8.0

RICHARDSON, TOM Thomas Mitchell B8.7.1883 Louisville IL D11.15.1939 Onawa IA BR/TR/6-0/190 d8.2

1917	StL A	1	1	0	0	0	0	0	0		0		.000	.000	.000	-99	0		—	0			/H		0.0

RICHARDSON, BILL William Henry B9.24.1878 Salem IN D11.6.1949 Sullivan IN BR/TR/5-11/200 d9.20

1901	StL N	15	52	7	11	2	0	2	7	6	0		.212	.293	.365	95	0	1	.981	-1	58	95	1b15		-0.2

RICHARDT, MIKE Michael Anthony B5.24.1958 Los Angeles CA BR/TR/6-0/170* [TexA78 S1/10] d8.30 Col Fresno (CA) City [DL 1985 Hou N 182]

1980	Tex A	22	71	2	16	2	0	0	8	1-0	0	7	.225	.236	.254	35	-7	0-0	.978	-3	92	75	2b20/D		-0.9
1982	Tex A	119	402	34	97	10	0	3	43	23-1	1	42	.241	.281	.289	60	-23	9-1	.988	11	105	101	2b98,D15,O6L	15	-0.5
1983	Tex A	22	83	9	13	2	1	1	7	2-0	0	11	.157	.174	.241	14	-10	2-1	.992	3	99	116	2b20	83	-0.6
1984	Tex A	6	9	0	1	0	0	0	0	1-0	0	1	.111	.200	.111	-11	-1	0-0	1.000	0	87	267	2b4		-0.1
	Hou N	16	15	1	4	1	0	0	2	0-0	0	1	.267	.267	.333	72	-1	0-0	—	0			/H	15	-0.1
Total	4	185	580	46	131	15	1	4	60	27-1	1	62	.226	.259	.276	50	-42	11-3	.988	11	102	102	2b142,D16,O6L	295	-2.2

RICHBOURG, LANCE Lance Clayton B12.18.1897 DeFuniak Springs FL D9.10.1975 Crestview FL BL/TR/5-10.5/160 d7.4 Col Florida

1921	Phi N	10	5	2	1	1	0	0	0	0	0	3	.200	.200	.400	51	0	1-1	1.000	1	175	0	2b4		0.0
1924	Was A	15	32	3	9	2	1	0	1	2	0	6	.281	.324	.406	90	0	1-0	1.000	1	100	240	O7R		0.0
1927	Bos N	115	450	57	139	12	9	2	34	22	1	30	.309	.342	.389	104	0	24	.953	-4	100	74	O110(0/3/107)		-1.3
1928	Bos N	148	612	105	206	26	12	2	52	62	2	39	.337	.399	.428	123	22	11	.972	4	114	52	O148R		1.3
1929	Bos N	139	557	76	170	24	13	3	56	42	1	26	.305	.355	.411	93	-7	7	.971	5	**108**	97	O134(2/0/132)		-1.3
1930	Bos N	130	529	81	161	23	8	3	54	19	2	31	.304	.331	.395	77	-21	13	.971	-2	105	56	O128R		-3.0
1931	Bos N	97	286	32	82	11	6	2	29	19	0	14	.287	.331	.388	96	-3	9	.981	-2	102	40	O71(15/0/56)		-0.9
1932	Chi N	44	148	22	38	2	2	1	21	8	0	6	.257	.295	.318	65	-8	0	.986	-2	91	58	O33(1/3/29)		-1.2
Total	8	698	2619	378	806	101	51	13	247	174	6	153	.308	.352	.400	97	-18	65-1	.970	-1	106	67	O631(18/6/607),2b4		-6.4

RICHIE, ROB Robert Eugene B9.5.1965 Reno NV BL/TR/6-2/190 [DetA87 2/53] d8.19 Col Nevada-Reno

1989	Det A	19	49	6	13	4	2	1	10	5-1	0	10	.265	.333	.490	132	2	0-1	.917	-1	88	139	O13(11/0/2),D4		0.1

RICHMOND, DON Donald Lester B10.27.1919 Gillett PA D5.24.1981 Elmira NY BL/TR/6-1/175* d9.16 Mil 1942-45

1941	Phi A	9	35	3	7	1	1	0	5	0	0	1	.200	.200	.286	28	-4	0-2	.957	-1	98	195	3b9		-0.5
1946	Phi A	16	62	3	18	3	0	1	9	0	0	10	.290	.290	.387	89	-1	1-0	.940	-1	90	27	3b16		-0.2
1947	Phi A	19	21	2	4	1	1	0	4	3	0	3	.190	.292	.333	72	-1	0-0	.500	-2	53	0	3b4/2		-0.3
1951	StL N	12	34	3	3	1	0	1	4	3	0	3	.088	.162	.206	-2	-5	0-1	1.000	3	119	163	3b11		-0.3
Total	4	56	152	11	32	6	2	2	22	6	0	17	.211	.241	.316	51	-11	1-3	.957	-2	99	91	3b40/2		-1.3

RICHMOND, LEE J Lee B5.5.1857 Sheffield OH D10.1.1929 Toledo OH TL/5-10/155 d9.27 Col Brown ▲

1879	Bos N	1	6	0	2	0	0	0				1	.333	.333	.333	118	0		1.000	0	106	0	/P		0.0
1880	Wor N	77	309	44	70	8	4	0	34	9		32	.227	.248	.278	72	-10		.827	-8	82	49	P74,O20(1/1/18)		-0.5
1881	Wor N	61	252	31	63	5	1	0	28	10		10	.250	.279	.278	71	-9		.937	1	113	79	P53,O11(0/2/9)		-0.2
1882	Wor N	55	228	50	64	8	9	2	28	9		11	.281	.308	.421	128	6		.889	3	124	66	P48,O11(1/1/9)		0.2
1883	Pro N	49	194	41	55	8	6	1	19	15		19	.284	.335	.402	120	4		.714	-8	37	0	O41(33/3/5),P12		-0.5
1886	Cin AA	8	29	3	8	0	0	0	3	3	0		.276	.344	.276	92	0	0	.400	-3	0	0	O7C,P3		-0.1
Total	6	251	1018	169	262	29	20	3	113	46	0	73	.257	.289	.334	94	-9	0	.886	-15	103	58	P191,O90(35/14/41)		-1.3

RICHMOND, JOHN John H. B3.5.1854 PA TR/5-9/170 d4.22

1875	Ath NA	29	125	29	25	2	0	0	12	1		4	.200	.206	.216	42	-8	1-0	.814	-3	79	136	2b17,O11(2/3/6),C3		-1.0
1879	Syr N	62	254	31	54	8	4	1	23	4		24	.213	.225	.287	76	-5		.875	-7	90	102	O35(4/29/2),S28,C2		-1.1
1880	Bos N	32	129	12	32	3	1	0	9	2		18	.248	.260	.287	88	-2		.844	-7	81	178	S31/OC		-0.7
1881	Bos N	27	98	13	27	2	2	1	12	6		7	.276	.317	.367	120	2		.969	-0	61	100	O25(0/24/1),S2		-0.4
1882	Cle N	41	140	12	24	6	0	0	11	11		27	.171	.232	.243	54	-6		.917	3	143	0	O41C		-0.1
	Phi N	18	65	8	12	2	2	0	4	11			.185	.303	.277	91	0		.892	0	94	0	O18(0/17/1)		3.8
1883	Col AA	92	385	63	109	7	8	0		25			.283	.327	.343	126	13		.866	-8	93	114	S105		-0.6
1884	Col AA	105	398	57	100	13	7	3		35	3		.251	.317	.342	125	14		.866	-9	89	102	S23,O11(0/8/3)		-1.1
1885	Pit AA	34	131	14	27	2	0	0	12	8	2		.206	.262	.252	64	-5		.849	-9	89	102	S280,O133(4/122/7),C2		1.1
Total	7	411	1600	210	385	43	28	5	71	102	5	76	.241	.288	.312	101	11		.866	0	99	104	S280,O133(4/122/7),C2		1.1

RICHTER, AL Allen Gordon B2.7.1927 Norfolk VA BR/TR/5-11/165* d9.23

1951	Bos A	5	11	1	1	0	0	0	0	3	0	0	.091	.286	.091	5	-1	0-0	1.000	2	112	232	S3		0.0
1953	Bos A	1	0	0	0	0	0	0	0	0	0	0					0	0-0	1.000	0	93	443	/S		0.0
Total	2	6	11	1	1	0	0	0	0	3	0	0	.091	.286	.091	5	-1	0-0	1.000	2	110	254	S4		0.0

RICHTER, JOHN John M. B2.8.1873 Louisville KY D10.4.1927 Louisville KY 6-0/178 d10.6

1898	Lou N	3	13	1	2	0	0	0	0	0	0		.154	.154	.154	-12	-2	0	.929	0	108	195	3b3		-0.3

RICKERT, JOE Joseph Francis "Diamond Joe" B12.12.1876 London OH D10.15.1943 Springfield OH BR/TR/5-10.5/165 d10.12

1898	Pit N	2	6	0	1	0	0	0	0	0	0		.167	.167	.167	-5	-1	0	1.000	1	0	0	O2L		-0.2
1901	Bos N	13	60	6	10	1	2	0	1	3	0		.167	.206	.250	29	-6	1	.974	2	107	231	O13L		-0.6
Total	2	15	66	6	11	1	2	0	1	3	0		.167	.203	.242	27	-7	1	.979	2	89	193	O15L		-0.8

RICKERT, MARV Marvin August "Twitch" B1.8.1921 Longbranch WA D6.3.1978 Oakville WA BL/TR/6-2/195* d9.10 Mil 1943-45

1942	Chi N	8	26	5	7	0	0	1	1	0	0	5	.269	.296	.269	69	-1	0	1.000	1	106	154	O6C		-0.1
1946	Chi N	111	392	44	103	18	3	7	47	28	1	54	.263	.314	.378	98	-3	3	.972	-4	97	59	O104(75/19/10)		-1.1
1947	Chi N	71	137	7	20	0	0	2	15	15	0	17	.146	.230	.190	13	-18	0	.982	1	99	106	O30(18/3/9),1b7		-1.9
1948	Cin N	8	6	0	1	0	0	0	0	0	0	1	.167	.167	.167	-10	-1	0	—	0			/H		-0.1
	†Bos N	3	13	1	3	0	0	0	2	0	1	1	.231	.286	.385	81	-1	0	1.000	1	109	324	O3L		-0.1
	Year	11	19	1	4	0	0	0	2	0	1	2	.211	.250	.316	54	-1	0	1.000	1	109	324	O3L		-0.1
1949	Bos N	100	277	44	81	18	3	6	49	23	0	38	.292	.347	.444	117	6	1	.981	5	107	162	O75(50/3/25),1b12		-0.3
1950	Pit N	17	20	0	3	0	0	0	4	0	0	4	.150	.150	.150	-20	-4	0	.968	-2	105	52	O78(18/0/63)/1		-2.0
	Chi A	84	278	38	66	9	2	4	27	21	0	42	.237	.291	.327	60	-18	0-1	.976	1	102	93	O299(164/31/110),1b20		-5.0
Total	6	402	1149	139	284	45	9	19	145	88	2	161	.247	.302	.352	79	-40	4-1	.976	1	102	93	O299(164/31/110),1b20		-5.0

RICKETTS, DAVE David William B7.12.1935 Pottstown PA BB/TR/6-2/195* d9.25 C19 b-Dick Col Duquesne

1963	StL N	3	8	0	2	0	0	0	0	0-0	0	2	.250	.250	.250	41	-1	0-0	1.000	-1	102	0	C3		-0.0
1965	StL N	11	29	1	7	0	0	0	1	1-0	0	3	.241	.267	.241	40	-2	0-0	.977	-4	51	0	C11		-0.1
1967	†StL N	52	99	11	27	0	0	1	14	4-0	0	7	.273	.295	.384	96	-1	0-0	1.000	-2	75	190	C21		-0.1
1968	†StL N	20	22	1	3	0	0	0	1	0-0	0	3	.136	.136	.136	-18	-3	0-0	1.000	0	33	0	/C		-0.1
1969	StL N	30	44	2	12	1	0	0	5	4-0	0	5	.273	.320	.295	77	-1	0-0	.983	-0	104	C8		-0.1
1970	Pit N	14	11	0	2	0	0	0	1	1-0	0	3	.182	.250	.182	18	-1	0-0	.988	-7	65	120	C51		-0.1
Total	6	130	213	15	53	9	0	1	20	10-0	0	23	.249	.278	.305	67	-9	0-0	.988	-7	65	120	C51		-0.1

RICKEY, BRANCH Wesley Branch "The Mahatma" B12.20.1881 Flat OH D12.9.1965 Columbia MO BL/TR/5-9/175 d6.16 M10 HF1967 Col Ohio Wesleyan

1905	StL A	1	3	0	0	0	0	0	0	0	0		.000	.000	.000	-99	-1	0	1.000	0	75	166	/C		-0.1
1906	StL A	65	201	22	57	7	3	3	24	16	3		.284	.345	.393	137	-1	8	.954	-6	86	93	C55/OR		-0.1
1907	NY A	52	137	16	25	1	3	0	15	11	2		.182	.253	.234	51	-8	4	.846	-4	40	0	O22(20/1/1),C11,1b9		-0.1
1914	StL A	2	2	0	0	0	0	0	0	0	0		.000	.000	.000	-99	0	0	—	0			/HM		-0.0
Total	4	120	343	38	82	8	6	3	39	27	5	1	.239	.304	.324	97	-2	8	.940	-11	88	90	C67,O23(20/1/2),1b9		-0.3

RICKLEY, CHRIS Christian B10.7.1859 Philadelphia PA D10.25.1911 Philadelphia PA 5-8/160 d6.9

1884	Phi U	6	25	5	5	0	0	0		2			.200	.259	.280	69	-2		.757	-0	111	156	S6		

YEAR	TM LG	G	AB	R	H	2B	3B	HR	RBI	BB-IB	HP	SO	AVG	OBP	SLG	AOPS	ABR	SB-CS	FA	FR	RNG	THR	GAMES AT POSITION	DL	BFW

RICKS, JOHN John B12.1866 St.Louis MO D8. 30 20St.Louis MO d9.21

YEAR	TM LG	G	AB	R	H	2B	3B	HR	RBI	BB-IB	HP	SO	AVG	OBP	SLG	AOPS	ABR	SB-CS	FA	FR	RNG	THR	GAMES AT POSITION	DL	BFW
1891	StL AA	5	18	3	3	0	0	0	0	0	0	2	.167	.167	.167	-4	-3	0	.810	-1	55	0	3b5		-0.3
1894	StL N	1	1	0	0	0	0	0	0	0	0	0	.000	.000	.000	-99	0	0	.250	-1	0	0	/3		-0.1
Total 2		6	19	3	3	0	0	0	0	0	0	2	.158	.158	.158	-9	-3	0	.720	-3	48	0	3b6		-0.4

RICO, FRED Alfredo (Cruz) B7.4.1944 Jerome AZ d9.1 Col Arizona St.

| 1969 | KC A | 12 | 26 | 2 | 6 | 2 | 0 | 0 | 2 | 9-1 | 0 | 10 | .231 | .429 | .308 | 107 | 1 | 0-1 | 1.000 | 4 | 167 | 319 | O9(0/2/7)/3 | | 0.4 |

RICO, ART Arthur Ramon B7.23.1895 Roxbury MA D1.3.1919 Boston MA BR/TR/5-9.5/185 d7.31 Mil 1918

1916	Bos N	4	4	0	0	0	0	0	0	0	0	0	.000	.000	.000	-99	-1	0	1.000	-0	109	118	C4		-0.1
1917	Bos N	13	14	1	4	1	0	0	2	0	0	2	.286	.286	.357	102	-1	0	.950	-1	104	82	C11,O2L		0.0
Total 2		17	18	1	4	1	0	0	2	0	0	2	.222	.222	.278	56	-1	0	.962	-1	105	90	C15,O2L		-0.1

RICONDA, HARRY Henry Paul B3.17.1897 New York NY D11.15.1958 Mahopac NY BR/TR/5-10/175 d4,19

1923	Phi A	55	175	23	46	11	4	0	12	12	2	18	.263	.317	.371	80	-6	4-2	.911	-1	108	98	3b47,S2		-0.3
1924	Phi A	83	281	34	71	16	3	1	21	27	2	43	.253	.323	.342	71	-13	3-4	.927	-3	97	108	3b73,S2		-1.1
1926	Bos N	4	12	1	2	0	0	0	2	0		2	.167	.286	.167	27	-1	0	.818	-1	46	0	3b4		-0.2
1928	Bro N	92	281	22	63	15	4	3	35	20	4	28	.224	.285	.338	63	-16	6	.957	0	94	64	2b53,3b21,S16		-1.3
1929	Pit N	8	15	3	7	2	0	0	0	0		0	.467	.467	.600	158	1	0	.840	-2	67	124	S4		0.0
1930	Cin N	1	1	0	0	0	0	0	0	0	0	0	.000	.000	.000	-99	0	0	—	0			/H		0.0
Total 6		243	765	83	189	44	11	4	70	61	8	91	.247	.309	.349	71	-35	13-6	.922	-7	101	95	3b145,2b53,S24		-2.9

RIDDLE, JOHN John H. B2.1864 PA D5.5.1931 Camden NJ BR/TR d9.18

1889	Was N	11	37	3	8	3	0	0	3	2	0	8	.216	.256	.297	58	-2	0	.841	1			C9,O2R		-0.1
1890	Phi AA	27	85	7	7	0	1	0	2	17	1		.082	.243	.106	3	-10	4	.914	-3	84	88	C13,O12(9/3/0),2b2/3		-1.1
Total 2		38	122	10	15	3	1	0	5	19	1	8	.123	.246	.164	20	-12	4	.880	-3	84	88	C22,O14(9/3/2),2b2/3		-1.2

RIDDLE, JOHNNY John Ludy "Mutt" B10.3.1905 Clinton SC D12.15.1998 Indianapolis IN BR/TR/5-11/190 d4.17 C11 b-Elmer

1930	Chi A	25	58	7	14	3	1	0	4	3	1	6	.241	.290	.328	58	-4	0-0	1.000	-1	91	132	C25		-0.4
1937	Was A	8	26	2	7	0	0	0	3	0	1	2	.269	.296	.269	46	-2	0-0	.971	-1	110	150	C8		-0.2
	Bos N	2	3	0	0	0	0	0	0	1		0	.000	.250	.000	-29	-1	0	1.000	1	0	243	C2		0.0
1938	Bos N	19	57	6	16	1	0	0	2	4	0	2	.281	.328	.298	81	-2	0	.951	3	162	125	C19		0.2
1941	Cin N	10	10	2	3	0	0	0	0	0	0	1	.300	.300	.300	69	0	0	1.000	1	0	95	C10		0.0
1944	Cin N	1	0	0	0	0	0	0	0	0			—	—	—		0	0	—	0	0	0	/C		0.0
1945	Cin N	23	45	0	8	0	0	0	2	4	0	6	.178	.245	.178	19	-5	0	1.000	0	0	0	/C		-0.2
1948	Pit N	10	15	1	3	0	0	0	0	1	0	2	.200	.250	.200	23	-2	0	1.000	0	151	99	C10		-0.1
Total 7		98	214	18	51	4	1	0	11	13	2	19	.238	.288	.266	51	-16	0-0	.983	5	114	124	C98		-0.7

RIEBE, HANK Harvey Donald B10.10.1921 Cleveland OH D4.16.2001 Cleveland OH BR/TR/5-9.5/175 d8.26 Mil 1943-45

1942	Det A	11	35	1	11	0	0	0	2	0	0	6	.314	.314	.371	85	-1	0-0	1.000	0	101	71	C11		0.0
1947	Det A	8	7	0	0	0	0	0	2	0	0	6	.000	.000	.000	-97	-2	0-0	1.000	-0	0	0	C3		-0.2
1948	Det A	25	62	0	12	0	0	0	5	3	0	5	.194	.231	.194	13	-8	0-1	1.000	0	108	50	C24		-0.7
1949	Det A	17	33	1	6	2	0	0	2	0	0	5	.182	.182	.242	12	-4	1-0	.960	-1	88	152	C11		-0.2
Total 4		61	137	2	29	4	0	0	11	3	0	18	.212	.229	.241	26	-15	1-1	.994	-1	101	73	C49		-0.5
																									-1.4

RIESGO, NIKCO Damon Nikco B1.11.1967 Long Beach CA BR/TR/6-2/185 d4.20 Col San Diego St.

| 1991 | Mon N | 4 | 7 | 1 | 1 | 0 | 0 | 0 | | 3-0 | 1 | 1 | .143 | .400 | .143 | 60 | 0 | 0 | .500 | -0 | 0 | 638 | O2R | 10 | -0.1 |

RIGGERT, JOE Joseph Aloysius B12.11.1886 Janesville WI D12.10.1973 Kansas City MO BR/TR/5-9.5/170 d5.12

1911	Bos A	50	146	19	31	4	4	2	13	12	4		.212	.290	.336	75	-6	5	.929	-3	99	37	O39(21/11/6)		-1.0
1914	Bro N	27	83	6	16	1	3	2	6	4	0	20	.193	.230	.349	70	-4	2	.972	-1	93	92	O20(1/0/20)		-0.6
	StL N	34	89	9	19	5	2	0	8	5	0	14	.213	.255	.315	70	-4	4	.961	-1	92	103	O30(9/19/2)		-0.6
	Year	61	172	15	35	6	5	2	14	9	0	34	.203	.243	.331	70	-8	6	.966	-1	92	98	O50(10/19/22)		-1.2
1919	Bos N	63	240	34	68	8	5	4	17	25	2	30	.283	.356	.408	135	10	9	.950	-2	103	72	O61C		0.5
Total 3		174	558	68	134	18	14	8	44	46	6	64	.240	.305	.366	98	-4	20	.950	-6	99	71	O150(31/91/28)		-1.7

RIGGS, ADAM Adam David B10.4.1972 Steubenville OH BR/TR/6-0/194* [LAN94 22/608] d8.7 Col South Carolina-Aiken [DL 1998 LA N 115]

1997	LA N	9	20	3	4	1	0	0	1	4-1	0	3	.200	.333	.250	59	-1	1-0	1.000	-1	98	81	2b8		-0.2
2001	SD N	12	36	2	7	1	0	0	1	2-0	0	8	.194	.237	.222	21	-4	1-1	1.000	-1	86	100	2b11/3		-0.5
2003	Ana A	24	61	11	15	4	1	3	5	9-0	0	10	.246	.343	.492	121	2	3-1	.976	2	170	74	1b10,O8L,2b3,D3		0.3
2004	†Ana A	16	36	2	7	3	0	0	3	1	0	10	.194	.216	.278	29	-4	1-0	1.000	2	138	454	O8L/12D		-0.2
Total 4		61	153	18	33	9	1	3	10	16-1	0	30	.216	.290	.346	69	-7	6-2	1.000	2	92	84	2b23,O16L,1b11,D7/3	115	-0.6

RIGGS, LEW Lewis Sidney B4.22.1910 Mebane NC D8.12.1975 Durham NC BL/TR/6-0/175 d4.28 Mil 1943-45

1934	StL N	2	1	0	0	0	0	0	0	0	0	1	.000	.000	.000	-94	0	0	—	0			/H		0.0
1935	Cin N	142	532	73	148	26	8	5	46	43	2	32	.278	.334	.385	96	-3	8	.928	8	110	99	3b135		0.9
1936	Cin N★	141	538	69	138	20	12	6	57	38	7	33	.257	.314	.372	90	-10	5	.968	13	116	**108**	3b140		0.7
1937	Cin N	122	384	43	93	17	5	6	45	24	1	17	.242	.289	.359	79	-13	4	.941	18	121	119	3b100,2b4/S		0.9
1938	Cin N	142	531	53	134	21	13	2	55	40	5	28	.252	.311	.352	84	-13	3	.947	-1	100	78	3b140		-0.9
1939	Cin N	22	38	5	6	1	0	0	1	5	0	4	.158	.256	.184	20	-4	1	.957	-0	102	75	3b11		-0.4
1940	†Cin N	41	72	8	21	7	1	1	9	2	0	4	.292	.311	.458	109	1	0	.943	1	118	145	3b11		0.2
1941	†Bro N	77	197	27	60	13	4	5	36	16	2	12	.305	.357	.487	131	7	1	.932	-8	83	56	3b43/12		0.1
1942	Bro N	70	180	20	50	5	0	3	22	13	2	9	.278	.333	.356	100	0	0	.944	-5	86	107	3b46/1		-0.4
1946	Bro N	1	4	0	0	0	0	0	0	0	0	0	.000	.000	.000	-99	-1	0	1.000	0	93	0	/3		-0.1
Total 10		760	2477	298	650	110	43	28	271	181	17	140	.262	.317	.375	91	-36	22	.945	26	107	97	3b627,2b5,1b2/S		1.0

RIGNEY, TOPPER Emory Elmo B1.7.1897 Groveton TX D6.6.1972 San Antonio TX BR/TR/5-9/150 d4.12 Col Texas A&M-Commerce

1922	Det A	**155**	536	68	161	17	7	2	63	68	1	44	.300	.380	.369	99	2	17-8	.938	-15	98	89	S155		0.5
1923	Det A	129	470	63	148	24	11	1	74	55	2	35	.315	.389	.419	115	11	7-5	.944	-10	99	73	S129		1.4
1924	Det A	147	499	81	144	29	9	4	94	102	1	39	.289	.410	.407	113	15	11-11	**.967**	8	106	103	S146		3.5
1925	Det A	62	146	21	36	5	2	2	18	21	0	15	.247	.341	.349	77	-5	2-2	.934	-9	91	36	S51,3b4		-1.0
1926	Bos A	148	525	71	142	32	6	4	53	108	0	31	.270	.395	.377	105	10	6-8	**.969**	21	114	97	S146		4.3
1927	Bos A	8	18	0	2	1	0	0	0	1	0	2	.111	.158	.167	-16	-1	0	1.000	-1	62	190	3b4/S		-0.4
	Was A	45	132	20	36	5	4	0	13	22	1	10	.273	.381	.371	97	0	0-0	.929	-2	93	123	S32,3b6		0.1
	Year	53	150	20	38	6	4	0	13	23	1	12	.253	.356	.347	84	-3	1-2	.932	-3	91	123	S33,3b10		-0.3
Total 6		694	2326	324	669	113	39	13	315	377	5	176	.288	.388	.387	104	30	44-36	.953	-8	103	90	S660,3b14		8.4

RIGNEY, BILL William Joseph "Specs","The Cricket" B1.29.1918 Alameda CA D2.20.2001 Walnut Creek CA BR/TR/6-1/178(165-178) d4.16 M18/C1

1946	NY N	110	360	38	85	9	1	3	31	36	1	29	.236	.307	.292	70	-14	9	.965	3	107	76	3b73,S33		-1.1
1947	NY N	130	531	84	142	24	3	17	59	51	5	54	.267	.337	.420	99	-1	7	.974	4	112	84	2b72,3b41,S24		0.7
1948	NY N★	113	424	72	112	17	3	10	43	47	3	54	.264	.342	.389	97	-2	4	.967	-7	99	80	2b105,S7		-0.3
1949	NY N	122	389	53	108	19	6	4	47	47	0	38	.278	.356	.404	103	2	3	.928	-11	95	80	S81,2b26,3b14		-0.3
1950	NY N	56	83	8	15	2	0	4	8	8	0	13	.181	.253	.205	22	-9	0	.966	3	107	130	2b23,3b11		-0.6
1951	†NY N	44	69	9	16	2	1	2	7	9	1	7	.232	.321	.435	100	0	0-1	.953	3	115	193	3b12,2b9		0.2
1952	NY N	60	90	13	27	5	1	1	14	11	2	6	.300	.388	.411	121	1	2-3	.889	-3	83	220	3b10,2b9,S4/1		0.2
1953	NY N	19	20	2	5	1	0	1	0	0	0	5	.250	.250	.250	30	-1	0-0	1.000	-0	52	0	3b2/2		-0.2
Total 8		654	1966	281	510	78	14	41	212	208	12	206	.259	.334	.376	91	-23	25-4	.971	-7	106	84	2b245,3b163,S149/1		-1.4

RIKARD, CULLEY Culley B5.9.1914 Oxford MS D2.25.2000 Memphis TN BL/TR/5-11/183 d9.20 Mil 1943-45

1941	Pit N	6	20	1	4	1	0	0	1	0	0	38	.200	.238	.250	38	1	1	1.000	1	129	0	O5(3/3/0)		-0.1
1942	Pit N	38	52	6	10	2	0	0	5	7	0	8	.192	.288	.269	62	-2	0	.958	-1	107	0	O16(2/14/0)		-0.3
1947	Pit N	109	324	57	93	16	4	4	32	50	1	39	.287	.384	.398	105	4	1	.978	-3	103	33	O79(5/28/45)		-0.1
Total 3		153	396	64	107	19	4	4	37	58	1	48	.270	.365	.374	97	4	1	.978	-3	105	28	O100(10/45/45)		-0.5

RILES, ERNEST Ernest B10.2.1960 Cairo GA BL/TR/6-1/180* [MilA81*S3/63] d5.14 Col Middle Georgia JC OF(2/0/3)

1985	Mil A	116	448	54	128	12	7	5	45	36-0	2	54	.286	.339	.377	97	-3	2-2	.957	-16	94	83	S115/D		-0.7
1986	Mil A	145	524	69	132	24	2	9	47	54-0	1	80	.252	.321	.357	92	-12	7-7	.964	-32	82	86	S142		-3.0
1987	Mil A	83	276	38	72	11	1	4	38	30-1	1	47	.261	.329	.351	80	-7	3-4	.935	-8	88	96	3b65,S21	83	-1.4

YEAR	TM LG	G	AB	R	H	2B	3B	HR	RBI	BB-IB	HP	SO	AVG	OBP	SLG	AOPS	ABR	SB-CS	FA	FR	RNG	THR	GAMES AT POSITION	DL	BFW
1988	Mil A	41	127	7	32	6	1	1	9	7-0	0	26	.252	.291	.339	75	-4	2-2	.958	-1	96	51	3b28,S9,D5		-0.6
	SF N	79	187	26	55	7	2	3	28	10-2	0	33	.294	.323	.401	114	2	1-2	.975	10	142	116	3b30,2b17,S16		1.3
1989	†SF N	122	302	43	84	13	2	7	40	28-3	2	50	.278	.339	.404	116	6	0-6	.962	-2	91	136	3b83,2b18,S7,O5(2/0/3)		0.2
1990	SF N	92	155	22	31	2	1	8	21	26-3	0	26	.200	.313	.381	92	1	0-0	.986	2	129	106	S26,2b24,3b10		0.1
1991	Oak A	108	281	30	60	8	4	5	32	31-3	1	42	.214	.290	.324	75	-10	3-2	.939	0	97	126	3b69,S20,2b7,1b5		-1.0
1992	Hou N	39	61	5	16	1	0	1	4	2-0	0	11	.262	.281	.328	76	-2	1-0	1.000	1	77	134	S6,3b5,1b4,2b2		-0.4
1993	Bos N	94	143	15	27	8	0	5	20	20-3	2	40	.189	.292	.350	69	-6	1-3	1.000	1	119	99	2b20,D15,3b11/1		-0.6
Total	9	919	2504	309	637	92	20	48	284	244-15	9	409	.254	.319	.365	89	-38	20-28	.964	-49	90	91	S362,3b301,2b88,D21,1b10,O5R	83	-6.1

RILEY, JIM James Joseph B11.10.1886 Buffalo NY D3.25.1949 Buffalo NY BR/TR/6-0/165 d8.2

YEAR	TM LG	G	AB	R	H	2B	3B	HR	RBI	BB-IB	HP	SO	AVG	OBP	SLG	AOPS	ABR	SB-CS	FA	FR	RNG	THR	GAMES AT POSITION	DL	BFW
1910	Bos N	1	1	0	0	0	0	0	0	1	0	1	.000	.500	.000	46	0	0	.600	-0	116	0	/OL		0.0

RILEY, JIM James Norman B5.25.1895 Bayfield NB, Can. D5.25.1969 Seguin TX BL/TR/5-10.5/185 d7.3

1921	StL A	4	11	0	0	0	0	0	1	0-0	0	3	.000	.083	.000	-73	-3	0-0	.818	-2	63	0	2b4		-0.5
1923	Was A	2	3	1	0	0	0	0	2	0-0	0	0	.000	.400	.000	12	0	0-0	.882	-1	0	191	1b2		-0.1
Total	2	6	14	1	0	0	0	0	3	0-0	0	3	.000	.176	.000	-50	-3	0-0	.818	-3	63	0	2b4,1b2		-0.6

RILEY, LEE Leon Francis B8.20.1906 Princeton NE D9.13.1970 Schenectady NY BL/TR/6-1/185 d4.19

| 1944 | Phi N | 4 | 12 | 1 | 1 | 0 | 1 | 0 | 1 | 0 | 0 | 0 | .083 | .083 | .167 | -32 | -2 | 0 | 1.000 | -1 | 50 | 0 | O3L | | -0.3 |

RILEY, BILLY William James "Pigtail Billy" B1855 Cincinnati OH D11.9.1887 Cincinnati OH BR/TR/5-10/160 d5.4

| 1875 | Wes NA | 8 | 33 | 4 | 5 | 0 | 0 | 0 | | 1 | | | .152 | .176 | .182 | 23 | -2 | 0-0 | .667 | -0 | 151 | 0 | O8R | | -0.2 |
| 1879 | Cle N | 43 | 161 | 14 | 23 | 2 | 0 | 0 | 9 | 2 | | 26 | .143 | .153 | .155 | 2 | -17 | | .850 | . 5 | 120 | 82 | O43L | | -1.4 |

RINGO, FRANK Frank C. B10.12.1860 Parkville MO D4.12.1889 Kansas City MO BR/5-11/175 d5.1

1883	Phi N	60	221	24	42	10	1	0	12	6		34	.190	.211	.244	42	-14		.847	-8			C39,O11(3/8/0),S6,3b5,2b2		-1.6
1884	Phi N	26	91	4	12	2	0	0	6	3		19	.132	.160	.154	-1	-10		.783	-14			C26		-2.1
	Phi AA	2	6	0	0	0	0	0		0	0		.000	.000	.000	-94	-1		.762	-1			C2		-0.2
1885	Det N	17	65	12	16	3	0	0	2	0		7	.246	.246	.292	73	-2		.852	3			C8,3b8/OC		-0.1
	Pit AA	3	11	0	2	0	0	0	0	0			.182	.182	.182	15	-1		.941	1			C3		0.1
1886	Pit AA	15	56	3	12	2	2	0	5	1	0		.214	.228	.321	72	-2	0	.934	0	87	190	1b9,C6		-0.2
	KC N	16	56	6	13	7	0	0	7	5		10	.232	.295	.357	92	0	0	.904	-4			C13,O2C/3		-0.3
Total	4	139	506	49	97	24	3	0	32	15		70	.192	.215	.251	46	-30		.844	-25			C97,3b14,O14(3/11/0),1b9,S6,2b2		-4.4

RINKER, BOB Robert John B4.21.1921 Audenried PA D12.19.2002 Hazleton PA BR/TR/6-0/190 d9.6

| 1950 | Phi A | 3 | 3 | 0 | 1 | 0 | 0 | 0 | 0 | | 0 | .333 | .333 | .333 | 72 | 0 | 0-0 | — | 0 | 0 | 0 | /C | | 0.0 |

RIOS, ALEX Alexis Israel B2.18.1981 Coffee Co. AL BR/TR/6-5/195* [TorA99 1/19] d5.27

2004	Tor A	111	426	55	122	24	7	1	28	31-0	2	84	.286	.338	.383	83	-11	15-3	.991	1	96	147	O111(0/3/108)		-1.2
2005	Tor A	146	481	71	126	23	6	10	59	28-1	5	101	.262	.306	.397	82	-13	14-9	.992	0	99	94	O142(0/5/138)/D		-1.9
Total	2	257	907	126	248	47	13	11	87	59-1	7	185	.273	.321	.390	82	-24	29-12	.992	2	98	119	O253(0/8/246)/D		-3.1

RIOS, ARMANDO Armando B9.13.1971 Santurce, PR BL/TL/5-9/185* d9.1 Col Louisiana St.

1998	SF N	12	7	3	4	0	0	2	3	3-0	0	1	.571	.700	1.429	465	4	0-0	1.000	0	167	0	O5(2/1/2)		0.4
1999	SF N	72	150	32	49	9	0	7	29	24-1	1	35	.327	.420	.527	148	12	7-4	.978	4	114	210	O53(14/2/39)	72	1.4
2000	†SF N	115	233	38	62	15	5	10	50	31-4	0	43	.266	.347	.502	120	7	3-2	.959	5	113	161	O93(19/0/76)/1		0.6
2001	SF N	93	316	38	82	17	3	14	49	34-6	3	73	.259	.330	.465	109	3	3-2	.971	7	114	125	O87(13/3/76)		0.6
	Pit N	2	3	0	1	0	0	0	1	2-0	0	1	.333	.500	.333	147	0	0-0	—	-1	0	0	O2R	67	0.6
	Year	95	319	38	83	17	3	14	50	36-6	3	74	.260	.332	.464	110	4	3-2	.971	6	112	123	O89(13/3/78)	77	-1.1
2002	Pit N	76	208	20	55	11	0	1	24	16-1	1	39	.264	.319	.332	74	-9	1-1	1.000	1	92	153	O56(11/0/47)		-1.0
2003	Chi A	49	104	4	22	3	0	2	11	5-0	0	13	.212	.245	.298	41	-9	0-1	.981	-1	92	91	O32(9/23/6),D4	216	1.1
Total	6	419	1021	135	275	55	8	36	167	115-12	2	206	.269	.341	.445	106	8	14-10	.975	15	107	146	O328(68/29/248),D4/1		

RIOS, JUAN Juan Onofre Velez (b Juan Onofre Velez (Rios)) B6.14.1942 Mayaguez, PR D8.28.1995 Mayaguez, PR BR/TR/6-3/185 d4.9

| 1969 | KC A | 87 | 196 | 20 | 44 | 5 | 1 | 1 | 5 | 7-2 | 3 | 19 | .224 | .262 | .276 | 50 | -14 | 1-3 | .967 | -19 | 76 | 77 | 2b46,S32,3b4 | | -3.1 |

RIPKEN, CAL Calvin Edwin Jr. B8.24.1960 Havre de Grace MD BR/TR/6-4/225(200-225) [BalA78 2/48] d8.10 b-Billy

1981	Bal A	23	39	1	5	0	0	0	0	1-0	0	8	.128	.150	.128	-19	-4	0-0	.946	-0	95	96	S12,3b6		-0.6
1982	Bal A	160	598	90	158	32	5	28	93	46-3	3	95	.264	.317	.475	116	11	3-3	.972	-3	99	89	S94,3b71		1.6
1983	†Bal A★	**162**	663	**121**	**211**	47	2	27	102	58-0	0	97	.318	.371	.517	144	40	0-4	.970	16	**105**	118	S162		7.0
1984	Bal A★	**162**	641	103	195	37	7	27	86	71-1	2	89	.304	.374	.510	145	40	2-1	.971	**39**	117	125	S162		9.4
1985	Bal A★	161	642	116	181	32	5	26	110	67-1	1	68	.282	.347	.469	125	22	2-3	.982	10	105	103	S162		4.5
1986	Bal A★	**162**	627	98	177	35	1	25	81	70-5	4	60	.282	.355	.461	122	20	4-2	.973	1	101	100	S161		4.6
1987	Bal A★	**162**	624	97	157	28	3	27	98	81-0	1	77	.252	.333	.436	106	6	3-5	.973	-5	102	104	S162		1.6
1988	Bal A★	161	575	87	152	25	1	23	81	102-7	2	69	.264	.372	.431	129	26	2-2	.973	4	103	109	S161		4.2
1989	Bal A★	**162**	646	80	166	30	0	21	93	57-5	3	72	.257	.317	.401	105	1	3-2	.990	5	107	112	S162		2.1
1990	Bal A★	161	600	78	150	28	4	21	84	82-18	5	66	.250	.341	.415	115	13	3-1	**.996**	-26	93	91	S161		8.5
1991	Bal A★	**162**	650	99	210	46	5	34	114	53-15	5	46	.323	.374	.566	163	54	6-1	**.986**	20	**109**	111	S162		-0.5
1992	Bal A★	**162**	637	73	160	29	1	14	72	64-14	7	50	.251	.323	.366	91	-7	4-3	.984	-10	91	**117**	S162		0.0
1993	Bal A★	**162**	641	87	165	26	3	24	90	65-19	6	58	.257	.329	.420	96	-5	1-4	.977	-5	101	100	S162		0.0
1994	Bal A★	112	444	71	140	19	3	13	75	32-3	4	41	.315	.364	.459	105	3	1-0	**.985**	-12	91	118	S112		0.6
1995	Bal A★	**144**	550	71	144	33	2	17	88	52-6	2	59	.262	.324	.422	92	-7	0-1	.989	3	97	118	S144		1.3
1996	†Bal A★	163	640	94	178	40	1	26	102	59-3	2	78	.278	.341	.466	102	2	1-2	.980	2	101	104	S158,3b6		-0.2
1997	†Bal A★	**162**	615	79	166	30	0	17	84	56-3	5	73	.270	.331	.402	94	-5	1-1	.949	0	97	95	3b161		-1.0
1998	Bal A★	161	601	65	163	27	1	14	61	51-0	4	68	.271	.331	.389	88	-11	0-2	**.979**	-0	97	95	3b161		-1.5
1999	Bal A★	86	332	51	113	27	0	18	57	13-3	3	31	.340	.368	.584	143	21	0-1	.932	-5	100	85	3b85	56	1.5
2000	Bal A*	83	309	43	79	16	0	15	56	23-0	2	37	.256	.310	.453	96	-3	0-0	.974	-7	107	131	3b73,D10	64	0.3
2001	Bal A	128	477	43	114	16	0	14	68	26-1	2	63	.239	.276	.361	71	-22	0-2	.956	4	102	119	3b111,D14		-1.8
Total	21	3001	11551	1647	3184	603	44	431	1695	1129-107	66	1305	.276	.340	.447	112	195	36-39	.979	54	102	109	S2302,3b675,D24	120	43.3

RIPKEN, BILLY William Oliver B12.16.1964 Havre de Grace MD BR/TR/6-1/186(178-190) [BalA82 11/286] d7.11 b-Cal

1987	Bal A	58	234	27	72	9	0	2	20	21-0	1	23	.308	.363	.372	98	0	4-1	.990	2	97	138	2b58		0.6
1988	Bal A	150	512	52	106	18	1	2	34	33-0	5	63	.207	.260	.258	47	-37	8-2	.984	-0	101	108	2b149,3b2/D	26	-3.3
1989	Bal A	115	318	31	76	11	2	2	26	22-0	1	53	.239	.284	.305	69	-14	1-2	.985	7	106	118	2b114/D	15	-0.1
1990	Bal A	129	406	48	118	28	1	3	38	28-2	1	43	.291	.342	.387	106	4	5-2	.987	8	98	104	2b127	31	-1.9
1991	Bal A	104	287	24	62	11	1	0	14	15-0	1	31	.216	.253	.261	45	-22	0-1	.986	1	100	117	2b103		-1.5
1992	Bal A	111	330	35	76	15	0	4	36	18-1	3	26	.230	.275	.312	63	-17	2-3	.993	0	102	99	2b108,D2	87	-1.0
1993	Tex A	50	132	12	25	4	0	0	11	11-0	1	19	.189	.270	.220	35	-12	0-2	.992	1	92	84	2b34,S18/3	42	-0.1
1994	Tex A	32	81	9	25	5	0	0		3-0	0	11	.309	.333	.370	80	-2	2-0	.970	1	95	113	3b18,2b12,S2/1		-0.1
1995	Cle A	8	17	4	7	0	0	2	3	0-0	1	3	.412	.412	.765	194	2	0-0	1.000	-3	50	42	2b7/3		-0.1
1996	Bal A	57	135	19	31	8	0	2	12	9-0	1	18	.230	.281	.333	55	-9	0-0	.968	1	105	113	2b30,3b25/1	34	-0.5
1997	Tex A	71	203	18	56	9	1	3	24	9-0	1	32	.276	.300	.374	72	-9	0-1	.971	1	93	92	S31,2b25,3b13,1b9	54	-0.6
1998	Det A	27	74	8	20	3	0	0	5	5-0	1	10	.270	.321	.311	66	-4	3-2	.926	-3	100	95	S21,1b2,2b2,3b2/D		-0.6
Total	12	912	2729	287	674	121	6	20	229	174-3	18	332	.247	.294	.318	69	-120	25-16	.987	-1	101	110	2b769,S72,3b62,1b13,D5	289	-9.6

RIPPLE, JIMMY James Albert B10.14.1909 Export PA D7.16.1959 Greensburg PA BL/TR/5-10/170 d4.20

1936	†NY N	96	311	42	95	17	2	7	47	28	1	15	.305	.365	.441	117	8	1	.980	-5	89	86	O76(0/75/1)		0.0
1937	†NY N	121	426	70	135	23	3	5	66	29	1	20	.317	.362	.420	110	6	3	.980	-9	86	63	O111(0/54/57)		-0.7
1938	NY N	134	501	68	131	21	4	3	60	49	5	21	.261	.333	.375	94	-2	2	.976	-4	90	112	O131(0/17/115)		-1.6
1939	NY N	66	123	10	28	4	0	1	12	8	1	7	.228	.286	.285	53	-8	0	1.000	-1	86	130	O23(9/4/10)		0.1
	Bro N	28	106	18	35	8	4	0	22	11	1	8	.330	.398	.481	131	5	0	1.000	-2	95	0	O28(12/1/15)		-0.9
	Year	94	229	28	63	12	4	1	34	19	2	15	.275	.339	.376	90	-3	0	1.000	-3	91	54	O51(21/5/25)		-0.1
1940	Bro N	7	13	0	3	0	0	0	1	1	0	2	.231	.333	.231	55	-1	0	1.000	0	135	0	O3(1/0/2)		-0.1
	†Cin N	32	101	15	31	10	0	2	20	13	0	5	.307	.397	.525	151	8	1	1.000	-3	85	0	O30(27/0/3)		0.3
	Year	39	114	15	34	10	0	2	20	15	0	7	.298	.389	.491	139	7	1	1.000	-1	88	60	O25(7/0/18)		-0.7
1941	Cin N	38	102	10	22	6	1	0	9	9		9	.216	.279	.324	69	-4	0	1.000	-3	99	76	O25(10/0/15)		-0.7

YEAR	TM	LG	G	AB	R	H	2B	3B	HR	RBI	BB-IB	HP	SO	AVG	OBP	SLG	AOPS	ABR	SB-CS	FA	FR	RNG	THR	GAMES AT POSITION	DL	BFW
1943	Phi	A	32	126	8	30	3	1	0	15	7	1	7	.238	.284	.278	65	-6	0-0	1.000	-2	92	0	O31(10/0/21)		-1.1
Total	7		554	1809	241	510	92	14	28	251	156	13	89	.282	.343	.395	101	4	7-0	.984	-27	89	72	O458(66/151/242)		-4.7

RISBERG, SWEDE   Charles August B10.13.1894 San Francisco CA D10.13.1975 Red Bluff CA   BR/TR/6-0/175   d4.11   Mil 1918

1917	†Chi	A	149	474	59	96	20	8	1	45	59	5	65	.203	.297	.285	76	-13	16	.913	-40	80	97	S146		-4.8
1918	Chi	A	82	273	36	70	12	3	1	27	23	3	32	.256	.321	.333	96	-1	5	.944	-7	93	122	S30,3b24,2b12,1b7,O3R		-0.7
1919	†Chi	A	119	414	48	106	19	6	2	38	35	2	38	.256	.317	.345	86	-8	19	.934	-12	95	119	S97,1b22		-1.5
1920	Chi	A	126	458	53	122	10	2	1	65	31	2	45	.266	.316	.369	81	-14	12-10	.934	-7	99	**127**	S124		-1.3
Total	4		476	1619	196	394	72	27	6	175	148	12	180	.243	.311	.332	83	-36	52-10	.928	-66	91	114	S397,1b29,3b24,2b12,O3R		-8.3

RISING, POP   Percival Sumner B1.2.1872 Industry PA D1.28.1938 Rochester PA   TR   d8.10

1905	Bos	A	11	29	2	3	1	1	0	2	2	0		.103	.161	.207	16	-3	0	1.000	0	152	0	O6R/3		-0.3

RITCHEY, CLAUDE   Claude Cassius "Little All Right" B10.5.1873 Emlenton PA D11.8.1951 Emlenton PA   BB/TR/5-6.5/167   d4.22

1897	Cin	N	101	337	58	95	12	4	0	41	42	5		.282	.370	.341	83	-7	11	.897	-11	92	87	S70,O22(10/1/11),2b8		-1.4
1898	Lou	N	151	551	65	140	10	4	5	51	46	9		.254	.322	.314	84	-12	19	.919	-16	87	95	S80,2b71		-1.9
1899	Lou	N	148	540	66	162	16	7	4	73	49	10		.300	.369	.378	105	-4	21	.938	-8	97	108	2b138,S11		0.3
1900	†Pit	N	123	476	62	139	17	8	1	67	29	5		.292	.339	.368	94	-4	18	.952	6	100	113	2b123		0.7
1901	Pit	N	**140**	540	66	160	20	4	1	74	47	5		.296	.358	.354	104	4	15	.941	4	99	**127**	2b139/S		0.9
1902	Pit	N	115	405	54	112	13	1	2	55	53	7		.277	.370	.328	112	9	10	**.966**	6	100	128	2b114/OR		1.7
1903	†Pit	N	138	506	60	145	28	10	0	59	55	3		.287	.360	.381	108	6	15	**.961**	17	115	106	2b137		2.3
1904	Pit	N	**156**	544	79	143	22	12	0	51	59	3		.263	.338	.347	109	7	12	.958	1	101	106	2b156,S2		1.0
1905	Pit	N	153	533	54	136	29	6	0	52	51	3		.255	.324	.332	93	-3	12	**.961**	-6	101	125	2b153,S2		-0.8
1906	Pit	N	152	484	46	130	21	5	1	62	68	9		.269	.369	.339	116	13	6	**.966**	-1	98	**130**	2b151		1.4
1907	Bos	N	144	499	45	127	17	4	2	51	50	5		.255	.329	.317	103	3	8	**.971**	13	109	106	2b144		1.9
1908	Bos	N	121	421	44	115	10	3	2	36	50	8		.273	.361	.325	121	13	7	.967	13	109	129	2b120		3.1
1909	Bos	N	30	87	4	15	1	0	0	3	8	0		.172	.242	.184	31	-7	1	.959	0	84	118	2b25		-0.8
Total	13		1672	5923	709	1619	216	68	18	675	607	72		.273	.348	.342	101	27	155	.957	18	101	116	2b1479,S166,O23(10/1/12)		8.4

RITTER, CHARLIE   Charles J.   d9.21

1885	Buf	N	2	6	1	0	0	0	0	0	0		2	.167	.167	.167	8	-1		.813	-0	82	105	2b2		-0.1

RITTER, FLOYD   Floyd Alexander B6.1.1870 Dorset OH D2.7.1943 Stevenson WA   BR/TR/5-8/155   d6.4

1890	Tol	AA	1	3	0	0	0	0	0	0	0		0	.000	.000	.000	-97	-1	0	.778	-0	120	207	/C		-0.1

RITTER, LEW   Lewis Elmer "Old Dog" B9.7.1875 Liverpool PA D5.27.1952 Harrisburg PA   BR/TR/5-9/150   d9.10

1902	Bro	N	16	57	5	12	1	0	0	2	1	1		.211	.237	.228	43	-4	2	.973	0	87	87	C16		-0.2
1903	Bro	N	78	259	26	61	9	6	0	37	19	1		.236	.290	.317	75	-9	9	.940	-22	67	88	C74,O2(1/1/0)		-2.3
1904	Bro	N	72	214	23	53	4	1	0	19	20	2		.248	.318	.276	86	-3	17	.966	7	99	107	C57,2b5/3		1.0
1905	Bro	N	92	311	32	68	10	5	1	28	15	0		.219	.255	.293	68	-14	16	.951	-15	75	98	C84,O4(0/1/3),3b2		-2.1
1906	Bro	N	73	226	22	47	5	0	0	15	16	1		.208	.263	.239	61	-11	6	.978	-5	91	93	C53,O9(5/0/5),1b3,3b2		-1.3
1907	Bro	N	93	271	15	55	6	1	0	17	18	1		.203	.255	.232	57	-14	5	.969	-6	88	91	C89		-1.2
1908	Bro	N	38	99	6	19	2	1	0	2	7	0		.192	.245	.232	55	-5	0	.961	-3	81	100	C37		-0.6
Total	7		462	1437	129	315	33	17	1	120	96	6		.219	.271	.268	67	-60	55	.960	-43	83	95	C410,O15(6/2/8),3b5,2b5,1b3		-6.7

RITTERSON, WHITEY   Edward West B4.26.1855 Philadelphia PA D7.28.1917 Sellersville PA   BR/TR/5-8/?   d5.2

1876	Phi	N	16	52	8	13	3	0	0	4	0		2	.250	.250	.308	86	-1		.671	-6			C14,O4(0/2/2)/3		-0.6

RITZ, JIM   James L. B1874 Pittsburgh PA D11.10.1896 Pittsburgh PA   5-8/160   d7.20

1894	Pit	N	1	4	1	0	0	0	0	0	0		0	.000	.200	.000	-49	-1	1	.750	-0	85	537	/3		-0.1

RIVAS, LUIS   Luis Wilfredo B8.30.1979 LaGuaira, Venez   BR/TR/5-10/175(175-190)   d9.16

2000	Min	A	16	58	8	18	4	1	0	6	2-0	0	4	.310	.323	.414	82	-2	2-0	.983	-3	75	86	2b14,S2		-0.3
2001	Min	A	153	563	70	150	21	6	7	47	40-0	6	99	.266	.319	.362	81	-20	31-11	.974	-52	81	72	2b150		-6.1
2002	†Min	A	93	316	46	81	23	4	4	35	19-2	3	51	.256	.305	.392	81	-9	9-4	.986	-29	79	92	2b93		-3.2
2003	†Min	A	135	475	69	123	16	9	8	43	30-0	5	65	.259	.308	.381	78	-16	17-7	.982	-31	87	80	2b134/D	61	-3.2
2004	†Min	A	109	336	44	86	19	5	10	34	13-0	1	53	.256	.283	.432	81	-11	15-1	.994	16	114	**126**	2b109	20	-3.9
2005	Min	A	59	136	21	35	3	1	1	12	9-0	2	17	.257	.311	.316	66	-7	4-0	.995	-6	94	106	2b53,S6	16	1.2
Total	6		565	1884	258	493	86	26	30	177	113-2	17	289	.262	.307	.383	78	-65	78-23	.984	-105	89	91	2b553,S8/D	97	-13.2

RIVERA, CARLOS   Carlos Alberto B6.10.1978 Fajardo, PR   BL/TL/5-11/230*   [PitN96 10/276]   d6.22

2003	Pit	N	78	95	12	21	5	0	3	10	8-2	1	28	.221	.283	.368	69	-5	0-0	.984	-1	91	109	1b60		-0.8
2004	Pit	N	7	15	1	3	0	0	0	1	1-1	0	3	.200	.250	.200	18	-2	0-0	1.000	0	69	158	1b7		-0.3
Total	2		85	110	13	24	5	0	3	11	9-3	1	31	.218	.279	.345	62	-7	0-0	.986	-2	87	117	1b67		-1.1

RIVERA, GERMAN   German (Diaz) B7.6.1960 Santurce, PR   BR/TR/6-2/195(170-195)   d9.2

1983	LA	N	13	17	1	6	1	0	0	2	0-0	0	2	.353	.421	.412	132	1	0-1	.929	1	130	0	3b8		0.1
1984	LA	N	94	227	20	59	12	2	2	17	21-5	1	30	.260	.321	.357	92	-2	0-0	.937	10	113	102	3b90		0.7
1985	Hou	N	13	36	3	7	2	1	0	2	4-1	0	8	.194	.275	.306	64	-2	0-0	.941	3	140	195	3b11		0.1
Total	3		120	280	24	72	15	3	2	19	27-6	1	40	.257	.322	.354	91	-3	1-1	.937	13	117	107	3b109		0.9

RIVERA, BOMBO   Jesus Manuel (Torres) B8.2.1952 Ponce, PR   BR/TR/5-10/187(170-195)   d4.17

1975	Mon	N	5	9	1	1	0	0	0	0	2-0	0	3	.111	.273	.111	9	-1	0-0	.889	-0	121	0	O5(4/0/2)		-0.1
1976	Mon	N	68	185	22	51	11	4	2	19	13-1	0	32	.276	.323	.411	102	0	1-0	.950	3	99	215	O56(44/0/15)		0.1
1978	Min	A	101	251	35	68	8	2	3	23	35-1	2	47	.271	.362	.355	100	1	5-3	.982	2	108	95	O94(32/0/72)/D		0.0
1979	Min	A	112	263	37	74	13	5	2	31	17-0	2	40	.281	.324	.392	88	-5	5-5	.989	9	114	222	O105(61/1/50),D2		0.1
1980	Min	A	44	113	13	25	7	0	3	10	4-0	1	20	.221	.248	.363	61	-6	6-0	.922	-2	98	45	O37(10/0/28)/D	76	-1.0
1982	KC	A	5	10	1	1	0	0	0	0	0-0	0	2	.100	.100	.100	-45	-2	0-0	1.000	-0	78	0	O3(2/0/1)		-0.3
Total	6		335	831	109	220	39	11	10	83	71-2	2	144	.265	.323	.374	89	-13	11-8	.970	13	107	151	O300(153/1/168),D4	76	-1.2

RIVERA, JUAN   Juan Luis B7.3.1978 Guarenas, Venez   BR/TR/6-2/170(170-205)   d9.4

2001	NY	A	3	4	0	0	0	0	0	0	0-0	0	0	.000	.000	.000	-99	-1	0-0	1.000	-0	37	0	O3(0/1/2)		-0.2
2002	†NY	A	28	83	9	22	5	0	1	6	6-0	0	10	.265	.311	.361	80	-2	1-1	.966	1	102	125	O28(15/0/15)	72	-0.3
2003	†NY	A	57	173	22	46	14	0	7	26	10-1	0	27	.266	.304	.468	101	0	0-0	.979	-1	97	108	O56(34/0/22)		-0.2
2004	Mon	N	134	391	48	120	24	1	12	49	34-7	1	45	.307	.364	.465	108	5	6-2	.986	4	95	**222**	O121(10/13/104)/D		0.5
2005	†LA	A	106	350	46	95	17	1	15	59	23-0	0	44	.271	.316	.454	103	1	1-9	.992	5	97	166	O282(92/18/181),D29	72	-0.7
Total	5		328	1001	125	283	60	2	35	140	73-8	1	126	.282	.331	.452	102	3	8-12	.984	5	97	166	O282(92/18/181),D29	72	-0.7

RIVERA, LUIS   Luis Antonio (Pedraza) B1.3.1964 Cidra, PR   BR/TR/5-9/170*   d8.3

1986	Mon	N	55	166	20	34	11	1	0	13	17-0	2	33	.205	.285	.283	58	-9	1-1	.953	-10	87	90	S55		-1.5
1987	Mon	N	18	32	0	5	2	0	0	1	1-0	0	8	.156	.182	.219	5	-4	0-0	.923	-0	109	86	S15		-0.4
1988	Mon	N	123	371	35	83	17	3	4	30	24-4	1	69	.224	.271	.318	66	-17	3-4	.962	-1	99	**128**	S116		-1.2
1989	Bos	A	93	323	35	83	17	1	5	29	20-1	1	81	.257	.301	.362	81	-8	2-3	.958	-8	92	104	S90/2D		-1.0
1990	†Bos	A	118	346	38	78	20	0	7	45	25-0	1	58	.225	.279	.344	70	-14	4-3	.965	5	101	97	S112,2b3/3		-0.1
1991	Bos	A	129	414	64	107	22	3	8	40	35-0	3	86	.258	.318	.384	89	-6	4-4	.959	7	102	113	S121,2b6		1.0
1992	Bos	A	102	288	17	62	11	1	0	29	26-0	1	56	.215	.287	.260	51	-19	4-3	.966	13	112	105	S93/23OLD		0.0
1993	Bos	A	62	130	13	27	8	1	1	7	11-0	1	36	.208	.273	.308	53	-9	1-2	.969	-4	102	108	2b27,S27,3b2,D7	42	-1.1
1994	NY	N	32	43	11	12	2	1	3	5	4-0	1	14	.279	.367	.581	144	3	0-1	.971	4	124	192	S11,2b5		0.6
1997	Hou	N	7	13	2	3	0	1	0	3	1-0	0	6	.231	.286	.385	76	-1	0-0	.875	-1	70	182	S6/2		-0.2
1998	KC	A	42	89	14	22	4	0	0	7	7-0	0	17	.247	.302	.292	53	-6	1-1	.961	4	115	126	S30,2b6,3b6		-0.1
Total	11		781	2215	249	516	114	12	28	209	171-5	14	443	.233	.291	.333	70	-90	20-22	.961	7	100	110	S684,2b44,3b10,D10/OL	42	-4.0

RIVERA, JIM   Manuel Joseph "Jungle Jim" B7.22.1922 New York NY   BL/TL/6-0/196*   d4.15

1952	StL	A	97	336	45	86	13	6	4	30	29	2	59	.256	.319	.366	88	-6	8-7	.976	6	112	103	O88(8/81/0)		-0.4
	Chi	A	53	201	27	50	7	3	3	18	21	0	27	.249	.320	.358	88	-4	13-2	.988	-1	102	67	O53C		-0.4
	Year		150	537	72	136	20	9	7	48	50	2	86	.253	.319	.363	88	-10	21-9	.980	5	108	81	O141(8/134/0)		-0.8
1953	Chi	A	**156**	567	79	147	26	**16**	11	78	53	6	70	.259	.329	.420	98	-4	22-15	.976	-8	90	110	O156(0/153/3)		-2.0
1954	Chi	A	145	490	64	140	16	8	13	61	49	6	68	.286	.354	.431	111	7	18-10	.959	-9	94	49	O143(3/28/128)		-0.7

YEAR	TM LG	G	AB	R	H	2B	3B	HR	RBI	BB-IB	HP	SO	AVG	OBP	SLG	AOPS	ABR	SB-CS	FA	FR	RNG	THR	GAMES AT POSITION	DL	BFW
1955	Chi A	147	454	71	120	24	4	10	52	62-6	1	59	.264	.352	.401	100	1	**25**-16	.981	.11	102	230	O143(2/50/115)		0.7
1956	Chi A	139	491	76	125	23	5	12	66	49-2	3	75	.255	.322	.395	88	-9	20-9	.976	2	104	96	O134(0/14/122)		-1.0
1957	Chi A	125	402	51	103	21	6	14	52	40-6	3	80	.256	.342	.443	108	4	18-2	.974	-4	100	105	O86(1/4/83),1b31		-0.2
1958	Chi A	116	276	37	62	8	4	9	35	24-5	1	49	.225	.282	.380	84	-7	21-3	.994	2	100	124	O99(54/1/45)		-0.5
1959	†Chi A	80	177	18	39	9	4	4	19	11-3	1	19	.220	.266	.384	78	-6	5-3	.976	0	88	186	O69(21/0/48)		-0.8
1960	Chi A	48	17	17	5	0	0	1	1	3-0	0	3	.294	.400	.471	136	1	4-0	1.000	-0	109	0	O24(9/1/14)		0.1
1961	Chi A	1	0	0	0	0	0	0	0	0-0	0	0	—	—	—	—	0	0-1	—	0			/H	44	0.0
	KC A	64	141	20	34	8	0	2	10	24-0	0	14	.241	.352	.340	84	-2	6-2	.981	-6	71	0	O43(0/7/36)		-1.0
	Year	65	141	20	34	8	0	2	10	24-0	0	14	.241	.352	.340	84	-2	6-3	.981	-6	71	0	O43(0/7/36)		-1.0
Total	10	1171	3552	503	911	155	56	83	422	365-22	23	523	.256	.328	.402	96	-25	160-70	.977	-7	98	111	O1038(98/392/594),1b31	44	-6.2

RIVERA, MIKE Michael R. B9.8.1976 Rio Piedras, PR BR/TR/6-0/190* d9.18 Col Troy St.

YEAR	TM LG	G	AB	R	H	2B	3B	HR	RBI	BB-IB	HP	SO	AVG	OBP	SLG	AOPS	ABR	SB-CS	FA	FR	RNG	THR	GAMES AT POSITION	DL	BFW
2001	Det A	4	12	2	4	2	0	0	1	0-0	0	2	.333	.333	.500	118	0	0-0	.929	1	70	347	C4		0.2
2002	Det A	39	132	11	30	8	1	1	11	4-0	1	35	.227	.254	.326	55	-9	0-0	.990	1	95	138	C37/D		-0.6
2003	SD N	19	53	2	9	1	0	1	2	5-0	0	11	.170	.241	.245	30	-6	0-0	.986	2	79	85	C19/1		-0.6
Total	3	62	197	15	43	11	1	2	14	9-0	1	48	.218	.255	.315	52	-15	0-0	.984	5	89	134	C60/1D		-0.6

RIVERA, RENE Rene B7.31.1983 Bayamon, PR BR/TR/5-10/190* [SeaA01 2/49] d9.22

YEAR	TM LG	G	AB	R	H	2B	3B	HR	RBI	BB-IB	HP	SO	AVG	OBP	SLG	AOPS	ABR	SB-CS	FA	FR	RNG	THR	GAMES AT POSITION	DL	BFW
2004	Sea A	2	1	0	0	0	0	0	0	0-0	0	1	.000	.000	.000	-99	-1	0-0	1.000	0	0	0	C2		-0.1
2005	Sea A	16	48	3	19	3	0	1	6	1-0	0	11	.396	.408	.521	155	4	0-0	.961	-1	164	72	C15		0.3
Total	2	18	51	3	19	3	0	1	6	1-0	0	12	.373	.385	.490	139	3	0-0	.962	-1	160	70	C17		0.2

RIVERA, RUBEN Ruben (Moreno) B11.14.1973 Chorrera, Pan BR/TR/6-3/200* d9.3 [DL 1997 NY A 59]

YEAR	TM LG	G	AB	R	H	2B	3B	HR	RBI	BB-IB	HP	SO	AVG	OBP	SLG	AOPS	ABR	SB-CS	FA	FR	RNG	THR	GAMES AT POSITION	DL	BFW
1995	NY A	5	1	0	0	0	0	0	0	0-0	0	1	.000	.000	.000	-99	0	0-0	1.000	0	174	0	O4L		0.0
1996	†NY A	46	88	17	25	6	1	2	16	13-0	2	26	.284	.381	.443	110	2	6-2	1.000	4	125	112	O45(13/14/19)		0.5
1997	SD N	17	20	2	5	1	0	0	1	2-0	0	9	.250	.318	.300	67	-1	2-1	1.000	1	140	0	O7(2/4/4)	75	0.0
1998	†SD N	95	172	31	36	7	2	6	29	28-0	2	52	.209	.325	.378	91	-2	5-1	.973	-0	100	86	O91(13/13/73)		-0.4
1999	SD N	147	411	65	80	16	1	23	46	55-1	5	143	.195	.295	.406	82	-14	18-7	.976	5	111	128	O143C		-0.6
2000	SD N	135	423	62	88	18	6	17	57	44-1	10	137	.208	.296	.400	79	-16	8-4	.984	1	102	97	O132(1/131/0)	22	-1.3
2001	Cin N	117	263	37	67	13	1	10	34	21-1	5	83	.255	.321	.426	86	-6	6-3	.983	1	107	97	O99(10/70/21)		-0.4
2002	Tex A	69	158	17	33	4	0	4	14	17-0	1	45	.209	.302	.310	63	-8	4-2	.983	4	120	71	O67C,D2		-0.3
2003	SF N	31	62	6	9	2	0	2	4	5-1	0	14	.180	.255	.340	52	-4	1-0	1.000	2	151	0	O27(9/13/6)		-0.1
Total	9	662	1586	237	343	67	11	64	203	185-4	29	510	.216	.307	.393	81	-49	50-20	.982	18	110	108	O615(52/455/123),D2	156	-2.6

RIVERS, MICKEY John Milton B10.31.1948 Miami FL BL/TL/5-10/165* [AtlN69 S2/40] d8.4 Mil 1971 Col Miami-Dade North (FL) CC

YEAR	TM LG	G	AB	R	H	2B	3B	HR	RBI	BB-IB	HP	SO	AVG	OBP	SLG	AOPS	ABR	SB-CS	FA	FR	RNG	THR	GAMES AT POSITION	DL	BFW
1970	Cal A	17	25	6	8	2	0	3	3	3-0	1	5	.320	.414	.400	129	1	1-0	1.000	0	107	0	O5R		0.1
1971	Cal A	79	268	31	71	12	2	1	12	19-1	1	38	.265	.316	.336	91	-4	13-1	.976	-2	94	110	O76(4/61/18)		-0.5
1972	Cal A	58	159	18	34	6	2	0	7	8-1	1	26	.214	.256	.277	62	-8	4-3	.981	1	116	0	O48(6/38/7)		-1.0
1973	Cal A	30	129	26	45	6	4	0	16	8-0	1	11	.349	.391	.457	149	8	8-3	.909	-6	81	0	O29C		0.2
1974	Cal A	118	466	69	133	19	**11**	3	31	39-0	1	47	.285	.341	.393	117	9	30-13	.994	3	106	115	O116C	43	1.2
1975	Cal A	155	616	70	175	17	**13**	1	53	43-5	2	42	.284	.331	.359	102	6	**70**-14	.977	1	100	125	O152(27/125/0)/D		0.6
1976	†NY A★	137	590	95	184	31	8	8	67	13-0	5	51	.312	.327	.432	123	13	43-7	.986	-1	104	57	O136C		1.6
1977	†NY A	138	565	79	184	18	5	12	69	18-4	4	45	.326	.350	.439	114	9	22-14	.982	7	110	118	O136C/D		1.4
1978	†NY A	141	559	78	148	25	8	11	48	29-3	3	51	.265	.302	.397	98	-4	25-5	.980	4	108	96	O138C	15	0.3
1979	NY A	74	286	37	82	18	5	3	25	13-2	1	21	.287	.315	.416	98	-1	3-7	.974	-7	82	92	O69C/D	20	-1.1
	Tex A	58	247	35	74	9	3	6	25	9-0	1	18	.300	.323	.433	104	0	7-2	.981	1	102	109	O57C		-1.0
	Year	132	533	72	156	27	8	9	50	22-2	2	39	.293	.319	.424	101	-1	10-9	.978	0	94	**208**	O141C,D4		1.7
1980	Tex A	147	630	96	210	32	6	7	60	20-1	1	34	.333	.353	.411	119	14	18-7	.978	-8	91	100	O97C		0.1
1981	Tex A	99	399	62	114	21	2	3	26	24-2	1	31	.286	.327	.371	106	3	9-5	.996	-1	88	**207**	O97C		-0.5
1982	Tex A	19	68	6	16	1	1	1	4	0-0	0	7	.235	.232	.324	54	-5	0-0	—	0	0	0	D16	146	-0.9
1983	Tex A	96	309	37	88	17	0	1	20	11-0	1	21	.285	.309	.350	82	-8	9-4	.980	0	110	62	D53,O23(15/0/8)		-0.7
1984	Tex A	102	313	40	94	13	1	4	33	9-1	0	23	.300	.320	.387	91	-4	5-5	1.000	1	92	177	D48,O30(26/2/2)		0.1
Total	15	1468	5629	785	1660	247	71	61	499	266-20	29	510	.295	.327	.397	106	23	267-90	.982	3	100	117	O1253(78/1145/40),D124	224	2.6

RIZZO, JOHNNY John Costa B7.30.1912 Houston TX D12.4.1977 Houston TX BR/TR/6-0/190 d4.19 Mil 1943-46

YEAR	TM LG	G	AB	R	H	2B	3B	HR	RBI	BB-IB	HP	SO	AVG	OBP	SLG	AOPS	ABR	SB-CS	FA	FR	RNG	THR	GAMES AT POSITION	DL	BFW
1938	Pit N	143	555	97	167	31	9	23	111	54	5	61	.301	.368	.514	139	29	1	.951	-11	90	43	O140L		0.9
1939	Pit N	94	330	49	86	23	3	6	55	42	3	27	.261	.349	.403	103	3	0	.974	-3	99	36	O86L		-0.6
1940	Pit N	9	28	1	5	1	0	0	2	5	1	5	.179	.324	.214	51	-2	0	.818	-2	65	0	O7L		-0.4
	Cin N	31	110	17	31	6	0	4	17	14	0	14	.282	.363	.445	121	3	1	.974	4	99	260	O30L		0.5
	Phi N	103	367	53	107	12	2	20	53	37	1	31	.292	.358	.499	130	18	2	.968	5	104	88	O91(56/23/15),3b7		1.9
	Year	143	505	71	143	19	2	24	72	56	2	50	.283	.357	.471	130	20	3	.964	7	101	126	O128(93/23/15),3b7		2.0
1941	Phi N	99	235	20	51	9	2	4	24	24	2	34	.217	.295	.323	77	-8	1	.968	2	103	170	O70(9/0/62)		-0.9
1942	Bro N	78	217	31	50	8	0	4	27	24	0	25	.230	.307	.323	83	-5	2	.977	2	108	118	O70(9/0/62)		-0.6
Total	5	557	1842	268	497	90	16	61	289	200	12	197	.270	.345	.435	116	38	7	.964	-3	98	89	O486(331/31/130),3b9		0.8

RIZZUTO, PHIL Philip Francis "Scooter" (b Fiero Francis Rizzuto) B9.25.1917 Brooklyn NY BR/TR/5-6/160* d4.14 Mil 1943-45 HF1994

YEAR	TM LG	G	AB	R	H	2B	3B	HR	RBI	BB-IB	HP	SO	AVG	OBP	SLG	AOPS	ABR	SB-CS	FA	FR	RNG	THR	GAMES AT POSITION	DL	BFW
1941	†NY A	133	515	65	158	20	9	3	46	27	1	36	.307	.343	.398	97	-5	14-5	.957	19	**108**	141	S128		2.4
1942	†NY A☆	144	553	79	157	24	7	4	68	44	6	40	.284	.343	.374	104	2	22-6	.962	**30**	108	149	S144		4.6
1946	NY A	126	471	53	121	17	1	2	38	34	6	39	.257	.315	.310	74	-16	14-7	.961	17	104	**129**	S125		0.9
1947	NY A	153	549	78	150	26	9	2	60	57	**8**	31	.273	.350	.364	100	0	11-6	.969	18	99	111	S151		2.8
1948	NY A	128	464	65	117	13	2	6	50	60	2	24	.252	.340	.328	79	-14	6-5	.973	-13	87	95	S128		-1.8
1949	†NY A	153	614	110	169	22	7	5	65	72	1	34	.275	.352	.358	88	-11	18-6	**.971**	3	94	101	S152		0.3
1950	†NY A★	**155**	617	125	200	36	7	7	66	92	7	39	.324	.418	.439	123	26	12-8	**.982**	8	95	108	S155		**4.0**
1951	†NY A★	144	540	87	148	21	6	2	43	58	5	27	.274	.350	.346	92	-4	17-6	.968	11	97	**116**	S144		1.7
1952	†NY A★	152	578	89	147	24	10	2	43	67	5	42	.254	.337	.341	95	-4	18-10	.976	21	**105**	127	S152		2.9
1953	†NY A★	134	413	54	112	21	3	2	54	71	4	39	.271	.383	.351	103	6	4-3	.963	3	103	127	S133		1.9
1954	NY A	127	307	47	60	11	0	2	15	41	1	23	.195	.291	.251	51	-20	3-2	.968	6	98	**137**	S126/2		-0.6
1955	†NY A	81	143	19	37	4	1	1	9	22-1	3	18	.259	.369	.322	88	-1	7-1	.957	-8	84	97	S79/2		-0.4
1956	NY A	31	52	6	12	0	0	0	6	6-0	0	5	.231	.310	.231	46	-4	3-0	.934	2	106	156	S30		0.0
Total	13	1661	5816	877	1588	239	62	38	563	651-1	49	398	.273	.351	.355	93	-46	149-58	.968	117	99	121	S1647,2b2		18.7

ROACH, MEL Melvin Earl B1.25.1933 Richmond VA BR/TR/6-1/190* d7.31 Mil 1955-56 Col Virginia

YEAR	TM LG	G	AB	R	H	2B	3B	HR	RBI	BB-IB	HP	SO	AVG	OBP	SLG	AOPS	ABR	SB-CS	FA	FR	RNG	THR	GAMES AT POSITION	DL	BFW
1953	Mil N	5	2	1	0	0	0	0	0	0-0	0	1	.000	.000	.000	-99	-1	0-0	—	-0	0	0	/2		-0.1
1954	Mil N	3	4	0	0	0	0	0	0	0-0	0	0	.000	.000	.000	-99	-1	0-0	1.000	-0	0	511	/1		-0.1
1957	Mil N	7	6	1	1	0	0	0	0	0-0	0	3	.167	.167	.167	-11	-1	0-0	1.000	-0	86	0	2b5		-0.1
1958	Mil N	44	136	14	42	7	0	3	10	6-0	0	15	.309	.336	.426	110	2	0-0	.993	1	109	76	2b27,O7(4/0/3)/1	52	0.4
1959	Mil N	19	31	1	3	0	0	0	0	2-0	0	9	.097	.152	.097	-35	-6	0-0	.880	-0	117	76	2b8,O4L/3	96	-0.6
1960	Mil N	48	140	12	42	12	0	3	18	6-1	1	19	.300	.329	.450	121	4	0-0	.975	-8	111	0	O21L,2b20/13		-0.4
1961	Mil N	13	36	3	6	1	0	1	6	2-0	2	4	.167	.244	.250	35	-3	1-0	1.000	-2	76	0	1b7,2b7		-1.0
	Chi N	23	39	1	5	2	0	0	1	3-0	0	9	.128	.190	.179	-1	-6	1-0	.981	-6	76	0	O9L,1b9,2b7		-1.6
	Year	36	75	4	11	3	0	1	7	5-0	2	13	.147	.217	.213	16	-9	1-0	1.000	-6	78	178	O9L,1b9,2b4,O3L		-1.3
1962	Phi N	65	105	9	20	4	0	0	8	5-0	0	19	.190	.225	.229	23	-11	0-0	.951	-2	98	77	3b26,2b9,1b4,O3L		-1.3
Total	8	227	499	42	119	25	0	7	43	24-1	0	75	.238	.275	.331	66	-23	1-0	.969	-15	94	66	2b77,O44(41/0/3),3b28,1b16	148	-3.8

ROACH, MIKE Michael Stephen B12.23.1869 Driftwood PA D11.12.1916 New York NY BR/TR/5-7/145 d8.10 b-John

YEAR	TM LG	G	AB	R	H	2B	3B	HR	RBI	BB-IB	HP	SO	AVG	OBP	SLG	AOPS	ABR	SB-CS	FA	FR	RNG	THR	GAMES AT POSITION	DL	BFW
1899	Was N	24	78	7	17	3	0	1	6	2-0	1	—	.218	.265	.231	37	-7	3	.964	-4	76	73	C20,1b3		-0.9

ROACH, ROXEY Wilbur Charles B11.28.1882 Anita PA D12.26.1947 Bay City MI BR/TR/5-11/160 d5.2

YEAR	TM LG	G	AB	R	H	2B	3B	HR	RBI	BB-IB	HP	SO	AVG	OBP	SLG	AOPS	ABR	SB-CS	FA	FR	RNG	THR	GAMES AT POSITION	DL	BFW
1910	NY A	70	220	27	47	9	4	0	20	29	0	—	.214	.313	.273	79	-4	15	.913	-4	96	139	S58,O9L		-0.7
1911	NY A	13	40	4	10	2	0	2	6	6	0	—	.250	.348	.350	89	0	0	.891	-2	86	179	S2,2b5		-0.1
1912	Was A	2	2	1	1	0	0	1	1	0	0	—	.500	.500	2.000	600	1	0	.500	-1	71	0	S2		-0.1
1915	Buf F	92	346	35	93	20	3	2	31	17	—	34	.269	.303	.361	85	-13	11	.959	17	108	104	S92		
Total	4	177	608	67	151	31	6	7	58	52	—	34	.248	.311	.334	85	11	26	.938	11	102	120	S160,O9L,2b5		

ROARKE, MIKE Michael Thomas B11.8.1930 West Warwick RI BR/TR/6-2/195* d4.19 C20 Col Boston College

YEAR	TM LG	G	AB	R	H	2B	3B	HR	RBI	BB-IB	HP	SO	AVG	OBP	SLG	AOPS	ABR	SB-CS	FA	FR	RNG	THR	GAMES AT POSITION	DL	BFW
1961	Det A	86	229	21	51	6	1	2	22	20-3	1	31	.223	.283	.284	51	-16	0-0	.988	1	132	104	C85		-1.?
1962	Det A	56	136	11	29	4	1	4	14	13-2	1	17	.213	.287	.346	67	-7	0-0	.982	3	87	143	C53		

YEAR	TM LG	G	AB	R	H	2B	3B	HR	RBI	BB-IB	HP	SO	AVG	OBP	SLG	AOPS	ABR	SB-CS	FA	FR	RNG	THR	GAMES AT POSITION	DL	BFW
1963	Det A	23	44	5	14	0	0	0	1	2-1	1	3	.318	.362	.318	89	-1	0-0	.986	0	116	117	C16		0.0
1964	Det A	29	82	4	19	1	0	0	7	10-0	0	10	.232	.315	.244	57	-4	0-0	.994	1	269	82	C27		-0.2
Total	4	194	491	41	113	11	2	6	44	45-6	2	61	.230	.296	.297	60	-28	0-0	.987	5	141	112	C181		-1.6

ROAT, FRED Frederick R. B11.10.1867 Oregon IL D9.24.1913 Oregon IL TR d5.10

1890	Pit N	57	215	18	48	0	2	0	17	16	3	22	.223	.286	.260	67	-8	7	.847	4	119	103	3b44,1b9,O4R		-0.4
1892	Chi N	8	31	4	6	1	0	2	2	2	0	3	.194	.242	.258	51	-2	2	.897	-3	97	32	2b8		-0.4
Total	2	65	246	22	54	1	2	2	19	18	3	25	.220	.281	.260	65	-10	9	.847	1	119	103	3b44,1b9,2b8,O4R		-0.8

ROBELLO, TONY Thomas Vardasco B2.9.1913 San Leandro CA D12.25.1994 Fort Worth TX BR/TR/5-10.5/175 d8.13

1933	Cin N	14	30	1	7	3	0	0	3	1	0	5	.233	.258	.333	69	-1		1.000	1	121	88	2b11,3b2		0.0
1934	Cin N	2	2	0	0	0	0	0	0	0	0	1	.000	.000	.000	-99	-1	0	—	0			/H		-0.1
Total	2	16	32	1	7	3	0	0	3	1	0	6	.219	.242	.313	58	-2	0	1.000	1	121	88	2b11,3b2		-0.1

ROBERGE, SKIPPY Joseph Albert Armand B5.19.1917 Lowell MA D6.7.1993 Lowell MA BR/TR/5-11/185 d7.18 Mil 1943-45

1941	Bos N	55	167	12	36	6	0	0	15	9	0	18	.216	.256	.251	45	-13	0	.978	4	111	123	2b46,3b5,S2		-0.6
1942	Bos N	74	172	10	37	7	0	1	12	9	1	19	.215	.258	.273	57	-10	1	.977	5	103	96	2b29,3b27,S6		-0.2
1946	Bos N	48	169	13	39	6	2	2	20	7	2	12	.231	.270	.325	68	-8	1	.973	2	95	174	3b48		-0.7
Total	3	177	508	35	112	19	2	3	47	25	3	49	.220	.261	.283	57	-31	2	.967	12	105	154	3b80,2b75,S8		-1.5

ROBERSON, KEVIN Kevin Lynn B1.29.1968 Decatur IL BB/TR/6-4/210* [ChiN88 16/404] d7.15 Col Parkland (IL) JC

1993	Chi N	62	180	23	34	4	0	9	27	12-0	3	48	.189	.251	.372	65	-10	0-1	.963	-5	83	56	O51(14/0/42)		-1.8
1994	Chi N	44	55	8	12	4	0	4	9	2-0	3	14	.218	.271	.509	97	-1	0-0	.800	-1	65	242	O9R		-0.1
1995	Chi N	32	38	5	7	1	0	4	6	6-0	1	14	.184	.311	.526	116	-1	0-1	1.000	-1	78	0	O11(10/0/1)	38	-0.1
1996	NY N	27	36	3	8	1	0	3	9	7-0	0	17	.222	.348	.500	131	2	0-0	1.000	-1	93	0	O10(1/0/9)		0.1
Total	4	165	309	44	61	10	1	20	51	27-0	7	93	.197	.275	.430	85	-8	0-2	.955	-6	82	61	O81(25/0/61)	38	-1.9

ROBERTS, BRIAN Brian Michael B10.9.1977 Durham NC BB/TR/5-9/170* [BalA99 1/50] d6.14 Col South Carolina-Aiken

2001	Bal A	75	273	42	69	12	3	2	17	13-0	0	36	.253	.284	.341	68	-14	12-3	.939	-4	102	84	S51,2b12,D7		-1.1
2002	Bal A	38	128	18	29	6	0	1	11	15-0	1	21	.227	.308	.297	67	-6	9-2	.976	1	105	117	2b25,D8		-0.3
2003	Bal A	112	460	65	124	22	4	5	41	46-1	1	58	.270	.337	.367	86	-9	23-6	.987	4	103	94	2b107,S2,D4		0.4
2004	Bal A	159	641	107	175	**50**	4	4	53	71-1	1	95	.273	.344	.376	89	-8	29-12	.988	-13	99	88	2b150,D6		-1.1
2005	Bal A★	143	561	92	176	45	7	18	73	67-5	3	83	.314	.387	.515	137	32	27-10	.988	9	105	97	2b141		4.8
Total	5	527	2063	324	573	135	16	30	195	212-7	6	293	.278	.344	.402	98	-5	100-33	.986	-3	102	94	2b435,S53,D25		2.7

ROBERTS, RED Charles Emory B8.8.1918 Carrollton GA D12.2.1998 Atlanta GA BR/TR/6-0/170 d9.3 Mil 1944-45

1943	Was A	9	23	1	6	1	0	1	3	4	0	2	.261	.370	.435	140	-4	0-0	.778	-4	59	39	S6/3		-0.2

ROBERTS, SKIPPER Clarence Ashley B1.11.1888 Wardner ID D12.24.1963 Long Beach CA BL/TR/5-10.5/175 d6.12

1913	StL N	26	41	6	6	2	0	0	3	3	0	13	.146	.205	.195	15	-5	1-2	.859	-3	84	53	C16		-0.8
1914	Pit F	33	55	7	12	1	1	0	4	1	1	11	.218	.246	.291	46	-5	2	.941	-1	107	77	C14		-0.6
	Chi F	4	3	0	1	0	0	0	1	1	0	1	.333	.500	.333	138	0	0	—	0			/H		0.0
	Pit F	19	39	5	10	2	1	1	4	1	1	8	.256	.293	.436	98	-1	1	.923	-2	107	77	C9/OR		-0.3
	Year	56	97	12	23	4	2	1	9	3	2	20	.237	.275	.351	70	-6	3	.935	-4	102	87	C23/OR		-0.9
Total	2	82	138	16	29	6	2	1	12	6	2	33	.210	.253	.304	54	-11	4-2	.906	-7	95	75	C39/OR		-1.7

ROBERTS, CURT Curtis Benjamin B8.16.1929 Pineland TX D11.14.1969 Oakland CA BR/TR/5-8/165* d4.13 Negro Lg 1947-50

1954	Pit N	134	496	47	115	18	7	1	36	55	2	49	.232	.309	.302	62	-28	6-3	.969	5	105	77	2b131		-1.3
1955	Pit N	6	17	1	2	1	0	0	0	2-0	0	1	.118	.211	.176	4	-2	0-0	.913	-0	112	120	2b6		-0.2
1956	Pit N	31	62	6	11	5	2	0	4	5-0	0	12	.177	.239	.323	50	-5	1-0	.988	-0	95	108	2b27		-0.4
Total	3	171	575	54	128	24	9	1	40	62-0	2	62	.223	.299	.301	59	-35	7-3	.969	4	104	82	2b164		-1.9

ROBERTS, DAVE David Leonard B6.30.1933 Panama City, Pan BL/TL/6-0/172* d9.5

1962	Hou N	16	53	3	13	3	0	1	10	8-0	1	8	.245	.349	.358	99	0	0-0	1.000	-0	115	0	O12(6/0/6),1b6		-0.1
1964	Hou N	61	125	9	23	4	1	1	7	14-1	1	28	.184	.270	.256	52	-8	0-1	.983	3	138	89	1b34,O4L		-0.7
1966	Pit N	14	16	3	2	1	0	0	0	0-0	0	7	.125	.125	.188	-15	-2	0-0	.950	0	168	126	1b2		-0.3
Total	3	91	194	15	38	8	1	2	17	22-1	2	43	.196	.282	.278	60	-10	0-1	.983	3	130	86	1b42,O16(10/0/6)		-1.1

ROBERTS, DAVE David Ray B5.31.1972 Okinawa, Japan BL/TL/5-10/175* [DetA94 28/781] d8.7 Col UCLA

1999	†Cle A	41	143	26	34	4	0	2	12	9-0	0	16	.238	.281	.308	48	-12	11-3	1.000	-1	105	0	O39(1/38/0)		-1.0
2000	Cle A	19	10	1	2	0	0	0	0	2-0	0	2	.200	.333	.200	38	-1	1-1	1.000	0	86	0	O17(12/5/1)		-0.1
2001	Cle A	15	12	3	4	1	0	0	2	1-0	0	2	.333	.385	.417	107	0	0-1	1.000	-0	102	0	O13(9/2/2),D2		-0.1
2002	LA N	127	422	63	117	14	4	3	34	48-0	2	51	.277	.353	.365	99	-3	45-10	**1.000**	-3	99	68	O117(3/115/0)	83	0.2
2003	LA N	107	388	56	97	6	5	2	16	43-1	4	39	.250	.331	.307	70	-17	40-14	.976	-1	96	78	O105C	39	-1.9
2004	LA N	68	233	45	59	4	7	2	21	28-0	4	31	.253	.340	.366	82	-6	33-1	.976	-1	104	63	O62(48/19/0)	23	-0.1
	†Bos A	45	86	19	22	10	0	2	14	10-0	1	17	.256	.330	.442	96	0	5-2	.982	0	103	73	O38(18/16/14)/D		0.0
2005	†SD N	115	411	65	113	19	10	8	38	53-3	1	59	.275	.356	.428	111	6	23-12	.992	-4	97	76	O109C	15	0.5
Total	7	537	1705	278	448	58	29	19	137	194-4	12	217	.263	.340	.364	88	-33	158-44	.989	-14	98	65	O500(91/409/17),D3	160	-2.4

ROBERTS, DAVE David Wayne B2.17.1951 Lebanon OR BR/TR/6-3/215(200-215) [SDN72 1/1] d6.7 C1 Col Oregon OF(3/6/0)

1972	SD N	100	418	38	102	17	0	5	33	18-1	0	64	.244	.275	.321	74	-16	7-2	.931	-13	97	130	3b84,2b20,S3/C		-3.0
1973	SD N	127	479	56	137	20	3	21	64	17-3	1	83	.286	.310	.472	124	11	11-2	.942	7	106	111	3b111,2b12		2.0
1974	SD N	113	318	26	53	10	1	5	18	32-6	2	69	.167	.246	.252	42	-26	2-0	.955	-8	88	72	3b103,S3/OL		-3.5
1975	SD N	33	113	7	32	2	0	2	12	13-3	2	19	.283	.367	.354	108	2	3-1	.925	-4	102	98	3b30,2b5		-0.2
1977	SD N	82	186	15	41	14	1	1	23	11-1	1	32	.220	.268	.323	64	-10	2-1	.982	-8	104	104	C63,2b2,3b2/S		-1.6
1978	SD N	54	97	7	21	4	1	1	12	12-6	1	25	.216	.309	.309	79	-3	0-0	.980	-3	122	87	C41,1b8,O2(1/1/0)		-0.5
1979	Tex A	44	84	12	22	2	1	3	14	7-0	0	17	.262	.319	.417	97	-1	1-0	.980	-3	112	107	C14,O11(1/5/5),2b8,1b6/3D	14	0.1
1980	Tex A	101	235	27	56	4	0	10	30	13-2	1	38	.238	.280	.383	82	-7	0-1	.930	-8	76	31	3b37,S33,C22,O5R,1b4,2b4	21	-1.4
1981	†Hou N	27	54	4	13	3	0	1	5	3-0	0	6	.241	.271	.352	83	-1	1-0	.958	-0	135	101	1b10,3b7,2b3/C		-0.2
1982	Phi N	28	33	2	6	1	0	0	1	4-0	0	5	.182	.289	.212	23	-3	0-1	.818	-2	102	0	3b11,C10,2b7		-0.6
Total	10	709	2017	194	483	77	7	49	208	128-22	8	361	.239	.286	.357	83	-54	27-8	.939	-36	97	97	3b386,C152,2b61,S40,1b28,O19R,D4	35	-8.9

ROBERTS, BIP Leon Joseph B10.27.1963 Berkeley CA BB/TR/5-7/165* [PitN82 S1/13] d4.7 Col Chabot (CA) JC OF(382/72/25)

1986	SD N	101	241	34	61	5	2	1	12	14-1	0	29	.253	.293	.303	66	-12	14-12	.971	-5	90	82	2b87	15	-1.3
1988	SD N	5	9	1	3	0	0	0	0	1-0	0	2	.333	.400	.333	115	0	0-2	.500	-1	33	0	3b2/2		-0.1
1989	SD N	117	329	81	99	15	8	3	25	49-0	1	45	.301	.391	.422	133	16	21-11	.976	5	104	147	O54(34/1/21),3b37,S14,2b9		2.3
1990	SD N	149	556	104	172	36	3	9	44	55-1	6	65	.309	.375	.433	121	18	46-12	.982	5	108	153	O75L,3b56,S18,2b8		2.9
1991	SD N	117	424	66	119	13	3	3	32	37-0	4	71	.281	.342	.347	92	-4	26-11	.978	-1	100	109	2b68,O46(19/29/0)		0.2
1992	Cin N★	147	532	92	172	34	6	4	45	62-4	2	54	.323	.393	.432	131	24	44-16	.993	-3	96	33	O79(69/16/0),2b42,3b36	23	-0.2
1993	Cin N	83	292	46	70	13	0	1	18	38-1	3	46	.240	.330	.295	69	-11	26-6	.984	1	96	30	2b64,O11(11/1/0),3b3/S	76	-0.4
1994	SD N	105	403	52	129	15	5	2	31	39-1	3	57	.320	.383	.397	108	9	21-7	.976	-12	86	82	2b90,O20(16/5/0)		-0.1
1995	SD N	73	296	40	90	14	0	2	25	17-1	2	36	.304	.346	.372	92	-3	20-2	.989	6	128	85	O50(48/4/0),2b25,S7	54	0.6
1996	KC A	90	339	39	96	21	2	2	52	25-8	2	25	.283	.331	.357	75	-12	12-9	.986	6	117	114	2b63,D16,O11(8/2/1)	64	-0.5
1997	KC A	97	346	44	107	17	2	1	36	21-2	1	53	.309	.348	.379	88	-6	15-3	.981	-2	101	108	O84(82/2/0),3b10	25	-0.8
	†Cle A	23	85	19	23	3	0	3	8	7-0	1	14	.271	.333	.412	92	-1	3-0	.932	1	100	129	2b13,O10L		0.1
	Year	120	431	63	130	20	2	4	44	28-2	3	67	.302	.345	.385	88	-7	18-3					2b13,D29,O24(10/12/3),3b3		-0.7
1998	Det A	34	113	17	28	6	0	0	9	16-0	2	14	.248	.351	.301	71	-4	6-1	1.000	-0	33	0	D29,O2L/2	36	-0.4
	Oak A	61	182	28	51	11	0	1	15	15-0	2	24	.280	.340	.357	79	-8	10-3	.970	-4	89	123	2b30,O22(8/12/3),3b3		-0.6
	Year	95	295	45	79	17	0	1	24	31-0	4	38	.268	.344	.336	79	-8	16-4	.971	-4	90	139	2b31,D29,O24(10/12/3),3b3		-1.0
Total	12	1202	4147	663	1220	203	31	30	352	396-19	30	548	.294	.358	.380	99	6	264-95	.977	-1	98	95	2b501,O464L,3b147,D45,S40	293	4.1

ROBERTS, LEON Leon Kauffman B1.22.1951 Vicksburg MI BR/TR/6-3/200* [DetA72 10/236] d9.3 C2 Col Michigan

1974	Det A	17	63	5	17	1	0	3	7	3-1	0	10	.270	.303	.381	92	-1	0-2	.926	-3	76	0	O17(0/1/16)		-0.6
1975	Det A	129	447	51	115	17	5	10	38	36-1	4	94	.257	.316	.385	94	-5	3-7	.982	5	112	97	O127R/D		-0.9
1976	Hou N	87	235	31	68	11	2	7	33	19-1	3	43	.289	.347	.443	135	10	1-0	.980	-4	89	25	O60(49/0/12)		0.4
1977	Hou N	19	27	1	2	0	0	0	1	1-0	0	8	.074	.107	.074	-55	-4	0-0	1.000	0	48	491	O9(4/0/6)		-0.7
1978	Sea A	134	472	78	142	21	7	22	92	41-2	2	52	.301	.364	.515	145	27	6-3	.975	6	112	105	O128R,D2		2.8
1979	Sea A	140	450	61	122	24	6	15	54	56-6	2	64	.271	.352	.451	113	9	3-3	.983	5	114	65	O136(67/0/69)/D		0.7

YEAR	TM LG	G	AB	R	H	2B	3B	HR	RBI	BB-IB	HP	SO	AVG	OBP	SLG	AOPS	ABR	SB-CS	FA	FR	RNG	THR	GAMES AT POSITION	DL	BFW
1980	Sea A	119	374	48	94	18	3	10	33	43-1	1	59	.251	.325	.396	96	-2	8-4	.984	3	111	81	O104(20/20/70),D4		-0.
1981	Tex A	72	233	26	65	17	2	4	31	25-2	1	38	.279	.345	.421	128	9	3-4	.992	-5	91	41	O71(25/3/46)		0.
1982	Tex A	31	73	7	17	3	0	1	6	4-1	1	14	.233	.278	.315	67	-3	0-0	1.000	-2	95	0	O28(11/2/17)/D		-0.
	Tor A	40	105	6	24	4	0	1	5	7-0	0	16	.229	.274	.295	53	-7	1-1	1.000	-2	74	0	O44(27/2/17),D22		-1.
	Year	71	178	13	41	7	0	2	11	11-1	1	30	.230	.276	.303	58	-10	1-1	1.000	-4	86	0	O76(41/3/35)/D		-0.
1983	KC A	84	213	24	55	7	0	8	24	17-1	1	27	.258	.313	.404	96	-2	1-1	.979	-2	107	63	O76(41/3/35)/D		-0.
1984	KC A	29	45	4	10	1	1	0	3	4-0	1	3	.222	.300	.289	63	-2	0-0	1.000	-0	107	0	O16(10/0/7)/PD	16	-0.
Total	11	901	2737	342	731	126	28	78	328	256-16	22	428	.267	.332	.419	108	27	26-25	.982	4	105	72	O788(243/29/533),D34/P	16	-0.

ROBERTSON, JIM   Alfred James B1.29.1928 Chicago IL   BR/TR/5-9/183*   d4.15   Col Bradley

YEAR	TM LG	G	AB	R	H	2B	3B	HR	RBI	BB-IB	HP	SO	AVG	OBP	SLG	AOPS	ABR	SB-CS	FA	FR	RNG	THR	GAMES AT POSITION	DL	BFW
1954	Phi N	63	147	9	27	8	0	0	8	23	0	25	.184	.298	.238	48	-10	0-0	.974	-3	94	68	C50		-1.
1955	KC A	6	8	1	2	0	0	0	0	1-0	0	2	.250	.333	.250	58	-0	0-0	1.000	0	0	251	C4		0.
Total	2	69	155	10	29	8	0	0	8	24-0	0	27	.187	.300	.239	49	-10	0-0	.975	-3	90	76	C54		-1.

ROBERTSON, ANDRE   Andre Levett B10.2.1957 Orange TX   BR/TR/5-10/160*   [TorA79 4/81]   d9.3   Col Texas

YEAR	TM LG	G	AB	R	H	2B	3B	HR	RBI	BB-IB	HP	SO	AVG	OBP	SLG	AOPS	ABR	SB-CS	FA	FR	RNG	THR	GAMES AT POSITION	DL	BFW
1981	†NY A	10	19	1	5	1	0	0	0	0-0	0	3	.263	.263	.316	67	-1	1-1	1.000	0	98	65	S8,2b3		0
1982	NY A	44	118	16	26	5	0	2	9	8-0	0	19	.220	.270	.314	60	-7	0-0	.966	3	98	153	S27,2b15,3b2		0
1983	NY A	98	322	37	80	16	3	1	22	8-0	3	54	.248	.271	.326	66	-16	2-4	.960	11	115	126	S78,2b29	46	0
1984	NY A	52	140	10	30	5	1	0	6	4-0	0	20	.214	.236	.264	40	-12	0-1	.930	3	105	130	S49,2b6		-0
1985	NY A	50	125	16	41	5	0	2	17	6-0	1	24	.328	.358	.416	115	2	1-2	.867	-6	82	136	S33,S14,2b2	51	-0
Total	5	254	724	80	182	32	4	5	54	26-0	4	120	.251	.279	.327	69	-34	4-8	.953	11	107	131	S176,2b55,3b35	97	-0

ROBERTSON, DARYL   Daryl Berdene B1.5.1936 Cripple Creek CO   BR/TR/6-0/184   d5.4

YEAR	TM LG	G	AB	R	H	2B	3B	HR	RBI	BB-IB	HP	SO	AVG	OBP	SLG	AOPS	ABR	SB-CS	FA	FR	RNG	THR	GAMES AT POSITION	DL	BFW
1962	Chi N	9	19	2	2	0	0	0	2	2-0	0	5	.105	.182	.105	-18	-3	0-0	1.000	-1	98	32	S6/3		-0

ROBERTSON, DAVE   Davis Aydelotte B9.25.1889 Portsmouth VA   D11.5.1970 Virginia Beach VA   BL/TL/6-0/186   d6.5   Def 1918   Col North Carolina St.

YEAR	TM LG	G	AB	R	H	2B	3B	HR	RBI	BB-IB	HP	SO	AVG	OBP	SLG	AOPS	ABR	SB-CS	FA	FR	RNG	THR	GAMES AT POSITION	DL	BFW
1912	NY N	3	2	1	1	0	0	0	1	0	0	1	.500	.500	.500	169	0	1	1.000	0	0	0	/1OL		0
1914	NY N	82	256	25	68	12	3	2	32	10	3	26	.266	.299	.359	99	-2	9	.950	2	97	141	O71(15/0/56)		-0
1915	NY N	141	544	72	160	17	10	3	58	22	4	52	.294	.326	.379	120	10	22-10	.956	-1	102	86	O138(16/0/123)		1
1916	NY N	150	587	88	180	18	8	12	69	14	3	56	.307	.326	.426	137	21	21-17	.960	-1	101	92	O144R		-0
1917	†NY N	142	532	64	138	16	9	12	54	10	2	47	.259	.276	.391	107	0	17	.942	-1	112	66	O140(0/1/140)		-0
1919	NY N	1	0	0	0	0	0	0	0	0	0	0	—	—	—	—	0	0	—	0			/R		-0
	Chi N	27	96	8	20	2	0	1	10	1	1	10	.208	.224	.260	45	-7	3	.932	-3	86	61	O25(1/24/0)		-1
	Year	28	96	8	20	2	0	1	10	1	1	10	.208	.224	.260	45	-7	3	.932	-3	86	61	O25(1/24/0)		-1
1920	Chi N	134	500	68	150	29	11	10	75	40	1	44	.300	.353	.462	130	19	17-23	.968	-11	87	69	O134L		-0
1921	Chi N	22	36	7	8	3	0	0	14	1	0	3	.222	.243	.306	44	-3	0-2	1.000	-1	90	0	O7(1/6/0)		-0
	Pit N	60	230	29	74	18	3	6	48	12	2	16	.322	.361	.504	123	8	4-5	.960	-4	107	26	O58(2/1/55)		-0
	Year	82	266	36	82	21	3	6	62	13	2	19	.308	.345	.477	113	5	4-7	.962	-5	105	24	O65(3/7/55)		-0
1922	NY N	42	47	5	13	2	0	1	3	3	1	8	.277	.320	.383	80	-1	0-0	.909	0	86	193	O8(1/6/1)		-
Total	9	804	2830	366	812	117	44	47	364	113	15	262	.287	.318	.409	117	45	94-57	.955	-18	100	79	O726(171/38/519)/1		-0

ROBERTSON, DON   Donald Alexander B10.15.1930 Harvey IL   BL/TL/5-10/180   d4.13

YEAR	TM LG	G	AB	R	H	2B	3B	HR	RBI	BB-IB	HP	SO	AVG	OBP	SLG	AOPS	ABR	SB-CS	FA	FR	RNG	THR	GAMES AT POSITION	DL	BFW
1954	Chi N	14	6	0	0	0	0	0	0	0	0	2	.000	.000	.000	-99	-2	0-0	1.000	0	152	0	O6R		-0

ROBERTSON, GENE   Eugene Edward B12.25.1898 St.Louis MO   D10.21.1981 Fallon NV   BL/TR/5-7/152   d7.4   Col St.Louis

YEAR	TM LG	G	AB	R	H	2B	3B	HR	RBI	BB-IB	HP	SO	AVG	OBP	SLG	AOPS	ABR	SB-CS	FA	FR	RNG	THR	GAMES AT POSITION	DL	BFW
1919	StL A	5	7	1	1	0	0	0	0	1	0	2	.143	.250	.143	11	-1	0	.750	-1	33	0	S2		-0
1922	StL A	18	27	2	8	2	1	0	1	1	0	1	.296	.321	.444	95	0	1-0	.875	-1	126	0	3b7,S6/2		-2
1923	StL A	78	251	36	62	10	1	0	17	21	2	7	.247	.310	.295	57	-16	4-2	.935	-12	79	50	3b74/2		-2
1924	StL A	121	439	70	140	25	4	4	52	36	2	14	.319	.373	.421	99	-1	3-5	.958	-9	91	122	3b111,2b2		-2
1925	StL A	154	582	97	158	26	5	14	76	81	4	30	.271	.364	.405	90	-8	10-7	.939	-4	94	127	3b154/S		-2
1926	StL A	78	247	23	62	12	6	1	19	17	1	10	.251	.302	.360	69	-12	5-1	.924	-3	102	98	3b55,S10,2b3		-2
1928	†NY A	83	251	29	73	9	0	1	36	14	0	6	.291	.328	.339	78	-8	2-4	.926	-11	83	42	3b70,2b3		-2
1929	NY A	90	309	45	92	15	6	0	35	28	1	6	.298	.358	.385	98	-1	3-3	.966	-10	83	45	3b77		-0
	Bos N	8	28	1	8	0	0	0	6	1	0	3	.286	.310	.286	51	-2	1	.875	-2	67	0	3b6/S		-0
1930	Bos N	21	59	7	11	1	0	0	7	5	0	3	.186	.250	.203	-12	-9	0	.949	-2	83	119	3b17		-
Total	9	656	2200	311	615	100	23	20	249	205	10	79	.280	.344	.373	83	-58	29-22	.941	-52	89	90	3b571,S20,2b10		-

ROBERTSON, MIKE   Michael Francis B10.9.1970 Norwich CT   BL/TL/6-0/180*   [ChiA91 3/98]   d9.6   Col USC

YEAR	TM LG	G	AB	R	H	2B	3B	HR	RBI	BB-IB	HP	SO	AVG	OBP	SLG	AOPS	ABR	SB-CS	FA	FR	RNG	THR	GAMES AT POSITION	DL	BFW
1996	Chi A	6	7	0	1	1	0	0	0	0-0	0	1	.143	.143	.286	5	-1	0-0	1.000	0	118	182	1b2,D2		-0
1997	Phi N	22	38	3	8	2	1	0	4	0-0	3	6	.211	.268	.316	53	-3	1-0	1.000	-1	61	56	1b5,O5(4/0/1)/D		-0
1998	Ari N	11	13	0	2	0	0	0	0	0-0	0	2	.154	.154	.154	-19	-2	0-0	—	0			D2		-0
Total	3	39	58	3	11	3	1	0	4	0-0	3	9	.190	.230	.276	32	-6	1-0	1.000	-1	82	102	1b7,O5(4/0/1),D5		-0

ROBERTSON, BOB   Robert Eugene B10.2.1946 Frostburg MD   BR/TR/6-1/210(195-210)   d9.18

YEAR	TM LG	G	AB	R	H	2B	3B	HR	RBI	BB-IB	HP	SO	AVG	OBP	SLG	AOPS	ABR	SB-CS	FA	FR	RNG	THR	GAMES AT POSITION	DL	BFW
1967	Pit N	9	35	4	6	0	0	2	4	3-0	0	12	.171	.237	.343	64	-2	0-0	.990	-0	90	115	1b9		
1969	Pit N	32	96	7	20	4	1	1	9	8-0	0	30	.208	.267	.302	61	-5	1-0	.996	1	108	97	1b26		
1970	†Pit N	117	390	69	112	19	4	27	82	51-2	2	98	.287	.367	.564	148	26	4-1	.995	2	115	131	1b99,3b5,O3L		
1971	†Pit N	131	469	65	127	18	2	26	72	60-8	4	101	.271	.356	.484	136	22	1-2	.993	8	157	124	1b89,O23L,3b11		
1972	Pit N	115	306	25	59	11	0	12	41	41-2	3	84	.193	.291	.346	83	-7	1-1	.993	4	113	96	1b107		
1973	Pit N	119	397	43	95	16	0	14	40	55-4	1	77	.239	.332	.385	101	7	0-0	.995	4	113	93	1b63		
1974	†Pit N	91	236	25	54	11	0	16	48	33-1	0	48	.229	.320	.479	126	7	0-0	.996	2	129	54	1b27		
1975	†Pit N	75	124	17	34	4	0	6	18	23-0	2	25	.274	.388	.452	134	7	0-0	.991	1	113	116	1b29	19	
1976	Pit N	61	129	10	28	5	1	2	25	16-0	0	23	.217	.299	.318	75	-4	0-1	1.000	-1	74	115	D29,1b18	17	
1978	Sea A	64	174	17	40	5	2	8	28	24-1	1	39	.230	.325	.420	108	2	0-0	1.000	1	168	106	1b9,D4		
1979	Tor A	15	29	1	3	0	0	1	3	3-0	0	9	.103	.188	.207	6	-4	0-0	1.000	1	123	106	1b16	36	
Total	11	829	2385	283	578	93	10	115	368	317-18	13	546	.242	.331	.434	113	43	7-9	.994	32	123	106	1b602,D33,O26L,3b16	36	

ROBERTSON, SHERRY   Sherrard Alexander B1.1.1919 Montreal QC, Can.   D10.23.1970 Houghton SD   BL/TR/6-0/180*   d9.8   Mil 1944-45   C1   Col Maryland-Baltimore Co.

YEAR	TM LG	G	AB	R	H	2B	3B	HR	RBI	BB-IB	HP	SO	AVG	OBP	SLG	AOPS	ABR	SB-CS	FA	FR	RNG	THR	GAMES AT POSITION	DL	BFW
1940	Was A	10	33	4	7	0	1	0	5	0	0	6	.212	.316	.273	58	-2	0-0	.940	1	103	137	S10		
1941	Was A	1	3	0	0	0	0	0	0	0	0	0	.000	.000	.000	-99	-1	0-0	.750	-0	95	0	/3		
1943	Was A	59	120	22	26	4	1	3	14	17	1	19	.217	.319	.342	97	0	3-1	.897	-3	92	23	3b27/S		
1946	Was A	74	230	30	46	6	3	6	19	30	0	42	.200	.292	.330	78	-8	6-2	.902	-7	97	108	3b38,2b14,S12/OR		
1947	Was A	95	266	25	62	9	3	4	23	32	1	52	.233	.318	.301	74	-9	4-5	.949	0	101	131	O51(1/1/49)		
1948	Was A	71	187	19	46	11	3	2	22	24	1	26	.246	.335	.369	90	-3	8-0	.939	-0	106	86	O51(1/1/49)		
1949	Was A	110	374	59	94	17	3	11	42	42	1	63	.251	.329	.401	95	-5	10-3	.947	-6	106	68	2b71,3b19,O13R		
1950	Was A	71	123	19	32	3	2	2	16	22	0	18	.260	.372	.382	98	0	1-1	.952	3	122	125	O22(1/0/21)		
1951	Was A	62	111	14	21	2	1	1	10	9	1	22	.189	.256	.252	38	-10	2-1	.949	2	122	125	O22(1/0/21)		
1952	Was A											0						0-0		0			/R		
	Phi A	43	60	8	12	3	0	2	5	21	0	15	.200	.407	.250	81	-0	1-2	.958	-2	89	56	2b8,O7R,3b2		
	Year	44	60	8	12	3	0	2	5	21	0	15	.200	.407	.250	81	0	1-2	.958	-2	89	56	2b8,O7R,3b2		
Total	10	597	1507	200	346	55	18	26	151	202	5	238	.230	.323	.342	83	-38	32-16	.946	-20	105	107	O163(57/1/105),2b109,3b98,S23		

ROBIDOUX, BILLY JO   William Joseph B1.13.1964 Ware MA   BL/TR/6-1/200*   [MilA82 6/157]   d9.11

YEAR	TM LG	G	AB	R	H	2B	3B	HR	RBI	BB-IB	HP	SO	AVG	OBP	SLG	AOPS	ABR	SB-CS	FA	FR	RNG	THR	GAMES AT POSITION	DL	BFW
1985	Mil A	18	51	5	9	2	0	3	8	12-0	0	16	.176	.333	.392	98	0	0-0	1.000	1	83	182	O11,1b6/D	72	
1986	Mil A	56	181	15	41	8	0	1	21	33-1	0	36	.227	.344	.287	72	-6	0-0	.986	-1	96	102	1b43,D10		
1987	Mil A	23	62	9	12	0	0	0	4	8-1	0	17	.194	.286	.194	30	-6	0-1	.983	-0	91	171	1b10,D10		
1988	Mil A	33	91	9	23	5	0	0	5	8-3	0	14	.253	.307	.308	74	-3	1-1	.983	2	130	102	1b30/D		
1989	Chi A	16	39	2	5	2	0	0	1	4-0	0	9	.128	.209	.179	11	-5	0-0	.990	-1	88	164	1b15/OL	62	
1990	Bos A	27	44	3	8	1	0	1	4	6-1	1	14	.182	.288	.341	73	-1	0-0	.986	0	104	113	1b115,D26,O12L	134	
Total	6	173	468	43	98	21	0	5	43	71-6	1	106	.209	.313	.286	70	-21	1-2	.986	0	104	113	1b115,D26,O12L	134	

ROBINSON, AARON   Aaron Andrew B6.23.1915 Lancaster SC   D3.9.1966 Lancaster SC   BL/TR/6-2/205*   d5.6   Mil 1943-45

YEAR	TM LG	G	AB	R	H	2B	3B	HR	RBI	BB-IB	HP	SO	AVG	OBP	SLG	AOPS	ABR	SB-CS	FA	FR	RNG	THR	GAMES AT POSITION	DL	BFW
1943	NY A	1	1	0	0	0	0	0	0	0	0	1	.000	.000	.000	-99	0	0-0	—	0			/H		
1945	NY A	50	160	19	45	6	1	8	24	21	1	23	.281	.368	.481	139	8	0-1	1.000	-4	74	73	C45		
1946	NY A	100	330	32	98	17	2	16	64	48	0	26	.297	.388	.506	146	21	0-1	.983	-3	112	101	C95		
1947	†NY A☆	82	252	23	68	11	5	5	36	40	0	26	.270	.370	.413	119	7	0-1	.997	-1	86	87	C74		
1948	Chi A	98	326	47	82	14	2	8	39	46	0	30	.252	.344	.380	96	-2	0-1	.989	-5	83	112	C92		

YEAR	TM LG	G	AB	R	H	2B	3B	HR	RBI	BB-IB	HP	SO	AVG	OBP	SLG	AOPS	ABR	SB-CS	FA	FR	RNG	THR	GAMES AT POSITION	DL	BFW
1949	Det A	110	331	38	89	12	0	13	56	73	1	21	.269	.402	.423	118	11	0-2	.986	-3	105	96	C108		1.3
1950	Det A	107	283	37	64	7	0	9	37	75	0	35	.226	.388	.346	86	-3	0-1	.993	-0	140	96	C103		0.2
1951	Det A	36	82	3	17	6	0	0	9	17	0	9	.207	.343	.280	70	-3	0-0	1.000	-2	75	116	C35		-0.3
	Bos A	26	74	9	15	1	1	2	7	17	0	10	.203	.352	.324	76	-2	0-0	.983	-0	116	84	C25		-0.1
	Year	62	156	12	32	7	1	2	16	34	0	19	.205	.347	.301	73	-5	0-0	.991	-2	95	100	C60		-0.4
Total 8		610	1839	208	478	74	11	61	272	337	3	194	.260	.375	.412	112	37	0-6	.990	-17	102	97	C577		4.9

ROBINSON, VAL Alfred Valentine B8.31.1848 Washington DC D8.2.1896 Washington DC d5.1

YEAR	TM LG	G	AB	R	H	2B	3B	HR	RBI	BB-IB	HP	SO	AVG	OBP	SLG	AOPS	ABR	SB-CS	FA	FR	RNG	THR	GAMES AT POSITION	DL	BFW
1872	Oly NA	7	30	6	6	0	0	0	4	1	1		.200	.226	.200	34	-2	0-0	.750	-0	135	0	O7R		-0.1

ROBINSON, BROOKS Brooks Calbert B5.18.1937 Little Rock AR BR/TR/6-1/190* d9.17 C1 HF1983

YEAR	TM LG	G	AB	R	H	2B	3B	HR	RBI	BB-IB	HP	SO	AVG	OBP	SLG	AOPS	ABR	SB-CS	FA	FR	RNG	THR	GAMES AT POSITION	DL	BFW
1955	Bal A	6	22	2	0	0	0	0	1	0-0	0	10	.091	.091	.091	-55	-5	0-0	.833	-1	89	106	3b6		-0.7
1956	Bal A	15	44	5	10	4	0	1	1	1-0	0	5	.227	.244	.386	70	-2	0-0	.944	0	109	131	3b14/2		-0.2
1957	Bal A	50	117	13	28	6	1	2	14	7-0	1	10	.239	.286	.359	81	-4	1-0	.971	1	101	91	3b47		-0.3
1958	Bal A	145	463	31	110	16	3	3	32	31-1	5	51	.238	.292	.305	68	-21	1-0	.953	5	99	**122**	3b140,2b16	58	-1.7
1959	Bal A	88	313	29	89	15	2	4	24	17-5	2	37	.284	.325	.383	96	-2	2-2	.955	5	105	170	3b87/2		0.2
1960	Bal A★	152	595	74	175	27	9	14	88	35-0	0	49	.294	.329	.440	109	5	2-2	**.977**	17	107	110	3b152,2b3		2.1
1961	Bal A★	**163**	668	89	192	38	7	7	61	47-2	4	57	.287	.334	.397	99	-2	2-2	**.972**	-6	94	108	3b163,2b2/S		-0.9
1962	Bal A★	162	634	77	192	29	9	23	86	42-3	1	70	.303	.342	.486	129	23	3-1	.979	8	104	111	3b162,S3,2b2		3.1
1963	Bal A★	161	589	67	148	26	4	11	67	46-4	1	84	.251	.305	.365	91	-8	2-3	.976	7	101	**148**	3b160/S		-0.2
1964	Bal A★	**163**	612	82	194	35	3	28	**118**	51-10	4	57	.317	.368	.521	146	38	1-0	.972	-1	98	**147**	3b160/S		3.8
1965	Bal A★	144	559	81	166	25	2	18	80	47-9	2	47	.297	.351	.445	123	17	3-0	.967	-8	95	129	3b143		0.9
1966	†Bal A★	157	620	91	167	35	2	23	100	56-11	5	36	.269	.333	.444	123	19	2-3	**.976**	1	94	93	3b157		2.0
1967	Bal A★	158	610	88	164	25	5	22	77	54-9	4	54	.269	.328	.434	126	19	1-3	.980	32	**120**	142	3b158		5.3
1968	Bal A★	**162**	608	65	154	36	6	17	75	44-11	4	55	.253	.304	.416	118	12	1-1	.970	19	**107**	115	3b162		3.3
1969	†Bal A★	156	598	73	140	21	3	23	84	56-10	3	55	.234	.298	.395	93	-8	1-2	**.976**	11	104	131	3b156		0.2
1970	†Bal A★	158	608	84	168	31	4	18	94	53-5	4	53	.276	.335	.429	108	6	1-1	.966	-7	93	104	3b156		-0.2
1971	†Bal A★	156	589	67	160	21	1	20	92	63-8	3	50	.272	.341	.413	110	10	0-0	.968	4	103	123	3b156		1.4
1972	Bal A★	153	556	48	139	23	2	8	64	43-4	2	45	.250	.303	.342	89	-8	1-0	**.977**	6	103	104	3b152		-0.2
1973	Bal A★	155	549	53	141	17	2	9	72	55-5	3	50	.257	.326	.344	89	-8	2-0	.970	5	107	98	3b154		-0.3
1974	†Bal A★	153	553	46	159	27	0	7	59	56-13	3	47	.288	.353	.374	113	11	2-0	.967	8	109	**137**	3b153		1.9
1975	Bal A	144	482	50	97	15	1	6	53	44-10	1	33	.201	.267	.274	57	-28	0-0	.979	-3	104	122	3b143		-3.2
1976	Bal A	71	218	16	46	8	2	3	11	8-0	1	24	.211	.240	.307	64	-11	0-0	.969	-3	94	108	3b71		-1.5
1977	Bal A	24	47	3	7	2	0	1	4	4-0	1	9	.149	.212	.255	29	-5	0-0	1.000	9	103	98	3b15		-0.5
Total 23		2896	10654	1232	2848	482	68	268	1357	860-120	53	990	.267	.322	.401	105	48	28-22	.971	100	102	121	3b2870,2b25,S5	58	14.3

ROBINSON, BRUCE Bruce Philip B4.16.1954 LaJolla CA BL/TR/6-1/194* [OakA75 1/21] d8.19 b-Dave Col Stanford [DL 1981 NY A 151]

YEAR	TM LG	G	AB	R	H	2B	3B	HR	RBI	BB-IB	HP	SO	AVG	OBP	SLG	AOPS	ABR	SB-CS	FA	FR	RNG	THR	GAMES AT POSITION	DL	BFW
1978	Oak A	28	84	5	21	3	1	0	8	3-0	0	8	.250	.276	.310	68	-4	0-0	.965	8	94	158	C28		0.5
1979	NY A	6	12	0	2	1	0	0	2	1-0	0	4	.167	.231	.167	9	-2	0-0	.943	1	75	61	C6		0.0
1980	NY A	4	5	0	0	0	0	0	0	0-0	0	4	.000	.000	.000	-99	-1	0-0	1.000	-0	0	0	C3		-0.1
Total 3		38	101	5	23	4	1	0	10	4-0	0	12	.228	.257	.277	51	-7	0-0	.962	9	88	137	C37	151	0.4

ROBINSON, CHARLIE Charles Henry B7.27.1856 Westerly RI D5.18.1913 BL/TR d8.2

YEAR	TM LG	G	AB	R	H	2B	3B	HR	RBI	BB-IB	HP	SO	AVG	OBP	SLG	AOPS	ABR	SB-CS	FA	FR	RNG	THR	GAMES AT POSITION	DL	BFW
1884	Ind AA	20	80	11	23	2	0	0		3	0		.287	.313	.313	108	1		.967	1			C17,S3/OR		0.3
1885	Bro AA	11	40	5	6	2	1	0	4	3	0		.150	.209	.250	44	-2		.840	-3			C11		-0.4
Total 2		31	120	16	29	4	1	0	4	6	0		.242	.278	.292	85	-1		.919	-2			C28,S3/OR		-0.1

ROBINSON, RABBIT Clyde B3.5.1882 Wellsburg WV D4.9.1915 Waterbury CT BR/TR/5-6/148 d4.22

YEAR	TM LG	G	AB	R	H	2B	3B	HR	RBI	BB-IB	HP	SO	AVG	OBP	SLG	AOPS	ABR	SB-CS	FA	FR	RNG	THR	GAMES AT POSITION	DL	BFW
1903	Was A	103	373	41	79	10	8	1	20	33	2		.212	.279	.290	69	-14	16	.917	4	113	112	2b45,O30(0/14/16),S24,3b5		-1.0
1904	Det A	101	320	30	77	13	6	0	37	29	5		.241	.314	.319	103	2	14	.925	2	106	78	S30,3b26,O20(7/0/13),2b19		0.6
1910	Cin N	2	7	0	0	0	0	0	1	1	0	0	.000	.125	.000	-66	-1	0	1.000	-0	78	0	3b2		-0.2
Total 3		206	700	71	156	23	14	1	58	63	7	0	.223	.294	.300	83	-13	30	.940	6	114	108	2b64,S54,O50(7/14/29),3b33		-0.6

ROBINSON, CRAIG Craig George B8.21.1948 Abington PA BR/TR/5-10/165* [PhiN70 11/252] d9.9 Col Wake Forest

YEAR	TM LG	G	AB	R	H	2B	3B	HR	RBI	BB-IB	HP	SO	AVG	OBP	SLG	AOPS	ABR	SB-CS	FA	FR	RNG	THR	GAMES AT POSITION	DL	BFW
1972	Phi N	5	15	0	3	1	0	0	0	1-0	0	2	.200	.250	.267	46	-1	0-0	1.000	2	147	199	S4		0.2
1973	Phi N	46	146	11	33	7	0	0	7	0-0	0	25	.226	.226	.274	37	-13	1-1	.945	-5	89	100	S42,2b4		-1.4
1974	Atl N	145	452	52	104	4	6	0	29	30-4	3	57	.230	.280	.265	52	-30	11-2	.956	-11	95	101	S142		-2.5
1975	Atl N	10	17	1	1	0	0	0	0	0-0	0	5	.059	.059	.059	-65	-4	0-0	1.000	-1	75	61	S7		-0.4
	SF N	29	29	4	2	1	0	0	0	2-0	0	6	.069	.129	.103	-34	-5	0-0	.941	-1	91	122	S12,2b9		-0.6
	Year	39	46	5	3	1	0	0	0	2-0	0	11	.065	.104	.087	-45	-9	0-0	.967	-2	84	95	S19,2b9		-1.0
1976	SF N	15	13	4	4	1	0	0	3	0-0	0	4	.308	.438	.385	131	1	0-1	.952	-0	132	98	2b7,3b2/S		0.0
	Atl N	15	17	4	4	0	0	0	3	5-0	0	2	.235	.391	.235	81	0	0-0	.952	0	107	43	2b5,S2/3		0.0
	Year	30	30	8	8	1	0	0	5	8-0	0	6	.267	.410	.300	103	1	0-1	.952	-0	121	75	2b12,3b3,S3		0.0
1977	Atl N	27	29	4	6	1	0	0	1	1-0	0	6	.207	.233	.242	25	-3	0-0	1.000	0	83	87	S23		0.0
Total 6		292	718	80	157	15	6	0	42	42-4	3	107	.219	.263	.256	44	-55	12-4	.956	-16	93	101	S233,2b25,3b3	42	-4.9

ROBINSON, DAVE David Tanner B5.22.1946 Minneapolis MN BB/TL/6-1/186* [SDN68 7/155] d9.10 b-Bruce Col San Diego St.

YEAR	TM LG	G	AB	R	H	2B	3B	HR	RBI	BB-IB	HP	SO	AVG	OBP	SLG	AOPS	ABR	SB-CS	FA	FR	RNG	THR	GAMES AT POSITION	DL	BFW
1970	SD N	15	38	5	12	2	0	2	6	5-1	0	4	.316	.395	.526	150	3	2-0	1.000	1	123	140	O13(12/1/0)		0.4
1971	SD N	7	6	0	0	0	0	0	0	1-0	0	3	.000	.143	.000	-60	-1	0-0	—	0			/H		-0.1
Total 2		22	44	5	12	2	0	2	6	6-1	0	7	.273	.360	.455	123	2	2-0	1.000	1	123	140	O13(12/1/0)		0.3

ROBINSON, EARL Earl John B11.3.1936 New Orleans LA BR/TR/6-1/190* d9.10 Col California-Davis

YEAR	TM LG	G	AB	R	H	2B	3B	HR	RBI	BB-IB	HP	SO	AVG	OBP	SLG	AOPS	ABR	SB-CS	FA	FR	RNG	THR	GAMES AT POSITION	DL	BFW
1958	LA N	8	15	3	3	0	0	0	1	0-0	0	4	.200	.200	.200	20	-2	0-0	1.000	1	130	0	3b6		-0.1
1961	Bal A	96	222	37	59	12	3	8	30	31-1	5	54	.266	.354	.455	119	6	4-3	.973	5	115	132	O82(6/1/78)		0.7
1962	Bal A	29	63	12	18	3	1	1	4	8-0	0	10	.286	.361	.413	116	2	2-0	1.000	0	119	0	O17(1/0/16)		0.1
1964	Bal A	37	121	11	33	5	1	3	10	7-0	0	24	.273	.310	.405	98	-1	1-2	.986	1	100	151	O34(16/20/0)		-0.2
Total 4		170	421	63	113	20	5	12	44	47-1	5	92	.268	.340	.425	109	5	7-5	.980	8	111	118	O133(23/21/94),3b6		0.5

ROBINSON, FLOYD Floyd Andrew B5.9.1936 Prescott AR BL/TR/5-9/175* d8.10

YEAR	TM LG	G	AB	R	H	2B	3B	HR	RBI	BB-IB	HP	SO	AVG	OBP	SLG	AOPS	ABR	SB-CS	FA	FR	RNG	THR	GAMES AT POSITION	DL	BFW
1960	Chi A	22	46	7	13	0	0	1	11	11-0	1	8	.283	.431	.282	98	1	2-3	.960	-2	90	0	O17(1/4/12)		-0.2
1961	Chi A	132	432	69	134	20	7	11	59	52-3	4	32	.310	.389	.465	129	19	7-4	.991	2	104	88	O106R		1.3
1962	Chi A	156	600	89	187	**45**	10	11	109	72-7	2	47	.312	.384	.475	131	29	4-2	.973	-1	90	141	O155(114/0/75)		1.8
1963	Chi A	146	527	71	149	21	6	13	71	62-4	4	43	.283	.361	.419	120	16	4-3	.984	-2	96	88	O137(36/0/119)		0.5
1964	Chi A	141	525	83	158	17	3	11	59	70-7	5	41	.301	.388	.408	125	21	9-5	.987	-6	93	63	O138(54/0/112)		0.7
1965	Chi A	156	577	70	153	16	6	14	66	76-6	5	51	.265	.352	.385	117	15	4-1	.985	-8	92	61	O153(6/1/148)		-0.4
1966	Chi A	127	342	44	81	11	2	6	35	44-4	5	32	.237	.330	.325	96	0	8-2	.962	-9	85	37	O113(4/0/111)		-1.6
1967	Cin N	55	130	19	31	6	2	1	10	14-1	0	14	.238	.310	.338	77	-3	3-1	.981	-0	100	0	O39(4/0/35)	42	-0.2
1968	Oak A	53	81	5	20	5	0	1	14	4-1	0	10	.247	.276	.346	93	-1	0-0	1.000	-1	81	117	O18L		-0.8
	Bos A	23	24	1	3	0	0	0	2	3-0	1	4	.125	.250	.125	15	-2	1-0	.833	-1	72	0	O10(5/0/5)		-0.4
	Year	76	105	6	23	5	0	1	16	7-1	1	14	.219	.270	.295	73	-3	1-0	.963	-1	79	90	O28(23/0/5)		-0.6
Total 9		1011	3284	458	929	140	36	67	426	408-33	27	282	.283	.365	.409	118	95	42-21	.981	-28	93	79	O886(242/5/723)	42	0.7

ROBINSON, FRANK Frank B8.31.1935 Beaumont TX BR/TR/6-1/195* d4.17 M15/C7 HF1982 OF(820/99/1281)

YEAR	TM LG	G	AB	R	H	2B	3B	HR	RBI	BB-IB	HP	SO	AVG	OBP	SLG	AOPS	ABR	SB-CS	FA	FR	RNG	THR	GAMES AT POSITION	DL	BFW
1956	Cin N★	152	572	**122**	166	27	6	38	83	64-7	**20**	95	.290	.379	.558	139	33	8-4	.976	-4	100	48	O152(143/10/0)		2.0
1957	Cin N★	150	611	97	197	29	5	29	75	44-5	12	92	.322	.376	.529	131	27	10-2	.989	15	115	116	O136(106/32/1),1b24		3.5
1958	Cin N	148	554	90	149	25	6	31	83	62-5	7	80	.269	.350	.504	116	13	10-1	.991	-1	99	109	O138(83/53/0),3b11		0.6
1959	Cin N★	146	540	106	168	31	4	36	125	69-9	**8**	93	.311	.391	.583	152	42	18-8	.984	-4	88	**111**	1b125,O40L		3.0
1960	Cin N	139	464	86	138	33	6	31	83	82-6	9	67	.297	.407	.595	148	36	13-6	.993	5	101	100	1b78,O51L/3		4.6
1961	†Cin N★	153	545	117	176	32	7	37	124	71-23	10	64	.323	.404	**.611**	164	52	22-3	.990	6	116	105	O150(52/3/99)/3		5.1
1962	Cin N★	**162**	609	**134**	208	**51**	2	39	136	76-16	11	62	.342	**.421**	**.624**	**172**	65	18-9	.994	4	111	74	O161(9/0/155)		5.7
1963	Cin N	140	482	79	125	19	3	21	91	81-20	14	69	.259	.379	.442	132	24	26-10	.984	7	105	149	O139(116/1/31)/1		2.7
1964	Cin N	156	568	103	174	38	6	29	96	79-20	14	67	.306	.396	.548	158	47	23-5	.986	3	108	67	O155(7/0/152)		4.5
1965	Cin N	156	582	109	172	33	5	33	113	70-18	18	100	.296	.386	.540	148	40	13-9	.990	-1	104	49	O155(7/0/152)		2.9
1966	†Bal A★	155	576	122	182	34	2	**49**	122	87-11	10	90	.316	.410	**.637**	**200**	78	8-5	.985	-7	93	46	O151(20/0/135),1b3		**6.3**
1967	Bal A★	129	479	83	149	23	7	30	94	71-4	7	84	.311	.403	.576	189	55	2-3	.990	-6	87	84	O126(31/0/95),1b2		4.3
1968	Bal A	130	421	69	113	27	1	15	52	73-4	12	84	.268	.390	.444	153	32	11-2	.962	-6	90	76	O117(55/0/78),1b3		2.2

YEAR	TM LG	G	AB	R	H	2B	3B	HR	RBI	BB-IB	HP	SO	AVG	OBP	SLG	AOPS	ABR	SB-CS	FA	FR	RNG	THR	GAMES AT POSITION	DL	BFW
1969	†Bal A★	148	539	111	166	19	5	32	100	88-11	13	62	.308	.415	.540	164	49	9-3	.987	-2	97	90	O134(1/0/134),1b19		4.2
1970	†Bal A★	132	471	88	144	24	1	25	78	69-9	7	70	.306	.398	.520	150	34	2-1	.987	1	99	113	O120R,1b7		2.9
1971	†Bal A★	133	455	82	128	16	2	28	99	72-11	9	62	.281	.384	.510	152	33	2-3	.973	-4	103	51	O92(1/0/91),1b37		2.4
1972	LA N	103	342	41	86	6	1	19	59	55-0	2	76	.251	.353	.442	128	13	2-3	.967	-2	95	88	O95(9/0/88)		0.6
1973	Cal A	147	534	85	142	29	0	30	97	82-12	10	93	.266	.372	.489	152	39	1-1	.976	3	121	265	D127,O17L		3.8
1974	Cal A★	129	427	75	107	26	2	20	63	75-14	10	85	.251	.371	.461	147	30	5-1	—	-0	0	0	D123/OL		2.8
	Cle A	15	50	6	10	1	0	2	5	10-0	0	10	.200	.328	.380	105	1	0-1	.958	-1	0	39	D11,1b4		-0.1
	Year	144	477	81	117	27	3	22	68	85-14	10	95	.245	.367	.453	143	30	5-2	.901	-1	0	0	D134,1b4/OL		2.7
1975	Cle A	49	118	19	28	5	0	9	24	29-3	0	15	.237	.385	.508	151	9	0-0	—	-0	0	0	D42,M	19	0.8
1976	Cle A	36	67	5	15	0	0	3	10	11-0	0	12	.224	.329	.358	103	0	0-0	1.000	-0	0	119	D18,1b2/OLM	18	-0.1
Total	21	2808	10006	1829	2943	528	72	586	1812	1420-218	198	1532	.294	.389	.537	153	764	204-77	.984	5	102	89	O2132R,D321,1b305,3b13	37	64.7

ROBINSON, FRED Frederic Henry B7.6.1856 South Acton MA D12.18.1933 Hudson MA BR/TR d4.17 b-Wilbert

YEAR	TM LG	G	AB	R	H	2B	3B	HR	RBI	BB-IB	HP	SO	AVG	OBP	SLG	AOPS	ABR	SB-CS	FA	FR	RNG	THR	GAMES AT POSITION	DL	BFW
1884	Cin U	3	13	1	3	0	0	0					.231	.231	.231	37	-1		.727	-2	84	0	2b3		-0.3

ROBINSON, JACKIE Jack Roosevelt B1.31.1919 Cairo GA D10.24.1972 Stamford CT BR/TR/5-11/204* d4.15 HF1962 Negro Lg 1945 Col UCLA OF(161/0/1)

YEAR	TM LG	G	AB	R	H	2B	3B	HR	RBI	BB-IB	HP	SO	AVG	OBP	SLG	AOPS	ABR	SB-CS	FA	FR	RNG	THR	GAMES AT POSITION	DL	BFW
1947	†Bro N	151	590	125	175	31	5	12	48	74	9	36	.297	.383	.427	111	11	29	.989	-3	94	119	1b151		0.3
1948	Bro N	147	574	108	170	38	8	12	85	57	7	37	.296	.367	.453	117	14	22	.980	0	97	115	2b116,1b30,3b6		2.0
1949	†Bro N★	156	593	122	203	38	12	16	124	86	8	27	.342	.432	.528	150	46	37	.981	-4	95	117	2b156		5.0
1950	Bro N★	144	518	99	170	39	4	14	81	80	5	24	.328	.423	.500	139	34	12	.986	19	104	130	2b150		7.3
1951	Bro N★	153	548	106	185	33	7	19	88	79	9	27	.338	.429	.527	153	45	25-8	.992	19	104	122	2b146		5.2
1952	†Bro N★	149	510	104	157	17	3	19	75	106	14	40	.308	.440	.465	149	42	24-7	.974	4	97	122	O76L,3b44,2b9,1b6/S		3.2
1953	†Bro N★	136	484	109	159	34	7	12	95	74	7	30	.329	.425	.502	137	31	17-4	.981	5	99	144	O74(73/0/1),3b50,2b4		1.9
1954	Bro N	124	386	62	120	22	4	15	59	63	7	20	.311	.413	.505	135	23	7-3	1.000	-1	93	109	3b84,O10L/12		1.
1955	†Bro N	105	317	51	81	6	2	8	36	61-5	3	18	.256	.378	.363	96	1	12-3	.966	11	116	132	3b72,2b22,1b9,O2L		2.
1956	†Bro N	117	357	61	98	15	2	10	43	60-2	5	32	.275	.382	.412	106	6	12-5	.967	19	132	141	3b72,2b56,1b197,O162L/S		34.
Total	10	1382	4877	947	1518	273	54	137	734	740-7	72	291	.311	.409	.474	131	253	197-30	.983	62	98	123	2b748,3b256,1b197,O162L/S		34.

ROBINSON, JACK John W. "Bridgeport" B7.15.1880 Portland ME D7.22.1921 Macon GA TR d9.6 Col Harvard

YEAR	TM LG	G	AB	R	H	2B	3B	HR	RBI	BB-IB	HP	SO	AVG	OBP	SLG	AOPS	ABR	SB-CS	FA	FR	RNG	THR	GAMES AT POSITION	DL	BFW
1902	NY N	4	9	0	0	0	0	0	0	0-0	0		.000	.000	.000	-99	-2	0	1.000	0	135	92	C3		-0.

ROBINSON, KERRY Kerry Keith B10.3.1973 St.Louis MO BL/TL/6-0/175* [StLN95 34/939] d9.22 Col Southeast Missouri

YEAR	TM LG	G	AB	R	H	2B	3B	HR	RBI	BB-IB	HP	SO	AVG	OBP	SLG	AOPS	ABR	SB-CS	FA	FR	RNG	THR	GAMES AT POSITION	DL	BFW
1998	TB A	2	3	0	0	0	0	0	0	0-0	0	1	.000	.000	.000	-98	-1	0-0	1.000	0	294	0	O2L		0.
1999	Cin N	9	1	4	0	0	0	0	0	0-0	0	1	.000	.000	.000	-97	0	0-1	—	-0	0	0	O2L		0.
2001	†StL N	114	186	34	53	6	1	1	15	12-0	2	20	.285	.330	.344	75	-7	11-2	.981	3	121	77	O74(42/22/17)		-0.
2002	†StL N	124	181	27	47	7	4	1	15	11-3	0	29	.260	.301	.359	76	-8	7-4	.977	-2	121	0	O76(52/10/17)/D		-1.
2003	StL N	116	208	19	52	6	3	1	16	8-3	1	27	.250	.281	.322	57	-14	6-1	1.000	1	122	0	O49(39/9/2),D2		-1.
2004	SD N	80	92	20	27	4	0	0	5	3-6	1	8	.293	.330	.337	79	-3	11-4	1.000	2	124	95	O291(173/61/75),D3		-2.
Total	6	445	671	104	179	23	8	3	51	36-6	4	86	.267	.305	.338	69	-33	35-12	.988	5	116	36	O291(173/61/75),D3		

ROBINSON, WILBERT Wilbert "Uncle Robby" B6.29.1863 Bolton MA D8.8.1934 Atlanta GA BR/TR/5-8.5/215 d4.19 M19/C3 HF1945 b-Fred

YEAR	TM LG	G	AB	R	H	2B	3B	HR	RBI	BB-IB	HP	SO	AVG	OBP	SLG	AOPS	ABR	SB-CS	FA	FR	RNG	THR	GAMES AT POSITION	DL	BFW
1886	Phi AA	87	342	57	69	11	3	1	30	21	3		.202	.254	.260	61	-16	33	.893	-7			C61,1b22,O5(0/4/1)		-1.
1887	Phi AA	68	264	28	60	6	2	1	24	14	1		.227	.269	.277	52	-18	15	.901	2			C67,1b3/OC		-0.
1888	Phi AA	66	254	32	62	7	2	1	31	9	0		.244	.270	.299	83	-6	11	.938	21			C65/1		1.
1889	Phi AA	69	264	31	61	13	2	0	28	6	1	34	.231	.251	.295	56	-16	9	.943	7			C82		-1
1890	Phi AA	82	329	32	78	13	4	4	42	16	3		.237	.279	.337	82	-10	20	.930	-15	84	80	C82		0.
	Bal AA	14	48	7	13	1	0	0	4	3	0		.271	.314	.292	75	-2	1	.989	6	119	64	C11,1b3		0.
	Year	96	377	39	91	14	4	4	46	19	3		.241	.283	.332	81	-11	21	.938	-9	88	78	C93,1b3		-1.
1891	Bal AA	93	334	25	72	8	5	2	46	16	2	37	.216	.251	.287	54	-23	18	.921	-14	95	84	C87,1b2/OR		-1
1892	Bal N	90	330	36	88	14	4	2	57	15	2	35	.267	.303	.352	95	-4	5	.942	-9	90	68	C93/1		0
1893	Bal N	95	359	49	120	21	3	3	57	26	2	22	.334	.382	.435	115	7	17	.944	-2	123	77	C109		1
1894	†Bal N	109	414	69	146	21	4	1	98	46	3	18	.353	.421	.430	101	2	12	.979	24	148	107	C75		1
1895	†Bal N	77	282	38	74	19	1	0	48	12	1	19	.262	.295	.337	61	-17	11	.948	4	111	73	C67		1
1896	†Bal N	67	245	43	85	9	6	2	38	14	1	13	.347	.385	.457	120	6	9	.965	-1	102	72	C48		1
1897	Bal N	48	181	25	57	9	0	0	23	8	1		.315	.347	.365		-3	0	.965	1	112	93	C77		-0
1898	Bal N	79	289	29	80	12	2	0	38	16	1		.277	.317	.332	84	-6	3	.969	1	117	79	C105		-0
1899	Bal N	108	356	40	101	15	2	0	47	31	2		.284	.344	.337	83	-8	5	.974	-7	94	103	C54		0
1900	StL N	60	210	26	52	5	1	0	28	11	2		.248	.291	.281	59	-12	7	.949	-0	107	81	C67		0
1901	Bal A	68	239	32	72	12	3	0	26	10	2		.301	.335	.377	93	-3	9	.949	-15	80	86	C87,M		-1
1902	Bal A	91	335	38	98	16	7	1	57	12	2		.293	.321	.391	93	-5	11	.941	16	109	81	C1316,1b32,O8(0/5/3)		0
Total	17	1371	5075	637	1388	212	51	18	722	286	27	178	.273	.316	.346	83	-134	196	.941	16	109	81	C1316,1b32,O8(0/5/3)		

ROBINSON, EDDIE William Edward B12.15.1920 Paris TX BL/TR/6-2.5/210* d9.9 Mil 1943-45 C3 Col Paris (TX) JC

YEAR	TM LG	G	AB	R	H	2B	3B	HR	RBI	BB-IB	HP	SO	AVG	OBP	SLG	AOPS	ABR	SB-CS	FA	FR	RNG	THR	GAMES AT POSITION	DL	BFW
1942	Cle A	8	8	1	1	0	0	0	2	1	0		.125	.222	.125	-1		0-0	1.000	-0	0	0	/1		-0
1946	Cle A	8	30	6	12	1	0	3	4	2	0	4	.400	.438	.733	238	5	0-0	.988	-2	17	53	1b8		-0
1947	Cle A	95	318	52	78	10	1	14	52	30	2	18	.245	.314	.415	105	0	1-0	.994	-3	88	109	1b87		-1
1948	†Cle A	134	493	53	125	18	5	16	83	36	4	42	.254	.307	.408	91	-10	1-0	.995	-1	94	114	1b131		-1
1949	Was A★	143	527	66	155	27	3	18	78	67	7	30	.294	.381	.459	125	18	3-4	.987	-2	97	82	1b143		-0
1950	Was A	36	129	21	30	4	2	1	13	25	2	4	.233	.365	.318	80	-3	0-0	1.000	-0	96	96	1b36		1
	Chi A	119	424	62	133	11	2	20	73	60	5	28	.314	.405	.491	132	21	0-0	.987	-5	88	88	1b155		0
	Year	155	553	83	163	15	4	21	86	85	7	32	.295	.395	.450	120	18	0-0	.990	-5	87	90	1b155		-1
1951	Chi A★	151	564	85	159	23	5	29	117	77	7	54	.282	.371	.495	135	27	2-5	.988	-8	78	106	1b155		-3
1952	Chi A★	155	594	79	176	33	4	22	104	70	12	49	.296	.382	.466	134	29	2-0	.988	-13	70	86	1b155		-3
1953	Phi A★	156	615	64	152	28	4	22	102	63	5	56	.247	.322	.413	94	-7	1-2	.980	1	118	97	1b29		-0
1954	NY A	85	142	11	37	9	0	3	27	19	0	21	.261	.344	.387	105	1	0-0	.995	-2	74	94	1b46		-0
1955	†NY A	88	173	25	36	1	0	16	42	36-7	3	26	.208	.358	.491	129	7	0-0	1.000	-1	76	112	1b14		-0
1956	NY A	26	54	9	12	1	0	5	11	5-1	3	3	.222	.323	.519	123	1	0-1	.977	-4	75	113	1b47		-0
	KC A	75	172	13	34	5	1	2	12	26-1	2	20	.198	.308	.273	55	-11	0-1	.983	-4	75	113	1b61		-0
	Year	101	226	20	46	6	1	7	23	31-2	5	23	.204	.312	.332	71	-10	0-1	1.000	-1	0	348	0		-0
1957	Det A	13	9	0	0	0	0	0	0	3-1	1	1	.000	.308	.000	-9	-1	0-0	1.000	-1	0	348	0	/1		-0
	Cle A	19	27	1	6	1	0	1	3	0-0	1	5	.222	.241	.370	68	-1	0-0	1.000	-0	106	60	1b7		-0
	Bal A	4	3	0	0	0	0	0	0	1-0	0	1	.000	.250	.000	-28	-1	0-0	—	-0	0	0	/H		-0
	Year	36	39	1	6	1	0	1	3	4-1	2	7	.154	.261	.256	44	-3	0-0	1.000	-1	128	60	1b8		-0
Total	13	1315	4282	546	1146	172	24	172	723	521-10	50	359	.268	.353	.440	113	74	10-12	.990	-48	84	98	1b1126		

ROBINSON, YANK William H. B9.19.1859 Philadelphia PA D8.25.1894 St.Louis MO BR/TR/5-6.5/170 d8.24 OF(52/2/2) ▲

YEAR	TM LG	G	AB	R	H	2B	3B	HR	RBI	BB-IB	HP	SO	AVG	OBP	SLG	AOPS	ABR	SB-CS	FA	FR	RNG	THR	GAMES AT POSITION	DL	BFW
1882	Det N	11	39	1	7	1	0	0	2	1		13	.179	.200	.205	30	-3		.800	-3	78	79	S10/OCP		-0
1884	Bal U	102	415	101	111	24	4	3		37			.267	.327	.366	100	-11		.831	10	122	128	3b71,S14,C11,P11,2b3		-0
1885	†StL AA	78	287	63	75	8	8	0	35	29	7		.261	.344	.345	113	5		.862	1	102	74	O52L,2b19,C5,3b2/1		-0
1886	†StL AA	133	481	89	132	26	9	3	71	64	15		.274	.377	.385	132	21	51	.888	-6	102	133	2b125,3b6/OCSP		-0
1887	†StL AA	.125	430	102	131	32	4	1	74	92	17		.305	.445	.405		20	75	.899	-12	101	117	2b117,3b6,O2R,S2/CP		-0
1888	†StL AA	134	455	111	105	17	6	3	50	116	12		.231	.400	.314	117	16	56	.895	-37	87	61	2b102,S34		-1
1889	StL AA	132	452	97	94	17	3	5	70	118	6	55	.208	.378	.292	81	-7	39	.887	-19	95	104	2b98		-1
1890	Pit P	98	306	59	70	9	0	0	38	101	10	33	.229	.434	.281	101	14	17	.887	-14	101	79	2b97		-1
1891	Cin N	97	342	48	61	9	4	1	37	68	8	51	.178	.328	.237	57	-18	23	.866	-15	100	78	2b98		-1
	StL AA	1	3	0	0	0	0	0	0	0	0		.000	.000	.000	-87	-1	0	.750	-1	0	0	/2		0
	Year	98	345	48	61	9	4	1	37	68	8	51	.177	.325	.235	56	-18	23	.866	-15	100	78	2b98		-1
1892	Was N	67	228	26	39	4	3	0	19	38	0	29	.171	.301	.225	60	-9	11	.852	-3	100	121	3b58,S5,2b4		-1
Total	10	978	3428	697	825	148	44	16	399	664	75	181	.241	.375	.324	101	27	272	.887	-124	95	99	2b698,3b143,S66,O56L,C17,P14/1		-0

ROBINSON, BILL William Henry B6.26.1943 McKeesport PA BR/TR/6-3/200(175-205) d9.20 C10

YEAR	TM LG	G	AB	R	H	2B	3B	HR	RBI	BB-IB	HP	SO	AVG	OBP	SLG	AOPS	ABR	SB-CS	FA	FR	RNG	THR	GAMES AT POSITION	DL	BFW
1966	Atl N	6	11	1	3	0	1	0	3	0-0	0	0	.273	.273	.455	96	0	0-0	.800	-1	79	0	O5(2/0/3)		
1967	NY A	116	342	31	67	6	1	7	29	28-4	2	56	.196	.259	.281	62	-17	2-2	.968	-2	90	159	O102(20/33/53)		
1968	NY A	107	342	34	82	16	7	6	40	26-3	2	54	.240	.294	.380	108	2	7-6	.985	-4	97	49	O98(6/51/44)		
1969	NY A	87	222	23	38	11	2	3	21	16-3	1	39	.171	.226	.279	42	-18	3-1	.963	1	94	126	O72(13/30/32)		
1972	Phi N	82	188	19	45	9	1	4	19	5-0	1	30	.239	.258	.426	89	-4	2-3	.982	1	104	63	O72(13/30/32)		

YEAR TM LG	G	AB	R	H	2B	3B	HR	RBI	BB-IB	HP	SO	AVG	OBP	SLG	AOPS	ABR	SB-CS	FA	FR	RNG	THR	GAMES AT POSITION	DL	BFW
973 Phi N	124	452	62	130	32	1	25	65	27-1	1	91	.288	.326	.529	130	17	5-4	.979	-0	110	104	O113(13/44/75),3b14	23	1.2
974 Phi N	100	280	32	66	14	1	5	29	17-4	1	61	.236	.280	.346	72	-11	5-3	.971	4	105	174	O87(40/40/19)		-1.0
975 †Pit N	92	200	26	56	12	2	6	33	11-4	0	36	.280	.313	.450	111	2	3-1	.991	2	112	93	O57(31/15/13)		0.2
976 Pit N	122	393	55	119	22	3	21	64	16-1	1	73	.303	.329	.534	140	18	2-4	.993	-12	95	141	O78(24/27/29),3b37,1b3		0.2
977 Pit N	137	507	74	154	32	1	26	104	25-3	3	92	.304	.337	.525	124	15	12-6	.992	-9	78	110	1b86,O43(41/2/1),3b17		0.1
978 Pit N	136	499	70	123	36	2	14	80	35-8	5	105	.246	.296	.411	93	-5	14-11	.988	4	105	90	O127(111/19/10),3b29,1b3	15	-0.7
979 †Pit N	148	421	59	111	17	6	24	75	24-11	1	81	.264	.302	.504	110	3	13-2	.982	-2	97	91	O125(119/0/6),1b28,3b3		-0.2
980 Pit N	100	272	28	78	10	1	12	36	15-2	0	45	.287	.320	.463	113	4	1-4	.985	-4	67	92	1b49,O41(28/0/14)	23	-0.6
981 Pit N	39	88	8	19	3	0	2	8	5-1	0	18	.216	.258	.318	60	-5	1-0	1.000	0	98	77	1b23,O7(1/0/6)/3	108	-0.6
982 Pit N	31	71	8	17	3	0	4	12	5-3	0	19	.239	.286	.451	100	0	0-1	1.000	0	117	0	O22(12/0/11)		-0.1
Phi N	35	69	6	18	6	0	3	19	7-1	0	15	.261	.321	.478	119	2	1-1	.960	2	85	316	O41(12/0/30),1b5		0.1
Year	66	140	14	35	9	0	7	31	12-4	0	34	.250	.303	.464	109	1	1-2	.984	1	103	140	O41(12/0/30),1b5		0.1
983 Phi N	10	7	0	1	0	0	0	2	1-0	0	4	.143	.250	.143	12	-1	0-0	1.000	-1	0	0	1b3,3b2/OL		-0.2
total 16	1472	4364	536	1127	229	29	166	641	263-49	16	820	.258	.300	.438	103	2	71-49	.979	-23	100	106	O1059(479/280/364),1b201,3b103	169	-8.1

ROBLES, OSCAR Oscar Manuel (Arenas) B4.9.1976 Tijuana, Baja California, Mexico BL/TR/5-11/155 d5.10

YEAR TM LG	G	AB	R	H	2B	3B	HR	RBI	BB-IB	HP	SO	AVG	OBP	SLG	AOPS	ABR	SB-CS	FA	FR	RNG	THR	GAMES AT POSITION	DL	BFW
005 LA N	110	364	44	99	18	1	5	34	31-0	2	33	.272	.332	.368	84	-9	0-8	.981	-3	93	91	S54,3b40/2		-1.0

ROBLES, RAFAEL Rafael Orlando (Natera) B10.20.1947 San Pedro de Macoris, D.R. D8.13.1998 New York NY BR/TR/6-0/160(150-170) d4.8

YEAR TM LG	G	AB	R	H	2B	3B	HR	RBI	BB-IB	HP	SO	AVG	OBP	SLG	AOPS	ABR	SB-CS	FA	FR	RNG	THR	GAMES AT POSITION	DL	BFW
969 SD N	6	20	1	2	0	0	0		1-0	0	3	.100	.143	.100	-32	-4	1-1	.895	-4	59	28	S6		-0.8
970 SD N	23	89	5	19	1	0	0	3	5-0	1	11	.213	.263	.225	33	-9	3-0	.968	6	122	101	S23		0.0
972 SD N	18	24	1	4	0	0	0	0	0-0	0	3	.167	.167	.167	-5	-3	0-0	.952	-3	89	0	S15/3		-0.6
total 3	47	133	7	25	1	0	0	3	6-0	1	17	.188	.229	.195	17	-16	4-1	.958	-1	106	71	S44/3		-1.4

ROBLES, SERGIO Sergio (Valenzuela) B4.16.1946 Magdalena de Kino, Sonora, Mexico BR/TR/6-2/190* d8.27

YEAR TM LG	G	AB	R	H	2B	3B	HR	RBI	BB-IB	HP	SO	AVG	OBP	SLG	AOPS	ABR	SB-CS	FA	FR	RNG	THR	GAMES AT POSITION	DL	BFW
972 Bal A	2	5	0	1	0	0	0	0	0-0	0	2	.200	.200	.200	19	-1	0-0	1.000	-1	0	0	/C		-0.1
973 Bal A	8	13	0	1	0	0	0	0	3-0	0	3	.077	.250	.077	-4	-2	0-0	1.000	2	0	0	C8		0.1
976 LA N	6	3	0	0	0	0	0	0	0-0	0	2	.000	.000	.000	-99	-1	0-0	1.000	-0	122	0	C6		-0.1
total 3	16	21	0	2	0	0	0	0	3-0	0	3	.095	.208	.095	-11	-4	0-0	1.000	1	28	0	C15		-0.1

ROBSON, TOM Thomas James B1.15.1946 Rochester NY BR/TR/6-3/220* [NYN67 50/859] d9.14 C13 Col Utah St. [DL 1976 NY A 23]

YEAR TM LG	G	AB	R	H	2B	3B	HR	RBI	BB-IB	HP	SO	AVG	OBP	SLG	AOPS	ABR	SB-CS	FA	FR	RNG	THR	GAMES AT POSITION	DL	BFW
974 Tex A	6	13	2	3	1	0	0	0	2-0	0	2	.231	.412	.308	112	2	0-0	1.000	-0	0	1016	/1D		0.1
975 Tex A	17	35	3	7	0	0	0	2	1-0	0	3	.200	.216	.200	20	-4	0-0	1.000	-0	79	202	1b5,D4	15	-0.4
total 2	23	48	5	10	1	0	0	2	5-0	0	6	.208	.278	.229	48	-3	0-0	1.000	-0	77	227	D9,1b6	38	-0.3

ROCAP, ADAM Adam B1854 Philadelphia PA D3.29.1892 Philadelphia PA 5-9/170 d5.5

YEAR TM LG	G	AB	R	H	2B	3B	HR	RBI	BB-IB	HP	SO	AVG	OBP	SLG	AOPS	ABR	SB-CS	FA	FR	RNG	THR	GAMES AT POSITION	DL	BFW
875 Ath NA	16	69	13	12	1	0	0	4	1		7	.174	.186	.188	27	-5	3-2	.839	-2	154	0	O12(0/5/7),2b4		-0.6

ROCCO, MICKEY Michael Dominick B3.2.1916 St.Paul MN D6.1.1997 St.Paul MN BL/TL/5-11/188 d6.5

YEAR TM LG	G	AB	R	H	2B	3B	HR	RBI	BB-IB	HP	SO	AVG	OBP	SLG	AOPS	ABR	SB-CS	FA	FR	RNG	THR	GAMES AT POSITION	DL	BFW
943 Cle A	108	405	43	97	14	4	5	46	51	2	40	.240	.328	.331	99	0	1-2	.995	-5	81	118	1b108		-1.2
944 Cle A	155	653	87	174	29	4	13	70	56	1	51	.266	.325	.392	108	3	4-8	.993	17	142	105	1b155		-1.2
945 Cle A	143	565	81	149	28	6	10	56	52	0	40	.264	.326	.388	111	6	0-4	.992	4	105	93	1b141		1.2
946 Cle A	34	98	8	24	2	0	2	14	15	0	15	.245	.345	.327	94	0	1-1	.996	5	155	79	1b27		0.1
total 4	440	1721	219	444	73	17	30	186	174	3	146	.258	.327	.372	106	11	6-15	.994	20	115	103	1b431		0.3

ROCHE, JACK John Joseph "Red" B11.22.1890 Los Angeles CA D3.30.1983 Peoria AZ BR/TR/6-1/178 d5.24

YEAR TM LG	G	AB	R	H	2B	3B	HR	RBI	BB-IB	HP	SO	AVG	OBP	SLG	AOPS	ABR	SB-CS	FA	FR	RNG	THR	GAMES AT POSITION	DL	BFW
14 StL N	12	9	1	6	2	1	0	3	0	1	1	.667	.700	1.111	441	4	1	.667	-1	63	0	C9		0.3
15 StL N	46	39	2	8	0	1	0	6	4	1	1	.205	.295	.256	68	-2	1	1.000	0	74	323	C4		-0.1
17 StL N	1	1	0	0	0	0	0	0	0	0	0	.000	.000	.000	-99	0	0	.000	-1	0	0	/C		-0.1
total 3	59	49	3	14	2	2	0	9	4	2	2	.286	.364	.408	133	2	2	.750	-2	60	119	C14		0.1

ROCHEFORT, BEN Bennett Harold (b Bennett Harold Rochefort Gilbert) B8.15.1896 Camden NJ D4.2.1981 Red Bank NJ BL/TR/6-2/185 d10.3 Col Temple

YEAR TM LG	G	AB	R	H	2B	3B	HR	RBI	BB-IB	HP	SO	AVG	OBP	SLG	AOPS	ABR	SB-CS	FA	FR	RNG	THR	GAMES AT POSITION	DL	BFW
14 Phi A	1	2	0	1	0	0	0	0	0-0	0	0	.500	.500	.500	209	0	1	1.000	-0	352	0	/1		0.1

ROCHELLI, LOU Louis Joseph B1.11.1919 Staunton IL D10.23.1992 Victoria TX BR/TR/6-1/175 d8.25 Mil 1944-46

YEAR TM LG	G	AB	R	H	2B	3B	HR	RBI	BB-IB	HP	SO	AVG	OBP	SLG	AOPS	ABR	SB-CS	FA	FR	RNG	THR	GAMES AT POSITION	DL	BFW
44 Bro N	5	17	0	3	0	1	0	2	2	0	6	.176	.263	.294	58	-1	0-0	.964	-1	100	30	2b5		-0.1

ROCK, LES Lester Henry (b Lester Henry Schwarzrock) B8.19.1912 Springfield MN D9.9.1991 Davis CA BL/TR/6-2/184 d9.11

YEAR TM LG	G	AB	R	H	2B	3B	HR	RBI	BB-IB	HP	SO	AVG	OBP	SLG	AOPS	ABR	SB-CS	FA	FR	RNG	THR	GAMES AT POSITION	DL	BFW
36 Chi A	1	0	0	0	0	0	0	0	0-0	0	0	.000	.000	.000	-97	0	0-0	—	0	0	0	1b2		0.0

ROCKENFIELD, IKE Isaac Broc B11.3.1876 Omaha NE D2.21.1927 San Diego CA BR/TR/5-7/150 d5.5

YEAR TM LG	G	AB	R	H	2B	3B	HR	RBI	BB-IB	HP	SO	AVG	OBP	SLG	AOPS	ABR	SB-CS	FA	FR	RNG	THR	GAMES AT POSITION	DL	BFW
05 StL A	95	322	40	70	12	0	0	16	46	14		.217	.340	.255	95	3	11	.926	-9	96	76	2b95		-0.6
06 StL A	27	89	3	21	4	0	0	8	1	4		.236	.277	.281	78	-2	0	.956	-6	81	60	2b26		-0.9
total 2	122	411	43	91	16	0	0	24	47	18		.221	.328	.260	91	1	11	.933	-15	93	72	2b121		-1.5

ROCKETT, PAT Patrick Edward B1.9.1955 San Antonio TX BR/TR/5-11/165* [AtlN73 1/10] d9.17

YEAR TM LG	G	AB	R	H	2B	3B	HR	RBI	BB-IB	HP	SO	AVG	OBP	SLG	AOPS	ABR	SB-CS	FA	FR	RNG	THR	GAMES AT POSITION	DL	BFW
76 Atl N	4	5	0	1	0	0	0	0	0-0	0	1	.200	.200	.200	13	-1	0-0	1.000	-1	55	0	S2		-0.1
77 Atl N	93	264	27	67	10	0	1	24	27-2	3	32	.254	.330	.303	64	-12	1-2	.940	-14	85	72	S84	42	-1.8
78 Atl N	55	142	6	20	2	0	0	4	13-3	0	12	.141	.212	.155	4	-18	1-2	.970	-18	71	61	S51		-3.5
total 3	152	411	33	88	12	0	1	28	40-5	3	45	.214	.288	.251	43	-31	2-4	.949	-32	80	68	S137	42	-5.4

RODGERS, ANDRE Kenneth Andre Ian "Andy" B12.2.1934 Nassau, Bahamas D12.13.2004 Nassau, Bahamas BR/TR/6-3/200(180-200) d4.16

YEAR TM LG	G	AB	R	H	2B	3B	HR	RBI	BB-IB	HP	SO	AVG	OBP	SLG	AOPS	ABR	SB-CS	FA	FR	RNG	THR	GAMES AT POSITION	DL	BFW
57 NY N	32	86	8	21	2	1	3	9	9-0	1	21	.244	.320	.395	92	-1	0-0	.950	3	104	110	S20,3b8		0.3
58 SF N	22	63	7	13	3	1	2	11	4-0	0	14	.206	.243	.381	67	-3	0-0	.972	-2	95	78	S18		-0.4
59 SF N	71	228	32	57	12	1	6	24	32-1	1	50	.250	.342	.390	98	0	2-1	.933	-10	93	89	S66		-0.5
60 SF N	81	217	22	53	8	5	2	22	24-4	3	44	.244	.325	.355	92	-2	1-1	.953	-4	92	105	S41,3b21,1b6,O2L		-0.4
61 Chi N	73	214	27	57	17	0	6	23	25-1	1	54	.266	.343	.430	103	-2	1-1	.983	-2	93	97	1b42,S24,O2R/2		-0.1
62 Chi N	138	461	40	128	20	8	5	44	44-3	4	93	.278	.343	.388	93	-4	5-6	.960	12	111	105	S133/1		1.8
63 Chi N	150	516	51	118	17	4	5	33	65-6	0	90	.229	.324	.306	79	-12	5-7	.954	-2	102	119	S150		-0.1
64 Chi N	129	448	50	107	17	3	12	46	53-5	0	88	.239	.317	.371	90	-5	5-1	.965	9	113	92	S126		1.6
65 Pit N	75	178	17	51	12	0	2	25	18-3	0	28	.287	.350	.388	108	3	2-1	.950	-1	101	137	S33,3b15,1b6/2		0.4
66 Pit N	36	49	6	9	1	0	0	4	8-0	0	7	.184	.293	.204	43	-4	0-1	.913	-1	101	201	S5,3b3,O3L,1b2		-0.5
67 Pit N	47	61	8	14	3	0	2	8	8-2	0	18	.230	.314	.377	90	0	1-1	1.000	1	158	84	1b9,3b5,S3,2b2	18	0.1
total 11	854	2521	268	628	112	23	45	245	290-26	18	507	.249	.328	.365	90	-26	22-20	.956	3	105	105	S619,1b66,3b52,O7(5/0/2),2b4	18	2.2

RODGERS, BUCK Robert Leroy B8.16.1938 Delaware OH BB/TR/6-2/195* d9.8 M13/C9

YEAR TM LG	G	AB	R	H	2B	3B	HR	RBI	BB-IB	HP	SO	AVG	OBP	SLG	AOPS	ABR	SB-CS	FA	FR	RNG	THR	GAMES AT POSITION	DL	BFW
1 LA A	16	56	8	18	2	0	2	13	1-0	0	6	.321	.333	.464	99	0	0-0	.965	-1	60	228	C14		-0.1
2 LA A	155	565	65	146	34	6	6	61	45-6	0	68	.258	.309	.372	86	-12	1-8	.989	5	129	116	C150		-0.1
3 LA A	100	300	24	70	6	0	4	23	29-2	0	35	.233	.303	.293	73	-11	2-2	.979	-6	118	127	C85		-1.3
4 LA A	148	514	38	125	18	3	4	54	40-11	4	71	.243	.299	.313	80	-15	4-3	.987	16	130	124	C146		0.8
5 Cal A	132	411	33	86	14	3	1	32	35-9	3	61	.209	.271	.265	56	-24	4-5	.991	8	116	85	C128		-1.1
6 Cal A	133	454	45	107	20	3	7	48	29-8	2	57	.236	.281	.339	81	-12	3-4	.992	-3	114	106	C133		-1.1
7 Cal A	139	429	29	94	13	3	6	41	34-5	2	55	.219	.277	.305	76	-14	1-4	.991	2	133	122	C134/OL		-0.8
8 Cal A	91	258	13	49	6	0	1	14	16-3	1	48	.190	.244	.225	45	-18	2-1	.985	-2	117	113	C87		-1.9
9 Cal A	18	46	4	9	1	0	0	2	5-1	1	8	.196	.288	.217	45	-3	0-0	1.000	-4	47	91	C18		-0.7
total 9	932	3033	259	704	114	18	31	288	234-45	17	409	.232	.288	.312	74	-109	17-27	.988	15	121	115	C895/OL		-6.3

RODGERS, BILL Wilbur Kincaid "Rawmeat Bill" B4.18.1887 Pleasant Ridge OH D12.24.1978 Goliad TX BL/TR/5-9.5/170 d4.15

YEAR TM LG	G	AB	R	H	2B	3B	HR	RBI	BB-IB	HP	SO	AVG	OBP	SLG	AOPS	ABR	SB-CS	FA	FR	RNG	THR	GAMES AT POSITION	DL	BFW
5 Cle A	16	45	4	14	2	0	0	7			7	.311	.415	.356	128	2	3-3	.945	-3	93	22	2b13		-0.1
Bos A	11	6	2	0	0	0	0	0	3	0	2	.000	.333	.000	-0	0	0	.900	1	162	0	2b6		0.0
Year	27	51	10	14	2	0	0	7	11	0	9	.255	.403	.314	115	2	3-3	.938	-2	114	141	2b19		-0.1
Cin N	72	213	20	51	13	0	0	12	11	7	29	.239	.299	.338	91	-2	8-5	.947	6	114	141	2b56,S6/3OR		0.5
Cin N	3	4	0	0	0	0	0	0	0	0	0	.000	.000	.000	-99	-1	0-0	1.000	-0	68	0	/S		-0.1
total 2	102	268	30	65	15	0		19	22	7	40	.243	.316	.328	93	-1	11-8	.943	3	111	116	2b75,S7/OR3		0.3

RODGERS, BILL William Sherman B12.5.1922 Harrisburg PA D5.13.2002 Worcester MA BL/TL/6-0/162 d9.27 Mil 1945

YEAR TM LG	G	AB	R	H	2B	3B	HR	RBI	BB-IB	HP	SO	AVG	OBP	SLG	AOPS	ABR	SB-CS	FA	FR	RNG	THR	GAMES AT POSITION	DL	BFW
4 Pit N	2	4	1	1	0	0	0	0			1	.250	.250	.250	39	0	0	—	-0	0	0	/OR		0.0
5 Pit N	1	1	1	1	0	0	0	0			0	1.000	1.000	1.000	440	0	0	—	0	0	0	/H		0.0
total 2	3	5	1	2	0	0	0	0			1	.400	.400	.400	120	0	0	.000	-0	0	0	/OR		0.0

RODIN, ERIC   Eric Chapman   B2.5.1930 Orange NJ   D1.4.1991 Somerville NJ   BR/TR/6-2/215   d9.7   Col Penn

YEAR	TM LG	G	AB	R	H	2B	3B	HR	RBI	BB-IB	HP	SO	AVG	OBP	SLG	AOPS	ABR	SB-CS	FA	FR	RNG	THR	GAMES AT POSITION	DL	BFW
1954	NY N	5	6	0	0	0	0	0	0	0		2	.000	.000	.000	-99	-2	0-0	1.000	0	109	0	O3(0/2/1)		-0.2

RODRIGUEZ, ALEX   Alexander Emmanuel "A-Rod"   B7.27.1975 New York NY   BR/TR/6-3/195(190-225)   [SeaA93 1/1]   d7.8

YEAR	TM LG	G	AB	R	H	2B	3B	HR	RBI	BB-IB	HP	SO	AVG	OBP	SLG	AOPS	ABR	SB-CS	FA	FR	RNG	THR	GAMES AT POSITION	DL	BFW
1994	Sea A	17	54	4	11	0	0	0	2	3-0	0	20	.204	.241	.204	17	-7	3-0	.915	-2	91	81	S17		-0.7
1995	†Sea A	48	142	15	33	6	2	5	19	6-0	0	42	.232	.264	.408	71	-7	4-2	.953	-4	92	52	S46/D		-0.8
1996	Sea A★	146	601	141	215	54	1	36	123	59-1	4	104	.358	.414	.631	160	56	15-4	.977	-6	95	94	S146	15	5.6
1997	†Sea A★	141	587	100	176	40	3	23	84	41-1	5	99	.300	.350	.496	118	15	29-6	.962	-3	94	90	S140/D	15	2.5
1998	Sea A★	161	686	123	213	35	5	42	124	45-0	10	121	.310	.360	.560	134	32	46-13	.975	-1	92	88	S160/D		4.4
1999	Sea A	129	502	110	143	25	0	42	111	56-2	5	109	.285	.357	.586	138	27	21-7	.977	1	99	107	S129	37	3.6
2000	†Sea A★	148	554	134	175	34	2	41	132	100-5	7	121	.316	.420	.606	160	55	15-4	.986	6	99	125	S148	15	6.6
2001	Tex A	162	632	133	201	34	1	52	135	75-6	16	131	.318	.399	.622	160	56	18-3	.987	12	104	96	S162		7.4
2002	Tex A★	162	624	125	187	27	2	57	142	87-12	10	122	.300	.392	.623	160	54	9-4	.989	13	106	98	S158/D		6.7
2003	Tex A★	161	607	124	181	30	6	47	118	87-10	15	126	.298	.396	.600	148	44	17-3	.965	-2	100	101	3b155,S2		2.9
2004	†NY A★	155	601	112	172	24	2	36	106	80-6	11	131	.286	.375	.512	129	27	28-4	.971	-6	93	91	3b161,S3/D		5.8
2005	†NY A★	162	605	124	194	29	1	48	130	91-8	16	139	.321	.421	.610	169	63	21-6	.977	10	98	99	S1272,3b316,D6	82	50.9
Total	12	1592	6195	1245	1901	338	25	429	1226	730-51	98	1265	.307	.385	.577	145	415	226-56	.977	10	98	99			

RODRIGUEZ, AURELIO   Aurelio (Ituarte)   B12.28.1947 Cananea, Sonora, Mexico   D9.23.2000 Detroit MI   BR/TR/5-10/180*   d9.1

YEAR	TM LG	G	AB	R	H	2B	3B	HR	RBI	BB-IB	HP	SO	AVG	OBP	SLG	AOPS	ABR	SB-CS	FA	FR	RNG	THR	GAMES AT POSITION	DL	BFW
1967	Cal A	29	130	14	31	3	1	1	8	2-0	0	21	.238	.250	.300	64	-7	1-0	.989	4	117	234	3b29		-0.2
1968	Cal A	76	223	14	54	10	1	1	16	17-2	1	36	.242	.299	.309	87	-3	0-2	.921	-8	87	162	3b70,2b2	26	-1.5
1969	Cal A	159	561	47	130	17	2	7	49	32-11	2	88	.232	.272	.307	66	-28	5-3	.954	15	109	135	3b159		-1.5
1970	Cal A	17	63	6	17	2	2	0	7	3-0	1	6	.270	.313	.365	89	-1	0-1	1.000	3	109	209	3b17		0.1
	Was A	142	547	64	135	31	5	19	76	37-5	7	81	.247	.300	.426	103	0	15-5	.961	13	117	118	3b136,S7		1.5
	Year	159	610	70	152	33	7	19	83	40-5	8	87	.249	.302	.420	102	-1	15-6	.965	16	116	128	3b153,S7		1.6
1971	Det A	154	604	68	153	30	7	15	39	27-6	3	93	.253	.288	.401	90	-11	4-6	.953	6	100	105	3b153/S		-0.8
1972	†Det A	153	601	65	142	23	5	13	56	28-4	2	104	.236	.272	.356	83	-15	2-3	.969	20	105	114	3b153,S2		0.5
1973	Det A	160	555	46	123	27	3	9	58	31-0	3	85	.222	.266	.330	63	-28	3-1	.971	5	97	102	3b160/S		-2.5
1974	Det A	159	571	54	127	23	5	5	49	26-2	1	70	.222	.255	.306	60	-31	2-0	.961	15	107	110	3b159		-1.7
1975	Det A	151	507	47	124	20	6	13	60	30-1	0	63	.245	.286	.385	85	-13	1-1	.953	27	116	105	3b151		1.3
1976	Det A	128	480	40	115	13	2	8	50	19-3	1	61	.240	.267	.325	71	-19	0-4	.978	8	102	92	3b128	35	-1.4
1977	Det A	96	306	30	67	14	1	10	32	16-1	0	36	.219	.257	.369	65	-16	1-1	.972	15	124	120	3b95/S	34	-0.2
1978	Det A	134	385	40	102	25	2	7	43	19-1	3	37	.265	.303	.395	92	-4	0-1	.987	6	109	101	3b131		-0.1
1979	Det A	106	343	27	87	18	0	5	36	11-0	1	40	.254	.277	.350	66	-17	0-2	.956	6	105	124	3b106/1		-1.3
1980	SD N	89	175	7	35	7	2	2	13	6-0	0	26	.200	.227	.297	48	-13	1-1	.965	2	106	139	3b88,S2		-2.2
	†NY A	52	164	14	36	6	1	3	14	7-1	0	35	.220	.251	.323	57	-10	0-0	.954	-11	75	57	3b20,2b3/1D		0.5
1981	†NY A	27	52	4	18	2	0	2	8	2-0	0	10	.346	.370	.500	150	3	0-0	.951	2	104	53	3b112,2b3,S2		-0.3
1982	Chi A	118	257	24	62	15	1	3	31	11-0	1	35	.241	.275	.350	68	-12	0-0	.969	9	107	103	3b112,2b3,S2		-1.6
1983	Bal A	45	67	3	8	1	0	1	0	0-0	1	13	.119	.143	.149	-31	-12	0-0	.969	-3	86	41	3b45		0.1
	†Chi A	22	20	1	4	0	0	1	3	0-0	0	3	.200	.200	.400	58	-1	0-0	1.000	2	117	299	3b22		-1.5
	Year	67	87	1	12	1	0	1	3	0-0	1	16	.138	.146	.184	-9	-13	0-0	.978	-1	94	108	3b67		
Total	17	2017	6611	612	1570	287	46	124	648	324-37	27	943	.237	.275	.351	75	-238	35-31	.964	134	106	114	3b1983,S16,2b14,D2,1b2	95	-12.

RODRIGUEZ, CARLOS   Carlos (Marquez)   B11.1.1967 Mexico City, Distrito Federal, Mexico   BB/TR/5-9/160*   d6.16

YEAR	TM LG	G	AB	R	H	2B	3B	HR	RBI	BB-IB	HP	SO	AVG	OBP	SLG	AOPS	ABR	SB-CS	FA	FR	RNG	THR	GAMES AT POSITION	DL	BFW
1991	NY A	15	37	1	7	0	0	0	2	1-0	0	2	.189	.211	.189	11	-5	1-0	.957	1	117	148	S11,2b3		-0.
1994	Bos A	57	174	15	50	14	1	1	13	11-0	0	13	.287	.330	.397	82	-4	1-0	.973	0	80	94	S32,2b20,3b4		-0.
1995	Bos A	13	30	5	10	2	0	0	5	2-0	1	2	.333	.394	.400	104	0	0-0	.960	0	94	84	2b7,S6/3		-0.
Total	3	85	241	21	67	16	1	1	20	14-0	1	17	.278	.320	.365	75	-9	1-0	.972	1	91	110	S49,2b30,3b5		-0.

RODRIGUEZ, EDWIN   Edwin (Morales)   B8.14.1960 Ponce, PR   BR/TR/5-11/175*   d9.28

YEAR	TM LG	G	AB	R	H	2B	3B	HR	RBI	BB-IB	HP	SO	AVG	OBP	SLG	AOPS	ABR	SB-CS	FA	FR	RNG	THR	GAMES AT POSITION	DL	BFW
1982	NY A	3	9	1	3	0	0	0	1	1-0	0	1	.333	.400	.333	105	0	0-0	.875	2	205	67	2b3		0.
1983	SD N	7	12	1	2	1	0	0	1	1-0	0	3	.167	.231	.250	34	-1	0-0	1.000	-2	79	92	2b5,S2/3		-0.
1985	SD N	1	1	0	0	0	0	0	0	0-0	0	0	.000	.000	.000	-99	0	0-0	—	0			/H		-0.
Total	3	11	22	3	5	1	0	0	2	2-0	0	4	.227	.292	.273	58	-1	0-0	.935	-0	127	83	2b8,S2/3		-0.

RODRIGUEZ, ELLIE   Eliseo (Delgado)   B5.24.1946 Fajardo, PR   BR/TR/5-11/185*   d5.26   [DL 1977 LA N 26]

YEAR	TM LG	G	AB	R	H	2B	3B	HR	RBI	BB-IB	HP	SO	AVG	OBP	SLG	AOPS	ABR	SB-CS	FA	FR	RNG	THR	GAMES AT POSITION	DL	BFW
1968	NY A	9	24	1	5	0	0	0	1	3-0	0	3	.208	.296	.208	57	-1	0-0	1.000	-1	128	133	C9		-0.
1969	KC ☆	95	267	27	63	10	0	2	20	31-6	8	26	.236	.333	.296	76	-7	3-2	.990	-7	136	108	C90		-1.
1970	KC A	80	231	25	52	8	2	1	15	27-2	4	35	.225	.312	.290	68	-9	2-1	.988	3	73	83	C75		-0.
1971	Mil A	115	319	28	67	10	1	1	30	41-5	8	51	.210	.311	.257	64	-13	1-1	.992	10	144	150	C114		0.
1972	Mil A ☆	116	355	31	101	14	2	2	35	52-5	7	43	.285	.382	.352	123	13	1-4	.983	-4	107	105	C114		1.
1973	Mil A	94	290	30	78	8	1	0	30	41-3	10	28	.269	.376	.303	95	1	4-3	.986	3	123	143	C75,D14		1.
1974	Cal A	140	395	48	100	20	0	7	36	69-6	6	56	.253	.373	.357	118	14	4-5	.992	2	127	119	C137/D		2.
1975	Cal A	90	226	20	53	6	0	3	20	49-0	6	37	.235	.380	.301	103	5	2-2	.991	-8	71	81	C90	29	0.
1976	Cal A	36	66	10	14	0	0	0	9	19-2	1	12	.212	.400	.212	81	0	0-0	.986	2	54	87	C33	17	0.
Total	9	775	2173	220	533	76	6	16	203	332-29	55	291	.245	.356	.308	94	3	17-18	.989	-0	112	114	C737,D15	72	3.

RODRIGUEZ, HECTOR   Hector Antonio (Ordenana)   B6.13.1920 Alquizar, Cuba   BR/TR/5-8/165   d4.15   Negro Lg 1939-44

YEAR	TM LG	G	AB	R	H	2B	3B	HR	RBI	BB-IB	HP	SO	AVG	OBP	SLG	AOPS	ABR	SB-CS	FA	FR	RNG	THR	GAMES AT POSITION	DL	BFW
1952	Chi A	124	407	55	108	14	0	1	40	47	3	22	.265	.346	.307	82	-8	7-6	.959	5	98	106	3b113		-0

RODRIGUEZ, HENRY   Henry Anderson (Lorenzo)   B11.8.1967 Santo Domingo, D.R.   BL/TL/6-1/205(180-225)   d7.5

YEAR	TM LG	G	AB	R	H	2B	3B	HR	RBI	BB-IB	HP	SO	AVG	OBP	SLG	AOPS	ABR	SB-CS	FA	FR	RNG	THR	GAMES AT POSITION	DL	BFW
1992	LA N	53	146	11	32	7	0	3	14	8-0	0	30	.219	.258	.329	66	-7	0-0	.960	2	84	290	O48(17/0/31)/1		-0
1993	LA N	76	176	20	39	10	0	8	23	11-2	0	39	.222	.266	.415	84	-5	1-0	.984	-2	78	108	O48(26/0/23),1b13		-0
1994	LA N	104	306	33	82	14	2	8	49	17-2	2	58	.268	.307	.405	90	-6	0-1	.986	3	105	95	O86(85/0/6),1b17		-0
1995	LA N	21	80	6	21	4	1	1	10	5-2	0	17	.262	.306	.375	84	-2	0-1	1.000	-1	103	0	O20R/1		-0
	Mon N	24	58	7	12	0	1	2	5	6-0	0	11	.207	.277	.259	42	-5	0-0	1.000	-1	117	116	1b10,O8(4/0/4)	75	-0
	Year	45	138	13	33	4	2	1	15	11-2	0	28	.239	.293	.326	65	-7	0-1	.977	-1	94	113	O28(4/0/24),1b11		-1
1996	Mon N★	145	532	81	147	42	1	36	103	37-7	3	160	.276	.325	.562	126	18	2-0	.947	-9	76	113	O89(88/0/2),1b51		-0
1997	Mon N	132	476	55	116	28	3	26	83	42-5	2	149	.244	.306	.479	103	0	3-3	.985	-4	92	53	O126(126/0/1),1b3		-0
1998	†Chi N	128	415	56	104	21	1	31	85	54-7	0	113	.251	.334	.530	119	10	1-3	.996	9	115	109	O114L,D5	15	1
1999	Chi N	130	447	72	136	29	0	26	87	56-6	1	76	.304	.381	.544	131	21	2-4	.983	-0	90	126	O70(70/0/1)		-0
2000	Chi N	76	259	37	65	15	1	18	51	22-2	3	76	.251	.314	.525	109	2	1-2	1.000	-2	82	63	O29(24/0/6)		-0
	Fla N	36	108	10	29	6	0	2	10	14-0	1	23	.269	.358	.380	91	-1	0-0	.987	-2	88	108	O99(94/0/7)		-0
	Year	112	367	47	94	21	1	20	61	36-2	4	99	.256	.327	.482	104	1	1-2					/D	52	-0
2001	NY A	5	8	0	0	0	0	0	0	0-0	0	4	.000	.000	.000	-99	-2	0-0	—	-1	0	0	O5(4/0/1)		-0
2002	Mon N	20	20	1	1	0	0	0	3	4-0	0	8	.050	.200	.050	-24	-4	0-0	.980	-4	94	103		142	-2
Total	11	950	3031	389	784	176	9	160	523	276-33	11	803	.259	.321	.481	107	19	10-14	.980	-4	94	103	O765(680/0/95),1b96,D8	142	-2

RODRIGUEZ, IVAN   Ivan (Torres) "Pudge"   B11.27.1971 Manati, PR   BR/TR/5-9/205(165-220)   d6.20

YEAR	TM LG	G	AB	R	H	2B	3B	HR	RBI	BB-IB	HP	SO	AVG	OBP	SLG	AOPS	ABR	SB-CS	FA	FR	RNG	THR	GAMES AT POSITION	DL	BFW
1991	Tex A	88	280	24	74	16	0	3	27	5-0	1	42	.264	.276	.354	74	-11	0-1	.983	11	138	132	C88	21	0
1992	Tex A★	123	420	39	109	16	1	8	37	24-2	1	73	.260	.300	.360	87	-9	0-0	.983	20	160	134	C116,D2		0
1993	Tex A★	137	473	56	129	28	4	10	66	29-3	4	70	.273	.315	.412	98	-2	8-7	.991	11	133	107	C134/D		0
1994	Tex A★	99	363	56	108	19	1	16	57	31-5	7	42	.298	.360	.488	116	8	6-3	.992	2	177	77	C99		0
1995	Tex A★	130	492	56	149	32	2	12	67	16-2	1	48	.303	.327	.449	97	-3	0-2	.990	13	198	108	C127/D		0
1996	†Tex A★	153	639	116	192	47	3	19	86	38-7	4	55	.300	.342	.473	110	4	5-3	.992	23	253	109	C143,D5		0
1997	Tex A★	150	597	98	187	34	4	20	77	38-7	8	89	.313	.360	.484	111	9	7-3	.994	16	262	109	C139,D6		0
1998	†Tex A★	145	579	88	186	40	4	21	91	32-4	3	88	.321	.358	.513	117	14	9-9	.994	7	248	96	C87/D	68	0
1999	†Tex A★	144	600	116	199	29	1	35	113	24-2	11	64	.332	.356	.558	122	17	25-12	.993	18	257	96	C141/D		0
2000	Tex A★	91	363	66	126	27	4	27	83	19-5	7	48	.347	.375	.667	156	29	5-5	.996	7	248	87	C87/D	53	0
2001	Tex A	111	442	70	136	24	2	25	65	23-3	4	75	.308	.347	.541	125	15	10-3	.990	13	308	118	C106,D5	51	0
2002	Tex A★	108	408	67	128	32	2	19	60	25-2	2	71	.314	.353	.542	130	17	5-4	.992	1	151	75	C138/D		0
2003	†Fla N	144	511	90	152	36	3	16	85	55-6	6	92	.297	.369	.474	124	11	10-6	.987	21	153	68	C124,D8		0
2004	†Det A★	135	527	72	176	32	2	19	86	41-6	3	91	.334	.383	.510	136	28	7-4	.995	14	191	130	C123,D3		0
2005	Det A★	129	504	71	139	33	5	14	50	11-2	2	93	.276	.290	.444	95	-5	7-3						193	3
Total	15	1887	7198	1085	2190	445	38	264	1050	411-56	50	1039	.304	.343	.487	113	123	104-53	.990	180	202	103	C1811,D46	193	3

YEAR	TM LG	G	AB	R	H	2B	3B	HR	RBI	BB-IB	HP	SO	AVG	OBP	SLG	AOPS	ABR	SB-CS	FA	FR	RNG	THR	GAMES AT POSITION	DL	BFW
RODRIGUEZ, JOHN	John Joseph B1.20.1978 New York NY BL/TL/6-0/205 d7.18																								
2005	†StL N	56	149	15	44	6	0	5	24	19-4	3	45	.295	.382	.436	113	3	2-0	.973	0	96	138	O45(40/0/9)		0.2
RODRIGUEZ, JOSE	Jose "El Hombre Goma" B2.23.1894 Havana, Cuba D1.21.1953 Havana, Cuba BR/TR/5-8/150 d10.5																								
1916	NY N	1	0	0	0	0	0	0	0	0-0	0	0	—	—	—	—	0	0	—	0			/R		0.0
1917	NY N	7	20	2	4	0	1	0	2	2	0	1	.200	.273	.300	78	-1	2	1.000	-1	36	71	1b7		-0.2
1918	NY N	50	125	15	20	0	2	0	15	12	1	3	.160	.239	.192	33	-10	6	.978	-0	91	104	2b40,1b8,3b2		-1.1
Total	3	58	145	17	24	0	3	0	17	14	1	4	.166	.244	.207	39	-11	8	.978	-0	91	104	2b40,1b15,3b2		-1.3
RODRIGUEZ, LIU	Liubiemithz B11.5.1976 Caracas, Venez BB/TR/5-9/170 d6.9																								
1999	Chi A	39	93	8	22	2	2	1	12	12-0	3	11	.237	.343	.333	72	-4	0-0	.985	-8	84	50	2b22,S14/3		-0.9
RODRIGUEZ, TONY	Luis Antonio B8.15.1970 Rio Piedras, PR BR/TR/5-11/178 [BosA91 10/278] d7.6 Col Charleston (WV)																								
1996	Bos A	27	67	7	16	1	0	1	9	4-0	1	8	.239	.292	.299	49	-5	0-0	.979	2	112	78	S21,3b5		-0.2
RODRIGUEZ, LUIS	Luis Orlando B6.27.1980 San Carlos, Venez BB/TR/5-9/180 d5.21																								
2005	Min A	79	175	21	47	10	2	2	18	18-0	1	23	.269	.335	.383	90	-2	2-2	1.000	1	102	149	2b40,3b27,S10,D3		0.0
RODRIGUEZ, RUBEN	Ruben Dario (Martinez) B8.4.1964 Cabrera, D.R. BR/TR/6-3/175(170-190) d9.15																								
1986	Pit N	2	3	0	0	0	0	0	0	0-0	0	1	.000	.000	.000	-97	-1	0-0	1.000	0	95	0	C2		-0.1
1988	Pit N	2	5	1	1	0	1	0	1	0-0	0	2	.200	.200	.600	123	0	0-0	1.000	1	0	0	C2		0.1
Total	2	4	8	1	1	0	1	0	1	0-0	0	3	.125	.125	.375	36	-1	0-0	1.000	1	45	0	C4		0.0
RODRIGUEZ, STEVE	Steven James B11.29.1970 Las Vegas NV BR/TR/5-8/170 [BosA92 5/142] d4.30 Col Pepperdine																								
1995	Bos A	6	8	1	1	0	0	0	0	1-0	0	1	.125	.222	.125	-6	-1	1-0	.667	-1	85	0	S4/2D		-0.2
	Det A	12	31	4	6	1	0	0	0	5-0	0	9	.194	.306	.226	41	-3	1-2	.982	-2	100	71	2b12/S		-0.4
	Year	18	39	5	7	1	0	0	0	6-0	0	10	.179	.289	.205	31	-4	2-2	.983	-3	98	66	2b13,S5/D		-0.6
RODRIGUEZ, VIC	Victor Manuel (Rivera) B7.14.1961 New York NY BR/TR/5-11/173* d9.5																								
1984	Bal A	11	17	4	7	3	0	0	2	0-0	0	2	.412	.412	.588	176	2	0-0	.958	-0	112	35	2b7/D		0.2
1989	Min A	6	11	2	5	2	0	0	0	0-0	1	1	.455	.455	.636	192	1	0-0	.900	0	103	202	3b5/D		0.2
Total	2	17	28	6	12	5	0	0	2	0-0	1	3	.429	.429	.607	182	3	0-0	.958	-0	112	35	2b7,3b5,D2		0.4
ROENICKE, GARY	Gary Steven B12.5.1954 Covina CA BR/TR/6-3/203* [MonN73 1/8] d6.8 b-Ron																								
1976	Mon N	29	90	9	20	3	1	2	5	4-0	1	18	.222	.260	.344	68	-4	0-0	.955	0	92	170	O25(3/0/22)		-0.6
1978	Bal A	27	58	5	15	3	0	3	8	8-0	1	3	.259	.348	.466	138	3	0-1	1.000	-1	74	104	O20L		0.1
1979	†Bal A	133	376	60	98	16	1	25	64	61-4	12	74	.261	.378	.508	142	16	1-3	.981	0	98	118	O130(114/26/8),D2		1.9
1980	Bal A	118	297	40	71	13	0	10	28	41-5	6	49	.239	.340	.384	100	1	2-0	**1.000**	3	103	119	O113(86/13/38)		0.1
1981	Bal A	85	219	31	59	16	0	3	20	23-1	2	29	.269	.340	.384	110	4	1-2	.983	5	123	43	O83(45/13/54)		0.5
1982	Bal A	137	393	58	106	25	1	21	74	70-2	9	73	.270	.392	.499	144	27	6-7	.990	9	118	98	O125(80/34/42),1b10		3.0
1983	†Bal A	115	323	45	84	13	0	19	64	30-2	4	35	.260	.326	.477	121	8	2-2	.982	-5	93	115	O100(79/8/23),1b7,3b2,D2		0.2
1984	Bal A	121	326	36	73	19	1	10	44	58-1	4	43	.224	.346	.380	103	4	1-2	.995	-3	93	69	O117(85/6/32)		-0.4
1985	Bal A	114	225	36	49	9	0	15	43	44-1	0	36	.218	.342	.458	120	7	2-2	.993	3	104	155	O89(76/9/9),D17		0.7
1986	NY A	69	136	11	36	5	0	3	18	27-0	1	30	.265	.388	.368	108	3	1-1	1.000	-2	72	172	O37(33/3/2),D15,3b3,1b2		0.7
1987	Atl N	67	151	25	33	8	0	9	28	32-0	1	23	.219	.353	.450	108	3	0-0	.968	-2	88	0	O44(40/0/4),1b9		-0.1
1988	Atl N	49	114	11	26	5	0	1	7	8-0	0	15	.228	.279	.298	63	-5	0-0	1.000	-2	92	0	O35(32/1/2)/1		-0.9
Total	12	1064	2708	367	670	135	4	121	406	406-16	41	428	.247	.351	.434	117	75	16-20	.988	7	101	101	O918(693/113/236),D36,1b29,3b5	35	4.5
ROENICKE, RON	Ronald Jon B8.19.1956 Covina CA BB/TL/6-0/180* [LAN77 S1/17] d9.2 C6 b-Gary Col UCLA																								
1981	LA N	22	47	6	11	0	0	0	6	6-0	0	9	.234	.321	.234	62	-2	1-1	1.000	2	133	98	O20(5/6/10)		-0.1
1982	LA N	109	143	18	37	8	0	1	12	21-3	2	32	.259	.359	.336	99	-1	5-0	.984	-3	84	43	O72(21/18/39)		-0.2
1983	LA N	81	145	12	32	4	0	2	12	14-1	0	26	.221	.287	.290	61	-8	3-2	.987	-1	98	43	O62(9/17/44)		-1.1
	Sea A	59	198	23	50	12	0	4	23	33-1	2	31	.253	.362	.374	100	2	6-2	.993	7	98	362	O54(16/38/4),1b8/D		0.7
1984	†SD N	12	20	4	6	1	0	1	2	2-1	0	5	.300	.364	.500	140	1	0-0	1.000	-1	86	0	O10(7/2/2)		0.0
1985	SF N	65	133	23	34	9	1	3	13	35-3	0	27	.256	.408	.406	139	9	0-0	.984	-1	106	0	O35(9/6/20)		0.7
1986	Phi N	102	275	42	68	13	1	5	42	61-4	0	52	.247	.381	.356	102	4	2-2	.989	-0	105	63	O83(24/63/8)		0.2
1987	Phi N	63	78	9	13	3	1	1	4	14-1	0	15	.167	.293	.269	49	-6	1-0	.964	0	102	138	O26(9/15/4)		-0.6
1988	Cin N	14	37	4	5	1	0	0	5	4-0	1	8	.135	.238	.162	16	-4	0-0	1.000	-1	82	0	O14(0/4/10)		-0.6
Total	8	527	1076	141	256	51	3	17	113	190-14	5	195	.238	.353	.338	92	-3	24-9	.989	2	100	109	O376(100/169/141),1b8/D		-1.0
ROETTGER, OSCAR	Oscar Frederick Louis "Okkie" B2.19.1900 St.Louis MO D7.4.1986 St.Louis MO BR/TR/6-0/170 d7.7 b-Wally ▲																								
1923	NY A	5	2	0	0	0	0	0	0	0-0	0	0	.000	.000	.000	-98	0	0-0	1.000	0	64	0	P5		0.0
1924	NY A	1	0	0	0	0	0	0	0	0-0	0	0	—	—	—	—	0	0-0	—	0	0	0	/P		0.0
1927	Bro N	5	4	0	0	0	0	0	0	0-0	0	0	.000	.000	.000		0	0-0	—	0	0	0	/P		-0.1
1932	Phi A	26	60	7	14	1	0	0	6	1	1	1	.233	.292	.250	40	-5	0-0	.978	-1	63	57	1b15		-0.8
Total	4	37	66	7	14	1	0	0	6	6	1	5	.212	.288	.227	34	-5	0-0	.978	-1	63	57	1b15,P6/OR		-0.9
ROETTGER, WALLY	Walter Henry B8.28.1902 St.Louis MO D9.14.1951 Champaign IL BR/TR/6-1.5/190 d5.1 b-Oscar Col Illinois																								
1927	StL N	5	1	0	0	0	0	0	0	0-0	0	0	.000	.500	.000	42	0	0-0	.500	-1	83	0	O3L		-0.1
1928	StL N	68	261	27	89	17	4	6	44	10	3	22	.341	.372	.506	125	9	2	.981	-3	101	31	O69(33/0/34)		0.1
1929	StL N	79	269	27	68	11	3	3	42	13	0	27	.253	.287	.349	56	-20	0	.993	-3	105	66	O69(7/0/62)		-2.2
1930	NY N	121	420	51	119	15	5	5	51	25	4	29	.283	.330	.379	72	-20	1	**.992**	-3	91	109	O114(28/85/4)		-2.5
1931	Cin N	44	185	25	65	11	4	1	20	7	1	9	.351	.378	.470	135	8	1	.990	-0	101	75	O44(18/2/24)		0.6
	†StL N	45	151	16	43	12	2	0	17	9	3	14	.285	.337	.391	92	-2	0	.974	-3	92	28	O42(8/7/27)		-0.7
	Year	89	336	41	108	23	6	1	37	16	4	23	.321	.360	.435	114	6	1	.983	-4	97	53	O86(26/9/51)		-0.1
1932	Cin N	106	347	26	96	18	3	3	43	23	1	24	.277	.323	.372	89	-5	0	.991	2	108	-53	O94(89/5/0)		-0.8
1933	Cin N	84	209	13	50	7	1	1	17	8	1	10	.239	.267	.297	62	-11	0	.977	2	111	88	O55(26/1/28)		-1.2
1934	Pit N	47	106	7	26	5	1	0	11	3	0	8	.245	.266	.311	53	-7	0	1.000	1	115	64	O23(19/0/4)		-0.7
Total	8	599	1949	192	556	96	23	19	245	99	12	143	.285	.324	.387	85	-48	4	.986	-4	102	68	O510(231/100/183)		-7.5
ROETZ, ED	Edward Bernard B8.6.1905 Philadelphia PA D3.16.1965 Philadelphia PA BR/TR/5-10/160 d5.26																								
1929	StL A	16	45	7	11	4	1	0	5	4	0	6	.244	.306	.378	72	-2	0-0	.909	-2	84	140	S8,1b5,2b2/3		-0.3
ROGELL, BILLY	William George B11.24.1904 Springfield IL D8.9.2003 Sterling Heights MI BB/TR/5-10.5/163 d4.14																								
1925	Bos A	58	169	12	33	5	1	0	17	11	0	17	.195	.244	.237	22	-21	0-3	.935	6	113	114	2b49,S6		-1.3
1927	Bos A	82	207	35	55	14	5	2	28	24	0	28	.266	.342	.420	99	-1	3-1	.966	6	123	73	3b53,2b2,O2(1/0/1)		0.8
1928	Bos A	102	296	33	69	10	4	0	29	22	4	47	.233	.295	.294	56	-19	2-6	.935	-2	104	84	S67,2b22,O6(1/2/3),3b3		-1.6
1930	Det A	54	144	20	24	4	0	2	9	15	1	23	.167	.250	.222	20	-18	1-2	.938	3	105	85	S33,3b13/OL		-1.1
1931	Det A	48	185	21	56	12	3	2	24	24	1	17	.303	.383	.432	110	3	8-8	.958	7	116	84	S48		1.2
1932	Det A	144	554	88	150	29	6	9	61	50	1	38	.271	.334	.394	84	-14	14-6	.944	11	105	104	S139,3b4		0.8
1933	Det A	155	587	67	173	42	11	0	57	79	3	33	.295	.381	.404	106	-8	6-9	.944	19	104	**133**	S155		3.4
1934	†Det A	154	592	114	175	32	8	3	100	74	0	36	.296	.374	.392	97	-1	13-3	.962	10	104	108	S154		2.1
1935	†Det A	150	560	88	154	23	11	6	71	80	1	29	.275	.367	.387	99	0	3-6	**.971**	11	104	**114**	S150		1.9
1936	Det A	146	585	85	160	27	5	6	68	73	3	41	.274	.357	.368	79	-19	14-10	**.965**	2	101	104	S146/3		-0.5
1937	Det A	146	536	85	148	30	8	7	64	83	4	48	.276	.376	.403	94	-3	5-5	**.967**	1	99	112	S146		0.7
1938	Det A	136	501	76	130	22	8	3	55	86	5	37	.259	.373	.353	78	-14	9-2	.959	10	**106**	109	S134		0.6
1939	Det A	74	174	24	40	6	3	2	23	26	0	14	.230	.330	.333	65	-9	3-1	.931	-0	95	115	S43,3b21,2b2		-0.5
1940	Chi N	33	59	7	8	0	1	0	8	6	1	4	.136	.164	.186	-4	-9	1	.900	-4	84	83	S14,3b9,2b3		-1.2
Total	14	1482	5149	755	1375	256	75	42	609	649	21	416	.267	.351	.370	84	-117	82-62	.956	80	104	109	S1235,3b104,2b78,O9(3/2/4)		5.3
ROGERS, EDDIE	Edward Antonio B8.29.1978 San Pedro de Macoris, D.R. BR/TR/6-1/165(165-190) d9.5																								
2002	Bal A	5	3	0	0	0	0	0	0	0-0	0	0	.000	.000	.000	-99	-1	0-0	1.000	1	226	196	S4		0.0
2005	Bal A	8	1	4	0	0	1	0	0	0-0	0	0	1.000	1.000	4.000	1134	1	0-2	—	-0	0	0	/SD		0.0
Total	2	13	4	4	0	0	1	0	0	0-0	0	0	.250	.250	1.000	218	0	0-2	1.000	1	176	152	S5,D2		0.0
ROGERS, EMMETT	Emmett E. B10.11.1870 Hot Springs AR D10.24.1941 Fort Smith AR BB/5-10/165 d4.19																								
1890	Tol AA	35	110	18	19	3	3	0	7	14	0		.173	.266	.255	52	-7	2	.924	5	115	96	C34/OL		0.1

YEAR	TM LG	G	AB	R	H	2B	3B	HR	RBI	BB-IB	HP	SO	AVG	OBP	SLG	AOPS	ABR	SB-CS	FA	FR	RNG	THR	GAMES AT POSITION	DL	BFW

ROGERS, FRALEY Fraley W. B1850 Brooklyn NY D5.10.1881 New York NY 5-8/184 d4.30

																									-0.3
1872	Bos NA	45	204	39	56	7	1	1	28	1		4	.275	.278	.333	83	-5	2-0	.790	-3	89	138	O41(4/0/38),1b6		0.0
1873	Bos NA	2	11	2	4	1	0	0	3	0		2	.364	.364	.455	131	0	0-0	.893	0	0	96	1b2		
Total	2 NA	47	215	41	60	8	1	1	31	1		6	.279	.282	.340	85	-5	2-0	.790	-3	89	138	O41(4/0/38),1b8		-0.3

ROGERS, JIM James F. B4.9.1872 Hartford CT 5-7.5/180 d4.17 M1

																									-0.4
1896	Was N	38	154	21	43	6	4	1	30	10		9	.279	.323	.390	87	-4	3	.882	-2	111	40	3b32,2b6/OC		-1.3
	Lou N	72	290	39	75	8	6	0	38	15	1	14	.259	.297	.328	67	-15	13	.971	-1	115	100	1b60,S12		-1.7
	Year	110	444	60	118	14	10	1	68	25	1	23	.266	.306	.349	74	-18	16	.971	-3	115	100	1b60,3b32,S12,2b6/OC		-1.5
1897	Lou N	42	153	22	22	3	2	2	22	23	1		.144	.260	.229	31	-16	4	.929	-3	98	89	2b40,1b3,M		-3.2
Total	2	152	597	82	140	17	12	3	90	48	2	23	.235	.294	.318	63	-35	20	.970	-6	114	97	1b63,2b46,3b32,S12/OC		

ROGERS, JAY Jay Lewis B8.3.1888 Sandusky NY D7.1.1964 Carlisle NY BR/TR/5-11.5/178 d5.22

| 1914 | NY A | 5 | 8 | 0 | 0 | 0 | 0 | 0 | 0 | 0 | | 4 | .000 | .000 | .000 | -99 | -2 | 0 | .923 | -0 | 121 | 49 | C4 | | -0.2 |

ROGERS, PACKY Stanley Frank (b Stanley Frank Hazinski) B4.26.1913 Swoyersville PA D5.15.1998 Elmira NY BR/TR/5-8/175 d7.12 Col Fordham

| | | | | | | | | | | | | | | | | | | | | | | | | | -0.3 |
| 1938 | Bro N | 23 | 37 | 3 | 7 | 1 | 1 | 0 | 5 | 6 | | 6 | .189 | .302 | .270 | 57 | -2 | 0 | 1.000 | -1 | 94 | 42 | S9,3b8,2b3/OL | | |

ROGODZINSKI, MIKE Michael George B2.22.1948 Evanston IL BL/TR/6-0/185* [PhiN69 2/30] d5.4 Col Southern Illinois

																									-0.1
1973	Phi N	66	80	13	19	3	0	2	7	12-1	0	19	.237	.333	.350	88	-1	0-0	.947	0	89	244	O16(5/0/13)		-0.3
1974	Phi N	17	15	1	1	0	0	0	1	2-0	0	3	.067	.176	.067	-29	-3	0-0		-0	0	0	/OR	12	-0.1
1975	Phi N	16	19	3	5	1	0	0	4	3-0	0	2	.263	.364	.316	85	0	0-1	.667	-1	51	0	O2L	12	-0.5
Total	3	99	114	17	25	4	0	2	12	17-1	0	24	.219	.318	.307	72	-4	0-1	.909	-0	82	199	O19(7/0/14)		

ROHDE, DAVE David Grant B5.8.1964 Los Altos CA BB/TR/6-2/182* [HouN86 5/120] d4.9 Col Arizona

																									-0.8
1990	Hou N	59	98	8	18	4	0	0	5	9-2	5	20	.184	.283	.224	43	-7	0-0	1.000	-1	108	105	2b32,3b4,S2		-0.4
1991	Hou N	29	41	3	5	0	0	0	5	5-0	0	8	.122	.217	.122	-2	-6	0-0	1.000	2	123	56	2b4,3b3,S3/1		0.0
1992	Cle A	5	7	0	0	0	0	0	0	2-1	0	3	.000	.222	.000	-33	-1	0-0	.900	1	131	248	3b5		-1.2
Total	3	93	146	11	23	4	0	0	5	16-3	5	31	.158	.262	.185	27	-14	0-0	1.000	1	110	98	2b36,3b12,S5/1		

ROHE, GEORGE George Anthony "Whitey" B9.15.1875 Cincinnati OH D6.10.1957 Cincinnati OH BR/TR/5-9/165 d5.7

																									-0.2
1901	Bal A	14	36	7	10	2	0	0	4	5		1	.278	.381	.333	95	-2	27	.912	-2	27	94	1b8,3b6		-0.3
1905	Chi A	34	113	14	24	1	0	1	12	12	4		.212	.310	.248	81	-2	2	.934	-1	89	191	2b17,3b17		0.5
1906	†Chi A	77	225	14	58	5	1	0	25	16	3		.258	.316	.289	92	-2	8	.926	5	114	133	3b57,2b5/OL		-1.6
1907	Chi A	144	494	46	105	11	2	2	51	39	3		.213	.274	.255	71	-15	16	.898	-2	108	199	3b76,2b39,S30		-1.6
Total	4	269	868	81	197	19	3	3	92	72	11		.227	.294	.266	79	-19	27	.917	-1	110	189	3b156,2b61,S30,1b8/OL		

ROHN, DAN Daniel Jay B1.10.1956 Alpena MI BL/TR/5-7/165* [ChiN77 4/90] d9.2 Col Central Michigan

																									0.3
1983	Chi N	23	31	3	12	3	2	0	6	2-0	0	2	.387	.424	.613	176	3	1-0	.923	-0	95	73	2b6/S		-0.5
1984	Chi N	25	31	1	4	0	0	1	3	1-0	0	6	.129	.152	.226	6	-4	0-0	1.000	-1	121	173	3b7,2b5,S5		0.0
1986	Cle A	6	10	1	2	0	0	0	2	1-0	0	1	.200	.273	.200	32	-1	0-0	.900	0	178	121	2b2,3b2/S	20	-0.2
Total	3	54	72	5	18	3	2	1	11	4-0	0	9	.250	.286	.389	82	-2	1-0	.930	-1	103	63	2b13,3b9,S7	20	

ROHRMEIER, DAN Daniel B9.27.1965 Cincinnati OH BR/TR/6-0/195 [ChiA87 5/115] d9.3 Col St. Thomas (FL)

| 1997 | Sea A | 7 | 9 | 4 | 3 | 0 | 0 | 0 | 2 | 2-0 | 0 | 4 | .333 | .455 | .333 | 110 | 0 | 0-0 | 1.000 | 0 | 295 | 0 | 1b3,D4 | | 0.0 |

ROHWER, RAY Ray B6.5.1895 Dixon CA D1.24.1988 Davis CA BL/TL/5-10/155 d4.13 Col California-Davis

																									-0.1
1921	Pit N	30	40	6	10	3	2	0	6	4	0	8	.250	.318	.425	93	-1	0-1	.842	0	100	218	O10(0/3/7)		-0.1
1922	Pit N	53	129	19	38	6	3	3	22	10	1	17	.295	.350	.457	105	1	1-0	.938	1	97	137	O30(0/2/28)		-0.2
Total	2	83	169	25	48	9	5	3	28	14	1	25	.284	.342	.450	102	0	1-1	.917	1	98	152	O40(0/5/35)		

ROIG, TONY Anton Ambrose B12.23.1927 New Orleans LA BR/TR/6-1/180* d9.13

																									0.0
1953	Was A	3	8	1	1	0	0	0	0	0	0	1	.125	.125	.250	-1	-1	0-0	1.000	1	114	126	2b2		-0.4
1955	Was A	29	57	3	13	1	0	4	2-0		0	15	.228	.254	.281	46	-5	0-0	.932	0	114	126	S21,3b8/2		0.
1956	Was A	44	119	10	25	5	2	0	7	20-0	0	29	.210	.321	.286	62	-6	2-0	.973	5	119	114	2b27,S19		0.
Total	3	76	184	14	39	7	2	0	11	22-0	0	45	.212	.295	.283	55	-12	2-0	.927	5	108	99	S40,2b30,3b8		0.

ROJAS, COOKIE Octavio Victor (Rivas) B3.6.1939 Havana, Cuba BR/TR/5-10/170* d4.10 M2/C14 OF(79/124/10)

																									-1.
1962	Cin N	39	86	9	19	2	0	0	9	9-1	1	4	.221	.302	.244	47	-6	3	.949	-7	76	84	2b30/3		0.
1963	Phi N	64	77	18	17	0	1	1	2	3-0	1	8	.221	.259	.286	57	-5	4-1	.991	7	127	116	2b25/OL		0.
1964	Phi N	109	340	58	99	19	5	2	31	22-0	1	27	.291	.334	.394	107	3	1-3	.967	-2	95	193	O70(23/54/1),2b20,S18/C3		2.
1965	Phi N★	142	521	78	158	25	3	3	42	42-3	3	33	.303	.356	.380	110	8	5-5	.986	6	99	106	2b84,O55(11/41/5),S11,C2/1		-1.
1966	Phi N	156	626	77	168	18	1	6	55	35-3	4	46	.268	.310	.329	78	-18	4-6	.983	-5	99	106	2b106,O56(30/28/3),S2		-0.
1967	Phi N	147	528	60	137	21	2	4	45	30-3	1	58	.259	.297	.330	79	-15	8-4	.977	-1	98	114	2b137,O9(8/1/1),C3,S2/P3		-0.
1968	Phi N	152	621	53	144	19	9	6	48	16-2	1	55	.232	.248	.306	67	-27	4-8	.987	16	103	118	2b150/C		-1.
1969	Phi N	110	391	35	89	11	1	4	30	23-1	1	28	.228	.269	.292	59	-22	1-6	.980	1	91	107	2b95,O2L		-0.
1970	StL N	23	47	2	5	0	0	0	2	3-0	1	4	.106	.176	.106	-22	-8	0-0	1.000	2	125	150	2b10,O3L,S2		-0.
	KC A	98	384	36	100	13	3	2	28	26-0	1	29	.260	.306	.326	71	-16	3-7	.982	4	105	114	2b97		-0.
1971	KC A★	115	414	56	124	22	2	6	59	39-3	2	35	.300	.357	.406	118	11	2-8	.986	-4	98	107	2b131,S2/OL	22	1.
1972	KC A★	137	487	49	127	25	0	3	53	41-5	1	35	.261	.315	.331	94	-3	2-8	.986	-9	105	102	2b133,3b6,S2		0.
1973	KC A★	139	551	78	152	29	3	6	69	37-1	1	38	.276	.320	.372	88	-8	18-4	.982	13	111	110	2b137		1.
1974	KC A☆	144	542	52	147	17	1	6	60	30-4	3	43	.271	.309	.339	83	-12	8-4	.987	-18	97	94	2b141		-2.
1975	KC A	120	406	34	103	14	1	2	37	30-2	1	24	.254	.304	.323	76	-13	2-0	.980	-10	95	88	2b40,3b6/1D		-1.
1976	†KC A	63	132	11	32	6	0	0	16	8-0	0	15	.242	.280	.288	68	-5	2-0	1.000	-6	76	88	2b40,3b6/1D		-1.
1977	†KC A	64	156	8	39	1	0	0	10	8-2	1	17	.250	.285	.321	64	-8	1-3	.944	-3	106	121	3b31,2b16,D6		-6
Total	16	1822	6309	714	1660	254	25	54	593	396-30	20	489	.263	.306	.337	83	-144	74-68	.984	-0	100	106	2b1447,O197C,3b46,S39,D16,C7,1b2/P22	-6	

ROJEK, STAN Stanley Andrew B4.21.1919 N.Tonawanda NY D7.9.1997 N.Tonawanda NY BR/TR/5-10/170* d9.22 Mil 1943-45

																							/R		0
1942	Bro N	1	0	1	0	0	0	0	0	0	0								.974	2	114	100	S15,2b6,3b4		0
1946	Bro N	45	47	11	13	2	1	0	2	4	0	0	.277	.333	.362	96	0	1	.971	5	111	131	S17,3b9,2b7		0
1947	Bro N	32	80	7	21	0	1	0	7	3	0	5	.262	.322	.287	61	-5	1	.971	4	106	97	S36,3b1		-2
1948	Pit N	156	641	85	186	27	5	4	51	61	3	41	.290	.355	.367	94	-5	24	.962	-4	102	105	S156		-1
1949	Pit N	144	557	72	136	19	2	0	31	50	2	31	.244	.309	.285	59	-32	4	.966	1	101	103	S144		-1
1950	Pit N	76	230	28	59	12	1	0	17	18	1	13	.257	.313	.317	64	-12	2	.967	-10	91	99	S68,2b3		-C
1951	Pit N	8	16	0	3	0	0	0	0	0	0	1	.188	.188	.188	1	-2	0-0	.900	-1	107	0	S8		-C
	StL N	51	186	21	51	7	3	0	14	10	2	10	.274	.318	.344	78	-6	0-3	.974	2	96	123	S51		-C
	Year	59	202	21	54	7	3	0	14	10	2	11	.267	.308	.332	72	-8	0-3	.968	1	97	113	S59		-C
1952	StL A	9	7	0	1	0	0	0	0	0	0	4	.143	.333	.143	35	-1	0-0	1.000	1	141	79	S4/2		-4
Total	8	522	1764	225	470	67	13	4	122	152	8	100	.266	.327	.326	74	-63	32-3	.965	-4	100	105	S463,2b17,3b13		

ROLEN, SCOTT Scott Bruce B4.4.1975 Evansville IN BR/TR/6-4/225(195-240) [PhiN93 2/46] d8.1

																									-C
1996	Phi N	37	130	10	33	7	0	4	18	13-0	1	27	.254	.322	.400	90	-2	0-2	.954	-7	72	68	3b37		-C
1997	Phi N	156	561	93	159	35	3	21	92	76-4	13	138	.283	.377	.469	123	21	16-6	.948	19	103	110	3b155		-C
1998	Phi N	160	601	120	174	45	4	31	110	93-6	11	141	.290	.391	.532	141	39	14-7	.970	13	105	98	3b159		
1999	Phi N	112	421	74	113	28	1	26	77	67-2	3	114	.268	.368	.525	122	15	12-2	.960	16	112	114	3b112		.15
2000	Chi N	128	483	88	144	32	6	26	89	51-9	5	99	.298	.370	.551	129	21	8-1	.971	5	102	63	3b128		
2001	Phi N	151	554	96	160	39	1	25	107	74-6	13	127	.289	.378	.498	132	29	16-5	.973	8	107	119	3b100		
2002	Phi N★	100	375	52	97	21	4	17	66	52-2	8	68	.259	.358	.472	129	14	5-2	.958	12	123	170	3b55		
	†StL N	55	205	37	57	8	4	14	44	20-2	4	34	.278	.354	.561	138	9	3-2	.967	8	103	83	3b55		
	Year	155	580	89	154	29	8	31	110	72-4	12	102	.266	.357	.503	132	23	8-4	.967	20	113	137	3b153		
2003	StL N★	154	559	98	160	49	3	28	104	82-5	9	104	.286	.382	.528	137	33	13-3	.969	-3	102	83	3b153		
2004	†StL N★	142	500	109	157	32	4	34	124	72-5	11	92	.314	.409	.598	150	43	4-3	.977	22	125	99	3b141	111	
2005	StL N★	56	196	28	46	12	1	5	28	25-1	1	28	.235	.323	.383	83	-5	1-2	.966	13	140	176	3b56	126	3
Total	10	1251	4585	805	1300	308	29	231	859	625-42	69	972	.284	.375	.515	131	200	88-36	.966	120	107	108	3b1247		

ROLFE, RED Robert Abial B10.17.1908 Penacook NH D7.8.1969 Gilford NH BL/TR/5-11.5/170 d6.29 M4/C1 Col Dartmouth

																									-C
1931	NY A	1	0	0	0	0	0	0	0	0	0						0-0	1.000	-0	0	0	/S		
1934	NY A	89	279	54	80	13	2	0	18	26		16	.287	.348	.348	86	-6	2-3	.944	-3	87	124	S46,3b26		

YEAR	TM LG	G	AB	R	H	2B	3B	HR	RBI	BB-IB	HP	SO	AVG	OBP	SLG	AOPS	ABR	SB-CS	FA	FR	RNG	THR	GAMES AT POSITION	DL	BFW
1935	NY A	**149**	639	108	192	33	9	5	67	57	3	39	.300	.361	.404	103	.2	7-3	**.964**	-7	91	96	3b136,S17		0.2
1936	†NY A	135	568	116	181	39	**15**	10	70	68	0	38	.319	.392	.493	121	19	3-0	**.957**	1	98	91	3b133		2.2
1937	†NY A★	154	648	143	179	34	10	4	62	90	1	53	.276	.365	.378	87	-11	4-2	.962	3	96	95	3b154		-0.2
1938	†NY A☆	151	631	132	196	36	8	10	80	74	3	44	.311	.386	.441	107	8	13-1	.959	-6	96	99	3b151		0.9
1939	†NY A★	**152**	648	**139**	213	46	10	14	80	81	1	41	.329	.404	.495	131	32	7-6	.958	-15	89	86	3b152		2.0
1940	NY A★	139	588	102	147	26	6	10	53	50	2	48	.250	.335	.366	78	-21	4-2	.949	0	99	96	3b138		-1.5
1941	†NY A	136	561	106	148	22	5	8	42	57	0	38	.264	.332	.364	85	-13	3-2	.946	-8	94	121	3b134		-1.5
1942	†NY A	69	265	42	58	8	2	8	25	23	0	18	.219	.281	.355	80	-9	1-1	.959	5	109	159	3b60		-0.2
Total	10	1175	4827	942	1394	257	67	69	497	526	10	335	.289	.360	.413	100	1	44-20	.956	-28	95	101	3b1084,S64		1.4

ROLISON, NATE   Nathan Mardis B3.27.1977 Hattiesburg MS BL/TR/6-6/240 [FlaN95 2/36] d9.5 [DL 2001 Fla N 190]
| 2000 | Fla N | 8 | 13 | 0 | 1 | 0 | 0 | 0 | 2 | 1-0 | 0 | 4 | .077 | .125 | .077 | -45 | -3 | 0-0 | 1.000 | 0 | 113 | 45 | 1b4 | | -0.3 |

ROLLING, RAY   Raymond Copeland B9.8.1886 Martinsburg MO D8.25.1966 St.Paul MN BR/TR-5-10.5/160 d9.6
| 1912 | StL N | 5 | 15 | 0 | 3 | 0 | 0 | 0 | 0 | 0 | 0 | 5 | .200 | .200 | .200 | 10 | -2 | 0 | .947 | -1 | 92 | 0 | 2b4 | | -0.2 |

ROLLINGS, RED   William Russell B3.21.1904 Mobile AL D12.31.1964 Mobile AL BL/TR/5-11/167 d4.17
1927	Bos A	82	184	19	49	4	1	0	9	12	4	10	.266	.325	.299	64	-10	3-1	.938	-3	98	27	3b44,1b10,2b2		-1.0
1928	Bos A	50	48	7	11	3	1	0	6	6	0	8	.229	.315	.333	72	-2	0-0	1.000	-2	0	222	1b5,2b4,O4(2/0/2)/3		-0.4
1930	Bos N	52	123	10	29	6	0	0	10	9	0	5	.236	.288	.285	40	-12	2	.973	1	113	119	3b28,2b10		-0.4
Total	3	184	355	36	89	13	2	0	28	27	4	23	.251	.311	.299	57	-24	5-1	.947	-5	103	64	3b73,2b16,1b15,O4(2/0/2)		-2.3

ROLLINS, JIMMY   James Calvin B11.27.1978 Oakland CA BB/TR/5-8/160(154-165) [PhiN96 2/46] d9.17
2000	Phi N	14	53	5	17	1	1	0	5	2-0	0	7	.321	.345	.377	83	-2	3-0	.978	3	66	125	S13		-0.3
2001	Phi N★	158	656	97	180	29	**12**	14	54	48-2	3	108	.274	.323	.419	95	-7	**46**-8	.979	-19	92	104	S157		-0.7
2002	Phi N★	154	637	82	156	33	**10**	11	60	54-3	4	103	.245	.306	.380	88	-16	31-13	.980	1	103	93	S152/2		-0.2
2003	Phi N	156	628	85	165	42	6	8	62	54-4	0	113	.263	.320	.387	90	-10	20-12	.979	-1	103	95	S154		0.1
2004	Phi N	154	657	119	190	43	**12**	14	73	57-3	2	73	.289	.348	.455	102	2	30-9	.986	-30	87	94	S154		-1.2
2005	Phi N★	158	677	115	196	38	11	12	54	47-8	4	71	.290	.338	.431	97	-4	41-6	.981	-11	92	86	S157		0.4
Total	6	794	3308	503	904	186	52	59	308	262-20	13	475	.273	.328	.414	95	-37	171-48	.981	-63	95	95	S787/2		-1.9

ROLLINS, RICH   Richard John "Red" B4.16.1938 Mount Pleasant PA BR/TR/5-10/185* d6.16 Col Kent St.
1961	Min A	13	17	3	5	1	0	0	3	2-0	1	2	.294	.400	.353	98	0	0-0	1.000	-1	80	74	2b5,3b4		-0.1
1962	Min A★	159	624	96	186	23	5	16	96	75-2	6	61	.298	.374	.428	112	13	3-1	.943	-8	94	118	3b159/S		0.5
1963	Min A	136	531	75	163	23	1	16	61	36-4	8	59	.307	.359	.444	122	16	2-0	.935	-8	94	96	3b132/2		0.8
1964	Min A	148	596	87	161	25	**10**	12	68	53-3	5	80	.270	.334	.406	104	3	2-5	.947	-7	95	66	3b146		-0.6
1965	†Min A	140	469	59	117	22	1	5	32	37-7	4	54	.249	.309	.333	79	-12	4-0	.958	-2	97	102	3b112,2b16		-1.4
1966	Min A	90	269	30	66	7	1	10	40	13-1	4	34	.245	.286	.390	88	-5	0-2	.953	-6	89	138	3b65,2b2/OL		-1.3
1967	Min A	109	339	31	83	11	2	6	37	27-4	3	58	.245	.305	.342	84	-6	1-1	.963	-6	84	99	3b97		-1.4
1968	Min A	93	203	14	49	6	0	6	30	10-2	3	34	.241	.287	.355	89	-3	3-1	.931	-0	105	56	3b56		-1.4
1969	Sea A	58	187	15	42	7	0	4	21	7-0	5	19	.225	.270	.326	67	-9	2-0	.948	5	115	60	3b47/S		-0.4
1970	Mil A	14	25	3	5	1	0	0	5	3-0	1	4	.200	.276	.240	42	-2	0-0	1.000	2	150	213	3b7	76	-0.4
	Cle A	42	43	6	10	0	0	2	4	3-0	0	5	.233	.283	.372	75	-2	0-0	1.000	-2	41	207	3b5		0.0
	Year	56	68	9	15	1	0	2	9	6-0	1	9	.221	.280	.324	65	-3	0-0	.900	0	113	211	3b12		-0.3
Total	10	1002	3303	419	887	125	20	77	399	266-23	39	410	.269	.328	.388	98	-7	17-10	.947	-32	95	96	3b830,2b24,S2/OL	76	-4.6

ROLLINSON, BILL   William (b William Henry Winslow) B6.10.1856 Fairfield ME D9.28.1938 Bristow VA d6.17
| 1884 | Was U | 1 | 3 | 0 | 0 | 0 | 0 | 0 | 0 | 0 | 0 | | .000 | .000 | .000 | -99 | -1 | | .714 | -0 | | | /C | | -0.1 |

ROLLS, DAMIAN   Damian Michael B9.15.1977 Manhattan KS BR/TR/6-2/205* [LAN96 1/23] d9.3
2000	TB A	4	3	0	1	0	0	0	0	0-0	0	1	.333	.333	.333	71	-0	0-0	—	-0	0	0	/3D		0.0
2001	TB A	81	237	33	62	11	1	2	12	10-0	0	47	.262	.291	.342	67	-12	12-4	.968	-2	99	79	2b42,O25(7/18/0)/3D	150	0.0
2002	TB A	21	89	15	26	6	1	0	6	3-0	2	16	.292	.330	.382	90	-1	2-5	.947	1	115	76	O21(4/4/13)		-1.0
2003	TB A	107	373	43	95	20	0	7	46	19-1	7	84	.255	.301	.365	77	-13	11-3	.972	7	109	128	3b73,O37(6/0/33),2b2	34	-0.5
2004	TB A	53	117	12	19	5	0	0	9	0-0	1	36	.162	.231	.205	16	-15	2-1	1.000	0	100	107	O24(16/5/5),3b19,2b2/1D	39	-0.9
Total	5	266	819	103	203	42	2	9	73	42-1	10	184	.248	.291	.337	67	-41	27-13	.980	7	102	81	O107(33/27/51),3b94,2b46,D12/1	223	-1.4

ROMAN, BILL   William Anthony B10.11.1938 Detroit MI BL/TL/6-4/190(190-205) d9.30 Col Michigan
1964	Det A	3	8	2	3	0	0	1	1-0	0	2	.375	.375	.750	201	1	0-0	1.000	0	103	169	1b2		0.1
1965	Det A	21	27	0	2	0	0	0	0	2-0	0	7	.074	.138	.074	-38	-5	0-0	1.000	-1	37	63	1b6		-0.6
Total	2	24	35	2	5	0	0	1	1	2-0	0	9	.143	.189	.229	17	-4	0-0	1.000	-1	54	91	1b8		-0.5

ROMANO, JASON   Jason Anthony B6.24.1979 Tampa FL BR/TR/6-0/185* [TexA97 1/39] d4.17
2002	Tex A	29	54	8	11	4	0	0	4	4-0	0	13	.204	.254	.278	42	-4	2-0	1.000	1	131	0	O18(11/8/0),2b8/3D		-0.3
	Col N	18	37	9	12	0	1	0	1	3-0	0	11	.324	.375	.378	90	-1	4-1	.952	-2	119	66	2b12,S5,O3C/3		-0.2
2003	LA N	37	36	3	3	0	0	0	0	1-0	0	9	.083	.108	.083	-51	-8	2-0	1.000	-1	93	0	O28(9/17/2)/2		-0.9
2004	TB A	4	8	0	1	0	0	0	1	0-0	0	2	.125	.125	.125	-35	-2	0-0	.500	-0	0	0	/2OL		-0.2
	Cin N	22	26	3	4	0	0	0	1	2-0	0	10	.154	.214	.269	24	-3	0-0	1.000	0	77	344	O11(0/5/6)	70	-0.3
2005	Cin N	19	30	3	8	2	0	1	3	3-0	1	9	.267	.353	.433	108	0	0-0	.941	0	92	229	O14(7/5/2)		0.0
Total	4	129	191	26	39	6	1	2	12	13-0	1	53	.204	.257	.277	40	-18	8-1	.989	-2	104	196	O75(28/38/10),2b22,S5,D4,3b2	70	-1.9

ROMANO, JOHNNY   John Anthony "Honey" B8.23.1934 Hoboken NJ BR/TR/5-11/205* d9.12
1958	Chi A	4	7	2	2	0	0	1	1-0	0	0	.286	.375	.286	86	0	0-0	1.000	0	0	C2		0.0
1959	†Chi A	53	126	20	37	5	1	5	25	23-0	1	18	.294	.407	.468	141	8	0-1	.979	8	80	113	C38		1.0
1960	Cle A	108	316	40	86	12	2	16	52	37-4	3	50	.272	.349	.475	126	11	0-0	.988	-9	81	97	C99		0.6
1961	Cle A★	142	509	76	152	29	1	21	80	61-3	5	69	.299	.377	.483	132	25	0-0	.989	-8	104	114	C141		2.3
1962	Cle A★	135	459	71	120	19	3	25	81	73-0	5	64	.261	.363	.479	130	21	0-1	.990	-4	99	115	C130		2.3
1963	Cle A	89	255	28	55	5	2	10	34	38-4	2	49	.216	.317	.369	94	-2	4-3	.993	-8	111	115	C71,O4L		-0.7
1964	Cle A	106	352	46	85	18	1	19	47	51-6	7	83	.241	.346	.460	124	8	1-1	.991	-4	80	99	C96/1	37	1.4
1965	Chi A	122	356	39	86	11	0	18	48	59-3	5	74	.242	.355	.424	129	15	0-2	.992	7	87	108	C111,O4L,1b2		2.7
1966	Chi A	122	329	33	76	12	0	15	47	58-7	1	72	.231	.344	.404	124	12	0-0	.993	10	80	83	C102		2.8
1967	StL N	24	58	1	7	1	0	0	2	13-0	0	15	.121	.282	.138	24	-5	1-0	.983	-2	139	20	C20		-0.6
Total		905	2767	355	706	112	10	129	417	414-27	29	485	.255	.354	.443	123	98	7-9	.990	-17	93	102	C810,O8L,1b3	37	11.8

ROMANO, TOM   Thomas Michael B10.25.1958 Syracuse NY BR/TR/5-10/170 [KCA80 17/432] d9.1 Col Coastal Carolina
| 1987 | Mon N | 7 | 3 | 1 | 0 | 0 | 0 | 0 | 0 | .000 | .000 | .000 | -96 | -1 | 0-0 | — | -0 | 0 | 0 | O3L | | -0.1 |

ROMERO, MANDY   Armando B10.29.1967 Miami FL BB/TR/5-11/190(180-200) [PitN88 19/486] d7.15 Col Brevard (FL) CC
1997	SD N	21	48	7	10	0	0	2	4	2-0	0	18	.208	.240	.333	51	-4	1-0	1.000	1	67	49	C19		-0.1
1998	SD N	6	9	1	0	0	0	0	0	1-0	0	3	.000	.100	.000	-76	-2	0-0	.963	1	86	127	C6		-0.2
	Bos A	12	13	2	3	1	0	0	1	3-0	0	3	.231	.375	.308	79	0	0-0	1.000	1	0	0	C4,D3		0.1
2003	Col N	3	7	2	3	1	0	0	0	0-0	2	1	.429	.556	.571	171	1	0-0	.938	1	49	232	C2		0.2
Total	3	42	77	12	16	2	0	2	5	6-0	2	25	.208	.282	.312	57	-5	1-0	.987	4	64	80	C31,D3		-0.0

ROMERO, ED   Edgardo Ralph (Rivera) B12.9.1957 Santurce, PR BR/TR/5-11/175(150-180) d7.16 OF(17/1/14)
1977	Mil A	10	25	4	6	0	0	1	0	2-0	0	3	.240	.379	.320	93	-0	0-0	.971	-3	91	56	S10		-0.2
1980	Mil A	42	104	20	27	7	0	1	10	9-0	0	11	.260	.319	.356	87	-2	2-0	.894	-2	102	115	S22,2b15,3b3		-0.1
1981	†Mil A	44	91	6	18	3	0	1	10	4-0	0	7	.198	.227	.264	44	-7	0-2	.949	5	92	122	S22,2b18,3b3		0.0
1982	Mil A	52	144	18	36	8	0	1	7	8-0	0	16	.250	.289	.326	72	-6	0-0	.975	-2	96	123	2b39,S10,3b2/OL		-0.5
1983	Mil A	59	145	17	46	7	0	1	18	8-0	0	9	.317	.348	.386	111	2	1-0	.962	-11	73	103	S22,O15(14/0/1),3b5,2b3,D5		-0.7
1985	Mil A	88	251	24	63	11	0	1	21	26-0	1	20	.251	.321	.303	72	-9	1-1	.977	6	108	113	S43,2b31,O14(2/0/12)/3		0.2
1986	†Bos A	100	233	41	49	11	0	2	23	18-0	5	21	.210	.270	.283	51	-16	2-0	.959	-8	85	84	S75,3b18,2b4/OC		-1.8
1987	Bos A	88	235	23	64	6	0	1	14	18-0	0	22	.272	.322	.294	64	-12	0-2	.973	-0	106	108	2b29,S24,3b24,1b8		0.2
1988	†Bos A	75	155	7	3	18	3	0	5	8-0	4	8	.240	.272	.280	54	-5	0-0	1.000	-2	66	66	3b15,S8,2b5/1D	45	-0.6
1989	Bos A	46	113	14	24	4	0	0	6	7-1	1	8	.212	.260	.248	42	-5	0-0	.983	7	105	106	2b22,3b14,S10,D2		-0.2
	Atl N	7	19	1	5	1	0	1		0-0	0	3	.263	.263	.474	104	0	0-0	.947	3	141	121	2b4,S2/3		0.4
	Mil A	15	50	3	10	0	0	0	5	4-0	0	5	.200	.200	.260	29	-5	0-0	1.000	-3	86	75	2b11,3b4/S		-0.8

(ROMERO, continued)

YEAR	TM LG	G	AB	R	H	2B	3B	HR	RBI	BB-IB	HP	SO	AVG	OBP	SLG	AOPS	ABR	SB-CS	FA	FR	RNG	THR	GAMES AT POSITION	DL	BFW
1990	Det A	32	70	8	16	3	0	0	4	6-1	0	4	.229	.286	.271	57	-4	0-0	.982	0	95	216	3b27,D3		-0.4
Total	12	730	1912	218	473	79	1	8	155	140-4	5	159	.247	.298	.302	67	-87	9-10	.958	-4	94	92	S288,2b192,3b176,032L,1b13,D13	45	-6.2

ROMINE, KEVIN Kevin Andrew B5.23.1961 Exeter NH BR/TR/5-11/185(171-204) [BosA82 1/29] d9.5 Col Arizona St.

YEAR	TM LG	G	AB	R	H	2B	3B	HR	RBI	BB-IB	HP	SO	AVG	OBP	SLG	AOPS	ABR	SB-CS	FA	FR	RNG	THR	GAMES AT POSITION	DL	BFW
1985	Bos A	24	28	3	6	2	0	0	1	1-0	0	4	.214	.241	.286	42	-2	1-0	1.000	1	114	179	O23(12/1/12)/D		-0.2
1986	Bos A	35	35	6	9	2	0	0	2	3-0	0	9	.257	.316	.314	72	-1	2-0	1.000	2	123	130	O33(0/28/5)		0.0
1987	Bos A	9	24	5	7	2	0	0	2	2-0	0	6	.292	.346	.375	89	0	0-0	1.000	0	74	294	O7(1/4/3),D2		0.0
1988	†Bos A	57	78	17	15	2	1	1	6	7-0	0	15	.192	.259	.282	49	-5	2-0	.957	-3	84	0	O45(5/9/38),D5		-0.9
1989	Bos A	92	274	30	75	13	0	1	23	21-1	2	53	.274	.327	.332	82	-6	1-1	.982	1	89	204	O89(9/48/32),D2		-0.7
1990	Bos A	70	136	21	37	7	0	2	14	12-0	1	27	.272	.331	.368	92	-1	4-0	.976	-3	92	0	O64(16/18/30)/D		-0.5
1991	Bos A	44	55	7	9	2	0	1	7	3-0	0	10	.164	.207	.255	25	-6	1-1	.964	-1	95	0	O23(10/4/10),D14		-0.8
Total	7	331	630	89	158	30	1	5	55	49-1	3	124	.251	.306	.325	73	-21	11-2	.980	-3	93	112	O284(53/112/130),D25		-3.0

RONAN, MARC Edward Marcus B9.19.1969 Ozark AL BL/TR/6-2/190 [StLN90 3/86] d9.21 Col Florida St.

YEAR	TM LG	G	AB	R	H	2B	3B	HR	RBI	BB-IB	HP	SO	AVG	OBP	SLG	AOPS	ABR	SB-CS	FA	FR	RNG	THR	GAMES AT POSITION	DL	BFW
1993	StL N	6	12	0	1	0	0	0	0	0-0	0	5	.083	.083	.083	-56	-3	0-0	1.000	2	0	0	C6		-0.1

RONDEAU, HENRI Henri Joseph B5.7.1887 Danielson CT D5.28.1943 Woonsocket RI BL/TR/5-11/175 d4.11

YEAR	TM LG	G	AB	R	H	2B	3B	HR	RBI	BB-IB	HP	SO	AVG	OBP	SLG	AOPS	ABR	SB-CS	FA	FR	RNG	THR	GAMES AT POSITION	DL	BFW
1913	Det A	36	70	5	13	2	0	0	5	14	0	16	.186	.321	.214	58	-3	1	1.000	-2	77	124	C16,1b6		-0.4
1915	Was A	14	40	3	7	0	0	0	4	4	0	3	.175	.250	.175	27	-4	1-2	1.000	2	131	136	O11L		-0.3
1916	Was A	50	162	20	36	5	3	1	28	18	3	18	.222	.311	.309	87	-3	7	.958	3	126	68	O48(31/0/17)		-0.2
Total	3	100	272	28	56	7	3	1	37	36	3	37	.206	.305	.265	71	-10	9-2	.967	3	127	82	O59(42/0/17),C16,1b6		-0.9

ROOF, GENE Eugene Lawrence B1.13.1958 Paducah KY BB/TR/6-2/180(180-195) [StLN76 12/279] d9.3 C4 b-Phil

YEAR	TM LG	G	AB	R	H	2B	3B	HR	RBI	BB-IB	HP	SO	AVG	OBP	SLG	AOPS	ABR	SB-CS	FA	FR	RNG	THR	GAMES AT POSITION	DL	BFW
1981	StL N	23	60	11	18	6	0	0	3	12-2	0	16	.300	.411	.400	127	3	5-1	.950	-1	109	0	O20L		0.2
1982	StL N	11	15	3	4	0	0	0	1	2-0	0	4	.267	.313	.267	62	-1	2-0	1.000	-0	102	0	O5(4/0/2)		-0.1
1983	StL N	6	3	1	0	0	0	0	0	0-0	0	0	.000	.000	.000	-99	-1	0-0	—	-0	0	0	/OL		-0.1
	Mon N	8	12	2	2	2	0	0	1	1-0	0	3	.167	.231	.333	55	-1	0-0	1.000	-0	81	0	O5(0/1/4)		-0.2
	Year	14	15	3	2	2	0	0	1	1-0	0	3	.133	.188	.267	24	-2	0-0	1.000	-0	77	0	O6(1/1/4)		-0.1
Total	3	48	90	17	24	8	0	0	5	14-2	0	23	.267	.362	.356	100	0	7-1	.958	-1	105	0	O31(25/1/6)		-0.1

ROOF, PHIL Phillip Anthony B3.5.1941 Paducah KY BR/TR/6-3/210(195-210) d4.29 C9 b-Gene

YEAR	TM LG	G	AB	R	H	2B	3B	HR	RBI	BB-IB	HP	SO	AVG	OBP	SLG	AOPS	ABR	SB-CS	FA	FR	RNG	THR	GAMES AT POSITION	DL	BFW
1961	Mil N	1	0	0	0	0	0	0	0	0-0	0	0					0	0-0	1.000	0	0	0	/C		0.0
1964	Mil N	1	2	0	0	0	0	0	0	0-0	0	1	.000	.000	.000	-99	-1	0-0	1.000	1	0	0	/C		0.0
1965	Cal A	9	22	1	3	0	0	0	0	0-0	0	6	.136	.136	.136	-23	-4	0-0	.983	4	286	69	C9		0.1
	Cle A	43	52	3	9	1	0	0	3	5-1	1	13	.173	.259	.192	30	-5	0-0	.994	8	153	174	C41		0.5
	Year	52	74	4	12	1	0	0	3	5-1	1	19	.162	.225	.176	15	-8	0-0	.992	12	189	145	C50		0.6
1966	KC A	127	369	33	77	14	3	7	44	37-6	0	95	.209	.285	.320	76	-11	2-5	.985	-1	89	100	C123,1b2		-0.9
1967	KC A	114	327	23	67	14	5	6	24	23-5	5	85	.205	.266	.333	79	-9	4-1	.991	-4	94	67	C113	45	-1.0
1968	Oak A	34	64	5	12	0	0	1	2	2-0	0	15	.188	.212	.234	37	-5	1-0	.968	-5	71	57	C32		-0.2
1969	Oak A	106	247	19	58	6	1	2	19	33-3	5	55	.235	.337	.291	80	-5	1-0	.983	-1	127	83	C106		-0.4
1970	Mil A	110	321	39	73	7	1	13	37	32-1	5	72	.227	.306	.377	88	-6	3-2	.988	-2	69	108	C107/1		-0.2
1971	Mil A	41	114	6	22	2	1	1	10	8-1	1	28	.193	.252	.254	44	-9	0-1	.975	5	196	161	C39		0.4
	Min A	31	87	6	21	4	0	0	6	8-0	0	18	.241	.305	.287	67	-4	0-1	.985	6	118	81	C29		0.2
	Year	72	201	12	43	6	1	1	16	16-1	1	46	.214	.275	.269	54	-12	0-1	.980	11	160	125	C68		-1.0
1972	Min A	61	146	16	30	11	1	3	12	6-0	0	27	.205	.235	.356	71	-6	0-0	.978	-5	133	75	C61		-0.5
1973	Min A	47	117	10	23	4	1	1	15	13-0	0	27	.197	.277	.274	53	-7	0-0	.992	1	91	95	C47		-0.2
1974	Min A	44	97	10	19	1	0	2	13	6-0	2	24	.196	.257	.268	50	-7	0-0	1.000	3	96	162	C44	37	0.9
1975	Min A	63	126	18	38	2	0	7	21	9-1	1	28	.302	.353	.484	133	5	0-0	.989	2	95	106	C63		0.1
1976	Min A	18	46	1	10	3	0	0	4	2-0	0	6	.217	.250	.283	55	-3	0-0	.962	3	50	184	C12/D		-0.2
	Chi A	4	9	0	1	0	0	0	0	0-0	0	3	.111	.111	.111	-35	-2	0-0	1.000	-0	0	164	C4		-0.2
	Year	22	55	1	11	3	0	0	4	2-0	0	9	.200	.228	.255	41	-4	0-0	.967	3	39	180	C16/D	63	-0.2
1977	Tor A	3	5	0	0	0	0	0	0	0-0	0	1	.000	.000	.000	-99	-1	0-0	1.000	-0	33	237	C3		-0.2
Total		857	2151	190	463	69	13	43	210	184-18	23	504	.215	.283	.319	73	-80	11-10	.986	15	104	100	C835,1b3/D	145	-3.7

ROOKS, GEORGE George Brinton McClellan (b George Brinton Mc Clellan Ruckser) B10.21.1863 Chicago IL D3.11.1935 Chicago IL BR/TR/5-11/170 d5.12 gs-Lou Possehl

YEAR	TM LG	G	AB	R	H	2B	3B	HR	RBI	BB-IB	HP	SO	AVG	OBP	SLG	AOPS	ABR	SB-CS	FA	FR	RNG	THR	GAMES AT POSITION	DL	BFW
1891	Bos N	5	16	1	2	0	0	0		4	0	1	.125	.300	.125	23	-1	0	1.000	1	121	0	O5L		-0.1

ROOMES, ROLANDO Rolando Audley B2.15.1962 Kingston, Jamaica BR/TR/6-3/180* d4.12

YEAR	TM LG	G	AB	R	H	2B	3B	HR	RBI	BB-IB	HP	SO	AVG	OBP	SLG	AOPS	ABR	SB-CS	FA	FR	RNG	THR	GAMES AT POSITION	DL	BFW
1988	Chi N	17	16	3	3	0	0	0	0	0-0	0	4	.188	.188	.188	8	-2	0-1	.833	-1	67	0	O5(4/0/1)		-0.4
1989	Cin N	107	315	36	83	18	5	7	34	13-0	3	100	.263	.296	.419	100	-1	12-8	.981	5	117	90	O100(45/29/37)		0.1
1990	Cin N	30	61	5	13	0	0	2	7	0-0	0	20	.213	.213	.311	41	-5	0-0	1.000	1	115	99	O19(12/0/7)		-0.5
	Mon N	16	14	1	4	0	1	0	1	1-1	0	6	.286	.333	.429	112	0	0-2	1.000	-0	85	0	O6(3/2/1)		-0.1
	Year	46	75	6	17	0	1	2	8	1-1	0	26	.227	.237	.333	54	-5	0-2	1.000	1	110	81	O25(15/2/8)		-0.6
Total	3	170	406	45	103	18	6	9	42	14-1	3	130	.254	.282	.394	88	-8	12-11	.980	5	114	85	O130(64/31/46)		-0.9

ROONEY, FRANK Frank (b Frank Rovny) B10.12.1884 Podebrady, Bohemia (Austria-Hungary) D4.6.1977 Bessemer MI d4.18

YEAR	TM LG	G	AB	R	H	2B	3B	HR	RBI	BB-IB	HP	SO	AVG	OBP	SLG	AOPS	ABR	SB-CS	FA	FR	RNG	THR	GAMES AT POSITION	DL	BFW
1914	Ind F	12	35	1	7	0	1	1	8	4	0		.200	.222	.343	47	-3	2	.980	-1	41	122	1b9		-0.5

ROONEY, PAT Patrick Eugene B11.28.1957 Chicago IL BR/TR/6-1/190 [MonN78 20/500] d9.9 Col Eastern Illinois

YEAR	TM LG	G	AB	R	H	2B	3B	HR	RBI	BB-IB	HP	SO	AVG	OBP	SLG	AOPS	ABR	SB-CS	FA	FR	RNG	THR	GAMES AT POSITION	DL	BFW
1981	Mon N	4	4	0	0	0	0	0	0	0-0	0	3	.000	.000	.000	-97	-1	0-0	1.000	-0	57	0	O2R		-0.2

ROQUE, JORGE Jorge (Vargas) B4.28.1950 Ponce, PR BR/TR/5-10/158* d9.4

YEAR	TM LG	G	AB	R	H	2B	3B	HR	RBI	BB-IB	HP	SO	AVG	OBP	SLG	AOPS	ABR	SB-CS	FA	FR	RNG	THR	GAMES AT POSITION	DL	BFW
1970	StL N	5	1	2	0	0	0	0	0	0-0	1	1	.000	.500	.000	45	0	0-0	—	-0	0	0	/OL		0.0
1971	StL N	3	10	2	3	0	0	0	1	0-0	0	3	.300	.300	.300	67	0	1-0	1.000	-0	86	0	O3C		-0.1
1972	StL N	32	67	3	7	2	1	1	5	6-0	0	19	.104	.176	.209	10	-8	1-1	.980	-0	112	0	O24(0/21/3)		-1.0
1973	Mon N	25	61	7	9	2	0	1	6	4-0	2	17	.148	.212	.230	22	-7	2-2	.878	-1	96	180	O24(1/23/0)		-0.9
Total	4	65	139	14	19	4	1	2	12	10-0	3	40	.137	.204	.223	20	-15	4-3	.934	-2	103	80	O52(2/47/3)		-2.0

ROSADO, LUIS Luis (Robles) B12.6.1955 Santurce, PR BR/TR/6-0/180* d9.8

YEAR	TM LG	G	AB	R	H	2B	3B	HR	RBI	BB-IB	HP	SO	AVG	OBP	SLG	AOPS	ABR	SB-CS	FA	FR	RNG	THR	GAMES AT POSITION	DL	BFW
1977	NY N	9	24	1	5	1	0	0	3	1-0	1	3	.208	.250	.250	42	-2	0-0	.980	-2	109	88	1b7/C		-0.4
1980	NY N	2	4	0	0	0	0	0	0	0-0	0	1	.000	.000	.000	-99	-1	0-0	1.000	-0	141		/1		-0.2
Total	2	11	28	1	5	1	0	0	3	1-0	1	4	.179	.219	.214	22	-3	0-0	.983	-2	95	95	1b8/C		-0.6

ROSAR, BUDDY Warren Vincent B7.3.1914 Buffalo NY D3.13.1994 Rochester NY BR/TR/5-9/190* d4.29 Def 1944-45

YEAR	TM LG	G	AB	R	H	2B	3B	HR	RBI	BB-IB	HP	SO	AVG	OBP	SLG	AOPS	ABR	SB-CS	FA	FR	RNG	THR	GAMES AT POSITION	DL	BFW
1939	NY A	43	105	18	29	5	1	0	12	13	0	10	.276	.356	.343	81	-3	4-0	.980	4	165	63	C35		0.3
1940	NY A	73	228	34	68	11	3	4	37	19	2	11	.298	.357	.425	106	2	7-1	.983	2	140	94	C63		0.8
1941	†NY A	67	209	25	60	17	2	1	36	22	0	11	.287	.355	.402	101	1	0-0	.996	1	138	83	C60		0.5
1942	†NY A☆	69	209	18	48	10	0	2	34	17	0	20	.230	.288	.306	68	-9	1-2	.996	6	177	86	C58		1.8
1943	Cle A☆	115	382	53	108	17	1	1	41	33	0	12	.283	.340	.340	106	3	0-4	.983	9	146	123	C114		1.8
1944	Cle A	99	331	29	87	9	3	0	30	34	4	17	.263	.339	.308	89	-4	1-3	.989	-0	93	113	C98		-1.7
1945	Phi A	92	300	23	63	12	1	1	25	20	1	16	.210	.262	.267	54	-18	2-1	.987	-3	88	108	C85		-1.4
1946	Phi A★	121	424	34	120	22	2	2	47	36	1	13	.283	.339	.358	96	-2	1-3	1.000	10	123	115	C117		1.2
1947	Phi A★	102	359	40	93	20	2	1	33	40	1	13	.259	.335	.334	85	-7	1-3	.996	13	139	129	C102		1.2
1948	Phi A★	90	302	30	77	13	0	4	41	39	2	12	.255	.344	.338	82	-7	0-2	.997	0	115	85	C90		-0.2
1949	Phi A	32	95	7	19	2	0	0	6	16	0	5	.200	.315	.221	45	-7	0-0	.992	-1	107	57	C31		-0.2
1950	Bos A	27	84	13	25	2	0	1	12	7	0	4	.298	.352	.357	75	-3	0-0	.991	-1	125	46	C25		-0.2
1951	Bos A	58	170	11	39	7	1	3	19	19	0	14	.229	.307	.288	56	-10	0-0	.996	0	124	55	C56		-0.2
Total	13	988	3198	335	836	147	15	18	367	315	10	161	.261	.330	.334	84	-64	17-18	.992	41	127	100	C934		2.4

ROSARIO, JIMMY Angel Ramon (Ferrer) B5.5.1945 Bayamon, PR BB/TR/5-10/155(155-170) [SFN65 8/180] d4.8

YEAR	TM LG	G	AB	R	H	2B	3B	HR	RBI	BB-IB	HP	SO	AVG	OBP	SLG	AOPS	ABR	SB-CS	FA	FR	RNG	THR	GAMES AT POSITION	DL	BFW
1971	†SF N	92	192	26	43	6	1	0	13	33-4	1	35	.224	.338	.266	75	-5	7-4	1.000	1	110	30	O67(9/60/1)		-0.
1972	SF N	7	2	1	0	0	0	0	0	0-0	0	1	.000	.000	.000	-98	-1	0-1	—	-0	0	0	/OC		-0.
1976	Mil A	15	37	4	7	0	0	1	5	3-0	0	8	.189	.250	.270	53	-2	1-3	1.000	-1	96	0	O12(11/2/0),D2		-1.
Total	3	114	231	31	50	6	1	1	18	36-4	1	43	.216	.322	.264	70	-8	8-8	1.000	0	108	25	O80(20/63/1),D2		

ROSARIO, MEL Melvin Gregorio B5.25.1973 Santo Domingo, D.R. BB/TR/6-0/191 d9.11

YEAR	TM LG	G	AB	R	H	2B	3B	HR	RBI	BB-IB	HP	SO	AVG	OBP	SLG	AOPS	ABR	SB-CS	FA	FR	RNG	THR	GAMES AT POSITION	DL	BFW
1997	Bal A	4	3	0	0	0	0	0	0	0-0	0	0	.000	.000	.000	-99	-1	0-0	.875	-1	87	0	C4		-0.

YEAR	TM LG	G	AB	R	H	2B	3B	HR	RBI	BB-IB	HP	SO	AVG	OBP	SLG	AOPS	ABR	SB-CS	FA	FR	RNG	THR	GAMES AT POSITION	DL	BFW

ROSARIO, SANTIAGO Santiago B7.25.1939 Guayanilla, PR BL/TL/5-11/165 d6.23
| 1965 | KC A | 81 | 85 | 8 | 20 | 3 | 0 | 2 | 8 | 6-0 | 1 | 16 | .235 | .287 | .341 | 81 | -2 | 0-0 | .991 | -1 | 81 | 47 | 1b31,O3(2/0/1) | | -0.4 |

ROSARIO, VICTOR Victor Manuel (Rivera) B8.26.1966 Hato Mayor Del Rey, D.R. BR/TR/5-11/155 d9.6
| 1990 | Atl N | 9 | 7 | 3 | 1 | 0 | 0 | 0 | 0 | 1-0 | 0 | 1 | .143 | .250 | .143 | 10 | -1 | 0-0 | 1.000 | -1 | 71 | 0 | S3/2 | | -0.2 |

ROSE, MIKE Michael John-Ferrero B8.25.1976 Sacramento CA BB/TR/6-1/185(185-225) [HouN95 5/137] d10.1
2004	Oak A	2	1	0	0	0	0	0	0	0-0	0	2	.000	.000	.000	-99	-1	0-0	1.000	-0	18	1179	C2		-0.1
2005	LA N	15	43	2	9	2	0	1	1	3-0	0	6	.209	.261	.326	53	-3	0-0	.978	-3	37	113	C13		-0.5
Total	2	17	45	2	9	2	0	1	1	3-0	0	8	.200	.250	.311	46	-4	0-0	.978	-3	37	141	C15		-0.6

ROSE, PETE Peter Edward Jr. B11.16.1969 Cincinnati OH BL/TR/6-1/180 [BalA88 12/295] d9.1 f-Pete
| 1997 | Cin N | 11 | 14 | 2 | 2 | 0 | 0 | 0 | 2 | 0-0 | 0 | 2 | .143 | .143 | .143 | 6 | -2 | 0-0 | .600 | -1 | 102 | 0 | 3b2/1 | | -0.3 |

ROSE, PETE Peter Edward Sr. "Charlie Hustle" B4.14.1941 Cincinnati OH BB/TR/5-11/200(185-203) d4.8 M6 s-Pete OF(671/70/594)
1963	Cin N	157	623	101	170	25	9	6	41	55-0	5	72	.273	.334	.371	101	1	13-15	.971	-16	86	88	2b157/OL		-0.4
1964	Cin N	136	516	64	139	13	2	4	34	36-0	2	51	.269	.319	.326	79	-14	4-10	.979	-9	88	94	2b128		-1.6
1965	Cin N★	162	670	117	209	35	11	11	81	69-2	1	76	.312	.382	.446	124	24	8-3	.975	-18	84	86	2b162		2.2
1966	Cin N	156	654	97	205	38	5	16	70	37-3	1	61	.313	.351	.460	113	12	4-9	.981	-8	84	84	2b140,3b16		1.5
1967	Cin N★	148	585	86	176	32	8	12	76	56-9	3	66	.301	.364	.444	117	15	11-6	.982	3	103	68	O123(123/1/0),2b35		1.4
1968	Cin N★	149	626	94	210	42	6	10	49	56-15	2	76	.335	.391	.470	149	39	3-7	.990	3	94	156	O148(0/7/144),2b3/1		3.4
1969	Cin N★	156	627	120	218	33	11	16	82	88-18	3	65	.348	.428	.512	155	50	7-10	.988	3	97	85	O156(0/56/101),2b2	21	4.0
1970	†Cin N	159	649	120	205	37	9	15	52	73-10	2	64	.316	.385	.470	128	27	12-7	.997	-1	100	72	O159(1/5/155)		1.8
1971	Cin N★	160	632	86	192	27	4	13	44	68-15	1	50	.304	.373	.421	126	23	13-9	.994	-0	94	108	O158(0/1/158)		1.5
1972	†Cin N★	154	645	107	198	31	11	6	57	73-4	7	46	.307	.382	.417	134	30	10-3	.994	10	103	129	O154L		3.4
1973	†Cin N★	160	680	115	230	36	8	5	64	65-6	6	42	.338	.401	.437	138	37	10-7	.992	8	102	127	O159L		3.5
1974	Cin N★	163	652	110	185	45	7	3	51	106-14	5	54	.284	.385	.388	119	23	2-4	.997	9	109	94	O163L		2.2
1975	†Cin N★	162	662	112	210	47	4	7	74	89-8	11	50	.317	.406	.432	131	33	0-1	.963	-22	86	99	3b137,O35L		0.9
1976	†Cin N★	162	665	130	215	42	6	10	63	86-7	6	54	.323	.404	.450	139	38	9-5	.969	-11	94	91	3b159/OR		2.8
1977	Cin N★	162	655	95	204	38	7	9	64	66-7	5	42	.311	.377	.432	114	15	16-4	.958	-19	86	76	3b161		-0.4
1978	Cin N★	159	655	103	198	51	3	7	52	62-6	3	30	.302	.362	.421	119	18	13-9	.961	-14	88	91	3b156,O7L,1b2		0.2
1979	Phi N	163	628	90	208	40	5	4	59	95-10	2	32	.331	.418	.430	127	30	20-11	.995	-2	94	104	1b159,3b5/2		1.9
1980	†Phi N★	162	655	95	185	42	1	1	64	66-5	6	33	.282	.352	.354	92	-3	12-8	.997	12	127	92	1b162		-0.2
1981	†Phi N★	107	431	73	140	18	5	0	33	46-5	1	26	.325	.391	.390	116	11	4-4	.996	11	132	82	1b107		1.6
1982	†Phi N	162	634	80	172	25	4	3	54	66-9	7	32	.271	.345	.338	89	-7	8-8	.995	6	107	97	1b162		-1.2
1983	†Phi N	151	493	52	121	14	3	0	45	52-5	2	28	.245	.316	.286	70	-19	7-7	.990	2	115	81	1b112,O35R		-2.7
1984	Mon N	95	278	34	72	6	2	0	23	31-3	1	20	.259	.334	.295	82	-6	1-1	.988	8	171	84	1b40,O28L		-0.1
	Cin N	26	96	9	35	9	0	0	11	9-1	2	7	.365	.430	.458	143	6	0-0	.990	-2	62	79	1b23,M		0.3
	Year	121	374	43	107	15	2	0	34	40-4	3	27	.286	.359	.337	99	1	1-1	.989	6	129	82	1b63,O28L		0.2
1985	Cin N★	119	405	60	107	12	2	2	46	86-5	4	35	.264	.395	.319	98	4	8-1	.995	1	99	94	1b110,M		0.0
1986	Cin N	72	237	15	52	8	2	0	25	30-0	4	21	.219	.316	.270	61	-12	3-0	.990	-1	101	117	1b61,M		0.0
Total	24	3562	14053	2165	4256	746	135	160	1314	1566-167	107	1143	.303	.375	.409	117	375	198-149	.991	-55	100	101	O1327L,1b939,3b634,2b628	16	-1.6
(Total) 37 24.4

ROSE, BOBBY Robert Richard B3.15.1967 Covina CA BR/TR/5-11/170(170-187) [CalA85 5/121] d8.12
1989	Cal A	14	38	4	8	1	2	1	3	2-0	1	10	.211	.268	.421	93	-1	0-0	.920	-2	91	69	3b10,2b3		-0.2
1990	Cal A	7	13	5	5	0	0	1	2	2-0	0	1	.385	.467	.615	204	2	0-0	1.000	-1	77	0	2b4,3b3		0.1
1991	Cal A	22	65	5	18	5	1	1	8	3-0	0	13	.277	.304	.431	102	0	0-0	1.000	1	118	116	2b8,O7(6/0/1),3b4,1b3	44	0.1
1992	Cal A	30	84	10	18	5	0	2	10	8-1	2	9	.214	.295	.345	79	-2	1-1	.953	9	142	115	2b28,1b2	38	0.1
Total	4	73	200	24	49	11	3	5	23	15-1	3	33	.245	.305	.405	97	-1	1-1	.965	8	132	106	2b43,3b17,O7(6/0/1),1b5	82	0.7

ROSEBORO, JOHNNY John Junior B5.13.1933 Ashland OH D8.16.2002 Los Angeles CA BL/TR/5-11.5/190(189-200) d6.14 C5
1957	Bro N	35	69	6	10	2	1	0	6	10-2	0	20	.145	.253	.261	35	-6	0-0	.972	2	151	68	C19,1b5		-0.4
1958	LA ☆	114	384	52	104	11	9	14	43	36-2	2	56	.271	.333	.456	104	1	11-8	.987	-7	132	108	C104,O5(4/1/0)		-0.2
1959	†LA N	118	397	39	92	14	7	10	38	52-11	3	69	.232	.322	.378	81	-1	7-5	.991	9	211	102	C117		0.4
1960	LA N	103	287	22	61	15	3	8	42	44-6	4	53	.213	.323	.369	84	-5	7-6	.993	14	130	91	C87/13		1.3
1961	LA N★	128	394	59	99	16	6	18	59	56-8	4	62	.251	.346	.459	104	2	6-4	.986	10	130	105	C125		1.8
1962	LA N★	128	389	45	97	16	7	5	55	50-11	7	60	.249	.341	.380	101	1	12-3	.985	-1	123	83	C128		0.9
1963	†LA N	135	470	50	111	13	7	9	49	36-3	3	50	.236	.291	.351	91	-7	7-6	.992	-1	136	73	C134		-0.2
1964	LA N	134	414	42	119	24	1	3	45	44-9	4	61	.287	.357	.372	115	11	3-3	.993	12	204	104	C128		3.0
1965	†LA N	136	437	42	102	10	3	8	57	34-7	2	51	.233	.289	.311	75	-15	1-6	.994	2	141	91	C131/3		-1.0
1966	†LA N★	142	445	47	123	23	2	9	53	44-13	5	51	.276	.343	.398	115	10	3-2	.993	13	132	83	C138		3.0
1967	LA N	116	334	37	91	18	2	4	24	38-12	2	33	.272	.348	.374	117	8	2-4	.984	-3	124	102	C107		1.0
1968	Min A	135	380	31	82	12	0	8	39	46-9	2	57	.216	.300	.311	82	-7	3-4	.991	4	108	75	C117		-0.1
1969	†Min A★	115	361	33	89	12	0	3	32	39-12	0	44	.246	.333	.321	93	0	5-5	.980	3	112	76	C111		-0.1
1970	Was A	46	86	7	20	4	0	1	6	18-5	0	10	.233	.365	.314	93	0	1-1	1.000	-2	71	33	C30		-0.1
Total	14	1585	4847	512	1206	190	44	104	548	547-110	36	677	.249	.326	.371	95	-26	67-56	.989	57	140	90	C1476,1b6,O5(4/1/0),3b2		9.6

ROSELLI, BOB Robert Edward B12.10.1931 San Francisco CA BR/TR/5-11/185(170-185) d8.16
1955	Mil N	6	9	1	2	1	0	0	1	1-0	1	4	.222	.364	.333	91	1	0-0	.917	-0	0	204	C2		0.0
1956	Mil N	4	2	1	1	0	0	1	1	0-0	1	1	.500	.500	2.000	564	1	0-0	1.000	1	0	0	C3		0.2
1958	Mil N	1	1	0	0	0	0	0	0	0-0	0	0	.000	.000	.000	-99	0	0-0	—	0			/H		0.0
1961	Chi A	22	38	2	10	3	0	0	4	0-0	0	11	.263	.263	.342	61	-2	0-0	1.000	-1	0	140	C10		-0.3
1962	Chi A	35	64	4	12	3	1	1	5	11-1	1	20	.188	.316	.313	70	-2	1-0	.988	-2	45	139	C20		-0.4
Total	5	68	114	8	25	7	1	2	10	12-1	2	31	.219	.305	.351	76	-3	1-0	.986	-3	27	139	C35		-0.5

ROSELLO, DAVE David (Rodriguez) B6.26.1950 Mayaguez, PR BR/TR/5-11/160(160-191) d9.10
1972	Chi N	5	12	3	3	0	1	0	3	3-0	0	2	.250	.400	.500	139	1	0-0	.846	-0	88	173	S5		0.1
1973	Chi N	16	38	4	10	3	0	0	3	2-0	0	4	.263	.300	.316	66	-2	2-2	.964	-1	85	78	2b13/S		-0.2
1974	Chi N	62	148	9	30	7	0	0	10	10-1	0	28	.203	.252	.250	39	-12	1-1	.972	-5	91	130	2b49,S12		-1.5
1975	Chi N	19	58	7	15	2	0	1	8	9-2	0	8	.259	.348	.345	91	0	0-0	.952	-3	92	58	S19		-0.1
1976	Chi N	91	227	27	55	5	1	1	11	41-8	1	33	.242	.359	.286	78	-4	1-2	.966	-5	95	100	S86/2		-0.1
1977	Chi N	56	82	18	18	2	1	1	9	12-1	0	12	.220	.319	.305	62	-4	0-0	.938	-3	108	103	3b21,S10,2b3		-0.7
1979	Cle A	59	107	20	26	6	1	3	14	15-0	0	27	.243	.328	.402	98	0	1-0	.976	-8	105	61	3b14,S11		-0.7
1980	Cle A	71	117	16	29	3	0	2	12	9-0	0	19	.248	.295	.325	71	-5	0-0	.980	-8	80	74	2b43,3b22,S3/D		-1.1
1981	Cle A	43	84	11	20	4	0	1	7	7-0	0	12	.238	.297	.321	79	-2	0-1	.979	-2	81	92	2b26,3b8,S4,D5		-0.3
Total	9	422	873	114	206	31	3	10	76	108-12	1	145	.236	.318	.313	73	-28	5-7	.975	-35	89	90	2b168,S151,3b65,D5		-4.7

ROSEMAN, CHIEF James John B1856 New York NY D7.4.1938 Brooklyn NY BR/TR/5-7/167 d5.1 M1 ▲
1882	Tro N	82	331	41	78	21	6	1	29	3		41	.236	.243	.344	90	-3			.853	-5	114	139	O82(1/0/81)		-0.8
1883	NY AA	93	398	48	100	13	6	0	11				.251	.271	.314	84	-8			.855	-6	102	169	O91(3/8/80),1b2		-1.3
1884	†NY AA	107	436	97	130	16	11	4	21				.298	.339	.413	148	23			.885	-4	58	0	O107(4/103/0)		1.4
1885	NY AA	101	410	72	114	13	14	4	46	25		10	.278	.335	.407	139	19			.865	-7	53	30	O101(1/99/1)/P		0.7
1886	NY AA	134	559	90	127	19	10	5	53	24			.227	.269	.324	93	-4	6		.891	-4	80	148	O134(88/44/3)/P		-1.1
1887	Phi AA	21	73	16	16	2	1	0	8	10	5		.219	.352	.274	76	-2	3		.821	-4	147	140	O21C		-0.2
	NY AA	60	241	30	55	10	1	1	27	9		1	.228	.265	.290	57	-14	3		.868	-5	69	93	O59(9/36/14),1b3,P2		-1.7
	Bro AA	1	3	2	1	0	0	0	1	0		1	.333	.500	.333	133	0	0		1.000	0	0	0	/OR		0.0
	Year	82	317	48	72	12	2	1	36	19		9	.227	.290	.287	63	-15	6		.856	-6	89	104	O81(9/57/15),1b3,P2		-1.9
1890	StL AA	80	302	47	103	26	2	2	58	30		29	.341	.449	.447	144	19	7		.819	-6	82	112	O58(17/40/1),1b22,M		0.9
	Lou AA	2	8	0	2	0	0	0	0	0			.250	.250	.250	48	-1	0		.864	-1	0	351	1b2		-0.1
	Year	82	310	47	105	26	2	2	58	30		29	.339	.444	.442	142	19	7		.819	-6	82	112	O58(17/40/1),1b24		0.8
Total	7	681	2761	443	726	120	49	17	222	133		62	41	.263	.312	.360	110	29	19		.866	-38	81	99	O654(123/351/181),1b29,P4		-2.2

ROSEN, AL Albert Leonard "Flip" B2.29.1924 Spartanburg SC BR/TR/5-10.5/180* d9.10 Col Florida
1947	Cle A	7	9	1	1	0	0	0	0	0		3	.111	.111	.111	-39	-2	0-0	—	1	0	0	3b2/OL		-0.1
1948	†Cle A	5	5	0	1	0	0	0	3	1-0	0	0	.200	.200	.200	7	-1	0-0	1.000	-0	93	0	3b2		-0.1
1949	Cle A	23	44	3	7	2	0	0	5	7	0	4	.159	.264	.205	-5	-1	0-1	1.000	-1	89	51	3b10		-0.6

YEAR TM LG	G	AB	R	H	2B	3B	HR	RBI	BB-IB	HP	SO	AVG	OBP	SLG	AOPS	ABR	SB-CS	FA	FR	RNG	THR	GAMES AT POSITION	BFW
1950 Cle A	**155**	554	100	159	23	4	**37**	116	100	10	72	.287	.405	.543	146	39	5-7	.969	6	107	79	3b154	4.0
1951 Cle A	154	573	82	152	30	1	24	102	85	2	71	.265	.362	.447	125	20	7-5	.958	-10	95	66	3b154	1.0
1952 Cle A★	148	567	101	171	32	5	28	**105**	75	4	54	.302	.387	.524	162	47	8-6	.958	-15	88	78	3b147,1b4,S3	3.3
1953 Cle A★	155	599	115	201	27	5	**43**	**145**	85	4	48	.336	.422	**.613**	181	68	8-7	.964	9	108	107	3b154/1S	7.4
1954 †Cle A★	137	466	76	140	20	2	24	102	85	3	43	.300	.404	.506	148	34	6-2	.959	-13	81	94	3b87,1b46/2S	1.9
1955 Cle A★	139	492	61	120	13	1	21	81	92-5	4	44	.244	.362	.402	103	4	4-2	.963	-1	89	84	3b106,1b41	0.1
1956 Cle A	121	416	64	111	18	2	15	61	58-4	0	44	.267	.351	.428	104	3	1-3	.945	-9	93	94	3b116	-0.7
Total 10	1044	3725	603	1063	165	20	192	717	587-9	27	385	.285	.384	.495	138	207	39-33	.961	-32	96	85	3b932,1b92,S5/2OL	16.2
ROSEN, GOODY Goodwin George B8.28.1912 Toronto ON, Can. D4.6.1994 Toronto ON, Can. BL/TL/5-10/155 d9.14																							
1937 Bro N	22	77	10	24	5	1	0	6	6	0	6	.312	.361	.403	106	1	2	.981	1	111	66	O21(8/13/0)	0.1
1938 Bro N	138	473	75	133	17	11	4	51	65	0	43	.281	.368	.389	106	5	0	.989	9	103	187	O113(13/43/59)	0.9
1939 Bro N	54	183	22	46	6	4	1	12	23	0	21	.251	.335	.344	80	-5	4	1.000	-3	97	0	O47(1/40/7)	-1.0
1944 Bro N	89	264	38	69	8	3	0	23	26	1	27	.261	.330	.314	83	-6	0	.991	11	119	210	O65(1/62/3)	0.4
1945 Bro N*	145	606	126	197	24	11	12	75	50	3	36	.325	.379	.460	134	26	6	.993	-4	101	59	O141C	1.8
1946 Bro N	3	3	0	1	0	0	0	0	0	0	1	.333	.333	.333	89	0	0	—	-0	0	0	/OC	0.0
NY N	100	310	39	87	11	4	5	30	48	0	32	.281	.377	.390	117	8	2	.976	-3	106	36	O84(0/30/52)	0.3
Year	103	313	39	88	11	4	5	30	48	0	33	.281	.377	.390	117	8	2	.976	-3	106	36	O85(0/31/52)	
Total 6	551	1916	310	557	71	34	22	197	218	4	166	.291	.364	.398	111	29	14	.989	11	105	101	O472(23/330/121)	2.5
ROSENBERG, HARRY Harry B6.22.1908 San Francisco CA D4.13.1997 San Mateo CA BR/TR/5-9.5/160 d7.15 b-Lou																							
1930 NY N	9	5	1	0	0	0	0	0	1	0	4	.000	.167	.000	-56	-1	0	1.000	0	118	0	O3(0/2/1)	-0.1
ROSENBERG, LOU Louis B3.5.1904 San Francisco CA D9.8.1991 Daly City CA BR/TR/5-7/155 d5.22 b-Harry																							
1923 Chi A	3	4	0	1	0	0	0	0	1	0	0	.250	.250	.250	32	0	0-1	1.000	-1	0	0	2b2	-0.1
ROSENFELD, MAX Max B12.23.1902 New York NY D3.10.1969 Miami FL BR/TR/5-8/175 d4.21 Col Alabama																							
1931 Bro N	3	9	0	2	1	0	0	1	0	0	1	.222	.300	.333	70	0	1	1.000	-0	100	0	O3C	-0.1
1932 Bro N	34	39	8	14	3	0	2	7	0	0	10	.359	.359	.590	153	3	2	.970	1	119	95	O30(1/10/19)	0.3
1933 Bro N	5	9	0	1	0	0	0	0	2	0	1	.111	.200	.111	-10	-1	0	1.000	0	110	0	O2(1/1/0)	-0.2
Total 3	42	57	8	17	4	0	2	7	2	0	12	.298	.322	.474	115	2	2	.978	1	115	66	O35(2/14/19)	0.0
ROSENTHAL, LARRY Lawrence John B5.21.1910 St.Paul MN D3.4.1992 Woodbury MN BL/TL/6-0.5/190 d6.20																							
1936 Chi A	85	317	71	89	15	8	3	46	59	0	37	.281	.394	.407	95	-1	2-0	.977	2	103	92	O80C	-0.1
1937 Chi A	58	97	20	28	5	3	0	9	15	0	20	.289	.355	.402	90	-2	1-0	.980	1	100	188	O25C	0.0
1938 Chi A	61	105	14	30	5	1	1	12	12	0	13	.286	.359	.381	83	-3	0-1	.959	-0	93	176	O22(0/22/2)	-0.3
1939 Chi A	107	324	50	86	21	5	10	51	53	0	46	.265	.369	.454	106	4	6-4	.990	-2	97	68	O93(0/20/75)	-0.3
1940 Chi A	107	276	46	83	14	5	6	42	64	0	32	.301	.432	.453	128	15	2-3	.977	4	116	67	O92(68/15/11)	1.4
1941 Chi A	20	59	9	14	4	0	0	1	12	0	10	.237	.306	.305	80	-1	0-0	.938	-0	82	203	O18(0/2/16)	-0.2
Cle A	45	75	10	14	3	1	1	8	9	0	10	.187	.274	.293	53	-5	1-0	1.000	0	106	-87	O14(5/8/1)/1	-0.5
Year	65	134	19	28	7	1	1	9	21	0	15	.209	.316	.299	66	-6	1-0	.986	2	111	91	O26(10/5/11)	-0.7
1944 NY A	36	101	9	20	3	0	0	9	19	0	15	.198	.325	.228	57	-5	1-0	.960	-1	106	0	O19(5/0/15)	-0.4
Phi A	32	54	5	11	2	0	1	6	5	0	9	.204	.271	.296	63	-3	0-0	.979	1	110	65	O45(15/5/26)	-0.9
Year	68	155	14	31	5	0	1	15	24	0	24	.200	.307	.252	60	-7	1-0	.971	-0	90	61	O21L	-0.6
1945 Phi A	28	75	6	15	3	0	0	8	9	0	8	.200	.286	.293	68	-3	0-1	1.000	1	90	61	O21L	-1.5
Total 8	579	1483	240	390	75	25	22	189	251	1	195	.263	.370	.392	96	-4	13-9	.979	5	103	89	O410(109/177/131)/1	-1.5
ROSENTHAL, SI Simon B11.13.1903 Boston MA D4.7.1969 Boston MA BL/TL/5-9/165 d9.8																							
1925 Bos A	19	72	6	19	5	2	0	8	7	0	3	.264	.329	.389	82	-2	1-0	.919	1	86	155	O17(7/0/10)	-0.4
1926 Bos A	104	285	34	76	12	3	4	34	19	2	18	.267	.317	.372	82	-9	4-1	.962	-10	81	0	O67(48/0/19)	-2.3
Total 2	123	357	40	95	17	5	4	42	26	2	21	.266	.319	.375	82	-11	5-1	.950	-10	82	35	O84(55/0/29)	-2.7
ROSER, BUNNY John William Joseph "Jack" B11.15.1901 St.Louis MO D5.6.1979 Rocky Hill CT BL/TL/5-11/175 d8.24																							
1922 Bos N	32	113	13	27	3	4	0	16	10	1	19	.239	.306	.336	69	-6	2-1	.915	-2	105	55	O32L	-0.9
ROSKOS, JOHN John Edward B11.19.1974 Victorville CA BR/TR/5-11/195* [FlaN93 2/69] d4.20																							
1998 Fla N	10	10	1	1	0	0	0	0	0	0	5	.100	.100	.100	-50	-2	0-0	1.000	0	0	0	/1	-0.2
1999 Fla N	13	12	0	2	2	0	0	1	1-0	0	7	.167	.231	.333	43	-1	0-0	1.000	0	0	0	/C	-0.1
2000 SD N	14	27	0	1	1	0	0	1	3-0	0	7	.037	.133	.074	-49	-6	0-0	.875	-1	72	0	O6(4/0/2),1b2	-0.7
Total 3	37	49	1	4	3	0	0	2	4-0	0	19	.082	.151	.143	-26	-9	0-0	.875	-0	72	0	O6(4/0/2),1b3/C	-1.0
ROSS, CHET Chester James B4.1.1917 Buffalo NY D2.21.1989 Buffalo NY BR/TR/6-1/195 d9.15 Mil 1945																							
1939 Bos N	11	31	4	10	1	1	0	2	0	0	10	.323	.364	.419	118	1	0	1.000	1	111	137	O8(1/1/7)	0.1
1940 Bos N	149	569	84	160	23	14	17	89	59	3	127	.281	.352	.460	130	21	4	.962	5	106	108	O149L	1.8
1941 Bos N	29	50	1	6	1	0	0	4	9	0	17	.120	.254	.140	14	-6	0-0	.992	0	105	52	O57(52/0/6)	-0.6
1942 Bos N	76	220	20	43	7	2	5	19	16	0	37	.195	.250	.314	66	-11	1	.977	2	104	111	O73L	-1.5
1943 Bos N	94	285	27	62	12	2	7	32	26	1	67	.218	.285	.409	84	-7	1	1.000	3	93	238	O38(25/0/15)	-1.0
1944 Bos N	54	154	20	35	9	2	5	26	12	1	23	.227	.287	.409	91	-3	1	.976	12	104	116	O12	-1.4
Total 6	413	1309	156	316	53	21	34	170	124	5	281	.241	.309	.392	100	-5	6	.976	12	104	116	O337(312/1/28)	-1.4
ROSS, CODY Cody Joseph B12.23.1980 Portales NM BR/TL/5-11/180* [DetA99 4/117] d7.4																							
2003 Det A	6	19	1	4	1	0	1	5	1-0	0	10	.211	.286	.421	87	0	0-0	.882	0	126	0	O6R	-0.1
2005 LA N	14	25	1	4	1	0	0	1	1-0	0	10	.160	.192	.200	3	-4	0-0	.933	1	105	585	O9R	-0.2
Total 2	20	44	2	8	2	0	1	6	2-0	0	13	.182	.234	.295	39	-4	0-0	.906	1	115	301	O15R	-0.3
ROSS, DAVID David Wade B3.19.1977 Bainbridge GA BR/TR/6-2/205* [LAN98 7/216] d6.29 Col Florida																							
2002 LA N	8	10	2	2	1	0	1	2	2-0	1	4	.200	.385	.600	167	1	0-0	1.000	0	0	125	C6	0.2
2003 LA N	40	124	19	32	7	0	10	18	13-0	2	42	.258	.336	.556	131	5	0-0	.986	-1	61	200	C38	0.7
2004 †LA N	70	165	13	28	3	1	5	15	15-1	5	62	.170	.253	.291	43	-15	0-0	.992	1	101	114	C67	-1.1
2005 Pit N	40	108	9	24	8	0	3	15	6-0	1	24	.222	.263	.380	68	-5	0-0	.986	4	324	136	C35	0.1
SD N	11	17	2	6	0	1	0	0	0	1	4	.353	.389	.471	130	1	0-0	1.000	0	180	0	C7	0.2
Year	51	125	11	30	8	1	3	15	6-0	2	28	.240	.279	.392	77	-5	0-0	.987	5	309	122	C42	0.1
Total 4	169	424	45	92	19	2	19	50	36-1	10	136	.217	.288	.406	81	-13	0-0	.989	5	145	141	C153	-0.0
ROSS, DON Donald Raymond B7.16.1914 Pasadena CA D3.28.1996 Arcadia CA BR/TR/6-2/200 d4.19																							
1938 Det A	77	265	22	69	7	1	1	30	29	0	11	.260	.333	.306	58	-17	1-0	.946	5	107	111	3b75	-0.8
1940 Bro N	10	38	4	11	2	0	1	8	3	0	3	.289	.341	.421	103	0	1	.879	-1	97	0	3b10	-0.3
1942 Det A	87	226	29	62	10	2	3	30	36	2	16	.274	.379	.376	104	3	2-1	.964	-4	96	135	O38(5/0/33),3b20	-0.3
1943 Det A	89	247	19	66	13	0	0	18	20	1	9	.267	.325	.320	82	-5	2-1	.985	-3	92	126	O38(6/0/32),S18,2b7/3	-1.4
1944 Det A	66	167	14	35	6	2	2	15	14	1	9	.210	.275	.240	54	-10	2-1	.958	-1	94	83	O37R,S2/1	0.4
1945 Det A	8	29	3	11	4	0	0	7	5	0	1	.379	.471	.517	175	3	0-0	.960	-0	104	0	3b8	-1.2
Cle A	106	363	26	95	15	1	2	43	42	1	15	.262	.340	.325	97	0	0-4	.958	-11	84	71	3b106	-0.8
Year	114	392	29	106	19	1	2	47	47	1	16	.270	.350	.339	104	3	0-4	.958	-11	85	66	3b114	-0.6
1946 Cle A	55	153	12	41	7	0	3	14	17	0	12	.268	.341	.373	106	1	0-0	.944	-7	73	66	3b41,O2R	-0.6
Total 7	498	1488	129	390	63	6	12	162	166	5	70	.262	.338	.334	86	-25	10-6	.946	-22	90	75	3b261,O115(11/0/104),S20,2b7/1	-4.9
ROSSI, JOE Joseph Anthony B3.13.1921 Oakland CA D2.20.1999 Oakland CA BR/TR/6-1/205 d4.20																							
1952 Cin N	55	145	14	32	0	1	1	6	20	1	20	.221	.319	.255	61	-7	1-0	.982	1	96	101	C46	-0.4
ROSSMAN, CLAUDE Claude R. B6.17.1881 Philmont NY D1.16.1928 Poughkeepsie NY BL/TL/6-0/188 d9.16																							
1904 Cle A	18	62	5	13	5	0	0	6	8	0		.210	.210	.290	58	-3	0	.933	-2	0	0	O17(0/1/16)	-0.6
1906 Cle A	118	396	49	122	13	2	1	53	17	1		.308	.338	.359	120	8	11	.984	-9	69	120	1b105/OC	-1.1
1907 †Det A	153	571	60	158	21	8	0	69	33	2		.277	.318	.342	107	3	20	.981	-14	64	81	1b153	2.2
1908 †Det A	138	524	45	154	33	8	2	71	27	1		.294	.330	.418	137	19	8	.981	6	120	110	1b138	
1909 Det A	82	287	16	75	10	0	0	39	13	0		.261	.293	.310	87	-5	10	.981	-6	77	84	1b75	-0.2
StL A	2	8	0	1	0	0	0	0	0	0		.125	.125	.125	-23	-1	0	1.000	-0	0	0	O2R	-1.1
Year	84	295	16	76	10	0	0	39	13	0		.258	.289	.305	84	-6	10	.981	-6	77	84	1b75,O2R	-1.1
Total 5	511	1848	175	523	80	26	3	238	90	4		.283	.318	.359	113	21	49	.982	-26	84	99	1b471,O20(0/2/18)	

YEAR	TM LG	G	AB	R	H	2B	3B	HR	RBI	BB-IB	HP	SO	AVG	OBP	SLG	AOPS	ABR	SB-CS	FA	FR	RNG	THR	GAMES AT POSITION	DL	BFW

ROSSY, RICO Elam Jose (Ramos) B2.16.1964 San Juan, PR BR/TR/5-10/175* [BalA85 33/803] d9.11 Col Purdue

1991	Atl N	5	1	0	0	0	0	0	0	0-0	0	1	.000	.000	.000	-95	0	0-0	—	-0	0	0	/S		0.0
1992	KC A	59	149	21	32	8	1	1	12	20-1	1	20	.215	.310	.302	70	-5	0-3	.961	1	104	137	S51,3b9,2b3		-0.2
1993	KC A	46	86	10	19	4	0	2	12	9-0	1	11	.221	.302	.337	67	-4	0-0	.987	-2	103	109	2b24,3b16,S11		-0.2
1998	Sea A	37	81	12	16	6	0	1	4	6-0	0	13	.198	.253	.309	45	-7	0-0	1.000	5	110	159	3b25,2b6,S4/D	15	-0.5
Total	4	147	317	43	67	18	1	4	28	35-1	2	45	.211	.293	.312	62	-16	0-3	.974	4	100	132	S67,3b50,2b33/D	15	-0.9

ROTH, FRANK Francis Charles B10.11.1878 Chicago IL D3.27.1955 Burlington WI BR/TR/5-10/160 d4.18 C7 b-Braggo

1903	Phi N	68	220	27	60	11	4	0	22	9	1		.273	.304	.359	92	-3	3	.935	-8	85	96	C60/3		-0.6
1904	Phi N	81	229	28	59	8	1	1	20	12	1		.258	.298	.314	92	-2	8	.958	-10	77	94	C67/12		-0.7
1905	StL A	35	107	9	25	3	0	0	7	6	0		.234	.274	.262	74	-3	1	.962	-6	69	110	C29		-0.7
1906	Chi A	16	51	4	10	1	1	0	7	3	0		.196	.241	.255	57	-3	1	.990	3	152	99	C15		0.2
1909	Cin N	56	147	12	35	7	2	0	16	6	4		.238	.287	.313	87	-3	5	.967	-2	92	90	C54		0.0
1910	Cin N	26	29	3	7	2	0	0	3	0	1	2	.241	.267	.310	71	-1	1	.938	-0	146	129	C4/OL		-0.1
Total	6	282	783	83	196	32	8	1	75	36	2		.250	.289	.315	86	-15	19	.956	-23	88	96	C229/OL213		-1.9

ROTH, BRAGGO Robert Frank B8.28.1892 Burlington WI D9.11.1936 Chicago IL BR/TR/5-7.5/170 d9.1 b-Frank

1914	Chi A	34	126	14	37	4	6	1	10	8		25	.294	.355	.444	142	6	3-3	.924	1	92	159	O34(0/12/22)		0.4
1915	Chi A	70	240	44	60	6	10	3	35	29	3	50	.250	.338	.396	116	4	12-6	.837	-12	68	22	3b35,O30(29/1/0)		-0.9
	Cle A	39	144	23	43	4	7	4	20	22	2	22	.299	.399	.507	168	12	14-4	.878	-4	78	105	O39C		0.7
	Year	109	384	67	103	10	17	7	55	51	5	72	.268	.361	.438	135	15	26-10	.906	-17	81	122	O69(29/40/0),3b35		-0.2
1916	Cle A	125	409	50	117	19	7	4	72	38	2	48	.286	.350	.396	117	8	29-14	.954	2	92	148	O112(0/9/103)		0.6
1917	Cle A	145	495	69	141	30	9	1	72	52	2	51	.285	.355	.388	118	11	51	.957	2	105	101	O135R		0.7
1918	Cle A	106	375	53	106	21	12	1	59	53	8	41	.283	.383	.411	127	14	36	.936	-4	91	109	O106(2/0/104)		0.6
1919	Phi A	48	195	33	63	13	8	5	29	15	2		.323	.377	.549	156	13	11	.975	-5	95	15	O48R		0.6
	Bos A	63	227	32	58	9	4	0	23	24	4	32	.256	.337	.330	93	-2	9	.943	-5	87	85	O58(1/57/0)		-1.1
	Year	111	422	65	121	22	12	5	52	39	6	53	.287	.355	.431	124	12	20	.955	-10	91	54	O106(1/57/48)		-0.5
1920	Was A	138	468	80	136	23	8	9	92	75	6	57	.291	.395	.432	122	18	24-12	.952	-8	85	92	O128(7/0/121)		0.5
1921	NY A	43	152	29	43	7	2	2	10	19	2	20	.283	.370	.408	96	0	1-2	.923	-4	88	63	O37(3/17/17)		-0.7
Total	8	811	2831	427	804	138	73	30	422	335	35	389	.284	.367	.416	122	84	190-41	.944	-37	92	104	O727(42/135/550),3b35		1.4

ROTHEL, BOB Robert Burton B9.17.1923 Columbia Station OH D3.21.1984 Huron OH BR/TR/5-10.5/170 d4.22

1945	Cle A	4	10	0	2	0	0	0	0	0-0	0		1	.200	.385	.200	75	0	0-0	.875	-1	81	0	3b4	-0.1

ROTHERMEL, BOBBY Edward Hill B12.18.1870 Fleetwood PA D2.11.1927 Detroit MI BR/5-6.5/148 d6.18

1899	Bal N	10	21	1	2	0	0	0	3	1	0		.095	.136	.095	-34	-4	0-0	.867	-2	93	0	2b5,3b2/S	-0.6

ROTHFUSS, JACK John Albert B4.18.1872 Newark NJ D4.20.1947 Basking Ridge NJ BR/TR/5-11.5/195 d8.2

1897	Pit N	35	115	20	36	3	1	2	18	5	2		.313	.352	.409	105	0	3	.984	-1	82	56	1b32	0.0

ROTHGEB, CLAUDE Claude James B1.1.1880 Milford IL D7.6.1944 Manitowoc WI BB/6-0.5/200 d6.17 Col Illinois

1905	Was A	7	16	2	2	0	0	0	1	1	0		.125	.176	.125	-22	-2	1	.833	0	259	0	O4R	-0.3

ROTHROCK, JACK John Huston B3.14.1905 Long Beach CA D2.2.1980 San Bernardino CA BB/TR/5-11.5/165 d7.28 OF(138/194/311)

1925	Bos A	22	55	6	19	3	3	0	7	3	0	7	.345	.379	.509	124	4	3	.893	-3	86	64	S22	0.0
1926	Bos A	15	17	3	5	1	0	0	2	3	0		.294	.400	.353	101	0	0-0	.692	-2	86	0	S2	-0.1
1927	Bos A	117	428	61	111	24	6	1	36	24	2	46	.259	.302	.360	73	-19	5-5	.953	4	100	115	S40,2b36,3b20,1b13	-1.0
1928	Bos A	117	344	52	92	9	4	3	22	33	1	40	.267	.333	.343	79	-11	12-6	.979	-8	93	22	O53(26/12/19),3b17,1b16,S13,2b2/PC	-2.0
1929	Bos A	143	473	70	142	19	7	6	59	43	2	47	.300	.361	.408	100	0	24-13	.970	3	104	95	O128(0/126/2)	-0.2
1930	Bos A	45	65	4	18	3	1	0	4	2	0	9	.277	.299	.354	67	-3	0-2	.947	1	105	129	O9(1/0/8)/3	-0.4
1931	Bos A	133	475	81	132	32	3	4	42	47	0	48	.278	.343	.383	96	-2	13-7	.982	-5	87	149	O79(75/2/2),2b23,1b8,3b2/S	-0.8
1932	Bos A	12	48	3	10	1	0	0	0	5	0	5	.208	.283	.229	35	-5	1-0	.973	1	112	91	O12L	-0.4
	Chi A	39	64	8	12	2	1	0	6	5	0	9	.188	.246	.250	31	-7	1-0	.929	-3	100	0	O19(12/1/6),3b8/1	-0.4
	Year	51	112	11	22	3	1	0	6	10	0	14	.196	.262	.241	33	-11	4-0	.961	-2	108	64	O31(24/1/6),3b8/1	-0.9
1934	†StL N	154	647	106	184	35	3	11	72	49	1	56	.284	.336	.399	90	-9	10	.975	3	109	72	O154(5/0/149)/2	-1.3
1935	StL N	129	502	76	137	18	5	3	56	57	0	29	.273	.347	.347	84	-10	7	.980	-2	109	38	O127(1/1/125)	-1.5
1937	Phi A	88	232	28	62	15	0	0	21	28	0	15	.267	.346	.332	73	-9	1-0	.992	-2	99	44	O58(6/52/0)/2	-1.1
Total	11	1014	3350	498	924	162	35	28	327	299	6	312	.276	.336	.370	85	-73	76-33	.976	-13	103	74	O639R,S78,2b63,3b48,1b38/CP	-10.4

ROUSH, EDD Edd J B5.8.1893 Oakland City IN D3.21.1988 Bradenton FL BL/TL/5-11/170 d8.20 C1 HF1962

1913	Chi A	9	10	2	1	0	0	0	0	0	0	2	.100	.100	.100	-42	-2	0	1.000	-0	109	0	O2C	-0.2
1914	Ind F	74	166	26	54	8	4	1	30	6	1	20	.325	.353	.440	104	-2	12	.989	3	124	86	O43(38/4/1),1b2	-0.1
1915	New F	145	551	73	164	20	11	3	60	38	6	25	.298	.350	.390	115	1	28	.972	-3	99	92	O144(0/143/1)	-1.3
1916	NY N	39	69	4	13	0	1	0	5	1	0	4	.188	.200	.217	30	-6	4	.952	0	86	145	O15(0/5/10)	-0.8
	Cin N	69	272	34	78	7	14	0	15	13	7	19	.287	.336	.415	133	9	15	.971	2	112	79	O69C	0.7
	Year	108	341	38	91	7	15	0	20	14	7	23	.267	.309	.375	114	3	19	.969	2	108	88	O84(0/74/10)	-0.1
1917	Cin N	136	522	82	178	19	14	4	67	27	5	24	.341	.379	.454	162	36	21	.962	-2	104	83	O134C	2.8
1918	Cin N	113	435	61	145	18	10	5	62	22	2	10	.333	.368	.455	153	25	24	.960	5	113	87	O113C	2.5
1919	†Cin N	133	504	73	162	19	12	4	71	42	6	19	.321	.380	.431	147	29	20	.989	5	100	126	O133C	2.8
1920	Cin N	149	579	81	196	22	16	4	90	42	3	22	.339	.386	.453	142	31	36-24	.975	10	114	88	O139C,1b11/2	3.1
1921	Cin N	112	418	68	147	27	12	4	71	31	2	8	.352	.403	.502	145	27	19-17	.980	-2	105	59	O108C	1.8
1922	Cin N	49	165	29	58	7	4	1	24	19	3	5	.352	.428	.461	132	9	5-3	.990	1	89	162	O43C	0.7
1923	Cin N	138	527	88	185	41	18	6	88	46	3	11	.351	.406	.531	149	37	10-15	.970	-10	91	77	O137C	1.8
1924	Cin N	121	483	67	168	23	21	3	72	22	0	11	.348	.376	.501	135	21	17-13	.959	-10	84	102	O119C	0.5
1925	Cin N	134	540	91	183	28	16	8	83	35	4	9	.339	.383	.494	125	19	22-20	.978	-5	90	115	O134C	0.6
1926	Cin N	144	563	95	182	37	10	7	79	38	0	17	.323	.366	.462	125	19	8	.955	-18	79	89	O143C/1	-0.5
1927	NY N	140	570	83	173	27	4	7	58	26	1	15	.304	.335	.402	97	-4	18	.975	-6	87	130	O138(0/137/1)	-1.6
1928	NY N	46	163	20	41	5	3	2	14	14	1	8	.252	.315	.356	75	-7	1	.955	0	93	198	O39C	-0.8
1929	NY N	115	450	76	146	19	7	8	52	45	2	16	.324	.390	.451	108	6	6	.982	-6	80	165	O107C	-0.4
1931	Cin N	101	376	46	102	6	5	1	41	17	3	5	.271	.308	.338	78	-13	2	.981	-3	95	86	O88(43/45/0)	-1.9
Total	18	1967	7363	1099	2376	339	182	68	981	484	53	260	.323	.369	.446	126	235	268-92	.972	-38	97	102	O1848(81/1754/13),1b14/2	9.7

ROUTCLIFFE, PHIL Philip John "Chicken" B10.24.1870 Oswego NY D10.4.1918 Oswego NY BR/TR/6-0/175 d4.21

1890	Pit N	1	4	1	1	0	0	0	1	0	1		.250	.400	.250	102	0	0	1.000	0	0	0	/OL	0.0

ROWAN, DAVE David (b David Drohan) B12.6.1882 Elora ON, Can. D7.30.1955 Toronto ON, Can. BL/TL/5-11/175 d5.27

1911	StL A	18	65	7	25	1	1	0	11	4	0		.385	.420	.431	143	4	0	.945	-1	99	59	1b18	0.2

ROWAND, AARON Aaron Ryan B8.29.1977 Portland OR BR/TR/6-1/200* [ChiA98 1/35] d6.16 Col Cal St.-Fullerton

2001	Chi A	63	123	21	36	5	0	4	28	15-0	4	28	.293	.385	.431	109	2	5-1	.991	3	109	127	O61(34/32/11)	0.5
2002	Chi A	126	302	41	78	16	2	7	29	12-1	6	54	.258	.298	.394	79	-10	0-1	.983	6	108	112	O120(40/76/7)	-0.5
2003	Chi A	93	157	22	45	8	0	6	24	7-0	3	21	.287	.327	.452	99	0	0-0	1.000	3	94	268	O87(24/65/12)	0.2
2004	Chi A	140	487	94	151	38	4	24	69	30-1	10	91	.310	.361	.544	128	20	17-5	.975	1	98	158	O137(0/126/12)	2.1
2005	†Chi A	157	578	77	156	30	5	13	69	32-3	21	116	.270	.329	.407	91	-8	16-5	.992	-8	96	38	O157C	-1.2
Total	5	579	1647	255	466	97	9	54	219	96-5	44	310	.283	.337	.451	102	4	38-12	.986	4	100	117	O562(98/456/42)	1.1

ROWDON, WADE Wade Lee B9.7.1960 Riverhead NY BR/TR/6-2/180* [ChiA81 8/188] d9.8 Col Stetson

1984	Cin N	4	7	0	2	0	0	0	1	0-0	0	1	.286	.286	.286	58	0	0-0	1.000	0	125	161	/S3	0.0
1985	Cin N	5	9	2	2	0	0	0	2	2-0	0	1	.222	.364	.222	64	0	0-0	.667	-1	64	0	3b4	-0.2
1986	Cin N	38	80	9	20	5	1	0	10	9-0	1	17	.250	.330	.338	82	-2	2-0	.889	-4	117	107	3b7,S6,O5L,2b3	-0.5
1987	Chi N	11	31	2	7	1	0	1	6	3-0	0	10	.226	.294	.419	83	-1	0-2	.818	-1	94	0	3b9	-0.3
1988	Bal A	20	30	1	3	0	0	0	1	0	0	6	.100	.100	.100	-45	-6	1-1	.947	3	179	141	3b8,O5L,D5	-0.3
Total	5	78	157	14	34	6	2	1	16	14-0	1	35	.217	.283	.299	59	-9	3-3	.866	-4	112	57	3b29,O10L,S7,D5,2b3	-1.3

ROWE, DAVE David Elwood B10.9.1854 Harrisburg PA D12.9.1930 Glendale CA BR/TR/5-9/180 d5.30 M2 b-Jack ▲

1877	Chi N	2	7	0	2	0	0	0		3			.286	.286	.286	72	0		.667	-0	0	0	O2R/P	-0.1
1882	Cle N	24	97	13	25	4	3	1	17	4		9	.258	.287	.392	119	2		.837	-3	63	103	O23(3/20/1)/P	-0.1

YEAR	TM LG	G	AB	R	H	2B	3B	HR	RBI	BB-IB	HP	SO	AVG	OBP	SLG	AOPS	ABR	SB-CS	FA	FR	RNG	THR	GAMES AT POSITION	DL	BFV
1883	Bal AA	59	256	40	80	11	6	0	2				.313	.318	.402	127	6		.798	-6	54	0	O50(2/0/48),S7,1b3/P		0.
1884	StL U	109	485	95	142	32	11	4	10				.293	.307	.429	116	-6		.947	-4	69	175	O92C,S14,2b2,1b2/P		-1.
1885	StL N	16	62	8	10	3	0	0	3	5		8	.161	.224	.210	44	-3		.906	-2	35	251	O16C		-0.
1886	KC N	105	429	53	103	24	8	3	57	15		43	.240	.266	.354	82	-11	2	.851	-9	61	63	O90(4/86/0),S11,2b4,M		-2.
1888	KC AA	32	122	14	21	3	4	0	13	6	1		.172	.217	.262	50	-8	2	.914	2	209	81	O32C,M		-0.
Total	7	347	1458	223	383	77	32	8	90	42	1	63	.263	.284	.376	99	-20	4	.878	-23	76	101	O305(9/246/51),S32,2b6,1b5,P4		-4.

ROWE, HARLAND   Harland Stimson "Hypie" B4.20.1896 Springvale ME D5.26.1969 Springvale ME BL/TR/6-1/170 d6.23 Col Maine

YEAR	TM LG	G	AB	R	H	2B	3B	HR	RBI	BB-IB	HP	SO	AVG	OBP	SLG	AOPS	ABR	SB-CS	FA	FR	RNG	THR	GAMES AT POSITION	DL	BFV
1916	Phi A	17	36	2	5	1	0	0	3	2	0	8	.139	.184	.167	6	-4	0	.842	-1	96	0	3b8/OR		-0.

ROWE, JACK   John Charles B12.8.1856 Hamburg PA D4.25.1911 St.Louis MO BL/TR/5-8/170 d9.6 M1 b-Dave

YEAR	TM LG	G	AB	R	H	2B	3B	HR	RBI	BB-IB	HP	SO	AVG	OBP	SLG	AOPS	ABR	SB-CS	FA	FR	RNG	THR	GAMES AT POSITION	DL	BFV
1879	Buf N	8	34	8	12	1	0	0		8		1	.353	.353	.382	139	1		.905	0			C6,O2R		0
1880	Buf N	79	326	43	82	10	6	1	36	6		17	.252	.265	.328	98	-1		.897	-14			C60,O25(2/6/19),3b3		-1.
1881	Buf N	64	246	30	82	11	11	1	43	1		12	.333	.336	.480	156	14		.900	-9			C46,S7,3b7,O5(0/1/4)		0.
1882	Buf N	75	308	43	82	14	5	1	42	12		0	.266	.294	.354	105	1		.950	-6			C49,O28L,S18,3b3		-1.
1883	Buf N	87	374	65	104	18	7	1	38	15		14	.278	.306	.372	102	1		.899	-16			C65,O30(17/12/1),S6		1.
1884	Buf N	93	400	85	126	14	14	4	61	23		14	.315	.352	.450	146	19		.834	-12	91	115	S65,C23,O12C		-0
1885	Buf N	98	421	62	122	28	8	2	51	13		19	.290	.311	.409	127	11		.880	-21	91	95	S110,C3		-0
1886	Det N	111	468	97	142	21	9	6	87	26		27	.303	.340	.425	127	14	12	.907	-24	92	95	S124		-0
1887	†Det N	124	537	135	171	30	10	6	96	39	3	11	.318	.368	.445	120	14	22	.861	-9	100	87	S105		-0
1888	Det N	105	451	62	125	19	8	2	74	19	3	28	.277	.311	.368	114	7	10	.896	-6	100	105	S75		-0
1889	Pit N	75	317	57	82	14	3	2	32	22	3	16	.259	.313	.341	91	-4	5	.896	-8	102	96	S125,M		-0
1890	Buf P	125	504	77	126	22	7	2	76	48	7	18	.250	.324	.333	83	-11	10	.901	4	95	96	S125,M		-0
Total	12	1044	4386	764	1256	202	88	28	644	224	16	177	.286	.323	.392	114	66	59	.882	-117			S657,C298,O103(47/32/26),3b20		-1

ROWELL, BAMA   Carvel William B1.13.1916 Citronelle AL D8.16.1993 Citronelle AL BL/TR/5-11/185 d9.4 Mil 1942-45 Col Louisiana St.

YEAR	TM LG	G	AB	R	H	2B	3B	HR	RBI	BB-IB	HP	SO	AVG	OBP	SLG	AOPS	ABR	SB-CS	FA	FR	RNG	THR	GAMES AT POSITION	DL	BFV
1939	Bos N	21	59	5	11	2	2	0	6	1	0	4	.186	.200	.288	32	-6	0	.853	-9	82	177	O16(0/13/3)		-0
1940	Bos N	130	486	46	148	19	8	3	58	18	1	22	.305	.331	.395	105	1	12	.953	-2	105	108	2b115,O7(0/1/6)		0
1941	Bos N	138	483	49	129	23	6	7	60	39		36	.267	.322	.383	102	0	11	.935	-8	98	120	2b112,O14(7/2/6),3b2		0
1946	Bos N	95	293	37	82	12	6	3	31	29		15	.280	.345	.392	108	2	5	.978	3	104	123	O85(71/14/0)		0
1947	Bos N	113	384	48	106	23	2	5	40	18		14	.276	.310	.385	86	-9	7	.945	-5	100	58	O100(99/2/0),2b7,3b4		-1
1948	Phi N	77	196	15	47	16	2	1	22	8		14	.240	.270	.357	70	-9	2	.821	-8	72	149	3b18,O17(14/0/3),2b12		-4
Total	6	574	1901	200	523	95	26	19	217	113	2	105	.275	.316	.382	95	-21	37	.945	-22	101	110	2b246,O239(191/32/18),3b24		-4

ROWEN, ED   W. Edward B10.22.1857 Bridgeport CT D2.22.1892 Bridgeport CT 5-6/155 d5.1

YEAR	TM LG	G	AB	R	H	2B	3B	HR	RBI	BB-IB	HP	SO	AVG	OBP	SLG	AOPS	ABR	SB-CS	FA	FR	RNG	THR	GAMES AT POSITION	DL	BFV
1882	Bos N	83	327	36	81	7	4	1	43	19		18	.248	.289	.303	90	-4		.885	-9	71	108	O48R,C34,S6/3		-0
1883	Phi AA	49	196	28	43	10	1	0	21	11			.219	.261	.281	68	-7		.855	-2			C44,O8(0/5/3)/32		-0
1884	Phi AA	4	15	4	6	1	0	0	1	1		1	.400	.471	.467	194	2		.806	-2			C4		0
Total	3	136	538	68	130	18	5	1	65	31		18	.242	.284	.299	85	-9		.866	-14			C82,O56(0/5/51),S6,3b2/2		-1

ROWLAND, CHUCK   Charlie Leland B7.23.1899 Warrenton NC D1.21.1992 Raleigh NC BR/TR/6-1/185 d5.11

YEAR	TM LG	G	AB	R	H	2B	3B	HR	RBI	BB-IB	HP	SO	AVG	OBP	SLG	AOPS	ABR	SB-CS	FA	FR	RNG	THR	GAMES AT POSITION	DL	BFV
1923	Phi A	5	6	0	0	0	0	0				2	.000	.000	.000	-99	-2	0-0	1.000	0	77	160	C4		-0

ROWLAND, RICH   Richard Garnet B2.25.1964 Cloverdale CA BR/TR/6-1/215* [DetA88 17/447] d9.7 Col Mendocino (CA) CC

YEAR	TM LG	G	AB	R	H	2B	3B	HR	RBI	BB-IB	HP	SO	AVG	OBP	SLG	AOPS	ABR	SB-CS	FA	FR	RNG	THR	GAMES AT POSITION	DL	BFV
1990	Det A	7	19	3	3	1	0	0	2-1	0		2	.158	.238	.211	26	-2	0-0	.967	-1	47	70	C5,D2		-
1991	Det A	4	4	0	1	0	0	0	1-0	0		2	.250	.333	.250	82	0	0-0	1.000	1	0	0	C2/D		-
1992	Det A	6	14	2	3	0	0	0	3-0	0		3	.214	.353	.214	61	-1	0-0	1.000	-1	74	0	C3/13D		-
1993	Det A	21	46	2	10	3	0	0	4	5-0		16	.217	.294	.283	56	-3	0-0	.988	1	94	63	C17,D3		-0
1994	Bos A	46	118	14	27	3	0	9	20	11-0		35	.229	.295	.483	92	-2	0-0	.972	-5	105	121	C39/1D		-0
1995	Bos A	14	29	1	5	1	0	0	1-0	0		11	.172	.172	.207	-2	-4	0-0	.977	-1	140	54	C11,D3		-
Total	6	98	230	22	49	8	0	9	26	22-1	0	71	.213	.281	.365	67	-12	0-0	.976	-4	101	92	C77,D15,1b2/3		-

ROXBURGH, JIM   James A. B1.17.1858 San Francisco CA D2.21.1934 San Francisco CA BR/TR/5-10/170 d5.30

YEAR	TM LG	G	AB	R	H	2B	3B	HR	RBI	BB-IB	HP	SO	AVG	OBP	SLG	AOPS	ABR	SB-CS	FA	FR	RNG	THR	GAMES AT POSITION	DL	BFV
1884	Bal AA	2	4	1	2	0	0	0	1	1			.500	.667	.500	275	-1		.824	-1			C2		-
1887	Phi AA	2	8	0	1	0	0	0	0			0	.125	.125	.125	-30	-1	0	.875	-2			C2/2		-
Total	2	4	12	1	3	0	0	0	1	1		0	.250	.357	.250	81	0	0	.840	-2			C4/2		-

ROYER, STAN   Stanley Dean B8.31.1967 Olney IL BR/TR/6-3/195(195-221) [OakA88 1/16] d9.11 Col Eastern Illinois

YEAR	TM LG	G	AB	R	H	2B	3B	HR	RBI	BB-IB	HP	SO	AVG	OBP	SLG	AOPS	ABR	SB-CS	FA	FR	RNG	THR	GAMES AT POSITION	DL	BFV
1991	StL N	9	21	1	6	1	0	0	1-0			4	.286	.318	.333	82	0	0-0	1.000	-1	51	0	3b5		-
1992	StL N	13	31	6	10	2	0	2	9	1-0		4	.323	.333	.581	161	2	0-0	.900	0	127	400	3b5,1b4		-
1993	StL N	24	46	4	14	2	0	1	8	2-0		14	.304	.333	.413	99	0	0-1	.857	-1	99	85	3b10,1b2		-
1994	StL N	39	57	3	10	5	0	1	2	1-0		18	.175	.175	.316	25	-6	0-0	.972	-1	105	57	1b11,3b5		-
	Bos A	4	9	1	1	0	0	0	1	1-0		3	.111	.111	.111	-41	-2	0-0	.833	-1	74	0	3b3/1		-
Total	4	89	164	14	41	10	0	4	21	4-0		41	.250	.266	.384	73	-6	0-1	.895	-3	92	92	3b28,1b18		-

ROYSTER, JERRY   Jeron Kennis B10.18.1952 Sacramento CA BR/TR/6-0/165* d8.14 M1/C4 OF(123/21/9)

YEAR	TM LG	G	AB	R	H	2B	3B	HR	RBI	BB-IB	HP	SO	AVG	OBP	SLG	AOPS	ABR	SB-CS	FA	FR	RNG	THR	GAMES AT POSITION	DL	BFV
1973	LA N	10	19	1	4	0	0	0	0-0			5	.211	.211	.211	18	-2	1-0	.842	0	121	115	3b6/2		-
1974	LA N	6	0	2					0-0	0		0	—	—	—		0	0-0	1.000	1	618	0	/23OR		-
1975	LA N	13	36	2	9	2	1	0	1	1-0		3	.250	.270	.361	77	-1	1-0	1.000	0	81	0	O7(1/0/6),2b4,3b3/S		-
1976	Atl N	149	533	65	132	13	1	5	45	52-4	1	53	.248	.313	.304	72	-19	24-13	.962	25	113	127	3b148,S2		-
1977	Atl N	140	445	64	96	10	2	6	28	38-3	1	67	.216	.278	.288	47	-33	28-10	.953	-12	94	79	3b56,S51,2b38/OC		-
1978	Atl N	140	529	67	137	17	8	2	35	56-2	3	49	.259	.331	.333	78	-14	27-17	.974	-4	91	84	2b75,S60/3		-
1979	Atl N	154	601	103	164	25	6	3	51	62-0	0	59	.273	.337	.349	84	-12	35-8	.948	29	124	83	3b80,2b77		-
1980	Atl N	123	392	42	95	17	5	1	20	37-1	0	48	.242	.309	.319	75	-13	22-13	.948	-7	90	107	2b49,3b48,O41L		-
1981	Atl N	64	93	13	19	4	1	0	9	7-0	0	14	.204	.257	.269	50	-6	7-5	.950	1	99	105	3b24,2b13		-
1982	†Atl N	108	261	43	77	13	2	2	25	22-1	2	36	.295	.351	.383	104	2	14-6	.943	0	89	61	3b62,O25L,2b16,S10	21	
1983	Atl N	91	268	32	63	10	3	3	30	28-2	0	35	.235	.305	.328	71	-10	11-7	.940	8	123	104	2b29,3b17,S16,O11L		
1984	Atl N	81	227	22	47	13	4	0	15	15-1	0	41	.207	.257	.295	52	-15	6-5	.973	10	128	101	2b58,3b29,S7,O2(0/1/1)		
1985	SD N	90	249	31	70	13	2	5	31	32-1	1	31	.281	.363	.410	117	7	6-5	.975	9	116	111	3b59,S24,2b21,O7L		
1986	SD N	118	257	31	66	12	0	5	26	32-3	0	45	.257	.336	.362	95	-1	3-5	.931	4	113	140	3b30,O13L,2b5,D4		
1987	Chi A	55	154	25	37	11	0	7	23	19-1	1	26	.240	.324	.448	100	0	2-1	.969	-4	87	88	3b13/2SOL		
	NY A	18	42	1	15	2	0	0	4	4-0	0	6	.357	.413	.405	119	1	2-1	.954	-3	97	121	3b43,O14L,2b6,D4/S		
	Year	73	196	26	52	13	0	7	27	23-1	1	32	.265	.342	.439	104	2	4-2	1.000	0	111	249	O26(7/19/1),3b10,2b2,S2		
1988	Atl N	68	102	8	18	3	0	0	6	6-1	0	16	.176	.222	.206	23	-10	0-0	.951	63	108	100	3b634,2b416,S187,O153L,D4	21	
Total	16	1428	4208	552	1049	165	33	40	352	411-20	11	534	.249	.315	.333	76	-126	189-95	.951	63	108	100	3b634,2b416,S187,O153L,D4	21	

ROYSTER, WILLIE   Willie Arthur B4.11.1954 Clarksville VA BR/TR/5-11/180 [BalA72 22/525] d9.3

YEAR	TM LG	G	AB	R	H	2B	3B	HR	RBI	BB-IB	HP	SO	AVG	OBP	SLG	AOPS	ABR	SB-CS	FA	FR	RNG	THR	GAMES AT POSITION	DL	BFV
1981	Bal A	4	4	0	0	0	0	0	0-0	0		2	.000	.000	.000	-99	-1	0-0	1.000	-0	0	0	C4		-

ROZNOVSKY, VIC   Victor Joseph B10.19.1938 Shiner TX BL/TR/6-1/180* d6.28

YEAR	TM LG	G	AB	R	H	2B	3B	HR	RBI	BB-IB	HP	SO	AVG	OBP	SLG	AOPS	ABR	SB-CS	FA	FR	RNG	THR	GAMES AT POSITION	DL	BFV
1964	Chi N	35	76	2	15	1	0	2	5	8-0	0	18	.197	.244	.211	29	-7	0-1	.976	-4	115	201	C26		-
1965	Chi N	71	172	9	38	4	1	3	15	16-1	3	30	.221	.295	.308	70	-7	1-0	.984	2	110	98	C63		-
1966	Bal A	41	97	4	23	5	0	1	10	9-4	1	11	.237	.308	.320	82	-2	0-0	.995	-4	82	96	C34		-
1967	Bal A	45	97	7	20	5	0	0	10	7-1	0	20	.206	.212	.258	39	-8	0-0	.993	-0	100	144	C23		-
1969	Phi N	13	13	0	3	0	0	0	1	1-0	0	4	.231	.286	.231	47	-1	0-0	1.000	1	0	0	C2		-
Total	5	205	455	22	99	15	1	4	38	32-5	4	83	.218	.273	.281	59	-25	1-1	.988	-5	102	121	C148		-

RUAN, WILKIN   Wilkin Chal B11.18.1978 Guaymate, D.R. BR/TR/6-0/170* d9.1

YEAR	TM LG	G	AB	R	H	2B	3B	HR	RBI	BB-IB	HP	SO	AVG	OBP	SLG	AOPS	ABR	SB-CS	FA	FR	RNG	THR	GAMES AT POSITION	DL	BFV
2002	LA N	12	11	2	3	1	0	0	0-0	0		2	.273	.273	.364	72	-1	0-0	1.000	-0	92	0	O5C		-
2003	LA N	21	41	2	9	2	1	0	2	0-0	0	7	.220	.220	.317	39	-4	1-0	1.000	-0	91	178	O20C		-
Total	2	33	52	4	12	3	1	0	2	0-0	0	9	.231	.231	.327	46	-5	1-0	1.000	-0	91	147	O25C		-

RUBELING, AL   Albert William B5.10.1913 Baltimore MD D1.28.1988 Baltimore MD BR/TR/6-0/185 d4.16 Col Towson

YEAR	TM LG	G	AB	R	H	2B	3B	HR	RBI	BB-IB	HP	SO	AVG	OBP	SLG	AOPS	ABR	SB-CS	FA	FR	RNG	THR	GAMES AT POSITION	DL	BFV
1940	Phi A	108	376	49	92	16	6	4	38	48	0	58	.245	.330	.351	78	-12	4-5	.933	-7	96	71	3b98,2b10		-
1941	Phi A	6	19	0	5	0	0	0	2	2		1	.263	.333	.263	61	-1	0	.833	-2	74	98	3b6		-
1943	Pit N	47	168	23	44	8	4	0	19	8		17	.262	.295	.357	85	-4	0	.974	0	109	106	2b44/3		-
1944	Pit N	92	184	22	45	7	2	4	30	19		19	.245	.322	.370	90	-2	4	1.000	1	106	72	O18(9/0/9),2b17,3b16		-
Total	4	253	747	94	186	31	12	8	79	77	2	95	.249	.321	.355	82	-19	8-5	.939	-7	97	88	3b121,2b71,O18(9/0/9)		-

YEAR	TM	LG	G	AB	R	H	2B	3B	HR	RBI	BB-IB	HP	SO	AVG	OBP	SLG	AOPS	ABR	SB-CS	FA	FR	RNG	THR	GAMES AT POSITION	DL	BFW

RUBERTO, SONNY John Edward B1.2.1946 Staten Island NY BR/TR/5-11/175* d5.25 C2

1969	SD	N	19	21	3	3	0	0	0	0	1-0	0	7	.143	.182	.143		-8	-3	0-0	1.000	1	105	98	C15		-0.2
1972	Cin	N	2	3	0	0	0	0	0	0	0-0	1	1	.000	.250	.000		-25	0	0-0	1.000	0	47	0	C2		-0.1
Total	2		21	24	3	3	0	0	0	0	1-0	1	8	.125	.192	.125		-10	-3	0-0	1.000	1	98	86	C17		-0.3

RUBLE, ART William Arthur "Speedy" B3.11.1903 Knoxville TN D11.1.1983 Maryville TN BL/TR/5-10.5/168 d4.18 Col Maryville

1927	Det	A	56	91	16	15	4	2	0	11	14	1	15	.165	.283	.253		39	-9	2-2	.970	1	104	110	O43(24/13/7)		-0.9
1934	Phi	N	19	54	7	15	4	0	0	8	7	0	3	.278	.361	.352		81	-1	0	.839	-1	86	179	O14(4/1/10)		-0.3
Total	2		75	145	23	30	8	2	0	19	21	1	18	.207	.311	.290		55	-9	2-2	.929	0	98	133	O57(28/14/17)		-1.2

RUCKER, JOHNNY John Joel B1.15.1917 Crabapple GA D8.7.1985 Moultrie GA BL/TR/6-2/175 d4.16 Col Georgia

1940	NY	N	86	277	38	82	7	5	4	23	7	0	32	.296	.313	.401		95	-4	4	.954	-7	85	64	O57C		-1.2
1941	NY	N	143	622	95	179	38	9	1	42	29	0	61	.288	.320	.383		95	-6	8	.967	-2	97	113	O142C		-1.2
1943	NY	N	132	505	56	138	19	4	2	46	22	0	44	.273	.304	.339		85	-12	4	.969	-4	98	81	O117C		-2.1
1944	NY	N	144	587	79	143	14	8	6	39	24	1	48	.244	.275	.325		69	-28	8	.985	-12	82	111	O139C		-4.6
1945	NY	N	105	429	58	117	19	11	7	51	20	0	36	.273	.305	.417		98	-4	7	.978	-5	95	73	O98C		-1.3
1946	NY	N	95	197	28	52	8	2	1	13	7	3	27	.264	.300	.340		81	-6	4	.948	-5	90	28	O54(0/50/6)		-1.3
Total	6		705	2617	354	711	105	39	21	214	109	4	248	.272	.300	.366		87	-60	35	.971	-35	92	89	O607(0/603/6)		-11.7

RUDDERHAM, JOHN John Edmund B8.30.1863 Quincy MA D4.3.1942 Randolph MA BR/TR/5-8/170 d9.18

| 1884 | Bos | U | 1 | 4 | 0 | 1 | 0 | 0 | 0 | | 0 | | 0 | .250 | .250 | .250 | | 53 | -1 | 0 | .000 | -1 | 0 | 0 | /OL | | -0.1 |

RUDI, JOE Joseph Oden B9.7.1946 Modesto CA BR/TR/6-2/200* d4.11 C2 [DL 1983 Oak A 182]

1967	KC	A	19	43	4	8	2	0	0	1	3-0	0	7	.186	.239	.233		41	-3	0-0	.984	-1	0	19	1b9,O6L		-0.6
1968	Oak	A	68	181	10	32	5	1	1	12	12-3	2	32	.177	.236	.232		44	-13	1-1	.987	-2	91	34	O56(55/1/1)		-2.1
1969	Oak	A	35	122	10	23	3	1	2	6	5-1	0	16	.189	.220	.279		40	-11	1-1	1.000	1	112	139	O18L,1b11		-1.2
1970	Oak	A	106	350	40	108	23	2	11	42	16-1	2	61	.309	.341	.480		128	12	3-1	.982	1	100	138	O63(58/1/12),1b28		0.8
1971	†Oak	A	127	513	62	137	23	4	10	52	28-2	2	62	.267	.304	.386		97	-4	3-2	.996	4	111	68	O121(115/0/9),1b5		-0.8
1972	†Oak	A★	147	593	94	181	32	9	19	75	37-6	2	62	.305	.345	.486		153	35	3-4	.992	-8	88	75	O147L/3		2.0
1973	Oak	A	120	437	53	118	25	1	12	66	30-4	2	72	.270	.315	.414		110	5	0-0	.992	2	106	75	O117L/1D	16	0.0
1974	†Oak	A★	158	593	73	174	39	4	22	99	34-6	5	92	.293	.334	.484		142	30	2-3	.984	-6	92	76	O140L,1b27,D2		1.4
1975	†Oak	A★	126	468	66	130	26	6	21	75	40-12	5	56	.278	.333	.494		135	20	2-1	.991	-7	69	102	1b91,O44L,D2	31	0.4
1976	Oak	A	130	500	54	135	32	3	13	94	41-10	3	71	.270	.323	.424		124	15	6-1	.991	-7	69	102	O126(126/0/1),1b2,D2		0.4
1977	Cal	A	64	242	48	64	13	2	13	53	22-4	4	48	.264	.333	.496		128	9	1-0	1.000	3	114	70	O61L,D3	99	0.9
1978	Cal	A	133	497	58	127	27	1	17	79	29-4	2	82	.256	.295	.416		102	-1	2-1	.992	2	105	57	O111L,D11,1b10		-0.5
1979	Cal	A	90	330	35	80	11	3	11	61	24-3	1	61	.242	.294	.394		87	-8	0-0	.989	2	106	85	O80(69/0/12),1b5,D3	43	-0.9
1980	Cal	A	104	372	42	88	17	1	16	53	17-2	5	84	.237	.277	.417		89	-7	1-0	.991	5	115	74	O90(89/0/1),1b6,D3	47	-0.6
1981	Bos	A	49	122	14	22	3	0	6	24	8-1	2	29	.180	.239	.352		65	-6	0-0	1.000	-1	30	44	D21,1b5/OR		-0.8
1982	Oak	A	71	193	21	41	6	1	5	18	24-0	1	35	.212	.301	.332		77	-6	0-0	.991	-5	65	74	1b49,O14(4/0/10),D3		-1.5
Total	16		1547	5556	684	1468	287	39	179	810	369-59	35	870	.264	.311	.427		112	67	25-15	.991	-16	101	74	O1195(1160/2/47),1b249,D51/3	418	-3.1

RUDOLPH, DUTCH John Herman B7.10.1882 Natrona PA D4.17.1967 Natrona PA BL/TL/5-10/160 d7.3

1903	Phi	N	1	1	0	0	0	0	0	0	0	0	0	.000	.000	.000		-99	0	0	—	0			/H		0.0
1904	Chi	N	2	3	0	1	0	0	0	0	0	0	0	.333	.333	.333		106	0	0	1.000	-0	0	0	O2R		0.0
Total	2		3	4	0	1	0	0	0	0	0	0	0	.250	.250	.250		52	0	0	1.000	-0	0	0	O2R		0.0

RUDOLPH, KEN Kenneth Victor B12.29.1946 Rockford IL BR/TR/6-1/185* [ChiN65 2/26] d4.20 Col Los Angeles (CA) City

1969	Chi	N	27	34	7	7	1	0	1	6	6-0	0	11	.206	.325	.324		73	-1	0-0	.977	-1	99	0	C11,O3L		-0.2
1970	Chi	N	20	40	4	4	1	0	0	2	1-1	0	12	.100	.122	.125		-30	-7	0-0	1.000	2	294	172	C16		-0.5
1971	Chi	N	25	76	5	15	3	0	0	7	6-0	1	20	.197	.265	.237		38	-6	0-0	1.000	3	371	219	C25		0.2
1972	Chi	N	42	106	10	25	1	0	2	9	6-0	1	14	.236	.283	.321		64	-5	1-2	.966	3	125	157	C41		-0.1
1973	Chi	N	64	170	12	35	8	1	2	17	7-0	1	25	.206	.239	.300		46	-13	1-4	.970	-5	89	148	C64	15	-1.8
1975	StL	N	44	80	5	16	2	0	1	8	21-5	1	15	.259	.350	.278		74	-5	0-0	.996	-1	91	69	C56		-0.3
1976	StL	N	27	50	1	8	3	0	0	5	1-0	0	7	.160	.176	.220		12	-6	0-0	.940	-0	103	111	C14		-0.8
1977	SF	N	11	15	1	3	0	0	0	1	1-1	0	7	.200	.250	.200		26	-2	0-0	.946	2	214	131	C11		-0.6
	Bal	A	11	14	2	4	1	0	0	2	2-0	0	4	.286	.286	.357		78	0	0-0	1.000	3	67	138	C11		0.2
Total	9		328	743	55	158	23	2	6	64	52-7	4	121	.213	.267	.273		48	-52	2-6	.980	9	140	130	C280,O3L	15	-3.9

RUEL, MUDDY Herold Dominic B2.20.1896 St.Louis MO D11.13.1963 Palo Alto CA BR/TR/5-9/150 d5.29 Mil 1918 M1/C14

1915	StL	A	10	14	0	4	1	0	0	1	5	0	5	.000	.263	.000		-22	-2	0	.958	-1	89	61	C6		
1917	NY	A	6	17	1	2	0	0	0	1	2	0	2	.118	.211	.118		-22	-2	1	1.000	0	130	96	C6		-0.3
1918	NY	A	3	6	0	2	0	0	0	1	2	0	1	.333	.500	.333		148	1	1	1.000	0	176	71	C2		-0.2
1919	NY	A	79	233	18	56	6	0	0	31	34	1	26	.240	.340	.266		71	-7	4	.975	-1	110	98	C79		0.1
1920	NY	A	82	261	30	70	14	1	1	15	15	1	18	.268	.310	.341		70	-11	4-2	.984	-1	114	66	C80		-0.2
1921	Bos	A	113	358	41	99	21	1	0	45	41	1	15	.277	.352	.349		82	-8	2-7	.977	-2	111	95	C109		-0.5
1922	Bos	A	116	361	34	92	15	1	0	28	41	1	26	.255	.333	.302		67	-16	4-2	.978	-1	86	84	C112		-1.0
1923	Was	A	136	449	63	142	24	3	0	54	55	3	21	.316	.394	.383		111	10	4-6	.980	15	102	123	C133		3.1
1924	†Was	A	149	501	50	142	20	2	0	57	62	7	20	.283	.370	.331		84	-9	7-11	.980	21	147	77	C147		1.9
1925	†Was	A	127	393	55	122	9	2	0	54	63	4	16	.310	.411	.344		95	1	4-5	.982	15	109	97	C126/1		2.1
1926	Was	A	117	368	42	110	22	5	1	53	61	2	14	.299	.401	.389		109	8	7-6	.989	1	98	93	C117		1.6
1927	Was	A	131	428	61	132	16	5	1	52	63	5	18	.308	.403	.376		104	6	9-6	.988	1	109	87	C128		1.4
1928	Was	A	108	350	31	90	18	2	0	55	44	1	14	.257	.342	.320		75	-11	12-10	.989	8	120	94	C101,1b2		0.3
1929	Was	A	69	188	16	46	4	2	0	20	31	7	10	.245	.352	.287		66	-9	0-5	.990	7	123	140	C62		0.1
1930	Was	A	66	198	18	50	3	4	0	26	24	3	13	.253	.342	.308		66	-10	1-0	.986	5	128	115	C60		0.1
1931	Bos	A	23	83	6	25	5	0	0	6	8	1	5	.301	.370	.361		98	0	0-0	.945	0	122	106	C30		-0.1
	Det	A	14	50	1	6	1	0	0	3	5	0	1	.120	.200	.140		-9	-8	0-0	.975	1	78	173	C14		0.2
	Year		47	133	7	31	6	0	0	9	14	1	7	.233	.306	.278		56	-8	0-0	.958	0	106	131	C44		-0.5
1932	Det	A	51	136	10	32	4	2	0	18	17	1	6	.235	.320	.294		58	-8	1-0	.989	-1	88	107	C49		-0.3
1933	StL	A	36	63	13	12	2	0	0	8	24	1	4	.190	.414	.222		68	-1	0-0	1.000	3	118	154	C28		-0.6
1934	Chi	A	22	57	4	12	1	1	0	7	8	0	1	.211	.308	.263		47	-4	0-0	.976	2	60	90	C21		-0.5
Total	19		1468	4514	494	1242	187	29	4	534	606	29	238	.275	.365	.332		84	-80	61-60	.982	72	111	97	C1410,1b3		7.0

RUETHER, DUTCH Walter Henry B9.13.1893 Alameda CA D5.16.1970 Phoenix AZ BL/TL/6-1.5/180 d4.13 Mil 1918 ▲

1917	Chi	N	31	44	3	12	1	0	0	11	8	0	11	.273	.385	.432		139	2	1	1.000	1	108	297	P10,1b5		0.1
	Cin	N	19	24	1	5	2	0	0	1	3	0	6	.208	.296	.292		84	2	1	.833	-0	98	0	P7		
	Year		50	68	4	17	3	0	0	12	11	0	17	.250	.354	.382		122	2	2	.920	0	103	149	P17,1b5		0.1
1918	Cin	N	2	3	0	0	0	0	0	0	0	0	2	.000	.000	.000		-99	0	0	1.000	-0	69	0	P2		0.0
1919	†Cin	N	42	92	8	24	2	3	0	6	4	0	18	.261	.292	.348		94	5	1	.971	-3	82	57	P33		0.0
1920	Cin	N	45	104	3	20	4	0	0	10	5	0	24	.192	.229	.231		33	-9	0-0	.952	-0	102	227	P37/1		-0.1
1921	Bro	N	49	97	12	34	5	2	2	13	4	1	9	.351	.376	.505		127	11	1-0	.966	-1	93	126	P36		0.0
1922	Bro	N	67	125	6	26	6	1	2	20	12	1	11	.208	.283	.320		56	-6	1.000		0	90	227	P35		0.0
1923	Bro	N	49	117	6	32	1	0	0	10	12	0	12	.274	.341	.282		68	-5	0-0	.968	-2	83	143	P34/1		-0.1
1924	Bro	N	34	62	5	15	1	1	0	4	5	0	2	.242	.299	.290		60	2		.981	1	112	154	P30		0.0
1925	†Was	A	55	108	18	36	3	2	1	19	11	0	8	.333	.390	.426		109	1	0-1	.962	-3	83	40	P30/1		-0.1
1926	Was	A	47	92	6	23	2	0	1	11	6	0	10	.250	.296	.304		58	4	0-0	.974	-2	84	86	P23		-0.1
	†NY	A	13	21	2	2	0	0	0	0	5	0	1	.095	.136	.095		-39	-2	0-0	.875	-1	55	0	P5		0.0
	Year		60	113	8	25	2	0	1	11	11	0	11	.221	.267	.265		40	2	0-0	.970	-3	79	71	P28		0.0
1927	NY	A	35	80	7	21	3	0	0	10	7	0	15	.262	.330	.338		76	5	0-0	1.000	0	104	103	P27		0.0
Total	11		488	969	83	250	30	12	7	111	77	2	129	.258	.314	.335		76	22	3-1	.970	-9	91	132	P309,1b8		-0.1

RUFER, RUDY Rudolph Joseph B10.28.1926 Ridgewood NY BR/TR/6-0.5/165* d9.22 Col Oklahoma

1949	NY	N	7	15	1	1	0	0	0	0	2	0	1	.067	.176	.067		-32	-2	0	.957	-0	94	79	S7		-0.3
1950	NY	N	15	11	1	1	0	0	0	0	0	1	1	.091	.091	.091		-52	-2	1	.889	1	165	120	S8		-0.2
Total	2		22	26	2	2	0	0	0	0	2	1	2	.077	.143	.077		-40	-5	1	.938	0	111	89	S15		-0.5

YEAR	TM LG	G	AB	R	H	2B	3B	HR	RBI	BB-IB	HP	SO	AVG	OBP	SLG	AOPS	ABR	SB-CS	FA	FR	RNG	THR	GAMES AT POSITION	DL	BFW
RUFFING, RED		Charles Herbert		B5.3.1905 Granville IL				D2.17.1986 Mayfield Hts. OH			BR/TR/6-1.5/205		d5.31		Mil 1943-44 C1		HF1967 ▲							
1924	Bos A	8	7	0	1	0	1	0	0	0	0	1	.143	.143	.429	44	0	0-0	1.000	-1	56	0	P8		0.0
1925	Bos A	37	79	6	17	4	2	0	11	1	1	22	.215	.235	.316	39	0	0-0	.983	-1	92	111	P37		0.0
1926	Bos A	37	51	8	10	1	0	1	5	2	0	12	.196	.226	.275	31	1	0-1	.978	-1	81	88	P37		0.0
1927	Bos A	29	55	5	14	3	1	0	4	0	1	6	.255	.268	.345	59	2	0-0	.978	0	93	49	P26		0.0
1928	Bos A	60	121	12	38	13	1	2	19	3	0	12	.314	.331	.488	115	13	0-0	.951	-3	78	102	P42		-0.1
1929	Bos A	60	114	9	35	9	0	2	17	2	1	13	.307	.325	.439	97	-1	0-0	.946	-1	88	36	P35,O2L		0.0
1930	Bos A	6	11	2	3	2	0	0	1	0	0	1	.273	.273	.455	84	1	0-0	.667	-1	41	0	P4		0.6
	NY A	52	99	15	37	6	2	4	21	7	0	7	.374	.415	.596	160	17	0-0	.914	-3	64	0	P38		0.0
	Year	58	110	17	40	8	2	4	22	7	0	8	.364	.402	.582	153	17	0-0	.914	-3	64	0	P38		-0.7
1931	NY A	48	109	14	36	8	1	3	12	1	0	13	.330	.336	.505	125	3	0-0	**1.000**	-3	66	42	P37/OR		0.0
1932	†NY A	55	124	20	38	6	1	3	19	6	0	10	.306	.338	.444	106	13	0-0	.955	-2	72	133	P35		0.0
1933	NY A	55	115	10	29	3	1	2	13	7	0	5	.252	.295	.348	74	8	0-0	.964	-0	89	178	P35		0.6
1934	NY A★	45	113	11	28	4	1	2	13	3	1	17	.248	.274	.327	58	6	0-0	**1.000**	-2	59	144	P30		0.6
1935	NY A	50	109	13	37	10	4	1	18	3	1	9	.339	.364	.486	125	13	0-0	.986	2	113	222	P33		0.6
1936	†NY A	53	127	14	37	5	0	5	22	11	0	12	.291	.348	.449	99	-15	0-0	.974	-4	58	91	P31		0.6
1937	†NY A	54	129	11	26	4	1	3	10	13	0	24	.202	.275	.248	32	2	0-0	**1.000**	-2	73	72	P31		0.6
1938	†NY A☆	45	107	12	24	4	1	3	17	17	0	21	.224	.331	.364	74	9	0-0	.952	-2	81	83	P28		0.6
1939	†NY A★	44	114	12	35	1	0	1	20	7	0	18	.307	.347	.342	78	8	1-0	.947	-3	73	86	P30		0.6
1940	NY A★	33	89	8	11	4	0	1	7	3	0	9	.124	.152	.202	-9	-3	0-0	**1.000**	-3	62	130	P23		0.6
1941	†NY A☆	38	89	10	27	8	1	2	22	4	0	13	.303	.333	.483	115	11	0-0	**1.000**	-3	66	170	P24		0.6
1942	†NY A☆	30	80	8	20	4	0	1	13	5	1	13	.250	.302	.338	81	6	0-0	.929	-2	65	94	P11		0.6
1945	NY A	21	46	4	10	1	0	1	5	0	0	8	.217	.217	.326	54	0	0-0	1.000	-1	57	157	P8	73	0.6
1946	NY A	8	25	1	3	1	0	0	1	1	0	8	.120	.154	.160	-12	-1	0-0	1.000	-1	82	174	P9	65	0.6
1947	Chi A	14	24	2	5	0	0	0	3	1	0	3	.208	.240	.208	26	0	1-1	.968	-37	76	104	P624,O3(2/0/1)	138	-0.
Total	22	882	1937	207	521	98	13	36	273	97	6	266	.269	.306	.389	81	123	1-1							
RUIZ, CHICO		Hiraldo (Sablon) (b (Hiraldo Sablon (Ruiz))		B12.5.1938 Santo Domingo, Cuba				D2.9.1972 San Diego CA			BB/TR/6-0/173*		d4.13		OF(11/0/3)									-2.
1964	Cin N	77	311	33	76	13	2	2	16	7-1	4	41	.244	.269	.318	63	-16	11-3	.942	-6	73	136	3b49,2b30		-0.
1965	Cin N	29	18	7	2	1	0	0	5	0-0	0	5	.111	.111	.167	-21	-3	1-2	.875	-0	96	0	3b4,S3	39	-0.
1966	Cin N	82	110	13	28	2	1	0	5	5-0	0	14	.255	.287	.291	56	-6	1-2	.927	-2	88	56	3b27,O8(7/0/1),S6		-1.
1967	Cin N	105	250	32	55	12	4	0	13	11-0	2	35	.220	.258	.300	53	-15	9-4	.969	-2	100	115	2b56,3b13,S11,O5(3/0/2)		-1.
1968	Cin N	85	139	15	36	2	1	0	9	12-0	0	18	.259	.316	.288	78	-4	4-3	.979	7	133	115	2b34,1b16,3b5,S3		0
1969	Cin N	88	196	19	48	4	1	0	13	14-3	0	28	.245	.292	.276	58	-11	4-2	.949	-6	99	105	2b39,S29,3b7,1b2/OL		-1
1970	Cal A	68	107	10	26	3	1	0	12	7-1	1	16	.243	.293	.290	64	-5	3-0	.985	-2	100	105	3b27,2b3,S3,1b2/C		-0
1971	Cal A	31	19	4	5	0	0	0	0	2-0	0	7	.263	.333	.263	76	-1	1-0	1.000	-2	45	0	3b3,2b2		-6
Total	8	565	1150	133	276	37	10	2	69	58-5	7	164	.240	.279	.295	60	-61	34-16	.966	-13	105	104	2b164,3b135,S55,1b20,O14L/C	39	-6
RUIZ, CHICO		Manuel (Cruz)		B11.1.1951 Santurce, PR				BR/TR/5-11.5/170*		d7.29															
1978	Atl N	18	46	3	13	3	0	0	2	2-1	0	7	.283	.313	.348	76	-1	0-0	.984	1	99	73	2b14/3		0
1980	Atl N	25	26	3	8	2	1	0	2	3-0	0	7	.308	.379	.462	132	1	0-1	.875	-0	146	0	3b16,S4,2b2		0
Total	2	43	72	6	21	5	1	0	4	5-1	0	14	.292	.338	.389	96	0	0-1	.880	3	133	0	3b17,2b16,S4		0
RULLO, JOE		Joseph Vincent		B6.16.1916 New York NY				D10.28.1969 Philadelphia PA			BR/TR/5-11/168		d9.22												
1943	Phi A	16	55	6	16	3	0	0	6	8	0	7	.291	.381	.345	114	1		.963	-1	111	89	2b16		0
1944	Phi A	35	96	5	16	0	0	0	5	6	1	19	.167	.223	.167	12	-11	1-0	.954	0	101	113	2b33/1OC		-1
Total	2	51	151	7	32	3	0	0	11	14	1	26	.212	.283	.232	50	-10	1-0	.957	-0	104	105	2b49/OC1		-0
RUMLER, WILLIAM		William George		B3.27.1891 Milford NE				D5.26.1966 Lincoln NE			BR/TR/6-1/190		d5.4		Mil 1918									-0
1914	StL A	34	46	2	8	1	0	0	6	3	1	12	.174	.240	.196	32	-4	2-2	1.000	-1	81	118	C10,O6R		-0
1916	StL A	27	37	6	12	3	0	0	10	3	0	7	.324	.375	.405	141	2	0	.971	0	83	61	C9		0
1917	StL A	78	88	7	23	3	4	1	16	8	0	9	.261	.323	.420	132	3	2	.938	1	97	194	O9(3/0/6)		0
Total	3	139	171	15	43	7	4	1	32	14	1	28	.251	.312	.357	107	1	4-2	.986	-0	82	90	C19,O15(3/0/12)		-0
RUNGE, PAUL		Paul William		B5.21.1958 Kingston NY				BR/TR/6-0/175*		[AtlN79 9/212]		d9.25		Col Jacksonville									-0
1981	Atl N	10	27	2	7	1	0	2	4	4-0	0	4	.259	.355	.296	86	0	0-0	.911	-2	95	91	S10		-0
1982	Atl N	4	2	0	0	0	0	0	0	0-0	0	1	.000	.000	.000	-98	-1	0-0	—	0			/H		-0
1983	Atl N	5	8	0	2	0	0	0	1	1-0	0	4	.250	.333	.250	60	0	0-0	1.000	-1	48	76	2b2		-0
1984	Atl N	28	90	5	24	3	1	0	3	10-0	0	14	.267	.340	.322	81	-2	5-3	.970	7	125	115	2b22,S7,3b3		-0
1985	Atl N	50	87	15	19	3	0	1	5	18-0	0	18	.218	.349	.287	76	-2	0-1	.929	2	133	72	3b28,S5,2b2		-0
1986	Atl N	7	8	1	2	0	0	0	0	2-0	0	4	.250	.400	.250	80	0	0-0	.923	-1	94	205	3b10,S9,2b2		-0
1987	Atl N	27	47	9	10	1	0	3	8	5-0	0	10	.213	.288	.426	73	-1	0-1	1.000	-6	84	89	3b19,2b7,S6		-0
1988	Atl N	52	76	11	16	5	0	0	7	14-0	0	21	.211	.330	.276	74	-2	0-0	.941	-2	111	101	3b60,2b40,S37		-0
Total	8	183	345	43	80	13	1	4	26	54-0	0	75	.232	.334	.310	78	-8	5-5							
RUNNELLS, TOM		Thomas William		B4.17.1955 Greeley CO				BB/TR/6-0/175*		d8.10		M2/C2		Col Northern Colorado									-0
1985	Cin N	28	35	3	7	1	0	0	0	3-0	0	4	.200	.263	.229	37	-3	0-0	1.000	-1	95	103	S11/2		-0
1986	Cin N	12	11	1	1	1	0	0	0	0-0	0	2	.091	.091	.182	-26	-2	0-0	1.000	0	165	160	2b4,3b3		-0
Total	2	40	46	4	8	2	0	0	0	3-0	0	6	.174	.224	.217	23	-5	0-0	1.000	-1	95	103	S11,2b5,3b3		-0
RUNNELS, PETE		James Edward (b James Edward Runnells)		B1.28.1928 Lufkin TX				D5.20.1991 Pasadena TX			BL/TR/6-0/170*		d7.1		M1/C2									-.
1951	Was A	78	273	31	76	12	2	0	25	31	1	24	.278	.354	.337	89	-3	0-3	.949	-15	86	77	S73		-.
1952	Was A	152	555	70	158	18	3	1	64	72	1	55	.285	.368	.333	99	2	0-10	.966	-13	95	100	S147/2		-.
1953	Was A	137	486	64	125	15	5	2	50	64	3	36	.257	.347	.321	83	-10	3-4	.958	-20	90	122	S121,2b11		-.
1954	Was A	139	488	75	131	17	15	3	56	78	4	60	.268	.368	.383	112	9	2-3	.953	-17	95	97	S107,2b27/OL		-.
1955	Was A	134	503	66	143	16	4	2	49	55-2	1	51	.284	.353	.344	94	-4	3-9	.976	4	103	95	2b132,S2		-.
1956	Was A	147	578	72	179	29	9	8	76	58-2	2	64	.310	.372	.433	113	11	5-5	.995	3	103	88	1b81,2b69,S3		-.
1957	Was A	134	473	53	109	18	4	2	33	55-5	2	51	.230	.310	.298	69	-20	2-3	.995	1	97	82	1b72,3b32,2b23		-.
1958	Bos A	147	568	103	183	32	5	8	59	87-0	6	49	.322	.416	.438	127	27	1-2	.985	5	**109**	94	2b106,1b42		-.
1959	Bos A★	147	560	95	176	33	6	6	57	95-1	1	48	.314	.415	.427	126	25	6-5	.982	6	97	111	2b101,1b44,S9		-.
1960	Bos A★	143	528	80	169	29	2	2	35	71-2	2	51	**.320**	.401	.394	112	13	5-2	**.995**	0	78	120	1b113,3b11,2b7/S		-.
1961	Bos A	143	360	49	114	20	3	3	38	46-2	3	32	.317	.396	.414	115	10	5-1	.993	-3	89	95	1b151		-.
1962	Bos A	152	562	80	183	33	5	10	60	79-11	3	57	**.326**	.408	.456	129	27	3-4	.993	1	88	66	1b70,2b36,3b3		-.
1963	Hou N	124	388	35	98	9	1	2	23	45-2	3	42	.253	.332	.296	89	-4	2-0	.986	-2	53	82	1b14		-.
1964	Hou N	22	51	3	10	1	0	2	8	8-1	0	7	.196	.305	.216	53	-3	0-0	.986	-2	53	82	1b14		-.
Total	14	1799	6373	876	1854	282	64	49	630	844-28	28	627	.291	.375	.378	106	80	37-51	.994	-48	89	96	1b644,2b642,S463,3b49/OL		-.
RUSHFORD, JIM		James Thomas		B3.24.1974 Chicago IL				BL/TL/6-1/225		d9.3		Col San Diego St.													
2002	Mil N	23	77	8	11	2	0	1	6	6-0	0	9	.143	.214	.208	14	-10	0-0	.956	-1	105	0	O22(1/0/21)		
RUSS, JOHN		John		B4.1.1858 Cannelton IN				D1.18.1912 Louisville KY			d7.4														
1882	Bal AA	1	3	0	1	0	0	0	0				.333	.333	.333	136	0		—	-0	0	0	/OCP		
RUSSELL, REB		Ewell Albert		B4.12.1889 Jackson MS				D9.30.1973 Indianapolis IN			BL/TL/5-11/185		d4.18 ▲												
1913	Chi A	54	106	9	20	5	3	1	7	1	1	29	.189	.204	.321	54	3	0	.953	-5	76	108	P52		
1914	Chi A	46	64	6	17	1	1	0	7	1	0	14	.266	.277	.313	78	3	0	.946	0	104	0	P38		
1915	Chi A	45	86	11	21	2	3	0	7	4	2	14	.244	.293	.337	86	4	1	.971	-2	83	48	P41		
1916	Chi A	56	91	9	13	2	0	0	6	0	1	18	.143	.152	.165	-5	-4	1	.974	-2	95	75	P56		
1917	†Chi A	39	68	4	19	3	0	0	9	2	1	10	.279	.300	.412	115	0	0	.984	-1	93	110	P35/OL		
1918	Chi A	27	50	2	7	3	0	0	3	0	1	6	.140	.157	.200	8	-6	0	1.000	-0	83	75	P19/OR		
1919	Chi A	1	0	0	0	0	0	0	0	0	0	0	—	—	—	—	0	0	—	0	0	0	/P		
1922	Pit N	60	220	51	81	14	8	12	75	14	7	18	.368	.423	.668	175	23	4-2	.968	-1	101	68	O60R		
1923	Pit N	94	291	49	84	18	7	9	58	20	3	21	.289	.341	.491	115	5	3-1	.970	0	110	50	O76(4/0/72)		
Total	9	422	976	141	262	48	25	22	172	42	15	130	.268	.309	.436	104	28	9-3	.968	-12	88	74	P242,O138(5/0/133)		

RUSSELL, RIP Glen David B1.26.1915 Los Angeles CA D9.26.1976 Los Alamitos CA BR/TR/6-1/180 d5.5

YEAR	TM LG	G	AB	R	H	2B	3B	HR	RBI	BB-IB	HP	SO	AVG	OBP	SLG	AOPS	ABR	SB-CS	FA	FR	RNG	THR	GAMES AT POSITION	DL	BFW
939	Chi N	143	542	55	148	24	5	9	79	36	0	56	.273	.318	.386	87	-11	2	.988	-5	87	85	1b143		-3.0
940	Chi N	68	215	15	53	7	2	5	33	8	1	23	.247	.277	.367	78	-8	2	.982	-6	59	55	1b51,3b3		-1.9
941	Chi N	6	17	1	5	1	0	0	1	1	0	5	.294	.333	.353	97	0	0	.975	0	119	118	1b5		0.0
942	Chi N	102	302	32	73	9	0	8	41	17	0	21	.242	.282	.351	88	-6	0	.974	-9	60	107	1b35,2b34,3b10,O3L		0.0
946	†Bos A	80	274	22	57	10	1	6	35	13	1	30	.208	.247	.318	54	-18	1-1	.942	-0	99	172	3b70,2b3		-1.8
947	Bos A	26	52	8	8	1	0	1	3	8	0	7	.154	.267	.231	36	-4	0-0	.923	1	121	90	3b13		-2.0
tal 6		425	1402	133	344	52	8	29	192	83	2	142	.245	.289	.356	77	-47	4-1	.984	-19	78	82	1b234,3b96,2b27,O3L		-9.1

RUSSELL, HARVEY Harvey Holmes B1.10.1887 Marshall VA D1.8.1980 Alexandria VA BL/TR/5-9.5/163 d4.17

YEAR	TM LG	G	AB	R	H	2B	3B	HR	RBI	BB-IB	HP	SO	AVG	OBP	SLG	AOPS	ABR	SB-CS	FA	FR	RNG	THR	GAMES AT POSITION	DL	BFW
914	Bal F	81	168	18	39	3	2	0	13	18	1	17	.232	.310	.274	58	-12	2	.956	-10	99	76	C47/SO(1/1/0)		-2.0
915	Bal F	53	73	5	19	1	0	0	11	14	4	5	.260	.407	.329	105	1	1	.989	-2	101	85	C21		0.0
tal 2		134	241	23	58	4	4	0	24	32	5	22	.241	.342	.290	73	-11	3	.965	-12	100	79	C68/O(1/1/0)S		-2.0

RUSSELL, JIM James William B10.1.1918 Fayette City PA D11.24.1987 Orlando FL BB/TR/6-1/181* d9.12

YEAR	TM LG	G	AB	R	H	2B	3B	HR	RBI	BB-IB	HP	SO	AVG	OBP	SLG	AOPS	ABR	SB-CS	FA	FR	RNG	THR	GAMES AT POSITION	DL	BFW
942	Pit N	5	14	2	1	0	0	0	0	1	0	4	.071	.133	.071	-38	-2	0	1.000	0	129	0	O3C		-0.3
943	Pit N	146	533	79	138	19	11	4	44	77	1	67	.259	.354	.358	102	3	12	.990	4	101	124	O134(133/2/2),1b6		-0.1
944	Pit N	152	580	109	181	34	14	8	66	79	5	63	.312	.399	.460	136	30	6	.986	9	102	164	O149(139/6/4)		3.1
945	Pit N	146	510	88	145	24	8	12	77	71	6	60	.284	.377	.433	120	15	15	.973	5	109	93	O140(139/1/0)		1.2
946	Pit N	146	516	68	143	29	6	8	50	67	2	54	.277	.362	.403	114	11	11	.966	-7	98	58	O134(67/68/0),1b5		-0.3
947	Pit N	128	478	68	121	21	8	6	51	63	2	58	.253	.343	.381	89	-7	7	.980	3	109	67	O119(1/102/19)		-0.7
948	Bos N	89	322	44	85	18	1	9	54	46	3	31	.264	.361	.410	110	6	4	.992	-2	103	46	O84(2/82/0)		0.2
949	Bos N	130	415	57	96	22	1	8	54	64	2	68	.231	.337	.347	88	-5	3	.975	-8	93	36	O120(30/93/0)		-1.8
950	Bro N	77	214	37	49	8	2	10	32	31	1	36	.229	.329	.425	95	-2	1	.993	4	119	80	O55(53/3/0)		-0.1
951	Bro N	16	13	2	0	0	0	0	0	4	1	6	.000	.278	.000	-18	-2	0-0	1.000	0	96	0	O4L		-0.2
tal 10		1035	3595	554	959	175	51	67	428	503	22	427	.267	.360	.400	108	47	59-0	.981	8	103	88	O942(568/360/25),1b11		1.0

RUSSELL, JOHN John William B1.5.1961 Oklahoma City OK BR/TR/6-0/200* [PhiN82 1/13] d6.22 C3 Col Oklahoma OF(88/0/36)

YEAR	TM LG	G	AB	R	H	2B	3B	HR	RBI	BB-IB	HP	SO	AVG	OBP	SLG	AOPS	ABR	SB-CS	FA	FR	RNG	THR	GAMES AT POSITION	DL	BFW
84	Phi N	39	99	11	28	8	1	2	11	12-2	0	33	.283	.351	.444	123	3	0-1	1.000	-1	100	53	O29(14/0/18),C2		0.1
85	Phi N	81	216	22	47	12	0	9	23	18-0	1	72	.218	.278	.398	85	-5	2-0	1.000	-5	72	131	O49L,1b18		-1.3
86	Phi N	93	315	35	76	21	2	13	60	25-2	3	103	.241	.300	.444	100	-1	0-1	.976	-11	67	98	C89		-0.9
87	Phi N	24	62	5	9	1	0	4	8	3-0	0	17	.145	.185	.306	26	-7	0-1	.955	-3	114	153	O10L,C7		-1.0
88	Phi N	22	49	5	12	1	0	2	4	3-0	1	15	.245	.302	.388	94	0	0-0	.945	1	49	161	C15		0.1
89	Atl N	74	159	14	29	2	0	2	8	8-1	1	53	.182	.225	.233	31	-15	0-0	.990	-1	122	153	C45,O14(1/0/15),1b2,3b2/P		-1.6
90	Tex A	68	128	16	35	4	0	2	9	11-2	0	41	.273	.331	.352	91	-3	1-0	.980	-1	49	30	C31,D19,O6L,1b3/3		-0.2
91	Tex A	22	27	3	3	0	0	0	1	1-0	0	7	.111	.138	.111	-29	-5	0-0	1.000	-1	68	0	O8(6/0/2),C5,D5		-0.6
92	Tex A	7	10	1	1	0	0	0	2	1-0	1	4	.100	.231	.100	2	-1	0-0	1.000	-1	54	243	C4,O2(1/0/1)/D	70	-0.6
93	Tex A	18	22	1	5	1	0	0	1	3	2-0	0	10	.227	.292	.409	89	0	0-0	1.000	-2	252	71	C11/13OL	102	-0.2
tal 10		448	1087	113	245	50	3	34	129	84-7	6	355	.225	.282	.371	79	-33	3-3	.979	-24	80	101	C209,O119L,D25,1b24,3b4/P	172	-5.8

RUSSELL, LLOYD Lloyd Opal B4.10.1913 Atoka OK D5.24.1968 Waco TX BR/TR/5-11/166 d4.26 Col Baylor

YEAR	TM LG	G	AB	R	H	2B	3B	HR	RBI	BB-IB	HP	SO	AVG	OBP	SLG	AOPS	ABR	SB-CS	FA	FR	RNG	THR	GAMES AT POSITION	DL	BFW
38	Cle A	2	0	0	0	0	0	0	0	0		—	—	—	—	—	—				0		/R		0.0

RUSSELL, PAUL Paul A. (b Benjamin Paul Sheeder) B3.23.1871 Reading PA D10.8.1957 Norristown PA d7.29

YEAR	TM LG	G	AB	R	H	2B	3B	HR	RBI	BB-IB	HP	SO	AVG	OBP	SLG	AOPS	ABR	SB-CS	FA	FR	RNG	THR	GAMES AT POSITION	DL	BFW
94	StL N	3	10	1	1	0	0	0	0	0	0	2	.100	.100	.100	-52	-3	0	1.000	-0	513	0	/OC32		-0.2

RUSSELL, BILL William Ellis B10.21.1948 Pittsburg KS BR/TR (BB 1971)/6-0/175(170-187) [LAN66 9/179] d4.7 M3/C9

YEAR	TM LG	G	AB	R	H	2B	3B	HR	RBI	BB-IB	HP	SO	AVG	OBP	SLG	AOPS	ABR	SB-CS	FA	FR	RNG	THR	GAMES AT POSITION	DL	BFW
69	LA N	98	212	35	48	6	2	5	15	22-1	1	45	.226	.301	.344	86	-4	4-1	.978	5	121	101	O86(7/24/62)		-0.2
70	LA N	81	278	30	72	11	9	0	28	16-1	3	28	.259	.303	.363	82	-9	9-1	.983	7	115	169	O79(2/23/57)/S		-0.4
71	LA N	91	211	29	48	7	4	2	15	11-2	0	39	.227	.265	.327	71	-9	6-3	.964	-0	108	94	2b41,O40(3/8/35),S6		-0.8
72	LA N	129	434	47	118	19	5	4	34	34-9	2	64	.272	.326	.366	98	-1	14-7	.949	10	109	104	S121,O6(1/1/4)		2.5
73	LA N★	162	615	55	163	26	3	4	56	34-20	1	63	.265	.301	.337	80	-18	15-7	.963	-1	101	118	S162		0.2
74	LA N	160	553	61	149	18	6	5	65	53-25	4	53	.269	.336	.351	96	-3	14-5	.946	-17	97	84	S160/OR		0.0
75	LA N	84	252	24	52	9	2	0	14	23-6	2	28	.206	.277	.258	51	-17	5-0	.967	-14	93	70	S83	73	-2.1
76	LA N★	149	554	53	152	17	3	5	65	21-9	3	46	.274	.301	.343	84	-13	15-5	.963	-9	98	108	S149		-0.4
77	†LA N	153	634	84	176	28	6	4	51	24-1	2	43	.278	.304	.360	77	-22	16-7	.963	17	108	130	S153		1.2
78	†LA N	155	625	72	179	32	4	3	46	30-8	2	34	.286	.320	.365	91	-8	10-6	.962	21	111	113	S155		3.0
79	LA N	153	627	72	170	26	4	7	56	24-2	1	43	.271	.297	.359	80	-19	6-9	.957	-15	98	79	S150		-2.1
80	LA N★	130	466	38	123	23	2	3	34	18-0	3	44	.264	.295	.341	79	-14	13-2	.968	-11	97	84	S129		-1.0
81	†LA N	82	262	20	61	9	2	0	22	19-3	1	20	.233	.284	.282	65	-12	2-1	.965	8	105	115	S80		0.4
82	†LA N	153	497	64	136	20	2	3	46	63-11	4	30	.274	.357	.340	100	2	10-2	.961	-2	104	82	S150		1.8
83	†LA N	131	451	47	111	13	1	1	30	33-4	4	31	.246	.302	.286	64	-22	13-9	.964	9	104	90	S127		-0.1
84	LA N	89	262	25	70	12	1	0	19	25-1	0	24	.267	.329	.321	84	-5	4-4	.965	-3	96	91	S65,O18C,2b5	36	-0.3
85	LA N	76	169	19	44	6	1	0	13	18-1	1	9	.260	.333	.308	83	-3	4-0	.919	-3	103	104	S23,O21L,2b8,3b5		-0.3
86	LA N	105	216	21	54	11	0	0	18	15-2	2	23	.250	.302	.301	72	-8	7-0	1.000	2	101	111	O48(28/1/20),S32,2b8/3		-0.3
tal 18		2181	7318	796	1926	293	57	46	627	483-106	36	667	.263	.310	.338	82	-185	167-69	.960	4	102	99	S1746,O299(62/75/179),2b62,3b6	109	1.0

SZKOWSKI, HANK Henry Alexander B11.10.1925 Cleveland OH D5.31.2000 Cleveland OH BR/TR/6-0/190 d9.26 Mil 1945-46 Col Dayton

YEAR	TM LG	G	AB	R	H	2B	3B	HR	RBI	BB-IB	HP	SO	AVG	OBP	SLG	AOPS	ABR	SB-CS	FA	FR	RNG	THR	GAMES AT POSITION	DL	BFW
4	Cle A	3	8	1	3	0	0	0	0	0	0	1	.375	.375	.375	119	0	0-0	1.000	-0	75	222	C2		0.0
5	Cle A	14	49	2	10	0	0	0	5	4	0	9	.204	.264	.204	38	-4	0-0	.975	2	95	158	C14		-0.1
7	Cle A	23	27	5	7	2	0	3	4	2	0	6	.259	.310	.667	172	2	0-0	1.000	-1	167	213	C16		0.2
al 3		40	84	8	20	2	0	3	10	6	0	16	.238	.289	.369	91	-2	0-0	.981	1	111	176	C32		0.1

TH, BABE George Herman "The Bambino","The Sultan of Swat" B2.6.1895 Baltimore MD D8.16.1948 New York NY BL/TL/6-2/215 d7.11 C1 HF1936 ▲

YEAR	TM LG	G	AB	R	H	2B	3B	HR	RBI	BB-IB	HP	SO	AVG	OBP	SLG	AOPS	ABR	SB-CS	FA	FR	RNG	THR	GAMES AT POSITION	DL	BFW
4	Bos A	5	10	1	2	1	0	0	2	0	0	4	.200	.200	.300	50	0		1.000	-0	106	0	P4		0.0
5	†Bos A	42	92	16	29	10	1	4	21	9	0	23	.315	.376	.576	191	16	0	.976	1	98	148	P32		0.0
6	Bos A	67	136	18	37	5	3	3	15	10	0	23	.272	.322	.419	122	13	0	.973	1	90	172	P44		0.0
7	Bos A	52	123	14	40	6	3	2	12	12	0	18	.325	.385	.472	163	17	0	.984	2	107	131	P41		0.0
8	†Bos A	95	317	50	95	26	11	11	66	58	2	58	.300	.411	.555	195	38	6	.949	0	92	95	O59(47/12/0),P20,1b13		2.7
9	Bos A	130	432	103	139	34	12	29	114	101	6	58	.322	.456	.657	224	76	7	.996	10	111	137	O111L,P17,1b5		7.3
0	NY A	142	458	158	172	36	9	54	137	150	3	80	.376	.532	.847	252	110	14-14	.936	-2	96	114	O141(36/20/85),1b2/P		9.3
1	†NY A	152	540	177	204	44	16	59	171	145	4	81	.378	.512	.846	236	118	17-13	.966	-0	100	87	O152(134/18/0),P2,1b2		9.4
2	†NY A	110	406	94	128	24	8	35	99	84	1	80	.315	.434	.672	181	49	2-5	.964	-2	96	99	O110(71/0/40)/1		3.5
3	†NY A	152	522	151	205	45	13	41	131	170	4	93	.393	.545	.764	238	119	17-21	.973	6	110	95	O148(68/7/73),1b4		10.1
4	NY A	153	529	143	200	39	7	46	121	142	4	81	.378	.513	.739	221	104	9-13	.962	3	109	90	O152(50/7/99)		8.4
5	NY A	98	359	61	104	12	2	25	66	59	2	68	.290	.393	.543	138	20	2-4	.974	6	105	140	O98(33/0/66)		1.5
6	†NY A	152	495	139	184	30	5	47	146	144	3	76	.372	.516	.737	228	103	11-9	.979	0	105	72	O149(82/0/68),1b2		8.5
7	†NY A	151	540	158	192	29	8	60	164	137	0	89	.356	.486	.772	229	108	7-6	.963	1	104	83	O151(56/0/95)		8.8
8	NY A	154	536	163	173	29	8	54	142	137	4	87	.323	.463	.709	211	92	4-5	.975	-4	102	59	O154(55/0/99)		7.1
9	NY A	135	499	121	172	26	6	46	154	72	3	60	.345	.430	.697	199	72	5-3	.984	-5	101	41	O133(55/0/78)		5.4
0	NY A	145	518	150	186	28	9	49	153	136	1	61	.359	.493	.732	216	100	10-10	.965	-1	102	86	O144(53/0/91)/P		7.6
1	†NY A	145	534	149	199	31	3	46	163	128	1	51	.373	.495	.700	223	104	5-4	.972	-7	95	46	O142(51/0/91)/1		8.1
2	NY A	133	457	120	156	13	5	41	137	130	2	62	.341	.489	.661	206	81	2-2	.961	-1	95	121	O128(44/0/87)/1		4.7
3	NY A★	137	459	97	138	21	3	34	103	114	2	90	.301	.442	.582	180	59	4-5	.970	0	101	91	O132(55/0/78)/P1		4.7
4	NY A★	125	365	78	105	17	4	22	84	104	2	63	.288	.448	.537	164	42	1-3	.962	-3	104	40	O111(34/0/77)		3.0
	Bos N	28	72	13	13	0	0	6	12	20	0	24	.181	.359	.431	121	3	0	.952	-1	96	69	O26(22/0/4)		0.1
22		2503	8399	2174	2873	506	136	714	2213	2062	43	1330	.342	.474	.690	209	1444	123-117	.968	5	102	87	O2241(1057/64/1131),P163,1b32		112.0

THERFORD, JIM James Hollis B9.26.1886 Stillwater MN D9.18.1956 Cleveland OH BL/TR/6-1/180 d7.12 Col Cornell

YEAR	TM LG	G	AB	R	H	2B	3B	HR	RBI	BB-IB	HP	SO	AVG	OBP	SLG	AOPS	ABR	SB-CS	FA	FR	RNG	THR	GAMES AT POSITION	DL	BFW
	Cle A	1	2	0	1	0	0	0	0	0	0	0	.500	.500	.500	210	0		1.000	0	109	0	/OC		0.0

TNER, MICKEY Milton B3.18.1920 Hempstead NY BR/TR/5-11/190 d9.11 Col St. Johns

YEAR	TM LG	G	AB	R	H	2B	3B	HR	RBI	BB-IB	HP	SO	AVG	OBP	SLG	AOPS	ABR	SB-CS	FA	FR	RNG	THR	GAMES AT POSITION	DL	BFW
	Phi A	12	48	4	12	1	0	1	4	3	0	2	.250	.294	.333	73	-2	0-0	.885	-2	99	118	3b11		-0.4

AL, MARK Mark Dwayne B4.28.1960 Henryetta OK BL/TL/6-1/185(180-197) [KCA78 3/77] d9.7

YEAR	TM LG	G	AB	R	H	2B	3B	HR	RBI	BB-IB	HP	SO	AVG	OBP	SLG	AOPS	ABR	SB-CS	FA	FR	RNG	THR	GAMES AT POSITION	DL	BFW
	KC A	6	13	0	1	0	0	0	0	1-0	0	3	.077	.143	.077	-37	-2	0-0	.900	-0	100	0	O5(4/1/0)		-0.3
	Chi A	12	33	3	5	0	0	0	3	3-0	1	3	.152	.222	.242	26	-3	0-0	1.000	-0	105	0	O12(12/1/0)		-0.4

YEAR	TM	LG	G	AB	R	H	2B	3B	HR	RBI	BB-IB	HP	SO	AVG	OBP	SLG	AOPS	ABR	SB-CS	FA	FR	RNG	THR	GAMES AT POSITION	DL	BFW
1986	Cal	A	13	32	6	12	0	0	2	5	2-1	0	4	.375	.412	.563	164	3	1-0	.900	-0	117	0	O6R,1b4,D2		0.2
1987	Cal	A	58	100	7	20	6	0	5	18	3-1	0	15	.200	.223	.410	65	-6	0-0	.955	-2	94	0	O21(6/0/15),1b4,D5		-0.8
1989	Phi	N	29	33	2	8	2	0	0	5	1-0	0	6	.242	.265	.303	62	-2	0-0	1.000	-0	0	0	1b4,O4(2/0/2)		-0.2
1990	Pit	N	9	12	0	1	0	0	0	0	0-0	0	3	.083	.083	.083	-56	-3	0-0	1.000	0	109	0	O4(3/0/2)		-0.3
Total	6		127	223	19	47	11	0	7	31	10-2	0	34	.211	.245	.354	61	-13	1-0	.957	-3	104	0	O52(27/25),1b12,D7		-1.8

RYAN, CONNIE Cornelius Joseph B2.27.1920 New Orleans LA D1.3.1996 Metairie LA BR/TR/5-11/175* d4.14 Mil 1944-45 M2/C8 Col Louisiana St.   0.2

YEAR	TM	LG	G	AB	R	H	2B	3B	HR	RBI	BB-IB	HP	SO	AVG	OBP	SLG	AOPS	ABR	SB-CS	FA	FR	RNG	THR	GAMES AT POSITION	DL	BFW
1942	NY	N	11	27	4	5	0	0	0	2	4	0	3	.185	.290	.185	40	-2	1	.944	3	122	102	2b11		-3.9
1943	Bos	N	132	457	52	97	10	2	1	24	58	0	56	.212	.301	.249	61	-22	7	.962	-20	95	67	2b100,3b30		2.3
1944	Bos	N★	88	332	56	98	18	5	4	25	36	0	40	.295	.364	.416	114	7	13	.974	12	110	117	2b80,3b14		-1.1
1946	Bos	N	143	502	55	121	28	8	1	48	55	1	63	.241	.317	.335	84	-10	7	.968	-6	95	85	2b120,3b24		0.0
1947	Bos	N	150	544	60	144	33	5	5	69	71	1	60	.265	.351	.371	94	-3	5	.973	-6	101	97	2b146		-0.3
1948	†Bos	N	51	122	14	26	3	0	0	10	21	1	16	.213	.333	.238	58	-6	0	.966	1	111	97	3b25,S18,2b16,1b3		0.3
1949	Bos	N	85	208	28	52	13	1	6	20	21	0	30	.250	.319	.409	99	-2	1	1.000	1	101	99	2b20		0.0
1950	Bos	N	20	72	12	14	2	0	3	6	12	0	9	.194	.326	.347	82	-2	0	.973	6	95	97	2b103		0.5
	Cin	N	106	367	45	95	18	5	3	43	52	1	46	.259	.352	.360	87	-5	4	.978	5	96	97	2b123		0.5
	Year		126	439	57	109	20	5	6	49	64	1	55	.248	.348	.358	87	-7	4							0.3
1951	Cin	N	136	473	75	112	17	4	16	53	79	3	72	.237	.350	.391	97	0	11-6	.970	-4	99	82	2b121,3b3,1b2/OR		-0.2
1952	Phi	N	154	577	81	139	24	6	12	49	69	5	72	.241	.327	.366	93	-5	13-5	.972	-7	103	101	2b154		0.8
1953	Phi	N	90	247	47	73	14	6	5	26	30	0	35	.296	.372	.462	116	6	5-1	.958	-3	97	101	2b65,1b2		-0.4
	Chi	A	17	54	6	12	1	0	0	6	9	0	12	.222	.333	.241	55	-3	2-0	.927	-2	91	27	3b16		0.0
1954	Cin	N	1	0	0	0	0	0	0	0	1	0	0	—	1.000	—	182	0	0-0	—	0			/H		
Total	12		1184	3982	535	988	181	42	56	381	518	14	514	.248	.337	.357	90	-46	69-12	.970	-22	100	93	2b980,3b116,S19,1b7/OR		-1.5

RYAN, CYCLONE Daniel R. B1866 Cappagh White, Ireland D1.30.1917 Medfield MA TR/6-0/200 d8.8   -0.2

YEAR	TM	LG	G	AB	R	H	2B	3B	HR	RBI	BB-IB	HP	SO	AVG	OBP	SLG	AOPS	ABR	SB-CS	FA	FR	RNG	THR	GAMES AT POSITION	DL	BFW
1887	NY	AA	8	32	4	7	1	0	0	3	3	0		.219	.286	.250	52	-2	1	.938	0	161	162	1b8,P2		0.0
1891	Bos	N	1	1	0	0	0	0	0	0	0	0		.000	.000	.000	-89	0	0	1.000	0	162	0	/P		0.0
Total	2		9	33	4	7	1	0	0	3	3	0		.212	.278	.242	48	-2	1	.938	0	161	162	1b8,P3		-0.2

RYAN, MIKE J. B St.Louis MO d7.25   -0.1

YEAR	TM	LG	G	AB	R	H	2B	3B	HR	RBI	BB-IB	HP	SO	AVG	OBP	SLG	AOPS	ABR	SB-CS	FA	FR	RNG	THR	GAMES AT POSITION	DL	BFW
1895	StL	N	2	2	0	0	0	0	0	0	0	0		.000	.000	.000	-99	-1	0	.000	-1	0	0	3b2		-0.1

RYAN, JIMMY James Edward "Pony" B2.11.1863 Clinton MA D10.26.1923 Chicago IL BR/TL/5-9/162 d10.8 Col Boston College OF(393/956/609) ▲   0.0

YEAR	TM	LG	G	AB	R	H	2B	3B	HR	RBI	BB-IB	HP	SO	AVG	OBP	SLG	AOPS	ABR	SB-CS	FA	FR	RNG	THR	GAMES AT POSITION	DL	BFW
1885	Chi	N	3	13	2	6	0	0	0	2	1		1	.462	.500	.538	207	3		.737	-1	129	0	S2/OC		0.0
1886	†Chi	N	84	327	58	100	17	6	4	53	12		28	.306	.330	.431	113	3	10	.828	-1	123	149	O70(38/8/24),S6,3b6,2b5,P5		-0.4
1887	Chi	N	126	508	117	145	23	10	11	74	53	6	19	.285	.360	.435	106	7	50	.857	-3	156	190	O122(1/97/24),P8,2b3		3.8
1888	Chi	N	129	549	115	182	33	10	16	64	35	5	50	.332	.377	.515	170	42	60	.878	3	162	117	O128(0/127/1),P8		2.5
1889	Chi	N	135	576	140	187	31	14	17	72	70	6	62	.325	.403	.516	149	36	45	.926	-4	168	243	O106(0/105/1),S29		1.3
1890	Chi	P	118	486	99	165	32	5	6	89	60	4	36	.340	.416	.463	129	22	30	.919	-1	114	123	O118C		1.3
1891	Chi	N	118	505	110	140	22	15	9	66	53	8	38	.277	.355	.434	129	18	27	.905	1	134	99	O117(43/74/0),S2,P2		1.8
1892	Chi	N	128	505	105	148	21	11	10	65	61	5	41	.293	.375	.438	144	27	27	.921	-1	130	72	O73(1/73/1),S10/P		0.7
1893	Chi	N	83	341	82	102	21	7	3	30	59	3	25	.299	.407	.428	124	15	8	.908	6	116	60	O110(0/5/106)		0.8
1894	Chi	N	110	482	133	172	37	7	3	62	51	3	22	.357	.422	.481	111	10	12	.908	6	116	85	O108R		0.1
1895	Chi	N	108	438	83	139	22	8	6	49	48	6	22	.317	.392	.445	109	5	18	.937	2	113	163	O128R		-0.6
1896	Chi	N	128	489	83	149	24	10	3	86	46	4	16	.305	.369	.413	102	1	29	.912	-1	146	177	O136R		0.8
1897	Chi	N	136	520	103	156	33	17	5	85	50	7		.300	.369	.458	113	9	27	.945	-8	96	43	O144(134/0/10)		1.4
1898	Chi	N	144	572	122	185	32	13	6	79	73	5		.323	.405	.446	144	35	29	.914	-2	90	116	O125L		-0.7
1899	Chi	N	125	525	91	158	20	10	3	68	43	3		.301	.357	.394	109	6	9	.956	-2	90	116	O120(2/105/13)		-1.0
1900	Chi	N	105	415	66	115	25	4	5	59	29	3		.277	.329	.393	102	1	19	.913	-5	87	83	O105(49/9/57)		1.5
1902	Was	A	120	484	92	155	32	6	4	44	43	7		.320	.384	.448	129	20	10	.949	1	102	0	O114C		-0.5
1903	Was	A	114	437	42	109	25	4	7	46	17	8		.249	.290	.373	96	-2	9	.970	-6	120	109	O114C		
Total	18		2014	8172	1643	2513	451	157	118	1093	804	83	362	.308	.375	.444	123	252	419	.918	-6	120	109	O1945C,S58,P24,2b8,3b6		12.8

RYAN, JACK John Bernard B11.12.1868 Haverhill MA D8.21.1952 Boston MA BR/TR/5-10.5/165 d9.2 C7 OF(4/4/7)   -1.1

YEAR	TM	LG	G	AB	R	H	2B	3B	HR	RBI	BB-IB	HP	SO	AVG	OBP	SLG	AOPS	ABR	SB-CS	FA	FR	RNG	THR	GAMES AT POSITION	DL	BFW
1889	Lou	AA	21	79	8	14	1	0	0	2	3	0	17	.177	.207	.190	14	-9	2	.864	-5			C15,O4(0/3/1),3b2		-1.1
1890	†Lou	AA	93	337	43	73	16	4	0	35	12	0		.217	.244	.288	58	-20	6	.932	15	136	110	C89,O3(1/0/2)/S1		0.
1891	Lou	AA	75	253	24	57	5	4	2	25	15	1	40	.225	.271	.300	64	-13	3	.930	-9	82	131	C56,1b11,3b6,O4(3/1/0),2b3		-1.
1894	Bos	N	53	201	39	54	12	7	1	29	13	1	16	.269	.316	.413	69	-12	3	.911	4	121	91	C51,1b2		-0.
1895	Bos	N	49	189	22	55	7	0	0	18	6	0	1	.291	.313	.328	61	-12	3	.951	5	129	106	C43,2b5/OR		-0.
1896	Bos	N	8	32	2	3	1	0	0	0	0	0		.094	.094	.125	-40	-7	0	.911	2	112	108	C8		-1.
1898	Bro	N	87	301	39	57	11	4	0	24	15	2		.189	.233	.252	39	-25	5	.960	-1	94	100	C84,3b4/1		0.
1899	Bal	N	2	4	0	2	0	0	0	1	0			.500	.500	.750	229	1	1	1.000	1	103	245	C2		-1.
1901	StL	N	83	300	27	59	6	5	0	31	7	1		.197	.218	.250	37	-25	5	.982	3	97	102	C65,2b9,1b5,O3R		-2.
1902	StL	N	76	267	23	48	4	4	0	14	4	1		.180	.195	.225	31	-23	2	.966	-6	88	100	C66,1b4,3b4,2b2/S		-2.
1903	StL	N	67	227	18	54	5	1	1	10	10	1		.238	.273	.282	60	-12	2	.971	-5	82	96	C47,1b18,S2		0.
1912	Was	A	1	1	0	0	0	0	0	0	0	0	0	.000	.000	.000	-99	0	0	1.000	0	107	0	/3		0.
1913	Was	A	1	1	0	0	0	0	0	0	0	0	0	.000	.000	.000	-98	0	0	1.000	0	0	424	/C		0.
Total	13		616	2192	245	476	69	29	4	189	85	7	80	.217	.249	.281	50	-157	32	.947	3	105	105	C527,1b42,2b19,3b17,O15R,S4		-10.

RYAN, BUDDY John Budd B10.6.1885 Denver CO D7.9.1956 Sacramento CA BL/TR/5-9.5/172 d4.11   0.

YEAR	TM	LG	G	AB	R	H	2B	3B	HR	RBI	BB-IB	HP	SO	AVG	OBP	SLG	AOPS	ABR	SB-CS	FA	FR	RNG	THR	GAMES AT POSITION	DL	BFW
1912	Cle	A	93	328	53	89	12	9	1	31	30	6		.271	.343	.372	101	0	12	.963	6	112	125	O90(56/0/34)		0.
1913	Cle	A	73	243	26	72	6	1	0	32	11	2	13	.296	.332	.329	91	-3	9	.986	-1	101	71	O68(3/65/0)/1		-0.
Total	2		166	571	79	161	18	10	1	63	41	8	13	.282	.339	.354	97	-3	21	.973	6	107	102	O158(59/65/34)/1		0.

RYAN, BLONDY John Collins B1.4.1906 Lynn MA D11.28.1959 Swampscott MA BR/TR/6-1/178 d7.13 Col Holy Cross   -0.

YEAR	TM	LG	G	AB	R	H	2B	3B	HR	RBI	BB-IB	HP	SO	AVG	OBP	SLG	AOPS	ABR	SB-CS	FA	FR	RNG	THR	GAMES AT POSITION	DL	BFW
1930	Chi	A	28	87	9	18	0	4	1	10	6	0	13	.207	.258	.333	50	-8	2-0	.875	-1	105	140	3b23,S2/2		-0.
1933	†NY	N	146	525	47	125	10	5	3	48	15	0	62	.238	.259	.293	58	-30	3	.950	17	107	117	S146		-0.
1934	NY	N	110	385	35	93	19	0	2	41	19	0	68	.242	.277	.306	57	-23	3	.953	10	120	91	3b65,S30,2b25		-0.
1935	Phi	N	39	129	13	34	3	0	1	10	7	2	20	.264	.312	.310	60	-7	1	.912	0	101	108	S35/23		-0.
	NY	A	30	105	12	25	1	3	0	11	3	0	10	.238	.259	.305	48	-9	0-0	.908	-6	90	79	S30		-0.1
1937	†NY	N	21	75	10	18	3	1	1	13	6	0	8	.240	.296	.347	73	-3	0	.941	2	100	138	S19/23		-0.
1938	NY	N	12	24	1	5	0	0	0	0	1	0	3	.208	.240	.208	24	-3	0	1.000	-1	118	27	2b5,3b3,S2		-0.
Total	6		386	1330	127	318	36	13	8	133	57	2	184	.239	.271	.304	57	-83	6-0	.936	21	103	114	S264,3b93,2b33		-0.

RYAN, JACK John Francis B5.5.1905 West Mineral KS D9.2.1967 Rochester MN BR/TR/6-0/185 d6.18   -0

YEAR	TM	LG	G	AB	R	H	2B	3B	HR	RBI	BB-IB	HP	SO	AVG	OBP	SLG	AOPS	ABR	SB-CS	FA	FR	RNG	THR	GAMES AT POSITION	DL	BFW
1929	Bos	A	2	3	0	0	0	0	0	0	0	0	0	.000	.000	.000	-99	-1	0-0	1.000	-0	61	0	O2(1/0/1)		-0

RYAN, JOHNNY John Joseph B10.1853 Philadelphia PA D3.22.1902 Philadelphia PA 5-7.5/150 d8.19 ▲   0

YEAR	TM	LG	G	AB	R	H	2B	3B	HR	RBI	BB-IB	HP	SO	AVG	OBP	SLG	AOPS	ABR	SB-CS	FA	FR	RNG	THR	GAMES AT POSITION	DL	BFW
1873	Phi	NA	2	8	1	2	0	0	0	1	0			.250	.250	.250	47	-1	0-0	.727	-0	488	247	/1OC		0
1874	Bal	NA	47	181	29	35	8	1	0	19	5		13	.193	.215	.249	49	-10	3-0	.862	13	105	69	O47L/P		-1
1875	NH	NA	37	146	17	23	2	2	0	8	3			.158	.174	.199	34	-8	10-4	.796	-8	21	97	O30L,P10,C4/S		-1
1876	Lou	N	64	241	32	61	5	1	1	18	6		23	.253	.271	.295	75	-8		.886	-8	9	50	O64(63/1/0)/P		-0
1877	Cin	N	6	26	2	4	1	0	1	2	1			.154	.185	.231	34	-2		.769	-1	72	79	O6(1/5/0)		-0
Total	3 NA		86	335	47	60	10	3	0	28	8		25	.179	.198	.227	43	-19	13-4	.850	5	72	79	O78(77/1/0),P11,C4/S1		-0
Total	2		70	267	34	65	5	2	1	20	7		28	.243	.263	.288	72	-10		.877	-9	8	46	O70(64/6/0)/P		-0

RYAN, JOHN John M. (Played 1 Game For Washington Under Real Name of Daniel Sheehan) B Washington DC d6.11   -0

YEAR	TM	LG	G	AB	R	H	2B	3B	HR	RBI	BB-IB	HP	SO	AVG	OBP	SLG	AOPS	ABR	SB-CS	FA	FR	RNG	THR	GAMES AT POSITION	DL	BFW
1884	Was	U	7	28	2	4	0	1	0		1			.143	.172	.214	17	-4		.667	-0	64	0	O7(2/3/2)/3		-0
	Wil	U	2	6	0	1	0	0	0		1			.167	.286	.167	39	-1		.800	-0	0	0	O2(1/1/0)/3		-0
	Year		9	34	2	5	0	1	0		2			.147	.194	.206	22	-4		.706	-1	47		O9(3/4/2)/3		-0

RYAN, MIKE Michael James B11.25.1941 Haverhill MA BR/TR/6-2/205(200-215) d10.3 C16   0

YEAR	TM	LG	G	AB	R	H	2B	3B	HR	RBI	BB-IB	HP	SO	AVG	OBP	SLG	AOPS	ABR	SB-CS	FA	FR	RNG	THR	GAMES AT POSITION	DL	BFW
1964	Bos	A	1	3	0	1	0	0	0	0	2-1	0	0	.333	.500	.333	131	0	0-0	1.000	-0	0	0	/C		0
1965	Bos	A	33	107	7	17	0	1	3	9	5-1	0	19	.159	.193	.262	27	-11	0-0	.981	-2	69	149	C33		-2
1966	Bos	A	116	369	27	79	15	3	2	32	29-3	0	68	.214	.271	.287	55	-21	1-0	.992	5	76	115	C114		-2
1967	†Bos	A	79	226	21	45	4	2	7	25	16-5	0	42	.199	.282	.261	58	-12	2-0	.988	3	132	87	C79		-2
1968	Phi	N	96	296	12	53	6	1	1	23	16-5	0	59	.179	.218	.216	31	-25	0-3	.991	-2	151	143	C96		0

YEAR	TM LG	G	AB	R	H	2B	3B	HR	RBI	BB-IB	HP	SO	AVG	OBP	SLG	AOPS	ABR	SB-CS	FA	FR	RNG	THR	GAMES AT POSITION	DL	BFW
1969	Phi N	133	446	41	91	17	2	12	44	30-4	2	66	.204	.256	.332	65	-22	1-1	.991	3	106	103	C132		-1.4
1970	Phi N	46	134	14	24	8	0	2	11	16-3	0	24	.179	.265	.284	49	-10	0-0	.992	-10	118	97	C46	98	-1.9
1971	Phi N	43	134	9	22	5	1	3	6	10-1	0	32	.164	.222	.284	42	-11	0-0	1.000	7	138	218	C43		-0.2
1972	Phi N	46	106	6	19	4	0	2	10	10-2	1	25	.179	.254	.274	49	-7	0-0	.992	3	111	110	C46		-0.2
1973	Phi N	28	69	7	16	1	2	1	5	6-0	0	19	.232	.289	.348	75	-3	0-0	.992	-0	213	103	C27		-0.2
1974	Pit N	15	30	2	3	0	0	0	0	4-0	0	16	.100	.206	.100	-13	-5	0-0	1.000	1	348	87	C15	28	-0.3
Total 11		636	1920	146	370	60	12	28	161	152-23	4	370	.193	.252	.280	51	-127	4-4	.991	-2	120	120	C632	126	-10.9

RYAN, MIKE Michael Sean B7.6.1977 Indiana PA BL/TR/5-10/182(182-215) [MinA96 5/127] d9.20

YEAR	TM LG	G	AB	R	H	2B	3B	HR	RBI	BB-IB	HP	SO	AVG	OBP	SLG	AOPS	ABR	SB-CS	FA	FR	RNG	THR	GAMES AT POSITION	DL	BFW
2002	Min A	7	11	3	1	0	0	0	0	0-0	0	2	.091	.091	.091	-50	-2	0-0	1.000	-1	51	0	O5(4/3/0)		-0.3
2003	†Min A	27	61	13	24	7	0	5	13	6-0	0	12	.393	.441	.754	202	9	2-1	1.000	-1	132	277	O16(4/0/12),D4		1.1
2004	Min A	36	71	9	17	2	1	0	7	4-1	0	16	.239	.280	.296	49	-6	1-1	.947	-1	94	0	O15(10/2/3),D11	36	-0.7
2005	Min A	57	117	7	27	5	0	2	13	9-1	0	22	.231	.283	.325	61	-7	1-2	1.000	-1	73	173	O25(16/0/10),D13/3		-1.0
Total 4		127	260	32	69	14	1	7	33	19-2	0	52	.265	.313	.408	86	-6	4-4	.989	0	92	155	O61(34/5/25),D28/3	36	-0.9

RYAN, ROB Robert James B6.24.1973 Havre MT BL/TL/5-11/190* [AriN96 26/785] d8.20 Col Washington St.

YEAR	TM LG	G	AB	R	H	2B	3B	HR	RBI	BB-IB	HP	SO	AVG	OBP	SLG	AOPS	ABR	SB-CS	FA	FR	RNG	THR	GAMES AT POSITION	DL	BFW
1999	Ari N	20	29	4	7	1	0	2	5	1-0	0	8	.241	.267	.483	84	-1	0-0	1.000	-0	103	0	O5(1/0/4)		-0.1
2000	Ari N	27	27	4	8	1	1	0	2	4-0	1	7	.296	.406	.407	103	0	0-0	1.000	-0	44	0	O2R/D		0.0
2001	Ari N	1	1	0	0	0	0	0	0	0-0	0	1	.000	.000	.000	-94	0	0-0	—	0			/H		0.0
	Oak A	7	7	0	0	0	0	0	0	0-0	0	5	.000	.000	.000	-99	-2	0-0	1.000	-0	71	0	O5(0/4/1)/D		-0.2
Total 3		55	64	8	15	2	1	2	7	5-0	1	21	.234	.300	.391	72	-3	0-0	1.000	-1	85		O12(1/4/7),D2		-0.3

RYDER, TOM Thomas B5.9.1863 Dubuque IA D7.18.1935 Dubuque IA BL d7.22

YEAR	TM LG	G	AB	R	H	2B	3B	HR	RBI	BB-IB	HP	SO	AVG	OBP	SLG	AOPS	ABR	SB-CS	FA	FR	RNG	THR	GAMES AT POSITION	DL	BFW
1884	StL U	8	28	4	7	1	0	0					.250	.300	.286	75	-2		.650	-1	140	0	O8(5/3/0)		-0.2

RYE, GENE Eugene Rudolph "Half-Pint" (b Eugene Rudolph Mercantelli) B11.15.1906 Chicago IL D1.21.1980 Park Ridge IL BL/TR/5-6/165 d4.22

YEAR	TM LG	G	AB	R	H	2B	3B	HR	RBI	BB-IB	HP	SO	AVG	OBP	SLG	AOPS	ABR	SB-CS	FA	FR	RNG	THR	GAMES AT POSITION	DL	BFW
1931	Bos A	17	39	3	7	0	0	0	5	.179			.220	.179	6	-5	0-0	.944	-1	94		O10L		-0.6

SABO, ALEX Alexander "Giz" (b Alexsander Szabo) B2.14.1910 New Brunswick NJ D1.3.2001 Tuckerton NJ BR/TR/6-0/192 d8.1 Col Fordham

YEAR	TM LG	G	AB	R	H	2B	3B	HR	RBI	BB-IB	HP	SO	AVG	OBP	SLG	AOPS	ABR	SB-CS	FA	FR	RNG	THR	GAMES AT POSITION	DL	BFW
1936	Was A	4	8	1	3	0	0	0	1	0	0	2	.375	.375	.375	91	0	0-0	.923	0	100	164	C4		0.0
1937	Was A	1	0	0	0	0	0	0	0	0	0	0	—	—	—		0	0-0	1.000	0	0	0	/C		0.0
Total 2		5	8	1	3	0	0	0	1	0	0	2	.375	.375	.375	91	0	0-0	.929	0	91	150	C5		0.0

SABO, CHRIS Christopher Andrew B1.19.1962 Detroit MI BR/TR/6-0/185* [CinN83 2/30] d4.4 Col Michigan

YEAR	TM LG	G	AB	R	H	2B	3B	HR	RBI	BB-IB	HP	SO	AVG	OBP	SLG	AOPS	ABR	SB-CS	FA	FR	RNG	THR	GAMES AT POSITION	DL	BFW
1988	Cin N★	137	538	74	146	40	2	11	44	29-1	6	52	.271	.314	.414	104	3	46-14	.966	10	108	149	3b135,S2		2.0
1989	Cin N	82	304	40	79	21	1	6	29	25-2	1	33	.260	.316	.395	99	0	14-9	.943	-5	97	96	3b76	66	-0.5
1990	†Cin N★	148	567	95	153	38	2	25	71	61-7	6	58	.270	.343	.476	119	15	25-10	.966	-8	96	83	3b146		1.0
1991	Cin N★	153	582	91	175	35	3	26	88	44-3	6	79	.301	.354	.505	134	26	19-6	.966	-16	86	98	3b151		1.2
1992	Cin N	96	344	42	84	19	3	12	43	30-1	1	54	.244	.302	.422	102	0	4-5	.961	-4	90	92	3b93		-0.5
1993	Cin N	148	552	86	143	33	2	21	82	43-5	6	105	.259	.315	.440	100	-1	6-4	.967	-12	91	67	3b148	15	-0.5
1994	Bal A	68	258	41	66	15	3	11	42	20-2	5	38	.256	.320	.465	94	-3	1-1	.958	-8	74	82	3b37,O22(9/0/13),D10	15	-1.2
1995	Chi A	20	71	10	18	5	0	1	8	3-1	2	12	.254	.295	.366	76	-3	2-0	.909	-1	0	118	D15/13		-0.4
	StL N	5	13	0	2	1	0	0	3	1-0	0	2	.154	.214	.231	17	-2	1-0	.929	-1	148	65	1b2/3	77	-0.2
1996	Cin N	54	125	15	32	7	1	3	16	18-0	0	27	.256	.354	.400	97	0	2-0	.961	5	112	112	3b43	27	0.5
Total 9		911	3354	494	898	214	17	116	426	274-22	32	460	.268	.326	.445	108	35	120-49	.963	-38	94	97	3b831,D25,O22(9/0/13),1b3,S2	215	0.8

SACKA, FRANK Frank B8.30.1924 Romulus MI D12.7.1994 Dearborn MI BR/TR/6-0/195* d4.29

YEAR	TM LG	G	AB	R	H	2B	3B	HR	RBI	BB-IB	HP	SO	AVG	OBP	SLG	AOPS	ABR	SB-CS	FA	FR	RNG	THR	GAMES AT POSITION	DL	BFW
1951	Was A	7	16	1	4	0	0	0	3	0	0	5	.250	.250	.250	36	-2	0-0	.962	1	163	166	C6		-0.1
1953	Was A	7	18	2	5	0	0	0	3	3	0	1	.278	.381	.278	82	0	0-0	1.000	1	141	138	C6		0.1
Total 2		14	34	3	9	0	0	0	6	3	0	6	.265	.324	.265	62	-2	0-0	.982	2	151	151	C12		0.0

SADEK, MIKE Michael George B5.30.1946 Minneapolis MN BR/TR (BB 1979p)/5-9/165* [MinA67 S5/83] d4.13 Col Minnesota

YEAR	TM LG	G	AB	R	H	2B	3B	HR	RBI	BB-IB	HP	SO	AVG	OBP	SLG	AOPS	ABR	SB-CS	FA	FR	RNG	THR	GAMES AT POSITION	DL	BFW
1973	SF N	39	66	6	11	1	0	0	4	11-0	0	8	.167	.282	.212	38	-5	1-0	.981	3	89	80	C35	15	-0.1
1975	SF N	42	106	14	25	5	2	0	9	14-1	0	14	.236	.322	.321	71	-3	1-0	.995	5	92	69	C38		0.3
1976	SF N	55	93	8	19	2	0	0	7	11-2	0	10	.204	.295	.226	48	-6	0-0	.985	3	95	108	C51		-0.2
1977	SF N	61	126	12	29	7	0	1	15	12-0	0	5	.230	.297	.310	63	-6	2-1	.992	6	96	151	C57		0.2
1978	SF N	40	109	15	26	3	0	2	9	10-2	1	16	.239	.303	.321	77	-4	1-0	.975	-3	67	68	C37	37	-0.5
1979	SF N	63	126	14	30	5	0	1	11	15-2	1	24	.238	.322	.302	77	-4	1-0	.993	-0	94	80	C60/OR		-0.2
1980	SF N	64	151	14	38	4	1	1	16	27-6	0	18	.252	.363	.311	94	0	0-0	.974	-1	108	103	C59	15	0.1
1981	SF N	19	36	5	6	3	0	0	3	8-0	0	7	.167	.318	.250	65	-1	0-0	.979	3	79	123	C19		0.3
Total 8		383	813	88	184	30	4	5	74	108-13	2	97	.226	.317	.292	71	-29	6-1	.985	16	92	98	C356/OR	67	-0.1

SADLER, DONNIE Donnie Lamont B6.17.1975 Clifton TX BR/TR/5-6/175* [BosA94 11/299] d4.1 OF(50/64/26)

YEAR	TM LG	G	AB	R	H	2B	3B	HR	RBI	BB-IB	HP	SO	AVG	OBP	SLG	AOPS	ABR	SB-CS	FA	FR	RNG	THR	GAMES AT POSITION	DL	BFW
1998	†Bos A	58	124	21	28	4	4	3	15	6-0	3	28	.226	.276	.395	71	-6	4-0	.972	-5	85	72	2b50,S4,D4		-0.8
1999	†Bos A	49	107	18	30	5	1	0	4	5-0	1	18	.280	.313	.346	66	-6	2-1	.930	-5	76	80	S14,2b10,3b9,O8(1/6/1),D3		-0.9
2000	Bos A	49	99	14	22	5	0	1	10	5-0	1	18	.222	.262	.303	43	-9	3-1	.958	1	116	78	S19,O17(3/13/1),2b12,3b3,D2		-0.6
2001	Cin N	39	84	9	17	3	0	1	3	9-0	0	20	.202	.280	.274	42	-7	3-3	.947	-1	105	109	2b15,S12,O8(6/2/2)/D		-0.8
	KC A	54	101	19	13	3	0	0	2	9-0	0	17	.129	.212	.158	0	-15	4-1	1.000	15	128	311	O16(5/4/7),3b15,2b13,S6		0.1
2002	Tex A	35	68	10	13	1	1	0	5	4-0	0	12	.191	.233	.235	23	-8	3-1	.957	-3	108	0	O15(11/0/4),3b11,2b4,S4,D3	24	-1.0
	Tex A	38	30	6	3	1	0	0	2	3-0	2	7	.100	.229	.133	-0	-4	2-2	1.000	1	126	327	O18(2/14/3),S12,3b4,2b2/D		-0.3
	Year	73	98	16	16	2	1	0	7	7-0	2	19	.163	.231	.204	17	-12	5-3	.976	-2	115	122	O33(13/14/7),S16,3b15,2b6,D4		-1.3
2003	Tex A	77	131	27	26	5	2	1	5	13-0	2	34	.198	.277	.290	48	-10	4-3	1.000	-1	95	215	O41(19/22/7),3b23,S19/2		-1.0
2004	Ari N	18	23	1	3	2	0	1	1	0-1	0	9	.130	.167	.217	-2	-3	0-0	1.000	-2	50	0	O6(3/3/1),S3,2b2,3b4		-1.0
Total 8		417	767	125	155	29	8	6	46	55-0	10	163	.202	.262	.284	40	-68	25-12	.982	-1	100	208	O129C,2b109,S93,3b67,D14	24	-5.8

SADLER, RAY Raymond Lee B9.19.1980 Clifton TX BR/TR/6-1/200 d5.8 Col Hill (TX) JC

YEAR	TM LG	G	AB	R	H	2B	3B	HR	RBI	BB-IB	HP	SO	AVG	OBP	SLG	AOPS	ABR	SB-CS	FA	FR	RNG	THR	GAMES AT POSITION	DL	BFW
2005	Pit N	3	8	1	2	0	0	1	1	0-0	0	4	.250	.250	.625	120	0	0-0	1.000	-0	89	0	O3L		0.0

SADOWSKI, ED Edward Roman B1.19.1931 Pittsburgh PA D11.6.1993 Garden Grove CA BR/TR/5-11/175* d4.20 b-Bob b-Ted

YEAR	TM LG	G	AB	R	H	2B	3B	HR	RBI	BB-IB	HP	SO	AVG	OBP	SLG	AOPS	ABR	SB-CS	FA	FR	RNG	THR	GAMES AT POSITION	DL	BFW
1960	Bos A	38	93	10	20	2	0	3	8	8-2	1	13	.215	.284	.333	64	-5	0-0	.995	5	242	125	C36	30	0.1
1961	LA A	69	164	16	38	13	0	4	12	11-1	0	33	.232	.278	.384	68	-7	2-3	.987	-1	106	54	C56		-0.6
1962	LA A	27	55	4	11	4	0	1	3	2-0	0	14	.200	.228	.327	49	-4	1-0	.968	-1	43	112	C18		-0.4
1963	LA A	80	174	24	30	1	4	4	15	17-5	0	33	.172	.245	.259	44	-14	2-1	.997	12	144	183	C68		0.1
1966	Atl N	3	9	1	1	0	0	0	1	1-0	0	1	.111	.200	.111	-10	-1	0-0	1.000	-0	62	366	C3		-0.1
Total 5		217	495	55	100	20	4	12	39	39-8	1	94	.202	.261	.319	56	-31	5-4	.991	15	140	128	C181	30	-0.9

SADOWSKI, BOB Robert Frank "Sid" B1.15.1937 St.Louis MO BL/TR/6-0/175* d9.16

YEAR	TM LG	G	AB	R	H	2B	3B	HR	RBI	BB-IB	HP	SO	AVG	OBP	SLG	AOPS	ABR	SB-CS	FA	FR	RNG	THR	GAMES AT POSITION	DL	BFW
1960	StL N	1	1	0	0	0	0	0	0	1-0	0	0	.000	.500	.000	47	0	0-0	.000	-1	0	0	/2		-0.1
1961	Phi N	16	54	4	7	0	0	0	4	4-0	0	7	.130	.203	.130	-9	-9	1-0	.971	0	102	125	3b14		-0.9
1962	Chi A	79	130	22	30	3	3	6	24	13-2	0	22	.231	.299	.438	97	-1	1-0	.955	4	120	0	3b16,2b12		0.3
1963	LA A	88	144	12	36	6	1	1	22	15-2	1	22	.250	.317	.313	83	-3	2-1	1.000	-2	111	0	3b36,O25(1/0/24),2b17		0.3
Total 4		184	329	38	73	9	7	7	46	33-4	1	63	.222	.292	.331	73	-13	3-1	.953	1	100	50	3b36,O25(1/0/24),2b17		-1.3

SAENZ, OLMEDO Olmedo (Sanchez) B10.8.1970 Chitre Herrera, Pan BR/TR/6-0/185(175-220) d5.28

YEAR	TM LG	G	AB	R	H	2B	3B	HR	RBI	BB-IB	HP	SO	AVG	OBP	SLG	AOPS	ABR	SB-CS	FA	FR	RNG	THR	GAMES AT POSITION	DL	BFW
1994	Chi A	5	14	2	2	0	0	0	0	0-0	0	5	.143	.143	.286	7	-2	0-0	1.000	-1	66	0	3b5		-0.3
1999	Oak A	97	255	41	70	18	0	11	41	22-1	15	47	.275	.363	.475	116	7	1-1	.938	1	102	165	3b56,1b28,D8	21	0.6
2000	†Oak A	76	214	40	67	12	0	9	33	25-2	7	40	.313	.401	.514	132	11	0-0	.923	-2	90	72	D27,3b18,1b17	48	0.6
2001	†Oak A	106	305	33	67	21	1	9	32	19-1	13	64	.220	.291	.384	76	-11	0-1	.986	-0	131	91	D58,1b28,3b14		-1.5
2002	†Oak A	68	156	15	43	10	0	6	18	13-1	7	21	.276	.354	.468	118	4	1-1	1.000	2	84	94	1b34,3b15,D7		0.4
2004	LA N	77	111	17	31	1	0	8	22	12-1	2	33	.279	.352	.505	122	9	0-1	.986	-1	132	146	1b25,3b2,D4		0.3
2005	LA N	109	319	39	84	24	0	15	63	27-1	3	73	.263	.325	.480	108	3	0-1	.998	-6	53	81	1b66,3b17,D8		-0.8
Total 7		538	1374	187	364	86	1	58	209	118-7	47	283	.265	.341	.461	107	15	3-4	.994	-5	88	94	1b198,3b127,D112	69	-0.7

SAFFELL, TOM Thomas Judson B7.26.1921 Etowah TN BL/TR/5-11/170* d7.2 Col Maryville

YEAR	TM LG	G	AB	R	H	2B	3B	HR	RBI	BB-IB	HP	SO	AVG	OBP	SLG	AOPS	ABR	SB-CS	FA	FR	RNG	THR	GAMES AT POSITION	DL	BFW
1949	Pit N	73	205	36	66	7	1	2	25	21	0	27	.322	.385	.395	107	3	5	.992	-2	96	59	O53(0/52/2)		-0.1
1950	Pit N	67	182	37	37	7	0	2	6	14	1	34	.203	.264	.275	41	-16	1	.993	4	110	135	O43(0/42/2)		-1.3
1951	Pit N	49	65	11	13	0	1	0	5	5	0	18	.200	.257	.246	35	-6	1-1	.929	-1	97	112	O17(1/13/3)		-0.7
1955	Pit N	73	113	21	19	1	0	1	3	15-3	0	22	.168	.266	.204	29	-12	1-0	.964	1	111	91	O47(6/37/4)		-1.2

YEAR	TM LG	G	AB	R	H	2B	3B	HR	RBI	BB-IB	HP	SO	AVG	OBP	SLG	AOPS	ABR	SB-CS	FA	FR	RNG	THR	GAMES AT POSITION	DL	BFW
	KC A	9	37	5	8	0	0	0	1	4-0	0	7	.216	.293	.216	38	-3	1-0	.962	-1	98	0	O9C		-0.4
Total	4	271	602	37	143	15	1	6	40	59-3	1	108	.238	.307	.296	60	-34	9-1	.980	2	104	90	O169(7/153/11)		-3.7

SAGE, HARRY   Harry "Doc" B3.16.1864 Rock Island IL   D5.27.1947 Rock Island IL   BR/TR/5-10/185   d4.17

| 1890 | Tol AA | 81 | 275 | 40 | 41 | 8 | 4 | 2 | 25 | 29 | 2 | | .149 | .235 | .229 | 36 | -23 | 10 | | .948 | 18 | 115 | 129 | C80/OC | | 0.1 |

SAGER, PONY   Samuel B. B1847 Marshalltown IA   ?/140   d5.6

| 1871 | Rok NA | 8 | 39 | 9 | 11 | 0 | 0 | 0 | 5 | 2 | | | 2 | .282 | .317 | .282 | 78 | -1 | 5-1 | .643 | -3 | 90 | 0 | S4,O4L | | -0.2 |

SAGMOEN, MARC   Marc Richard B4.16.1971 Seattle WA   BL/TL/5-11/185   [TexA93 13/367]   d4.15   Col Nebraska

| 1997 | Tex A | 21 | 43 | 2 | 6 | 2 | 0 | 3 | 4 | 2-0 | 0 | 13 | .140 | .174 | .256 | 11 | -6 | 0-0 | 1.000 | -1 | 99 | 0 | O17(2/0/16)/1D | | -0.7 |

SAIER, VIC   Victor Sylvester B5.4.1891 Lansing MI   D5.14.1967 E.Lansing MI   BL/TR/5-11/185   d5.3

1911	Chi N	86	259	42	67	15	1	1	37	25	7	37	.259	.340	.336	89	-3	11	.980	-4	81	115	1b73		-0.9
1912	Chi N	122	451	74	130	25	14	2	61	34	1	65	.288	.340	.419	107	3	11	.992	-5	77	105	1b120		-0.6
1913	Chi N	149	519	94	150	15	21	14	92	62	5	62	.289	.370	.480	141	27	26-20	.983	-5	87	101	1b149		1.7
1914	Chi N	153	537	87	129	24	8	18	72	94	4	61	.240	.357	.415	130	22	19	.986	-11	69	78	1b153		0.9
1915	Chi N	144	497	74	131	35	11	11	64	64	2	62	.264	.350	.445	140	25	29-9	.983	-5	87	88	1b139		2.1
1916	Chi N	147	498	60	126	25	3	7	50	79	1	68	.253	.356	.357	108	9	20-17	.984	-1	103	97	1b147		0.4
1917	Chi N	6	21	5	5	1	0	0	2	2	0	1	.238	.304	.286	75	-1	0	1.000	2	224	85	1b6		0.1
1919	Pit N	58	166	19	37	3	3	2	17	18	2	13	.223	.306	.313	83	-3	5	.985	-5	61	77	1b51		-1.0
Total	8	865	2948	455	775	143	61	55	395	378	22	369	.263	.351	.409	119	79	121-46	.986	-33	84	94	1b838		2.7

ST.CLAIRE, EBBA   Edward Joseph B8.5.1921 Whitehall NY   D8.22.1982 Whitehall NY   BB/TR/6-1/219*   d4.17   s-Randy   Col Colgate

1951	Bos N	72	220	22	62	17	2	1	25	12	1	24	.282	.322	.391	98	-1	2-0	.977	-0	82	100	C62	31	0.2
1952	Bos N	39	108	5	23	2	0	2	4	8	0	12	.213	.267	.287	56	-7	0-1	.972	1	101	135	C34		-0.5
1953	Mil N	33	80	7	16	3	0	2	5	3		9	.200	.229	.313	42	-7	0-0	.992	2	90	144	C27		-0.4
1954	NY N	20	42	5	11	1	0	2	6	12	1	7	.262	.436	.429	126	2	0-0	.975	1	134	107	C16		0.4
Total	4	164	450	39	112	23	2	7	40	35	2	52	.249	.306	.356	81	-13	2-1	.978	4	94	117	C139	31	-0.3

SAKATA, LENN   Lenn Haruki B6.8.1954 Honolulu HI   BR/TR/5-9/160(160-174)   [MilA75*S1/10]   d7.21   Col Gonzaga

1977	Mil A	53	154	13	25	2	0	2	12	9-0	1	22	.162	.209	.214	15	-18	1-3	.985	6	110	132	2b53		-1.0
1978	Mil A	30	78	8	15	4	0	0	3	8-1	0	11	.192	.267	.244	44	-6	1-0	.975	-5	94	79	2b29		-0.9
1979	Mil A	4	14	1	7	2	0	0	1	0-0	0	1	.500	.500	.643	205	2	0-0	1.000	1	110	184	2b4		0.3
1980	Bal A	43	83	12	16	3	2	1	9	6-0	0	10	.193	.244	.313	53	-6	2-1	.984	1	101	112	2b34,S4/D		-0.4
1981	Bal A	61	150	19	34	4	0	5	15	11-0	1	15	.227	.282	.353	83	-4	4-0	.963	-5	102	107	2b60/CD		0.6
1982	Bal A	136	343	40	89	18	1	6	31	30-2	4	39	.259	.323	.370	91	-4	7-4	.977	-13	93	95	2b83,S56		-0.8
1983	†Bal A	66	134	23	34	7	0	3	12	16-0	1	17	.254	.338	.373	97	0	8-4	.990	-3	95	128	2b60/CD		-0.1
1984	Bal A	81	157	23	30	1	0	3	11	6-2	0	15	.191	.221	.255	32	-15	4-1	.988	5	117	112	2b76/OL		-0.8
1985	Bal A	55	97	15	22	3	0	3	6	6-0	1	15	.227	.279	.351	73	-4	3-2	.960	-5	94	83	2b50/D		0.4
1986	Oak A	17	34	4	12	2	0	0	5	3-0	0	6	.353	.386	.412	132	2	0-1	.984	2	119	55	2b16/D		-0.1
1987	NY A	19	45	5	12	0	1	2	4	2-0	1	8	.267	.313	.444	98	0	0-1	.929	-0	113	54	3b12,2b6		-0.1
Total	11	565	1289	163	296	46	4	25	109	97-5	8	158	.230	.286	.330	71	-53	30-17	.982	-8	103	109	2b431,S102,3b12,D4/OLC	82	-3.5

SALAS, MARK   Mark Bruce B3.8.1961 Montebello CA   BL/TR/6-0/205(180-205)   [StLN79 18/448]   d6.19

1984	StL N	14	20	1	2	1	0	0	1	0-0	0	3	.100	.100	.150	-31	-4	0-0	1.000	-1	50	108	C4,O3(2/0/1)		-0.4
1985	Min A	120	360	51	108	20	5	9	41	18-5	1	37	.300	.332	.458	108	3	0-1	.991	8	100	121	C115,D3		1.5
1986	Min A	91	258	28	60	7	4	8	33	18-2	1	32	.233	.282	.384	78	-9	3-1	.980	0	92	110	C69,D8	24	-0.6
1987	Min A	22	45	8	17	2	0	3	9	5-1	0	4	.378	.431	.622	171	5	0-0	.989	-0	41	28	C14		0.4
	NY A	50	115	13	23	4	0	3	12	10-0	3	17	.200	.279	.313	58	-7	0-0	1.000	-0	102	120	C41/OLD		-0.6
	Year	72	160	21	40	6	0	6	21	15-1	3	21	.250	.322	.400	90	-2	0-1	.996	-0	85	95	C55,D4/OL		-0.2
1988	Chi A	75	196	17	49	7	0	3	9	12-2	3	17	.250	.303	.332	78	-6	0-0	.979	-1	98	121	C69/D		-0.3
1989	Cle A	30	77	4	17	4	1	2	7	5-1	1	13	.221	.277	.377	81	-2	0-0	1.000	0	57	396	C57/3D		-0.3
1990	Det A	74	164	18	38	3	0	9	24	21-2	1	28	.232	.323	.415	103	0	0-0	.988	-6	81	107	C57/3D		-1.0
1991	Det A	33	57	2	5	1	0	1	7	0-0	2	10	.088	.117	.158	-24	-10	0-0	1.000	-0	68	140	C11,1b5,D8	24	-1.0
Total	8	509	1292	142	319	49	10	38	143	89-13	12	163	.247	.300	.389	86	-30	3-3	.987	1	92	114	C385,D47,1b5,O4(3/0/1)/3	24	-1.6

SALAZAR, ANGEL   Argenis Antonio (Yepez) B11.4.1961 Anaco, Venez   BR/TR/6-0/173*   d8.10

1983	Mon N	36	37	5	8	1	1	0	1	1-0	0	8	.216	.231	.297	47	-3	0-0	.966	-4	69	117	S34		-0.6
1984	Mon N	80	174	12	27	4	1	0	12	4-0	1	38	.155	.178	.201	7	-22	1-1	.960	-7	91	113	S80		-2.5
1986	KC A	117	298	24	73	20	2	0	24	7-0	2	47	.245	.266	.326	59	-17	1-1	.978	-2	107	87	S115/2		-0.9
1987	KC A	116	317	24	65	7	0	2	21	6-0	0	46	.205	.219	.246	23	-36	4-4	.981	20	120	98	S116	22	-0.6
1988	Chi N	34	60	4	15	1	0	0	1	1-1	0	11	.250	.262	.300	58	-3	0-0	.966	1	95	106	S29,2b2/3		-0.1
Total	5	383	886	69	188	33	4	2	59	19-1	3	150	.212	.230	.270	35	-81	6-6	.974	9	106	99	S374,2b3/3	22	-4.1

SALAZAR, LUIS   Luis Ernesto (Garcia) B5.19.1956 Barcelona, Venez   BR/TR/5-9/180*   d8.15   C1   OF(161/114/36)

1980	SD N	44	169	28	57	4	7	1	25	9-1	1	25	.337	.372	.462	141	8	11-2	.944	-1	99	111	3b42,O4(0/3/1)		0.8
1981	SD N	109	400	37	121	19	6	3	38	16-2	1	72	.303	.329	.403	117	6	11-8	.955	-1	101	106	3b94,O23(1/10/14)		0.1
1982	SD N	145	524	55	127	15	5	8	62	23-10	2	80	.242	.274	.336	75	-20	32-9	.938	-2	107	147	3b129,S18/OC		-2.5
1983	SD N	134	481	52	124	16	2	14	45	17-8	2	80	.258	.285	.387	87	-11	24-9	.949	-5	110	98	3b118,S19		-0.8
1984	†SD N	93	228	20	55	7	2	3	17	6-1	0	38	.241	.261	.329	64	-12	11-7	.970	-4	105	77	3b58,O24(4/19/2),S4	27	-0.9
1985	Chi N	122	327	39	80	18	2	10	45	12-2	0	60	.245	.267	.404	78	-11	14-4	.968	-6	83	87	O84(26/68/1),3b39,1b6,D8	167	-1.1
1986	Chi A	4	7	1	1	0	0	0	0	1-0	0	1	.143	.250	.143	10	-1	0-0	—	0			D2		-1.1
1987	SD N	84	189	13	48	5	0	3	17	14-2	0	30	.254	.302	.328	70	-8	3-3	.957	-6	101	93	3b38,S22,O10(4/6/2),P2/1		-1.1
1988	Det A	130	452	61	122	14	1	12	62	21-2	3	72	.270	.305	.385	96	-4	6-0	.992	-1	107	127	O68(60/5/5),S37,3b31,2b5,1b4		-0.1
1989	SD N	95	246	27	66	7	2	8	22	11-3	1	44	.268	.302	.411	102	4	1-3	.968	4	112	123	3b72,O14(2/2/10),S9,1b2		-0.1
	†Chi N	26	80	7	26	5	0	1	12	4-0	0	13	.325	.357	.425	115	2	0-1	.921	-4	81	93	3b25,O2L		-0.2
	Year	121	326	34	92	12	2	9	34	15-3	1	57	.282	.316	.414	105	1	1-4	.959	0	104	101	3b97,O16(4/2/10),S9,1b2		-0.2
1990	Chi N	115	410	44	104	13	3	12	47	19-3	4	59	.254	.293	.388	80	-12	3-1	.950	-9	90	91	3b91,O28L		-2.2
1991	Chi N	103	333	38	86	14	1	14	38	15-1	1	45	.258	.292	.432	97	-3	0-3	.956	-3	106	99	3b86,1b7/OL		-0.2
1992	Chi N	98	255	20	53	7	2	5	25	11-2	0	34	.208	.237	.310	53	-17	1-1	.935	5	126	144	3b40,O34(33/0/1),S12,1b5		-1.6
Total	13	1302	4101	438	1070	144	33	94	455	179-37	15	653	.261	.293	.381	88	-84	117-51	.950	-14	104	100	3b863,O293L,S121,1b25,D10,2b5,P2194		-10.4

SALAZAR, OSCAR   Oscar Enrique B6.27.1978 Maracay, Venez   BR/TR/5-11/175   d4.10

| 2002 | Det A | 8 | 21 | 2 | 4 | 1 | 0 | 1 | 3 | 1-0 | 0 | 2 | .190 | .227 | .381 | 60 | -1 | 0-0 | .938 | -2 | 69 | 105 | 2b6/3S | | -0.2 |

SALES, ED   Edward A. B1861 Harrisburg PA   D8.10.1912 New Haven CT   BL/TR   d7.15

| 1890 | Pit N | 51 | 189 | 19 | 43 | 7 | 1 | 1 | 23 | 16 | 3 | 15 | .228 | .298 | .312 | 88 | -2 | 3 | .871 | -12 | 91 | 44 | S51 | | -1.2 |

SALKELD, BILL   William Franklin B3.8.1917 Pocatello ID   D4.22.1967 Los Angeles CA   BL/TR/5-10/190*   d4.18   gs-Roger

1945	Pit N	95	267	45	83	16	1	15	52	50	0	16	.311	.420	.547	161	24	2	.973	-6	84	100	C86		2.1
1946	Pit N	69	160	18	47	8	0	3	19	39	0	16	.294	.432	.400	133	10	2	.972	-3	68	128	C51		1.1
1947	Pit N	47	61	5	13	2	0	0	8	6	0	8	.213	.284	.246	41	-5	0	.971	-2	82	101	C15		-0.1
1948	†Bos N	78	198	26	48	8	1	8	28	42	1	37	.242	.378	.414	116	6	1	.990	-3	91	114	C59		1.1
1949	Bos N	66	161	17	41	5	0	5	25	44	1	24	.255	.417	.379	121	8	1	.980	-2	97	75	C63		0.1
1950	Chi A	1	3	0	0	0	0	0	0	1	0	0	.000	.250	.000	-33	-1	0	1.000	0			/C		0
Total	6	356	850	111	232	39	2	31	132	182	2	101	.273	.402	.433	129	42	6-0	.979	-10	85	103	C275		4.4

SALMON, CHICO   Ruthford Eduardo B12.3.1940 Colon, Pan   D9.17.2000 Bocas Del Toro, Pan   BR/TR/5-10/170(155-170)   d6.28   OF(56/5/64)

1964	Cle A	86	283	43	87	17	4	25	13-0	2	37	.307	.340	.424	113	5	10-6	1.000	-0	104	43	O53(1/0/52),2b32,1b13		0.6
1965	Cle A	79	120	20	29	8	0	3	12	5-0	2	19	.242	.281	.383	87	-2	7-4	.985	-3	65	83	1b28,O17(10/1/6),2b5,3b5		-0.1
1966	Cle A	126	422	46	108	13	2	7	40	21-2	0	41	.256	.289	.346	82	-11	10-1	.958	-7	88	100	S61,2b28,1b24,O10(9/0/1),3b6		-1.8
1967	Cle A	90	203	19	46	13	1	2	19	17-1	1	29	.227	.288	.330	82	-4	10-4	1.000	9	139	123	O28(24/4/3),1b24,2b24,S14,3b4		-0.2
1968	Cle A	103	276	24	59	8	1	3	12	12-0	3	30	.214	.253	.283	64	-13	7-7	.971	-8	87	87	2b45,3b18,S15,O13(11/0/2),1b11	21	-2.0
1969	Bal A	52	91	18	27	5	0	3	12	10-1	1	22	.297	.375	.451	130	4	0-1	1.000	-6	60	106	1b17,2b9,S9,3b3/OL		-0.3
1970	†Bal A	63	172	19	43	4	0	2	22	8-0	1	30	.250	.287	.395	94	-3	2-2	.946	-14	79	79	S33,2b12,3b11,1b2		-1.6
1971	Bal A	42	84	11	15	1	0	2	7	3-0	1	21	.179	.205	.262	32	-8	0-0	1.000	-1	57	93	1b9,2b9,3b6,S5		-1.5

YEAR	TM LG	G	AB	R	H	2B	3B	HR	RBI	BB-IB	HP	SO	AVG	OBP	SLG	AOPS	ABR	SB-CS	FA	FR	RNG	THR	GAMES AT POSITION	DL	BFW
1972	Bal A	17	16	2	1	1	0	0	0	0-0	0	4	.063	.063	.125	-43	-3	0-0	1.000	-0	0	601	1b2/3		-0.3
Total	9	658	1667	202	415	70	6	31	149	89-4	11	233	.249	.290	.354	84	-36	46-24	.959	-29	96	80	2b164,S137,1b130,O122R,3b54	21	-5.8

SALMON, TIM   Timothy James   B8.24.1968 Long Beach CA   BR/TR/6-3/220(200-241)   [CalA89 3/69]   d8.21 Col Grand Canyon   [DL 2005 Ala A 183]

YEAR	TM LG	G	AB	R	H	2B	3B	HR	RBI	BB-IB	HP	SO	AVG	OBP	SLG	AOPS	ABR	SB-CS	FA	FR	RNG	THR	GAMES AT POSITION	DL	BFW
1992	Cal A	23	79	8	14	1	0	2	6	11-1	1	23	.177	.283	.266	55	-5	1-1	.953	-2	86	67	O21R		-0.7
1993	Cal A	142	515	93	146	35	1	31	95	82-5	5	135	.283	.382	.536	141	31	5-6	.980	9	110	113	O140(0/1/140)/D		3.1
1994	Cal A	100	373	67	107	18	2	23	70	54-2	5	102	.287	.382	.531	131	18	1-3	.966	4	105	121	O99R	16	1.4
1995	Cal A	143	537	111	177	34	3	34	105	91-2	6	111	.330	.429	.594	165	55	5-5	.988	7	113	74	O142R/D		5.0
1996	Cal A	156	581	90	166	27	4	30	98	93-7	4	125	.286	.386	.501	121	20	4-2	.975	0	96	121	O153R,D3		1.1
1997	Ana A	157	582	95	172	28	1	33	129	95-5	7	142	.296	.394	.517	137	34	9-12	.971	10	107	147	O153R,D4		3.2
1998	Ana A	136	463	84	139	28	1	26	88	90-5	3	100	.300	.410	.533	142	33	0-1	.959	1	126	75	D111,O19R	16	2.5
1999	Ana A	98	353	60	94	24	2	17	69	63-2	0	82	.266	.372	.490	119	12	4-1	.981	5	110	108	O89R,D7	74	1.1
2000	Ana A	158	568	108	165	36	2	34	97	104-5	6	139	.290	.404	.540	133	32	0-2	.979	6	105	134	O124R,D33		2.6
2001	Ana A	137	475	63	108	21	1	17	49	96-4	8	121	.227	.365	.383	96	1	9-3	.989	6	102	156	O125R,D12	19	0.1
2002 †Ana A	138	483	84	138	37	1	22	88	71-3	7	102	.286	.380	.503	136	28	6-3	.986	-4	95	60	O111R,D25	18	1.6
2003	Ana A	148	528	78	145	35	4	19	72	77-3	10	93	.275	.374	.464	125	22	3-1	.958	-1	98	102	O78R,D68		1.3
2004	Ana A	60	186	15	47	7	0	2	23	14-0	2	41	.253	.306	.323	69	-9	1-0	1.000	1	126	264	D39,O8(3/0/6)	41	-0.9
Total	13	1596	5723	956	1618	331	22	290	989	941-44	64	1316	.283	.386	.500	129	272	48-40	.978	42	105	115	O1262(3/1/1260),D304	367	21.4

SALTZGAVER, JACK   Otto Hamlin   B1.23.1903 Croton IA   D2.1.1978 Keokuk IA   BL/TR/5-11/165   d4.12

YEAR	TM LG	G	AB	R	H	2B	3B	HR	RBI	BB-IB	HP	SO	AVG	OBP	SLG	AOPS	ABR	SB-CS	FA	FR	RNG	THR	GAMES AT POSITION	DL	BFW
1932	NY A	20	47	10	6	2	1	0	5	10	0	10	.128	.281	.213	31	-5	1-1	.958	-3	72	64	2b16		-0.6
1934	NY A	94	350	64	95	8	1	6	36	48	0	28	.271	.359	.351	90	-4	8-1	.953	-11	84	74	3b84,1b4		-1.1
1935	NY A	61	149	17	39	6	1	3	18	23	1	12	.262	.368	.362	95	0	0-2	.937	-9	86	60	2b25,3b18,1b6		-0.8
1936	NY A	34	90	14	19	5	0	1	13	13	0	18	.211	.311	.300	53	-7	0-0	.972	-4	90	53	3b16,2b6,1b4		-0.8
1937	NY A	17	11	6	2	0	0	0	3	4	0	4	.182	.357	.182	40	-1	0-0	1.000	0	98	281	1b4		-0.1
1945	Pit N	52	117	20	38	5	3	0	10	8	1	8	.325	.368	.419	114	2	0	.963	-2	95	83	2b31/3		0.2
Total	6	278	764	131	199	26	5	10	82	105	2	80	.260	.351	.347	85	-15	9-4	.957	-28	83	79	3b119,2b78,1b18		-3.2

SAMCOFF, ED   Edward William   B9.1.1924 Sacramento CA   BR/TR/5-10/165   d4.21

YEAR	TM LG	G	AB	R	H	2B	3B	HR	RBI	BB-IB	HP	SO	AVG	OBP	SLG	AOPS	ABR	SB-CS	FA	FR	RNG	THR	GAMES AT POSITION	DL	BFW
1951	Phi A	4	11	0	0	0	0	0	0	1	0	0	.000	.083	.000	-75	-3	0-0	1.000	-0	80	178	2b3		-0.3

SAMFORD, RON   Ronald Edward   B2.28.1930 Dallas TX   BR/TR/5-11/156*   d4.15

YEAR	TM LG	G	AB	R	H	2B	3B	HR	RBI	BB-IB	HP	SO	AVG	OBP	SLG	AOPS	ABR	SB-CS	FA	FR	RNG	THR	GAMES AT POSITION	DL	BFW
1954	NY N	12	5	2	0	0	0	0	0	1	0	1	.000	.000	.000	-99	-1	0-1	1.000	0	124	0	2b3		-0.1
1955	Det A	1	1	0	0	0	0	0	0	0-0	0	1	.000	.000	.000	-99	-0	0-0	1.000	0	193	0	/S		0.0
1957	Det A	54	91	6	20	1	2	0	5	6-0	1	15	.220	.276	.275	49	-7	1-0	.964	4	109	133	S35,2b11,3b4		-0.1
1959	Was A	91	237	23	53	13	0	5	22	11-0	2	29	.224	.262	.342	65	-12	1-0	.947	2	107	96	S64,2b23		-0.4
Total	4	158	334	31	73	14	2	5	27	17-0	3	46	.219	.261	.317	58	-20	2-1	.952	6	108	106	S100,2b37,3b4		-0.6

SAMPLE, BILL   William Amos   B4.2:1955 Roanoke VA   BR/TR/5-9/175*   [TexA76 10/228]   d9.2 Col James Madison

YEAR	TM LG	G	AB	R	H	2B	3B	HR	RBI	BB-IB	HP	SO	AVG	OBP	SLG	AOPS	ABR	SB-CS	FA	FR	RNG	THR	GAMES AT POSITION	DL	BFW
1978	Tex A	8	15	2	7	2	0	0	3	0-0	0	3	.467	.467	.600	197	2	1-0	—	-0	0	0	O2L,D3		0.2
1979	Tex A	128	325	64	95	21	2	5	35	37-1	2	28	.292	.365	.415	112	7	8-6	1.000	1	96	113	O103(91/10/5),D9		0.4
1980	Tex A	99	204	29	53	10	0	4	19	18-2	6	15	.260	.335	.368	96	-1	8-5	.973	-4	91	53	O72(15/18/40),D4		-0.6
1981	Tex A	66	230	36	65	16	0	3	25	17-1	7	21	.283	.346	.391	119	6	4-1	.993	-2	92	87	O64(62/5/0)		0.2
1982	Tex A	97	360	56	94	14	2	10	29	27-0	3	35	.261	.318	.394	99	-1	10-2	.981	-1	98	105	O91(85/9/0)/D		-0.4
1983	Tex A	147	554	80	152	28	3	12	57	44-2	5	46	.274	.331	.401	102	2	44-8	.988	2	103	70	O146(144/2/1)		0.4
1984	Tex A	130	489	67	121	20	2	5	33	29-1	0	46	.247	.286	.327	68	-22	18-6	.986	-4	99	37	O122(72/51/3),D2		-2.8
1985	NY A	59	139	18	40	5	0	1	15	9-0	2	10	.288	.336	.345	90	-2	2-1	.989	-1	104	39	O55(51/4/0)		-0.4
1986	Atl N	92	200	23	57	11	0	6	14	14-1	1	26	.285	.338	.430	106	2	4-2	.986	-4	88	30	O56(10/0/48)/2		-0.4
Total	9	826	2516	371	684	127	9	46	230	195-8	28	230	.272	.329	.384	97	-7	98-31	.987	-12	97	70	O711(532/99/97),D19/2	27	-3.4

SAMUEL, AMADO   Amado Ruperto   B12.6.1938 San Pedro de Macoris, D.R.   BR/TR/6-1/170*   d4.10

YEAR	TM LG	G	AB	R	H	2B	3B	HR	RBI	BB-IB	HP	SO	AVG	OBP	SLG	AOPS	ABR	SB-CS	FA	FR	RNG	THR	GAMES AT POSITION	DL	BFW
1962	Mil N	76	209	16	43	10	0	3	20	12-1	0	54	.206	.248	.297	47	-16	0-2	.958	-10	84	81	S36,2b28,3b3		-2.3
1963	Mil N	15	17	0	3	1	0	0	0	0-0	0	4	.176	.176	.235	18	-2	0-1	.786	-2	76	118	S7,2b4		-0.4
1964	NY N	53	142	7	33	7	0	0	5	4-0	2	24	.232	.264	.282	55	-8	0-1	.945	1	105	144	S34,3b17,2b3		-0.6
Total	3	144	368	23	79	18	0	3	25	16-1	2	82	.215	.251	.288	49	-26	0-4	.953	-11	92	109	S77,2b35,3b20		-3.3

SAMUEL, JUAN   Juan Milton   B12.9.1960 San Pedro de Macoris, D.R.   BR/TR/5-11/170(163-190)   d8.24   C7   OF(34/197/40)

YEAR	TM LG	G	AB	R	H	2B	3B	HR	RBI	BB-IB	HP	SO	AVG	OBP	SLG	AOPS	ABR	SB-CS	FA	FR	RNG	THR	GAMES AT POSITION	DL	BFW
1983 †Phi N	18	65	14	18	1	2	2	5	4-1	1	16	.277	.324	.446	114	1	3-2	.916	3	110	87	2b18		0.5
1984	Phi N	160	701	105	191	36	19	15	69	28-2	7	168	.272	.307	.442	107	2	72-15	.962	-15	95	78	2b160		0.7
1985	Phi N	161	663	101	175	31	13	19	74	33-2	6	141	.264	.303	.436	102	-1	53-19	.983	1	99	79	2b159		1.4
1986	Phi N	145	591	90	157	36	12	16	78	26-3	8	142	.266	.302	.448	102	-2	42-14	.967	-5	105	92	2b143	19	0.6
1987	Phi N★	160	655	113	178	37	15	28	100	60-5	5	162	.272	.335	.502	115	12	35-15	.978	-12	97	94	2b160		1.1
1988	Phi N	157	629	68	153	32	9	12	67	39-6	12	151	.243	.298	.380	92	-8	33-10	.978	-21	87	93	2b152,O3(0/2/1)/3		-2.3
1989	Phi N	51	199	32	49	1	9	8	20	18-1	1	45	.246	.311	.392	100	-1	11-3	.993	1	109	80	O50C	16	0.2
	NY N	86	333	37	76	13	1	3	28	24-1	10	75	.228	.299	.300	75	-11	31-9	.986	1	103	98	O84C		-0.8
	Year	137	532	69	125	16	2	11	48	42-2	11	120	.235	.303	.335	85	-11	42-12	.989	2	105	91	O134C		-0.6
1990	LA N	143	492	62	119	24	3	13	52	51-5	5	126	.242	.316	.382	94	-4	38-20	.972	-12	86	92	2b108,O31C		-1.2
1991	LA N★	153	594	74	161	22	6	12	58	49-4	3	133	.271	.328	.389	103	1	23-8	.978	-5	96	95	2b152		0.3
1992	LA N	47	122	7	32	3	1	0	15	7-3	1	22	.262	.303	.303	74	-4	2-2	.974	-2	86	70	2b38/OR	44	-0.1
	KC A	29	102	15	29	5	3	0	8	7-1	1	27	.284	.336	.392	100	0	6-1	.903	-1	78	183	O18R,2b10		-0.1
	Year	76	224	22	61	8	4	0	23	14-4	2	49	.272	.319	.350	87	-4	8-3	.940	-3	82	127	2b48,O18R		-0.2
1993	Cin N	103	261	31	60	10	4	4	26	23-3	3	53	.230	.298	.345	72	-11	9-7	.971	-2	91	87	2b70,1b6,3b4,O3(2/0/1)		-1.0
1994	Det A	59	136	32	42	9	5	5	21	10-0	3	26	.309	.364	.559	133	6	5-2	1.000	1	92	76	O27(2/25/0),D10,2b8,1b2		0.7
1995	Det A	76	171	28	48	10	1	10	34	24-0	2	38	.281	.376	.526	132	8	5-4	.983	-1	109	93	1b37,D16,O9L,2b6		0.3
	KC A	15	34	3	6	0	0	2	5	5-1	0	11	.176	.282	.353	63	-2	1-0	1.000	-1	39	0	O5L/1D		0.0
	Year	91	205	31	54	10	1	12	39	29-1	2	49	.263	.360	.498	120	6	6-4	.984	-2	105	90	1b38,D23,O14L,2b6		-0.3
1996	Tor A	69	188	34	48	8	3	8	26	15-0	5	65	.255	.319	.457	94	-3	9-1	1.000	-5	117	0	O24(8/5/15),D24,1b17	15	-0.8
1997	Tor A	45	95	13	27	5	4	3	15	10-0	3	28	.284	.364	.516	126	3	5-3	1.000	-3	49	155	D15,3b9,1b7,2b4,O2R		0.0
1998	Tor A	43	50	14	9	2	1	0	7	3-0	1	13	.180	.293	.280	50	-1	13-8	.882	-3	98	0	D11,O10(8/0/2),1b3,2b2		-0.5
Total	16	1720	6081	878	1578	287	102	161	703	440-38	74	1442	.259	.315	.420	100	-18	396-143	.973	-76	95	88	2b1190,O267C,D83,1b73,3b14	94	-1.8

SAMUELS, IKE   Samuel Earl   B2.20.1874 Quincy IL   D2.22.1964 New York NY   BR/TR   d8.3

YEAR	TM LG	G	AB	R	H	2B	3B	HR	RBI	BB-IB	HP	SO	AVG	OBP	SLG	AOPS	ABR	SB-CS	FA	FR	RNG	THR	GAMES AT POSITION	DL	BFW
1895	StL N	24	74	5	17	3	0	0	5	5	0	7	.230	.278	.257	39	-7	5	.750	-6	92	32	3b21,S3		-1.0

SANCHEZ, ALEJANDRO   Alejandro (Pimentel)   B2.14.1959 San Pedro de Macoris, D.R.   BR/TR/6-0/185*   d9.6

YEAR	TM LG	G	AB	R	H	2B	3B	HR	RBI	BB-IB	HP	SO	AVG	OBP	SLG	AOPS	ABR	SB-CS	FA	FR	RNG	THR	GAMES AT POSITION	DL	BFW
1982	Phi N	7	14	3	4	1	0	2	4	0-0	0	4	.286	.286	.786	184	1	0-0	1.000	-0	107	0	O4R		0.1
1983	Phi N	8	7	2	2	0	0	0	2	0-0	0	2	.286	.286	.286	59	0	0-0	.500	-0	62	0	O7R		-0.1
1984	SF N	13	41	3	8	0	1	0	2	0-0	0	12	.195	.195	.244	23	-5	2-3	.952	1	91	280	O11(3/0/9)		-0.5
1985	Det A	71	169	19	33	6	2	6	12	0-0	0	39	.248	.248	.459	89	-3	2-2	.923	-1	93	82	O14R,D28		-0.6
1986	Min A	8	16	1	0	0	0	0	1	1-0	0	8	.125	.176	.125	-16	-3	0-0	—	-0	0	0	/OLD		-0.3
1987	Oak A	2	3	0	0	0	0	0	0	0-0	0	1	.000	.000	.000	-99	-1	0-0	1.000	-0	91	0	/ORD		-0.1
Total	6	109	214	28	49	7	3	8	21	1-0	0	66	.229	.233	.402	71	-11	4-5	.929	-2	92	128	O50(9/2/40),D32		-1.5

SANCHEZ, ALEX   Alexis   B8.26.1976 Havana, Cuba   BL/TL/5-10/180*   [TBA96 5/154]   d6.15 Col Miami-Dade Wolfson (FL) CC

YEAR	TM LG	G	AB	R	H	2B	3B	HR	RBI	BB-IB	HP	SO	AVG	OBP	SLG	AOPS	ABR	SB-CS	FA	FR	RNG	THR	GAMES AT POSITION	DL	BFW
2001	Mil N	30	68	5	14	3	2	0	4	5-0	0	13	.206	.260	.309	47	-6	6-2	.963	-1	72	237	O19(3/14/3)	15	-0.5
2002	Mil N	112	394	55	114	10	7	1	33	31-0	2	62	.289	.343	.358	89	-9	37-14	.982	6	126	19	O100(16/86/0)	28	0.1
2003	Mil N	43	163	15	46	10	3	0	10	7-0	2	28	.282	.316	.380	82	-5	8-6	.990	3	116	152	O36C		-0.1
	Det A	101	394	43	114	13	5	1	22	18-0	1	46	.289	.320	.355	82	-11	44-18	.979	-1	107	0	O99C		-0.7
2004	Det A	79	332	41	107	9	3	2	26	7-0	0	50	.322	.335	.386	91	-6	19-13	.952	-6	92	53	O78C	77	-1.1
2005	TB A	43	133	28	46	8	1	2	13	7-1	0	25	.346	.373	.466	127	5	6-3	.957	-1	99	66	O31(0/18/14),D7		0.4
	SF N	19	43	4	11	2	0	0	1	0-0	0	9	.256	.289	.326	58	-3	2-2	.870	0	105	215	O10(0/4/6)/D	15	-0.3
Total	5	427	1527	193	452	56	21	6	111	76-1	5	233	.296	.330	.372	87	-35	122-58	.971	0	108	58	O373(19/335/23),D8	135	-2.3

SANCHEZ, CELERINO   Celerino (Perez)   B2.3.1944 El Guayabal, Veracruz, Mexico   D5.1.1992 Leon, Guanajuato, Mexico   BR/TR/5-11/160*   d6.13

YEAR	TM LG	G	AB	R	H	2B	3B	HR	RBI	BB-IB	HP	SO	AVG	OBP	SLG	AOPS	ABR	SB-CS	FA	FR	RNG	THR	GAMES AT POSITION	DL	BFW
1972	NY A	71	250	18	62	8	0	0	22	12-1	4	30	.248	.292	.304	80	-7	0-0	.939	2	114	98	3b68		-0.6
1973	NY A	34	64	12	14	3	0	1	9	2-0	0	12	.219	.239	.313	57	-4	1-1	1.000	-0	99	0	3b11,D11,S2,O2R		-0.5
Total	2	105	314	30	76	11	3	1	31	14-1	4	42	.242	.281	.306	75	-11	1-1	.943	2	113	89	3b79,D11,O2R,S2		-1.1

YEAR	TM LG	G	AB	R	H	2B	3B	HR	RBI	BB-IB	HP	SO	AVG	OBP	SLG	AOPS	ABR	SB-CS	FA	FR	RNG	THR	GAMES AT POSITION	DL	BFW

SANCHEZ, FREDDY   Frederick Philip   B12.21.1977 Hollywood CA   BR/TR/5-11/185*   d9.10   Col Oklahoma City

2002	Bos A	12	16	3	3	2	0	0	2	0-0	0	3	.188	.278	.188	27	-2	0-0	1.000	-1	93	51	2b5,S5		-0.
2003	Bos A	20	34	6	8	2	0	0	2	0-0	1	8	.235	.235	.294	37	-3	0-0	1.000	2	158	0	3b7,S6,2b3		-0.
2004	Pit N	9	19	-2	3	0	0	0	2	0-0	0	3	.158	.158	.158	-18	-3	0-0	.800	-3	75	0	S4,2b3/3	96	0
2005	Pit N	132	453	54	132	26	4	5	35	27-1	5	36	.291	.336	.400	93	-5	2-2	.977	10	114	176	3b65,2b58,S11		0
Total	4	173	522	65	146	28	4	5	41	29-1	5	50	.280	.322	.377	83	-13	2-2	.979	8	117	162	3b73,2b69,S26	96	-0.

SANCHEZ, ORLANDO   Orlando (Marquez)   B9.7.1956 Canovanas, PR   BL/TR/6-1/185*   d5.6

1981	StL N	27	49	5	14	2	1	0	6	2-1	0	6	.286	.308	.367	89	-1	1-0	.926	-3	71	44	C18		-0.
1982	StL N	26	37	6	7	0	1	0	3	5-0	0	5	.189	.286	.243	48	-3	0-0	1.000	-3	49	0	C15		-0.
1983	StL N	6	6	0	0	0	0	0	0	0-0	0	4	.000	.000	.000	-99	-2	0-0	1.000	0	0	0	/C		-0.
1984	KC A	10	10	0	1	1	0	0	2	0-0	0	2	.100	.100	.200	-19	-2	0-0	1.000	0	113	158	C4		-0.
	Bal A	4	8	0	2	0	0	0	1	0-0	0	1	.250	.250	.250	40	-1	0-0	1.000	0	107	149	C5		-0
	Year	14	18	0	3	1	0	0	3	0-0	0	3	.167	.167	.222	6	-2	0-0	1.000	0	108	155	C9		-0
Total	4	73	110	11	24	3	2	0	12	7-1	0	19	.218	.263	.282	52	-9	1-0	.962	-6	65	36	C39		-1

SANCHEZ, REY   Rey Francisco (Guadalupe)   B10.5.1967 Rio Piedras, PR   BR/TR/5-9/170*   [TexA86 13/319]   d9.8

1991	Chi N	13	23	1	6	0	0	0	2	4-0	0	3	.261	.370	.261	77	-1	0-0	1.000	-1	80	27	S10,2b2		-0
1992	Chi N	74	255	24	64	14	3	1	19	10-1	3	17	.251	.285	.341	75	-9	2-1	.974	10	104	142	S68,2b4	15	0
1993	Chi N	105	344	35	97	11	2	0	28	15-7	3	22	.282	.316	.326	73	-13	1-1	.969	27	122	116	S98		2
1994	Chi N	96	291	26	83	13	1	0	24	20-4	7	29	.285	.345	.337	79	-8	2-5	.993	20	108	84	2b50,S30,3b17	16	-1
1995	Chi N	114	428	57	119	22	2	3	27	14-2	1	48	.278	.301	.360	74	-17	6-4	.987	2	109	87	2b111,S4	66	0
1996	Chi N	95	289	28	61	9	0	1	12	22-6	3	42	.211	.272	.253	39	-26	7-1	.977	21	119	103	S92		0
1997	Chi N	97	205	14	51	9	0	1	12	11-2	0	26	.249	.287	.307	54	-14	4-2	.964	-7	91	63	S63,2b32/3		-1
†NY A		38	138	21	43	12	0	1	15	5-0	1	21	.312	.338	.420	98	0	0-4	.976	2	108	98	2b37,S6		0
1998	SF N	109	316	44	90	14	2	2	30	16-0	4	47	.285	.325	.361	85	-7	0-0	.977	12	109	97	S76,2b36		1
1999	KC A	134	479	66	141	18	6	2	56	22-2	4	48	.294	.329	.370	75	-19	11-5	.982	29	119	115	S134		1
2000	KC A	143	509	68	139	18	2	1	38	28-0	4	55	.273	.314	.322	59	-32	7-3	.994	19	112	108	S143		-0
2001	KC A	100	390	46	118	14	5	0	28	11-0	2	34	.303	.322	.364	74	-15	9-1	.994	32	126	158	S100		-2
†Atl N		49	154	-10	35	4	1	0	9	4-1	0	15	.227	.245	.266	32	-16	2-0	.986	8	113	122	S48		-0
2002	Bos A	107	357	46	102	12	3	1	38	17-1	2	31	.286	.318	.345	76	-13	2-2	.991	4	100	111	2b100,S10	37	-1
2003	NY A	56	174	11	36	3	1	0	12	8-2	0	18	.207	.240	.236	26	-20	1-1	.989	-1	99	87	S42,2b12	41	-0
	Sea A	46	170	22	50	5	1	0	11	8-1	0	21	.294	.330	.335	81	-5	1-0	.979	-3	88	128	S46		-0
2004	TB A	91	285	23	70	14	3	2	26	12-0	3	28	.246	.281	.337	62	-17	0-1	.987	4	103	104	2b87,S4	115	0
2005	NY A	23	43	7	12	1	0	0	2	1-0	1	3	.279	.326	.302	68	-2	0-1	.955	-3	112	141	S10,2b9/3D	290	3
Total	15	1490	4850	549	1317	193	32	15	389	229-29	40	508	.272	.308	.334	68	-234	55-32	.981	183	113	117	S984,2b480,3b19,D2		

SAND, HEINIE   John Henry   B7.3.1897 San Francisco CA   D11.3.1958 San Francisco CA   BR/TR/5-8/160   d4.17

1923	Phi N	132	470	85	107	16	5	4	32	82	4	56	.228	.347	.309	67	-20	7-3	.934	-3	98	106	S120,3b11		-0
1924	Phi N	137	539	79	132	21	6	6	40	52	4	57	.245	.316	.340	67	-24	5-4	.959	2	100	97	S137		-0
1925	Phi N	148	496	69	138	30	7	3	55	64	3	65	.278	.364	.385	84	-10	1-1	.928	-6	94	100	S143		-0
1926	Phi N	149	567	99	154	30	5	4	37	66	2	56	.272	.350	.363	88	-8	2	.939	-0	102	85	S149		-0
1927	Phi N	141	535	87	160	22	8	1	49	58	1	59	.299	.369	.376	98	0	5	.949	-4	92	65	S86,3b58		-0
1928	Phi N	141	426	38	90	26	1	0	38	60	1	47	.211	.310	.277	53	-28	1	.951	-0	98	95	S137		-1
Total	6	848	3033	457	781	145	32	18	251	382	15	340	.258	.343	.344	77	-90	21-8	.943	-12	98	93	S772,3b69		-0

SANDBERG, GUS   Gustave E.   B2.23.1895 Long Island City NY   D2.3.1930 Los Angeles CA   BR/TR/6-1/189   d5.11

1923	Cin N	7	17	1	3	1	0	0	1	1	0	1	.176	.222	.235	21	-2	0-0	1.000	-0	117	113	C5		-0
1924	Cin N	24	52	1	9	0	0	0	3	2	0	7	.173	.204	.173	2	-7	0-0	1.000	0	94	83	C24		-0
Total	2	31	69	2	12	1	0	0	4	3	0	8	.174	.208	.188	7	-9	0-0	1.000	-0	99	89	C29		-0

SANDBERG, JARED   Jared Lawrence   B3.2.1978 Olympia WA   BR/TR/6-3/212(185-212)   [TBA96 16/484]   d8.7

2001	TB A	39	136	13	28	7	0	1	15	10-0	1	45	.206	.265	.279	45	-11	1-0	.944	-1	93	101	3b38/1		-8
2002	TB A	102	358	55	82	21	1	18	54	39-3	1	139	.229	.305	.444	98	-2	3-2	.948	-2	98	107	3b97,1b3,D2		-8
2003	TB A	55	136	15	29	10	1	6	23	16-1	2	52	.213	.305	.434	94	-1	0-0	.956	1	106	56	3b50/1S		-8
Total	3	196	630	83	139	38	2	25	92	65-4	4	236	.221	.297	.406	86	-14	4-2	.949	-2	99	94	3b185,1b5,D2/S		

SANDBERG, RYNE   Ryne Dee   B9.18.1959 Spokane WA   BR/TR/6-2/180(175-190)   [PhiN78 20/511]   d9.2   HF2005

1981	Phi N	13	6	2	1	0	0	0	0	0-0	0	1	.167	.167	.167	-5	-1	0-0	1.000	1	85	0	S5/2		
1982	Chi N	156	635	103	172	33	5	7	54	36-3	4	90	.271	.312	.372	88	-11	32-12	.970	15	112	88	3b133,2b24		
1983	Chi N	158	633	94	165	25	4	8	48	51-3	3	79	.261	.316	.351	81	-16	37-11	.986	44	121	123	2b157/S		
1984	†Chi N★	156	636	114	200	36	19	19	84	52-3	3	101	.314	.367	.520	136	29	32-7	.993	22	112	103	2b156		
1985	Chi N★	153	609	113	186	31	6	26	83	57-5	1	97	.305	.364	.504	128	23	54-11	.986	13	108	95	2b153/S		
1986	Chi N★	154	627	68	178	28	5	14	76	46-6	0	79	.284	.330	.411	97	-3	34-11	.994	4	104	84	2b153		
1987	Chi N★	132	523	81	154	25	2	16	59	59-4	2	79	.294	.367	.442	109	8	21-2	.985	5	98	93	2b131		
1988	Chi N★	155	618	77	163	23	8	19	69	54-3	1	91	.264	.322	.419	107	4	25-10	.987	12	111	82	2b153		
1989	†Chi N★	157	606	104	176	25	5	30	76	59-8	4	85	.290	.356	.497	132	25	15-5	.992	-1	103	92	2b155		
1990	Chi N★	155	615	116	188	30	3	40	100	50-8	1	84	.306	.354	.559	139	31	25-7	.989	4	106	93	2b154		
1991	Chi N★	158	585	104	170	32	2	26	100	87-4	2	89	.291	.379	.485	137	31	22-8	.995	-3	108	77	2b157		
1992	Chi N★	158	612	100	186	32	8	26	87	68-11	4	73	.304	.371	.510	144	35	17-6	.990	12	112	100	2b157	25	
1993	Chi N★	117	456	67	141	20	0	9	45	37-1	2	62	.309	.359	.412	108	-1	9-2	.988	1	105	111	2b115		
1994	Chi N	57	223	36	53	9	5	5	24	23-0	1	40	.238	.312	.390	81	-7	2-3	.987	6	115	98	2b57		
1996	Chi N	150	554	85	135	28	4	25	92	54-4	7	116	.244	.316	.444	95	-5	12-8	.991	-16	101	94	2b146		
1997	Chi N	135	447	54	118	26	0	12	64	28-3	2	94	.264	.308	.403	82	-12	7-4	.984	-20	90	81	2b126/D	52	3
Total	16	2164	8385	1318	2386	403	76	282	1061	761-59	34	1260	.285	.344	.452	113	137	344-107	.989	99	107	94	2b1995,3b133,S7/D		

SANDERS, BEN   Alexander Bennett   B2.16.1865 Catharpin VA   D8.29.1930 Memphis TN   BR/TR/6-0/210   d6.6   Col Roanoke ▲

1888	Phi N	57	236	26	58	11	2	1	25	8	2	12	.246	.276	.322	86	-4	13	.929	3	125	81	P31,O25(13/6/7)/3		
1889	Phi N	44	169	21	47	8	2	0	21	6	1	11	.278	.307	.367	76	-6	4	.879	-2	84	36	P44,O3(1/2/0)		
1890	Phi P	52	189	31	59	6	6	0	30	10	0	10	.312	.347	.407	99	-2	2	.924	1	103	171	P43,O10(0/3/7)		
1891	Phi AA	40	156	24	39	6	4	1	19	7	2	12	.250	.291	.359	86	-4	2	.839	-4	0	0	O22(10/0/13),P19		
1892	Lou N	54	198	30	54	12	2	3	18	16	1	17	.273	.330	.399	131	7	6	.930	-3	90	150	P31,1b15,O9R		
Total	5	247	948	132	257	43	16	5	113	47	6	62	.271	.310	.376	95	-9	27	.916	-5	99	107	P168,O69(24/11/36),1b15/3		

SANDERS, ANTHONY   Anthony Marcus   B3.2.1974 Tucson AZ   BR/TR/6-2/200*   [TorA92 7/205]   d4.26

1999	Tor A	3	7	1	2	1	0	0	2	0-0	0	2	.286	.286	.429	78	-0	0-0	1.000	-0	49	0	/OLD		
2000	Sea A	1	1	1	1	0	0	0	0	0-0	0	0	1.000	1.000	1.000	416	0	0-0	1.000	0	431	0	/OR		
2001	Sea A	9	17	1	3	2	0	0	2	2-0	0	3	.176	.263	.294	49	-1	0-0	1.000	0	121	0	O9(8/0/1)		
Total	3	13	25	3	6	3	0	0	4	2-0	0	5	.240	.296	.360	73	-1	0-0	1.000	0	115	0	O11(9/0/2),D2		

SANDERS, DEION   Deion Luwynn   B8.9.1967 Ft.Myers FL   BL/TL/6-1/195*   [NYA88 30/781]   d5.31   Col Florida St.   [DL 2000 Cin N 59]

1989	NY A	14	47	7	11	2	0	3	7	3-1	0	8	.234	.280	.404	91	-1	1-0	.969	-0	95	144	O14(3/11/0)		
1990	NY A	57	133	24	21	2	2	3	9	13-0	1	27	.158	.236	.271	42	-11	8-2	.973	-3	83	92	O42(29/15/0),D4		
1991	Atl N	54	110	16	21	1	2	4	13	12-0	1	23	.191	.270	.345	68	-5	11-3	.952	-1	93	169	O44(41/5/1)		
1992	†Atl N	97	303	54	92	6	14	8	28	18-0	2	52	.304	.346	.495	128	9	26-9	.983	-1	99	100	O75(12/60/9)	15	
1993	†Atl N	95	272	42	75	18	6	6	28	16-3	2	42	.276	.321	.452	102	-0	19-7	.986	-3	95	33	O60(5/55/0)		
1994	Atl N	46	191	32	55	10	4	4	21	16-1	1	28	.288	.343	.403	91	-2	19-7	.980	-4	91	0	O46C		
	Cin N	46	184	26	51	7	4	0	7	16-0	2	35	.277	.342	.359	83	-5	19-9	1.000	1	104	86	O45C		
	Year	92	375	58	106	17	4	4	28	32-1	3	63	.283	.342	.381	87	-7	38-16	.991	-4	97	42	O91C	45	
1995	Cin N	33	129	19	31	2	3	1	10	9-0	2	18	.240	.296	.326	64	-7	16-3	.968	-3	93	0	O52C		
	SF N	52	214	29	61	9	5	5	18	18-0	2	42	.285	.344	.444	109	2	8-6	.984	-3	101	0	O85C		
	Year	85	343	48	92	11	8	6	28	27-0	4	60	.268	.327	.399	92	-5	24-9	.977	-0	107	45	O85C		
1997	Cin N	115	465	53	127	13	7	5	23	34-2	1	67	.273	.329	.363	80	-14	56-13	.982	-2	109	404	O16(12/4/1),D2		
2001	Cin N	32	75	6	13	0	2	0	4	2-0	0	8	.173	.235	.240	22	-9	3-4	1.000	3	109	0	O540(139/403/11),D6	119	
Total	9	641	2123	308	558	72	43	39	168	159-7	21	352	.263	.319	.392	88	-43	186-63	.982	-11	99	76	O540(139/403/11),D6		

YEAR	TM LG	G	AB	R	H	2B	3B	HR	RBI	BB-IB	HP	SO	AVG	OBP	SLG	AOPS	ABR	SB-CS	FA	FR	RNG	THR	GAMES AT POSITION	DL	BFW

SANDERS, JOHN   John Frank B11.20.1945 Grand Island NE BR/TR/6-2/200 d4.13

| 1965 | KC A | 1 | 0 | 0 | 0 | 0 | 0 | 0 | 0 | 0-0 | 0 | 0 | — | — | — | — | 0 | 0-0 | — | 0 | | | /R | | 0.0 |

SANDERS, RAY   Raymond Floyd B12.4.1916 Bonne Terre MO D10.28.1983 Washington MO BL/TR/6-2/185 d4.14 [DL 1947 Bos N 114]

1942	†StL N	95	282	37	71	17	2	5	39	42	1	31	.252	.351	.379	106	3	2	.991	-3	79	107	1b77		-0.7
1943	†StL N	144	478	69	134	21	5	11	73	77	1	33	.280	.381	.414	124	17	1	.995	-5	80	130	1b141		0.5
1944	†StL N	154	601	87	177	34	9	12	102	71	2	50	.295	.371	.441	126	21	2	.994	-12	64	136	1b152		0.1
1945	StL N	143	537	85	148	29	3	8	78	83	2	55	.276	.375	.385	109	10	3	.986	-5	92	113	1b142		-0.2
1946	Bos N	80	259	43	63	12	0	6	35	50	1	38	.243	.368	.359	105	4	0	.988	3	116	106	1b77		0.5
1948	†Bos N	5	4	0	1	0	0	0	2	1	0	0	.250	.400	.250	81	0	0	—	0			/H		0.5
1949	Bos N	9	21	0	3	1	0	0	0	4	0	9	.143	.280	.190	30	-2	0	.984	2	250	40	1b7	136	0.0
Total	7	630	2182	321	597	114	19	42	329	328	7	216	.274	.370	.401	115	53	8	.991	-20	85	121	1b596	250	0.2

SANDERS, REGGIE   Reginald Jerome B9.9.1949 Birmingham AL BR/TR/6-2/205 d9.1

| 1974 | Det A | 26 | 99 | 12 | 27 | 7 | 0 | 3 | 10 | 5-2 | 0 | 20 | .273 | .308 | .434 | 108 | 1 | 1-0 | .987 | 1 | 119 | 82 | 1b25/D | | 0.0 |

SANDERS, REGGIE   Reginald Laverne B12.1.1967 Florence SC BR/TR/6-1/196(180-205) [CinN87 7/180] d8.22 Col Spartanburg Methodist (SC) JC

1991	Cin N	9	40	6	8	0	0	1	3	0-0	0	9	.200	.200	.275	31	-4	1-1	1.000	-0	105	0	O9C	27	-0.5
1992	Cin N	116	385	62	104	26	6	12	36	48-2	4	98	.270	.356	.462	127	15	16-7	.978	11	112	212	O110(53/77/0)	32	2.6
1993	Cin N	138	496	90	136	16	4	20	83	51-7	5	118	.274	.343	.444	109	6	27-10	.975	2	117	29	O137(0/4/135)		0.4
1994	Cin N	107	400	66	105	20	8	17	62	41-1	2	114	.262	.332	.480	109	4	21-9	.975	6	107	155	O104R		0.5
1995	†Cin N★	133	484	91	148	36	6	28	99	69-4	8	122	.306	.397	.579	153	39	36-12	.983	4	101	128	O130(0/16/125)		4.0
1996	Cin N	81	287	49	72	17	1	14	33	44-4	2	86	.251	.353	.463	112	6	24-8	.988	4	106	131	O80R	60	0.7
1997	Cin N	86	312	52	79	19	2	19	56	42-3	2	95	.253	.347	.510	119	8	13-7	.974	3	113	63	O85R	76	0.7
1998	Cin N	135	481	83	129	18	6	14	59	51-2	7	137	.268	.344	.418	99	-1	20-9	.978	-4	102	53	O131(0/88/57)		-0.5
1999	SD N	133	478	92	136	24	5	26	72	65-1	6	108	.285	.376	.527	136	25	36-13	.975	-3	98	54	O129(97/15/41)/D	15	2.0
2000	†Atl N	103	340	43	79	23	1	11	37	32-2	2	78	.232	.302	.403	77	-13	21-4	.964	-1	92	127	O96(69/1/27)	39	-1.4
2001	†Ari N	126	441	84	116	21	3	33	90	46-7	5	126	.263	.337	.549	116	9	14-10	.996	1	102	67	O119R	7	0.4
2002	†SF N	140	505	75	126	23	6	23	85	47-3	12	121	.250	.324	.455	110	3	18-6	.984	9	112	154	O137R		0.7
2003	Pit N	130	453	74	129	27	4	31	87	38-4	5	110	.285	.345	.567	132	19	15-5	.983	-1	100	80	O120(39/0/91),D2		1.4
2004	†StL N	135	446	64	116	27	3	22	67	33-5	4	118	.260	.315	.482	101	-1	21-5	.981	-3	95	90	O119(38/0/81)/D		-0.5
2005	†StL N	93	295	49	80	14	2	21	54	28-1	4	75	.271	.340	.546	125	10	14-1	.983	-5	75	138	O81(80/0/1)/D	58	0.5
Total	15	1665	5843	980	1563	311	59	292	923	635-46	69	1513	.267	.344	.491	116	125	297-107	.980	23	103	101	O1587(376/210/1083),D5	314	11.1

SANDLOCK, MIKE   Michael Joseph B10.17.1915 Old Greenwich CT BB/TR (BL 1944)/6-1/185* d9.19

1942	Bos N	2	1	0	1	0	0	0	0	0-0	0	0	1.000	1.000	1.000	496	0	0	—	-0	0	0	S2		0.0
1944	Bos N	30	30	1	3	0	0	0	2	5	1	0	.100	.250	.100	1	-4	0	.956	4	143	55	3b22,S7		0.0
1945	Bro N	80	195	21	55	14	2	2	17	18	1	19	.282	.346	.405	109	2	2	.991	-1	108	79	C47,S22,2b4,3b2		0.5
1946	Bro N	19	34	1	5	0	0	0	3	0	0	4	.147	.216	.147	4	-4	0	.973	4	130	167	C17/3		0.0
1953	Pit N	64	186	10	43	5	0	0	12	12	1	19	.231	.281	.258	42	-16	0-0	.991	7	76	170	C64		-0.5
Total	5	195	446	34	107	19	2	2	31	38	4	45	.240	.304	.305	66	-22	2-0	.989	14	94	135	C128,S31,3b25,2b4		0.0

SANDOVAL, DANNY   Danny E. B4.7.1979 Lara, Venez BB/TR/5-11/190 d7.17

| 2005 | Phi N | 3 | 2 | 1 | 0 | 0 | 0 | 0 | 1 | 0-0 | 0 | 1 | .000 | .000 | .000 | -97 | -1 | 0-0 | 1.000 | 0 | 305 | 0 | /S | | 0.0 |

SANDS, CHARLIE   Charles Duane B12.17.1947 Newport News VA BL/TR/6-2/215(200-215) [BalA65 11/380] d6.21

1967	NY A	1	1	0	0	0	0	0	0	0-0	0	1	.000	.000	.000	-99	0	0-0	—	0			/H		0.0
1971	†Pit N	28	25	4	5	2	0	1	5	7-1	0	6	.200	.375	.400	119	1	0-0	1.000	-0	41	225	C3		0.1
1972	Pit N	1	1	0	0	0	0	0	0	0-0	0	0	.000	.000	.000	-99	0	0-0	—	0			/H		0.0
1973	Cal A	17	33	5	9	2	1	1	5	5-1	0	10	.273	.368	.485	149	2	0-0	.917	-5	83	0	C10		-0.3
1974	Cal A	43	83	6	16	2	0	4	13	23-2	1	17	.193	.370	.361	118	3	0-0	1.000	-0	174	0	D21,C5	64	0.3
1975	Oak A	3	2	0	1	0	0	0	0	1-0	0	1	.500	.667	.500	238	1	0-0	—	0			/D	64	0.1
Total	6	93	145	15	31	6	1	6	23	36-4	1	35	.214	.372	.393	125	7	0-0	.955	-5	98	34	D22,C18	64	0.2

SANDT, TOMMY   Thomas James B12.22.1950 Brooklyn NY BR/TR/5-11/175* [OakA69 2/33] d6.29 C16

1975	Oak A	1	0	0	0	0	0	0	0	0-0	0	0	—	—	—	—	-0	0	0		/2			0.0
1976	Oak A	41	67	6	14	1	0	0	3	7-0	0	9	.209	.284	.224	52	-4	0-0	.966	-4	88	100	S29,2b9,3b2		-0.6
Total	2	42	67	6	14	1	0	0	3	7-0	0	9	.209	.284	.224	52	-4	0-0	.966	-4	88	100	S29,2b10,3b2		-0.6

SANFORD, CHANCE   Chance Steven B6.2.1972 Houston TX BL/TR/5-10/175* [PitN92 27/763] d4.30 Col San Jacinto North (TX) JC

1998	Pit N	14	28	3	4	1	0	0	3	1-0	0	5	.143	.172	.250	9	-4	0-0	.900	-3	49	217	3b5/2S		-0.7
1999	LA N	5	8	1	2	0	0	0	2	0-0	0	1	.250	.250	.250	28	-1	0-0	1.000	-1	34	0	2b2		-0.2
Total	2	19	36	4	6	1	0	0	5	1-0	0	7	.167	.189	.250	13	-5	0-0	.900	-4	49	217	3b5,2b3/S		-0.9

SANFORD, JACK   John Doward B6.23.1917 Chatham VA D1.4.2005 Greensboro NC BR/TR/6-3/195 d8.24 Mil 1942-45 Col Richmond

1940	Was A	34	122	5	24	4	2	0	10	6	0	17	.197	.234	.262	30	-13	0-0	.993	-2	76	132	1b34		-1.7
1941	Was A	3	5	1	2	0	1	0	1	1	0	0	.400	.500	.800	251	1	0-0	1.000	-0	0	97	/1		0.1
1946	Was A	10	26	7	6	0	1	0	1	2	0	6	.231	.286	.308	70	-1	0-0	.971	-2	23	116	1b6		-0.3
Total	3	47	153	13	32	4	4	0	11	9	0	24	.209	.253	.288	44	-13	0-0	.989	-4	65	128	1b41		-1.9

SANGUILLEN, MANNY   Manuel De Jesus (Magan) B3.21.1944 Colon, Pan BR/TR/6-0/193* d7.23

1967	Pit N	30	96	6	24	4	0	0	8	4-3	0	12	.271	.300	.313	75	-3	0-1	.986	-3	179	106	C28		-0.5
1969	Pit N	129	459	62	139	21	6	5	57	12-4	3	48	.303	.324	.407	106	2	8-4	.981	6	99	115	C113		1.3
1970	†Pit N	128	486	63	158	19	7	7	61	17-9	0	45	.325	.344	.444	111	5	2-3	.988	10	155	101	C125		2.0
1971	†Pit N☆	138	533	60	170	26	5	7	81	19-13	3	32	.319	.345	.426	117	10	6-4	.994	12	172	112	C135		3.0
1972	†Pit N★	136	520	55	155	18	8	7	71	21-11	3	38	.298	.322	.404	108	2	1-2	.988	4	157	74	C127,O2L		1.2
1973	†Pit N	149	589	64	166	26	7	12	65	17-8	3	39	.282	.301	.411	99	-4	2-5	.983	4	100	73	C89,O59R		-0.1
1974	†Pit N	151	596	77	171	21	4	7	68	21-9	5	27	.287	.313	.371	94	-7	2-2	.985	1	128	105	C151		0.0
1975	†Pit N☆	133	481	60	158	24	4	9	58	48-15	3	31	.328	.391	.451	133	22	5-4	.987	1	114	67	C132		3.0
1976	Pit N	114	389	52	113	16	6	2	36	28-14	2	18	.290	.338	.378	102	1	2-4	.978	-2	119	103	C111		0.3
1977	Oak A	152	571	42	157	17	5	6	58	22-4	2	35	.275	.302	.354	80	-18	2-5	.985	-3	68	139	C77,D58,O9R,1b7		-2.1
1978	Pit N	85	220	15	58	5	1	3	16	9-2	2	10	.264	.296	.336	73	-8	2-2	1.000	-4	68	93	1b40,C18		-1.5
1979	†Pit N	56	74	8	17	5	2	0	9	2-2	0	5	.230	.247	.351	59	-4	0-0	.947	0	72	155	C8,1b5		-0.4
1980	Pit N	47	48	2	12	3	0	0	3	3-2	0	5	.250	.294	.313	67	-2	3-2	.956	-0	127	111	1b5		-0.3
Total	13	1448	5062	566	1500	205	57	65	585	223-96	23	331	.296	.326	.398	102	-4	35-38	.986	26	129	97	C1114,O70(2/0/68),D58,1b57		5.9

SANICKI, ED   Edward Robert "Butch" B7.7.1923 Wallington NJ D7.6.1998 Old Bridge NJ BR/TR/5-9/175* d9.14

1949	Phi N	7	13	4	3	0	0	3	7	1	0	4	.231	.286	.923	217	2	0	1.000	0	121	0	O6(0/1/5)		0.2
1951	Phi N	13	4	1	2	1	0	0	1	1	0	1	.500	.600	.750	265	1	1-0	1.000	0	101	0	O10L		0.1
Total	2	20	17	5	5	1	0	3	8	2	0	5	.294	.368	.882	231	3	1-0	1.000	0	119	0	O16(10/1/5)		0.3

SANKEY, BEN   Benjamin Turner B9.2.1907 Nauvoo AL D10.14.2001 Washington GA BR/TR/5-10/155 d10.5 Col Auburn-Montgomery

1929	Pit N	2	7	1	1	0	0	0	0	0	0	3	.143	.143	.143	-28	-2	0	.909	0	101	81	S2		-0.2
1930	Pit N	13	30	6	5	0	0	0	2	3	0	3	.167	.219	.167	-5	-5	0	.871	-1	104	56	S6,2b4		-0.5
1931	Pit N	57	132	14	30	2	5	0	14	14	0	10	.227	.301	.318	67	-7	0	.920	-8	100	95	S49,2b2,3b2		-1.1
Total	3	72	169	21	36	2	5	0	14	16	0	14	.213	.281	.284	49	-13	0	.914	-9	100	96	S57,2b6,3b2		-1.8

SANTANA, ANDRES   Andres Confesor (Belonis) B2.5.1968 San Pedro de Macoris, D.R. BB/TR/5-11/160 d9.16 [DL 1992 SF N 182]

| 1990 | SF N | 6 | 2 | 0 | 0 | 0 | 0 | 0 | 0 | 0-0 | 0 | 0 | .000 | .000 | .000 | -99 | -1 | 0-0 | 1.000 | 1 | 35 | 177 | S3 | | -0.1 |

SANTANA, PEDRO   Pedro B9.21.1976 San Pedro de Macoris, D.R. BR/TR/5-11/160 d7.16

| 2001 | Det A | 1 | 0 | 0 | 0 | 0 | 0 | 0 | 0 | 0-0 | 0 | 0 | — | — | — | — | 0 | 0-0 | 1.000 | 0 | 0 | 0 | /2 | | 0.0 |

SANTANA, RAFAEL   Rafael Francisco (De La Cruz) B1.31.1958 LaRomana, D.R. BR/TR/6-1/165* d4.5 C2 [DL 1989 NY A 182]

1983	StL N	30	14	1	3	0	0	0	1	2-0	1	2	.214	.353	.214	60	-1	0-1	.857	-3	61	70	2b9,S6,3b4		-0.4
1984	NY N	51	152	14	42	8	1	1	12	9-0	0	17	.276	.317	.382	97	-1	0-3	.970	-2	79	132	S50	15	0.1
1985	NY N	154	529	41	136	19	1	1	29	29-12	1	54	.257	.295	.302	69	-23	1-0	.965	-16	84	96	S153		-2.4
1986	†NY N	139	394	38	86	11	0	1	28	36-12	2	43	.218	.285	.254	51	-26	0-0	.973	10	103	107	S137/2		-0.4

YEAR	TM LG	G	AB	R	H	2B	3B	HR	RBI	BB-IB	HP	SO	AVG	OBP	SLG	AOPS	ABR	SB-CS	FA	FR	RNG	THR	GAMES AT POSITION	DL	BFW
1987	NY N	139	439	41	112	21	2	5	44	29-10	1	57	.255	.302	.346	74	-17	1-1	.973	13	104	113	S138		0.9
1988	NY A	148	480	50	115	12	1	4	38	33-0	1	61	.240	.289	.294	64	-24	1-2	.966	-14	98	102	S148		-2.8
1990	Cle A	7	13	3	3	0	0	1	3	0-0	0	0	.231	.231	.462	89	0	0-0	1.000	-2	78	77	S7		-0.2
Total	7	668	2021	188	497	74	5	13	156	138-34	5	234	.246	.295	.307	68	-92	3-7	.969	-14	95	106	S639,2b10,3b4	197	-5.2

SANTANGELO, F. P. Frank-Paul B10.24.1967 Livonia MI BB/TR/5-10/180(165-180) [MonN89 20/514] d8.2 Col Miami OF(217/195/88)

YEAR	TM LG	G	AB	R	H	2B	3B	HR	RBI	BB-IB	HP	SO	AVG	OBP	SLG	AOPS	ABR	SB-CS	FA	FR	RNG	THR	GAMES AT POSITION	DL	BFW
1995	Mon N	35	98	11	29	5	1	1	9	12-0	2	9	.296	.384	.398	103	1	1-1	.979	-2	115		O25(20/2/7),2b5		-0.2
1996	Mon N	152	393	54	109	20	5	7	56	49-4	11	61	.277	.369	.407	103	4	5-2	.983	10	119	83	O124(33/76/18),3b23,2b5/S		1.3
1997	Mon N	130	350	56	87	19	5	5	31	50-1	25	73	.249	.379	.374	100	3	8-5	1.000	1	111	83	O99(40/13/51),3b32,2b7/S		0.7
1998	Mon N	122	383	53	82	18	0	4	23	44-1	23	72	.214	.330	.292	68	-16	7-3	.983	-2	110	124	O92(72/23/1),2b35/3	15	-1.8
1999	SF N	113	254	49	66	17	3	3	26	53-0	11	54	.260	.406	.386	110	8	12-4	.993	-2	99	123	O81(26/49/9),2b11,3b3/S		0.7
2000	LA N	81	142	19	28	4	0	1	9	21-0	6	33	.197	.322	.246	50	-10	3-2	.983	-3	90	0	O50(26/27/1),2b7	44	-1.3
2001	†Oak A	32	71	16	14	4	0	0	8	11-0	5	17	.197	.341	.254	61	-3	1-1	1.000	-2	96	81	2b20,O6(0/5/1),3b3,D2		-0.4
Total	7	665	1691	258	415	87	14	21	162	240-6	83	319	.245	.364	.351	89	-13	37-18	.988	1	109	85	O477L,2b90,3b62,S3,D2	59	-1.5

SANTIAGO, BENITO Benito (Rivera) B3.9.1965 Ponce, PR BR/TR/6-1/182(180-200) d9.14

YEAR	TM LG	G	AB	R	H	2B	3B	HR	RBI	BB-IB	HP	SO	AVG	OBP	SLG	AOPS	ABR	SB-CS	FA	FR	RNG	THR	GAMES AT POSITION	DL	BFW
1986	SD N	17	62	10	18	2	0	3	6	2-0	0	13	.290	.308	.468	115	1	0-1	.946	-5	107	44	C17		-0.4
1987	SD N	146	546	64	164	33	2	18	79	16-2	5	112	.300	.324	.467	111	6	21-12	.976	1	122	98	C146		1.4
1988	SD N	139	492	49	122	22	2	10	46	24-2	1	82	.248	.282	.362	86	-11	15-7	.985	19	213	93	C136		0.8
1989	SD N★	129	462	50	109	16	3	16	62	26-6	5	89	.236	.277	.387	88	-9	11-6	.975	5	205	73	C127		0.4
1990	SD N*	100	344	42	93	8	5	11	53	27-2	3	55	.270	.323	.419	103	0	5-5	.980	4	138	92	C98	56	1.0
1991	SD N★	152	580	60	155	22	3	17	87	23-5	4	114	.267	.296	.403	93	-8	8-10	.985	8	137	95	C151/OL		0.8
1992	SD N★	106	386	37	97	21	0	10	42	21-1	0	52	.251	.287	.383	88	-7	2-5	.982	-7	113	110	C103	41	-1.0
1993	Fla N	139	469	49	108	19	6	13	50	37-2	5	88	.230	.291	.380	74	-18	10-7	.987	-4	103	92	C136/OL		-1.
1994	Fla N	101	337	35	92	14	2	11	41	25-1	1	57	.273	.322	.424	90	-6	1-2	.991	10	141	135	C97		0.9
1995	†Cin N	81	266	40	76	20	0	11	44	24-1	4	48	.286	.351	.485	117	7	2-2	.996	7	150	60	C75,1b8	57	1.
1996	Phi N	136	481	71	127	21	2	30	85	49-7	1	104	.264	.332	.503	116	9	2-0	.987	2	136	81	C114,1b14		1.
1997	Tor A	97	341	31	83	10	0	13	42	17-1	2	80	.243	.279	.387	72	-15	1-0	.997	-1	128	103	C95/D	15	-0.8
1998	Tor A	15	29	3	9	5	0	0	4	1-0	0	6	.310	.333	.483	108	0	0-0	1.000	-4	53	0	C15	156	-0.1
1999	Chi N	109	350	28	87	18	3	7	36	32-6	2	71	.249	.313	.377	74	-14	1-1	.990	-10	175	85	C107/1		-1.
2000	Cin N	89	252	22	66	11	4	8	45	19-8	1	45	.262	.310	.409	79	-9	2-2	.994	6	221	71	C84		0.
2001	SF N	133	477	39	125	25	4	6	45	23-0	2	78	.262	.295	.369	76	-19	5-4	.995	-2	122	75	C125		-1.
2002	†SF N★	126	478	56	133	24	5	16	74	27-8	2	73	.278	.315	.450	106	-4	4-2	.995	-2	124	44	C106	15	0.4
2003	†SF N	108	401	53	112	21	2	11	56	29-0	2	69	.279	.329	.424	94	-4	0-1	.993	-7	118	118	C49	107	-1.
2004	KC A	49	175	15	48	10	0	6	23	8-0	2	32	.274	.312	.434	92	-2	1-2	.996	-1	88	72	C47	23	0.
2005	Pit N	6	23	1	6	1	0	0	0	0-0	2	3	.261	.261	.391	68	-1	0-0	1.000	-4	95	0	C6		0.
Total	20	1978	6951	755	1830	323	41	217	920	430-52	38	1270	.263	.307	.415	92	-100	91-69	.987	3	142	87	C1917,1b25,O2L/D	470	1.

SANTIAGO, RAMON Ramon D. B8.31.1979 Las Matas de Farfan, D.R. BB/TR/5-11/150(150-175) d5.17

YEAR	TM LG	G	AB	R	H	2B	3B	HR	RBI	BB-IB	HP	SO	AVG	OBP	SLG	AOPS	ABR	SB-CS	FA	FR	RNG	THR	GAMES AT POSITION	DL	BFW
2002	Det A	65	222	33	54	5	5	4	20	13-0	8	48	.243	.306	.365	81	-7	8-5	.977	5	114	95	S63/D	39	0.
2003	Det A	141	444	41	100	18	1	2	29	33-0	10	66	.225	.292	.284	56	-28	10-4	.975	-2	106	116	S85,2b53		-2.
2004	Sea A	19	39	8	7	1	0	0	2	3-0	1	3	.179	.256	.205	23	-4	0-0	.946	-1	89	105	S16,D2		-0.
2005	Sea A	8	8	2	1	0	0	0	0	1-0	3	2	.125	.417	.125	58	0	0-0	1.000	-2	71	0	2b2,S2		-0.
Total	4	233	713	84	162	24	6	6	51	50-0	22	119	.227	.297	.303	62	-39	18-9	.973	0	108	107	S166,2b55,D3	39	-2.

SANTO, RON Ronald Edward B2.25.1940 Seattle WA BR/TR/6-0/190* d6.26 OF(7/0/1)

YEAR	TM LG	G	AB	R	H	2B	3B	HR	RBI	BB-IB	HP	SO	AVG	OBP	SLG	AOPS	ABR	SB-CS	FA	FR	RNG	THR	GAMES AT POSITION	DL	BFW
1960	Chi N	95	347	44	87	24	2	9	44	34-5	0	44	.251	.311	.409	97	-2	0-3	.945	-22	79	35	3b94		-2.
1961	Chi N	154	578	84	164	32	6	23	83	73-7	0	77	.284	.362	.479	120	18	2-3	.937	4	103	133	3b153		2.
1962	Chi N	162	604	44	137	20	4	17	83	65-5	2	94	.227	.302	.358	74	-22	4-1	.955	13	114	107	3b157,S8		3.
1963	Chi N★	162	630	79	187	29	6	25	99	42-7	4	92	.297	.339	.481	128	22	6-4	.951	14	116	106	3b162		7.
1964	Chi N☆	161	592	94	185	33	13	30	114	86-5	2	96	.313	.398	.564	162	51	3-4	.963	20	119	117	3b161		8.
1965	Chi N★	164	608	88	173	30	4	33	101	88-7	5	109	.285	.378	.510	144	38	3-1	.957	22	119	97	3b164		6.
1966	Chi N★	155	561	93	175	21	8	30	94	95-7	6	78	.312	.412	.538	161	51	4-5	.956	25	115	116	3b152,S8		7.
1967	Chi N	161	586	107	176	23	4	31	98	96-9	3	103	.300	.395	.512	153	44	1-5	.971	20	115	112	3b162		4
1968	Chi N★	162	577	86	142	17	3	26	98	96-7	3	106	.246	.354	.421	125	21	3-4	.947	-1	103	85	3b160		3.
1969	Chi N★	160	575	97	166	18	4	29	123	96-7	2	97	.289	.384	.485	128	24	1-3	.947	7	103	85	3b160		2.
1970	Chi N★	154	555	83	148	30	4	26	114	92-6	1	108	.267	.369	.476	112	11	2-0	.945	18	109	135	3b152/OR		2
1971	Chi N★	154	555	77	148	22	1	21	88	79-8	0	95	.267	.354	.423	105	6	4-0	.958	1	97	120	3b149,O6L		0
1972	Chi N★	133	464	68	140	25	5	17	74	69-5	4	75	.302	.391	.487	135	24	1-4	.948	14	116	94	3b129,2b3/SOL		3
1973	Chi N★	149	536	65	143	29	2	20	77	63-8	4	97	.267	.348	.440	109	7	1-2	.950	-3	99	61	3b146		0
1974	Chi A	117	375	29	83	12	1	5	41	37-1	2	72	.221	.293	.299	69	-15	0-2	.970	-1	101	136	D47,2b39,3b28,1b3/S		-1
Total	15	2243	8143	1138	2254	365	67	342	1331	1108-94	38	1343	.277	.362	.464	123	278	35-41	.954	165	109	105	3b2130,D47,2b42,S18,O8L,1b3	44	

SANTO DOMINGO, RAFAEL Rafael (Molina) B11.24.1955 Orocovis, PR BB/TR/6-0/160 d9.7

YEAR	TM LG	G	AB	R	H	2B	3B	HR	RBI	BB-IB	HP	SO	AVG	OBP	SLG	AOPS	ABR	SB-CS	FA	FR	RNG	THR	GAMES AT POSITION	DL	BFW
1979	Cin N	7	6	1	1	0	0	0	0	1-0	0	1	.167	.286	.167	27	-1	0-0	—	0			/H		-0

SANTOS, ANGEL Angel Ramon B8.14.1979 Rio Piedras, PR BB/TR/5-11/185* [BosA97 4/131] d9.8

YEAR	TM LG	G	AB	R	H	2B	3B	HR	RBI	BB-IB	HP	SO	AVG	OBP	SLG	AOPS	ABR	SB-CS	FA	FR	RNG	THR	GAMES AT POSITION	DL	BFW
2001	Bos A	9	16	2	2	1	0	0	1	2-0	0	7	.125	.211	.188	10	-2	0-0	.905	-1	90	0	2b6		-0
2003	Cle A	32	76	9	17	3	1	3	6	3-0	0	18	.224	.253	.408	71	-4	1-1	.981	1	108	123	2b28,3b4		-0
Total	2	41	92	11	19	4	1	3	7	5-0	0	25	.207	.245	.370	60	-6	1-1	.968	-1	105	102	2b34,3b4		-0

SANTOS, FRANCISCO Francisco Alejandro B3.9.1974 Santo Domingo, D.R. BL/TL/6-1/175 d6.18

YEAR	TM LG	G	AB	R	H	2B	3B	HR	RBI	BB-IB	HP	SO	AVG	OBP	SLG	AOPS	ABR	SB-CS	FA	FR	RNG	THR	GAMES AT POSITION	DL	BFW
2003	SF N	8	15	2	3	2	0	1	1	0-0	1	3	.200	.200	.533	81	0	0-0	1.000	-0	102	0	O3R/1		-0

SANTOVENIA, NELSON Nelson Gil (Mayol) B7.27.1961 Pinar Del Rio, Cuba BR/TR/6-3/215(205-220) [MonN82 S1/19] d9.16 Col Miami

YEAR	TM LG	G	AB	R	H	2B	3B	HR	RBI	BB-IB	HP	SO	AVG	OBP	SLG	AOPS	ABR	SB-CS	FA	FR	RNG	THR	GAMES AT POSITION	DL	BFW
1987	Mon N	2	1	0	0	0	0	0	0	0-0	0	0	.000	.000	.000	-96	0	0-0	1.000	0	0		/C	16	0
1988	Mon N	92	309	26	73	20	2	8	41	24-3	3	77	.236	.294	.392	92	-3	2-3	.983	1	93	108	C86/1	31	0
1989	Mon N	97	304	30	76	14	1	5	31	24-2	5	37	.250	.307	.352	88	-5	2-1	.981	8	84	135	C89/1	50	-0
1990	Mon N	59	163	13	31	3	1	6	28	8-0	0	31	.190	.222	.331	54	-12	0-3	.980	-3	73	74	C51		-0
1991	Mon N	41	96	7	24	5	0	2	14	2-2	0	18	.250	.255	.365	76	-3	0-0	.976	-1	93	102	C30,1b7		-0
1992	Chi A	2	3	1	1	0	0	1	2	0-0	0	1	.333	.333	1.333	349	0	1-0	1.000	-1	0	261	C2		-0
1993	KC A	4	8	0	1	0	0	0	0	0-0	0	2	.125	.222	.125	-4	-1	0-0	1.000	-1	177	0	C4		-0
Total	7	297	884	77	206	42	4	22	116	59-7	6	165	.233	.281	.364	82	-23	4-7	.981	4	87	110	C263,1b9	97	-0

SANTRY, EDWARD Edward B Chicago IL D3.6.1899 Chicago IL d8.7

YEAR	TM LG	G	AB	R	H	2B	3B	HR	RBI	BB-IB	HP	SO	AVG	OBP	SLG	AOPS	ABR	SB-CS	FA	FR	RNG	THR	GAMES AT POSITION	DL	BFW
1884	Det N	6	22	1	4	0	0	0	1			2	.182	.217	.182	29	-2		.821	-1	82	77	S5/2		-0

SARDINHA, DANE Dane K. B4.8.1969 Honolulu HI BR/TR/6-0/210* [CinN00 2/46] d9.6 Col Pepperdine

YEAR	TM LG	G	AB	R	H	2B	3B	HR	RBI	BB-IB	HP	SO	AVG	OBP	SLG	AOPS	ABR	SB-CS	FA	FR	RNG	THR	GAMES AT POSITION	DL	BFW
2003	Cin N	1	2	0	0	0	0	0	0	0-0	0	1	.000	.000	.000	-99	-1	0-0	1.000	-0	0	0	/C		-0
2005	Cin N	1	3	0	0	0	0	0	0	0-0	0	1	.000	.000	.000	-99	-1	0-0	1.000	-0	0	0	/C		-0
Total	2	2	5	0	0	0	0	0	0	0-0	0	2	.000	.000	.000	-99	-2	0-0	1.000	-0	0	0	C2		-0

SARGENT, JOE Joseph Alexander "Horse Belly" B9.24.1893 Rochester NY D7.5.1950 Rochester NY BR/TR/5-10/165 d4.27

YEAR	TM LG	G	AB	R	H	2B	3B	HR	RBI	BB-IB	HP	SO	AVG	OBP	SLG	AOPS	ABR	SB-CS	FA	FR	RNG	THR	GAMES AT POSITION	DL	BFW
1921	Det A	66	178	21	45	8	5	2	24		0	26	.253	.342	.388	86	-4	2-3	.927	-2	91	102	2b24,3b23,S19		-0

SARNI, BILL William Florine B9.19.1927 Los Angeles CA D4.15.1983 Creve Coeur MO BR/TR/5-11/187* d5.9 C1

YEAR	TM LG	G	AB	R	H	2B	3B	HR	RBI	BB-IB	HP	SO	AVG	OBP	SLG	AOPS	ABR	SB-CS	FA	FR	RNG	THR	GAMES AT POSITION	DL	BFW
1951	StL N	36	86	7	15	1	0	0	2	9	1	13	.174	.253	.186	20	-10	1-0	.984	1	119	68	C35		
1952	StL N	3	5	1	1	0	0	0	0		0	2	.200	.200	.200	11	-1	0-0	0	0	0	C3		
1954	StL N	123	380	40	114	18	4	9	70	25	0	42	.300	.337	.439	101	0	3-3	.996	-8	141	79	C118		
1955	StL N	107	325	32	83	15	2	3	34	27-0	1	33	.255	.313	.342	74	-12	1-1	.987	-6	107	105	C99		
1956	StL N	43	148	12	43	7	2	6	22	8-2	1	15	.291	.329	.466	111	2	1-0	.992	1	97	102	C41		
	NY N	78	238	16	55	9	3	5	23	20-2	1	31	.231	.290	.357	74	-9	0-1	.993	-0	118	101	C78		
	Year	121	386	28	98	16	5	11	45	28-4	2	46	.254	.305	.399	88	-7	1-1	.992	1	110	101	C119		
Total	5	390	1182	107	311	50	11	22	151	89-4	3	135	.263	.313	.380	84	-30	6-5	.991	-10	119	92	C374		

SASSER, MACKEY Mack Daniel B8.3.1962 Fort Gaines GA BL/TR/6-1/210(190-210) [SFN84*5/114] d7.17 Col Troy St.

YEAR	TM LG	G	AB	R	H	2B	3B	HR	RBI	BB-IB	HP	SO	AVG	OBP	SLG	AOPS	ABR	SB-CS	FA	FR	RNG	THR	GAMES AT POSITION	DL	BFW
1987	SF N	2	4	0	0	0	0	0	0	0-0	0	0	.000	.000	.000	-99	-1	0-0	1.000	0	0	0	/C		
	Pit N	12	23	3	5	0	0	0	0	0-0	0	1	.217	.217	.217	15	-3	0-0	1.000	-0	104	5	C5		

YEAR	TM LG	G	AB	R	H	2B	3B	HR	RBI	BB-IB	HP	SO	AVG	OBP	SLG	AOPS	ABR	SB-CS	FA	FR	RNG	THR	GAMES AT POSITION	DL	BFW
	Year	14	27	2	5	0	0	0	2	0-0	0	2	.185	.185	.185	-1	-4	0-0	1.000	-0	79	0	C6		-0.4
1988	†NY N	60	123	9	35	10	1	1	17	6-4	0	9	.285	.313	.407	111	2	0-0	.977	1	61	116	C42/3OR		0.5
1989	NY N	72	182	17	53	14	2	1	22	7-4	0	15	.291	.316	.407	110	2	0-1	.992	-3	89	93	C62/3		0.1
1990	NY N	100	270	31	83	14	0	6	41	15-9	1	19	.307	.344	.426	111	4	0-0	.975	-5	67	**150**	C87/1		0.3
1991	NY N	96	228	18	62	14	2	5	35	9-2	1	19	.272	.298	.417	101	-1	0-2	.994	-7	88	95	C43,O21(7/0/14),1b10		-0.3
1992	NY N	92	141	7	34	6	0	2	18	3-0	0	19	.241	.248	.326	65	-7	0-0	.989	-8	49	73	C27,1b12,O9(7/0/2)		-1.6
1993	Sea A	83	188	18	41	10	2	1	21	15-6	1	30	.218	.274	.309	57	-12	1-0	.946	-2	83	156	O37(26/0/11),D19,C4/1	16	-1.5
1994	Sea A	3	4	0	0	0	0	0	0	0-0	0	0	.000	.000	.000	-98	-1	0-0	—	-1	0	0	/COL	22	-0.2
1995	Pit N	14	26	1	4	0	0	0	1	0-0	0	0	.154	.154	.192	-9	-4	0-0	1.000	-0	118	157	C11		-0.4
Total	9	534	1189	103	317	69	7	16	156	55-25	3	104	.267	.296	.377	88	-21	1-3	.983	-19	74	115	C283,O69(41/0/28),1b24,D19,3b2	38	-3.5

SASSER, ROB   Robert Doffell   B3.9.1975 Philadelphia PA   BR/TR/6-3/205   [AtlN93 10/292] d7.31

| 1998 | Tex A | 1 | 1 | 0 | 0 | 0 | 0 | 0 | 0 | 0-0 | 0 | 0 | .000 | .000 | .000 | -95 | 0 | 0-0 | — | 0 | | | /H | | 0.0 |

SATRIANO, TOM   Thomas Victor Nicholas   B8.28.1940 Pittsburgh PA   BL/TR/6-1/190*   d7.23   Col USC

1961	LA A	35	96	15	19	5	1	1	8	12-0	1	16	.198	.294	.302	53	-6	2-0	.915	1	113	135	3b23,2b10/S		-0.4
1962	LA A	10	19	4	8	2	0	2	6	0-0	0	7	.421	.421	.842	238	3	0-0	.833	2	125	163	3b5		0.4
1963	LA A	23	50	1	9	1	0	0	2	9-2	0	10	.180	.305	.200	48	-3	0-0	.952	4	159	98	3b13,C2/1		0.0
1964	LA A	108	255	18	51	9	0	1	17	30-3	0	37	.200	.282	.247	55	-15	0-2	.917	-3	114	86	3b38,1b32,C25,S2/2		-2.1
1965	Cal A	47	79	8	13	2	0	1	4	10-1	0	10	.165	.258	.228	40	-6	1-1	1.000	-6	78	80	3b15,C12,2b12,1b3		-0.7
1966	Cal A	103	226	16	54	5	3	0	24	27-2	0	32	.239	.320	.288	78	-6	3-3	.991	-9	64	73	C43,1b36,3b25,2b4		-1.5
1967	Cal A	90	201	13	45	7	0	4	21	28-3	0	25	.224	.319	.318	92	-1	1-0	.962	-2	95	89	3b38,C23,2b15,1b5		-0.2
1968	Cal A	111	297	20	75	9	0	8	35	37-5	1	44	.253	.337	.364	116	6	0-0	.989	-4	109	**142**	C85,2b14,3b11/1		0.8
1969	Cal A	41	108	5	28	2	0	1	16	18-1	1	15	.259	.364	.306	95	0	0-2	1.000	2	107	97	C36,1b5,2b2		0.3
	Bos A	47	127	9	24	2	0	0	11	22-7	2	12	.189	.310	.205	47	-8	0-0	.978	0	104	81	C44		-0.7
	Year	88	235	14	52	4	0	1	27	40-8	3	27	.221	.335	.251	68	-8	0-2	.987	2	105	88	C80,1b5,2b2		-0.4
1970	Bos A	59	165	21	39	9	1	3	13	21-3	1	23	.236	.326	.358	83	-3	0-0	.985	1	105	68	C51		0.0
Total	10	674	1623	130	365	53	5	21	157	214-27	6	225	.225	.316	.303	79	-39	7-8	.987	-11	100	107	C321,3b168,1b83,2b58,S3		-4.1

SATURRIA, LUIS   Luis Arturo   B7.21.1976 San Pedro de Macoris, D.R.   BR/TR/6-2/165*   d9.11

2000	StL N	12	5	1	0	0	0	0	1	0-0	0	3	.000	.167	.000	-52	-1	0-0	1.000	-1	59	0	O9(0/5/4)		-0.2
2001	StL N	13	5	0	1	1	0	0	1	0-0	0	1	.200	.200	.400	48	0	1-0	1.000	-0	75	0	O9(3/3/3)		0.0
Total	2	25	10	1	1	1	0	0	1	1-0	0	4	.100	.182	.200	-3	-1	1-0	1.000	-1	65	0	O18(3/8/7)		-0.2

SAUCIER, FRANK   Francis Field   B5.28.1926 Leslie MO   BL/TR/6-1/180   d7.21   Mil 1952-54   Col Westminster (MO)

| 1951 | StL A | 18 | 14 | 4 | 1 | 1 | 0 | 0 | 1 | 3 | 1 | 4 | .071 | .278 | .143 | 16 | -2 | 0-0 | .714 | -0 | 126 | 0 | O3(1/0/2) | | -0.2 |

SAUER, ED   Edward "Horn"   B1.3.1919 Pittsburgh PA   D7.1.1988 Thousand Oaks CA   BR/TR/6-1/188   d9.17   b-Hank   Col Elon

1943	Chi N	14	55	3	15	3	0	0	9	3	1	6	.273	.322	.327	89	-1	1	1.000	0	108	64	O13L		-0.2
1944	Chi N	23	50	3	11	4	0	0	5	2	0	6	.220	.250	.300	55	-3	0	.960	-0	96	119	O12L		-0.4
1945	†Chi N	49	93	8	24	4	1	2	11	8	0	23	.258	.317	.387	97	-1	2	1.000	1	106	70	O26(21/2/3)		-0.1
1949	StL N	24	45	5	10	2	1	0	1	3	0	8	.222	.271	.311	53	-3	0	1.000	-0	76	146	O10(4/0/7)		-0.4
	Bos N	79	214	26	57	12	6	3	31	17	1	34	.266	.323	.364	89	-3	0	.972	0	106	64	O71(29/20/25)		-0.6
	Year	103	259	31	67	14	1	3	32	20	1	42	.259	.314	.355	82	-7	0	.974	-0	102	74	O81(33/20/32)		-1.0
Total	4	189	457	45	117	25	2	5	57	33	2	77	.256	.309	.352	83	-11	3	.981	0	103	76	O132(79/22/35)		-1.7

SAUER, HANK   Henry John   B3.17.1917 Pittsburgh PA   D8.24.2001 Burlingame CA   BR/TR/6-4/199*   d9.9   Mil 1944-45   C1   b-Ed

1941	Cin N	9	33	4	10	4	0	0	5	1	0	4	.303	.324	.424	109	0	0	.957	1	102	152	O8L		0.0
1942	Cin N	7	20	4	5	0	0	2	4	2	0	2	.250	.318	.550	152	1	0	.976	0	149	254	1b4		0.1
1945	Cin N	31	116	18	34	1	0	5	20	6	0	16	.293	.328	.431	112	1	2	.972	0	109	0	O28L,1b3		-0.1
1948	Cin N	145	530	78	138	22	1	35	97	60	4	85	.260	.340	.504	130	20	2	.973	5	100	137	O132L,1b12		1.5
1949	Cin N	42	152	22	36	6	0	4	16	18	0	19	.237	.318	.355	79	-4	0	.956	4	110	169	O39L/1		-0.4
	Chi N	96	357	59	104	17	1	27	83	37	3	47	.291	.363	.571	151	24	0	.981	1	95	127	O96L		1.7
	Year	138	509	81	140	23	1	31	99	55	3	66	.275	.349	.507	129	19	0	.972	4	100	140	O135L/1		1.3
1950	Chi N★	145	540	85	148	32	2	32	103	60	3	67	.274	.350	.519	127	20	1	.965	-4	85	125	O125L,1b18		0.6
1951	Chi N	141	525	77	138	19	4	30	89	45	3	77	.263	.325	.486	113	7	2-1	.981	8	102	**165**	O132(131/0/1)		0.6
1952	Chi N★	151	567	89	153	31	3	**37**	**121**	77	4	92	.270	.361	.531	143	33	1-2	.983	10	107	147	O151L		3.1
1953	Chi N	108	395	61	104	16	5	19	60	50	2	56	.263	.349	.473	109	5	0-0	.970	-1	106	59	O105(42/0/64)		0.0
1954	Chi N	142	520	98	150	18	1	41	103	70	6	68	.288	.375	.563	140	30	2-1	.963	-3	103	64	O141(9/0/140)		2.2
1955	Chi N	79	261	29	55	8	1	12	28	26-0	2	47	.211	.286	.387	77	-9	0-0	.984	0	100	88	O68(67/0/1)		-1.3
1957	NY N	127	378	46	98	14	1	26	76	49-2	5	31	.259	.343	.508	126	13	1-0	1.000	-1	90	97	O37(35/0/2)		0.4
1958	SF N	88	236	27	59	8	0	12	46	35-2	4	37	.250	.354	.436	111	4	0-0	.950	-4	86	72	O67L		0.0
1959	SF N	13	15	1	1	0	0	1	1	0-0	0	7	.067	.067	.267	-17	-3	0-0	—	-0	0	0	/OL		-0.3
Total	15	1399	4796	709	1278	200	19	288	876	561-7	34	714	.266	.347	.496	123	149	11-4	.974	10	98	110	O1228(1029/0/208),1b38		7.8

SAUNDERS, DOUG   Douglas Long   B12.13.1969 Yorba Linda CA   BR/TR/6-0/172   [NYN88 3/78]   d6.13

| 1993 | NY N | 28 | 67 | 8 | 14 | 2 | 0 | 0 | 0 | 3-0 | 0 | 4 | .209 | .243 | .239 | 30 | -7 | 0-0 | .956 | 2 | 107 | 178 | 2b22,3b4/S | | -0.4 |

SAUNDERS, RUSTY   Russell Collier   B3.12.1906 Trenton NJ   D11.24.1967 Trenton NJ   BR/TR/6-2/205   d9.24

| 1927 | Phi A | 5 | 15 | 2 | 2 | 1 | 0 | 0 | 2 | 3 | 0 | 2 | .133 | .278 | .200 | 24 | -2 | 0-0 | .818 | -0 | 78 | 205 | O4L | | -0.2 |

SAUTER, AL   Albert C.   B9.2.1868 Philadelphia PA   D7.15.1928 Ocean City NJ   d9.8

| 1890 | Phi AA | 14 | 41 | 4 | 4 | 0 | 0 | 0 | 0 | 11 | 0 | | .098 | .288 | .098 | 14 | -4 | 0 | .850 | -3 | 87 | 0 | 3b11,O2C,2b2 | | -0.6 |

SAVAGE, DON   Donald Anthony   B3.5.1919 Bloomfield NJ   D12.25.1961 Montclair NJ   BR/TR/6-0/180   d4.18   Col Rutgers

1944	NY A	71	239	31	63	7	5	4	24	20	1	41	.264	.323	.385	98	-1	1-1	.946	-8	84	100	3b60		-1.0
1945	NY A	34	58	5	13	1	0	0	3	3	0	14	.224	.262	.241	44	-4	1-0	.891	0	103	135	3b14,O2L		-0.4
Total	2	105	297	36	76	8	5	4	27	23	1	55	.256	.312	.357	88	-5	2-1	.935	-8	87	106	3b74,O2L		-1.4

SAVAGE, JIMMIE   James Harold   B8.29.1883 Southington CT   D6.26.1940 New Castle PA   BB/TR/5-5/150   d9.3   Col Villanova

1912	Phi N	2	3	1	0	0	0	0	0	1	0	0	.000	.250	.000	-27	-1	0	.750	-0	99	0	/2		-0.1
1914	Pit F	132	479	81	136	9	9	1	26	67	0	32	.284	.372	.347	97	-7	17	.963	-4	103	108	O93(22/5/66),3b29,S11,2b3		-1.4
1915	Pit F	14	21	0	3	0	0	0	0	1	0	0	.143	.182	.143	-8	-3	0	1.000	1	113	0	O3R/3		-0.5
Total	3	148	503	82	139	9	9	1	26	69	0	32	.276	.364	.336	92	-11	17	.964	-5	103	105	O96(22/5/69),3b30,S11,2b4		-2.0

SAVAGE, TED   Theodore Edmund (b Ephesian Savage)   B2.21.1936 Venice IL   BR/TR/6-1/185*   d4.9   Col Lincoln Missouri

1962	Phi N	127	335	54	89	11	2	7	39	40-0	2	66	.266	.345	.373	96	-1	16-5	.974	4	114	63	O109(92/12/10)		-0.1
1963	Pit N	85	149	22	29	2	1	5	14	14-1	1	31	.195	.268	.322	69	-6	4-3	.943	-1	81	147	O47(36/9/2)	30	-1.0
1965	StL N	30	63	7	10	3	0	1	4	6-1	0	9	.159	.232	.254	34	-5	1-1	.938	-1	96	88	O20R		-0.8
1966	StL N	16	29	4	5	2	1	0	3	4-0	0	7	.172	.273	.310	61	-1	4-0	1.000	0	80	0	O7(0/2/5)		-0.2
1967	StL N	9	8	1	1	0	0	0	0	1-0	0	3	.125	.222	.125	2	-1	0-0	—	0			/H		-0.1
	Chi N	96	225	40	49	10	1	5	33	40-6	5	54	.218	.346	.338	93	0	7-6	.979	-0	98	104	O86(0/23/66)/3		-0.5
	Year	105	233	41	50	10	1	5	33	41-6	5	57	.215	.342	.330	90	-1	7-6	.979	-0	98	104	O86(0/23/66)/3		-0.6
1968	Chi N	3	8	0	2	0	0	0	0	0-0	0	1	.250	.250	.250	47	-1	0-1	1.000	-0	79	0	O2(0/1/2)		-0.2
	LA N	61	126	7	26	6	1	2	7	10-0	1	20	.206	.270	.317	82	-3	1-2	.985	4	122	185	O39(18/0/24)		-0.2
	Year	64	134	7	28	6	1	2	7	10-0	1	21	.209	.269	.313	80	-4	1-3	.986	4	119	174	O41(18/1/26)		-0.4
1969	Cin N	68	110	20	25	7	0	2	11	20-0	0	27	.227	.344	.345	90	-1	3-0	.983	1	116	0	O42(28/12/4)/2		0.0
1970	Mil A	114	276	43	77	10	5	12	50	57-1	2	44	.279	.402	.482	144	19	10-6	.953	-6	87	66	O92(34/22/33)/1		1.0
1971	Mil A	14	17	2	3	0	0	0	1	5-0	0	4	.176	.364	.176	58	-1	0-0	1.000	-0	87	0	O6(6/0/1)		-0.1
	KC A	19	29	2	5	0	0	0	2	3-0	0	6	.172	.250	.172	22	-3	2-0	1.000	0	36	539	O9(5/1/3)	37	-0.3
	Year	33	46	2	8	0	0	0	3	8-0	0	10	.174	.296	.174	36	-4	3-0	1.000	-0	51	380	O15(11/0/6)	67	-0.4
Total	9	642	1375	202	321	51	11	34	163	200-9	11	272	.233	.334	.361	95	-4	49-24	.970	-1	100	93	O449(219/81/172)/123	67	-2.5

SAVERINE, BOB   Robert Paul "Rabbit"   B6.2.1941 Norwalk CT   BB/TR/5-9/165*   d9.12

1959	Bal A	1	0	1	0	0	0	0	0	0-0	0		—	—	—	0	0	0-0	—	0			/R		0.0
1962	Bal A	8	21	2	5	2	0	0	3	1-0	0	3	.238	.273	.333	66	-1	0-2	1.000	0	113	79	2b7		-0.1
1963	Bal A	115	167	21	39	1	2	1	12	25-0	0	44	.234	.332	.281	77	-5	8-3	.976	0	91	86	O59(1/58/0),2b19,S13		-0.1

YEAR	TM LG	G	AB	R	H	2B	3B	HR	RBI	BB-IB	HP	SO	AVG	OBP	SLG	AOPS	ABR	SB-CS	FA	FR	RNG	THR	GAMES AT POSITION	DL	BFW
1964	Bal A	46	34	14	5	1	0	0	0	3-0	0	6	.147	.216	.176	11	-4	3-1	1.000	-4	77	26	S15,O2C		-0.7
1966	Was A	120	406	54	102	10	4	5	24	27-1	2	62	.251	.300	.333	83	-10	4-3	.972	-5	98	87	2b70,3b26,S11,O9(5/0/4)		-1.0
1967	Was A	89	233	22	55	13	0	0	8	17-1	0	34	.236	.287	.292	75	-7	8-0	.957	-12	94	95	2b48,S10,3b8,O2L		-1.5
Total	6	379	861	114	206	27	6	6	47	73-2	2	149	.239	.299	.299	88	-27	23-9	.971	-19	97	88	2b144,O72(8/60/4),S49,3b34		-3.4

SAWATSKI, CARL   Carl Ernest "Swats"   B11.4.1927 Shickshinny PA   D11.24.1991 Little Rock AR   BL/TR/5-10/210(205-220)   d9.29   Mil 1951-52

YEAR	TM LG	G	AB	R	H	2B	3B	HR	RBI	BB-IB	HP	SO	AVG	OBP	SLG	AOPS	ABR	SB-CS	FA	FR	RNG	THR	GAMES AT POSITION	DL	BFW
1948	Chi N	2	2	0	0	0	0	0	0	0-0	0	0	.000	.000	.000	-99	-1	0					/H		-0.1
1950	Chi N	38	103	4	18	1	0	1	7	11	0	19	.175	.254	.214	25	-11	0	.983	-1	64	165	C32		-1.1
1953	Chi N	43	59	5	13	3	0	1	5	7	0	7	.220	.303	.322	62	-3	0-0	.943	-1	88	114	C15		-0.4
1954	Chi A	43	109	6	20	3	3	1	12	15	0	20	.183	.276	.294	56	-7	0-0	.987	1	108	123	C33		-0.5
1957	†Mil N	58	105	13	25	4	0	6	17	10-2	2	15	.238	.316	.448	110	1	0-0	.986	4	100	153	C28		0.6
1958	Mil N	10	10	1	1	0	0	0	1	2-0	0	5	.100	.231	.100	-3	-1	0-0	1.000	1	0	280	C3		-0.1
	Phi N.	60	183	12	42	4	1	5	12	16-4	3	42	.230	.300	.344	72	-8	0-0	.986	-4	89	65	C56		-1.0
	Year	70	193	13	43	4	1	5	13	18-4	3	47	.223	.296	.332	68	-9	0-0	.987	-3	86	72	C56		-1.1
1959	Phi N	74	198	15	58	10	0	9	43	32-11	1	36	.293	.392	.480	129	10	0-0	.993	-6	70	116	C67		0.5
1960	StL N	78	179	16	41	4	0	6	27	22-2	0	24	.229	.310	.352	75	-6	0-0	.993	-6	92	92	C67		0.2
1961	StL N	86	174	23	52	8	0	10	33	25-7	0	17	.299	.385	.517	125	7	0-0	.996	-3	56	83	C60/OC		0.6
1962	StL N	85	222	26	56	9	1	13	42	36-5	0	38	.252	.351	.477	111	4	0-0	.997	1	102	69	C70		0.8
1963	StL N	56	105	12	25	0	0	6	14	15-7	0	14	.238	.333	.410	103	1	2-0	.986	-4	53	112	C27		-0.2
Total	11	633	1449	133	351	46	5	58	213	191-38	6	251	.242	.330	.401	92	-14	2-0	.988	-9	87	102	C457/OC		-0.7

SAWYER, CARL   Carl Everett "Huck"   B10.19.1890 Seattle WA   D1.17.1957 Los Angeles CA   BR/TR/5-11/160   d9.11

YEAR	TM LG	G	AB	R	H	2B	3B	HR	RBI	BB-IB	HP	SO	AVG	OBP	SLG	AOPS	ABR	SB-CS	FA	FR	RNG	THR	GAMES AT POSITION	DL	BFW
1915	Was A	10	32	8	8	1	0	0	3	4	1	5	.250	.351	.281	88	0	2	.964	-2	96	96	2b6,S4		-0.2
1916	Was A	16	31	3	6	1	0	0	2	4	1	4	.194	.306	.226	60	-1	3	.963	-0	91	151	2b6,S5/3		-0.1
Total	2	26	63	11	14	2	0	0	5	8	2	9	.222	.329	.254	74	-1	5	.964	-2	94	71	2b12,S9/3		-0.3

SAX, DAVE   David John   B9.22.1958 Sacramento CA   BR/TR/6-0/185*   d9.1   b-Steve

YEAR	TM LG	G	AB	R	H	2B	3B	HR	RBI	BB-IB	HP	SO	AVG	OBP	SLG	AOPS	ABR	SB-CS	FA	FR	RNG	THR	GAMES AT POSITION	DL	BFW
1982	LA N	2	2	0	0	0	0	0	0	0-0	0	0	.000	.000	.000	-99	-1	0-0	1.000	0	454	0	/OL		0.0
1983	LA N	7	8	0	0	0	0	0	1	0-0	0	0	.000	.000	.000	-99	-2	0-0	.917	-1	30	0	C4		-0.3
1985	Bos A	22	36	2	11	3	0	0	6	3-0	0	3	.306	.350	.389	100	0	0-1	.985	-4	52	28	C16,O4(2/0/2)		-0.3
1986	Bos A	4	11	1	5	1	0	1	1	0-0	0	1	.455	.455	.818	236	2	0-0	1.000	-0	114	172	C2/1		0.2
1987	Bos A	2	3	0	0	0	0	0	0	0-0	0	1	.000	.000	.000	-97	-1	0-0	1.000	1	0	0	C2		0.0
Total	5	37	60	3	16	4	0	1	8	3-0	0	5	.267	.297	.383	84	-2	0-1	.980	-4	55	41	C24,O5(3/0/2)/1		-0.4

SAX, OLLIE   Erik Oliver   B11.5.1904 Branford CT   D3.21.1982 Newark NJ   BR/TR/5-8/164   d4.13

YEAR	TM LG	G	AB	R	H	2B	3B	HR	RBI	BB-IB	HP	SO	AVG	OBP	SLG	AOPS	ABR	SB-CS	FA	FR	RNG	THR	GAMES AT POSITION	DL	BFW
1928	StL A	16	17	4	3	0	0	0	0	5	0	4	.176	.364	.176	45	-1	0-0	.955	2	138	210	3b9		0.1

SAX, STEVE   Stephen Louis   B1.29.1960 Sacramento CA   BR/TR/5-11/185(175-189)   [LAN78 9/229]   d8.18   b-Dave

YEAR	TM LG	G	AB	R	H	2B	3B	HR	RBI	BB-IB	HP	SO	AVG	OBP	SLG	AOPS	ABR	SB-CS	FA	FR	RNG	THR	GAMES AT POSITION	DL	BFW
1981	†LA N	31	119	15	33	2	0	2	9	7-1	0	14	.277	.317	.345	92	-2	5-7	.975	4	108	135	2b29		0.3
1982	LA N★	150	638	88	180	23	7	4	47	49-1	2	53	.282	.335	.359	97	-3	49-19	.977	3	103	96	2b149		1.3
1983	†LA N	155	623	94	175	18	5	5	41	58-3	1	73	.281	.342	.350	92	-6	56-30	.961	-19	90	80	2b152		-1.5
1984	LA N	145	569	70	138	24	4	1	35	47-3	1	53	.243	.300	.304	71	-22	34-19	.973	23	109	112	2b135/3	15	1.0
1985	†LA N	136	488	62	136	8	4	1	42	54-12	3	43	.279	.352	.318	91	-5	27-11	.969	-5	94	103	2b135/3		4.9
1986	LA N★	157	633	91	210	43	4	6	56	59-5	3	58	.332	.390	.441	138	35	40-17	.980	2	96	74	2b154		0.5
1987	LA N	157	610	84	171	22	7	6	46	44-5	3	61	.280	.331	.369	88	-12	37-11	.982	4	95	96	2b152/3OL		-1.6
1988	†LA N	160	632	70	175	19	4	5	57	45-6	1	51	.277	.325	.343	90	-1	42-12	.981	-19	92	81	2b158		2.1
1989	NY A★	158	651	88	205	26	3	5	63	52-2	1	44	.315	.364	.387	113	12	43-17	.987	1	103	107	2b158		-1.3
1990	NY A★	155	615	70	160	24	2	4	42	49-3	4	46	.260	.316	.325	80	-16	43-9	.987	-7	101	93	2b154		1.3
1991	NY A	158	652	85	198	38	2	10	56	41-2	3	38	.304	.345	.414	109	8	31-11	.990	-2	100	104	2b149,3b5,D4		-4.4
1992	Chi A	143	567	74	134	26	4	4	47	43-4	2	42	.236	.290	.317	71	-22	30-12	.972	-26	92	78	2b141/D		-1.1
1993	Chi A	57	119	20	28	5	0	1	8	8-0	1	20	.235	.283	.303	58	-7	7-3	1.000	-2	78	0	O32(26/0/6),D21/2	95	0.0
1994	Oak A	7	24	2	6	0	1	0	1	0-0	0	2	.250	.250	.333	53	-2	0-0	1.000	2	111	79	2b6		0.0
Total	14	1769	6940	913	1949	278	47	54	550	556-47	24	584	.281	.335	.358	95	-47	444-178	.978	-39	98	94	2b1679,O33(27/0/6),D26,3b7	110	1.5

SAY, JIMMY   James I.   B1862 Baltimore MD   D6.23.1894 Baltimore MD   d7.22   b-Lou

YEAR	TM LG	G	AB	R	H	2B	3B	HR	RBI	BB-IB	HP	SO	AVG	OBP	SLG	AOPS	ABR	SB-CS	FA	FR	RNG	THR	GAMES AT POSITION	DL	BFW
1882	Lou AA	1	4	1	1	0	0	0				0	.250	.250	.250	73	0		.333	-1	0	0	/3		-0.1
	Phi AA	22	82	12	17	2	0	1				1	.207	.217	.268	59	-4		.884	4	105	200	S22		0.1
	Year	23	86	13	18	2	0	1				1	.209	.218	.267	59	-4		.884	3	105	200	S22/3		0.0
1884	Wil U	16	59	3	13	1	2	0				1	.220	.233	.305	60	-5		.733	-3	75	116	3b16		-0.7
	KC U	2	8	0	2	0	0	0				0	.250	.250	.250	60	-1		.200	-2	0	0	3b2		-0.9
	Year	18	67	3	15	1	2	0				1	.224	.235	.299	60	-6		.680	-4	72	106	3b18		0.1
1887	Cle AA	16	64	9	24	5	3	0	12			3	.375	.385	.547	163	5	0	.714	-4	85	109	3b16		-0.8
Total	3	57	217	25	57	8	5	1	12			3	.263	.273	.359	91	-5		.690	-6	76	104	3b35,S22		-0.8

SAY, LOU   Louis I.   B2.4.1854 Baltimore MD   D6.5.1930 Fallston MD   BR/TR/5-7/145   d4.14   b-Jimmy

YEAR	TM LG	G	AB	R	H	2B	3B	HR	RBI	BB-IB	HP	SO	AVG	OBP	SLG	AOPS	ABR	SB-CS	FA	FR	RNG	THR	GAMES AT POSITION	DL	BFW
1873	Mar NA	3	12	1	2	0	0	0	2	0			.167	.167	.167	-1	-1	0-0	.667	0	0	0	S2/OR		-0.1
1874	Bal NA	18	66	4	14	3	0	0	5	0		1	.212	.212	.258	50	-3	0-0	.786	6	140	0	S18		0.2
1875	Was NA	11	38	4	10	0	0	0	2	0		7	.263	.263	.263	87	0	0-0	.698	-3	104	0	S8,2b2/OC		-0.3
1880	Cin N	48	191	14	38	8	1	0	15	4		31	.199	.215	.251	58	-8		.832	-4	101	76	S48		-0.9
1882	Phi AA	49	199	35	45	4	3	1	28	8			.226	.256	.291	79	-5		.867	3	107	56	S49		0.1
1883	Bal AA	74	324	52	83	13	2	1	10				.256	.278	.318	89	-4		.794	3	113	70	S74		0.1
1884	Bal U	78	339	65	81	14	2	2	11				.239	.263	.310	66	-24		.795	-2	100	119	S78		-2.1
	KC U	17	70	6	14	2	0	1	2				.200	.222	.271	56	-6		.860	7	134	91	S16/2		0.1
	Year	95	409	71	95	16	2	3	13				.232	.256	.303	65	-30		.808	5	106	114	S94/2		-2.0
Total	3 NA	32	116	9	26	3	0	0	9	0			.224	.224	.250	57	-4	0-0	.750	3	127	0	S28,2b2,O2(0/1/1)		-0.2
Total	4	266	1123	172	261	41	8	5	43	35		31	.232	.256	.297	73	-47		.820	8	107	84	S265/2		-2.8

SCALA, JERRY   Gerard Michael   B9.27.1924 Bayonne NJ   D12.14.1993 Fallston MD   BL/TR/5-11/178*   d4.22

YEAR	TM LG	G	AB	R	H	2B	3B	HR	RBI	BB-IB	HP	SO	AVG	OBP	SLG	AOPS	ABR	SB-CS	FA	FR	RNG	THR	GAMES AT POSITION	DL	BFW
1948	Chi A	3	6	1	0	0	0	0	0	0-0	0	3	.000	.000	.000	-99	-2	0-0	1.000	0	135	0	O2C		-0.2
1949	Chi A	37	120	17	30	7	1	1	13	17	1	19	.250	.348	.350	88	-2	3-3	.988	-2	96	45	O37(2/35/0)		-0.5
1950	Chi A	40	67	8	13	2	1	0	6	10	0	10	.194	.299	.254	44	-6	0-0	1.000	1	109	81	O23(1/22/0)		-1.2
Total	3	80	193	26	43	9	2	1	19	27	1	32	.223	.321	.306	67	-10	3-3	.993	-1	101	55	O62(3/59/0)		-1.2

SCALZI, SKEETER   Frank John   B6.16.1913 Lafferty OH   D8.25.1984 Pittsburgh PA   BR/TR/5-6/160   d7.21   Col Alabama

YEAR	TM LG	G	AB	R	H	2B	3B	HR	RBI	BB-IB	HP	SO	AVG	OBP	SLG	AOPS	ABR	SB-CS	FA	FR	RNG	THR	GAMES AT POSITION	DL	BFW
1939	NY N	11	18	3	6	0	0	0	0	3	0	2	.333	.429	.333	106	0	1	.875	1	119	96	S5/3		0.1

SCALZI, JOHNNY   John Anthony   B3.22.1907 Stamford CT   D9.27.1962 Port Chester NY   BR/TR/5-7/170   d6.19   Col Georgetown

YEAR	TM LG	G	AB	R	H	2B	3B	HR	RBI	BB-IB	HP	SO	AVG	OBP	SLG	AOPS	ABR	SB-CS	FA	FR	RNG	THR	GAMES AT POSITION	DL	BFW
1931	Bos N	2	1	0	0	0	0	0	0	0	0	1	.000	.000	.000	-99	0	0	—	0			/H		0.0

SCANLAN, MORT   Mortimer J.   B3.18.1861 Chicago IL   D12.29.1928 Chicago IL   6-1/186   d4.21

YEAR	TM LG	G	AB	R	H	2B	3B	HR	RBI	BB-IB	HP	SO	AVG	OBP	SLG	AOPS	ABR	SB-CS	FA	FR	RNG	THR	GAMES AT POSITION	DL	BFW
1890	NY N	3	10	0	1	0	0	0	0	0	0		.100	.167	.100	-50	-2	1	1.000	-0	0	135	1b3		-0.2

SCANLAN, PATRICK   Patrick J.   B3.25.1861 Halifax NS, Can.   D7.17.1913 Springfield MA   BL/6-0/180   d7.4

YEAR	TM LG	G	AB	R	H	2B	3B	HR	RBI	BB-IB	HP	SO	AVG	OBP	SLG	AOPS	ABR	SB-CS	FA	FR	RNG	THR	GAMES AT POSITION	DL	BFW
1884	Bos U	6	24	2	7	1	0	0	0				.292	.292	.333	90	-1		.800	0	129	0	O6L		-0.1

SCANLON, PAT   James Patrick   B9.23.1952 Minneapolis MN   BL/TR/6-0/170*   [MonN70 5/101]   d9.27

YEAR	TM LG	G	AB	R	H	2B	3B	HR	RBI	BB-IB	HP	SO	AVG	OBP	SLG	AOPS	ABR	SB-CS	FA	FR	RNG	THR	GAMES AT POSITION	DL	BFW
1974	Mon N	2	4	1	1	0	0	0	0	0-0	0	1	.250	.250	.250	38	0	0-0	1.000	0	195	0	/3		0.0
1975	Mon N	60	109	5	20	3	1	2	15	17-3	1	25	.183	.294	.284	58	-6	0-1	.957	1	118	94	3b28/1		-0.5
1976	Mon N	11	27	2	5	1	0	1	2	2-0	0	5	.185	.241	.333	59	-2	0-0	.842	-0	112	0	3b7/1		-0.2
1977	SD N	47	79	9	15	3	0	1	11	12-3	0	20	.190	.297	.266	58	-5	0-0	.957	-2	99	62	3b47,2b15,1b2/OL		-0.6
Total	4	120	219	17	41	7	1	4	28	31-6	1	51	.187	.288	.283	58	-13	0-1	.938	-0	118	77	3b47,2b15,1b2/OL		-1.3

SCARRITT, RUSS   Stephen Russell Mallory   B1.14.1903 Pensacola FL   D12.4.1994 Pensacola FL   BL/TR/5-10.5/165   d4.18   Col Florida

YEAR	TM LG	G	AB	R	H	2B	3B	HR	RBI	BB-IB	HP	SO	AVG	OBP	SLG	AOPS	ABR	SB-CS	FA	FR	RNG	THR	GAMES AT POSITION	DL	BFW
1929	Bos A	151	540	69	159	26	17	1	71	34	1	38	.294	.337	.411	94	-7	13-11	.944	-2	96	111	O145(134/1/10)		-2.0
1930	Bos A	113	447	48	129	17	8	2	48	12	3	49	.289	.312	.376	76	-18	4-7	.967	-0	107	56	O110L		-2.6
1931	Bos A	10	39	2	6	1	0	0	1	2	0	2	.154	.195	.179	-1	-6	0-0	1.000	0	98	135	O9L		-0.6
1932	Phi N	11	11	0	2	0	0	0	0	1	0	2	.182	.250	.182	16	-1	0	1.000	0	135	0	/OL		-0.1
Total	4	285	1037	119	296	44	25	3	120	49	4	91	.285	.320	.385	82	-32	17-18	.956	-2	101	O265(254/1/10)			-5.3

YEAR	TM LG	G	AB	R	H	2B	3B	HR	RBI	BB-IB	HP	SO	AVG	OBP	SLG	AOPS	ABR	SB-CS	FA	FR	RNG	THR	GAMES AT POSITION	DL	BFW

SCARSELLA, LES   Leslie George B11.23.1913 Santa Cruz CA D12.16.1958 San Francisco CA BL/TL/5-11/185   d9.15   Col St. Marys (CA)

1935	Cin N	6	10	4	2	1	0	0	3	0			1	.200	.385	.300	89	0	0	1.000	1	238	130	1b2		0.1
1936	Cin N	115	485	63	152	21	9	3	65	14	2	36	.313	.335	.412	107	2	6	.989	2	108	94	1b115		-0.7
1937	Cin N	110	329	35	81	11	4	3	34	17	1	26	.246	.285	.331	70	-15	5	.984	-3	89	106	1b65,O14(12/0/2)		-2.4
1939	Cin N	16	14	0	2	0	0	0	2	0			2	.143	.143	.143	-23	-2	0	—	0			/H		-0.2
1940	Bos N	18	60	7	18	1	3	0	8	3	1	5	.300	.344	.417	115	1	2	.986	-1	78	137	1b15		-0.2
Total	5	265	898	109	255	34	16	6	109	37	4	70	.284	.315	.378	92	-14	13	.988	-1	101	101	1b197,O14(12/0/2)		-3.4

SCARSONE, STEVE   Steven Wayne B4.11.1966 Anaheim CA BR/TR/6-2/195(170-195) [PhiN86*2/34]   d5.15   Col Santa Ana (CA) JC OF(1/1/0)

1992	Phi N	7	13	1	2	1	0	0	0	0	0	6	.154	.214	.154	-6	-2	0-0	1.000	-2	48	74	2b3		-0.4
	Bal A	11	17	2	3	0	0	0	1	0-0	0	6	.176	.222	.176	13	-2	0-0	.889	-1	54	251	2b5,3b2/S		-0.3
1993	SF N	44	103	16	26	9	0	2	15	4-0	0	32	.252	.278	.398	82	-4	0-2	1.000	-4	73	110	2b20,3b8,1b6	57	-0.7
1994	SF N	52	103	21	28	8	0	2	13	10-1	0	27	.272	.330	.408	96	0	0-2	.990	8	118	176	2b22,3b8,1b6/S		0.7
1995	SF N	80	233	33	62	10	3	11	29	18-0	6	82	.266	.333	.476	113	4	3-2	.927	-6	84	113	3b50,2b13,1b11		-0.2
1996	SF N	105	283	28	62	12	1	5	23	25-0	2	91	.219	.286	.322	62	-16	2-3	.973	-4	91	106	2b74,3b14/1S		-1.7
1997	StL N	5	10	0	1	0	0	0	0	2-0	0	5	.100	.250	.100	-4	-2	1-0	1.000	-3	33	0	2b2,O2(1/1/0)/3		-0.4
1999	KC A	46	68	2	14	5	0	0	6	9-0	1	24	.206	.295	.279	47	-5	1-0	.977	2	123	126	S16,1b12,2b9,3b3,D2		-0.2
Total	7	350	830	103	198	44	4	20	86	70-1	8	266	.239	.302	.373	79	-26	7-8	.975	-10	91	120	S16,1b12,2b9,3b3,D2,O2L	57	-3.2

SCHAAL, PAUL   Paul B3.3.1943 Pittsburgh PA BR/TR/5-11/180(165-185)   d9.3

1964	LA A	17	32	3	4	0	0	0	0	2-0	0	5	.125	.176	.125	-16	-5	0-1	1.000	-0	155	151	2b9,3b9		-0.6
1965	Cal A	155	483	48	108	12	3	9	45	61-8	1	88	.224	.310	.313	80	-12	6-3	.970	-12	100	67	3b153/2		-2.6
1966	Cal A	138	386	59	94	15	7	6	24	68-0	5	56	.244	.362	.365	113	10	6-4	.948	-3	104	99	3b131		0.7
1967	Cal A	99	272	31	51	9	1	6	20	38-3	1	39	.188	.286	.294	76	-3	2-2	.970	-1	98	74	3b88,S2/2		-1.0
1968	Cal A	60	219	22	46	7	1	2	16	29-0	2	25	.210	.307	.279	81	-4	5-7	.958	12	123	132	3b58	94	0.7
1969	KC A	61	205	22	54	6	0	1	13	25-2	2	27	.263	.346	.307	84	-3	2-1	.897	-16	81	33	3b49,2b6,S6		-2.0
1970	KC A	124	380	50	102	12	3	5	35	43-1	1	39	.268	.343	.355	93	-3	7-4	.938	-17	87	64	3b97,S10,2b6		-2.0
1971	KC A	161	548	80	150	31	6	11	63	103-5	2	51	.274	.387	.412	129	26	7-5	.940	-8	101	95	3b161		1.8
1972	KC A	127	435	47	99	19	3	6	41	61-1	2	59	.228	.323	.326	95	-1	1-3	.947	-11	97	67	3b123/S		-1.6
1973	KC A	121	396	61	114	14	3	8	42	63-0	5	45	.288	.389	.399	115	11	5-6	.913	-10	100	57	3b121	17	-0.1
1974	KC A	12	34	3	6	2	0	1	4	5-0	1	5	.176	.286	.324	75	-1	0-0	.949	1	109	161	3b12		-0.1
	Cal A	53	165	10	41	5	0	2	20	18-1	0	24	.248	.322	.315	89	-2	2-2	.903	-9	79	87	3b51		0.0
	Year	65	199	13	47	7	0	3	24	23-1	1	32	.236	.316	.317	86	-3	2-2	.914	-8	85	102	3b63		-1.2
Total	11	1128	3555	436	869	132	26	57	323	516-21	22	466	.244	.341	.344	98	8	43-38	.943	-75	99	78	3b1053,2b23,S19	111	-7.9

SCHAEFER, GERMANY   Herman A. B2.4.1877 Chicago IL D5.16.1919 Saranac Lake NY BR/TR/5-9/175   d10.5   C1   OF(18/13/46)

1901	Chi N	2	5	0	3	1	0	0	2	0				.600	.714	.800	352	2	0	1.000	0	77	318	/23		0.2
1902	Chi N	81	291	32	57	2	3	0	14	19	2			.196	.250	.223	48	-18	12	.864	-12	93	116	3b75,1b3,O2R/S		-3.0
1905	Det A	153	554	64	135	17	9	2	47	45	1			.244	.302	.318	96	-3	19	.955	9	96	87	2b151,S3		0.8
1906	Det A	124	446	48	106	14	3	2	42	32	1			.238	.290	.296	81	-10	31	.948	7	101	100	2b114,S7		-0.1
1907	†Det A	109	372	44	96	12	3	1	32	30	0			.258	.313	.315	97	-3	21	.961	-10	90	92	2b74,S18,3b14/OR		-1.1
1908	†Det A	153	584	96	151	20	10	3	52	37	1			.259	.304	.342	106	2	40	.918	-2	103	150	2b86/OR		0.5
1909	Det A	87	280	26	70	12	0	0	22	14	0			.250	.286	.293	79	-7	12	.966	8	114	92	2b66/OR		0.2
	Was A	37	128	13	31	5	1	1	4	6	1			.242	.281	.320	94	-1	2	.941	1	107	144	2b32/3		0.0
	Year	124	408	39	101	17	1	1	26	20	1			.248	.284	.301	84	-8	14	.960	9	112	106	2b118/OR3		0.2
1910	Was A	74	229	27	63	6	1	0	14	25	2			.275	.352	.345	124	7	17	.953	3	108	130	2b35,O26(8/13/5),3b2		1.0
1911	Was A	125	440	73	147	14	7	0	45	57	1			.334	.412	.398	129	20	22	.980	2	105	116	1b108,O7L		1.8
1912	Was A	60	166	21	41	7	3	0	19	23	1			.247	.342	.325	90	-1	11	.900	-7	74	221	O19R,1b15,2b15/P		-0.9
1913	Was A	54	100	17	32	1	1	0	7	15	2	12		.320	.419	.350	123	4	6	.926	-3	91	110	2b16,1b6,3b2/POR		0.1
1914	Was A	30	29	6	7	1	0	0	2	3	0			.241	.313	.276	74	-1	4-1	1.000	0	45	0	2b3,O3R		0.0
1915	New F	59	154	26	33	5	3	0	8	25	1	11		.214	.328	.286	78	-6	3	.952	-0	76	172	O17(3/0/14),1b13,3b9,2b2		-0.8
1916	NY A	1	1	0	0	0	0	0	0	0				.000	.000	.000	-98	0	0	—	0	0	0	/O		0.0
1918	Cle A	1	5	2	0	0	0	0	0	0				.000	.000	.000	-91	-1	1	1.000	-0	87	0	/2		-0.2
Total	15	1150	3784	495	972	117	48	9	308	333	13	28		.257	.319	.320	96	-14	201-1	.954	-3	99	100	2b588,1b145,3b133,S97,O78R,P2		-1.5

SCHAEFER, JEFF   Jeffrey Scott B5.31.1960 Patchogue NY BR/TR/5-10/170* [BalA81 12/310]   d4.7   Col Maryland-Baltimore Co.

1989	Chi A	15	10	2	1	0	0	0	0	0-0	0	2	.100	.100	.100	-44	-2	1-1	.900	1	130	353	S5,2b4,3b4/D		-0.2
1990	Sea A	55	107	11	22	3	0	0	6	3-0	0	25	.206	.239	.234	33	-10	4-1	.933	6	127	218	3b26,S24,2b3		-0.3
1991	Sea A	84	164	19	41	7	1	1	11	5-0	0	25	.250	.272	.323	64	-7	3-1	.968	-7	81	102	S46,3b30,2b11/D		-1.2
1992	Sea A	65	70	5	8	2	0	1	3	2-0	0	10	.114	.139	.186	-10	-11	0-1	.922	1	107	50	S33,3b21,2b7,D2		-0.9
1994	Oak A	6	8	0	1	0	0	0	0	0-0	0	1	.125	.125	.125	-38	-2	0-0	.800	-1	56	0	S3,S2/1		-0.3
Total	5	225	359	37	73	12	1	2	20	10-0	2	49	.203	.228	.259	35	-34	8-4	.957	-1	91	95	S110,3b84,2b25,D4/1		-2.8

SCHAFER, HARRY   Harry C. "Silk Stocking" B8.14.1846 Philadelphia PA D2.28.1935 Philadelphia PA BR/TR/5-9.5/143   d5.5

1871	Bos NA	31	149	38	42	7	5	0	28	3				.282	.296	.396	94	-2	13-4	.684	3	116	190	3b31		0.1
1872	Bos NA	48	226	51	65	10	4	1	35	0		8		.288	.288	.381	98	-2	3	.792	4	111	145	3b31		0.1
1873	Bos NA	60	296	65	79	12	2	2	42	3		4		.267	.274	.341	75	-11	14-7	.703	-15	67	169	3b47,O13L		-1.9
1874	Bos NA	71	327	69	87	10	2	1	45	1		5		.266	.268	.318	83	-7	2-4	.785	6	105	188	3b71/S		-0.4
1875	Bos NA	52	222	49	64	9	0	0	17	1		8		.288	.291	.329	111	2		.795	3	105	87	3b51/OC		0.3
1876	Bos N	70	286	47	72	11	0	0	35	4		11		.252	.262	.290	82	-5		.810	4	104	122	3b70		0.1
1877	Bos N	33	141	20	39	5	2	0	13	0		7		.277	.277	.340	90	-2		.621	-11	26	0	O23(1/0/22),3b9/S		-1.1
1878	Bos N	2	8	0	1	0	0	0	0	0		1		.125	.125	.125	-16	-1		1.000	-0	0	0	O2R		-1.1
Total	5 NA	262	1220	272	337	48	13	4	167	8		26		.276	.284	.347	90	-20	35-17	.758	0	100	156	3b243,O19(18/1/0),C2/S		-1.8
Total	3	105	435	67	112	16	2	0	48	4		19		.257	.264	.303	83	-8		.810	-4	95	120	3b79,O25(1/0/24)/S		-1.1

SCHAFFER, JIMMIE   Jimmie Ronald B4.5.1936 Limeport PA BR/TR/5-9/185*   d5.20   C10

1961	StL N	68	153	15	39	7	0	1	16	9-1	1	29	.255	.301	.320	59	-9	0-0	.996	0	129	126	C68		-0.6
1962	StL N	70	66	7	16	2	1	0	6	6-0	0	16	.242	.301	.303	58	-4	1-0	.993	-4	122	109	C69		-0.6
1963	Chi N	57	142	17	34	7	0	7	19	11-2	0	35	.239	.294	.437	102	0	0-0	.996	-0	224	127	C54		0.2
1964	Chi N	54	122	9	25	6	1	2	9	17-4	1	17	.205	.307	.320	74	-4	2-4	.970	-6	144	48	C43	30	-1.0
1965	Chi A	17	31	4	6	1	2	0	5	3-0	0	4	.194	.265	.355	79	-1	0-0	1.000	2	177	170	C14		0.2
	NY N	24	37	0	5	2	0	1	3	1-0	0	15	.135	.158	.189	-3	-5	0-0	.968	-2	103	0	C21		-0.7
1966	Phi N	8	15	2	2	1	0	1	4	1-0	0	7	.133	.188	.400	58	-1	0-0	.952	-2	64	157	C6		-0.3
1967	Phi N	2	2	1	0	0	0	0	0	1-1	0	1	.000	.333	.000	3	0	0-0	1.000	0	0	0	/C		0.0
1968	Cin N	4	6	0	1	0	0	0	0	0-0	0	3	.167	.167	.167	-0	-1	0-0	1.000	0	17	0	C2		-0.2
Total	8	304	574	53	128	28	3	11	56	49-8	2	127	.223	.286	.340	69	-25	3-4	.989	-12	153	103	C278	30	-3.0

SCHAIVE, JOHNNY   John Edward B2.25.1934 Springfield IL BR/TR/5-8/175*   d9.19

1958	Was A	7	24	3	6	1	0	1	1-0	0	4		.250	.280	.250	48	-1	0-0	1.000	-1	78	80	2b6		-0.2
1959	Was A	16	59	3	9	2	0	2	0-0	1	7		.153	.167	.186	-3	-8	0-0	.977	2	120	94	2b16		-0.5
1960	Was A	6	12	1	3	0	0	0	0-0	0	3		.250	.250	.333	57	-1	0-0	.917	-1	91	109	2b4		-0.1
1962	Was A	82	225	20	57	15	1	6	29	6-1	0	25	.253	.270	.409	81	-7	0-1	.967	-2	108	82	3b49,2b6		-0.1
1963	Was A	3	3	0	0	0	0	0	0-0	0	1		.000	.000	.000	-99	-1	0-0	—	0			/H		-0.1
Total	5	114	323	25	75	18	1	6	32	7-1	1	40	.232	.249	.350	61	-19	0-1	.967	3	108	82	3b49,2b32		-1.4

SCHALK, ROY   Le Roy John B11.9.1908 Chicago IL D3.11.1990 Gainesville TX BR/TR/5-10/168   d9.17   Mil 1943

1932	NY A	3	12	3	3	1	0	0	0	0		2		.250	.357	.333	84	0		.867	-1	92	55	2b3		-0.1
1944	Chi A	146	587	69	128	19	14	4	44	45	1	52		.218	.276	.262	55	-35	5-4	.964	-10	97	111	2b142,S5		-3.9
1945	Chi A	133	513	50	127	18	1	1	65	32	1	41		.248	.293	.302	75	-17	3-6	.977	10	105	100	2b133		-0.1
Total	3	282	1112	100	259	38	5	2	109	79	2	95		.233	.285	.281	64	-52	8-10	.970	-0	101	105	2b278,S5		-4.1

SCHALK, RAY   Raymond William "Cracker" B8.12.1892 Harvel IL D5.19.1970 Chicago IL BR/TR/5-9/165   d8.11   M2/C2   HF1955

1912	Chi A	23	63	7	18	2	0	0	8	4	4			.286	.357	.317	96	0	2	.917	1	107	109	C23		0.3
1913	Chi A	129	401	38	98	15	5	1	38	27	3	36		.244	.297	.314	80	-11	14	.980	10	129	82	C125		1.0
1914	Chi A	136	392	30	106	13	4	0	36	38	8	24		.270	.347	.314	100	1	24-11	.974	14	128	94	C125		3.0
1915	Chi A	135	413	46	110	14	4	1	54	62	3	21		.266	.366	.327	104	5	15-18	.984	13	173	85	C134		2.8

YEAR	TM LG	G	AB	R	H	2B	3B	HR	RBI	BB-IB	HP	SO	AVG	OBP	SLG	AOPS	ABR	SB-CS	FA	FR	RNG	THR	GAMES AT POSITION	DL	BFW
1916	Chi A	129	410	36	95	12	9	0	41	41	6	31	.232	.311	.305	84	-8	30-13	.988	23	154	73	C124		3.0
1917	†Chi A	140	424	48	96	12	5	2	51	59	7	27	.226	.331	.292	88	-4	19	.981	16	140	95	C139		2.7
1918	Chi A	108	333	35	73	6	3	0	22	36	3	22	.219	.301	.255	67	-13	12	.978	1	124	77	C106		-0.3
1919	†Chi A	131	394	57	111	9	3	0	34	51	2	25	.282	.367	.320	93	-1	11	.981	4	118	95	C129		1.4
1920	Chi A	151	485	64	131	25	5	1	61	68	2	19	.270	.362	.348	89	-5	10-4	.986	6	150	93	C151		1.4
1921	Chi A	128	416	32	105	24	4	0	47	40	7	36	.252	.328	.329	69	-19	3-4	.985	4	87	121	C126		-0.7
1922	Chi A	142	442	57	124	22	3	4	60	67	4	36	.281	.379	.371	97	1	12-4	.989	19	114	121	C142		2.9
1923	Chi A	123	382	42	87	12	2	1	44	39	4	28	.228	.306	.277	55	-25	7-4	.983	1	78	91	C121		-1.5
1924	Chi A	57	153	15	30	4	2	1	11	21	2	10	.196	.301	.268	49	-12	1-5	.959	3	83	128	C56		-0.7
1925	Chi A	125	343	44	94	18	1	0	52	57	3	27	.274	.382	.332	87	-3	11-5	.983	7	186	119	C125		1.1
1926	Chi A	82	226	26	60	9	1	0	32	27	2	11	.265	.349	.314	77	-7	5-1	.977	-2	133	85	C80		0.0
1927	Chi A	16	26	2	6	2	0	0	2	2	1	0	.231	.286	.308	55	-2	0-0	1.000	1	117	139	C15,M		0.0
1928	Chi A	2	1	0	1	0	0	0	1	0	0	0	1.000	1.000	1.000	433	0	1-0	1.000	1	0	0	/CM		0.1
1929	NY N	5	2	0	0	0	0	0	0	0	0	0	.000	.000	.000	-99	-1	0	1.000	1	0	0	/C5		0.0
Total	18	1762	5306	579	1345	199	49	11	594	638	59	355	.253	.340	.316	83	-104	177-69	.981	121	130	96	C1727		16.1

SCHALL, GENE Eugene David B6.5.1970 Abington PA BR/TR/6-3/190(190-206) [PhiN91 4/109] d6.16 Col Villanova

YEAR	TM LG	G	AB	R	H	2B	3B	HR	RBI	BB-IB	HP	SO	AVG	OBP	SLG	AOPS	ABR	SB-CS	FA	FR	RNG	THR	GAMES AT POSITION	DL	BFW
1995	Phi N	24	65	2	15	0	0	5		6-1	1	16	.231	.306	.262	51	-4	0-0	.984	-1	105	87	1b14,O4L		-0.6
1996	Phi N	28	66	7	18	5	1	2	10	12-0	1	15	.273	.392	.470	125	3	0-0	.986	-2	68	118	1b19		0.0
Total	2	52	131	9	33	7	1	2	15	18-1	2	31	.252	.351	.366	89	-1	0-0	.985	-2	84	105	1b33,O4L		-0.6

SCHALLER, BIFF Walter B9.23.1889 Chicago IL D10.9.1939 Emeryville CA BL/TR/5-11/168 d4.30

YEAR	TM LG	G	AB	R	H	2B	3B	HR	RBI	BB-IB	HP	SO	AVG	OBP	SLG	AOPS	ABR	SB-CS	FA	FR	RNG	THR	GAMES AT POSITION	DL	BFW
1911	Det A	40	60	8	8	0	1	1	7	4		1	.133	.200	.217	15	-7	1	1.000	2	126	114	O16(7/9/0)/1		-0.6
1913	Chi A	36	96	12	21	3	0	0	4	20		16	.219	.353	.250	78	-1	5	.918	-5	88	5	O32L		-0.8
Total	2	76	156	20	29	3	1	1	11	24	1	16	.186	.298	.237	54	-8	6	.949	-2	98	31	O48(39/9/0)/1		-1.4

SCHANG, BOBBY Robert Martin B12.7.1886 Wales Center NY D8.29.1966 Sacramento CA BR/TR/5-7/165 d9.23 b-Wally

YEAR	TM LG	G	AB	R	H	2B	3B	HR	RBI	BB-IB	HP	SO	AVG	OBP	SLG	AOPS	ABR	SB-CS	FA	FR	RNG	THR	GAMES AT POSITION	DL	BFW
1914	Pit N	11	35	0	8	1	0	1	1	0	0	10	.229	.229	.314	64	-2	0	.964	-1	107	74	C10		-0.2
1915	Pit N	56	125	13	23	6	3	0	4	14	1	32	.184	.271	.280	68	-5	2-2	.974	-4	81	104	C45		-0.7
	NY N	12	21	1	3	0	0	0	1	4	0	5	.143	.280	.143	31	-2	1	.875	-3	82	73	C6		-0.4
	Year	68	146	14	26	6	3	0	5	18	1	37	.178	.273	.260	63	-6	3-2	.960	-7	81	100	C51		-1.1
1927	StL N	3	5	0	1	0	0	0	0	0	0	0	.200	.200	.200	7	-1	0	1.000	-0	56	0	C3		-0.1
Total	3	82	186	14	35	7	4	0	6	18	1	47	.188	.263	.269	62	-10	3-2	.962	-8	86	93	C64		-1.4

SCHANG, WALLY Walter Henry B8.22.1889 S.Wales NY D3.6.1965 St.Louis MO BB/TR/5-10/180 d5.9 C3 b-Bobby

YEAR	TM LG	G	AB	R	H	2B	3B	HR	RBI	BB-IB	HP	SO	AVG	OBP	SLG	AOPS	ABR	SB-CS	FA	FR	RNG	THR	GAMES AT POSITION	DL	BFW
1913	†Phi A	79	207	32	55	16	3	3	30	34	9	44	.266	.392	.415	139	13	4	.967	-3	111	95	C72		1.6
1914	†Phi A	107	307	44	88	11	8	3	45	32	9	33	.287	.371	.404	138	14	7-7	.956	-6	90	110	C100		1.7
1915	Phi A	116	359	64	89	9	11	1	44	66	14	47	.248	.385	.343	122	14	18-3	.890	-2	99	104	3b43,O41(20/21/0),C26		1.6
1916	Phi A	110	338	41	90	15	8	7	38	38	10	44	.266	.358	.420	140	16	14	.966	-3	100	121	O61(58/3/0),C36		1.1
1917	Phi A	118	316	41	90	14	9	3	36	29	9	24	.285	.362	.415	139	14	6	.956	-10	72	120	C80,3b12,O6(2/0/4)		1.1
1918	†Bos A	88	225	36	55	7	1	0	20	46	2	35	.244	.377	.284	101	4	4	.962	-7	101	73	C57,O16(14/2/0),3b5/S		0.3
1919	Bos A	113	330	43	101	16	3	5	55	71	5	42	.306	.436	.373	136	23	15	.972	-1	98	108	C103		3.1
1920	Bos A	122	387	58	118	30	4	5	51	64	7	37	.305	.413	.450	134	23	7-7	.958	-7	76	92	C73,O40(0/39/1)		1.8
1921	†NY A	134	424	77	134	30	5	6	55	78	5	35	.316	.428	.453	122	19	7-4	.969	-4	101	88	C132		1.9
1922	†NY A	124	408	46	130	21	7	1	53	53	6	36	.319	.405	.412	111	9	12-6	.976	1	135	112	C119		-0.5
1923	†NY A	84	272	39	75	8	2	2	29	27	9	17	.276	.360	.342	84	-6	5-2	.970	-5	120	86	C81		1.0
1924	NY A	114	356	46	104	19	7	5	52	48	4	43	.292	.382	.427	109	5	2-6	.972	2	96	135	C58		-0.4
1925	NY A	73	167	17	40	8	1	2	24	17	0	20	.240	.310	.335	65	-9	2-1	.974	1	126	144	C82,O3L		1.8
1926	StL A	103	285	36	94	19	5	8	50	32	4	20	.330	.405	.516	133	14	5-5	.968	1	126	144	C82,O3L		1.8
1927	StL A	97	264	40	84	15	2	5	42	41	2	33	.318	.414	.447	119	9	3-2	.976	-5	98	147	C75		0.9
1928	StL A	91	245	41	70	10	5	3	39	68	4	26	.286	.448	.404	121	13	8-2	.984	-9	84	74	C82		1.0
1929	StL A	94	249	43	59	10	5	5	36	74	7	22	.237	.424	.378	104	6	1-4	.988	-0	134	89	C85		1.0
1930	Phi A	45	92	16	16	4	1	1	9	17	1	15	.174	.309	.272	47	-7	0-0	.973	1	103	103	C36		-0.4
1931	Det A	30	76	9	14	2	0	0	2	14		11	.184	.311	.211	38	-6	1-0	.965	-1	72	137	C30		-0.5
Total	19	1842	5307	769	1506	264	90	59	710	849	107	573	.284	.393	.401	117	168	121-49	.967	-57	102	107	C1435,O167(97/65/5),3b60/S		20.4

SCHAREIN, ART Arthur Otto "Scoop" B6.30.1905 Decatur IL D7.2.1969 San Antonio TX BR/TR/5-11/155 d7.6 b-George

YEAR	TM LG	G	AB	R	H	2B	3B	HR	RBI	BB-IB	HP	SO	AVG	OBP	SLG	AOPS	ABR	SB-CS	FA	FR	RNG	THR	GAMES AT POSITION	DL	BFW
1932	StL A	81	303	43	92	19	2	0	42	25	3	10	.304	.363	.380	87	-5	4-8	.965	15	114	160	3b77,S3,2b2		1.0
1933	StL A	123	471	49	96	13	3	0	26	41	1	21	.204	.269	.244	35	-45	7-9	.949	16	117	181	3b95,S24,2b7		-2.4
1934	StL A	1	2	0	1	0	0	0	2	0	0	0	.500	.500	.500	146	0	0-0	—		0		/H		0.0
Total	3	205	776	92	189	32	5	0	70	66	4	31	.244	.306	.298	56	-50	11-17	.956	31	116	171	3b172,S27,2b9		-1.4

SCHAREIN, GEORGE George Albert "Tom" B11.21.1914 Decatur IL D12.23.1981 Decatur IL BR/TR/6-1/174 d4.19 b-Art

YEAR	TM LG	G	AB	R	H	2B	3B	HR	RBI	BB-IB	HP	SO	AVG	OBP	SLG	AOPS	ABR	SB-CS	FA	FR	RNG	THR	GAMES AT POSITION	DL	BFW
1937	Phi N	146	511	44	123	20	1	0	57	36	2	47	.241	.293	.284	53	-33	13	.947	8	102	104	S146		-1.4
1938	Phi N	117	390	47	93	16	4	1	29	16	1	33	.238	.268	.308	60	-23	11	.921	-5	96	80	S77,2b39/3		-2.1
1939	Phi N	118	399	35	95	17	1	1	33	13	0	40	.238	.262	.293	50	-29	4	.958	-11	91	83	S117		-3.3
1940	Phi N	7	17	0	5	0	0	0	0	0	0	3	.294	.294	.294	65	-1	0	.839	-2	82	64	S7		-0.2
Total	4	388	1317	126	316	53	6	2	119	65	2	123	.240	.277	.294	54	-86	28	.943	-10	97	91	S347,2b39/3		-7.0

SCHARF, NICK Edward T. B7.18.1858 Baltimore MD D5.11.1937 Baltimore MD TR d5.18

YEAR	TM LG	G	AB	R	H	2B	3B	HR	RBI	BB-IB	HP	SO	AVG	OBP	SLG	AOPS	ABR	SB-CS	FA	FR	RNG	THR	GAMES AT POSITION	DL	BFW
1882	Bal AA	10	39	4	8	1	1	1		0			.205	.205	.359	94	0		.727	-2	44	0	O9(1/7/1)/3		-0.2
1883	Bal AA	3	13	1	2	1	0	0		1			.154	.214	.231	42	-1		.643	-2	62	118	S3		-0.3
Total	2	13	52	5	10	2	1	1		1			.192	.208	.327	79	-1		.727	-4	44	0	O9(1/7/1),S3/3		-0.5

SCHEER, AL Allen George B10.27.1888 Groveport OH D5.6.1959 Logansport IN BL/TR/5-9/165 d8.2

YEAR	TM LG	G	AB	R	H	2B	3B	HR	RBI	BB-IB	HP	SO	AVG	OBP	SLG	AOPS	ABR	SB-CS	FA	FR	RNG	THR	GAMES AT POSITION	DL	BFW
1913	Bro N	6	22	3	5	0	0	0	2	0		4	.227	.227	.227	48	-1	1	.800	-1	45	192	O6R		-0.2
1914	Ind F	120	363	63	111	23	6	3	45	49	5	39	.306	.396	.427	112	4	9	.926	-1	103	91	O102(46/2/54),2b4/S		-0.2
1915	New F	155	546	75	146	25	14	2	60	65	7	38	.267	.353	.375	111	0	31	.971	-4	97	77	O155L		-1.1
Total	3	281	931	141	262	48	20	5	105	116	12	81	.281	.368	.392	110	3	41	.953	-5	98	84	O263(201/2/60),2b4/S		-1.5

SCHEER, HEINIE Henry B7.31.1900 New York NY D3.21.1976 New Haven CT BR/TR/5-8/146 d4.20

YEAR	TM LG	G	AB	R	H	2B	3B	HR	RBI	BB-IB	HP	SO	AVG	OBP	SLG	AOPS	ABR	SB-CS	FA	FR	RNG	THR	GAMES AT POSITION	DL	BFW
1922	Phi A	51	135	10	23	3	0	4	12	3	0	25	.170	.188	.281	21	-17	1-0	.976	6	126	55	2b30,3b10		-0.9
1923	Phi A	69	210	26	50	8	1	2	21	17	2	41	.238	.301	.314	61	-12	3-4	.971	-5	93	92	2b61		-1.6
Total	2	120	345	36	73	11	1	6	33	20	2	66	.212	.259	.301	46	-29	4-4	.973	1	103	80	2b91,3b10		-2.5

SCHEEREN, FRITZ Frederick "Dutch" B9.8.1891 Kokomo IN D6.17.1973 Kittaning PA BR/TR/6-0/180 d9.14 Col Lafayette

YEAR	TM LG	G	AB	R	H	2B	3B	HR	RBI	BB-IB	HP	SO	AVG	OBP	SLG	AOPS	ABR	SB-CS	FA	FR	RNG	THR	GAMES AT POSITION	DL	BFW
1914	Pit N	11	31	4	9	2	1	0	1	2	1	6	.290	.313	.452	132	1	1	.824	-2	95	0	O10(0/4/7)		-0.1
1915	Pit N	4	3	0	0	0	0	0	0	0		0	.000	.000	.000	-99	-1	0	—	-0	0	0	/OC		-0.1
Total	2	15	34	4	9	2	1	0	1	2	1	6	.265	.286	.412	111	0	1	.824	-2	94	0	O11(0/5/7)		-0.2

SCHEFFING, BOB Robert Boden B8.11.1913 Overland MO D10.26.1985 Phoenix AZ BR/TR/6-2/189* d4.27 Mil 1943-45 M6/C5

YEAR	TM LG	G	AB	R	H	2B	3B	HR	RBI	BB-IB	HP	SO	AVG	OBP	SLG	AOPS	ABR	SB-CS	FA	FR	RNG	THR	GAMES AT POSITION	DL	BFW
1941	Chi N	51	132	9	32	6	0	1	20	5	0	19	.242	.270	.326	70	-6	2	.966	-3	91	93	C34		-0.7
1942	Chi N	44	102	7	20	3	0	2	12	7	0	11	.196	.248	.284	58	-6	2	.986	2	111	94	C32		-0.3
1946	Chi N	63	115	8	32	4	1	0	18	12	0	18	.278	.346	.330	94	-1	0	1.000	-3	117	69	C40		-0.8
1947	Chi N	110	363	33	96	11	5	5	50	25	0	25	.264	.312	.364	82	-11	0	.984	-1	111	104	C97		-0.4
1948	Chi N	102	293	23	88	18	2	5	45	22	1	27	.300	.351	.427	114	5	0	.989	-3	94	113	C78		0.7
1949	Chi N	79	268	23	72	3	1	3	19	19		9	.268	.314	.383	88	-3	0	.977	-3	63	115	C40		-0.4
1950	Chi N	12	16	0	3	1	0	0	2			2	.188	.188	.250	14	-2	0	.917	-0	64	0	C3		-0.2
	Cin N	21	47	4	13	0	1	0	7	4	0	4	.277	.333	.404	93	-3	0	1.000	-2	70	45	C11		-0.5
	Year	33	63	4	16	1	1	0	9	4	0	4	.254	.299	.365	74	-3	0	.982	-3	69	36	C14		-0.7
1951	Cin N	47	122	9	31	2	0	2	14	16	1		.254	.345	.320	79	-3	0-0	.976	-4	76	50	C41		-0.5
	StL N	12	18	0	2	0	0	0	2	3	0	2	.111	.238	.111	-3	-3	0-0	1.000	1	119	68	C11		-0.1
	Year	59	140	9	33	2	0	2	16	19	1	14	.236	.331	.293	68	-6	0-0	.980	-3	83	64	C52		-0.6
Total	8	517	1357	105	357	53	9	20	187	103	3	127	.263	.316	.360	86	-31	6-0	.984	-18	96	95	C387		-3.4

YEAR	TM LG	G	AB	R	H	2B	3B	HR	RBI	BB-IB	HP	SO	AVG	OBP	SLG	AOPS	ABR	SB-CS	FA	FR	RNG	THR	GAMES AT POSITION	DL	BFW

SCHEFFLER, TED Theodore J. B4.5.1864 New York NY D2.24.1949 Jamaica NY BR/TR/5-10/160 d8.7

YEAR	TM LG	G	AB	R	H	2B	3B	HR	RBI	BB-IB	HP	SO	AVG	OBP	SLG	AOPS	ABR	SB-CS	FA	FR	RNG	THR	GAMES AT POSITION	DL	BFW
1888	Det N	27	94	17	19	3	1	0	4	9	2	9	.202	.286	.255	73	-2	4	.847	-4	22	120	O27(4/23/0)		-0.8
1890	Roc AA	119	445	111	109	12	6	3	34	78	14		.245	.374	.319	113	14	77	.911	8	**140**	131	O119(2/0/117)/C		1.8
Total	2	146	539	128	128	15	7	3	38	87	16	9	.237	.360	.308	106	12	81	.899	4	118	129	O146(6/23/117)/C		1.0

SCHEIBECK, FRANK Frank S. B6.28.1865 Detroit MI D10.22.1956 Detroit MI BR/TR/5-7/145 d5.9 ▲

YEAR	TM LG	G	AB	R	H	2B	3B	HR	RBI	BB-IB	HP	SO	AVG	OBP	SLG	AOPS	ABR	SB-CS	FA	FR	RNG	THR	GAMES AT POSITION	DL	BFW
1887	Cle AA	3	9	2	2	0	0	0	2		0		.222	.364	.222	67	0	0	.500	-2	84	0	/S3P		-0.1
1888	Det N	1	4	0	0	0	0	0	0		0		.000	.000	.000	-99	-1	0	.500	-1	0	0	/S		-0.2
1890	Tol AA	**134**	485	72	117	13	5	1	49	76	5		.241	.350	.295	88	-5	57	.883	2	95	91	S134		0.1
1894	Pit N	28	102	20	36	2	3	1	10	11	0		.353	.416	.461	112	2	7	.891	-6	71	87	S11,O9(8/1/0),3b3,2b2		-0.3
	Was N	52	196	49	45	4	1	0	17	45	4	24	.230	.384	.281	64	-9	11	.876	-9	119	63	S52		0.2
	Year	80	298	69	81	4	7	1	27	56	4	33	.272	.394	.342	81	-7	18	.878	3	111	67	S63,O9(8/1/0),3b3,2b2		-0.1
1895	Was N	49	172	18	31	5	2	0	25	17	1		.180	.258	.233	27	-19	5	.889	1	101	92	S45,3b2,2b2		-1.3
1899	Was N	27	94	19	27	4	0	0	9	11	1		.287	.368	.351	99	0	5	.877	-6	91	29	S27		-0.4
1901	Cle A	93	329	33	70	11	3	0	38	18	2		.213	.258	.264	47	-24	3	.897	-11	92	70	S92		-2.9
1906	Det A	3	10	1	1	0	0	0	0	2	0		.100	.250	.100	11	-1	0	.889	-0	92	178	2b3		-0.1
Total	8	390	1401	214	329	37	18	2	148	182	13	56	.235	.328	.291	69	-57	88	.884	-14	97	77	S363,O9(8/1/0),2b7,3b6/P		-5.0

SCHEINBLUM, RICHIE Richard Alan B11.5.1942 New York NY BB/TR/6-1/180* d9.1 Col Long Island-C.W.Post

YEAR	TM LG	G	AB	R	H	2B	3B	HR	RBI	BB-IB	HP	SO	AVG	OBP	SLG	AOPS	ABR	SB-CS	FA	FR	RNG	THR	GAMES AT POSITION	DL	BFW
1965	Cle A	4	1	1	0	0	0	0	0	0	0		.000	.000	.000	-99	0	0-0		0			/H		0.0
1967	Cle A	18	66	8	21	4	2	0	6	5-1	0	10	.318	.361	.439	136	3	0-2	.943	-1	109	0	O18R		0.0
1968	Cle A	19	55	3	12	5	0	0	5	0	1	8	.218	.281	.309	85	-1	0-0	1.000	1	140	0	O16(6/0/11)		0.0
1969	Cle A	102	199	13	37	5	1	1	13	19-0	0	30	.186	.253	.236	38	-17	0-2	.974	1	98	132	O50(32/3/15)		-2.0
1971	Was A	27	49	5	7	3	0	0	4	8-0	0	5	.143	.263	.204	35	-4	0-0	.933	4	112	720	O13(7/0/6)		-0.1
1972	KC A★	134	450	60	135	21	4	8	66	58-3	4	40	.300	.383	.418	139	24	0-1	.965	-5	96	71	O119(2/0/119)		1.5
1973	Cin N	29	54	5	12	2	0	1	8	10-1	0	4	.222	.338	.315	87	-1	0-0	.960	0	90	178	O19(1/0/18)		-0.1
	Cal A	77	229	28	75	10	2	3	21	35-6	1	27	.328	.417	.428	149	17	0-0	.969	1	97	93	O54(6/0/49),D7		1.4
1974	Cal A	10	26	1	4	0	0	0	2	1-0	0	2	.154	.185	.154	-2	-4	0-0	.929	0	132	0	O8(4/0/5)/D		-0.4
	KC A	36	83	7	15	2	0	2		8-0	0	1	.181	.253	.205	31	-7	0-1	—	0	0	0	D17,O2L		-0.9
	Year	46	109	8	19	2	0	2	4	9-0	0	10	.174	.237	.193	24	-11	0-1	.929	0	127	0	D18,O10(6/0/5)		-1.3
	StL N	6	6	0	2	0	0	0	0	0-0	0	2	.333	.333	.333	87	0	0-0	—	0	0	0	/H		0.0
Total	8	462	1218	131	320	52	9	13	127	149-11	6	135	.263	.343	.352	103	10	0-6	.965	0	101	104	O299(60/3/241),D25		-0.6

SCHELL, DANNY Clyde Daniel B12.26.1927 Fostoria MI D5.11.1972 Mayville MI BR/TR/6-1/195* d4.13

YEAR	TM LG	G	AB	R	H	2B	3B	HR	RBI	BB-IB	HP	SO	AVG	OBP	SLG	AOPS	ABR	SB-CS	FA	FR	RNG	THR	GAMES AT POSITION	DL	BFW
1954	Phi N	92	272	25	77	14	3	7	33	17	2	31	.283	.327	.434	97	-2	0-3	.974	0	103	89	O69(60/3/6)		-0.6
1955	Phi N	2	2	0	0	0	0	0	0	0			.000	.000	.000	-99	-1	0-0	—	0			/H		-0.1
Total	2	94	274	25	77	14	3	7	33	17-0	2	32	.281	.324	.431	96	-3	0-3	.974	0	103	89	O69(60/3/6)		-0.7

SCHELLHASE, AL Albert Herman "Schelley" B9.13.1864 Evansville IN D1.3.1919 Evansville IN BR/TR/5-8/148 d5.7

YEAR	TM LG	G	AB	R	H	2B	3B	HR	RBI	BB-IB	HP	SO	AVG	OBP	SLG	AOPS	ABR	SB-CS	FA	FR	RNG	THR	GAMES AT POSITION	DL	BFW
1890	Bos N	9	29	1	4	0	0	0	1	0		10	.138	.167	.138	-10	-4	0	.778	-1	253	0	O5R,C2/S3		-0.4
1891	Lou AA	6	16	3	2	0	0	0	1	1	1		.125	.176	.125	-14	-2	2	.929	-1	83	127	C6		-0.3
Total	2	15	45	4	6	0	0	0	1		2	11	.133	.170	.133	-11	-6	2	.909	-2	95	121	C8,O5R/3S		-0.7

SCHEMER, MIKE Michael "Lefty" B11.20.1917 Baltimore MD D4.22.1983 Miami FL BL/TL/6-0/180 d8.8

YEAR	TM LG	G	AB	R	H	2B	3B	HR	RBI	BB-IB	HP	SO	AVG	OBP	SLG	AOPS	ABR	SB-CS	FA	FR	RNG	THR	GAMES AT POSITION	DL	BFW
1945	NY N	31	108	10	36	3	1	1	10	6	0	1	.333	.368	.407	114	2	2	.993	4	145	104	1b27		0.4
1946	NY N	1	1	0	0	0	0	0	0	0			.000	.000	.000	-99	0	0	—	0			/H		0.0
Total	2	32	109	10	36	3	1	1	10	6	0	1	.330	.365	.404	112	2	2	.993	4	145	104	1b27		0.4

SCHENCK, BILL William G. B7.1854 Brooklyn NY D1.29.1934 Brooklyn NY 5-7/171 d5.29 ▲

YEAR	TM LG	G	AB	R	H	2B	3B	HR	RBI	BB-IB	HP	SO	AVG	OBP	SLG	AOPS	ABR	SB-CS	FA	FR	RNG	THR	GAMES AT POSITION	DL	BFW
1882	Lou AA	60	231	37	60	11	3	0		8			.260	.285	.333	114	4		.814	-5	91	73	3b58,S2,P2		0.0
1884	Ric AA	42	151	14	31	4	0	3		1	1		.205	.216	.291	65	-6		.836	-2	104	79	S40,2b2		-0.6
1885	Bro AA	1	4	0	0	0	0	0		0			.000	.000	.000	-99	-1		1.000	0	59	0	/3		-0.1
Total	3	103	386	51	91	15	3	3		9	1		.236	.255	.313	92	-3		.817	-7	90	72	3b59,S42,2b2,P2		-0.7

SCHENZ, HANK Henry Leonard B4.11.1919 New Richmond OH D5.12.1988 Cincinnati OH BR/TR/5-9.5/175* d9.18

YEAR	TM LG	G	AB	R	H	2B	3B	HR	RBI	BB-IB	HP	SO	AVG	OBP	SLG	AOPS	ABR	SB-CS	FA	FR	RNG	THR	GAMES AT POSITION	DL	BFW
1946	Chi N	6	11	0	2	0	0	0	1	0			.182	.182	.182	3	-1	1	1.000	0	98	317	3b5		-0.1
1947	Chi N	7	14	2	1	0	0	0	0	2	1		.071	.235	.071	-16	-2	0	.917	0	130	0	3b5		-0.2
1948	Chi N	96	337	43	88	17	1	1	14	18	4	15	.261	.306	.326	74	-13	3	.974	-1	96	100	2b78,3b5		-1.0
1949	Chi N	7	14	2	6	0	0	0	1	0			.429	.467	.429	146	1	2	1.000	1	132	405	3b5		0.2
1950	Pit N	58	101	17	23	4	2	1	5	6	0	7	.228	.271	.337	57	-7	0	.987	3	107	150	2b21,3b12,S4		-0.3
1951	Pit N	25	61	5	13	1	0	0	3	0	1	2	.213	.226	.230	22	-7	0-2	.961	-1	87	146	2b19,3b2		-0.8
	†NY N	8	0	0	0	0	0	0	0	0			—	—	—	—	0	0-0	—	0			/R		0.0
	Year	33	61	6	13	1	0	0	3	0	1	2	.213	.226	.230	22	-7	0-2	.961	-1	87	146	2b19,3b2		-0.8
Total	6	207	538	70	133	22	3	2	24	27	6	25	.247	.291	.310	63	-29	6-2	.974	2	96	113	2b118,3b34,S4		-2.2

SCHEPNER, JOE Joseph Maurice "Gentleman Joe" B8.10.1895 Aliquippa PA D7.25.1959 Mobile AL BR/TR/5-10/160 d9.11

YEAR	TM LG	G	AB	R	H	2B	3B	HR	RBI	BB-IB	HP	SO	AVG	OBP	SLG	AOPS	ABR	SB-CS	FA	FR	RNG	THR	GAMES AT POSITION	DL	BFW
1919	StL A	14	48	2	10	0	6	1		0		5	.208	.224	.292	43	-4	0	.947	-0	84	121	3b13		-0.4

SCHERBARTH, BOB Robert Elmer B1.18.1926 Milwaukee WI BR/TR/6-0/180 d4.23

YEAR	TM LG	G	AB	R	H	2B	3B	HR	RBI	BB-IB	HP	SO	AVG	OBP	SLG	AOPS	ABR	SB-CS	FA	FR	RNG	THR	GAMES AT POSITION	DL	BFW
1950	Bos A	1	0	0	0	0	0	0	0	0							0	0-0	—	0	0	0	/C		0.0

SCHERER, HARRY Harry d7.24

YEAR	TM LG	G	AB	R	H	2B	3B	HR	RBI	BB-IB	HP	SO	AVG	OBP	SLG	AOPS	ABR	SB-CS	FA	FR	RNG	THR	GAMES AT POSITION	DL	BFW
1889	Lou AA	1	3	0	1	0	0	0		0			.333	.333	.333	92	0	0	.500	-1	0	0	/OC		-0.1

SCHIAPPACASSE, LOU Louis Joseph B3.29.1881 Ann Arbor MI D9.20.1910 Ann Arbor MI BR/TR d9.7

YEAR	TM LG	G	AB	R	H	2B	3B	HR	RBI	BB-IB	HP	SO	AVG	OBP	SLG	AOPS	ABR	SB-CS	FA	FR	RNG	THR	GAMES AT POSITION	DL	BFW
1902	Det A	2	5	0	0	0	0	0	0	1			.000	.167	.000	-50	-1	0	.000	-1	0	0	O2R		-0.2

SCHICK, MORRIE Maurice Francis B4.17.1892 Chicago IL D10.25.1979 Hazel Crest IL BR/TR/5-11/170 d4.15 Mil 1918

YEAR	TM LG	G	AB	R	H	2B	3B	HR	RBI	BB-IB	HP	SO	AVG	OBP	SLG	AOPS	ABR	SB-CS	FA	FR	RNG	THR	GAMES AT POSITION	DL	BFW
1917	Chi N	14	34	3	5	0	0	0	3	3	0	10	.147	.216	.147	11	-4	0	.960	2	103	257	O12(2/10/0)		-0.3

SCHILLING, CHUCK Charles Thomas B10.25.1937 Brooklyn NY BR/TR/5-11/170* d4.11 Col Manhattan

YEAR	TM LG	G	AB	R	H	2B	3B	HR	RBI	BB-IB	HP	SO	AVG	OBP	SLG	AOPS	ABR	SB-CS	FA	FR	RNG	THR	GAMES AT POSITION	DL	BFW
1961	Bos A	158	646	87	167	25	2	5	62	78-0	2	77	.259	.340	.327	77	-19	7-6	**.991**	15	103	105	2b158		0.9
1962	Bos A	119	413	48	95	17	1	7	35	29-5	4	48	.230	.286	.327	63	-22	1-0	.985	7	100	107	2b118	30	-0.5
1963	Bos A	146	576	63	135	25	0	8	33	41-0	5	72	.234	.291	.319	69	-24	3-2	.985	-13	93	85	2b143		-2.5
1964	Bos A	47	163	18	32	6	0	0	7	15-0	0	22	.196	.263	.233	38	-13	0-1	.974	-1	92	73	2b42		-1.2
1965	Bos A	71	171	14	41	3	2	3	9	13-0	0	17	.240	.292	.333	73	-6	0-1	.976	10	118	91	2b41		0.7
Total	5	541	1969	230	470	76	5	23	146	176-5	11	236	.239	.304	.317	68	-84	11-10	.985	18	100	96	2b502	30	-2.6

SCHINDLER, BILL William Gibbons B7.10.1896 Perryville MO D2.6.1979 Perryville MO BR/TR/5-11/160 d9.3

YEAR	TM LG	G	AB	R	H	2B	3B	HR	RBI	BB-IB	HP	SO	AVG	OBP	SLG	AOPS	ABR	SB-CS	FA	FR	RNG	THR	GAMES AT POSITION	DL	BFW
1920	StL N	1	2	0	0	0	0	0	0	0			.000	.000	.000	-99	0	0-0	1.000	-0	0	0	/C		-0.1

SCHIRICK, DUTCH Harry Ernest B6.15.1890 Ruby NY D11.12.1968 Kingston NY BR/TR/5-8/160 d9.17

YEAR	TM LG	G	AB	R	H	2B	3B	HR	RBI	BB-IB	HP	SO	AVG	OBP	SLG	AOPS	ABR	SB-CS	FA	FR	RNG	THR	GAMES AT POSITION	DL	BFW
1914	StL A	1	0	0	0	0	0	0	0	0			—	1.000	—	212	0	2	—	0			/H		0.1

SCHLAFLY, LARRY Harry Fenton B9.19.1878 Port Washington OH D6.27.1919 Beach City OH BR/TR/5-11/182 d9.18 M2

YEAR	TM LG	G	AB	R	H	2B	3B	HR	RBI	BB-IB	HP	SO	AVG	OBP	SLG	AOPS	ABR	SB-CS	FA	FR	RNG	THR	GAMES AT POSITION	DL	BFW
1902	Chi N	10	31	5	10	0	3	0	5	6	0		.323	.432	.516	198	4	2	1.000	-2	0		O5R,2b4,3b2		0.2
1906	Was A	123	426	60	105	13	8	2	30	50	14		.246	.345	.329	117	11	29	.961	16	103	93	2b123		3.1
1907	Was A	24	74	10	10	0	0	1	4	22			.135	.354	.176	75	0	7	.928	-8	68	60	2b24		-0.2
1914	Buf F	51	127	16	33	7	1	2	19	12	3		.260	.338	.378	93	-3	3	.951	1	106	89	2b23,1b7/C3OLM		-0.2
Total	4	208	658	91	158	20	12	5	58	90	20	22	.240	.349	.330	111	12	41	.954	8	98	86	2b174,1b7,O6(1/0/5),3b3/C		2.3

SCHLEI, ADMIRAL George Henry B1.12.1878 Cincinnati OH D1.24.1958 Huntington WV BR/TR/5-8.5/179 d4.24

YEAR	TM LG	G	AB	R	H	2B	3B	HR	RBI	BB-IB	HP	SO	AVG	OBP	SLG	AOPS	ABR	SB-CS	FA	FR	RNG	THR	GAMES AT POSITION	DL	BFW
1904	Cin N	97	291	25	69	8	3	0	32	17	8		.237	.297	.285	74	-9	7	.977	9	107	101	C88		0.9
1905	Cin N	99	314	32	71	8	3	1	36	22	4		.226	.285	.280	62	-15	9	.962	11	101	113	C89,1b6		0.5
1906	Cin N	116	388	44	95	13	6	4	54	29	4		.245	.304	.351	100	-1	7	.961	7	102	108	C91,1b21		1.6
1907	Cin N	84	246	28	67	3	2	0	27	28	0		.272	.347	.301	99	1	5	.980	6	103	117	C67,1b3,O2(1/0/1)		1.4
1908	Cin N	92	300	31	66	6	4	1	22	22	2		.220	.278	.277	79	-7	2	.962	-3	106	94	C88		-0.2
1909	NY N	92	279	25	68	12	0	0	30	40	2		.244	.343	.287	94	0	4	.963	3	113	109	C89		1.3
1910	NY N	55	99	10	19	2	1	0	8	14	2	10	.192	.304	.232	57	-5	4	.986	0	96	106	C49		-0.2

YEAR	TM LG	G	AB	R	H	2B	3B	HR	RBI	BB-IB	HP	SO	AVG	OBP	SLG	AOPS	ABR	SB-CS	FA	FR	RNG	THR	GAMES AT POSITION	DL	BFW
1911	NY N	1	1	0	0	0	0	0	0	0-0	0	1	.000	.000	.000	-97	0	0-0	—	0			/H		0.0
Total	8	636	1918	195	455	52	21	6	209	172	22	11	.237	.307	.296	83	-36	38	.968	33	105	107	C561,1b30,O2(1/0/1)		5.3

SCHLESINGER, RUDY William Cordes B11.5.1941 Cincinnati OH BR/TR/6-2/175 d5.4 Col Cincinnati

YEAR	TM LG	G	AB	R	H	2B	3B	HR	RBI	BB-IB	HP	SO	AVG	OBP	SLG	AOPS	ABR	SB-CS	FA	FR	RNG	THR	GAMES AT POSITION	DL	BFW
1965	Bos A	1	1	0	0	0	0	0	0	0-0	0	0	.000	.000	.000	-94	0	0-0	—	0			/H		0.0

SCHLIEBNER, DUTCH Frederick Paul B5.19.1891 Charlottenburg, Germany D4.15.1975 Toledo OH BR/TR/5-10/180 d4.17

YEAR	TM LG	G	AB	R	H	2B	3B	HR	RBI	BB-IB	HP	SO	AVG	OBP	SLG	AOPS	ABR	SB-CS	FA	FR	RNG	THR	GAMES AT POSITION	DL	BFW
1923	Bro N	19	76	11	19	4	0	0	4	5	0	7	.250	.296	.303	60	-4	1-0	.981	2	165	118	1b19		-0.3
	StL A	127	444	50	122	19	6	4	52	39	4	60	.275	.339	.372	82	-12	3-2	.989	-0	98	110	1b127		-2.0
Total	1	146	520	61	141	23	6	4	56	44	4	67	.271	.333	.362	79	-16	4-2	.988	2	107	111	1b146		-2.3

SCHLUETER, JAY Jay D B7.31.1949 Phoenix AZ BR/TR/6-0/182 d6.18

YEAR	TM LG	G	AB	R	H	2B	3B	HR	RBI	BB-IB	HP	SO	AVG	OBP	SLG	AOPS	ABR	SB-CS	FA	FR	RNG	THR	GAMES AT POSITION	DL	BFW
1971	Hou N	7	3	1	1	0	0	0	0	0-0	0	1	.333	.333	.333	92	0	0-0	1.000	0	278	0	O2L		0.0

SCHLUETER, NORM Norman John "Duke" B9.25.1916 Belleville IL D10.6.2004 Belleville IL BR/TR/5-10/175 d5.28

YEAR	TM LG	G	AB	R	H	2B	3B	HR	RBI	BB-IB	HP	SO	AVG	OBP	SLG	AOPS	ABR	SB-CS	FA	FR	RNG	THR	GAMES AT POSITION	DL	BFW
1938	Chi A	35	118	11	27	5	1	0	7	4	0	15	.229	.254	.288	35	-12	1-0	.952	-2	112	62	C34		-1.1
1939	Chi A	34	56	5	13	2	1	0	8	1	0	11	.232	.246	.304	39	-5	2-0	.988	0	103	23	C32		-0.4
1944	Cle A	49	122	2	15	4	0	0	11	12	0	22	.123	.201	.156	3	-16	0-2	.985	-6	84	50	C43		-2.1
Total	3	118	296	18	55	11	2	0	26	17	0	48	.186	.230	.236	24	-33	3-2	.974	-7	99	49	C109		-3.6

SCHMANDT, RAY Raymond Henry B1.25.1896 St.Louis MO D2.2.1969 St.Louis MO BR/TR/6-1/175 d6.24 Col St.Louis

YEAR	TM LG	G	AB	R	H	2B	3B	HR	RBI	BB-IB	HP	SO	AVG	OBP	SLG	AOPS	ABR	SB-CS	FA	FR	RNG	THR	GAMES AT POSITION	DL	BFW
1915	StL A	3	4	0	0	0	0	0	0	0	0	1	.000	.000	.000	-99	-1	0	1.000	-0	-0	-0	/1		-0.1
1918	Bro N	34	114	11	35	5	4	0	18	7	0	7	.307	.347	.421	134	4	1	.934	-3	92	61	2b34		0.2
1919	Bro N	47	127	8	21	4	0	0	10	4	0	15	.165	.191	.197	16	-13	0	.911	-1	102	93	2b18,1b12,3b6		-1.6
1920	†Bro N	28	63	7	15	2	1	0	7	3	0	4	.238	.273	.302	63	-3	1-1	.995	3	175	159	1b20		-0.1
1921	Bro N	95	350	42	107	8	5	1	43	11	1	22	.306	.329	.366	81	-10	3-4	.989	4	119	106	1b92		-1.7
1922	Bro N	110	396	54	106	17	3	2	44	21	1	28	.268	.306	.341	67	-20	6-6	.989	4	119	106	1b110		-2.2
Total	6	317	1054	122	284	36	13	3	122	46	2	75	.269	.301	.337	72	-43	11-11	.990	4	116	113	1b235,2b52,3b6		-5.5

SCHMEES, GEORGE George Edward "Rocky" B9.6.1924 Cincinnati OH D10.30.1998 San Jose CA BL/TL/6-0/195 d4.15

YEAR	TM LG	G	AB	R	H	2B	3B	HR	RBI	BB-IB	HP	SO	AVG	OBP	SLG	AOPS	ABR	SB-CS	FA	FR	RNG	THR	GAMES AT POSITION	DL	BFW
1952	StL A	34	61	9	8	1	1	0	3	2	0	18	.131	.159	.180	-6	-9	0-0	.932	1	127	90	O19(9/2/8),1b2		-0.9
	Bos A	42	64	8	13	3	0	0	3	10	0	11	.203	.311	.250	53	-4	0-1	1.000	0	97	98	O29(0/18/11),P2,1b2		-0.5
	Year	76	125	17	21	4	1	0	6	12	0	29	.168	.241	.216	26	-13	0-1	.960	1	113	94	O48(9/20/19),1b4,P2		-1.4

SCHMIDT, BOSS Charles B9.12.1880 Coal Hill AR D11.14.1932 Altus AR BB/TR/5-11/200 d4.30 b-Walter

YEAR	TM LG	G	AB	R	H	2B	3B	HR	RBI	BB-IB	HP	SO	AVG	OBP	SLG	AOPS	ABR	SB-CS	FA	FR	RNG	THR	GAMES AT POSITION	DL	BFW
1906	Det A	68	216	13	47	4	3	0	16	6	1		.218	.242	.264	57	-11	1	.958	8	111	116	C67		0.3
1907	†Det A	104	349	32	85	6	6	0	23	5	7		.244	.269	.295	77	-11	8	.944	5	107	103	C103		0.4
1908	†Det A	122	419	45	111	14	3	1	38	16	3		.265	.297	.320	96	-3	5	.951	2	97	119	C121		1.3
1909	†Det A	84	253	21	53	8	2	1	28	7	3		.209	.240	.269	58	-13	7	.955	-6	99	111	C81/OR		-1.2
1910	Det A	71	197	22	51	7	7	1	23	2	3		.259	.277	.381	99	-2	2	.973	-3	99	94	C66		0.0
1911	Det A	28	46	4	13	2	1	0	2	0	1		.283	.298	.370	82	-1	0	1.000	-1	90	95	C9/OR		-0.2
Total	6	477	1480	137	360	41	22	3	124	36	18		.243	.270	.307	79	-41	23	.955	4	102	110	C447,O2R		0.6

SCHMIDT, BUTCH Charles John "Butcher Boy" B7.19.1886 Baltimore MD D9.4.1952 Baltimore MD BL/TL/6-1.5/200 d5.11

YEAR	TM LG	G	AB	R	H	2B	3B	HR	RBI	BB-IB	HP	SO	AVG	OBP	SLG	AOPS	ABR	SB-CS	FA	FR	RNG	THR	GAMES AT POSITION	DL	BFW
1909	NY A	1	2	0	0	0	0	0	0	0	0		.000	.000	.000	-99	-0	0	.500	0	65	0	/P		0.0
1913	Bos N	22	78	6	24	2	1	0	14	2	1	5	.308	.333	.423	113	1	1	.983	1	123	54	1b22		0.1
1914	†Bos N	147	537	67	153	17	9	1	71	43	11	55	.285	.350	.356	111	7	14	.990	2	106	144	1b147		0.6
1915	Bos N	127	458	48	115	26	7	2	60	36	9	59	.251	.318	.352	107	4	3-10	.987	-4	87	119	1b127		-0.6
Total	4	297	1075	119	292	45	18	4	145	81	21	119	.272	.335	.358	109	12	18-10	.988	-1	99	128	1b296/P		0.1

SCHMIDT, DAVE David Frederick B12.22.1956 Mesa AZ BR/TR/6-1/205 [BosA75 2/39] d4.28

YEAR	TM LG	G	AB	R	H	2B	3B	HR	RBI	BB-IB	HP	SO	AVG	OBP	SLG	AOPS	ABR	SB-CS	FA	FR	RNG	THR	GAMES AT POSITION	DL	BFW
1981	Bos A	15	42	6	10	1	2	3	7-0	0		17	.238	.347	.405	109	1	0-0	1.000	-3	109	66	C15		-0.2

SCHMIDT, MIKE Michael Jack B9.27.1949 Dayton OH BR/TR/6-2/203* [PhiN71 2/30] d9.12 HF1995 Col Ohio U.

YEAR	TM LG	G	AB	R	H	2B	3B	HR	RBI	BB-IB	HP	SO	AVG	OBP	SLG	AOPS	ABR	SB-CS	FA	FR	RNG	THR	GAMES AT POSITION	DL	BFW
1972	Phi N	13	34	2	7	0	0	1	3	5-0	1	15	.206	.325	.294	75	-1	0-0	.964	2	114	208	3b11/2		0.1
1973	Phi N	132	367	43	72	11	0	18	52	62-3	9	136	.196	.324	.373	91	-3	8-2	.954	18	112	136	3b125,2b4,1b2,S2	16	1.6
1974	Phi N★	162	568	108	160	28	7	36	116	106-14	4	138	.282	.395	.546	155	44	23-12	.954	28	117	118	3b162		7.3
1975	Phi N	158	562	93	140	34	3	38	95	101-10	4	180	.249	.367	.523	138	30	29-12	.954	19	110	119	3b151,S10		5.9
1976	†Phi N★	160	584	112	153	31	4	38	107	100-8	11	149	.262	.376	.524	149	40	14-9	.961	18	107	109	3b160		6.4
1977	†Phi N★	154	544	114	149	27	11	38	101	104-8	4	122	.274	.393	.574	149	40	15-8	.964	27	119	144	3b149,S2/2		2.8
1978	†Phi N	145	513	93	129	27	2	21	78	91-12	4	103	.251	.364	.435	121	18	19-6	.963	9	106	162	3b139/S		5.6
1979	Phi N	160	541	109	137	25	4	45	114	120-12	3	115	.253	.386	.564	151	41	9-5	.954	17	113	134	3b157,S2		6.8
1980	†Phi N★	150	548	104	157	25	8	48	121	89-10	2	119	.286	.380	.624	167	49	12-5	.946	19	115	135	3b149		7.1
1981	†Phi N★	102	354	78	112	19	2	31	91	73-18	4	71	.316	.435	.644	193	46	12-4	.950	19	109	122	3b148	15	6.3
1982	Phi N★	148	514	108	144	26	3	35	87	107-17	3	131	.280	.403	.547	159	45	14-7	.954	19	109	122	3b148		6.4
1983	†Phi N★	154	534	104	136	16	4	40	109	128-17	1	148	.255	.399	.524	156	45	7-8	.959	22	110	122	3b153,S2		4.7
1984	Phi N★	151	528	93	146	23	3	36	106	92-14	4	116	.277	.383	.536	155	40	5-7	.941	9	112	85	3b145,1b2/S		3.7
1985	Phi N	158	549	89	152	31	5	33	93	87-8	3	117	.277	.375	.532	148	37	1-3	.993	7	122	100	1b106,3b54/S		3.0
1986	Phi N★	160	552	97	160	29	1	37	119	89-25	7	84	.290	.390	.547	151	41	1-2	.980	-8	95	134	3b124,1b35		3.7
1987	Phi N★	147	522	88	153	28	0	35	113	83-15	2	80	.293	.388	.548	141	32	2-1	.971	8	110	122	3b138,1b9,S3	15	3.7
1988	Phi N	108	390	52	97	21	2	12	62	49-10	6	42	.249	.337	.405	111	7	3-0	.939	5	106	89	3b104,1b3	51	1.3
1989	Phi N★	42	148	19	30	7	0	6	28	21-4	0	17	.203	.297	.372	91	-2	0-1	.918	-4	91	118	3b42		-0.6
Total	18	2404	8352	1506	2234	408	59	548	1595	1507-201	79	1883	.267	.380	.527	146	549	174-92	.955	237	111	123	3b2212,1b157,S24,2b6	97	77.3

SCHMIDT, BOB Robert Benjamin B4.22.1933 St.Louis MO BR/TR/6-2/205(190-205) d4.16

YEAR	TM LG	G	AB	R	H	2B	3B	HR	RBI	BB-IB	HP	SO	AVG	OBP	SLG	AOPS	ABR	SB-CS	FA	FR	RNG	THR	GAMES AT POSITION	DL	BFW
1958	SF N☆	127	393	46	96	20	2	14	54	33-5	2	59	.244	.306	.412	90	-6	0-1	.982	-2	113	128	C123		-0.3
1959	SF N	71	181	17	44	7	1	5	20	13-4	1	24	.243	.296	.376	80	-6	0-2	1.000	2	100	116	C70		-0.2
1960	SF N	110	344	31	92	12	1	8	37	26-4	0	51	.267	.317	.378	96	-3	0-3	.981	-2	81	51	C108		-0.1
1961	SF N	2	6	0	1	0	0	0	1	0-0	0	1	.167	.143	.167	-12	-1	0-0	1.000	1	0	227	C2		0.0
	Cin N	27	70	4	9	0	0	1	5	8-1	0	14	.129	.218	.171	5	-10	0-0	.993	-1	55	76	C27		-1.0
	Year	29	76	4	10	0	0	1	5	8-1	0	15	.132	.212	.171	4	-11	0-0	.994	-0	50	89	C29		-1.1
1962	Was A	88	256	28	62	14	0	10	31	14-2	1	37	.242	.281	.414	86	-6	0-0	.997	-1	162	123	C88		-0.4
1963	Was A	9	15	3	3	1	0	0	3	3-0	0	5	.200	.333	.267	71	-0	0-0	1.000	-1	118	0	C6		0.0
1965	NY A	20	40	4	10	1	0	1	3	3-1	0	8	.250	.302	.350	85	-1	0-0	.990	0	118	0	C20		-0.1
Total	7	454	1305	133	317	55	4	39	150	100-17	5	199	.243	.297	.381	84	-33	0-6	.988	-4	109	97	C444		-2.1

SCHMIDT, WALTER Walter Joseph B3.20.1887 Coal Hill AR D7.4.1973 Modesto CA BR/TR/5-9/159 d4.13 b-Boss

YEAR	TM LG	G	AB	R	H	2B	3B	HR	RBI	BB-IB	HP	SO	AVG	OBP	SLG	AOPS	ABR	SB-CS	FA	FR	RNG	THR	GAMES AT POSITION	DL	BFW
1916	Pit N	64	184	16	35	1	2	2	15	10	1	13	.190	.236	.250	49	-12	3	.976	-0	84	115	C57		-0.1
1917	Pit N	72	183	9	45	7	0	0	17	11	2	11	.246	.296	.284	76	-5	4	.978	1	77	132	C61		0.3
1918	Pit N	105	323	31	77	8	7	0	27	17	2	19	.238	.281	.276	68	-13	7	.981	24	160	116	C104		2.2
1919	Pit N	85	267	23	67	9	2	0	29	23	0	9	.251	.310	.300	81	-6	5	.982	5	129	102	C85		0.6
1920	Pit N	94	310	22	86	8	4	0	20	24	4	15	.277	.337	.329	89	-4	9-3	.971	-4	94	94	C92		-0.1
1921	Pit N	114	393	30	111	9	3	0	38	12	2	13	.282	.307	.321	65	-20	10-6	.986	8	138	88	C111		-0.7
1922	Pit N	40	152	21	50	11	1	0	22	1	0	5	.329	.333	.414	91	-2	2-1	.995	-3	92	50	C40		-0.3
1923	Pit N	97	335	39	83	7	2	0	37	22	3	12	.248	.300	.281	53	-23	10-5	.981	-2	117	86	C96		-1.2
1924	Pit N	58	177	16	43	3	2	0	20	13	0	5	.243	.295	.299	59	-11	6-1	.986	4	145	92	C57		0.3
1925	StL N	37	87	9	22	2	1	0	9	4	1	3	.253	.293	.299	51	-7	1-0	.967	5	122	144	C31		0.6
Total	10	766	2411	216	619	63	20	3	234	137	15	105	.257	.301	.303	68	-103	57-16	.980	38	120	100	C734		-0.7

SCHMULBACH, HANK Henry Alrives B1.17.1925 E.St.Louis IL D5.3.2001 Belleville IL BL/TR/5-11/165 d9.27 Mil 1944-46 Col Washington-St.Louis

YEAR	TM LG	G	AB	R	H	2B	3B	HR	RBI	BB-IB	HP	SO	AVG	OBP	SLG	AOPS	ABR	SB-CS	FA	FR	RNG	THR	GAMES AT POSITION	DL	BFW
1943	StL A	1	0	1	0	0	0	0	0	0	0		—	—	—		0	0-0	—	0			/R		0.0

SCHNECK, DAVE David Lee B6.18.1949 Allentown PA BL/TL/5-10/200* d7.14

YEAR	TM LG	G	AB	R	H	2B	3B	HR	RBI	BB-IB	HP	SO	AVG	OBP	SLG	AOPS	ABR	SB-CS	FA	FR	RNG	THR	GAMES AT POSITION	DL	BFW
1972	NY N	37	123	7	23	3	2	3	10	10-2	1	26	.187	.254	.317	62	-7	0-1	.985	-2	97	49	O33(1/17/16)		-1.1
1973	NY N	13	36	2	7	0	1	0	1	1-1	0	4	.194	.216	.250	29	-4	0-0	1.000	1	137	0	O12C		-0.3
1974	NY N	93	254	23	52	11	1	5	24	16-2	1	43	.205	.254	.315	59	-15	4-1	.974	5	109	161	O84(23/59/9)		-1.1
Total	3	143	413	32	82	14	4	8	35	27-5	2	73	.199	.251	.310	57	-26	4-2	.979	5	108	115	O129(24/88/25)		-2.5

SCHNEIDER, BRIAN
Brian Duncan B11.26.1976 Jacksonville FL BL/TR/6-1/200* [MonN95 5/143] d5.26

YEAR	TM LG	G	AB	R	H	2B	3B	HR	RBI	BB-IB	HP	SO	AVG	OBP	SLG	AOPS	ABR	SB-CS	FA	FR	RNG	THR	GAMES AT POSITION	DL	BFW
2000	Mon N	45	115	6	27	6	0	0	11	7-2	0	24	.235	.276	.287	43	-10	0-1	.974	-2	71	111	C43		-1.0
2001	Mon N	27	41	4	13	3	0	1	6	6-1	0	3	.317	.396	.463	125	2	0-0	1.000	3	136	148	C14		0.5
2002	Mon N	73	207	21	57	19	2	5	29	21-8	0	41	.275	.339	.459	106	1	1-2	.993	3	129	130	C65,O2(1/0/1)		0.8
2003	Mon N	108	335	34	77	26	1	9	46	37-8	2	75	.230	.309	.394	80	-10	0-2	.996	24	195	127	C98,D2		2.0
2004	Mon N	135	436	40	112	20	3	12	49	42-10	1	83	.257	.325	.399	83	-11	0-1	.998	15	185	138	C133		1.1
2005	Was N	116	369	38	99	20	1	10	44	29-7	6	48	.268	.330	.409	99	-1	1-0	.993	5	117	147	C113		1.2
Total	6	504	1503	143	385	94	7	37	185	142-36	11	254	.256	.323	.402	87	-29	2-6	.994	48	153	135	C466,D2,O2(1/0/1)		4.6

SCHOENDIENST, RED
Albert Fred B2.2.1923 Germantown IL BB/TR/6-0/170* d4.17 M14/C17 HF1989

YEAR	TM LG	G	AB	R	H	2B	3B	HR	RBI	BB-IB	HP	SO	AVG	OBP	SLG	AOPS	ABR	SB-CS	FA	FR	RNG	THR	GAMES AT POSITION	DL	BFW
1945	StL N	137	565	89	157	22	6	1	47	21	1	17	.278	.305	.343	78	-19	26	.983	1	105	110	O118L,S10/2		-2.5
1946	†StL N★	142	606	94	170	28	5	0	34	37	0	27	.281	.322	.343	85	-13	12	.984	2	98	121	2b128,3b12,S4		-0.3
1947	StL N★	151	659	91	167	25	9	3	48	48	0	27	.253	.304	.332	66	-33	6	.976	-2	99	118	2b142,3b5/OL		-2.7
1948	StL N★	119	408	64	111	21	4	4	36	28	0	16	.272	.319	.373	82	-11	1	.980	7	106	108	2b96		0.1
1949	StL N★	151	640	102	190	25	2	3	54	51	2	18	.297	.351	.356	86	-12	8	.987	27	114	116	2b138,S14,3b6,O2C		2.4
1950	StL N★	153	642	81	177	43	9	7	63	33	2	32	.276	.313	.403	83	-17	3	.985	12	104	114	2b143,S10/3		0.3
1951	StL N★	135	553	88	160	32	7	6	54	35	3	23	.289	.335	.405	98	-3	0-1	.990	17	110	116	2b124,S8		2.1
1952	StL N☆	152	620	91	188	40	7	7	67	42	0	30	.303	.347	.424	113	10	9-6	.977	36	109	119	2b142,3b11,S3		-5.4
1953	StL N★	146	564	107	193	35	5	15	79	60	0	23	.342	.405	.502	135	31	3-3	.983	29	111	112	2b140		6.5
1954	StL N★	148	610	98	192	38	8	5	79	54	1	22	.315	.366	.428	107	7	4-2	.980	28	113	123	2b144		4.5
1955	StL N★	145	553	68	148	21	3	11	51	54-5	4	28	.268	.335	.376	89	-8	7-7	.985	-14	97	95	2b142		-1.2
1956	StL N	40	153	22	48	9	0	0	15	13-0	0	5	.314	.365	.373	100	1	0-1	.995	1	93	114	2b36		0.4
	NY N	92	334	39	99	12	3	2	14	28-1	2	10	.296	.352	.368	95	-2	1-2	.993	-6	94	93	2b85		0.2
	Year	132	487	61	147	21	3	2	29	41-1	2	15	.302	.356	.370	97	-1	1-3	.993	-5	94	99	2b121		0.2
1957	NY N	57	254	35	78	8	4	9	33	10-0	2	2	.307	.337	.476	116	5	2-1	.984	-0	102	107	2b57		0.9
	†Mil N★	93	394	56	122	23	4	6	32	23-1	1	7	.310	.348	.434	117	9	2-3	.987	9	108	119	2b92,O2C		2.4
	Year	150	648	91	200	31	8	15	65	33-1	3	15	.309	.344	.451	117	14	4-4	.986	9	106	114	2b149,O2C		3.3
1958	†Mil N	106	427	47	112	23	1	1	24	31-0	1	21	.262	.313	.328	77	-14	3-1	.987	4	104	114	2b105		-0.2
1959	Mil N	5	3	0	0	0	0	0	0	0-0	0	0	.000	.000	.000	-99	-1	0-0	.667	-1	63	0	2b4	119	-0.2
1960	Mil N	68	226	21	58	9	1	1	19	17-4	1	13	.257	.311	.319	79	-7	1-0	.964	-5	98	100	2b62		-0.8
1961	StL N	72	120	9	36	9	1	0	12	12-2	0	6	.300	.364	.400	93	0	1-0	.955	-7	76	71	2b32		-0.5
1962	StL N	98	143	21	43	4	0	2	12	9-2	1	12	.301	.346	.371	84	-3	0-0	.986	3	118	130	2b21,3b4		0.1
1963	StL N	6	5	0	0	0	0	0	0	0-0	0	0	.000	.000	.000	-91	-1	0-0	—	0			/H		-0.1
Total	19	2216	8479	1223	2449	427	78	84	773	606-15	21	346	.289	.337	.387	93	-81	89-27	.983	140	105	113	2b1834,O123(119/4/0),S49,3b39	119	16.5

SCHOENECK, JUMBO
Louis N. B3.3.1862 Chicago IL D1.20.1930 Chicago IL BR/TR/6-3/223 d4.20

YEAR	TM LG	G	AB	R	H	2B	3B	HR	RBI	BB-IB	HP	SO	AVG	OBP	SLG	AOPS	ABR	SB-CS	FA	FR	RNG	THR	GAMES AT POSITION	DL	BFW
1884	CP U	90	366	56	116	22	2	2	8				.317	.332	.404	123	0		.956	0	90	93	1b90		-0.7
	Bal U	16	60	5	15	2	0	0	8				.250	.250	.283	56	-5		.962	2	152	53	1b16		-0.4
	Year	106	426	61	131	24	2	2	8				.308	.320	.387	113	-6		.957	2	99	87	1b106		-1.1
1888	Ind N	48	169	15	40	4	0	0	20	9	2	24	.237	.283	.260	73	-5	11	.974	-1	93	75	1b48,P2		-1.0
1889	Ind N	16	62	3	15	2	0	0	8	3	2		.242	.299	.339	76	-2	1	.978	2	174	79	1b16		-0.1
Total	3	170	657	79	186	30	4	2	28	20	4	27	.283	.308	.350	99	-12	12	.964	3	104	83	1b170,P2		-2.2

SCHOFIELD, DICK
John Richard "Ducky" B1.7.1935 Springfield IL BB/TR/5-9/165(155-170) d7.3 s-Dick gs-Jayson Werth

YEAR	TM LG	G	AB	R	H	2B	3B	HR	RBI	BB-IB	HP	SO	AVG	OBP	SLG	AOPS	ABR	SB-CS	FA	FR	RNG	THR	GAMES AT POSITION	DL	BFW
1953	StL N	33	39	9	7	0	0	2	4	2	0	11	.179	.220	.333	42	-4	0-0	.917	5	137	147	S15		0.2
1954	StL N	43	7	17	1	0	1	0	1	0	0	1	.143	.143	.429	42	-1	1-1	1.000	1	144	217	S11		0.0
1955	StL N	12	4	3	0	0	0	0	0	0-0	0	1	.000	.000	.000	-99	-1	0-0	1.000	1	145	0	S3		-0.1
1956	StL N	16	30	3	3	0	0	0	1	0-0	0	6	.100	.100	.167	-30	-5	0-0	.923	-1	85	120	S9		-0.6
1957	StL N	65	56	10	9	0	0	0	1	7-0	0	13	.161	.254	.161	14	-7	1-3	.948	5	137	148	S23		-0.8
1958	StL N	39	108	16	23	4	0	1	8	23-0	0	15	.213	.348	.278	67	-4	0-2	.932	-6	95	65	S27		-0.8
	Pit N	26	27	4	4	0	0	0	2	3-0	0	6	.148	.226	.222	22	-3	0-1	1.000	0	100	149	S5,3b2		-0.3
	Year	65	135	20	27	4	0	1	10	26-0	0	21	.200	.325	.267	59	-7	0-3	.943	-5	96	78	S32,3b2		-1.1
1959	Pit N	81	145	21	34	10	1	1	16	16-0	0	22	.234	.311	.338	73	-5	1-1	.980	4	113	134	2b28,S8,O3R		0.1
1960	†Pit N	65	102	9	34	4	1	0	10	16-4	1	20	.333	.429	.392	126	5	0-1	.947	1	108	147	S23,2b10/3		0.8
1961	Pit N	60	78	16	15	2	1	0	2	10-0	1	19	.192	.284	.244	42	-7	0-1	.923	-4	149	77	3b11,S9,2b5,O3(2/0/2)		-0.2
1962	Pit N	54	104	19	30	3	0	1	10	17-0	0	22	.288	.382	.375	106	2	0-1	.933	-4	77	58	3b20,2b2/S		-0.3
1963	Pit N	138	541	54	133	18	2	3	32	69-1	3	83	.246	.333	.303	84	-8	2-4	.966	17	108	138	S117,2b20/3		2.1
1964	Pit N	121	398	50	98	22	5	3	36	54-3	7	60	.246	.345	.349	97	1	1-2	.950	12	108	122	S111		2.3
1965	Pit N	31	109	13	25	5	0	0	6	15-1	0	19	.229	.317	.275	70	-4	1-0	.974	5	113	155	S28		0.4
	SF N	101	379	39	77	16	1	2	19	33-0	3	50	.203	.272	.251	47	-26	2-4	.984	-1	98	101	S93		-1.5
	Year	132	488	52	102	15	1	2	25	48-1	3	69	.209	.282	.256	52	-30	3-4	.981	6	102	114	S121		-1.9
1966	SF N	11	16	4	1	0	0	0	0	2-0	0	2	.063	.167	.063	-32	-3	0-0	1.000	1	100	118	S8		-0.2
	NY A	25	58	5	9	0	0	2		9-0	0	8	.155	.265	.190	36	-5	0-0	.909	2	118	103	S19		-0.2
	LA N	20	70	10	18	0	0	0	4	8-0	2	8	.257	.350	.257	78	-2	1-1	.923	-2	100	4	3b19,S3		-0.3
1967	LA N	84	232	23	50	10	1	2	15	31-4	2	40	.216	.307	.293	79	-5	1-2	.976	8	110	106	S69,2b4,3b2		0.8
1968	†StL N	69	127	14	28	1	1	1	8	13-2	1	31	.220	.303	.315	87	-2	1-2	.973	5	96	64	S43,2b23		0.7
1969	Bos A	94	226	30	58	9	3	2	20	29-1	4	44	.257	.349	.350	92	-1	0-2	.981	5	120	97	2b15,S11,3b9,O5(3/0/2)		0.6
1970	Bos A	76	139	16	26	1	0	1	14	21-2	1	26	.187	.249	.245	48	-10	0-1	.969	-2	97	70	2b15,3b15,S3		-1.1
1971	Mil A	23	28	2	3	2	0	0	1	2-0	1	6	.107	.194	.179	6	-3	0-0	1.000	-1	96	203	3b12,S4,2b2		-0.5
	StL N	34	60	7	13	2	0	1	6	10-0	2	9	.217	.347	.300	81	-1	0-0	.935	4	110	103	S17,2b13,3b3		0.4
Total	19	1321	3083	394	699	113	20	21	211	390-18	26	526	.227	.317	.297	73	-99	12-29	.961	64	106	117	S660,2b159,3b95,O11(5/0/7)		1.6

SCHOFIELD, DICK
Richard Craig B11.21.1962 Springfield IL BR/TR/5-10/178* [CalA81 1/3] d9.8 f-Dick

YEAR	TM LG	G	AB	R	H	2B	3B	HR	RBI	BB-IB	HP	SO	AVG	OBP	SLG	AOPS	ABR	SB-CS	FA	FR	RNG	THR	GAMES AT POSITION	DL	BFW
1983	Cal A	21	54	4	11	2	0	3	4	6-0	1	8	.204	.295	.407	91	-1	0-0	.929	-2	111	78	S21		0.0
1984	Cal A	140	400	39	77	10	3	4	21	33-0	6	79	.192	.264	.262	46	-30	5-2	.982	10	107	117	S140		-0.5
1985	Cal A	147	438	50	96	19	3	8	41	35-0	2	70	.219	.287	.331	69	-19	11-4	.963	11	104	130	S147	23	0.7
1986	†Cal A	139	458	67	114	17	6	13	57	48-2	5	55	.249	.321	.397	97	-2	23-5	.972	17	105	134	S137		3.1
1987	Cal A	134	479	52	120	17	3	9	46	37-0	2	63	.251	.305	.355	77	-16	19-3	.984	-18	92	101	S131,2b2/D		-1.6
1988	Cal A	155	527	61	126	11	6	6	34	40-0	9	57	.239	.303	.317	76	-18	20-5	.983	22	110	118	S155	29	1.8
1989	Cal A	91	302	42	69	11	2	4	26	27-0	3	47	.228	.299	.318	75	-10	9-3	.983	-2	102	105	S90		-0.4
1990	Cal A	99	310	41	79	8	1	1	18	52-3	2	61	.255	.363	.297	89	-2	3-4	.966	10	106	114	S99	65	1.5
1991	Cal A	134	427	44	96	9	3	0	31	50-2	3	69	.225	.310	.260	59	-23	8-4	.975	4	99	107	S133	58	-0.9
1992	Cal A	1	3	0	1	0	0	0	0	0-0	0	0	.333	.500	.333	136	0	0-0	1.000	-1	31	0	/S		0.0
	NY N	142	420	52	86	18	2	4	36	60-4	0	71	.205	.309	.286	71	-14	11-4	.988	15	104	110	S141		1.3
1993	Tor A	36	110	11	21	1	2	0	5	16-0	0	25	.191	.294	.236	44	-9	3-0	.977	5	104	102	S36		-0.1
1994	Tor A	95	325	38	83	14	1	4	32	34-0	1	62	.255	.332	.342	74	-12	7-7	.972	-8	84	97	S95	111	-1.3
1995	LA N	9	10	1	1	0	0	0	0	1-0	0	3	.100	.182	.100	-25	-2	0-0	1.000	3	227	401	S3/3		0.1
	Cal A	12	20	1	5	0	0	0	2	4-0	0	7	.250	.375	.250	67	-1	0-0	1.000	-4	83	35	S12		-0.3
1996	Cal A	13	20	3	4	0	0	0	1	1-0	0	1	.250	.294	.250	39	-2	1-0	.889	-2	36	50	S7,2b2/3D	133	-0.8
Total	14	1368	4299	505	989	137	32	56	353	446-11	48	684	.230	.308	.316	73	-161	120-41	.976	59	102	113	S1348,2b4,3b2,D2	419	3.1

SCHOMBERG, OTTO
Otto H. (b Otto H. Shambrick) B11.14.1864 Milwaukee WI D5.3.1927 Ottawa KS BL/TL d7.7

YEAR	TM LG	G	AB	R	H	2B	3B	HR	RBI	BB-IB	HP	SO	AVG	OBP	SLG	AOPS	ABR	SB-CS	FA	FR	RNG	THR	GAMES AT POSITION	DL	BFW
1886	Pit AA	72	246	56	67	6	6	1	29	57	4		.272	.417	.358	144	17	7	.966	7	26	109	1b72		0.4
1887	Ind N	112	419	91	129	18	16	5	83	56	6	32	.308	.397	.463	143	27	21	.958	-10	70	111	1b112/OR		0.6
1888	Ind N	30	112	11	24	5	1	1	10	10	2	12	.214	.290	.304	88	-1	6	.857	-3	144	0	O15R,1b15		-0.6
Total	3	214	777	155	220	29	23	7	122	123	12	44	.283	.389	.407	136	43	34	.961	-20	49	110	1b199,O16R		0.4

SCHOONMAKER, JERRY
Jerald Lee B12.14.1933 Seymour MO BR/TR/5-11/190* d6.11 Mil 1956 Col Missouri

YEAR	TM LG	G	AB	R	H	2B	3B	HR	RBI	BB-IB	HP	SO	AVG	OBP	SLG	AOPS	ABR	SB-CS	FA	FR	RNG	THR	GAMES AT POSITION	DL	BFW
1955	Was A	20	46	5	7	0	1	1	4	5-0	1	11	.152	.235	.261	35	-5	1-0	.960	0	92	231	O15(5/3/7)		-0.5
1957	Was A	30	23	5	2	1	0	0	2	2-0	0	11	.087	.160	.130	-20	-4	0-0	1.000	1	156	0	O13(5/8/0)		-0.3
Total	2	50	69	10	9	1	1	1	6	7-0	1	22	.130	.211	.217	16	-9	1-0	.975	1	109	168	O28(10/11/7)		-0.8

SCHRAMKA, PAUL
Paul Edward B3.22.1928 Milwaukee WI BL/TL/6-0/185 d4.14 Col San Francisco

YEAR	TM LG	G	AB	R	H	2B	3B	HR	RBI	BB-IB	HP	SO	AVG	OBP	SLG	AOPS	ABR	SB-CS	FA	FR	RNG	THR	GAMES AT POSITION	DL	BFW
1953	Chi N	2	0	0	0	0	0	0	0	0-0	0	0	—	—	—			0-0	—	-0	0	0	/OL		0.0

YEAR	TM LG	G	AB	R	H	2B	3B	HR	RBI	BB-IB	HP	SO	AVG	OBP	SLG	AOPS	ABR	SB-CS	FA	FR	RNG	THR	GAMES AT POSITION	DL	BFW

SCHRECKENGOST, OSSEE Ossee Freeman (aka Ossee Schreck) (b Schrecongost) B4.11.1875 New Bethlehem PA D7.9.1914 Philadelphia PA BR/TR/5-10/180 d9.8

1897	Lou N	1	3	0	0	0	0	0	0	0	0		.000	.000	.000	-99	-1	0	1.000	0	117	147	/C		-0.1
1898	Cle N	10	35	5	11	2	3	0	10	0	0		.314	.314	.543	146	1	1	.860	0	116	84	C9		0.2
1899	StL N	6	8	0	0	0	0	0	0	1	0		.000	.111	.000	-67	-2	0	1.000	-0	0	0	/1OR		-0.7
	Cle N	43	150	15	47	8	3	0	10	6	2		.313	.348	.407	115	3	4	.911	-14	59	124	C39/1SOR		-0.7
	StL N	66	269	42	77	12	2	2	37	14	1		.286	.324	.368	88	-5	14	.963	-3	0	0	1b41,C25/2		-0.5
	Year	115	427	57	124	20	5	2	47	21	3		.290	.328	.375	94	-5	18	.927	-17	87	122	C64,1b43,O2R/S2		-1.4
1901	Bos A	86	280	37	85	13	5	0	38	19	4		.304	.356	.386	108	3	6	.926	4	105	100	C72,1b4		1.3
1902	Cle N	18	74	5	25	0	0	0	9	0	0		.338	.338	.338	91	-1	2	.975	-1	86	62	1b17		-0.2
	Phi A	79	284	45	92	17	2	2	43	9	1		.324	.347	.419	107	2	3	.960	17	108	105	C71,1b7/OC		2.4
	Year	97	358	50	117	17	2	2	52	9	1		.327	.345	.402	104	1	5	.960	16	108	105	C71,1b24/OC		2.2
1903	Phi A	92	306	26	78	13	4	3	30	11	2		.255	.285	.353	87	-6	0	.975	12	107	105	C77,1b10		1.4
1904	Phi A	95	311	23	58	9	4	1	21	5	0		.186	.199	.232	34	-24	3	.979	3	109	81	C84,1b9		-1.3
1905 †Phi A	123	420	30	114	19	6	0	45	3	1		.271	.278	.345	96	-4	9	**.984**	9	117	84	C114,1b2		1.7
1906	Phi A	98	338	29	96	20	1	1	41	10	0		.284	.305	.358	104	1	5	.971	8	97	90	C89,1b4		1.9
1907	Phi A	101	356	30	97	16	3	0	38	17	0		.272	.306	.334	102	0	4	**.985**	10	97	103	C99,1b2		2.3
1908	Phi A	71	207	16	46	7	1	0	16	6	1		.222	.248	.266	63	-9	1	.978	1	74	112	C65/1		-0.2
	Chi A	6	16	1	3	0	0	0	0	1	0		.188	.235	.188	38	-1	0	.982	2	155	46	C6		0.2
	Year	77	223	17	49	7	1	0	16	7	1		.220	.247	.260	61	-10	1	.978	3	83	105	C71/1		0.0
Total	11	895	3057	304	829	136	31	9	338	102	12		.271	.297	.345	90	-43	52	.970	49	102	98	C751,1b99,O3(0/1/2)/2S		8.

SCHREIBER, HANK Henry Walter B7.12.1891 Cleveland OH D2.23.1968 Indianapolis IN BR/TR/5-11/165 d4.14 Mil 1918

1914	Chi A	1	2	0	0	0	0	0	0	0	0	1	.000	.000	.000	-99	-0	0	—	-0	0	0	/OL		-0.
1917	Bos N	2	7	1	2	0	0	0	0	0	0		.286	.286	.286	80	0	0	1.000	-1	39	0	/S3		-0.
1919	Cin N	19	58	5	13	4	0	0	4	0	0	12	.224	.224	.293	56	-3	0	.984	5	134	281	3b17,S2		0.
1921	NY N	4	6	2	2	0	0	0	2	1	0		.333	.429	.333	104	0	0-0	.500	-1	0	0	2b2,S2/3		-0.
1926	Chi N	10	18	2	1	1	0	0	0	0	0		.056	.056	.111	-55	-4	0	1.000	0	148	0	S3,3b3/2		-0.
Total	5	36	91	10	18	5	0	0	6	1	0	16	.198	.207	.253	34	-7	0-0	.986	4	126	233	3b22,S8,2b3/OL		-0.

SCHREIBER, TED Theodore Henry B7.11.1938 Brooklyn NY BR/TR/5-11/175 d4.14 Col St. Johns

1963	NY N	39	50	1	8	0	0	0	2	4-0	1	14	.160	.236	.160	16	-5	0-1	.977	5	138	158	3b17,S9,2b3		-0.

SCHRIVER, POP William Frederick B7.11.1865 Brooklyn NY D12.27.1932 New York NY BR/TR/5-9.5/172 d4.29 OF(8/10/5)

1886	Bro AA	8	21	1	0	0	0	0	2	0			.048	.130	.048	-43	-3	0	.667	-1	264	0	O5(2/0/3),C3		-0.
1888	Phi N	40	134	15	26	5	2	1	23	7	3	21	.194	.250	.284	66	-5	2	.870	-7			C27,S6,3b6/OR		-1.
1889	Phi N	55	211	24	56	10	0	1	19	16	2	8	.265	.323	.327	75	-8	5	.920	1			C48,2b6/3		0.
1890	Phi N	57	223	37	61	9	6	0	35	22	0	15	.274	.339	.368	103	0	9	.916	-2	105	98	C34,1b10,3b8,2b3,O2L		0.
1891	Chi N	27	90	15	30	6	4	0	21	10	2	9	.333	.412	.467	156	6	1	.964	3	132	84	C27,1b2		1.
1892	Chi N	92	326	40	73	10	6	1	34	27	7	25	.224	.297	.301	80	-8	4	.929	-3	105	100	C82,O10C		-0.
1893	Chi N	64	229	49	65	8	3	4	34	14	4	9	.284	.336	.397	96	-2	4	.926	1	90	108	C56,O5(4/0/1)		0.
1894	Chi N	98	354	56	97	12	3	3	49	32	6	21	.274	.344	.350	64	-22	9	.920	-5	80	109	C90,S3,3b3,1b2		-1.
1895	NY N	24	92	16	29	2	1	1	16	9	1	10	.315	.382	.391	102	1	3	.898	-3	94	126	C16,1b6		0.
1897	Cin N	61	178	29	54	12	4	1	30	19	1		.303	.374	.433	106	1	3	.959	-5	155	84	C53		0.
1898	Pit N	95	315	25	72	15	3	0	32	23	3		.229	.287	.295	68	-13	0	.957	-2	105	90	C92/1		0.
1899	Pit N	92	302	31	85	19	5	1	49	24	5		.281	.344	.387	101	1	4	.958	9	121	88	C78,1b9		1.
1900 †Pit N	37	92	12	27	7	0	1	12	10	3		.293	.381	.402	115	3	0	.959	-1	127	67	C24/1		0.
1901	StL N	53	166	17	45	7	3	1	23	12	4		.271	.330	.353	109	2	2	.971	2	95	139	C24,1b19		0.
Total	14	803	2733	368	721	117	40	16	377	227	41	118	.264	.330	.353	88	-47	46	.934	-2	107	98	C656,1b50,O23C,3b18,2b9,S9		0.

SCHRODER, BOB Robert James B12.30.1944 Ridgefield NJ BL/TR/6-0/175* d4.20 Col Loyola-New Orleans

1965	SF N	31	9	4	2	0	0	0	1	1-0	0	1	.222	.300	.222	48	-1	0-0	1.000	1	172	151	2b4/3		0.
1966	SF N	10	33	0	8	0	0	0	2	0-0	0	2	.242	.242	.242	34	-3	0-0	.963	-5	69	45	S9		-0
1967	SF N	62	135	20	31	4	0	0	7	15-3	0	15	.230	.307	.259	64	-6	1-0	.993	-6	95	64	2b45,3b4		-0.
1968	SF N	35	44	5	7	1	1	0	2	7-0	1	3	.159	.283	.227	56	-2	0-0	.960	-5	80	50	2b12,S4,3b2		-0.
Total	4	138	221	29	48	5	1	0	12	23-3	1	21	.217	.293	.249	58	-12	1-0	.989	-14	95	64	2b61,S13,3b7		-2.

SCHROEDER, BILL Alfred William B9.7.1958 Baltimore MD BR/TR/6-2/200* [MilA79 8/205] d7.13 Col Clemson

1983	Mil A	23	73	7	13	2	1	3	7	3-0	1	23	.178	.221	.356	60	-5	0-1	.980	-4	97	71	C23		-0.
1984	Mil A	61	210	29	54	6	0	14	25	8-2	2	54	.257	.288	.486	115	3	0-1	.987	-9	67	90	C58/1D		-0.
1985	Mil A	53	194	18	47	8	0	8	25	12-1	1	61	.242	.290	.407	89	-3	0-1	.987	-7	78	84	C48/1D		-0.
1986	Mil A	64	217	32	46	14	0	7	19	9-0	6	59	.212	.262	.373	68	-10	1-0	.995	-3	84	74	C35,1b19,D10	27	-1.
1987	Mil A	75	250	35	83	12	0	14	42	16-0	3	56	.332	.379	.548	137	13	5-2	.995	-11	94	64	C67,1b4,D2		-0.
1988	Mil A	41	122	9	19	2	0	5	10	6-0	2	36	.156	.208	.295	39	-11	0-0	1.000	3	89	99	C30,1b10/D	19	-0.
1989	Cal A	41	138	16	28	2	0	6	15	3-0	0	44	.203	.220	.348	59	-9	0-0	.991	9	80	81	C33,1b8	18	-0.
1990	Cal A	18	58	7	13	3	0	4	9	1-0	0	10	.224	.237	.483	98	-1	0-0	1.000	-1	64	130	C15,1b3	84	-0.
Total	8	376	1262	153	303	49	1	61	152	58-3	16	343	.240	.281	.426	91	-23	6-5	.992	-22	82	82	C309,1b46,D20	205	-3.

SCHU, RICK Richard Spencer B1.26.1962 Philadelphia PA BR/TR/6-0/170(170-194)* d9.1 C1 Col Sacramento (CA) City

1984	Phi N	17	29	12	8	2	1	2	5	6-0	0	6	.276	.389	.621	180	3	0-0	.952	-2	68	209	3b15		0.
1985	Phi N	112	416	54	105	21	4	7	24	38-3	2	78	.252	.318	.373	90	-5	8-6	.933	-15	82	94	3b111		-2.
1986	Phi N	92	208	32	57	10	1	8	25	18-1	2	44	.274	.335	.447	110	3	2-2	.913	-1	101	75	3b58		0.
1987	Phi N	92	196	24	46	6	3	7	23	20-1	2	36	.235	.311	.403	85	-5	0-2	.905	-6	93	37	3b45,1b28	15	-1.
1988	Bal A	89	270	22	69	9	4	4	20	21-0	3	49	.256	.316	.363	92	-4	6-4	.937	-8	89	59	3b72,1b4,D9	47	-1.
1989	Bal A	1	0	0	0	0	0	0	0	0-0	0	0	—	—	—			0-0	1.000	-0	0	0	/2		0
	Det A	98	266	25	57	11	0	7	21	24-0	0	37	.214	.278	.335	74	-10	1-2	.934	-3	94	89	3b83,2b5,1b3,S3,D9		-1
	Year	99	266	25	57	11	0	7	21	24-0	0	37	.214	.278	.335	74	-10	1-2	.934	-3	94	89	3b83,D9,2b6,1b3,S3		-1
1990	Cal A	61	157	19	42	8	0	6	14	11-0	0	25	.268	.314	.433	109	1	0-0	.918	1	115	154	3b38,1b15,O4L/2		-0
1991	Phi N	17	22	1	2	0	0	0	2	1-0	0	7	.091	.125	.091	-37	-4	0-0	.667	-1	0	0	3b3/1		-0
1996	Mon N	1	4	0	0	0	0	0	0	0-0	0	0	.000	.000	.000	-98	-1	0-0	.667	-0	94	0	/3		-0
Total	9	580	1568	189	386	67	13	41	134	139-5	9	282	.246	.310	.384	92	-22	17-16	.926	-35	91	87	3b426,1b51,D18,2b7,O4L,S3	62	-6

SCHUBLE, HEINIE Henry George B11.1.1906 Houston TX D10.2.1990 Baytown TX BR/TR/5-9/152 d7.8

1927	StL N	65	218	29	56	6	2	4	28	7	1	27	.257	.288	.358	69	-11	0	.915	-5	100	110	S65		-1
1929	Det A	92	258	35	60	11	7	2	28	19	1	23	.233	.288	.353	64	-15	3-2	.886	-16	94	82	S86,3b2		-2
1932	Det A	102	340	58	92	20	6	5	52	24	0	37	.271	.319	.409	84	-9	14-5	.941	5	106	80	3b76,S16		-0
1933	Det A	49	96	12	21	4	1	0	6	5	0	17	.219	.257	.281	42	-8	2-0	.951	0	113	29	3b23,S2/2		-0
1934	Det A	11	15	2	4	2	0	0	2	1	0	4	.267	.313	.400	83	-1	0-0	1.000	0	98	0	S3,3b2/2		0
1935	Det A	11	8	3	2	0	0	0	0	1	0	0	.250	.333	.250	55	-1	0-0	.714	0	158	1142	3b2/2		0
1936	StL N	2	0	0	0	0	0	0	0	0	0	0	—	—	—		-0	0-0	—	-0	0	0	/3		0
Total	7	332	935	139	235	43	16	11	116	57	2	108	.251	.296	.367	70	-44	19-7	.906	-16	97	97	S172,3b106,2b3		-3

SCHULMERICH, WES Edward Wesley B8.21.1901 Hillsboro OR D6.26.1985 Corvallis OR BR/TR/5-11/210 d5.1 Col Oregon St.

1931	Bos N	95	327	36	101	17	7	2	43	28	0	30	.309	.348	.422	115	6	0	.966	-4	101	56	O87R		-0
1932	Bos N	119	404	47	105	22	5	11	57	27	5	61	.260	.314	.421	99	-1	5	.968	1	100	101	O101R		-0
1933	Bos N	29	85	10	21	6	1	1	13	5	0	10	.247	.289	.376	91	-1	0	.980	1	102	148	O21R		-0
	Phi N	97	365	53	122	19	4	8	59	32	4	45	.334	.394	.474	130	16	1	.977	-1	100	78	O97L		1
	Year	126	450	63	143	25	5	9	72	37	4	55	.318	.375	.456	126	16	1	.978	-0	100	90	O118(97/0/21)		-0
1934	Phi N	15	52	2	13	1	0	0	4	1	0	8	.250	.316	.269	51	-3	0	.963	-0	100	96	O13(3/0/10)		-0
	Cin N	74	209	21	55	8	3	5	19	22	0	43	.263	.333	.402	98	-1	1	.976	-2	104	35	O56(16/0/53)		-0
	Year	89	261	23	68	9	3	5	23	23	0	51	.261	.330	.375	88	-3	1	.974	-2	104	35	O69(16/0/53)		-0
Total	4	429	1442	169	417	73	20	27	192	118	10	197	.289	.347	.424	109	16	7	.971	-5	101	75	O375(113/0/262)		-1

SCHULT, ART Arthur William "Dutch" B6.20.1928 Brooklyn NY BR/TR/6-4/220* d5.17 Col Georgetown

1953	NY A	7	0	3	0	0	0	0	0	0-0	0	0	—	—	—			0-0	—	0			/R		0
1956	Cin N	5	7	3	3	0	0	0	2	1-0	0	1	.429	.500	.429	144	0	0-0	—	0	0	0	/OL		-0
1957	Cin N	21	34	4	9	2	0	0	4	0-0	1	2	.265	.286	.324	59	-2	0-0	1.000	1	134	0	O5L		-0

YEAR	TM LG	G	AB	R	H	2B	3B	HR	RBI	BB-IB	HP	SO	AVG	OBP	SLG	AOPS	ABR	SB-CS	FA	FR	RNG	THR	GAMES AT POSITION	DL	BFW
	Was A	77	247	30	65	14	0	4	35	14-0	1	30	.263	.303	.368	84	-6	0-1	.987	-3	60	111	1b35,O31(14/1/17)		-1.3
1959	Chi N	42	118	17	32	7	0	2	14	7-0	2	14	.271	.320	.381	88	-2	0-0	.985	-3	57	130	1b23,O15(12/0/6)		-0.6
1960	Chi N	12	15	1	2	1	0	0	1	1-1	0	3	.133	.188	.200	6	-2	0-0	1.000	-0	80	0	O4L/1		-0.2
Total	5	164	421	58	111	24	0	6	56	23-1	4	50	.264	.300	.363	81	-11	0-1	.987	-6	59	117	1b59,O56(36/1/23)		-2.3

SCHULTE, FRANK Frank M. "Wildfire" B9.17.1882 Cohocton NY D10.2.1949 Oakland CA BL/TR/5-11/170 d9.21

YEAR	TM LG	G	AB	R	H	2B	3B	HR	RBI	BB-IB	HP	SO	AVG	OBP	SLG	AOPS	ABR	SB-CS	FA	FR	RNG	THR	GAMES AT POSITION	DL	BFW
1904	Chi N	20	84	16	24	4	3	2	13	2	1		.286	.310	.476	141	3	1	.949	-0	111	0	O20L		0.2
1905	Chi N	123	493	67	135	15	14	1	47	32	6		.274	.326	.367	102	0	16	.981	-6	86	0	O123(107/0/16)		-1.4
1906	†Chi N	146	563	77	158	18	13	7	60	31	5		.281	.324	.396	118	8	25	.975	-2	96	183	O146R		-0.1
1907	†Chi N	97	342	44	98	14	7	2	32	22	5		.287	.339	.386	120	7	7	.973	-3	89	38	O92(1/0/91)		0.1
1908	†Chi N	102	386	42	91	20	2	1	43	29	3		.236	.294	.306	88	-5	15	.994	-6	71	0	O102(12/1/89)		-1.8
1909	Chi N	140	538	57	142	16	11	4	60	24	2		.264	.298	.357	101	-3	23	.968	-12	73	27	O140R		-2.4
1910	†Chi N	151	559	93	168	29	15	10	68	39	3	57	.301	.349	.460	137	22	22	.968	-6	91	87	O150R		1.0
1911	Chi N	154	577	105	173	30	21	21	107	76	3	71	.300	.384	.534	156	40	23	.971	-7	92	86	O154R		2.5
1912	Chi N	139	553	90	146	27	11	12	64	53	7	70	.264	.336	.418	106	3	17	.952	-5	94	92	O139R		-0.9
1913	Chi N	132	497	85	138	28	6	9	68	39	5	68	.278	.336	.412	113	8	21-19	.956	-6	92	84	O130(1/0/129)		-0.7
1914	Chi N	137	465	54	112	22	7	5	61	39	5	55	.241	.306	.351	95	-3	16	.954	-3	92	58	O134(134/0/2)		-1.9
1915	Chi N	151	550	66	137	20	6	12	62	49	2	68	.249	.313	.373	107	4	19-17	.962	5	97	139	O147(146/0/4)		0.0
1916	Chi N	72	230	31	68	11	1	5	27	20	0	35	.296	.352	.417	123	7	9	.951	-1	94	127	O67(66/0/1)		0.4
	Pit N	55	177	12	45	5	3	0	14	17	1	19	.254	.323	.316	96	-1	5	.968	-2	109	37	O48(20/0/28)		-0.5
	Year	127	407	43	113	16	4	5	41	37	1	54	.278	.339	.373	111	6	14	.958	-2	101	88	O115(86/0/29)		-0.1
1917	Pit N	30	103	11	22	5	1	0	7	10	0	14	.214	.283	.282	71	-3	5	.963	-0	105	87	O28(3/0/25)		-0.5
	Phi N	64	149	21	32	10	0	1	15	16	2	22	.215	.299	.302	81	-2	4	.923	-6	74	24	O42(20/7/15)		-1.2
	Year	94	252	32	54	15	1	1	22	26	2	36	.214	.293	.294	77	-6	9	.943	-8	88	52	O70(23/7/40)		-1.7
1918	Was A	93	267	35	77	14	3	0	44	47	6	36	.288	.406	.363	135	15	5	.969	2	105	98	O75(14/1/60)		1.4
Total	15	1806	6533	906	1766	288	124	92	792	545	56	515	.270	.332	.395	114	100	233-36	.966	-64	90	82	O1737(544/9/1189)		-5.8

SCHULTE, FRED Fred William "Fritz" (b Fred William Schult) B1.13.1901 Belvidere IL D5.20.1983 Belvidere IL BR/TR/6-1/183 d4.15

YEAR	TM LG	G	AB	R	H	2B	3B	HR	RBI	BB-IB	HP	SO	AVG	OBP	SLG	AOPS	ABR	SB-CS	FA	FR	RNG	THR	GAMES AT POSITION	DL	BFW
1927	StL A	60	189	32	60	16	5	3	34	20	0	14	.317	.383	.503	124	7	5-3	.916	-2	102	67	O49C		0.2
1928	StL A	146	556	90	159	44	6	7	85	51	1	60	.286	.347	.424	99	-1	6-5	.973	10	108	130	O143C		0.2
1929	StL A	121	446	63	137	24	5	3	71	59	1	44	.307	.389	.404	101	3	8-3	.989	6	107	93	O116C		0.4
1930	StL A	113	392	59	109	23	5	5	62	41	1	44	.278	.348	.401	86	-8	12-8	.966	-5	94	70	O98C,1b5		-1.6
1931	StL A	134	553	100	168	32	7	9	65	56	1	49	.304	.369	.436	107	6	6-8	.971	-1	96	119	O134C		0.0
1932	StL A	146	565	106	166	35	6	9	73	71	0	44	.294	.373	.425	100	2	5-9	.986	-4	96	85	O129(3/126/0),1b5		-0.8
1933	†Was A	144	550	98	162	30	7	5	87	61	1	27	.295	.366	.402	104	4	10-12	.980	8	112	94	O142C		0.6
1934	Was A	136	524	72	156	32	6	3	73	53	1	34	.298	.363	.399	100	1	3-7	.986	-4	101	46	O134C		-0.8
1935	Was A	76	226	33	60	6	4	2	23	26	1	22	.265	.344	.354	83	-6	0-3	.980	-2	97	55	O56(12/19/26)		-1.0
1936	Pit N	74	238	28	62	7	3	1	17	20	1	20	.261	.320	.328	73	-9	1	.977	-3	96	28	O55(1/54/0)		-1.3
1937	Pit N	29	20	3	5	2	0	0	3	4	1	3	.100	.280	.100	7	-2	0	.800	-0	116	0	O4(1/1/2)		-0.3
Total	11	1179	4259	686	1241	249	54	47	593	462	9	361	.291	.362	.408	98	-3	56-58	.976	2	102	87	O1060(17/1016/28),1b10		-4.4

SCHULTE, HAM Herman Joseph (b Herman Joseph Schultehenrich) B9.1.1912 St.Louis MO D12.21.1993 St.Charles MO BR/TR/5-8.5/158 d4.16 b-Len

YEAR	TM LG	G	AB	R	H	2B	3B	HR	RBI	BB-IB	HP	SO	AVG	OBP	SLG	AOPS	ABR	SB-CS	FA	FR	RNG	THR	GAMES AT POSITION	DL	BFW
1940	Phi N	120	436	44	103	18	2	1	21	32		1	.236	.288	.294	63	-22	3	.980	-9	91	98	2b119/S		-2.4

SCHULTE, JOHNNY John Clement B9.8.1896 Fredericktown MO D6.28.1978 St.Louis MO BL/TR/5-11/190 d4.18 C18

YEAR	TM LG	G	AB	R	H	2B	3B	HR	RBI	BB-IB	HP	SO	AVG	OBP	SLG	AOPS	ABR	SB-CS	FA	FR	RNG	THR	GAMES AT POSITION	DL	BFW
1923	StL A	7	3	1	0	0	0	0	1	4	0	0	.000	.571	.000	56	0	0-0	1.000	1	0	289	/C1		0.1
1927	StL N	64	156	35	45	8	2	9	32	47	1	19	.288	.456	.538	160	17	1	.956	0	91	131	C59		2.0
1928	Phi N	65	113	14	28	2	2	4	17	15	0	12	.248	.336	.407	90	-2	0	.949	-4	77	137	C34		-0.4
1929	Chi N	31	69	6	18	3	0	0	9	7	0	11	.261	.329	.304	58	-4	0	.978	1	129	133	C30		-0.2
1932	StL A	15	24	2	5	2	0	0	3	1	0	6	.208	.240	.292	35	-2	0-0	.864	-1	176	0	C6		-0.2
	Bos N	10	9	1	2	0	1	0	2	2	0	1	.222	.364	.556	149	1	0	1.000	1	135	0	C10		0.1
Total	5	192	374	59	98	15	4	14	64	76	1	49	.262	.388	.436	112	10	1-0	.957	-3	99	124	C140/1		1.4

SCHULTE, JACK John Herman Frank B11.15.1881 Cincinnati OH D8.17.1975 Roseville MI BR/TR/5-9/180 d8.19

YEAR	TM LG	G	AB	R	H	2B	3B	HR	RBI	BB-IB	HP	SO	AVG	OBP	SLG	AOPS	ABR	SB-CS	FA	FR	RNG	THR	GAMES AT POSITION	DL	BFW
1906	Bos N	2	7	0	0	0	0	0	0	0	0		.000	.000	.000	-99	-2	0	1.000	-1	69	0	S2		-0.3

SCHULTE, LEN Leonard Bernard (b Leonard Bernard Schultehenrich) B12.5.1916 St.Charles MO D5.6.1986 Orlando FL BR/TR/5-10/160 d9.27 b-Herman Col Iowa

YEAR	TM LG	G	AB	R	H	2B	3B	HR	RBI	BB-IB	HP	SO	AVG	OBP	SLG	AOPS	ABR	SB-CS	FA	FR	RNG	THR	GAMES AT POSITION	DL	BFW
1944	StL A	1	0	0	0	0	0	0	0	1	0	0	–	1.000	–	188	0	0-0	–		0		/H		0.0
1945	StL A	119	430	37	106	16	1	0	36	24	0	35	.247	.286	.288	64	-20	0-3	.961	-10	101	69	3b71,2b37,S14		-3.0
1946	StL A	4	5	1	2	0	1	0	2	0	0	0	.400	.400	.400	118	0	0-0	1.000	0	75	0	/23		0.0
Total	3	124	435	38	108	16	1	0	38	25	0	35	.248	.289	.290	65	-20	0-3	.962	-9	102	68	3b72,2b38,S14		-3.0

SCHULTZ, HOWIE Howard Henry "Stretch","Steeple" B7.3.1922 St.Paul MN BR/TR/6-6/200 d8.16 Col Hamline

YEAR	TM LG	G	AB	R	H	2B	3B	HR	RBI	BB-IB	HP	SO	AVG	OBP	SLG	AOPS	ABR	SB-CS	FA	FR	RNG	THR	GAMES AT POSITION	DL	BFW
1943	Bro N	45	182	20	49	12	6	1	34	6	2	24	.269	.300	.352	88	-3	3	.986	1	113	69	1b45		-0.4
1944	Bro N	138	526	59	134	32	3	11	83	24	2	67	.255	.290	.390	92	-8	6	.988	-0	98	77	1b136		-1.6
1945	Bro N	39	142	18	34	8	2	1	19	10	1	14	.239	.294	.345	78	-5	2	.984	2	126	123	1b38		-0.4
1946	Bro N	90	249	27	63	14	1	3	27	16	1	34	.253	.298	.353	84	-6	2	.989	5	124	122	1b87		-0.4
1947	Bro N	2	1	0	0	0	0	0	0	0	0	0	.000	.000	.000	-96	-0	0	1.000	-0	0	0	/1		0.0
	Phi N	114	403	30	90	19	1	6	35	21	1	70	.223	.264	.320	56	-27	0	.993	-1	95	105	1b114		-3.2
	Year	116	404	30	90	19	1	6	35	21	1	70	.223	.263	.319	56	-27	0	.993	-1	95	105	1b115		-3.2
1948	Phi N	6	13	0	1	0	0	0	1	1	0	2	.077	.143	.077	-40	-3	0	1.000	-0	118	153	1b3		-0.3
	Cin N	36	72	9	12	0	0	2	9	4	0	7	.167	.211	.250	25	-8	2	.982	-3	45	103	1b26		-1.1
	Year	42	85	9	13	0	0	2	10	5	0	9	.153	.200	.224	15	-11	2	.984	-3	54	109	1b29		-1.4
Total	6	470	1588	163	383	85	7	24	208	82	6	218	.241	.281	.349	75	-60	15	.989	4	103	97	1b450		-7.4

SCHULTZ, JOE Joseph Charles Jr. "Dode" B8.29.1918 Chicago IL D1.10.1996 St.Louis MO BL/TR/5-11/184 d9.27 M2/C14 f-Joe

YEAR	TM LG	G	AB	R	H	2B	3B	HR	RBI	BB-IB	HP	SO	AVG	OBP	SLG	AOPS	ABR	SB-CS	FA	FR	RNG	THR	GAMES AT POSITION	DL	BFW
1939	Pit N	4	14	3	4	0	0	2	2	0	0	0	.286	.375	.429	117	0	0	1.000	0	148	0	C4		0.1
1940	Pit N	16	36	2	7	0	1	0	4	2	0	1	.194	.237	.250	35	-3	0	.917	-2	75	82	C13		-0.5
1941	Pit N	2	2	1	1	0	0	0	0	0	0	0	.500	.500	.500	183	0	0	–	0	0	0	C2		0.0
1943	StL A	46	92	6	22	5	0	0	8	9	0	8	.239	.307	.293	74	-3	0-1	.979	-4	61	70	C26		-0.7
1944	StL A	3	8	1	2	0	0	0	2	0	0	1	.250	.250	.250	41	-1	0-0	.818	-1	101	0	C3		-0.1
1945	StL A	41	44	1	13	2	0	0	8	3	0	1	.295	.340	.341	93	0	0-0	.941	0	121	0	C4		0.0
1946	StL A	42	57	5	22	4	0	0	14	11	0	2	.386	.485	.456	156	5	0-0	1.000	-3	59	0	C17		0.3
1947	StL A	43	42	3	7	0	1	1	4	5	0	5	.184	.262	.263	45	-3	0-0	–	0			/H		-0.3
1948	StL A	43	37	0	7	0	0	0	9	6	0	3	.189	.302	.189	32	-4	0-0	–	0			/H		-0.3
Total	9	240	328	18	85	13	1	1	46	37	0	21	.259	.334	.314	81	-9	0-1	.964	-10	77	42	C69		-1.5

SCHULTZ, JOE Joseph Charles Sr. "Germany" B7.24.1893 Pittsburgh PA D4.13.1941 Columbia SC BR/TR/5-11.5/172 d9.28 s-Joe OF(104/9/307)

YEAR	TM LG	G	AB	R	H	2B	3B	HR	RBI	BB-IB	HP	SO	AVG	OBP	SLG	AOPS	ABR	SB-CS	FA	FR	RNG	THR	GAMES AT POSITION	DL	BFW
1912	Bos N	4	12	1	3	1	0	0	4	0	0	2	.250	.250	.333	58	-1	0	.824	-1	99	80	2b4		-0.1
1913	Bos N	9	18	2	4	0	0	1	0	2	0	7	.222	.333	.222	58	-1	0	1.000	0	121	0	O5(0/2/3)/2		-0.1
1915	Bro N	56	120	13	35	3	2	0	4	10	0	18	.292	.346	.350	109	1	3-4	.894	-4	77	80	3b27/S		-0.3
	Chi N	7	8	1	2	0	0	0	3	0	0	2	.250	.250	.250	51	-1	0	.857	-0	93	0	3b2		-0.1
	Year	63	128	14	37	3	2	0	7	10	0	20	.289	.341	.344	106	1	3-4	.894	-5	77	80	3b27,2b2/S		-0.4
1916	Pit N	77	204	18	53	8	2	0	22	7	4	14	.260	.298	.319	88	-3	6	.840	-15	89	24	2b24,3b24,O6(4/0/3)/S		-2.0
1919	StL N	88	229	24	58	9	1	2	21	11	0	7	.253	.287	.328	90	-3	4	1.000	0	97	0	O49(2/2/46),2b6/3		-0.9
1920	StL N	99	320	38	84	5	5	0	32	21	0	11	.262	.308	.309	81	0	5-4	.945	-3	101	72	O80(2/0/79)		-1.7
1921	StL N	92	275	37	85	20	3	6	45	15	1	11	.309	.347	.469	116	6	4-3	.977	1	109	90	O67R,3b3,1b2		0.2
1922	StL N	112	344	50	108	13	4	2	64	19	0	10	.314	.350	.392	96	-3	3-1	.976	-3	113	65	O89(33/3/53)		-0.7
1923	StL N	2	7	0	2	0	0	0	1	1	0	0	.286	.375	.286	78	0	0-0	1.000	0	117	0	O2R		0.0
1924	StL N	12	12	0	2	0	0	0	2	3	0	0	.167	.333	.167	39	-1	0-0	1.000	-0	41	0	O2(1/1/0)		-0.1
	Phi N	88	284	35	80	15	1	5	29	20	0	18	.282	.329	.394	83	-7	6-2	.960	-3	94	92	O76(54/1/25)		-1.4
	Year	100	296	35	82	15	1	5	31	23	0	18	.277	.329	.385	82	-7	6-2	.960	-3	93	91	O78(55/2/25)		-1.5
1925	Phi N	24	64	10	22	6	0	0	8	4	0	1	.344	.382	.438	100	0	1-1	.923	0	106	0	O20(3/0/17)		-0.1
	Cin N	33	62	6	20	3	1	0	13	3	1	1	.323	.354	.403	95	-1	3-1	.950	-1	79	150	O15(5/0/12)/2		-0.2
	Year	57	126	16	42	9	1	0	21	7	1	2	.333	.368	.421	99	0	4-2	.932	-1	95	117	O35(8/0/29)/2		-0.3
Total	11	703	1959	235	558	83	19	15	249	116	6	102	.285	.327	.370	93	-23	35-16	.966	-26	103	83	O411R,3b55,2b38,1b2,S2		-7.5

YEAR	TM LG	G	AB	R	H	2B	3B	HR	RBI	BB-IB	HP	SO	AVG	OBP	SLG	AOPS	ABR	SB-CS	FA	FR	RNG	THR	GAMES AT POSITION	DL	BFW

SCHULZ, JEFF   Jeffrey Alan B6.2.1961 Evansville IN   BL/TR/6-1/190*   [KCA83 23/586]   d9.2   Col Southern Indiana
1989	KC A	7	9	0	2	0	0	0	1	0-0	0	2	.222	.222	.222	26	-1	0-0	1.000	0	150	0	O5L		-0.1
1990	KC A	30	66	5	17	5	1	0	6	6-2	0	13	.258	.319	.364	92	-1	0-0	.943	-1	98	0	O22(8/0/16)/D	29	-0.3
1991	Pit N	3	3	0	0	0	0	0	0	0-0	0	2	.000	.000	.000	-99	-1	0-0	—	0			/H		-0.1
Total 3		40	78	5	19	5	1	0	7	6-2	0	17	.244	.298	.333	77	-3		.951	-1	103	0	O27(12/0/16)/D	29	-0.5

SCHULZE, JOHN   John H. B4.1866 St.Louis MO   D5.19.1941 St.Louis MO   d8.7
| 1891 | StL AA | 1 | 2 | 0 | 0 | 0 | 0 | 0 | 0 | 0-0 | 0 | 0 | .000 | .000 | .000 | -87 | 0 | 0 | 1.000 | -0 | 88 | 186 | /C | | 0.0 |

SCHUMAKER, SKIP   Jared Michael B2.3.1980 Torrance CA   BL/TR/5-10/175   d6.8   Col California-Santa Barbara
| 2005 | StL N | 27 | 24 | 9 | 6 | 1 | 0 | 0 | 2 | 2-0 | 0 | 2 | .250 | .308 | .292 | 57 | -1 | 1-0 | 1.000 | 0 | 121 | 0 | O21(14/4/7) | | -0.1 |

SCHUSTER, BILL   William Charles "Broadway Bill" B8.4.1912 Buffalo NY   D6.28.1987 El Monte CA   BR/TR/5-9/164   d9.29
1937	Pit N	3	6	2	3	0	0	0	1	0	0	0	.500	.571	.500	193	1	0	1.000	1	120	216	S2		0.2
1939	Bos N	2	3	0	0	0	0	0	0	0	0	0	1.000	.000	.000	-99	-1	0	.833	1	100	0	/S3		-0.1
1943	Chi N	13	51	3	15	2	1	0	3	0	0	2	.294	.333	.373	105	0	3	.977	4	109	165	S13		0.6
1944	Chi N	60	154	14	34	7	1	1	14	12	0	16	.221	.277	.299	62	-8	4	.946	-1	101	100	S38,2b6		-0.6
1945	†Chi N	45	47	8	9	2	0	0	2	7	0	4	.191	.296	.277	61	-2	2	.949	4	99	142	S22,2b3/3		0.2
Total 5		123	261	27	61	11	3	1	17	23	0	23	.234	.296	.310	72	-10	6	.954	7	103	126	S76,2b9,3b2		0.3

SCHWARTZ, RANDY   Douglas Randall B2.9.1944 Los Angeles CA   BL/TL/6-3/230*   d9.8   Col UCLA
1965	KC A	6	7	0	2	0	0	0	1	0-0	0	4	.286	.286	.286	64	0	0-0	1.000	1	237	0	1b2		0.0
1966	KC A	10	11	0	1	0	0	0	1	1-0	0	3	.091	.167	.091	-24	-2	0-0	1.000	-0	148	52	1b2		-0.2
Total 2		16	18	0	3	0	0	0	2	1-0	0	7	.167	.211	.167	10	-2	0-0	1.000	-0	145	58	1b4		-0.2

SCHWARTZ, BILL   William August "Pop","Scooper Bill" B4.3.1864 Jamestown KY   D12.22.1940 Newport KY   BR/TR/6-1/195   d5.3
1883	Col AA	2	4	0	1	0	0	0	0				.250	.250	.250	67	0	0	.600	-2	0	0	/1C		-0.1
1884	Cin U	29	106	14	25	4	0	1	3				.236	.257	.302	64	-8		.837	-6			C25,O3(2/1/1)/3		-1.0
Total 2		31	110	14	26	4	0	1	3				.236	.257	.300	64	-8		.828	-7			C26,O3(2/1/1)/31		-1.1

SCHWARTZ, BILL   William Charles "Blab" B4.22.1884 Cleveland OH   D8.29.1961 Nashville TN   BR/TR/6-2/185   d5.2
| 1904 | Cle A | 24 | 86 | 5 | 13 | 2 | 0 | 0 | 0 | 0 | 0 | | .151 | .151 | .174 | 3 | -10 | 4 | .980 | -4 | 36 | 43 | 1b22/3 | | -1.7 |

SCHWEITZER, AL   Albert Caspar "Cheese" B12.23.1882 Cleveland OH   D1.27.1969 Newark OH   BR/TR/5-6/170   d4.30
1908	StL A	64	182	22	53	4	2	1	14	20	4		.291	.374	.352	135	8	6	.952	6	247	202	O55(0/28/27)		1.4
1909	StL A	27	76	7	17	2	0	0	2	5	3		.224	.298	.250	79	-2	3	.933	-1	88	0	O22(6/7/9)		-0.4
1910	StL A	113	379	30	87	11	2	2	37	36	4		.230	.303	.285	90	-4	26	.937	-2	93	106	O109(1/32/76)		-1.2
1911	StL A	76	237	31	51	11	4	0	34	43	1		.215	.338	.295	80	-4	12	.934	1	97	118	O68(9/8/51)		-0.7
Total 4		280	874	97	208	28	8	3	87	104	12		.238	.327	.299	95	-2	47	.940	4	127	122	O254(16/75/163)		-0.9

SCHWERT, PI   Pius Louis B11.22.1892 Angola NY   D3.11.1941 Washington DC   BR/TR/5-10.5/160   d8.20   Col Penn
1914	NY A	3	6	0	0	0	0	0	2		0	3	.000	.250	.000	-24	-1	0	.923	0	85	231	C3		0.0
1915	NY A	9	18	6	5	3	0	0	6	1	0	6	.278	.316	.444	128	0	0	.972	0	102	108	C9		0.1
Total 2		12	24	6	5	3	0	0	6	3	0	9	.208	.296	.333	89	0	0	.959	0	97	142	C12		0.1

SCHWIND, ART   Arthur Edwin B11.4.1889 Ft.Wayne IN   D1.13.1968 Sullivan IL   BB/TR/5-8/150   d10.3
| 1912 | Bos N | 1 | 2 | 1 | 1 | 0 | 0 | 0 | 0 | | 0 | 0 | .500 | .500 | .500 | 171 | 0 | 0 | — | -0 | 0 | 0 | /3 | | 0.0 |

SCHYPINSKI, JERRY   Gerald Albert B9.16.1931 Detroit MI   BL/TR/5-10/170   d8.31   Col Detroit Mercy
| 1955 | KC A | 22 | 69 | 7 | 15 | 2 | 0 | 0 | 5 | 1-0 | 0 | 6 | .217 | .229 | .246 | 27 | -7 | 0-0 | .932 | -2 | 99 | 95 | S21,2b2 | | -0.8 |

SCIOSCIA, MIKE   Michael Lorri B11.27.1958 Upper Darby PA   BL/TR/6-2/220(200-229)   [LAN76 1/19]   d4.20   M6/C2   [DL 1993 SD N 182]
1980	LA N	54	134	8	34	5	1	1	8	12-2	0	9	.254	.313	.328	82	-3	1-0	.992	-1	84	112	C54		-0.2
1981	†LA N	93	290	27	80	10	0	2	29	36-8	1	18	.276	.353	.331	101	2	0-2	.987	1	114	101	C91		0.6
1982	LA N	129	365	31	80	11	1	5	38	44-11	1	31	.219	.302	.296	71	-14	2-0	.986	-3	112	88	C123		-1.2
1983	LA N	12	35	3	11	3	0	1	7	5-1	0	2	.314	.400	.486	144	2	0-0	1.000	0	277	123	C11	141	0.3
1984	LA N	114	341	29	93	18	0	5	38	52-10	1	26	.273	.367	.370	109	7	2-1	.985	15	113	127	C112	15	2.7
1985	†LA N	141	429	47	127	26	3	7	53	77-9	5	21	.296	.407	.420	135	25	3-3	.986	10	138	91	C139		4.2
1986	LA N	122	374	36	94	18	1	5	26	62-4	3	23	.251	.359	.345	103	4	3-3	.982	4	125	84	C119	35	1.3
1987	LA N	142	461	44	122	26	1	6	38	55-9	1	23	.265	.343	.364	90	-5	7-4	.989	16	132	104	C138	15	1.6
1988	†LA N	130	408	29	105	18	0	3	35	38-12	0	31	.257	.318	.324	88	-6	0-3	.991	15	132	130	C123		1.6
1989	LA N★	133	408	40	102	16	0	10	40	54-12	3	29	.250	.338	.363	102	2	0-2	.988	20	131	107	C130		3.0
1990	LA N★	135	435	46	115	25	0	12	66	55-14	3	31	.264	.348	.405	110	7	4-1	.989	8	112	86	C132	15	2.4
1991	LA N	119	345	39	91	16	2	8	40	47-3	3	32	.264	.353	.391	112	7	4-3	.990	5	106	71	C115		1.8
1992	LA N	117	348	19	77	6	3	3	24	32-4	1	31	.221	.286	.282	63	-18	3-2	.988	11	88	120	C108		0.0
Total 13		1441	4373	398	1131	198	12	68	446	567-101	22	307	.259	.344	.356	99	10	29-24	.988	100	120	101	C1395	403	18.1

SCOFFIC, LOU   Louis "Weaser" B5.20.1913 Herrin IL   D8.28.1997 Herrin IL   BR/TR/5-10/182   d4.16
| 1936 | StL N | 4 | 7 | 2 | 3 | 0 | 0 | 1 | | 2 | 0 | 2 | .429 | .500 | .429 | 153 | 1 | 0 | .875 | -0 | 129 | 0 | O3R | | 0.0 |

SCONIERS, DARYL   Daryl Anthony B10.3.1958 San Bernardino CA   BL/TL/6-2/195(185-199)   [AnaA77*3/59]   d9.13   Col Orange Coast (CA) JC
1981	Cal A	15	52	6	14	1	1	1	7	1-0	0	10	.269	.283	.385	90	-1	0-0	1.000	1	116	124	1b12,D3		-0.1
1982	Cal A	12	13	0	2	0	0	0	2	2-0	0	1	.154	.267	.154	19	-1	0-0	1.000	-0	82	332	1b3/D		-0.2
1983	Cal A	106	314	49	86	19	3	8	46	17-2	0	41	.274	.310	.430	102	0	4-2	.986	-6	72	99	1b57,D27/OL		-0.9
1984	Cal A	57	160	14	39	4	0	4	17	13-2	0	17	.244	.301	.344	78	-5	1-2	.990	-2	90	82	1b41/D	92	-1.0
1985	Cal A	44	98	14	28	6	1	2	12	15-0	0	18	.286	.371	.429	121	3	2-1	.973	-1	30	57	D20,1b6	48	0.2
Total 5		234	637	83	169	30	5	15	84	48-4	0	87	.265	.315	.399	96	-4	7-5	.989	-8	81	98	1b119,D52/OL	140	-2.0

SCOTT   d7.16
| 1884 | Bal U | 13 | 53 | 10 | 12 | 1 | 1 | 1 | | 2 | | | .226 | .255 | .340 | 71 | -4 | | .909 | -1 | 42 | 257 | O13R/3 | | -0.4 |

SCOTT, TONY   Anthony B9.18.1951 Cincinnati OH   BB/TR/6-0/175(163-195)   [MonN69 71/1017]   d9.1   C3
1973	Mon N	11	1	2	0	0	0	0	0	0-0	0	1	1.000	.000	.000	-96	0	0-0	.000	-1	0	0	O3(1/1/1)		-0.1
1974	Mon N	19	7	2	2	0	0	0	1	1-0	0	3	.286	.375	.286	82	0	1-1	1.000	-0	101	0	O16(2/1/14)		-0.1
1975	Mon N	92	143	19	26	4	2	0	11	12-2	2	38	.182	.258	.238	37	-12	5-6	.962	4	110	194	O71(45/4/28)		-1.3
1977	StL N	95	292	38	85	16	3	3	41	33-4	2	48	.291	.368	.397	106	4	13-10	.996	5	115	95	O89(3/82/6)	45	0.7
1978	StL N	96	219	28	50	5	2	1	14	14-1	2	41	.228	.278	.283	58	-13	5-6	.946	-0	93	166	O77(38/31/10)		-1.7
1979	StL N	153	587	69	152	22	10	6	68	34-4	5	92	.259	.301	.361	80	-18	37-17	.984	6	107	120	O151(0/140/14)		-1.7
1980	StL N	143	415	52	104	19	3	0	28	35-9	2	68	.251	.308	.311	70	-16	22-10	.997	1	105	63	O134C		-1.5
1981	StL N	45	176	21	40	5	2	2	17	5-0	1	22	.227	.253	.313	57	-11	10-7	1.000	-1	100	63	O44C		-1.3
	†Hou N	55	225	28	66	13	2	2	22	15-1	0	32	.293	.338	.396	114	4	8-3	.985	-2	92	138	O55C		0.2
	Year	100	401	49	106	18	4	4	39	20-1	1	54	.264	.301	.359	87	-8	18-10	.992	-3	96	105	O99C		-1.1
1982	Hou N	132	460	43	110	16	3	1	29	15-4	1	56	.239	.262	.293	61	-26	18-4	.982	-5	95	103	O129(2/125/3)		-3.2
1983	Hou N	80	186	20	42	6	1	2	17	11-0	0	39	.226	.264	.301	61	-11	5-4	1.000	-1	99	79	O61(7/30/28)		-1.3
1984	Hou N	25	21	2	4	1	0	0	0	4-1	0	3	.190	.320	.238	63	-1	0-0	1.000	-0	98	0	O6(1/5/0)		-0.1
	Mon N	45	71	8	18	4	0	0	5	7-1	0	21	.254	.316	.310	81	-2	1-1	1.000	-0	91	106	O17(16/1/2)		-0.2
	Year	70	92	10	22	5	0	0	5	11-2	0	24	.239	.317	.293	77	-2	1-1	1.000	-0	93	83	O23(17/6/2)		-0.3
Total 11		991	2803	331	699	111	28	17	253	186-27	16	464	.249	.297	.327	74	-102	125-69	.986	6	102	107	O853(115/653/106)	45	-11.2

SCOTT, DONNIE   Donald Malcolm B8.16.1961 Dunedin FL   BB/TR/5-11/185(185-200)   [TexA79 2/43]   d9.30
1983	Tex A	2	4	0	0	0	0	0	0	0-0	0	0	.000	.000	.000	-99	-1	0-0	1.000	1	0	273	C2		0.0
1984	Tex A	81	235	16	52	9	0	3	20	20-1	0	44	.221	.280	.298	58	-13	0-1	.974	4	117	100	C80		-0.7
1985	Sea A	80	185	18	41	13	0	4	23	15-0	0	41	.222	.278	.357	72	-7	1-1	.981	-2	82	125	C74		-0.7
1991	Cin N	10	19	0	3	0	0	0	0	0-0	0	2	.158	.158	.158	-11	-3	0-0	1.000	-4	49	0	C8		-0.7
Total 4		173	443	34	96	22	0	7	43	35-1	0	87	.217	.271	.314	60	-24	1-2	.977	-2	100	108	C164		-2.1

SCOTT, PETE   Floyd John B12.21.1898 Woodland CA   D5.3.1953 Daly City CA   BR/TR/5-11.5/175   d4.13   Col St. Marys (CA)
| 1926 | Chi N | 77 | 189 | 34 | 54 | 13 | 1 | 3 | 34 | 22 | 1 | 31 | .286 | .363 | .413 | 107 | 3 | 3 | .968 | 2 | 108 | 118 | O59(34/0/29)/3 | | 0.1 |
| 1927 | Chi N | 71 | 156 | 28 | 49 | 18 | 1 | 0 | 21 | 19 | 1 | 18 | .314 | .392 | .442 | 123 | 6 | 1 | .986 | -1 | 98 | 73 | O36(1/1/35) | | 0.3 |

YEAR	TM LG	G	AB	R	H	2B	3B	HR	RBI	BB-IB	HP	SO	AVG	OBP	SLG	AOPS	ABR	SB-CS	FA	FR	RNG	THR	GAMES AT POSITION	DL	BFW
1928	Pit N	60	177	33	55	10	4	5	33	18	1	14	.311	.378	.497	122	5	1	.979	3	112	155	O42(29/0/13),1b8		0.5
Total	3	208	522	95	158	41	6	8	88	59	3	63	.303	.377	.450	117	14	5	.976	5	107	117			0.9

SCOTT, GARY Gary Thomas B8.22.1968 New Rochelle NY BR/TR/6-0/175* [ChiN89 2/38] d4.9 Col Villanova

YEAR	TM LG	G	AB	R	H	2B	3B	HR	RBI	BB-IB	HP	SO	AVG	OBP	SLG	AOPS	ABR	SB-CS	FA	FR	RNG	THR	GAMES AT POSITION	DL	BFW
1991	Chi N	31	79	8	13	3	0	1	5	13-4	3	14	.165	.305	.241	53	-4	0-1	.969	-1	101	136	3b31		-0.6
1992	Chi N	36	96	8	15	2	0	2	11	5-1	0	14	.156	.198	.240	23	-10	0-1	.922	-4	85	68	3b29,S2		-1.6
Total	2	67	175	16	28	5	0	3	16	18-5	3	28	.160	.250	.240	38	-14	0-2	.946	-5	93	102	3b60,S2		-2.2

SCOTT, GEORGE George Charles "Boomer" B3.23.1944 Greenville MS BR/TR/6-2/215(205-225) d4.12

YEAR	TM LG	G	AB	R	H	2B	3B	HR	RBI	BB-IB	HP	SO	AVG	OBP	SLG	AOPS	ABR	SB-CS	FA	FR	RNG	THR	GAMES AT POSITION	DL	BFW
1966	Bos A★	162	601	73	147	18	7	27	90	65-13	8	152	.245	.324	.433	105	4	4-0	.991	-1	98	98	1b158,3b5		-0.7
1967	†Bos A	159	565	74	171	21	7	19	82	63-10	4	119	.303	.373	.465	136	27	10-8	.987	-8	86	107	1b152,3b2		1.0
1968	Bos A	124	350	23	60	14	0	3	25	26-3	5	88	.171	.236	.237	42	-24	3-5	.987	-1	95	95	1b112,3b6		-3.7
1969	Bos A	152	549	63	139	14	5	16	52	61-12	4	74	.253	.331	.384	95	-4	4-3	.954	-8	93	121	3b109,1b53		-1.7
1970	Bos A	127	480	50	142	24	5	16	63	44-5	2	95	.296	.355	.467	118	11	4-11	.934	-9	80	90	3b68,1b59	30	-0.6
1971	Bos A	-146	537	72	141	16	4	24	78	41-5	5	102	.263	.317	.441	106	-6	0-3	.992	-6	82	96	1b143		-1.8
1972	Mil A	152	578	71	154	24	4	20	88	43-4	4	130	.266	.321	.426	123	14	16-4	.992	-3	92	96	1b139,3b23		0.3
1973	Mil A	158	604	98	185	30	4	24	107	61-6	2	94	.306	.370	.488	142	34	9-5	.994	3	110	100	1b157/D		2.5
1974	Mil A	158	604	74	170	36	2	17	82	59-5	3	90	.281	.345	.432	124	19	9-9	.992	7	125	105	1b148,D9		1.4
1975	Mil A★	158	617	86	176	26	4	36	109	51-7	3	97	.285	.341	.515	139	28	6-5	.989	2	109	92	1b144,D12,3b5		1.9
1976	Mil A	156	606	73	166	21	5	18	77	53-6	5	118	.274	.334	.414	121	-15	0-1	.991	-1	99	100	1b155		0.1
1977	Bos A★	157	584	103	157	26	5	33	95	57-4	6	112	.269	.337	.500	113	10	1-1	.985	-3	97	118	1b157		-0.4
1978	Bos A	120	412	51	96	16	4	12	54	44-3	0	86	.233	.305	.379	83	-10	1-1	.991	-11	68	107	1b113,D7		-2.9
1979	Bos A	45	156	18	35	9	1	4	23	17-1	0	22	.224	.299	.372	76	-5	0-0	.986	-4	77	107	1b41		-1.1
	KC A	44	146	19	39	8	2	1	20	12-1	2	32	.267	.329	.370	87	-3	1-1	.989	-3	82	81	1b41/3D		-0.7
	NY A	16	44	9	14	3	1	1	6	2-0	0	7	.318	.340	.500	128	2	1-0	1.000	0	0	0	D15/1		0.1
	Year	105	346	46	88	20	4	6	49	31-2	2	61	.254	.317	.387	87	-6	2-1	.987	-6	79	95	1b83,D17/3		-1.7
Total	14	2034	7433	957	1992	306	60	271	1051	699-85	53	1418	.268	.333	.435	113	121	69-57	.990	-46	96	101	1b1773,3b219,D46	30	-6.3

SCOTT, JIM James Walter B9.22.1888 Shenandoah PA D5.12.1972 S.Pasadena FL BR/TR/5-9.5/165 d4.22

YEAR	TM LG	G	AB	R	H	2B	3B	HR	RBI	BB-IB	HP	SO	AVG	OBP	SLG	AOPS	ABR	SB-CS	FA	FR	RNG	THR	GAMES AT POSITION	DL	BFW
1914	Pit F	8	24	2	6	1	0	0	1	5	0		.250	.379	.292	85	-1	1	.800	-3	88	150	S8		-0.3

SCOTT, JOHN John Henry B1.24.1952 Jackson MS BR/TR/6-2/165* [SDN70*1/2] d9.7

YEAR	TM LG	G	AB	R	H	2B	3B	HR	RBI	BB-IB	HP	SO	AVG	OBP	SLG	AOPS	ABR	SB-CS	FA	FR	RNG	THR	GAMES AT POSITION	DL	BFW
1974	SD N	14	15	3	1	0	0	0	0	0-0	0	4	.067	.067	.067	-66	-2	1-0	1.000	1	86	361	O8(5/2/1)		-0.3
1975	SD N	25	9	6	0	0	0	0	0	0-0	0	2	.000	.000	.000	-99	-3	2-0	—	-0	0	0	/OC		-0.2
1977	Tor A	79	233	26	56	9	0	2	15	8-0	0	39	.240	.266	.305	54	-15	10-8	.963	-4	90	72	O67(27/41/0),D2		-2.1
Total	3	118	257	35	57	9	0	2	15	8-0	0	45	.222	.245	.280	43	-21	13-8	.965	-3	89	91	O76(32/44/1),D2		-2.6

SCOTT, LE GRANT Le Grant Edward B7.25.1910 Cleveland OH D11.12.1993 Birmingham AL BL/TL/5-8.5/170 d4.19 Col Alabama

YEAR	TM LG	G	AB	R	H	2B	3B	HR	RBI	BB-IB	HP	SO	AVG	OBP	SLG	AOPS	ABR	SB-CS	FA	FR	RNG	THR	GAMES AT POSITION	DL	BFW
1939	Phi N	76	232	31	65	15	1	1	26	22		14	.280	.343	.366	93	-2	5	.959	1	99	139	O55(1/1/54)		-0.4

SCOTT, EVERETT Lewis Everett "Deacon" B11.19.1892 Bluffton IN D11.2.1960 Fort Wayne IN BR/TR/5-8/148 d4.14

YEAR	TM LG	G	AB	R	H	2B	3B	HR	RBI	BB-IB	HP	SO	AVG	OBP	SLG	AOPS	ABR	SB-CS	FA	FR	RNG	THR	GAMES AT POSITION	DL	BFW
1914	Bos A	144	539	66	129	15	6	2	37	32	3	43	.239	.286	.301	76	-18	9-14	.949	-11	95	106	S143		-2.4
1915	†Bos A	100	359	25	72	11	0	0	28	17		21	.201	.237	.231	41	-27	4-7	.961	0	99	96	S100		-2.3
1916	†Bos A	123	366	37	85	19	2	0	27	23	3	24	.232	.283	.295	73	-13	8	.967	5	102	96	S121/23		0.0
1917	Bos A	157	528	40	127	24	7	0	50	20	0	46	.241	.268	.313	78	-17	12	.953	8	103	105	S157		0.3
1918	†Bos A	126	443	40	98	11	5	0	43	12		16	.221	.242	.269	55	-27	11	.976	21	108	79	S126		0.2
1919	Bos A	138	507	41	141	19	0	0	38	19	1	26	.278	.306	.316	79	-16	8	.976	11	104	128	S138		0.4
1920	Bos A	154	569	41	153	21	12	4	61	21	4	35	.269	.300	.369	80	-20	4-11	.973	14	102	112	S154		0.1
1921	Bos A	154	576	65	151	21	9	1	62	27	0	21	.262	.295	.335	62	-36	5-9	.972	41	110	135	S154		1.9
1922	†NY A	154	557	64	150	23	5	3	45	23	5	22	.269	.304	.345	67	-28	2-3	.966	17	107	104	S154		0.5
1923	†NY A	152	533	48	131	16	4	6	60	13	2	19	.246	.266	.325	54	-39	1-3	.961	-13	95	99	S152		-3.6
1924	NY A	153	548	56	137	12	6	4	64	21	0	15	.250	.278	.316	53	-42	3-7	.966	-10	99	110	S153		-1.6
1925	NY A	22	60	3	13	.0	0	0	4	2	0	2	.217	.242	.217	17	-8	0-1	.988	-3	92	173	S18		-0.4
	Was A	33	103	10	28	6	1	0	18	4	0	4	.272	.299	.350	65	-6	1-2	.932	-1	95	112	S30,3b2		-0.4
	Year	55	163	13	41	6	1	0	22	6	0	6	.252	.278	.301	48	-14	1-3	.952	-3	94	134	S48,3b2		-0.8
1926	Chi A	40	143	15	36	10	1	0	13	9	0	8	.252	.296	.336	67	-7	1-3	.955	5	111	105	S39		0.0
	Cin N	4	6	1	4	0	0	0	1	0		0	.667	.667	.667	267	1	0	.875	-1	77	0	S4		0.0
Total	13	1654	5837	552	1455	208	58	20	551	243	18	282	.249	.281	.315	65	-303	69-60	.965	108	102	108	S1643,3b3/2		-7.2

SCOTT, LUKE Luke Brandon B6.25.1978 DeLeon Springs FL BL/TR/6-0/210 d4.5 Col Oklahoma St.

YEAR	TM LG	G	AB	R	H	2B	3B	HR	RBI	BB-IB	HP	SO	AVG	OBP	SLG	AOPS	ABR	SB-CS	FA	FR	RNG	THR	GAMES AT POSITION	DL	BFW
2005	†Hou A	34	80	6	15	4	2	0	9	9-1	0	23	.188	.270	.287	46	-7	1-1	.963	-2	68	186	O24(21/1/4)		-0.9

SCOTT, MILT Milton Parker "Mikado Milt" B1.17.1861 Chicago IL D11.3.1938 Baltimore MD BR/5-9/160 d9.30

YEAR	TM LG	G	AB	R	H	2B	3B	HR	RBI	BB-IB	HP	SO	AVG	OBP	SLG	AOPS	ABR	SB-CS	FA	FR	RNG	THR	GAMES AT POSITION	DL	BFW
1882	Chi N	1	5	1	2	0	0	0	0	0			.400	.400	.400	150	0		1.000	0	0	0	/1		0.0
1884	Det N	110	438	29	108	17	5	3	50	9		62	.247	.262	.329	90	-5		.968	-1	82	68	1b110		-1.4
1885	Det N	38	148	14	39	7	0	0	12	4		16	.264	.283	.311	92	-1		.967	2	136	82	1b38		-0.3
	Pit AA	55	210	.15	52	7	1	0	18	5	2		.248	.272	.290	79	-5		.986	3	108	106	1b55		-0.7
1886	Bal AA	137	484	48	92	11	4	2	52	22	9		.190	.239	.242	52	-27	11	.974	8	137	57	1b137/P		-2.7
Total	4	341	1285	107	293	42	10	5	132	40	11	78	.228	.257	.288	74	-38	11	.973	12	114	71	1b341/P		-5.1

SCOTT, DICKIE Richard Edward B7.19.1962 Ellsworth ME BR/TR/6-1/170 d5.19

YEAR	TM LG	G	AB	R	H	2B	3B	HR	RBI	BB-IB	HP	SO	AVG	OBP	SLG	AOPS	ABR	SB-CS	FA	FR	RNG	THR	GAMES AT POSITION	DL	BFW
1989	Oak A	3	2	0	0	0	0	0	0	0-0	0	0	.000	.000	.000	-99	-1	0-0	—	-0	0	0	S3		-0.1

SCOTT, RODNEY Rodney Darrell B10.16.1953 Indianapolis IN BB/TR (BR 1975)/6-0/160* [KCA72 11/258] d4.11 OF(0/10/1)

YEAR	TM LG	G	AB	R	H	2B	3B	HR	RBI	BB-IB	HP	SO	AVG	OBP	SLG	AOPS	ABR	SB-CS	FA	FR	RNG	THR	GAMES AT POSITION	DL	BFW
1975	KC A	48	15	13	1	0	0	0	0	1-0	0	3	.067	.125	.067	-43	-3	4-2	1.000	-2	39	88	D22,2b9,S8/R		-0.5
1976	Mon N	7	10	3	4	0	0	0	0	1-0	0	1	.400	.455	.400	137	1	2-0	1.000	1	63	86	2b6,S3		0.0
1977	Oak A	133	364	56	95	4	4	0	20	43-0	2	50	.261	.342	.294	77	-11	33-18	.963	-10	96	75	2b71,S70,3b5/ORD		-1.3
1978	Chi N	78	227	41	64	5	1	0	15	43-0	4	41	.282	.403	.313	91	0	27-10	.929	-3	102	176	3b59,O10C,2b6,S6		-0.1
1979	Mon N	151	562	69	134	12	5	3	42	66-2	2	82	.238	.319	.294	69	-24	39-12	.980	-5	102	105	2b113,S39		-1.4
1980	Mon N	154	567	84	127	13	13	0	46	70-0	1	75	.224	.307	.293	68	-24	63-13	.982	-8	96	92	2b129,S21		-1.5
1981	†Mon N	95	336	43	69	9	3	0	26	50-0	1	35	.205	.308	.250	58	-17	30-7	.983	-12	94	79	2b93		-2.2
1982	Mon N	14	25	2	5	0	0	0	1	3-0	0	2	.200	.286	.200	37	-2	5-0	.971	-2	74	72	2b12		-0.3
	NY A	10	26	5	5	0	0	0	0	4-0	0	2	.192	.300	.192	39	-2	2-0	.963	-0	100	159	S6,2b4		-0.1
Total	8	690	2132	316	504	43	26	3	150	281-2	10	291	.236	.326	.285	70	-82	205-62	.979	-42	96	88	2b443,S153,3b64,D23,O11C		-7.4

SCRANTON, JIM James Dean B4.5.1960 Torrance CA BR/TR/6-0/175* d9.5 Col Arizona

YEAR	TM LG	G	AB	R	H	2B	3B	HR	RBI	BB-IB	HP	SO	AVG	OBP	SLG	AOPS	ABR	SB-CS	FA	FR	RNG	THR	GAMES AT POSITION	DL	BFW
1984	KC A	2	2	0	0	0	0	0	0	0-0	0	0	.000	.000	.000	-99	-1	0-0	1.000	0	142	753	/S3		0.0
1985	KC A	6	4	1	0	0	0	0	0	0-0	0	0	.000	.000	.000	-99	-1	0-0	1.000	1	148	89	S5		0.0
Total	2	8	6	1	0	0	0	0	0	0-0	0	0	.000	.000	.000	-99	-2	0-0	1.000	1	147	163	S6/3		0.0

SCRIVENER, CHUCK Wayne Allison B10.3.1947 Alexandria VA BR/TR/5-9/170* [DetA68*S2/23] d9.18 Col CC of Baltimore (MD)

YEAR	TM LG	G	AB	R	H	2B	3B	HR	RBI	BB-IB	HP	SO	AVG	OBP	SLG	AOPS	ABR	SB-CS	FA	FR	RNG	THR	GAMES AT POSITION	DL	BFW
1975	Det A	4	16	0	4	1	0	0	0	0-0	0	1	.250	.250	.313	56	-1	1-0	1.000	-1	81	0	3b3,S2		-0.2
1976	Det A	80	222	28	49	7	1	2	16	19-0	0	34	.221	.282	.288	65	-10	1-0	.976	13	116	89	2b43,S37,3b5		1.0
1977	Det A	61	72	10	6	0	0	0	2	5-0	0	9	.083	.143	.083	-35	-14	0-0	.981	0	98	102	S50,2b8,3b3		-1.1
Total	3	145	310	38	59	8	1	2	18	24-0	0	44	.190	.249	.242	40	-25	2-0	.970	12	103	116	S89,2b51,3b11		-0.3

SCRUGGS, TONY Anthony Raymond B3.19.1966 Riverside CA BR/TR/6-1/210 [TexA87 7/181] d4.8 Col UCLA

YEAR	TM LG	G	AB	R	H	2B	3B	HR	RBI	BB-IB	HP	SO	AVG	OBP	SLG	AOPS	ABR	SB-CS	FA	FR	RNG	THR	GAMES AT POSITION	DL	BFW
1991	Tex A	5	6	1	0	0	0	0	0	0-0	0	1	.000	.000	.000	-99	-2	0-0	1.000	0	111	0	O5(5/1/0)		-0.2

SCUTARO, MARCO Marcos B10.30.1975 San Felipe, Venez BR/TR/5-10/170* d7.21

YEAR	TM LG	G	AB	R	H	2B	3B	HR	RBI	BB-IB	HP	SO	AVG	OBP	SLG	AOPS	ABR	SB-CS	FA	FR	RNG	THR	GAMES AT POSITION	DL	BFW
2002	NY N	27	36	2	8	0	1	9	6	0-0	0	11	.222	.216	.361	56	-3	0-1	1.000	-2	84	0	2b12,S6,3b3/OL		-0.5
2003	NY N	48	75	10	16	4	0	2	6	13-2	1	14	.213	.333	.347	82	-2	2-0	.981	-5	83	81	2b39/S		-0.5
2004	Oak A	137	455	50	124	32	1	7	43	16-1	0	58	.273	.297	.393	78	-15	0-0	.995	8	104	13	2b123,S16/3		-0.1
2005	Oak A	118	381	48	94	22	3	9	37	36-1	0	48	.247	.310	.391	84	-9	5-2	.976	4	98	112	S81,2b30,3b5,O2L		0.3
Total	4	330	947	110	242	58	5	19	92	65-4	1	131	.256	.303	.388	80	-29	7-3	.993	5	100	104	2b204,S104,3b9,O3L		-0.8

YEAR	TM LG	G	AB	R	H	2B	3B	HR	RBI	BB-IB	HP	SO	AVG	OBP	SLG	AOPS	ABR	SB-CS	FA	FR	RNG	THR	GAMES AT POSITION	DL	BFW

SEABOL, SCOTT   Scott Anthony B5.17.1975 McKeesport PA BR/TR/6-4/200* [NYA96 88/1718] d4.8 Col West Virginia [DL 1998 NY A 28]   0.0

2001	NY A	1	1	0	0	0	0	0	0	0-0	0	0	.000	.000	.000	-99	-0	0-0					/D		-0.5
2005	StL N	59	105	11	23	5	0	1	10	8-0	0	23	.219	.272	.295	48	-8	0-0	.929	3	132	244	3b20,2b8,1b5,O4(2/0/2),D3		-0.5
Total	2	60	106	11	23	5	0	1	10	8-0	0	23	.217	.270	.292	47	-8	0-0	.929	3	132	244	3b20,2b8,1b5,O4(2/0/2),D4	28	-0.5

SEARS, KEN   Kenneth Eugene "Ziggy" B7.6.1917 Streator IL D7.17.1968 Bridgeport TX BL/TR/6-1/200 d5.2 Mil 1944-45 Col Alabama   0.4

1943	NY A	60	187	22	52	7	0	2	22	11	3	18	.278	.328	.348	97	-1	1-3	.974	2	177	96	C50		-0.1
1946	StL A	7	15	1	5	0	0	0	1	3	0	0	.333	.444	.333	114	1	0-0	1.000	-2	54	0	C4		0.3
Total	2	67	202	23	57	7	0	2	23	14	3	18	.282	.338	.347	99	0	1-3	.975	1	170	90	C54		

SEARS, TODD   Todd Andrew B10.23.1975 Des Moines IA BL/TR/6-5/215* [ColN97 3/102] d9.17 Col Nebraska   0.0

2002	Min A	7	12	2	4	1	0	0	0	0-0	1	.333	.333	.500	113	0	0-0	1.000	0	102	128	1b6		-0.3
2003	Min A	24	65	7	16	2	0	2	11	7-0	1	15	.246	.324	.369	81	-2	0-0	.990	-0	96	81	1b14,D6		-0.3
	SD N	9	8	2	2	1	0	0	0	3	.250	.250	.375	66	0	0-0	1.000	-0	0	1013	/1		-0.3
Total	2	40	85	11	22	5	0	2	11	7-0	1	19	.259	.319	.388	84	-2	0-0	.992	-0	97	99	1b21,D6		-0.3

SEBRING, JIMMY   James Dennison B3.22.1882 Liberty PA D12.22.1909 Williamsport PA BL/TR/6-0/180 d9.8 Col Bucknell   0.6

1902	Pit N	19	80	15	26	4	4	0	15	5	0	.325	.365	.475	154	4	2	.974	3	173	312	O19R		-0.4
1903	†Pit N	124	506	71	140	16	13	6	64	32	4	.277	.325	.383	98	-4	20	.927	5	114	279	O124R		0.2
1904	Pit N	80	305	28	82	11	7	0	32	17	0	.269	.307	.351	100	-1	8	.959	6	150	162	O80R		-0.8
	Cin N	56	222	22	50	9	2	0	24	14	0	.225	.271	.284	65	-9	8	1.000	4	159	158	O56R		-0.6
	Year	136	527	50	132	20	9	0	56	31	0	.250	.292	.323	85	-10	16	.974	10	154	160	O136R		-0.8
1905	Cin N	58	217	31	62	10	5	2	28	14	0	.286	.329	.406	107	1	11	.885	-4	90	116	O56R		-1.1
1909	Bro N	25	81	11	8	1	1	0	5	11	0	.099	.207	.123	7	-9	3	.951	9	144	150	O25(0/21/4)		0.0
	Was A	1	0	0	0	0	0	0	0	0	0	—	—	—		-0		-0	-0	0	0	/OC		-2.1
Total	5	363	1411	178	368	51	32	6	168	93	4	.261	.308	.355	93	-18	52	.945	13	131	204	O361(0/22/339)		

SECORY, FRANK   Frank Edward B8.24.1912 Mason City IA D4.7.1995 Port Huron MI BR/TR/6-1/200 d4.28 U19 Col Western Michigan   0.0

1940	Det A	1	1	0	0	0	0	0	0	1	0	.000	.000	.000	-91	-0	0					/H		-0.1
1942	Cin N	2	5	1	0	0	0	0	0	3	0	.000	.375	.000	14	0	0	.857	-1	106	0	O2L		0.3
1944	Chi N	22	56	10	18	1	0	4	17	6	0	.321	.387	.554	163	4	1	1.000	-0	112	0	O17(17/1/0)		-0.9
1945	†Chi N	35	57	4	9	1	0	0	6	2	0	.158	.186	.175	1	-8	0	1.000	-0	104	0	O12(10/0/2)		-0.7
1946	Chi N	33	43	6	10	3	0	3	12	6	0	.233	.327	.512	139	2	0	.833	-1	84	0	O9L		-0.7
Total	5	93	162	21	37	5	0	7	36	17	0	.228	.302	.389	95	-2	1-0	.964	-2	105	0	O40(38/1/2)		

SEE, CHARLIE   Charles Henry "Chad" B10.13.1896 Pleasantville NY D7.19.1948 Bridgeport CT BL/TR/5-10.5/175 d8.6   -0.1

1919	Cin N	8	14	1	4	0	0	0	0	0	.286	.333	.286	89	0	0	.833	-1	90	0	O4(2/2/0)		0.1
1920	Cin N	47	82	9	25	4	0	0	15	1	2	.305	.329	.354	97	0	2-4	1.000	3	125	130	O17(0/14/4)/P		-0.6
1921	Cin N	37	106	11	26	5	1	1	7	7	1	.245	.298	.340	72	-4	3-2	.954	1	101	108	O30(0/11/18)		-0.6
Total	3	92	202	21	55	9	1	1	23	9	3	.272	.313	.342	83	-4	5-6	.967	3	109	110	O51(2/27/22)/P		

SEE, LARRY   Ralph Laurence B6.20.1960 Norwalk CA BR/TR/6-1/195* [LAN80*3/62] d9.3 Col Cerritos (CA) JC   0.0

1986	LA N	13	20	1	5	2	0	0	2	2-0	0	7	.250	.318	.350	90	0	0-0	.979	1	171	76	1b9		-0.4
1988	Tex A	13	23	0	3	0	0	0	0	1-0	0	8	.130	.167	.130	-15	-4	0-0	1.000	-1	0	0	C2,1b2/3D		
Total	2	26	43	1	8	2	0	0	2	3-0	0	15	.186	.239	.233	32	-4	0-0	.967	0	178	109	1b11,D7,C2/3		

SEEDS, BOB   Ira Robert "Suitcase Bob" B2.24.1907 Ringgold TX D10.28.1993 Erick OK BR/TR/6-0/180 d4.19   -1.1

1930	Cle A	85	277	37	79	11	3	3	32	12	0	22	.285	.315	.379	72	-12	1-3	.953	1	102	117	O70(48/21/1)		-0.7
1931	Cle A	48	134	26	41	4	1	1	10	11	0	11	.306	.359	.373	88	-2	1-0	.966	-1	98	37	O33(3/1/29),1b2		-0.3
1932	Cle A	2	4	0	0	0	0	0	0	0	0	0	.000	.000	.000	-94	-1	0-0	—	-0	0	0	/OR		-1.8
	Chi A	116	434	53	126	18	6	6	45	31	3	37	.290	.342	.373	91	-6	5-7	.964	-4	96	82	O112(34/34/53)		-1.6
	Year	118	438	53	126	18	6	6	45	31	3	37	.288	.340	.370	89	-8	5-7	.964	-4	96	82	O113(34/34/54)		-1.8
1933	Bos A	82	230	26	56	13	4	0	23	21	1	20	.243	.310	.335	71	-10	1-3	.985	-0	89	107	1b41,O32(17/0/16)		-1.1
1934	Cle A	8	6	0	1	0	0	0	0	0	0	1	.167	.167	.167	-13	-1	0-0	—	-0	0	0	/OR		-1.1
	Cle A	61	186	28	46	8	1	0	18	21	1	14	.247	.327	.301	62	-10	2-1	.977	-2	93	56	O48(26/2/21)		-1.1
	Year	69	192	28	47	8	1	0	19	21	1	14	.245	.322	.297	59	-11	2-1	.977	-3	93	56	O49(26/2/22)		0.
1936	†NY A	13	42	12	11	1	0	4	10	5	0	3	.262	.340	.571	126	1	3-1	1.000	1	115	125	O9(1/0/8),3b3		0.
1938	NY N	81	296	35	86	12	3	9	52	20	1	33	.291	.338	.443	112	4	0	.987	-4	87	100	O76(37/40/1)		-0.
1939	NY N	63	173	33	46	5	1	5	26	22	1	31	.266	.352	.393	99	0	1	.975	-4	81	66	O50(12/38/0)		-0.
1940	NY N	56	155	18	45	9	2	4	16	17	1	19	.290	.371	.426	118	4	0	.985	-2	82	116	O40(16/24/0)		0.
Total	9	615	1937	268	537	77	21	28	233	160	10	190	.277	.336	.382	89	-33	14-15	.970	-16	93	93	O472(194/160/131),1b43,3b3		-7.

SEEREY, PAT   James Patrick B3.17.1923 Wilburton OK D4.28.1986 Jennings MO BR/TR/5-10/200 d6.9   -0.

1943	Cle A	26	72	8	16	3	0	1	5	4	0	19	.222	.263	.306	70	-3	0-0	.974	1	99	235	O16L		-0.
1944	Cle A	101	342	39	80	6	10	15	39	19	1	99	.234	.276	.412	99	-3	0-2	.986	1	100	109	O86(63/19/4)		-0.
1945	Cle A	126	414	56	98	22	2	14	56	66	0	97	.237	.342	.401	120	12	1-2	.975	-4	97	69	O117(38/28/68)		-0.
1946	Cle A	117	404	57	91	17	2	26	62	65	1	101	.225	.334	.470	131	16	2-3	.981	-4	103	50	O115(39/40/43)		-0.
1947	Cle A	82	216	24	37	4	1	11	29	34	0	66	.171	.284	.352	78	-7	0-1	.957	-1	85	181	O68(53/1/16)		-0.
1948	Cle A	10	23	7	6	0	0	1	6	7	0	8	.261	.433	.391	123	1	0-0	1.000	-1	62	0	O7R		
	Chi A	95	340	44	78	11	0	18	64	61	0	94	.229	.347	.421	107	3	0-0	.981	0	93	130	O93(82/12/0)		-0.
	Year	105	363	51	84	11	0	19	70	68	0	102	.231	.353	.419	108	4	0-0	.982	-1	92	124	O100(82/12/7)		-0.
1949	Chi A	4	1	4	1	0	0	0	0	3	0	1	1.000	.429	.000	19	0	0-0	1.000	-0	61	0	O2R		
Total	7	561	1815	236	406	73	5	86	261	259	2	485	.224	.321	.412	109	19	3-8	.978	-5	96	101	O504(291/100/140)		

SEERY, EMMETT   John Emmett B2.13.1861 Princeville IL D8.7.1930 Saranac Lake NY BL/TR/5-7/145 d4.17   -0.

1884	Bal U	105	463	113	144	25	7	2		20			.311	.340	.408	114	-6		.828	3	96	68	O103(99/0/5),C3,3b2		-0.
	KC U	1	4	2	1	0	0	0		1			.500	.600	.750	353	1		—	-0	0	0	/OL		0.
	Year	106	467	115	146	26	7	2		21			.313	.342	.411	116	-5		.828	3	96	68	O104(100/0/5),C3,3b2		-1.
1885	StL N	59	216	20	35	7	0	1	14	16		37	.162	.220	.208	42	-13		.874	5	139	63	O59(49/0/10)/3		-1.
1886	StL N	126	453	73	108	22	6	2	48	57		82	.238	.324	.327	105	7	24	.883	4	82	51	O126(122/1/1)/S		-1.
1887	Ind N	122	465	104	104	19	15	4	28	71	4	68	.224	.331	.353	93	-2	48	.891	7	114	45	O122(122/1/1)/S		2.
1888	Ind N	133	500	87	110	20	15	6	50	64	6	73	.220	.316	.330	104	5	80	.939	9	87	126	O133L/S		1.
1889	Ind N	127	526	123	165	26	12	8	59	59	10	59	.314	.401	.454	136	26	19	.909	2	83	88	O127L		2.
1890	Bro P	104	394	78	88	12	7	1	50	70	5	36	.223	.348	.297	69	-17	44	.894	6	105	71	O104L		-1.
1891	Cin AA	97	372	77	106	15	10	4	36	81	8	52	.285	.423	.411	128	17	19	.898	1	98	77	O97(17/1/80)		-0.
1892	Lou N	42	154	18	31	6	1	0	15	24	0	19	.201	.309	.253	76	-3	6	.962	4	149	72	O42R		-0.
Total	9	916	3547	695	893	152	68	27	300	471	33	426	.252	.345	.356	104	15	240	.896	31	100	75	O914(778/2/138),3b3,C3,S2,P2		

SEFCIK, KEVIN   Kevin John B2.10.1971 Tinley Park IL BR/TR/5-10/181* [PhiN93 33/916] d9.8 Col St. Xavier   -0.

1995	Phi N	5	4	1	0	0	0	0	0-0	0	2	.000	.000	.000	-99	-1	0-0	1.000	0	86	1057	3b2		-0.
1996	Phi N	44	116	10	33	5	3	0	9	9-3	2	16	.284	.341	.379	91	-2	3-0	.986	-2	109	101	S21,3b2b2/0		-0.
1997	Phi N	61	119	11	32	5	1	0	6	4-0	1	9	.269	.298	.345	69	-6	1-2	.961	-4	97	59	2b22,S10,3b4		-0.
1998	Phi N	104	169	27	53	7	2	3	11	20-0	7	32	.314	.412	.432	125	8	4-2	.989	1	114	39	O60(35/8/20),3b2/2		-0.
1999	Phi N	111	209	28	58	15	3	1	11	29-0	1	24	.278	.368	.392	91	-2	9-4	.986	-4	90	46	O64(31/19/17),2b15		-0.
2000	Phi N	99	153	15	36	6	2	0	16	13-0	2	19	.235	.300	.301	54	-11	4-2	1.000	1	116	0	O50(25/20/9)/D		-1.
2001	Col N	1	1	0	0	0	0	0	0-0	0	0	.000	.000	.000	-83	-0	0-0					/H		-0.
Total	7	425	771	92	212	36	10	6	56	80-3	13	102	.275	.351	.371	87	-14	21-10	.991	-7	106	30	O174(91/47/46),2b39,S31,3b28/D		

SEGRIST, KAL   Kal Hill B4.14.1931 Greenville TX BR/TR/6-0/180* d7.16 Col Texas   -0.

1952	NY A	13	23	1	1	0	0	0	1	3	0	1	.043	.154	.043	-46	-5	0-0	.971	0	107	115	2b11/3		-0.
1955	Bal A	7	9	3	3	0	0	0	2	0	.333	.455	.333	123	0	0-0	1.000	1	162	0	3b3/12		
Total	2	20	32	4	4	0	0	0	1	5-0	0	1	.125	.243	.125	4	-5	0-0	.971	1	109	111	2b12,3b4/1		

SEGUI, DAVID   David Vincent B7.19.1966 Kansas City KS BB/TL/6-1/202(170-220) [BalA87 18/455] d5.8 f-Diego Col Louisiana Tech

1990	Bal A	40	123	14	30	7	0	2	15	11-2	1	15	.244	.311	.350	87	-2	0-0	.990	0	105	85	1b36,D4		-0.
1991	Bal A	86	212	15	59	7	0	2	22	12-0	1	19	.278	.316	.340	85	-5	1-1	.996	1	125	104	1b42,O33(28/0/5),D4		
1992	Bal A	115	189	21	44	9	0	1	17	20-3	0	23	.233	.306	.296	67	-8	1-0	.998	1	104	117	1b95,O18(3/0/15)		

YEAR	TM	LG	G	AB	R	H	2B	3B	HR	RBI	BB-IB	HP	SO	AVG	OBP	SLG	AOPS	ABR	SB-CS	FA	FR	RNG	THR	GAMES AT POSITION	DL	BFW
1993	Bal	A	146	450	54	123	27	0	10	60	58-4	0	53	.273	.351	.400	98	0	2-1	.996	4	109	111	1b144/D		-0.8
1994	NY	N	92	336	46	81	17	1	10	43	33-6	1	43	.241	.308	.387	81	-10	0-0	.996	-4	95	115	1b78,O21(19/0/2)	15	-2.0
1995	NY	N	33	73	9	24	3	1	2	11	12-1	1	9	.329	.420	.479	144	5	1-3	1.000	-2	57	224	O18L,1b7		0.2
	Mon	N	97	383	59	117	22	3	10	57	28-4	2	38	.305	.355	.457	108	4	1-4	.997	3	109	92	1b97,O2L		-0.2
	Year		130	456	68	141	25	4	12	68	40-5	3	47	.309	.367	.461	115	10	2-7	.997	2	107	93	1b104,O20L		0.0
1996	Mon	N	115	416	69	119	30	1	11	58	60-4	0	54	.286	.375	.442	112	10	4-4	.993	7	119	94	1b113	43	0.6
1997	Mon	N	125	459	75	141	22	3	21	68	57-12	1	66	.307	.380	.505	132	22	1-0	.995	-1	96	111	1b125	17	1.0
1998	Sea	A	143	522	79	159	36	1	19	84	49-4	0	80	.305	.359	.487	118	14	3-1	.999	17	145	98	1b134/OL		1.8
1999	Sea	A	90	345	43	101	22	3	9	39	32-4	1	43	.293	.352	.452	105	3	1-2	.996	6	130	102	1b90		0.0
	Tor	A	31	95	14	30	5	0	5	13	8-0	0	17	.316	.365	.526	123	3	0-0	.955	-0	111	108	D25,1b4	25	0.1
	Year		121	440	57	131	27	3	14	52	40-4	1	60	.298	.355	.468	109	6	1-2	.995	6	130	102	1b94,D25		0.1
2000	Tex	A	93	351	52	118	29	1	11	57	34-1	0	51	.336	.391	.519	127	15	0-1	1.000	2	121	99	D52,1b38		1.0
	Cle	A	57	223	41	74	13	0	8	46	19-1	1	33	.332	.384	.498	118	6	0-0	1.000	4	148	68	1b35,D16,O7R		0.5
	Year		150	574	93	192	42	1	19	103	53-2	1	84	.334	.388	.510	123	22	0-1	1.000	6	134	84	1b73,D68,O7R		1.5
2001	Bal	A	82	292	48	88	18	1	10	46	49-5	4	61	.301	.406	.473	139	19	1-1	.983	-6	74	93	1b65,D16	41	0.7
2002	Bal	A	26	95	10	25	4	0	2	16	11-0	0	22	.263	.336	.368	93	-1	0-0	1.000	0	110	225	D19,1b7	135	-0.2
2003	Bal	A	67	224	26	59	10	1	5	25	26-2	1	47	.263	.341	.384	92	-2	1-0	1.000	1	130	121	D53,1b8	86	-0.5
2004	Bal	A	18	59	8	20	3	0	1	7	5-1	1	13	.339	.400	.441	120	2	0-1	1.000	-1	0	55	D15,1b2	154	0.0
Total	15		1456	4847	683	1412	284	16	139	684	524-56	14	687	.291	.359	.443	110	75	17-19	.995	34	113	102	1b1120,D205,O100(71/0/29)	516	-0.0

SEGUIGNOL, FERNANDO Fernando Alfredo B1.19.1975 Bocas Del Toro, Pan BB/TR/6-5/230(190-230) d9.5

YEAR	TM	LG	G	AB	R	H	2B	3B	HR	RBI	BB-IB	HP	SO	AVG	OBP	SLG	AOPS	ABR	SB-CS	FA	FR	RNG	THR	GAMES AT POSITION	DL	BFW
1998	Mon	N	16	42	6	11	4	0	2	3	3-0	0	15	.262	.304	.500	112	1	0-0	1.000	3	189	0	O9(8/0/1),1b7		0.2
1999	Mon	N	35	105	14	27	9	0	5	10	5-1	1	33	.257	.328	.486	108	1	0-0	.989	-2	79	121	1b23,O8(6/0/3)	58	-0.5
2000	Mon	N	76	162	22	45	8	0	10	22	9-0	3	46	.278	.326	.512	107	1	0-1	.987	-3	87	103	1b30,O30(17/0/14)/D		-0.5
2001	Mon	N	46	50	0	7	2	0	0	5	2-1	1	17	.140	.185	.180	-4	-8	0-0	1.000	1	100	356	O13(7/0/7),1b7		-0.7
2003	NY	A	5	7	0	1	0	0	0	0	1-0	0	3	.143	.250	.143	8	-1	0-0	1.000	1	290	0	1b3/D		0.0
Total	5		178	366	42	91	23	0	17	40	20-2	11	114	.249	.303	.451	91	-6	0-1	.986	-1	101	106	1b70,O60(38/0/25),D2	58	-1.3

SEIBERT, KURT Kurt Elliott B10.16.1955 Cheverly MD BB/TR/6-0/190 [ChiN76 3/55] d9.3 Col Clemson

YEAR	TM	LG	G	AB	R	H	2B	3B	HR	RBI	BB-IB	HP	SO	AVG	OBP	SLG	AOPS	ABR	SB-CS	FA	FR	RNG	THR	GAMES AT POSITION	DL	BFW
1979	Chi	N	7	2	2	0	0	0	0	0	0-0	0	1	.000	.000	.000	-91	-1	0-0	1.000	0	0	0	/2		-0.1

SEIBOLD, SOCKS Harry B5.31.1896 Philadelphia PA D9.21.1965 Philadelphia PA BR/TR/5-8.5/162 d9.18 Mil 1918 ▲

YEAR	TM	LG	G	AB	R	H	2B	3B	HR	RBI	BB-IB	HP	SO	AVG	OBP	SLG	AOPS	ABR	SB-CS	FA	FR	RNG	THR	GAMES AT POSITION	DL	BFW
1915	Phi	A	10	26	3	4	1	0	0	2	4	0	4	.115	.233	.154	16	-3	0	.714	-4	94	33	S7		-0.6
1916	Phi	A	5	12	0	2	1	0	0	1	0	0	4	.167	.167	.250	26	-1	0	1.000	1	160	0	P3/OC		0.1
1917	Phi	A	36	59	6	13	1	1	0	5	4	1	8	.220	.281	.271	70	-2	1	.978	-1	89	111	P33,O2L		-0.1
1919	Phi	A	15	13	1	2	0	0	0	1	0	0	4	.154	.154	.154	-13	-1	0	.941	0	90	159	P14		0.0
1929	Bos	N	33	70	6	20	2	0	0	9	6	0	6	.286	.342	.314	67	5	0	1.000	-1	87	107	P33		0.0
1930	Bos	N	36	90	6	19	2	0	1	5	6	0	6	.211	.260	.267	29	0	0	.941	-3	75	88	P36		0.0
1931	Bos	N	33	70	3	9	0	0	0	2	1	0	9	.129	.141	.129	-28	-4	0	1.000	-0	102	183	P33		0.0
1932	Bos	N	28	46	2	7	0	0	0	2	2	0	5	.152	.188	.152	-8	-2	0	1.000	2	123	235	P28		0.0
1933	Bos	N	11	9	0	1	0	0	0	0	2	0	2	.111	.273	.111	14	0	0	1.000	0	123	0	P11		0.0
Total	9		207	395	27	76	7	1	1	27	25	1	43	.192	.242	.223	25	-8	1	.982	-5	95	131	P191,S7,O3(2/1/0)		-0.6

SEILHEIMER, RICKY Ricky Allen B8.30.1960 Brenham TX BL/TR/5-11/185 [ChiA79 1/19] d7.5

YEAR	TM	LG	G	AB	R	H	2B	3B	HR	RBI	BB-IB	HP	SO	AVG	OBP	SLG	AOPS	ABR	SB-CS	FA	FR	RNG	THR	GAMES AT POSITION	DL	BFW
1980	Chi	A	21	52	4	11	3	1	0	3	4-1	0	15	.212	.268	.365	72	-2	1-0	.946	-8	40	71	C21		-0.9

SEITZER, KEVIN Kevin Lee B3.26.1962 Springfield IL BR/TR/5-11/190(180-195) [KCA83 11/283] d9.3 Col Eastern Illinois OF(14/1/1)

YEAR	TM	LG	G	AB	R	H	2B	3B	HR	RBI	BB-IB	HP	SO	AVG	OBP	SLG	AOPS	ABR	SB-CS	FA	FR	RNG	THR	GAMES AT POSITION	DL	BFW
1986	KC	A	28	96	16	31	4	1	2	11	19-0	1	14	.323	.440	.448	139	5	0-0	.987	1	102	94	1b22,O5L,3b3		0.5
1987	KC	A★	161	641	105	207	33	8	15	83	80-0	2	85	.323	.399	.470	126	26	12-7	.947	10	105	120	3b141,1b25,O3L/D		3.2
1988	KC	A	149	559	90	170	32	5	5	60	72-4	6	64	.304	.387	.406	121	20	10-8	.938	4	104	135	3b147/OLD		2.3
1989	KC	A	160	597	78	168	17	2	4	48	102-7	5	76	.281	.387	.337	107	12	17-8	.950	-3	95	111	3b159,S6,O3(2/1/0),1b2		1.0
1990	KC	A	158	622	91	171	31	5	6	38	67-2	2	66	.275	.346	.370	102	3	7-5	.953	7	101	113	3b152,2b10		1.0
1991	KC	A	85	234	28	62	11	3	1	25	29-3	2	21	.265	.350	.350	94	-1	4-1	.940	6	115	69	3b68,D3	34	0.6
1992	Mil	A	148	540	74	146	35	1	5	71	57-4	2	44	.270	.337	.367	100	2	13-11	.969	-5	100	81	3b146,2b2/1		-0.4
1993	Oak	A	73	255	24	65	10	2	4	27	27-1	1	33	.255	.324	.357	89	-4	4-7	.933	-6	85	71	3b46,1b24,O3L,2b2/PDS		-1.3
	Mil	A	47	162	21	47	6	0	7	30	17-0	1	15	.290	.359	.457	119	4	3-0	.942	-1	100	124	3b33,1b7/2ORD		0.3
	Year		120	417	45	112	16	2	11	57	44-1	2	48	.269	.338	.396	101	0	7-7	.937	-7	91	93	3b79,1b31,D6,O4(3/0/1),2b3/PS		-1.0
1994	Mil	A	80	309	44	97	24	2	5	49	30-1	1	38	.314	.375	.453	108	4	2-1	.924	-1	95	95	3b43,1b35,D4	35	0.1
1995	Mil	A★	132	492	56	153	33	3	5	69	64-2	6	57	.311	.395	.421	107	8	2-0	.968	4	114	128	3b88,1b36,D14		0.9
1996	Mil	A	132	490	74	155	35	3	12	62	73-6	4	68	.316	.406	.453	113	13	6-1	.996	2	118	102	1b65,D56,3b12		0.7
	†Cle	A	22	83	11	32	10	0	1	16	14-1	1	11	.386	.480	.542	158	9	0-0	1.000	4	252	24	D17,1b5		0.9
	Year		154	573	85	187	35	3	13	78	87-7	5	79	.326	.416	.466	119	21	6-1	.995	4	128	96	D73,1b70,3b12		1.6
1997	†Cle	A	64	198	27	53	14	0	2	24	18-0	0	25	.268	.326	.369	79	-6	0-0	1.000	1	112	118	D24,1b19,3b13		-0.7
Total	12		1439	5278	739	1557	285	35	74	613	669-31	35	617	.295	.375	.404	110	97	80-49	.949	21	104	107	3b1051,1b241,D126,O16L,2b15,S7/P	69	9.1

SELBACH, KIP Albert Karl B3.24.1872 Columbus OH D2.17.1956 Columbus OH BR/TR/5-7/190 d4.24

YEAR	TM	LG	G	AB	R	H	2B	3B	HR	RBI	BB-IB	HP	SO	AVG	OBP	SLG	AOPS	ABR	SB-CS	FA	FR	RNG	THR	GAMES AT POSITION	DL	BFW
1894	Was	N	97	372	69	114	21	17	7	51		0	20	.306	.390	.511	119	11	21	.915	-6	62	59	O80(45/2/33),S19		0.0
1895	Was	N	130	519	116	168	22	22	6	55	71	1	28	.324	.406	.486	131	24	31	.913	16	119	88	O119(118/0/1),S6,2b5		2.4
1896	Was	N	127	487	100	148	17	13	5	100	76	2	28	.304	.405	.423	118	16	49	.946	8	74	61	O126(124/0/2)		1.1
1897	Was	N	124	448	113	152	25	16	5	59	80	4		.313	.414	.461	131	25	46	.955	12	79	55	O124L		2.2
1898	Was	N	132	515	88	156	28	11	3	60	64	3		.303	.383	.417	130	22	25	.948	20	130	123	O131(127/4/0)/S		2.8
1899	Cin	N	141	525	105	156	28	11	6	87	70	6		.297	.386	.410	116	14	38	.953	11	116	166	O141(101/40/0)		1.2
1900	NY	N	141	523	98	176	29	12	4	68	72	8		.337	.425	.461	151	41	36	.951	12	132	141	O141L		3.7
1901	NY	N	125	502	89	145	29	6	1	56	45	2		.289	.350	.376	115	11	8	.942	-9	70	46	O125L		-0.4
1902	Bal	A	128	503	86	161	27	9	3	60	58	2		.320	.393	.427	122	17	22	.941	10	105	79	O127L		1.9
1903	Was	A	140	533	68	134	23	12	3	49	41	0		.251	.305	.356	96	-3	20	.956	-1	66	49	O140(120/0/20)/3		-1.2
1904	Was	A	48	178	15	49	8	4	0	14	24	0		.275	.361	.365	132	8	9	.931	1	86	57	O48L		0.6
	Bos	A	98	376	50	97	19	8	0	30	48	3		.258	.347	.351	114	8	10	.961	1	72	81	O98L		0.4
	Year		146	554	65	146	27	12	0	44	72	3		.264	.351	.356	120	16	19	.950	2	77	73	O146L		1.0
1905	Bos	A	121	418	54	103	16	6	4	47	67	3		.246	.355	.342	120	13	12	.928	-6	60	35	O112(0/20/92)		0.2
1906	Bos	A	67	228	15	49	9	7	0	23	18	3		.215	.277	.268	71	-7	7	.966	0	79	122	O58L		-1.1
Total	13		1612	6165	1066	1807	301	149	44	779	785	42	76	.293	.377	.412	121	200	334	.944	71	85	85	O1570(1356/66/148),S26,2b5/3		13.8

SELBY, BILL William Frank B6.11.1970 Monroeville AL BL/TR/5-9/195* [BosA92 13/366] d4.19 Col Southern Mississippi

YEAR	TM	LG	G	AB	R	H	2B	3B	HR	RBI	BB-IB	HP	SO	AVG	OBP	SLG	AOPS	ABR	SB-CS	FA	FR	RNG	THR	GAMES AT POSITION	DL	BFW
1996	Bos	A	40	95	12	26	4	0	3	6	9-1	1	11	.274	.337	.411	86	-2	1-1	.980	-6	80	56	2b14,3b14,O6L		-0.7
2000	Cle	A	30	46	8	11	1	0	0	4	1-0	1	9	.239	.271	.261	34	-5	0-0	1.000	-1	119	0	O10(4/0/6),2b6,3b4,D6		-0.5
2001	Cin	N	36	92	7	21	7	1	2	12	5-1	1	13	.228	.273	.391	66	-5	0-0	1.000	-2	99	114	2b21,3b8,1b2		-0.6
2002	Cle	A	65	159	15	34	7	2	6	21	15-2	0	27	.214	.278	.396	76	-6	0-1	.933	-2	95	59	3b33,O18(13/0/5),2b6		-0.8
2003	Cle	A	27	39	3	4	1	0	0	5	3-0	0	11	.103	.163	.128	-21	-7	0-0	.926	3	159	197	3b10/12OLD		-0.4
Total	5		198	431	45	96	20	3	11	48	33-4	2	71	.223	.279	.360	63	-25	1-2	.917	-7	96	87	3b69,2b48,O35(24/0/11),D8,1b3		-3.0

SELF, TODD Todd Douglas B11.9.1978 Shreveport LA BL/TR/6-5/215 d5.12 Col Louisiana-Monroe

YEAR	TM	LG	G	AB	R	H	2B	3B	HR	RBI	BB-IB	HP	SO	AVG	OBP	SLG	AOPS	ABR	SB-CS	FA	FR	RNG	THR	GAMES AT POSITION	DL	BFW
2005	Hou	N	21	45	7	9	2	0	1	4	3-0	0	9	.200	.250	.311	46	-4	0-0	1.000	0	118	0	O15(5/0/10)		-0.4

SELKIRK, GEORGE George Alexander "Twinkletoes" B1.4.1908 Huntsville ON, Can. D1.19.1987 Ft.Lauderdale FL BL/TR/6-1/182 d8.12 Mil 1943-45

YEAR	TM	LG	G	AB	R	H	2B	3B	HR	RBI	BB-IB	HP	SO	AVG	OBP	SLG	AOPS	ABR	SB-CS	FA	FR	RNG	THR	GAMES AT POSITION	DL	BFW
1934	NY	A	46	176	23	55	7	1	5	38	15	1	17	.313	.370	.449	118	4	1-5	.989	1	105	86	O46(43/0/7)		0.3
1935	NY	A	128	491	64	153	29	12	11	94	44	3	36	.312	.372	.487	128	13	2-7	.975	5	114	98	O127R		1.3
1936	†NY	A★	137	493	93	152	28	9	18	107	94	1	60	.308	.420	.511	133	29	13-7	.974	2	106	80	O135(18/0/118)		2.0
1937	†NY	A	78	256	49	84	13	5	18	68	34	2	24	.328	.411	.629	157	22	8-2	.987	4	104	138	O69R		2.0
1938	†NY	A	99	335	58	85	12	5	10	62	68	3	52	.254	.384	.409	99	1	9-4	.973	-3	91	104	O95L		-0.6
1939	†NY	A★	128	418	103	128	17	4	21	101	103	8	49	.306	.452	.517	149	38	12-5	.989	-4	98	47	O124(86/0/38)		2.6
1940	NY	A	118	379	68	102	17	5	19	71	84	3	45	.269	.406	.491	137	24	3-6	.962	-0	95	111	O111(79/2/31)		1.5
1941	†NY	A	70	164	30	36	5	0	6	25	28	2	30	.220	.340	.360	86	-3	1-0	.967	0	99	107	O47(19/0/28)		-0.5
1942	†NY	A	42	78	15	15	3	0	0	8	18	0	8	.192	.330	.231	65	-4	0-0	1.000	0	109	0	O19R		-0.5
Total	9		846	2790	503	810	131	41	108	556	486	23	319	.290	.400	.483	128	130	49-32	.977	4	102	89	O773(340/2/437)		8.1

YEAR	TM LG	G	AB	R	H	2B	3B	HR	RBI	BB-IB	HP	SO	AVG	OBP	SLG	AOPS	ABR	SB-CS	FA	FR	RNG	THR	GAMES AT POSITION	DL	BFW

SELLERS, RUBE Oliver B3.7.1881 Duquesne PA D1.14.1952 Pittsburgh PA BR/TR/5-10/180 d8.12

| 1910 | Bos N | 12 | 32 | 3 | 5 | 0 | 0 | 0 | 2 | 6 | 0 | 5 | .156 | .289 | .156 | 29 | -3 | 1 | 1.000 | -1 | 86 | 0 | O9(8/0/1) | | -0.4 |

SELLMAN, FRANK Charles Francis (aka Frank C. Williams 1871-75) B1852 Baltimore MD D5.6.1907 Baltimore MD d5.4 ▲

1871	Kek NA	14	65	14	15	3	0	1	10	4		0	.231	.275	.323	70	-2	1-0	.711	-2	38	157	3b14,C5,S2		-0.3
1872	Oly NA	9	42	3	10	2	0	0	1	0		1	.238	.238	.286	64	-1	0-2	.788	-3			C7,3b2		-0.3
1873	Mar NA	1	3	1	1	0	0	0	0	0		0	.333	.333	.333	129	0	0-0	.000	0	0	0	/P		0.0
1874	Bal NA	12	54	9	16	3	2	0	7	0		2	.296	.296	.426	130	2	2-0	.304	-15			C6,S6,2b2,3b2,O2(0/1/1)		-1.0
1875	Was NA	1	3	0	1	0	0	0	0	0		0	.333	.333	.333	137	0	0-0	1.000	0	0	0	/1		0.0
Total	5 NA	37	167	27	43	8	2	1	18	4		3	.257	.275	.347	88	-1	3-2	.657	-20			C18,3b18,S8,O2(0/1/1),2b2/1P		-1.6

SELPH, CAREY Carey Isom B12.5.1901 Donaldson AR D2.24.1976 Houston TX BR/TR/5-9.5/175 d5.25 Col Ouachita Baptist

1929	StL N	25	51	8	12	1	1	0	7	6	0	4	.235	.316	.294	52	-4	1	.981	-3	85	47	2b16		-0.6
1932	Chi A	116	396	50	112	19	8	0	51	31	4	9	.283	.341	.371	90	-6	7-6	.910	-4	91	109	3b71,2b26		-0.7
Total	2	141	447	58	124	20	9	0	58	37	4	13	.277	.338	.362	85	-10	8-6	.910	-7	91	109	3b71,2b42		-1.3

SEMBER, MIKE Michael David B2.24.1953 Hammond IN BR/TR/6-0/185* [ChiN74 2/31] d8.18 Col Tulsa

1977	Chi N	3	4	0	1	0	0	0	0	0-0	0	2	.250	.250	.250	31	0	0-0	1.000	0	84	209	/2		0.0
1978	Chi N	9	3	2	1	0	0	0	0	1-0	0	1	.333	.500	.333	122	0	0-0	.667	-0	86	0	3b7/S		0.0
Total	2	12	7	2	2	0	0	0	0	1-0	0	3	.286	.375	.286	75	0	0-0	.667	-0	86	0	3b7/S2		0.0

SEMINICK, ANDY Andrew Wasil B9.12.1920 Pierce WV D2.22.2004 Melbourne FL BR/TR/5-11/187(187-198) d9.14 C5

1943	Phi N	22	72	9	13	2	0	2	5	7	0	22	.181	.253	.292	60	-4	0	.930	-0	96	113	C22/OL		-0.3
1944	Phi N	22	63	9	14	2	1	0	4	6	1	17	.222	.300	.286	68	-3	0	.963	1	118	114	C11,O7L		-0.2
1945	Phi N	80	188	18	45	7	2	6	26	18	2	38	.239	.313	.394	98	-1	3	.979	-4	69	121	C70,3b4/OL		-0.2
1946	Phi N	124	406	55	107	15	5	12	52	39	4	86	.264	.334	.414	115	6	2	.974	-3	93	93	C118		1.0
1947	Phi N	111	337	48	85	16	2	13	50	58	5	69	.252	.370	.427	115	9	4	.978	1	72	120	C107		1.6
1948	Phi N	125	391	49	88	11	3	13	44	58	2	68	.225	.328	.368	90	-6	4	.965	-2	63	153	C124		0.6
1949	Phi N★	109	334	52	81	11	2	24	68	69	15	74	.243	.380	.503	138	20	0	.975	3	86	120	C98		2.7
1950	†Phi N	130	393	55	113	15	3	24	68	68	6	50	.288	.400	.524	143	27	0	.976	4	104	80	C124		3.6
1951	Phi N	101	291	42	66	8	1	11	37	63	3	67	.227	.370	.375	102	3	1-0	.979	-1	109	92	C91		0.6
1952	Cin N	108	336	38	86	16	1	14	50	35	2	65	.256	.330	.435	111	4	1-3	.973	-3	92	103	C99		0.7
1953	Cin N	119	387	46	91	12	0	19	64	49	1	82	.235	.323	.413	90	-6	2-2	.982	-3	130	67	C112		0.7
1954	Cin N	86	247	26	58	9	4	7	30	48	2	39	.235	.362	.389	93	-1	0-0	.989	4	172	115	C82		-0.1
1955	Cin N	6	15	1	2	0	0	1	1	0-0	0	3	.133	.133	.333	18	-2	0-0	1.000	1	128	0	C5		-0.1
	Phi N	93	289	32	71	12	1	11	34	32-2	6	59	.246	.333	.408	97	-1	1-2	.994	11	112	79	C88		1.4
	Year	99	304	33	73	12	1	12	35	32-2	6	62	.240	.325	.405	93	-3	1-2	.994	12	113	75	C93		1.3
1956	Phi N	60	161	16	32	7	1	7	23	31-7	1	38	.199	.332	.360	88	-2	3-0	.976	-8	72	109	C54		-0.7
1957	Phi N	8	11	0	1	0	0	0	0	1	0	5	.091	.167	.091	-29	-2	0-0	1.000	0	101	0	C8		-0.2
Total	15	1304	3921	495	953	139	26	164	556	582-9	40	780	.243	.347	.417	107	41	23-7	.977	3	98	104	C1213,O9L,3b4		10.3

SENERCHIA, SONNY Emanuel Robert B4.6.1931 Newark NJ D11.1.2003 Freehold NJ BR/TR/6-1/195 d8.22 Col Montclair St.

| 1952 | Pit N | 29 | 100 | 5 | 22 | 5 | 0 | 3 | 11 | 4 | 0 | 21 | .220 | .250 | .360 | 66 | -5 | 0-3 | .953 | -5 | 70 | 72 | 3b28 | | -1.1 |

SENSENDERFER, COUNT John Phillips Jenkins B12.28.1847 Philadelphia PA D5.3.1903 Philadelphia PA 5-9/170 d5.20

1871	Ath NA	25	127	38	41	5	2	0	23	0		1	.323	.323	.394	106	1	5-3	.814	-3	68	196	O25C		-0.1
1872	Ath NA	1	5	2	2	0	0	0	1	0		0	.400	.400	.400	146	0	0-1	.827	0	0	38	/OR		0.0
1873	Ath NA	20	86	12	24	1	0	0	8	0		2	.279	.279	.291	65	-4	0-2	.827	-1	0	0	O19C/1		-0.4
1874	Ath NA	5	16	3	3	0	0	0	2	0		0	.188	.188	.188	19	-2	0-0	.625	-1	0	0	O5(0/1/4)		-0.2
Total	4 NA	51	234	55	70	6	2	0	34	0		3	.299	.299	.342	85	-5	5-6	.807	-3	51	103	O50(0/45/5)/1		-0.7

SENTELL, PAUL Leopold Theodore B8.27.1879 New Orleans LA D4.27.1923 Cincinnati OH BR/TR/5-9/176 d4.12 U2

1906	Phi N	63	192	19	44	5	1	1	14	14	3		.229	.292	.281	79	-5	15	.887	-9	99	26	3b33,2b19,O2R/S		-1.5
1907	Phi N	3	3	0	0	0	0	0	0	1	0		.000	.250	.000	-22	0	0	1.000	-1	57	0	S2/OR		-0.1
Total	2	66	195	19	44	5	1	1	14	15	3		.226	.291	.277	77	-5	15	.887	-10	99	26	3b33,2b19,S3,O3R		-1.6

SEPKOWSKI, TED Theodore Walter (b Theodore Walter Sczepkowski) B11.9.1923 Baltimore MD D3.8.2002 Severna Park MD BL/TR/5-11/190 d9.9 Mil 1944-45

1942	Cle A	5	10	1	1	0	0	0	0	0	0	3	.100	.100	.100	-46	-2	1	.824	-1	113	0	2b2		-0.3
1946	Cle A	2	8	2	4	1	0	1	0	0	0	0	.500	.500	.625	228	1	0-0	.833	-1	49	225	3b2		0.1
1947	Cle A	10	8	0	1	0	0	0	1	1	0	1	.125	.222	.250	32	-1	0-0	—	0		0	/OR		0.0
	NY A	2	0	1	0	0	0	0	0	0	0	0						0-1	—	-0	0	0	/R		-0.1
	Year	12	8	1	1	0	0	0	1	1	0	1	.125	.222	.250	32	-1	0-1	—	-0	0	0	/OR		-0.1
Total	3	19	26	3	6	1	0	1	1	1	0	4	.231	.259	.308	61	-2	0-1	.833	-1	49	225	3b2,2b2/OR		-0.3

SERENA, BILL William Robert B10.2.1924 Alameda CA D4.17.1996 Hayward CA BR/TR/5-9.5/175* d9.16

1949	Chi N	12	37	3	8	3	0	1	7	5	0	9	.216	.341	.378	95	0	1	.923	-3	76	0	3b11		-0.3
1950	Chi N	127	435	56	104	20	4	17	61	65	1	75	.239	.339	.421	100	0	1	.945	-3	102	86	3b125		-0.4
1951	Chi N	13	39	8	13	3	1	1	4	11	1	4	.333	.490	.538	173	4	0-2	.941	-2	75	37	3b12	40	0.2
1952	Chi N	122	390	49	107	21	5	15	61	39	3	83	.274	.345	.469	122	11	1-0	.971	-5	90	53	3b58,2b49		1.0
1953	Chi N	93	275	30	69	10	5	10	52	41	1	46	.251	.350	.433	100	0	0-0	.983	-11	88	68	2b49,3b28		-0.7
1954	Chi N	41	63	8	10	0	1	4	13	14	1	18	.159	.316	.381	81	-2	0-0	.933	-2	107	0	3b12,2b2		-0.4
Total	6	408	1239	154	311	57	16	48	198	177	7	235	.251	.348	.439	108	14	2-2	.951	-25	96	73	3b246,2b100	40	-0.5

SERNA, PAUL Paul David B11.16.1958 El Centro CA BR/TR/5-8/170* d9.1 Col Azusa Pacific

1981	Sea A	30	94	11	24	2	0	4	9	3-0	2	11	.255	.293	.404	95	-1	2-3	.954	-3	105	45	S23,2b7		-0.2
1982	Sea A	65	169	15	38	3	0	3	8	4-0	1	13	.225	.246	.296	47	-13	0-5	.936	-3	101	100	S31,2b18,3b15,D2		-1.5
Total	2	95	263	26	62	5	0	7	17	7-0	3	24	.236	.263	.335	63	-14	2-8	.945	-6	103	73	S54,2b25,3b15,D2		-1.6

SERVAIS, SCOTT Scott Daniel B6.4.1967 LaCrosse WI BR/TR/6-2/205(195-210) [HouN88 3/64] d7.12 Col Creighton

1991	Hou N	16	37	0	6	3	0	0	6	0	0	8	.162	.244	.243	39	-3	0-0	.988	1	180	91	C14	34	-0.1
1992	Hou N	77	205	12	49	9	0	0	15	11-2	5	25	.239	.294	.283	67	-9	0-0	.995	-1	97	67	C73		-0.6
1993	Hou N	85	258	24	63	11	0	11	32	22-2	5	45	.244	.313	.415	97	-2	0-0	.996	4	100	71	C82		0.7
1994	Hou N	78	251	27	49	15	1	9	41	10-0	4	44	.195	.235	.371	58	-17	0-0	.996	-2	92	61	C78		-1.4
1995	Hou N	28	89	7	20	10	0	1	12	9-2	1	15	.225	.300	.371	82	-2	0-1	.977	-1	73	71	C28	24	-0.1
	Chi N	52	175	31	50	12	0	12	35	23-6	2	37	.286	.371	.560	143	11	2-1	.981	-1	85	120	C52		1.4
	Year	80	264	38	70	22	0	13	47	32-8	3	52	.265	.348	.496	123	9	2-2	.980	-1	81	103	C80		1.3
1996	Chi N	129	445	42	118	20	0	11	63	30-1	14	75	.265	.337	.384	85	-9	0-2	.988	1	99	102	C128/1		-0.8
1997	Chi N	122	385	36	100	21	0	6	45	24-7	6	56	.260	.311	.361	73	-15	0-1	.990	-0	92	117	C118/1D		-2.0
1998	†Chi N	113	325	35	72	15	1	9	36	26-6	5	51	.222	.289	.338	62	-18	1-0	.994	-8	92	94	C110/1	22	-0.5
1999	SF N	69	198	21	54	10	0	5	21	13-2	3	31	.273	.327	.399	88	-4	0-0	.992	-5	88	75	C62/1	57	-0.5
2000	Col N	33	101	6	22	4	0	1	13	7-2	1	16	.218	.273	.287	34	-10	0-1	.987	6	80	102	C32		-0.5
	SF N	7	8	1	2	0	0	0	0	2-1	0	1	.250	.400	.250	74	0	0-0	1.000	0	0	0	C6		-0.0
	Year	40	109	7	24	4	0	1	13	9-3	1	17	.220	.283	.284	38	-10	0-1	.988	7	74	94	C38	20	-0.5
2001	Hou N	11	16	1	6	0	0	0	2	2-0	0	5	.375	.444	.375	107	1	0-0	1.000	2	212	0	C9	20	0.2
Total	11	820	2493	243	611	130	4	63	319	183-31	46	407	.245	.306	.375	79	-78	3-6	.991	-9	94	90	C792,1b4,D2	157	-3.5

SESSI, WALTER Walter Anthony "Watsie" B7.23.1918 Finleyville PA D4.18.1998 Mobile AL BL/TL/6-3/225 d9.18 Mil 1942-45

1941	StL N	5	13	2	0	0	0	0	0	0	0	2	.000	.071	.000	-74	-3	0	.750	-1	65	0	O3R		-0.4
1946	StL N	15	14	2	2	0	0	1	2	1	0	4	.143	.200	.357	54	-1	0	—	0			/H		-0.0
Total	2	20	27	4	2	0	0	1	2	1	0	6	.074	.138	.185	-9	-4	0	.750	-1	65	0	O3R		-0.4

SEVCIK, JOHN John Joseph B7.11.1942 Oak Park IL BR/TR/6-2/205 d4.24 Col Missouri

| 1965 | Min A | 12 | 16 | 1 | 1 | 0 | 0 | 0 | 0 | 1 | 0 | 5 | .063 | .118 | .125 | -30 | -3 | 0-0 | 1.000 | 2 | 29 | 218 | C11 | | -0.1 |

SEVEREID, HANK Henry Levai B6.1.1891 Story City IA D12.17.1968 San Antonio TX BR/TR/6-0/175 d5.15 Mil 1918

1911	Cin N	37	56	5	17	6	1	0	3	1		6	.304	.350	.446	127	2	0	.913	-1	129	79	C22		0
1912	Cin N	50	114	10	27	0	3	0	13	8		11	.237	.287	.289	60	-7	0	.943	-6	88	63	C20,1b7,O6(5/1/0)		-0
1913	Cin N	8	6	0	0	0	0	0	0	1		0	.000	.143	.000	-58	-1	0	1.000	-0	56	0	C2/OL		0

YEAR	TM LG	G	AB	R	H	2B	3B	HR	RBI	BB-IB	HP	SO	AVG	OBP	SLG	AOPS	ABR	SB-CS	FA	FR	RNG	THR	GAMES AT POSITION	DL	BFW
1915	StL A	80	203	12	45	6	1	1	22	16	0	25	.222	.279	.276	69	-8	2-1	.966	-7	87	91	C64		-1.1
1916	StL A	100	293	23	80	8	2	0	34	26	4	17	.273	.341	.314	102	1	3	.976	-15	80	85	C89/13		-0.8
1917	StL A	143	501	45	133	23	4	1	57	28	1	20	.265	.306	.333	99	-3	6	.966	-20	81	100	C139/1		-1.2
1918	StL A	51	133	8	34	4	0	0	11	18	3	4	.256	.357	.286	97	1	4	.946	-6	80	95	C42		-0.2
1919	StL A	112	351	16	87	12	2	0	36	21	4	13	.248	.298	.293	65	-17	2	.983	-2	96	85	C103		-1.0
1920	StL A	123	422	46	117	14	5	2	49	33	4	11	.277	.336	.348	79	-13	5-3	.983	-1	95	98	C117		-0.3
1921	StL A	143	472	66	153	23	4	3	78	42	0	9	.324	.379	.415	97	-2	7-2	.972	-1	106	97	C126		0.6
1922	StL A	137	517	49	166	32	7	3	78	28	0	12	.321	.356	.427	100	-1	1-4	.984	9	119	120	C133		1.6
1923	StL A	122	432	50	133	27	6	3	51	31	1	11	.308	.356	.419	98	-2	3-0	.972	1	98	98	C116		1.4
1924	StL A	137	432	37	133	23	2	4	48	36	1	15	.308	.362	.398	90	-6	1-6	.989	-3	93	118	C130		-0.2
1925	StL A	34	109	15	40	9	0	1	21	11	0	2	.367	.425	.477	122	4	0-2	.993	-1	85	109	C31		0.4
	†Was A	50	110	11	39	8	1	0	14	13	0	6	.355	.423	.445	123	5	0-0	.986	3	114	63	C35		0.8
	Year	84	219	26	79	17	1	1	35	24	0	8	.361	.424	.461	123	9	0-2	.990	2	99	87	C66		1.2
1926	Was A	22	34	2	7	1	0	0	4	3	0	2	.206	.270	.235	34	-3	0-0	.977	-0	104	96	C16		-0.3
	†NY A	41	127	13	34	8	1	0	13	13	0	4	.268	.336	.346	79	-4	1-1	.988	-2	82	96	C40		-0.3
	Year	63	161	15	41	9	1	0	17	16	0	6	.255	.322	.323	70	-7	1-1	.985	-2	86	96	C56		-0.3
Total	15	1390	4312	408	1245	204	42	17	539	331	19	169	.289	.342	.367	91	-54	35-19	.978	-43	96	99	C1225,1b9,O7(6/1/0)/3		-1.7

SEVERSON, RICH Richard Allen B1.18.1945 Artesia CA BR/TR/6-0/170(160-174) d4.10

YEAR	TM LG	G	AB	R	H	2B	3B	HR	RBI	BB-IB	HP	SO	AVG	OBP	SLG	AOPS	ABR	SB-CS	FA	FR	RNG	THR	GAMES AT POSITION	DL	BFW
1970	KC A	77	240	22	60	11	1	1	22	16-2	1	33	.250	.300	.317	70	-10	0-0	.962	0	107	120	S50,2b25		-0.3
1971	KC A	16	30	4	9	0	2	0	1	3-0	0	5	.300	.344	.433	126	1	0-0	1.000	4	154	225	2b6,S6/3		0.5
Total	2	93	270	26	69	11	3	1	23	19-2	1	38	.256	.307	.330	76	-9	0-0	.958	4	108	124	S56,2b31/3		0.2

SEWARD, GEORGE George T. B St.Louis MO D3.28.1904 St.Louis MO 5-7.5/145 d5.19

YEAR	TM LG	G	AB	R	H	2B	3B	HR	RBI	BB-IB	HP	SO	AVG	OBP	SLG	AOPS	ABR	SB-CS	FA	FR	RNG	THR	GAMES AT POSITION	DL	BFW
1875	StL NA	25	96	12	24	2	0	0	8	1		1	.250	.258	.271	92	0	1-0	.817	-2			C18,O7(3/1/3),2b2		-0.2
1876	NY N	1	3	0	0	0	0	0	0	0		0	.000	.000	.000	-99	-1		1.000	0	118	0	/2		0.0
1882	StL AA	38	144	23	31	1	1	0		12			.215	.276	.236	71	-4		.776	0	150	118	O35(6/2/27),C5		-0.4
Total	2	39	147	23	31	1	1	0	0	12		0	.211	.270	.231	68	-5		.817	0			O35(6/2/27),C5/2		-0.4

SEWELL, LUKE James Luther B1.5.1901 Titus AL D5.14.1987 Akron OH BR/TR/5-9/160 d6.30 M10/C4 b-Joe b-Tommy Col Alabama

YEAR	TM LG	G	AB	R	H	2B	3B	HR	RBI	BB-IB	HP	SO	AVG	OBP	SLG	AOPS	ABR	SB-CS	FA	FR	RNG	THR	GAMES AT POSITION	DL	BFW
1921	Cle A	3	6	0	0	0	0	0	1	0	0	3	.000	.000	.000	-99	-2	0-0	1.000	1	112	109	C3		-0.1
1922	Cle A	41	87	14	23	5	0	0	10	5	1	8	.264	.312	.322	65	-4	1-1	.963	-2	88	63	C39		-0.5
1923	Cle A	10	10	2	2	0	1	0	1	1	0	1	.200	.273	.400	76	-1	0-0	.833	-2	145	173	C7		0.0
1924	Cle A	63	165	27	48	9	1	0	17	22	4	13	.291	.387	.358	92	-1	1-0	.959	1	103	87	C57		0.4
1925	Cle A	74	220	30	51	10	2	0	18	33	2	18	.232	.337	.295	61	-12	6-2	.971	4	135	90	C66,O2L		-0.3
1926	Cle A	126	433	41	103	16	4	0	46	36	4	27	.238	.302	.293	55	-29	9-3	.983	9	173	63	C125		-1.0
1927	Cle A	128	470	52	138	27	6	0	53	20	4	23	.294	.328	.377	82	-14	9-8	.963	3	117	146	C126		-0.4
1928	Cle A	122	411	52	111	16	9	3	52	26	3	27	.270	.318	.375	81	-13	4-4	.972	2	106	124	C118		0.3
1929	Cle A	124	406	41	96	16	3	1	39	29	0	26	.236	.287	.298	49	-31	6-6	.966	2	92	111	C124		-2.1
1930	Cle A	76	292	40	75	21	2	1	43	14	1	9	.257	.293	.353	61	-18	5-2	.974	-4	86	91	C76		-1.4
1931	Cle A	108	375	45	103	30	4	1	53	36	2	7	.275	.344	.384	86	-7	1-1	.980	-6	103	108	C104		-0.7
1932	Cle A	87	300	36	76	20	2	2	52	38	2	24	.253	.337	.353	74	-11	4-5	.978	3	125	85	C84		-0.3
1933	†Was A	141	474	65	125	30	4	2	61	48	3	24	.264	.335	.357	84	-10	7-2	.990	5	181	61	C141		0.0
1934	Was A	72	207	21	49	7	3	2	21	22	1	10	.237	.313	.329	68	-10	0-1	.994	0	150	121	C50,O7(2/0/5),1b6/23		-0.8
1935	Chi A	118	421	52	120	19	3	2	67	32	5	18	.285	.336	.359	78	-14	3-2	.988	7	85	99	C112		0.0
1936	Chi A	128	451	59	113	20	5	5	73	54	1	16	.251	.332	.350	66	-25	11-2	.984	13	122	113	C126		-0.2
1937	Chi A☆	122	412	51	111	21	6	1	61	46	0	18	.269	.343	.357	77	-15	4-5	.985	9	118	93	C118		0.1
1938	Chi A	65	211	23	45	4	1	0	27	20	1	20	.213	.284	.242	32	-23	0-0	.985	8	118	130	C65		-1.0
1939	Cle A	16	20	1	3	1	0	0	1	3	0	1	.150	.261	.200	20	-2	0-0	.966	-1	90	126	C15/1		-0.2
1942	StL A	6	12	1	1	0	0	0	0	1	0	5	.083	.154	.083	-32	-2	0-0	.944	0	84	170	C6,M		-0.2
Total	20	1630	5383	653	1393	272	56	20	696	486	27	307	.259	.323	.341	70	-244	66-44	.978	56	121	100	C1562,O9(4/0/5),1b7/32		-8.4

SEWELL, JOE Joseph Wheeler B10.9.1898 Titus AL D3.6.1990 Mobile AL BL/TR/5-6.5/155 d9.10 C2 HF1977 b-Luke b-Tommy Col Alabama

YEAR	TM LG	G	AB	R	H	2B	3B	HR	RBI	BB-IB	HP	SO	AVG	OBP	SLG	AOPS	ABR	SB-CS	FA	FR	RNG	THR	GAMES AT POSITION	DL	BFW
1920	†Cle A	22	70	14	23	4	1	0	12	9	1	4	.329	.412	.414	116	2	1-0	.884	1	106	104	S22		0.4
1921	Cle A	154	572	101	182	36	12	4	93	80	11	17	.318	.412	.444	116	18	7-6	.944	2	99	107	S154		3.0
1922	Cle A	153	558	80	167	28	7	2	83	73	6	20	.299	.386	.385	101	4	10-12	.939	9	102	96	S139,2b12		2.6
1923	Cle A	153	553	98	195	41	10	3	109	98	7	12	.353	.456	.479	147	45	9-6	.930	5	106	104	S151		6.2
1924	Cle A	153	594	99	188	45	5	4	106	67	2	13	.316	.388	.429	109	10	3-3	.960	22	110	95	S153		4.5
1925	Cle A	155	608	78	204	37	7	1	98	64	4	4	.336	.402	.424	109	11	7-6	.967	16	111	85	S153,2b3		3.9
1926	Cle A	154	578	91	187	41	5	4	85	65	8	6	.324	.399	.433	116	16	17-7	.955	1	101	110	S154		3.4
1927	Cle A	153	569	83	180	48	5	1	92	51	7	9	.316	.382	.424	108	9	3-16	.962	1	100	88	S154		2.4
1928	Cle A	155	588	79	190	40	2	4	70	58	7	9	.323	.391	.418	111	13	7-1	.963	20	119	119	S137,3b19		5.3
1929	Cle A	152	578	90	182	38	3	7	73	48	5	4	.315	.372	.427	102	3	6-6	.975	14	115	92	3b152		2.4
1930	Cle A	109	353	44	102	17	6	0	48	41	7	3	.289	.374	.371	86	-6	1-4	.950	0	109	92	3b97		-0.1
1931	NY A	130	484	102	146	22	1	6	64	61	9	8	.302	.390	.388	111	12	1-1	.952	-6	92	66	3b121/2		0.9
1932	†NY A	125	503	95	137	21	3	11	68	56	4	3	.272	.349	.392	96	-2	0-2	.974	1	93	76	3b123		0.2
1933	NY A	135	524	87	143	18	1	2	54	71	1	4	.273	.361	.323	87	-6	2-2	.964	4	95	120	3b131		0.1
Total	14	1903	7132	1141	2226	436	68	49	1055	842	80	114	.312	.391	.413	109	129	74-72	.951	94	105	101	S1216,3b643,2b16		35.2

SEWELL, TOMMY Thomas Wesley B4.16.1906 Titus AL D7.30.1956 Montgomery AL BL/TR/5-7.5/155 d6.21 b-Luke b-Joe Col Alabama

YEAR	TM LG	G	AB	R	H	2B	3B	HR	RBI	BB-IB	HP	SO	AVG	OBP	SLG	AOPS	ABR	SB-CS	FA	FR	RNG	THR	GAMES AT POSITION	DL	BFW
1927	Chi N	1	1	0	0	0	0	0	0	0	0	0	.000	.000	.000	-99	0	0	—	0			/H		0.0

SEXSON, RICHIE Richmond Lockwood B12.29.1974 Portland OR BR/TR/6-7/225(206-235) [CleA93 24/671] d9.14

YEAR	TM LG	G	AB	R	H	2B	3B	HR	RBI	BB-IB	HP	SO	AVG	OBP	SLG	AOPS	ABR	SB-CS	FA	FR	RNG	THR	GAMES AT POSITION	DL	BFW
1997	Cle A	5	11	1	3	0	0	0	0	0-0	0	2	.273	.273	.273	41	-1	0-0	1.000	-0	74	0	1b2/D		-0.1
1998	†Cle A	49	174	28	54	14	1	11	35	6-0	1	42	.310	.344	.592	132	8	1-1	.984	2	126	102	1b45,O3L,D2		0.5
1999	†Cle A	134	479	72	122	17	7	31	116	34-0	4	117	.255	.305	.514	100	-4	3-3	.988	3	146	96	1b61,O49(48/0/3),D24		-0.9
2000	Cle A	91	324	45	83	16	1	16	44	25-0	4	96	.256	.315	.460	90	-6	1-0	1.000	-0	76	99	O58L,1b27,D10		-1.0
	Mil N	57	213	44	63	14	0	14	47	34-2	1	63	.296	.398	.559	140	14	1-0	.991	9	164	102	1b57		1.7
2001	Mil N	158	598	94	162	24	3	45	125	60-5	6	178	.271	.342	.547	128	22	2-4	.995	9	121	95	1b158		1.5
2002	Mil N★	157	570	86	159	37	2	29	102	70-7	8	136	.279	.363	.504	130	23	0-0	.995	10	125	99	1b154/D		1.9
2003	Mil N★	162	606	97	165	28	2	45	124	98-7	9	151	.272	.379	.548	139	36	2-3	.993	9	124	89	1b162		2.9
2004	Ari N	23	90	20	21	4	0	9	23	14-0	0	21	.233	.337	.578	122	3	0-0	.996	5	185	91	1b23		0.6
2005	Sea A	156	558	99	147	36	1	39	121	89-4	6	167	.263	.369	.541	126	41	1-1	.995	10	126	94	1b151,D5	156	10.6
Total	9	992	3623	586	979	190	17	239	737	430-25	43	973	.270	.352	.530	126	136	11-12	.993	57	131	94	1b840,O110(109/0/3),D43	156	10.6

SEXTON, CHRIS Christopher Philip B8.3.1971 Cincinnati OH BR/TR/5-11/180* [CinN93 10/288] d5.3 Col Miami-Ohio

YEAR	TM LG	G	AB	R	H	2B	3B	HR	RBI	BB-IB	HP	SO	AVG	OBP	SLG	AOPS	ABR	SB-CS	FA	FR	RNG	THR	GAMES AT POSITION	DL	BFW
1999	Col N	35	59	9	14	0	1	1	7	11-1	0	10	.237	.357	.322	59	-4	4-2	1.000	0	72	264	O13(3/9/1),2b10,S6		-0.3
2000	Cin N	35	100	9	21	4	0	0	10	13-1	2	12	.210	.310	.250	43	-8	4-2	.954	-5	97	72	S14,2b12,3b3		-1.1
Total	2	70	159	18	35	4	1	1	17	24-2	2	22	.220	.328	.277	50	-12	8-4	.976	-4	93	78	2b22,S20,O13(3/9/1),3b3		-1.4

SEXTON, JIMMY Jimmy Dale B12.15.1951 Mobile AL BR/TR/5-10/175(160-175) d9.2

YEAR	TM LG	G	AB	R	H	2B	3B	HR	RBI	BB-IB	HP	SO	AVG	OBP	SLG	AOPS	ABR	SB-CS	FA	FR	RNG	THR	GAMES AT POSITION	DL	BFW
1977	Sea A	14	37	5	8	1	1	0	3	2-0	0	6	.216	.256	.378	71	-2	1-1	.929	2	124	147	S12		0.1
1978	Hou N	88	141	17	29	3	2	2	6	13-1	0	28	.206	.273	.298	63	-8	16-2	.981	-10	80	82	S58,3b8,2b3		-1.1
1979	Hou N	52	69	8	9	0	0	0	1	7-0	0	7	.130	.320	.209	50	-3	1-3	.943	0	107	159	S11,3b4,2b2		-0.3
1981	Oak A	7	3	3	0	0	0	0	0	0-0	0	2	.000	.000	.000	-99	-1	2-0	1.000	1	344	0	/3D		-0.3
1982	Oak A	69	139	19	34	4	0	2	14	9-0	1	24	.245	.289	.317	70	-6	16-0	.957	-10	86	68	S47,3b8,D5		-0.9
1983	StL N	6	9	1	1	0	0	0	0	1-1	0	1	.111	.200	.222	17	-1	0-0	1.000	1	143	205	S4,3b2		0.1
Total	6	236	372	53	81	9	3	5	24	32-2	1	71	.218	.279	.298	63	-21	36-6	.962	-16	90	91	S132,3b23,D6,2b5		-2.1

SEXTON, TOM Thomas William B3.14.1865 Rock Island IL D2.8.1934 Rock Island IL BL d9.27

YEAR	TM LG	G	AB	R	H	2B	3B	HR	RBI	BB-IB	HP	SO	AVG	OBP	SLG	AOPS	ABR	SB-CS	FA	FR	RNG	THR	GAMES AT POSITION	DL	BFW
1884	Mil U	12	47	9	11	2	0	0					.234	.294	.277	136			.853	-1	61	91	S12		0.1

SEYBOLD, SOCKS Ralph Orlando B11.23.1870 Washingtonville OH D12.22.1921 Greensburg PA BR/TR/5-11/175 d8.20

YEAR	TM LG	G	AB	R	H	2B	3B	HR	RBI	BB-IB	HP	SO	AVG	OBP	SLG	AOPS	ABR	SB-CS	FA	FR	RNG	THR	GAMES AT POSITION	DL	BFW
1899	Cin N	22	85	13	19	5	1	0	8	6	1		.224	.306	.306	60	-5	2	.917	0	119		O22(3/0/19)		-0.5
1901	Phi A	114	449	74	150	24	14	8	90	40	7		.334	.397	.503	142	25	15	.954	-5	79	68	O100(2/25/74),1b14		1.4
1902	Phi A	137	522	91	165	27	12	16	97	43	6		.316	.375	.506	137	24	6	.963	-1	61	81	O136(0/16/120)		1.6
1903	Phi A	137	522	76	156	45	8	8	84	38	6		.299	.353	.462	137	24	5	.964	-1	70	126	O120(0/1/119),1b18		1.8

YEAR	TM LG	G	AB	R	H	2B	3B	HR	RBI	BB-IB	HP	SO	AVG	OBP	SLG	AOPS	ABR	SB-CS	FA	FR	RNG	THR	GAMES AT POSITION	DL	BFW
1904	Phi A	143	510	56	149	26	9	3	64	42	4		.292	.351	.396	129	18	12	.975	2	87	145	O129R,1b13		1.6
1905	†Phi A	133	492	64	135	37	4	6	59	42	8		.274	.341	.402	133	20	5	.983	8	87	153	O133R		2.4
1906	Phi A	116	411	41	130	23	2	5	59	30	3		.316	.367	.418	141	20	9	.925	-3	73	102	O114R		1.3
1907	Phi A	147	564	58	153	29	4	5	92	40	4		.271	.324	.363	116	10	10	.973	0	100	171	O147R		0.5
1908	Phi A	48	130	5	28	7	0	0	3	12	1		.215	.287	.231	64	-5	2	.921	-1	96	0	O34R		-0.8
Total	9	997	3685	478	1085	218	54	51	556	293	40		.294	.353	.424	129	131	66	.961	-1	82	117	O935(5/42/889),1b45		9.3

SEYMOUR, CY James Bentley B12.9.1872 Albany NY D9.20.1919 New York NY BL/TL/6-0/200 d4.22 OF(20/1094/224) ▲

YEAR	TM LG	G	AB	R	H	2B	3B	HR	RBI	BB-IB	HP	SO	AVG	OBP	SLG	AOPS	ABR	SB-CS	FA	FR	RNG	THR	GAMES AT POSITION	DL	BFW
1896	NY N	12	32	2	7	0	0	0	0	0		7	.219	.219	.219	16	-4	0	.857	1	109	164	P11/OC		0.0
1897	NY N	45	141	13	34	5	1	2	14	4			.241	.262	.333	58	-9	3	.853	7	**158**	241	P39,O6(2/4/0)		0.2
1898	NY N	80	297	41	82	5	2	4	23	9	1		.276	.300	.347	88	-6	8	.887	6	127	233	P45,O35(10/12/15)/2		-0.3
1899	NY N	50	159	25	52	3	2	2	27	4	0		.327	.344	.409	110	1	2	.839	2	130	43	P32,O8(2/1/5),1b3/3		0.0
1900	NY N	23	40	9	12	0	0	0	2	-3	0		.300	.349	.300	84	-1	0	.828	-0	150	0	P13,O3(1/1/2)/1		-0.1
1901	Bal A	**134**	547	84	166	19	8	1	77	28	2		.303	.337	.373	90	-7	38	.945	14	135	99	O133(4/0/131)/1		0.1
1902	Bal A	72	280	38	75	8	3	4	41	18	2		.268	.317	.386	90	-5	12	.956	2	99	94	O72(0/3/70)		-0.6
	Cin N	62	244	27	83	8	2	2	37	12	3		.340	.378	.414	132	9	8	.920	2	118	137	O61C/P3		0.8
1903	Cin N	135	558	85	191	25	5	7	72	33	3		.342	.382	.478	130	19	25	.902	3	76	46	O135C		1.5
1904	Cin N	131	531	71	166	26	13	5	58	29	3		.313	.352	.439	132	18	11	.951	9	121	88	O149C		2.1
1905	Cin N	149	581	95	**219**	**40**	**21**	8	**121**	51	2		**.377**	**.429**	**.559**	**175**	**52**	21	.947	10	128	**237**	O79C		5.6
1906	Cin N	79	307	35	79	7	2	4	38	24	3		.257	.317	.332	98	-1	9	.968	1	97	118	O72C		0.2
	NY N	72	269	35	86	12	3	4	42	18	1		.320	.365	.431	145	13	20	.978	-2	81	150	O151C		0.9
	Year	151	576	70	165	19	5	8	80	42	4		.286	.339	.378	120	12	29	.972	5	90	133	O126C		1.1
1907	NY N	131	473	46	139	25	8	3	75	36	5		.294	.350	.400	131	16	21	.975	-0	4	59	O155C		1.1
1908	NY N	156	587	60	157	23	2	5	92	30	3		.267	.306	.339	101	0	18	.949	5	145	**208**	O74(1/71/1)		-0.3
1909	NY N	80	280	37	87	12	5	1	30	25	1		.311	.369	.400	137	12	14	.968	-1	107	138	O76C		0.8
1910	NY N	79	287	32	76	9	4	1	40	23	2	18	.265	.324	.334	92	-4	10	.936	-7	84	93	O18C		-1.5
1913	Bos N	39	73	2	13	2	0	0	10	7	1	7	.178	.259	.205	33	-6	2-1	.950	1	95	189	O16C		-0.6
Total	16	1529	5686	737	1724	229	96	52	799	354	30	32	.303	.347	.405	117	97	222-1	.945	58	102	126	O1333C,P141,1b5,3b2/2		9.9

SHABALA, ADAM Adam Jason B2.6.1978 Streator IL BL/TR/6-1/190 d6.16 Col Nebraska

YEAR	TM LG	G	AB	R	H	2B	3B	HR	RBI	BB-IB	HP	SO	AVG	OBP	SLG	AOPS	ABR	SB-CS	FA	FR	RNG	THR	GAMES AT POSITION	DL	BFW
2005	SF N	6	15	1	3	0	0	0	4	1-0		5	.200	.235	.200	19	-2	0-0	.875	-0	107	0	O5(4/0/1)		-0.2

SHAFER, TILLIE Arthur Joseph B3.22.1889 Los Angeles CA D1.10.1962 Los Angeles CA BB/TR/5-10/165 d4.24 Col Santa Clara

YEAR	TM LG	G	AB	R	H	2B	3B	HR	RBI	BB-IB	HP	SO	AVG	OBP	SLG	AOPS	ABR	SB-CS	FA	FR	RNG	THR	GAMES AT POSITION	DL	BFW
1909	NY N	38	84	11	15	2	1	0	7	14	0		.179	.296	.226	61	-3	6	.750	-3	91	82	3b16,2b13,O2(0/1/1)		-0.6
1910	NY N	29	21	5	4	1	0	0	1	0	0	6	.190	.190	.238	25	-2	0	.889	2	183	478	3b8,2b2,S2		0.0
1912	†NY N	78	163	48	47	4	1	0	23	30	3	19	.288	.408	.325	99	2	22	.879	-5	81	81	S31,3b16,2b15		0.4
1913	†NY N	138	508	74	146	17	12	5	52	61	5	55	.287	.369	.398	118	13	32-29	.903	-10	89	118	3b79,2b25,S16,O15(4/12/0)		-0.2
Total	4	283	776	138	212	24	14	5	83	105	8	80	.273	.366	.360	106	10	60-29	.903	-14	95	110	3b119,2b55,S49,O17(4/13/1)		-0.2

SHAFER, ORATOR George W. B10.1851 Philadelphia PA D1.21.1922 Philadelphia PA BL/TR/5-9/165 d5.23 b-Taylor

YEAR	TM LG	G	AB	R	H	2B	3B	HR	RBI	BB-IB	HP	SO	AVG	OBP	SLG	AOPS	ABR	SB-CS	FA	FR	RNG	THR	GAMES AT POSITION	DL	BFW
1874	Har NA	9	35	6	8	0	1	0	3	0		4	.229	.229	.314	69	-2	0-0	.710	-2	0	0	O9(8/0/1)		-0.2
	Mut NA	1	5	1	1	0	0	0	0	0		4	.200	.200	.200	28	0	0-0	—	0	0	0	/OR		0.0
	Year	10	40	7	9	0	1	0	3	0		4	.225	.225	.300	64	-2	0-0	.710	-2	0	0	O10(8/0/2)		-0.2
1875	Phi NA	19	70	10	17	2	1	0	6	0		4	.243	.243	.300	84	-1	2-0	.769	-2	55	307	O12(3/8/1),3b5,1b2		1.0
1877	Lou N	**61**	260	38	74	9	5	3	34	9		17	.285	.309	.392	101	-1		.835	13	179	56	O60(0/1/60)/1		**3.3**
1878	Ind N	**63**	266	48	90	19	6	0	30	13		20	.338	.369	.455	**196**	29		.842	8	172	80	O63(1/0/63)		2.0
1879	Chi N	73	316	53	96	13	0	0	35	6		28	.304	.317	.345	126	9		.901	19	**304**	169	O72R/3		2.3
1880	Cle N	83	338	62	90	14	9	0	21	17		36	.266	.301	.361	126	9		.901	15	180	156	O83R		2.3
1881	Cle N	**85**	343	48	88	13	6	1	34	23		20	.257	.303	.338	107	4		.880	-0	105	124	O85R		0.3
1882	Cle N	**84**	313	37	67	14	2	3	28	27		27	.214	.276	.300	88	-2		.805	-10	90	52	O84(2/1/83)		-1.2
1883	Buf N	95	401	67	117	11	3	0	41	27		39	.292	.336	.334	103	1		.861	16	186	87	O95R		1.5
1884	StL U	106	467	130	168	**40**	10	2		30			.360	.398	.501	165	25		.870	-3	99	95	O100(6/0/96),2b7/1		1.9
1885	StL N	69	257	30	50	11	2	0	18	19		31	.195	.250	.253	67	-8		.918	10	213	0	O69(0/1/68)		0.1
	Phi AA	2	9	1	2	0	1	0	1	1	0		.222	.300	.444	125	0		1.000	-0	0	0	O2C		0.0
1886	Phi AA	21	82	15	22	3	0	0	8	8	0		.268	.333	.378	121	2	3	.815	0	114	286	O21(0/18/4)		0.7
1890	Phi AA	100	390	55	110	15	5	1	58	47	5		.282	.367	.354	113	8	29	.958	2	102	137	O98R,1b3		-0.4
Total	2 NA	29	110	17	26	2	1	0	9	0		8	.236	.236	.300	76	-4	2-0	.737	-4	29	161	O22(11/8/3),3b5,1b2		-0.4
Total	11	842	3442	584	974	162	52	10	308	227	5	218	.283	.328	.369	119	70	32	.865	70	157	103	O832(9/23/807),2b7,1b5/3		12.

SHAFER, RALPH Ralph Newton B3.17.1894 Cincinnati OH D2.5.1950 Akron OH 5-11/? d7.25 Col Cincinnati

YEAR	TM LG	G	AB	R	H	2B	3B	HR	RBI	BB-IB	HP	SO	AVG	OBP	SLG	AOPS	ABR	SB-CS	FA	FR	RNG	THR	GAMES AT POSITION	DL	BFW
1914	Pit N	1	0	0	0	0	0	0	0	0			—	—	—		0	0	—	0			/H		0.

SHAFER, TAYLOR Zachary Taylor B7.13.1866 Philadelphia PA D10.27.1945 Glendale CA 5-7/155 d4.24 b-Orator

YEAR	TM LG	G	AB	R	H	2B	3B	HR	RBI	BB-IB	HP	SO	AVG	OBP	SLG	AOPS	ABR	SB-CS	FA	FR	RNG	THR	GAMES AT POSITION	DL	BFW
1884	Alt U	19	74	11	21	2	0	0		3			.284	.312	.311	88	-3		.889	-2	54	0	O17(9/7/1),C2/3		-0.
	KC U	44	164	18	28	3	2	0		15			.171	.240	.213	44	-16		.768	-3	115	0	O41R,C2/2S3		-1.
	Bal U	3	13	1	1	0	0	0		0			.077	.077	.077	-48	-3		.750	-0	148	0	O3(1/0/3)		-2.
	Year	66	251	30	50	5	2	0		18			.199	.253	.235	53	-22		.796	-6	101	0	O61(10/7/45),C4,3b2/2S		-1.
1890	Phi AA	69	261	28	45	3	4	0	21	28	2		.172	.258	.215	40	-20	19	.921	-3	93	103	2b69		-1.
Total	2	135	512	58	95	8	6	0	21	46	2		.186	.255	.225	46	-42	19	.920	-8	92	102	2b70,O61(10/7/45),C4,3b2/S		-4.

SHAFFER d9.15

YEAR	TM LG	G	AB	R	H	2B	3B	HR	RBI	BB-IB	HP	SO	AVG	OBP	SLG	AOPS	ABR	SB-CS	FA	FR	RNG	THR	GAMES AT POSITION	DL	BFW
1875	Atl NA	1	4	0	0	0	0	0	0	0		0	.000	.000	.000	-99	-1	0-0	.500	-0	0	0	/OR		-0.

SHAMSKY, ART Arthur Louis B10.14.1941 St.Louis MO BL/TL/6-1/175(168-180) d4.17 Col Missouri

YEAR	TM LG	G	AB	R	H	2B	3B	HR	RBI	BB-IB	HP	SO	AVG	OBP	SLG	AOPS	ABR	SB-CS	FA	FR	RNG	THR	GAMES AT POSITION	DL	BFW
1965	Cin N	64	96	13	25	4	3	2	10	0	0	29	.260	.330	.427	104	0	1-0	.966	2	120	251	O18(3/0/15)/1		0.
1966	Cin N	96	234	41	54	5	0	21	47	32-1	0	45	.231	.321	.521	120	6	0-2	.973	-0	101	73	O74(42/0/33)		0.
1967	Cin N	76	147	6	29	3	1	3	13	15-5	1	34	.197	.274	.293	56	-8	0-1	.984	1	111	97	O40(18/0/25)		-1.
1968	Cin N	116	345	30	82	14	4	12	48	21-6	7	58	.238	.292	.406	108	2	1-0	.993	3	111	129	O82(71/0/12),1b17		0.
1969	†NY N	100	303	42	91	9	3	14	47	36-2	3	32	.300	.375	.488	138	16	1-2	.992	-4	96	41	O78(16/0/63),1b9	22	0.
1970	NY N	122	403	48	118	19	2	11	49	49-13	3	33	.293	.371	.432	114	9	1-1	1.000	3	115	60	O58(4/0/54),1b56	27	0.
1971	NY N	68	135	13	25	2	5	5	18	21-2	1	18	.185	.299	.370	89	-2	1-1	.984	5	112	320	O38(12/0/27)/1		-0.
1972	Chi N	15	16	1	2	0	0	1	0	3-0	0	3	.125	.263	.125	12	-2	0-0	1.000	-0	66	54	1b4		-0.
	Oak A	8	7	0	0	0	0	0	1	1-0	0	2	.000	.125	.000	-64	-1	0-0	—	0			/H	49	-0.
Total	8	665	1686	194	426	60	15	68	233	188-29	15	254	.253	.330	.427	109	20	5-7	.987	9	107	108	O388(166/0/229),1b88		0.

SHANABROOK, WARREN Warren Hilton B11.30.1880 Massillon OH D3.10.1964 N.Canton OH BR/TR/6-0/170 d8.13

YEAR	TM LG	G	AB	R	H	2B	3B	HR	RBI	BB-IB	HP	SO	AVG	OBP	SLG	AOPS	ABR	SB-CS	FA	FR	RNG	THR	GAMES AT POSITION	DL	BFW
1906	Was A	1	2	0	0	0	0	0	0	0		5	.000	.000	.000	-99	0	0	1.000	-0	88	0	/3		-0.

SHANDLEY, JIM James H. B NY D11.4.1904 Brooklyn NY d5.3

YEAR	TM LG	G	AB	R	H	2B	3B	HR	RBI	BB-IB	HP	SO	AVG	OBP	SLG	AOPS	ABR	SB-CS	FA	FR	RNG	THR	GAMES AT POSITION	DL	BFW
1876	NY N	2	8	0	1	0	0	0	0	0		5	.125	.125	.125	-19	-1		.600	-1	0	0	O2(0/1/1)		-0.

SHANER, WALLY Walter Dedaker "Skinny" B5.24.1900 Lynchburg VA D11.13.1992 Las Vegas NV BR/TR/6-2/195 d5.4 Col VPI

YEAR	TM LG	G	AB	R	H	2B	3B	HR	RBI	BB-IB	HP	SO	AVG	OBP	SLG	AOPS	ABR	SB-CS	FA	FR	RNG	THR	GAMES AT POSITION	DL	BFW
1923	Cle A	3	4	1	1	0	0	0	0	1		0	.250	.400	.250	74	0	0-0	1.000	-0	102	0	O2L/3		0.
1926	Bos A	69	191	20	54	12	2	0	21	17	2	13	.283	.348	.366	89	-3	1-0	.965	-2	97	58	O48L		-0.
1927	Bos A	122	406	54	111	33	6	3	49	21	1	35	.273	.311	.406	87	-10	11-4	.955	-1	94	121	O108(85/25/10)/1		-1.
1929	Cin N	13	28	5	9	0	0	1	4	4		5	.321	.406	.429	112	1	1	1.000	-1	26	187	1b8,O2L		0.
Total	4	207	629	80	175	45	8	4	74	43		54	.278	.327	.394	89	-12	13-4	.959	-4	95	98	O160(137/25/10),1b9/3		-2.

SHANKS, HOWIE Howard Samuel "Hank" B7.21.1890 Chicago IL D7.30.1941 Monaca PA BR/TR/5-11/170 d5.9 C5 OF(603/55/44)

YEAR	TM LG	G	AB	R	H	2B	3B	HR	RBI	BB-IB	HP	SO	AVG	OBP	SLG	AOPS	ABR	SB-CS	FA	FR	RNG	THR	GAMES AT POSITION	DL	BFW
1912	Was A	116	399	52	92	14	7	1	48	40	3		.231	.305	.308	75	-13	21	.962	-2	91	102	O114(112/0/2)		-1.
1913	Was A	109	390	38	99	11	5	1	37	15	3	40	.254	.284	.315	75	-14	24	.978	2	104	89	O109L		-3.
1914	Was A	143	500	44	112	22	12	4	64	29	3	51	.224	.269	.332	78	-16	18-16	.954	-2	102	74	O139(94/43/2)		-3.
1915	Was A	141	492	52	123	19	8	0	47	30	3	42	.250	.297	.321	83	-12	12-14	.982	7	110	141	O80(75/1/4),3b49,2b10		0.
1916	Was A	140	471	45	119	15	7	1	48	41	4	34	.253	.317	.321	92	-5	23-12	.987	7	117	167	O88(72/3/13),3b31,S8,1b7		0.
1917	Was A	126	430	45	87	15	5	0	28	33	4	37	.202	.269	.260	62	-20	15	.929	7	92	110	S90,O26(21/5/0),1b2		-0.
1918	Was A	120	436	42	112	19	4	1	56	31	4	21	.257	.312	.326	94	-4	23	.957	-6	114	80	O64(54/2/8),2b48,3b3		-3.
1919	Was A	135	491	33	122	8	7	1	54	25	3	48	.248	.289	.299	79	-24	13	.922	-16	88	70	S94,2b34,O6L		-3.

YEAR	TM	LG	G	AB	R	H	2B	3B	HR	RBI	BB-IB	HP	SO	AVG	OBP	SLG	AOPS	ABR	SB-CS	FA	FR	RNG	THR	GAMES AT POSITION	DL	BFW
1920	Was	A	128	444	56	119	16	7	4	37	29	2	43	.268	.316	.363	82	-13	11-6	.951	-4	90	37	3b63,O35(32/0/3),1b14,2b5/S		-1.6
1921	Was	A	154	562	81	170	24	**18**	7	69	57	3	38	.302	.370	.447	113	9	11-10	**.960**	3	96	**124**	3b154/2		1.9
1922	Was	A	84	272	35	77	10	9	1	32	25	4	25	.283	.352	.397	100	-1	6-0	.920	5	106	151	3b54,O27(21/0/6)		0.6
1923	Bos	A	131	464	38	118	19	5	3	57	19	1	37	.254	.285	.316	63	-27	6-6	.939	-11	99	103	3b83,2b38,O6(4/1/1)/S		-3.3
1924	Bos	A	72	193	22	50	16	3	0	25	21	1	12	.259	.332	.373	81	-5	1-0	.972	6	96	114	S41,3b22,O4R,1b2,2b2		0.5
1925	NY	A	66	155	15	40	3	1	1	18	20	1	15	.258	.343	.310	68	-7	1-0	.938	-2	70	51	3b26,2b21,O4(3/0/1)		-0.9
Total	14		1665	5699	604	1440	211	96	25	620	415	37	443	.253	.308	.337	82	-152	185-64	.971	-8	115	109	O702L,3b485,S235,2b159,1b25		-16.5

SHANLEY, DOC Harry Root B1890 Granbury TX D12.13.1934 St.Petersburg FL BR/TR/6-0/174 d9.15 Col Washington-St. Louis

YEAR	TM	LG	G	AB	R	H	2B	3B	HR	RBI	BB-IB	HP	SO	AVG	OBP	SLG	AOPS	ABR	SB-CS	FA	FR	RNG	THR	GAMES AT POSITION	DL	BFW
1912	StL	A	5	8	1	0	0	0	0	1	2	0		.000	.000	.000	-43	-1	-5	.833	-1	43	130	S4		-0.3

SHANNON, DAN Daniel Webster B3.23.1865 Bridgeport CT D10.24.1913 Bridgeport CT 5-9/175 d4.17 M2

YEAR	TM	LG	G	AB	R	H	2B	3B	HR	RBI	BB-IB	HP	SO	AVG	OBP	SLG	AOPS	ABR	SB-CS	FA	FR	RNG	THR	GAMES AT POSITION	DL	BFW
1889	Lou	AA	121	498	90	128	22	12	4	48	42	0	52	.257	.315	.373	97	-3	26	.910	5	**113**	90	2b121,M		0.5
1890	Phi	P	19	75	15	18	5	1	1	16	4	0	12	.240	.278	.373	72	-4	4	.926	-3	96	48	2b19		-0.5
	NY	P	83	324	59	70	7	8	3	44	25	1	34	.216	.274	.315	53	-25	21	.908	0	111	98	2b77,S6		-1.8
	Year		102	399	74	88	.12	9	4	60	29	1	46	.221	.275	.326	56	-29	25	.911	-3	108	89	2b96,S6		-2.3
1891	Was	AA	19	67	7	9	2	0	0	3	6	0	9	.134	.205	.164	6	-8	3	.878	1	101	114	S14,2b5/M		-0.6
Total	3		242	964	171	225	36	21	8	111	77	1	107	.233	.291	.339	73	-40	54	.911	2	110	88	2b222,S20		-2.4

SHANNON, FRANK John Francis B12.3.1873 San Francisco CA D2.27.1934 Boston MA 5-3/155 d10.1

YEAR	TM	LG	G	AB	R	H	2B	3B	HR	RBI	BB-IB	HP	SO	AVG	OBP	SLG	AOPS	ABR	SB-CS	FA	FR	RNG	THR	GAMES AT POSITION	DL	BFW
1892	Was	N	1	4	0	1	0	0	0	2	0	0	2	.250	.250	.250	53	0	0	.625	-1	52	0	/S		-0.1
1896	Lou	N	31	115	14	18	1	1	1	15	13	1	15	.157	.248	.209	22	-13	3	.830	-13	79	52	S28,3b3		-2.1
Total	2		32	119	14	19	1	1	1	17	13	1	17	.160	.248	.210	23	-13	3	.820	-13	78	50	S29,3b3		-2.2

SHANNON, JOE Joseph Aloysius B2.11.1897 Jersey City NJ D7.28.1955 Jersey City NJ BR/TR/5-11/170 d7.7 twb-Red Col Seton Hall

YEAR	TM	LG	G	AB	R	H	2B	3B	HR	RBI	BB-IB	HP	SO	AVG	OBP	SLG	AOPS	ABR	SB-CS	FA	FR	RNG	THR	GAMES AT POSITION	DL	BFW
1915	Bos	N	5	10	3	2	0	0	0	1	0	0	3	.200	.200	.200	22	-1	0	.750	-1	68	0	O4(1/1/0)/2		-0.2

SHANNON, RED Maurice Joseph B2.11.1897 Jersey City NJ D4.12.1970 Jersey City NJ BB/TR/5-11/170 d10.7 twb-Joe Col Seton Hall

YEAR	TM	LG	G	AB	R	H	2B	3B	HR	RBI	BB-IB	HP	SO	AVG	OBP	SLG	AOPS	ABR	SB-CS	FA	FR	RNG	THR	GAMES AT POSITION	DL	BFW
1915	Bos	N	1	0	0	0	0	0	0	0	0	0	0	.000	.000	.000	-99	-1	0	.857	0	104	260	/2		-0.1
1917	Phi	A	11	35	8	10	0	0	0	7	6	0	9	.286	.390	.286	108	1	2	.875	-1	103	43	S10		0.1
1918	Phi	A	72	225	23	54	6	5	0	16	42	3	52	.240	.367	.311	103	3	5	.898	1	97	139	S45,2b26		0.8
1919	Phi	A	39	155	14	42	7	2	0	14	12	2	28	.271	.331	.342	88	-2	4	.948	-2	106	60	2b37		-0.4
	Bos	A	80	290	36	75	11	7	0	17	17	6	42	.259	.313	.345	90	-5	7	.973	-1	98	126	2b79		-0.5
	Year		119	445	50	117	18	9	0	31	29	8	70	.263	.320	.344	89	-7	11	.965	-3	101	105	2b116		-0.9
1920	Was	A	62	222	30	64	8	7	0	30	22	0	32	.288	.352	.387	98	-1	2-5	.919	-13	83	118	S31,2b16,3b15		-1.3
	Phi	A	25	88	4	15	1	0	0	3	4	0	12	.170	.207	.205	9	-12	1-1	.945	1	106	95	S24		-0.9
	Year		87	310	34	79	9	8	0	33	26	0	44	.255	.313	.335	73	-13	3-6	.931	-12	93	108	S55,2b16,3b15		-2.2
1921	Phi	A	1	1	0	0	0	0	0	0	0	0	0	.000	.000	.000	-99	-1	0-0	—	0			/H		0.0
1926	Chi	N	19	51	9	17	5	0	0	4	6	1	3	.333	.414	.431	126	2	0	.957	-1	100	77	S13		0.3
Total	7		310	1070	124	277	38	22	0	91	109	12	178	.259	.334	.336	89	-15	21-6	.957	-16	103	99	2b159,S123,3b15		-2.0

SHANNON, OWEN Owen Dennis Ignatius B12.22.1879 Omaha NE D4.10.1918 Omaha NE BR/TR d9.6

YEAR	TM	LG	G	AB	R	H	2B	3B	HR	RBI	BB-IB	HP	SO	AVG	OBP	SLG	AOPS	ABR	SB-CS	FA	FR	RNG	THR	GAMES AT POSITION	DL	BFW
1903	StL	A	9	28	1	6	2	0	0	3	1	0		.214	.241	.286	59	-1	0	.957	-0	133	63	C8/1		-0.1
1907	Was	A	4	7	0	0	0	0	0	0	0	0		.143	.143	.143	-10	-1	0	1.000	2	134	235	C4		0.1
Total	2		13	35	1	7	2	0	0	3	1	0		.200	.222	.257	47	-2	0	.970	1	133	107	C12/1		0.0

SHANNON, MIKE Thomas Michael "Moonman" B7.5.1939 St.Louis MO BR/TR/6-3/195* d9.11 Col Missouri

YEAR	TM	LG	G	AB	R	H	2B	3B	HR	RBI	BB-IB	HP	SO	AVG	OBP	SLG	AOPS	ABR	SB-CS	FA	FR	RNG	THR	GAMES AT POSITION	DL	BFW
1962	StL	N	10	15	3	2	0	0	0		1-0	0	3	.133	.188	.133	-11	-2	0-0	1.000	0	87	296	O7(5/0/2)		-0.2
1963	StL	N	32	26	3	8	0	0	1	2	0-0	1	6	.308	.333	.423	106	-2	0-0	.944	1	99	329	O26(13/1/12)		0.0
1964	†StL	N	88	253	30	66	8	2	9	43	19-1	0	54	.261	.310	.415	95	-2	4-0	.983	-1	88	138	O88(9/6/76)		-0.8
1965	StL	N	124	244	32	54	17	3	3	25	28-1	2	46	.221	.305	.352	78	-6	2-1	.994	9	132	108	O101(1/14/87),C4		-0.1
1966	StL	N	137	459	61	132	20	6	16	64	37-0	0	106	.288	.339	.462	120	12	8-4	.985	5	109	114	O129(14/7/112)/C		1.0
1967	†StL	N	130	482	53	118	18	3	12	77	37-6	4	89	.245	.302	.369	93	-5	2-4	.919	-13	93	92	3b122,O6(2/2/5)		-2.2
1968	†StL	N	156	576	62	153	29	2	15	79	37-5	2	114	.266	.309	.401	114	9	1-2	.952	-13	95	92	3b156		-0.6
1969	StL	N	150	551	51	140	15	5	12	55	49-7	1	87	.254	.315	.365	89	-9	1-4	.945	-18	86	88	3b149		-3.0
1970	StL	N	55	174	18	37	9	0	2	22	16-4	0	20	.213	.275	.287	51	-12	1-1	.919	-19	61	42	3b51		-3.2
Total	9		882	2780	313	710	116	23	68	367	224-24	10	525	.255	.311	.387	96	-15	19-17	.938	-48	88	86	3b478,O357(44/30/294),C5	82	-9.1

SHANNON, WALLY Walter Charles B1.23.1933 Cleveland OH D2.8.1992 Creve Coeur MO BL/TR/6-0/178* d7.9

YEAR	TM	LG	G	AB	R	H	2B	3B	HR	RBI	BB-IB	HP	SO	AVG	OBP	SLG	AOPS	ABR	SB-CS	FA	FR	RNG	THR	GAMES AT POSITION	DL	BFW
1959	StL	N	47	95	5	27	5	0	0		0-0	1	12	.284	.292	.337	63	-5	0-0	1.000	-6	50	98	S21,2b10		-1.0
1960	StL	N	18	23	2	4	0	0	0	1	3-1	1	6	.174	.296	.174	30	-2	0-0	1.000	3	157	122	2b15/S		0.2
Total	2		65	118	7	31	5	0	0	6	3-1	2	18	.263	.293	.305	54	-7	0-0	.955	-3	124	79	2b25,S22		-0.8

SHANNON, SPIKE William Porter B2.7.1878 Pittsburg PA D5.16.1940 Minneapolis MN BB/TR/5-11/180 d4.15 U2 Col Grove City

YEAR	TM	LG	G	AB	R	H	2B	3B	HR	RBI	BB-IB	HP	SO	AVG	OBP	SLG	AOPS	ABR	SB-CS	FA	FR	RNG	THR	GAMES AT POSITION	DL	BFW
1904	StL	N	134	500	84	140	10	3	1	26	50	3		.280	.349	.318	111	9	34	**.978**	5	101	**203**	O133(13/3/117)		0.7
1905	StL	N	140	544	73	146	16	3	0	41	47	0		.268	.327	.309	92	-4	27	**.984**	1	38	65	O140L		-1.2
1906	StL	N	80	302	36	78	4	0	0	25	36	0		.258	.337	.272	94	-1	15	.972	4	84	113	O80L		-0.2
	NY	N	76	287	42	73	5	1	0	25	34	4		.254	.342	.279	91	-1	18	.958	-5	44	96	O76L		-1.2
	Year		156	589	78	151	9	1	0	50	70	4		.256	.339	.275	93	-2	33	.966	-2	66	105	O156L		-1.4
1907	NY	N	**155**	585	**104**	155	12	5	1	33	82	8		.265	.363	.308	107	9	33	.977	2	84	96	O155L		0.3
1908	NY	N	77	268	34	60	.2	1	1	21	28	7		.224	.314	.250	77	-6	13	.976	-3	84	146	O74(60/0/15)		-1.5
	Pit	N	32	127	10	25	0	2	0	12	9	0		.197	.250	.228	53	-7	5	.947	-1	43	0	O32(8/20/7)		-1.1
	Year		109	395	44	85	2	3	1	33	37	7		.215	.294	.243	69	-13	18	.964	-4	71	98	O106(68/20/22)		-2.6
Total	5		694	2613	383	677	49	15	3	183	286	22		.259	.337	.293	96	-1	145	.974	2	72	106	O690(532/23/139)		-4.2

SHANTZ, BILLY Wilmer Ebert B7.31.1927 Pottstown PA D12.13.1993 Lauderhill FL BR/TR/6-1/160* d4.13 b-Bobby

YEAR	TM	LG	G	AB	R	H	2B	3B	HR	RBI	BB-IB	HP	SO	AVG	OBP	SLG	AOPS	ABR	SB-CS	FA	FR	RNG	THR	GAMES AT POSITION	DL	BFW
1954	Phi	A	51	164	13	42	9.	1	1	17	17	0	23	.256	.326	.366	89	-3	0-0	.975	-9	*83*	*106*	C51		-1.0
1955	KC	A	79	217	18	56	4	1	1	12	11-1	0	14	.258	.293	.300	59	-13	0-0	.990	-7	117	67	C78		-1.7
1960	NY	A	1	0	0	0	0	0	0	0	0	0	0	—	—	—		0	0-0	1.000	0	0	0	/C		0.0
Total	3		131	381	31	98	13	4	2	29	28-1	0	37	.257	.307	.328	72	-16	0-0	.984	-15	103	83	C130		-2.7

SHARMAN, RALPH Ralph Edward "Bally" B4.11.1895 Cleveland OH D5.24.1918 Camp Sheridan AL BR/TR/5-11/176 d9.10

YEAR	TM	LG	G	AB	R	H	2B	3B	HR	RBI	BB-IB	HP	SO	AVG	OBP	SLG	AOPS	ABR	SB-CS	FA	FR	RNG	THR	GAMES AT POSITION	DL	BFW
1917	Phi	A	13	37	2	11	2	1	0	2	3	1	2	.297	.366	.405	137	2	1	.941	-2	72	68	O10(2/3/5)		-0.1

SHARON, DICK Richard Louis B4.15.1950 San Mateo CA BR/TR/6-2/195* [PitN68 1/9] d5.13

YEAR	TM	LG	G	AB	R	H	2B	3B	HR	RBI	BB-IB	HP	SO	AVG	OBP	SLG	AOPS	ABR	SB-CS	FA	FR	RNG	THR	GAMES AT POSITION	DL	BFW
1973	Det	A	91	178	20	43	9	0	7	16	10-0	0	31	.242	.280	.410	87	-4	2-0	.970	4	115	137	O91(19/7/71)		-0.2
1974	Det	A	60	129	12	28	4	0	2	10	14-0	0	23	.217	.292	.295	67	-5	4-4	.989	1	103	159	O56(23/14/19)		-0.7
1975	SD	N	91	160	14	31	7	0	4	26	26-0	0	35	.194	.306	.313	77	-5	0-2	.948	-2	102	32	O57(39/12/7)		-0.7
Total	3		242	467	46	102	20	0	13	46	50-0	0	89	.218	.293	.345	79	-14	6-6	.969	3	108	97	O204(81/33/97)		-1.9

SHARP, BILL William Howard B1.18.1950 Lima OH BL/TL/5-10/178* [ChiA71 2/25] d5.26 Col Ohio St.

YEAR	TM	LG	G	AB	R	H	2B	3B	HR	RBI	BB-IB	HP	SO	AVG	OBP	SLG	AOPS	ABR	SB-CS	FA	FR	RNG	THR	GAMES AT POSITION	DL	BFW
1973	Chi	A	77	196	23	54	8	3	4	22	19-2	3	28	.276	.345	.408	109	2	2-3	.981	5	101	238	O70(11/59/0)/D		0.5
1974	Chi	A	100	320	45	81	13	2	4	24	25-2	2	37	.253	.309	.344	86	-6	0-3	.986	1	110	43	O99(13/7/85)		-1.1
1975	Chi	A	18	35	1	7	0	0	0	3	2-0	0	6	.200	.243	.200	26	-3	0-0	.941	-2	76	0	O14(2/1/11)		-0.6
	Mil	A	125	373	37	95	27	1	0	34	19-2	1	26	.255	.289	.351	81	-10	0-3	.994	13	113	157	O124(43/82/23)		-0.2
	Year		143	408	38	102	27	3	1	38	21-2	1	29	.250	.285	.338	76	-13	0-3	.991	11	110	143	O138(45/83/34)		-0.8
1976	Mil	A	78	180	16	44	4	0	0	11	10-0	1	15	.244	.288	.267	64	-8	1-3	.975	6	117	224	O56(11/10/37),D7		-0.5
Total	4		398	1104	122	281	52	8	9	95	75-6	7	109	.255	.304	.341	83	-25	3-12	.985	23	109	142	O363(80/159/156),D8		-1.9

SHARPE, BUD Bayard Heston B8.6.1881 West Chester PA D5.31.1916 Haddock GA BR/TR/6-1/170 d4.14 Col Penn St.

YEAR	TM	LG	G	AB	R	H	2B	3B	HR	RBI	BB-IB	HP	SO	AVG	OBP	SLG	AOPS	ABR	SB-CS	FA	FR	RNG	THR	GAMES AT POSITION	DL	BFW
1905	Bos	N	46	170	8	31	3	2	0	11	7	0		.182	.215	.224	31	-15	0	.904	2	205	223	O42R,C3/1		-1.6
1910	Pit	N	4	16	2	3	0	1	0	2	0	0	2	.188	.188	.313	43	-1	0	1.000	0	131	0	1b4		-0.1
	Bos	N	115	439	30	105	14	3	0	29	14	1	31	.239	.264	.285	58	-25	4	.987	8	128	103	1b113		-2.1
	Year		119	455	32	108	14	4	0	30	14	1	33	.237	.262	.286	57	-27	4	.987	8	**128**	99	1b117		-2.2
Total	2		165	625	40	139	17	6	0	41	21	1	33	.222	.249	.269	50	-41	4	.987	10	127	99	1b118,O42R,C3		-3.8

YEAR	TM LG	G	AB	R	H	2B	3B	HR	RBI	BB-IB	HP	SO	AVG	OBP	SLG	AOPS	ABR	SB-CS	FA	FR	RNG	THR	GAMES AT POSITION	DL	BFW

SHARPERSON, MIKE Michael Tyrone B10.4.1961 Orangeburg SC D5.26.1996 Las Vegas NV BR/TR/6-3/191(185-205) [TorA81 S1/11] d4.6 Col Georgia Perimeter JC

YEAR	TM LG	G	AB	R	H	2B	3B	HR	RBI	BB-IB	HP	SO	AVG	OBP	SLG	AOPS	ABR	SB-CS	FA	FR	RNG	THR	GAMES AT POSITION	DL	BFW
1987	Tor A	32	96	4	20	4	1	0	9	7-0	1	15	.208	.269	.271	43	-8	2-1	.971	-4	85	91	2b32		-1.0
	LA N	10	33	7	9	2	0	0	4	4-1	0	5	.273	.351	.333	85	-1	0-0	1.000	1	131	3	3b7,2b6		0.0
1988	†LA N	46	59	8	16	1	0	0	4	1-0	1	12	.271	.290	.288	70	-2	0-1	.949	-2	102	128	2b20,3b6,S4		-0.5
1989	LA N	27	28	2	7	3	0	0	5	4-1	0	7	.250	.333	.357	102	0	0-1	1.000	1	50	142	2b4,1b2,3b2/S		-0.1
1990	LA N	129	357	42	106	14	2	3	36	46-6	1	39	.297	.376	.373	110	7	15-6	.949	11	107	91	3b106,S15,2b9,1b6		1.9
1991	LA N	105	216	24	60	11	2	2	20	25-0	1	24	.278	.355	.375	107	3	1-3	.981	-3	85	70	3b68,S16,1b10,2b5		0.1
1992	LA N★	128	317	48	95	21	0	3	36	47-1	1	33	.300	.387	.394	124	13	2-2	.979	18	114	107	2b63,3b60,S2		3.4
1993	LA N	73	90	13	23	4	0	2	10	5-0	1	17	.256	.299	.367	82	-2	2-0	.945	-0	87	127	2b17,3b6,S3/1OR		-0.2
1995	Atl N	7	7	1	1	0	0	0	2	0-0	0	2	.143	.143	.286	9	-1	0-0	—	-0	0	0	/3		-0.1
Total	8	557	1203	149	337	61	5	10	123	139-9	5	154	.280	.355	.364	102	9	22-14	.952	21	104	77	3b256,2b156,S41,1b19/OR	22	3.5

SHARROTT, JACK John Henry B8.13.1869 Bangor ME D12.31.1927 Los Angeles CA BR/TR/5-9/165 d4.22 ▲

YEAR	TM LG	G	AB	R	H	2B	3B	HR	RBI	BB-IB	HP	SO	AVG	OBP	SLG	AOPS	ABR	SB-CS	FA	FR	RNG	THR	GAMES AT POSITION	DL	BFW
1890	NY N	32	109	16	22	3	2	0	14	0		14	.202	.202	.266	36	-10	6	.932	-1	129	0	P25,O9(5/0/4)		-0.3
1891	NY N	10	30	5	10	2	0	1	7	1	0	2	.333	.355	.500	154	4	3	.950	1	105	0	P10		0.0
1892	NY N	4	8	1	1	0	0	0	0	0	0	1	.125	.125	.125	-25	-1	0	.333	-1	0	0	O3R/P		-0.2
1893	Phi N	50	152	25	38	4	3	1	22	8	0	14	.250	.287	.336	65	-9	6	.824	-1	114	0	O33(24/9/5),P12		-0.9
Total	4	96	299	47	71	9	5	2	43	9		31	.237	.260	.321	61	-16	15	.927	-2	120	0	P48,O45(29/9/12)		-1.4

SHAUGHNESSY, SHAG Francis Joseph B4.8.1883 Amboy IL D5.15.1969 Montreal QC, Can. BR/TR/6-1.5/185 d4.17 C1 Col Notre Dame

YEAR	TM LG	G	AB	R	H	2B	3B	HR	RBI	BB-IB	HP	SO	AVG	OBP	SLG	AOPS	ABR	SB-CS	FA	FR	RNG	THR	GAMES AT POSITION	DL	BFW
1905	Was A	1	3	0	0	0	0	0			1		.000	.250	.000	-19	0	0	.667	-0	0	0	/OR		-0.1
1908	Phi A	8	29	2	9	0	0	0	1	2		0	.310	.355	.310	109	0	3	1.000	-0	0	0	O8C		-0.1
Total	2	9	32	2	9	0	0	0	1	2	1		.281	.343	.281	97	0	3	.938	-1	0	0	O9(0/8/1)		-0.2

SHAVE, JON Jonathan Taylor B11.4.1967 Waycross GA BR/TR/6-0/185* [TexA90 5/144] d5.15 Col Mississippi St. [DL 1994 Tex A 16]

YEAR	TM LG	G	AB	R	H	2B	3B	HR	RBI	BB-IB	HP	SO	AVG	OBP	SLG	AOPS	ABR	SB-CS	FA	FR	RNG	THR	GAMES AT POSITION	DL	BFW
1993	Tex A	17	47	3	15	2	0	0	7	0-0	0	8	.319	.306	.362	85	-1	1-3	.917	-2	93	131	S9,2b8		-0.3
1998	Min A	19	40	7	10	3	0	1	5	3-0	0	10	.250	.302	.400	79	-1	1-2	1.000	-0	103	124	3b15/1SD		-0.2
1999	Tex A	43	73	10	21	4	0	0	9	5-0	2	17	.288	.350	.342	73	-3	1-0	.953	2	112	118	S24,1b9,3b6/2D		0.1
Total	3	79	160	20	46	9	0	1	21	8-0	2	35	.287	.326	.363	78	-5	3-5	.942	-0	106	121	S34,3b21,1b10,2b9,D4	16	-0.4

SHAW, AL Albert Simpson B3.1.1881 Toledo OH D12.30.1974 Danville IL BL/TR/5-8.5/165 d9.28

YEAR	TM LG	G	AB	R	H	2B	3B	HR	RBI	BB-IB	HP	SO	AVG	OBP	SLG	AOPS	ABR	SB-CS	FA	FR	RNG	THR	GAMES AT POSITION	DL	BFW
1907	StL N	9	25	2	7	0	0	0	1	3	1		.280	.379	.280	110	1	1	.947	-1	84	0	O9C		0.0
1908	StL N	107	367	40	97	13	4	1	19	25	0		.264	.311	.330	110	3	9	.931	5	200	237	O91(2/67/22),S4/3		0.4
1909	StL N	114	331	45	82	12	7	2	34	55	0		.248	.355	.344	125	12	15	.940	-4	106	30	O92(0/90/2)		0.3
1914	Bro F	112	376	81	122	27	7	5	49	44	0	59	.324	.395	.473	137	15	24	.955	2	102	109	O102C		1.1
1915	KC F	132	448	67	126	22	10	6	67	46	0	45	.281	.348	.415	119	4	15	.942	-12	83	71	O124(120/4/0)		-1.4
Total	5	474	1547	235	434	74	28	14	170	173	1	104	.281	.353	.392	123	35	64	.942	-9	119	106	O418(122/272/24),S4/3		0.4

SHAW, AL Alfred "Shoddy" B10.3.1874 Burslem, England D3.25.1958 Uhrichsville OH BR/TR/5-8/170 d6.8

YEAR	TM LG	G	AB	R	H	2B	3B	HR	RBI	BB-IB	HP	SO	AVG	OBP	SLG	AOPS	ABR	SB-CS	FA	FR	RNG	THR	GAMES AT POSITION	DL	BFW
1901	Det A	55	171	20	46	7	0	1	23	10	3		.269	.321	.327	76	-5	2	.938	1	119	96	C42,1b9,3b2/S		-0.1
1907	Bos A	76	198	10	38	1	3	0	7	18	3		.192	.269	.227	59	-9	4	.971	11	124	105	C73/1		1.0
1908	Chi A	32	49	0	4	1	0	0	2	2	0		.082	.118	.102	-29	-7	0	.953	0	129	72	C29		-0.6
1909	Bos N	18	41	1	4	0	0	0	0	5	1		.098	.213	.098	-3	-5	0	.975	2	92	123	C14		-0.2
Total	4	181	459	31	92	9	3	1	32	35	7		.200	.267	.240	53	-26	6	.961	14	120	100	C158,1b10,3b2/S		0.1

SHAW, BEN Benjamin Nathaniel B6.18.1893 LaCenter KY D3.16.1959 Cleveland OH BR/TR/5-11.5/190 d4.11 Mil 1918 Col Rhodes

YEAR	TM LG	G	AB	R	H	2B	3B	HR	RBI	BB-IB	HP	SO	AVG	OBP	SLG	AOPS	ABR	SB-CS	FA	FR	RNG	THR	GAMES AT POSITION	DL	BFW
1917	Pit N	2	2	0	0	0	0	0	0	0	0	0	.000	.000	.000	-97	0	0					/H		-0.1
1918	Pit N	21	36	5	7	1	0	0	2	2	2	2	.194	.275	.222	51	-2	0	.981	-1	31	108	1b9,C5		-0.3
Total	2	23	38	5	7	1	0	0	2	2	2	2	.184	.262	.211	43	-2	0	.981	-1	31	108	1b9,C5		-0.4

SHAW, HUNKY Royal N B9.29.1884 Yakima WA D7.3.1969 Yakima WA BB/TR/5-8/165 d5.16 Col Washington

YEAR	TM LG	G	AB	R	H	2B	3B	HR	RBI	BB-IB	HP	SO	AVG	OBP	SLG	AOPS	ABR	SB-CS	FA	FR	RNG	THR	GAMES AT POSITION	DL	BFW
1908	Pit N	1	1	0	0	0	0	0	0	0	0	0	.000	.000	.000	-99	0	0	—		0		/H		0.0

SHAY, MARTY Arthur Joseph B4.25.1896 Boston MA D2.20.1951 Worcester MA BR/TR/5-7.5/148 d9.16

YEAR	TM LG	G	AB	R	H	2B	3B	HR	RBI	BB-IB	HP	SO	AVG	OBP	SLG	AOPS	ABR	SB-CS	FA	FR	RNG	THR	GAMES AT POSITION	DL	BFW
1916	Chi N	2	7	0	2	0	0	0	0	0	0	1	.286	.286	.286	68	0	0	.917	-0	76	237	S2		0.0
1924	Bos N	19	68	4	16	3	1	0	2	5	1	5	.235	.297	.309	65	-3	2-1	.950	-8	69	96	2b19/S		-1.1
Total	2	21	75	4	18	3	1	0	2	5	1	6	.240	.296	.307	66	-3	2-1	.950	-8	69	96	2b19,S3		-1.1

SHAY, DANNY Daniel C. B11.8.1876 Springfield OH D12.1.1927 Kansas City MO BR/TR/5-10/? d4.30

YEAR	TM LG	G	AB	R	H	2B	3B	HR	RBI	BB-IB	HP	SO	AVG	OBP	SLG	AOPS	ABR	SB-CS	FA	FR	RNG	THR	GAMES AT POSITION	DL	BFW
1901	Cle A	19	75	4	17	2	2	0	10	2	2		.227	.266	.307	61	-4	0	.901	-3	89	39	S19		-0.6
1904	StL N	99	340	45	87	11	1	1	18	39	3		.256	.338	.303	103	3	36	.911	-8	105	93	S97,2b2		-0.2
1905	StL N	78	281	30	67	12	1	0	28	35	4		.238	.331	.288	88	-2	11	.953	-15	99	106	2b39,S39		-1.6
1907	NY N	35	79	10	15	1	1	1	6	12	1		.190	.304	.266	76	-2	5	.931	-6	70	24	2b13,S9,O2C		-0.9
Total	4	231	775	89	186	26	5	2	62	88	10		.240	.325	.294	90	-5	52	.902	-33	98	75	S164,2b54,O2C		-3.3

SHEA, GERRY Gerald J. B7.26.1881 St.Louis MO D5.3.1964 Berkeley MO TR/5-7/160 d10.1 Col Creighton

YEAR	TM LG	G	AB	R	H	2B	3B	HR	RBI	BB-IB	HP	SO	AVG	OBP	SLG	AOPS	ABR	SB-CS	FA	FR	RNG	THR	GAMES AT POSITION	DL	BFW
1905	StL N	2	6	0	2	0	0	0			0		.333	.333	.333	102	0	0	.917	0	85	144	C2		

SHEA, NAP John Edward "Napoleon" B5.23.1874 Ware MA D7.8.1968 Bloomfield Hills MI BR/TR/5-5/155 d9.11

YEAR	TM LG	G	AB	R	H	2B	3B	HR	RBI	BB-IB	HP	SO	AVG	OBP	SLG	AOPS	ABR	SB-CS	FA	FR	RNG	THR	GAMES AT POSITION	DL	BFW
1902	Phi N	3	8	1	1	0	0	0	0	1			.125	.300	.125	32	-1	0	1.000	-1	75	82	C3		-0.1

SHEA, MERV Mervyn David John B9.5.1900 San Francisco CA D1.27.1953 Sacramento CA BR/TR/5-11/175 d4.23 C8

YEAR	TM LG	G	AB	R	H	2B	3B	HR	RBI	BB-IB	HP	SO	AVG	OBP	SLG	AOPS	ABR	SB-CS	FA	FR	RNG	THR	GAMES AT POSITION	DL	BFW
1927	Det A	34	85	5	15	6	3	0	9	7	1	15	.176	.239	.318	43	-8	0-0	.949	-2	97	72	C31		-0.7
1928	Det A	39	85	8	20	2	3	0	9	9	1	11	.235	.316	.329	69	-4	2-1	.951	1	107	183	C30		-0.5
1929	Det A	50	162	23	47	6	0	3	24	19	0	18	.290	.365	.383	92	-1	2-1	.964	-0	70	120	C46		-0.5
1933	Bos A	16	56	1	8	0	0	0	8	4	0	5	.143	.200	.196	14	-8	0-0	1.000	-1	69	145	C16		-0.3
	StL A	94	279	26	73	11	1	1	27	43	0	26	.262	.360	.319	76	-8	2-0	.995	9	121	113	C85		0.5
	Year	110	335	27	81	14	1	1	35	47	0	33	.242	.335	.299	65	-15	2-0	.996	9	114	117	C101		0.1
1934	Chi A	62	176	8	28	3	0	0	5	24	0	19	.159	.260	.176	14	-23	0-1	.972	-3	64	128	C60		-2.7
1935	Chi A	46	122	8	28	2	0	0	13	30	0	9	.230	.382	.246	64	-5	0-0	.990	6	93	100	C43		-0.5
1936	Chi A	14	24	3	3	0	0	0	2	6	0	5	.125	.300	.125	8	-3	0-0	1.000	1	116	49	C14		-0.5
1937	Chi A	25	71	7	15	1	0	0	5	15	0	10	.211	.349	.225	48	-5	1-0	.966	3	126	144	C25		-0.5
1938	Bro N	48	120	14	22	5	0	0	12	28	0	20	.183	.338	.225	56	-6	1	.977	-0	86	90	C47		-0.5
1939	Det A	4	2	0	0	0	0	0	0	0	0	1	.000	.000	.000	-93	-1	0-0	.500	-1	0	0	C4		-0.4
1944	Phi N	7	15	2	4	0	0	0	1	4	0	0	.267	.421	.467	155	1	0	.952	-0	143	94	C6		-0.2
Total	11	439	1197	105	263	39	7	5	115	189	1	145	.220	.327	.277	58	-71	8-3	.976	7	95	116	C407		-3.4

SHEAFFER, DANNY Danny Todd B8.2.1961 Jacksonville FL BR/TR/6-0/202(185-202) [BosA81*1/20] d4.9 Col Clemson OF(20/2/9)

YEAR	TM LG	G	AB	R	H	2B	3B	HR	RBI	BB-IB	HP	SO	AVG	OBP	SLG	AOPS	ABR	SB-CS	FA	FR	RNG	THR	GAMES AT POSITION	DL	BFW
1987	Bos A	25	66	5	8	1	0	1	5	5-0	0	14	.121	.119	.182	-21	-12	0-0	.977	-5	104	88	C25		-1.1
1989	Cle A	7	16	1	1	0	0	0	0	2-0	0	2	.063	.167	.063	-32	-3	0-0	—	-0	0	0	3b2/OLD		-0.5
1993	Col N	82	216	26	60	9	1	4	32	8-0	1	15	.278	.299	.384	72	-9	2-3	.994	-1	114	82	C65,1b7,O2L/3		-0.4
1994	Col N	44	110	11	24	4	0	1	12	10-0	0	11	.218	.283	.282	41	-9	0-2	.995	2	77	107	C30,1b2/OL		-0.1
1995	StL N	76	208	24	48	10	1	5	30	23-2	3	38	.231	.306	.361	74	-8	0-0	.993	9	114	99	C67,1b3/3		-0.2
1996	†StL N	79	198	10	45	9	3	2	20	9-0	1	17	.227	.271	.333	58	-13	3-3	.983	-2	102	62	3b30,O22(13/2/9),C9,2b3		-1.3
1997	StL N	76	132	10	33	5	0	0	11	8-0	1	17	.250	.296	.288	54	-9	1-0	.957	-2	102	62	C243,3b51,O29L,1b18,2b3,D3		-4.3
Total	8	389	946	87	219	38	5	13	110	60-2	5	122	.232	.278	.323	56	-63	6-8	.990	7	93	94	C243,3b51,O29L,1b18,2b3,D3		-4.7

SHEALY, RYAN Ryan Nelson B8.29.1979 Fort Lauderdale FL BR/TR/6-5/240 d6.14 Col Florida

YEAR	TM LG	G	AB	R	H	2B	3B	HR	RBI	BB-IB	HP	SO	AVG	OBP	SLG	AOPS	ABR	SB-CS	FA	FR	RNG	THR	GAMES AT POSITION	DL	BFW
2005	Col N	36	91	14	30	7	0	2	16	13-0	0	22	.330	.413	.473	115	3	1-0	1.000	-1	73	47	1b19,D5		0.0

SHEAN, DAVE David William B7.9.1883 Arlington MA D5.22.1963 Boston MA BR/TR/5-11/175 d9.10 Col Fordham

YEAR	TM LG	G	AB	R	H	2B	3B	HR	RBI	BB-IB	HP	SO	AVG	OBP	SLG	AOPS	ABR	SB-CS	FA	FR	RNG	THR	GAMES AT POSITION	DL	BFW
1906	Phi A	22	75	7	16	3	2	0	3	5	2		.213	.304	.307	81	-2	6	.980	-1	94	70	2b22		-0.4
1908	Phi N	14	48	4	7	2	0	0	2	2	1		.146	.180	.188	17	-4	1	.871	-5	80	52	S14		-1.1
1909	Phi N	36	112	14	26	2	2	0	4	14	1		.232	.323	.286	88	-1	3	.982	-2	95	78	2b14,1b11,O3C/S		-0.0
	Bos N	75	267	32	66	11	4	1	29	17	2		.247	.297	.330	90	-4	14	.956	7	106	120	2b72		0.5
	Year	111	379	46	92	13	6	1	33	31	3		.243	.305	.317	90	-5	17	.960	6	104	118	2b86,1b11,O3C/S		0.5
1910	Bos N	150	543	52	130	12	7	3	36	42	0	45	.239	.294	.304	71	-22	16	.953	43	116	132	2b148		2.2
1911	Chi N	54	145	17	28	4	0	0	15	8	1		.193	.240	.221	29	-14	4	.947	1	106	59	2b23,S19/3		-1.8

YEAR	TM LG	G	AB	R	H	2B	3B	HR	RBI	BB-IB	HP	SO	AVG	OBP	SLG	AOPS	ABR	SB-CS	FA	FR	RNG	THR	GAMES AT POSITION	DL	BFW
1912	Bos N	4	10	1	3	0	0	0	1		1	2	.300	.417	.300	96	0	0	.917	-0	106	170	S4		0.0
1917	Cin N	131	442	36	93	9	5	2	35	22	1	39	.210	.249	.267	61	-22	10	.961	17	**106**	112	2b131		-0.3
1918	†Bos A	115	425	58	112	16	3	0	34	40	3	25	.264	.331	.315	97	-1	11	.967	-4	97	85	2b115		-0.4
1919	Bos A	29	100	4	14	0	0	0	8	5	1	7	.140	.189	.140	-7	-15	1	.981	3	100	155	2b29		
Total 9		630	2167	225	495	59	23	6	166	155	13	133	.228	.284	.285	70	-85	66	.961	59	106	111	2b554,S38,1b11,O3C/3		-1.2 / -1.9

SHEARER, RAY   Ray Solomon B9.19.1929 Jacobus PA D2.21.1982 York PA BR/TR/6-0/200 d9.18

YEAR	TM LG	G	AB	R	H	2B	3B	HR	RBI	BB-IB	HP	SO	AVG	OBP	SLG	AOPS	ABR	SB-CS	FA	FR	RNG	THR	GAMES AT POSITION	DL	BFW
1957	Mil N	2	2	1	1	0	0	0	0	1-0	0	1	.500	.667	.500	237	1	0-0	—	-0	0	0	/OL		0.1

SHEARON, JOHN   John M. B1870 Pittsburgh PA D2.1.1923 Bradford PA d7.28 ▲

YEAR	TM LG	G	AB	R	H	2B	3B	HR	RBI	BB-IB	HP	SO	AVG	OBP	SLG	AOPS	ABR	SB-CS	FA	FR	RNG	THR	GAMES AT POSITION	DL	BFW
1891	Cle N	30	124	10	30	1	1	0	13	1	0	15	.242	.248	.266	48	-9	6	.814	-1	160	0	O25(4/14/10),P6		-0.8
1896	Cle N	16	64	6	11	0	1	0	3	4	0	6	.172	.221	.203	11	-9	3	.818	-4	0	0	O16R		-1.1
Total 2		46	188	16	41	1	2	0	16	5	0	21	.218	.238	.245	34	-18	9	.815	-5	94	0	O41(4/14/26),P6		-1.9

SHECKARD, JIMMY   Samuel James Tilden B11.23.1878 Upper Chanceford PA D1.15.1947 Lancaster PA BL/TR/5-9/175 d9.14 OF(1843/22/214)

YEAR	TM LG	G	AB	R	H	2B	3B	HR	RBI	BB-IB	HP	SO	AVG	OBP	SLG	AOPS	ABR	SB-CS	FA	FR	RNG	THR	GAMES AT POSITION	DL	BFW
1897	Bro N	13	49	12	14	3	2	3	14	6	0		.286	.364	.612	164	4	5	.753	-6	100	108	S11,O2R		
1898	Bro N	105	408	51	113	17	9	4	64	37	8		.277	.349	.392	113	6	8	.926	-7	76	52	O105(101/4/0)/3		-0.1
1899	Bal N	147	536	104	158	18	10	3	75	56	18		.295	.380	.382	104	5	**77**	.943	19	146	244	O146(0/1/146)/1		-0.9
1900	Bro N	85	273	74	82	19	10	3	39	42	12		.300	.414	.454	132	14	30	.925	3	125	108	O78(67/6/5)		1.5
1901	Bro N	133	554	116	196	29	**19**	11	104	47	5		.354	.409	**.534**	168	47	35	.944	5	96	121	O121(120/1/0),3b12		1.0
1902	Bal A	4	15	3	4	0	0	0	1	0	5		.267	.313	.333	76	0	1	1.000	-1	0	0	O4C		4.3
	Bro N	123	486	86	129	20	10	4	37	57	5		.265	.349	.372	122	14	23	.964	9	71	128	O123(122/1/0)		-0.1
1903	Bro N	139	515	99	171	29	9	**9**	75	75	6		.332	.423	.476	161	**45**	**67**	.951	**25**	**190**	154	O139L		1.6
1904	Bro N	143	507	70	121	23	6	1	46	56	2		.239	.317	.314	97	0	21	.956	9	92	95	O141L,2b2		5.8
1905	Bro N	130	480	58	140	20	11	3	41	61	7		.292	.380	.398	142	28	23	.967	17	144	130	O129L		0.1
1906	†Chi N	149	549	90	144	27	10	1	45	67	6		.262	.348	.353	112	10	30	.986	-2	68	26	O149L		3.8
1907	†Chi N	143	484	76	129	23	1	1	36	76	6		.267	.373	.324	112	12	31	.975	-8	68	49	O142L		0.0
1908	†Chi N	115	403	54	93	18	3	2	22	62	2		.231	.336	.305	101	4	18	.955	-4	85	89	O115L		-0.5
1909	Chi N	148	525	81	134	29	5	1	43	72	1		.255	.346	.335	109	8	15	.967	-5	84	122	O148L		-0.9
1910	†Chi N	144	507	82	130	27	6	5	51	83	5	53	.256	.366	.363	114	12	22	.976	8	107	117	O143L		-0.5
1911	Chi N	156	539	**121**	149	26	11	4	50	**147**	3	58	.276	**.434**	.388	130	34	32	.963	15	107	144	O156L		1.3
1912	Chi N	146	523	85	128	22	10	3	47	**122**	5	81	.245	.392	.342	102	9	15	.962	9	107	119	O146L		4.1
1913	StL N	52	136	18	27	2	1	0	17	41	1	25	.199	.388	.228	79	0	5-7	.953	-0	98	105	O46(16/0/36)		1.2
	Cin N	47	116	16	22	1	3	0	7	27	0	16	.190	.343	.250	71	-3	6-5	.969	-0	99	96	O38(9/5/25)		-0.4
	Year	99	252	34	49	3	4	0	24	68	1	41	.194	.368	.238	76	-4	11-12	.960	-0	98	101	O84(25/5/61)		-0.6
Total 17		2122	7605	1296	2084	354	136	56	813	1135	92	233	.274	.375	.378	120	249	465-12	.958	87	104	113	O2071L,3b13,S11,2b2/1		-1.0 / 20.7

SHEEHAN, JIM   James Thomas "Big Jim" B6.3.1913 New Haven CT D12.2.2003 New Haven CT BR/TR/6-2/196 d9.26 Col Alabama

YEAR	TM LG	G	AB	R	H	2B	3B	HR	RBI	BB-IB	HP	SO	AVG	OBP	SLG	AOPS	ABR	SB-CS	FA	FR	RNG	THR	GAMES AT POSITION	DL	BFW
1936	NY N	1	4	0	0	0	0	0	0	0	0	2	.000	.000	.000	-99	-1	0	.833	-0	0	0	/C		-0.1

SHEEHAN, JACK   John Thomas B4.15.1893 Chicago IL D5.29.1987 W.Palm Beach FL BB/TR/5-8.5/165 d9.11 Col Fordham

YEAR	TM LG	G	AB	R	H	2B	3B	HR	RBI	BB-IB	HP	SO	AVG	OBP	SLG	AOPS	ABR	SB-CS	FA	FR	RNG	THR	GAMES AT POSITION	DL	BFW
1920	†Bro N	3	5	0	2	1	0	0	0	1	0	1	.400	.500	.600	208	1	0-0	.875	-0	120	0	S2/3		0.1
1921	Bro N	5	12	2	0	0	0	0	0	0	0	1	.000	.000	.000	-97	-3	0-0	.900	-0	84	112	2b2/S3		-0.4
Total 2		8	17	2	2	1	0	0	0	1	0	1	.118	.167	.176	-7	-2	0-0	.909	-1	105	0	S3,2b2,3b2		-0.3

SHEEHAN, TOMMY   Thomas H. B11.6.1877 Sacramento CA D5.22.1959 Panama City, Pan BR/TR/5-8/160 d8.2

YEAR	TM LG	G	AB	R	H	2B	3B	HR	RBI	BB-IB	HP	SO	AVG	OBP	SLG	AOPS	ABR	SB-CS	FA	FR	RNG	THR	GAMES AT POSITION	DL	BFW
1900	NY N	1	2	0	0	0	0	0	0	0	0		.000	.000	.000	-99	-1	0	—	-0	0	0	/S		-0.1
1906	Pit N	95	315	28	76	6	3	1	34	18	1		.241	.284	.289	75	-10	13	.947	-4	97	122	3b90		-1.2
1907	Pit N	75	226	23	62	2	3	0	25	23	0		.274	.341	.310	103	1	10	.941	1	115	42	3b57,S10		0.4
1908	Bro N	146	468	45	100	18	2	0	29	53	6		.214	.302	.261	83	-6	9	.930	-4	97	73	3b145		-0.8
Total 4		317	1011	96	238	26	8	1	88	94	7		.235	.305	.280	85	-16	32	.938	-7	101	82	3b292,S11		-1.7

SHEEHAN, BIFF   Timothy James B2.13.1868 Hartford CT D10.21.1923 Hartford CT BL/TR/5-9/165 d7.22

YEAR	TM LG	G	AB	R	H	2B	3B	HR	RBI	BB-IB	HP	SO	AVG	OBP	SLG	AOPS	ABR	SB-CS	FA	FR	RNG	THR	GAMES AT POSITION	DL	BFW
1895	StL N	52	180	24	57	3	6	1	18	20	3	6	.317	.394	.417	111	3	7	.940	-0	135	80	O41(0/2/39),1b11		0.1
1896	StL N	6	19	0	3	0	0	0	1	4	0	0	.158	.304	.158	25	-2	0	1.000	-0	0	0	O6(1/0/5)		-0.2
Total 2		58	199	24	60	3	6	1	19	24	3	6	.302	.385	.392	103	1	7	.948	-0	117	69	O47(1/2/44),1b11		-0.1

SHEELY, EARL   Earl Homer "Whitey" B2.12.1893 Bushnell IL D9.16.1952 Seattle WA BR/TR/6-3.5/195 d4.14 s-Bud

YEAR	TM LG	G	AB	R	H	2B	3B	HR	RBI	BB-IB	HP	SO	AVG	OBP	SLG	AOPS	ABR	SB-CS	FA	FR	RNG	THR	GAMES AT POSITION	DL	BFW
1921	Chi A	**154**	563	68	171	25	6	11	95	57	7	34	.304	.375	.428	106	5	4-9	.988	6	**119**	108	1b154		-0.1
1922	Chi A	149	526	72	167	37	4	6	80	60	5	27	.317	.393	.437	117	15	4-6	.993	2	102	96	1b149		0.6
1923	Chi A	**156**	570	84	169	25	3	4	88	79	5	30	.296	.387	.372	102	5	5-5	.992	-1	95	97	1b156		-0.7
1924	Chi A	146	535	84	171	34	3	3	103	95	4	28	.320	.426	.411	120	23	7-4	.991	-11	75	85	1b146		0.3
1925	Chi A	153	600	93	189	43	3	9	111	68	6	23	.315	.384	.442	117	17	3-3	.988	-6	88	109	1b153		0.1
1926	Chi A	145	525	77	157	40	2	6	89	75	7	13	.299	.394	.417	116	16	3-3	**.995**	-1	93	86	1b144		0.6
1927	Chi A	45	129	11	27	3	0	2	16	20	1	5	.209	.320	.279	58	-8	3-1	**.995**	-1	93	86	1b44		0.6
1929	Pit N	139	485	63	142	22	4	6	88	75	4	24	.293	.392	.392	93	-8	1-3	**.996**	-1	93	94	1b139		-1.4
1931	Bos N	147	538	30	147	15	2	1	77	34	2	21	.273	.319	.314	73	-21	0	.992	-2	93	93	1b143		-1.2
Total 9		1234	4471	572	1340	244	27	48	747	563	40	205	.300	.383	.399	104	49	33-31	.991	-18	94	96	1b1220		-3.6 / -5.4

SHEELY, BUD   Hollis Kimball B11.26.1920 Spokane WA D10.17.1985 Sacramento CA BL/TR/6-1/200* d7.26 f-Earl Col St. Marys (CA)

YEAR	TM LG	G	AB	R	H	2B	3B	HR	RBI	BB-IB	HP	SO	AVG	OBP	SLG	AOPS	ABR	SB-CS	FA	FR	RNG	THR	GAMES AT POSITION	DL	BFW
1951	Chi A	34	89	2	16	2	0	0	7	6	1	7	.180	.240	.202	21	-10	0-0	.986	2	86	63	C33		-0.6
1952	Chi A	36	75	4	18	2	0	0	3	12	1	7	.240	.352	.267	73	-2	0-1	.992	-1	72	97	C31		-0.3
1953	Chi A	31	46	4	10	1	0	0	2	9	0	8	.217	.345	.239	58	-2	0-0	1.000	0	84	41	C17		-0.1
Total 3		101	210	7	44	5	0	0	12	27	2	22	.210	.305	.233	49	-14	0-1	.991	2	81	73	C81		-1.0

SHEERIN, CHUCK   Charles Joseph B4.17.1909 Brooklyn NY D9.27.1986 Valley Stream NY BR/TR/5-11.5/198 d4.21 Col Fordham

YEAR	TM LG	G	AB	R	H	2B	3B	HR	RBI	BB-IB	HP	SO	AVG	OBP	SLG	AOPS	ABR	SB-CS	FA	FR	RNG	THR	GAMES AT POSITION	DL	BFW
1936	Phi N	39	72	4	19	4	0	0	4	7	0	18	.264	.329	.319	68	-3	0	.942	-1	103	33	2b17,3b13,S5		-0.3

SHEETS, ANDY   Andrew Mark B11.19.1971 Baton Rouge LA BR/TR/6-2/180* [SeaA92 4/110] d4.22 Col Louisiana St.

YEAR	TM LG	G	AB	R	H	2B	3B	HR	RBI	BB-IB	HP	SO	AVG	OBP	SLG	AOPS	ABR	SB-CS	FA	FR	RNG	THR	GAMES AT POSITION	DL	BFW
1996	Sea A	47	110	18	21	8	0	0	9	10-1	1	41	.191	.262	.264	34	-11	2-0	.947	3	99	186	3b25,2b18,S7		-0.7
1997	†Sea A	32	89	18	22	3	0	4	9	7-0	1	34	.247	.299	.416	85	-2	2-0	.872	-5	84	120	3b21,S9,2b2		-0.5
1998	†SD N	88	194	31	47	5	3	7	29	21-3	1	62	.242	.318	.407	96	-2	7-2	.964	1	109	106	S39,3b23,2b22,1b2		0.2
1999	Ana N	87	244	22	48	10	0	3	29	14-0	0	59	.197	.236	.275	31	-26	1-2	.966	-22	85	77	S76,2b7/3		-4.1
2000	Bos A	12	21	1	2	0	0	0	1	0-0	0	3	.095	.095	.095	-50	-5	0-0	1.000	1	108	122	S10/1D		-0.3
2001	TB A	49	153	10	30	8	0	1	14	12-0	1	35	.196	.251	.268	39	-14	2-0	.990	0	94	96	S49		-0.9
2002	TB A	41	149	18	37	4	0	4	22	12-0	1	41	.248	.301	.356	76	-5	2-3	.992	3	96	137	2b26,S11,3b4		-0.1
Total 7		356	960	118	207	38	3	19	113	76-3	2	275	.216	.271	.321	55	-65	16-7	.975	-19	95	88	S201,2b75,3b74,1b3,D2		-6.4

SHEETS, LARRY   Larry Kent B12.6.1959 Staunton VA BL/TR/6-3/225(215-236) [BalA78 2/29] d9.18 OF(192/0/144)

YEAR	TM LG	G	AB	R	H	2B	3B	HR	RBI	BB-IB	HP	SO	AVG	OBP	SLG	AOPS	ABR	SB-CS	FA	FR	RNG	THR	GAMES AT POSITION	DL	BFW
1984	Bal A	8	16	3	7	1	0	1	2	1-0	0	3	.438	.471	.688	202	3	0-0	1.000	1	126	350	O7R		0.3
1985	Bal A	113	328	43	86	8	0	17	50	18-2	1	52	.262	.323	.442	110	3	0-1	.875	-1	63	0	D93,O9(1/0/8)/1		-0.1
1986	Bal A	112	338	42	92	17	1	18	60	21-3	2	56	.272	.317	.488	117	7	2-0	.984	-1	111	57	D58,O32(21/0/11),C6,1b4,3b2	17	0.3
1987	Bal A	135	469	74	148	23	0	31	94	31-1	3	67	.316	.358	.563	143	28	1-1	.975	-5	60		O124(72/0/58),D7		1.6
1988	Bal A	136	452	38	104	19	1	10	47	42-4	3	72	.230	.302	.343	83	-10	1-6	.974	-3	94	215	O76(42/0/36),D50,1b3		-1.4
1989	Bal A	102	304	33	74	12	1	7	33	26-10	3	58	.243	.305	.359	90	-4	1-1	—	0	0	0	D88		-0.7
1990	Det A	131	360	40	94	17	2	10	52	24-2	2	42	.261	.308	.403	97	-2	1-3	.981	-2	80	178	O79(56/0/23),D44		-0.9
1993	Sea A	11	9	1	0	2	1	0	0	2-0	1	6	.118	.250	.176	16	-2	0-0	1.000	-2	0	86	/ORD		-0.2
Total 8		748	2284	273	607	98	5	94	339	175-22	19	351	.266	.321	.437	108	23	6-12	.976	-3	93	125	D345,O328L,1b11,C6,3b2	17	-1.1

SHEFFIELD, GARY   Gary Antonian B11.18.1968 Tampa FL BR/TR/5-11/190(190-205) [MilA86 1/6] d9.3 OF(428/0/1114)

YEAR	TM LG	G	AB	R	H	2B	3B	HR	RBI	BB-IB	HP	SO	AVG	OBP	SLG	AOPS	ABR	SB-CS	FA	FR	RNG	THR	GAMES AT POSITION	DL	BFW
1988	Mil A	24	80	12	19	1	0	4	12	7-0	0	7	.237	.295	.400	93	-11		.967	-11	67	64	S24		-1.0
1989	Mil A	95	368	34	91	18	0	5	32	27-0	4	33	.247	.303	.337	81	-9	10-6	.959	-11	93	91	S70,3b21,D4	57	-1.5
1990	Mil A	125	487	67	143	30	1	10	67	44-1	3	41	.294	.350	.421	117	12	25-10	.934	-1	105	69	3b125		1.3
1991	Mil A	50	175	25	34	12	2	2	22	19-1	3	15	.194	.277	.320	68	-7	5-5	.922	-9	80	85	3b43,D5		-1.7
1992	SD N★	146	557	87	184	34	3	33	100	48-5	6	40	**.330**	.385	.580	168	49	5-6	.961	9	106	109	3b144	95	6.0
1993	SD N	68	258	34	76	12	2	10	36	18-0	3	30	.295	.344	.473	116	5	5-1	.905	-2	89	102	3b67		-0.1
	Fla N★	72	236	33	69	8	3	10	37	29-6	3	34	.292	.378	.479	122	8	12-4	.894	-3	103	37	3b66		0.6
	Year	140	494	67	145	20	5	20	73	47-6	9	64	.294	.361	.476	119	13	17-5	.899	-10	96	70	3b133		0.5

YEAR	TM LG	G	AB	R	H	2B	3B	HR	RBI	BB-IB	HP	SO	AVG	OBP	SLG	AOPS	ABR	SB-CS	FA	FR	RNG	THR	GAMES AT POSITION	DL	BFW
1994	Fla N	87	322	61	89	16	1	27	78	51-11	6	50	.276	.380	.584	142	21	12-6	.970	-3	91	107	O87R	30	1.3
1995	Fla N	63	213	46	69	8	0	16	46	55-8	4	45	.324	.467	.587	174	19	16-9	.942	-1	95	116	O61(3/0/59)	82	2.4
1996	Fla N★	161	519	118	163	33	1	42	120	142-19	10	66	.314	**.465**	**.624**	**190**	79	16-9	.976	-14	80	77	O161R	15	5.6
1997	†Fla N	135	444	86	111	22	1	21	71	121-11	15	79	.250	.424	.446	135	32	11-7	.980	2	96	152	O132R/D		2.7
1998	Fla N	40	136	21	37	11	1	6	28	26-1	2	16	.272	.392	.500	142	10	4-2	.986	0	94	118	O37R		0.8
	LA N★	90	301	52	95	16	1	16	57	69-11	6	30	.316	.428	.535	166	34	18-5	.994	-2	91	103	O89R		2.9
	Year	130	437	73	132	27	2	22	85	95-12	8	46	.302	.428	.524	159	44	22-7	.991	-2	92	107	O126R		3.7
1999	LA N★	152	549	103	165	20	0	34	101	101-4	4	64	.301	.407	.523	142	38	11-5	.972	-8	84	79	O145L,D3		2.4
2000	LA N★	141	501	105	163	24	3	43	109	101-7	4	71	.325	.438	.643	178	64	4-6	.954	-8	83	64	O139L,D2		4.6
2001	LA N	143	515	98	160	28	2	36	100	94-13	4	67	.311	.417	.583	166	54	10-4	.972	-3	77	189	O141(141/0/2),D2	15	4.5
2002	†Atl N	135	492	82	151	26	0	25	84	72-2	11	53	.307	.404	.512	144	32	12-2	.984	-6	90	81	O127R,D4		2.1
2003	†Atl N★	155	576	126	190	37	2	39	132	86-6	8	55	.330	.419	.604	165	58	18-4	.983	-5	95	70	O153R		4.7
2004	†NY A★	154	573	117	166	30	1	36	121	92-7	11	83	.290	.393	.534	140	37	5-6	.983	7	100	122	O136R,D18,3b2		2.7
2005	†NY A★	154	584	104	170	27	0	34	123	78-7	8	76	.291	.379	.512	134	30	10-2	.988	-4	95	68	O131R,D23		1.9
Total	18	2190	7886	1411	2345	413	24	449	1476	1280-120	118	955	.297	.399	.527	146	573	215-95	.977	-83	89	102	O1539R,3b468,S94,D62	294	42.2

SHELBY, JOHN   John T. B2.23.1958 Lexington KY   BB/TR/6-1/175* [BalA77*1/19] d9.15 C8 Col Columbia St. (TN) CC

YEAR	TM LG	G	AB	R	H	2B	3B	HR	RBI	BB-IB	HP	SO	AVG	OBP	SLG	AOPS	ABR	SB-CS	FA	FR	RNG	THR	GAMES AT POSITION	DL	BFW
1981	Bal A	7	2	2	1	0	0	0	0	0-0	0	1	1.000	.000	.000	-99	-1	2-0	1.000	0	46	0	O4C		0.0
1982	Bal A	26	35	8	11	3	0	1	2	0-0	0	5	.314	.314	.486	117	1	0-1	1.000	-1	75	152	O15C/D		-0.1
1983	†Bal A	126	325	52	84	15	2	5	27	18-2	0	64	.258	.297	.363	82	-9	15-2	.981	0	93	185	O124(0/118/9)		-0.7
1984	Bal A	128	383	44	80	12	5	6	30	20-0	0	71	.209	.248	.313	55	-25	12-4	.993	-1	96	136	O124(0/118/9)		-2.6
1985	Bal A	69	205	28	58	6	2	7	27	7-0	0	44	.283	.307	.434	102	-1	5-1	.981	4	117	95	O59(9/43/10)/2D		0.4
1986	Bal A	135	404	54	92	14	4	11	49	18-0	2	75	.228	.263	.364	64	-19	18-6	.978	-2	97	84	O121(49/56/31),D2		-2.2
1987	Bal A	21	32	4	6	0	0	1	3	1-0	0	13	.188	.212	.281	30	-3	0-1	1.000	0	113	0	O19(0/4/15)/D		-0.4
	LA N	120	476	61	132	26	0	21	69	31-2	1	97	.277	.317	.464	108	4	16-6	.972	-1	98	138	O117C		0.3
1988	†LA N	140	494	65	130	23	6	10	64	44-5	1	128	.263	.320	.395	108	4	16-5	.982	-3	96	116	O140C	20	0.2
1989	LA N	108	345	26	63	11	1	1	12	25-5	0	92	.183	.237	.229	34	-30	10-7	.991	-6	92	61	O98C		-4.0
1990	LA N	25	24	2	6	1	0	0	2	0-0	0	7	.250	.250	.292	50	-2	1-0	1.000	0	121		O12(7/1/4)		-0.2
	Det A	78	222	22	55	9	3	4	20	10-0	0	51	.248	.280	.369	79	-7	3-5	.973	2	100	146	O68(24/35/13),D5		-0.8
1991	Det A	53	143	19	22	8	1	3	8	8-1	0	23	.154	.204	.287	34	-13	0-2	.982	4	120	183	O47(25/26/3),D4		-1.1
Total	11	1036	3090	389	739	128	24	70	313	182-15	4	671	.239	.281	.364	78	-101	98-40	.982	-3	98	120	O948(114/781/85),D16/2	20	-11.2

SHELDON, BOB   Bob Mitchell B11.27.1950 Montebello CA BL/TR/6-0/170* [MilA72 22/507] d4.10 Col Loyola Marymount

YEAR	TM LG	G	AB	R	H	2B	3B	HR	RBI	BB-IB	HP	SO	AVG	OBP	SLG	AOPS	ABR	SB-CS	FA	FR	RNG	THR	GAMES AT POSITION	DL	BFW
1974	Mil A	10	17	4	2	1	1	0	4	0-0	0	2	.118	.286	.294	67	-1	0-1	1.000	-1	97	0	2b3,D4		-0.2
1975	Mil A	53	181	17	52	3	0	3	14	13-0	0	14	.287	.338	.337	92	-2	0-3	.977	1	105	113	2b44,D6		0.0
1977	Mil A	31	64	9	13	4	1	0	3	6-0	0	9	.203	.268	.297	55	-4	0-0	1.000	-1	80	78	D17,2b5		-0.6
Total	3	94	262	30	67	8	5	0	21	23-0	0	25	.256	.317	.324	81	-7	0-4	.979	-1	103	106	2b52,D27		-0.8

SHELDON, SCOTT   Scott Patrick B11.28.1968 Hammond IN BR/TR/6-3/215(185-215) [OakA91 8/229] d5.18 Col Houston OF(4/1/2)

YEAR	TM LG	G	AB	R	H	2B	3B	HR	RBI	BB-IB	HP	SO	AVG	OBP	SLG	AOPS	ABR	SB-CS	FA	FR	RNG	THR	GAMES AT POSITION	DL	BFW
1997	Oak A	13	24	2	6	0	0	1	2	1-0	1	6	.250	.308	.375	77	-1	0-0	.939	-3	71	68	S12/23		-0.3
1998	Tex A	7	16	0	2	0	0	0	1	1-0	1	6	.125	.176	.125	-19	-3	0-0	1.000	2	157	849	3b3,S2/1D		0.0
1999	Tex A	2	1	0	0	0	0	0	0	0-0	0	0	.000	.000	.000	-94	0	0-0	1.000	1	497	0	3b2		0.1
2000	Tex A	58	124	21	35	11	0	4	19	10-0	1	37	.282	.336	.468	101	0	0-0	.970	-0	94	56	S22,3b15,2b12,1b10,C3,O2(2/1/1)/P		0.1
2001	Tex A	61	120	11	24	5	0	3	11	3-0	0	35	.200	.216	.317	38	-11	1-1	.951	4	102	18	3b38,S16,O3(2/0/1)/C		-0.7
Total	5	141	285	34	67	16	0	8	33	15-0	3	84	.235	.275	.375	65	-15	1-1	.961	4	114	112	3b59,S52,2b13,1b11,O5L,C4/PD		-0.8

SHELLEY, HUGH   Hubert Leneirre B10.26.1910 Rogers TX D6.16.1978 Beaumont TX BR/TR/6-0/170 d6.25

YEAR	TM LG	G	AB	R	H	2B	3B	HR	RBI	BB-IB	HP	SO	AVG	OBP	SLG	AOPS	ABR	SB-CS	FA	FR	RNG	THR	GAMES AT POSITION	DL	BFW
1935	Det A	7	8	1	2	0	0	0	2	0-0	0	1	.250	.400	.250	74	0	0-0	1.000	0	119	0	O5(3/1/1)		0.0

SHELTON, SKEETER   Andrew Kemper B6.29.1888 Huntington WV D1.9.1954 Huntington WV BR/TR/5-11/175 d8.25 Col West Virginia

YEAR	TM LG	G	AB	R	H	2B	3B	HR	RBI	BB-IB	HP	SO	AVG	OBP	SLG	AOPS	ABR	SB-CS	FA	FR	RNG	THR	GAMES AT POSITION	DL	BFW
1915	NY A	10	40	1	1	0	0	0	0	2	0	10	.025	.071	.025	-71	-9	0	1.000	0	87	141	O10C		-1.0

SHELTON, BEN   Benjamin Davis B9.21.1969 Chicago IL BR/TL/6-3/210 [PitN87 2/34] d6.16

YEAR	TM LG	G	AB	R	H	2B	3B	HR	RBI	BB-IB	HP	SO	AVG	OBP	SLG	AOPS	ABR	SB-CS	FA	FR	RNG	THR	GAMES AT POSITION	DL	BFW
1993	Pit N	15	24	3	6	1	0	2	7	3-0	0	3	.250	.333	.542	130	1	0-0	.889	0	90	326	O6L,1b2		0.1

SHELTON, CHRIS   Christopher Bob B6.26.1980 Salt Lake City UT BR/TR/6-0/220* [PitN01 33/984] d4.15 Col Utah

YEAR	TM LG	G	AB	R	H	2B	3B	HR	RBI	BB-IB	HP	SO	AVG	OBP	SLG	AOPS	ABR	SB-CS	FA	FR	RNG	THR	GAMES AT POSITION	DL	BFW
2004	Det A	27	46	6	9	1	0	1	3	9-0	0	14	.196	.321	.283	64	-2	0-0	1.000	0	219	119	D11,1b8,C6/OR	40	-0.3
2005	Det A	107	388	61	116	22	3	18	59	34-0	5	101	.299	.360	.510	132	18	0-0	.993	3	116	122	1b84,D15/OL		1.2
Total	2	134	434	67	125	23	3	19	62	43-0	5	115	.288	.355	.486	125	16	0-0	.993	3	120	122	1b92,D26,C6,O2(1/0/1)	40	0.9

SHEMO, STEVE   Stephen Michael B4.9.1915 Swoyersville PA D4.13.1992 Eden NC BR/TR/5-11/175 d4.18

YEAR	TM LG	G	AB	R	H	2B	3B	HR	RBI	BB-IB	HP	SO	AVG	OBP	SLG	AOPS	ABR	SB-CS	FA	FR	RNG	THR	GAMES AT POSITION	DL	BFW
1944	Bos N	18	31	3	9	2	0	0	1	1	0	3	.290	.313	.355	84	1	0	.966	2	124	74	2b16,3b2		0.2
1945	Bos N	17	46	4	11	1	0	0	7	1	0	6	.239	.255	.261	43	-4	0	.921	-5	67	23	2b12,3b3/S		-0.8
Total	2	35	77	7	20	3	0	0	8	2	0	9	.260	.278	.299	60	-5	0	.948	-3	98	51	2b28,3b5/S		-0.6

SHEPARD, JACK   Jack Leroy B5.13.1932 Clovis CA D12.31.1994 Atherton CA BR/TR/6-2/195* d6.19 Col Stanford

YEAR	TM LG	G	AB	R	H	2B	3B	HR	RBI	BB-IB	HP	SO	AVG	OBP	SLG	AOPS	ABR	SB-CS	FA	FR	RNG	THR	GAMES AT POSITION	DL	BFW
1953	Pit N	2	4	0	1	0	0	0	0	0-0	0	2	.250	.250	.250	31	0	0-0	.750	-1	0	0	C2		-0.1
1954	Pit N	82	227	24	69	8	2	3	22	26-?	0	33	.304	.370	.396	103	2	0-0	.977	-2	56	166	C67		0.3
1955	Pit N	94	264	24	63	10	2	2	23	33-3	0	25	.239	.321	.314	71	-10	1-0	.982	-7	72	127	C77		-1.4
1956	Pit N	100	256	24	62	11	2	7	30	25-5	0	37	.242	.309	.383	87	-5	1-1	.990	3	102	118	C86,1b2		0.1
Total	4	278	751	72	195	29	6	12	75	84-8	0	97	.260	.331	.362	86	-13	2-1	.982	-7	77	135	C232,1b2		-1.1

SHEPARDSON, RAY   Raymond Francis B5.3.1897 Little Falls NY D11.8.1975 Little Falls NY BR/TR/5-11.5/170 d9.19

YEAR	TM LG	G	AB	R	H	2B	3B	HR	RBI	BB-IB	HP	SO	AVG	OBP	SLG	AOPS	ABR	SB-CS	FA	FR	RNG	THR	GAMES AT POSITION	DL	BFW
1924	StL N	3	6	1	0	0	0	0	0	0-0	0	3	.000	.000	.000	-99	-2	0-0	1.000	0	97	121	C3		-0.2

SHEPHERD, RON   Ronald Wayne B10.27.1960 Longview TX BR/TR/6-4/175* [TorA79 2/29] d9.5 [DL 1988 Mon N 131]

YEAR	TM LG	G	AB	R	H	2B	3B	HR	RBI	BB-IB	HP	SO	AVG	OBP	SLG	AOPS	ABR	SB-CS	FA	FR	RNG	THR	GAMES AT POSITION	DL	BFW
1984	Tor A	12	4	0	0	0	0	0	0	0-0	0	3	.000	.000	.000	-96	-1	0-1	1.000	1	86	1367	O5L,D4		-0.1
1985	Tor A	38	35	7	4	2	0	0	1	2-0	0	12	.114	.162	.171	-8	-5	3-0	1.000	-0	107	0	O16(3/13/1),D15	14	-0.5
1986	Tor A	65	69	16	14	4	0	2	4	3-0	0	22	.203	.236	.348	55	-5	0-0	1.000	-3	71	0	O32(12/10/11),D16		-0.9
Total	3	115	108	23	18	6	0	2	5	5-0	0	37	.167	.204	.278	29	-11	3-1	1.000	-3	83	50	O53(20/23/12),D35	145	-1.5

SHEPPARD, JOHN   John B Baltimore MD d6.27

YEAR	TM LG	G	AB	R	H	2B	3B	HR	RBI	BB-IB	HP	SO	AVG	OBP	SLG	AOPS	ABR	SB-CS	FA	FR	RNG	THR	GAMES AT POSITION	DL	BFW
1873	Mar NA	3	11	1	0	0	0	0	0	0	0	1	.000	.000	.000	-99	-3	0-0	.500	-2	0	0	O2(1/0/1)/C		-0.3

SHERIDAN   d10.9

YEAR	TM LG	G	AB	R	H	2B	3B	HR	RBI	BB-IB	HP	SO	AVG	OBP	SLG	AOPS	ABR	SB-CS	FA	FR	RNG	THR	GAMES AT POSITION	DL	BFW
1875	Atl NA	1	4	0	0	0	0	0	0	0	0	1	.000	.000	.000	-99	-1	0-0	—	-0	0	0	/OL		-0.1

SHERIDAN, RED   Eugene Anthony B11.14.1896 Brooklyn NY D11.25.1975 Queens Village NY BR/TR/5-10.5/160 d7.3 Mil 1918

YEAR	TM LG	G	AB	R	H	2B	3B	HR	RBI	BB-IB	HP	SO	AVG	OBP	SLG	AOPS	ABR	SB-CS	FA	FR	RNG	THR	GAMES AT POSITION	DL	BFW
1918	Bro N	2	4	1	1	0	0	0	0	0-0	0	0	.250	.400	.250	100	0	1	1.000	-1	58	0	2b2		0.0
1920	Bro N	3	2	0	0	0	0	0	0	1	0	1	.000	.000	.000	-97	-1	0-0	1.000	1	113	591	S3		0.0
Total	2	5	6	1	1	0	0	0	0	1	0	1	.167	.286	.167	37	-1	1-0	1.000	0	113	591	S3,2b2		0.0

SHERIDAN, NEILL   Neill Rawlins "Wild Horse" B11.20.1921 Sacramento CA BR/TR/6-1.5/195 d9.19 Col San Francisco

YEAR	TM LG	G	AB	R	H	2B	3B	HR	RBI	BB-IB	HP	SO	AVG	OBP	SLG	AOPS	ABR	SB-CS	FA	FR	RNG	THR	GAMES AT POSITION	DL	BFW
1948	Bos A	2	1	0	0	0	0	0	0	0-0	0	1	.000	.000	.000	-95	0	0-0	—	—	—		/H		0.0

SHERIDAN, PAT   Patrick Arthur B12.4.1957 Ann Arbor MI BL/TR/6-3/175(175-195) [KCA79 3/73] d9.16 Col Eastern Michigan

YEAR	TM LG	G	AB	R	H	2B	3B	HR	RBI	BB-IB	HP	SO	AVG	OBP	SLG	AOPS	ABR	SB-CS	FA	FR	RNG	THR	GAMES AT POSITION	DL	BFW
1981	KC A	3	1	0	0	0	0	0	0	0-0	0	0	1.000	.000	.000	-99	0	0-0	1.000	0	158	0	O3(1/0/2)		0.0
1983	KC A	109	333	43	90	12	2	7	36	20-0	0	64	.270	.312	.381	89	-6	12-3	.988	6	115	93	O100(28/36/48)		-0.8
1984	†KC A	138	481	64	136	24	4	8	53	41-3	1	91	.283	.338	.399	103	2	19-6	.986	-4	93	98	O134(0/35/101)	44	-1.6
1985	†KC A	78	206	18	47	9	2	3	19	21-3	1	38	.228	.307	.335	76	-7	11-3	.983	-1	97	76	O69R/D		-1.1
1986	Det A	98	236	41	56	9	1	6	19	21-4	1	57	.237	.300	.360	79	-7	9-2	.977	-3	99	23	O90(11/51/32),D5		-1.8
1987	†Det A	141	421	57	109	19	3	6	49	44-4	1	64	.259	.327	.361	87	-8	18-13	.976	-2	102	78	O137(0/26/124),D3		0.2
1988	Det A	127	347	47	88	9	5	11	47	44-4	0	64	.254	.339	.403	111	5	8-6	.981	-2	103	38	O111(92/9/12),D3		-0.7
1989	Det A	50	120	16	29	3	0	3	15	17-0	0	21	.242	.333	.342	93	-7	4-0	.982	-1	88	119	O35(19/7/9),D6		-0.6
	†SF N	70	161	20	33	3	4	3	14	13-1	0	45	.205	.264	.329	71	-7	4-1	.983	3	118	70	O66(8/3/58)		-0.6
1991	NY A	62	113	13	23	3	0	4	7	13-1	0	30	.204	.286	.336	71	-5	1-1	1.000	0	90	183	O34(3/6/26),D2		-0.5
Total	9	876	2419	319	611	91	21	51	257	236-19	6	501	.253	.319	.371	90	-34	86-35	.983	-3	101	77	O779(162/173/481),D19	44	-0.1

YEAR TM LG	G	AB	R	H	2B	3B	HR	RBI	BB-IB	HP	SO	AVG	OBP	SLG	AOPS	ABR	SB-CS	FA	FR	RNG	THR	GAMES AT POSITION	DL	BFW

SHERLING, ED Edward Creech "Shine" B7.17.1897 Coalburg AL D11.16.1965 Enterprise CA BR/TR/6-1/185 d8.13 Col Auburn-Montgomery

YEAR TM LG	G	AB	R	H	2B	3B	HR	RBI	BB-IB	HP	SO	AVG	OBP	SLG	AOPS	ABR	SB-CS	FA	FR	RNG	THR	GAMES		BFW
1924 Phi A	4	2	1	1	0	0	0	0	0-0	0	0	.500	.500	1.000	278	1	0-0	—	0			/H		0.1

SHERLOCK, MONK John Clinton B10.26.1904 Buffalo NY D11.26.1985 Buffalo NY BR/TR/5-10/175 d4.20 b-Vince

| 1930 Phi N | 92 | 299 | 51 | 97 | 18 | 2 | 0 | 38 | 27 | 0 | 28 | .324 | .380 | .398 | 83 | -7 | 0 | .990 | 3 | 123 | 77 | 1b70,2b5/OC | | -0.7 |

SHERLOCK, VINCE Vincent Thomas "Baldy" B3.27.1910 Buffalo NY D5.11.1997 Cheektowaga NY BR/TR/6-0/180 d9.18 b-Monk

| 1935 Bro N | 9 | 26 | 4 | 12 | 1 | 1 | 0 | 6 | 1 | 0 | 2 | .462 | .481 | .500 | 168 | 3 | 1 | .907 | -2 | 76 | 27 | 2b8 | | 0.1 |

SHERMAN, DARRELL Darrell Edward B12.4.1967 Los Angeles CA BL/TL/5-9/160 [SDN89 6/156] d4.8 Col Cal St.-Long Beach

| 1993 SD N | 37 | 63 | 8 | 14 | 1 | 0 | 0 | 2 | 6-0 | 3 | 8 | .222 | .315 | .238 | 51 | -4 | 2-1 | 1.000 | -2 | 143 | 0 | O26(24/6/1) | | -0.2 |

SHERRILL, DENNIS Dennis Lee B3.3.1956 Miami FL BR/TR/6-0/165* [NYA74 1/12] d9.4

1978 NY A	2	1	1	0	0	0	0	0	0-0	0	0	1.000	.000	.000	-99	0	0-0	—	-0	0		/3D		-0.1
1980 NY A	3	4	0	1	0	0	0	0	0-0	0	2	.250	.250	.250	38	0	0-0	1.000	-1	0	0	S2/2		-0.1
Total 2	5	5	1	1	0	0	0	0	0-0	0	2	.200	.200	.200	11	0	0-0	1.000	-1	0	0	S2/2D3		-0.2

SHERRY, NORM Norman Burt B7.16.1931 New York NY BR/TR/5-11/181* d4.12 M2/C16 b-Larry

1959 LA N	2	3	0	1	0	0	0	0	2-0	1	0	.333	.500	.333	119	0	0-0	1.000	-0	0	0	C2		0.0
1960 LA N	47	138	22	39	4	1	8	19	12-3	3	29	.283	.353	.500	122	4	0-0	.993	-3	148	48	C44		0.3
1961 LA N	47	121	10	31	2	0	5	16	9-2	0	30	.256	.308	.397	78	-4	0-0	.993	0	62	67	C45		0.0
1962 LA N	35	88	7	16	2	0	3	16	6-0	1	17	.182	.240	.307	49	-4	0-0	.992	5	120	89	C34	33	-0.2
1963 NY N	63	147	6	20	1	0	2	11	10-1	3	26	.136	.205	.184	13	-17	1-0	.980	-2	120	129	C61		0.0
Total 5	194	497	45	107	9	1	18	69	37-6	8	102	.215	.279	.346	69	-24	1-0	.989	1	114	85	C186	33	-1.7 -1.6

SHETRONE, BARRY Barry Stevan B7.6.1938 Baltimore MD D7.18.2001 Bowie MD BL/TR/6-2/190* d7.27

1959 Bal A	33	79	8	16	1	1	0	5	5-1	0	9	.203	.247	.241	36	-7	3-0	.947	-2	86	0	O23(5/17/1)		-1.0
1960 Bal A	1	0	1	0	0	0	0	0	0-0	0	0					-0			0			/R		0.0
1961 Bal A	3	7	0	1	0	0	0	0	0-0	0	2	.143	.143	.143	-24	-1	0-0	1.000	-0	91	0	O2C		-0.1
1962 Bal A	21	24	3	6	1	0	1	1	0-0	0	5	.250	.250	.417	81	-1	0-0	1.000	1	153	0	O6(3/2/1)		-0.1
1963 Was A	2	2	0	0	0	0	0	0	0-0	0	0	.000	.000	.000	-99	-1	0-0	—	0			/H		-0.1
Total 5	60	112	12	23	2	1	1	7	5-1	0	16	.205	.237	.268	39	-10	3-0	.962	-2	97	0	O31(8/21/2)		-1.2

SHETZLINE, JOHN John Henry B1852 Philadelphia PA D12.15.1892 Philadelphia PA 5-11.5/190 d5.2

| 1882 Bal AA | 73 | 282 | 23 | 62 | 8 | 3 | 0 | | 5 | | | .220 | .233 | .270 | 75 | -7 | | .800 | 4 | 106 | 138 | 3b52,2b20/ORS | | -0.1 |

SHEVLIN, JIMMY James Cornelius B7.9.1909 Cincinnati OH D10.30.1974 Ft.Lauderdale FL BL/TL/5-10.5/155 d6.29 Col Holy Cross

1930 Det A	28	14	4	2	0	0	0	2	2	0	3	.143	.250	.143	2	-2	0-0	1.000	0	115	0	1b25		-0.2
1932 Cin N	7	24	3	5	2	0	0	4	4	1	4	.208	.345	.292	76	-1	0-0	.985	-0	85	58	1b7		-0.2
1934 Cin N	18	39	6	12	0	0	0	6	6	0	5	.308	.400	.359	107	1	0	1.000	1	124	119	1b10		0.1
Total 3	53	77	13	19	4	0	0	12	12	1	12	.247	.356	.299	77	-2	4-0	.995	1	108	70	1b42		-0.3

SHIELDS, PETE Francis Leroy B9.21.1891 Swiftwater MS D2.11.1961 Jackson MS BR/TR/6-0/175 d4.14 Col U. of Mississippi

| 1915 Cle A | 23 | 72 | 4 | 15 | 6 | 0 | 0 | 6 | 4 | 0 | 14 | .208 | .250 | .292 | 61 | -4 | 3-3 | .974 | -0 | 107 | 47 | 1b23 | | -0.5 |

SHIELDS, TOMMY Thomas Charles B8.14.1964 Fairfax VA BL/TR/6-0/180* [PitN86 15/368] d7.25 Col Notre Dame

1992 Bal A	2	0	0	0	0	0	0	0	0-0	0	0	—	—					—	0			/R		0.0
1993 Chi N	20	34	4	6	1	0	0	1	2-0	0	10	.176	.222	.206	16	-4	0-0	1.000	2	143	173	2b7,3b7/1OL		-0.2
Total 2	22	34	4	6	1	0	0	1	2-0	0	10	.176	.222	.206	16	-4	0-0	1.000	2	104	136	3b7,2b7/OL1		-0.2

SHILLING, JIM James Robert B5.14.1914 Tulsa OK D9.12.1986 Tulsa OK BR/TR/5-11/175 d4.21

1939 Cle A	31	98	8	27	7	2	0	12	7	0	9	.276	.324	.388	84	-3	1-0	.935	0	105	105	2b27,S3		0.0
Phi N	11	33	3	10	1	0	0	4	1	0	4	.303	.324	.515	126	1	0	.944	-2	79	85	2b5,S3,3b3/OL		-0.1
Total 1	42	131	11	37	8	2	0	16	8	0	13	.282	.324	.420	94	-2	1-0	.936	-2	102	103	2b32,S6,3b3/OL		-0.1

SHINAULT, GINGER Enoch Erskine B9.7.1892 Benton AR D12.29.1930 Denver CO BR/TR/5-11/170 d7.4

1921 Cle A	22	29	5	11	1	0	0	4	6	0	5	.379	.486	.414	129	2	1-0	.917	1	103	142	C20		0.3
1922 Cle A	13	15	1	2	1	0	0	0	0	0	2	.133	.133	.200	-14	-3	0-0	.400	-3	60	0	C11		-0.5
Total 2	35	44	6	13	2	0	0	4	6	0	7	.295	.380	.341	85	-1	1-0	.868	-2	95	114	C31		-0.2

SHINDLE, BILLY William D. B12.5.1860 Gloucester NJ D6.3.1936 Lakeland NJ BR/TR/5-8.5/155 d10.5

1886 Det N	7	26	4	7	0	0	0	4	0		5	.269	.269	.269	62	-1	2	.900	0	118	61	S7		
1887 Det N	22	84	17	24	3	2	0	12	7		5	.286	.341	.369	93	-1	13	.818	-3	83	180	3b21/OL		-0.1
1888 Bal AA	135	514	61	107	14	8	1	53	20	8		.208	.249	.272	69	-19	52	.922	38	120	128	3b135		-0.3
1889 Bal AA	138	567	122	178	24	7	3	64	42	7	37	.314	.369	.397	116	11	56	.862	23	113	105	3b138		2.0
1890 Phi P	132	584	127	189	21	21	10	90	40	4	30	.324	.371	.483	124	15	51	.856	8	103	125	S130,3b2		3.0
1891 Phi N	103	415	68	87	13	1	0	38	33	6	39	.210	.278	.246	51	-26	17	.874	4	106	156	3b100,S3		2.2
1892 Bal N	143	619	100	156	20	18	3	50	35	8	34	.252	.301	.357	96	-7	24	.882	37	130	114	3b134,S9		-1.7
1893 Bal N	125	521	100	136	22	11	1	75	66	8	17	.261	.353	.351	86	-10	17	.885	10	108	103	3b125		3.0
1894 Bro N	117	480	94	142	22	9	4	96	29	6	21	.296	.344	.404	86	-12	19	.896	1	96	62	3b117		0.1
1895 Bro N	117	481	92	135	21	2	3	70	47	11	28	.281	.358	.351	91	-3	17	.895	-0	106	98	3b117		-0.7
1896 Bro N	131	516	75	144	24	9	1	61	24	4	20	.279	.316	.366	84	-13	24	.912	-11	93	105	3b131		-0.1
1897 Bro N	134	542	83	154	32	6	4	105	35	7		.284	.336	.387	96	-3	23	.904	-14	90	76	3b134		-1.8
1898 Bro N	120	466	50	105	10	3	1	41	10	5		.225	.249	.266	48	-33	3	.911	4	107	128	3b120		-1.3
Total 13	1424	5815	993	1564	226	97	31	759	388	74	241	.269	.323	.357	88	-102	318	.892	96	107	108	3b1274,S149/OL		-2.6 1.7

SHINES, RAZOR Anthony Raymond "Ray" B7.18.1956 Durham NC BB/TR/6-1/210* [MonN78 18/451] d9.9 Col St. Augustines

1983 Mon N	3	2	0	1	0	0	0	0	0-0	0	0	.500	.500	.500	178	0	0-0	—	-0	0	0	/OL		0.0
1984 Mon N	12	20	1	6	1	0	0	2	0-0	0	3	.300	.286	.350	86	0	0-0	1.000	-1	0	91	1b3/3		-0.2
1985 Mon N	47	50	0	6	0	0	0	3	4-0	0	9	.120	.185	.120	-14	-8	0-0	.950	0	167	37	1b5/P		-0.8
1987 Mon N	6	9	0	2	0	0	0	3	1-0	1	0	.222	.364	.222	58	0	1-0	1.000	0	82	169	1b2		-0.2
Total 4	68	81	0	15	1	0	0	8	5-0	1	12	.185	.239	.198	24	-8	1-1	.975	-1	88	83	1b10/P3OL		-1.0

SHINJO, TSUYOSHI Tsuyoshi B1.28.1972 Fukuoka, Japan BR/TR/6-1/185* d4.3

2001 NY N	123	400	46	107	23	1	10	56	25-3	7	70	.268	.320	.405	93	-5	4-5	.989	13	117	190	O119(46/53/39)	28	0.4
2002 †SF N	118	362	42	86	15	3	9	37	24-2	6	46	.238	.294	.370	80	-14	5-0	.980	12	121	179	O117(1/108/10)	18	0.0
2003 NY N	62	114	10	22	3	0	1	7	6-1	1	22	.193	.238	.246	28	-13	0-1	.972	7	129	275	O54(7/50/1)		-0.6
Total 3	303	876	98	215	41	4	20	100	55-6	14	128	.245	.299	.370	79	-32	9-6	.982	31	120	197	O290(54/211/50)	46	-0.2

SHINNERS, RALPH Ralph Peter B10.4.1895 Monches WI D7.23.1962 Milwaukee WI BR/TR/6-0/180 d4.12 Col Marquette

1922 NY N	56	135	16	34	4	2	0	15	5	6	22	.252	.308	.311	60	-8	3-5	.915	-4	94	46	O37(1/30/6)		-1.4
1923 NY N	33	13	5	2	1	0	0	0	0		3	.154	.267	.231	33	-1	0-0	1.000	1	171	0	O6(2/1/3)		-0.1
1925 StL N	74	251	39	74	9	2	7	36	12	1	19	.295	.330	.430	90	-5	8-5	.982	-2	103	34	O66(3/56/7)		-0.9
Total 3	163	399	60	110	14	4	7	51	17	7	44	.276	.320	.383	78	-14	11-10	.959	-5	101	38	O109(6/87/16)		-2.4

SHINNICK, TIM Timothy James "Dandy","Good Eye" B11.6.1867 Exeter NH D5.18.1944 Exeter NH BB/TR/5-9/150 d4.19

1890 †Lou AA	133	493	87	126	16	11	1	82	62	8		.256	.348	.339	105	4	62	.925	-31	92	87	2b130,3b3		-1.9
1891 Lou AA	126	436	77	96	9	11	1	52	54	5	46	.220	.313	.298	76	-14	36	.913	-21	95	94	2b118,3b7/S		-2.7
Total 2	259	929	164	222	25	22	2	134	116	13	46	.239	.332	.320	91	-10	98	.919	-52	93	90	2b248,3b10/S		-4.6

SHIPKE, BILL William Martin "Skipper Bill","Muskrat Bill" (b William Martin Shipkrethaver) B11.18.1882 St.Louis MO D9.10.1940 Omaha NE BR/TR/5-7/145 d4.23

1906 Cle A	2	6	0	0	0	0	0	0	0-0	0	0	.000	.000	.000	-99	-1	0-0	.933	1	124	294	2b2		
1907 Was A	64	189	17	37	3	2	1	9	3-0		2	.196	.262	.249	68	-7	6	.944	8	117	33	3b63		-0.1
1908 Was A	111	341	40	71	7	8	0	20	38		5	.208	.297	.276	94	-1	15	.932	-4	96	103	3b110/2		0.3
1909 Was A	9	16	2	2	1	0	0	0	5		0	.125	.222	.188	31	-1	0	.905	2	137	154	3b6,S2		-0.3
Total 4	186	552	59	110	11	10	1	29	46	7	21	.199	.280	.261	81	-10	21	.935	6	105	80	3b179,2b3,S2		-0.1

SHIPLEY, CRAIG Craig Barry B1.7.1963 Parramatta, New South Wales, Australia BR/TR/6-1/185(168-190) d6.22 Col Alabama OF(4/4/4)

| 1986 LA N | 12 | 27 | 3 | 3 | 1 | 0 | 0 | 1 | 2-1 | 0 | 9 | .111 | .200 | .148 | -6 | -3 | 0-0 | .914 | -3 | 61 | 80 | S10/23 | | -0.7 |
| 1987 LA N | 26 | 35 | 3 | 9 | 1 | 0 | 0 | 1 | 2-0 | 1 | 6 | .257 | .257 | .286 | 45 | -3 | 0-0 | .949 | -2 | 95 | 39 | S18,3b6 | | -0.4 |

YEAR	TM LG	G	AB	R	H	2B	3B	HR	RBI	BB-IB	HP	SO	AVG	OBP	SLG	AOPS	ABR	SB-CS	FA	FR	RNG	THR	GAMES AT POSITION	DL	BFW
1989	NY N	4	7	3	1	0	0	0	0	0-0	0	1	.143	.143	.143	-19	-1	0-0	1.000	-1	47	0	S3,3b2		-0.2
1991	SD N	37	91	6	25	3	0	1	6	2-0	1	14	.275	.298	.341	77	-3	0-1	.902	-4	75	83	S19,2b14		-0.6
1992	SD N	52	105	7	26	6	0	0	7	2-1	0	21	.248	.282	.305	59	-6	1-1	.986	5	113	183	S23,2b11,3b8		0.1
1993	SD N	105	230	25	54	9	0	4	22	10-0	3	31	.235	.275	.326	60	-14	12-3	.936	-3	96	51	S38,3b37,2b12,O5(2/3/0)	17	-1.5
1994	SD N	81	240	32	80	14	4	4	30	9-1	3	28	.333	.362	.475	121	7	6-6	.982	-3	90	67	3b53,S14,2b13,O2(1/1/0)/1	25	0.4
1995	Hou N	92	232	23	61	8	1	3	24	8-3	2	28	.263	.291	.345	72	-10	6-1	.985	3	114	87	3b65,S11,2b4/1	90	0.5
1996	SD N	33	92	13	29	5	0	1	7	2-1	0	15	.315	.337	.402	100	7	7-0	.947	-4	96	59	2b17,S7,3b4,O3R	66	-0.3
1997	SD N	63	139	22	38	5	0	5	19	7-0	0	22	.273	.306	.446	101	-1	1-1	.963	2	80	26	S21,2b16,1b4,3b2	33	-0.5
1998	Ana A	77	147	18	38	7	1	2	17	5-0	5	22	.259	.304	.361	71	-6	0-4	.963	-14	90	76	3b48,2b11,1b8,S5,O2(1/0/1)	231	-1.1
Total	11	582	1345	155	364	63	6	20	138	47-7	17	191	.271	.302	.371	80	-41	33-17	.963	-14	90	76	3b226,S169,2b99,1b14,O12L	231	-4.3

SHIRES, ART Charles Arthur "Art the Great" B8.13.1907 Italy TX D7.13.1967 Italy TX BL/TR/6-1/195 d8.20

YEAR	TM LG	G	AB	R	H	2B	3B	HR	RBI	BB-IB	HP	SO	AVG	OBP	SLG	AOPS	ABR	SB-CS	FA	FR	RNG	THR	GAMES AT POSITION	DL	BFW
1928	Chi A	33	123	20	42	6	1	1	11	13	1	10	.341	.409	.431	122	5	0-3	.990	3	138	90	1b32		0.4
1929	Chi A	100	353	41	110	20	7	3	41	32	1	20	.312	.370	.433	108	4	4-5	.991	-0	107	110	1b90,2b3		-0.3
1930	Chi A	37	128	14	33	5	1	0	18	6	0	6	.258	.291	.336	61	-8	2-0	.979	-2	81	67	1b33		-1.1
	Was A	38	84	11	31	5	0	1	19	5	0	5	.369	.404	.464	119	3	1-3	.982	0	113	151	1b21		0.1
	Year	75	212	25	64	10	1	2	37	11	0	11	.302	.336	.387	84	-5	3-3	.980	-1	92	96	1b54		-1.0
1932	Bos N	82	298	32	71	9	3	5	30	25	1	21	.238	.299	.339	74	-11	1	.988	-1	95	100	1b80		-2.1
Total		290	986	118	287	45	12	11	119	81	3	62	.291	.347	.395	95	-7	8-11	.988	-1	104	101	1b256,2b3		-3.0

SHIRLEY, BART Barton Arvin B1.4.1940 Corpus Christi TX BR/TR/5-10/183* d9.14 Col Texas

YEAR	TM LG	G	AB	R	H	2B	3B	HR	RBI	BB-IB	HP	SO	AVG	OBP	SLG	AOPS	ABR	SB-CS	FA	FR	RNG	THR	GAMES AT POSITION	DL	BFW
1964	LA N	18	62	6	17	1	0	1	7	4-2	0	8	.274	.318	.323	87	-1	0-0	.900	-2	51	0	3b10,S8		-0.3
1966	LA N	12	5	2	1	0	0	0	0	0-0	0	2	.200	.200	.200	13	-1	0-0	1.000	-0	61	0	S5		-0.1
1967	NY N	6	12	1	0	0	0	0	0	0-0	0	5	.000	.000	.000	-99	-3	0-0	.917	-1	108	53	2b3		-0.4
1968	LA N	39	83	6	15	3	0	0	4	10-1	0	13	.181	.269	.217	51	-5	0-1	.903	-0	94	180	S21,2b18,3b10		-0.3
Total	4	75	162	15	33	4	1	0	14	14-3	0	28	.204	.267	.241	52	-10	0-1	.936	-4	105	153	S34,2b21,3b10		-1.1

SHIRLEY, MULE Ernest Raeford B5.21.1901 Snow Hill NC D8.3.1955 Goldsboro NC BL/TL/5-11/180 d5.6 Col North Carolina-Asheville

YEAR	TM LG	G	AB	R	H	2B	3B	HR	RBI	BB-IB	HP	SO	AVG	OBP	SLG	AOPS	ABR	SB-CS	FA	FR	RNG	THR	GAMES AT POSITION	DL	BFW
1924	†Was A	30	77	12	18	2	2	0	16	3	0	7	.234	.262	.312	49	-6	0-0	.984	0	103	133	1b25		-0.7
1925	Was A	14	23	2	3	1	0	0	2	1	0	7	.130	.167	.174	-14	-4	0-0	1.000	0	92	104	1b9		-0.4
Total	2	44	100	14	21	3	2	0	18	4	0	14	.210	.240	.280	34	-10	0-0	.988	0	101	127	1b34		-1.1

SHIVER, IVEY Ivey Merwin "Chick" B1.22.1906 Sylvester GA D8.31.1972 Savannah GA BR/TR/6-1.5/190 d4.14 Col Georgia

YEAR	TM LG	G	AB	R	H	2B	3B	HR	RBI	BB-IB	HP	SO	AVG	OBP	SLG	AOPS	ABR	SB-CS	FA	FR	RNG	THR	GAMES AT POSITION	DL	BFW
1931	Det A	2	9	2	1	0	0	0	0	0	0	3	.111	.111	.111	-40	-2	0-0	1.000	-0	64	0	O2C		-0.2
1934	Cin N	19	59	6	12	1	0	2	6	3	0	15	.203	.242	.322	51	-4	1	1.000	-1	94	0	O15R		-0.6
Total	2	21	68	8	13	1	0	2	6	3	0	18	.191	.225	.294	38	-6	1-0	1.000	-2	91	0	O17(0/2/15)		-0.8

SHOCH, GEORGE George Quintus B1.6.1859 Philadelphia PA D9.30.1937 Philadelphia PA BR/TR/5-6/158 d9.10 OF(99/41/159)

YEAR	TM LG	G	AB	R	H	2B	3B	HR	RBI	BB-IB	HP	SO	AVG	OBP	SLG	AOPS	ABR	SB-CS	FA	FR	RNG	THR	GAMES AT POSITION	DL	BFW
1886	Was N	26	95	11	28	2	1	1	18	2		13	.295	.309	.368	114	-3		.882	-3	47	0	O25(1/0/24)/S		-0.2
1887	Was N	70	264	47	63	9	1	1	18	21	4	16	.239	.304	.292	71	-9	29	.897	4	124	137	O63(11/3/49),S6/2		-0.5
1888	Was N	90	317	46	58	6	3	2	24	25	9	22	.183	.262	.240	65	-11	23	.900	6	111	39	S52,O35(9/0/26)/2P		-0.5
1889	Was N	30	109	12	26	2	0	0	11	20	6	5	.239	.385	.257	86	0	9	.905	3	145	86	O29(16/0/13)/S		-0.1
1891	Mil AA	34	127	29	40	7	1	1	16	18	6	19	.315	.435	.409	118	4	12	.932	3	107	52	S25,3b9		0.2
1892	Bal N	76	308	42	85	15	3	1	50	24	6	13	.276	.340	.354	107	3	14	.872	-3	105	73	S57,O12(8/4/0),3b7		-0.5
1893	Bro N	94	327	53	86	17	1	2	54	48	5	13	.263	.366	.339	92	-1	9	.892	-3	87	0	O46(32/0/15),3b37,S11,2b3		-0.5
1894	Bro N	65	243	47	77	6	5	1	37	26	5	6	.317	.394	.395	97	1	16	.926	0	86	77	O35(1/28/6),3b14,2b9,S7		0.2
1895	Bro N	61	216	49	56	9	7	1	29	32	5	9	.259	.368	.366	97	1	7	.952	-4	81	77	O39(16/2/21),2b13,S6,3b3		0.2
1896	Bro N	76	250	36	73	7	4	1	28	33	3	10	.292	.381	.364	103	3	11	.941	-3	104	98	2b62,O10(2/3/5),3b3/S		0.2
1897	Bro N	85	284	42	79	9	2	0	38	49	5		.278	.393	.324	96	3	6	.941	-3	96	67	2b68,S13,O4(3/1/0)		-0.4
Total	11	707	2540	414	671	89	28	10	323	298	57	115	.264	.354	.333	93	-5	138	.912	-4	96	67	O298R,S180,2b157,3b73/P		-0.4

SHOCKLEY, COSTEN John Costen B2.8.1942 Georgetown DE BL/TL/6-2/195* d7.17

YEAR	TM LG	G	AB	R	H	2B	3B	HR	RBI	BB-IB	HP	SO	AVG	OBP	SLG	AOPS	ABR	SB-CS	FA	FR	RNG	THR	GAMES AT POSITION	DL	BFW
1964	Phi N	11	35	4	8	0	0	1	2	2-0	0	8	.229	.263	.314	65	-2	0-0	.968	-1	78	119	1b9		-0.1
1965	Cal A	40	107	5	20	2	0	2	17	9-0	1	16	.187	.252	.262	49	-7	0-0	.996	1	106	124	1b31/OR		-1.
Total	2	51	142	9	28	2	0	3	19	11-0	1	24	.197	.255	.275	53	-9	0-0	.991	-0	100	123	1b40/OR		-1.

SHOEMAKER, CHARLIE Charles Landis B8.10.1939 Los Angeles CA D5.31.1990 Mount Penn PA BL/TR/5-10/155* d9.9 Col Arizona

YEAR	TM LG	G	AB	R	H	2B	3B	HR	RBI	BB-IB	HP	SO	AVG	OBP	SLG	AOPS	ABR	SB-CS	FA	FR	RNG	THR	GAMES AT POSITION	DL	BFW
1961	KC A	7	26	5	10	2	0	0	1	2-0	0	2	.385	.429	.462	135	3	0-0	1.000	1	112	64	2b6		0.
1962	KC A	5	11	1	2	0	0	0	0	0-0	0	0	.182	.182	.182	-2	-2	0-0	1.000	-1	144	67	2b4		0.
1964	KC A	16	52	6	11	2	2	0	3	0-0	0	9	.212	.212	.327	46	-4	0-0	.964	-8	63	39	2b14		0.
Total	3	28	89	12	23	4	2	0	4	2-0	0	13	.258	.275	.348	67	-5	0-0	.981	-6	84	48	2b24		0.

SHOFNER, STRICK Frank Strickland B7.23.1919 Crawford TX D10.10.1998 Crawford TX BL/TR/5-10.5/187 d4.19

YEAR	TM LG	G	AB	R	H	2B	3B	HR	RBI	BB-IB	HP	SO	AVG	OBP	SLG	AOPS	ABR	SB-CS	FA	FR	RNG	THR	GAMES AT POSITION	DL	BFW
1947	Bos A	5	13	1	2	0	1	0	0	0-0	0	3	.154	.154	.308	25	-2	0-0	1.000	1	118	182	3b4		-0.

SHOKES, EDDIE Edward Christopher B1.27.1920 Charleston SC D9.14.2002 Winchester VA BL/TL/6-0/170 d6.9 Mil 1943-45 Col Duke

YEAR	TM LG	G	AB	R	H	2B	3B	HR	RBI	BB-IB	HP	SO	AVG	OBP	SLG	AOPS	ABR	SB-CS	FA	FR	RNG	THR	GAMES AT POSITION	DL	BFW
1941	Cin N	1	0	0	0	0	0	0	0	0	0	0	.000	.000	.000	-99	0	0	—	0			/H		-1
1946	Cin N	31	83	3	10	1	0	0	5	18	0	21	.120	.277	.133	19	-8	1	.996	-2	76	138	1b29		-1
Total	2	32	84	3	10	1	0	0	5	18	0	22	.119	.275	.131	18	-8	1	.996	-2	76	138	1b29		-1

SHOOK, RAY Raymond Curtis B11.18.1889 Perry OH D9.16.1970 South Bend IN BR/TR/5-7.5/155 d4.16

YEAR	TM LG	G	AB	R	H	2B	3B	HR	RBI	BB-IB	HP	SO	AVG	OBP	SLG	AOPS	ABR	SB-CS	FA	FR	RNG	THR	GAMES AT POSITION	DL	BFW
1916	Chi A	1	0	0	0	0	0	0	0	0	0	0	—	—	—	0	0	—		0			/R		

SHOOP, RON Ronald Lee B9.19.1931 Rural Valley PA D3.14.2003 Rural Valley PA BR/TR/5-11/185 d8.22

YEAR	TM LG	G	AB	R	H	2B	3B	HR	RBI	BB-IB	HP	SO	AVG	OBP	SLG	AOPS	ABR	SB-CS	FA	FR	RNG	THR	GAMES AT POSITION	DL	BFW
1959	Det A	3	7	1	1	0	0	0	0	0-0	0	1	.143	.143	.143	-20	-1	0	1.000	-0	0	0	C3		-0

SHOPAY, TOM Thomas Michael B2.21.1945 Bristol CT BL/TR/5-9.5/160* [NYA65 16/633] d9.17 Col Dean (MA) JC

YEAR	TM LG	G	AB	R	H	2B	3B	HR	RBI	BB-IB	HP	SO	AVG	OBP	SLG	AOPS	ABR	SB-CS	FA	FR	RNG	THR	GAMES AT POSITION	DL	BFW
1967	NY A	8	27	2	8	1	0	2	6	1-1	0	5	.296	.310	.556	161	2	2-0	.917	0	69	393	O7L		0
1969	NY A	28	48	2	4	0	1	0	2	2-1	0	10	.083	.120	.125	-33	-9	0-1	1.000	1	137	0	O11(7/0/5)		-1
1971	†Bal A	47	74	10	19	2	0	0	5	3-1	0	7	.257	.286	.284	61	-4	2-1	1.000	-0	90	146	O13(4/0/9)	43	-0
1972	Bal A	49	40	3	9	0	0	0	2	5-0	0	12	.225	.311	.225	59	-2	3-0	1.000	-1	100	0	O3L		-0
1975	Bal A	40	31	4	5	1	0	0	2	4-0	0	7	.161	.257	.194	31	-3	3-0	1.000	-1	75	0	O13(1/6/6)/CD		-0
1976	Bal A	14	20	4	4	0	0	0	1	3-0	0	3	.200	.304	.200	53	-1	1-0	1.000	-1			O11(6/2/3)/C		-0
1977	Bal A	67	69	15	13	3	0	1	4	8-0	0	7	.188	.273	.275	53	-4	3-3	1.000	2	111	134	O52(25/28/14),D2		-0
Total	7	253	309	40	62	7	1	3	20	26-3	0	51	.201	.262	.259	50	-21	11-5	.993	4	104	121	O110(53/36/37),D5,C2	43	-0

SHOPPACH, KELLY Kelly Brian B4.29.1980 Fort Worth TX BR/TR/6-1/210 d5.28 Col Baylor

YEAR	TM LG	G	AB	R	H	2B	3B	HR	RBI	BB-IB	HP	SO	AVG	OBP	SLG	AOPS	ABR	SB-CS	FA	FR	RNG	THR	GAMES AT POSITION	DL	BFW
2005	Bos A	9	15	1	0	0	0	0	0	1-0	0	7	.000	.063	.000	-77	-4	0-0	1.000	-2	90	0	C7,D2		-0

SHORT, DAVE David Orvis B5.11.1917 Magnolia AR D11.22.1983 Shreveport LA BL/TR/5-11.5/162 d9.16 Mil 1941-45 Col Louisiana Tech

YEAR	TM LG	G	AB	R	H	2B	3B	HR	RBI	BB-IB	HP	SO	AVG	OBP	SLG	AOPS	ABR	SB-CS	FA	FR	RNG	THR	GAMES AT POSITION	DL	BFW
1940	Chi A	4	3	1	1	0	0	0	0	0-0	0	2	.333	.500	.333	119	0	0-0	—	0			/H		0
1941	Chi A	3	8	0	1	0	0	0	0	2	0	1	.125	.300	.125	-44	-2	0-0	.800	-1	80	0	O2L		0
Total	2	7	11	1	2	0	0	0	0	2	0	3	.091	.286	.091	-2	-2	0-0	.800	-1	80	0	O2L		0

SHORT, RICK Richard Ryan B12.6.1972 Elgin IL BR/TR/6-0/200 d6.10 Col Western Illinois

YEAR	TM LG	G	AB	R	H	2B	3B	HR	RBI	BB-IB	HP	SO	AVG	OBP	SLG	AOPS	ABR	SB-CS	FA	FR	RNG	THR	GAMES AT POSITION	DL	BFW
2005	Was N	11	15	4	6	2	0	1	4	1-0	1	1	.400	.471	.933	274	4	0-0	.938	-1	78	88	2b6/1	9	0

SHORTEN, CHICK Charles Henry B4.19.1892 Scranton PA D10.23.1965 Scranton PA BL/TL/6-0/175 d9.22 Mil 1918

YEAR	TM LG	G	AB	R	H	2B	3B	HR	RBI	BB-IB	HP	SO	AVG	OBP	SLG	AOPS	ABR	SB-CS	FA	FR	RNG	THR	GAMES AT POSITION	DL	BFW
1915	Bos A	6	14	1	3	0	0	0	0	0-0	0	0	.214	.214	.286	51	-1	1	1.000	1	98	254	O5(0/4/1)		
1916	†Bos A	53	112	14	33	2	1	0	11	10	0	8	.295	.352	.330	105	-1	1	1.000	-3	95	0	O33(13/19/1)		
1917	Bos A	69	168	12	30	4	2	0	16	10	0	10	.179	.229	.226	39	-13	2	.977	-3	100	37	O43(16/20/7)		
1919	Det A	95	270	37	85	9	5	0	22	22	0	13	.315	.366	.404	110	4	5	.973	-6	100	115	O75(0/18/57)		
1920	Det A	116	364	35	105	19	6	1	40	28	0	14	.288	.339	.354	86	-8	2-4	.989	-1	92	115	O99(0/31/68)		
1921	Det A	92	217	33	59	11	3	0	23	20	0	11	.272	.333	.350	75	-8	2-3	.981	-2	98	52	O31(4/16/12)		
1922	StL A	55	131	22	36	5	2	0	16	16	0	2	.275	.354	.328	114	2	0-1	1.000	-1	71	104	O15(11/0/4)		
1924	Cin N	41	69	7	19	3	0	0	6	4	0	1	.275	.315	.319	71	-3	0-0	1.000	-1	104	62	O15(0/15/0)		
Total	8	527	1345	161	370	51	20	3	134	110	0	68	.275	.330	.349	87	-26	12-8	.985	-14	96	62	O352(47/144/162)		

YEAR	TM	LG	G	AB	R	H	2B	3B	HR	RBI	BB-IB	HP	SO	AVG	OBP	SLG	AOPS	ABR	SB-CS	FA	FR	RNG	THR	GAMES AT POSITION	DL	BFW

SHOTTON, BURT Burton Edwin "Barney" B10.18.1884 Brownhelm OH D7.29.1962 Lake Wales FL BL/TR/5-11/175 d9.13 M11/C8

YEAR	TM	LG	G	AB	R	H	2B	3B	HR	RBI	BB-IB	HP	SO	AVG	OBP	SLG	AOPS	ABR	SB-CS	FA	FR	RNG	THR	GAMES AT POSITION	DL	BFW
1909	StL	A	17	61	5	16	0	1	0	0	5	1		.262	.328	.295	104	0	3	.915	0	85	0	O17(2/15/0)		-0.1
1911	StL	A	139	572	84	146	11	8	0	36	51	1		.255	.317	.302	76	-19	26	.950	3	111	87	O139(18/121/0)		-2.5
1912	StL	A	154	580	87	168	15	8	2	40	86	9		.290	.390	.353	117	18	35	.941	4	112	90	O154C		1.2
1913	StL	A	147	549	105	163	23	8	1	28	99	1	63	.297	.405	.373	132	28	43	.951	7	104	118	O146C		2.7
1914	StL	A	154	579	82	156	19	9	0	38	64	2	66	.269	.344	.333	108	6	40-29	.940	-4	103	74	O152C		-1.1
1915	StL	A	156	559	93	158	18	11	1	30	118	2	62	.283	.409	.360	135	32	43-32	.931	-3	103	78	O154(138/5/11)		2.2
1916	StL	A	156	614	97	174	23	6	1	36	110	0	65	.283	.392	.345	128	27	41-28	.950	8	107	117	O156L		3.0
1917	StL	A	118	398	48	89	9	1	0	20	62	1	47	.224	.330	.259	83	-5	16	.923	-12	28	36	O107L		-2.5
1918	Was	A	126	505	68	132	16	7	0	21	67	1	28	.261	.349	.321	104	4	25	.942	-1	105	81	O122(67/1/54)		-0.4
1919	StL	N	85	270	35	77	13	5	1	20	22	1	25	.285	.341	.381	125	8	16	.927	-4	83	124	O67L		0.2
1920	StL	N	62	180	28	41	5	0	1	12	18	2	14	.228	.305	.272	69	-7	5-1	.959	2	93	175	O51(41/2/6)		-0.6
1921	StL	N	38	48	9	12	1	1	1	7	7	1	4	.250	.357	.375	96	0	0-2	.958	1	107	181	O11(1/10/0)		-0.3
1922	StL	N	34	30	5	6	1	0	0	2	4	0	6	.200	.294	.233	39	-3	0-1	1.000	0	398	0	O3(1/1/1)		-0.3
1923	StL	N	1	0	1	0	0	0	0	0	0	0	0						0-0		0			/R		
Total		14	1387	4945	747	1338	154	65	9	290	713	22	380	.271	.365	.333	110	89	293-93	.942	2	98	92	O1279(598/607/72)		1.8

SHOUPE, JOHN John F. B9.30.1851 Cincinnati OH D2.13.1920 Cincinnati OH BL/TL/5-7/140 d5.3

YEAR	TM	LG	G	AB	R	H	2B	3B	HR	RBI	BB-IB	HP	SO	AVG	OBP	SLG	AOPS	ABR	SB-CS	FA	FR	RNG	THR	GAMES AT POSITION	DL	BFW
1879	Tro	N	11	44	5	4	0	0	0		1	0	3	.091	.091	.091	-43	-6		.820	-3	101	0	S10/2		-0.8
1882	StL	AA	2	7	1	0	0	0	0		0			.000	.000	.000	-96	-1		1.000	1	130	0	2b2		-0.1
1884	Was	U	1	4	1	3	0	0	0		0			.750	.750	.750	368	1		.857	2	354	1092	/OC		0.2
Total		3	14	55	7	7	0	0	0		1	0	3	.127	.127	.127	-17	-6		.820	-0	101	0	S10,2b3/OC		-0.7

SHOVLIN, JOHN John Joseph "Brode" B1.14.1891 Drifton PA D2.16.1976 Bethesda MD BR/TR/5-7/163 d6.21

YEAR	TM	LG	G	AB	R	H	2B	3B	HR	RBI	BB-IB	HP	SO	AVG	OBP	SLG	AOPS	ABR	SB-CS	FA	FR	RNG	THR	GAMES AT POSITION	DL	BFW
1911	Pit	N	2	1	0	0	0	0	0	0	0	0	1	.000	.000	.000	-96	-1	0	—	0			/H		0.0
1919	StL	A	9	35	4	7	0	0	0	1	5	0	2	.200	.300	.200	41	-3	0	.936	-1	92	134	2b9		-0.4
1920	StL	A	7	7	2	2	0	0	0	2	0	0	0	.286	.286	.286	50	-1	0-0	1.000	0	117	0	S5		0.0
Total		3	18	43	7	9	0	0	0	3	5	0	3	.209	.292	.209	39	-4	0-0	.936	-1	92	134	2b9,S5		-0.4

SHUBA, GEORGE George Thomas "Shotgun" B12.13.1924 Youngstown OH BL/TR/5-11/180* d7.2

YEAR	TM	LG	G	AB	R	H	2B	3B	HR	RBI	BB-IB	HP	SO	AVG	OBP	SLG	AOPS	ABR	SB-CS	FA	FR	RNG	THR	GAMES AT POSITION	DL	BFW
1948	Bro	N	63	161	21	43	6	4	32	34		0	31	.267	.395	.379	107	3	1	.936	-4	91	28	O56(55/2/1)		-0.4
1949	Bro	N	1	0	0	0	0	0	0	0	0	0	0							—	0			/H		
1950	Bro	N	34	111	15	23	8	2	3	12	13	2	22	.207	.302	.396	80	-3	2	.984	3	105	219	O27L		-0.2
1952	†Bro	N	94	256	40	78	12	1	9	40	38	1	29	.305	.395	.465	136	14	1-3	.992	-2	92	36	O67(66/0/1)		0.7
1953	†Bro	N	74	169	19	43	12	1	5	23	17	1	20	.254	.326	.426	92	-2	1-2	.984	-3	92	36	O44(43/0/1)		-0.7
1954	Bro	N	45	65	3	10	5	0	2	10	7	1	10	.154	.240	.323	46	-5	0-0	.913	-1	100	0	O13(7/0/5)		-0.7
1955	†Bro	N	44	51	8	14	2	0	1	8	11-1	1	2	.275	.422	.373	110	-5	0-0	.909	-1	80	0	O9(7/1/2)		
Total		7	355	814	106	211	45	4	24	125	120-1	6	122	.259	.358	.413	104	9	5-5	.967	-8	96	59	O216(205/3/10)		-1.3

SHUGART, FRANK Frank Harry (b Frank Harry Shugarts) B12.10.1866 Luthersburg PA D9.9.1944 Clearfield PA BL/TR (BB 1897)/5-8/170 d8.23

YEAR	TM	LG	G	AB	R	H	2B	3B	HR	RBI	BB-IB	HP	SO	AVG	OBP	SLG	AOPS	ABR	SB-CS	FA	FR	RNG	THR	GAMES AT POSITION	DL	BFW
1890	Chi	P	29	106	8	22	6	1	1	13	18	1	13	.189	.232	.330	47	-9	5	.881	-3	87	110	S25,O5(0/1/4)		-0.9
1891	Pit	N	75	320	57	88	19	8	3	33	20	3	26	.275	.324	.412	117	5	21	.902	2	92	131	S75		0.8
1892	Pit	N	137	554	94	148	19	14	0	62	47	4	48	.267	.329	.352	105	2	28	.886	6	104	89	S134,C2/OR		1.4
1893	Pit	N	52	210	37	55	7	3	1	32	19	3	15	.262	.332	.338	80	-6	12	.882	-3	103	77	S51/O(2/1/0)		-0.5
	StL	N	59	246	41	69	10	4	0	28	22	6	10	.280	.354	.354	88	-4	13	.907	-6	183	49	O28(0/19/9),S23,3b9		-0.8
	Year		111	456	78	124	17	7	1	60	41	9	25	.272	.344	.346	84	-10	25	.868	-8	100	80	S74,O29(2/20/9),3b9		-1.3
1894	StL	N	133	527	103	154	19	18	7	72	38	9	37	.292	.350	.436	89	-13	21	.912	-9	125	41	O122C,S7,3b7		-2.3
1895	Lou	N	113	473	61	125	14	13	4	70	31	4	25	.264	.315	.374	84	-14	14	.874	-18	88	97	S88,O27(0/22/5)		-2.4
1897	Phi	N	40	163	20	41	8	2	5	25	8	0		.252	.287	.417	87	-4	5	.872	-10	88	92	S40		-1.0
1901	Chi	A	107	415	62	104	9	12	2	47	28	2		.251	.301	.345	81	-12	12	.885	-11	96	85	S107		-1.8
Total		8	745	3014	483	804	110	79	22	384	218	32	174	.267	.323	.378	90	-55	131	.883	-51	95	95	S550,O184(2/165/19),3b16,C2		-7.5

SHUMPERT, TERRY Terrance Darnell B8.16.1966 Paducah KY BR/TR/5-11/185(185-200) [KCA87 2/41] d5.1 Col Kentucky OF(84/9/15)

YEAR	TM	LG	G	AB	R	H	2B	3B	HR	RBI	BB-IB	HP	SO	AVG	OBP	SLG	AOPS	ABR	SB-CS	FA	FR	RNG	THR	GAMES AT POSITION	DL	BFW
1990	KC	A	32	91	7	25	6	1	0	8	2-0	1	17	.275	.292	.363	85	-2	3-3	.977	-2	89	79	2b29,D3		-0.4
1991	KC	A	144	369	45	80	16	4	5	34	30-0	5	75	.217	.283	.322	67	-17	17-11	.975	-8	93	94	2b144	99	-2.2
1992	KC	A	36	94	6	14	5	1	1	11	3-0	0	17	.149	.175	.255	19	-11	2-2	.969	-9	87	85	2b33/SD	31	-2.0
1993	KC	A	8	10	0	1	0	0	0	0	2-0	0	2	.100	.250	.100	-9	-1	1-0	1.000	1	95	119	2b8		0.0
1994	KC	A	64	183	28	44	6	2	8	24	13-0	0	39	.240	.289	.426	78	-7	18-3	.964	-5	102	71	2b38,3b24/SD		-0.7
1995	Bos	A	21	47	6	11	3	0	0	3	4-0	0	13	.234	.294	.298	63	-3	3-1	1.000	2	82	97	2b8,3b5,S3/D		0.0
1996	Chi	N	27	31	5	7	1	0	2	6	2-0	1	11	.226	.286	.452	90	-1	0-0	.923	-1	48	0	3b10,2b4/S	15	-0.2
1997	SD	N	13	33	4	9	3	0	1	6	3-0	0	4	.273	.344	.455	111	1	0-0	.973	-1	78	89	2b7,O3(2/0/1),3b2	70	0.0
1998	Col	N	23	26	3	6	1	0	1	2	2-0	0	8	.231	.286	.385	61	-1	0-0	1.000	3	211	188	2b6		0.1
1999	Col	N	92	262	58	91	26	3	10	37	31-2	6	41	.347	.413	.584	120	9	14-0	.988	8	116	99	2b54,O19(6/9/4),3b14,S2		2.1
2000	Col	N	115	263	52	68	11	7	9	40	28-1	6	40	.259	.340	.456	81	0	8-4	.967	-2	104	104	O40L,2b23,3b15,S7,1b6/D		-0.9
2001	Col	N	114	242	37	70	14	5	4	24	15-2	4	41	.289	.337	.438	82	-6	14-3	.968	-2	108	122	2b41,O24L,3b12,S4		-0.1
2002	Col	N	106	234	30	55	12	1	6	21	21-0	4	41	.235	.304	.372	71	-10	4-1	.974	-1	104	93	2b60,O8(7/0/1),S3/3		-0.9
2003	TB	A	59	84	14	16	5	2	2	10	10-0	2	17	.190	.289	.369	74	-3	1-0	.978	-3	89	48	D17,2b14,O14(5/0/9),3b11/S	33	-0.7
Total		14	854	1969	295	497	109	26	49	223	166-5	24	369	.252	.315	.409	80	-60	85-29	.977	-17	98	93	2b467,O108L,3b94,D25,S23,1b6	248	-5.9

SHUPE, VINCE Vincent William B9.5.1921 E.Canton OH D4.5.1962 Canton OH BL/TL/5-11/180 d7.7

YEAR	TM	LG	G	AB	R	H	2B	3B	HR	RBI	BB-IB	HP	SO	AVG	OBP	SLG	AOPS	ABR	SB-CS	FA	FR	RNG	THR	GAMES AT POSITION	DL	BFW
1945	Bos	N	78	283	22	76	8	0	0	15	17	1	16	.269	.312	.297	69	-12	3	.989	1	107	147	1b77		-1.5

SICKING, ED Edward Joseph B3.30.1897 St.Bernard OH D8.30.1978 Madeira OH BR/TR/5-9.5/165 d8.26 Mil 1918

YEAR	TM	LG	G	AB	R	H	2B	3B	HR	RBI	BB-IB	HP	SO	AVG	OBP	SLG	AOPS	ABR	SB-CS	FA	FR	RNG	THR	GAMES AT POSITION	DL	BFW
1916	Chi	N	1	0	0	0	0	0	0	0	0	0	0	.000	.000	.000		0	0	—	0			/H		0.0
1918	NY	N	46	132	9	33	4	0	0	12	6	0	11	.250	.283	.280	73	-4	2	.917	-7	83	0	3b24,2b18,S3		-1.2
1919	NY	N	6	15	2	5	0	0	0	3	1	1	0	.333	.412	.333	127	1	0	.971	2	133	147	S6		0.3
	Phi	N	61	185	16	40	2	1	0	15	8	1	17	.216	.253	.238	45	-12	4	.925	3	101	167	S35,2b22		-0.8
	Year		67	200	18	45	2	1	0	18	9	2	17	.225	.265	.245	51	-12	4	.933	5	106	164	S41,2b22		-0.5
1920	NY	N	46	134	11	23	3	1	0	9	10	1	10	.172	.234	.209	28	-12	6-2	.915	-1	101	0	3b28,2b15,S3		-1.2
	Cin	N	37	123	12	33	3	0	0	17	13	0	5	.268	.338	.293	83	-2	2-3	.955	-2	105	77	2b25,S9,3b2		-0.4
	Year		83	257	23	56	6	1	0	26	23	1	15	.218	.285	.249	55	-14	8-5	.952	-2	103	122	2b40,3b30,S12		-1.6
1927	Pit	N	6	7	1	1	0	0	0	3	1	0	0	.143	.250	.286	40	-1	0	1.000	1	112	89	2b5		0.0
Total		5	203	597	51	135	13	2	0	59	39	3	43	.226	.277	.255	57	-30	14-5	.965	-3	97	113	2b85,S56,3b54		-3.3

SIDDALL, JOE Joseph Todd B10.25.1967 Windsor ON, Can. BL/TR/6-1/197* d7.28

YEAR	TM	LG	G	AB	R	H	2B	3B	HR	RBI	BB-IB	HP	SO	AVG	OBP	SLG	AOPS	ABR	SB-CS	FA	FR	RNG	THR	GAMES AT POSITION	DL	BFW
1993	Mon	N	19	20	0	2	1	0	0	1	1-1	0	5	.100	.143	.150	-21	-3	0-0	1.000	-1	75	135	C15/1OL		-0.4
1995	Mon	N	7	10	4	3	0	0	0	1	3-0	1	1	.300	.500	.300	113	1	0-0	.882	-4	35	0	C7		-0.3
1996	Fla	N	18	47	0	7	3	0	0	3	2-0	0	8	.149	.184	.170	-6	-7	0-0	.977	-2	86	147	C18		-0.8
1998	Det	A	29	65	3	12	3	0	1	6	7-0	0	25	.185	.264	.277	40	-6	0-0	.994	6	116	162	C27/OR		0.2
Total		4	73	142	7	24	6	0	1	11	13-1	1	41	.169	.244	.225	24	-15	0-0	.983	-1	95	142	C67,O2(1/0/1)/1		-1.3

SIEBERN, NORM Norman Leroy B7.26.1933 St.Louis MO BL/TR/6-3/205* d6.15

YEAR	TM	LG	G	AB	R	H	2B	3B	HR	RBI	BB-IB	HP	SO	AVG	OBP	SLG	AOPS	ABR	SB-CS	FA	FR	RNG	THR	GAMES AT POSITION	DL	BFW
1956	†NY	A	54	162	27	33	1	4	4	21	19-0	0	38	.204	.286	.333	66	-9	1-1	.971	-1	104	27	O51L		-1.4
1958	†NY	A	134	460	79	138	19	5	14	55	66-3	1	87	.300	.388	.454	136	25	5-8	.982	-0	98	103	O133(127/11/0)		1.5
1959	NY	A	120	380	52	103	17	0	11	53	41-2	2	71	.271	.341	.403	108	7	3-1	.989	-0	94	17	O93(82/5/9),1b2		-0.5
1960	KC	A	144	520	69	145	31	6	19	69	72-6	2	78	.279	.364	.471	125	19	0-0	.987	-2	100	78	O75L,1b69		0.9
1961	KC	A	153	560	68	166	36	5	18	98	82-3	1	91	.296	.384	.475	127	24	2-4	.989	1	100	86	1b109,O47L		1.5
1962	KC	A★	162	600	114	185	25	6	25	117	110-9	1	88	.308	.412	.495	138	36	3-1	.994	2	101	87	1b162		2.9
1963	KC	A☆	152	556	80	151	25	2	16	83	79-6	0	82	.272	.358	.410	110	10	1-4	.991	-3	103	88	1b131,O16(16/0/1)		0.1
1964	Bal	A★	150	478	92	117	24	2	12	56	106-3	2	87	.245	.379	.379	114	15	2-3	.995	4	108	114	1b149		0.9
1965	Bal	A	106	297	44	76	8	4	8	32	50-7	1	49	.256	.364	.407	117	8	1-2	.991	-0	104	121	1b76		0.4
1966	Cal	A	125	336	29	83	14	1	5	41	63-7	0	61	.247	.361	.387	107	6	0-1	.992	3	115	138	1b99		0.4
1967	SF	N	46	58	6	9	1	0	0	4	14-0	1	13	.155	.319	.207	54	-3	0-0	1.000	-0	85	94	1b15,O2L		-0.4
1968	†Bos	A	33	44	2	9	1	0	0	5	6-1	0	14	.205	.300	.295	71	-2	0-0	.981	1	105	43	1b13/OL		-0.2
	Bos	A	27	30	4	2	0	0	0	1	5	0	9	.067	.067	.067	-56	-6	0-0	1.000	0	141	114	1b2,O2(1/0/1)		-0.9
Total		12	1406	4481	662	1217	206	38	132	636	708-47	10	748	.272	.369	.423	119	128	18-25	.992	3	103	101	1b827,O420(402/16/11)		5.4

YEAR	TM LG	G	AB	R	H	2B	3B	HR	RBI	BB-IB	HP	SO	AVG	OBP	SLG	AOPS	ABR	SB-CS	FA	FR	RNG	THR	GAMES AT POSITION	DL	BFW
SIEBERT, DICK	Richard Walther B2.19.1912 Fall River MA D12.9.1978 Minneapolis MN BL/TL/6-0/170 d9.7 s-Paul Col Concordia (TX)																								
1932	Bro N	6	7	1	2	0	0	0	0	0	0	2	.286	.444	.286	104	0	0	1.000	-0	0	0	1b2		0.0
1936	Bro N	2	2	0	0	0	0	0	0	0	0	0	.000	.000	.000	-99	-1	0	1.000	1	0	2806	/OR		-0.4
1937	StL N	22	38	3	7	2	0	0	2	4	0	8	.184	.279	.237	41	-3	1	.979	-1	75	44	1b7		0.0
1938	StL N	1	1	0	1	0	0	0	0	0	0	0	1.000	1.000	1.000	427	0	0	—		0		/H		-0.7
	Phi A	48	194	24	55	8	3	0	28	10	3	9	.284	.329	.356	73	-9	2-3	1.000	5	136	81	1b46		-0.9
1939	Phi A	101	402	58	118	28	3	6	47	21	0	22	.294	.329	.423	93	-6	4-1	.991	5	123	81	1b99		-2.0
1940	Phi A	**154**	595	69	170	31	6	5	77	33	2	34	.286	.325	.383	85	-15	8-6	.985	8	125	84	1b154		1.0
1941	Phi A	123	467	63	156	28	8	5	79	37	2	22	.334	.385	.460	126	17	1-3	.990	-2	94	80	1b152		-4.1
1942	Phi A	153	612	57	159	25	7	2	74	24	3	17	.260	.291	.333	76	-23	4-5	.989	-1	108	89	1b145		-2.2
1943	Phi A★	146	558	50	140	26	7	1	72	33	2	21	.251	.295	.328	83	-14	6-7	.990	3	108	89	1b74,O58(42/0/17)		1.9
1944	Phi A	132	468	52	143	27	5	6	52	62	2	17	.306	.387	.423	133	22	2-0	.993	8	117	98	1b147		-0.3
1945	Phi A	147	573	62	153	29	4	1	51	50	2	33	.267	.328	.358	99	-1	2-7	.991	8	113	88	1b59,O59(42/0/18)		-7.7
Total	11	1035	3917	439	1104	204	43	32	482	276	15	185	.282	.332	.379	96	-33	30-32	.990	33	113	88	1b949,O59(42/0/18)		-7.5
SIEFKE, ED	Frederick Edwin B3.27.1870 New York NY D4.18.1893 New York NY 5-11/168 d5.2																								
1890	Bro AA	16	58	1	8	2	0	0	3	5	0		.138	.206	.172	12	-6	2	.811	-1	124	69	3b16		-0.6
SIEGEL, JOHN	John B York PA d6.9																								
1884	Phi U	8	31	4	7	2	0	0		1			.226	.250	.290	69	-2		.533	-4	61	0	3b8		-0.6
SIEGLE, JOHNNY	John Herbert B7.8.1874 Urbana OH D2.12.1968 Urbana OH BR/TR/5-10/165 d9.15																								
1905	Cin N	17	56	9	17	1	2	1	8	7	1		.304	.391	.446	135	2	0	.960	-1	51	0	O16R		0.1
1906	Cin N	22	68	4	8	2	2	0	7	3	2		.118	.178	.206	19	-7	0	.959	0	39	157	O21(7/14/0)		-0.9
Total	2	39	124	13	25	3	4	1	15	10	3		.202	.277	.315	75	-5	0	.959	-1	44	91	O37(7/14/16)		-0.8
SIEMER, OSCAR	Oscar Sylvester "Cotton" B8.14.1901 St.Louis MO D12.5.1959 St.Louis MO BR/TR/5-9/162 d5.20																								
1925	Bos N	16	46	5	14	0	1	1	6	1	0	0	.304	.319	.413	94	-1	0	.900	-2	112	99	C16		-0.2
1926	Bos N	31	73	3	15	1	0	0	5	2	0	7	.205	.227	.219	22	-8	0	.920	-3	83	65	C30		-1.0
Total	2	47	119	8	29	1	1	1	11	3	0	7	.244	.262	.294	51	-9	0-0	.913	-5	94	78	C46		-1.2
SIERRA, RUBEN	Ruben Angel (Garcia) B10.6.1965 Rio Piedras, PR BB/TR/6-1/200(175-215) d6.1																								
1986	Tex A	113	382	50	101	13	10	16	55	22-3	1	65	.264	.302	.476	106	1	7-8	.972	-2	95	109	O107(44/21/68),D3		-0.6
1987	Tex A	158	643	97	169	35	4	30	109	39-4	2	114	.263	.302	.470	101	-1	16-11	.963	-1	92	159	O157(0/4/156)		-1.0
1988	Tex A	156	615	77	156	32	2	23	91	44-10	1	91	.254	.301	.424	99	-2	18-4	.979	-0	96	118	O153R/D		-0.5
1989	Tex A★	**162**	634	101	194	35	14	29	119	43-2	2	82	.306	.347	**.543**	146	35	8-2	.973	-1	98	112	O162(0/2/161)		3.0
1990	Tex A	159	608	70	170	37	2	16	96	49-13	1	86	.280	.330	.426	111	8	9-0	.967	-3	92	94	O151R,D7		-0.3
1991	Tex A★	161	661	110	203	44	5	25	116	56-7	0	91	.307	.357	.502	138	33	16-4	.979	-3	92	126	O161(0/3/161)		2.7
1992	Tex A★	124	500	66	139	30	6	14	87	31-6	0	59	.278	.315	.446	116	8	12-4	.970	-6	93	75	O119R,D4		-0.1
	†Oak A	27	101	17	28	4	1	3	17	14-6	0	9	.277	.359	.426	127	4	2-0	1.000	-6	116	0	O25R,D2		0.4
	Year	151	601	83	167	34	7	17	87	45-12	0	68	.278	.323	.443	118	12	14-4	.976	-6	97	62	O144R,D6		0.3
1993	Oak A	158	630	77	147	23	5	22	101	52-16	0	97	.233	.288	.390	86	-16	25-5	.977	1	105	89	O133R,D25		-1.9
1994	Oak A★	110	426	71	114	21	1	23	92	23-4	0	64	.268	.298	.484	107	2	8-5	.948	-6	85	119	O98(0/1/97),D10		-0.9
1995	Oak A	70	264	40	70	17	0	12	42	24-2	1	42	.265	.323	.466	108	3	4-4	.957	-7	82	27	O62R,D7	15	-0.7
	†NY A	56	215	33	56	15	0	7	44	22-2	0	34	.260	.322	.428	96	-1	1-0	.950	0	104	170	D46,O10R		-1.0
	Year	126	479	73	126	32	0	19	86	46-4	1	76	.263	.323	.449	103	1	5-4	.956	-5	85	46	O72R,D53		-1.1
1996	NY A	96	360	39	93	17	1	11	52	40-11	0	58	.258	.327	.403	85	-9	1-3	.984	2	95	243	D61,O33(32/0/1)		-1.1
	Det A	46	158	22	35	9	1	1	20	20-1	0	25	.222	.306	.310	57	-10	3-1	.914	-0	109	60	O23(4/0/19),D20		-2.2
	Year	142	518	61	128	26	2	12	72	60-12	0	83	.247	.320	.375	76	-19	4-4	.950	2	101	164	D81,O56(36/0/20)		-0.4
1997	Cin N	25	90	6	22	5	1	2	7	6-1	0	21	.244	.292	.389	75	-4	0-0	1.000	-8	97	0	O7(6/0/2),D6		-0.4
	Tor A	14	48	4	10	0	2	1	5	3-1	1	13	.208	.250	.354	57	-4	0-0	.929	-1	90	0	O14(2/0/12),D5		-0.3
1998	Chi A	27	74	7	16	4	1	4	11	3-0	0	11	.216	.247	.459	80	-3	2-0	1.000	-1	82	122	D14		-0.6
2000	Tex A	20	60	5	14	0	0	1	7	4-0	0	9	.233	.281	.283	43	-5	1-0	—	0	0	0	D14		-0.5
2001	Tex A	94	344	55	100	22	1	23	67	19-0	0	52	.291	.322	.561	124	11	2-0	.937	-3	92	35	O60(59/0/1),D52	15	0.3
2002	Sea A	122	419	47	113	23	0	13	60	31-5	0	66	.270	.319	.418	97	-2	4-0	.962	-3	94	92	O23(20/0/4),D15		-0.6
2003	Tex A	43	133	14	35	9	0	3	12	14-1	0	20	.263	.333	.398	86	-2	1-1	1.000	-4	84	0	D32,O17(6/0/11)		-0.3
	†NY A	63	174	19	48	8	1	6	31	13-2	1	27	.276	.323	.437	100	0	0-0	.978	-4	73	55	D47,O40(26/0/15)		-0.9
	Year	106	307	33	83	17	1	9	43	27-3	1	47	.270	.327	.420	94	-3	1-1	.977	-1	99	74	D56,O29(8/0/22)		-0.8
2004	†NY A	107	307	40	75	12	1	17	65	25-4	0	55	.244	.296	.456	94	-4	1-0	.958	-2	86	0	D30,O18(8/0/10)	73	-1.2
2005	†NY A	61	170	14	39	12	0	4	29	9-1	0	41	.229	.265	.371	67	-8	0-0	.958	-2	86	0	D30,O18(8/0/10)	103	-0.8
Total	19	2172	8016	1081	2147	427	59	306	1318	606-102	7	1232	.268	.316	.450	105	34	142-52	.970	-43	94	100	O1622(202/31/1425),D446	103	-7.5
SIEVERS, ROY	Roy Edward "Squirrel" B11.18.1926 St.Louis MO BR/TR/6-1/195* d4.21 C1																								
1949	StL A	140	471	84	144	28	1	16	91	70	2	75	.306	.398	.471	124	18	1-5	.973	5	101	162	O125(51/76/0),3b7		1.4
1950	StL A	113	370	46	88	20	4	10	57	34	2	42	.238	.305	.395	75	-16	1-3	.983	4	106	183	O78(10/68/0),3b21		-1.4
1951	StL A	31	89	10	20	2	1	1	11	9	1	21	.225	.303	.303	62	-5	0-0	.985	0	111	48	O25(9/19/0)	139	-0.5
1952	StL A	11	30	3	6	3	0	0	5	1	0	4	.200	.226	.300	44	-2	0-0	.968	-1	63	123	1b7		-1.0
1953	StL A	92	285	37	77	15	0	8	35	32	0	47	.270	.344	.407	100	0	0-1	.971	8	110	117	O133L,1b8		1.3
1954	Was A	145	514	75	119	26	6	24	102	80	2	77	.232	.331	.446	120	13	2-1	.988	-3	101	49	O129L,1b17,3b2		1.3
1955	Was A	144	509	74	138	20	8	25	106	73-3	1	66	.271	.364	.489	136	25	1-2	.988	1	98	52	O78L,1b76		0.9
1956	Was A	152	550	92	139	27	4	29	95	100-10	5	88	.253	.370	.467	140	30	1-1	.985	-2	96	86	O130L,1b21		3.9
1957	Was A☆	152	572	99	172	23	5	**42**	**114**	76-11	7	55	.301	.388	.579	163	49	1-1	.993	-4	92	70	O114L,1b33		2.2
1958	Was A	148	550	85	162	18	4	39	108	53-2	6	63	.295	.357	.544	148	34	3-1	.991	-4	87		1b93,O13L		0.7
1959	Was A★	115	385	55	93	19	0	21	49	53-6	2	62	.242	.333	.455	116	8	1-1	.989	5	124	95	1b93,O13L		2.3
1960	Chi A	127	444	87	131	22	0	28	93	74-8	3	69	.295	.396	.534	152	34	1-1	.993	-4	87	**114**	1b114,O6L		2.7
1961	Chi A★	141	492	76	145	26	4	27	92	61-4	6	62	.295	.377	.537	144	31	1-0	.993	4	109	89	1b132		0.8
1962	Phi N	144	477	62	125	19	1	21	80	56-3	7	80	.262	.346	.455	117	11	2-1	.991	4	114	98	1b130,O7(3/0/4)		-0.3
1963	Phi N	138	450	46	108	19	2	19	82	43-5	1	72	.240	.308	.418	110	6	0-2	.989	-0	97	106	1b126		-0.3
1964	Phi N	49	120	7	22	3	1	4	16	13-1	1	20	.183	.265	.325	67	-5	0-0	.992	-1	80	101	1b33		0.0
	Was A	33	58	5	10	1	0	4	11	9-2	0	14	.172	.284	.397	87	-1	0-0	1.000	2	151	166	1b15		-0.2
1965	Was A	12	21	3	4	1	0	0	4-0		0	1	.190	.320	.238	62	-1	0-0	1.000	-1	35	155	1b7		0.0
Total	17	1887	6387	945	1703	292	42	318	1147	841-55	51	920	.267	.354	.475	124	217	14-19	.991	9	101	102	1b888,O838(676/163/4),3b30	139	12.8
SIFFELL, FRANK	Frank B1860 , Germany D10.26.1909 Philadelphia PA d6.14																								
1884	Phi AA	7	17	3	3	1	0	0	3	0	1		.176	.222	.235	46	-1		.875	-2			C7		-0.2
1885	Phi AA	3	10	0	1	0	0	0	0	0			.100	.100	.100	-35	-2		.750	-2			C2/OR		-0.3
Total	2	10	27	3	4	1	0	0	3	0	1		.148	.179	.185	16	-3		.841	-4			C9/OR		-0.5
SIGAFOOS, FRANK	Francis Leonard B3.21.1904 Easton PA D4.12.1968 Indianapolis IN BR/TR/5-9/170 d9.3 Col Purdue																								
1926	Phi A	13	43	4	11	0	0	0	2	0	0	3	.256	.256	.256	32	-4	0-0	.915	-2	99	95	S12		-0.5
1929	Det A	14	23	3	4	1	0	0	2	5	0	2	.174	.321	.217	41	-2	0-2	.909	-2	66	0	3b6,S5		0.0
	Chi A	7	3	1	1	0	0	0	1	2	0	1	.333	.600	.333	148	-1	0-0	1.000	1	172	114	2b6		0.0
	Year	21	26	4	5	1	0	0	3	7	0	3	.192	.364	.231	56	-1	0-2	.909	-2	66	0	3b6,2b6,S5		0.0
1931	Cin N	21	65	6	11	2	0	0	8	0	1	8	.169	.182	.200	3	-9	0-0	.881	-2	89	79	3b15,2b6		-1.0
Total	3	55	134	14	27	3	0	0	13	7	1	14	.201	.246	.224	25	-14	0-2	.887	-5	85	64	3b21,S19,2b6		-1.5
SIGLIN, PADDY	Wesley Peter B9.24.1891 Aurelia IA D8.5.1956 Oakland CA BR/TR/5-10/160 d9.12																								
1914	Pit N	14	39	4	6	0	0	0		6			.154	.233	.154	16	-4	1	.911	-5	61	30	2b11		-1.0
1915	Pit N	6	7	1	2	0	0	0	1	2			.286	.375	.286	103	0	0	.800	-0	117	0	/2		0.0
1916	Pit N	3	4	0	1	0	0	0	1	2			.250	.250	.250	53	0	0	.857	0	55	596	2b3		0.0
Total	3	23	50	5	9	0	0	0	2	5			.180	.255	.180	32	-4	2	.895	-5	65	89	2b15		-1.0
SIGMAN, TRIPP	Wesley Triplett B1.17.1899 Mooresville NC D3.8.1971 Augusta GA BL/TR/6-0/180 d9.18																								
1929	Phi N	10	29	8	15	2	1	2	9	3	0	1	.517	.563	.759	210	5	0	.944	-1	102	0	O10(5/5/0)		0.0
1930	Phi N	52	100	15	27	4	1	4	6	6	2	9	.270	.324	.450	79	-4	1	.932	-0	95	156	O19(3/16/0)		-0.0
Total	2	62	129	23	42	5	1	6	15	9	2	10	.326	.379	.519	108	1	1	.935	-1	97	109	O29(8/21/0)		0.0

YEAR	TM LG	G	AB	R	H	2B	3B	HR	RBI	BB-IB	HP	SO	AVG	OBP	SLG	AOPS	ABR	SB-CS	FA	FR	RNG	THR	GAMES AT POSITION	DL	BFW

SILBER, EDDIE Edward James B6.6.1914 Philadelphia PA D10.26.1976 Dunedin FL BR/TR/5-11/170 d9.3 Col Temple

1937	StL A	22	83	10	26	2	0	0	4	5	0	13	.313	.352	.337	74	-3	0-2	.871	-4	73	0	O21(2/6/15)		-0.8
1939	StL A	1	1	0	0	0	0	0	0	0	0	1	.000	.000	.000	-98	0	0-0		0			/H		0.0
Total	2	23	84	10	26	2	0	0	4	5	0	14	.310	.348	.333	72	-3	0-2	.871	-4	73	0	O21(2/6/15)		-0.8

SILCH, ED Edward "Baldy" B2.22.1865 St.Louis MO D1.15.1895 St.Louis MO TR/6-/180 d4.29

| 1888 | Bro AA | 14 | 48 | 5 | 13 | 4 | 0 | 0 | | 3 | 4 | 0 | | .271 | .327 | .354 | 118 | 1 | 4 | .870 | -1 | 51 | 0 | O14(0/6/8) | | 0.0 |

SILVA, DANNY Daniel James B10.5.1896 Everett MA D4.4.1974 Hyannis MA BR/TR/6-0/170 d8.11

| 1919 | Was A | 1 | 4 | 0 | 1 | 0 | 0 | 0 | 0 | | 0 | 0 | .250 | .250 | .250 | 41 | 0 | | 1.000 | 1 | 155 | 0 | /3 | | 0.0 |

SILVERA, AL Aaron Albert B8.26.1935 San Diego CA D7.24.2002 Los Angeles CA BR/TR/6-0/180* d6.12 Col USC

1955	Cin N	13	7	3	1	0	0	0	2	0-0	0	1	.143	.143	.143	-23	-1	0-0		-0	0	0	/OL		-0.1
1956	Cin N	1	0	0	0	0	0	0	0	0-0	0		—	—	—	—	0	0-0	—	0			/R		0.0
Total	2	14	7	3	1	0	0	0	2	0-0	0	1	.143	.143	.143	-23	-1	0-0		-0	0	0	/OL		-0.1

SILVERA, CHARLIE Charles Anthony Ryan "Swede" B10.13.1924 San Francisco CA BR/TR/5-10/175* d9.29 C6

1948	NY A	4	14	1	8	0	0	0	1		0	1	.571	.571	.714	243	3	0-0	1.000	-0	102	126	C4		0.3
1949	†NY A	58	130	8	41	2	0	0	13	18	1	5	.315	.403	.331	95	0	2-1	.985	4	82	117	C51		0.5
1950	NY A	18	25	2	4	0	0	0	1	1	0	2	.160	.192	.160	-9	-4	0-0	.959	2	148	0	C15		-0.2
1951	NY A	18	51	5	14	3	0	1	7	5	0	3	.275	.339	.392	101	0	0-0	1.000	1	132	93	C18		0.2
1952	NY A	20	55	4	18	3	0	0	11	5	0	2	.327	.383	.382	121	2	0-3	1.000	-1	92	126	C20		0.0
1953	NY A	42	82	11	23	3	1	0	12	9	0	5	.280	.352	.341	91	-1	0-1	.992	4	121	112	C39/3		0.0
1954	NY A	20	37	1	10	1	0	0	4	3	1	0	.270	.341	.297	79	-1	0-1	.962	-3	172	77	C18		0.4
1955	NY A	14	26	1	5	0	0	0	1	6-0	0	4	.192	.344	.192	48	-2	0-0	1.000	2	184	126	C11		0.2
1956	NY A	7	9	0	2	0	0	0		2-0	0	3	.222	.364	.222	60	0	0-0	.909	-1	58	0	C7		0.1
1957	Chi N	26	53	1	11	0	0	0	5	4-0	0	5	.208	.263	.264	43	-4	0-0	.982	1	88	214	C26		-0.2
Total	10	227	482	34	136	15	2	1	52	53-0	2	32	.282	.356	.328	86	-7	2-6	.985	14	113	116	C209/3		1.2

SILVERIO, LUIS Luis Pascual (Delmonte) B10.23.1956 Villa Gonzalez, D.R. BR/TR/5-11/165 d9.9 C3

| 1978 | KC A | 8 | 11 | 7 | 6 | 2 | 1 | 0 | 3 | 2-0 | 0 | 3 | .545 | .615 | .909 | 314 | 3 | 1-1 | .833 | -1 | 71 | 0 | O6(4/0/2),D2 | | 0.2 |

SILVERIO, TOM Tomas Roberto (Veloz) B10.14.1945 Santiago, D.R. BL/TL/5-10/170* d4.30

1970	Cal A	15	15	1	0	0	0	0	0	2-1	0	4	.000	.118	.000	-67	-4	0-1	1.000	-1	30	0	O5(1/4/0)/1		-0.5
1971	Cal A	3	3	0	1	0	0	0	0	0-0	0	0	.333	.333	.333	96	0	0-0	1.000	-0	0	0	/OC		0.0
1972	Cal A	13	12	1	2	0	0	0	0	0-0	0	5	.167	.167	.167	-1	-2	0-0	1.000	-0	36	0	O4(2/1/1)		-0.2
Total	3	31	30	2	3	0	0	0	0	2-1	0	9	.100	.156	.100	-27	-6	0-1	1.000	-1	32	0	O10(3/6/1)/1		-0.7

SILVESTRI, DAVE David Joseph B9.29.1967 St.Louis MO BR/TR/6-0/196(180-196) [HouN88 2/52] d4.27 Col Missouri

1992	NY A	7	13	3	4	0	0	1	0	0-0	1	1	.308	.308	.615	153	1	0-0	.889	0	113	127	S6		0.1
1993	NY A	7	21	4	6	1	0	1	4	5-0	0	9	.286	.423	.476	145	2	0-0	.955	0	93	153	S4,3b3		0.2
1994	NY A	12	18	3	2	0	1	1	2	4-0	0	9	.111	.261	.389	70	-1	0-1	1.000	-0	84	74	2b9,3b2/S		0.1
1995	NY A	17	21	4	2	0	0	1	4	4-0	1	9	.095	.259	.238	34	-2	0-0	1.000	1	150	61	2b7,1b4/SD		-0.1
	Mon N	39	72	12	19	6	0	2	7	9-0	0	27	.264	.341	.431	99	0	2-0	1.000	1	150	22	S9,3b8,1b4,2b3,O3L	17	-0.1
1996	Mon N	86	162	16	33	4	0	1	17	34-6	0	41	.204	.340	.247	57	-9	2-1	.913	-3	102	83	3b47,S10,O2(1/1/0)/12		-1.0
1997	Tex A	2	4	0	0	0	0	0	0	0-0	0	1	.000	.000	.000	-94	-1	0-0	—	-1	0	0	/3S		-0.2
1998	TB A	8	14	0	1	0	0	0	0	0-0	0	2	.071	.071	.071	-61	-3	0-0	1.000	-0	61	0	3b3,2b2/SD		-0.3
1999	Ana A	3	11	0	1	1	0	0	1	0-0	0	1	.091	.091	.182	-33	-2	0-0	1.000	-1	127	0	/2SOL		-0.3
Total	8	181	336	42	68	12	1	6	36	56-6	1	96	.202	.315	.310	65	-15	4-2	.912	-5	106	67	3b64,S34,2b23,1b9,O6(5/1/0),D6	17	-1.8

SILVESTRI, KEN Kenneth Joseph "Hawk" B5.3.1916 Chicago IL D3.31.1992 Tallahassee FL BB/TR/6-1/200* d4.18 Mil 1942-45 M1/C17

1939	Chi A	22	75	6	13	3	0	2	5	6	1	13	.173	.244	.293	36	-8	0-1	.947	0	96	152	C20		-0.6
1940	Chi A	28	24	5	6	3	0	2	10	4	0	7	.250	.357	.583	138	1	0-1	1.000	-0	0	0	/C		0.1
1941	NY A	17	40	6	10	5	0	1	4	7	0	6	.250	.362	.450	115	1	0-0	1.000	0	129	112	C13		0.1
1946	NY A	13	21	4	6	1	0	0	1	3	0	7	.286	.375	.333	98	0	0-0	.977	1	111	53	C12		0.2
1947	NY A	3	10	0	2	0	0	0	0	2	0	2	.200	.333	.200	51	-1	0-0	1.000	-1	76	0	C3		-0.1
1949	Phi N	4	4	1	0	0	0	0	0	2	0	1	.000	.333	.000	-3	0	0-0	1.000	0	48	268	/C2S		-0.1
1950	†Phi N	11	20	2	5	1	0	0	4	4	1	3	.250	.400	.350	101	0	0-0	1.000	-1	86	0	C9		-0.1
1951	Phi N	4	9	2	2	0	0	0	1	3	0	2	.222	.417	.222	78	0	0-0	1.000	-1	68	0	C3/2		-0.2
Total	8	102	203	26	44	11	1	5	25	31	2	41	.217	.326	.355	78	-7	0-1	.974	-2	100	102	C62,2b2/S		-0.5

SIMMONS, AL Aloysius Harry "Bucketfoot Al" (b Aloys Szymanski) B5.22.1902 Milwaukee WI D5.26.1956 Milwaukee WI BR/TR/5-11/190 d4.15 C11 HF1953

1924	Phi A	**152**	594	69	183	31	9	8	102	30	2	60	.308	.343	.431	98	-5	16-15	.976	-2	95	106	O152(51/101/0)		-1.7
1925	Phi A	153	654	122	**253**	43	12	24	129	35	1	41	.387	.419	.599	146	43	7-14	.966	-6	103	47	O153C		2.5
1926	Phi A	147	583	90	199	53	10	19	109	48	1	49	.341	.392	.564	139	32	11-3	.975	-10	88	76	O147C		1.6
1927	Phi A	106	406	86	159	36	11	15	108	31	1	30	.392	.436	.645	168	39	10-2	.985	-1	98	99	O105(10/94/1)		3.3
1928	Phi A	119	464	78	163	33	9	15	107	31	1	30	.351	.396	.558	144	28	1-4	.988	-0	97	94	O114L		1.7
1929	†Phi A	143	581	114	212	41	9	34	**157**	31	1	38	.365	.398	.642	158	46	4-3	.989	20	**124**	145	O142L		5.1
1930	†Phi A	138	554	**152**	211	41	16	36	165	39	1	34	**.381**	.423	.708	173	58	9-2	**.990**	2	101	100	O136(129/7/0)		4.5
1931	†Phi A	128	513	105	200	37	13	22	128	47	3	45	**.390**	.444	.641	172	52	3-3	.987	6	108	108	O128(125/3/0)		4.6
1932	Phi A	**154**	670	144	**216**	28	9	35	151	47	3	76	.322	.368	.548	129	25	4-2	.980	-6	91	79	O154(154/1/0)		1.0
1933	Chi A★	146	605	85	200	29	10	14	119	39	2	49	.331	.373	.481	130	24	5-1	.990	9	111	97	O145(144/1/0)		2.4
1934	Chi A★	138	558	102	192	36	7	18	104	53	2	58	.344	.403	.530	135	28	3-2	.987	-4	100	122	O138(136/2/0)		2.3
1935	Chi A★	128	525	68	140	22	7	16	79	33	2	43	.267	.313	.427	87	-13	4-6	.981	-4	100	49	O126(11/115/0)		-2.1
1936	Det A	143	568	96	186	38	6	13	112	49	2	35	.327	.383	.484	112	10	6-4	**.986**	-5	97	68	O138(7/134/0)/1		0.2
1937	Was A	103	419	60	117	21	10	8	84	21	2	35	.279	.329	.434	95	-6	3-2	.984	4	109	86	O102(98/4/0)		-0.7
1938	Was A	125	470	79	142	23	6	21	95	38	2	40	.302	.357	.511	123	14	2-1	.983	-5	96	47	O117(112/8/0)		0.3
1939	Bos N	93	330	39	93	17	5	7	43	22	2	40	.282	.331	.427	110	3	0-1	.982	1	95	141	O82(81/1/0)		-0.1
	†Cin N	9	21	0	3	0	0	1	2	0	0	1	.143	.217	.143	-1	-3	0-0	.938	1	90	97	O5L		-0.1
	Year	102	351	39	96	17	5	7	44	24	2	43	.274	.324	.410	103	0	0-0	.978	1	95	149	O87(86/1/0)		-0.3
1940	Phi A	37	81	7	25	4	0	1	19	4	0	8	.309	.341	.395	92	-1	0-0	.963	2	125	73	O18L		0.0
1941	Phi A	9	24	1	3	1	0	0	1	1	0	2	.125	.160	.167	-14	-4	0-0	1.000	1	128	0	O5L		-0.4
1943	Bos A	40	133	9	27	5	0	1	12	8	0	21	.203	.248	.263	49	-9	0-1	.986	-1	91	117	O33L		-1.3
1944	Phi A	4	6	1	3	0	0	0	2	0	0	0	.500	.500	.500	189	1	0-0	1.000	0	120	0	O2		0.1
Total	20	2215	8759	1507	2927	539	149	307	1827	615	30	737	.334	.380	.535	132	362	88-65	.982	9	101	91	O2142(1377/771/1)/1		23.0

SIMMONS, BRIAN Brian Lee B9.4.1973 Lebanon PA BB/TR/6-2/185* [ChiA95 2/55] d9.21 Col Michigan [DL 2000 Chi A 181]

1998	Chi A	5	19	4	7	0	0	2	6	0-0	0	2	.368	.368	.684	168	2	0-1	1.000	0	111	0	O5(2/4/0)		0.1
1999	Chi A	54	126	14	29	3	3	4	17	9-0	0	30	.230	.281	.397	69	-7	4-0	.976	2	113	93	O46(28/11/9),D3	23	-0.5
2001	Tor A	60	107	8	19	5	0	2	8	8-0	1	26	.178	.239	.299	36	-10	1-0	1.000	1	110	69	O37(19/12/7),D2		-0.9
Total	3	119	252	26	55	8	3	8	31	17-0	1	58	.218	.269	.369	62	-15	5-1	.987	3	112	77	O88(49/27/16),D5	204	-1.3

SIMMONS, HACK George Washington B1.29.1885 Brooklyn NY D4.26.1942 Arverne NY BR/TR/5-8/179 d4.15

1910	Det A	42	110	12	25	3	1	0	9	10		2	.227	.303	.273	75	-3	1	.984	-0	104	97	1b22,3b7,O2(0/1/1)		-0.4
1912	NY A	110	401	45	96	17	2	0	41	33	7		.239	.308	.292	68	-16	19	.946	-17	90	75	2b88,1b13,S4		-3.2
1914	Bal F	114	352	50	95	16	5	1	38	32	6	26	.270	.341	.352	86	-11	7	.894	-3	84	103	O73(61/0/12),2b26,1b4,S2/3		-1.7
1915	Bal F	39	88	8	18	7	1	0	14	10	1	9	.205	.293	.341	76	-4	1	1.000	-2	103	0	2b13,O13L		-0.7
Total	4	305	951	115	234	43	9	2	102	85	16	35	.246	.318	.317	76	-34	28	.953	-21	93	68	2b127,O88(74/1/13),1b39,3b8,S6		-6.0

SIMMONS, JOHN John Earl B7.7.1924 Birmingham AL BR/TR/6-1.5/192 d4.22 Col NYU

| 1949 | Was A | 62 | 93 | 12 | 20 | 0 | 0 | 0 | 5 | 11 | 0 | 6 | .215 | .298 | .215 | 38 | -8 | 0-0 | 1.000 | -1 | 95 | 75 | O26(18/0/8) | | -1.0 |

SIMMONS, JOE Joseph S. (b Joseph S. Chabriel) B6.13.1845 New York NY D7.24.1901 Jersey City NJ 5-9/166 d5.8 M2

1871	Chi NA	27	129	29	28	6	1	0	17	1		0	.217	.223	.279	39	-11		.894	-1	34	0	O25(0/9/17),1b2		-0.7
1872	Cle NA	18	90	11	23	5	1	0		0		0	.256	.264	.333	87	-1	1-0	.938	1	164	168	1b15,O3(1/0/2)		0.1
1875	Wes NA	**13**	53	5	9	1	0	0	4	0		2	.170	.170	.189	23	-4	1-2	.733	-1	0	75	O10(0/9/1),1b3,M		-0.4
Total	3 NA	58	272	45	60	12	2	0	30	2		4	.221	.226	.279	51	-16	6-3	.855	-0	44	0	O38(1/18/20),1b20		-1.0

YEAR	TM LG	G	AB	R	H	2B	3B	HR	RBI	BB-IB	HP	SO	AVG	OBP	SLG	AOPS	ABR	SB-CS	FA	FR	RNG	THR	GAMES AT POSITION	DL	BFW

SIMMONS, NELSON   Nelson Bernard B6.27.1963 Washington DC   BB/TR/6-1/195*   [DetA81 2/43]   d9.4   0.3

1984	Det A	9	30	4	13	1	0	0	3	2-1	0	5	.433	.469	.500	168	3	1-0	1.000	-0	92	0	O5(2/0/4),D4		-0.6
1985	Det A	75	251	31	60	11	0	10	33	26-5	0	41	.239	.306	.402	94	-2	1-0	.945	-2	92	88	O38(25/0/13),D31	21	-0.1
1987	Bal A	16	49	3	13	1	1	1	4	3-0	0	8	.265	.296	.388	99	-1	0-1	1.000	1	104	239	O13R/D		-0.1
Total	3	100	330	38	86	14	1	11	40	31-6	0	54	.261	.319	.409	99	0	2-1	.963	-1	95	115	O56(27/0/30),D36	21	-0.4

SIMMONS, TED   Ted Lyle B8.9.1949 Highland Park MI   BB/TR/6-0/200(187-200)   [StLN67 1/10]   d9.21   Mil 1970   OF(37/0/3)   0.0

1968	StL N	2	3	0	1	0	0	0	0	1-0	0	1	.333	.500	.333	156	0	0-0	1.000	0	0	0	C2		-0.1
1969	StL N	5	14	0	3	0	1	0	3	1-0	0	1	.214	.250	.357	73	-1	0-0	.957	-0	64	0	C4		-1.2
1970	StL N	82	284	29	69	8	2	3	24	37-5	2	37	.243	.333	.317	73	-10	2-2	.990	-5	109	118	C79		0.9
1971	StL N	133	510	64	155	32	4	7	77	36-3	3	50	.304	.347	.424	114	10	1-3	.989	-7	135	96	C130		2.7
1972	StL N☆	152	594	70	180	36	6	16	96	29-8	2	57	.303	.336	.465	127	18	1-3	.991	3	79	97	C135,1b6,O2R		3.9
1973	StL N★	161	619	62	192	36	2	13	91	61-15	2	47	.310	.370	.438	124	21	2-2	.987	10	85	112	C141,1b12		1.1
1974	StL N☆	152	599	66	163	33	6	20	103	47-8	1	35	.272	.327	.447	116	11	0-0	.986	-6	90	80	C154,1b2,O2L		3.5
1975	StL N	157	581	80	193	32	3	18	100	63-16	1	35	.332	.396	.491	139	32	1-3	.983	-4	90	80	C113,1b30,O7L,3b2		1.4
1976	StL N	150	546	60	159	35	3	5	75	73-19	0	35	.291	.371	.394	116	15	0-7	.993	-2	122	129	C143/OR		3.3
1977	StL N★	150	516	82	164	25	3	21	90	79-25	2	37	.318	.408	.500	144	35	2-6	.987	-6	112	97	C134,O23L		4.0
1978	StL N★	152	516	71	148	40	5	22	80	77-17	3	39	.287	.377	.512	149	36	1-1	.988	-2	77	142	C122	29	2.6
1979	StL N	123	448	68	127	22	0	26	87	61-22	0	34	.283	.369	.507	135	27	0-1	.985	-3	92	87	C129,O5L		2.7
1980	StL N	145	495	84	150	33	4	21	98	59-13	2	45	.303	.375	.505	138	27	1-0	.980	-8	95	102	C75,D22,1b4		-1.5
1981	†Mil A★	100	380	45	82	13	3	14	61	23-2	3	32	.216	.262	.376	87	-9	0-1	.995	-4	77	129	C121,D15		0.8
1982	†Mil A	137	539	73	145	29	0	23	97	32-5	2	40	.269	.309	.451	112	7	0-0	.975	-6	69	123	C86,D66		1.9
1983	Mil A★	153	600	76	185	39	3	13	108	41-6	3	51	.308	.341	.448	128	23	4-2	.995	-3	93	104	D77,1b37,3b14		-3.6
1984	Mil A	132	497	44	110	23	2	4	52	30-3	3	40	.221	.269	.300	59	-28	3-0	.992	-2	82	92	D99,1b28,C15,3b2		-0.3
1985	Mil A	143	528	60	144	28	2	12	76	57-9	1	32	.273	.342	.402	104	4	1-1	.992	-2	85	125	1b14,C10,3b9		-0.6
1986	Atl N	76	127	14	32	6	4	0	25	12-5	1	14	.252	.313	.386	90	-2	1-0	.964	-3	112	130	1b28,C15,3b2		-0.3
1987	Atl N	73	177	20	49	8	0	4	30	21-5	0	23	.277	.350	.390	93	-1	1-1	.984	-1	138	125	1b19,C10	16	-0.5
1988	Atl N	78	107	6	21	6	0	2	11	15-2	1	9	.196	.293	.308	71	-4	0-0	.993	-0	97	107	1b19,C10	45	20.2
Total	21	2456	8680	1074	2472	483	47	248	1389	855-188	39	694	.285	.348	.437	117	207	21-33	.987	-57	97	107	C1771,D279,1b195,O40L,3b29	45	20.2

SIMMS, MIKE   Michael Howard B1.12.1967 Orange CA   BR/TR/6-4/185(185-230)   [HouN85 6/144]   d9.5   [DL 2000 Tex A 165]   0.0

1990	Hou N	12	13	3	4	1	0	1	2	4-0	0	5	.308	.308	.615	151	1	0-0	1.000	-0	55	123	1b6		-0.1
1991	Hou N	49	123	18	25	5	0	3	16	18-0	0	38	.203	.301	.317	79	-3	1-0	.889	-2	75	176	O41(1/0/41)		-0.1
1992	Hou N	15	24	1	6	1	0	1	3	2-0	1	9	.250	.333	.417	116	0	0-0	1.000	-0	58	556	O9R/1		-0.1
1994	Hou N	6	12	1	1	1	0	0	1	0-0	0	5	.083	.083	.167	-39	-2	0-0	.857	-0	111	0	O3R		-0.0
1995	Hou N	50	121	14	31	4	0	9	24	13-0	3	28	.256	.341	.512	130	5	1-2	.995	-1	105	93	1b25,O12R		-0.0
1996	Hou N	49	68	6	12	2	1	1	8	4-0	0	16	.176	.233	.279	37	-7	0-1	1.000	-0	0	115	O12(9/0/3),1b5		-0.1
1997	Tex A	59	111	19	28	6	0	5	22	8-1	3	27	.252	.298	.459	89	-2	0-1	.958	-0	86	52	O43(3/0/40),D26,1b16		-0.0
1998	†Tex A	86	186	36	55	11	0	16	46	24-0	3	47	.296	.381	.613	146	13	0-1	1.000	-2	0	1401	/1ORD	155	-0.0
1999	†Tex A	4	2	0	1	0	0	0	0	0-0	0	2	.500	.500	.500	147	-0	0-0	1.000	-0	0	0	/1ORD	320	-1.
Total	9	330	660	92	163	33	2	36	121	69-1	8	175	.247	.323	.464	108	5	4-4	.954	-5	87	104	O140(15/0/126),D56,1b56		

SIMON, HANK   Henry Joseph B8.25.1862 Hawkinsville NY   D1.1.1925 Albany NY   BR/TR/5-6/155   d10.7   -0.

1887	Cle AA	3	10	1	1	0	0	0	0	0-0	2		.100	.100	.100	-45	-2	0	1.000	-0	0	0	O3L		-0.
1890	Bro AA	89	373	66	96	17	11	0	38	34	2		.257	.323	.362	105	1	23	.951	5	108	99	O89L		-1.
	Syr AA	38	156	33	47	5	3	2	23	17	0		.301	.370	.410	145	9	12	.941	-2	33	70	O38(36/2/0)		1.
	Year	127	529	99	143	22	14	2	61	51	2		.270	.337	.376	116	10	35	.948	3	87	91	O127(125/2/0)		
Total	2	130	539	100	144	22	14	2	61	51	2		.267	.333	.371	113	8	35	.949	3	86	90	O130(128/2/0)		

SIMON, MIKE   Michael Edward B4.13.1883 Hayden IN   D6.10.1963 Los Angeles CA   BR/TR/5-11/188   d6.27   Col Indiana   0

1909	Pit N	12	18	2	3	0	0	0	2	1	0		.167	.211	.167	16	-2	0	.917	-0	171	71	C9		-0.
1910	Pit N	22	50	3	10	0	1	0	5	1	0		.200	.216	.240	31	-5	1	1.000	-1	104	74	C14		-0
1911	Pit N	71	215	19	49	4	3	0	22	10	4	14	.228	.275	.274	52	-15	1	.968	-3	118	86	C68		-0
1912	Pit N	42	113	10	34	2	1	0	11	5	0	9	.301	.331	.336	84	-0	1	.991	3	135	102	C40		0
1913	Pit N	92	255	23	63	6	2	1	17	10	2	15	.247	.281	.298	68	-11	3-2	.975	9	94	117	C92		-1
1914	StL F	93	276	24	57	11	2	0	12	9	3	21	.207	.263	.261	41	-27	2	.984	2	88	102	C78		-3
1915	Bro F	47	142	7	25	5	1	0	6	9	0	12	.176	.225	.225	27	-16	1	.992	-4	82	110	C45		-3
Total	7	379	1069	85	241	28	10	1	90	54	9	73	.225	.269	.273	51	-79	9-2	.979	14	102	102	C346		

SIMON, RANDALL   Randall Carlito B5.25.1975 Willemstad, Curacao   BL/TL/6-0/180(180-240)   d9.1   0

1997	Atl N	13	14	2	6	1	0	1	1	1-0	0	2	.429	.467	.500	151	1	0-0	1.000	0	109	110	1b6		-0
1998	Atl N	7	16	2	3	0	0	0	4	0-0	1	1	.188	.176	.188	-1	-2	0-0	.994	-1	42	122	1b4		-0
1999	Atl N	90	218	26	69	16	0	5	25	17-6	1	25	.317	.367	.459	109	3	2-2	.992	-1	96	109	1b43,D29		-0
2001	Det A	81	256	28	78	14	2	5	29	18-5	1	28	.305	.341	.445	108	3	0-1	.988	-5	76	99	1b59		-1
2002	Det A	130	482	51	145	17	1	19	82	13-5	4	30	.301	.320	.459	109	4	0-1	.994	1	109	94	1b80		-1
2003	Pit N	91	307	34	84	14	0	10	52	12-1	1	30	.274	.305	.417	85	-8	0-0	.991	2	120	95	1b29		-1
	†Chi N	33	103	13	29	3	0	6	21	4-1	2	7	.282	.318	.485	104	1	0-0	.994	3	112	109	1b109		-1
	Year	124	410	47	113	17	0	16	72	16-2	3	37	.276	.309	.434	90	-4	0-0	.992	0	101	113	1b46,D4	33	-1
2004	Pit N	61	175	14	34	6	0	3	14	15-5	2	17	.194	.264	.280	41	-16	0-0		0	0	0	/1D	49	-5
	TB A	8	17	2	2	0	0	0	3	3-0	1	2	.118	.286	.118	11	-2	0-0	.992	-5	94	99	1b338,D104		
Total	7	514	1588	172	450	71	3	49	235	80-20	12	142	.283	.320	.424	94	-17	2-4	.992	-5	94	99	1b338,D104		

SIMON, SYL   Sylvester Adam "Sammy" B12.14.1897 Evansville IN   D2.28.1973 Chandler IN   BR/TR/5-10.5/170   d10.1   -0

1923	StL A	1	1	0	0	0	0	0	0	0-0	0	0	.000	.000	.000	-95	-0	0-0		0			/H		-0
1924	StL A	23	32	5	8	1	1	0	6	3	0	5	.250	.314	.344	66	-2	0-0	.889	-1	55	228	3b6,S5		-0
Total	2	24	33	5	8	1	1	0	6	3	0	5	.242	.306	.333	61	-2	0-0	.889	-1	55	228	3b6,S5		-0

SIMONS, MEL   Melbern Ellis "Butch" B7.1.1900 Carlyle IL   D11.10.1974 Paducah KY   BL/TR/5-10/175   d4.14   -0

1931	Chi A	68	189	24	52	9	0	0	12	12	0	17	.275	.318	.323	73	-7	1-1	.950	-1	101	89	O59(15/45/0)		-0
1932	Chi A	7	5	0	0	0	0	0	0	0	0	1	.000	.000	.000	-99	-2	0-0	.951	-1	91	0	O6(4/2/0)		-0
Total	2	75	194	24	52	9	0	0	12	12	0	18	.268	.311	.314	69	-9	1-1	.951	-1	100	87	O65(19/47/0)		-0

SIMPSON, HARRY   Harry Leon "Suitcase","Goody" B12.3.1925 Atlanta GA   D4.3.1979 Akron OH   BL/TR/6-1/180*   d4.21   Negro Lg 1946-48   -C

1951	Cle A	122	332	51	76	7	0	7	24	45	2	48	.229	.325	.313	77	-10	6-4	.971	-4	105	65	O68(5/8/58),1b50		-C
1952	Cle A	146	545	66	145	21	10	10	65	56	2	82	.266	.337	.396	111	6	5-3	.988	-4	101	112	O127(0/11/117),1b28		-C
1953	Cle A	82	242	25	55	3	1	7	22	18	1	27	.227	.284	.335	68	-12	0-0	.968	-2	100	74	O69(1/7/62),1b2		-C
1955	Cle A	3	1	0	0	0	0	0	0	2-0	0	1	.000	.667	.000	88	0		—	0			/H		
	KC A	112	396	42	119	16	7	6	52	34-4	2	61	.301	.356	.414	106	3	3-5	.978	-5	94	75	O100(4/91/10),1b3		
	Year	115	397	42	119	16	7	6	52	36-4	2	61	.300	.358	.413	106	3	3-5	.978	-5	94	75	O100(4/91/10),1b3		
1956	KC A★	141	543	76	159	22	11	21	105	47-8	1	82	.293	.347	.490	119	12	2-3	.965	-13	85	38	O111(0/19/96),1b32		
1957	KC A	50	179	24	53	9	6	7	39	24-12	2	28	.296	.339	.514	128	6	0-1	.996	1	135	83	1b27,O21R		
	†NY A	75	224	27	56	7	3	7	24	12-2	0	36	.250	.307	.402	94	-3	1-0	.957	-1	79	155	O63(16/0/47),1b48		
	Year	125	403	51	109	16	9	13	63	31-2	2	64	.270	.321	.452	110	3	1-1	.975	-1	98		O15(8/0/9)		
1958	NY A	24	51	1	11	2	1	0	6	6-0	1	12	.216	.310	.294	70	-2	0-0	1.000	0	94	65	1b4		
	KC A	78	212	21	56	7	1	7	27	26-3	0	33	.264	.345	.406	104	1	0-2	.990	-4	67	113	1b43,O11(9/0/2)		
	Year	102	263	22	67	9	2	7	33	32-3	1	45	.255	.338	.384	98	-1	0-2	.990	-4	67	113	1b43,O26(17/0/11)		
1959	KC A	8	14	1	4	1	0	1	3	0-0	0	4	.286	.389	.500	146	1	0-0	1.000	0	94	65	1b4		
	Chi A	38	75	5	14	2	1	2	13	4-0	1	14	.187	.228	.360	59	-5	0-0	.947	-2	86	0	O12R/1		
	Year	46	89	6	18	3	1	3	16	4-0	1	18	.202	.258	.382	75	-4	0-0	1.000	-2	111	0	O12R,1b5		
	Pit N												.000	.000	.000		0		1.000	-0	111	0	O3(1/0/2)		
Total	8	888	2829	343	752	101	41	73	381	271-17	10	429	.266	.331	.408	102	-4	17-18	.974	-34	95	81	O579(44/136/415),1b211		

SIMPSON, JOE   Joe Allen B12.31.1951 Purcell OK   BL/TL/6-3/175(175-190)   [LAN73 3/66]   d9.2   Col Oklahoma

1975	LA N	9	6	3	2	0	0	0	0	0-0	0	2	.333	.333	.333	89	0	0-0	1.000	-0	89	0	O6C		
1976	LA N	23	30	2	4	1	0	0	1	1-0	0	6	.133	.161	.167	-7	-4	0-1	1.000	-0	102	0	O20(5/6/9)		
1977	LA N	29	23	4	4	0	0	0	2	2-0	0	6	.174	.240	.174	13	-3	1-1	.957	0	92	131	O28(5/7/16)/1		

YEAR	TM LG	G	AB	R	H	2B	3B	HR	RBI	BB-IB	HP	SO	AVG	OBP	SLG	AOPS	ABR	SB-CS	FA	FR	RNG	THR	GAMES AT POSITION	DL	BFW
1978	LA N	10	5	1	2	0	0	0	1	0-0	0	2	.400	.400	.400	124	-2	0-0	1.000	0	133	0	O10(3/2/6)		0.0
1979	Sea A	120	265	29	75	11	0	2	27	11-1	1	21	.283	.312	.347	77	-9	6-3	.966	5	106	183	O105(27/5/73),D3		-0.7
1980	Sea A	129	365	42	91	15	3	3	34	28-3	1	43	.249	.302	.332	73	-14	17-4	.977	-1	92	139	O119(24/36/63),1b3		-1.6
1981	Sea A	91	288	32	64	11	3	2	30	15-0	1	41	.222	.261	.302	60	-16	12-3	.978	2	105	106	O88(0/86/2)		-1.4
1982	Sea A	105	296	39	76	14	4	2	23	22-4	2	48	.257	.312	.351	79	-9	8-14	.984	-2	90	108	O97(32/59/10)		-1.5
1983	KC A	91	119	16	20	2	2	0	8	11-2	2	21	.168	.248	.218	30	-12	1-1	.995	6	128	115	1b54,O38(4/19/19),P2/D		-0.8
Total 9		607	1397	166	338	54	12	9	124	90-10	7	190	.242	.289	.317	66	-67	45-27	.978	10	100	140	O511(100/226/198),1b58,D4,P2		-6.9

SIMPSON, MARTY Martin B Baltimore MD d5.14

YEAR	TM LG	G	AB	R	H	2B	3B	HR	RBI	BB-IB	HP	SO	AVG	OBP	SLG	AOPS	ABR	SB-CS	FA	FR	RNG	THR	GAMES AT POSITION	DL	BFW
1873	Mar NA	4	15	4	2	0	0	0	2		0		.133	.133	.133	-27	-2	0-0	.792	1	181	0	2b3/C		-0.1

SIMPSON, DICK Richard Charles B7.28.1943 Washington DC BR/TR/6-4/176* d9.21

YEAR	TM LG	G	AB	R	H	2B	3B	HR	RBI	BB-IB	HP	SO	AVG	OBP	SLG	AOPS	ABR	SB-CS	FA	FR	RNG	THR	GAMES AT POSITION	DL	BFW
1962	LA A	6	8	1	2	0	0	0	0	2-0	0	3	.250	.400	.375	114	0	0-0	1.000	1	162	0	O4(4/0/1)		0.1
1964	LA A	21	50	11	7	1	0	2	4	8-0	0	15	.140	.259	.280	55	-3	2-2	1.000	-2	80	17	O16C		-0.7
1965	Cal A	8	27	2	6	1	0	0	3	2-0	0	8	.222	.267	.259	54	-2	1-0	.875	-2	72	0	O8C		-0.4
1966	Cin N	92	84	26	20	2	0	4	14	10-0	1	32	.238	.333	.405	96	0	0-1	.921	-4	74	0	O64(9/10/46)		-0.7
1967	Cin N	44	54	8	14	3	0	1	6	7-1	0	11	.259	.339	.370	94	0	0-1	.973	2	118	186	O26(1/4/21)		0.0
1968	StL N	26	56	11	13	0	0	3	8	8-2	0	12	.232	.333	.393	117	1	0-1	1.000	-1	82	71	O22R		-0.2
	Hou N	59	177	25	33	7	2	3	11	20-2	4	61	.186	.282	.299	77	-5	4-4	.970	-6	71	60	O49(13/16/23)		-1.6
	Year	85	233	36	46	7	2	6	19	28-4	4	82	.197	.292	.322	86	-4	4-5	.979	-7	74	63	O71(13/16/45)		-1.8
1969	NY A	6	11	2	3	2	0	0	4	3-0	0	6	.273	.429	.455	152	1	0-0	1.000	-0	53	386	O5(3/2/0)		0.1
	Sea A	26	51	8	9	2	0	2	5	4-0	0	17	.176	.236	.333	58	-3	3-1	1.000	-1	86	0	O17(1/16/0)		-0.5
	Year	32	62	10	12	4	0	2	9	7-0	0	23	.194	.275	.355	76	-2	3-1	1.000	-1	78	92	O22(4/18/0)		-0.4
Total 7		288	518	94	107	19	2	15	56	64-5	6	174	.207	.299	.338	84	-11	10-10	.967	-15	81	57	O211(31/72/113)	76	-3.9

SIMS, DUKE Duane B B6.5.1941 Salt Lake City UT BL/TR/6-2/205(197-209) d9.22

YEAR	TM LG	G	AB	R	H	2B	3B	HR	RBI	BB-IB	HP	SO	AVG	OBP	SLG	AOPS	ABR	SB-CS	FA	FR	RNG	THR	GAMES AT POSITION	DL	BFW
1964	Cle A	2	6	0	0	0	0	0	0	0-0	0	3	.000	.000	.000	-99	-2	0-0	1.000	0	0	0	/C		-0.1
1965	Cle A	48	118	9	21	0	0	6	15	15-2	0	33	.178	.271	.331	69	-5	0-0	.980	-0	120	145	C40		-0.4
1966	Cle A	52	133	12	35	2	2	6	19	11-1	4	31	.263	.338	.444	122	4	0-1	.975	1	123	53	C48	44	0.6
1967	Cle A	88	272	25	55	8	2	12	37	30-2	6	64	.202	.294	.379	97	-1	3-3	.989	-6	77	102	C85		-0.4
1968	Cle A	122	361	48	90	21	0	11	44	62-11	5	68	.249	.366	.399	134	18	1-3	.983	-6	77	102	C84,1b31,O4(2/0/2)		2.1
1969	Cle A	114	326	40	77	8	0	18	45	66-5	6	59	.236	.374	.426	120	11	1-3	.983	-6	77	102	C84,1b31,O4(2/0/2)		2.1
1970	Cle A	110	345	46	91	12	0	23	56	46-5	6	80	.264	.360	.499	128	13	0-4	.993	8	123	96	C102,O3(2/0/1)/1		2.3
1971	LA N	90	230	23	63	7	2	6	25	30-7	1	59	.274	.357	.400	121	7	0-1	.991	1	120	62	C39,O36(26/0/10),1b29		1.3
1972	LA N	51	151	7	29	7	0	2	11	17-3	1	23	.192	.278	.278	59	-8	0-0	.992	2	105	94	C74		1.1
1973	†Det A	38	98	11	31	4	0	4	19	19-0	1	18	.316	.432	.480	165	9	0-0	.989	1	100	71	C48		-0.6
	Det A	80	252	31	61	10	0	8	30	30-1	2	36	.242	.324	.377	92	-2	1-2	.994	-5	70	41	C25,O4R		0.6
	NY A	4	9	3	3	0	0	1	1	3-0	0	1	.333	.500	.667	132	1	2-0	.979	-1	79	121	C68,O6(5/0/1)		0.6
	Year	84	261	34	64	10	0	9	31	33-1	2	37	.245	.331	.387	97	-1	1-2	1.000	1	0	288	/CD		-0.1
1974	NY A	5	15	1	2	1	0	0	1	1-0	0	5	.133	.188	.200	12	-2	0-0	.979	-0	78	124	C69,O6(5/0/1),D2		0.3
	Tex A	39	106	7	22	0	0	3	8	8-1	3	24	.208	.280	.292	67	-5	0-0	1.000	0	52	0	/CD		-0.2
	Year	44	121	8	24	1	0	3	8	9-1	3	29	.198	.269	.281	60	-6	0-0	.970	-1	55	139	C30/ORD		-0.4
Total 11		843	2422	263	580	80	6	100	310	338-34	35	483	.239	.340	.401	111	39	6-16	.986	-0	98	96	C646,1b61,O54(35/0/19),D7	44	6.1

SIMS, GREG Gregory Emmett B6.28.1946 San Francisco CA BB/TR/6-0/190 d4.15 Col Sacramento (CA) City

YEAR	TM LG	G	AB	R	H	2B	3B	HR	RBI	BB-IB	HP	SO	AVG	OBP	SLG	AOPS	ABR	SB-CS	FA	FR	RNG	THR	GAMES AT POSITION	DL	BFW
1966	Hou N	7	6	1	0	0	0	0	0	0-0	0	3	.167	.286	.167	32	-1	0-0	.500	-0	126	0	/OL		-0.1

SINATRO, MATT Matthew Stephen B3.22.1960 Hartford CT BR/TR/5-9/175* (AtlN78 2/27) d9.22 C11

YEAR	TM LG	G	AB	R	H	2B	3B	HR	RBI	BB-IB	HP	SO	AVG	OBP	SLG	AOPS	ABR	SB-CS	FA	FR	RNG	THR	GAMES AT POSITION	DL	BFW
1981	Atl N	12	32	4	9	1	0	1	4	5-1	0	4	.281	.378	.375	114	1	1-0	1.000	4	215	140	C12		0.6
1982	Atl N	37	81	10	11	2	0	1	4	4-0	0	9	.136	.176	.198	4	-11	0-1	1.000	3	72	101	C35		-1.2
1983	Atl N	7	12	0	2	0	0	0	2	2-0	0	1	.167	.286	.167	26	-1	0-0	.967	0	67	210	C7		-0.1
1984	Atl N	2	4	0	0	0	0	0	0	0-0	0	0	.000	.000	.000	-93	-1	0-0	1.000	-1	33	0	C2		-0.2
1987	Oak A	6	3	0	0	0	0	0	0	0-0	0	1	.000	.000	.000	-99	-1	0-0	1.000	-1	60	0	C6		-0.1
1988	Oak A	10	9	1	3	2	0	0	1	0-0	0	3	.333	.300	.556	149	-1	0-0	1.000	1	0	0	C9		-0.1
1989	Det A	13	25	2	3	0	0	1	1	1-0	1	3	.120	.185	.120	-13	-4	0-0	1.000	-4	63	104	C13	15	0.2
1990	Sea A	30	50	2	15	1	0	0	4	10-0	1	10	.300	.352	.320	88	-1	1-0	.992	3	94	186	C28		-0.7
1991	Sea A	5	8	1	2	0	0	0	1	1-0	0	1	.250	.333	.250	64	-0	0-0	1.000	1	181	0	C5		0.4
1992	Sea A	18	28	0	3	0	0	0	1	1-0	1	5	.107	.167	.107	-35	-5	0-0	1.000	-2	183	82	C18		0.1
Total 10		140	252	20	48	6	1	1	21	17-1	1	35	.190	.244	.234	34	-22	2-1	.996	1	106	117	C135	141	-1.7

SINNER, HOSEA Hosea John B3.20.1885 Shelburn IN D6.10.1948 Sullivan IN BR/TR/5-10.5/185 d7.28

YEAR	TM LG	G	AB	R	H	2B	3B	HR	RBI	BB-IB	HP	SO	AVG	OBP	SLG	AOPS	ABR	SB-CS	FA	FR	RNG	THR	GAMES AT POSITION	DL	BFW
1909	Bos N	10	23	1	3	0	0	0	1	2	0		.130	.200	.130	3	-3	0	.909	-1	83	238	3b5/2S		-0.4

SINGLETON, CHRIS Christopher Verdell B8.15.1972 Martinez CA BL/TL/6-2/210(195-210) [SFN93 2/48] d4.10 Col Nevada-Reno

YEAR	TM LG	G	AB	R	H	2B	3B	HR	RBI	BB-IB	HP	SO	AVG	OBP	SLG	AOPS	ABR	SB-CS	FA	FR	RNG	THR	GAMES AT POSITION	DL	BFW
1999	Chi A	133	496	72	149	31	6	17	72	22-1	1	45	.300	.328	.490	104	1	20-5	.990	12	118	113	O127(11/121/1),D2		1.5
2000	†Chi A	147	511	83	130	22	5	11	62	35-2	1	85	.254	.301	.382	69	-25	22-7	.992	5	106	129	O145(19/143/0)		-1.6
2001	Chi A	140	392	57	117	21	5	7	45	20-2	1	61	.298	.331	.431	94	-4	12-11	.991	7	111	124	O133(19/121/3),D2		0.2
2002	Bal A	136	466	67	122	30	6	9	50	21-0	4	83	.262	.296	.410	91	-8	20-2	.986	-11	88	44	O126C/D		-1.3
2003	†Oak A	120	306	38	75	24	1	1	36	26-4	1	55	.245	.301	.340	70	-13	7-2	.969	-12	81	24	O113(4/102/8)		-2.3
2005	TB A	28	59	9	16	5	0	0	11	6-0	1	14	.271	.348	.356	91	-0	0-0	.973	2	126	144	O19(2/6/11),D4		0.1
Total 6		704	2230	326	609	133	23	45	276	130-9	9	343	.273	.312	.414	86	-49	81-27	.987	3	103	93	O663(55/619/23),D9		-3.4

SINGLETON, DUANE Duane Earl B8.6.1972 Staten Island NY BL/TR/6-1/170* [MilA90 5/142] d8.4

YEAR	TM LG	G	AB	R	H	2B	3B	HR	RBI	BB-IB	HP	SO	AVG	OBP	SLG	AOPS	ABR	SB-CS	FA	FR	RNG	THR	GAMES AT POSITION	DL	BFW
1994	Mil A	2	0	0	0	0	0	0	0	0-0	0	0						0-0	1.000	0	155	0	O2C		0.0
1995	Mil A	13	31	0	2	0	0	0	0	1-0	0	10	.065	.094	.065	-55	-7	1-0	1.000	-0	86	193	O11(3/9/0)		-0.7
1996	Det A	18	56	5	9	1	0	0	3	4-0	1	15	.161	.230	.179	5	-8	0-2	1.000	-1	85	354	O13(3/15/0)		-0.7
Total 3		33	87	5	11	1	0	0	3	5-0	1	25	.126	.183	.138	-16	-15	1-2	1.000	1	87	281	O28(6/26/0)		-1.4

SINGLETON, KEN Kenneth Wayne B6.10.1947 New York NY BB/TR/6-4/213* [NYN67*1/3] d6.24 Col Hofstra

YEAR	TM LG	G	AB	R	H	2B	3B	HR	RBI	BB-IB	HP	SO	AVG	OBP	SLG	AOPS	ABR	SB-CS	FA	FR	RNG	THR	GAMES AT POSITION	DL	BFW
1970	NY N	69	198	22	52	8	0	5	26	30-1	1	48	.263	.361	.379	98	0	1-1	.968	-1	107	30	O51(26/0/26)		-0.3
1971	NY N	115	298	34	73	5	0	13	46	61-9	2	64	.245	.374	.393	118	10	0-1	.974	-3	93	89	O96(10/3/85)		0.2
1972	Mon N	142	507	77	139	23	2	14	50	70-5	2	99	.274	.363	.410	118	14	5-10	.972	-4	86	91	O137(111/0/29)		0.0
1973	Mon N	162	560	100	169	26	2	23	103	123-13	2	91	.302	**.425**	.479	146	42	2-8	.983	-0	89	133	O161(2/0/161)		3.2
1974	Mon N	148	511	68	141	20	2	9	74	93-12	0	84	.276	.385	.376	108	10	5-2	.955	-13	86	71	O143R		-1.1
1975	Bal A	155	586	88	176	37	4	15	55	118-12	1	82	.300	.415	.454	155	51	3-5	.990	-12	87	65	O155R		2.9
1976	Bal A	154	544	62	151	25	2	13	70	79-6	0	76	.278	.366	.403	133	26	2-2	.983	-1	99	91	O155R		0.0
1977	Bal A★	152	536	90	176	24	0	24	99	107-13	2	101	.328	.438	.507	167	58	0-1	.986	-3	93	76	O150R/D		1.7
1978	Bal A	149	502	67	147	21	2	20	81	98-5	2	94	.293	.409	.462	**154**	40	0-0	.976	-11	93	11	O140(4/0/139),D5		4.6
1979	†Bal A★	159	570	93	168	29	1	35	111	109-**16**	1	118	.295	.405	.533	157	51	3-1	.981	-9	88	78	O143(7/0/136),D16		2.4
1980	Bal A	156	583	85	177	28	3	24	104	92-1	1	94	.304	.397	.485	143	38	0-2	.984	-12	88	28	O151R,D5		3.4
1981	Bal A★	103	363	48	101	16	1	13	49	61-6	0	59	.278	.380	.436	136	19	0-0	**1.000**	-3	95	43	O72(0/1/72),D30		1.8
1982	Bal A	156	561	71	141	27	2	14	77	86-2	2	93	.251	.349	.381	102	5	0-0	1.000	1	149	0	O148,O5(2/0/3)		1.3
1983	†Bal A	151	507	52	140	21	3	18	84	99-**19**	1	83	.276	.393	.436	130	26	0-2	—	0	0	0	D103		0.0
1984	Bal A	111	363	28	78	7	1	6	36	37-5	0	60	.215	.286	.289	61	-19	0-0	—	0	0	0	D150	16	2.0
Total 15		2082	7189	985	2029	317	25	246	1065	1263-125	17	1246	.282	.388	.436	132	372	21-36	.980	-71	91	71	O1538(242/4/1313),D477	16	19.8

SINGTON, FRED Frederic William B2.24.1910 Birmingham AL D8.20.1998 Birmingham AL BR/TR/6-2/215 d9.23 Col Alabama

YEAR	TM LG	G	AB	R	H	2B	3B	HR	RBI	BB-IB	HP	SO	AVG	OBP	SLG	AOPS	ABR	SB-CS	FA	FR	RNG	THR	GAMES AT POSITION	DL	BFW
1934	Was A	9	35	2	10	2	0	0	6	4	0	3	.286	.359	.343	85	-1	0-1	.933	-0	81	155	O9(3/0/6)		-0.2
1935	Was A	20	22	1	4	0	0	0	3	5	0	1	.182	.333	.182	38	-2	0-1	.889	-0	96	335	O4(2/0/2)		-0.2
1936	Was A	25	94	13	30	8	0	1	28	15	0	19	.319	.413	.436	116	3	0-0	.946	-1	102	43	O25R		0.1
1937	Was A	78	228	27	54	15	4	3	36	37	2	33	.237	.348	.377	87	-4	1-1	.961	-0	77	64	O64(14/0/50)		-0.7
1938	Bro N	17	53	10	19	6	1	2	13	5	1	5	.358	.493	.623	200	9	1-1	1.000	-1	104	0	O17R		0.7
1939	Bro N	32	84	13	23	5	0	1	7	15	0	5	.274	.384	.369	100	1	0-0	.978	-4	98	55	O22(7/0/15)		-0.1
Total 6		181	516	66	140	36	5	7	85	89	3	66	.271	.382	.401	104	6	2-2	.961	-3	92	70	O141(26/0/115)		-0.4

SIPEK, DICK Richard Francis B1.16.1923 Chicago IL D7.17.2005 Quincy IL BL/TR/5-9/170 d4.28

YEAR	TM LG	G	AB	R	H	2B	3B	HR	RBI	BB-IB	HP	SO	AVG	OBP	SLG	AOPS	ABR	SB-CS	FA	FR	RNG	THR	GAMES AT POSITION	DL	BFW
1945	Cin N	82	156	14	38	6	2	0	13	9	4	15	.244	.302	.308	71	-6	0	.972	0	105	78	O31(14/0/17)		-0.8

YEAR	TM LG	G	AB	R	H	2B	3B	HR	RBI	BB-IB	HP	SO	AVG	OBP	SLG	AOPS	ABR	SB-CS	FA	FR	RNG	THR	GAMES AT POSITION	DL	BFW

SIPIN, JOHN   John White   B8.29.1946 Watsonville CA   BR/TR/6-1.5/175   [StLN65 23/782]   d5.24   -0.7
| 1969 | SD N | 68 | 229 | 22 | 51 | 12 | 2 | 2 | 9 | 8-1 | 1 | 44 | .223 | .251 | .319 | 61 | -13 | 2-0 | .976 | 2 | 113 | 108 | 2b60 | | |

SISCO, STEVE   Steven Michael   B12.2.1969 Thousand Oaks CA   BR/TR/5-10/190   [KCA92 16/442]   d5.6   Col Cal St.-Fullerton   -0.2
| 2000 | Atl N | 25 | 27 | 4 | 5 | 0 | 0 | 1 | 2 | 3-0 | 0 | 4 | .185 | .267 | .296 | 42 | -3 | 0-0 | 1.000 | 0 | 140 | 1423 | O6(5/0/1),2b5,3b2/D | | |

SISLER, GEORGE   George Harold "Georgeous George"   B3.24.1893 Manchester OH   D3.26.1973 Richmond Heights MO   BL/TL/5-11/170   d6.28   M3/C1   HF1939   s-Dave s-Dick   Col Michigan   OF(12/10/15)   ▲   -0.6
1915	StL A	81	274	28	78	10	2	3	29	7	2	27	.285	.307	.369	106	0	10-9	.989	-2	84	102	1b36,O29(6/8/15),P15		1.4
1916	StL A	151	580	83	177	21	11	4	76	40	5	37	.305	.355	.400	133	20	34-26	.985	-2	97	107	1b133,2b2		4.0
1917	StL A	135	539	60	190	30	9	2	52	30	3	19	.353	.390	.453	163	38	37	.985	5	121	117	1b133,2b2		4.0
1918	StL A	114	452	69	154	21	9	2	41	40	5	17	.341	.400	.440	159	32	45	.990	8	124	94	1b114,P2		4.4
1919	StL A	132	511	96	180	31	15	10	83	27	5	20	.352	.390	.530	153	33	28	.991	13	135	88	1b131		7.9
1920	StL A	**154**	631	137	**257**	49	18	19	122	46	2	19	**.407**	.449	.632	179	69	42-17	.990	15	**137**	91	1b154/P		3.1
1921	StL A	138	582	125	216	38	18	12	104	34	5	27	.371	.411	.560	137	31	**35**-11	.993	8	119	89	1b138		6.3
1922	StL A	142	586	**134**	246	42	18	8	105	49	3	14	**.420**	.467	.594	169	**60**	**51**-19	.988	12	**131**	**122**	1b141		-2.2
1924	StL A	151	636	94	194	27	10	9	74	31	3	29	.305	.340	.421	90	-12	19-17	.984	1	106	103	1b151,M		0.3
1925	StL A	150	649	100	224	21	15	12	105	27	0	24	.345	.371	.479	109	-1	11-12	.983	11	**129**	91	1b150/PM		-2.9
1926	StL A	150	613	78	178	21	12	7	71	30	3	30	.290	.327	.398	84	-17	12-8	.987	-3	97	**116**	1b149/PM		0.4
1927	StL A	149	614	87	201	32	8	5	97	24	1	15	.327	.357	.430	100	-2	**27**-7	.984	12	**132**	110	1b149		-0.7
1928	Was A	20	49	1	12	1	0	0	2	1	0	2	.245	.260	.265	39	-5	0-1	1.000	7	**129**	90	1b118/P		1.2
	Bos N	118	491	71	167	26	4	4	68	30	2	15	.340	.380	.434	119	13	11	.988	4	116	100	1b154		-0.8
1929	Bos N	**154**	629	67	205	40	8	2	79	33	4	17	.326	.363	.424	98	-2	6	.982	4	116	100	1b107		-1.3
1930	Bos N	116	431	54	133	15	7	3	67	23	2	15	.309	.346	.397	82	-13	7	.987	5	123	105	1b107		24.8
Total	15	2055	8267	1284	2812	425	164	102	1175	472	48	327	.340	.379	.468	124	250	375-<u>127</u>	.987	93	120	102	1b1971,O37R,P24,2b2,3b2		

SISLER, DICK   Richard Allan   B11.2.1920 St.Louis MO   D11.20.1998 Nashville TN   BL/TR/6-2/205*   d4.16   M2/C13   b-Dave f-George   -0.7
1946	†StL N	83	235	17	61	11	2	3	42	14	2	28	.260	.307	.362	86	-5	0	.988	2	119	117	1b37,O29L		-0.8
1947	StL N	46	74	4	15	2	1	0	9	3	0	8	.203	.234	.257	29	-8	0	.976	1	119	49	1b10,O5L		-0.5
1948	Phi N	121	446	60	122	21	3	11	56	47	1	46	.274	.344	.408	105	3	1	.983	-4	93	96	1b120		-1.3
1949	Phi N	121	412	42	119	19	6	7	50	25	2	38	.289	.333	.415	102	0	0	.987	-9	67	92	1b96		0.3
1950	†Phi N★	141	523	79	155	29	4	13	83	64	0	50	.296	.373	.442	115	13	1	.987	1	100	89	O137L		-0.5
1951	Phi N	125	428	46	123	20	5	8	52	40	2	39	.287	.351	.414	107	4	1-0	.968	-1	99	83	O111L		-0.2
1952	Cin N	11	27	3	5	1	1	0	4	3	0	5	.185	.267	.296	56	-2	0-0	1.000	4	115	122	1b114		-0.3
	StL N	119	418	48	109	14	5	13	60	29	2	35	.261	.312	.411	99	-3	3-3	.985	3	115	122	1b114,O7(3/0/4)		-0.5
	Year	130	445	51	114	15	6	13	64	32	2	40	.256	.309	.404	96	-4	3-3	.985		1	179	112	1b10		-0.2
1953	StL N	32	43	3	11	1	1	0	4	1	0	2	.256	.273	.326	55	-3	0-0	1.000	1	179	112	1b10		-4.2
Total	8	799	2606	302	720	118	28	55	360	226	9	253	.276	.336	.406	101	-1	6-3	.985	-7	97	104	1b387,O289(285/0/4)		

SISTI, SIBBY   Sebastian Daniel   B7.26.1920 Buffalo NY   BR/TR/5-11/175*   d7.21   Mil 1943-45   C2   OF(29/14/35)   -1.3
1939	Bos N	63	215	19	49	7	1	1	11	12	0	38	.228	.269	.284	52	-15	4	.994	-1	88	118	2b34,3b17,S10		-0.5
1940	Bos N	123	459	73	115	19	5	6	34	36	4	64	.251	.311	.353	87	-9	4	.936	-1	99	124	3b102,2b16		-1.6
1941	Bos N	140	541	72	140	24	3	1	45	38	1	76	.259	.309	.320	81	-15	7	.916	-6	101	105	3b137,2b2,S2		-1.0
1942	Bos N	129	407	50	86	11	4	4	35	45	4	55	.211	.296	.287	73	-14	5	.970	-2	101	90	2b124/OC		0.0
1946	Bos N	1	0	0	0	0	0	0	0	0	0	0	—	—	—		0	0	—	-0	0	0	/3		-0.4
1947	Bos N	56	153	22	43	8	0	2	15	20	1	17	.281	.371	.373	100	1	2	.947	-8	88	96	S51/2	57	-1.0
1948	†Bos N	83	221	30	54	6	2	0	21	31	1	34	.244	.340	.290	73	-7	0	.972	-6	96	88	2b44,S26		-0.8
1949	Bos N	101	268	39	69	12	0	5	22	34	1	42	.257	.343	.358	93	-2	1	.989	-6	101	64	O48(21/3/17),2b21,S18/3		-1.0
1950	Bos N	69	105	21	18	3	1	2	11	16	1	19	.171	.287	.276	52	-7	1	.931	-3	79	85	S23,2b19,3b13/1OR		-1.3
1951	Bos N	114	362	46	101	20	2	2	38	32	2	50	.279	.341	.362	96	-2	4-5	.944	-16	81	75	2b33,O23(8/0/16),S18,3b9		-2.3
1952	Bos N	90	245	19	52	10	1	4	24	14	0	43	.212	.255	.310	58	-15	2-0	.966	-9	90	75	2b13,S6,3b4		0.1
1953	Mil N	38	23	8	5	1	0	0	4	5	0	2	.217	.357	.261	69	-1	0-0	1.000	2	107	51	2b13,S6,3b4		0.0
1954	Mil N	9	0	2	0	0	0	0	0	0	0	0	—	—	—		0	0-0	—	0			/R	57	-11.
Total	13	1016	2999	401	732	121	19	27	260	283	16	440	.244	.313	.324	79	-86	30-5	.973	-56	96	86	2b359,3b290,S209,O74R,1b2		

SIXSMITH, ED   Edward   B2.26.1863 Philadelphia PA   D12.12.1926 Philadelphia PA   BR/TR   d9.11   -0.
| 1884 | Phi N | 1 | 2 | 0 | 0 | 0 | 0 | 0 | 0 | 0 | 0 | 0 | .000 | .000 | .000 | -99 | 0 | | 1.000 | -1 | | | /C | | |

SIZEMORE, GRADY   Grady   B8.2.1982 Seattle WA   BL/TL/6-2/200*   [MonN00 3/75]   d7.21   -0.
2004	Cle A	43	138	15	34	6	2	4	24	14-0	5	34	.246	.333	.406	96	-1	2-0	.991	-1	105	0	O42C		1.
2005	Cle A	158	640	111	185	37	11	22	81	52-1	7	132	.289	.348	.484	123	20	22-10	.992	-9	94	39	O155C		1.
Total	2	201	778	126	219	43	13	26	105	66-1	12	166	.281	.345	.470	118	19	24-10	.992	-10	96	31	O197C		

SIZEMORE, TED   Theodore Crawford   B4.15.1945 Gadsden AL   BR/TR/5-10/165(155-170)   [LAN66 15/299]   d4.7   Col Michigan   0.
1969	LA N	159	590	69	160	20	5	4	46	45-7	5	40	.271	.328	.342	94	-6	5-5	.979	1	101	112	2b118,S46/OL		0.
1970	LA N	96	340	40	104	10	1	1	34	34-6	1	19	.306	.367	.350	97	0	5-1	.984	-3	101	95	2b86,O9(8/0/1),S2	29	1.
1971	StL N	135	478	53	126	14	5	3	42	42-5	1	26	.264	.322	.333	82	-11	4-6	.976	17	102	99	2b111		0.
1972	StL N	120	439	53	116	17	4	2	38	37-1	2	34	.264	.324	.335	95	0	6-4	.981	7	**106**	93	2b139,3b3	19	1.
1973	StL N	142	521	69	147	22	1	1	54	68-0	2	37	.282	.365	.334	95	0	6-4	.980	15	108	**129**	2b128/SOR	16	1.
1974	StL N	129	504	68	126	17	0	2	47	70-2	0	37	.250	.339	.296	79	-11	8-4	.980	15	108	83	2b153		-4.
1975	StL N	153	562	56	135	23	1	3	49	45-2	2	37	.240	.296	.301	64	-27	1-5	.972	-21	90	83	2b153		-0.
1976	LA N	84	266	18	64	8	1	0	18	15-1	0	22	.241	.280	.278	60	-15	2-3	.986	5	103	133	2b71,3b3,C2		1.
1977	†Phi N	152	519	64	146	20	3	4	47	52-21	1	40	.281	.345	.355	84	-10	8-11	.986	15	107	121	2b152	52	1.
1978	†Phi N	108	351	38	77	12	0	0	25	25-8	3	25	.219	.270	.254	47	-25	8-1	.978	10	108	113	2b107		1
1979	Chi N	98	330	36	82	17	0	2	24	32-7	1	29	.248	.318	.318	68	-13	3-3	.973	23	111	109	2b96		1
	Bos A	26	88	12	23	7	0	1	6	4-0	1	5	.261	.301	.375	77	-3	1-0	.993	8	117	150	2b26,C2		0
1980	Bos A	9	23	1	5	1	0	0	0	0-0	1	3	.217	.217	.261	29	-2	0-0	.927	-1	96	132	2b8	116	3
Total	12	1411	5011	577	1311	188	21	23	430	469-60	20	350	.262	.325	.321	79	-129	59-46	.979	81	104	108	2b1288,S88,O26(16/0/10),3b7,C4		

SKAFF, FRANK   Francis Michael   B9.30.1910 LaCrosse WI   D4.12.1988 Towson MD   BR/TR/5-10/185   d9.11   M1/C4   Col Villanova   0
1935	Bro N	6	11	4	6	1	1	0	3	0	0	2	.545	.545	.818	267	2	0	.857	-1	54	0	3b3		0
1943	Phi A	32	64	8	18	2	1	1	8	6	0	11	.281	.343	.391	115	1	0-0	.976	1	142	111	1b18,3b3/S		0
Total	2	38	75	12	24	3	2	1	11	6	0	13	.320	.370	.453	138	3	0-0	.976	0	142	111	1b18,3b6/S		

SKAGGS, DAVE   David Lindsey   B6.12.1951 Santa Monica CA   BR/TR/6-2/200(190-205)   [BalA69 6/135]   d4.17   -0
1977	Bal A	80	216	22	62	9	1	1	24	20-0	0	34	.287	.345	.352	97	-3	116	93	.995	C80		-0
1978	Bal A	36	86	6	13	1	1	0	9	9-1	0	14	.151	.232	.186	20	-9	0-1	.988	2	112	106	C35		-0
1979	†Bal A	63	137	9	34	8	0	1	14	13-0	0	14	.248	.313	.328	76	-4	0-0	.984	-4	82	74	C63		-0
1980	Bal A	2	5	0	1	0	0	0	1	0-0	0	1	.200	.200	.200	10	-1	0-0	1.000	0	53	0	C2		-0
	Cal A	24	66	7	13	0	0	1	9	9-0	0	13	.197	.289	.242	49	-5	0-0	.971	-8	87	28	C24	105	-1
	Year	26	71	7	14	0	0	1	9	9-0	0	14	.197	.284	.239	47	-5	0-0	.988	-14	102	81	C204	105	-2
Total	4	205	510	44	123	18	2	3	49	51-1	0	76	.241	.309	.302	71	-20	0-1	.988	-14	102	81	C204		

SKETCHLEY, BUD   Harry Clement   B3.30.1919 Virden MB, Can.   D12.19.1979 Los Angeles CA   BL/TL/5-10/180   d4.14   Col UCLA
| 1942 | Chi A | 13 | 36 | 1 | 7 | 1 | 0 | 0 | 3 | 7 | 0 | 4 | .194 | .326 | .222 | 57 | -2 | 0-1 | .952 | 0 | 98 | 141 | O12R | | |

SKIDMORE, ROE   Robert Roe   B10.30.1945 Decatur IL   BR/TR/6-3/188   [AtlN66 47/780]   d9.17   Col Millikin
| 1970 | Chi N | 1 | 1 | 0 | 1 | 0 | 0 | 0 | 0 | 0-0 | 0 | 0 | 1.000 | 1.000 | 1.000 | 390 | 0 | | — | 0 | | | /H | | C |

SKIFF, BILL   William Franklin   B10.16.1895 New Rochelle NY   D12.25.1976 Bronxville NY   BR/TR/5-10/170   d5.17
1921	Pit N	16	45	7	13	2	0	0	11	0	0	4	.289	.289	.333	63	-2	1-1	.982	-0	140	56	C13		-0
1926	NY A	6	11	0	1	0	0	0	0	0	0	1	.091	.091	.091	-53	-3	0-0	1.000	-0	61	0	C6		-0
Total	2	22	56	7	14	2	0	0	11	0	0	5	.250	.250	.286	40	-5	1-1	.984	-1	127	47	C19		-0

YEAR	TM LG	G	AB	R	H	2B	3B	HR	RBI	BB-IB	HP	SO	AVG	OBP	SLG	AOPS	ABR	SB-CS	FA	FR	RNG	THR	GAMES AT POSITION	DL	BFW

SKINNER, ALEXANDER Alexander B8.14.1856 Chicago IL D3.5.1901 Washington MA d7.12

YEAR	TM LG	G	AB	R	H	2B	3B	HR	RBI	BB-IB	HP	SO	AVG	OBP	SLG	AOPS	ABR	SB-CS	FA	FR	RNG	THR	GAMES AT POSITION	DL	BFW
1884	Bal U	1	3	0	1	0	0	0	0				.333	.333	.333	93	0		1.000	0	0	0	/OR		0.0
	CP U	1	3	1	1	0	0	0	0				.333	.333	.333	104	0		—	-0	0	0	/OC		0.0
Year		2	6	1	2	0	0	0	0				.333	.333	.333	98	0		1.000	—	0	0	O2(0/1/1)		0.0

SKINNER, CAMP Elisha Harrison B6.25.1897 Douglasville GA D8.4.1944 Douglasville GA BL/TR/5-11/165 d5.2

YEAR	TM LG	G	AB	R	H	2B	3B	HR	RBI	BB-IB	HP	SO	AVG	OBP	SLG	AOPS	ABR	SB-CS	FA	FR	RNG	THR	GAMES AT POSITION	DL	BFW
1922	NY A	27	33	1	6	0	0	0	2	0	1	4	.182	.206	.182	2	-5	1-0	1.000	0	118	0	O4(1/3/0)		-0.5
1923	Bos A	7	13	1	3	2	0	0	1	0	0	0	.231	.231	.385	60	-1	1-0	—	-0	0	0	O2C		-0.1
Total 2		34	46	2	9	2	0	0	3	0	1	4	.196	.213	.239	18	-6	1-0	1.000	-0	114	0	O6(1/5/0)		-0.6

SKINNER, JOEL Joel Patrick B2.21.1961 LaJolla CA BR/TR/6-4/204* (PitN79 37/842) d6.12 M1/C5 f-Bob [DL 1992 Cle A 182, 1993 Cle A 182]

YEAR	TM LG	G	AB	R	H	2B	3B	HR	RBI	BB-IB	HP	SO	AVG	OBP	SLG	AOPS	ABR	SB-CS	FA	FR	RNG	THR	GAMES AT POSITION	DL	BFW
1983	Chi A	6	11	3	3	0	0	0	1	0-0	0	1	.273	.273	.273	49	-1	0-0	.960	1	113	174	C6		0.1
1984	Chi A	43	80	4	17	2	0	0	3	7-0	0	19	.213	.273	.237	41	-6	1-0	.989	1	78	70	C43		-0.1
1985	Chi A	22	44	9	15	4	1	1	5	5-0	0	13	.341	.408	.545	151	3	0-0	.971	-0	95	130	C21		0.4
1986	Chi A	60	149	17	30	5	1	4	20	9-0	1	43	.201	.250	.329	54	-10	1-0	.988	-11	115	68	C60		-1.9
	NY A	54	166	6	43	4	0	1	17	7-0	1	40	.259	.287	.301	61	-9	0-4	.981	8	147	97	C54		-0.7
Year		114	315	23	73	9	1	5	37	16-0	1	83	.232	.269	.314	58	-19	1-4	.984	-10	131	83	C114		-2.6
1987	NY A	64	139	9	19	4	0	3	14	8-0	1	46	.137	.187	.230	11	-18	0-0	.984	-8	97	108	C64		-2.4
1988	NY A	88	251	23	57	15	0	4	23	14-0	1	72	.227	.267	.335	68	-11	0-0	.990	-8	**217**	53	C85,O2(1/0/1)/1		-1.5
1989	Cle A	79	178	10	41	10	0	1	13	9-0	1	42	.230	.271	.303	60	-9	1-1	.990	-8	100	92	C79		-1.4
1990	Cle A	49	139	16	35	4	1	2	16	7-0	0	44	.252	.288	.338	74	-5	0-0	.996	-4	140	89	C49		-0.7
1991	Cle A	99	284	23	69	14	0	1	24	14-1	1	67	.243	.279	.303	61	-15	0-2	.991	-0	107	96	C99		-1.1
Total 9		564	1441	119	329	62	3	17	136	80-1	4	387	.228	.269	.311	59	-81	3-7	.988	-33	129	86	C560,O2(1/0/1)/1	364	-9.3

SKINNER, BOB Robert Ralph B10.3.1931 LaJolla CA BL/TR/6-4/190* d4.13 M3/C19 s-Joel

YEAR	TM LG	G	AB	R	H	2B	3B	HR	RBI	BB-IB	HP	SO	AVG	OBP	SLG	AOPS	ABR	SB-CS	FA	FR	RNG	THR	GAMES AT POSITION	DL	BFW
1954	Pit N	132	470	67	117	15	9	8	46	47-0	0	59	.249	.316	.370	80	-15	4-0	.986	-2	98	76	1b118,O2R		-2.4
1956	Pit N	113	233	29	47	8	3	6	29	26-1	1	50	.202	.282	.326	65	-12	1-1	.977	-5	91	125	O36(26/0/10),1b23/3		-2.0
1957	Pit N	126	387	58	118	12	6	13	45	38-6	2	50	.305	.370	.468	127	14	10-4	.963	3	100	154	O93L,1b9/3		1.3
1958	Pit N★	144	529	93	170	33	9	13	70	58-7	2	55	.321	.387	.491	135	28	12-4	.977	7	94	206	O141L		2.8
1959	Pit N	143	547	78	153	18	4	13	61	67-8	0	65	.280	.357	.399	102	3	10-7	.964	-3	97	75	O142L/1		-1.0
1960	†Pit N★	145	571	61	156	33	6	15	86	59-11	1	86	.273	.340	.431	109	8	11-8	.981	-2	93	109	O141L		-0.3
1961	Pit N	119	381	61	102	20	3	3	42	51-9	4	49	.268	.358	.360	91	-2	3-5	.973	-2	101	65	O97L		-0.9
1962	Pit N	144	510	87	154	29	7	20	75	76-5	4	89	.302	.395	.504	140	31	10-4	.960	-6	89	64	O139L		1.8
1963	Pit N	34	122	18	33	5	5	0	8	13-1	0	22	.270	.341	.393	110	2	4-1	.983	0	103	49	O32L		0.0
	Cin N	72	194	25	49	10	2	3	17	21-1	2	42	.253	.332	.371	99	0	1-2	1.000	1	97	105	O51L		-0.2
Year		106	316	43	82	15	7	3	25	34-2	2	64	.259	.335	.380	103	2	5-3	.993	1	99	82	O83L		-0.2
1964	Cin N	25	59	6	13	3	0	3	5	4-0	0	12	.220	.270	.424	89	-1	0-0	.913	1	109	144	O12L		-0.1
	†StL N	55	118	10	32	5	0	1	16	11-2	0	20	.271	.333	.339	83	-2	0-0	.938	1	103	177	O31(4/0/27)		-0.3
Year		80	177	16	45	8	0	4	21	15-2	0	32	.254	.313	.367	85	-3	0-0	.930	1	105	166	O43(16/0/27)		-0.4
1965	StL N	80	152	25	47	5	4	5	26	12-2	0	30	.309	.360	.493	126	5	1-0	.935	1	92	93	O33(15/0/19)		0.1
1966	StL N	49	45	2	7	1	0	1	5	2-0	1	17	.156	.208	.244	25	-5	0-0	—	0			/H		-0.5
Total 12		1381	4318	642	1198	197	58	103	531	485-53	17	646	.277	.351	.421	108	54	67-36	.969	-9	96	106	O950(893/0/58),1b151,3b2		-1.7

SKIZAS, LOU Louis Peter "The Nervous Greek" B6.2.1932 Chicago IL BR/TR/5-11/175* d4.19

YEAR	TM LG	G	AB	R	H	2B	3B	HR	RBI	BB-IB	HP	SO	AVG	OBP	SLG	AOPS	ABR	SB-CS	FA	FR	RNG	THR	GAMES AT POSITION	DL	BFW
1956	NY A	6	6	0	1	0	0	0	0	0-0	0	2	.167	.167	.167	-12	-1	0-0	—	0			/H		-0.1
	KC A	83	297	39	94	11	3	11	39	15-1	0	17	.316	.346	.485	118	6	3-1	.975	3	100	161	O74(57/0/18)		0.5
Year		89	303	39	95	11	3	11	40	15-1	0	19	.314	.343	.479	116	5	3-1	.975	3	100	161	O74(57/0/18)		0.4
1957	KC A	119	376	34	92	14	1	18	44	27-1	2	15	.245	.297	.431	95	-4	5-2	.976	-2	88	95	O76(14/0/69),3b32		-1.0
1958	Det A	23	33	4	8	2	0	1	2	5-1	0	1	.242	.342	.394	95	0	0-0	.750	-1	78	0	O5(4/0/1),3b4		-0.1
1959	Chi A	8	13	3	1	0	0	0	0	3-0	0	2	.077	.250	.077	-6	-2	0-0	1.000	0	84	438	O6(5/0/1)		-0.2
Total 4		239	725	80	196	27	4	30	86	50-3	2	37	.270	.317	.443	102	-1	8-3	.973	-0	93	133	O161(80/0/89),3b36		-0.9

SKOWRON, BILL William Joseph "Moose" B12.18.1930 Chicago IL BR/TR/5-11/195* d4.13 Col Purdue

YEAR	TM LG	G	AB	R	H	2B	3B	HR	RBI	BB-IB	HP	SO	AVG	OBP	SLG	AOPS	ABR	SB-CS	FA	FR	RNG	THR	GAMES AT POSITION	DL	BFW
1954	NY A	87	215	37	73	12	9	7	41	19-1	1	18	.340	.392	.577	170	19	2-1	.986	-0	98	126	1b61,3b5,2b2		1.7
1955	†NY A	108	288	46	92	17	3	12	61	21-4	3	32	.319	.369	.524	141	15	1-1	.989	-2	94	115	1b74,3b3		1.0
1956	†NY A	134	464	78	143	21	6	23	90	50-3	6	60	.308	.382	.528	143	27	4-4	.993	4	**112**	**131**	1b120,3b2		2.3
1957	†NY A★	122	457	54	139	15	5	17	88	31-6	3	60	.304	.347	.470	125	14	3-2	.992	6	119	**113**	1b115		1.3
1958	†NY A★	126	465	61	127	22	3	14	73	28-1	4	69	.273	.317	.424	107	3	1-1	**.993**	-2	99	**106**	1b118,3b2		-0.7
1959	NY A	74	282	39	84	11	5	15	59	20-0	3	47	.298	.349	.539	145	16	1-0	.991	-0	97	115	1b72		1.2
1960	†NY A★	146	538	63	166	34	3	26	91	38-2	2	95	.309	.353	.528	144	31	2-3	.991	10	128	107	1b142	65	3.1
1961	†NY A☆	150	561	76	150	23	4	28	89	35-9	8	108	.267	.318	.472	115	8	0-1	.993	1	100	**126**	1b149		0.0
1962	†NY A	140	478	63	129	16	6	23	80	36-4	5	99	.270	.325	.473	116	8	0-1	.991	-5	86	104	1b135		-0.5
1963	†LA N	89	237	19	48	8	0	4	19	13-4	3	49	.203	.252	.287	59	-13	0-1	.991	-0	95	104	1b66/3		-1.9
1964	Was A	73	262	28	71	10	0	13	41	11-2	3	56	.271	.306	.458	110	3	0-0	.994	-1	95	79	1b66		-0.3
	Chi A	73	273	19	80	11	3	4	38	19-4	1	36	.293	.337	.399	108	3	0-0	.998	-1	93	112	1b70		-0.2
Year		146	535	47	151	21	3	17	79	30-6	4	92	.282	.322	.428	109	5	0-0	.996	-2	94	96	1b136		-0.5
1965	Chi A★	146	559	63	153	24	3	18	78	32-4	5	77	.274	.316	.424	116	9	1-3	.994	-6	83	117	1b145		-0.7
1966	Chi A	120	337	27	84	15	2	6	29	26-4	3	45	.249	.308	.359	98	-1	1-1	.991	3	116	135	1b98		-0.4
1967	Chi A	8	8	0	0	0	0	0	1	0-0		1	.000	.000	.000	-99	-2	0-0	—	0			/H		-0.2
	Cal A	62	123	8	27	2	1	1	10	4-1	4	18	.220	.267	.276	63	-6	0-0	.988	-1	93	82	1b32		-0.9
Year		70	131	8	27	2	1	1	11	4-1	4	19	.206	.252	.260	53	-8	0-0	.988	-1	93	82	1b32		-1.1
Total 14		1658	5547	681	1566	243	53	211	888	383-48	54	870	.282	.332	.459	121	134	16-18	.992	5	102	114	1b1463,3b13,2b2	65	4.8

SKUBE, BOB Robert Jacob B10.8.1957 Northridge CA BL/TL/6-0/182* [MilA79 13/335] d9.17 Col USC

YEAR	TM LG	G	AB	R	H	2B	3B	HR	RBI	BB-IB	HP	SO	AVG	OBP	SLG	AOPS	ABR	SB-CS	FA	FR	RNG	THR	GAMES AT POSITION	DL	BFW
1982	Mil A	4	3	0	2	0	0	0	0	0-0	0	0	.667	.667	.667	282	1	0-0	—	-0	0	0	/OCD		0.1
1983	Mil A	12	25	2	5	1	1	0	9	4-0	0	7	.200	.310	.320	79	-1	0-0	1.000	-0	111	0	O8(0/4/4)/1D		-0.1
Total 2		16	28	2	7	1	1	0	9	4-0	0	7	.250	.344	.357	100	0	0-0	1.000	-0	109	0	O9(0/5/4),D3/1		0.0

SLADE, GORDON Gordon Leigh "Oskie" B10.9.1904 Salt Lake City UT D1.2.1974 Long Beach CA BR/TR/5-10.5/160 d4.21 Col Oregon

YEAR	TM LG	G	AB	R	H	2B	3B	HR	RBI	BB-IB	HP	SO	AVG	OBP	SLG	AOPS	ABR	SB-CS	FA	FR	RNG	THR	GAMES AT POSITION	DL	BFW
1930	Bro N	25	37	8	8	2	0	1	2	3	0	5	.216	.275	.351	51	-3	0	.938	6	137	183	S21		0.4
1931	Bro N	85	272	27	65	13	2	1	29	23	0	53	.239	.310	.313	68	-12	2	.947	10	107	105	S82,3b2		0.4
1932	Bro N	79	250	23	60	15	1	1	23	11	3	26	.240	.280	.320	62	-13	3	.943	8	100	108	S55,3b23		-0.1
1933	StL N	39	62	6	7	1	0	0	3	6	0	7	.113	.191	.129	-7	-9	1	.941	0	102	95	S31/2		-0.8
1934	Cin N	138	555	61	158	19	8	4	52	25	4	34	.285	.320	.369	86	-12	6	.952	5	105	103	S97,2b39		0.2
1935	Cin N	71	196	22	55	10	0	1	14	16	2	16	.281	.341	.347	88	-3	0	.927	-5	91	94	S30,2b19,O8L,3b7		-0.5
Total 6		437	1372	147	353	60	11	8	123	84	14	116	.257	.307	.335	73	-52	12	.945	25	104	106	S316,2b59,3b32,O8L		-0.4

SLADEN, ART Arthur B10.28.1860 Dracut MA D2.28.1914 Dracut MA d4.22

YEAR	TM LG	G	AB	R	H	2B	3B	HR	RBI	BB-IB	HP	SO	AVG	OBP	SLG	AOPS	ABR	SB-CS	FA	FR	RNG	THR	GAMES AT POSITION	DL	BFW
1884	Bos U	2	7	0	0	0	0	0	0	0-0	0		.000	.000	.000	-99	-2		1.000	-0	0	0	O2R		-0.2

SLAGLE, JIMMY James Franklin "Rabbit","Shorty" B7.11.1873 Worthville PA D5.10.1956 Chicago IL BL/TR/5-10.5/144 d4.17

YEAR	TM LG	G	AB	R	H	2B	3B	HR	RBI	BB-IB	HP	SO	AVG	OBP	SLG	AOPS	ABR	SB-CS	FA	FR	RNG	THR	GAMES AT POSITION	DL	BFW
1899	Was N	147	599	92	163	15	8	0	41	55	5		.272	.338	.324	83	-13	22	.953	18	91	120	O146C		-0.4
1900	Phi N	141	574	115	165	16	9	0	45	60	3		.287	.358	.347	96	-2	34	.922	0	112	90	O141L		-1.3
1901	Phi N	48	183	20	37	6	2	0	20	16	3		.202	.277	.273	59	-9	5	.930	5	187	206	O44L		-0.7
	Bos N	66	255	35	69	7	0	0	7	34	1		.271	.359	.298	84	-4	14	.935	-2	133	157	O66(0/5/61)		-0.8
Year		114	438	55	106	13	2	1	27	50	4		.242	.325	.288	74	-13	19	.932	3	**157**	178	O114(48/5/61)		-1.5
1902	Chi N	117	463	66	146	11	4	1	28	53	0		.315	.386	.356	133	20	41	.965	4	90	125	O115(94/22/0)		1.8
1903	Chi N	139	543	104	162	20	6	0	44	81	4		.298	.393	.357	117	18	33	.936	-3	78	176	O139(115/24/0)		0.7
1904	Chi N	120	481	73	125	12	10	1	31	41	3		.260	.322	.333	102	1	28	.921	-5	94	166	O120(102/18/0)		-1.2
1905	Chi N	155	568	96	153	19	4	0	37	97	3		.269	.379	.317	104	1	27	.962	-5	105	135	O155(33/123/0)		0.1
1906	Chi N	127	498	71	119	8	6	0	33	63	1		.239	.324	.279	83	-8	25	.976	-1	129	137	O127(4/123/0)		-1.9
1907	†Chi N	136	489	71	126	6	9	0	32	76	1		.258	.359	.294	99	3	28	.962	-10	83	131	O136(4/132/0)		-1.5
1908	Chi N	104	352	38	78	4	1	0	26	43	0		.222	.306	.239	71	-10	17	.976	-6	48	73	O101(26/75/0)		-2.5
Total 10		1300	5005	781	1343	124	56	2	344	619	23		.268	.352	.317	97	5	274	.950	-2	95	135	O1294(567/668/61)		-7.7

YEAR	TM LG	G	AB	R	H	2B	3B	HR	RBI	BB-IB	HP	SO	AVG	OBP	SLG	AOPS	ABR	SB-CS	FA	FR	RNG	THR	GAMES AT POSITION	DL	BFW

SLATTERY, JACK John Terrence B1.6.1878 S.Boston MA D7.17.1949 Boston MA BR/TR/6-2/191 d9.28 M1/C2 Col Fordham

YEAR	TM LG	G	AB	R	H	2B	3B	HR	RBI	BB-IB	HP	SO	AVG	OBP	SLG	AOPS	ABR	SB-CS	FA	FR	RNG	THR	GAMES AT POSITION	DL	BFW
1901	Bos A	1	3	1	1	0	0	0	1		0		.333	.500	.333	137	0	0	1.000	0	124	102	/C		0.1
1903	Cle A	4	11	1	0	0	0	0	0		0		.000	.000	.000	-99	-3	0	.885	-1	71	280	1b2		-0.4
	Chi A	63	211	8	46	3	2	0	20	2	2		.218	.233	.251	47	-14	2	.974	-4	109	80	C56,1b5		-1.4
	Year	67	222	9	46	3	2	0	20	2	2		.207	.221	.239	40	-17	2	.974	-5	109	80	C56,1b7		-1.8
1906	StL N	3	7	0	2	0	0	0	0	1	0		.286	.375	.286	111	0	0	1.000	-1	68	45	C2		0.0
1909	Was A	32	56	4	12	2	0	0	6	2	1		.214	.254	.250	62	-2	1	.953	-1	128	51	1b11,C6		-0.4
Total	4	103	288	14	61	5	2	0	27	6	3		.212	.236	.243	47	-19	3	.974	-6	106	79	C65,1b18		-2.1

SLATTERY, MIKE Michael J. B11.26.1866 Boston MA D10.16.1904 Boston MA BL/TL/6-2/210 d4.17

YEAR	TM LG	G	AB	R	H	2B	3B	HR	RBI	BB-IB	HP	SO	AVG	OBP	SLG	AOPS	ABR	SB-CS	FA	FR	RNG	THR	GAMES AT POSITION	DL	BFW
1884	Bos U	106	413	60	86	6	2	0		4			.208	.216	.232	36	-45		.802	4	112	89	O96(1/96/0),1b11		-4.1
1888	†NY N	103	391	50	96	12	6	1	35	13	1	28	.246	.272	.315	87	-6	26	.919	-0	93	101	O103(4/90/9)		-1.0
1889	†NY N	12	48	7	14	2	0	1	12	4	3	2	.292	.346	.396	107	0	2	.852	-1	86	241	O12(4/7/1)		-0.1
1890	NY P	97	411	80	126	20	11	5	67	27	2	25	.307	.352	.445	103	-2	18	.905	-12	28	29	O97(53/39/9)		-1.3
1891	Cin N	41	158	24	33	3	2	1	16	10	0	10	.209	.256	.272	53	-10	1	.941	-2	62	92	O41(4/37/0)		-1.2
	Was AA	15	60	8	17	1	0	0	5	4	3		.283	.358	.300	93	0	6	.862	-3	42	163	O15(3/12/0)		-0.2
Total	5	374	1481	229	372	44	21	8	135	62	6	71	.251	.284	.325	77	-63	53	.883	-13	75	85	O364(69/281/19),1b11		-7.9

SLAUGHT, DON Donald Martin B9.11.1958 Long Beach CA BR/TR/6-1/190* [KCA80 7/172] d7.6 Col UCLA

YEAR	TM LG	G	AB	R	H	2B	3B	HR	RBI	BB-IB	HP	SO	AVG	OBP	SLG	AOPS	ABR	SB-CS	FA	FR	RNG	THR	GAMES AT POSITION	DL	BFW
1982	KC A	43	115	14	32	6	0	3	8	9-0	0	12	.278	.331	.409	101	0	0-0	.994	2	147	70	C43	16	0.3
1983	KC A	83	276	21	86	13	4	0	28	11-0	0	21	.312	.336	.388	98	-1	3-1	.964	-7	90	95	C79/D		-0.4
1984	†KC A	124	409	48	108	27	4	4	42	20-4	2	55	.264	.297	.379	86	-8	0-0	.982	-1	99	105	C123/D	17	-0.4
1985	Tex A	102	343	34	96	17	4	8	35	20-1	6	41	.280	.331	.423	102	1	5-4	.990	-4	97	95	C102	47	-0.7
1986	Tex A	95	314	39	83	17	1	13	46	16-0	5	59	.264	.308	.449	101	-1	3-2	.993	-11	60	104	C91,D2		-0.9
1987	Tex A	95	237	25	53	15	2	8	16	24-3	1	54	.224	.298	.405	83	-6	0-3	.985	-5	71	111	C85,D5	36	0.8
1988	NY A	97	322	33	91	25	1	9	43	24-3	3	54	.283	.334	.450	149	8	1-1	.979	-9	92	64	C94/D		0.9
1989	NY A	117	350	34	88	21	3	5	38	30-3	5	57	.251	.315	.371	95	-2	1-1	.991	0	123	112	C105,D3	16	1.1
1990	†Pit N	84	230	27	69	18	3	4	29	27-2	3	27	.300	.375	.457	134	12	0-1	.979	2	116	107	C69/3	22	1.9
1991	†Pit N	77	220	19	65	17	1	1	29	21-1	3	32	.295	.363	.395	115	5	1-0	.987	2	116	104	C79	17	2.8
1992	†Pit N	87	255	26	88	17	3	4	37	17-5	2	23	.345	.384	.482	146	16	2-2	.988	1	120	47	C105		0.8
1993	Pit N	116	377	34	113	19	2	10	55	29-2	6	56	.300	.356	.440	113	7	2-1	.993	-8	98	76	C74		0.5
1994	Pit N	76	240	21	69	7	0	2	21	34-2	3	31	.287	.381	.342	89	-2	0-0	.994	0	98	62	C33	89	0.3
1995	Pit N	35	112	13	34	6	0	0	13	9-2	1	8	.304	.361	.357	88	-2	0-0	.996	1	72	62	C24	15	-0.1
1996	Cal A	62	207	23	67	9	0	6	32	13-0	2	20	.324	.366	.454	105	2	0-0	.992	-5	62	126	C59/D		-0.5
	Chi A	14	36	2	9	1	0	0	4	2-0	0	2	.250	.289	.278	46	-3	0-0	.986	-3	56	34	C12/D		-0.2
	Year	76	243	25	76	10	0	6	36	15-0	2	22	.313	.355	.428	97	-1	0-0	.991	-8	61	110	C71,D2		-0.7
1997	SD N	20	20	2	0	0	0	0	0	5-0	0	4	.000	.200	.000	-45	-4	0-0	1.000	-1	104	0	C6		-0.5
Total	16	1327	4063	415	1151	235	26	77	476	311-28	42	559	.283	.338	.412	104	22	18-15	.987	-45	95	95	C1237,D15/3	275	3.9

SLAUGHTER, ENOS Enos Bradsher "Country" B4.27.1916 Roxboro NC D8.12.2002 Durham NC BL/TR/5-9/192* d4.19 Mil 1943-45 HF1985

YEAR	TM LG	G	AB	R	H	2B	3B	HR	RBI	BB-IB	HP	SO	AVG	OBP	SLG	AOPS	ABR	SB-CS	FA	FR	RNG	THR	GAMES AT POSITION	DL	BFW
1938	StL N	112	395	59	109	20	10	8	58	32		38	.276	.330	.438	104	1	1	.970	-0	103	90	O92(1/20/75)		-0.2
1939	StL N	149	604	95	193	52	5	12	86	44	5	53	.320	.371	.482	120	18	2	.968	13	118	132	O149R		1.3
1940	StL N	140	516	96	158	25	13	17	73	50	2	35	.306	.370	.504	131	21	8	.989	5	111	81	O132R		3.3
1941	StL N★	113	425	71	132	22	9	13	76	53		28	.311	.390	.496	139	22	4	.987	0	98	112	O151R		3.1
1942	†StL N★	152	591	100	188	31	17	13	98	88	6	30	.318	.412	.494	153	42	9	.981	2	92	146	O156R		2.7
1946	†StL N★	156	609	100	183	30	8	18	130	69		27	.300	.374	.465	131	25	9	.982	2	96	129	O142(110/0/32)		1.4
1947	StL N★	147	551	100	162	31	13	10	86	59	4	29	.294	.366	.452	111	9	4	.971	2	107	77	O146(107/0/39)		0.7
1948	StL N★	146	549	91	176	27	11	11	90	81	1	37	.321	.409	.470	130	25	4	.983	-1	100	78	O150L		2.1
1949	StL N★	151	568	92	191	34	13	13	96	79	1	37	.336	.418	.511	141	36	3	.978	-6	94	81	O145(20/0/125)		-1.1
1950	StL N★	148	556	82	161	26	7	10	101	66	2	33	.290	.367	.415	100	2	3	.995	1	101	109	O106R		0.4
1951	StL N★	123	409	48	115	17	8	4	64	67	3	25	.281	.386	.391	109	8	7-2	.989	-2	98	89	O137R		1.3
1952	StL N★	140	510	73	153	17	12	11	101	70	1	25	.300	.386	.445	130	21	6-1	.996	-8	95	21	O137R		0.6
1953	StL N★	143	492	64	143	34	9	6	89	80	5	28	.291	.395	.433	116	16	0-2	.974	-3	84	0	O30(3/0/29)	45	-0.2
1954	NY A	69	125	19	31	4	2	1	19	28	0	8	.248	.386	.336	102	2	0-0	—	0			/H		-0.4
1955	NY A	10	9	1	1	0	0	1	1	1-0	0	1	.111	.200	.111	-15	-1	0-0	.985	-1	98	95	O77R		-0.0
	KC A	108	267	49	86	12	4	5	34	40-4	2	17	.322	.408	.453	132	13	2-3	.985	-1	98	95	O77R		-0.1
	Year	118	276	50	87	12	4	5	35	41-4	2	18	.315	.401	.442	127	12	2-3	.985	-1	98	95	O56(19/1/37)		-0.1
1956	KC A	91	223	37	62	14	3	2	23	29-1	1	20	.278	.362	.395	100	1	1-0	1.000	-3	98	75	O20(17/0/4)		-0.0
	†NY A	24	83	15	24	4	2	0	4	5-0	0	6	.289	.330	.386	91	-1	1-1	1.000	-1	80	38	O76(36/1/41)		-0.1
	Year	115	306	52	86	18	5	2	27	34-1	1	26	.281	.354	.392	97	-1	2-1	.985	-4	93	38	O64(56/0/9)		-0.1
1957	†NY A	96	209	24	53	7	1	5	34	40-5	1	19	.254	.369	.368	105	3	0-2	1.000	-3	85	64	O35(16/0/20)		-0.0
1958	†NY A	77	138	21	42	4	1	4	19	21-0	0	16	.304	.396	.435	133	7	2-0	.957	-2	88	53	O36(5/0/31)		-0.1
1959	NY A	74	99	10	17	2	0	1	21	13-1	0	21	.172	.265	.374	77	-4	1-0	1.000	-0	85	0	O5L		-0.4
	Mil N	11	18	0	3	0	0	1		3-0	0	3	.167	.286	.167	27	-2	0-0	1.000	-0	85	0	O2		-0.1
Total	19	2380	7946	1247	2383	413	148	169	1304	1018-11	37	538	.300	.382	.453	122	264	71-15	.980	-17	99	89	O2064(513/21/1541)	45	14.4

SLAYBACK, SCOTTIE Elbert B10.5.1901 Paducah KY D11.30.1979 Cincinnati OH BR/TR/5-8/165 d9.26

YEAR	TM LG	G	AB	R	H	2B	3B	HR	RBI	BB-IB	HP	SO	AVG	OBP	SLG	AOPS	ABR	SB-CS	FA	FR	RNG	THR	GAMES AT POSITION	DL	BFW
1926	NY N	2	8	0	0	0	0	0	0	0-0	0		.000	.000	.000	-99	-1	0-0	.889	-1	68	0	2b2		-0.1

SLEDGE, TERRMEL Terrmel B3.18.1977 Fayetteville NC BL/TL/6-0/185* [SeaA99 8/245] d4.6 Col Cal St.-Long Beach

YEAR	TM LG	G	AB	R	H	2B	3B	HR	RBI	BB-IB	HP	SO	AVG	OBP	SLG	AOPS	ABR	SB-CS	FA	FR	RNG	THR	GAMES AT POSITION	DL	BFW
2004	Mon N	133	398	45	107	20	6	15	62	40-4	1	66	.269	.336	.462	100	-1	3-3	.987	5	112	84	O114(79/4/43),1b10	153	0.3
2005	Was N	20	37	7	9	0	1	1	8	7-1	0	8	.243	.348	.378	102	0	2-1	1.000	1	113	181	O13(12/0/1)	153	0.1
Total	2	153	435	52	116	20	7	16	70	47-5	1	74	.267	.337	.455	100	-1	5-4	.988	6	112	92	O127(91/4/44),1b10		0.3

SLOAN, BRUCE Bruce Adams "Fatso" B10.4.1914 McAlester OK D9.24.1973 Oklahoma City OK BL/TL/5-9/195 d4.29 Col Oklahoma City

YEAR	TM LG	G	AB	R	H	2B	3B	HR	RBI	BB-IB	HP	SO	AVG	OBP	SLG	AOPS	ABR	SB-CS	FA	FR	RNG	THR	GAMES AT POSITION	DL	BFW
1944	NY N	59	104	7	28	4	1	1	9	13	0	8	.269	.350	.356	99	0	0	.935	-2	91	0	O21(3/0/18)		-0.2

SLOAN, TOD Yale Yeastman B12.24.1890 Madisonville TN D9.12.1956 Akron OH BL/TR/6-0/175 d9.22 Mil 1918

YEAR	TM LG	G	AB	R	H	2B	3B	HR	RBI	BB-IB	HP	SO	AVG	OBP	SLG	AOPS	ABR	SB-CS	FA	FR	RNG	THR	GAMES AT POSITION	DL	BFW
1913	StL A	7	26	2	7	1	0	0	2	1		9	.269	.321	.308	87	0	1	.950	1	125	147	O7R		-0.1
1917	StL A	109	313	32	72	6	2	2	25	28	1	34	.230	.307	.281	83	-6	8	.963	-1	93	99	O77(16/1/60)		-0.2
1919	StL A	27	63	9	15	1	3	0	6	12	1	3	.238	.368	.349	99	0	0	.933	1	79	221	O20R		0.1
Total	3	143	402	43	94	8	5	2	33	41		46	.234	.319	.294	86	-6	9	.957	1	94	123	O104(16/1/87)		-0.2

SLOCUM, RON Ronald Reece B7.2.1945 Modesto CA BR/TR/6-2/185* d9.8

YEAR	TM LG	G	AB	R	H	2B	3B	HR	RBI	BB-IB	HP	SO	AVG	OBP	SLG	AOPS	ABR	SB-CS	FA	FR	RNG	THR	GAMES AT POSITION	DL	BFW
1969	SD N	13	24	6	7	1	0	1	5	0-0	1	5	.292	.280	.458	111	0	0-0	.938	-1	133	0	2b4,3b4/S		-0.1
1970	SD N	60	71	8	10	2	1	1	11	8-1	1	24	.141	.237	.268	36	-7	0-1	.978	6	75	111	C19,S17,3b11,2b9		-0.2
1971	SD N	7	18	1	0	0	0	0	0	0-0	1	8	.000	.053	.000	-90	-5	0-0	.905	0	103	0	3b6		-0.3
Total	3	80	113	15	17	3	2	2	16	8-1	2	37	.150	.218	.265	33	-12	0-1	.887	6	119	123	3b21,C19,S18,2b13		-0.6

SMAJSTRLA, CRAIG Craig Lee B6.19.1962 Houston TX BB/TR/5-9/165 [ChiA81 4/84] d9.6

YEAR	TM LG	G	AB	R	H	2B	3B	HR	RBI	BB-IB	HP	SO	AVG	OBP	SLG	AOPS	ABR	SB-CS	FA	FR	RNG	THR	GAMES AT POSITION	DL	BFW
1988	Hou N	8	3	2	0	0	0	0	0	0-0	0	1	.000	.000	.000	-99	-1	0-0	1.000	-0	0	0	2b2		-0.0

SMALL, CHARLIE Charles Albert B10.24.1905 Auburn ME D1.14.1953 Auburn ME BL/TL/5-11/180 d7.7 Col Bates

YEAR	TM LG	G	AB	R	H	2B	3B	HR	RBI	BB-IB	HP	SO	AVG	OBP	SLG	AOPS	ABR	SB-CS	FA	FR	RNG	THR	GAMES AT POSITION	DL	BFW
1930	Bos A	25	18	1	3	1	0	0	2		0	5	.167	.250	.222	22	-2	1-0	1.000	0	153	0	/OC		-0.2

SMALL, HANK George Henry B7.31.1953 Atlanta GA BR/TR/6-3/205 [AtlN75 4/90] d9.27 Col South Carolina-Aiken

YEAR	TM LG	G	AB	R	H	2B	3B	HR	RBI	BB-IB	HP	SO	AVG	OBP	SLG	AOPS	ABR	SB-CS	FA	FR	RNG	THR	GAMES AT POSITION	DL	BFW
1978	Atl N	1	4	0	0	0	0	0	0	0-0	0		.000	.000	.000	-90	-1	0-0	1.000	0	156	119	/1		-0.1

SMALL, JIM James Arthur Patrick B3.8.1937 Portland OR BL/TL/6-1.5/180* d6.22

YEAR	TM LG	G	AB	R	H	2B	3B	HR	RBI	BB-IB	HP	SO	AVG	OBP	SLG	AOPS	ABR	SB-CS	FA	FR	RNG	THR	GAMES AT POSITION	DL	BFW
1955	Det A	12	4	0	0	0	0	0	0	1-0	0	1	.000	.200	.000	-44	-1	0-0	1.000	1	117	1449	O4(3/0/1)		-0.1
1956	Det A	58	91	13	29	4	2	0	10	6-0	0	10	.319	.361	.407	102	0	0-0	.940	-2	121	0	O26(4/12/10)		0.1
1957	Det A	36	42	9	9	2	0	0	0	3-0	0	11	.214	.250	.262	39	-4	0-2	1.000	0	126	0	O14(8/1/5)		-0.2
1958	KC A	2	4	0	0	0	0	0	0	1-0	0	0	.000	.200	.000	-39	-1	0-0	1.000	-0	99	0	/OR		-0.0
Total	4	108	141	22	38	6	2	0	10	10-0	0	22	.270	.318	.340	75	-6	0-2	.957	1	121	46	O45(15/13/17)		-0.2

YEAR	TM	LG	G	AB	R	H	2B	3B	HR	RBI	BB-IB	HP	SO	AVG	OBP	SLG	AOPS	ABR	SB-CS	FA	FR	RNG	THR	GAMES AT POSITION	DL	BFW

SMALLEY, ROY Roy Frederick III B10.25.1952 Los Angeles CA BB/TR/6-1/185* [TexA74*1/1] d4.30 f-Roy Col USC

1975	Tex	A	78	250	22	57	8	0	3	33	30-1	0	42	.228	.309	.296		73	-8	4-0	.941	1	112	96	S59,2b19/C		0.1
1976	Tex	A	41	129	15	29	2	0	1	8	29-3	0	27	.225	.363	.264		85	-1	2-0	.963	-11	86	77	2b38,S5		-0.9
	Min	A	103	384	46	104	16	3	2	36	47-1	2	79	.271	.353	.344		103	3	0-4	.967	10	105	104	S103		2.5
	Year		144	513	61	133	18	3	3	44	76-4	2	106	.259	.356	.324		98	2	2-4	.966	-1	104	104	S108,2b38		1.6
1977	Min	A	150	584	93	135	21	5	6	56	74-1	1	89	.231	.316	.315		74	-19	5-5	.958	20	112	125	S150		1.5
1978	Min	A	158	586	80	160	31	3	19	77	85-3	1	70	.273	.362	.433		121	19	2-8	.970	18	108	123	S157		5.1
1979	Min	A★	162	621	94	168	28	3	24	95	80-8	4	80	.271	.362	.441		109	9	2-3	.968	33	111	130	S161/1		5.6
1980	Min	A	133	486	64	135	24	1	12	63	65-4	2	63	.278	.359	.405		103	4	3-3	.975	26	113	122	S125,1b3,D3		4.2
1981	Min	A	56	167	24	44	7	1	7	22	31-5	0	24	.263	.375	.443		128	7	0-0	.946	-13	81	56	S37,D15/1		-0.2
1982	Min	A	4	13	2	2	1	0	0	0	3-1	0	4	.154	.313	.231		50	-1	0-0	1.000	1	124	78	S4		0.1
	NY	A	142	486	55	125	14	2	20	67	68-7	0	100	.257	.346	.418		111	8	0-1	.977	-15	89	85	S89,3b53/2D		0.1
	Year		146	499	57	127	15	2	20	67	71-8	0	104	.255	.345	.413		109	7	0-1	.979	-14	91	85	S93,3b53,D4/2		0.2
1983	NY	A	130	451	70	124	24	1	18	62	58-2	2	68	.275	.357	.452		126	17	3-3	.959	-14	87	82	S91,3b26,1b22		1.0
1984	NY	A	67	209	17	50	8	1	7	26	15-2	0	35	.239	.286	.388		89	-4	2-1	.905	-2	108	120	3b35,S13,1b5,D5		-0.6
	Chi	A	47	135	15	23	4	0	4	13	22-1	0	30	.170	.286	.289		57	-4	0-0	.947	-4	93	105	3b38,S3/1D		-1.2
	Year		114	344	32	73	12	1	11	39	37-3	0	65	.212	.286	.349		75	-12	3-2	.923	-5	101	113	3b73,S16,D7,1b6		-1.8
1985	Min	A	129	388	57	100	20	0	12	45	60-3	1	65	.258	.357	.402		102	3	0-2	.987	-3	82	67	D56,S49,3b14/1		0.1
1986	Min	A	143	459	59	113	20	4	20	57	68-4	0	80	.246	.342	.438		108	5	1-3	.963	-1	73	64	D114,S19,3b8		0.1
1987	†Min	A	110	309	32	85	16	1	8	34	36-1	1	52	.275	.352	.411		98	0	2-0	.850	-5	52	0	D73,3b14,S4		-0.6
total	13		1653	5657	745	1454	244	25	163	694	771-47	14	908	.257	.345	.395		102	34	27-34	.966	43	104	109	S1069,D272,3b188,2b58,1b34/C		16.9

SMALLEY, ROY Roy Frederick Jr. B6.9.1926 Springfield MO BR/TR/6-3/190* d4.20 s-Roy

1948	Chi	N	124	361	25	78	14	4	36	23		1	76	.216	.265	.302		55	-24	0	.941	11	107	112	S124		-0.7
1949	Chi	N	135	477	57	117	21	10	8	35	36	4	77	.245	.304	.382		85	-12	2	.947	18	108	107	S132		1.3
1950	Chi	N	154	557	58	128	21	9	21	85	49	4	114	.230	.297	.413		85	-15	2	.945	20	111	104	S154		1.4
1951	Chi	N	79	238	24	55	7	4	8	31	25	2	53	.231	.304	.395		85	-6	0-0	.953	-8	94	92	S74		1.4
1952	Chi	N	87	261	36	58	14	1	5	30	29	2	58	.222	.305	.341		78	-8	0-0	.952	-13	91	69	S82		-1.7
1953	Chi	N	82	253	20	63	9	0	6	25	28	1	57	.249	.329	.356		77	-8	0-0	.932	-8	81	57	S77		-1.0
1954	Mil	N	25	36	5	8	0	0	1	7	4	1	9	.222	.310	.306		67	-2	0-0	.950	2	99	242	S9,2b7,1b2		0.1
1955	Phi	N	92	260	33	51	11	1	7	39	39-2	2	58	.196	.304	.327		69	-11	0-0	.974	-12	91	70	S87/23		-1.7
1956	Phi	N	65	168	14	38	9	3	0	16	23-4	1	29	.226	.323	.315		74	-6	0-0	.949	-3	99	104	S60		-0.4
1957	Phi	N	28	31	5	5	0	1	1	1	1-0	1	9	.161	.212	.323		42	-3	0-0	.941	-0	97	114	S20		-0.3
1958	Phi	N	1	2	0	0	0	0	0	0	0-0	0	1	.000	.000	.000		-99	-1		.714	0	73	160	/S		-0.1
total	11		872	2644	277	601	103	33	61	305	257-6	18	541	.227	.300	.360		77	-96	4-0	.947	7	101	96	S820,2b8,1b2/3	53	-4.1

SMALLEY, WILL William Darwin "Deacon" B6.27.1871 Oakland CA D10.11.1891 Bay City MI BR/TR d4.19

1890	Cle	N	136	502	62	107	11	1	0	42	60	5	44	.213	.303	.239		60	-23	10	.895	20	118	116	3b136		-0.1
1891	Was	AA	11	38	5	6	0	1	0	3	5	0	2	.158	.256	.211		35	-3	0	.762	-1	102	58	3b9,2b2		-0.4
total	2		147	540	67	113	11	2	0	45	65	5	46	.209	.300	.237		58	-26	10	.887	19	117	112	3b145,2b2		-0.5

SMAZA, JOE Joseph Paul B7.7.1923 Detroit MI D5.30.1979 Royal Oak MI BL/TL/5-11/175 d9.18 Col Western Michigan

| 1946 | Chi | A | 2 | 5 | 2 | 1 | 0 | 0 | 0 | 0 | | 0 | 0 | .200 | .200 | .200 | | 12 | -1 | 0-0 | — | -0 | 0 | 0 | /OR | | -0.1 |

SMILEY, BILL William B. B1856 Baltimore MD D7.11.1884 Baltimore MD d10.13

1874	Bal	NA	2	7	0	0	0	0	0	0		0	0	.000	.000	.000		-99	-2	0-0	.786	0	75	0	3b2		-0.1
1882	StL	AA	59	240	30	51	4	2	0	6		0		.213	.232	.246		59	-11		.885	-8	94	81	2b57,O2(1/0/1)		-1.6
	Bal	AA	16	61	3	9	0	0	0			0		.148	.148	.148		-0	-6		.843	1	123	96	2b16,S2		-0.4
	Year		75	301	33	60	4	2	0	6		0		.199	.215	.226		48	-16		.874	-7	100	84	2b73,O2(1/0/1),S2		-2.0

SMITH, EDGAR Albert Edgar B10.15.1860 North Haven CT TR/6-0/200 d6.20 Col Yale

| 1883 | Bos | N | 30 | 115 | 10 | 25 | 5 | 3 | 0 | 16 | 5 | | 11 | .217 | .250 | .313 | | 68 | -5 | | .905 | -0 | 46 | 325 | O30C/C | | -0.5 |

SMITH, ALECK Alexander Benjamin "Broadway Aleck" B1871 New York NY D7.9.1919 New York NY TR d4.23 OF(35/13/10)

1897	Bro	N	66	237	36	71	13	1	1	39	4	2		.300	.317	.376		87	-5	12	.903	-6	89	118	C43,O18(14/2/2),1b6		-0.7
1898	Bro	N	52	199	25	52	6	5	0	23	3	1		.261	.276	.342		77	-7	7	.909	-8	0	135	O26(17/5/5),C20,3b2,2b2/1		-1.4
1899	Bro	N	17	61	6	11	0	1	0	6	2	0		.180	.206	.213		15	-7	0	.917	-2	92	69	C17		-0.7
	Bal	N	41	120	17	46	6	4	0	25	4	3		.383	.417	.500		144	7	7	.951	-1	118	71	C36,O2R/1		0.8
	Year		58	181	23	57	6	5	0	31	6	3		.315	.347	.403		101	-1	7	.939	-3	110	70	C53,O2R/1		0.1
1900	Bro	N	7	25	2	6	0	0	0	6	0	0		.240	.269	.240		39	-2	2	.875	-2	74	0	3b6/C		-0.4
1901	NY	N	26	78	5	11	0	0	0	6	0	0		.141	.141	.141		-19	-12	2	.962	-2	86	85	C24		-1.2
1902	Bal	A	41	145	10	34	3	0	0	21	8	0		.234	.275	.255		45	-11	5	.947	-6	78	100	C27,1b7,O4L,2b3/3		-1.4
1903	Bos	A	11	33	4	10	1	0	0	4	0	0		.303	.303	.333		86	-1	0	.932	0	131	96	C10		0.1
1906	NY	N	16	28	0	5	0	0	0	2	1	0		.179	.207	.179		20	-3	1	1.000	1	104	70	O6C/C3		-0.3
total	9		287	955	107	252	30	11	1	130	26	6		.264	.288	.321		69	-42	37	.933	-27	96	94	C187,O57L,1b3b/OR		-5.4

SMITH, AL Alphonse Eugene "Fuzzy" B2.7.1928 Kirkwood MO D1.3.2002 Hammond IN BR/TR/6-0/191* d7.10 Negro Lg 1946-48

1953	Cle	A	47	150	28	36	9	0	3	14	20	3	25	.240	.341	.360		92	-1	2-0	.920	-4	92	59	O39(4/0/35),3b2		-0.6
1954	†Cle	A	131	481	101	135	29	6	11	50	88	7	65	.281	.398	.435		126	22	2-9	.984	-8	94	100	O109(98/0/17),3b21,S4		0.5
1955	Cle	A★	154	607	123	186	27	4	22	77	93-1	15	77	.306	.407	.473		132	32	11-6	.977	-13	92	57	O120(7/9/111),3b45,S1/2		1.4
1956	Cle	A	141	526	87	144	26	5	16	71	84-7	8	72	.274	.378	.433		112	12	6-3	.981	-7	101	69	O122(50/23/58),3b28/2		0.0
1957	Cle	A	135	507	78	125	23	5	11	49	79-3	4	70	.247	.348	.377		100	2	12-6	.913	-9	87	91	3b84,O58(18/41/6)		-0.9
1958	Chi	A	139	480	61	121	25	3	12	58	48-2	5	77	.252	.323	.396		94	0	3-3	.970	-4	93	92	O138(77/2/63)/3		-1.2
1959	†Chi	A	129	472	65	112	16	4	17	55	46-3	5	74	.237	.311	.396		94	-5	7-5	.980	-0	99	89	O128(84/3/45)/3		-1.3
1960	Chi	A★	142	536	80	169	31	3	12	72	50-3	3	65	.315	.374	.451		124	19	8-3	.966	-9	94	55	O141(3/5/139)		0.6
1961	Chi	A	147	532	88	148	29	4	28	93	56-2	5	67	.278	.348	.506		128	20	4-4	.948	-6	101	83	3b80,O71(10/3/59)		1.0
1962	Chi	A	142	511	62	149	23	8	16	82	57-7	3	60	.292	.363	.462		122	16	3-3	.935	-11	96	47	3b105,O39(38/0/2)		0.2
1963	Bal	A	120	368	45	100	17	1	10	39	32-1	3	74	.272	.335	.405		110	5	9-0	.971	-1	97	104	O97(7/0/92)		0.2
1964	Cle	A	61	136	15	22	1	1	4	9	8-1	1	32	.162	.214	.272		34	-13	0-1	1.000	1	114	104	O48(1/1/46)/3		-1.5
	Bos	A	29	51	10	11	4	0	2	7	13-0	1	10	.216	.385	.412		116	2	0-0	.917	0	74	0	3b10,O8(2/0/6)		0.2
	Year		90	187	25	33	5	1	6	16	21-1	2	42	.176	.267	.310		59	-11	0-1	.987	2	113	89	O56(3/1/52),3b11		-1.3
total	12		1517	5357	843	1458	258	46	164	676	674-30	63	768	.272	.358	.429		113	111	67-43	.974	-70	95	86	O1118(399/87/679),3b378,S9,2b2		-1.6

SMITH, TONY Anthony B5.14.1884 Chicago IL D2.27.1964 Galveston TX BR/TR/5-9/150 d8.12

1907	Was	A	51	139	12	26	1	9	0	18	8	1		.187	.285	.209		63	-5	3	.920	-5	92	71	S51		-0.9
1910	Bro	N	106	321	31	58	10	1	1	16	69	2	53	.181	.329	.227		65	-10	9	.941	9	101	136	S101,3b6		0.2
1911	Bro	N	13	40	3	6	1	0	0	2	8	0	7	.150	.292	.175		33	-3	1	.870	-1	114	133	S10,2b3		-0.2
total	3		170	500	46	90	12	2	1	26	95	3	60	.180	.314	.218		62	-18	13	.931	3	99	117	S162,3b6,2b3		-1.0

SMITH, KLONDIKE Armstrong Frederick B1.4.1887 London, England D11.15.1959 Springfield MA BL/TL/5-9/160 d9.28

| 1912 | NY | A | 7 | 27 | 0 | 5 | 0 | 0 | 0 | 0 | 0 | | | .185 | .185 | .222 | | 15 | -3 | 1 | 1.000 | -1 | 93 | 0 | O7(0/5/2) | | -0.4 |

SMITH, BILLY Billy Edward B7.14.1953 Jonesboro LA BB/TR/6-2.5/185(165-185) d4.13

1975	Cal	A	59	143	10	29	5	1	0	14	12-0	0	27	.203	.263	.252		50	-10	1-3	.932	-12	75	73	S50,1b6,3b2,D4		-1.8
1976	Cal	A	13	8	0	3	0	0	0	0	0-0	0	2	.375	.375	.375		128	0	0-0	.625	-2	81	90	S10/D		-0.1
1977	Bal	A	109	367	44	79	12	2	5	29	33-2	1	71	.215	.281	.300		62	-20	3-2	.991	9	102	130	2b104,S5,1b2/3		-0.5
1978	Bal	A	85	250	29	65	12	2	5	30	27-3	1	40	.260	.333	.384		108	0	3-0	.986	-1	99	128	2b63,S2		-0.1
1979	†Bal	A	68	189	18	47	9	4	6	33	15-1	2	33	.249	.309	.434		102	0	1-0	.980	-5	95	106	2b63,S5	19	0.7
	SF	N	36	61	6	11	0	1	0	5	0	0	16	.180	.180	.262		49	-4	0-0	.971	1	101	118	S21,2b5,3b3		-0.2
total	6		370	1018	107	234	38	9	17	111	96-6	4	189	.230	.297	.335		79	-31	8-5	.987	-8	100	114	2b255,S93,1b8,3b6,D5	19	-2.0

SMITH, BOBBY GENE Bobby Gene B5.28.1934 Hood River OR BR/TR/5-11/185* d4.16

1957	StL	N	93	185	24	39	7	1	3	18	13-3	0	35	.211	.260	.308		52	-13	1-1	.973	3	106	156	O79(0/61/18)		-1.2
1958	StL	N	28	88	8	25	3	0	2	5	8-0	1	18	.284	.304	.386		79	-3	1.000	1.000	5	113	0	O27(0/25/2)		-0.3
	StL	N	43	60	11	13	1	1	1	7	1-0	0	9	.217	.230	.317		41	-5	0-0	.971	2	112	289	O32(11/6/15)		-0.4
	Phi	N	98	217	24	62	8	2	4	27	10-1	0	28	.286	.317	.382		90	-4	2-3	1.000	5	121	93	O70(65/6/0)/3		-0.2

YEAR TM LG	G	AB	R	H	2B	3B	HR	RBI	BB-IB	HP	SO	AVG	OBP	SLG	AOPS	ABR	SB-CS	FA	FR	RNG	THR	GAMES AT POSITION	DL	BFW
1961 Phi N	79	174	16	44	7	0	2	18	15-2	1	32	.253	.313	.328	72	-7	0-1	.971	8	126	250	O47(33/3/12)		-0.2
1962 NY N	8	22	1	3	0	1	0	2	3-0	0	2	.136	.240	.227	26	-2	0-1	1.000	-0	106	0	O6(0/3/4)		-0.3
Chi N	13	29	3	5	0	0	1	2	2-0	0	6	.172	.219	.276	33	-3	0-1	1.000	-1	58	211	O7(0/6/1)		-0.4
StL N	91	130	13	30	9	0	0	12	7-0	0	14	.231	.270	.300	48	-9	1-1	1.000	-1	89	144	O80(66/13/7)		-1.1
Year	112	181	17	38	9	1	1	16	12-0	0	22	.210	.258	.287	43	-15	1-3	1.000	-1	87	137	O93(66/22/12)		-1.8
1965 Cal A	23	57	1	13	3	0	0	5	2-0	1	10	.228	.262	.281	57	-3	0-1	1.000	0	99	132	O15(14/0/1)		-0.4
Total 7	476	962	101	234	35	5	13	96	55-6	3	154	.243	.284	.331	64	-49	5-9	.986	19	108	157	O363(189/123/60)/3		-4.5

SMITH, BRICK Brick Dudley B5.2.1959 Charlotte NC BR/TR/6-4/225* [SeaA81 5/104] d9.13 Col Wake Forest

YEAR TM LG	G	AB	R	H	2B	3B	HR	RBI	BB-IB	HP	SO	AVG	OBP	SLG	AOPS	ABR	SB-CS	FA	FR	RNG	THR	GAMES AT POSITION	DL	BFW
1987 Sea A	5	8	1	1	0	0	0	0	2-0	0	4	.125	.300	.125	18	-1	0-0	.963	-0	117	52	1b3/D		-0.1
1988 Sea A	4	10	1	1	0	0	0	1	0-0	0	1	.100	.100	.100	-42	-2	0-0	1.000	1	172	110	1b4		-0.1
Total 2	9	18	2	2	0	0	0	1	2-0	0	5	.111	.200	.111	-12	-3	0-0	.983	1	148	85	1b7/D		-0.2

SMITH, BERNIE Calvin Bernard B9.4.1941 Ponchatoula LA BR/TR/5-9/164* d7.31 Col Southern A&M

YEAR TM LG	G	AB	R	H	2B	3B	HR	RBI	BB-IB	HP	SO	AVG	OBP	SLG	AOPS	ABR	SB-CS	FA	FR	RNG	THR	GAMES AT POSITION	DL	BFW
1970 Mil A	44	76	8	21	3	1	1	6	11-1	2	12	.276	.382	.382	111	2	1-3	.979	0	119	0	O39(2/11/27)		0.0
1971 Mil A	15	36	1	5	1	0	1	3	0-0	1	5	.139	.162	.250	15	-4	0-0	.923	-1	68	178	O12(3/1/9)		-0.6
Total 2	59	112	9	26	4	1	2	9	11-1	3	17	.232	.317	.339	83	-2	1-3	.967	-1	104	54	O51(5/12/36)		-0.6

SMITH, REGGIE Carl Reginald B4.2.1945 Shreveport LA BB/TR/6-0/195(170-195) d9.18 Mil 1963 C5 OF(3/808/874)

YEAR TM LG	G	AB	R	H	2B	3B	HR	RBI	BB-IB	HP	SO	AVG	OBP	SLG	AOPS	ABR	SB-CS	FA	FR	RNG	THR	GAMES AT POSITION	DL	BFW
1966 Bos A	6	26	1	4	1	0	0	0	0-0	0	5	.154	.154	.192	-1	-3	0-0	.944	0	121	0	O6C		-0.4
1967 †Bos A	158	565	78	139	24	6	15	61	57-11	1	95	.246	.315	.389	99	0	16-6	.983	3	103	117	O144C,2b6		0.1
1968 Bos A	155	558	78	148	37	5	15	69	64-13	4	77	.265	.342	.430	126	19	22-18	.985	2	107	77	O155C		1.7
1969 Bos A★	143	543	87	168	29	7	25	93	54-7	1	67	.309	.368	.527	142	30	7-13	.959	-4	100	91	O139(3/136/0)		1.9
1970 Bos A	147	580	109	176	32	7	22	74	51-1	4	60	.303	.361	.497	126	20	10-7	.977	7	108	167	O145C		2.4
1971 Bos A	159	618	85	175	33	2	30	96	63-4	5	82	.283	.352	.489	127	22	11-3	.966	7	108	144	O159(0/87/74)		2.6
1972 Bos A★	131	467	75	126	25	4	21	74	68-12	4	63	.270	.365	.475	141	25	15-4	.981	0	103	89	O129(0/4/125)		2.4
1973 Bos A	115	423	79	128	23	2	21	69	68-7	1	49	.303	.398	.515	147	29	3-2	.983	4	110	112	O104C/1D		3.0
1974 StL N★	143	517	79	160	26	9	23	100	71-10	1	70	.309	.389	.528	156	39	4-3	.976	0	107	95	O132R/1		3.4
1975 StL N★	135	477	67	144	26	3	19	76	63-9	3	59	.302	.382	.488	136	24	9-7	.963	-5	103	69	O69(0/1/68),1b66/3		1.1
1976 StL N	47	170	20	37	7	1	8	23	14-2	1	28	.218	.281	.412	93	-2	1-2	.985	7	112	62	O58(0/1/57)/3		0.7
LA N	65	225	35	63	8	4	10	26	18-4	1	42	.280	.335	.484	132	8	2-0	.989	8	113	130	O74(0/4/70),1b17,3b14		3.7
Year	112	395	55	100	15	5	18	49	32-6	2	70	.253	.312	.453	115	5	3-2	.980	-7	93	69	O140(0/9/138)		3.0
1977 †LA N★	148	488	104	150	27	4	32	87	104-11	3	76	.307	.427	.576	167	51	7-5	.950	-5	95	82	O62(0/5/59)		1.4
1978 †LA N★	128	447	82	132	27	2	29	93	70-8	1	90	.295	.382	.559	163	39	12-5	.988	8	137	104	O62(0/5/59)	42	2.7
1979 LA N★	68	234	41	64	13	1	10	32	31-3	2	50	.274	.359	.466	127	9	6-5	.994	0	98	216	O84(0/7/82)	42	0.0
1980 LA N★	92	311	47	100	13	0	15	55	41-1	1	63	.322	.392	.508	157	25	5-6	1.000	0	104	92	1b2		1.7
1981 †LA N	41	35	5	7	1	0	1	8	7-3	0	8	.200	.318	.314	88	0	0-0	.982	5	128	92	1b99	15	1.7
1982 SF N	106	349	51	99	11	0	18	56	46-9	0	46	.284	.364	.470	134	16	7-0	.976	32	105	110	O1668R,1b186,3b15,D8,2b6		
Total 17	1987	7033	1123	2020	363	57	314	1092	890-115	33	1030	.287	.366	.489	136	351	137-86	.976	32	105	110	O1668R,1b186,3b15,D8,2b6	99	31.6

SMITH, CHARLIE Charles J. B12.11.1840 Brooklyn NY D11.15.1897 Great Neck NY 5-10.5/150 d5.18

YEAR TM LG	G	AB	R	H	2B	3B	HR	RBI	BB-IB	HP	SO	AVG	OBP	SLG	AOPS	ABR	SB-CS	FA	FR	RNG	THR	GAMES AT POSITION	DL	BFW
1871 Mut NA	14	72	15	19	2	1	0	5	1		1	.264	.274	.319	77	-1	6-0	.688	-1	96	73	3b12,2b3		-0.1

SMITH, POP Charles Marvin B10.12.1856 Digby NS, Can. D4.18.1927 Boston MA BR/TR/5-11/170 d5.1 U1

YEAR TM LG	G	AB	R	H	2B	3B	HR	RBI	BB-IB	HP	SO	AVG	OBP	SLG	AOPS	ABR	SB-CS	FA	FR	RNG	THR	GAMES AT POSITION	DL	BFW
1880 Cin N	83	334	35	69	10	9	0	27	6		36	.207	.221	.290	72	-10		.855	-9	92	85	2b83		-1.4
1881 Cle N	10	34	1	4	0	0	0	3	0		8	.118	.118	.118	-27	-5		.838	-3	73	0	3b10		-0.7
Buf N	3	11	0	0	0	0	0	1	3		5	.000	.214	.000	-27	-1		.840	-1	64	215	2b3		-0.2
Wor N	11	41	1	3	0	0	0	2	3		5	.073	.136	.073	-31	-6		.955	2	176	265	O8(1/4/3),2b3		-0.4
Year	24	86	2	7	0	0	0	6	6		18	.081	.141	.081	-28	-12		.732	-0	93	0	3b11,S4,O3(0/2/1),2b2		-1.3
1882 Phi AA	20	65	10	6	0	0	0	2	12			.092	.234	.092	13	-6		.778	-1	91	0	S3		-0.1
Lou AA	3	11	1	2	0	0	0	0	0			.182	.182	.182	24	-1		.732	-1	93	0	3b11,S7,O3(0/2/1),2b2		-0.6
Year	23	76	11	8	0	0	0	2	12			.105	.227	.105	15	-6		.732	-1	93	0	3b11,S7,O3(0/2/1),2b2		-0.5
1883 Col AA	97	405	82	106	14	17	4		22			.262	.300	.410	137	17		.889	19	117	119	2b73,3b24,P3		4.1
1884 Col AA	108	445	78	106	18	10	6		20		12	.238	.289	.364	122	12		.905	30	115	135	2b106		2.8
1885 Pit AA	106	453	85	113	11	13	0	35	25		3	.249	.293	.331	98	-1	38	.922	29	114	123	S98,2b28/C		1.3
1886 Pit AA	126	483	75	105	20	9	2	57	42		6	.217	.288	.308	87	-7	30	.895	18	112	108	2b89,S33		-2.5
1887 Pit N	122	456	69	98	12	7	2	54	30	13	48	.215	.283	.285	63	-22	30	.914	-12	100	85	S75,2b56		-0.9
1888 Pit N	131	481	61	99	15	2	4	52	22	6	78	.206	.248	.270	71	-14	37	.901	1	110	85	S58,2b9,3b3,O3(1/0/2)		-0.5
1889 Pit N	72	258	26	54	10	2	5	27	24	6	38	.209	.292	.322	79	-7	12	.897	-1	103	107	S59		-0.6
Bos N	59	208	21	54	13	4	0	32	23	4	30	.260	.345	.361	92	-2	11	.890	-6	86	112	S117,2b9,3b3,O3(1/0/2)		-1.1
Year	131	466	47	108	23	6	5	59	47	10	68	.232	.315	.339	85	-9	23	.894	-7	94	110	2b134/S		-1.8
1890 Bos N	134	463	82	106	16	12	1	53	80	9	81	.229	.353	.322	90	-5	39	.919	4	103	112	2b19,S5,3b4		0.0
1891 Was AA	27	90	13	16	2	2	0	13	13	2	16	.178	.295	.244	57	-5	2	.903	50	105	106	P3/C		2.0
Total 12	1112	4238	634	941	141	87	24	358	325	60	345	.222	.287	.313	86	-63	169	.903	50	105	106	2b713,S336,3b52,O14(2/6/6),P3/C		2.0

SMITH, CHARLEY Charles William B9.15.1937 Charleston SC D11.29.1994 Reno NV BR/TR/6-0/177* d9.8

YEAR TM LG	G	AB	R	H	2B	3B	HR	RBI	BB-IB	HP	SO	AVG	OBP	SLG	AOPS	ABR	SB-CS	FA	FR	RNG	THR	GAMES AT POSITION	DL	BFW
1960 LA N	18	60	2	10	1	0	1	5	1-0	0	15	.167	.172	.217	-8	-8	0-0	.953	-1	87	77	3b18		-0.9
1961 LA N	9	24	4	6	1	0	2	3	1-0	0	6	.250	.280	.542	103	0	0-0	1.000	-1	40	138	3b4,S3		-0.1
Phi N	112	411	43	102	13	4	9	47	23-3	5	76	.248	.294	.365	75	-16	3-4	.924	-3	110	101	3b94,S14		-1.9
Year	121	435	47	108	14	4	11	50	24-3	5	82	.248	.293	.375	77	-16	3-4	.926	-5	107	102	3b98,S17		-2.0
1962 Chi A	65	145	11	30	4	0	2	17	9-0	1	32	.207	.256	.276	44	-12	0-1	.944	-3	97	173	3b54		0.2
1963 Chi A	4	7	0	2	0	1	0	1	0-0	0	2	.286	.286	.571	136	0	0-0	1.000	2	168	724	/S		0.2
1964 Chi A	2	7	1	1	0	1	0	1	1-0	0	1	.143	.250	.429	87	0	0-0	1.000	3	234	640	3b2		-1.3
NY N	127	443	44	106	12	4	20	58	19-1	3	101	.239	.275	.402	90	-8	2-2	.917	-5	109	65	3b85,S36,O13L		0.5
1965 NY N	135	499	49	122	20	3	16	62	17-3	4	123	.244	.273	.393	89	-10	2-1	.957	15	114	125	3b131,S6/2		-1.2
1966 StL N	116	391	34	104	13	4	10	43	22-4	0	81	.266	.301	.396	93	-5	0-2	.964	-5	94	134	3b107/S		0.3
1967 NY A	135	425	38	95	15	3	9	38	32-6	1	110	.224	.278	.336	84	-9	0-2	.947	8	115	116	3b115	32	0.3
1968 NY A	46	70	2	16	4	1	1	7	5-2	0	18	.229	.280	.357	95	-1	0-0	.961	3	120	141	3b13		-0.1
1969 Chi N	2	2	0	0	0	0	0	0	0-0	0	0	.000	.000	.000	-89	0	0-0	—	0			/H		
Total 10	771	2484	228	594	83	18	69	281	130-19	14	565	.239	.279	.370	82	-69	7-12	.945	12	108	117	3b623,S61,O13L/2	32	-6.1

SMITH, CHRIS Christopher William B7.18.1957 Torrance CA BB/TR/6-0/185* [TexA78 11/280] d5.14 Col USC

YEAR TM LG	G	AB	R	H	2B	3B	HR	RBI	BB-IB	HP	SO	AVG	OBP	SLG	AOPS	ABR	SB-CS	FA	FR	RNG	THR	GAMES AT POSITION	DL	BFW
1981 Mon N	7	7	0	0	0	0	0	0	0-0	0	2	.000	.000	.000	-97	-2	0-0	1.000	0	270	0	/2		-0.2
1982 Mon N	2	2	0	0	0	0	0	0	0-0	0	1	.000	.000	.000	-97	-1	0-0	—	0			/H		-0.1
1983 SF N	22	67	13	22	6	1	1	11	7-1	2	12	.328	.403	.493	153	5	0-0	.976	-2	81	56	1b15,O4L/3		0.0
Total 3	31	76	13	22	6	1	1	11	7-1	2	15	.289	.360	.434	124	2	0-0	.976	-1	81	56	1b15,O4L/32		0.0

SMITH, EARL Earl Calvin B3.14.1928 Sunnyside WA BR/TR/6-0/185 d4.14 Col Cal St.-Fresno

YEAR TM LG	G	AB	R	H	2B	3B	HR	RBI	BB-IB	HP	SO	AVG	OBP	SLG	AOPS	ABR	SB-CS	FA	FR	RNG	THR	GAMES AT POSITION	DL	BFW
1955 Pit N	5	16	1	1	1	0	0	0	4-0	1	1	.063	.286	.063	-1	-2	0-0	1.000	-0	99	0	O5C		-0.

SMITH, EARL Earl Leonard "Sheriff" B1.20.1891 Oak Hill OH D3.14.1943 Portsmouth OH BB/TR/5-11/170 d9.12

YEAR TM LG	G	AB	R	H	2B	3B	HR	RBI	BB-IB	HP	SO	AVG	OBP	SLG	AOPS	ABR	SB-CS	FA	FR	RNG	THR	GAMES AT POSITION	DL	BFW
1916 Chi N	14	27	2	7	1	1	0	4	2	0	5	.259	.310	.370	98	0	1	.800	-1	52	0	O7(6/0/1)		-0.
1917 StL A	52	199	31	56	7	7	0	10	15	4	21	.281	.332	.387	124	4	5	.977	3	93	155	O51(22/29/0)		-0.
1918 StL A	89	286	28	77	10	5	0	32	13	1	16	.269	.303	.339	97	-3	13	.952	1	95	127	O81(54/25/2)		-0.
1919 StL A	88	252	21	63	12	5	1	34	18	0	27	.250	.300	.349	80	-7	1	.916	-4	98	18	3b70,O15(4/2/9)		-0
1920 StL A	103	353	45	108	21	8	3	55	13	1	18	.306	.336	.436	100	-1	11-4	.878	-3	80	0	3b13,O4C		-0
1921 StL A	25	78	7	26	4	2	0	14	3	1	13	.333	.366	.513	115	1	0-0	.949	1	108	180	O43(3/4/36)/3		-1.
Was A	59	180	20	39	5	2	2	12	10	2		.217	.266	.300	46	-16	1-1	.944	1	107	166	O47(3/8/36),3b14		-1.
Year	84	258	27	65	9	4	2	26	13	3	23	.252	.296	.364	69	-14	1-1	.917	3	107	167	O47(47/0/2),3b2		-1.
1922 Was A	65	205	22	53	12	2	1	23	8	9	17	.259	.311	.375	90	-32	36-8	.952	8	100	150	O318(136/68/114),3b86		-3
Total 7	495	1580	176	429	72	32	9	186	82		127	.272	.311	.375			36-8							

SMITH, EARL Earl Sutton "Oil" B2.14.1897 Hot Springs AR D6.8.1963 Little Rock AR BL/TR/5-10.5/180 d4.24

YEAR TM LG	G	AB	R	H	2B	3B	HR	RBI	BB-IB	HP	SO	AVG	OBP	SLG	AOPS	ABR	SB-CS	FA	FR	RNG	THR	GAMES AT POSITION	DL	BFW
1919 NY N	21	36	5	9	2	1	0	8	3	0	3	.250	.308	.361	102	0	1	.973	-2	88	86	C14/2		-0.
1920 NY N	91	262	20	77	7	1	0	30	18	0	16	.294	.344	.340	98	0	5-2	.976	1	124	76	C82		0
1921 NY N	89	229	35	77	8	4	10	51	20	1	8	.336	.409	.537	148	16	4-3	.965	-5	114	92	C78		1
1922 †NY N	90	234	29	65	11	4	9	39	37	3	12	.278	.383	.474	119	7	1-1	.978	1	133	72	C75		1

YEAR	TM LG	G	AB	R	H	2B	3B	HR	RBI	BB-IB	HP	SO	AVG	OBP	SLG	AOPS	ABR	SB-CS	FA	FR	RNG	THR	GAMES AT POSITION	DL	BFW
1923	NY N	24	34	2	7	1	1	1	4	4	0	1	.206	.289	.382	77	-1	0-0	.975	1	164	100	C12		0.0
	Bos N	72	191	22	55	15	1	3	19	22	1	10	.288	.364	.424	112	4	0-1	.975	-2	82	125	C54		0.5
	Year	96	225	24	62	16	2	4	23	26	1	11	.276	.353	.418	106	3	0-1	.975	-1	93	122	C66		0.5
1924	Bos N	33	59	1	16	3	0	0	8	6	0	3	.271	.338	.322	81	-1	0-1	.946	-2	83	109	C13		-0.2
	Pit N	39	111	12	41	10	1	4	21	13	0	4	.369	.435	.586	168	11	2-0	.974	2	154	60	C35		1.5
	Year	72	170	13	57	13	1	4	29	19	0	7	.335	.402	.494	140	11	2-1	.967	0	136	72	C48		1.3
1925	†Pit N	109	329	34	103	22	3	8	64	31	1	13	.313	.374	.471	107	4	4-1	.968	11	142	87	C96		2.0
1926	Pit N	105	292	29	101	17	2	2	46	28	2	7	.346	.407	.438	121	10	1	.964	5	119	84	C98		2.0
1927	†Pit N	66	189	16	51	3	1	5	25	21	1	11	.270	.346	.376	87	-3		.986	-0	135	61	C61		0.0
1928	Pit N	32	85	8	21	6	0	2	11	11	0	7	.247	.333	.388	85	-2		.967	-3	80	71	C28		-0.3
	†StL N	24	58	3	13	2	0	0	7	5	0	4	.224	.286	.259	42	-5	0	1.000	-0	127	58	C18		-0.4
	Year	56	143	11	34	8	0	2	18	16	0	11	.238	.314	.336	68	-6	0	.980	-3	98	66	C46		-0.7
1929	StL N	57	145	9	50	8	0	1	22	18	0	6	.345	.417	.421	107	3	0	.962	-3	115	80	C50		0.2
1930	StL N	8	10	0	0	0	0	0	0	3	0	1	.000	.231	.000	-36	-2	0	.913	0	128	200	C6		-0.1
Total	12	860	2264	225	686	115	19	46	355	247	11	106	.303	.374	.432	111	41	18-9	.971	5	123	83	C720/2		8.6

SMITH, EDGAR   Edgar Eugene B6.12.1862 Providence RI D11.3.1892 Providence RI BR/TR/5-10/160 d5.25 ▲

1883	Pro N	2	9	2	2	1	0	0	1	0		2	.222	.222	.333	64	0		1.000	-0	0	0	1b2,O2L		-0.1
	Phi N	1	4	1	3	0	0	0	1	0		0	.750	.750	.750	393	1		.000	-1	0	0	/POL		0.0
	Year	3	13	3	5	1	0	0	2	0		2	.385	.385	.462	158	1		1.000	-1	0	0	O3L,1b2/P		-0.1
1884	Was AA	14	57	5	5	0	1	0		1	0		.088	.103	.123	-30	-8		.794	4	350	814	O12R,P3		-0.2
1885	Pro N	1	4	0	1	0	0	0	0	0		0	.250	.250	.250	64	0		.750	0	148	0	/P		0.0
1890	Cle N	8	24	2	7	0	1	0	4	4	0	1	.292	.393	.375	126	1	0	.900	2	202	0	P6,O2R		0.1
Total	4	26	98	10	18	1	2	0	6	5	0	3	.184	.223	.235	47	-6	0	.816	5	286	828	O17(3/0/14),P11,1b2		-0.2

SMITH, MAYO   Edward Mayo B1.17.1915 New London MO D11.24.1977 Boynton Beach FL BL/TR/6-0/183 d6.24 M9

| 1945 | Phi A | 73 | 203 | 18 | 43 | 5 | 0 | 0 | 11 | 36 | 1 | 13 | .212 | .333 | .236 | 67 | -7 | 0-1 | .976 | -3 | 91 | 80 | O65(33/27/7) | | -1.4 |

SMITH, ELMER   Elmer Ellsworth B3.23.1868 Pittsburgh PA D11.3.1945 Pittsburgh PA BL/TL/5-11/178 d9.10 ▲

1886	Cin AA	9	28	6	8	1	1	0	2	9	0		.286	.459	.393	163	3	0	.600	-2	24	0	P9/OL		-0.1
1887	Cin AA	52	186	26	47	10	6	0	23	11	1		.253	.298	.371	84	-5	5	.851	-6	74	105	P52,O2C		-0.2
1888	Cin AA	40	129	15	29	4	1	0	9	20	0		.225	.329	.271	88	-1	2	.838	-6	76	0	P40,O2C		-0.3
1889	Cin AA	29	83	12	23	3	1	2	17	7	2	18	.277	.348	.410	112	5	1	.821	-4	52	0	P29		0.0
1892	Pit N	138	511	86	140	16	14	4	63	82	1	43	.274	.375	.384	129	20	22	.885	-7	73	0	O124(115/2/7),P17		0.0
1893	Pit N	128	518	121	179	26	23	7	103	77	5	23	.346	.435	.525	158	44	26	.921	4	92	160	O128L		2.9
1894	Pit N	126	490	128	175	33	19	6	74	68	5	12	.357	.440	.533	136	31	34	.933	2	83	154	O126(121/5/0)/P		1.7
1895	Pit N	125	484	89	146	15	12	1	81	55	6	25	.302	.380	.388	104	5	34	.897	-3	85	48	O124L		-0.7
1896	Pit N	122	484	121	175	21	14	6	94	74	8	18	.362	.454	.500	158	46	33	.946	8	80	137	O122L		3.6
1897	Pit N	123	467	99	145	19	17	6	54	70	2		.310	.408	.463	136	25	25	.904	3	110	30	O123L		1.6
1898	Cin N	123	486	79	166	21	10	1	66	69	2		.342	.425	.432	136	26	20	.949	2	84	120	O123L/P		1.6
1899	Cin N	88	343	65	101	13	6	1	24	47	1		.294	.381	.376	106	4	10	.923	-2	88	85	O88(38/28/22)		-0.3
1900	Cin N	29	111	14	31	4	4	1	18	18	2		.279	.389	.414	125	4	5	.930	-1	74	95	O27L		-0.1
	NY N	85	312	47	81	9	7	2	34	24	2		.260	.317	.353	89	-6	14	.953	-6	95	63	O83R		0.1
	Year	114	423	61	112	13	11	3	52	42	4		.265	.337	.369	99	-1	19	.944	-7	89	72	O110(27/0/83)		-1.4
1901	Pit N	4	4	0	0	0	0	0	0	2	0		.000	.333	.000	1	0		1.000	-0	0	0	/OL		-1.3
	Bos N	16	57	5	10	2	1	0	3	6	0		.175	.254	.246	41	-4	2	.833	-2	55	0	O15(4/0/11)		0.0
	Year	20	61	5	10	2	1	0	3	8	0		.164	.261	.230	40	-5	2	.846	-2	52	0	O16(5/0/11)		-0.7
Total	14	1237	4693	913	1456	197	136	37	665	639	42	139	.310	.398	.434	126	198	233	.922	-21	86	89	O1089(927/39/123),P149		7.8

SMITH, ELMER   Elmer John B9.21.1892 Sandusky OH D8.3.1984 Columbia KY BL/TR/5-10/165 d9.20 Mil 1918

1914	Cle A	13	53	5	17	3	0	0	8	2	0	11	.321	.345	.377	113	1	1-1	1.000	1	103	122	O13C		0.0
1915	Cle A	144	476	37	118	23	12	3	67	36	0	35	.248	.301	.366	97	-4	10-11	.923	-0	105	101	O123(21/0/102)		-1.3
1916	Cle A	79	213	25	59	15	3	3	40	18	1	35	.277	.336	.418	119	5	3	.966	-0	94	111	O57(1/0/56)		0.2
	Was A	45	168	12	36	10	3	2	27	18	2	28	.214	.298	.345	94	-2	4	.988	2	111	101	O45(10/0/35)		-0.2
	Year	124	381	37	95	25	6	5	67	36	3	63	.249	.319	.386	108	3	7	.976	2	102	107	O102(11/0/91)		0.0
1917	Was A	35	117	8	26	4	3	0	17	5	1	14	.222	.260	.308	74	-4	1	.901	-0	107	103	O29(27/0/2)		-0.7
	Cle A	64	161	21	42	5	1	3	22	13	0	18	.261	.316	.360	90	-1	6	.986	0	100	99	O40(8/0/32)		-0.2
	Year	99	278	29	68	9	4	3	39	18	1	32	.245	.293	.338	89	-5	7	.943	0	103	101	O69(35/0/34)		-0.9
1919	Cle A	114	395	60	110	24	6	9	54	41	5	30	.278	.354	.438	115	8	15	.957	-4	90	83	O111R		-0.2
1920	†Cle A	129	456	82	144	37	10	12	103	53	2	46	.316	.391	.520	135	23	5-4	.970	-6	101	48	O129R		1.0
1921	Cle A	129	431	98	125	28	9	16	85	56	2	46	.290	.374	.508	121	13	0-2	.971	-3	90	104	O127(1/0/126)		0.0
1922	Bos A	73	231	43	66	13	6	6	32	25	1	21	.286	.358	.472	116	5	0-3	.947	3	112	104	O58(0/1/57)		0.2
	†NY A	21	27	1	5	0	0	1	5	3	0	5	.185	.267	.296	46	-2	0-0	.933	1	116	145	O11(2/0/9)		-0.2
	Year	94	258	44	71	13	6	7	37	28	1	26	.275	.348	.453	108	2	0-3	.945	3	112	112	O69(2/1/66)		0.0
1923	NY A	70	183	30	56	6	2	7	35	21	0	21	.306	.377	.475	121	5	3-1	.948	1	107	91	O47R		0.3
1925	Cin N	96	284	47	77	13	7	8	46	28	1	20	.271	.339	.451	102	0	6-5	.967	-1	94	105	O80(53/2/26)		-0.6
Total	10	1012	3195	469	881	181	62	70	541	319	16	359	.276	.344	.437	112	47	54-27	.957	-9	100	93	O870(123/16/732)		-1.7

SMITH, MIKE   Elwood Hope B11.16.1904 Norfolk VA D5.31.1981 Chesapeake VA BL/TR/5-11.5/170 d9.4 Col William and Mary

| 1926 | NY N | 4 | 7 | 0 | 1 | 0 | 0 | 0 | 0 | 2 | 0 | 2 | .143 | .143 | .143 | -23 | -1 | 0 | 1.000 | 0 | 129 | 0 | /OL | | -0.1 |

SMITH, CARR   Emanuel Carr B4.8.1901 Kernersville NC D4.14.1989 Miami FL BR/TR/6-1/175 d9.23

1923	Was A	5	9	0	1	0	0	0		0	0	0	.111	.111	.222	-14	-2	0-0	1.000	-0	86	0	O4C		-0.2
1924	Was A	5	10	1	2	0	0	0	0	1	0	3	.200	.200	.200	-3	-1	0-0	1.000	-0	97	0	O4R		-0.2
Total	2	10	19	1	3	0	0	0	1	0	0	3	.158	.158	.211	-5	-3	0-0	1.000	-1	91	0	O8(0/4/4)		-0.4

SMITH, ERNIE   Ernest Henry "Kansas City Kid" B10.11.1899 Totowa NJ D4.6.1973 Brooklyn NY BR/TR/5-8/155 d4.17

| 1930 | Chi A | 24 | 79 | 5 | 19 | 3 | 0 | 0 | 3 | 5 | 0 | 6 | .241 | .286 | .278 | 45 | -7 | | .920 | -2 | 95 | 64 | S21 | | -0.6 |

SMITH, FRANK   Frank L. B11.24.1857 Fonthill ON, Can. D10.11.1928 Canandaigua NY BR/5-10/175 d8.6

| 1884 | Pit AA | 10 | 36 | 3 | 9 | 0 | 1 | 0 | 0 | 0 | | | .250 | .250 | .306 | 81 | -1 | | .930 | -1 | | | C7,O3(1/1/1) | | -0.2 |

SMITH, FRED   Fred Vincent B7.29.1886 Cleveland OH D5.28.1961 Cleveland OH BR/TR/5-11.5/185 d4.17 b-Charlie

1913	Bos N	92	285	35	65	9	3	0	27	29	1	55	.228	.302	.281	65	-12	7-11	.920	-10	82	55	3b59,2b14,S11,O4(2/1/1)		-2.3
1914	Buf F	145	473	48	104	12	10	2	45	49	3	78	.220	.297	.300	62	-34	24	.930	-3	95	75	3b127,S19/1		-3.4
1915	Buf F	35	114	8	27	2	4	0	11	13	1	15	.237	.320	.325	80	-5	2	.920	3	101	111	S32/3		0.0
	Bro F	110	385	41	95	16	6	5	58	25	3	49	.247	.298	.358	85	-15	21	.920	-2	101	63	S94,3b15		-1.1
	Year	145	499	49	122	18	10	5	69	38	4	64	.244	.303	.351	84	-20	23	.920	1	101	75	S126,3b16		-1.1
1917	StL N	56	165	11	30	0	1	1	17	17	1	22	.182	.262	.224	51	-9	4	.920	6	112	63	3b51,2b2/S		-0.3
Total	4	438	1422	143	321	39	25	8	158	133	9	219	.226	.296	.305	69	-75	58-11	.932	-7	98	76	3b253,S157,2b16,O4(2/1/1)/1		-7.1

SMITH, GEORGE   George Cornelius B7.7.1937 St.Petersburg FL D6.15.1987 St.Petersburg FL BR/TR/5-10/168* d8.4 Col Michigan St.

1963	Det A	52	171	16	37	8	2	0	17	18-1	2	34	.216	.298	.287	63	-8	4-0	.982	7	112	89	2b52		0.4
1964	Det A	5	7	1	2	0	0	0	2	1-0	0	1	.286	.375	.286	86	0	1-0	1.000	-0	94	160	2b3		0.0
1965	Det A	32	53	6	5	0	0	1	1	3-0	0	18	.094	.143	.151	-16	-7	0-0	.984	-2	88	123	2b22,S3,3b3		-1.0
1966	Bos A	128	403	41	86	19	4	8	37	37-6	3	89	.213	.283	.340	77	-15	4-0	.969	2	99	110	2b109,S19		-0.2
Total	4	217	634	64	130	27	6	9	57	59-7	5	142	.205	.277	.309	62	-31	9-0	.974	6	102	105	2b186,S22,3b3		-0.8

SMITH, HEINIE   George Henry B10.24.1871 Pittsburgh PA D6.25.1939 Buffalo NY BR/TR/5-9.5/160 d9.8 M1 ▲

1897	Lou N	21	76	7	20	3	0	1	7	3	1		.263	.300	.342	72	-3		.928	-2	93	111	2b21		-0.4
1898	Lou N	35	121	14	23	4	0	0	13	6	3		.190	.246	.223	35	-10	6	.910	-7	92	64	2b33		-1.5
1899	Pit N	15	53	9	15	3	1	0	12	5	0		.283	.345	.377	98	-5	2	.851	-5	96	51	2b15/S		-0.4
1901	NY N	9	29	5	6	2	1	0	4	1	0		.207	.233	.448	99	0	1	.969	-1	93	0	2b7,P2		-0.1
1902	NY N	140	517	48	129	19	2	0	34	17	3		.250	.277	.294	77	-15	32	.954	5	98	113	2b140,M		-0.9
1903	Det A	93	336	36	75	11	3	1	22	19	3		.223	.271	.283	68	-13	12	.928	-1	98	89	2b93		-1.3
Total	6	313	1132	119	268	42	7	3	92	51	10		.237	.276	.294	71	-41	54	.935	-11	97	95	2b309,P2/S		-4.6

YEAR	TM LG	G	AB	R	H	2B	3B	HR	RBI	BB-IB	HP	SO	AVG	OBP	SLG	AOPS	ABR	SB-CS	FA	FR	RNG	THR	GAMES AT POSITION	DL	BFW

SMITH, GERMANY George J. B4.21.1863 Pittsburgh PA D12.1.1927 Altoona PA BR/TR/6-0/175 d4.17

YEAR	TM LG	G	AB	R	H	2B	3B	HR	RBI	BB-IB	HP	SO	AVG	OBP	SLG	AOPS	ABR	SB-CS	FA	FR	RNG	THR	GAMES AT POSITION	DL
1884	Alt U	25	108	9	34	8	1	0		1			.315	.321	.407	118	-1		.871	5	122	20	S25/P	0.5
	Cle N	72	291	31	74	14	4	4	26	2		45	.254	.275	.371	93	-3		.879	6	96	123	2b42,S30	0.5
1885	Bro AA	108	419	63	108	17	11	6	62	10	0		.258	.275	.379	105	0		.884	40	127	77	S108	3.9
1886	Bro AA	105	426	66	105	17	6	2	45	19	0		.246	.279	.329	89	-7	22	.860	12	112	94	S105/OLC	0.8
1887	Bro AA	103	435	79	128	19	16	4	72	13	1		.294	.316	.439	108	1	26	.886	30	123	84	S101,3b2	2.7
1888	Bro AA	103	402	47	86	10	7	3	61	22	0		.214	.255	.296	76	-12	27	.844	1	103	130	S103/2	-0.7
1889	†Bro AA	121	446	89	103	22	3	3	53	40	1	42	.231	.296	.314	73	-16	35	.899	-6	99	92	S120/OR	-1.6
1890	†Bro N	129	481	76	92	6	5	1	47	42	3	23	.191	.260	.231	43	-36	24	.904	1	106	114	S129	-2.7
1891	Cin N	138	512	50	103	11	5	3	53	38	1	32	.201	.258	.260	50	-34	16	.920	23	119	113	S139	2.4
1892	Cin N	139	506	58	123	13	6	3	63	42	0	52	.243	.301	.340	95	-5	19	.920	23	119	113	S139	-0.6
1893	Cin N	130	500	63	118	18	6	4	56	38	2	20	.236	.293	.320	61	-30	14	.934	16	110	124	S130	-0.3
1894	Cin N	129	492	73	130	34	6	3	79	41	2	28	.264	.323	.376	66	-29	15	.910	19	116	130	S129	-0.3
1895	Cin N	127	503	75	151	23	6	4	74	34	0	24	.300	.345	.394	87	-12	13	.923	1	104	110	S127	-1.4
1896	Cin N	120	456	65	131	21	9	3	71	28	1	22	.287	.330	.393	84	-13	22	.926	-10	100	102	S120	-4.3
1897	Bro N	112	428	47	86	17	3	0	29	14	4		.201	.233	.255	30	-44	1	.908	-11	106	84	S112	-1.1
1898	StL N	51	157	16	25	2	1	1	9	24	1		.159	.275	.204	37	-12	1	.904	-6	105	67	S51	-4.2
Total	15	1712	6562	907	1597	252	95	47	800	408	16	288	.243	.289	.332	74	-253	235	.902	135	111	100	S1667,2b43,3b2,O2(1/0/1)/CP

SMITH, JUD Grant Judson B1.13.1869 Green Oak MI D12.7.1947 Los Angeles CA BR/TR/6-0/185 d5.21 Col Ohio St.

YEAR	TM LG	G	AB	R	H	2B	3B	HR	RBI	BB-IB	HP	SO	AVG	OBP	SLG	AOPS	ABR	SB-CS	FA	FR	RNG	THR	GAMES AT POSITION	DL
1893	Cin N	17	43	7	10	1	0	0	5	9	0	5	.233	.365	.326	82	-1	1	.750	-1	82	0	O9(1/0/8),3b6/S	-0.1
	StL N	4	13	1	1	0	0	0	0	1	1	2	.077	.200	.077	-25	-2	0	.889	1	100	296	3b4	-0.1
	Year	21	56	8	11	1	0	0	5	10	1	7	.196	.328	.268	58	-3	1	.844	-1	117	381	3b10,O9(1/0/8)/S	-0.1
1896	Pit N	10	35	6	12	2	1	0	4	2	1	2	.343	.378	.457	129	2	3	.909	0	88	178	3b10	0.1
1898	Was N	66	234	33	71	7	5	3	28	28	6		.303	.378	.415	127	8	11	.903	-6	79	85	3b47,S10,1b7/2	0.1
1901	Pit N	6	21	1	3	1	0	0	0	3	0		.143	.250	.190	28	-2	0	.947	0	106	0	3b6	-0.1
Total	4	103	346	48	97	11	6	3	41	37	8	9	.280	.363	.382	109	5	15	.900	-7	87	126	3b73,S11,O9(1/0/8),1b7/2

SMITH, GREG Gregory Alan B4.5.1967 Baltimore MD BB/TR/5-11/170* [ChiN85 2/52] d9.2

YEAR	TM LG	G	AB	R	H	2B	3B	HR	RBI	BB-IB	HP	SO	AVG	OBP	SLG	AOPS	ABR	SB-CS	FA	FR	RNG	THR	GAMES AT POSITION	DL
1989	Chi N	4	5	1	2	0	0	0	2	0-0	1	0	.400	.500	.400	150	0	0-0	.778	-1	68	118	2b2	0.1
1990	Chi N	18	44	9	9	2	1	0	5	2-0	0	5	.205	.234	.295	43	-4	1-0	1.000	3	118	105	2b7,S7	-0.1
1991	LA N	5	3	1	0	0	0	0	0	0-0	0	2	.000	.000	.000	-99	-1	0-0	—	0	0	0	/2	-0.1
Total	3	27	52	6	11	2	1	0	7	2-0	1	7	.212	.250	.288	47	-5	1-0	.944	2	105	106	2b10,S7

SMITH, HAL Harold Raymond "Cura" B6.1.1931 Barling AR BR/TR/5-11/189* d5.2 C8

YEAR	TM LG	G	AB	R	H	2B	3B	HR	RBI	BB-IB	HP	SO	AVG	OBP	SLG	AOPS	ABR	SB-CS	FA	FR	RNG	THR	GAMES AT POSITION	DL	BFW
1956	StL N	75	227	27	64	11	0	5	23	15-4	0	22	.282	.326	.401	94	-2	1-0	.982	-2	90	98	C66		-0.1
1957	StL N☆	100	333	25	93	12	3	2	37	18-2	0	18	.279	.314	.351	78	-11	2-2	.990	0	107	97	C97		-0.1
1958	StL N	77	220	13	50	4	1	1	24	14-4	0	14	.227	.272	.268	42	-18	0-0	.989	-3	67	75	C71		-0.1
1959	StL N★	142	452	35	122	15	3	13	50	15-6	1	28	.270	.295	.403	78	-15	2-6	.989	15	133	120	C124		0
1960	StL N	127	337	20	77	16	0	2	28	29-13	1	33	.228	.291	.294	56	-20	0-0	.990	15	126	118	C45		1.1
1961	StL N	45	125	6	31	4	1	0	10	11-4	1	12	.248	.309	.296	57	-7	0-0	1.000	1	0	0	C4	104	0
1965	Pit N	4	3	0	0	0	0	0	0	0-0	0	1	.000	.000	.000	-99	-1	0-0	1.000	0	0	0		104	-2
Total	7	570	1697	126	437	63	8	23	172	102-33	3	128	.258	.300	.345	69	-74	6-8	.989	32	105	108	C548

SMITH, HAL Harold Wayne B12.7.1930 W.Frankfort IL BR/TR/6-0/195* d4.11

YEAR	TM LG	G	AB	R	H	2B	3B	HR	RBI	BB-IB	HP	SO	AVG	OBP	SLG	AOPS	ABR	SB-CS	FA	FR	RNG	THR	GAMES AT POSITION	DL
1955	Bal A	135	424	41	115	23	4	4	52	30-2	2	21	.271	.318	.373	93	-6	1-3	.986	-4	77	141	C125	0
1956	Bal A	77	229	16	60	14	0	3	18	17-3	1	22	.262	.315	.362	85	-5	1-0	.994	3	74	108	C71	0
	KC A	37	142	15	39	9	2	2	24	3-0	0	12	.275	.284	.408	82	-4	1-1	.986	1	86	121	C37	0
	Year	114	371	31	99	23	2	5	42	20-3	1	34	.267	.303	.380	85	-10	2-1	.991	4	79	113	C108	0
1957	KC A	107	360	41	109	26	0	13	44	14-0	1	44	.303	.328	.483	118	-8	2-2	.983	-1	89	74	C103	1
1958	KC A	99	315	32	86	19	2	5	46	25-2	2	47	.273	.323	.394	97	-1	0-0	.949	-2	97	99	3b43,C31,1b14	0
1959	KC A	108	292	36	84	12	0	5	31	34-0	3	39	.288	.367	.380	104	3	0-3	.953	2	95	87	3b77,C22	0
1960	†Pit N	77	258	37	76	18	2	11	45	22-0	2	48	.295	.351	.508	132	11	1-1	.985	-4	150	52	C71	-1
1961	Pit N	67	193	12	43	10	0	3	26	11-1	1	38	.223	.267	.321	55	-12	0-0	.990	-4	75	107	C92,3b6,1b2	-1
1962	Hou N	109	345	32	81	14	0	12	35	24-1	2	55	.235	.286	.380	84	-9	0-0	.986	-2	149	62	C11	-0
1963	Hou N	31	58	1	14	2	0	0	2	4-1	0	15	.241	.290	.276	48	-2	0-0	.983	-6	96	106	C20	-1
1964	Cin N	32	66	6	8	1	0	0	3	12-2	0	20	.121	.256	.136	14	-7	1-0	.983	-6	96	106	C20	-1
Total	10	879	2682	269	715	148	10	58	323	196-12	14	361	.267	.317	.394	94	-24	7-10	.986	-18	100	95	C648,3b126,1b16

SMITH, HARRY Harry Thomas B10.31.1874 Yorkshire, England D2.17.1933 Salem NJ BR/TR/5-8.5/165 d7.11 M1

YEAR	TM LG	G	AB	R	H	2B	3B	HR	RBI	BB-IB	HP	SO	AVG	OBP	SLG	AOPS	ABR	SB-CS	FA	FR	RNG	THR	GAMES AT POSITION
1901	Phi A	11	34	3	11	1	0	0	3	2	1		.324	.378	.353	99	0	1	.969	-2	83	110	C9/OR
1902	Pit N	50	185	14	35	4	1	0	12	4	1		.189	.211	.222	32	-15	4	.972	2	146	77	C50
1903	†Pit N	61	212	15	37	3	2	0	19	12	1		.175	.222	.208	22	-22	2	.974	1	136	90	C60/OR
1904	Pit N	47	141	17	35	3	1	0	18	16	5		.248	.346	.284	92	0	5	.964	-1	104	111	C44,O3(2/0/1)
1905	Pit N	1	3	0	0	0	0	0	0	0	0		.000	.000	.000	-98	-1	1	1.000	0	117	105	/C
1906	Pit N	1	1	0	0	0	0	0	0	0	0		.000	.000	.000	-96	0	0	.800	1	0	0	/C
1907	Pit N	18	38	4	10	1	0	0	1	4	2		.263	.364	.289	103	1	0	.939	-1	124	106	C18
1908	Bos N	41	130	13	32	2	1	1	16	7	1		.246	.295	.315	96	-1	2	.975	-2	89	112	C38
1909	Bos N	43	113	9	19	4	1	0	4	5	0		.168	.203	.221	30	-10	3	.972	1	87	98	C31,M
1910	Bos N	70	147	8	35	4	0	1	15	5	0	14	.238	.263	.286	57	-8	5	.949	-2	87	127	C38
Total	10	343	1004	83	214	22	7	2	89	55	12	14	.213	.262	.255	54	-56	23	.967	-4	113	100	C290,O5(2/0/3)

SMITH, HARRY Harry W. B2.5.1856 N.Vernon IN D6.4.1898 Queensville IN BR/TR/6-0/175 d5.8

YEAR	TM LG	G	AB	R	H	2B	3B	HR	RBI	BB-IB	HP	SO	AVG	OBP	SLG	AOPS	ABR	SB-CS	FA	FR	RNG	THR	GAMES AT POSITION
1877	Chi N	24	94	7	19	1	0	0	3	4		6	.202	.235	.213	37	-7		.853	-7	80	45	2b14,O10(0/7/3)
	Cin N	10	36	4	9	2	1	0	3	1		5	.250	.270	.361	109	1		.879	-1			C8,2b3,O3C
	Year	34	130	11	28	3	1	0	6	5		11	.215	.244	.254	54	-7		.837	-8	78	40	2b17,O13(0/10/3),C8
1889	Lou AA	1	2	0	1	0	0	0	1	0	0	1	.500	.500	.500	189	0	0	—	-1	0	0	/OCC
Total	2	35	132	11	29	3	1	0	7	5	0	12	.220	.248	.258	56	-6	0	.853	-9	78	40	2b17,O14(0/11/3),C9

SMITH, HARVEY Harvey Fetterhoff B7.24.1871 Union Deposit PA D11.12.1962 Harrisburg PA BL/TR/5-8/160 d8.19 Col Bucknell

YEAR	TM LG	G	AB	R	H	2B	3B	HR	RBI	BB-IB	HP	SO	AVG	OBP	SLG	AOPS	ABR	SB-CS	FA	FR	RNG	THR	GAMES AT POSITION
1896	Was N	36	131	21	36	7	2	0	17	12	2	7	.275	.345	.359	86	-3	9	.861	1	117	85	3b36

SMITH, HAPPY Henry Joseph B7.14.1883 Coquille OR D2.26.1961 San Jose CA BR/TR/6-0/185 d4.15

YEAR	TM LG	G	AB	R	H	2B	3B	HR	RBI	BB-IB	HP	SO	AVG	OBP	SLG	AOPS	ABR	SB-CS	FA	FR	RNG	THR	GAMES AT POSITION
1910	Bro N	35	76	6	18	2	0	0	6	14	2	4	.237	.275	.263	59	-4	4	.974	2	106	172	O16(0/5/11)

SMITH, JACK Jack B6.23.1895 Chicago IL D5.2.1972 Westchester IL BL/TL/5-8/165 d9.30 Mil 1918

YEAR	TM LG	G	AB	R	H	2B	3B	HR	RBI	BB-IB	HP	SO	AVG	OBP	SLG	AOPS	ABR	SB-CS	FA	FR	RNG	THR	GAMES AT POSITION
1915	StL N	4	16	3	2	0	1	0	1	0	0	5	.188	.235	.313	65	-1	0	1.000	-1	70	0	O4(3/1/0)
1916	StL N	130	357	43	87	6	5	6	34	20	4	50	.244	.291	.339	94	-4	24-16	.949	-4	92	98	O120(1/109/11)
1917	StL N	137	462	64	137	16	11	3	34	38	1	65	.297	.351	.398	133	18	25	.961	-11	86	72	O128(27/65/37)
1918	StL N	42	166	24	35	2	1	0	4	7	4	21	.211	.260	.235	53	-9	5	.941	0	85	167	O42C
1919	StL N	119	408	47	91	16	3	0	15	26	1	29	.223	.271	.277	69	-15	30	.960	2	95	132	O111(1/36/76)
1920	StL N	91	313	53	104	22	5	1	28	25	2	23	.332	.385	.444	143	18	14-9	.963	2	89	128	O83(18/57/14)
1921	StL N	116	411	86	135	22	9	7	33	21	0	24	.328	.361	.477	122	12	11-6	.951	-5	98	73	O136(17/79/40)
1922	StL N	143	510	117	158	23	12	8	46	50	3	30	.310	.375	.449	117	13	18-7	.974	7	113	106	O109(77/10/23)
1923	StL N	124	407	98	126	16	6	5	41	27	2	20	.310	.356	.415	105	2	32-11	.974	8	108	140	O114(25/14/77)
1924	StL N	124	459	91	130	18	6	2	33	33	1	27	.283	.333	.362	88	-3	24-16	.958	1	105	104	O64(5/38/28)
1925	StL N	80	243	53	61	11	4	4	31	19	1	14	.251	.308	.379	73	-11	20-2	—	0			/H
1926	StL N	1	1	0	0	0	0	0	0	0	0	1	.000	.000	.000	-96	0		.973	2	105	99	O83(10/59/15)
	Bos N	96	322	46	100	15	2	2	25	28	2	13	.311	.369	.388	114	7	11	.973	2	105	99	O83(10/59/15)
	Year	97	323	46	100	15	2	2	25	28	2	14	.310	.368	.387	113	7	11	.950	2	106	137	O48(3/14/32)
1927	Bos N	84	183	27	58	6	4	1	24	16	1	12	.317	.375	.410	119	5	8	.988	2	109	75	O65(18/40/7)
1928	Bos N	96	254	30	71	9	2	1	32	20	0	14	.280	.335	.343	82	-7	6	.833	-1	108	0	O9(2/4/3)
1929	Bos N	19	20	2	5	0	0	0	0	2	2	2	.250	.318	.250	45	-2	0					
Total	15	1406	4532	783	1301	182	71	40	382	334	22	348	.287	.339	.385	103	18	228-67	.961	-1	99	104	O1219(207/587/447)

YEAR	TM LG	G	AB	R	H	2B	3B	HR	RBI	BB-IB	HP	SO	AVG	OBP	SLG	AOPS	ABR	SB-CS	FA	FR	RNG	THR	GAMES AT POSITION	DL	BFW

SMITH, STUB   James A.   B11.26.1876 Elmwood IL   BL/TR/5-6/145   d9.10

| 1898 | Bos N | 3 | 10 | 1 | 1 | 0 | 0 | 0 | 0 | 0 | 0 | | .100 | .100 | .100 | -41 | -2 | 0 | .933 | 0 | 111 | 0 | S3 | | -0.2 |

SMITH, RED   James Carlisle   B4.6.1890 Greenville SC   D10.11.1966 Atlanta GA   BR/TR/5-11/165   d9.5   Col Auburn-Montgomery

1911	Bro N	28	111	10	29	6	1	0	19	5	1	13	.261	.299	.333	80	-3	5	.900	-2	99	178	3b28		-0.4
1912	Bro N	128	486	75	139	28	6	4	57	54	4	51	.286	.362	.393	111	8	22	.938	7	106	95	3b125		1.8
1913	Bro N	151	540	70	160	40	10	6	76	45	7	67	.296	.358	.441	124	17	22-19	.933	-2	103	65	3b151		1.8
1914	Bro N	90	330	39	81	10	8	4	48	30	1	26	.245	.310	.361	97	-2	11	.937	13	108	129	3b90		1.4
	Bos N	60	207	30	65	17	1	3	37	28	2	24	.314	.401	.449	153	15	4	.937	6	108	139	3b60		2.4
	Year	150	537	69	146	27	9	7	85	58	3	50	.272	.346	.395	119	13	15	.937	18	108	133	3b150		3.8
1915	Bos N	**157**	549	66	145	34	4	2	65	67	3	49	.264	.345	.352	116	14	10-5	.947	-6	94	129	3b157		1.4
1916	Bos N	150	509	48	132	16	10	3	60	53	3	55	.259	.333	.348	114	9	13	.928	-5	97	75	3b150		1.0
1917	Bos N	147	505	60	149	31	6	2	62	53	6	61	.295	.369	.392	142	27	16	.925	-23	85	111	3b147		1.0
1918	Bos N	119	429	55	128	20	3	2	65	45	6	47	.298	.373	.373	133	19	8	.922	3	**110**	78	3b119		2.9
1919	Bos N	87	241	24	59	6	1	0	25	40	3	22	.245	.359	.282	98	-2	1	.981	2	104	55	O48(17/30/3),3b23		0.2
Total 9		1117	3907	477	1087	208	49	27	514	420	34	415	.278	.353	.377	120	106	117-24	.932	-6	100	101	3b1050,O48(17/30/3)		13.5

SMITH, HARRY   James Harry   B5.15.1890 Brooklyn NY   D4.1.1922 Charlotte NC   BR/TR/5-10/180   d9.21

1914	NY N	5	7	0	3	0	0	0	2	3	0	1	.429	.600	.429	215	1	1	1.000	1	166	76	C4		0.3
1915	NY N	21	32	1	4	0	1	0	3	6	0	12	.125	.263	.188	40	-2	0-1	.967	-2	87	69	C18		-0.4
	Bro F	28	65	5	13	0	1	0	4	7	0	16	.200	.278	.246	48	-6	2	.967	-4	77	95	C19/OR		-0.9
1917	Cin N	8	17	0	2	0	0	0	1	2	0	7	.118	.211	.118	2	-2	0	.978	2	119	130	C7		0.1
1918	Cin N	13	27	4	5	1	2	0	4	3	0	6	.185	.267	.370	95	0	1	1.000	-5	49	0	C6/OC		-0.1
Total 4		75	148	10	27	1	3	1	14	21	0	42	.182	.284	.250	59	-9	4-1	.975	-4	96	87	C54,O2(0/1/1)		-1.0

SMITH, JIMMY   James Lawrence "Greenfield Jimmy"   B5.15.1895 Pittsburgh PA   D1.1.1974 Pittsburgh PA   BB/TR (BR 1914)/5-9/152   d9.26   Col Duquesne

1914	Chi F	3	6	1	3	1	0	0	1	0	0	0	.500	.500	.667	229	1	0	1.000	1	113	434	S3		0.2
1915	Chi F	95	318	32	69	11	4	4	30	14	0	65	.217	.250	.314	62	-24	4	.904	-15	91	89	S92/2		-3.6
	Bal F	33	108	9	19	1	1	1	11	11	1	23	.176	.258	.231	37	-11	3	.883	-3	90	33	S33		-1.3
	Year	128	426	41	88	12	5	5	41	25	1	88	.207	.252	.293	55	-35	7	.898	-18	91	83	S125/2		-4.9
1916	Pit N	36	96	4	18	1	1	0	5	6	3	22	.188	.257	.219	44	-6	0	.929	-2	96	66	S27,3b6		-0.7
1917	NY N	36	96	12	22	5	1	0	9	9	0	18	.229	.295	.302	86	-1	6	.971	-1	105	60	2b29,S7		-0.2
1918	Bos N	34	102	8	23	3	4	1	14	3	1	13	.225	.255	.363	91	-2	1	1.000	-3	73	47	2b10,S9,O6(2/3/1),3b5		-0.5
1919	†Cin N	28	40	9	11	1	3	1	10	4	0	8	.275	.341	.525	163	3	1	1.000	-1	114	0	3b6,S5,2b4,O4(1/0/3)		0.2
1921	Phi N	67	247	31	57	8	1	4	22	11	1	28	.231	.266	.320	50	-18	2-8	.971	11	119	60	3b66		-0.8
1922	Phi N	38	114	13	25	1	0	1	6	5	1	9	.219	.258	.254	30	-12	1-3	.952	-1	93	120	S23,2b13/3		-1.2
Total 8		370	1127	119	247	32	15	12	108	63	7	186	.219	.265	.306	60	-70	18-11	.910	-15	92	89	S199,2b123,3b18,O10(3/3/4)		-7.9

SMITH, JIM   James Lorne   B9.8.1954 Santa Monica CA   BR/TR/6-3/185   (BalA76 6/140)   d4.12   Col Cal St.-Long Beach

| 1982 | Pit N | 42 | 42 | 5 | 10 | 2 | 1 | 0 | 4 | 5-0 | 0 | 7 | .238 | .313 | .333 | 79 | -1 | 0-1 | .929 | 0 | 94 | 101 | S29,2b3/3 | | 0.0 |

SMITH, JASON   Jason William   B7.24.1977 Meridian MS   BL/TR/6-3/195*   (ChiN96 23/682)   d6.17   Col Meridian (MS) CC

2001	Chi N	2	1	0	1	0	0	0	0	0-0	0	0	1.000	1.000	1.000		0	0	1.000	0	0	0	/S		0.0
2002	TB A	26	65	9	13	1	2	1	6	2-0	0	24	.200	.224	.323	44	-6	3-0	.962	-3	102	169	3b12,S9/2		-0.7
2003	TB A	1	4	0	1	0	0	0	0	0-0	0	0	.250	.250	.250	33	0	0	.500	-0	123	607	/3		-0.1
2004	Det A	61	155	20	37	7	4	5	19	8-0	1	37	.239	.280	.432	85	-4	1-2	.987	5	107	110	2b34,S20,3b5,D2		0.2
2005	Det A	27	58	4	11	1	2	0	2	0-0	1	16	.190	.203	.276	27	-6	2-1	1.000	4	129	131	S15,2b6,3b3/1D		-0.1
Total 5		117	283	33	62	9	8	6	27	10-0	2	78	.219	.251	.371	62	-16	6-3	.955	7	104	87	S45,2b41,3b21,D3/1		-0.7

SMITH, JOHN   John B Baltimore MD   d4.14

1873	Mar NA	5	19	2	2	0	0	0	1	0		1	.105	.105	.105	-49	-3	0-0	.773	-1	91	0	S3,O2L		-0.3
1874	Bal NA	6	21	2	4	1	0	0	1	0		1	.190	.190	.238	37	-1	0-0	.731	-2	64	0	S6		-0.3
Total 3	NA	1	3	0	0	0	0	0	0	1			.000	.250	.000	-6	0	0-0	.500	-1	58	0	/S		-0.1
	3 NA	12	43	4	6	1	0	0	2	1		2	.140	.159	.163	1	-4	0-0	.722	-4	73	0	S10,O2L		-0.7

SMITH, DWIGHT   John Dwight   B11.8.1963 Tallahassee FL   BL/TR/5-11/175(175-195)   (ChiN84 S3/62)   d5.1   Col Spartanburg Methodist (SC) JC

1989	†Chi N	109	343	52	111	19	6	9	52	31-0	2	51	.324	.382	.493	139	17	9-4	.975	4	104	141	O102(75/0/32)		2.0
1990	Chi N	117	290	34	76	15	0	6	27	28-2	2	46	.262	.329	.376	88	-4	11-6	.986	-0	98	82	O81(59/3/22)		-0.6
1991	Chi N	90	167	16	38	7	2	3	21	11-2	1	32	.228	.279	.347	72	-7	2-3	.962	0	100	126	O42(5/13/28)		-0.8
1992	Chi N	109	217	28	60	10	3	3	24	13-0	1	51	.276	.318	.392	98	-1	9-8	.979	-3	86	76	O63(20/27/22)		-0.7
1993	Chi N	111	310	51	93	17	5	11	35	25-1	3	51	.300	.355	.494	126	11	8-6	.955	-2	95	115	O89(14/53/28)		-0.7
1994	Cal A	45	122	19	32	5	1	5	18	7-0	0	20	.262	.300	.443	87	-3	2-3	.912	-1	98	107	O31L,D2	28	0.8
	Bal A	28	74	12	23	2	1	3	12	5-1	1	17	.311	.363	.486	110	1	0-1	.939	-3	81	0	O22(20/2/1),D3		-0.5
	Year	73	196	31	55	7	2	8	30	12-1	1	37	.281	.324	.459	96	-2	2-4	.922	-4	91	63	O53(51/2/1),D5		-0.8
1995	†Atl N	103	131	16	33	8	2	3	21	13-1	2	35	.252	.327	.412	90	-2	0-3	.923	-2	80	0	O25(11/0/14)		-0.6
1996	Atl N	101	153	16	31	6	1	3	16	17-1	1	42	.203	.285	.294	50	-11	1-3	.962	2	124	73	O29(3/0/26)		-0.6
Total 8		813	1807	244	497	88	20	46	226	150-8	13	334	.275	.333	.422	101	1	42-37	.964	-5	97	98	O484(238/98/173),D5	28	-1.8

SMITH, JACK   John Joseph "Big"   B1858 New York NY   D1.6.1899 San Francisco CA   BL/TR/5-11/210   d5.1

1882	Tro N	35	149	27	36	4	3	0	14	3		24	.242	.257	.309	84	-3		.960	-0	95	95	1b35		-0.5
	Wor N	19	70	10	17	3	2	0	5	5		10	.243	.293	.343	101	-3		.939	1	199	101	1b19		-0.1
	Year	54	219	37	53	7	5	0	19	8		34	.242	.269	.320	90	-3		.952	1	131	97	1b54		-0.6

SMITH, JACK   John Joseph (b John Joseph Coffey)   B8.8.1893 Oswayo PA   D12.4.1962 New York NY   BR/TR/5-9/?   d5.18

| 1912 | Det A | 1 | 0 | 0 | 0 | 0 | 0 | 0 | 0 | 0 | 0 | | — | — | — | — | 0 | | 1.000 | 0 | 86 | 1159 | /3 | | 0.0 |

SMITH, JOHN   John Marshall   B9.27.1906 Washington DC   D5.9.1982 Silver Spring MD   BR/TR/6-1/180   d9.17

| 1931 | Bos A | 4 | 15 | 2 | 2 | 0 | 0 | 0 | 1 | 2 | 0 | 1 | .133 | .235 | .133 | -1 | -2 | 1-0 | 1.000 | -1 | 0 | 31 | 1b4 | | -0.3 |

SMITH, KEITH   Keith Lavarne   B5.3.1953 Palmetto FL   BR/TR/5-9/175*   (TexA72 S4/48)   d8.2   Col Manatee (FL) CC

1977	Tex A	23	67	13	16	4	0	2	6	4-0	2	7	.239	.301	.388	85	-1	2-0	.975	-0	97	70	O22L		-0.2
1979	StL N	6	13	1	3	0	0	0	0	0-0	0	1	.231	.231	.231	26	-1	0-1	1.000	2	197	365	O5L		0.0
1980	StL N	24	31	3	4	1	0	0	2	2-1	0	2	.129	.182	.161	-3	-4	0-1	1.000	-0	109	0	O7(4/1/2)		-0.5
Total 3		53	111	17	23	5	0	2	8	6-1	2	10	.207	.261	.306	54	-6	2-1	.985	2	112	96	O34(31/1/2)		-0.7

SMITH, KEN   Kenneth Earl   B2.12.1958 Youngstown OH   BL/TR/6-1/195(195-213)   (AtlN76 1/3)   d9.22

1981	Atl N	5	3	0	1	1	0	0	0	0-0	0	1	.333	.333	.667	178	0	0-0	1.000	0	118	0	1b4		0.0
1982	Atl N	48	41	6	12	1	0	0	3	6-0	0	13	.293	.383	.317	96	0	0-0	1.000	-1	88	0	1b6,O3L		-0.1
1983	Atl N	30	12	2	2	0	0	0	2	1-0	0	5	.167	.231	.417	71	-1	1-0	1.000	2	277	132	1b13		0.1
Total 3		83	56	8	15	2	0	1	5	7-0	0	19	.268	.349	.357	95	-1	1-0	1.000	1	193	69	1b23,O3L		0.0

SMITH, L.   L.   d9.7

| 1882 | Bal AA | 1 | 3 | 0 | 0 | 0 | 0 | 0 | | 0 | | | .000 | .000 | .000 | -99 | -1 | | .500 | -1 | 0 | 0 | /OC | | -0.1 |

SMITH, PADDY   Lawrence Patrick   B5.16.1894 Pelham NY   D12.2.1990 New Rochelle NY   BL/TR/6-0/195   d7.6   Col Fordham

| 1920 | Bos A | 2 | 2 | 0 | 0 | 0 | 0 | 0 | 0 | 0 | 0 | | .000 | .000 | .000 | -99 | -1 | 0 | — | -0 | 0 | 0 | /C | | -0.1 |

SMITH, BULL   Lewis Oscar   B8.20.1880 Plum WV   D5.1.1928 Charleston WV   BR/TR/6-0/180   d8.30   Col West Virginia

1904	Pit N	13	42	2	6	0	1	0	3	0			.143	.163	.190	9	-5	0	.857	-0	123	0	O13(11/0/2)		-0.6
1906	Chi N	1	0	1	0	0	0	0	0	0	0		.000	.000	.000	-95	0	0	—	0			/H		0.0
1911	Was A	1	1	0	0	0	0	0	0	0			.000	.000	.000		0	0	—	0			/R		0.0
Total 3		15	43	3	6	0	1	0	3	0			.140	.159	.186	6	-5	0	.857	-0	123	0	O13(11/0/2)		-0.6

SMITH, LEO   Lionel H.   B5.13.1859 Brooklyn NY   D8.30.1935 Brooklyn NY   5-6/142   d8.28

| 1890 | Roc AA | 35 | 112 | 11 | 21 | 7 | 3 | 0 | 11 | 14 | 1 | | .188 | .283 | .250 | 62 | -5 | 1 | .948 | 6 | 104 | 146 | S35 | | 0.2 |

SMITH, LONNIE   Lonnie "Skates"   B12.22.1955 Chicago IL   BR/TR/5-9/170(170-195)   (PhiN74 1/3)   d9.2

| 1978 | Phi N | 17 | 4 | 6 | 1 | 0 | 0 | 0 | 0 | 4-0 | 0 | 0 | — | .500 | .000 | 49 | -1 | 4-0 | 1.000 | 1 | 94 | 529 | O11(10/1/1) | | 0.2 |
| 1979 | Phi N | 17 | 30 | 4 | 5 | 2 | 0 | 0 | 3 | 1-0 | 0 | 7 | .167 | .194 | .233 | 15 | -4 | 2-1 | 1.000 | 1 | 113 | 180 | O11(3/5/4) | | -0.3 |

YEAR	TM LG	G	AB	R	H	2B	3B	HR	RBI	BB-IB	HP	SO	AVG	OBP	SLG	AOPS	ABR	SB-CS	FA	FR	RNG	THR	GAMES AT POSITION	DL	BFW
1980	†Phi N	100	298	69	101	14	4	3	20	26-2	4	48	.339	.397	.443	126	12	33-13	.969	-7	88	37	O82(52/9/23)		0.5
1981	†Phi N	62	176	40	57	14	3	2	11	18-1	5	14	.324	.402	.472	139	10	21-10	.971	6	104	338	O51(8/23/24)		1.7
1982	†StL N★	156	592	**120**	182	35	8	8	69	64-2	9	74	.307	.381	.434	130	22	68-26	.970	1	95	135	O149(135/36/0)		2.5
1983	StL N	130	492	83	158	31	5	8	45	41-2	9	55	.321	.381	.453	130	21	43-18	.941	1	93	148	O126L	27	2.1
1984	StL N	145	504	77	126	20	4	6	49	70-0	9	90	.250	.349	.341	98	1	50-13	.948	-5	76	179	O140L		-0.3
1985	StL N	28	96	15	25	2	2	0	7	15-0	3	20	.260	.377	.323	98	1	12-6	1.000	-1	94	57	O28L		-0.9
	†KC A	120	448	77	115	23	4	6	41	41-0	4	69	.257	.321	.366	88	-7	40-7	.958	-4	88	143	O119L	21	0.2
1986	KC A	134	508	80	146	25	7	8	44	46-0	10	78	.287	.357	.411	106	5	26-9	.965	-0	105	68	O118L,D10		-0.6
1987	KC A	48	167	26	42	7	1	3	8	24-0	4	31	.251	.355	.359	89	-2	9-4	.915	-3	85	94	O32L,D15		-0.3
1988	Atl N	43	114	14	27	3	0	3	9	10-0	1	25	.237	.296	.342	80	-3	4-2	.968	1	104	113	O35L	24	4.8
1989	Atl N	134	482	89	152	34	4	21	79	76-3	11	95	.315	**.415**	.533	167	46	25-12	.993	3	110	41	O132L		1.5
1990	Atl N	135	466	72	142	27	9	9	42	58-3	6	69	.305	.384	.459	125	18	10-10	.956	9	110	73	O122L	20	-0.1
1991	†Atl N	122	353	58	97	19	1	7	44	50-3	5	64	.275	.377	.394	111	8	9-5	.965	-7	81	103	O99L		1.3
1992	†Atl N	84	158	23	39	8	2	6	33	17-1	3	37	.247	.324	.437	109	2	4-0	.954	1	110	153	O35L		1.1
1993	Pit N	94	199	35	57	5	4	6	24	43-2	5	42	.286	.422	.442	133	12	9-4	.981	-0	112	28	O60(58/3/0)		0.1
	Bal A	9	24	8	5	1	0	2	3	8-0	0	10	.208	.406	.500	136	2	0-0	1.000	0	66	442	O4L,D5	23	-0.4
1994	Bal A	35	59	13	12	3	0	0	2	11-0	1	20	.203	.333	.254	53	-4	1-0	1.000	1	61	839	D30,O2R		12.1
Total	17	1613	5170	909	1488	273	58	98	533	623-19	92	849	.288	.371	.420	117	140	370-140	.964	-9	96	114	O1356(1257/77/54),D60	115	

SMITH, MARK
Mark Edward B5.7.1970 Pasadena CA BR/TR/6-3/195(195-235) [BalA91 1/9] d5.14 Col USC

YEAR	TM LG	G	AB	R	H	2B	3B	HR	RBI	BB-IB	HP	SO	AVG	OBP	SLG	AOPS	ABR	SB-CS	FA	FR	RNG	THR	GAMES AT POSITION	DL	BFW
1994	Bal A	3	7	1	1	0	0	0	2	0-0	0	2	.143	.143	.143	-25	-1	0-0	1.000	1	190	0	O3R		-0.1
1995	Bal A	37	104	11	24	5	0	3	15	12-2	1	22	.231	.314	.365	75	-4	3-0	1.000	1	107	105	O32(15/0/17),D3		-0.3
1996	Bal A	27	78	9	19	2	0	4	10	3-0	1	20	.244	.298	.423	80	-3	0-2	.980	2	137	0	O20(12/0/8),D6	69	-0.2
1997	Pit N	71	193	29	55	13	1	9	35	28-1	0	36	.285	.374	.503	125	8	3-1	1.000	-0	83	169	O24(16/0/9),1b9,D5	23	0.5
1998	Pit N	59	128	18	25	6	0	2	13	10-0	3	26	.195	.264	.289	47	-10	7-0	.977	0	110	0	O24(16/0/9),1b6,D3	15	-1.0
2000	Fla N	104	192	22	47	8	1	5	27	17-1	2	54	.245	.310	.375	77	-8	2-0	1.000	1	105	62	O60(54/6/4)/1	24	-0.7
2001	Mon N	80	194	28	47	13	1	6	18	23-0	2	38	.242	.326	.412	91	-3	0-2	1.000	-1	104	0	O15(12/0/3)		-0.4
2003	Mil N	33	63	8	15	4	0	3	10	4-0	0	13	.238	.275	.444	86	-2	0-0	.960	-1	104	0	O15(12/0/3)		-0.3
Total	8	414	959	125	233	51	3	32	130	97-4	11	211	.243	.316	.403	85	-23	15-5	.993	6	104	91	O245(159/6/91),D18,1b16	131	-2.5

SMITH, RED
Marvin Harold B7.17.1899 Ashley IL D2.19.1961 Los Angeles CA BL/TR/5-7/165 d4.14

YEAR	TM LG	G	AB	R	H	2B	3B	HR	RBI	BB-IB	HP	SO	AVG	OBP	SLG	AOPS	ABR	SB-CS	FA	FR	RNG	THR	GAMES AT POSITION	DL	BFW
1925	Phi A	20	14	1	4	0	0	0	1	2	0	5	.286	.375	.286	65	-1	0-0	.864	-1	113	0	S16,3b2		-0.1

SMITH, MILT
Milton B3.27.1929 Columbus GA D4.11.1997 San Diego CA BR/TR/5-10/165 d7.21 Negro Lg 1949-50

YEAR	TM LG	G	AB	R	H	2B	3B	HR	RBI	BB-IB	HP	SO	AVG	OBP	SLG	AOPS	ABR	SB-CS	FA	FR	RNG	THR	GAMES AT POSITION	DL	BFW
1955	Cin N	36	102	15	20	3	1	3	8	13-0	1	24	.196	.293	.333	62	-6	2-2	.915	-1	105	87	3b28,2b5		-0.7

SMITH, NATE
Nathaniel Beverly B4.26.1935 Chicago IL BR/TR/5-11/170 d9.19 Col Tennessee St.

YEAR	TM LG	G	AB	R	H	2B	3B	HR	RBI	BB-IB	HP	SO	AVG	OBP	SLG	AOPS	ABR	SB-CS	FA	FR	RNG	THR	GAMES AT POSITION	DL	BFW
1962	Bal A	5	9	3	2	1	0	0	1	0-0	1	4	.222	.364	.333	95	0	0-0	1.000	-0	48	0	C3		0.0

SMITH, OLLIE
Orlin Hudson B10.19.1865 Mt.Vernon OH D2.14.1954 Torrance CA BL/TL d7.11

YEAR	TM LG	G	AB	R	H	2B	3B	HR	RBI	BB-IB	HP	SO	AVG	OBP	SLG	AOPS	ABR	SB-CS	FA	FR	RNG	THR	GAMES AT POSITION	DL	BFW
1894	Lou N	39	137	27	41	6	1	3	20	29	3	15	.299	.432	.423	115	6	13	.883	-3	78	0	O39R		0.1

SMITH, OZZIE
Osborne Earl "The Wizard of Oz" B12.26.1954 Mobile AL BB/TR/5-11/150(150-180) [SDN77 4/86] d4.7 HF2002 Col Cal Poly-San Luis Obispo

YEAR	TM LG	G	AB	R	H	2B	3B	HR	RBI	BB-IB	HP	SO	AVG	OBP	SLG	AOPS	ABR	SB-CS	FA	FR	RNG	THR	GAMES AT POSITION	DL	BFW
1978	SD N	159	590	69	152	17	6	1	46	47-0	0	43	.258	.311	.312	81	-17	40-12	.976	30	113	115	S159		3.5
1979	SD N	156	587	77	124	18	6	0	27	37-5	2	37	.211	.260	.262	46	-46	28-7	.976	20	112	96	S155		-0.7
1980	SD N	158	609	67	140	18	5	0	35	71-1	5	49	.230	.313	.276	71	-22	57-15	.974	39	117	117	S158		4.2
1981	SD N★	110	450	53	100	11	2	0	21	41-1	5	37	.222	.294	.256	62	-22	22-12	.976	22	115	98	S110		1.3
1982	†StL N★	140	488	58	121	24	1	2	43	68-12	1	32	.248	.339	.314	82	-8	25-5	.984	36	119	125	S139		4.7
1983	StL N★	159	552	69	134	30	6	3	50	64-9	1	36	.243	.321	.335	82	-12	34-7	.975	16	110	107	S158		2.6
1984	StL N	124	412	53	106	20	5	1	44	56-5	2	17	.257	.347	.337	96	0	35-7	.982	32	116	132	S124	36	5.0
1985	†StL N★	158	537	70	148	22	3	6	54	65-11	2	27	.276	.355	.361	102	3	31-8	.983	18	109	124	S158		4.3
1986	StL N★	153	514	67	144	19	4	0	54	79-13	2	27	.280	.376	.333	98	2	31-7	.978	-12	101	122	S144		1.1
1987	StL N★	158	600	104	182	40	4	0	75	89-3	1	36	.303	.392	.383	104	9	43-9	.987	12	108	122	S158		4.6
1988	StL N★	153	575	80	155	27	1	3	51	74-2	1	43	.270	.350	.336	97	1	57-9	.972	21	115	96	S150	12	2.7
1989	StL N★	155	593	82	162	30	8	2	50	55-3	2	33	.273	.335	.361	96	-2	29-7	.976	12	112	99	S153		-1.2
1990	StL N★	143	512	61	130	21	1	1	50	61-4	1	33	.254	.330	.305	77	-14	32-6	.980	-12	96	90	S140		2.1
1991	StL N★	150	550	96	157	30	3	3	50	83-2	1	36	.285	.380	.367	110	12	35-9	.985	16	111	125	S132	15	3.9
1992	StL N★	132	518	73	153	20	2	0	31	59-4	1	34	.295	.367	.342	104	5	43-9	.985	23	113	129	S134		2.5
1993	StL N★	141	545	75	157	22	6	1	53	43-1	1	18	.288	.337	.356	87	-9	21-8	.982	2	103	110	S96		-0.3
1994	StL N★	98	381	51	100	18	3	3	30	38-3	0	26	.262	.326	.349	77	-13	6-3	.982	3	105	130	S96	92	-0.5
1995	StL N★	44	156	16	31	5	1	0	11	17-0	2	12	.199	.282	.244	41	-13	4-3	.964	5	109	123	S41	20	0.8
1996	†StL N★	82	227	36	64	10	2	2	18	25-0	2	9	.282	.358	.370	92	-2	7-5	.969	7	106	121	S52		-0.3
Total	19	2573	9396	1257	2460	402	69	28	793	1072-79	33	589	.262	.337	.328	87	-148	580-148	.978	279	110	113	S2511	175	44.9

SMITH, KEITH
Patrick Keith B10.20.1961 Los Angeles CA BB/TR/6-1/175* [NYA79 15/389] d4.12

YEAR	TM LG	G	AB	R	H	2B	3B	HR	RBI	BB-IB	HP	SO	AVG	OBP	SLG	AOPS	ABR	SB-CS	FA	FR	RNG	THR	GAMES AT POSITION	DL	BFW
1984	NY A	2	4	0	0	0	0	0	0	0-0	1	2	.000	.200	.000	-41	-1	0-0	.923	1	167	83	S2		0.1
1985	NY A	4	0	0	0	0	0	0	0	0-0	0	0	—	—	—	—	0	0-0	1.000	-0	100	0	S3		0.0
Total	2	6	4	0	0	0	0	0	0	0-0	1	2	.000	.200	.000	-41	-1	0-0	.929	1	157	71	S5		0.1

SMITH, PAUL
Paul Leslie B3.19.1931 New Castle PA BL/TL/5-8/165* d4.14 Mil 1955-56

YEAR	TM LG	G	AB	R	H	2B	3B	HR	RBI	BB-IB	HP	SO	AVG	OBP	SLG	AOPS	ABR	SB-CS	FA	FR	RNG	THR	GAMES AT POSITION	DL	BFW
1953	Pit N	118	389	41	110	12	7	4	44	24	3	23	.283	.329	.380	85	-9	3-0	.985	-1	100	75	1b74,O19L		-1.4
1957	Pit N	81	150	12	38	4	0	3	11	12-1	1	17	.253	.313	.340	78	-5	0-2	1.000	1	102	106	O33(16/1/20)/1		-0.6
1958	Pit N	6	3	0	1	0	0	0	0	3-0	0	0	.333	.667	.333	180	1	0-0	—	—	—	—	/H		0.1
	Chi N	18	20	1	3	0	0	0	1	3-0	0	4	.150	.261	.150	13	-3	0-0	.941	0	142	0	1b4		-0.3
	Year	24	23	1	4	0	0	0	1	6-0	0	4	.174	.345	.174	44	-2	0-0	.941	0	142	0	1b4		-0.2
Total	3	223	562	54	152	16	7	7	56	42-1	4	44	.270	.326	.361	81	-16	3-0	.984	-0	101	73	1b79,O52(35/1/20)		-2.2

SMITH, PAUL
Paul Stoner B5.7.1888 Mt.Zion IL D7.3.1958 Decatur IL BL/TR/6-1/190 d9.19 Col Millikin

YEAR	TM LG	G	AB	R	H	2B	3B	HR	RBI	BB-IB	HP	SO	AVG	OBP	SLG	AOPS	ABR	SB-CS	FA	FR	RNG	THR	GAMES AT POSITION	DL	BFW
1916	Cin N	10	44	5	10	0	1	0	1	2-0	0	8	.227	.244	.273	20	-2	3	1.000	-1	79	111	O10L		-0.4

SMITH, RAY
Raymond Edward B9.18.1955 Glendale CA BR/TR/6-1/185* d4.9 Col Oregon

YEAR	TM LG	G	AB	R	H	2B	3B	HR	RBI	BB-IB	HP	SO	AVG	OBP	SLG	AOPS	ABR	SB-CS	FA	FR	RNG	THR	GAMES AT POSITION	DL	BFW
1981	Min A	15	40	4	8	1	0	1	1	0-0	0	3	.200	.200	.300	40	-3	0-0	1.000	-0	158	63	C15	150	
1982	Min A	9	23	1	5	1	0	1	0	1-0	0	3	.217	.250	.304	50	-2	0-0	1.000	-0	167	71	C9		
1983	Min A	59	152	11	34	5	0	0	8	10-0	1	12	.224	.274	.257	46	-11	1-0	.984	8	92	150	C59		
Total	3	83	215	16	47	6	1	1	10	11-0	1	18	.219	.259	.270	45	-16	1-0	.988	8	113	125	C83	150	

SMITH, DICK
Richard Arthur B5.17.1939 Lebanon OR BR/TR/6-2/205* d7.20

YEAR	TM LG	G	AB	R	H	2B	3B	HR	RBI	BB-IB	HP	SO	AVG	OBP	SLG	AOPS	ABR	SB-CS	FA	FR	RNG	THR	GAMES AT POSITION	DL	BFW
1963	NY N	20	42	4	10	0	1	0	3	5-2	0	10	.238	.319	.286	74	-1	3-2	1.000	-1	79	0	O10(3/7/0),1b2		
1964	NY N	46	94	14	21	6	1	0	3	1-0	2	29	.223	.247	.309	57	-5	6-2	.987	-1	103	85	1b18,O13(12/1/1)		
1965	LA N	10	6	0	0	0	0	0	1	0-0	0	3	.000	.000	.000	-99	-2	0-0	1.000	-1	19	0	O9(5/4/1)		
Total	3	76	142	18	31	6	2	0	7	6-2	2	42	.218	.260	.289	56	-8	9-4	1.000	-3	72	0	O32(20/12/2),1b20		

SMITH, DICK
Richard Harrison B7.21.1927 Blandburg PA BR/TR/5-8/160* d9.14 Col Lock Haven

YEAR	TM LG	G	AB	R	H	2B	3B	HR	RBI	BB-IB	HP	SO	AVG	OBP	SLG	AOPS	ABR	SB-CS	FA	FR	RNG	THR	GAMES AT POSITION	DL	BFW
1951	Pit N	12	46	2	8	0	0	0	4	8	0	8	.174	.296	.174	29	-4	0-2	.936	2	115	188	3b12		
1952	Pit N	29	66	8	7	1	0	0	3	6-0	0	8	.106	.213	.121	-5	-9	0-0	.958	3	111	118	3b16,2b4,S4		
1953	Pit N	13	43	4	7	0	1	0	2	6	0	6	.163	.265	.209	26	-5	0-1	.961	3	111	101	S13		
1954	Pit N	12	31	2	3	1	0	0	0	6	0	5	.097	.243	.194	16	-4	0-0	.933	1	121	171	3b9		
1955	Pit N	4	0	1	0	0	0	0	0	1-0	0	0	—	1.000	—	198	0	0-0	—	-0	0	0	/S		
Total	5	70	186	17	25	2	2	0	13	30-0	0	22	.134	.255	.167	15	-22	0-3	.944	10	115	156	3b37,S18,2b4		

SMITH, DICK
Richard Kelly B8.25.1944 Lincolnton NC BR/TR/6-5/200 d8.20 Col Lenoir-Rhyne

YEAR	TM LG	G	AB	R	H	2B	3B	HR	RBI	BB-IB	HP	SO	AVG	OBP	SLG	AOPS	ABR	SB-CS	FA	FR	RNG	THR	GAMES AT POSITION	DL	BFW
1969	Was A	21	28	2	3	0	0	0	2	4-1	0	7	.107	.242	.107	1	-4	0-0	.909	-1	82	0	O9L		

SMITH, RED
Richard Paul B5.18.1904 Brokaw WI D3.8.1978 Sylvania OH BR/TR/5-10/185 d5.31 C4 Col Notre Dame

YEAR	TM LG	G	AB	R	H	2B	3B	HR	RBI	BB-IB	HP	SO	AVG	OBP	SLG	AOPS	ABR	SB-CS	FA	FR	RNG	THR	GAMES AT POSITION	DL	BFW
1927	NY N	1	0	0	0	0	0	0	0	0-0	0	0	—	—	—	—	0	0	1.000	-0	0	0	/C		

YEAR	TM LG	G	AB	R	H	2B	3B	HR	RBI	BB-IB	HP	SO	AVG	OBP	SLG	AOPS	ABR	SB-CS	FA	FR	RNG	THR	GAMES AT POSITION	DL	BFW

SMITH, BOB Robert Eldridge B4.22.1895 Rogersville TN D7.19.1987 Waycross GA BR/TR/5-10/175 d4.19 ▲

YEAR	TM LG	G	AB	R	H	2B	3B	HR	RBI	BB-IB	HP	SO	AVG	OBP	SLG	AOPS	ABR	SB-CS	FA	FR	RNG	THR	GAMES AT POSITION	DL	BFW
1923	Bos N	115	375	30	94	16	3	0	40	17	1	35	.251	.285	.309	59	-23	4-9	.944	12	106	110	S101,2b8		-0.3
1924	Bos N	106	347	32	79	12	3	2	38	15	0	26	.228	.260	.297	51	-25	5-2	.958	4	103	103	S80,3b23		-1.1
1925	Bos N	58	174	17	49	9	4	0	23	5	0	6	.282	.302	.379	80	-6	2-2	.906	-1	111	110	S21,2b15,P13/OC		-0.3
1926	Bos N	40	84	10	25	6	2	0	13	2	0	4	.298	.314	.417	105	8	0	.972	2	120	207	P33		0.0
1927	Bos N	54	109	10	27	3	1	1	10	2	0	4	.248	.261	.321	60	5	0	.966	2	110	101	P41		0.0
1928	Bos N	39	92	11	23	2	0	1	8	1	0	6	.250	.258	.304	49	3	2	.965	2	116	142	P38		0.0
1929	Bos N	39	99	12	17	4	2	1	8	2	0	8	.172	.188	.283	16	-14	0	.986	3	109	96	P34,S5		0.1
1930	Bos N	39	81	7	19	2	0	0	4	0	0	5	.235	.235	.259	20	-1	0	.984	1	106	100	P38		0.0
1931	Chi N	36	87	7	19	2	0	0	4	5	0	2	.218	.261	.241	35	1	0	1.000	1	109	118	P36		0.0
1932	†Chi N	36	42	5	10	4	1	0	4	0	0	2	.238	.238	.381	64	-2	1	1.000	2	105	206	P34,2b2		0.2
1933	Cin N	23	25	2	5	1	0	0	1	1	0	0	.200	.231	.240	35	-2	1	.882	-1	92	471	P16/S		-0.1
	Bos N	14	20	1	4	0	1	0	2	0	0	1	.200	.200	.300	45	0	0	1.000	1	146	0	P14		-0.1
	Year	37	45	3	9	1	1	0	3	1	0	1	.200	.217	.267	39	-4	1	.946	0	116	262	P30/S		-0.1
1934	Bos N	42	36	5	9	1	0	0	3	0	0	5	.250	.250	.278	44	1	0	1.000	1	119	139	P39		0.0
1935	Bos N	47	63	3	17	0	0	0	4	0	0	5	.270	.281	.270	53	3	0	.980	-1	91	40	P46		0.0
1936	Bos N	35	45	1	10	2	0	0	4	0	0	4	.222	.222	.267	33	0	0	1.000	1	118	105	P35		0.0
1937	Bos N	19	10	1	2	0	0	0	0	1	0	1	.200	.273	.200	33	0	0	1.000	-1	63	0	P18		0.0
Total 15		742	1689	154	409	64	17	5	166	52	1	110	.242	.265	.309	53	-52	16-13	.981	29	109	125	P435,S208,2b25,3b23/OC		-1.5

SMITH, BOBBY Robert Eugene B4.10.1974 Oakland CA BR/TR/6-3/190* [AtlN92 11/313] d3.31

YEAR	TM LG	G	AB	R	H	2B	3B	HR	RBI	BB-IB	HP	SO	AVG	OBP	SLG	AOPS	ABR	SB-CS	FA	FR	RNG	THR	GAMES AT POSITION	DL	BFW
1998	TB A	117	370	44	102	15	3	11	55	34-0	6	110	.276	.343	.422	96	-2	5-3	.963	10	109	85	3b97,S7,2b6,D7	15	0.8
1999	TB A	68	199	18	36	4	1	3	19	16-0	1	64	.181	.244	.256	28	-23	4-4	.933	5	115	149	3b59,2b13		-1.6
2000	TB A	49	175	21	41	8	0	6	26	14-1	1	59	.234	.293	.383	71	-8	2-2	.970	2	107	86	2b45,3b5		-0.4
2001	TB A	6	19	1	2	0	0	1		3-0	1	0	10	.105	.227	.105	-8	-3	0-0	.958	-2	66	77	2b6	43	-0.5
2002	TB A	18	63	4	11	2	0	1	6	3-0	0	25	.175	.212	.254	24	-7	0-0	.897	1	101	159	3b10,1b6,O2(1/0/1)/D		-0.6
Total 5		258	826	88	192	29	4	21	107	70-1	8	268	.232	.297	.354	67	-43	11-9	.947	15	111	110	3b171,2b70,D8,S7,1b6,O2(1/0/1)	58	-2.3

SMITH, JOE Salvatore Joseph (b Salvatore Persico) B12.29.1893 New York NY D1.12.1974 Yonkers NY BR/TR/5-7/170 d7.7 Col California-Davis

YEAR	TM LG	G	AB	R	H	2B	3B	HR	RBI	BB-IB	HP	SO	AVG	OBP	SLG	AOPS	ABR	SB-CS	FA	FR	RNG	THR	GAMES AT POSITION	DL	BFW
1913	NY A	14	32	1	5	0	0	0	2	1	0	14	.156	.182	.156	-1	-4	1	.952	-1	71	126	C14		-0.5

SMITH, SKYROCKET Samuel J. B3.19.1868 St.Louis MO D4.26.1916 St.Louis MO BR/6-2/170 d4.18

YEAR	TM LG	G	AB	R	H	2B	3B	HR	RBI	BB-IB	HP	SO	AVG	OBP	SLG	AOPS	ABR	SB-CS	FA	FR	RNG	THR	GAMES AT POSITION	DL	BFW
1888	Lou AA	58	206	27	49	9	4	1	31	24	11		.238	.349	.335	122	7	5	.970	-0	105	56	1b58		0.2

SMITH, SYD Sydney E. B8.31.1883 Smithville SC D6.5.1961 Orangeburg SC BR/TR/5-10/190 d4.14 Col South Carolina-Aiken

YEAR	TM LG	G	AB	R	H	2B	3B	HR	RBI	BB-IB	HP	SO	AVG	OBP	SLG	AOPS	ABR	SB-CS	FA	FR	RNG	THR	GAMES AT POSITION	DL	BFW
1908	Phi A	46	128	8	26	8	0	1	10	4	1		.203	.233	.289	65	-5	0	.975	-2	70	102	C31,1b6/OC		-0.5
	StL A	27	76	6	14	4	0	0	5	4	0		.184	.225	.237	50	-4	2	.977	6	142	89	C24		0.4
	Year	73	204	14	40	12	0	1	15	8	1		.196	.230	.270	60	-9	2	.976	4	103	96	C55,1b6/OC		-0.1
1910	Cle A	9	27	1	9	1	0	0	3	3	0		.333	.400	.370	140	1	0	.958	-1	82	114	C9		0.2
1911	Cle A	58	154	8	46	8	1	1	21	11	2		.299	.353	.383	104	1	0	.979	5	93	94	C48/13		0.9
1914	Pit N	5	11	1	3	0	0	0	1	0	0		.273	.273	.273	65	-1	0	1.000	-0	101	82	C3		0.0
1915	Pit N	1	1	0	0	0	0	0	0	0	0		.000	.000	.000	-99	0	0	—				/H		0.0
Total 5		146	397	24	98	21	1	2	40	22	3	1	.247	.291	.320	83	-8	2	.977	8	97	96	C115,1b7/3OC		1.0

SMITH, TOM Thomas N. B1851 Guelph ON, Can. D3.28.1889 Detroit MI BR/5-8/141 d9.15

YEAR	TM LG	G	AB	R	H	2B	3B	HR	RBI	BB-IB	HP	SO	AVG	OBP	SLG	AOPS	ABR	SB-CS	FA	FR	RNG	THR	GAMES AT POSITION	DL	BFW
1875	Atl NA	3	13	0	1	0	0	0	0	0	0		.077	.077	.077	-53	-2	0	.783	-0	116	0	2b3		-0.2

SMITH, TOMMY Tommy Alexander B8.1.1948 Albemarle NC BL/TR/6-3/215* [CleA70 5/100] d9.6 Col North Carolina St.

YEAR	TM LG	G	AB	R	H	2B	3B	HR	RBI	BB-IB	HP	SO	AVG	OBP	SLG	AOPS	ABR	SB-CS	FA	FR	RNG	THR	GAMES AT POSITION	DL	BFW
1973	Cle A	14	41	6	10	2	0	2	3	1-0	0	2	.244	.262	.439	92	-1	1-0	1.000	-1	93		O13(1/11/1)		-0.2
1974	Cle A	23	31	4	3	1	0	0	2	2-1	1	7	.097	.176	.129	-11	-4	0-0	.938	2	133	141	O17(9/4/4)/D		-0.4
1975	Cle A	8	8	0	1	0	0	0	2	0-0		1	.125	.111	.125	-29	-1	0-0	1.000	0	135		O3(1/0/2),D3		-0.1
1976	Cle A	55	164	17	42	14	1	2	12	8-2	0	8	.256	.289	.323	80	-5	8-0	.979	1	104	131	O50(12/0/38),D2		-0.4
1977	Sea A	21	27	1	7	1	0	0	2	1-0	0	6	.259	.259	.370	70	-1	0-1	1.000	2	86	711	O14(1/0/14)		0.0
Total 5		121	271	28	63	7	2	4	21	11-3	2	24	.232	.263	.317	67	-12	9-1	.977	4	105	156	O97(24/15/59),D6		-1.1

SMITH, VINNIE Vincent Ambrose B12.7.1915 Richmond VA D12.14.1979 Virginia Beach VA BR/TR/6-1/176 d9.10 Mil 1942-45 U9 [DL 1947 Pit N 162]

YEAR	TM LG	G	AB	R	H	2B	3B	HR	RBI	BB-IB	HP	SO	AVG	OBP	SLG	AOPS	ABR	SB-CS	FA	FR	RNG	THR	GAMES AT POSITION	DL	BFW
1941	Pit N	9	33	3	10	1	0	0	5	1	0	5	.303	.324	.333	86	-1	0	.941	-1	92	84	C9		-0.1
1946	Pit N	7	21	2	4	0	0	0	1	0	0	5	.190	.227	.190	19	-2	0	.967	0	80	109	C7	115	-0.2
Total 2		16	54	5	14	1	0	0	5	2	0	10	.259	.286	.278	59	-3	0	.953	-1	87	94	C16	277	-0.3

SMITH, WALLY Wallace H. B3.13.1888 Philadelphia PA D6.10.1930 Florence AZ BR/TR/5-11.5/180 d4.17

YEAR	TM LG	G	AB	R	H	2B	3B	HR	RBI	BB-IB	HP	SO	AVG	OBP	SLG	AOPS	ABR	SB-CS	FA	FR	RNG	THR	GAMES AT POSITION	DL	BFW
1911	StL N	81	194	23	42	6	5	2	19	21	3	33	.216	.303	.330	79	-6	5	.936	2	108	30	3b26,S25,2b8/OC		-0.2
1912	StL N	75	219	22	56	5	5	0	26	29	3	27	.256	.351	.324	87	-3	4	.949	1	106	69	3b32,S22,1b6		-0.1
1914	Was A	45	97	11	19	4	1	0	8	3	2	12	.196	.235	.258	46	-7	3-4	.955	-3	57	99	2b12,1b7,S7,3b5/OR		-1.2
Total 3		201	510	56	117	15	11	2	53	53	8	72	.229	.312	.314	77	-16	12-4	.947	-1	107	63	3b63,S54,2b20,1b13,O2(0/1/1)		-1.5

SMITH, WIB Wilbur Floyd B8.30.1886 Evart MI D11.18.1959 Fargo ND BL/TR/5-10.5/165 d5.31 Col Albion

YEAR	TM LG	G	AB	R	H	2B	3B	HR	RBI	BB-IB	HP	SO	AVG	OBP	SLG	AOPS	ABR	SB-CS	FA	FR	RNG	THR	GAMES AT POSITION	DL	BFW
1909	StL A	17	42	3	8	0	0	0	2	4	0		.190	.190	.190	22	-4	0	.836	-7	82	78	C13/1		-1.1

SMITH, RED Willard Jehu B4.11.1892 Logansport IN D7.17.1972 Noblesville IN BR/TR/5-8/165 d9.17

YEAR	TM LG	G	AB	R	H	2B	3B	HR	RBI	BB-IB	HP	SO	AVG	OBP	SLG	AOPS	ABR	SB-CS	FA	FR	RNG	THR	GAMES AT POSITION	DL	BFW
1917	Pit N	11	21	1	3	1	0	0	4			4	.143	.250	.190	35	-1	1	1.000	1	79	163	C6		0.0
1918	Pit N	15	24	1	4	1	0	0	3			4	.167	.259	.208	42	-2	0	.939	0	142	45	C10		-0.1
Total 2		26	45	2	7	2	0	0	5	6			.156	.255	.200	39	-3	1	.969	1	113	99	C16		-0.1

SMITH, BILL William E. B3.1860 E.Liverpool OH D8.9.1886 Toronto ON, Can. 5-11/178 d9.17

YEAR	TM LG	G	AB	R	H	2B	3B	HR	RBI	BB-IB	HP	SO	AVG	OBP	SLG	AOPS	ABR	SB-CS	FA	FR	RNG	THR	GAMES AT POSITION	DL	BFW
1884	Cle N	1	3	0	0	0	0	0	0	0		2	.000	.000	.000	-97	-1		—	0	0	0	/OL		-0.1

SMITH, BILL William J. B Baltimore MD D8.9.1886 d4.14 M1

YEAR	TM LG	G	AB	R	H	2B	3B	HR	RBI	BB-IB	HP	SO	AVG	OBP	SLG	AOPS	ABR	SB-CS	FA	FR	RNG	THR	GAMES AT POSITION	DL	BFW
1873	Mar NA	6	23	2	4	0	0	0	0				.174	.174	.174	5	-2	0-0	.500	-3	0	0	O3C,C2/2M		-0.3

SMITH, WILLIE Willie B2.11.1939 Anniston AL BL/TL/6-0/190(178-190) d6.18 ▲

YEAR	TM LG	G	AB	R	H	2B	3B	HR	RBI	BB-IB	HP	SO	AVG	OBP	SLG	AOPS	ABR	SB-CS	FA	FR	RNG	THR	GAMES AT POSITION	DL	BFW
1963	Det A	17	8	2	1	0	0	0		0-0	0	1	.125	.125	.125	-29	0	0-0	1.000	0	118	0	P11		0.0
1964	LA A	118	359	46	108	14	6	11	51	8-1	2	39	.301	.317	.465	128	10	7-5	.977	-5	88	45	O87(58/3/31),P15		0.0
1965	Cal A	136	459	52	120	14	9	14	57	32-10	1	60	.261	.308	.423	109	3	9-8	.980	2	92	145	O123(123/0/1),1b2		-0.3
1966	Cal A	90	195	18	36	3	1		20	12-2	1	37	.185	.239	.236	39	-16	1-0	.974	1	98	164	O52(32/0/22)		-1.8
1967	Cle A	21	30		7	2	0	0	2	1-0	0	10	.219	.242	.281	54	-2	0-2	.800	-1	74	0	O4L,1b3		-0.4
1968	Cle A	33	42	1	6	2	0	0	3	3-2	1	14	.143	.213	.190	25	-4	0-0	1.000	-0	65	149	1b7,P2/OL		-0.5
	Chi N	55	142	13	39	8	2	5	25	12-2	1	33	.275	.333	.465	130	5	0-0	1.000	-2	81	49	O38L,1b4/P		0.1
1969	Chi N	103	195	21	48	9	1	9	25	25-3	0	49	.246	.330	.441	102	1	1-0	.929	-5	64	0	O33(32/0/1),1b24		-0.7
1970	Chi N	87	167	15	36	9	1	5	24	11-0	1	32	.216	.267	.371	62	-9	2-1	.994	-5	45	120	1b43/OR		-1.7
1971	Cin N	31	55	3	9	2	0	1	4	3-0	0	9	.164	.207	.255	30	-5	0-0	1.000	1	150	138	1b10		-0.5
Total 9		691	1654	171	410	63	21	46	211	107-20	9	284	.248	.295	.395	94	-17	20-16	.975	-13	88	95	O339(288/3/56),1b93,P29		-5.8

SMITHERMAN, STEPHEN Stephen Lydell B9.1.1978 McAlester OK BR/TR/6-4/230 [CinN00 23/693] d7.1 Col Arkansas-Little Rock

YEAR	TM LG	G	AB	R	H	2B	3B	HR	RBI	BB-IB	HP	SO	AVG	OBP	SLG	AOPS	ABR	SB-CS	FA	FR	RNG	THR	GAMES AT POSITION	DL	BFW
2003	Cin N	21	44	3	7	2	0	1	8	2-0	0	9	.159	.213	.273	27	-5	1-0	.917	1	83	0	O14L		-0.6

SMOOT, HOMER Homer Vernon "Doc" B3.23.1878 Galestown MD D3.25.1928 Salisbury MD BL/TR/5-10/180 d4.17 Col Washington College

YEAR	TM LG	G	AB	R	H	2B	3B	HR	RBI	BB-IB	HP	SO	AVG	OBP	SLG	AOPS	ABR	SB-CS	FA	FR	RNG	THR	GAMES AT POSITION	DL	BFW
1902	StL N	129	518	58	161	19	4	3	48	23	8		.311	.350	.380	131	18	20	.931	-2	80	102	O129C		1.0
1903	StL N	129	500	67	148	22	8	4	49	32	3		.296	.342	.396	114	8	17	.942	-7	82	67	O129C		-0.5
1904	StL N	137	520	58	146	23	6	3	66	37	2		.281	.331	.365	120	12	23	.966	-2	98	125	O137C		0.4
1905	StL N	139	534	73	166	21	16	4	58	33	7		.311	.359	.433	140	24	21	.975	-0	101	134	O138C		1.8
1906	StL N	86	343	41	85	9	10	0	31	11	9		.248	.289	.332	98	-3	4	.953	-2	70	140	O55(31)		-1.1
	Cin N	60	220	11	57	8	1	1	17	13	5		.259	.315	.318	93	-2	0	.944	1	145	0	O59(4/55/0)		-0.3
	Year	146	563	52	142	17	11	1	48	24	14		.252	.300	.327	96	-5	3	.950	-2	98	87	O145(4/110/31)		-1.4
Total 5		680	2635	308	763	102	45	15	269	149	34		.290	.336	.380	120	57	84	.953	-12	92	103	O678(4/643/31)		1.3

SMOYER, HENRY Henry Neitz "Hennie" (b Henry Neitz Smowery) B4.24.1890 Fredericksburg PA D2.28.1958 DuBois PA BR/TR/5-6/? d8.14 Col Albright

YEAR	TM LG	G	AB	R	H	2B	3B	HR	RBI	BB-IB	HP	SO	AVG	OBP	SLG	AOPS	ABR	SB-CS	FA	FR	RNG	THR	GAMES AT POSITION	DL	BFW
1912	StL A	6	14	1	3	0	0	0	0	2	0		.214	.313	.214	53	-1	0	1.000	0	125	0	S4,3b2		0.0

YEAR	TM LG	G	AB	R	H	2B	3B	HR	RBI	BB-IB	HP	SO	AVG	OBP	SLG	AOPS	ABR	SB-CS	FA	FR	RNG	THR	GAMES AT POSITION	DL	BFW

SMYKAL, FRANK   Frank John (b Frank John Smejkal) B10.13.1889 Chicago IL D8.11.1950 Chicago IL BR/TR/5-7/150 d8.30 Col Illinois
| | | | | | | | | | | | | | | | | | | | | | | | | | 0.1 |
| 1916 | Pit N | 6 | 10 | 1 | 3 | 0 | 0 | 0 | 2 | 3 | 1 | 1 | .300 | .500 | .300 | 147 | 1 | 1 | .842 | -1 | 114 | 66 | S5/3 | | |

SMYRES, CLANCY   Clarence Melvin B5.24.1922 Culver City CA BB/TR/5-11.5/175 d4.18
| | | | | | | | | | | | | | | | | | | | | | | | | | -0.1 |
| 1944 | Bro N | 5 | 2 | 1 | 0 | 0 | 0 | 0 | 0 | 0 | 0 | 0 | .000 | .000 | .000 | -99 | -1 | 0 | — | 0 | | | /H | | |

SMYTH, RED   James Daniel B1.30.1891 Holly Springs MS D4.14.1958 Inglewood CA BL/TR/5-9/152 d8.11
																									-0.1
1915	Bro N	19	22	3	3	1	0	0	3	4	0	3	.136	.269	.182	37	-1	1-2	1.000	1	126	154	O9(6/2/1)		-0.2
1916	Bro N	2	5	0	0	0	0	0	0	0	0	3	.000	.000	.000	-97	-1	0	1.000	-0	60	240	2b2		-0.4
1917	Bro N	29	24	5	3	0	0	0	1	4	0	6	.125	.250	.125	16	-2	0	.667	-2	47	297	3b4,O2C		-0.8
	StL N	38	72	5	15	0	2	0	4	4	2	9	.208	.269	.264	66	-3	3	.889	-3	73	50	O23(12/4/5)		-1.2
	Year	67	96	10	18	0	2	0	5	8	2	15	.188	.264	.229	52	-5	3	.871	-4	77	48	O25(12/6/5),3b4		-0.5
1918	StL N	40	113	19	24	1	2	0	4	16	1	11	.212	.315	.257	78	-2	3	.956	-1	86	99	O25(2/0/22),2b11		-2.0
Total	4	128	236	32	45	2	4	0	12	28	3	31	.191	.285	.233	60	-9	7-2	.934	-4	87	88	O59(20/8/28),2b13,3b4		

SNEAD, ESIX   Esix B6.7.1976 Fort Myers FL BB/TR/5-10/175* [StLN98 18/528] d9.3 Col Central Florida
																									0.0
2002	NY N	17	13	3	4	0	0	1	3	1-0	0	4	.308	.357	.538	143	1	4-3	1.000	-0	88	0	O6(1/5/0)		0.0
2004	NY N	1	0	1	0	0	0	0	0	0-0	0	0	—	—	—	—	0	0-0	—	-0	0	0	/OL		0.0
Total	2	18	13	4	4	0	0	1	3	1-0	0	4	.308	.357	.538	143	1	4-3	1.000	-0	84	0	O7(2/5/0)		

SNEED, JOHN   John Law B1861 Shelby Co. TN D1.4.1899 Memphis TN BL/5-8/160 d5.1
																									-0.3
1884	Ind AA	27	102	14	22	4	0	1		6		0	.216	.259	.284	79	-2		.817	-1	79	0	O27(0/21/6)		0.1
1890	Tol AA	9	30	3	6	0	0	0	4	8		0	.200	.368	.200	66	-1	5	.889	2	332	315	O9R		1.3
	Col AA	128	484	114	141	13	15	2	65	63		9	.291	.383	.393	138	26	39	.883	-9	92	121	O126(26/3/97),S2		1.4
	Year	137	514	117	147	13	15	2	69	71		9	.286	.382	.381	133	25	44	.883	-7	108	134	O135(26/3/106),S2		-0.1
1891	Col AA	99	366	66	94	9	6	1	61	55		8	29	.257	.366	.322	103	5	24	.894	-5	59	114	O99R		-1.1
Total	3	263	982	197	263	26	21	4	130	132		17	29	.268	.364	.349	117	29		.879	-13	86	113	O261(26/24/211),S2		

SNELL, CHARLIE   Charles Anthony (b Charles Anthony Schnell) B11.29.1893 Hampstead MD D4.4.1988 Reading PA BR/TR/5-11/160 d7.19
| | | | | | | | | | | | | | | | | | | | | | | | | | 0.1 |
| 1912 | StL A | 8 | 19 | 0 | 4 | 1 | 0 | 0 | 3 | | | | .211 | .348 | .263 | 78 | 0 | 0 | .941 | 0 | 98 | 116 | C8 | | |

SNELL, WALLY   Walter Henry "Doc" B5.19.1889 W.Bridgewater MA D7.23.1980 Providence RI BR/TR/5-10/170 d8.1 Col Brown
| | | | | | | | | | | | | | | | | | | | | | | | | | 0.1 |
| 1913 | Bos N | 6 | 12 | 1 | 3 | 0 | 0 | 0 | 1 | | | | .250 | .250 | .250 | 45 | -1 | 1 | .923 | -0 | 140 | 88 | C2 | | |

SNELLING, CHRIS   Christopher Doyle B12.3.1981 North Miami FL BL/TL/5-10/165(165-205) d5.25 [DL 2003 Sea A 30, 2004 Sea A 183]
																								117	-0.1
2002	Sea A	8	27	2	4	0	0	1	1	2-0	0	4	.148	.207	.259	24	-3	0-0	1.000	0	113	0	O8(6/0/2)	63	-0.1
2005	Sea A	15	29	4	8	2	0	1	3	5-0	0	2	.276	.382	.448	128	1	0-2	1.000	2	111	402	O10(7/0/3)	393	-0.1
Total	2	23	56	6	12	2	0	2	4	7-0	0	6	.214	.302	.357	78	-2	0-2	1.000	2	112	224	O18(13/0/5)		

SNIDER, DUKE   Edwin Donald "The Silver Fox" B9.19.1926 Los Angeles CA BL/TR/6-0/190(185-206) d4.17 C2 HF1980
																									-0.1
1947	Bro N	40	83	6	20	3	1	0	5	3	1	24	.241	.276	.301	51	-6	2	.980	-1	108	0	O25(4/13/7)		-0.1
1948	Bro N	53	160	22	39	6	6	5	21	12	0	27	.244	.297	.450	96	-2	4	.989	1	93	188	O47(0/41/7)		0.4
1949	†Bro N★	146	552	100	161	28	7	23	92	56	4	92	.292	.361	.493	122	16	12	.984	-1	96	121	O151C		0.7
1950	Bro N★	152	620	109	199	31	10	31	107	58	0	79	.321	.379	.553	139	33	16	.983	-1	96	121	O150C		3.4
1951	Bro N★	150	606	96	168	26	6	29	101	62	0	97	.277	.344	.483	118	14	14-10	.987	-6	95	92	O150C		2.1
1952	†Bro N☆	144	534	80	162	25	7	21	92	55	1	77	.303	.368	.494	136	25	7-4	.992	-5	94	95	O151C		3.0
1953	†Bro N★	153	590	132	198	38	4	42	126	82	3	90	.336	.419	**.627**	165	58	16-7	.987	-11	91	52	O151C		6.2
1954	†Bro N★	149	584	120	199	39	10	40	130	84	4	96	.341	.423	.647	169	61	6-6	.981	-10	97	72	O148C		5.6
1955	†Bro N★	148	538	126	136	34	6	42	136	104-19	1	87	.309	.418	.628	169	57	9-7	.989	-3	97	95	O150C		3.3
1956	†Bro N★	151	542	112	158	33	2	**43**	101	99-26	1	101	.292	**.399**	**.598**	152	**43**	3-3	.984	-4	94	104	O136C		5.0
1957	Bro N	139	508	91	139	25	7	40	92	77-12	1	104	.274	.368	.587	139	28	3-4	.990	-12	87	63	O139C		-0.2
1958	LA N	106	327	45	102	12	3	15	58	32-4	1	49	.312	.371	.505	126	12	2-2	.987	-9	81	66	O92(6/78/11)		0.1
1959	†LA N	126	370	59	114	11	2	23	88	58-13	0	71	.308	.400	.535	137	21	1-0	.965	-6	83	63	O75(0/48/35)		0.0
1960	LA N	101	235	38	57	13	5	14	36	46-8	1	54	.243	.366	.519	131	11	1-0	.975	3	107	133	O66(0/24/51)	30	0.0
1961	LA N	85	233	35	69	8	3	16	56	29-3	0	46	.296	.375	.562	133	11	1-1	.975	-0	92	113	O39(15/2/24)		-0.1
1962	LA N	80	158	28	44	11	3	5	30	36-6	2	32	.278	.418	.481	150	14	2-0	.986	-6	84	77	O106(34/13/62)		-0.1
1963	NY N★	129	354	44	86	8	3	14	45	56-9	1	74	.243	.345	.401	113	7	0-1	.979	-2	78	88	O43(19/0/25)		-1.1
1964	SF N	91	167	16	35	7	0	4	17	22-4	0	40	.210	.302	.323	85	-4	0-0	.979	-2	78	87	O1918(78/1590/293)	30	-2.2
Total	18	2143	7161	1259	2116	358	85	407	1333	971-104	21	1237	.295	.380	.540	138	398	99-50	.985	-88	92	87	O1918(78/1590/293)		

SNIDER, VAN   Van Voorhees B8.11.1963 Birmingham AL BL/TR/6-3/185(185-205) d9.2
																									-0.0
1988	Cin N	11	28	4	6	1	0	1	6	0-0	0	13	.214	.207	.357	59	-2	0-1	1.000	0	111	0	O8(6/0/3)		-0.0
1989	Cin N	8	7	1	1	0	0	0	0	0-0	0	5	.143	.143	.143	-18	-1	0-0	1.000	0	138	0	O6(5/0/2)		-0.0
Total	2	19	35	5	7	1	0	1	6	0-0	0	18	.200	.194	.314	44	-3	0-1	1.000	0	117	0	O14(11/0/5)		

SNIPES, ROXY   Wyatt Eure "Rock" B10.28.1896 Marion SC D5.1.1941 Fayetteville NC BL/TR/6-0/185 d7.15 Col South Carolina-Aiken
| | | | | | | | | | | | | | | | | | | | | | | | | | -0.0 |
| 1923 | Chi A | 1 | 1 | 0 | 0 | 0 | 0 | 0 | 0 | | | 0 | .000 | .000 | .000 | -99 | 0 | 0-0 | — | | | | /H | | |

SNODGRASS, CHAPPIE   Amzie Beal B3.18.1870 Springfield OH D9.9.1951 New York NY BR/TR/5-10/165 d5.15
| | | | | | | | | | | | | | | | | | | | | | | | | | -0.0 |
| 1901 | Bal A | 3 | 10 | 1 | 1 | 0 | 0 | 0 | 1 | | | | .100 | .100 | .100 | -43 | -2 | 0 | .500 | -1 | 0 | 0 | O2L | | |

SNODGRASS, FRED   Frederick Carlisle "Snow" B10.19.1887 Ventura CA D4.5.1974 Ventura CA BR/TR/5-11.5/175 d6.4 OF(108/666/73)
																									-0.0
1908	NY N	6	4	2	1	0	0	0	1	0		0	.250	.250	.250	57	0	1	1.000	1	0	192	C3		-0.0
1909	NY N	28	70	10	21	5	0	1	6	7		3	.300	.387	.414	146	4	7	.921	9	153	181	O20(15/3/1),C2/1		-0.0
1910	NY N	123	396	69	127	22	8	2	44	71	13	52	.321	.440	.432	154	33	33	.970	-2	97	85	O101(31/70/22),1b9/C3		-0.0
1911	†NY N	151	534	83	157	27	10	1	77	72	15	59	.294	.393	.388	115	14	51	.973	6	91	**153**	O149(1/149/0)/13		-0.0
1912	†NY N	146	535	91	144	24	9	3	69	70	8	65	.269	.362	.364	96	-1	43	.948	-3	88	140	O116(52/66/5),1b27/2		-0.0
1913	†NY N	141	457	65	133	21	6	3	49	53	7	44	.291	.373	.383	115	11	27-18	.968	-2	97	100	O133C,1b3/2		-0.0
1914	NY N	113	392	54	103	20	4	4	37	44	6	43	.263	.336	.334	103	2	25	.977	-4	109	87	O96(9/47/40),1b14/23		-0.0
1915	NY N	80	252	36	49	9	0	0	20	35	6	33	.194	.307	.230	68	-8	11-12	.935	-0	94	46	O18C,1b5		-0.0
	Bos N	23	79	10	22	2	0	0	9	7	2	9	.278	.352	.304	104	1	0-4	.938	-2	104	0	O93(0/88/5),1b5		-0.0
	Year	103	331	46	71	11	0	0	29	42	8	42	.215	.318	.248	76	-7	11-16	.935	-2	96	118	O110C		-0.0
1916	Bos N	112	382	33	95	13	5	0	32	34	5	54	.249	.318	.317	100	0	14	.983	9	106	142	O110C		-0.0
Total	9	923	3101	453	852	143	42	11	351	386		359	.275	.367	.359	110	56	212-34	.965	10	98	121	O818C,1b60,C6,2b3,3b3		

SNOPEK, CHRIS   Christopher Charles B9.20.1970 Cynthiana KY BR/TR/6-1/185* [ChiA92 6/176] d7.31 Col U. of Mississippi
																									-0.1
1995	Chi A	22	68	12	22	4	1	1	9-0		0	12	.324	.403	.426	121	3	1-0	1.000	-3	50	0	3b17,S6		-0.0
1996	Chi A	46	104	18	27	6	1	6	18	6-0	1	16	.260	.304	.510	106	0	0-1	.939	2	103	152	3b82,S12,D3		-0.0
1997	Chi A	86	298	27	65	15	0	5	35	18-0	1	51	.218	.263	.319	53	-21	3-2	.915	-15	79	80	3b82,S4		-0.1
1998	Chi A	53	125	17	26	2	0	1	14	14-0	1	24	.208	.291	.248	43	-10	3-0	.972	1	111	87	S33,2b12,3b3/1ORD		-0.0
	Bos A	8	12	2	2	0	0	0		2-0		5	.167	.286	.167	21	-1	0-0	.750	-1	120	0	2b3,3b3,D2		-0.0
	Year	61	137	19	28	2	0	1	14	16-0	1	29	.204	.290	.241	41	-12	3-0	.972	0	111	81	S33,2b15,3b6,D4/1OR		-0.0
Total	4	215	607	76	142	27	1	13	66	49-0	3	108	.234	.293	.346	67	-29	7-3	.928	-15	79	81	3b132,S55,2b15,D6/OR1		

SNOW, CHARLIE   Charles M. B8.3.1849 Lowell MA D8.27.1929 Brooklyn NY d10.1
| | | | | | | | | | | | | | | | | | | | | | | | | | -0.0 |
| 1874 | Atl NA | 1 | 1 | 0 | 1 | 0 | 0 | 0 | 0 | | | 0 | 1.000 | 1.000 | 1.000 | 615 | 1 | 0-0 | .000 | -1 | | | /C | | |

SNOW, J.T.   Jack Thomas B2.26.1968 Long Beach CA BL/TL (BB 1992-98)/6-2/202* [NYA89 5/129] d9.20 Col Arizona
1992	NY A	7	14	1	2	1	0	0	2	5-1	0	5	.143	.368	.214	67	-0	0-0	1.000	-0	62	177	1b6/D		
1993	Cal A	129	419	60	101	18	2	16	57	55-4	2	88	.241	.328	.408	95	-3	3-0	.995	2	106	98	1b129		
1994	Cal A	61	223	22	49	4	0	8	30	19-1	3	48	.220	.289	.345	62	-14	0-1	.996	1	103	105	1b61		
1995	Cal A	143	544	80	157	22	1	24	102	52-4	3	91	.289	.353	.465	112	9	2-1	.997	-13	61	88	1b143		
1996	Cal A	155	575	69	148	20	1	17	67	56-6	5	96	.257	.327	.384	78	-20	1-6	.993	3	106	95	1b154		
1997	†SF N	157	531	81	149	36	1	28	104	96-13	1	124	.281	.387	.510	137	32	6-4	**.999**	4	110	105	1b156		
1998	SF N	138	435	65	108	29	1	15	79	58-3	0	84	.248	.332	.423	103	3	1-2	.996	11	**127**	99	1b136		
1999	SF N	161	570	93	156	25	2	24	98	86-7	1	125	.274	.370	.487	115	14	0-4	.995	-0	98	114	1b160		
2000	†SF N	155	536	82	152	33	2	19	96	66-6	11	129	.284	.365	.459	116	15	1-3	.995	-0	98	114	1b153		
2001	SF N	101	285	43	70	12	1	8	34	55-10	2	81	.246	.371	.379	102	3	0-0	.999	-0	98	120	1b92	54	

YEAR	TM LG	G	AB	R	H	2B	3B	HR	RBI	BB-IB	HP	SO	AVG	OBP	SLG	AOPS	ABR	SB-CS	FA	FR	RNG	THR	GAMES AT POSITION	DL	BFW
2002	†SF N	143	422	47	104	26	2	6	53	59-5	7	90	.246	.344	.360	93	-4	0-0	.993	1	105	112	1b135		-1.4
2003	†SF N	103	330	48	90	18	3	8	51	55-0	8	55	.273	.387	.418	109	7	1-2	.994	5	122	110	1b97		
2004	SF N	107	346	62	113	32	1	12	60	58-0	7	61	.327	.429	.529	142	26	4-0	.995	-2	93	92	1b100	30	0.3
2005	SF N	117	367	40	101	17	2	4	40	32-1	7	61	.275	.343	.365	83	-8	1-0	.997	0	101	75	1b108	34	1.6
Total	14	1677	5597	793	1500	293	19	189	873	752-61	63	1134	.268	.357	.428	105	60	20-23	.996	13	102	102	1b1630/D	118	-6.9

SNYDER, BERNIE   Bernard Austin B8.25.1913 Philadelphia PA D4.15.1999 Havertown PA BR/TR/6-0/165 d9.15

1935	Phi A	10	32	5	11	1	0	0	2				.344	.364	.375	92	0	0-0	.880	-3	66	33	2b5,S4		-0.3

SNYDER, CHARLES   Charles B Camden NJ D3.3.1901 Philadelphia PA BR/TR d9.19

1890	Phi AA	9	33	5	9	1	0	0	4	2	0		.273	.314	.303	82	-1	0	.583	-4	95	0	O5(1/0/4),C5		-0.4

SNYDER, POP   Charles N. B10.6.1854 Washington DC D10.29.1924 Washington DC BR/TR/5-11.5/184 d6.16 M4/U7

1873	Was NA	28	107	16	21	3	0	0	3	3		4	.196	.218	.215	30	-9	0-1	.819	-2			C28,O3C		-0.8
1874	Bal NA	39	151	24	33	4	0	1	17	1		2	.219	.224	.265	56	-7	0-0	.789	-2			C39		-0.7
1875	Phi NA	66	263	38	64	8	2	1	25	4		9	.243	.255	.300	89	-3	3-8	.825	4			C66/1		-0.1
1876	Lou N	56	224	21	44	4	1	1	9	2		7	.196	.204	.237	39	-16		.833	12			C55,O4(0/3/1)		-0.2
1877	Lou N	61	248	23	64	7	2	2	28	3		14	.258	.267	.327	73	-9		.910	15			C61/ORS		0.6
1878	Bos N	60	226	21	48	5	0	0	14	1		19	.212	.216	.235	44	-14		.912	7			C58,O2R		-0.5
1879	Bos N	81	329	42	78	16	3	2	35	5		31	.237	.249	.322	85	-5		.925	25			C80,O2R		2.0
1881	Bos N	62	219	14	50	8	0	0	16	3		23	.228	.239	.265	61	-9		.897	3			C60/ORS2		-0.5
1882	Cin AA	72	309	49	90	12	2	1	50	9			.291	.311	.353	117	5		.916	18			C70,1b2/ORM		2.5
1883	Cin AA	58	250	38	64	14	6	0	34	8			.256	.276	.360	99	-1		.919	13			C57,S2,M		1.5
1884	Cin AA	67	268	32	69	9	9	0	39	7	0		.257	.276	.358	101	-1		.922	26			C65,1b2/ORM		2.7
1885	Cin AA	39	152	13	36	4	1	0	19	6	1		.237	.270	.283	85	-3		.880	2			C38/1		0.2
1886	Cin AA	60	220	33	41	8	3	0	28	13	3		.186	.242	.250	52	-13	11	.874	-4			C41,1b19/OC		-1.3
1887	Cle AA	74	282	33	72	12	6	0	27	9			.255	.281	.340	75	-11	5	.905	16			C63,1b13		0.8
1888	Cle AA	64	237	22	51	7	3	0	14	6	1		.215	.238	.270	64	-11	9	.901	10			C58,1b4,O3R		0.4
1889	Cle N	22	83	5	16	3	0	0	12	2	1	12	.193	.221	.229	26	-9	4	.907	3			C22		-0.3
1890	Cle P	13	48	5	9	1	0	0	12	1	1	9	.188	.220	.208	16	-6	1	.958	-1	71	108	C13		-0.3
1891	Was NA	8	27	4	5	0	1	0	2	0	2	3	.185	.241	.259	45	-2	0	1.000	0	73	0	1b4,C3/ORM		-0.4
Total	3 NA	133	521	78	118	14	2	2	45	8			.226	.238	.273	66	-19	3-9	.814	-0			C133,O3C/1		-1.6
Total	15	797	3122	355	737	110	39	7	339	75	10	118	.236	.256	.303	73	-104	30	.904	144	74	111	C744,1b45,O17(0/4/13),S4/2		7.3

SNYDER, CHRIS   Christopher Ryan B2.12.1981 Houston TX BR/TR/6-3/220* [AriN02 2/68] d8.21 Col Houston

2004	Ari N	29	96	10	23	6	0	5	15	13-1	0	25	.240	.327	.458	95	-1	0-0	1.000	4	118	102	C29		0.5
2005	Ari N	115	326	24	66	14	0	6	28	40-5	4	87	.202	.297	.301	55	-21	0-1	.997	-7	119	76	C113		-2.2
Total	2	144	422	34	89	20	0	11	43	53-6	4	112	.211	.304	.336	64	-22	0-1	.998	-3	119	82	C142		-1.7

SNYDER, EARL   Earl Clifford B5.6.1976 New Britain CT BR/TR/6-0/207* [NYN98 36/1084] d4.28 Col Hartford

2002	Cle A	18	55	5	11	2	0	1	4	6-0	0	21	.200	.279	.291	51	-4	0-0	.981	0	119	31	1b12,3b2/D		-0.5
2004	Bos A	1	4	0	1	0	0	0	0	0-0	0	1	.250	.250	.250	2	0	0-0	1.000	1	172	0	/3		0.0
Total	2	19	59	5	12	2	0	1	4	6-0	0	22	.203	.277	.288	49	-4	0-0	.981	1	119	31	1b12,3b3/D		-0.5

SNYDER, REDLEG   Emanuel Sebastian (b Emanuel Sebastian Schneider) B12.12.1854 Camden NJ D11.24.1932 Camden NJ BR/TR/5-10/175 d4.25

1876	Cin N	55	205	10	31	3	1	0	12	1		19	.151	.155	.176	12	-17		.825	4	62	39	O55(54/0/1)		-1.5
1884	Wil U	17	52	4	10	0	0	0	1				.192	.208	.192	21	-7		.976	1	111	136	1b16/OL		-0.6
Total	2	72	257	14	41	3	1	0	12	2		19	.160	.166	.179	14	-24		.825	5	62	39	O56(55/0/1),1b16		-2.1

SNYDER, COONEY   Frank C. B1872 Toronto ON, Can. D3.9.1917 Toronto ON, Can. BR/6-3/180 d5.19

1898	Lou N	17	61	4	10	0	0	0	6	3	1		.164	.215	.164	9	-7	0	.935	-5	83	100	C17		-1.0

SNYDER, FRANK   Frank Elton "Pancho" B5.27.1894 San Antonio TX D1.5.1962 San Antonio TX BR/TR/6-2/185 d8.25 Mil 1918 C9

1912	StL N	11	18	2	2	0	0	0	2	0	0	7	.111	.200	.111	-14	-3	1	.919	-1	80	122	C11		-0.3
1913	StL N	7	21	1	4	0	1	0	2	0		4	.190	.190	.286	35	-2	0	.956	0	85	126	C7		-0.1
1914	StL N	100	326	19	75	15	4	1	25	13	1	28	.230	.262	.310	71	-13	1	.979	4	104	96	C98		-0.1
1915	StL N	144	473	41	141	22	7	4	55	39	1	49	.298	.353	.387	124	13	3-6	.983	11	111	109	C142		3.8
1916	StL N	132	406	23	105	12	4	0	39	18		31	.259	.290	.308	84	-9	7	.973	7	83	100	C72,1b46/S		0.4
1917	StL N	115	313	18	74	9	2	1	33	27	2	43	.236	.301	.288	83	-6	4	.975	3	121	117	C94/2		0.5
1918	StL N	39	112	5	28	7	1	0	10	6		13	.250	.288	.330	92	-1	4	.959	-1	86	112	C27,1b3		0.1
1919	StL N	50	154	7	28	4	2	0	14	5	1	13	.182	.213	.234	36	-12	2	.983	4	103	143	C48/1		-0.5
	NY N	32	92	7	21	6	0	0	11	8	1	9	.228	.297	.293	79	-2	1	.983	-3	93	93	C31		-0.3
	Year	82	246	14	49	10	2	0	25	13	2	22	.199	.245	.256	53	-14	3	.983	1	99	123	C79/1		-0.8
1920	NY N	87	264	26	66	13	4	3	27	17	0	18	.250	.295	.364	89	-4	2-2	.978	4	128	90	C84		0.7
1921	†NY N	108	309	36	99	13	2	8	45	27		24	.320	.382	.453	120	10	3-4	.985	4	121	112	C101		1.9
1922	†NY N	104	318	34	109	21	5	5	51	23		25	.343	.387	.487	123	11	1-5	.980	2	129	74	C97		1.6
1923	†NY N	120	402	37	103	13	6	5	63	24		29	.256	.298	.356	73	-17	5-3	.990	7	164	85	C112		-0.3
1924	†NY N	118	354	37	107	18	3	5	53	30		43	.302	.357	.412	109	5	3-0	.987	-11	95	84	C110		0.1
1925	NY N	55	148	10	32	3	2	5	16	13		13	.216	.280	.375	70	-16	0-0	.985	2	93	108	C96		-0.8
1926	NY N	55	148	10	32	3	2	5	16	13		13	.216	.280	.365	73	-6	0	.981	-1	85	105	C55		-0.4
1927	StL N	63	194	7	50	5	0	1	30	9		18	.258	.291	.299	56	-12	0	.981	-0	90	108	C62		-0.4
Total	16	1392	4229	331	1122	170	44	47	525	281	11	416	.265	.313	.360	90	-64	37-20	.981	32	111	101	C1247,1b50/2S		5.4

SNYDER, JERRY   Gerald George B7.21.1929 Jenks OK BR/TR/6-0/170* d5.8

1952	Was A	36	57	5	9	2	0	0	2	5	0	8	.158	.226	.193	18	-6	1-0	.965	2	118	117	2b19,S4		-0.4
1953	Was A	29	62	10	21	4	0	0	4	5		8	.339	.388	.403	117	2	1-1	.988	3	117	109	S17,2b4		0.5
1954	Was A	64	154	17	36	3	1	0	17	15		18	.234	.298	.266	60	-9	3-0	.978	3	107	106	S48,2b3		-0.1
1955	Was A	46	107	7	24	5	0	0	6	6-0	0	6	.224	.265	.271	47	-8	1-1	.977	1	108	122	2b22,S20		-0.5
1956	Was A	43	148	14	40	3	1	2	14	10-0	1	9	.270	.321	.345	76	-6	1-0	.968	-1	106	93	S35,2b7		-0.3
1957	Was A	42	93	6	14	1	0	1	4	4-0	0		.151	.186	.194	4	-13	0-1	.966	1	112	96	S15,2b13/3		-1.1
1958	Was A	6	9	1	1	0	0	1	0	1-0		1	.111	.200	.111	-12	-1	0-0	1.000	-1	37	62	2b2/S		-0.2
Total	7	266	630	60	145	18	2	3	47	46-0	1	59	.230	.283	.279	54	-41	7-3	.971	8	106	106	S140,2b70/3		-2.1

SNYDER, JIM   James C. A. B9.15.1847 Brooklyn NY D12.1.1922 Rockaway Beach NY 5-7/130 d5.7

1872	Eck N	25	103	16	30	2	0	0	1				.291	.291	.369	120	4	0-2	.755	3	123	62	S24/COR		0.4

SNYDER, CORY   James Cory B11.11.1962 Inglewood CA BR/TR/6-3/185(175-206) [CleA84 1/4] d6.13 Col Brigham Young OF(99/17/793)

1986	Cle A	103	416	58	113	21	1	24	69	16-0	0	123	.272	.299	.500	114	6	2-3	.987	-5	106	82	O74(6/0/70),S34,3b11/D		-0.1
1987	Cle A	157	577	74	136	24	2	33	82	31-4	2	166	.236	.273	.456	88	-13	5-1	.971	4	105	165	O139(15/0/134),S18		-1.4
1988	Cle A	142	511	71	139	24	3	26	75	42-7	1	101	.272	.326	.483	121	12	5-1	.985	10	105	187	O141(1/3/139)/D		1.9
1989	Cle A	132	489	49	105	17	0	18	59	23-1	2	134	.215	.251	.360	69	-22	6-5	.997	16	107	184	O125R,S7,D2	16	-1.1
1990	Chi A	50	117	10	22	4	0	3	11	6-1	0	41	.188	.228	.299	45	-9	0-0	.975	-2	96	133	O120R,S5		-1.7
1991	Tor A	21	49	4	7	0	1	0	6	3-0	0	19	.143	.189	.184	4	-7	0-0	1.000	-1	62	145	O14R,1b4,3b3,D3		-1.2
	Year	71	166	14	29	4	1	3	17	9-1	0	60	.175	.216	.265	34	-16	0-0	.985	-3	92	88	O43(13/0/31),1b22,3b3,D3		-2.0
1992	SF N	124	390	48	105	22	2	14	57	23-2	2	96	.269	.311	.444	118	7	4-4	.992	-0	93	181	O70(22/13/48),1b2/7,3b14,2b4,S3		0.4
1993	LA N	143	516	61	137	33	1	11	56	47-3	2	147	.266	.331	.397	99	0	4-1	.979	-11	81	170	O115(2/1/113),3b23,1b12,S2		-0.7
1994	LA N	73	153	18	36	6	0	6	18	14-4	1	42	.235	.300	.392	84	-4	0-0	.967	-2	94	50	O50(40/0/13),1b9,3b6,S4,2b3	11	-0.7
Total	9	1068	3656	439	902	178	13	149	488	226-25	13	992	.247	.291	.426	95	-40	28-19	.983	7	99	155	O877R,S73,1b70,3b57,2b7,D7	27	-6.3

SNYDER, JIM   James Robert B8.15.1932 Dearborn MI BR/TR/6-1/185* d9.15 M1/C4 Col Eastern Michigan

1961	Min A	3	5	0	0	0	0	0	0			1	.000	.000	.000	-95	-1		1.000	-0	79	97	2b3		-0.1
1962	Min A	12	10	1	1	0	0	0	0			1	.100	.100	.100	-44	-2	0-1	.941	-4	96	152	2b5/1		-0.2
1964	Min A	26	71	9	11	1	0	0	4	4-0	1	11	.155	.208	.225	17	-7	0-1	.990	-4	84	109	2b25		-1.0
Total	3	41	86	10	12	1	0	0	4	4-0	1	12	.140	.185	.198	6	-11	0-1	.984	-4	85	113	2b33/1		-1.3

YEAR	TM	LG	G	AB	R	H	2B	3B	HR	RBI	BB-IB	HP	SO	AVG	OBP	SLG	AOPS	ABR	SB-CS	FA	FR	RNG	THR	GAMES AT POSITION	DL	BFW

SNYDER, JACK John William B10.6.1886 Lincoln PA D12.13.1981 Brownsville PA BR/TR/5-9/168 d6.13

1914	Buf	F	1	0	0	0	0	0	0	0	0-0	0		—	1.000	—		183	0	0	—	-0	0	0	/C		0.0
1917	Bro	N	7	11	1	3	0	0	0	1	0	0	2	.273	.273	.273		66	0	0	1.000	0	114	113	C5		0.0
Total	2		8	11	1	3	0	0	0	1	1	0	2	.273	.333	.273		84	0	0	1.000	0	109	108	C6		0.0

SNYDER, JOSH Joshua M. B3.1844 Brooklyn NY D4.21.1881 Brooklyn NY d5.18

1872	Eck	NA	9	37	4	6	2	0	0	1	1		3	.162	.184	.216		27	-2	0-0	.788	2	291	0	O9L		0.0

SNYDER, RUSS Russell Henry B6.22.1934 Oak NE BL/TR/6-1/190* d4.18

1959	KC	A	73	243	41	76	13	2	3	21	19-0	2	29	.313	.367	.420	113	5	6-2	.986	5	100	241	O64(27/30/12)		0.7
1960	KC	A	125	304	45	79	10	5	4	26	20-1	1	28	.260	.306	.365	81	-9	7-3	.986	-2	96	87	O91(21/16/62)		-1.4
1961	Bal	A	115	312	46	91	13	5	1	13	20-0	0	32	.292	.333	.375	92	-4	5-3	.966	-2	101	53	O108(75/28/22)		-1.0
1962	Bal	A	139	416	47	127	19	4	9	40	17-0	2	46	.305	.335	.435	113	5	7-4	.974	4	105	146	O121(43/41/45)		0.4
1963	Bal	A	148	429	51	110	21	4	7	36	40-1	0	48	.256	.321	.364	95	-2	18-5	.988	0	106	71	O130(32/74/57)		-0.5
1964	Bal	A	56	93	11	27	3	0	1	7	11-1	0	22	.290	.362	.355	102	1	0-2	.971	-3	80	0	O40(31/8/3)	76	-0.4
1965	Bal	A	132	345	49	93	11	2	1	29	27-1	1	38	.270	.323	.322	83	-8	3-4	1.000	5	114	82	O106(36/36/52)		-0.9
1966	†Bal	A	117	373	66	114	21	5	3	41	38-1	0	37	.306	.368	.413	127	14	2-1	.986	3	108	106	O104(59/86/4)		1.4
1967	Bal	A	108	275	40	65	8	2	4	23	32-0	1	48	.236	.314	.324	91	-3	5-2	.985	-0	103	73	O69(24/25/27)		-0.7
1968	Chi	A	38	82	2	11	2	0	1	5	4-1	0	16	.134	.172	.195	12	-9	0-0	1.000	-3	71	0	O22(9/1/16)		-1.5
	Cle	A	68	217	30	61	8	2	2	23	25-0	0	21	.281	.354	.364	120	0	1-1	.991	5	121	142	O54(5/11/43)/1		0.8
	Year		106	299	32	72	10	2	3	28	29-1	0	37	.241	.306	.318	90	-3	1-1	.992	2	108	106	O76(14/12/59)/1		-0.7
1969	Cle	A	122	266	26	66	10	0	2	24	25-3	0	33	.248	.312	.308	72	-10	3-2	.966	-3	99	23	O106(43/40/26)		-2.3
1970	Mil	A	124	276	34	64	11	0	4	31	16-1	0	40	.232	.270	.315	62	-15	1-3	.981	12	105	17	O1099(442/424/390)/1	76	-6.5
Total	12		1365	3631	488	984	150	29	42	319	294-10	9	438	.271	.325	.363	94	-29	58-32	.981	12	105	17			

SOCKALEXIS, CHIEF Louis Francis B10.24.1871 Old Town ME D12.24.1913 Burlington ME BL/TR/5-11/185 d4.22 Col Holy Cross

1897	Cle	N	66	278	43	94	9	8	3	42	18	1		.338	.385	.460	116	5	16	.888	-0	103	173	O66(0/1/66)		0.1
1898	Cle	N	21	67	11	15	2	0	0	10	1	1		.224	.246	.254	44	-5	0	.964	3	299	693	O16(4/4/8)		-0.3
1899	Cle	N	7	22	0	6	1	0	0	3	1	0		.273	.304	.318	76	-1	0	.818	3	228	323	O5R		-0.1
Total	3		94	367	54	115	12	8	3	55	20		4	.313	.355	.414	103	-1	16	.896	3	143	267	O87(4/5/79)		-0.3

SODD, BILL William B9.18.1914 Ft.Worth TX D5.14.1998 Fort Worth TX BR/TR/6-2/210 d9.27 Col Texas A&M-Commerce

1937	Cle	A	1	1	0	0	0	0	0	0	0	0	1	.000	.000	.000	-99	-0	0-0		—	-0	0	0	/H		0.0

SODERHOLM, ERIC Eric Thane B9.24.1948 Cortland NY BR/TR/5-11/187(187-202) [MinA68*S1/1] d9.3 Col South Georgia JC [DL 1976 Min A 179, 1981 NY A 180]

1971	Min	A	21	64	9	10	4	0	1	4	10-1	3	17	.156	.299	.266	59	-3	0-1	.942	2	112	47	3b20		-0.2
1972	Min	A	93	287	28	54	10	0	13	39	19-2	1	48	.188	.245	.359	75	-10	3-3	.942	1	104	116	3b79		-1.1
1973	Min	A	35	111	22	33	7	2	1	9	21-0	1	16	.297	.414	.423	130	6	1-2	.921	2	110	86	3b33/S		0.7
1974	Min	A	141	464	63	128	18	3	10	51	48-1	5	68	.276	.349	.392	110	7	7-3	.956	4	101	68	3b130/S		1.1
1975	Min	A	117	419	62	120	17	2	11	58	53-1	0	66	.286	.365	.415	119	12	3-5	.969	15	114	61	3b113,D3	39	2.5
1977	Chi	A	130	460	77	129	20	3	25	67	47-5	4	47	.280	.350	.500	129	18	2-4	.978	-1	98	73	3b126,D3		1.4
1978	Chi	A	143	457	57	118	17	1	20	67	39-2	4	44	.258	.318	.431	109	4	2-2	.964	5	96	73	3b128,D11/2		0.6
1979	Chi	A	56	210	31	53	8	2	6	34	19-1	0	19	.252	.313	.395	90	4	0-1	.986	13	118	109	3b56		0.8
	Tex	A	63	147	15	40	6	0	4	19	12-0	1	9	.272	.325	.395	96	-1	0-0	.944	0	99	116	3b37,D14,1b2		-0.2
	Year		119	357	46	93	14	2	10	53	31-1	1	28	.261	.318	.395	92	-4	0-1	.975	13	112	111	3b93,D14,1b2		0.6
1980	†NY	A	95	275	38	79	13	1	11	35	27-2	1	25	.287	.353	.462	123	9	0-0	.952	-1	100	71	D51,3b37	398	6.
Total	9		894	2894	402	764	120	14	102	383	295-15	22	359	.264	.335	.421	110	38	18-21	.962	39	104	79	3b759,D82,1b2,S2/2		

SOFIELD, RICK Richard Michael B12.16.1956 Cheyenne WY BL/TR/6-1/193* [MinA75 1/13] d4.6

1979	Min	A	35	93	8	28	5	0	0	12	12-0	0	27	.301	.381	.355	96	-1	2-3	.954	-1	99	48	O35(7/6/22)		-0.
1980	Min	A	131	417	52	103	18	4	9	49	24-2	2	92	.247	.287	.374	75	-15	4-5	.979	-2	100	84	O126(74/49/9),D2		-2.
1981	Min	A	41	102	9	18	2	0	0	5	8-0	0	22	.176	.234	.196	24	-10	3-2	.983	1	85	242	O34(33/0/1)		-1.
Total	3		207	612	69	149	25	4	9	66	44-2	2	141	.243	.293	.342	71	-25	9-10	.975	-2	97	105	O195(114/55/32),D2		-3.

SOJO, LUIS Luis Beltran (Sojo) B1.3.1965 Caracas, Venez BR/TR/5-11/175(165-185) d7.14 C2

1990	Tor	A	33	80	14	18	5	0	1	9	5-0	0	5	.225	.271	.300	58	-5	1-1	.969	-4	62	57	2b15,S5,O5L,3b4,D3		-0.
1991	Cal	A	113	364	38	94	14	1	3	20	14-0	5	26	.258	.295	.327	72	-15	4-2	.981	27	115	118	2b107,S2/3OLD		1.
1992	Cal	A	106	368	37	100	12	3	7	43	14-0	1	24	.272	.299	.378	88	-8	7-11	.985	14	112	121	2b96,3b9,S5		0.
1993	Tor	A	19	47	5	8	2	0	0	6	4-0	0	2	.170	.231	.213	21	-5	0-0	1.000	-0	81	67	2b8,S8,3b3	20	-0.
1994	Sea	A	63	213	32	59	9	2	6	22	8-0	2	25	.277	.308	.423	84	-6	2-1	.973	18	117	97	2b40,S24/3D	16	-1.
1995	†Sea	A	102	339	50	98	18	2	7	39	23-0	1	19	.289	.335	.416	93	-4	4-2	.983	-14	82	70	3b33,2b27,S19		-2.
1996	Sea	A	77	247	20	52	8	1	1	16	10-0	1	13	.211	.244	.263	28	-28	2-2	.940	5	113	147	2b53,3b19,S21		-2.
	†NY	A	18	40	3	11	2	0	0	5	1-0	0	4	.275	.286	.325	56	-3	0-0	1.000	3	127	147	2b14,S4/3		0.
	Year		95	287	23	63	10	1	1	21	11-0	1	17	.220	.250	.272	32	-31	2-2	.986	7	104	111	2b72,S4,3b3,1b2	45	-2.
1997	NY	A	77	215	27	66	6	1	2	25	16-0	1	14	.307	.355	.372	92	-3	3-1	.982	4	101	104	S20,1b19,2b8,3b6,D2	27	-1.
1998	†NY	A	54	147	16	34	3	1	0	14	4-0	1	15	.231	.250	.265	36	-14	1-0	.973	0	91	132	3b20,2b16,S6,1b4,D2		-0
1999	†NY	A	49	127	20	32	6	0	2	16	4-0	1	17	.252	.275	.346	58	-8	1-0	.960	4	120	58	3b50/2	21	-0.
2000	Pit	N	61	176	14	50	11	0	5	20	11-3	1	16	.284	.328	.432	90	-3	1-0	.989	-3	100	51	2b25,3b10,1b7,S2		-0.
	†NY	A	34	125	19	36	7	1	2	17	6-0	1	6	.288	.321	.408	84	-3	1-0	.933	-2	100	119	3b17,1b8,2b7,S5/D		-0.
2001	NY	A	39	79	5	13	2	0	0	9	4-0	1	12	.165	.214	.190	8	-11	1-0		-0	0	0	/12D		-0.
2003	NY	A	3	4	0	0	0	0	0	0	0-0	0	0	.000	.000	.000	-99	-1	0-0	—	-0	0	0	/D		-0.
Total	13		848	2571	300	671	103	12	36	261	124-3	13	198	.261	.297	.352	71	-117	28-20	.982	53	108	106	2b456,S184,3b158,1b41,D12,O12L	129	-3

SOLAITA, TONY Tolia B1.15.1947 Nuuuli, American Samoa D2.10.1990 Tafuna, American Samoa BL/TL/6-0/215* d9.16

1968	NY	A	1	1	0	1	0	0	0	0	0-0	0	0	1.000	1.000	1.000	-99	0	0-0	1.000	-0	0	407	/1		0
1974	KC	A	96	239	31	64	12	0	7	30	35-5	1	70	.268	.361	.406	115	6	0-3	.991	1	113	72	1b65,D14/OR		-0
1975	KC	A	93	231	35	60	11	0	16	44	39-1	2	79	.260	.369	.515	145	14	0-1	.994	3	130	99	D37,1b35		-0
1976	Cal	A	31	68	4	16	4	0	0	6	6-0	0	17	.235	.286	.294	73	-2	0-0	.974	0	126	38	D14,1b5		1
	Cal	A	63	215	25	58	9	0	9	33	34-3	0	44	.270	.367	.437	144	13	1-1	.998	8	147	76	1b54,D7		-0
	Year		94	283	29	74	13	0	9	42	40-3	0	61	.261	.348	.403	126	10	1-1	.996	8	146	74	1b59,D21		0
1977	Cal	A	116	324	40	78	15	0	14	53	56-6	7	77	.241	.349	.417	113	7	1-3	.990	1	127	106	D18,1b11		-0
1978	Cal	A	60	94	10	21	3	0	1	14	16-3	0	25	.223	.336	.287	79	-2	0-0	.989	0	108	100	1b13		-0
1979	Mon	N	29	42	5	12	4	0	1	7	11-0	0	16	.286	.434	.452	142	3	0-0	1.000	0	133	195	D26,1b6		C
	Tor	A	36	102	14	27	8	1	2	15	16-3	0	25	.265	.364	.422	112	2	0-0	1.000	1	91	106	D18,1b11		C
Total	7		525	1316	164	336	66	1	50	203	214-18	3	345	.255	.357	.421	120	41	2-8	.993	16	122	82	1b281,D122/OR		3

SOLOMON, MOSE Mose Hirsch "The Rabbi of Swat" B12.8.1900 New York NY D6.25.1966 Miami FL BL/TL/5-9.5/180 d9.30

1923	NY	N	2	8	0	3	1	0	0	1	0	0	1	.375	.375	.500	131	0	0-0	.833	-1	70	74	O2R		-0

SOLTERS, MOOSE Julius Joseph (b Julius Joseph Soltesz) B3.22.1906 Pittsburgh PA D9.28.1975 Pittsburgh PA BR/TR/6-0/190 d4.17

1934	Bos	A	101	365	61	109	25	4	7	58	18	1	50	.299	.333	.447	93	-5	9-4	.933	-1	94	155	O89(6/57/26)		-0
1935	Bos	A	24	79	15	19	6	1	0	8	2	1	7	.241	.268	.342	53	-6	1-1	.966	2	120	108	O21(10/0/11)		-0
	StL	A	127	552	79	182	39	6	18	104	34		35	.330	.369	.520	122	16	10-1	.989	12	107	158	O127(116/12/0)		2
	Year		151	631	94	201	45	7	18	112	36		42	.319	.356	.498	113	10	11-2	.985	13	109	151	O148(126/12/11)		1
1936	StL	A	152	628	100	183	45	7	17	134	41		76	.291	.336	.467	93	-10	3-0	.956	13	118	125	O147(145/6/0)		-1
1937	Cle	A	152	589	90	190	42	11	20	109	42		56	.323	.372	.533	125	20	6-9	.953	2	93	171	O149L		-2
1938	Cle	A	67	199	30	40	6	3	2	19	9		28	.201	.250	.291	36	-21	4-1	.969	2	104	126	O46(40/0/6)		-2
1939	Cle	A	41	102	19	28	7	2	3	19	9		15	.275	.333	.441	100	0	2-1	.915	-2	93	69	O25(17/0/8)		-0
	StL	A	40	131	14	27	6	1	0	14	10		20	.206	.262	.267	35	-13	1-0	.935	-1	101	89	O30(22/1/7)		-0
	Year		81	233	33	55	13	3	3	33	19		35	.236	.294	.343	63	-14	3-1	.927	-2	98	80	O55(39/1/15)		-1
1940	Chi	A	116	428	65	132	28	5	7	80	27		54	.308	.351	.472	110	5	3-3	.971	6	115	77	O107L		-1
1941	Chi	A	76	251	24	65	9	4	4	43	18		31	.259	.305	.375	80	-8	3-2	.966	-0	95	133	O63(62/0/1)		-1
1943	Chi	A	42	97	6	15	0	0	1	8	7		5	.155	.212	.186	17	-11	0-1	.941	-1	81	152	O21(13/0/8)		-1
Total	9		938	3421	503	990	213	42	83	599	221		377	.289	.334	.449	96	-33	42-23	.960	31	104	133	O825(687/76/67)		

YEAR	TM	LG	G	AB	R	H	2B	3B	HR	RBI	BB-IB	HP	SO	AVG	OBP	SLG	AOPS	ABR	SB-CS	FA	FR	RNG	THR	GAMES AT POSITION	DL	BFW

SOMERLOTT, JOCK John Wesley B10.26.1882 Flint IN D4.21.1965 Butler IN BR/TR/6-0/160 d9.19
1910	Was	A	16	63	6	14	0	0	0	2	3	0		.222	.258	.222	53	-4	2	.994	0	91	59	1b16		-0.4
1911	Was	A	13	40	2	7	0	0	0	2	0	1		.175	.195	.175	4	-5	2	.992	2	140	135	1b12		-0.4
Total	2		29	103	8	21	0	0	0	4	3	1		.204	.234	.204	32	-9	4	.993	2	111	91	1b28		-0.8

SOMERVILLE, ED Edward G. B3.1.1853 Philadelphia PA D10.1.1877 London ON, Can. BR/TR/5-7/158 d4.21
1875	Cen	NA	14	57	6	13	3	0	0	6	1		3	.228	.241	.281	88		1-0	.771	-6	84	34	2b14/S		-0.6
	NH	NA	33	136	14	29	5	0	0	7	1		3	.213	.219	.250	72	-2	1-2	.802	13	139	123	2b29,3b2/1S		0.7
	Year		47	193	20	42	8	0	0	13	2		6	.218	.226	.259	77	-2	2-2	.794	7	121	94	2b43,S2,3b2/1		0.1
1876	Lou	N	64	256	29	48	5	1	0	14	1		6	.188	.191	.215	30	-20		.870	28	131	115	2b64		0.9

SOMMER, JOE Joseph John B11.20.1858 Covington KY D1.16.1938 Cincinnati OH BR/TR d7.8 OF(567/15/132) ▲
1880	Cin	N	24	88	10	16	1	0	0			2		.182	.182	.193	28	-7		.913	-1	88	110	O22(14/8/0)/S3C		-0.7
1882	Cin	AA	80	354	82	102	12	6	1	29	24			.288	.333	.364	128	10		.925	3	47	121	O80L		1.0
1883	Cin	AA	97	413	79	115	5	7	3	52	20			.278	.312	.346	106	1		.854	-3	58	53	O94(82/0/12),3b3/P		-0.3
1884	Bal	AA	107	479	96	129	11	10	4		8		8	.269	.293	.359	107	2		.841	3	94	95	3b97,O9(0/2/7)/2		0.6
1885	Bal	AA	110	471	84	118	23	6	1	44	24	3		.251	.291	.331	98	0		.920	12	77	54	O107(105/2/0),S2,3b2,P2/1		0.8
1886	Bal	AA	139	560	79	117	18	4	1	52	24	3		.209	.245	.261	60	-26	31	.900	7	73	131	O95L,2b32,3b11,S3/P		-1.8
1887	Bal	AA	131	463	88	123	11	5	0	65	63	4		.266	.358	.311	93	0	29	.902	-3	81	102	O110L,2b13,3b10,S2/P		-0.4
1888	Bal	AA	79	297	31	65	10	0	0	35	18	1		.219	.266	.253	68	-10	13	.871	-2	106	65	O44(30/0/14),S34,2b2/1		-1.1
1889	Bal	AA	106	386	51	85	13	2	1	36	42	1	49	.220	.298	.272	62	-19	18	.929	9	119	157	O105(4/3/99)/S		-0.9
1890	Cle	N	9	35	4	8	1	0	0	0	2	0	2	.229	.270	.257	55	-2	0	.789	-2	0	0	O9L/P		-0.3
	Bal	AA	38	129	13	33	4	2	0	23	13	0		.256	.324	.318	85	-3	10	.892	2	80	221	O38L		-0.2
Total	10		920	3675	617	911	109	42	11	342	238	20	53	.248	.297	.309	88	-54	101	.901	27	83	108	O713L,3b124,2b48,S43,P6,1b2/C		-3.3

SOMMERS, PETE Joseph Andrews B10.26.1866 Cleveland OH D7.22.1908 Cleveland OH BR/TR/5-11.5/181 d4.27
1887	NY	AA	33	116	9	21	3	0	1	12	7	1		.181	.234	.233	32	-11	6	.830	-7			C31/OR1		-1.3
1888	Bos	N	4	13	1	3	1	0	0	0	0	0	3	.231	.231	.308	69	0	0	.880	-1			C4		-0.1
1889	Chi	N	12	45	5	10	5	0	0	8	2	1	8	.222	.271	.333	65	-2	0	.836	-4			C11/OR		-0.5
	Ind	N	23	84	12	21	2	2	2	14	1	1	16	.250	.267	.393	82	-3	2	.905	-4			C21,O2C		-0.4
	Year		35	129	17	31	7	2	2	22	3	2	24	.240	.269	.372	76	-5	2	.882	-8	0	0	C32,O3(0/2/1)		-0.9
1890	NY	N	17	47	4	5	1	0	0	1	4	1	13	.106	.192	.170	6	-6	0	.837	-1	98	148	C11,1b5,O2R		-0.5
	Cle	N	9	34	4	7	1	0	1	2	0	3	.206	.250	.294	60	-2	0	.906	1	119	117	C8/OC		0.0
Total	4		98	339	35	67	13	4	3	36	16	4	43	.198	.242	.286	50	-24	8	.865	-15	108	133	C86,O7(0/3/4),1b6		-2.8

SOMMERS, BILL William Dunn B2.17.1923 Brooklyn NY D9.22.2000 Palm City FL BR/TR/6-0/180 d4.25
| 1950 | StL | A | 65 | 137 | 24 | 35 | 5 | 1 | 0 | 14 | 25 | 0 | 14 | .255 | .370 | .307 | 72 | -5 | 0 | .917 | -7 | 95 | 76 | 3b37,2b21 | | -1.1 |

SORENSEN, ZACH Zach Hart B1.3.1977 Salt Lake City UT BB/TR/6-0/190* [CleA98 2/63] d6.3 Col Wichita St.
2003	Cle	A	36	37	2	5	1	0	1	2	7-0	0	13	.135	.273	.243	38	-3	0-3	.944	-1	90	96	2b14,S3/3OLD		-0.5
2005	LA	A	12	12	3	2	1	0	0	0	0-0	0	2	.167	.167	.250	9	-2	0-0	1.000	-1	61	59	2b5/3		-0.2
Total	2		48	49	5	7	2	0	1	2	7-0	0	15	.143	.250	.245	32	-5	0-3	.955	-3	83	87	2b19,S3,3b2/DOL		-0.7

SORIANO, ALFONSO Alfonso Guilleard B1.7.1976 San Pedro de Macoris, D.R. BR/TR/6-1/180(160-180) d9.14
1999	NY	A	9	8	2	1	0	1	1	0-0	0	3	.125	.125	.500	50	-1	0-1	.500	-1	37	166	/SD		-0.2
2000	NY	A	22	50	5	9	3	0	2	3	1-0	0	15	.180	.196	.360	37	-5	2-0	.846	-6	77	153	3b10,S9/2D		-0.9
2001	†NY	A	158	574	77	154	34	3	18	73	29-0	3	125	.268	.304	.432	91	-9	43-14	.973	-12	84	99	2b156,D2		-0.8
2002	†NY	A★	156	696	128	209	51	2	39	102	23-1	14	157	.300	.332	.547	130	28	41-13	.968	-13	92	90	2b155/D		2.6
2003	†NY	A★	156	682	114	198	36	5	38	91	38-7	12	130	.290	.338	.525	125	22	35-8	.975	3	100	91	2b155		3.5
2004	Tex	A★	145	608	77	170	32	4	28	91	33-4	5	121	.280	.324	.484	103	1	18-5	.969	6	102	109	2b142,D3		1.6
2005	Tex	A★	156	637	102	171	43	2	36	104	33-3	7	125	.268	.309	.512	110	7	30-2	.972	-11	100	90	2b153,D2		0.9
Total	7		802	3255	505	912	199	16	162	465	157-15	46	676	.280	.320	.509	111	43	169-43	.971	-33	95	96	2b762,D15,3b10,S10		6.7

SORRELL, BILL William B10.14.1940 Morehead KY BL/TR/6-0/190* d9.2
1965	Phi	N	10	13	2	5	0	0	1	2	2-0	0	1	.385	.467	.615	206	2	0-0	—	-1	0	0	/3		0.1
1967	SF	N	18	17	1	3	1	0	0	1	3-0	0	2	.176	.300	.235	56	-1	0-0	1.000	1	28	0	O5L		-0.2
1970	KC	A	57	135	12	36	2	0	4	14	10-4	0	13	.267	.317	.370	89	-2	1-0	.873	-6	87	57	3b29,O4(2/0/2),1b3		-0.9
Total	3		85	165	15	44	3	0	5	17	15-4	0	16	.267	.328	.376	95	-1	1-0	.873	-8	82	57	3b30,O9(7/0/2),1b3		-1.0

SORRELLS, CHICK Raymond Edwin B7.31.1896 Stringtown OK D7.20.1983 Terrell TX BR/TR/5-9/155 d9.18 Col St. Edwards
| 1922 | Cle | A | 1 | 0 | 0 | 0 | 0 | 0 | 0 | 0 | 0-0 | 0 | 0 | .000 | .000 | .000 | — | 0 | 0-0 | 1.000 | 0 | 205 | 0 | /S | | 0.0 |

SORRENTO, PAUL Paul Anthony B11.17.1965 Somerville MA BL/TR/6-2/210(200-223) d9.8 Col Florida St.
1989	Min	A	14	21	2	5	0	0	0	1	5-1	0	4	.238	.370	.238	74	0	0-0	1.000	0	82	1b5,D5		-0.1
1990	Min	A	41	121	11	25	4	1	5	13	12-0	1	31	.207	.281	.380	79	-4	1-1	.992	-1	71	109	D23,1b15		-0.7
1991	†Min	A	26	47	6	12	2	0	4	13	4-2	0	11	.255	.314	.553	129	2	0-0	1.000	1	119	106	1b13,D2		0.1
1992	Cle	A	140	458	52	123	24	1	18	60	51-7	1	89	.269	.341	.443	120	12	0-3	.993	-2	96	107	1b121,D11		0.1
1993	Cle	A	148	463	75	119	26	1	18	65	58-11	2	121	.257	.340	.434	107	5	3-1	.995	-1	98	95	1b144,O3R/D		-0.7
1994	Cle	A	95	322	43	90	14	0	14	62	34-6	0	68	.280	.345	.453	104	1	0-1	.995	-1	95	104	1b84,D8		-0.7
1995	†Cle	A	104	323	50	76	14	0	25	79	51-6	0	71	.235	.336	.511	115	6	1-1	.992	-4	88	128	1b91,D11		-0.5
1996	Sea	A	143	471	67	136	32	1	23	93	57-10	7	103	.289	.370	.507	119	15	1-0	.990	-0	100	86	1b138		0.2
1997	†Sea	A	146	457	68	123	19	0	31	80	51-9	3	112	.269	.345	.514	121	13	0-2	.996	8	120	86	1b139/D		0.9
1998	TB	A	137	435	40	98	27	0	17	57	54-1	5	133	.225	.313	.405	83	-11	2-3	1.000	3	138	102	D86,1b27,O18(4/0/14)		-1.5
1999	TB	A	99	294	40	69	14	1	11	42	49-1	1	101	.235	.351	.401	90	-4	1-1	.957	-5	89	63	O57L,1b27,D9	15	-1.2
Total	11		1093	3412	454	876	176	5	166	565	426-54	21	844	.257	.340	.457	107	35	8-15	.994	-2	100	102	1b806,D157,O78(61/0/17)	15	-4.1

SOSA, JUAN Juan Luis (Encarnacion) B8.19.1975 San Francisco de Macoris, D.R. BR/TR/6-1/175* d9.10
1999	Col	N	11	9	3	2	0	0	0	0	2-0	0	2	.222	.364	.222	42	-1	0-0	1.000	0	81	0	O6(1/5/0),S2		0.0
2001	Ari	N	2	1	0	0	0	0	0	0	0-0	0	1	.000	.000	.000	-94	0	0-0	1.000	0	454	0	/3		0.0
Total	2		13	10	3	2	0	0	0	0	2-0	0	3	.200	.333	.200	32	-1	0-0	1.000	1	81	0	O6(1/5/0),S2/3		0.0

SOSA, SAMMY Samuel Peralta "Slammin' Sammy" B11.12.1968 San Pedro de Macoris, D.R. BR/TR/6-0/190(165-230) d6.16
1989	Tex	A	25	84	8	20	3	0	1	3	0-0	2	20	.238	.238	.310	52	-6	0-2	.944	-1	96	116	O19(12/8/1),D6		-0.7
	Chi	A	33	99	19	27	5	0	3	10	11-2	2	27	.273	.351	.414	119	3	7-3	.969	-4	81	55	O13(1/25/9)		-0.1
	Year		58	183	27	47	8	0	4	13	11-2	2	47	.257	.303	.366	89	-3	7-5	.960	-4	86	77	O52(13/33/10),D6		-0.8
1990	Chi	A	153	532	72	124	26	10	15	70	33-4	6	150	.233	.282	.404	93	-8	32-16	.962	4	106	133	O152(0/1/152)		-0.7
1991	Chi	A	116	316	39	64	10	1	10	33	14-2	2	98	.203	.240	.335	59	-19	13-6	.973	3	110	92	O111(0/13/102),D2		-0.9
1992	Chi	N	67	262	41	68	7	2	8	25	19-1	4	63	.260	.317	.393	98	-1	15-7	.961	-8	83	105	O67C		-0.9
1993	Chi	N	159	598	92	156	25	5	33	93	38-6	4	135	.261	.309	.485	110	5	36-11	.976	3	97	160	O158(0/70/114)		0.7
1994	Chi	N	105	426	59	128	17	6	25	70	25-1	2	92	.300	.339	.545	126	14	22-13	.973	6	114	63	O105(0/15/98)		1.2
1995	Chi	N★	144	564	89	151	17	3	36	119	58-11	5	134	.268	.340	.500	119	13	34-7	.962	8	113	121	O143R		1.8
1996	Chi	N	124	498	84	136	21	2	40	100	34-6	6	134	.273	.323	.564	125	14	18-5	.964	6	105	174	O124R		1.6
1997	Chi	N★	162	642	90	161	31	4	36	119	45-9	2	174	.251	.300	.480	97	-6	22-12	.977	7	108	134	O161R	40	-0.6
1998	†Chi	N★	159	643	134	198	20	0	66	158	73-14	1	171	.308	.377	.647	158	51	18-9	.975	7	110	130	O159(0/7/156)		5.0
1999	Chi	N★	162	625	114	180	24	2	63	141	78-8	3	171	.288	.367	.635	148	43	7-8	.978	9	118	75	O162(0/25/146)		4.1
2000	Chi	N★	156	604	106	193	38	1	50	138	91-19	2	168	.320	.406	.634	160	57	7-4	.970	-6	100	30	O156(0/0/156)		4.0
2001	Chi	N★	160	577	146	189	34	5	64	160	116-37	6	153	.328	.437	.737	204	90	0-2	.982	6	112	82	O160R		8.6
2002	Chi	N★	150	556	122	160	19	2	49	108	103-15	3	144	.288	.399	.594	162	48	2-0	.980	2	108	77	O150R		4.2
2003	†Chi	N	137	517	99	144	22	0	40	103	62-9	5	143	.279	.358	.553	131	23	0-1	.977	-10	90	25	O137R	20	0.5
2004	Chi	N★	126	478	69	121	21	0	35	80	56-4	2	133	.253	.332	.517	112	7	0-0	.984	1	105	67	O124R,D2	33	0.1
2005	Bal	A	102	380	39	84	15	1	14	45	39-3	2	84	.221	.295	.376	77	-13	1-1	.976	-2	93	80	O66R,D35	57	-2.0
Total	17		2240	8401	1422	2304	355	44	588	1575	895-151	58	2319	.274	.345	.537	128	319	234-107	.973	29	105	97	O2187(13/233/1999),D45	234	25.0

SOTHERN, DENNY Dennis Elwood (b Dennis Elwood Southern) B1.20.1904 Washington DC D12.7.1977 Durham NC BR/TR/5-11/175 d9.10
| 1926 | Phi | N | 14 | 53 | 5 | 13 | 1 | 0 | 3 | 10 | 4 | 1 | 10 | .245 | .310 | .434 | 94 | -1 | | .975 | 1 | 117 | 70 | O13(11/3/0) | | -0.1 |
| 1928 | Phi | N | 141 | 579 | 82 | 165 | 27 | 5 | 5 | 38 | 34 | 2 | 53 | .285 | .327 | .375 | 80 | -17 | 17 | .964 | 5 | 101 | 161 | O136(8/127/1) | | -1.8 |

YEAR	TM LG	G	AB	R	H	2B	3B	HR	RBI	BB-IB	HP	SO	AVG	OBP	SLG	AOPS	ABR	SB-CS	FA	FR	RNG	THR	GAMES AT POSITION	DL	BFW
1929	Phi N	76	294	52	90	21	3	5	27	16	2	24	.306	.346	.449	90	-5	13	.967	2	102	132	O71(2/63/6)		-0.6
1930	Phi N	90	347	66	97	26	1	5	36	22	2	37	.280	.326	.403	70	-17	6	.967	7	100	226	O84(3/81/0)		-1.2
	Pit N	17	51	4	9	4	0	1	4	3	0	4	.176	.222	.314	28	-6	2	.971	0	114	0	O13(0/12/1)		-0.6
	Year	107	398	70	106	30	1	6	40	25	2	41	.266	.305	.392	65	-23	8	.967	7	102	199	O97(3/93/1)		-1.8
1931	Bro N	19	31	10	5	1	0	0	0	4	0	8	.161	.257	.194	23	-3	0	.958	0	120	0	O10(3/7/0)		-0.3
Total	5	357	1355	219	379	80	9	19	115	83	7	136	.280	.325	.394	77	-49	38	.966	15	103	158	O327(27/293/8)		-4.6

SOTO, GEOVANY Geovany B1.20.1983 San Juan, PR BR/TR/6-1/230 d9.23

YEAR	TM LG	G	AB	R	H	2B	3B	HR	RBI	BB-IB	HP	SO	AVG	OBP	SLG	AOPS	ABR	SB-CS	FA	FR	RNG	THR	GAMES AT POSITION	DL	BFW
2005	Chi N	1	1	0	0	0	0	0	0	0-0	0	1	.000	.000	.000	-97	0	0-0	—	0			/H		0.0

SOUCHOCK, STEVE Stephen "Bud" B3.3.1919 Yatesboro PA D7.28.2002 Westland MI BR/TR/6-2.5/203* d5.25

YEAR	TM LG	G	AB	R	H	2B	3B	HR	RBI	BB-IB	HP	SO	AVG	OBP	SLG	AOPS	ABR	SB-CS	FA	FR	RNG	THR	GAMES AT POSITION	DL	BFW
1946	NY A	47	86	15	26	3	3	2	10	7	1	13	.302	.342	.477	131	3	0-3	.964	-2	71	123	1b20		-0.1
1948	NY A	44	118	11	24	3	1	3	11	7	0	13	.203	.248	.322	51	-9	3-0	.988	-2	73	101	1b32		-1.1
1949	Chi A	84	252	29	59	13	5	7	37	25	0	38	.234	.303	.409	90	-6	5-2	.951	1	108	33	O39L,1b30		-0.8
1951	Det A	91	188	33	46	10	3	11	28	18	1	27	.245	.314	.505	118	3	0-2	.941	-1	101	94	O59(30/0/29),3b3/12		-0.1
1952	Det A	92	265	40	66	16	4	13	45	21	0	28	.249	.304	.487	117	4	1-0	.964	2	110	106	O56(16/1/41),3b13,1b9		0.4
1953	Det A	89	278	29	84	13	3	11	46	8	2	35	.302	.326	.489	119	5	5-1	.962	-2	105	122	O80(39/0/44)/1		0.5
1954	Det A	25	39	6	7	0	1	3	8	2	0	10	.179	.220	.462	84	-2	1-1	1.000	0	115	0	O9L,3b2		-0.2
1955	Det A	1	1	0	1	0	0	0	1	0-0	0	0	1.000	1.000	1.000	449	0	0-0	—	0			/H		0.0
Total	8	473	1227	163	313	58	20	50	186	88-0	4	164	.255	.307	.457	106	-2	15-9	.957	0	106	92	O243(133/1/114),1b93,3b18/2	34	-1.4

SOUTHWICK, CLYDE Clyde Aubra B11.3.1886 Maxwell IA D10.14.1961 Freeport IL BL/TR/6-0/180 d8.22 Col Iowa St.

YEAR	TM LG	G	AB	R	H	2B	3B	HR	RBI	BB-IB	HP	SO	AVG	OBP	SLG	AOPS	ABR	SB-CS	FA	FR	RNG	THR	GAMES AT POSITION	DL	BFW
1911	StL A	4	12	3	3	0	0	0	0				.250	.308	.250	58	-1	0	.938	-1	75	82	C4		-0.1

SOUTHWORTH, BILL William Frederick B11.10.1945 Madison WI BR/TR/6-2/205 d10.2

YEAR	TM LG	G	AB	R	H	2B	3B	HR	RBI	BB-IB	HP	SO	AVG	OBP	SLG	AOPS	ABR	SB-CS	FA	FR	RNG	THR	GAMES AT POSITION	DL	BFW
1964	Mil N	3	7	2	2	0	0	1	2	0-0	2	3	.286	.444	.714	219	1	0-0	1.000	-1	48	0	3b2		0.0

SOUTHWORTH, BILLY William Harrison B3.9.1893 Harvard NE D11.15.1969 Columbus OH BL/TR/5-9/170 d8.4 M13/C1

YEAR	TM LG	G	AB	R	H	2B	3B	HR	RBI	BB-IB	HP	SO	AVG	OBP	SLG	AOPS	ABR	SB-CS	FA	FR	RNG	THR	GAMES AT POSITION	DL	BFW
1913	Cle A	1	0	0	0	0	0	0	0	0	0	0	—	—	—	—	0	0		0	0	0	/O		0.0
1915	Cle A	60	177	25	39	2	5	0	8	36	0	12	.220	.352	.288	90	-1	2-4	.942	1	96	117	O44(10/30/4)		-0.5
1918	Pit N	64	246	37	84	5	7	2	43	26	2	9	.341	.409	.443	154	16	19	.980	6	119	112	O64R		2.1
1919	Pit N	121	453	56	127	14	14	4	61	32	1	22	.280	.329	.400	114	6	23	.968	6	110	105	O121(75/0/46)		0.7
1920	Pit N	146	546	64	155	17	13	6	53	52	2	20	.284	.348	.374	104	3	23-25	.991	7	121	64	O142R		-0.1
1921	Bos N	141	569	86	175	25	15	7	79	36	2	13	.308	.351	.441	115	10	22-20	.975	5	101	123	O141R		0.2
1922	Bos N	43	158	27	51	4	4	4	18	18	1	1	.323	.392	.475	128	7	4-1	.955	4	118	126	O41R		0.7
1923	Bos N	153	611	95	195	29	16	6	78	61	2	23	.319	.383	.448	124	21	14-16	.943	3	103	122	O151R,2b2		0.9
1924	†NY N	94	281	40	72	13	0	3	36	32	0	16	.256	.332	.335	81	-6	1-6	.935	-6	94	63	O75(1/51/19)		-1.8
1925	NY N	123	473	79	138	19	5	6	44	51	2	11	.292	.363	.391	97	-1	6-13	.964	-15	85	59	O119(0/117/2)		-2.3
1926	NY N	36	116	23	38	6	1	5	30	7	0	1	.328	.366	.526	139	6	1	.970	-2	93	67	O29(7/16/8)		0.3
	†StL N	99	391	76	124	22	6	11	69	26	3	9	.317	.364	.488	123	12	13	.971	-3	109	36	O99R		0.1
	Year	135	507	99	162	28	7	16	99	33	3	10	.320	.365	.497	127	18	14	.971	-5	105	43	O128(7/16/107)		0.4
1927	StL N	92	306	52	92	15	5	2	39	23	0	7	.301	.350	.402	98	-1	10	.970	-4	95	64	O83R		-1.1
1929	StL N	19	32	1	6	2	0	0	3	2	0	4	.188	.235	.250	20	-4	0	1.000	4	118	0	O5R,M		-0.4
Total	13	1192	4359	661	1296	173	91	52	561	402	14	148	.297	.359	.415	111	68	138-85	.965	3	104	88	O1115(93/214/805),2b2		-1.2

SOWDERS, LEN Leonard B6.29.1861 Louisville KY D11.19.1888 Indianapolis IN 5-11.5/172 d9.10 b-John b-Bill

YEAR	TM LG	G	AB	R	H	2B	3B	HR	RBI	BB-IB	HP	SO	AVG	OBP	SLG	AOPS	ABR	SB-CS	FA	FR	RNG	THR	GAMES AT POSITION	DL	BFW
1886	Bal AA	23	76	10	20	3	1	0	14	12	0		.263	.364	.329	121	3	6	.889	0	121	0	O23C/1		0.?

SPALDING, AL Albert Goodwill B9.2.1850 Byron IL D9.9.1915 San Diego CA BR/TR/6-1/170 d5.5 M2 HF1939 ▲

YEAR	TM LG	G	AB	R	H	2B	3B	HR	RBI	BB-IB	HP	SO	AVG	OBP	SLG	AOPS	ABR	SB-CS	FA	FR	RNG	THR	GAMES AT POSITION	DL	BFW
1871	Bos NA	31	144	43	39	10	1	1	31	8		1	.271	.309	.375	93	-1	2-0	.776	-1	108	105	P31,O9C		0.?
1872	Bos NA	48	237	60	84	12	5	0	47	3		1	.354	.363	.447	140	10	3-0	.902	8	148	111	P48,O7C		0.?
1873	Bos NA	60	323	83	106	15	1	1	71	3		2	.328	.334	.390	106	0	9-0	.885	10	154	197	P60,O14C		0.?
1874	Bos NA	71	362	80	119	13	1	0	54	3		0	.329	.334	.370	119	6	2-1	.854	3	124	144	P71,O6C		0.?
1875	Bos NA	74	343	68	107	15	3	0	56	3		1	.312	.318	.373	134	11	2-2	.906	3	112	223	P72,O18(1/9/9),1b4		0.?
1876	Chi N	66	292	54	91	14	2	0	44	6		3	.312	.326	.373	118	4		.951	4	110	306	P61,O10(9/1/0),1b3/SM		0.?
1877	Chi N	60	254	29	65	7	6	0	35	3		16	.256	.265	.331	77	-8		.959	5	155	116	1b45,2b13,P4,3b2,M		-0.?
1878	Chi N	1	4	0	2	0	0	0	0	0		0	.500	.500	.500	215	0		.429	-2	0	0	/2		-0.?
Total	5 NA	284	1409	334	455	65	11	2	259	20		7	.323	.332	.389	120	26	18-3	.875	25	130	164	P282,O54(1/45/9),1b4		1.?
Total	3	127	550	83	158	21	8	0	79	9		19	.287	.299	.355	99	-4		.948	7	114	300	P65,1b48,2b14,O10(9/1/0),3b2/S		-0.?

SPALDING, DICK Charles Harry B10.13.1893 Philadelphia PA D2.3.1950 Philadelphia PA BL/TL/5-11/185 d4.18 C6

YEAR	TM LG	G	AB	R	H	2B	3B	HR	RBI	BB-IB	HP	SO	AVG	OBP	SLG	AOPS	ABR	SB-CS	FA	FR	RNG	THR	GAMES AT POSITION	DL	BFW
1927	Phi N	115	442	68	131	16	3	0	25	38	0	40	.296	.352	.346	86	-3	5	.992	2	109	68	O113L		-1.?
1928	Was A	16	23	1	8	0	0	0	0	0	0	4	.348	.348	.348	84	-1	0-2	1.000	-0	105	0	O11(8/0/3)		-0.?
Total	2	131	465	69	139	16	3	0	25	38	0	44	.299	.352	.346	86	-9	5-2	.993	2	109	66	O124(121/0/3)		-1.?

SPANGLER, AL Albert Donald B7.8.1933 Philadelphia PA BL/TL/6-0/175* d9.16 C3 Col Duke

YEAR	TM LG	G	AB	R	H	2B	3B	HR	RBI	BB-IB	HP	SO	AVG	OBP	SLG	AOPS	ABR	SB-CS	FA	FR	RNG	THR	GAMES AT POSITION	DL	BFW
1959	Mil N	6	12	3	5	0	1	0	0	1	0	1	.417	.462	.583	192	1	1-0	1.000	-0	98	0	O4(1/3/0)		0.?
1960	Mil N	101	105	26	28	5	2	0	6	14-1	0	17	.267	.355	.352	103	1	6-2	.989	5	126	129	O92(90/1/1)		0.?
1961	Mil N	68	97	23	26	2	0	0	6	28-2	0	9	.268	.432	.289	102	3	4-2	1.000	-0	98	95	O44(23/21/1)		0.?
1962	Hou N	129	418	51	119	10	9	5	35	70-6	3	46	.285	.389	.388	119	14	7-6	.960	-3	91	96	O121(93/28/0)		0.?
1963	Hou N	120	430	52	121	25	4	4	27	50-5	3	38	.281	.355	.386	122	14	5-8	.987	0	102	70	O113(87/33/3)		0.?
1964	Hou N	135	449	51	110	18	5	4	38	41-1	4	43	.245	.311	.334	88	-7	7-8	.964	-6	89	41	O127(113/18/0)		-2.?
1965	Hou N	38	112	18	24	1	1	1	9	14-2	1	8	.214	.299	.268	66	-5	1-1	.956	-1	81	192	O33(31/1/1)		-0.?
	Cal A	51	96	17	25	1	0	1	8	8-0	0	9	.260	.317	.271	70	-4	4-0	.973	-2	91	0	O24(4/17/6)		-0.?
1966	Cal A	6	9	2	6	0	0	0	2	0-0	0	2	.667	.727	.667	312	0	0-0	1.000	-0	71	0	O3R		0.?
1967	Chi N	62	130	18	33	7	0	0	13	23-4	0	17	.254	.361	.308	91	0	2-2	.986	-1	104	0	O41(0/7/34)		-0.?
1968	Chi N	88	177	21	48	9	3	2	18	20-2	1	24	.271	.343	.390	114	4	0-1	.973	-2	93	62	O48(1/7/42)		-0.?
1969	Chi N	82	213	23	45	8	1	1	23	21-0	1	16	.211	.284	.315	60	-11	0-2	.950	-6	84	26	O58(0/1/57)		-2.?
1970	Chi N	21	14	2	2	0	0	0	1	3-0	0	3	.143	.294	.429	81	0	0-0	1.000	0	164	0	O6(3/0/3)		0.?
1971	Chi N	5	5	0	2	0	0	0	0	0	0	1	.400	.400	.400	111	0	0	—	0			/H		0.?
Total	13	912	2267	307	594	87	26	21	175	295-23	11	234	.262	.347	.351	100	13	37-32	.973	-16	95	68	O714(446/137/151)		-4.?

SPEAKE, BOB Robert Charles "Spook" B8.22.1930 Springfield MO BL/TL/6-1/178* d4.16

YEAR	TM LG	G	AB	R	H	2B	3B	HR	RBI	BB-IB	HP	SO	AVG	OBP	SLG	AOPS	ABR	SB-CS	FA	FR	RNG	THR	GAMES AT POSITION	DL	BFW
1955	Chi N	95	261	36	57	9	5	12	43	28-4	3	71	.218	.300	.429	91	-4	3-4	.959	-1	94	110	O55(49/0/8),1b8		-0.?
1957	Chi N	129	418	65	97	14	5	16	50	38-1	3	68	.232	.299	.404	89	-8	5-6	.974	0	92	111	O60(20/40/0),1b39		-1.?
1958	SF N	66	71	9	15	3	0	3	10	13-1	0	15	.211	.333	.380	90	-1	0-1	.938	1	91	363	O10L		-0.?
1959	SF N	15	11	0	1	0	0	0	1	1-0	0	4	.091	.167	.091	-30	-2	0-0	—	0			/H		-0.?
Total	4	305	761	110	170	26	10	31	104	80-6	6	158	.223	.301	.406	88	-15	8-11	.966	0	93	126	O125(79/40/8),1b47		-2.?

SPEAKER, TRIS Tristram E "The Grey Eagle" B4.4.1888 Hubbard TX D12.8.1958 Lake Whitney TX BL/TL/5-11.5/193 d9.12 M8 HF1937 Col Texas Wesleyan

YEAR	TM LG	G	AB	R	H	2B	3B	HR	RBI	BB-IB	HP	SO	AVG	OBP	SLG	AOPS	ABR	SB-CS	FA	FR	RNG	THR	GAMES AT POSITION	DL	BFW
1907	Bos A	7	19	0	3	0	0	0	1	1			.158	.200	.158	14	-2	0	1.000	1	394	930	O4R		-0.?
1908	Bos A	31	116	12	26	2	2	0	9	4	2		.224	.262	.276	73	-4	3	1.000	4	254	314	O31(1/30/0)		-0.?
1909	Bos A	143	544	73	168	26	13	7	77	38	7		.309	.362	.443	151	30	35	.973	19	195	298	O142C		4.?
1910	Bos A	141	538	92	183	20	14	7	65	52	6		.340	.404	.468	169	43	35	.957	9	117	96	O140C		3.?
1911	Bos A	141	500	88	167	34	13	8	70	59	13		.334	.418	.502	158	41	25	.956	3	100	118	O138C		3.?
1912	†Bos A	153	580	136	222	53	12	10	90	82	6		.383	.464	.567	185	68	52	.958	7	110	157	O153C		7.?
1913	Bos A	141	520	94	189	35	22	3	71	65	7	22	.363	.441	.533	180	54	46	.942	19	122	137	O139C		6.?
1914	Bos A	158	571	101	193	46	18	4	90	77	9	25	.338	.423	.503	178	57	42-29	.968	23	121	142	O156C/P1		7.?
1915	†Bos A	150	547	108	176	25	12	0	69	81	7	14	.322	.416	.411	152	39	29-25	.976	8	108	97	O151C		5.?
1916	Cle A	151	546	102	211	41	8	2	79	82	4	20	.386	.470	.502	181	60	35-27	.975	6	103	117	O151C		7.?
1917	Cle A	142	523	90	184	42	11	2	60	67	7	14	.352	.432	.486	168	45	30	.980	2	101	107	O127C		5.?
1918	Cle A	127	471	73	150	33	11	0	61	64	1	9	.318	.403	.435	140	25	27	.973	8	118	83	O134C,M		4.?
1919	Cle A	134	494	83	146	38	12	2	63	73	4	12	.296	.395	.433	125	20	19	.983	15	112	130	O134C,M		5.?
1920	†Cle A	150	552	137	214	50	11	8	107	97	5	13	.388	.483	.562	171	64	10-13	.977	6	102	130	O148C,M		7.?
1921	Cle A	132	506	107	183	52	14	3	75	68	2	11	.362	.439	.538	146	38	2-4	.984	9	115	0	O109C,M		4.?
1922	Cle A	131	426	85	161	48	8	11	71	77	1	11	.378	.474	.606	178	55	8-3	.983	3	101	114	O109C,M		4.?
1923	Cle A	150	574	133	218	59	11	17	130	93	2	15	.380	.469	.610	183	74	8-9	.968	3	94	148	O150C,M		7.?

YEAR	TM LG	G	AB	R	H	2B	3B	HR	RBI	BB-IB	HP	SO	AVG	OBP	SLG	AOPS	ABR	SB-CS	FA	FR	RNG	THR	GAMES AT POSITION	DL	BFW
924	Cle A	135	486	94	167	36	9	9	65	72	4	13	.344	.432	.510	141	32	5-7	.963	1	94	164	O128(0/127/1),M		2.5
925	Cle A	117	429	79	167	35	5	12	87	70	4	12	.389	.479	.578	166	48	5-2	.967	4	99	130	O109C,M		**4.3**
926	Cle A	150	539	96	164	52	8	7	86	94	0	15	.304	.408	.469	127	26	6-1	.981	4	98	130	O149C,M		2.4
927	Was A	141	523	71	171	43	6	2	73	55	4		.327	.395	.444	119	17	9-8	.967	-3	94	103	O120(0/119/1),1b17		0.7
928	Phi A	64	191	28	51	22	2	3	30	10	2	5	.267	.310	.450	95	-2	5-1	.975	1	94	162	O50(1/49/0)		-0.2
total 22		2789	10195	1882	3514	792	222	117	1529	1381	103	220	.345	.428	.500	156	828	436-129	.970	161	113	136	O2698(2/2690/6),1b18/P		82.7

SPEED, HORACE Horace Arthur B10.4.1951 Los Angeles CA BR/TR/6-1/180* [SFN69 3/66] d4.10

YEAR	TM LG	G	AB	R	H	2B	3B	HR	RBI	BB-IB	HP	SO	AVG	OBP	SLG	AOPS	ABR	SB-CS	FA	FR	RNG	THR	GAMES AT POSITION	DL	BFW
975	SF N	17	15	2	2	1	0	0	1	1-0	1		.133	.235	.200	21	-2	0-0	.900	-0	105	0	O9(5/0/5)		-0.2
978	Cle A	70	106	13	24	4	1	0	4	14-1	1	31	.226	.320	.283	72	-3	2-4	.977	-1	99	39	O61(12/23/30),D3		-0.7
979	Cle A	26	14	6	2	0	0	0	1	5-0		7	.143	.368	.143	44	-1	2-1	.875	-1	102	0	O16(10/3/3),D4	26	-0.7
total 3		113	135	21	28	5	1	0	6	20-1	2	46	.207	.316	.259	63	-6	4-5	.956	-2	100	30	O86(27/26/38),D7	26	-1.1

SPEHR, TIM Timothy Joseph B7.2.1966 Excelsior Springs MO BR/TR/6-2/200* [KCA88 5/127] d7.18 Col Arizona St.

YEAR	TM LG	G	AB	R	H	2B	3B	HR	RBI	BB-IB	HP	SO	AVG	OBP	SLG	AOPS	ABR	SB-CS	FA	FR	RNG	THR	GAMES AT POSITION	DL	BFW
991	KC A	37	74	7	14	5	0	3	14	9-0	1	18	.189	.282	.378	81	-2	1-0	.986	9	126	167	C37		0.9
993	Mon N	53	87	14	20	6	0	2	10	6-1	1	20	.230	.281	.368	71	-4	2-0	.954	1	49	170	C49		-0.1
994	Mon N	52	36	8	9	3	1	0	5	4-0	0	11	.250	.325	.389	84	-1	2-0	1.000	5	108	27	C46,O2L		0.6
995	Mon N	41	35	4	9	1	0	1	3	6-0	0	7	.257	.366	.486	118	1	0-0	.990	4	69	147	C38		0.6
996	Mon N	63	44	4	4	1	0	1	3	3-0	1	15	.091	.167	.182	-8	-7	1-0	.985	-1	79	39	C58/OR	63	0.6
997	KC A	17	35	3	6	0	0	1	2	2-0	1	12	.171	.237	.257	28	-4	0-0	1.000	3	59	118	C17	19	-0.7
	Atl N	8	14	2	3	1	0	1	4	0-0	1	4	.214	.214	.500	79	-1	0-0	.947	1	159	273	C7		-0.1
998	NY N	21	51	3	7	1	0	0	3	7-1	2	16	.137	.267	.157	15	-6	1-0	1.000	2	89	147	C21/1		0.1
	KC A	11	25	5	6	2	0	1	2	8-0	2	3	.240	.457	.440	130	2	0-0	1.000	-2	150	58	C11	114	-0.3
999	KC A	60	155	26	32	7	0	9	26	22-0	6	47	.206	.324	.426	87	-3	1-0	.990	-9	93	49	C59		0.0
total 8		363	556	76	110	31	1	19	72	67-2	14	153	.198	.298	.360	71	-25	9-0	.985	11	92	106	C343,O3(2/0/1)/1	196	0.2

SPEIER, CHRIS Chris Edward B6.28.1950 Alameda CA BR/TR (BB 1972p)/6-1/182* [SFN70*S1/2] d4.7 C4 s-Justin Col California-Santa Barbara

YEAR	TM LG	G	AB	R	H	2B	3B	HR	RBI	BB-IB	HP	SO	AVG	OBP	SLG	AOPS	ABR	SB-CS	FA	FR	RNG	THR	GAMES AT POSITION	DL	BFW
971	†SF N	157	601	74	141	17	6	8	46	56-6	7	90	.235	.307	.323	79	-16	4-7	.958	-4	103	102	S156		-0.4
972	SF N★	150	562	74	151	25	2	15	71	82-2	3	92	.269	.361	.400	115	14	9-4	.974	1	107	76	S150		3.7
973	SF N★	153	542	58	135	17	4	11	71	66-4	2	69	.249	.332	.356	87	-9	4-5	.956	0	102	103	S150/2		0.9
974	SF N☆	141	501	55	125	19	5	9	53	62-8	4	64	.250	.336	.361	91	-5	3-2	.969	10	107	105	S135,2b4		2.1
975	SF N	141	487	60	132	30	5	10	69	70-7	1	50	.271	.362	.415	112	10	4-5	**.982**	9	98	96	S136/3		3.5
976	SF N	145	495	51	112	18	4	3	40	60-1	4	52	.226	.311	.297	72	-17	2-2	.974	3	104	95	S135,2b7,3b5/1		0.2
977	SF N	6	17	1	3	1	0	0	0	0-0	0	3	.176	.176	.235	9	-2	0-0	.920	2	153	82	S5		0.0
	Mon N	139	531	58	125	30	6	5	38	67-3	1	78	.235	.321	.343	80	-14	1-2	.970	-8	99	94	S138		-0.8
	Year	145	548	59	128	31	6	5	38	67-3	1	81	.234	.317	.339	78	-16	1-2	.968	-6	101	94	S143		-0.8
978	Mon N	150	501	47	126	18	5	4	51	60-10	1	75	.251	.329	.329	86	-8	1-0	.975	-2	99	114	S148		0.6
979	Mon N	113	344	31	78	13	1	7	26	43-10	3	45	.227	.317	.331	77	-10	0-0	.970	1	101	88	S112	19	0.6
980	Mon N	128	388	35	103	14	4	1	32	52-18	0	38	.265	.351	.330	90	-4	0-3	.965	0	102	88	S127/3		0.9
981	†Mon N	96	307	33	69	10	2	2	25	38-10	0	29	.225	.310	.290	69	-12	1-2	.964	-6	94	108	S96		0.9
982	Mon N	156	530	41	136	26	4	7	60	47-12	1	67	.257	.316	.360	86	-9	1-6	.982	-14	86	94	S155		-0.9
983	Mon N	88	261	31	67	12	2	2	22	29-4	2	37	.257	.332	.341	88	-4	2-1	.962	-6	99	83	S74,3b12,2b2	15	-0.3
984	Mon N	25	40	1	6	0	0	0	1	1-0	0	8	.150	.171	.150	-10	-6	0-0	.960	1	98	126	S13,3b4		-0.5
	StL N	38	118	9	21	7	1	3	8	9-1	1	19	.178	.242	.331	61	-7	0-0	.983	7	121	129	S34,3b2		0.4
	Year	63	158	10	27	7	1	3	9	10-1	1	27	.171	.225	.285	44	-12	0-0	.980	8	85	93	S47,3b6		
	Min A	12	33	2	7	0	0	0	1	3-0	0	7	.212	.278	.212	36	-3	0-0	.977	-3	85	93	S12	16	-0.5
985	Chi N	106	218	16	53	11	0	4	24	17-0	0	34	.243	.295	.349	73	-8	1-3	.964	5	113	151	S58,3b31,2b13		0.0
986	Chi N	95	155	21	44	8	0	6	23	15-3	1	32	.284	.349	.452	111	2	2-2	.984	3	92	71	3b53,S23,2b7		0.0
987	†SF N	111	317	39	79	13	0	11	39	42-5	3	51	.249	.342	.394	99	0	4-7	.989	4	90	94	2b55,3b44,S22		0.7
988	SF N	82	171	26	37	9	1	3	18	23-2	1	39	.216	.311	.333	89	-2	3-3	.985	4	105	117	2b45,3b2,S12		0.5
989	SF N	28	37	7	9	4	0	0	2	5-0	0	9	.243	.333	.351	99	0	0-0	1.000	-1	82	0	3b9,S9,2b4/1	119	0.3
total 19		2260	7156	770	1759	302	50	112	720	847-106	35	988	.246	.327	.349	87	-110	42-54	.970	6	101	99	S1900,3b184,2b138,1b2	169	9.6

SPENCE, BOB John Robert B2.10.1946 San Diego CA BL/TR/6-4/215* [ChiA67*S1/4] d9.5 Col Santa Clara

YEAR	TM LG	G	AB	R	H	2B	3B	HR	RBI	BB-IB	HP	SO	AVG	OBP	SLG	AOPS	ABR	SB-CS	FA	FR	RNG	THR	GAMES AT POSITION	DL	BFW
69	Chi A	12	26	0	4	1	0	0	3	0-0	1	9	.154	.148	.192	-4	-4	0-0	1.000	-0	73	130	1b6		-0.5
70	Chi A	46	130	11	29	4	1	4	15	11-0	1	32	.223	.285	.362	75	-5	0-0	.994	3	133	122	1b37		-0.5
71	Chi A	14	27	2	4	0	0	0	1	5-0	0	6	.148	.273	.148	24	-3	0-0	.986	-1	50	109	1b7		-0.4
total 3		72	183	13	37	5	1	4	19	16-0	1	47	.202	.265	.306	57	-12	0-0	.993	2	114	121	1b50		-1.4

SPENCE, STAN Stanley Orville B3.20.1915 S.Portsmouth KY D1.9.1983 Kinston NC BL/TL/5-10.5/180 d6.8 Mil 1945

YEAR	TM LG	G	AB	R	H	2B	3B	HR	RBI	BB-IB	HP	SO	AVG	OBP	SLG	AOPS	ABR	SB-CS	FA	FR	RNG	THR	GAMES AT POSITION	DL	BFW
40	Bos A	51	68	5	19	2	1	2	13	4	0	9	.279	.319	.426	88	-2	0-1	1.000	-1	97	0	O15(6/0/9)		-0.3
41	Bos A	86	203	22	47	10	3	2	28	18	3	14	.232	.304	.340	68	-10	1-0	1.000	3	103	161	O52(27/10/16)/1		-0.8
42	Was A☆	149	629	94	203	27	**15**	4	79	62	1	16	.323	.384	.432	131	25	5-2	.973	-7	97	63	O149C		1.5
43	Was A	149	570	72	152	23	10	12	88	84	5	39	.267	.366	.405	94	23	8-1	.983	-1	99	104	O148C		2.1
44	Was A★	153	592	83	187	31	8	18	100	69	4	28	.316	.391	.486	157	44	3-7	.989	15	103	197	O150C,1b3		5.4
46	Was A★	152	578	83	169	50	10	16	87	62	4	31	.292	.365	.497	148	36	1-7	.982	2	99	142	O150C		3.3
47	Was A	147	506	62	141	22	6	16	73	81	0	41	.279	.378	.441	131	22	2-2	.984	6	105	131	O142C		2.5
48	Bos A	114	391	71	92	17	4	12	61	82	0	33	.235	.368	.391	97	0	0-2	.977	-3	101	57	O92(24/0/70),1b16		-0.8
49	Bos A	7	20	3	3	1	0	0	1	6	0	1	.150	.346	.200	43	-1	0-0	1.000	1	102	196	O5(0/2/3)		-0.1
	StL A	104	314	46	77	13	3	13	45	52	2	36	.245	.356	.430	103	1	1-1	.995	4	100	168	O87(33/50/6)/1		0.1
	Year	111	334	49	80	14	3	13	46	58	2	37	.240	.355	.416	99	-1	1-1	.996	4	100	170	O92(33/52/9)/1		0.0
total 9		1112	3871	541	1090	196	60	95	575	520	19	248	.282	.369	.437	126	138	21-23	.984	19	100	125	O990(90/801/104),1b19		12.9

SPENCER d6.3

YEAR	TM LG	G	AB	R	H	2B	3B	HR	RBI	BB-IB	HP	SO	AVG	OBP	SLG	AOPS	ABR	SB-CS	FA	FR	RNG	THR	GAMES AT POSITION	DL	BFW
72	Nat NA	1	4	1	0	0	0	0	0	0		0	.000	.000	.000	-86	-1	0-0	.429	-1	99	0	/S		-0.1

SPENCER, CHET Chester Arthur B3.4.1883 S.Webster OH D11.10.1938 Portsmouth OH BL/TR/6-0/180 d8.22

YEAR	TM LG	G	AB	R	H	2B	3B	HR	RBI	BB-IB	HP	SO	AVG	OBP	SLG	AOPS	ABR	SB-CS	FA	FR	RNG	THR	GAMES AT POSITION	DL	BFW
06	Bos N	8	27	1	4	1	0	0	0	0		0	.148	.148	.185	4	-1	3	.875	-1	144	0	O8(1/3/3)		-0.5

SPENCER, DARYL Daryl Dean "Big Dee" B7.13.1929 Wichita KS BR/TR/6-2/190(185-197) d9.17 Mil 1954-55 Col Wichita St.

YEAR	TM LG	G	AB	R	H	2B	3B	HR	RBI	BB-IB	HP	SO	AVG	OBP	SLG	AOPS	ABR	SB-CS	FA	FR	RNG	THR	GAMES AT POSITION	DL	BFW
52	NY N	7	17	0	5	0	1	0	3	1	0	4	.294	.333	.412	105	0	0-0	1.000	1	116	59	S3,3b3		0.1
53	NY N	118	408	55	85	18	5	20	56	42	3	74	.208	.287	.424	81	-13	0-1	.927	-8	103	86	S53,3b36,2b32		-1.6
56	NY N	146	489	46	108	13	2	14	42	35-2	3	65	.221	.275	.342	66	-25	1-3	.974	-8	95	80	2b70,S66,3b12		-2.5
57	NY N	148	534	65	133	31	2	11	50	50-0	1	50	.249	.313	.376	85	-11	3-1	.950	11	105	**132**	S110,2b36,3b6		1.2
58	SF N	148	539	71	138	20	5	17	74	73-4	3	60	.256	.343	.406	101	2	1-0	.955	-5	104	100	S134,2b17		1.0
59	SF N	152	555	59	147	20	1	12	62	58-4	1	67	.265	.332	.369	89	-8	5-0	.970	1	99	89	S147		0.4
60	StL N	148	507	70	131	20	3	16	58	81-7	5	74	.258	.365	.404	102	4	1-1	.946	-18	87	90	S138,2b16		-0.2
61	StL N	37	130	19	33	4	0	8	27	23-3	1	17	.254	.366	.377	89	-1	1-0	.956	1	100	108	S37		0.3
	LA N	60	189	27	46	7	0	8	27	20-1	4	35	.243	.327	.407	88	-3	0-1	.964	2	91	141	3b57,S3		-0.3
	Year	97	319	46	79	11	0	12	48	43-4	5	52	.248	.343	.395	88	-5	1-1	.964	2	91	141	3b57,S40		0.0
62	LA N	77	157	24	37	5	1	2	12	32-4	2	31	.236	.365	.318	91	0	1-0	.925	-2	98	49	3b57,S10		-0.1
63	LA N	7	9	0	1	0	0	0	0	3-0	0	2	.111	.333	.111	37	-1	0-0	1.000	-1	60	0	3b3		-0.1
	Cin N	50	155	21	37	7	0	1	23	31-0	1	37	.239	.359	.303	93	1	1-0	.979	4	99	135	3b48		0.5
	Year	57	164	21	38	7	0	1	23	34-0	1	39	.232	.358	.293	91	0	1-0	.979	3	97	128	3b51		0.3
total 10		1098	3689	457	901	145	20	105	428	449-25	20	516	.244	.327	.380	88	-55	13-7	.953	-24	98	102	S558,2b322,3b222		-1.4

SPENCER, TUBBY Edward Russell B1.26.1884 Oil City PA D2.1.1945 San Francisco CA BR/TR/5-10/215 d7.23

YEAR	TM LG	G	AB	R	H	2B	3B	HR	RBI	BB-IB	HP	SO	AVG	OBP	SLG	AOPS	ABR	SB-CS	FA	FR	RNG	THR	GAMES AT POSITION	DL	BFW
05	StL A	35	115	6	27	1	1	0	7	7	1		.235	.285	.278	83	-5	2	.962	-6	71	107	C34		-0.6
06	StL A	58	188	15	33	6	1	0	17	7	1		.176	.205	.218	34	-15	4	.935	-6	88	100	C54		-1.7
07	StL A	71	230	27	61	11	1	1	28	7	1		.265	.299	.335	102	0	1	.957	-5	93	99	C63		0.2
08	StL A	91	286	19	60	11	0	1	28	17	0		.210	.254	.238	60	-13	1	.983	5	121	91	C88		-0.6
09	Bos A	28	74	6	12	1	0	0	9	6	1		.162	.225	.176	26	-6	2	.992	-1	108	82	C26		0.1
11	Phi N	11	32	2	5	1	0	1	3	3	0	7	.156	.229	.281	49	-2	0	.925	-2	88	114	C11		-0.4
16	Det A	19	54	7	20	1	1	1	10	6	1	6	.370	.443	.481	172	5	2	.988	-5	77	114	C19		0.1
17	Det A	70	192	13	46	8	3	0	22	15	**9**	15	.240	.324	.313	95	-1	0	.978	-4	89	89	C62		0.1

YEAR	TM LG	G	AB	R	H	2B	3B	HR	RBI	BB-IB	HP	SO	AVG	OBP	SLG	AOPS	ABR	SB-CS	FA	FR	RNG	THR	GAMES AT POSITION	DL	BFV
1918	Det A	66	155	11	34	8	1	0	8	19	2	18	.219	.313	.284	83	-3	1	.966	-11	73	91	C48/1		-1.
Total	9	449	1326	106	298	43	10	3	133	87	17	46	.225	.281	.279	76	-39	13	.966	-33	94	96	C405/1		-3.9

SPENCER, TOM   Hubert Thomas   B2.28.1951 Gallipolis OH   BR/TR/6-0/170   [CinN69 20/468]   d7.17   C5

YEAR	TM LG	G	AB	R	H	2B	3B	HR	RBI	BB-IB	HP	SO	AVG	OBP	SLG	AOPS	ABR	SB-CS	FA	FR	RNG	THR	GAMES AT POSITION	DL	BFV
1978	Chi A	29	65	3	12	1	0	0	4	2-0	0	9	.185	.209	.200	15	-7	0-1	1.000	2	115	173	O27(6/19/2),D2		-0.

SPENCER, JIM   James Lloyd   B7.30.1947 Hanover PA   D2.10.2002 Ft.Lauderdale FL   BL/TL/6-2/195(190-206)   [AnaA65 1/11]   d9.7   gf-Ben

YEAR	TM LG	G	AB	R	H	2B	3B	HR	RBI	BB-IB	HP	SO	AVG	OBP	SLG	AOPS	ABR	SB-CS	FA	FR	RNG	THR	GAMES AT POSITION	DL	BFV
1968	Cal A	19	68	2	13	1	0	0	5	3-0	1	10	.191	.233	.206	36	-5	0-0	.994	3	155	107	1b19		-0.9
1969	Cal A	113	386	39	98	14	3	10	31	26-6	2	53	.254	.304	.383	95	-4	1-0	.991	-1	94	100	1b107		-1.
1970	Cal A	146	511	61	140	20	4	15	68	28-6	0	61	.274	.309	.399	98	-4	0-2	**.995**	-0	97	**123**	1b142		-1.
1971	Cal A	148	510	50	121	21	2	18	59	48-7	3	63	.237	.304	.392	104	1	0-1	**.996**	2	104	99	1b145		-1.
1972	Cal A	82	212	13	47	5	0	1	14	12-1	0	25	.222	.262	.259	59	-11	0-1	.990	0	126	99	1b35,O24L		-1.
1973	Cal A	29	87	10	21	4	2	2	11	9-1	1	24	.241	.316	.402	110	1	0-0	1.000	-3	46	109	1b26,D2		-0.
	Tex A★	102	352	35	94	12	3	4	43	34-6	1	41	.267	.332	.352	97	-2	0-3	.999	5	113	93	1b99/D		-0.
	Year	131	439	45	115	16	5	6	54	43-7	2	50	.262	.329	.362	99	-1	0-3	**.999**	2	99	94	1b125,D3		-0.
1974	Tex A	118	352	36	98	11	4	7	44	22-3	3	27	.278	.323	.392	108	3	1-2	.998	0	93	94	1b60,D54		-0.
1975	Tex A	132	403	50	107	18	1	11	47	35-6	2	43	.266	.327	.397	105	2	0-1	.995	3	111	124	1b99,D25		-0.
1976	Chi A	150	518	53	131	13	2	14	70	49-**19**	1	55	.253	.315	.367	100	-1	6-4	**.998**	9	119	96	1b143,D2		-0.
1977	Chi A	128	470	56	116	16	1	18	69	36-11	2	50	.247	.300	.400	90	-8	1-2	.991	2	105	70	1b125	15	-1.
1978	†NY A	71	150	12	34	9	1	7	24	15-3	0	32	.227	.299	.440	107	1	0-1	1.000	0	106	55	D35,1b15	16	-0.
1979	NY A	106	295	60	85	15	9	23	53	38-11	0	25	.288	.367	.593	157	23	0-2	.992	-0	96	155	D71,1b26		1.
1980	†NY A	97	259	38	61	9	0	13	43	30-2	1	44	.236	.313	.421	102	0	1-0	.990	2	109	91	1b75,D15		-0.
1981	NY A	25	63	6	9	2	0	2	4	9-2	0	7	.143	.250	.270	50	-4	0-0	1.000	3	140	107	1b25		-0.
	†Oak A	54	171	14	35	6	0	2	9	10-1	0	20	.205	.246	.275	53	-11	1-0	.997	1	107	79	1b48		-1
	Year	79	234	20	44	8	0	4	13	19-3	0	27	.188	.247	.274	52	-15	1-0	.998	4	117	88	1b73		-1
1982	Oak A	33	101	6	17	3	1	2	5	3-1	0	20	.168	.190	.277	28	-11	0-0	.992	1	120	82	1b32	21	-1.
Total	15	1553	4908	541	1227	179	27	146	599	407-86	17	582	.250	.307	.387	99	-30	11-19	.995	26	106	100	1b1221,D205,O24L	52	-10

SPENCER, BEN   Lloyd Benjamin   B5.15.1890 Patapsco MD   D9.1.1970 Finksburg MD   BL/TL/5-8/160   d9.8   gs-Jim

YEAR	TM LG	G	AB	R	H	2B	3B	HR	RBI	BB-IB	HP	SO	AVG	OBP	SLG	AOPS	ABR	SB-CS	FA	FR	RNG	THR	GAMES AT POSITION	DL	BFV
1913	Was A	8	21	2	6	1	1	0	4	4		4	.286	.348	.429	124	1	0	.917	-0	87	120	O8(7/1/0)		0.

SPENCER, SHANE   Michael Shane   B2.20.1972 Key West FL   BR/TR/5-11/210(210-225)   [NYA90 28/750]   d4.10

YEAR	TM LG	G	AB	R	H	2B	3B	HR	RBI	BB-IB	HP	SO	AVG	OBP	SLG	AOPS	ABR	SB-CS	FA	FR	RNG	THR	GAMES AT POSITION	DL	BFV
1998	†NY A	27	67	18	25	6	0	10	27	5-0	0	12	.373	.411	.910	242	13	0-1	1.000	-1	83	94	O22(9/0/15)/1D		1
1999	†NY A	71	205	25	48	8	0	8	20	18-0	2	51	.234	.301	.390	76	-8	0-4	1.000	3	104	146	O64(46/0/22),D3	24	-0
2000	NY A	73	248	33	70	11	3	9	40	19-0	2	45	.282	.330	.460	101	-1	1-2	.989	4	118	142	O40(33/0/7),D33	81	-0
2001	†NY A	80	283	40	73	14	2	10	46	21-0	4	58	.258	.315	.428	93	-3	4-1	.993	7	117	183	O68(44/0/28),D14	28	0
2002	†NY A	94	288	32	71	15	2	6	34	31-4	4	62	.247	.324	.375	87	-5	0-3	.975	-1	97	105	O91(40/0/55)/D		-1
2003	Cle A	64	210	23	57	10	0	8	26	16-0	1	52	.271	.328	.433	100	0	2-0	.987	-3	92	84	O43(16/0/30),1b11,D7		-0
	Tex A	55	185	16	42	10	0	4	23	27-0	2	40	.227	.329	.346	74	-6	0-0	.982	0	102	65	O54(50/0/12)/D		-0
	Year	119	395	39	99	20	0	12	49	45-0	3	92	.251	.328	.392	88	-7	2-0	.984	-3	98	73	O97(66/0/42),1b11,D8		-1
2004	NY N	74	185	21	52	10	1	4	26	13-0	2	37	.281	.332	.411	94	-2	6-0	.974	4	127	77	O62(43/6/19)/1	8	0
Total	7	538	1671	208	438	84	6	59	242	152-4	17	357	.262	.326	.428	96	-12	13-11	.986	13	106	116	O444(281/6/188),D63,1b13	141	-2

SPENCER, ROY   Roy Hampton   B2.22.1900 Scranton NC   D2.8.1973 Port Charlotte FL   BR/TR/5-10/168   d4.19

YEAR	TM LG	G	AB	R	H	2B	3B	HR	RBI	BB-IB	HP	SO	AVG	OBP	SLG	AOPS	ABR	SB-CS	FA	FR	RNG	THR	GAMES AT POSITION	DL	BFV
1925	Pit N	14	28	1	6	1	0	0	2	1	0	3	.214	.241	.250	24	-1	0-0	.905	-1	138	0	C11		-0
1926	Pit N	28	43	5	17	3	0	0	4	1	0	0	.395	.409	.465	128	2	0	.970	-0	125	34	C12		0
1927	†Pit N	38	92	9	26	3	1	0	13	3	0	3	.283	.305	.337	67	-4	0	.974	2	134	58	C34		0
1929	Was A	50	116	18	18	4	0	1	9	8	0	15	.155	.222	.216	13	-15	0-0	.967	-0	116	99	C41		-1
1930	Was A	93	321	32	82	11	4	0	36	18	4	27	.255	.303	.315	57	-22	3-0	.989	6	127	97	C93		-0
1931	Was A	145	483	48	133	16	3	1	60	35	2	21	.275	.327	.327	72	-20	0-1	.985	7	126	82	C145		-C
1932	Was A	102	317	28	78	9	0	1	41	24	1	17	.246	.301	.284	53	-22	0-1	.978	-4	**152**	87	C98		-2
1933	Cle A	75	227	26	46	5	2	0	23	23	2	17	.203	.282	.242	38	-20	0-0	.990	6	136	116	C72		-1
1934	Cle A	5	7	0	1	1	0	0	2	0	0	1	.143	.143	.286	8	-1	0	1.000	1	78	224	C4		-0
1936	NY N	19	18	3	5	1	0	0	3	2	0	0	.278	.350	.333	86	0	0	1.000	1	141	82	C14		-C
1937	Bro N	51	117	5	24	2	0	0	8	8	0	17	.205	.256	.256	39	-10	0	1.000	6	85	115	C45		-C
1938	Bro N	16	45	2	12	1	0	0	6	5	0	6	.267	.340	.333	84	-1	0	.968	-1	84	73	C16		-C
Total	12	636	1814	177	448	57	13	3	203	128	11	130	.247	.301	.298	56	-116	4-1	.984	21	128	91	C585		-6

SPENCER, VERN   Vernon Murray   B2.4.1894 Wixom MI   D6.3.1971 Wixom MI   BL/TR/5-7/165   d7.4

YEAR	TM LG	G	AB	R	H	2B	3B	HR	RBI	BB-IB	HP	SO	AVG	OBP	SLG	AOPS	ABR	SB-CS	FA	FR	RNG	THR	GAMES AT POSITION	DL	BFV
1920	NY N	45	140	15	28	2	3	0	19	11	0	17	.200	.258	.257	49	-10	4-3	.932	4	119	169	O40(38/1/2)		-C

SPERAW, PAUL   Paul Bachman "Polly","Birdie"   B10.5.1893 Annville PA   D2.22.1962 Cedar Rapids IA   BR/TR/5-8.5/145   d9.15

YEAR	TM LG	G	AB	R	H	2B	3B	HR	RBI	BB-IB	HP	SO	AVG	OBP	SLG	AOPS	ABR	SB-CS	FA	FR	RNG	THR	GAMES AT POSITION	DL	BFV
1920	StL A	1	2	0	0	0	0	0	0	0	0	0	.000	.000	.000	-97	-1	0-0	1.000	-0	76	0	/3		-0

SPERBER, ED   Edwin George   B1.21.1895 Cincinnati OH   D1.5.1976 Cincinnati OH   BL/TL/5-11/175   d4.16

YEAR	TM LG	G	AB	R	H	2B	3B	HR	RBI	BB-IB	HP	SO	AVG	OBP	SLG	AOPS	ABR	SB-CS	FA	FR	RNG	THR	GAMES AT POSITION	DL	BFV
1924	Bos N	24	59	8	17	2	0	1	12	10	1	9	.288	.400	.373	113	2	3-1	.897	-2	82	56	O17(2/1/14)		-C
1925	Bos N	2	2	0	0	0	0	0	0	0	0	0	.000	.000	.000	-99	-1	0-0	—	0			/H		-C
Total	2	26	61	8	17	2	0	1	12	10	1	9	.279	.389	.361	106	1	3-1	.897	-2	82	56	O17(2/1/14)		-C

SPERRING, ROB   Robert Walter   B10.10.1949 San Francisco CA   BR/TR/6-1/175*   [ChiN71 5/112]   d8.11   Col Pacific (CA)

YEAR	TM LG	G	AB	R	H	2B	3B	HR	RBI	BB-IB	HP	SO	AVG	OBP	SLG	AOPS	ABR	SB-CS	FA	FR	RNG	THR	GAMES AT POSITION	DL	BFV
1974	Chi N	42	107	9	22	3	0	1	5	9-1	0	28	.206	.267	.262	46	-8	1-2	.952	-4	104	83	2b35,S8		-1
1975	Chi N	65	144	25	30	4	1	1	9	16-3	1	31	.208	.288	.271	54	-9	0-2	.946	4	124	60	3b22,2b17,S16,O8(2/0/6)		-C
1976	Chi N	43	93	8	24	3	0	0	7	9-0	0	17	.258	.320	.290	69	-4	0-2	.955	-11	36	34	3b20,S15,2b4,O3L		-1
1977	Hou N	58	129	6	24	3	0	1	9	12-2	0	31	.186	.254	.233	35	-12	0-0	.940	-5	63	113	S22,2b20,3b11		-1
Total	4	208	473	48	100	13	1	3	30	46-6	1	107	.211	.281	.262	50	-33	1-6	.964	-15	102	66	2b76,S61,3b53,O11(5/0/6)		-4

SPERRY, STAN   Stanley Kenneth   B2.19.1914 Evansville WI   D9.27.1962 Evansville WI   BL/TR/5-10.5/164   d7.28

YEAR	TM LG	G	AB	R	H	2B	3B	HR	RBI	BB-IB	HP	SO	AVG	OBP	SLG	AOPS	ABR	SB-CS	FA	FR	RNG	THR	GAMES AT POSITION	DL	BFV
1936	Phi N	20	37	2	5	3	0	0	4	3	0	5	.135	.200	.216	11	-5	0	.900	-3	78	72	2b15		-1
1938	Phi A	60	253	28	69	6	3	0	27	15	0	9	.273	.313	.320	61	-16	1-2	.959	-5	105	60	2b60		-1
Total	2	80	290	30	74	9	3	0	31	18	0	14	.255	.299	.307	54	-21	1-2	.951	-8	102	62	2b75		-2

SPIERS, BILL   William James   B6.5.1966 Orangeburg SC   BL/TR/6-2/190*   [MilA87 1/13]   d4.7   Col Clemson   OF(33/11/20)

YEAR	TM LG	G	AB	R	H	2B	3B	HR	RBI	BB-IB	HP	SO	AVG	OBP	SLG	AOPS	ABR	SB-CS	FA	FR	RNG	THR	GAMES AT POSITION	DL	BFV
1989	Mil A	114	345	44	88	9	3	4	33	21-1	1	63	.255	.298	.333	79	-11	10-2	.962	10	107	110	S89,3b12,2b4,1b2,D4		-1
1990	Mil A	112	363	44	88	15	3	2	36	16-0	1	45	.242	.274	.317	66	-18	11-6	.976	-7	103	99	S111	36	-1
1991	Mil A	133	414	71	117	13	6	8	54	34-0	2	55	.283	.337	.401	106	3	14-8	.970	-12	93	116	S128/OCD	149	-1
1992	Mil A	12	16	2	5	2	0	0	2	1-0	0	4	.313	.353	.438	122	1	1-1	1.000	-4	19	0	S5,2b4/3D		-1
1993	Mil A	113	340	43	81	8	4	2	36	29-2	4	51	.238	.302	.303	65	-17	9-8	.971	-23	83	86	2b104,O7(2/2/4),S4/D		-1
1994	Mil A	73	214	27	54	10	1	0	11	19-1	1	42	.252	.316	.308	59	-13	7-1	.947	4	104	96	3b35,S35,O2R/1D		-1
1995	NY N	63	72	5	15	2	1	0	11	12-1	0	15	.208	.314	.264	58	-4	0-1	.794	3	128	180	3b11,2b6	41	-1
1996	Hou N	122	218	27	55	10	1	6	26	20-4	5	34	.252	.320	.390	93	-3	7-0	.959	-0	109	119	3b77,2b7,1b4,S4,O2(0/1/1)		-1
1997	†Hou N	132	291	51	93	27	4	4	48	61-6	1	42	.320	.438	.481	145	24	14-5	.935	18	119	130	3b84,S28,1b8,2b4		-0
1998	†Hou N	123	384	66	105	27	4	4	43	45-0	2	62	.273	.356	.396	100	2	11-2	.966	-5	97	64	3b99,2b9,1b7,S2		-0
1999	†Hou N	127	393	56	113	18	5	4	39	47-2	0	45	.288	.363	.389	92	-4	10-5	.958	13	128	118	O31(25/7/9),S13,2b4/1		-0
2000	Hou N	124	355	41	107	13	3	3	43	49-3	1	38	.301	.386	.392	91	-3	7-4	.959	9	124	108	3b51,S27,2b26,O10(6/0/4)		-1
2001	Hou N	4	3	0	1	0	0	0	0	1-1	0	0	.333	.500	.333	114	0	0-0	—	0			/H	182	-1
Total	13	1252	3408	477	922	158	35	37	388	355-21	18	496	.271	.341	.370	90	-43	97-43	.970	7	101	113	S446,3b441,2b168,O53L,1b23,D11	408	

SPIES, HARRY   Henry   B6.12.1866 New Orleans LA   D7.7.1942 Los Angeles CA   BL/TR/5-9/170   d4.20

YEAR	TM LG	G	AB	R	H	2B	3B	HR	RBI	BB-IB	HP	SO	AVG	OBP	SLG	AOPS	ABR	SB-CS	FA	FR	RNG	THR	GAMES AT POSITION	DL	BFV
1895	Cin N	14	50	2	11	0	1	0	5	3	0	2	.220	.264	.260	44	-5	0	.867	2	103	165	C12,1b2		-C
	Lou N	72	276	42	74	14	7	2	35	11	7	19	.268	.313	.391	86	-7	4	.981	-6	90	98	1b47,C26/S		-C
	Year	86	326	44	85	14	8	2	40	14	7	21	.261	.305	.371	78	-12	4	.979	-4	96	106	1b49,C38/S		-C

SPIEZIO, ED   Edward Wayne   B10.31.1941 Joliet IL   BR/TR/5-11/180*   d7.23   s-Scott   Col Lewis

YEAR	TM LG	G	AB	R	H	2B	3B	HR	RBI	BB-IB	HP	SO	AVG	OBP	SLG	AOPS	ABR	SB-CS	FA	FR	RNG	THR	GAMES AT POSITION	DL	BFV
1964	StL N	12	12	0	4	0	0	0	0-0	0	1	.333	.333	.333	81	0	0-0	—	0			/H			
1965	StL N	10	18	0	3	0	0	0	5	1-0	1	4	.167	.250	.167	18	-2	0-0	1.000	0	128	0	3b3		
1966	StL N	26	73	4	16	5	1	2	10	5-1	0	11	.219	.269	.397	82	-2	1-0	.885	-5	80	87	3b19		
1967	†StL N	55	105	9	22	2	0	3	10	7-0	1	18	.210	.265	.314	66	-5	2-1	.962	1	103	156	3b19,O7(2/0/6)		
1968	†StL N	29	51	1	8	1	0	0	2	5-0	0	6	.157	.228	.157	19	-5	1-1	1.000	1	107	127	O11(3/0/9),3b2		

YEAR	TM LG	G	AB	R	H	2B	3B	HR	RBI	BB-IB	HP	SO	AVG	OBP	SLG	AOPS	ABR	SB-CS	FA	FR	RNG	THR	GAMES AT POSITION	DL	BFW
1969	SD N	121	355	29	83	9	0	13	43	38-3	4	64	.234	.313	.369	94	-3	1-2	.939	0	105	55	3b98/OL		-0.5
1970	SD N	110	316	45	90	18	1	12	42	43-2	4	42	.285	.373	.462	128	14	4-0	.953	2	108	59	3b93		1.6
1971	SD N	97	308	16	71	10	1	7	36	22-3	4	50	.231	.286	.338	83	-8	6-5	.962	1	101	83	3b91/OL		-0.8
1972	SD N	20	29	2	4	2	0	0	4	1-0	0	6	.138	.161	.207	6	-4	1-0	1.000	-1	57	158	3b5		-0.5
	Chi A	74	277	20	66	10	1	2	22	13-3	2	43	.238	.276	.303	71	-10	0-1	.952	6	106	75	3b74		-0.6
Total	10	554	1544	126	367	56	4	39	174	135-12	16	245	.238	.303	.355	88	-25	16-10	.949	5	104	72	3b404,O20(7/0/15)		-2.7

SPIEZIO, SCOTT Scott Edward B9.21.1972 Joliet IL BB/TR/6-2/225(195-225) [OakA93 6/181] d9.14 f-Ed Col Illinois OF(29/0/19)

YEAR	TM LG	G	AB	R	H	2B	3B	HR	RBI	BB-IB	HP	SO	AVG	OBP	SLG	AOPS	ABR	SB-CS	FA	FR	RNG	THR	GAMES AT POSITION	DL	BFW
1996	Oak A	9	29	6	9	2	0	2	8	4-1	0	4	.310	.394	.586	145	2	0-1	.846	-1	67	0	3b5,D4		0.1
1997	Oak A	147	538	58	131	28	4	14	65	44-2	1	75	.243	.300	.388	79	-18	9-3	.990	-8	99	88	2b146/3	17	-1.8
1998	Oak A	114	406	54	105	19	1	9	50	44-3	2	56	.259	.333	.377	85	-8	1-3	.975	-3	101	103	2b112/D	46	-0.7
1999	Oak A	89	247	31	60	24	0	8	33	29-3	2	36	.243	.324	.437	95	-1	0-0	.984	5	127	111	2b42,3b31,1b10,D6		0.4
2000	Ana A	123	297	47	72	11	2	17	49	40-2	3	56	.242	.334	.465	98	-2	1-2	.993	-2	35	74	D50,1b29,3b15,O10(8/0/2),2b2		-0.8
2001	Ana A	139	457	57	124	29	4	13	54	34-4	5	65	.271	.326	.438	98	-2	5-2	.999	6	125	86	1b105,D20,O18(10/0/8),3b10		-0.5
2002	†Ana A	153	491	80	140	34	2	12	82	67-7	4	52	.285	.371	.436	117	15	6-7	.997	-8	72	106	1b143,3b20,O10(8/0/2)/2		-0.5
2003	Ana A	158	521	69	138	36	7	16	83	46-8	5	66	.265	.326	.453	108	6	6-3	.994	-10	89	83	1b114,3b52,O10(3/0/7)		-1.2
2004	Sea A	112	367	38	79	12	3	10	41	36-2	4	60	.215	.288	.346	69	-18	4-1	.964	5	104	136	3b66,1b42,D2	13	-1.4
2005	Sea A	29	47	2	3	1	0	1	4	4-0	0	18	.064	.137	.149	-25	-9	0-0	1.000	-2	32	350	3b6,1b4/2D	73	-0.1
Total	10	1073	3400	442	861	196	23	102	466	348-32	26	488	.253	.324	.414	93	-35	32-22	.996	-20	90	91	1b447,2b304,3b206,D88,O48L	149	-7.6

SPIKES, CHARLIE Leslie Charles B1.23.1951 Bogalusa LA BR/TR/6-3/220(205-220) [NYA69 1/11] d9.1

YEAR	TM LG	G	AB	R	H	2B	3B	HR	RBI	BB-IB	HP	SO	AVG	OBP	SLG	AOPS	ABR	SB-CS	FA	FR	RNG	THR	GAMES AT POSITION	DL	BFW
1972	NY A	14	34	2	5	0	0	0	0	0-0	0	13	.147	.171	.176	4	-4	0-1	1.000	0	91	176	O9R		-0.5
1973	Cle A	140	506	68	120	12	3	23	73	45-1	0	103	.237	.303	.409	98	-4	5-3	.964	3	94	174	O111(90/0/22),D26		-0.8
1974	Cle A	155	568	63	154	23	1	22	80	34-2	7	100	.271	.319	.431	115	9	10-7	.968	-2	94	135	O154R		0.0
1975	Cle A	111	345	41	79	13	3	11	33	30-3	0	51	.229	.291	.380	88	-7	7-6	.974	4	96	176	O103(31/0/72),D2		-0.9
1976	Cle A	101	334	34	79	11	5	3	31	23-3	5	50	.237	.294	.326	82	-8	5-6	.985	1	102	108	O98(2/0/96),D2		-1.4
1977	Cle A	32	95	13	22	2	0	3	11	11-0	2	17	.232	.321	.347	85	-2	0-2	.972	-3	74	60	O27R,D2		-0.6
1978	Det A	10	28	1	7	1	0	0	2	2-1	0	6	.250	.344	.286	76	-1	0-0	.909	-1	58	178	O9R		-0.2
1979	Atl N	66	93	12	26	8	0	3	21	5-1	0	30	.280	.310	.462	104	0	0-0	.842	-2	72	0	O15(12/0/3)		-0.2
1980	Atl N	41	36	6	10	1	0	0	2	3-2	1	18	.278	.350	.306	84	-1	0-0	1.000	0	91	0	O7(1/0/6)		-0.1
Total	9	670	2039	240	502	72	12	65	256	154-13	22	388	.246	.304	.389	96	-18	27-25	.969	0	94	140	O533(136/0/398),D32		-4.7

SPILBORGHS, RYAN Ryan Adam B9.5.1979 Santa Barbara CA BR/TR/6-1/190 d7.16 Col California-Santa Barbara

YEAR	TM LG	G	AB	R	H	2B	3B	HR	RBI	BB-IB	HP	SO	AVG	OBP	SLG	AOPS	ABR	SB-CS	FA	FR	RNG	THR	GAMES AT POSITION	DL	BFW
2005	Col N	1	4	0	2	0	0	0	1	0-0	0	1	.500	.500	.500	142	0	0-0	1.000	2	337	1904	/OR		0.2

SPILMAN, HARRY William Harry B7.18.1954 Albany GA BL/TR/6-1/190* d9.11 C6

YEAR	TM LG	G	AB	R	H	2B	3B	HR	RBI	BB-IB	HP	SO	AVG	OBP	SLG	AOPS	ABR	SB-CS	FA	FR	RNG	THR	GAMES AT POSITION	DL	BFW
1978	Cin N	4	4	1	1	0	0	0	0	0-0	0	1	.250	.250	.250	40	0	0-0	—	0			/H		-0.1
1979	†Cin N	43	56	7	12	3	0	0	5	7-2	2	5	.214	.323	.268	63	-2	0-0	1.000	-0	42	54	1b12,3b4		-0.3
1980	Cin N	65	101	14	27	4	0	4	19	9-1	1	19	.267	.327	.426	113	2	0-0	.986	1	131	99	1b18,O2L/C3		0.1
1981	Cin N	23	24	4	4	1	0	0	3	3-0	0	7	.167	.259	.208	34	-2	0-0	1.000	-0	58	0	3b3,1b2		-0.2
	†Hou N	28	34	5	10	0	0	0	1	2-0	0	3	.294	.333	.294	84	-1	0-1	1.000	-1	54	81	1b13		-0.2
	Year	51	58	9	14	1	0	0	4	5-0	0	10	.241	.302	.259	62	-3	0-1	1.000	-1	64	65	1b15,3b3		-0.4
1982	Hou N	38	61	7	17	2	0	3	11	5-0	0	12	.279	.333	.459	130	2	0-0	.989	-1	71	73	1b11		0.1
1983	Hou N	42	78	7	13	3	0	1	9	5-0	0	12	.167	.212	.244	29	-8	0-0	1.000	-2	75	52	1b19,C6		-1.1
1984	Hou N	32	72	14	19	2	0	2	15	12-0	0	11	.264	.356	.375	117	2	0-0	.978	-4	62	127	1b18,C8	77	-0.3
1985	Hou N	44	66	3	9	1	0	0	4	3-0	0	7	.136	.174	.197	4	-9	0-0	1.000	-1	45	141	1b19,C2		-1.2
1986	Det A	24	49	6	12	2	0	3	8	3-0	0	8	.245	.288	.469	102	0	0-0	1.000	-0	66	0	D11,3b2/C1		-0.1
	SF N	58	94	12	27	7	0	2	22	12-3	0	13	.287	.368	.426	124	3	0-0	.994	1	126	70	1b19,3b5/C2OL		-0.4
1987	†SF N	83	90	5	24	5	0	1	14	9-0	0	20	.267	.327	.356	87	-2	1-1	.875	-2	75	152	3b10,1b9/C		-0.4
1988	SF N	40	40	4	7	1	1	0	3	4-1	0	6	.175	.250	.325	67	-2	0-0	1.000	0	68	218	1b6,C2/OL		-0.2
	Hou N	7	5	0	0	0	0	0	0	0-0	0	3	.000	.000	.000	-99	-1	0-0	1.000	-0	0	0	/1		-0.2
	Year	47	45	4	7	1	1	0	3	4-1	0	9	.156	.224	.289	48	-3	0-0	1.000	0	56	178	1b7,C2/OL		-0.4
1989	Hou N	32	36	7	10	3	0	0	3	7-1	0	2	.278	.395	.361	122	2	0-0	1.000	0	120	58	1b9/C		0.1
Total	12	563	810	96	192	34	1	18	117	81-8	3	126	.237	.306	.348	85	-16	1-2	.991	-11	82	91	1b157,3b25,C23,D11,O4L/2	77	-3.6

SPINDEL, HAL Harold Stewart B5.27.1913 Chandler OK D7.28.2002 San Clemente CA BR/TR/6-0/185 d4.23 Col UCLA

YEAR	TM LG	G	AB	R	H	2B	3B	HR	RBI	BB-IB	HP	SO	AVG	OBP	SLG	AOPS	ABR	SB-CS	FA	FR	RNG	THR	GAMES AT POSITION	DL	BFW
1939	StL A	48	119	13	32	3	1	0	11	8	0	7	.269	.315	.311	59	-7	0-2	.993	-2	82	100	C32		-0.8
1945	Phi N	36	87	7	20	3	0	0	8	6	0	7	.230	.280	.264	53	-6	0	.964	-1	68	119	C31		-0.5
1946	Phi N	1	3	0	1	0	0	0	1	0	0	0	.333	.333	.333	92	0	0	1.000	0	0	0	/C		0.0
Total	3	85	209	20	53	6	1	0	20	14	0	14	.254	.300	.292	57	-13	0-2	.982	-3	75	107	C64		-1.3

SPIVEY, JUNIOR Ernest Lee B1.28.1975 Oklahoma City OK BR/TR/6-0/185(185-200) [AriN96 36/1085] d6.2 Col Cowley Co. (KS) CC [DL 2000 Ari N 98]

YEAR	TM LG	G	AB	R	H	2B	3B	HR	RBI	BB-IB	HP	SO	AVG	OBP	SLG	AOPS	ABR	SB-CS	FA	FR	RNG	THR	GAMES AT POSITION	DL	BFW
2001	Ari N	72	163	33	42	6	3	5	21	23-0	2	47	.258	.354	.423	94	-1	3-0	.985	-2	88	112	2b66/S		0.0
2002	†Ari N★	143	538	103	162	34	6	16	78	65-5	16	100	.301	.389	.476	119	15	11-6	.977	1	94	78	2b143	16	2.3
2003	Ari N	106	365	52	93	22	2	13	50	33-1	7	95	.255	.326	.433	89	-6	4-3	.982	2	98	89	2b98/OC	36	0.1
2004	Mil N	59	228	33	62	13	0	7	28	25-0	7	48	.272	.359	.421	101	1	5-3	.963	2	106	114	2b58/S	93	0.6
2005	Mil N	49	182	22	43	8	1	5	17	18-1	1	57	.236	.308	.374	77	-6	7-3	.968	-3	92	91	2b48		-0.6
	Was N	28	77	15	17	7	0	2	7	11-1	2	26	.221	.330	.390	95	0	2-0	1.000	-4	95	97	2b22	70	-0.2
	Year	77	259	37	60	15	1	7	24	29-2	3	83	.232	.315	.378	83	-7	9-3	.978	-6	93	93	2b70		-0.8
Total	5	457	1553	258	419	90	12	48	201	175-6	35	373	.270	.354	.436	101	3	32-15	.974	-3	96	92	2b435,S2/OC	313	2.2

SPOGNARDI, ANDY Andrea Ettore B10.18.1908 Boston MA D1.1.2000 Dedham MA BR/TR/5-9.5/160 d9.2 Col Boston College

YEAR	TM LG	G	AB	R	H	2B	3B	HR	RBI	BB-IB	HP	SO	AVG	OBP	SLG	AOPS	ABR	SB-CS	FA	FR	RNG	THR	GAMES AT POSITION	DL	BFW
1932	Bos A	17	34	9	10	1	0	0	1	6	0	4	.294	.400	.324	92	0	1	.979	2	130	110	2b9,S3,3b2		0.3

SPOHRER, AL Alfred Ray B12.3.1902 Philadelphia PA D7.17.1972 Plymouth NH BR/TR/5-10.5/175 d4.13

YEAR	TM LG	G	AB	R	H	2B	3B	HR	RBI	BB-IB	HP	SO	AVG	OBP	SLG	AOPS	ABR	SB-CS	FA	FR	RNG	THR	GAMES AT POSITION	DL	BFW
1928	NY N	2	2	0	0	0	0	0	0	0	0	0	.000	.000	.000	-99	-1	1	1.000	0	0	0	C2		0.0
	Bos N	51	124	15	27	3	0	0	9	5	1	11	.218	.254	.242	32	-13	1	.976	-5	90	89	C48		-1.5
	Year	53	126	15	27	3	0	0	9	5	1	11	.214	.250	.238	30	-13	1	.977	-5	89	88	C50		-1.5
1929	Bos N	114	342	42	93	21	8	2	48	26	2	35	.272	.327	.398	82	-11	1	.954	-5	105	90	C109		-0.9
1930	Bos N	112	356	44	113	22	8	2	37	22	3	24	.317	.361	.441	96	-3	3	.957	-10	115	61	C108		-0.6
1931	Bos N	114	350	23	84	17	5	0	27	22	0	27	.240	.285	.317	64	-19	2	.982	1	106	79	C111		-1.1
1932	Bos N	104	335	31	90	12	2	0	33	15	0	26	.269	.300	.316	69	-15	2	.991	8	138	101	C100		-0.1
1933	Bos N	67	184	11	46	6	1	0	12	11	0	13	.250	.292	.310	78	-6	3	.972	-3	196	73	C65		-0.6
1934	Bos N	100	265	25	59	15	0	0	17	14	0	18	.223	.262	.279	49	-20	1	.977	-1	112	106	C98		-1.6
1935	Bos N	92	260	22	63	7	1	1	16	9	2	12	.242	.273	.288	55	-17	0	.958	-10	88	100	C90		-2.2
Total	8	756	2218	213	575	103	25	6	199	124	7	166	.259	.301	.336	70	-105	13	.972	-25	117	87	C731		-8.6

SPOTTS, JIM James Russell B4.10.1909 Honey Brook PA D6.15.1964 Medford NJ BR/TR/5-10.5/175 d4.23 Col Marshall

YEAR	TM LG	G	AB	R	H	2B	3B	HR	RBI	BB-IB	HP	SO	AVG	OBP	SLG	AOPS	ABR	SB-CS	FA	FR	RNG	THR	GAMES AT POSITION	DL	BFW
1930	Phi N	3	2	1	0	0	0	0	0	0	0	1	.000	.000	.000	-93	-1	0	1.000	0	0	0	C2		0.0

PRAGUE, CHARLIE Charles Wellington B10.10.1864 Cleveland OH D12.31.1912 Des Moines IA BL/TL/5-11/150 d9.17 ▲

YEAR	TM LG	G	AB	R	H	2B	3B	HR	RBI	BB-IB	HP	SO	AVG	OBP	SLG	AOPS	ABR	SB-CS	FA	FR	RNG	THR	GAMES AT POSITION	DL	BFW
1887	Chi N	3	13	0	2	0	0	0		0		0	.154	.154	.154	-13	-2	0	.667	-1	48	0	P3/OC		0.0
1889	Cle N	2	7	2	1	0	0	0	1	1	0	0	.143	.250	.143	11	0	1	.857	1	180	780	P2		0.0
1890	Tol AA	55	199	25	47	5	6	1	19	16	3		.236	.303	.337	86	-5	10	.892	-4	84	79	O40(24/10/6),P19		-0.6
Total	3	60	219	27	50	5	6	1	20	17	3	2	.228	.293	.320	77	-7	11	.892	-4	83	78	O41(24/11/6),P24		-0.6

PRAGUE, ED Edward Nelson Jr. B7.25.1967 Castro Valley CA BR/TR/6-2/205* [TorA88 1/25] d5.7 f-Ed Col Stanford OF(14/0/2)

YEAR	TM LG	G	AB	R	H	2B	3B	HR	RBI	BB-IB	HP	SO	AVG	OBP	SLG	AOPS	ABR	SB-CS	FA	FR	RNG	THR	GAMES AT POSITION	DL	BFW
1991	Tor A	61	160	17	44	7	0	4	20	19-2	3	43	.275	.361	.394	105	-2	0-3	.870	-2	101	38	3b35,1b22,C2,D2		-0.3
1992	†Tor A	22	47	6	11	2	0	1	7	3-0	0	7	.234	.280	.340	70	-2	0-0	.985	0	104	26	C15,1b4/3D		-0.1
1993	†Tor A	150	546	50	142	31	1	12	73	32-1	10	85	.260	.310	.386	85	-12	1-0	.955	-6	88	79	3b150		-1.6
1994	Tor A	109	405	38	97	19	1	11	44	23-1	5	95	.240	.296	.373	71	-19	1-0	.946	-10	74	107	3b107,1b3		-2.6
1995	Tor A	144	521	77	127	27	2	18	74	58-3	15	96	.244	.333	.407	92	-6	0-0	.958	-1	94	78	3b139,1b7,D2		-0.6
1996	Tor A	159	591	88	146	35	2	36	101	60-3	12	146	.247	.325	.496	105	3	0-0	.956	-9	87	115	3b148,D10		-0.6
1997	Tor A	138	504	63	115	29	1	14	48	51-0	6	102	.228	.306	.385	79	-16	0-1	.945	-4	90	93	3b129,D8	25	-1.9
1998	Tor A	105	382	49	91	20	0	17	51	24-1	11	73	.238	.301	.424	86	-9	0-2	.924	-6	90	52	3b105		-1.4
	Oak A	27	87	8	13	5	0	3	7	2-1	2	17	.149	.187	.310	27	-10	1-0	.909	-1	95	59	3b23/1		-1.0
	Year	132	469	57	104	25	0	20	58	26-2	13	90	.222	.280	.403	75	-19	1-2	.921	-6	91	53	3b128/1		-2.4

YEAR	TM LG	G	AB	R	H	2B	3B	HR	RBI	BB-IB	HP	SO	AVG	OBP	SLG	AOPS	ABR	SB-CS	FA	FR	RNG	THR	GAMES AT POSITION	DL	BFW
1999	Pit N★	137	490	71	131	27	2	22	81	50-6	17	93	.267	.352	.465	105	4	3-6	.920	-1	103	99	3b134	14	0.2
2000	SD N	53	117	17	32	10	0	0	25	10-2	2	28	.274	.336	.336	144	7	0-0	.964	-8	69	83	1b24,3b5,O5(4/0/1)		-0.4
	Bos A	33	111	11	24	4	0	2	9	12-0	0	18	.216	.306	.306	51	-9	0-0	.972	0	96	22	3b30,1b3/D		-0.8
	SD N	20	40	2	9	2	0	0	2	3-0	1	12	.225	.295	.275	48	-3	0-0	1.000	-9	27	0	3b5,O2L/12		-1.4
2001	†Sea A	45	94	9	28	7	0	2	16	11-1	1	18	.298	.374	.436	120	3	0-0	.981	-2	43	79	1b12,O9(8/0/1),3b8/CD	24	0.0
Total	11	1203	4095	506	1010	225	12	152	558	358-21	91	833	.247	.318	.419	90	-67	6-12	.942	-59	90	85	3b1019,1b77,D34,C18,O16L/2	63	-12.3

SPRATT, HARRY   Henry Lee   B7.10.1887 Bradford VA   D7.3.1969 Washington DC   BL/TR/5-8.5/175   d4.13   Col Emory & Henry

1911	Bos N	62	154	22	37	4	4	2	13	13	0	25	.240	.299	.357	77	-6	1	.892	-9	82	70	S26,2b5,3b4,O4(0/3/1)		-1.3
1912	Bos N	27	89	6	23	3	2	3	15	7	0	11	.258	.313	.438	102	0	2	.842	-10	88	65	S23		-0.9
Total	2	89	243	28	60	7	6	5	28	20	0	36	.247	.304	.387	86	-6	3	.871	-18	85	68	S49,2b5,O4(0/3/1),3b4		-2.2

SPRIGGS, GEORGE   George Herman   B5.22.1941 Jewell MD   BL/TR/5-11/175*   d9.15

1965	Pit N	9	2	5	1	0	0	0		0-0	0	0	.500	.500	.500	182	0	2-0	—	-0	0	0	/OR		0.1
1966	Pit N	9	7	0	1	0	0	0		0-0	0	3	.143	.143	.143	-20	-1	0-0	—	0			/H		-0.1
1967	Pit N	38	57	14	10	1	1	0	5	6-0	0	20	.175	.246	.228	39	-5	3-0	1.000	-1	85	0	O13(10/0/3)		-0.6
1969	KC A	23	29	4	4	2	1	0	3	4-0	1	8	.138	.242	.276	44	-2	0-0	1.000	-1	82	0	O6(4/1/1)		-0.3
1970	KC A	51	130	12	27	2	3	1	7	14-0	0	32	.208	.283	.292	59	-8	4-3	.953	1	98	188	O36R		-0.9
Total	5	130	225	35	43	5	5	1	12	23-0	1	63	.191	.266	.271	51	-16	9-3	.965	-1	93	128	O56(14/1/41)		-1.8

SPRINGER, STEVE   Steven Michael   B2.11.1961 Long Beach CA   BR/TR/6-0/190*   [NYN82 20/501]   d5.22   Col Utah

1990	Cle A	4	12	1	2	0	0	0	1	0-0	0	6	.167	.154	.167	-7	-2	0-0	1.000	-1	57	0	3b3/D		-0.3
1992	NY N	4	5	0	2	1	0	0	0	0-0	0	1	.400	.400	.600	181	1	0-0	1.000	-0	37	182	/23		0.0
Total	2	8	17	1	4	1	0	0	1	0-0	0	7	.235	.222	.294	48	-1	0-0	1.000	-1	55	0	3b4/2D		-0.3

SPRINZ, JOE   Joseph Conrad "Mule"   B8.3.1902 St.Louis MO   D1.11.1994 Fremont CA   BR/TR/5-11/185   d7.16

1930	Cle A	17	45	5	8	1	0	0	2	4	0	4	.178	.245	.200	14	-6	0-0	1.000	4	108	116	C17		-0.1
1931	Cle A	1	3	0	0	0	0	0	0	0	0	0	.000	.000	.000	-95	-1	0-0	1.000	0	0	411	/C		-0.1
1933	StL N	3	5	1	1	0	0	0	0	1	0	1	.200	.333	.200	53	0	0-0	1.000	1	74	159	C3		0.1
Total	3	21	53	6	9	1	0	0	2	5	0	5	.170	.241	.189	12	-7	0-0	1.000	4	99	133	C21		-0.1

SPURGEON, FREDDY   Fred   B10.9.1900 Wabash IN   D11.5.1970 Kalamazoo MI   BR/TR/5-11.5/160   d9.19   Col Valparaiso

1924	Cle A	3	7	1	1	0	0	0	0	0	0	1	.143	.250	.286	37	-1	0-0	.882	-0	125	0	2b3		-0.1
1925	Cle A	107	376	50	108	9	3	0	32	15	0	21	.287	.315	.327	62	-23	8-5	.927	-3	110	119	3b56,2b46,S3		-2.0
1926	Cle A	149	614	101	181	31	3	0	49	27	2	36	.295	.327	.355	77	-22	7-2	.962	-6	100	119	2b149		-2.3
1927	Cle A	57	179	30	45	6	1	1	19	18	1	14	.251	.323	.313	65	-9	8-1	.938	-6	93	91	2b52		-1.2
Total	4	316	1176	181	335	47	7	1	100	60	4	71	.285	.322	.339	70	-55	23-8	.958	-16	99	104	2b250,3b56,S3		-5.6

SPURNEY, ED   Edward Frederick   B1.19.1872 Cleveland OH   D10.12.1932 Cleveland OH   d6.26

1891	Pit N	3	7	2	2	1	0	0	0	2	0	1	.286	.444	.429	158	1	0	.889	-0	109	0	S3		0.0

SQUIRES, MIKE   Michael Lynn   B3.5.1952 Kalamazoo MI   BL/TL/5-11/185(185-198)   [ChiA73 18/429]   d9.1 C4   Col Western Michigan

1975	Chi A	20	65	5	15	0	0	0	4	8-2	0	5	.231	.311	.231	56	-4	3-0	.988	0	108	82	1b20		-0.4
1977	Chi A	3	3	0	0	0	0	0	0	0-0	0	1	.000	.000	.000	-99	-1	0-0	1.000	0	418	0	/1		-0.1
1978	Chi A	46	150	25	42	9	2	0	19	16-0	0	21	.280	.343	.367	100	1	4-4	.997	-2	75	83	1b45		-0.5
1979	Chi A	122	295	44	78	10	1	2	22	22-3	2	9	.264	.318	.325	74	-11	15-5	.995	5	123	84	1b110/OL		-0.9
1980	Chi A	131	343	38	97	11	3	2	33	33-1	1	24	.283	.347	.350	92	-3	8-9	.995	6	123	90	1b114,C2		-0.5
1981	Chi A	92	294	35	78	9	0	0	25	22-0	0	17	.265	.312	.296	78	-8	7-2	.992	4	118	101	1b88/OL		-0.9
1982	Chi A	116	195	33	52	9	3	1	21	14-3	0	13	.267	.316	.359	84	-4	3-3	.995	5	134	119	1b109		-0.3
1983	†Chi A	143	153	21	34	4	1	1	11	22-3	2	11	.222	.326	.281	67	-6	3-3	.996	3	119	131	1b124/3D		-0.7
1984	Chi A	104	82	9	15	1	0	0	6	6-1	0	7	.183	.239	.195	21	-9	2-2	1.000	-1	93	155	1b77,3b13,O3(0/1/1)/P		-1.0
1985	Chi A	2	0	1	0	0	0	0	0	0-0	0	0	—	—	—		-0	0-0	—	0			/R		0.0
Total	10	779	1580	211	411	53	10	6	141	143-13	5	108	.260	.321	.318	78	-45	45-28	.995	23	117	102	1b688,3b14,D5,O5(2/1/1),C2/P		-5.3

STABELL, JOE   Joseph F.   B Buffalo NY   D7.10.1923 Buffalo NY   5-11.5/?   d9.19

1885	Buf N	7	22	0	1	0	0	0	0	0	0	9	.045	.045	.045	-68	-4		.545	-2	0	0	O6(0/6/1)/2		-0.6

STAEHLE, MARV   Marvin Gustave   B3.13.1942 Oak Park IL   BL/TR/5-10/172(165-176)   d9.15

1964	Chi A	6	5	0	2	0	0	0	2	0-0	0	0	.400	.400	.400	127	0	1-0	—	0			/H		0.0
1965	Chi A	7	7	0	3	0	0	0	2	0-0	0	0	.429	.429	.429	154	0	0-0	—	0			/H		0.0
1966	Chi A	8	15	2	2	0	0	0	0	4-0	0	2	.133	.316	.133	37	-1	1-0	1.000	1	121	202	2b6		0.1
1967	Chi A	32	54	1	6	1	0	0	1	4-0	0	8	.111	.172	.130	-10	-7	1-1	1.000	-3	107	48	2b17,S5		-1.0
1969	Mon N	6	17	4	7	2	0	1	1	2-0	0	0	.412	.474	.706	225	3	0-0	.944	-1	103	73	2b4		0.3
1970	Mon N	104	321	41	70	9	1	0	26	39-1	3	21	.218	.306	.252	52	-21	1-3	.963	-17	89	94	2b91/S		-3.4
1971	Atl N	22	36	5	4	0	0	0	1	5-0	0	4	.111	.238	.111	2	-5	0-0	1.000	4	132	113	2b7/3		0.0
Total	7	185	455	53	94	12	1	1	33	54-1	4	35	.207	.295	.244	49	-31	4-4	.971	-15	95	94	2b125,S6/3		-4.0

STAFFORD, HEINIE   Henry Alexander   B11.1.1891 Orleans VT   D1.29.1972 Lake Worth FL   BR/TR/5-7/160   d10.5   Col Tufts

1916	NY N	1	1	0	0	0	0	0	0	0-0	0	0	.000	.000	.000	-99	0	0-0	—	0			/H		0.0

STAFFORD, GENERAL   James Joseph "Jamsey"   B7.9.1868 Webster MA   D9.18.1923 Worcester MA   BR/TR/5-8/165   d8.27 b-John   OF(96/111/44) ▲

1890	Buf P	15	49	11	7	1	0	0	3	7	0	8	.143	.250	.163	13	-6	2	.893	-2	82	207	P12,O4(1/1/2)		-0.2
1893	NY N	67	281	58	79	7	4	5	27	25	2	31	.281	.344	.388	94	-4	19	.901	-7	72	173	O67C		-1.3
1894	NY N	14	46	10	10	1	1	0	4	10	1	7	.217	.368	.283	59	-3	2	.750	-4	75	104	3b6,O5R/21		-0.5
1895	NY N	124	463	79	129	12	5	3	73	40	6	32	.279	.344	.346	80	-14	42	.911	-7	99	97	2b110,O12L,3b2		-1.4
1896	NY N	59	230	28	66	9	1	0	40	13	3	18	.287	.333	.335	79	-7	15	.897	-2	133	116	O53L,S6		-1.1
1897	NY N	7	23	0	2	0	0	0	3	3				.087	.192	.087	-26	-4	0	1.000	-3		0	O5L,S2		-0.6
	Lou N	113	441	68	122	16	5	7	54	31		3		.277	.328	.383	91	-7	15	.886	-10	101	82	S105,O7(4/2/1)/3		-1.1
	Year	120	464	68	124	16	5	7	57	34		3		.267	.321	.369	85	-11	15	.881	-12	100	83	S107,O12(9/2/1)/3		-1.7
1898	Lou N	49	181	26	54	3	0	1	25	19		1		.298	.368	.331	102	1	7	.901	-5	95	56	2b28,O22(6/7/9)/3		-0.8
	Bos N	37	123	21	32	2	0	1	8	4		1		.260	.298	.301	66	-6	3	.909	-3	22	0	O35(9/1/25)/1		-1.1
	Year	86	304	47	86	5	0	2	33	23		2		.283	.337	.319	87	-5	10	.924	-8	69	170	O57(15/8/34),2b28/31		-1.8
1899	Bos N	55	182	29	55	4	2	3	40	7		0		.302	.328	.396	89	-4	9	.956	-8	0		O41(6/33/2),2b5,S5		-2.1
	Was N	31	118	11	29	5	1	1	14	5		0		.246	.276	.331	67	-6	4	.951	-4	85	39	2b17,S13,3b2		-0.5
	Year	86	300	40	84	9	3	4	54	12		0		.280	.308	.370	81	-10	13	.956	-12	0		O41(6/33/2),2b22,S18,3b2		-2.6
Total	8	571	2137	341	585	60	19	21	291	164	17	96	.274	.330	.349	82	-60	118	.911	-54	69	111	O251C,2b161,S131,3b12,P12,1b2		-9.0

STAFFORD, BOB   Robert M.   B6.26.1872 Oak Ridge NC   D8.20.1916 Moores Springs NC   6-0/180   d10.12

1890	Phi AA	1	2	0	0	0	0	0	0	0	0	0	.000	.000	.000	-99	-1	0	—	-0	0	0	/OR		-0.1

STAGGS, STEVE   Stephen Robert   B5.6.1951 Anchorage AK   BR/TR/5-9/155*   [KCA71 A2/33]   d7.1   Col Cerritos (CA) JC

1977	Tor A	72	290	37	75	11	6	2	28	36-0	0	38	.259	.339	.359	90	-4	5-9	.965	-13	88	67	2b72		-1.1
1978	Oak A	47	78	10	19	2	0	0	0	19-0	0	17	.244	.392	.321	108	2	2-3	.976	-3	90	64	2b40,S2,3b2,D2		0.1
Total	2	119	368	47	94	13	8	2	28	55-0	0	55	.255	.351	.351	94	-2	7-12	.968	-16	88	66	2b112,D2,3b2,S2		-1.0

STAHL, CHICK   Charles Sylvester   B1.10.1873 Avilla IN   D3.28.1907 W.Baden IN   BL/TL/5-10/160   d4.19 M1

1897	†Bos N	114	469	112	166	30	13	4	97	38	3		.354	.406	.499	130	19	18	.928	-5	104	141	O111(1/0/110)		0.9
1898	Bos N	125	467	72	144	21	8	3	52	46	4		.308	.375	.407	118	11	6	.968	-3	79	110	O125(8/0/118)		0.2
1899	Bos N	148	576	122	202	23	19	7	52	72	4		.351	.426	.493	138	31	33	.969	-2	112	110	O148(1/1/146)/P		2.3
1900	Bos N	136	553	88	163	23	16	5	82	34	0		.295	.336	.421	96	-6	27	.968	5	110	80	O135(64/1/71)		-1.0
1901	Bos A	131	515	105	156	20	16	6	72	54	7		.303	.377	.439	128	20	29	.957	-5	70	89	O131(0/130/1)		0.9
1902	Bos A	127	508	92	164	22	11	2	58	37	5		.323	.386	.421	117	12	24	.953	-6	119	68	O125C		-0.5
1903	†Bos A	77	299	60	82	12	6	2	44	28	1		.274	.338	.375	108	3	10	.961	-3	134	106	O74C		-0.2
1904	Bos A	157	587	83	170	27	19	3	67	64	7		.290	.366	.416	139	28	18	.961	-18	34	0	O157C		-1.4
1905	Bos A	134	500	61	129	17	19	3	60	47	50	5	.258	.332	.308	102	3	18	.977	-6	77	133	O134C		-1.1
1906	Bos A	155	595	63	170	24	6	4	51	47	8		.286	.346	.366	123	17	13	.961	7	124	216	O155C,M		1.4
Total	10	1304	5069	858	1546	219	118	36	622	470	44		.305	.369	.416	121	138	189	.961	-31	94	104	O1295(74/777/446)/P		3.4

YEAR	TM	LG	G	AB	R	H	2B	3B	HR	RBI	BB-IB	HP	SO	AVG	OBP	SLG	AOPS	ABR	SB-CS	FA	FR	RNG	THR	GAMES AT POSITION	DL	BFW

STAHL, JAKE Garland B4.13.1879 Elkhart IL D9.18.1922 Monrovia CA BR/TR/6-2/195 d4.20 M4 Col Illinois

YEAR	TM	LG	G	AB	R	H	2B	3B	HR	RBI	BB-IB	HP	SO	AVG	OBP	SLG	AOPS	ABR	SB-CS	FA	FR	RNG	THR	GAMES AT POSITION	DL	BFW
1903	Bos	A	40	92	14	22	3	5	2	8	4	2		.239	.286	.446	111	1	1	.956	0	119	89	C28/OL		0.3
1904	Was	A	142	520	54	136	29	12	3	50	21	15		.262	.309	.381	119	11	25	.978	4	115	90	1b119,O23C		1.3
1905	Was	A	141	501	66	125	22	12	5	66	28	**17**		.250	.311	.371	121	11	41	.986	2	104	86	1b140,M		1.1
1906	Was	A	137	482	38	107	9	8	0	51	21	8		.222	.266	.274	73	-17	30	.983	-2	93	82	1b136,M		-2.3
1908	NY	A	75	274	34	70	18	5	2	42	11	8		.255	.304	.380	120	6	17	.933	4	177	123	O68(64/4/0),1b6		0.7
	Bos		78	262	29	64	9	11	0	23	20	15		.244	.333	.363	123	7	13	.984	-2	88	98	1b78		0.4
	Year		153	536	63	134	27	16	2	.65	31	**23**		.250	.319	.371	122	13	30	.984	2	87	91	1b84,O68(64/4/0)		1.1
1909	Bos	A	127	435	62	128	19	12	6	60	'43	15		.294	.377	.434	153	27	16	.986	-12	64	93	1b126		1.5
1910	Bos	A	144	531	68	144	19	16	**10**	77	42	8		.271	.334	.424	134	18	22	.985	-7	75	75	1b142		0.9
1912	†Bos	A	95	326	40	98	21	6	3	60	31	6		.301	.372	.429	123	10	13	.980	-2	92	96	1b92,M		0.6
1913	Bos	A	2	2	0	0	0	0	0	0	0	0	1	.000	.000	.000	-98	-1	0	—	0			/HM		-0.1
Total 9			981	3425	405	894	149	87	31	437	221	94	1	.261	.323	.382	120	73	178	.983	-13	90	87	1b839,O92(65/27/0),C28		4.4

STAHL, LARRY Larry Floyd B6.29.1941 Belleville IL BL/TL/6-1/185* d9.11

YEAR	TM	LG	G	AB	R	H	2B	3B	HR	RBI	BB-IB	HP	SO	AVG	OBP	SLG	AOPS	ABR	SB-CS	FA	FR	RNG	THR	GAMES AT POSITION	DL	BFW
1964	KC	A	15	46	7	12	1	0	3	6	1	0	10	.261	.277	.478	102	0	0-0	.955	1	102	171	O10(5/4/1)		0.0
1965	KC	A	28	81	9	16	2	1	4	14	5-0	1	16	.198	.250	.395	82	-2	1-0	1.000	2	119	98	O21(8/12/4)		-0.2
1966	KC	A	119	312	37	78	11	5	5	34	17-3	1	63	.250	.289	.365	90	-5	5-3	.980	1	98	123	O94(69/2/27)		-1.0
1967	NY	N	71	155	9	37	5	0	1	18	8-0	2	25	.239	.283	.290	66	-7	2-2	.969	5	129	204	O43(3/32/8)		-0.3
1968	NY	N	53	183	15	43	7	2	3	10	21-1	0	38	.235	.314	.344	97	0	3-0	.983	7	128	168	O47(13/30/19),1b9		0.5
1969	SD	N	95	162	10	32	6	2	3	10	17-3	1	31	.198	.278	.315	68	-7	3-3	.981	4	99	192	O37(27/4/5),1b13		-0.6
1970	SD	N	52	66	5	12	2	0	0	3	2-0	0	14	.182	.206	.212	13	-8	2-2	1.000	-0	82	129	O20(17/0/4)		-1.0
1971	SD	N	114	308	27	78	13	4	8	36	26-4	0	59	.253	.310	.399	107	1	4-3	.987	7	94	208	O75(46/8/26),1b7		0.4
1972	SD	N	107	297	31	67	9	3	7	20	31-3	0	67	.226	.298	.347	89	-5	1-3	.986	-1	98	78	O76(26/10/42)/1		-1.2
1973	†Cin	N	76	111	17	25	2	2	2	12	14-3	1	34	.225	.315	.333	84	-3	1-0	1.000	-1	68	176	O29(3/4/24),1b2		-0.4
Total 10			730	1721	167	400	58	19	36	163	142-17	6	357	.232	.292	.351	86	-36	22-16	.983	23	103	150	O452(217/106/160),1b32		-3.8

STAHOVIAK, SCOTT Scott Edmund B3.6.1970 Waukegan IL BL/TR/6-5/222(210-230) [MinA91 1/27] d9.10 Col Creighton

YEAR	TM	LG	G	AB	R	H	2B	3B	HR	RBI	BB-IB	HP	SO	AVG	OBP	SLG	AOPS	ABR	SB-CS	FA	FR	RNG	THR	GAMES AT POSITION	DL	BFW
1993	Min	A	20	55	7	11	4	0	0	1	3-0	0	23	.193	.233	.263	33	-5	0-2	.922	2	129	35	3b19		-0.4
1995	Min	A	94	263	28	70	19	0	3	23	30-1	1	61	.266	.341	.373	86	-5	5-1	.998	7	144	94	1b69,3b22/D		-0.2
1996	Min	A	130	405	72	115	30	3	13	61	59-7	2	114	.284	.376	.469	111	8	3-3	.994	10	134	89	1b114,D9		0.7
1997	Min	A	91	275	33	63	17	0	10	33	24-1	6	73	.229	.301	.400	81	-8	5-2	.990	4	124	110	1b81,D5	44	-1.0
1998	Min	A	9	19	1	2	0	0	1	1	0-0	0	7	.105	.105	.263	-8	-3	0-0	.975	0	145	117	1b4/OR		-0.3
Total 5			344	1019	135	261	70	3	27	119	116-9	9	277	.256	.335	.410	90	-13	13-8	.994	23	134	97	1b268,3b41,D15/OR	44	-1.2

STAIGER, ROY Roy Joseph B1.6.1950 Tulsa OK BR/TR/6-0/195* [NYN70*S1/24] d9.12 Col Bacone

YEAR	TM	LG	G	AB	R	H	2B	3B	HR	RBI	BB-IB	HP	SO	AVG	OBP	SLG	AOPS	ABR	SB-CS	FA	FR	RNG	THR	GAMES AT POSITION	DL	BFW
1975	NY	N	13	19	2	3	1	0	0	0	0-0	0	4	.158	.158	.211	2	-3	0-0	1.000	-1	79	0	3b13		-0.4
1976	NY	N	95	304	23	67	8	1	2	26	25-6	1	35	.220	.278	.273	61	-16	3-3	.967	13	111	132	3b93/S		-0.4
1977	NY	N	40	123	16	31	9	0	2	11	4-0	0	20	.252	.276	.374	75	-5	1-0	.934	4	116	85	3b36/S		-0.1
1979	NY	A	4	11	1	3	1	0	0	1	1-0	0	0	.273	.308	.364	89	-0	0-0	1.000	-0	90	158	3b4		0.0
Total 4			152	457	42	104	19	1	4	38	30-6	1	59	.228	.274	.300	63	-24	4-3	.960	16	110	115	3b146,S2		-0.9

STAINBACK, TUCK George Tucker B8.4.1911 Los Angeles CA D11.29.1992 Camarillo CA BR/TR/5-11.5/175 d4.17

YEAR	TM	LG	G	AB	R	H	2B	3B	HR	RBI	BB-IB	HP	SO	AVG	OBP	SLG	AOPS	ABR	SB-CS	FA	FR	RNG	THR	GAMES AT POSITION	DL	BFW
1934	Chi	N	104	359	47	110	14	3	2	46	8	1	42	.306	.327	.379	90	-6	7	.955	-3	97	64	O96(60/22/15)/3		-1.3
1935	Chi	N	47	94	16	24	4	0	3	11	0	2	13	.255	.271	.394	76	-4	1	.932	-1	99	49	O28(1/1/26)		-0.6
1936	Chi	N	44	75	13	13	3	0	1	5	6	0	14	.173	.235	.253	31	-7	1	1.000	1	110	79	O26(15/6/5)		-0.7
1937	Chi	N	72	160	18	37	7	1	0	14	7	1	16	.231	.268	.287	49	-11	3	.981	2	105	126	O49(9/39/1)		-1.1
1938	StL	N	6	10	2	0	0	0	0	0	0	0	3	.000	.000	.000	-95	-3	0	1.000	0	133	0	O2(1/1/0)		-0.3
	Phi	N	30	81	9	21	3	0	1	11	3	1	3	.259	.294	.333	74	-3	1	.980	1	117	63	O25(13/4/9)		-0.0
	Bro	N	35	104	15	34	6	3	0	20	2	1	4	.327	.346	.442	113	1	1	.981	-1	99	56	O23(2/21/0)		-0.0
	Year		71	195	26	55	9	3	1	31	5	2	10	.282	.307	.374	86	-4	2	.982	0	109	56	O50(16/26/9)		-0.6
1939	Bro	N	68	201	22	54	7	0	3	19	4	1	23	.269	.290	.348	68	-10	0	.938	-4	103	0	O55(10/39/7)		-1.5
1940	Det	A	15	40	4	9	2	0	1	1	1	1	9	.225	.262	.275	36	-4	0	.968	2	99	542	O9(1/8/0)		-0.2
1941	Det	A	94	200	19	49	8	1	2	10	3	1	21	.245	.260	.325	49	-15	6-3	.948	-1	103	69	O80(39/6/36)		-1.9
1942	†NY	A	15	10	0	2	0	0	0	0	0	0	2	.200	.200	.200	13	-1	0-0	1.000	1	122	0	O3(2/0/1)		-0.1
1943	†NY	A	71	231	31	60	11	2	0	10	7	1	16	.260	.285	.325	77	-8	3-3	.993	-0	101	71	O60(12/43/5)		-1.1
1944	NY	A	30	78	13	17	3	0	0	5	3	0	7	.218	.247	.256	42	-6	1-0	.957	-0	104	84	O24(4/4/17)		-0.8
1945	NY	A	95	327	40	84	12	2	5	32	13	2	20	.257	.289	.352	82	-9	0-4	.968	5	107	137	O83(2/72/9)		-0.9
1946	Phi	A	91	291	35	71	10	2	0	20	7	1	20	.244	.264	.292	56	-19	3-2	.963	2	110	98	O66(11/18/37)		-2.0
Total 13			817	2261	284	585	90	14	17	204	64	16	213	.259	.284	.333	68	-105	27-12	.965	3	104	88	O629(182/284/168)/3		-12.8

STAIRS, MATT Matthew Wade B2.27.1968 St.John NB, Can. BL/TR/5-9/206(175-217) d5.29

YEAR	TM	LG	G	AB	R	H	2B	3B	HR	RBI	BB-IB	HP	SO	AVG	OBP	SLG	AOPS	ABR	SB-CS	FA	FR	RNG	THR	GAMES AT POSITION	DL	BFW
1992	Mon	N	13	30	2	5	2	0	0	5	7-0	0	7	.167	.316	.233	61	-1	0-0	.933	-1	93	0	O10L		-0.2
1993	Mon	N	6	8	1	3	1	0	0	2	0-0	1		.375	.375	.500	126	0	0-0	1.000	-0	88	0	/OL		0.0
1995	†Bos	A	39	88	8	23	7	1	1	17	4-0	1	14	.261	.298	.398	78	-3	0-1	.913	-4	48	150	O23(17/0/6),D2		-0.8
1996	Oak	A	61	137	21	38	5	1	10	23	19-2	1	23	.277	.367	.547	129	6	1-1	.985	4	86	339	O44(16/0/29)/1D		0.8
1997	Oak	A	133	352	62	105	19	0	27	73	50-1	3	66	.298	.386	.582	150	26	3-2	.977	-3	83	109	O89(28/0/63),D16,1b7		1.7
1998	Oak	A	149	523	88	154	33	4	26	106	59-4	6	93	.294	.370	.511	128	22	8-3	1.000	4	102	449	D120,O12(11/0/2),1b6		1.8
1999	Oak	A	146	531	94	137	26	3	38	102	89-6	2	124	.258	.366	.533	129	24	2-7	.981	-4	89	133	O139(0/1/139)/1D		1.0
2000	†Oak	A	143	476	74	108	26	0	21	81	78-4	1	122	.227	.333	.414	90	-7	5-2	.979	-4	94	103	O103(0/1/102),D37/1		-1.6
2001	Chi	N	128	340	48	85	21	0	17	61	52-7	7	76	.250	.358	.462	114	8	2-3	.993	3	105	69	1b89,O22(22/0/1)/2D		0.4
2002	Mil	N	107	270	41	66	15	0	16	41	36-4	8	50	.244	.349	.478	119	7	2-0	.993	1	98	134	O84(35/0/51)	18	0.5
2003	Pit	N	121	305	49	89	20	1	20	57	45-3	5	64	.292	.389	.561	143	20	0-1	.987	-6	81	131	O55(8/0/47),1b31,D2	22	0.9
2004	KC	A	126	439	48	117	21	3	18	66	49-2	5	92	.267	.345	.451	106	4	1-0	.986	-2	96	116	O71(14/0/57),1b30,D22	15	-0.4
2005	KC	A	127	396	55	109	26	1	13	66	60-4	5	69	.275	.373	.444	125	17	1-2	.993	-2	97	103	1b64,D40,O15(2/0/13)		0.7
Total 13			1299	3895	591	1039	222	11	207	700	548-37	44	795	.267	.361	.489	120	123	25-22	.982	-12	89	133	O668(164/2/510),D251,1b230/2	55	4.8

STALEY, GALE George Gaylord B5.2.1899 DePere WI D4.19.1989 Walnut Creek CA BL/TR/5-8.5/167 d9.16

YEAR	TM	LG	G	AB	R	H	2B	3B	HR	RBI	BB-IB	HP	SO	AVG	OBP	SLG	AOPS	ABR	SB-CS	FA	FR	RNG	THR	GAMES AT POSITION	DL	BFW
1925	Chi	N	7	26	2	11	2	0	2	8	1-1	0	1	.423	.464	.500	144	2	0-1	.979	3	117	171	2b7		0.4

STALLCUP, VIRGIL Thomas Virgil "Red" B1.3.1922 Ravensford NC D5.2.1989 Greenville SC BR/TR/6-3/185* d4.18

YEAR	TM	LG	G	AB	R	H	2B	3B	HR	RBI	BB-IB	HP	SO	AVG	OBP	SLG	AOPS	ABR	SB-CS	FA	FR	RNG	THR	GAMES AT POSITION	DL	BFW
1947	Cin	N	8	1	0	0	0	0	0	0	0-0	0	1	.000	.000	.000	-99	-0	0	—	-0	0	0	/S		0.0
1948	Cin	N	149	539	40	123	30	4	3	65	18	0	52	.228	.253	.315	55	-36	2	.956	-0	98	99	S148		-2.8
1949	Cin	N	141	575	49	146	28	5	3	45	9	2	44	.254	.268	.336	60	-34	1	.962	-14	96	99	S141		-3.9
1950	Cin	N	136	483	44	121	23	2	6	54	17	0	39	.251	.276	.356	65	-26	4	**.973**	-5	95	89	S136		-2.3
1951	Cin	N	121	428	33	103	17	2	8	49	6	0	40	.241	.251	.346	58	-27	2-4	**.969**	-6	99	87	S117		-2.7
1952	Cin	N	2	1	0	0	0	0	0	0	0-0	0	0	.000	.000	.000	-99	-0	0	—	-0	0	0	/S		0.0
	StL	N	29	31	4	4	0	0	0	1	1	0	5	.129	.156	.161	-12	-5	0-0	1.000	2	134	159	S12		-0.3
	Year		31	32	4	4	1	0	0	1	1	0	5	.125	.152	.156	-15	-5	0-0	1.000	2	130	155	S13		-0.3
1953	StL	N	1	1	0	0	0	0	0	0	0	0	0	.000	.000	.000	-99	-0	0	—	0			/H		0.0
Total 7			587	2059	171	497	99	13	22	214	51	2	181	.241	.260	.334	58	-128	9-4	.965	-23	97	94	S556		-12.0

STALLER, GEORGE George Walborn "Stopper" B4.1.1916 Rutherford Heights PA D7.3.1992 Harrisburg PA BL/TL/5-11/190 d9.14 Mil 1944-45 C9

YEAR	TM	LG	G	AB	R	H	2B	3B	HR	RBI	BB-IB	HP	SO	AVG	OBP	SLG	AOPS	ABR	SB-CS	FA	FR	RNG	THR	GAMES AT POSITION	DL	BFW
1943	Phi	A	21	85	14	23	3	2	1	12	5	2	12	.271	.326	.459	129	2	1-0	.977	-0	101	68	O20R		0.1

STALLINGS, GEORGE George Tweedy "Gentleman George" B11.17.1867 Augusta GA D5.13.1929 Haddock GA BR/TR/6-1/187 d5.22 M13

YEAR	TM	LG	G	AB	R	H	2B	3B	HR	RBI	BB-IB	HP	SO	AVG	OBP	SLG	AOPS	ABR	SB-CS	FA	FR	RNG	THR	GAMES AT POSITION	DL	BFW
1890	Bro	N	4	11	1	3	0	0	0	0	0	1	3	.000	.154	.000	-54	-2	0	.933	-1	85	29	C4		-0.3
1897	Phi	N	2	9	1	2	1	0	0	0	0	0		.222	.222	.333	47	-1	0	1.000	10	431	0	/OR1M		0.0
1898	Phi	N	1	0	1	0	0	0	0	0	0	0		—	—	—	—	0	0	—	0			/HM		0.0
Total 3			7	20	3	5	1	0	0	0	1	1	3	.100	.182	.150	-7	-3	0	.933	-1	85	29	C4/1OR		-0.3

STANAGE, OSCAR Oscar Harland B3.17.1883 Tulare CA D11.11.1964 Detroit MI BR/TR/5-9.5/185 d5.19 C5

YEAR	TM	LG	G	AB	R	H	2B	3B	HR	RBI	BB-IB	HP	SO	AVG	OBP	SLG	AOPS	ABR	SB-CS	FA	FR	RNG	THR	GAMES AT POSITION	DL	BFW
1906	Cin	N	1	1	0	0	0	0	0	0	0	0		.000	.000	.000	-96	-0	0	1.000	-0	0	0	/C		0.0
1909	†Det	A	77	252	17	66	8	6	0	21	11	2		.262	.298	.341	98	-2	2	.964	-5	98	88	C77		0.1
1910	Det	A	88	275	24	57	7	4	2	25	20	2		.207	.266	.284	68	-11	1	.952	-1	103	113	C84		-0.4
1911	Det	A	141	503	45	133	13	7	3	51	20	3		.264	.297	.336	73	-21	3	.952	-10	103	105	C141		-1.8

YEAR	TM LG	G	AB	R	H	2B	3B	HR	RBI	BB-IB	HP	SO	AVG	OBP	SLG	AOPS	ABR	SB-CS	FA	FR	RNG	THR	GAMES AT POSITION	DL	BFW
1912	Det A	121	394	35	103	9	4	0	41	34	4		.261	.326	.305	83	-8	3	.950	-34	75	106	C120		-3.3
1913	Det A	80	241	19	54	13	2	0	21	21	2	35	.224	.292	.295	73	-8	5	.960	-12	81	108	C77		-1.5
1914	Det A	122	400	16	77	8	4	0	25	24	2	58	.192	.242	.233	41	-30	2-1	.960	-13	91	104	C122		-3.6
1915	Det A	100	300	27	67	9	2	1	31	20	1	41	.223	.274	.277	62	-15	5-1	.964	-9	97	92	C100		-1.7
1916	Det A	94	291	16	69	17	3	0	30	17	3	48	.237	.286	.316	78	-8	3	.969	-13	88	87	C94		-1.5
1917	Det A	99	297	19	61	14	1	0	30	20	3	35	.205	.262	.259	59	-15	3	.977	-6	88	88	C95		-1.5
1918	Det A	54	186	9	47	4	0	1	14	11	0	18	.253	.294	.290	80	-5	2	.980	-9	76	90	C47,1b5/S		-1.2
1919	Det A	38	120	9	29	4	1	1	15	7	2	12	.242	.295	.317	73	-5	1	.974	-0	89	90	C36/1		-0.2
1920	Det A	78	238	12	55	17	0	0	17	14	1	21	.231	.277	.303	55	-16	0-0	.958	-9	87	105	C77		-1.9
1925	Det A	3	5	0	1	0	0	0	0	0	0	0	.200	.200	.200	2	-1	0-0	1.000	-1	52	0	C3		-0.1
Total	14	1096	3503	248	819	123	34	8	321	219	25	268	.234	.284	.295	69	-145	30-2	.961	-123	91	99	C1074,1b6/S		-18.6

STANDAERT, JERRY   Jerome John B11.2.1901 Chicago IL D8.4.1964 Chicago IL BR/TR/5-10/168 d4.16

YEAR	TM LG	G	AB	R	H	2B	3B	HR	RBI	BB-IB	HP	SO	AVG	OBP	SLG	AOPS	ABR	SB-CS	FA	FR	RNG	THR	GAMES AT POSITION	DL	BFW
1925	Bro N	1	1	0	0	0	0	0	0	0	0	1	.000	.000	.000	-99	0	0-0	—	0			/H		0.0
1926	Bro N	66	113	13	39	8	2	0	14	5	1	9	.345	.378	.451	124	4	0-0	.918	-7	72	57	2b21,3b14,S6		-0.3
1929	Bos A	19	18	1	3	2	0	0	4	3	0	0	.167	.286	.278	47	-1	0-0	.958	0	121	90	1b10		-0.1
Total	3	86	132	14	42	10	2	0	18	8	1	10	.318	.362	.424	111	3	0-0	.918	-7	72	57	2b21,3b14,1b10,S6		-0.4

STANICEK, PETE   Peter Louis B4.18.1963 Harvey IL BB/TR/5-11/185* [BalA85 9/229] d9.1 b-Steve Col Stanford [DL 1989 Bal A 34]

YEAR	TM LG	G	AB	R	H	2B	3B	HR	RBI	BB-IB	HP	SO	AVG	OBP	SLG	AOPS	ABR	SB-CS	FA	FR	RNG	THR	GAMES AT POSITION	DL	BFW
1987	Bal A	30	113	9	31	3	0	0	9	8-1	2	19	.274	.333	.301	72	-4	8-1	.975	-4	83	129	2b19,D10,3b2		-0.6
1988	Bal A	83	261	29	60	7	1	4	17	28-0	4	45	.230	.313	.310	77	-8	12-6	.985	-1	100	114	O65L,2b16/D	8	-1.0
Total	2	113	374	38	91	10	1	4	26	36-1	6	64	.243	.319	.307	75	-12	20-7	.985	-5	100	114	O65L,2b35,D11,3b2	42	-1.6

STANICEK, STEVE   Stephen Blair B6.19.1961 Lake Forest IL BR/TR/6-0/190* [SFN82 1/11] d9.16 b-Pete Col Nebraska [DL 1988 Mil A 66]

YEAR	TM LG	G	AB	R	H	2B	3B	HR	RBI	BB-IB	HP	SO	AVG	OBP	SLG	AOPS	ABR	SB-CS	FA	FR	RNG	THR	GAMES AT POSITION	DL	BFW
1987	Mil A	4	7	2	2	0	0	0	1	0-0	0	2	.286	.286	.286	51	-1	0-0	—	0			/D		-0.2
1989	Phi N	9	9	0	1	0	0	0	1	0-0	0	3	.111	.111	.111	-36	-2	0-0	—	0			/H		-0.2
Total	2	13	16	2	3	0	0	0	1	0-0	0	5	.188	.188	.188	4	-3	0-0		0	0	0	/D	66	-0.3

STANKARD, TOM   Thomas Francis B3.20.1882 Waltham MA D6.13.1958 Waltham MA BR/TR/6-0/190 d7.2 Col Holy Cross

YEAR	TM LG	G	AB	R	H	2B	3B	HR	RBI	BB-IB	HP	SO	AVG	OBP	SLG	AOPS	ABR	SB-CS	FA	FR	RNG	THR	GAMES AT POSITION	DL	BFW
1904	Pit N	2	2	0	0	0	0	0	0	0	0		.000	.000	.000	-97	0	0	1.000	-0	69	0	/S3		-0.1

STANKIEWICZ, ANDY   Andrew Neal B8.10.1964 Inglewood CA BR/TR/5-9/165* [NYA86 12/314] d4.11 Col Pepperdine

YEAR	TM LG	G	AB	R	H	2B	3B	HR	RBI	BB-IB	HP	SO	AVG	OBP	SLG	AOPS	ABR	SB-CS	FA	FR	RNG	THR	GAMES AT POSITION	DL	BFW
1992	NY A	116	400	52	107	22	2	2	25	38-0	5	42	.268	.338	.348	93	-3	9-5	.973	11	108	102	S81,2b34/D	15	1.5
1993	NY A	16	9	5	0	0	0	0	0	0-0	0	0	1.000	.100	.000	-73	-2	0-0	1.000	2	143	245	2b6,3b4/SD		0.0
1994	Hou N	37	54	10	14	3	0	1	5	12-0	1	12	.259	.403	.370	109	2	1-1	1.000	-2	107	77	S17,2b6/3	32	-0.1
1995	Hou N	43	52	6	6	1	0	0	7	12-2	0	19	.115	.281	.135	15	-6	4-2	.985	4	137	81	S14,2b6,3b3	28	-0.3
1996	Mon N	64	77	12	22	5	1	0	9	6-1	3	12	.286	.356	.377	93	-1	1-0	.969	-2	111	54	2b19,S13/3	20	-0.2
1997	Mon N	76	107	11	24	9	0	1	5	4-0	0	22	.224	.250	.336	53	-8	1-0	.957	1	118	109	2b25,S14,3b3,D2	31	-1.5
1998	Ari N	77	145	9	30	5	0	0	8	7-0	2	33	.207	.252	.241	31	-15	1-0	.994	-6	98	80	2b61		-1.1
Total	7	429	844	105	203	45	3	4	59	80-3	11	141	.241	.313	.315	72	-33	17-9	.986	9	107	93	2b157,S140,3b12,D4	126	-1.6

STANKY, EDDIE   Edward Raymond "The Brat","Muggsy" B9.3.1916 Philadelphia PA D6.6.1999 Fairhope AL BR/TR/5-8/170* d4.21 M8/C2

YEAR	TM LG	G	AB	R	H	2B	3B	HR	RBI	BB-IB	HP	SO	AVG	OBP	SLG	AOPS	ABR	SB-CS	FA	FR	RNG	THR	GAMES AT POSITION	DL	BFW
1943	Chi N	142	510	92	125	15	1	0	47	92	2	42	.245	.363	.278	88	-3	4	.966	12	104	102	2b131,S12,3b2		1.1
1944	Chi N	13	25	4	6	1	0	0	2	2	0		.240	.296	.320	74	-1	1	.875	1	67	344	2b3,S3,3b3		-0.1
	Bro N	89	261	32	72	9	2	0	16	44	1	13	.276	.382	.326	102	3	3	.961	-16	89	81	2b58,S35/3		-0.1
	Year	102	286	36	78	9	3	0	16	46	1		.273	.375	.325	100	2	4	.958	-15	88	88	2b61,S38,3b4		-0.2
1945	Bro N	153	555	128	143	29	5	1	39	148	4	42	.258	.417	.333	111	21	6	.962	9	97	117	2b153/S		3.1
1946	Bro N	144	483	98	132	24	7	0	36	137	2	56	.273	.436	.352	124	27	8	.977	-6	92	110	2b141		2.8
1947	†Bro N★	146	559	97	141	24	5	3	53	103	5	39	.252	.373	.329	85	-7	3	.985	8	98	130	2b146		0.8
1948	†Bos N*	67	247	49	79	14	2	4	29	61	2	13	.320	.455	.417	140	19	3	.981	3	106	123	2b66	60	2.7
1949	Bos N	138	506	90	144	24	5	1	42	113	2	41	.285	.417	.358	116	20	3	.979	-7	95	100	2b135		1.2
1950	NY N☆	152	527	115	158	25	5	8	51	144	12	50	.300	.460	.412	131	37	9	.976	4	99	124	2b151		4.2
1951	†NY N	145	515	88	127	17	2	14	43	127	6	63	.247	.401	.369	108	13	8-5	.977	0	100	118	2b140		0.8
1952	StL N	53	83	13	19	4	0	0	7	19	0	9	.229	.373	.277	83	-1	0-0	1.000	2	103	90	2b20,M		0.7
1953	StL N	17	30	5	8	0	0	0	1	6	1	4	.267	.405	.267	80	0	0-0	1.000	1	117	85	2b8,M	30	0.3
Total	11	1259	4301	811	1154	185	35	29	364	996	35	374	.268	.410	.348	109	128	48-5	.975	11	98	114	2b1152,S51,3b6	90	20.0

STANLEY, FRED   Frederick Blair B8.13.1947 Farnhamville IA BR/TR (BB 1969-71)/5-10/167(155-170) [HouN66 8/143] d9.11 C1

YEAR	TM LG	G	AB	R	H	2B	3B	HR	RBI	BB-IB	HP	SO	AVG	OBP	SLG	AOPS	ABR	SB-CS	FA	FR	RNG	THR	GAMES AT POSITION	DL	BFW
1969	Sea A	17	43	2	12	2	1	0	4	3-0	0	8	.279	.319	.372	96	0	1-0	.962	-6	70	94	S15/2		-0.1
1970	Mil A	6	6	1	0	0	0	0	0	0-0	0	1	.225	.361	.302	82	-2	1-0	1.000	0	147	0	2b2		0.1
1971	Cle A	60	129	14	29	4	0	2	12	27-3	1	25	.225	.361	.302	82	-2	1-0	.971	4	110	99	S65,2b3		-0.3
1972	Cle A	6	12	1	2	1	0	0	0	2-0	0	3	.167	.286	.250	58	-1	0-0	.917	-2	56	0	S5/2		-0.2
	SD N	39	85	15	17	2	0	0	2	12-1	1	19	.200	.306	.224	57	-4	1-0	.989	0	106	124	2b21,S17,3b4		-0.2
1973	NY A	26	66	6	14	0	1	1	5	7-0	0	16	.212	.288	.288	64	-3	0-0	.981	2	107	95	S21,2b3		-0.1
1974	NY A	33	38	2	7	0	0	0	3	3-0	0	7	.184	.244	.184	25	-4	1-2	.973	-6	117	90	S19,2b15		-0.1
1975	NY A	117	252	34	56	5	1	0	15	21-0	1	27	.222	.283	.250	53	-16	3-1	.977	-3	91	95	S83,2b33/3		-1.4
1976	†NY A	110	260	32	62	2	2	1	20	34-0	1	29	.238	.329	.273	78	-6	1-0	.983	-23	88	74	S110,2b3		-2.5
1977	†NY A	48	46	6	12	0	1	0	7	8-0	0	6	.261	.370	.326	92	0	1-1	.958	-3	91	65	S42,3b3,2b2		-0.2
1978	†NY A	81	160	14	35	7	0	1	9	25-0	0	31	.219	.324	.281	73	-5	0-0	.959	-8	89	84	S71,2b11,3b4		-0.3
1979	NY A	57	100	9	20	1	0	2	14	5-0	0	17	.200	.236	.270	37	-9	0-1	.978	4	114	152	S31,3b16,2b8/1OL		-0.9
1980	NY A	49	86	13	18	3	0	0	5	5-0	2	5	.209	.266	.244	42	-7	0-0	.923	-0	105	110	S19,2b17,3b12	37	-2.0
1981	†Oak A	66	145	15	28	4	0	0	7	16-0	0	23	.193	.269	.221	44	-10	2-0	.986	-18	75	78	S62,2b6		-2.0
1982	Oak A	101	228	33	44	7	0	2	17	29-0	1	32	.193	.287	.250	51	-15	0-1	.963	-19	91	81	S98,2b2		-2.6
Total	14	816	1650	197	356	38	5	10	120	196-4	7	243	.216	.301	.263	61	-82	11-6	.971	-66	91	87	S648,2b128,3b40/OL1	37	-9.2

STANLEY, JIM   James F. B1889 BB/TR/5-6/148 d4.19

YEAR	TM LG	G	AB	R	H	2B	3B	HR	RBI	BB-IB	HP	SO	AVG	OBP	SLG	AOPS	ABR	SB-CS	FA	FR	RNG	THR	GAMES AT POSITION	DL	BFW
1914	Chi F	54	98	13	19	3	0	0	4	19	4	14	.194	.347	.224	61	-6	2	.878	-8	85	110	S40,3b3/2OL		-1.0

STANLEY, JOE   Joseph B NJ d4.24

YEAR	TM LG	G	AB	R	H	2B	3B	HR	RBI	BB-IB	HP	SO	AVG	OBP	SLG	AOPS	ABR	SB-CS	FA	FR	RNG	THR	GAMES AT POSITION	DL	BFW
1884	Bal U	6	21	3	5	1	0	0		0			.238	.238	.286	53	-2		.444	-2	77	0	O6(0/4/2)		-0.0

STANLEY, JOE   Joseph Bernard B4.2.1881 Washington DC D9.13.1967 Detroit MI BB/TR/5-9.5/150 d9.11 b-Buck

YEAR	TM LG	G	AB	R	H	2B	3B	HR	RBI	BB-IB	HP	SO	AVG	OBP	SLG	AOPS	ABR	SB-CS	FA	FR	RNG	THR	GAMES AT POSITION	DL	BFW
1897	Was N	1	1	0	0	0	0	0	0	0	0		.000	.000	.000	-99	0	0	—	-0	0		/P		0.0
1902	Was A	3	12	2	4	0	0	0	1	0	0		.333	.333	.333	85	0	1	.833	-1	0		O3L		-0.0
1903	Bos N	86	308	40	77	12	5	1	47	18	7		.250	.306	.331	85	-7	10	.902	2	197	74	O77(11/32/34)/PS		-0.0
1904	Bos N	3	8	0	0	0	0	0	0	0	0		.000	.000	.000	-99	-2	0	.800	1	633	0	O3(1/0/2)		-0.0
1905	Was A	28	92	13	24	2	1	1	17	7	0		.261	.313	.337	111	1	4	.944	1	140	0	O27(13/9/5)		-0.0
1906	Was A	73	221	18	36	0	4	0	9	20	1		.163	.236	.199	38	-16	6	.934	-3	97	0	O63(0/7/56)/P		-0.0
1909	Chi N	22	52	4	7	1	0	0	2	6	0		.135	.224	.154	17	-5	0	.947	-1	60	0	O16(5/4/9)		-0.0
Total	7	216	694	77	148	15	10	2	76	51	8		.213	.275	.272	66	-29	20	.918	-2	150	32	O189(33/52/106),P3/S		-0.4

STANLEY, MICKEY   Mitchell Jack B7.20.1942 Grand Rapids MI BR/TR/6-1/195(180-195) d9.13 Col Grand Rapids (MI) CC OF(44/1171/82)

YEAR	TM LG	G	AB	R	H	2B	3B	HR	RBI	BB-IB	HP	SO	AVG	OBP	SLG	AOPS	ABR	SB-CS	FA	FR	RNG	THR	GAMES AT POSITION	DL	BFW
1964	Det A	4	11	3	3	0	0	0	1	0-0	0	1	.273	.273	.273	52	-1	0-0	1.000	-0	89	0	O4(3/1/1)		-0.0
1965	Det A	30	117	14	28	6	0	3	13	3-0	0	12	.239	.256	.368	75	-4	1-0	.986	0	106	81	O29C	33	-0.5
1966	Det A	92	235	28	68	15	4	3	19	17-4	0	20	.289	.336	.426	115	5	2-1	1.000	4	108	153	O82C		0.8
1967	Det A	145	333	38	70	7	3	7	24	29-2	0	46	.210	.275	.372	71	-13	9-2	.982	2	114	59	O129(2/126/2),1b8		-1.1
1968	†Det A	153	583	88	151	16	6	11	60	42-1	4	57	.259	.311	.364	102	-3	4-3	1.000	-1	101	83	O130C,1b15,S9/2		-0.4
1969	Det A	149	592	73	139	28	1	16	70	52-1	2	56	.235	.299	.367	82	-15	8-4	.985	-13	103	39	O132C,1b9		-2.6
1970	Det A	142	568	83	143	21	11	13	47	45-1	0	56	.252	.305	.396	92	-9	10-1	1.000	-2	106	37	O132C,1b9		-1.1
1971	Det A	139	401	43	117	14	5	7	41	24-5	0	44	.292	.329	.404	103	-3	1-3	.988	9	114	142	O139C		0.4
1972	†Det A	142	435	45	102	16	6	14	55	29-8	0	49	.234	.278	.395	97	-4	1-0	.994	2	103	114	O139C		0.3
1973	Det A	157	602	81	147	23	5	17	57	48-4	0	65	.244	.297	.384	96	-13	0-4	.992	5	104	63	O91(1/90/0),1b2/2	44	-0.6
1974	Det A	99	394	40	87	13	2	6	34	26-1	1	63	.221	.270	.325	68	-17	5-3	.983	0	102	58	O28(14/15/0),1b14,3b7/D	59	-1.7
1975	Det A	52	164	26	42	7	3	2	19	15-2	1	27	.256	.320	.390	96	-1	1-1	.983	3	90	101	O38(15/19/4),1b17,3b11,S3,2b2,D2		-0.4
1976	Det A	84	214	34	55	17	1	6	23	14-1	1	36	.257	.300	.402	102	2	2-0	.969	3	90	101	O38(15/19/4),1b17,3b11,S3,2b2,D2		-0.4
1977	Det A	75	222	30	51	9	1	8	23	18-2	0	30	.230	.284	.387	78	-7	0-0	.972	-5	89	51	O57(7/10/44),1b3,S3,D2		-0.8

YEAR	TM LG	G	AB	R	H	2B	3B	HR	RBI	BB-IB	HP	SO	AVG	OBP	SLG	AOPS	ABR	SB-CS	FA	FR	RNG	THR	GAMES AT POSITION	DL	BFW
1978	Det A	53	151	15	40	9	0	3	8	9-0	0	19	.265	.306	.384	90	-2	0-1	.960	-4	79	49	O34(2/4/28),1b12		-0.8
Total	15	1516	5022	641	1243	201	48	117	500	371-32	8	564	.248	.298	.377	89	-81	44-23	.991	2	105	83	O1290C,1b94,S74,3b18,D5,2b4	136	-11.4

STANLEY, MIKE Robert Michael B6.25.1963 Ft.Lauderdale FL BR/TR/6-1/185(185-205) [TexA85 16/395] d6.24 C1 Col Florida

YEAR	TM LG	G	AB	R	H	2B	3B	HR	RBI	BB-IB	HP	SO	AVG	OBP	SLG	AOPS	ABR	SB-CS	FA	FR	RNG	THR	GAMES AT POSITION	DL	BFW
1986	Tex A	15	30	4	10	3	0	1	1	3-0	0	7	.333	.394	.533	145	2		.857	-2	86	143	3b7,C4/OLD		0.1
1987	Tex A	78	216	34	59	8	1	6	37	31-0	1	48	.273	.361	.403	103	2	3-0	.980	-21	53	57	C61,1b12/OLD		-1.6
1988	Tex A	94	249	21	57	8	0	3	27	37-0	0	62	.229	.323	.297	75	-7	0-0	.991	-8	58	73	C64,D18,1b6,3b2		-0.7
1989	Tex A	67	122	9	30	3	1	1	11	12-1	2	29	.246	.324	.311	78	-3	1-0	.978	-8	122	60	C25,D21,1b7,3b3	21	-1.3
1990	Tex A	103	189	21	47	8	1	2	19	30-2	0	25	.249	.350	.333	92	-1	1-0	.985	-8	65	85	C63,D14,3b8,1b6	15	-1.1
1991	Tex A	95	181	25	45	13	1	3	25	34-0	1	44	.249	.372	.381	111	5	0-0	.980	-13	75	53	C58,1b12,3b6/OLD		-0.7
1992	NY A	68	173	24	43	7	0	8	27	33-0	1	45	.249	.372	.428	124	7	0-0	.980	-2	90	102	C55,1b4,D6		0.7
1993	NY A	130	423	70	129	17	1	26	84	57-4	5	85	.305	.389	.534	151	31	1-1	.996	-5	124	65	C122,D2		3.2
1994	NY A	82	290	54	87	20	0	17	57	39-2	2	56	.300	.384	.545	142	19	0-0	.993	-5	162	102	C72,1b7,D4		2.4
1995	†NY A★	118	399	63	107	29	1	18	83	57-1	5	106	.268	.360	.481	119	13	1-1	.993	-4	93	101	C107,D10		1.3
1996	Bos A	121	397	73	107	24	1	24	69	69-3	5	62	.270	.383	.506	120	14	2-0	.985	-28	65	72	C105,D10		-0.7
1997	Bos A	97	260	45	78	17	0	13	53	39-0	6	50	.300	.394	.515	135	15	0-1	.996	-3	103	110	D53,1b31,C15		0.7
	†NY A	28	87	16	25	8	0	3	12	15-4	0	22	.287	.388	.483	128	4	0-0	1.000	-1	55	110	D16,1b12		0.2
	Year	125	347	61	103	25	0	16	65	54-4	6	72	.297	.393	.507	133	19	0-1	.997	-4	91	110	D69,1b43,C15		0.9
1998	Tor A	98	341	49	82	13	0	22	47	56-3	5	86	.240	.353	.472	112	7	2-1	.995	-2	74	78	D73,1b22/OL		-0.1
	†Bos A	47	156	25	45	12	0	7	32	26-2	2	43	.288	.388	.500	128	8	1-0	1.000	-1	70	150	D34,1b13		0.4
	Year	145	497	74	127	25	0	29	79	82-5	7	129	.256	.364	.481	117	14	3-1	.997	-2	73	103	D107,1b35/OL		0.3
1999	†Bos A	136	427	59	120	22	0	19	72	70-3	11	94	.281	.393	.466	115	13	0-0	.988	-1	94	88	1b111,D20		0.1
2000	Bos A	58	185	22	41	5	0	10	28	30-0	1	44	.222	.327	.411	84	-5	0-0	.997	-8	138	93	1b39,D18	20	-0.5
	Oak A	32	97	11	26	7	0	4	18	14-0	1	21	.268	.363	.464	110	2	0-0	.988	0	111	109	1b19,D8		0.0
	Year	90	282	33	67	12	0	14	46	44-0	1	65	.238	.339	.429	93	-3	0-0	.993	-4	129	98	1b58,D26		-0.5
Total	15	1467	4222	625	1138	220	7	187	702	652-25	48	929	.270	.370	.458	117	126	13-4	.988	-98	93	80	C751,D321,1b301,3b26,O4L	71	2.5

STANSBURY, JACK John James B12.6.1885 Phillipsburg NJ D12.26.1970 Easton PA BR/TR/5-9/165 d6.30

YEAR	TM LG	G	AB	R	H	2B	3B	HR	RBI	BB-IB	HP	SO	AVG	OBP	SLG	AOPS	ABR	SB-CS	FA	FR	RNG	THR	GAMES AT POSITION	DL	BFW
1918	Bos A	20	47	3	6	1	0	0	2	6	1	3	.128	.241	.149	18	-5	0	.980	2	118	192	3b18,O2C		-0.2

STANTON, BUCK George Washington B6.19.1906 Stantonsburg NC D1.1.1992 San Antonio TX BL/TL/5-10/150 d9.5 Col North Carolina-Asheville

YEAR	TM LG	G	AB	R	H	2B	3B	HR	RBI	BB-IB	HP	SO	AVG	OBP	SLG	AOPS	ABR	SB-CS	FA	FR	RNG	THR	GAMES AT POSITION	DL	BFW
1931	StL A	13	15	3	3	2	0	0	0	0-0	0	6	.200	.200	.333	37	-1	0-0	.750	-0	100	0	/OR		-0.2

STANTON, HARRY Harry Andrew B St.Louis MO TR d10.14

YEAR	TM LG	G	AB	R	H	2B	3B	HR	RBI	BB-IB	HP	SO	AVG	OBP	SLG	AOPS	ABR	SB-CS	FA	FR	RNG	THR	GAMES AT POSITION	DL	BFW
1900	StL N	1	0	0	0	0	0	0	0	0	0	0	—	—	—		0	0	—	0	0	0	/C		0.0

STANTON, LEROY Leroy Bobby B4.10.1946 Latta SC BR/TR/6-1/195* d9.10

YEAR	TM LG	G	AB	R	H	2B	3B	HR	RBI	BB-IB	HP	SO	AVG	OBP	SLG	AOPS	ABR	SB-CS	FA	FR	RNG	THR	GAMES AT POSITION	DL	BFW
1970	NY N	4	4	0	1	0	1	0	0	0-0	0	0	.250	.250	.750	155	0	0-0	1.000	0	404	0	/OC		0.0
1971	NY N	5	21	2	4	1	0	0	2	2-1	0	4	.190	.261	.238	42	-2	0-0	1.000	-1	90	0	O5R		-0.3
1972	Cal A	127	402	44	101	15	3	12	39	22-4	4	100	.251	.295	.393	110	2	2-3	.983	2	109	78	O124(0/2/123)		-0.2
1973	Cal A	119	306	41	72	9	2	8	34	27-2	2	88	.235	.300	.356	91	-5	3-3	.965	-1	99	89	O107(36/0/76)		-1.1
1974	Cal A	118	415	48	111	21	2	11	62	33-3	5	107	.267	.325	.407	117	9	10-8	.975	5	107	139	O114(0/10/110)	35	0.7
1975	Cal A	137	440	67	115	20	3	14	82	52-4	6	85	.261	.345	.416	123	14	18-6	.961	3	98	165	O131(0/5/127)/D		1.3
1976	Cal A	93	231	12	44	13	1	2	25	24-1	1	57	.190	.266	.281	65	-10	2-6	.985	-6	90	22	O79(33/31/27),D4		-2.2
1977	Sea A	133	454	56	125	24	1	27	90	42-2	5	115	.275	.341	.511	130	18	0-1	.953	4	105	148	O91(8/0/84),D33		1.6
1978	Sea A	93	302	24	55	11	0	3	34	26-1	1	80	.182	.265	.248	46	-21	1-0	1.000	2	117	62	D59,O30(30/0/1)		-2.3
Total	9	829	2575	294	628	114	13	77	358	236-18	24	636	.244	.311	.388	103	5	36-27	.972	8	103	110	O682(107/49/553),D97	35	-2.5

STANTON, TOM Thomas Patrick B10.25.1874 St.Louis MO D1.17.1957 St.Louis MO BB/TR/5-10/175 d4.19

YEAR	TM LG	G	AB	R	H	2B	3B	HR	RBI	BB-IB	HP	SO	AVG	OBP	SLG	AOPS	ABR	SB-CS	FA	FR	RNG	THR	GAMES AT POSITION	DL	BFW
1904	Chi N	1	3	0	0	0	0	0	0	0-0	0	0	.000	.000	.000	-99	-1	0	1.000	-0	99	118	/C		-0.1

STAPLETON, DAVE David Leslie B1.16.1954 Fairhope AL BR/TR/6-1/178(170-185) [BosA75 10/231] d5.30 Col South Alabama OF(5/0/2)

YEAR	TM LG	G	AB	R	H	2B	3B	HR	RBI	BB-IB	HP	SO	AVG	OBP	SLG	AOPS	ABR	SB-CS	FA	FR	RNG	THR	GAMES AT POSITION	DL	BFW
1980	Bos A	106	449	45	144	33	5	7	45	13-1	1	32	.321	.338	.463	112	7	3-2	.979	11	111	132	2b94,1b8,O6(4/0/2),3b2,D3		2.2
1981	Bos A	93	355	45	101	17	1	10	42	21-1	1	22	.285	.325	.423	107	3	0-4	.948	-7	89	82	S33,3b25,2b23,1b12,D3		-0.2
1982	Bos A	150	538	66	142	28	1	14	65	31-5	3	40	.264	.305	.398	87	-10	2-4	.991	5	113	108	1b106,S27,2b9,3b5/OLD		-1.0
1983	Bos A	151	542	54	134	31	1	10	66	40-2	2	44	.247	.297	.363	76	-17	1-1	.993	-0	102	97	1b145,2b5		-2.7
1984	Bos A	13	39	4	9	2	0	0		3-1	0	3	.231	.286	.282	55	-2	0-0	1.000	1	111	57	1b10/D		-0.2
1985	Bos A	30	66	4	15	6	0	0	2	4-0	0	11	.227	.271	.318	58	-4	0-0	1.000	-1	91	88	2b14,1b8,D5		-0.2
1986	†Bos A	39	39	4	5	1	0	0	2	2-0	0	10	.128	.171	.154	-11	-6	0-0	1.000	0	89	126	1b29,2b6,3b2		-0.7
Total	7	582	2028	238	550	118	8	41	224	114-10	7	162	.271	.310	.398	90	-29	6-11	.993	9	105	105	1b318,2b151,S60,3b34,D16,O7L	22	-3.0

STARGELL, WILLIE Wilver Dornel "Pops" B3.6.1940 Earlsboro OK D4.9.2001 Wilmington NC BL/TL/6-2.5/225(190-228) d9.16 C4 HF1988

YEAR	TM LG	G	AB	R	H	2B	3B	HR	RBI	BB-IB	HP	SO	AVG	OBP	SLG	AOPS	ABR	SB-CS	FA	FR	RNG	THR	GAMES AT POSITION	DL	BFW
1962	Pit N	10	31	1	9	3	1	0	4	3-1	0	10	.290	.353	.452	114	1	0-1	.929	-0	86	165	O9(2/1/6)		0.0
1963	Pit N	108	304	34	74	11	6	11	47	19-0	2	85	.243	.290	.428	104	0	0-1	.953	-8	74	74	O65(35/6/24),1b16		-1.4
1964	Pit N	117	421	53	115	19	7	21	78	17-2	2	92	.273	.304	.501	123	10	1-1	.900	-6	90	60	O59(57/1/2),1b50		-0.2
1965	Pit N★	144	533	68	145	25	8	27	107	39-3	7	127	.272	.328	.501	130	19	1-1	.965	-1	90	156	O137(125/0/19),1b7		1.1
1966	Pit N★	140	485	84	153	30	0	33	102	48-16	1	96	.315	.381	.581	164	42	2-3	.945	-5	88	110	O127(121/0/7),1b15		3.0
1967	Pit N	134	462	54	125	18	6	20	73	67-25	3	103	.271	.365	.465	136	23	1-0	.938	-2	86	198	O98(92/0/6),1b37		1.5
1968	Pit N	128	435	57	103	15	1	24	67	47-11	6	105	.237	.315	.441	129	15	5-0	.945	-5	78	165	O113(108/0/5),1b13		0.5
1969	Pit N	145	522	89	160	31	6	29	92	61-14	6	120	.307	.382	.556	164	45	1-0	.970	-5	90	69	O116(115/0/1),1b23		3.3
1970	†Pit N	136	474	70	125	18	3	31	85	44-11	5	119	.264	.329	.511	123	13	0-1	.976	3	90	187	O125(123/0/2)/1		0.8
1971	†Pit N★	141	511	104	151	26	0	48	125	83-20	7	154	.295	.398	.628	186	59	0-0	.984	-4	88	85	O138L		4.9
1972	†Pit N★	138	495	75	145	28	2	33	112	65-15	2	129	.293	.373	.558	165	42	1-1	.984	-12	67	133	1b101,O32L		2.1
1973	Pit N★	148	522	106	156	43	3	44	119	80-22	3	129	.299	.392	.646	187	63	0-0	.975	2	91	145	O142L		5.7
1974	†Pit N	140	508	90	153	37	4	25	96	87-21	6	106	.301	.407	.537	168	49	0-2	.967	-4	95	80	O135L/1		3.7
1975	†Pit N	124	461	71	136	32	2	22	90	58-6	3	109	.295	.375	.516	145	29	0-0	.992	-7	75	116	1b122		1.2
1976	Pit N★	117	428	54	110	20	3	20	65	50-6	5	101	.257	.339	.458	123	13	2-0	.988	-8	76	86	1b111		-0.4
1977	Pit N	63	186	29	51	12	0	13	35	31-10	2	52	.274	.383	.548	143	12	0-1	.986	-1	98	73	1b55		0.8
1978	Pit N★	122	390	60	115	18	2	28	97	50-13	7	93	.295	.382	.567	155	29	3-2	.994	-2	91	95	1b112		2.2
1979	†Pit N	126	424	60	119	19	0	32	82	47-12	3	105	.281	.352	.552	136	20	0-1	.997	-8	88	124	1b113		0.6
1980	Pit N	67	202	28	53	10	1	11	38	26-10	2	52	.262	.351	.485	127	8	0-0	.992	0	100	143	1b54	71	0.5
1981	Pit N	38	60	2	9	0	0	5	9	5-1	0	24	.283	.333	.350	91	-1	0-0	1.000	-2	143	169	1b9		-0.4
1982	Pit N	74	73	6	17	4	0	3	17	10-1	0		.233	.318	.411	100	0	0-0	1.000	0	104	143	1b8		-0.4
Total	21	2360	7927	1195	2232	423	55	475	1540	937-227	78	1936	.282	.360	.529	147	491	17-16	.961	-73	88	123	O1296(1225/8/72),1b848	146	29.5

TARK, MATT Matthew Scott B1.21.1965 Whittier CA BR/TR/6-4/225* [TorA83 1/9] d4.8 [DL 1988 Tor A 74]

YEAR	TM LG	G	AB	R	H	2B	3B	HR	RBI	BB-IB	HP	SO	AVG	OBP	SLG	AOPS	ABR	SB-CS	FA	FR	RNG	THR	GAMES AT POSITION	DL	BFW
1987	Tor A	5	12	0	1	0	0	0	0	0-0	0	3	.083	.083	.083	-54	-3	0-0	1.000	-0	41	89	C5	20	-0.3
1990	Chi A	8	16	0	4	1	0	0	3	1-0	0	6	.250	.294	.313	71	-1	0-0	—	-0			D6		-0.1
Total	2	13	28	0	5	1	0	0	3	1-0	0	6	.179	.207	.214	15	-4	0-0	1.000	-0	41	89	D6,C5	94	-0.4

TARK, DOLLY Monroe Randolph B1.19.1885 Ripley MS D12.1.1924 Memphis TN BR/TR/5-9/160 d9.12

YEAR	TM LG	G	AB	R	H	2B	3B	HR	RBI	BB-IB	HP	SO	AVG	OBP	SLG	AOPS	ABR	SB-CS	FA	FR	RNG	THR	GAMES AT POSITION	DL	BFW
1909	Cle N	19	60	4	12	0	0	0	1	6	0		.200	.273	.200	48	-3	4	.875	-7	73	52	S19		-1.2
1910	Bro N	30	103	7	17	3	0	0	8	1	1	19	.165	.225	.194	23	-10	4	.893	-2	98	106	S30		-1.2
1911	Bro N	70	193	25	57	4	1	0	19	20	3	24	.295	.370	.326	100	1	6	.910	-4	96	101	S34,2b18,3b3		-0.1
1912	Bro N	8	22	2	4	0	0	0	2	1	0	3	.182	.217	.182	10	-3		.892	-1	98	113	S7		-0.3
Total	4	127	378	38	90	7	1	0	30	34	4	46	.238	.308	.262	66	-15	14	.896	-14	92	94	S90,2b18,3b3		-2.3

TARNAGLE, GEORGE George Henry (b George Henry Steuernagel) B10.6.1873 Belleville IL D2.15.1946 Belleville IL BR/TR/5-11/175 d9.14

YEAR	TM LG	G	AB	R	H	2B	3B	HR	RBI	BB-IB	HP	SO	AVG	OBP	SLG	AOPS	ABR	SB-CS	FA	FR	RNG	THR	GAMES AT POSITION	DL	BFW
1902	Cle N	1	3	0	0	0	0	0	0	0	0	0	.000	.000	.000	-99	-1	0	.667	-1	83	0	/C		-0.1

TARR, CHARLIE Charles Watkin B8.30.1878 Pike Co. OH D10.18.1937 Pasadena CA TR/5-10.5/165 d4.29

YEAR	TM LG	G	AB	R	H	2B	3B	HR	RBI	BB-IB	HP	SO	AVG	OBP	SLG	AOPS	ABR	SB-CS	FA	FR	RNG	THR	GAMES AT POSITION	DL	BFW
1905	StL A	26	97	9	20	0	0	0	6	7	0		.206	.260	.206	51	-5	0	.938	-2	109	27	2b18,3b6		-0.8
1908	Pit N	20	59	8	11	2	0	0	8	13	1		.186	.342	.220	80	0	6	.926	-4	99	95	2b12,S5,3b2		-0.5
1909	Bos N	61	216	16	48	2	0	0	6	31	5		.222	.323	.259	80	-4	7	.931	-4	100	99	2b24,S6,3b3		-0.8
	Phi N	3	3	0	0	0	0	0	0	0	0		.000	.000	.000	-99	-1	0	—				/H		-0.1
	Year	64	219	16	48	2	0	0	6	31	5		.219	.329	.256	78	-4	7	.931	-4	100	99	2b54,S6,3b3		-0.9
Total	3	110	375	33	79	4	0	0	20	51	6		.211	.315	.237	72	-10	13	.931	-10	102	85	2b84,S11,3b11		-2.2

YEAR	TM LG	G	AB	R	H	2B	3B	HR	RBI	BB-IB	HP	SO	AVG	OBP	SLG	AOPS	ABR	SB-CS	FA	FR	RNG	THR	GAMES AT POSITION	DL	BFW

STARR, BILL William B2.26.1911 Brooklyn NY D8.12.1991 LaJolla CA BR/TR/6-1/175 d8.23

1935	Was A	12	24	1	5	0	0	0	0	0	0	1	.208	.208	.208	8	-3	0-0	.971	0	92	157	C12		-0.3
1936	Was A	1	0	0	0	0	0	0	0	0	0	0	—	—	—	—	0	0-0	—	0	0	0	/C		0.0
Total	2	13	24	1	5	0	0	0	0	0	0	1	.208	.208	.208	8	-3	0-0	.971	0	91	155	C13		-0.3

START, JOE Joseph "Old Reliable","Rocks" B10.14.1842 New York NY D3.27.1927 Providence RI BL/TL/5-9/165 d5.18 M1

1871	Mut NA	33	161	35	58	5	1	1	34	3		0	.360	.372	.422	140	10	4-2	.921	-2	38	82	1b33		0.6
1872	Mut NA	54	277	60	75	5	0	0	48	0		0	.271	.271	.289	77	-6	3-3	.958	2	0	139	1b54		-0.2
1873	Mut NA	53	252	42	67	8	3	1	29	4		0	.266	.277	.333	81	-6	1-0	.943	6	150	88	1b53,O2R,M		0.1
1874	Mut NA	63	306	67	96	13	3	2	46	4		0	.314	.323	.395	125	8	5-0	.961	5	108	67	1b63,O2(1/1/0)		1.2
1875	Mut NA	69	314	58	90	10	5	4	30	3		0	.287	.293	.389	128	7	1-4	.948	2	88	72	1b69		0.8
1876	NY N	56	264	40	73	6	0	0	21	1		2	.277	.279	.299	107	3		.964	3	99	48	1b56		0.4
1877	Har N	60	271	55	90	3	6	1	21	6		2	.332	.347	.399	150	16		.964	-2	52	98	1b60		0.9
1878	Chi N	61	285	58	100	12	5	1	27	2		3	.351	.355	.439	150	14		.957	-2	75	103	1b61		0.8
1879	Pro N	66	317	70	101	11	5	2	37	7		4	.319	.333	.404	144	14		.973	0	65	88	1b65/OR		1.1
1880	Pro N	82	345	53	96	14	6	0	27	13		20	.278	.304	.354	126	10		.971	-3	45	93	1b82		0.3
1881	Pro N	79	348	56	114	12	6	0	29	9		7	.328	.345	.397	135	13		.963	-4	59	111	1b79		0.5
1882	Pro N	82	356	58	117	8	10	0	48	11		7	.329	.349	.407	142	15		.974	-1	102	126	1b87		-0.5
1883	Pro N	87	370	63	105	16	7	1	57	22		16	.284	.324	.373	108	3		.957	-1	92	100	1b69		0.3
1884	†Pro N	93	381	80	105	10	5	2	32	35		25	.276	.337	.344	117	9		.980	1	75	91	1b93		0.1
1885	Pro N	101	374	47	103	11	4	0	41	39		10	.275	.344	.326	121	11		.972	1	104	83	1b101		-0.9
1886	Was N	31	122	10	27	4	0	0	17	5		13	.221	.252	.270	64	-5	4	.973	-2	58	92	1b31		-0.3
Total	5 NA	272	1310	262	386	41	12	8	187	14		0	.295	.302	.363	109	13	14-9	.948	13	81	89	1b272,O4(1/1/2)		2.5
Total	11	798	3433	590	1031	107	55	7	357	150			.300	.330	.370	127	103	4	.968	-7	77	100	1b797/OR		3.9

STATON, DAVE David Alan B4.12.1968 Seattle WA BR/TR/6-5/215* [SDN89 5/130] d9.8 Col Cal St.-Fullerton

1993	SD N	17	42	7	11	3	0	5	9	3-0	1	12	.262	.326	.690	162	3	0-0	1.000	3	200	137	1b12		0.5
1994	SD N	29	66	6	12	2	0	4	6	10-0	0	18	.182	.289	.394	78	-2	0-0	1.000	3	150	65	1b20		-0.1
Total	2	46	108	13	23	5	0	9	15	13-0	1	30	.213	.303	.509	111	1	0-0	1.000	6	167	90	1b32		0.4

STATON, JOE Joseph B3.8.1948 Seattle WA BL/TL/6-3/175* d9.5

1972	Det A	6	2	1	0	0	0	0	0	0-0	0	1	.000	.000	.000	-97	0	0-1	1.000	-0	0	0	1b2		-0.1
1973	Det A	9	17	2	4	0	0	0	3	0-0	0	3	.235	.235	.235	31	-2	1-0	.969	1	257	30	1b5		0.0
Total	2	15	19	3	4	0	0	0	3	0-0	0	4	.211	.211	.211	18	-2	1-1	.973	1	213	25	1b7		-0.1

STATZ, JIGGER Arnold John B10.20.1897 Waukegan IL D3.16.1988 Corona Del Mar CA BR/TR (BB 1922p)/5-7.5/150 d7.30 Col Holy Cross

1919	NY N	21	60	7	18	2	1	0	6	3		8	.300	.333	.367	112	1		.977	-1	115	0	O18(3/7/8),2b5		-0.1
1920	NY N	16	30	0	4	0	1	0	5	2		9	.133	.188	.200	11	-4	0-1	.944	-2	69	76	O12C		-0.7
	Bos A	2	3	0	0	0	0	0	0	0		0	.000	.000	.000	-99	-1		1.000	-0	98	0	O2R		-0.1
1922	Chi N	110	462	77	137	19	5	1	34	41		31	.297	.355	.366	85	-10	16-13	.959	1	100	113	O110C		-1.4
1923	Chi N	154	655	110	209	33	8	10	70	56		42	.319	.375	.440	114	14	29-23	.975	11	106	128	O154C		1.6
1924	Chi N	135	549	69	152	22	5	3	49	37		50	.277	.325	.352	80	-15	13-9	.961	8	104	154	O131C/2		-1.3
1925	Chi N	38	148	21	38	6	3	2	14	11		16	.257	.317	.378	76	-6	4-0	.943	-1	104	82	O37C		-0.7
1927	Bro N	130	507	64	139	24	7	1	21	26		43	.274	.310	.355	77	-17	10	.990	10	111	108	O122(3/118/1)/2		-1.3
1928	Bro N	77	171	28	40	8	1	0	16	18		12	.234	.311	.292	59	-10	3	.965	-1	99	83	O52(2/49/1)/2		-1.3
Total	8	683	2585	376	737	114	31	17	215	194		9	211	.285	.337	.373	87	-48	77-46	.969	25	105	117	O638(8/618/12),2b8		-5.3

STAUB, RUSTY Daniel Joseph B4.1.1944 New Orleans LA BL/TR/6-2/200(190-230) d4.9 C1

1963	Hou N	150	513	43	115	17	4	6	45	59-8	5	58	.224	.309	.308	84	-10	0-0	.989	-3	81	71	1b109,O49(0/1/48)		-2.3
1964	Hou N	89	292	26	63	10	2	8	35	21-4	3	31	.216	.272	.346	78	-9	1-1	.992	-2	79	95	1b49,O38(0/7/31)		-1.8
1965	Hou N	131	410	43	105	20	1	14	63	52-5	2	57	.256	.339	.412	120	12	3-0	.951	2	100	157	O112(1/2/110)/1		0.7
1966	Hou N	153	554	60	155	28	3	13	81	58-13	1	61	.280	.345	.412	119	15	2-1	.962	8	112	127	O148(55/1/105)/1		1.4
1967	Hou N★	149	546	71	182	44	1	10	74	60-21	3	47	.333	.398	.473	155	42	0-4	.962	1	105	98	O144R		3.4
1968	Hou N★	161	591	54	172	37	1	6	72	73-24	7	57	.291	.373	.387	132	27	2-0	.992	0	100	84	1b147,O15R		2.1
1969	Mon N☆	158	549	89	166	26	5	29	79	110-11	3	61	.302	.426	.526	165	54	3-4	.966	2	99	140	O156R		4.8
1970	Mon N★	160	569	98	156	23	7	30	94	112-11	3	93	.274	.394	.497	138	34	12-11	.985	6	105	130	O160R		3.0
1971	Mon N☆	162	599	94	186	34	6	19	97	74-13	9	42	.311	.392	.482	145	32	9-5	.945	2	96	173	O162(1/0/162)		3.4
1972	NY N	66	239	32	70	11	2	9	38	31-7	2	13	.293	.372	.452	137	13	0-1	.982	-3	91	80	O65R		1.3
1973	†NY N	152	585	77	163	36	1	15	76	74-10	3	52	.279	.361	.421	117	16	1-1	.978	5	102	126	O152R		0.6
1974	NY N	151	561	65	145	22	2	19	78	77-12	9	39	.258	.347	.406	112	10	2-1	.983	3	92	185	O147R		2.0
1975	NY N	155	574	93	162	30	4	19	105	77-14	9	55	.282	.371	.448	132	26	2-0	.986	1	92	146	O153R		1.4
1976	Det A★	161	589	73	176	28	3	15	96	83-13	4	49	.299	.386	.433	136	30	3-1	.970	-10	82	86	O126R,D36		0.2
1977	Det A	158	623	84	173	34	3	22	101	59-4	1	47	.278	.336	.448	107	7	1-1	—	0	0	0	D156		1.1
1978	Det A	162	642	75	175	30	1	24	121	76-5	3	35	.273	.347	.435	116	15	3-1	—	0	0	0	D162		-0.3
1979	Det A	68	246	32	58	12	1	9	40	32-1	5	18	.236	.331	.402	95	-1	1-0	.994	-2	64	79	1b22/OR		-0.1
	Mon N	38	86	9	23	3	0	3	14	14-3	0	10	.267	.366	.407	111	2	0-0	.977	-0	58	109	D57,1b30,O14(3/0/11)	35	1.1
1980	Tex A	109	340	42	102	23	2	9	55	39-3	2	18	.300	.370	.459	131	16	1-1	.989	-0	77	87	1b41		0.7
1981	NY N	70	161	9	51	9	0	5	21	22-3	1	12	.317	.398	.466	146	11	0-0	.959	2	91	212	O27(12/0/15),1b18		-0.6
1982	NY N	112	219	11	53	9	0	3	27	24-1	0	10	.242	.309	.324	79	-6	0-0	.976	-1	132	148	1b5,O5(3/0/2)		0.3
1983	NY N	104	115	5	34	6	0	3	28	14-3	1	10	.296	.371	.426	123	4	0-0	1.000	-1	0	168	1b3		0.2
1984	NY N	78	72	2	19	4	0	1	18	10-3	1	9	.264	.291	.361	87	-1	0-0	1.000	-0	0	168	1b3		0.2
1985	NY N	54	45	1	12	3	0	1	8	10-3	0	4	.267	.400	.400	127	2	0-0	—	0	0	0	/OR		0.2
Total	23	2951	9720	1189	2716	499	47	292	1466	1255-193	79	888	.279	.362	.431	124	347	47-33	.969	12	99	138	O1675(75/11/1604),D477,1b426	77	23.1

STEARNS, ECKY Daniel Eckford B10.17.1861 Buffalo NY D6.28.1944 Glendale CA BL/TR/6-1/185 d8.17 U1 OF(7/3/28)

1880	Buf N	28	104	8	19	6	1	0	13	3		23	.183	.206	.260	55	-5		.774	-5	88	142	O20(6/1/15),C8,3b5/S		-1.0
1881	Det N	3	11	1	1	1	0	0	0	0		2	.091	.091	.182	-16	-1		.714	-1	100	115	S3		-0.2
1882	Cin AA	49	214	28	55	10	2	0	35	6			.257	.277	.322	96	-1		.931	-3	57	126	1b35,O12R,2b2/S		-0.7
1883	Bal AA	93	382	54	94	10	9	1	34				.246	.308	.327	101	1		.947	3	141	79	1b92/OL		-0.4
1884	Bal AA	100	396	61	94	12	3	3		28	6		.237	.298	.306	94	-2		.949	4	139	78	1b100/2		-0.7
1885	Bal AA	67	253	40	47	3	8	1	29	38	6		.186	.306	.273	85	-2		.973	2	115	102	1b63,O3(0/2/1),C2		-0.8
	Buf N	30	105	7	21	6	1	0	9	8		23	.200	.257	.276	70	-3		.821	-7	75	59	S19,1b12,C2		-1.0
1889	KC AA	139	560	96	160	24	12	3	87	56		0	69	.286	.351	.387	104	1	67	.967	0	117	91	1b135,3b4		-0.9
Total	7	509	2025	295	491	72	36	8	173	173		12	117	.242	.306	.325	94	-12	67	.956	-7	122	89	1b437,O36R,S24,C12,3b9,2b3		-5.4

STEARNS, JOHN John Hardin B8.21.1951 Denver CO BR/TR/6-0/185* [PhiN73 1/2] d9.22 C5 Col Colorado

1974	Phi N	1	2	0	1	0	0	0	0	0-0	0	0	.500	.500	.500	172	0	0-0	1.000	0	0	0	/C		0.0
1975	NY N	59	169	25	32	5	1	3	10	17-4	2	15	.189	.268	.284	56	-11	4-1	.994	3	76	167	C54		-0.5
1976	NY N	32	103	13	27	6	0	2	10	16-0	1	11	.262	.364	.379	117	3	1-2	.987	6	138	172	C30		1.6
1977	NY N★	139	431	52	108	25	1	12	55	77-7	7	76	.251	.370	.397	110	10	9-8	.982	10	117	103	C127,1b6		2.4
1978	NY N	143	477	65	126	24	4	15	73	72-6	4	57	.264	.364	.413	121	16	25-13	.985	3	126	106	C141/3		2.2
1979	NY N☆	155	538	58	131	29	2	9	66	52-5	4	57	.243	.312	.355	84	-11	15-15	.983	-0	87	117	C121,1b16,3b11,O6L		-0.8
1980	NY N★	91	319	42	91	15	1	0	45	33-1	1	24	.285	.346	.370	104	3	7-3	.985	9	108	92	C74,1b16/3	71	1.4
1981	NY N	80	273	25	74	12	1	1	24	24-2	0	17	.271	.329	.333	89	4	12-2	.983	1	123	93	C66,1b9,3b4	17	0.2
1982	NY N★	98	352	46	103	25	3	4	28	30-2	2	35	.293	.349	.415	113	7	17-7	.987	-4	100	146	C81,3b12	147	0.2
1983	NY N	4	4	0	0	0	0	0	0	0-0	0	0	—	—	—	—	0	0-0	—	0			/R	144	0.0
1984	NY N	8	17	6	3	1	0	1	1	4-0	0	2	.176	.333	.235	63	-1	1-0	1.000	-0	89	0	C4,1b2	379	0.0
Total	11	810	2681	334	696	152	10	46	312	323-25	25	294	.260	.341	.375	101	12	91-51	.985	27	109	116	C699,1b49,3b29,O6L	379	7.1

STEDRONSKY, JOHN John B Troy NY d9.26

1879	Chi N	4	12	0	1	0	0	0	0	0		3	.083	.083	.083	-42	-2		.789	1	144	233	3b4		-0.1

STEELMAN, FARMER Morris James B6.29.1875 Millville NJ D9.16.1944 Merchantville NJ TR d9.15

1899	Lou N	4	15	2	1	0	1	0	2	2		3	-2	.067	.176	.200	3	-2	0	.929	-1	111	46	C4		-0.1
1900	Bro N	1	4	0	0	0	0	0	0	0		1	.000	.000	.000	-94	-1	0	1.000	0	81	153	/C		-0.1
1901	Bro N	1	3	0	1	0	0	0	0	0		0	.333	.333	.333	91	0	0	.875	0	126	199	/C		-0.1

YEAR	TM LG	G	AB	R	H	2B	3B	HR	RBI	BB-IB	HP	SO	AVG	OBP	SLG	AOPS	ABR	SB-CS	FA	FR	RNG	THR	GAMES AT POSITION	DL	BFW
	Phi A	27	88	5	23	2	0	0	7	10	2		.261	.350	.284	74	-3	4	1.000	3	100	132	C14,O12R		0.1
1902	Phi A	10	32	1	6	1	0	0	6	2	0		.188	.235	.219	25	-3	2	1.000	1	94	80	C5,O5R		-0.2
Total	4	43	142	8	31	3	1	0	15	14	2		.218	.297	.254	52	-9	6	.985	3	101	114	C25,O17R		-0.5

STEELS, JAMES James Earl B5.30.1961 Jackson MS BL/TL/5-10/185* [SDN79 8/196] d4.6

YEAR	TM LG	G	AB	R	H	2B	3B	HR	RBI	BB-IB	HP	SO	AVG	OBP	SLG	AOPS	ABR	SB-CS	FA	FR	RNG	THR	GAMES AT POSITION	DL	BFW
1987	SD N	62	68	9	13	1	1	0	6	11-0	0	14	.191	.300	.235	47	-5	3-2	.960	-0	95	129	O28(17/6/7)		-0.6
1988	Tex A	36	53	4	10	1	0	0	5	0-0	0	15	.189	.185	.208	11	-6	2-0	1.000	-1	79	0	O17(9/1/7),1b7,D7		-0.7
1989	SF N	13	12	0	1	0	0	0	0	2-1	0	4	.083	.214	.083	-12	-2	0-0	1.000	1	177	0	1b3/OR		-0.1
Total	3	111	133	13	24	2	1	0	11	13-1	0	33	.180	.250	.211	28	-13	5-2	.973	-0	91	82	O46(26/7/15),1b10,D7		-1.4

STEERE, GENE Frederick Eugene B8.16.1872 S.Scituate RI D3.13.1942 San Francisco CA d8.29 Col Brown

YEAR	TM LG	G	AB	R	H	2B	3B	HR	RBI	BB-IB	HP	SO	AVG	OBP	SLG	AOPS	ABR	SB-CS	FA	FR	RNG	THR	GAMES AT POSITION	DL	BFW
1894	Pit N	10	39	3	8	0	0	0	4	2	0	1	.205	.244	.205	9	-6	2	.896	-2	93	105	S10		-0.6

STEFERO, JOHN John Robert B9.22.1959 Sumter SC BL/TR/5-8/185* d6.24

YEAR	TM LG	G	AB	R	H	2B	3B	HR	RBI	BB-IB	HP	SO	AVG	OBP	SLG	AOPS	ABR	SB-CS	FA	FR	RNG	THR	GAMES AT POSITION	DL	BFW
1983	Bal A	9	11	2	5	1	0	0	4	3-0	0	2	.455	.571	.545	212	2	0-0	.920	0	84	164	C9		0.3
1986	Bal A	52	120	14	28	2	0	2	13	16-0	0	25	.233	.321	.300	72	-4	0-1	.984	-4	65	145	C50/2		-0.7
1987	Mon N	18	56	4	11	0	0	1	3	3-1	0	17	.196	.237	.250	28	-6	0-0	.981	1	76	57	C17		-0.5
Total	3	79	187	20	44	3	0	3	20	22-1	0	44	.235	.314	.299	67	-8	0-1	.979	-2	69	124	C76/2		-0.9

STEGMAN, DAVE David William B1.30.1954 Inglewood CA* BR/TR/5-11/190* [DetA76 S1/2] d9.4 Col Arizona

YEAR	TM LG	G	AB	R	H	2B	3B	HR	RBI	BB-IB	HP	SO	AVG	OBP	SLG	AOPS	ABR	SB-CS	FA	FR	RNG	THR	GAMES AT POSITION	DL	BFW
1978	Det A	8	14	3	4	2	0	1	3	1-0	0	1	.286	.313	.643	163	1	0-0	1.000	-1	91	0	O7(0/5/3)		0.0
1979	Det A	12	31	8	6	0	0	3	5	2-0	0	3	.194	.242	.484	88	-1	1-1	1.000	1	131	0	O12(0/11/1)		0.0
1980	Det A	65	130	12	23	5	0	2	9	14-0	0	23	.177	.255	.262	41	-11	1-1	.988	-4	85	34	O57(14/27/23),D2		-1.6
1982	NY A	2	0	0	0	0	0	0	0	0-0	0	0	—	—	—	—	0	0-0	—	0			/D		0.0
1983	Chi A	30	53	5	9	2	0	0	4	10-0	0	9	.170	.292	.208	41	-4	0-1	1.000	-2	74	93	O29(5/19/5)		-0.7
1984	Chi A	55	92	13	24	1	2	2	11	4-0	2	18	.261	.306	.380	84	-2	3-0	.985	-2	89	54	O46(11/27/8),D3		-0.4
Total	6	172	320	39	66	10	2	8	32	31-0	2	55	.206	.277	.325	64	-17	5-3	.991	-8	89	44	O151(30/89/40),D6		-2.7

STEIN, JUSTIN Justin Marion "Ott" B8.9.1911 St.Louis MO D5.1.1992 Creve Coeur MO BR/TR/5-11/180 d5.28 Col St. Louis

YEAR	TM LG	G	AB	R	H	2B	3B	HR	RBI	BB-IB	HP	SO	AVG	OBP	SLG	AOPS	ABR	SB-CS	FA	FR	RNG	THR	GAMES AT POSITION	DL	BFW
1938	Phi N	11	39	6	10	0	1	0	2	2	0	4	.256	.293	.308	67	-2	0	.880	-1	104	199	3b7,2b3		-0.2
	Cin N	11	18	3	6	1	0	0	1	0	0	1	.333	.333	.389	101	0	0	.857	-0	117	97	S7,2b2		0.0
	Year	22	57	9	16	1	1	0	3	2	0	5	.281	.305	.333	78	-2	0	.857	-1	104	199	3b7,S7,2b5		-0.2

STEIN, BILL William Allen B1.21.1947 Battle Creek MI BR/TR/5-10/170* [StLN69 4/90] d9.6 Col Southern Illinois OF(15/0/14)

YEAR	TM LG	G	AB	R	H	2B	3B	HR	RBI	BB-IB	HP	SO	AVG	OBP	SLG	AOPS	ABR	SB-CS	FA	FR	RNG	THR	GAMES AT POSITION	DL	BFW
1972	StL N	14	35	2	11	0	1	2	3	0-0	0	7	.314	.314	.543	140	1	1-0	1.000	-3	48	0	3b4,O4(4/0/1)		-0.1
1973	StL N	32	55	4	12	2	1	0	3	7-0	0	18	.218	.306	.255	57	-3	0-0	1.000	-3	105	0	O10(2/0/8),1b2/3		-0.5
1974	Chi A	13	43	5	12	1	0	0	5	7-2	0	8	.279	.380	.302	96	0	0-0	.871	-3	80	0	3b11,D2		-0.3
1975	Chi A	76	226	23	61	7	1	3	21	18-0	1	32	.270	.327	.350	90	-3	2-2	.974	-1	115	82	2b28,3b24,D18/OL		-0.4
1976	Chi A	117	392	32	105	15	2	4	36	22-3	2	67	.268	.310	.347	92	-5	4-2	.960	-5	96	95	2b58,3b58/1SORD		-0.7
1977	Sea A	151	556	53	144	26	5	13	67	29-2	5	79	.259	.299	.394	88	-10	3-4	.964	-9	89	70	3b147,S2,D3		-2.2
1978	Sea A	114	403	41	105	24	4	4	37	37-3	0	56	.261	.318	.370	94	-3	1-0	.929	-1	108	91	3b111/D		-0.6
1979	Sea A	88	250	28	62	9	2	7	27	17-1	2	28	.248	.297	.384	82	-7	1-2	.959	-1	99	113	3b67,2b17,S3	21	-0.8
1980	Sea A	67	198	16	53	5	1	5	27	16-4	1	25	.268	.321	.379	91	-3	1-1	.972	6	112	60	3b34,2b14,1b8,D5	50	0.3
1981	Tex A	53	115	21	38	6	0	2	22	7-3	0	15	.330	.360	.435	137	5	1-2	1.000	7	109	82	1b20,O8(7/0/1),3b7,2b3/S		0.4
1982	Tex A	85	184	14	44	8	0	1	16	12-0	2	23	.239	.293	.299	66	-9	0-0	.957	7	117	149	2b34,3b28,S6,1b2/OLD		-0.1
1983	Tex A	78	232	21	72	15	1	2	33	8-0	0	31	.310	.331	.409	104	1	2-3	.975	1	84	122	2b32,1b23,3b10,D6		0.1
1984	Tex A	27	43	3	12	1	0	0	3	5-2	1	9	.279	.354	.302	81	-1	0-0	.967	-2	91	74	2b11,1b3,3b3,D4	64	-0.3
1985	Tex A	44	79	5	20	3	1	1	12	1-1	0	15	.253	.272	.354	68	-4	0-0	.952	2	109	73	3b11,1b8,2b3,O3R,D6	15	-0.3
Total	14	959	2811	268	751	122	18	44	311	186-21	14	413	.267	.313	.370	90	-41	16-20	.950	-9	98	80	3b516,2b200,1b67,D49,O28L,S13	150	-5.5

STEINBACH, TERRY Terry Lee B3.2.1962 New Ulm MN BR/TR/6-1/195(195-212) [OakA83 9/215] d9.12 Col Minnesota

YEAR	TM LG	G	AB	R	H	2B	3B	HR	RBI	BB-IB	HP	SO	AVG	OBP	SLG	AOPS	ABR	SB-CS	FA	FR	RNG	THR	GAMES AT POSITION	DL	BFW
1986	Oak A	6	15	3	5	0	0	2	4	1-0	0	5	.333	.375	.733	207	2	0-0	.962	0	35	357	C5		0.2
1987	Oak A	122	391	66	111	16	3	16	56	32-2	9	66	.284	.349	.463	121	12	1-2	.986	-4	115	118	C107,3b10/1D		1.1
1988	†Oak A	104	351	42	93	19	1	9	51	33-2	6	47	.265	.334	.402	110	5	3-0	.983	7	104	161	C84,3b9,1b8/OLD	26	1.7
1989	†Oak A★	130	454	37	124	13	1	7	42	30-2	5	66	.273	.319	.352	93	-5	1-2	.985	2	166	88	C103,O14(6/0/8),1b10,3b3,D4		0.1
1990	†Oak A	114	379	32	95	15	2	9	57	19-1	4	66	.251	.291	.372	88	-8	0-1	.988	-2	115	75	C83,D25,1b3	25	-0.6
1991	Oak A	129	456	50	125	31	1	6	67	22-4	7	70	.274	.312	.386	99	-1	2-2	.980	-16	87	101	C117,1b9,D2		-1.2
1992	†Oak A★	128	438	48	122	20	1	12	53	45-3	1	58	.279	.345	.411	117	10	2-3	.985	-1	122	125	C124,1b5,D2	15	1.7
1993	Oak A★	104	389	47	111	19	1	10	43	25-1	3	65	.285	.333	.416	106	2	3-3	.989	-15	86	111	C86,1b15,D6	49	-0.9
1994	Oak A	103	369	51	105	21	2	11	57	26-4	0	62	.285	.327	.442	105	2	2-1	.998	9	119	144	C93,1b6,D6		1.5
1995	Oak A	114	406	43	113	26	1	15	65	25-4	3	74	.278	.322	.458	106	2	1-3	.993	7	112	132	C111,1b2	16	1.4
1996	Oak A	145	514	79	140	25	1	35	100	49-5	6	115	.272	.342	.529	117	12	0-1	.991	-7	102	94	C137/1D		1.2
1997	Min A	122	447	60	111	27	1	12	54	35-2	1	106	.248	.302	.394	79	-14	6-1	.993	-0	124	80	C116,1b2/D		-0.6
1998	Min A	124	422	45	102	25	2	14	54	38-0	4	89	.242	.310	.410	83	-11	0-1	.990	-1	131	91	C119,D3		-0.4
1999	Min A	101	338	35	96	16	4	4	42	38-1	2	54	.284	.358	.391	87	-6	2-2	.991	-5	124	53	C96/D	34	-0.5
Total	14	1546	5369	638	1453	273	21	162	745	418-31	48	938	.271	.326	.420	101	-2	23-22	.989	-24	116	105	C1381,D69,1b62,3b22,O15(7/0/8)	165	4.7

STEINBACHER, HANK Henry John B3.22.1913 Sacramento CA D4.3.1977 Sacramento CA BL/TR/5-11/180 d4.21

YEAR	TM LG	G	AB	R	H	2B	3B	HR	RBI	BB-IB	HP	SO	AVG	OBP	SLG	AOPS	ABR	SB-CS	FA	FR	RNG	THR	GAMES AT POSITION	DL	BFW
1937	Chi A	26	73	13	19	4	1	1	9	4	0	7	.260	.299	.384	71	-4	2-0	.960	-1	90	0	O15L		-0.5
1938	Chi A	106	399	59	132	23	8	4	61	41	0	19	.331	.393	.459	110	6	1-3	.963	-4	96	74	O101(0/8/93)		-0.7
1939	Chi A	71	111	16	19	2	1	1	15	21	0	8	.171	.303	.234	38	-10	0-0	1.000	-1	64	0	O22(1/0/21)		-1.1
Total	3	203	583	88	170	29	10	6	85	66	0	34	.292	.364	.407	92	-8	3-3	.968	-6	95	65	O138(16/8/114)		-2.0

STEINBRENNER, GENE Eugene Gass B11.17.1892 Pittsburgh PA D4.25.1970 Pittsburgh PA BR/TR/5-8.5/155 d4.25

YEAR	TM LG	G	AB	R	H	2B	3B	HR	RBI	BB-IB	HP	SO	AVG	OBP	SLG	AOPS	ABR	SB-CS	FA	FR	RNG	THR	GAMES AT POSITION	DL	BFW
1912	Phi N	3	9	0	2	1	0	0	0	0	0		.222	.222	.333	48	-1	0	.900	-0	87	122	2b3		-0.1

STEINECKE, BILL William Robert B2.7.1907 Cincinnati OH D7.20.1986 St.Augustine FL BR/TR/5-8.5/175 d9.16 Col DePaul

YEAR	TM LG	G	AB	R	H	2B	3B	HR	RBI	BB-IB	HP	SO	AVG	OBP	SLG	AOPS	ABR	SB-CS	FA	FR	RNG	THR	GAMES AT POSITION	DL	BFW
1931	Pit N	4	4	0	0	0	0	0	0	0	0	1	.000	.000	.000	-99	-1	0		0	0	0	/C		-0.1

STEINER, BEN Benjamin Saunders B7.28.1921 Alexandria VA D10.27.1988 Venice FL BL/TR/5-11/165 d4.17

YEAR	TM LG	G	AB	R	H	2B	3B	HR	RBI	BB-IB	HP	SO	AVG	OBP	SLG	AOPS	ABR	SB-CS	FA	FR	RNG	THR	GAMES AT POSITION	DL	BFW
1945	Bos A	78	304	39	78	8	3	3	20	31	1	29	.257	.327	.332	89	-4	10-6	.967	-2	96	118	2b77		-0.2
1946	Bos A	3	4	1	1	0	0	0	0	0	0	0	.250	.250	.250	38	0	0-0	.750	-1	54	0	/3		-0.1
1947	Det A	1	0	1	0	0	0	0	0	0	0	0	—	—	—	—	0	0-0	—	0			/R		0.0
Total	3	82	308	41	79	8	3	3	20	31	1	29	.256	.326	.331	89	-4	10-6	.967	-2	96	118	2b77/3		-0.3

STEINER, RED James Harry B1.7.1915 Los Angeles CA D11.16.2001 Gardena CA BL/TR/6-0/185 d5.11

YEAR	TM LG	G	AB	R	H	2B	3B	HR	RBI	BB-IB	HP	SO	AVG	OBP	SLG	AOPS	ABR	SB-CS	FA	FR	RNG	THR	GAMES AT POSITION	DL	BFW
1945	Cle A	12	20	0	3	0	0	0	2	1	0	4	.150	.190	.150	-1	-3	0-0	1.000	1	68	95	C4		-0.2
	Bos A	26	59	6	12	1	0	0	4	14	0	2	.203	.356	.220	67	-2	0-0	.986	-3	90	94	C24		-0.3
	Year	38	79	6	15	1	0	0	6	15	0	6	.190	.319	.203	52	-4	0-0	—	-2	86	94	C28		-0.5

STEINFELDT, HARRY Harry M. B9.29.1877 St.Louis MO D8.17.1914 Bellevue KY BR/TR/5-9.5/180 d4.22 OF(15/16/4)

YEAR	TM LG	G	AB	R	H	2B	3B	HR	RBI	BB-IB	HP	SO	AVG	OBP	SLG	AOPS	ABR	SB-CS	FA	FR	RNG	THR	GAMES AT POSITION	DL	BFW
1898	Cin N	88	308	47	91	18	6	0	43	43	2		.295	.354	.393	107	2	9	.917	-7	96	97	2b31,O29(14/15/0),3b22,S5,1b4		-0.5
1899	Cin N	108	390	63	96	16	8	0	43	40	6		.246	.326	.328	78	-11	19	.888	-8	94	67	3b60,2b40,S8,O2(0/1/1)		-1.5
1900	Cin N	134	510	57	125	29	7	2	66	27	7		.245	.292	.341	76	-17	14	.922	16	100	110	3b67,2b64,O2R,S2		0.3
1901	Cin N	105	382	40	95	18	7	6	47	28	2		.249	.303	.380	104	1	10	.886	7	116	76	3b55,2b50		1.0
1902	Cin N	129	479	53	133	19	4	2	49	24	3		.278	.316	.355	98	-2	12	.912	22	118	174	3b129/OR		2.4
1903	Cin N	118	439	71	137	32	12	6	83	47	2		.312	.386	.481	132	18	13	.937	6	101	104	3b104,S14		2.6
1904	Cin N	99	349	35	85	14	1	1	52	29	6		.244	.313	.318	87	-5	17	.887	-10	85	128	3b98		-1.3
1905	Cin N	114	384	49	104	16	9	1	39	30	3		.271	.329	.367	97	-2	15	.919	12	111	122	3b103/12OL		1.3
1906	†Chi N	151	539	81	176	27	10	3	83	47	14		.327	.395	.430	149	32	29	.954	-20	84	88	3b150/2		1.7
1907	†Chi N	152	542	52	144	25	5	1	70	37	9		.266	.323	.336	100	1	19	.967	-7	96	104	3b151		-0.3
1908	†Chi N	150	539	63	130	20	6	1	62	36	4		.241	.294	.306	88	-2	16	.940	-13	91	89	3b150		-1.9
1909	Chi N	151	528	73	133	27	6	2	59	57	5		.252	.331	.337	105	4	22	.940	1	99	101	3b151		1.0
1910	†Chi N	129	448	70	113	21	1	3	58	46	11	29	.252	.323	.317	88	-6	10	.946	1	102	97	3b128		-0.3
1911	Bos N	19	63	5	16	4	1	0	8	6	2	3	.254	.338	.365	89	-1	1	.810	-5	79	70	3b19		-0.1
Total	14	1647	5900	759	1578	284	90	27	762	471	79	32	.267	.330	.360	101	5	202	.926	-5	98	106	3b1387,2b187,O35C,S29,1b5		4.0

STELLBAUER, BILL
William Jennings B3.20.1894 Bremond TX D2.16.1974 New Braunfels TX BR/TR/5-10/175 d4.12 Col Baylor

YEAR	TM LG	G	AB	R	H	2B	3B	HR	RBI	BB-IB	HP	SO	AVG	OBP	SLG	AOPS	ABR	SB-CS	FA	FR	RNG	THR	GAMES AT POSITION	DL	BFW
1916	Phi A	25	48	2	13	2	1	0	5	6	0	7	.271	.352	.354	118	1	2	.857	-3	79	0	O14L		-0.2

STELMASZEK, RICK
Richard Francis B10.8.1948 Chicago IL BL/TR/6-1/195* [TexA67 11/205] d6.25 C25

YEAR	TM LG	G	AB	R	H	2B	3B	HR	RBI	BB-IB	HP	SO	AVG	OBP	SLG	AOPS	ABR	SB-CS	FA	FR	RNG	THR	GAMES AT POSITION	DL	BFW
1971	Was A	6	9	0	0	0	0	0	0	0-0	0	3	.000	.000	.000	-99	-2	0-0	1.000	-1	0	243	C3		-0.3
1973	Tex A	7	9	0	1	0	0	0	0	1-0	0	2	.111	.200	.111	-11	-1	0-0	1.000	-1	157	0	C7		-0.2
	Cal A	22	26	2	4	1	0	0	3	6-0	0	7	.154	.313	.192	48	-1	0-0	1.000	-4	124	105	C22		-0.5
	Year	29	35	2	5	1	0	0	3	7-0	0	9	.143	.286	.171	33	-3	0-0	1.000	-4	131	83	C29		-0.7
1974	Chi A	25	44	2	10	2	0	1	7	10-0	0	6	.227	.364	.341	96	0	0-0	.983	-5	70	61	C16		-0.4
Total	3	60	88	4	15	3	0	1	10	17-0	0	18	.170	.302	.239	54	-4	0-0	.993	-10	99	83	C48		-1.4

STEM, FRED
Frederick Boothe B9.22.1885 Oxford NC D9.5.1964 Darlington SC BL/TR/6-2/160 d9.15 Col North Carolina-Asheville

YEAR	TM LG	G	AB	R	H	2B	3B	HR	RBI	BB-IB	HP	SO	AVG	OBP	SLG	AOPS	ABR	SB-CS	FA	FR	RNG	THR	GAMES AT POSITION	DL	BFW
1908	Bos N	20	72	9	20	0	1	0	3	2	0		.278	.297	.306	94	-1	1	.995	-1	80	111	1b19		-0.2
1909	Bos N	73	245	13	51	2	3	0	11	12	3		.208	.254	.241	51	-15	5	.989	11	172	86	1b68		-0.6
Total	2	93	317	22	71	2	4	0	14	14	3		.224	.263	.256	60	-16	6	.990	10	152	91	1b87		-0.8

STENGEL, CASEY
Charles Dillon "The Old Professor" B7.30.1890 Kansas City MO D9.29.1975 Glendale CA BL/TL/5-11/175 d9.17 Mil 1918 M25/C2 HF1966

YEAR	TM LG	G	AB	R	H	2B	3B	HR	RBI	BB-IB	HP	SO	AVG	OBP	SLG	AOPS	ABR	SB-CS	FA	FR	RNG	THR	GAMES AT POSITION	DL	BFW
1912	Bro N	17	57	9	18	1	0	1	13	15	1	9	.316	.466	.386	140	5	5	.902	-2	94	40	O17C		0.1
1913	Bro N	124	438	60	119	16	8	7	43	56	1	58	.272	.356	.393	110	7	19-17	.960	-4	95	95	O119(0/117/2)		-0.8
1914	Bro N	126	412	55	130	13	10	4	60	56	5	55	.316	**.404**	.425	143	24	19	.964	-7	89	81	O121(0/2/119)		1.2
1915	Bro N	132	459	52	109	20	12	3	50	34	3	46	.237	.294	.353	94	-5	5-10	.959	-1	102	86	O129(1/0/128)		-1.7
1916	†Bro N	127	462	66	129	27	8	8	53	33	1	51	.279	.329	.424	127	14	11	.965	5	112	101	O121R		1.5
1917	Bro N	150	549	69	141	23	12	6	73	60	5	62	.257	.336	.375	115	11	18	.969	11	102	157	O150(0/1/149)		1.6
1918	Pit N	39	122	18	30	4	1	1	12	16	2	14	.246	.343	.320	99	1	11	.973	3	112	133	O37R		0.2
1919	Pit N	89	321	38	94	10	10	4	43	35	1	35	.293	.364	.424	131	12	12	.957	1	118	53	O87R		0.9
1920	Phi N	129	445	53	130	25	6	9	50	38	6	35	.292	.356	.436	121	13	7-13	.954	-2	97	110	O118(1/5/113)		0.2
1921	Phi N	24	59	7	18	3	1	0	4	6	0	7	.305	.369	.390	94	0	1-1	.969	2	93	251	O15R		0.1
	NY N	18	22	4	5	1	0	0	2	1	0	5	.227	.261	.273	41	-2	0-1	.875	-1	107	0	O8(0/2/6)		-0.3
	Year	42	81	11	23	4	1	0	6	7	0	12	.284	.341	.358	81	-2	1-2	.950	1	95	207	O23(0/2/21)		-0.2
1922	†NY N	84	250	48	92	8	10	7	48	21	9	17	.368	.436	.564	155	20	4-2	.969	-4	94	79	O77(0/75/2)		1.3
1923	†NY N	75	218	39	74	11	5	5	43	20	2	18	.339	.400	.505	139	12	6-2	.983	-6	83	59	O57(6/51/0)		0.4
1924	Bos N	131	461	57	129	20	6	3	39	45	3	39	.280	.348	.382	100	0	13-13	.978	-6	89	84	O126(0/5/121)		-1.7
1925	Bos N	12	13	0	1	0	0	0	2	1	0	2	.077	.143	.077	-46	-3	0-1	1.000	-0	68	0	/OR		-0.3
Total	14	1277	4288	575	1219	182	89	60	535	437	39	453	.284	.356	.410	109		131-60	.964	-10	99	98	O1183(8/275/901)		2.7

STENHOUSE, MIKE
Michael Steven B5.29.1958 Pueblo CO BL/TR/6-1/195* [MonN80*S1/4] d10.3 f-Dave Col Harvard

YEAR	TM LG	G	AB	R	H	2B	3B	HR	RBI	BB-IB	HP	SO	AVG	OBP	SLG	AOPS	ABR	SB-CS	FA	FR	RNG	THR	GAMES AT POSITION	DL	BFW
1982	Mon N	1	1	0	0	0	0	0	0	0-0	0	1	.000	.000	.000	-97	0	0-0	1.000	-1	99	0	/H		0.0
1983	Mon N	24	40	2	5	1	0	0	2	4-0	0	10	.125	.205	.150	-0	-5	0-0	.986	-1	90	139	O9(3/0/7),1b5		
1984	Mon N	80	175	14	32	8	0	4	16	26-4	1	32	.183	.289	.297	69	-7	0-0	.929	2	95	248	O48(30/0/19),1b14		
1985	Min A	81	179	23	40	5	0	5	21	29-1	0	18	.223	.330	.335	78	-5	1-0	.929	2	95	248	D27,O16(8/0/9),1b8		
1986	Bos A	21	21	1	2	1	0	0	1	12-0	0	5	.095	.424	.143	62	0	0-0	1.000	1	105	0	O4(2/0/2),1b3		
Total	5	207	416	40	79	15	0	9	40	71-5	1	66	.190	.308	.291	67	-17	1-0	.973	0	92	146	O77(43/0/37),1b30,D27		

STENNETT, RENNIE
Renaldo Antonio (Porte) B4.5.1951 Colon, Pan BR/TR/5-11/175(154-188) d7.10

YEAR	TM LG	G	AB	R	H	2B	3B	HR	RBI	BB-IB	HP	SO	AVG	OBP	SLG	AOPS	ABR	SB-CS	FA	FR	RNG	THR	GAMES AT POSITION	DL	BFW
1971	Pit N	50	153	24	54	5	4	1	15	7-0	0	9	.353	.377	.458	136	6	1-1	.954	6	114	106	2b36		
1972	†Pit N	109	370	43	106	14	5	3	30	9-1	2	43	.286	.307	.376	94	-5	4-3	.977	11	110	145	2b49,O41(31/5/10),S6		
1973	Pit N	128	466	45	113	18	5	3	55	16-3	0	63	.242	.265	.358	73	-19	2-3	.981	17	107	119	2b84,S43,O5(3/0/2)		
1974	†Pit N	157	673	84	196	29	3	7	56	32-8	2	51	.291	.322	.374	98	-4	8-9	.980	21	112	113	2b154,O2R		
1975	†Pit N	148	616	89	176	25	7	7	62	33-1	4	42	.286	.324	.383	96	-6	5-4	.979	26	**114**	107	2b144		
1976	†Pit N	157	654	59	168	31	9	2	60	19-2	1	32	.257	.277	.341	74	-25	18-6	.981	24	111	111	2b157,S4		
1977	Pit N	116	453	53	152	20	4	5	51	29-4	2	24	.336	.376	.430	112	8	28-18	.982	1	103	109	2b113	42	
1978	Pit N	106	333	30	81	9	2	3	35	13-6	2	24	.243	.274	.309	60	-19	2-1	.971	-4	99	91	2b80,3b6		
1979	†Pit N	108	319	31	76	13	2	0	24	24-6	0	25	.238	.289	.292	56	-19	1-4	.974	0	107	115	2b102		
1980	SF N	120	397	34	97	13	2	2	37	22-10	2	31	.244	.286	.302	67	-18	4-4	.973	-7	98	80	2b111		
1981	SF N	38	87	8	20	0	0	1	7	3-0	1	6	.230	.264	.264	52	-6	2-1	1.000	-3	81	77	2b19		
Total	11	1237	4521	500	1239	177	41	41	432	207-41	16	348	.274	.306	.359	85	-107	75-54	.978	91	107	108	2b1049,S53,O48(34/5/14),3b6	42	

STENSON, DERNELL
Dernell Renauld B6.17.1978 LaGrange GA D11.4.2003 Chandler AZ BL/TL/6-1/230 [BosA96 3/91] d8.13

YEAR	TM LG	G	AB	R	H	2B	3B	HR	RBI	BB-IB	HP	SO	AVG	OBP	SLG	AOPS	ABR	SB-CS	FA	FR	RNG	THR	GAMES AT POSITION	DL	BFW
2003	Cin N	37	94	10	24	2	0	4	16	11-0	0	24	.247	.333	.420	101	0	0-0	.979	2	114	156	O22(18/0/7)/1		

STENZEL, JAKE
Jacob Charles (b Jacob Charles Stelzle) B6.24.1867 Cincinnati OH D1.6.1919 Cincinnati OH BR/TR/5-10/168 d6.16

YEAR	TM LG	G	AB	R	H	2B	3B	HR	RBI	BB-IB	HP	SO	AVG	OBP	SLG	AOPS	ABR	SB-CS	FA	FR	RNG	THR	GAMES AT POSITION	DL	BFW
1890	Chi N	11	41	3	11	1	0	0	3	1	0		.268	.286	.293	66	-2	0	.857	-1	0	0	O6R,C6		
1892	Pit N	3	9	0	0	0	0	0	0	1	0		.000	.100	.000	-69	-2	1	1.000	0	273	0	O2(1/1/0)/C		
1893	Pit N	60	224	57	81	13	4	4	37	24	0		.362	.423	.509	150	16	16	.905	-7	55	138	O45(4/18/23),C12/S2		
1894	Pit N	132	525	150	185	39	20	13	121	76	6		.352	.440	.577	145	40	61	.926	-3	104	112	O130C		
1895	Pit N	130	518	134	192	38	13	7	97	57	11		.371	.444	.535	160	50	53	.909	-10	116	137	O130C		
1896	Pit N	114	479	104	173	26	14	2	82	32	8		.361	.410	.486	142	29	57	.922	-8	79	121	O114C/1		
1897	†Bal N	131	536	113	189	**43**	7	4	116	36	10		.353	.404	.481	133	26	69	.932	-15	63	58	O131C		
1898	Bal N	35	138	33	35	5	2	0	22	12	6		.254	.340	.319	87	-2	4	.926	-1	139	111	O35C		
	StL N	108	404	64	114	15	11	1	33	41	13		.282	.367	.381	112	7	21	.943	-3	53	54	O108C		
	Year	143	542	97	149	20	13	1	55	53	19		.275	.360	.365	106	5	25	.940	-3	72	67	O143C		
1899	StL N	35	128	21	35	9	0	1	19	16	3		.273	.367	.367	99	1	8	.949	-2	56	74	O33(8/21/4)		
	Cin N	9	29	5	9	1	0	0	3	4	1		.310	.412	.345	106	1	2	1.000	-1	0	0	O7C		
	Year	44	157	26	44	10	0	1	22	20	4		.280	.376	.363	101	1	10	.957	-3	48	63	O40(8/28/4)		
Total	9	768	3031	664	1024	190	71	32	533	300	58	<u>71</u>	.338	.408	.479	135	164	292	.927	-49	83	98	O743(18/692/33),C19/12S		5

STEPHENS, RAY
Carl Ray B9.22.1962 Houston TX BR/TR/6-0/190* [StLN85 6/150] d9.20 Col Troy St.

YEAR	TM LG	G	AB	R	H	2B	3B	HR	RBI	BB-IB	HP	SO	AVG	OBP	SLG	AOPS	ABR	SB-CS	FA	FR	RNG	THR	GAMES AT POSITION	DL	BFW
1990	StL N	5	15	1	2	1	0	1	3		0	3	.133	.133	.400	40	-1	0-0	1.000	-1	35	0	C5		-0
1991	StL N	6	7	0	2	0	0	0	0	1-0	0	3	.286	.375	.286	87	0	0-0	1.000	1	51	81	C6		-0
1992	Tex A	8	13	0	2	0	0	0	0	0-0	0	5	.154	.154	.154	-14	-2	0-0	1.000	-2	120	248	C6/D		-0
Total	3	19	35	2	6	1	0	1	3	1-0	0	11	.171	.194	.286	32	-3	0-0	1.000	-3	65	97	C17/D		-0

STEPHENS, GENE
Glen Eugene B1.20.1933 Gravette AR BL/TR/6-3.5/175* d4.16

YEAR	TM LG	G	AB	R	H	2B	3B	HR	RBI	BB-IB	HP	SO	AVG	OBP	SLG	AOPS	ABR	SB-CS	FA	FR	RNG	THR	GAMES AT POSITION	DL	BFW
1952	Bos A	21	53	10	12	5	0	0	5	3	0	8	.226	.268	.321	59	-3	4-2	.962	0	107	104	O13(2/0/11)		-0
1953	Bos A	78	221	30	45	6	2	3	18	29	2	56	.204	.302	.290	57	-13	3-3	.966	-3	95	46	O72(71/0/3)		-2
1955	Bos A	109	157	25	46	9	4	3	18	20-0	2	34	.293	.374	.459	114	3	0-0	.947	3	100	220	O75(71/4/0)		0
1956	Bos A	104	63	22	17	2	0	1	7	12-0	0	12	.270	.387	.349	85	-1	0-1	.983	4	137	130	O71(69/2/2)		0
1957	Bos A	120	173	25	46	4	4	3	26	26-1	0	20	.266	.353	.399	102	1	0-2	.975	-0	85	174	O90(75/6/11)		-1
1958	Bos A	134	270	38	59	10	1	9	26	22-1	1	46	.219	.279	.363	71	-11	1-2	.975	1	100	115	O110(92/26/3)		-1
1959	Bos A	92	270	34	75	13	1	3	39	29-0	1	33	.278	.353	.367	95	-1	5-2	.981	4	93	103	O85(62/17/7)	42	-0
1960	Bos A	35	109	9	25	4	0	2	11	14-0	1	25	.229	.312	.321	71	-4	5-1	.951	-5	91	103	O31(21/4/8)		-0
	Bal A	84	193	38	46	11	0	5	11	25-0	1	25	.238	.327	.373	91	-2	4-2	.992	5	118	149	O77(36/19/42)		-0
	Year	119	302	47	71	15	0	7	22	39-0	1	47	.235	.322	.354	83	-6	9-3	.979	5	109	132	O108(57/23/50)		-0
1961	Bal A	32	58	4	11	2	0	0	2	14-0	0	7	.190	.347	.224	58	-3	1-1	1.000	-0	86	141	O30(27/5/5)		-0
	KC A	62	183	22	38	6	1	4	26	16-0	2	27	.208	.279	.317	58	-11	3-2	.968	4	110	194	O54(6/28/25)		-1
	Year	94	241	26	49	8	1	4	28	30-0	2	34	.203	.297	.295	59	-14	4-3	.975	4	103	178	O84(33/33/30)		-1
1962	KC A	5	4	0	0	0	0	0	0	1-0	0	1	.000	.200	.000	-39	-1	0-0	—	0			/H	127	0
1963	Chi A	6	18	5	7	0	0	1	2	1-0	0	3	.389	.421	.556	174	2	0-0	.909	1	88	614	O5(2/0/3)		0
1964	Chi A	82	141	21	33	4	4	3	17	21-3	2	28	.234	.335	.355	97	0	1-2	.969	3	122	89	O69(32/25/6)	169	-0
Total	12	964	1913	283	430	78	17	33	207	233-<u>5</u>	14	322	.240	.325	.350	82	-44	27-20	.973	20	102	152	O772(566/136/126)		-5

STEPHENS, JIM
James Walter "Little Nemo" B12.10.1883 Salineville OH D1.2.1965 Oxford AL BR/TR/5-6.5/157 d4.11 Col Villanova

YEAR	TM LG	G	AB	R	H	2B	3B	HR	RBI	BB-IB	HP	SO	AVG	OBP	SLG	AOPS	ABR	SB-CS	FA	FR	RNG	THR	GAMES AT POSITION	DL	BFW
1907	StL A	58	173	15	35	6	3	0	11	15	1		.202	.270	.272	73	-5	3	.967	-5	91	96	C56		-0
1908	StL A	47	150	14	30	4	1	0	6	9	2		.200	.255	.240	61	-6	0	.960	2	121	107	C45		-0
1909	StL A	79	223	18	49	5	0	1	18	13	5		.220	.278	.283	83	-5	5	.980	2	96	109	C72		-0
1910	StL A	99	289	24	62	3	7	0	23	16	2		.215	.261	.273	72	-11	2	.971	-1	82	**113**	C96		-0

YEAR	TM LG	G	AB	R	H	2B	3B	HR	RBI	BB-IB	HP	SO	AVG	OBP	SLG	AOPS	ABR	SB-CS	FA	FR	RNG	THR	GAMES AT POSITION	DL	BFW
1911	StL A	70	212	11	49	5	5	0	17	17	4		.231	.300	.302	71	-9	1	.949	-8	75	102	C66		-1.1
1912	StL A	75	205	13	51	7	5	0	22	7	0		.249	.274	.332	76	-8	3	.954	-1	88	119	C66		-0.4
Total 6		428	1252	95	276	30	21	3	97	77	14		.220	.273	.285	73	-44	14	.965	-11	90	108	C401		-1.9

STEPHENS, VERN   Vernon Decatur "Junior","Buster" B10.23.1920 McAlister NM D11.4.1968 Long Beach CA   BR/TR/5-10/185*   d9.13 Col Long Beach (CA) City

YEAR	TM LG	G	AB	R	H	2B	3B	HR	RBI	BB-IB	HP	SO	AVG	OBP	SLG	AOPS	ABR	SB-CS	FA	FR	RNG	THR	GAMES AT POSITION	DL	BFW
1941	StL A	3	2	1	0	0	0	0	0	0	0	0	.500	.500	.500	160	0	0-0	.500	-0	103	0	/S		0.0
1942	StL A	145	575	84	169	26	6	14	92	41	0	53	.294	.341	.433	115	9	1-3	.944	-13	98	92	S144		0.6
1943	StL A	137	512	75	148	27	3	22	91	54	0	73	.289	.357	.482	142	25	3-2	.943	-22	91	62	S123,O11(9/0/3)		1.3
1944	†StL A*	145	559	91	164	32	1	20	109	62	0	54	.293	.365	.462	128	21	2-2	.954	-5	102	76	S143		2.8
1945	StL A★	149	571	90	165	27	3	24	89	55	1	70	.289	.352	.473	132	21	2-1	.961	-18	94	80	S144,3b4		1.6
1946	StL A★	115	450	67	138	19	4	14	64	35	0	49	.307	.357	.460	121	11	0-1	.950	-1	103	93	S112		1.7
1947	StL A	150	562	74	157	18	4	15	83	70	0	61	.279	.359	.406	110	8	8-4	.970	13	108	103	S149		3.1
1948	Bos A★	155	635	114	171	25	8	29	137	77	2	56	.269	.350	.471	112	7	1-0	.971	9	110	99	S155		2.5
1949	Bos A★	155	610	113	177	31	2	39	159	101	0	73	.290	.391	.539	135	20	2-2	.966	2	105	108	S155		3.9
1950	Bos A☆	149	628	125	185	34	6	30	144	65	0	43	.295	.361	.511	110	7	1-0	.981	1	97	102	S146		1.6
1951	Bos A	109	377	62	113	21	2	17	78	38	0	33	.300	.364	.501	120	10	1-2	.978	12	111	102	3b89,S2		2.0
1952	Bos A	92	295	35	75	13	2	7	44	39	1	31	.254	.343	.383	95	-2	2-2	.957	4	104	119	S53,3b29		0.5
1953	Chi A	44	129	14	24	6	0	1	14	13	0	18	.186	.261	.256	39	-11	2-0	.990	-0	99	97	3b38,S3		-1.1
	StL A	46	165	16	53	8	0	4	17	18	0	24	.321	.388	.442	121	5	0-0	.954	-2	95	77	3b46		0.3
	Year	90	294	30	77	14	0	5	31	31	0	42	.262	.332	.361	85	-6	2-0	.968	-2	97	85	3b84,S3		-0.8
1954	Bal A	101	365	31	104	17	1	8	46	17	0	36	.285	.311	.403	104	0	0-3	.966	-2	98	101	3b96		-0.3
1955	Bal A	3	6	0	1	0	0	0	0	0-0		1	0	.167	.286	.167	26	-1	0-0	1.000	-0	96	0	3b2		-0.1
	Chi A	22	56	10	14	3	0	3	7	7-0		0	11	.250	.328	.464	110	1	0-0	1.000	2	113	137	3b18		0.3
	Year	25	62	10	15	3	0	3	7	7-0		1	11	.242	.324	.435	102	0	0-0	1.000	2	112	129	3b20		0.2
Total 15		1720	6497	1001	1859	307	42	247	1174	692-0		6	685	.286	.355	.460	118	141	25-22	.960	-20	101	92	S1330,3b322,O11(9/0/3)		20.7

STEPHENSON, RIGGS   Jackson Riggs "Old Hoss" B1.5.1898 Akron AL D11.15.1985 Tuscaloosa AL   BR/TR/5-10/185   d4.13 Col Alabama

YEAR	TM LG	G	AB	R	H	2B	3B	HR	RBI	BB-IB	HP	SO	AVG	OBP	SLG	AOPS	ABR	SB-CS	FA	FR	RNG	THR	GAMES AT POSITION	DL	BFW
1921	Cle A	65	206	45	68	17	2	1	34	23	4	15	.330	.408	.461	119	7	4-1	.942	-4	95	115	2b54,3b2		0.5
1922	Cle A	86	233	47	79	24	5	2	32	27	6	18	.339	.421	.511	141	16	3-0	.952	-4	96	75	3b34,2b25,O3(2/0/1)		1.4
1923	Cle A	91	301	48	96	20	6	5	65	15	3	15	.319	.357	.475	118	6	5-5	.970	11	106	124	2b66,O3R,3b2		1.8
1924	Cle A	71	240	33	89	20	0	4	44	27	2	10	.371	.439	.504	141	16	1-2	.961	-11	102	58	2b58,O7R		0.6
1925	Cle A	19	54	8	16	3	1	1	9	7	1	3	.296	.387	.444	110	1	1-1	.946	1	112	124	O16R		0.0
1926	Chi N	82	281	40	95	18	3	3	44	31	0	16	.338	.404	.456	129	13	2	.950	-4	90	105	O74(73/0/1)		0.4
1927	Chi N	152	579	101	199	46	9	7	82	65	6	28	.344	.415	.491	142	37	8	.975	-0	96	129	O146L,3b6		2.5
1928	Chi N	137	512	75	166	36	9	8	90	68	3	29	.324	.407	.477	132	26	8	.982	-2	97	98	O135L		1.4
1929	†Chi N	136	495	91	179	36	6	17	110	67	7	21	.362	.445	.562	147	40	10	.984	-2	93	105	O130L		2.5
1930	Chi N	109	341	56	125	21	1	5	68	32	0	20	.367	.421	.478	116	11	2	.958	-3	91	99	O80L		0.2
1931	Chi N	80	263	34	84	14	4	1	52	37	1	11	.319	.405	.414	119	9	1	.985	-2	98	29	O66L		0.3
1932	†Chi N	147	583	86	189	49	4	4	85	54	2	27	.324	.383	.443	123	21	3	.984	-7	92	77	O147L		0.7
1933	Chi N	97	346	45	114	17	4	4	51	34	5	16	.329	.397	.436	138	19	5	.985	-1	99	73	O91L		1.3
1934	Chi N	38	74	5	16	0	0	0	7	7	1	5	.216	.293	.216	39	-6	0	1.000	-2	93	327	O15L		-0.5
Total 14		1310	4508	714	1515	321	54	63	773	494	41	247	.336	.407	.473	130	216	53-9	.978	-25	95	98	O913(885/0/28),2b203,3b44		13.1

STEPHENSON, JOHN   John Herman B4.13.1941 S.Portsmouth KY   BL/TR/5-11/180*   d4.14 Col William Carey

YEAR	TM LG	G	AB	R	H	2B	3B	HR	RBI	BB-IB	HP	SO	AVG	OBP	SLG	AOPS	ABR	SB-CS	FA	FR	RNG	THR	GAMES AT POSITION	DL	BFW
1964	NY N	37	57	2	9	0	0	1	2	2-0	1	18	.158	.226	.211	24	-6	0-0	.800	-0	130	80	3b14,O8(5/3/0)		-0.7
1965	NY N	62	121	9	26	5	0	4	15	8-2	1	19	.215	.264	.355	75	-4	0-1	.981	-3	78	98	C47,O2R		-0.7
1966	NY N	63	143	17	28	1	1	1	11	8-0	2	28	.196	.248	.238	37	-13	0-0	.973	2	75	116	C52/OL		-0.9
1967	Chi N	18	49	3	11	3	1	0	5	1-1	0	5	.224	.255	.327	62	-2	0-0	1.000	-1	58	172	C13		-0.3
1968	Chi N	2	2	0	0	0	0	0	0	0-0	0	0	.000	.000	.000	-94	0	0-0	—	0			/H		-0.1
1969	SF N	22	27	2	6	2	0	0	3	0-0	0	4	.222	.214	.296	45	-2	0-0	.941	-3	35	0	C9/3		-0.5
1970	SF N	23	43	3	3	1	0	0	6	2-0	0	7	.070	.109	.093	-45	-9	0-0	1.000	1	74	90	C9/OL		-0.7
1971	Cal A	98	279	24	61	17	0	3	25	22-6	3	21	.219	.281	.312	73	-10	0-0	.992	-2	106	61	C88		-0.9
1972	Cal A	66	146	14	40	3	1	2	17	11-5	2	8	.274	.342	.349	112	2	0-0	.993	-4	67	79	C56		0.0
1973	Cal A	60	122	9	30	5	0	1	9	7-1	1	7	.246	.292	.311	75	-4	0-0	.980	-4	94	54	C56		-0.7
Total 10		451	989	83	214	37	3	12	93	63-15	12	118	.216	.271	.296	64	-48	0-1	.986	-14	85	82	C330,3b15,O12(7/3/2)		-5.5

STEPHENSON, JOE   Joseph Chester B6.30.1921 Detroit MI D9.20.2001 Fullerton CA   BR/TR/6-2/185   d9.19 Mil 1944-45   s-Jerry Col Western Michigan

YEAR	TM LG	G	AB	R	H	2B	3B	HR	RBI	BB-IB	HP	SO	AVG	OBP	SLG	AOPS	ABR	SB-CS	FA	FR	RNG	THR	GAMES AT POSITION	DL	BFW
1943	NY N	9	24	4	6	1	0	0	4	1	0	5	.250	.250	.292	56	-1	0	.973	1	98	194	C6		0.0
1944	Chi N	4	8	1	1	0	0	0	0	1	0	3	.125	.222	.125	-1	-1	1	1.000	1	77	174	C3		0.0
1947	Chi A	16	35	3	5	0	0	0	3	1	2	7	.143	.211	.143	-1	-5	0-0	.959	-1	94	118	C13		-0.5
Total 3		29	67	8	12	1	0	0	4	2	2	15	.179	.225	.194	19	-7	1-0	.970	1	93	151	C22		-0.5

STEPHENSON, PHIL   Phillip Raymond B9.19.1960 Guthrie OK   BL/TL/6-1/195*   [OakA82 3/80]   d4.5 Col Wichita St.

YEAR	TM LG	G	AB	R	H	2B	3B	HR	RBI	BB-IB	HP	SO	AVG	OBP	SLG	AOPS	ABR	SB-CS	FA	FR	RNG	THR	GAMES AT POSITION	DL	BFW
1989	Chi N	17	21	0	3	0	0	0	0	2-0	0	3	.143	.217	.143	5	-3	1-0	1.000	-1	57	0	O3L	15	-0.3
	SD N	10	17	4	6	2	0	2	2	3-0	0	2	.353	.450	.706	225	3	0-0	.977	0	121	90	1b8		0.3
	Year	27	38	4	9	2	0	2	2	5-0	0	5	.237	.326	.395	100	0	1-0	.977	-0	121	90	1b8,O3L		0.0
1990	SD N	103	182	26	38	9	1	4	19	30-1	0	43	.209	.319	.335	80	-4	2-1	.997	2	116	111	1b60		-0.5
1991	SD N	11	7	0	2	0	0	0	0	2-0	0	3	.286	.444	.286	106	0	0-0	—	0			/H	153	-0.0
1992	SD N	53	71	5	11	2	1	0	8	10-0	0	11	.155	.259	.211	34	-6	0-0	1.000	1	79	0	O15(10/0/6),1b7		-0.9
Total 5		194	298	35	60	11	2	6	29	47-1	0	62	.201	.309	.312	73	-10	3-2	.993	1	117	107	1b75,O18(13/0/6)	168	-1.4

STEPHENSON, DUMMY   Reuben Crandol B9.22.1869 Petersburg NJ D12.1.1924 Trenton NJ   BR/TR/5-11.5/180   d9.9

YEAR	TM LG	G	AB	R	H	2B	3B	HR	RBI	BB-IB	HP	SO	AVG	OBP	SLG	AOPS	ABR	SB-CS	FA	FR	RNG	THR	GAMES AT POSITION	DL	BFW
1892	Phi N	8	37	4	10	3	0	0	5	0	1	2	.270	.289	.351	94	0	1	.800	-1	84	0	O8C		-0.2

STEPHENSON, BOB   Robert Lloyd B8.11.1928 Blair OK   BR/TR/6-0/165   d4.14 Col Oklahoma

YEAR	TM LG	G	AB	R	H	2B	3B	HR	RBI	BB-IB	HP	SO	AVG	OBP	SLG	AOPS	ABR	SB-CS	FA	FR	RNG	THR	GAMES AT POSITION	DL	BFW
1955	StL N	67	111	19	27	3	0	0	6	5-0	0	18	.243	.274	.270	46	-9	2-1	.938	-2	89	122	S48,2b7/3		-0.8

STEPHENSON, WALTER   Walter McQueen "Tarzan" B3.27.1911 Saluda NC D7.4.1993 Shreveport LA   BR/TR/6-0/180   d4.29

YEAR	TM LG	G	AB	R	H	2B	3B	HR	RBI	BB-IB	HP	SO	AVG	OBP	SLG	AOPS	ABR	SB-CS	FA	FR	RNG	THR	GAMES AT POSITION	DL	BFW
1935	†Chi N	16	26	2	10	1	1	0	2	1	0	5	.385	.407	.500	142	1	0	1.000	1	126	299	C6		0.3
1936	Chi N	6	12	0	1	0	0	0	1	0	0	5	.083	.083	.083	-54	-3	0	1.000	0	65	0	C4		-0.2
1937	Phi N	10	23	1	6	0	0	0	2	2	0	3	.261	.320	.261	55	-1	0	.967	0	102	112	C7		-0.1
Total 3		32	61	3	17	1	1	0	5	3	0	13	.279	.313	.328	70	-3	0	.984	2	104	156	C17		0.0

STERN, ADAM   Adam James B2.12.1980 London ON, Can.   BL/TR/5-11/180   d7.7 Col Nebraska

YEAR	TM LG	G	AB	R	H	2B	3B	HR	RBI	BB-IB	HP	SO	AVG	OBP	SLG	AOPS	ABR	SB-CS	FA	FR	RNG	THR	GAMES AT POSITION	DL	BFW
2005	Bos A	36	15	4	2	0	0	1	2	0-0	1	4	.133	.188	.333	33	-2	1-1	1.000	-1	81	0	O21(2/6/13)	110	-0.2

TERRETT, DUTCH   Charles Hurlbut B10.1.1889 Milroy PA D12.9.1965 Baltimore MD   BR/TR/5-11.5/165   d6.20 Col Princeton

YEAR	TM LG	G	AB	R	H	2B	3B	HR	RBI	BB-IB	HP	SO	AVG	OBP	SLG	AOPS	ABR	SB-CS	FA	FR	RNG	THR	GAMES AT POSITION	DL	BFW
1912	NY A	66	230	30	61	4	7	1	32	11	4		.265	.310	.357	85	-6	8	.972	-5	96	63	O37(0/31/6),1b17,C10/2		-1.3
1913	NY A	21	35	0	6	0	0	0	3	1	1	5	.171	.216	.171	14	-4	1	1.000	-1	68	38	1b6/C		-0.5
Total 2		87	265	30	67	4	7	1	35	12	5		.253	.298	.332	77	-10	9	.972	-5	96	63	O37(0/31/6),1b23,C11/2		-1.8

STEVENS, CHUCK   Charles Augustus B7.10.1918 Van Houten NM   BB/TL/6-1/180   d9.16 Mil 1943-45

YEAR	TM LG	G	AB	R	H	2B	3B	HR	RBI	BB-IB	HP	SO	AVG	OBP	SLG	AOPS	ABR	SB-CS	FA	FR	RNG	THR	GAMES AT POSITION	DL	BFW
1941	StL A	4	13	2	2	0	0	0	2	0	0	1	.154	.154	.154	-18	-2	0-0	.966	-1	0	121	1b4		-0.4
1946	StL A	122	432	53	107	17	4	3	27	47	2	62	.248	.324	.326	78	-12	4-6	.995	4	110	90	1b120		-1.4
1948	StL A	85	287	34	75	12	4	1	26	41	0	26	.261	.354	.341	83	-6	2-2	.991	1	103	101	1b85		-0.9
Total 3		211	732	89	184	29	8	4	55	88	2	89	.251	.333	.329	79	-20	6-8	.993	3	106	95	1b209		-2.7

STEVENS, LEE   De Wain Lee B7.10.1967 Kansas City MO   BL/TL/6-4/219(205-235)   [CalA86 1/22]   d7.16

YEAR	TM LG	G	AB	R	H	2B	3B	HR	RBI	BB-IB	HP	SO	AVG	OBP	SLG	AOPS	ABR	SB-CS	FA	FR	RNG	THR	GAMES AT POSITION	DL	BFW
1990	Cal A	67	248	28	53	10	2	7	32	22-3	0	75	.214	.275	.339	73	-10	1-1	.994	-2	85	105	1b67		-1.7
1991	Cal A	18	58	8	17	7	0	0	9	6-0	2	12	.293	.364	.414	113	1	1-2	.989	-0	113	72	1b11,O9(1/0/8)		0.0
1992	Cal A	106	312	25	69	19	0	7	37	29-6	1	64	.221	.288	.349	77	-10	1-4	.995	-1	92	121	1b91,D2		-1.9
1996	Tex A	27	78	6	18	2	3	3	12	6-0	1	22	.231	.291	.449	79	-3	0-0	.994	0	122	143	1b18,O5L		-0.4
1997	Tex A	137	426	58	128	24	2	21	74	23-2	1	83	.300	.336	.514	111	5	1-3	.994	-4	89	93	1b62,D38,O22(3/0/19)		-0.7
1998	†Tex A	120	344	52	91	17	4	20	59	31-4	0	93	.265	.324	.512	107	2	0-2	.996	0	94	56	D72,1b37,O7R	24	-0.8
1999	†Tex A	146	517	76	146	31	1	24	81	52-10	2	132	.282	.344	.485	103	2	2-3	.994	-9	73	109	1b133,D8		-1.8
2000	Mon N	123	449	60	119	27	2	22	75	48-5	1	105	.265	.337	.481	103	1	0-0	.991	0	102	97	1b123		-0.9
2001	Mon N	152	542	77	133	35	1	25	95	74-12	5	157	.245	.337	.452	103	4	2-1	.986	-4	94	94	1b152		-1.4

YEAR	TM LG	G	AB	R	H	2B	3B	HR	RBI	BB-IB	HP	SO	AVG	OBP	SLG	AOPS	ABR	SB-CS	FA	FR	RNG	THR	GAMES AT POSITION	DL	BFW
2002	Mon N	63	205	28	39	6	1	10	31	39-5	0	57	.190	.318	.376	81	-7	1-0	.993	4	125	101	1b58		-0.8
	Cle A	53	153	22	34	7	1	5	26	15-0	0	32	.222	.285	.379	75	-6	0-0	.987	-1	58	96	1b25,O16(11/0/5),D3		-0.9
Total	10	1012	3332	440	847	185	15	144	531	345-50	10	832	.254	.323	.448	97	-21	9-16	.992	-17	92	102	1b777,D123,O59(20/0/39)	52	-10.9

STEVENS, ED Edward Lee "Big Ed" B1.12.1925 Galveston TX BL/TL/6-1/190* d8.9 C1

YEAR	TM LG	G	AB	R	H	2B	3B	HR	RBI	BB-IB	HP	SO	AVG	OBP	SLG	AOPS	ABR	SB-CS	FA	FR	RNG	THR	GAMES AT POSITION	DL	BFW
1945	Bro N	55	201	29	55	14	3	4	29	32	1	20	.274	.376	.433	125	8	0	.987	0	103	97	1b55		0.5
1946	Bro N	103	310	34	75	13	7	10	60	27	0	44	.242	.303	.426	104	0	2	.986	-4	84	90	1b99		-0.8
1947	Bro N	5	13	0	2	1	0	0	1	0	0	5	.154	.214	.231	18	-2	0	.971	1	193	79	1b4		-0.1
1948	Pit N	128	429	47	109	19	6	10	69	35	2	53	.254	.313	.396	89	-8	0	.996	4	112	114	1b117		-0.7
1949	Pit N	67	221	22	58	10	1	4	32	22	1	24	.262	.332	.371	86	-4	1	.995	10	167	131	1b58	62	0.4
1950	Pit N	17	46	2	9	2	0	0	3	4	0	5	.196	.260	.239	31	-5	0	1.000	1	115	109	1b12		-0.4
Total	6	375	1220	134	308	59	17	28	193	121	4	151	.252	.322	.398	95	-11	7	.992	12	114	107	1b345	62	-1.1

STEVENS, R C R C B7.22.1934 Moultrie GA BL/TR/6-5/219(200-219) d4.15

YEAR	TM LG	G	AB	R	H	2B	3B	HR	RBI	BB-IB	HP	SO	AVG	OBP	SLG	AOPS	ABR	SB-CS	FA	FR	RNG	THR	GAMES AT POSITION	DL	BFW
1958	Pit N	59	90	16	24	3	1	7	18	5-0	0	25	.267	.320	.556	129	3	0-0	.991	2	128	138	1b52		0.4
1959	Pit N	3	7	2	2	0	0	1	1	0-0	0	0	.286	.286	.714	157	0	0-0	1.000	0	113	100	/1		0.0
1960	Pit N	9	3	1	0	0	0	0	0	0-0	0	1	.000	.000	.000	-99	-1	0-0	1.000	1	229	216	1b7		0.0
1961	Was A	33	62	2	8	1	0	0	2	7-0	0	15	.129	.217	.145	-1	-9	1-0	1.000	3	166	128	1b25		-0.7
Total	4	104	162	21	34	4	1	8	21	12-0	0	41	.210	.273	.395	77	-7	1-0	.995	6	145	135	1b85		-0.3

STEVENS, ROBERT Robert d5.4

YEAR	TM LG	G	AB	R	H	2B	3B	HR	RBI	BB-IB	HP	SO	AVG	OBP	SLG	AOPS	ABR	SB-CS	FA	FR	RNG	THR	GAMES AT POSITION	DL	BFW
1875	Was NA	1	4	0	1	0	0	0	0	0			.250	.250	.250	77	0	0-0	.000	-0	0	0	/OR		0.0

STEVENS, BOBBY Robert Jordan B4.17.1907 Chevy Chase MD BL/TR/5-8/149 d7.3

YEAR	TM LG	G	AB	R	H	2B	3B	HR	RBI	BB-IB	HP	SO	AVG	OBP	SLG	AOPS	ABR	SB-CS	FA	FR	RNG	THR	GAMES AT POSITION	DL	BFW
1931	Phi N	12	35	3	12	0	0	0	4	2	2	2	.343	.410	.343	97	0	0	.870	-4	73	77	S10		-0.3

STEVERSON, TODD Todd Anthony B11.15.1971 Los Angeles CA BR/TR/6-2/195* [TorA92 1/25] d4.28 Col Arizona St.

YEAR	TM LG	G	AB	R	H	2B	3B	HR	RBI	BB-IB	HP	SO	AVG	OBP	SLG	AOPS	ABR	SB-CS	FA	FR	RNG	THR	GAMES AT POSITION	DL	BFW
1995	Det A	30	42	11	11	0	0	2	6	6-0	0	10	.262	.340	.405	97	0	2-0	1.000	-2	73	100	O27(17/1/10)/D	77	-0.2
1996	SD N	1	1	0	0	0	0	0	0	0-0	0	1	.000	.000	.000	-99	0	0-0	—	0			/H		0.0
Total	2	31	43	11	11	0	0	2	6	6-0	0	11	.256	.333	.395	93	0	2-0	1.000	-2	73	100	O27(17/1/10)/D	77	-0.2

STEWART, ANDY Andrew David B12.5.1970 Oshawa ON, Can. BR/TR/5-11/205 d9.6

YEAR	TM LG	G	AB	R	H	2B	3B	HR	RBI	BB-IB	HP	SO	AVG	OBP	SLG	AOPS	ABR	SB-CS	FA	FR	RNG	THR	GAMES AT POSITION	DL	BFW
1997	KC A	5	8	1	2	1	0	0	0	0			.250	.250	.375	58	0	0-0	1.000	0	113	185	C4/D		0.0

STEWART, ACE Asa B2.14.1869 Terre Haute IN D4.17.1912 Terre Haute IN BR/TR/5-10/176 d4.18

YEAR	TM LG	G	AB	R	H	2B	3B	HR	RBI	BB-IB	HP	SO	AVG	OBP	SLG	AOPS	ABR	SB-CS	FA	FR	RNG	THR	GAMES AT POSITION	DL	BFW
1895	Chi N	97	365	52	88	8	10	8	76	39	0	40	.241	.314	.384	75	-17	14	.911	-9	94	124	2b97		-1.7

STEWART, TUFFY Charles Eugene B7.31.1883 Chicago IL D11.18.1934 Chicago IL BL/TL/5-10/167 d8.8

YEAR	TM LG	G	AB	R	H	2B	3B	HR	RBI	BB-IB	HP	SO	AVG	OBP	SLG	AOPS	ABR	SB-CS	FA	FR	RNG	THR	GAMES AT POSITION	DL	BFW
1913	Chi N	9	8	1	1	0	0	2	2		0	5	.125	.300	.250	58	0	1	1.000	0	152	0	/OR		0.0
1914	Chi N	2	1	0	0	0	0	0	0		0	0	.000	.000	.000	-99	0	0	—	0			/H		0.0
Total	2	11	9	1	1	0	0	2	2		0	5	.111	.273	.222	43	0	1	1.000	0	152	0	/OR		0.0

STEWART, BUD Edward Perry B6.15.1916 Sacramento CA D6.21.2000 Palo Alto CA BL/TR/5-11/170* d4.19 Def 1943 Mil 1944-45 Col UCLA

YEAR	TM LG	G	AB	R	H	2B	3B	HR	RBI	BB-IB	HP	SO	AVG	OBP	SLG	AOPS	ABR	SB-CS	FA	FR	RNG	THR	GAMES AT POSITION	DL	BFW
1941	Pit N	73	172	27	46	7	0	0	10	12	0	17	.267	.315	.308	76	-5	3	.962	1	97	176	O41(15/4/24)		-0.6
1942	Pit N	82	183	21	40	8	4	0	20	22	0	16	.219	.302	.306	76	-5	2	1.000	-1	110	42	O34(19/0/16),3b10,2b6		-0.9
1948	NY A	6	5	1	1	1	0	0	0	0	0	0	.200	.200	.400	58	0	0-0	—	0			/H		0.0
	Was A	118	401	56	112	17	13	7	69	49	2	27	.279	.361	.439	115	7	8-9	.975	-1	104	60	O114(10/37/72)		0.1
	Year	124	406	57	113	18	13	7	69	49	2	27	.278	.359	.438	115	7	8-9	.975	-1	104	60	O114(10/37/72)		0.1
1949	Was A	118	388	58	110	23	4	8	43	49	3	33	.284	.368	.425	112	7	6-4	.982	-3	91	103	O105(75/16/20)		-0.3
1950	Was A	118	378	46	101	15	6	4	35	46	1	33	.267	.348	.370	88	-7	5-4	.991	2	99	126	O100(42/0/66)		-0.9
1951	Chi A	95	217	40	60	13	5	6	40	29	2	9	.276	.367	.465	127	8	1-6	.983	-1	93	97	O63(52/1/14)		0.1
1952	Chi A	92	225	23	60	10	0	5	30	28	1	17	.267	.350	.378	102	1	3-0	.982	-1	102	31	O60(57/0/3)		-0.3
1953	Chi A	53	59	16	16	2	0	2	13	14	0	3	.271	.411	.407	118	2	1-0	1.000	-1	83		O16(11/0/5)	51	0.1
1954	Chi A	18	13	0	1	0	0	0	3	3	0	2	.077	.250	.077	-7	-2	0-0	1.000	0	175	0	O2R	51	-0.2
Total	9	773	2041	288	547	96	32	32	260	252	9	157	.268	.351	.393	102	6	29-23	.982	-6	99	89	O535(281/58/222),3b10,2b6	51	-2.9

STEWART, GLEN Glen Weldon "Gabby" B9.29.1912 Tullahoma TN D2.11.1997 Memphis TN BR/TR/6-0/175 d6.26 Col Ohio St.

YEAR	TM LG	G	AB	R	H	2B	3B	HR	RBI	BB-IB	HP	SO	AVG	OBP	SLG	AOPS	ABR	SB-CS	FA	FR	RNG	THR	GAMES AT POSITION	DL	BFW
1940	NY N	15	29	1	4	1	0	0	1	1	0	2	.138	.167	.172	-6	-4	0	.875	0	133	6	3b6,S5		-0.4
1943	Phi N	110	336	25	71	10	1	2	24	32	2	41	.211	.284	.265	61	-17	1	.947	-12	94	90	S77,2b18,1b8/C		-2.4
1944	Phi N	118	377	32	83	11	5	0	29	28	0	40	.220	.274	.276	57	-23	0	.963	1	105	88	3b83,S32/2		-1.9
Total	3	243	742	56	158	22	6	2	53	61	2	83	.213	.275	.267	56	-44	1	.953	-11	97	90	S114,3b89,2b19,1b8/C		-4.7

STEWART, JIMMY James Franklin B6.11.1939 Opelika AL BB/TR/6-0/165(160-175) d9.3 Col Austin Peay OF(176/43/11)

YEAR	TM LG	G	AB	R	H	2B	3B	HR	RBI	BB-IB	HP	SO	AVG	OBP	SLG	AOPS	ABR	SB-CS	FA	FR	RNG	THR	GAMES AT POSITION	DL	BFW
1963	Chi N	13	37	1	11	2	0	0	1	1-0	0	7	.297	.316	.351	87	-1	1-1	.973	2	112	165	S9/2		0.2
1964	Chi N	132	415	59	105	17	3	0	33	49-0	2	61	.253	.331	.316	81	-8	10-8	.981	6	109	114	2b61,S45,O4C/3		0.6
1965	Chi N	116	282	26	63	9	4	0	19	30-1	2	53	.223	.301	.284	65	-13	13-3	.955	-2	97	156	O55(47/8/0),S48		-1.4
1966	Chi N	57	90	4	16	4	1	0	4	7-0	2	12	.178	.253	.244	38	-7	1-1	1.000	-2	118	116	O15(4/11/1),2b4,S2,3b2		-1.0
1967	Chi N	6	6	1	1	0	0	0	0	0-0	1	0	.167	.167	.167	-4	-1	0-0	—	0			/H		-0.1
	Chi A	24	18	5	3	0	0	0	1	0-0	0	6	.167	.211	.167	13	-2	1-0	1.000	1	0	1192	O6L,2b5,S2		-0.1
1969	Cin N	119	221	26	56	3	4	4	24	19-3	0	33	.253	.311	.357	83	-6	4-2	.973	1	93	176	O66(55/10/1),2b18,3b6/S		-0.6
1970	†Cin N	101	105	15	28	3	1	1	8	8-1	1	13	.267	.322	.343	78	-3	5-3	1.000	2	73	120	O48(41/2/5),2b18,3b9/C1		-0.1
1971	Cin N	80	82	7	19	2	2	0	9	9-1	0	12	.232	.308	.305	75	-3	3-1	1.000	2	45	0	O19(11/6/3),3b9,2b6		-0.4
1972	Hou N	68	96	14	21	5	2	0	9	6-2	0	9	.219	.257	.313	65	-5	0-1	1.000	-2	80	0	O11(9/2/1),1b9,2b8,3b2		-0.8
1973	Hou N	61	68	4	13	0	0	0	3	9-1	0	12	.191	.295	.191	38	-6	0-0	1.000	1	118	151	3b8,O3L/2	15	-0.5
Total	10	777	1420	164	336	45	14	5	112	139-9	8	218	.237	.306	.305	71	-55	38-20	.969	6	91	150	O227L,2b122,S107,3b37,1b10/C	15	-4.2

STEWART, STUFFY John Franklin B1.31.1894 Jasper FL D12.30.1980 Lake City FL BR/TR/5-9.5/160 d9.3

YEAR	TM LG	G	AB	R	H	2B	3B	HR	RBI	BB-IB	HP	SO	AVG	OBP	SLG	AOPS	ABR	SB-CS	FA	FR	RNG	THR	GAMES AT POSITION	DL	BFW
1916	StL N	9	17	1	3	0	0	0	0	0	0	3	.176	.176	.176	9	-2	0	.833	-1	75	112	2b8		-0.4
1917	StL N	13	9	4	0	0	0	0	0	0	0	4	.000	.000	.000	-99	-2	0	1.000	0	64	511	O7(2/3/2),2b2		-0.2
1922	Pit N	3	13	3	2	0	0	0	0	0	0	1	.154	.154	.154	-20	-2	0-0	.875	-1	84	122	2b3		-0.4
1923	Bro N	4	11	3	4	1	0	1	1	1	0	1	.364	.417	.727	202	2	0-0	.786	-1	86	68	2b3		0.0
1925	Was A	7	17	3	6	1	0	0	3	1	0	2	.353	.389	.412	105	0	1-0	.929	1	112	133	3b5/2		0.1
1926	Was A	62	63	27	17	6	1	0	9	6	0	6	.270	.333	.397	92	-1	8-4	.975	4	112	111	2b25/3		0.3
1927	Was A	56	129	24	31	6	2	0	4	8	0	15	.240	.285	.318	57	-9	12-2	.939	-0	102	96	2b37,3b2		-0.6
1929	Was A	22	6	10	0	0	0	0	0	0	0	0	.000	.143	.000	-60	-1	0-1	1.000	1	176	0	2b3		-0.1
Total	8	176	265	74	63	14	3	1	18	17	0	32	.238	.284	.325	61	-15	21-7	.932	1	101	99	2b82,3b8,O7(2/3/2)		-1.1

STEWART, MARK Mark "Big Slick" B10.11.1889 Whitlock TN D1.17.1932 Memphis TN BL/TR/6-1/180 d10.4 Col Washington and Lee

YEAR	TM LG	G	AB	R	H	2B	3B	HR	RBI	BB-IB	HP	SO	AVG	OBP	SLG	AOPS	ABR	SB-CS	FA	FR	RNG	THR	GAMES AT POSITION	DL	BFW
1913	Cin N	1	1	0	0	0	0	0	0	0	0	0	.000	.000	.000	-99	0	-	-0	0	0	0	/C		0.0

STEWART, SHANNON Shannon Harold B2.25.1974 Cincinnati OH BR/TR/6-1/205(190-210) [TorA92 1/19] d9.2

YEAR	TM LG	G	AB	R	H	2B	3B	HR	RBI	BB-IB	HP	SO	AVG	OBP	SLG	AOPS	ABR	SB-CS	FA	FR	RNG	THR	GAMES AT POSITION	DL	BFW
1995	Tor A	12	38	2	8	0	0	1	5	5-0	1	4	.211	.318	.211	41	-3	2-0	.955	-1	76	196	O12C		-0.4
1996	Tor A	7	17	2	3	1	0	0	2	1-0	0	4	.176	.222	.235	16	-2	1-0	.800	-2	43	0	O6C		-0.1
1997	Tor A	44	168	25	48	13	7	0	22	19-1	4	24	.286	.368	.446	112	3	10-3	.980	-2	99	50	O41(2/39/0)/D		0.1
1998	Tor A	144	516	90	144	29	4	12	55	67-1	15	77	.279	.377	.417	106	7	51-18	.980	0	104	51	O144(110/44/0)		0.9
1999	Tor A	145	608	102	185	28	2	11	67	59-0	8	83	.304	.371	.411	98	0	37-14	.981	-10	91	44	O142(140/7/0),D2		-1.3
2000	Tor A	136	583	107	186	43	5	21	69	37-1	6	79	.319	.363	.518	116	14	20-5	.993	2	106	61	O136(136/1/0)	14	1.2
2001	Tor A	155	640	103	202	44	7	12	60	46-1	11	72	.316	.371	.463	115	15	27-10	.981	-7	88	79	O142L,D13		0.1
2002	Tor A	141	577	103	175	38	6	10	45	54-2	9	60	.303	.371	.442	111	11	14-2	.990	-4	92	51	O99L,D38		0.1
2003	Tor A	71	303	47	89	22	2	7	35	27-2	2	30	.294	.347	.449	106	3	1-2	.974	-0	103	72	O69L,D2	25	0.1
	†Min A	65	270	43	87	22	0	6	38	25-1	4	36	.322	.384	.470	121	9	3-4	.993	4	115	113	O58(46/0/14),D6		1.1
	Year	136	573	90	176	44	2	13	73	52-3	6	66	.307	.364	.459	113	13	4-6	.983	5	108	90	O127(115/0/14),D8		1.1
2004	†Min A	92	378	46	115	17	2	11	47	47-4	1	40	.304	.380	.447	112	4	6-3	.972	-10	73	50	O71L,D21	58	-0.5
2005	Min A	132	551	69	151	27	3	10	56	34-2	6	73	.274	.323	.388	87	-11	7-5	.985	-2	96	99	O125L,D5	112	-1.0
Total	11	1144	4649	739	1393	284	37	100	497	425-15	69	573	.300	.364	.441	107	54	179-66	.983	-29	96	67	O1045(940/109/14),D88	112	0.5

STEWART, NEB Walter Nesbitt B5.21.1918 S.Charleston OH D6.8.1990 London OH BR/TR/6-1/195 d9.8

YEAR	TM LG	G	AB	R	H	2B	3B	HR	RBI	BB-IB	HP	SO	AVG	OBP	SLG	AOPS	ABR	SB-CS	FA	FR	RNG	THR	GAMES AT POSITION	DL	BFW
1940	Phi N	10	31	3	4	0	0	0	0	1	0	5	.129	.156	.129	-21	-5	0	.944	1	86	342	O9(8/1/0)		-0.0

YEAR	TM LG	G	AB	R	H	2B	3B	HR	RBI	BB-IB	HP	SO	AVG	OBP	SLG	AOPS	ABR	SB-CS	FA	FR	RNG	THR	GAMES AT POSITION	DL	BFW

STEWART, BILL William Wayne B4.15.1928 Bay City MI BR/TR/5-11/200 d4.17 Col Michigan St.

YEAR	TM LG	G	AB	R	H	2B	3B	HR	RBI	BB-IB	HP	SO	AVG	OBP	SLG	AOPS	ABR	SB-CS	FA	FR	RNG	THR	GAMES AT POSITION	DL	BFW
1955	KC A	11	18	2	2	1	0	0	0	1-0	0	6	.111	.158	.167	-13	-3	0-0	1.000	1	103	361	O6(4/0/2)		-0.2

STILLMAN, ROYLE Royle Eldon B1.2.1951 Santa Monica CA BL/TL/5-11/180(165-180) [LAN69 22/510] d6.22

1975	Bal A	13	14	1	6	0	0	0	1	1-0	0	3	.429	.467	.429	163	1	0-0	1.000	0	141	0	O2(0/1/1)		0.1
1976	Bal A	20	22	0	2	0	0	0	1	3-1	0	4	.091	.200	.091	-14	-3	0-0	1.000	-0	0	0	1b2,D5		-0.3
1977	Chi A	56	119	18	25	7	1	3	13	17-1	0	21	.210	.307	.361	82	-3	2-1	.977	0	122	0	O26(19/0/8),D13/1		-0.4
Total	3	89	155	19	33	7	1	3	15	21-2	0	28	.213	.305	.329	77	-5	2-1	.978	0	123	0	O28(19/1/9),D18,1b3		-0.6

STILLWELL, KURT Kurt Andrew B6.4.1965 Glendale CA BB/TR/5-11/175(165-190) [CinN83 1/2] d4.13 f-Ron

1986	Cin N	104	279	31	64	6	1	0	26	30-1	2	47	.229	.309	.258	56	-16	6-2	.951	-5	99	100	S80		-1.4
1987	Cin N	131	395	54	102	20	7	4	33	32-2	1	50	.258	.316	.375	79	-12	4-6	.914	-19	80	80	S51,2b37,3b20		-2.6
1988	KC A★	128	459	63	115	28	5	10	53	47-0	3	76	.251	.322	.399	100	0	6-5	.976	-10	97	78	S124		-0.1
1989	KC A	130	463	52	121	20	7	7	54	42-2	1	64	.261	.325	.380	99	-1	9-6	.970	-19	89	84	S130	28	-1.1
1990	KC A	144	506	60	126	35	4	3	51	39-1	4	60	.249	.304	.352	85	-10	0-2	.957	-12	94	88	S141		-1.3
1991	KC A	122	385	44	102	17	1	6	51	33-5	1	56	.265	.322	.361	89	-6	3-4	.959	-14	87	99	S118	16	-1.3
1992	SD N	114	379	35	86	15	3	2	24	26-9	1	58	.227	.274	.298	62	-19	4-1	.970	-12	87	105	2b111	15	-3.0
1993	SD N	57	121	9	26	4	0	1	11	11-2	1	22	.215	.286	.273	50	-9	4-3	.921	-5	82	77	S30,3b3	22	-1.2
	Cal A	22	61	2	16	2	2	0	3	4-0	0	11	.262	.299	.361	76	-2	2-0	.952	1	106	62	2b18,S7		0.0
1996	Tex A	46	77	12	21	4	0	1	4	10-0	1	11	.273	.364	.364	80	-2	0-0	.964	-9	68	40	2b21,S9,3b6/1D	28	-1.0
Total	9	998	3125	362	779	151	30	34	310	274-22	18	455	.249	.311	.349	82	-77	38-29	.958	-104	92	87	S690,2b187,3b29/D1	109	-13.0

STILLWELL, RON Ronald Roy B12.3.1939 Los Angeles CA BR/TR/5-11/170* d7.3 s-Kurt Col USC

1961	Was A	8	16	3	2	1	0	0	1	0-0	0	4	.125	.176	.188	-3	-2	0-0	.929	-3	66	131	S5		-0.5
1962	Was A	6	22	5	6	0	0	0	2	2-0	0	2	.273	.333	.273	66	-1	0-0	1.000	-1	79	80	2b6/S		-0.2
Total	2	14	38	8	8	1	0	0	3	2-0	0	6	.211	.268	.237	37	-3	0-0	1.000	-4	79	80	2b6,S6		-0.7

STIMAC, CRAIG Craig Steven B11.18.1954 Oak Park IL BR/TR/6-2/185* [SDN76 9/197] d8.12 Col Denver

1980	SD N	20	50	5	11	0	0	0	7	1-0	0	6	.220	.222	.260	41	-4	0-0	.982	1	52	151	C11,3b2		-0.3
1981	SD N	9	9	0	1	0	0	0	0	0-0	0	3	.111	.111	.111	-40	-2	0-0	—	0			/H		-0.2
Total	2	29	59	5	12	0	0	0	7	1-0	0	9	.203	.206	.237	29	-6	0-0	.982	1	52	151	C11,3b2		-0.5

STINNETT, KELLY Kelly Lee B2.14.1970 Lawton OK BR/TR/5-11/195(195-225) [CleA89 11/281] d4.5 Col Seminole St. (OK) JC

1994	NY N	47	150	20	38	6	2	4	14	11-1	5	28	.253	.323	.360	79	-6	2-0	.979	-6	122	87	C44		-0.8
1995	NY N	77	196	23	43	8	1	4	18	29-3	6	65	.219	.338	.332	80	-5	2-0	.983	-10	67	86	C67		-1.1
1996	Mil A	14	26	1	2	0	0	0	0	2-0	1	11	.077	.172	.077	-33	-5	0-0	.960	-1	75	84	C14/D		-0.6
1997	Mil A	30	36	2	9	4	0	0	3	3-0	1	9	.250	.308	.361	73	-1	0-0	.989	3	250	84	C25/D	37	0.3
1998	Ari N	92	274	35	71	14	1	11	34	35-3	6	74	.259	.353	.438	107	3	0-1	.984	-6	104	124	C86/D		0.3
1999	†Ari N	88	284	36	66	13	0	14	38	24-2	5	83	.232	.302	.426	81	-9	2-1	.990	-8	86	120	C86		-1.1
2000	Ari N	76	240	22	52	7	0	8	33	19-4	6	56	.217	.291	.346	58	-16	0-1	.990	5	81	117	C74		-0.7
2001	Cin N	63	187	27	48	11	0	9	25	17-3	5	61	.257	.333	.460	97	-1	2-2	.966	-7	72	84	C59/D	33	-0.4
2002	Cin N	34	93	10	21	5	0	3	13	15-1	0	25	.226	.333	.376	87	-2	0-0	.990	2	83	95	C30	100	0.2
2003	Cin N	60	179	14	41	13	0	3	19	13-3	4	51	.229	.294	.352	72	-8	0-0	.993	-6	116	86	C50		-1.0
	Phi N	7	7	0	3	0	0	0	0	1-0	0	1	.429	.500	.429	157	1	0-0	1.000	1	0	0	/C		0.1
	Year	67	186	14	44	13	0	3	19	14-3	4	52	.237	.302	.355	75	-7	0-0	.993	-5	115	85	C51		-0.9
2004	KC A	20	59	10	18	0	0	3	7	5-0	2	16	.305	.379	.458	117	1	0-0	.971	-3	84	120	C20	106	-0.1
2005	Ari N	59	129	15	32	4	0	6	12	12-3	1	32	.248	.317	.419	87	-3	0-0	.977	-5	98	87	C56	21	-0.6
Total	12	667	1860	215	444	85	4	63	216	186-23	41	512	.239	.320	.390	83	-50	10-5	.984	-42	94	102	C612,D4	297	-5.5

STINSON, BOB Gorrell Robert B10.11.1945 Elkin NC BB/TR (BR 1969 BL 1980p)/5-11.5/185* [LAN66 S1/15] d9.23 Col Miami-Dade North (FL) CC

1969	LA N	4	8	1	3	0	0	0	2	0-0	2	3	.375	.375	.375	118	0	0-1	.952	-1	65	115	C4		-0.1
1970	LA N	4	3	1	0	0	0	0	0	0-0	0	1	.000	.000	.000	-99	-1	0-0	1.000	-1	0	0	C3		-0.1
1971	StL N	17	19	3	4	1	0	0	1	1-0	0	7	.211	.250	.263	43	-1	0-0	.971	0	63	189	C6,O3(1/0/2)		-0.1
1972	Hou N	27	35	3	6	1	0	0	1	1-0	1	6	.171	.211	.200	19	-4	0-0	.964	-2	40	0	C12,O3(2/0/1)		-0.6
1973	Mon N	48	111	12	29	6	1	3	12	17-2	3	15	.261	.374	.414	114	3	0-1	.979	-4	98	71	C35/3		0.0
1974	Mon N	38	87	4	15	2	0	1	6	15-3	0	16	.172	.294	.230	45	-6	1-1	1.000	3	140	98	C29	39	-0.2
1975	KC A	63	147	18	39	9	1	1	18	18-1	1	29	.265	.345	.361	98	0	1-0	.993	7	110	105	C59/12ORD		1.0
1976	†KC A	79	209	26	55	7	1	2	25	25-2	1	29	.263	.342	.335	99	0	3-1	.979	-3	98	80	C79		0.1
1977	Sea A	105	297	27	80	11	1	8	32	37-4	6	50	.269	.360	.404	106	4	0-3	.984	-8	68	73	C99/D		-0.1
1978	Sea A	124	364	46	94	14	3	11	55	45-1	6	42	.258	.346	.404	111	6	2-1	.987	-18	71	117	C123/D	17	-0.7
1979	Sea A	95	247	19	60	8	0	6	28	33-3	4	38	.243	.338	.348	85	-4	1-2	.978	-10	71	71	C91		-1.1
1980	Sea A	48	107	6	23	2	0	1	8	9-0	1	26	.215	.277	.262	49	-7	0-0	.979	-8	55	78	C45		-1.5
Total	12	652	1634	166	408	61	7	33	180	201-16	23	254	.250	.337	.356	93	-10	8-10	.984	-46	81	89	C585,O7(3/0/4),D3/213	56	-3.4

STIRES, GAT Garrett B10.13.1849 Hunterdon Co. NJ D6.13.1933 Byron IL BL/TR/5-8/180 d5.6

| 1871 | Rok NA | 25 | 110 | 23 | 30 | 4 | 2 | 4 | 24 | 7 | | 5 | .273 | .316 | .473 | 129 | 4 | 3-0 | .837 | -0 | 101 | 0 | O25R | | 0.4 |

STIRNWEISS, SNUFFY George Henry B10.26.1918 New York NY D9.15.1958 Newark Bay NJ BR/TR/5-8.5/175* d4.22 Col North Carolina-Asheville

1943	†NY A	83	274	34	60	8	4	1	25	47	0	37	.219	.333	.288	82	-5	11-9	.938	-2	99	129	S68,2b4		-0.2
1944	NY A	154	643	125	205	35	16	8	43	73	1	87	.319	.389	.460	137	32	55-11	.982	18	105	104	2b154		6.8
1945	NY A★	152	632	107	195	32	22	10	64	78	1	62	.309	.385	.476	143	34	33-17	.970	25	110	126	2b152		7.2
1946	NY A★	129	487	75	122	19	7	0	37	66	0	58	.251	.340	.318	83	-9	18-6	.991	6	103	118	3b79,2b46,S4		0.1
1947	†NY A	148	571	102	146	18	8	5	41	89	2	47	.256	.358	.342	96	-1	5-3	.983	-8	92	107	2b148		-0.1
1948	NY A	141	515	90	130	20	7	3	32	86	1	62	.252	.360	.360	87	-8	5-4	.993	-8	88	107	2b141		-0.8
1949	†NY A	70	157	29	41	8	2	0	11	29	1	20	.261	.380	.338	90	-1	3-2	.974	-2	91	105	2b51,3b4		0.3
1950	NY A	7	2	0	0	0	0	0	0	0	0	0	.000	.000	.000	-99	-1	0-0	1.000	0	203	0	2b4		0.3
	StL A	93	326	32	71	16	2	1	24	51		49	.218	.324	.288	56	-21	3-3	.975	-17	90	83	2b62,3b31,S5		-3.3
	Year	100	328	32	71	16	2	1	24	51		49	.216	.322	.287	55	-22	3-3	.975	-16	91	82	2b66,3b31,S5		-3.3
1951	Cle A	50	88	10	19	1	0	1	4	22	1	16	.216	.373	.261	78	-1	1-0	.992	5	116	116	2b25,3b2		0.5
1952	Cle A	1	0	0	0	0	0	0	0	0		0					-0	0-0	—	-0	-0	0	/3		0.0
Total	10	1028	3695	604	989	157	68	29	281	541	6	447	.268	.362	.371	102	19	134-55	.980	21	99	109	2b787,3b117,S77		10.5

STIVETTS, JACK John Elmer "Happy Jack" B3.31.1868 Ashland PA D4.18.1930 Ashland PA BR/TR/6-2/185 d6.26 OF(41/33/69) ▲

1889	StL AA	27	79	12	18	2	2	0	7	3	1	13	.228	.265	.304	55	-5	0	.896	-1	81	0	P26/OR		-0.1
1890	StL AA	67	226	36	65	15	6	4	43	16	1		.288	.337	.500	128	5	0	.894	3	102	119	P54,O10C,1b3		0.2
1891	StL AA	85	302	45	92	10	2	7	54	10	1	32	.305	.331	.421	100	-3	4	.898	4	104	63	P64,O24(1/0/23)		0.1
1892	†Bos N	71	240	40	71	14	2	3	36	27	1	28	.296	.369	.408	124	7	8	.904	1	103	177	P54,O18(16/2/0)/1		0.1
1893	Bos N	50	172	32	51	5	6	3	25	12		14	.297	.342	.448	101	-2	6	.955	-4	79	105	P38,O8(3/0/5),3b3		-0.3
1894	Bos N	68	244	55	80	12	7	8	64	16	1	21	.328	.369	.533	107	0	3	.943	-4	74	46	P45,O16(8/2/6),1b4		-0.2
1895	Bos N	46	158	20	30	6	4	0	24	6		18	.190	.220	.278	26	-19	1	.961	-2	76	49	P38,1b5,O2(0/1/1)		-0.4
1896	Bos N	67	222	43	77	9	6	3	49	12	1	10	.347	.383	.482	120	5	4	.946	-7	70	113	P42,O12(3/2/7),1b5/3		-0.3
1897	†Bos N	61	199	41	73	9	9	2	37	15	2		.367	.417	.533	141	1	2	.926	-3	75	144	O29(6/10/14),P18,2b1,1b2		-0.7
1898	Bos N	41	111	16	28	1	1	2	16	10	1		.252	.314	.333	81	-3	1	.909	-4	59	0	O14(2/5/8),1b10,S4,2b2,P2		-0.7
1899	Cle N	18	39	8	8	1	1	0	2	6	1		.205	.326	.282	73	-1	0	1.000	1	112	0	O7(2/1/4),P7/S3		0.0
Total	11	601	1992	348	593	84	46	35	357	133	9	136	.298	.344	.439	104	-15	91	.924	-15	91	86	P388,O141R,1b30,S5,3b5,2b4		-1.4

STOCK, MILT Milton Joseph B7.11.1893 Chicago IL D7.16.1977 Fairhope AL BR/TR/5-8/154 d9.29 C9

1913	NY N	7	17	2	3	0	0	0	1	1		1	.176	.263	.235	43	-1	2	.838	0	108	223	S7		0.0
1914	NY N	115	365	50	96	17	1	4	43	34	4	21	.263	.333	.340	103	2	11	.939	13	122	122	3b113/S		1.9
1915	†Phi N	69	227	37	59	7	3	1	15	22	0	26	.260	.325	.330	98	0	6-2	.971	-0	96	102	3b55,S4		0.2
1916	Phi N	132	509	61	143	25	6	1	43	27		33	.281	.320	.360	105	3	21-26	.955	-2	93	142	3b117,S15		0.1
1917	Phi N	150	564	76	149	27	6	3	53	51	1	34	.264	.326	.349	105	3	25	.942	-8	92	76	3b133,S19		0.0
1918	Phi N	123	481	62	132	14	1	1	42	35		22	.274	.325	.314	89	-5	20	.946	-5	102	74	3b123		0.0
1919	StL N	135	492	56	151	16	4	0	52	49		21	.307	.371	.356	127	18	17	.966	19	109	98	2b77,3b58		4.4
1920	StL N	155	639	85	204	28	6	0	76	40	1	27	.319	.360	.382	117	15	15-17	.939	-10	97	78	3b155		0.7
1921	StL N	149	587	96	180	27	6	3	84	48	1	26	.307	.360	.388	100	2	11-3	.940	-20	83	73	3b149		-0.8

YEAR	TM LG	G	AB	R	H	2B	3B	HR	RBI	BB-IB	HP	SO	AVG	OBP	SLG	AOPS	ABR	SB-CS	FA	FR	RNG	THR	GAMES AT POSITION	DL	BFW
1922	StL N	151	581	85	177	33	9	5	79	42	0	29	.305	.352	.418	103	2	7-12	.950	-8	89	90	3b149/S		0.1
1923	StL N	151	603	63	174	33	3	2	96	40	1	21	.289	.334	.363	86	-12	9-6	.955	-15	91	90	3b150/2		-1.7
1924	Bro N	142	561	66	136	14	4	2	52	26	1	32	.242	.277	.292	54	-37	3-8	.931	-21	78	61	3b142		-5.2
1925	Bro N	146	615	98	202	28	9	1	62	38	0	28	.328	.368	.408	101	1	8-1	.978	-1	98	85	2b141,3b5		0.5
1926	Bro N	3	8	0	0	0	0	0	0	1	0	0	.000	.111	.000	-69	-2	0	.923	-0	98	70	2b3		-0.2
Total	14	1628	6249	839	1806	270	58	22	696	455	13	321	.289	.339	.361	98	-11	155-75	.945	-57	94	92	3b1349,2b222,S47		-0.8

STOCKER, KEVIN Kevin Douglas B2.13.1970 Spokane WA BB/TR/6-1/175* [PhiN91 2/54] d7.7 Col Washington

YEAR	TM LG	G	AB	R	H	2B	3B	HR	RBI	BB-IB	HP	SO	AVG	OBP	SLG	AOPS	ABR	SB-CS	FA	FR	RNG	THR	GAMES AT POSITION	DL	BFW
1993	†Phi N	70	259	46	84	12	3	3	31	30-11	8	43	.324	.409	.417	124	11	5-0	.958	-4	91	101	S70		1.3
1994	Phi N	82	271	38	74	11	2	2	28	44-8	7	41	.273	.383	.351	93	-0	2-2	.959	-1	102	90	S82	34	0.5
1995	Phi N	125	412	42	90	14	3	1	32	43-9	7	75	.218	.304	.274	54	-27	6-1	.969	-5	106	100	S125		-1.2
1996	Phi N	119	394	46	100	22	6	5	41	43-9	8	89	.254	.336	.378	88	-6	6-4	.975	7	102	112	S119		0.9
1997	Phi N	149	504	51	134	23	5	4	40	51-7	2	91	.266	.335	.355	82	-13	11-6	.981	-12	90	83	S147		-1.4
1998	TB A	112	336	37	70	11	3	6	25	27-1	8	80	.208	.282	.313	53	-24	5-3	.979	11	100	**117**	S110	29	-0.4
1999	TB A	79	254	39	76	11	2	1	27	24-0	4	41	.299	.369	.370	88	-4	9-7	.957	4	100	97	S76	74	0.5
2000	TB A	40	114	20	30	7	1	2	8	19-0	2	27	.263	.378	.395	97	0	1-2	.933	-5	102	99	S40		-0.2
	Ana A	70	229	21	45	13	3	0	16	32-0	2	54	.197	.299	.279	47	-19	0-3	.978	-3	110	112	S69	14	-1.1
	Year	110	343	41	75	20	4	2	24	51-0	4	81	.219	.326	.318	63	-18	1-5	.962	-2	107	107	S109		-1.3
Total	8	846	2773	340	703	124	28	23	248	313-45	50	541	.254	.338	.343	78	-82	45-28	.969	9	100	101	S838	151	-1.1

STOCKWELL, LEN Leonard Clark B8.25.1859 Cordova IL D1.28.1905 Niles CA BR/TR/5-11/165 d5.17

YEAR	TM LG	G	AB	R	H	2B	3B	HR	RBI	BB-IB	HP	SO	AVG	OBP	SLG	AOPS	ABR	SB-CS	FA	FR	RNG	THR	GAMES AT POSITION	DL	BFW
1879	Cle N	2	6	0	0	0	0	0	0	0		2	.000	.000	.000	-99	-1		1.000	1	471	1934	O2(0/1/1)		0.0
1884	Lou AA	2	9	0	1	0	0	0	0	0			.111	.111	.111	-29	-1		.667	-1	0		O2(1/1/0)/C		-0.2
1890	Cle N	2	7	2	2	1	0	0	0	3			.286	.286	.429	110	-1		1.000	0	518		O/OL1		0.0
Total	3	6	22	2	3	1	0	0	0	5			.136	.136	.182	-1	-2	0	.900	1	307	765	O5(2/2/1)/1C		-0.2

STODDARD d9.25

YEAR	TM LG	G	AB	R	H	2B	3B	HR	RBI	BB-IB	HP	SO	AVG	OBP	SLG	AOPS	ABR	SB-CS	FA	FR	RNG	THR	GAMES AT POSITION	DL	BFW
1875	Atl NA	2	9	1	1	1	0	0	0	0		1	.111	.111	.222	15	-1	0-0	.800	-1	0		O2(1/1/0)		-0.1

STOKES, AL Albert John (b Albert John Stocek) B1.1.1900 Chicago IL D12.19.1986 Grantham NH BR/TR/5-9/175 d5.10

YEAR	TM LG	G	AB	R	H	2B	3B	HR	RBI	BB-IB	HP	SO	AVG	OBP	SLG	AOPS	ABR	SB-CS	FA	FR	RNG	THR	GAMES AT POSITION	DL	BFW
1925	Bos A	17	52	7	11	0	1	0	1	4	0	8	.212	.268	.250	32	-6	0-0	.969	1	76	153	C17		-0.3
1926	Bos A	30	86	7	14	3	3	0	6	8	0	28	.163	.234	.267	32	-9	0-0	.931	-5	61	106	C29		-1.3
Total	2	47	138	14	25	3	4	0	7	12	0	36	.181	.247	.261	32	-15	0-0	.946	-4	67	124	C46		-1.6

STONE, GENE Eugene Daniel B1.16.1944 Burbank CA BL/TL/5-11/190 d5.13

YEAR	TM LG	G	AB	R	H	2B	3B	HR	RBI	BB-IB	HP	SO	AVG	OBP	SLG	AOPS	ABR	SB-CS	FA	FR	RNG	THR	GAMES AT POSITION	DL	BFW
1969	Phi N	18	28	4	6	0	1	0	0	4-1	0	9	.214	.313	.286	70	-1	0-0	1.000	-1	33	69	1b5		-0.2

STONE, GEORGE George Robert B9.3.1877 Lost Nation IA D1.3.1945 Clinton IA BL/TL/5-9/175 d4.20

YEAR	TM LG	G	AB	R	H	2B	3B	HR	RBI	BB-IB	HP	SO	AVG	OBP	SLG	AOPS	ABR	SB-CS	FA	FR	RNG	THR	GAMES AT POSITION	DL	BFW
1903	Bos A	2	2	0	0	0	0	0	0	0		0	.000	.000	.000	-95	0	0	—		0		/H		0.0
1905	StL A	154	632	76	**187**	25	13	7	52	44		5	.296	.347	.410	147	32	26	.954	2	88	127	O154L		2.8
1906	StL A	154	581	91	208	25	20	6	71	52		7	**.358**	**.417**	**.501**	195	63	35	.968	0	52	79	O155L		5.9
1907	StL A	155	596	77	191	13	11	4	59	59		6	.320	.387	.399	151	36	23	.970	-3	60	112	O155L		2.6
1908	StL A	148	588	89	165	21	8	5	31	55		3	.281	.345	.369	131	21	20	.947	0	64	67	O148L		1.4
1909	StL A	83	310	33	89	5	4	1	15	24		1	.287	.340	.339	123	8	8	.928	-1	70	149	O81(63/0/18)		0.2
1910	StL A	152	562	60	144	17	12	0	40	48		0	.256	.315	.329	108	4	20	.972	-1	92	107	O145(139/1/5)		-0.5
Total	7	848	3271	426	984	106	68	23	268	282		22	.301	.360	.396	145	164	132	.958	-2	71	104	O837(813/1/23)		12.4

STONE, RON Harry Ronald B9.9.1942 Corning CA BL/TL/6-2/195(185-200) d4.13 Col Cal St.-Sacramento

YEAR	TM LG	G	AB	R	H	2B	3B	HR	RBI	BB-IB	HP	SO	AVG	OBP	SLG	AOPS	ABR	SB-CS	FA	FR	RNG	THR	GAMES AT POSITION	DL	BFW
1966	KC A	26	22	2	6	1	0	0	0	0	3		.273	.273	.318	71	-1	1-1	1.000	0	84	0	O4(2/2/1),1b3		-0.1
1969	Phi N	103	222	22	53	7	1	1	24	29-8	3	28	.239	.332	.293	79	-5	3-1	.978	-1	86	164	O69(37/2/32)		-0.9
1970	Phi N	123	321	30	84	12	5	3	39	38-1	1	45	.262	.338	.358	90	-4	5-6	.968	-1	102	87	O99(51/0/48),1b6		-1.1
1971	Phi N	95	185	16	42	8	1	2	23	25-3	0	36	.227	.315	.314	79	-4	2-2	.964	1	100	179	O51(22/1/33),1b3		-0.6
1972	Phi N	41	54	3	9	0	1	0	3	9-1	0	11	.167	.286	.204	40	-4	0-0	1.000	3	143	464	O15(6/1/9)		-0.1
Total	5	388	804	73	194	28	8	6	89	101-13	4	122	.241	.326	.318	81	-18	11-10	.973	3	99	147	O238(118/6/123),1b12		-2.8

STONE, JEFF Jeffrey Glen B12.26.1960 Kennett MO BL/TR/6-0/175* d9.9

YEAR	TM LG	G	AB	R	H	2B	3B	HR	RBI	BB-IB	HP	SO	AVG	OBP	SLG	AOPS	ABR	SB-CS	FA	FR	RNG	THR	GAMES AT POSITION	DL	BFW
1983	Phi N	9	4	2	3	0	2	0	3	0-0	0	1	.750	.750	1.750	578	2	4-0	—	-0	0	0	/OC		0.3
1984	Phi N	51	185	27	67	4	6	1	15	9-0	2	26	.362	.394	.465	139	9	27-5	.916	-4	94	29	O46L	30	0.8
1985	Phi N	88	264	36	70	4	3	3	11	15-0	1	50	.265	.307	.337	78	-9	15-5	.966	-4	78	98	O69L		-1.5
1986	Phi N	82	249	32	69	6	4	6	19	20-0	4	52	.277	.341	.406	101	0	19-6	.982	1	89	224	O58(37/25/0)		0.1
1987	Phi N	66	125	19	32	7	1	1	16	8-0	3	38	.256	.316	.352	74	-5	3-1	1.000	0	80	221	O25(20/5/1)	34	-0.5
1988	Bal A	26	61	4	10	1	0	0	1	4-0	0	11	.164	.215	.180	12	-7	4-1	.963	0	70	331	O21(18/0/3)/D	44	-0.7
1989	Tex A	22	36	5	6	1	2	0	5	3-0	1	5	.167	.250	.306	55	-2	2-1	—	-1	0		O15,O3(1/1/1)		-0.4
	Bos A	18	15	3	3	0	0	0	1	1-1	0	2	.200	.235	.200	27	-1	1-0	1.000	-0	106		O11(0/4/7),D3		-0.1
	Year	40	51	8	9	1	2	0	6	4-1	1	7	.176	.246	.275	46	-3	3-1	1.000	-1	75		O18,O14(1/5/8)		-0.5
1990	Bos A	10	2	1	1	0	0	0	0	0-0	0	1	.500	.500	.500	172	0	0-1	—		0		D2		0.0
Total	8	372	941	129	261	23	18	11	72	60-1	11	186	.277	.327	.375	92	-13	75-20	.963	-8	84	146	O234(191/36/12),D21	108	-2.0

STONE, JOHN John Thomas "Rocky" B10.10.1905 Mulberry TN D11.30.1955 Shelbyville TN BL/TR/6-1/178 d8.31 Col Maryville

YEAR	TM LG	G	AB	R	H	2B	3B	HR	RBI	BB-IB	HP	SO	AVG	OBP	SLG	AOPS	ABR	SB-CS	FA	FR	RNG	THR	GAMES AT POSITION	DL	BFW
1928	Det A	26	113	20	40	10	3	2	21	5	1	8	.354	.387	.549	141	6	1-0	.962	-1	90	83	O26L		0.3
1929	Det A	51	150	23	39	11	2	2	15	11	0	13	.260	.311	.400	81	-5	1-1	.986	2	104	132	O36(35/0/2)		-0.5
1930	Det A	127	425	60	132	29	11	3	56	32	1	49	.311	.360	.462	102	1	6-9	.966	-1	102	63	O109(93/11/6)		-0.9
1931	Det A	147	584	86	191	28	11	10	76	56	2	48	.327	.388	.464	119	16	13-13	.959	5	108	107	O147(143/5/0)		1.1
1932	Det A	145	582	106	173	35	12	17	108	58	0	64	.297	.361	.486	113	10	2-1	.961	-1	99	99	O142(90/53/0)		0.2
1933	Det A	148	574	86	161	33	11	11	80	54	2	37	.280	.344	.434	103	1	1-4	.970	-2	100	84	O141(18/0/124)		-1.0
1934	Was A	113	419	77	132	28	7	7	67	52	3	26	.315	.395	.465	126	17	1-2	.966	5	103	144	O112(0/16/98)		1.4
1935	Was A	125	455	78	143	27	18	1	78	39	3	29	.314	.372	.459	118	10	10-4	.955	2	100	130	O114(19/7/90)		0.5
1936	Was A	123	437	95	149	22	11	15	90	60	0	26	.341	.421	.545	145	31	8-0	.967	6	108	121	O114(109/0/6)		2.8
1937	Was A	139	542	84	179	33	15	6	88	66	0	36	.330	.403	.480	127	23	6-4	.984	7	107	121	O137(37/7/95)		2.1
1938	Was A	56	213	32	52	14	4	3	28	30	1	16	.244	.337	.380	85	-5	2-1	.974	-1	95	110	O53(29/1/26)		-0.8
Total	11	1200	4494	739	1391	268	105	77	707	463	12	352	.310	.376	.467	116	105	45-40	.967	20	103	108	O1131(599/100/447)		5.2

STONE, TIGE William Arthur B9.18.1901 Macon GA D1.1.1960 Jacksonville FL BR/TR/5-8/145 d8.23 Col Mercer

YEAR	TM LG	G	AB	R	H	2B	3B	HR	RBI	BB-IB	HP	SO	AVG	OBP	SLG	AOPS	ABR	SB-CS	FA	FR	RNG	THR	GAMES AT POSITION	DL	BFW
1923	StL N	5	1	0	1	0	0	0	0	2		0	1.000	1.000	1.000	438	1	0-0	—	0	0	0	O4(2/2/0)/P		0.0

STONEHAM, JOHN John Andrew B11.8.1908 Wood River IL D1.1.2004 Owasso OK BL/TR/5-9.5/168 d9.18 Col Washington-St. Louis

YEAR	TM LG	G	AB	R	H	2B	3B	HR	RBI	BB-IB	HP	SO	AVG	OBP	SLG	AOPS	ABR	SB-CS	FA	FR	RNG	THR	GAMES AT POSITION	DL	BFW
1933	Chi A	10	25	4	3	0	0	1	3	2	0		.120	.185	.240	12	-3	0-0	1.000	-0	100	0	O9(1/1/7)		-0.4

STORIE, HOWIE Howard Edward "Sponge" B5.15.1911 Pittsfield MA D7.27.1968 Pittsfield MA BR/TR/5-10/175 d9.7

YEAR	TM LG	G	AB	R	H	2B	3B	HR	RBI	BB-IB	HP	SO	AVG	OBP	SLG	AOPS	ABR	SB-CS	FA	FR	RNG	THR	GAMES AT POSITION	DL	BFW
1931	Bos A	6	17	2	2	0	0	0	3	2			.118	.250	.118	-1	-2	0-0	1.000	0	145	49	C6		-0.2
1932	Bos A	6	8	0	3	0	0	0	0	0		2	.375	.375	.375	98	0	0-0	1.000	0	97	0	C5		0.0
Total	2	12	25	2	5	0	0	0	0	2			.200	.286	.200	31	-2	0-0	1.000	0	131	35	C11		-0.2

STORKE, ALAN Alan Marshall B9.27.1884 Auburn NY D3.18.1910 Newton MA BR/TR/6-1/? d9.24 Col Amherst

YEAR	TM LG	G	AB	R	H	2B	3B	HR	RBI	BB-IB	HP	SO	AVG	OBP	SLG	AOPS	ABR	SB-CS	FA	FR	RNG	THR	GAMES AT POSITION	DL	BFW
1906	Pit N	5	12	1	3	1	0	0	0	3			.250	.308	.333	96	0		1.000	0	121	770	3b2/S		0.0
1907	Pit N	112	357	24	92	6	6	1	39	16	3		.258	.294	.317	90	-6	6	.925	-9	94	128	3b67,1b23,2b7,S5		-1.4
1908	Pit N	64	202	20	51	5	3	1	12	9	0		.252	.284	.322	93	-2	4	.988	-6	56	96	1b49,3b6/2		-1.1
1909	Pit N	37	118	12	30	5	2	0	12	7	1		.254	.302	.331	89	-2	1	.994	-1	75	137	1b18,3b14		-0.3
	StL N	48	174	11	49	5	0	0	10	12	0		.282	.328	.310	105	1	5	.958	-1	99	81	S44,2b4/1		0.2
	Year	85	292	23	79	10	2	0	22	19	1		.271	.317	.319	97	-1	6	.958	-1	99	81	S44,1b19,3b14,2b4		-0.1
Total	4	266	863	68	225	22	11	2	74	45	4		.261	.300	.319	94	-9	17	.990	-15	68	99	1b91,3b89,S50,2b12		-2.6

STORTI, LIN Lindo Ivan B12.5.1906 Santa Monica CA D7.24.1982 Ontario CA BB/TR/5-11/165 d9.18

YEAR	TM LG	G	AB	R	H	2B	3B	HR	RBI	BB-IB	HP	SO	AVG	OBP	SLG	AOPS	ABR	SB-CS	FA	FR	RNG	THR	GAMES AT POSITION	DL	BFW
1930	StL A	7	28	6	9	1	1	0	2	2	0	6	.321	.367	.429	98	0	0-0	.975	1	96	201	2b6		0.1
1931	StL A	86	273	32	60	15	4	3	26	15	1	50	.220	.263	.337	55	-19	0-2	.926	5	105	168	3b67,2b7		-1.2
1932	StL A	53	193	19	50	11	2	3	26	5	0	20	.259	.278	.383	66	-11	1-0	.956	-0	96	104	3b51		-0.8
1933	StL A	70	210	26	41	7	4	3	21	25	0	31	.195	.281	.310	53	-15	2-2	.934	1	102	198	3b32,2b24		-1.1
Total	4	216	704	83	160	34	11	9	75	47	1	107	.227	.277	.345	59	-45	3-4	.936	7	102	154	3b150,2b37		-3.0

YEAR	TM LG	G	AB	R	H	2B	3B	HR	RBI	BB-IB	HP	SO	AVG	OBP	SLG	AOPS	ABR	SB-CS	FA	FR	RNG	THR	GAMES AT POSITION	DL	BFW

STOUCH, TOM Thomas Carl B12.2.1869 Perrysville OH D10.7.1956 Lancaster PA BR/TR/6-2/165 d7.7

| 1898 | Lou N | 4 | 16 | 4 | 5 | 1 | 0 | 0 | 6 | 1 | 0 | | .313 | .353 | .375 | 110 | 0 | 0 | .850 | -2 | 78 | 66 | 2b4 | | -0.1 |

STOVALL, DA ROND Da Rond Tyrone B1.3.1973 St.Louis MO BB/TL/6-1/185 [StLN91 5/129] d4.1

| 1998 | Mon N | 62 | 78 | 11 | 16 | 2 | 1 | 2 | 6 | 6-0 | 0 | 29 | .205 | .262 | .333 | 57 | -5 | 1-0 | .925 | -1 | 91 | 157 | O47(27/14/7) | | -0.6 |

STOVALL, GEORGE George Thomas "Firebrand" B11.23.1877 Leeds MO D11.5.1951 Burlington IA BR/TR/6-2/180 d7.4 M5 b-Jesse

1904	Cle A	52	181	18	54	10	1	1	31	2	3		.298	.317	.381	121	4	3	.978	-1	93	115	1b38,2b9,O3(2/1/0)/3		0.3
1905	Cle A	112	423	41	115	31	1	1	47	13	1		.272	.295	.357	105	2	13	.973	-3	133	115	1b60,2b46,O4C		-0.2
1906	Cle A	116	443	54	121	19	5	0	37	8	1		.273	.288	.339	97	-3	15	.985	-1	111	214	1b55,3b30,2b19		-0.6
1907	Cle A	124	466	38	110	17	6	1	36	18	2		.236	.267	.305	82	-11	13	.983	-3	89	168	1b122,3b2		-1.8
1908	Cle A	138	534	71	156	29	6	2	45	17	2		.292	.316	.380	126	13	14	**.990**	2	104	146	1b132,O5C/S		1.4
1909	Cle A	145	565	60	139	17	10	2	49	6	4		.246	.259	.322	80	-16	25	.988	10	**126**	119	1b145		-1.0
1910	Cle A	142	521	49	136	19	4	0	52	14	3		.261	.284	.313	86	-11	16	.988	7	**121**	94	1b132,2b2		-0.7
1911	Cle A	126	458	48	124	17	7	0	79	21	2		.271	.306	.338	79	-15	11	.986	7	118	103	1b118,2b2,M		-1.1
1912	StL A	116	398	35	101	17	5	0	45	14	4		.254	.286	.322	76	-14	11	.983	5	125	139	1b94,M		-1.1
1913	StL A	89	303	34	87	14	3	1	24	7	1	23	.287	.305	.363	98	-3	7	.988	8	143	91	1b76,M		0.3
1914	KC F	124	450	51	128	20	5	7	75	23	4	35	.284	.325	.398	100	-9	6	.989	5	117	**131**	1b116/3M		-0.8
1915	KC F	130	448	48	111	21	3	0	44	31	6	36	.231	.286	.287	64	-31	8	.987	5	**121**	91	1b129,M		-3.2
Total	12	1414	5222	547	1382	231	56	15	564	174	33	94	.265	.293	.339	91	-94	142	.986	40	117	125	1b1217,2b78,3b34,O12(2/9/0)/S		-8.5

STOVEY, HARRY Harry Duffield (b Harry Duffield Stowe) B12.20.1856 Philadelphia PA D9.20.1937 New Bedford MA BR/TR/5-11.5/175 d5.1 M2 ▲

1880	Wor N	83	355	76	94	21	**14**	6	28	12		46	.265	.289	.454	136	12		.860	-6	54	54	O46(5/42/0),1b37,P2		0.2
1881	Wor N	75	341	57	92	25	7	2	30	12		23	.270	.295	.442	111	4		.955	-5	79	75	1b57,O18(1/0/17),M		-0.4
1882	Wor N	**84**	360	90	104	13	10	-5	26	22		34	.289	.330	.422	136	14		.956	3	111	81	1b43,O41L		1.1
1883	Phi AA	94	421	**110**	128	**31**	6	**14**	66	27			.304	.346	**.506**	156	25		**.965**	1	81	74	1b93,O3C/P		1.5
1884	Phi AA	104	448	**124**	146	22	**23**	10	83	26	4		.326	.384	.545	182	38		.960	-1	90	99	1b104		2.5
1885	Phi AA	112	486	**130**	153	27	9	**13**	75	39	4		.315	.371	.488	160	32		.967	4	**128**	106	1b82,O30C,M		2.5
1886	Phi AA	123	489	115	144	28	11	7	59	64	1		.294	.377	.440	154	32	68	.870	-1	106	178	O63(0/46/17),1b62/P		2.0
1887	Phi AA	124	497	125	142	31	12	4	77	56	7		.286	.366	.421	119	14	74	.902	7	109	32	O80(49/29/2),1b46		1.1
1888	Phi AA	130	530	127	152	25	**20**	9	65	62	3		.287	.365	.460	165	**39**	87	.943	4	61	102	O118L,1b13		**3.5**
1889	Phi AA	137	556	**152**	171	38	13	**19**	**119**	77	1	68	.308	.393	**.525**	162	46	63	.897	18	146	153	O137L/1		**5.0**
1890	Bos P	118	481	142	144	25	11	12	84	81	5	38	.299	.406	.472	126	18	**97**	.921	0	109	64	O117(1/0/116)/1		1.3
1891	Bos N	134	544	118	152	31	**20**	**16**	95	79	2	69	.279	.373	.498	137	23	57	.910	7	101	123	O134(39/0/96)/1		2.4
1892	Bos N	38	146	21	24	8	1	0	12	14	3	19	.164	.252	.233	43	-10	20	.901	4	49	85	O38L		-1.3
	Bal N	74	283	58	77	14	11	4	55	40	1	32	.272	.364	.442	140	13	20	.913	-2	61	81	O64L,1b10		0.5
	Year	112	429	79	101	22	12	4	67	54	4	51	.235	.326	.371	105	2	40	.908	-2	56	83	O102L,1b10		-0.8
1893	Bal N	8	26	4	4	2	0	0	5	8	0	3	.154	.353	.231	55	-1	1	.864	0	71	0	O7L		-0.2
	Bro N	48	175	43	44	6	6	1	29	44	0	11	.251	.402	.371	111	5	22	.901	-4	35	0	O48(19/26/3)		-0.2
	Year	56	201	47	48	8	6	1	34	52	0	14	.239	.395	.353	103	4	23	.895	-4	40	0	O55(26/26/3)		-0.4
Total	14	1486	6138	1492	1771	347	174	122	908	663	31	343	.289	.361	.461	141	304	509	.896	23	96	97	O944(519/176/251),1b550,P4		21.5

STOVIAK, RAY Raymond Thomas B6.6.1915 Scottdale PA D2.23.1998 Nicoya, Costa Rica BL/TL/6-1/195 d6.5 Col Villanova

| 1938 | Phi N | 10 | 10 | 1 | 0 | 0 | 0 | 0 | 0 | 0 | | 3 | .000 | .000 | .000 | -99 | -3 | 0 | 1.000 | 1 | 57 | 1233 | O4R | | -0.2 |

STOWERS, CHRIS Christopher James B8.18.1974 St.Louis MO BL/TL/6-3/195 [MonN96 17/490] d7.10 Col Georgia

| 1999 | Mon N | 4 | 2 | 0 | 0 | 0 | 0 | 0 | 0 | 0 | | 0 | .000 | .000 | .000 | -99 | -1 | 0-0 | 1.000 | 0 | 127 | 0 | O2(0/1/1) | | -0.1 |

STRAIN, JOE Joseph Allan B4.30.1954 Denver CO BR/TR/5-10/169* d6.28 Col Northern Colorado

1979	SF N	67	257	27	62	6	1	1	12	13-0	3	21	.241	.285	.292	62	-14	8-4	.982	7	110	75	2b67/3		-0.4
1980	SF N	77	189	26	54	6	0	0	10	10-0	1	10	.286	.320	.317	82	-5	1-2	.989	-5	95	63	2b42,3b6/S	31	-0.9
1981	Chi N	25	74	7	14	1	0	0	1	5-0	1	7	.189	.250	.203	28	-7	0-0	.975	9	142	83	2b20	15	0.3
Total	3	169	520	60	130	15	1	1	29	28-0	4	38	.250	.292	.288	64	-26	9-6	.983	11	110	72	2b129,3b7/S	46	-1.0

STRAND, PAUL Paul Edward B12.19.1893 Carbonado WA D7.2.1974 Salt Lake City UT BR/TL/6-0.5/190 d5.15 ▲

1913	Bos N	7	6	0	1	0	0	0	0	0		0	.167	.167	.167	-5	0	0	.875	0	137	0	P7		0.0
1914	Bos N	18	24	2	8	2	0	0	3	0		2	.333	.333	.417	123	2	0	.813	-0	89	237	P16		0.0
1915	Bos N	24	22	3	2	0	0	0	2	0		4	.091	.091	.091	-47	-4	0	.750	-1	32	0	P6,O5(2/1/0)		-0.2
1924	Phi A	47	167	15	38	9	4	0	13	4	2	9	.228	.254	.329	49	-14	3-3	.988	-3	83	81	O44(0/39/5)		-1.9
Total	4	96	219	20	49	11	4	0	18	4	2	15	.224	.244	.311	47	-16	3-3	.989	-4	82	98	O49(2/40/5),P29		-2.1

STRANDS, LARRY John Lawrence B12.5.1885 Chicago IL D1.19.1957 Forest Park IL BR/TR/5-10.5/165 d4.25

| 1915 | New F | 35 | 75 | 7 | 14 | 3 | 1 | 1 | 11 | 6 | 0 | 11 | .187 | .247 | .293 | 55 | -6 | 1 | .852 | -4 | 83 | 161 | 3b12,2b9,O2R | | -1.1 |

STRANG, SAMMY Samuel Nicklin "The Dixie Thrush" (b Samuel Strang Nicklin) B12.16.1876 Chattanooga TN D3.13.1932 Chattanooga TN BB/TR/5-8/160 d7.10 OF(11/63/92)

1896	Lou N	14	46	6	12	0	0	0	7	6	0	6	.261	.346	.261	64	-2	4	.803	-6	78	90	S14		-0.6
1900	Chi N	27	102	15	29	3	0	0	9	8	2		.284	.348	.314	86	-1	1	.887	-7	93	160	3b16,S9,2b2		-0.7
1901	NY N	135	493	55	139	14	6	1	34	59	5		.282	.364	.341	109	9	40	.877	8	113	155	3b91,2b37,O5R,S4		1.9
1902	Chi A	137	536	108	158	18	5	3	46	76	5		.295	.387	.364	114	15	38	.890	5	**109**	93	3b137		2.2
	Chi N	3	11	1	4	0	0	0	0	0	0		.364	.364	.364	128	0	1	1.000	-1	59	996	2b2,3b2		0.0
1903	Bro N	135	508	101	138	21	5	0	38	75	10		.272	.376	.333	106	9	46	.914	-5	100	105	3b124,O8C,2b3		-0.6
1904	Bro N	77	271	28	52	11	0	1	9	45	4		.192	.316	.244	75	-5	16	.910	-29	84	63	2b63,3b12/S		-3.6
1905	†NY N	111	294	51	76	9	4	3	29	58	5		.259	.389	.347	117	10	23	.915	-7	97	81	2b47,O38(4/7/27),S9/13		0.3
1906	NY N	113	313	50	100	16	4	4	49	54	2		.319	.442	.435	164	27	21	.944	6	111	78	2b57,O39(5/17/17),S4,3b3/1		3.4
1907	NY N	123	306	56	77	20	4	4	30	60	8		.252	.388	.382	137	18	21	.947	-0	138	229	O70(1/28/41),2b13,3b7,1b5/S		1.6
1908	NY N	28	53	8	5	0	0	0	2	23	2		.094	.385	.094	52	0	5	.863	-3	98	138	2b14,O5(1/3/2),S3		-0.4
Total	10	903	2933	479	790	112	28	16	253	464	43	6	.269	.377	.343	113	80	216	.891	-38	106	119	3b393,2b238,O165R,S45,1b7		4.8

STRANGE, ALAN Alan Cochrane "Inky" B11.7.1906 Philadelphia PA D6.27.1994 Seattle WA BR/TR/5-9/162 d4.17 Col Penn St.

1934	StL A	127	430	39	100	14	2	1	45	48	0	28	.233	.310	.288	51	-31	3-1	.955	5	100	104	S125		-1.6
1935	StL A	49	147	8	34	6	1	0	17	17	0	7	.231	.311	.286	53	-10	0-0	.960	3	101	96	S49		-0.4
	Was A	20	54	3	10	2	1	0	5	4	0	1	.185	.241	.259	30	-6	0-0	.974	4	113	119	S16		-0.3
	Year	69	201	11	44	8	2	0	22	21	0	8	.219	.293	.279	47	-16	0-0	.963	5	104	102	S65		-0.7
1940	StL A	54	167	26	31	8	3	0	22	21	1	12	.186	.284	.269	43	-14	2-1	.962	5	115	105	S35,2b4		-0.6
1941	StL A	45	112	14	26	4	0	0	11	15	0	5	.232	.323	.268	56	-7	0-0	.973	0	98	174	S32,1b2/3		-0.4
1942	StL A	19	37	3	10	2	0	0	5	3	0	1	.270	.325	.324	82	-1	0-0	.935	2	142	218	3b10,S3/2		0.1
Total	5	314	947	93	211	39	7	1	89	109	1	54	.223	.304	.282	50	-69	6-3	.959	17	103	101	S260,3b11,2b5,1b2		-3.2

STRANGE, DOUG Joseph Douglas B4.13.1964 Greenville SC BB/TR/6-1/185(170-185) [DetA85 7/184] d7.13 Col North Carolina St. OF(18/0/2) [DL 1999 Pit N 182]

1989	Det A	64	196	16	42	4	1	1	14	17-0	1	36	.214	.280	.260	54	-14	3-3	.878	-1	100	118	3b54,2b9,S9/D		-1.4
1991	Chi N	3	9	0	4	1	0	0	0	0-0	1		.444	.455	.556	188	1	1-0	.800	-2	53	0	3b3		0.0
1992	Chi N	52	94	7	15	1	0	1	5	10-2	0	15	.160	.240	.202	26	-9	1-0	.900	-2	93	57	3b33,2b12		-1.2
1993	Tex A	145	484	58	124	29	0	7	60	43-3	3	69	.256	.318	.360	85	-10	6-4	.980	4	102	95	2b135,3b9/S		0.0
1994	Tex A	73	226	26	48	12	1	5	26	15-0	3	38	.212	.268	.341	56	-16	1-3	.970	3	107	114	2b53,3b13,O3(2/0/1)	15	-1.0
1995	†Sea A	74	155	19	42	9	2	2	21	10-0	1	25	.271	.323	.394	84	-4	0-3	.948	6	120	39	3b41,2b5,O4L/D		0.2
1996	Sea A	88	183	19	43	7	1	3	23	14-0	1	31	.235	.290	.333	58	-12	1-0	.961	-6	80	65	3b39,O11(10/0/1),D10,1b3,2b3		-1.7
1997	Mon N	118	327	40	84	16	2	12	47	36-9	2	76	.257	.332	.428	99	-1	0-2	.947	0	99	85	3b105,2b3,O2L/1		-0.1
1998	Pit N	90	185	9	32	8	0	0	14	10-1	3	29	.173	.217	.216	15	-23	0-0	.940	-4	83	51	3b42,2b9,1b3	29	-2.6
Total	9	707	1859	194	434	87	7	31	211	155-15	14	330	.233	.295	.338	69	-86	14-15	.927	-1	98	82	3b339,2b229,O20L,D12,S10,1b7	241	-7.8

STRATTON, ASA Asa Evans B2.10.1853 Grafton MA D8.14.1925 Fitchburg MA d6.17 Col Boston College

| 1881 | Wor N | 1 | 4 | 0 | 1 | 0 | 0 | 0 | 0 | 0 | | | .250 | .250 | .250 | 55 | 0 | | .333 | -1 | 38 | 0 | /S | | -0.1 |

STRATTON, SCOTT Chilton Scott B10.2.1869 Campbellsburg KY D3.8.1939 Louisville KY BL/TR/6-0/180 d4.21 ▲

1888	Lou AA	67	249	35	64	8	1	1	29	12	7		.257	.310	.309	101	1	10	.825	-1	146	0	O38(28/7/3),P33		-0.1
1889	Lou AA	62	229	30	66	7	5	4	34	13	2	36	.288	.332	.415	114	3	10	.915	6	173	75	O29(10/4/15),P19,1b17		0.4
1890	†Lou AA	55	189	29	61	3	5	0	24	16	3		.323	.385	.423	132	7	8	**.977**	5	128	88	P50,O5C		0.2

YEAR	TM LG	G	AB	R	H	2B	3B	HR	RBI	BB-IB	HP	SO	AVG	OBP	SLG	AOPS	ABR	SB-CS	FA	FR	RNG	THR	GAMES AT POSITION	DL	BFW
1891	Pit N	2	8	1	1	0	0	0	0	0	0	3	.125	.125	.125	-28	-1	0	.900	1	242	0	P2		0.0
	Lou AA	34	115	20	27	2	0	0	8	11	1	13	.235	.307	.252	61	-6	8	.939	.3	133	378	P20,1b8,O6(2/3/1)		-0.1
1892	Lou N	63	219	22	56	2	9	0	23	17	3	21	.256	.318	.347	103	0	2	.915	2	109	152	P42,O17(1/0/16),1b6		0.1
1893	Lou N	61	221	34	50	8	5	0	16	25	1	15	.226	.308	.308	69	-10	6	.975	2	131	79	P37,O24R/1		-0.1
1894	Lou N	13	37	9	12	1	2	0	4	4	0	2	.324	.390	.459	112	1	1	.929	2	123	0	P7,O5R		0.1
	Chi N	24	99	30	37	5	4	3	23	7	1	1	.374	.421	.596	135	5	3	.938	-0	98	230	P16,O5R,1b2		0.1
	Year	37	136	39	49	6	6	3	27	11	1	3	.360	.412	.559	131	6	4	.935	1	105	169	P23,O10R,1b2		0.2
1895	Chi N	10	24	3	7	1	1	0	2	4	0	2	.292	.393	.417	102	0	1	.833	-0	147	0	P5,O4C		-0.1
Total	8	391	1390	202	381	37	32	8	163	109	18	93	.274	.335	.364	103	2	56	.938	22	120	143	P231,O133(41/23/68),1b34		0.5

STRAUB, JOE Joseph B1.19.1858 , Germany D2.13.1929 Pueblo CO BR/TR/5-10/160 d6.24

YEAR	TM LG	G	AB	R	H	2B	3B	HR	RBI	BB-IB	HP	SO	AVG	OBP	SLG	AOPS	ABR	SB-CS	FA	FR	RNG	THR	GAMES AT POSITION	DL	BFW
1880	Tro N	3	12	1	3	0	0	0		1		3	.250	.308	.250	87	0		.815	0			C3		0.0
1882	Phi AA	8	32	2	6	2	0	0	1	1			.188	.212	.250	52	-2		.830	-1			C7/OR		-0.2
1883	Col AA	27	100	4	13	0	0	0		4			.130	.163	.130	-5	-11		.860	-2			C14,1b12/OC		-1.1
Total	3	38	144	7	22	2	0	0	1	6		3	.153	.187	.167	17	-13		.843	-3			C24,1b12,O2(0/1/1)		-1.3

STRAUSS, JOE Joseph "Dutch","The Socker" (b Joseph Strasser) B11.16.1858 Cincinnati OH D6.24.1906 Cincinnati OH BR/TR d7.27

YEAR	TM LG	G	AB	R	H	2B	3B	HR	RBI	BB-IB	HP	SO	AVG	OBP	SLG	AOPS	ABR	SB-CS	FA	FR	RNG	THR	GAMES AT POSITION	DL	BFW
1884	KC U	16	60	4	12	3	0	0		1			.200	.213	.250	46	-6		.833	-2	81	0	O10(8/2/0),C3,2b2/3		-0.7
1885	Lou AA	2	6	0	1	0	0	0					.167	.167	.167	6	-1		—	0	0	0	/OLC		-0.2
1886	Lou AA	74	297	36	64	5	6	1	31	8	1		.215	.239	.283	60	-16	25	.857	3	158	0	O73(67/6/1),P2/C		-1.3
	Bro AA	9	36	6	9	1	1	0	5	1	0		.250	.270	.333	88	-1	4	1.000	1	108	0	O7L,C2		0.0
	Year	83	333	42	73	6	7	1	36	9	1		.219	.242	.288	63	-17	29	.866	4	154	0	O80(74/6/1),C3,P2		-1.3
Total	3	101	399	46	86	9	7	1	36	10	1		.216	.237	.281	59	-24	29	.861	1	146	0	O91(83/8/1),C7,P2,2b2/3		-2.2

STRAWBERRY, DARRYL Darryl Eugene B3.12.1962 Los Angeles CA BL/TL/6-6/200(190-215) [NYN80 1/1] d5.6 [DL 1994 LA N 52]

YEAR	TM LG	G	AB	R	H	2B	3B	HR	RBI	BB-IB	HP	SO	AVG	OBP	SLG	AOPS	ABR	SB-CS	FA	FR	RNG	THR	GAMES AT POSITION	DL	BFW
1983	NY N	122	420	63	108	15	7	26	74	47-9	4	128	.257	.336	.512	133	17	19-6	.984	0	104	94	O117R		1.3
1984	NY N★	147	522	75	131	27	4	26	97	75-15	0	131	.251	.343	.467	128	20	27-8	.980	0	101	120	O146(0/21/134)		1.7
1985	NY N★	111	393	78	109	15	4	29	79	73-13	1	96	.277	.389	.557	166	36	26-11	.991	-4	95	68	O110(0/27/100)	47	3.0
1986	†NY N★	136	475	76	123	27	5	27	93	72-9	6	141	.259	.358	.507	140	27	28-12	.975	-3	93	95	O131(1/0/130)		1.9
1987	NY N★	154	532	108	151	32	5	39	104	97-13	7	122	.284	.398	.583	163	51	36-12	.972	-4	99	60	O151R		4.2
1988	†NY N★	153	543	101	146	27	3	39	101	85-21	3	127	.269	.366	.545	166	48	29-14	.971	3	109	59	O150R		4.9
1989	NY N★	134	476	69	107	26	1	29	77	61-13	1	105	.225	.312	.466	126	15	11-4	.972	5	114	61	O131R		1.8
1990	NY N★	152	542	92	150	18	1	37	108	70-15	4	110	.277	.361	.518	140	29	15-8	.989	1	97	106	O149R		2.7
1991	LA N★	139	505	86	134	22	4	28	99	75-4	3	125	.265	.361	.491	140	28	10-8	.978	-9	81	109	O136R	15	1.5
1992	LA N	43	156	20	37	8	0	5	25	19-4	1	34	.237	.322	.385	101	0	3-1	.986	-2	88	77	O42(2/0/40)	95	-0.3
1993	LA N	32	100	12	14	2	0	5	12	16-1	2	19	.140	.267	.310	58	-6	1-0	.905	-5	69	48	O29(4/0/25)	132	-1.3
1994	SF N	29	92	13	22	3	1	4	17	19-4	2	22	.239	.363	.424	110	2	0-3	.969	2	126	54	O27R		0.1
1995	†NY A	32	87	15	24	4	1	3	13	10-1	2	22	.276	.364	.448	111	1	0-0	.909	1	110	358	D15,O11(1/0/10)		0.1
1996	†NY A	63	202	35	53	13	0	11	36	31-5	1	55	.262	.359	.490	113	4	6-5	1.000	-2	82	53	O34(26/0/8),D26		-0.1
1997	NY A	11	29	1	3	1	0	0	2	3-0	1	9	.103	.188	.138	-13	-5	0-0	1.000	-1	78	0	O4L,D4	130	-0.5
1998	NY A	101	295	44	73	11	2	24	57	46-4	1	90	.247	.354	.542	134	14	8-7	.905	-2	88	0	D81,O16L		0.7
1999	†NY A	24	49	10	16	5	0	3	6	17-0	0	16	.327	.500	.612	185	8	2-0	—	0	0	0	D17		0.7
Total	17	1583	5418	898	1401	256	38	335	1000	816-131	38	1352	.259	.357	.505	138	289	221-99	.977	-18	98	84	O1384(54/48/1308),D143	471	22.4

STREET, GABBY Charles Evard "Old Sarge" B9.30.1882 Huntsville AL D2.6.1951 Joplin MO BR/TR/5-11/180 d9.13 M6/C2

YEAR	TM LG	G	AB	R	H	2B	3B	HR	RBI	BB-IB	HP	SO	AVG	OBP	SLG	AOPS	ABR	SB-CS	FA	FR	RNG	THR	GAMES AT POSITION	DL	BFW
1904	Cin N	11	33	1	4	1	0	0		1		0	.121	.147	.152	-7	-4	2	.973	3	127	109	C11		0.0
1905	Cin N	2	2	0	0	0	0	0		2		0	.000	.500	.000	48	0	1	1.000	0	118	207	/C		0.1
	Bos N	3	12	0	2	0	0	0				0	.167	.167	.167	-1	-2	1	.778	-2	69	89	C3		-0.4
	Cin N	29	91	8	23	5	1	0	8	6		1	.253	.306	.330	81	-2	1	.975	2	118	207	C26		0.3
	Year	34	105	8	25	5	1	0	8	8		1	.238	.298	.305	73	-3	2	.957	1	96	120	C30		0.0
1908	Was A	131	394	31	81	12	7	1	32	40		6	.206	.289	.279	92	-2	5	.973	4	109	103	C128		1.5
1909	Was A	137	407	25	86	12	1	0	29	26		2	.211	.262	.246	63	-17	2	.981	1	88	100	C137		-0.3
1910	Was A	89	257	13	52	6	0	1	16	23		2	.202	.273	.237	63	-11	1	.978	8	103	111	C86		0.6
1911	Was A	72	216	16	48	7	1	0	14	14		3	.222	.279	.264	53	-14	4	.973	9	105	92	C71		0.1
1912	NY A	29	88	4	16	1	1	0	6	7		2	.182	.258	.216	34	-8	1	.958	-1	89	109	C29		-0.7
1931	StL N	1	1	0	0	0	0	0	0	0		0	.000	.000	.000	-96	0	0	1.000	0	0	0	/CM		0.0
Total	8	504	1501	98	312	44	11	2	105	108		16	.208	.273	.256	66	-60	17	.974	25	100	103	C493		1.2

STREULI, WALT Walter Herbert B9.26.1935 Memphis TN BR/TR/6-2/195* d9.25 Col Rhodes

YEAR	TM LG	G	AB	R	H	2B	3B	HR	RBI	BB-IB	HP	SO	AVG	OBP	SLG	AOPS	ABR	SB-CS	FA	FR	RNG	THR	GAMES AT POSITION	DL	BFW
1954	Det A	1	0	0	0	0	0	0	0		0	0	—	1.000	—	195	0	0-0	1.000	-0	0	0	/C		0.0
1955	Det A	2	4	1	1	1	0	0	1	0-0	0	0	.250	.200	.500	100	0	0-0	1.000	-0	0	0	C2		0.0
1956	Det A	3	8	0	2	1	0	0	1	1-0	0	2	.250	.333	.375	87	0	0-0	.933	-0	204	53	C3		0.0
Total	3	6	12	1	3	2	0	0	2	2-0	0	2	.250	.333	.417	106	0	0-0	.957	-0	0	122	C6		0.0

STRICK, CHARLES Charles E. (b Charles E. Streck) B9.15.1858 Erie PA D11.18.1933 Erie PA d5.18

YEAR	TM LG	G	AB	R	H	2B	3B	HR	RBI	BB-IB	HP	SO	AVG	OBP	SLG	AOPS	ABR	SB-CS	FA	FR	RNG	THR	GAMES AT POSITION	DL	BFW
1882	Lou AA	32	110	17	18	6	1	0		9			.164	.227	.236	60	-4		.898	1			C21,O6C,2b6/S1		-0.1

STRICKER, CUB John A. (b John A. Streaker) B2.15.1860 Philadelphia PA D11.19.1937 Philadelphia PA BR/TR/5-3/138 d5.2 M1 OF(0/1/19) ▲

YEAR	TM LG	G	AB	R	H	2B	3B	HR	RBI	BB-IB	HP	SO	AVG	OBP	SLG	AOPS	ABR	SB-CS	FA	FR	RNG	THR	GAMES AT POSITION	DL	BFW
1882	Phi AA	72	272	34	59	6	1	0	18	15			.217	.258	.246	66	-10		.904	23	123	101	2b72,P2/OR		1.4
1883	Phi AA	89	330	67	90	8	0	1	40	19			.273	.312	.306	91	-4		.837	-22	86	68	2b88,C2		-2.0
1884	Phi AA	107	399	59	92	16	11	1		19		1	.231	.267	.333	89	-6		.870	-36	77	92	2b107/OCCP		-3.5
1885	Phi AA	106	398	71	93	9	3	1	41	21		7	.234	.284	.279	74	-12		.879	-14	92	86	2b106		-2.0
1887	Cle AA	131	534	122	141	19	4	2	53	53		3	.264	.334	.326	87	-7	86	.912	11	97	97	2b126,S6,P3		0.7
1888	Cle AA	127	493	80	115	13	6	1	33	50		6	.233	.311	.290	96	0	60	.929	24	102	121	2b122,O6R,P2		2.6
1889	Cle N	136	566	83	142	10	4	1	47	58		2	18	.251	.323	.288	73	-21	32	.932	8	96	108	2b135/S		-0.7
1890	Cle P	127	544	93	133	19	8	2	65	54		5	16	.244	.318	.320	77	-16	24	.905	3	104	98	2b109,S20		-0.7
1891	Bos AA	139	514	96	111	15	4	0	46	63		6	34	.216	.309	.261	64	-22	54	.942	24	101	148	2b139		0.5
1892	StL N	28	98	12	20	1	0	0	11	10		3	7	.204	.297	.214	58	-4	5	.939	-2	92	70	2b27/SM		-0.5
	Bal N	75	269	45	71	5	5	3	37	32		1	18	.264	.344	.353	108	3	13	.918	2	98	85	2b75		0.7
	Year	103	367	57	91	6	5	3	48	42		4	25	.248	.332	.316	95	-2	18	.923	-1	96	81	2b102/S		0.2
1893	Was N	59	218	28	39	7	1	0	20	20		0	12	.179	.248	.220	25	-24	4	.903	6	104	105	2b39,O12R,S4,3b4		-1.4
Total	11	1196	4635	790	1106	128	47	12	411	444		34	105	.239	.306	.294	78	-123	278	.907	26	97	103	2b1145,S32,O20R,P8,3b4,C3		-4.9

STRICKLAND, GEORGE George Bevan "Bo" B1.10.1926 New Orleans LA BR/TR/6-1/180* d5.7 M2/C11

YEAR	TM LG	G	AB	R	H	2B	3B	HR	RBI	BB-IB	HP	SO	AVG	OBP	SLG	AOPS	ABR	SB-CS	FA	FR	RNG	THR	GAMES AT POSITION	DL	BFW
1950	Pit N	23	27	0	3	0	0	0	2			8	.111	.226	.111	-8	-4	0	.978	1	93	126	S19/3		-0.2
1951	Pit N	138	454	59	98	12	7	9	47	65		3	83	.216	.318	.333	73	-17	4-2	.943	9	105	104	S125,2b13		-0.5
1952	Pit N	76	232	17	41	6	2	5	22	21		1	45	.177	.248	.284	46	-18	4-2	.953	11	112	103	2b45,S28/13		-1.2
	Cle A	31	88	8	19	4	0	1	8	14			15	.216	.324	.295	78	-2	0-0	.964	6	115	103	S30/2		0.6
1953	Cle A	123	419	43	119	17	4	5	47	51		0	52	.284	.362	.379	103	3	0-0	.974	21	109	135	S122/1		3.2
1954	†Cle A	112	361	42	77	12	3	6	37	55		1	62	.213	.314	.313	72	-13	2-1	.961	-13	95	95	S112		-1.5
1955	Cle A	130	388	34	81	9	5	2	34	49-0		3	60	.209	.302	.273	54	-25	1-0	.976	7	95	115	S128		-1.3
1956	Cle A	85	211	22	36	1	2	3	17	22-0		1	27	.211	.299	.292	56	-11	0-1	.986	8	106	128	2b28,S28,3b26		0.1
1957	Cle A	89	201	21	47	8	2	1	19	26-1		1	24	.234	.323	.308	75	-7	0-3	.980	7	99	78	2b48,S23,3b19		0.4
1959	Cle A	132	441	55	105	15	2	8	48	51-2		0	64	.238	.313	.302	74	-15	1-1	.971	-8	90	89	3b80,S50,2b41		-1.4
1960	Cle A	32	42	4	7	0	0	0	3	4-1		1	8	.167	.255	.238	35	-4	0-0	.962	-2	120	155	S14,3b12,2b2		-0.2
Total	10	971	2824	305	633	84	27	36	284	361-4		11	453	.224	.313	.311	70	-113	12-10	.963	45	102	115	S679,2b141,3b139,1b2		-1.7

STRIEF, GEORGE George Andrew B10.16.1856 Cincinnati OH D4.1.1946 Cleveland OH BR/TR/5-7/172 d5.1 U1

YEAR	TM LG	G	AB	R	H	2B	3B	HR	RBI	BB-IB	HP	SO	AVG	OBP	SLG	AOPS	ABR	SB-CS	FA	FR	RNG	THR	GAMES AT POSITION	DL	BFW
1879	Cle N	71	264	24	46	7	1	0	15	10			23	.174	.204	.208	37	-17		.918	-8	64	0	O55(1/54/1),2b16		-2.1
1882	Pit AA	79	297	45	58	9	2	0		13			.195	.229	.286	76	-7		.917	0	91	93	2b78/S		-0.5
1883	StL AA	82	302	22	68	9	0	1	22	12			.225	.255	.265	64	-12		.899	5	104	127	2b67,O15(11/1/3)		-0.9
1884	StL AA	48	184	22	37	5	2	2		13		0	.201	.254	.283	72	-6		.848	-4	95	112	O44(43/1/0),2b3/1		-0.6
	KC U	15	56	6	6	0	0	0		4			.107	.167	.196	11	-8		.900	5	119	153	2b15		-0.6
	CP U	15	53	6	11	5	0	0		3			.208	.250	.302	67	-4		.905	-1	88	25	2b15		-0.2
	Year	30	109	11	17	10	0	0		7			.156	.207	.248	40	-11		.902	4	105	94	2b30		-0.8
	Cle N	8	29	2	7	2	0	0	0	0			.241	.241	.310	70	-1		1.000	1	240	0	O6L,3b2		0.0

YEAR	TM LG	G	AB	R	H	2B	3B	HR	RBI	BB-IB	HP	SO	AVG	OBP	SLG	AOPS	ABR	SB-CS	FA	FR	RNG	THR	GAMES AT POSITION	DL	BFW
1885	Phi AA	44	175	19	48	8	5	0	27	9	0		.274	.310	.377	110	1		.828	0	98	0	3b19,S10,O8(0/4/4),2b7		0.2
Total	5	362	1360	145	281	50	14	5	64	64	0	28	.207	.242	.275	67	-54		.899	-2	96	108	2b201,O128(61/60/8),3b21,S11/1		-4.6

STRINGER, LOU Louis Bernard B5.13.1917 Grand Rapids MI BR/TR/5-11/173* d4.15 Mil 1943-45

1941	Chi N	145	512	59	126	31	4	5	53	59	0	86	.246	.324	.352	94	-4	3	.960	24	114	101	2b137,S7		2.9
1942	Chi N	121	406	45	96	10	5	9	41	31	1	55	.236	.292	.352	92	-7	3	.955	-1	106	85	2b113/3		0.0
1946	Chi N	80	209	26	51	13	1	3	19	26	0	34	.244	.328	.311	83	-5	0	.956	-9	95	54	2b62/S3		-1.1
1948	Bos A	4	11	1	1	0	0	1	1	0	0	3	.091	.091	.364	17	-2	0-0	.947	2	146	231	2b2		0.0
1949	Bos A	35	41	10	11	4	0	1	6	5	0	10	.268	.348	.439	100	0	0-0	.978	2	96	208	2b9		0.3
1950	Bos A	24	17	7	5	1	0	0	2	0	0	4	.294	.294	.353	59	-1	1-0	.778	1	141	334	3b3/2S		0.0
Total	6	409	1196	148	290	49	10	19	122	121	1	192	.242	.313	.348	90	-19	7-0	.958	20	108	91	2b324,S9,3b5		2.1

STRIPP, JOE Joseph Valentine "Jersey Joe" B2.3.1903 Harrison NJ D6.10.1989 Orlando FL BR/TR/5-11.5/175 d7.2 OF(10/0/12)

1928	Cin N	42	139	18	40	7	3	1	17	8	3	8	.288	.340	.403	95	-1	0	.931	-4	92	0	O21(10/0/11),3b17/S		-0.5
1929	Cin N	64	187	24	40	3	2	3	20	24	3	15	.214	.313	.299	55	-13	2	.960	-3	115	52	3b55,2b2		-0.6
1930	Cin N	130	464	74	142	37	6	3	64	51	2	37	.306	.377	.431	100	2	15	.996	-0	83	113	1b75,3b48		0.0
1931	Cin N	105	426	71	138	26	2	3	42	21	2	31	.324	.359	.415	114	8	5	.957	6	108	126	3b96,1b9		1.7
1932	Bro N	138	534	94	162	36	9	6	64	36	2	30	.303	.350	.438	113	9	14	.954	16	115	133	3b93,1b43		2.4
1933	Bro N	141	537	69	149	20	7	1	51	26	1	23	.277	.312	.346	92	-7	5	.967	7	99	86	3b140		0.5
1934	Bro N	104	384	50	121	19	6	1	40	22	1	20	.315	.344	.404	108	4	2	.941	-4	90	159	3b96,1b7/S		0.2
1935	Bro N	109	373	44	114	13	5	3	43	22	1	15	.306	.344	.391	99	-1	2	.962	7	116	142	3b88,1b15/OR		0.7
1936	Bro N	110	439	51	139	31	1	1	60	22	1	12	.317	.351	.399	100	1	2	.968	7	97	99	3b106		1.1
1937	Bro N	90	300	37	73	10	2	1	26	20	1	18	.243	.291	.300	60	-17	1	.971	-4	89	52	3b66,1b14,S3		-2.0
1938	StL N	54	199	24	57	7	0	0	18	18	1	10	.286	.349	.322	81	-5	0	.977	-4	82	113	3b51		-0.7
	Bos N	59	229	19	63	10	0	1	19	10	0	7	.275	.305	.332	84	-6	2	.966	-1	100	126	3b58		-0.4
	Year	113	428	43	120	17	0	1	37	28	1	17	.280	.326	.327	82	-10	2	.971	-4	92	120	3b109		-1.1
Total	11	1146	4211	575	1238	219	43	24	464	280	16	226	.294	.340	.384	96	-26	50	.961	30	102	108	3b914,1b163,O22R,S5,2b2		2.4

STRITTMATTER, MARK Mark Arthur B4.4.1969 Huntington NY BR/TR/6-1/210 [ColN92 28/795] d9.3 Col Virginia Commonwealth

| 1998 | Col N | 4 | 4 | 0 | 0 | 0 | 0 | 0 | 0 | 0-0 | 0 | 3 | .000 | .000 | .000 | -83 | -1 | 0-0 | 1.000 | 1 | 72 | 0 | C3 | | 0.0 |

STROBEL, ALLIE Albert Irving B6.11.1884 Boston MA D2.10.1955 Hollywood FL BR/TR/6-0/160 d8.29 Col Boston College

1905	Bos N	5	19	1	2	0	0	0	2	0	0		.105	.105	.105	-38	-3	0	1.000	0	101	228	3b4/OL		-0.3
1906	Bos N	100	317	28	64	10	3	1	24	29	2		.202	.273	.262	69	-12	2	.946	-6	95	98	2b93,S6/OC		-1.8
Total	2	105	336	29	66	10	3	1	26	29	2		.196	.264	.253	63	-15	2	.946	-6	95	98	2b93,S6,3b4,O2(1/1/0)		-2.1

STRONER, JIM James Melvin B5.29.1901 Chicago IL D12.6.1975 Tarboro NC BR/TR/5-10/175 d5.1

| 1929 | Pit N | 6 | 8 | 0 | 3 | 1 | 0 | 0 | 0 | 0 | 0 | | .375 | .444 | .500 | 130 | 0 | | .571 | -1 | 88 | 0 | 3b2 | | 0.0 |

STRONG, JAMAL Jamal Najar B8.5.1978 Pasadena CA BR/TR/5-10/180* [SeaA00 6/176] d9.2 Col Nebraska

2003	Sea A	12	2	2	0	0	0	0	0	0-0	0	0	.000	.000	.000	-99	-1	0-0	—	-0	0	0	O2C,D7		-0.1
2005	Sea A	16	20	6	5	0	1	0	2	2-0	1	6	.250	.333	.350	93	0	0-0	1.000	0	87	327	O11(7/4/1),D3	21	0.0
Total	2	28	22	8	5	0	1	0	2	2-0	1	6	.227	.308	.318	76	-1	0-0	1.000	0	82	309	O13(7/6/1),D10	21	-0.1

STROUD, ED Edwin Marvin B10.31.1939 Lapine AL BL/TR/5-11/180* d9.11

1966	Chi A	12	36	3	6	2	0	0	1	2-0	1	8	.167	.231	.222	33	-3	3-0	1.000	0	120	0	O11(4/0/7)		-0.3
1967	Chi A	20	27	6	8	0	1	0	3	1-0	1	6	.296	.345	.370	116	0	7-2	1.000	2	106	395	O12(11/0/5)		0.3
	Was A	87	204	36	41	5	3	1	10	25-0	1	29	.201	.289	.270	69	-8	8-6	.983	-7	88	28	O79(1/79/0)		-1.8
	Year	107	231	42	49	5	4	1	13	26-0	2	34	.212	.295	.281	75	-7	15-8	.985	-5	90	69	O91(12/79/5)		-1.5
1968	Was A	105	306	41	73	10	10	4	23	20-1	0	50	.239	.284	.376	102	-1	9-3	.979	-1	105	45	O84(25/7/58)		-0.6
1969	Was A	123	206	35	52	5	6	4	29	30-1	0	33	.252	.353	.393	114	4	12-2	.982	1	117	25	O85(28/1/58)		0.4
1970	Was A	129	433	69	115	11	5	5	32	40-2	3	79	.266	.331	.349	92	-5	29-8	.993	3	105	113	O118(9/106/9)	21	-0.2
1971	Chi A	53	141	19	25	4	3	0	12	11-0	0	20	.177	.237	.248	37	-12	6-4	1.000	-6	72	0	O44(8/22/20)		-2.2
Total	6	529	1353	209	320	37	28	14	100	129-4	8	224	.237	.306	.336	87	-25	72-26	.988	-7	101	62	O433(86/215/157)	21	-4.4

STROUGHTER, STEVE Stephen Lewis B3.15.1952 Visalia CA BL/TR/6-2/190 [SFN71 A1/6] d4.7 Col Sequoias (CA) [JC]

| 1982 | Sea A | 26 | 47 | 4 | 8 | 1 | 0 | 1 | 3 | 3-1 | 1 | 9 | .170 | .235 | .255 | 33 | -4 | 0-0 | 1.000 | 1 | 194 | 975 | O3L,D9 | | -0.3 |

STRUEVE, AL Albert Frederick B6.26.1860 Cincinnati OH D1.28.1929 Buckskin Twp. OH d6.22

| 1884 | StL AA | 2 | 7 | 2 | 2 | 0 | 0 | 0 | 0 | 0 | 0 | | .286 | .286 | .286 | 84 | 0 | | — | 1 | 0 | 0 | /OCC | | 0.1 |

STRUNK, AMOS Amos Aaron B1.22.1889 Philadelphia PA D7.22.1979 Llanerch PA BL/TL/5-11.5/175 d9.24

1908	Phi A	12	34	4	8	1	0	0	4	0	0		.235	.316	.265	83	0	0	.903	0	74	271	O11(1/10/0)		-0.1
1909	Phi A	11	35	1	4	0	0	0	2	1	0		.114	.139	.114	-20	-5	2	1.000	0	245	0	O9(1/8/0)		-0.6
1910	Phi A	16	48	9	16	0	1	0	2	3	0		.333	.373	.375	135	2	4	1.000	1	121	51	O14C		0.2
1911	†Phi A	74	215	42	55	7	2	1	21	35	0		.256	.363	.321	93	0	13	.958	-2	104	116	O62(19/43/0),1b2		-0.2
1912	Phi A	122	412	58	119	13	12	3	63	47	3		.289	.366	.400	123	13	29	.990	8	112	99	O116(65/51/0)		1.4
1913	†Phi A	94	292	30	89	11	12	0	46	29	0	23	.305	.368	.425	135	12	14	.962	-2	100	74	O81C		0.4
1914	†Phi A	122	404	58	111	15	5	4	45	57	0	38	.275	.364	.342	117	11	25-22	.987	6	111	93	O120(12/108/0)		0.8
1915	Phi A	132	485	76	144	28	16	1	45	56	1	45	.297	.371	.427	144	25	17-19	.980	10	106	165	O111(0/59/52),1b19		2.6
1916	Phi A	150	544	71	172	30	9	3	49	66	3	59	.316	.393	.421	152	36	21-23	.978	0	98	108	O143(6/119/18),1b7		2.5
1917	Phi A	148	540	83	152	26	7	1	45	68	1	37	.281	.363	.361	123	17	16	.986	-5	100	146	O146C		0.1
1918	†Bos A	114	413	50	106	18	9	0	35	36	0	13	.257	.316	.364	101	-1	20	.988	-6	90	85	O113(1/112/0)		-1.6
1919	Bos A	48	184	27	50	11	3	0	17	13	1	13	.272	.323	.364	98	-1	3	.968	-4	94	55	O48C		-0.9
	Phi A	60	194	15	41	6	4	0	13	23	1	15	.211	.298	.284	63	-10	3	.981	-1	97	0	O52(0/10/42)		-1.4
	Year	108	378	42	91	17	7	0	30	36	2	28	.241	.310	.323	79	-11	6	.974	-5	96	75	O100(0/58/42)		-2.3
1920	Phi A	58	202	23	60	9	3	0	20	21	0	9	.297	.363	.371	94	-1	0-6	.990	-4	97	29	O54(6/10/38)		-1.0
	Chi A	53	188	33	45	8	1	1	16	28	0	15	.239	.338	.309	72	-7	1-0	.981	-1	109	47	O49(3/7/38)		-1.0
	Year	111	390	56	105	17	4	1	36	49	0	24	.269	.351	.341	83	-8	1-6	.985	-5	103	38	O103(9/17/76)		-2.0
1921	Chi A	121	401	68	133	19	10	3	69	38	1	27	.332	.391	.451	116	10	7-10	.970	-6	93	76	O111(9/69/33)		-0.4
1922	Chi A	92	311	36	90	11	4	0	33	33	0	28	.289	.358	.350	85	-6	9-6	.989	1	99	117	O74(14/56/4),1b7		-0.9
1923	Chi A	54	54	7	17	0	0	0	8	8	0	5	.315	.403	.315	92	0	1-0	1.000	0	136	0	O5(2/3/0),1b2		0.0
1924	Chi A	1	1	0	0	0	0	0	0	0	0	0	.000	.000	.000	-99	-0		—	0			/H		0.0
	Phi A	30	42	5	6	0	0	0	1	7	0	4	.143	.265	.143	7	-6	0-0	1.000	-1	62	0	O8(4/1/3)		-0.7
	Year	31	43	5	6	0	0	0	1	7	0	4	.140	.260	.140	5	-6	0-0	1.000	-1	62	0	O8(4/1/3)		-0.7
Total	17	1512	4999	696	1418	213	96	15	530	573	12	331	.284	.359	.374	112	89	185-86	.980	-2	102	92	O1327(143/955/228),1b37		-0.8

STUART, LUKE Luther Lane B5.23.1892 Alamance Co. NC D6.15.1947 Winston-Salem NC BR/TR/5-8/165 d7.28 Col Guilford

| 1921 | StL A | 3 | 3 | 2 | 1 | 0 | 0 | 1 | 2 | 0 | 0 | 1 | .333 | .333 | 1.333 | 291 | 1 | 0-0 | 1.000 | -0 | 58 | 0 | 2b3 | | 0.0 |

STUART, DICK Richard Lee "Dr. Strangeglove" B11.7.1932 San Francisco CA D12.15.2002 Redwood City CA BR/TR/6-4/212(200-215) d7.10

1958	Pit N	67	254	38	68	12	5	16	48	11-1	5	75	.268	.310	.543	124	7	0-0	.973	-1	109	124	1b64		0.2
1959	Pit N	118	397	64	118	15	2	27	78	42-7	2	86	.297	.362	.549	141	23	1-1	.976	0	113	108	1b105/OL		1.7
1960	†Pit N	122	438	48	114	17	5	23	83	39-5	0	107	.260	.317	.479	115	7	0-0	.986	0	106	117	1b108		0.2
1961	Pit N★	138	532	83	160	28	8	35	117	34-1	4	121	.301	.344	.581	140	28	0-3	.983	1	107	123	1b132/OL		1.9
1962	Pit N	114	394	52	90	11	4	16	64	32-1	2	94	.228	.286	.398	83	-11	0-1	.982	2	112	119	1b101		-1.6
1963	Bos A	157	612	81	160	25	4	42	118	44-2	1	144	.261	.312	.521	125	17	0-1	.979	7	118	81	1b155		1.5
1964	Bos A	156	603	73	168	27	1	33	114	37-7	3	130	.279	.321	.491	117	12	0-0	.981	-0	100	80	1b155		0.3
1965	Phi N	149	538	53	126	19	1	28	95	39-8	3	136	.234	.287	.429	101	-1	1-0	.986	-3	109	47	1b143/3		-0.6
1966	NY N	31	87	7	19	0	0	4	9	8-2	0	29	.218	.292	.356	81	-2	0-1	.974	-1	96	109	1b23	17	-0.6
	†LA N	38	91	4	24	1	0	3	9	11-0	2	17	.264	.356	.374	112	2	0-1	.991	4	166	104	1b25		0.4
	Year	69	178	11	43	1	0	7	22	20-2	2	43	.242	.325	.365	97	-1	0-2	.982	3	131	106	1b48		-0.2
1969	Cal A	22	51	3	8	2	0	1	4	3-0	2	21	.157	.204	.255	29	-5	0-0	.991	-1	54	128	1b13		-0.8
Total	10	1112	3997	506	1055	157	30	228	743	301-34	22	957	.264	.316	.489	114	77	2-7	.982	13	110	102	1b1024,O2L/3	17	2.6

YEAR	TM LG	G	AB	R	H	2B	3B	HR	RBI	BB-IB	HP	SO	AVG	OBP	SLG	AOPS	ABR	SB-CS	FA	FR	RNG	THR	GAMES AT POSITION	DL	BFW

STUART, BILL William Alexander "Chauncey" B8.28.1873 Boalsburg PA D10.14.1928 Fort Worth TX 5-11/170 d8.15 Col Penn St.

1895	Pit N	19	77	5	19	3	0	0	10	2	1	6	.247	.275	.286	47	-6	2	.913	-1	99	72	S17,2b2		-0.5
1899	NY N	1	3	0	0	0	0	0	0	0	0		.000	.000	.000	-99	-1	0	1.000	0	93	0	/2		-0.1
Total	2	20	80	5	19	3	0	0	10	2	1	6	.237	.265	.286	42	-7	2	.913	-1	99	72	S17,2b3		-0.6

STUBBS, FRANKLIN Franklin Lee B10.21.1960 Richlands NC BL/TL/6-2/215* [LAN82 1/19] d4.28 Col VPI

1984	LA N	87	217	22	42	2	3	8	17	24-3	0	63	.194	.273	.341	72	-9	2-2	.993	2	138	94	1b51,O20(6/3/13)		-1.2
1985	LA N	10	9	0	2	0	0	0	2	0-0	0	3	.222	.222	.222	25	-1	0-0	1.000	-0	0	117	1b4		-0.1
1986	LA N	132	420	55	95	11	1	23	58	37-11	2	107	.226	.291	.421	101	-2	7-1	.969	3	101	140	O124(108/23/15),1b13		-0.3
1987	LA N	129	386	48	90	16	3	16	52	31-9	1	85	.233	.290	.415	87	-9	8-1	.994	6	117	90	1b111,O18(13/0/6)	21	-0.8
1988	†LA N	115	242	30	54	13	0	8	34	23-3	1	61	.223	.288	.376	93	-2	11-3	.978	4	126	99	1b84,O13(7/1/6)		-0.2
1989	LA N	69	103	11	30	6	0	4	15	16-2	0	27	.291	.387	.466	145	7	3-2	.948	4	117	262	O28(22/5/3),1b7	43	1.0
1990	Hou N	146	448	59	117	23	2	23	71	48-3	2	114	.261	.334	.475	124	14	19-6	.991	-7	89	100	1b72,O71(67/0/5)		0.2
1991	Mil A	103	362	48	77	16	2	11	38	35-3	2	71	.213	.282	.359	79	-11	13-4	.991	4	124	100	1b92,O4L,D4		-1.2
1992	Mil A	92	288	37	66	11	1	9	42	27-3	1	68	.229	.297	.368	87	-6	11-8	.987	5	134	92	1b68,D16/OR		-0.7
1995	Det A	62	116	13	29	11	0	2	19	19-1	1	27	.250	.358	.397	97	-0	0-1	.972	-2	56	111	1b20,O20L,D3	26	-0.5
Total	10	945	2591	323	602	109	12	104	348	260-38	10	626	.232	.303	.404	96	-19	74-28	.989	16	118	96	1b522,O299(247/32/49),D23	90	-3.8

STUBING, MOOSE Lawrence George B3.31.1938 Bronx NY BL/TL/6-3/220 d8.14 M1/C6

1967	Cal A	5	5	0	0	0	0	0	0	0-0	0	4	.000	.000	.000	-99	-1	0-0	—	0			/H		-0.1

STUDLEY, SEEM Seymour L. "Warhorse" B5.1841 Byron NY D7.19.1901 Grand Island NE 5-7.5/180 d4.20

1872	Nat NA	5	21	3	2	0	0	0	2	0		1	.095	.095	.095	-35	-4	0	.571	-2	0	0	O5C		-0.4

STUMPF, GEORGE George Frederick B12.15.1910 New Orleans LA D3.6.1993 Metairie LA BL/TL/5-8/155 d9.19

1931	Bos A	7	28	2	7	1	1	0	4	1	0	2	.250	.276	.357	69	-2	0-0	1.000	-0	96	0	O7(6/2/0)		-0.2
1932	Bos A	79	169	18	34	2	2	1	18	18	0	21	.201	.278	.254	40	-16	1-1	.952	-2	95	65	O51(17/2/32)		-1.9
1933	Bos A	22	41	8	14	3	0	0	5	4	0	2	.341	.400	.415	117	1	4-0	1.000	-0	110	0	O15(3/8/4)		0.2
1936	Chi A	10	22	3	6	1	0	0	1	3	0	1	.273	.333	.318	59	-1	0-0	1.000	0	93	243	O4L		-0.1
Total	4	118	260	31	61	7	3	1	32	25	0	26	.235	.302	.296	57	-18	5-1	.969	-2	97	63	O77(30/12/36)		-2.0

STUMPF, BILL William Frederick B3.21.1892 Baltimore MD D2.14.1966 Crownsville MD BR/TR/6-0.5/175 d5.11

1912	NY A	42	129	8	31	0	0	0	10	6	1		.240	.279	.240	46	-9	5	.892	-6	95	109	S26,2b8,3b5/1OC		-1.3
1913	NY A	12	29	5	6	1	0	0	1	3	0	3	.207	.281	.241	53	-2	0	.818	-3	96	0	S6,2b4/OR		-0.4
Total	2	54	158	13	37	1	0	0	11	9	1	3	.234	.280	.241	47	-11	5	.877	-8	95	87	S32,2b12,3b5,O2(0/1/1)/1		-1.7

STURDY, GUY Guy B8.7.1899 Sherman TX D5.4.1965 Marshall TX BL/TL/6-0.5/180 d9.30

1927	StL A	5	21	5	9	1	0	0	5	1	0	0	.429	.455	.476	137	1	2-0	.974	-0	69	54	1b5		0.1
1928	StL A	54	45	3	10	1	0	1	8	8	0	4	.222	.340	.311	70	-2	1-0	1.000	-0	0	0	/1		-0.2
Total	2	59	66	8	19	2	0	1	13	9	0	4	.288	.373	.364	91	-1	3-0	.975	-1	66	51	1b6		-0.1

STURGEON, BOBBY Robert Howard B8.6.1919 Clinton IN BR/TR/6-0/175 d4.16 Mil 1943-45

1940	Chi N	7	21	1	4	1	0	0	2	0	0	1	.190	.190	.238	18	-2	0	.848	-1	91	123	S7		-0.3
1941	Chi N	129	433	45	106	15	3	0	25	9	0	30	.245	.260	.293	58	-26	5	.956	-0	101	98	S126/23		-1.9
1942	Chi N	63	162	8	40	7	1	0	7	4	1	13	.247	.269	.302	70	-7	2	.988	13	125	106	2b32,S29,3b2		1.0
1946	Chi N	100	294	26	87	12	2	1	21	10	0	18	.296	.319	.361	94	-4	0	.934	-10	90	92	S72,2b21		-1.0
1947	Chi N	87	232	16	59	10	5	0	21	7	0	12	.254	.276	.341	66	-13	0	.975	11	108	104	S45,2b30,3b5		0.1
1948	Bos N	34	78	10	17	3	1	0	4	4	0	5	.218	.256	.308	46	-6	0	.938	-4	97	113	2b18,S4,3b4		-0.9
Total	6	420	1220	106	313	48	12	1	80	34	1	79	.257	.277	.318	68	-58	7	.951	9	100	100	S283,2b102,3b12		-3.0

STURGIS, DEAN Dean Donnell B12.1.1892 Beloit KS D6.4.1950 Uniontown PA BR/TR/6-1/180 d5.1 Col Bucknell

1914	Phi A	4	4	1	1	0	0	0	2	1	0		.250	.400	.250	100	0	1.000	0	87	138	/C		0.0

STURM, JOHNNY John Peter Joseph B1.23.1916 St.Louis MO D10.8.2004 St.Louis MO BL/TL/6-1/185 d4.14 Mil 1942-45

1941	†NY A	124	524	58	125	17	3	3	36	37	3	50	.239	.293	.300	58	-33	3-5	.990	-2	94	117	1b124		-4.2

STUTZ, GEORGE George "Kid","Satan" B2.12.1893 Philadelphia PA D12.29.1930 Philadelphia PA BR/TR/5-5/150 d8.17

1926	Phi N	6	9	0	0	0	0	0	0	0	0		.000	.000	.000	-95	-2	0	.938	0	95	127	S5		-0.2

STYLES, LENA William Graves B11.27.1899 Gurley AL D3.14.1956 Hunstville AL BR/TR/6-1/185 d9.10 Col Alabama

1919	Phi A	8	22	0	6	1	0	0	5	1	0	6	.273	.304	.318	74	-1	0	.974	-0	76	93	C8		-0.1
1920	Phi A	24	50	1	13	3	1	0	5	6	0	7	.260	.339	.360	84	-1	1-0	.966	1	111	195	C9,1b7		0.6
1921	Phi A	4	5	0	1	0	0	0	0	0	0	2	.200	.200	.200	2	-1	0-0	.333	-1	0	237	C2		-0.0
1930	Cin N	7	12	2	3	0	1	0	1	1	1	2	.250	.357	.417	91	-0	0-0	.875	-0	70	184	C5/1		0.0
1931	Cin N	34	87	7	21	3	0	0	5	8	1	7	.241	.313	.276	63	-4	0	.949	-5	84	51	C31		-0.8
Total	5	77	176	14	44	7	2	0	16	16	2	24	.250	.320	.313	71	-7	1-0	.929	-6	83	93	C55,1b8		-1.1

STYNES, CHRIS Christopher Desmond B1.19.1973 Queens NY BR/TR/5-10/185(175-205) [TorA91 3/94] d5.19 OF(134/2/22)

1995	KC A	22	35	7	6	1	0	0	4	4-0	0	3	.171	.256	.200	20	-4	0-0	.982	0	111	204	2b17,D2		-0.1
1996	KC A	36	92	8	27	6	0	0	6	2-0	0	5	.293	.309	.359	68	-5	5-2	.939	-3	93	91	O19L,2b5,3b2,D3		-0.2
1997	Cin N	49	198	31	69	7	1	6	28	11-1	4	13	.348	.394	.485	126	7	11-2	.976	3	112	204	O38L,2b8,3b3		1.6
1998	Cin N	123	347	52	88	10	1	6	27	32-1	4	36	.254	.323	.340	74	-13	15-1	1.000	5	108	100	O80(64/2/20),3b22,2b11,S2		-0.8
1999	Cin N	73	113	18	27	1	0	2	14	12-1	5	17	.239	.310	.301	54	-8	5-2	.956	-9	82	70	2b43,3b8,O4L		-1.4
2000	Cin N	119	380	71	127	24	1	12	40	32-2	2	54	.334	.386	.497	118	11	5-2	.966	-4	88	106	3b77,2b15,O8(6/0/2)		0.7
2001	Bos A	96	361	52	101	19	2	8	33	20-0	3	56	.280	.322	.410	91	-5	4-5	.949	-4	81	64	3b46,2b43,O3L	46	-0.1
2002	Chi N	98	195	25	47	9	1	5	26	21-1	1	29	.241	.314	.374	85	-5	1-1	.921	-3	74	48	3b40,2b20		-0.7
2003	Col N	138	443	71	113	31	3	11	73	48-1	6	76	.255	.335	.413	83	-10	3-1	.972	3	104	99	3b119,2b5		-0.8
2004	Pit N	74	162	16	35	10	0	1	16	9-2	2	25	.216	.266	.296	45	-13	0-0	.992	1	100	106	3b71		-1.7
Total	10	828	2326	351	640	118	9	51	265	191-9	22	308	.275	.335	.399	87	-45	49-16	.965	-10	95	93	3b388,2b167,O152L,D5,S2	46	-4.4

STYNES, NEIL Cornelius William B12.10.1868 Arlington MA D3.26.1944 Somerville MA BR/TR/6-0/165 d9.8

1890	Cle P	2	8	0	0	0	0	0	0	0	0	0	.000	.000	.000	-99	-2	0	.786	-1	70	0	C2		-0.0

SUAREZ, KEN Kenneth Raymond B4.12.1943 Tampa FL BR/TR/5-9/175* d4.14 Col Florida St.

1966	KC A	35	69	5	10	1	0	2	5	10-1	0	26	.145	.298	.174	41	-5	2-0	.954	-1	58	175	C34		-0.1
1967	KC A	39	63	7	15	1	0	2	9	16-1	1	11	.238	.387	.413	143	5	1-0	.979	5	93	175	C36		1.1
1968	Cle A	17	10	1	1	0	0	0	1	0-0	0	3	.100	.182	.100	-13	-0	0-0	1.000	0	0	0	C12/23OL		-0.5
1969	Cle A	36	85	7	25	5	0	1	9	15-5	0	12	.294	.400	.388	118	3	1-0	.991	1	176	123	C36		0.5
1971	Cle A	50	123	10	25	7	0	1	9	18-3	2	15	.203	.310	.285	65	-5	0-1	.993	1	121	113	C48		-0.5
1972	Tex A	25	33	2	5	1	0	0	4	1-0	0	4	.152	.167	.182	7	-4	0-0	.965	1	318	147	C17		-0.5
1973	Tex A	93	278	25	69	11	0	1	27	33-0	5	16	.248	.334	.299	84	-4	1-2	.989	-2	91	111	C90		-0.5
Total	7	295	661	57	150	29	1	5	60	99-9	7	97	.227	.330	.247	81	-11	5-3	.984	5	111	127	C273/OL32		0.0

SUAREZ, LUIS Luis Abelardo B8.24.1916 Alto Songo, Cuba D6.5.1991 Havana, Cuba BR/TR/5-11/170 d5.28

1944	Was A	1	2	0	0	0	0	0	0	0	0	0	.000	.000	.000	-99	-1	0-0	1.000	0	159	0	/3		0.0

SUCK, TONY Anthony (b Charles Anthony Zuck) B6.11.1858 Chicago IL D1.29.1895 Chicago IL 5-9/164 d8.9

1883	Buf N	2	7	1	0	0	0	0		0		4	.000	.125	.000	-56	-1		—	-2	0	0	/OLC		-0.0
1884	CP U	53	188	18	28	2	0	0		13			.149	.204	.160	12	-26		.904	-4			C28,S15,O12(1/10/1)/3		-2.?
	Bal U	3	10	2	3	0	0	0		0			.300	.300	.300	75	-1		.882	1			C3		0.0
	Year	56	198	20	31	2	0	0		13			.157	.209	.167	15	-27		.901	-4			C31,S15,O12(1/10/1)/3		-2.?
Total	2	58	205	21	31	2	0	0		14		4	.151	.205	.161	12	-28		.894	-5			C32,S15,O13(2/10/1)/3		0.0

SUDAKIS, BILL William Paul "Suds" B3.27.1946 Joliet IL BB/TR/6-1/190* d9.3

1968	LA N	24	87	11	24	3	1	3	12	15-1	0	14	.276	.382	.471	167	8	1-0	.953	4	116	69	3b24		1.1
1969	LA N	132	462	50	108	17	5	14	53	40-5	1	94	.234	.294	.383	95	-5	3-2	.946	10	110	136	3b121		0.0
1970	LA N	94	269	37	71	11	0	14	44	35-4	3	46	.264	.352	.461	121	8	4-0	.983	-4	54	24	C38,3b37,O3R/1		0.0
1971	LA N	41	83	10	16	3	0	1	7	12-2	1	22	.193	.302	.337	85	-2	0-1	1.000	2	143	128	C19,3b3/1O(1/0/1)	49	0.0
1972	NY N	18	49	3	7	0	1	1	7	6-0	1	14	.143	.236	.204	27	-5	0-0	.967	1	186	59	1b7,C5	86	0.0

YEAR	TM LG	G	AB	R	H	2B	3B	HR	RBI	BB-IB	HP	SO	AVG	OBP	SLG	AOPS	ABR	SB-CS	FA	FR	RNG	THR	GAMES AT POSITION	DL	BFW
1973	Tex A	82	235	32	60	11	0	15	43	23-1	0	53	.255	.320	.494	131	9	0-1	.962	-2	89	19	3b29,1b24,C9,O2R,D8		0.5
1974	NY A	89	259	26	60	8	0	7	39	25-1	1	48	.232	.296	.344	86	-5	0-0	.990	1	126	120	D39,1b33,3b3/C		-0.8
1975	Cal A	30	58	4	7	2	0	1	6	12-3	1	15	.121	.274	.207	43	-4	1-1	.941	-0	14	186	D13,C5,1b2		-0.5
	Cle A	20	46	4	9	0	0	1	3	4-1	0	7	.196	.260	.261	47	-3	0-1	1.000	-0	58	118	1b12,C6		-0.5
	Year	50	104	8	16	2	0	2	9	16-4	1	22	.154	.268	.231	45	-7	1-2	1.000	-1	50	102	1b14,D13,C11		-1.0
Total 8		530	1548	177	362	56	7	59	214	172-18	7	313	.234	.311	.393	102	1	9-6	.942	11	112	116	3b217,C83,1b80,D60,O6(1/0/6)	135	0.6

SUDER, PETE Peter "Pecky" B4.16.1916 Aliquippa PA BR/TR/6-0/175* d4.15 Mil 1944-45

YEAR	TM LG	G	AB	R	H	2B	3B	HR	RBI	BB-IB	HP	SO	AVG	OBP	SLG	AOPS	ABR	SB-CS	FA	FR	RNG	THR	GAMES AT POSITION	DL	BFW
1941	Phi A	139	531	45	130	20	9	4	52	19	0	47	.245	.271	.339	62	-33	1-3	.957	-6	97	95	3b136,S3		-3.3
1942	Phi A	128	476	46	122	20	4	4	54	24	0	39	.256	.293	.340	78	-16	4-4	.954	-1	97	69	S69,3b34,2b31		-0.9
1943	Phi A	131	475	30	105	14	5	3	41	14	0	40	.221	.243	.291	56	-29	1-1	.971	-9	95	84	2b95,3b32,S5		-3.6
1946	Phi A	128	455	38	128	20	3	2	50	18	0	37	.281	.309	.352	85	-11	1-1	.959	2	102	85	S67,3b33,2b12,1b3,O2R		-0.4
1947	Phi A	145	528	45	127	28	4	5	60	35	2	44	.241	.290	.337	73	-21	0-3	.986	-21	97	96	2b140,S3,3b2		-3.7
1948	Phi A	148	519	64	125	23	5	7	60	60	1	60	.241	.321	.345	77	-18	1-3	.988	-4	101	103	2b148		-1.4
1949	Phi A	118	445	44	119	24	6	10	75	23	0	35	.267	.306	.416	93	-9	0-1	.975	5	107	122	2b89,3b36,S2		0.0
1950	Phi A	77	248	34	61	10	0	8	35	23	0	31	.246	.310	.383	78	-9	2-2	.979	2	106	120	2b47,3b11,S10,1b4		-0.4
1951	Phi A	123	440	46	108	18	1	1	42	30	1	42	.245	.295	.298	59	-26	5-5	.987	11	107	119	2b103,S18,3b3		-0.9
1952	Phi A	74	228	22	55	7	2	1	20	16	0	17	.241	.291	.303	61	-12	1-1	.991	1	98	109	2b43,S17,3b16		-0.9
1953	Phi A	115	454	44	130	11	3	4	35	17	0	35	.286	.312	.350	76	-17	3-3	.974	3	109	103	3b72,2b38,S7		-1.2
1954	Phi A	69	205	8	41	11	1	0	16	7	0	16	.200	.225	.263	34	-19	0-0	.961	4	105	102	2b35,3b20,S2		-1.4
1955	KC A	26	81	3	17	4	1	0	1	2-0	0	13	.210	.229	.284	37	-8	0-1	.990	-2	88	106	2b24		-0.9
Total 13		1421	5085	469	1268	210	44	49	541	288-0	7	456	.249	.290	.337	71	-228	19-28	.982	-15	101	103	2b805,3b395,S203,1b7,O2R		-19.0

SUERO, WILLIAM Williams (Urban) B11.7.1966 Santo Domingo, D.R. D11.30.1995 Santo Domingo, D.R. BR/TR/5-9/175* d4.9

YEAR	TM LG	G	AB	R	H	2B	3B	HR	RBI	BB-IB	HP	SO	AVG	OBP	SLG	AOPS	ABR	SB-CS	FA	FR	RNG	THR	GAMES AT POSITION	DL	BFW
1992	Mil A	18	16	4	3	1	0	0	0	2-0	1	1	.188	.316	.250	61	-1	1-1	.971	2	134	154	2b15/SD		0.1
1993	Mil A	15	14	0	4	0	0	0	0	1-0	0	3	.286	.333	.286	69	-1	0-1	.944	1	137	50	2b8/3		0.0
Total 2		33	30	4	7	1	0	0	0	3-0	1	4	.233	.324	.267	65	-2	1-2	.962	3	135	117	2b23,D2/3S		0.1

SUGDEN, JOE Joseph B7.31.1870 Philadelphia PA D6.28.1959 Philadelphia PA BB/TR/5-10/180 d7.20 C7

YEAR	TM LG	G	AB	R	H	2B	3B	HR	RBI	BB-IB	HP	SO	AVG	OBP	SLG	AOPS	ABR	SB-CS	FA	FR	RNG	THR	GAMES AT POSITION	DL	BFW
1893	Pit N	27	92	20	24	4	3	0	12	10	1	11	.261	.340	.370	90	-1	1	.956	1	99	103	C27		0.1
1894	Pit N	39	139	23	46	13	2	2	23	14	3	2	.331	.404	.496	117	4	3	.910	-5	103	89	C31,3b4,S3/OC		0.2
1895	Pit N	50	158	28	48	4	1	1	17	16	3	12	.304	.379	.361	97	0	4	.901	-3	88	122	C50		0.1
1896	Pit N	80	301	42	89	5	7	0	36	19	5	9	.296	.348	.359	90	-5	5	.952	-5	84	100	C70,1b7,O4C		-0.3
1897	Pit N	84	288	31	64	6	4	0	38	18	3		.222	.275	.271	46	-23	9	.941	-12	83	94	C81,1b3		-2.4
1898	StL N	89	289	29	73	7	1	0	34	23	3		.253	.314	.284	70	-11	5	.937	-6	74	137	C60,O15(0/1/14),1b8		-1.2
1899	Cle N	76	250	19	69	5	1	0	14	11	0		.276	.307	.304	73	-10	2	.935	-18	59	129	C66,O4R,1b3/3		-2.0
1901	Chi A	48	153	21	42	7	1	0	19	13	2		.275	.339	.333	89	-2	4	.970	5	115	103	C42,1b5		0.7
1902	StL A	68	200	25	50	7	2	0	15	20	4		.250	.306	.305	78	-5	2	.956	-0	110	100	C61,1b4/P		0.0
1903	StL A	79	241	18	51	4	0	0	22	25	1		.212	.288	.228	58	-11	4	.983	7	121	102	C66,1b8		0.3
1904	StL A	105	348	25	93	6	3	0	30	28	5		.267	.331	.302	107	4	6	.989	-3	94	100	C79,1b28		0.9
1905	StL A	90	266	21	46	4	0	0	23	23	3		.173	.247	.188	41	-17	3	.983	7	81	118	C76,1b9		-0.3
1912	Det A	1	4	1	1	0	0	0	0	0	0		.250	.250	.250	44	0	0	.941	1	410	0	/1		0.0
Total 13		836	2729	303	696	72	25	3	283	220	33	34	.255	.318	.303	78	-77	48	.957	-32	91	109	C709,1b76,O24(0/6/18),3b5,S3/P		-3.9

SUHR, GUS August Richard B1.3.1906 San Francisco CA D1.15.2004 Scottsdale AZ BL/TR/6-0/180 d4.15

YEAR	TM LG	G	AB	R	H	2B	3B	HR	RBI	BB-IB	HP	SO	AVG	OBP	SLG	AOPS	ABR	SB-CS	FA	FR	RNG	THR	GAMES AT POSITION	DL	BFW
1930	Pit N	151	542	93	155	26	14	17	107	80	2	56	.286	.380	.480	106	5	11	.992	-7	83	97	1b151		-1.0
1931	Pit N	87	270	26	57	13	4	4	32	38	0	25	.211	.308	.333	73	-10	4	.993	-0	100	118	1b76		-1.7
1932	Pit N	154	581	78	153	31	16	5	81	63	2	39	.263	.337	.398	99	-1	7	.988	-10	79	92	1b154		-2.6
1933	Pit N	154	566	72	151	31	11	10	75	72	0	52	.267	.350	.413	117	14	2	.991	-3	91	97	1b154		-0.4
1934	Pit N	151	573	67	162	36	13	13	103	66	3	52	.283	.360	.459	115	13	4	.994	-4	85	94	1b151		-0.5
1935	Pit N	153	529	68	144	33	12	10	81	70	0	54	.272	.357	.437	109	8	6	.989	-7	80	86	1b149,O2R		-1.2
1936	Pit N☆	156	583	111	182	33	12	11	118	95	2	34	.312	.410	.467	133	31	8	.993	-5	86	86	1b156		1.1
1937	Pit N	151	575	69	160	28	14	5	97	83	0	42	.278	.369	.402	109	10	2	.993	-4	85	94	1b151		-0.9
1938	Pit N	145	530	82	156	35	14	3	64	87	0	37	.294	.394	.430	126	22	4	.993	-10	77	124	1b145		-0.2
1939	Pit N	63	204	23	59	10	2	1	31	25	0	23	.289	.367	.373	101	1	4	.993	-5	66	88	1b52		-0.9
	Phi N	60	198	21	63	12	2	3	24	34	1	14	.318	.421	.444	137	12	1	.995	0	98	90	1b60		0.7
	Year	123	402	44	122	22	4	4	55	59	1	37	.303	.394	.408	118	13	5	.994	-4	83	89	1b112		-0.2
1940	Phi N	10	25	4	4	0	0	2	5	5	0	5	.160	.300	.400	95	-0	2	.967	-2	25	96	1b7		-0.2
Total 11		1435	5176	714	1446	288	114	84	818	718	10	433	.279	.368	.428	112	105	53	.992	-56	84	97	1b1406,O2R		-7.8

SUKEFORTH, CLYDE Clyde Leroy "Sukey" B11.30.1901 Washington ME D9.3.2000 Waldoboro ME BL/TR/5-10/155 d5.23 M1/C15 Col Georgetown

YEAR	TM LG	G	AB	R	H	2B	3B	HR	RBI	BB-IB	HP	SO	AVG	OBP	SLG	AOPS	ABR	SB-CS	FA	FR	RNG	THR	GAMES AT POSITION	DL	BFW
1926	Cin N	1	1	0	0	0	0	0	0	0	0	0	1.000	.000	.000	-99	0	0	—	0			/H		0.0
1927	Cin N	38	58	12	11	2	0	0	2	7	0	2	.190	.277	.224	37	-5	2	.970	-0	81	77	C24		-0.4
1928	Cin N	33	53	5	7	2	1	0	3	3	0	5	.132	.179	.208	1	-8	0	.966	0	99	83	C26		-0.7
1929	Cin N	84	237	31	84	16	2	1	33	17	0	6	.354	.398	.451	115	6	8	.981	-2	109	100	C76		0.8
1930	Cin N	94	296	30	84	9	3	1	19	17	1	12	.284	.325	.345	65	-17	0	.976	-2	92	109	C82		-1.2
1931	Cin N	112	351	22	90	15	4	0	25	38	3	13	.256	.334	.322	82	-8	0	.965	-9	84	97	C106		-1.1
1932	Bro N	59	111	14	26	4	0	0	12	6	1	10	.234	.280	.342	68	-6	1	.991	-2	93	89	C36		-0.6
1933	Bro N	20	36	1	2	0	0	0	0	1	0	1	.056	.105	.056	-55	-7	0	.983	2	85	103	C18		-0.5
1934	Bro N	27	43	5	7	1	0	0	1	1	0	6	.163	.182	.186	-1	-6	0	1.000	-0	83	112	C18		-0.6
1945	Bro N	18	51	2	15	1	0	0	1	4	0	1	.294	.345	.314	85	-1	0	.947	-2	98	0	C13		-0.3
Total 10		486	1237	122	326	50	14	2	96	95	5	57	.264	.319	.331	71	-52	12	.974	-16	92	95	C399		-4.6

SULARZ, GUY Guy Patrick B11.7.1955 Minneapolis MN BR/TR/5-11/165* [SFN74 10/235] d9.2

YEAR	TM LG	G	AB	R	H	2B	3B	HR	RBI	BB-IB	HP	SO	AVG	OBP	SLG	AOPS	ABR	SB-CS	FA	FR	RNG	THR	GAMES AT POSITION	DL	BFW
1980	SF N	25	65	3	16	1	1	0	3	9-1	0	6	.246	.333	.292	80	-2	1-0	.975	7	125	114	2b21,3b5		0.7
1981	SF N	10	20	0	4	0	0	0	2	2-0	1	4	.200	.292	.200	47	-1	0-1	1.000	2	118	95	2b6/3		0.1
1982	SF N	63	101	15	23	3	0	1	7	9-0	0	11	.228	.291	.287	63	-5	3-0	.961	6	111	166	S37,3b14,2b9		0.4
1983	SF N	10	20	3	2	0	0	0	0	3-0	0	2	.100	.217	.100	-10	-3	0-0	.917	1	98	83	S6,3b4		-0.1
Total 4		108	206	21	45	4	1	1	12	23-1	1	23	.218	.297	.262	60	-11	4-1	.954	16	109	153	S43,2b36,3b24		1.1

SULIK, ERNIE Ernest Richard "Dave" B7.7.1910 San Francisco CA D5.31.1963 Oakland CA BL/TL/5-10/178 d4.15 Col San Francisco

YEAR	TM LG	G	AB	R	H	2B	3B	HR	RBI	BB-IB	HP	SO	AVG	OBP	SLG	AOPS	ABR	SB-CS	FA	FR	RNG	THR	GAMES AT POSITION	DL	BFW
1936	Phi N	122	404	69	116	14	4	6	36	40	1	22	.287	.353	.386	90	-5	4	.971	-3	97	85	O105(41/65/1)		-1.1

SULLIVAN B Bristol RI d5.15

YEAR	TM LG	G	AB	R	H	2B	3B	HR	RBI	BB-IB	HP	SO	AVG	OBP	SLG	AOPS	ABR	SB-CS	FA	FR	RNG	THR	GAMES AT POSITION	DL	BFW
1875	NH NA	2	8	3	3	0	0	0	2	0		1	.375	.375	.375	185	1	1-0	1.000	-0	0	0	O2R		0.1

SULLIVAN, ANDY Andrew Raymond B8.30.1884 Southborough MA D2.14.1920 Framingham MA TR d9.13

YEAR	TM LG	G	AB	R	H	2B	3B	HR	RBI	BB-IB	HP	SO	AVG	OBP	SLG	AOPS	ABR	SB-CS	FA	FR	RNG	THR	GAMES AT POSITION	DL	BFW
1904	Bos N	1	1	0	0	0	0	0	0	0	0	1	.000	.000	.000	-64	0	0	1.000	-0	0	0	/S		0.0

SULLIVAN, JACKIE Carl Mancel B2.22.1918 Princeton TX D10.15.1992 Dallas TX BR/TR/5-11/172 d7.6

YEAR	TM LG	G	AB	R	H	2B	3B	HR	RBI	BB-IB	HP	SO	AVG	OBP	SLG	AOPS	ABR	SB-CS	FA	FR	RNG	THR	GAMES AT POSITION	DL	BFW
1944	Det A	1	1	0	0	0	0	0	0	0	0	0	.000	.000	.000	-95	0	0-0	1.000	-0	0	0	/2		0.0

SULLIVAN, CORY Cory B8.20.1979 Tulsa OK BL/TL/6-0/180 d4.4 Col Wake Forest

YEAR	TM LG	G	AB	R	H	2B	3B	HR	RBI	BB-IB	HP	SO	AVG	OBP	SLG	AOPS	ABR	SB-CS	FA	FR	RNG	THR	GAMES AT POSITION	DL	BFW
2005	Col N	139	378	64	111	15	4	4	30	28-0	3	83	.294	.343	.386	80	-10	12-3	.986	3	103	148	O114(24/83/8)		-0.6

SULLIVAN, DAN Daniel C. "Link" B5.9.1857 Providence RI D10.26.1893 Providence RI TR/5-11/194 d5.2

YEAR	TM LG	G	AB	R	H	2B	3B	HR	RBI	BB-IB	HP	SO	AVG	OBP	SLG	AOPS	ABR	SB-CS	FA	FR	RNG	THR	GAMES AT POSITION	DL	BFW
1882	Lou AA	67	286	44	78	8	2	0		9			.273	.295	.315	112	4		.878	5			C54,3b10,O4(0/3/1)/S		1.3
1883	Lou AA	36	145	8	31	5	2	0		3			.214	.230	.276	67	-5		.900	-6			C31,O2C,3b2/S		-0.7
1884	Lou AA	63	247	27	59	8	6	0	26	9	1		.239	.268	.320	95	-1		.930	-14			C63/OL		-0.9
1885	Lou AA	13	44	3	8	1	0	0	3	6	0		.182	.234	.205	40	-3		.948	-2			C13		-0.4
	StL AA	17	60	4	7	2	0	0	3	6	0		.117	.197	.150	10	-6		.956	2			C13,1b4		-0.3
	Year	30	104	7	15	3	0	0	6	12	0		.144	.213	.173	22	-9		.952	-0			C26,1b4		-0.7
1886	Pit AA	1	4	0	0	0	0	0	0	0	0		.000	.000	.000	-99	-1	0	.600	-1			/C		-0.2
Total 5		197	786	86	183	24	10	0	33	29	2		.233	.262	.289	84	-12	0	.909	-16			C175,3b12,O7(1/5/1),1b4,S2		-1.2

YEAR	TM LG	G	AB	R	H	2B	3B	HR	RBI	BB-IB	HP	SO	AVG	OBP	SLG	AOPS	ABR	SB-CS	FA	FR	RNG	THR	GAMES AT POSITION	DL	BFW

SULLIVAN, DENNY — Dennis J. B6.26.1858 Boston MA D12.31.1925 Boston MA TR/5-9/170 d8.25 Col Holy Cross

YEAR	TM LG	G	AB	R	H	2B	3B	HR	RBI	BB-IB	HP	SO	AVG	OBP	SLG	AOPS	ABR	SB-CS	FA	FR	RNG	THR	GAMES AT POSITION	BFW
1879	Pro N	5	19	5	5	2	0	0	2	1		1	.263	.300	.368	121	1		.429	-3	63	0	3b4/OR	-0.2
1880	Bos N	1	4	1	1	0	0	0	2	0		1	.250	.250	.250	72	0		.857	-0			/C	-0.1
Total	2	6	23	6	6	2	0	0	4	1		2	.261	.292	.348	113	1		.429	-4			3b4/COR	-0.3

SULLIVAN, DENNY — Dennis William B9.28.1882 Hillsboro WI D6.2.1956 W.Los Angeles CA BL/TR/5-10/? d4.22

YEAR	TM LG	G	AB	R	H	2B	3B	HR	RBI	BB-IB	HP	SO	AVG	OBP	SLG	AOPS	ABR	SB-CS	FA	FR	RNG	THR	GAMES AT POSITION	BFW
1905	Was A	3	11	0	0	0	0	0	0	0			.000	.083	.000	-76	-2	0	1.000	-0	0		O3R	-0.3
1907	Bos A	144	551	73	135	18	0	1	26	44	12		.245	.315	.283	92	-3	16	.975	-1	89	79	O143C	-1.2
1908	Bos A	101	355	33	85	7	8	0	25	14	4		.239	.276	.304	86	-7	4	.981	5	152	132	O97(0/92/5)	-0.8
	Cle A	4	6	0	0	0	0	0	0	0			.000	.000	.000	-99	-1	0	1.000	-0	0		O2(1/0/1)	-0.2
	Year	105	361	33	85	7	8	0	25	14	4		.235	.272	.299	83	-8	4	.982	4	150	130	O99(1/92/6)	-1.0
1909	Cle A	3	2	0	1	0	0	0	0	0			.500	.500	.500	207	0	0	—	0	0		O2R	0.0
Total	4	255	925	106	221	25	8	1	51	59	16		.239	.296	.286	87	-13	20	.978	3	113	99	O247(1/235/11)	-2.5

SULLIVAN, HAYWOOD — Haywood Cooper B12.15.1930 Donalsonville GA D2.12.2003 Fort Myers FL BR/TR/6-4/215* d9.20 M1 s-Marc Col Florida [DL 1958 Bos A 168]

YEAR	TM LG	G	AB	R	H	2B	3B	HR	RBI	BB-IB	HP	SO	AVG	OBP	SLG	AOPS	ABR	SB-CS	FA	FR	RNG	THR	GAMES AT POSITION	DL	BFW
1955	Bos A	2	6	1	0	0	0	0	0	0-0		1	1.000	.000	.000	-92	-2	0-0	1.000	1	0	0	C2		-0.1
1957	Bos A	2	1	0	0	0	0	0	0	0-0			.000	.000	.000	-95	0	0-0	1.000	0			/C		0.0
1959	Bos A	4	2	0	0	0	0	0	0	1-0		1	.000	.333	.000	-0	0	0-0	1.000	0	0		C2		0.0
1960	Bos A	52	124	9	20	1	0	3	10	16-2		24	.161	.255	.242	35	-12	0-0	.992	3	104	78	C50		-0.7
1961	KC A	117	331	42	80	16	2	6	40	46-0		45	.242	.333	.356	83	-7	1-0	.984	-3	106	106	C88,1b16,O5(2/0/3)		-0.7
1962	KC A	95	274	33	68	7	2	4	29	31-5		54	.248	.325	.332	74	-10	1-0	.980	-8	82	80	C94/1		-1.4
1963	KC A	40	113	9	24	6	1	0	15	15-2		15	.212	.300	.283	62	-5	0-0	.992	2	41	126	C37		-0.1
Total	7	312	851	94	192	30	5	13	87	109-9	1	140	.226	.312	.318	69	-36	2-0	.985	-5	87	94	C274,1b17,O5(2/0/3)	168	-3.0

SULLIVAN, JOHN — John Eugene B2.16.1873 IL D6.5.1924 St.Paul MN BR/TR/5-10/170 d4.19

YEAR	TM LG	G	AB	R	H	2B	3B	HR	RBI	BB-IB	HP	SO	AVG	OBP	SLG	AOPS	ABR	SB-CS	FA	FR	RNG	THR	GAMES AT POSITION	BFW
1905	Det A	13	32	4	5	0	0	0	4	4		0	.156	.250	.156	29	-2	0	.964	1	80	165	C12	-0.1
1908	Pit N	1	1	0	0	0	0	0	0	0		0	.000	.000	.000	-99	0	0	1.000	0	0	321	/C	0.0
Total	2	14	33	4	5	0	0	0	4	4		0	.152	.243	.152	26	-2	0	.965	1	78	169	C13	-0.1

SULLIVAN, CHUB — John Frank B1.12.1856 Boston MA D9.24.1881 Boston MA BR/TR/6-0/164 d9.24

YEAR	TM LG	G	AB	R	H	2B	3B	HR	RBI	BB-IB	HP	SO	AVG	OBP	SLG	AOPS	ABR	SB-CS	FA	FR	RNG	THR	GAMES AT POSITION	BFW
1877	Cin N	8	32	4	8	0	0	0	4	1			.250	.273	.250	74	-1		.944	-1	44	24	1b8	-0.1
1878	Cin N	61	244	29	63	4	2	0	20	2		9	.258	.264	.291	91	-1		.975	5	133	125	1b61	0.0
1880	Wor N	43	166	22	43	6	3	0	4	4		6	.259	.276	.331	97	-1		.983	3	108	104	1b43	0.0
Total	3	112	442	55	114	10	5	0	24	7		15	.258	.269	.303	92	-4		.976	7	118	110	1b112	-0.1

SULLIVAN, JOHN — John Lawrence B3.21.1890 Williamsport PA D4.1.1966 Milton PA BR/TR/5-11/180 d4.18

YEAR	TM LG	G	AB	R	H	2B	3B	HR	RBI	BB-IB	HP	SO	AVG	OBP	SLG	AOPS	ABR	SB-CS	FA	FR	RNG	THR	GAMES AT POSITION	BFW
1920	Bos N	81	250	36	74	14	4	1	28	29		2 29	.296	.374	.396	126	10	3-2	.977	-2	89	123	O66(16/5/45),1b6	0.5
1921	Bos N	5	5	0	0	0	0	0	0	0		0 0	.000	.000	.000	-99	-1	0-0	—	0			/H	-0.1
	Chi N	76	240	28	79	14	4	4	41	19		1 26	.329	.381	.471	124	9	3-5	.962	-5	94	40	O66(63/1/1)	-0.2
	Year	81	245	28	79	14	4	4	41	19		1 26	.322	.374	.461	120	7	3-5	.962	-5	94	40	O66(63/1/1)	-0.3
Total	2	162	495	64	153	28	8	5	69	48		3 55	.309	.374	.428	123	18	6-7	.972	-7	91	83	O132(79/6/46),1b6	0.2

SULLIVAN, JOHN — John Paul B11.2.1920 Chicago IL BR/TR/5-10/170 d6.7 Mil 1945-46 C15 Col Wisconsin-Madison

YEAR	TM LG	G	AB	R	H	2B	3B	HR	RBI	BB-IB	HP	SO	AVG	OBP	SLG	AOPS	ABR	SB-CS	FA	FR	RNG	THR	GAMES AT POSITION	BFW
1942	Was A	94	357	38	84	16	1	0	42	25		30	.235	.285	.286	61	-19	2-0	.936	-10	90	81	S92	-2.3
1943	Was A	134	456	49	95	12	2	1	55	57	1	59	.208	.298	.250	63	-20	6-2	.946	9	109	99	S133	0.0
1944	Was A	138	471	49	118	12	1	0	30	52		43	.251	.325	.280	77	-13	3-3	.934	-13	94	94	S138	-1.5
1947	Was A	49	133	13	34	0	1	0	5	22		14	.256	.361	.271	79	-3	0-2	.963	2	104	91	S40/2	0.1
1948	Was A	85	173	25	36	4	1	0	12	22		25	.208	.297	.243	46	-13	2-2	.951	-3	98	91	S57,2b4	-1.3
1949	StL A	105	243	29	55	8	3	0	18	38		35	.226	.331	.284	61	-13	5-2	.942	-7	91	78	S71,3b23,2b6	-1.6
Total	6	605	1833	203	422	52	9	1	162	216	1	206	.230	.312	.270	66	-81	18-11	.942	-22	98	91	S531,3b23,2b11	-6.6

SULLIVAN, JOHN — John Peter B1.3.1941 Somerville NJ BL/TR/6-0/195* d9.20

YEAR	TM LG	G	AB	R	H	2B	3B	HR	RBI	BB-IB	HP	SO	AVG	OBP	SLG	AOPS	ABR	SB-CS	FA	FR	RNG	THR	GAMES AT POSITION	BFW
1963	Det A	3	5	0	0	0	0	0		2-0	0	1	.000	.286	.000	-11	-1	0-0	1.000	-0	51	0	C2	-0.1
1964	Det A	2	3	0	0	0	0	0	0	0-0	0		.000	.000	.000	-99	-1	0-0	1.000	-1	0	905	C2	-0.1
1965	Det A	34	86	5	23	0	0	2	11	9-0	1	13	.267	.340	.337	93	-1	0-0	.994	-0	221	111	C29	0.1
1967	NY N	65	147	4	32	5	0	0	6	6-3		26	.218	.248	.252	44	-11	0-2	.991	-6	60	119	C57	-1.7
1968	Phi N	12	18	0	4	0	0	0	1	2-0		4	.222	.300	.222	59	-1	0-0	.967	1	0	191	C8	0.0
Total	5	116	259	9	59	5	0	2	18	19-3	1	45	.228	.282	.270	59	-15	0-2	.991	-5	116	131	C98	-1.8

SULLIVAN, JOE — Joseph Daniel B1.6.1870 Charlestown MA D11.2.1897 Charlestown MA 5-10/178 d4.27

YEAR	TM LG	G	AB	R	H	2B	3B	HR	RBI	BB-IB	HP	SO	AVG	OBP	SLG	AOPS	ABR	SB-CS	FA	FR	RNG	THR	GAMES AT POSITION	BFW
1893	Was N	128	508	72	134	16	13	2	64	36	8	24	.264	.322	.358	83	-14	7	.860	-29	91	56	S128	-3.0
1894	Was N	17	60	7	15	3	0	0	5	6	4	2	.250	.357	.300	62	-3	3	.900	-2	106	24	2b8,S6/3OR	-0.4
	Phi N	77	312	65	110	10	8	3	63	24	5	10	.353	.408	.465	112	6	12	.886	-18	85	99	S77	-0.6
	Year	94	372	72	125	13	8	3	68	30	9	12	.336	.399	.438	104	3	15	.883	-20	84	96	S83,2b8/3OR	-1.0
1895	Phi N	94	373	75	126	7	3	2	50	24	11	20	.338	.395	.389	102	2	15	.879	-19	89	83	S89,O6(3/2/1)	-1.1
1896	Phi N	48	191	45	48	5	3	2	24	18	10	12	.251	.341	.340	82	-4	9	.962	-3	52	0	O45(8/37/0),S2/3	-0.8
	StL N	51	212	25	62	4	2	2	21	9	10	12	.292	.351	.358	91	-3	5	.955	-4	66	60	O45L,2b7/3	-0.8
	Year	99	403	70	110	9	5	4	45	27	20	24	.273	.349	.350	87	-7	14	.959	-6	59	31	O90(53/37/0),2b7,S2,3b2	-1.6
Total	4	415	1656	289	495	45	29	11	227	117	48	80	.299	.362	.381	93	-16	51	.871	-74	88	75	S302,O97(56/39/2),2b15,3b3	-6.7

SULLIVAN, MARC — Marc Cooper B7.25.1958 Quincy MA BR/TR/6-4/205(198-213) [BosA79 2/52] d10.1 f-Haywood Col Florida

YEAR	TM LG	G	AB	R	H	2B	3B	HR	RBI	BB-IB	HP	SO	AVG	OBP	SLG	AOPS	ABR	SB-CS	FA	FR	RNG	THR	GAMES AT POSITION	DL	BFW
1982	Bos A	2	3	0	1	0	0	0		0-0	0	1	.333	.333	.333	79	0	0-0	1.000	1	0	166	C2		0.1
1984	Bos A	2	6	1	3	0	0	0		1-0	0		.500	.571	.500	190	1	0-0	.950	1	114	0	C2		0.2
1985	Bos A	32	69	10	12	2	0	2	3	6-0	1	32	.174	.240	.290	42	-6	0-0	.993	-2	140	105	C32	46	-0.6
1986	Bos A	41	119	15	23	4	0	1	14	7-0	4	32	.193	.260	.252	40	-10	0-0	.986	-7	102	59	C41		-1.5
1987	Bos A	60	160	11	27	5	0	2	10	4-0	2	43	.169	.198	.237	33	-20	0-0	.994	-3	109	140	C60		-2.0
Total	5	137	360	37	67	11	0	5	28	18-0	6	92	.186	.236	.258	33	-35	0-0	.990	-10	112	105	C137	46	-3.8

SULLIVAN, MARTY — Martin C. B10.20.1862 Lowell MA D1.6.1894 Lowell MA BR/TR d4.30

YEAR	TM LG	G	AB	R	H	2B	3B	HR	RBI	BB-IB	HP	SO	AVG	OBP	SLG	AOPS	ABR	SB-CS	FA	FR	RNG	THR	GAMES AT POSITION	BFW
1887	Chi N	115	472	98	134	13	16	3	77	36	4	53	.284	.340	.424	98	-4	35	.847	-9	47	0	O115(111/3/1)/P	-1.4
1888	Chi N	75	314	40	74	12	6	7	39	15	1	32	.236	.273	.379	99	-2	9	.927	3	102	272	O75(74/1/0)	-0.1
1889	Ind N	69	256	45	73	11	3	4	35	50	1	31	.285	.404	.398	122	10	15	.910	-6	74	176	O64(0/63/1),1b5	0.1
1890	Bos N	121	505	82	144	19	7	6	61	56		48	.285	.357	.386	108	4	33	.951	4	64	26	O120L/3	0.4
1891	Bos N	17	67	15	15	1	0	2	7	5		3	.224	.288	.328	71	-3	7	.926	-1	43	0	O17L	-0.4
	Cle N	1	4	0	1	0	0	0	1	0		0	.250	.250	.250	44	0	0	—	0	0		/OR	0.0
	Year	18	71	15	16	1	0	2	8	5		3	.225	.286	.324	69	-3	7	.926	-1	43	0	O18(17/0/1)	-0.4
Total	5	398	1618	280	441	56	32	26	220	162	7	168	.273	.341	.395	104	5	99	.909	-9	67	89	O392(322/67/3),1b5/3P	-1.4

SULLIVAN, MIKE — Michael Joseph B6.10.1860 Webster MA D6.16.1929 Webster MA BR/TR/5-8.5/165 d4.26

YEAR	TM LG	G	AB	R	H	2B	3B	HR	RBI	BB-IB	HP	SO	AVG	OBP	SLG	AOPS	ABR	SB-CS	FA	FR	RNG	THR	GAMES AT POSITION	BFW
1888	Phi AA	28	112	20	31	5	6	1	19	3			.277	.296	.455	140	4	10	.742	-7	36	0	O18(16/0/2),3b10	-0.3

SULLIVAN, PAT — Patrick B. B5.1861 Milwaukee WI D4.14.1901 Milwaukee WI TR/5-11/165 d7.17

YEAR	TM LG	G	AB	R	H	2B	3B	HR	RBI	BB-IB	HP	SO	AVG	OBP	SLG	AOPS	ABR	SB-CS	FA	FR	RNG	THR	GAMES AT POSITION	BFW
1884	KC U	31	114	15	22	3	1	0		4			.193	.220	.237	44	-11		.767	1	108	231	3b21,O9(1/8/0)/CP	

SULLIVAN, RUSS — Russell Guy B2.19.1923 Fredericksburg VA BL/TR/6-0/196* d9.8

YEAR	TM LG	G	AB	R	H	2B	3B	HR	RBI	BB-IB	HP	SO	AVG	OBP	SLG	AOPS	ABR	SB-CS	FA	FR	RNG	THR	GAMES AT POSITION	BFW
1951	Det A	7	26	2	5	1	0	1	2	2		0	.192	.250	.346	60	-2	0-0	.938	0	91	187	O7(6/0/1)	-0.2
1952	Det A	15	52	7	17	2	1	3	5	3	1	5	.327	.375	.577	161	4	1-0	.826	-1	75	227	O14(6/0/9)	
1953	Det A	23	72	7	18	5	1	1	6	13	2	5	.250	.359	.389	109	2	0-0	.958	2	98	261	O20L	
Total	3	45	150	16	40	8	2	5	12	18	3	11	.267	.357	.447	118	4	1-0	.920	1	90	238	O41(32/0/10)	

SULLIVAN, SUTER — Suter Grant B10.14.1872 Baltimore MD D4.19.1925 Baltimore MD 6-0/170 d7.24

YEAR	TM LG	G	AB	R	H	2B	3B	HR	RBI	BB-IB	HP	SO	AVG	OBP	SLG	AOPS	ABR	SB-CS	FA	FR	RNG	THR	GAMES AT POSITION	BFW
1898	StL N	42	144	10	32	3	0	1	12	13			.222	.300	.243	55	-8	1	.875	-10	78	59	S23,O10R,2b6/1P	-1.4
1899	Cle N	127	473	37	116	16	3	0	55	25		10	.245	.297	.292	67	-21	16	.938	12	115	118	3b101,O20(1/0/20),S3,1b3,2b2	-0.1
Total	2	169	617	47	148	19	3	0	67	38		13	.240	.298	.280	64	-29	17	.938	2	115	118	3b101,O30(1/0/30),S26,2b8,1b4/P	-2.4

SULLIVAN, TOM — Thomas Brandon B12.19.1906 Nome AK D8.16.1944 Seattle WA BR/TR/6-0/190 d6.14

YEAR	TM LG	G	AB	R	H	2B	3B	HR	RBI	BB-IB	HP	SO	AVG	OBP	SLG	AOPS	ABR	SB-CS	FA	FR	RNG	THR	GAMES AT POSITION	BFW
1925	Cin N	1	1	0	0	0	0	0	0	0		0 0	.000	.000	.000	-99	0	0-0	1.000	-0	0	0	/C	

YEAR	TM LG	G	AB	R	H	2B	3B	HR	RBI	BB-IB	HP	SO	AVG	OBP	SLG	AOPS	ABR	SB-CS	FA	FR	RNG	THR	GAMES AT POSITION	DL	BFW

SULLIVAN, SLEEPER Thomas Jefferson "Old Iron Hands" B1859 , Ireland D10.13.1909 St.Louis MO BR/TR/?/175 d5.3

1881	Buf N	35	121	13	23	4	0	0	15	1		21	.190	.197	.223	32	-9		.853	-11			C31,O5(0/2/4)		-1.9
1882	StL AA	51	188	24	34	3	3	0		3			.181	.194	.229	40	-12		.840	-18			C51		-2.4
1883	StL AA	8	27	2	6	0	1	0		0			.222	.222	.296	62	-1		.939	3			C6,O2(0/1/1)		0.2
	Lou AA	1	2	0	0	0	0	0		0			.000	.000	.000	-99	0		.667	-0			/C		-0.1
	Year	9	29	2	6	0	1	0		0			.207	.207	.276	52	-2		.923	3			C7,O2(0/1/1)		0.1
1884	StL U	2	9	0	1	0	0	0		0			.111	.111	.111	-31	-2		—	-1	0	0	/ORCP		-0.1
Total	4	97	347	39	64	7	4	0	15	4		21	.184	.194	.228	36	-24		.851	-27			C90,O8(0/3/6)/P		-4.3

SULLIVAN, TED Timothy Paul B1851 Co. Clare, Ireland D7.5.1929 Washington DC d9.9 M3/U2

| 1884 | KC U | 3 | 9 | 3 | 3 | 0 | 0 | 0 | | 1 | | | .333 | .400 | .333 | 143 | 0 | | 1.000 | -1 | 0 | 0 | O2R/SM | | -0.1 |

SULLIVAN, BILL William B7.4.1853 , Ireland D11.13.1884 Holyoke MA d8.9

| 1878 | Chi N | 2 | 6 | 1 | 1 | 0 | 0 | 0 | | 0 | | 0 | .167 | .167 | .167 | 9 | -1 | | 1.000 | -0 | 0 | 0 | O2L | | -0.1 |

SULLIVAN, BILLY William Joseph Jr. B10.23.1910 Chicago IL D1.4.1994 Sarasota FL BL/TR/6-0/170 d6.9 Mil 1944-46 f-Billy Col Notre Dame/Portland OF(33/0/33)

1931	Chi A	92	363	48	100	16	5	2	33	20		14	.275	.315	.364	83	-10	4-4	.912	-6	97	58	3b83,O2R/1		-1.3
1932	Chi A	93	307	31	97	16	1	0	45	20	0	11	.316	.358	.384	99	-1	1-3	.990	-2	114	95	1b52,3b17,C5,O3(1/0/2)		-0.7
1933	Chi A	54	125	9	24	0	1	0	13	10		5	.192	.252	.208	24	-14	0-0	.982	-3	108	138	1b22,C8		-1.8
1935	Cin N	85	241	29	64	9	4	2	36	19	2	16	.266	.324	.361	87	-5	4	.992	3	135	125	1b40,3b15,2b6		-0.4
1936	Cle A	93	319	39	112	32	6	2	48	16	0	15	.351	.382	.508	117	8	5-2	.968	-1	96	117	C72,3b5,1b3/O(1/0/1)		1.1
1937	Cle A	72	168	26	48	12	3	3	22	17	1	7	.286	.355	.446	100	-1	1-4	.949	-5	81	116	C38,1b5/3		-0.4
1938	StL A	111	375	35	104	16	1	9	49	20	1	10	.277	.316	.381	74	-17	8-5	.990	0	77	123	C99,1b6		-1.0
1939	StL A	118	332	53	96	17	5	5	50	34	4	18	.289	.362	.416	96	-2	3-3	.954	3	104	152	C59(31/0/28),C19,1b4		-0.4
1940	†Det A	78	220	36	68	14	4	3	41	31	2	11	.309	.399	.450	109	4	2-0	.976	3	104	99	C57,3b6		1.0
1941	Det A	85	234	29	66	15	1	3	29	35		11	.282	.375	.393	94	-1	0-3	.976	3	90	77	C63		0.5
1942	Bro N	43	101	11	27	2	1	1	14	12		6	.267	.345	.337	98	0	1-1	.962	0	153	77	C41		0.2
1947	Pit N	38	55	1	14	3	0	0	8	6	0	3	.255	.328	.309	68	-2	1	1.000	0	93	90	C12		-0.1
Total	12	962	2840	347	820	152	32	29	388	240	11	119	.289	.346	.395	91	-40	30-24	.972	-7	94	102	C414,1b133,3b127,O65L,2b6		-3.3

SULLIVAN, BILLY William Joseph Sr. B2.1.1875 Oakland WI D1.28.1965 Newberg OR BR/TR/5-9/155 d9.13 M1 s-Billy

1899	Bos N	22	74	10	20	2	0	2	12	1	1		.270	.308	.378	80	-2	3	.952	4	120	87	C22		0.3
1900	Bos N	72	238	36	65	6	0	8	41	9	1		.273	.302	.399	83	-7	4	.974	4	101	85	C66/S2		0.2
1901	Chi A	98	367	54	90	15	6	4	56	10	3		.245	.271	.351	74	-15	12	.967	5	110	98	C97/3		0.0
1902	Chi A	76	263	36	64	12	3	1	26	6	3		.243	.268	.323	66	-13	11	.967	4	121	106	C70,1b2,O2(1/0/1)		-0.2
1903	Chi A	32	111	10	21	4	0	1	7	5	0		.189	.224	.252	45	-7	3	.988	-1	108	104	C31		-0.5
1904	Chi A	108	371	29	85	18	4	1	44	11	1		.229	.255	.307	81	-9	11	.964	6	128	107	C107		0.9
1905	Chi A	98	323	25	65	10	3	2	26	13	3		.201	.239	.269	64	-14	14	.974	7	127	94	C92,1b2/3		-0.3
1906	†Chi A	118	387	37	83	18	4	2	33	22	3		.214	.262	.297	77	-11	10	.974	6	145	92	C118		0.7
1907	Chi A	112	329	30	59	8	4	0	36	21	3		.179	.285	.228	49	-19	6	.983	2	118	92	C108/2		-0.8
1908	Chi A	137	430	40	82	8	4	0	29	22	3		.191	.235	.228	51	-24	15	.985	-12	109	97	C137		-2.7
1909	Chi A	97	265	11	43	3	0	0	16	17	5		.162	.226	.174	28	-22	11	.983	1	96	98	C97,M		-1.3
1910	Chi A	45	142	10	26	4	1	0	6	7	1		.183	.227	.225	43	-10	0	.976	9	130	92	C45		0.4
1911	Chi A	89	256	26	55	9	3	0	31	16	2		.215	.266	.273	52	-17	1	.986	7	147	91	C89		-0.3
1912	Chi A	41	91	9	19	2	1	0	15	9	1		.209	.287	.253	57	-5	0	.975	2	97	105	C41		-0.1
1914	Chi A	1	0	0	0	0	0	0	0	0	0	0	—	—	—	—	0	0	1.000	-0	0	0	/C		0.0
1916	Det A	1	0	0	0	0	0	0	0	0	0	0	—	—	—	—	0	0	—	0	0	0	/C		0.0
Total	16	1147	3647	363	777	119	33	21	378	170	32	0	.213	.254	.281	63	-175	98	.976	39	120	96	C1122,1b4,O2(1/0/1),3b2,2b2/S		-3.7

SUMMA, HOMER Homer Wayne B11.3.1898 Gentry MO D1.29.1966 Los Angeles CA BL/TR/5-10.5/170 d9.13 Col Missouri

1920	Pit N	10	22	7	7	1	0	1	3	1	0	1	.318	.400	.455	141	1	1-0	.950	0	112	110	O6(1/5/0)		0.2
1922	Cle A	12	46	9	16	3	3	1	6	1	3		.348	.400	.609	154	4	1-2	1.000	1	78	271	O12R		0.3
1923	Cle A	137	525	92	172	27	6	3	69	33	6	20	.328	.374	.419	109	6	9-13	.951	-12	81	84	O136(0/3/133)		-1.9
1924	Cle A	111	390	55	113	21	6	2	38	11		16	.290	.311	.390	79	-15	4-2	.941	-3	101	81	O95(0/3/92)		-2.3
1925	Cle A	75	224	28	74	10	1	0	25	13		3	.330	.375	.384	92	-2	3-2	.966	-5	94	42	O54(18/1/35),3b2		-1.0
1926	Cle A	154	581	84	179	31	6	4	74	47	8	9	.308	.368	.403	100	0	15-8	.975	6	109	102	O154R		-0.6
1927	Cle A	145	574	72	164	41	7	4	74	32		18	.286	.331	.402	89	-11	6-5	.955	-9	89	78	O145(0/1/144)		-3.0
1928	Cle A	134	504	60	143	26	3	3	57	20	6	15	.284	.319	.365	78	-17	4-2	.977	-6	90	88	O132R		-3.3
1929	†Phi A	37	81	12	22	4	0	0	10	2	1		.272	.298	.321	57	-5	1-1	.980	1	126	53	O24(18/0/16)		-0.5
1930	Phi A	25	54	10	15	2	1	1	5	4	1	1	.278	.339	.407	85	-1	0-0	.938	0	117	87	O15(3/0/12)		-0.2
Total	10	840	3001	413	905	166	34	18	361	166	36	88	.302	.344	.392	92	-40	44-35	.968	-27	95	87	O773(40/13/730),3b2		-12.3

SUMMERS, CHAMP John Junior B6.15.1946 Bremerton WA BL/TR/6-2/205* d5.4 C2 Col Southern Illinois Edwardsville

1974	Oak A	20	24	2	3	1	0	0	3	1-0		5	.125	.160	.167	-6	-3	0-0	1.000	-1	78	0	O12(8/0/4),D2		-0.4
1975	Chi N	76	91	14	21	1	1	1	16	10-0	1	13	.231	.311	.341	78	-3	0-0	.889	-2	80	1	O18(15/0/3)		-0.5
1976	Chi N	83	126	11	26	2	0	3	13	13-1	1	31	.206	.284	.294	59	-7	1-0	.964	-1	87	90	O26(19/0/7),1b10/C		-1.0
1977	Cin N	59	76	11	13	4	0	3	6	6-1	1	16	.171	.238	.342	53	-5	0-0	1.000	1	113	127	O16(3/0/13)/3		-0.5
1978	Cin N	13	35	4	9	2	1	1	3	7-1	0	4	.257	.381	.400	118	1	2-1	.933	-2	67	0	O12R		-0.2
1979	Cin N	27	60	10	12	3	1	1	11	13-0		15	.200	.351	.317	84	-1	0-1	.941	-1	74	119	O13(4/0/9),1b6		-0.3
	Det A	90	246	47	77	12	1	20	51	40-4		33	.313	.414	.614	168	24	7-6	.989	-8	75	70	O69(2/0/67),D10,1b4		1.2
1980	Det A	120	347	61	103	19	1	17	60	52-6	5	52	.297	.393	.504	141	22	4-3	.953	-5	81	37	D64,O47(21/0/26)/1		1.3
1981	Det A	64	165	16	42	8	1	2	21	19-3		35	.255	.339	.358	98	0	1-1	.964	-1	92	99	D37,O18R		-0.2
1982	SF N	70	125	15	31	5	0	4	19	16-0	3	17	.248	.342	.384	105	1	0-1	.913	-3	74	89	O31(30/0/1),1b3		-0.4
1983	SF N	29	22	3	3	0	0	0	3	7-0	0	6	.136	.333	.136	39	-1	0-0	1.000	0	179	0	/OL	66	-0.1
1984	†SD N	47	54	5	10	3	0	1	12	4-1	0	15	.185	.254	.296	54	-3	0-0	1.000	-1	30	196	1b8		-0.5
Total	11	698	1371	199	350	63	4	54	218	188-17	19	244	.255	.350	.425	111	25	15-13	.959	-22	80	67	O263(103/0/160),D113,1b32/3C	81	-1.6

SUMMERS, KID William B1868 Toronto ON, Can. D10.16.1895 Toronto ON, Can. BR/TR/5-10/169 d8.5

| 1893 | StL N | 2 | 1 | 0 | 0 | 0 | 0 | 0 | 1 | 0 | | 0 | .000 | .000 | .000 | 37 | 0 | 0 | .500 | -1 | 0 | 0 | /OLC | | 0.0 |

SUMNER, CARL Carl Ringdahl "Lefty" B9.28.1908 Cambridge MA D2.8.1999 Chatham MA BL/TL/5-8/170 d7.28

| 1928 | Bos A | 16 | 29 | 6 | 8 | 1 | 0 | 3 | 5 | 0 | | 6 | .276 | .382 | .379 | 103 | 0 | 0-0 | .923 | -1 | 86 | 0 | O10(5/4/1) | | -0.1 |

SUNDAY, ART Arthur (b August Hawker) B1.21.1862 Springfield IL D10.2.1926 Reno NV BL/TL/5-9/193 d5.5

| 1890 | Bro P | 24 | 83 | 26 | 22 | 5 | 1 | 0 | 7 | 9 | | 9 | .265 | .419 | .349 | 100 | 1 | 0 | .909 | -3 | 57 | 0 | O24(0/5/20) | | -0.1 |

SUNDAY, BILLY William Ashley "Parson","The Evangelist" B11.19.1862 Ames IA D11.6.1935 Chicago IL BL/TR/5-10/160 d5.22

1883	Chi N	14	54	6	13	4	0	0		1		18	.241	.255	.315	70	-2		.647	-9	40	0	O14(1/0/13)		-0.5
1884	Chi N	43	176	25	39	4	1	4	28	4		36	.222	.239	.324	70	-7		.663	-9	94	72	O43(0/9/34)		-1.5
1885	†Chi N	46	172	36	44	3	3	2	20	12		33	.256	.304	.343	96	-2		.825	-5	81	222	O46(1/4/43)		-0.7
1886	Chi N	28	103	16	25	2	2	0		7		26	.243	.291	.301	70	-4	10	.914	-1	49	0	O28(1/0/27)		-0.5
1887	Chi N	50	199	41	58	6	6	3	32	21	1	20	.291	.362	.427	105	0	34	.766	-10	42	119	O50(2/23/25)		-0.9
1888	Pit N	120	505	69	119	14	3	0	15	12		36	.236	.256	.275	76	-13	71	.939	15	133	125	O120(1/117/3)		-0.2
1889	Pit N	81	321	62	77	10	6	2	25	27	4	33	.240	.307	.327	85	-7	47	.946	8	110	73	O81(1/0/80)		0.0
1890	Pit N	86	358	58	92	9	2	1	33	32	5	20	.257	.327	.302	94	-1	56	.883	9	150	217	O86(0/51/35)/P		0.5
	Phi N	31	119	26	31	3	1	0	6	18	2	7	.261	.367	.303	93	0	28	.950	2	129	174	O31C		0.1
	Year	117	477	84	123	12	3	1	39	50	7	27	.258	.337	.302	94	-1	84	.900	11	145	206	O117(0/82/35)/P		0.6
Total	8	499	2007	339	498	55	24	12	170	134	14	229	.248	.301	.332	86	-36	246	.883	4	108	129	O499(7/235/260)/P		-3.7

SUNDBERG, JIM James Howard B5.18.1951 Galesburg IL BR/TR/6-0/195* [TexA73*S1/2] d4.4 Col Iowa

1974	Tex A☆	132	368	45	91	13	3	3	36	62-0	1	61	.247	.354	.323		2-4		.990	6	114	93	C132		1.3
1975	Tex A	155	472	45	94	9	0	6	36	51-4	4	77	.199	.283	.256	54	-29	3-1	.981	10	135	104	C155		-1.2
1976	Tex A	140	448	33	102	24	2	3	34	37-0	0	61	.228	.285	.310	73	-15	0-0	.991	20	127	112	C140		1.2
1977	Tex A	149	453	61	132	20	3	6	65	53-0	2	77	.291	.365	.389	105	5	2-3	.994	32	197	100	C149		4.2
1978	Tex A★	149	518	54	144	23	6	6	58	64-6	3	70	.278	.355	.380	108	7	2-5	.997	17	118	126	C148/D		3.0
1979	Tex A	150	495	50	136	23	4	9	64	51-5	5	51	.275	.345	.368	94	-3	3-3	.995	15	107	104	C150		1.8
1980	Tex A	151	505	59	138	24	1	10	63	64-3	1	67	.273	.353	.384	106	6	2-2	.993	-1	92	104	C151		1.1

YEAR	TM	LG	G	AB	R	H	2B	3B	HR	RBI	BB-IB	HP	SO	AVG	OBP	SLG	AOPS	ABR	SB-CS	FA	FR	RNG	THR	GAMES AT POSITION	DL	BFW
1981	Tex	A	102	339	42	94	17	2	3	28	50-6	1	48	.277	.369	.366	119	11	2-5	.996	3	146	107	C98,O2L		1.7
1982	Tex	A	139	470	37	118	22	5	10	47	49-2		57	.251	.322	.383	97	-2	2-6	.991	4	104	113	C132/OL		0.6
1983	Tex	A	131	378	30	76	14	0	2	28	35-0	2	64	.201	.272	.254	46	-27	0-4	.993	4	101	132	C131		-2.0
1984	Mil	A★	110	348	43	91	19	4	7	43	38-2	0	63	.261	.332	.399	106	3	1-1	.995	12	142	129	C109		-0.1
1985	†KC	A	115	367	38	90	12	4	10	35	33-3	1	67	.245	.308	.381	87	-7	0-2	.992	2	114	73	C112		-1.4
1986	KC	A	140	429	41	91	9	1	12	42	57-1	0	91	.212	.303	.322	69	-18	1-1	.995	-1	118	102	C134		-0.1
1987	Chi	N	61	139	9	28	2	0	4	15	19-3	2	40	.201	.306	.302	60	-8	0-0	.994	4	90	108	C57		-0.1
1988	Chi	N	24	54	8	13	1	0	2	9	8-0	0	15	.241	.333	.370	99	-2	0-0	1.000	-2	99	116	C20		-0.1
	Tex	A	38	91	13	26	4	0	4	13	5-0	0	17	.286	.323	.462	114	1	0-0	1.000	-4	95	76	C36		-0.1
1989	Tex	A	76	147	13	29	7	1	2	8	23-0	1	37	.197	.304	.299	70	-5	0-0	.992	-1	107	127	C73/D		-0.3
Total	16		1962	6021	621	1493	243	36	95	624	699-31	22	963	.248	.327	.348	89	-79	20-37	.993	120	123	108	C1927,O3L,D2	26	11.4

SURHOFF, B.J. William James B8.4.1964 Bronx NY BL/TR/6-1/200(190-215) [MilA85 1/1] d4.8 b-Rich Col North Carolina-Asheville OF(904/5/94)

YEAR	TM	LG	G	AB	R	H	2B	3B	HR	RBI	BB-IB	HP	SO	AVG	OBP	SLG	AOPS	ABR	SB-CS	FA	FR	RNG	THR	GAMES AT POSITION	DL	BFW
																										1.2
1987	Mil	A	115	395	50	118	22	3	7	68	36-1	0	30	.299	.350	.423	103	2	11-10	.984	8	105	116	C98,3b10/1D		-1.1
1988	Mil	A	139	493	47	121	21	0	5	38	31-9	3	49	.245	.292	.318	71	-20	21-6	.990	0	113	89	C106,D12,3b6		-1.3
1989	Mil	A	126	436	42	108	17	4	5	55	25-1	3	29	.248	.287	.339	78	-14	14-12	.985	-4	84	88	C106,D12,3b6		0.3
1990	Mil	A	135	474	55	131	21	4	6	59	41-5	1	37	.276	.331	.376	99	-1	18-7	.985	-5	84	78	C125,3b11		0.0
1991	Mil	A	143	505	57	146	19	4	5	68	26-2	0	33	.289	.319	.372	94	-6	5-8	.995	0	88	91	C127,3b5,O2(0/1/1)/2D		0.7
1992	Mil	A	139	480	63	121	19	1	4	62	46-8	2	41	.252	.314	.321	81	-12	14-8	.990	13	122	107	C109,1b17,O7(5/1/1),3b3,D9		-1.0
1993	Mil	A	148	552	66	151	38	3	7	79	36-5	2	47	.274	.318	.391	91	-7	12-9	.949	-2	100	92	3b121,O24(12/0/14),1b8,C3/D		-0.8
1994	Mil	A	40	134	20	35	11	2	5	22	16-0	0	14	.261	.336	.485	104	1	0-1	.923	-9	53		3b18,C12,1b8,O3R/D	82	-0.8
1995	Mil	A	117	415	72	133	26	3	13	73	37-4	4	43	.320	.378	.492	118	11	7-3	.993	6	107	232	O60(54/3/9),1b55,C18,D3		1.2
1996	†Bal	A	143	537	74	157	27	6	21	82	47-8	5	79	.292	.352	.482	109	6	0-1	.948	-7	90	118	3b106,O27L,D10,1b2	15	-0.2
1997	†Bal	A	147	528	80	150	30	4	18	88	49-14	5	60	.284	.345	.458	112	9	1-1	.992	4	99	136	O133L,1b3,3b3,D9		0.7
1998	Bal	A	162	573	79	160	34	1	22	92	49-9	1	81	.279	.332	.450	106	4	5-1	.989	4	87	137	O157L/1		-0.5
1999	Bal	A★	162	673	104	207	38	1	28	107	43-1	2	78	.308	.347	.492	116	14	5-1	1.000	7	96	171	O148L,D13,3b2		1.4
2000	†Bal	A	103	411	56	120	27	0	13	57	29-3	2	46	.292	.341	.453	104	2	7-2	.987	4	107	83	O102L/D		0.2
	†Atl	N	44	128	13	37	9	2	1	11	12-0	1	12	.289	.352	.414	94	-1	3-0	1.000	-2	87	52	O32L		-0.3
2001	†Atl	N	141	484	68	131	33	1	10	58	38-5	1	48	.271	.321	.405	86	-10	9-3	.986	-3	91	99	O129L,D3		-1.6
2002	Atl	N	25	75	5	22	5	0	0	9	9-0	0	5	.293	.369	.360	97	0	1-3	1.000	3	105	140	1b11,O9R	155	0.0
2003	Bal	A	93	319	32	94	20	0	5	41	29-3	1	29	.295	.353	.404	101	1	2-2	.978	-4	80	0	D39,O27(24/0/3),1b22	42	-0.1
2004	Bal	A	100	343	49	106	12	1	8	50	30-2	1	46	.309	.365	.420	105	3	2-0	.986	1	103	75	O70(34/0/38),D18,1b10	38	-0.1
2005	Bal	A	91	303	30	78	11	2	5	34	11-1	1	32	.257	.282	.356	69	-14	0-0	.991	1	103	101	O60(46/0/16),1b18,D7	33	-1.7
Total	19		2313	8258	1062	2326	440	42	188	1153	640-81	33	839	.282	.332	.413	98	-32	141-84	.989	5	96	124	O991L,C704,3b316,1b158,D139/2S	365	-3.7

SUSCE, GEORGE George Cyril Methodius "Good Kid" B8.13.1907 Pittsburgh PA D2.25.1986 Sarasota FL BR/TR/5-11.5/200 d4.23 C29 s-George Col St. Bonaventure

YEAR	TM	LG	G	AB	R	H	2B	3B	HR	RBI	BB-IB	HP	SO	AVG	OBP	SLG	AOPS	ABR	SB-CS	FA	FR	RNG	THR	GAMES AT POSITION	DL	BFW
1929	Phi	N	17	17	5	5	3	0	1	1	1	1	2	.294	.368	.647	137	1	0	.900	-2	82	0	C11		0.0
1932	Det	A	2	0	0	0	0	0	0	0	0							0	0-0	1.000	-0	0	0	C2		0.0
1939	Pit	N	31	75	8	17	3	1	1	4	12		5	.227	.333	.333	81	-2	0	.984	1	111	92	C31		0.1
1940	StL	N	61	113	6	24	4	0	0	13	9	2	9	.212	.282	.248	38	-10	0-0	.984	1	111	84	C61		-0.6
1941	Cle	A	1	0	0	0	0	0	0	0	0							0	0-0	1.000	-0	0	0	/C		0.1
1942	Cle	A	2	1	1	1	0	0	0	1	0		0	1.000	1.000	1.000	492	1	0-0	1.000	0	0	838	C3		0.1
1943	Cle	A	3	1	0	0	0	0	0	0	0		0	.000	.000	.000	-99	-0	0-0	1.000	-0	0	0	C3		-0.4
1944	Cle	A	29	61	3	14	1	0	0	4	2		5	.230	.254	.246	45	-5	0-0	.948	-1	103	121	C29		-0.4
Total	8		146	268	23	61	11	1	2	22	25		21	.228	.301	.299	60	-15	1-0	.974	0	107	93	C140		

SUSKO, PETE Peter Jonathan B7.2.1904 Laura OH D5.22.1978 Jacksonville FL BL/TL/5-11/172 d8.1

YEAR	TM	LG	G	AB	R	H	2B	3B	HR	RBI	BB-IB	HP	SO	AVG	OBP	SLG	AOPS	ABR	SB-CS	FA	FR	RNG	THR	GAMES AT POSITION	DL	BFW
1934	Was	A	58	224	25	64	5	3	2	25	18	1	10	.286	.342	.362	85	-6	3-4	.988	3	129	112	1b58		-0.9

SUTCLIFFE, BUTCH Charles Inigo B7.22.1915 Fall River MA D3.2.1994 Fall River MA BR/TR/5-8.5/165 d8.28

YEAR	TM	LG	G	AB	R	H	2B	3B	HR	RBI	BB-IB	HP	SO	AVG	OBP	SLG	AOPS	ABR	SB-CS	FA	FR	RNG	THR	GAMES AT POSITION	DL	BFW
1938	Bos	N	4	4	1	1	0	0	0	2	2		1	.250	.500	.250	124	0	0-0	.800	-0	0	0	C3		0.0

SUTCLIFFE, SY Elmer Ellsworth B4.15.1862 Wheaton IL D2.13.1893 Wheaton IL BL/TL/6-2/170 d10.2 OF(10/5/43)

YEAR	TM	LG	G	AB	R	H	2B	3B	HR	RBI	BB-IB	HP	SO	AVG	OBP	SLG	AOPS	ABR	SB-CS	FA	FR	RNG	THR	GAMES AT POSITION	DL	BFW
1884	Chi	N	4	15	4	3	1	0	0	2	2		4	.200	.294	.267	72	0		.976	1			C4		0.1
1885	Chi	N	11	43	5	8	1	1	0	4	3		10	.186	.222	.256	48	-3		.838	-4			C11/OR		-0.5
	StL	N	16	49	2	6	1	0	0	4	5		10	.122	.204	.143	15	-4		.881	-3			C14,O2R		-0.6
	Year		27	92	7	14	2	1	0	8	7		15	.152	.212	.196	32	-7		.862	-7			C25,O3R		-1.1
1888	Det	N	49	191	19	49	5	3	0	23	5		14	.257	.276	.314	87	-3	6	.901	3	111	85	S24,C14,1b5,O4R,2b2		0.1
1889	Cle	N	46	161	17	40	3	2	1	21	14		6	.248	.309	.311	75	-6	5	.892	6			C37,1b8/OR		0.3
1890	Cle	P	99	386	62	127	14	8	2	60	33	0	16	.329	.382	.422	125	14	10	.883	-19	70	124	C84,O15(1/0/14),S4,3b2		1.0
1891	Was	AA	53	201	29	71	8	2	0	33	17	2	17	.353	.409	.453	154	14	8	.918	-4	107	71	O35(9/5/21),C22,S3/3		-0.6
1892	Bal	N	66	276	41	77	10	7	1	27	14	1	5	.279	.316	.377	106	0	12	.958	-7	71	92	1b66		-0.6
Total	7		344	1322	177	381	43	24	6	174	92	3	87	.288	.336	.371	107	12	41	.887	-25	73	129	C186,1b79,O58R,S31,3b3,2b2		0.0

SUTHERLAND, GARY Gary Lynn B9.27.1944 Glendale CA BR/TR/6-0/185* d9.17 b-Darrell Col USC OF(31/0/6)

YEAR	TM	LG	G	AB	R	H	2B	3B	HR	RBI	BB-IB	HP	SO	AVG	OBP	SLG	AOPS	ABR	SB-CS	FA	FR	RNG	THR	GAMES AT POSITION	DL	BFW
1966	Phi	N	3	3	0	0	0	0	0	0	0-0		0	.000	.000	.000	-99	-1	0-0	1.000	1	282	745	/S		0.0
1967	Phi	N	103	231	23	57	12	1	1	19	17-5	0	22	.247	.298	.320	76	-7	0-3	.928	-2	91	144	S66,O25L		-0.9
1968	Phi	N	67	138	16	38	7	0	0	15	8-0	0	15	.275	.313	.326	93	-1	0-0	.968	-1	103	76	2b17,S10,3b10,O7(2/0/5)		-0.1
1969	Mon	N	141	544	63	130	26	1	3	35	37-5	2	31	.239	.289	.307	67	-24	0-0	.971	11	101	114	2b139,S15/OR	21	-0.6
1970	Mon	N	116	359	37	74	10	0	3	26	31-1	2	22	.206	.271	.259	43	-29	2-2	.975	-3	105	123	2b97,S15/3		-2.1
1971	Mon	N	111	304	25	78	7	4	2	26	18-3	2	12	.257	.302	.332	79	-9	3-4	.963	-3	108	121	2b56,S46,O4L,3b2		-0.8
1972	Hou	N	5	8	1	1	0	0	0	0	0-0	0	0	.125	.125	.125	-30	-1	0-0	—	0	0	0	/23		-0.1
1973	Hou	N	16	54	9	14	5	0	0	3	3-0	0	5	.259	.298	.352	80	-1	0-0	.971	-2	81	123	2b14/S		-0.3
1974	Det	A	149	619	60	157	20	1	5	49	26-1	0	37	.254	.282	.313	69	-26	1-3	.976	-11	94	90	2b147,S10,3b4		-2.9
1975	Det	A	129	503	51	130	12	3	6	39	45-3	3	41	.258	.321	.330	81	-12	0-2	.968	-3	98	91	2b128		-0.8
1976	Det	A	42	117	10	24	5	0	2	6	7-0	0	12	.205	.248	.282	53	-7	0-1	.984	5	112	125	2b42		-0.6
	Mil	A	59	115	9	25	4	1	0	9	8-2	1	9	.217	.268	.261	58	-6	0-2	.955	-9	101	105	2b45,1b2,D8	17	-0.6
	Year		101	232	19	49	9	1	2	15	15-2	1	21	.211	.258	.272	56	-13	0-3	.970	-4	105	114	2b87,D8,1b2		-0.8
1977	SD	N	80	103	5	25	3	0	1	11	7-0	0	15	.243	.291	.301	65	-5	0-0	.943	-3	98	100	2b30,3b21,1b4		-0.5
1978	StL	N	5	6	0	1	0	0	0	0	0-0	0	1	.167	.167	.167	-7	-1	0-0	1.000	1	437	0	/2		-0.1
Total	13		1031	3104	308	754	109	10	24	239	207-20	10	219	.243	.291	.308	69	-130	11-24	.971	-2	100	105	2b717,S164,3b39,O37L,D8,1b6	38	-9.6

SUTHERLAND, LEO Leonardo (Cantin) B4.6.1958 Santiago de Cuba, Cuba BL/TL/5-10/165* [ChiA76*S1/3] d8.11 Col Golden West (CA) JC

YEAR	TM	LG	G	AB	R	H	2B	3B	HR	RBI	BB-IB	HP	SO	AVG	OBP	SLG	AOPS	ABR	SB-CS	FA	FR	RNG	THR	GAMES AT POSITION	DL	BFW
1980	Chi	A	34	89	9	23	4	0	0	5	1-1	0	11	.258	.264	.292	53	-6	4-1	.943	-1	110	0	O23(16/7/0)		-0.2
1981	Chi	A	11	12	6	2	0	0	0	0	3-0	0	1	.167	.333	.167	49	-1	2-1	1.000	-1	66	0	O7(4/4/0)		-0.1
Total	2		45	101	15	25	3	0	0	5	4-1	0	12	.248	.274	.277	53	-7	6-2	.949	-2	103	0	O30(20/11/0)		-0.1

SUTKO, GLENN Glenn Edward B5.9.1968 Atlanta GA BR/TR/6-3/225* [CinN87 45/1103] d10.3 Col Spartanburg Methodist (SC) JC

YEAR	TM	LG	G	AB	R	H	2B	3B	HR	RBI	BB-IB	HP	SO	AVG	OBP	SLG	AOPS	ABR	SB-CS	FA	FR	RNG	THR	GAMES AT POSITION	DL	BFW
1990	Cin	N	1	1	0	1	0	0	0	0	0-0		0	1.000	1.000	1.000	-96	0	0-0	1.000	0	0	0	/C		0.0
1991	Cin	N	10	10	0	1	0	0	0	1	2-0	0	6	.100	.250	.100	2	-1	0-0	.875	-1	61	265	C9		-0.2
Total	2		11	11	0	2	0	0	0	1	2-0	0	6	.091	.231	.091	-6	-1	0-0	.889	-1	54	236	C10		-0.2

SUTTON, EZRA Ezra Ballou B9.17.1850 Palmyra NY D6.20.1907 Braintree MA BR/TR/5-8.5/153 d5.4 OF NA(0/1/2) OF(29/7/30)

YEAR	TM	LG	G	AB	R	H	2B	3B	HR	RBI	BB-IB	HP	SO	AVG	OBP	SLG	AOPS	ABR	SB-CS	FA	FR	RNG	THR	GAMES AT POSITION	DL	BFW
1871	Cle	NA	29	128	35	45	3	7	3	23	1		0	.352	.357	.555	166	11	3-1	.795	-0	89	89	3b29,O2(0/1/1)/C		-0.
1872	Cle	NA	22	107	30	30	6	1	0	10	1		1	.280	.287	.355	102	1	1-0	.718	-6	77	67	3b22		-0.
1873	Ath	NA	51	243	51	81	7	6	0	34	2		2	.333	.339	.412	113	2	2-3	.803	-1	103	53	3b43,S8,2b2		-0.
1874	Ath	NA	55	243	54	71	10	3	0	28	0		2	.292	.292	.358	99	-2	6-4	.827	0	87	97	3b36,S20		1.
1875	Ath	NA	75	358	83	116	11	7	1	59	1		2	.324	.326	.402	136	10	13-10	.803	13	115	147	3b73,P2,1b2/SOR		1.
1876	Phi	N	54	236	45	70	12	7	1	31	3		2	.297	.305	.419	141	9		.915	-5	201	77	1b29,2b15,3b8,O4R		1.
1877	Bos	N	58	253	43	74	10	6	0	39	4		10	.292	.304	.379	110	2		.882	-1	93	77	S36,3b22		-0.
1878	Bos	N	60	239	31	54	9	3	1	29	2		14	.226	.232	.301	69	-9		.888	-2	93	121	3b59/S		-0.
1879	Bos	N	84	339	54	84	13	4	0	34	2		18	.248	.252	.310	82	-7		.884	-9	99	147	S51,3b33		-0.
1880	Bos	N	76	288	41	72	9	2	0	25	6		7	.250	.268	.295	94	-2		.896	2	101	132	S39,3b37		-0.
1881	Bos	N	83	333	42	97	12	4	0	31	13		6	.291	.318	.351	116	6		.877	-1	99	82	3b81,S2		-2.
1882	Bos	N	81	319	44	80	13	2	3	38	24		25	.251	.303	.301	94	-1		.856	-5	89	67	3b77,S4		-2.
1883	Bos	N	94	414	101	134	28	15	3	73	17		2	.324	.350	.486	147	22		.866	-0	83	131	3b93/ORS		-0.

YEAR	TM LG	G	AB	R	H	2B	3B	HR	RBI	BB-IB	HP	SO	AVG	OBP	SLG	AOPS	ABR	SB-CS	FA	FR	RNG	THR	GAMES AT POSITION	DL	BFW
1884	Bos N	110	468	102	**162**	28	7	3	61	29			22	.346	.346	.455	164	35		**.908**	-5	86	63	3b110		2.8
1885	Bos N	110	457	78	143	23	8	4	47	17			25	.313	.338	.425	151	25		.875	3	93	150	3b91,S16,2b2/1		2.8
1886	Bos N	116	499	83	138	21	6	3	48	26			21	.277	.321	.361	107	4	18	.859	-9	55	71	O43(20/7/16),S28,3b28,2b18		-0.3
1887	Bos N	77	326	61	99	14	9	3	46	13	6	6	.304	.342	.429	112	4	17	.875	10	124	71	S37,O18(9/0/9),2b13,3b11		1.4
1888	Bos N	28	110	16	24	3	1	1	16	7	2	3	.218	.277	.291	79	-2	10	.859	-3	92	116	3b27/S		
Total	5 NA	232	1079	253	343	37	24	4	154	5			.318	.321	.408	122	22	25-18	.795	5	100	101	3b203,S29,O3R,1b2,P2,2b2/C		1.6
Total	13	1031	4281	741	1231	190	73	21	518	164	8	174	.288	.315	.381	117	18	87	.871	-34	88	102	3b677,S216,O66R,2b48,1b30		6.6

SUTTON, LARRY Larry James B5.14.1970 West Covina CA BL/TL/6-0/185* [KCA92 21/582] d8.17 Col Illinois

YEAR	TM LG	G	AB	R	H	2B	3B	HR	RBI	BB-IB	HP	SO	AVG	OBP	SLG	AOPS	ABR	SB-CS	FA	FR	RNG	THR	GAMES AT POSITION	DL	BFW
1997	KC A	27	69	9	20	2	0	2	8	5-0		12	.290	.338	.406	90	-1	0-0	1.000	0	99	105	1b12/OLD		-0.2
1998	KC A	111	310	29	76	14	2	5	42	29-3	3	46	.245	.311	.352	70	-14	3-3	.987	-0	100	80	O79(39/0/47),1b6,D3		-1.7
1999	KC A	43	102	14	23	6	0	2	15	13-0	0	17	.225	.308	.343	65	-5	1-0	.987	-1	97	88	1b30/ORD		-0.8
2000	StL N	23	25	5	8	0	0	1	6	5-0		7	.320	.406	.440	119	-1	0-0	1.000	0	101	89	1b6,O4(3/0/1)	51	0.1
2001	StL N	33	42	3	5	1	0	1	3	1-0		10	.119	.140	.214	-10	-7	0-0	1.000	1	214	108	1b11,O3R		-0.7
2002	Oak A	7	19	3	3	2	0	0	3	1-0		8	.158	.190	.263	7	-3	0-0	1.000	-0	0	0	1b6,O3(2/0/1)		-0.3
2004	Fla N	5	5	0	1	0	0	0	0	1-0		2	.200	.333	.200	45	0	0-0	1.000	-0	0	0	/1		0.0
Total	7	252	572	63	135	23	2	12	78	55-3	3	102	.236	.302	.346	66	-29	4-3	.988	-0	99	94	O91(45/0/53),1b72,D11	51	-3.6

SUZUKI, ICHIRO Ichiro B10.22.1973 Kasugai, Japan BL/TR/5-9/160* d4.2

YEAR	TM LG	G	AB	R	H	2B	3B	HR	RBI	BB-IB	HP	SO	AVG	OBP	SLG	AOPS	ABR	SB-CS	FA	FR	RNG	THR	GAMES AT POSITION	DL	BFW
2001	†Sea A★	157	692	127	**242**	34	8	8	69	30-10	8	53	**.350**	.381	.457	127	26	**56**-14	.997	7	113	80	O152R,D4		3.1
2002	Sea A★	157	647	111	208	27	8	8	51	68-**27**	5	62	.321	.388	.425	121	21	31-15	.991	7	113	87	O152(0/3/150),D4		2.1
2003	Sea A	159	679	111	212	29	8	13	62	36-7	6	69	.312	.352	.436	112	10	34-8	.994	9	109	135	O159R		1.5
2004	Sea A★	161	704	101	**262**	24	5	8	60	49-**19**	4	63	**.372**	.414	.455	133	35	36-11	.992	9	110	109	O158R,D3		3.7
2005	Sea A★	162	679	111	206	21	12	15	68	48-23	4	66	.303	.350	.436	116	13	33-8	.995	13	117	105	O158R,D3		2.1
Total	5	796	3401	561	1130	135	41	52	310	231-86	27	313	.332	.377	.442	122	105	190-56	.994	45	112	104	O779(0/3/777),D14		12.5

SVEUM, DALE Dale Curtis B11.23.1963 Richmond CA BB/TR/6-3/185(185-212) [MilA82 1/25] d5.12 C2 [DL 1989 Mil A 182]

YEAR	TM LG	G	AB	R	H	2B	3B	HR	RBI	BB-IB	HP	SO	AVG	OBP	SLG	AOPS	ABR	SB-CS	FA	FR	RNG	THR	GAMES AT POSITION	DL	BFW
1986	Mil A	91	317	35	78	13	2	7	35	32-0	1	63	.246	.316	.366	83	-8	4-3	.865	-12	95	70	3b65,2b13,S13	17	-1.8
1987	Mil A	153	535	86	135	27	3	25	95	40-4	1	133	.252	.303	.454	95	-6	2-6	.965	-20	88	96	S142,2b13		-1.2
1988	Mil A	129	467	41	113	14	4	9	51	21-0	1	122	.242	.274	.347	72	-19	1-0	.955	-2	99	125	S127/2D		-1.2
1990	Mil A	48	117	15	23	7	0	1	12	12-0	2	30	.197	.278	.282	59	-6	0-1	.918	-7	77	57	3b22,2b16,1b5,S5		-1.4
1991	Mil A	90	266	33	64	19	1	4	43	32-0	1	78	.241	.320	.365	92	-2	2-4	.968	-5	104	92	S51,3b38,2b2,D3		-0.5
1992	Phi N	54	135	13	24	4	0	2	16	16-4	0	39	.178	.261	.252	47	-9	0-0	.948	5	109	105	S34,3b5,1b4		-0.2
	Chi N	40	114	15	25	9	0	2	12	12-0	0	29	.219	.287	.351	80	-3	1-1	.944	-6	97	90	S37,1b2,3b2	15	-0.7
1993	Oak A	30	79	12	14	2	1	2	6	16-1	1	21	.177	.316	.304	71	-3	0-0	.976	-5	53	95	1b14,3b7,2b4/SOLD		-0.1
1994	Sea A	10	27	3	5	0	0	1	2	2-0	0	10	.185	.241	.296	37	-3	0-0	.909	2	181	0	3b3,D4		-0.1
1996	Pit N	12	34	9	12	5	0	1	5	6-0	0	6	.353	.450	.588	165	4	0-0	.913	-1	100	73	3b10		0.3
1997	Pit N	126	306	30	80	20	1	12	47	27-2	0	81	.261	.319	.451	98	-2	0-3	.941	-5	107	58	3b47,S28,1b21,2b2		-0.1
1998	NY A	30	58	6	9	3	0	1	13	4-0	0	16	.155	.203	.155	-3	-9	0-0	.975	-1	125	110	1b21,3b6,D3		-1.1
1999	Pit N	49	71	7	15	5	1	3	13	7-1	0	28	.211	.278	.437	78	-3	0-0	.944	0	109	0	3b12,1b4,S4,2b2/OL		-0.3
Total	12	862	2526	305	597	125	13	69	340	227-12	6	656	.236	.298	.378	82	-69	10-18	.960	-51	97	105	S442,3b217,1b71,2b53,D13,O2L	214	-9.2

SWACINA, HARRY Harry Joseph "Swats" B8.22.1881 St.Louis MO D6.21.1944 Birmingham AL BR/TR/6-2/190 d9.13

YEAR	TM LG	G	AB	R	H	2B	3B	HR	RBI	BB-IB	HP	SO	AVG	OBP	SLG	AOPS	ABR	SB-CS	FA	FR	RNG	THR	GAMES AT POSITION	DL	BFW
1907	Pit N	26	95	9	19	1	1	0	10	4	1		.200	.240	.232	47	-6	1	.996	-1	76	73	1b26		-0.9
1908	Pit N	53	176	7	38	6	1	0	13	5	0		.216	.238	.261	59	-9	4	.983	-5	63	95	1b50		-1.7
1914	Bal F	158	617	70	173	26	8	0	90	14	1	23	.280	.297	.348	73	-34	15	.985	10	**128**	93	1b158		-2.9
1915	Bal F	85	301	24	74	13	1	1	38	9	0	11	.246	.268	.306	59	-21	9	.986	6	137	111	1b75/2		-1.9
Total	4	322	1189	110	304	46	11	1	151	32	2	34	.256	.276	.315	60	-70	29	.986	10	115	96	1b309/2		-7.4

SWAN, ANDY Andrew J. B8.1858 Falls PA d7.23

YEAR	TM LG	G	AB	R	H	2B	3B	HR	RBI	BB-IB	HP	SO	AVG	OBP	SLG	AOPS	ABR	SB-CS	FA	FR	RNG	THR	GAMES AT POSITION	DL	BFW
1884	Was AA	5	21	3	3	1	0	0		0			.143	.143	.190	19	-2		.824	-2	0	0	1b3,3b2		-0.4
	Ric AA	3	10	2	5	0	0	0		0			.500	.500	.500	230	1		1.000	-0	0	0	1b3		0.1
	Year	8	31	5	8	1	0	0		0			.258	.258	.290	85	0		.902	-2	0	0	1b6,3b2		-0.3

SWANDELL, MARTY John Martin (b Martin Schwendel) B1841 Baden, Germany D10.25.1906 Brooklyn NY TL/5-10.5/146 d5.7 U1

YEAR	TM LG	G	AB	R	H	2B	3B	HR	RBI	BB-IB	HP	SO	AVG	OBP	SLG	AOPS	ABR	SB-CS	FA	FR	RNG	THR	GAMES AT POSITION	DL	BFW
1872	Eck NA	14	52	8	12	1	0	0	4	4		1	.231	.286	.250	78	-0	0-1	.564	-5	69	100	3b6,O5(0/4/1),2b2/1		-0.4
1873	Res NA	2	9	1	1	0	0	0	1	0		0	.111	.111	.111	-37	-1	0-0	.909	-0	0	0	1b2		-0.1
Total	2 NA	16	61	9	13	1	0	0	5	4		1	.213	.262	.230	60	-1	0-1	.564	-5	69	100	3b6,O5(0/4/1),1b3,2b2		-0.5

SWANDER, PINKY Edward Ottis B7.4.1880 Portsmouth OH D10.24.1944 Springfield MA BL/TL/5-9/180 d9.18

YEAR	TM LG	G	AB	R	H	2B	3B	HR	RBI	BB-IB	HP	SO	AVG	OBP	SLG	AOPS	ABR	SB-CS	FA	FR	RNG	THR	GAMES AT POSITION	DL	BFW
1903	StL A	14	51	9	14	2	2	0	6	10	2		.275	.413	.392	146	4	0	.833	-1	142	0	O14R		0.2
1904	StL A	1	1	0	0	0	0	0	0	0	0		.000	.000	.000	-99	-0	0	—	-0	0	0	/H		0.0
Total	2	15	52	9	14	2	2	0	6	10	2		.269	.406	.385	142	4	0	.833	-1	142	0	O14R		0.2

SWANN, PEDRO Pedro Maurice B10.27.1970 Wilmington DE BL/TR/6-0/195* [AtlN91 26/673] d9.9 Col Delaware St.

YEAR	TM LG	G	AB	R	H	2B	3B	HR	RBI	BB-IB	HP	SO	AVG	OBP	SLG	AOPS	ABR	SB-CS	FA	FR	RNG	THR	GAMES AT POSITION	DL	BFW
2000	Atl N	4	2	0	0	0	0	0	0	0-0		2	.000	.000	.000	-99	-0	0-0	—	-0	0	0	O3(1/1/2)		-0.1
2002	Tor A	13	12	3	1	0	0	0	1	1-0		6	.083	.154	.083	-33	-2	0-0	—	-0	0	0	/ORD		-0.2
2003	Bal A	8	14	3	3	1	0	1	2	1-0		4	.214	.267	.500	96	0	0-0	1.000	-0	94	500	O6L/D		0.0
Total	3	25	28	6	4	1	0	1	3	2-0		12	.143	.200	.286	26	-3	0-0	1.000	-1	75	0	O10(7/1/3),D4		-0.3

SWANSON, EVAR Ernest Evar B10.15.1902 DeKalb IL D7.17.1973 Galesburg IL BR/TR/5-9/170 d4.18 Col Knox

YEAR	TM LG	G	AB	R	H	2B	3B	HR	RBI	BB-IB	HP	SO	AVG	OBP	SLG	AOPS	ABR	SB-CS	FA	FR	RNG	THR	GAMES AT POSITION	DL	BFW
1929	Cin N	148	574	100	172	35	12	4	43	41	6	47	.300	.353	.423	96	-5	33	.970	-4	97	82	O142(91/51/0)		-1.6
1930	Cin N	95	301	43	93	15	3	2	22	11	1	17	.309	.335	.399	81	-10	4	.963	-1	101	92	O71(3/68/0)		-1.2
1932	Chi A	14	52	9	16	3	1	0	8	8	0	3	.308	.400	.404	116	2	3-1	.960	-2	87	0	O14L		0.1
1933	Chi A	144	539	102	165	25	7	1	63	93	3	35	.306	.411	.384	117	19	19-11	.973	-10	93	51	O139(6/8/129)		-1.4
1934	Chi A	117	426	71	127	9	5	0	34	59	1	31	.298	.385	.343	86	-7	10-3	.980	-3	98	51	O105(4/1/100)		-4.1
Total	5	518	1892	325	573	87	28	7	170	212	11	133	.303	.376	.390	98	-1	69-15	.971	-19	96	65	O471(118/128/229)		-4.1

SWANSON, KARL Karl Edward B12.17.1900 N.Henderson IL D4.3.2002 Rock Island IL BL/TR/5-10/155 d8.12

YEAR	TM LG	G	AB	R	H	2B	3B	HR	RBI	BB-IB	HP	SO	AVG	OBP	SLG	AOPS	ABR	SB-CS	FA	FR	RNG	THR	GAMES AT POSITION	DL	BFW
1928	Chi A	22	64	2	9	1	0	0	6	4	0	7	.141	.191	.156	-8	-10	3-0	.943	-1	110	81	2b21		-1.0
1929	Chi A	2	1	0	0	0	0	0	0	0	0	0	.000	.000	.000	-99	-0	0-0	—	0			/H		0.0
Total	2	24	65	2	9	1	0	0	6	4	0	7	.138	.188	.154	-9	-10	3-0	.943	-1	110	81	2b21		-1.0

SWANSON, STAN Stanley Lawrence B5.19.1944 Yuba City CA BR/TR/5-11/178 d6.23

YEAR	TM LG	G	AB	R	H	2B	3B	HR	RBI	BB-IB	HP	SO	AVG	OBP	SLG	AOPS	ABR	SB-CS	FA	FR	RNG	THR	GAMES AT POSITION	DL	BFW
1971	Mon N	49	106	14	26	3	2	1	13	.245		.310	.330	80	-3	1-3	1.000	-1	95	0	O38(24/16/2)		-0.6

SWANSON, BILL William Andrew B10.12.1888 New York NY D10.14.1954 New York NY BB/TR/5-6/156 d9.2

YEAR	TM LG	G	AB	R	H	2B	3B	HR	RBI	BB-IB	HP	SO	AVG	OBP	SLG	AOPS	ABR	SB-CS	FA	FR	RNG	THR	GAMES AT POSITION	DL	BFW
1914	Bos A	11	20	0	4	2	0	0	3	0		4	.200	.304	.300	82	-0	1	.875	-3	81	0	2b6,3b3/S		-0.4

SWARTWOOD, ED Cyrus Edward B1.12.1859 Rockford IL D5.15.1924 Pittsburgh PA BL/TL/5-11/198 d8.11 U4

YEAR	TM LG	G	AB	R	H	2B	3B	HR	RBI	BB-IB	HP	SO	AVG	OBP	SLG	AOPS	ABR	SB-CS	FA	FR	RNG	THR	GAMES AT POSITION	DL	BFW
1881	Buf N	1	3	0	1	0	0	0	1			0	.333	.500	.333	170	0		.500	-1	0	0	/OR		0.0
1882	Pit AA	76	325	**86**	107	**18**	11	4		21			.329	.370	.489	197	33		.788	-12	49	112	O73(0/29/44),1b4		1.8
1883	Pit AA	94	412	86	**147**	24	8	3		25			**.357**	**.394**	.476	**186**	41		.936	-1	131	87	1b60,O37(0/31/6),C3		2.8
1884	Pit AA	102	399	74	115	19	6	0		33	**15**		.288	.365	.366	141	21		.804	-5	141	71	O79(0/2/77),1b22/3P		1.2
1885	Bro AA	99	399	80	106	8	9	0	49	36	5		.266	.334	.331	110	5		.851	-12	47	0	O95(47/0/48),1b4/SC		-0.8
1886	Bro AA	122	471	95	132	13	10	3	58	**70**	5		.280	.377	.369	133	21	37	.884	5	154	101	O122(0/20/103)/C		2.1
1887	Bro AA	91	363	72	92	14	8	1	54	46	3		.253	.344	.344	91	-4	29	.835	1	155	149	O91R		-0.3
1890	Tol AA	126	462	106	151	23	11	3	64	80	17		.327	.444	.444	157	38	53	.925	6	105	0	O126(0/7/119)/P		3.8
1892	Pit N	13	42	8	10	1	0	0	4	13		11	.238	.418	.262	106	2	1	.933	3	262	405	O13R		0.4
Total	9	724	2876	607	861	120	63	14	229	325	43	11	.299	.379	.400	142	157	120	.856	-15	114	78	O637(47/89/502),1b90,C5,P2/S3		11.0

SWEASY, CHARLIE Charles James (b Charles James Swasey) B11.2.1847 Newark NJ D3.30.1908 Newark NJ BR/TR/5-9/160 d5.19 M1

YEAR	TM LG	G	AB	R	H	2B	3B	HR	RBI	BB-IB	HP	SO	AVG	OBP	SLG	AOPS	ABR	SB-CS	FA	FR	RNG	THR	GAMES AT POSITION	DL	BFW
1871	Oly NA	5	19	5	4	1	0	0	4	1		0	.211	.250	.263	-1	0-0		.788	-1	95	0	2b5		-0.2
1872	Cle NA	12	57	8	16	0	0	0	6	2		1	.281	.305	.281	86	-1	1-0	.833	2	116	74	2b11/OR		0.1
1873	Bos NA	1	4	0	1	0	0	0	0	0			.250	.250	.250	45	0	0-0	.714	0	140	244	/2		
1874	Bal NA	8	33	2	8	0	0	0	4	2		0	.242	.286	.242	72	-1	0-0	.646	-6	53	96	2b8/OR		-0.6
	Atl NA	10	44	4	5	1	0	0	7	2		0	.114	.114	.136	-23	-5	0-0	.879	6	174	106	2b10		0.0
	Year	18	77	6	13	1	0	0	11	4		0	.169	.190	.182	-6		0-0	.781	-0	117	101	2b18/OR		-0.6

YEAR	TM LG	G	AB	R	H	2B	3B	HR	RBI	BB-IB	HP	SO	AVG	OBP	SLG	AOPS	ABR	SB-CS	FA	FR	RNG	THR	GAMES AT POSITION	DL	BFW
1875	RS NA	19	76	7	13	1	0	0	4	3		1	.171	.203	.184	39	-4	2-4	.828	-5	78	76	2b19,M		-1.0
1876	Cin N	56	225	18	46	5	2	0	10	2		5	.204	.211	.244	60	-8		.864	1	98	130	2b55/OR		-0.3
1878	Pro N	55	212	23	37	3	0	0	8	7		23	.175	.201	.189	29	-16		.846	-8	97	87	2b55		-2.1
Total	5 NA	55	233	26	47	3	0	0	21	8		2	.202	.228	.215	47	-12	3-4	.808	-4	101	80	2b54,O2R		-1.7
Total	2	111	437	41	83	8	2	0	18	9		28	.190	.206	.217	44	-24		.855	-7	98	109	2b110/OR		-2.4

SWEENEY, BUCK Charles Francis B4.15.1890 Pittsburgh PA D3.13.1955 Pittsburgh PA 5-8/165 d9.28

YEAR	TM LG	G	AB	R	H	2B	3B	HR	RBI	BB-IB	HP	SO	AVG	OBP	SLG	AOPS	ABR	SB-CS	FA	FR	RNG	THR	GAMES AT POSITION	DL	BFW
1914	Phi A	1	1	0	0	0	0	0	0	0		1	.000	.000	.000	-99	-1		1.000	0	161	0	/OL		0.0

SWEENEY, CHARLIE Charles J. B4.13.1863 San Francisco CA D4.4.1902 San Francisco CA BR/TR/5-10.5/181 d5.11 ▲

YEAR	TM LG	G	AB	R	H	2B	3B	HR	RBI	BB-IB	HP	SO	AVG	OBP	SLG	AOPS	ABR	SB-CS	FA	FR	RNG	THR	GAMES AT POSITION	DL	BFW
1882	Pro N	1	4	0	0	0	0	0	0	0		1	.000	.000	.000	-99	-1		.500	0	443	0	/OR		-0.1
1883	Pro N	22	87	9	19	3	0	0	15	2		10	.218	.236	.253	47	-5		.863	1	128	144	P20,O7(2/3/2)		-0.2
1884	Pro N	41	168	24	50	9	0	1	19	11		17	.298	.341	.369	126	6		.940	0	104	89	P27,O17(0/5/13)/1		0.1
	StL U	45	171	31	54	14	2	1		10			.316	.354	.439	134	3		.943	5	124	267	P33,O13L/1		0.3
1885	StL N	71	267	27	55	7	1	0	24	12		33	.206	.240	.240	59	-11		.827	-4	70	100	O39(14/19/6),P35		-1.0
1886	StL N	17	64	4	16	2	0	0	7	3		10	.250	.284	.281	77	-2	2	.929	-0	104	159	P11,O4C,S2		-0.1
1887	Cle AA	36	133	22	30	4	4	0	19	21	0		.226	.331	.316	83	-2	11	.936	-1	79	35	1b20,O10(1/0/9),P3,S2,3b2		-0.6
Total	6	233	894	117	224	39	7	2	84	59		71	.251	.297	.317	90	-12	11	.909	-1	111	155	P129,O91(30/31/31),1b22,S4,3b2		-1.6

SWEENEY, DAN Daniel J. B1.28.1868 Philadelphia PA D7.13.1913 Louisville KY 5-5/160 d4.18

YEAR	TM LG	G	AB	R	H	2B	3B	HR	RBI	BB-IB	HP	SO	AVG	OBP	SLG	AOPS	ABR	SB-CS	FA	FR	RNG	THR	GAMES AT POSITION	DL	BFW
1895	Lou N	22	90	18	24	5	1	0	16	17	1	2	.267	.389	.356	99	1	2	.800	-3	65	0	O22(0/1/21)		-0.2

SWEENEY, ED Edward Francis "Jeff" B7.19.1888 Chicago IL D7.4.1947 Chicago IL BR/TR/6-1/200 d5.16 Col Loyola-Chicago

YEAR	TM LG	G	AB	R	H	2B	3B	HR	RBI	BB-IB	HP	SO	AVG	OBP	SLG	AOPS	ABR	SB-CS	FA	FR	RNG	THR	GAMES AT POSITION	DL	BFW
1908	NY A	32	82	4	12	0	0	0	2	5		19	.146	.195	.171	19	-7	0	.955	-3	84	92	C25/1OR		-0.9
1909	NY A	67	176	18	47	3	0	0	21	16		0	.267	.328	.284	93	-1	3	.947	-1	94	114	C62,1b3		0.4
1910	NY A	78	215	25	43	4	0	0	13	17		4	.200	.271	.256	62	-10	12	.974	2	105	104	C77		-0.8
1911	NY A	83	229	17	53	6	5	0	18	14		8	.231	.299	.301	63	-12	8	.964	-3	94	95	C83		-0.6
1912	NY A	110	351	40	94	12	1	0	30	27		3	.268	.325	.308	77	-10	6	.955	-5	89	109	C108		-0.6
1913	NY A	117	351	35	93	10	2	0	40	37	8	41	.265	.348	.322	96	0	11	.964	-7	72	114	C112/1OC		0.3
1914	NY A	87	258	25	55	8	1	1	22	35	4	30	.213	.316	.264	75	-7	19-6	.960	2	92	98	C78		0.5
1915	NY A	53	137	12	26	2	0	0	5	25	1	12	.190	.319	.204	57	-6	3-3	.975	-4	91	92	C53		-0.6
1919	Pit N	17	42	0	4	1	0	0		5	0	6	.095	.191	.119	-5	-5	1	.944	-1	113	111	C15		-0.6
Total	9	644	1841	173	427	48	13	3	151	181	28	89	.232	.310	.277	73	-58	63-9	.964	-19	90	104	C613,1b5,O2(0/1/1)		-2.3

SWEENEY, HANK Henry Leon B12.28.1915 Franklin TN D5.6.1980 Columbia TN BL/TL/6-0/185 d10.1

YEAR	TM LG	G	AB	R	H	2B	3B	HR	RBI	BB-IB	HP	SO	AVG	OBP	SLG	AOPS	ABR	SB-CS	FA	FR	RNG	THR	GAMES AT POSITION	DL	BFW
1944	Pit N	1	2	0	0	0	0	0	0	0			.000	.000	.000	-96	-1		1.000	0	197	0	/1		0.0

SWEENEY, JERRY Jeremiah H. B1860 Boston MA D8.25.1891 Boston MA 5-9.5/157 d8.22

YEAR	TM LG	G	AB	R	H	2B	3B	HR	RBI	BB-IB	HP	SO	AVG	OBP	SLG	AOPS	ABR	SB-CS	FA	FR	RNG	THR	GAMES AT POSITION	DL	BFW
1884	KC U	31	129	16	34	3	0	0		4			.264	.286	.287	85	-6		.958	3	156	119	1b31		-0.5

SWEENEY, ROONEY John J. B11.1.1858 New York NY 5-8/155 d7.25

YEAR	TM LG	G	AB	R	H	2B	3B	HR	RBI	BB-IB	HP	SO	AVG	OBP	SLG	AOPS	ABR	SB-CS	FA	FR	RNG	THR	GAMES AT POSITION	DL	BFW
1883	Bal AA	25	101	13	21	5	2	0		4			.208	.238	.297	69	-3		.878	-0			C23,O3R		-0.2
1884	Bal U	48	186	37	42	7	1	0		15			.226	.284	.274	63	-14		.917	-5			C33,O16(0/6/10)/3		-1.5
1885	StL N	3	11	1	1	0	0	0	0	0		4	.091	.091	.091	-44	-2		.750	-0	0	0	O2(1/1/0)/C		-0.2
Total	3	76	298	51	64	12	3	0	0	19		4	.215	.262	.275	62	-19		.905	-6			C57,O21(1/7/13)/3		-1.9

SWEENEY, MARK Mark Patrick B10.26.1969 Framingham MA BL/TL/6-1/215(195-215) [CalA91 9/246] d8.4 Col Maine

YEAR	TM LG	G	AB	R	H	2B	3B	HR	RBI	BB-IB	HP	SO	AVG	OBP	SLG	AOPS	ABR	SB-CS	FA	FR	RNG	THR	GAMES AT POSITION	DL	BFW
1995	StL N	37	77	5	21	2	0	2	13	10-0	0	15	.273	.348	.377	92	-1	1-1	.994	-1	90	145	1b19/OL		-0.3
1996	†StL N	98	170	32	45	9	0	3	22	33-2	1	29	.265	.387	.371	101	2	3-0	.984	-0	106	55	O43(36/0/7),1b15		-0.1
1997	StL N	44	61	5	13	0	0	2	4	9-1	1	14	.213	.319	.262	56	-4	0-1	1.000	-1	100	0	O25(10/0/15),1b4		-0.5
	SD N	71	103	11	33	4	0	2	19	11-0	0	18	.320	.383	.417	118	2	3-2	.944	-2	74	0	O20(6/1/13),1b7		0.0
	Year	115	164	16	46	7	0	2	23	20-1	1	32	.280	.358	.360	93	-1	3-3	.976	-3	87	0	O45(16/1/28),1b11		-0.5
1998	†SD N	122	192	17	45	8	3	2	15	26-0	1	37	.234	.324	.339	82	-5	1-2	1.000	-3	99	0	O34(5/0/29),1b21/D		-1.1
1999	Cin N	37	31	6	11	3	0	2	7	4-1	0	9	.355	.429	.645	152	3	0-0	1.000	0	601	0	/1OL		0.3
2000	Mil N	71	73	9	16	6	0	1	6	12-1	1	18	.219	.337	.342	73	-3	0-0	1.000	1	315	0	O3L,1b2,D4	60	-0.2
2001	Mil N	48	89	9	23	1	3	1	11	12-0	1	23	.258	.347	.404	98	0	2-1	.968	-2	86	0	O20(20/0/3),1b2		-0.3
2002	SD N	48	65	3	11	3	0	1	4	4-0	0	19	.169	.217	.262	30	-7	0-0	.946	0	95	116	1b11,O5R/D	20	-0.8
2003	Col N	67	97	13	25	9	0	2	14	9-1	0	27	.258	.321	.412	79	-3	0-1	1.000	-2	77	0	O17(7/0/11),1b8/D		-0.6
2004	Col N	122	177	25	47	12	2	9	40	32-2	2	51	.266	.377	.508	114	5	1-0	1.000	3	111	248	O28(9/0/20),1b15,D4		0.6
2005	†Col N	135	221	31	65	12	1	8	40	40-3	0	58	.294	.395	.466	133	12	4-0	.988	-2	82	80	1b53,O6(1/1/4),D5	80	0.8
Total	11	900	1356	166	355	74	6	35	195	202-11	6	318	.262	.356	.404	99	2	14-8	.981	-11	100	50	O203(99/2/107),1b158,D16	80	-2.2

SWEENEY, MIKE Michael John B7.22.1973 Orange CA BR/TR/6-2/215(195-235) [KCA91 10/262] d9.4

YEAR	TM LG	G	AB	R	H	2B	3B	HR	RBI	BB-IB	HP	SO	AVG	OBP	SLG	AOPS	ABR	SB-CS	FA	FR	RNG	THR	GAMES AT POSITION	DL	BFW
1995	KC A	4	4	1	1	0	0	0	0	0-0	0	1	.250	.250	.250	30	0	0-0	.875	0	0	0	C4		0.0
1996	KC A	50	165	23	46	10	0	4	24	18-0	4	21	.279	.358	.412	95	-1	0-0	.994	2	139	120	C26,D22		0.1
1997	KC A	84	240	30	58	8	0	7	31	17-0	6	33	.242	.306	.363	72	-10	3-2	.993	9	136	110	C76,D3		-0.5
1998	KC A	92	282	32	73	18	0	8	35	24-1	2	34	.259	.320	.408	85	-6	2-3	.984	-3	114	80	C91		0.8
1999	KC A	150	575	101	185	44	6	22	102	54-0	10	48	.322	.387	.520	124	23	6-1	.981	-4	95	110	D71,1b74,C4		1.4
2000	KC A★	159	618	105	206	30	4	29	144	71-5	15	67	.333	.407	.523	128	29	8-3	.991	3	112	103	1b114,D45		1.4
2001	KC A★	147	559	97	170	46	0	29	99	64-13	2	64	.304	.374	.542	125	22	10-3	.989	0	115	136	1b108,D38	30	3.2
2002	KC A★	126	471	81	160	31	4	24	86	61-10	6	56	.340	.417	.563	141	30	9-7	.991	14	159	107	1b102,D24	48	5.1
2003	KC A★	108	392	62	115	18	1	16	83	64-5	2	56	.293	.391	.467	118	13	3-2	.990	2	126	78	D62,1b45	48	0.7
2004	KC A	106	411	56	118	23	0	22	79	33-9	6	44	.287	.347	.504	119	11	3-2	.992	1	116	92	1b55,D48	43	0.8
2005	KC A★	122	470	63	141	39	0	21	83	33-7	4	61	.300	.347	.517	135	5	3-0	.998	-1	93	61	D73,1b49	15	1.0
Total	11	1148	4187	651	1273	267	4	182	766	439-50	57	478	.304	.374	.500	120	135	48-25	.990	27	119	104	1b547,D386,C201	136	14.0

SWEENEY, PETE Peter Jay B12.31.1863 CA D8.22.1901 San Francisco CA BR/TR/5-9/170 d9.28

YEAR	TM LG	G	AB	R	H	2B	3B	HR	RBI	BB-IB	HP	SO	AVG	OBP	SLG	AOPS	ABR	SB-CS	FA	FR	RNG	THR	GAMES AT POSITION	DL	BFW
1888	Was N	11	44	3	8	0	1	0	5	2		0	.182	.182	.227	32	-4	0	.784	-1	68	77	3b8,O3L		-0.5
1889	Was N	49	193	13	44	7	3	1	23	11	4	26	.228	.284	.311	70	-8	8	.802	-10	87	65	3b47/2OR		-1.8
	StL AA	9	38	8	14	2	0	0	8	1	2	5	.368	.415	.421	122	1	2	.780	-2	81	71	3b8/OC		0.1
1890	StL AA	49	190	23	34	3	2	0	10	17	7		.179	.271	.216	38	-16	9	.880	-6	94	71	2b23,3b21,1b3,O2R		-1.3
	Lou AA	2	7	1	1	1	0	0	1	1		0	.143	.250	.286	59	-0	1	.889	-1	33	0	S2		-0.0
	Phi AA	14	49	5	8	1	0	0	7	1	1		.163	.281	.224	49	-3	0	.915	-4	79	23	2b9,O4C,3b2		-0.8
	Year	65	246	29	43	5	3	0	11	25	8		.175	.272	.220	41	-19	9	.889	-11	90	58	2b32,3b23,O6(0/4/2),1b3,S2		-2.2
Total	3	134	521	53	109	14	7	1	47	37	14	35	.209	.280	.257	57	-30	19	.799	-24	77	79	3b86,2b33,O11(3/5/3),1b3,S2		-4.4

SWEENEY, BILL William John B3.6.1886 Covington KY D5.26.1948 Cambridge MA BR/TR/5-11/175 d6.14 OF(9/1/1)

YEAR	TM LG	G	AB	R	H	2B	3B	HR	RBI	BB-IB	HP	SO	AVG	OBP	SLG	AOPS	ABR	SB-CS	FA	FR	RNG	THR	GAMES AT POSITION	DL	BFW
1907	Chi N	3	10	1	1	0	0	0		1			.100	.182	.100	-11	-1	1	.571	-3	66	0	S3		-0.1
	Bos N	58	191	24	50	2	0	0	18	15		0	.262	.316	.272	85	-3	8	.871	-0	108	153	3b23,S15,O11(9/1/1),2b5/1		-1.0
	Year	61	201	25	51	2	0	0	19	16		0	.254	.309	.264	79	-5	9	.871	-4	108	153	3b23,S18,O11(9/1/1),2b5/1		-1.1
1908	Bos N	127	418	44	102	15	3	0	40	45		0	.244	.317	.294	97	0	17	.930	12	114	92	3b123,S3/2		0.9
1909	Bos N	138	493	44	120	19	3	1	36	37		0	.243	.296	.300	81	-11	25	.903	7	109	90	3b112,S26		-0.1
1910	Bos N	150	499	43	133	22	4	1	46	61		2	.267	.349	.357	101	2	25	.903	-4	91	113	S110,3b21,1b17		0.2
1911	Bos N	137	523	92	164	33	6	3	63	77		26	.314	.404	.417	120	17	33	.944	11	104	87	2b136		2.0
1912	Bos N	153	593	84	204	31	13	1	100	68		34	.344	.416	.445	133	30	27	.959	26	104	108	2b153		5.0
1913	Bos N	139	502	65	129	17	6	0	47	66		50	.257	.347	.315	88	-5	18-18	.939	1	101	79	2b137		-0.1
1914	Chi N	134	463	45	101	14	5	1	38	53		15	.218	.298	.276	71	-16	18	.954	16	107	79	2b134		0.9
Total	8	1039	3692	442	1004	153	40	11	389	423		12	153	.272	.349	.344	100	13	172-18	.949	66	104	88	2b566,3b279,S157,1b18,O11L		9.1

SWEENEY, BILL William Joseph B12.29.1904 Cleveland OH D4.18.1957 San Diego CA BR/TR/5-11/180 d4.13 C2

YEAR	TM LG	G	AB	R	H	2B	3B	HR	RBI	BB-IB	HP	SO	AVG	OBP	SLG	AOPS	ABR	SB-CS	FA	FR	RNG	THR	GAMES AT POSITION	DL	BFW
1928	Det A	89	309	47	78	15	5	0	19	15		28	.252	.287	.333	62	-18	12-8	.993	4	120	88	1b75,O3L		-1.3
1930	Bos A	88	243	25	72	15	3	0	4	8		15	.296	.333	.412	91	-4	5-3	.993	1	93	113	1b56/3		-0.3
1931	Bos A	131	498	48	147	28	3	5	58	20		30	.295	.322	.373	87	-10	5-12	.993	8	132	92	1b124		0.6
Total	3	308	1050	120	297	58	8	5	107	44		73	.286	.314	.370	80	-32	22-23	.994	12	120	95	1b255,O3L/3		-1.0

SWEET, RICK Ricky Joe B9.7.1952 Longview WA BB/TR (BL 1978p)/6-1/190(187-200) [SDN75*S3/65] d4.8 C2 Col Gonzaga

YEAR	TM LG	G	AB	R	H	2B	3B	HR	RBI	BB-IB	HP	SO	AVG	OBP	SLG	AOPS	ABR	SB-CS	FA	FR	RNG	THR	GAMES AT POSITION	DL	BFW
1978	SD N	88	226	15	50	8	0	1	11	27-7	1	22	.221	.306	.270	67	-9	1-4	.984	6	164	111	C76		-0.8
1982	NY N	3	3	0	1	0	0	0	0	0-0	1	0	.333	.333	.333	87	0		—	0	0		/H		0.0

YEAR	TM LG	G	AB	R	H	2B	3B	HR	RBI	BB-IB	HP	SO	AVG	OBP	SLG	AOPS	ABR	SB-CS	FA	FR	RNG	THR	GAMES AT POSITION	DL	BFW
1983	Sea A	88	258	29	66	6	1	4	24	20-0	2	24	.256	.311	.333	75	-9	3-0	.993	1	116	92	C83		-0.4
1983	Sea A	93	249	18	55	9	0	1	22	13-1	0	26	.221	.259	.269	44	-19	2-2	.987	5	81	131	C85		-1.2
Total	3	272	736	62	172	23	1	6	57	60-8	3	73	.234	.292	.292	62	-37	6-6	.988	11	119	111	C244	11	-1.8

SWEIGERT, HAM Hampton d10.12

1890	Phi AA	1	1	0	0	0	0	0	0	0-0		0	.000	.500	.000	48	0	1	1.000	1	722	0	/OL		0.1

SWENTOR, AUGIE August William B11.21.1899 Seymour CT D11.10.1969 Waterbury CT BR/TR/6-0/185 d9.12 Col Colgate

1922	Chi A	1	1	0	0	0	0	0	0	0-0		0	.000	.000	.000	-99	0	0-0	—	0			/H		0.0

SWETT, POP William E. B4.16.1870 San Francisco CA D11.22.1934 San Francisco CA 6-0/175 d5.3

1890	Bos P	37	94	16	18	4	3	1	12	16	2	26	.191	.321	.330	69	-4	4	.820	-2	151	44	C34,O3R		-0.4

SWIFT, BOB Robert Virgil B3.6.1915 Salina KS D10.17.1966 Detroit MI BR/TR/5-11.5/180* d4.16 M2/C10

1940	StL A	130	398	37	97	20	1	0	39	28	1	39	.244	.295	.299	53	-27	1-0	.980	-15	93	79	C128		-3.4
1941	StL A	63	170	13	44	7	0	0	21	22	0	11	.259	.344	.300	69	-7	2-0	.985	-4	96	81	C58		-0.7
1942	StL A	29	76	9	15	4	0	1	8	3	0	5	.197	.228	.289	44	-6	0-2	1.000	-1	78	76	C28		-0.7
	Phi A	60	192	9	44	3	0	0	15	13	0	17	.229	.278	.245	48	-14	1-2	.970	-2	76	132	C60		-1.3
	Year	89	268	12	59	7	0	1	23	16	0	22	.220	.264	.257	47	-20	1-4	.977	-4	77	117	C88		-2.0
1943	Phi A	77	224	16	43	5	1	1	11	35	0	16	.192	.301	.237	58	-11	0-0	.976	-5	76	98	C77		-1.3
1944	Det A	80	247	15	63	11	1	1	19	27	1	27	.255	.331	.340	82	-5	2-0	.982	7	172	151	C76		0.7
1945	†Det A	95	279	19	65	5	0	0	24	26	0	22	.233	.298	.251	56	-15	1-0	.988	5	115	120	C94		-0.6
1946	Det A	42	107	13	25	2	0	0	10	14	0	7	.234	.322	.308	72	-4	0-0	.980	-3	98	59	C42		-0.5
1947	Det A	97	279	23	70	11	0	1	23	33	0	16	.251	.330	.301	74	-9	2-2	.989	3	120	95	C97		-0.2
1948	Det A	113	292	23	65	6	0	4	33	51	0	23	.223	.338	.284	65	-14	1-0	.991	3	100	89	C112		-0.5
1949	Det A	74	189	16	45	6	0	2	18	26	0	20	.238	.330	.302	68	-9	0-0	.989	-1	105	110	C69		-0.6
1950	Det A	67	132	14	30	4	0	2	9	25	0	6	.227	.350	.303	66	-6	0-0	.995	5	149	90	C66		0.1
1951	Det A	44	104	8	20	1	0	0	5	12	0	10	.192	.276	.192	28	-11	0-0	.982	-0	76	89	C43		-0.9
1952	Det A	28	58	3	8	1	0	0	4	7	1	7	.138	.242	.155	12	-7	0-0	.977	3	124	120	C28		-0.3
1953	Det A	2	3	0	1	1	0	0	1	2	0	1	.333	.600	.667	245	1	0-0	1.000	0			C2		0.1
Total	14	1001	2750	212	635	86	3	14	238	324	3	233	.231	.313	.280	61	-144	10-6	.985	-5	107	100	C980	50	-10.1

SWINDELLS, CHARLIE Charles Jay "Swin" B10.26.1878 Rockford IL D7.22.1940 Portland OR BR/TR/5-11.5/180 d9.7 Col Stanford

1904	StL N	3	8	0	1	0	0	0	0	0		0	.125	.125	.125	-24	-1	0	1.000	0	101	39	C3		-0.1

SWISHER, NICK Nicholas Thompson B1.25.1980 Columbus OH BB/TL/6-0/195* [OakA02 1/16] d9.3 f-Steve Col Ohio St.

2004	Oak A	20	60	11	15	4	0	2	8	8-0	2	11	.250	.352	.417	102	0	0-1	.889	-3	84		O16(12/1/4),1b3,D2		-0.3
2005	Oak A	131	462	66	109	32	1	21	74	55-3	4	110	.236	.322	.446	100	1	0-1	.990	-6	85	88	O121R,1b21	23	-1.3
Total	2	151	522	77	124	36	1	23	82	63-3	6	121	.238	.325	.443	100	1	0-1	.978	-9	85	78	O137(12/1/125),1b24,D2	23	-1.6

SWISHER, STEVE Steven Eugene B8.9.1951 Parkersburg WV BR/TR/6-2/205* [ChiA73 1/21] d6.14 C4 s-Nick Col Ohio U.

1974	Chi N	90	280	21	60	5	0	5*	27	37-1	2	63	.214	.307	.286	69	-13	0-3	.987	-3	113	96	C90		-1.3
1975	Chi N	93	254	20	54	16	3	1	22	30-7	1	82	.213	.301	.303	66	-11	1-0	.979	-11	104	95	C93		-1.9
1976	Chi N☆	109	359	29	89	13	3	5	42	20-3	2	82	.236	.275	.326	65	-18	2-1	.983	-4	119	104	C107		-1.8
1977	Chi N	74	205	21	39	7	0	5	15	9-5	2	47	.190	.229	.298	37	-19	0-0	.976	-4	100	103	C72		-2.1
1978	StL N	45	115	11	32	5	1	1	10	8-0	1	14	.278	.331	.365	95	-1	1-0	.991	-2	84	86	C42		-0.1
1979	StL N	38	73	4	11	1	1	1	3	6-0	0	17	.151	.211	.233	22	-8	0-0	.974	-4	140	58	C33		-1.1
1980	StL N	18	24	2	6	1	0	0	2	1-0	0	9	.250	.280	.292	57	-1	0-0	.957	-1	86	103	C8		-0.2
1981	SD N	16	28	2	4	0	0	0	0	2-0	1	11	.143	.200	.143	-2	-4	0-0	.971	-1	110	39	C10	26	-0.5
1982	SD N	26	58	2	10	1	0	2	3	9-0	1	24	.172	.238	.293	51	-4	0-0	.981	-3	89	64	C26	43	-0.6
Total	9	509	1414	108	305	49	7	20	124	118-16	11	322	.216	.279	.303	59	-79	4-4	.982	-32	109	94	C481	69	-9.6

SWOBODA, RON Ronald Alan "Rocky" B6.30.1944 Baltimore MD BR/TR/6-2/205(195-215) d4.12 Col Maryland-Baltimore Co.

1965	NY N	135	399	52	91	15	3	19	50	33-3	3	102	.228	.291	.424	102	0	2-3	.947	2	101	153	O112(73/26/15)		-0.4
1966	NY N	112	342	34	76	9	4	8	50	31-4	5	76	.222	.296	.342	79	-10	4-2	.987	-1	89	109	O97(88/0/10)		-1.7
1967	NY N	134	449	47	126	17	3	13	53	41-4	1	96	.281	.340	.419	119	11	3-1	.957	1	101	105	O108R,1b20		0.4
1968	NY N	132	450	46	109	14	6	11	59	52-1	4	113	.242	.325	.373	109	5	8-1	.975	1	97	136	O125R		0.0
1969	†NY N	109	327	38	77	10	2	9	52	43-4	2	90	.235	.326	.361	90	-4	1-1	.988	-1	100	76	O97(22/0/77)		-1.0
1970	NY N	115	245	29	57	8	2	9	40	40-0	1	72	.233	.340	.392	95	-1	2-4	.984	-2	93	60	O100(1/0/100)		-0.8
1971	Mon N	39	75	7	19	4	3	0	6	11-0	2	16	.253	.364	.387	111	1	0-1	.977	2	98	286	O26(10/17/3)		0.2
	NY A	54	138	17	36	2	1	2	20	27-1	3	35	.261	.391	.333	113	4	0-0	.965	-1	97	47	O47(7/1/39)		0.1
1972	NY A	63	113	9	28	8	0	1	12	17-1	0	29	.248	.341	.345	108	2	0-1	.983	-0	96	99	O35(0/5/35),1b2		0.0
1973	NY A	35	43	6	5	0	1	0	5	8-1	1	18	.116	.191	.186	7	-6	0-0	1.000	-1	98	0	O20(0/8/12),D4		-0.7
Total	9	928	2581	285	624	87	24	73	344	299-18	21	647	.242	.324	.379	100	2	20-14	.972	0	97	111	O767(201/57/524),1b22,D4		-3.9

SYLVESTER, LOU Louis J. B2.14.1855 Springfield IL D5.5.1936 Brooklyn NY BR/TR/5-6/165 d4.18 ▲

1884	Cin U	82	333	67	89	13	8	2		18			.267	.305	.372	96	-12		.792	-3	110	71	O81(54/6/22),P6,S2		-1.3
1886	Lou AA	45	154	41	35	5	3	0	17	29	0		.227	.350	.299	98	1	3	.913	1	140	258	O45C		0.0
	Cin AA	17	55	10	10	0	0	3	8	7	1		.182	.286	.345	94	0	2	.909	1	144	367	O17(7/7/3)		0.0
	Year	62	209	51	45	5	3	3	25	36	1		.215	.333	.311	97	0	5	.912	2	141	291	O62(7/52/3)		0.0
1887	StL AA	29	112	20	25	4	3	1	18	13	1		.223	.310	.339	73	-5	13	.923	2	148	323	O29(12/4/13)/2		-0.3
Total	3	173	654	138	159	22	14	6	43	67	2		.243	.315	.347	93	-16	18	.854	2	127	186	O172(73/62/38),P6,S2/2		-1.6

ZEKELY, JOE Joseph B2.2.1925 Cleveland OH D10.16.1995 Paris TX BR/TR/5-11/180 d9.13 Col Baylor

1953	Cin N	5	13	0	1	0	0	0	0	0	0	3	.077	.077	.077	-59	-3	0-0	1.000	1	72	942	O3R		-0.2

ZOTKIEWICZ, KEN Kenneth John B2.25.1947 Wilmington DE BL/TR/6-0/165 [DetA68*S1/3] d4.7 Col Georgia Southern

1970	Det A	47	84	9	9	1	0	3	9	12-2	0	29	.107	.216	.226	23	-9	0-0	.971	3	111	106	S44	50	-0.3

ABB, JERRY Jerry Lynn B3.17.1952 Altus OK BL/TR/6-2/195* [ChiN73 1/16] d9.8 Col Tulsa [DL 1979 Oak A 47]

1976	Chi N	11	24	2	7	0	0	0	3	3-0	0	2	.292	.370	.292	82	0	0-0	1.000	-0	64	112	1b6		-0.1
1977	Oak A	51	144	8	32	3	0	6	19	10-2	0	26	.222	.269	.368	74	-6	0-1	.993	-2	77	98	1b36,D5		-1.0
1978	Oak A	12	9	0	1	0	0	0	1	2-1	0	5	.111	.273	.111	12	-1	0-0	1.000	-0	0	0	1b2,D2		-0.1
Total	3	74	177	10	40	3	0	6	20	15-3	0	33	.226	.284	.345	72	-7	0-1	.994	-2	74	98	1b44,D7	47	-1.2

ABLER, PAT Patrick Sean B2.2.1958 Hamilton OH BR/TR/6-2/200* [NYA76 1/16] d8.21 OF(204/0/80)

1981	Chi N	35	101	11	19	3	1	1	5	13-0	1	26	.188	.281	.267	53	-6	0-1	.982	-2	94	82	2b35		-0.7
1982	Chi N	25	85	9	20	4	2	1	7	6-0	1	20	.235	.287	.365	80	-2	0-0	.949	-5	72	75	3b25		-0.8
1983	Cle A	124	430	56	125	23	6	6	65	56-1	1	63	.291	.370	.409	111	8	2-4	.948	-5	95	59	O88(87/0/1),3b25,2b2,D6		-0.2
1984	Cle A	144	473	66	137	21	3	10	68	47-2	3	62	.290	.354	.410	110	7	3-1	.998	-6	93	95	1b67,O43L,3b36/2D		-0.4
1985	Cle A	117	404	47	111	18	3	5	59	27-2	2	55	.275	.321	.371	90	-6	0-0	.983	3	119	99	1b92,D18,3b4/2		-1.1
1986	Cle A	130	473	61	154	29	2	6	48	29-3	3	75	.326	.368	.433	119	13	3-1	.990	-1	103	93	1b107,D18		0.5
1987	Cle A★	151	553	66	170	34	3	11	86	51-6	6	84	.307	.369	.439	113	12	5-2	.984	6	134	72	1b82,D66	19	1.1
1988	Cle A	41	143	16	32	5	1	1	17	23-1	1	27	.224	.333	.294	75	-4	1	1.000	-0	80	66	D29,1b10		-0.6
	KC A	89	301	37	93	17	2	1	49	23-0	2	41	.309	.358	.389	109	4	2-3	.986	-1	101	52	D40,O37(28/0/9),1b7/3		0.6
	Year	130	444	53	125	22	3	2	66	46-1	3	68	.282	.349	.358	98	0	3-3	.986	-2	101	52	D69,O37(28/0/9),1b17/3		-0.6
1989	KC A	123	390	36	101	11	1	2	42	37-0	2	42	.259	.325	.308	80	-10	0-0	.970	5	94	258	O55(26/0/28),D39,1b20,2b3/3		-0.8
1990	KC A	75	195	12	53	14	0	1	19	20-2	1	21	.272	.338	.359	98	0	0-2	.986	1	105	179	O42(11/0/31),D15,3b6,1b5		-0.1
	NY N	17	43	6	12	1	1	1	10	3-0	1	5	.279	.340	.419	107	0	0-0	1.000	1	116	168	O10(3/0/8)		0.1
1991	†Tor A	82	185	20	40	5	1	2	21	29-5	1	25	.216	.318	.270	64	-8	0-0	.985	0	103	70	D57,1b20/OL		-1.2
1992	†Tor A	49	135	11	34	7	0	0	16	11-0	0	14	.252	.306	.304	65	-6	0-0	1.000	0	98	81	1b34,O8(5/0/3)/3D		-0.8
Total	12	1202	3911	454	1101	190	25	47	512	375-22	24	559	.282	.345	.379	99	2	16-20	.988	-3	111	90	1b444,D291,O284L,3b99,2b42	19	-5.0

ABOR, GREG Gregory Steven B5.21.1961 Castro Valley CA BR/TR/6-0/165 [TexA81*1/10] d9.10 Col Chabot (CA) JC

1987	Tex A	9	9	4	1	1	0	0	1	0-0	0	4	.111	.111	.222	-15	-1	0-0	.938	1	146	113	2b4/D		0.0

YEAR	TM	LG	G	AB	R	H	2B	3B	HR	RBI	BB-IB	HP	SO	AVG	OBP	SLG	AOPS	ABR	SB-CS	FA	FR	RNG	THR	GAMES AT POSITION	DL	BFW

TABOR, JIM   James Reubin "Rawhide" B11.5.1916 New Hope AL D8.22.1953 Sacramento CA BR/TR/6-2/175 d8.2 Mil 1944-45 Col Alabama

YEAR	TM	LG	G	AB	R	H	2B	3B	HR	RBI	BB-IB	HP	SO	AVG	OBP	SLG	AOPS	ABR	SB-CS	FA	FR	RNG	THR	GAMES AT POSITION	DL	BFW
1938	Bos	A	19	57	8	18	3	2	1	8	1	0	6	.316	.328	.491	98	-1	0-1	.889	-1	100	91	3b11,S2		-0.1
1939	Bos	A	149	577	76	167	33	8	14	95	40	1	54	.289	.337	.447	95	-7	16-10	.923	4	108	107	3b148		0.3
1940	Bos	A	120	459	73	131	28	6	21	81	42	0	58	.285	.334	.510	114	8	14-10	.926	2	103	99	3b120		1.4
1941	Bos	A	126	498	65	139	29	3	16	101	36	0	48	.279	.328	.446	100	-2	17-9	.930	0	104	99	3b125		0.4
1942	Bos	A	139	508	56	128	18	2	12	75	37	0	47	.252	.303	.366	85	-12	6-13	.924	-8	90	103	3b138		-1.9
1943	Bos	A	137	537	57	130	26	3	13	85	43	1	54	.242	.299	.374	95	-5	7-7	.938	-7	100	125	3b133,O2L		-1.3
1944	Bos	A	116	438	58	125	25	3	13	72	31	1	38	.285	.334	.445	123	11	4-4	.950	4	105	63	3b124		1.7
1946	Phi	N	124	463	53	124	15	2	10	50	36	1	51	.268	.322	.374	100	-2	3	.954	-2	94	89	3b124		-0.5
1947	Phi	N	75	251	27	59	14	0	4	31	20	2	21	.235	.297	.339	71	-11	2	.916	-12	79	73	3b67		-2.3
Total	9		1005	3788	473	1021	191	29	104	598	286	6	377	.270	.322	.418	99	-21	69-54	.933	-18	99	97	3b980,O2L,S2		-2.3

TACKETT, JEFF   Jeffrey Wilson B12.1.1965 Fresno CA BR/TR/6-2/200* [BalA84 2/53] d9.11

YEAR	TM	LG	G	AB	R	H	2B	3B	HR	RBI	BB-IB	HP	SO	AVG	OBP	SLG	AOPS	ABR	SB-CS	FA	FR	RNG	THR	GAMES AT POSITION	DL	BFW
1991	Bal	A	6	8	1	1	0	0	0	0	2-0	0	2	.125	.300	.125	23	-1	0-0	1.000	-1	75	0	C6		-0.1
1992	Bal	A	65	179	21	43	8	1	5	24	17-1	2	28	.240	.307	.380	90	-3	0-0	.997	3	134	81	C64/3		0.4
1993	Bal	A	39	87	8	15	3	0	0	9	13-0	0	28	.172	.277	.207	32	-8	0-0	.989	-1	93	150	C38/P		-0.7
1994	Bal	A	26	53	5	12	3	1	2	9	5-0	2	13	.226	.317	.434	86	-1	0-0	.980	-3	114	68	C26		-0.3
Total	4		136	327	35	71	14	2	7	42	37-1	4	71	.217	.300	.336	72	-13	0-0	.992	-1	118	95	C134/P3		-0.7

TAGUCHI, SO   So B7.22.1969 Hyogo, Japan BR/TR/5-10/163* d6.10

YEAR	TM	LG	G	AB	R	H	2B	3B	HR	RBI	BB-IB	HP	SO	AVG	OBP	SLG	AOPS	ABR	SB-CS	FA	FR	RNG	THR	GAMES AT POSITION	DL	BFW
2002	StL	N	19	15	4	6	0	0	0	2	1-0	0	1	.400	.471	.400	136	1	1-0	.929	2	115	803	O14(8/6/0)		0.
2003	StL	N	43	54	9	14	3	1	3	13	4-1	0	11	.259	.310	.519	112	1	0-0	1.000	1	102	246	O38(11/16/13)/2		0.
2004	†StL	N	109	179	26	52	10	2	3	25	12-1	2	23	.291	.337	.419	94	-2	6-3	.980	-3	92	35	O103(53/31/28)		-1.4
2005	†StL	N	143	396	45	114	21	2	8	53	20-2	2	62	.288	.322	.412	90	-7	11-2	.989	-6	86	88	O131(50/52/57)		-1.5
Total	4		314	644	84	186	34	5	14	93	38-4	4	97	.289	.329	.422	94	-7	18-5	.985	-6	90	102	O286(122/105/98)/2		

TAITT, DOUG   Douglas John "Poco" B8.3.1902 Bay City MI D12.12.1970 Portland OR BL/TR/6-0/176 d4.10

YEAR	TM	LG	G	AB	R	H	2B	3B	HR	RBI	BB-IB	HP	SO	AVG	OBP	SLG	AOPS	ABR	SB-CS	FA	FR	RNG	THR	GAMES AT POSITION	DL	BFW
1928	Bos	A	143	482	51	144	28	14	3	61	36	0	32	.299	.350	.434	107	3	13-6	.975	6	102	140	O139(9/0/130)/P		-0.
1929	Bos	A	26	65	6	18	4	0	0	6	8	1	5	.277	.365	.338	84	-1	0-1	.955	1	106	163	O21(11/0/11)		-1.
	Chi	A	47	124	11	21	7	0	0	12	8	0	13	.169	.220	.226	15	-16	0-1	.966	1	101	141	O30R		-1.
	Year		73	189	17	39	11	0	0	18	16	1	18	.206	.272	.265	39	-17	0-1	.961	2	103	150	O51(11/0/41)		-1.
1931	Phi	N	38	151	13	34	4	2	1	15	4	0	14	.225	.245	.298	42	-13	0	.990	4	113	190	O38L		-1.
1932	Phi	N	4	4	0	0	0	0	0	1	2	0	0	.000	.500	.000	43	0	0	—	0			/H		0.
Total	4		258	824	81	217	43	16	4	95	58	3	64	.263	.314	.369	79	-27	13-7	.975	12	104	151	O228(58/0/171)/P		

TALBOT, BOB   Robert Dale B6.6.1927 Visalia CA BR/TR/6-0/170* d9.16

YEAR	TM	LG	G	AB	R	H	2B	3B	HR	RBI	BB-IB	HP	SO	AVG	OBP	SLG	AOPS	ABR	SB-CS	FA	FR	RNG	THR	GAMES AT POSITION	DL	BFW
1953	Chi	N	8	30	5	10	1	0	0	0	6		0	.333	.333	.400	88	-1	1-0	1.000	2	98	442	O7C		0.
1954	Chi	N	114	403	45	97	15	4	1	19	16	3	25	.241	.274	.305	50	-30	3-6	.985	-3	91	132	O111C		-4.
Total	2		122	433	50	107	15	5	1	19	22	3	53	.247	.278	.312	53	-31	4-6	.986	-1	91	153	O118C		-3

TALTON, TIM   Marion Lee B1.14.1939 Pikeville NC BL/TR/6-3/200* d7.8 Col East Carolina

YEAR	TM	LG	G	AB	R	H	2B	3B	HR	RBI	BB-IB	HP	SO	AVG	OBP	SLG	AOPS	ABR	SB-CS	FA	FR	RNG	THR	GAMES AT POSITION	DL	BFW
1966	KC	A	37	53	8	18	3	1	2	6	1-0	0	5	.340	.364	.547	163	4	0-1	1.000	-1	46	166	C14,1b9	41	-0.
1967	KC	A	46	59	7	15	3	1	0	5	7-1	0	13	.254	.328	.339	102	0	0-0	.971	-4	37	79	C22/1	41	-0.
Total	2		83	112	15	33	6	2	2	11	8-1	0	18	.295	.344	.438	131	4	0-1	.980	-2	40	108	C36,1b10	41	0.

TAMARGO, JOHN   John Felix B11.7.1951 Tampa FL BB/TR/5-10/180(168-180) [StLN73 6/132] d9.3 C6 Col Georgia Southern

YEAR	TM	LG	G	AB	R	H	2B	3B	HR	RBI	BB-IB	HP	SO	AVG	OBP	SLG	AOPS	ABR	SB-CS	FA	FR	RNG	THR	GAMES AT POSITION	DL	BFW
1976	StL	N	10	10	2	3	0	0	0	1	3-0	0	2	.300	.429	.300	117	-1	0-0	1.000	-1	70	0	/C		0.
1977	StL	N	4	4	0	0	0	0	0	0	0-0	0	2	.000	.000	.000	-99	-1	0-0	1.000	0	0	0	/C		-0.
1978	StL	N	6	6	0	0	0	0	0	0	0-0	0	2	.000	.000	.000	-99	-2	0-0	—	-0	0	0	/C		-0.
	SF	N	36	92	6	22	4	1	1	8	18-5	0	7	.239	.360	.337	100	1	1-1	.965	-5	63	29	C31		-0.
	Year		42	98	6	22	4	1	1	8	18-5	0	9	.224	.342	.316	88	-1	1-1	.965	-5	63	29	C32		-0.
1979	SF	N	30	60	7	12	3	0	2	6	4-0	0	3	.200	.239	.350	67	-3	0-0	.985	-3	101	128	C17		-0.
	Mon	N	12	21	0	8	2	0	0	5	3-0	0	3	.381	.440	.476	155	-2	0-0	1.000	-2	45	61	C4		-0.
	Year		42	81	7	20	5	0	2	11	7-0	0	6	.247	.293	.383	91	-5	0-0	.989	-5	87	111	C21		-0.
1980	Mon	N	37	51	4	14	3	0	1	13	6-0	0	5	.275	.345	.392	105	-1	0-0	.975	-2	45	72	C12	25	-1.
Total	5		135	244	19	59	12	1	4	33	34-5	0	27	.242	.326	.348	92	-1	1-1	.974	-12	68	60	C67	25	-1

TANKERSLEY, LEO   Lawrence William B6.8.1901 Terrell TX D9.18.1980 Dallas TX BR/TR/6-0/176 d7.2 Col TCU

YEAR	TM	LG	G	AB	R	H	2B	3B	HR	RBI	BB-IB	HP	SO	AVG	OBP	SLG	AOPS	ABR	SB-CS	FA	FR	RNG	THR	GAMES AT POSITION	DL	BFW
1925	Chi	A	1	3	0	0	0	0	0	0	0	0		.000	.000	.000	-99	-1	0-0	—	-0	0	0	/C		-0

TANNEHILL, JESSE   Jesse Niles "Powder" B7.14.1874 Dayton KY D9.22.1956 Dayton KY BB/TL (BL 1903)/5-8/150 d6.17 C1 b-Lee ▲

YEAR	TM	LG	G	AB	R	H	2B	3B	HR	RBI	BB-IB	HP	SO	AVG	OBP	SLG	AOPS	ABR	SB-CS	FA	FR	RNG	THR	GAMES AT POSITION	DL	BFW
1894	Cin	N	5	11	0	0	0	0	0	0	2			.000	.083	.000	-76	-2		.600	-1	37	0	P5		
1897	Pit	N	56	184	22	49	8	2	0	22	18	2		.266	.338	.332	80	-5	4	.900	4	151	0	P43(4/27/2),P21		
1898	Pit	N	60	152	25	44	9	3	1	17	7	0		.289	.321	.408	110	1	4	.956	3	116	81	P43,O7(3/4/0)		
1899	Pit	N	48	136	18	34	5	3	0	11	8	0		.250	.301	.331	74	-5	2	.955	3	124	311	P41/OL		
1900	Pit	N	34	110	19	37	7	0	0	12	6	0		.336	.365	.400	110	2	2	.924	1	109	0	P29,O4R		
1901	Pit	N	42	135	19	33	3	3	1	12	6	0		.244	.277	.333	74	-5	0	.917	-2	78	0	P32,O10(9/0/1)		
1902	Pit	N	44	148	27	43	6	1	1	17	12	1		.291	.348	.365	116	3	3	.969	-1	96	197	P26,O16(5/0/11)		
1903	NY	A	40	111	18	26	6	2	1	13	8	1		.234	.292	.351	87	-2	1	.969	2	115	124	P32,O5(4/1/0)		
1904	Bos	A	45	122	14	24	2	6	0	6	9	0		.197	.252	.311	73	-4	1	.991	2	117	173	P33,O2L		
1905	Bos	A	37	93	11	21	2	0	1	12	16	0		.226	.339	.280	96	6	1	.946	6	103	141	P37		
1906	Bos	A	31	79	12	22	2	2	0	6	6	0		.278	.329	.354	114	6	1	.948	9	98	63	P27		
1907	Bos	A	21	51	2	10	3	1	0	6	2	1		.196	.241	.294	71	1	0	.981	0	103	285	P18		
1908	Bos	A	1	2	0	1	0	0	0	0	0	0		.500	.500	.500	219	0	0	1.000	0	196	0	/P		
	Was	A	26	43	1	11	1	0	0	3	2	0		.256	.289	.279	92	2	0	.897	1	141	339	P10		
	Year		27	45	1	12	1	0	0	3	2	0		.267	.298	.289	99	3	0	.907	2	145	317	P11		
1909	Was	A	16	36	2	6	1	0	0	1	5	1		.167	.286	.194	55	-2	0	1.000	-0	0	0	O9R,P3		
1911	Cin	N	1	0	0	0	0	0	0	0	0	0		1.000	.000	.000	-99	-0	0	1.000	-0	93	0	/P		
Total	15		507	1414	190	361	55	23	5	142	105	8	3	.255	.310	.337	89	-4	19	.953	15	111	140	P359,O87(28/32/27)		

TANNEHILL, LEE   Lee Ford B10.26.1880 Dayton KY D2.16.1938 Live Oak FL BR/TR/5-11/170 d4.22 b-Jesse

YEAR	TM	LG	G	AB	R	H	2B	3B	HR	RBI	BB-IB	HP	SO	AVG	OBP	SLG	AOPS	ABR	SB-CS	FA	FR	RNG	THR	GAMES AT POSITION	DL	BFW
1903	Chi	A	**138**	503	48	113	14	3	2	50	25	1		.225	.263	.276	65	-22	10	.908	-9	103	118	S138		
1904	Chi	A	153	547	50	125	31	5	0	61	20	3		.229	.260	.303	81	-12	14	.947	27	123	172	3b153		
1905	Chi	A	142	480	38	96	17	2	0	39	45	3		.200	.274	.244	67	-16	8	.931	25	124	156	3b142		
1906	†Chi	A	116	378	26	69	8	3	0	33	31	5		.183	.254	.220	50	-21	7	.951	32	136	139	3b99,S17		
1907	Chi	A	33	108	9	26	2	0	0	11	8	0		.241	.293	.259	79	-3	3	.912	4	125	97	3b31,S2		
1908	Chi	A	141	482	44	104	15	3	0	35	25	2		.216	.257	.259	69	-17	6	.935	17	122	112	3b136,S5		
1909	Chi	A	155	531	39	118	21	5	0	47	31	3		.222	.269	.281	77	-15	2	.941	7	92	112	3b91,S64		
1910	Chi	A	67	230	17	51	10	1	0	21	11	2		.222	.263	.278	73	-8	3	.947	7	114	134	S38,1b23,3b6		
1911	Chi	A	141	516	60	131	16	6	0	49	32	2		.254	.300	.310	73	-20	1	.957	36	114	109	S102,2b27,3b7,1b5		
1912	Chi	A	3	3	0	0	0	0	0	0	0	1		.000	.400	.000	18	0	1	.667	-1	66	504	3b3/S		
Total	10		1090	3778	331	833	135	27	3	346	229	23		.220	.269	.273	70	-133	63	.938	147	120	141	3b668,S367,1b28,2b27		

TANNER, CHUCK   Charles William B7.4.1929 New Castle PA BL/TL/6-0/185* d4.12 M19 s-Bruce

YEAR	TM	LG	G	AB	R	H	2B	3B	HR	RBI	BB-IB	HP	SO	AVG	OBP	SLG	AOPS	ABR	SB-CS	FA	FR	RNG	THR	GAMES AT POSITION	DL	BFW
1955	Mil	N	97	243	27	60	9	3	6	27	27-3	0	32	.247	.319	.383	91	-4	0-0	.981	-2	91	94	O62(52/0/11)		
1956	Mil	N	60	63	6	15	3	0	1	4	10-2	1	10	.238	.342	.317	84	-1	0-0	.800	-1	53	0	O8(7/0/1)		
1957	Mil	N	22	69	5	17	3	0	2	5	5-0	0	4	.246	.297	.377	86	-2	0-0	1.000	-1	103	0	O18L		
	Chi	N	95	318	42	91	16	2	7	44	23-2	2	20	.286	.336	.415	103	1	0-2	.988	-2	93	95	O82(59/25/0)		
	Year		117	387	47	108	19	2	9	48	28-2	2	24	.279	.329	.408	100	0	0-2	.990	-2	95	78	O100(77/25/0)		
1958	Chi	N	73	103	10	27	4	0	1	17	9-2	1	15	.262	.321	.437	100	1	1-0	.955	-2	86	0	O15(2/3/10)		
1959	Cle	A	14	48	6	12	2	1	2	9	1-0	0	7	.250	.280	.458	76	-2	0-0	1.000	-1	84	0	O10(3/7/0)		
1960	Cle	A	21	25	2	7	0		4	0	4-0	0	5	.280	.367	.320	94	-0	1-0	1.000	-0	84	0	O4L		49
1961	LA	A	7	8	1	1	0	0	0		4-0	0	2	.125	.300	.125	16	-1	0-0	—	-0	0	0	/OR		
1962	LA	A	7	7	2	0	0	0	0		1-0	0	3	.125	.125	.125	-34	-2	0-0	—	-0	0	0	O2(1/0/1)		
Total	8		396	885	98	231	39	5	21	105	82-9	4	93	.261	.323	.388	93	-11	2-2	.983	-9	91	70	O202(146/35/24)		49

YEAR	TM LG	G	AB	R	H	2B	3B	HR	RBI	BB-IB	HP	SO	AVG	OBP	SLG	AOPS	ABR	SB-CS	FA	FR	RNG	THR	GAMES AT POSITION	DL	BFW

TAPPAN, WALTER   Walter Van Dorn "Tap"   B10.8.1890 Carlinville IL   D12.19.1967 Lynwood CA   BR/TR/5-8/158   d4.16

| 1914 | KC F | 18 | 39 | 1 | 8 | 1 | 0 | 1 | 3 | 1 | 0 | | .205 | .225 | .308 | | 46 | -4 | 1 | .875 | -2 | 126 | 80 | S8,3b6/2 | | -0.5 |

TAPPE, EL   Elvin Walter   B5.21.1927 Quincy IL   D10.10.1998 Quincy IL   BR/TR/5-11/180*   d4.24   M2/C8

1954	Chi N	46	119	5	22	3	0	0	4	10	0	9	.185	.246	.210		21	-14	0-0	.986	1	62	113	C46		-1.1
1955	Chi N	2	0	0	0	0	0	0	0	0-0	0		—	—	—		—	0*	0-0	1.000	1	0	0	C2		0.1
1956	Chi N	3	1	0	0	0	0	0	0	1-0	0	0	.000	.500	.000		51	0	0-0	1.000	0	0	0	C3		0.1
1958	Chi N	17	28	2	6	0	0	0	4	3-2	0	1	.214	.290	.214		37	-3	0-0	.962	-1	88	123	C16	167	0.0
1960	Chi N	51	103	11	24	7	0	0	3	11-1	0	12	.233	.313	.301		70	-4	0-1	.992	1	65	219	C49		-0.3
1962	Chi N	26	53	3	11	0	0	0	6	4-0	2	3	.208	.288	.208		34	-5	0-1	1.000	1	92	107	C26,M		-0.3
Total 6		145	304	21	63	10	0	0	17	29-3	3	25	.207	.282	.240		41	-26	0-1	.989	2	70	149	C142	167	-1.7

TAPPE, TED   Theodore Nash   B2.2.1931 Seattle WA   D2.13.2004 Wenatchee WA   BL/TR/6-3/185*   d9.14   Col Washington St.

1950	Cin N	7	5	1	1	0	0	0	1	0	1	1	.200	.333	.800	187	1	0	—	0			/H		0.1
1951	Cin N	4	3	0	1	0	0	0	0	0	0	0	.333	.333	.333	79	1	0	—	0			/H		0.0
1955	Chi N	23	50	12	13	2	0	4	10	11-3	2	11	.260	.413	.540	151	4	0-0	1.000	-1	81	101	O15R	120	0.3
Total 3		34	58	13	15	2	0	5	11	12-3	4	12	.259	.403	.552	151	5	0-0	1.000	-1	81	101	O15R	120	0.4

TARASCO, TONY   Anthony Giacinto   B12.9.1970 New York NY   BL/TR/6-1/205*   [AtlN88 15/372]   d4.30

1993	†Atl N	24	35	6	8	2	0	2	0-0		1	5	.229	.243	.286	42	-3	0-1	1.000	-1	82	0	O12(4/0/8)		-0.4
1994	Atl N	87	132	16	36	6	0	5	19	9-1	0	17	.273	.313	.432	90	-2	5-0	1.000	-1	94	63	O45(26/0/22)		-0.3
1995	Mon N	126	438	64	109	18	4	14	40	51-12	2	78	.249	.329	.404	89	-7	24-3	.979	2	103	86	O116(11/0/105)		-0.7
1996	†Bal A	31	84	14	20	3	0	1	9	7-0	0	15	.238	.297	.310	54	-6	5-3	1.000	2	126	75	O23(0/1/22),D6		-0.4
1997	Bal A	100	166	26	34	8	1	7	26	25-1	1	33	.205	.313	.392	85	-4	2-2	.991	2	105	132	O81(7/8/68),D2	19	-0.4
1998	Cin N	15	24	5	5	2	0	1	4	3-0	0	5	.208	.296	.417	84	-1	0-0	1.000	0	114	0	O7(4/1/2)		-0.1
1999	NY A	14	31	5	5	2	0	0	3	3-0	0	5	.161	.229	.226	19	-4	1-0	1.000	-2	66	0	O12(9/0/5)		-0.5
2002	NY N	60	96	15	24	5	0	6	15	8-0	0	13	.250	.305	.490	115	1	2-1	.977	3	128	286	O29(18/2/13),1b7,D2		0.4
Total 8		457	1006	151	241	46	5	34	118	106-14	4	171	.240	.313	.397	84	-26	39-10	.987	7	104	98	O325(79/12/245),D10,1b7	19	-2.4

TARBERT, ARLIE   Wilbur Arlington   B9.10.1904 Cleveland OH   D11.27.1946 Cleveland OH   BR/TR/6-0/160   d6.18   Col Ohio St.

1927	Bos A	33	69	5	13	1	0	0	5	3	3	12	.188	.253	.203	20	-8	0-0	.944	1	85	222	O27(10/3/14)		-0.9
1928	Bos A	6	17	1	3	1	0	0	2	1	0	2	.176	.222	.235	21	-2	1-0	.900	0	91	202	O6R		-0.2
Total 2		39	86	6	16	2	0	0	7	4	3	13	.186	.247	.209	20	-10	1-0	.935	1	86	218	O33(10/3/20)		-1.1

TARTABULL, DANNY   Danilo (Mora)   B10.30.1962 San Juan, PR   BR/TR/6-1/205(185-210)   [CinN80 3/71]   d9.7   f-Jose   OF(15/0/904)

1984	Sea A	10	20	3	6	1	0	2	7	2-0	1	3	.300	.375	.650	183	2	0-0	.931	2	120	109	S8/2		0.5
1985	Sea A	19	61	8	20	7	1	1	7	8-0	0	14	.328	.406	.525	151	5	1-0	.940	2	100	127	S16,3b4		0.8
1986	Sea A	137	511	76	138	25	6	25	96	61-2	1	157	.270	.347	.489	124	16	4-8	.953	-3	77	100	O101(14/0/87),2b31/3D	15	0.7
1987	KC A	158	582	95	180	27	3	34	101	79-2	1	136	.309	.390	.541	140	35	9-4	.976	-13	78	105	O149R,D6		1.4
1988	KC A	146	507	80	139	38	3	26	102	76-4	4	119	.274	.369	.515	144	32	8-5	.963	-8	84	103	O130R,D13		2.0
1989	KC A	133	441	54	118	22	0	18	62	69-2	3	123	.268	.369	.440	128	18	4-2	.982	-9	75	57	O71R,D55	15	0.6
1990	KC A	88	313	41	84	19	0	15	60	36-0	0	93	.268	.341	.473	128	12	1-1	.965	-5	88	30	O52R,D32		0.4
1991	KC A★	132	484	78	153	35	3	31	100	65-6	3	121	.316	.397	.593	170	47	6-3	.965	-14	80	46	O124R,D6	54	0.4
1992	NY A	123	421	72	112	19	0	25	85	103-14	0	115	.266	.409	.489	151	34	2-2	.980	-3	97	62	O69(1/0/68),D53	35	2.9
1993	NY A	138	513	87	128	33	2	31	102	92-9	2	156	.250	.363	.503	135	27	0-0	.978	-4	83	80	D88,O50R	21	2.8
1994	NY A	104	399	68	102	24	1	19	67	66-3	1	111	.256	.360	.464	115	10	1-1	1.000	-3	79	51	D78,O26R		1.5
1995	NY A	59	192	25	43	12	0	6	28	33-1	1	54	.224	.335	.380	88	-3	0-0	1.000	-3	47	0	D39,O18R		0.2
	Oak A	24	88	9	23	4	0	2	7	10-0	0	28	.261	.337	.375	89	-1	0-2	1.000	0	115	0	D22/OR		-0.5
	Year	83	280	34	66	16	0	8	35	43-1	1	82	.236	.335	.379	88	-4	0-2	.911	-3	91	95	D61,O19R	29	-0.3
1996	Chi A	132	472	58	120	23	3	27	101	64-4	0	128	.254	.340	.487	111	7	1-2	.973	1	109	49	O122R,D10		-0.8
1997	Phi N	3	7	2	0	0	0	0	0	4	0	4	.000	.364	.000		-5	0-0	1.000	-1	47	0	O3R		0.1
Total 14		1406	5011	756	1366	289	22	262	925	768-47	17	1362	.273	.368	.496	133	240	37-30	.971	-58	85	75	O916R,D405,2b32,S24,3b5	343	13.0

TARTABULL, JOSE   Jose Milages (Guzman)   B11.27.1938 Cienfuegos, Cuba   BL/TL/5-11/165*   d4.10   s-Danny

1962	KC A	107	310	49	86	6	9	0	22	20-0	1	19	.277	.321	.329	73	-12	19-5	.974	4	111	176	O85(1/85/0)		-0.9
1963	KC A	79	242	27	58	8	5	1	19	17-0	0	17	.240	.290	.326	68	-11	16-1	.986	-4	95	78	O71(1/70/0)		-1.4
1964	KC A	104	100	9	20	2	0	0	3	5-0	0	12	.200	.238	.220	28	-10	4-0	.978	2	104	252	O59(44/13/5)		-0.9
1965	KC A	68	218	28	68	11	4	1	19	18-0	0	20	.312	.361	.413	122	6	11-5	.986	8	128	182	O54(26/27/8)		1.3
1966	KC A	37	127	13	30	2	3	0	4	11-0	0	13	.236	.297	.299	74	-5	8-1	1.000	-2	92	50	O32(1/32/0)		-0.7
	Bos A	68	195	28	54	7	4	0	11	6-0	0	11	.277	.297	.354	79	-6	4-4	.989	-4	89	38	O47C		-1.1
	Year	105	322	41	84	9	7	0	15	17-0	0	24	.261	.297	.332	77	-10	19-4	.994	-7	90	43	O79(1/79/0)		-1.8
1967	†Bos A	115	247	36	55	1	2	0	10	23-0	0	26	.223	.287	.243	54	-14	6-6	.989	-3	83	82	O83(12/19/55)		-2.4
1968	Bos A	72	139	24	39	6	0	0	6	6-0	0	11	.281	.306	.324	87	-2	2-3	.984	1	111	58	O43(12/11/20)		-0.4
1969	Oak A	75	266	28	71	11	1	0	11	9-0	0	11	.267	.290	.316	72	-11	3-4	.993	-1	101	47	O63(28/36/0)	25	-1.6
1970	Oak A	24	13	5	3	2	0	0	2	0-0	0	2	.231	.231	.385	69	-1	1-0	1.000	0	66	0	O6(4/2/0)		-0.1
Total 9		749	1857	247	484	56	24	2	107	115-0	1	136	.261	.303	.320	74	-66	81-28	.986	-1	102	104	O543(129/342/88)	25	-8.2

TARVER, LA SCHELLE   La Schelle   B1.30.1959 Modesto CA   BL/TL/5-11/165   d7.12   Col Cal St.-Sacramento

| 1986 | Bos A | 13 | 25 | 3 | 3 | 0 | 0 | 0 | 0 | 4 | 0 | 4 | .120 | .154 | .120 | | -24 | -4 | 0-1 | 1.000 | -0 | 98 | 0 | O9(3/7/0) | | -0.5 |

TASBY, WILLIE   Willie   B1.8.1933 Shreveport LA   BR/TR/5-11/175*   d9.9

1958	Bal A	18	50	6	10	3	0	1	1	7-0	1	15	.200	.310	.320	78	-1	1-1	1.000	-1	102	0	O16(6/12/5)		-0.3
1959	Bal A	142	505	69	126	16	5	13	48	34-0	6	80	.250	.303	.378	88	-10	3-5	.968	-4	92	137	O137(5/132/1)		-2.2
1960	Bal A	39	85	9	18	2	1	0	3	9-1	1	12	.212	.295	.259	52	-6	1-0	.980	-1	94	63	O36(17/9/18)		-0.8
	Bos A	105	385	68	108	17	1	7	37	51-0	5	54	.281	.371	.384	101	3	3-1	.979	-3	98	102	O102C		-0.5
	Year	144	470	77	126	19	2	7	40	60-1	6	66	.268	.358	.362	93	-2	4-1	.979	-5	97	94	O138(17/111/18)		-1.3
1961	Was A	141	494	54	124	13	2	17	63	58-2	2	94	.251	.330	.389	93	-5	4-10	.985	-7	97	67	O139(0/138/1)		-1.9
1962	Was A	11	34	4	7	0	0	0	0	2-0	0	5	.206	.250	.206	24	-4	0-0	.933	-1	80	0	O10(7/3/0)		-0.5
	Cle A	75	199	25	48	7	0	4	17	25-0	0	41	.241	.326	.337	81	-5	0-2	1.000	-4	91	38	O66(12/57/10)/3		-1.1
	Year	86	233	29	55	7	0	4	17	27-0	0	47	.236	.315	.318	73	-9	0-2	.992	-5	91	33	O76(19/60/10)/3		-1.6
1963	Cle A	52	116	11	26	3	1	4	15	15-4	1	25	.224	.318	.371	93	-1	0-1	.981	-3	87	0	O37(18/7/13)/2		-0.7
Total 6		583	1868	246	467	61	10	46	174	201-7	16	327	.250	.327	.367	89	-29	12-20	.980	-24	94	83	O543(65/460/48)/23		-8.0

TATE, POP   Edward Christopher "Dimples"   B12.22.1860 Richmond VA   D6.25.1932 Richmond VA   BR/TL/5-10/178   d9.26

1885	Bos N	4	13	1	2	0	0	0	2	1		3	.154	.214	.154	21	-1		.865	1			C4		0.0
1886	Bos N	31	106	13	24	3	1	0	3	7		17	.226	.274	.274	69	-4	0	.885	-5			C31		-0.6
1887	Bos N	60	231	34	60	7	3	0	27	8	4		.260	.296	.307	67	-11	7	.924	13			C53,O8R		0.6
1888	Bos N	41	148	18	34	7	1	1	6	8	2	7	.230	.278	.311	85	-2	7	.854	-4			C41/OR		-0.2
1889	Bal AA	72	253	28	46	6	3	1	27	13	5	37	.182	.236	.241	55	-22	4	.938	0			C62,1b10		-1.5
1890	Bal AA	19	71	7	13	1	1	0	6		6		.183	.284	.225	48	-5	3	.923	0	118	124	C11,1b8		-0.4
Total 6		227	822	101	179	22	9	2	71	41	17	73	.218	.269	.274	58	-45	17	.905	5	118	124	C202,1b18,O9R		-2.1

TATE, BENNIE   Henry Bennett   B12.3.1901 Whitwell TN   D10.27.1973 W.Frankfort IL   BL/TR/5-8/165   d4.29

1924	†Was A	21	43	2	13	2	0	0	7	1	0	2	.302	.318	.349	74	-2	0-0	.841	-2	129	48	C14		-0.3
1925	Was A	16	27	4	13	3	0	0	7	2	0	2	.481	.517	.593	185	4	0-0	.955	2	137	85	C14		0.5
1926	Was A	59	142	17	38	5	2	1	13	15	0	1	.268	.338	.352	82	-4	0-0	.960	-3	89	134	C45		-0.5
1927	Was A	61	131	12	41	5	1	1	24	8	1	1	.313	.357	.389	95	-1	0-3	.977	3	123	81	C39		-0.4
1928	Was A	57	122	10	30	6	0	0	15	10	0	4	.246	.303	.295	58	-7	0-4	.985	-2	123	100	C30		-0.4
1929	Was A	81	265	26	78	13	0	3	30	16	0	8	.294	.335	.362	79	-9	2-6	.971	1	116	107	C74		-0.5
1930	Was A	14	20	1	5	0	0	0	2	0	0		.250	.250	.250	27	-2	0-0	.933	-1	157	89	C9		-0.2
	Chi A	72	230	26	73	11	2	0	27	18	0	10	.317	.367	.383	94	-2	2-1	.981	-6	90	92	C70		-0.3
	Year	86	250	27	78	11	2	0	29	18	0	11	.312	.358	.372	88	-4	2-1	.978	-6	94	92	C79		-0.5
1931	Chi A	89	273	27	73	12	3	0	22	26	0	10	.267	.331	.333	80	-8	1-1	.987	-0	71	105	C85		-0.3
1932	Chi A	4	10	1	1	0	0	0	0	0	0	0	.100	.182	.100	-27	-2	0-0	1.000	0	117	223	C4		-0.2
	Bos A	81	273	21	67	12	5	2	26	20	0	6	.245	.297	.348	68	-14	0-1	.974	-6	63	110	C76		-1.5
	Year	85	283	22	68	12	5	2	26	21	0	6	.240	.293	.339	-16	-16	0-1	.975	-6	65	114	C80		-1.7

YEAR	TM LG	G	AB	R	H	2B	3B	HR	RBI	BB-IB	HP	SO	AVG	OBP	SLG	AOPS	ABR	SB-CS	FA	FR	RNG	THR	GAMES AT POSITION	DL	BFW
1934	Chi N	11	24	1	3	0	0	0		.1	0	3	.125	.160	.125	-23	-4	0	1.000	-1	116	119	C8		-0.5
Total	10	566	1560	144	435	68	16	4	173	118	1	51	.279	.330	.351	78	-51	5-16	.974	-12	93	104	C468		-4.0

TATE, HUGHIE
Hugh Henry B5.19.1880 Everett PA D8.7.1956 Greenville PA BR/TR/5-11/190 d9.21 Col Penn

YEAR	TM LG	G	AB	R	H	2B	3B	HR	RBI	BB-IB	HP	SO	AVG	OBP	SLG	AOPS	ABR	SB-CS	FA	FR	RNG	THR	GAMES AT POSITION	DL	BFW
1905	Was A	4	13	1	4	0	1	0	2		0	3	.308	.308	.462	149	0	1	1.000	0	0	0	O3L		0.0

TATE, LEE
Lee Willie "Skeeter" B3.18.1932 Black Rock AR BR/TR/5-10/165* d9.12

YEAR	TM LG	G	AB	R	H	2B	3B	HR	RBI	BB-IB	HP	SO	AVG	OBP	SLG	AOPS	ABR	SB-CS	FA	FR	RNG	THR	GAMES AT POSITION	DL	BFW
1958	StL N	10	35	4	7	2	0	0	1	4-0	0	3	.200	.282	.257	42	-3	0-0	.950	-3	78	74	S9		-0.5
1959	StL N	41	50	5	7	1	1	1	4	5-1	1	7	.140	.232	.260	29	-5	0-0	.927	-1	93	88	S39,2b2,3b2		-0.5
Total	2	51	85	9	14	3	1	1	5	9-1	1	10	.165	.253	.259	34	-8	0-0	.934	-4	87	83	S48,3b2,2b2		-1.0

TATIS, FERNANDO
Fernando B1.1.1975 San Pedro de Macoris, D.R. BR/TR/5-10/170* d7.26

YEAR	TM LG	G	AB	R	H	2B	3B	HR	RBI	BB-IB	HP	SO	AVG	OBP	SLG	AOPS	ABR	SB-CS	FA	FR	RNG	THR	GAMES AT POSITION	DL	BFW
1997	Tex A	60	223	29	57	9	0	8	29	14-0	1	42	.256	.297	.404	76	-8	3-0	.951	-10	81	46	3b60		-1.7
1998	Tex A	95	330	41	89	17	2	3	32	12-2	4	66	.270	.303	.361	68	-16	6-2	.945	11	116	102	3b94		-0.3
	StL N	55	202	28	58	16	2	8	26	24-1	2	57	.287	.367	.505	127	8	7-3	.928	1	114	71	3b55,S3		1.0
1999	StL N	149	537	104	160	31	2	34	107	82-4	16	128	.298	.404	.553	137	33	21-9	.958	-9	94	115	3b147		2.5
2000	†StL N	96	324	59	82	21	1	18	64	57-1	10	94	.253	.379	.491	116	9	2-3	.953	-12	85	102	3b91/1D	60	-0.2
2001	Mon N	41	145	20	37	9	0	2	11	16-0	4	43	.255	.339	.359	83	-3	0-0	.889	-9	78	29	3b41	142	-1.2
2002	Mon N	114	381	43	87	18	1	15	55	35-1	8	90	.228	.303	.399	82	-12	2-2	.948	-2	102	91	3b99,D4	29	-1.3
2003	Mon N	53	175	15	34	6	0	2	15	16-0	3	40	.194	.281	.263	42	-15	2-1	.968	1	102	110	3b49	105	-1.4
Total	7	663	2317	339	604	127	8	90	339	258-9	47	560	.261	.344	.439	99	-4	43-20	.947	-29	97	91	3b636,D6,S3/1	336	-2.6

TATUM, JIM
James Ray B10.9.1967 Grossmont CA BR/TR/6-2/200* [SDN85 3/76] d9.18

YEAR	TM LG	G	AB	R	H	2B	3B	HR	RBI	BB-IB	HP	SO	AVG	OBP	SLG	AOPS	ABR	SB-CS	FA	FR	RNG	THR	GAMES AT POSITION	DL	BFW
1992	Mil A	5	8	0	1	0	0	0		1-0	0	2	.125	.222	.125	-0	-1	0-0	1.000	-1	39	0	3b5		-0.2
1993	Col N	92	98	7	20	5	0	1	12	5-0	1	27	.204	.245	.286	37	-9	0-0	.978	-2	111	136	1b12,3b6,O3(2/0/1)		-1.1
1995	Col N	34	34	4	8	1	1	0	4	1-0	0	7	.235	.257	.324	40	-3	0-0	1.000	-1	95	0	O2L/C		-0.3
1996	Bos A	2	8	1	1	0	0	0	0	0-0	0	2	.125	.125	.125	-36	-2	0-0	1.000	-0	53	0	3b2		-0.2
	SD N	5	3	0	0	0	0	0	0	0-0	0	1	.000	.000	.000	-99	-1	0-0	—	-0	0	0	/3		-0.1
1998	NY N	35	50	4	9	1	2	2	13	3-0	0	19	.180	.211	.400	62	-3	0-0	1.000	-4	77	91	1b9,C4,O4L,3b3/D		-0.4
Total	5	173	201	16	39	7	3	3	30	10-0	1	58	.194	.229	.303	37	-19	0-0	.987	-4	77	91	1b21,3b17,O9(8/0/1),C5/D		-2.3

TATUM, JARVIS
Jarvis B10.11.1946 Fresno CA D1.6.2003 Los Angeles CA BR/TR/6-0/185* [AnaA65 12/405] d9.7

YEAR	TM LG	G	AB	R	H	2B	3B	HR	RBI	BB-IB	HP	SO	AVG	OBP	SLG	AOPS	ABR	SB-CS	FA	FR	RNG	THR	GAMES AT POSITION	DL	BFW
1968	Cal A	17	51	7	9	0	0	0	0	9-0	0	9	.176	.176	.196	13	-6	0-0	1.000	-1	94	0	O11C		-0.8
1969	Cal A	10	22	2	7	0	0	0	0	0-0	0	6	.318	.318	.318	82	-1	0-1	.857	-1	86	0	O5R		-0.2
1970	Cal A	75	181	28	43	7	0	0	6	17-1	0	35	.238	.302	.276	63	-9	1-0	.982	0	105	68	O58(8/43/12)		-1.1
Total	3	102	254	37	59	8	0	0	8	17-1	0	50	.232	.279	.264	55	-16	1-1	.979	-2	102	51	O74(8/54/17)		-2.1

TATUM, TOMMY
V T B7.16.1919 Decatur TX D11.7.1989 Oklahoma City OK BR/TR/6-0/185 d8.1 Mil 1942-45

YEAR	TM LG	G	AB	R	H	2B	3B	HR	RBI	BB-IB	HP	SO	AVG	OBP	SLG	AOPS	ABR	SB-CS	FA	FR	RNG	THR	GAMES AT POSITION	DL	BFW
1941	Bro N	8	12	1	2	1	0	0	1	0-0	0	3	.167	.231	.250	34	-1	0	1.000	-0	90	0	O4(1/3/0)		-0.1
1947	Bro N	4	6	0	0	0	0	0	0	0-0	0	1	.000	.000	.000	-96	-2	0	1.000	-0	90	0	O3(2/0/1)		-0.2
	Cin N	69	176	19	48	5	2	1	16	16	0	16	.273	.333	.341	80	-5	7	1.000	6	112	198	O49(9/37/4)/2		-0.1
	Year	73	182	19	48	5	2	1	16	16	0	17	.264	.323	.330	74	-7	7	1.000	5	111	193	O52(11/37/5)/2		-0.3
Total	2	81	194	20	50	6	2	1	17	17	0	20	.258	.318	.325	72	-8	7	1.000	5	111	185	O56(12/40/5)/2		-0.4

TAUBENSEE, EDDIE
Edward Kenneth B10.31.1968 Beeville TX BL/TR/6-4/205(205-230) [CinN86 6/150] d5.18 [DL 2002 Cle A 183]

YEAR	TM LG	G	AB	R	H	2B	3B	HR	RBI	BB-IB	HP	SO	AVG	OBP	SLG	AOPS	ABR	SB-CS	FA	FR	RNG	THR	GAMES AT POSITION	DL	BFW
1991	Cle A	26	66	5	16	2	1	0	8	5-1	0	16	.242	.288	.303	65	-3	0-0	.979	-8	70	45	C25		-1.1
1992	Hou N	104	297	23	66	15	0	5	28	31-3	2	78	.222	.299	.323	80	-8	2-1	.992	5	106	102	C103		0.1
1993	Hou N	94	288	26	72	11	0	9	42	21-5	0	44	.250	.299	.389	86	-7	1-0	.992	5	122	78	C90		0.4
1994	Hou N	5	10	0	1	0	0	0	0	0-0	0	3	.100	.100	.100	-50	-2	0-0	1.000	1	183	114	C5		-0.1
	Cin N	61	177	29	52	8	2	8	21	15-2	0	28	.294	.345	.497	117	4	2-0	.990	-4	82	99	C61		0.4
	Year	66	187	29	53	8	2	8	21	15-2	0	31	.283	.333	.476	109	2	2-0	.990	-3	87	100	C66		0.3
1995	†Cin N	80	218	32	62	14	2	9	44	22-2	2	52	.284	.354	.491	119	6	2-2	.983	-5	95	64	C65,1b3		0.3
1996	Cin N	108	327	46	95	20	0	12	48	26-5	2	64	.291	.338	.462	108	4	3-4	.981	-5	68	109	C94		0.3
1997	Cin N	108	254	26	68	18	0	10	34	22-2	1	66	.268	.323	.457	101	0	0-1	.987	-1	76	67	C64,O11(6/0/5),1b7,D3		0.2
1998	Cin N	130	431	61	120	27	0	11	72	52-6	0	93	.278	.352	.418	102	2	1-0	.988	-9	89	71	C126		1.1
1999	Cin N	126	424	58	132	22	2	21	87	30-1	1	67	.311	.354	.521	115	9	0-2	.989	-3	83	50	C76	61	-0.9
2000	Cin N	81	266	29	71	12	0	6	24	21-1	2	44	.267	.324	.380	75	-10	0-0	.989	-3	81	73	C38,D5	40	-1.0
2001	Cle A	52	116	16	29	2	1	3	11	10-1	1	19	.250	.315	.362	75	-4	0-0	.986	-8	72	82	C51		-0.4
Total	11	975	2874	351	784	151	9	94	419	255-29	9	574	.273	.331	.430	98	-9	11-10	.988	-40	89	78	C871,O11(6/0/5),1b10,D8	284	-0.4

TAUBY, FRED
Frederick Joseph (b Frederick Joseph Taubensee) B3.27.1906 Canton OH D11.23.1955 Concord CA BR/TR/5-9.5/168 d9.1

YEAR	TM LG	G	AB	R	H	2B	3B	HR	RBI	BB-IB	HP	SO	AVG	OBP	SLG	AOPS	ABR	SB-CS	FA	FR	RNG	THR	GAMES AT POSITION	DL	BFW
1935	Chi A	13	32	5	4	1	0	0	2	2	0	3	.125	.176	.156	-13	-6	0-0	1.000	1	97	323	O7(1/1/5)		-0.4
1937	Phi N	11	20	2	0	0	0	0	3	0	0	5	.000	.000	.000	-93	-5	1	1.000	-0	105	0	O7(3/3/1)		-0.6
Total	2	24	52	7	4	1	0	0	5	2	0	8	.077	.111	.096	-43	-11	1-0	1.000	1	100	221	O14(4/4/6)		-1.0

TAUSSIG, DON
Donald Franklin B2.19.1932 New York NY BR/TR/6-0/180* d4.23 Col Hofstra

YEAR	TM LG	G	AB	R	H	2B	3B	HR	RBI	BB-IB	HP	SO	AVG	OBP	SLG	AOPS	ABR	SB-CS	FA	FR	RNG	THR	GAMES AT POSITION	DL	BFW
1958	SF N	39	50	10	10	0	0	1	4	3-1	0	8	.200	.245	.260	35	-5	0-0	1.000	0	112	0	O36(27/0/11)		-0.2
1961	StL N	98	188	27	54	14	5	2	25	16-0	0	34	.287	.338	.447	98	0	2-2	.992	5	116	133	O87(48/20/30)		-0.2
1962	Hou N	16	25	1	5	0	0	1	1	2-0	0	11	.200	.259	.320	59	-2	0-0	1.000	1	146	0	O4L		-0.1
Total	3	153	263	38	69	14	5	4	30	21-1	0	53	.262	.314	.399	84	-7	2-2	.994	6	117	102	O127(79/20/41)		-0.5

TAVAREZ, JESUS
Jesus Rafael (Alcantaras) B3.26.1971 Santo Domingo, D.R. BB/TR/6-0/170* d5.23

YEAR	TM LG	G	AB	R	H	2B	3B	HR	RBI	BB-IB	HP	SO	AVG	OBP	SLG	AOPS	ABR	SB-CS	FA	FR	RNG	THR	GAMES AT POSITION	DL	BFW
1994	Fla N	17	39	4	7	0	0	0	1	4-0	0	5	.179	.200	.179	-0	-6	1-1	1.000	3	168	177	O11(1/2/8)		-0.4
1995	Fla N	63	190	31	55	6	2	2	13	16-1	1	27	.289	.346	.374	89	-3	7-5	1.000	7	102	34	O61(4/47/32)	16	-0.4
1996	Fla N	98	114	14	25	3	0	0	6	7-0	0	18	.219	.264	.246	37	-11	5-1	.980	0	105	0	O65(25/30/12)		-0.8
1997	Bos A	42	69	12	12	3	1	0	9	4-0	0	9	.174	.216	.246	21	-8	0-0	.980	-0	99	89	O35(4/29/4),D2		-0.5
1998	Bal A	8	11	2	2	0	0	1	1	2-0	0	3	.182	.308	.455	96	0	1	1.000	-1	77	0	O8(0/5/4)	16	-2.
Total	5	228	423	63	101	12	3	3	33	30-1	1	62	.239	.289	.303	56	-28	13-8	.996	2	106	45	O180(34/113/60),D2	16	-2.

TAVENER, JACKIE
John Adam "Rabbit" B12.27.1897 Celina OH D9.14.1969 Fort Worth TX BL/TR/5-5/138 d9.24

YEAR	TM LG	G	AB	R	H	2B	3B	HR	RBI	BB-IB	HP	SO	AVG	OBP	SLG	AOPS	ABR	SB-CS	FA	FR	RNG	THR	GAMES AT POSITION	DL	BFW
1921	Det A	2	4	0	0	0	0	0	0	0-0	0	1	.000	.000	.000	-99	-1	0	1.000	0	113	0	S2		-0.
1925	Det A	134	453	45	111	11	11	0	47	39	3	60	.245	.309	.318	60	-30	5-4	.963	3	104	96	S134		-1.
1926	Det A	156	532	65	141	22	14	1	58	52	1	53	.265	.332	.365	80	-17	8-7	.952	7	103	106	S156		0.
1927	Det A	116	419	60	115	22	9	5	59	36	1	38	.274	.333	.406	90	-8	19-8	.948	2	100	116	S114		1.
1928	Det A	132	493	59	123	24	15	5	52	33	4	51	.260	.314	.406	86	-12	13-8	.944	12	106	101	S131		0.
1929	Cle A	92	250	25	53	9	4	2	27	26	1	28	.212	.289	.304	51	-19	1-4	.945	22	123	125	S89		0.
Total	6	632	2131	254	543	88	53	13	243	186	10	231	.255	.318	.364	75	-87	46-31	.951	46	106	107	S626		

TAVERAS, ALEX
Alejandro Antonio (Betances) B10.9.1955 Santiago, D.R. BR/TR/5-10/155(145-170) d9.9

YEAR	TM LG	G	AB	R	H	2B	3B	HR	RBI	BB-IB	HP	SO	AVG	OBP	SLG	AOPS	ABR	SB-CS	FA	FR	RNG	THR	GAMES AT POSITION	DL	BFW
1976	Hou N	14	46	3	10	0	0	0	2	2-0	0	11	.217	.250	.217	36	-4	1-2	.923	3	116	50	2b7,S7		-0.
1982	LA N	11	3	1	1	1	0	0	2	0-0	0	1	.333	.333	.667	179	0	0-0	1.000	2	102	0	2b4,3b4,S2		0.
1983	LA N	10	4	0	0	0	0	0	0	0-0	0	1	.000	.000	.000	-99	-1	0-0	—	0	0	0	S3,2b2/3		0.
Total	3	35	53	4	11	1	0	0	4	2-0	0	13	.208	.236	.226	34	-5	1-2	.938	4	109	38	2b13,S12,3b5		-0.

TAVERAS, FRANK
Franklin Crisostomo (Fabian) B12.24.1949 Las Matas de Santa Cruz, D.R. BR/TR/6-0/168(150-170) d9.25

YEAR	TM LG	G	AB	R	H	2B	3B	HR	RBI	BB-IB	HP	SO	AVG	OBP	SLG	AOPS	ABR	SB-CS	FA	FR	RNG	THR	GAMES AT POSITION	DL	BFW
1971	Pit N	1								0-0	0						0	0-0					/R		-0.
1972	Pit N	4	3	0	0	0	0	0	0	0-0	0	1	.000	.250	.000	-24	0	0-0	1.000	-1	56	155	S4		-0.
1974	†Pit N	126	333	33	82	4	2	0	26	25-2	2	41	.246	.300	.270	63	-17	13-4	.941	-18	93	97	S124		-2.
1975	†Pit N	134	378	44	80	9	4	0	23	37-0	2	42	.212	.284	.257	51	-25	17-6	.953	-8	95	110	S132		-2.
1976	Pit N	144	519	76	134	8	6	0	24	44-1	4	79	.258	.319	.297	75	-17	58-11	.952	4	**108**	94	S141		-2.
1977	Pit N	147	544	72	137	20	10	1	29	38-2	6	71	.252	.306	.331	69	-24	70-18	.962	-22	97	84	S146		-2.
1978	Pit N	157	654	81	182	31	9	0	38	29-3	5	60	.278	.313	.353	82	-14	46-25	.946	-26	91	92	S157		-2.
1979	Pit N	11	45	4	11	3	0	0	1	0	0	2	.244	.244	.311	48	-3	2-1	.935	-3	80	70	S11		-2.
	NY N	153	635	89	167	26	9	0	33	33-1	2	72	.263	.301	.330	76	-23	42-19	.966	-20	91	95	S153		-2.
	Year	164	680	93	178	29	9	0	34	33-1	2	74	.262	.298	.335	74	-26	44-20	.964	-24	90	93	S164		-2.
1980	NY N	141	562	65	157	27	0	0	25	23-0	1	64	.279	.308	.327	79	-16	32-18	.959	-25	82	79	S140		-2.
1981	NY N	84	283	30	65	11	3	0	11	12-0	1	58	.230	.263	.290	58	-16	16-4	.931	-12	89	99	S79		-2.

YEAR	TM LG	G	AB	R	H	2B	3B	HR	RBI	BB-IB	HP	SO	AVG	OBP	SLG	AOPS	ABR	SB-CS	FA	FR	RNG	THR	GAMES AT POSITION	DL	BFW
1982	Mon N	48	87	9	14	5	1	0	4	7-0	0	6	.161	.221	.241	29	-8	4-0	.947	-2	56	103	S26,2b19		-0.8
Total	11	1150	4043	503	1029	144	44	2	214	249-9	24	474	.255	.301	.313	70	-166	300-106	.953	-131	93	93	S1113,2b19		-16.7

TAVERAS, WILLY Willy B12.25.1981 Tenares, D.R. BR/TR/6-0/160* d9.6

YEAR	TM LG	G	AB	R	H	2B	3B	HR	RBI	BB-IB	HP	SO	AVG	OBP	SLG	AOPS	ABR	SB-CS	FA	FR	RNG	THR	GAMES AT POSITION	DL	BFW
2004	Hou N	10	1	2	0	0	0	0	0-0	0	1	.000	.000	.000	-97	-1	1-0	1.000	-0	40	0	O7(2/4/1)		0.0
2005	†Hou N	152	592	82	172	13	4	3	29	25-1	7	103	.291	.325	.341	75	-23	34-11	.991	2	101	140	O148C		-1.6
Total	2	162	593	84	172	13	4	3	29	25-1	7	104	.290	.324	.341	75	-23	35-11	.991	2	100	139	O155(2/152/1)		-1.6

TAYLOR, TONY Antonio Nemesio (Sanchez) B12.19.1935 Central Alara, Cuba BR/TR/5-9/179(170-185) d4.15 C9

YEAR	TM LG	G	AB	R	H	2B	3B	HR	RBI	BB-IB	HP	SO	AVG	OBP	SLG	AOPS	ABR	SB-CS	FA	FR	RNG	THR	GAMES AT POSITION	DL	BFW
1958	Chi N	140	497	63	117	15	3	6	27	40-0	7	93	.235	.299	.314	64	-26	21-6	.968	12	104	106	2b137/3		-0.2
1959	Chi N	150	624	96	175	30	8	8	38	45-0	6	86	.280	.331	.393	94	-6	23-9	.970	7	107	113	2b149,S2		1.5
1960	Chi N	19	76	14	20	3	3	1	9	8-0	1	12	.263	.337	.421	108	1	2-0	.977	-3	92	158	2b19		0.0
	Phi N★	127	505	66	145	22	4	4	35	33-2	2	86	.287	.330	.370	92	-5	24-11	.968	-6	102	87	2b123,3b4		-0.1
	Year	146	581	80	165	25	7	5	44	41-2	3	98	.284	.331	.377	94	-5	26-11	.969	-8	101	97	2b142,3b4		-0.1
1961	Phi N	106	400	47	100	17	3	2	26	29-4	2	59	.250	.304	.322	67	-19	11-5	.980	-1	97	105	2b91,3b3	30	-1.2
1962	Phi N	152	625	87	162	21	5	7	43	68-4	5	82	.259	.336	.342	85	-12	20-9	.972	-14	90	99	2b150,S2		-1.2
1963	Phi N	157	640	102	180	20	10	5	49	42-1	7	99	.281	.330	.367	102	1	23-9	.986	-2	95	99	2b149,3b13		1.5
1964	Phi N	154	570	62	143	13	6	4	46	46-8	13	74	.251	.320	.316	81	-14	13-7	.977	-23	84	106	2b150		-2.5
1965	Phi N	106	323	41	74	14	3	3	27	22-0	12	58	.229	.302	.319	77	-10	5-4	.958	-8	92	97	2b86,3b5		-1.2
1966	Phi N	125	434	47	105	14	8	5	40	31-0	1	56	.242	.294	.346	77	-14	8-4	.988	1	100	89	2b68,3b52		-0.8
1967	Phi N	132	462	55	110	16	6	2	34	42-8	5	74	.238	.308	.312	77	-13	10-9	.991	-9	87	126	1b58,3b44,2b42,S3		-2.5
1968	Phi N	145	547	59	137	20	2	3	38	39-7	3	60	.250	.302	.311	85	-10	22-5	.966	13	111	95	3b138,2b5/1		0.7
1969	Phi N	138	557	68	146	24	5	3	30	42-1	4	62	.262	.317	.339	86	-10	19-10	.967	-1	112	66	3b71,2b57,1b10		-0.9
1970	Phi N	124	439	74	132	26	9	9	55	50-9	1	67	.301	.374	.462	126	17	9-11	.996	6	88	114	2b59,3b38,O18L/S		2.3
1971	Phi N	36	107	14	25	2	1	1	5	9-2	0	10	.234	.291	.299	68	-5	2-2	1.000	3	106	146	2b14,3b11,1b2		-0.1
	Det A	55	181	27	52	10	2	3	19	12-1	1	11	.287	.335	.414	107	1	5-1	.995	-0	95	97	2b51,3b3		0.5
1972	†Det A	78	228	33	69	12	4	1	20	14-0	2	34	.303	.346	.404	119	5	5-1	.966	-2	87	84	2b67,3b8/1		0.8
1973	Det A	84	275	35	63	9	3	5	24	17-0	1	29	.229	.276	.338	68	-13	9-5	.987	-6	95	85	2b72,1b6,3b4/OLD		-1.5
1974	Phi N	62	64	5	21	4	0	2	13	6-0	1	6	.328	.389	.484	138	3	0-0	1.000	-1	63	0	1b7,3b5,2b4		0.2
1975	Phi N	79	103	13	25	5	1	1	17	17-2	1	18	.243	.350	.340	89	-1	3-3	.913	2	125	52	3b16,1b4,2b3		0.0
1976	Phi N	26	23	2	6	1	0	0	3	1-0	1	7	.261	.320	.304	75	-1	0-0	—	-0	0	0	2b2/3	98	-0.1
Total	19	2195	7680	1005	2007	298	86	75	598	613-49	78	1083	.261	.321	.352	88	-131	234-111	.976	-32	95	102	2b1498,3b417,1b89,O19L,S8,D2	128	-4.8

TAYLOR, BEN Benjamin Eugene B9.30.1924 Metropolis IL D5.11.1999 Alma OK BL/TL/6-0/185* d7.29

YEAR	TM LG	G	AB	R	H	2B	3B	HR	RBI	BB-IB	HP	SO	AVG	OBP	SLG	AOPS	ABR	SB-CS	FA	FR	RNG	THR	GAMES AT POSITION	DL	BFW
1951	StL A	33	93	14	24	2	1	3	6	9	2	22	.258	.337	.398	95	-1	1-1	.972	-2	82	78	1b25		-0.4
1952	Det A	7	18	0	3	0	0	0	0	0	0	5	.167	.167	.167	-7	-3	0-0	1.000	-0	78	112	1b4		-0.3
1955	Mil N	12	10	2	1	0	0	0	0	2-0	0	4	.100	.250	.100	-3	-1	0-0	1.000	-0	0	0	/1		-0.2
Total	3	52	121	16	28	2	1	3	6	11-0	2	31	.231	.306	.339	73	-5	1-1	.976	-2	81	82	1b30		-0.9

TAYLOR, CHINK C L B2.9.1898 Burnet TX D7.7.1980 Temple TX BR/TR/5-9/160 d4.18

YEAR	TM LG	G	AB	R	H	2B	3B	HR	RBI	BB-IB	HP	SO	AVG	OBP	SLG	AOPS	ABR	SB-CS	FA	FR	RNG	THR	GAMES AT POSITION	DL	BFW
1925	Chi N	8	6	2	0	0	0	0	0	0-0	0	0	.000	.000	.000	-99	-2	0-0	1.000	-0	138	0	O2(1/0/1)		-0.2

TAYLOR, CARL Carl Means B1.20.1944 Sarasota FL BR/TR/6-2/207* d4.11

YEAR	TM LG	G	AB	R	H	2B	3B	HR	RBI	BB-IB	HP	SO	AVG	OBP	SLG	AOPS	ABR	SB-CS	FA	FR	RNG	THR	GAMES AT POSITION	DL	BFW
1968	Pit N	44	71	5	15	1	0	0	7	10-3	0	10	.211	.309	.225	63	-3	1-0	.979	-8	51	120	C29,O2(1/0/1)		-1.1
1969	Pit N	104	221	30	77	10	1	4	33	31-0	3	36	.348	.432	.457	153	18	0-1	.914	1	107	171	O36(19/0/19),1b24		1.6
1970	StL N	104	245	39	61	12	2	6	45	41-0	1	30	.249	.358	.388	97	0	5-2	.986	-3	85	106	O46R,1b15/3		0.0
1971	Pit N	7	12	1	2	0	1	0	0	0-0	0	5	.167	.167	.333	38	-1	0-0	1.000	-0	121	0	/OR		-0.1
	KC A	20	39	3	7	0	0	0	3	5-0	0	13	.179	.244	.179	30	-4	0-1	.964	1	145	0	O12(6/0/6)		-0.4
1972	KC A	63	113	17	30	2	1	0	11	17-1	0	16	.265	.361	.301	101	2	4-1	.982	-2	78	60	C21,O7(1/0/6),1b6,3b5		0.0
1973	KC A	69	145	18	33	6	1	0	16	32-0	0	20	.228	.363	.283	79	-2	2-2	.980	-2	84	56	C63,1b2/D		-0.2
Total	6	411	846	113	225	31	6	10	115	136-4	5	130	.266	.367	.352	102	9	12-7	.980	-12	76	71	C113,O104(27/0/79),1b47,3b6/D		-0.7

TAYLOR, DANNY Daniel Turney B12.23.1900 Lash PA D10.11.1972 Latrobe PA BR/TR/5-10/190 d6.30

YEAR	TM LG	G	AB	R	H	2B	3B	HR	RBI	BB-IB	HP	SO	AVG	OBP	SLG	AOPS	ABR	SB-CS	FA	FR	RNG	THR	GAMES AT POSITION	DL	BFW
1926	Was A	21	50	10	15	0	1	1	5	5	0	7	.300	.364	.400	102	0	1-2	1.000	-0	95	98	O12(0/1/11)		-0.1
1929	Chi N	2	3	0	0	0	0	0	0	1	0	0	1.000	.250	.000	-32	-1	0-0	1.000	-0	82	0	/OR		-0.1
1930	Chi N	74	219	43	62	14	3	2	37	27	0	34	.283	.364	.402	84	-5	0-0	.971	-1	97	86	O52L		-0.9
1931	Chi N	88	270	48	81	13	6	5	41	31	0	46	.300	.372	.448	117	7	4	.989	0	105	64	O67(39/22/4)		0.4
1932	Chi N	6	22	3	5	2	0	0	3	3	0	1	.227	.320	.318	-73	-1	1	.900	-1	96	0	O6(0/4/2)		-0.2
	Year	105	395	84	128	22	7	11	48	33	1	41	.324	.378	.499	136	20	13	.989	-1	100	91	O96C		1.7
	Bro N	111	417	87	133	24	7	11	51	36	1	42	.319	.374	.489	133	19	14	.983	-2	100	85	O102(0/100/2)		1.5
1933	Bro N	103	358	75	102	21	9	9	40	47	0	45	.285	.368	.469	144	21	11	.977	-2	101	62	O91C		1.7
1934	Bro N	120	405	62	121	24	6	7	57	63	2	47	.299	.396	.440	130	20	12	.975	-2	90	121	O108(89/21/0)		1.3
1935	Bro N	112	352	51	102	19	5	7	59	46	0	32	.290	.372	.432	118	10	6	.970	-3	96	60	O99L		0.2
1936	Bro N	43	116	12	34	6	0	2	15	11	1	14	.293	.359	.397	102	1	2	.981	-0	94	107	O31Ł		-0.1
Total	9	674	2190	388	650	121	37	44	305	267	5	268	.297	.374	.446	121	72	56-2	.979	-11	98	82	O563(310/235/18)		3.9

TAYLOR, DWIGHT Dwight Bernard B3.24.1960 Los Angeles CA BL/TL/5-9/166 [CleA81 7/168] d4.14 Col Arizona

YEAR	TM LG	G	AB	R	H	2B	3B	HR	RBI	BB-IB	HP	SO	AVG	OBP	SLG	AOPS	ABR	SB-CS	FA	FR	RNG	THR	GAMES AT POSITION	DL	BFW
1986	KC A	4	2	1	0	0	0	0	0	0-0	0	0	.000	.000	.000	-98	-1	0-0	—	-0	0	0	/OCD		-0.1

TAYLOR, ED Edward James B11.17.1901 Chicago IL D1.30.1992 Chula Vista CA BR/TR/5-6.5/160 d4.14

YEAR	TM LG	G	AB	R	H	2B	3B	HR	RBI	BB-IB	HP	SO	AVG	OBP	SLG	AOPS	ABR	SB-CS	FA	FR	RNG	THR	GAMES AT POSITION	DL	BFW
1926	Bos N	92	272	37	73	8	2	0	33	38	5	26	.268	.368	.313	93	0	4	.945	-1	98	102	3b62,S33		0.4

TAYLOR, LIVE OAK Edward S. B2.3.1851 Belfast ME 5-9/170 d8.21

YEAR	TM LG	G	AB	R	H	2B	3B	HR	RBI	BB-IB	HP	SO	AVG	OBP	SLG	AOPS	ABR	SB-CS	FA	FR	RNG	THR	GAMES AT POSITION	DL	BFW
1877	Har N	2	8	0	3	0	0	0	0		2	.375	.375	.375	153	0		1.000	-0	0	0	O2L		0.0
1884	Pit AA	41	152	22	32	4	1	0	6	.3	.211	.255	.250	66	-5		.798	-2	87	0	O41C		-0.8
Total	2	43	160	22	35	4	1	0	6	3	2	.219	.260	.256	70	-5		.802	-3	83	0	O43(2/41/0)		-0.8

TAYLOR, FRED Frederick Rankin B12.3.1924 Zanesville OH D1.6.2002 Columbus OH BL/TR/6-3/201* d9.12 Col Ohio St.

YEAR	TM LG	G	AB	R	H	2B	3B	HR	RBI	BB-IB	HP	SO	AVG	OBP	SLG	AOPS	ABR	SB-CS	FA	FR	RNG	THR	GAMES AT POSITION	DL	BFW
1950	Was A	6	16	1	2	0	0	0	1	0	2	.125	.176	.125	-23	-3	0-0	.968	0	144	147	1b3		-0.3
1951	Was A	6	12	1	2	0	0	0	0	0	2	.167	.167	.250	12	-2	0-0	.962	-1	57	165	1b2		-0.2
1952	Was A	10	19	3	5	2	0	0	3	0	2	.263	.364	.316	93	0	0-0	1.000	1	177	99	1b5		0.1
Total	3	22	47	5	9	2	0	0	4	4	0	6	.191	.255	.234	33	-5	0-0	.979	1	137	130	1b10		-0.4

TAYLOR, HARRY Harry Leonard B4.4.1866 Halsey Valley NY D7.12.1955 Buffalo NY BL/6-2/160 d4.18 Col Cornell OF(23/0/50)

YEAR	TM LG	G	AB	R	H	2B	3B	HR	RBI	BB-IB	HP	SO	AVG	OBP	SLG	AOPS	ABR	SB-CS	FA	FR	RNG	THR	GAMES AT POSITION	DL	BFW
1890	†Lou AA	134	553	115	169	7	7	0	53	68	1		.306	.383	.344	117	14	45	.982	3	104	100	1b118,S12,2b4/C		0.6
1891	Lou AA	91	348	80	103	7	3	2	35	55	4	30	.296	.398	.351	116	10	15	.978	2	118	106	1b90/32C		0.4
1892	Lou N	125	493	66	128	7	1	0	34	58	4	23	.260	.342	.278	96	1	24	.923	-6	81	116	O73(23/0/50),1b34,2b14,3b5,S2		-0.8
1893	Bal N	88	360	50	102	9	1	1	54	32	3	11	.283	.347	.322	77	-12	24	.976	-3	88	100	1b88		-1.2
Total	4	438	1754	311	502	30	12	3	176	213	12	64	.286	.367	.322	102	13	108	.979	-3	104	104	1b330,O73R,2b19,S14,3b6,C2		-1.0

TAYLOR, HARRY Harry Warren B12.26.1907 McKeesport PA D4.27.1969 Toledo OH BL/TL/6-1.5/185 d4.14

YEAR	TM LG	G	AB	R	H	2B	3B	HR	RBI	BB-IB	HP	SO	AVG	OBP	SLG	AOPS	ABR	SB-CS	FA	FR	RNG	THR	GAMES AT POSITION	DL	BFW
1932	Chi N	10	8	1	1	0	0	0	0	1	0	1	.125	.222	.125	-4	-1	0	1.000	-0	0	0	/1		-0.1

TAYLOR, SANDY James B. 5-10.5/175 d8.11

YEAR	TM LG	G	AB	R	H	2B	3B	HR	RBI	BB-IB	HP	SO	AVG	OBP	SLG	AOPS	ABR	SB-CS	FA	FR	RNG	THR	GAMES AT POSITION	DL	BFW
1879	Tro N	24	97	10	21	4	0	0	8	1		8	.216	.224	.258	63	-3		.765	-3	37	0	O24L		-0.8

TAYLOR, ZACK James Wren B7.27.1898 Yulee FL D9.19.1974 Orlando FL BR/TR/5-11.5/180 d6.15 M5/C8 Col Rollins

YEAR	TM LG	G	AB	R	H	2B	3B	HR	RBI	BB-IB	HP	SO	AVG	OBP	SLG	AOPS	ABR	SB-CS	FA	FR	RNG	THR	GAMES AT POSITION	DL	BFW
1920	Bro N	9	13	5	2	0	0	5	0	0	2	.385	.385	.538	158	1	0	.882	-1	86	89	C9		0.0
1921	Bro N	30	102	6	20	0	2	0	6	1	0	1	.196	.212	.235	17	-12	2-0	.965	-0	86	96	C30		-1.0
1922	Bro N	7	14	0	3	0	0	0	2	0	0	0	.214	.267	.214	26	-2	0-0	.950	-1	79	99	C6		-0.2
1923	Bro N	96	337	29	97	11	6	0	46	9	3	13	.288	.312	.356	78	-12	0-1	.967	7	84	136	C84		-0.1
1924	Bro N	99	345	36	100	9	4	1	39	14	1	14	.290	.319	.348	81	-10	0-1	.988	-4	88	121	C93		-0.9
1925	Bro N	109	343	33	109	16	4	3	50	22	0	19	.318	.343	.403	92	-5	0-0	.959	-10	68	173	C96		-0.9
1926	Bos N	125	432	36	110	22	3	0	42	28	2	25	.255	.303	.319	74	-16	1	.985	-0	81	134	C123		-0.8
1927	Bos N	30	96	8	23	2	1	1	14	8	0	5	.240	.298	.313	69	-5	0	.988	6	100	127	C27		0.3
	NY N	83	258	18	60	7	3	0	21	17	1	20	.233	.283	.283	52	-18	2	.972	-3	119	92	C81		-1.6
	Year	113	354	26	83	9	4	1	35	25	1	25	.234	.287	.291	56	-23	2	.978	3	113	102	C108		-1.3
1928	Bos N	125	399	36	100	15	1	2	30	33	3	29	.251	.313	.308	66	-20	2	.985	-12	90	99	C124		-2.4

YEAR	TM LG	G	AB	R	H	2B	3B	HR	RBI	BB-IB	HP	SO	AVG	OBP	SLG	AOPS	ABR	SB-CS	FA	FR	RNG	THR	GAMES AT POSITION	DL	BFW
1929	Bos N	34	101	8	25	7	0	0	10	7	1	9	.248	.303	.317	56	-7	0	.965	4	104	164	C31		-0.1
	†Chi N	64	215	29	59	16	3	1	31	19	1	18	.274	.336	.391	79	-7	0	.979	2	129	89	C64		-0.1
	Year	98	316	37	84	23	3	1	41	26	2	27	.266	.326	.367	72	-14	0	.974	6	120	115	C95		-0.2
1930	Chi N	32	95	12	22	2	1	1	11	2	1	12	.232	.255	.305	34	-11	0	1.000	0	121	137	C28		-0.8
1931	Chi N	8	4	0	1	0	0	0	0	2	0	1	.250	.500	.250	106	0	0	1.000	2	269	229	C5		0.1
1932	Chi N	21	30	2	6	1	0	0	3	1	0	4	.200	.226	.233	24	-3	0	1.000	2	269	92	C14		-0.1
1933	Chi N	16	11	0	0	0	0	0	0	0	0	1	.000	.000	.000	-99	-3	0	1.000	0	0	0	C12		-0.3
1934	NY A	4	7	0	1	0	0	0	0	0	0	1	.143	.143	.143	-28	-1	0-0	1.000	-0	55	321	C3		-0.1
1935	Bro N	26	54	2	7	3	0	0	5	2	1	8	.130	.175	.185	-3	-8	0	.970	1	111	170	C26		-0.6
Total 16		918	2865	258	748	113	28	9	311	161	16	192	.261	.304	.329	68	-139	9-7	.977	-10	95	124	C856		-9.5

TAYLOR, JOE Joe Cephus B3.2.1926 Chapman AL D3.18.1993 Pittsburgh PA BR/TR/6-1/185* d8.26 Negro Lg 1949-50

YEAR	TM LG	G	AB	R	H	2B	3B	HR	RBI	BB-IB	HP	SO	AVG	OBP	SLG	AOPS	ABR	SB-CS	FA	FR	RNG	THR	GAMES AT POSITION	DL	BFW
1954	Phi A	18	58	5	13	1	1	1	8	2	0	9	.224	.250	.328	57	-4	0-1	.943	0	110	99	O16(9/0/8)		-0.5
1957	Cin N	33	107	14	28	7	0	4	9	6-0	0	24	.262	.301	.439	89	-2	0-1	.971	3	121	159	O27(19/0/8)		0.0
1958	StL N	18	23	2	7	3	0	1	3	2-0	0	4	.304	.346	.565	135	1	0-0	1.000	0	120	0	O5(2/2/1)		0.0
	Bal A	36	77	11	21	4	0	2	9	7-1	0	19	.273	.333	.403	107	1	0-0	.972	-0	101	78	O21(3/4/15)		-0.2
1959	Bal A	14	32	2	5	1	0	1	2	11-0	0	5	.156	.372	.281	84	0	0-0	1.000	-1	70	0	O12(2/0/10)		-0.2
Total 4		119	297	34	74	16	1	9	31	28-1	0	61	.249	.313	.401	92	-4	0-2	.969	2	108	101	O81(35/6/42)		-0.6

TAYLOR, LEO Leo Thomas "Chink" B5.13.1901 Walla Walla WA D5.20.1982 Seattle WA BR/TR/5-10.5/150 d5.3

YEAR	TM LG	G	AB	R	H	2B	3B	HR	RBI	BB-IB	HP	SO	AVG	OBP	SLG	AOPS	ABR	SB-CS	FA	FR	RNG	THR	GAMES AT POSITION	DL	BFW
1923	Chi A	1	0	0	0	0	0	0	0	0	0	—	—	—	—	-1	0-0	—	0			/R		0.0

TAYLOR, REGGIE Reginald Tremain B1.12.1977 Newberry SC BL/TR/6-1/178* [PhiN95 1/14] d9.17

YEAR	TM LG	G	AB	R	H	2B	3B	HR	RBI	BB-IB	HP	SO	AVG	OBP	SLG	AOPS	ABR	SB-CS	FA	FR	RNG	THR	GAMES AT POSITION	DL	BFW
2000	Phi N	9	11	1	1	0	0	0	0	0-0	0	8	.091	.091	.091	-54	-3	1-0	.800	-1	76	0	O3C		-0.3
2001	Phi N	5	7	1	0	0	0	0	0	1-0	0	1	.000	.125	.000	-67	-2	0-0	1.000	-0	96	0	O2C		-0.2
2002	Cin N	135	287	41	73	15	4	9	38	14-3	2	79	.254	.291	.429	87	-8	11-8	.973	1	109	49	O103(34/68/5)		-0.8
2003	Cin N	100	180	17	39	5	4	5	19	11-0	1	68	.217	.266	.350	62	-11	7-0	.990	1	107	89	O60(13/49/3)	34	-0.9
2005	TB A	11	22	2	4	2	0	0	1	2-0	0	7	.182	.250	.273	40	-2	2-0	1.000	0	116	0	O10(0/9/1)		-0.1
Total 5		260	507	62	117	22	6	14	58	28-3	3	163	.231	.274	.381	71	-26	21-8	.977	2	108	58	O178(47/131/9)	34	-2.3

TAYLOR, HAWK Robert Dale B4.3.1939 Metropolis IL BR/TR/6-2/190* d6.9

YEAR	TM LG	G	AB	R	H	2B	3B	HR	RBI	BB-IB	HP	SO	AVG	OBP	SLG	AOPS	ABR	SB-CS	FA	FR	RNG	THR	GAMES AT POSITION	DL	BFW
1957	Mil N	7	1	2	0	0	0	0	0	0-0	0	0	.000	.000	.000	-99	0	0-0	—	0	0	0	/C		0.0
1958	Mil N	4	8	1	1	1	0	0	0	0-0	0	3	.125	.125	.250	-4	-1	0-0	1.000	0	119	0	O4L		-0.1
1961	Mil N	20	26	1	5	0	0	1	1	3-0	0	11	.192	.276	.308	58	-2	0-1	1.000	1	127	128	O11(7/0/4)		-0.3
1962	Mil.N	20	47	3	12	0	0	0	2	2-0	0	10	.255	.286	.255	48	-4	0-1	.960	1	113	0	O8(4/3/1)		-0.7
1963	Mil N	16	29	1	2	0	0	0	1	0-0	0	9	.069	.100	.069	-51	-6	0-0	1.000	0	113	0	O8(4/3/1)	69	-1.0
1964	NY N	92	225	20	54	8	0	4	23	8-1	2	33	.240	.272	.329	70	-9	0-0	.981	-1	59	179	C45,O16L		-0.5
1965	NY N	25	46	5	7	0	0	4	10	1-0	0	8	.152	.167	.413	61	-3	0-0	.962	-2	29	93	C15/1		-1.4
1966	NY N	53	109	5	19	2	0	3	12	3-0	1	19	.174	.204	.275	32	-10	0-1	1.000	-3	61	172	C29,1b13		-0.3
1967	NY N	13	37	3	9	3	0	0	4	2-1	0	8	.243	.282	.324	74	-1	0-0	.955	-2	63	237	C12		0.6
	Cal A	23	52	5	16	3	0	1	3	4-0	0	8	.308	.357	.423	135	2	0-0	1.000	3	291	177	C19		0.1
1969	KC A	64	89	7	24	5	0	3	21	6-0	0	18	.270	.313	.427	105	0	0-0	.909	1	122	148	O18(2/0/16),C6		-0.6
1970	KC A	57	55	3	9	3	0	0	6	6-2	1	16	.164	.258	.218	33	-5	0-0	1.000	-1	67	0	C3/1	69	-0.4
Total 11		394	724	56	158	25	0	16	82	44	4	146	.218	.258	.319	62	-39	0-3	.984	-4	91	171	C131,O62(37/3/22),1b15		-4.4

TAYLOR, BOB Robert Lee B3.20.1944 Leland MS BL/TR/5-9/170 d4.9

YEAR	TM LG	G	AB	R	H	2B	3B	HR	RBI	BB-IB	HP	SO	AVG	OBP	SLG	AOPS	ABR	SB-CS	FA	FR	RNG	THR	GAMES AT POSITION	DL	BFW
1970	SF N	63	84	12	16	0	0	2	10	12-0	1	13	.190	.320	.262	58	-5	0-0	1.000	-1	85	80	O26(22/0/5)/C		-0.6

TAYLOR, SAMMY Samuel Douglas B2.27.1933 Woodruff SC BL/TR/6-2/185* d4.20

YEAR	TM LG	G	AB	R	H	2B	3B	HR	RBI	BB-IB	HP	SO	AVG	OBP	SLG	AOPS	ABR	SB-CS	FA	FR	RNG	THR	GAMES AT POSITION	DL	BFW
1958	Chi N	96	301	30	78	12	6	2	36	27-4	0	46	.259	.319	.372	84	-7	2-1	.988	-9	78	63	C87		-1.2
1959	Chi N	110	353	41	95	13	2	13	43	35-13	1	47	.269	.336	.428	103	1	1-0	.982	-20	53	80	C109	30	-1.4
1960	Chi N	74	150	14	31	9	0	3	17	6-0	1	18	.207	.241	.327	55	-10	0-1	.978	-3	97	130	C43		-1.2
1961	Chi N	89	235	26	56	8	2	8	23	23-7	4	39	.238	.316	.391	86	-5	0-0	.989	-7	76	74	C75		-0.9
1962	Chi N	7	15	0	2	1	0	1	1	3-1	0	3	.133	.278	.200	30	-1	0-0	1.000	-1	207	0	C6	41	-1.0
	NY N	68	158	12	35	4	2	3	20	23-1	2	17	.222	.323	.329	76	-5	0-0	.991	-7	81	130	C50		-1.2
	Year	75	173	12	37	5	2	3	21	26-2	2	20	.214	.319	.318	72	-6	0-0	.992	-7	93	118	C56		0.3
1963	NY N	22	35	3	9	0	1	0	6	5-1	0	7	.257	.341	.314	91	0	0-0	1.000	2	78	93	C13		-0.3
	Cin N	3	6	0	0	0	0	0	0	0-0	0	2	.000	.000	.000	-97	-2	0-0	.833	-1	0	0	C2		0.0
	Year	25	41	3	9	0	1	0	6	5-1	0	9	.220	.298	.268	65	-2	0-0	.984	1	0	376	C15		0.0
	Cle A	4	10	1	3	0	0	1	0	0-0	0	3	.300	.300	.300	69	0	0-0	1.000	0	0	376	C2	71	-5.9
Total 6		473	1263	127	309	47	9	33	147	122-27	8	181	.245	.314	.375	84	-29	3-2	.986	-44	73	86	C387		-5.9

TAYLOR, TOMMY Thomas Livingstone Carlton B9.17.1892 Mexia TX D4.5.1956 Greenville MS BR/TR/5-8.5/160 d7.9

YEAR	TM LG	G	AB	R	H	2B	3B	HR	RBI	BB-IB	HP	SO	AVG	OBP	SLG	AOPS	ABR	SB-CS	FA	FR	RNG	THR	GAMES AT POSITION	DL	BFW
1924	†Was A	26	73	11	19	3	1	0	8	3-0	2	9	.260	.289	.329	61	-5	2-0	.923	-4	60	191	3b16,2b2/OC		-0.8

TAYLOR, BILLY William H. B12.1870 Butler KY D9.12.1905 Cincinnati OH TR/5-10/160 d9.19

YEAR	TM LG	G	AB	R	H	2B	3B	HR	RBI	BB-IB	HP	SO	AVG	OBP	SLG	AOPS	ABR	SB-CS	FA	FR	RNG	THR	GAMES AT POSITION	DL	BFW
1898	Lou N	9	24	2	6	1	0	0	2	1	1		.250	.308	.292	73	-1	1	.909	-1	115	0	3b7/2		-0.8

TAYLOR, BILLY William Henry "Bollicky Bill" B1855 Washington DC D5.14.1900 Jacksonville FL BR/TR/5-11.5/204 d5.21 OF(24/15/38) ▲

YEAR	TM LG	G	AB	R	H	2B	3B	HR	RBI	BB-IB	HP	SO	AVG	OBP	SLG	AOPS	ABR	SB-CS	FA	FR	RNG	THR	GAMES AT POSITION	DL	BFW
1881	Wor N	6	28	3	3	1	0	0	2	0		2	.107	.107	.143	-21	-4		.882	-0	59	0	O5R/P		-0.3
	Det N	1	4	0	2	0	0	0	1	0		0	.500	.500	1.000	346	1		.750	-0	99	0	/3		0.1
	Cle N	24	103	6	25	1	0	0	12	0		8	.243	.243	.252	59	-5		.859	-2	61	108	O23L/P3		-0.8
	Year	31	135	9	30	4	0	0	15	0		10	.222	.222	.252	50	-8		.862	-8			C27,1b23,3b14,O8(0/6/2)/P		0.5
1882	Pit AA	70	299	40	84	16	13	3		7			.281	.297	.452	157	17		.747	-16	134	135	O37(0/8/29),C33,P19,1b9		-1.0
1883	Pit AA	83	369	43	96	13	7	2		9			.260	.278	.350	105	2		.872	2	86	138	P33,1b10,O4(1/1/2)		0.0
1884	StL U	43	186	44	68	23	1	3		7			.366	.389	.548	174	12		.788	2	126	95	P30		0.5
	Phi AA	30	111	8	28	6	2	0		2	1		.252	.272	.342	93	3		.556	-1	58	0	P6		0.4
1885	Phi AA	6	21	4	4	0	0	0	2	0			.190	.190	.190	19	-1		.556	-1	58	0	P6		-0.2
1886	Bal AA	10	39	4	12	0	1	0	8	1			.308	.325	.359	117	0	1	.800	-1	97	0	P8/1C		0.0
1887	Phi AA	1	4	0	1	0	0	0		0			.250	.250	.250	40	0	0	1.000	-0	55	0	/P		-0.1
Total 7		274	1164	148	323	62	24	8	26	26	1	10	.277	.294	.393	121	25	1	.822	-28			P100,O77R,C61,1b43,3b16		-1.0

TAYLOR, BILL William Michael B12.30.1929 Alhambra CA BL/TR/6-3/212* d4.14

YEAR	TM LG	G	AB	R	H	2B	3B	HR	RBI	BB-IB	HP	SO	AVG	OBP	SLG	AOPS	ABR	SB-CS	FA	FR	RNG	THR	GAMES AT POSITION	DL	BFW
1954	NY N	55	65	4	12	1	0	2	10	3		15	.185	.239	.292	38	-6	0-0	1.000	-1	66	0	O9(7/0/2)		-0.1
1955	NY N	65	64	9	17	4	0	4	12	1-0	0	16	.266	.273	.516	104	0	0-0	—	-0	0	0	O2R		-0.1
1956	NY N	1	4	0	1	1	0	0	0	0-0	0	1	.250	.250	.500	96	0	0-0	1.000	0	67	0	/OR		0.0
1957	NY N	11	9	0	0	0	0	0	0	1-0	0	2	.000	.100	.000	-70	-2	0-0	—	0	0	0	/H		0.0
	Det A	9	23	4	8	2	0	1	3	0-0	1	3	.348	.348	.565	142	1	0-0	1.000	0	74	0	O5L		0.1
1958	Det A	8	8	0	3	0	0	0	1	0-0	0	2	.375	.375	.375	100	1	0-0	1.000	0	155	0	/OR		0.0
Total 5		149	173	17	41	8	0	7	26	5-0	2	39	.237	.264	.405	74	-7	0-0	1.000	-1	72	0	O18(12/0/6)		0.0

TAYLOR, ZACHARY Zachary H. d9.10

YEAR	TM LG	G	AB	R	H	2B	3B	HR	RBI	BB-IB	HP	SO	AVG	OBP	SLG	AOPS	ABR	SB-CS	FA	FR	RNG	THR	GAMES AT POSITION	DL	BFW
1874	Bal NA	13	48	3	12	0	0	0	3	0		1	.250	.250	.250	61	-2	0-0	.914	-1	112	17	1b13		-0.1

TEAHEN, MARK Mark Thomas B9.6.1981 Redlands CA BL/TR/6-3/210 d4.4 Col St. Marys (CA)

YEAR	TM LG	G	AB	R	H	2B	3B	HR	RBI	BB-IB	HP	SO	AVG	OBP	SLG	AOPS	ABR	SB-CS	FA	FR	RNG	THR	GAMES AT POSITION	DL	BFW
2005	KC A	130	447	60	110	29	4	7	55	40-2	1	107	.246	.309	.376	86	-9	7-2	.947	9	105	95	3b128	21	0.0

TEBBETTS, BIRDIE George Robert B11.10.1912 Burlington VT D3.24.1999 Manatee FL BR/TR/5-11.5/170(170-190) d9.16 Mil 1943-45 M11 Col Providence

YEAR	TM LG	G	AB	R	H	2B	3B	HR	RBI	BB-IB	HP	SO	AVG	OBP	SLG	AOPS	ABR	SB-CS	FA	FR	RNG	THR	GAMES AT POSITION	DL	BFW
1936	Det A	10	33	7	10	1	2	1	4	5	0	3	.303	.395	.545	129	1	0-0	.982	1	158	76	C10		0.0
1937	Det A	50	162	15	31	4	3	2	16	10	0	13	.191	.238	.290	32	-18	0-0	.963	-4	89	91	C48		-1.3
1938	Det A	53	143	16	42	6	2	1	25	12	0	20	.294	.348	.385	79	-5	1-2	.985	-1	131	89	C53		0.0
1939	Det A	106	341	37	89	22	4	6	53	25	2	20	.261	.315	.372	70	-16	2-1	.970	11	114	126	C100		0.6
1940	†Det A	111	379	46	112	24	4	4	46	35	1	14	.296	.357	.412	90	-5	4-5	.975	15	112	149	C107		1.2
1941	Det A☆	110	359	28	102	19	4	2	47	38	1	29	.284	.354	.376	85	-7	1-2	.977	7	102	107	C97		0.2
1942	Det A★	99	308	24	76	11	0	1	27	39	2	17	.247	.339	.292	71	-10	4-0	.977	-0	105	86	C87		-0.6
1946	Det A	87	280	20	68	11	2	1	34	28	0	23	.243	.312	.307	69	-11	1-3	.982	-0	105	86	C20		-0.5
1947	Det A	20	53	1	5	1	0	0	2	3	0	9	.094	.143	.113	-27	-9	0-1	1.000	5	139	158	C20		-0.5
	Bos A	90	291	22	87	10	4	1	28	21	0	30	.299	.346	.344	86	-5	2-4	.974	-1	88	75	C89		-0.1

YEAR	TM LG	G	AB	R	H	2B	3B	HR	RBI	BB-IB	HP	SO	AVG	OBP	SLG	AOPS	ABR	SB-CS	FA	FR	RNG	THR	GAMES AT POSITION	DL	BFW
	Year	110	344	23	92	11	0	1	30	24	0	33	.267	.315	.308	69	-14	2-5	.980	4	97	90	C109		-0.7
1948	Bos A★	128	446	54	125	26	2	5	68	62	1	32	.280	.371	.381	95	-1	5-2	.981	-8	116	68	C126		-0.1
1949	Bos A★	122	403	42	109	14	0	5	48	62	1	22	.270	.369	.342	83	-8	8-1	.980	-2	130	67	C118		-0.2
1950	Bos A	79	268	33	83	10	1	8	45	29	0	26	.310	.377	.444	100	0	1-1	.988	1	110	90	C74		0.0
1951	Cle A	55	137	8	36	6	0	2	18	8	1	7	.263	.308	.350	82	-4	0-0	.977	1	93	118	C44		-0.1
1952	Cle A	42	101	4	25	4	0	1	8	12	2	9	.248	.339	.317	89	-1	0-1	.986	-2	93	98	C37		-0.2
Total	14	1162	3704	357	1000	169	22	38	469	389	12	261	.270	.341	.358	81	-99	29-23	.978	23	108	100	C1108		-1.9

TEBEAU, PUSSY Charles Alston B2.22.1870 Worcester MA D3.25.1950 Pittsfield MA BR/TR/5-10/175 d7.22

1895	Cle N	2	6	3	3	0	0	0	1	2		0	1	.500	.625	.500	182	1	1	1.000	1	303	0	O2R		0.1

TEBEAU, GEORGE George E. "White Wings" B12.26.1861 St.Louis MO D2.4.1923 Denver CO BR/TR/5-9/175 d4.16 b-Patsy ▲

1887	Cin AA	85	318	57	94	12	5	4	33	31	3		.296	.364	.403	111	5	37	.887	1	95	68	O84(80/1/3)/P		0.3
1888	Cin AA	121	411	72	94	12	12	3	51	61	7		.229	.338	.338	111	6	37	.911	2	99	72	O121L		0.5
1889	Cin AA	135	496	110	125	21	11	7	70	69	6	62	.252	.350	.381	105	3	61	.887	-7	69	53	O134L/1		-0.6
1890	Tol AA	94	381	71	102	16	10	1	36	51	3		.268	.359	.370	112	6	55	.951	1	87	30	O94(1/93/0)/P		0.3
1894	Was N	61	222	41	50	10	6	0	28	37	2	20	.225	.341	.324	63	-13	17	.857	-5	90	43	O61(8/53/0)		-1.7
	Cle N	40	150	32	47	9	4	0	25	25	0	18	.313	.411	.427	98	0	9	.928	-5	24	213	O27(4/23/0),1b12/3		-0.5
	Year	101	372	73	97	19	10	0	53	62	2	38	.261	.369	.366	78	-12	26	.880	-10	69	97	O88(12/76/0),1b12/3		-2.2
1895	Cle N	92	341	58	111	16	6	0	68	50	1	29	.326	.413	.408	106	5	12	.873	-7	48	0	O49(1/0/48),1b43		-0.4
Total	6	628	2319	441	623	96	54	15	311	324	22	129	.269	.364	.376	103	12	228	.900	-20	81	58	O570(349/170/51),1b56,P2/3		-2.1

TEBEAU, PATSY Oliver Wendell B12.5.1864 St.Louis MO D5.15.1918 St.Louis MO BR/TR/5-8/163 d9.20 M11 b-George

1887	Chi N	20	68	8	11	3	0	0	10	4	0	4	.162	.208	.206	14	-8	8	.855	1	96	147	3b20		-0.8
1889	Cle N	136	521	72	147	20	6	8	76	37	2	41	.282	.332	.390	103	0	26	.897	1	100	110	3b136		0.3
1890	Cle P	110	450	86	134	26	6	5	74	34	3	20	.298	.351	.416	114	9	14	**.872**	13	103	120	3b110,M		1.9
1891	Cle N	61	249	38	65	8	3	1	41	16	3	13	.261	.313	.329	84	-6	12	.884	6	107	137	3b61/OLM		0.1
1892	†Cle N	86	340	47	83	13	3	2	49	23	8	34	.244	.307	.318	86	-6	6	.911	-3	94	172	3b74,2b5,1b4,S3,M		-0.7
1893	Cle N	116	486	90	160	32	8	2	102	32	4	11	.329	.375	.440	110	5	19	.980	5	128	82	1b57,3b56,2b3,M		0.8
1894	Cle N	125	523	82	158	23	7	3	89	35	1	35	.302	.347	.390	74	-24	30	.977	-5	75	100	1b115,2b10,3b2/SM		-2.2
1895	†Cle N	63	264	50	84	13	2	2	52	16	2	18	.318	.362	.405	92	-4	8	.992	3	76	113	1b49,2b9,3b6,M		0.0
1896	†Cle N	132	543	56	146	22	6	2	94	21	3	22	.269	.300	.343	65	-30	20	.985	3	112	**130**	1b122,3b7,2b5/SPM		-2.3
1897	Cle N	109	412	62	110	15	9	0	59	30	4		.267	.323	.347	73	-17	11	**.994**	1	89	107	1b92,2b18,3b2/SM		-1.4
1898	Cle N	131	477	53	123	11	4	1	63	53	7		.258	.341	.304	86	-7	5	.984	3	97	85	1b91,2b34,S7,3b3,M		-0.2
1899	StL N	77	281	27	69	10	3	1	26	18	5		.246	.303	.313	67	-13	5	.980	-3	73	96	1b65,S11/32M		-1.4
1900	StL N	1	4	0	0	0	0	0	0	0	0		.000	.000	.000	-99	-1	0	.700	-1	65	0	/SM		-0.2
Total	13	1167	4618	671	1290	196	57	27	735	319	42	198	.279	.332	.364	86	-102	164	.984	23	94	104	1b595,3b478,2b85,S25/POL		-6.1

TEED, DICK Richard Leroy B3.8.1926 Springfield MA BB/TR/5-11/180 d7.24

| 1953 | Bro N | 1 | 1 | 0 | 0 | 0 | 0 | 0 | 0 | 0 | 0 | 1 | 1.000 | .000 | .000 | -98 | 0 | 0-0 | — | 0 | | | /H | | 0.0 |

TEIXEIRA, MARK Mark Charles B4.11.1980 Annapolis MD BB/TR/6-3/220* [TexA01 1/5] d4.1 Col Georgia Tech

2003	Tex A	146	529	66	137	29	5	26	84	44-5	14	120	.259	.331	.480	104	2	1-2	.996	-3	96	96	1b116,O25(14/0/11),3b15,D5		-1.1
2004	Tex A	145	545	101	153	34	2	38	112	68-12	10	117	.281	.370	.560	133	27	4-1	.992	2	109	95	1b142,O7R,D2		1.5
2005	Tex A★	**162**	644	112	194	41	3	43	144	72-5	11	124	.301	.379	.575	144	42	4-0	**.998**	1	101	87	1b155,D8	16	2.8
Total	3	453	1718	279	484	104	10	107	340	184-22	35	361	.282	.362	.541	128	71	9-3	.996	0	102	92	1b413,O32(14/0/18),D15,3b15	16	3.2

TEJADA, MIGUEL Miguel Odalis (Martinez) B5.25.1976 Bani, D.R. BR/TR/5-9/188(170-215) d8.27

1997	Oak A	26	99	10	20	3	2	2	10	2-0	1	22	.202	.240	.333	48	-8	2-0	.968	-1	93	94	S26		-0.7
1998	Oak A	105	365	53	85	20	1	11	45	28-0	7	86	.233	.298	.384	77	-13	5-6	.951	3	106	110	S104		-0.3
1999	Oak A	159	593	93	149	33	4	21	84	57-3	10	94	.251	.325	.427	90	-7	8-7	.973	9	103	100	S159		1.2
2000	†Oak A	160	607	105	167	32	1	30	115	66-6	4	102	.275	.349	.479	109	7	6-0	.972	2	105	101	S160		2.0
2001	†Oak A	162	622	107	166	31	3	31	113	43-5	13	89	.267	.326	.476	108	5	11-5	.973	7	102	102	S162		2.4
2002	†Oak A★	162	662	108	204	30	0	34	131	38-3	11	84	.308	.354	.508	127	24	7-2	.975	8	107	107	S162		4.3
2003	†Oak A	162	636	98	177	42	0	27	106	53-7	6	65	.278	.336	.472	110	10	10-0	.972	7	104	97	S162		3.0
2004	Bal A★	162	653	107	203	40	2	34	**150**	48-6	10	73	.311	.360	.534	132	30	4-1	.970	28	**113**	106	S162		**6.6**
2005	Bal A★	162	654	89	199	**50**	5	26	98	40-9	7	83	.304	.349	.515	126	24	5-1	.971	14	**104**	99	S160,D2		4.8
Total	9	1260	4891	770	1370	261	18	216	852	375-39	71	698	.280	.338	.477	111	72	58-22	.970	77	105	102	S1257,D2	50	23.3

TEJADA, WILFREDO Wilfredo Aristides (Andujar) B11.12.1962 Santo Domingo, D.R. BR/TR/6-0/175* d9.9

1986	Mon N	10	25	2	6	2	0	0	2	2-1	0	4	.240	.296	.280	60	-1	0-0	1.000	-2	93	117	C10		-0.3
1988	Mon N	8	15	1	4	0	0	0	2	0-0	0	8	.267	.250	.400	85	0	0-0	1.000	0	94	0	C7		0.0
Total	2	18	40	2	10	3	0	0	4	2-1	0	12	.250	.279	.325	69	-1	0-0	1.000	-1	93	71	C17		-0.3

TEMPLE, JOHNNY John Ellis B8.8.1927 Lexington NC D1.9.1994 Anderson SC BR/TR/5-11/175(154-175) d4.15 C1 Col Catawba

1952	Cin N	30	97	8	19	3	0	1	5	5	0	1	.196	.235	.258	37	-9	2-1	.984	-0	92	117	2b22		-0.8
1953	Cin N	63	110	14	29	4	0	1	9	7	1	12	.264	.314	.327	67	-5	1-0	.964	7	127	110	2b44		0.4
1954	Cin N	146	505	60	155	14	8	0	44	62	2	32	.307	.384	.366	94	-2	21-7	.973	-4	93	107	2b144		0.6
1955	Cin N	150	588	94	165	20	3	0	50	80-0	1	32	.281	.365	.325	81	-12	19-4	.971	2	99	**118**	2b149/S		0.3
1956	Cin N★	154	632	88	180	18	3	2	41	58-0	1	40	.285	.344	.332	78	-17	14-14	.981	-7	99	87	2b154/OR		-1.1
1957	Cin N★	145	557	85	158	24	4	0	37	94-0	4	34	.284	.387	.341	92	0	19-5	.974	-19	89	85	2b154/1		-0.6
1958	Cin N	141	542	82	166	31	6	3	47	91-0	0	41	.306	.405	.402	109	13	15-8	.979	-14	90	91	2b141/1		0.9
1959	Cin N★	149	598	102	186	35	6	8	67	72-2	2	40	.311	.380	.430	114	15	14-3	.974	-25	92	98	2b149		0.3
1960	Cle A	98	381	50	102	13	1	2	19	32-0	1	20	.268	.326	.323	79	-11	11-5	.974	-28	75	93	2b77,3b17		-3.4
1961	Cle A★	129	518	73	143	22	3	3	30	61-1	0	36	.276	.351	.347	90	-6	9-5	.969	-31	91	90	2b129		-2.5
1962	Bal A	78	270	28	71	8	1	1	17	36-0	1	22	.263	.352	.311	85	-4	7-4	.981	-11	90	96	2b71		-0.9
	Hou N	31	95	14	25	4	0	0	12	7-0	0	11	.263	.311	.305	72	-4	1-0	.941	-5	95	43	2b26/3		-0.7
1963	Hou N	100	322	29	85	12	1	1	17	41-1	0	24	.264	.347	.317	99	1	7-2	.970	-11	92	59	2b61,3b29		-0.5
1964	Cin N	6	3	0	0	0	0	0	0	2-1	0	1	.000	.400	.000	23	0	0-0	—	0			/H		0.0
Total	13	1420	5218	720	1484	208	36	22	395	648-5	13	338	.284	.363	.351	91	-41	140-48	.974	-145	93	95	2b1312,3b47/1ORS		-8.0

TEMPLETON, GARRY Garry Lewis B3.24.1956 Lockney TX BB/TR/5-11/190(170-209) [StLN74 1/13] d8.9

1976	StL N	53	213	32	62	8	2	1	17	7-0	1	33	.291	.314	.362	90	-3	11-7	.922	5	104	127	S53		0.8
1977	StL N★	153	621	94	200	19	**18**	8	79	15-3	1	70	.322	.336	.449	110	5	28-24	.958	3	99	121	S151		2.1
1978	StL N	155	647	82	181	31	**13**	2	47	22-3	1	87	.280	.303	.377	90	-12	34-11	.953	**33**	111	124	S155		4.2
1979	StL N★	154	672	105	**211**	32	**19**	9	62	18-4	1	91	.314	.331	.458	111	7	26-10	.960	24	**113**	121	S150		4.9
1980	StL N	118	504	83	161	19	9	4	43	18-6	0	43	.319	.342	.417	106	2	31-15	.959	36	**122**	**125**	S115	36	5.3
1981	StL N	80	333	47	96	16	8	1	33	14-3	0	55	.288	.315	.393	96	-3	8-12	.960	11	113	**123**	S76	17	1.4
1982	SD N	141	563	76	139	25	8	6	64	26-7	1	81	.247	.279	.352	81	-7	27-16	.961	-23	94	95	S136		-2.7
1983	SD N	126	460	39	121	20	2	3	40	21-7	0	57	.263	.294	.335	76	-16	16-6	.960	-7	95	98	S123		-1.0
1984	†SD N	148	493	40	127	19	3	2	35	39-**23**	1	81	.258	.312	.320	78	-14	8-3	.960	-24	92	99	S146	19	-2.4
1985	SD N★	148	546	63	154	30	4	6	55	41-**24**	2	85	.282	.332	.377	99	-1	16-6	.968	-4	101	115	S148		1.3
1986	SD N	147	510	42	126	21	2	2	44	35-21	1	86	.247	.296	.308	68	-23	10-5	.966	-25	88	74	S144		-3.5
1987	SD N	148	510	42	113	13	5	5	48	42-11	1	79	.222	.281	.296	55	-34	14-3	.972	13	106	92	S105,3b2		-0.4
1988	SD N	110	362	35	90	15	7	3	36	20-10	1	50	.249	.286	.354	85	-9	8-2	.968	9	106	118	S105,3b2		1.0
1989	SD N	142	509	43	129	25	6	6	40	23-12	0	63	.253	.286	.354	82	-13	1-3	.970	13	105	112	S140		1.0
1990	SD N	144	505	45	125	25	3	9	59	24-7	0	59	.248	.280	.362	75	-19	1-4	.957	-9	96	107	S135		-1.9
1991	SD N	32	57	5	11	1	1	1	6	1-0	0	9	.193	.203	.298	39	-5	0-1	.950	3	86	131	3b15/S		-0.8
	NY N	80	219	20	50	9	1	2	20	9-3	0	29	.228	.257	.306	58	-13	3-1	.963	8	112	117	S40,1b25,3b2,O2R		-0.4
	Year	112	276	25	61	10	2	3	26	10-3	0	38	.221	.246	.304	54	-18	3-2	.963	5	110	115	S41,1b25,3b17,O2R		-1.2
Total	16	2079	7721	893	2096	329	106	70	728	375-144	9	1092	.271	.304	.369	87	-168	242-129	.961	61	103	109	S1964,1b25,3b19,O2R	72	8.9

TENACE, GENE Fury Gene (b Fiore Gino Tennaci) B10.10.1946 Russellton PA BR/TR/6-0/190* [OakA65 11/340] d5.29 M1/C10 OF(1/0/10)

1969	Oak A	16	38	4	6	1	0	1	1	15	0		.158	.200	.237	23	-4	0-0	1.000	1	99	70	C13		-0.3
1970	Oak A	38	105	19	32	6	0	7	20	23-2	0	30	.305	.430	.562	177	12	0-2	.990	1	51	127	C30		1.7
1971	†Oak A	65	179	26	49	7	1	7	25	29-0	2	34	.274	.381	.430	132	9	2-1	.994	-2	132	67	C52/OL		0.9
1972	†Oak A	82	227	22	51	6	2	5	32	24-2	3	42	.225	.307	.339	97	-1	0-0	.979	-5	102	69	C49,O9R,1b7,2b2,3b2		-0.5

YEAR	TM LG	G	AB	R	H	2B	3B	HR	RBI	BB-IB	HP	SO	AVG	OBP	SLG	AOPS	ABR	SB-CS	FA	FR	RNG	THR	GAMES AT POSITION	DL	BFW
1973	†Oak A	160	510	83	132	18	2	24	84	101-8	10	94	.259	.387	.443	141	33	2-2	.989	-6	86	107	1b134,C33/2D		1.8
1974	†Oak A	158	484	71	102	17	1	26	73	110-6	12	105	.211	.367	.411	132	26	2-9	.995	5	80	107	1b106,C79,2b3		2.4
1975	†Oak A★	158	498	83	127	17	0	29	87	106-2	12	127	.255	.395	.464	146	36	7-4	.984	2	104	79	C125,1b68/D		4.0
1976	Oak A	128	417	64	104	19	1	22	66	81-2	4	91	.249	.373	.458	149	29	5-4	.995	-12	69	95	1b70,C65,D2	27	1.6
1977	SD N	147	437	66	102	24	6	15	61	125-10	13	119	.233	.415	.410	136	33	5-3	.980	1	96	129	C99,1b36,3b14		3.6
1978	SD N	142	401	60	90	18	4	16	61	101-8	11	98	.224	.392	.409	134	25	6-5	.993	4	95	118	1b80,C71/3		2.9
1979	SD N	151	463	61	122	16	4	20	67	105-4	7	106	.263	.403	.445	141	32	2-6	.998	8	140	126	C94,1b72		3.9
1980	SD N	133	316	46	70	11	1	17	50	92-11	4	63	.222	.399	.424	140	23	4-4	.979	-4	94	109	C104,1b19		2.3
1981	StL N	58	129	26	30	7	0	5	22	38-2	4	26	.233	.416	.403	129	8	0-0	.980	-6	94	82	C38,1b7		0.4
1982	†StL N	66	124	18	32	9	0	7	18	36-1	4	31	.258	.436	.500	158	13	1-1	.994	2	92	118	C37,1b7	32	1.6
1983	Pit N	53	62	7	11	5	0	0	6	12-0	1	17	.177	.348	.258	68	-2	0-1	.989	-0	76	83	1b19,C3/OR	24	-0.3
Total 15		1555	4390	653	1060	179	20	201	674	984-58	91	998	.241	.388	.429	137	272	36-42	.986	-8	105	100	C892,1b625,3b17,O11R,D6,2b6	83	26.0

TENNANT, TOM   Thomas Francis   B7.3.1882 Monroe WI   D2.15.1955 San Carlos CA   BL/TL/5-11/165   d4.18   Col Northern Illinois

1912	StL A	2	2	1	0	0	0	0	0				.000	.000	.000	-99	-1	0			0		/H		-0.1

TENNEY, FRED   Fred Clay   B7.9.1859 Marlborough NH   D6.15.1919 Fall River MA   d4.28   Col Brown ▲

1884	Was U	32	119	17	28	3	1	0		6			.235	.272	.277	69	-8		.867	0	85	209	O27(0/1/26),1b6		-0.8
	Bos U	4	17	1	2	0	0	0		0			.118	.118	.118	-29	-3		.750	-1	51	0	P4		0.0
	Wil U	1	3	0	0	0	0	0		0			.000	.000	.000	-97	-1		1.000	0	55	1698	/P		0.0
	Year	37	139	18	30	3	1	0		6			.216	.248	.252	54	-12		.867	-1	85	209	O27(0/1/26),1b6,P5		-0.8

TENNEY, FRED   Frederick   B11.26.1871 Georgetown MA   D7.3.1952 Boston MA   BL/TL/5-9/155   d6.16   M4   Col Brown

1894	Bos N	27	86	23	34	7	1	2	21	12	0	9	.395	.469	.570	139	6	6	.893	2	120	108	C20,O6(3/2/1)/1		0.7
1895	Bos N	49	173	35	47	9	1	1	21	24	0	5	.272	.360	.353	78	-5	6	.885	2	160	129	O28(25/3/0),C21		-0.3
1896	Bos N	88	348	64	117	14	3	2	49	36	1	12	.336	.400	.411	108	4	18	.957	4	121	57	O60(7/0/53),C27		0.8
1897	†Bos N	132	566	125	180	24	3	1	85	49	4		.318	.376	.376	93	-5	34	.988	5	111	109	1b128,O4R		1.2
1898	Bos N	117	488	106	160	25	5	0	62	63	3		.328	.370	.400	114	9	23	.980	5	115	115	1b117/C		2.4
1899	Bos N	150	603	115	209	19	17	1	67	63	3		.347	.411	.439	122	18	28	.978	10	131	134	1b150		3.7
1900	Bos N	112	437	77	122	13	5	1	56	39	6		.279	.346	.339	80	-12	17	.981	9	131	85	1b111		-0.4
1901	Bos N	115	451	66	127	13	1	1	22	37	5		.282	.340	.322	85	-8	15	.976	7	132	112	1b113,C2		-0.2
1902	Bos N	134	489	88	154	18	3	2	30	73	5		.315	.409	.376	141	29	21	.985	12	135	104	1b134		4.6
1903	Bos N	122	447	79	140	22	3	3	41	70	8		.313	.415	.396	137	28	21	.974	9	131	93	1b122		3.2
1904	Bos N	147	533	76	144	17	9	1	37	57	9		.270	.351	.341	118	14	17	.986	8	120	95	1b144,O4(0/1/3)		3.2
1905	Bos N	149	549	84	158	18	3	0	28	67	3		.288	.368	.332	111	12	15	.982	22	160	87	1b148/PM		3.4
1906	Bos N	143	544	61	148	12	8	1	28	58	5		.273	.357	.340	121	14	17	.983	11	130	107	1b143,M		2.8
1907	Bos N	150	554	83	151	18	8	0	26	82	5		.273	.371	.334	121	18	15	.989	9	122	104	1b149,M		1.7
1908	NY N	156	583	101	149	20	1	2	49	72	7		.256	.344	.304	102	6	17	.990	10	121	111	1b98		0.6
1909	NY N	101	375	43	88	8	2	3	30	52	3		.235	.333	.291	92	-2	8	.986	4	120	74	1b96,O2(0/1/1),M		-0.5
1911	Bos N	102	369	52	97	13	4	1	36	50	1	17	.263	.352	.358	84	-1	5	.985	4	120	104	1b96,O104(35/7/62),C71/P		-0.7
Total 17		1994	7595	1278	2231	270	77	22	688	874	63	43	.294	.371	.358	109	119	285	.983	135	128	104	1b1810,O104(35/7/62),C71/P		23.9

TEPEDINO, FRANK   Frank Ronald   B11.23.1947 Brooklyn NY   BL/TL/5-11/192*   [BalA65 3/55]   d5.12

1967	NY A	9	5	0	2	0	0	0	0	1-0	0	1	.400	.500	.400	175	1	0-0	1.000	-0	0	0	/1		0.0
1969	NY A	13	39	6	9	0	0	0	4	4-0	0	4	.231	.302	.231	53	-2	1-0	.950	-1	99	0	O13R		0.0
1970	NY A	16	19	2	6	2	0	0	2	1-0	0	2	.316	.350	.421	117	0	0-1	1.000	-1	0	0	/1OL		0.0
1971	NY A	6	6	0	0	0	0	0	0	0-0	0	0	.000	.000	.000	-99	-2	0-0	1.000	0	224	0	/OL		-0.1
	Mil A	53	106	11	21	0	0	2	7	4-0	1	17	.198	.234	.264	41	-9	2-2	.986	2	144	96	1b28		-0.9
	Year	59	112	11	21	0	0	2	7	4-0	1	17	.188	.222	.250	34	-10	2-2	.986	3	144	96	1b28/OL		-1.0
1972	NY A	8	8	0	0	0	0	0	0	0-0	0	1	.000	.000	.000	-99	-2	0-0	—	0	0	0	/H		-0.1
1973	Atl N	74	148	20	45	5	0	4	29	13-3	0	21	.304	.354	.419	107	2	0-0	.992	1	108	91	1b58		0.5
1974	Atl N	78	169	11	39	5	1	0	16	9-2	1	13	.231	.272	.272	51	-11	1-2	.988	-0	103	128	1b46		-1.0
1975	Atl N	8	8	0	1	0	0	0	0	0-0	0	2	.000	.125	.000	-61	-2	0-0	—	0	0	0	/H		-0.3
Total 8		265	507	50	122	13	1	6	58	33-5	2	61	.241	.288	.306	65	-25	4-5	.989	2	113	105	1b134,O15(2/0/13)		-1.9

TEPSIC, JOE   Joseph John   B9.18.1923 Slovan PA   BR/TR/5-9/170   d7.12   Col Penn St.

| 1946 | Bro N | 15 | 5 | 2 | 0 | 0 | 0 | 0 | 0 | 0-0 | 0 | 1 | .000 | .167 | .000 | -50 | -1 | 0 | 1.000 | 0 | 138 | 0 | /OL | | -0.1 |

TERRELL, JERRY   Jerry Wayne   B7.13.1946 Waseca MN   BR/TR (BB 1974p)/6-0/170*   [MinA68 18/412]   d4.14   Col Mankato St.   OF(12/1/11)

1973	Min A	124	438	43	116	15	2	1	32	21-0	1	56	.265	.297	.315	70	-18	13-7	.962	-12	87	74	S81,3b30,2b14/ORD		-0.9
1974	Min A	116	229	43	56	4	6	0	19	11-1	2	27	.245	.279	.314	68	-10	3-2	.960	12	109	105	S34,2b26,3b21,D12,O3L,1b2		-0.5
1975	Min A	108	385	48	110	16	2	1	36	19-0	3	27	.286	.324	.345	88	-6	4-4	.947	2	98	131	S41,2b39,1b15,3b12,O6R,D2		-0.3
1976	Min A	89	171	29	42	3	1	0	6	9-0	1	15	.246	.286	.275	64	-8	11-2	.988	2	88	101	2b31,3b26,S16,D12,O6(3/1/2)		-0.3
1977	Min A	93	214	32	48	6	0	1	20	11-1	1	21	.224	.263	.266	46	-16	10-4	.953	1	101	115	2b34,3b25,S11,1b5		-0.9
1978	KC A	73	133	14	27	1	0	0	8	4-0	0	13	.203	.225	.211	23	-14	8-4	1.000	-2	95	68	2b31,3b25,S11,1b5		0.0
1979	KC A	31	40	5	12	3	0	1	2	1-0	0	1	.300	.317	.450	102	0	1-0	.963	-1	97	54	3b19,2b7/PSD	50	0.1
1980	KC A	23	16	4	1	0	0	0	1	0-0	0	3	.063	.063	.063	-65	-4	0-0	1.000	1	112	0	O7(6/0/1),1b3,2b3/PD		0.0
Total 8		657	1626	218	412	48	11	4	125	76-2	6	160	.253	.288	.304	66	-76	50-23	.961	3	102	132	3b192,S191,2b165,D39,1b26,O24,P250		-1.9

TERRELL, TOM   John Thomas   B6.19.1867 Louisville KY   D7.9.1893 Louisville KY   d10.5

| 1886 | Lou AA | 1 | 4 | 0 | 1 | 0 | 0 | 0 | 0 | 0 | | | .250 | .250 | .250 | 54 | 0 | 0 | — | -1 | 0 | 0 | /OLC | | -0.0 |

TERRERO, LUIS   Luis Enrique   B5.18.1980 Santa Cruz de Barahona, D.R.   BR/TR/6-2/206*   d7.10

2003	Ari N	5	4	0	1	0	0	0	1	1	0	1	.250	.400	.250	69	0	0-0	1.000	-0	68	0	O3(0/2/1)		-0.1
2004	Ari N	62	229	21	56	14	0	4	14	20-2	5	78	.245	.319	.354	70	-10	10-2	.938	-3	86	170	O61(1/57/4)		-1.1
2005	Ari N	88	161	23	37	6	1	4	19	14-0	6	40	.230	.313	.354	72	-7	3-2	.984	-4	104	38	O77(1/74/2)	22	-1.2
Total 3		155	394	44	94	20	1	8	34	34-2	12	119	.239	.317	.355	71	-17	13-4	.961	-4	94	110	O141(2/133/7)	22	-2.5

TERRY, WALLACE   Wallace W.   B10.1850 Attleborough (now Langhorne) PA   D1.21.1916 Philadelphia PA   d4.26

| 1875 | Was NA | 6 | 22 | 0 | 4 | 0 | 1 | 0 | 2 | 0 | | 1 | .182 | .182 | .273 | 58 | -1 | 0 | .810 | -3 | 0 | 0 | 1b4,O3(0/1/2) | | -0.4 |

TERRY, ADONIS   William H   B8.7.1864 Westfield MA   D2.24.1915 Milwaukee WI   BR/TR/5-11.5/168   d5.1   U1 ▲

1884	Bro AA	67	236	15	55	10	3	0		8	0		.233	.258	.301	81	-5		.764	-2	83		P56,O13(2/7/4)		-0.3
1885	Bro AA	71	264	23	45	1	3	0	1	20	9	0		.170	.201	.208	29	-22		.883	1	120	133	O47(26/11/10),P25/3		-1.1
1886	Bro AA	75	299	34	71	8	9	0		20	19	1		.237	.265	.344	89	-6	17	.934	1	128	127	P34,O32(10/11/11),S13		0.8
1887	Bro AA	86	352	56	103	6	10	3	65	16	0			.293	.323	.392	98	-4	27	.895	2	62	55	O49(12/4/33),P40,S2		1.0
1888	Bro AA	30	115	13	29	6	0	0	8	5	0			.252	.283	.304	89	-1	7	.909	3	93	203	P23,O7(2/4/1),1b2		0.5
1889	Bro AA	49	160	29	48	6	4	2	26	14	0	14	.300	.356	.450	129	5	4	.963	5	125	113	P41,1b10		0.8
1890	†Bro N	99	363	63	101	17	9	4	59	40	4	34	.278	.356	.408	122	10	32	.930	-3	40	103	O54(42/5/7),P46/1		1.8
1891	Bal N	1	4	0	0	0	0	0	0	0			1	.000	.000	.000	-97	-1	0	1.000	-1	0	149	0	P		-0.0
1892	Pit N	31	100	10	16	0	4	2	11	10	3		11	.160	.236	.300	62	-6	2	.938	-1	90	170	P30/OC		-0.5
	Year	32	104	10	16	0	4	2	11	10			12	.154	.228	.288	56	-7	2	.940	-1	92	0	P31/OC		-0.6
1893	Pit N	26	71	9	18	6	1	0	11	3	1		12	.254	.293	.394	84	2	1	.920	-0	98	170	/P		0.4
1894	Pit N	1	1	0	0	0	0	0	0			—	—	—	—	—	—	—	—		—		0	/P		-0.0
	Chi N	30	95	19	33	4	2	0	17	11	0	12	.347	.415	.432	99	3	2	.875	-1	85	70	P23,O7R,1b2		1.0
	Year	31	95	19	33	4	2	0	17	11	0	12	.347	.415	.432	99	3	2	.875	-1	84	0	P24,O7R,1b2		1.0
1895	Chi N	40	137	18	30	3	1	2	10	2	1	17	.219	.236	.292	33	-15	1	.895	1	115	123	P38,O2R		-0.4
1896	Chi N	30	99	14	26	5	1	0	11	12		12	.263	.324	.343	73	2	4	.968	-2	74	0	P30		-0.1
1897	Chi N	1	3	1	0	0	0	0	0	0			1	.000	.000	.000	-96	-1	0	.903	1	101	69	/P		-0.0
Total 14		667	2389	314	594	76	54	15	287	146		139	.249	.295	.344	85	-44	106	.903	11	101		P440,O216(94/43/79),S16,1b15/3		4.3

TERRY, BILL   William Harold "Memphis Bill"   B10.30.1898 Atlanta GA   D1.9.1989 Jacksonville FL   BL/TL/6-1/200   d9.24   M10   HF1954

1923	NY N	3	7	1	1	0	0	0		0		0	.143	.333	.143	30	-1	0-0	1.000	-4	67		1b2		-0.1
1924	†NY N	77	163	26	39	7	2	5	24	17		18	.239	.311	.399	91	-2	1-1	.988	7	120	133	1b35		0.0
1925	NY N	133	489	75	156	31	6	11	70	42		52	.319	.371	.454	117	5	3	.990	4	113	84	1b126		2.9
1926	NY N	98	225	26	65	12	5	5	43	22		17	.289	.352	.453	117	5	3	.979	4	140	124	1b38,O14(1/0/13)		0.9

YEAR	TM LG	G	AB	R	H	2B	3B	HR	RBI	BB-IB	HP	SO	AVG	OBP	SLG	AOPS	ABR	SB-CS	FA	FR	RNG	THR	GAMES AT POSITION	DL	BFW
1927	NY N	150	580	101	189	32	13	20	121	46	2	53	.326	.377	.529	141	31	1	.993	5	111	111	1b150		2.6
1928	NY N	149	568	100	185	36	11	17	101	64	0	36	.326	.394	.518	136	30	7	.993	-2	93	123	1b149		1.8
1929	NY N	150	607	103	226	39	5	14	117	48	0	35	.372	.418	.522	132	31	10	.994	7	118	129	1b149/OL		2.5
1930	NY N	154	633	139	254	39	15	23	129	57	1	33	.401	.452	.619	159	61	8	.990	14	137	94	1b154		2.5
1931	NY N	153	611	121	213	43	20	9	112	47	2	36	.349	.397	.529	150	42		.990	10	129	89	1b153		5.6
1932	NY N	154	643	124	225	42	11	28	117	32	1	23	.350	.382	.580	158	49	4	.991	15	135	99	1b153		3.7
1933	†NY N★	123	475	68	153	20	5	6	58	40	0	23	.322	.375	.423	129	19	3	.992	1	101	120	1b117,M		4.8
1934	NY N★	153	602	109	213	30	6	8	83	60	1	47	.354	.414	.463	138	35	0	.994	6	115	123	1b153,M		0.9
1935	NY N★	145	596	91	203	32	8	6	64	41	0	55	.341	.383	.451	126	22	7	.996	6	113	109	1b143,M		2.5
1936	†NY N	79	229	36	71	10	5	2	39	19	0	19	.310	.363	.424	112	4	0	.996	3	120	142	1b56,M		1.4
Total	14	1721	6428	1120	2193	373	112	154	1078	537	9	449	.341	.393	.506	137	341	56-6	.992	72	117	110	1b1579,O15(2/0/13)		26.7

TERRY, ZEB   Zebulon Alexander B6.17.1891 Denison TX D3.14.1988 Los Angeles CA BR/TR/5-8/129 d4.12 Mil 1918 Col Stanford

YEAR	TM LG	G	AB	R	H	2B	3B	HR	RBI	BB-IB	HP	SO	AVG	OBP	SLG	AOPS	ABR	SB-CS	FA	FR	RNG	THR	GAMES AT POSITION	DL	BFW
1916	Chi A	94	269	20	51	8	4	0	17	33	6	36	.190	.292	.249	62	-12	4	.935	-9	93	130	S93		-1.7
1917	Chi A	2	1	0	0	0	0	0	0	2	0	0	.000	.667	.000	102	0		1.000	-0	74	0	/S		0.0
1918	Bos N	28	105	17	32	2	2	0	8	8	1	14	.305	.360	.362	125	3	1	.977	7	115	116	S27		1.3
1919	Pit N	129	472	46	107	12	6	0	27	31	4	26	.227	.280	.278	65	-20	12	.960	-31	90	84	S127		-4.7
1920	Chi N	133	496	56	139	26	9	0	52	44	2	22	.280	.341	.369	102	2	12-16	.962	17	107	99	S70,2b63		2.4
1921	Chi N	123	488	59	134	18	1	2	45	27	4	19	.275	.318	.328	71	-20	1-13	.972	5	103	94	2b122		-1.2
1922	Chi N	131	496	56	142	24	2	0	67	34	2	16	.286	.335	.343	74	-19	2-11	.964	5	102	111	2b125,S4,3b3		-1.2
Total	7	640	2327	254	605	90	24	2	216	179	19	133	.260	.318	.322	78	-66	32-40	.964	-3	97	103	S322,2b310,3b3		-5.1

TERWILLIGER, WAYNE   Willard Wayne "Twig" B6.27.1925 Clare MI BR/TR/5-11/170* d8.6 C18 Col Western Michigan

YEAR	TM LG	G	AB	R	H	2B	3B	HR	RBI	BB-IB	HP	SO	AVG	OBP	SLG	AOPS	ABR	SB-CS	FA	FR	RNG	THR	GAMES AT POSITION	DL	BFW
1949	Chi N	36	112	11	25	2	1	0	10	16	1	22	.223	.326	.313	74	-4	0	.978	4	119	48	2b34		0.2
1950	Chi N	133	480	63	116	22	3	10	32	43	5	63	.242	.311	.363	77	-16	13	.967	-7	106	78	2b126/13OC		-1.6
1951	Chi N	50	192	26	41	6	0	0	10	29	0	21	.214	.317	.245	52	-12	3-1	.969	-2	99	93	2b49		-1.1
	Bro N	37	50	11	14	1	0	0	4	8	1	7	.280	.390	.300	87	0	1-0	.949	4	126	102	2b24/3		0.4
	Year	87	242	37	55	7	0	0	14	37	1	28	.227	.332	.256	59	-12	4-1	.964	1	104	95	2b73/3		-0.7
1953	Was A	134	464	62	117	24	4	4	46	46	3	65	.252	.343	.347	89	-6	7-4	.982	7	107	112	2b133		1.1
1954	Was A	106	337	42	70	10	1	3	24	32	3	40	.208	.282	.270	55	-22	3-3	.972	10	117	115	2b90,3b10,S3		-0.6
1955	NY N	80	257	36	66	16	1	1	18	36-1	1	42	.257	.348	.339	84	-4	2-4	.985	17	112	128	2b78/S3		1.7
1956	NY N	14	18	0	4	1	0	0	1	0-0	0	5	.222	.222	.278	34	-2	0-0	.958	1	88	151	2b6		-0.1
1959	KC A	74	180	27	48	11	0	2	18	19-0	0	31	.267	.335	.361	90	-2	2-2	.972	12	115	109	2b63,S2/3		1.4
1960	KC A	2	1	0	0	0	0	0	0	0-0	0	0	.000	.000	.000	-99	-1	0-0	1.000	0	78	282	2b2		0.0
Total	9	666	2091	271	501	93	10	22	162	247-1	11	296	.240	.323	.325	76	-68	31-14	.974	45	110	102	2b605,3b14,S6/OC1		1.4

ESCH, AL   Albert John "Tiny" B1.27.1891 Jersey City NJ D8.3.1947 Jersey City NJ BB/TR/5-10/155 d8.21

YEAR	TM LG	G	AB	R	H	2B	3B	HR	RBI	BB-IB	HP	SO	AVG	OBP	SLG	AOPS	ABR	SB-CS	FA	FR	RNG	THR	GAMES AT POSITION	DL	BFW
1915	Bro F	8	7	2	2	1	0	0	2	0	0	0	.286	.286	.429	88	0		.867	1	176	151	2b3		0.1

ESTA, NICK   Nicholas B6.29.1928 New York NY BR/TR/5-8/180 d4.23 C1 Col Florida

YEAR	TM LG	G	AB	R	H	2B	3B	HR	RBI	BB-IB	HP	SO	AVG	OBP	SLG	AOPS	ABR	SB-CS	FA	FR	RNG	THR	GAMES AT POSITION	DL	BFW
1958	SF N	1	0	0	0	0	0	0	0-0	0	0	—	—	—	--	0	0-0		.000	-0	0	0	/C		0.0

ETTELBACH, DICK   Richard Morley "Tut" B6.26.1929 New Haven CT D1.26.1995 E.Harwich MA BR/TR/6-0/195* d9.25 Col Yale

YEAR	TM LG	G	AB	R	H	2B	3B	HR	RBI	BB-IB	HP	SO	AVG	OBP	SLG	AOPS	ABR	SB-CS	FA	FR	RNG	THR	GAMES AT POSITION	DL	BFW
1955	NY A	2	5	0	0	0	0	0	0-0	0	0		.000	.000	.000	-99	-1	0-0	1.000	0	1288	0	O2L		-0.1
1956	Was A	18	64	10	10	1	2	1	9	14-0	0	15	.156	.304	.281	56	-4	0-1	1.000	1	98	137	O18L		-0.5
1957	Was A	9	11	2	2	0	0	0	1	4-0	0	2	.182	.375	.182	65	0	0-0	.900	-2	124	0	O3(2/2/0)		0.0
Total	3	29	80	12	12	1	2	1	10	18-0	0	17	.150	.300	.250	49	-5	0-1	.980	1	98	164	O23(22/2/0)		-0.6

ETTLETON, MICKEY   Mickey Lee B9.16.1960 Oklahoma City OK BB/TR/6-2/212(195-214) [OakA81 5/118] d6.30 Col Oklahoma St.

YEAR	TM LG	G	AB	R	H	2B	3B	HR	RBI	BB-IB	HP	SO	AVG	OBP	SLG	AOPS	ABR	SB-CS	FA	FR	RNG	THR	GAMES AT POSITION	DL	BFW
1984	Oak A	33	76	10	20	1	1	1	5	11-0	0	21	.263	.352	.355	104	1	0-0	.992	1	155	97	C32		0.2
1985	Oak A	78	211	23	53	12	0	3	15	28-0	2	59	.251	.344	.351	98	1	2-2	.989	-9	72	107	C76/D		-0.5
1986	Oak A	90	211	26	43	9	0	10	35	39-0	1	51	.204	.325	.389	102	2	7-1	.984	-8	80	111	C89	21	-0.2
1987	Oak A	82	211	19	41	3	0	8	26	30-0	1	65	.194	.292	.322	68	-10	1-1	.987	-6	94	72	C80/1D	38	-1.3
1988	Bal A	86	283	31	74	11	1	11	37	28-2	2	70	.261	.330	.424	113	5	0-1	.992	-7	80	101	C80	15	0.1
1989	Bal A★	117	411	72	106	21	2	26	65	73-4	1	117	.258	.369	.509	149	29	3-2	.994	-6	91	95	C75,D43		2.6
1990	Bal A	135	444	68	99	21	2	15	51	106-3	5	160	.223	.376	.381	116	15	2-4	.991	-6	103	71	C90,D40,1b5/OR	28	1.2
1991	Det A	154	501	85	132	17	2	31	89	101-9	2	131	.263	.387	.491	139	30	3-3	.990	-2	114	100	C125,D24,O3(2/0/1)/1		3.3
1992	Det A	157	525	82	125	25	0	32	83	122-18	1	137	.238	.379	.469	135	30	0-6	.996	-9	111	96	C113,D40,1b3,O2(1/0/1)		2.4
1993	Det A★	152	522	79	128	25	4	32	110	109-12	0	139	.245	.372	.492	131	25	3-7	.992	-9	84	113	1b59,C56,O55(18/0/39),D4		1.1
1994	Det A	107	339	57	84	18	2	17	51	97-10	5	96	.248	.419	.463	126	19	0-1	.992	-14	66	72	C53,1b24,D22,O18(1/0/17)		0.5
1995	Tex A	134	429	76	102	19	1	32	78	107-5	7	110	.238	.396	.510	130	22	0-0	.972	-3	92	81	O63(2/0/61),D58,1b9,C3		1.2
1996	†Tex A	143		78	121	26	1	24	83	95-8	3	137	.246	.366	.450	100	2	2-1	.977	-2	77	76	D115,1b23	68	-0.7
1997	Tex A	17	44	5	4	1	0	3	6	13-1	1	12	.091	.167	.318	21	-6	0-0	—	0	0	0	D13		-0.6
Total	14	1485	4698	711	1132	210	16	245	732	949-72	30	1307	.241	.369	.449	121	165	23-29	.991	-80	95	90	C872,D361,O142(24/0/120),1b125	170	9.3

EUFEL, TIM   Timothy Shawn B7.7.1958 Greenwich CT BR/TR/6-0/175* [MinA80 2/38] d9.3 Col Clemson

YEAR	TM LG	G	AB	R	H	2B	3B	HR	RBI	BB-IB	HP	SO	AVG	OBP	SLG	AOPS	ABR	SB-CS	FA	FR	RNG	THR	GAMES AT POSITION	DL	BFW
1983	Min A	21	78	11	24	7	1	3	6	2-0	0	8	.308	.325	.538	127	3	0-0	.990	2	105	102	2b18/SD		0.6
1984	Min A	157	568	76	149	30	3	14	61	76-8	2	73	.262	.349	.400	102	4	1-3	.984	-6	103	82	2b157		0.6
1985	Min A	138	434	58	113	24	3	10	50	48-2	3	70	.260	.335	.399	95	-2	4-2	.980	-24	91	78	2b137/D		-1.9
1986	†NY N	93	279	35	69	20	1	4	31	32-1	1	42	.247	.324	.369	93	-2	1-2	.971	-22	80	69	2b84,1b3/3	15	-2.2
1987	NY N	97	299	55	92	29	0	14	61	44-2	2	53	.308	.398	.545	154	25	3-2	.972	-7	96	93	2b92/1		-2.2
1988	†NY N	90	273	45	64	20	4	0	31	29-1	1	41	.234	.306	.352	93	-2	0-1	.981	16	107	133	2b84,1b3	25	2.2
1989	NY N	83	219	27	56	7	2	2	15	32-1	1	50	.256	.350	.333	101	1	1-3	.960	-0	95	80	2b40,1b33		1.7
1990	NY N	80	175	28	43	11	0	10	24	15-1	0	33	.246	.304	.480	112	2	0-0	.991	-6	93	125	1b24,2b4,3b10	18	-0.1
1991	NY N	20	34	2	4	0	0	1	2	2-0	1	8	.118	.167	.206	4	-5	1-1	1.000	0	59	32	1b6,3b5/2		-0.5
	SD N	97	307	39	70	16	0	11	42	49-4	1	69	.228	.334	.388	100	1	8-2	.987	-15	81	84	2b65,3b48		-1.2
	Year	117	341	41	74	16	0	12	44	51-4	1	77	.217	.319	.370	91	-3	9-3	.987	-15	82	83	2b66,3b53,1b6		-1.7
1992	SD N	101	246	23	55	10	0	6	25	31-3	1	45	.224	.312	.337	83	-5	2-1	.987	-3	98	77	2b52,3b26,1b5		-0.7
1993	SD N	96	200	26	50	11	2	7	31	27-0	0	39	.250	.338	.430	103	1	0-0	.990	-4	94	86	2b52,3b9,1b8		-0.1
Total	11	1073	3112	415	789	185	12	86	379	387-23	12	531	.254	.336	.404	103	21	23-19	.990	-69	94	86	2b806,3b99,1b83,D2/S	58	-2.1

EXTOR, GEORGE   George Bernhardt B12.27.1888 Newport KY D3.10.1954 Massillon OH BB/TR/5-10.5/174 d4.19

YEAR	TM LG	G	AB	R	H	2B	3B	HR	RBI	BB-IB	HP	SO	AVG	OBP	SLG	AOPS	ABR	SB-CS	FA	FR	RNG	THR	GAMES AT POSITION	DL	BFW
1914	Ind F	22	57	2	9	2	0	0	9	2-0	0	9	.175	.230	.175	10	-8	0-0	.955	1	87	141	C21		-0.6
1915	New F	3	6	1	2	0	0	0	0	0-0	0	0	.333	.333	.333	93	0	0-0	1.000	-1	73	85	C3		-0.1
Total	2	25	63	3	12	0	0	0	4	2-0	0	9	.190	.239	.190	17	-8	0-0	.957	1	86	137	C24		-0.7

HACKER, MOE   Morris Benton B5.21.1934 Louisville KY D11.13.1997 Louisville KY BR/TR/6-3/210(195-210) d8.3

YEAR	TM LG	G	AB	R	H	2B	3B	HR	RBI	BB-IB	HP	SO	AVG	OBP	SLG	AOPS	ABR	SB-CS	FA	FR	RNG	THR	GAMES AT POSITION	DL	BFW
1958	Chi N	11	24	4	6	1	0	2	3	1-1	0	7	.250	.269	.542	113	0	0-0	.952	0	105	233	C9		0.1
1960	Chi N	54	90	5	14	1	0	0	6	14-5	1	20	.156	.269	.167	23	-9	1-1	.980	0	127	151	C50		-0.8
1961	Chi N	25	35	3	6	0	0	0	2	11-1	1	11	.171	.383	.171	53	-2	0-0	.973	-2	176	62	C25		-0.3
1962	Chi N	65	107	8	20	1	0	0	9	14-1	1	40	.187	.287	.234	40	-9	0-1	.996	7	69	231	C65		-0.3
1963	StL N	3	4	0	0	0	0	0	0	0-0	0	0	.000	.000	.000	-91	-1	0-0	1.000	0	65	208	C3		-0.1
Total	5	158	260	20	46	7	0	2	20	40-8	2	81	.177	.290	.227	41	-21	1-2	.984	6	107	178	C152		-1.1

HAKE, AL   Albert B9.21.1849 Wymondham, England D9.1.1872 Brooklyn NY 6-0/? d6.13

YEAR	TM LG	G	AB	R	H	2B	3B	HR	RBI	BB-IB	HP	SO	AVG	OBP	SLG	AOPS	ABR	SB-CS	FA	FR	RNG	THR	GAMES AT POSITION	DL	BFW
1872	Atl NA	18	78	14	23	2	2	0	15	0-?		2	.295	.295	.372	88	-2	2-0	.808	-1	50	0	O18L/2		-0.2

HAMES, MARCUS   Marcus Markley B3.6.1977 Louisville MS BR/TR/6-2/205* [NYA96 30/899] d6.10 Col East Central (MO) JC

YEAR	TM LG	G	AB	R	H	2B	3B	HR	RBI	BB-IB	HP	SO	AVG	OBP	SLG	AOPS	ABR	SB-CS	FA	FR	RNG	THR	GAMES AT POSITION	DL	BFW
1992	NY A	7	13	2	3	1	0	1	2	0-0	0	4	.231	.231	.538	97	0	0-0	1.000	-0	104	0	O7(3/0/4)		0.0
1993	Tex A	30	73	12	15	2	0	1	4	8-0	1	18	.205	.298	.274	50	-5	0-1	1.000	-1	91	85	O24(4/0/20),D4		-0.7
1994	Det A	61	165	24	42	12	0	10	33	16-0	2	42	.255	.326	.509	118	4	0-1	1.000	3	114	123	O52(40/0/12),D5		0.5
1995	Det A	38	107	11	21	2	0	7	16	9-1	1	38	.196	.263	.411	78	-4	0-0	.978	-3	83	95	O31(21/0/10),D4		-0.8
Total	4	136	358	49	81	17	0	19	55	33-1	5	102	.226	.298	.433	90	-5	0-2	.995	-1	100	74	O114(68/0/46),D13		-1.0

YEAR	TM LG	G	AB	R	H	2B	3B	HR	RBI	BB-IB	HP	SO	AVG	OBP	SLG	AOPS	ABR	SB-CS	FA	FR	RNG	THR	GAMES AT POSITION	DL	BFW

THEOBALD, RON Ronald Merrill B7.28.1943 Oakland CA BR/TR/5-8/165* d4.12 Col Arizona

																									1.0
1971	Mil A	126	388	50	107	12	1	0	23	38-0	1	39	.276	.342	.325	91	-3	11-8	.973	7	105	117	2b111/S3		-1.1
1972	Mil A	125	391	45	86	11	0	1	19	68-2	5	38	.220	.342	.256	81	-5	0-7	.988	-9	104	99	2b113		-0.1
Total	2	251	779	95	193	23	2	2	42	106-2	8	77	.248	.342	.290	87	-8	11-15	.980	-2	104	108	2b224/3S		

THEODORE, GEORGE George Basil B11.13.1946 Salt Lake City UT BR/TR/6-4/190* d4.14 Col Utah

1973	†NY N	45	116	14	30	4	0	1	15	10-0	1	13	.259	.320	.319	79	-3	1-0	.984	3	118	169	O33(28/4/1),1b4	59	-0.2
1974	NY N	60	76	7	12	1	0	1	1	8-0	1	14	.158	.247	.211	29	-7	0-0	.990	-2	35	87	1b14,O12(8/0/4)		-1.1
Total	2	105	192	21	42	5	0	2	16	18-0	2	27	.219	.291	.276	59	-10	1-0	.958	1	107	188	O45(36/4/5),1b18	59	-1.3

THERIOT, RYAN Ryan Stewart B12.7.1979 Baton Rouge LA BR/TR/5-11/175 d9.13 Col Louisiana St.

2005	Chi N	9	13	3	2	1	0	0	1	1-0	0	2	.154	.214	.231	16	-2	0-0	1.000	1	143	0	2b3		-0.1

THEVENOW, TOMMY Thomas Joseph B9.6.1903 Madison IN D7.29.1957 Madison IN BR/TR/5-10/155 d9.4

1924	StL N	23	89	4	18	4	1	0	7	1	0	6	.202	.211	.270	28	-9	1-3	.951	4	110	87	S23		-0.3
1925	StL N	50	175	17	47	7	2	0	17	7	1	20	.269	.301	.331	60	-11	3-0	.950	1	104	60	S50		-0.4
1926	†StL N	156	563	64	144	15	5	2	63	27	1	26	.256	.291	.311	60	-33	8	.956	16	111	106	S156		-0.8
1927	StL N	59	191	23	37	6	1	0	4	14	0	12	.194	.249	.236	29	-19	2	.945	5	111	124	S59		-1.5
1928	†StL N	69	171	11	35	8	3	0	13	20	0	12	.205	.288	.287	50	-13	0	.931	-8	96	99	S64,3b3/1		-2.2
1929	Phi N	90	317	30	72	11	0	0	35	25	2	26	.227	.288	.262	35	-32	3	.953	-1	101	87	S90		-2.2
1930	Phi N	156	573	57	164	21	6	0	78	23	2	26	.286	.316	.326	52	-44	1	.941	-6	104	84	S156		-3.0
1931	Pit N	120	404	35	86	12	1	0	38	28	1	22	.213	.266	.248	39	-35	0	.964	5	109	114	S120		-1.4
1932	Pit N	59	194	12	46	3	0	0	26	7	0	12	.237	.264	.284	48	-15	0	.918	-1	91	111	S29,3b22		-1.1
1933	Pit N	73	253	20	79	5	1	0	34	3	0	5	.312	.320	.340	89	-5	0	.975	-8	94	94	2b61,S3/3		-1.8
1934	Pit N	122	446	37	121	16	2	0	54	20	2	26	.271	.306	.316	65	-22	0	.969	-14	89	82	2b75,3b44/S		-3.0
1935	Pit N	110	408	38	97	9	0	0	47	12	1	23	.238	.261	.304	50	-30	1	.951	4	107	93	3b82,S13,2b8		-2.2
1936	Cin N	106	321	25	75	7	2	0	36	15	0	23	.234	.268	.268	48	-25	2	.945	-3	96	87	S12,3b6,2b2		-2.0
1937	Bos N	21	34	5	4	0	1	0	2	4	0	2	.118	.211	.176	7	-5	0	1.000	2	129	44	2b9,S4/3		-0.0
1938	Pit N	15	25	2	5	0	0	0	2	4	1	0	.200	.333	.200	49	-2	0	1.000	4	105	98	2b9,S4/3		-0.0
Total	15	1229	4164	380	1030	124	32	2	456	210	11	222	.247	.285	.294	52	-300	23-3	.951	-4	105	98	S848,2b188,3b171/1		-20.0

THOMAS, ANDRES Andres Perez (b Andres Perez (Thomas)) B11.10.1963 Boca Chica, D.R. BR/TR/6-1/185(170-185) d9.3

1985	Atl N	15	18	6	5	0	0	0	2	0-0	0	2	.278	.278	.278	53	-1	0-0	.920	1	128	69	S10		0.0
1986	Atl N	102	323	26	81	17	2	6	32	8-2	1	49	.251	.267	.372	71	-14	4-6	.958	25	121	124	S97	79	-0.1
1987	Atl N	82	324	29	75	11	0	5	39	14-0	2	50	.231	.268	.312	51	-23	6-5	.953	11	115	111	S81		-1.0
1988	Atl N	153	606	54	153	22	2	13	68	14-6	1	95	.252	.268	.360	76	-21	7-3	.959	-8	101	98	S150		-1.0
1989	Atl N	141	554	41	118	18	0	13	57	12-3	0	83	.213	.228	.316	53	-36	3-3	.956	9	102	119	S138	17	-1.1
1990	Atl N	84	278	26	61	8	0	5	30	11-2	0	43	.219	.248	.302	48	-20	2-1	.967	-1	97	101	S72,3b5	96	-4.0
Total	6	577	2103	182	493	76	4	42	228	59-13	3	301	.234	.255	.334	62	-115	22-18	.958	36	106	110	S548,3b5		

THOMAS, CHARLES Charles Wesley B12.26.1978 Fairfield CA BL/TL/6-0/190* [AtlN00 19/580] d6.23 Col Western Carolina

2004	†Atl N	83	236	35	68	8	4	7	31	21-9	9	45	.288	.368	.445	108	3	3-1	.993	7	114	189	O71(70/1/2)		-0.0
2005	Oak A	30	46	4	5	0	0	1	1	5-0	4	8	.109	.185	.109	2	-6	0-1	.951	1	117	120	O27(13/9/8)		-0.0
Total	2	113	282	39	73	8	4	7	32	26-9	13	53	.259	.349	.390	91	-3	3-2	.984	8	115	176	O98(83/10/10)		

THOMAS, PINCH Chester David B1.24.1888 Camp Point IL D12.24.1953 Modesto CA BL/TR/5-9.5/173 d4.24

1912	Bos A	13	30	0	6	0	0	0	5	2	0		.200	.250	.200	28	-3	1	.966	1	129	118	C8		0.0
1913	Bos A	38	91	6	26	1	2	1	15	2	1	11	.286	.309	.374	97	-1	1	.983	0	92	108	C31		0.0
1914	Bos A	66	130	9	25	1	0	1	5	18	0	17	.192	.291	.200	48	-8	1	.966	2	127	72	C64/1		0.0
1915	†Bos A	86	203	21	48	4	4	0	21	13	1	20	.236	.286	.296	76	-7	3-2	.969	7	122	89	C82		0.0
1916	†Bos A	99	216	23	57	10	1	1	21	33	1	21	.264	.364	.333	109	4	4	.981	2	135	75	C90		1.0
1917	Bos A	83	202	24	48	7	1	0	24	27	0	9	.238	.333	.272	86	-2	2	**.986**	4	127	80	C77		0.0
1918	Cle A	32	73	2	18	0	1	0	5	6	0	6	.247	.304	.274	68	-3	0	.948	1	130	83	C24		-0.0
1919	Cle A	34	46	2	5	0	0	0	2	4	0	3	.109	.180	.109	-17	-7	0	.980	-1	131	79	C21		-0.0
1920	†Cle A	9	9	0	3	1	0	0	3	1	0	1	.333	.500	.444	147	1	0-0	1.000	1	183	60	C7		-0.0
1921	Cle A	21	35	1	9	3	0	0	4	10	0	2	.257	.422	.343	96	1	0-0	.882	-4	72	24	C19		0.0
Total	10	481	1035	88	245	27	8	2	102	118	5	82	.237	.318	.284	78	-25	12-2	.973	11	124	81	C423/1		0.0

THOMAS, DAN Danny Lee B5.9.1951 Birmingham AL D6.12.1980 Mobile AL BR/TR/6-2/190* [MilA72 1/6] d9.2 Col Southern Illinois

1976	Mil A	32	105	13	29	5	1	4	15	14-1	2	28	.276	.372	.457	144	6	1-2	.955	-1	92	132	O32L		0.0
1977	Mil A	22	70	11	19	3	2	2	11	8-2	1	11	.271	.350	.457	119	2	0-2	1.000	1	126	0	O9L,D9		0.0
Total	2	54	175	24	48	8	3	6	26	22-3	3	39	.274	.363	.457	134	8	1-4	.966	-0	100	103	O41L,D9		

THOMAS, DERREL Derrel Osbon B1.14.1951 Los Angeles CA BB/TR/6-0/160* [HouN69*1/1] d9.14 OF(93/394/65)

1971	Hou N	5	5	0	0	0	0	0	0	0-0	0	2	.000	.000	.000	-99	-1	0-1	1.000	-0	64	148	/2		-0.0
1972	SD N	130	500	48	115	15	5	5	36	41-1	2	73	.230	.290	.310	76	-17	9-9	.967	-6	99	91	2b83,S49,O3(0/2/1)		-1.0
1973	SD N	113	404	41	96	7	1	0	22	34-3	2	52	.238	.299	.260	61	-21	15-5	.914	4	106	91	S74,2b47		-0.0
1974	SD N	141	523	48	129	24	6	3	41	51-7	1	58	.247	.313	.333	85	-11	7-8	.976	2	103	52	2b104,3b22,O20(1/19/0),S5		-0.0
1975	SF N	144	540	99	149	21	9	6	48	57-0	3	56	.276	.347	.381	-1	28-13		.974	0	92	108	2b141/OR		65	-0.0
1976	SF N	81	272	38	63	5	4	2	19	29-0	4	26	.232	.313	.301	73	-9	10-11	.964	6	108	118	2b69,O2(0/1/1)/S3		-0.0
1977	SF N	148	506	75	135	13	10	8	44	46-1	2	70	.267	.328	.379	90	-9	15-13	.991	19	119	246	O77(12/67/0),2b40,3b26,1b14		-0.0
1978	SD N	128	352	36	80	10	2	0	26	35-3	2	37	.227	.301	.293	72	-13	11-6	.991	2	106	139	O119C,3b18,2b5,S3/1		-0.0
1979	LA N	141	406	47	104	15	4	5	44	41-7	5	49	.256	.330	.350	88	-6	18-5	.996	2	106	139	O52(4/40/8),S49,2b18,C5,3b4		-0.0
1980	LA N	117	297	32	79	18	3	4	22	26-3	1	48	.266	.326	.357	93	-2	7-9	.987	-1	119	114	2b30,S26,O18(3/10/6),3b10	68	-0.0
1981	†LA N	80	218	25	54	4	0	4	24	25-2	0	23	.248	.322	.321	88	-3	7-2	.986	-6	102	102	2b30,S26,O18(3/10/6),3b10		-0.0
1982	LA N	66	98	13	26	2	1	0	10	10-1	0	12	.265	.333	.306	82	-2	2-3	1.000	-0	108	142	O82(15/42/29),S13,2b9,3b7	32	-0.0
1983	†LA N	118	192	38	48	6	2	8	27-2		2	36	.250	.345	.375	100	-3	9-3	.990	-0	91	98	S62,O48(41/0/7),2b15,3b4/1		-0.0
1984	Mon N	108	243	26	62	12	2	0	20	20-1	0	33	.255	.308	.321	81	-6	0-4	.963	-11	83	111	O7(2/2/4),S4,3b3		-0.0
	Cal N	14	29	3	4	0	1	0	2	3-0	0	4	.138	.219	.207	19	-3	0-0	.889	-3	75	24	S21,O7(5/2/0)/C23		-0.0
1985	Phi N	63	92	16	19	4	0	2	12	11-1	0	14	.207	.291	.359	79	-3	0-0	.906	-2	92	98	2b608,O542C,S339,3b116,1b19,C6	184	-0.0
Total	15	1597	4677	585	1163	154	54	43	456-32		25	593	.249	.317	.332	83	-107	140-92	.970	5	99	98			

THOMAS, FRANK Frank Edward "The Big Hurt" B5.27.1968 Columbus GA BR/TR/6-5/257(240-275) [ChiA89 1/7] d8.2 Col Auburn-Montgomery

1990	Chi A	60	191	39	63	11	3	7	31	44-0	2	54	.330	.454	.529	179	24	0-1	.989	-4	77	133	1b51,D8		-0.0
1991	Chi A	158	559	104	178	31	2	32	109	**138**-13	1	112	.318	**.453**	.553	**181**	71	1-2	.996	-4	70	100	D101,1b56		-0.0
1992	Chi A	160	573	108	185	**46**	2	24	115	**122**-6	5	88	.323	**.439**	.536	175	66	6-3	.992	-11	80	82	1b158,D2		-0.0
1993	†Chi A★	153	549	106	174	36	0	41	128	112-23	2	54	.317	.426	.607	179	67	4-2	.989	-11	77	104	1b150,D4		-0.0
1994	Chi A★	113	399	**106**	141	34	1	38	101	**109**-12	2	61	.353	**.487**	**.729**	**212**	75	2-3	.991	-8	68	99	1b99,D13		-0.0
1995	Chi A★	**145**	493	102	152	27	0	40	111	**136**-29	6	74	.308	.454	.606	183	70	3-2	.991	-11	56	82	1b90,D54	22	-0.0
1996	Chi A★	141	527	110	184	26	0	40	134	109-**26**	5	70	.349	.459	.626	180	72	1-1	.992	-9	89	90	1b139	15	-0.0
1997	Chi A★	146	530	110	184	35	0	35	125	109-9	3	69	**.347**	**.456**	.611	**183**	72	1-1	.986	-6	79	87	1b97,D49		-0.0
1998	Chi A	160	585	109	155	35	2	29	109	110-2	6	93	.265	.381	.480	126	26	7-0	.984	-1	72	107	D146,1b14		-0.0
1999	Chi A	135	486	74	148	36	0	15	77	87-13	6	66	.305	.414	.471	125	24	3-3	.990	-4	65	90	D82,1b49		-0.0
2000	Chi A	159	582	115	191	44	0	43	143	112-18	5	94	.328	.436	.625	160	58	1-3	.996	-5	83	145	D127,1b30	161	-0.0
2001	Chi A	20	68	8	15	3	0	4	10	10-2	0	12	.221	.316	.441	92	-1	0-0	.955	-0	66	106	D16,1b3		-0.0
2002	Chi A	148	523	77	132	29	1	28	92	88-2	7	115	.252	.361	.472	124	17	3-0	.955	-0	176	175	D140,1b4		-0.0
2003	Chi A	153	546	87	146	35	0	42	105	100-4	12	115	.267	.390	.562	142	37	0-0	1.000	-3	56	101	D124,1b27	89	-0.0
2004	Chi A	74	240	53	65	16	0	18	49	64-3	6	57	.271	.434	.563	152	23	0-2	—	0	0	0	D28	131	-0.0
2005	Chi A	34	105	19	22	3	0	12	26	16-0	0	31	.219	.315	.590	129	4	0-0	—	0	0	0	D28	418	-4
Total	16	1959	6956	1327	2136	447	11	448	1465	1466-162	71	1165	.307	.427	.568	161	703	32-23	.991	-67	76	96	1b971,D959		

THOMAS, FRANK Frank Joseph B6.11.1929 Pittsburgh PA BR/TR/6-3/205* d8.17 OF(709/308/48)

1951	Pit N	39	148	21	39	9	2	2	16	9	0	15	.264	.306	.392	84	-4	0-2	1.000	0	92	163	O37C		
1952	Pit N	6	21	1	2	0	0	0	1	1	0	6	.095	.136	.095	-34	-4	0-0	1.000	0	77	254	O5C		
1953	Pit N	128	455	68	116	23	1	30	102	50	2	93	.255	.331	.505	115	9	1-2	.976	6	102	**166**	O118(6/96/16)		
1954	Pit N★	153	577	81	172	32	7	23	94	51	**10**	74	.298	.359	.497	124	20	3-2	.989	7	106	122	O153(48/109/0)		

YEAR	TM LG	G	AB	R	H	2B	3B	HR	RBI	BB-IB	HP	SO	AVG	OBP	SLG	AOPS	ABR	SB-CS	FA	FR	RNG	THR	GAMES AT POSITION	DL	BFW
1955	Pit N★	142	510	72	125	16	2	25	72	60-10	2	76	.245	.324	.431	101	0	0-0	.984	-2	99	77	O139(86/59/0)		-0.9
1956	Pit N	**157**	588	69	166	24	3	25	80	36-5	5	61	.282	.326	.461	112	8	0-5	.942	-4	91	117	3b111,O56L,2b4		0.0
1957	Pit N	151	594	72	172	30	1	23	89	44-9	3	66	.290	.335	.460	116	13	3-1	.977	-4	99	93	1b71,O59(46/2/19),3b31		1.0
1958	Pit N★	149	562	89	158	26	4	35	109	42-2	1	79	.281	.334	.528	129	21	0-1	.926	-26	86	78	3b139,O8(5/0/3),1b2		-0.6
1959	Cin N	108	374	41	84	18	2	12	47	27-6	3	56	.225	.278	.380	72	-16	0-2	.927	-5	95	82	3b64,O33L,1b14		-2.4
1960	Chi N	135	479	54	114	12	1	21	64	28-4	0	74	.238	.280	.399	84	-13	1-0	.983	-5	100	93	1b50,O49(44/0/6),3b33		-2.4
1961	Chi N	15	50	7	13	2	0	2	6	2-0	0	8	.260	.288	.420	84	-1	0-0	1.000	-1	57	288	O10L,1b6		-0.3
	Mil N	124	423	58	120	13	3	25	67	29-7	6	70	.284	.335	.500	128	15	2-4	.954	-5	97	44	O109L,1b11		0.3
	Year	139	473	65	133	15	3	27	73	31-7	6	78	.281	.331	.497	123	13	2-4	.956	-5	94	62	O119L,1b17		0.0
1962	NY N	156	571	69	152	23	3	34	94	48-4	8	95	.266	.329	.496	117	12	2-1	.962	2	97	159	O126L,1b11,3b10		0.6
1963	NY N	126	420	34	109	9	1	15	60	33-5	3	48	.260	.317	.393	102	0	0-0	.988	3	101	138	O96L,1b15/3		-0.3
1964	NY N	60	197	19	50	6	1	3	19	10-1	2	29	.254	.295	.340	81	-5	1-1	1.000	4	106	99	O31L,1b19,3b2		-0.5
	Phi N	39	143	20	42	11	0	7	26	5-2	0	12	.294	.311	.517	132	6	0-1	.976	1	117	134	1b36		0.4
	Year	99	340	39	92	17	1	10	45	15-3	2	41	.271	.302	.415	103	0	1-2	.982	4	120	118	1b55,O31L,3b2		-0.1
1965	Phi N	35	77	7	20	4	0	1	7	4-0	0	10	.260	.289	.351	83	-2	0-0	1.000	-0	103	300	O12(9/0/4),1b11/3		-0.3
	Hou N	23	58	7	10	2	0	3	9	3-0	0	15	.172	.210	.362	63	-3	0-0	.984	-2	68	114	1b16,3b2/OL		-0.6
	Mil N	15	33	3	7	3	0	0	1	2-0	0	11	.212	.250	.303	57	-2	0-0	.979	-1	81	66	1b6,O3L		-0.3
	Year	73	168	17	37	9	0	4	17	9-0	0	36	.220	.254	.345	71	-7	0-0	.985	-3	70	111	1b33,O16(13/0/4),3b3		-1.2
1966	Chi N	5	5	0	0	0	0	0	0	0-0	0	1	.000	.000	.000	-99	-1	0-0	—	0			/H		-0.1
Total	16	1766	6285	792	1671	262	31	286	962	484-55	51	894	.266	.320	.454	108	53	15-22	.978	-22	100	129	O1045L,3b394,1b268,2b4		-4.6

THOMAS, FRED Frederick Harvey "Tommy" B12.19.1892 Milwaukee WI D1.15.1986 Rice Lake WI BR/TR/5-10/160 d4.22 Mil 1918

YEAR	TM LG	G	AB	R	H	2B	3B	HR	RBI	BB-IB	HP	SO	AVG	OBP	SLG	AOPS	ABR	SB-CS	FA	FR	RNG	THR	GAMES AT POSITION	DL	BFW
1918	†Bos A	44	144	19	37	2	1	1	11	15	1	20	.257	.331	.306	94	-1	4	.968	2	105	52	3b41/S		0.3
1919	Phi A	124	453	42	96	11	10	2	23	43	2	52	.212	.283	.294	61	-25	12	.945	-3	94	63	3b124		-2.6
1920	Phi A	76	255	27	59	6	3	1	11	26	2	18	.231	.307	.290	58	-15	8-4	.960	2	101	86	3b61,S12		-1.0
	Was A	3	7	0	1	0	0	0	0	0	0	1	.143	.143	.143	-25	-1	0-1	1.000	1	189	61	3b2		-1.0
	Year	79	262	27	60	6	3	1	11	26	2	18	.229	.303	.286	56	-17	8-5	.962	4	104	83	3b63,S12		-1.0
Total	3	247	859	88	193	19	14	4	45	84	5	90	.225	.297	.293	65	-42	24-5	.954	3	99	66	3b228,S13		-3.3

THOMAS, GEORGE George Edward B11.29.1937 Minneapolis MN BR/TR/6-3.5/190* d9.11 C1 Col Minnesota OF(136/170/186)

YEAR	TM LG	G	AB	R	H	2B	3B	HR	RBI	BB-IB	HP	SO	AVG	OBP	SLG	AOPS	ABR	SB-CS	FA	FR	RNG	THR	GAMES AT POSITION	DL	BFW
1957	Det A	1	1	0	0	0	0	0	0	0-0	0	1	.000	.000	.000	-97	0	0-0	.000	-1	0	0	/3		-0.1
1958	Det A	1	0	0	0	0	0	0	0	0-0	0					-97	0	0-0	—	-0	0	0	/OR		0.0
1961	Det A	17	6	2	0	0	0	0	0	0-0	0	4	.000	.000	.000	-97	-2	0-0	—	-0	0	0	O2R/S		-0.2
	LA A	79	282	39	79	12	1	13	59	21-1	3	66	.280	.334	.468	101	0	3-6	.986	-9	90	45	O45(24/17/4),3b38		-1.2
	Year	96	288	41	79	12	1	13	59	21-1	3	70	.274	.328	.458	99	-1	3-6	.986	-9	89	0	O47(24/17/6),3b38/S		-1.4
1962	LA A	56	181	13	43	10	2	4	21	21-0	1	37	.238	.320	.381	91	-2	0-0	.957	2	109	141	O51(3/8/45)		-0.4
1963	LA A	53	167	14	35	7	1	4	15	9-1	1	32	.210	.254	.335	68	-5	0-0	.941	-1	101	45	O39(3/1/35),3b10,1b4		-1.2
	Det A	49	109	13	26	4	1	1	11	11-0	1	22	.239	.306	.321	76	-3	2-1	1.000	1	122	0	O40(2/30/9)/2		-0.4
	Year	102	276	27	61	11	2	5	26	20-1	2	54	.221	.276	.330	71	-11	2-1	.974	-0	111	23	O79(5/31/44),3b10,1b4/2		-1.6
1964	Det A	105	308	39	88	15	2	12	44	18-0	3	56	.286	.329	.464	117	6	4-1	.988	0	101	80	O90(17/57/19)/3		0.3
1965	Det A	79	169	19	36	5	1	3	10	12-1	1	39	.213	.269	.308	64	-8	2-3	.948	0	103	173	O59(5/26/28)/2		-1.2
1966	Bos A	69	173	25	44	9	0	5	20	23-1	2	33	.237	.332	.347	87	-2	1-0	1.000	3	99	163	O48(10/25/15),3b6,C2,1b2		-0.2
1967	†Bos A	65	89	10	19	2	0	1	6	3-0	2	23	.213	.255	.270	51	-5	0-1	.973	-1	93	0	O43(20/3/20),1b3/C		-0.9
1968	Bos A	12	10	3	2	0	0	1	1	1-0	0	5	.200	.273	.500	123	0	1-0	1.000	-0	144	0	O9(5/2/2)	23	0.1
1969	Bos A	29	51	9	18	3	1	0	8	3-0	1	11	.353	.400	.451	131	2	0-0	1.000	0	154	0	O12(1/8/3),1b10/C3	69	0.1
1970	Bos A	38	99	13	34	8	0	2	13	11-0	2	12	.343	.420	.485	139	6	0-0	.972	-4	109	0	O26(25/0/1),3b6		0.1
1971	Bos A	9	13	0	1	0	0	0	1	1-0	0	4	.077	.143	.077	-34	-2	0-0	1.000	-1	37	0	O5(3/0/2)		-0.4
	Min A	23	30	4	8	1	0	0	2	4-0	0	9	.267	.353	.300	84	0	0-0	1.000	-2	51	0	O11L/13		-0.3
	Year	32	43	4	9	1	0	0	3	5-0	0	13	.209	.292	.233	48	-3	0-0	1.000	-2	45	0	O16(14/0/2)/13		-0.7
Total	13	685	1688	203	430	71	9	46	202	138-4	18	343	.255	.316	.389	92	-18	13-12	.976	-12	102	79	O481R,3b64,1b20,C4,2b2/S	92	-5.9

THOMAS, HERB Herbert Mark B5.26.1902 Sampson City FL D12.4.1991 Starke FL BR/TR/5-4.5/157 d8.28

YEAR	TM LG	G	AB	R	H	2B	3B	HR	RBI	BB-IB	HP	SO	AVG	OBP	SLG	AOPS	ABR	SB-CS	FA	FR	RNG	THR	GAMES AT POSITION	DL	BFW
1924	Bos N	32	127	12	28	4	1	0	6	3	1	9	.220	.288	.291	58	-8	5-2	.983	6	119	165	O32C		-0.3
1925	Bos N	5	17	2	4	0	1	0	0	2	1	0	.235	.350	.353	88	0	0-1	.963	-1	97	35	2b5		-0.2
1927	Bos N	24	74	11	17	6	1	0	6	3	1	9	.230	.269	.338	67	-4	2	.972	-7	80	75	2b17,S2		-1.0
	NY N	13	17	2	3	1	1	0	1	1	1	9	.176	.263	.353	64	-1	0	.900	-0	125	0	O3(1/0/2)/S		-0.1
	Year	37	91	13	20	7	2	0	7	4	2	18	.220	.268	.341	65	-5	2	.972	-7	80	75	2b17,S3,O3(1/0/2)		-1.1
Total	3	74	235	27	52	11	4	1	15	15	6	18	.221	.285	.315	63	-13	7-3	.976	-2	120	150	O35(1/32/2),2b22,S3		-1.6

THOMAS, IRA Ira Felix B1.22.1881 Ballston Spa NY D10.11.1958 Philadelphia PA BR/TR/6-2/200 d5.18 C6

YEAR	TM LG	G	AB	R	H	2B	3B	HR	RBI	BB-IB	HP	SO	AVG	OBP	SLG	AOPS	ABR	SB-CS	FA	FR	RNG	THR	GAMES AT POSITION	DL	BFW
1906	NY A	44	115	12	23	1	2	0	15	8	1		.200	.258	.243	52	-3		.938	-3	103	97	C42		-0.7
1907	NY A	80	208	20	40	5	4	1	24	10	3		.192	.240	.269	52	-5	5	.953	5	95	127	C61,1b2		0.0
1908	†Det A	40	101	6	31	1	0	0	8	5	1		.307	.346	.317	111	1	0	.972	-3	90	51	C29		0.1
1909	Phi A	84	269	22	57	9	3	0	31	18	7		.223	.292	.281	79	-6	4	**.985**	14	**127**	91	C84		1.9
1910	†Phi A	60	180	14	50	8	2	1	19	6	0		.278	.301	.361	108	1	2	.967	7	114	96	C60		1.4
1911	†Phi A	103	297	33	81	14	3	0	39	23	8		.273	.341	.340	92	-3	4	.974	6	116	**110**	C103		1.1
1912	Phi A	48	139	14	30	4	2	1	13	8	2		.216	.268	.295	63	-7	3	.971	2	131	89	C48		-0.1
1913	Phi A	22	53	3	15	4	1	0	6	4	0	8	.283	.333	.396	116	1	0	.983	2	120	97	C21		0.4
1914	Phi A	2	3	0	0	0	0	0	0	0	0		.000	.000	.000	-99	-1	0	1.000	0	101	118	/C		-0.1
1915	Phi A	1	0	0	0	0	0	0	0	—			—	—	—	-99	-0	0	1.000	0	0	498	/C		0.0
Total	10	484	1352	124	327	46	17	3	155	82	22	8	.242	.296	.308	82	-30	20	.970	29	114	99	C450,1b2		4.0

THOMAS, GORMAN James Gorman B12.12.1950 Charleston SC BR/TR/6-2/210(190-215) [MilA69 1/21] d4.6

YEAR	TM LG	G	AB	R	H	2B	3B	HR	RBI	BB-IB	HP	SO	AVG	OBP	SLG	AOPS	ABR	SB-CS	FA	FR	RNG	THR	GAMES AT POSITION	DL	BFW
1973	Mil A	59	155	16	29	7	1	2	11	14-1	0	61	.187	.254	.284	52	-10	5-5	.957	-3	99	32	O50(4/1/46)/3D		-1.6
1974	Mil A	17	46	10	12	4	0	2	11	8-0	0	15	.261	.357	.478	143	3	4-0	1.000	-1	101	0	O13(4/1/8),D2		0.3
1975	Mil A	121	240	34	43	12	2	10	28	31-0	1	84	.179	.268	.371	80	-7	4-2	.961	-1	102	86	O113(23/92/1),D6		-1.0
1976	Mil A	99	227	27	45	9	2	8	36	31-1	1	67	.198	.294	.361	94	-2	2-3	.986	5	114	76	O94(1/66/29)/3D		0.0
1978	Mil A	137	452	70	111	24	4	32	86	73-4	2	133	.246	.351	.515	140	25	3-4	.983	-13	90	55	O137C		1.1
1979	Mil A	156	557	97	136	29	4	**45**	123	98-6	2	175	.244	.356	.539	138	31	1-5	.991	-7	98	37	O152C,D4		2.0
1980	Mil A	**162**	628	78	150	26	3	38	105	58-4	2	170	.239	.304	.471	112	7	8-5	.985	-9	97	51	O160C,D2		-0.3
1981	†Mil A★	103	363	50	94	22	0	21	65	50-8	2	85	.259	.348	.493	147	23	4-5	.979	-1	95	122	O97(0/49/49),D6		1.8
1982	†Mil A	158	567	96	139	29	1	**39**	112	84-5	4	143	.245	.343	.506	138	30	3-7	.991	-2	97	101	O157C		2.4
1983	Mil A	46	164	21	30	6	1	5	18	23-0	1	50	.183	.284	.323	73	-6	2-1	.992	-4	94	0	O46C		-1.1
	Cle A	106	371	51	82	17	0	17	51	57-2	1	98	.221	.322	.404	96	-1	8-3	.982	4	108	107	O106C		0.3
	Year	152	535	72	112	23	1	22	69	80-2	2	148	.209	.310	.379	89	-7	10-4	.985	0	104	74	O152C		-0.8
1984	Sea A	35	108	6	17	3	0	1	13	28-0	1	27	.157	.322	.213	56	-5	0-3	1.000	-3	73	99	O34L/D	138	0.4
1985	Sea A	135	484	76	104	16	1	32	87	84-6	1	126	.215	.330	.450	111	8	3-2	—	0	0	0	D133	20	-0.4
1986	Sea A	57	170	24	33	4	0	10	26	27-3	1	55	.194	.308	.394	88	-3	1-2	—	0	0	0	D52		-0.5
	Mil A	44	145	21	26	4	1	6	10	31-1	0	50	.179	.324	.345	79	-4	2-2	.980	-1	71	63	D36,1b6		-0.5
	Year	101	315	45	59	8	1	16	36	58-4	1	105	.187	.316	.371	84	-7	3-4	.980	-1	71	63	D88,1b6		-1.1
Total	13	1435	4677	681	1051	212	13	268	782	697-41	18	1339	.225	.324	.448	113	89	50-49	.984	-35	98	70	O1159(66/967/133),D246,1b6,3b2	158	2.1

THOMAS, LEE James Leroy B2.5.1936 Peoria IL BL/TR/6-2/198(187-198) d4.22 C2

YEAR	TM LG	G	AB	R	H	2B	3B	HR	RBI	BB-IB	HP	SO	AVG	OBP	SLG	AOPS	ABR	SB-CS	FA	FR	RNG	THR	GAMES AT POSITION	DL	BFW
1961	NY A	2	2	0	1	0	0	0	0	0-0	0	1	.500	.500	.500	177	0	0-0	—	0			/H		0.0
	LA A	130	450	77	128	11	5	24	70	47-2	2	74	.284	.353	.491	111	6	0-5	.966	-1	104	152	O86(26/0/65),1b34		-0.4
	Year	132	452	77	129	11	5	24	70	47-2	2	74	.285	.353	.491	111	6	0-5	.966	-1	104	152	O86(26/0/65),1b34		-0.4
1962	LA A★	160	583	88	169	21	2	26	104	55-3	6	74	.290	.355	.467	124	19	6-1	.982	-10	71	92	1b90,O74(17/18/42)		0.0
1963	LA A	149	528	52	116	12	6	9	55	53-6	9	82	.220	.301	.316	78	-16	6-0	.996	2	113	107	1b104,O43(2/0/41)		-2.3
1964	LA A	47	172	14	47	8	1	2	24	18-1	0	22	.273	.340	.366	108	-1	2-1	.949	-1	89	144	O47(1/0/46)/1		-0.3
	Bos A	107	401	44	103	19	2	13	42	34-4	4	29	.257	.319	.411	97	-1	2-1	.995	1	102	100	O107R/1		-0.8
	Year	154	573	58	150	27	3	15	66	52-5	4	51	.262	.325	.398	100	0	3-1	.981	-1	98	113	O154(1/0/153),1b2		-1.1
1965	Bos A	151	521	74	141	27	4	22	75	72-8	4	42	.271	.361	.464	126	19	6-2	.984	4	**115**	83	1b127,O20(14/0/6)		1.5
1966	Atl N	39	126	11	25	1	1	6	10	10-1	1	15	.198	.265	.341	71	-5	1-1	.987	-2	122	81	1b36		-0.6
	Chi N	75	149	15	36	4	0	1	9	14-1	3	15	.242	.319	.289	70	-6	0-0	.992	-1	107	121	1b20,O17(16/1/0)		-0.8
	Year	114	275	26	61	5	1	7	24	24-2	4	30	.222	.293	.324	71	-11	1-1	.989	1	118	92	1b56,O17(16/1/0)		-1.4

YEAR	TM LG	G	AB	R	H	2B	3B	HR	RBI	BB-IB	HP	SO	AVG	OBP	SLG	AOPS	ABR	SB-CS	FA	FR	RNG	THR	GAMES AT POSITION	DL	BFW
1967	Chi N	77	191	16	42	4	1	2	23	15-5	3	22	.220	.284	.283	61	-10	1-0	.969	-3	83	70	O43(0/1/43),1b10		-1.7
1968	Hou N	90	201	14	39	4	0	1	11	14-4	1	22	.194	.249	.229	45	-13	2-1	.973	0	88	147	O48(7/0/42),1b2		-1.9
Total	8	1027	3324	405	847	111	22	106	428	332-35	32	397	.255	.327	.397	99	-5	25-11	.975	-8	95	113	O485(83/20/392),1b425		-7.3

THOMAS, BUD John Tillman B3.10.1929 Sedalia MO BR/TR/6-0/180 d9.2

1951	StL A	14	20	3	7	0	0	1	0	0	0	3	.350	.350	.500	124	0	2-0	1.000	1	108	82	S14		0.2

THOMAS, KITE Keith Marshall B4.27.1923 Kansas City KS D1.7.1995 Rocky Mount NC BR/TR/6-1.5/195* d4.19 Col Kansas St.

1952	Phi A	75	116	24	29	6	1	6	18	20	1	27	.250	.365	.474	124	4	0-1	.957	-1	101	60	O29(12/0/17)		0.2
1953	Phi A	24	49	1	6	0	0	0	2	3	0	6	.122	.173	.122	-18	-4	0-0	1.000	0	121		O15(6/0/9)		-0.9
	Was A	38	58	10	17	3	2	1	12	11	1	7	.293	.414	.466	141	4	0-0	1.000	-1	84	0	O8(3/0/5)/C		0.2
	Year	62	107	11	23	3	2	1	14	14	1	13	.215	.311	.308	68	-5	0-0	1.000	-1	108	0	O23(9/0/14)/C		-0.7
Total	2	137	223	35	52	9	3	7	32	34	2	40	.233	.340	.395	98	0	0-1	.978	-2	104	32	O52(21/0/31)/C		-0.5

THOMAS, LEO Leo Raymond "Tommy" B7.26.1923 Turlock CA D3.5.2001 Concord CA BR/TR/5-11.5/178* d4.29

1950	StL A	35	121	19	24	6	1	0	9	20	0	14	.198	.312	.273	49	-9	0-1	.964	-2	102	83	3b35		-1.1
1952	StL A	41	124	12	29	5	1	0	12	17	2	7	.234	.336	.290	73	-4	2-0	.934	2	106	106	3b37,S3/2		-0.2
	Chi A	19	24	1	4	0	0	0	6	6	0	4	.167	.333	.167	42	-2	0-0	.952	1	116	75	3b9		-0.1
	Year	60	148	13	33	5	1	0	18	23	2	11	.223	.335	.270	68	-5	2-0	.936	2	107	101	3b46,S3/2		-0.2
Total	2	95	269	32	57	11	1	0	27	43	2	25	.212	.325	.271	59	-15	2-1	.948	0	105	93	3b81,S3/2		-1.4

THOMAS, RAY Raymond Joseph B7.9.1910 Dover NH D12.6.1993 Wilson NC BR/TR/5-10.5/175 d7.22 Col Western Michigan

1938	Bro N	3	3	1	1	0	0	0	0	0	0	0	.333	.333	.333	82	0	0-0	1.000	0	0	0	/C		0.0

THOMAS, RED Robert William B4.25.1898 Hargrove AL D3.22.1962 Fremont OH BR/TR/5-11/165 d9.13

1921	Chi N	8	30	5	8	3	0	1	5	4	1	5	.267	.371	.467	120	1	0-0	.962	-0	103	76	O8C		0.0

THOMAS, ROY Roy Allen B3.24.1874 Norristown PA D11.20.1959 Norristown PA BL/TL/5-11/150 d4.14 C1 b-Bill Col Penn

1899	Phi N	150	547	137	178	12	4	0	47	115	17		.325	.457	.362	130	37	42	.952	1	107	150	O135C,1b14		2.8
1900	Phi N	140	531	**132**	168	13	4	0	33	**115**	15		.316	.451	.335	119	27	37	.958	-6	98	110	O139C/P		1.8
1901	Phi N	129	479	102	148	5	2	1	28	**100**			.309	.437	.334	123	23	27	.967	-3	56	55	O129C		2.3
1902	Phi N	**138**	500	89	143	4	7	0	24	**107**	2		.286	**.414**	.322	127	25	17	.974	5	126	60	O138C		2.0
1903	Phi N	130	477	88	156	11	2	1	27	**107**	3		.327	.453	.365	139	35	17	.963	12	106	65	O130C		3.8
1904	Phi N	139	496	92	144	6	6	3	29	**102**	5		.290	.416	.345	141	33	28	.974	13	123	70	O139C		4.1
1905	Phi N	147	562	118	178	11	6	0	31	93			.317	.417	.358	137	33	23	.983	15	137	128	O147C		4.4
1906	Phi N	142	493	81	125	10	7	0	16	**107**	6		.254	.393	.302	117	18	22	**.986**	8	69	167	O142C		2.1
1907	Phi N	121	419	70	102	15	3	1	23	**83**			.243	.374	.301	113	13	11	.980	2	89	100	O121C		1.1
1908	Phi N	6	24	2	4	0	0	0	2		0		.167	.231	.167	26	-2	0	1.000	-1	0	0	O6C		-0.1
	Pit N	102	386	52	99	11	10	1	24	49	5		.256	.348	.345	121	11	11	.975	-1	54	136	O101C		-0.1
	Year	108	410	54	103	11	10	1	24	51	5		.251	.341	.341	116	9	11	.976	-1	51	129	O107C		-0.0
1909	Bos N	82	281	36	74	9	1	0	11	47	1	5	.263	.369	.302	104	4	5	.976	1	88	39	O76(75/2/0)		-0.0
1910	Phi N	23	71	7	13	0	0	0	4	8		6	.183	.266	.239	46	-5	4	1.000	1	96	249	O11R		-0.3
1911	Phi N	21	30	5	5	2	0	0	2	8	71	11	.167	.342	.233	61	-1	0	.972	49	97	101			0.2
Total	13	1470	5296	1011	1537	100	53	7	299	1042	71	11	.290	.413	.333	124	251	244	.972	49	97	101	O1434(75/1349/11),1b14/P		22.?

THOMAS, VALMY Valmy B10.21.1928 Santurce, PR BR/TR/5-9/165* d4.16

1957	NY N	88	241	30	60	10	3	6	31	16-1	1	29	.249	.296	.390	83	-6	0-0	.991	2	129	80	C88		
1958	SF N	63	143	14	37	5	0	3	16	13-0	1	24	.259	.321	.357	82	-4	1-0	.992	1	116	110	C61		
1959	Phi N	66	140	5	28	2	0	1	9	9-2	1	19	.200	.253	.236	31	-14	1-0	.980	8	89	150	C65/3		
1960	Bal A	8	16	0	1	0	0	0	0	1-0	0	0	.063	.118	.063	-51	-3	0-1	1.000	0	178	167	C8		
1961	Cle A	27	86	7	18	3	0	2	4	6-0	0	7	.209	.261	.314	54	-6	0-0	.988	7	177	157	C27		
Total	5	252	626	56	144	20	3	12	60	45-3	3	79	.230	.283	.329	64	-33	2-1	.988	18	123	115	C249/3		

THOMAS, BILL William Miskey B12.8.1877 Norristown PA D1.14.1950 Evansburg PA BR/TR/5-10/190 d5.1 b-Roy Col Ursinus

1902	Phi N	6	17	1	2	0	0	0	1	0	0		.118	.167	.118	-12	-2	0	.500	-1	0	1195	O3(2/0/1)/12		-0.?

THOMAS, WALT William Walter "Tommy" B4.28.1884 Foot Of Ten PA D6.6.1950 Altoona PA BR/TR/5-8/156 d9.18

1908	Bos N	5	13	2	2	0	0	0	1	3	0		.154	.313	.154	51	-1	2	.864	-1	96	83	S5		-0.?

THOMASON, ART Arthur Wilson B2.12.1889 Liberty MO D5.2.1944 Kansas City MO BL/TL/5-8/150 d8.10

1910	Cle A	20	70	4	12	2	0	0	5	0	2	5	.171	.227	.200	33	-6	3	.944	2	98	174	O20(0/1/19)		-0.?

THOMASSON, GARY Gary Leah B7.29.1951 San Diego CA BL/TL/6-1/180(170-195) [SFN69 7/160] d9.5

1972	SF N	10	27	5	9	1	0	1	0	0	0	7	.333	.357	.444	124	1	0-0	1.000	-1	28	146	1b7,O2L		-0
1973	SF N	112	235	35	67	10	4	4	30	22-2	0	43	.285	.345	.413	105	1	2-0	.992	-3	76	64	1b47,O43(23/11/9)		-0
1974	SF N	120	315	41	77	14	3	6	29	38-2	0	56	.244	.325	.327	80	-8	7-1	.981	2	102	89	O76(20/32/26),1b15		-0
1975	SF N	114	326	44	74	12	5	4	32	37-1	1	48	.227	.304	.347	79	-10	9-3	.978	8	115	194	O74(27/34/18),1b17		-0
1976	SF N	103	328	45	85	20	5	8	36	30-7	1	45	.259	.321	.424	107	3	8-3	.959	-4	106	27	O113(62/49/20),1b31		-0
1977	SF N	145	446	63	114	24	6	17	71	75-8	1	102	.256	.358	.451	117	12	16-4	.959	-1	108		O44R,1b5		-0
1978	Oak A	47	154	17	31	4	1	5	20	15-2	0	44	.201	.272	.338	74	-6	4-1	.969	1	101	126	O50(24/16/12)/D		-0
†NY A		55	116	20	32	4	1	3	16	13-0	0	22	.276	.346	.405	113	2	4-3	.971	7	112	147	O94(24/16/56),1b5/D		-0
	Year	102	270	37	63	8	2	8	36	28-2	0	66	.233	.304	.367	91	-4	8-4	.980	-3	99		O100(10/61/43)/1		-0
1979	LA N	115	315	39	78	11	1	14	45	43-4	1	70	.248	.339	.422	109	4	2-0	.974	-1	90	71	O31(9/9/15)/1		-0
1980	LA N	80	111	6	24	3	0	1	12	17-3	1	26	.216	.326	.270	70	-4	0-0	.974	-1	90			34	-2
Total	9	901	2373	315	591	103	25	61	294	291-29	5	463	.249	.330	.391	98	-5	50-16	.970	3	106	90	O587(182/247/206),1b163/D	34	

THOME, JIM James Howard B8.27.1970 Peoria IL BL/TR/6-4/225(200-245) [CleA89 13/333] d9.4 Col Illinois Central JC

1991	Cle A	27	98	7	25	4	2	1	9	5-1	1	16	.255	.298	.367	82	-1	0-0	.900	-1	108	109	3b27		-0
1992	Cle A	40	117	8	24	3	1	2	12	10-2	2	34	.205	.275	.299	63	-6	2-0	.882	-7	86	48	3b40		68
1993	Cle A	47	154	28	41	11	0	7	22	29-0	4	36	.266	.385	.474	132	9	2-1	.950	1	105	122	3b47		
1994	Cle A	98	321	58	86	20	1	20	52	46-5	2	84	.268	.359	.523	123	11	3-3	.940	7	115	83	3b94		
1995	†Cle A	137	452	92	142	29	3	25	73	97-3	5	113	.314	.438	.558	154	42	4-3	.948	-9	94	106	3b134/D		
1996	†Cle A	151	505	122	157	28	5	38	116	123-8	6	141	.311	.450	.612	166	57	2-2	.953	2	106	98	3b150/D		
1997	†Cle A★	147	496	104	142	25	0	40	102	120-9	3	146	.286	.423	.579	154	44	1-1	.993	-0	98	101	1b145		
1998	†Cle A	123	440	89	129	34	2	30	85	89-8	4	141	.293	.413	.584	151	37	1-0	.991	-0	98	117	1b117,D6		39
1999	†Cle A★	146	494	101	137	27	2	33	108	127-13	4	171	.277	.426	.540	138	34	0-0	.994	7	123	96	1b111,D34		
2000	Cle A	158	557	106	150	33	1	37	106	118-4	4	171	.269	.398	.531	129	28	1-0	.995	10	130	105	1b107,D48		
2001	†Cle A	156	526	101	153	26	1	49	124	111-14	4	185	.291	.416	.624	163	52	0-1	.992	-5	81	83	1b148,D6		
2002	Cle A	147	480	101	146	19	2	52	118	122-18	5	139	.304	.445	**.677**	190	68	1-2	.991	-1	94	104	1b128,D18		
2003	Phi N	159	578	111	154	30	3	**47**	131	111-11	4	182	.266	.385	.573	158	51	0-3	.997	-6	83	103	1b156,D2		
2004	Phi N★	143	508	97	139	28	1	42	105	104-26	2	144	.274	.396	.581	144	36	0-2	.994	-2	97	91	1b52,D5	114	-?
2005	Phi N	59	193	26	40	7	0	7	30	45-4	2	59	.207	.360	.352	86	-2	0-0	1.000	-4	99	98	1b52,D5	221	3?
Total	15	1738	5919	1151	1665	324	24	430	1193	1257-127	50	1762	.281	.408	.562	147	458	18-19	.994	-4	99	98	1b1098,3b492,D127		

THOMPSON, ANDREW Andrew d4.26

1875	Was NA	11	41	3	4	0	1	0	3	0		1	.098	.098	.146	-17	-5	0-0	.624	-8			C11/OR		

THOMPSON, ANDY Andrew John B10.8.1975 Oconomowoc WI BR/TR/6-3/215 [TorA94 23/651] d5.2 [DL 2001 Tor A 45]

2000	Tor A	2	6	2	1	0	0	0	3-0			2	.167	.444	.167	62	-0	0-0	1.000	-1	47	0	O2L		

THOMPSON, BOBBY Bobby La Rue B11.3.1953 Charlotte NC BB/TR/5-11/175 [TexA72 19/436] d4.16

1978	Tex A	64	120	23	27	3	4	2	12	9-1	2	26	.225	.284	.350	79	-4	7-2	.982	1	109	40	O52(8/37/10),D3		37

THOMPSON, TIM Charles Lemoine B3.1.1924 Coalport PA BL/TR/5-11/190* d4.28 C1

1954	Bro N	10	13	2	2	1	0	0	1	0	0	2	.154	.214	.231	15	-2	0-0	.909	-1	0	0	C2/OL		
1956	KC A	92	268	21	73	13	2	1	27	17-1	2	23	.272	.319	.347	76	-10	2-4	.981	1	88	120	C68		
1957	KC A	81	230	25	47	10	0	7	19	18-6	0	26	.204	.262	.339	62	-13	0-0	.993	-1	87	70	C62		
1958	Det A	4	6	1	1	0	0	0	0	3-0		1	.167	.444	.167	70	-0	0-0	1.000	-1	54	229	C4		
Total	4	187	517	49	123	24	2	8	47	39-7	2	52	.238	.293	.338	68	-25	2-4	.986	-1	86	97	C136/OL		

YEAR	TM LG	G	AB	R	H	2B	3B	HR	RBI	BB-IB	HP	SO	AVG	OBP	SLG	AOPS	ABR	SB-CS	FA	FR	RNG	THR	GAMES AT POSITION	DL	BFW

THOMPSON, DANNY Danny Leon B2.1.1947 Wichita KS D12.10.1976 Rochester MN BR/TR/6-0/183* [MinA68 S1/18] d6.25 Col Oklahoma St.

1970	†Min A	96	302	25	66	9	0	0	22	7-0	0	39	.219	.234	.248	33	-28	0-0	.986	-0	105	83	2b81,3b37,S6		-2.4
1971	Min A	48	57	10	15	2	0	0	7	7-0	0	12	.263	.338	.298	81	-1	0-0	.897	-2	95	113	3b17,2b3/S		-0.3
1972	Min A	144	573	54	158	22	6	4	48	34-1	2	57	.276	.314	.356	96	-4	3-4	.957	-5	102	90	S144		0.9
1973	Min A	99	347	29	78	13	2	1	36	16-3	2	41	.225	.259	.282	51	-23	1-0	.950	8	111	85	S95/3D		-0.4
1974	Min A	97	264	25	66	6	1	4	25	22-0	2	29	.250	.311	.326	81	-6	1-1	.963	-9	83	91	S88,3b5/D		-0.6
1975	Min A	112	355	25	96	11	2	5	37	18-2	1	30	.270	.302	.355	85	-8	0-3	.941	-7	95	76	S100,3b7/2D	24	-0.7
1976	Min A	34	124	9	29	4	0	0	6	3-0	1	8	.234	.256	.266	53	-8	1-1	.988	-0	97	106	S34		-0.6
	Tex A	64	196	12	42	3	0	1	13	13-0	1	19	.214	.264	.245	49	-13	2-2	.976	-8	84	56	3b39,2b14,S10/D		-2.1
	Year	98	320	21	71	7	0	1	19	16-0	2	27	.222	.261	.253	51	-20	3-3	.981	-9	95	102	S44,3b39,2b14/D		-2.5
Total	7	694	2218	189	550	70	11	15	194	120-6	8	235	.248	.287	.310	70	-91	8-11	.956	-24	99	87	S478,3b106,2b99,D6	24	-6.0

THOMPSON, DON Donald Newlin B12.28.1923 Swepsonville NC BL/TL/6-0/185* d4.24

1949	Bos N	7	11	0	2	0	0	0	0	0	0	2	.182	.182	.182	-2	-2	0	.800	-0	116	0	O2R		-0.2
1951	Bro N	80	118	25	27	3	0	0	6	12	1	12	.229	.305	.254	51	-8	2-8	.987	2	110	110	O61(56/6/0)		-1.0
1953	†Bro N	96	153	25	37	5	0	1	12	14	1	13	.242	.310	.294	57	-9	2-3	.989	2	105	155	O81(51/8/25)		-0.9
1954	Bro N	34	25	2	1	0	0	0	1	5	1	5	.040	.226	.040	-25	-5	0-0	1.000	1	99	230	O29(27/2/0)		-0.5
Total	4	217	307	52	67	8	0	1	19	31	3	32	.218	.296	.254	46	-24	4-11	.984	5	107	140	O173(134/16/27)		-2.6

THOMPSON, FRANK Frank d9.11

| 1875 | Atl NA | 1 | 5 | 1 | 2 | 0 | 0 | 0 | | | 0 | | .400 | .400 | .400 | 205 | 1 | 0-0 | .000 | -1 | 0 | | /OR | | 0.0 |

THOMPSON, FRANK Frank E B7.2.1895 Springfield MO D6.27.1940 Jasper Co. MO BR/TR/5-8/155 d5.6

| 1920 | StL A | 22 | 53 | 7 | 9 | 0 | 0 | 0 | 3 | 1 | 0 | 3 | .170 | .343 | .170 | 38 | -4 | 1-1 | .878 | -4 | 88 | 44 | 3b14,2b2 | | -0.7 |

THOMPSON, HANK Henry Curtis B12.8.1925 Oklahoma City OK D9.30.1969 Fresno CA BL/TR/5-9/174* d7.17 Negro Lg 1943-48 Mil 1944-45

1947	StL A	27	78	10	20	1	0	0	5	10	1	7	.256	.341	.295	76	-2	2-1	.957	0	97	104	2b19		-0.1
1949	NY N	75	275	51	77	10	4	9	34	42	1	30	.280	.377	.444	120	8	5	.961	-6	91	97	2b69/3		0.6
1950	NY N	148	512	82	148	17	6	20	91	83	3	60	.289	.391	.463	123	19	8	.944	10	108	165	3b138,O10(0/2/9)		2.7
1951	†NY N	87	264	37	62	8	4	8	33	43	4	23	.235	.342	.386	95	-2	1-2	.925	-9	88	111	3b71		-1.2
1952	NY N	128	423	67	110	13	9	17	67	50	4	38	.260	.344	.444	119	10	4-4	.979	1	102	74	O72(20/51/1),3b46,2b4		0.7
1953	NY N	114	388	80	117	15	8	24	74	60	4	39	.302	.400	.567	146	27	6-5	.956	3	108	83	3b101,O9(1/0/8)/2		2.8
1954	†NY N	136	448	76	118	18	1	26	86	90	5	58	.263	.389	.482	146	20	3-0	.945	-2	98	114	3b130,2b2/OL		1.8
1955	NY N	135	432	65	106	13	1	17	63	84-4	4	56	.245	.367	.398	105	6	2-2	.943	1	106	99	3b124,2b7/S		0.7
1956	NY N	83	183	24	43	9	0	8	29	31-2	1	26	.235	.346	.415	105	2	2-1	.908	1	117	104	3b44,O10(8/0/3)/S		0.3
Total	9	933	3003	492	801	104	34	129	482	493-6	22	337	.267	.372	.453	118	88	33-15	.941	-2	104	116	3b655,O102(30/53/21),2b102,S2		8.3

THOMPSON, HOMER Homer Thomas B6.1.1891 Spring City TN D9.12.1957 Atlanta GA BR/TR/5-9/160 d10.5 b-Tommy Col Georgia

| 1912 | NY A | 1 | 0 | 0 | 0 | 0 | 0 | 0 | | | | | — | — | — | | 0 | 0 | .500 | -0 | 0 | 0 | /C | | 0.0 |

THOMPSON, SHAG James Alfred B4.29.1893 Haw River NC D1.7.1990 Black Mountain NC BL/TR/5-8.5/165 d6.8 Col North Carolina-Asheville

1914	Phi A	16	29	3	5	1	0	0	2	7	1	8	.172	.351	.241	82	0	1	.941	2	90	335	O8(2/6/0)		0.1
1915	Phi A	17	33	5	11	2	0	0	2	4	0	6	.333	.405	.394	144	2	0-1	1.000	1	87	257	O7C		0.2
1916	Phi A	15	17	4	0	0	0	0	0	7	0	6	.000	.292	.000	-12	-2	1	1.000	0	136	0	O8(1/6/1)		-0.2
Total	3	48	79	12	16	2	1	0	4	18	1	20	.203	.357	.253	87	0	2-1	.978	3	103	206	O23(3/19/1)		0.1

THOMPSON, JASON Jason Dolph B7.6.1954 Hollywood CA BL/TL/6-3/210(200-220) [DetA75 4/75] d4.23 Col Cal St.-Northridge

1976	Det A	123	412	45	90	12	1	17	54	68-6	1	72	.218	.328	.376	102	3	2-4	.994	4	112	103	1b117		-0.4
1977	Det A☆	158	585	87	158	24	5	31	105	73-2	1	91	.270	.347	.487	120	16	0-1	.991	-6	88	101	1b158		-0.1
1978	Det A★	153	589	79	169	25	3	26	96	74-3	0	96	.287	.364	.472	130	24	0-0	.993	-9	82	123	1b151		0.6
1979	Det A	145	492	58	121	16	1	20	79	70-8	1	90	.246	.338	.404	97	-1	2-0	.994	-1	94	115	1b140,D2		-1.0
1980	Det A	36	126	10	27	5	0	4	20	13-1	1	26	.214	.289	.349	73	-5	0-1	1.000	3	128	103	1b36		-0.4
	Cal A	102	312	59	99	14	0	17	70	70-9	0	60	.317	.439	.526	167	33	2-0	1.000	-3	71	1b47,D45		2.6
	Year	138	438	69	126	19	0	21	90	83-10	1	86	.288	.398	.475	140	28	2-1	1.000	0	96	88	1b83,D45		2.2
1981	Pit N	86	223	36	54	13	0	15	42	59-1	0	49	.242	.396	.502	147	17	0-0	.989	-2	93	115	1b78		1.1
1982	Pit N★	156	550	87	156	32	2	31	101	101-7	2	107	.284	.391	.511	145	38	1-0	.993	-9	88	1b155		2.9
1983	Pit N	152	517	70	134	20	1	18	76	99-7	1	128	.259	.376	.406	114	14	1-0	.993	-5	84	113	1b151		0.1
1984	Pit N	154	543	61	138	22	0	17	74	87-14	2	73	.254	.357	.389	110	10	0-0	.990	-8	79	99	1b152		-0.8
1985	Pit N	123	402	42	97	17	1	12	61	84-10	1	58	.241	.369	.378	111	10	0-0	.992	1	101	114	1b114		0.4
1986	Mon N	30	51	6	10	4	0	0	4	18-2	0	16	.196	.406	.275	92	1	0-1	.962	-3	45	81	1b15		-0.3
Total	11	1418	4802	640	1253	204	12	208	782	816-70	9	862	.261	.366	.438	121	160	8-27	.992	-28	91	103	1b1314,D47		4.7

THOMPSON, JASON Jason Michael B6.13.1971 Orlando FL BL/TL/6-4/205 [SDN93 9/254] d6.9 Col Arizona

| 1996 | SD N | 13 | 49 | 4 | 11 | 4 | 0 | 2 | 6 | 1-0 | 0 | 14 | .224 | .235 | .429 | 75 | -2 | 0-0 | .964 | 1 | 136 | 63 | 1b13 | | -0.2 |

THOMPSON, TUG John Parkinson B9.8.1856 London ON, Can. D8.1.1938 Guelph ON, Can. BR/TR/5-8/160 d8.31

1882	Cin AA	1	5	0	1	0	0	0		0			.200	.200	.200	33	0		.000	-1	0	0	/OC		-0.1
1884	Ind AA	24	97	10	20	3	0	0		2	0		.206	.222	.237	51	-5		.429	-9	95	0	O12(0/7/5),C12		-1.2
Total	2	25	102	10	21	3	0	0		2	0		.206	.221	.235	50	-5		.409	-9	88	0	O13(0/8/5),C12		-1.3

THOMPSON, FRESCO Lafayette Fresco "Tommy" B6.6.1902 Centreville AL D11.20.1968 Fullerton CA BR/TR/5-8/150 d9.5 Col Columbia

1925	Pit N	14	37	4	9	2	1	0	8	4	0	1	.243	.317	.351	66	-2	2-1	.977	-1	88	135	2b12		-0.2
1926	NY N	2	8	1	5	0	0	0	1	2	0	0	.625	.700	.625	262	2	1	1.000	-0	113	0	2b2		0.2
1927	Phi N	153	597	78	181	32	14	1	70	34	2	36	.303	.343	.409	99	-2	19	.963	1	94	98	2b153		0.3
1928	Phi N	152	634	99	182	34	11	3	50	42	1	27	.287	.332	.390	85	-15	19	.966	8	101	91	2b152		-0.3
1929	Phi N	148	623	115	202	41	4	4	53	75	1	34	.324	.398	.419	96	0	16	.965	11	103	98	2b148		1.4
1930	Phi N	122	478	77	135	34	4	4	46	35	0	29	.282	.331	.395	70	-23	7	.955	-3	100	101	2b112		-2.1
1931	Bro N	74	181	26	48	6	1	1	21	23	1	16	.265	.351	.326	84	-3	5	.946	-2	94	138	2b43,S10,3b5		-0.2
1932	Bro N	3	0	0	0	0	0	0	0	0	0	0	.000	.000	.000	-99	0		—	0			/H		0.0
1934	NY N	1	0	0	0	0	0	0	0	0	0	0	.000	.000	.000	-99	0		—	0			/H		0.0
Total	9	669	2560	400	762	149	34	13	249	215	5	143	.298	.353	.398	88	-43	69-1	.962	13	99	100	2b622,S10,3b5		-0.9

THOMPSON, MILT Milton Bernard B1.5.1959 Washington DC BL/TR/5-11/170(160-203) [AtlN79*2/29] d9.4 C2 Col Howard

1984	Atl N	25	99	16	30	1	0	2	4	11-1	0	11	.303	.373	.374	103	1	14-2	.956	1	75	302	O25L		0.3
1985	Atl N	73	182	17	55	7	2	0	6	7-0	3	36	.302	.339	.363	91	-2	9-4	.964	1	112	78	O49(23/5/27)		-0.3
1986	Phi N	96	299	38	75	7	1	6	23	26-1	1	62	.251	.311	.341	77	-10	19-4	.991	2	117	22	O89C		-0.6
1987	Phi N	150	527	86	159	26	9	7	43	42-2	1	87	.302	.351	.425	101	1	46-10	.989	4	114	54	O146(1/145/1)		1.0
1988	Phi N	122	378	53	109	16	2	2	33	39-6	1	59	.288	.354	.357	103	3	17-9	.983	5	114	116	O112(0/112/5)		1.0
1989	StL N	155	545	60	158	28	8	4	68	39-5	4	91	.290	.340	.393	106	4	27-8	.978	-4	99	66	O147(23/123/3)		0.1
1990	StL N	135	418	42	91	14	7	6	30	39-5	5	60	.218	.292	.328	70	-18	25-5	.971	-4	100	116	O116(12/14/96)		-2.2
1991	StL N	115	326	55	100	16	5	6	34	32-7	5	53	.307	.368	.442	125	11	16-9	.991	9	116	160	O91(72/12/12)		1.9
1992	StL N	109	208	31	61	9	1	4	17	16-3	2	39	.293	.350	.404	114	4	18-6	.974	-3	89	47	O45(35/1/11)		0.2
1993	†Phi N	129	340	42	89	14	2	4	44	40-9	2	57	.262	.341	.350	87	-5	9-4	.994	-1	97	93	O106(102/4/0)		-0.9
1994	Phi N	87	220	29	60	7	0	3	30	23-4	2	28	.273	.348	.345	81	-6	7-2	1.000	1	100	27	O79(72/12/0)		-0.8
	Hou N	9	21	5	6	0	0	0	3	1-0	0	2	.286	.318	.429	97	0	2-0	1.000	0	82	306	O6R		0.0
	Year	96	241	34	66	7	0	3	33	24-4	2	30	.274	.346	.353	82	-6	9-2	1.000	1	99	46	O85(72/12/6)		-0.8
1995	Hou N	92	132	14	29	9	0	2	19	14-1	1	37	.220	.297	.333	71	-5	4-2	.979	2	109	137	O34(15/1/21)		-0.5
1996	LA N	48	51	2	6	1	0	0	6-0		0	10	.118	.211	.137	-6	-8	1-1	1.000	1	87	0	O17L		-0.9
	Col N	14	15	1	1	0	0	0	3	1-0	0	3	.067	.125	.133	-26	-3	0-0	1.000	0	135	0	/OL		-0.3
	Year	62	66	3	7	1	0	0	9-0		0	13	.106	.192	.106	-12	-11	1-1	1.000	1	91	0	O18L		-1.2
Total	13	1359	3761	491	1029	156	37	47	357	336-46	22	635	.274	.335	.372	93	-33	214-66	.984	13	105	81	O1063(398/518/182)		-2.0

THOMPSON, RICH Richard Charles B4.23.1979 Reading PA BL/TR/6-3/180 [TorA00 6/178] d4.7 Col James Madison

| 2004 | KC A | 6 | 1 | 1 | 0 | 0 | 0 | 0 | 0 | 0-0 | 0 | 1 | .000 | .000 | .000 | -99 | -0 | 1-0 | 1.000 | 0 | 166 | 0 | O3(1/0/2) | | 0.0 |

THOMPSON, ROBBY   Robert Randall   B5.10.1962 W.Palm Beach FL   BR/TR/5-11/170*   [SFN83 S1/2]   d4.8   C4   Col Florida

YEAR	TM LG	G	AB	R	H	2B	3B	HR	RBI	BB-IB	HP	SO	AVG	OBP	SLG	AOPS	ABR	SB-CS	FA	FR	RNG	THR	GAMES AT POSITION	DL	BFW
1986	SF N	149	549	73	149	27	3	7	47	42-0	5	112	.271	.328	.370	97	-3	12-15	.976	-3	101	116	2b149/S		0.0
1987	†SF N*	132	420	62	110	26	5	10	44	40-3	8	91	.262	.338	.419	104	2	16-11	.972	4	99	**138**	2b126	15	1.2
1988	SF N*	138	477	66	126	24	6	7	48	40-0	4	111	.264	.307	.384	108	1	14-5	.978	-3	99	**128**	2b134		0.7
1989	†SF N*	148	547	91	132	26	**11**	13	50	51-0	13	133	.241	.321	.400	108	5	12-2	.989	-2	100	116	2b148		0.9
1990	SF N	144	498	67	122	22	3	15	56	34-1	6	95	.245	.299	.392	92	-7	14-4	.989	20	112	127	2b142		1.9
1991	SF N	144	492	74	129	24	5	19	48	63-2	8	75	.262	.352	.447	127	18	14-7	.985	12	102	133	2b144		3.6
1992	SF N	128	443	54	115	25	1	14	49	43-1	8	75	.260	.333	.415	118	10	5-9	.978	**26**	109	**144**	2b120	23	3.9
1993	SF N*	128	494	85	154	30	2	19	65	45-0	7	97	.312	.375	.496	136	26	10-4	.988	17	106	**138**	2b128	17	4.8
1994	SF N	35	129	13	27	8	2	2	7	15-0	1	32	.209	.290	.349	69	-6	3-1	.989	5	114	114	2b35	86	0.0
1995	SF N	95	336	51	75	15	0	8	23	42-1	4	76	.223	.317	.339	75	-12	1-2	.993	-19	93	87	2b91	15	-2.7
1996	SF N	63	227	35	48	11	1	5	21	24-0	5	69	.211	.301	.335	69	-10	2-2	.976	-6	94	99	2b62	85	-1.4
Total	11	1304	4612	671	1187	238	39	119	458	439-8	66	987	.257	.329	.403	105	27	103-62	.983	50	103	124	2b1279/S	241	12.9

THOMPSON, TOMMY   Rupert Lockhart   B5.19.1910 Elkhart IL   D5.24.1971 Auburn CA   BL/TR/5-9.5/155   d9.3

YEAR	TM LG	G	AB	R	H	2B	3B	HR	RBI	BB-IB	HP	SO	AVG	OBP	SLG	AOPS	ABR	SB-CS	FA	FR	RNG	THR	GAMES AT POSITION	DL	BFW
1933	Bos N	24	97	6	18	1	0	0	6	4	0	6	.186	.218	.196	21	-10	0	1.000	2	105	146	O24(1/13/10)		-1.
1934	Bos N	105	343	40	91	12	3	0	37	13	0	19	.265	.300	.318	71	-15	2	.964	8	113	152	O82(6/1/75)		-1.
1935	Bos N	112	297	34	81	7	1	4	30	36	1	17	.273	.353	.343	96	-1	2	.965	5	111	120	O85(12/12/62)		0.
1936	Bos N	106	266	37	76	9	0	4	36	31	1	12	.286	.362	.365	103	2	3	1.000	-1	99	96	O39(10/22/7),1b25		-0.
1938	Chi A	19	18	2	2	0	0	0	2	1	0	5	.111	.158	.111	-31	-4	0-0	1.000	-0	0	483	/1		-0.
1939	Chi A	1	0	0	0	0	0	0	0	0	0	0	—	—	—		0	0-0	—	0			/H		0.
	StL A	30	86	23	26	5	0	1	7	23	1	7	.302	.455	.395	117	4	0-0	.977	0	90	172	O23R		0.
	Year	31	86	23	26	5	0	1	8	23	1	7	.302	.455	.395	117	4	0-0							
Total	6	397	1107	142	294	34	4	9	119	108	7	63	.266	.335	.328	84	-24	7-0	.975	13	107	135	O253(29/48/177),1b26		-2.

THOMPSON, RYAN   Ryan Orlando   B11.4.1967 Chestertown MD   BR/TR/6-3/215(200-215)   [TorA87 13/335]   d9.1

YEAR	TM LG	G	AB	R	H	2B	3B	HR	RBI	BB-IB	HP	SO	AVG	OBP	SLG	AOPS	ABR	SB-CS	FA	FR	RNG	THR	GAMES AT POSITION	DL	BFW
1992	NY N	30	108	15	24	7	1	3	10	8-0	0	24	.222	.274	.389	87	1	2-2	.988	2	117	126	O29(0/26/10)		0.
1993	NY N	80	288	34	72	19	2	11	26	19-4	3	81	.250	.302	.444	98	-2	2-7	.987	5	114	100	O76C		0.
1994	NY N	98	334	39	75	14	1	18	59	28-7	10	94	.225	.301	.434	91	-6	3-1	.989	3	108	90	O98C		-0.
1995	NY N	75	267	39	67	13	0	7	31	19-1	0	77	.251	.306	.378	83	-7	0-0	.985	7	123	86	O74(11/38/31)	66	-0.
1996	Cle A	8	22	2	7	0	0	1	5	1-0	0	6	.318	.348	.455	101	0	0-0	1.000	-2	37	0	O8C		-0.
1999	Hou N	12	20	2	4	1	0	1	5	2-0	0	7	.200	.273	.400	68	-1	0-0	1.000	-0			O31(20/9/6)		-0.
2000	NY A	33	50	12	13	3	0	3	14	5-0	1	12	.260	.339	.500	110	1	0-1	.923	-1	62	193	O16(1/4/12)		-0.
2001	Fla N	18	31	6	9	5	0	2	10	2-0	0	8	.290	.313	.452	97	0	0-0	1.000	-0	101	99	O51(34/5/14)		0.
2002	Mil N	62	137	16	34	9	2	8	24	7-0	2	38	.248	.295	.518	112	1	1-0	.985	0	101	99	O393(68/269/76)	66	-0.
Total	9	416	1257	165	305	71	6	52	176	90-12	20	347	.243	.301	.433	94	-16	9-12	.986	13	109	96	O393(68/269/76)	66	-0.

THOMPSON, SAM   Samuel Luther "Big Sam"   B3.5.1860 Danville IN   D11.7.1922 Detroit MI   BL/TL/6-2/207   d7.2   HF1974

YEAR	TM LG	G	AB	R	H	2B	3B	HR	RBI	BB-IB	HP	SO	AVG	OBP	SLG	AOPS	ABR	SB-CS	FA	FR	RNG	THR	GAMES AT POSITION	DL	BFW
1885	Det N	63	254	58	77	11	9	7	44	16		22	.303	.344	.500	170	19		.885	6	203	0	O63R		2
1886	Det N	122	503	101	156	18	13	8	89	35		31	.310	.355	.445	137	21	13	.945	8	117	**329**	O122R		4
1887	†Det N	**127**	545	118	**203**	29	**23**	10	**166**	32	9	19	.372	.416	**.565**	164	45	22	.909	6	107	179	O127R		0
1888	Det N	56	238	51	67	10	8	6	40	23		3	.282	.352	.466	157	16	5	.882	-8	41	0	O56R		2
1889	Phi N	128	533	103	158	36	4	**20**	111	36		6	.296	.348	.492	123	12	24	.939	0	126	103	O132R		1
1890	Phi N	132	549	116	**172**	**41**	9	4	102	42		8	.313	.371	.443	133	22	25	.937	18	153	164	O133(0/2/131)		2
1891	Phi N	133	554	108	163	23	10	7	90	52		8	.294	.363	.410	122	15	29	.937	1	112	138	O153(3/0/150)		2
1892	Phi N	153	609	109	186	28	11	9	104	59	11	19	.305	.377	.432	145	33	28	.931	-12	78	65	O131R/1		2
1893	Phi N	131	600	130	**222**	**37**	13	11	126	50		6	.370	.424	.530	153	44	18	**.972**	-4	73	50	O102R		3
1894	Phi N	102	451	114	187	32	28	13	**147**	41	1	13	.415	.465	**.696**	181	57	27	.943	12	**179**	49	O118R		1
1895	Phi N	119	538	131	211	45	21	**18**	**165**	31	5	11	.392	.430	**.654**	177	57	27	**.974**	18	**169**	242	O119R		1
1896	Phi N	119	517	103	154	28	7	12	100	28		6	.298	.341	.449	108	4	12	.833	0	224	0	O3R		
1897	Phi N	3	13	2	3	0	1	0	3	1		0	.231	.286	.385	78	-1	0	1.000	3	281	0	O14R		
1898	Phi N	14	63	14	22	5	3	1	15	4		0	.349	.388	.571	182	6	2	1.000	3	180	0	O8R		
1906	Det A	8	31	4	7	0	1	0	3	1		0	.226	.250	.290	67	-1	0	1.000	-0	0	0	O8R		
Total	15	1410	5998	1262	1988	343	161	126	1305	451	63	<u>226</u>	.331	.384	.505	146	349	232	.934	41	121	133	O1409(3/2/1404)/1		29

THOMPSON, SCOT   Vernon Scot   B12.7.1955 Grove City PA   BL/TL/6-3/195(175-195)   [ChiN74 1/7]   d9.3

YEAR	TM LG	G	AB	R	H	2B	3B	HR	RBI	BB-IB	HP	SO	AVG	OBP	SLG	AOPS	ABR	SB-CS	FA	FR	RNG	THR	GAMES AT POSITION	DL	BFW
1978	Chi N	19	36	7	15	3	0	0	2	2-0	0	4	.417	.447	.500	147	2	0-0	1.000	-1	50	0	O5(0/5/1),1b2		
1979	Chi N	128	346	36	100	13	5	2	29	17-1	0	37	.289	.322	.373	82	-9	4-3	.971	-1	98	112	O100(12/26/72),1b12		
1980	Chi N	102	226	26	48	10	1	2	13	28-3	1	31	.212	.301	.292	61	-11	6-6	.963	-3	89	90	O66(1/14/52),1b12	31	
1981	Chi N	57	115	8	19	5	0	0	8	7-1	0	21	.165	.208	.209	19	-12	2-0	.980	-4	78	54	O30(3/20/8),1b3		
1982	Chi N	49	74	11	27	5	1	0	5	5-0	0	14	.365	.405	.459	136	4	0-1	1.000	3	130	186	O23(20/1/4),1b4	34	
1983	Chi N	53	88	4	17	3	1	0	10	3-0	1	28	.193	.220	.250	28	-9	0-0	1.000	-3	92	93	O29(23/0/6)/1		
1984	SF N	120	245	30	75	7	1	3	31	30-5	2	26	.306	.376	.355	111	5	5-3	.998	-2	92	93	1b87,O6(2/0/4)		
1985	SF N	64	111	8	23	4	0	0	6	2-0	1	20	.207	.224	.252	34	-10	0-0	.995	2	146	94	1b24		
	Mon N	34	32	2	9	1	0	0	4	3-0	0	7	.281	.333	.313	89	0	0-0	1.000	1	114	100	1b3,O3R		
	Year	98	143	10	32	5	0	0	10	5-0	1	27	.224	.248	.266	46	-11	0-0	.995	3	144	94	1b27,O3R	65	
Total	8	626	1273	132	333	52	9	5	110	97-10	5	141	.262	.312	.328	76	-40	17-13	.973	-6	92	96	O262(61/66/150),1b136	65	

THOMSON, BOBBY   Robert Brown "The Staten Island Scot"   B10.25.1923 Glasgow, Scotland   BR/TR/6-2/185*   d9.9

YEAR	TM LG	G	AB	R	H	2B	3B	HR	RBI	BB-IB	HP	SO	AVG	OBP	SLG	AOPS	ABR	SB-CS	FA	FR	RNG	THR	GAMES AT POSITION	DL	BFW
1946	NY N	18	54	8	17	4	1	2	9	4	0	5	.315	.362	.537	152	3	0	.935	-0	94	0	3b16		
1947	NY N	138	545	105	154	26	5	29	85	40	4	78	.283	.336	.508	121	13	1	.980	-3	96	132	O127C,2b9		
1948	NY N★	138	471	75	117	20	2	16	63	30	2	77	.248	.296	.401	87	-11	2	.970	3	105	105	O125(64/57/4)		
1949	NY N★	**156**	641	99	198	35	9	27	109	44	2	45	.309	.355	.518	132	25	10	.982	8	111	87	O156C		
1950	NY N	149	563	79	142	22	7	25	85	55	5	45	.252	.324	.449	101	-2	3	.978	3	101	121	O149C		
1951	†NY N	148	518	89	152	27	8	32	101	73	4	57	.293	.385	.562	150	37	5-5	.966	-10	97	48	O77(33/43/3),3b69		
1952	NY N★	153	608	89	164	29	**14**	24	108	52	3	74	.270	.331	.482	122	15	5-2	.940	-5	104	87	3b91,O63C		
1953	NY N	154	608	80	175	22	6	26	106	43	3	57	.288	.338	.472	106	4	4-2	.983	1	93	198	O26L		
1954	Mil N	43	99	7	23	3	0	2	15	12	0	29	.232	.315	.323	71	-4	0-0	.980	1	93	198	O26L	91	
1955	Mil N	101	343	40	88	12	3	12	56	34-4	0	52	.257	.319	.414	99	-1	2-1	.969	-3	97	72	O91(88/3/0)		
1956	Mil N	142	451	59	106	10	4	20	74	43-4	2	75	.235	.302	.408	95	-5	2-4	.974	-0	100	84	O136(128/18/0),3b3		
1957	Mil N	41	148	15	35	5	3	4	23	8-0	0	27	.236	.285	.392	86	-5	2-1	.988	-0	99	75	O38(36/5/1)		
	NY N	81	215	24	52	7	4	8	38	19-2	0	39	.242	.302	.423	93	-3	1-2	.992	-0	103	47	O71(54/3/17)/3		
	Year	122	363	39	87	12	7	12	61	27-2	0	66	.240	.295	.410	90	-7	3-3	.990	-1	101	58	O109(90/8/18)/3		
1958	Chi N	152	547	67	155	27	5	21	82	56-7	4	76	.283	.351	.466	117	13	0-2	.989	-5	94	111	O148(7/143/1),3b4		
1959	Chi N	122	374	55	97	15	2	11	52	35-6	2	50	.259	.322	.398	93	-4	1-0	.987	3	102	120	O116(62/49/29)		
1960	Bos A	40	114	12	30	3	1	5	20	11-0	0	15	.263	.323	.439	102	0	0-1	.971	-1	116	62	O27(12/13/2)/1		
	Bal A	3	6	0	0	0	0	0	0	0-0	0	3	.000	.000	.000	-99	-2	0-0		-1	0	0	2(1/0/1)		
	Year	43	120	12	30	3	1	5	20	11-0	0	18	.250	.308	.417	93	-2	0-1	.971	0	111	59	O29(13/13/3)/1		
Total	15	1779	6305	903	1705	267	74	264	1026	559-<u>23</u>	34	804	.270	.332	.462	111	74	38-<u>20</u>	.980	-13	100	98	O1506(511/982/59),3b184,2b9/1	91	

THON, DICKIE   Richard William   B6.20.1958 South Bend IN   BR/TR/5-11/175(150-178)   d5.22

YEAR	TM LG	G	AB	R	H	2B	3B	HR	RBI	BB-IB	HP	SO	AVG	OBP	SLG	AOPS	ABR	SB-CS	FA	FR	RNG	THR	GAMES AT POSITION	DL	BFW
1979	†Cal A	35	56	6	19	3	0	0		5-0	0	10	.339	.393	.393	116	2	0-0	.923	-3	84	114	2b24,S8/3D		
1980	Cal A	80	267	32	68	12	2	0	15	10-0	1	28	.255	.282	.315	65	-13	7-5	.928	-11	99	80	S22,2b21,D15,3b10/1		
1981	†Hou N	49	95	13	26	6	0	0	3	9-1	0	13	.274	.337	.337	97	0	6-1	.950	-10	63	93	2b28,S13,3b5		
1982	Hou N	136	496	73	137	31	**10**	3	36	37-2	1	48	.276	.327	.397	110	6	37-8	.966	22	111	**128**	S154		
1983	Hou N★	154	619	81	177	28	9	20	79	54-10	2	73	.286	.341	.457	128	21	34-16	.966	22	111	128	S154	175	
1984	Hou N	5	17	3	6	0	1	0	0	1-0	0	4	.353	.389	.471	150	1	0-1	1.000	-0	94	40	S5	20	
1985	Hou N	84	251	26	63	6	1	6	29	18-4	0	50	.251	.299	.355	85	-6	8-3	.967	2	101	115	S79	17	
1986	Hou N	106	278	24	69	13	1	3	21	29-5	0	49	.248	.318	.335	83	-6	6-5	.972	5	87	95	S104	21	
1987	Hou N	32	66	6	14	1	0	1	3	16-3	0	13	.212	.366	.273	75	-2	3-0	.954	-11	92	87	S70,2b2/3		
1988	SD N	95	258	36	68	12	2	1	18	33-0	1	49	.264	.347	.337	100	1	19-4	.972	20	**113**	102	S129		
1989	Phi N	136	435	45	118	18	4	15	60	33-6	6	81	.271	.321	.434	115	7	6-3	.964	2	105	85	S148		
1990	Phi N	149	552	54	141	20	4	8	48	50-7	3	84	.255	.283	.351	79	-17	11-5	.964	2	105	85	S146		
1991	Phi N	146	539	44	136	18	4	9	44	25-6	3	84	.252	.283	.351	78	-8	12-2	.969	-9	96	85	S146		
1992	Tex A	95	275	30	68	15	3	4	37	20-1	0	40	.247	.293	.367	88	-5	2	.958	-2	98	72	S87		37

YEAR	TM LG	G	AB	R	H	2B	3B	HR	RBI	BB-IB	HP	SO	AVG	OBP	SLG	AOPS	ABR	SB-CS	FA	FR	RNG	THR	GAMES AT POSITION	DL	BFW
1993	Mil A	85	245	23	66	10	1	1	33	22-3	0	39	.269	.324	.331	79	-7	6-5	.966	-9	96	62	S28,3b25,2b22,D14	16	-1.5
Total	15	1387	4449	496	1176	193	42	71	435	348-51	9	658	.264	.317	.374	95	-34	167-63	.965	1	102	101	S1143,2b98,3b50,D30/1	286	7.7

THONEY, JACK   John "Bullet Jack" (b John Thoeny) B12.8.1879 Ft.Thomas KY D10.24.1948 Covington KY   BR/TR/5-10/175   d4.26

YEAR	TM LG	G	AB	R	H	2B	3B	HR	RBI	BB-IB	HP	SO	AVG	OBP	SLG	AOPS	ABR	SB-CS	FA	FR	RNG	THR	GAMES AT POSITION	DL	BFW
1902	Cle A	28	105	14	30	7	1	0	11	9	0		.286	.342	.371	102	1	4	.891	-11	102	21	2b14,S11,O2R		-1.0
	Bal A	3	11	1	0	0	0	0	1	9	0		.000	.083	.000	-72	-3	1	.778	-1	68	0	3b3		-0.4
	Year	31	116	15	30	7	1	0	11	10	0		.259	.317	.336	84	-2	5	.891	-12	102	21	2b14,S11,3b3,O2R		-1.4
1903	Cle A	32	122	10	25	3	0	1	9	2	0		.205	.218	.254	42	-9	7	.889	-1	217	148	O24(0/23/1),2b5,3b2		-1.1
1904	Was A	17	70	6	21	3	0	0	6	1	0		.300	.310	.343	108	0	2	.860	0	180	299	O17(0/8/9)		0.0
	NY A	36	128	17	24	4	2	0	12	8	1		.188	.241	.250	53	-7	9	.826	-2	82	100	3b26,O10C		-1.0
	Year	53	198	23	45	7	2	0	18	9	1		.227	.264	.283	71	-7	11	.886	-1	234	194	O27(0/18/9),3b26		-1.0
1908	Bos A	109	416	58	106	5	9	2	30	13	3		.255	.282	.325	94	-5	16	.948	4	94	58	O101(87/11/3)		-0.8
1909	Bos A	13	40	1	5	1	0	0	2	0	0		.125	.167	.150	0	-5	2	.960	1	67	297	O10L		-0.6
1911	Bos A	26	20	5	5	0	0	0	2	0	0		.250	.250	.250	40	-2	1	—	0			/H		-0.2
Total	4	264	912	112	216	23	12	3	73	36	4		.237	.269	.298	75	-30	42	.929	-10	132	108	O164(97/52/15),3b31,2b19,S11		-5.1

THORNTON, ANDY   Andre B8.13.1949 Tuskegee AL   BR/TR/6-2/205*   d7.28   [DL 1980 Cle A 109]

YEAR	TM LG	G	AB	R	H	2B	3B	HR	RBI	BB-IB	HP	SO	AVG	OBP	SLG	AOPS	ABR	SB-CS	FA	FR	RNG	THR	GAMES AT POSITION	DL	BFW
1973	Chi N	17	35	4	7	0	0	2	7	7-0	1		.200	.333	.286	68	-1	0-0	.989	2	177	44	1b9		0.0
1974	Chi N	107	303	41	79	16	4	10	46	48-4	4	50	.261	.368	.439	120	9	2-1	.992	7	131	84	1b90/3		1.0
1975	Chi N	120	372	70	109	21	4	18	60	88-12	4	63	.293	.428	.516	155	33	3-2	.988	0	102	90	1b113,3b2		2.5
1976	Chi N	27	85	8	17	6	0	2	14	20-1	2	14	.200	.361	.341	93	0	2-0	.987	1	114	89	1b25	27	0.0
	Mon N	69	183	20	35	5	2	9	24	28-0	3	32	.191	.304	.388	92	-2	2-1	.994	-0	103	126	1b43,O11R	21	-0.6
	Year	96	268	28	52	11	2	11	38	48-1	5	46	.194	.323	.373	93	-2	4-1	.991	0	107	112	1b68,O11R		-0.6
1977	Cle A	131	433	77	114	20	5	28	70	70-1	11	82	.263	.378	.527	148	31	3-4	.995	-4	84	100	1b117,D9		1.8
1978	Cle A	145	508	97	133	22	4	33	105	93-4	6	72	.262	.377	.516	152	37	4-7	.995	7	116	87	1b145		3.5
1979	Cle A	143	515	89	120	31	1	26	93	90-2	4	93	.233	.347	.449	114	12	5-4	.994	-3	88	82	1b130,D13		0.0
1981	Cle A	69	226	22	54	12	0	6	30	23-1	0	37	.239	.303	.372	96	-1	3-1	.986	-1	74	78	D53,1b11		-0.4
1982	Cle A★	161	589	90	161	26	1	32	116	109-18	2	81	.273	.386	.484	137	34	6-7	1.000	-0	78	63	D152,1b8	24	-0.4
1983	Cle A	141	508	78	143	27	1	17	77	87-14	2	72	.281	.383	.439	122	19	4-2	.991	1	114	83	D114,1b27		2.7
1984	Cle A★	155	587	91	159	26	0	33	99	91-11	2	79	.271	.366	.484	132	27	6-5	.979	0	108	113	D144,1b11		1.6
1985	Cle A	124	461	49	109	13	0	22	88	47-1	0	75	.236	.304	.408	94	-5	3-2	—	0	0	0	D122		2.2
1986	Cle A	120	401	49	92	14	0	17	66	65-0	1	67	.229	.333	.392	99	1	4-1	—	0	0	0	D110	17	-0.8
1987	Cle A	36	85	8	10	2	0	5	9	8-0	0	25	.118	.206	.141	-4	-13	1-0	—	0	0	0	D21		-0.2
Total	14	1565	5291	792	1342	244	22	253	895	876-69	41	851	.254	.360	.452	122	181	48-37	.992	9	104	90	D738,1b729,O11R,3b3	198	12.0

THORNTON, LOU   Louis B4.26.1963 Montgomery AL   BL/TR/6-2/185*   [NYN81 19/471]   d4.8

YEAR	TM LG	G	AB	R	H	2B	3B	HR	RBI	BB-IB	HP	SO	AVG	OBP	SLG	AOPS	ABR	SB-CS	FA	FR	RNG	THR	GAMES AT POSITION	DL	BFW
1985	†Tor A	56	72	18	17	1	1	1	8	2-0	1	24	.236	.267	.319	58	-4	1-0	.957	-2	99	0	O35(16/0/20),D16		-0.7
1987	Tor A	12	2	1	1	0	0	0	0	1-1	0	1	.500	.667	.500	211	0	0-1	—	-0	0	0	O4L,D6		0.0
1988	Tor A	11	2	1	0	0	0	0	0	0-0	0	1	.000	.000	.000	-99	-1	0-0	1.000	-1	30	0	O10(9/0/1)/D		-0.1
1989	NY N	13	13	5	4	1	0	0	1	0-0	0	1	.308	.308	.385	101	0	2-0	1.000	1	149	0	O6(3/1/2)		0.1
1990	NY N	3	0	0	0	0	0	0	0	—	0		—	—	—		0	0-0	1.000	0	134	0	O2(0/1/1)		0.0
Total	5	95	89	29	22	2	1	1	9	3-1	1	25	.247	.280	.326	65	-5	3-1	.965	-2	98	0	O57(32/2/24),D23		-0.7

THORNTON, OTIS   Otis Benjamin B6.30.1945 Docena AL   BR/TR/6-1/186   d7.6

YEAR	TM LG	G	AB	R	H	2B	3B	HR	RBI	BB-IB	HP	SO	AVG	OBP	SLG	AOPS	ABR	SB-CS	FA	FR	RNG	THR	GAMES AT POSITION	DL	BFW
1973	Hou N	2	3	0	0	0	0	0	0	0-0	0		.000	.000	.000	-99	-1	0-0	1.000	0	27	0	C2		-0.1

THORNTON, WALTER   Walter Miller B2.18.1875 Lewiston ME   D7.14.1960 Los Angeles CA   BL/TL/6-1/180   d7.1   Col Cornell ▲

YEAR	TM LG	G	AB	R	H	2B	3B	HR	RBI	BB-IB	HP	SO	AVG	OBP	SLG	AOPS	ABR	SB-CS	FA	FR	RNG	THR	GAMES AT POSITION	DL	BFW
1895	Chi N	8	22	4	7	1	0	1	7	3	0		.318	.400	.500	123	1	0	.900	-1	55	0	P7/1		0.0
1896	Chi N	9	22	6	8	0	1	0	1	5	0	2	.364	.481	.455	142	2	2	.800	-1	50	0	P5,O3(0/2/1)		0.0
1897	Chi N	75	265	39	85	9	6	0	55	30	6		.321	.402	.400	108	4	13	.781	-9	102	0	O59(48/8/3),P16		-0.9
1898	Chi N	62	210	34	62	5	2	0	14	22	0		.295	.362	.338	101	1	8	.877	-3	111	199	O34(2/26/6),P28		-0.3
Total	4	154	519	83	162	15	9	1	77	60	6	3	.312	.390	.382	108	8	23	.821	-14	101	71	O96(50/36/10),P56/1		-1.2

THORPE, BOB   Benjamin Robert B11.19.1926 Caryville FL   D10.30.1996 Waveland MS   BR/TR/6-1.5/190*   d4.19

YEAR	TM LG	G	AB	R	H	2B	3B	HR	RBI	BB-IB	HP	SO	AVG	OBP	SLG	AOPS	ABR	SB-CS	FA	FR	RNG	THR	GAMES AT POSITION	DL	BFW
1951	Bos N	2	2	1	1	0	1	0	1	0	0		.500	.500	1.500	448	1	0-0	—	0			/H		0.1
1952	Bos N	81	292	20	76	8	2	3	26	5	1	42	.260	.275	.332	70	-13	3-1	.972	-2	98	140	O72(8/0/70)		-1.5
1953	Mil N	27	37	1	6	1	0	0	5	1	0	6	.162	.184	.189	-3	-6	0-1	1.000	-1	96	0	O18(10/0/8)		-0.7
Total	3	110	331	22	83	9	3	3	32	6	1	48	.251	.266	.323	64	-18	3-2	.975	1	98	128	O90(18/0/78)		-2.1

THORPE, JIM   James Francis B5.28.1887 Prague OK   D3.28.1953 Long Beach CA   BR/TR (BB 1915)/6-1/185   d4.14

YEAR	TM LG	G	AB	R	H	2B	3B	HR	RBI	BB-IB	HP	SO	AVG	OBP	SLG	AOPS	ABR	SB-CS	FA	FR	RNG	THR	GAMES AT POSITION	DL	BFW
1913	NY N	19	35	6	5	0	1	0	2	1	0	9	.143	.167	.229	12	-4	2-1	.944	1	92	202	O9(3/7/0)		-0.4
1914	NY N	30	31	5	6	1	0	0	2	0	0	4	.194	.194	.226	25	-3	1	.750	-0	101	0	O4(0/2/2)		-0.4
1915	NY N	17	52	8	12	3	1	0	1	2	0	16	.231	.259	.327	82	-1	4-2	.933	-2	99	0	O10(13/2)		-0.4
1917	Cin N	77	251	29	62	2	8	4	36	6	1	35	.247	.267	.367	98	-3	11	.962	2	111	80	O69(38/0/33)		-0.6
	†NY N	26	57	12	11	3	2	0	4	0	0	10	.193	.303	.316	93	-1	0	.939	-1	111	0	O18(6/1/13)		-0.2
	Year	103	308	41	73	5	10	4	40	14	2	45	.237	.275	.360	97	-3	12	.958	1	111	66	O87(44/1/46)		-0.8
1918	NY N	58	113	15	28	4	4	1	11	4	2	18	.248	.286	.381	106	0	9	.983	-2	92	53	O44(2/33/12)		-0.5
1919	NY N	2	3	0	1	0	0	0	1	0	0		.333	.333	.333	102	0	0	1.000	-0	98	0	O2(1/1/0)		0.0
	Bos N	60	156	16	51	7	3	1	25	6	2	30	.327	.360	.429	143	7	7	.926	-4	98	43	O38(22/12/7),1b2		0.2
	Year	62	159	16	52	7	3	1	26	6	2	30	.327	.359	.428	142	7	7	.928	-4	98	42	O40(23/13/7),1b2		0.2
Total	6	289	698	91	176	20	18	7	82	27	6	122	.252	.286	.362	99	-4	29-3	.951	-7	103	59	O199(72/69/69),1b2		-2.3

THRASHER, BUCK   Frank Edward B8.6.1889 Watkinsville GA   D6.12.1938 Cleveland OH   BL/TR/5-11/182   d9.27

YEAR	TM LG	G	AB	R	H	2B	3B	HR	RBI	BB-IB	HP	SO	AVG	OBP	SLG	AOPS	ABR	SB-CS	FA	FR	RNG	THR	GAMES AT POSITION	DL	BFW
1916	Phi A	7	29	4	9	2	1	0	4	2	0	1	.310	.355	.448	148	1	0	1.000	-1	98	0	O7R		0.1
1917	Phi A	23	77	5	18	2	1	0	2	3	1	12	.234	.272	.286	71	-3	0	.938	-3	85	36	O22R		-0.8
Total	2	30	106	9	27	4	2	0	6	5	1	13	.255	.295	.330	92	-2	0	.951	-3	88	28	O29R		-0.7

THRONEBERRY, MARV   Marvin Eugene "Marvelous Marv" B9.2.1933 Collierville TN   D6.23.1994 Fisherville TN   BL/TL/6-0/197(185-197)   d9.25   b-Maynard

YEAR	TM LG	G	AB	R	H	2B	3B	HR	RBI	BB-IB	HP	SO	AVG	OBP	SLG	AOPS	ABR	SB-CS	FA	FR	RNG	THR	GAMES AT POSITION	DL	BFW
1955	NY A	1	2	1	2	1	0	0	3	0-0	0		1.000	.667	1.500	574	1	1-0	1.000	0	281	0	/1		0.2
1958	†NY A	60	150	30	34	5	2	7	19	19-0	1	40	.227	.316	.427	107	1	1-1	.991	-1	99	134	1b40,O5R		-0.2
1959	NY A	80	192	27	46	5	0	8	22	18-1	0	51	.240	.302	.391	93	-3	0-0	.989	0	111	123	1b54,O13(1/0/12)		-0.3
1960	KC A	104	236	29	59	9	2	11	41	23-1	0	60	.250	.315	.445	103	0	0-0	.991	0	104	103	1b71		-0.3
1961	KC A	40	130	17	31	2	1	6	24	19-1	0	30	.238	.336	.408	96	-1	0-0	.996	2	130	119	1b30,O10R		-0.2
	Bal A	56	96	9	20	3	0	5	11	12-0	0	20	.208	.296	.396	86	-2	0-0	.923	-1	53	0	O15R,1b11		-0.5
	Year	96	226	26	51	5	1	11	35	31-1	0	50	.226	.319	.403	93	-3	0-0	.991	0	144	117	1b41,O25R		-0.7
1962	Bal A	9	9	1	0	0	0	0	0	4-0	0	6	.000	.308	.000	-9	-1	0-0	1.000	0	120	0	O2R		-0.7
	NY N	116	357	29	87	11	3	16	49	34-4	0	83	.244	.306	.426	94	-1	1-3	.981	4	125	104	1b97		-0.7
1963	NY N	14	14	0	2	1	0	0	1	1-0	0	5	.143	.200	.214	19	-1	0-0	1.000	-0	93	1b3			-0.2
Total	7	480	1186	143	281	37	8	53	170	130-7	1	295	.237	.311	.416	96	-10	3-4	.987	6	117	112	1b307,O45(1/0/44)		-2.3

THRONEBERRY, FAYE   Maynard Faye B6.22.1931 Fisherville TN   D4.26.1999 Memphis TN   BL/TR/6-0/190(185-199)   d4.15   Mil 1953-54   b-Marv

YEAR	TM LG	G	AB	R	H	2B	3B	HR	RBI	BB-IB	HP	SO	AVG	OBP	SLG	AOPS	ABR	SB-CS	FA	FR	RNG	THR	GAMES AT POSITION	DL	BFW
1952	Bos A	98	310	38	80	11	3	5	23	33	1	67	.258	.331	.361	86	-6	16-7	.955	1	98	148	O86(11/4/71)		-0.7
1955	Bos A	60	144	20	37	7	3	6	27	14-1	1	31	.257	.323	.472	104	0	0-0	.960	3	101	104	O34(32/0/3)		-0.2
1956	Bos A	24	50	6	11	2	0	1	3	3-0	0	16	.220	.264	.320	48	-4	0-0	.909	-2	86	0	O13(8/2/3)	56	-0.6
1957	Was A	1	1	0	0	0	0	0	0	1-0	0	1	.000	.000	.000	-95	-0	0-0	—	0			/H		0.0
	Was A	68	195	21	36	8	2	2	12	17-0	1	37	.185	.252	.277	45	-15	0-1	.983	-1	99	62	O58(14/48/2)		-2.0
	Year	69	196	21	36	8	2	2	12	17-0	1	38	.184	.251	.276	45	-15	0-1	.983	-1	99	62	O58(14/48/2)		-2.0
1958	Was A	44	87	12	16	1	1	4	7	4-0	3	28	.184	.245	.356	64	-5	0-1	1.000	-1	93	88	O25(5/13/8)		-0.7
1959	Was A	117	327	36	82	11	3	10	42	33-3	3	61	.251	.322	.388	95	-2	6-4	.953	-2	92	151	O86(16/1/71)		-0.7
1960	Was A	85	157	18	39	7	1	6	23	18-3	1	33	.248	.326	.522	78	-4	1-1	.947	-2	87	104	O34(12/7/17)		-0.8
1961	LA A	24	31	1	6	1	0	0	5	5-0	1	10	.194	.306	.226	40	-3	0-0	1.000	0	91	294	O5(3/0/2)		-0.2
Total	8	521	1302	152	307	48	12	29	137	127-7	10	284	.236	.307	.358	79	-39	23-14	.962	-5	95	120	O342(101/75/177)	56	-6.0

THURMAN, GARY   Gary Montez B11.12.1964 Indianapolis IN   BR/TR/5-10/175(165-180)   [KCA83 1/21]   d8.30

YEAR	TM LG	G	AB	R	H	2B	3B	HR	RBI	BB-IB	HP	SO	AVG	OBP	SLG	AOPS	ABR	SB-CS	FA	FR	RNG	THR	GAMES AT POSITION	DL	BFW
1987	KC A	27	81	12	24	2	0	0	5	8-0	0	20	.296	.360	.321	80	-2	7-2	.971	5	120	320	O27(22/6/0)		0.2
1988	KC A	35	66	6	11	1	0	2	4	4-0	0	20	.167	.214	.182	12	-8	5-1	.949	2	77	93	O32(22/11/0),D		-1.0
1989	KC A	72	87	24	17	2	1	0	5	15-0	0	26	.195	.311	.241	64	-4	16-0	.949	-4	73	104	O60(12/28/24),D4	56	-0.6

YEAR	TM LG	G	AB	R	H	2B	3B	HR	RBI	BB-IB	HP	SO	AVG	OBP	SLG	AOPS	ABR	SB-CS	FA	FR	RNG	THR	GAMES AT POSITION	DL	BFW
1990	KC A	23	60	5	14	3	0	0	3	2-0	0	12	.233	.258	.283	52	-4	1-1	1.000	-1	98	0	O21(5/2/15)		-0.6
1991	KC A	80	184	24	51	9	0	2	13	11-0	1	42	.277	.320	.359	87	-3	15-5	.970	4	122	67	O72(39/9/29)	34	-0.1
1992	KC A	88	200	25	49	6	3	0	20	9-0	1	34	.245	.281	.305	62	-11	9-6	.986	5	117	132	O67(7/2/59),D9		-0.8
1993	Det A	75	89	22	19	2	2	0	13	11-0	0	30	.213	.297	.281	57	-6	7-0	.950	-3	77	161	O53(17/21/15),D9		-0.7
1995	Sea A	13	25	3	8	2	0	0	3	1-0	0	3	.320	.333	.400	92	0	5-2	1.000	0	113	0	O9(5/1/4)		0.0
1997	NY N	11	6	0	1	0	0	0	0	0-0	0	1	.167	.167	.167	-13	-1	0-1	1.000	0	157	0	O7(3/4/1)		-0.1
Total	9	424	798	121	194	27	6	2	64	61-0	2	187	.243	.297	.299	65	-39	65-18	.971	3	103	121	O348(132/84/147),D23	90	-3.5

THURMAN, BOB Robert Burns B5.14.1917 Wichita KS D10.31.1998 Wichita KS BL/TL/6-1/205* d4.14 Negro Lg 1946-49 Mil 1942-45

YEAR	TM LG	G	AB	R	H	2B	3B	HR	RBI	BB-IB	HP	SO	AVG	OBP	SLG	AOPS	ABR	SB-CS	FA	FR	RNG	THR	GAMES AT POSITION	DL	BFW
1955	Cin N	82	152	19	33	2	3	7	22	17-2	0	26	.217	.296	.408	80	-5	0-2	.949	-0	99	98	O36L		-0.8
1956	Cin N	80	139	25	41	5	2	8	22	10-2	1	14	.295	.340	.532	123	4	0-0	.953	-1	92	109	O29(9/0/20)		0.2
1957	Cin N	74	190	38	47	4	2	16	40	15-0	1	33	.247	.306	.542	114	3	0-0	.987	1	104	115	O44(29/0/15)		0.2
1958	Cin N	94	178	23	41	7	4	4	20	20-1	4	38	.230	.330	.382	81	-5	1-2	.976	1	110	69	O41(33/0/8)		-0.6
1959	Cin N	4	4	1	1	0	0	0	2	0-0	1		.250	.250	.250	33	0	0-0	—	0			/H		0.0
Total	5	334	663	106	163	18	11	35	106	62-5	5	112	.246	.314	.465	99	-3	1-4	.970	2	103	96	O150(107/0/43)		-1.0

THURSTON, JOE Joseph William B9.29.1979 Fairfield CA BL/TR/5-11/175(175-190) [LAN99 4/134] d9.2 Col Sacramento (CA) City

YEAR	TM LG	G	AB	R	H	2B	3B	HR	RBI	BB-IB	HP	SO	AVG	OBP	SLG	AOPS	ABR	SB-CS	FA	FR	RNG	THR	GAMES AT POSITION	DL	BFW
2002	LA N	8	13	1	6	1	0	0	1	0-0	0	1	.462	.429	.538	176	1	0-0	1.000	0	104	229	2b4		0.2
2003	LA N	12	10	2	2	0	0	0	1-0	0	1		.200	.273	.200	27	-1	0-0	.857	1	206	478	2b3		0.0
2004	LA N	17	17	1	3	1	1	0	1	0-0	0	5	.176	.167	.353	33	-2	0-0	1.000	-0	88	135	2b4		-0.2
Total	3	37	40	4	11	2	1	0	2	1-0	0	7	.275	.279	.375	76	-2	0-0	.955	1	116	242	2b11		0.0

TIEMEYER, EDDIE Edward Carl B5.9.1885 Cincinnati OH D9.27.1946 Cincinnati OH BR/TR/5-11.5/185 d8.19

YEAR	TM LG	G	AB	R	H	2B	3B	HR	RBI	BB-IB	HP	SO	AVG	OBP	SLG	AOPS	ABR	SB-CS	FA	FR	RNG	THR	GAMES AT POSITION	DL	BFW
1906	Cin N	5	11	3	2	0	0	0	1	0			.182	.250	.182	33	-1	0	1.000	0	133	377	3b3/P		0.0
1907	Cin N	1	0	1	0	0	0	0	0	1	0		—	1.000	—	206	0	0	—	0			/H		0.0
1909	NY A	3	8	1	3	1	0	0	1	0			.375	.444	.500	197	1	0	.962	-1	0	0	1b3		0.0
Total	3	9	19	5	5	1	0	0	3	0			.263	.364	.316	110	0	0	.962	-0	0	0	1b3,3b3/P		0.0

TIERNAN, MIKE Michael Joseph "Silent Mike" B1.21.1867 Trenton NJ D11.7.1918 New York NY BL/TL/5-11/165 d4.30 ▲

YEAR	TM LG	G	AB	R	H	2B	3B	HR	RBI	BB-IB	HP	SO	AVG	OBP	SLG	AOPS	ABR	SB-CS	FA	FR	RNG	THR	GAMES AT POSITION	DL	BFW
1887	NY N	103	407	82	117	13	12	10	62	32		3	31	.287	.344	.452	125	13	28	.865	-7	58	101	O103(34/11/58),P5		0.4
1888	†NY N	113	443	75	130	16	8	9	52	42		7	42	.293	.364	.427	153	28	52	.960	-1	83	60	O113(0/1/112)		2.5
1889	†NY N	122	499	147	167	23.	14	10	73	96		5	32	.335	.447	.497	163	47	33	.896	-3	82	48	O122(0/1/122)		3.7
1890	NY N	133	553	132	168	25	21	13	59	68		5	53	.304	.385	.495	156	37	56	.896	-15	59	105	O133(2/131/1)		1.6
1891	NY N	134	542	111	166	30	12	16	73	69		3	52	.306	.388	.494	163	44	53	.901	-8	78	116	O134(0/4/130)		3.0
1892	NY N	116	450	79	130	16	10	5	66	57		2	46	.289	.371	.402	136	21	20	.899	-4	81	49	O116R		0.3
1893	NY N	125	511	114	158	19	12	16	102	72		4	24	.309	.399	.476	131	23	26	.927	-11	56	45	O125R		0.6
1894	†NY N	113	429	87	120	20	13	5	79	55		1	21	.280	.363	.422	89	-8	28	.923	-12	48	24	O112R		-2.6
1895	NY N	120	476	127	165	23	21	7	70	66		1	19	.347	.427	.527	149	35	36	.946	-5	46	51	O119R		1.9
1896	NY N	133	521	132	192	24	16	7	89	77		2	18	.369	.452	.516	159	48	35	.970	-2	82	86	O133R		3.6
1897	NY N	128	532	123	174	29	10	5	72	61		1		.327	.397	.447	126	22	40	.931	-13	59	57	O128(38/0/90)		0.5
1898	NY N	103	415	90	116	15	11	5	49	43		7		.280	.357	.405	122	12	19	.973	-10	85	57	O103(96/0/7)		-0.6
1899	NY N	35	137	17	35	4	2	0	7	10		0		.255	.306	.314	73	-5	2	.938	-4	58	61	O35R		-1.1
Total	13	1478	5915	1316	1838	257	162	106	853	748	41	318	.311	.392	.463	138	317	428	.924	-96	68	67	O1476(170/148/1160),P5		14.

TIERNEY, COTTON James Arthur B2.10.1894 Kansas City KS D4.18.1953 Kansas City MO BR/TR/5-8/175 d9.23

YEAR	TM LG	G	AB	R	H	2B	3B	HR	RBI	BB-IB	HP	SO	AVG	OBP	SLG	AOPS	ABR	SB-CS	FA	FR	RNG	THR	GAMES AT POSITION	DL	BFW
1920	Pit N	12	46	4	11	5	0	0	8	3		2	4	.239	.286	.348	79	-1	1-1	.964	-1	104	91	2b10,S2		-0.0
1921	Pit N	117	442	49	132	22	8	3	52	24		2	31	.299	.338	.405	93	-5	4-6	.965	-28	78	108	2b72,3b32,O4R,S3		-1.3
1922	Pit N	122	441	58	152	26	14	7	86	22		2	40	.345	.378	.515	127	16	7-8	.964	-30	86	97	2b105,O2R/S3		-1.5
1923	Pit N	29	120	22	35	5	2	2	23	2		1	10	.292	.309	.417	88	-3	2-1	.941	-2	95	130	2b29		-0.3
	Phi N	121	480	68	152	31	1	11	65	24		2	42	.317	.352	.454	100	0	3-4	.975	19	112	106	2b115,O7(3/0/4),3b2		1.9
	Year	150	600	90	187	36	3	13	88	26		3	52	.312	.343	.447	97	-3	5-5	.968	17	108	111	2b144,O7(3/0/4),3b2		1.
1924	Bos N	136	505	38	131	16	4	6	58	22		4	37	.259	.296	.331	71	-22	11-8	.964	-8	99	112	2b115,3b22		-2.
1925	Bro N	93	265	27	68	14	4	2	39	12		2	23	.257	.294	.362	68	-13	0-3	.963	-3	94	54	3b61/12		-1.
Total	6	630	2299	266	681	119	30	31	331	109	13	187	.296	.332	.415	93	-28	28-31	.966	-52	96	107	2b447,3b118,O13(3/0/10),S6/1		-6.

TIERNEY, BILL William J. B5.14.1858 Boston MA D9.21.1898 Boston MA d5.2

YEAR	TM LG	G	AB	R	H	2B	3B	HR	RBI	BB-IB	HP	SO	AVG	OBP	SLG	AOPS	ABR	SB-CS	FA	FR	RNG	THR	GAMES AT POSITION	DL	BFW
1882	Cin AA	1	5	1	0	0	0	0	0					.000	.000	.000	-95	-1		.917	0	317	0	/1		0
1884	Bal U	1	3	0	1	0	0	0	1					.333	.500	.333	143	0		1.000	0	0	0	/OR		0
Total	2	2	8	1	1	0	0	0	1					.125	.222	.125	13	-1		1.000	0	0	0	/OR1		-0

TIFFEE, TERRY Terry R. B4.21.1979 North Little Rock AR BB/TR/6-3/210* [MinA99 26/779] d9.1 Col Pratt (KS) CC

YEAR	TM LG	G	AB	R	H	2B	3B	HR	RBI	BB-IB	HP	SO	AVG	OBP	SLG	AOPS	ABR	SB-CS	FA	FR	RNG	THR	GAMES AT POSITION	DL	BFW
2004	Min A	17	44	7	12	4	0	2	8	3-0	1	3	.273	.333	.500	110	1	0-0	.966	-1	86	0	3b12/1D		0.
2005	Min A	54	150	9	31	8	1	1	15	8-1	0	15	.207	.245	.293	42	-13	1-0	.912	-2	87	188	3b24,1b13,D10		-1
Total	2	71	194	16	43	12	1	3	23	11-1	1	18	.222	.266	.340	58	-12	1-0	.930	-3	87	123	3b36,1b14,D11		-1

TILLEY, JOHN John C. B New York NY BR/5-7/154 d8.23

YEAR	TM LG	G	AB	R	H	2B	3B	HR	RBI	BB-IB	HP	SO	AVG	OBP	SLG	AOPS	ABR	SB-CS	FA	FR	RNG	THR	GAMES AT POSITION	DL	BFW
1882	Cle N	15	56	2	5	1	1	0	4	2		11	.089	.121	.143	-16	-7		.857	1	110	135	O15(14/1/0)		-0
1884	Tol AA	17	56	5	10	2	0	0	4	1	1		.179	.246	.214	50	-3		.632	-3	0	0	O17L		-0
	StP U	9	26	2	4	1	0	0	3				.154	.241	.192	60	-2		.938	1	51	0	O9L		-1
Total	2	41	138	9	19	4	1	0	4	9	1	11	.138	.196	.181	23	-12		.818	-5	58	58	O41(40/1/0)		-1

TILLMAN, BOB John Robert B3.24.1937 Nashville TN D6.23.2000 Gallatin TN BR/TR/6-4/205* d4.15 Col Middle Tennessee

YEAR	TM LG	G	AB	R	H	2B	3B	HR	RBI	BB-IB	HP	SO	AVG	OBP	SLG	AOPS	ABR	SB-CS	FA	FR	RNG	THR	GAMES AT POSITION	DL	BFW
1962	Bos A	81	249	28	57	6	4	14	38	19-0	1	65	.229	.283	.454	93	-4	0-0	.983	-7	79	98	C66		-0
1963	Bos A	96	307	24	69	10	2	8	32	34-8	1	64	.225	.304	.349	80	-8	0-0	.992	-7	75	52	C95		-0
1964	Bos A	131	425	43	118	18	1	17	61	49-11	0	74	.278	.352	.445	114	9	0-0	.989	-7	70	93	C131		-1
1965	Bos A	111	368	20	79	10	3	6	35	40-3	1	69	.215	.288	.307	66	-16	0-0	.988	-6	90	83	C106		-1
1966	Bos A	78	204	12	47	8	0	3	24	22-3	0	35	.230	.303	.314	71	-7	0-0	.990	-8	53	98	C72		-1
1967	Bos A	30	64	4	12	1	0	1	4	3-0	0	17	.188	.224	.250	37	-5	0-0	.977	-3	42	78	C26		-0
	NY A	22	63	5	16	1	0	2	9	7-1	0	17	.254	.324	.365	109	1	0-0	.970	-2	62	124	C15		-0
	Year	52	127	9	28	2	0	3	13	10-1	0	35	.220	.275	.307	70	-5	0-0	.974	-5	51	100	C41		-0
1968	Atl N	86	236	16	52	4	0	5	20	16-2	1	55	.220	.278	.301	74	-8	1-0	.990	-7	76	88	C75		-1
1969	†Atl N	69	190	18	37	5	0	12	29	18-1	0	47	.195	.263	.411	86	-5	0-0	.988	-9	90	26	C69		-0
1970	Atl N	71	223	19	53	5	0	11	30	20-4	0	66	.238	.299	.408	83	-6	0-0	.988	-5	72	54	C70		-0
Total	9	775	2329	189	540	68	10	79	282	228-33	5	510	.232	.300	.371	85	-49	1-0	.988	-60	75	77	C725		-8

TILLMAN, RUSTY Kerry Jerome B8.29.1960 Jacksonville FL BR/TR/6-0/185(175-190) [NYN79*10/201] d6.6 Col Florida JC

YEAR	TM LG	G	AB	R	H	2B	3B	HR	RBI	BB-IB	HP	SO	AVG	OBP	SLG	AOPS	ABR	SB-CS	FA	FR	RNG	THR	GAMES AT POSITION	DL	BFW
1982	NY N	12	13	4	2	1	0	0	0	0-0	0	4	.154	.154	.231	6	-2	1-0	1.000	-1	51	0	O3R		-0
1986	Oak A	22	39	6	10	1	0	1	6	3-0	0	11	.256	.310	.359	87	1	2-0	.952	-1	97	0	O17(8/0/10)		-0
1988	SF N	4	4	1	1	0	0	1	3	2-0	0	1	.250	.500	1.000	335	1	0-0	1.000	0	143	0	/OL		-0
Total	3	38	56	11	13	2	0	2	9	5-0	0	16	.232	.295	.375	87	-2	3-0	.958	-1	91	0	O21(9/0/13)		-0

TIMMONS, OZZIE Osborne Llewellyn B9.18.1970 Tampa FL BR/TR/6-2/225* [ChiN91 5/137] d4.26 Col Tampa

YEAR	TM LG	G	AB	R	H	2B	3B	HR	RBI	BB-IB	HP	SO	AVG	OBP	SLG	AOPS	ABR	SB-CS	FA	FR	RNG	THR	GAMES AT POSITION	DL	BFW
1995	Chi N	77	171	30	45	10	1	8	28	13-2	0	30	.263	.314	.474	105	-3	3-0	.970	-3	88	41	O55(49/0/6)		-0
1996	Chi N	65	140	18	28	4	0	7	16	15-0	1	30	.200	.282	.379	70	-7	1-0	1.000	1	111	50	O47(25/0/22)		-0
1997	Cin N	6	9	1	3	1	0	0	0	0-0	0	1	.333	.333	.444	100	0	0-0	.000	0	0	0	/OL		-0
1999	Sea A	26	44	4	5	2	0	1	3	4-0	0	12	.114	.188	.227	5	-7	0-1	1.000	-2	69	0	O17(12/0/5)/1D		-0
2000	TB A	12	41	9	14	3	0	4	13	1-0	0	9	.341	.357	.707	163	4	0-0	1.000	-2	45	0	O9(2/0/7)/D		-0
Total	5	186	405	62	95	20	1	20	60	33-2	1	82	.235	.293	.437	87	-10	4-1	.980	-6	89	35	O129(89/0/40),D6/1		-0

TINGLEY, RON Ronald Irvin B5.27.1959 Presque Isle ME BR/TR/6-2/194(160-195) [SDN77 10/242] d9.25

YEAR	TM LG	G	AB	R	H	2B	3B	HR	RBI	BB-IB	HP	SO	AVG	OBP	SLG	AOPS	ABR	SB-CS	FA	FR	RNG	THR	GAMES AT POSITION	DL	BFW
1982	SD N	8	20	2	2	0	0	0	0	0-0	0	7	.100	.100	.100	-47	-4	0-0	.957	-1	40	72	C8		
1988	Cle A	9	24	1	4	1	0	1	2	0-0	0	8	.167	.231	.292	44	-2	0-0	1.000	-2	55	133	C9		
1989	Cal A	4	3	1	1	0	0	0	1	0-0	0	2	.333	.500	.333	141	0	0-0	.889	-1	32	0	C4		
1990	Cal A	5	3	0	0	0	0	0	0	1-0	0	1	.000	.250	.000	-25	0	0-0	1.000	-0	0	0	C5		
1991	Cal A	45	115	11	23	7	0	1	13	8-0	1	34	.200	.258	.287	50	-8	1-1	.988	6	117	184	C45		28
1992	Cal A	71	127	15	25	2	1	3	8	13-0	2	35	.197	.282	.299	62	-7	0-1	.987	7	121	139	C69		
1993	Cal A	58	90	7	18	7	0	0	12	9-0	1	22	.200	.277	.278	49	-6	1-2	.995	4	155	84	C58		

YEAR	TM LG	G	AB	R	H	2B	3B	HR	RBI	BB-IB	HP	SO	AVG	OBP	SLG	AOPS	ABR	SB-CS	FA	FR	RNG	THR	GAMES AT POSITION	DL	BFW
1994	Fla N	19	52	9	3	1	1	2		5-0	0	18	.173	.246	.327	46	-4	0-0	.990	2	173	144	C18		-0.1
	Chi A	5	5	0	0	0	0	0		0-0	0	2	.000	.000	.000	-99	-2	0-0	1.000	-0	50	0	C5		-0.2
1995	Det A	54	124	14	28	8	1	4		15-0	0	38	.226	.307	.403	84	-3	0-1	.991	-5	113	118	C53/1	19	-0.2
Total	9	278	563	52	110	27	3	10	55	54-0	4	165	.195	.270	.307	56	-36	2-5	.989	15	121	127	C274/1	47	-0.8

TINKER, JOE   Joseph Bert   B7.27.1880 Muscotah KS   D7.27.1948 Orlando FL   BR/TR/5-9/175   d4.17   M4   HF1946

YEAR	TM LG	G	AB	R	H	2B	3B	HR	RBI	BB-IB	HP	SO	AVG	OBP	SLG	AOPS	ABR	SB-CS	FA	FR	RNG	THR	GAMES AT POSITION	DL	BFW
1902	Chi N	133	501	55	132	19	5	2	55	26	0		.263	.300	.333	98	-3	27	.908	1	108	113	S126,3b8		0.3
1903	Chi N	124	460	67	134	21	7	2	70	37	1		.291	.345	.380	110	5	27	.906	0	105	106	S107,3b19		0.9
1904	Chi N	141	488	55	108	12	13	3	41	29	2		.221	.268	.318	80	-13	41	.925	16	105	120	S140/OR		0.7
1905	Chi N	149	547	70	135	18	8	2	66	34	1		.247	.292	.320	79	-15	31	.940	12	105	**130**	S149		0.2
1906	†Chi N	148	523	75	122	18	4	1	64	43	1		.233	.293	.289	77	-14	30	**.944**	-0	100	131	S147/3		-1.1
1907	†Chi N	117	402	36	89	11	3	1	36	25	1		.221	.269	.271	65	-17	20	.939	13	**111**	**135**	S113		0.1
1908	†Chi N	157	548	67	146	22	14	6	68	32	0		.266	.307	.391	117	8	30	**.958**	26	109	106	S157		4.5
1909	Chi N	143	516	56	132	26	11	4	57	17	0		.256	.280	.372	100	-4	23	.940	18	**105**	112	S143		2.1
1910	†Chi N	134	473	48	136	25	9	3	69	24	0	35	.288	.322	.397	110	3	30	.942	14	104	113	S132		2.3
1911	Chi N	144	536	61	149	24	12	4	69	39	0	31	.278	.327	.390	100	-2	30	**.937**	22	109	103	S143		2.9
1912	Chi N	142	550	80	155	24	7	0	75	38	2	21	.282	.331	.351	87	-11	25	.943	**26**	106	132	S142		2.5
1913	Cin N	110	382	47	121	20	13	1	57	20	1	26	.317	.352	.445	127	12	10-12	.968	21	111	95	S101,3b9,M		**3.8**
1914	Chi F	126	438	50	112	21	7	2	46	38	1	30	.256	.317	.349	86	-1	17	.947	12	109	**123**	S125,M		0.5
1915	Chi F	31	67	7	18	2	1	0	9	13	0	5	.269	.387	.328	109	1	3	.914	-2	109	50	S16,2b5,3b4,M		0.0
1916	Chi N	7	10	0	1	0	0	0	0	1	0	1	.100	.182	.100	-11	-1	0	.909	-0	106	0	S4,3b2,M		-0.2
Total	15	1806	6441	774	1690	263	114	31	783	416	10	149	.262	.308	.353	95	-68	336-12	.938	180	107	117	S1745,3b43,2b5/OR		19.5

TINSLEY, LEE   Lee Owen   B3.4.1969 Shelbyville KY   BB/TR/5-10/185(185-198)   [OakA87 1/11]   d4.6

YEAR	TM LG	G	AB	R	H	2B	3B	HR	RBI	BB-IB	HP	SO	AVG	OBP	SLG	AOPS	ABR	SB-CS	FA	FR	RNG	THR	GAMES AT POSITION	DL	BFW
1993	Sea A	11	19	2	3	1	0	2		2-0	0	9	.158	.238	.368	59	-1	0-0	.900	0	147	0	O6(5/1/1),D2		-0.1
1994	Bos A	78	144	27	32	4	0	2	14	19-1	1	36	.222	.315	.292	56	-9	13-0	.991	1	111	35	O60(27/26/11),D10		-0.6
1995	†Bos A	100	341	61	97	17	1	7	41	39-1	1	74	.284	.359	.402	95	-2	18-9	.979	-0	103	93	O97C		-1.1
1996	Phi N	31	52	1	7	0	0	0	2	4-0	1	22	.135	.196	.135	-11	-9	2-4	.960	0	107	0	O22(18/7/0)	36	0.0
	Bos A	92	192	28	47	6	1	3	14	13-0	2	56	.245	.298	.333	59	-13	6-8	.993	1	94	237	O83(4/79/0)	16	-1.0
1997	Sea A	49	122	12	24	6	2	0	6	11-0	3	34	.197	.263	.279	42	-11	2-0	1.000	1	105	98	O41(34/6/2),D5	107	-1.0
Total	5	361	870	131	210	34	4	13	79	88-2	4	231	.241	.313	.334	66	-45	41-20	.985	3	103	112	O309(88/216/14),D17	159	-3.8

TIPPER, JIM   James   B6.18.1849 Middletown CT   D4.21.1895 New Haven CT   5-5.5/148   d4.26

YEAR	TM LG	G	AB	R	H	2B	3B	HR	RBI	BB-IB	HP	SO	AVG	OBP	SLG	AOPS	ABR	SB-CS	FA	FR	RNG	THR	GAMES AT POSITION	DL	BFW
1872	Man NA	24	110	24	29	4	0	0	18	0		1	.264	.264	.300	77	-2	0-0	.773	-2	141	0	O20L,3b5		-0.3
1874	Har NA	45	197	36	60	8	0	0	19	1		7	.305	.308	.345	104	0	0-1	.812	-1	78	77	O45L		0.1
1875	NH NA	41	159	10	25	1	0	0	4	1		6	.157	.162	.164	16	-12	1-0	.790	-3	94	73	O41(8/32/3)		-1.2
Total	3 NA	110	466	70	114	13	0	0	41	2		14	.245	.248	.273	72	-14	1-1	.798	-6	96	61	O106(73/32/3),3b5		-1.4

TIPTON, ERIC   Eric Gordon "Dukie","Blue Devil"   B4.20.1915 Petersburg VA   D8.29.2001 Newport News VA   BR/TR/5-11/190   d6.9   Col Duke

YEAR	TM LG	G	AB	R	H	2B	3B	HR	RBI	BB-IB	HP	SO	AVG	OBP	SLG	AOPS	ABR	SB-CS	FA	FR	RNG	THR	GAMES AT POSITION	DL	BFW
1939	Phi A	47	104	12	24	4	2	1	14	13	0	7	.231	.316	.337	68	-5	2-0	.942	-0	114	0	O34(33/0/2)		-0.6
1940	Phi A	2	8	2	1	0	1	0	0	1	0	1	.125	.222	.375	53	-1	2-0	1.000	-0	85	0	O2L		-0.1
1941	Phi A	1	4	0	2	0	0	0	0	0	0	0	.500	.500	.500	169	0	0-0	1.000	-0	96	0	/OL		0.0
1942	Cin N	63	207	22	46	5	5	4	18	25	1	14	.222	.309	.353	94	-2	1	.977	-2	97	67	O58(38/20/1)		-0.8
1943	Cin N	140	493	82	142	26	7	9	49	85	2	36	.288	.395	.424	138	28	1	.984	-5	99	57	O139L		1.6
1944	Cin N	140	479	62	144	28	3	6	36	59	2	32	.301	.380	.390	121	16	5	.983	2	107	73	O139L		1.0
1945	Cin N	108	331	32	80	17	1	5	34	40	2	37	.242	.327	.344	89	-4	11	.970	-2	102	32	O83L		-1.2
Total	7	501	1626	212	439	90	19	22	151	223	7	127	.270	.360	.383	112	32	20-0	.977	-8	103	55	O456(435/20/3)		-0.1

TIPTON, JOE   Joe Hicks   B2.18.1922 McCaysville GA   D3.1.1994 Birmingham AL   BR/TR/5-11/185*   d5.2

YEAR	TM LG	G	AB	R	H	2B	3B	HR	RBI	BB-IB	HP	SO	AVG	OBP	SLG	AOPS	ABR	SB-CS	FA	FR	RNG	THR	GAMES AT POSITION	DL	BFW
1948	†Cle A	47	90	11	26	3	0	1	13	4	2	10	.289	.333	.356	85	-2	0-0	.971	2	125	123	C40		0.1
1949	Chi A	67	191	20	39	5	3	3	19	27	1	17	.204	.306	.309	65	-10	1-1	.992	1	85	113	C53		-0.6
1950	Phi A	64	184	15	49	5	1	6	20	19	0	16	.266	.335	.402	90	-4	0-0	.987	-4	88	71	C59		-0.5
1951	Phi A	72	213	23	51	9	0	3	20	51	1	25	.239	.389	.324	92	1	1-1	.969	5	149	149	C72		0.9
1952	Phi A	23	68	6	13	4	0	3	8	15	0	10	.191	.337	.382	94	0	0-0	.990	-1	121	174	C23		0.0
	Cle A	43	105	15	26	2	0	6	22	21	2	21	.248	.383	.438	137	6	1-0	.971	-5	85	110	C35		0.3
	Year	66	173	21	39	6	0	9	30	36	2	31	.225	.365	.416	119	6	1-0	.979	-6	100	137	C58		0.3
1953	Cle A	47	109	17	25	2	0	4	13	22	3	13	.229	.359	.413	111	2	0-0	1.000	-3	82	91	C46		0.0
1954	Was A	54	157	9	35	6	1	1	10	30	2	30	.223	.353	.293	83	-2	0-1	.992	0	93	98	C52		0.1
Total	7	417	1117	116	264	36	5	29	125	186	11	142	.236	.351	.355	91	-9	3-3	.984	-5	105	114	C380		0.3

ISCHINSKI, TOM   Thomas Arthur   B7.12.1944 Kansas City MO   BR/TR/5-10/190(180-200)   d4.11

YEAR	TM LG	G	AB	R	H	2B	3B	HR	RBI	BB-IB	HP	SO	AVG	OBP	SLG	AOPS	ABR	SB-CS	FA	FR	RNG	THR	GAMES AT POSITION	DL	BFW
1969	Min A	37	47	2	9	0	0	2		8-0	0	8	.191	.300	.191	42	-3	0-0	1.000	-3	198	69	C32		-0.6
1970	Min A	24	46	2	9	0	1	0	2	9-1	0	9	.196	.327	.261	63	-2	0-0	.990	-2	120	110	C22		-0.3
1971	Min A	21	23	0	3	2	0	0	2	1-0	1	4	.130	.200	.217	18	-2	0-0	.982	-0	55	124	C21		-0.3
Total	3	82	116	8	21	2	1	2	12	18	1	18	.181	.296	.224	44	-7	0-0	.992	-5	136	97	C75		-1.2

ITUS, JOHN   John Franklin "Silent John"   B2.21.1876 St.Clair PA   D1.8.1943 St.Clair PA   BL/TL/5-9/156   d6.8

YEAR	TM LG	G	AB	R	H	2B	3B	HR	RBI	BB-IB	HP	SO	AVG	OBP	SLG	AOPS	ABR	SB-CS	FA	FR	RNG	THR	GAMES AT POSITION	DL	BFW
1903	Phi N	72	280	38	80	15	6	2	34	19	4		.286	.340	.404	115	5	5	.952	3	129	77	O72(34/2/36)		0.4
1904	Phi N	146	504	60	148	25	5	4	55	46	8		.294	.362	.387	136	23	15	.952	10	122	122	O140(105/2/33)		2.7
1905	Phi N	147	548	99	169	36	14	2	89	69	12		.308	.397	.436	154	40	11	.962	7	122	86	O147R		4.1
1906	Phi N	145	484	67	129	22	5	1	57	78	9		.267	.378	.339	124	19	12	.974	7	131	118	O142(0/8/134)		2.1
1907	Phi N	145	523	72	144	23	12	3	63	47	9		.275	.345	.382	130	18	9	.928	-5	107	64	O142R		0.7
1908	Phi N	149	539	75	154	24	5	2	48	53	14		.286	.360	.360	127	19	27	.963	-4	116	69	O149R		1.0
1909	Phi N	151	540	69	146	22	6	3	46	66	16		.270	.367	.350	121	17	23	.971	4	108	130	O149R		1.5
1910	Phi N	143	535	91	129	26	5	3	35	93	4		.241	.358	.325	96	2	20	.976	1	94	107	O142(1/0/142)		-0.6
1911	Phi N	76	236	35	67	14	1	8	26	32	1	16	.284	.372	.453	129	9	3	.979	-1	87	125	O60(1/0/59)		0.6
1912	Phi N	45	157	43	43	9	5	3	22	33	1	14	.274	.403	.452	125	7	6	.917	-5	85	36	O42R		-0.1
	Bos N	96	345	56	112	23	6	2	48	49	9	20	.325	.422	.443	134	20	5	.965	-3	96	86	O96(1/0/96)		1.1
	Year	141	502	99	155	32	11	5	70	82	10	34	.309	.416	.446	131	26	11	.952	-9	93	72	O138(1/0/138)		1.0
1913	Bos N	87	269	33	80	14	2	5	38	35	7	22	.297	.392	.420	129	12	4-7	.919	-5	85	93	O75R		0.2
Total	11	1402	4960	738	1401	253	72	38	562	620	94	116	.282	.373	.385	127	191	140-7	.959	5	110	96	O1356(142/12/1204)		13.7

OBIN, JOHNNY   John Martin "Tip"   B9.15.1906 Jamaica Plain MA   D8.6.1983 Rhinebeck NY   BR/TR/6-3/187   d9.22   Col Fordham

YEAR	TM LG	G	AB	R	H	2B	3B	HR	RBI	BB-IB	HP	SO	AVG	OBP	SLG	AOPS	ABR	SB-CS	FA	FR	RNG	THR	GAMES AT POSITION	DL	BFW
1932	NY N	1	1	0	0	0	0	0	0	0	0	0	.000	.000	.000	-99	0						/H		0.0

OBIN, JOHNNY   John Patrick "Jackie"   B1.8.1921 Oakland CA   D1.18.1982 Oakland CA   BL/TR/6-0/165   d4.20   b-Jim   Col St.Marys (CA)

YEAR	TM LG	G	AB	R	H	2B	3B	HR	RBI	BB-IB	HP	SO	AVG	OBP	SLG	AOPS	ABR	SB-CS	FA	FR	RNG	THR	GAMES AT POSITION	DL	BFW
1945	Bos A	84	278	25	70	6	2	0	21	26	2	24	.252	.320	.288	75	-9	2-6	.951	7	112	121	3b72,2b5/OC		-0.2

OBIN, JACK   John Thomas   B5.4.1892 St.Louis MO   D12.10.1969 St.Louis MO   BL/TL/5-8/142   d4.16   C3

YEAR	TM LG	G	AB	R	H	2B	3B	HR	RBI	BB-IB	HP	SO	AVG	OBP	SLG	AOPS	ABR	SB-CS	FA	FR	RNG	THR	GAMES AT POSITION	DL	BFW
1914	StL F	139	529	81	143	24	10	7	35	51	5	53	.270	.340	.393	94	-12	20	.952	6	94	151	O132(12/7/113)		-1.4
1915	StL F	158	625	92	**184**	26	13	6	51	68	3	42	.294	.366	.406	111	2	31	.965	-1	100	99	O158(0/31/128)		-0.9
1916	StL A	77	150	16	32	4	1	0	10	12	0	13	.213	.272	.253	61	-8	7	.842	-5	86	51	O41(0/6/35)		-1.6
1918	StL A	122	480	59	133	19	5	0	36	48	5	26	.277	.349	.338	111	7	13	.971	-5	86	114	O122(43/78/1)		-0.6
1919	StL A	127	486	54	159	22	7	6	57	36	2	24	.327	.376	.438	125	15	8	.953	1	97	124	O123L		1.3
1920	StL A	147	593	94	202	34	10	4	62	39	2	23	.341	.393	.452	117	14	21-13	.960	3	109	91	O147(34/0/113)		1.0
1921	StL A	150	671	132	236	31	**18**	8	59	45	3	22	.352	.395	.487	117	16	7-12	.956	5	98	134	O150(0/8/143)		0.5
1922	StL A	146	625	122	207	34	8	13	66	56	2	22	.331	.388	.474	119	18	7-9	.940	9	85	94	O145(0/1/144)		-0.5
1923	StL A	151	637	91	202	32	15	13	73	42	4	33	.317	.363	.476	113	9	8-7	.969	-10	90	69	O151R		-1.4
1924	StL A	136	569	87	170	30	8	2	48	50	2	12	.299	.357	.390	87	-11	6-10	.957	-1	101	101	O132(1/1/130)		-2.3
1925	StL A	77	193	25	58	11	0	2	27	9	1	5	.301	.335	.389	79	-6	8-2	1.000	-3	98	29	O39(1/1/38),1b3		-1.0
1926	Was A	27	33	5	7	0	0	0	2	6	0	4	.212	.282	.212	26	-4	0-0	1.000	0	118	0	O7(0/4/3)		-0.4
	Bos A	51	209	26	57	9	0	1	14	16	0	3	.273	.324	.330	73	-8	6-5	.966	-4	79	118	O51(1/0/51)		-1.6
	Year	78	242	31	64	9	1	1	16	16	0	3	.264	.310	.342	67	-12	6-5	.970	-4	82	110	O58(1/4/54)		-2.0
1927	Bos A	111	374	52	116	18	3	2	40	36	0	9	.310	.371	.390	100	0	5-4	.947	-3	89	103	O93(5/0/89)		-1.0
Total	13	1619	6174	936	1906	294	99	64	581	508	29	267	.309	.364	.420	106	32	147-62	.957	-26	95	104	O1491(220/137/1139),1b3		-10.1

YEAR	TM LG	G	AB	R	H	2B	3B	HR	RBI	BB-IB	HP	SO	AVG	OBP	SLG	AOPS	ABR	SB-CS	FA	FR	RNG	THR	GAMES AT POSITION	DL	BFW

TOBIN, BILL William F. B10.10.1854 Hartford CT D10.10.1912 Hartford CT BL d7.21

1880	Wor N	5	16	1	2	0	0	0	3	0		5	.125	.125	.125	-14	-2		1.000	-0	0	99	1b5		-0.2
	Tro N	33	136	14	22	1	1	0	8	4		20	.162	.186	.184	24	-11		.950	-1	94	160	1b33		-1.3
	Year	38	152	15	24	1	1	0	11	4		25	.158	.179	.178	20	-13		.958	-1	82	152	1b38		-1.5

TOCA, JORGE Jorge Luis B1.7.1975 Remedios, Cuba BR/TR/6-3/220* d9.12 [DL 2002 NY N 61]

1999	NY N	4	3	0	1	0	0	0	0	0-0	0		.333	.333	.333	73		0-0	1.000	0	0	0	/1		0.0
2000	NY N	8	7	1	3	0	0	0	4	0-0	0	1	.429	.429	.571	158	1	0-0	1.000	-0	0	0	1b5/OL		0.0
2001	NY N	13	17	3	3	0	0	0	1	0-0	0	8	.176	.176	.176	-9	-3	0-0	1.000	0	113	93	1b3,O2L		-0.3
Total 3		25	27	4	7	1	0	0	5	0-0	0	11	.259	.259	.296	45	-2	0-0	1.000	-0	64	53	1b9,O3L	61	-0.3

TODD, AL Alfred Chester B1.7.1902 Troy NY D3.8.1985 Elmira NY BR/TR/6-1/198 d4.25 Col Mansfield

1932	Phi N	33	70	8	16	5	0	0	9	1	2	9	.229	.260	.300	45	-5	1	.899	-4	90	46	C25		-0.8
1933	Phi N	73	136	13	28	4	0	0	10	4	2	18	.206	.239	.235	32	-12	1	.983	1	72	150	C34,O2L		-0.9
1934	Phi N	91	302	33	96	22	2	4	41	10	2	39	.318	.344	.444	96	-1	3	.976	1	119	84	C82		0.4
1935	Phi N	107	328	40	95	18	3	3	42	19	3	35	.290	.334	.390	85	-6	3	.968	-7	99	82	C87		-0.8
1936	Pit N	76	267	28	73	10	5	2	28	11	2	24	.273	.307	.371	80	-9	4	.976	1	76	88	C70		-0.5
1937	Pit N	133	514	51	158	18	10	8	86	16	1	36	.307	.330	.428	104	0	2	.972	-7	61	104	C128		0.1
1938	Pit N	133	491	52	130	19	7	7	75	18	4	31	.265	.296	.375	83	-14	2	.985	8	101	121	C132		0.3
1939	Bro N	86	245	28	68	10	0	5	32	13	1	16	.278	.317	.380	83	-6	1	.985	6	107	104	C73		0.4
1940	Chi N	104	381	31	97	13	2	6	42	11	2	29	.255	.280	.383	74	-15	1	.984	-4	101	95	C104		-1.3
1941	Chi N	6	6	1	1	0	0	0	0	0		1	.167	.167	.167	-6	-1	0	—	0			/H		-0.1
1943	Chi N	21	45	1	6	0	0	0	1	1		5	.133	.152	.133	-17	-7	0	.986	3	133	64	C17		-0.5
Total 11		863	2785	286	768	119	29	35	366	104	21	243	.276	.307	.377	82	-76	18	.977	-5	93	99	C752,O2L		-3.7

TODT, PHIL Philip Julius "Hook" B8.9.1901 St.Louis MO D11.15.1973 St.Louis MO BL/TL/6-0/175 d4.25

1924	Bos A	52	103	17	27	8	2	1	14	6	1	9	.262	.309	.408	84	-3	0-1	.983	-1	91	63	1b18,O4(0/2/2)		-0.5
1925	Bos A	141	544	62	151	29	13	11	75	44	10	29	.278	.343	.439	97	-5	3-2	.991	3	105	103	1b140		-1.1
1926	Bos A	154	599	56	153	19	12	7	69	40	4	38	.255	.306	.362	76	-25	3-2	.988	10	**130**	97	1b154		-2.4
1927	Bos A	140	516	55	122	22	6	6	52	28	3	23	.236	.280	.337	61	-33	6-2	.991	8	121	106	1b139		-3.1
1928	Bos A	144	539	61	136	31	8	12	73	26	3	47	.252	.290	.406	83	-17	6-5	**.997**	3	102	87	1b144		-2.3
1929	Bos A	153	534	49	140	38	10	4	64	31	2	28	.262	.305	.393	80	-18	6-7	.991	3	108	101	1b153		-2.5
1930	Bos A	111	383	49	103	22	5	11	62	24	1	33	.269	.312	.439	92	-7	4-1	.993	2	**109**	105	1b104		-1.0
1931	†Phi A	62	197	23	48	14	2	5	44	8	0	22	.244	.273	.411	73	-9	1-1	.995	-4	53	117	1b52		-1.6
Total 8		957	3415	372	880	183	58	57	453	207	23	229	.258	.305	.395	81	-117	29-21	.992	23	109	100	1b904,O4(0/2/2)		-14.5

TOLAN, BOBBY Robert B11.19.1945 Los Angeles CA BL/TL/5-11/170* d9.3 C5 [DL 1971 Cin N 179]

1965	StL N	17	69	8	13	2	0	6	6	0-0	1	4	.188	.197	.217	16	-8	2-1	.970	-1	99	0	O17R		-1.1
1966	StL N	43	93	10	16	5	1	1	6	6-2	2	15	.172	.233	.280	43	-7	1-2	.952	-1	95	61	O26(10/0/16)/1		-0.4
1967	†StL N	110	265	35	67	7	3	6	32	19-0	4	43	.253	.309	.370	96	-2	12-7	.992	1	103	119	O80(6/54/25),1b13		-1.3
1968	†StL N	92	278	28	64	12	1	5	17	13-3	4	42	.230	.272	.335	82	-7	9-5	.967	-0	101	61	O67(2/9/57),1b9		1.4
1969	Cin N	152	637	104	194	25	10	21	93	27-2	6	94	.305	.347	.474	122	16	26-12	.974	2	112	55	O150(0/88/62)		2.6
1970	†Cin N	152	589	112	186	34	6	16	80	62-3	8	94	.316	.384	.475	129	26	**57-20**	.978	-2	103	82	O150C		-3.5
1972	†Cin N	149	604	88	171	28	5	8	82	44-5	6	88	.283	.334	.386	110	8	42-15	.990	3	103	94	O149C		-0.3
1973	Cin N	129	457	42	94	14	2	9	51	27-2	5	68	.206	.251	.304	57	-29	15-10	.966	3	103	99	O120(0/76/65)		-3.8
1974	SD N	95	357	45	95	16	1	4	40	20-4	2	41	.266	.320	.384	101	0	7-9	.971	-3	98	86	O88(1/9/81)		-0.5
1975	SD N	147	506	58	129	19	4	5	43	28-3	10	45	.255	.306	.338	84	-12	11-13	.971	-1	96	56	O120(90/16/19),1b27		-2.0
1976	†Phi N	110	272	32	71	7	0	5	35	7-3	0	39	.261	.285	.342	76	-10	10-5	.992	-6	50	114	1b50,O35(20/10/5)		-2.1
1977	Phi N	15	16	1	2	0	0	0	1	1-0	0	4	.125	.176	.125	-17	-3	0-0	.944	-0	104	79	1b5		-0.6
	Pit N	49	74	7	15	4	0	2	9	4-0	0	10	.203	.241	.300	52	-5	1-1	1.000	0	93	109	1b20,O2L		-0.5
	Year	64	90	8	17	4	0	2	10	5-0	0	14	.189	.229	.300	40	-8	1-1	.995	0	232	172	1b5/OR		-0.2
1979	SD N	22	21	2	4	0	1	0	2	1-0	0	3	.190	.190	.286	30	-2	0-0	1.000	0			/H		-0.2
Total 11		1282	4238	572	1121	173	34	86	497	258-27	65	587	.265	.314	.382	96	-35	193-100	.976	-10	102	77	O1005(131/561/348),1b130	237	-9.1

TOLENTINO, JOSE Jose (Franco) B6.3.1961 Mexico City, Distrito Federal, Mexico BL/TL/6-1/195 [OakA83 7/163] d7.28 Col Texas

1991	Hou N	44	54	6	14	4	0	1	6	4-0	0	9	.259	.305	.389	101	0	0-0	.982	1	112	74	1b10/OL		-0.3

TOLLESON, WAYNE Jimmy Wayne B11.22.1955 Spartanburg SC BB/TR/5-9/160* [TexA78 8/202] d9.1 Col Western Carolina

1981	Tex A	14	24	6	4	0	0	0	1	1-0	0	5	.167	.200	.167	7	-3	2-0	1.000	-2	71	0	3b6,S2		-0.1
1982	Tex A	38	70	6	8	1	0	0	2	5-0	0	14	.114	.173	.129	-16	-11	1-1	.958	1	96	140	S26,3b4/2		-0.7
1983	Tex A	134	470	64	122	13	2	3	20	40-0	2	68	.260	.319	.315	76	-15	33-10	.972	-6	97	95	2b112,S26/D		-2.1
1984	Tex A	118	338	35	72	9	2	0	9	27-0	3	47	.213	.276	.251	46	-25	22-4	.979	-9	94	96	S81,2b29,3b12,D6		-2.2
1985	Tex A	123	323	45	101	9	5	1	18	21-0	0	46	.313	.353	.381	99	-1	21-12	.972	-3	95	86	S83,S18,O2(1/1/0),D2		-1.4
1986	Chi A	81	260	39	65	7	3	3	29	38-0	0	43	.250	.342	.335	83	-5	13-6	.955	-6	97	95	S3b65,S18,O2(1/1/0),D2		-0.3
	NY A	60	215	22	61	9	0	0	14	14-0	2	33	.284	.332	.344	85	-10	4-4	.981	3	110	108	S74,3b72,2b3,O2(1/1/0),D2		-0.1
	Year	141	475	61	126	16	3	3	43	52-0	2	76	.265	.338	.339	84	-10	17-10	.981	3	100	100	S119,3b3	15	-1.3
1987	NY A	121	349	48	77	4	0	1	22	43-0	0	72	.221	.306	.241	48	-26	5-3	.970	-3	100	103	S119,3b3	144	-1.8
1988	NY A	21	59	8	15	2	0	0	5	8-0	0	11	.254	.338	.288	79	-1	1-0	.981	6	136	120	2b12,3b10/S		-0.1
1989	NY A	80	140	16	23	5	2	1	9	16-0	1	23	.164	.255	.250	43	-11	1-0	.912	2	89	128	S45,2b13,3b3,D5	13	-0.9
1990	NY A	73	74	12	11	1	1	0	4	16-0	1	21	.149	.210	.189	13	-9	1-0	.983	7	129	176	S42,2b13,3b3,D5		-0.3
Total 10		863	2322	301	559	60	17	9	133	219-0	8	384	.241	.307	.293	65	-111	108-41	.974	-3	103	104	S409,2b292,3b143,D25,O3(1/2/0)	172	-12.0

TOLMAN, TIM Timothy Lee B4.20.1956 Santa Monica CA BR/TR/6-0/195* [HouN78 12/297] d9.9 Col USC

1981	Hou N	4	8	0	1	0	0	0	0	0-0	0	1	.125	.125	.125	-31	-1	0-0	1.000	-0	65	0	O3(3/0/1)		-0.1
1982	Hou N	15	26	4	5	2	0	1	3	4-0	0	1	.192	.300	.385	98	0	0-1	1.000	-1	77	0	O5(4/0/1)/1		-0.1
1983	Hou N	43	56	4	11	0	0	2	10	6-0	0	9	.196	.270	.375	83	-1	0-1	1.000	-1	48	141	1b7,O3L		-0.1
1984	Hou N	14	17	2	3	1	0	0	4	0-0	0	3	.176	.176	.235	16	-2	0-0	1.000	0	123	0	O3(1/0/2)/1		-0.1
1985	Hou N	31	43	4	6	2	0	2	8	1-0	1	10	.140	.178	.302	33	-4	1-1	1.000	1	122	0	O9(6/0/3),1b6		-0.2
1986	Det A	16	34	4	6	0	0	2	6	6-0	0	4	.176	.293	.294	41	-3	1-1	1.000	-0	138	0	O4R,1b3,D9		-0.1
1987	Det A	9	12	3	1	0	0	0	0	7-1	1	2	.083	.429	.167	76	0	0-0	1.000	-1	80	0	O7(2/0/5),D2		0.1
Total 7		132	196	21	33	10	0	5	24	24-1	2	31	.168	.262	.296	58	-11	1-3	1.000	-2	97	0	O34(19/0/16),1b18,D11		-0.6

TOLSON, CHICK Charles Julius "Toby" B11.6.1898 Washington DC D4.16.1965 Washington DC BR/TR/6-0/185 d7.3

1925	Cle A	3	12	0	3	0	0	0	2	0		0	.250	.357	.250	56	-1	0-0	1.000	-0	93	36	1b3		-0.1
1926	Chi N	57	80	4	25	6	1	1	8	5	0	9	.313	.353	.450	113	1	0	.991	-1	112	128	1b13		-0.1
1927	Chi N	39	54	6	16	4	0	2	17	4	0	9	.296	.345	.481	119	1	0	1.000	0	106	49	1b8		-0.1
1929	†Chi N	32	109	13	28	5	0	1	19	9	2	16	.257	.325	.330	63	-6	0	.978	-2	83	88	1b31		-0.4
1930	Chi N	13	20	0	6	1	0	0	1	5	0	5	.300	.462	.350	99	1	1	.979	-3	141	145	1b5		0.0
Total 5		144	275	23	78	16	1	4	45	26			.284	.350	.393	90	-4	1-0	.985	-1	97	92	1b60		-0.8

TOMBERLIN, ANDY Andy Lee B11.7.1966 Monroe NC BL/TL/5-11/180(160-185) d8.12

1993	Pit N	27	42	4	12	0	1	1	5	2-0	1	14	.286	.318	.405	97	0	0-0	1.000	-0	68	194	O7(6/0/1)	47	-0.0
1994	Bos A	18	36	1	7	0	1	1	1	6-0	0	12	.194	.310	.333	63	-2	1-0	1.000	1	75	345	O11(5/0/6)/PD		-0.0
1995	Oak A	46	85	15	18	0	0	4	10	5-0	0	22	.212	.256	.353	59	-6	4-1	.979	-2	58	214	O42(5/18/20),D2		-0.2
1996	NY N	63	66	12	17	4	0	3	10	9-0	1	27	.258	.355	.455	118	2	0-0	1.000	-1	58	214	O17(9/0/8)/1	173	-0.0
1997	NY N	6	7	0	2	0	0	0	0	3-0	0	3	.286	.375	.286	80	0	0-0	1.000	0	111	0	O2(1/0/1)		-0.0
1998	Det A	32	69	8	15	2	0	2	12	1-0	3	25	.217	.280	.333	58	-4	1-0	.989	-2	78	154	O84(30/18/37),D29/1P	220	-0.1
Total 6		192	305	40	71	6	2	11	38	26-1	5	103	.233	.304	.374	77	-10	6-1	.989	-2	78	154	O84(30/18/37),D29/1P	220	-0.1

TOMER, GEORGE George Clarence B11.26.1895 Perry IA D12.15.1984 Perry IA BL/TR/6-0/180 d9.17

1913	StL A	1	1	0	0	0	0	0	0	0		0	1.000	.000	.000	-99	0		—	0			/H		-0.0

TOMNEY, PHIL Philip Howard "Buster" B7.17.1863 Reading PA D3.18.1892 Reading PA BR/TR/5-7/155 d9.7

1888	Lou AA	34	120	15	18	3	0	0	4				.150	.197	.175	20	-11	11	.882	6	114	87	S34		-0.7
1889	Lou AA	112	376	61	80	8	5	4	38	46	3	47	.213	.304	.293	71	-14	26	.857	22	**115**	121	S112		-0.8
1890	†Lou AA	108	386	72	107	21	7	1	58	43	5		.277	.357	.376	119	10	27	**.902**	15	112	111	S108		-0.5
Total 3		254	882	148	205	32	12	5	100	96	8	47	.232	.313	.313	86	-15	64	.878	43	114	112	S254		-2.0

YEAR	TM LG	G	AB	R	H	2B	3B	HR	RBI	BB-IB	HP	SO	AVG	OBP	SLG	AOPS	ABR	SB-CS	FA	FR	RNG	THR	GAMES AT POSITION	DL	BFW

TONIS, MIKE Michael Timothy B2.9.1979 Sacramento CA BR/TR/6-3/220 [KCA00 2/44] d6.20 Col California
| 2004 | KC A | 2 | 6 | 0 | 0 | 0 | 0 | 0 | 1-0 | 0 | 0 | 1-0.0 | .000 | .143 | .000 | -58 | -1 | 0-0 | 1.000 | 0 | 101 | 0 | C2 | | -0.1 |

TONNEMAN, TONY Charles Richard B9.10.1881 Chicago IL D8.4.1951 Prescott AZ BR/TR/5-10.5/175 d9.19
| 1911 | Bos A | 2 | 5 | 0 | 1 | 1 | 0 | 0 | 3 | 1 | 0 | | .200 | .333 | .400 | 105 | 0 | 0 | .900 | 0 | 106 | 77 | C2 | | 0.0 |

TOOLEY, BERT Albert R. B8.30.1886 Howell MI D8.17.1976 Marshall MI BR/TR/5-10/155 d4.12
1911	Bro N	119	433	55	89	11	3	1	29	53	2	63	.206	.295	.252	56	-25	18	.925	-6	98	94	S114		-2.4
1912	Bro N	77	265	34	62	6	5	2	37	19	0	21	.234	.285	.317	67	-13	12	.885	-17	90	74	S76		-2.5
Total 2		196	698	89	151	17	8	3	66	72	2	84	.216	.291	.277	60	-38	30	.909	-23	95	86	S190		-4.9

TOPORCER, SPECS George B2.9.1899 New York NY D5.17.1989 Huntington Station NY BL/TR/5-10.5/165 d4.13
1921	StL N	22	53	4	14	1	0	0	2	3	0	4	.264	.304	.283	57	-3	1-0	.938	-0	98	111	2b12,S2		-0.3
1922	StL N	116	352	56	114	25	6	3	36	24	2	18	.324	.370	.455	117	9	2-1	.939	-14	91	71	S91,3b6/2OR		0.3
1923	StL N	97	303	45	77	11	3	3	35	41	3	14	.254	.349	.340	84	-6	4-3	.945	-14	88	120	2b52,S33/13		-1.5
1924	StL N	70	198	30	62	10	3	1	24	11	4	14	.313	.362	.409	108	2	2-3	.974	-8	96	36	3b33,S25,2b3		-0.3
1925	StL N	83	268	38	76	13	4	2	26	36	2	15	.284	.373	.384	92	-2	7-2	.960	-1	97	95	S66,2b7		-0.9
1926 †StL N	64	88	13	22	3	2	0	9	8	2	9	.250	.327	.330	74	-3	1	.983	-6	81	44	2b27,S5/3		-0.9
1927	StL N	86	290	37	72	13	4	0	19	27	1	16	.248	.314	.321	68	-13	5	.980	-8	92	101	3b54,S27,2b2/1		-1.5
1928	StL N	8	14	0	0	0	0	0	0	0	0	3	.000	.000	.000	-98	-4	0	1.000	0	536	0	/12		-0.4
Total 8		546	1566	223	437	76	22	9	151	150	14	93	.279	.347	.373	90	-20	22-9	.946	-51	93	87	S249,2b105,3b95,1b3/OR		-4.1

TORBORG, JEFF Jeffrey Allen B11.26.1941 Plainfield NJ BR/TR/6-0.5/195* d5.10 M11/C13 Col Rutgers
1964	LA N	28	43	4	10	1	0	4	3-1	1	8	.233	.302	.302	75	-2	0-0	.977	-6	48	86	C27		-0.7
1965	LA N	56	150	8	36	5	1	3	13	10-4	1	26	.240	.290	.347	85	-3	0-0	.991	3	101	71	C53		0.1
1966	LA N	46	120	4	27	3	0	1	13	10-3	0	23	.225	.278	.275	61	-6	0-0	.986	4	133	103	C45		0.0
1967	LA N	76	196	11	42	4	1	2	12	13-3	1	31	.214	.265	.276	60	-11	1-3	.989	4	147	108	C75		-0.5
1968	LA N	37	93	2	15	2	0	0	4	6-2	0	10	.161	.212	.183	21	-9	0-0	.991	4	109	143	C37		-0.5
1969	LA N	51	124	7	23	4	0	0	7	9-5	0	17	.185	.241	.218	31	-12	1-0	.996	3	102	100	C50		-0.7
1970	LA N	64	134	11	31	8	0	1	17	14-6	0	15	.231	.300	.313	68	-6	1-1	.983	4	128	91	C63		0.0
1971	Cal A	55	123	6	25	5	0	0	5	3-1	0	6	.203	.220	.244	34	-11	0-0	.987	-4	76	92	C49	32	-1.4
1972	Cal A	59	153	5	32	3	0	0	8	14-4	1	21	.209	.280	.229	55	-8	0-0	.998	6	67	115	C58	23	0.0
1973	Cal A	102	255	20	56	7	0	1	18	21-0	0	32	.220	.278	.259	56	-15	0-2	.991	2	80	77	C102	28	-1.0
Total 10		574	1391	78	297	42	3	8	101	103-29	4	189	.214	.268	.265	56	-83	3-6	.990	19	101	97	C559	83	-4.7

TORCATO, TONY Anthony Dale B10.25.1979 Woodland CA BL/TL/6-1/195(195-220) [SFN98 1/19] d7.26
2002	SF N	5	11	0	3	1	0	0	0	0-0	0	2	.273	.273	.364	71	-1	0-0	1.000	-1	40	0	O3R		-0.1
2003	SF N	14	16	0	3	1	0	0	1	0-0	1	4	.188	.235	.250	26	-2	0-0	.833	-0	106	0	O6(4/0/2)		-0.2
2004	SF N	13	9	1	5	0	0	0	2	1-0	1	0	.556	.583	.556	205	2	0-0	—	0			/H		0.1
2005	SF N	11	11	1	3	0	0	0	0	1-0	0	2	.273	.333	.273	59	-1	0-0	1.000	0	145	0	/OR		-0.1
Total 4		43	47	2	14	2	0	0	3	2-0	2	8	.298	.346	.340	82	-2	0-0	.889	-1	78	0	O10(4/0/6)		-0.3

TORGESON, EARL Clifford Earl "The Earl of Snohomish" B1.1.1924 Snohomish WA D11.8.1990 Everett WA BL/TL/6-3/180* d4.15 C1
1947	Bos N	128	399	73	112	20	6	16	78	82	0	59	.281	.403	.481	137	24	11	.984	-1	106	100	1b117		1.9
1948 †Bos N	134	438	70	111	23	5	10	67	81	2	54	.253	.372	.397	110	9	19	.993	0	101	103	1b129		0.5
1949	Bos N	25	100	17	26	5	1	4	19	13	4	.260	.345	.450	118	2	4	.988	-3	50	94	1b25	122	-0.2
1950	Bos N	**156**	576	**120**	167	30	3	23	87	119	1	69	.290	.412	.472	141	41	15	.986	0	104	87	1b156		3.5
1951	Bos N	**155**	581	99	153	21	4	24	92	102	2	70	.263	.375	.437	127	25	20-11	.988	0	100	90	1b155		2.0
1952	Bos N	122	382	49	88	17	0	5	34	81	1	38	.230	.366	.314	94	1	11-7	.988	-1	99	90	1b105,O5(2/0/3)		-0.3
1953	Phi N	111	379	58	104	25	4	11	64	53	2	57	.274	.366	.470	117	9	7-1	.987	-4	89	98	1b105		0.2
1954	Phi N	135	490	63	133	22	6	5	54	75	0	52	.271	.364	.371	93	-2	7-1	.990	-1	74	93	1b133		-2.0
1955	Phi N	47	150	29	40	5	3	1	17	32-1	0	20	.267	.393	.360	104	3	2-3	.995	-2	84	78	1b43		-0.2
	Det A	89	300	58	85	10	1	9	50	61-2	0	29	.283	.397	.413	123	9	9-0	.992	-1	98	111	1b83		0.9
1956	Det A	117	318	61	84	9	3	12	42	78-0	0	47	.264	.406	.425	120	13	6-4	.992	-6	65	84	1b83		0.2
1957	Det A	30	50	5	12	2	1	1	5	12-0	0	11	.240	.387	.380	108	1	0-0	1.000	0	95	107	1b17		0.6
	Chi A	86	251	53	74	11	2	7	46	49-0	0	44	.295	.406	.438	131	13	7-3	.998	-4	72	126	1b70/OR		0.6
	Year	116	301	58	86	13	3	8	51	61-0	0	55	.286	.403	.429	127	14	7-3	.999	-4	75	122	1b87/OR		0.6
1958	Chi A	96	188	37	50	8	0	10	30	48-1	0	29	.266	.415	.468	146	15	7-2	.978	-3	91	116	1b73		1.0
1959 †Chi A	127	277	40	61	5	3	9	45	62-1	0	55	.220	.359	.357	100	2	7-6	.983	-7	74	92	1b103		-1.0
1960	Chi A	68	57	12	15	2	0	2	9	21-2	0	8	.263	.462	.404	137	5	1-0	.983	0	126	66	1b10		0.5
1961	Chi A	20	15	1	1	0	0	0	1	3-0	0	5	.067	.211	.067	-19	-3	0-0	1.000	0	0	0	/1		-0.3
	NY A	22	18	3	2	0	0	0	0	8-0	0	3	.111	.385	.111	42	-1	0-1	.969	-0	70	217	1b8		-0.2
	Year	42	33	4	3	0	0	0	1	11-0	0	8	.091	.311	.091	16	-3	0-1	.970	-0	68	211	1b9		-0.5
Total 15		1668	4969	848	1318	215	46	149	740	980-7	8	653	.265	.385	.417	118	171	133-39	.989	-41	91	97	1b1416,O6(2/0/4)	122	7.1

TORPHY, RED Walter Anthony B11.6.1891 Fall River MA D2.11.1980 Fall River MA BR/TR/5-11/169 d9.25
| 1920 | Bos N | 3 | 15 | 1 | 3 | 0 | 0 | 0 | 3 | 0-0 | 0 | 3 | .200 | .200 | .200 | 54 | -1 | 0-0 | .969 | -1 | 0 | 95 | 1b3 | | -0.2 |

TORRE, FRANK Frank Joseph B12.30.1931 Brooklyn NY BL/TL/6-3/205* d4.20 b-Joe
1956	Mil N	111	159	17	41	6	0	0	16	11-2	0	6	.258	.304	.296	67	-7	1-0	.993	5	142	108	1b89		-0.5
1957 †Mil N	129	364	46	99	19	5	5	40	29-1	9	19	.272	.339	.393	104	2	0-0	**.996**	2	106	116	1b117		-0.1
1958 †Mil N	138	372	41	115	22	5	6	55	42-7	3	14	.309	.386	.444	131	18	2-0	**.994**	6	118	104	1b122		1.9
1959	Mil N	115	263	23	60	15	1	1	33	35-6	3	12	.228	.321	.304	75	-8	0-0	.994	-0	98	81	1b87		-1.2
1960	Mil N	21	44	2	9	1	0	0	5	3-1	0	2	.205	.245	.227	36	-4	0-0	1.000	-2	48	128	1b17		-0.6
1962	Phi N	108	168	13	52	8	2	0	20	24-1	4	6	.310	.404	.381	117	6	1-1	.980	2	119	102	1b76		0.5
1963	Phi N	92	112	8	28	7	2	1	10	11-2	4	5	.250	.333	.375	105	1	0-0	.989	3	141	118	1b56		0.3
Total 7		714	1482	150	404	78	15	13	179	155-20	26	64	.273	.349	.372	101	8	4-1	.993	16	114	105	1b564		0.3

TORRE, JOE Joseph Paul B7.18.1940 Brooklyn NY BR/TR/6-2/212* d9.25 M24 b-Frank
1960	Mil N	2	2	0	1	0	0	0	0	0-0	0	1	.500	.500	.500	189	0	0-0	—	0			/H		0.0
1961	Mil N	113	406	40	113	21	4	10	42	28-4	4	60	.278	.330	.424	105	2	3-5	.982	-5	138	113	C112		0.1
1962	Mil N	80	220	23	62	8	1	5	26	24-2	2	24	.282	.355	.395	105	2	0-0	.986	8	128	122	C63		1.3
1963	Mil N★	142	501	57	147	19	4	14	71	42-4	5	79	.293	.350	.431	126	17	1-5	.994	3	134	79	C105,1b37,O2L		2.2
1964	Mil N★	154	601	87	193	36	5	20	109	36-4	7	67	.321	.365	.498	140	31	2-4	**.995**	0	142	77	C96,1b70		3.2
1965	Mil N★	148	523	68	152	21	1	27	80	61-7	8	79	.291	.372	.489	140	23	0-1	.991	9	84	96	C100,1b49		2.3
1966	Atl N★	148	546	83	172	20	3	36	101	60-8	2	61	.315	.382	.560	157	42	0-4	.984	0	129	112	C114,1b36		4.5
1967	Atl N★	135	477	67	132	18	1	20	68	49-7	3	75	.277	.345	.444	127	7	2-2	.991	0	143	—	C114,1b23		2.2
1968	StL N	115	424	45	115	11	2	10	55	34-7	5	72	.271	.332	.377	112	6	1-0	**.996**	-5	78	68	C92,1b29		0.5
1969	StL N	159	602	72	174	29	6	18	101	66-13	5	85	.289	.361	.447	125	21	0-0	.996	-5	91	**108**	1b144,C17		0.5
1970	StL N★	161	624	89	203	27	9	21	100	70-10	7	91	.325	.398	.498	135	32	2-2	.987	-10	93	96	C90,3b73/1		2.6
1971	StL N★	161	634	97	**230**	34	8	24	**137**	63-20	4	70	**.363**	.421	.555	167	57	4-1	.951	-22	82	73	3b161		3.7
1972	StL N★	149	544	71	157	26	6	11	81	54-13	8	74	.289	.357	.419	122	16	3-0	.963	-9	86	88	3b117,1b27		0.5
1973	StL N★	141	519	67	149	17	2	13	69	65-14	10	78	.287	.376	.403	116	13	2-0	.993	-10	96	108	1b114,3b58		-0.4
1974	StL N	147	529	59	149	28	1	11	70	69-9	8	88	.282	.371	.401	116	14	1-2	.992	2	**119**	**130**	1b139,3b18		0.5
1975	NY N	114	361	33	89	16	3	6	35	35-3	2	55	.247	.317	.357	89	-6	0-0	.950	1	95	126	1b78,3b4		-0.7
1976	NY N	114	310	36	95	10	3	5	31	21-1	5	35	.306	.358	.406	123	4	1-3	.989	3	116	82	1b78,3b4		0.5
1977	NY N	26	51	2	9	1	0	1	9	6-1	1	6	.176	.204	.294	34	-5	0-0	.989	2	118	—	1b16/3M		-0.8
Total 18		2209	7874	996	2342	344	59	252	1185	779-127	85	1094	.297	.365	.452	128	297	23-29	.990	-60	115	102	C903,1b787,3b515,O2L	21	22.7

TORREALBA, STEVE Steven Alexander B2.24.1978 Barquisimeto, Venez BR/TR/6-0/175* d10.6 f-Pablo [DL 2003 StL N 65]
2001 †Atl N	2	2	0	1	0	0	0	0	0-0	0	1	.500	.500	.500	158	0	0-0	1.000	0	0	0	C2		0.0
2002	Atl N	13	17	1	1	0	0	0	0	0-0	0	3	.059	.200	.059	-26	-3	0-0	1.000	-1	75	97	C12		-0.4
Total 2		15	19	1	2	0	0	0	0	3-0	0	4	.105	.227	.105	-7	-3	0-0	1.000	-1	75	54	C14	65	-0.4

TORREALBA, YORVIT Yorvit Adolfo B7.19.1978 Caracas, Venez BR/TR/5-11/190(180-200) d9.5
| 2001 | SF N | 3 | 4 | 0 | 2 | 0 | 0 | 0 | 2 | 0-0 | 0 | 1 | .500 | .500 | 1.000 | 291 | 1 | 0-0 | 1.000 | -0 | 0 | 0 | C3 | | 0.1 |
| 2002 | SF N | 53 | 136 | 12 | 38 | 10 | 0 | 2 | 14 | 14-2 | 3 | 20 | .279 | .355 | .397 | 105 | 1 | 0-0 | .993 | 2 | 86 | 96 | C53 | | 0.5 |

YEAR	TM LG	G	AB	R	H	2B	3B	HR	RBI	BB-IB	HP	SO	AVG	OBP	SLG	AOPS	ABR	SB-CS	FA	FR	RNG	THR	GAMES AT POSITION	DL	BFW
2003 †SF N		66	200	22	52	10	2	4	29	14-1	2	39	.260	.312	.390	81	-6	1-0	.997	7	130	151	C66/OL		0.5
2004 SF N		64	172	19	39	7	3	6	23	17-3	2	31	.227	.302	.407	79	-6	2-0	.995	6	129	86	C59		0.4
2005 SF N		34	93	18	21	8	0	1	7	9-1	1	25	.226	.301	.344	66	-4	1-0	1.000	2	129	192	C27/D		-0.1
Sea A		42	108	14	26	4	0	2	8	7-0	1	25	.241	.293	.333	71	-5	0-0	1.000	3	72	125	C41		0.1
Total 5		262	713	90	178	39	6	15	83	61-7	8	140	.250	.315	.384	82	-19	4-0	.997	20	110	124	C249/DOL		1.5

TORRES, ANDRES Andres Vungo (Feliciano) B1.26.1978 Aguadilla, PR BB/TR/5-10/175(175-190) [DetA98 4/117] d4.7 Col Miami-Dade Wolfson (FL) CC

2002 Det A		19	70	7	14	1	1	0	3	6-0	1	16	.200	.266	.243	40	-6	2-2	.981	-1	104	0	O19C		-0.7
2003 Det A		59	168	23	37	4	3	1	9	10-0	0	35	.220	.263	.298	50	-13	5-5	.991	-0	91	179	O50(1/36/16),D3		-1.4
2004 Det A		3	0	1	0	0	0	0	0	0-0	0	0	—	—	—	—	0	1-0	—	-0	0	0	/OCD		0.0
2005 Tex A		8	19	2	3	1	0	0	1	1-0	0	6	.158	.190	.211	9	-2	1-0	1.000	0	125	0	O5(0/4/2)		-0.2
Total 4		89	257	33	54	6	4	1	13	17-0	1	57	.210	.258	.276	44	-21	9-7	.988	-1	96	118	O75(1/60/18),D5		-2.3

TORRES, GIL Don Gilberto (Nunez) B8.23.1915 Regla, Cuba D1.10.1983 Regla, Cuba BR/TR/6-0/155 d4.25 f-Ricardo ▲

1940 Was A		2	0	0	0	0	0	0	0	0-0	0	0	—	—	—	—	0	0-0	1.000	0	184	0	P2		0.0
1944 Was A		134	524	42	140	20	6	0	58	21	1	24	.267	.297	.328	82	-15	10-7	.952	8	110	107	3b123,2b10,1b4		-0.1
1945 Was A		147	562	39	133	12	5	0	48	21	1	29	.237	.264	.276	62	-31	7-4	.953	-24	93	76	S145,3b2		-4.1
1946 Was A		63	185	18	47	8	0	0	13	11	0	12	.254	.296	.297	70	-8	3-2	.939	-2	97	88	S31,3b18,2b7,P3		-0.1
Total 4		346	1271	99	320	40	11	0	119	53	2	65	.252	.282	.301	72	-54	20-13	.951	-18	94	78	S176,3b143,2b17,P5,1b4		-6.2

TORRES, FELIX Felix (Sanchez) B5.1.1932 Ponce, PR BR/TR/5-11/165(165-180) d4.10

1962 LA A		127	451	44	117	19	4	11	74	28-5	4	73	.259	.306	.392	90	-8	0-0	.938	-0	105	88	3b123		-0.1
1963 LA A		138	463	40	121	32	1	4	51	30-0	3	73	.261	.307	.361	93	-4	1-0	.939	1	107	129	3b122,1b2		-0.1
1964 LA A		100	277	25	64	10	0	12	28	13-0	1	56	.231	.266	.397	91	-5	1-3	.970	-0	96	85	3b72,1b3		-0.1
Total 3		365	1191	109	302	61	5	27	153	71-5	8	202	.254	.297	.381	91	-17	2-3	.945	-1	104	103	3b317,1b5		-1.1

TORRES, HECTOR Hector Epitacio (Marroquin) B9.16.1945 Monterrey, Nuevo Leon, Mexico BR/TR/6-0/175* d4.10 C2

1968 Hou N		128	466	44	104	11	1	1	24	18-2	0	64	.223	.252	.258	54	-27	2-3	.958	-3	100	77	S127/2		-2.1
1969 Hou N		34	69	5	11	1	0	1	8	2-0	0	12	.159	.183	.217	12	-8	0-0	.944	-3	74	71	S22	21	-1.0
1970 Hou N		31	65	6	16	1	2	0	5	6-0	0	8	.246	.310	.323	73	-3	0-0	.947	-4	92	71	S18,2b4		-0.5
1971 Chi N		31	58	4	13	3	0	0	2	4-0	0	10	.224	.274	.276	49	-4	0-0	.962	-4	97	76	S18,2b4		-0.5
1972 Mon N		83	181	14	28	4	1	2	7	13-1	1	26	.155	.215	.221	24	-19	0-2	.965	-7	95	94	2b60,S16,O2(1/0/1)/P3		-2.?
1973 Hou N		38	66	3	6	1	0	0	2	7-0	1	13	.091	.189	.106	-16	-11	0-1	.952	1	124	73	S22,2b13		-0.?
1975 SD N		112	352	31	91	12	0	5	26	22-3	0	32	.259	.297	.335	82	-10	2-3	.971	8	124	109	S75,3b42,2b16		0.9
1976 SD N		74	215	9	42	6	0	4	15	16-3	1	31	.195	.254	.279	56	-13	2-1	.949	-20	86	84	S63,3b4,2b3		-2.?
1977 Tor A		91	266	33	64	7	3	5	26	16-1	1	33	.241	.282	.346	70	-12	1-1	.980	-0	99	79	S68,2b23,3b2		-0.?
Total 9		622	1738	148	375	46	7	18	116	104-10	4	229	.216	.260	.281	55	-107	7-11	.962	-32	101	83	S433,2b126,3b49,O2(1/0/1)/P	21	-10.?

TORRES, RICARDO Ricardo J. (Martinez) B4.16.1891 Regla, Cuba D4.17.1960 Regla, Cuba BR/TR/5-11/160 d5.18 s-Gil

1920 Was A		16	30	8	10	1	0	0	3	1	0	4	.333	.355	.367	94	-0	0-0	1.000	-1	42	45	1b7,C5		-0.?
1921 Was A		2	3	1	1	0	0	0	1	1	0	1	.333	.500	.333	122	0	0-0	.750	-1	0	0	C2		0.0
1922 Was A		4	4	0	0	0	0	0	0	0	0	1	.000	.000	.000	-99	-1	0-0	1.000	1	0	256	C3		0.0
Total 3		22	37	9	11	1	0	0	4	3	0	6	.297	.333	.324	76	-1	0-0	.955	-1	44	91	C10,1b7		-0.?

TORRES, RUSTY Rosendo (Hernandez) B9.30.1948 Aguadilla, PR BB/TR/5-10/180* [NYA66 54/811] d9.20

1971 NY A		9	26	5	10	3	0	2	3	0-0	0	8	.385	.385	.731	220	4	0-1	1.000	0	122	0	O5(0/1/4)		0.?
1972 NY A		80	199	15	42	7	0	3	13	18-3	1	44	.211	.280	.291	72	-3	0-4	.978	-3	83	105	O62(1/1/60)		-1.?
1973 Cle A		122	312	31	64	8	1	7	28	50-5	3	62	.205	.317	.304	75	-9	6-5	.976	-2	92	136	O114(1/37/77)		-1.?
1974 Cle A		108	150	19	28	2	0	3	12	13-1	0	26	.187	.248	.260	48	-10	2-1	.959	-2	92	220	O94(35/38/24)/D		-1.?
1976 Cal A		120	264	37	54	16	3	6	27	36-3	0	39	.205	.299	.356	97	0	4-4	.990	-4	92	88	O105(0/104/1)/3D		-0.?
1977 Cal A		58	77	9	12	1	1	3	10	10-0	0	18	.156	.250	.312	55	-5	0-1	.984	-1	92	55	O54(4/40/10)	41	-0.?
1978 Chi A		16	44	7	14	3	0	3	6	6-0	0	7	.318	.400	.591	173	4	0-1	.964	-1	98	0	O14(4/5/8)		0.?
1979 Chi A		90	170	26	43	5	0	8	24	23-1	2	37	.253	.349	.424	107	2	0-0	.976	-0	98	103	O85(36/17/35)	15	-0.?
1980 KC A		51	72	10	12	0	0	3	8	8-0	0	7	.167	.250	.167	16	-8	1-3	.973	5	130	221	O40(15/8/21)/D		-0.?
Total 9		654	1314	159	279	45	5	35	126	164-13	6	246	.212	.301	.334	82	-29	13-20	.977	-5	94	122	O573(96/251/240),D8/3	56	-5.?

TORVE, KELVIN Kelvin Curtis B1.10.1960 Rapid City SD BL/TR/6-3/205(190-205) [SFN81 2/36] d6.25 Col Oral Roberts

1988 Min A		12	16	1	3	0	0	1	2	1-0	0	2	.188	.235	.375	66	-1	0-1	1.000	-0	58	50	1b4/D		-0.?
1990 NY N		20	38	0	11	4	0	0	2	4-0	2	5	.289	.386	.395	115	1	0-0	1.000	-2	0	118	1b9/OL		-0.?
1991 NY N		10	8	0	0	0	0	0	0	0-0	0	1	.000	.000	.000	-99	-2	0-0	1.000	1	2399	0	/1		-0.?
Total 3		42	62	1	14	4	0	1	4	5-0	2	12	.226	.304	.339	77	-2	0-1	1.000	-1	40	101	1b14/OLD		-0.?

TOVAR, CESAR Cesar Leonardo "Pepito" (b Cesar Leonard Perez (Tovar)) B7.3.1940 Caracas, Venez D7.14.1994 Caracas, Venez BR/TR/5-9/155* d4.12 OF(378/471/205)

1965 Min A		18	25	3	5	2	0	0	2	2-0	0	3	.200	.259	.240	41	-2	2-0	.800	1	136	197	2b4,3b2,O2C/S		-0.?
1966 Min A		134	465	57	121	19	5	2	41	44-1	4	50	.260	.325	.335	86	-7	16-6	.978	-4	104	79	2b76,S31,O24(4/20/0)		-0.?
1967 Min A		164	649	98	173	32	7	6	47	46-0	13	51	.267	.325	.365	97	-2	19-11	.994	-8	118	124	O74(10/64/5),3b70,2b36,S9		-0.?
1968 Min A		157	613	89	167	31	6	6	47	34-0	17	41	.272	.326	.372	106	6	35-13	.966	6	123	110	O78(39/34/10),3b75,S35,2b18/PC1		-0.?
1969 Min A		158	535	99	154	25	5	11	52	37-3	9	37	.288	.342	.415	109	6	45-12	.983	3	117	152	O113(39/70/8),2b41,3b20		-0.?
1970 †Min A		161	650	120	195	36	13	10	54	52-5	8	47	.300	.356	.442	118	15	30-15	.977	1	111	127	O151(39/134/2),2b8,3b4		-0.?
1971 Min A		157	657	94	204	29	3	1	45	45-5	3	39	.311	.356	.368	103	3	18-14	.986	13	118	150	O154(98/44/47),3b7,2b2		-0.?
1972 Min A		141	548	86	145	20	6	2	31	39-6	14	34	.265	.329	.334	93	-4	21-10	.983	4	108	97	O139(38/5/101)		-0.?
1973 Phi N		97	328	49	88	18	4	1	21	29-2	5	35	.268	.335	.357	90	-4	6-4	.928	-3	71	90	3b46,O24(6/3/16),2b22	18	-0.?
1974 Tex A		138	562	78	164	24	6	4	58	47-0	9	33	.292	.354	.377	114	11	13-9	.986	6	103	137	O135(66/87/11),D3		-0.?
1975 Tex A		102	427	53	110	16	0	3	28	27-0	3	25	.258	.306	.316	77	-13	16-11	.919	-4	84	46	D66,O31(25/6/1)/2	15	-2.?
†Oak A		19	26	5	6	1	0	0	3	3-0	0	3	.231	.310	.269	66	-1	4-0	1.000	-1	29	0	2b4,3b3/SD		-0.?
Year		121	453	58	116	17	0	3	31	30-0	3	28	.256	.306	.313	76	-14	20-11	.896	-6	84	46	D73,O31(25/6/1),2b5,3b3/S		-2.?
1976 Oak A		29	45	1	8	0	0	0	4	4-0	2	4	.178	.275	.178	36	-4	1-2	.958	-1	88	0	O20(14/2/4),D4	73	-0.?
NY A		13	39	2	6	1	0	0	2	4-1	1	3	.154	.250	.179	27	-3	0-1	1.000	4	149	189	D10,2b3		-0.?
Year		42	84	3	14	1	0	0	6	8-1	3	7	.167	.263	.179	32	-7	1-3	.958	-0	88	0	O20(14/2/4),D14,2b3		-0.?
Total 12		1488	5569	834	1546	253	55	46	435	413-23	88	410	.278	.335	.368	99	0	226-108	.980	17	111	124	O945C,3b227,2b215,D90,S77/1CP	106	?

TOWNE, BABE Jay King B3.12.1880 Coon Rapids IA D10.29.1938 Des Moines IA BR/TR/5-10/180 d8.1

| 1906 †Chi A | | 14 | 36 | 3 | 10 | 0 | 0 | 0 | 5 | 6 | 7 | 0 | .278 | .395 | .278 | 115 | 1 | 0 | .923 | -2 | 141 | 69 | C13 | | 0.? |

TOWNSEND, GEORGE George Hodgson "Sleepy" B6.4.1867 Hartsdale NY D3.15.1930 New Haven CT BR/TR/5-7.5/180 d6.25 Col NYU

1887 Phi AA		31	109	12	21	3	0	0	14	3	0		.193	.214	.220	21	-12	8	.865	-5			C28,O3(1/0/2)		-0.?
1888 Phi AA		42	161	13	25	6	0	0	12	4	1		.155	.181	.193	20	-14	2	.912	1			C42		-0.?
1890 Bal AA		18	67	6	16	4	1	0	9	4	0		.239	.282	.328	76	-2	3	.930	4	116	139	C18		-0.?
1891 Bal AA		61	204	29	39	5	4	0	18	20	5	21	.191	.279	.255	53	-13	3	.909	2	141	94	C58,O3(0/1/2)		-0.?
Total 4		152	541	60	101	18	5	0	53	31	6	21	.187	.239	.238	40	-41	16	.905	3	135	105	C146,O6(1/1/4)		-0.?

TOY, JIM James Madison B2.20.1858 Beaver Falls PA D3.13.1919 Cresson PA 5-6/160 d4.20

1887 Cle AA		109	423	56	94	20	5	1	56	17	2		.222	.256	.300	56	-26	8	.975	4	113	111	1b82,O11(2/2/7),C10,3b8,S3		-0.?
1890 Bro AA		44	160	11	29	3	0	0	7	11	1		.181	.238	.200	30	-14	2	.867	-7	82	121	C44		-0.?
Total 2		153	583	67	123	23	5	1	63	28	3		.211	.251	.273	50	-40	10	.975	-4	113	111	1b82,C54,O11(2/2/7),3b8,S3		-0.?

TRABER, JIM James Joseph B12.26.1961 Columbus OH BL/TL/6-0/194(194-215) [BalA82 21/544] d9.21 Col Oklahoma St.

1984 Bal A		10	21	3	5	0	0	2	2	2-0	0	4	.238	.292	.238	53	-1	0-0	—	0		0	D9		-0.?
1986 Bal A		65	212	28	54	7	0	13	44	18-2	5	31	.255	.321	.472	116	4	0-0	.988	2	98	121	1b29,D21,O8(7/0/1)		-0.?
1988 Bal A		103	352	25	78	6	0	10	45	19-3	1	42	.222	.261	.324	65	-18	1-2	.990	7	141	105	1b57,D30,O11(2/0/8)		-0.?
1989 Bal A		86	234	14	49	8	0	4	26	19-1	0	41	.209	.266	.295	60	-13	4-3	.998	5	132	119	1b69,D5		-0.?
Total 4		264	819	70	186	21	0	27	117	58-6	6	118	.227	.279	.352	77	-28	5-5	.993	13	129	114	1b155,D65,O19(9/0/9)		-0.?

TRACEWSKI, DICK Richard Joseph B2.3.1935 Eynon PA BR/TR/5-11/167* d4.12 M1/C24

1962 LA N		15	2	3	0	0	0	0	0	0-0	0	0	.000	.000	.000	—	0	0-0	1.000	1	186	0	S4		-0.?
1963 †LA N		104	217	23	49	7	1	1	10	19-1	0	39	.226	.287	.258	63	-11	2-3	.957	-0	101	91	S81,2b23		-0.?
1964 LA N		106	304	31	75	13	4	1	26	31-4	0	61	.247	.315	.326	88	-5	3-3	.970	-8	89	81	2b56,3b30,S19		-0.?
1965 †LA N		78	186	17	40	6	0	1	29	25-4	2	30	.215	.313	.263	69	-7	2-6	.950	-2	110	96	3b53,2b14,S7		-0.?

YEAR	TM LG	G	AB	R	H	2B	3B	HR	RBI	BB-IB	HP	SO	AVG	OBP	SLG	AOPS	ABR	SB-CS	FA	FR	RNG	THR	GAMES AT POSITION	DL	BFW
1966	Det A	81	124	15	24	1	1	0	7	10-0	0	32	.194	.252	.218	36	-10	1-1	.947	1	100	118	2b70,S3		-0.7
1967	Det A	74	107	19	30	4	2	1	9	8-0	0	20	.280	.325	.383	107	1	1-1	.965	6	105	136	S44,2b12,3b10		0.9
1968	†Det A	90	212	30	33	3	1	4	15	24-0	0	51	.156	.239	.236	44	-14	3-0	.982	-8	94	102	S51,3b16,2b14		-2.0
1969	Det A	66	79	10	11	2	0	0	4	15-1	0	20	.139	.277	.165	25	-8	3-0	.957	5	97	153	S41,2b13,3b6		0.0
Total	8	614	1231	148	262	31	9	8	91	134-10	2	253	.213	.289	.272	65	-54	15-14	.958	-6	101	106	S250,2b202,3b115		-4.1

TRACY, ANDY Andrew Michael B12.11.1973 Bowling Green OH BL/TR/6-3/220* [MonN96 16/460] d4.25 Col Bowling Green

2000	Mon N	83	192	29	50	8	1	11	32	22-1	2	61	.260	.339	.484	105	1	1-0	.882	-5	86	46	3b34,1b27		-0.5
2001	Mon N	38	55	4	6	1	0	2	8	6-0	0	26	.109	.190	.236	11	-8	0-0	1.000	1	83	0	3b11,1b3,D2		-0.9
2004	Col N	15	16	1	3	1	0	0	1	1-0	0	8	.188	.235	.250	23	-2	0-0	1.000	-0	71	0	/3		-0.2
Total	3	136	263	34	59	10	1	13	41	29-1	2	95	.224	.302	.418	81	-9	1-0	.913	-7	86	34	3b46,1b30,D2		-1.6

TRACY, CHAD Chad Austin B5.22.1980 Charlotte NC BL/TR/6-2/200* [AriN01 7/218] d4.21 Col East Carolina

2004	Ari N	143	481	45	137	29	3	8	53	35-3	0	60	.285	.343	.407	88	-8	2-3	.935	11	104	116	3b135,1b11/OL		0.3
2005	Ari N	145	503	73	155	34	4	27	72	35-4	2	78	.308	.359	.553	130	21	3-4	.996	-1	100	113	1b80,O51(6/0/47)/D		1.1
Total	2	288	984	118	292	63	7	35	125	80-7	2	138	.297	.351	.482	109	13	5-4	.935	10	104	116	3b135,1b91,O52(7/0/47)/D		1.4

TRACY, JIM James Edwin B12.31.1955 Hamilton OH BL/TR/6-3/193* [ChiN77*4/88] d7.20 M5/C6 Col Marietta

1980	Chi N	42	122	12	31	3	3	3	9	13-1	0	37	.254	.326	.402	94	-1	2-2	.950	-6	66	0	O31(22/0/14)/1		-1.0
1981	Chi N	45	63	6	15	2	1	0	5	12-0	0	14	.238	.355	.302	84	-1	1-0	1.000	-2	76	0	O11(10/0/1)		-0.3
Total	2	87	185	18	46	5	4	3	14	25-1	0	51	.249	.336	.368	91	-2	3-2	.964	-8	69	0	O42(32/0/15)/1		-1.3

RAFFLEY, JOHN John M. B1862 Chicago IL D5.15.1900 Baltimore MD d6.15 b-Bill

1889	Lou AA	1	2	0	1	0	0	0	0	0-0	0	0	.500	.500	.500	189	0	0	.000	-0	0	0	/OR		0.0

RAFFLEY, BILL William Franklin B12.21.1859 Staten Island NY D6.23.1908 Des Moines IA BR/TR/5-11.5/185 d7.27 b-John

1878	Chi N	2	9	1	1	0	0	0	1	0-0		1	.111	.111	.111	-25	-1		1.000	-1			C2		-0.2
1883	Cin N	30	105	17	21	5	0	0	8	4			.200	.229	.248	51	-6		.851	0			C29,S2		-0.3
1884	Bal AA	53	210	25	37	4	6	0		3	1		.176	.192	.252	42	-14		.926	-4			C47,O6R/1		-1.3
1885	Bal AA	69	254	27	39	4	5	1	20	17	3		.154	.215	.220	38	-18		**.943**	4			C61,O10(0/5/5),2b3		-0.8
1886	Bal AA	25	85	15	18	0	1	0	7	10	0		.212	.295	.235	68	-3	8	.952	-3			C25		-0.3
Total	5	179	663	85	116	13	12	1	36	34	4	1	.175	.220	.235	45	-42	8	.927	-3			C164,O16(0/5/11),2b3,S2/1		-2.9

RAGESSER, WALT Walter Joseph B6.14.1887 Lafayette IN D12.14.1970 Lafayette IN BR/TR/6-0/175 d7.30 Mil 1918 Col Purdue

1913	Bos N	2	0	0	0	0	0	0	0	0	0	—	—	—	—	0	0	0	1.000	-0	-0	0	C2		0.0
1915	Bos N	7	7	1	0	0	0	0	0	0	0	2	.000	.000	.000	-99	-2	0	.944	1	231	51	C7		-0.1
1916	Bos N	41	54	3	11	1	0	0	4	5	1	10	.204	.283	.222	59	-2	0	.971	4	178	113	C29		0.3
1917	Bos N	98	297	23	66	10	2	0	25	15	2	36	.222	.264	.269	68	-12	5	.971	0	113	91	C94		-0.4
1918	Bos N	7	1	0	0	0	0	0	0	0	0	0	.000	.000	.000	-99	-0	0	.833	1	0	156	C7		0.0
1919	Bos N	20	40	3	7	0	0	0	3	2	1	10	.175	.233	.175	39	-3	1	.959	-1	92	150	C14		-0.3
	Phi N	35	114	7	27	7	0	0	8	9	1	31	.237	.298	.298	74	-3	4	.953	-2	90	106	C34		-0.2
	Year	55	154	10	34	9	0	0	11	11	2	41	.221	.281	.279	67	-6	5	.954	-3	90	115	C48		-0.5
1920	Phi N	62	176	17	37	11	1	6	26	6	2	36	.210	.236	.386	73	-7	4-0	.944	-10	76	77	C52		-1.2
Total	7	272	689	54	148	31	3	6	66	35	7	125	.215	.260	.295	67	-29	14-0	.961	-7	105	95	C239		-1.9

RAMBACK, RED Stephen Joseph B11.1.1915 Iselin PA D12.28.1979 Buffalo NY BL/TL/6-0/175 d9.15

1940	NY N	2	4	0	1	0	0	0	0	0	0	1	.250	.400	.250	82	0	1	.667	-0	79	0	/OR		-0.1

RAMMELL, ALAN Alan Stuart B2.21.1958 Garden Grove CA BR/TR/6-0/175(160-185) [DetA76 2/26] d9.9 M3/C4

1977	Det A	19	43	6	8	0	0	0	4	4-0	2	12	.186	.255	.186	21	-5	0-0	.961	-8	74	57	S19		-1.1
1978	Det A	139	448	49	120	14	6	2	34	45-0	2	56	.268	.335	.339	88	-7	3-1	.979	5	103	118	S139		1.3
1979	Det A	142	460	68	127	11	4	6	50	43-0	0	55	.276	.335	.357	85	-10	17-14	.961	-4	92	109	S142		-0.1
1980	Det A★	146	560	107	168	21	5	9	65	69-2	3	63	.300	.376	.404	112	11	12-12	.980	-18	92	92	S144		0.7
1981	Det A	105	392	52	101	15	3	2	31	49-2	3	31	.258	.342	.327	91	-3	10-3	.983	13	107	102	S105		2.2
1982	Det A	157	489	66	126	34	3	9	57	57-2	1	47	.258	.325	.395	97	-1	19-8	.978	1	99	111	S157		1.7
1983	Det A	142	505	83	161	31	2	14	66	57-2	0	64	.319	.385	.471	138	28	30-10	.979	-8	90	92	S140		3.7
1984	†Det A✻	139	555	85	174	34	5	14	69	60-2	3	63	.314	.382	.468	134	28	19-13	.980	-3	95	110	S114,D22	22	3.5
1985	Det A★	149	605	79	156	21	7	13	57	50-4	2	71	.258	.312	.380	90	-9	14-5	.977	-13	93	98	S149		-0.5
1986	Det A	151	574	107	159	33	7	21	75	59-4	5	57	.277	.347	.469	120	16	25-12	.969	14	110	113	S149,D2		4.5
1987	†Det A★	151	597	109	205	34	3	28	105	60-8	3	47	.343	.402	.551	157	50	21-2	.971	-4	99	109	S149		6.1
1988	Det A✻	128	466	73	145	24	1	15	69	46-8	4	46	.311	.373	.464	139	25	7-4	.980	-1	100	91	S125	18	3.4
1989	Det A	121	449	54	109	20	3	5	43	45-1	4	46	.243	.314	.334	85	-6	10-2	.985	16	**112**	85	S117,D2	19	1.8
1990	Det A★	146	559	71	170	37	1	14	89	68-7	1	55	.304	.377	.449	130	24	12-10	.979	1	99	107	S142,D3		3.5
1991	Det A	101	375	57	93	20	0	9	55	37-1	0	39	.248	.320	.373	90	-5	11-2	.979	4	111	101	S92,D6	27	0.7
1992	Det A	29	102	11	28	7	1	1	11	15-0	1	4	.275	.370	.392	113	2	2-2	.977	-0	101	90	S27/D	142	0.4
1993	Det A	112	401	72	132	25	3	12	60	38-2	2	38	.329	.388	.496	136	21	12-8	.989	-6	104	64	S63,3b35,O8(4/4/0),D6	12	1.9
1994	Det A	76	292	38	78	17	1	8	28	16-1	1	35	.267	.307	.414	83	-8	3-0	.968	2	101	108	S63,D11		-0.3
1995	Det A	74	223	28	60	12	0	2	23	27-4	0	19	.269	.345	.350	82	-5	3-1	.980	-4	100	87	S60,D6	11	-0.5
1996	Det A	66	193	16	45	2	0	1	16	10-0	0	27	.233	.267	.259	35	-20	6-0	.976	-4	101	51	S2,b11,3b8/OL	55	-1.8
Total	20	2293	8288	1231	2365	412	55	185	1003	850-48	37	874	.285	.352	.415	110	124	236-109	.977	-19	100	100	S2139,D59,3b43,2b11,O9(5/4/0)	306	31.1

RAMMELL, BUBBA Thomas Bubba B11.6.1971 Knoxville TN BR/TR/6-2/220(205-220) [DetA94 11/305] d4.1 Col Tennessee

1997	Det A	44	123	14	28	5	0	4	13	15-0	0	35	.228	.307	.366	76	-4	3-1	1.000	0	104	63	O28(13/0/16),D15		-0.6
1998	TB A	59	199	28	57	18	1	12	35	16-0	0	45	.286	.338	.568	127	7	0-2	1.000	-2	77	140	O37(23/0/16),D19		0.2
1999	TB A	82	283	49	82	19	0	14	39	43-1	1	37	.290	.384	.505	123	11	0-2	.993	-1	103	44	O74(61/0/20),D6		0.6
2000	TB A	66	189	19	52	11	2	7	33	21-0	2	30	.275	.352	.466	107	2	3-0	1.000	-4	78	75	O48(26/0/24),D9		-0.3
	†NY N	36	56	9	13	2	0	3	12	6-0	1	19	.232	.323	.429	94	-1	1-0	.963	0	96	121	O25(11/0/16)		-0.1
2001	SD N	142	490	66	128	20	3	25	92	48-2	4	78	.261	.330	.467	112	7	2-2	.985	2	108	61	O132(34/0/102),D3		0.2
2002	SD N	133	403	54	98	16	1	17	56	53-2	3	71	.243	.333	.414	109	2	1-3	.973	-6	90	60	O122(23/0/104),D2		-1.0
2003	NY A	22	55	4	11	5	0	0	5	6-0	0	10	.200	.279	.291	51	-4	0-0	1.000	1	184	0	D15,O3L		-0.4
Total	7	584	1798	243	469	96	7	82	285	210-5	9	10	325	.261	.339	.459	109	20	10-10	.986	-10	97	67	O469(194/0/298),D69	-1.4

RAVIS, CECIL Cecil Howell B8.8.1913 Riverdale GA BL/TR/6-1.5/185 d5.16 Mil 1942-45

1933	Was A	18	43	7	13	1	0	0	2	2	1	5	.302	.348	.326	80	-1	0-0	.974	2	132	52	3b15		0.1
1934	Was A	109	392	48	125	22	4	1	53	24	2	37	.319	.361	.403	101	0	1-5	.937	4	113	128	3b99		0.5
1935	Was A	138	534	85	170	27	8	0	61	41	9	24	.318	.377	.399	104	4	4-2	.963	21	**118**	**173**	3b114,O16L		2.6
1936	Was A	138	517	77	164	34	10	2	92	39	1	21	.317	.366	.433	102	-1	4-4	.938	-5	98	119	S71,O53(1/0/52),2b4,3b2		-0.1
1937	Was A	135	526	72	181	27	7	3	66	39	5	14	.344	.395	.439	115	12	3-2	.965	-8	98	**122**	S129		1.3
1938	Was A☆	146	567	96	190	30	5	5	67	58	4	22	.335	.401	.432	117	16	6-5	.950	-4	102	110	S143		2.1
1939	Was A	130	476	55	139	20	9	5	63	34	2	25	.292	.342	.403	97	-4	0-3	.958	-5	101	106	S118		-0.1
1940	Was A★	136	528	60	170	37	11	2	76	48	2	23	.322	.381	.445	121	17	0-1	.934	11	108	**127**	3b113,S23		3.1
1941	Was A★	152	608	106	218	39	19	2	101	52	1	25	.359	.410	.520	152	44	2-2	.964	-0	98	104	S136,3b16		5.1
1945	Was A	15	54	4	13	2	1	0	10	4	1	5	.241	.293	.315	83	-1	0-1	.920	-1	94	154	3b14		-0.2
1946	Was A	137	465	45	117	22	3	1	56	45	4	47	.252	.323	.318	85	-9	2-4	.959	-18	95	95	S75,3b56		-2.5
1947	Was A	74	204	10	44	4	1	1	10	16	0	19	.216	.273	.260	50	-14	1-3	.932	-2	104	95	3b39,S15		-1.7
Total		1328	4914	665	1544	265	78	27	657	402	31	291	.314	.370	.416	109	65	23-32	.955	-4	99	110	S710,3b468,O69(17/0/52),2b4		10.2

RAXLER, BRIAN Brian Lee B9.26.1967 Waukegan IL D11.19.2004 San Antonio TX BL/TL/5-10/200 [LAN88 16/400] d4.24 Col New Orleans

1990	LA N	9	11	0	1	0	0	0	1	2-0	0	4	.091	.091	.182	-28	-2	0-0	1.000	1	226	0	1b3		-0.2

RAY, JIM James (b James Trahey) B2.14.1860 Jackson MI D7.28.1905 Jackson MI 5-11/180 d9.6

1884	Ind AA	6	21	2	6	0	0	0		2	0		.286	.348	.286	112	0		.857	-2			C4,1b2		-0.1

RAYNOR, PIE Harold Joseph B11.11.1899 Framingham MA D3.16.1972 Pittsburgh PA BR/TR/6-0/170 d9.15 M6 HF1948

1920	Pit N	17	52	6	11	3	1	0	2	3	1	6	.212	.268	.308	63	-2	1-3	.860	-7	74	61	S17		-1.1
1921	Pit N	7	19	0	5	0	0	0	2	1	0	2	.263	.300	.263	49	-1	0-0	.917	-0	104	0	3b3/S		-0.9
1922	Pit N	142	571	89	161	17	12	4	81	27	4	28	.282	.319	.375	77	-21	17-3	.945	-8	89	105	3b124,S18		-1.6
1923	Pit N	153	616	108	208	19	**19**	12	101	34	5	19	.338	.377	.489	106	19	28-13	.950	9	103	115	3b152/S		3.6

YEAR	TM LG	G	AB	R	H	2B	3B	HR	RBI	BB-IB	HP	SO	AVG	OBP	SLG	AOPS	ABR	SB-CS	FA	FR	RNG	THR	GAMES AT POSITION	DL	BFW
1924	Pit N	142	545	86	160	26	13	6	82	37	1	26	.294	.340	.417	100	-1	24-18	.968	6	102	**144**	3b141		1.
1925	†Pit N	150	591	114	189	39	14	6	106	52	2	19	.320	.377	.464	106	6	15-9	**.957**	23	107	154	3b150/S		3.
1926	Pit N	152	574	83	182	25	17	3	92	38	1	14	.317	.361	.436	108	5	8	.952	6	99	128	3b148,S3		2.
1927	†Pit N	149	573	93	196	32	9	5	106	22	3	11	.342	.370	.455	112	9	11	.962	14	100	109	3b143,S9		2.
1928	Pit N	144	569	91	192	38	12	3	124	28	1	10	.337	.370	.462	112	9	12	.946	6	103	57	3b144		1.
1929	Pit N	130	540	94	192	27	12	4	108	30	3	7	.356	.393	.472	111	8	13	.951	3	95	127	3b130		1.
1930	Pit N	130	497	90	182	22	11	9	119	48	1	19	.366	.423	.509	124	20	7	.941	5	109	74	3b130		2.
1931	Pit N	**155**	615	81	183	37	15	2	103	54	0	28	.298	.336	.416	107	6	6	.925	-10	97	76	3b155		0.
1932	Pit N	135	513	74	169	27	10	2	68	32	4	20	.329	.373	.433	118	13	6	.936	-2	94	66	3b127		1.
1933	Pit N★	**154**	624	85	190	27	6	1	82	35	1	24	.304	.342	.372	104	3	5	.946	-2	98	77	3b154		0.
1934	Pit N★	119	444	62	137	22	10	1	61	21	1	27	.309	.341	.410	98	-2	3	.954	-10	84	**108**	3b110,M		-0.
1935	Pit N	57	204	24	57	10	3	1	36	10	3	17	.279	.323	.373	84	-5	2	.888	-3	94	28	3b49/1M		-0.
1937	Pit N	5	12	3	2	0	0	0	0	0	0	1	.167	.167	.167	-9	-2	0	1.000	1	152	0	3b3,M		-0.
Total 17		1941	7559	1183	2416	371	164	58	1273	472	31	278	.320	.362	.435	107	64	158-46	.947	25	99	101	3b1863,S50/1		18.

TREACEY, FRED   Frederick S. B1847 Brooklyn NY 5-9.5/145 d5.16 b-Pete

1871	Chi NA	25	124	39	42	7	5	**4**	33	2		5	.339	.349	.573	144	5	13-5	**.918**	7	229	201	O25L		0*
1872	Ath NA	**47**	236	53	65	7	3	2	31	5		10	.275	.290	.356	97	-1	7-5	.814	-2	59	108	O47C		-0.
1873	Phi NA	51	243	49	62	7	2	1	31	5		7	.255	.270	.313	70	-10	4-3	.761	2	140	316	O51(2/50/0)		-0.
1874	Chi NA	35	148	18	28	5	0	0	12	2		6	.189	.200	.223	35	-10	4-4	.790	7	302	350	O35(2/11/24)		0.
1875	Cen NA	11	46	9	12	3	0	0	2	2		0	.261	.292	.326	124	2	1-0	.848	1	108	214	O11L		-0.
	Phi NA	43	179	23	38	3	3	0	15	1		3	.212	.217	.263	63	-7	6-3	.858	5	54	103	O54(53/1/0)		-0.
	Year	54	225	32	50	6	3	0	17	3		3	.222	.232	.276	75	-6	7-3	.856	3	64	126	O57(52/0/5)		-0.
1876	NY N	**57**	256	47	54	5	1	0	18	1		9	.211	.214	.238	58	-9		.844	9	84	36	O57(52/0/5)		-0.
Total 5 NA		212	976	191	247	32	13	7	124	17		31	.253	.266	.334	84	-21	35-20	.823	16	135	205	O212(82/109/24)		-0.

TREACEY, PETE   Peter B1852 Brooklyn NY d8.5 b-Fred Col Fordham

| 1876 | NY N | 2 | 5 | 1 | 0 | 0 | 0 | 0 | 0 | 1 | | | .000 | .167 | .000 | -46 | -1 | | .750 | -1 | 84 | 0 | S2 | | -0. |

TREADAWAY, RAY   Edgar Raymond B10.31.1907 Ragland AL D10.12.1935 Chattanooga TN BL/TR/5-7/150 d9.17

| 1930 | Was A | 6 | 19 | 1 | 4 | 2 | 0 | 0 | 1 | 0 | | 3 | .211 | .211 | .316 | 31 | -2 | 0-0 | .833 | -1 | 63 | 147 | 3b4 | | -0. |

TREADWAY, GEORGE   George B. B11.11.1866 Greenup Co. KY BL/TL/6-0/185 d4.27

1893	Bal N	115	458	78	119	16	17	1	67	58	4	50	.260	.348	.376	91	-7	24	.901	8	141	94	O115(1/0/114)		-0.
1894	Bro N	124	482	125	159	28	26	4	102	73	2	43	.330	.420	.521	135	29	27	.893	-1	75	39	O123(121/0/2)/1		-1.
1895	Bro N	87	343	56	89	14	3	8	57	33	2	22	.259	.328	.388	91	-4	9	.886	-8	58	157	O87R		-0.
1896	Lou N	2	7	0	1	0	0	0	1	1	0	0	.143	.250	.143	5	-1	0	.500	-1	0	0	/OR1		-0.
Total 4		328	1290	259	368	58	46	13	227	165	8	115	.285	.370	.432	108	17	60	.891	-2	94	87	O326(122/0/204),1b2		-0.

TREADWAY, JEFF   Hugh Jeffery B1.22.1963 Columbus GA BL/TR/5-11/170* d9.4 Col Georgia

1987	Cin N	23	84	9	28	4	0	2	4	2-0		6	.333	.356	.452	108	1	1-0	.958	-4	85	113	2b21		-0.
1988	Cin N	103	301	30	76	19	4	2	29	27-7	3	30	.252	.315	.362	92	-3	2-0	.984	7	109	104	2b97,3b2	27	0.
1989	Atl N	134	473	58	131	18	3	8	40	30-3	3	38	.277	.317	.378	97	-3	3-2	.981	6	98	121	2b123,3b6		0.
1990	Atl N	128	474	56	134	20	2	11	59	25-1	3	42	.283	.320	.403	93	-5	3-4	.976	24	**116**	107	2b122		1.
1991	†Atl N	106	306	41	98	17	2	3	32	23-1	2	19	.320	.368	.418	115	7	2-2	.960	1	105	92	2b93		0.
1992	†Atl N	61	126	5	28	6	1	0	5	9-4	0	16	.222	.274	.286	55	-7	1-2	.993	1	103	145	2b45/3	81	-0.
1993	Cle A	97	221	25	67	14	1	2	27	14-2	1	21	.303	.347	.403	101	-1	1-1	.933	-1	99	83	3b42,2b19,D4		0.
1994	LA N	52	67	14	20	3	0	0	5	5-0	1	8	.299	.351	.343	88	-1	1-1	.950	1	106	104	2b24,3b3	23	-0.
1995	LA N	17	17	2	2	0	1	0	3	0-0	1	2	.118	.118	.235	-11	-3	0-0	—	0	0	0	3b2/2		-0.
	Mon N	41	50	4	12	2	0	0	10	5-1	0	2	.240	.309	.280	55	-3	0-1	1.000	-0	57	2b11/3		18	-0.
	Year	58	67	6	14	2	1	0	13	5-1	1	4	.209	.264	.269	41	-6	0-1	1.000	-0	99	83	2b12,3b3		-0.
Total 9		762	2119	244	596	103	14	28	208	140-19	12	184	.281	.326	.383	94	-16	14-13	.975	36	106	109	2b556,3b57,D4	149	3.

TREADWAY, RED   Thadford Leon B4.28.1920 Athlone (now Bowlens Creek) NC D5.26.1994 Atlanta GA BL/TR/5-10/175 d7.25 Col Barton

1944	NY N	50	170	23	51	5	2	0	5	13	0	11	.300	.350	.353	98	0	2	.957	-0	106	77	O38(10/2/27)		-0.
1945	NY N	88	224	31	54	4	2	4	23	20	0	13	.241	.303	.330	75	-8	3	.940	-4	91	72	O60(27/18/18)		-1.
Total 2		138	394	54	105	9	4	4	28	33	0	24	.266	.323	.340	85	-8	5	.948	-4	98	74	O98(37/20/45)		-.

TREANOR, MATT   Matthew Aaron B3.3.1976 Garden Grove CA BR/TR/6-2/220* d6.2

2004	Fla N	29	55	7	13	2	0	1	4	2	2	13	.236	.311	.273	56	-4	0-0	.976	-2	81	87	C27		-0.
2005	Fla N	58	134	10	27	8	0	0	13	16-1	3	28	.201	.301	.261	52	-9	0-0	.985	-1	89	103	C55		-0.
Total 2		87	189	17	40	10	0	1	14	20-1	5	41	.212	.304	.265	53	-13	0-0	.982	-3	87	98	C82		-0.

TRECHOCK, FRANK   Frank Adam B12.24.1915 Windber PA D1.16.1989 Minneapolis MN BR/TR/5-10/175 d9.19

| 1937 | Was A | 1 | 4 | 0 | 2 | 0 | 0 | 0 | 0 | 1 | | | .500 | .500 | .500 | 160 | -0 | | .750 | -0 | 100 | 249 | /S | | -. |

TREMARK, NICK   Nicholas Joseph B10.15.1912 Yonkers NY D9.7.2000 Tomball TX BL/TL/5-5/150 d8.9 Col Manhattan

1934	Bro N	17	28	3	7	1	0	0	6	2	0	2	.250	.300	.286	61	-2		1.000	0	123	0	O9(8/1/0)		-.
1935	Bro N	10	13	1	3	1	0	0	3	1	0	1	.231	.286	.308	61	-1	0	1.000	0	129	0	O4R		-.
1936	Bro N	8	32	6	8	2	0	0	1	3	1	2	.250	.333	.313	74	-1	0	1.000	1	97	261	O8(0/2/6)		-.
Total 3		35	73	10	18	4	0	0	10	6	1	5	.247	.313	.301	67	-4	0	1.000	1	111	128	O21(8/3/10)		-.

TREMIE, CHRIS   Christopher James B10.17.1969 Houston TX BR/TR/6-0/200(200-215) [ChiA92 39/1100] d7.1 Col Houston

1995	Chi A	10	24	0	4	0	0	0	0	1-0		2	.167	.200	.167	-3	-4	0-0	.976	-4	48	94	C9/D		-.
1998	Tex A	2	3	2	1	0	0	0	0	1-0		1	.333	.500	.667	189	1	0-0	—	0			D2		-.
1999	Pit N	9	14	1	1	0	0	0	0	2-0		4	.071	.188	.071	-31	-3	0-0	1.000	0	61	159	C8		-.
2004	Hou N	1	0	0	0	0	0	0	0	0-0		—	—	—	—		-0	0-0	—	-0	0	0	/C		-.
Total 4		22	41	3	6	1	0	0	1	4-0		7	.146	.222	.171	3	-6	0-0	.986	-4	52	116	C18,D3		-.

TREMPER, OVERTON   Carlton Overton B3.22.1906 Brooklyn NY D1.9.1996 Clearwater FL BR/TR/5-10/163 d6.16 Col Penn

1927	Bro N	26	60	4	14	0	0	0	1	2		1	.233	.246	.233	29	-6	0-0	1.000	-1	62	210	O18L		-.
1928	Bro N	10	31	1	6	2	1	0	1	0		1	.194	.194	.323	33	-3	0-0	1.000	1	79	378	O9(7/1/1)		-.
Total 2		36	91	5	20	2	1	0	5	0		3	.220	.228	.264	30	-9	0-0	1.000	-0	69	275	O27(25/1/1)		-.

TRENWITH, GEORGE   George W. B1851 Philadelphia PA D2.1.1890 Philadelphia PA d4.21

1875	Cen NA	10	45	5	8	2	0	0	4	1		2	.178	.196	.222	49	-2	0-0	.583	-6	58	0	3b10		-.
	NH NA	6	25	1	6	2	0	0	3	0		1	.240	.240	.320	106	0	0-0	.692	-2	78	0	3b6		-.
	Year	16	70	6	14	4	0	0	7	1		3	.200	.211	.257	69	-1	0-0	.629	-7	66	0	3b16		-.

TRESH, MIKE   Michael B2.23.1914 Hazleton PA D10.4.1966 Detroit MI BR/TR/5-11/170 d9.4 s-Tom

1938	Chi A	10	29	3	7	2	0	0	2	8	0	4	.241	.405	.310	80	0	0-0	.978	1	114	110	C10		-.
1939	Chi A	119	352	49	91	5	4	0	38	64	3	30	.259	.377	.284	70	-13	3-2	.985	2	94	100	C119		-.
1940	Chi A	135	480	62	135	15	5	1	64	49	1	40	.281	.349	.340	78	-15	9	.983	9	111	80	C135		-.
1941	Chi A	115	390	38	98	10	1	0	33	38	1	27	.251	.319	.282	61	-22	1-0	.981	10	103	125	C115		-.
1942	Chi A	72	233	21	54	8	1	0	15	28	0	24	.232	.314	.275	68	-9	2-0	.977	-3	100	69	C72		-.
1943	Chi A	86	279	20	60	3	0	0	25	37	0	25	.215	.307	.226	57	-14	2-1	.982	1	99	90	C85		-.
1944	Chi A	93	312	22	81	8	1	0	20	37	2	15	.260	.342	.292	83	-6	0-3	.981	-1	119	92	C93		-.
1945	Chi A★	150	458	50	114	12	0	0	47	65	2	37	.249	.346	.275	82	-8	6-3	.984	2	**148**	114	C150		-.
1946	Chi A	80	217	28	47	5	2	0	21	36	3	14	.217	.336	.258	70	-7	0-2	.995	10	91	109	C79		-.
1947	Chi A	90	274	19	66	6	2	0	26	26	2	26	.241	.311	.277	67	-12	2-0	.975	-6	74	94	C89		-.
1948	Chi A	39	108	10	27	1	0	1	11	9	0	7	.250	.308	.287	61	-6	0-0	.983	-2	83	112	C34		-.
1949	Cle A	38	37	4	8	0	0	0	5	5	0	7	.216	.310	.216	41	-3	0-0	1.000	4	203	123	C38		-.
Total 12		1027	3169	326	788	75	14	2	297	402	12	263	.249	.335	.283	71	-115	19-21	.983	28	108	99	C1019		-.

TRESH, TOM   Thomas Michael B9.20.1937 Detroit MI BB/TR/6-0/191(175-192) d9.3 f-Mike Col Central Michigan

1961	NY A	9	8	1	2	0	0	0	0	0		3	.250	.250	.250	36	-1	0-0	1.000	1	160	119	S3		-.
1962	†NY A★	157	622	94	178	26	5	20	93	67-3	8	74	.286	.359	.441	119	17	4-8	.970	-15	94	77	S111,O43L		-.
1963	†NY A★	145	520	91	140	28	5	25	71	83-5	4	79	.269	.371	.487	140	31	3-3	.981	-5	99	65	O144(46/101/0)		-.

YEAR TM LG	G	AB	R	H	2B	3B	HR	RBI	BB-IB	HP	SO	AVG	OBP	SLG	AOPS	ABR	SB-CS	FA	FR	RNG	THR	GAMES AT POSITION	DL	BFW
1964 †NY A	153	533	75	131	25	5	16	73	73-3	7	110	.246	.342	.402	105	5	13-0	.996	-7	88	80	O146(106/69/6)		-0.6
1965 NY A	156	602	94	168	29	6	26	74	59-4	5	92	.279	.348	.477	133	25	5-2	.970	-4	91	135	O154(100/105/18)		1.5
1966 NY A	151	537	76	125	12	4	27	68	86-5	6	89	.233	.341	.421	123	18	5-4	.985	27	115	230	O84(69/18/0),3b64		4.2
1967 NY A	130	448	45	98	23	3	14	53	50-0	4	86	.219	.301	.377	104	2	1-0	.972	-1	91	107	O118L		-0.6
1968 NY A	152	507	60	99	18	3	11	52	76-8	4	97	.195	.304	.308	89	-5	10-5	.951	14	117	114	S119,O27L		2.1
1969 NY A	45	143	13	26	5	2	1	9	17-2	0	23	.182	.269	.266	52	-9	2-1	.980	1	100	94	S41		-0.4
Det A	94	331	46	74	13	1	13	37	39-0	2	47	.224	.305	.387	90	-5	2-2	.965	-11	84	95	S77,O11(7/0/4)/3		-0.8
Year	139	474	59	100	18	3	14	46	56-2	2	70	.211	.294	.350	79	-14	4-3	.971	-10	90	95	S118,O11(7/0/4)/3		-1.2
Total 9	1192	4251	595	1041	179	34	153	530	550-30	40	698	.245	.335	.411	113	78	45-25	.979	-0	95	112	O727(516/293/28),S351,3b65		8.3

REVINO, ALEX Alejandro (Castro) B8.26.1957 Monterrey, Nuevo Leon, Mexico BR/TR/5-11/170(165-179) d9.11 b-Bobby

1978 NY N	6	12	3	3	0	0	0	1-0		0	2	.250	.308	.250	59	-1	0-0	1.000	1	0	368	C5/3		0.0
1979 NY N	79	207	24	56	11	1	0	20	20-2	1	27	.271	.338	.333	86	-3	2-2	.976	8	111	162	C36,3b27,2b8		0.6
1980 NY N	106	355	26	91	11	2	0	37	13-1	1	41	.256	.281	.299	64	-18	0-3	.977	-1	128	143	C86,3b14/2		-1.8
1981 NY N	56	149	17	39	2	0	0	10	13-0	1	19	.262	.323	.275	72	-5	3-0	.963	5	164	83	C45,2b4,O2(2/0/1)/3		0.2
1982 Cin N	120	355	24	89	10	3	1	33	34-11	3	24	.251	.318	.304	76	-11	3-1	.979	9	110	80	C116,3b2		0.3
1983 Cin N	74	167	14	36	8	1	1	13	17-6	0	20	.216	.285	.293	59	-9	0-0	.987	12	143	93	C63,3b4/2		0.6
1984 Cin N	6	6	0	1	0	0	0	0-0		0	2	.167	.167	.167	46	-0	0-0	1.000	-0	29	0	C4		-0.1
Atl N	79	266	36	65	16	0	3	28	16-1	1	27	.244	.289	.338	71	-10	5-2	.989	13	92	143	C79		0.6
Year	85	272	36	66	16	0	3	28	16-1	1	29	.243	.286	.335	69	-11	5-2	.989	13	91	142	C83		0.5
1985 SF N	57	157	17	34	10	1	6	19	20-0	0	24	.217	.303	.408	102	0	0-0	.978	-7	105	74	C55/3		-0.4
1986 LA N	89	202	31	53	13	0	4	26	27-2	1	35	.262	.351	.386	111	4	0-0	.969	-3	123	138	C63/1		-0.8
1987 LA N	72	144	16	32	7	1	3	16	6-2	4	28	.222	.271	.347	64	-8	1-0	.987	-2	125	103	C45,O2(1/0/1)/3		-0.8
1988 Hou N	78	193	19	48	17	0	2	13	24-4	3	29	.249	.341	.368	108	3	5-2	.977	-16	73	60	C74/OL		-0.9
1989 Hou N	59	131	15	38	7	1	2	16	7-0	1	18	.290	.329	.405	113	2	0-0	.989	-2	148	72	C32,1b2,3b2		0.2
1990 Hou N	42	69	3	13	3	0	1	10	6-1	2	11	.188	.266	.275	53	-4	0-1	.992	4	106	94	C30/1		0.1
NY N	9	10	0	3	1	0	0	2	1-0	0	0	.300	.333	.400	110	0	0-0	.929	-0	88	92	C7		0.0
Cin N	7	7	3	3	1	0	0	1	0-0	1	0	.429	.500	.571	186	1	0-0	1.000	0	0	0	C39/1		0.1
Year	58	86	3	19	5	0	1	13	7-1	3	11	.221	.293	.314	71	-3	0-1	.982	5	98	89	C39/1		0.2
Total 13	939	2430	245	604	117	10	23	244	205-30	19	317	.249	.310	.333	81	-60	19-11	.979	23	115	106	C742,3b53,2b14,O5(4/0/2),1b4		-0.9

REVINO, BOBBY Carlos (Castro) B8.15.1943 Monterrey, Nuevo Leon, Mexico BR/TR/6-2/185 d5.22 b-Alex

1968 Cal A	17	40	1	9	1	0	0	1	2-0	0	9	.225	.262	.250	57	-2	0-1	.962	1	123	169	O11(1/7/5)		-0.2

RIANDOS, GUS Gus B7.30.1930 San Francisco CA BR/TR/6-3/215(205-220) d8.13 Col St. Marys (CA)

1953 NY A	18	51	5	8	2	0	1	6	3	0	9	.157	.204	.255	24	-6	0-0	.991	-0	90	85	1b12,C5		-0.6
1954 NY A	2	1	0	0	0	0	0	0	0	0	1	.000	.000	.000	-99	-0	0-0	—	0	0	0	/C		0.0
1955 Bal A	140	481	47	133	17	3	12	65	40-4	2	55	.277	.333	.399	104	1	0-0	.989	-1	109	102	1b103,C36/3		-0.4
1956 Bal A	131	452	47	126	18	1	21	88	48-4	2	73	.279	.348	.462	122	13	0-0	.989	9	76	120	C89,1b52		2.2
1957 Bal A☆	129	418	44	106	21	1	19	72	38-7	3	73	.254	.317	.445	114	6	0-0	.992	-2	107	135	C120		1.0
1958 Bal A★	137	474	59	116	10	0	30	79	60-4	1	65	.245	.327	.456	120	12	1-0	.987	7	164	77	C132		2.6
1959 Bal A★	126	393	43	85	7	1	25	73	65-6	3	56	.216	.330	.430	110	5	0-0	.981	3	135	133	C125		1.4
1960 Bal A	109	364	36	98	18	0	12	54	41-5	1	62	.269	.343	.418	107	4	0-0	.989	1	141	75	C105		1.0
1961 Bal A	115	397	35	97	21	0	17	63	44-7	1	60	.244	.320	.426	101	0	0-0	.989	11	177	94	C114	34	1.6
1962 Bal A	66	207	20	33	7	0	6	23	29-2	1	43	.159	.262	.280	49	-15	0-0	.985	-0	98	131	C63	34	-1.2
1963 Det A	106	327	28	78	13	0	14	41	32-4	6	67	.239	.315	.407	98	-1	0-0	.998	-4	143	85	C90		0.0
1964 Phi N	73	188	17	47	9	0	8	33	26-5	1	41	.250	.339	.426	117	-5	0-0	.985	1	84	102	C64/1		0.9
1965 Phi N	30	82	5	14	2	0	0	4	9-1	0	17	.171	.253	.195	29	-8	0-0	.975	-4	87	152	C28		-1.2
Hou N	24	72	5	13	2	0	2	7	5-0	1	14	.181	.244	.292	54	-5	0-0	.970	-3	94	99	C20		-0.7
Year	54	154	8	27	4	0	2	11	14-1	1	31	.175	.249	.240	40	-12	0-0	.973	-7	90	127	C48		-1.9
Total 13	1206	3907	389	954	147	6	167	608	440-49	21	636	.244	.322	.413	103	11	1-0	.987	17	127	105	C992,1b168/3	68	6.6

RILLO, MANNY Jesus Manuel Marcano (b Jesus Manuel Marcano (Trillo)) B12.25.1950 Caripito, Venez BR/TR/6-1/164(150-165) d6.28

1973 Oak A	17	12	0	3	2	0	0	3	0-0	0	4	.250	.250	.417	89	0	0-0	.941	1	111	137	2b16		0.1
1974 †Oak A	21	33	3	5	0	0	0	2	2-0	1	9	.152	.222	.152	10	-4	0-0	.949	4	133	118	2b21	34	0.1
1975 Chi N	154	545	55	135	12	2	7	70	45-3	3	70	.248	.306	.316	70	-22	1-7	.967	18	108	95	2b153/S		0.3
1976 Chi N	158	582	42	139	24	3	4	59	53-4	3	70	.239	.304	.311	69	-23	17-6	.981	9	105	97	2b156/S		-0.2
1977 Chi N★	152	504	51	141	18	5	7	57	44-6	5	58	.280	.339	.377	84	-11	3-5	.970	30	114	98	2b149		2.6
1978 Chi N	152	552	53	144	17	5	4	55	50-3	2	67	.261	.320	.332	75	-18	0-7	.978	29	117	109	2b149		1.8
1979 Phi N	118	431	40	112	22	1	6	42	20-3	4	59	.260	.296	.357	75	-15	4-7	.985	14	112	116	2b118	43	0.3
1980 †Phi N	141	531	68	155	25	9	7	43	32-8	3	46	.292	.334	.412	101	0	8-3	.987	24	111	101	2b140	17	3.4
1981 †Phi N★	94	349	37	100	14	3	6	36	26-3	3	37	.287	.338	.395	103	1	10-4	.987	18	104	107	2b94		2.6
1982 Phi N★	149	549	52	149	24	1	0	39	33-3	3	53	.271	.316	.319	76	-17	8-10	.994	14	97	114	2b149		0.3
1983 Cle A★	88	320	33	87	13	1	1	29	21-2	0	46	.272	.315	.328	75	-11	1-3	.989	8	107	95	2b87	15	0.0
Mon N	31	121	16	32	8	0	2	16	10-0	2	18	.264	.331	.380	96	0	0-0	.979	-4	92	126	2b31		-0.2
1984 SF N	98	401	45	102	21	1	4	36	25-0	3	55	.254	.300	.342	83	-9	0-0	.988	-0	101	101	2b96,3b4	55	-0.5
1985 SF N	125	451	36	101	16	2	3	25	40-0	1	44	.224	.287	.288	65	-22	2-0	.981	12	106	94	2b120/3		-0.3
1986 Chi N	81	152	22	45	10	0	1	19	16-0	1	21	.296	.359	.382	98	0	0-2	.949	-3	89	59	3b53,1b11,2b6	38	-0.4
1987 Chi N	108	214	27	63	8	0	8	26	25-0	0	37	.294	.364	.444	110	3	0-3	.994	-5	89	106	1b47,3b35,2b10,S6		-0.5
1988 Chi N	76	164	15	41	5	0	1	14	8-0	0	32	.250	.283	.299	65	-8	2-0	.994	-1	54	61	1b24,3b17,2b13,S7		-0.9
1989 Cin N	17	39	3	8	0	0	0	6	2-0	1	9	.205	.262	.205	34	-3	0-0	1.000	-4	72	39	2b10,1b3/S		-0.8
Total 17	1780	5950	598	1562	239	33	61	571	452-35	34	742	.263	.316	.345	80	-159	56-57	.981	167	104	103	2b1518,3b110,1b85,S16	202	8.2

RIPLETT, COAKER Herman Coaker B12.18.1911 Boone NC D1.30.1992 Boone NC BR/TR/5-11/185 d4.19 Col Appalachian St.

1938 Chi N	12	36	4	9	2	0	0	1	1-0	0	2	.250	.250	.361	65	-2	0	1.000	1	94	169	O9(6/2/1)		-0.2
1941 StL N	76	185	29	53	6	3	3	21	18	0	27	.286	.350	.400	104	1	0	.965	-0	93	140	O46(38/0/8)		-0.2
1942 StL N	64	154	18	42	7	4	1	23	17	0	15	.273	.345	.390	107	1	1	.966	2	114	86	O46(45/0/1)		0.1
1943 StL N	9	25	1	2	0	0	1	4	1	0	6	.080	.115	.200	-9	-4	2	1.000	-0	116	0	O6(2/0/4)		-0.5
Phi N	105	360	45	98	16	4	14	52	28	0	28	.272	.325	.456	129	11	2	.970	3	103	133	O90L		0.9
Year	114	385	46	100	16	4	15	56	29	0	34	.260	.312	.439	120	7	2	.972	3	104	125	O96(92/0/4)		0.4
1944 Phi N	84	184	15	43	5	1	1	25	19	0	10	.234	.305	.288	70	-7	1	.989	0	100	92	O44(41/1/2)		-1.0
1945 Phi N	120	363	36	87	11	1	7	40	40	0	27	.240	.315	.333	83	-9	6	.945	-3	103	46	O92(92/0/2)		-1.7
Total 6	470	1307	148	334	47	14	27	173	123	0	114	.256	.320	.375	97	-9	10	.965	2	103	95	O333(314/3/18)		-2.6

ROSKY, HAL Harold Arthur Sr. (b Harold Arthur Trojovsky) B11.11.1912 Norway IA D6.18.1979 Cedar Rapids IA BL/TR (BB 1935p)/6-2/207 d9.11 s-Hal

1933 Cle A	11	44	6	13	1	2	1	8	2	1	12	.295	.340	.477	110	0	0-0	.990	-1	73	82	1b11		-0.1
1934 Cle A	154	625	117	206	45	9	35	142	58	2	49	.330	.388	.598	149	42	2-2	.986	0	104	110	1b154		2.5
1935 Cle A	154	632	84	171	33	7	26	113	46	1	60	.271	.321	.468	100	-4	1-2	.993	1	102	106	1b153		-1.7
1936 Cle A	151	629	124	216	45	9	42	162	63	3	58	.343	.382	.644	148	41	6-5	.985	1	107	96	1b151/2		2.4
1937 Cle A	153	601	104	179	36	4	32	128	65	1	60	.298	.367	.547	127	22	3-1	.993	-2	89	99	1b152		0.5
1938 Cle A	150	554	106	185	40	4	19	110	67	4	40	.334	.407	.542	138	33	5-1	.993	4	103	88	1b148		2.1
1939 Cle A	122	448	89	150	31	4	25	104	52	1	28	.335	.405	.589	157	38	2-3	.992	12	137	100	1b118		3.4
1940 Cle A	140	522	85	154	39	4	25	93	79	4	45	.295	.392	.529	140	33	1-2	.991	-6	79	117	1b139		1.3
1941 Cle A	89	310	43	91	17	0	11	51	44	1	21	.294	.383	.455	127	13	1-2	.989	-1	93	108	1b85		0.3
1944 Chi A	135	497	55	120	32	2	10	70	62	1	30	.241	.327	.374	101	2	3-2	.993	-9	71	107	1b130		-1.5
1946 Chi A	88	299	22	76	12	3	4	31	34	0	37	.254	.330	.334	89	-4	4-3	.991	-7	68	97	1b80		-1.5
Total 11	1347	5161	835	1561	331	58	228	1012	545	16	440	.302	.371	.522	130	216	28-23	.991	-8	96	103	1b1321/2		7.7

ROST, MIKE Michael J. B1866 Philadelphia PA D3.24.1901 Philadelphia PA TR/6-0.5/180 d8.21

1890 StL AA	17	51	10	13	2	0	1	7	6	1		.255	.345	.353	93	-1	4	.890	-1	99	84	C13,O4(0/3/1)		-0.1
1895 Lou N	3	12	1	1	0	0	0	1	0	0	1	.083	.083	.083	-61	-3	1	1.000	-0	0	63	1b3		-0.3
Total 2	20	63	11	14	2	0	1	8	6	1		.222	.300	.302	66	-4	5	.890	-2	99	84	C13,O4(0/3/1),1b3		-0.4

ROTT, SAM Samuel W. B3.1859 MD D6.5.1925 Catonsville MD BL/TL/5-9/190 d5.29 M1

1890 Bos N	39	125	14	26	4	1	0		5			.208	.227	.256	65	-4		.893	5			C36,O4(1/3/0)		0.1
1891 Det N	6	25	3	5	2	1	0	2	1			.200	.231	.360	80	-1		.868	-1			C6		-0.2

YEAR	TM LG	G	AB	R	H	2B	3B	HR	RBI	BB-IB	HP	SO	AVG	OBP	SLG	AOPS	ABR	SB-CS	FA	FR	RNG	THR	GAMES AT POSITION	DL	BFW
1882	Det N	32	129	11	31	7	1	0	12	0		13	.240	.240	.310	75	-4		.890	2			C23,S3,2b3,1b3,O2L/3		0.1
1883	Det N	75	295	27	72	14	1	0	29	10		23	.244	.269	.298	76	-8		.882	-15	82	97	2b42,C34,O6(0/1/5)/1		-1.6
1884	Bal AA	71	284	36	73	17	9	3		4	2		.257	.272	.412	116	4		.931	11			C60,2b6,O5(1/1/3)		1.8
1885	Bal AA	21	88	12	24	2	2	0	12	5	0		.273	.312	.341	108	1		.882	-3			C17,O4R,2b2/S		-0.1
1887	Bal AA	85	300	44	77	16	3	0	37	27	2		.257	.322	.330	87	-4	8	.915	2			C69,2b11,O3L,1b2/S		0.3
1888	Bal AA	31	108	19	30	11	4	0	22	4	0		.278	.304	.454	145	5	1	.908	-5			C27,O3(1/0/2)/21		0.2
Total	8	360	1354	166	338	73	22	3	123	54		44	.250	.280	.343	93	-11	9	.906	-4			C272,2b65,O27(8/5/14),1b7,S5/3		0.6

TROUPPE, QUINCY   Quincy Thomas   B12.25.1912 Dublin GA   D8.12.1993 Creve Coeur MO   BB/TR/6-2.5/225   d4.30   Negro Lg 1930-51

1952	Cle A	6	10	1	1	0	0	0	1	0		3	.100	.182	.100	-22	-2	0-0	1.000	0	110	106	C6		0.0

TROY, DASHER   John Joseph   B5.8.1856 New York NY   D3.30.1938 Ozone Park NY   BR/TR/5-5/154   d8.23

1881	Det N	11	44	2	15	3	0	0	4	3		8	.341	.383	.409	143	2		.792	-1	103	0	3b7,2b4		0.1
1882	Det N	40	152	22	37	7	2	0	14	5		10	.243	.268	.316	86	-2		.847	-17	80	65	2b31,S11		-1.7
	Pro N	4	17	1	4	0	0	0	1	0		1	.235	.235	.235	52	-1		.750	-1	96	93	S4		-0.2
	Year	44	169	23	41	7	2	0	15	5		11	.243	.264	.308	83	-3		.847	-19	80	65	2b31,S15		-1.9
1883	NY N	85	316	37	68	7	5	0	20	9		33	.215	.237	.269	-54	-18		.879	-12	97	71	2b73,S12		-2.4
1884	†NY AA	107	421	80	111	22	10	2		19	3		.264	.300	.378	123	11		.879	-20	93	66	2b107		-0.5
1885	NY AA	45	177	24	39	3	3	2	12	5	4		.220	.258	.305	81	-4		.866	-12	80	90	2b42,O2R/S		-1.3
Total	5	292	1127	166	274	42	20	4	51	41	7	52	.243	.274	.327	91	-12		.873	-64	90	73	2b257,S28,3b7,O2R		-6.0

TRUAX, FRED   Frederick W.   B1868   D12.18.1899 Omaha NE   d8.18

1890	Pit N	1	3	0	1	0	0	0	1	1		1	.333	.500	.333	163	0	0	1.000	0		0	3185 /OL		0.0

TRUBY, CHRIS   Christopher John   B12.9.1973 Palm Springs CA   BR/TR/6-2/190*   d6.16   [DL 2005 KC A 38]

2000	Hou N	78	258	28	67	15	4	11	59	10-1		56	.260	.295	.477	85	-7	2-1	.926	3	105	116	3b74		-0.4
2001	†Hou N	48	136	11	28	6	1	8	23	13-2	1	38	.206	.276	.441	77	-5	1-2	.923	-4	91	72	3b35/1		-0.5
2002	Mon N	35	105	12	27	5	2	2	7	5-1	1	27	.257	.297	.400	80	-4	1-1	.924	-3	95	75	3b31,1b2/OL		-0.7
	Det A	89	277	23	55	13	2	2	15	5-1	2	71	.199	.215	.282	33	-28	1-1	.958	10	116	147	3b89	25	-1.7
2003	TB A	13	43	4	12	3	0	3	5	0-0		13	.279	.354	.349	88	0	0-0	.976	4	138	170	3b13		0.1
Total	4	263	819	78	189	42	9	23	107	38-4	9	205	.231	.269	.388	67	-44	5-5	.942	9	108	119	3b242,1b3/OL	63	-3.2

TRUBY, HARRY   Harry Garvin "Bird Eye"   B5.12.1870 Ironton OH   D3.21.1953 Ironton OH   TR/5-11/185   d8.21   U1

1895	Chi N	33	119	17	40	3	0	0	16	10		7	.336	.402	.361	92	-1	7	.950	-0	90	143	2b33		0.6
1896	Chi N	29	109	13	28	2	2	2	31	6		3	.257	.314	.367	76	-4	4	.935	0	93	141	2b28		-0.1
	Pit N	8	32	1	5	0	0	0	3	2		4	.156	.206	.156	-4	-5	1	.949	-2	69	215	2b8		-0.4
	Year	37	141	14	33	2	2	2	34	8		3	.234	.289	.319	59	-9	5	.938	-2	88	157	2b36		-0.5
Total	2	70	260	31	73	5	2	2	50	18		16	.281	.342	.338	75	-10	12	.944	-2	89	150	2b69		-0.2

TRUESDALE, FRANK   Frank Day   B3.31.1884 St.Louis MO   D8.27.1943 Albuquerque NM   BB/TR/5-8/145   d4.27

1910	StL A	123	415	39	91	7	1	0	25	48		21	.219	.303	.253	79	-8	29	.914	-2	100	91	2b122		-1.1
1911	StL A	1	0	1	0	0	0	0	0	0			—	—	—		0	0	—	0			/R		0.0
1914	NY A	77	217	22	46	4	0	0	13	39	3	35	.212	.340	.230	72	-5	11-11	.947	3	109	106	2b67,3b4		-0.5
1918	Bos A	15	36	6	10	1	0	0	2	4	0	5	.278	.350	.306	99	0	1	.913	-1	106	59	2b10		-0.1
Total	4	216	668	68	147	12	2	1	40	91	5	40	.220	.318	.249	78	-13	41-11	.924	0	103	94	2b199,3b4		-1.6

TRUMBULL, ED   Edward J. (b Edward J. Trembly)   B11.3.1860 Chicopee MA   D1.14.1937 Kingston PA   d5.10 ▲

1884	Was AA	25	86	5	10	2	0	0		2			.116	.136	.140	-11	-10		.828	0	154	202	O15(2/8/5),P10		-0.7

TUBBS, GREG   Gregory Alan   B8.31.1962 Smithville TN   BR/TR/5-9/185   [AtIN84 22/565]   d8.1   Col Austin Peay

1993	Cin N	35	59	10	11	0	0	1	2	14-0	1	10	.186	.351	.237	61	-3	3-1	.975	1	105	109	O21(11/14/2)		-0.2

TUCKER, EDDIE   Eddie Jack "Scooter"   B11.18.1966 Greenville MS   BR/TR/6-2/205*   [SFN88 5/126]   d6.14   Col Delta St.

1992	Hou N	20	50	5	6	1	0	0	3	3-0	2	13	.120	.200	.140	-2	-7	1-1	.976	6	83	71	C19		-0.1
1993	Hou N	9	26	1	5	1	0	0	3	2-0	0	3	.192	.250	.231	31	-3	0-0	1.000	3	171	86	C8		0.0
1995	Hou N	5	7	1	2	0	0	1	1	0-0	0	0	.286	.286	.714	164	0	0-0	1.000	0	85	274	C3		-0.0
	Cle A	17	20	2	0	0	0	0	0	5-0	1	4	.000	.231	.000	-33	-4	0-0	.982	-0	108	125	C17		-0.0
Total	3	51	103	9	13	2	0	1	7	10-0	3	20	.126	.224	.175	11	-14	1-1	.986	-3	109	96	C47		-1.2

TUCKER, MICHAEL   Michael Anthony   B6.25.1971 S.Boston VA   BL/TR/6-2/185(185-210)   [KCA92 1/10]   d4.26   Col Longwood   OF(285/195/781)

1995	KC A	62	177	23	46	10	0	4	17	18-2	1	51	.260	.332	.384	84	-4	2-3	.986	1	98	133	O36(30/1/5),D22		-0.5
1996	KC A	108	339	55	88	18	4	12	53	40-1	6	69	.260	.346	.442	98	-1	10-4	.989	-2	97	97	O98(28/0/73),1b9,D5	50	-0.5
1997	†Atl N	138	499	80	141	25	7	14	56	44-0	6	116	.283	.347	.445	104	3	12-7	.980	1	104	68	O129(53/0/102)		-0.2
1998	†Atl N	130	414	54	101	27	3	13	46	49-10	3	112	.244	.327	.418	95	-3	8-3	.995	-1	97	72	O118R		-0.9
1999	Cin N	133	296	55	75	8	5	11	44	37-3	3	81	.253	.338	.426	90	-5	11-4	.990	7	115	158	O120(41/28/67)/2		-0.5
2000	Cin N	148	270	55	72	13	4	15	36	44-1	7	64	.267	.381	.511	120	9	13-6	.969	-0	99	109	O127(75/76/25),1b4		-0.1
2001	Cin N	86	231	31	56	10	1	7	30	23-1	1	55	.242	.308	.385	75	-9	12-5	.978	3	100	188	O70(37/32/19)		-0.6
	Chi N	63	205	31	54	9	7	5	31	23-3	1	47	.263	.339	.449	105	1	4-3	.991	2	103	72	O57(38/44/6),1b4		-0.0
	Year	149	436	62	110	19	8	12	61	46-4	2	102	.252	.322	.415	88	-9	16-8	.984	5	101	133	O127(75/76/25),1b4		-0.5
2002	KC A	144	475	65	118	27	6	12	56	56-1	3	105	.248	.330	.406	84	-11	23-9	.991	4	102	142	O108(33/14/67),D23,1b5,2b2		-1.3
2003	KC A	104	389	61	102	20	5	13	55	39-3	2	88	.262	.331	.440	95	-3	8-10	.989	-3	88	145	O85(21/30/47),D15	50	-0.6
2004	SF N	140	464	77	119	21	6	13	62	70-3	2	106	.256	.353	.412	95	-3	4-0	.978	0	109	28	O124(0/25/106)		-0.8
2005	SF N	104	250	32	60	16	1	5	33	28-3	2	48	.240	.317	.372	78	-8	4-0	.983	0	92	178	O72(4/7/64)		-1.2
	Phi N	22	18	3	4	0	0	0	3	3-0	0	4	.222	.333	.222	48	-1	0-0	—	-0	0	0	/OCD		-0.1
	Year	126	268	35	64	16	1	5	36	31-3	2	52	.239	.318	.362	76	-9	4-0	.983	0	92	178	O73(4/8/64),D4		-1.2
Total	11	1382	4027	622	1036	204	49	124	522	474-31	38	946	.257	.339	.425	94	-35	112-56	.985	11	101	105	O1132R,D69,1b18,2b3	100	-6.4

TUCKER, OLLIE   Oliver Dinwiddie   B1.27.1902 Radiant VA   D7.13.1940 Radiant VA   BL/TR/5-11/180   d4.17

1927	Was A	20	24	1	5	2	0	0	8	4	0	2	.208	.321	.292	61	-1	0-0	1.000	0	122	0	O5R		-0.0
1928	Cle A	14	47	5	6	0	0	1	2	7	1	3	.128	.255	.191	19	-6	0-2	1.000	0	77	231	O14R		-0.0
Total	2	34	71	6	11	2	0	1	10	11	1	5	.155	.277	.225	33	-7	0-2	1.000	0	88	175	O19R		-0.0

TUCKER, TOMMY   Thomas Joseph "Foghorn"   B10.28.1863 Holyoke MA   D10.22.1935 Montague MA   BB/TR/5-11/165   d4.16

1887	Bal AA	136	524	114	144	15	9	6	84	29	29		.275	.347	.372	107	7	85	.976	4	113	75	1b136		-0.7
1888	Bal AA	136	520	74	149	17	12	6	61	16	18		.287	.330	.400	137	20	43	.975	3	126	105	1b129,O7(2/0/5)/P		1.4
1889	Bal AA	134	527	110	196	22	11	5	99	42	33	26	.372	.450	.484	163	46	63	.964	-1	103	93	1b123,O12(0/11/1)		3.2
1890	Bos N	132	539	104	159	17	8	1	62	56	25	22	.295	.387	.362	110	8	43	.979	-2	85	85	1b132		-0.2
1891	Bos N	140	548	103	148	16	5	2	69	37	29	30	.270	.349	.328	87	-9	26	.976	-3	87	100	1b140/P		-0.8
1892	†Bos N	149	542	85	153	15	7	1	62	45	26	35	.282	.365	.341	104	4	22	.972	-12	65	129	1b149		-2.5
1893	Bos N	121	486	83	138	13	2	7	91	27		20	.284	.347	.362	82	-14	8	.980	-11	58	128	1b121		-2.6
1894	Bos N	123	500	112	165	24	6	3	100	53	17	21	.330	.412	.420	94	-4	18	.985	2	99	108	1b123/OC		-1.3
1895	Bos N	126	465	87	115	19	6	3	73	63	19	29	.247	.360	.333	74	-17	15	.978	5	118	111	1b126		-1.0
1896	Bos N	122	474	74	144	27	6	2	72	30	14	29	.304	.363	.395	94	-4	8	.985	3	108	102	1b122		-0.9
1897	Bos N	4	14	0	3	0	0	0	2	0			.214	.313	.357	72	-1	0	.957	0	172	0	1b4		-0.0
	Was N	93	352	52	119	18	5	2	61	27	11		.338	.403	.460	128	15	18	.984	-3	81	110	1b93		-0.7
	Year	97	366	52	122	20	5	2	65	29	11		.333	.399	.456	126	14	18	.982	-2	85	105	1b97		-0.7
1898	Bro N	73	283	35	79	9	4	1	34	12	7		.279	.325	.350	94	-3	1	.991	7	138	97	1b73		-0.3
	StL N	72	252	18	60	7	2	0	20	18	12		.238	.319	.282	71	-9	1	.973	-2	105	89	1b72		-0.9
	Year	145	535	53	139	16	6	1	54	30	19		.260	.322	.318	83	-12	2	.982	7	122	93	1b145		-1.2
1899	Cle N	127	456	40	110	19	3	0	49	24	12		.241	.297	.296	68	-20	3	.977	-9	91	77	1b127		-4.3
Total	13	1688	6482	1084	1882	240	85	42	932	481	272	223	.290	.364	.373	101	19	352	.978	-8	98	101	1b1670,O20(2/12/6),P2		-4.3

TUCKER, THURMAN   Thurman Lowell "Joe E."   B9.26.1917 Gordon TX   D5.7.1993 Oklahoma City OK   BL/TR/5-11/170*   d4.14   Mil 1945

1942	Chi A	7	24	2	7	0	0	0	1	0	0	4	.125	.125	.208	-7	-4	0-0	.900	7	71	326	O5C		
1943	Chi A	139	528	81	124	15	6	3	39	79	1	72	.235	.336	.303	87	-6	29-17	.988	9	109	133	O132C		
1944	Chi A★	124	446	59	128	15	6	2	46	57	0	40	.287	.368	.361	110	7	13-12	.991	11	115	96	O120C		
1946	Chi A	121	438	62	126	20	3	4	36	54	1	45	.288	.367	.354	106	5	9-10	.990	-2	93	145	O110C		
1947	Chi A	89	254	28	60	11	7	1	17	38	0	25	.236	.334	.346	85	-5	10-4	.978	-1	96	119	O65C		

YEAR	TM LG	G	AB	R	H	2B	3B	HR	RBI	BB-IB	HP	SO	AVG	OBP	SLG	AOPS	ABR	SB-CS	FA	FR	RNG	THR	GAMES AT POSITION	DL	BFW
1948	†Cle A	83	242	52	63	13	2	1	19	31	1	17	.260	.347	.343	86	-4	11-2	1.000	-0	97	98	O66C		-0.4
1949	Cle A	80	197	28	48	5	2	0	14	18	0	19	.244	.307	.289	59	-12	4-2	.984	-2	98	64	O42(4/38/0)		-1.5
1950	Cle A	57	101	13	18	2	0	1	7	14	1	14	.178	.284	.228	34	-10	1-0	.968	1	103	107	O34(15/16/4)		-1.0
1951	Cle A	1	1	0	0	0	0	0	0	0	0	0	.000	.000	.000	-99	0		—	-0			/H		0.0
Total 9		701	2231	325	570	79	24	9	179	291	4	237	.255	.342	.325	89	-29	77-47	.988	16	103	117	O574(19/552/4)		-2.8

TURANG, BRIAN Brian Craig B6.14.1967 Long Beach CA BR/TR/5-10/170* [SeaA89 52/1299] d8.13 Col Loyola Marymount

YEAR	TM LG	G	AB	R	H	2B	3B	HR	RBI	BB-IB	HP	SO	AVG	OBP	SLG	AOPS	ABR	SB-CS	FA	FR	RNG	THR	GAMES AT POSITION	DL	BFW
1993	Sea A	40	140	22	35	11	1	0	7	17-0	2	20	.250	.340	.343	82	-3	6-2	.986	-2	91	98	O38(26/14/1),3b2/2D		-0.5
1994	Sea A	38	112	9	21	5	1	1	8	7-0	1	25	.188	.242	.277	32	-12	3-1	.978	-2	98	77	O30(20/12/0),2b5,D4	16	-1.2
Total 2		78	252	31	56	16	2	1	15	24-0	3	45	.222	.297	.313	60	-15	9-3	.983	-4	94	90	O68(46/26/1),2b6,D5,3b2	16	-1.7

TURBIDY, JERRY Jeremiah B7.4.1852 Dudley MA D9.5.1920 Webster MA 5-8/165 d7.27

YEAR	TM LG	G	AB	R	H	2B	3B	HR	RBI	BB-IB	HP	SO	AVG	OBP	SLG	AOPS	ABR	SB-CS	FA	FR	RNG	THR	GAMES AT POSITION	DL	BFW
1884	KC U	13	49	5	11	4	0	0		3			.224	.269	.306	85	-2		.830	4	125	141	S13		0.2

TURCHIN, EDDIE Edward Lawrence "Smiley" B2.10.1917 New York NY D2.8.1982 Brookhaven NY BR/TR/5-10/165 d5.9 Col Brooklyn

YEAR	TM LG	G	AB	R	H	2B	3B	HR	RBI	BB-IB	HP	SO	AVG	OBP	SLG	AOPS	ABR	SB-CS	FA	FR	RNG	THR	GAMES AT POSITION	DL	BFW
1943	Cle A	11	13	4	3	0	0	0	1	3	0	1	.231	.375	.231	84	0	1-0	1.000	1	118	257	3b4,S2		0.1

TURGEON, PETE Eugene Joseph B1.3.1897 Minneapolis MN D1.24.1977 Wichita Falls TX BR/TR/5-6/145 d9.20

YEAR	TM LG	G	AB	R	H	2B	3B	HR	RBI	BB-IB	HP	SO	AVG	OBP	SLG	AOPS	ABR	SB-CS	FA	FR	RNG	THR	GAMES AT POSITION	DL	BFW
1923	Chi N	3	6	1	1	0	0	0	0	0	0	0	.167	.167	.167	-12	-1	0-0	.875	-0	64	258	S2		-0.1

TURNER, CHRIS Christopher Wan B3.23.1969 Bowling Green KY BR/TR/6-3/200* [CalA91 7/194] d8.27 Col Western Kentucky

YEAR	TM LG	G	AB	R	H	2B	3B	HR	RBI	BB-IB	HP	SO	AVG	OBP	SLG	AOPS	ABR	SB-CS	FA	FR	RNG	THR	GAMES AT POSITION	DL	BFW
1993	Cal A	25	75	9	21	5	0	1	9	9-0	1	16	.280	.360	.387	99	0	1-1	.992	-1	62	63	C25		0.0
1994	Cal A	58	149	23	36	7	1	1	12	10-0	1	29	.242	.290	.322	58	-10	3-0	.997	1	91	91	C57		-0.5
1995	Cal A	5	10	0	1	0	0	0	1	0-0	0	3	.100	.100	.100	-48	-2	0-0	1.000	1	0	0	C4/D		-0.1
1996	Cal A	4	3	1	1	0	0	0	1	1-0	0	1	.333	.400	.333	195	0	0-0	1.000	1	0	791	C3/OL		0.1
1997	Ana A	13	23	4	6	1	1	1	2	5-0	0	8	.261	.393	.522	136	1	0-0	1.000	-4	53	0	C8,1b2/ORD	100	-0.2
1998	KC A	4	9	0	0	0	0	0	0	1-0	1	4	.000	.100	.000	-68	-2	0-0	1.000	-0	177	0	C4		-0.2
1999	Cle A	12	21	3	4	0	0	0	1	0-0	1	8	.190	.227	.190	8	-3	1-0	.964	-1	87	90	C12		-0.3
2000	NY A	37	89	9	21	3	0	1	9	10-0	1	21	.236	.320	.303	60	-5	0-1	1.000	-3	78	47	C36/1		-0.7
Total 8		158	379	49	90	16	2	4	36	36-0	4	89	.237	.307	.322	63	-21	5-2	.994	-7	79	69	C149,1b3,O2(1/0/1),D2	100	-1.9

TURNER, EARL Earl Edwin B5.6.1923 Pittsfield MA D10.20.1999 Lee MA d9.25

YEAR	TM LG	G	AB	R	H	2B	3B	HR	RBI	BB-IB	HP	SO	AVG	OBP	SLG	AOPS	ABR	SB-CS	FA	FR	RNG	THR	GAMES AT POSITION	DL	BFW
1948	Pit N	2	1	0	0	0	0	0	0	0	0	0	.000	.000	.000	-98	0	0	—	0	0	0	/C		0.0
1950	Pit N	40	74	10	18	0	0	3	5	4	0	13	.243	.282	.365	66	-4	1	.974	1	127	99	C34		-0.2
Total 2		42	75	10	18	0	0	3	5	4	0	13	.240	.278	.360	64	-4	1	.974	1	126	98	C35		-0.2

TURNER, TUCK George A. B2.13.1873 W.New Brighton NY D7.16.1945 Staten Island NY BB/TL/5-6.5/155 d8.18

YEAR	TM LG	G	AB	R	H	2B	3B	HR	RBI	BB-IB	HP	SO	AVG	OBP	SLG	AOPS	ABR	SB-CS	FA	FR	RNG	THR	GAMES AT POSITION	DL	BFW
1893	Phi N	36	155	32	50	4	3	1	13	9	1	19	.323	.364	.406	105	-	7	.933	1	94	178	O36(1/35/0)		-0.1
1894	Phi N	82	347	95	145	21	9	1	84	24	2	13	.418	.458	.539	143	25	11	.902	-5	58	34	O80(56/3/22)/P		1.1
1895	Phi N	59	210	51	81	8	6	2	43	25	1	11	.386	.453	.510	147	16	14	.847	-4	70	0	O55(31/9/15)		0.6
1896	Phi N	13	32	12	7	2	0	0	8		0	5	.219	.375	.281	75	-1	6	.905	2	387	0	O8(1/7/0)		0.1
	StL N	51	203	30	50	7	8	1	27	14	1	21	.246	.298	.374	80	-7	6	.961	-3	64	57	O51R		-1.1
	Year	64	235	42	57	9	8	1	27	22	1	26	.243	.310	.362	79	-8	12	.948	-1	110	49	O59(1/7/51)		-1.0
1897	StL N	103	416	58	121	17	12	2	41	35	3		.291	.350	.404	101	-1	8	.945	-4	75	98	O102R		-0.8
1898	StL N	35	141	20	28	8	0	0	7	14	2		.199	.280	.255	53	-8	1	.929	-3	42	85	O34R		-1.3
Total 6		379	1504	298	482	67	38	7	215	129	10	69	.320	.378	.430	111	24	53	.916	-18	75	69	O366(89/54/224)/P		-1.5

TURNER, JERRY John Webber B1.17.1954 Texarkana AR BL/TL/5-9/180* [SDN72 10/217] d9.2

YEAR	TM LG	G	AB	R	H	2B	3B	HR	RBI	BB-IB	HP	SO	AVG	OBP	SLG	AOPS	ABR	SB-CS	FA	FR	RNG	THR	GAMES AT POSITION	DL	BFW
1974	SD N	17	48	4	14	1	0	0	2	3-0	0	5	.292	.333	.313	85	-1	2-1	1.000	-1	68	135	O13L		-0.2
1975	SD N	11	22	1	6	0	0	0	2	1-0	0	1	.273	.333	.273	74	-1	0-0	.909	0	131	0	O4L		-0.1
1976	SD N	105	281	41	75	16	5	5	37	32-3	0	38	.267	.339	.413	123	8	12-6	.960	-2	89	128	O74L		0.3
1977	SD N	118	289	43	71	16	1	10	48	31-1	0	43	.246	.316	.412	105	1	12-4	.947	4	97	246	O69(65/4/2)		0.4
1978	SD N	106	225	28	63	9	1	8	37	21-5	3	32	.280	.348	.436	127	8	6-4	.970	-1	90	137	O58(28/17/24)		0.5
1979	SD N	138	448	55	111	23	2	9	61	34-0	2	58	.248	.301	.368	88	-9	4-2	.958	-2	97	85	O115(114/0/2)		-1.6
1980	SD N	85	153	22	44	5	0	3	18	10-4	2	18	.288	.335	.379	107	1	8-3	1.000	-1	91	93	O34(5/0/30)	52	0.0
1981	SD N	33	31	5	7	0	0	2	6	4-1	0	9	.226	.314	.419	116	0	0-0	.833	-0	107	0	O4R		0.0
	Chi N	10	12	1	2	0	0	0	2	1-0	0	2	.167	.231	.167	16	-1	0-0	1.000	0	106	0	/OR		-0.1
1982	Det A	85	210	21	52	3	0	8	27	20-1	0	37	.248	.310	.376	88	-4	1-3	.909	-2	58	0	D50,O13(2/0/12)		-0.9
1983	SD N	25	23	1	3	0	0	0	1	1-1	0	8	.130	.167	.130	-17	-4	0-0	—	-0	0	0	/OR		-0.4
Total 10		733	1742	222	448	73	9	45	238	159-17	7	245	.257	.319	.387	101	-2	45-24	.959	-5	93	129	O386(305/21/76),D50	52	-2.1

TURNER, SHANE Shane Lee B1.8.1963 Los Angeles CA BL/TR/5-10/180* [NYA85 6/155] d8.19 Col Cal St.-Fullerton

YEAR	TM LG	G	AB	R	H	2B	3B	HR	RBI	BB-IB	HP	SO	AVG	OBP	SLG	AOPS	ABR	SB-CS	FA	FR	RNG	THR	GAMES AT POSITION	DL	BFW
1988	Phi N	18	35	1	6	0	0	0	1	5-0	0	9	.171	.275	.171	30	-3	0-0	.941	-3	83	76	3b8,S5		-0.6
1991	Bal A	4	1	0	0	0	0	0	0	0-0	0	0	.000	.000	.000	-99	0	1-0	1.000	0	290	0	/2D		0.0
1992	Sea A	34	74	8	20	5	0	0	6	14-0	0	15	.270	.341	.338	92	0	2-1	.881	-1	99	193	3b18,O15(15/0/1)		-0.1
Total 3		56	110	9	26	5	0	0	6	14-0	0	24	.236	.317	.282	71	-3	2-1	.898	-3	94	153	3b26,O15(15/0/1),S5/D2		-0.7

TURNER, TERRY Terrence Lamont "Cotton Top" B2.28.1881 Sandy Lake PA D7.18.1960 Cleveland OH BR/TR/5-8/149 d8.25 C1

YEAR	TM LG	G	AB	R	H	2B	3B	HR	RBI	BB-IB	HP	SO	AVG	OBP	SLG	AOPS	ABR	SB-CS	FA	FR	RNG	THR	GAMES AT POSITION	DL	BFW
1901	Pit N	2	7	0	3	0	0	0	1	0		0	.429	.429	.429	145	0	0	.833	1	151	0	3b2		0.1
1904	Cle A	111	404	41	95	9	6	1	45	11		0	.235	.255	.295	74	-13	5	.940	3	106	85	S111		-0.8
1905	Cle A	155	586	49	155	16	14	4	72	14		-6	.265	.289	.360	104	-1	17	.946	-25	94	106	S155		-2.4
1906	Cle A	147	584	85	170	27	7	2	62	35		6	.291	.348	.372	124	16	27	.960	19	114	141	S147		4.2
1907	Cle A	140	524	57	127	20	7	0	46	19		2	.242	.272	.307	84	-11	27	.950	-2	100	155	S139		-1.0
1908	Cle A	60	201	21	48	11	1	0	19	15		2	.239	.298	.303	95	-1	18	.952	-3	57	0	O36(0/2/34),S17		-0.5
1909	Cle A	53	208	25	52	7	4	0	16	14		2	.250	.304	.322	94	-2	14	.969	10	125	78	2b26,S26		1.0
1910	Cle A	150	574	71	132	14	6	0	33	53		5	.230	.301	.275	79	-13	31	.973	-1	102	113	S94,3b46,2b9		-1.1
1911	Cle A	117	417	59	105	16	9	0	28	34		1	.252	.310	.333	78	-13	29	.970	1	108	72	3b94,2b14,S10		-0.9
1912	Cle A	103	370	54	114	14	4	0	33	31		1	.308	.363	.368	106	3	19	.951	3	97	144	3b103		0.8
1913	Cle A	120	388	60	96	13	4	0	44	55	5	35	.247	.348	.302	88	-4	13	.954	13	99	272	3b71,2b25,S21		1.4
1914	Cle A	121	428	43	105	14	9	1	33	44	2	36	.245	.319	.327	91	-5	17-13	.963	22	113	140	3b104,2b17		2.1
1915	Cle A	75	262	35	66	14	1	0	14	29	1	13	.252	.329	.313	90	-2	12-11	.965	-4	94	58	2b51,3b20		-0.7
1916	Cle A	124	428	52	112	15	3	0	38	40	0	29	.262	.325	.311	86	-7	15	.963	9	112	70	3b77,2b42		0.5
1917	Cle A	69	180	16	37	7	0	0	15	14	0	19	.206	.263	.244	51	-10	4	.980	-0	91	68	3b40,2b23/S		-1.1
1918	Cle A	74	233	24	58	7	2	0	23	22	1	15	.249	.316	.296	77	-6	6	.969	2	110	84	3b46,2b26/S		-0.4
1919	Phi A	38	127	7	24	3	0	0	6	5	0	9	.189	.220	.213	21	-14	2	.946	3	117	155	S19,2b17/3		-0.9
Total 17		1659	5921	699	1499	207	77	8	528	435	34	156	.253	.308	.318	89	-83	256-24	.951	49	103	123	S741,3b604,2b250,O36(0/2/34)		0.3

TURNER, TOM Thomas Richard B9.8.1916 Custer Co. OK D5.14.1986 Kennewick WA BR/TR/6-2/195 d4.25 Mil 1945

YEAR	TM LG	G	AB	R	H	2B	3B	HR	RBI	BB-IB	HP	SO	AVG	OBP	SLG	AOPS	ABR	SB-CS	FA	FR	RNG	THR	GAMES AT POSITION	DL	BFW
1940	Chi A	37	96	11	20	1	0	0	6	3	1	12	.208	.240	.260	29	-11	1-0	.969	2	116	83	C29		-0.7
1941	Chi A	38	126	7	30	5	0	0	8	9	0	15	.238	.289	.278	51	-9	2-0	.979	3	104	101	C35		-0.3
1942	Chi A	56	182	18	44	9	1	3	21	19	0	15	.242	.313	.352	89	-3	1-0	.971	-0	101	81	C54		0.0
1943	Chi A	51	154	16	37	7	1	2	11	13	0	21	.240	.299	.338	86	-3	1-0	.978	3	105	92	C49		0.3
1944	Chi A	36	113	9	26	6	0	2	13	5	0	16	.230	.263	.336	71	-5	0-1	.958	-2	119	87	C36		-0.5
	†StL A	15	25	2	8	1	0	0	4	2	0	5	.320	.370	.360	103	0	0-0	.969	-1	97	56	C11		0.0
	Year	51	138	11	34	7	0	2	17	7	0	21	.246	.283	.341	77	-5	0-1	.960	-2	115	82	C47		-0.5
Total 5		233	696	63	165	29	4	7	63	51	1	84	.237	.290	.320	70	-31	5-1	.972	5	107	88	C214		-1.2

TUTTLE, BILL William Robert B7.4.1929 Elwood IL D7.27.1998 Anoka MN BR/TR/6-0/190* d9.10 Col Bradley

YEAR	TM LG	G	AB	R	H	2B	3B	HR	RBI	BB-IB	HP	SO	AVG	OBP	SLG	AOPS	ABR	SB-CS	FA	FR	RNG	THR	GAMES AT POSITION	DL	BFW
1952	Det A	7	25	2	6	0	0	1	2	0	0	1	.240	.240	.240	34	-2	0-0	1.000	0	115	0	O6(3/3/0)		-0.3
1954	Det A	147	530	64	141	20	11	7	58	62	2	60	.266	.343	.385	102	1	5-8	.985	-2	93	133	O145(1/144/0)		-1.0
1955	Det A	154	603	102	168	23	4	14	78	76-2	1	76	.279	.358	.400	107	6	6-3	.985	5	104	127	O154C		0.4
1956	Det A	140	546	61	138	22	4	9	65	38-1	1	48	.253	.301	.378	73	-23	5-4	.976	3	102	149	O137C		-2.6
1957	Det A	133	451	49	113	12	4	5	47	44-4	1	41	.251	.316	.328	75	-16	2-0	.982	-1	105	57	O128C		-2.5
1958	KC A	148	511	77	118	19	4	9	11	74-1	1	58	.231	.327	.358	88	-8	7-9	.988	-4	93	125	O145(0/107/46)		-2.1
1959	KC A	126	463	74	139	19	6	7	43	48-2	5	38	.300	.369	.413	113	9	10-6	.984	9	103	221	O121C		1.3
1960	KC A	151	559	75	143	21	3	8	40	66-2	2	52	.256	.336	.347	85	-11	1-5	.988	8	108	183	O148C		-1.1
1961	KC A	25	84	15	22	2	0	1	8	5	0	9	.262	.333	.333	77	-3	0-0	.951	-2	104	0	O25C		-0.5

YEAR	TM LG	G	AB	R	H	2B	3B	HR	RBI	BB-IB	HP	SO	AVG	OBP	SLG	AOPS	ABR	SB-CS	FA	FR	RNG	THR	GAMES AT POSITION	DL	BFW
	Min A	113	370	38	91	12	3	5	38	43-4	0	41	.246	.321	.335	73	-14	1-3	.943	-1	98	95	3b85,O64(0/63/6),2b2		-1.7
	Year	138	454	53	113	14	5	5	46	52-4	0	50	.249	.323	.335	72	-17	1-3	.970	-2	105	36	O89(0/88/6),3b85,2b2		-2.2
1962	Min A	110	123	21	26	4	1	1	13	19-1	0	14	.211	.317	.285	62	-6	1-0	.973	-6	75	98	O104(0/95/15)		-1.3
1963	Min A	16	3	0	0	0	0	0	0	1-1	0	0	.000	.250	.000	-22	0	0-0	1.000	1	156	823	O14C		0.1
Total	11	1270	4268	578	1105	149	47	67	443	480-18	13	416	.259	.334	.363	88	-67	38-44	.983	12	100	135	O1191(4/1139/67),3b85,2b2		-11.3

TUTWILER, GUY   Guy Isbel "King Tut"   B7.17.1888 Coalburg AL   D8.15.1930 Birmingham AL   BL/TR/6-0/175   d8.29

YEAR	TM LG	G	AB	R	H	2B	3B	HR	RBI	BB-IB	HP	SO	AVG	OBP	SLG	AOPS	ABR	SB-CS	FA	FR	RNG	THR	GAMES AT POSITION	DL	BFW
1911	Det A	13	32	3	6	0	0	0	3	2	0		.188	.235	.250	34	-3	0	.778	-4	75	0	2b6,O3L		-0.6
1913	Det A	14	47	4	10	0	1	0	7	4	0	12	.213	.275	.255	56	-3	2	.987	1	127	135	1b14		-0.3
Total	2	27	79	7	16	0	1	0	10	6	0	12	.203	.259	.253	47	-6	2	.987	-3	127	135	1b14,2b6,O3L		-0.9

TWINEHAM, ART   Arthur S. "Old Hoss"   B11.26.1866 Galesburg IL   BL/TL/6-1.5/190   d9.11

YEAR	TM LG	G	AB	R	H	2B	3B	HR	RBI	BB-IB	HP	SO	AVG	OBP	SLG	AOPS	ABR	SB-CS	FA	FR	RNG	THR	GAMES AT POSITION	DL	BFW
1893	StL N	14	48	8	15	2	0	0	11	1	1	2	.313	.340	.354	84	-1	0	.928	1	85	120	C14		0.0
1894	StL N	38	127	22	40	4	1	1	16	9	6	11	.315	.387	.386	87	-2	2	.939	3	106	103	C38		0.3
Total	2	52	175	30	55	6	1	1	27	10	7	13	.314	.375	.377	86	-3	2	.936	3	100	107	C52		0.3

TWITCHELL, LARRY   Lawrence Grant   B2.18.1864 Cleveland OH   D8.23.1930 Cleveland OH   BR/TR/6-0/185   d4.30 ▲

YEAR	TM LG	G	AB	R	H	2B	3B	HR	RBI	BB-IB	HP	SO	AVG	OBP	SLG	AOPS	ABR	SB-CS	FA	FR	RNG	THR	GAMES AT POSITION	DL	BFW
1886	Det N	4	16	0	1	0	0	0	0	0		2	.063	.063	.063	-60	-3	0	1.000	0	155	693	P4,O2(1/1/0)		-0.1
1887	†Det N	65	264	44	88	14	6	5	51	8	2	19	.333	.358	.432	114	4	12	.871	-5	45	64	O53(44/9/0),P15		-0.2
1888	Det N	131	524	71	128	19	4	5	87	28	3	45	.244	.286	.324	93	-4	14	.885	-9	59	98	O131L,P2		-1.6
1889	Cle N	134	549	73	151	16	11	4	95	29	3	37	.275	.315	.366	92	-10	17	.916	-10	39	0	O134L/P		-1.9
1890	Cle P	56	233	33	52	6	3	2	36	17	1	17	.223	.279	.300	60	-14	4	.821	-7	86	49	O56(1/0/56)		-1.7
	Buf P	44	172	24	38	3	1	2	17	23	1	12	.221	.316	.285	67	-7	4	.918	1	64	90	O32(4/0/28),P13,1b3		-0.4
	Year	100	405	57	90	9	4	4	53	40	2	29	.222	.295	.294	63	-21	8	.857	-5	79	63	O88(5/0/84),P13,1b3		-2.1
1891	Col AA	57	224	32	62	9	4	2	35	20	2	28	.277	.341	.379	113	3	10	.887	-7	46	0	O56L,P6		-0.4
1892	Was N	51	192	20	42	9	5	0	20	11	4	31	.219	.275	.318	82	-5	8	.897	-3	73	65	O48(46/0/2),S3/3		-1.0
1893	Lou N	45	187	37	58	11	3	2	31	17	3	20	.310	.377	.433	125	7	7	.874	-2	77	0	O45(43/0/2)		0.1
1894	Lou N	52	210	28	56	16	3	2	32	15	0	20	.267	.316	.400	77	-8	8	.908	7	179	189	O51L/P		-0.4
Total	9	639	2571	362	676	103	40	19	384	168	19	231	.263	.313	.356	91	-37	84	.890	-34	67	57	O608(511/10/88),P42,S3,1b3/3		-7.6

TWOMBLY, BABE   Clarence Edward   B1.18.1896 Jamaica Plain MA   D11.23.1974 San Clemente CA   BL/TR/5-10/185   d4.14   b-George   Col Lehigh

YEAR	TM LG	G	AB	R	H	2B	3B	HR	RBI	BB-IB	HP	SO	AVG	OBP	SLG	AOPS	ABR	SB-CS	FA	FR	RNG	THR	GAMES AT POSITION	DL	BFW
1920	Chi N	78	183	25	43	1	1	2	14	17	1	20	.235	.303	.284	68	-7	5-9	.970	0	101	107	O45(5/15/25),2b2		-1.3
1921	Chi N	87	175	22	66	8	1	1	18	11	0	10	.377	.414	.451	129	8	4-6	.968	4	94	220	O45(10/29/6)		0.8
Total	2	165	358	47	109	9	2	3	32	28	1	30	.304	.357	.366	98	1	9-15	.969	4	98	158	O90(15/44/31),2b2		-0.5

TWOMBLY, GEORGE   George Frederick "Silent George"   B6.4.1892 Boston MA   D2.17.1975 Lexington MA   BR/TR/5-9/165   d7.9   b-Babe

YEAR	TM LG	G	AB	R	H	2B	3B	HR	RBI	BB-IB	HP	SO	AVG	OBP	SLG	AOPS	ABR	SB-CS	FA	FR	RNG	THR	GAMES AT POSITION	DL	BFW
1914	Cin N	68	240	22	56	0	5	0	19	14	3	27	.233	.284	.275	64	-11	12	.968	1	91	138	O68(68/0/1)		-1.5
1915	Cin N	46	66	5	13	0	1	0	5	8	1	8	.197	.293	.227	57	-3	5-3	1.000	1	106	129	O24(10/13/1)		-0.3
1916	Cin N	3	5	0	0	0	0	0	0	1	0		.000	.167	.000	-48	-1	0	1.000	-0	101	-0	/OL		-0.1
1917	Bos N	32	102	8	19	1	1	0	9	18	1	5	.186	.314	.226	68	-3	4	.943	-4	87	30	O29(1/21/7)/1		-1.0
1919	Was A	1	4	0	0	0	0	0	0	0	0		.000	.000	.000	-99	-1	0	—	-0	0	0	/OL		-0.1
Total	5	150	417	35	88	1	7	0	33	41	5	41	.211	.289	.247	62	-19	21-3	.967	-2	92	109	O123(81/34/9)/1		-3.0

TYACK, JIM   James Frederick   B1.9.1911 Florence MT   D1.3.1995 Bakersfield CA   BL/TR/6-2/195   d4.20

YEAR	TM LG	G	AB	R	H	2B	3B	HR	RBI	BB-IB	HP	SO	AVG	OBP	SLG	AOPS	ABR	SB-CS	FA	FR	RNG	THR	GAMES AT POSITION	DL	BFW
1943	Phi A	54	155	11	40	8	1	0	23	14	0	9	.258	.320	.323	88	-2	1-1	.977	1	103	144	O38(9/2/27)		-0.4

TYLER, FRED   Frederick Franklin "Clancy"   B12.16.1891 Derry NH   D10.14.1945 E.Derry NH   BR/TR/5-10.5/180   d10.3   b-Lefty

YEAR	TM LG	G	AB	R	H	2B	3B	HR	RBI	BB-IB	HP	SO	AVG	OBP	SLG	AOPS	ABR	SB-CS	FA	FR	RNG	THR	GAMES AT POSITION	DL	BFW
1914	Bos N	6	19	2	2	0	0	0	2	1	0	5	.105	.150	.105	-24	-3	0	1.000	-0	117	107	C6		-0.3

TYLER, JOHNNIE   John Anthony "Ty Ty","Katz" (b John Tylka)   B7.30.1906 Mt.Pleasant PA   D7.11.1972 Mt.Pleasant PA   BB/TR/6-0/175   d9.16

YEAR	TM LG	G	AB	R	H	2B	3B	HR	RBI	BB-IB	HP	SO	AVG	OBP	SLG	AOPS	ABR	SB-CS	FA	FR	RNG	THR	GAMES AT POSITION	DL	BFW
1934	Bos N	3	6	0	1	0	0	0	1	0	0	3	.167	.167	.167	-11	-1	0	1.000	1	82	989	/OC		0.0
1935	Bos N	13	47	7	16	1	2	1	11	4	1	3	.340	.404	.553	168	4	0	.893	-0	100	127	O11L		0.3
Total	2	16	53	7	17	1	2	1	12	4	1	6	.321	.379	.509	148	3	0	.906	0	98	225	O12(11/1/0)		0.3

TYNER, JASON   Jason Renyt   B4.23.1977 Bedford TX   BL/TL/6-1/170(170-185)   [NYN98 1/21]   d6.5   Col Texas A&M-Commerce

YEAR	TM LG	G	AB	R	H	2B	3B	HR	RBI	BB-IB	HP	SO	AVG	OBP	SLG	AOPS	ABR	SB-CS	FA	FR	RNG	THR	GAMES AT POSITION	DL	BFW
2000	NY N	13	41	3	8	2	0	0	5	1-0	1	4	.195	.222	.244	22	-5	1-1	.920	1	124	167	O12(12/2/0)		-0.4
	TB A	37	83	6	20	2	0	0	8	4-0	1	12	.241	.281	.265	41	-8	6-1	1.000	2	97	286	O31(27/4/0)/D		-0.5
2001	TB A	105	396	51	111	8	5	0	21	15-0	3	42	.280	.311	.326	70	-19	31-6	.978	4	106	147	O100(57/47/3)		-1.1
2002	TB A	44	168	17	36	1	0	0	9	7-0	1	19	.214	.249	.238	31	-17	7-1	.990	2	113	80	O42(41/1/0)/D		-1.5
2003	TB A	46	90	12	25	7	0	0	6	10-0	0	12	.278	.350	.356	89	-1	2-1	.962	-0	101	72	O32(9/2/23),D4		-0.2
2005	Min A	18	56	8	18	1	1	0	5	4-0	0	4	.321	.367	.375	96	0	2-0	1.000	0	112	0	O15(12/2/2),D3		0.0
Total	5	263	834	97	218	22	7	0	54	41-0	6	93	.261	.299	.305	61	-50	49-10	.980	9	107	133	O232(158/58/28),D9		-3.7

TYREE, EARL   Earl Carlton "Ty"   B3.4.1890 Huntsville IL   D5.17.1954 Rushville IL   BR/TR/5-8/160   d10.5

YEAR	TM LG	G	AB	R	H	2B	3B	HR	RBI	BB-IB	HP	SO	AVG	OBP	SLG	AOPS	ABR	SB-CS	FA	FR	RNG	THR	GAMES AT POSITION	DL	BFW
1914	Chi N	1	4	1	0	0	0	0	0	0	0	0	.000	.000	.000	-99	-1	0	1.000	-1	91	137	/C		-0.2

TYRONE, JIM   James Vernon   B1.29.1949 Alice TX   BR/TR/6-1/185*   [ChiN71 7/162]   d8.27   b-Wayne   Col Texas-Pan American

YEAR	TM LG	G	AB	R	H	2B	3B	HR	RBI	BB-IB	HP	SO	AVG	OBP	SLG	AOPS	ABR	SB-CS	FA	FR	RNG	THR	GAMES AT POSITION	DL	BFW
1972	Chi N	13	8	1	0	0	0	0	0	0-0	0	3	.000	.000	.000	-90	-2	1-0	1.000	1	180	839	O4(3/0/1)		-0.1
1974	Chi N	57	81	19	15	0	1	3	3	6-0	0	18	.185	.241	.321	54	-6	1-1	.962	-1	85	98	O32(21/1/12)/3		-0.8
1975	Chi N	11	22	0	5	0	1	0	3	1-0	0	4	.227	.250	.318	57	-1	1-1	1.000	0	73	271	O8L		-0.2
1977	Oak A	96	294	32	72	11	1	5	26	25-2	0	52	.245	.300	.340	76	-10	3-1	.950	1	107	90	O81(10/4/70)/1SD		-1.3
Total	4	177	405	52	92	11	3	8	32	32-2	0	77	.227	.281	.328	67	-19	6-3	.955	1	103	113	O125(42/5/83),D4/S13		-2.4

TYRONE, WAYNE   Oscar Wayne   B8.1.1950 Alice TX   BR/TR/6-1/185   [ChiN72 20/470]   d7.15   b-Jim   Col Texas-Pan American

YEAR	TM LG	G	AB	R	H	2B	3B	HR	RBI	BB-IB	HP	SO	AVG	OBP	SLG	AOPS	ABR	SB-CS	FA	FR	RNG	THR	GAMES AT POSITION	DL	BFW
1976	Chi N	30	57	3	13	1	0	1	8	3-2	0	21	.228	.262	.298	55	-3	0-0	1.000	-1	35	0	O7(6/0/1),1b5,3b5		-0.5

TYSON, TY   Albert Thomas   B6.1.1892 Wilkes-Barre PA   D8.16.1953 Buffalo NY   BR/TR/5-11/169   d4.13

YEAR	TM LG	G	AB	R	H	2B	3B	HR	RBI	BB-IB	HP	SO	AVG	OBP	SLG	AOPS	ABR	SB-CS	FA	FR	RNG	THR	GAMES AT POSITION	DL	BFW
1926	NY N	97	335	40	98	16	1	3	35	15	3	28	.293	.329	.373	90	-1	9	.980	1	99	105	O92(12/83/0)		-0.9
1927	NY N	43	159	24	42	7	2	1	17	10	0	19	.264	.308	.352	76	-6	5	.929	-2	87	132	O41(40/1/2)		-1.1
1928	Bro N	59	210	25	57	11	1	1	21	10	4	14	.271	.317	.348	75	-8	3	.965	-0	97	123	O55(1/41/14)		-1.1
Total	3	199	704	89	197	34	4	5	73	35	7	61	.280	.320	.361	82	-19	14	.966	-1	96	116	O188(53/125/16)		-3.1

TYSON, TURKEY   Cecil Washington "Slim"   B12.6.1914 Elm City NC   D2.17.2000 Elm City NC   BL/TR/6-5.5/225   d4.23

YEAR	TM LG	G	AB	R	H	2B	3B	HR	RBI	BB-IB	HP	SO	AVG	OBP	SLG	AOPS	ABR	SB-CS	FA	FR	RNG	THR	GAMES AT POSITION	DL	BFW
1944	Phi N	1	1	0	0	0	0	0	0	0	0	0	.000	.000	.000	-99	0	0	—	0			/H		0.0

TYSON, MIKE   Michael Ray   B1.13.1950 Rocky Mount NC   BR/TR (BB 1972p, 76p, 79p, 80p)/5-9/170*   [StLN70*3/60]   d9.5   Col Indian River (FL) CC

YEAR	TM LG	G	AB	R	H	2B	3B	HR	RBI	BB-IB	HP	SO	AVG	OBP	SLG	AOPS	ABR	SB-CS	FA	FR	RNG	THR	GAMES AT POSITION	DL	BFW
1972	StL N	13	37	1	7	1	0	0	0	9	1	9	.189	.211	.216	22	-4	0-1	.981	2	121	56	2b11,S2		-0.7
1973	StL N	144	469	48	114	15	4	1	33	23-10	2	66	.243	.279	.299	60	-26	2-5	.944	-10	94	94	S128,2b16		-2.3
1974	StL N	151	422	35	94	14	5	1	37	22-9	3	70	.223	.264	.287	55	-27	4-2	.955	7	103	145	S143,2b12		-0.4
1975	StL N	122	368	45	98	16	3	2	37	24-4	3	39	.266	.316	.342	79	-11	5-2	.971	-8	91	83	S95,2b24,3b5		-0.8
1976	StL N	76	245	26	70	12	6	0	28	16-5	0	34	.286	.326	.445	116	4	3-1	.971	10	116	113	2b74	68	1.9
1977	StL N	138	418	42	103	15	2	7	57	30-11	2	48	.246	.299	.342	72	-17	3-4	.979	24	118	134	2b135		1.1
1978	StL N	125	377	26	88	16	0	3	26	24-7	0	41	.233	.277	.300	62	-20	2-0	.977	8	90	116	2b124		-2.5
1979	StL N	75	190	18	42	8	2	5	20	13-6	1	28	.221	.272	.363	71	-8	2-1	.975	2	106	120	2b71	33	-0.7
1980	Chi N	123	341	34	81	19	3	3	25	15-3	2	61	.238	.273	.337	64	-16	1-2	.968	10	106	103	2b117		-0.7
1981	Chi N	50	92	6	17	2	0	2	8	7-1	1	15	.185	.248	.272	45	-7	1-0	.940	-3	97	85	2b36/S		-0.6
Total	10	1017	2959	281	714	118	28	27	269	175-56	14	411	.241	.285	.327	69	-132	23-18	.973	25	107	115	2b620,S369,3b5	101	-4.3

UECKER, BOB   Robert George   B1.26.1935 Milwaukee WI   BR/TR/6-1/190*   d4.13

YEAR	TM LG	G	AB	R	H	2B	3B	HR	RBI	BB-IB	HP	SO	AVG	OBP	SLG	AOPS	ABR	SB-CS	FA	FR	RNG	THR	GAMES AT POSITION	DL	BFW
1962	Mil N	33	64	5	16	2	0	1	8	7-0	0	15	.250	.324	.328	78	-2	0-0	.982	3	428	112	C24		0.2
1963	Mil N	13	16	3	4	2	0	0	3	2-0	0	5	.250	.333	.375	105	0	0-0	.958	1	116	119	C6		0.2
1964	StL N	40	106	8	21	1	0	1	6	11-0	1	24	.198	.315	.236	53	-6	0-1	.987	1	102	93	C40		-0.4
1965	StL N	53	145	17	33	7	0	1	10	24-1	1	27	.228	.345	.317	80	-3	0-1	.985	-7	60	107	C49		-0.7
1966	Phi N	78	207	15	43	6	0	7	30	22-6	0	36	.208	.279	.338	72	-8	0-0	.985	-2	91	112	C76		-0.5
1967	Phi N	18	35	3	6	2	0	0	3	5	0	9	.171	.275	.229	45	-2	0-0	.973	-1	48	105	C17		-0.5
	Atl N	62	158	14	23	2	0	3	13	19-4	1	51	.146	.236	.215	31	-14	0-1	.972	-5	77	55	C59		-1.5
	Year	80	193	17	29	4	0	3	16	24-5	1	60	.150	.243	.218	33	-17	0-1	.972	-6	72	64	C76		-2.0
Total	6	297	731	65	146	22	0	14	74	96-12	3	167	.200	.293	.287	63	-35	0-3	.981	-10	108	95	C271		-3.6

YEAR	TM LG	G	AB	R	H	2B	3B	HR	RBI	BB-IB	HP	SO	AVG	OBP	SLG	AOPS	ABR	SB-CS	FA	FR	RNG	THR	GAMES AT POSITION	DL	BFW

UGUETO, LUIS   Luis Enrique B2.15.1979 Caracas, Venez   BB/TR/5-11/170*   d4.3

YEAR	TM LG	G	AB	R	H	2B	3B	HR	RBI	BB-IB	HP	SO	AVG	OBP	SLG	AOPS	ABR	SB-CS	FA	FR	RNG	THR	GAMES AT POSITION	DL	BFW
2002	Sea A	62	23	19	5	0	0	1	1	2-0	0	8	.217	.280	.348	68	-1	8-4	.960	2	118	119	D16,2b11,S8/3	24	0.0
2003	Sea A	12	5	4	1	0	0	0	1	1-0	0	0	.200	.333	.200	48	0	2-0	1.000	-0	98	334	2b4/3SD		0.0
Total	2	74	28	23	6	0	0	1	2	3-0	0	8	.214	.290	.321	65	-1	10-4	.967	1	114	161	D19,2b15,S9,3b2	24	0.0

UHALT, FRENCHY   Bernard Bartholomew B4.27.1910 Bakersfield CA   D9.3.2004 Walnut Creek CA   BL/TR/5-10/180   d4.17

YEAR	TM LG	G	AB	R	H	2B	3B	HR	RBI	BB-IB	HP	SO	AVG	OBP	SLG	AOPS	ABR	SB-CS	FA	FR	RNG	THR	GAMES AT POSITION	DL	BFW
1934	Chi A	57	165	28	40	5	1	0	16	29	1	12	.242	.359	.285	66	-7	6-5	.935	-2	96	62	O40(4/14/22)		-1.1

UHLAENDER, TED   Theodore Otto B10.21.1940 Chicago Heights IL   BL/TR/6-2/190*   d9.4   C2   Col Baylor

YEAR	TM LG	G	AB	R	H	2B	3B	HR	RBI	BB-IB	HP	SO	AVG	OBP	SLG	AOPS	ABR	SB-CS	FA	FR	RNG	THR	GAMES AT POSITION	DL	BFW
1965	Min A	13	22	1	4	0	0	1	0	0-0	0	2	.182	.182	.182	3	-3	1-0	1.000	1	118	496	O4L		-0.2
1966	Min A	105	367	39	83	12	2	2	22	27-1	1	33	.226	.280	.286	60	-19	10-2	.985	3	113	66	O100(4/96/0)		-1.9
1967	Min A	133	415	41	107	19	7	6	49	13-1	3	45	.258	.285	.381	88	-7	4-4	.996	2	107	95	O118C		-1.1
1968	Min A	140	488	52	138	21	5	7	52	28-3	3	46	.283	.324	.389	110	5	16-7	.986	-7	96	36	O129C		-0.5
1969	†Min A	152	554	93	151	18	2	8	62	44-4	4	52	.273	.328	.356	89	-8	15-9	.997	-8	89	85	O150(44/108/1)		-2.2
1970	Cle A	141	473	56	127	21	2	11	46	39-3	1	44	.268	.321	.391	92	-5	3-6	.991	-11	83	66	O134(24/116/8)		-2.3
1971	Cle A	141	500	52	144	20	3	2	47	38-5	0	44	.288	.336	.352	87	-7	3-6	.992	-1	99	79	O131(87/33/13)		-1.7
1972	†Cin N	73	113	9	18	3	0	0	6	13-3	0	11	.159	.246	.186	25	-11	0-1	.976	-0	86	185	O27(3/2/23)		-1.4
Total	8	898	2932	343	772	114	21	36	285	202-20	12	277	.263	.311	.353	86	-55	52-35	.991	-21	97	76	O793(166/602/45)		-11.3

UHLE, GEORGE   George Ernest "The Bull" B9.18.1898 Cleveland OH   D2.26.1985 Lakewood OH   BR/TR/6-0/190   d4.30   C4 ▲

YEAR	TM LG	G	AB	R	H	2B	3B	HR	RBI	BB-IB	HP	SO	AVG	OBP	SLG	AOPS	ABR	SB-CS	FA	FR	RNG	THR	GAMES AT POSITION	DL	BFW
1919	Cle A	26	43	7	13	2	1	0	6	1	0	5	.302	.318	.395	94	3	0	.915	0	97	67	P26		0.0
1920	†Cle A	27	32	4	11	0	0	2	2	2	0	2	.344	.382	.344	91	2	1-0	1.000	0	96	0	P27		0.0
1921	Cle A	48	94	21	23	2	3	1	18	6	0	9	.245	.290	.362	64	3	0	.938	-3	75	102	P41		0.0
1922	Cle A	56	109	21	29	8	2	0	14	13	1	6	.266	.350	.376	88	9	1-2	.932	-3	75	153	P50		0.0
1923	Cle A	58	144	23	52	10	3	0	22	7	0	10	.361	.391	.472	127	17	2-1	.982	-0	96	184	P54		0.0
1924	Cle A	59	107	10	33	6	1	1	19	4	1	8	.308	.339	.411	92	7	0-1	1.000	1	92	220	P28		0.0
1925	Cle A	55	101	10	29	3	0	1	13	7	1	7	.287	.339	.376	81	6	0-0	.943	-3	72	80	P29		0.0
1926	Cle A	50	132	16	30	3	0	1	11	10	1	12	.227	.287	.273	46	4	2-2	.933	-0	84	77	P39		0.0
1927	Cle A	43	79	4	21	7	1	0	14	5	0	12	.266	.310	.380	78	5	0-1	.974	-1	82	159	P25		0.0
1928	Cle A	55	98	9	28	3	2	1	17	8	0	4	.286	.340	.388	90	7	0-0	.972	2	122	127	P31		0.0
1929	Det A	40	108	18	37	1	1	0	13	6	0	6	.343	.377	.370	93	8	0-0	.929	-3	73	64	P32		0.0
1930	Det A	59	117	15	36	4	2	2	21	8	0	13	.308	.352	.427	95	8	0-0	.975	-3	60	75	P33		0.0
1931	Det A	53	90	8	22	6	0	2	7	8	0	8	.244	.306	.378	76	5	0-1	1.000	-1	97	47	P29		0.0
1932	Det A	38	55	2	10	3	1	0	4	6	0	5	.182	.262	.273	37	1	0-0	1.000	-1	84	111	P33		0.0
1933		1	0	0	0	0	0	0	0	0	0	—	—	—	—	—	0	0-0	—	0	0	0	/P		0.0
	NY N	8	5	1	0	0	0	0	0	1	0	3	.000	.167	.000	-50	0	0-0	1.000	0	130	0	P6		0.0
	NY A	12	20	1	8	1	0	0	1	4	0	2	.400	.500	.450	163	4	0-0	1.000	-1	69	137	P12		0.0
1934	NY A	10	5	1	3	1	0	0	1	0	0	0	.600	.600	1.000	329	2	0-0	1.000	-0	32	0	P10		0.0
1936	Cle A	24	21	1	8	1	0	1	4	2	0	0	.381	.435	.571	145	4	0-0	—	-1	0	0	P7		0.0
Total	17	722	1360	172	393	60	21	9	187	98	4	112	.289	.339	.384	86	95	6-8	.960	-16	84	111	P513		0.0

UHLER, MAURY   Maurice William B12.14.1886 Pikesville MD   D5.4.1918 Baltimore MD   BR/TR/5-11/165   d4.14

YEAR	TM LG	G	AB	R	H	2B	3B	HR	RBI	BB-IB	HP	SO	AVG	OBP	SLG	AOPS	ABR	SB-CS	FA	FR	RNG	THR	GAMES AT POSITION	DL	BFW
1914	Cin N	46	56	12	12	2	0	3	5	0	11	.214	.279	.250	56	-3	4	.932	0	118	47	O36(22/11/3)		-0.4

UHLIR, CHARLIE   Charles Karel B7.30.1912 Chicago IL   D7.9.1984 Spirit Lake IA   BL/TL/5-7.5/150   d8.3

YEAR	TM LG	G	AB	R	H	2B	3B	HR	RBI	BB-IB	HP	SO	AVG	OBP	SLG	AOPS	ABR	SB-CS	FA	FR	RNG	THR	GAMES AT POSITION	DL	BFW
1934	Chi A	14	27	3	4	0	0	0	3	2	0	6	.148	.207	.148	-7	-4	0-0	1.000	-0	96	0	O6L		-0.5

ULICNEY, MIKE   Michael Edward "Slugs" B9.28.1917 Greenwald PA   D9.22.2005 New Smyrna FL   BR/TR/5-9/165   d5.5

YEAR	TM LG	G	AB	R	H	2B	3B	HR	RBI	BB-IB	HP	SO	AVG	OBP	SLG	AOPS	ABR	SB-CS	FA	FR	RNG	THR	GAMES AT POSITION	DL	BFW
1945	Bos N	11	18	4	7	1	0	1	4	1	0	0	.389	.421	.611	184	2	0	.714	-1	92	165	C4		0.1

ULLGER, SCOTT   Scott Matthew B6.10.1956 New York NY   BR/TR/6-2/200   [MinA77 18/456]   d4.17   C11   Col St. Johns

YEAR	TM LG	G	AB	R	H	2B	3B	HR	RBI	BB-IB	HP	SO	AVG	OBP	SLG	AOPS	ABR	SB-CS	FA	FR	RNG	THR	GAMES AT POSITION	DL	BFW
1983	Min A	35	79	8	15	4	0	0	5	5-0	1	21	.190	.247	.241	33	-7	0-2	.990	-2	57	69	1b30,3b3/D		-1.1

ULRICH, GEORGE   George T. B6.5.1869 Philadelphia PA   d5.1

YEAR	TM LG	G	AB	R	H	2B	3B	HR	RBI	BB-IB	HP	SO	AVG	OBP	SLG	AOPS	ABR	SB-CS	FA	FR	RNG	THR	GAMES AT POSITION	DL	BFW
1892	Was N	6	24	1	7	1	0	0	0	0	0	4	.292	.292	.333	91	0	2	.889	0	71	0	3b3,S2,C2		0.0
1893	Cin N	1	3	0	0	0	0	0	0	0	1	0	.000	.250	.000	-31	-1	1	1.000	-0	0	0	/OC		-0.1
1896	NY N	14	45	4	8	1	0	0	1	1	2	1	.178	.229	.200	14	-6	0	.920	0	194	253	O11L,3b3		-0.6
Total	3	21	72	5	15	2	0	0	1	1	3	5	.208	.250	.236	35	-7	3	.923	0	183	238	O12(11/1/0),3b6,C2,S2		-0.7

UMPHLETT, TOM   Thomas Mullen B5.12.1930 Scotland Neck NC   BR/TR/6-2/180*   d4.16

YEAR	TM LG	G	AB	R	H	2B	3B	HR	RBI	BB-IB	HP	SO	AVG	OBP	SLG	AOPS	ABR	SB-CS	FA	FR	RNG	THR	GAMES AT POSITION	DL	BFW
1953	Bos A	137	495	53	140	27	5	3	59	34	2	30	.283	.331	.376	86	-10	4-2	.983	-1	100	100	O136C		-1.7
1954	Was A	114	342	21	75	8	3	1	33	17	4	42	.219	.255	.269	46	-27	1-2	.989	3	92	190	O101(12/4/86)		-3.0
1955	Was A	110	323	34	70	10	0	2	19	24-0	0	35	.217	.271	.266	47	-25	2-1	.988	5	108	128	O103(18/62/23)		-2.5
Total	3	361	1160	108	285	45	8	6	111	75-0	2	107	.246	.292	.314	65	-62	7-5	.986	7	100	133	O340(30/202/109)		-7.2

UNGLAUB, BOB   Robert Alexander B7.31.1881 Baltimore MD   D11.29.1916 Baltimore MD   BR/TR/5-11/178   d4.15   M1   Col Maryland-Baltimore Co.

YEAR	TM LG	G	AB	R	H	2B	3B	HR	RBI	BB-IB	HP	SO	AVG	OBP	SLG	AOPS	ABR	SB-CS	FA	FR	RNG	THR	GAMES AT POSITION	DL	BFW
1904	NY A	6	19	2	4	0	0	0	2	0				.211	.211	.211	32	-2	0	.786	-1	88	290	3b4/S		-0.3
	Bos A	9	13	1	2	1	0	0	2	1	0		.154	.214	.231	39	-1	0	.625	-2	21	0	2b3,3b2/S		-0.4
	Year	15	32	3	6	1	0	0	4	1	0		.188	.212	.219	35	-2	0	.842	-3	85	218	3b6,2b3,S2		-0.7
1905	Bos A	43	121	18	27	5	1	0	11	6	0		.223	.260	.281	71	-4	2	.928	-1	102	131	3b21,2b7,1b2		-0.5
1907	Bos A	139	544	49	138	17	13	1	62	23	0		.254	.284	.338	99	-3	14	.986	-1	96	117	1b139,M		-0.8
1908	Bos A	72	266	23	70	11	3	1	25	7	2		.263	.287	.338	100	-1	6	.980	2	112	69	1b72		-0.1
	Was A	72	276	23	85	10	5	0	29	8	0		.308	.327	.380	142	11	8	.928	6	115	43	3b39,2b27,1b4		2.0
	Year	144	542	46	155	21	8	1	54	15	2		.286	.308	.360	120	9	14	.981	7	115	78	1b76,3b39,2b27		1.9
1909	Was A	130	480	43	127	14	9	3	41	22	3		.265	.301	.350	111	3	15	.992	2	109	111	1b57,O42(8/0/34),2b25,3b4		0.3
	Was A	124	431	29	101	9	4	0	44	21	0		.234	.270	.274	74	-15	21	.985	6	119	99	1b124		-1.2
Total	6	595	2150	188	554	67	35	6	216	88	5		.258	.288	.328	99	-12	66	.986	10	108	103	1b398,3b70,2b62,O42(8/0/34),S2		-1.0

UNROE, TIM   Timothy Brian B10.7.1970 Round Lake Beach IL   BR/TR/6-3/200*   [MilA92 28/780]   d5.30   Col Lewis

YEAR	TM LG	G	AB	R	H	2B	3B	HR	RBI	BB-IB	HP	SO	AVG	OBP	SLG	AOPS	ABR	SB-CS	FA	FR	RNG	THR	GAMES AT POSITION	DL	BFW
1995	Mil A	2	4	0	1	0	0	0	0	0-0	0	1	.250	.250	.250	29	0	0-0	1.000	-0	0	233	1b2		-0.1
1996	Mil A	14	16	5	3	0	0	0	0	4-0	0	5	.188	.350	.188	40	-1	0-0	.976	2	117	1b11,3b3/OLD		0.0
1997	Mil A	32	16	3	4	1	0	2	5	2-0	0	9	.250	.333	.688	155	1	2-0	.969	1	129	88	1b23,3b2,O2(1/0/1)/2		0.2
1999	Ana A	27	54	5	13	2	0	1	6	4-0	1	16	.241	.305	.333	63	-3	0-0	1.000	-2	67	150	O12(4/0/8),3b3/2D		-0.5
2000	Atl N	4	5	0	0	0	0	0	0	1-0	0	2	.000	.167	.000	-54	-1	0-0	1.000	1	278	0	1b2/OL		-0.1
Total	5	79	95	13	21	3	0	3	11	11-0	1	32	.221	.308	.347	67	-4	2-1	.977	1	92	104	1b38,O16(7/0/9),D9,3b8,2b2		-0.5

UNSER, AL   Albert Bernard B10.12.1912 Morrisonville IL   D7.7.1995 Decatur IL   BR/TR/6-1/175   d9.14   s-Del

YEAR	TM LG	G	AB	R	H	2B	3B	HR	RBI	BB-IB	HP	SO	AVG	OBP	SLG	AOPS	ABR	SB-CS	FA	FR	RNG	THR	GAMES AT POSITION	DL	BFW
1942	Det A	4	8	2	3	0	0	0	0	0	0	2	.375	.375	.375	103	0	0-0	1.000	1	110	130	C4		0.1
1943	Det A	38	101	14	25	5	0	0	4	15	1	15	.248	.350	.297	84	-1	0-1	.982	-1	90	113	C37		0.0
1944	Det A	11	25	2	3	0	1	1	5	3	0	2	.120	.214	.320	49	-2	0-0	.864	-3	57	66	2b5/C		-0.5
1945	Cin N	67	204	23	54	10	3	3	21	14	2	24	.265	.318	.387	98	-1	0	.956	-2	86	85	C61		0.0
Total	4	120	338	41	85	15	4	4	30	32	3	43	.251	.322	.355	90	-4	0-1	.967	-5	88	95	C103,2b5		-0.4

UNSER, DEL   Delbert Bernard B12.9.1944 Decatur IL   BL/TL/6-1/180*   d4.10   C4   f-Al   Col Mississippi St.

YEAR	TM LG	G	AB	R	H	2B	3B	HR	RBI	BB-IB	HP	SO	AVG	OBP	SLG	AOPS	ABR	SB-CS	FA	FR	RNG	THR	GAMES AT POSITION	DL	BFW
1968	Was A	156	635	66	146	13	7	1	30	46-1	2	66	.230	.282	.277	73	-22	11-6	.988	10	100	200	O156C/1		-1.9
1969	Was A	153	581	69	166	19	8	7	57	58-3	0	54	.286	.349	.382	110	7	8-10	.972	-3	102	89	O149C		-0.1
1970	Was A	119	322	37	83	5	1	5	30	30-0	1	29	.258	.319	.326	82	-8	1-1	.983	3	102	151	O103(11/43/50)		-0.9
1971	Was A	153	581	63	148	19	6	9	41	59-10	2	68	.255	.325	.355	97	-3	11-6	.981	10	113	103	O151(8/105/68)		0.1
1972	Cle A	132	383	29	91	12	0	1	17	28-4	1	46	.238	.288	.277	67	-15	5-6	.989	4	104	146	O119(14/85/23)		-1.5
1973	Phi N	136	440	64	127	20	4	11	52	47-7	1	55	.289	.354	.427	114	9	5-8	.988	14	119	194	O132C		1.9
1974	Phi N	142	454	72	120	18	5	11	61	50-9	1	62	.264	.337	.399	101	0	6-4	.981	1	98	173	O135C		-0.3
1975	NY N	147	531	65	156	18	2	10	53	37-6	0	76	.294	.337	.392	106	2	4-3	.987	9	109	158	O144C		0.8
1976	NY N	77	276	28	63	13	2	5	25	18-1	0	40	.228	.275	.344	79	-9	4-4	.995	-1	98	112	O77(2/75/0)		-1.3
	Mon N	69	220	29	50	6	2	7	15	11-1	0	44	.227	.261	.368	74	-9	3-3	.982	-3	89	116	O65(29/13/34)		-1.5
	Year	146	496	57	113	19	4	12	40	29-2	0	84	.228	.269	.355	77	-17	7-7	.990	-3	94	114	O142(31/88/34)		-2.8
1977	Mon N	113	289	33	79	14	1	12	40	33-7	2	41	.273	.346	.453	115	6	2-5	.976	-6	86	45	O72(11/34/27),1b27		-0.4
1978	Mon N	130	179	16	35	10	0	2	15	24-5	1	29	.196	.293	.257	55	-10	2-0	.994	2	93	111	1b64,O33(7/12/14)		-1.1

YEAR	TM LG	G	AB	R	H	2B	3B	HR	RBI	BB-IB	HP	SO	AVG	OBP	SLG	AOPS	ABR	SB-CS	FA	FR	RNG	THR	GAMES AT POSITION	DL	BFW
1979	Phi N	95	141	26	42	8	0	6	29	14-2	0	33	.298	.354	.482	123	4	2-0	.978	-1	102	0	O30(16/11/3),1b22		0.
1980	†Phi N	96	110	15	29	6	4	0	10	10-1	0	21	.264	.320	.391	93	-1	0-1	1.000	5	268	114	1b31,O23(13/12/1)		0.
1981	Phi N	62	59	5	9	3	0	0	6	13-1	0	9	.153	.301	.203	44	-4	0-0	1.000	1	146	96	1b18,O16(7/6/4)		-0.
1982	Phi N	19	14	0	0	0	0	0	0	3-1	0	2	.000	.176	.000	-45	-3	0-0	1.000	0	177	171	1b5,O2R		-0.
Total	15	1799	5215	617	1344	179	42	87	481	481-62	9	675	.258	.319	.358	93	-56	64-60	.984	46	104	136	O1407(118/1112/226),1b168		-6.

UPHAM, JOHN John Leslie B12.29.1941 Windsor ON, Can. BL/TL/6-0/180* d4.16

YEAR	TM LG	G	AB	R	H	2B	3B	HR	RBI	BB-IB	HP	SO	AVG	OBP	SLG	AOPS	ABR	SB-CS	FA	FR	RNG	THR	GAMES AT POSITION	DL	BFW
1967	Chi N	8	3	1	2	0	0	0	0	0-0	0	0	.667	.667	.667	270	1	0-0	—	0	0	0	P5		0.
1968	Chi N	13	10	0	2	0	0	0	0	0-0	0	3	.200	.200	.200	19	-1	0-0	1.000	-0	262	0	P2,O2(1/1/0)		-0.
Total	2	21	13	1	4	0	0	0	0	0-0	0	3	.308	.308	.308	78	0	0-0	1.000	-0	229	0	P7,O2(1/1/0)		-0.

UPRIGHT, DIXIE Roy T. B5.30.1926 Kannapolis NC D11.13.1986 Concord NC BL/TL/6-0/175 d4.18

YEAR	TM LG	G	AB	R	H	2B	3B	HR	RBI	BB-IB	HP	SO	AVG	OBP	SLG	AOPS	ABR	SB-CS	FA	FR	RNG	THR	GAMES AT POSITION	DL	BFW
1953	StL A	9	8	3	2	0	0	1	1	0-0	0	3	.250	.333	.625	151	0	0-0	—	0			/H		0.

UPSHAW, WILLIE Willie Clay B4.27.1957 Blanco TX BL/TL/6-0/185* [NYA75 5/115] d4.9 C4

YEAR	TM LG	G	AB	R	H	2B	3B	HR	RBI	BB-IB	HP	SO	AVG	OBP	SLG	AOPS	ABR	SB-CS	FA	FR	RNG	THR	GAMES AT POSITION	DL	BFW
1978	Tor A	95	224	26	53	8	2	1	17	21-0	0	35	.237	.298	.304	69	-9	4-6	.943	-5	86	68	O52(46/6/1),D18,1b10		-1.
1980	Tor A	34	61	10	13	1	1	1	5	6-1	0	14	.213	.284	.344	68	-3	1-0	.983	1	160	178	1b14,D12/OL		-0.
1981	Tor A	61	111	15	19	3	1	4	10	11-0	1	16	.171	.252	.324	61	-6	2-1	1.000	-1	105	119	D15,1b14,O14(6/0/8)		-0.
1982	Tor A	160	580	77	155	25	7	21	75	52-8	1	91	.267	.327	.443	101	0	8-8	.989	-6	89	95	1b155,D5		-1.
1983	Tor A	160	579	99	177	26	7	27	104	61-8	5	98	.306	.373	.515	134	27	10-7	.985	-2	98	95	1b159/D		1.
1984	Tor A	152	569	79	158	31	9	19	84	55-14	5	86	.278	.345	.464	117	13	10-4	.990	-8	84	105	1b151/D		-0.
1985	†Tor A	148	501	79	138	31	4	15	65	48-7	4	71	.275	.342	.447	111	8	8-8	.992	-0	106	106	1b147/D		-0.
1986	Tor A	155	573	85	144	28	6	9	60	78-4	2	87	.251	.341	.368	91	-5	23-5	.992	4	107	95	1b154/D		-0.
1987	Tor A	150	512	68	125	22	4	15	58	58-4	3	78	.244	.324	.391	86	-10	10-11	.993	13	129	107	1b146		-0.
1988	Cle A	149	493	58	121	22	3	11	50	62-4	2	66	.245	.330	.369	93	-3	12-9	.991	2	108	84	1b144		-1.
Total	10	1264	4203	596	1103	199	45	123	528	452-50	23	642	.262	.335	.419	102	12	88-59	.990	-2	102	98	1b1094,O67(53/6/9),D54		-6.

UPTON, B.J. Melvin Emanuel B8.21.1984 Norfolk VA BR/TR/6-3/180 [TBA02 1/2] d8.2

YEAR	TM LG	G	AB	R	H	2B	3B	HR	RBI	BB-IB	HP	SO	AVG	OBP	SLG	AOPS	ABR	SB-CS	FA	FR	RNG	THR	GAMES AT POSITION	DL	BFW
2004	TB A	45	159	19	41	8	2	4	12	15-0	1	46	.258	.324	.409	92	-2	4-1	.901	-9	89	76	S16,D14,3b13/OL		-0.

UPTON, TOM Thomas Herbert "Muscles" B12.29.1926 Esther MO BR/TR/6-0/160* d4.19 b-Bill Col Penn

YEAR	TM LG	G	AB	R	H	2B	3B	HR	RBI	BB-IB	HP	SO	AVG	OBP	SLG	AOPS	ABR	SB-CS	FA	FR	RNG	THR	GAMES AT POSITION	DL	BFW
1950	StL A	124	389	50	92	5	6	2	30	52	1	45	.237	.328	.296	58	-25	7-2	.946	-9	103	73	S115,2b2/3		-2.
1951	StL A	52	131	9	26	4	3	0	12	12	1	22	.198	.271	.275	46	-10	1-1	.949	-4	93	100	S47		-1.
1952	Was A	5	5	1	0	0	0	0	0	1	0	0	.000	.167	.000	-53	-1	0-0	1.000	1	156	85	S3		0.
Total	3	181	525	60	118	9	9	2	42	65	2	67	.225	.313	.288	55	-36	8-3	.948	-12	101	80	S165,2b2/3		-3.

URBAN, LUKE Louis John B3.22.1898 Fall River MA D12.7.1980 Somerset MA BR/TR/5-8/168 d7.19 Col Boston College

YEAR	TM LG	G	AB	R	H	2B	3B	HR	RBI	BB-IB	HP	SO	AVG	OBP	SLG	AOPS	ABR	SB-CS	FA	FR	RNG	THR	GAMES AT POSITION	DL	BFW
1927	Bos N	35	111	11	32	5	0	0	10	3	1	6	.288	.313	.333	79	-3	1	.947	-4	98	172	C34		-0.
1928	Bos N	15	17	0	3	0	0	0	2	0	1	1	.176	.222	.176	6	-2	0	1.000	0	92	202	C10		-0.
Total	2	50	128	11	35	5	0	0	12	3	2	7	.273	.301	.313	69	-5	1	.955	-4	97	176	C44		-0.

URBANSKI, BILLY William Michael B6.5.1903 Linoleumville (now Travis) NY D7.12.1973 Perth Amboy NJ BR/TR/5-8/165 d7.4

YEAR	TM LG	G	AB	R	H	2B	3B	HR	RBI	BB-IB	HP	SO	AVG	OBP	SLG	AOPS	ABR	SB-CS	FA	FR	RNG	THR	GAMES AT POSITION	DL	BFW
1931	Bos N	82	303	22	72	13	4	0	17	10	5	32	.238	.274	.307	58	-19	3	.961	6	111	131	3b68,S19		-0.
1932	Bos N	136	563	80	153	25	8	8	46	28	1	60	.272	.307	.387	89	-11	6	.946	-6	98	107	S136		-0.
1933	Bos N	144	566	65	142	21	4	0	35	33	5	48	.251	.298	.302	78	-17	4	.953	-5	101	108	S143		-1.
1934	Bos N	146	605	104	177	30	6	7	53	56	5	37	.293	.357	.397	110	9	4	.961	-10	99	146	S146		1.
1935	Bos N	132	514	53	118	17	0	4	30	40	1	32	.230	.286	.286	59	-30	3	.939	-22	94	69	S129		-4.
1936	Bos N	122	494	55	129	17	5	0	26	31	4	42	.261	.310	.316	74	-19	2	.937	-12	87	114	S80,3b38		-2.
1937	Bos N	1	1	0	0	0	0	0	0	0	0	1	.000	.000	.000	-99	-1	0	—	0			/H		0.
Total	7	763	3046	379	791	123	27	19	207	198	21	252	.260	.309	.337	81	-87	24	.949	-49	96	99	S653,3b106		-8.

URIBE, JOSE Jose Altagracia (Played Under Real Name of Jose Altagracia Gonzalez (Uribe) in 1984) B1.21.1959 San Cristobal, D.R. BB/TR (BR 1984, 89p)/5-10/165(160-184) d9.13

YEAR	TM LG	G	AB	R	H	2B	3B	HR	RBI	BB-IB	HP	SO	AVG	OBP	SLG	AOPS	ABR	SB-CS	FA	FR	RNG	THR	GAMES AT POSITION	DL	BFW
1984	StL N	8	19	4	4	0	0	0	3	0-0	0	2	.211	.211	.211	19	-2	1-0	.955	-0	99	149	S5/2		-0.
1985	SF N	147	476	46	113	20	4	3	26	30-8	1	57	.237	.285	.315	71	-20	8-2	.961	-1	98	91	S145/2		-0.
1986	SF N	157	453	46	101	15	1	3	43	61-19	0	76	.223	.315	.280	69	-18	22-11	.977	13	103	118	S156		-1.
1987	†SF N	95	309	44	90	16	5	5	30	24-9	1	35	.291	.343	.424	107	3	12-2	.971	9	105	121	S95	71	2
1988	SF N	141	493	47	124	10	7	3	35	36-10	1	69	.252	.301	.318	82	-13	14-10	.970	-6	98	108	S140	16	-1
1989	†SF N	151	453	34	100	12	6	1	30	34-12	0	74	.221	.273	.280	61	-24	6-6	.973	17	113	130	S150		0
1990	SF N	138	415	35	103	8	6	1	24	29-13	0	49	.248	.297	.304	68	-20	5-9	.965	9	113	113	S134		-0
1991	SF N	90	231	23	51	8	4	1	12	20-6	1	33	.221	.283	.303	67	-11	3-4	.966	-0	105	98	S87	46	-0
1992	SF N	66	162	24	39	9	1	2	13	14-3	1	25	.241	.299	.346	87	-3	2-2	.971	4	107	138	S62	17	0
1993	Hou N	45	53	4	13	1	0	0	3	8-4	1	5	.245	.355	.264	71	-2	1-0	.944	2	92	187	S41		0
Total	10	1038	3064	307	738	99	34	19	219	256-84	4	425	.241	.300	.314	74	-110	74-46	.969	47	105	115	S1015,2b2	150	1

URIBE, JUAN Juan C. (Tena) B7.22.1979 Bani, D.R. BR/TR/5-11/173(173-215) d4.8

YEAR	TM LG	G	AB	R	H	2B	3B	HR	RBI	BB-IB	HP	SO	AVG	OBP	SLG	AOPS	ABR	SB-CS	FA	FR	RNG	THR	GAMES AT POSITION	DL	BFW
2001	Col N	72	273	32	82	15	11	8	53	8-1	2	55	.300	.325	.524	95	-3	3-0	.983	-5	92	103	S69		-0
2002	Col N	155	566	69	136	25	7	6	49	34-1	5	120	.240	.286	.341	60	-35	9-2	.966	27	114	115	S155		0
2003	Col N	87	316	45	80	19	3	10	33	17-0	3	60	.253	.297	.427	76	-12	7-2	.972	27	121	118	S74,2b11/OC	65	2
2004	Chi A	134	502	82	142	31	6	23	74	32-1	3	96	.283	.327	.506	110	5	9-11	.984	20	103	109	2b77,S38,3b27,D2		2
2005	†Chi A	146	481	58	121	23	3	16	71	34-0	4	77	.252	.301	.412	85	-11	4-6	.977	2	100	113	S146		0
Total	5	594	2138	286	561	113	30	63	280	125-3	17	408	.262	.310	.436	84	-56	32-21	.974	71	108	116	S482,2b88,3b27,D2/OC	65	5

URY, LON Louis Newton "Old Sleep" B1877 Ft.Scott KS D3.4.1918 Kansas City MO TR/6-0/? d9.9

YEAR	TM LG	G	AB	R	H	2B	3B	HR	RBI	BB-IB	HP	SO	AVG	OBP	SLG	AOPS	ABR	SB-CS	FA	FR	RNG	THR	GAMES AT POSITION	DL	BFW
1903	StL N	2	7	0	1	0	0	0	0	0	0		.143	.143	.143	-19	-1	0	1.000	0	88	95	1b2		-0

USHER, BOB Robert Royce B3.1.1925 San Diego CA BR/TR/6-1.5/180* d4.16

YEAR	TM LG	G	AB	R	H	2B	3B	HR	RBI	BB-IB	HP	SO	AVG	OBP	SLG	AOPS	ABR	SB-CS	FA	FR	RNG	THR	GAMES AT POSITION	DL	BFW
1946	Cin N	92	152	16	31	5	1	1	14	13	1	27	.204	.271	.270	56	-9	2	.982	3	100	190	O80(23/32/25)/3		-0
1947	Cin N	9	22	2	4	0	0	1	1	2	0	7	.182	.250	.318	50	-2	0	1.000	1	116	249	O8(3/5/0)		-0
1950	Cin N	106	321	51	83	17	0	6	35	27	0	38	.259	.316	.368	79	-10	3	.985	-1	96	108	O93(4/80/12)		-1
1951	Cin N	114	303	27	63	12	2	5	25	19	1	36	.208	.257	.310	51	-22	4-5	.974	2	102	125	O98(14/82/2)		-0
1952	Chi N	1	0	0	0	0	0	0	0	1	0	0	—	1.000	—	197	0	0-0	—	0			/H		0
1957	Cle A	10	8	1	1	0	0	0	0	1-0	0	3	.125	.222	.125	-3	-1	0-0	1.000	-0	102	0	O4(1/3/0)/3		-0
	Was A	96	295	36	77	7	1	5	27	27-2	2	30	.261	.324	.342	84	-7	0-0	.979	2	105	116	O95(1/93/2)		-0
	Year	106	303	37	78	7	1	5	27	28-2	2	33	.257	.321	.337	82	-8	0-0	.979	2	105	114	O99(2/96/2)/3		-1
Total	6	428	1101	133	259	41	4	18	102	90-2	4	136	.235	.295	.329	69	-51	9-5	.980	7	101	129	O378(46/295/41),3b2		-5

USSAT, DUTCH William August B4.11.1904 Dayton OH D5.29.1959 Dayton OH BR/TR/6-1/170 d9.13

YEAR	TM LG	G	AB	R	H	2B	3B	HR	RBI	BB-IB	HP	SO	AVG	OBP	SLG	AOPS	ABR	SB-CS	FA	FR	RNG	THR	GAMES AT POSITION	DL	BFW
1925	Cle A	1	1	0	0	0	0	0	0	0	0	0	.000	.000	.000	-99	0	0-0	1.000	0	142	0	/2		0
1927	Cle A	4	16	4	3	0	1	0	2	2	0	1	.188	.278	.313	53	-1	0-0	1.000	-0	82	134	3b4		-0
Total	2	5	17	4	3	0	1	0	2	2	0	1	.176	.263	.294	44	-1	0-0	1.000	-0	82	134	3b4/2		-0

UTLEY, CHASE Chase Cameron B12.17.1978 Pasadena CA BL/TR/6-1/170(170-185) [PhiN00 1/15] d4.4 Col UCLA

YEAR	TM LG	G	AB	R	H	2B	3B	HR	RBI	BB-IB	HP	SO	AVG	OBP	SLG	AOPS	ABR	SB-CS	FA	FR	RNG	THR	GAMES AT POSITION	DL	BFW
2003	Phi N	43	134	13	32	10	1	2	21	11-0	6	22	.239	.322	.373	88	-2	2-0	.983	3	106	134	2b37		0
2004	Phi N	94	267	36	71	11	2	13	57	15-1	2	40	.266	.308	.468	94	-4	4-1	.982	-2	95	102	2b50,1b13		-0
2005	Phi N	147	543	93	158	39	6	28	105	69-5	9	109	.291	.376	.540	133	28	16-3	.978	6	95	86	2b135,1b8		4
Total	3	284	944	142	261	60	9	43	183	95-6	17	171	.276	.350	.496	116	22	22-4	.980	7	97	97	2b222,1b21		4

VACHE, TEX Ernest Lewis B11.17.1888 Santa Monica CA D6.11.1953 Los Angeles CA BR/TR/6-1/200 d4.16

YEAR	TM LG	G	AB	R	H	2B	3B	HR	RBI	BB-IB	HP	SO	AVG	OBP	SLG	AOPS	ABR	SB-CS	FA	FR	RNG	THR	GAMES AT POSITION	DL	BFW
1925	Bos A	110	252	41	79	15	7	3	48	21	7	33	.313	.382	.464	114	5	2-2	.908	-7	84	37	O53(52/0/1)		-0

VADEBONCOEUR, GENE Onesime Eugene B7.15.1858 Louiseville QC, Can. BR/TR/5-6/150 d7.11

YEAR	TM LG	G	AB	R	H	2B	3B	HR	RBI	BB-IB	HP	SO	AVG	OBP	SLG	AOPS	ABR	SB-CS	FA	FR	RNG	THR	GAMES AT POSITION	DL	BFW
1884	Phi N	4	14	1	3	0	0	0		2			.214	.267	.214	56	-1		.846	-1			C4		-0

VAHRENHORST, HARRY Harry Henry "Van" B2.13.1885 St.Louis MO D10.10.1943 St.Louis MO BR/TR/6-1/175 d9.21

YEAR	TM LG	G	AB	R	H	2B	3B	HR	RBI	BB-IB	HP	SO	AVG	OBP	SLG	AOPS	ABR	SB-CS	FA	FR	RNG	THR	GAMES AT POSITION	DL	BFW
1904	StL A	1	1	0	0	0	0	0	0	0	0		.000	.000	.000	-99	0	0	—	0			/H		

VAIL, MIKE Michael Lewis B11.10.1951 San Francisco CA BR/TR/6-0/185* [StLN71*A4/86] d8.18

YEAR	TM LG	G	AB	R	H	2B	3B	HR	RBI	BB-IB	HP	SO	AVG	OBP	SLG	AOPS	ABR	SB-CS	FA	FR	RNG	THR	GAMES AT POSITION	DL	BFW
1975	NY N	38	162	17	49	8	1	3	17	9-1	0	37	.302	.339	.420	113	2	0-0	.971	9	127	315	O36(35/1/0)		
1976	NY N	53	143	9	31	5	1	0	9	6-0	1	31	.217	.243	.266	52	-8	0-1	.941	1	103	40	O35(2/0/33)	68	

YEAR	TM LG	G	AB	R	H	2B	3B	HR	RBI	BB-IB	HP	SO	AVG	OBP	SLG	AOPS	ABR	SB-CS	FA	FR	RNG	THR	GAMES AT POSITION	DL	BFW
1977	NY N	108	279	29	73	12	1	8	35	19-0	2	58	.262	.310	.398	93	-4	0-7	.965	5	123	98	O85(2/0/83)		-0.4
1978	Cle A	14	34	2	8	2	1	0	2	1-1	0	9	.235	.250	.353	71	2	1-1	1.000	1	142	0	O9(2/0/7)/D		-0.1
	Chi N	74	180	15	60	6	2	4	33	3-0	0	24	.333	.341	.456	109	1	0-1	.981	-5	74	34	O45(7/0/39)/3		-0.6
1979	Chi N	87	179	28	60	8	2	7	35	14-1	0	27	.335	.379	.520	131	8	0-2	.964	-3	81	112	O39(1/0/38),3b2		0.3
1980	Chi N	114	312	30	93	17	2	6	47	14-1	1	77	.298	.330	.423	100	0	2-5	.963	-1	101	91	O77(19/0/61)		-0.6
1981	Cin N	31	31	1	5	0	0	0	3	0-0	0	9	.161	.161	.161	-8	-5	0-0	1.000	4	130	0	O3R		-0.5
1982	Cin N	78	189	9	48	10	1	4	29	6-1	0	33	.254	.274	.381	82	-5	0-0	.988	3	95	227	O52(50/0/2)		-0.4
1983	SF N	18	26	1	4	1	0	0	3	0-0	1	7	.154	.185	.192	5	-3	0-0	1.000	-1	0	0	1b4,O2L		-0.5
	Mon N	34	53	5	15	2	0	2	4	8-0	1	10	.283	.387	.434	127	2	0-0	.958	2	91	501	O15(3/0/12)/13		0.4
	Year	52	79	6	19	3	0	2	7	8-0	2	17	.241	.326	.354	89	-1	0-0	.960	1	88	463	O17(5/0/12),1b5/3		-0.1
1984	LA N	16	16	1	1	0	0	0	2	1-0	0	7	.063	.118	.063	-48	-3	0-0	—	-0	0	0	/OL		-0.4
Total	10	665	1604	146	447	71	11	34	219	81-5	5	317	.279	.313	.400	94	-19	3-17	.968	10	103	137	O399(124/1/278),1b5,3b4/D	68	-3.4

VALDERRAMA, CARLOS Carlos Alberto B11.30.1977 Bachaquero, Venez BR/TR/6-0/180 d6.21

2003	SF N	7	7	0	1	0	0	0	0	0-0	0	1	.143	.143	.143	-25	-1	1-0	1.000	0	147	0	O5(4/2/0)/D		-0.1

VALDES, PEDRO Pedro Jose (Manzo) B6.29.1973 Fajardo, PR BL/TL/6-1/180* [ChiN90 12/340] d5.15

1996	Chi N	9	8	2	1	1	0	0	2	1-0	0	5	.125	.222	.250	25	-1	0-0	1.000	0	150	0	O2R		-0.1
1998	Chi N	14	23	1	5	1	1	0	2	1-0	0	3	.217	.250	.348	53	-2	0-1	1.000	0	134	0	O7(6/0/1)	57	-0.2
2000	Tex A	30	54	4	15	5	0	1	8	6-0	0	7	.278	.350	.426	94	0	0-0	1.000	-1	92	0	O14(1/0/13),D5		-0.1
Total	3	53	85	7	21	7	1	1	8	8-0	0	15	.247	.312	.388	77	-3	0-0	1.000	-0	106	0	O23(7/0/16),D5	57	-0.4

VALDES, ROY Rogelio Lazaro (Rojas) B2.20.1920 Havana, Cuba BR/TR/5-11/185 d5.3

1944	Was A	1	1	0	0	0	0	0	0	0-0	0	0	.000	.000	.000	-99	0	0-0	—	0		0	/H		0.0

VALDESPINO, SANDY Hilario (Borroto) B1.14.1939 San Jose de las Lajas, Cuba BL/TL/5-8/170* d4.12

1965	†Min A	108	245	38	64	8	2	1	22	20-3	2	28	.261	.319	.322	80	-6	7-4	.990	2	103	127	O57(43/0/17)		-0.7
1966	Min A	52	108	11	19	1	1	2	9	4-0	1	24	.176	.211	.259	33	-10	2-2	1.000	-1	99	0	O23(22/1/0)		-1.3
1967	Min A	99	97	9	16	2	0	1	3	5-1	0	22	.165	.204	.216	23	-9	3-1	.977	1	96	186	O65(64/0/1)		-1.0
1968	Atl N	36	86	8	20	1	0	1	4	10-5	1	20	.233	.320	.279	81	-2	0-0	.976	0	119	0	O20L		-0.3
1969	Hou N	41	119	17	29	4	0	0	12	15-0	0	19	.244	.326	.277	72	-4	2-2	.976	1	91	228	O29L		-0.5
	Sea N	20	38	3	8	1	0	0	2	1-0	1	7	.211	.250	.237	37	-3	0-1	.889	2	166	177	O7L		-0.2
1970	Mil A	8	9	0	0	0	0	0	0	0-0	0	4	.000	.000	.000	-99	-2	0-0	—	-0	0	0	/OL		-0.3
1971	KC A	18	63	10	20	6	0	2	15	2-0	0	5	.317	.338	.508	138	3	0-0	.950	-2	65	109	O15(13/0/2)		0.0
Total	7	382	765	96	176	23	3	7	67	57-9	5	129	.230	.286	.295	65	-33	14-10	.974	4	101	121	O217(199/1/20)		-4.3

VALDEZ, JULIO Julio Julian (b Julio Julian Castillo (Valdez) B6.3.1956 San Cristobal, D.R. BB/TR (BR 1980)/6-2/160* d9.2

1980	Bos A	8	19	4	5	1	0	0	4	0-0	1	5	.263	.300	.474	103	-2	2-0	.935	4	132	225	S8		0.5
1981	Bos A	17	23	1	5	0	0	0	3	0-0	0	7	.217	.208	.217	24	-2	0-1	.955	0	114	54	S17		-0.1
1982	Bos A	28	20	3	5	1	0	0	1	0-0	0	7	.250	.250	.300	47	-1	1-0	.976	1	102	108	S22,D3		0.1
1983	Bos A	12	25	3	3	0	0	0	0	1-0	1	4	.120	.185	.120	-13	-4	0-0	.939	-3	74	57	2b9,S2/D		-0.7
Total	4	65	87	11	18	2	0	0	8	1-0	2	23	.207	.231	.264	36	-7	3-1	.955	1	115	120	S49,2b9,D3		-0.2

VALDEZ, MARIO Mario A. B11.19.1974 Ciudad Obregon, Sonora, Mexico BL/TL/6-2/190(190-210) [ChiA93 48/1333] d6.15 Col Miami-Dade North (FL) CC [DL 2002 Oak A 36]

1997	Chi A	54	115	11	28	7	0	1	13	17-0	3	39	.243	.350	.330	83	-4	1-0	1.000	-4	51	62	1b47/3D		-0.9
2000	Oak A	5	12	0	0	0	0	0	0	0-0	0	3	.000	.000	.000	-99	-4	0-0	1.000	0	96	68	1b4	25	-0.4
2001	Oak A	32	54	7	15	1	0	1	8	12-1	1	18	.278	.418	.352	106	1	0-0	1.000	0	98	312	D12,O7L,1b6	132	0.1
Total	3	91	181	18	43	8	0	2	21	29-1	4	60	.238	.352	.315	79	-5	1-0	1.000	-4	53	67	1b57,D14,O7L/3	193	-1.2

VALDEZ, WILSON Wilson Antonio B5.20.1978 Nizao, D.R. BR/TR/5-11/160* d9.7

2004	Chi A	19	43	8	10	1	0	1	4	2-0	0	5	.233	.267	.326	52	-3	1-2	.973	-4	87	53	S12,2b5		-0.6
2005	Sea A	42	126	9	25	5	1	0	8	6-0	0	25	.198	.235	.254	32	-13	2-2	.973	-1	99	87	S42		-1.1
	SD N	9	13	0	3	2	0	0	1	0-0	0	1	.231	.333	.385	92	0	0-0	.944	-2	60	68	S8		-0.2
Total	2	70	182	17	38	8	1	1	13	8-0	0	31	.209	.250	.280	42	-16	3-4	.970	-7	93	79	S62,2b5		-1.9

VALDIVIELSO, JOSE Jose (Lopez) (b Jose Martinez De Valdivielso (Lopez)) B5.22.1934 Matanzas, Cuba BR/TR/6-1/175* d6.21

1955	Was A	94	294	32	65	12	5	2	28	21-1	3	38	.221	.277	.316	63	-17	1-2	.956	11	110	106	S94		0.1
1956	Was A	90	246	18	58	8	2	4	29	29-1	3	36	.236	.318	.333	72	-10	3-1	.947	9	110	97	S90		0.5
1959	Was A	24	14	1	4	0	0	0	1	1-1	0	3	.286	.333	.286	72	-1	0-0	1.000	3	128	205	S21		0.3
1960	Was A	117	268	23	57	1	1	2	19	20-0	4	36	.213	.276	.246	43	-22	1-2	.954	5	104	112	S115/3		-1.0
1961	Min A	76	149	15	29	5	1	0	8	8-0	0	19	.195	.234	.248	28	-15	1-1	.971	-12	80	78	S43,2b15,3b14		-2.5
Total	5	401	971	89	213	26	9	8	85	79-3	8	132	.219	.282	.290	55	-65	6-6	.955	15	105	104	S363,2b15,3b15		-2.6

VALENT, ERIC Eric Christian B4.4.1977 LaMirada CA BL/TL/6-0/191* [PhiN98 1/42] d6.8 Col UCLA

2001	Phi N	22	41	3	4	2	0	0	4	4-0	1	11	.098	.196	.146	-10	-7	0-0	1.000	3	191	517	O8(7/0/1),D4		-0.4
2002	Phi N	7	10	1	2	0	0	0	0	0-0	0	3	.200	.200	.200	8	-1	0-0	—	-1	0	0	O2R/1		-0.2
2003	Cin N	18	42	3	9	0	0	0	1	2-0	0	9	.214	.250	.214	24	-5	0-0	1.000	1	122	181	O8R		-0.4
2004	NY N	130	270	39	72	15	2	13	34	28-4	1	61	.267	.337	.481	111	4	0-1	1.000	1	90	48	O46(32/0/14),1b27		0.1
2005	NY N	28	43	4	8	3	0	1	7	3-0	0	7	.186	.300	.256	49	-3	0-0	.955	0	118	0	O12(2/2/8)		-0.3
Total	5	205	406	50	95	20	2	13	37	41-7	2	101	.234	.307	.389	81	-12	0-1	.992	4	107	104	O76(41/2/33),1b28,D4		-1.2

VALENTIN, JOHN John William B2.18.1967 Mineola NY BR/TR/6-0/180(170-185) [BosA88 5/121] d7.27 Col Seton Hall

1992	Bos A	58	185	21	51	13	0	5	25	20-0	2	17	.276	.351	.427	109	3	1-0	.963	6	106	125	S58		1.3
1993	Bos A	144	468	50	130	40	3	11	66	49-2	2	77	.278	.346	.447	105	4	3-4	.971	16	**105**	**113**	S144	15	2.9
1994	Bos A	84	301	53	95	26	2	9	49	42-1	3	38	.316	.400	.505	127	4	3-1	.979	4	100	104	S83/D	33	2.2
1995	†Bos A	135	520	108	155	37	2	27	102	81-2	10	67	.298	.399	.533	137	31	20-5	.973	6	103	107	S135		4.6
1996	Bos A	131	527	84	156	29	3	13	59	63-0	5	59	.296	.374	.436	103	6	9-10	.971	6	102	100	S118,3b12/D	15	1.7
1997	Bos A	143	575	95	176	**47**	5	18	77	58-5	5	66	.306	.372	.499	123	20	7-4	.976	18	111	120	2b79,3b64		4.0
1998	Bos A	153	588	113	145	44	1	23	73	77-3	9	82	.247	.340	.442	100	1	4-5	.965	18	**112**	132	3b153/2		1.9
1999	†Bos A	113	450	58	114	27	1	12	70	40-2	4	68	.253	.315	.398	79	-15	0-1	.954	12	109	100	3b111,D2	38	-0.4
2000	Bos A	10	35	6	9	1	0	2	2	2-0	0	5	.257	.297	.457	85	-1	0-1	1.000	-3	52	0	3b10	161	-0.4
2001	Bos A	20	60	8	12	2	0	1	5	9-0	1	14	.200	.314	.283	59	-3	0-0	.970	-1	98	92	S18,3b3	161	-0.3
2002	NY N	114	208	18	50	15	0	3	30	22-0	10	37	.240	.339	.356	92	-2	0-0	.971	-1	108	93	S24,1b22,3b18,2b3,D2	17	-0.4
Total	11	1105	3917	614	1093	281	17	124	558	463-15	53	524	.279	.360	.454	108	56	47-31	.972	82	103	108	S580,3b371,2b83,1b22,D6	440	17.3

VALENTIN, JOSE Jose Antonio B10.12.1969 Manati, PR BB/TR (BL 2004)/5-10/166(166-195) d9.17 b-Javier OF(22/24/1)

1992	Mil A	4	3	1	0	0	0	0	0	0-0	0	0	.000	.000	.000	-99	-1	0-0	.667	-2	36	0	/2S		-0.3
1993	Mil A	19	53	10	13	1	2	1	7	7-1	1	16	.245	.344	.396	99	0	1-0	.922	-5	97	79	S19		-0.3
1994	Mil A	97	285	47	68	19	0	11	46	38-1	2	75	.239	.330	.421	88	-5	12-3	.954	21	**123**	119	S83,2b18/3		2.2
1995	Mil A	112	338	62	74	23	3	11	49	37-0	0	83	.219	.293	.402	75	-13	16-8	.971	6	111	**119**	S104/3D		0.1
1996	Mil A	154	552	90	143	33	7	24	95	66-9	0	145	.259	.336	.475	98	-3	17-4	.950	1	107	112	S151		1.0
1997	Mil A	136	494	58	125	23	1	17	58	39-4	4	109	.253	.310	.407	85	-12	19-8	.967	5	102	106	S134/D	21	0.4
1998	Mil N	151	428	65	96	24	0	16	49	63-8	1	105	.224	.323	.393	86	-4	10-7	.963	0	103	91	S139/D		0.1
1999	Mil N	89	256	45	58	9	5	10	38	48-7	2	52	.227	.347	.418	94	-2	3-2	.937	-8	100	78	S85	66	-0.4
2000	†Chi A	144	568	107	155	37	6	25	92	59-1	4	106	.273	.343	.491	105	3	19-2	.950	17	108	124	S141/OR		3.1
2001	Chi A	124	438	74	113	22	2	28	68	50-2	3	114	.258	.336	.509	112	7	9-6	.926	12	106	97	3b66,S43,O24C	15	2.1
2002	Chi A	135	474	70	118	26	4	25	75	43-2	3	114	.249	.311	.473	103	0	3-3	.952	5	107	112	3b83,S50/D		0.8
2003	Chi A	144	503	79	119	26	4	28	74	54-4	3	114	.237	.313	.463	97	-3	8-3	.969	14	102	**114**	S143		2.1
2004	Chi A	125	450	73	97	20	3	30	70	43-4	3	139	.216	.287	.473	91	-9	8-6	.965	17	110	**117**	S122,D2	18	1.6
2005	LA N	56	147	17	25	4	2	2	14	31-2	4	38	.170	.326	.395	59	-8	3-1	1.000	2	117	0	3b29,O22L/S	88	-0.7
Total	14	1490	4989	798	1204	267	37	228	736	578-45	29	1195	.241	.321	.447	94	-54	128-53	.959	86	107	112	S1216,3b180,O47C,2b19,D9	208	11.9

VALENTIN, JAVIER Jose Javier (Rosario) B9.19.1975 Manati, PR BB/TR/5-10/192(185-210) [MinA93 3/93] d9.13 b-Jose

1997	Min A	4	7	1	2	0	0	0	0	0-0	0	3	.286	.286	.286	49	-1	0-0	1.000	1	111	363	C4		0.0
1998	Min A	55	162	11	32	7	1	3	18	11-1	0	30	.198	.247	.309	43	-14	0-0	.983	-3	97	67	C53/D		-1.3
1999	Min A	78	218	22	54	12	1	5	28	22-0	1	39	.248	.313	.381	74	-9	0-0	.998	6	159	108	C76		0.1
2002	Min A	4	2	0	2	0	0	0	0	0-0	0	0	.500	.500	.500	162		0-0	1.000	2	0	0	C4		0.2

YEAR	TM LG	G	AB	R	H	2B	3B	HR	RBI	BB-IB	HP	SO	AVG	OBP	SLG	AOPS	ABR	SB-CS	FA	FR	RNG	THR	GAMES AT POSITION	DL	BFW
2003	TB A	49	135	13	30	7	1	3	15	5-0	1	31	.222	.254	.356	60	-8	0-0	1.000	2	115	85	C42,D6		-0.4
2004	Cin N	82	202	18	47	10	1	6	20	17-3	1	36	.233	.293	.381	75	-8	0-0	.988	-0	93	122	C55,1b7		-0.5
2005	Cin N	76	221	36	62	11	0	14	50	30-3	0	37	.281	.362	.520	133	11	0-0	.992	-7	121	80	C62,1b2		0.8
Total	7	348	949	101	229	47	4	31	131	85-7	3	176	.241	.302	.397	80	-29	0-0	.992	1	119	95	C296,1b9,D7		-1.1

VALENTINE, ELLIS   Ellis Clarence   B7.30.1954 Helena AR   BR/TR/6-4/207(207-218)   [MonN72 2/29]   d9.3   [DL 1984 Cal A 182]

YEAR	TM LG	G	AB	R	H	2B	3B	HR	RBI	BB-IB	HP	SO	AVG	OBP	SLG	AOPS	ABR	SB-CS	FA	FR	RNG	THR	GAMES AT POSITION	DL	BFW
1975	Mon N	12	33	2	12	4	0	1	3	2-0	0	4	.364	.400	.576	160	1	0-0	.867	-1	67	158	O11R		0.1
1976	Mon N	94	305	36	85	15	2	7	39	30-0	0	51	.279	.339	.410	108	3	14-1	.972	-2	82	210	O88(2/55/31)		0.1
1977	Mon N★	127	508	63	149	28	2	25	76	30-3	0	58	.293	.331	.504	123	14	13-5	.972	-5	95	91	O126R		0.4
1978	Mon N	151	570	75	165	35	2	25	76	35-3	2	88	.289	.330	.489	127	19	13-8	.970	11	103	**198**	O146(0/3/145)		2.3
1979	Mon N	146	548	73	151	29	3	21	82	22-3	1	74	.276	.303	.454	104	0	11-9	.983	-4	96	82	O144R		-1.2
1980	Mon N	86	311	40	98	22	2	13	67	25-0	3	44	.315	.367	.524	144	18	5-5	.970	-3	102	86	O83R		1.2
1981	Mon N	22	76	8	16	3	0	3	15	6-0	0	11	.211	.259	.368	77	-3	0-1	1.000	-1	87	125	O21R	16	-0.5
	NY N	48	169	15	35	8	1	5	21	5-0	0	38	.207	.227	.355	64	-9	0-3	.957	1	97	163	O47R		-1.3
	Year	70	245	23	51	11	1	8	36	11-0	0	49	.208	.238	.359	68	-12	0-4	.969	0	94	152	O68R		-1.8
1982	NY N	111	337	33	97	14	1	8	48	5-0	1	38	.288	.294	.407	96	-4	1-3	.983	-4	101	167	O98(14/4/82)		-1.2
1983	Cal A	86	271	30	65	10	2	13	43	18-0	0	48	.240	.283	.435	96	-3	2-1	.963	-4	92	82	O85(11/0/80)	32	-1.1
1985	Tex A	11	38	5	8	1	0	2	4	2-0	0	8	.211	.250	.395	72	-2	0-1	1.000	-1	64	0	O7R,D4		-0.5
Total	10	894	3166	380	881	169	15	123	474	180-9	7	462	.278	.315	.458	112	36	59-37	.972	-3	96	132	O856(27/62/777),D4	266	-0.2

VALENTINE, FRED   Fred Lee "Squeaky"   B1.19.1935 Clarksdale MS   BB/TR/6-1/190*   d9.7   Col Tennessee St.

YEAR	TM LG	G	AB	R	H	2B	3B	HR	RBI	BB-IB	HP	SO	AVG	OBP	SLG	AOPS	ABR	SB-CS	FA	FR	RNG	THR	GAMES AT POSITION	DL	BFW
1959	Bal A	12	19	0	6	0	0	1	3	0-0	0	4	.316	.409	.316	104	0	0-1	.889	0	81	368	O8(3/0/6)		0.1
1963	Bal A	26	41	5	11	1	0	0	1	8-0	0	5	.268	.388	.293	98	0	0-0	1.000	0	98	0	O10(1/0/10)		-0.1
1964	Was A	102	212	20	48	5	0	4	20	21-0	3	44	.226	.304	.307	71	-8	4-2	.978	-2	91	68	O57(22/14/22)		-1.4
1965	Was A	12	29	6	7	0	0	0	1	4-0	1	5	.241	.353	.241	73	-1	3-0	1.000	2	160	0	O11(5/6/1)		0.1
1966	Was A	146	508	77	140	29	4	16	59	51-1	10	63	.276	.351	.455	132	22	22-10	.980	3	109	76	O138(32/63/70),1b2		2.2
1967	Was A	151	457	52	107	16	1	11	44	56-1	10	76	.234	.330	.346	104	4	17-3	.989	-2	100	55	O136(26/70/55)		-0.5
1968	Was A	37	101	11	24	2	0	3	7	6-0	2	11	.238	.291	.347	97	-1	1-0	1.000	-1	81	145	O27(0/1/26)		-0.5
	Bal A	47	91	9	17	3	2	2	5	7-0	1	20	.187	.253	.330	75	-3	0-0	.972	1	97	183	O26(6/6/14)		-0.1
	Year	84	192	20	41	5	2	5	12	13-0	3	31	.214	.273	.339	86	-4	1-0	.986	-0	88	162	O53(6/7/40)		-0.6
Total	7	533	1458	180	360	56	10	36	138	156-2	27	228	.247	.330	.373	106	13	47-16	.983	-1	102	88	O413(95/160/204),1b2		-0.5

VALENTINE, BOB   Robert   d5.20

YEAR	TM LG	G	AB	R	H	2B	3B	HR	RBI	BB-IB	HP	SO	AVG	OBP	SLG	AOPS	ABR	SB-CS	FA	FR	RNG	THR	GAMES AT POSITION	DL	BFW
1876	NY N	1	3	0	0	0	0	0		0-0		0	.000	.000	.000	-99	-1		.333	-1			/C		

VALENTINE, BOBBY   Robert John   B5.13.1950 Stamford CT   BR/TR/5-10/189*   [LAN68 1/5]   d9.2   M15/C4   OF(87/18/26)

YEAR	TM LG	G	AB	R	H	2B	3B	HR	RBI	BB-IB	HP	SO	AVG	OBP	SLG	AOPS	ABR	SB-CS	FA	FR	RNG	THR	GAMES AT POSITION	DL	BFW
1969	LA N	5	.0	3	0	0	0	0	0	0-0	0	0	—	—	—								/R		0.1
1971	LA N	101	281	32	70	10	2	1	25	15-0	2	20	.249	.287	.310	74	-10	5-3	.961	-6	99	119	S37,3b23,2b21,O11(0/3/8)		-1.1
1972	LA N	119	391	42	107	11	2	3	32	27-2	2	33	.274	.319	.335	89	-6	5-5	.976	1	110	107	2b49,3b39,O16(5/8/4),S10		0.3
1973	Cal A	32	126	12	38	5	2	1	13	5-0	0	9	.302	.323	.397	111	1	6-1	.948	-2	84	65	S25,O8(1/7/0)	138	0.1
1974	Cal A	117	371	39	97	10	3	3	39	25-0	3	25	.261	.308	.329	89	-6	8-5	.950	2	116	59	O62L,S36,3b15/2D	15	-0.4
1975	Cal A	26	57	5	16	2	0	0	5	4-0	1	3	.281	.323	.316	92	0	0-2	.958	-1	0	108	D13,1b3,3b2,O2(1/0/1)		-0.1
	SD N	7	15	1	2	0	0	1	1	4-0	0	3	.133	.316	.333	86	0	1-0	1.000	-1	54	0	O4L		-0.1
1976	SD N	15	49	3	18	4	0	0	6	6-0	0	2	.367	.436	.449	164	2	0-1	1.000	2	104	297	O10(7/0/5),1b4		0.8
1977	SD N	44	67	5	12	3	0	1	10	7-1	0	10	.179	.253	.269	46	-5	0-0	.962	-1	94	34	S10,3b10/1		-1.4
	NY N	42	83	8	11	1	0	1	3	6-0	0	9	.133	.191	.181	0	-12	0-0	1.000	-1	72	51	1b15,S14,3b4		-1.2
	Year	86	150	13	23	4	0	2	13	13-1	0	19	.153	.220	.220	20	-18	0-0	.969	-2	88	92	S24,1b16,3b14		-2.6
1978	NY N	69	160	17	43	7	0	1	18	19-1	1	18	.269	.346	.331	94	-1	1-1	.977	-2	100	71	2b45,3b9		-0.2
1979	Sea A	62	98	9	27	6	0	0	7	22-1	0	18	.276	.405	.337	101	2	1-2	.971	-4	73	42	S29,O15(7/0/8),2b4,3b4,C2/D		-0.4
Total	10	639	1698	176	441	59	6	12	157	140-5	9	134	.260	.315	.329	86	-32	27-20	.957	-12	93	76	S161,O128L,2b120,3b106,1b23,D18,C2153-3.

VALENZUELA, BENNY   Benjamin Beltran "Papelero"   B6.2.1933 Los Mochis, Sinaloa, Mexico   BR/TR/5-10/175   d4.27

YEAR	TM LG	G	AB	R	H	2B	3B	HR	RBI	BB-IB	HP	SO	AVG	OBP	SLG	AOPS	ABR	SB-CS	FA	FR	RNG	THR	GAMES AT POSITION	DL	BFW
1958	StL N	10	14	0	3	1	0	0	0	0-0	0	4	.214	.267	.286	45	-1	0-0	.875	-0	89	0	3b3		-0.1

VALERA, YOHANNY   Yohanny   B8.17.1976 Santo Domingo, D.R.   BR/TR/6-1/205   d9.13

YEAR	TM LG	G	AB	R	H	2B	3B	HR	RBI	BB-IB	HP	SO	AVG	OBP	SLG	AOPS	ABR	SB-CS	FA	FR	RNG	THR	GAMES AT POSITION	DL	BFW
2000	Mon N	7	10	1	0	0	0	0	1	1-0	1	5	.000	.167	.000	-53	-2	0-0	1.000	1	99	112	C7		-0.

VALLE, DAVE   David   B10.30.1960 Bayside NY   BR/TR/6-2/200(200-220)   [SeaA78 2/32]   d9.7

YEAR	TM LG	G	AB	R	H	2B	3B	HR	RBI	BB-IB	HP	SO	AVG	OBP	SLG	AOPS	ABR	SB-CS	FA	FR	RNG	THR	GAMES AT POSITION	DL	BFW
1984	Sea A	13	27	4	8	1	0	1	4	1-0	0	5	.296	.321	.444	110	0	0-0	1.000	1	113	116	C13		0
1985	Sea A	31	70	2	11	1	0	0	4	1-0	1	17	.157	.181	.171	-3	-10	0-0	.976	-2	93	31	C31	84	-1
1986	Sea A	22	53	10	18	3	0	5	15	7-0	0	7	.340	.417	.679	190	7	0-0	.982	-4	104	32	C12,1b4		0
1987	Sea A	95	324	40	83	16	3	12	53	15-2	3	46	.256	.292	.435	86	-4	2-0	.989	6	134	98	C75,D14,1b2/OR	15	0.
1988	Sea A	93	290	29	67	15	2	10	50	18-0	1	32	.231	.295	.400	84	-5	0-1	.989	9	106	120	C84/1D	41	0.
1989	Sea A	94	316	32	75	10	3	7	34	29-2	6	32	.237	.311	.354	85	-6	0-0	.993	7	131	**125**	C93	37	0.
1990	Sea A	107	308	37	66	15	0	7	33	45-0	7	48	.214	.328	.331	84	-5	1-2	**.997**	1	97	85	C104/1	30	0.
1991	Sea A	132	324	38	63	8	1	8	32	34-0	5	49	.194	.286	.299	63	-17	0-0	.992	10	149	85	C129,1b2		-0
1992	Sea A	124	367	39	88	16	1	9	30	27-1	8	58	.240	.305	.362	85	-8	0-0	.990	-7	98	96	C122	17	-0
1993	Sea A	135	423	48	109	19	0	13	63	48-4	**17**	56	.258	.354	.395	100	1	1-0	.995	12	129	118	C135		2
1994	Bos A	30	76	6	12	2	1	1	5	5-1	1	5	.158	.256	.250	30	-8	0-1	.982	-3	94	67	C28,1b2		-1
	Mil A	16	36	8	14	6	0	1	5	13-1	0	4	.389	.522	.583	188	6	0-1	1.000	-2	84	67	C12,D2	15	0
	Year	46	112	14	26	8	1	2	10	18-2	1	22	.232	.348	.375	83	-2	0-2	.986	-5	94	67	C40,1b2,D2		-0
1995	Tex A	36	75	7	18	3	0	0	5	6-0	1	18	.240	.305	.280	52	-5	1-0	.993	2	122	94	C29,1b7		-0
1996	Tex A	42	86	14	26	6	1	3	10	9-0	0	17	.302	.368	.500	110	1	0-0	.994	2	96	102	C35,1b5/D		-0
Total	13	970	2775	314	658	121	12	77	350	258-11	63	413	.237	.314	.373	85	-57	5-7	.992	32	118	100	C902,1b24,D20/OR	239	1

VALLE, HECTOR   Hector Jose   B10.27.1940 Vega Baja, PR   BR/TR/5-9/180   d6.6

YEAR	TM LG	G	AB	R	H	2B	3B	HR	RBI	BB-IB	HP	SO	AVG	OBP	SLG	AOPS	ABR	SB-CS	FA	FR	RNG	THR	GAMES AT POSITION	DL	BFW
1965	LA N	9	13	1	4	0	0	0	2	2-0	0	3	.308	.400	.308	110	0	0-0	1.000	-2	36	114	C6		

VALO, ELMER   Elmer William   B3.5.1921 Ribnik, Czechoslovakia   D7.19.1998 Palmerton PA   d9.22   Mil 1943-45   C2   BL/TR/5-11/190*

YEAR	TM LG	G	AB	R	H	2B	3B	HR	RBI	BB-IB	HP	SO	AVG	OBP	SLG	AOPS	ABR	SB-CS	FA	FR	RNG	THR	GAMES AT POSITION	DL	BFW
1940	Phi A	6	23	6	8	0	0	0	3		0	0	.348	.423	.348	104	0	2-0	1.000	-0	123	0	O6L		C
1941	Phi A	15	50	13	21	0	1	2	6	4	0	2	.420	.463	.580	179	5	0-0	1.000	-0	103	0	O10L		C
1942	Phi A	133	459	64	115	13	10	2	40	70	4	21	.251	.355	.336	95	-1	13-8	.964	-1	**108**	55	O122(1/1/120)		-0
1943	Phi A	77	249	31	55	6	2	3	18	35	1	13	.221	.319	.297	81	-5	2-6	.986	-0	101	85	O63(9/0/54)		-0
1946	Phi A	108	348	59	107	21	6	0	31	60	0	18	.307	.411	.411	131	18	9-8	.974	2	108	0	O90(5/0/85)		-0
1947	Phi A	112	370	60	111	12	6	5	36	64	2	21	.300	.406	.405	123	14	11-3	.973	0	101	120	O104R		C
1948	Phi A	113	383	72	117	17	4	3	46	81	4	13	.305	.432	.394	120	17	10-6	.983	-4	98	0	O109R		-0
1949	Phi A	150	547	86	155	27	12	5	85	119	2	32	.283	.413	.404	121	22	14-11	.981	10	**118**	71	O150L		2
1950	Phi A	129	446	62	125	16	5	10	46	82	7	22	.280	.400	.406	109	9	12-7	.982	2	106	91	O117(33/0/85)		-0
1951	Phi A	123	444	75	134	27	8	7	55	75	8	20	.302	.412	.446	129	22	11-6	.981	-3	101	57	O116(1/22/95)		-0
1952	Phi A	129	388	69	109	26	4	5	47	101	2	16	.281	.432	.407	126	21	12-11	.962	-4	100	73	O121(2/11/108)		-0
1953	Phi A	50	85	15	19	3	0	0	9	22	0	7	.224	.383	.259	73	-2	0-1	1.000	0	107	55	O25(10/0/15)		-C
1954	Phi A	95	224	28	48	11	6	1	33	51	2	18	.214	.356	.330	90	-1	2-1	.965	1	111	72	O62(34/0/30)		-C
1955	KC A	112	283	50	103	17	4	3	37	52-2	1	16	.364	.460	.484	153	25	5-3	.987	1	104	90	O72(46/4/23)		-C
1956	KC A	9	9	1	2	0	0	0	1	4-0	1	0	.222	.273	.222	40	-1	0-0	—	-0	0	0	/OL		-C
	Phi N	98	291	40	84	13	3	5	37	48-6	3	21	.289	.392	.405	118	10	7-6	.966	-1	107	54	O87R		-C
1957	Bro N	81	161	14	44	10	1	4	26	25-2	1	16	.273	.370	.422	104	2	0-1	1.000	-2	94	0	O36(26/0/14)		-C
1958	LA N	65	101	9	25	2	1	1	14	12-0	0	11	.248	.322	.317	69	-4	0-1	1.000	-2	84	0	O26(16/0/13)		-C
1959	Cle A	34	24	3	7	0	0	0	5	7-1	0	4	.292	.424	.292	113	1	0-0	1.000	0	165	0	O2R		C
1960	NY A	8	5	1	0	0	0	0		2-0	0	1	.000	.286	.000	-17	-0	0-0	1.000	-0	0	0	O2R		-C
	Was A	76	64	6	18	3	0	0	16	17-0	1	4	.281	.424	.328	112	3	0-0	1.000	1	116	671	O6(1/0/5)		-C
	Year	84	69	7	18	3	0	0	16	19-0	1	5	.261	.413	.304	103	2	0-0	1.000	1	93	537	O8(1/0/7)		-C
1961	Min A	33	32	0	5	0	0	0	4	5-0	0	3	.156	.250	.219	25	-3	0-0	1.000	0	189	0	/OL		-C
	Phi N	50	43	4	8	2	0	1	8	8-0	1	6	.186	.327	.302	69	-2	0-0	—	-0	0	0	/OR		-C
Total	20	1806	5029	768	1420	228	73	58	601	942-12	38	284	.282	.398	.391	114	149	110-79	.977	0	105	71	O1329(352/38/952)		C

YEAR	TM LG	G	AB	R	H	2B	3B	HR	RBI	BB-IB	HP	SO	AVG	OBP	SLG	AOPS	ABR	SB-CS	FA	FR	RNG	THR	GAMES AT POSITION	DL	BFW

Van BUREN, DEACON   Edward Eugene   B12.14.1870 LaSalle Co. IL   D6.29.1957 Portland OR   BL/TR/5-10/175   d4.21

1904	Bro N	1	1	0	0	0	0	0	0	0-0	0		1.000	1.000	1.000	531	0		—	0			/H		0.0
	Phi N	12	43	2	10	2	0	0	3	3	0		.233	.283	.279	76	-1	2	.962	1	131	197	O12L		-0.1
	Year	13	44	2	11	2	0	0	3	3	0		.250	.298	.295	86	-1	2	.962	1	131	197	O12L		-0.1

Van BURKLEO, TY   Tyler Lee   B10.7.1963 Oakland CA   BL/TL/6-5/225*   d7.28

1993	Cal A	12	33	2	5	3	0	1	1	6-0	0	9	.152	.282	.333	63	-2	1-0	1.000	-1	46	90	1b12		-0.4
1994	Col N	2	5	0	0	0	0	0	0	0-0	0	1	1.000	.000	.000	-86	-1	0-0	1.000	0	127	104	1b2		-0.1
Total 2		14	38	2	5	3	0	1	1	6-0	0	10	.132	.250	.289	42	-3	1-0	1.000	-1	53	91	1b14		-0.5

Van CAMP, AL   Albert Joseph   B9.7.1903 Moline IL   D2.2.1981 Davenport IA   BR/TR/5-11.5/175   d9.11

1928	Cle A	5	17	0	4	0	0	0	1		0	1	.235	.235	.294	38	-2	1-0	.980	-1	37	27	1b5		-0.2
1931	Bos A	101	324	34	89	15	4	0	33	20	1	24	.275	.319	.346	79	-11	3-2	.973	-2	89	73	O59(58/3/2),1b25		-1.6
1932	Bos A	34	103	10	23	4	2	0	6	4	0	17	.223	.252	.301	44	-9	0-0	.985	1	118	88	1b25		-1.0
Total 3		140	444	44	116	20	6	0	41	24	1	42	.261	.301	.333	69	-22	4-2	.973	-2	89	73	O59(58/3/2),1b55		-2.8

VANDAGRIFT, CARL   Carl William   B4.22.1883 Cantrall IL   D10.9.1920 Fort Wayne IN   BR/TR/5-8/155   d5.19   Col Illinois

| 1914 | Ind F | 43 | 136 | 25 | 34 | 4 | 0 | 0 | 15 | | 0 | | .250 | .301 | .279 | 53 | -11 | 7 | .925 | -5 | 83 | 72 | 2b28,3b12,S5 | | -1.6 |

VANDER WAL, JOHN   John Henry   B4.29.1966 Grand Rapids MI   BL/TL/6-2/198(190-205)   [MonN87 3/70]   d9.6   Col Western Michigan

1991	Mon N	21	61	4	13	4	1	1	8	1-0	0	18	.213	.222	.361	63	-3	0-0	1.000	-1	99	0	O17L		-0.5
1992	Mon N	105	213	21	51	8	2	4	20	24-2	0	36	.239	.316	.352	90	-3	3-0	.981	3	112	96	O57(55/0/4),1b7		-0.1
1993	Mon N	106	215	34	50	7	4	5	30	27-2	1	30	.233	.320	.372	81	-6	6-3	.988	-6	74	90	1b42,O38(27/2/10)		-1.4
1994	Col N	91	110	12	27	3	1	5	15	10-0	0	31	.245	.339	.427	85	-2	2-1	1.000	-2	37	111	1b14,O7(5/0/2)		-0.5
1995	†Col N	105	101	15	35	8	1	5	21	16-5	0	23	.347	.432	.594	131	5	1-1	.957	1	95	85	1b10,O10(7/0/3)		0.5
1996	Col N	104	151	20	38	6	2	5	31	19-2	1	38	.252	.335	.417	79	-4	2-2	1.000	-2	91	0	O26(25/0/1),1b10		-0.8
1997	Col N	76	92	7	16	2	0	1	11	10-0	0	33	.174	.255	.228	23	-10	1-1	.923	-1	104	0	O9(2/0/7),1b5,D2		-1.2
1998	Col N	89	104	18	30	10	1	5	20	16-0	0	29	.288	.380	.548	117	3	0-0	1.000	1	88	237	O25(3/0/22),1b2		0.3
	†SD N	20	25	3	6	3	0	0	0	6-0	0	5	.240	.387	.360	105	1	0-0	1.000	3	169	0	O5(2/0/3),1b3,D3		0.1
	Year	109	129	21	36	13	1	5	20	22-0	0	34	.279	.382	.512	115	4	0-0	1.000	1	101	200	O30(5/0/25),1b5,D3		0.4
1999	SD N	132	246	26	67	18	0	6	41	37-1	2	59	.272	.368	.419	108	4	2-1	1.000	0	96	0	O48(45/0/3),1b28/D		0.2
2000	Pit N	134	384	74	115	29	0	24	94	72-5	2	92	.299	.410	.563	143	28	11-2	.965	-6	96	0	O78(13/0/65),1b33,D3		1.7
2001	Pit N	97	313	39	87	22	3	11	50	42-6	1	84	.278	.361	.473	111	6	7-4	.973	-8	78	44	O73(20/0/56),1b13,D7		-0.6
	SF N	49	139	19	35	6	1	3	20	26-3	0	38	.252	.370	.374	99	1	1-2	1.000	2	115	43	O41(3/0/38)/1		0.0
	Year	146	452	58	122	28	4	14	70	68-9	1	122	.270	.364	.442	108	7	8-6	.985	-7	91	44	O114(23/0/94),1b14,D7		-0.6
2002	†NY A	84	219	30	57	17	1	6	23	23-3	0	58	.260	.327	.429	101	1	1-1	.978	-4	99	0	O57(8/0/49),D16,1b6		-0.6
2003	Mil N	117	327	50	84	25	1	14	45	46-3	1	104	.257	.350	.468	112	6	1-2	.984	3	110	75	O89(6/0/83)		0.4
2004	Cin N	42	51	6	9	2	0	2	4	4-0	0	18	.176	.182	.275	16	-7	0-0	1.000	1	123	315	O7R,1b4		-0.6
Total 14		1372	2751	374	717	170	18	97	430	385-32	8	698	.261	.351	.441	102	20	38-20	.982	-19	100	61	O587(238/2/353),1b178,D32		-3.1

Van DUSEN, FRED   Frederick William   B7.31.1937 Jackson Heights NY   BL/TL/6-3/180   d9.11

| 1955 | Phi N | 1 | 0 | 0 | 0 | 0 | 0 | 0 | 0 | 0-0 | 1 | 0 | — | 1.000 | — | 199 | 0 | 0-0 | — | 0 | | | /H | | 0.0 |

Van DYKE, BILL   William Jennings   B12.15.1863 Paris IL   D5.5.1933 El Paso TX   BR/TR/5-8/170   d4.17

1890	Tol AA	129	502	74	129	14	11	2	54	25	3		.257	.296	.341	85	-13	73	.924	-6	80	0	O110(109/1/0),3b18,2b2/C		-1.9
1892	StL N	4	16	2	2	0	0	0	1	0	0	1	.125	.125	.125	-26	-2	0	.875	-2	41	0	O4C		-0.3
1893	Bos N	3	12	2	3	1	0	0	1	0	0	1	.250	.250	.333	50	-1	1	1.000	-0	0	0	O3L		-0.1
Total 3		136	530	78	134	15	11	2	56	25	3	2	.253	.290	.334	81	-16	74	.924	-7	76	0	O117(112/5/0),3b18,2b2/C		-2.3

Van GORDER, DAVE   David Thomas   B3.27.1957 Los Angeles CA   BR/TR/6-2/205*   [CinN78 2/43]   d6.15   Col USC

1982	Cin N	51	137	4	25	3	1	0	7	14-2	1	19	.182	.263	.219	36	-12	1-0	.986	-8	78	49	C51		-1.9
1984	Cin N	38	101	10	23	2	0	0	6	12-2	0	17	.228	.310	.248	56	-6	0-0	1.000	-1	97	67	C36/1		-0.6
1985	Cin N	73	151	12	36	7	0	2	24	9-2	1	19	.238	.280	.325	67	-7	0-0	.989	-8	111	61	C70		-1.3
1986	Cin N	9	10	0	0	0	0	0	0	1-0	0	2	.000	.091	.000	-70	-2	0-0	1.000	0	135	0	C7	15	-0.2
1987	Bal A	12	21	4	5	0	0	1	1	3-0	0	6	.238	.333	.381	91	0	0-0	.978	-3	55	0	C12	42	-0.3
Total 5		183	420	30	89	12	1	3	38	39-6	2	63	.212	.280	.267	52	-27	1-0	.990	-19	94	53	C176/1	57	-4.3

Van HALTREN, GEORGE   George Edward Martin "Rip"   B3.30.1866 St.Louis MO   D9.29.1945 Oakland CA   BL/TL/5-11/170   d6.27   M1   OF(313/1376/149) ▲

1887	Chi N	45	172	30	35	4	0	3	17	15	1	15	.203	.271	.279	47	-13	12	.927	-3	23	131	O27(4/0/23),P20		-0.9
1888	Chi N	81	318	46	90	9	14	4	34	22	0	34	.283	.329	.437	133	10	21	.872	0	102	0	O57(47/4/7),P30		0.4
1889	Chi N	134	543	126	175	20	10	9	81	82	5	23	.322	.416	.446	134	26	28	.898	-5	98	68	O130(115/15/0),S3/2		1.5
1890	Bro P	92	376	84	126	8	9	5	54	41	3	23	.335	.405	.444	119	9	35	.896	4	130	39	O67(6/12/49),P28,S3		0.7
1891	Bal AA	139	546	136	180	14	15	9	83	71	4	46	.318	.398	.443	139	28	75	.882	-15	146	234	O81(79/0/2),S59,P6,2b2		1.1
1892	Bal N	135	556	105	168	20	12	7	57	70	2	34	.302	.382	.419	138	26	49	.850	-12	128	94	O129(16/62/53),P4,3b3,1b2,S2,M		1.4
	Pit N	13	55	10	11	2	2	0	5	6	0	9	.200	.279	.309	77	-2	6	.905	-2	56	261	O13C		-0.4
	Year	148	611	115	179	22	14	7	62	76	2	34	.293	.373	.409	133	25	55	.854	-4	122	107	O142(16/75/53),P4,3b3,1b2,S2		1.0
1893	Pit N	124	529	129	179	14	11	3	79	75	2	25	.338	.422	.423	128	24	37	.869	-11	126	78	O111C,S12,2b2		0.5
1894	†NY N	139	528	109	175	22	4	7	105	55	4	23	.331	.399	.428	100	1	43	.915	-6	125	96	O139C		-1.0
1895	NY N	131	521	113	177	23	19	8	103	57	3	36	.340	.408	.503	137	28	32	.914	-5	134	69	O131C/P		1.2
1896	NY N	133	562	136	197	18	21	5	74	55	2	36	.351	.410	.484	139	31	39	.952	4	139	87	O133C,P2		2.3
1897	NY N	130	566	119	186	22	9	3	64	42	1		.329	.372	.415	112	9	50	.938	7	166	114	O130C		0.7
1898	NY N	156	654	129	204	28	16	2	68	59	4		.312	.372	.413	129	24	36	.917	-8	97	88	O156(17/138/3)		0.5
1899	NY N	152	607	118	183	22	3	2	58	75	1		.301	.379	.357	106	9	31	.932	-0	134	110	O152(23/129/0)		-0.1
1900	NY N	141	571	114	180	30	7	1	51	50	1		.315	.371	.398	116	15	45	.939	8	148	123	O141C/P		1.3
1901	NY N	135	543	82	182	23	6	1	47	51	4		.335	.396	.405	138	29	24	.941	5	139	109	O135C/P		2.6
1902	NY N	26	96	14	24	1	2	0	7	17	0		.250	.363	.302	107	2	6	.929	1	164	108	O26(3/13/10)		0.1
1903	NY N	84	280	42	72	6	1	0	28	28	1		.257	.327	.286	72	-9	14	.959	-5	31	44	O75(3/70/2)		-1.7
Total 17		1990	8043	1642	2544	286	161	69	1015	871	38	306	.316	.386	.418	122	247	583	.915	-33	124	96	O1833C,P93,S79,2b5,3b3,1b2		10.2

Van MANN, JOHN   John Silas   B6.7.1890 Fairland OK   D6.10.1958 Shreveport LA   BR/TR/?/186   d6.11

| 1913 | StL N | 1 | 0 | 0 | 0 | 0 | 0 | 0 | 0 | 0-0 | 0 | 0 | 1.000 | .000 | .000 | -99 | 0 | 0 | — | 0 | | | /H | | 0.0 |

Van NOY, JAY   Jay Lowell   B11.4.1928 Garland UT   BL/TR/6-1/200   d6.18   Col Utah St.

| 1951 | StL N | 6 | 7 | 1 | 0 | 0 | 0 | 0 | 0 | 1 | 0 | 6 | .000 | .125 | .000 | -63 | -2 | 0-0 | 1.000 | 0 | 126 | 0 | /OR | | -0.2 |

Van ROBAYS, MAURICE   Maurice Rene "Bomber"   B11.15.1914 Detroit MI   D3.1.1965 Detroit MI   BR/TR/6-0.5/190   d9.7   Mil 1944-45

1939	Pit N	27	105	13	33	9	0	2	16	6	0	10	.314	.351	.457	118	3	0	.919	-2	76	78	O25L/3		-0.1
1940	Pit N	145	572	82	156	27	7	11	116	33	3	58	.273	.316	.402	98	-4	2	.963	-5	90	96	O143(137/0/6)/1		-1.7
1941	Pit N	129	457	62	129	23	5	4	78	41	1	29	.282	.343	.381	104	2	0	.974	6	108	105	O121L		0.2
1942	Pit N	100	328	29	76	13	5	1	46	30	1	24	.232	.298	.311	76	-10	0	.986	4	108	103	O84L		-1.1
1943	Pit N	69	236	32	68	17	7	1	35	18	2	19	.288	.344	.432	119	5	0	.940	-3	97	80	O60(15/0/45)		-0.1
1946	Pit N	59	146	14	31	5	1	1	12	11	1	15	.212	.272	.308	63	-8	0	.955	-2	95	34	O37(21/3/13),1b2		-1.3
Total 6		529	1844	232	493	94	27	20	303	139	8	155	.267	.321	.380	97	-12	2	.966	-2	99	93	O470(403/3/64),1b3/3		-4.1

Van SLYKE, ANDY   Andrew James   B12.21.1960 Utica NY   BL/TR/6-2/192*   [StLN79 1/6]   d6.17

1983	StL N	101	309	51	81	15	5	8	38	46-5	1	64	.262	.357	.421	115	7	21-7	.974	-1	97	99	O69(50/7/23),3b30,1b9		0.5
1984	StL N	137	361	45	88	16	4	7	50	63-9	0	71	.244	.354	.368	106	5	28-5	1.000	2	79	133	O81(34/15/35),3b32,1b30		0.8
1985	†StL N	146	424	61	110	25	6	13	55	47-6	2	54	.259	.335	.439	116	9	34-6	.996	6	101	160	O142(4/10/133),1b2		1.5
1986	StL N	137	418	48	113	23	7	13	61	47-5	1	85	.270	.343	.452	118	10	21-8	.969	8	108	148	O110(1/27/87),1b38		1.5
1987	Pit N	157	564	93	165	36	11	21	82	56-4	4	122	.293	.359	.507	125	20	34-8	.988	1	101	118	O150(0/114/37)/1		2.3
1988	Pit N★	154	587	101	169	23	15	25	100	57-2	1	126	.288	.345	.506	145	31	30-9	.991	5	102	170	O152C		4.1
1989	Pit N	130	476	64	113	18	9	9	53	47-3	3	100	.237	.308	.370	97	-3	16-4	.989	4	104	135	O123C,1b2	25	0.2
1990	†Pit N	136	493	67	140	26	6	17	77	66-2	1	89	.284	.367	.465	132	23	14-4	.976	-8	90	86	O133C		1.6
1991	†Pit N	138	491	87	130	24	7	17	83	71-1	2	85	.265	.355	.460	127	19	10-3	.996	-11	86	110	O135C		0.9
1992	†Pit N★	154	614	103	199	45	12	14	89	58-4	1	99	.324	.381	.505	151	41	12-3	.989	-3	98	117	O154C		4.1
1993	Pit N	83	323	42	100	13	4	8	50	24-5	2	40	.310	.357	.449	116	7	11-2	.995	-3	98	48	O78C	73	0.7
1994	Pit N★	105	374	41	92	18	3	6	30	52-7	2	72	.246	.340	.358	81	-9	7-0	.992	2	99	170	O99C		-0.5

YEAR	TM LG	G	AB	R	H	2B	3B	HR	RBI	BB-IB	HP	SO	AVG	OBP	SLG	AOPS	ABR	SB-CS	FA	FR	RNG	THR	GAMES AT POSITION	DL	BFW
1995	Bal A	17	63	6	10	1	0	3	8	5-1	0	15	.159	.221	.317	37	-6	0-0	.978	1	104	247	O17(0/16/1)	31	-0.5
	Phi N	63	214	26	52	10	2	3	16	28-1	2	41	.243	.333	.350	81	-5	7-0	.984	-1	91	171	O56C	26	-0.4
Total	13	1658	5711	835	1562	293	91	164	792	667-55	27	1063	.274	.349	.443	119	149	245-59	.988	3	98	130	O1499(89/1119/316),1b82,3b62	155	16.8

Van ZANDT, IKE   Charles Isaac   B2.1876 Brooklyn NY   D9.14.1908 Nashua NH   BL/TL   d8.5 ▲

YEAR	TM LG	G	AB	R	H	2B	3B	HR	RBI	BB-IB	HP	SO	AVG	OBP	SLG	AOPS	ABR	SB-CS	FA	FR	RNG	THR	GAMES AT POSITION	DL	BFW
1901	NY N	3	6	1	1	0	0	0	0				.167	.167	.167	-3	-1	0	.333	-1	0	0	P2/OL		-0.1
1904	Chi N	3	11	0	0	0	0	0	0				.000	.000	.000	-99	-3	0	1.000	0	0	0	O3R		-0.3
1905	StL A	94	322	31	75	15	1	1	20	7		1	.233	.252	.295	77	-9	7	.874	-11	93	0	O75(0/29/45)/P1		-2.6
Total	3	100	339	32	76	15	1	1	20	7		1	.224	.242	.283	69	-13	7	.868	-13	89	0	O79(1/29/46),P3/1		-3.0

Van ZANT, DICK   Richard "Foghorn Dick"   B11.1864 IN   D8.6.1912 Wayne Co. IN   6-0/?   d10.4

YEAR	TM LG	G	AB	R	H	2B	3B	HR	RBI	BB-IB	HP	SO	AVG	OBP	SLG	AOPS	ABR	SB-CS	FA	FR	RNG	THR	GAMES AT POSITION	DL	BFW
1888	Cle AA	10	31	1	8	1	0	1	1	,1		1	.258	.303	.290	93	0	1	.784	0	122	150	3b10		0.0

VARGAS, EDDIE   Hediberto (Rodriguez)   B2.23.1959 Guanica, PR   BR/TR/6-4/205*   d9.8   [DL 1983 Pit N 81]

YEAR	TM LG	G	AB	R	H	2B	3B	HR	RBI	BB-IB	HP	SO	AVG	OBP	SLG	AOPS	ABR	SB-CS	FA	FR	RNG	THR	GAMES AT POSITION	DL	BFW
1982	Pit N	8	8	1	3	1	0	0	3	0-0		2	.375	.333	.500	136	0	0-0	1.000	-0	69	65	1b5		0.0
1984	Pit N	18	31	3	7	2	0	0	3	3-0		5	.226	.294	.290	65	-1	0-0	.982	-0	91	115	1b13		-0.2
Total	2	26	39	4	10	3	0	0	6	3-0		7	.256	.302	.333	80	-1	0-0	.986	-0	86	104	1b18	81	-0.2

VARITEK, JASON   Jason Andrew   B4.11.1972 Rochester MN   BB/TR/6-2/220(210-230)   [SeaA94 1/14]   d9.24   Col Georgia Tech

YEAR	TM LG	G	AB	R	H	2B	3B	HR	RBI	BB-IB	HP	SO	AVG	OBP	SLG	AOPS	ABR	SB-CS	FA	FR	RNG	THR	GAMES AT POSITION	DL	BFW
1997	Bos A	1	1	0	1	0	0	0	0	0-0	0	0	1.000	1.000	1.000	415	0	0-0	1.000	0	0	0	/C		0.0
1998	†Bos A	86	221	31	56	13	0	7	33	17-1	2	45	.253	.309	.407	83	-6	2-2	.988	-1	88	97	C75,D3		-0.3
1999	†Bos A	144	483	70	130	39	2	20	76	46-2	2	85	.269	.330	.482	102	1	1-2	.990	9	69	110	C140,D2		1.7
2000	Bos A	139	448	55	111	31	1	10	65	60-3	3	84	.248	.342	.388	83	-10	1-1	.992	0	71	107	C128/D		-0.2
2001	Bos A	51	174	19	51	11	1	7	25	21-3	1	35	.293	.371	.489	124	7	0-0	.996	11	72	122	C50	122	1.9
2002	Bos A	132	467	58	124	27	0	10	61	41-3	7	95	.266	.332	.392	91	-6	4-3	.996	12	82	99	C127/D		1.4
2003	†Bos A☆	142	451	63	123	31	1	25	85	51-8	7	106	.273	.351	.512	120	14	3-2	.990	-7	111	79	C137,D4		1.4
2004	†Bos A	137	463	67	137	30	1	18	73	62-9	10	126	.296	.390	.482	118	15	10-3	.998	9	82	78	C130/D		3.2
2005	†Bos A★	133	470	70	132	30	1	22	70	62-3	3	117	.281	.366	.489	119	14	2-0	.990	-5	104	72	C130		1.7
Total	9	965	3178	433	865	212	8	119	488	360-32	38	693	.272	.350	.456	105	29	23-13	.993	27	86	93	C918,D12	122	10.8

VARNER, BUCK   Glen Gann   B8.17.1930 Hixson TN   D4.29.2000 Chattanooga TN   BL/TR/5-10/170   d9.19

YEAR	TM LG	G	AB	R	H	2B	3B	HR	RBI	BB-IB	HP	SO	AVG	OBP	SLG	AOPS	ABR	SB-CS	FA	FR	RNG	THR	GAMES AT POSITION	DL	BFW
1952	Was A	2	4	0	0	0	0	0	1	0-0	0	1	.000	.000	.000	-43	-1	0-0	1.000	-0	78	0	/OR		-0.1

VARNEY, PETE   Richard Fred   B4.10.1949 Roxbury MA   BR/TR/6-3/235*   [ChiA71 A1/1]   d8.26   Col Harvard

YEAR	TM LG	G	AB	R	H	2B	3B	HR	RBI	BB-IB	HP	SO	AVG	OBP	SLG	AOPS	ABR	SB-CS	FA	FR	RNG	THR	GAMES AT POSITION	DL	BFW
1973	Chi A	5	4	0	0	0	0	0	0	1-0	0	1	.000	.200	.000	-38	-0	0-0	1.000	0	0	0	C5		0.0
1974	Chi A	9	28	1	7	0	0	0	2	1-0	0	8	.250	.267	.250	51	-2	0-0	.981	2	245	169	C9		0.0
1975	Chi A	36	107	12	29	5	1	2	8	6-1	0	28	.271	.316	.393	98	-2	1-0	.988	-2	100	114	C34,D2		-0.1
1976	Chi A	14	41	5	10	2	0	3	5	2-0	0	9	.244	.279	.512	128	1	0-0	.988	-1	57	57	C14		0.0
	Atl N	5	10	0	1	0	0	0	0	0-0	1	4	.100	.100	.100	-41	-2	0-0	1.000	-1	27	153	C5		-0.2
Total	4	69	190	18	47	7	1	5	15	10-1	1	47	.247	.287	.374	87	-5	2-0	.988	-2	106	107	C67,D2		-0.3

VARSHO, GARY   Gary Andrew   B6.20.1961 Marshfield WI   BL/TR/5-11/190*   [ChiN82 5/107]   d7.6   C4   Col Wisconsin-Oshkosh

YEAR	TM LG	G	AB	R	H	2B	3B	HR	RBI	BB-IB	HP	SO	AVG	OBP	SLG	AOPS	ABR	SB-CS	FA	FR	RNG	THR	GAMES AT POSITION	DL	BFW
1988	Chi N	46	73	6	20	3	0	0	5	1-0	0	6	.274	.280	.315	68	-3	5-0	.906	-0	116	0	O18(10/0/8)		-0.3
1989	Chi N	61	87	10	16	4	2	0	6	4-1	0	13	.184	.220	.276	38	-7	3-0	.929	-1	86	125	O21(17/0/4)		-0.8
1990	Chi N	46	48	10	12	4	0	0	1	1-1	0	6	.250	.265	.333	59	-3	2-0	1.000	0	83	0	O3(2/0/1)		-0.2
1991	†Pit N	99	187	23	51	11	2	4	23	19-2	1	34	.273	.344	.417	115	4	9-2	.989	-0	100	67	O54(5/5/45),1b3		0.4
1992	†Pit N	103	162	22	36	6	3	4	22	10-1	2	32	.222	.266	.370	79	-5	5-2	.984	-1	101	54	O44(14/2/28)		-0.7
1993	Cin N	77	95	8	22	6	0	2	11	9-0	1	19	.232	.302	.358	76	-3	1-0	1.000	0	99	96	O22(13/0/9)		-0.6
1994	Pit N	67	82	15	21	6	3	0	5	4-1	2	19	.256	.307	.402	81	-2	0-1	.926	-2	85	18	O36(18/2/18)/1		-0.6
1995	Phi N	72	103	7	26	1	1	0	11	7-1	2	17	.252	.310	.282	58	-6	2-0	.939	-3	113	0	O25(9/0/16)	23	-0.7
Total	8	571	837	101	204	41	11	10	84	55-7	7	146	.244	.294	.355	78	-25	27-5	.963	-4	100	52	O223(88/9/129),1b4	23	-3.2

VATCHER, JIM   James Ernest   B5.27.1965 Santa Monica CA   BR/TR/5-9/165*   [PhiN87 20/520]   d5.30   Col Cal St.-Northridge

YEAR	TM LG	G	AB	R	H	2B	3B	HR	RBI	BB-IB	HP	SO	AVG	OBP	SLG	AOPS	ABR	SB-CS	FA	FR	RNG	THR	GAMES AT POSITION	DL	BFW
1990	Phi N	36	46	5	12	1	0	1	4	4-0	0	6	.261	.320	.348	84	-1	0-0	1.000	-1	96	0	O24(12/0/12)		-0.2
	Atl N	21	27	2	7	1	1	0	3	1-0	0	9	.259	.286	.370	75	-1	0-0	1.000	1	129	0	O6(2/0/4)		-0.1
	Year	57	73	7	19	2	1	1	7	5-0	0	15	.260	.308	.356	80	-2	0-0	1.000	-0	103	0	O30(14/0/16)		-0.3
1991	SD N	17	20	3	4	0	0	0	2	4-0	0	6	.200	.333	.200	52	-1	1-0	.900	-1	76	253	O11(2/0/9)		-0.1
1992	SD N	13	16	1	4	1	0	0	3	2-0	1	6	.250	.368	.313	93	-0	0-0	1.000	1	95	229	O13(0/1/12)		0.0
Total	3	87	109	11	27	3	1	1	12	11-0	1	27	.248	.322	.321	77	-3	1-0	.980	-0	95	117	O54(16/1/37)		-0.4

VAUGHAN, GLENN   Glenn Edward "Sparky"   B2.16.1944 Compton CA   D12.18.2004 Houston TX   BB/TR/5-11/170   d9.20   Col Houston

YEAR	TM LG	G	AB	R	H	2B	3B	HR	RBI	BB-IB	HP	SO	AVG	OBP	SLG	AOPS	ABR	SB-CS	FA	FR	RNG	THR	GAMES AT POSITION	DL	BFW
1963	Hou N	9	30	1	5	0	0	0	0	2-0	0	5	.167	.219	.167	14	-3	1-0	.914	-2	91	25	S9/3		-0.5

VAUGHAN, ARKY   Joseph Floyd   B3.9.1912 Clifty AR   D8.30.1952 Eagleville CA   BL/TR/5-10.5/175   d4.17   HF1985

YEAR	TM LG	G	AB	R	H	2B	3B	HR	RBI	BB-IB	HP	SO	AVG	OBP	SLG	AOPS	ABR	SB-CS	FA	FR	RNG	THR	GAMES AT POSITION	DL	BFW
1932	Pit N	129	497	71	158	15	10	4	61	39	6	26	.318	.375	.412	113	10	10	.934	-16	96	101	S128		0.3
1933	Pit N	152	573	85	180	29	**19**	9	97	64	5	23	.314	.388	.478	146	35	3	.945	-10	98	104	S152		3.8
1934	Pit N★	149	558	115	186	41	11	12	94	**94**	2	38	**.333**	**.431**	.511	148	43	10	.952	3	101	91	S149		5.5
1935	Pit N★	137	499	108	192	34	10	19	99	**97**	7	18	**.385**	**.491**	**.607**	187	69	4	.950	-9	101	79	S137		6.6
1936	Pit N☆	**156**	568	**122**	190	30	11	9	78	**118**	5	21	.335	**.453**	.474	146	46	6	.945	-9	97	93	S156		4.7
1937	Pit N★	126	469	71	151	17	**17**	5	72	54	2	22	.322	.394	.463	132	21	7	.956	5	100	93	S108,O12L		2.1
1938	Pit N☆	148	541	88	174	35	5	7	68	104	2	17	.322	.433	.444	140	38	14	.961	17	108	118	S147		6.4
1939	Pit N★	152	595	94	182	30	11	6	62	70	6	20	.306	.385	.424	119	18	12	.962	11	**107**	96	S152		4.0
1940	Pit N★	**156**	594	**113**	178	40	**15**	7	95	88	3	25	.300	.393	.453	134	31	12	.942	9	**109**	91	S155,3b2		5.1
1941	Pit N★	106	374	69	118	20	7	6	38	50	2	13	.316	.399	.455	141	21	8	.958	-8	100	77	S97,3b3		2.1
1942	Bro N★	128	495	82	137	18	4	2	49	51	3	17	.277	.348	.341	100	1	8	.959	-10	88	89	3b119,S5/2		-0.5
1943	Bro N	149	610	**112**	186	39	6	5	66	60	3	13	.305	.374	.413	126	21	**20**	.965	-15	93	89	S99,3b55		1.6
1947	†Bro N	64	126	24	41	5	2	2	25	27	0	11	.325	.444	.444	132	7	4	1.000	1	112	0	O22L,3b10		0.7
1948	Bro N	65	123	19	30	3	0	3	22	21	0	8	.244	.354	.341	86	2	7	.951	2	93	210	O26L,3b8		-0.2
Total	14	1817	6622	1173	2103	356	128	96	926	937	46	276	.318	.406	.453	136	359	118	.951	-29	100	93	S1485,3b197,O60L/2		43.3

VAUGHN, FRED   Frederick Thomas "Muscles"   B10.18.1918 Coalinga CA   D3.2.1964 Near Lake Wales FL   BR/TR/5-10/185   d8.20

YEAR	TM LG	G	AB	R	H	2B	3B	HR	RBI	BB-IB	HP	SO	AVG	OBP	SLG	AOPS	ABR	SB-CS	FA	FR	RNG	THR	GAMES AT POSITION	DL	BFW
1944	Was A	30	109	10	28	6	1	1	21	9	1	24	.257	.319	.321	87	-2	2-2	.942	-2	100	90	2b26,3b3		-0.3
1945	Was A	80	268	28	63	7	4	1	25	23	1	48	.235	.298	.302	81	-7	0-3	.946	-11	94	84	2b76/S		-1.8
Total	2	110	377	38	91	9	5	2	46	32	2	72	.241	.304	.308	83	-9	2-5	.945	-13	96	86	2b102,3b3/S		-2.2

VAUGHN, GREG   Gregory Lamont   B7.3.1965 Sacramento CA   BR/TR/6-0/202(193-205)   [MilA86 S1/4]   d8.10   Col Miami

YEAR	TM LG	G	AB	R	H	2B	3B	HR	RBI	BB-IB	HP	SO	AVG	OBP	SLG	AOPS	ABR	SB-CS	FA	FR	RNG	THR	GAMES AT POSITION	DL	BFW
1989	Mil A	38	113	18	30	3	0	5	23	13-0	0	23	.265	.336	.425	115	2	4-1	.943	-2	83	90	O24L,D13		-0.3
1990	Mil A	120	382	51	84	26	2	17	61	33-1	1	91	.220	.280	.432	98	-3	7-4	.967	-1	95	124	O106L,D8	15	-0.3
1991	Mil A	145	542	81	132	24	5	27	98	62-2	-1	125	.244	.319	.456	115	9	2-2	.994	6	110	65	O135(134/0/1),D10		1.8
1992	Mil A	141	501	77	114	18	2	23	78	60-1	5	123	.228	.313	.409	103	1	15-15	.990	-2	99	65	O131(131/0/0),D7		0.5
1993	Mil A★	154	569	97	152	28	2	30	97	89-14	5	118	.267	.369	.482	128	24	10-7	.986	-1	106	17	O94L,D58		1.1
1994	Mil A	95	370	59	94	24	1	19	55	51-6	1	93	.254	.345	.478	104	3	9-5	.982	-3	92	82	O81(81/1/0),D14	19	-0.4
1995	Mil A	108	392	67	88	19	1	17	59	55-3	1	89	.224	.317	.408	83	-10	10-4	—	0	0	0	D104		-1.4
1996	Mil A☆	102	375	78	105	16	0	31	95	58-4	4	99	.280	.378	.571	136	18	5-2	.980	-4	94	72	O100(98/3/0)/D		1.8
	†SD N	43	141	20	29	3	1	10	22	24-2	2	31	.206	.329	.454	109	1	4-1	.974	1	109	92	O39L		0.1
1997	SD N	120	361	60	78	10	0	18	57	56-1	2	110	.216	.322	.393	92	-4	7-4	.994	0	92	120	O94L,D3		-0.4
1998	†SD N★	158	573	112	156	28	4	50	119	79-6	3	121	.272	.363	.597	159	47	11-4	.993	1	100	53	O151L,D4		4.6
1999	Cin N	153	550	104	135	20	2	45	118	85-3	3	137	.245	.347	.535	116	11	15-2	.986	1	109	82	O144L,D6		2.1
2000	TB A	127	461	83	117	27	1	28	74	80-3	2	128	.254	.365	.499	118	13	8-1	.993	1	95	138	O72L,D52	21	-0.8
2001	TB A★	136	485	74	113	25	0	24	82	71-7	2	130	.233	.333	.433	102	2	11-5	.978	6	120	124	D76,O57L		0.3
2002	TB A	69	251	28	41	10	2	8	29	41-1	5	82	.163	.286	.315	61	-14	3-2	.987	3	119	110	D38,O31L	70	-1.8
2003	Col N	6	27	4	7	3	0	3	6	5-0	0	13	.189	.326	.514	102	0	0-0	1.000	1	144	0	O7(6/0/1),D3		0.1
Total	15	1731	6103	1017	1475	284	23	355	1072	865-54	37	1513	.242	.337	.470	112	99	121-59	.986	7	101	82	O1266(1261/4/3),D397	125	4

VAUGHN, FARMER   Harry Francis   B3.1.1864 Ruraldale OH   D2.21.1914 Cincinnati OH   BR/TR/6-3/177   d10.7   OF(59/14/35)

YEAR	TM LG	G	AB	R	H	2B	3B	HR	RBI	BB-IB	HP	SO	AVG	OBP	SLG	AOPS	ABR	SB-CS	FA	FR	RNG	THR	GAMES AT POSITION	DL	BFW
1886	Cin AA	1	3	0	0	0	0	0	0				.000	.000	.000	-19	-0	0	.917	0	0	0	/C		
1888	Lou AA	51	189	15	37	4	2	1	21	4		1	.196	.216	.254	52	-11	4	.863	-1	95	207	O28(22/1/5),C25		
1889	Lou AA	90	360	39	86	11	5	3	45	7		0	41	.239	.253	.322	65	-19	13	.900	-2			C54,O20(5/9/4),1b18,3b3		

YEAR	TM LG	G	AB	R	H	2B	3B	HR	RBI	BB-IB	HP	SO	AVG	OBP	SLG	AOPS	ABR	SB-CS	FA	FR	RNG	THR	GAMES AT POSITION	DL	BFW
1890	NY P	44	166	27	44	7	0	1	22	10	0	9	.265	.307	.325	63	-9	6	.877	-8	99	66	C30,O12(8/1/3)/32		-1.2
1891	Cin AA	51	175	21	45	1	1	1	14	14	1	15	.257	.316	.326	77	-6	7	.923	4	89	129	C44,O6(3/1/2),1b2,3b2/P		0.1
	Mil AA	25	99	13	33	7	0	0	9	4	0	5	.333	.359	.404	98	-1	1	.924	5	120	67	C20,1b4/OL		0.4
	Year	76	274	34	78	14	1	1	23	18	1	20	.285	.331	.354	86	-7	8	.923	9	100	107	C64,O7(4/1/2),1b6,3b2/P		0.5
1892	Cin N	91	346	45	88	10	5	2	50	16	4	13	.254	.295	.329	90	-6	10	.929	-6	118	73	C67,1b14,O11(4/0/7),3b6		-0.6
1893	Cin N	121	483	68	135	17	12	1	108	35	3	17	.280	.332	.371	85	-13	16	.969	1	110	84	C80,O23(12/1/10),1b21		-0.5
1894	Cin N	72	284	50	88	15	5	8	64	12	0	11	.310	.338	.482	93	-6	6	.918	-3	98	87	C43,1b27,O8(4/1/3),S3		-0.4
1895	Cin N	92	334	60	102	23	5	1	48	17	0	10	.305	.339	.413	90	-6	15	.934	10	102	107	C77,1b15/32		0.9
1896	Cin N	114	433	71	127	20	9	2	66	16	1	7	.293	.320	.395	82	-14	7	.984	12	98	114	1b57,C57		0.3
1897	Cin N	54	199	21	58	13	5	0	30	2			.291	.299	.407	80	-7		.986	1	85	101	1b35,C15		-0.4
1898	Cin N	78	275	35	84	12	4	1	46	11	3		.305	.339	.389	101	-1	4	.979	0	51	111	1b39,C33		0.3
1899	Cin N	31	108	9	19	1	0	0	2	3	0		.176	.198	.185	5	-14	2	.982	3	124	82	1b21,C7/OR		-1.0
Total	13	915	3454	474	946	147	53	21	525	151	14	128	.274	.307	.365	80	-113	92	.926	17	117	91	C553,1b253,O110L,3b13,S3,2b2/P		-4.7

VAUGHN, MO   Maurice Samuel B12.15.1967 Norwalk CT BL/TR/6-1/240(225-268) [BosA89 1/23] d6.27 Col Seton Hall [DL 2001 Ana A 190, 2004 NY N 183]

YEAR	TM LG	G	AB	R	H	2B	3B	HR	RBI	BB-IB	HP	SO	AVG	OBP	SLG	AOPS	ABR	SB-CS	FA	FR	RNG	THR	GAMES AT POSITION	DL	BFW
1991	Bos A	74	219	21	57	12	0	4	32	26-2	2	43	.260	.339	.370	92	-1	2-1	.985	-1	93	127	1b49,D16		-0.6
1992	Bos A	113	355	42	83	16	2	13	57	47-7	3	67	.234	.326	.400	96	-2	3-3	.982	-1	102	108	1b85,D20		-1.0
1993	Bos A	152	539	86	160	34	1	29	101	79-23	8	130	.297	.390	.525	136	30	4-3	.987	-11	75	98	1b131,D19		0.6
1994	Bos A	111	394	65	122	25	1	26	82	57-20	10	112	.310	.408	.576	144	27	4-4	.989	-5	82	112	1b106/D		1.1
1995	†Bos A★	140	550	98	165	28	3	39	126	68-17	14	150	.300	.388	.575	143	35	11-4	.992	-3	94	106	1b138,D2		1.9
1996	Bos A★	161	635	118	207	29	1	44	143	95-19	14	154	.326	.420	.583	149	50	2-0	.988	-12	71	86	1b146,D15		2.2
1997	Bos A	141	527	91	166	24	0	35	96	86-17	12	154	.315	.420	.560	150	42	2-2	.988	-7	85	99	1b131,D9	23	2.2
1998	†Bos A✱	154	609	107	205	31	2	40	115	61-13	8	144	.337	.402	.591	151	46	0-0	.991	-4	90	83	1b142,D12		2.7
1999	Ana A	139	524	63	147	20	0	33	108	54-7	11	127	.281	.358	.508	118	13	0-0	.995	-2	88	102	1b72,D67	15	0.1
2000	Ana A	161	614	93	167	31	0	36	117	79-11	14	181	.272	.365	.498	113	13	2-0	.990	-12	74	120	1b147,D14		-1.2
2002	NY N	139	487	67	126	18	0	26	72	59-6	10	145	.259	.349	.456	120	11	0-1	.984	-15	59	89	1b134	15	-1.5
2003	NY N	27	79	10	15	2	0	3	15	14-2	2	22	.190	.323	.329	75	-3	0-0	.974	-3	64	117	1b24	149	-0.7
Total	12	1512	5532	861	1620	270	10	328	1064	725-144	108	1429	.293	.383	.523	131	261	30-18	.988	-74	81	101	1b1305,D175	575	5.8

VAUGHN, BOBBY   Robert B6.4.1885 Stamford NY D4.11.1965 Seattle WA BR/TR/5-9/150 d6.12 Col Princeton

YEAR	TM LG	G	AB	R	H	2B	3B	HR	RBI	BB-IB	HP	SO	AVG	OBP	SLG	AOPS	ABR	SB-CS	FA	FR	RNG	THR	GAMES AT POSITION	DL	BFW
1909	NY A	5	14	1	2	0	0	0	1	0		0	.143	.200	.143	8	-1	1	.882	-3	46	0	2b4/S		-0.5
1915	StL F	144	521	69	146	19	9	0	32	58	3	38	.280	.356	.351	94	-10	24	.953	-7	97	94	2b127,S12,3b8		-1.5
Total	2	149	535	70	148	19	9	0	32	59	3	38	.277	.352	.346	92	-11	25	.951	-10	96	91	2b131,S13,3b8		-2.0

VAZQUEZ, RAMON   Ramon Luis B8.21.1976 Aibonito, PR BL/TR/5-11/170* [SeaA95 27/734] d9.7 Col Indian Hills (IA) CC

YEAR	TM LG	G	AB	R	H	2B	3B	HR	RBI	BB-IB	HP	SO	AVG	OBP	SLG	AOPS	ABR	SB-CS	FA	FR	RNG	THR	GAMES AT POSITION	DL	BFW
2001	†Sea A	17	35	5	8	0	0	0	3	2-0	0	3	.229	.222	.229	22	-4	0-0	1.000	-5	56	99	S10,2b6,3b2		-0.8
2002	SD N	128	423	50	116	21	5	2	32	45-3	1	79	.274	.344	.362	98	-3	7-2	.985	9	102	99	2b81,S41,3b20		1.2
2003	SD N	116	422	56	110	17	4	3	30	52-2	2	88	.261	.342	.341	88	-7	10-3	.969	-13	92	85	S108,3b4,2b3	36	-1.0
2004	SD N	52	115	12	27	3	1	1	11	11-2	0	24	.235	.297	.322	65	-6	1-1	.983	-6	79	56	S22,2b10,3b9,1b3	31	-1.1
2005	Bos A	27	61	6	12	2	0	0	4	3-0	0	14	.197	.234	.230	23	-7	0-0	.969	-5	66	56	S12,3b8,2b4/D		-1.0
	Cle A	12	24	1	6	3	0	0	1	2-0	0	3	.250	.308	.375	83	0	0-0	1.000	-0	68	163	2b8,S2		0.0
	Year	39	85	7	18	5	0	0	5	5-0	0	17	.212	.256	.271	39	-7	0-0	.974	-5	70	63	S14,2b12,3b8/D		-1.0
Total	5	352	1080	130	279	46	11	6	84	113-7	3	211	.258	.328	.338	83	-27	18-6	.974	-19	92	80	S195,2b112,3b43,1b3/D	67	-2.7

VEACH, BOBBY   Robert Hayes B6.29.1888 Island KY D8.7.1945 Detroit MI BL/TR/5-11/160 d9.6

YEAR	TM LG	G	AB	R	H	2B	3B	HR	RBI	BB-IB	HP	SO	AVG	OBP	SLG	AOPS	ABR	SB-CS	FA	FR	RNG	THR	GAMES AT POSITION	DL	BFW
1912	Det A	23	79	8	27	5	1	0	15	5	1		.342	.388	.430	138	4	2	.927	1	97	162	O22L		0.4
1913	Det A	137	491	54	132	22	10	0	64	53	5	31	.269	.346	.354	107	5	22	.917	-5	98	86	O135L		-0.7
1914	Det A	149	531	56	146	19	14	1	72	50	3	29	.275	.341	.369	110	5	20-20	.965	3	100	103	O145L		-0.1
1915	Det A	152	569	81	178	40	10	3	112	68	4	43	.313	.390	.434	140	29	16-19	.975	7	100	97	O152L		2.2
1916	Det A	150	566	92	173	33	15	3	91	52	3	41	.306	.367	.433	135	23	24-15	.967	3	109	70	O150L		2.1
1917	Det A	154	571	79	182	31	12	8	103	61	9	44	.319	.393	.457	160	41	21	.956	2	111	77	O154L		4.0
1918	Det A	127	499	59	139	21	13	3	78	35	4	23	.279	.331	.391	123	11	21	.977	2	107	83	O127(124/1/2)/P		0.8
1919	Det A	139	538	87	191	45	17	3	101	33	5	33	.355	.398	.519	160	41	19	.967	9	117	95	O138L		4.5
1920	Det A	154	612	92	188	39	15	11	113	36	7	22	.307	.353	.474	121	15	11-7	.967	14	112	129	O154L		2.1
1921	Det A	150	612	110	207	43	13	16	128	48	1	31	.338	.387	.529	133	29	14-10	.974	13	115	108	O149L		2.7
1922	Det A	155	618	96	202	34	13	9	126	42	8	27	.327	.377	.468	123	20	9-1	.982	10	116	84	O154L		1.8
1923	Det A	114	293	45	94	13	2	2	39	29	3	21	.321	.388	.406	111	5	10-3	.943	-6	88	72	O85(46/13/26)		-0.4
1924	Bos A	142	519	77	153	35	9	5	99	47	5	41	.295	.359	.426	102	1	5-5	.956	-4	97	82	O130L		-1.3
1925	Bos A	1	5	0	1	0	0	0	1	0	0	1	.200	.333	.200	38	0	0-0	1.000	-0	101	0	/OL		-0.1
	NY A	56	116	13	41	10	2	0	15	8	1	3	.353	.400	.474	123	4	1-4	.957	2	253	186	O33(13/0/30)		0.3
	†Was A	18	37	4	9	3	0	0	8	3	0	3	.243	.300	.324	60	-2	0-0	.923	-1	90	0	O11(4/0/7)		-0.4
	Year	75	158	17	51	13	2	0	25	12	1		.323	.374	.430	106	1	1-4	.952	1	88	186	O45(18/0/37)		-0.2
Total	14	1821	6656	953	2063	393	147	64	1166	571	59	367	.310	.370	.442	127	231	195-84	.964	43	106	94	O1740(1671/14/65)/P		17.9

VEACH, PEEK-A-BOO   William Walter B6.15.1862 Indianapolis IN D11.12.1937 Indianapolis IN 6-0/175 d8.24 ▲

YEAR	TM LG	G	AB	R	H	2B	3B	HR	RBI	BB-IB	HP	SO	AVG	OBP	SLG	AOPS	ABR	SB-CS	FA	FR	RNG	THR	GAMES AT POSITION	DL	BFW
1884	KC U	27	82	9	11	1	0	1		9			.134	.220	.183	27	-10		.833	2	150	268	O14(11/2/1),P12/21		-0.3
1887	Lou AA	1	3	0	0	0	0	0		0			.000	.250	.000	-26	0		.750	0	55	0	/P		0.0
1890	Cle N	64	238	24	56	10	5	0	32	33	3	28	.235	.336	.319	93	-1	9	.971	6	184	105	1b64		0.0
	Pit N	8	30	6	9	1	2	5	8		0	3	.300	.447	.600	231	6	0	.968	0	136	17	1b8		0.4
	Year	72	268	30	65	11	6	2	37	41	3	31	.243	.349	.351	107	4	9	.971	7	178	95	1b72		0.4
Total	3	100	353	39	76	12	6	3	37	51	3	31	.215	.319	.309	90	-5	9	.971	8	175	93	1b73,O14(11/2/1),P13/2		0.1

VEAL, COOT   Orville Inman B7.9.1932 Sandersville GA BR/TR/6-1/165* d7.30 Col Auburn-Montgomery

YEAR	TM LG	G	AB	R	H	2B	3B	HR	RBI	BB-IB	HP	SO	AVG	OBP	SLG	AOPS	ABR	SB-CS	FA	FR	RNG	THR	GAMES AT POSITION	DL	BFW
1958	Det A	58	207	29	53	10	2	0	16	14-0	1	21	.256	.304	.324	69	-9	1-1	.981	-5	92	82	S58		-1.0
1959	Det A	77	89	12	18	1	0	1	15	8-1	1	7	.202	.273	.247	42	-7	0-0	.962	5	107	94	S72		0.1
1960	Det A	27	64	8	19	5	1	0	8	11-0	0	7	.297	.400	.406	115	2	0-0	.988	-3	97	92	S22,3b3/2		0.0
1961	Was A	69	218	21	44	10	0	0	19	19-0	3	29	.202	.273	.248	41	-18	1-8	.974	5	103	116	S63		-1.0
1962	Pit N	1	1	0	0	0	0	0	0	0-0	0	1	.000	.000	.000	-99	0	0-0	—	0			/H		0.0
1963	Det A	15	32	5	7	0	0	0	4	4-0	0	4	.219	.297	.219	48	-2	0-0	.980	2	126	19	S12		0.0
Total	6	247	611	75	141	26	3	1	51	56-1	5	69	.231	.298	.288	59	-34	2-9	.976	4	101	93	S227,3b3/2		-1.9

VEGA, JESUS   Jesus Anthony (Morales) B10.14.1955 Bayamon, PR BR/TR/6-1/176(176-190) d9.5

YEAR	TM LG	G	AB	R	H	2B	3B	HR	RBI	BB-IB	HP	SO	AVG	OBP	SLG	AOPS	ABR	SB-CS	FA	FR	RNG	THR	GAMES AT POSITION	DL	BFW
1979	Min A	4	7	0	0	0	0	0	0	0-0	0	2	.000	.000	.000	-96	-2	0-0	—	0			D3		-0.2
1980	Min A	12	30	3	5	0	0	0	4	3-0	0	7	.167	.242	.167	13	-4	1-0	1.000	-2	1b2,D9				-0.3
1982	Min A	71	199	23	53	6	0	5	29	8-1	0	19	.266	.289	.372	79	-6	6-1	.974	-2	78	63	D39,1b18/OL		-0.9
Total	3	87	236	26	58	6	0	5	33	11-1	0	28	.246	.275	.335	65	-12	7-1	.975	-1	87	62	D51,1b20/OL		-1.4

VELANDIA, JORGE   Jorge Luis (Macias) B1.12.1975 Caracas, Venez BR/TR/5-9/185(160-185) d6.20

YEAR	TM LG	G	AB	R	H	2B	3B	HR	RBI	BB-IB	HP	SO	AVG	OBP	SLG	AOPS	ABR	SB-CS	FA	FR	RNG	THR	GAMES AT POSITION	DL	BFW
1997	SD N	14	29	0	3	2	0	0	1-0	0	7		.103	.133	.172	-22	-5	0-0	.941	-2	92	139	S6,2b5,3b3		-0.6
1998	Oak A	8	4	0	1	0	0	0	0	0-0	0	1	.250	.250	.250	31	0	0-0	.909	1	173	112	S7/2		0.1
1999	Oak A	63	48	4	9	1	0	0	2	2-0	1	13	.188	.235	.208	15	-6	2-0	.989	8	118	119	2b52,S8,3b2/D	58	0.3
2000	Oak A	18	24	1	3	1	0	0	2	0-0	0	6	.125	.160	.167	-17	-4	0-0	1.000	1	111	124	2b14,S4		-0.3
	NY N	15	7	1	0	0	0	0	0	2-0	0	2	.000	.222	.000	-50	-2	0-0	1.000	-2	77	100	S8/3	71	-0.3
2001	NY N	9	9	1	0	0	0	0	0	0-0	0	1	.000	.182	.000	-52	0	0-0	1.000	-2	77	100	S8/3	71	-0.3
2003	NY N	23	58	6	11	3	0	0	8	10-1	0	15	.190	.304	.276	56	-4	0-0	.972	3	110	96	S23		0.1
Total	6	150	179	13	27	7	0	0	12	17-1	2	45	.151	.231	.201	4	-23	2-0	.987	8	108	104	2b79,S63,3b9/D	129	-0.9

VELARDE, RANDY   Randy Lee B11.24.1962 Midland TX BR/TR/6-0/190(183-200) [ChiA85 19/475] d8.20 Col Lubbock Christian OF(97/4/12)

YEAR	TM LG	G	AB	R	H	2B	3B	HR	RBI	BB-IB	HP	SO	AVG	OBP	SLG	AOPS	ABR	SB-CS	FA	FR	RNG	THR	GAMES AT POSITION	DL	BFW
1987	NY A	8	22	1	4	0	0	0	0	0-0	0	6	.182	.182	.182	-3	-3	0-0	.933	-1	100	76	S8		-0.4
1988	NY A	48	115	18	20	6	0	5	12	8-0	2	24	.174	.240	.357	65	-6	1-1	.967	3	109	168	2b24,S14,3b11		-0.2
1989	NY A	33	100	12	34	4	2	2	11	7-0	1	14	.340	.389	.480	145	6	0-3	.954	-3	87	154	3b27,S9	20	0.5
1990	NY A	95	229	21	48	6	2	5	19	20-0	3	53	.210	.275	.319	65	-11	0-3	.945	-8	113	105	3b74,S15,O5L,2b3,D3		-0.3
1991	NY A	80	184	19	45	11	1	1	15	18-0	0	43	.245	.322	.332	81	-4	3-1	.935	10	118	114	3b50,S31,O2L		0.8
1992	NY A	121	412	57	112	24	1	7	46	38-1	2	78	.272	.333	.386	102	1	7-2	.974	-1	103	91	S75,3b26,O23(14/2/7),2b3		0.6
1993	NY A	85	226	28	68	13	2	7	24	18-2	1	39	.301	.360	.469	125	8	2-2	.932	1	101	103	O50(48/2/0),S26,3b16/D	54	0.9
1994	NY A	77	280	47	78	16	1	9	34	22-0	4	61	.279	.338	.439	103	1	4-2	.944	2	107	116	S49,3b27,O7(6/0/1),2b5		0.5

YEAR	TM LG	G	AB	R	H	2B	3B	HR	RBI	BB-IB	HP	SO	AVG	OBP	SLG	AOPS	ABR	SB-CS	FA	FR	RNG	THR	GAMES AT POSITION	DL	BFW
1995	†NY A	111	367	60	102	19	1	7	46	55-0	4	64	.278	.375	.392	102		5-1	.976	-2	89	72	2b62,S28,O20(20/0/1),3b19		0.6
1996	Cal A	136	530	82	151	27	3	14	54	70-0	5	118	.285	.372	.426	100	2	7-7	.982	-17	81	99	2b114,3b28,S7		-1.0
1997	Ana A	1	0	0	0	0	0	0	0	0-0	0		—	—	—	—		0-0	—	0				175	0.0
1998	Ana A	51	188	29	49	13	1	4	26	34-0	1	42	.261	.375	.404	101	2	7-2	.982	-4	95	79	2b51	123	0.0
1999	Ana A	95	376	57	115	15	4	9	48	43-1	4	56	.306	.383	.439	109	6	13-4	.986	6	110	94	2b95		1.6
	Oak A	61	255	48	85	10	3	7	28	27-1	2	42	.333	.401	.478	127	11	11-4	.977	-3	100	102	2b61		1.0
	Year	156	631	105	200	25	7	16	76	70-2	6	98	.317	.390	.455	116	17	24-8	.983	2	106	97	2b156		2.6
2000	†Oak A	122	485	82	135	23	0	12	41	54-0	3	95	.278	.354	.400	92	-5	9-3	.982	22	115	111	2b122	34	2.1
2001	Tex A	78	296	46	88	16	2	9	31	29-0	5	73	.297	.369	.456	113	6	4-2	.988	0	100	109	2b52,1b9,3b7,O2R,D6	48	0.7
	†NY A	15	46	4	7	3	0	1	5	5-0	1	13	.152	.278	.217	33	-4	2-0	.952	2	135	106	3b7,O3(2/0/1)/1D		-0.2
	Year	93	342	50	95	19	2	9	32	34-0	6	86	.278	.356	.424	102	2	6-2	.988	3	100	109	2b52,3b14,D11,1b10,O5(2/0/3)		0.5
2002	†Oak A	56	133	22	30	8	0	2	8	15-1	5	32	.226	.325	.331	76	-4	3-0	.981	4	108	121	2b38,1b5/3D	29	0.2
Total	16	1273	4244	633	1171	214	23	100	445	463-6	49	853	.276	.352	.408	100	9	78-37	.980	31	101	102	2b630,3b293,S262,O112L,D20,1b15	483	7.5

VELASQUEZ, GUILLERMO Guillermo (Burgara) B4.23.1968 Mexicali, Baja California, Mexico BL/TR/6-3/220* d9.14

YEAR	TM LG	G	AB	R	H	2B	3B	HR	RBI	BB-IB	HP	SO	AVG	OBP	SLG	AOPS	ABR	SB-CS	FA	FR	RNG	THR	GAMES AT POSITION	DL	BFW
1992	SD N	15	23	1	7	0	0	1	5	1-0	0	7	.304	.333	.435	114	0	0-0	.933	-1	82	83	1b3,O2L		0.0
1993	SD N	79	143	7	30	2	0	3	20	13-2	0	35	.210	.274	.287	50	-10	0-0	.984	-1	99	91	1b38,O6(4/0/2)		-1.4
Total	2	94	166	8	37	2	0	4	25	14-2	0	42	.223	.282	.307	59	-10	0-0	.981	-1	98	91	1b41,O8(6/0/1)		-1.4

VELAZQUEZ, FREDDIE Federico Antonio (Velasquez) B12.6.1937 Santo Domingo, D.R. BR/TR/6-1/185* d4.20

YEAR	TM LG	G	AB	R	H	2B	3B	HR	RBI	BB-IB	HP	SO	AVG	OBP	SLG	AOPS	ABR	SB-CS	FA	FR	RNG	THR	GAMES AT POSITION	DL	BFW
1969	Sea A	6	16	1	2	2	0	0	2	1-0	0	3	.125	.176	.250	18	-2	0-0	1.000	-2	40	0	C5		-0.3
1973	Atl N	15	23	2	8	1	0	0	3	1-0	0	3	.348	.375	.391	105	0	0-0	.975	1	146	60	C11		0.1
Total	2	21	39	3	10	3	0	0	5	2-0	0	6	.256	.293	.333	71	-2	0-0	.985	-1	102	35	C16		-0.2

VELEZ, OTTO Otoniel (Franceschi) B11.29.1950 Ponce, PR BR/TR/6-0/195(170-195) d9.4

YEAR	TM LG	G	AB	R	H	2B	3B	HR	RBI	BB-IB	HP	SO	AVG	OBP	SLG	AOPS	ABR	SB-CS	FA	FR	RNG	THR	GAMES AT POSITION	DL	BFW
1973	NY A	23	77	9	15	4	0	2	7	15-0	0	24	.195	.326	.325	86	-1	0-1	.959	-0	99	128	O23R		-0.3
1974	NY A	27	67	9	14	1	1	2	10	15-1	1	24	.209	.345	.343	102	1	0-0	.986	-3	48	54	1b21,O3R,3b2		-0.4
1975	NY A	6	8	0	2	0	0	0	1	2-0	0	0	.250	.400	.250	88	0	0-0	1.000	-0	0	124	/1D		0.0
1976	†NY A	49	94	11	25	6	0	2	10	23-1	0	26	.266	.410	.394	137	6	0-0	.979	-1	107	66	O24(6/0/19),1b8/3D		0.4
1977	Tor A	120	360	50	92	19	3	16	62	65-1	1	87	.256	.366	.458	123	14	4-2	.973	0	100	98	O79R,D28		0.9
1978	Tor A	91	248	29	66	14	2	9	38	45-1	2	41	.266	.380	.448	130	12	1-3	.982	9	112	202	O74(39/0/39)/1D		1.7
1979	Tor A	99	274	45	79	21	0	15	48	46-2	3	45	.288	.396	.529	145	19	0-1	.971	-1	102	65	O73(43/0/34),1b6,D9		1.5
1980	Tor A	104	357	54	96	12	3	20	62	54-8	2	86	.269	.365	.487	127	14	0-0	.975	0	118	55	D97,1b3	38	1.1
1981	Tor A	80	240	32	51	9	2	11	28	55-3	3	60	.213	.363	.404	115	7	0-3	1.000	-0	0	0	D74/1		-0.2
1982	Tor A	28	52	4	10	1	0	1	5	13-0	1	15	.192	.354	.269	68	-2	1-0	—	0	0	0	D24	31	-0.2
1983	Cle A	10	25	1	2	0	0	0	1	3-0	0	6	.080	.179	.080	-25	-4	0-0	—	0	0	0	D8		-0.5
Total	11	637	1802	244	452	87	11	78	272	336-17	11	414	.251	.369	.441	122	66	6-10	.973	3	104	122	O276(88/0/197),D255,1b41,3b3	69	4.5

VELTMAN, PAT Arthur Patrick B3.24.1906 Mobile AL D10.1.1980 San Antonio TX BR/TR/6-0/175 d4.17

YEAR	TM LG	G	AB	R	H	2B	3B	HR	RBI	BB-IB	HP	SO	AVG	OBP	SLG	AOPS	ABR	SB-CS	FA	FR	RNG	THR	GAMES AT POSITION	DL	BFW
1926	Chi A	5	4	1	1	0	0	0		1			.250	.400	.250	75	0	0-0	1.000	0	151	0	/S		0.0
1928	NY A	1	3	1	1	0	1	0		1			.333	.500	1.000	282	1	0	1.000	-0	95	0	/OC		0.1
1929	NY N	2	1	1	0	0	0	0	2				.000	.667	.000	81	0	0	1.000	-0	0	0	/C		0.1
1931	Bos N	1	1	0	0	0	0	0					.000	.000	.000	-99	0		—	0			/H		0.0
1932	NY N	2	1	0	0	0	0	0					.000	.000	.000	-99	0		—	0			/H		0.0
1934	Pit N	12	28	4	3	0	0	0		1			.107	.107	.107	-41	-6	0-0	1.000	-1	65	0	C11		-0.8
Total	6	23	38	7	6	0	1	0		5			.132	.214	.184	7	-5	0-0	1.000	-1	62	0	C12/OCS		-0.5

VENABLE, MAX William McKinley B6.6.1957 Phoenix AZ BL/TR/5-10/185(180-193) [LAN76 3/67] d4.8

YEAR	TM LG	G	AB	R	H	2B	3B	HR	RBI	BB-IB	HP	SO	AVG	OBP	SLG	AOPS	ABR	SB-CS	FA	FR	RNG	THR	GAMES AT POSITION	DL	BFW
1979	SF N	55	85	12	14	1	1	0	3	10-1	1	18	.165	.260	.200	29	-8	3-3	.914	-2	78	127	O25(6/2/21)		-1.2
1980	SF N	64	138	13	37	5	0	0	10	15-0	1	22	.268	.333	.304	84	-2	8-2	1.000	-3	94	0	O40(16/14/11)		-0.5
1981	SF N	18	32	2	6	0	2	0	1	4-0	0	3	.188	.278	.313	69	-2	3-1	1.000	-0	102	0	O5(0/2/3)		-0.5
1982	SF N	71	125	17	28	2	1	1	7	7-0	0	16	.224	.265	.280	53	-4	9-3	.986	4	102	258	O53(33/12/8)	41	-0.5
1983	SF N	94	228	28	50	7	4	6	27	22-1	3	34	.219	.295	.364	84	-6	15-2	.993	6	117	139	O66(32/25/14)		0.1
1984	Mon N	38	71	7	17	2	0	2	7	3-1	1	7	.239	.276	.352	80	-2	1-0	1.000	-0	107	0	O27(23/3/3)		-0.3
1985	Cin N	77	135	21	39	12	3	0	10	6-0	1	17	.289	.315	.422	100	0	11-3	1.000	-0	116	157	O39(31/7/3)		-0.2
1986	Cin N	108	147	17	31	7	1	2	15	17-2	0	24	.211	.289	.313	65	-7	7-2	.969	-0	111	0	O57(49/8/3)		-0.2
1987	Cin N	7	7	2	1	0	0	0	2	0-0	0	0	.143	.143	.143	-23	-1	0-0	1.000	-0	72	0	O4C		-0.2
1989	Cal A	20	53	7	19	4	0	0	4	1-0	0	16	.358	.370	.434	128	2	0-0	1.000	-1	86	0	O13(4/4/7)		0.0
1990	Cal A	93	189	26	49	9	3	4	21	24-2	0	31	.259	.340	.402	109	3	5-1	.975	-1	96	101	O77(40/33/10)/D		-1.2
1991	Cal A	82	187	24	46	8	2	3	21	11-2	0	30	.246	.292	.358	80	-6	2-1	.967	-5	76	101	O65(13/27/30),D3		-1.2
Total	12	727	1397	176	337	57	17	18	128	120-9	7	218	.241	.302	.345	81	-37	64-18	.982	-1	99	100	O471(247/141/113),D4	41	-4.4

VENTO, MIKE Michael B5.25.1978 Albuquerque NM BR/TR/6-0/195 d9.13 Col San Ana (CA) JC

YEAR	TM LG	G	AB	R	H	2B	3B	HR	RBI	BB-IB	HP	SO	AVG	OBP	SLG	AOPS	ABR	SB-CS	FA	FR	RNG	THR	GAMES AT POSITION	DL	BFW
2005	NY A	2	2	0	0	0	0	0	0	0-0	0	0	1.000	.000	.000	-99	0	0-0	1.000	1	125	2139	O2R		0.0

VENTURA, ROBIN Robin Mark B7.14.1967 Santa Maria CA BL/TR/6-1/198(185-200) [ChiA88 1/10] d9.12 Col Oklahoma St.

YEAR	TM LG	G	AB	R	H	2B	3B	HR	RBI	BB-IB	HP	SO	AVG	OBP	SLG	AOPS	ABR	SB-CS	FA	FR	RNG	THR	GAMES AT POSITION	DL	BFW
1989	Chi A	16	45	5	8	3	0	0	7	8-0	1	6	.178	.298	.244	61	-3	0-0	.962	2	110	73	3b16		0.0
1990	Chi A	150	493	48	123	17	1	5	54	55-2	1	53	.249	.324	.318	83	-11	1-4	.939	3	100	133	3b147/1		0.0
1991	Chi A	157	606	92	172	25	1	23	100	80-3	4	67	.284	.367	.442	126	24	2-4	.959	1	99	111	3b151,1b31		2.3
1992	Chi A★	157	592	85	167	38	1	16	93	93-9	0	71	.282	.375	.431	127	25	2-4	.957	26	119	106	3b157,1b2		5.1
1993	†Chi A	157	554	85	145	27	1	22	94	105-16	3	82	.262	.379	.433	121	20	1-6	.965	-2	97	97	3b155,1b4		0.8
1994	Chi A	109	401	57	113	15	1	18	78	61-15	2	69	.282	.373	.459	116	11	3-1	.935	-3	90	143	3b108,1b3/S		0.8
1995	Chi A	135	492	79	145	22	0	26	93	75-11	0	98	.295	.384	.498	134	26	4-3	.948	-0	94	70	3b121,1b18/D		2.4
1996	Chi A	158	586	96	168	31	2	34	105	78-14	2	81	.287	.368	.520	128	25	1-3	.974	5	93	132	3b150,1b14		2.5
1997	Chi A	54	183	27	48	10	1	6	26	34-5	0	21	.262	.373	.426	113	5	0-0	.956	3	101	120	3b54	114	0.0
1998	Chi A	161	590	84	155	31	4	21	91	79-15	1	111	.263	.349	.436	105	5	1-1	.966	14	112	154	3b161		1.8
1999	†NY N	161	588	80	177	38	0	32	120	74-10	3	109	.301	.379	.529	133	31	1-1	.980	19	107	137	3b160/1		4.
2000	†NY N	141	469	60	109	23	0	24	84	75-12	2	91	.232	.338	.439	100	0	3-5	.954	5	99	122	3b137/1	14	0.
2001	NY N	142	456	70	108	20	0	21	61	88-10	1	101	.237	.359	.419	108	2	8-2	.957	9	105	117	3b139		1.
2002	†NY A★	141	465	68	115	17	0	27	93	90-9	2	101	.247	.368	.458	120	16	3-1	.941	11	105	109	3b137,1b5		0.
2003	NY A	89	283	31	71	13	0	9	42	40-2	2	62	.251	.344	.392	95	-1	0-0	.974	-0	100	74	3b80/2D		-0.
	LA N	49	109	11	24	5	1	5	13	18-2	1	25	.220	.331	.422	97	-1	0-0	.993	-2	92	118	1b42,3b3		-0.
2004	†LA N	102	152	19	37	3	0	5	28	22-1	1	31	.243	.337	.362	83	-4	0-0	1.000	1	92	82	1b40,3b11/P		-0.
Total	16	2079	7064	1006	1885	338	14	294	1182	1075-132	23	1179	.267	.362	.444	115	177	24-38	.958	89	102	119	3b1887,1b162,D5/P2S	128	25.

VENTURA, VINCE Vincent B4.18.1917 New York NY D9.11.2001 Lake Worth FL BR/TR/6-1.5/190 d5.8

YEAR	TM LG	G	AB	R	H	2B	3B	HR	RBI	BB-IB	HP	SO	AVG	OBP	SLG	AOPS	ABR	SB-CS	FA	FR	RNG	THR	GAMES AT POSITION	DL	BFW
1945	Was N	18	58	4	12	0	0	2	4					.207	.258	.207	39	-5	0-0	.886	-1	99	78	O15L	-0.

VERAS, QUILVIO Quilvio Alberto (Perez) B4.3.1971 Santo Domingo, D.R. BB/TR/5-9/166(166-183) d4.25

YEAR	TM LG	G	AB	R	H	2B	3B	HR	RBI	BB-IB	HP	SO	AVG	OBP	SLG	AOPS	ABR	SB-CS	FA	FR	RNG	THR	GAMES AT POSITION	DL	BFW
1995	Fla N	124	440	86	115	20	7	5	32	80-0	9	68	.261	.384	.373	99	4	56-21	.986	5	93	110	2b122,O2(0/1/1)		1.
1996	Fla N	73	253	40	64	8	1	4	14	51-1	2	42	.253	.381	.340	95	1	8-8	.986	10	102	126	2b67	42	1.
1997	SD N	145	539	74	143	23	1	3	45	72-0	7	87	.265	.357	.328	87	-5	33-12	.984	-5	103	71	2b142		-0.
1998	†SD N	138	517	79	138	24	2	6	45	84-2	6	78	.267	.373	.356	101	5	24-9	.987	20	108	131	2b131		3.
1999	SD N	132	475	95	133	25	2	6	41	65-0	2	88	.280	.368	.379	97	0	30-17	.983	16	103	110	2b118	15	2.
2000	Atl N	84	298	56	92	15	0	5	37	51-0	5	50	.309	.413	.409	111	9	25-12	.984	4	109	91	2b82	78	1.
2001	Atl N	71	258	39	65	14	2	3	25	24-1	7	57	.252	.330	.357	77	-8	7-4	.991	5	106	102	2b67	17	0.
Total	7	767	2780	469	750	129	15	32	239	427-4	38	462	.270	.372	.362	96	4	183-83	.985	55	103	102	2b729,O2(0/1/1)	152	9.

VERAS, WILTON Wilton Andres B1.19.1978 Monte Cristi, D.R. BR/TR/6-2/198(186-198) d7.1

YEAR	TM LG	G	AB	R	H	2B	3B	HR	RBI	BB-IB	HP	SO	AVG	OBP	SLG	AOPS	ABR	SB-CS	FA	FR	RNG	THR	GAMES AT POSITION	DL	BFW
1999	Bos A	36	118	14	34	6	1	2	13	5-0	2	14	.288	.323	.398	81	-4	0-2	.929	0	95	141	3b35		-0.
2000	Bos A	49	164	21	40	6	1	1	14	7-0	2	20	.244	.278	.299	46	-14	0-0	.907	4	109	145	3b49		-1.
Total	2	85	282	35	74	12	2	3	27	12-0	4	34	.262	.297	.340	61	-18	0-2	.916	4	103	143	3b84		-1.

VERBAN, EMIL Emil Matthew "Dutch","Antelope" B8.27.1915 Lincoln IL D6.8.1989 Quincy IL BR/TR/5-11/165* d4.18

YEAR	TM LG	G	AB	R	H	2B	3B	HR	RBI	BB-IB	HP	SO	AVG	OBP	SLG	AOPS	ABR	SB-CS	FA	FR	RNG	THR	GAMES AT POSITION	DL	BFW
1944	†StL N	146	498	51	128	14	2	0	43	19	2	14	.257	.287	.293	62	-26	0	.968	-5	94	150	2b146		-3
1945	StL N★	155	597	59	166	22	8	0	72	19	3	15	.278	.304	.342	71	-21	4	.978	-21	88	118	2b155		-3
1946	StL N	1	1	0	0	0	0	0	0		0	0	.000	.000	.000	-96	0	0					/H		0

YEAR	TM LG	G	AB	R	H	2B	3B	HR	RBI	BB-IB	HP	SO	AVG	OBP	SLG	AOPS	ABR	SB-CS	FA	FR	RNG	THR	GAMES AT POSITION	DL	BFW
	Phi N★	138	473	44	130	17	5	0	34	21	0	18	.275	.306	.332	83	-13	5	.963	-2	100	100	2b138		-0.8
	Year	139	474	44	130	17	5	0	34	21	0	18	.274	.305	.331	83	-13	5	.963	-2	100	100	2b138		-0.8
1947	Phi N★	155	540	50	154	14	8	0	42	23	1	8	.285	.316	.341	77	-20	5	.982	18	104	111	2b155		0.6
1948	Phi N	55	169	14	39	5	1	0	11	11	1	5	.231	.282	.272	51	-12	0	.975	-2	100	91	2b54		-1.2
	Chi N	56	248	37	73	15	1	1	16	4	1	7	.294	.308	.375	88	-5	4	.964	5	106	134	2b56		0.3
	Year	111	417	51	112	20	2	1	27	15	2	12	.269	.297	.333	72	-17	4	.969	3	103	115	2b110		-0.9
1949	Chi N	98	343	39	99	11	1	0	22	8	2	2	.289	.309	.327	72	-14	3	.965	6	107	98	2b88		-0.4
1950	Chi N	45	37	7	4	1	0	0	1	3	0	5	.108	.175	.135	-17	-6	0	.966	3	165	202	2b8,S3/3OC		-0.3
	Bos N	4	5	1	0	0	0	0	0	0	0	0	.000	.000	.000	-99	-2	0	.833	-0	72	175	2b2		-0.2
	Year	49	42	8	4	1	0	0	1	3	0	5	.095	.156	.119	-27	-8	0	.927	3	138	194	2b10,S3/3OC		-0.2
Total	7	853	2911	301	793	99	26	1	241	108	10	74	.272	.301	.325	73	-119	21	.971	-1	99	117	2b802,S3/OC3		-7.8

VERBLE, GENE Gene Kermit "Satchel" B6.29.1928 Concord NC BR/TR/5-10/163* d4.17

YEAR	TM LG	G	AB	R	H	2B	3B	HR	RBI	BB-IB	HP	SO	AVG	OBP	SLG	AOPS	ABR	SB-CS	FA	FR	RNG	THR	GAMES AT POSITION	DL	BFW
1951	Was A	68	177	16	36	3	2	0	15	18	0	10	.203	.277	.243	42	-15	1-1	.978	-3	99	99	S28,2b19/3		-1.5
1953	Was A	13	21	4	4	0	0	0	2	2	0	1	.190	.261	.190	24	-2	0-0	1.000	1	113	126	S8		-0.1
Total	2	81	198	20	40	3	2	0	17	20	0	11	.202	.275	.237	40	-17	1-1	.981	-2	101	104	S36,2b19/3		-1.6

VERDI, FRANK Frank Michael B6.2.1926 Brooklyn NY BR/TR/5-10.5/170 d5.10

YEAR	TM LG	G	AB	R	H	2B	3B	HR	RBI	BB-IB	HP	SO	AVG	OBP	SLG	AOPS	ABR	SB-CS	FA	FR	RNG	THR	GAMES AT POSITION	DL	BFW
1953	NY A	1	0	0	0	0	0	0	0	0	0	0	—	—	—	—	0	0-0	—	-0	0	0	/S		0.0

VERGEZ, JOHNNY John Louis B7.9.1906 Oakland CA D7.15.1991 Davis CA BR/TR/5-8/165 d4.14

YEAR	TM LG	G	AB	R	H	2B	3B	HR	RBI	BB-IB	HP	SO	AVG	OBP	SLG	AOPS	ABR	SB-CS	FA	FR	RNG	THR	GAMES AT POSITION	DL	BFW
1931	NY N	152	565	67	157	24	2	13	81	29	6	65	.278	.320	.396	94	-7	11	.932	-6	92	95	3b152		-0.7
1932	NY N	118	376	42	98	21	3	6	43	25	2	36	.261	.310	.380	86	-8	1	.935	5	107	123	3b111/S		0.1
1933	NY N	123	458	57	124	21	6	16	72	39	3	66	.271	.332	.448	123	13	1	.928	-13	91	108	3b123		0.4
1934	NY N	108	320	31	64	18	1	7	27	28	2	55	.200	.269	.328	60	-18	1	.943	9	116	102	3b104		-0.6
1935	Phi N	148	546	56	136	27	4	9	63	46	4	67	.249	.312	.363	73	-20	8	.953	-4	88	102	3b148,S2		-1.9
1936	Phi N	15	40	4	11	2	0	1	5	3	0	11	.275	.326	.400	86	-1	0	.964	1	98	154	3b12		0.0
	StL N	8	18	1	3	1	0	0	1	1	0	3	.167	.211	.222	17	-2	0	.929	-0	76	166	3b8		-0.2
	Year	23	58	5	14	3	0	1	6	4	0	14	.241	.290	.345	66	-3	0	.952	0	91	158	3b20		-0.2
Total	6	672	2323	258	593	114	16	52	292	171	17	303	.255	.311	.385	87	-43	22	.939	-8	97	106	3b658,S3		-2.9

VERNON, MICKEY James Barton B4.22.1918 Marcus Hook PA BL/TL/6-2/180* d7.8 Mil 1944-45 M3/C6 Col Villanova

YEAR	TM LG	G	AB	R	H	2B	3B	HR	RBI	BB-IB	HP	SO	AVG	OBP	SLG	AOPS	ABR	SB-CS	FA	FR	RNG	THR	GAMES AT POSITION	DL	BFW
1939	Was A	76	276	23	71	15	4	1	30	24	0	28	.257	.317	.351	76	-10	1-1	.985	-3	91	119	1b75		-1.9
1940	Was A	5	19	0	3	0	0	0	3	0	0	3	.158	.158	.158	-19	-3	0-0	1.000	-0	72	122	1b4		-0.4
1941	Was A	138	531	73	159	27	11	9	93	43	0	51	.299	.352	.443	114	9	9-3	.992	-7	81	101	1b132		-1.0
1942	Was A	151	621	76	168	34	6	9	86	59	3	63	.271	.337	.388	104	3	25-6	.982	-9	84	76	1b151		-1.8
1943	Was A	145	553	89	148	29	8	7	70	67	10	55	.268	.357	.387	122	17	24-8	.990	-11	75	99	1b143		0.1
1946	Was A★	148	587	88	207	51	8	8	85	49	0	64	.353	.403	.508	163	49	14-10	.990	-2	100	96	1b147		4.3
1947	Was A	154	600	77	159	29	12	7	85	49	0	42	.265	.320	.388	99	-4	12-12	.987	-3	94	83	1b154		-1.4
1948	Was A★	150	558	78	135	27	7	3	48	54	1	43	.242	.310	.332	73	-23	15-11	.989	5	114	83	1b150		-2.4
1949	Cle A	153	584	72	170	27	4	18	83	58	2	51	.291	.357	.443	113	8	9-7	.991	16	134	116	1b153		1.8
1950	Cle A	28	90	8	17	0	0	0	10	12	0	10	.189	.284	.189	24	-10	2-0	.996	1	102	126	1b25		-1.0
	Was A	90	327	47	100	17	3	9	65	50	4	29	.306	.404	.459	127	15	6-1	.990	2	111	104	1b85		1.4
	Year	118	417	55	117	17	3	9	75	62	4	39	.281	.379	.400	104	4	8-1	.991	3	109	109	1b110		0.4
1951	Was A	141	546	69	160	30	7	9	87	53	2	45	.293	.358	.423	112	9	7-6	.994	-5	86	87	1b137		-0.1
1952	Was A	154	569	71	143	33	9	10	80	89	0	66	.251	.353	.394	111	10	7-7	.993	-4	93	94	1b153		0.0
1953	Was A★	152	608	101	205	43	11	15	115	63	4	57	.337	.403	.518	151	43	4-6	.992	-3	93	116	1b152		3.0
1954	Was A★	151	597	90	173	33	14	20	97	61	5	61	.290	.357	.492	140	30	1-4	.992	-6	84	105	1b148		1.4
1955	Was A	150	538	74	162	23	8	14	85	74-9	3	50	.301	.384	.452	133	26	0-4	.994	-6	81	97	1b144		1.0
1956	Bos A★	119	403	67	125	28	4	15	84	57-6	7	40	.310	.403	.511	125	16	1-0	.989	-5	85	99	1b108		0.6
1957	Bos A	102	270	36	65	18	1	7	38	41-2	5	35	.241	.350	.393	97	1	0-0	.992	3	115	74	1b70		-0.1
1958	Cle A★	119	355	49	104	22	3	8	55	44-3	2	56	.293	.372	.439	126	14	0-4	.987	-2	93	104	1b96		0.5
1959	Mil N	74	91	8	20	4	0	3	14	7-1	1	20	.220	.283	.363	77	-3	0-0	.983	-0	108	71	1b10,O4(2/0/2)		-0.4
1960	Pit N	9	8	1	1	0	0	0	1	1-1	0	0	.125	.222	.125	-2	-1	0-0	—	0			/H		-0.1
Total	20	2409	8731	1196	2495	490	120	172	1311	955-22	49	869	.286	.359	.428	116	196	137-90	.990	-39	94	97	1b2237,O4(2/0/2)		3.5

VERSALLES, ZOILO Zoilo Casanova (Rodriguez) "Zorro" B12.18.1939 Veldado, Cuba D6.9.1995 Bloomington MN BR/TR/5-10/150(150-165) d8.1

YEAR	TM LG	G	AB	R	H	2B	3B	HR	RBI	BB-IB	HP	SO	AVG	OBP	SLG	AOPS	ABR	SB-CS	FA	FR	RNG	THR	GAMES AT POSITION	DL	BFW
1959	Was A	29	59	4	9	0	0	1	4	4-0	1	15	.153	.219	.203	17	-7	1-0	.943	2	102	108	S29		-0.3
1960	Was A	15	45	2	6	2	2	0	4	2-0	0	5	.133	.170	.267	16	-6	0-0	.935	-0	100	67	S15		-0.5
1961	Min A	129	510	65	143	25	5	7	53	25-2	1	61	.280	.314	.390	83	-13	16-9	.952	6	100	95	S129		0.4
1962	Min A	160	568	69	137	18	3	17	67	37-8	2	71	.241	.287	.373	74	-22	5-5	.970	35	106	137	S160		2.6
1963	Min A★	159	621	74	162	31	13	10	54	33-2	5	66	.261	.303	.401	94	-7	7-4	.961	-4	95	101	S159		0.4
1964	Min A	160	659	64	171	33	10	20	64	42-1	8	88	.259	.311	.431	103	1	14-4	.957	-22	89	95	S160		-0.5
1965	†Min A★	160	666	126	182	45	12	19	77	41-3	7	122	.273	.319	.462	115	12	27-5	.950	2	105	123	S160		3.3
1966	Min A	137	543	73	135	20	6	7	36	40-2	7	85	.249	.307	.346	82	-12	10-12	.942	-10	95	97	S135		-1.3
1967	Min A	160	581	63	116	16	7	6	50	33-2	6	113	.200	.249	.282	53	-35	5-3	.958	8	101	101	S159		-1.6
1968	LA N	122	403	29	79	16	3	2	24	26-4	0	84	.196	.244	.266	57	-22	6-4	.954	9	102	98	S119		-0.3
1969	Cle A	72	217	21	49	11	1	1	13	21-1	2	47	.226	.298	.300	66	-9	3-1	.975	-7	89	66	2b46,3b30,S3		-1.4
	Was A	31	75	9	20	2	1	0	6	3-0	1	13	.267	.304	.320	79	-2	1-0	.935	-1	110	34	S13,2b6,3b5		-0.2
	Year	103	292	30	69	13	2	1	19	24-1	3	60	.236	.299	.305	69	-12	4-1	.978	-8	91	64	2b52,3b35,S16		-1.6
†1971	Atl N	66	194	21	37	11	0	5	17	11-2	0	40	.191	.233	.325	53	-12	2-1	.902	-14	84	41	3b30,S24/2		-2.6
Total	12	1400	5141	650	1246	230	63	95	471	318-26	40	810	.242	.290	.367	82	-134	97-48	.956	4	99	105	S1265,3b65,2b53		-2.0

VERYZER, TOM Thomas Martin B2.11.1953 Port Jefferson NY BR/TR/6-1/185(170-185) [DetA71 1/11] d8.14

YEAR	TM LG	G	AB	R	H	2B	3B	HR	RBI	BB-IB	HP	SO	AVG	OBP	SLG	AOPS	ABR	SB-CS	FA	FR	RNG	THR	GAMES AT POSITION	DL	BFW
1973	Det A	18	20	1	6	0	0	0	2	2-0	1	4	.300	.364	.400	108	0	1-0	.857	-4	63	28	S18		-0.3
1974	Det A	22	55	4	13	2	0	2	9	5-0	0	8	.236	.300	.382	92	-1	1-0	.927	-8	69	43	S20		-0.7
1975	Det A	128	404	37	102	13	1	5	48	23-1	5	76	.252	.297	.327	74	-14	2-6	.960	-3	96	79	S128		-0.5
1976	Det A	97	354	31	83	8	2	1	25	21-1	4	44	.234	.286	.277	63	-16	1-4	.966	4	102	89	S97		-0.3
1977	Det A	125	350	31	69	12	1	2	28	16-0	0	44	.197	.230	.254	31	-34	0-1	.969	12	112	95	S124		-1.0
1978	Cle A	130	421	48	114	18	4	1	32	13-0	5	44	.271	.298	.340	80	-12	1-2	.963	-11	98	75	S129		-1.1
1979	Cle A	149	449	41	99	9	3	0	34	34-0	4	54	.220	.279	.254	45	-35	2-5	.974	2	100	90	S148		-1.8
1980	Cle A	109	358	28	97	12	0	2	28	10-1	8	25	.271	.303	.321	71	-14	0-5	.971	4	100	81	S108		-0.1
1981	Cle A	75	221	13	54	4	0	0	14	10-1	1	10	.244	.278	.262	57	-12	1-0	.970	-1	94	98	S75		-0.6
1982	NY N	40	54	6	18	2	0	0	4	3-2	0	4	.333	.362	.370	107	1	1-0	.962	-11	107	66	2b26,S16	90	-0.9
1983	Chi N	59	88	5	18	3	0	1	3	3-1	1	13	.205	.231	.273	37	-8	0-0	.978	1	115	140	S28,3b17		-0.5
1984	†Chi N	44	74	5	14	1	0	0	4	3-1	4	11	.189	.259	.203	29	-7	0-0	.966	-3	82	89	S36,3b5,2b4	82	-0.5
Total	12	996	2848	250	687	84	12	14	231	143-8	33	329	.241	.283	.294	61	-152	9-23	.966	-17	99	85	S927,2b30,3b22	218	-8.6

VICK, ERNIE Henry Arthur B7.2.1900 Toledo OH D7.16.1980 Ann Arbor MI BR/TR/5-9.5/185 d6.29 Col Michigan

YEAR	TM LG	G	AB	R	H	2B	3B	HR	RBI	BB-IB	HP	SO	AVG	OBP	SLG	AOPS	ABR	SB-CS	FA	FR	RNG	THR	GAMES AT POSITION	DL	BFW
1922	StL N	3	6	1	2	2	0	0	0	0	0	0	.333	.333	.667	159	1	0-0	.875	-0	92	0	C3		0.0
1924	StL N	16	23	2	8	1	0	0	3	3	0	1	.348	.423	.391	122	1	0-0	.974	2	115	153	C16		0.3
1925	StL N	14	32	3	6	2	1	0	3	3	0	1	.188	.257	.313	44	-3	0-0	.929	-0	115	56	C9		-0.2
1926	StL N	24	51	6	10	2	0	0	4	3	0	4	.196	.241	.235	27	-5	0-0	.944	0	128	101	C23		-0.4
Total	4	57	112	12	26	7	1	0	7	9	0	6	.232	.289	.313	58	-6	0-0	.944	1	120	97	C51		-0.3

VICK, SAMMY Samuel Bruce B4.12.1895 Batesville MS D8.17.1986 Memphis TN BR/TR/5-10.5/163 d9.20 Mil 1918 Col Millsaps

YEAR	TM LG	G	AB	R	H	2B	3B	HR	RBI	BB-IB	HP	SO	AVG	OBP	SLG	AOPS	ABR	SB-CS	FA	FR	RNG	THR	GAMES AT POSITION	DL	BFW
1917	NY A	10	36	4	10	3	0	2	1	6	0	6	.278	.297	.361	100	0	1-0	.882	-1	95	83	O10R		-0.1
1918	NY A	2	3	1	2	0	0	0	1	0	0	0	.667	.667	.667	296	1	0-0	—	-0			/OR		0.1
1919	NY A	106	407	59	101	15	9	2	27	35	0	55	.248	.308	.344	82	-11	9	.952	-6	92	78	O100R		-2.3
1920	NY A	51	118	21	26	7	1	0	11	14	2	20	.220	.313	.297	60	-6	1-1	.949	-2	113	0	O33(4/1/28)		-1.0
1921	Bos A	44	77	5	19	3	1	0	11	2	0	10	.247	.269	.325	52	-6	0-1	1.000	-0	104	65	O14R		-0.7
Total	5	213	641	90	159	28	11	2	50	51	2	91	.248	.305	.335	76	-22	12-2	.951	-8	97	63	O158(4/1/153)		-4.0

YEAR	TM LG	G	AB	R	H	2B	3B	HR	RBI	BB-IB	HP	SO	AVG	OBP	SLG	AOPS	ABR	SB-CS	FA	FR	RNG	THR	GAMES AT POSITION	DL	BFW

VICO, GEORGE   George Steve "Sam" B8.9.1923 San Fernando CA   D1.14.1994 Redondo Beach CA   BL/TR/6-4/200   d4.20

1948	Det A	144	521	50	139	23	9	8	58	39	7	39	.267	.326	.392	88	-11	2-2	.988	-2	94	88	1b142		-1.7
1949	Det A	67	142	15	27	5	2	4	18	21	4	17	.190	.311	.338	72	-6	0-0	.985	1	112	93	1b53		-0.6
Total	2	211	663	65	166	28	11	12	76	60	11	56	.250	.323	.380	85	-17	2-2	.987	-0	98	89	1b195		-2.3

VICTORINO, SHANE   Shane Patrick B11.30.1980 Wailuku HI   BB/TR/5-9/160*   [LAN99 6/194]   d4.2

2003	SD N	36	73	8	11	2	0	0	4	7-0	1	17	.151	.232	.178	11	-10	7-2	1.000	1	91	241	O32(15/16/3)		-0.9
2005	Phi N	21	17	5	5	0	0	2	8	0-0	0	3	.294	.263	.647	133	1	0-0	—	-1	0	0	O12(4/5/3)		0.0
Total	2	57	90	13	16	2	0	2	12	7-0	1	20	.178	.238	.267	36	-9	7-2	1.000	0	84	223	O44(19/21/6)		-0.9

VIDAL, JOSE   Jose (Nicolas) "Papito" B4.3.1940 Batey Lechuga, D.R.   BR/TR/6-0/190*   d9.5

1966	Cle A	17	32	4	6	1	0	3	5-0		0	11	.188	.297	.281	67	-1	0-1	1.000	-1	91	0	O11(0/3/8)		-0.3
1967	Cle A	16	34	4	4	0	0	0	7-0		0	12	.118	.268	.118	17	-3	0-1	1.000	1	106	162	O10(8/6/1)		-0.4
1968	Cle A	37	54	5	9	0	0	2	5	2-0	0	15	.167	.196	.278	43	-4	3-0	1.000	-1	75	0	O26(11/0/15)/1		-0.4
1969	Sea A	18	26	7	5	0	1	1	2	4-0	1	8	.192	.323	.385	98	0	1-1	.917	-0	107	0	O6(1/0/5)		-0.1
Total	4	88	146	20	24	1	2	3	10	18-0	1	46	.164	.261	.260	53	-8	4-3	.985	-1	92	42	O53(20/9/29)/1		-1.4

VIDRO, JOSE   Jose Angel (Cetty) B8.27.1974 Mayaguez, PR   BB/TR/5-11/190*   [MonN92 6/155]   d6.8

1997	Mon N	67	169	19	42	12	1	2	17	11-0	2	20	.249	.297	.367	75	-6	1-0	.958	-2	90	123	3b36,2b5,D5		-0.8
1998	Mon N	83	205	24	45	12	0	3	18	27-0	4	33	.220	.318	.278	61	-10	2-2	.975	-1	91	82	2b56,3b7		-1.9
1999	Mon N	140	494	67	150	45	2	12	59	29-2	4	51	.304	.346	.476	110	7	0-4	.982	-16	91	84	2b121,1b14,O3L,3b2		-0.6
2000	Mon N★	153	606	101	200	51	2	24	97	49-4	2	69	.330	.379	.540	129	27	5-4	.986	-1	105	101	2b153		3.1
2001	Mon N	124	486	82	155	34	1	15	59	31-2	10	49	.319	.371	.486	120	15	4-1	.983	-13	95	85	2b121,D2	23	0.8
2002	Mon N★	152	604	103	190	43	3	19	96	60-1	3	70	.315	.378	.490	124	19	2-1	.986	-1	103	94	2b152		0.8
2003	Mon N★	144	509	77	158	36	0	15	65	69-6	7	50	.310	.397	.470	123	21	3-2	.983	-18	98	87	2b137		0.8
2004	Mon N	110	412	51	121	24	0	14	60	49-7	0	43	.294	.367	.454	107	5	3-1	.987	-15	92	109	2b105,D4	39	-0.5
2005	Was N	87	309	38	85	21	2	7	32	31-3	1	30	.275	.339	.424	107	3	0-0	.985	-23	84	77	2b79	61	-1.6
Total	9	1060	3794	562	1146	278	11	108	503	356-25	33	415	.302	.364	.467	114	81	20-15	.984	-92	97	91	2b929,3b45,1b14,D11,O3L	123	2.5

VILLANUEVA, HECTOR   Hector (Balasquide) B10.2.1964 Rio Piedras, PR   BR/TR/6-1/220*   d6.1   Col Alabama-Birmingham

1990	Chi N	52	114	14	31	4	1	7	18	4-2	2	27	.272	.308	.509	113	1	1-0	.991	3	729	50	C23,1b14		0.5
1991	Chi N	71	192	23	53	10	1	13	32	21-1	0	30	.276	.346	.542	140	10	0-0	.979	-5	91	86	C55,1b6	13	0.7
1992	Chi N	51	112	9	17	6	0	2	13	11-2	0	24	.152	.228	.259	36	-9	0-0	.978	5	97	116	C28,1b6		-0.4
1993	StL N	17	55	7	8	1	0	3	9	4-1	0	17	.145	.203	.327	40	-5	0-0	1.000	-3	70	92	C17		-0.7
Total	4	191	473	53	109	21	2	25	72	40-6	2	98	.230	.293	.442	98	-3	1-0	.984	0	189	89	C123,1b26	13	0.1

VINA, FERNANDO   Fernando B4.16.1969 Sacramento CA   BL/TR/5-9/170(160-180)   [NYN90 9/253]   d4.10   Col Arizona St.   [DL 2005 Det A 183]

1993	Sea A	24	45	5	10	2	0	0	2	4-0	3	3	.222	.327	.267	60	-2	6-0	1.000	1	108	144	2b16,S4,D2		0.1
1994	NY N	79	124	20	31	6	0	0	6	12-0	12	11	.250	.372	.298	78	-3	3-1	.979	1	118	105	2b13,3b12,S9,O6L	15	-0.1
1995	Mil A	113	288	46	74	7	3	3	29	22-0	9	28	.257	.327	.361	75	-11	6-3	.983	12	107	136	2b99,S6,3b2		0.5
1996	Mil A	140	554	94	157	19	10	7	46	38-3	13	35	.283	.342	.392	82	-16	16-7	.979	18	108	121	2b137		0.8
1997	Mil A	79	324	37	89	12	2	4	28	12-1	7	23	.275	.312	.361	75	-13	8-7	.982	8	106	114	2b77/D	89	-0.2
1998	Mil A★	159	637	101	198	39	7	7	45	54-2	25	46	.311	.386	.427	112	14	22-16	.986	28	107	128	2b158		4.7
1999	Mil A	37	154	17	41	7	0	1	16	14-0	4	6	.266	.339	.331	71	-6	5-2	.995	2	103	122	2b37	137	-0.2
2000	†StL N	123	487	81	146	24	6	4	31	36-0	28	35	.300	.380	.398	95	-2	10-8	.988	11	100	118	2b122	16	1.4
2001	†StL N	154	631	95	191	30	8	9	56	32-3	22	35	.303	.357	.418	98	-2	17-7	.987	-4	94	114	2b151		0.2
2002	†StL N	150	622	75	168	29	5	1	54	44-2	18	36	.270	.333	.338	81	-19	17-11	.981	-16	94	109	2b150		-2.9
2003	StL N	61	259	36	65	14	4	4	23	11-0	11	24	.251	.309	.382	80	-8	4-4	.974	-9	87	108	2b60	96	-1.5
2004	Det A	29	115	21	26	5	0	0	7	9-0	5	9	.226	.308	.270	55	-7	2-1	.970	6	109	123	2b29	145	0.0
Total	12	1148	4240	627	1196	194	49	40	343	288-11	157	292	.282	.348	.379	88	-75	116-67	.984	57	101	119	2b1049,S19,3b14,O6L,D3	681	2.8

VINSON, CHARLIE   Charles Anthony "Chuck" B1.5.1944 Washington DC   BL/TL/6-3/207   d9.19

| 1966 | Cal A | 13 | 22 | 3 | 4 | 0 | 0 | 1 | 9 | .182 | | 5 | .357 | .409 | 123 | 1 | 0-0 | 1.000 | -1 | 40 | 130 | 1b11 | | -0.1 |

VINSON, RUBE   Ernest Augustus B3.20.1879 Dover DE   D10.12.1951 Chester PA   BL/TR/5-9/168   d9.27

1904	Cle A	15	49	12	15	1	0	0	2	10		3	.306	.433	.327	143	3	2	1.000	4	370	0	O15L		0.7
1905	Cle A	39	134	12	26	3	1	0	9	7		2	.194	.245	.231	51	-8	4	.930	-2	27	0	O36(27/9/0)		-1.3
1906	Chi A	10	24	2	6	0	0	0	3	2		0	.250	.308	.250	77	-1	1	.600	-2	0	0	O7L		-0.4
Total	3	64	207	26	47	4	1	0	14	19		3	.227	.301	.256	77	-6	7	.919	-1	116	0	O58(49/9/0)		-1.0

VIOX, JIM   James Harry B12.30.1890 Lockland OH   D1.6.1969 Erlanger KY   BR/TR/5-7/150   d5.9

1912	Pit N	33	70	8	13	2	3	1	7	3	0	9	.186	.219	.343	53	-5	2	.957	-3	114	0	3b10,S8,O3R/2		-0.8
1913	Pit N	137	492	86	156	32	8	2	65	64	3	28	.317	.399	.427	142	30	14-14	.959	-40	85	59	2b124,S10		-0.9
1914	Pit N	143	506	52	134	18	5	1	57	63	4	33	.265	.351	.326	106	6	9	.939	-22	99	88	2b138,S2,O2R		-1.4
1915	Pit N	150	503	56	129	17	8	2	45	75	4	31	.256	.357	.334	111	10	12-8	.954	-20	95	69	2b134,3b13,O2C		-0.9
1916	Pit N	43	132	12	33	7	0	1	17	17	1	11	.250	.340	.326	104	2	2	.937	-11	82	64	2b25,3b11		-1.0
Total	5	506	1703	214	465	76	24	7	191	222	12	112	.273	.361	.358	116	43	39-22	.949	-96	93	72	2b422,3b34,S20,O7(0/2/5)		-5.0

VIRDON, BILL   William Charles B6.9.1931 Hazel Park MI   BL/TR/6-0/175*   d4.12   M13/C8

1955	StL N	144	534	58	150	18	6	17	68	36-3	1	64	.281	.322	.433	100	-2	2-4	.966	-5	99	63	O142(1/109/34)		-1.5
1956	StL N	24	71	10	15	2	0	2	9	5-2	1	8	.211	.269	.324	60	-4	0-1	.982	-1	90	121	O24C		-0.7
	Pit N	133	509	67	170	21	10	8	37	33-7	1	63	.334	.374	.462	126	18	6-6	.989	2	102	110	O130C		1.4
	Year	157	580	77	185	23	10	10	46	38-9	2	71	.319	.361	.445	118	14	6-7	.988	1	100	112	O154C		0.7
1957	Pit N	144	561	59	141	28	11	8	50	33-5	0	69	.251	.291	.383	82	-16	3-3	.986	7	108	127	O141C		-1.6
1958	Pit N	144	604	75	161	24	11	9	46	52-5	1	70	.267	.324	.387	90	-10	5-3	.993	-2	105	93	O143C		-1.3
1959	Pit N	144	519	67	132	24	2	8	41	55-11	2	65	.254	.327	.355	83	-12	7-4	.979	14	114	190	O144C		-0.5
1960	†Pit N	120	409	60	108	16	9	8	40	40-2	0	44	.264	.326	.406	99	-1	8-2	.983	5	107	132	O109C		0.0
1961	Pit N	146	599	81	156	22	8	9	58	49-1	2	45	.260	.313	.369	81	-17	5-8	.985	-1	108	55	O145C		-2.4
1962	Pit N	156	663	82	164	27	10	6	47	36-0	1	65	.247	.286	.345	69	-31	5-13	.976	-3	98	107	O156C		-4.3
1963	Pit N	142	554	58	149	22	6	8	53	43-4	0	55	.269	.321	.370	99	-1	1-2	.988	-4	99	65	O142C		-1.0
1964	Pit N	145	473	59	115	11	3	3	27	30-1	0	48	.243	.287	.298	66	-22	1-5	.976	-7	95	67	O134C		-3.7
1965	Pit N	135	481	58	134	22	5	4	24	30-0	1	49	.279	.322	.370	94	-4	4-3	.970	-5	99	44	O128(1/127/0)		-1.4
1968	Pit N	6	3	1	1	0	0	0	0	0-0	0	2	.333	.333	.333	388	1	0-0	1.000	-0	80	0	O4(1/0/3)		-0.0
Total	12	1583	5980	735	1596	237	81	91	502	442-41	8	647	.267	.316	.379	89	-101	47-54	.982	4	103	96	O1542(3/1504/37)		-17.1

VIRGIL, OZZIE   Osvaldo Jose Jr. B12.7.1956 Mayaguez, PR   BR/TR/6-1/205*   [PhiN76 6/137]   d10.5   f-Ozzie

1980	Phi N	1	5	1	1	0	0	0	0-0	0	1	.200	.200	.400	60	0	0-0	1.000	-2	21	0	/C		-0.2
1981	Phi N	6	6	0	0	0	0	0	0-0	0	0	.000	.000	.000	-95	-2	0-0	1.000	0	0	0	/C		-0.
1982	Phi N	49	101	11	24	6	0	3	8	10-0	0	26	.238	.306	.386	90	-1	0-1	.964	1	80	59	C35		0.0
1983	†Phi N	55	140	11	30	7	0	6	23	8-0	3	34	.214	.272	.393	83	-4	0-2	.966	-11	63	97	C51		-1.5
1984	Phi N	141	456	61	119	21	4	18	68	45-5	5	91	.261	.331	.434	113	7	1-1	.992	-3	107	77	C137		1.
1985	Phi N★	131	426	47	105	16	3	19	55	49-6	5	85	.246	.330	.432	109	5	0-0	.994	-9	81	84	C120		1.
1986	Atl N	114	359	45	80	9	1	15	48	63-5	4	73	.223	.343	.373	94	-2	1-0	.984	13	75	132	C111		1.
1987	Atl N★	123	429	57	106	13	1	27	72	47-4	2	81	.247	.331	.471	105	2	0-1	.989	-4	85	93	C122		0.
1988	Atl N	107	320	23	82	10	0	9	31	22-1	5	54	.256	.313	.372	92	-3	2-0	.990	-6	102	93	C96		-0.
1989	Tor A	9	11	2	2	1	0	0	1	4-0	0	3	.182	.400	.545	166	1	0-0	1.000	0	0	0	/CD		0.
1990	Tor A	5	3	0	0	0	0	0	0	0-0	0	3	.000	.000	.000	-98	-1	0-0	1.000	-1	0	0	C2/D		-0.
Total	11	739	2258	258	549	84	6	98	307	248-21	29	453	.243	.324	.416	101	-7	4-5	.983	-27	88	93	C677,D7		-0.

VIRGIL, OZZIE   Osvaldo Jose Sr. (Pichardo) B5.17.1933 Monte Cristi, D.R.   BR/TR/6-0/175*   d9.23   C19   s-Ozzie   OF(8/0/18)

1956	NY N	3	12	2	5	0	0	0	0-0	0	1	.417	.417	.667	186	1	1-0	.800	-1	22	259	3b3		0.
1957	NY N	96	226	26	53	12	4	4	24	14-1	1	27	.235	.278	.305	57	-15	2-3	.926	8	142	133	3b62,O24(8/0/16)/S		-0.
1958	Det A	49	193	19	47	10	2	3	19	8-0	0	20	.244	.272	.363	69	-9	1-0	.981	4	102	73	3b49		0.
1960	Det A	62	132	16	30	4	2	3	13	4-1	0	14	.227	.248	.356	60	-8	1-1	.974	3	102	159	3b42,2b8,S5/C		-0.
1961	Det A	20	30	1	4	0	0	0	1	1-0	0	5	.133	.161	.133	4	-4	0-0	.938	-3	48	179	3b9,C3/2S		-0.
	KC A	11	21	1	3	0	0	0	0	1-0	0	3	.143	.143	.143	-23	-4	0-0	.818	-1	137	180	3b4,C3		-0.
	Year	31	51	2	7	0	0	1	1	1-0	0	8	.137	.154	.196	-7	-8	0-0	.889	-3	74	179	3b13,C6/2S		-1.

YEAR	TM LG	G	AB	R	H	2B	3B	HR	RBI	BB-IB	HP	SO	AVG	OBP	SLG	AOPS	ABR	SB-CS	FA	FR	RNG	THR	GAMES AT POSITION	DL	BFW
1962	Bal A	1	0	0	0	0	0	0	0	1-1	0	0	—	1.000	—	209	0	0-0		0			/H		0.0
1965	Pit N	39	49	3	13	2	0	1	5	2-0	0	10	.265	.294	.367	85	-1	0-0	1.000	-0	137	65	C15,3b7,2b5		-0.1
1966	SF N	42	89	7	19	2	0	2	9	4-1	0	12	.213	.245	.303	51	-6	1-1	.984	-1	91	34	C13,3b13,1b5,2b2,O2R		-0.7
1969	SF N	1	1	0	0	0	0	0	0	0-0	0	0	.000	.000	.000	-99	-0	0-0	—	0			/H		0.0
Total	9	324	753	75	174	19	7	14	73	34-4	0	91	.231	.263	.331	59	-46	6-5	.951	9	114	114	3b189,C35,O26R,2b16,S7,1b5		-3.8

VIRTUE, JAKE   Jacob Kitchline "Guesses"   B3.2.1865 Philadelphia PA   D2.3.1943 Camden NJ   BB/TL/5-9.5/165   d7.21

1890	Cle N	62	223	39	68	6	5	2	25	49	1	15	.305	.432	.404	147	17	9	.982	0	99	96	1b62		1.0
1891	Cle N	139	517	82	135	19	14	2	72	75	1	8	.261	.363	.364	107	6	15	.972	-10	71	89	1b139		-1.5
1892	†Cle N	147	557	98	157	15	20	2	89	84	4	68	.282	.380	.391	128	20	14	.984	-4	78	85.	1b147		1.4
1893	Cle N	97	378	87	100	16	10	1	60	54	1	14	.265	.358	.368	88	-7	11	.975	1	115	108	1b73,O13(0/9/4),S5,3b5/P		-0.6
1894	Cle N	29	89	15	23	4	1	0	10	13	1	3	.258	.359	.326	64	-5	1	.885	-2	93	0	O21(0/16/5),2b3,1b2/P		-0.6
Total	5	474	1764	321	483	60	50	7	256	275	15	140	.274	.376	.376	111	31	50	.978	-15	85	92	1b423,O34(0/25/9),3b5,S5,2b3,P2		-0.3

VISNER, JOE   Joseph Paul (b Joseph Paul Vezina)   B9.27.1859 Minneapolis MN   D6.17.1945 Fosston MN   BL/TR/5-11/180   d7.4

1885	Bal AA	4	13	2	3	0	0	0	2	2	0		.231	.333	.231	82	0		.750	-1	0	0	O4(0/2/2)		-0.1
1889	†Bro AA	80	295	56	76	12	10	8	68	36	1	36	.258	.346	.447	125	9	13	.871	-11			C53,O29(2/0/27)		0.1
1890	Pit P	127	521	110	139	15	22	3	71	76	8	44	.267	.369	.397	114	13	18	.893	-7	78	91	O127R		0.4
1891	Was AA	18	68	13	19	2	3	1	7	8	0	7	.279	.355	.441	134	3	2	.806	-3	67	0	O17R/C3		0.0
	StL AA	6	27	2	4	0	1	0	1	0	0	3	.148	.148	.222	5	-4	0	1.000	1	112	0	O6R		-0.3
	Year	24	95	15	23	2	4	1	8	8	0	10	.242	.301	.379	94	-2	2	.846	-2	77	0	O23R/C3		-0.3
Total	4	235	924	183	241	29	36	12	149	122	12	90	.261	.354	.409	115	21	33	.892	-20			O183(2/2/179),C54/3		0.1

VITIELLO, JOE   Joseph David   B4.11.1970 Cambridge MA   BR/TR/6-3/230(215-230)   [KCA91 1/7]   d4.29   Col Alabama

1995	KC A	53	130	13	33	4	0	7	21	8-0	4	25	.254	.317	.446	94	-2	0-0	.982	-1	80	69	D38,1b8		-0.4
1996	KC A	85	257	29	62	15	1	8	40	38-2	3	69	.241	.342	.401	88	-4	2-0	1.000	0	120	76	D70,1b9/OR		-0.7
1997	KC A	51	130	11	31	6	0	5	18	14-1	2	37	.238	.322	.400	84	-3	0-0	.980	-0	111	0	O28(12/0/16),D12/1	92	-0.5
1998	KC A	3	7	0	1	0	0	0	0	1-0	0	1	.143	.250	.143	6	-1	0-0	—	0			D2	40	-0.1
1999	KC A	13	41	4	6	1	0	1	4	2-0	2	9	.146	.222	.244	18	-5	0-0	1.000	1	132	128	1b10,D2		-0.5
2000	SD N	39	52	7	13	3	0	2	8	10-0	2	9	.250	.365	.423	107	1	0-0	.966	-1	95	128	1b17/OR		-0.1
2003	Mon N	38	76	12	26	6	0	3	13	7-0	2	14	.342	.407	.539	142	5	0-0	1.000	-1	76	0	O15L,1b12/D		0.3
Total	7	282	693	76	172	35	1	26	104	80-3	13	165	.248	.335	.414	90	-9	2-0	.983	-1	112	108	D125,1b57,O45(27/0/18)	132	-2.0

VITT, OSSIE   Oscar Joseph   B1.4.1890 San Francisco CA   D1.31.1963 Oakland CA   BR/TR/5-10/150   d4.11   M3

1912	Det A	76	273	39	67	4	4	0	19	18	2		.245	.297	.289	70	-11	17	.929	0	87	53	O28(26/1/1),3b24,2b15		-1.2
1913	Det A	99	359	45	86	11	3	2	33	31	2	18	.240	.304	.304	79	-10	5	.960	2	107	84	2b78,3b17,O2C		-0.7
1914	Det A	66	195	35	49	7	0	0	8	31	0	8	.251	.354	.287	90	-1	10-8	.964	3	117	90	2b36,3b16,O2L/S		0.3
1915	Det A	152	560	116	140	18	13	1	48	80	4	22	.250	.348	.334	99	1	26-18	.964	13	112	81	3b151,2b2		1.8
1916	Det A	153	597	88	135	17	12	0	42	75	1	28	.226	.314	.295	80	-14	18	.964	26	118	107	3b151,S2		1.8
1917	Det A	140	512	65	130	13	6	0	47	56	1	15	.254	.329	.303	80	-4	18	.940	-17	88	86	3b140		-1.8
1918	Det A	81	267	29	64	7	2	0	17	32	0	6	.240	.321	.273	83	-5	5	.953	3	97	108	3b66,2b9,O3C		-0.1
1919	Bos A	133	469	64	114	10	3	0	40	44	1	11	.243	.309	.277	69	-19	9	.970	18	113	115	3b133		0.3
1920	Bos A	87	296	50	65	10	4	1	28	43	1	10	.220	.321	.291	65	-14	5-4	.986	-1	104	51	3b64,2b21		-1.3
1921	Bos A	78	232	29	44	11	1	0	13	45	0	9	.190	.321	.246	48	-17	1-2	.962	-3	99	122	3b71,O3L,1b2		-1.5
Total	10	1065	3760	560	894	106	48	4	295	455	12	131	.238	.322	.295	80	-94	114-32	.960	45	107	96	3b833,2b161,O38(31/6/1),S3,1b2		-2.4

VIZCAINO, JOSE   Jose Luis (Pimental)   B3.26.1968 San Cristobal, D.R.   BB/TR/6-1/180(150-190)   d9.10

1989	LA N	7	10	2	2	0	0	0	0	0-0	0	1	.200	.200	.200	15	-1	0-0	.882	1	114	148	S5		0.0
1990	LA N	37	51	3	14	1	1	0	2	4-1	0	8	.275	.327	.333	84	-1	1-1	.956	1	104	120	S11,2b6		0.0
1991	Chi N	93	145	7	38	5	0	0	10	5-0	0	18	.262	.283	.297	61	-8	2-1	.947	1	86	37	3b57,S33,2b9		-0.5
1992	Chi N	86	285	25	64	10	4	1	17	14-2	0	35	.225	.260	.298	56	-17	3-0	.969	7	115	117	S50,3b29,2b5	37	-0.6
1993	Chi N	151	551	74	158	19	4	4	54	46-2	3	71	.287	.340	.358	89	-8	12-9	.968	15	114	93	S81,3b44,2b34		1.4
1994	NY N	103	410	47	105	13	3	3	33	33-3	2	62	.256	.310	.324	68	-20	1-11	.970	-10	100	92	S102		-2.6
1995	NY N	135	509	66	146	21	5	3	56	35-4	1	76	.287	.332	.365	87	-10	8-3	.984	15	109	112	S134/2		1.5
1996	NY N	96	363	47	110	12	6	1	32	28-0	3	58	.303	.356	.377	99	-1	9-5	.986	1	100	123	2b93		0.5
	†Cle A	48	179	23	51	5	2	0	13	7-0	0	24	.285	.310	.335	64	-10	8-8	.981	-4	92	122	2b45,S4/D		-1.1
1997	†SF N	151	568	97	151	19	7	5	50	48-1	0	87	.266	.323	.350	78	-20	8-8	.976	6	106	110	S147,2b5		-0.4
1998	LA N	67	237	30	62	9	0	3	29	17-0	1	35	.262	.311	.338	75	-9	7-3	.985	-3	93	88	S66	79	-0.7
1999	LA N	94	266	27	67	9	0	1	29	20-0	1	23	.252	.304	.297	56	-18	2-1	.966	4	100	75	S44,2b30,3b9/OL	18	-1.0
2000	LA N	40	93	9	9	2	1	0	4	10-3	1	15	.204	.288	.247	39	-9	1-0	1.000	1	105	68	S19,3b12,2b3/1D		-0.6
	†NY A	73	174	23	48	8	1	0	10	12-0	0	28	.276	.319	.333	68	-9	5-7	.990	-2	94	94	2b62,3b6,S2,D4		-0.9
2001	†Hou N	107	256	38	71	8	3	1	14	15-0	2	33	.277	.322	.344	67	-13	3-2	.937	-3	102	90	S53,2b18,3b7		-1.2
2002	Hou N	125	406	53	123	19	2	5	37	24-2	1	40	.303	.342	.397	90	-7	3-5	.980	2	96	112	S58,3b30,2b25,1b5		-0.2
2003	Hou N	91	189	14	47	7	3	3	26	8-3	0	22	.249	.281	.365	64	-11	0-1	.963	-1	86	103	S32,2b20,3b2/1	53	-1.0
2004	†Hou N	138	358	34	98	21	3	3	33	20-5	0	39	.274	.311	.374	74	-4	1-1	.969	5	104	86	S64,2b37,3b21,1b8		-0.4
2005	†Hou N	50	187	16	46	10	2	1	23	15-0	1	30	.246	.299	.337	67	-9	2-0	1.000	2	109	190	2b23,S17,1b13,3b8		-0.6
Total	17	1740	5237	614	1420	198	47	34	472	361-30	16	715	.271	.318	.346	75	-195	74-60	.973	37	105	101	S922,2b416,3b225,1b28,D6/OL	187	-8.4

VIZQUEL, OMAR   Omar Enrique (Gonzalez)   B4.24.1967 Caracas, Venez   BB/TR/5-9/165(155-185)   d4.3

1989	Sea A	143	387	45	85	7	3	1	20	28-0	1	40	.220	.273	.261	50	-26	1-4	.971	5	100	119	S143		-1.3
1990	Sea A	81	255	19	63	3	2	2	18	18-0	0	22	.247	.295	.298	66	-12	4-1	.980	4	103	95	S81	34	-0.2
1991	Sea A	142	426	42	98	16	4	1	41	45-0	0	37	.230	.302	.293	66	-20	7-2	.980	26	108	128	S138/2		1.7
1992	Sea A	136	483	49	142	20	4	0	21	32-0	2	38	.294	.340	.352	93	-5	15-13	.989	8	99	100	S136	28	1.2
1993	Sea A	158	560	68	143	14	2	2	31	50-2	4	71	.255	.319	.298	66	-27	12-14	.980	20	103	112	S155,D2		0.2
1994	Cle A	69	286	39	78	10	1	1	33	23-0	0	23	.273	.325	.325	68	-14	13-4	.981	2	102	117	S69	51	-0.5
1995	†Cle A	136	542	87	144	28	0	6	56	59-0	1	59	.266	.333	.351	78	-16	29-11	.986	5	104	103	S136		0.1
1996	Cle A	151	542	98	161	36	1	9	64	56-0	4	42	.297	.362	.417	98	0	35-9	.971	4	105	97	S150		1.7
1997	Cle A	153	565	89	158	23	6	5	49	57-1	2	58	.280	.347	.368	84	-13	43-12	.985	10	102	100	S152		1.3
1998	†Cle A★	151	576	86	166	30	6	2	50	62-1	4	64	.288	.358	.372	88	-9	37-12	.993	8	102	96	S151		1.3
1999	†Cle A★	144	574	112	191	36	4	5	66	65-0	1	50	.333	.397	.436	108	10	42-9	.976	-0	98	93	S143/OR		2.4
2000	†Cle A	156	613	101	176	27	3	7	66	87-0	5	72	.287	.377	.375	89	-7	22-10	.995	-0	92	94	S156		0.5
2001	†Cle A	155	611	84	156	26	8	2	50	61-0	2	72	.255	.323	.334	71	-25	13-9	.989	6	98	90	S154		-0.8
2002	Cle A★	151	582	85	160	31	5	14	72	56-3	8	64	.275	.341	.418	100	1	18-10	.990	13	102	95	S150		2.4
2003	Cle A	64	250	43	61	13	2	2	19	29-0	0	20	.244	.331	.336	74	-9	8-3	.978	13	111	146	S64	98	0.9
2004	Cle A	148	567	82	165	28	3	7	59	57-0	1	62	.291	.353	.388	98	-1	19-6	.982	-7	97	98	S147		0.5
2005	SF N	152	568	66	154	28	4	3	45	56-0	5	58	.271	.341	.350	79	-16	24-10	.988	-8	98	91	S150		-1.2
Total	17	2290	8387	1195	2301	376	58	69	760	841-7	40	852	.274	.341	.358	83	-189	342-139	.984	106	101	102	S2275,D2/OR2	211	10.2

VOGEL, OTTO   Otto Henry   B10.26.1899 Mendota IL   D7.19.1969 Iowa City IA   BR/TR/6-0/195   d6.5   Col Illinois

1923	Chi N	41	81	10	17	0	1	1	6	7	3	11	.210	.297	.272	51	-6	2-3	.929	0	96	143	O24(3/0/21)/3		-0.7
1924	Chi N	70	172	28	46	11	2	1	24	10	3	26	.267	.319	.372	84	-4	4-4	.956	3	107	128	O53(12/1/40),3b2		-0.5
Total	2	111	253	38	63	11	3	2	30	17	6	37	.249	.312	.340	73	-10	6-7	.948	3	104	132	O77(15/1/61),3b3		-1.2

VOIGT, JACK   John David   B5.17.1966 Sarasota FL   BR/TR/6-1/175*   [BalA87 9/221]   d8.3   Col Louisiana St.

1992	Bal A	1	0	0	0	0	0	0	0	0-0	0	0	—	—	—		0	0-0	—	0			/R		0.0
1993	Bal A	64	152	32	45	11	4	6	23	25-0	0	33	.296	.395	.500	133	8	1-0	.987	-0	99	121	O43(22/0/23),1b5,3b3,D9		0.6
1994	Bal A	59	141	15	34	5	0	3	20	18-1	1	25	.241	.327	.340	70	-6	0-0	.989	1	107	68	O54(17/1/37),1b6,D2		-0.7
1995	Bal A	3	1	1	1	0	0	0	0	0-0	0	0	1.000	1.000	1.000	415	1	0-0	1.000	0	409	0	/1D		0.1
	Tex A	33	62	8	10	3	0	2	8	10-0	0	14	.161	.274	.306	50	-5	0-0	1.000	-0	103	84	O25(8/0/17),1b5,D2		-0.6
	Year	36	63	9	11	3	0	2	8	10-0	0	14	.175	.284	.317	55	-4	0-0	1.000	-0	103	84	O25(8/0/17),1b6,D3		-0.5
1996	Tex A	5	9	1	1	0	0	0	0	0-0	0	5	.111	.111	.111	-41	-2	0-0	1.000	0	151	0	O3(2/0/1)/3		-0.2
1997	Mil A	72	151	20	37	9	2	8	22	19-2	1	36	.245	.331	.490	110	2	1-2	.985	-0	103	266	O40(35/2/5),1b19,3b6/D		-0.1
1998	Oak A	57	72	7	10	4	0	1	10	6-0	0	23	.139	.205	.236	15	-9	5-1	.987	-0	40	128	1b27,O20(9/10/2),3b2,D3		-0.9
Total	7	294	588	84	138	32	6	20	83	78-3	2	129	.235	.324	.401	86	-12	7-3	.990	1	103	143	O185(93/13/85),1b63,D18,3b12		-1.8

VOLLMER, CLYDE
Clyde Frederick B9.24.1921 Cincinnati OH BR/TR/6-1/190* d5.31 Mil 1943-45

YEAR	TM LG	G	AB	R	H	2B	3B	HR	RBI	BB-IB	HP	SO	AVG	OBP	SLG	AOPS	ABR	SB-CS	FA	FR	RNG	THR	GAMES AT POSITION	DL	BFW
1942	Cin N	12	43	2	4	0	0	1	4	1	0	5	.093	.114	.163	-20	-7	0	1.000	0	113	0	O11(10/1/0)		-0.8
1946	Cin N	9	22	1	4	0	0	0	1	1	0	3	.182	.217	.182	14	-3	2	1.000	-1	75	0	O7(5/3/1)		-0.4
1947	Cin N	78	155	19	34	10	0	1	13	9	1	18	.219	.267	.303	51	-11	0	.984	4	123	72	O66(8/58/0)		-0.8
1948	Cin N	7	9	0	1	0	0	0	0	0	0	1	.111	.200	.111	-14	-1	0	—	-0	0	0	O2(0/1/1)		-0.2
	Was A	1	5	1	2	0	0	0	0	0	0	1	.400	.400	.400	116	0	0-0	1.000	-0	74	0	/OC		0.0
1949	Was A	129	443	58	112	17	1	14	59	53	2	62	.253	.335	.391	94	-6	1-2	.982	1	109	37	O114(0/99/15)		-0.8
1950	Was A	6	14	4	4	0	0	0	1	2	0	3	.286	.375	.286	75	0	1-0	1.000	0	79	458	O3L		0.0
	Bos A	57	169	35	48	10	0	7	37	21	0	35	.284	.363	.467	102	0	1-0	.954	-2	93	98	O39(17/11/11)		-0.3
	Year	63	183	39	52	10	0	7	38	23	0	38	.284	.364	.454	100	0	2-0	.957	-1	92	123	O42(20/11/11)		-0.3
1951	Bos A	115	386	66	97	9	2	22	85	55	1	66	.251	.346	.456	105	2	0-0	.986	-4	97	66	O106(2/8/97)		-0.5
1952	Bos A	90	250	35	66	12	4	11	50	39	3	47	.264	.370	.476	124	9	2-2	1.000	1	104	66	O72(43/9/21)		0.5
1953	Bos A	1	0	0	0	0	0	0	0	1	0	0	—	1.000	—	180	0	0-0	—	0			/H		0.0
	Was A	118	408	54	106	15	3	11	74	48	3	59	.260	.342	.392	100	0	0-2	.979	3	103	102	O106(104/0/2)		-0.5
	Year	119	408	54	106	15	3	11	74	49	3	59	.260	.343	.392	101	0	0-2	.979	3	103	102	O106(104/0/2)		-0.5
1954	Was A	62	117	8	30	4	0	2	15	12	1	28	.256	.331	.342	89	-2	0-0	1.000	-1	80	131	O26(5/0/21)		-0.4
Total	10	685	2021	283	508	77	10	69	339	243	11	328	.251	.335	.402	95	-19	7-6	.984	0	103	72	O551(197/191/169)		-4.2

VON KOLNITZ, FRITZ
Alfred Holmes B5.20.1893 Charleston SC D3.18.1948 Mount Pleasant SC BR/TR/5-10.5/175 d4.18 Col South Carolina-Aiken

YEAR	TM LG	G	AB	R	H	2B	3B	HR	RBI	BB-IB	HP	SO	AVG	OBP	SLG	AOPS	ABR	SB-CS	FA	FR	RNG	THR	GAMES AT POSITION	BFW
1914	Cin N	41	104	8	23	2	0	0	6	6	1	16	.221	.270	.240	51	-6	4	.914	-1	112	72	3b20,O11(2/7/2),C2/1	-0.8
1915	Cin N	50	78	6	15	4	1	0	6	7	0	11	.192	.259	.269	59	-4	1-3	.933	-3	85	191	3b18,S6,1b3,C2/OR	-0.8
1916	Chi A	24	44	1	10	3	0	0	7	2	0	6	.227	.261	.295	42	-2	0	.909	-3	64	74	3b13	-0.5
Total	3	115	226	15	48	9	1	0	19	15	1	33	.212	.264	.261	56	-12	5-3	.918	-7	94	107	3b51,O12(2/7/3),S6,1b4,C4	-2.1

VOSMIK, JOE
Joseph Franklin B4.4.1910 Cleveland OH D1.27.1962 Cleveland OH BR/TR/6-0/185 d9.13

YEAR	TM LG	G	AB	R	H	2B	3B	HR	RBI	BB-IB	HP	SO	AVG	OBP	SLG	AOPS	ABR	SB-CS	FA	FR	RNG	THR	GAMES AT POSITION	BFW
1930	Cle A	9	26	1	6	2	0	0	4	1	0	1	.231	.259	.308	42	-1	0-0	.933	0	88	237	O5(1/4/0)	-0.2
1931	Cle A	149	591	80	189	36	14	7	117	38	2	30	.320	.363	.464	110	7	7-7	.970	4	104	116	O147(147/1/0)	0.1
1932	Cle A	153	621	106	194	39	12	10	97	58	5	42	.312	.376	.462	109	8	2-3	.989	19	124	99	O153L	1.6
1933	Cle A	119	438	53	115	20	10	4	56	42	3	13	.263	.331	.381	84	-11	0-2	.985	3	97	130	O113L	-1.4
1934	Cle A	104	405	71	138	33	2	6	78	35	0	10	.341	.393	.477	122	14	1-1	.976	-4	93	80	O104L	-0.9
1935	Cle A★	152	620	93	216	47	20	10	110	59	4	30	.348	.408	.537	140	36	2-1	.986	3	110	41	O150L	2.8
1936	Cle A	138	506	76	145	29	7	6	94	79	0	21	.287	.383	.413	96	-2	5-1	.978	-3	95	95	O136(136/0/1)	-1.0
1937	StL A	144	594	81	193	47	9	4	93	49	1	38	.325	.377	.455	108	8	2-3	.972	7	109	107	O143L	0.6
1938	Bos A	146	621	121	201	37	6	9	86	59	2	26	.324	.384	.446	103	3	0-3	.978	4	100	131	O146(146/1/0)	-0.2
1939	Bos A	145	554	89	153	29	6	7	84	66	3	33	.276	.356	.388	87	-10	4-3	.974	-6	92	90	O144L	-2.2
1940	Bro N	116	404	45	114	14	6	1	42	22	1	21	.282	.321	.354	81	-11	0	.976	1	98	123	O99(99/9/51)	-1.6
1941	Bro N	25	56	0	11	0	0	0	4	4	0	4	.196	.250	.196	26	-6	0-0	1.000	-2	71	0	O18(2/0/16)	-0.4
1944	Was A	14	36	2	7	2	0	0	9	2	0	3	.194	.237	.250	41	-3	0-0	1.000	-0	102	0	O12(5/0/7)	-0.4
Total	13	1414	5472	818	1682	363	92	65	874	514	21	272	.307	.369	.438	104	25	23-24	.979	26	103	100	O1370(1283/15/75)	-2.3

VOSS, ALEX
Alexander B5.16.1858 Roswell GA D8.31.1906 Cincinnati OH BR/TR/6-1/180 d4.17 ▲

YEAR	TM LG	G	AB	R	H	2B	3B	HR	RBI	AVG	OBP	SLG	AOPS	ABR	FA	FR	RNG	THR	GAMES AT POSITION	BFW
1884	Was U	63	245	33	47	9	0	0	5	.192	.208	.229	33	-27	.848	6	126	156	P27,3b16,1b15,O13(0/7/6)/S	-1.3
	KC U	14	45	1	4	0	0	0	0	.089	.089	.089	-53	-10	.867	2	134	359	O8(5/3/0),P7	-0.3
	Year	77	290	34	51	9	0	0	5	.176	.190	.207	21	-37	.859	7	126	174	P34,O21(5/10/6),3b16,1b15/S	-1.6

VOSS, BILL
William Edward B10.31.1943 Glendale CA BL/TL/6-2/160* d9.14

YEAR	TM LG	G	AB	R	H	2B	3B	HR	RBI	BB-IB	HP	SO	AVG	OBP	SLG	AOPS	ABR	SB-CS	FA	FR	RNG	THR	GAMES AT POSITION	DL	BFW
1965	Chi A	11	33	4	6	0	1	1	3	3-1	0	5	.182	.250	.333	68	-2	0-0	1.000	-1	76	0	O10R		-0.4
1966	Chi A	2	2	0	0	0	0	0	0	0-0	0	2	.000	.000	.000	-99	-1	0-0	1.000	0	95	0	/OL		-0.1
1967	Chi A	13	22	4	2	0	0	0	0	0-0	0	1	.091	.091	.091	-48	-4	1-1	1.000	0	113	0	O11(1/2/9)		-0.5
1968	Chi A	61	167	14	26	2	1	2	15	16-1	2	34	.156	.238	.216	38	-13	5-3	.963	-1	86	179	O55(5/2/53)	52	-1.9
1969	Cal A	133	349	33	91	11	4	2	40	35-6	0	40	.261	.327	.332	89	-5	5-3	.995	7	110	161	O111(6/4/104),1b2		-0.3
1970	Cal A	80	181	21	44	4	3	3	30	23-2	2	18	.243	.327	.348	91	-2	2-1	.979	3	99	224	O55R	32	-0.7
1971	Mil A	97	275	31	69	4	0	10	30	24-1	1	45	.251	.312	.375	95	-3	2-2	.987	-1	109	22	O79(4/13/67)		-0.7
1972	Mil A	27	36	1	3	1	0	0	1	5-0	0	4	.083	.195	.111	-7	-5	0-1	.929	-1	97	0	O11(3/0/9)		-0.7
	Oak A	40	97	10	22	5	1	1	9	9-3	1	16	.227	.296	.330	91	-1	0-0	1.000	1	102	158	O34(1/13/21)		-0.1
	Year	67	133	11	25	6	1	1	6	14-3	1	20	.188	.268	.271	63	-6	0-1	.987	0	92	0	O45(4/13/30)		-0.8
	StL N	11	15	1	4	2	0	0	3	2-0	0	2	.267	.333	.400	114	0	0-0	1.000	-0	92	0	O2C		0.0
Total	8	475	1177	119	267	29	10	19	127	117-14	6	167	.227	.298	.317	78	-36	15-11	.986	7	102	128	O369(21/36/328),1b2	84	-4.8

VOYLES, PHIL
Philip Vance B5.12.1900 Murphy NC D11.3.1972 Marlborough MA BL/TR/5-11.5/175 d9.4

YEAR	TM LG	G	AB	R	H	2B	3B	HR	RBI	BB-IB	HP	SO	AVG	OBP	SLG	AOPS	ABR	SB-CS	FA	FR	RNG	THR	GAMES AT POSITION	BFW
1929	Bos N	20	68	9	16	4	2	0	14	6	0	8	.235	.297	.294	49	-6	0	.922	-1	92	116	O20(1/19/0)	-0.7

VUKOVICH, GEORGE
George Stephen B6.24.1956 Chicago IL BL/TR/6-0/198* [PhiN77 4/100] d4.13 Col Southern Illinois

YEAR	TM LG	G	AB	R	H	2B	3B	HR	RBI	BB-IB	HP	SO	AVG	OBP	SLG	AOPS	ABR	SB-CS	FA	FR	RNG	THR	GAMES AT POSITION	BFW
1980	†Phi N	78	58	6	13	1	1	0	8	6-0	0	9	.224	.297	.276	57	-3	0-0	.933	-0	112	0	O28(13/0/15)	-0.4
1981	†Phi N	20	26	5	10	0	1	1	4	1-0	0	0	.385	.407	.500	148	1	1-0	1.000	0	118	0	O9(3/1/5)	0.2
1982	Phi N	123	335	41	91	18	2	6	42	32-14	0	47	.272	.334	.391	99	0	2-9	.977	1	108	67	O102(15/0/100)	-0.7
1983	Cle A	124	312	31	77	13	2	3	44	24-4	2	37	.247	.301	.330	72	-12	3-4	.986	0	111	44	O122(20/3/107)	-1.7
1984	Cle A	134	437	38	133	22	5	9	60	34-3	1	61	.304	.354	.439	116	10	1-4	.994	19	128	172	O130(16/0/124)	2.1
1985	Cle A	149	434	43	106	22	10	27	45	30-6	1	75	.244	.292	.350	76	-15	2-2	.988	20	105	51	O137(10/0/131)	-2.1
Total	6	628	1602	164	430	76	10	27	203	127-27	4	229	.268	.322	.379	91	-19	9-19	.988	20	114	86	O528(77/4/482)	-2.8

VUKOVICH, JOHN
John Christopher B7.31.1947 Sacramento CA BR/TR/6-1/190* [PhiN66*1/10] d9.11 M2/C23 Col American River (CA) CC

YEAR	TM LG	G	AB	R	H	2B	3B	HR	RBI	BB-IB	HP	SO	AVG	OBP	SLG	AOPS	ABR	SB-CS	FA	FR	RNG	THR	GAMES AT POSITION	BFW
1970	Phi N	3	8	1	1	0	0	0	0	1-0	0	1	.125	.222	.125	-4	-1	0-0	.778	0	72	95	S2/3	-0.1
1971	Phi N	74	217	11	36	5	0	0	14	12-1	1	34	.166	.211	.189	15	-25	2-1	.956	4	107	75	3b74	-2.3
1973	Mil A	55	128	10	16	3	0	2	9	9-0	0	40	.125	.182	.195	6	-16	0-2	.948	-4	94	42	3b40,1b13/S	-2.3
1974	Mil A	38	80	5	15	1	0	3	11	1-0	0	16	.188	.193	.313	45	-6	2-1	.945	-5	102	92	S12,3b12,2b11,1b4	-1.0
1975	Cin N	31	38	4	8	3	0	0	2	4-1	0	5	.211	.286	.289	59	-2	0-0	.925	0	109	148	3b31	-0.2
1976	Phi N	4	8	2	1	0	0	1	2	0-0	0	2	.125	.125	.500	69	-1	0-0	1.000	-1	48	0	3b4/1	-0.2
1977	Phi N	2	2	0	0	0	0	0	0	0-0	0	1	.000	.000	.000	-95	-1	0-0	—	0			/H	-0.1
1979	Phi N	10	15	0	3	1	0	0	1	0-0	0	3	.200	.200	.267	25	-2	0-0	1.000	0	164	218	3b7,2b3	-0.2
1980	Phi N	49	62	4	10	1	1	0	5	2-1	1	7	.161	.197	.210	14	-7	0-1	.958	-4	84	0	3b34,2b9,S5/1	-1.3
1981	Phi N	11	1	0	0	0	0	0	0	0-0	0	1	.000	.000	.000	-95	-0	0-0	.800	-1	105	0	3b9/12	-0.1
Total	10	277	559	37	90	14	1	6	49	29-3	2	109	.161	.203	.222	20	-60	4-5	.951	-12	103	62	3b212,2b24,1b20,S20	-7.8

WADDEY, FRANK
Frank Orum B8.21.1905 Memphis TN D10.21.1990 Knoxville TN BL/TL/5-10.5/185 d4.16 Col Georgia Tech

YEAR	TM LG	G	AB	R	H	2B	3B	HR	RBI	BB-IB	HP	SO	AVG	OBP	SLG	AOPS	ABR	SB-CS	FA	FR	RNG	THR	GAMES AT POSITION	BFW
1931	StL A	14	22	3	6	1	0	0	2	0	0	3	.273	.333	.318	70	-1	0-0	1.000	-1	71	0	O7(1/5/1)	-0.2

WADE, HAM
Abraham Lincoln B12.20.1880 Spring City PA D7.21.1968 Riverside NJ BR/TR/5-8/155 d9.9

YEAR	TM LG	G	AB	R	H	2B	3B	HR	RBI	BB-IB	HP	SO	AVG	OBP	SLG	AOPS	ABR	SB-CS	FA	FR	RNG	THR	GAMES AT POSITION	BFW
1907	NY N	1	0	0	0	0	0	0	0			1-	—	1.000	—	208	0	0	1.000	0	0	0	/OL	0.0

WADE, GALE
Galeard Lee B1.20.1929 Hollister MO BL/TR/6-1.5/185* d4.11

YEAR	TM LG	G	AB	R	H	2B	3B	HR	RBI	BB-IB	HP	SO	AVG	OBP	SLG	AOPS	ABR	SB-CS	FA	FR	RNG	THR	GAMES AT POSITION	BFW
1955	Chi N	9	33	5	6	1	0	1	1	4-0	0	3	.182	.270	.303	52	-2	0-0	.867	-2	62	175	O9C	-0.4
1956	Chi N	10	12	0	0	0	0	0	0	1-0	0	0	.000	.077	.000	-78	-3	0-0	.875	-0	119	0	O3C	-0.3
Total	2	19	45	5	6	1	0	1	1	5-0	0	3	.133	.220	.222	18	-5	0-0	.870	-2	75	134	O12C	-0.7

WADE, RIP
Richard Frank B1.12.1898 Duluth MN D7.15.1957 Duluth MN BL/TR/5-11/174 d4.19

YEAR	TM LG	G	AB	R	H	2B	3B	HR	RBI	BB-IB	HP	SO	AVG	OBP	SLG	AOPS	ABR	SB-CS	FA	FR	RNG	THR	GAMES AT POSITION	BFW
1923	Was A	33	69	8	16	2	2	0	10				.232	.284	.406	84	-2	0-0	.967	0	82	190	O19(5/12/2)	-0.3

WAGENHORST, WOODY
Ellwood Otto B6.3.1863 Kutztown PA D2.12.1946 Washington DC 5-11/165 d6.25 Col Princeton

YEAR	TM LG	G	AB	R	H	2B	3B	HR	RBI	BB-IB	HP	SO	AVG	OBP	SLG	AOPS	ABR	SB-CS	FA	FR	RNG	THR	GAMES AT POSITION	BFW
1888	Phi N	2	8	0	1	0	0	0	1			1	.125	.125	.125	-19	-1	0	.800	-1	53	414	3b2	-0.2

WAGNER, BUTTS
Albert B9.17.1871 Chartiers (now Carnegie) PA D11.26.1928 Pittsburgh PA BR/TR/5-10/170 d4.27 b-Honus

YEAR	TM LG	G	AB	R	H	2B	3B	HR	RBI	BB-IB	HP	SO	AVG	OBP	SLG	AOPS	ABR	SB-CS	FA	FR	RNG	THR	GAMES AT POSITION	BFW
1898	Was N	63	223	20	50	11	2	1	31	14		3	.224	.279	.305	67	-10	4	.833	-9	84	79	3b39,O10(1/9/0),S8,2b5	-1.7
	Bro N	11	38	2	9	1	1	0	3	2		3	.237	.275	.316	69	-2	0	.813	-3	88	53	3b11	-0.4
	Year	74	261	22	59	12	3	1	34	16		3	.226	.279	.307	68	-11	4	.828	-12	85	73	3b50,O10(1/9/0),S8,2b5	-2.1

YEAR	TM LG	G	AB	R	H	2B	3B	HR	RBI	BB-IB	HP	SO	AVG	OBP	SLG	AOPS	ABR	SB-CS	FA	FR	RNG	THR	GAMES AT POSITION	DL	BFW

WAGNER, HEINIE Charles F. B9.23.1880 New York NY D3.20.1943 New Rochelle NY BR/TR/5-9/183 d7.1 M1/C7

YEAR	TM LG	G	AB	R	H	2B	3B	HR	RBI	BB-IB	HP	SO	AVG	OBP	SLG	AOPS	ABR	SB-CS	FA	FR	RNG	THR	GAMES AT POSITION	DL	BFW
1902	NY N	17	56	4	12	1	0	0	2	0	0		.214	.214	.232	38	-4	3	.862	-4	86	91	S17		-0.8
1906	Bos A	9	32	1	9	0	0	0	4	1	0		.281	.303	.281	83	-1	2	.943	1	129	65	2b9		0.1
1907	Bos A	111	385	29	82	10	4	2	21	31	2		.213	.275	.275	76	-10	20	.931	-6	99	92	S109/23		-1.4
1908	Bos A	153	526	62	130	11	5	1	46	27	3		.247	.288	.293	86	-9	20	.939	32	108	108	S153		3.2
1909	Bos A	124	430	53	110	16	7	1	49	35	3		.256	.316	.333	103	1	18	.933	10	105	97	S123/2		1.7
1910	Bos A	142	491	61	134	26	7	1	52	44	2		.273	.335	.360	115	9	26	.927	-13	94	83	S140		0.0
1911	Bos A	80	261	34	67	13	8	1	38	29	4		.257	.340	.379	101	6	15	.946	-6	92	81	2b40,S32		-0.3
1912	†Bos A	144	504	75	138	25	6	2	68	62	4		.274	.358	.359	100	2	21	.922	-13	87	102	S144		-0.1
1913	Bos A	110	365	43	83	14	8	2	34	40	7	29	.227	.316	.326	86	-7	9	.937	-0	91	85	S103,2b5/3		0.0
1915	Bos A	84	267	38	64	11	2	0	29	37	3	34	.240	.339	.296	93	-1	8-4	.927	-15	87	70	2b79/3OL		-1.6
1916	Bos A	6	8	2	4	1	0	0	0	3	0	0	.500	.636	.625	278	2	2	1.000	1	149	0	3b4/2S		0.4
1918	Bos A	3	8	1	1	0	0	0	0	1	0	0	.125	.222	.125	5	-1	0	.900	-0	113	254	2b2/3		-0.1
Total	12	983	3333	402	834	128	47	10	343	310	28	63	.250	.319	.326	95	-19	144-4	.928	-14	97	96	S822,2b138,3b8/OL		1.1

WAGNER, HAL Harold Edward B7.2.1915 E.Riverton NJ D8.7.1979 Riverside NJ BL/TR/6-0/165 d10.3 Mil 1944-45 Col Duke

YEAR	TM LG	G	AB	R	H	2B	3B	HR	RBI	BB-IB	HP	SO	AVG	OBP	SLG	AOPS	ABR	SB-CS	FA	FR	RNG	THR	GAMES AT POSITION	DL	BFW
1937	Phi A	1	0	0	0	0	0	0	0	0	0	0	—	—	—	—		0-0	1.000	0	0	0	/C		0.0
1938	Phi A	33	88	10	20	2	1	0	8	8	1	9	.227	.299	.273	45	-8	0-0	.972	-2	78	136	C30		-0.7
1939	Phi A	5	8	0	1	0	0	0	0	0	0	3	.125	.125	.125	-37	-2	0-0	1.000	1	127	264	C5		-0.1
1940	Phi A	34	75	9	19	5	1	0	10	11	0	6	.253	.356	.347	85	-1	0-0	.964	-1	69	121	C28		0.1
1941	Phi A	46	131	18	29	8	2	1	15	19	0	9	.221	.320	.336	75	-4	1-0	.976	-1	89	91	C42		-0.2
1942	Phi A☆	104	288	26	68	17	1	1	30	24	4	29	.236	.304	.313	74	-10	1-0	.986	-6	74	110	C94		-1.0
1943	Phi A	111	289	22	69	17	1	1	26	36	2	17	.239	.327	.315	89	-3	3-3	.980	-10	75	88	C99		-0.9
1944	Phi A	5	4	0	1	0	0	0	0	0	0	0	.250	.250	.250	44	0	0-0	1.000	0	0	1076	/C		0.0
	Bos A	66	223	21	74	13	4	1	38	29	4	14	.332	.418	.439	147	15	1-1	.970	-2	101	80	C64		1.8
	Year	71	227	21	75	13	4	1	38	29	4	14	.330	.415	.436	145	15	1-1	.971	-2	100	85	C65		1.8
1946	†Bos A★	117	370	39	85	12	2	6	52	69	2	32	.230	.354	.322	85	-5	3-1	.983	-5	133	61	C116		-0.4
1947	Bos A	21	65	5	15	3	0	0	6	9	0	5	.231	.324	.277	.63	-3	0-0	.978	-1	87	59	C21		0.9
	Det A	71	191	19	55	10	0	5	33	28	1	16	.288	.382	.419	119	6	0-1	.990	-0	119	70	C71		0.9
	Year	92	256	24	70	13	0	5	39	37	1	21	.273	.367	.383	105	3	0-1	.987	-1	111	67	C92		0.6
1948	Det A	54	109	10	22	3	0	0	10	20	0	11	.202	.326	.229	48	-8	1-0	.989	-2	95	51	C52		-0.7
	Phi N	3	4	0	0	0	0	0	0	0	0	0	.000	.000	.000	-99	-1	0	1.000	1	0	540	/C		-0.1
1949	Phi N	1	4	0	0	0	0	0	0	0	0	0	.000	.000	.000	-99	-1	0	.750	-0	0	0	/C		-0.2
Total	12	672	1849	179	458	90	12	15	228	253	15	152	.248	.343	.334	87	-25	10-6	.981	-26	97	85	C626		-1.8

WAGNER, HONUS John Peter "The Flying Dutchman" B2.24.1874 Chartiers (now Carnegie) PA D12.6.1955 Carnegie PA BR/TR/5-11/200 d7.19 M1/C19 HF1936 b-Butts OF(35/67/272)

YEAR	TM LG	G	AB	R	H	2B	3B	HR	RBI	BB-IB	HP	SO	AVG	OBP	SLG	AOPS	ABR	SB-CS	FA	FR	RNG	THR	GAMES AT POSITION	DL	BFW
1897	Lou N	62	242	38	81	18	4	2	39	15	1		.335	.376	.467	126	9	20	.912	4	233	330	O53(1/53/0),2b9		0.8
1898	Lou N	151	588	80	176	29	3	10	105	31	6		.299	.341	.410	117	11	27	.972	-1	113	95	1b75,3b65,2b10		1.1
1899	Lou N	148	575	100	196	45	13	7	114	40	11		.341	.395	.501	145	35	37	.920	4	104	97	3b76,O61(3/0/58),2b7,1b4		3.4
1900	†Pit N	135	527	107	201	45	22	4	100	41	8		.381	.434	.573	175	53	38	.965	-3	71	109	O118R,3b9,2b7,1b3/P		4.1
1901	Pit N	140	549	101	194	37	11	6	126	53	7		.353	.417	.494	159	43	49	.918	3	99	139	S61,O54(1/0/53),3b24/2		4.4
1902	Pit N	136	534	105	176	30	16	3	91	43	14		.330	.394	.463	159	37	42	1.000	3	119	97	O61(20/11/30),S44,1b32/P2		3.9
1903	†Pit N	129	512	97	182	30	19	5	101	44	7		.355	.414	.518	160	39	46	.933	18	106	132	S111,O12(1/0/11),1b6		5.6
1904	Pit N	132	490	97	171	44	14	4	75	59	4		.349	.423	.520	186	52	53	.929	-4	97	110	S121,O8(6/2/0),1b3,2b2		5.3
1905	Pit N	147	548	114	199	32	14	6	101	54	7		.363	.427	.505	173	50	57	.935	19	108	117	S145,O2L		7.5
1906	Pit N	142	516	103	175	38	9	2	71	58	10		.339	.416	.459	166	42	53	.941	20	109	137	S137,O2R/3		7.2
1907	Pit N	142	515	98	180	38	14	6	82	46	5		.350	.408	.513	186	50	61	.938	6	102	73	S138,1b4		6.7
1908	Pit N	151	568	100	201	39	19	10	109	54	5		.354	.415	.542	205	66	53	.943	-11	93	106	S151		6.9
1909	†Pit N	137	495	92	168	39	10	5	100	66	3		.339	.420	.489	168	42	35	.940	5	99	134	S136/OL		5.6
1910	Pit N	150	556	90	178	34	8	4	81	59		47	.320	.390	.432	132	24	24	.935	5	97	119	S138,1b11,2b2		3.5
1911	Pit N	130	473	87	158	23	16	9	89	67	6	34	.334	.423	.507	154	35	20	.932	-0	97	153	S101,1b28/OC		4.1
1912	Pit N	145	558	91	181	35	20	7	102	59	6	38	.324	.395	.496	145	34	26	.962	17	100	137	S143		5.9
1913	Pit N	114	413	51	124	18	4	3	56	26	5	40	.300	.349	.385	114	7	21-11	.962	9	96	120	S105		2.5
1914	Pit N	150	552	60	139	15	9	1	50	51	2	51	.252	.317	.317	93	-5	23	.950	8	102	102	S132,3b17/1		1.2
1915	Pit N	156	566	68	155	32	17	6	78	39	4	64	.274	.325	.422	127	16	22-15	.948	1	97	105	S131,2b12,1b10		2.8
1916	Pit N	123	432	45	124	15	9	1	39	34	8	36	.287	.350	.370	120	11	11	.942	-14	86	79	S92,1b24,2b4		0.3
1917	Pit N	74	230	15	61	7	1	0	24	24	1	17	.265	.337	.304	94	0	5	.985	-4	89	93	1b47,3b18,2b2/SM		-0.6
Total	21	2794	10439	1739	3420	643	252	101	1733	963	125	327	.328	.391	.467	150	651	723-26	.940	84	100	116	S1887,O373R,1b248,3b210,2b57,P2		82.2

WAGNER, JOE Joseph Bernard B4.24.1889 New York NY D11.15.1948 Bronx NY BR/TR/5-11/165 d4.25

YEAR	TM LG	G	AB	R	H	2B	3B	HR	RBI	BB-IB	HP	SO	AVG	OBP	SLG	AOPS	ABR	SB-CS	FA	FR	RNG	THR	GAMES AT POSITION	DL	BFW
1915	Cin N	75	197	17	35	5	2	0	13				.178	.210	.223	31	-17	4-6	.961	6	101	162	2b46,S12,3b2		-1.3

WAGNER, LEON Leon Lamar "Daddy Wags" B5.13.1934 Chattanooga TN D1.3.2004 Los Angeles CA BL/TR/6-1/195(192-205) d6.22 Col Tuskegee

YEAR	TM LG	G	AB	R	H	2B	3B	HR	RBI	BB-IB	HP	SO	AVG	OBP	SLG	AOPS	ABR	SB-CS	FA	FR	RNG	THR	GAMES AT POSITION	DL	BFW
1958	SF N	74	221	31	70	9	0	13	35	18-3	1	34	.317	.371	.534	139	12	1-0	.949	-1	89	130	O57L		0.8
1959	SF N	87	129	20	29	4	3	5	22	25-6	3	24	.225	.361	.419	110	2	0-0	.941	-1	105	0	O28L		0.0
1960	StL N	39	98	12	21	2	0	4	11	17-3	1	17	.214	.333	.357	83	-2	0-1	.963	1	98	182	O32(29/0/4)		-0.3
1961	LA A	133	453	74	127	19	2	28	79	48-2	3	65	.280	.348	.517	116	10	5-1	.971	0	89	148	O116(104/0/14)		0.4
1962	LA A★	160	612	96	164	21	5	37	107	50-4	5	87	.268	.326	.500	123	16	7-5	.972	-8	88	76	O156(102/0/62)		-0.1
1963	LA A★	149	550	73	160	11	1	26	90	49-8	1	73	.291	.352	.456	134	24	5-7	.960	-4	92	71	O141(136/0/7)		1.0
1964	Cle A	163	641	94	162	19	2	31	100	56-12	6	121	.253	.316	.434	108	5	14-2	.959	-6	92	63	O163L		-0.8
1965	Cle A	144	517	90	152	18	1	28	79	60-8	3	52	.294	.369	.495	143	29	12-2	.957	-12	78	40	O134L		1.2
1966	Cle A	150	549	70	153	20	0	23	66	46-9	1	69	.279	.334	.441	121	14	5-2	.990	-10	82	51	O139L		-0.2
1967	Cle A	135	433	56	105	15	1	15	54	37-6	12	76	.242	.317	.386	107	4	3-3	.980	-7	79	58	O117L		-1.1
1968	Cle A	38	49	5	9	4	0	0	6	6-0	1	6	.184	.273	.265	65	-2	0-0	.500	-3	27	0	O10(7/0/3)		-0.5
	Chi A	69	162	14	46	8	0	1	18	21-2	0	31	.284	.366	.352	117	4	2-1	.941	-6	72	0	O46(9/1/36)		-0.5
	Year	107	211	19	55	12	0	1	24	27-2	1	37	.261	.345	.332	105	3	2-1	.895	-9	65	0	O56(16/1/39)		-1.0
1969	SF N	11	12	0	4	0	0	0	2	2-1	1	1	.333	.467	.333	129	1	0-0	1.000	0	164	0	/OL		0.1
Total	12	1352	4426	636	1202	150	15	211	669	435-64	43	656	.272	.340	.455	121	117	54-24	.964	-56	86	72	O1140(1026/1/126)		-0.0

WAGNER, MARK Mark Duane B3.4.1954 Conneaut OH BR/TR/6-1/175* [DetA72 19/452] d8.20

YEAR	TM LG	G	AB	R	H	2B	3B	HR	RBI	BB-IB	HP	SO	AVG	OBP	SLG	AOPS	ABR	SB-CS	FA	FR	RNG	THR	GAMES AT POSITION	DL	BFW
1976	Det A	39	115	9	30	2	3	0	12	6-0	0	18	.261	.298	.330	80	-3	0-2	.947	7	116	110	S39		0.8
1977	Det A	22	48	4	7	0	1	1	3	4-0	1	12	.146	.222	.250	28	-5	0-1	.923	-1	118	107	S21/2		-0.4
1978	Det A	39	109	10	26	1	0	0	6	3-0	2	11	.239	.272	.284	55	-7	1-0	.964	-3	92	107	S35,2b4		-0.7
1979	Det A	75	146	16	40	3	0	1	13	16-0	0	25	.274	.341	.315	77	-4	3-2	.974	-6	96	98	S41,2b29,3b2/D		-0.7
1980	Det A	45	72	5	17	1	0	0	5	7-0	0	11	.236	.304	.250	52	-5	0-1	.935	-10	71	49	S28,3b9,2b6	21	-1.3
1981	Tex A	50	85	15	22	4	1	1	14	8-0	0	13	.259	.323	.365	102	0	1-1	.964	0	92	89	S43,2b4,3b2		0.3
1982	Tex A	60	179	14	43	4	1	0	8	10-0	1	28	.240	.280	.274	55	-11	1-0	.955	2	110	88	S60	73	-0.3
1983	Tex A	2	2	0	0	0	0	0	0	0-0	1	1	.000	.000	.000	-99	-1	0-0	1.000	0	193	0	S2	18	0.0
1984	Oak A	82	87	8	20	1	2	0	10	12-0	1	12	.230	.284	.310	69	-4	2-0	.951	-4	86	84	S57,3b15,2b8/PD	112	-0.4
Total	9	414	843	81	205	20	9	3	71	61-0	3	130	.243	.295	.299	66	-40	8-7	.953	-13	100	92	S326,2b52,3b28,D4/P		-2.6

WAGNER, BILL William Joseph B1.2.1894 Jesup IA D1.11.1951 Waterloo IA BR/TR/6-0/187 d7.16

YEAR	TM LG	G	AB	R	H	2B	3B	HR	RBI	BB-IB	HP	SO	AVG	OBP	SLG	AOPS	ABR	SB-CS	FA	FR	RNG	THR	GAMES AT POSITION	DL	BFW
1914	Pit N	3	1	0	0	0	0	0	0	0	0	0	.000	.000	.000	-99	0	0	1.000	0	0	316	C3		0.0
1915	Pit N	5	5	0	0	0	0	0	1	0	-1	0	2	.000	.167	.000	-48	-1	0	1.000	1	135	252	C3	0.1
1916	Pit N	19	38	2	9	0	0	0	2	5	0	8	.237	.326	.342	104	0	3	.936	9	139	C15		0.0
1917	Pit N	53	151	15	31	7	2	0	9	11	1	22	.205	.264	.278	64	-6	1	.958	-6	72	117	C37,1b12		-1.1
1918	Bos N	13	47	2	10	0	0	1	5	2	0	5	.213	.275	.277	71	-2	0	.917	-4	88	78	C13		-0.5
Total	5	93	242	19	50	7	4	1	18	21	0	37	.207	.273	.281	69	-9	1	.947	-9	81	117	C71,1b12		-1.5

WAHL, KERMIT Kermit Emerson B11.18.1922 Columbia SD D9.16.1987 Tucson AZ BR/TR/5-11/170* d6.23 Col Indiana

YEAR	TM LG	G	AB	R	H	2B	3B	HR	RBI	BB-IB	HP	SO	AVG	OBP	SLG	AOPS	ABR	SB-CS	FA	FR	RNG	THR	GAMES AT POSITION	DL	BFW
1944	Cin N	4	1	0	0	0	0	0	0	0	0	0	.000	.000	.000	-99	-1	0	—	0	0	0	/3		0.0
1945	Cin N	71	194	18	39	8	2	0	10	23	0	22	.201	.286	.263	54	-12	3	.948	-1	101	82	2b32,S31,3b7		-0.9
1947	Cin N	39	81	8	14	0	1	1	4	6	1	12	.173	.239	.210	20	-10	0	.964	3	97	70	3b20,S9,2b2		-0.7
1950	Phi A	89	280	26	72	12	3	2	27	30	1	30	.257	.331	.343	74	-11	1-1	.946	4	108	77	3b61,S18,2b2		-0.6
1951	Phi A	20	59	4	11	2	0	0	6	9	0	5	.186	.294	.203	40	-5	0-0	.967	2	110	117	3b18		-0.3

YEAR	TM LG	G	AB	R	H	2B	3B	HR	RBI	BB-IB	HP	SO	AVG	OBP	SLG	AOPS	ABR	SB-CS	FA	FR	RNG	THR	GAMES AT POSITION	DL	BFW
	StL A	8	27	2	9	1	1	0	3	0	0	3	.333	.333	.444	106	0	0-0	.950	1	103	205	3b6		0.0
	Year	28	86	6	20	3	1	0	9	9	0	8	.233	.305	.291	60	-5	0-0	.962	2	108	141	3b24		-0.3
Total	5	231	642	58	145	23	6	3	50	68	2	72	.226	.302	.294	60	-38	3-1	.949	8	107	86	3b113,S58,2b36		-2.5

WAITKUS, EDDIE Edward Stephen B9.4.1919 Cambridge MA D9.16.1972 Jamaica Plain MA BL/TL/6-1/175* d4.15 Mil 1942-45 Col Boston College

YEAR	TM LG	G	AB	R	H	2B	3B	HR	RBI	BB-IB	HP	SO	AVG	OBP	SLG	AOPS	ABR	SB-CS	FA	FR	RNG	THR	GAMES AT POSITION	DL	BFW
1941	Chi N	12	28	1	5	0	0	0	0	0	1	3	.179	.207	.179	10	-3	0	.949	-1	71	141	1b9		-0.6
1946	Chi N	113	441	50	134	24	5	4	55	23	1	14	.304	.340	.408	114	6	3	.996	3	105	89	1b106		0.6
1947	Chi N	130	514	60	150	28	6	2	35	32	2	17	.292	.336	.381	94	-6	3	.994	8	124	101	1b126		-0.1
1948	Chi N★	139	562	87	166	27	10	7	44	43	2	19	.295	.348	.416	110	7	11	.992	7	123	84	1b116,O20L		0.8
1949	Phi N*	54	209	41	64	16	3	1	28	33	1	12	.306	.403	.426	126	10	3	.994	1	106	114	1b54	93	0.8
1950	†Phi N	154	641	102	182	32	5	2	44	55	1	29	.284	.341	.359	86	-13	3	.993	-3	91	107	1b154		-2.1
1951	Phi N	145	610	65	157	27	4	1	46	53	0	22	.257	.317	.320	73	-23	0-3	.992	-3	92	91	1b144		-3.2
1952	Phi N	146	499	51	144	29	4	2	49	64	1	23	.289	.371	.375	108	-3	2-2	.991	-3	94	104	1b146		0.0
1953	Phi N	81	247	24	72	9	2	1	16	13	1	23	.291	.330	.356	79	-8	1-1	.989	-1	94	141	1b59		-1.2
1954	Bal A	95	311	35	88	17	4	2	33	28	1	25	.283	.341	.383	107	2	0-1	1.000	-0	91	104	1b78		-0.3
1955	Bal A	38	85	2	22	1	1	0	9	11-3	0	10	.259	.344	.294	78	-2	2-0	.974	-3	68	80	1b26	36	-0.6
	Phi N	33	107	10	30	5	0	2	14	17-1	1	7	.280	.379	.383	105	2	0-1	.996	0	96	126	1b31		-0.1
Total	11	1140	4254	528	1214	215	44	24	373	372-4	11	204	.285	.344	.374	96	-20	28-8	.993	5	101	101	1b1049,O20L	129	-6.0

WAITT, CHARLIE Charles C. B10.14.1853 Hallowell ME D10.21.1912 San Francisco CA TR/5-11/165 d5.25

YEAR	TM LG	G	AB	R	H	2B	3B	HR	RBI	BB-IB	HP	SO	AVG	OBP	SLG	AOPS	ABR	SB-CS	FA	FR	RNG	THR	GAMES AT POSITION	DL	BFW
1875	StL N	30	113	14	23	10	0	0	12	2		7	.204	.217	.292	83	0	3-2	.787	-2	72	284	O28(2/7/23),1b4		-0.1
1877	Chi N	10	41	2	4	0	0	0	2	0		3	.098	.098	.098	-34	-6		.793	1	135	264	O10N		-0.5
1882	Bal AA	72	250	19	39	4	0	0		13		2	.156	.198	.172	28	-17		.874	0	65	100	O72(60/0/12)		-1.7
1883	Phi N	1	3	0	1	0	0	0	0	0		1	.333	.333	.333	114	0		.333	-1	0	0	/OC		-0.1
Total	3	83	294	21	44	4	0	0	2	13		4	.150	.186	.163	18	-23		.855	0	74	122	O83(60/1/22)		-2.3

WAKAMATSU, DON Wilbur Donald B2.22.1963 Hood River OR BR/TR/6-2/200 [CinN85 11/266] d5.22 C3 Col Arizona St.

YEAR	TM LG	G	AB	R	H	2B	3B	HR	RBI	BB-IB	HP	SO	AVG	OBP	SLG	AOPS	ABR	SB-CS	FA	FR	RNG	THR	GAMES AT POSITION	DL	BFW
1991	Chi A	18	31	2	7	0	0	0		1-0	0	6	.226	.250	.226	33	-3	0-0	1.000	-3	325	60	C18		-0.5

WAKEFIELD, HOWARD Howard John B4.2.1884 Bucyrus OH D4.16.1941 Chicago IL BR/TR/6-1/185 d9.18 s-Dick

YEAR	TM LG	G	AB	R	H	2B	3B	HR	RBI	BB-IB	HP	SO	AVG	OBP	SLG	AOPS	ABR	SB-CS	FA	FR	RNG	THR	GAMES AT POSITION	DL	BFW
1905	Cle A	10	26	3	4	0	0	1	0	1	1		.154	.185	.154	8	-3	0	.926	-2	96	108	C8		-0.4
1906	Was A	77	211	17	59	9	1	1	21	7			.280	.303	.355	111	2	6	.946	-13	74	92	C60		-0.7
1907	Cle A	26	37	4	5	2	0	0	3	3	0		.135	.200	.189	24	-3	0	.930	-1	111	32	C11		-0.3
Total	3	113	274	24	68	11	2	1	25	10	1		.248	.277	.314	89	-4	6	.943	-15	80	87	C79		-1.4

WAKEFIELD, DICK Richard Cummings B5.6.1921 Chicago IL D8.26.1985 Redford MI BL/TR/6-4/210* d6.26 Mil 1944-45 f-Howard Col Michigan

YEAR	TM LG	G	AB	R	H	2B	3B	HR	RBI	BB-IB	HP	SO	AVG	OBP	SLG	AOPS	ABR	SB-CS	FA	FR	RNG	THR	GAMES AT POSITION	DL	BFW
1941	Det A	7	7	0	1	0	0	0	0	0		1	.143	.143	.143	-22	0	0-0	1.000	0	114	0	/OR		-0.1
1943	Det A★	155	633	91	200	38	8	7	79	62	0	60	.316	.377	.434	127	22	4-5	.959	-7	92	90	O155(140/0/15)		0.5
1944	Det A	78	276	53	98	15	5	12	53	55	1	29	.355	.464	.576	186	34	2-2	.963	-5	93	46	O78L		2.4
1946	Det A	111	396	64	106	11	5	12	59	59	1	55	.268	.364	.412	110	6	3-5	.964	-2	96	87	O104L		-0.6
1947	Det A	112	368	59	104	15	5	8	51	80	1	44	.283	.412	.416	127	17	1-4	.950	-2	90	148	O101L		0.7
1948	Det A	110	322	50	89	20	5	11	53	70	0	55	.276	.406	.472	129	16	0-1	.948	-2	105	47	O86L		0.7
1949	Det A	59	126	17	26	3	1	6	19	32	0	24	.206	.367	.389	100	1	0-0	1.000	2	103	131	O32L		0.0
1950	NY A	3	2	1	1	0	0	0	1	1	0	1	.500	.667	.500	208	1	0-0	—	0			/H		0.0
1952	NY N	3	2	0	0	0	0	0	0	1	0	1	.000	.333	.000	-0	0	0-0	—	0			/H		0.0
Total	9	638	2132	334	625	102	29	56	315	360	3	270	.293	.396	.447	130	96	10-17	.959	-16	95	89	O557(541/0/16)		3.6

WAKELAND, CHRIS Christopher Robert B6.15.1974 Huntington Beach CA BL/TL/6-0/185 [DetA96 15/431] d9.4 Col Oregon St.

YEAR	TM LG	G	AB	R	H	2B	3B	HR	RBI	BB-IB	HP	SO	AVG	OBP	SLG	AOPS	ABR	SB-CS	FA	FR	RNG	THR	GAMES AT POSITION	DL	BFW
2001	Det A	10	36	5	9	2	0	2	6	0	0	13	.250	.250	.472	86	-1	0-0	.941	2	164	0	O10R		0.0

WALBECK, MATT Matthew Lovick B10.2.1969 Sacramento CA BB/TR/5-11/206(188-206) [ChiN87 8/192] d4.7

YEAR	TM LG	G	AB	R	H	2B	3B	HR	RBI	BB-IB	HP	SO	AVG	OBP	SLG	AOPS	ABR	SB-CS	FA	FR	RNG	THR	GAMES AT POSITION	DL	BFW
1993	Chi N	11	30	2	6	2	0	1	6	1-0	0	6	.200	.226	.367	56	-2	0-0	1.000	-1	74	37	C11		-0.2
1994	Min A	97	338	31	69	12	0	5	35	17-1	2	37	.204	.246	.284	36	-33	1-1	.993	-3	94	149	C95/D		-2.9
1995	Min A	115	393	40	101	18	1	1	44	25-2	1	71	.257	.302	.316	61	-23	3-1	.991	-14	107	68	C113		-2.7
1996	Min A	63	215	25	48	10	0	2	24	9-0	0	34	.223	.252	.298	38	-21	3-1	.994	-3	106	93	C61	77	-1.9
1997	Det A	47	137	18	38	3	0	3	10	12-0	0	19	.277	.331	.365	83	-4	3-3	.988	-3	94	98	C44	81	-0.4
1998	Ana A	108	338	41	87	15	2	6	46	30-0	2	68	.257	.317	.367	77	-12	1-1	.990	2	72	131	C104,D2		-0.3
1999	Ana A	107	288	26	69	8	1	3	22	26-1	3	46	.240	.308	.306	58	-19	2-3	.989	-9	91	116	C97/D		-2.1
2000	Ana A	47	146	17	29	5	0	6	12	7-0	1	22	.199	.240	.356	47	-13	0-0	.991	-4	73	165	C44,1b2/D	14	-1.3
2001	Phi N	1	1	0	1	0	0	0	0	0-0	0	0	1.000	1.000	1.000	441	0	0-0	—	0			/H		0.0
2002	Det A	27	85	4	20	2	0	3	3	3-0	0	14	.235	.258	.259	41	-7	0-0	.993	-1	229	32	C27		-0.7
2003	Det A	59	138	11	24	4	1	1	6	3-0	1	26	.174	.197	.239	15	-18	0-1	.979	-11	66	115	C55/D		-2.5
Total	11	682	2109	215	492	79	5	28	208	133-4	10	343	.233	.280	.315	54	-152	13-12	.991	-46	96	110	C651,D6,1b2	172	-15.0

WALCZAK, ED Edwin Joseph "Husky" B9.21.1918 Arctic RI D3.10.1998 Norwich CT BR/TR/5-11/180 d9.3

YEAR	TM LG	G	AB	R	H	2B	3B	HR	RBI	BB-IB	HP	SO	AVG	OBP	SLG	AOPS	ABR	SB-CS	FA	FR	RNG	THR	GAMES AT POSITION	DL	BFW
1945	Phi N	20	57	6	12	0	0	0	5	3-0	0	9	.211	.286	.263	55	-3	0	.966	0	91	134	2b17,S2		-0.2

WALDEN, FRED Thomas Fred B6.25.1890 Fayette MO D9.27.1955 Jefferson Barracks MO BR/TR d6.3

YEAR	TM LG	G	AB	R	H	2B	3B	HR	RBI	BB-IB	HP	SO	AVG	OBP	SLG	AOPS	ABR	SB-CS	FA	FR	RNG	THR	GAMES AT POSITION	DL	BFW
1912	StL A	1	0	0	0	0	0	0	0	0	0	0	—	—	—		0	0	.000	-1	34	0	/C		-0.1

WALDRON, IRV Irving J. B1.21.1876 Hillside NY D7.22.1944 Worcester MA BL/TR/5-5.5/155 d4.25

YEAR	TM LG	G	AB	R	H	2B	3B	HR	RBI	BB-IB	HP	SO	AVG	OBP	SLG	AOPS	ABR	SB-CS	FA	FR	RNG	THR	GAMES AT POSITION	DL	BFW
1901	Mil A	62	266	48	79	8	6	0	29	16	2		.297	.342	.372	103	1	12	.883	-2	112	0	O62R		-0.4
	Was A	79	332	54	107	14	3	0	23	22	2		.322	.368	.383	110	5	8	.955	-3	76	0	O78(0/69/9)		-0.1
	Year	141	598	102	186	22	9	0	52	38	4		.311	.356	.378	107	6	20	.923	-6	93	0	O140(0/69/71)		-0.5

WALEWANDER, JIM James B5.2.1962 Chicago IL BB/TR/5-10/160* [DetA83 9/225] d5.31 Col Iowa St.

YEAR	TM LG	G	AB	R	H	2B	3B	HR	RBI	BB-IB	HP	SO	AVG	OBP	SLG	AOPS	ABR	SB-CS	FA	FR	RNG	THR	GAMES AT POSITION	DL	BFW
1987	Det A	53	54	24	13	3	1	1	4	7-0	0	6	.241	.328	.389	93	-1	2-1	1.000	2	112	136	2b24,3b17,S3,D8		0.2
1988	Det A	88	175	23	37	5	0	0	6	12-0	0	26	.211	.261	.240	43	-13	11-4	.977	-5	93	109	2b61,S8,3b3,D9		-1.6
1990	NY A	9	5	1	1	0	0	0	1	0-0	0	0	.200	.200	.200	63	0	1-1	1.000	-0	50	0	2b3,3b/SD		0.0
1993	Cal A★	12	8	2	1	0	0	0	3	5-0	0	1	.125	.429	.125	64	0	1-1	1.000	1	114	163	S6,2b2,D3		0.1
Total	4	162	242	50	52	9	1	1	14	24-0	0	33	.215	.284	.273	57	-14	15-7	.982	-2	95	112	2b89,D22,3b22,S18		-1.3

WALKER, RUBE Albert Bluford B5.16.1926 Lenoir NC D12.12.1992 Morganton NC BL/TR/6-1/185(185-208) d4.20 C21

YEAR	TM LG	G	AB	R	H	2B	3B	HR	RBI	BB-IB	HP	SO	AVG	OBP	SLG	AOPS	ABR	SB-CS	FA	FR	RNG	THR	GAMES AT POSITION	DL	BFW
1948	Chi N	79	171	17	47	8	0	5	26	24	2	17	.275	.371	.409	115	4	0	.980	-2	97	123	C44		0.4
1949	Chi N	56	172	11	42	4	1	3	22	9	0	18	.244	.282	.331	66	-9	0	.964	-5	64	124	C43	70	-1.2
1950	Chi N	74	213	19	49	7	1	6	16	18	0	34	.230	.290	.357	70	-10	0	.975	-2	66	129	C62		-0.8
1951	Chi N	37	107	9	25	4	0	2	5	12	0	13	.234	.311	.327	71	-4	0-0	.969	-4	57	107	C31		-0.3
	Bro N	36	74	6	18	4	0	2	9	6	0	14	.243	.300	.378	80	-2	0-0	.972	-2	242	102	C23		-0.3
	Year	73	181	15	43	8	0	4	14	18	0	27	.238	.307	.348	74	-7	0-0	.970	-6	121	105	C54		-1.0
1952	Bro N	46	139	9	36	8	0	1	19	8	1	11	.259	.304	.338	77	-4	0-0	.987	2	169	105	C40		-0.1
1953	Bro N	43	95	12	23	6	0	3	19	9	1	17	.242	.301	.400	79	-3	0-0	.978	1	161	123	C28		-0.6
1954	Bro N	50	155	12	28	7	0	5	23	9	1	17	.181	.291	.323	59	-9	0-0	.996	1	152	84	C47		-0.6
1955	Bro N	48	103	6	26	5	0	2	13	15-4	0	11	.252	.342	.359	86	-2	1-0	.987	2	116	73	C35		0.1
1956	†Bro N	54	146	5	31	6	1	3	20	7-2	0	18	.212	.245	.329	50	-11	0-1	.986	1	139	123	C43		-0.8
1957	Bro N	60	166	12	30	8	0	2	23	15-4	0	33	.181	.243	.265	35	-15	2-0	.992	-0	115	97	C50		-1.3
1958	LA N	25	44	3	5	2	0	1	7	5-2	0	10	.114	.200	.227	14	-6	0-0	.985	-1	156	158	C20		-0.7
Total	11	608	1585	114	360	69	3	35	192	150-12	5	213	.227	.294	.341	68	-71	3-1	.982	-8	117	111	C466	70	-5.9

WALKER, TONY Anthony Bruce B7.1.1959 San Diego CA BR/TR/6-2/205 d4.8

YEAR	TM LG	G	AB	R	H	2B	3B	HR	RBI	BB-IB	HP	SO	AVG	OBP	SLG	AOPS	ABR	SB-CS	FA	FR	RNG	THR	GAMES AT POSITION	DL	BFW
1986	Hou N	84	90	19	20	2	0	0	6	15			.222	.307	.367	87	-1	11-3	.986	0	119	0	O68C		0.0

WALKER, FRANK Charles Franklin B9.22.1894 Enoree SC D9.16.1974 Bristol TN BR/TR/5-11/165 d9.6 Col Randolph-Macon

YEAR	TM LG	G	AB	R	H	2B	3B	HR	RBI	BB-IB	HP	SO	AVG	OBP	SLG	AOPS	ABR	SB-CS	FA	FR	RNG	THR	GAMES AT POSITION	DL	BFW
1917	Det A	2	2	0	0	0	0	0	0	0		1	.000	.000	.000	-99	0	0	—	0			/H		-0.1
1918	Det A	55	167	10	33	10	3	1	20	7	1	29	.198	.234	.311	67	-8	3	.922	-2	103	80	O45(3/34/9)		-1.4
1920	Phi A	24	91	10	21	2	2	0	10	5	2	14	.231	.286	.297	54	-6	0-2	.983	-2	98	33	O24C		-1.1
1921	Phi A	19	66	6	15	3	1	0	6	8	1	11	.227	.311	.318	60	-4	1-0	.961	0	97	122	O19(3/16/0)		-0.4
1925	NY N	39	81	12	18	1	0	3	5	9	1	11	.222	.308	.272	51	-6	1-1	.960	-1	86	162	O21(0/21/1)		-0.7
Total	5	139	407	38	87	16	5	3	41	29	4	66	.214	.273	.300	58	-24	5-3	.949	-4	98	91	O109(6/95/10)		-3.7

YEAR	TM LG	G	AB	R	H	2B	3B	HR	RBI	BB-IB	HP	SO	AVG	OBP	SLG	AOPS	ABR	SB-CS	FA	FR	RNG	THR	GAMES AT POSITION	DL	BFW
WALKER, TILLY Clarence William B9.4.1887 Telford TN D9.20.1959 Unicoi TN BR/TR/5-11/165 d6.10 Col Washington College																									
1911	Was A	95	356	44	99	6	4	2	39	15	2		.278	.311	.334	82	-10	12	.917	-2	98	98	O94L		-1.6
1912	Was A	39	110	22	30	2	1	0	9	8	2		.273	.333	.309	83	-2	11	.837	-1	80	164	O34(4/7/23)/2		-0.5
1913	StL A	23	85	7	25	4	1	0	11	2	0	9	.294	.310	.365	100	-1	5	.911	0	86	165	O23L		-0.2
1914	StL A	151	517	67	154	24	16	6	78	51	4	72	.298	.365	.441	148	28	29-17	.972	17	112	144	O145L		4.2
1915	StL A	144	510	53	137	20	7	5	49	36	5	77	.269	.323	.365	110	4	20-17	.940	9	106	135	O139(1/119/19)		0.1
1916	†Bos A	128	467	68	124	29	11	3	46	23	2	45	.266	.303	.394	109	2	14	.959	-5	101	69	O128(3/125/0)		-1.3
1917	Bos A	106	337	41	83	18	7	2	37	25	1	38	.246	.300	.359	102	-1	6	.972	4	96	144	O96C		-0.4
1918	Phi A	114	414	56	122	20	0	**11**	48	41	1	44	.295	.360	.423	135	17	8	.953	3	94	155	O109C		1.3
1919	Phi A	125	456	47	133	30	6	10	64	26	0	41	.292	.330	.450	116	8	8	.933	-4	98	89	O115(28/85/2)		-0.3
1920	Phi A	149	585	79	157	23	7	17	82	41	4	59	.268	.321	.419	94	-8	8-3	.940	-0	94	127	O149(123/26/0)		-1.5
1921	Phi A	142	556	89	169	32	5	23	101	73	4	41	.304	.389	.504	125	22	3-5	.955	5	102	125	O142L		1.3
1922	Phi A	153	565	111	160	31	4	37	99	61	4	67	.283	.357	.549	130	22	4-3	.956	-2	95	103	O148(137/11/0)		0.8
1923	Phi A	52	109	12	30	5	2	2	16	14	2	11	.275	.368	.413	104	1	1-2	1.000	-1	102	34	O26L		-0.2
Total	13	1421	5067	696	1423	244	71	118	679	416	31	504	.281	.339	.427	115	82	129-47	.949	23	99	119	O1348(726/578/44)/2		1.7
WALKER, CHICO Cleotha B11.25.1958 Jackson MS BB/TR/5-9/179(160-185) [BosA76 22/525] d9.2																									
1980	Bos A	19	57	3	12	0	0	1	5	6-1	1	10	.211	.292	.263	52	-4	3-2	.958	-2	101	98	2b11,D7		-0.5
1981	Bos A	6	17	3	6	0	0	0	2	1-0	0	1	.353	.389	.353	108	-3	0-2	1.000	-2	81	35	2b5		-0.3
1983	Bos A	4	5	2	2	0	2	0	1	0-0	0	0	.400	.400	1.200	298	1	0-0	1.000	1	146	977	O3L		0.2
1984	Bos A	3	2	0	0	0	0	0	1	0-0	0	1	.000	.000	.000	-95	-1	0-0	1.000	0	146		/2		-0.1
1985	Chi N	21	12	3	1	0	0	0	0	0-0	0	5	.083	.083	.083	-48	-2	1-0	1.000	-0	92		O6(3/0/3),2b2		-0.3
1986	Chi N	28	101	21	28	3	2	1	7	10-0	0	20	.277	.339	.376	91	-1	15-4	.956	-3	83	56	O26(1/11/22)		-0.3
1987	Chi N	47	105	15	21	4	0	0	7	12-1	0	23	.200	.277	.238	38	-9	11-4	.974	-4	74	0	O33(25/3/5),3b2		-1.4
1988	Cal A	33	78	8	12	1	0	0	2	6-0	0	15	.154	.214	.167	8	-10	2-1	.933	-2	76	149	O17(5/12/0),2b7,3b2		-1.2
1991	Chi N	124	374	51	96	10	1	6	34	33-2	0	57	.257	.315	.337	80	-10	13-5	.929	-7	87	99	3b57,O53(20/36/8),2b6		-1.7
1992	Chi N	19	26	2	3	0	0	0	2	3-0	0	4	.115	.200	.115	-6	-4	1-0	1.000	-1	206		O6(6/0/1),2b2,3b2		-0.3
	NY N	107	227	24	70	12	1	4	36	24-3	0	46	.308	.369	.423	127	8	14-1	.971	-0	102	-44	3b36,2b16,O15(9/4/2)		1.2
	Year	126	253	26	73	12	1	4	38	27-3	0	50	.289	.351	.391	112	5	15-1	.960	1	105	42	3b38,O21(15/4/2),2b18		0.9
1993	NY N	115	213	18	48	7	1	5	19	14-0	0	29	.225	.271	.338	63	-12	7-0	.976	-4	113	98	2b24,3b23,O15(15/0/1)		-0.6
Total	11	526	1217	150	299	37	7	17	116	109-7	1	212	.246	.305	.329	75	-44	67-19	.968	-14	84	127	O174(87/66/42),3b122,2b74,D7		-5.3
WALKER, DUANE Duane Allen B3.13.1957 Pasadena TX BL/TL/6-0/185* [CinN76*S1/22] d5.25 Col San Jacinto North (TX) JC																									
1982	Cin N	86	239	26	52	10	0	5	22	27-0	2	58	.218	.298	.322	74	-8	9-3	.992	1	94	150	O69(40/2/31)		-0.9
1983	Cin N	109	225	14	53	12	1	2	29	20-4	0	43	.236	.296	.324	70	-9	6-3	.956	3	113	114	O60(35/0/26)		-0.9
1984	Cin N	83	195	35	57	10	3	10	28	33-2	0	35	.292	.391	.528	150	14	7-3	.950	-0	105	77	O68(51/13/9)	.43	1.2
1985	Cin N	37	48	5	8	2	1	2	6	6-1	0	18	.167	.259	.375	72	-2	1-0	.882	-0	120	0	O10(8/0/2)		-0.2
	Tex A	53	132	14	23	2	0	5	11	15-0	1	29	.174	.264	.303	54	-9	2-1	1.000	3	94	340	O32(12/0/23),D10		-0.7
1988	StL N	24	22	1	4	1	0	0	3	2-0	0	7	.182	.250	.227	37	-0	1-0	—	-1	0	0	O4(2/0/2)/1		-0.3
Total	5	392	861	95	197	37	5	24	99	103-7	3	190	.229	.311	.367	87	-16	25-10	.967	6	102	142	O243(148/15/93),D10/1	43	-1.8
WALKER, ERNIE Ernest Robert B9.17.1890 Blossburg AL D4.1.1965 Pell City AL BL/TR/6-0/165 d4.13 b-Dixie																									
1913	StL A	7	14	0	3	0	0	0	2	0	0	5	.214	.214	.214	26	-1	0	1.000	-0	113	0	O2C		-0.2
1914	StL A	74	131	19	39	5	3	1	14	13	1	26	.298	.366	.405	137	6	6-4	.960	-1	96	87	O38(21/9/10)		0.4
1915	StL A	50	109	15	23	4	2	0	9	23	0	32	.211	.348	.284	93	0	5-8	.881	-3	89	32	O33(3/3/27)		-0.6
Total	3	131	254	34	65	9	5	1	25	36	1	63	.256	.351	.343	112	5	11-12	.928	-4	93	57	O73(24/14/37)		-0.4
WALKER, DIXIE Fred "The People's Cherce" B9.24.1910 Villa Rica GA D5.17.1982 Birmingham AL BL/TR/6-1/175 d4.28 C5 b-Harry f-Dixie																									
1931	NY A	2	10	1	3	2	0	0	1	0	0	4	.300	.300	.500	113	0	0-0	1.000	-0	74	0	O2(1/0/1)		0.0
1933	NY A	98	328	68	90	15	7	15	51	26	1	28	.274	.330	.500	125	9	2-2	.962	1	102	117	O77(15/60/3)		0.6
1934	NY A	17	17	2	2	0	0	0	0	1	0	3	.118	.167	.118	-27	-3	0-0	1.000	-0	87	0	/OL		-0.3
1935	NY A	8	13	1	2	1	0	0	1	0	0	1	.154	.154	.231	-2	-2	0-0	.750	-0	85	0	O2L		-0.2
1936	NY A	6	20	3	7	0	2	1	5	1	0	3	.350	.381	.700	167	2	1-1	1.000	-0	90	0	O5C		0.1
	Chi A	26	70	12	19	2	0	0	11	14	1	6	.271	.400	.300	73	-2	1-0	1.000	1	101	134	O17(0/16/1)		-0.2
	Year	32	90	15	26	2	2	1	16	15	1	9	.289	.396	.389	92	-1	2-1	1.000	0	99	109	O22(0/21/1)		-0.1
1937	Chi A	**154**	593	105	179	28	**16**	9	95	78	0	26	.302	.383	.449	109	8	1-2	.952	-10	92	70	O154R		-1.0
1938	Det A	127	454	84	140	27	6	6	43	65	1	32	.308	.396	.434	102	3	5-4	.979	-3	94	96	O114(94/26/0)		-0.5
1939	Det A	43	154	30	47	4	5	4	19	15	0	8	.305	.367	.474	106	0	4-3	.970	2	105	138	O37(23/4/11)		0.1
	Bro N	61	225	27	63	6	4	2	38	20	0	10	.280	.339	.369	87	-4	1	.968	-1	97	104	O59C		-0.7
1940	Bro N	143	556	75	171	37	8	6	66	42	1	21	.308	.357	.435	111	8	3	.973	-5	102	50	O136(14/112/20)		-0.1
1941	†Bro N	148	531	88	165	32	8	9	71	70	0	18	.311	.391	.452	131	24	4	.976	10	106	160	O146(22/22/105)		2.6
1942	Bro N	118	393	57	114	28	1	6	54	47	0	15	.290	.367	.412	126	14	1	.986	0	103	87	O110(0/7/104)		0.9
1943	Bro N★	138	540	83	163	32	6	5	71	49	3	24	.302	.363	.411	123	16	3	.969	4	99	152	O136(57/0/82)		1.3
1944	Bro N★	147	535	77	191	37	8	13	91	72	4	27	**.357**	.434	.529	173	55	6	.962	2	100	124	O140(19/0/125)		4.9
1945	Bro N★	154	607	102	182	42	9	8	**124**	75	5	16	.300	.381	.438	128	25	6	.992	10	109	124	O153R		2.4
1946	Bro N★	150	576	80	184	29	9	9	116	67	1	28	.319	.391	.448	136	28	14	.969	-9	85	103	O149R		1.6
1947	†Bro N★	148	529	77	162	31	3	9	94	97	1	26	.306	.415	.427	119	20	6	.964	-8	92	74	O147R		0.7
1948	Pit N	129	408	39	129	19	3	2	54	52	0	18	.316	.393	.392	111	9	1	.977	-6	91	57	O112(1/1/110)		0.0
1949	Pit N	88	181	26	51	4	1	1	18	26	0	11	.282	.372	.331	88	-2	0	.984	-2	93	60	O39R,1b3		-0.5
Total	18	1905	6740	1037	2064	376	96	105	1023	817	16	325	.306	.383	.437	121	208	59-10	.972	-14	98	102	O1736(249/312/1204),1b3		11.7
WALKER, GEE Gerald Holmes B3.19.1908 Gulfport MS D3.20.1981 Whitfield MS BR/TR/5-11/188 d4.14 C1 b-Hub Col U. of Mississippi																									
1931	Det A	59	189	20	56	17	2	1	28	14	0	21	.296	.345	.423	98	-1	10-7	.953	-5	86	59	O44(1/41/1)		-0.6
1932	Det A	127	480	71	155	32	6	8	78	13	3	48	.323	.346	.465	104	1	30-6	.949	1	105	96	O116(39/79/0)		0.2
1933	Det A	127	483	68	135	29	7	9	64	15	2	49	.280	.304	.424	89	-10	26-9	.942	-4	94	89	O113(92/8/13)		-1.7
1934	†Det A	98	347	54	104	19	2	6	39	19	2	20	.300	.340	.418	94	-4	20-9	.947	-0	104	80	O80(9/48/23)		-0.6
1935	†Det A	98	362	52	109	22	6	7	53	15	0	21	.301	.330	.453	104	0	46-4	.954	-3	103	31	O85(29/45/11)		-0.6
1936	Det A	134	550	105	194	55	5	12	93	23	8	30	.353	.387	.536	125	21	17-8	.948	1	101	117	O125(2/21/103)		1.4
1937	Det A★	151	635	105	213	42	4	18	113	41	5	74	.335	.380	.499	117	16	23-7	.956	-3	98	69	O151(88/11/54)		0.4
1938	Chi A	120	442	69	135	23	6	16	87	30	8	32	.305	.360	.493	109	4	9-4	.958	-5	91	102	O107(50/0/57)		-0.5
1939	Chi A	149	598	95	174	30	11	13	111	28	7	43	.291	.330	.443	94	-9	17-6	.967	8	110	108	O147L		-0.8
1940	Was A	140	595	87	175	29	7	13	96	24	3	58	.294	.325	.432	101	-3	21-4	.967	-2	96	100	O140L		-0.8
1941	Cle A	121	445	56	126	26	11	6	48	18	1	46	.283	.313	.431	100	-4	12-6	.982	5	111	98	O105(103/2/0)		-0.4
1942	Cin N	119	422	40	97	20	2	5	50	31	5	44	.230	.290	.322	79	-12	11	.973	-2	103	68	O110(20/74/19)		-1.9
1943	Cin N	114	429	48	105	23	2	3	54	12	3	48	.245	.270	.329	74	-16	6	.980	-6	91	79	O106(15/75/17)		-2.9
1944	Cin N	121	478	56	133	21	3	5	62	23	5	48	.278	.318	.366	96	-4	7	.967	-9	100	24	O117(1/59/61)		-1.9
1945	Cin N	106	316	30	80	11	2	2	21	16	0	38	.253	.289	.320	71	-14	8	.962	-5	93	67	O67(6/0/61),3b3		-2.3
Total	15	1784	6771	954	1901	399	76	124	997	330	52	600	.294	.331	.430	99	-35	223-70	.961	-31	100	82	O1613(742/463/420),3b3		-13.0
WALKER, GREG Gregory Lee B10.6.1959 Douglas GA BL/TR/6-3/210(198-212) [PhiN77 20/511] d9.18 C3																									
1982	Chi A	11	17	3	7	2	1	2	7	2-0	2	1	.412	.474	1.000	291	3	0-0	—	0			D4		0.4
1983	†Chi A	118	307	32	83	16	3	10	55	28-3	2	57	.270	.332	.440	107	3	2-1	.985	-5	62	105	1b59,D21		-0.6
1984	Chi A	136	442	62	130	29	2	24	75	35-3	2	66	.294	.344	.532	133	19	8-5	.995	-5	78	93	1b101,D21		0.8
1985	Chi A	**163**	601	77	155	38	4	24	92	44-6	2	100	.258	.309	.454	102	5	5-2	.994	-1	91	91	1b151,D7		-0.9
1986	Chi A	78	282	37	78	10	6	13	51	29-4	2	44	.277	.345	.493	121	8	1-2	.993	-1	94	93	1b77/D	93	0.1
1987	Chi A	157	566	85	145	33	2	27	94	75-7	5	112	.256	.346	.465	110	9	2-1	.994	-15	71	112	1b154,D3		-1.5
1988	Chi A	99	377	45	93	22	1	8	42	29-3	5	50	.247	.304	.374	89	-5	0-1	.993	-13	58	106	1b98	65	-2.7
1989	Chi A	77	233	25	49	14	0	5	26	23-2	3	50	.210	.286	.335	77	-7	0-0	.987	-5	59	101	1b48,D23	16	-1.7
1990	Chi A	2	5	0	1	0	0	0	0	2-0	1	2	.200	.200	.200	12	-1	0-0	1.000	0	155	264	/1D		-0.1
	Bal A	14	34	2	5	0	0	0	2	3-0	1	9	.147	.237	.147	10	-4	1-0	—	0	0	0	D11		-0.4
	Year	16	39	2	6	0	0	0	2	3-0	1	11	.154	.233	.154	0	-5	1-0	1.000	0	155	264	D12/1		-0.5
Total	9	855	2864	368	746	164	19	113	444	268-28	20	520	.260	.326	.449	107	26	19-12	.993	-45	76	101	1b689,D92	174	-6.6

YEAR	TM LG	G	AB	R	H	2B	3B	HR	RBI	BB-IB	HP	SO	AVG	OBP	SLG	AOPS	ABR	SB-CS	FA	FR	RNG	THR	GAMES AT POSITION	DL	BFW

WALKER, HARRY   Harry William "Harry the Hat"   B10.22.1916 Pascagoula MS   D8.8.1999 Birmingham AL   BL/TR/6-2/190*   d9.25   Mil 1944-45   M9/C4   b-Dixie f-Dixie

1940	StL N	7	27	2	5	2	0	0	6	0	0	2	.185	.185	.259	20	-3	0	1.000	2	125	350	O7(2/5/1)		-0.1
1941	StL N	7	15	3	4	1	0	0	1	2	0	1	.267	.353	.333	88	0	0	.875	-0	94	0	O5L		-0.1
1942	†StL N	74	191	38	60	12	2	0	16	11	1	14	.314	.355	.398	112	3	2	.968	2	104	145	O56(12/43/3),2b2		-0.9
1943	†StL N★	148	564	76	166	28	6	2	53	40	1	24	.294	.341	.376	102	1	5	.965	-6	92	111	O144(0/143/1)/2		-1.2
1946	†StL N	112	346	53	82	14	6	3	27	30	1	29	.237	.300	.338	77	-11	12	.974	3	102	146	O92(13/79/0),1b8		-1.2
1947	StL N	10	25	2	5	1	0	0	0	4	0	2	.200	.310	.240	46	-2	0	.938	-1	87	0	O10(2/7/0)		-0.3
	Phi N★	130	488	79	181	28	16	1	41	59	4	37	.371	.443	.500	156	41	13	.966	5	103	167	O127C,1b4		4.1
	Year	140	513	81	186	29	16	1	41	63	4	39	.363	.436	.487	150	39	13	.964	4	102	159	O137(2/134/0),1b4		3.8
1948	Phi N	112	332	34	97	11	2	2	23	33	1	30	.292	.358	.355	95	-2	4	.981	2	106	108	O81(21/58/3),1b4/3		-0.2
1949	Chi N	42	159	20	42	6	3	1	14	11	0	8	.264	.312	.358	81	-5	2	.947	-3	85	92	O39(27/0/13)		-1.0
	Cin N	86	314	53	100	15	2	1	23	34	0	17	.318	.385	.389	107	4	4	.963	-2	97	106	O77(22/26/29)/1		0.0
	Year	128	473	73	142	21	5	2	37	45	0	23	.300	.361	.378	99	0	6	.959	-4	93	101	O116(49/26/42)/1		-1.0
1950	StL N	60	150	17	31	5	0	0	7	18	0	12	.207	.292	.240	40	-13	0	.969	-0	101	101	O46(9/30/3),1b2		-1.4
1951	StL N	8	26	6	8	1	0	0	2	2	0	1	.308	.357	.346	90	0	0-0	1.000	-1	84	0	O6(2/4/0)/1		-0.1
1955	StL N	11	14	2	5	2	0	0	1	1-0	0	0	.357	.400	.500	137	0	0-0	1.000	1	79	1064	/OLM		0.2
Total	11	807	2651	385	786	126	37	10	214	245-0	7	175	.296	.358	.383	103	14	42-0	.968	2	99	128	O691(116/522/53),1b20,2b3/3		-0.7

WALKER, HUB   Harvey Willos   B8.17.1906 Gulfport MS   D11.26.1982 San Jose CA   BL/TR/5-10.5/175   d4.15   Mil 1942-44   b-Gee   Col U. of Mississippi

1931	Det A	90	252	27	72	13	1	0	16	23	0	4	.286	.355	.345	82	-6	10-1	.961	-2	98	78	O66(4/60/2)		-0.7
1935	Det A	9	25	4	4	3	0	0	1	3	0	4	.160	.250	.280	38	-2	0-0	1.000	0	112	0	O7C		-0.2
1936	Cin N	92	258	49	71	18	1	4	23	35	2	32	.275	.366	.399	113	6	8	.970	-0	101	85	O73(25/47/2)/C1		0.4
1937	Cin N	78	221	33	55	9	4	1	19	34	0	24	.249	.349	.339	92	-1	7	.993	1	101	110	O58(17/40/1),2b3		-0.2
1945	†Det A	28	23	4	3	0	0	0	1	9	0	4	.130	.375	.130	46	-1	1-0	1.000	-0	89	0	O7(5/0/2)		-0.1
Total	5	297	779	117	205	43	6	5	60	104	6	89	.263	.354	.353	92	-4	26-1	.975	-1	100	86	O211(51/154/7),2b3/1C		-0.8

WALKER, JOHNNY   John Miles   B12.11.1896 Toulon IL   D8.19.1976 Hollywood FL   BR/TR/6-0/175   d9.19

1919	Phi A	3	9	0	0	0	0	0	0	0	0	1	.000	.000	.000	-99	-2	0	.941	-1	73	56	C3		-0.3
1920	Phi A	9	22	0	5	1	0	0	5	0	0	1	.227	.227	.273	32	-2	0-0	.960	-0	106	102	C6		-0.2
1921	Phi A	113	423	41	109	14	5	2	46	9	3	29	.258	.278	.329	54	-31	5-0	.989	-7	75	99	1b99,C7		-4.2
Total	3	125	454	41	114	15	5	2	51	9	3	32	.251	.270	.319	50	-35	5-0	.989	-8	75	99	1b99,C16		-4.7

WALKER, SPEED   Joseph Richard   B1.23.1898 Munhall PA   D6.20.1959 W.Mifflin PA   BR/TR/6-0/170   d9.15

| 1923 | StL N | 2 | 7 | 1 | 2 | 0 | 0 | 0 | 1 | 0 | 0 | 1 | .286 | .286 | .286 | 52 | -1 | | 1.000 | -0 | 0 | 69 | 1b2 | | -0.1 |

WALKER, LARRY   Larry Kenneth Robert   B12.1.1966 Maple Ridge BC, Can.   BL/TR/6-3/225(205-237)   d8.16   [DL 1988 Mon N 182]

1989	Mon N	20	47	4	8	0	0	0	4	5-0	1	13	.170	.264	.170	26	-4	1-1	1.000	0	78	292	O15(2/0/13)		-0.5
1990	Mon N	133	419	59	101	18	3	19	51	49-5	5	112	.241	.326	.434	112	6	21-7	.985	6	105	145	O124R		1.1
1991	Mon N	137	487	59	141	30	2	16	64	42-2	5	102	.290	.349	.458	127	18	14-9	.991	8	119	86	O102(0/5/99),1b39	15	2.1
1992	Mon N★	143	528	85	159	31	4	23	93	41-10	6	97	.301	.353	.506	143	29	18-6	.993	9	98	169	O139R		3.4
1993	Mon N	138	490	85	130	24	5	22	86	80-20	6	76	.265	.371	.469	119	15	29-7	.979	4	102	128	O132R,1b4	15	1.6
1994	Mon N	103	395	76	127	44	2	19	86	47-5	4	74	.322	.394	.587	151	32	15-5	.973	-0	102	97	O68R,1b35		2.6
1995	†Col N	131	494	96	151	31	5	36	101	49-13	14	72	.306	.381	.607	122	16	16-3	.988	-1	91	140	O129(0/4/129)		1.1
1996	Col N	83	272	58	75	18	4	18	58	20-2	9	58	.276	.342	.570	110	4	18-2	.994	-1	97	101	O83(0/54/33)	66	0.5
1997	Col N★	153	568	143	208	46	4	49	130	78-14	14	90	.366	.452	.720	164	56	33-8	.992	-9	83	107	O151(0/2/150),1b3/D		4.3
1998	Col N★	130	454	113	165	46	3	23	67	64-2	4	61	.363	.445	.630	148	35	14-4	.984	2	104	100	O123(0/3/123)/23D	15	3.2
1999	Col N★	127	438	108	166	26	4	37	115	57-8	12	52	.379	.458	.710	152	37	11-4	.982	3	95	182	O114R/D	9	3.3
2000	Col N	87	314	64	97	21	7	9	51	46-4	9	40	.309	.409	.506	106	4	5-5	.994	7	104	202	O83(31/0/52),D3	70	0.7
2001	Col N★	142	497	107	174	35	3	38	123	82-6	14	103	.350	.449	.662	153	43	14-5	.984	-1	94	95	O129R,D5		3.6
2002	Col N	136	477	95	161	40	4	26	104	65-6	7	73	.338	.421	.602	150	35	6-5	.984	4	95	172	O123R,D7		3.2
2003	Col N	143	454	86	129	25	7	16	79	98-14	11	87	.284	.422	.476	118	17	7-4	.983	-5	90	93	O131R,D2		0.5
2004	Col N	38	108	22	35	9	3	6	20	25-2	4	23	.324	.464	.630	160	11	2-0	1.000	3	103	202	O34R	78	1.2
	†StL N	44	150	29	42	7	1	11	27	24-1	4	34	.280	.393	.560	141	10	4-0	.983	-1	77	40	O41(0/1/41)/D		0.4
	Year	82	258	51	77	16	4	17	47	49-3	8	57	.298	.424	.589	149	21	6-0	.992	-2	88	111	O75(0/1/75)/D		1.6
2005	Col N	100	315	66	91	20	1	15	52	41-3	9	64	.289	.384	.502	128	14	2-1	.983	-8	73	114	O83(0/1/83),D6	28	0.2
Total	17	1988	6907	1355	2160	471	62	383	1311	913-117	138	1231	.313	.400	.565	136	378	230-76	.986	14	96	130	O1804(33/70/1716),1b81,D27/32	478	32.5

WALKER, FLEET   Moses Fleetwood   B10.7.1856 Mt.Pleasant OH   D5.11.1924 Cleveland OH   BR/TR/?/159   d5.1   b-Welday   Col Michigan

| 1884 | Tol AA | 42 | 152 | 23 | 40 | 2 | 3 | 0 | | 8 | 6 | | .263 | .325 | .316 | 106 | 1 | | .887 | -5 | | | C41/OL | | 0.0 |

WALKER, OSCAR   Oscar   B3.18.1854 Brooklyn NY   D5.20.1889 Brooklyn NY   BL/TL/5-10/166   d9.17

1875	Atl NA	1	2	0	0	0	0	0	1		0		.000	.333	.000	30	-0	0-0	.400	-0	0	366	/1OR		0.0
1879	Buf N	72	287	35	79	15	6	1	35	8		38	.275	.295	.380	118	5		.946	3	165	181	1b72		0.4
1880	Buf N	34	126	12	29	4	2	1	15	6		18	.230	.265	.317	95	-1		.917	-1	115	130	1b24,O11(3/7/1)		-0.4
1882	StL AA	76	318	48	76	15	7	7		10			.239	.262	.396	115	4		.846	6	101	212	O75(1/74/0)/21		0.6
1884	Bro AA	95	382	59	103	12	8	2		9	3		.270	.292	.359	114	0		.868	1	114	0	O59(16/43/0),1b36		-0.1
1885	Bal AA	4	13	1	0	0	0	0		0	0		.000	.000	.000	-99	-3		.667	-1	0	0	O4R		-0.4
Total	5	281	1126	155	287	46	23	11	51	33	3	56	.255	.278	.366	109	8		.850	7	105	126	O149(20/124/5),1b133/2		0.1

WALKER, TODD   Todd Arthur   B5.25.1973 Bakersfield CA   BL/TR/6-0/181(170-185)   [MlnA94 1/8]   d8.30   Col Louisiana St.

1996	Min A	25	82	8	21	6	0	0	6	3-0	0	13	.256	.281	.329	55	-6	2-0	.956	-0	103	100	3b20,2b4/D		-0.5
1997	Min A	52	156	15	37	7	1	3	16	11-1	1	26	.237	.288	.353	66	-8	7-0	.969	-1	106	67	3b40,2b8,D2		-0.7
1998	Min A	143	528	85	167	41	3	12	62	47-9	2	65	.316	.372	.473	116	13	19-7	.978	-20	96	86	2b140/D		0.1
1999	Min A	143	531	62	148	37	4	6	46	52-5	1	83	.279	.343	.397	84	-12	18-10	.984	-12	97	86	2b103/D34		-1.9
2000	Min A	23	77	14	18	1	0	2	8	7-0	1	10	.234	.287	.325	54	-4	3-0	.946	-4	78	105	2b19,D2		-0.8
	Col N	57	171	28	54	10	4	7	36	20-0	1	19	.316	.385	.544	108	4	4-1	.975	-6	96	84	2b52		-0.2
2001	Col N	85	290	52	86	18	2	12	43	25-1	0	40	.297	.349	.497	96	-1	1-3	.981	7	108	108	2b77		0.8
	Cin N	66	261	41	77	17	0	5	32	26-0	1	42	.295	.361	.418	95	-1	0-5	.987	-6	97	83	2b65/S		-0.5
	Year	151	551	93	163	35	2	17	75	51-1	1	82	.296	.355	.459	96	-2	1-8	.984	1	103	96	2b142/S		0.3
2002	Cin N	155	612	79	183	42	3	11	64	50-7	3	81	.299	.353	.431	105	-3	8-5	.989	-7	100	91	2b154		0.3
2003	†Bos N	144	587	92	166	38	4	13	85	48-0	1	54	.283	.333	.428	96	-3	1-1	.975	-7	95	88	2b139,D2		-0.4
2004	Chi N	129	372	60	102	19	4	15	50	43-8	4	50	.274	.352	.468	107	4	0-3	.981	-12	86	63	2b89,1b5/OL		-0.7
2005	Chi N	110	397	50	121	25	3	12	40	31-1	1	40	.305	.355	.474	111	6	1-1	.985	-4	92	77	2b97,1b4,D2	44	0.7
Total	10	1132	4064	586	1180	261	28	98	488	364-32	15	529	.290	.348	.441	99	-9	64-36	.981	-72	96	86	2b947,3b60,D44,1b9/OLS	44	-3.6

WALKER, WALLIE   Walter S.   B3.12.1860 Berlin (now Marne) MI   D2.28.1922 Pontiac MI   TR/5-10.5/162   d5.8

| 1884 | Det N | 1 | 4 | 1 | 1 | 0 | 0 | 0 | | 0 | 0 | | .250 | .250 | .250 | 61 | -0 | | .750 | -1 | | | /C | | -0.1 |

WALKER, WELDAY   Welday Wilberforce   B6.1859 Steubenville OH   D11.23.1937 Steubenville OH   d7.15   b-Fleet   Col Michigan

| 1884 | Tol AA | 5 | 18 | 1 | 4 | 1 | 0 | 0 | | 2 | 0 | | .222 | .222 | .278 | 60 | -1 | 0 | .667 | -1 | 0 | 0 | O5(4/1/0) | | -0.2 |

WALKER, CURT   William Curtis   B7.3.1896 Beeville TX   D12.9.1955 Beeville TX   BL/TR/5-9.5/170   d9.17   Col Southwestern (TX)

1919	NY A	1	1	0	0	0	0	0	1	0	0	0	.000	.000	.000	-99	0	0	—	0			/H		0.0
1920	NY N	8	14	0	1	0	0	0	0	1	0	3	.071	.133	.071	-41	-3	0-0	1.000	-1	80	0	O4(1/2/1)		-0.2
1921	NY N	64	192	30	55	13	5	2	35	15	0	21	.286	.338	.453	107	2	4-3	.978	3	98	150	O58(0/46/13)		0.3
	Phi N	21	77	11	26	2	1	0	8	5	0	5	.338	.378	.390	96	0	0-1	.970	-2	79	85	O21(7/7/10)		0.2
	Year	85	269	41	81	15	6	2	43	20	0	13	.301	.349	.435	104	1	4-5	.976	1	93	133	O79(7/53/23)		0.5
1922	Phi N	148	581	102	196	36	11	12	89	56	4	46	.337	.399	.499	119	17	11-4	.955	5	100	125	O147R		1.
1923	Phi N	140	548	77	154	28	16	5	66	45	0	31	.281	.337	.378	79	-15	12-12	.947	3	102	121	O137(12/0/125)/1		-2.
1924	Phi N	24	71	11	21	6	1	0	8	7	0	4	.296	.359	.451	103	1	0-1	.900	-2	84	53	O20R		0.
	Cin N	109	397	55	119	21	10	4	46	44	1	15	.300	.371	.433	117	10	7-5	.978	1	97	116	O109(3/23/86)		0.
	Year	133	468	66	140	27	11	4	54	51	1	19	.299	.369	.436	114	10	7-6	.969	-1	93	102	O129(3/23/106)		0.
1925	Cin N	145	509	86	162	22	16	6	71	57	0	31	.318	.387	.460	118	11	14-11	.983	0	109	61	O141(4/15/124)		1.
1926	Cin N	155	571	83	175	24	20	6	78	60	0	31	.306	.372	.450	104	8	3	.961	-0	99	0	O152(1/0/151)		0.
1927	Cin N	148	527	60	154	16	10	6	80	47	0	19	.292	.350	.395	102	1	5-3	.957	-2	107	87	O141R		0.
1928	Cin N	123	427	64	119	15	12	6	73	49	1	14	.279	.354	.412	101	0	19	.955	2	107	70	O122R		0.

YEAR	TM LG	G	AB	R	H	2B	3B	HR	RBI	BB-IB	HP	SO	AVG	OBP	SLG	AOPS	ABR	SB-CS	FA	FR	RNG	THR	GAMES AT POSITION	DL	BFW
1929	Cin N	141	492	76	154	28	15	7	83	85	2	17	.313	.416	.474	126	23	17	.969	-4	98	75	O138R		0.8
1930	Cin N	134	472	74	145	26	11	8	51	64	1	30	.307	.391	.460	110	9	4	.965	-3	102	49	O120(77/2/42)		-0.2
Total	12	1359	4858	718	1475	235	117	64	688	535	9	254	.304	.374	.440	110	77	96-38	.963	3	102	91	O1310(105/95/1120)/1		-2.1

WALL, HOWARD   Howard Cornelius   B12.1854 Washington DC   D3.15.1909 Washington DC   d9.13

YEAR	TM LG	G	AB	R	H	2B	3B	HR	RBI	BB-IB	HP	SO	AVG	OBP	SLG	AOPS	ABR	SB-CS	FA	FR	RNG	THR	GAMES AT POSITION	DL	BFW
1873	Was NA	1	3	1	1	0	0	0	1				.333	.500	.333	158	0	0-0	.000	-1	0	0	/S		-0.1

WALL, JOE   Joseph Francis "Gummy"   B7.24.1873 Brooklyn NY   D7.17.1936 Brooklyn NY   BL/TL   d9.22

YEAR	TM LG	G	AB	R	H	2B	3B	HR	RBI	BB-IB	HP	SO	AVG	OBP	SLG	AOPS	ABR	SB-CS	FA	FR	RNG	THR	GAMES AT POSITION	DL	BFW
1901	NY N	4	8	0	4	0	0	0	1	0			.500	.500	.500	198	1	0	1.000	-1	48	0	C2/OR		0.0
1902	NY N	6	14	2	5	2	0	0	2	0			.357	.438	.500	191	2	0	1.000	0	327	0	O3R		0.2
	Bro N	5	18	0	3	0	0	0	3	1			.167	.318	.167	50	-1	0	.893	-3	75	41	C5		-0.3
	Year	11	32	2	8	2	0	0	5	1			.250	.368	.313	111	1	0	.893	-3	75	41	C5,O3R		-0.1
Total	2	15	40	2	12	2	0	0	6	1			.300	.391	.350	127	2	0	.903	-4	70	33	C7,O4R		-0.1

WALLACE, JACK   Clarence Eugene   B8.6.1890 Winnfield LA   D10.15.1960 Winnfield LA   BR/TR/5-10.5/175   d9.27   Col Louisiana St.

YEAR	TM LG	G	AB	R	H	2B	3B	HR	RBI	BB-IB	HP	SO	AVG	OBP	SLG	AOPS	ABR	SB-CS	FA	FR	RNG	THR	GAMES AT POSITION	DL	BFW
1915	Chi N	2	7	1	2	0	0	0	1	0		1	.286	.375	.286	101	0	0	1.000	1	116	151	C2		0.1

WALLACE, DON   Donald Allen   B8.25.1940 Sapulpa OK   BL/TR/5-8/165   d4.12   Col Oklahoma St.

YEAR	TM LG	G	AB	R	H	2B	3B	HR	RBI	BB-IB	HP	SO	AVG	OBP	SLG	AOPS	ABR	SB-CS	FA	FR	RNG	THR	GAMES AT POSITION	DL	BFW
1967	Cal A	23	6	0	0	0	0	0	0	3-0	0	2	.000	.333	.000	6	0	0-1	1.000	-0	81	122	2b4/13		-0.1

WALLACE, DOC   Frederick Renshaw "Jesse"   B9.30.1893 Church Hill MD   D12.31.1964 Haverford PA   BR/TR/6-5/135   d5.2   Col Washington College

YEAR	TM LG	G	AB	R	H	2B	3B	HR	RBI	BB-IB	HP	SO	AVG	OBP	SLG	AOPS	ABR	SB-CS	FA	FR	RNG	THR	GAMES AT POSITION	DL	BFW
1919	Phi N	2	4	0	1	0	0	0	0	0			.250	.250	.250	47	0	0	.875	-0	104	0	S2		0.0

WALLACE, JIM   James Leo   B11.14.1881 Boston MA   D5.16.1953 Revere MA   BL/TL/5-9/150   d8.24

YEAR	TM LG	G	AB	R	H	2B	3B	HR	RBI	BB-IB	HP	SO	AVG	OBP	SLG	AOPS	ABR	SB-CS	FA	FR	RNG	THR	GAMES AT POSITION	DL	BFW
1905	Pit N	7	29	3	6	1	0	0	3	3			.207	.281	.241	55	-2	2	.929	1	291	0	O7R		-0.1

WALLACE, BOBBY   Rhoderick John   B11.4.1873 Pittsburgh PA   D11.3.1960 Torrance CA   BR/TR/5-8/170   d9.15   M3/C1/U1   HF1953   OF(4/6/16) ▲

YEAR	TM LG	G	AB	R	H	2B	3B	HR	RBI	BB-IB	HP	SO	AVG	OBP	SLG	AOPS	ABR	SB-CS	FA	FR	RNG	THR	GAMES AT POSITION	DL	BFW
1894	Cle N	4	13	0	2	1	0	0	1	0		1	.154	.154	.231	-8	-1	0	1.000	1	184	0	P4		0.0
1895	Cle N	30	98	16	21	2	3	0	10	6	2	17	.214	.274	.296	44	-3	0	.910	3	127	129	P30		0.0
1896	†Cle N	45	149	19	35	6	3	1	17	11	0	21	.235	.287	.336	60	-9	2	.950	-2	102	0	O23(3/6/15),P22/1		-0.7
1897	Cle N	130	516	99	173	33	21	4	112	48	2		.335	.394	.504	129	20	14	.928	4	99	68	3b130/OL		2.2
1898	Cle N	154	593	81	160	25	13	3	99	63	4		.270	.344	.371	106	5	7	.936	18	109	103	3b141,2b13		2.4
1899	StL N	151	577	91	170	28	14	12	108	54	2		.295	.357	.454	119	13	17	.919	30	109	107	S100,3b52		4.4
1900	StL N	126	485	70	130	25	9	4	70	40	3		.268	.328	.381	96	-3	7	.934	6	98	64	S126/3		0.8
1901	StL N	134	550	69	178	34	15	2	91	20	3		.324	.351	.451	138	24	15	.929	27	116	131	S134		5.4
1902	StL A	133	494	71	141	32	9	1	63	45	4		.285	.350	.393	107	6	18	.948	7	104	118	S131/POR		1.6
1903	StL A	135	511	63	136	21	7	1	54	28	4		.266	.309	.341	97	-2	10	.924	18	109	117	S135		2.2
1904	StL A	139	541	57	149	29	4	2	69	42	2		.275	.330	.355	124	16	20	.947	3	105	84	S139		2.6
1905	StL A	156	587	67	159	25	9	1	59	45	1		.271	.324	.349	120	13	13	.935	21	108	82	S156		4.2
1906	StL A	139	476	64	123	21	7	2	67	58	4		.258	.345	.345	121	14	24	.949	2	99	115	S138		2.3
1907	StL A	147	538	56	138	20	7	0	70	54	1		.257	.328	.320	107	6	16	.941	8	105	116	S147		2.0
1908	StL A	137	487	59	123	24	4	1	60	52	2		.253	.327	.324	111	8	5	.951	15	107	108	S137		3.1
1909	StL A	116	403	36	96	12	2	0	35	38	4		.238	.310	.278	92	-2	7	.946	11	100	113	S87,3b29		1.4
1910	StL A	138	508	47	131	19	7	0	37	49	1		.258	.324	.323	110	6	12	.948	23	108	91	S99,3b39		3.6
1911	StL A	125	410	35	95	12	2	0	31	46	2		.232	.312	.271	66	-18	8	.943	4	107	101	S124/2M		-0.5
1912	StL A	100	323	39	78	14	5	0	31	43	1		.241	.332	.316	89	-3	3	.942	8	104	102	S87,3b10,2b2,M		1.1
1913	StL A	55	147	11	31	5	0	0	21	14	3	16	.211	.293	.245	59	-7	1	.931	-4	93	59	S39,3b7		-0.9
1914	StL A	26	73	3	16	2	1	0	5	5	0	13	.219	.269	.274	66	-3	1-1	.889	-7	89	30	S19,3b2		-1.0
1915	StL A	9	13	1	3	0	1	0	4	5	0	0	.231	.444	.385	154	1	0-1	.848	1	108	198	S9		0.2
1916	StL A	14	18	0	5	0	0	0	1	2	0	1	.278	.350	.278	93	0	0	.958	3	167	97	3b9,S5		0.3
1917	StL N	8	10	0	1	0	0	0	2	0	0	1	.100	.100	.100	-40	-2	0	1.000	-1	0	0	3b5,S2		-0.3
1918	StL N	32	98	3	15	1	0	0	3	4	0	9	.153	.202	.163	12	-10	1	.959	1	110	113	2b17,S12/3		-1.0
Total	25	2383	8618	1057	2309	391	143	34	1121	774	47	79	.268	.332	.358	106	69	201-2	.938	201	105	102	S1826,3b426,P57,2b33,O25R/1		35.4

WALLACH, TIM   Timothy Charles   B9.14.1957 Huntington Park CA   BR/TR/6-3/200(200-220)   [MonN79 1/10]   d9.6   C2   Col Cal St.-Fullerton   OF(4/0/36)

YEAR	TM LG	G	AB	R	H	2B	3B	HR	RBI	BB-IB	HP	SO	AVG	OBP	SLG	AOPS	ABR	SB-CS	FA	FR	RNG	THR	GAMES AT POSITION	DL	BFW
1980	Mon N	5	11	1	2	0	0	1	2	1-0	0	5	.182	.250	.455	91	0	0-0	1.000	-1	57	0	O3(2/0/1)/1		-0.1
1981	†Mon N	71	212	19	50	9	1	4	13	15-2	4	37	.236	.299	.344	79	-6	0-1	1.000	-2	92	116	O35(1/0/34),1b16,3b15		-1.1
1982	Mon N	158	596	89	160	31	3	28	97	36-4	4	81	.268	.313	.471	113	8	6-4	.948	2	96	97	3b156,O2(1/0/1)/1		0.7
1983	Mon N	156	581	54	156	33	3	19	70	55-8	6	97	.269	.335	.434	112	10	0-3	.956	-3	93	103	3b156		0.4
1984	Mon N★	160	582	55	143	25	4	18	72	50-6	7	101	.246	.311	.395	102	0	3-7	.959	22	110	118	3b160/S		1.9
1985	Mon N★	155	569	70	148	36	3	22	81	38-8	5	79	.260	.310	.450	117	10	9-9	.967	36	123	132	3b154		4.4
1986	Mon N	134	480	50	112	22	1	18	71	44-8	10	72	.233	.308	.396	94	-5	8-4	.958	18	117	126	3b132		1.2
1987	Mon N★	153	593	89	177	42	4	26	123	37-5	7	98	.298	.343	.514	120	16	9-5	.952	7	102	88	3b150/P		2.0
1988	Mon N	159	592	52	152	32	5	12	69	38-7	3	88	.257	.302	.389	93	-6	2-6	.962	19	114	131	3b153/2		1.3
1989	Mon N★	154	573	76	159	42	0	13	77	58-10	1	81	.277	.341	.419	115	13	3-7	.958	9	104	82	3b153/P		2.2
1990	Mon N★	161	626	69	185	37	5	21	98	42-11	3	80	.296	.339	.471	126	20	6-9	.954	5	103	102	3b161		2.4
1991	Mon N	151	577	60	130	22	1	13	73	50-8	6	100	.225	.292	.334	77	-18	2-4	.968	6	105	110	3b149		-1.4
1992	Mon N	150	537	53	120	29	1	9	59	50-2	8	90	.223	.296	.331	79	-14	2-2	.964	19	122	133	3b85,1b71		-0.1
1993	LA N	133	477	42	106	19	1	12	62	32-2	3	70	.222	.271	.342	68	-24	0-2	.958	9	106	70	3b130/1		-1.4
1994	LA N	113	414	68	116	21	1	23	78	46-2	1	80	.280	.356	.502	128	17	0-2	.959	-4	94	63	3b113		1.2
1995	†LA N	97	327	24	87	22	2	9	38	27-4	4	69	.266	.326	.428	105	2	0-0	.976	-6	90	72	3b96/1	40	-0.3
1996	Cal A	57	190	23	45	7	0	8	20	18-2	1	47	.237	.306	.400	76	-8	1-0	.941	3	110	52	3b46,1b3,D8		-0.4
	†LA N	45	162	14	37	3	1	4	22	10-1	1	32	.228	.286	.333	67	-9	0-1	.971	-6	74	44	3b45		-1.5
Total	17	2212	8099	908	2085	432	36	260	1125	649-89	77	1307	.257	.316	.416	102	6	51-66	.959	150	105	100	3b2054,1b94,O40R,D8,P2/2S	62	11.4

WALLAESA, JACK   John   B8.31.1919 Easton PA   D12.27.1986 Easton PA   BB/TR (BR 1940)/6-3/191   d9.22   Mil 1943-45

YEAR	TM LG	G	AB	R	H	2B	3B	HR	RBI	BB-IB	HP	SO	AVG	OBP	SLG	AOPS	ABR	SB-CS	FA	FR	RNG	THR	GAMES AT POSITION	DL	BFW
1940	Phi A	6	20	1	3	0	0	0	2	1-0	0	2	.150	.150	.150	-22	-4	0-0	.903	-0	113	81	S6		-0.3
1942	Phi A	36	117	13	30	4	1	2	13	8	2	26	.256	.315	.359	90	-2	0-1	.920	-6	86	80	S36		-0.7
1946	Phi A	63	194	16	38	4	2	5	11	14	0	47	.196	.250	.314	57	-12	1-0	.916	-10	85	87	S59		-2.1
1947	Chi A	81	205	25	40	9	1	7	32	23	1	51	.195	.279	.351	78	-7	2-2	.968	6	113	114	S27,O22L/3		-0.2
1948	Chi A	33	48	2	9	0	0	1	3	1	0	12	.188	.204	.250	21	-6	0-0	1.000	1	107	124	S5/OL		-0.5
Total	5	219	584	56	120	17	4	15	61	46	3	138	.205	.267	.325	65	-31	3-3	.933	-10	94	92	S133,O23L/3		-3.8

WALLEN, NORM   Norman Edward (b Norman Edward Walentoski)   B2.13.1917 Milwaukee WI   D6.20.1994 Milwaukee WI   BR/TR/5-11.5/175   d4.20

YEAR	TM LG	G	AB	R	H	2B	3B	HR	RBI	BB-IB	HP	SO	AVG	OBP	SLG	AOPS	ABR	SB-CS	FA	FR	RNG	THR	GAMES AT POSITION	DL	BFW
1945	Bos N	4	15	1	2	0	1	0	1	1	0	1	.133	.188	.267	25	-2	0	.800	-1	73	0	3b4		-0.3

WALLER, TY   Elliott Tyrone   B3.14.1957 Fresno CA   BR/TR/6-0/180*   [StLN77*4/82]   d9.6   C1   Col San Diego (CA) City

YEAR	TM LG	G	AB	R	H	2B	3B	HR	RBI	BB-IB	HP	SO	AVG	OBP	SLG	AOPS	ABR	SB-CS	FA	FR	RNG	THR	GAMES AT POSITION	DL	BFW
1980	StL N	5	12	3	1	0	0	0	0	1-0	0	5	.083	.154	.083	-31	-2	0-0	1.000	-3	27	0	3b5		-0.5
1981	Chi N	30	71	10	19	2	1	3	13	4-1	0	11	.268	.303	.451	106	0	2-0	.978	0	100	68	3b22,2b3,O3C		0.1
1982	Chi N	17	21	4	5	0	0	0	1	2-0	0	5	.238	.304	.238	52	-1	0-0	1.000	-0	84	0	O7(1/5/1)/3		-0.2
1987	Hou N	11	6	1	1	1	0	0	0	0-0	0	1	.167	.167	.333	29	-1	0-0	1.000	-0	0	0	3b(1/2/0)		0.0
Total	4	63	110	18	26	3	1	3	14	7-1	0	31	.236	.280	.364	77	-4	2-0	.961	-2	89	55	3b28,O13(2/10/1),2b3		-0.6

WALLING, DENNY   Dennis Martin   B4.17.1954 Neptune NJ   BL/TR/6-1/185*   [OakA75 S1/1]   d9.7   C5   Col Clemson

YEAR	TM LG	G	AB	R	H	2B	3B	HR	RBI	BB-IB	HP	SO	AVG	OBP	SLG	AOPS	ABR	SB-CS	FA	FR	RNG	THR	GAMES AT POSITION	DL	BFW
1975	Oak A	6	8	0	1	1	0	0	2	0-0	0	4	.125	.125	.250	4	-1	0-0	1.000	-0	88	0	O3(1/2/0)		-0.1
1976	Oak A	3	11	3	3	0	0	0	0	0-0	0	1	.273	.273	.273	62	-1	0-0	.889	-0	108	0	O3(2/2/0)		0.0
1977	Oak A	6	21	1	6	0	1	0	6	2-0	0	4	.286	.348	.381	103	0	0-1	1.000	0	125	0	O5(1/2/2)		0.0
1978	Hou N	120	247	30	62	11	3	3	36	30-3	1	24	.251	.332	.356	100	0	9-2	.980	4	116	81	O78(66/7/4)		0.3
1979	Hou N	82	147	21	48	8	4	3	31	17-2	0	21	.327	.394	.497	151	10	3-2	.985	-0	103	75	O42(7/0/35)		0.8
1980	†Hou N	100	284	30	85	6	5	3	29	35-4	0	26	.299	.374	.387	124	9	4-3	.989	-5	81	114	1b63,O19(1/0/18)		0.3
1981	†Hou N	65	158	23	37	6	0	5	23	28-1	0	17	.234	.346	.367	110	3	2-0	1.000	-4	58	118	1b27,O27(5/1/21)		-0.3
1982	Hou N	85	146	22	30	4	1	4	14	23-3	0	19	.205	.312	.267	69	-5	4-2	1.000	-0	89	218	O32(4/11/18),1b20		-0.7
1983	Hou N	100	135	29	40	5	3	1	19	15-1	0	16	.296	.366	.444	131	5	1-2	.992	-1	76	112	1b42,3b13,O13(2/0/12)		0.3
1984	Hou N	87	249	37	70	11	5	3	31	16-2	1	31	.281	.325	.402	111	2	7-1	.956	6	116	202	3b52,1b16,O6(3/3/0)	22	0.8
1985	Hou N	119	345	44	93	20	1	7	45	25-2	0	26	.270	.316	.394	101	0	5-2	.938	2	111	112	3b51,1b46,O13(6/0/7)		-0.1
1986	†Hou N	130	382	54	119	23	3	13	58	36-5	0	31	.312	.367	.479	136	19	1-1	.960	3	95	49	3b102,O11(6/0/5),1b4	11	2.0
1987	Hou N	110	325	45	92	21	4	5	33	39-1	0	37	.283	.356	.418	109	4	5-1	.948	0	83	122	3b79,1b16,O7(6/0/2)		0.4

YEAR	TM LG	G	AB	R	H	2B	3B	HR	RBI	BB-IB	HP	SO	AVG	OBP	SLG	AOPS	ABR	SB-CS	FA	FR	RNG	THR	GAMES AT POSITION	DL	BFW
1988	Hou N	65	176	19	43	10	2	1	20	15-3	0	18	.244	.304	.341	88	-3	1-0	.950	8	115	207	3b51,1b3/OL	47	0.5
	StL N	19	58	3	13	3	0	0	1	2-0	0	7	.224	.250	.276	50	-4	1-0	1.000	-1	65	0	O11(10/0/1),3b5/1		-0.5
	Year	84	234	22	56	13	2	1	21	17-3	0	25	.239	.291	.325	79	-7	2-0	.941	7	118	118	3b56,O12(11/0/1),1b4		0.0
1989	StL N	69	79	9	24	7	0	1	11	14-2	0	12	.304	.304	.430	135	5	0-0	.969	4	87	89	1b20,3b9,O6(3/0/3)	15	-0.9
1990	StL N	78	127	7	28	5	0	1	19	8-0	0	15	.220	.265	.283	51	-9	0-0	1.000	1	92	63	1b15,3b11,O8(3/0/5)		-0.3
1991	Tex A	24	44	1	4	1	0	0	2	3-0	2	8	.091	.184	.114	-16	-7	0-0	.950	-1	97	0	3b14,O5(3/0/2)	21	-0.8
1992	Hou N	3	3	1	1	0	0	0	0	0-0	0	0	.333	.333	.333	93	0	0-0	—	0			/H	177	0.0
Total	18	1271	2945	372	799	142	30	49	380	308-29	4	316	.271	.339	.390	107	28	44-18	.947	8	101	119	3b387,O290(131/27/135),1b273	293	1.6

WALLIS, JOE
Harold Joseph   B1.9.1952 E.St.Louis IL   BB/TR/5-10/195(180-195)   [ChiN73 6/136]   d9.2   Col Southern Illinois

YEAR	TM LG	G	AB	R	H	2B	3B	HR	RBI	BB-IB	HP	SO	AVG	OBP	SLG	AOPS	ABR	SB-CS	FA	FR	RNG	THR	GAMES AT POSITION	DL	BFW
1975	Chi N	16	56	9	16	2	2	1	4	5-0	0	14	.286	.344	.446	113	1	2-0	1.000	-0	98	123	O15(0/14/1)		0.1
1976	Chi N	121	338	51	86	11	5	5	21	33-3	1	62	.254	.322	.361	86	-6	3-9	.976	2	94	198	O90(10/68/16)		-1.1
1977	Chi N	56	80	14	20	3	0	2	8	16-1	0	25	.250	.375	.363	89	-1	0-1	.974	-3	69	146	O35C	29	-0.4
1978	Chi N	28	55	7	17	2	1	1	6	5-1	0	13	.309	.367	.436	110	1	0-2	1.000	1	86	110	O25C		-0.1
	Oak A	85	279	28	66	16	1	6	26	26-1	0	42	.237	.300	.366	91	-3	1-4	.980	3	102	146	O80(5/55/23)/D		-0.3
1979	Oak A	23	78	6	11	2	0	1	3	10-1	1	18	.141	.247	.205	25	-8	1-0	1.000	-1	93	62	O23(0/1/23)	109	-1.0
Total	5	329	886	115	216	36	9	16	68	95-7	2	174	.244	.317	.359	86	-16	7-16	.982	1	94	153	O268(15/198/63)/D	138	-2.8

WALLS, LEE
Ray Lee   B1.6.1933 San Diego CA   D10.11.1993 Los Angeles CA   BR/TR/6-3/205(190-205)   d4.21   C5   Col Pasadena (CA) City

YEAR	TM LG	G	AB	R	H	2B	3B	HR	RBI	BB-IB	HP	SO	AVG	OBP	SLG	AOPS	ABR	SB-CS	FA	FR	RNG	THR	GAMES AT POSITION	DL	BFW
1952	Pit N	32	80	6	15	0	1	2	5	8	0	22	.188	.261	.287	51	-6	0-0	1.000	-0	96	116	O19(1/18/0)		-0.6
1956	Pit N	143	474	72	130	20	11	11	54	50-0	1	83	.274	.345	.432	110	6	3-5	.967	4	109	101	O133(74/10/56)/3		0.3
1957	Pit N	8	22	3	4	1	0	0	0	2-0	0	5	.182	.250	.227	30	-2	1-0	1.000	1	111	250	O7L		-0.2
	Chi N	117	366	42	88	10	5	6	33	27-1	1	67	.240	.292	.344	72	-15	5-3	.984	-2	94	102	O94(67/29/6)/3		-2.3
	Year	125	388	45	92	11	5	6	33	29-1	1	72	.237	.290	.338	70	-18	6-3	.985	-1	95	111	O101(74/29/6)/3		-2.5
1958	Chi N★	136	513	80	156	19	3	24	72	47-0	8	62	.304	.370	.493	128	21	4-4	.992	1	99	91	O132R		1.4
1959	Chi N	120	354	43	91	18	3	8	33	42-1	5	73	.257	.342	.393	97	-1	0-2	.967	-6	102	12	O119R		-1.1
1960	Cin N	29	84	12	23	3	2	1	7	17-1	0	20	.274	.392	.393	115	3	2-0	.960	0	106	97	O24(12/0/12),1b2		0.2
	Phi N	65	181	19	36	6	1	3	19	14-1	0	32	.199	.253	.293	50	-13	3-2	.947	-4	102	65	3b34,O13(8/0/5),1b7		-1.8
	Year	94	265	31	59	9	3	4	26	31-2	0	52	.223	.303	.325	72	-10	5-2	.958	-4	102	65	O37(20/0/17),3b34,1b9		-1.6
1961	Phi N	91	261	32	73	6	4	8	30	19-1	0	48	.280	.329	.425	99	-1	2-2	.987	-3	100	126	1b28,3b26,O17(11/1/8)		-0.7
1962	LA N	60	109	9	29	3	1	0	17	10-0	1	21	.266	.325	.312	77	-3	1-0	.929	-1	64	127	O17(15/0/3),1b11,3b4		-0.6
1963	LA N	64	86	12	20	1	0	3	11	7-1	0	25	.233	.290	.349	89	-2	0-0	1.000	2	137	0	O18(10/0/8),1b5,3b2		0.0
1964	LA N	37	28	1	5	1	0	0	3	2-0	1	12	.179	.233	.214	29	-3	0-0	1.000	-0	88	0	O6(3/0/3)/C		-0.3
Total	10	902	2558	331	670	88	31	66	284	245-6	16	470	.262	.329	.398	96	-16	21-18	.977	-10	101	81	O599(208/58/352),3b68,1b53/C		-5.7

WALSH, AUSTIN
Austin Edward   B9.1.1891 Cambridge MA   D1.26.1955 Glendale CA   BL/TL/5-11/175   d4.19

YEAR	TM LG	G	AB	R	H	2B	3B	HR	RBI	BB-IB	HP	SO	AVG	OBP	SLG	AOPS	ABR	SB-CS	FA	FR	RNG	THR	GAMES AT POSITION	DL	BFW
1914	Chi F	57	121	14	29	6	1	1	10	4	0	25	.240	.264	.331	65	-9	0	1.000	-0	98	83	O30(21/1/8)		-1.0

WALSH, JIMMY
James Charles   B9.22.1885 Kallila, Ireland   D7.3.1962 Syracuse NY   BL/TR/5-10.5/170   d8.26   Mil 1918

YEAR	TM LG	G	AB	R	H	2B	3B	HR	RBI	BB-IB	HP	SO	AVG	OBP	SLG	AOPS	ABR	SB-CS	FA	FR	RNG	THR	GAMES AT POSITION	DL	BFW
1912	Phi A	31	107	11	27	8	2	0	15	12	0		.252	.328	.364	101	0	7	.947	-0	115	25	O30L		-0.1
1913	Phi A	97	303	56	77	16	5	0	27	38	2	40	.254	.341	.340	102	2	15	.961	2	109	87	O90(39/44/13)		-0.1
1914	NY A	43	136	13	26	1	3	1	11	29	0	21	.191	.333	.265	80	-2	6-9	.977	-1	103	69	O41(37/4/0)		0.0
†Phi A	68	216	35	51	11	6	3	36	30	4	27	.236	.340	.384	123	6	6-12	.966	-0	101	101	O56(25/26/6),1b3,3b3/S		-0.7
	Year	111	352	48	77	12	9	4	47	59	4	48	.219	.337	.338	106	4	12-21	.971	-2	102	85	O97(62/30/6),1b3,3b3/S		-1.2
1915	Phi A	117	417	48	86	15	6	1	20	57	3	64	.206	.306	.278	78	-11	22-12	.976	5	110	105	O109(29/44/36),3b2/1		-0.8
1916	Phi A	114	390	42	91	13	6	1	27	54	2	36	.233	.330	.305	95	-1	27-14	.939	-1	101	100	O113(0/6/107)/1		-0.2
†Bos A	14	17	5	3	1	0	0	2	4	0	2	.176	.333	.235	71	0	3-2	1.000	-1	104	0	O6(1/3/2),3b2		-0.1
	Year	128	407	47	94	14	6	1	29	58	2	38	.231	.330	.302	94	-1	30-16	.940	-2	101	98	O119(1/9/109),3b2/1		-0.9
1917	Bos A	57	185	25	49	6	3	0	12	25	0	14	.265	.352	.330	109	3	6	.982	-1	91	117	O47(2/43/2)		-0.2
Total	6	541	1771	235	410	71	31	6	150	249	11	204	.232	.330	.317	96	-3	92-49	.964	3	105	92	O492(163/170/166),3b7,1b5/S		-3.2

WALSH, JOHN
John Gabriel   B3.25.1879 Wilkes-Barre PA   D4.25.1947 Jamaica NY   BR/TR/5-8.5/162   d6.22   Col Notre Dame

YEAR	TM LG	G	AB	R	H	2B	3B	HR	RBI	BB-IB	HP	SO	AVG	OBP	SLG	AOPS	ABR	SB-CS	FA	FR	RNG	THR	GAMES AT POSITION	DL	BFW
1903	Phi N	1	3	0	0	0	0	0	0	0	0		.000	.000	.000	-99	-1		1.000	-0	123	0	/3		-0.1

WALSH, JOE
Joseph Francis   B10.14.1886 Minersville PA   D1.6.1967 Buffalo NY   BR/TR/6-2/170   d10.8   Col Villanova

YEAR	TM LG	G	AB	R	H	2B	3B	HR	RBI	BB-IB	HP	SO	AVG	OBP	SLG	AOPS	ABR	SB-CS	FA	FR	RNG	THR	GAMES AT POSITION	DL	BFW
1910	NY A	1	4	0	2	1	0	0	2	0	0		.500	.500	.750	275	-0		.900	-0	167	74	/C		0.1
1911	NY A	4	9	2	2	1	0	0	0	0	0		.222	.222	.333	51	-1	0	1.000	-2	71	58	C4		-0.2
Total	2	5	13	2	4	2	0	0	2	0	0		.308	.308	.462	114	0	0	.933	-2	115	65	C5		-0.1

WALSH, JOE
Joseph Patrick "Tweet"   B3.13.1917 Boston MA   D10.5.1996 Boston MA   BR/TR/5-10/155   d7.1

YEAR	TM LG	G	AB	R	H	2B	3B	HR	RBI	BB-IB	HP	SO	AVG	OBP	SLG	AOPS	ABR	SB-CS	FA	FR	RNG	THR	GAMES AT POSITION	DL	BFW
1938	Bos N	4	8	0	0	0	0	0	0	0	0	2	.000	.000	.000	-99	-2	0	.900	-1	50	86	S4		-0.3

WALSH, JOE
Joseph R. "Reddy"   B11.5.1864 Chicago IL   D8.8.1911 Omaha NE   BL/TR   d9.3

YEAR	TM LG	G	AB	R	H	2B	3B	HR	RBI	BB-IB	HP	SO	AVG	OBP	SLG	AOPS	ABR	SB-CS	FA	FR	RNG	THR	GAMES AT POSITION	DL	BFW
1891	Bal AA	26	100	14	21	0	1	1	10	6	0	18	.210	.255	.260	47	-8	4	.865	1	85	215	S13,2b13		-0.5

WALSH, DEE
Leo Thomas   B3.28.1890 St.Louis MO   D7.14.1971 St.Louis MO   BB/TR/5-9.5/165   d4.10

YEAR	TM LG	G	AB	R	H	2B	3B	HR	RBI	BB-IB	HP	SO	AVG	OBP	SLG	AOPS	ABR	SB-CS	FA	FR	RNG	THR	GAMES AT POSITION	DL	BFW
1913	StL A	23	53	8	9	0	1	0	5	6	4	11	.170	.302	.208	51	-3	3	.933	0	112	81	S22/3		-0.2
1914	StL A	7	23	1	2	0	0	0	1	2	0	4	.087	.160	.087	-27	-4	1-1	.919	-0	97	188	S7		-0.4
1915	StL A	59	150	13	33	5	0	0	6	14	5	25	.220	.308	.253	71	-5	6-6	.951	4	95	227	O45(0/21/24),3b2/P2S		-0.4
Total	3	89	226	22	44	5	1	0	12	22	9	40	.195	.292	.226	56	-12	10-7	.951	4	95	227	O45(0/21/24),S30,3b3/2P		-1.0

WALSH, JIMMY
Michael Timothy "Runt"   B3.25.1886 Lima OH   D1.21.1947 Baltimore MD   BR/TR/5-9/174   d4.25   OF(29/16/33)

YEAR	TM LG	G	AB	R	H	2B	3B	HR	RBI	BB-IB	HP	SO	AVG	OBP	SLG	AOPS	ABR	SB-CS	FA	FR	RNG	THR	GAMES AT POSITION	DL	BFW
1910	Phi N	88	242	28	60	8	3	3	31	25	2	38	.248	.323	.343	91	-3	5	.947	-4	113	82	2b26,O26(7/14/6),S9,3b5		-0.8
1911	Phi N	94	289	29	78	20	3	1	31	21	2	30	.270	.324	.370	93	-3	5	.962	-3	92	50	O48(22/2/25),2b14,S9,3b7,C4/P1		-0.7
1912	Phi N	51	150	16	40	6	3	2	19	8	0	20	.267	.304	.387	83	-4	3	.944	1	108	81	2b31,3b12,C5		-0.2
1913	Phi N	26	30	3	10	4	0	0	5	1	0	5	.333	.355	.467	128	1	0	1.000	-0	90	219	2b6,S3/3OR		0.0
1914	Bal F	120	428	54	132	25	4	10	65	22	2	56	.308	.345	.456	113	0	18	.932	3	102	103	3b113/2SOR		0.7
1915	Bal F	106	401	43	121	20	1	9	60	21	4	44	.302	.340	.424	111	-1	12	.936	-5	94	91	3b106		-0.2
StL F	17	31	3	6	1	0	0	1	3	0	4	.194	.306	.226	48	-2	1	.913	-0	106	0	3b9		-0.2
	Year	123	432	48	127	21	1	9	61	24	4	48	.294	.337	.410	106	-3	13	.934	-5	95	85	3b115		-0.4
Total	6	502	1571	178	447	84	14	25	212	101	10	197	.285	.332	.404	102	-12	45	.925	-8	97	95	3b253,2b78,O76R,S22,C9/1P		-1.7

WALSH, TOM
Thomas Joseph   B2.28.1886 Davenport IA   D3.16.1963 Naples FL   BR/TR/5-11/170   d8.15

YEAR	TM LG	G	AB	R	H	2B	3B	HR	RBI	BB-IB	HP	SO	AVG	OBP	SLG	AOPS	ABR	SB-CS	FA	FR	RNG	THR	GAMES AT POSITION	DL	BFW
1906	Chi N	2	1	0	0	0	0	0	0	0	0		.000	.000	.000	-95	-0	0	1.000	-0	0	323	C2		0.0

WALSH, WALT
Walter William   B4.30.1897 Newark NJ   D1.15.1966 Avon By The Sea NJ   BR/TR/5-11/170   d5.4

YEAR	TM LG	G	AB	R	H	2B	3B	HR	RBI	BB-IB	HP	SO	AVG	OBP	SLG	AOPS	ABR	SB-CS	FA	FR	RNG	THR	GAMES AT POSITION	DL	BFW
1920	Phi N	2	0	0	0	0	0	0	0	0	0		—	—	—	—	-0	0	—	0			/R		0.0

WALTERS, ROXY
Alfred John   B11.5.1892 San Francisco CA   D6.3.1956 Alameda CA   BR/TR/5-8.5/160   d9.16

YEAR	TM LG	G	AB	R	H	2B	3B	HR	RBI	BB-IB	HP	SO	AVG	OBP	SLG	AOPS	ABR	SB-CS	FA	FR	RNG	THR	GAMES AT POSITION	DL	BFW
1915	NY A	2	6	2	2	0	0	0	0	0	0		.333	.333	.333	100	0		1.000	1	141	189	C2		0.
1916	NY A	66	203	13	54	9	3	0	23	14	2	42	.266	.320	.340	96	-1	2	.974	12	143	139	C65		1.
1917	NY A	61	171	16	45	2	2	0	14	9	1	22	.263	.304	.275	76	-5	2	.968	8	139	105	C57		0.
1918	NY A	64	191	18	38	5	1	0	12	9	1	18	.199	.239	.236	42	-14	3	.953	-2	120	76	C50,O9R		-0.
1919	Bos A	48	135	7	26	2	0	0	9	7	5	15	.193	.259	.207	33	-12	1	.982	3	105	109	C47		-0.
1920	Bos A	88	258	25	51	11	3	0	28	30	2	21	.198	.303	.248	49	-18	2-2	.980	5	77	100	C85,1b2		-0.
1921	Bos A	54	169	17	34	4	1	0	14	10	2	11	.201	.254	.237	27	-19	3-0	.990	11	128	111	C36		-0.
1922	Bos A	38	98	4	19	2	0	0	6	3	1	6	.194	.240	.214	19	-12	0-0	.977	3	99	90	C36		-0.
1923	Bos A	40	104	5	26	4	0	0	5	2	0	6	.250	.264	.288	45	-9	0-2	.974	-3	90	135	C36/2		-0.
1924	Cle A	32	74	5	19	2	0	0	5	10	0	6	.257	.345	.284	63	-4	0-1	.979	3	104	129	C25,2b7		-0.
1925	Cle A	5	19	0	2	0	0	0	0	3	0	2	.105	.227	.105	6	-3	0-0	1.000	0	124	197	C5		-0.
Total	11	498	1426	119	317	41	6	0	116	97	20	151	.222	.281	.259	51	-97	13-5	.975	46	113	111	C462,O9R,2b8,1b2		-0.

WALTERS, DAN
Daniel Gene   B8.15.1966 Brunswick ME   BR/TR/6-4/225*   [HouN84 5/123]   d6.1

YEAR	TM LG	G	AB	R	H	2B	3B	HR	RBI	BB-IB	HP	SO	AVG	OBP	SLG	AOPS	ABR	SB-CS	FA	FR	RNG	THR	GAMES AT POSITION	DL	BFW
1992	SD N	57	179	14	45	11	1	4	22	10-0	2	28	.251	.295	.391	92	-2	1-0	.992	3	85	97	C55		-0.1
1993	SD N	27	94	6	19	3	0	1	10	7-2	0	13	.202	.255	.266	40	-8	0-0	.970	-5	75	140	C26		-0.1
Total	2	84	273	20	64	14	1	5	32	17-2	2	41	.234	.281	.348	73	-10	1-0	.985	-2	81	112	C81		

YEAR	TM LG	G	AB	R	H	2B	3B	HR	RBI	BB-IB	HP	SO	AVG	OBP	SLG	AOPS	ABR	SB-CS	FA	FR	RNG	THR	GAMES AT POSITION	DL	BFW
WALTERS, FRED			Fred James "Whale"			B9.4.1912 Laurel MS			D2.1.1980 Laurel MS			BR/TR/6-1/210		d4.17		Col Mississippi St.								
1945	Bos A	40	93	2	16	2	0	0	5	10		9	.172	.252	.194	29	-8	1-1	.993	3	115	196	C38		-0.4
WALTERS, KEN			Kenneth Rogers			B11.11.1933 Fresno CA			BR/TR/6-1/180*			d4.12												
1960	Phi N	124	426	42	102	10	0	8	37	16-3	1	50	.239	.266	.319	60	-25	4-3	.988	9	108	166	O119(5/2/116)		-2.1
1961	Phi N	86	180	23	41	8	2	2	14	5-0	1	25	.228	.251	.328	53	-13	2-2	.975	0	100	112	O56(0/4/53),1b5/3		-1.6
1963	Cin N	49	75	6	14	2	0	1	7	4-1	1	14	.187	.237	.253	40	-6	0-2	.889	-2	73	0	O21(11/0/10)/1		-1.1
Total	3	259	681	71	157	20	2	11	58	25-4	3	89	.231	.259	.314	56	-44	6-7	.979	7	103	139	O196(16/6/179),1b6/3		-4.8
WALTERS, BUCKY			William Henry			B4.19.1909 Philadelphia PA			D4.20.1991 Abington PA			BR/TR/6-1/180*		d9.18 M2/C8 ▲										
1931	Bos N	9	38	2	8	2	0	0	0	0	0	3	.211	.211	.263	28	-4	0	.947	1	113	0	3b6,2b3		-0.3
1932	Bos N	22	75	8	14	3	1	0	4	2	0	18	.187	.208	.253	24	-8	0	.910	0	106	213	3b22		-0.8
1933	Bos N	52	195	27	50	8	3	4	28	19	1	24	.256	.326	.390	90	-5	1-1	.940	1	106	143	3b43,2b7		-0.1
1934	Bos A	23	88	10	19	4	4	4	18	3	0	12	.216	.242	.489	79	-4	0-0	.906	3	112	129	3b23		0.0
	Phi N	83	300	36	78	20	3	4	38	19	2	54	.260	.308	.387	75	-10	1	.950	-6	91	106	3b80,2b3,P2		-1.4
1935	Phi N	49	96	14	24	2	1	0	6	9	0	12	.250	.314	.292	58	-6	0	1.000	2	126	211	P24,O5L,2b2/3		0.0
1936	Phi N	64	121	12	29	10	1	1	16	7	0	15	.240	.281	.364	66	-6	0	.974	2	176	149	P40/23		0.4
1937	Phi N★	56	137	15	38	6	0	1	16	5	0	16	.277	.303	.343	69	-6	0	.988	5	143	237	P37,3b8		0.2
1938	Phi N	15	35	6	10	1	0	0	3	1	0	5	.286	.306	.429	103	3	1	.955	0	107	250	P12		0.0
	Cin N	36	64	10	9	1	0	0	5	7	1	18	.141	.236	.156	10	0	0	.981	2	141	100	P27		0.0
	Year	51	99	16	19	3	0	1	8	8	1	23	.192	.259	.253	42	3	1	.973	3	130	150	P39		0.0
1939	†Cin N☆	40	120	16	39	8	1	1	16	5	1	12	.325	.357	.433	111	13	1	.979	4	118	291	P39		0.0
1940	†Cin N★	37	117	11	24	3	0	1	18	4	0	14	.205	.231	.256	34	2	2	.945	-1	91	233	P36		0.0
1941	Cin N	39	106	6	20	6	0	0	9	7	0	13	.189	.239	.245	36	2	0	.977	2	109	153	P37		0.0
1942	Cin N★	40	99	13	24	6	1	2	13	3	0	13	.242	.265	.384	89	-2	0	.961	1	110	198	P34/OL		0.1
1943	Cin N	37	90	11	24	7	1	1	12	6	0	18	.267	.313	.400	107	8	0	.971	1	97	206	P34		0.0
1944	Cin N★	37	107	9	30	4	0	0	13	8	0	16	.280	.330	.318	86	8	0	1.000	0	101	241	P34		0.0
1945	Cin N	24	61	11	14	3	0	3	8	3	0	14	.230	.266	.426	93	5	2	.975	-0	100	165	P22		0.0
1946	Cin N	24	55	6	7	2	0	0	5	4	0	12	.127	.186	.164	-0	-1	2	.940	2	123	371	P22		0.0
1947	Cin N	20	45	3	12	2	0	0	4	2	0	13	.267	.298	.311	62	3	0	.962	-1	83	0	P20		0.0
1948	Cin N	7	15	1	4	0	0	0	2	0	0	2	.267	.267	.267	46	1	0	1.000	1	169	0	P7,M	60	0.0
1950	Bos N	1	2	0	0	0	0	0	0	0	0	0	.000	.000	.000	-99	-0	0	1.000	-0	-0	0	/P		0.0
Total	19	715	1966	227	477	99	16	23	234	114	5	303	.243	.286	.344	69	-5	12-1	.974	24	117	205	P428,3b184,2b16,O6L	60	-1.9
WALTON, DANNY			Daniel James "Mickey"			B7.14.1947 Los Angeles CA			BR/TR (BB 1975-80)/6-0/200(185-200)			[HouN65 8/192]		d4.20										
1968	Hou N	2	2	0	0	0	0	0	0	0-0	0	1	.000	.000	.000	-99	0	0-0	—	0			/H		-0.1
1969	Sea A	23	92	12	20	1	2	3	10	5-0	2	26	.217	.275	.370	81	-3	2-0	.976	-2	87	0	O23L		-0.7
1970	Mil A	117	397	32	102	20	1	17	66	51-4	6	126	.257	.349	.441	117	10	2-3	.965	-5	86	62	O114L		-0.2
1971	Mil A	30	69	5	14	3	0	2	9	7-0	1	22	.203	.286	.333	76	-2	0-0	.923	-3	75	0	O19(19/1/0)/3		-0.7
	NY A	5	14	1	2	0	0	1	2	0-0	0	7	.143	.143	.357	40	-1	0-0	1.000	1	62	0	O4(1/0/3)		-0.2
	Year	35	83	6	16	3	0	3	11	7-0	1	29	.193	.264	.337	70	-4	0-0	.933	-3	73	0	O23(20/1/3)/3		-0.9
1973	Min A	37	96	13	17	1	1	4	8	17-0	0	28	.177	.301	.333	75	-3	0-0	1.000	-2	61	0	O18(15/0/3),D11/3		-0.7
1975	Min A	42	63	4	11	2	0	1	8	4-2	0	18	.175	.224	.254	34	-6	0-0	.962	-0	52	169	1b7,C2,D6		-0.7
1976	LA N	18	15	0	2	0	0	0	2	1-0	0	5	.133	.176	.133	-8	-2	0-0	—	0			/H		-0.3
1977	Hou N	13	21	0	4	0	0	1	0	0-0	1	5	.190	.190	.190	3	-3	0-0	.956	1	85	37	1b5		-0.4
1980	Tex A	10	10	2	2	0	0	0	1	3-0	0	5	.200	.385	.200	67	0	0-0	—	0			/D		0.0
Total	9	297	779	69	174	27	4	28	107	88-6	10	240	.223	.309	.376	90	-10	4-3	.966	-14	82	39	O178(172/1/6),D18,1b12,C2,3b2		-3.9
WALTON, JEROME			Jerome O'Terrell			B7.8.1965 Newnan GA			BR/TR/6-1/175(175-200)			[ChiN86*2/36]		d4.4 Col Enterprise St. (AL) JC										
1989	†Chi N	116	475	64	139	23	3	5	46	27-1	6	77	.293	.335	.385	100	0	24-7	.990	-5	99	34	O115C	31	-0.3
1990	Chi N	101	392	63	103	16	2	2	21	50-1	4	70	.263	.350	.329	83	-7	14-7	.977	-5	99	56	O98C	45	-1.3
1991	Chi N	123	270	42	59	13	1	5	17	19-0	3	55	.219	.275	.330	67	-12	7-3	.983	-2	104	53	O101(0/100/1)		-1.4
1992	Chi N	30	55	7	7	0	1	0	1	9-0	2	13	.127	.273	.164	26	-5	1-2	.944	-1	90	0	O24(22/1/1)	18	-0.8
1993	Cal A	5	2	0	0	0	0	0	0	1-0	0	2	.000	.333	.000	-2	0	1-0	1.000	0	174	0	/OLD		0.0
1994	Cin N	46	68	10	21	4	0	1	9	4-0	0	12	.309	.347	.412	97	0	1-3	1.000	-0	107	166	O26(16/5/6),1b7	38	-0.2
1995	†Cin N	102	162	32	47	12	1	8	22	17-0	4	25	.290	.368	.525	132	8	10-7	.982	3	116	82	O89(36/50/8),1b3		0.9
1996	Atl N	37	47	9	16	5	0	1	4	5-0	0	10	.340	.389	.511	131	2	0-0	1.000	2	157	0	O28(23/1/5)	123	0.4
1997	†Bal A	26	68	8	20	1	0	3	9	4-0	0	10	.294	.333	.441	103	0	0-0	1.000	-0	111	0	O19(9/2/11),1b5,D2	129	-0.1
1998	TB A	12	34	4	11	3	0	0	3	2-0	0	6	.324	.361	.412	98	0	0-0	1.000	2	124	581	O8(4/0/4),D3	19	0.2
Total	10	598	1573	241	423	77	8	25	132	138-2	19	280	.269	.333	.385	97	-14	58-29	.984	-6	105	56	O509(111/373/36),1b15,D9	403	-2.6
WALTON, REGGIE			Reginald Sherard			B10.24.1952 Kansas City MO			BR/TR/6-3/205*			[SFN72*2/44]		d6.13 Col Compton (CA) CC										
1980	Sea A	31	83	8	23	6	0	2	7	1-0	1	10	.277	.307	.422	97	-0	2-2	.929	-1	0	118	O17(6/0/11),D11		-0.2
1981	Sea A	12	6	1	0	0	0	0	0	1-0	0	2	.000	.143	.000	-53	-1	0-0	—	-0	0	0	O4(3/0/1)/D	23	-0.2
1982	Pit N	13	15	1	3	1	0	0	0	1-0	1	1	.200	.294	.267	55	-1	0-0	—	-0	0	0	O2L		-0.1
Total	3	56	104	10	26	7	0	2	9	5-0	2	13	.250	.295	.375	82	-2	2-2	.929	-1	101	0	O23(11/0/12),D12	23	-0.5
WAMBSGANSS, BILL			William Adolph			B3.19.1894 Cleveland OH			D12.8.1985 Lakewood OH			BR/TR/5-11/175		d8.4 Mil 1918										
1914	Cle A	43	143	12	31	6	2	0	12	8	4	24	.217	.277	.287	67	-6	2-7	.921	-2	103	105	S36,2b4		-0.8
1915	Cle A	121	375	30	73	4	4	0	21	36	4	50	.195	.272	.227	48	-24	8-9	.938	-2	104	81	2b78,3b35		-2.7
1916	Cle A	136	475	57	117	14	4	0	45	41	5	40	.246	.313	.293	77	-13	13	.925	-5	100	95	S106,2b24,3b5		-1.1
1917	Cle A	141	499	52	127	17	6	0	43	37	7	42	.255	.315	.313	85	-9	16	.951	15	111	126	2b137,1b3		0.9
1918	Cle A	87	315	34	93	15	2	0	40	21	3	21	.295	.345	.356	102	1	16	.952	-1	97	98	2b87		0.1
1919	Cle A	139	526	60	146	17	6	2	60	32	3	24	.278	.323	.344	82	-13	18	.963	11	103	109	2b139		0.0
1920	†Cle A	153	565	83	138	16	11	1	55	54	5	26	.244	.316	.317	66	-28	9-18	.960	8	101	114	2b153		-2.2
1921	Cle A	107	410	80	117	28	5	2	47	44	3	27	.285	.359	.393	90	-5	13-7	.963	-16	82	101	2b103,3b2		-1.7
1922	Cle A	142	538	89	141	22	6	0	47	60	4	26	.262	.341	.325	74	-19	17-10	.961	-7	98	101	2b125,S16		-2.1
1923	Cle A	101	345	59	100	20	4	1	59	43	3	15	.290	.373	.380	99	1	10-9	.963	7	105	92	2b88,3b4		0.9
1924	Bos A	156	636	93	174	41	5	0	49	54	4	33	.274	.334	.354	77	-21	14-8	.963	13	100	110	2b156		-0.3
1925	Bos A	111	360	50	83	12	4	1	41	52	1	21	.231	.329	.294	59	-22	3-5	.957	8	106	98	2b103,1b6		-1.1
1926	Phi A	54	54	11	19	3	0	0	1	8	1	6	.352	.444	.407	117	2	1-1	.923	0	107	122	S17,2b8		0.3
Total	13	1491	5241	710	1359	215	59	7	520	490	47	357	.259	.328	.327	78	-156	140-74	.958	29	101	105	2b1205,S175,3b46,1b9		-9.8
WANER, LLOYD			Lloyd James "Little Poison"			B3.16.1906 Harrah OK			D7.22.1982 Oklahoma City OK			BL/TR/5-9/150		d4.12 Def 1943 HF1967 b-Paul Col East Central										
1927	†Pit N	150	629	133	223	17	6	2	27	37	6	23	.355	.396	.410	108	9	14	.976	-4	103	58	O150(42/109/0)/2		-0.3
1928	Pit N	152	659	121	221	22	14	5	61	40	4	13	.335	.377	.434	107	6	8	.980	-1	99	107	O152(10/143/0)		-0.2
1929	Pit N	151	662	134	234	28	20	5	74	37	9	20	.353	.395	.479	113	12	6	.987	7	101	140	O151C		1.1
1930	Pit N	68	260	32	94	8	3	1	36	5	1	5	.362	.378	.427	93	-3	3	.983	3	105	120	O65C		-0.5
1931	Pit N	154	681	90	214	25	13	1	57	39	1	16	.314	.352	.407	104	2	7	.979	0	105	143	O153C/2		0.9
1932	Pit N	134	565	90	188	27	11	2	38	31	0	11	.333	.367	.430	116	12	6	.986	9	116	76	O131C		1.7
1933	Pit N	121	500	59	138	14	5	0	26	22	0	8	.276	.307	.324	80	-14	3	.982	-1	101	107	O114(65/49/0)		-1.9
1934	Pit N	140	611	95	173	27	6	1	48	38	3	12	.283	.326	.352	80	-17	6	.979	7	113	81	O139C		-1.3
1935	Pit N	122	537	83	166	22	14	0	46	22	0	10	.309	.336	.402	95	-6	1	.989	2	108	50	O121C		-0.7
1936	Pit N	106	414	67	133	13	8	1	31	31	0	5	.321	.369	.399	104	3	1	.984	-3	100	30	O92C		-0.3
1937	Pit N	129	537	80	177	22	4	1	45	34	0	12	.330	.370	.393	107	6	3	.988	5	102	80	O123C		0.3
1938	Pit N☆	147	619	79	194	25	7	5	57	28	1	13	.313	.343	.401	103	1	5	.986	-5	92	121	O144C		-0.9
1939	Pit N	112	379	49	108	15	3	0	24	17	3	13	.285	.321	.340	79	-12	0	.992	5	105	130	O92C/3		-1.1
1940	Pit N	72	166	30	43	3	0	0	3	5	1	5	.259	.285	.277	56	-10	2	.989	0	101	102	O42(1/41/0)		-1.1
1941	Pit N	3	4	2	1	0	0	0	0	2	0	0	.250	.500	.250	116	0	0	1.000	0	114	0	/OC		0.0
	Bos N	19	51	7	21	1	0	0	5	4	0	3	.412	.434	.431	151	4	1	.969	-1	104	106	O15(3/11/1)		0.3
	Cin N	55	164	17	42	4	1	0	6	8	0	8	.256	.291	.293	64	-8	0	.986	-1	93	101	O44(0/13/31)		-1.1
	Year	77	219	26	64	5	1	0	11	12	0	11	.292	.329	.324	85	-5	1	.981	-1	96	99	O60(3/25/32)		-0.8
1942	Phi N	101	287	23	75	7	3	0	10	16	0	6	.261	.300	.307	82	-8	1	.967	-2	100	92	O75C		-1.2
1944	Pit N	15	14	3	4	0	0	0	2	2	0	0	.286	.412	.286	116	1	0	1.000	-0	97	0	O4C		0.0
	Pit N	19	14	2	5	0	0	0	2	1	0	0	.357	.438	.357	120	1	0	1.000	1	162	0	O7(1/6/0)		0.1

YEAR	TM LG	G	AB	R	H	2B	3B	HR	RBI	BB-IB	HP	SO	AVG	OBP	SLG	AOPS	ABR	SB-CS	FA	FR	RNG	THR	GAMES AT POSITION	DL	BF
	Year	34	28	5	9	0	0	0	3	5	0	0	.321	.424	.321	100	1	0	1.000	1	139	0	O11(1/10/0)		0.
1945	Pit N	23	19	5	5	0	0	0	1	1	0	0	.263	.300	.263	55	-1	0	1.000	1	104	1380	O3(2/0/1)		0
Total	18	1993	7772	1201	2459	281	118	27	598	420	26	173	.316	.353	.393	99	-25	67	.983	31	103	97	O1818(124/1663/33),2b2/3		-5

WANER, PAUL Paul Glee "Big Poison" B4.16.1903 Harrah OK D8.29.1965 Sarasota FL BL/TL/5-8.5/153 d4.13 Mil 1945 C1 HF1952 b-Lloyd Col East Central

YEAR	TM LG	G	AB	R	H	2B	3B	HR	RBI	BB-IB	HP	SO	AVG	OBP	SLG	AOPS	ABR	SB-CS	FA	FR	RNG	THR	GAMES AT POSITION	DL	BF
1926	Pit N	144	536	101	180	35	**22**	8	79	66	4	19	.336	**.413**	.528	154	34	11	.976	4	103	0	O139(6/0/133)		2
1927	†Pit N	155	623	114	**237**	42	18	9	**131**	60	3	14	.380	.437	.549	152	47	5	.980	5	107	112	O143R,1b14		3.
1928	Pit N	152	602	**142**	223	**50**	19	6	86	77	5	16	.370	.446	.547	152	49	6	.975	3	107	105	O131R,1b24		3.
1929	Pit N	151	596	131	200	43	15	15	100	89	4	18	.336	.424	.534	133	33	15	.986	1	101	95	O143R,1b7		3
1930	Pit N	145	589	117	217	32	18	8	77	57	4	18	.368	.428	.525	128	28	18	.959	-4	106	50	O143(0/5/138)		0
1931	Pit N	150	559	88	180	35	10	6	70	73	4	21	.322	.404	.453	131	28	6	.976	13	107	153	O138R,1b10		3
1932	Pit N	**154**	630	107	215	**62**	10	8	82	56	2	24	.341	.397	.510	144	42	13	.974	1	105	81	O154(0/9/145)		4
1933	Pit N★	**154**	618	101	191	38	16	7	70	60	2	20	.309	.372	.456	136	29	3	.981	3	103	105	O154R		4
1934	Pit N★	146	599	**122**	**217**	32	16	14	90	68	2	24	**.362**	.428	.539	154	47	8	.985	7	108	113	O145R		1
1935	Pit N★	139	549	98	176	29	12	11	78	61	3	22	.321	.392	.477	128	23	2	.983	1	103	91	O136R		2
1936	Pit N	148	585	107	218	53	9	5	94	74	3	29	**.373**	.446	.520	156	51	7	.960	-9	107	95	O150R,1b3		4
1937	Pit N★	**154**	619	94	219	30	9	2	74	63	0	34	.354	.413	.441	132	30	4	.970	-6	95	79	O147(0/1/148)		0
1938	Pit N	148	625	77	175	31	6	6	69	47	1	28	.280	.331	.378	94	-6	2	.977	-5	95	79	O106R		0
1939	Pit N	125	461	62	151	30	6	3	45	35	0	18	.328	.375	.438	120	13	0	.978	1	97	122	O106R		-0
1940	Pit N	89	238	32	69	16	1	1	32	23	0	14	.290	.352	.378	102	2	0	.985	-1	92	109	O45R,1b8		-0
1941	Bro N	11	35	5	6	0	0	0	4	8	0	0	.171	.326	.171	41	-2	0	.923	-1	83	0	O9R		-0
	Bos N	95	294	40	82	10	2	2	46	47	0	14	.279	.384	.347	110	6	1	.965	-1	95	120	O77(10/3/66),1b7		-0
	Year	106	329	45	88	10	2	2	50	55	0	14	.267	.372	.328	102	3	1	.961	-2	94	108	O86(10/3/75),1b7		-0
1942	Bos N	114	333	43	86	17	1	1	39	62	0	20	.258	.376	.324	108	7	2	.969	-5	90	78	O94R		-0
1943	Bro N	82	225	29	70	16	0	1	26	35	1	9	.311	.406	.396	132	12	0	.960	-1	106	70	O57(1/0/56)		-0
1944	Bro N	83	136	16	39	4	1	0	16	27	0	7	.287	.405	.331	111	4	0	.983	1	108	112	O32(1/0/31)		-0
	NY A	9	7	1	1	0	0	1	2	0	0	0	.143	.333	.143	37	0	1-0	—	0			/H		C
1945	NY A	1	0	0	0	0	0	0	0	1	0	0	—	1.000	—	191	0	0	—	0			/H		C
Total	20	2549	9459	1627	3152	605	191	113	1309	1091	38	376	.333	.404	.473	133	477	104-0	.975	29	103	99	O2288(18/18/2256),1b73		33

WANNER, JACK Clarence Curtis "Johnny" B11.29.1885 Geneseo IL D5.28.1919 Geneseo IL BR/TR/5-11.5/190 d9.28

YEAR	TM LG	G	AB	R	H	2B	3B	HR	RBI	BB-IB	HP	SO	AVG	OBP	SLG	AOPS	ABR	SB-CS	FA	FR	RNG	THR	GAMES AT POSITION	DL	BF
1909	NY A	3	8	0	1	0	0	0	2	0	0		.125	.300	.125	35	0	1	.600	-2	80	143	S2		-0

WANNINGER, PEE-WEE Paul Louis B12.12.1902 Birmingham AL D3.7.1981 N.Augusta SC BL/TR/5-7/150 d4.22

YEAR	TM LG	G	AB	R	H	2B	3B	HR	RBI	BB-IB	HP	SO	AVG	OBP	SLG	AOPS	ABR	SB-CS	FA	FR	RNG	THR	GAMES AT POSITION	DL	BF
1925	NY A	117	403	35	95	13	6	1	22	11	0	34	.236	.256	.305	43	-38	3-5	.944	-5	93	98	S111,3b3/2		-3
1927	Bos A	18	60	4	12	0	0	1	6	1	1	2	.200	.284	.200	28	-6	2-4	.890	-1	104	125	S15		-C
	Cin N	28	93	14	23	2	2	0	8	6	0	7	.247	.293	.312	64	-5	0	.953	3	107	131	S28		-C
Total	2	163	556	53	130	15	8	1	31	23	1	43	.234	.266	.295	45	-49	5-9	.941	-3	97	107	S154,3b3/2		-5

WARD, AARON Aaron Lee B8.28.1896 Booneville AR D1.30.1961 New Orleans LA BR/TR/5-10.5/160 d8.14 Mil 1918 Col Ouachita Baptist

YEAR	TM LG	G	AB	R	H	2B	3B	HR	RBI	BB-IB	HP	SO	AVG	OBP	SLG	AOPS	ABR	SB-CS	FA	FR	RNG	THR	GAMES AT POSITION	DL	BF
1917	NY A	8	26	0	3	0	0	0	1	1	0	5	.115	.148	.115	-19	-4	0	.926	-1	75	126	S7		-C
1918	NY A	20	32	2	4	1	0	0	1	2	0	7	.125	.176	.156	0	-4	0	.941	3	121	186	S12,O4C,2b3		-C
1919	NY A	27	34	5	7	2	0	0	2	5	0	6	.206	.308	.265	61	-2	0	1.000	3	94	261	1b5,3b3,S2/2		-C
1920	NY A	127	496	62	127	18	7	11	54	33	1	84	.256	.304	.387	79	-17	7-5	.965	17	110	127	3b114,S12		-C
1921	†NY A	153	556	77	170	30	16	5	75	42	3	68	.306	.363	.423	98	-2	6-8	.961	19	110	136	2b124,3b33		-C
1922	†NY A	154	558	69	149	19	5	7	68	46	6	64	.267	.328	.357	77	-20	6-4	**.980**	10	105	107	2b152		-C
1923	†NY A	152	567	79	161	26	11	10	82	56	3	65	.284	.351	.422	101	-1	8-8	**.980**	15	105	107	2b152		-C
1924	NY A	120	440	42	101	13	10	8	66	40	2	45	.253	.324	.395	85	-12	1-4	.973	8	104	92	2b120/S		-C
1925	NY A	125	439	41	108	22	3	4	38	49	3	49	.246	.326	.337	70	-20	1-1	.966	-14	91	92	2b113,3b10		-C
1926	NY A	22	31	5	10	2	0	0	3	2	0	6	.323	.364	.387	97	0	0	1.000	-3	50	0	2b4/3		-C
1927	Chi A	145	463	75	125	25	8	5	56	63	2	56	.270	.360	.391	97	-1	6-5	.963	-24	95	85	2b139,3b6		-2
1928	Cle A	6	9	0	1	0	0	0	0	1	0	2	.111	.200	.111	-16	-2	0	.818	1	80	414	3b3,S2/2		-C
Total	12	1059	3611	457	966	158	54	50	446	339	25	457	.268	.335	.383	85	-85	36-38	.970	17	101	89	2b809,3b172,S36,1b5,O4C		-C

WARD, CHUCK Charles William B7.30.1894 St.Louis MO D4.4.1969 Indian Rocks FL BR/TR/5-11.5/170 d4.11 Mil 1918

YEAR	TM LG	G	AB	R	H	2B	3B	HR	RBI	BB-IB	HP	SO	AVG	OBP	SLG	AOPS	ABR	SB-CS	FA	FR	RNG	THR	GAMES AT POSITION	DL	BF
1917	Pit N	125	423	25	100	12	3	0	43	32	8	43	.236	.302	.279	76	-11	5	.912	-26	87	98	S112,2b8,3b5		-0
1918	Bro N	2	6	0	2	0	0	0	3	0	0	0	.333	.333	.333	104	0	0	1.000	-1	103	0	3b2		-0
1919	Bro N	45	150	7	35	1	2	0	8	5	2	11	.233	.277	.267	62	-7	0	.920	-7	88	0	3b45		-0
1920	Bro N	19	71	7	11	1	0	0	4	3	1	9	.155	.200	.169	6	-9	0	.928	-7	71	63	S19		-0
1921	Bro N	12	28	1	2	1	0	0	0	4	0	2	.071	.188	.107	-19	-5	0-0	.937	-3	110	143	S12		-0
1922	Bro N	33	91	12	25	5	1	0	14	5	1	8	.275	.320	.352	74	-4	1-1	.934	-4	94	81	S31,3b2		-0
Total	6	236	769	52	175	20	6	0	72	51	12	67	.228	.286	.269	63	-36	7-1	.919	-40	88	94	S174,3b54,2b8		-0

WARD, CHRIS Chris Gilbert B5.18.1949 Oakland CA BL/TL/6-0/180* d9.10 Col Chabot (CA) JC

YEAR	TM LG	G	AB	R	H	2B	3B	HR	RBI	BB-IB	HP	SO	AVG	OBP	SLG	AOPS	ABR	SB-CS	FA	FR	RNG	THR	GAMES AT POSITION	DL	BF
1972	Chi N	1	1	0	0	0	0	0	0	0	0	0	.000	.000	.000	-90	0	0-0	—	0			/H		-C
1974	Chi N	92	137	8	28	4	0	1	15	18-3	0	13	.204	.293	.255	53	-8	0-2	.977	2	122	84	O22(21/0/1),1b6		-C
Total	2	93	138	8	28	4	0	1	15	18-3	0	13	.203	.291	.254	52	-8	0-2	.977	2	122	84	O22(21/0/1),1b6		-C

WARD, DARYLE Daryle Lamar B6.27.1975 Lynwood CA BL/TL/6-2/230(230-245) [DetA94 15/417] d5.14 f-Gary Col Santa Ana (CA) JC

YEAR	TM LG	G	AB	R	H	2B	3B	HR	RBI	BB-IB	HP	SO	AVG	OBP	SLG	AOPS	ABR	SB-CS	FA	FR	RNG	THR	GAMES AT POSITION	DL	BF
1998	Hou N	4	3	1	1	0	0	0	1-0	0	2	.333	.500	.333	128	0	0-0	.944	-3	74	70	O31L,1b10,D3		
1999	†Hou N	64	150	11	41	6	0	8	30	9-0	0	31	.273	.311	.473	97	-2	0-0	.986	-3	88	40	O47(43/0/4),1b19,D4		
2000	Hou N	119	264	36	68	10	2	20	47	15-2	0	61	.258	.295	.538	97	-3	0-0	.985	-2	89	82	O42(27/0/15),1b9,D3		
2001	†Hou N	95	213	21	56	15	0	9	39	19-4	1	48	.263	.323	.460	93	-2	0-0	.981	-5	76	141	O122L/D		
2002	Hou N	136	453	41	125	31	0	12	72	33-5	1	82	.276	.324	.424	91	-7	1-3	.992	-0	146	171	1b13,O11L		19
2003	LA N	52	109	6	20	1	0	9	3-0	1	19	.183	.211	.193	7	-15	0-0	.992	-8	95	0	1b28,D6		50
2004	Pit N	79	293	39	73	17	2	15	57	22-3	2	45	.249	.305	.474	98	-2	0-2	.991	-5	82	134	1b71,O12R		
2005	Pit N	133	407	46	106	21	1	12	63	37-10	1	60	.260	.318	.405	90	-6	0-2	.994	7	131	124	1b109		69
Total	8	682	1892	201	490	101	5	76	317	139-24	7	348	.259	.309	.438	89	-37	1-5	.980	-11	79	95	O265(234/0/31),1b231,D11		

WARD, PIGGY Frank Gray B4.16.1867 Chambersburg PA D10.24.1912 Altoona PA BB/TR/5-9.5/196 d6.12

YEAR	TM LG	G	AB	R	H	2B	3B	HR	RBI	BB-IB	HP	SO	AVG	OBP	SLG	AOPS	ABR	SB-CS	FA	FR	RNG	THR	GAMES AT POSITION	DL	BF
1883	Phi N	1	5	0	0	0	0	0	2		.000	.000	.000	-99	-1		1.000	-0	111	0	/3		
1889	Phi N	7	25	4	4	1	0	0	4	0	0	7	.160	.160	.200	-3	1	2b6/OC	.848	-2	98	0	2b6/OC		
1891	Pit N	6	18	3	6	0	0	0	2	3	1		.333	.455	.333	134	1		.833	-1	0	0	O5L		
1892	Bal N	56	186	28	54	6	5	1	33	31	4	18	.290	.403	.392	137	10	10	.892	3	205	251	O43R,2b7,S5/C		
1893	Bal N	11	49	11	12	1	3	0	5	5	1	2	.245	.327	.388	88	-1	4	.862	-1	55	0	O9L,1b2		
	Cin N	42	150	44	42	4	1	0	10	37	6	10	.280	.440	.320	101	4	27	.827	-2	125	295	O40(1/0/39)/1		
	Year	53	199	55	54	5	4	0	15	42	7	12	.271	.415	.337	99	2	31	.837	-3	119	214	O49(10/0/39),1b3		
1894	Was N	98	347	86	105	11	7	0	36	80	11	31	.303	.447	.375	103	7	41	.900	-14	99	54	2b79,O12(6/3/3),S3/3		
Total	6	221	780	172	223	23	16	1	90	156	23	73	.286	.419	.360	105	19	86	.854	-17	134	224	O110(21/4/85),2b92,S8,1b3,3b2/C		

WARD, GARY Gary Lamell B12.6.1953 Los Angeles CA BR/TR/6-2/202* d9.3 C3 s-Daryle OF(848/181/111)

YEAR	TM LG	G	AB	R	H	2B	3B	HR	RBI	BB-IB	HP	SO	AVG	OBP	SLG	AOPS	ABR	SB-CS	FA	FR	RNG	THR	GAMES AT POSITION	DL	BF
1979	Min A	10	14	2	4	0	0	1	3-0	0	5	.286	.412	.286	88	0	0-1	1.000	0	138	0	O5(1/0/4),D3		
1980	Min A	13	41	11	19	6	2	1	10	3-1	0	6	.463	.489	.780	229	7	0-0	1.000	-2	68	0	O12L		
1981	Min A	85	295	42	78	7	6	3	29	28-4	0	48	.264	.325	.359	92	-3	5-2	.975	4	103	151	O150(61/19/1),D2		
1982	Min A	152	570	85	165	33	7	28	91	37-4	1	105	.289	.330	.519	126	18	13-1	.989	11	111	142	O150(127/4/25),D2		
1983	Min A★	157	623	76	173	34	6	19	88	44-2	3	98	.278	.326	.440	105	8	8-1	.978	19	112	194	O152L,D2		
1984	Tex A	155	602	97	171	21	7	21	79	55-3	3	95	.284	.343	.447	113	9	7-5	.987	5	105	110	O148(58/59/36),D5		
1985	Tex A★	154	593	77	170	28	7	15	70	39-3	1	97	.287	.329	.433	105	3	26-7	.969	-2	94	116	O153(139/21/1)/D		
1986	Tex A	105	380	54	120	15	2	5	51	31-3	4	72	.316	.372	.405	109	5	12-8	.996	10	116	128	O104(102/4/0)/D		
1987	NY A	146	529	65	131	22	1	16	78	33-2	7	78	.248	.291	.384	78	-18	9-1	.985	0	109	38	O54(69/30/5),D36,1b15		
1988	NY A	91	231	26	52	8	0	4	24	24-4	2	41	.225	.302	.312	73	-8	0-1	.992	-1	109	0	O6R/D		
1989	NY A	8	17	3	5	1	0	1	3-1	1	5	.294	.400	.353	115	1	0-0	1.000	-1	64	0	O6R/D		
	Det A	105	275	24	69	13	2	9	29	21-1	0	54	.251	.301	.375	100	-1	0-1	.990	1	119	78	O51(35/5/14),1b26,D26		
	Year	113	292	27	74	14	2	9	30	24-2	1	59	.253	.306	.397	100	-1	0-1	.991	0	113	69	O57(35/5/20),D27,1b26		
1990	Det A	106	309	32	79	11	2	9	46	30-0	1	50	.256	.322	.392	98	-1	2-0	.988	-1	102	41	O85(75/0/16),D13,1b2		15
Total	12	1287	4479	594	1236	196	41	130	597	351-28	13	775	.276	.328	.425	104	14	83-30	.984	45	107	114	O1094L,D101,1b54,D15		15

EAR	TM LG	G	AB	R	H	2B	3B	HR	RBI	BB-IB	HP	SO	AVG	OBP	SLG	AOPS	ABR	SB-CS	FA	FR	RNG	THR	GAMES AT POSITION	DL	BFW

WARD, JIM   James H. H. B3.2.1855 Boston MA D6.4.1886 Boston MA d8.3

| 876 | Phi N | 1 | 4 | 1 | 2 | 0 | 0 | 0 | 1 | 0 | | 1 | .500 | .500 | .500 | 236 | | | .750 | -1 | | | /C | | 0.0 |

WARD, RUBE   John Andrew B2.6.1879 New Lexington OH D1.17.1945 Akron OH 5-7/152 d4.28 Col Holy Cross

| 902 | Bro N | 13 | 31 | 4 | 9 | 1 | 0 | 0 | 2 | 2 | 0 | | .290 | .333 | .323 | 102 | 0 | 0 | .850 | -0 | 88 | 0 | O11(6/1/4) | | -0.1 |

WARD, JOHN   John E. B Washington DC d5.23

| 884 | Was U | 1 | 4 | 0 | 1 | 0 | 0 | 0 | | 0 | | | .250 | .250 | .250 | 54 | 0 | | .000 | -1 | 0 | 0 | /OC | | -0.1 |

WARD, JAY   John Francis B9.9.1938 Brookfield MO BR/TR/6-1/185* d5.6 C3

963	Min A	9	15	0	1	1	0	0	2	1-0	0	5	.067	.125	.133	-27	-3	0-0	1.000	-2	61	0	3b4/OL		-0.4
964	Min A	12	31	4	7	2	0	0	2	6-1	0	13	.226	.351	.290	80	0	0-0	.977	0	93	73	2b9,O3L		0.0
970	Cin N	6	3	0	0	0	0	0	0	2-0	0	1	.000	.400	.000	17	0	0-0	1.000	0	114	0	3b2/12		0.0
tal	3	27	49	4	8	3	0	0	4	9-1	0	19	.163	.293	.224	46	-3	0-0	.977	-1	92	72	2b10,3b6,O4L/1		-0.4

WARD, JOHN   John Montgomery B3.3.1860 Bellefonte PA D3.4.1925 Augusta GA BL/TR (TL 1884p, BB 1888)/5-9/165 d7.15 M7 HF1964 Col Penn St. OF(4/110/100) ▲

878	Pro N	37	138	14	27	5	4	1	15	2		13	.196	.207	.312	69	1		.866	2	107	179	P37		0.0
879	Pro N	83	364	71	104	9	4	2	41	7		14	.286	.299	.349	115	5		.938	4	109	86	P70,3b16,O8(4/0/4)		0.3
880	Pro N	86	356	53	81	12	2	0	27	6		16	.228	.240	.272	76	-9		.983	14	112	55	P70,3b25,O2R,M		0.9
881	Pro N	85	357	56	87	18	6	0	53	5		10	.244	.254	.328	83	-7		.887	3	126	0	O40(0/4/36),P39,S13		-0.3
882	Pro N	83	355	58	87	10	3	1	39	13		22	.245	.272	.299	83	-7		.824	5	174	142	O49(0/2/47),P34,S4		-0.1
883	NY N	88	380	76	97	18	7	7	54	8		25	.255	.271	.395	100	-1		.859	14	198	88	O56(0/45/11),P34,3b5,S2/2		0.9
884	NY N	113	482	98	122	11	8	2	51	28		47	.253	.294	.322	91	-6		.847	10	105	93	O59C,2b47,P9,M		0.4
885	NY N	111	446	72	101	8	9	0	37	17		39	.226	.255	.285	75	-13		.904	4	95	127	S111		-0.6
886	NY N	122	491	82	134	17	5	2	81	19		46	.273	.300	.340	93	-5	36	.890	11	99	113	S122		0.9
887	NY N	129	545	114	184	16	5	1	53	29	4	12	.338	.359	.391	119	15	111	.919	32	109	136	S129		4.3
888	†NY N	122	510	70	128	14	5	2	49	9	1	13	.251	.265	.310	84	-10	38	.857	-4	90	129	S122		-1.1
889	†NY N	114	479	87	143	13	4	1	67	27	2	7	.299	.339	.349	92	7	62	.890	9	95	104	S108,2b7		0.4
890	Bro P	128	561	134	188	15	12	4	60	51	2	22	.335	.393	.426	112	7	63	.878	17	104	105	S128,M		2.2
891	Bro N	105	441	85	122	13	5	0	39	36	3	10	.277	.335	.329	94	-3	57	.878	3	104	93	S87,2b18,M		0.2
892	Bro N	148	614	109	163	13	3	1	47	82	3	19	.265	.355	.301	103	6	88	.920	-2	101	79	2b148,M		1.0
893	NY N	135	588	129	193	27	9	2	77	47	1	5	.328	.379	.415	110	8	46	.918	4	105	65	2b134,M		1.4
894	†NY N	138	549	102	146	12	5	0	79	35	1	6	.266	.311	.306	49	-46	39	.923	1	104	90	2b138,M		-3.1
tal	17	1827	7656	1410	2107	231	96	26	869	421	17	326	.275	.314	.341	93	-72	540	.887	123	99	115	S826,2b493,P293,O214C,3b46		7.7

WARD, JOE   Joseph A. B9.2.1884 Philadelphia PA D8.11.1934 Philadelphia PA TR d4.24

906	Phi N	35	129	12	38	8	6	0	11	5	0		.295	.321	.450	140	5	2	.929	-5	80	66	3b27,2b3/S		0.0
909	NY A	9	28	3	5	0	0	0	0	1	1		.179	.233	.179	30	-2	2	.846	-4	75	41	2b7/1		-0.7
	Phi N	74	184	21	49	8	2	0	23	9	1		.266	.304	.332	96	-1	7	.944	-6	95	126	2b48,S8,1b5,O2(1/1/0)		-0.8
910	Phi N	48	124	11	18	2	1	0	13	3	2	11	.145	.178	.177	4	-16	1	.975	2	133	62	1b32/S3		-1.6
tal	3	166	465	47	110	18	9	0	47	18	4	11	.237	.271	.314	78	-14	12	.929	-13	91	102	2b58,1b38,3b28,S10,O2(1/1/0)		-3.1

WARD, HAP   Joseph Nichols B11.15.1885 Leesburg NJ D9.13.1979 Elmer NJ 5-5.5/166 d5.18

| 912 | Det A | 1 | 2 | 0 | 0 | 0 | 0 | 0 | | 0 | | | .000 | .000 | .000 | -99 | -1 | 0 | 1.000 | 0 | 0 | 0 | /OR | | 0.0 |

WARD, KEVIN   Kevin Michael B9.28.1961 Lansdale PA BR/TR/6-1/195* [PhiN83 6/154] d5.10 Col Arizona

991	SD N	44	107	13	26	7	2	2	8	9-0	1	27	.243	.308	.402	95	-1	1-4	.982	-1	102	0	O33(31/0/2)		-0.4
992	SD N	81	147	12	29	5	0	3	12	14-0	2	38	.197	.274	.293	60	-8	2-3	.946	-1	96	116	O51(36/9/8)		-1.1
tal	2	125	254	25	55	12	2	5	20	23-0	3	65	.217	.288	.339	75	-9	3-7	.961	-2	99	66	O84(67/9/10)		-1.5

WARD, PETE   Peter Thomas B7.26.1939 Montreal QC, Can. BL/TR/6-1/200(185-205) d9.21 C1 Col Lewis & Clark OF(139/0/54)

962	Bal A	8	21	1	3	2	0	0	2	4-0	0	5	.143	.280	.238	44	-2	0-0	1.000	-0	91	0	O6(2/0/4)		-0.2
963	Chi A	157	600	80	177	34	6	22	84	52-1	5	77	.295	.353	.482	135	27	7-6	.923	-8	95	99	3b154/2S		1.9
964	Chi A	144	539	61	152	28	3	23	94	56-11	2	76	.282	.348	.473	131	22	1-1	.958	4	106	113	3b138		2.7
965	Chi A	138	507	62	125	25	3	10	57	56-11	6	83	.247	.327	.367	104	3	2-4	.952	4	114	91	3b134/2		0.6
966	Chi A	84	251	22	55	7	1	3	28	24-0	3	49	.219	.290	.291	74	-8	3-1	.989	4	94	99	O59(44/0/18),3b16,1b5		-0.8
967	Chi A	146	467	49	109	16	2	18	62	61-9	11	109	.233	.334	.392	119	12	3-2	.991	-10	72	52	O89(74/0/19),1b39,3b22	47	-0.5
968	Chi A	125	399	43	86	15	0	15	50	76-8	10	85	.216	.354	.366	117	12	4-3	.946	-2	105	57	3b77,1b31,O22(16/0/7)		0.9
969	Chi A	105	199	22	49	7	0	6	32	33-1	3	38	.246	.359	.372	101	1	0-0	.994	0	107	76	1b25,3b21,O9(3/0/6)		0.0
970	NY A	66	77	5	20	2	2	1	18	9-0	0	17	.260	.333	.377	101	1	0-0	1.000	-1	48	97	1b13		-0.2
tal	9	973	3060	345	776	136	17	98	427	371-41	40	539	.254	.339	.405	116	67	20-17	.945	-9	106	96	3b562,O185L,1b113,2b2/S	47	4.4

WARD, PRESTON   Preston Meyer B7.24.1927 Columbia MO BL/TR/6-3/198* d4.20 Mil 1951-52

948	Bro N	42	146	9	38	9	2	1	21	15	0	23	.260	.329	.370	86	-3	0	.990	-1	86	79	1b38		-0.5
950	Chi N	80	285	31	72	11	2	6	33	27		42	.253	.317	.368	81	-8	3	.995	9	142	106	1b76	61	-0.2
953	Chi N	33	100	10	23	5	0	4	12	18	0	21	.230	.347	.400	92	-1	3-1	.961	-4	89	0	O27C,1b7		-0.5
	Year	121	381	35	59	7	1	8	27	44		1	39	.210	.319	.327	69	-12	1-3	.991	3	117	88	1b78		-1.4
954	Pit N	117	360	37	97	16	2	7	48	39	0	61	.269	.337	.383	90	-5	0-0	.984	6	141	80	1b48,O42R,3b11		-0.3
955	Pit N	84	179	16	38	7	4	5	25	22-4	1	28	.212	.296	.380	80	-6	0-0	.998	2	113	100	1b48/OR		-0.6
956	Pit N	16	30	3	10	0	1	1	11	6-0	0	4	.333	.432	.500	157	3	0-0	1.000	-2	47	0	3b5,O5R		0.1
	Cle A	87	150	18	38	10	0	6	21	16-0	0	20	.253	.325	.440	98	-1	0-0	.988	5	127	0	1b60,O17(14/0/3)		0.0
957	Cle A	10	11	2	2	1	0	0	0	0-0		2	.182	.182	.273	23	-1	0-0	1.000	-0	0	0	/1		-0.1
958	Cle A	48	148	22	50	3	1	4	21	10-1	1	27	.338	.379	.453	133	6	0-1	.957	-1	85	59	3b24,1b21		0.4
	KC A	81	268	28	68	10	1	6	24	27-2	0	36	.254	.319	.366	87	-5	0-1	.989	6	92	77	1b39,3b34,O2L		-1.4
	Year	129	416	50	118	13	2	10	45	37-3	1	63	.284	.340	.397	103	1	0-2	.992	-8	98	75	1b60,3b58,O2L		-1.0
959	KC A	58	109	8	27	4	1	2	19	7-1	0	12	.248	.286	.358	76	-4	0-0	.982	-3	60	83	1b22/OL		-0.8
tal	9	744	2067	219	522	83	15	50	262	231-8	2	315	.253	.326	.380	88	-37	7-6	.992	6	115	90	1b438,O95(17/27/51),3b74	61	-5.3

WARD, TURNER   Turner Max B4.11.1965 Orlando FL BB/TR/6-2/200(182-204) [NYA86 18/470] d9.10 Col South Alabama

990	Cle A	14	46	10	16	2	1	1	10	3-0	0	8	.348	.388	.500	147	3	3-0	.957	0	88	251	O13R/D		0.3
991	Cle A	40	100	11	23	7	0	0	5	10-0	0	16	.230	.300	.300	66	-4	0-0	1.000	-1	101	45	O38(0/2/36)		-0.6
	Tor A	8	13	1	4	0	0	0	2	1-0	0	2	.308	.357	.308	82	0	0-0	1.000	-1	64	0	O6(1/0/5)		-0.1
	Year	48	113	12	27	7	0	0	7	11-0	0	18	.239	.306	.301	68	-5	0-0	1.000	-1	97	40	O44(1/2/41)		-0.7
992	Tor A	18	29	7	10	3	0	1	3	4-0	0	4	.345	.424	.552	163	2	0-1	1.000	-1	104	208	O12(2/4/6)		0.3
993	Tor A	72	167	20	32	4	2	4	28	23-2	1	26	.192	.287	.311	61	-9	3-3	.990	-2	93	65	O65(33/10/22)/1	30	-1.4
994	Mil A	102	367	55	85	15	2	9	45	52-4	3	68	.232	.328	.357	74	-14	6-2	.985	6	109	125	O99(35/52/25)/3		-0.8
995	Mil A	44	129	19	34	3	1	4	16	14-1	1	21	.264	.338	.395	86	-3	6-1	.989	3	106	202	O40(26/7/19)/D	102	-0.1
996	Mil A	43	67	7	12	2	1	2	10	13-0	0	17	.179	.309	.328	60	-4	3-0	1.000	3	135	76	O32(15/3/18)/D	99	-0.1
997	Pit N	71	167	33	59	16	1	7	33	18-2	2	17	.353	.420	.587	158	15	4-1	1.000	-2	85	94	O54(11/31/23)		1.2
998	Pit N	123	282	33	74	13	3	9	46	27-1	4	40	.262	.328	.426	98	-1	5-4	.983	7	115	165	O97(41/48/22)/D	15	0.4
999	Pit N	49	91	2	19	2	0	0	8	13-0	1	9	.209	.311	.231	41	-8	2-2	.955	-2	82	78	O34(5/22/13)	63	-1.0
	†Ari N	10	23	6	8	1	0	2	7	2-0	0	6	.348	.385	.652	159	2	0-0	1.000	0	113	0	O5(0/2/4)	15	0.2
	Year	59	114	8	27	3	0	2	15	15-0	1	15	.237	.326	.316	64	-6	2-2	.964	-2	87	65	O39(5/24/17)		-0.8
000	Ari N	14	52	5	9	4	0	0	4	5-0	0	7	.173	.241	.250	25	-6	1-1	1.000	1	121	0	O15(0/1/14)		-0.6
001	Phi N	17	15	1	4	1	0	0	2	1-1	0	6	.267	.353	.333	83	0	0-0	—	0			/H		-0.1
tal	12	626	1548	210	389	73	11	39	219	186-11	13	247	.251	.332	.388	87	-26	33-15	.988	13	104	115	O510(169/182/220),D4/31	324	-2.3

WARES, BUZZY   Clyde Ellsworth B3.23.1886 Vandalia MI D5.26.1964 South Bend IN BR/TR/5-10/150 d9.15 C22

913	StL A	11	35	5	10	2	0	0	1	0	0		.286	.306	.343	92	0	2	.973	-2	71	139	2b9		-0.3
914	StL A	81	215	20	45	10	1	0	23	28		0	35	.209	.300	.265	73	-6	10-10	.903	-6	103	93	S68,2b8		-1.0
tal	2	92	250	25	55	12	1	0	24	29		0	38	.220	.301	.276	76	-6	12-10	.903	-8	103	93	S68,2b17		-1.3

WARNER, FRED   Frederick John Rodney B1855 Philadelphia PA D2.13.1886 Philadelphia PA 5-7/155 d4.21

875	Cen NA	14	57	11	14	4	0	0		2			.246	.259	.316	107	1		.784	-1	86	0	O14C		0.0
876	Phi N	1	3	0	0	0	0	0	0	0			.000	.000	.000	-99	-1		.600	-1	0	0	/OC		-0.1
878	Ind N	43	165	19	41	4	0	0	10	2		15	.248	.257	.273	72	-2		.907	-5	92	92	S41,O2L		-0.5

YEAR	TM LG	G	AB	R	H	2B	3B	HR	RBI	BB-IB	HP	SO	AVG	OBP	SLG	AOPS	ABR	SB-CS	FA	FR	RNG	THR	GAMES AT POSITION	DL	BFW
1879	Cle N	76	316	32	77	11	4	0	22	2		20	.244	.248	.304	82	-6		.827	1	99	72	3b54,O21(13/7/1)/1		-0.5
1883	Phi N	39	141	13	32	6	1	0	13	5		21	.227	.253	.284	69	-5		.775	-6	82	70	3b38/OR		-0.9
1884	Bro AA	84	352	40	78	4	0	1		17	1		.222	.259	.241	64	-14		.824	1	97	133	3b84		-1.7
Total	5	243	977	104	228	25	5	1	45	24		56	.233	.254	.272	73	-28		.815	-17	95	102	3b176,S41,O25(15/8/2)/1		-3.7

WARNER, HOOKS Hoke Hayden B5.22.1894 Del Rio TX D2.19.1947 San Francisco CA BL/TR/5-10.5/170 d8.21 Mil 1918

YEAR	TM LG	G	AB	R	H	2B	3B	HR	RBI	BB-IB	HP	SO	AVG	OBP	SLG	AOPS	ABR	SB-CS	FA	FR	RNG	THR	GAMES AT POSITION	DL	BFW
1916	Pit N	44	168	12	40	1	1	2	14	6		19	.238	.264	.292	70	-7	6	.899	-10	67	82	3b42/2		-1.8
1917	Pit N	3	5	1	1	0	0	0	0	0		1	.200	.200	.200	22	0	0	1.000	0	65	0	/3		0.0
1919	Pit N	6	8	0	1	0	0	0	2	3		0	.125	.364	.125	48	0	0	.818	-1	104	0	3b3		-0.1
1921	Chi N	14	38	4	8	1	0	0	3	2	1	1	.211	.268	.237	35	-4	1-1	.957	0	114	65	3b10		-0.3
Total	4	67	219	16	50	2	1	2	19	11	1	22	.228	.268	.274	61	-11	7-1	.906	-10	76	73	3b56/2		-2.2

WARNER, JOHN John Joseph B8.15.1872 New York NY D12.21.1943 Far Rockaway NY BL/TR/5-11/165 d4.23

YEAR	TM LG	G	AB	R	H	2B	3B	HR	RBI	BB-IB	HP	SO	AVG	OBP	SLG	AOPS	ABR	SB-CS	FA	FR	RNG	THR	GAMES AT POSITION	DL	BFW
1895	Bos N	3	7	2	1	0	0	0	1	1		1	.143	.333	.143	24	-1	0	.917	1	135	168	C3		0.0
	Lou N	67	232	20	62	4	2	1	20	11	7	16	.267	.320	.315	68	-11	10	.931	-11	91	80	C64,1b3/2		-1.4
	Year	70	239	22	63	4	2	1	21	12	8	16	.264	.320	.310	67	-12	10	.930	-11	93	83	C67,1b3/2		-1.4
1896	Lou N	33	110	9	25	1	1	0	10	10	2	10	.227	.303	.255	50	-8	3	.939	2	78	120	C32/1		-0.3
	NY N	19	54	9	14	1	0	0	3	3	1	7	.259	.310	.278	57	-3	1	.922	-2	95	89	C19		-0.6
	Year	52	164	18	39	2	1	0	13	13	3	17	.238	.306	.262	52	-11	4	.934	-0	84	109	C51/1		-0.6
1897	NY N	111	400	50	109	6	3	2	51	26	16		.273	.342	.318	77	-13	8	.953	32	169	111	C111		2.5
1898	NY N	110	373	40	96	14	5	0	42	22	10		.257	.316	.322	86	-7	9	.968	9	91	111	C109/OR		1.0
1899	NY N	88	293	38	78	8	1	0	19	15	6		.266	.315	.300	72	-11	15	.952	-0	86	122	C82,1b3		0.3
1900	NY N	34	108	15	27	4	0	0	8	8	3		.250	.319	.287	71	-4	1	.948	4	111	109	C31		0.3
1901	NY N	87	291	19	70	6	1	0	20	3	8		.241	.268	.268	58	-16	3	.967	-0	84	112	C84		-1.2
1902	Bos A	65	222	19	52	5	7	0	12	13	3		.234	.286	.320	66	-11	0	.979	8	128	92	C64		0.3
1903	NY N	89	285	38	81	8	5	0	34	7	7		.284	.322	.347	88	-6	5	**.986**	12	119	108	C85		1.3
1904	NY N	86	287	29	57	5	1	1	15	14	7		.199	.253	.233	48	-17	7	**.982**	8	140	108	C86		-0.1
1905	StL N	41	137	9	35	4	2	0	12	6	3		.255	.301	.321	88	-2	2	.958	-2	90	116	C41		-0.4
	Det A	36	119	12	24	2	3	0	7	8	0		.202	.252	.269	65	-5	2	.974	-2	75	98	C36		-0.7
1906	Det A	50	153	15	37	4	2	0	10	12	7		.242	.326	.294	92	-1	4	.978	9	110	120	C49		0.2
	Was A	32	103	5	21	4	1	0	9	2	1		.204	.226	.291	65	-5	3	.968	3	86	149	C32		1.5
	Year	82	256	20	58	8	3	1	19	14	8		.227	.288	.293	82	-5	7	.974	11	100	132	C81		-0.4
1907	Was A	72	207	11	53	5	0	0	17	12	3		.256	.306	.280	95	-1	3	.971	-8	84	100	C64		0.6
1908	Was A	51	116	8	28	2	1	0	8	8	4		.241	.313	.276	100	0	7	.982	2	112	83	C41/1		3.1
Total	14	1074	3497	348	870	81	35	6	303	181	91	33	.249	.303	.297	73	-122	83	.966	60	108	108	C1033,1b8/OR2		

WARNER, JACKIE John Joseph B8.1.1943 Monrovia CA BR/TR/6-0/180 d4.12

YEAR	TM LG	G	AB	R	H	2B	3B	HR	RBI	BB-IB	HP	SO	AVG	OBP	SLG	AOPS	ABR	SB-CS	FA	FR	RNG	THR	GAMES AT POSITION	DL	BFW
1966	Cal A	45	123	22	26	4	1	7	16	9-0		55	.211	.263	.431	99	-1	0-0	.984	-2	94	51	O37R		-0.

WARNER, JACK John Ralph B8.29.1903 Evansville IN D3.13.1986 Mt.Vernon IL BR/TR/5-9.5/165 d9.24

YEAR	TM LG	G	AB	R	H	2B	3B	HR	RBI	BB-IB	HP	SO	AVG	OBP	SLG	AOPS	ABR	SB-CS	FA	FR	RNG	THR	GAMES AT POSITION	DL	BFW
1925	Det A	10	39	7	13	0	0	0	2	3	0	6	.333	.381	.333	84	-1	0-0	1.000	-1	101	204	3b10		-0.
1926	Det A	100	311	41	78	8	9	0	34	38	5	24	.251	.342	.315	71	-13	8-4	.956	-1	97	62	3b95,S3		-0.
1927	Det A	139	559	78	149	22	9	1	45	47	6	45	.267	.330	.343	74	-22	14-4	.947	-4	99	116	3b138		-1.
1928	Det A	75	206	33	44	4	0	1	13	16	1	15	.214	.274	.272	43	-18	4-5	.944	4	109	64	3b52/S		-1.
1929	Bro N	17	62	3	17	2	0	0	4	7	0	6	.274	.348	.306	65	-3	3	.945	-2	93	72	S17		-0.
1930	Bro N	21	25	4	8	1	0	0	6	2	0	7	.320	.370	.360	79	-1	1	1.000	1	137	0	3b8		-0.
1931	Bro N	4	2	2	1	0	0	0	0	0	0	1	.500	.500	.500	200	1	0	1.000	1	211	0	S2/3		0.
1933	Phi N	107	340	31	76	15	1	0	22	28	1	33	.224	.285	.274	53	-20	31-13	.973	4	102	98	2b71,3b30/S		-1.
Total	8	478	1546	199	387	52	20	1	120	142	13	137	.250	.319	.312	65	-77	31-13	.950	2	103	100	3b334,2b71,S30		-4.

WARNOCK, HAL Harold Charles B1.6.1912 New York NY D2.8.1997 Tucson AZ BL/TR/6-2/180 d9.2 Col Arizona

YEAR	TM LG	G	AB	R	H	2B	3B	HR	RBI	BB-IB	HP	SO	AVG	OBP	SLG	AOPS	ABR	SB-CS	FA	FR	RNG	THR	GAMES AT POSITION	DL	BFW
1935	StL A	6	7	1	2	0	0	0	0	1		0	.286	.286	.571	112	0	0-0	1.000	-0	59	0	O2(1/1/0)		0.

WARREN, BENNIE Bennie Louis B3.2.1912 Elk City OK D5.11.1994 Oklahoma City OK BR/TR/6-1/184 d9.13 Mil 1943-45

YEAR	TM LG	G	AB	R	H	2B	3B	HR	RBI	BB-IB	HP	SO	AVG	OBP	SLG	AOPS	ABR	SB-CS	FA	FR	RNG	THR	GAMES AT POSITION	DL	BFW
1939	Phi N	18	56	4	13	0	1	1	7	7	0	7	.232	.317	.286	65	-3	0	.958	-3	53	100	C17		-0.
1940	Phi N	106	289	33	71	6	1	12	34	40	1	46	.246	.339	.398	107	3	1	.975	-3	92	110	C97/1		-1.
1941	Phi N	121	345	34	74	13	2	9	35	44	3	66	.214	.309	.342	86	-6	0	.973	-5	73	140	C110		-1.
1942	Phi N	90	225	19	47	6	3	7	20	24	1	36	.209	.288	.356	92	-3	0	.972	-6	67	132	C78/1		-0.
1946	NY N	39	69	7	11	1	4	1	8	14	0	21	.159	.301	.377	91	-1	0	.965	-0	86	67	C30		-0.
1947	NY N	3	5	0	1	0	0	0	0	0	0	1	.200	.200	.200	6	-1	0	1.000	-0	0	0	C3		-0.
Total	6	377	989	97	217	26	11	33	104	129	5	177	.219	.313	.360	92	-11	1	.972	-17	77	122	C335,1b2		-5.

WARREN, BILL William Hackney "Hack" B2.11.1883 MO D1.28.1960 Whiteville TN BR/TR/5-8/165 d4.30

YEAR	TM LG	G	AB	R	H	2B	3B	HR	RBI	BB-IB	HP	SO	AVG	OBP	SLG	AOPS	ABR	SB-CS	FA	FR	RNG	THR	GAMES AT POSITION	DL	BFW
1914	Ind F	26	50	5	12	2	0	5	5	5	0	7	.240	.309	.280	55	-1	2	.931	-3	81	84	C23		-0.
1915	New F	5	3	0	1	0	0	0	0	0	0	0	.333	.333	.333	93	0	0	1.000	-0	0	0	/C1		-0.
Total	2	31	53	5	13	2	0	5	5	5	0	7	.245	.310	.283	57	-1	2	.932	-3	80	83	C24/1		-0.

WARSTLER, RABBIT Harold Burton B9.13.1903 N.Canton OH D5.31.1964 N.Canton OH BR/TR/5-7.5/150 d7.24

YEAR	TM LG	G	AB	R	H	2B	3B	HR	RBI	BB-IB	HP	SO	AVG	OBP	SLG	AOPS	ABR	SB-CS	FA	FR	RNG	THR	GAMES AT POSITION	DL	BFW
1930	Bos A	54	162	16	30	2	3	1	13	20		21	.185	.275	.253	36	-16	0-2	.947	-1	103	103	S54		-1.
1931	Bos A	66	181	20	44	5	3	0	10	15	2	27	.243	.308	.304	65	-10	2-3	.933	-0	115	89	2b42,S19/3		-0.
1932	Bos A	115	388	26	82	15	5	0	34	42	3	43	.211	.259	.276	40	-36	9-6	.939	23	115	114	S107		-1.
1933	Bos A	92	322	44	70	13	1	1	17	42	0	36	.217	.308	.273	55	-20	2-4	.951	-1	103	82	S87		-1.
1934	Phi A	117	419	56	99	19	3	1	36	51	1	30	.236	.321	.303	64	-22	9-3	.969	16	117	116	2b107,S2		0
1935	Phi A	138	496	62	124	20	7	3	59	56	2	53	.250	.326	.337	72	-21	0-0	.959	-1	105	94	2b136,3b2		-1
1936	Phi A	66	236	27	59	8	6	1	24	36	2	16	.250	.354	.347	75	-7	4	.973	9	121	94	2b66		-0
	Bos N	74	304	27	64	6	0	0	7	22	1	33	.211	.266	.230	37	-27	2	.948	7	114	120	S74		-2
1937	Bos N	149	555	57	124	20	6	0	36	51	2	62	.223	.291	.276	60	-30	4	.942	-9	106	104	S149		-2
1938	Bos N	142	467	37	108	11	3	0	40	48	0	38	.231	.303	.270	65	-22	3	.937	-7	103	94	S135,2b7		-1
1939	Bos N	114	342	34	83	11	3	0	24	40	0	31	.243	.292	.292	62	-19	2	.953	2	100	116	S49,2b43,3b21		-1
1940	Bos N	33	57	6	12	0	0	0	4	10	0	5	.211	.328	.211	54	-3	0	.974	0	100	161	2b24,3b2/S		-0
	Chi N	45	159	19	36	4	1	0	18	8	0	19	.226	.263	.283	52	-11	1	.939	-0	103	113	S28,2b17		-1
	Year	78	216	25	48	4	1	0	22	18	0	24	.222	.282	.264	53	-14	1	.960	-0	103	113	2b41,S29,3b2		-1
Total	11	1205	4088	431	935	133	36	11	332	405	11	414	.229	.300	.287	59	-246	42-22	.942	41	106	102	S705,2b442,3b26		-12

WARWICK, CARL Carl Wayne B2.27.1937 Dallas TX BR/TL/5-10/170* d4.11 Col TCU

YEAR	TM LG	G	AB	R	H	2B	3B	HR	RBI	BB-IB	HP	SO	AVG	OBP	SLG	AOPS	ABR	SB-CS	FA	FR	RNG	THR	GAMES AT POSITION	DL	BFW
1961	LA N	19	11	2	1	0	0	1	2	2-0	0	3	.091	.231	.091	-9	-2	0-0	1.000	-1	38	0	O12(6/5/1)		-0
	StL N	55	152	27	38	6	2	4	16	18-0	0	33	.250	.324	.395	83	-4	3-0	.970	0	110	64	O48(15/34/10)		-0
	Year	74	163	29	39	6	2	4	17	20-0	0	36	.239	.317	.374	77	-5	3-0	.970	-1	105	60	O60(21/39/11)		-0
1962	StL N	13	23	4	8	0	0	1	4	2-0	0	2	.348	.385	.478	123	1	0-0	1.000	-1	92	217	O10(1/0/9)		-0
	Hou N	130	477	63	124	17	1	16	60	38-1	0	77	.260	.312	.400	98	-3	2-3	.986	2	98	150	O138(16/116/18)		-1
	Year	143	500	67	132	17	1	17	64	40-1	0	79	.264	.315	.404	98	-3	4-3	.986	2	98	153	O138(16/116/18)		-1
1963	Hou N	150	528	49	134	19	5	7	63	49-4	2	70	.254	.319	.348	98	-1	3-3	.988	-2	101	70	O149(11/0/41)		-1
1964	†StL N	88	158	14	41	7	1	3	15	11-1	0	30	.259	.306	.373	92	0	0-0	.933	-0	94	130	O49(11/0/41)		-0
1965	StL N	50	77	3	12	2	1	0	6	4-0	0	18	.156	.198	.208	13	-9	1-0	.960	-1	105	129	O21(4/2/15),1b4		-0
	Bal A	9	14	3	0	0	0	0	0	3-0	0	2	.000	.176	.000	-44	-3	0-0	1.000	0	69	0	O3(1/0/2)		-0
1966	Chi N	16	22	3	5	0	0	1	4	0-0	0	6	.227	.227	.227	36	-0	0-0	.980	-1	99	108	O422(79/175/201),1b6		-0
Total	6	530	1462	168	363	51	10	31	149	127-6	2	241	.248	.307	.360	87	-26	13-6	.980	-1	99	108	O422(79/175/201),1b6		-0

WARWICK, BILL Firmin Newton B11.26.1897 Philadelphia PA D12.19.1984 San Antonio TX BR/TR/6-0.5/180 d7.18 Col Penn

YEAR	TM LG	G	AB	R	H	2B	3B	HR	RBI	BB-IB	HP	SO	AVG	OBP	SLG	AOPS	ABR	SB-CS	FA	FR	RNG	THR	GAMES AT POSITION	DL	BFW
1921	Pit N	1	1	0	0	0	0	0	0	0-0	0	0	.000	.000	.000	-97	-0	0	.500	-0	0	470	/C		-0
1925	StL N	13	41	8	12	1	2	1	6	5	0	5	.293	.370	.488	114	1	0-1	1.000	0	91	47	C13		-0
1926	StL N	9	14	0	5	0	0	0	2	0	0	2	.357	.357	.357	89	1	0-0	.923	1	120	107	C9		-0
Total	3	23	56	8	17	1	2	1	8	5	0	7	.304	.361	.446	105	1	0-1	.954	-1	99	76	C23		-0

WASDELL, JIMMY James Charles B5.15.1914 Cleveland OH D8.6.1983 New Port Richey FL BL/TL/5-11/185 d9.3

YEAR	TM LG	G	AB	R	H	2B	3B	HR	RBI	BB-IB	HP	SO	AVG	OBP	SLG	AOPS	ABR	SB-CS	FA	FR	RNG	THR	GAMES AT POSITION	DL	BFW
1937	Was A	32	110	13	28	4	4	2	12	7		13	.255	.299	.418	82	-4	0-1	.995	0	85	99	1b21,O7(3/0/4)		
1938	Was A	53	140	19	33	4	1	2	16	12		12	.236	.296	.307	55	-10	5-2	.996	-2	79	119	1b26,O6R		

YEAR	TM LG	G	AB	R	H	2B	3B	HR	RBI	BB-IB	HP	SO	AVG	OBP	SLG	AOPS	ABR	SB-CS	FA	FR	RNG	THR	GAMES AT POSITION	DL	BFW
1939	Was A	29	109	12	33	5	1	0	13	9	1	16	.303	.361	.367	94	-1	3-1	.964	-2	90	100	1b28		-0.5
1940	Was A	10	35	3	3	1	0	0	2	0	0	7	.086	.135	.114	-37	-7	0-0	1.000	-1	38	103	1b8		-0.9
	Bro N	77	230	35	64	14	4	3	37	18	1	24	.278	.333	.413	99	-1	4	.947	-5	93	33	O42(1/1/40),1b17		-0.9
1941	†Bro N	94	265	39	79	14	3	4	48	16	3	15	.298	.345	.419	110	3	2	.956	-3	97	54	O54(8/0/46),1b15		-0.4
1942	Pit N	122	409	44	106	11	2	3	38	47	1	22	.259	.337	.318	90	-4	1	.957	-2	99	102	O97(36/2/61),1b7		-1.3
1943	Pit N	4	2	0	1	0	0	0	1	2	0	0	.500	.750	.500	256	1	0	—	0			/H		0.1
	Phi N	141	522	54	136	19	6	4	67	46	2	22	.261	.323	.343	96	-4	6	.988	1	110	91	1b82,O56(39/22/5)		-0.9
	Year	145	524	54	137	19	6	4	68	48	2	22	.261	.326	.344	97	-3	6	.988	1	110	91	1b82,O56(39/22/5)		-0.8
1944	Phi N	133	451	47	125	20	3	3	40	45	1	17	.277	.344	.355	100	1	0	.980	-6	96	66	O121(118/5/3),1b4		-1.2
1945	Phi N	134	500	65	150	19	8	7	60	32	3	11	.300	.346	.412	113	7	7	.967	-1	103	74	O65(17/13/37),1b63		-0.1
1946	Phi N	26	51	7	13	0	1	0	5	3	1	2	.255	.309	.392	101	0	0	.923	-1	79	0	O11(4/0/6),1b2		-0.2
	Cle A	32	41	1	11	0	0	0	4	4	0	4	.268	.333	.268	74	-1	1-0	.939	-1	105	223	1b4,O3(1/0/2)		-0.2
1947	Cle A	1	1	0	0	0	0	0	0	0	0	0	.000	.000	.000	-99	0	0	—	0			/H		0.0
Total	11	888	2866	339	782	109	34	29	341	243	13	165	.273	.332	.365	96	-20	29-4	.966	-22	98	75	O462(227/43/210),1b277		-8.5

WASEM, LINK Lincoln William B1.30.1911 Birmingham OH D3.6.1979 S.Laguna CA BR/TR/5-9.5/180 d5.5

1937	Bos N	2	1	0	0	0	0	0	0	0	0	0	.000	.000	.000	-99	0	0	1.000	0	0	0	C2		0.0

WASHBURN, LIBE Libeus B6.16.1874 Lyme NH D3.22.1940 Malone NY BB/TL/5-10/180 d5.30 Col Brown ▲

1902	NY N	6	9	1	4	0	0	0		2	2		.444	.615	.444	230	2	1	1.000	-0	0	0	O3(0/2/1)		0.2
1903	Phi N	8	18	1	3	0	0	1	1	0			.167	.211	.167	-2	-0	1	1.000	-1	73	0	P4,O2L		-0.1
Total	2	14	27	2	7	0	0	1	1	3	2		.259	.375	.259	89	0	1	1.000	-1	0	0	O5(1/2/1),P4		0.1

WASHINGTON, CLAUDELL Claudell B8.31.1954 Los Angeles CA BL/TL/6-0/190* d7.5

1974	†Oak A	73	221	16	63	10	5	0	19	13-1	1	44	.285	.326	.376	108	2	6-8	.985	1	110	107	D38,O32(14/10/10)		-0.1
1975	†Oak A★	148	590	86	182	24	7	10	77	32-9	5	80	.308	.345	.424	120	13	40-15	.978	-5	96	73	O148(112/35/11)		0.4
1976	Oak A	134	490	65	126	20	6	5	53	30-1	3	90	.257	.302	.353	96	-4	37-20	.963	-3	97	105	O126(0/30/105),D6		-1.3
1977	Tex A	129	521	63	148	31	2	12	68	25-9	2	112	.284	.318	.420	99	-2	21-8	.978	-2	92	120	O127(93/41/4)/D	16	-0.6
1978	Tex A	12	42	1	7	0	0	0	2	1-0	0	12	.167	.186	.167	-0	-6	0-1	.917	-2	71	0	O7(1/0/6),D4	15	-0.8
	Chi A	86	314	33	83	16	5	6	31	12-2	1	57	.264	.290	.440	93	-4	5-5	.959	-2	94	106	O82(15/8/63)/D	25	-1.1
	Year	98	356	34	90	16	5	6	33	13-2	1	69	.253	.278	.376	82	-10	5-6	.957	-4	92	97	O89(16/8/69),D5		-1.9
1979	Chi A	131	471	79	132	33	5	13	66	28-7	3	93	.280	.322	.454	107	4	19-11	.974	1	104	80	O122(0/1/121),D3		-0.1
1980	Chi A	32	90	15	26	4	2	1	12	5-0	1	19	.289	.333	.411	103	0	4-2	.933	-1	101	67	O23(21/0/3),D2		-0.1
	NY N	79	284	38	78	16	4	10	42	20-5	1	63	.275	.324	.465	120	4	17-5	.978	4	97	214	O70(23/1/58)		0.9
1981	Atl N	85	320	37	93	22	3	5	37	15-1	4	47	.291	.328	.425	113	5	12-6	.993	-3	94	74	O79R		-0.3
1982	†Atl N	150	563	94	150	24	6	16	80	50-9	6	107	.266	.330	.416	106	4	33-10	.950	-11	84	88	O139R		-1.2
1983	Atl N	134	496	75	138	24	3	10	44	35-6	0	103	.278	.322	.413	97	-3	31-9	.974	-3	97	94	O128R		-0.9
1984	Atl N★	120	416	62	119	21	2	17	61	59-8	1	77	.286	.374	.469	127	16	21-9	.967	-10	86	57	O107R	15	0.3
1985	Atl N	122	398	62	110	14	6	15	43	40-11	6	76	.276	.342	.455	115	7	14-4	.962	-15	67	45	O99R		-1.2
1986	Atl N	40	137	17	37	11	0	5	14	14-0	1	26	.270	.336	.460	113	2	4-7	.957	-5	75	39	O38R	29	-0.6
	NY A	54	135	19	32	5	0	6	16	7-0	2	33	.237	.285	.407	86	-3	6-1	.985	-2	100	9	O39(11/20/9)		-0.5
1987	NY A	102	312	42	87	17	0	9	44	27-2	0	54	.279	.336	.420	99	-0	10-1	.988	0	101	102	O72(2/69/1),D13	15	0.1
1988	NY A	126	455	62	140	22	3	11	64	24-2	2	74	.308	.342	.442	119	10	15-6	.984	2	103	93	O117(13/103/8)		1.2
1989	Cal A	110	418	53	114	18	4	13	42	27-3	2	84	.273	.319	.428	111	4	13-5	.975	-5	90	80	O100(0/2/99),D7	17	-0.3
1990	Cal A	12	34	3	6	1	0	1	3	2-0	1	5	.176	.222	.294	44	-3	1-0	1.000	1	111	168	O9R		-0.2
	NY A	33	80	4	13	1	1	0	6	2-1	0	17	.162	.181	.200	7	-10	3-1	1.000	1	103	157	O21(19/0/4),D2	107	-1.0
	Year	45	114	7	19	2	1	1	9	4-1	1	22	.167	.193	.228	18	-13	4-1	1.000	2	105	157	O30(19/0/13),D2		-1.2
Total	17	1912	6787	926	1884	334	69	164	824	468-77	36	1266	.278	.325	.420	106	38	312-134	.973	-57	93	90	O1685(324/320/1101),D77	304	-7.4

WASHINGTON, HERB Herbert Lee B11.16.1951 Belzoni MS BR/TR/6-0/170* d4.4

1974	†Oak A	92	0	29	0	0	0	0	0	0-0	0		—	—	—	0	29-16		—	0			/R		-0.2
1975	Oak A	13	0	4	0	0	0	0	0	0-0	0		—	—	—	0	2-1		—	0			/R		0.0
Total	2	105	0	33	0	0	0	0	0	0-0	0		—	—	—	0	31-17		—	0					-0.2

WASHINGTON, LA RUE La Rue B9.7.1953 Long Beach CA BR/TR/6-0/170* [TexA75 23/540] d9.7 Col Cal St.-Dominguez Hills

1978	Tex A	3	3	0	0	0	0	0	0	0-0	0	1	.000	.000	.000	-99	-1	0-0	1.000	1	202	399	2b2/D		0.0
1979	Tex A	25	18	5	5	0	0	0	2	4-0	0	5	.278	.409	.278	90	-1	2-1	1.000	-0	93	0	O13(0/12/1)/3D		0.0
Total	2	28	21	5	5	0	0	0	2	4-0	0	6	.238	.360	.238	66	-1	2-1	1.000	1	93	0	O13(0/12/1),D2,2b2/3		0.0

WASHINGTON, RON Ronald B4.29.1952 New Orleans LA BR/TR/5-11/163(155-170) d9.10 C10

1977	LA N	10	19	4	7	0	0	0	0	0-0	1	2	.368	.400	.368	107	0	1-1	.857	-3	83	73	S10		-0.2
1981	Min A	28	84	8	19	3	1	0	5	0-0	1	14	.226	.270	.286	57	-5	4-1	.951	4	100	107	S26,O2C		0.2
1982	Min A	119	451	48	122	17	6	5	39	14-0	0	79	.271	.291	.368	77	-15	3-3	.972	-22	77	79	S91,2b37/3		-2.8
1983	Min A	99	317	28	78	7	3	4	26	22-1	1	50	.246	.296	.325	68	-14	10-5	.962	-11	89	100	S81,2b14/3D		-1.6
1984	Min A	88	197	25	58	11	5	3	23	4-0	1	31	.294	.307	.447	102	0	1-1	.978	-8	91	78	S71,2b9,3b2,D4		-0.4
1985	Min A	70	135	24	37	6	4	1	14	8-0	0	15	.274	.308	.400	89	-3	5-1	.951	-2	102	62	S31,2b24,3b7/1D		-0.2
1986	Min A	48	74	15	19	3	0	4	11	3-0	0	21	.257	.278	.459	96	-1	1-2	.917	-2	68	71	2b16,D15,S7,3b3		-0.3
1987	Bal A	26	79	7	16	3	1	1	6	1-0	0	15	.203	.213	.304	36	-8	0-1	1.000	2	123	93	3b20,2b3,O2L/SD		-0.6
1988	Cle A	69	223	30	57	14	2	2	21	9-0	5	35	.256	.292	.363	82	-5	3-3	.933	-6	96	81	S54,3b8,2b7/D		-0.8
1989	Hou N	7	7	1	1	0	0	0	0	0-0	1	4	.143	.143	.286	20	-1	0-0	—	-0	0	0	/23		-0.1
Total	9	564	1586	190	414	65	22	20	146	65-1	9	266	.261	.292	.368	78	-52	28-18	.958	-47	89	87	S372,2b111,3b43,D30,O4(2/2/0)/1		-6.8

WASHINGTON, GEORGE Sloan Vernon "Vern" B6.4.1907 Linden TX D2.17.1985 Linden TX BL/TR/5-11.5/190 d4.17

1935	Chi A	108	339	40	96	22	3	8	47	10	3	18	.283	.310	.437	89	-7	1-0	.974	-2	96	162	O79R		-0.9
1936	Chi A	20	49	6	8	2	0	1	5	1	0	4	.163	.180	.265	8	-7	0-0	.938	0	75	248	O12R		-0.7
Total	2	128	388	46	104	24	3	9	52	11	3	22	.268	.294	.415	78	-14	1-0	.970	-2	94	171	O91R		-1.6

WASHINGTON, U L U L B10.27.1953 Stringtown OK BB/TR/5-11/175(170-185) d9.6 Col Murray St. (OK) JC

1977	KC A	10	20	0	4	1	1	0	1	5-0	0	4	.200	.360	.350	93	-1	98	101	S9					0.0
1978	KC A	69	129	10	34	2	1	0	9	10-0	0	20	.264	.314	.295	71	-5	12-6	.927	-14	69	55	S49,2b19/D		-1.5
1979	KC A	101	268	32	68	12	5	2	25	20-1	0	44	.254	.299	.358	77	-9	10-7	.970	-2	101	114	S50,2b46/3D		-0.5
1980	†KC A	153	549	79	150	16	11	6	53	53-0	0	78	.273	.336	.375	94	-5	20-7	.957	-20	98	88	S152		-0.8
1981	†KC A	98	339	40	77	19	1	2	29	41-1	0	43	.227	.310	.307	78	-8	10-10	.973	-20	93	92	S98		-2.0
1982	KC A	119	437	64	125	19	3	10	60	38-0	0	48	.286	.338	.412	105	3	23-7	.961	-4	102	96	S117/D		1.4
1983	KC A	144	547	76	129	19	6	5	41	48-0	1	78	.236	.298	.320	70	-23	40-7	.947	-8	103	104	S140/D	23	-0.8
1984	†KC A	63	170	18	38	6	0	1	10	14-0	0	31	.224	.281	.276	55	-10	4-6	.961	-2	99	127	S61	63	-0.8
1985	Mon N	68	193	24	48	9	4	1	17	15-1	0	33	.249	.301	.352	87	-4	6-3	.978	-5	96	96	2b43,S9,3b3	36	-0.7
1986	Pit N	72	135	14	27	0	4	1	9	15-2	0	27	.200	.278	.259	48	-10	6-0	.947	-1	98	135	S51,2b3		-0.6
1987	Pit N	10	10	1	3	0	0	0	0	0-0	0	3	.300	.417	.300	93	0	0-0	.833	-0	133	0	/S3		0.0
Total	11	907	2797	358	703	103	36	27	255	261-6	1	409	.251	.313	.343	81	-71	132-53	.956	-77	98	100	S737,2b111,D6,3b5	122	-6.5

WASINGER, MARK Mark Thomas B8.4.1961 Monterey CA BR/TR/6-0/165* [SDN82 3/57] d5.27 Col Old Dominion

1986	SD N	3	8	0	0	0	0	0	0	0-0	0	2	.000	.000	.000	-99	-2	0-0	.500	-2	57	325	3b3/2		-0.4
1987	SF N	44	80	16	22	3	0	1	3	8-0	0	14	.275	.341	.350	88	-1	2-0	.973	1	99	161	3b21,2b10,S2		0.0
1988	SF N	3	2	1	0	0	0	0	0	0-0	0	0	.000	.000	.000	-99	-1	0-0	—	0	0	0	/3		-0.1
Total	3	50	90	17	22	3	0	1	3	8-0	0	16	.244	.306	.311	68	-4	2-0	.907	-0	94	179	3b25,2b11,S2		-0.5

WASZGIS, B.J. Robert Michael B8.24.1970 Omaha NE BR/TR/6-2/215 [BalA91 10/264] d7.29 Col McNeese St.

| 2000 | Tex A | 24 | 45 | 6 | 10 | 1 | 0 | 2 | 6 | 3-0 | 1 | 22 | .222 | .294 | .244 | 40 | -4 | 0-0 | 1.000 | -4 | 265 | 30 | C23,1b3 | | -0.7 |

WATERMAN, FRED Frederick A. B12.16.1845 New York NY D12.16.1899 Cincinnati OH 5-7.5/148 d5.5 M1

1871	Oly NA	32	158	46	50	7	4	0	17	10		0	.316	.357	.411	127	7	11-3	.695	2	117	200	3b28,C6		0.6
1872	Oly NA	9	45	13	17	1	2	0	6	0		0	.378	.378	.489	173	4	0-0	.843	4	170	260	3b7,C2,M		0.5
1873	Was NA	15	80	20	28	1	1	0	12	1		1	.350	.358	.387	102	-1	0-0	.649	-6	70	0	S9,O4(0/3/1),3b2		-0.3
1875	Chi NA	5	20	2	6	0	0	0	3	0		2	.300	.300	.300	108	0	0-1	.545	-3	72	221	3b5		-0.3
	4 NA	61	303	81	101	9	7	0	38	11		3	.333	.357	.409	132	13	11-4	.707	-3	118	204	3b42,S9,C8,O4(0/3/1)		0.5

YEAR	TM LG	G	AB	R	H	2B	3B	HR	RBI	BB-IB	HP	SO	AVG	OBP	SLG	AOPS	ABR	SB-CS	FA	FR	RNG	THR	GAMES AT POSITION	DL	BFW

WATHAN, DUSTY Dustin James B8.22.1973 Jacksonville FL BR/TR/6-4/215 d9.24 f-John Col Cerritos (CA) JC

2002	KC A	3	5	1	3	1	0	0	1	0-0		1	.600	.667	.800	256	1	0-0	1.000	1	82	0	C3		0.2

WATHAN, JOHN John David B10.4.1949 Cedar Rapids IA BR/TR/6-2/205* [KCA71*1/4] d5.26 M6/C4 s-Dusty Col San Diego

1976	†KC A	27	42	5	12	1	0	0	5	2-0	1	5	.286	.333	.310	88	-1	0-2	.984	-1	103	63	C23,1b3	34	-0.1
1977	†KC A	55	119	18	39	5	3	2	21	5-1	0	8	.328	.346	.471	121	3	2-0	.993	1	94	32	C35,1b5,D2		0.3
1978	†KC A	67	190	19	57	10	1	2	28	3-1	4	12	.300	.320	.395	98	-1	2-1	1.000	1	102	76	1b47,C21	21	-0.2
1979	†KC A	90	199	26	41	7	3	2	28	7-1	0	24	.206	.227	.302	42	-17	2-1	.993	-3	98	118	1b49,C23,D11,O3(2/0/1)		-2.7
1980	†KC A	126	453	57	138	14	7	6	58	50-6	3	42	.305	.377	.406	113	9	17-3	.982	-9	76	83	C77,O35(19/0/17),1b12		0.4
1981	†KC A	89	301	24	76	9	3	1	19	19-1	2	25	.252	.298	.312	77	-9	11-6	.979	-5	89	73	C73,O16(3/0/13)/1		-1.2
1982	KC A	121	448	79	121	11	3	3	51	48-0	2	46	.270	.343	.328	85	-8	36-9	.980	-9	108	102	C120,1b3	35	-0.8
1983	KC A	128	437	49	107	18	3	2	32	27-0	1	56	.245	.289	.314	66	-21	28-7	.985	1	99	102	C92,1b37,O9(3/0/6)		-1.4
1984	KC A	97	171	17	31	7	1	2	10	21-0	0	34	.181	.271	.269	49	-12	6-6	.985	-2	92	86	C59,1b33/OLD		-1.3
1985	KC A	60	145	11	34	8	1	1	9	17-0	1	15	.234	.319	.324	76	-4	1-1	.986	12	126	121	C49,1b6,D2		0.9
Total	10	860	2505	305	656	90	25	21	261	199-10	14	265	.262	.318	.343	82	-61	105-36	.982	-17	100	88	C572,1b196,O64(28/0/37),D19	90	-5.5

WATKINS, DAVE David Roger B3.15.1944 Owensboro KY BR/TR/5-10/185 d4.9

1969	Phi N	69	148	17	26	2	1	4	12	22-0	1	53	.176	.291	.284	63	-7	2-3	.981	-4	79	124	C54,O5(5/0/1)/3		-1.

WATKINS, GEORGE George Archibald B6.4.1900 Freestone Co. TX D6.1.1970 Houston TX BL/TR/6-0/175 d4.15

1930	†StL N	119	391	85	146	32	7	17	87	24		49	.373	.415	.621	141	26	5	.956	-3	91	100	O89(3/1/85),1b13/2		0.1
1931	†StL N	131	503	93	145	30	13	13	51	31	5	66	.288	.336	.477	112	6	15	.958	-3	99	83	O129(0/9/121)		-0.
1932	StL N	127	458	67	143	35	3	9	63	45	8	62	.312	.384	.461	122	17	18	.949	-2	99	106	O120(38/19/62)		-0.
1933	StL N	138	525	66	146	24	5	5	62	39	12	62	.278	.342	.371	98	0	11	.953	1	109	74	O135R		-0.
1934	NY N	105	296	38	73	18	4	6	33	24	6	34	.247	.316	.389	90	-4	2	.944	-8	86	54	O81(8/68/5)		-1.
1935	Phi N	150	600	80	162	25	5	17	76	40	4	78	.270	.320	.413	87	-12	3	.958	-3	96	163	O148(128/20/1)		-0.
1936	Phi N	19	70	7	17	4	2	2	5	5	0	13	.243	.293	.386	74	-3	2	.889	-2	75	93	O17L		-0.
	Bro N	105	364	54	93	24	6	4	43	39	5	34	.255	.334	.387	93	-3	5	.969	-3	99	67	O98(72/1/25)		-0.
	Year	124	434	61	110	28	8	6	48	43	5	47	.253	.328	.387	90	-6	7	.959	-4	96	70	O115(89/1/25)		
Total	7	894	3207	490	925	192	42	73	420	246	44	382	.288	.347	.443	105	27	61	.954	-16	98	97	O817(266/118/434),1b13/2		

WATKINS, ED James Edward B6.21.1877 Philadelphia PA D3.29.1933 Kelvin AZ d9.6

1902	Phi N	1	3	0	0	0	0	0	0	1	0		.000	.250	.000	-22	0	0	1.000	-0	0	0	/OL		-0.

WATKINS, BILL William Henry B5.5.1858 Brantford ON, Can. D6.9.1937 Port Huron MI BR/5-10/156 d8.1 M9

1884	Ind AA	34	127	16	26	4	0	0		5			.205	.241	.236	58	-5		.845	-4	74	40	3b23,2b9,S2,M		-0.

WATKINS, PAT William Patrick B9.2.1972 Raleigh NC BR/TR/6-2/195* [CinN93 S1/32] d9.9 Col East Carolina

1997	Cin N	17	29	2	6	2	0	0	0-0	1	5	.207	.207	.276	25	-3	1-0	1.000	-1	69	299	O15C		-0.
1998	Cin N	83	147	11	39	8	1	2	15	8-0	1	26	.265	.300	.374	77	-5	1-3	.971	0	111	38	O77(13/39/28)		-0.
1999	Col N	16	19	2	1	0	0	0	2-0	0	5	.053	.143	.053	-38	-4	0-0	1.000	0	113	0	O10(4/1/5)		-1
Total	3	116	195	15	46	10	1	2	15	10-0	1	36	.236	.271	.328	56	-12	2-3	.976	0	106	70	O102(17/55/33)		

WATLINGTON, NEAL Julius Neal B12.25.1922 Yanceyville NC BL/TR/6-0/195 d7.10

1953	Phi A	21	44	4	7	1	0	0	3	6	0	8	.159	.213	.182	7	-6	0-1	.978	0	117	174	C9		-0.

WATSON, ART Arthur Stanhope "Watty" B1.11.1884 Jeffersonville IN D5.9.1950 Buffalo NY BL/TR/5-10/175 d5.19

1914	Bro F	22	46	7	13	4	1	1	3	1	0	6	.283	.298	.478	110	0	0	.977	-0	89	113	C18		C
1915	Bro F	9	19	3	5	0	0	0	1	3	0	4	.263	.364	.579	164	1	0	.957	-2	74	72	C7		C
	Buf F	22	30	6	14	1	0	1	13	0	0	4	.467	.467	.600	195	3	0	.778	-3	59	91	C6/OL		C
	Year	31	49	10	19	1	0	1	14	3	0	8	.388	.423	.592	182	4	0	.878	-5	68	80	C13/OL		C
Total	2	53	95	17	32	5	1	2	17	4	0	14	.337	.364	.537	147	4	0	.946	-5	80	100	C31/OL		

WATSON, BRANDON Brandon Eric B9.30.1981 Los Angeles CA BL/TR/6-1/170 d8.9

2005	Was N	25	40	8	7	1	1	0	5	0-0	0	8	.175	.250	.325	53	-3	0-2	.933	-0	78	205	O13(12/1/0)		-0

WATSON, JOHNNY John Thomas B1.16.1908 Tazewell VA D4.29.1965 Huntington WV BL/TR/6-0/175 d9.26 Col Marshall

1930	Det A	4	12	1	3	2	0	0	3	1	0	2	.250	.308	.417	80	0	0-0	.933	-1	73	151	S4		-0

WATSON, MATT Matthew Kyle B9.5.1978 Lancaster PA BL/TR/5-11/190* [MonN99 16/480] d9.12 Col Xavier

2003	NY N	15	23	0	4	0	0	0	2	1-0	0	5	.174	.208	.261	22	-3	0-0	.846	0	181	0	O5L		-0
2005	Oak A	19	48	4	9	3	0	0	5	2-0	0	4	.188	.220	.250	24	-5	0-0	1.000	1	127	0	O17(14/0/3)		-0
Total	2	34	71	4	13	5	0	0	7	3-0	0	9	.183	.216	.254	24	-8	0-0	.953	1	139	0	O22(19/0/3)		

WATSON, BOB Robert Jose "Bull" B4.10.1946 Los Angeles CA BR/TR/6-2/205(200-218) d9.9 C3

1966	Hou N	1	1	0	0	0	0	0	0	0-0	0	0	.000	.000	.000	-99	0	0-0	—	0			/H		
1967	Hou N	6	14	1	3	0	0	1	2	0-0	0	3	.214	.214	.429	82	0	0-0	.958	0	117	0	1b3		
1968	Hou N	45	140	13	32	7	0	2	8	13-1	1	32	.229	.297	.321	88	-2	1-0	.885	-5	77	0	O40(40/0/1)	58	
1969	Hou N	20	40	3	11	3	0	0	3	6-0	2	5	.275	.396	.350	112	1	0-0	1.000	1	90	0	O6L,1b5/C		
1970	Hou N	97	327	48	89	19	2	11	61	24-1	4	59	.272	.324	.443	109	3	1-1	.992	-6	70	81	1b83,C6/OL		
1971	Hou N	129	468	49	135	17	3	9	67	41-5	2	56	.288	.347	.395	114	8	0-3	.985	-10	79	35	O87L,1b45		
1972	Hou N	147	548	74	171	27	4	16	86	53-5	8	83	.312	.378	.464	143	31	1-1	.978	-10	80	61	O143L,1b2		
1973	Hou N★	158	573	97	179	24	3	16	94	85-8	4	73	.312	.403	.449	137	33	1-4	.969	-4	99	84	O142L,1b26,C3		
1974	Hou N	150	524	69	156	19	4	11	67	60-9	3	61	.298	.370	.412	125	18	3-4	.981	-7	83	79	O140L,1b35		
1975	Hou N★	132	485	67	157	27	1	18	85	40-10	3	50	.324	.375	.495	152	32	3-5	.993	-2	92	107	1b118,O9L		
1976	Hou N	157	585	76	183	31	6	16	102	62-10	4	64	.313	.377	.458	150	39	5-0	.994	10	126	0	1b146		
1977	Hou N	151	554	77	160	38	6	22	110	57-11	7	69	.289	.360	.498	139	30	5-0	.992	8	122	68	1b128		
1978	Hou N	139	461	51	133	25	4	14	79	51-16	4	57	.289	.357	.451	135	22	3-1	.993	3	121	77	1b44		
1979	Hou N	49	163	15	39	4	0	3	18	16-1	0	23	.239	.304	.319	92	-6	0-0	.993	3	121	77	1b58,D26		
	Bos A	84	312	48	105	19	4	13	53	29-7	5	33	.337	.401	.548	145	20	3-2	.988	1	111	119	1b84,D21		
1980	†NY A	130	469	62	144	25	4	13	68	48-5	1	56	.307	.368	.456	128	19	2-1	.990	3	113	105	1b104,D21	23	
1981	†NY A	59	156	15	33	3	6	12	24-2	0	17	.212	.317	.385	102	0	0-0	1.000	-1	0	144	D59,1b6/D		
1982	NY A	7	17	3	4	0	0	3	3-0	0	5	.235	.350	.412	110	0	0-0	1.000	0	0	144	1b6/D		
	Atl N	57	114	16	28	3	1	5	22	14-2	1	20	.246	.323	.421	106	1	1-1	.984	-4	49	93	1b27,O2L		
1983	Atl N	65	114	14	24	7	0	6	37	18-3	0	23	.309	.376	.490	131	7	0-2	.984	-2	81	93	1b34	18	
1984	Atl N	49	85	4	18	5	0	1	12	9-2	0	12	.212	.287	.329	68	-4	0-0	.983	0	114	147	1b19		
Total	19	1832	6185	802	1826	307	41	184	989	653-98	48	796	.295	.364	.447	130	252	27-28	.991	-29	99	95	1b1088,O570(570/0/1),D54,C10	99	

WATT, ALLIE Albert Bailey B12.12.1899 Philadelphia PA D3.15.1968 Norfolk VA BR/TR/5-8/154 d10.3 b-Frank

1920	Was A	1	1	0	1	0	1	1	0	0			1.000	1.000	2.000	700	1	0-0	1.000	0	143	0	/2		

WATWOOD, JOHNNY John Clifford "Lefty" B8.17.1905 Alexander City AL D3.1.1980 Goodwater AL BL/TL/6-1/186 d4.16 Col Auburn-Montgomery

1929	Chi A	85	278	33	84	12	6	2	28	22	1	21	.302	.355	.410	98	-1	6-3	.942	-1	102	90	O77(1/53/23)		
1930	Chi A	133	427	75	129	25	4	2	51	52	3	35	.302	.382	.393	100	3	5-7	.989	3	117	116	1b62,O52(1/36/14)		
1931	Chi A	128	367	51	104	16	6	1	47	56	1	30	.283	.380	.368	103	4	9-3	.944	5	105	161	O102(4/76/24),1b4		
1932	Chi A	13	49	5	15	2	0	0	1	1		3	.306	.333	.347	82	-1	0-0	.960	-0	91	107	O13(4/1/11)		
	Bos A	95	266	26	66	11	0	0	30	20		11	.248	.301	.289	55	-18	7-4	.945	-2	92	88	O46(7/25/14),1b18		
	Year	108	315	31	81	13	0	0	30	21	1	14	.257	.306	.298	59	-19	7-4	.948	-2	92	92	O59(11/26/25),1b18		
1933	Bos A	13	30	2	4	0	0	0	2	3		3	.133	.212	.133	-7	-5	0-0	.950	-4	119	0	O9(5/0/4)		
1939	Phi N	2	6	1	1	0	0	0	0	1		0	.167	.167	.167	-11	-1	0-0	.933	-1	0	0	1b2		
Total	6	469	1423	192	403	66	16	5	158	154	6	103	.283	.356	.363	89	-19	27-17	.948	5	101	119	O299(22/191/90),1b86		

WAUXHAM d6.22

1872	Eck NA	1	2	0	0	0	0	0	0	0			1.000	.000	.000	-99	0	0-0	.500	-1	122	0	/2		

WAY, BOB Robert Clinton B4.2.1906 Emlenton PA D6.20.1974 Pittsburgh PA BR/TR/5-10.5/168 d4.12

1927	Chi A	5	3	1	1	0	0	0	0	1		0	.333	.333	.333	75	0	0-0	1.000	-0	0	0	/2		

YEAR	TM LG	G	AB	R	H	2B	3B	HR	RBI	BB-IB	HP	SO	AVG	OBP	SLG	AOPS	ABR	SB-CS	FA	FR	RNG	THR	GAMES AT POSITION	DL	BFW

WEATHERLY, ROY   Cyril Roy "Stormy"   B2.25.1915 Warren TX   D1.19.1991 Woodville TX   BL/TR/5-6.5/170*   d6.27   Mil 1944-45

1936	Cle A	84	349	64	117	28	6	8	53	16		0	29	.335	.364	.519	115	6	3-8	.973	5	97	197	O84(3/5/80)		0.4
1937	Cle A	53	134	19	27	4	0	5	13	6	2	14	.201	.246	.343	47	-12	1-1	.964	1	84	227	O38(7/0/32)/3		-1.2
1938	Cle A	83	210	32	55	14	3	2	18	14	0	14	.262	.308	.386	74	-9	8-5	.975	2	97	170	O55(6/41/8)		-0.8
1939	Cle A	95	323	43	100	16	6	1	32	19	0	23	.310	.348	.406	95	-3	7-2	.961	-5	91	58	O76(36/27/14)		-0.9
1940	Cle A	135	578	90	175	35	11	12	59	27	1	26	.303	.335	.464	108	4	9-8	.969	2	103	101	O135(1/134/0)		0.1
1941	Cle A	102	363	59	105	21	5	3	37	32	2	20	.289	.350	.399	103	1	2-5	.968	-8	94	15	O88(0/87/1)		-0.9
1942	Cle A	128	473	61	122	23	7	5	39	35	1	25	.258	.310	.368	96	-5	8-13	.991	2	104	82	O117C		-0.8
1943	†NY A	77	280	37	74	8	3	7	28	18	1	9	.264	.311	.389	104	0	4-7	.983	-4	97	39	O68C		-0.8
1946	NY A	2	2	0	1	0	0	0	0	0	0		.500	.500	.500	178	0	0-0	—	0			/H		0.0
1950	NY N	52	69	10	18	3	3	0	11	13	0	10	.261	.378	.391	102	1	0	1.000	1	95	261	O15(12/1/2)		0.1
Total	10	811	2781	415	794	152	44	43	290	180	7	170	.286	.331	.418	99	-17	42-49	.975*	-3	98	101	O676(65/480/137)/3		-4.8

WEAVER, ART   Arthur Coggshall "Six O'Clock"   B4.7.1879 Wichita KS   D3.23.1917 Denver CO   TR/6-1/160   d9.14

1902	StL N	11	33	2	6	2	0	0	3	1	0		.182	.206	.242	40	-2	0	.983	0	99	136	C11		-0.1
1903	StL N	16	49	4	12	0	0	0	5	4	0		.245	.302	.245	58	-3	1	.969	1	94	124	C16		0.0
	Pit N	16	48	8	11	0	1	0	3	2	0		.229	.260	.271	50	-3	0	.978	0	142	85	C11,1b5		-0.3
	Year	32	97	12	23	0	1	0	8	6	0		.237	.282	.258	54	-6	1	.972	1	111	111	C27,1b5		-0.3
1905	StL A	28	92	5	11	2	1	0	3	1	0		.120	.129	.163	-8	-12	0	.962	1	79	113	C28		-0.8
1908	Chi A	15	35	1	7	1	0	0	1	1	0		.200	.222	.229	47	-2	0	.953	-3	92	78	C15		-0.5
Total	4	86	257	20	47	5	2	0	15	9	0		.183	.211	.218	31	-22	1	.967	0	94	111	C81,1b5		-1.7

WEAVER, BUCK   George Daniel   B8.18.1890 Pottstown PA   D1.31.1956 Chicago IL   BB/TR (BR 1912)/5-11/170   d4.11

1912	Chi A	147	523	55	117	21	8	1	43	9	6		.224	.245	.300	58	-32	13	.915	-7	93	115	S147		-2.9
1913	Chi A	151	533	51	145	17	8	4	52	15	8	60	.272	.302	.356	94	-8	20	.929	36	111	132	S151		4.0
1914	Chi A	136	541	64	133	20	9	2	28	20	5	40	.246	.279	.327	83	-14	14-20	.928	6	96	108	S134		-0.3
1915	Chi A	148	563	83	151	18	11	3	49	32	7	58	.268	.316	.355	98	-5	24-20	.939	-1	103	112	S148		0.4
1916	Chi A	151	582	78	132	27	6	3	38	30	13	48	.227	.280	.309	76	-19	22-13	.941	-0	100	145	3b85,S66		-1.3
1917	†Chi A	118	447	64	127	16	5	3	32	27	5	29	.284	.332	.362	110	4	19	.949	2	95	120	3b107,S10		1.0
1918	Chi A	112	420	37	126	12	5	0	29	11	3	24	.300	.323	.352	103	-1	20	.941	1	103	134	S98,3b11/2		0.7
1919	†Chi A	140	571	89	169	33	9	3	75	11	5	21	.296	.315	.401	100	-3	22	.963	-3	97	96	3b97,S43		0.0
1920	Chi A	151	629	102	208	34	8	2	74	28	6	23	.331	.365	.420	107	6	19-17	.933	-15	91	75	3b127,S25		-0.5
Total	9	1254	4809	623	1308	198	69	21	420	183	58	303	.272	.307	.355	92	-72	173-70	.935	19	100	121	S822,3b427/2		1.1

WEAVER, JIM   James Francis   B10.10.1959 Kingston NY   BL/TL/6-3/200*   [MinA80 2/35]   d4.10   Col Florida St.

1985	Det A	12	7	2	1	1	0	0	0	1-0	0	4	.143	.250	.286	46	-0	0-1	1.000	-0	43	0	O4(0/3/1),D4		-0.1
1987	Sea A	7	4	2	0	0	0	0	0	2-0	0	3	.000	.333	.000	-1	-1	1-1	1.000	1	83	751	O4(1/2/2)		0.0
1989	SF N	12	20	2	4	3	0	0	2	0-0	0	7	.200	.200	.350	56	-1	1-0	1.000	-1	73	0	O8(1/0/7)		-0.2
Total	3	31	31	6	5	4	0	0	2	3-0	0	14	.161	.235	.290	47	-2	2-2	1.000	-1	72	210	O16(2/5/10),D4		-0.3

WEAVER, FARMER   William B.   B3.23.1865 Parkersburg WV   D1.23.1943 Akron OH   BL/5-10/170   d9.16   OF(132/406/111)

1888	Lou AA	26	112	12	28	1	1	0	8	3	1		.250	.276	.277	79	-3	12	.878	-1	158	0	O26C		-0.4
1889	Lou AA	124	499	62	145	17	6	0	60	40	7	22	.291	.352	.349	102	2	21	.918	1	136	71	O123C,C2/32		-0.1
1890	†Lou AA	130	557	101	161	27	9	3	67	29	8		.289	.333	.386	114	8	45	.933	-6	101	96	O127(0/126/1),S2/3		-0.2
1891	Lou AA	133	556	74	157	25	7	1	53	33	11	23	.282	.335	.358	99	-2	30	.958	13	139	141	O130C,C4		0.6
1892	Lou N	138	551	58	140	15	4	0	57	40	9	17	.254	.315	.296	92	-4	30	.902	-10	94	75	O122(109/1/12),C15/1.		-2.1
1893	Lou N	106	439	79	128	17	7	2	49	27	11	12	.292	.348	.376	100	0	17	.913	2	119	60	O85(20/0/65),C21		0.0
1894	Lou N	64	244	19	54	5	2	3	24	7	2	11	.221	.249	.295	33	-28	17	.958	1	133	0	O35(2/0/33),C17,1b10/2		-2.1
	Pit N	30	115	16	40	7	2	0	24	6	5	1	.348	.405	.443	105	1	4	.943	-8	100	96	C14,S12,3b5/OL		-0.4
	Year	94	359	35	94	12	4	3	48	13	7	12	.262	.301	.343	58	-26	7	.947	-7	128	0	O36(3/0/33),C31,S12,1b10,3b5/2		-2.5
Total	7	751	3073	421	853	114	38	9	342	185	54	86	.278	.330	.348	95	-26	162	.927	-8	120	83	O649C,C73,S14,1b11,3b7,2b2		-4.7

WEBB, SKEETER   James Laverne   B11.4.1909 Meridian MS   D7.8.1986 Meridian MS   BR/TR/5-9.5/150   d7.20   Col U. of Mississippi

1932	StL N	1	0	0	0	0	0	0	0	0	0		—	—	—		0	0	—	-0	0	0	/S		0.0
1938	Cle A	20	58	11	16	2	0	0	2	8	0	7	.276	.364	.310	72	-2	1-0	.964	-2	85	94	S13,3b3,2b2		-0.3
1939	Cle A	81	269	28	71	14	1	2	26	15	1	24	.264	.305	.346	68	-13	1-1	.932	-8	89	91	S81		-1.4
1940	Chi A	84	334	33	79	11	2	1	29	30	0	33	.237	.299	.290	53	-23	3-6	.969	-9	100	95	2b74,S7/3		-2.8
1941	Chi A	29	84	7	16	2	0	0	6	3	1	9	.190	.227	.214	18	-10	1-0	.940	-0	103	121	2b18,S5,3b3		-0.9
1942	Chi A	32	94	5	16	2	1	0	4	4	0	13	.170	.204	.213	18	-11	1-2	.951	0	111	85	2b29		-0.9
1943	Chi A	58	213	15	50	5	2	0	22	6	0	19	.235	.256	.277	56	-13	5-4	.963	0	111	95	2b54		-1.1
1944	Chi A	139	513	44	108	19	6	0	30	20	1	39	.211	.242	.271	47	-38	7-3	.944	-3	106	95	S135,2b5		-3.2
1945	†Det A	118	407	43	81	12	2	0	21	30	0	35	.199	.254	.238	41	-31	8-7	.957	16	106	115	S104,2b11		-0.8
1946	Det A	64	169	22	37	1	1	0	17	9	0	18	.219	.258	.237	37	-15	3-3	.972	6	112	100	2b50,S8		-0.5
1947	Det A	50	79	13	16	3	0	0	6	7	0	9	.203	.267	.241	41	-6	3-0	.992	1	125	62	2b30,S6		0.1
1948	Phi A	23	54	5	8	2	0	0	3	0	0	9	.148	.148	.185	-12	-9	0-0	1.000	2	97	199	2b9,S8		-0.6
Total	12	699	2274	216	498	73	15	3	166	132	3	215	.219	.263	.268	46	-171	33-26	.946	11	102	99	S368,2b282,3b7		-12.4

WEBB, EARL   William Earl   B9.17.1897 Bon Air TN   D5.23.1965 Jamestown TN   BL/TR/6-1/185   d8.13

1925	NY N	4	3	0	0	0	0	0	1	0	0	1	1.000	1.000	1.000	-31	-1	0-0		0			/H		-0.1
1927	Chi N	102	332	58	100	18	4	14	52	48	1	31	.301	.391	.506	138	19	3	.959	-0	93	133	O86(8/0/78)		1.2
1928	Chi N	62	140	22	35	7	3	3	23	14	0	17	.250	.318	.407	90	-3	0	.986	1	99	127	O31R		-0.4
1930	Bos A	127	449	61	145	30	6	16	66	44	1	56	.323	.385	.523	133	22	2-1	.959	-6	92	75	O116R		0.7
1931	Bos A	151	589	96	196	67	3	14	103	70	0	51	.333	.404	.528	151	47	2-2	.948	-5	86	136	O151R		3.0
1932	Bos A	52	192	23	54	9	1	5	27	25	0	15	.281	.364	.417	105	2	0-0	.964	-1	78	190	O50R,1b2		-0.2
	Det A	88	338	49	97	19	8	3	51	39	0	18	.287	.361	.417	97	-1	1-1	.955	0	98	125	O85R		-0.6
	Year	140	530	72	151	28	9	8	78	64	0	33	.285	.362	.417	100	1	1-1	.958	-1	91	148	O135R,1b2		-0.8
1933	Det A	6	11	1	3	0	0	0	3	3	0	2	.273	.429	.273	87	0	0-0	1.000	-0	38	0	O2R		0.0
	Chi A	58	107	16	31	5	0	1	8	16	0	13	.290	.382	.364	103	1	0-0	1.000	-2	92	197	O18(5/0/11),1b10		-0.2
	Year	64	118	17	34	5	0	1	11	19	0	13	.288	.387	.356	101	1	0-0	1.000	-2	86	174	O18(5/0/13),1b10		-0.2
Total	7	650	2161	326	661	155	25	56	333	260	2	202	.306	.381	.478	125	86	8-4	.958	-13	90	126	O537(13/0/524),1b12		3.4

WEBB, BILL   William Joseph   B6.25.1895 Chicago IL   D1.12.1943 Chicago IL   BR/TR/5-10/161   d9.17   Mil 1918 C5

| 1917 | Pit N | 5 | 15 | 1 | 3 | 0 | 0 | 0 | 2 | 0 | 0 | 3 | .200 | .294 | .200 | 51 | -1 | 0 | 1.000 | 0 | 104 | 82 | 2b4/S | | -0.1 |

WEBER, HARRY   Henry J.   B3.1.1862 NY   D12.22.1926 Indianapolis IN   d7.22

| 1884 | Ind AA | 3 | 8 | 0 | 0 | 0 | 0 | 0 | | 0 | | 1 | .000 | .111 | .000 | -62 | -1 | | .794 | -1 | | | C3 | | -0.2 |

WEBER, JOE   Joseph Edward   B2.15.1862 Hamilton ON, Can.   D12.15.1921 Hamilton ON, Can.   BR/5-9/167   d5.30

| 1884 | Det N | 2 | 8 | 0 | 0 | 0 | 0 | 0 | | 0 | | 2 | .000 | .000 | .000 | -99 | -2 | | .750 | 0 | 227 | 0 | O2(1/0/1) | | -0.2 |

WEBSTER, LENNY   Leonard Irell   B2.10.1965 New Orleans LA   BR/TR/5-9/191(185-202)   [MinA85 21/535]   d9.1   Col Grambling St.

1989	Min A	14	20	3	6	2	0	0	3	3-0	0	1	.300	.391	.400	116	1	0-0	1.000	-3	50	74	C14		-0.2
1990	Min A	2	6	1	2	1	0	0	0	0	0	1	.333	.429	.500	149	0	0-0	1.000	-3	68	0	C2		0.0
1991	Min A	18	34	7	10	1	0	1	8	6-0	0	10	.294	.390	.588	162	3	0-0	.986	4	128	62	C17		0.7
1992	Min A	53	118	10	33	10	1	1	13	9-0	0	11	.280	.331	.407	102	0	0-2	.995	-6	91	69	C49/D		-0.4
1993	Min A	49	106	14	21	2	0	1	8	11-1	0	9	.198	.274	.245	-9	-10	1-0	1.000	-1	111	94	C45/D		-0.8
1994	Mon N	57	143	13	39	10	0	5	23	16-1	0	24	.273	.370	.448	113	3	0-0	.996	-3	73	110	C46		0.2
1995	Phi N	49	150	18	40	8	0	4	14	16-0	0	27	.267	.337	.407	95	-1	0-0	.990	-8	68	51	C43		-0.6
1996	Mon N	78	174	18	40	10	0	2	17	25-2	2	21	.230	.332	.322	72	-6	0-0	.998	10	124	123	C63		0.7
1997	†Bal A	98	259	29	66	8	1	7	37	22-0	1	46	.255	.317	.375	82	-7	0-1	.995	-3	78	112	C97/D		-0.6
1998	Bal A	108	309	37	88	16	0	10	46	15-0	0	38	.285	.317	.434	95	-3	0-0	.993	-13	73	92	C102,D4		-1.0
1999	Bal A	16	36	1	6	1	0	0	3	1	0	5	.167	.333	.194	41	-3	0	.986	2	88	131	C12,D2	64	0.0
	Bos A	6	14	0	0	0	0	0	1	2-0	1	2	.000	.176	.000	-48	-3	0-0	1.000	-1	71	73	C6		-0.3
	Year	22	50	1	6	1	0	0	4	10-0	2	7	.120	.290	.140	15	-6	0-0	.990	1	83	113	C18,D2		-0.3
2000	Mon N	39	81	6	17	3	0	0	5	6-1	0	14	.210	.264	.247	30	-9	0-0	1.000	-5	74	50	C32	31	-0.2
Total	12	587	1450	157	368	73	2	33	176	140-5	12	209	.254	.324	.375	84	-34	1-3	.995	-26	85	91	C528,D9	95	-3.3

YEAR TM LG	G	AB	R	H	2B	3B	HR	RBI	BB-IB	HP	SO	AVG	OBP	SLG	AOPS	ABR	SB-CS	FA	FR	RNG	THR	GAMES AT POSITION	DL	BFV

WEBSTER, MITCH   Mitchell Dean B5.16.1959 Larned KS BB/TL/6-1/185(180-191) [LAN77 23/581] d9.2

YEAR TM LG	G	AB	R	H	2B	3B	HR	RBI	BB-IB	HP	SO	AVG	OBP	SLG	AOPS	ABR	SB-CS	FA	FR	RNG	THR	GAMES AT POSITION	DL	BFV
1983 Tor A	11	11	2	2	0	0	0	0	1-0	0	1	.182	.250	.182	20	-1	0-0	1.000	-1	52	0	O7C,D2		-0
1984 Tor A	26	22	9	5	2	1	0	4	1-0	0	7	.227	.261	.409	79	-1	0-0	.875	-0	119	0	O10(3/7/0)/1D		-0
1985 Tor A	4	1	0	0	0	0	0	0	0-0	0	0	.000	.000	.000	-97	0	0-1	—	-0	0	0	O2L,D2		-0
Mon N	74	212	32	58	8	2	11	30	20-3	0	33	.274	.335	.486	134	9	15-9	.993	0	101	86	O64(4/52/20)		-0
1986 Mon N	151	576	89	167	31	13	8	49	57-4	4	78	.290	.355	.431	117	13	36-15	.977	0	100	130	O146(8/118/44)		-0
1987 Mon N	156	588	101	165	30	8	15	63	70-5	6	95	.281	.361	.435	106	7	33-10	.982	-4	91	59	O71(12/53/12)		-0
1988 Mon N	81	259	33	66	5	2	2	13	36-2	5	37	.255	.354	.313	89	-2	12-10	.994	-3	91	59	O71(12/53/12)		-0
Chi N	70	264	36	70	11	6	4	26	19-0	3	50	.265	.319	.398	101	0	10-4	.982	1	109	33	O65(8/52/10)		-0
Year	151	523	69	136	16	8	6	39	55-2	8	87	.260	.337	.356	95	-2	22-14	.982	-3	100	47	O130(20/105/22)		-0
1989 †Chi N	98	272	40	70	12	4	3	19	30-5	1	55	.257	.331	.364	93	-2	14-2	.965	3	116	82	O74(52/13/21)	15	-0
1990 Cle A	128	437	58	110	20	6	12	55	20-1	3	61	.252	.285	.407	93	-7	22-6	.991	8	122	17	O118(25/95/0),1b3,D3		-0
1991 Cle A	13	32	2	4	0	0	0	0	3-0	0	5	.125	.200	.125	-8	-5	-2-2	1.000	0	115	0	O10(6/1/6)		-0
Pit N	36	97	9	17	3	4	1	9	9-1	0	31	.175	.245	.320	58	-6	0-0	.963	-1	94	116	O29(2/9/20)		-0
LA N	58	74	12	21	5	1	1	10	9-1	0	21	.284	.361	.419	121	2	0-1	1.000	1	120	0	O36(29/4/7)/1		-0
Year	94	171	21	38	8	5	2	19	18-2	0	52	.222	.296	.363	85	-4	0-1	.978	0	103	74	O65(31/13/27)/1		-0
1992 LA N	135	262	33	70	12	5	6	35	27-3	2	49	.267	.334	.420	115	5	11-5	.977	-2	103	0	O90(36/8/56)		-0
1993 LA N	88	172	26	42	6	2	1	14	11-2	2	24	.244	.293	.337	73	-7	4-6	.950	-2	97	35	O56(32/2/27)		
1994 LA N	82	84	16	23	4	0	4	12	8-1	1	13	.274	.344	.464	114	2	1-2	1.000	-1	95	0	O48(45/0/6)	21	
1995 †LA N	54	56	6	10	1	1	1	3	4-1	1	14	.179	.246	.286	43	-5	0-0	1.000	-1	72	0	O25(11/4/11)	36	-1
Total 13	1265	3419	504	900	150	55	70	342	325-28	28	578	.263	.330	.401	101	2	160-73	.980	-3	103	63	O1004(275/425/393),D16,1b5		

WEBSTER, RAY   Ramon Alberto B8.31.1942 Colon, Pan BL/TL/6-0/185* d4.11

YEAR TM LG	G	AB	R	H	2B	3B	HR	RBI	BB-IB	HP	SO	AVG	OBP	SLG	AOPS	ABR	SB-CS	FA	FR	RNG	THR	GAMES AT POSITION	DL	BFV
1967 KC A	122	360	41	92	15	4	11	51	32-1	2	44	.256	.320	.411	118	7	5-3	.989	-3	76	75	1b83,O15(14/0/2)		-0
1968 Oak A	66	196	17	42	11	1	3	23	12-6	1	24	.214	.258	.327	80	-5	3-0	.988	-3	79	91	1b55		
1969 Oak A	64	77	5	20	0	1	1	13	12-5	1	8	.260	.359	.325	98	0	0-0	1.000	0	104	69	1b13		
1970 SD N	95	116	12	30	3	0	2	11	11-0	0	12	.259	.323	.336	80	-3	1-1	.981	-1	83	134	1b15/OL		
1971 SD N	10	8	0	1	0	0	0	0	2-0	0	1	.125	.300	.125	26	-1	0-0	—	0			/H		
Oak A	7	5	0	0	0	0	0	0	0-0	0	1	.000	.000	.000	-99	-1	0-0	1.000	0	0	0	/1		
Chi N	16	16	1	5	2	0	0	0	1-0	0	3	.313	.353	.438	107	0	0-0	1.000	0	316	266	/1		
Total 5	380	778	76	190	31	6	17	98	70-12	5	94	.244	.308	.365	98	-3	9-4	.989	-7	80.	85	1b168,O16(15/0/2)		

WEBSTER, RAY   Raymond George B11.15.1937 Grass Valley CA BR/TR/6-0/175(160-175) d4.17

YEAR TM LG	G	AB	R	H	2B	3B	HR	RBI	BB-IB	HP	SO	AVG	OBP	SLG	AOPS	ABR	SB-CS	FA	FR	RNG	THR	GAMES AT POSITION	DL	BFV
1959 Cle A	40	74	10	15	2	1	2	10	5-0	0	7	.203	.253	.338	63	-4	1-0	.929	-2	99	109	2b24,3b4		
1960 Bos A	7	3	1	0	0	0	0	0	1-0	0	0	.000	.200	.000	-25	-1	0-0	1.000	0	76	265	/2		
Total 2	47	77	11	15	2	1	2	11	6-0	0	7	.195	.250	.325	59	-5	1-0	.931	-2	98	114	2b25,3b4		

WECKBECKER, PETE   Peter B8.30.1864 Butler PA D5.16.1935 Hampton VA 5-7/150 d10.5

YEAR TM LG	G	AB	R	H	2B	3B	HR	RBI	BB-IB	HP	SO	AVG	OBP	SLG	AOPS	ABR	SB-CS	FA	FR	RNG	THR	GAMES AT POSITION	DL	BFV
1889 Ind N	1	1	0	0	0	0	0	0	0-0	0		.000	.000	.000	-98	0	0	1.000	-0			/C		
1890 †Lou AA	32	101	17	24	1	0	0	11	8-1	1		.238	.300	.248	63	-5	7	.941	4	*135*	73	C32		
Total 2	33	102	17	24	1	0	0	11	8-1	1		.235	.297	.245	61	-5	7	.941	4	*135*	*73*	C33		

WEDGE, ERIC   Eric Michael B1.27.1968 Fort Wayne IN BR/TR/6-3/215* [BosA89 3/83] d10.5 M3 Col Wichita St.

YEAR TM LG	G	AB	R	H	2B	3B	HR	RBI	BB-IB	HP	SO	AVG	OBP	SLG	AOPS	ABR	SB-CS	FA	FR	RNG	THR	GAMES AT POSITION	DL	BFV
1991 Bos A	1	1	0	1	0	0	0	0	0-0	0	0	1.000	1.000	1.000	431	0	0-0	—	0			/D		
1992 Bos A	27	68	11	17	2	0	5	11	13-0	3	18	.250	.370	.500	132	3	0-0	1.000	-1	77	0	D20,C5		
1993 Col N	9	11	2	2	0	0	0	4	1-0	0	4	.182	.182	.182	-2	-2	0-0	1.000	0	75	300	/C	111	
1994 Bos A	2	6	0	0	0	0	0	0	1-0	0	3	.000	.143	.000	-56	-1	0-0	—	0			D2		
Total 4	39	86	13	20	2	0	5	12	14-0	3	25	.233	.340	.430	103	0	0-0	1.000	-1	77	61	D23,C6	111	

WEEDEN, BERT   Charles Albert B12.21.1882 Northwood NH D1.7.1939 Northwood NH BL/TR/6-0/200 d6.4

YEAR TM LG	G	AB	R	H	2B	3B	HR	RBI	BB-IB	HP	SO	AVG	OBP	SLG	AOPS	ABR	SB-CS	FA	FR	RNG	THR	GAMES AT POSITION	DL	BFV
1911 Bos N	1	1	0	0	0	0	0	0	0-0	0	0	.000	.000	.000	-93	0	0	—	0			/H		

WEEKLY, JOHNNY   Johnny B6.14.1937 Waterproof LA D11.24.1974 Walnut Creek CA BR/TR/6-0/200(180-200) d4.13 Col Diablo Valley (CA) JC [DL 1960 SF N 102]

YEAR TM LG	G	AB	R	H	2B	3B	HR	RBI	BB-IB	HP	SO	AVG	OBP	SLG	AOPS	ABR	SB-CS	FA	FR	RNG	THR	GAMES AT POSITION	DL	BFV
1962 Hou N	13	26	3	5	1	0	2	7	7-0	0	4	.192	.364	.462	129	1	0-0	1.000	-1	73	0	O7(4/0/4)		
1963 Hou N	34	80	4	18	3	0	3	14	7-0	1	14	.225	.292	.375	98	0	0-0	1.000	2	113	160	O23(15/0/8)	33	
1964 Hou N	6	15	0	2	0	0	0	3	1-0	0	3	.133	.167	.133	-8	-2	0-0	1.000	1	124	321	O5R		
Total 3	53	121	7	25	4	0	5	19	15-0	1	21	.207	.293	.364	92	-1	0-0	1.000	2	106	148	O35(19/0/17)	135	

WEEKS, RICKIE   Rickie Darnell B9.13.1982 Altamonte Springs FL BR/TR/6-0/195* d9.15 Col Southern

YEAR TM LG	G	AB	R	H	2B	3B	HR	RBI	BB-IB	HP	SO	AVG	OBP	SLG	AOPS	ABR	SB-CS	FA	FR	RNG	THR	GAMES AT POSITION	DL	BFV
2003 Mil N	7	12	1	2	1	0	0	1	1-0	1	6	.167	.286	.250	42	-1	0-0	.667	-4	15	0	2b4		
2005 Mil N	96	360	56	86	13	2	13	42	40-2	11	96	.239	.333	.394	90	-6	15-2	.951	-13	88	97	2b95		
Total 2	103	372	57	88	14	2	13	42	41-2	12	102	.237	.331	.390	88	-7	15-2	.949	-16	86	95	2b99		

WEHNER, JOHN   John Paul B6.29.1967 Pittsburgh PA BR/TR/6-3/206* [PitN88 7/174] d7.17 Col Indiana OF(69/29/54)

YEAR TM LG	G	AB	R	H	2B	3B	HR	RBI	BB-IB	HP	SO	AVG	OBP	SLG	AOPS	ABR	SB-CS	FA	FR	RNG	THR	GAMES AT POSITION	DL	BFV
1991 Pit N	37	106	15	36	7	0	0	7	7-0	0	17	.340	.381	.406	122	5	3-0	.936	5	118	223	3b36	39	
1992 †Pit N	55	123	11	22	6	0	0	4	12-2	0	22	.179	.252	.228	37	-10	3-0	.961	2	130	223	3b34,1b13,2b5		
1993 Pit N	29	35	3	5	0	0	0	1	6-1	0	10	.143	.268	.143	14	-4	0-0	1.000	2	121	294	O13(4/8/2),2b3,3b3	23	
1994 Pit N	2	4	1	1	1	0	0	0	0-0	0	1	.250	.250	.500	88	0	0-0	1.000	0	122	0	/3		
1995 Pit N	52	107	13	33	6	0	3	10	10-1	0	17	.308	.361	.364	92	-1	3-1	1.000	0	104	137	O29(9/13/8),3b24,2b12/C		
1996 Pit N	86	139	19	36	9	1	2	13	8-1	0	22	.259	.299	.381	75	-5	1-5	.971	-1	100	113	O27(10/1/19),3b6	65	
1997 †Fla N	44	36	8	10	2	0	0	3	2-0	1	5	.278	.333	.333	79	-1	1-0	1.000	1	93	214	O23(12/2/11),3b8		
1998 Fla N	53	88	10	20	6	0	2	12	7-0	0	12	.227	.281	.250	45	-7	1-0	.958	-1	100	0	O17(12/2/6),3b2,S2/2		
1999 Pit N	39	65	6	12	2	0	1	4	7-0	0	12	.185	.264	.262	33	-7	1-0	.973	1	100	0	3b16/OL		
2000 Pit N	21	50	10	15	3	0	1	4	4-0	0	6	.300	.352	.420	94	0	0-0	1.000	-0	37	52	1b11,O8(3/1/5),3b6/C2	28	
2001 Pit N	43	51	3	10	1	0	2	10	0-2	1	12	.196	.328	.216	44	-4	2-1	1.000	0	112	154	3b155,O141L,1b24,2b22,S3,C3	155	
Total 11	461	804	99	200	33	4	4	54	73-5	1	136	.249	.311	.315	68	-36	15-7	.964	8	112	154	3b155,O141L,1b24,2b22,S3,C3		

WEIGEL, RALPH   Ralph Richard "Wig" B10.2.1921 Coldwater OH D4.15.1992 Memphis TN BR/TR/6-1/180 d9.18

YEAR TM LG	G	AB	R	H	2B	3B	HR	RBI	BB-IB	HP	SO	AVG	OBP	SLG	AOPS	ABR	SB-CS	FA	FR	RNG	THR	GAMES AT POSITION	DL	BFV
1946 Cle A	6	12	1	2	0	0	0	0	0-0	0	2	.167	.167	.167	-7	-2	0-0	1.000	-1	*90*	0	C6		
1948 Chi A	66	163	8	38	7	3	0	26	13-1	1	18	.233	.294	.313	64	-9	1-2	.969	-4	78	105	C39,O2L		
1949 Was A	34	60	4	14	2	0	0	4	8-0	0	6	.233	.324	.267	58	-3	0-1	.985	-1	89	137	C21		
Total 3	106	235	12	54	9	3	0	30	21-1	1	26	.230	.296	.294	59	-14	2-3	.976	-6	*82*	108	C66,O2L		

WEIHE, PODGE   John Garibaldi B11.13.1862 Cincinnati OH D4.15.1914 Cincinnati OH BR/TR/5-11/175 d8.6

YEAR TM LG	G	AB	R	H	2B	3B	HR	RBI	BB-IB	HP	SO	AVG	OBP	SLG	AOPS	ABR	SB-CS	FA	FR	RNG	THR	GAMES AT POSITION	DL	BFV
1883 Cin AA	1	4	1	1	0	0	0		0-0	0		.250	.250	.250	58	0		1.000	0	0	0	/OC		
1884 Ind AA	63	256	29	65	13	2	4		9	0		.254	.279	.367	112	4		.860	-0	124	105	O58(1/23/35),2b4,1b3		
Total 2	64	260	30	66	13	2	4		9	0		.254	.279	.365	111	4		.864	-0	121	102	O59(1/24/35),2b4,1b3		

WEINGARTNER, ELMER   Elmer William "Dutch" B8.13.1918 Cleveland OH BR/TR/5-11/178 d4.19

YEAR TM LG	G	AB	R	H	2B	3B	HR	RBI	BB-IB	HP	SO	AVG	OBP	SLG	AOPS	ABR	SB-CS	FA	FR	RNG	THR	GAMES AT POSITION	DL	BFV
1945 Cle A	20	39	5	9	0	0	0	4	11	0	2	.231	.302	.256	66	-2	0-0	.871	-3	81	90	S20		

WEINTRAUB, PHIL   Philip "Mickey" B10.12.1907 Chicago IL D6.21.1987 Palm Springs CA BL/TL/6-1/195 d9.5 Col Loyola-Chicago

YEAR TM LG	G	AB	R	H	2B	3B	HR	RBI	BB-IB	HP	SO	AVG	OBP	SLG	AOPS	ABR	SB-CS	FA	FR	RNG	THR	GAMES AT POSITION	DL	BFV
1933 NY N	8	15	2	3	1	1	0	3	2-0	0	10	.200	.333	.400	110	0	0	.667	-1	58	0	O6R		
1934 NY N	31	74	13	26	2	0	0	15	15-0	0	10	.351	.461	.378	130	5	0	.944	-3	82	0	O20(12/9/0)		
1935 NY N	64	112	18	27	3	1	1	6	17	0	13	.241	.341	.348	87	-2	0	.975	-0	107	79	1b19,O7(1/0/6)		
1937 Cin N	49	177	27	48	10	4	3	20	19	1	25	.271	.345	.424	113	3	1	.976	-2	90	89	O47(41/0/6)		
NY N	6	9	3	3	2	0	0	1	2	0	1	.333	.400	.556	155	1	0	1.000	-0	51	0	/OL		
Year	55	186	30	51	12	4	3	21	20	1	26	.274	.348	.430	115	4	1	.976	-2	89	87	O48(42/0/6)		
1938 Phi N	100	351	51	109	23	4	6	45	64	4	43	.311	.422	.422	137	23	1	.988	3	112	73	1b98		
1944 NY N	104	361	55	114	18	9	13	77	59	0	59	.316	.412	.524	162	31	0	.992	3	109	88	1b99		
1945 NY N	82	283	45	77	9	1	10	42	54	0	29	.272	.389	.417	122	10	2	.993	2	107	84	1b77		
Total 7	444	1382	215	407	67	19	32	207	232	5	182	.295	.398	.440	133	71	4	.990	2	109	81	1b293,O81(55/9/18)		

WEIS, AL   Albert John B4.2.1938 Franklin Square NY BB/TR (BR 1969-71)/6-0/170* d9.15

YEAR TM LG	G	AB	R	H	2B	3B	HR	RBI	BB-IB	HP	SO	AVG	OBP	SLG	AOPS	ABR	SB-CS	FA	FR	RNG	THR	GAMES AT POSITION	DL	BFV
1962 Chi A	7	12	2	1	0	0	0	0	0-0	0	1	.083	.267	.083	-1	-2	1-0	.882	-1	122	0	S4/23		
1963 Chi A	99	210	41	57	9	0	0	18	18-1	2	37	.271	.333	.314	85	-4	15-1	.990	6	110	139	2b48,S27/3		
1964 Chi A	133	328	36	81	4	4	2	23	22-0	3	41	.247	.299	.302	70	-14	22-7	.966	3	111	**134**	2b116,S9,O2C		

YEAR	TM LG	G	AB	R	H	2B	3B	HR	RBI	BB-IB	HP	SO	AVG	OBP	SLG	AOPS	ABR	SB-CS	FA	FR	RNG	THR	GAMES AT POSITION	DL	BFW
965	Chi A	103	135	29	40	4	3	1	12	12-1	2	22	.296	.360	.393	122	4	4-1	.975	5	109	111	2b74,S7,3b2,O2C		1.4
966	Chi A	129	187	20	29	4	1	0	9	17-3	2	50	.155	.233	.187	24	-19	3-5	.987	13	120	142	2b96,S18		-0.1
967	Chi A	50	53	9	13	2	0	0	4	1-0	1	7	.245	.273	.283	27	-2	3-3	.986	-2	115	24	2b32,S13		-0.1
968	NY N	90	274	15	47	6	0	1	14	21-3	0	63	.172	.234	.204	33	-22	3-1	.958	-3	96	92	S59,2b29,3b2	88	-0.3
969	†NY N	103	247	20	53	9	2	2	23	15-1	0	51	.215	.259	.291	33	-16	3-3	.960	-2	93	117	S52,2b43/3		-2.1
970	NY N	75	121	20	25	7	1	1	11	7-1	1	21	.207	.254	.306	49	-9	1-1	.952	-12	73	58	2b44,S15		-1.2
971	NY N	11	11	3	0	0	0	0	1	0		4	.000	.143	.000	-53	-2	0-0	1.000	-0	53	81	2b5,3b2		-1.8
otal 10		800	1578	195	346	45	11	7	115	117-11	7		.219	.278	.275	59	-86	55-22	.975	7	107	119	2b488,S204,3b9,O4C	88	-3.5

WEIS, BUTCH   Arthur John   B3.2.1901 St.Louis MO   D5.4.1997 St.Louis MO   BL/TL/5-11/180   d4.15

YEAR	TM LG	G	AB	R	H	2B	3B	HR	RBI	BB-IB	HP	SO	AVG	OBP	SLG	AOPS	ABR	SB-CS	FA	FR	RNG	THR	GAMES AT POSITION	DL	BFW
922	Chi N	2	2	1	1	0	0	0	0	0			.500	.500	.500	156	0	0-0	—		0		/H		0.0
923	Chi N	22	26	2	6	1	0	0	2	5	0	8	.231	.355	.269	67	-1	0-1	1.000	-0	110	0	O6(4/0/2)		-0.2
924	Chi N	37	133	19	37	8	1	0	23	15	1	14	.278	.355	.353	90	-1	4-5	.978	4	102	178	O36(14/0/22)		-0.2
925	Chi N	67	180	16	48	5	3	2	25	23	0	22	.267	.350	.361	81	-5	2-4	.964	-3	88	76	O47(45/0/2)		-0.2
otal 4		128	341	39	92	14	4	2	44		1	44	.270	.353	.352	82	-7	6-10	.973	0	96	120	O89(63/0/26)		-1.1
																									-1.5

WEISER, BUD   Harry Budson   B1.8.1891 Shamokin PA   D7.31.1961 Shamokin PA   BR/TR/5-11/165   d4.29

YEAR	TM LG	G	AB	R	H	2B	3B	HR	RBI	BB-IB	HP	SO	AVG	OBP	SLG	AOPS	ABR	SB-CS	FA	FR	RNG	THR	GAMES AT POSITION	DL	BFW
915	Phi N	37	64	6	9	2	0	0	8	7	1	12	.141	.236	.172	24	-6	2-2	.897	-3	83	0	O20(4/16/0)		-1.1
916	Phi N	4	10	1	3	1	0	0	1	0	0	3	.300	.300	.400	110	0	0	1.000	-0	110	0	O4L		0.0
otal 2		41	74	7	12	3	0	0	9		1	15	.162	.244	.203	36	-6	2-2	.912	-3	87	0	O24(8/16/0)		-1.1

WEISS, GARY   Gary Lee   B12.27.1955 Brenham TX   BB/TR (BR 1980)/5-10/170*   [LAN78 19/486]   d9.13   Col Houston

YEAR	TM LG	G	AB	R	H	2B	3B	HR	RBI	BB-IB	HP	SO	AVG	OBP	SLG	AOPS	ABR	SB-CS	FA	FR	RNG	THR	GAMES AT POSITION	DL	BFW
980	LA N	8	0	0					0	0-0								0-0					/R		0.0
981	LA N	14	19	4	2	0	0	0	1	1-0	0	4	.105	.143	.105	-28	-3	0-0	.920	-4	49	209	S13		-0.7
otal 2		22	19	4	2	0	0	0	1	1-0	0	4	.105	.143	.105	-28	-3	0-0	.920	-4	49	209	S13		-0.7

WEISS, JOE   Joseph Harold   B1.27.1894 Chicago IL   D7.7.1967 Cedar Rapids IA   BR/TR/6-0/165   d8.29

YEAR	TM LG	G	AB	R	H	2B	3B	HR	RBI	BB-IB	HP	SO	AVG	OBP	SLG	AOPS	ABR	SB-CS	FA	FR	RNG	THR	GAMES AT POSITION	DL	BFW
915	Chi F	29	85	6	19	1	2	0	11	3	0	24	.224	.250	.282	53	-7	0	.992	-1	75	58	1b29		-1.0

WEISS, WALT   Walter William   B11.28.1963 Tuxedo NY   BB/TR/6-0/175(175-188)   [OakA85 1/11]   d7.12   Col North Carolina-Asheville

YEAR	TM LG	G	AB	R	H	2B	3B	HR	RBI	BB-IB	HP	SO	AVG	OBP	SLG	AOPS	ABR	SB-CS	FA	FR	RNG	THR	GAMES AT POSITION	DL	BFW
87	Oak A	16	26	3	12	4	0	0	1	2-0	1	2	.462	.500	.615	207	1	1-2	.974	1	125	81	S11,D2		0.6
88	†Oak A	147	452	44	113	17	3	8	39	35-1	9	56	.250	.312	.321	81	-11	4-4	.979	10	104	95	S147		0.9
89	†Oak A	84	236	30	55	11	0	3	21	21-0	1	39	.233	.298	.318	76	-11	6-1	.953	-14	87	99	S84	74	-1.5
90	†Oak A	138	445	50	118	17	1	2	35	46-5	4	53	.265	.337	.321	89	-5	9-3	.979	-15	98	101	S137	15	-0.9
91	Oak A	40	133	15	30	6	1	0	13	12-0	1	14	.226	.286	.286	63	-7	6-0	.970	-3	92	86	S40	137	-0.6
92	†Oak A	103	316	36	67	5	2	0	21	43-1	1	39	.212	.305	.241	58	-17	6-3	.956	-19	94	89	S103	58	-2.2
93	Fla N	158	500	50	133	14	2	1	39	79-13	3	73	.266	.367	.308	79	-11	7-3	.977	-18	91	86	S153		-1.7
94	Col N	110	423	58	106	11	4	1	32	56-0	0	58	.251	.336	.303	59	-24	12-7	.973	7	105	94	S110		-0.9
95	†Col N	137	427	65	111	17	3	1	25	98-5	8	57	.260	.403	.321	73	-12	15-3	.974	14	107	**119**	S136		1.4
96	Col N	155	517	89	146	20	2	8	48	80-5	6	78	.282	.381	.375	82	-10	10-2	.957	-2	104	87	S155		0.0
97	Col N	121	393	52	106	23	5	4	38	66-3	2	56	.270	.377	.384	82	-8	5-2	.983	19	**117**	118	S119	17	1.9
98	†Atl N★	96	347	64	97	18	2	0	27	50-0	3	53	.280	.386	.343	95	1	7-1	.967	-1	96	130	S96		0.8
99	†Atl N	110	279	38	63	13	4	2	29	35-1	3	48	.226	.315	.323	63	-16	7-3	.963	-10	90	95	S102	24	-1.8
00	†Atl N	80	192	29	50	6	3	1	18	26-1	1	32	.260	.353	.313	72	-8	1-1	.949	-9	113	110	S69	16	0.4
al 14		1495	4686	623	1207	182	31	25	386	658-38	44	658	.258	.351	.326	77	-131	96-35	.949	-16	101	100	S1462,D2	341	-3.6

ELAJ, JOHNNY   John Ludwig   B5.27.1914 Moss Creek PA   D9.13.2003 Arlington TX   BR/TR/6-0/164   d5.2   Mil 1943-45

YEAR	TM LG	G	AB	R	H	2B	3B	HR	RBI	BB-IB	HP	SO	AVG	OBP	SLG	AOPS	ABR	SB-CS	FA	FR	RNG	THR	GAMES AT POSITION	DL	BFW
39	Was A	63	201	23	55	11	2	1	33	13	0	20	.274	.318	.363	80	-7	13-2	.975	0	106	55	O55(13/17/26)		-0.6
40	Was A	88	215	31	55	9	0	3	21	19	2	20	.256	.322	.340	77	-7	8-7	.978	1	111	28	O53(15/35/3)		-0.9
41	Was A	49	96	16	20	4	0	0	5	6	0	16	.208	.255	.250	36	-9	3-1	.979	0	120	0	O19(13/3/3)		-0.9
43	Phi A	93	281	45	68	16	1	0	15	15	0	17	.242	.280	.306	72	-11	12-5	.960	0	110	54	O72(15/27/32)		-1.4
al 4		293	793	115	198	40	3	4	74	53	2	73	.250	.298	.323	71	-34	36-15	.970	1	110	42	O199(56/82/64)		-3.8

ELCH, CURT   Curtis Benton   B2.10.1862 Williamsport OH   D8.29.1896 E.Liverpool OH   BR/TR/5-10/175   d5.1   OF(17/1059/0)

YEAR	TM LG	G	AB	R	H	2B	3B	HR	RBI	BB-IB	HP	SO	AVG	OBP	SLG	AOPS	ABR	SB-CS	FA	FR	RNG	THR	GAMES AT POSITION	DL	BFW
84	Tol AA	109	425	61	95	24	5	0		10	4		.224	.248	.304	76	-11		.888	14	119	97	O107(1/106/0),2b2,C2/1		0.0
85	†StL AA	112	432	84	117	18	8	3	69	23	7		.271	.318	.370	112	5		.946	12	130	159	O112C		1.2
86	†StL AA	138	563	114	158	31	13	2	95	29	14		.281	.332	.393	121	12	59	.952	10	83	109	O138C,2b2		1.5
87	†StL AA	131	544	98	151	32	7	3	108	25	11		.278	.322	.379	86	-13	89	.941	12	140	172	O123C,2b8/1		-0.4
88	Phi AA	136	549	125	155	22	8	1	61	33	29		.282	.355	.357	129	20	95	.952	12	104	135	O135C,2b3		1.5
89	Phi AA	125	516	134	140	**39**	6	0	39	67	19	30	.271	.375	.370	114	15	66	.923	5	124	183	O125C		1.3
90	Phi AA	103	396	100	106	21	4	2	40	49	32		.268	.392	.356	121	16	64	.919	11	104	149	O103C/P		1.3
	Bal N	19	68	16	9	4	0	0	5	9	2		.132	.253	.191	30	-6	8	.974	1	97	149	O17C,1b2		2.0
	Year	122	464	116	115	25	4	2	45	58	**34**		.248	.372	.332	107	9	72	.926	10	129	149	O120C,1b2/P		1.5
92	Bal N	132	514	122	138	22	10	3	55	77	**36**	42	.268	.400	.368	119	18	50	.946	13	111	97	O113(1/112/0),2b21,S2		2.4
	Cin N	25	94	14	19	0	2	1	7	7	6	8	.202	.299	.277	75	-3	7	.905	-4	41	41	O63C		-0.7
	Year	88	331	56	75	1	5	2	29	43	17	17	.227	.345	.278	84	-3	21	.911	-5	43	63	O88(1/88/0)		-1.2
93	Lou N	14	47	5	8	1	0	0	2	16	2	4	.170	.400	.191	64	2		.912	0	84	0	O14L		-0.1
al 10		1107	4385	915	1152	215	66	16	503	381	173	93	.263	.345	.353	107	53	453	.933	74	110	130	O1075C,2b36,1b4,S2,C2/P		7.7

ELCH, FRANK   Frank Tiguer "Bugger"   B8.10.1897 Birmingham AL   D7.25.1957 Birmingham AL   BR/TR/5-9/175   d9.9

YEAR	TM LG	G	AB	R	H	2B	3B	HR	RBI	BB-IB	HP	SO	AVG	OBP	SLG	AOPS	ABR	SB-CS	FA	FR	RNG	THR	GAMES AT POSITION	DL	BFW
9	Phi A	15	54	5	9	1	1	2	7	7	0	10	.167	.262	.333	66	-3	0	.909	-0	103	95	O15C		-0.5
0	Phi A	100	360	43	93	17	5	4	40	26	2	41	.258	.312	.367	78	-12	2-9	.937	-5	89	117	O97(0/84/16)		-2.6
1	Phi A	115	403	48	115	18	6	7	45	34	2	43	.285	.347	.412	92	-5	2-0	.943	-2	95	116	O104(3/93/8)		-1.1
2	Phi A	114	375	43	97	17	3	11	49	40	3	40	.259	.335	.408	90	-6	3-4	.949	1	104	109	O104(4/6/94)		-1.3
3	Phi A	125	421	56	125	19	4	4	55	48	4	40	.297	.374	.413	106	4	1-4	.967	6	**116**	88	O117R		-0.1
4	Phi A	94	293	47	85	13	2	5	31	35	3	27	.290	.372	.399	98	1	2-3	.985	1	88	147	O74(0/2/72)		-0.6
5	Phi A	85	202	40	56	5	4	4	41	29	2	14	.277	.361	.431	90	-3	2-1	.968	-2	86	110	O57R		-0.8
6	Phi A	75	174	26	49	8	1	4	23	26	2	9	.282	.381	.408	100	1	2-5	.975	-1	92	96	O49(28/3/20)		-0.5
7	Bos A	15	28	2	5	2	0	0	4	5	0	6	.179	.303	.250	46	-2	0-2	1.000	1	80	466	O6R		-0.1
al 9		738	2310	310	634	100	31	41	295	250	20	225	.274	.350	.398	92	-26	18-28	.955	-2	98	115	O623(35/203/390)		-7.6

ELCH, HERB   Herbert M. "Dutch"   B10.19.1898 RoEllen TN   D4.13.1967 Memphis TN   BL/TR/5-6/154   d9.15

YEAR	TM LG	G	AB	R	H	2B	3B	HR	RBI	BB-IB	HP	SO	AVG	OBP	SLG	AOPS	ABR	SB-CS	FA	FR	RNG	THR	GAMES AT POSITION	DL	BFW
5	Bos A	13	38	2	11	0	1	0	2	0	0	6	.289	.289	.342	60	-3	0-0	.893	3	124	125	S13		0.1

LCH, TUB   James T.   B7.3.1866 St.Louis MO   TR/5-11/230   d6.12

YEAR	TM LG	G	AB	R	H	2B	3B	HR	RBI	BB-IB	HP	SO	AVG	OBP	SLG	AOPS	ABR	SB-CS	FA	FR	RNG	THR	GAMES AT POSITION	DL	BFW
0	Tol AA	35	108	15	31	3	1	1	14	8	4		.287	.358	.361	109	1	7	.930	1	114	116	C25,1b10		0.3
5	Lou N	47	153	18	37	4	1	1	8	13	2	7	.242	.310	.301	62	-9	2	.888	-3	91	106	C28,1b20		-0.8
2		82	261	33	68	7	2	2	22	21	6	7	.261	.330	.326	81	-8	9	.911	-2	102	111	C53,1b30		-0.5

LCH, MILT   Milton Edward   B7.26.1924 Farmersville IL   BR/TR/5-10/175   d6.5

YEAR	TM LG	G	AB	R	H	2B	3B	HR	RBI	BB-IB	HP	SO	AVG	OBP	SLG	AOPS	ABR	SB-CS	FA	FR	RNG	THR	GAMES AT POSITION	DL	BFW
5	Det N	1	2	0	0	0	0	0	0	0	0		.000	.000	.000	-94	0		1.000	0	0	0	/C		0.0

LCHONCE, HARRY   Harry Monroe "Welch"   B11.20.1883 North Point PA   D2.26.1977 Arcadia CA   BL/TR/6-0/170   d4.17

YEAR	TM LG	G	AB	R	H	2B	3B	HR	RBI	BB-IB	HP	SO	AVG	OBP	SLG	AOPS	ABR	SB-CS	FA	FR	RNG	THR	GAMES AT POSITION	DL	BFW
	Phi N	26	66	9	14	4	0	0	6	7	0	8	.212	.288	.273	56	-4	0	.929	-2	91	49	O17(1/6/11)		-0.6

LDAY, MIKE   Lyndon Earl   B12.19.1879 Conway IA   D5.28.1942 Leavenworth KS   BL/TL/5-8/165   d4.21

YEAR	TM LG	G	AB	R	H	2B	3B	HR	RBI	BB-IB	HP	SO	AVG	OBP	SLG	AOPS	ABR	SB-CS	FA	FR	RNG	THR	GAMES AT POSITION	DL	BFW
	Chi A	24	35	2	8	1	0	0	6		0		.229	.341	.314	113	1	0	.938	0	177	0	O15(4/8/3)		0.0
	Chi A	29	74	3	14	0	1	0	5	10	0		.189	.231	.189	34	-6	2	.886	-0	148	182	O20(7/10/3)		-0.8
2		53	109	5	22	1	1	0	5	10	0		.202	.269	.229	60	-5	2	.900	-0	157	128	O35(11/18/6)		-0.5

LF, OLLIE   Oliver Henry   B1.17.1889 Cleveland OH   D6.15.1967 Cleveland OH   BR/TL/5-9/160   d8.30   Col Ohio St.

YEAR	TM LG	G	AB	R	H	2B	3B	HR	RBI	BB-IB	HP	SO	AVG	OBP	SLG	AOPS	ABR	SB-CS	FA	FR	RNG	THR	GAMES AT POSITION	DL	BFW
	Cle A	1	0	0	0	0	0	0	0	0	0		—	—	—		0	0	—		0		/R		0.0

LLMAN, BRAD   Brad Eugene   B8.17.1959 Lodi CA   BR/TR/6-0/170*   d9.4

YEAR	TM LG	G	AB	R	H	2B	3B	HR	RBI	BB-IB	HP	SO	AVG	OBP	SLG	AOPS	ABR	SB-CS	FA	FR	RNG	THR	GAMES AT POSITION	DL	BFW
	SF N	6	4	1	1	0	0	0	0	1			.250	.250	.250	41	0	0-0	1.000	-1	48	0	2b2		-0.1
	SF N	82	182	15	39	3	0	1	16	22-1	0	39	.214	.296	.247	54	-11	5-3	.965	-8	99	74	2b74,S2		-1.6
	SF N	93	265	23	60	9	1	2	25	19-0	0	41	.226	.274	.291	62	-14	10-5	.977	6	109	71	2b54,S34,3b9		-0.3

YEAR	TM LG	G	AB	R	H	2B	3B	HR	RBI	BB-IB	HP	SO	AVG	OBP	SLG	AOPS	ABR	SB-CS	FA	FR	RNG	THR	GAMES AT POSITION	DL	BFW
1985	SF N	71	174	16	41	11	1	0	16	4-1	4	33	.236	.268	.310	64	-9	5-2	.983	-7	79	63	2b36,3b25,S3	29	-1.5
1986	SF N	12	13	0	2	0	0	0	1	0-0	0	2	.154	.214	.154	3	-2	0-0	1.000	-0	87	0	S8/23		-0.2
1987	LA N	3	4	1	1	0	0	0	1	0-0	0	1	.250	.250	.250	34	0	0-0	1.000	1	296	0	/2S3	30	0.0
1988	KC A	71	107	11	29	3	0	1	6	6-0	1	23	.271	.322	.327	81	-3	1-2	.972	2	111	118	2b46,S15,3b4,D3		0.0
1989	KC A	103	178	30	41	4	0	2	12	7-0	1	36	.230	.263	.287	55	-11	5-3	.995	1	107	109	2b64,S34,3b3/D	15	-0.8
Total	8	441	927	97	214	30	2	6	59	59-2	7	176	.231	.280	.287	61	-50	26-15	.978	-6	102	85	2b278,S97,3b43,D4	74	-4.5

WELLMAN, BOB Robert Joseph B7.15.1925 Norwood OH D12.20.1994 Villa Hills KY BR/TR/6-4/210* d9.23

YEAR	TM LG	G	AB	R	H	2B	3B	HR	RBI	BB-IB	HP	SO	AVG	OBP	SLG	AOPS	ABR	SB-CS	FA	FR	RNG	THR	GAMES AT POSITION	DL	BFW
1948	Phi A	4	10	1	2	0	1	0	3	0	0	3	.200	.385	.400	109	0	0-0	1.000	-0	77	106	1b2/OR		0.0
1950	Phi A	11	15	1	5	0	1	1	3	1	0	3	.333	.333	.533	121	0	0-0	1.000	0	119	0	O2R		0.0
Total	2	15	25	2	7	0	2	1	6	1	0	6	.280	.357	.480	117	0	0-0	.889	-0	110	0	O3R,1b2		0.0

WELLS, GREG Gregory De Wayne B4.25.1954 McIntosh AL BR/TR/6-5/218* d8.10

YEAR	TM LG	G	AB	R	H	2B	3B	HR	RBI	BB-IB	HP	SO	AVG	OBP	SLG	AOPS	ABR	SB-CS	FA	FR	RNG	THR	GAMES AT POSITION	DL	BFW
1981	Tor A	32	73	7	18	5	0	0	5	5-0	0	12	.247	.295	.315	71	-3	0-2	.994	-1	81	65	1b22,D3		-0.6
1982	Min A	15	54	5	11	1	2	0	3	1-0	0	8	.204	.211	.296	38	-5	0-0	.962	-2	33	72	1b10,D5		-0.8
Total	2	47	127	12	29	6	2	0	8	6-0	0	20	.228	.259	.307	58	-8	0-2	.983	-3	64	68	1b32,D8		-1.4

WELLS, JAKE Jacob B8.9.1863 Memphis TN D3.16.1927 Hendersonville NC BR/TR/5-11/167 d8.10

YEAR	TM LG	G	AB	R	H	2B	3B	HR	RBI	BB-IB	HP	SO	AVG	OBP	SLG	AOPS	ABR	SB-CS	FA	FR	RNG	THR	GAMES AT POSITION	DL	BFW
												5						0	.917	2			C16		-0.3
1888	Det N	16	57	5	9	1	0	0				5	.158	.158	.175	6	-6		.941	2	99	102	C28,O3L		0.0
1890	StL AA	30	105	17	25	3	0	0	12	10	5		.238	.333	.267	67	-4	1	.932	5	99	102	C44,O3L		-0.3
Total	2	46	162	22	34	4	0	0	14	10	5	5	.210	.277	.235	50	-10	1	.932	5	99	102	C44,O3L		-0.3

WELLS, LEO Leo Donald B7.18.1917 Kansas City KS BR/TR/5-9/170 d4.16 Mil 1943-45

YEAR	TM LG	G	AB	R	H	2B	3B	HR	RBI	BB-IB	HP	SO	AVG	OBP	SLG	AOPS	ABR	SB-CS	FA	FR	RNG	THR	GAMES AT POSITION	DL	BFW
1942	Chi A	35	62	8	12	4	0	0	4	4	0	5	.194	.242	.274	46	-5	1-0	1.000	7	149	157	S12,3b6		0.3
1946	Chi A	45	127	11	24	4	1	1	11	12	0	34	.189	.259	.260	47	-9	3-4	.942	4	117	91	3b38,S2		-0.7
Total	2	80	189	19	36	6	1	1	15	16	0	39	.190	.254	.265	47	-14	4-4	.938	11	119	104	3b44,S14		-0.4

WELLS, VERNON Vernon M. B12.8.1978 Shreveport LA BR/TR/6-1/215(210-225) [TorA97 1/5] d8.30

YEAR	TM LG	G	AB	R	H	2B	3B	HR	RBI	BB-IB	HP	SO	AVG	OBP	SLG	AOPS	ABR	SB-CS	FA	FR	RNG	THR	GAMES AT POSITION	DL	BFW
1999	Tor A	24	88	8	23	5	0	1	8	4-0	0	18	.261	.293	.352	63	-5	1-1	1.000	0	84	272	O24C		-0.
2000	Tor A	3	2	0	0	0	0	0	0	0	0	2	.000	.000	.000	-97	-1	0-0	1.000	0	96	0	O3C		-0.
2001	Tor A	30	96	14	30	8	0	1	6	5-0	1	15	.313	.350	.427	102	0	5-0	.969	-1	96	135	O30(0/27/3)		-0.
2002	Tor A	159	608	87	167	34	4	23	100	27-0	3	85	.275	.305	.457	96	-5	9-4	.992	-3	96	120	O159(0/146/13)		-0.
2003	Tor A★	161	678	118	215	49	5	33	117	42-2	7	80	.317	.359	.550	131	30	4-1	.990	-13	90	41	O161C		1.8
2004	Tor A	134	536	82	146	34	2	23	67	51-2	3	83	.272	.337	.472	102	1	9-2	.997	-2	99	77	O131C,D3	30	0.
2005	Tor A	156	620	78	167	30	3	28	97	47-3	5	86	.269	.320	.463	100	-1	8-3	1.000	-6	87	154	O155C,D2	30	0.
Total	7	667	2628	387	748	160	14	109	395	176-7	16	367	.285	.330	.481	106	19	36-11	.994	-25	93	106	O663(0/647/16),D5		0.

WELSH, JIMMY James Daniel B10.9.1902 Denver CO D10.30.1970 Oakland CA BL/TR/6-1/174 d4.14

YEAR	TM LG	G	AB	R	H	2B	3B	HR	RBI	BB-IB	HP	SO	AVG	OBP	SLG	AOPS	ABR	SB-CS	FA	FR	RNG	THR	GAMES AT POSITION	DL	BFW
1925	Bos N	122	484	69	151	25	6	3	63	20	8	24	.312	.350	.440	110	6	7-4	.960	5	93	157	O116(7/1/109),2b3		0.
1926	Bos N	134	490	69	136	18	11	3	57	33	8	28	.278	.333	.378	100	-1	6	.965	8	105	129	O129R		-0.
1927	Bos N	131	497	72	143	26	7	9	54	23	8	27	.288	.330	.423	109	4	11	.969	8	101	161	O117(6/110/1)		-0.
1928	NY N	124	476	77	146	22	6	4	54	29	8	30	.307	.357	.431	104	2	4	.981	-3	98	76	O117(6/110/1)		-0.
1929	NY N	38	129	25	32	7	0	2	8	9	7	9	.248	.331	.349	69	-6	3	.940	-3	65	181	O35(30/7/0)		-0.
	Bos N	53	186	24	54	8	7	2	16	13	4	9	.290	.350	.441	98	-1	1	.979	5	116	110	O51(1/49/2)		-0.
	Year	91	315	49	86	15	7	4	24	22	11	12	.273	.342	.403	86	-8	4	.970	2	98	135	O86(31/56/2)		-1.
1930	Bos N	113	432	51	116	21	9	3	36	29	4	23	.275	.327	.389	75	-18	5	.980	7	113	90	O110C		-1.
Total	6	715	2684	387	778	127	47	35	288	156	47	144	.290	.340	.411	98	-14	37-4	.971	26	101	126	O687(45/398/252),2b3/1		-1.

WENDELL, LEW Lewis Charles B3.22.1892 New York NY D7.11.1953 Brooklyn NY BR/TR/5-11/178 d6.10

YEAR	TM LG	G	AB	R	H	2B	3B	HR	RBI	BB-IB	HP	SO	AVG	OBP	SLG	AOPS	ABR	SB-CS	FA	FR	RNG	THR	GAMES AT POSITION	DL	BFW
1915	NY N	20	36	0	8	1	1	0	5	2	0	7	.222	.263	.306	76	-1	0	.920	-4	76	115	C18		-0.
1916	NY N	2	2	0	0	0	0	0	0	0	0	0	.000	.000	.000	-99	-0	0	—	0			/H		-0.
1924	Phi N	21	32	3	8	1	0	0	2	3	0	5	.250	.314	.281	54	-2	0-0	1.000	-1	93	77	C17		-0.
1925	Phi N	18	26	0	2	0	0	0	3	1	0	3	.077	.111	.077	-47	-6	0-0	.909	-1	99	92	C9		-0.
1926	Phi N	1	4	0	0	0	0	0	0	0	0	2	.000	.000	.000	-95	-1	0	.333	-1	0	319	/C		-0.
Total	5	62	100	3	18	2	1	0	10	6	0	17	.180	.226	.220	23	-10	0-0	.925	-6	84	104	C45		-0.

WENTZ, JACK John George (b John George Wernz) B3.4.1863 Louisville KY D9.14.1907 Louisville KY BR/TR/5-10.5/175 d4.15

YEAR	TM LG	G	AB	R	H	2B	3B	HR	RBI	BB-IB	HP	SO	AVG	OBP	SLG	AOPS	ABR	SB-CS	FA	FR	RNG	THR	GAMES AT POSITION	DL	BFW
1891	Lou AA	1	4	1	1	0	0	0	0	0	0		.250	.250	.250	44	0	0	.667	-1	59	0	/2		-0.

WENTZEL, STAN Stanley Aaron B1.13.1917 Lorane PA D11.28.1991 St.Lawrence PA BR/TR/6-1/200 d9.23

YEAR	TM LG	G	AB	R	H	2B	3B	HR	RBI	BB-IB	HP	SO	AVG	OBP	SLG	AOPS	ABR	SB-CS	FA	FR	RNG	THR	GAMES AT POSITION	DL	BFW
1945	Bos N	4	19	3	4	1	0	0	6	0	0	3	.211	.211	.316	45	-2	-1	1.000	-1	80	0	O4C		-0.

WERA, JULIE Julian Valentine B2.9.1902 Winona MN D12.12.1975 Rochester MN BR/TR/5-8/164 d4.14

YEAR	TM LG	G	AB	R	H	2B	3B	HR	RBI	BB-IB	HP	SO	AVG	OBP	SLG	AOPS	ABR	SB-CS	FA	FR	RNG	THR	GAMES AT POSITION	DL	BFW
1927	NY A	38	42	7	10	3	1	1	8	1	1	5	.238	.273	.381	70	-2	0-0	1.000	0	86	0	3b19		-0.
1929	NY A	5	12	1	5	0	0	2	2	1	0		.417	.462	.417	137	1	0-0	1.000	-0	114	0	3b4		0.
Total	2	43	54	8	15	3	1	2	10	2	1		.278	.316	.389	85	-1	0-0	1.000	-0	92	0	3b23		-0.

WERBER, BILLY William Murray B6.20.1908 Berwyn MD BR/TR/5-10/170 d6.25 Col Duke

YEAR	TM LG	G	AB	R	H	2B	3B	HR	RBI	BB-IB	HP	SO	AVG	OBP	SLG	AOPS	ABR	SB-CS	FA	FR	RNG	THR	GAMES AT POSITION	DL	BFW
1930	NY A	4	14	5	4	0	0	0	2	3	0	1	.286	.412	.286	84	0	0-0	.955	0	82	133	S3/3		-1
1933	NY A	3	2	0	0	0	0	0	0	0	0	0	.000	.000	.000	-99	-1	0-0	—	-0	0	0	/3		-1
	Bos A	108	425	64	110	30	6	3	39	33	0	39	.259	.312	.379	83	-11	15-5	.910	-14	90	90	S71,3b38,2b2		-1
	Year	111	427	64	110	30	6	3	39	33	0	39	.258	.311	.377	82	-12	15-5	.910	-14	90	90	S71,3b39,2b2		-1
1934	Bos A	152	623	129	200	41	10	11	67	77	4	37	.321	.397	.472	115	15	40-15	.941	17	122	97	3b130,S22		-1
1935	Bos A	124	462	84	118	30	3	14	61	69	4	41	.255	.357	.424	95	-3	29-7	.942	-14	109	118	3b123		-1
1936	Bos A	145	535	84	147	29	6	10	67	89	4	37	.275	.382	.407	90	-7	23-13	.935	-11	81	104	3b101,O45(38/0/7)/2		-1
1937	Phi A	128	493	85	144	31	4	7	70	74	1	39	.292	.386	.414	103	5	35-13	.958	4	104	99	3b125,O3(1/2/0)		0
1938	Phi A	134	499	92	129	7	11	4	69	93	2	37	.259	.377	.397	96	0	19-15	.933	9	104	128	3b147		2
1939	†Cin N	147	599	115	175	35	5	5	57	91	6	46	.289	.388	.389	109	12	15	.962	6	107	126	3b143		2
1940	†Cin N	143	584	105	162	35	5	12	48	68	2	40	.277	.361	.416	113	12	16	.959	10	108	150	3b107		0
1941	Cin N	109	418	56	100	9	2	4	46	53	2	24	.239	.328	.299	77	-12	14	.959	10	108	88	3b93		0
1942	NY N	98	370	56	74	11	2	4	13	51	2	22	.205	.308	.249	64	-15	9	.927	13	126	88	3b93		0
Total	11	1295	5024	875	1363	271	50	78	539	701	32	363	.271	.364	.392	97	-5	215-68	.944	50	106	111	3b1143,S96,O48(39/2/7),2b3		-1

WERDEN, PERRY Percival Wheritt B7.21.1865 St.Louis MO D1.9.1934 Minneapolis MN BR/TR/6-2/220 d4.24 ▲

YEAR	TM LG	G	AB	R	H	2B	3B	HR	RBI	BB-IB	HP	SO	AVG	OBP	SLG	AOPS	ABR	SB-CS	FA	FR	RNG	THR	GAMES AT POSITION	DL	BFW
1884	StL U	18	76	7	18	2	0	0	2				.237	.256	.263	56	-6		.893	0	113	128	P16,O6(4/1/1)		
1888	Was N	3	10	0	3	0	0	0	1				.300	.364	.300	121	0	0	.857	-0	0	0	O3L		
1890	Tol AA	128	498	113	147	22	20	6	72	78	13		.295	.404	.456	149	32	59	.972	5	121	93	1b124,O5(0/4/1)		
1891	Bal AA	139	552	102	160	20	18	6	104	52	11	59	.290	.363	.424	124	15	40	.980	-1	101	102	1b139		
1892	StL N	149	598	73	154	22	6	1	84	59	4	52	.258	.328	.355	109	3	11	.968	2	118	99	1b124/OR		
1893	StL N	125	500	73	138	29	1	4	94	49	7	25	.276	.349	.442	109	3	15	.984	19	163	94	1b133		
1897	Lou N	133	512	76	154	24	14	5	83	41	12		.301	.366	.426	112	9	15	.978	14	127	96	1b669,P16,O15(7/5/3)		
Total	7	695	2746	444	774	109	87	26	439	282	47	140	.282	.359	.413	119	62	151	.978	40	127	96	1b669,P16,O15(7/5/3)		

WERHAS, JOHNNY John Charles "Peaches" B2.7.1938 Highland Park MI BR/TR/6-2/200* d4.14 Col USC

YEAR	TM LG	G	AB	R	H	2B	3B	HR	RBI	BB-IB	HP	SO	AVG	OBP	SLG	AOPS	ABR	SB-CS	FA	FR	RNG	THR	GAMES AT POSITION	DL	BFW
1964	LA N	29	83	6	16	2	1	0	8	13-0	0	12	.193	.296	.241	59	-4	0-0	.952	-0	91	100	3b28		-0
1965	LA N	4	3	1	0	0	0	0	0	1-0	0	2	.000	.250	.000	-24	-1	0-0	1.000	-0	0		/1		-0
1967	LA N	7	7	0	1	0	0	0	0	0-0	0	3	.143	.143	.143	-20	-1	0-0		0			/H		-0
	Cal A	49	75	8	12	1	1	2	6	10-0	1	22	.160	.264	.280	64	-3	0-0	.963	-0	98	0	3b30,1b4/OL		-0
Total	3	89	168	15	29	3	2	2	14	24-0	1	39	.173	.276	.250	57	-8	0-0	.956	-0	94	62	3b58,1b5/OL		-0

WERNER, DON Donald Paul B3.8.1953 Appleton WI BR/TR/6-1/185(170-185) [CinN71 5/120] d9.2

YEAR	TM LG	G	AB	R	H	2B	3B	HR	RBI	BB-IB	HP	SO	AVG	OBP	SLG	AOPS	ABR	SB-CS	FA	FR	RNG	THR	GAMES AT POSITION	DL	BFW
1975	Cin N	7	8	0	1	0	0	0	0	0-0	0	1	.125	.222	.125	-2	-1	0-0	.923	-2	31	0	C7		
1976	Cin N	3	4	2	2	0	0	1	3	1-0	0	0	.500	.600	.750	274	1	0-0	1.000	-0	54	0	C3		
1977	Cin N	10	23	3	4	0	0	2	4	2-1	0	3	.174	.231	.435	75	-1	0-1	1.000	-0	88	68	C10		
1978	Cin N	50	113	7	19	2	0	0	11	14-2	1	30	.162	.250	.186	22	-12	0-0	.987	-4	81	87	C49		
1980	Cin N	24	64	3	11	2	0	0	5	7-0	1	10	.172	.260	.203	33	-6	1-0	.962	-5	94	46	C24		
1981	Tex A	2	8	1	2	0	0	0	0	0-0	0	2	.250	.250	.250	47	-1	0-1	—	0			D2		

YEAR	TM LG	G	AB	R	H	2B	3B	HR	RBI	BB-IB	HP	SO	AVG	OBP	SLG	AOPS	ABR	SB-CS	FA	FR	RNG	THR	GAMES AT POSITION	DL	BFW
1982	Tex A	22	59	4	12	2	0	0	3	3-0	0	7	.203	.242	.237	34	-5	0-0	.980	-1	120	30	C22		-0.6
Total	7	118	279	17	49	7	1	2	24	27-3	3	53	.176	.251	.229	36	-25	2-2	.979	-12	84	59	C115,D2		-3.5

WERRICK, JOE   Joseph Abraham   B10.25.1861 St.Paul MN   D5.10.1943 St.Peter MN   BR/TR/5-9/151   d9.27

YEAR	TM LG	G	AB	R	H	2B	3B	HR	RBI	BB-IB	HP	SO	AVG	OBP	SLG	AOPS	ABR	SB-CS	FA	FR	RNG	THR	GAMES AT POSITION	DL	BFW
1884	StP U	**9**	27	3	2	0	0	0		1			.074	.107	.074	-81	-7		.756	1	112	0	S9		
1886	Lou AA	136	561	75	140	20	14	3	62	33			.250	.294	.351	96	-6	19	.853	-2	94	47	3b136		-0.5
1887	Lou AA	136	533	90	152	21	13	7	99	38			.285	.336	.413	106	2	49	.831	-2	103	61	3b136		0.2
1888	Lou AA	111	413	49	89	12	7	0	51	30	3		.215	.274	.278	79	-10	15	.811	-15	92	69	3b89,S11,2b8,O3L		-2.1
Total	4	392	1534	217	383	53	34	10	212	102	8		.250	.300	.348	94	-21	83	.834	-18	97	58	3b361,S20,2b8,O3L		-2.9

WERT, DON   Donald Ralph   B7.29.1938 Strasburg PA   BR/TR/5-9/165*   d5.11   Col Franklin & Marshall

YEAR	TM LG	G	AB	R	H	2B	3B	HR	RBI	BB-IB	HP	SO	AVG	OBP	SLG	AOPS	ABR	SB-CS	FA	FR	RNG	THR	GAMES AT POSITION	DL	BFW
1963	Det A	78	251	31	65	6	2	7	25	24-2	2	51	.259	.326	.382	95	-2	3-3	.957	5	111	75	3b47,2b21,S8		0.5
1964	Det A	148	525	63	135	18	5	9	55	50-5	1	74	.257	.325	.362	91	-6	3-4	.965	2	101	121	3b142,S4		-0.6
1965	Det A	**162**	609	81	159	22	2	12	54	73-4	3	71	.261	.341	.363	100	1	5-6	**.976**	3	96	105	3b161,S3/2		0.3
1966	Det A	150	559	56	150	20	2	11	70	64-3	2	69	.268	.342	.370	103	4	6-3	.972	-19	83	74	3b150		-1.7
1967	Det A	142	534	60	137	23	6	6	40	44-2	1	59	.257	.320	.341	93	-4	1-1	.978	2	98	100	3b140/S		-0.2
1968	†Det A★	150	536	44	107	15	1	12	37	37-7	5	79	.200	.258	.299	66	-23	0-3	.966	-6	90	90	3b150,S2		-3.5
1969	Det A	132	423	46	95	11	1	14	50	49-6	1	60	.225	.303	.355	81	-11	3-1	.966	1	97	81	3b129		-1.1
1970	Det A	128	363	34	79	13	0	6	33	44-7	4	56	.218	.307	.303	69	-15	1-3	.953	-11	83	88	3b117,2b2		-2.8
1971	Was A	20	40	2	2	1	0	0	2	4-1	1	6	.050	.156	.075	-35	-7	0-0	1.000	-4	92	30	S7,3b7/2	15	-1.1
Total	9	1110	3840	417	929	129	15	77	366	389-37	31	529	.242	.314	.343	87	-63	22-24	.968	-22-4	94	30	3b1043,S25,2b25	15	-10.2

WERTH, DENNIS   Dennis Dean   B12.29.1952 Lincoln IL   BR/TR/6-1/200*   [NYA74 19/437]   d9.17   s-Jayson   Col Southern Illinois Edwardsville

YEAR	TM LG	G	AB	R	H	2B	3B	HR	RBI	BB-IB	HP	SO	AVG	OBP	SLG	AOPS	ABR	SB-CS	FA	FR	RNG	THR	GAMES AT POSITION	DL	BFW
1979	NY A	3	4	1	1	0	0	0	0-0		1		.250	.250	.250	36	0	0-0	1.000	0	329	0	/1		0.0
1980	NY A	39	65	15	20	3	0	3	12	12-0	1	19	.308	.416	.492	150	5	0-1	1.000	-1	63	126	1b12,O8(3/0/5)/C3D		0.3
1981	NY A	34	55	7	6	1	0	0	1	12-2		12	.109	.269	.127	17	-5	1-0	1.000	2	145	86	1b19,O8(4/0/4),C3,D4		-0.5
1982	KC A	41	15	5	2	0	0	0	2	4-0		2	.133	.316	.133	29	-1	1-0	.990	-1	169	135	1b35,C2	77	-0.1
Total	4	117	139	28	29	4	0	3	15	28-2	2	33	.209	.341	.302	82	-1	1-1	.996	2	132	112	1b67,O16(7/0/9),D12,C6/3	77	-0.3

WERTH, JAYSON   Jayson Richard Gowan   B5.20.1979 Springfield IL   BR/TR/6-5/215*   [BalA97 1/22]   d9.1   f-Dennis   gf-John Schofield

YEAR	TM LG	G	AB	R	H	2B	3B	HR	RBI	BB-IB	HP	SO	AVG	OBP	SLG	AOPS	ABR	SB-CS	FA	FR	RNG	THR	GAMES AT POSITION	DL	BFW
2002	Tor A	15	46	4	12	1	0	0	6	6-0	0	11	.261	.340	.348	82	-1	1-0	1.000	1	117	118	O15(4/1/10)		0.0
2003	Tor A	26	48	7	10	4	0	2	10	3-0	0	22	.208	.255	.417	70	-2	1-0	1.000	1	108	144	O20(0/1/19),D3		0.0
2004	†LA N	89	290	56	76	11	3	16	47	30-0	4	85	.262	.338	.486	111	4	4-1	.974	3	108	145	O79(65/6/14)/D	12	-0.2
2005	LA N	102	337	46	79	22	2	7	43	48-2	6	114	.234	.338	.374	87	-5	11-2	.987	6	113	110	O101(64/30/43)/D	59	0.5
Total	4	232	721	113	177	39	6	25	106	87-2	10	232	.245	.333	.420	96	-4	17-3	.984	11	111	127	O215(133/38/86),D5	138	0.3

WERTZ, DEL   Dwight Lyman Moody   B10.11.1888 Canton OH   D5.16.1958 Sarasota FL   BR/TR/5-10/160   d5.23   Col Case Western Reserve

YEAR	TM LG	G	AB	R	H	2B	3B	HR	RBI	BB-IB	HP	SO	AVG	OBP	SLG	AOPS	ABR	SB-CS	FA	FR	RNG	THR	GAMES AT POSITION	DL	BFW
1914	Buf F	3	0	1	0	0	0	0		0		0					0	0	1.000	-0	0	0	/S		0.0

WERTZ, VIC   Victor Woodrow   B2.9.1925 York PA   D7.7.1983 Detroit MI   BL/TR/6-0/186(186-203)   d4.15

YEAR	TM LG	G	AB	R	H	2B	3B	HR	RBI	BB-IB	HP	SO	AVG	OBP	SLG	AOPS	ABR	SB-CS	FA	FR	RNG	THR	GAMES AT POSITION	DL	BFW
1947	Det A	102	333	60	96	22	4	6	44	47	0	66	.288	.376	.432	121	11	2-0	.965	-2	95	106	O83(38/2/43)		0.5
1948	Det A	119	391	49	97	19	9	7	67	48	3	70	.248	.335	.396	92	-6	0-0	.954	1	96	158	O98(64/1/36)		-1.0
1949	Det A★	155	608	96	185	26	6	20	133	80	0	61	.304	.385	.465	124	20	2-3	.981	-2	98	95	O155R		1.3
1950	Det A	149	559	99	172	37	4	27	123	91	4	55	.308	.408	.533	135	31	0-1	.967	-11	95	39	O145R		1.4
1951	Det A★	138	501	86	143	24	4	27	94	78	1	61	.285	.383	.511	139	28	0-3	.989	0	103	79	O131R		2.2
1952	Det A☆	85	285	46	70	15	3	17	51	46	1	50	.246	.352	.498	134	13	1-0	.986	2	103	136	O79R		1.3
	StL A	37	130	22	45	5	0	6	19	23	0	20	.346	.444	.523	164	12	0-0	.955	-3	103		O36R		0.9
	Year	122	415	68	115	20	3	23	70	69	1	64	.277	.381	.506	143	25	1-0	.976	-0	103		O115R		2.2
1953	StL A	128	440	61	118	18	6	19	70	72	4	44	.268	.376	.466	124	16	1-4	.974	4	103	134	O121(0/1/120)		1.4
1954	Bal A	29	94	5	19	1	0	1	13	11	0	17	.202	.283	.245	50	-7	0-0	.963	3	103	277	O27R		-0.5
	†Cle A	94	295	33	81	14	2	14	48	34	0	40	.275	.344	.478	123	9	0-2	.989	1	109	108	1b83,O5(2/0/3)		0.5
	Year	123	389	38	100	15	2	15	61	45	0	57	.257	.330	.422	106	2	0-2	.989	4	109	108	1b83,O32(2/0/30)		-0.2
1955	Cle A	74	257	30	65	11	2	14	55	32-3	1	33	.253	.332	.475	112	4	1-1	.984	-2	86	100	1b63,O9(1/0/8)		1.2
1956	Cle A	136	481	65	127	22	0	32	106	75-10	5	87	.264	.364	.509	127	19	0-0	.991	1	98	95	1b133		1.8
1957	Cle A★	144	515	84	145	21	0	28	105	78-6	2	88	.282	.371	.485	136	27	2-3	.988	-1	98	89	1b139		0.2
1958	Cle A	25	43	5	12	1	0	3	12	5-0	0	5	.279	.354	.512	139	2	0-0	.980	0	131	82	1b8	98	0.0
1959	Bos A	94	247	38	68	13	0	7	49	22-5	2	32	.275	.337	.413	101	1	0-0	.992	2	116	94	1b64		0.0
1960	Bos A	131	443	45	125	22	0	19	103	37-4	1	54	.282	.335	.460	110	6	0-2	.987	3	110	86	1b117		0.2
1961	Bos A	99	317	33	83	16	2	11	60	38-3	2	45	.262	.339	.429	103	2	0-0	.991	4	117	95	1b86		0.1
	Det A	8	6	1	1	0	0	1		1-0	0	1	.167	.167	.167	-10	-1	0-0	—	0		/H		-0.1
	Year	107	323	33	84	16	2	11	61	38-3	2	46	.260	.336	.424	101	1	0-0	.991	4	117	95	1b86		0.0
1962	Det A	74	105	7	34	2	0	5	18	5-0	1	13	.324	.357	.486	121	4	0-0	.988	0	100	48	1b16		0.0
1963	Det A	6	5	0	0	0	0	0	0	0-0	0	1	.000	.000	.000	-97	-1	0-0	—	0		/H		0.2
	Min A	35	44	3	6	0	0	0	7	6-2	0	1	.136	.240	.341	59	-3	0-0	1.000	1	149	53	1b6		-0.2
	Year	41	49	3	6	0	0	0	7	6-2	0	6	.122	.218	.306	44	-4	0-0	1.000	1	149	53	1b6		-0.3
Total	17	1862	6099	867	1692	289	42	266	1178	828-33	27	842	.277	.364	.469	121	185	9-19	.973	3	99	102	O889(105/4/783),1b715	98	11.1

WESSINGER, JIM   James Michael   B9.25.1955 Utica NY   BR/TR/5-10/165   [AtlN76 6/123]   d8.4   Col LeMoyne (NY)

YEAR	TM LG	G	AB	R	H	2B	3B	HR	RBI	BB-IB	HP	SO	AVG	OBP	SLG	AOPS	ABR	SB-CS	FA	FR	RNG	THR	GAMES AT POSITION	DL	BFW
1979	Atl N	10	7	2	0	0	0	0	0	4-0	0	4	.000	.125	.000	-2	-1	0-0	.833	-1	66	0	2b2		-0.3

WESSON, BARRY   Barry Jarvis   B4.6.1977 Tupelo MS   BR/TR/6-2/195*   [HouN95 14/389]   d7.15

YEAR	TM LG	G	AB	R	H	2B	3B	HR	RBI	BB-IB	HP	SO	AVG	OBP	SLG	AOPS	ABR	SB-CS	FA	FR	RNG	THR	GAMES AT POSITION	DL	BFW
2002	Hou N	15	20	1	4	0	1	0		1-0	0	5	.200	.238	.250	40	-2	0-0	1.000	-1	81	0	O15(3/9/3)		-0.3
2003	Ana A	10	11	2	2	0	0	1	3	0-0	0	4	.182	.182	.455	62	-1	1-0	1.000	1	130	0	O9(5/0/4)/D		0.0
Total	2	25	31	3	6	0	1	1	4	1-0	0	9	.194	.219	.355	47	-3	1-0	1.000	-1	98	0	O24(8/9/7)/D		-0.3

WEST, MAX   Max Edward   B11.28.1916 Dexter MO   D12.31.2003 Sierra Madre CA   BL/TR/6-1.5/182   d4.19   Mil 1943-45

YEAR	TM LG	G	AB	R	H	2B	3B	HR	RBI	BB-IB	HP	SO	AVG	OBP	SLG	AOPS	ABR	SB-CS	FA	FR	RNG	THR	GAMES AT POSITION	DL	BFW
1938	Bos N	123	418	47	98	16	5	10	63	38	1	38	.234	.300	.368	92	-6	5	.986	-4	94	70	O109(75/0/36),1b7		-1.7
1939	Bos N	130	449	67	128	26	6	19	82	51	5	55	.285	.364	.497	139	24	1	.974	1	104	80	O124(44/46/54)		1.9
1940	Bos N★	139	524	72	137	27	5	7	72	65	1	54	.261	.344	.372	103	4	2	.975	5	98	199	O102(4/59/49),1b36		0.1
1941	Bos N	138	484	63	134	28	4	12	68	72	2	68	.277	.373	.426	130	21	5	.981	5	101	135	O132(126/5/5)		2.0
1942	Bos N	134	452	54	115	22	4	16	56	68	1	72	.254	.354	.409	126	16	4	.991	-1	97	108	1b85,O50(36/2/13)		0.6
1946	Bos N	1	0	0	0	0	0	0	0	0	0	1	.000	.000	.000	-99	0		1.000	-0		0	/1		0.0
	Cin N	72	202	16	43	13	0	5	18	32	1	36	.213	.323	.351	95	-1	1	.952	-3	86	112	O58(54/3/1)		-0.8
	Year	73	203	16	43	13	0	5	18	32	1	37	.212	.322	.350	94	-1	1	.952	-3	86	112	O58(54/3/1)/1		-0.8
1948	Pit N	87	146	19	26	4	0	8	21	27	1	29	.178	.310	.370	82	-1		.975	4	123	78	1b32,O16(3/0/13)		-0.4
Total	7	824	2676	338	681	136	20	77	380	353	13	340	.254	.344	.407	114	54	19	.975	4	98	117	O591(342/115/171),1b161		1.7

WEST, BUCK   Milton Douglas   B8.29.1860 Spring Mill OH   D1.13.1929 Mansfield OH   BL/TR/5-10/200   d8.24

YEAR	TM LG	G	AB	R	H	2B	3B	HR	RBI	BB-IB	HP	SO	AVG	OBP	SLG	AOPS	ABR	SB-CS	FA	FR	RNG	THR	GAMES AT POSITION	DL	BFW
1884	Cin AA	33	131	20	32	6	1	1		15	2		.244	.256	.405	107	-4		.825	-4	19	0	O33C		-0.5
1890	Cle N	37	151	20	37	6	1	2	29	7	1	11	.245	.283	.338	82	-4	4	.831	-4	147	73	O37(0/4/33)		-0.5
Total	2	70	282	40	69	8	9	3	44	9	1	11	.245	.271	.369	94	-4	4	.828	-8	92	42	O70(0/37/33)		-1.0

WEST, DICK   Richard Thomas   B11.24.1915 Louisville KY   D3.13.1996 Fort Wayne IN   BR/TR/6-2/180   d9.28   Mil 1944-45   Col Georgia Southwestern

YEAR	TM LG	G	AB	R	H	2B	3B	HR	RBI	BB-IB	HP	SO	AVG	OBP	SLG	AOPS	ABR	SB-CS	FA	FR	RNG	THR	GAMES AT POSITION	DL	BFW
1938	Cin N	1	1	0	0	0	0	0		0-0	0	0	.000	.000	.000	-99	0			0			/H		0.0
1939	Cin N	8	19	1	4	0	0	0	4	1-0	0	4	.211	.250	.211	25	-2	0	1.000	-0	90	0	O5L/C		-0.3
1940	Cin N	7	28	4	11	3	0	1	3	0-0	0	2	.393	.393	.571	161	2	1	1.000	-1	102	60	CF		0.1
1941	Cin N	67	172	15	37	5	2	1	17	6	1	23	.215	.246	.285	49	-12	4	.970	-4	77	84	C64		-1.4
1942	Cin N	33	79	9	14	3	0	1	8	5	0	13	.177	.226	.253	40	-6	1	.989	1	92	150	C17,O6L		-0.4
1943	Cin N												—	—	—	—	—			0			/R		0.0
Total	6	119	299	30	66	11	2	4	35	12	2	42	.221	.253	.298	55	-18	6	.977	-4	82	97	C89,O11L		-2.0

WEST, SAM   Samuel Filmore   B10.5.1904 Longview TX   D11.23.1985 Lubbock TX   BL/TL/5-11/165   d4.17   Mil 1943-45   C3

YEAR	TM LG	G	AB	R	H	2B	3B	HR	RBI	BB-IB	HP	SO	AVG	OBP	SLG	AOPS	ABR	SB-CS	FA	FR	RNG	THR	GAMES AT POSITION	DL	BFW
1927	Was A	38	67	9	16	0	1	0	8	8	0	8	.239	.320	.328	69	-3	1-0	.939	1	95	223	O18(5/8/5)		-0.3
1928	Was A	125	378	59	114	30	7	3	40	20	1	23	.302	.338	.442	104	1	5-6	**.996**	2	97	138	O116(53/60/6)		-0.3
1929	Was A	142	510	60	136	16	8	3	75	45	0	41	.267	.326	.347	73	-22	10-8	.978	13	103	**178**	O139(4/136/0)		-1.4
1930	Was A	120	411	75	135	22	10	6	67	37	1	34	.328	.385	.474	116	10	5-5	.972	3	103	99	O118(1/117/0)		0.7
1931	Was A	132	526	77	175	43	13	3	91	30	0	37	.333	.369	.481	121	15	6-8	.990	14	**115**	128	O127C		2.2

YEAR	TM LG	G	AB	R	H	2B	3B	HR	RBI	BB-IB	HP	SO	AVG	OBP	SLG	AOPS	ABR	SB-CS	FA	FR	RNG	THR	GAMES AT POSITION	DL	BFW
1932	Was A	146	554	88	159	27	12	6	83	48	1	57	.287	.345	.412	96	-4	4-5	.979	15	115	126	O143C		0.6
1933	StL A★	133	517	93	155	25	12	11	48	59	-1	49	.300	.373	.458	112	8	10-8	.988	5	102	157	O127C		0.9
1934	StL A★	122	482	90	157	22	10	9	55	62	0	55	.326	.403	.469	115	11	3-5	.972	5	101	151	O120C		1.1
1935	StL A☆	138	527	93	158	37	4	10	70	75	0	46	.300	.388	.442	109	9	1-6	.989	11	118	65	O148C		1.4
1936	StL A	152	533	78	148	26	4	7	70	94	0	70	.278	.386	.381	87	-8	2-0	.983	6	110	77	O105C		-0.4
1937	StL A★	122	457	68	150	31	4	7	58	46	0	28	.328	.390	.473	115	12	1-1	.987	9	103	169	O105C		1.7
1938	StL A	44	165	17	51	8	2	1	27	14	0	9	.309	.363	.400	91	-2	1-0	.971	-3	102		O41C		-0.5
	Was A	92	344	51	104	19	5	5	47	33	0	21	.302	.363	.430	105	2	1-1	.983	-3	98	50	O85(1/84/0)		-0.3
	Year	136	509	68	155	27	7	6	74	47	0	30	.305	.363	.420	100	0	2-1	.979	-6	99	34	O126(1/125/0)		-0.8
1939	Was A	115	390	52	110	20	8	3	52	67	0	29	.282	.387	.397	109	8	1-1	.992	1	104	98	O89(23/55/11),1b17		0.4
1940	Was A	57	99	7	25	6	1	1	18	16	0	13	.253	.357	.364	93	0	0-2	.990	0	100	127	1b12,O9(0/3/6)		-0.2
1941	Was A	26	37	3	10	0	0	0	6	11	0	2	.270	.438	.270	95	1	1-0	1.000	0	116	0	O8(4/1/3)		0.1
1942	Chi A	49	151	14	35	5	0	0	25	31	0	18	.232	.363	.265	80	-2	2-0	.983	-1	101	33	O45(1/44/0)		-0.4
Total	16	1753	6148	934	1838	347	101	75	838	696	5	540	.299	.371	.425	103	36	54-56	.983	79	106	115	O1573(92/1454/31),1b29		5.3

WEST, MAX   Walter Maxwell   B7.14.1904 Sunset TX   D4.25.1971 Houston TX   BR/TR/5-11/165   d9.18   Col North Texas

YEAR	TM LG	G	AB	R	H	2B	3B	HR	RBI	BB-IB	HP	SO	AVG	OBP	SLG	AOPS	ABR	SB-CS	FA	FR	RNG	THR	GAMES AT POSITION	DL	BFW
																									0.1
1928	Bro N	7	21	4	6	1	0	0	1	1	0	1	.286	.400	.429	118	1	0	.882	1	78	544	O6(1/4/1)		-0.1
1929	Bro N	5	8	1	2	1	0	0	1	5	0	0	.250	.333	.375	77	0	0	1.000	-0	68	0	O2(1/1/0)		0.0
Total	2	12	29	5	8	2	1	0	2	5	0	1	.276	.382	.414	107	1	0	.895	1	76	453	O8(2/5/1)		0.0

WEST, BILLY   William O.   B8.15.1853 Williamsburg NY   D10.27.1928 Richmond Hill NY   d5.22

YEAR	TM LG	G	AB	R	H	2B	3B	HR	RBI	BB-IB	HP	SO	AVG	OBP	SLG	AOPS	ABR	SB-CS	FA	FR	RNG	THR	GAMES AT POSITION	DL	BFW
1874	Atl NA	9	35	4	8	1	0	0		1		2	.229	.250	.257	71	-1	0-0	.707	-2	139	75	2b9/CS		-0.2
1876	NY N	1	4	0	0	0	0	0	0	0		0	.000	.000	.000	-99	-1		1.000	0	118	281	/2		-0.1

WESTERBERG, OSCAR   Oscar William   B7.8.1882 Alameda CA   D4.17.1909 Alameda CA   BB/TR/6-0/186   d9.5   Col St. Marys (CA)

YEAR	TM LG	G	AB	R	H	2B	3B	HR	RBI	BB-IB	HP	SO	AVG	OBP	SLG	AOPS	ABR	SB-CS	FA	FR	RNG	THR	GAMES AT POSITION	DL	BFW
1907	Bos N	2	6	0	2	0	0	0	1	1	0		.333	.429	.333	139	-1		1.000	-0	72	199	S2		0.0

WESTLAKE, JIM   James Patrick   B7.3.1930 Sacramento CA   D1.3.2003 Sacramento CA   BL/TL/6-1/190   d4.16   b-Wally

YEAR	TM LG	G	AB	R	H	2B	3B	HR	RBI	BB-IB	HP	SO	AVG	OBP	SLG	AOPS	ABR	SB-CS	FA	FR	RNG	THR	GAMES AT POSITION	DL	BFW
1955	Phi N	1	1	0	0	0	0	0	0	0-0	1		.000	.000	.000	1	0	0-0	—	0			/H		0.0

WESTLAKE, WALLY   Waldon Thomas   B11.8.1920 Gridley CA   BR/TR/6-0/186*   d4.15   b-Jim

YEAR	TM LG	G	AB	R	H	2B	3B	HR	RBI	BB-IB	HP	SO	AVG	OBP	SLG	AOPS	ABR	SB-CS	FA	FR	RNG	THR	GAMES AT POSITION	DL	BFW
1947	Pit N	112	407	59	111	17	4	17	69	27	4	63	.273	.324	.459	103	0	5	.988	3	109	89	O109(0/12/97)		0.0
1948	Pit N	132	428	78	122	10	6	17	65	46	4	40	.285	.360	.456	117	9	2	.976	-2	98	91	O125(1/67/57)		0.4
1949	Pit N	147	525	77	148	24	8	23	104	45	6	78	.282	.345	.490	118	12	6	.982	3	104	103	O143(0/51/92)		0.8
1950	Pit N	139	477	69	136	15	6	24	95	48	7	78	.285	.359	.493	118	11	1	.991	1	108	40	O123(5/97/26)		1.0
1951	Pit N	50	181	28	51	4	0	16	45	9	2	26	.282	.323	.569	131	6	0-1	.908	5	120	136	3b34,O11(10/1/0)		1.0
	StL N★	73	267	36	68	8	5	6	39	24	4	42	.255	.325	.390	91	-4	1-2	.982	-1	96	113	O68(11/29/28)		-0.7
	Year	123	448	64	119	12	5	22	84	33	6	68	.266	.324	.462	107	2	1-3	.984	4	95	129	O79(21/30/28),3b34		0.3
1952	StL N★	21	74	7	16	3	0	0	10	8		11	.216	.293	.257	93	1		1.000	3	122	161	O15C		-0.2
	Cin N	59	183	29	37	4	3	9	14	31	2	29	.202	.324	.273	67	-7	0-2	.992	-1	98	98	O56(5/43/10)		-1.1
	Year	80	257	36	53	7	3	9	24	39	2	40	.206	.315	.268	63	-12	1-3	.995	2	100	245	O71(5/58/10)		-1.3
	Cle A	29	69	11	16	4	1	9	8		1		.232	.362	.362	93	-1	1-0	1.000	2	100	245	O28(12/4/20)		-1.0
1953	Cle A	82	218	42	72	7	1	9	46	35	2	29	.330	.427	.495	153	18	2-0	.963	-2	99	59	O70(49/10/14)		1.4
1954	†Cle A	85	240	36	63	9	2	11	42	26	2	37	.262	.337	.454	114	4	0-1	1.000	1	107	339	O7(4/3/0)		0.4
1955	Cle A	16	20	2	5	1	0	0	3	3-1	0	5	.250	.348	.300	73	-1	0-0	1.000	-1	76	0	O7(2/0/5)		-0.3
	Bal A	8	24	0	3	1	0	0	6-0		1	6	.125	.300	.167	30	-2	0-0	1.000	-0	90	151	O14(6/3/5)		-0.3
	Year	24	44	2	8	2	0	0	9-1		1	11	.182	.321	.227	49	-3	0-0	—	0			/H		-0.5
1956	Phi N	5	4	0	0	0	0	0	0	0-0	0	3	.000	.200	.000	-41	-1	0-0	—	0			/H		-0.1
Total	10	958	3117	474	848	107	33	127	539	317-1	33	453	.272	.345	.450	111	40	19-7	.983	8	102	88	O834(137/344/385),3b34		

WESTON, AL   Alfred John   B12.11.1905 Lynn MA   D11.13.1997 San Diego CA   BR/TR/6-0/195   d7.7   Col Boston College

YEAR	TM LG	G	AB	R	H	2B	3B	HR	RBI	BB-IB	HP	SO	AVG	OBP	SLG	AOPS	ABR	SB-CS	FA	FR	RNG	THR	GAMES AT POSITION	DL	BFW
1929	Bos N	3	3	0	0	0	0	0	0	0	0	2	.000	.000	.000	-99	-1	0	—	0			/H		-0.1

WESTRUM, WES   Wesley Noreen   B11.28.1922 Clearbrook MN   D5.28.2002 Clearbrook MN   BR/TR/5-11/185*   d9.17   M5/C12

YEAR	TM LG	G	AB	R	H	2B	3B	HR	RBI	BB-IB	HP	SO	AVG	OBP	SLG	AOPS	ABR	SB-CS	FA	FR	RNG	THR	GAMES AT POSITION	DL	BFW
1947	NY N	6	12	1	5	1	0	0	2		0	0	.417	.417	.500	142	1	0	1.000	0	0	202	C2		0
1948	NY N	66	125	14	20	3	1	4	16	20		36	.160	.276	.296	54	-8	3	.981	5	120	104	C63		0
1949	NY N	64	169	23	41	4	1	7	28	37	2	39	.243	.385	.402	111	4	1	.980	-0	90	59	C62		2
1950	NY N	140	437	68	103	13	6	23	71	92	2	73	.236	.371	.437	111	9	2	.999	14	153	98	C139		2
1951	†NY N	124	361	59	79	12	0	20	70	104	5	93	.219	.400	.418	119	16	1-0	.987	8	142	123	C122		0
1952	NY N	114	322	47	71	11	0	14	43	76	1	73	.220	.374	.385	110	8	1-2	.978	2	182	88	C112		1
1953	NY N☆	107	290	40	65	5	0	12	30	56	1	73	.224	.352	.366	86	-3	2-0	.982	5	138	109	C106/3		-0
1954	†NY N	98	246	25	46	3	1	8	27	45	3	60	.187	.315	.305	63	-13	0-1	.985	10	157	105	C98		-0
1955	NY N	69	137	11	29	1	0	4	18	24-3	1	41	.212	.327	.307	71	-5	0-1	.987	5	130	105	C68		-0
1956	NY N	68	132	10	29	5	2	3	8	25-5	1	28	.220	.346	.356	91	-1	0-0	.982	8	132	111	C67		-0
1957	NY N	63	91	4	15	1	0	1	2	10-1	1	24	.165	.255	.209	27	-9	0-1	.966	1	132	134	C63		-0
Total	11	919	2322	302	503	59	8	96	315	489-9	19	514	.217	.356	.373	95	-3	10-5	.985	58	144	104	C902/3		-0

WETHERBY, JEFF   Jeffrey Barrett   B10.18.1963 Granada Hills CA   BL/TL/6-2/195   [AtlN85 21/536]   d6.7   Col USC

YEAR	TM LG	G	AB	R	H	2B	3B	HR	RBI	BB-IB	HP	SO	AVG	OBP	SLG	AOPS	ABR	SB-CS	FA	FR	RNG	THR	GAMES AT POSITION	DL	BFW
1989	Atl N	52	48	5	10	2	1	1	7	4-0	0	6	.208	.264	.354	75	-2	1-0	1.000	-0	100	0	O9(7/0/2)		-0

WETZEL, DUTCH   Franklin Burton   B7.7.1893 Columbus IN   D3.5.1942 Hollywood CA   BR/TR/5-9.5/177   d9.15

YEAR	TM LG	G	AB	R	H	2B	3B	HR	RBI	BB-IB	HP	SO	AVG	OBP	SLG	AOPS	ABR	SB-CS	FA	FR	RNG	THR	GAMES AT POSITION	DL	BFW
1920	StL A	7	21	5	9	1	1	0	5	4	0	1	.429	.520	.571	183	3	0-1	.875	-0	96	121	O6(5/1/0)		-1
1921	StL A	61	119	16	25	2	0	2	10	9	1	20	.210	.271	.277	38	-11	0-1	.981	0	115	35	O27(12/4/11)		-1
Total	2	68	140	21	34	3	1	2	15	13	1	21	.243	.312	.321	59	-8	0-1	.957	-0	111	54	O33(17/5/11)		-0

WHALEY, BILL   William Carl   B2.10.1899 Indianapolis IN   D3.3.1943 Indianapolis IN   BR/TR/5-11/178   d4.18

YEAR	TM LG	G	AB	R	H	2B	3B	HR	RBI	BB-IB	HP	SO	AVG	OBP	SLG	AOPS	ABR	SB-CS	FA	FR	RNG	THR	GAMES AT POSITION	DL	BFW
1923	StL A	23	50	5	12	2	1	0	4	4	1	2	.240	.309	.320	62	-3	0-0	1.000	1	96	160	O13(4/9/0)		-0

WHALING, BERT   Albert James   B6.22.1888 Los Angeles CA   D1.21.1965 Los Angeles CA   BR/TR/6-0/185   d4.22

YEAR	TM LG	G	AB	R	H	2B	3B	HR	RBI	BB-IB	HP	SO	AVG	OBP	SLG	AOPS	ABR	SB-CS	FA	FR	RNG	THR	GAMES AT POSITION	DL	BFW
1913	Bos N	79	211	22	51	8	2	0	25	10	2	32	.242	.283	.299	65	-10	3-3	.990	1	101	101	C77		-0
1914	Bos N	60	172	18	36	7	0	0	12	21	2	28	.209	.303	.250	66	-8	0-1	.981	10	142	106	C59		-0
1915	Bos N	72	190	10	42	6	2	0	13	8	3	38	.221	.264	.274	66	-8	2-0	.986	5	144	82	C69		-0
Total	3	211	573	50	129	21	4	0	50	39	7	98	.225	.283	.276	65	-24	5-4	.986	15	128	96	C205		-0

WHEAT, MACK   McKinley Davis   B6.9.1893 Polo MO   D8.14.1979 Los Banos CA   BR/TR/5-11.5/167   d4.14   b-Zack

YEAR	TM LG	G	AB	R	H	2B	3B	HR	RBI	BB-IB	HP	SO	AVG	OBP	SLG	AOPS	ABR	SB-CS	FA	FR	RNG	THR	GAMES AT POSITION	DL	BFW
1915	Bro N	8	14	0	1	0	0	0	0	0		5	.071	.071	.071	-56	-3	0	.957	-1	95	63	C8		-0
1916	Bro N	2	2	0	0	0	0	0	0	1		1	.000	.000	.000	-97	-0		1.000	-0	70	0	C2		-0
1917	Bro N	29	60	2	8	1	0	1	0	1		12	.133	.161	.150	-4	-7	1	.968	2	108	130	C18,O9(9/1/0)		-0
1918	Bro N	57	157	11	34	7	1	1	8	8		24	.217	.255	.293	67	-6	2	.966	-1	87	109	C38,O7(1/1/4)		-0
1919	Bro N	41	112	5	23	3	0	0	4	0		22	.205	.246	.232	43	-8	1	.944	-3	86	100	C38		-0
1920	Phi N	78	230	15	52	10	3	0	20	8	3	35	.226	.261	.335	67	-10	3-1	.961	2	90	119	C9		-0
1921	Phi N	10	27	1	5	0	1	0	3	1		3	.185	.241	.333	47	-2	0-0	.980	-0	89	110	C187,O16(10/2/4)		-0
Total	7	225	602	34	123	23	5	4	35	19	10	102	.204	.241	.279	52	-36	7-1	.961	2	90				-0

WHEAT, ZACK   Zachary Davis "Buck"   B5.23.1888 Hamilton MO   D3.11.1972 Sedalia MO   BL/TR/5-10/170   d9.11   HF1959   b-Mack

YEAR	TM LG	G	AB	R	H	2B	3B	HR	RBI	BB-IB	HP	SO	AVG	OBP	SLG	AOPS	ABR	SB-CS	FA	FR	RNG	THR	GAMES AT POSITION	DL	BFW
1909	Bro N	26	102	15	31	7	3	0	4	6	0		.304	.343	.431	145	5	1	.952	1	126	105	O26(25/1/0)		
1910	Bro N	**156**	606	78	172	36	15	2	55	47	6	80	.284	.341	.403	120	14	16	.962	5	105	99	O156L		
1911	Bro N	140	534	55	153	26	13	6	76	29	7		.287	.332	.412	112	5	21	.955	-3	105	62	O136(135/1/0)		
1912	Bro N	123	453	70	138	28	7	8	65	39	4	40	.305	.367	.450	128	17	16	.968	3	108	70	O120L		
1913	Bro N	138	535	64	161	28	10	7	58	25	2	45	.301	.335	.430	114	8	19-20	.978	5	111	81	O135L		
1914	Bro N	145	533	66	170	26	9	9	89	47	3	42	.319	.377	.452	143	28	24	.962	15	121	118	O144L		
1915	Bro N	146	528	64	136	15	12	5	66	52	5	42	.258	.330	.360	107	4	21-14	.953	9	115	101	O144L		
1916	†Bro N	149	568	76	177	32	13	9	73	43	6	49	.312	.366	**.461**	149	33	19	.975	6	**114**	88	O149(149/1/0)		
1917	Bro N	109	362	38	113	15	11	1	41	20	2	17	.312	.363	.423	133	13	5	.979	-3	105	98	O105L		
1918	Bro N	105	409	39	137	15	5	0	51	16	6	17	**.335**	.369	.386	131	15	15	.979	4	103	98	O105L		
1919	Bro N	137	536	70	159	23	11	5	62	33	6	27	.297	.344	.409	123	14	15	.971	-3	100	63	O148L		
1920	†Bro N	148	583	89	191	26	13	9	73	48	2	19	.328	.385	.463	138	29	8-10	.965	-3	92	103	O148L		
1921	Bro N	148	568	91	182	31	10	14	85	44	3	19	.320	.372	.484	121	17	11-8	.965	-3	92	103	O148L		

YEAR	TM LG	G	AB	R	H	2B	3B	HR	RBI	BB-IB	HP	SO	AVG	OBP	SLG	AOPS	ABR	SB-CS	FA	FR	RNG	THR	GAMES AT POSITION	DL	BFW
1922	Bro N	152	600	92	201	29	12	16	112	45	7	22	.335	.388	.503	129	25	9-6	.991	1	104	76	O152L		1.3
1923	Bro N	98	349	63	131	13	5	8	65	23	2	12	.375	.417	.510	148	23	3-3	.908	-8	86	57	O87(85/0/2)		0.8
1924	Bro N	141	566	92	212	41	8	14	97	49	4	18	.375	.428	.549	165	54	3-4	.965	4	106	97	O139L		4.5
1925	Bro N	150	616	125	221	42	14	14	103	45	1	22	.359	.403	.541	143	39	3-1	.962	-2	106	54	O149L		2.4
1926	Bro N	111	411	68	119	31	2	5	35	21	1	14	.290	.326	.411	99	-1	4	.955	1	105	99	O102L		-0.8
1927	Phi A	88	247	34	80	12	1	1	38	18	4	5	.324	.379	.393	95	-1	2	.983	-1	86	137	O62(57/2/3)		-0.7
Total 19		2410	9106	1289	2884	476	172	132	1248	650	77	559	.317	.367	.450	129	341	205-69	.966	34	107	84	O2337(2328/5/5)		24.1

WHEATON, WOODY Elwood Pierce B10.3.1914 Philadelphia PA D12.11.1995 Lancaster PA BL/TL/5-8.5/160 d9.28 ▲

1943	Phi A	7	30	2	6	2	0	0	2	3	1	2	.200	.294	.267	65	-1	0-0	1.000	1	103	178	O7C		-0.1
1944	Phi A	30	59	1	11	2	0	0	5	5	0	3	.186	.250	.220	35	-5	1-2	1.000	0	56	0	P11,O8C		-0.4
Total 2		37	89	3	17	4	0	0	7	8	1	5	.191	.265	.236	45	-6	1-2	.981	1	103	192	O15C,P11		-0.5

WHEELER, DON Donald Wesley "Scott" B9.29.1922 Minneapolis MN D12.10.2003 Bloomington MN BR/TR/5-10/175 d4.23

| 1949 | Chi A | 67 | 192 | 17 | 46 | 9 | 2 | 3 | 27 | 20 | 1 | 19 | .240 | .333 | .323 | 76 | -6 | 2-0 | .976 | 1 | 88 | 125 | C58 | | -0.2 |

WHEELER, ED Edward B6.15.1878 Sherman MI D8.15.1960 Ft.Worth TX BB/TR/5-10/160 d5.10

| 1902 | Bro N | 30 | 96 | 4 | 12 | 0 | 0 | 0 | 5 | 3 | 0 | | .125 | .152 | .125 | -14 | -13 | 1 | .863 | -6 | 74 | 0 | 3b11,2b10,S5 | | -2.0 |

WHEELER, ED Edward Raymond B5.24.1915 Los Angeles CA D8.4.1983 Centralia WA BR/TR/5-9/160 d4.19 Col Loyola Marymount

| 1945 | Cle A | 46 | 72 | 12 | 14 | 2 | 0 | 0 | 2 | 8 | 0 | 13 | .194 | .275 | .222 | 47 | -5 | 1-1 | .912 | -6 | 56 | 0 | 3b14,S11,2b3 | | -1.1 |

WHEELER, GEORGE George Harrison "Heavy" B11.10.1881 Shelburn IN D6.13.1918 Clinton IN BL/TR/5-9.5/180 d7.27

| 1910 | Cin N | 3 | 3 | 0 | 0 | 0 | 0 | 0 | 0 | 0 | 0 | | .000 | .000 | .000 | -99 | -1 | | — | 0 | 0 | 0 | /H | | -0.1 |

WHEELER, HARRY Harry Eugene B3.3.1858 Versailles IN D10.9.1900 Cincinnati OH BR/TR/5-11/165 d6.19 M1 ▲

1878	Pro N	7	27	7	4	0	0	0		1		15	.148	.207	.148	18	-1		.875	-2	39	0	P7		0.0
1879	Cin N	1	3	0	0	0	0	0	0	0			.000	.000	.000	-99	-1		1.000	-0	0	0	/ORP		-0.1
1880	Cle N	1	4	0	1	0	0	0	0	0			.250	.250	.250	72	0		1.000	-0	0	0	/OL		0.0
	Cin N	17	65	6	6	2	0	0		2		15	.092	.092	.123	-28	-8		.750	1	116	116	O17(16/1/0)		-0.9
	Year	18	69	6	7	2	0	0	0	2		15	.101	.101	.130	-22	-8		.759	0	107	107	O18(17/1/0)		-0.9
1882	Cin AA	76	344	59	86	11	11	1	29	7			.250	.265	.355	102	-1		.808	-7	72	76	O64R,1b12,P4		-0.9
1883	Col AA	82	371	42	84	6	7	0		6			.226	.239	.280	72	-11		.803	-2	83	48	O82L/2P		-0.9
1884	StL AA	5	19	0	5	2	0	0	1		0		.263	.300	.368	113	0		.600	-2	0	0	O5(4/1/0)		-1.3
	KC U	14	62	11	16	1	0	0		3			.258	.292	.274	84	-3		.769	-1	27	0	O13(12/0/1)/PM		-0.1
	CP U	37	158	29	36	5	3	1		4			.228	.247	.316	70	-11		.774	-5	35	0	O37C		-0.4
	Bal U	17	69	3	18	2	0	0		0			.261	.261	.290	61	-5		.815	-1	99	0	O17(0/1/16)		-1.6
	Year	68	289	43	70	8	3	1		7			.242	.260	.301	70	-20		.781	-7	49	0	O67(12/38/17)/P		-2.6
Total 6		257	1122	152	256	29	21	2	32	23	32		.228	.244	.297	74	-41		.791	-19	70	46	O237(115/40/82),P14,1b12/2		-5.9

WHEELER, DICK Richard (b Richard Wheeler Maynard) B1.14.1898 Keene NH D2.12.1962 Lexington MA BR/TR/5-11/185 d6.17 Col Amherst

| 1918 | StL N | 3 | 6 | 0 | 0 | 0 | 0 | 0 | 0 | 0 | | | .000 | .000 | .000 | -99 | -1 | | — | -0 | 0 | 0 | O2R | | -0.2 |

WHEELOCK, BOBBY Warren H. B8.6.1864 Charlestown MA D3.13.1928 Boston MA BR/TR/5-8/160 d5.19

1887	Bos N	48	166	32	42	4	2	2	15	15		0	.253	.315	.337	80	-4	20	.878	-2	25	0	O28(9/1/18),S20,2b4		-0.5
1890	Col AA	52	190	24	45	6	1	1	16	25		0	.237	.326	.295	89	-2	34	.885	-4	95	89	S52		0.0
1891	Col AA	136	498	82	114	15	1	0	39	78	2	55	.229	.336	.263	76	-11	52	.899	16	110	144	S136		0.8
Total 3		236	854	138	201	25	4	3	70	118	2	70	.235	.330	.285	80	-17	106	.894	14	107	125	S208,O28(9/1/18),2b4		0.3

WHELAN, JIMMY James Francis B5.11.1890 Kansas City MO D11.29.1929 Dayton OH BR/TR/5-8.5/165 d4.24

| 1913 | StL N | 1 | 1 | 0 | 0 | 0 | 0 | 0 | 0 | 0 | | 0 | .000 | .000 | .000 | -99 | -0 | | — | 0 | | 0 | /H | | 0.0 |

WHELAN, TOM Thomas Joseph B1.3.1894 Lynn MA D6.26.1957 Boston MA BR/TR/5-11/175 d8.13 Col Georgetown

| 1920 | Bos N | 1 | 1 | 1 | 0 | 0 | 0 | 0 | 0 | 0 | | 0 | .000 | .500 | .000 | .54 | 0 | 0-0 | 1.000 | -0 | 0 | 0 | /1 | | 0.0 |

WHISENANT, PETE Thomas Peter B12.14.1929 Asheville NC D3.22.1996 Port Charlotte FL BR/TR/6-2/200* d4.16 C2

1952	Bos N	24	52	3	10	2	0	0	7	4	0	13	.192	.250	.231	35	-5	1-1	.973	2	118	184	O14(9/5/0)		-0.4
1955	StL N	58	115	10	22	5	1	2	9	5-0		29	.191	.223	.304	39	-11	2-0	.964	3	116	162	O40(12/11/19)		-0.8
1956	Chi N	103	314	37	75	16	3	11	46	24-1	1	36	.239	.292	.414	89	-5	8-2	.992	2	105	93	O93(6/84/0)		-0.7
1957	Cin N	67	90	18	19	3	2	5	11	5-0		24	.211	.250	.456	80	-3	0-1	.982	2	132	0	O43(24/9/12)		-0.3
1958	Cin N	85	203	33	48	9	2	11	40	18-0	0	37	.236	.292	.463	93	-3	2-3	1.000	3	116	68	O66(26/2/42)/2		-0.2
1959	Cin N	36	71	13	17	2	0	5	11	8-0	0	18	.239	.316	.479	105	-3	0-0	.966	-0	97	86	O21(5/0/16)		-0.1
1960	Cin N	1	1	0	0	0	0	0	0	0-0	0	0	.000	.000	.000	-98	0		—	0			/H		0.0
	Cle A	7	6	0	1	0	0	0	0	0-0	0	1	.167	.167	.167	-10	-1	0-0	1.000	-0	139	0	O2L		0.0
	Was A	58	115	19	26	9	0	3	9	19-0	0	14	.226	.336	.383	95	0	2-1	1.000	-1	93	96	O47(23/31/1)		-0.1
	Year	65	121	19	27	9	0	3	9	19-0	0	16	.223	.329	.372	90	-1	2-1	1.000	-1	93	95	O49(25/31/1)		-0.3
1961	Min A	7	0	1	0	0	0	0	0	0-0	0	0	—	—	—		0	0-0	1.000	-0	0	0	O5L		-0.4
	Cin N	26	15	6	3	0	0	1	2	1-0		4	.200	.143	.200	34	-1	1-0	1.000	-1	0	96	O5L		-0.1
Total 8		475	988	140	221	46	8	37	134	86-1	1	196	.224	.284	.399	80	-30	17-5	.988	10	109	92	O343(122/142/92)/3C2		-3.0

WHISENTON, LARRY Larry B7.3.1956 St.Louis MO BL/TL/6-1/190* [AtlN75 2/42] d9.17

1977	Atl N	4	4	1	1	0	0	0	1	0-0	0	3	.250	.250	.250	31	0	0-0	—	0.			/H		-0.1
1978	Atl N	6	16	1	3	1	0	0	1	1-0	0	3	.188	.235	.250	32	-1	0-0	1.000	-1	67	0	O4R		-0.3
1979	Atl N	13	37	3	9	2	1	0	1	3-0	0	5	.243	.300	.351	73	-1	1-0	1.000	4	138	371	O13(9/0/4)		0.2
1981	Atl N	9	5	1	1	0	0	0	0	2-0	0	1	.200	.429	.200	83	0	0-0	.000	-0	0	0	O2(1/0/1)		0.0
1982	†Atl N	84	143	21	34	7	2	4	17	23-3		33	.238	.339	.399	105	1	2-2	.964	-2	88	42	O34(29/0/5)		-0.2
Total 5		116	205	27	48	10	3	4	21	29-3	0	42	.234	.326	.371	91	-1	3-2	.968	0	97	115	O53(39/0/14)		-0.4

WHISTLER, LEW Lewis W. (b Lewis Wissler) B3.10.1868 St.Louis MO D12.30.1959 St.Louis MO TR/5-10.5/178 d8.7 OF(15/5/12)

1890	NY N	45	170	27	49	9	7	2	29	20	1	37	.288	.366	.459	140	8	8	.982	-2	62	111	1b45		0.2
1891	NY N	72	265	39	65	8	7	3	38	24	3	45	.245	.315	.362	101	0	4	.852	-14	91	60	S33,O22(14/5/3),1b7,2b6,3b5		-1.2
1892	Bal N	52	209	32	47	6	4	2	21	18	3	22	.225	.296	.340	90	-4	12	.973	-1	97	62	1b51/OL		-0.4
	Lou N	80	285	42	67	4	7	5	34	30	2	45	.235	.312	.351	109	3	14	.978	-2	84	131	1b72,2b10		0.1
	Year	132	494	74	114	10	13	7	55	48	5	67	.231	.305	.362	101	-1	26	.976	-3	89	102	1b123,2b10/OL		-0.3
1893	Lou N	13	47	5	10	1	1	0	9	5	1	5	.213	.302	.277	59	-3	1	.946	-1	116	93	1b13		-0.3
	StL N	10	38	5	9	1	0	0	2	3		2	.237	.293	.263	48	-3	0	.923	-1	82	0	O9R/1		-0.3
	Year	23	85	10	19	2	1	0	11	8	1	7	.224	.298	.271	54	-6	1	.949	-2	107	98	1b14,O9R		-0.6
Total 4		272	1014	152	247	29	28	12	133	100	10	156	.244	.318	.363	103	1	39	.976	-19	82	104	1b189,S33,O32L,2b16,3b5		-1.9

WHITAKER, LOU Louis Rodman B5.12.1957 Brooklyn NY BL/TR/5-11/160(155-180) [DetA75 5/99] d9.9

1977	Det A	11	32	5	8	1	0	0	2	4-0	0	6	.250	.333	.281	66	-1	2-2	1.000	-4	71	37	2b9		-0.5
1978	Det A	139	484	71	138	12	7	3	58	61-0	1	65	.285	.361	.357	101	2	7-7	.978	20	111	115	2b136,D2		2.9
1979	Det A	127	423	75	121	14	8	3	42	78-2	1	66	.286	.395	.378	107	8	20-10	.986	17	102	125	2b126		3.1
1980	Det A	145	477	68	111	19	1	1	45	73-0	0	79	.233	.331	.283	69	-17	8-4	.985	-1	97	92	2b143	15	-1.0
1981	Det A	109	335	48	88	14	4	5	36	40-3	1	42	.263	.340	.373	102	2	5-3	.985	7	105	111	2b108		1.6
1982	Det A	152	560	76	160	22	8	15	65	48-4	1	58	.286	.341	.434	111	8	11-3	.988	13	104	125	2b149/D		3.0
1983	Det A★	161	643	94	206	40	6	12	72	67-8	0	70	.320	.380	.457	133	31	17-10	.983	-9	90	92	2b160		2.1
1984	†Det A★	143	558	90	161	25	1	13	56	62-0	0	63	.289	.357	.407	112	10	6-5	.979	-5	94	100	2b142		1.3
1985	Det A★	152	609	102	170	29	8	21	73	80-9	1	56	.279	.362	.456	123	21	6-4	.985	-14	89	103	2b150		1.5
1986	Det A★	144	584	95	157	26	6	20	73	63-5	0	70	.269	.338	.437	109	7	13-8	.976	-11	97	106	2b148		2.1
1987	†Det A★	149	604	110	160	38	6	16	59	71-2	1	108	.265	.341	.427	107	7	13-5	.984	6	106	113	2b141		0.5
1988	Det A	115	403	54	111	18	2	12	55	66-5	0	61	.275	.376	.419	127	17	2-0	.984	-9	93	82	2b110		1.2
1989	Det A	148	509	77	128	21	1	28	85	89-6	3	59	.251	.361	.462	124	26	6-3	.985	6	98	99	2b146,D2		3.5
1990	Det A	132	472	75	112	22	2	18	60	74-7	3	71	.237	.338	.420	107	6	8-2	.985	-6	97	107	2b130/D		2.8
1991	Det A	138	470	94	131	26	2	23	78	90-6	2	45	.279	.391	.489	141	30	4-2	.991	18	106	114	2b130/D		2.8
1992	Det A	130	453	77	126	26	0	19	71	81-5	1	46	.278	.386	.461	135	25	6-4	.984	-13	94	90	2b119,D10		1.4
1993	Det A	119	383	72	111	32	1	9	67	78-4	4	46	.290	.412	.449	132	23	3-3	.981	18	114	112	2b110		4.3
1994	Det A	92	322	67	97	21	2	12	43	41-4	1	47	.301	.377	.491	132	11	2-0	.970	-1	110	88	2b83,D5		1.3

YEAR	TM LG	G	AB	R	H	2B	3B	HR	RBI	BB-IB	HP	SO	AVG	OBP	SLG	AOPS	ABR	SB-CS	FA	FR	RNG	THR	GAMES AT POSITION	DL	BFW
1995	Det A	84	249	36	73	14	0	14	44	31-4	2	41	.293	.372	.518	130	11	4-0	.985	-1	105	83	2b63,D8	17	1.3
Total	19	2390	8570	1386	2369	420	65	244	1084	1197-79	20	1099	.276	.363	.426	116	227	143-75	.984	24	100	104	2b2308,D32	32	35.2

WHITAKER, STEVE   Stephen Edward   B5.7.1943 Tacoma WA   BL/TR/6-1/187*   d8.23

YEAR	TM LG	G	AB	R	H	2B	3B	HR	RBI	BB-IB	HP	SO	AVG	OBP	SLG	AOPS	ABR	SB-CS	FA	FR	RNG	THR	GAMES AT POSITION	DL	BFW
1966	NY A	31	114	15	28	3	2	7	15	9-0	1	24	.246	.304	.491	130	4	0-0	.955	-1	91	159	O31(4/20/10)		0.1
1967	NY A	122	441	37	107	13	3	11	50	23-2	1	89	.243	.283	.358	92	-6	2-5	.982	2	94	153	O114(26/12/78)		-1.5
1968	NY A	28	60	3	7	2	0	0	3	8-0	0	18	.117	.221	.150	14	-6	0-1	.917	-2	66	209	O14(6/7/2)		-1.0
1969	Sea A	69	116	15	29	2	1	6	13	12-1	1	29	.250	.323	.440	113	1	2-0	.962	1	87	227	O39(22/0/18)		0.1
1970	SF N	16	27	3	3	1	0	0	4	2-0	0	14	.111	.167	.148	-13	-4	0-0	.857	-1	58	0	O9L		-0.6
Total	5	266	758	73	174	20	6	24	85	54-3	5	174	.230	.283	.367	91	-11	4-6	.967	-1	89	164	O207(67/39/108)		-2.9

WHITE, FUZZ   Albert Eugene   B6.27.1916 Springfield MO   D4.24.2003 Springfield MO   BL/TR/6-0/175   d9.17

YEAR	TM LG	G	AB	R	H	2B	3B	HR	RBI	BB-IB	HP	SO	AVG	OBP	SLG	AOPS	ABR	SB-CS	FA	FR	RNG	THR	GAMES AT POSITION	DL	BFW
1940	StL A	2	2	0	0	0	0	0	0	0-0	0	0	.000	.000	.000	-98	-1	0-0	—	0			/H		-0.1
1947	NY N	7	13	3	3	0	0	0	0	0-0	0	0	.231	.231	.231	23	-1	0	1.000	1	153	0	O5R		-0.1
Total	2	9	15	3	3	0	0	0	0	0-0	0	0	.200	.200	.200	6	-2	0-0	1.000	1	153	0	O5R		-0.2

WHITE, C. B.   C. B.   B Wakeman OH   d6.1

YEAR	TM LG	G	AB	R	H	2B	3B	HR	RBI	BB-IB	HP	SO	AVG	OBP	SLG	AOPS	ABR	SB-CS	FA	FR	RNG	THR	GAMES AT POSITION	DL	BFW
1883	Phi N	1	1	1	0	0	0	0	0	0		0	.000	.000	.000	-99	0		.667	-0	0	0	/S3		0.0

WHITE, CHARLIE   Charles   B8.12.1928 Kinston NC   D5.26.1998 Seatac WA   BL/TR/5-11/192*   d4.18   Negro Lg 1950

YEAR	TM LG	G	AB	R	H	2B	3B	HR	RBI	BB-IB	HP	SO	AVG	OBP	SLG	AOPS	ABR	SB-CS	FA	FR	RNG	THR	GAMES AT POSITION	DL	BFW
1954	Mil N	50	93	14	22	4	0	1	8	9	0	8	.237	.304	.312	65	-1	0-0	.981	-1	101	27	C28		-0.2
1955	Mil N	12	30	3	7	1	0	0	4	5-0	1	7	.233	.361	.267	74	-1	0-0	1.000	-1	127	50	C10	—	-0.2
Total	2	62	123	17	29	5	0	1	12	14-0	1	15	.236	.319	.301	67	-6	0-0	.986	-2	109	34	C38		-0.7

WHITE, DERRICK   Derrick Ramon   B10.12.1969 San Rafael CA   BR/TR/6-1/220*   [MonN91 6/165]   d7.22   Col Oklahoma

YEAR	TM LG	G	AB	R	H	2B	3B	HR	RBI	BB-IB	HP	SO	AVG	OBP	SLG	AOPS	ABR	SB-CS	FA	FR	RNG	THR	GAMES AT POSITION	DL	BFW
1993	Mon N	17	49	6	11	3	0	2	4	2-1	1	12	.224	.269	.408	75	-2	2-0	.993	-1	87	162	1b17		-0.3
1995	Det A	39	48	3	9	2	0	0	2	0-0	0	8	.188	.188	.229	8	-7	0-0	.981	-1	137	83	1b16,D11,O9(4/0/5)		-0.9
1998	Chi N	11	10	1	1	0	0	0	2	0-0	0	5	.100	.100	.400	23	-1	0-0	1.000	0	113	0	O2L/D		-0.2
	Col N	9	9	0	0	0	0	0	0	0-0	0	4	.000	.000	.000	-8	-3	0-0	1.000	0	90	0	O3L/D		-0.3
	Year	20	19	1	1	0	0	0	2	0-0	0	9	.053	.053	.211	-31	-4	0-0	1.000	0	90	0			-0.5
Total	3	76	116	10	21	5	0	3	8	2-1	1	28	.181	.202	.302	29	-12	3-0	.990	-2	101	140	1b33,O12(8/0/5),D12		-1.5

WHITE, DEVON   Devon Markes   B12.29.1962 Kingston, Jamaica   BB/TR/6-2/182(170-195)   [CalA81 6/132]   d9.2

YEAR	TM LG	G	AB	R	H	2B	3B	HR	RBI	BB-IB	HP	SO	AVG	OBP	SLG	AOPS	ABR	SB-CS	FA	FR	RNG	THR	GAMES AT POSITION	DL	BFW
1985	Cal A	21	7	7	1	0	0	0	1	1-0	1	3	.143	.333	.142	36	-1	3-1	1.000	1	100	350	O16(14/1/3)		0.0
1986	†Cal A	29	51	8	12	1	1	1	3	6-0	0	15	.235	.316	.353	82	-1	6-0	.961	1	125	0	O28(17/7/5)		0.1
1987	Cal A	159	639	103	168	33	5	24	87	39-2	2	135	.263	.306	.443	99	-3	32-11	.980	18	120	156	O159(66/64/120)	34	0.3
1988	Cal A	122	455	76	118	22	2	11	51	23-1	2	84	.259	.296	.389	93	-6	17-8	.976	9	113	128	O116C		-1.2
1989	Cal A★	156	636	86	156	18	13	12	56	31-3	2	129	.245	.282	.371	84	-17	44-16	.989	3	103	118	O154C/D		-1.2
1990	Cal A	125	443	57	96	17	3	11	44	44-5	3	116	.217	.290	.343	78	-14	21-6	.972	3	100	186	O122C		-1.0
1991	†Tor A	156	642	110	181	40	10	17	60	55-1	5	135	.282	.342	.455	115	12	33-10	.998	5	107	98	O156C		1.9
1992	†Tor A	153	641	98	159	26	7	17	60	47-0	5	133	.248	.303	.390	89	-11	37-4	.985	7	111	98	O152C/D		0.1
1993	†Tor A★	146	598	116	163	42	6	15	52	57-1	7	127	.273	.341	.438	106	-5	34-4	.993	5	115	64	O98C		1.6
1994	Tor A	100	403	67	109	24	6	13	49	21-3	5	80	.270	.313	.457	95	-5	11-3	.978	5	115	0	O99C		0.2
1995	Tor A	101	427	61	121	23	5	10	53	29-1	5	97	.283	.334	.431	98	-2	11-2	.989	2	102	142	O139C		0.0
1996	Fla N	146	552	77	151	37	6	17	84	38-6	8	99	.274	.325	.455	107	4	22-6	.987	-8	91	71	O139C		0.0
1996	Fla N	146	552	77	151	37	6	17	84	38-6	8	99	.274	.325	.455	107	4	22-6	.987	0	102	128	O71C	85	-0.1
1997	†Fla N	74	265	37	66	13	1	6	34	32-2	7	65	.249	.338	.370	90	-3	13-5	.987	-2	109	33	O144C		-1.3
1998	Ari N★	146	563	84	157	32	1	22	85	42-4	9	102	.279	.335	.456	106	5	22-8	.986	-11	90	45	O128C/D		-1.3
1999	LA N	134	474	60	127	20	2	14	68	39-2	11	88	.268	.337	.407	92	-7	19-5	.972	-4	84	99	O40C	80	-1.0
2000	LA N	47	158	26	42	5	1	4	13	9-0	1	30	.266	.310	.380	78	-6	3-6	1.000	-7	90	58	O100(13/86/2)		-1.0
2001	Mil N	126	390	52	108	25	2	14	47	28-1	12	95	.277	.343	.459	107	4	18-3	.986	25	105	100	O1867(50/1722/130),D3	199	1.5
Total	17	1941	7344	1125	1934	378	71	208	846	541-32	87	1526	.263	.319	.419	97	-46	346-98	.986	25	105	100	O1867(50/1722/130),D3	199	1.5

WHITE, DON   Donald William   B1.8.1919 Everett WA   D6.15.1987 Carlsbad CA   BR/TR/6-1/195   d4.19

YEAR	TM LG	G	AB	R	H	2B	3B	HR	RBI	BB-IB	HP	SO	AVG	OBP	SLG	AOPS	ABR	SB-CS	FA	FR	RNG	THR	GAMES AT POSITION	DL	BFW
1948	Phi A	86	253	29	62	14	2	1	28	19	2	16	.245	.303	.328	68	-12	0-1	.957	0	100	84	O54(33/7/17),3b17		-1.5
1949	Phi A	57	169	12	36	6	0	0	10	14	0	12	.213	.273	.249	40	-15	2-0	.989	1	106	103	O48(6/0/43),3b4		-1.5
Total	2	143	422	41	98	20	2	1	38	33	2	28	.232	.291	.296	57	-27	2-1	.971	1	103	93	O102(39/7/60),3b21		-3.0

WHITE, ED   Edward Perry   B4.6.1926 Anniston AL   D9.28.1982 Lakeland FL   BR/TR/6-2/200   d9.16   Col Alabama

YEAR	TM LG	G	AB	R	H	2B	3B	HR	RBI	BB-IB	HP	SO	AVG	OBP	SLG	AOPS	ABR	SB-CS	FA	FR	RNG	THR	GAMES AT POSITION	DL	BFW
1955	Chi A	3	4	0	2	0	0	0	0	1-0	0	1	.500	.600	.500	193	1	0-0	1.000	0	115	0	O2R		0.1

WHITE, ELDER   Elder Lafayette   B12.23.1934 Colerain NC   BR/TR/5-11/165   d4.10

YEAR	TM LG	G	AB	R	H	2B	3B	HR	RBI	BB-IB	HP	SO	AVG	OBP	SLG	AOPS	ABR	SB-CS	FA	FR	RNG	THR	GAMES AT POSITION	DL	BFW
1962	Chi N	23	53	4	8	2	0	0	2	8-0	1	11	.151	.274	.189	26	-5	3-0	.986	-1	102	63	S15/3		-0.4

WHITE, FRANK   Frank   B9.4.1950 Greenville MS   BR/TR/5-11/170(170-190)   d6.12   C8

YEAR	TM LG	G	AB	R	H	2B	3B	HR	RBI	BB-IB	HP	SO	AVG	OBP	SLG	AOPS	ABR	SB-CS	FA	FR	RNG	THR	GAMES AT POSITION	DL	BFW
1973	KC A	51	139	20	31	6	1	0	5	8-0	0	23	.223	.262	.281	50	-9	3-1	.937	5	103	139	S37,2b11		0.0
1974	KC A	99	204	19	45	6	3	1	18	5-0	0	33	.221	.239	.294	50	-14	3-4	.962	7	102	106	2b50,S29,3b16,D3		-0.3
1975	KC A	111	304	43	76	10	2	7	36	20-0	1	39	.250	.297	.365	85	-7	11-3	.987	4	104	92	2b67,S42,3b4/CD		0.5
1976	†KC A	152	446	39	102	17	6	2	46	19-0	3	42	.229	.263	.307	67	-20	20-11	.973	18	114	105	2b130,S37		1.0
1977	†KC A	152	474	59	116	21	5	5	50	25-0	2	67	.245	.284	.342	69	-21	23-5	.989	-1	101	95	2b152,S4		-1.1
1978	†KC A★	143	461	66	127	24	6	7	50	26-1	1	59	.275	.317	.399	98	-2	13-10	.978	-8	96	112	2b140		-0.3
1979	KC A★	127	467	73	124	26	4	10	48	25-3	1	54	.266	.300	.403	87	-10	28-8	.982	15	92	90	2b125	33	-1.4
1980	†KC A	154	560	70	148	23	4	7	60	19-0	2	69	.264	.289	.357	75	-20	19-6	.988	-10	93	109	2b93		-1.2
1981	†KC A★	94	364	35	91	17	1	9	38	19-0	1	50	.250	.285	.376	90	-6	4-2	.988	-10	93	109	2b144		2.0
1982	KC A★	145	524	71	156	45	6	11	56	16-1	2	65	.298	.318	.469	113	8	10-7	.978	4	102	107	2b144		2.0
1983	KC A	146	549	52	143	35	6	11	77	20-4	0	51	.260	.283	.406	87	-11	13-5	.985	29	118	124	2b129	15	3.7
1984	†KC A	129	479	58	130	22	5	17	56	27-3	2	72	.271	.311	.445	106	2	5-5	.990	22	109	118	2b149		2.0
1985	†KC A	149	563	62	140	25	1	22	69	28-2	1	86	.249	.284	.414	88	-11	10-4	.980	23	114	101	2b151/S3		2.6
1986	KC A★	151	566	76	154	37	3	22	84	43-5	2	88	.272	.322	.465	110	7	4-4	.987	13	107	98	2b152/D		1.5
1987	KC A	154	563	67	138	32	2	17	78	51-5	2	86	.245	.308	.400	84	-13	1-2	.994	21	110	98	2b148,D3		-0.1
1988	KC A	150	537	48	126	25	1	8	58	21-3	4	67	.235	.266	.330	66	-26	7-3	.985	14	109	83	2b132/OC		0.6
1989	KC A	135	418	34	107	22	1	2	36	30-0	1	52	.256	.307	.328	57	-14	1-0	.978	9	96	98	2b79/OR	17	-1.2
1990	KC A	82	241	20	52	14	1	2	21	10-0	3	32	.216	.253	.299	45	-9	1-3	.984	147	105	102	2b79	65	-1.2
Total	18	2324	7859	912	2006	407	58	160	886	412-27	30	1035	.255	.293	.383	85	-178	178-83	.984	147	105	102	2b2150,S150,3b21,D8,O2(0/1/1)/C	65	9.2

WHITE, DOC   Guy Harris   B4.9.1879 Washington DC   D2.19.1969 Silver Spring MD   BL/TL/6-1/150   d4.22   Col Georgetown ▲

YEAR	TM LG	G	AB	R	H	2B	3B	HR	RBI	BB-IB	HP	SO	AVG	OBP	SLG	AOPS	ABR	SB-CS	FA	FR	RNG	THR	GAMES AT POSITION	DL	BFW
1901	Phi N	31	98	15	27	3	1	1	10	2	1		.276	.297	.357	87	-2	1	.951	2	119	0	P31/OL		0.1
1902	Phi N	61	179	17	47	3	1	1	15	11	0		.263	.305	.307	89	-3	5	.931	-1	107	0	P36,O19(17/0/2)		-0.3
1903	Chi A	38	99	10	20	3	0	0	5	19	0		.202	.331	.232	74	-2	1	.969	2	108	236	P37/OC		0.0
1904	Chi A	33	76	7	12	2	0	0	2	10	0		.158	.256	.184	42	-5	3	.951	1	92	101	P36/OL		0.2
1905	Chi A	37	90	7	15	1	0	0	7	9	0		.167	.202	.233	40	-6	3	.953	-4	101	104	P28/OC		0.2
1906	†Chi A	29	65	11	12	1	0	2	13		0		.185	.321	.231	75	-1	3	.986	5	113	43	P46,O2R/2		-0.1
1907	Chi A	48	90	12	20	1	0	0	2	9	0		.222	.314	.233	77	1	2	.986	7	128	326	P41,O3(0/2/1)		-0.1
1908	Chi A	51	109	12	25	1	0	0	10	12	0		.229	.306	.239	79	-2	4	.926	-3	158	0	O40(1/35/4),P24		0.1
1909	Chi A	72	192	24	45	13	1	0	7	33	0		.234	.347	.292	106	4	2	.972	3	100	222	P33,O14(0/10/4)		0.1
1910	Chi A	56	126	14	25	1	2	0	8	14	0		.198	.279	.238	65	-5	2	.919	-1	97	133	P34,1b2/OR		0.0
1911	Chi A	39	78	12	20	1	1	0	6	7	0		.256	.318	.295	74	-1	0	1.000	-1	92	74	P32		-0.2
1912	Chi A	32	56	5	7	1	1	0	3	1	0		.125	.222	.179	15	-2	3	.959	3	142	0	P19/1		0.0
1913	Chi A	21	25	1	5	1	0	0	0	3	1		.217	.298	.259	74	-33	32	.959	20	108	111	P427,O85(20/51/14),1b3/2		-0.1
Total	13	548	1283	147	278	22	13	2	75	147	1		.217	.298	.259	74	-33	32	.959	20	108	111	P427,O85(20/51/14),1b3/2		

WHITE, DEACON   James Laurie   B12.7.1847 Caton NY   D7.7.1939 Aurora IL   BL/TR/5-11/175   d5.4   M2   b-Will   OF(8/5/101) ▲

YEAR	TM LG	G	AB	R	H	2B	3B	HR	RBI	BB-IB	HP	SO	AVG	OBP	SLG	AOPS	ABR	SB-CS	FA	FR	RNG	THR	GAMES AT POSITION	DL	BFW
1871	Cle NA	29	146	40	47	6	5	1	21	4			.322	.340	.452	132	7	2-2	.821	-4			C29,S2/23OR		
1872	Cle NA	22	109	21	37	2	2	0	22	4			.339	.363	.394	140	6	0-1	.882	1			C14,2b7,O5(2/1/3),M		
1873	Bos NA	60	311	79	122	7	8	1	77	0			.392	.392	.508	153	17	19-3	.842	-0			C56,O12(2/2/8)		
1874	Bos NA	70	352	75	106	5	7	3	52	5			.301	.311	.381	114	3	1-1	.839	1			C75,O14R/1		
1875	Bos NA	80	371	76	136	23	3	1	60	3			2	.367	.372	.453	178	28	2-3	.880	19			C63,O3L,1b3/3P		
1876	Chi N	66	303	66	104	18	1	1	60	7			3	.343	.358	.419	141	12		.844	8			C63,O3L,1b3/3P		

YEAR	TM LG	G	AB	R	H	2B	3B	HR	RBI	BB-IB	HP	SO	AVG	OBP	SLG	AOPS	ABR	SB-CS	FA	FR	RNG	THR	GAMES AT POSITION	DL	BFW
1877	Bos N	59	266	51	**103**	14	**11**	2	49	8			3	**.387**	.405	**.545**	190	**26**		.963	1	119	117	1b35,O19R,C7		2.2
1878	Cin N	**61**	258	41	81	4	1	0	29	10			5	.314	.340	.337	136	11		.909	0			C48,O16R/3		1.1
1879	Cin N	78	333	55	110	16	6	1	52	6			9	.330	.342	.423	159	21		.901	6			C59,O21(0/4/18),1b2,M		2.5
1880	Cin N	35	141	21	42	4	2	0	7	6			7	.298	.340	.355	137	6		.738	-4	115	64	O33(0/1/33),1b3/2		0.2
1881	Buf N	78	319	58	99	24	4	0	53	9			12	.310	.329	.411	133	12		.943	-9	91	67	1b26,2b25,O17(2/0/15),3b7,C4		0.4
1882	Buf N	83	337	51	95	17	0	1	33	15			16	.282	.313	.341	108	3		.837	-11	85	77	3b63,C20		-0.4
1883	Buf N	94	391	62	114	14	5	0	47	23			18	.292	.331	.353	106	3		.797	-14	85	82	3b77,C22		-0.7
1884	Buf N	110	452	82	147	16	11	5	74	32			13	.325	.370	.442	149	25		.825	-5	98	88	3b108,C3		1.9
1885	Buf N	98	404	54	118	6	6	0	57	12			11	.292	.313	.337	106	1		.888	2	103	83	3b98		0.4
1886	Det N	124	491	65	142	19	5	1	76	31			35	.289	.331	.354	105	3	9	.847	-9	97	141	3b124		-0.4
1887	†Det N	111	449	71	136	20	11	3	75	26	9		15	.303	.353	.416	109	5	20	.848	1	105	110	3b106,O3L,1b2		0.6
1888	Det N	125	527	75	157	22	5	4	71	21	9		24	.298	.336	.381	127	6	12	.857	-3	100	122	3b125		1.4
1889	Pit N	55	225	35	57	10	1	0	26	16	4		18	.253	.341	.307	82	-5	2	.872	-8	88	79	3b52,1b3		-1.1
1890	Buf P	122	439	62	114	13	4	0	47	67	19		30	.260	.381	.308	93	-3	3	.905	18	117	140	3b4,1b57/SP		1.3
Total	5 NA	261	1289	291	448	53	25	6	232	16			6	.348	.356	.441	146	61	24-9	.854	16			C232,O53(4/3/47),2b8,1b2,S2/3		6.3
Total	15	1299	5335	849	1619	217	73	18	756	292			41	.303	.344	.382	122	142	46	.853	-27			3b826,C226,1b131,O112R,2b26,P2/S		11.3

WHITE, JERRY   Jerome Cardell B8.23.1952 Shirley MA BB/TR/5-11/165(160-175) [MonN70 14/322] d9.16 C10

YEAR	TM LG	G	AB	R	H	2B	3B	HR	RBI	BB-IB	HP	SO	AVG	OBP	SLG	AOPS	ABR	SB-CS	FA	FR	RNG	THR	GAMES AT POSITION	DL	BFW
1974	Mon N	9	10	4	4	1	2	0	2	1-0	0	0	.400	.400	.700	193	1	3-0	1.000	-1	76	0	O7(5/2/0)		0.1
1975	Mon N	39	97	14	29	4	1	2	7	10-1	0	7	.299	.364	.423	112	2	5-2	.976	2	120	58	O30(7/24/0)		0.4
1976	Mon N	114	278	32	68	11	4	2	21	27-2	0	31	.245	.316	.313	75	-8	15-7	.982	-3	94	90	O92(27/67/0)		-1.4
1977	Mon N	16	21	4	4	0	0	0	1	1-0	0	3	.190	.227	.190	14	-1	1-0	1.000	-0	73	0	O8(7/0/1)		-0.3
1978	Mon N	18	10	2	2	0	0	0	0	1-0	0	0	.200	.273	.200	34	-1	1-0	—	-0	0	0	O3(1/0/2)		-0.1
	Chi N	59	136	22	37	6	1	1	10	23-1	0	16	.272	.373	.338	90	0	4-3	.981	1	99	178	O54C		0.0
	Year	77	146	24	39	6	1	1	10	24-1	0	19	.267	.366	.329	89	-1	5-3	.981	1	98	176	O57(1/54/2)	23	0.0
1979	Mon N	88	138	30	41	7	1	3	18	21-2	1	23	.297	.391	.428	124	5	8-4	.983	-3	82	81	O43(6/13/26)		-0.1
1980	Mon N	110	214	22	56	9	3	7	23	30-0	1	37	.262	.351	.430	116	5	8-7	.946	-1	96	122	O84(62/7/18)		0.2
1981	†Mon N	59	119	11	26	5	1	3	11	13-0	0	17	.218	.293	.353	81	-3	5-2	.952	-1	97	86	O39(7/13/20)		0.1
1982	Mon N	69	115	13	28	6	1	2	13	8-1	2	26	.243	.304	.365	83	-3	3-3	1.000	0	100	72	O30(21/9/2)	15	-0.6
1983	Mon N	40	34	4	5	1	0	0	6	12-0	1	8	.147	.383	.176	60	-1	4-0	1.000	0	104	0	O13(2/5/6)		-0.4
1986	StL N	25	24	1	3	0	0	1	3	0-0	0	3	.125	.179	.250	21	-3	0-0	1.000	0	154	0	O6(3/0/3)		0.0
Total	11	646	1196	155	303	50	9	21	109	148-7	7	174	.253	.337	.363	93	-9	57-28	.974	-5	97	98	O409(148/194/78)	38	-2.3

WHITE, JACK   John Peter B8.31.1905 New York NY D6.19.1971 Flushing NY BB/TR/5-7.5/150 d6.22 Col Fordham

YEAR	TM LG	G	AB	R	H	2B	3B	HR	RBI	BB-IB	HP	SO	AVG	OBP	SLG	AOPS	ABR	SB-CS	FA	FR	RNG	THR	GAMES AT POSITION	DL	BFW
1927	Cin N	5	4	1	0	0	0	0	0	0		0	.000	.000	.000	-99	-1	0	1.000	0	117	146	2b3,S2		-0.1
1928	Cin N	1	3	0	0	0	0	0	0	0		0	.000	.000	.000	-99	-1	0	.833	-1	0	0	/2		-0.2
Total	2	6	7	1	0	0	0	0	0	0		1	.000	.000	.000	-99	-2	0	.929	-1	68	85	2b4,S2		-0.3

WHITE, JACK   John Wallace B1.19.1878 Traders Point IN D9.30.1963 Indianapolis IN BR/TR/5-6/? d6.26

YEAR	TM LG	G	AB	R	H	2B	3B	HR	RBI	BB-IB	HP	SO	AVG	OBP	SLG	AOPS	ABR	SB-CS	FA	FR	RNG	THR	GAMES AT POSITION	DL	BFW
1904	Bos N	1	5	1	0	0	0	0	0	0		0	.000	.000	.000	-99	-1	0	1.000	1	497	0	/OL		-0.1

WHITE, JO-JO   Joyner Clifford B6.1.1909 Red Oak GA D10.9.1986 Tacoma WA BL/TR/5-11/165 d4.15 M1/C10 s-Mike

YEAR	TM LG	G	AB	R	H	2B	3B	HR	RBI	BB-IB	HP	SO	AVG	OBP	SLG	AOPS	ABR	SB-CS	FA	FR	RNG	THR	GAMES AT POSITION	DL	BFW
1932	Det A	80	208	25	54	6	3	2	21	22	0	19	.260	.330	.346	73	-9	6-8	.962	2	96	176	O48(16/17/16)		-1.0
1933	Det A	91	234	43	59	9	5	2	34	27	3	26	.252	.337	.359	83	-6	5-5	.977	-1	98	93	O54(16/32/6)		-0.9
1934	†Det A	115	384	97	120	18	5	0	44	69	1	39	.313	.419	.385	108	9	28-6	.959	-0	98	123	O100(1/93/6)		0.9
1935	†Det A	114	412	82	99	13	12	2	32	68	0	42	.240	.348	.345	83	-10	19-10	.962	-4	94	94	O98C		-1.5
1936	Det A	58	51	11	14	3	0	0	6	9	0	10	.275	.383	.333	78	-1	2-0	.938	0	96	211	O18(0/18/1)		-0.1
1937	Det A	94	305	50	75	5	7	0	21	50	1	40	.246	.354	.308	67	-15	12-7	.973	-5	96	51	O82(3/79/0)		-2.0
1938	Det A	78	206	40	54	6	1	0	15	30	1	15	.262	.359	.301	63	-11	3-4	.967	-1	106	85	O55(21/34/1)		-1.2
1943	Phi A	139	500	69	124	17	7	1	30	61	4	51	.248	.335	.316	91	-5	12-4	.966	-5	97	80	O133(2/131/0)		-1.3
1944	Phi A	85	267	30	59	4	2	1	21	40	3	27	.221	.329	.262	71	-9	5-4	.949	0	106	93	O74(10/9/57)/S		-1.4
	Cin N	24	85	9	20	2	-0	0	5	10	0	7	.235	.316	.259	65	-4	0-0	1.000	1	99	177	O23(4/11/10)		-0.1
Total	9	878	2652	456	678	83	42	8	229	386	13	276	.256	.353	.328	82	-61	92-48	.965	-11	98	98	O685(73/522/97)/S		-8.8

WHITE, MIKE   Joyner Michael B12.18.1938 Detroit MI BR/TR/5-8/160* d9.21 f-Jo-Jo Col American River (CA) CC

YEAR	TM LG	G	AB	R	H	2B	3B	HR	RBI	BB-IB	HP	SO	AVG	OBP	SLG	AOPS	ABR	SB-CS	FA	FR	RNG	THR	GAMES AT POSITION	DL	BFW
1963	Hou N	3	7	0	2	0	0	0	0	0-0	0	0	.286	.286	.286	69	0	0-0	1.000	-0	53	0	2b2		0.0
1964	Hou N	89	280	30	76	11	3	-0	27	20-0	0	47	.271	.319	.332	89	-4	0-0	.978	7	99	100	O72(9/55/8),2b10,3b3		0.1
1965	Hou N	8	9	0	0	0	0	0	0	1-0	0	2	.000	.100	.000	-74	-2	0-0	1.000	-0	81	0	/3		-0.3
Total	3	100	296	30	78	11	3	0	27	21-0	0	49	.264	.311	.321	84	-6	1-1	.978	6	99	100	O72(9/55/8),2b12,3b4		-0.2

WHITE, MYRON   Myron Alan B8.1.1957 Long Beach CA BL/TL/5-11/180 [LAN75 2/48] d9.4

YEAR	TM LG	G	AB	R	H	2B	3B	HR	RBI	BB-IB	HP	SO	AVG	OBP	SLG	AOPS	ABR	SB-CS	FA	FR	RNG	THR	GAMES AT POSITION	DL	BFW
1978	LA N	7	4	1	2	0	0	0	1	0-0	0	1	.500	.500	.500	180	0	0-1	1.000	-0	75	0	O4(1/0/3)		0.0

WHITE, RONDELL   Rondell Bernard B2.23.1972 Milledgeville GA BR/TR/6-1/210(205-225) [MonN90 1/24] d9.1

YEAR	TM LG	G	AB	R	H	2B	3B	HR	RBI	BB-IB	HP	SO	AVG	OBP	SLG	AOPS	ABR	SB-CS	FA	FR	RNG	THR	GAMES AT POSITION	DL	BFW
1993	Mon N	23	73	9	19	3	1	2	15	7-0	0	16	.260	.321	.411	91	-1	1-2	1.000	-2	88	0	O21(19/5/0)		-0.4
1994	Mon N	40	97	16	27	10	1	2	13	9-0	1	18	.278	.358	.464	111	-2	1-1	.946	-2	80	75	O29(25/4/0)		-0.1
1995	Mon N	130	474	87	140	33	4	13	57	41-1	6	87	.295	.356	.464	111	8	25-5	.986	-3	99	78	O119(8/111/0)		1.0
1996	Mon N	88	334	35	98	19	4	6	41	22-0	2	53	.293	.340	.428	99	-1	14-6	.990	-0	98	121	O86C		0.1
1997	Mon N	151	592	84	160	29	5	28	82	31-3	10	111	.270	.316	.478	106	-2	16-8	.992	3	109	83	O151C		0.7
1998	Mon N	97	357	54	107	21	2	17	58	30-2	7	57	.300	.363	.513	131	16	16-7	.996	9	120	117	O96(15/83/0)/D	69	2.6
1999	Mon N	138	539	83	168	26	6	22	62	32-2	11	85	.312	.359	.505	121	15	10-6	.964	-0	91	135	O135(102/73/0)	30	1.2
2000	Mon N	75	290	52	89	24	0	11	54	28-0	2	67	.307	.370	.503	118	8	5-1	.994	6	117	92	O74L	23	1.2
	Chi N	19	67	7	22	2	0	2	7	5-0	2	12	.328	.392	.448	113	1	0-2	1.000	9	133	0	O18L	40	0.2
	Year	94	357	59	111	26	0	13	61	33-0	4	79	.311	.374	.493	117	10	5-3	.995	8	120	75	O92L		1.4
2001	Chi N	95	323	43	99	19	1	17	50	26-4	7	56	.307	.371	.529	133	16	1-2	.979	-0	97	82	O90L		1.2
2002	†NY A	126	455	59	109	21	0	14	62	25-1	8	86	.240	.288	.378	77	-16	1-2	**1.000**	4	114	47	O113(113/1/0),D11	65	-1.7
2003	SD N★	115	413	49	115	17	3	18	66	25-2	8	71	.278	.330	.465	115	7	1-4	.978	1	99	104	O104L,D3		0.3
	KC A	22	75	13	26	6	1	4	21	6-0	2	8	.347	.400	.613	154	6	0-0	.978	2	144	0	O17L,D4		0.7
2004	Det A	121	448	76	121	21	2	19	67	39-4	8	77	.270	.337	.453	108	5	1-2	.977	-4	94	51	O74L,D43		-0.4
2005	Det A	97	344	49	114	24	3	12	53	17-0	5	48	.313	.348	.489	123	12	1-0	1.000	-3	98		O65L,D30	49	0.5
Total	13	1337	4911	716	1417	275	33	187	710	343-19	81	852	.289	.343	.472	112	80	93-46	.986	13	105	78	O1192(724/514/0),D92	355	7.1

WHITE, ROY   Roy Hilton B12.27.1943 Los Angeles CA BB/TR/5-10/172* d9.7 C5 OF(1520/63/56)

YEAR	TM LG	G	AB	R	H	2B	3B	HR	RBI	BB-IB	HP	SO	AVG	OBP	SLG	AOPS	ABR	SB-CS	FA	FR	RNG	THR	GAMES AT POSITION	DL	BFW
1965	NY A	14	42	7	14	2	0	0	3	4-0	1	7	.333	.404	.381	125	-2	2-1	1.000	-0	84	0	O10(0/1/9)/2		0.1
1966	NY A	115	316	39	71	13	2	7	20	37-1	1	43	.225	.308	.345	91	-3	14-7	.957	-1	105	61	O82(72/12/0),2b2		-0.8
1967	NY A	70	214	22	48	8	2	2	18	19-0	1	25	.224	.287	.290	75	-7	10-4	.968	-7	96	36	O36(5/0/31),3b17		-1.7
1968	NY A	159	577	89	154	20	7	17	62	73-6	-3	50	.267	.350	.414	136	26	20-11	.997	2	93	134	O154(119/25/12)	A M...	2.2
1969	NY A★	130	448	50	130	30	5	7	74	81-4	1	51	.290	.392	.456	136	26	18-10	.989	6	110	88	O126L		2.6
1970	NY A☆	162	609	109	180	30	6	22	94	95-11	0	66	.296	.387	.473	143	39	24-10	.994	0	107	88	O162L		2.6
1971	NY A	147	524	86	153	22	7	19	84	86-7	0	66	.292	.388	.469	152	39	14-7	1.000	5	107	84	O145L		3.8
1972	NY A	**155**	556	76	150	29	0	10	54	99-10	5	59	.270	.384	.376	122	17	23-7	.994	2	109	62	O155L		2.5
1973	NY A	**162**	639	88	157	22	3	18	60	78-3	2	81	.246	.329	.374	100	0	16-9	.977	-1	104	35	O162L		-1.0
1974	NY A	136	473	68	130	19	8	7	43	67-5	4	44	.275	.367	.393	121	15	15-6	.993	1	106	43	O67L,D53		1.2
1975	NY A	148	556	81	161	32	5	12	59	72-1	2	50	.290	.372	.430	128	22	16-15	.984	-7	113	110	O135L,1b7,D2		1.9
1976	†NY A	156	626	**104**	179	34	3	14	65	83-1	0	52	.286	.365	.409	128	25	31-13	.987	-0	103	73	O156(140/21/1)		1.9
1977	†NY A	143	519	72	139	25	2	14	52	75-9	0	58	.268	.358	.405	109	9	18-11	.981	4	111	69	O135(133/1/2),D4		0.7
1978	†NY A	103	346	44	93	13	3	8	42	42-7	2	35	.269	.349	.393	111	6	10-4	.992	-8	97	62	O74(73/3/0),D23	15	-1.1
1979	NY A	24	51	2	11	2	0	0	3	27	2-1	0	21	.215	.290	.288	59	-12	2-2	1.000	-1	86	154	O29,O27L		-1.4
Total	15	1881	6650	964	1803	300	51	160	758	934-66	29	708	.271	.360	.404	121	214	233-117	.988	11	104	74	O1625L,D111,3b17,1b7,2b3	15	14.8

WHITE, SAMMY   Samuel Charles B7.7.1927 Wenatchee WA D9.4.1991 Princeville HI BR/TR/6-3/195* d9.26 Col Washington

YEAR	TM LG	G	AB	R	H	2B	3B	HR	RBI	BB-IB	HP	SO	AVG	OBP	SLG	AOPS	ABR	SB-CS	FA	FR	RNG	THR	GAMES AT POSITION	DL	BFW
1951	Bos A	4	11	0	2	0	0	0	2	1-0	0	2	.182	.182	.182	-2	0	0-0	1.000	1	105	0	C4		-0.1
1952	Bos A	115	381	35	107	22	9	4	49	16	0	43	.281	.310	.423	95	-4	2-3	.983	3	124	93	C110		0.4
1953	Bos A☆	136	476	59	130	34	2	13	64	29	2	50	.273	.318	.435	96	-4	3-2	.986	10	106	93	C131		1.3
1954	Bos A	137	493	46	139	25	2	14	75	21	0	50	.282	.307	.426	90	-8	1-3	.979	5	81	99	C133		0.2
1955	Bos A	143	544	65	142	30	4	11	64	44-4	7	58	.261	.323	.392	84	-12	1-2	.984	-2	82	106	C143		-0.7

YEAR	TM LG	G	AB	R	H	2B	3B	HR	RBI	BB-IB	HP	SO	AVG	OBP	SLG	AOPS	ABR	SB-CS	FA	FR	RNG	THR	GAMES AT POSITION	DL	BFW
1956	Bos A	114	392	28	96	15	2	5	44	35-7	0	40	.245	.304	.332	61	-22	2-1	.984	3	124	102	C114		-1.3
1957	Bos A	111	340	24	73	10	1	3	31	25-6	0	38	.215	.267	.276	46	-25	0-1	.985	-1	139	87	C111		-2.3
1958	Bos A	102	328	25	85	15	3	6	35	21-4	1	37	.259	.304	.378	81	-9	1-1	.988	-2	128	103	C102		-0.6
1959	Bos A	119	377	34	107	13	4	1	42	23-6	1	39	.284	.324	.347	81	-10	4-2	.990	4	132	90	C119		-0.1
1961	Mil N	21	63	1	14	1	0	1	5	2-0	0	9	.222	.242	.286	43	-5	0-0	.975	0	82	152	C20		-0.2
1962	Phi N	41	97	7	21	4	0	2	12	2-0	1	16	.216	.238	.320	50	-7	0-0	.975	2	113	97	C40		-0.6
Total	11	1043	3502	324	916	167	20	66	421	218-27	12	381	.262	.305	.377	79	-108	14-15	.984	22	113	97	C1027		-4.0

WHITE, SAM Samuel Lambeth B8.23.1892 Greater Preston, England D11.11.1929 Philadelphia PA BL/TR/6-0/185 d9.8

| 1919 | Bos N | 1 | 1 | 0 | 0 | 0 | 0 | 0 | 0 | 0-0 | 0 | 0 | .000 | .000 | .000 | -99 | 0 | 0 | 1.000 | 1 | 0 | 650 | /C | | 0.1 |

WHITE, ELMER Willard Elmer B12.7.1849 Caton NY D3.17.1872 Caton NY d5.4

| 1871 | Cle NA | 15 | 70 | 13 | 18 | 2 | 0 | 0 | 9 | | 1 | 6 | .257 | .268 | .286 | 63 | -3 | 0-1 | .783 | -1 | 62 | 0 | O15R,C3 | | -0.2 |

WHITE, BARNEY William Barney "Bear" B6.25.1923 Paris TX D7.24.2002 Tyler TX BR/TR/5-11/186 d6.5

| 1945 | Bro N | 4 | 1 | 2 | 0 | 0 | 0 | 0 | 1 | | 0 | 1 | .000 | .500 | .000 | 46 | 0 | | 1.000 | 0 | 93 | 0 | /S3 | | 0.0 |

WHITE, BILL William De Kova B1.28.1934 Lakewood FL BL/TL/6-0/195(185-200) d5.7 Mil 1957-58 Col Hiram

1956	NY N	138	508	63	130	23	7	22	59	47-3	4	72	.256	.321	.459	108	5	15-8	.989	5	113	91	1b138,O2(1/0/1)		0.2
1958	SF N	26	29	5	7	1	0	1	4	7-1	0	5	.241	.389	.379	107	1	0-0	1.000	-0	69	100	1b3,O2(1/0/1)		-0.5
1959	StL N☆	138	517	77	156	33	9	12	72	34-1	2	61	.302	.344	.470	108	6	15-10	.962	-3	108	32	O92(86/9/0),1b71		-1.0
1960	StL N★	144	554	81	157	27	10	16	79	42-1	2	83	.283	.334	.455	105	3	12-6	.990	-5	79	121	1b123,O29(3/28/0)		-0.7
1961	StL N★	153	591	89	169	28	11	20	90	64-4	1	84	.286	.354	.472	107	6	8-11	.989	2	98	104	1b146,O27(8/0/19)		1.1
1962	StL N★	159	614	93	199	31	3	20	102	58-6	6	69	.324	.386	.482	120	19	9-7	.993	2	99	103	1b162		1.5
1963	StL N★	162	658	106	200	26	8	27	109	59-9	0	100	.304	.360	.491	131	26	10-9	.996	1	98	103	1b160		1.8
1964	†StL N★	160	631	92	191	37	4	21	102	52-7	1	103	.303	.355	.474	121	19	7-6	.992	5	113	101	1b144		1.6
1965	StL N	148	543	82	157	26	3	24	73	63-11	4	86	.289	.364	.481	125	18	3-3	.994	5	109	95	1b158		1.6
1966	Phi N	159	577	85	159	23	6	22	103	68-12	3	109	.276	.352	.451	122	5	16-6	.993	-0	96	127	1b95		1.8
1967	Phi N	110	308	29	77	6	2	8	33	52-9	1	61	.250	.359	.360	107	5	6-1	.994	6	118	114	1b111		0.8
1968	Phi N	127	385	34	92	16	2	9	40	39-6	2	79	.239	.309	.361	102	1	0-1	1.000	1	126	106	1b15		-0.2
1969	StL N	49	57	7	12	1	0	0	4	11-0	0	15	.211	.338	.228	61	-2	1-0	.992	12	101	102	1b1477,O152(99/37/21)		4.6
Total	13	1673	5972	843	1706	278	65	202	870	596-70	28	927	.286	.351	.455	115	126	103-68							

WHITE, BILL William Dighton B5.1.1860 Bridgeport OH D12.29.1924 Bellaire OH TR d5.3

1884	Pit AA	74	291	25	66	7	10	0		13		1		.227	.262	.320	90	-4		.807	-9	102	72	S60,3b10,O4R		-1.6
1886	Lou AA	135	557	96	143	17	10	1	66	37		1		.257	.304	.329	93	-7	14	.871	17	99	123	S135/P		1.5
1887	Lou AA	132	512	85	129	7	9	2	79	47		0		.252	.315	.313	74	-19	41	.869	18	103	137	S132		0.
1888	Lou AA	49	198	35	55	6	5	1	30	7		3		.278	.313	.374	122	4	15	.816	1	105	51	S38,3b11		-2.
	†StL AA	76	275	31	48	2	3	2	30	21		2		.175	.184	.225	44	-18	6	.892	-5	86	69	S74,2b2		-1.
	Year	125	473	66	103	8	8	3	60	28		5		.218	.238	.288	74	-16	21	.864	-5	93	63	S112,3b11,2b2		-1.
Total	4	466	1833	272	441	39	37	6	205	125		7		.241	.292	.312	82	-44	76	.860	20	99	105	S439,3b21,O4R,2b2/P		-1.

WHITE, BILL William Edward B Milner GA d6.21 Col Brown

| 1879 | Pro N | 1 | 4 | 1 | 1 | 0 | 0 | 0 | 0 | 0 | 0 | 0 | .250 | .250 | .250 | 67 | 0 | | 1.000 | 0 | 0 | 242 | /1 | | 0. |

WHITE, WARREN William Warren (aka William Warren) B1844 Washington DC D6.12.1890 Little Rock AR 5-10.5/170 d6.17 M2

1871	Oly NA	1	4	0	0	0	0	0	0	0		0	.000	.000	.000	-99	-1	0-0	1.000	-0	54	0	/2		-0.
1872	Nat NA	10	45	7	12	0	0	0	4	0		0	.267	.267	.267	55	-3	0-0	.861	7	148	120	3b9/SM		0
1873	Was NA	39	158	29	43	3	4	0	20	0		1	.272	.272	.342	84	-3	2-1	.728	25	175	82	3b45,C3,M		1
1874	Bal NA	45	211	21	57	1	0	0	17	2			.270	.277	.275	78	-5	1-0	.782	5	111	70	3b59,S5,O5C,2b2		-0.
1875	Chi NA	69	287	37	71	9	0	0	23	0			.247	.247	.279	82	-5	5-10	.813	-2	59		3b2/S2		-0.
1884	Was U	4	18	1	1	0	0	0	0	0			.056	.056	.056	-69	-4		.692	-2	59	0	3b2/S2		1
Total	5 NA	164	705	94	183	13	4	0	64	2		6	.260	.262	.289	78	-17	8-11	.783	40	133	90	3b150,S9,O5C,C3,2b3		1

WHITED, ED Edward Morris B2.9.1964 Bristol PA BR/TR/6-3/195 [HouN86 18/458] d7.5 Col Rider

| 1989 | Atl N | 36 | 74 | 5 | 12 | 3 | 0 | 1 | 4 | 6-2 | 0 | 15 | .162 | .222 | .243 | 33 | -7 | 1-0 | .914 | -3 | 78 | 59 | 3b29,1b3 | | -0. |

WHITEHEAD, BURGESS Burgess Urquhart "Whitey" B6.29.1910 Tarboro NC D11.25.1993 Windsor NC BR/TR/5-10.5/160 d4.30 Mil 1942-45 Col North Carolina-Asheville

1933	StL N	12	7	2	2	0	0	0	1	0	0	1	.286	.286	.286	60	0		1.000	0	74	128	S9,2b3		0
1934	†StL N	100	332	55	92	13	5	1	24	12	4	19	.277	.310	.355	73	-13	5	.962	-1	106	119	2b48,S29,3b28		-1
1935	StL N★	107	338	45	89	10	2	0	33	11	1	14	.263	.289	.305	57	-21	5	.980	1	97	119	2b80,3b8,S6		2
1936	†NY N★	154	632	99	176	31	3	4	47	29	7	32	.278	.317	.356	82	-17	14	.974	28	107	126	2b152		2
1937	†NY N★	152	574	64	164	15	4	5	52	28	4	20	.286	.323	.359	84	-14	7	.970	23	116	100	2b91,S4/3		2
1939	NY N	95	335	31	80	6	3	2	24	24	5	17	.239	.299	.293	59	-20	1	.947	11	91	46	3b74,2b57,S4		1
1940	NY N	133	568	68	160	9	4	4	36	26	2	14	.282	.319	.340	81	-16	9	.970	3	97	82	2b104/3		2
1941	NY N	116	403	41	92	15	4	1	23	14	2	21	.228	.258	.293	54	-26	7	.963	-3	92	92	2b30,3b4/S		-2
1946	Pit N	55	127	10	28	1	2	0	5	6	1	7	.220	.261	.260	47	-9	3	.972	94	106	116	2b3,3b4/S		-0
Total	9	924	3316	415	883	100	31	17	245	150	29	138	.266	.304	.331	72	-136	51					2b718,3b116,S53		

WHITEHEAD, MILT Milton P. B1862 Toronto ON, Can. D8.15.1901 Highland CA BB/TR d4.20

1884	StL U	99	393	61	83	15	1	1		8			.211	.227	.262	46	-38		.803	-12	98	151	S94,O2C/P23		-1
	KC U	5	22	2	3	0	0	0					.136	.136	.136	-20	-4		.857	0	141	0	2b3/CS3		-1
	Year	104	415	63	86	15	1	1		8			.207	.222	.255	43	-41		.804	-12	98	150	S95,2b4,O2C,3b2/PC		

WHITEHOUSE, GIL Gilbert Arthur B10.15.1893 Somerville MA D2.14.1926 Brewer ME BB/TR/5-10/170 d6.20

1912	Bos N	2	3	0	0	0	0	0	0	0		0	.000	.000	.000	-98	-1	0	.667	-1	120	0	C2		-0
1915	New F	35	120	16	27	6	2	0	9	6	1	16	.225	.268	.308	66	-8	3	.949	-0	70	206	O28(0/2/26),PC		-0
Total	2	37	123	16	27	6	2	0	9	6	1	19	.220	.262	.301	61	-9	3	.949	-1	70	206	O28(0/2/26),C3/P		

WHITELEY, GUERDON Guerdon W. B10.5.1859 Hopkinton RI D11.23.1925 Cranston RI 5-11/190 d8.7

1884	Cle N	8	34	4	5	0	0	0	1		8		.147	.171	.147	1	-4		.800	1	196	764	O8(4/3/1)		-0
1885	Bos N	33	135	14	25	2	2	1	7	1		25	.185	.191	.252	44	-9		.781	-3	123	218	O32(8/0/24)/C		-0
Total	2	41	169	18	30	2	2	1	7	2		33	.178	.187	.231	34	-13		.785	-2	136	316	O40(12/3/25)/C		

WHITEMAN, GEORGE George "Lucky" B12.23.1882 Peoria IL D2.10.1947 Houston TX BR/TR/5-7/160 d9.13

1907	Bos A	4	12	0	2	0	0	0	1	0		0	.167	.167	.167	6	-1	0	1.000	-0	0	0	O2L		-0
1913	NY A	11	32	8	11	3	1	0	7			2	.344	.462	.500	181	4	2	.938	-0	114	50	O11(4/4/3)		
1918	†Bos A	71	214	24	57	14	0	1	28	20	2	9	.266	.335	.346	107	2	9	.935	-8	68	68	O69(65/0/4)		
Total	3	86	258	32	70	17	1	1	36		2	11	.271	.345	.357	113	5	11	.936	-6	89	63	O82(71/4/7)		

WHITEN, MARK Mark Anthony B11.25.1966 Pensacola FL BB/TR/6-3/215(210-235) [TorA86*5/130] d7.12 Col Pensacola (FL) JC

1990	Tor A	33	88	12	24	1	2	7		7-0	0	14	.273	.323	.375	94	-1	1-0	1.000	3	115	165	O30(3/0/27),D2		
1991	Tor A	46	149	12	33	4	3	2	19	11-1	1	35	.221	.274	.329	65	-8	0-1	1.000	1	107	67	O42R		
	Cle A	70	258	34	66	14	4	7	26	19-1	2	50	.256	.310	.422	100	-1	4-2	.962	10	119	230	O67(0/8/63),D3		
	Year	116	407	46	99	18	7	9	45	30-2	3	85	.243	.297	.388	100	-9	4-3	.975	11	114	168	O109(0/8/105),D3		
1992	Cle A	148	508	73	129	19	4	9	43	72-10	2	102	.254	.347	.360	100	2	16-12	.980	5	103	137	O144R,D2		
1993	StL N	152	562	81	142	13	4	25	99	58-9	6	110	.253	.323	.423	99	-3	15-8	.964	11	128	130	O90R	17	
1994	StL N	92	334	57	98	18	2	14	53	37-9	0	75	.293	.364	.485	119	10	10-5	1.000	5	95	213	O31R/D	18	
1995	Bos A	32	108	13	20	3	0	1	11	23-1	0	23	.185	.239	.241	25	-12	1-0	.965	-1	98	100	O55R		
	Phi N	60	212	38	57	10	1	11	37	31-1	1	62	.269	.365	.481	120	7	7-0	.945	3	107	199	O51(0/8/44)		
1996	Phi N	60	182	33	43	8	0	7	21	33-2	1	49	.236	.356	.396	98	0	13-3	.933	-2	90	63	O29R		
	Atl N	36	90	12	21	5	1	3	17	16-2	0	38	.233	.349	.444	104	1	15-8	.942	1	116	149	O80(0/8/73)		
	Year	96	272	45	64	13	1	10	38	49-2	1	87	.243	.359	.408	100	1	15-8	.969	3	116	149	O109(36/0/4)		
	Sea A	40	140	31	42	7	0	12	33	21-4	2	40	.300	.399	.607	149	11	2-1	.954	-2	100	60	O57(44/0/16),D6		
1997	Sea A	69	215	34	57	9	0	12	30	30-5	2	47	.265	.360	.386	96	1	4-2	.970	2	99	194	O72(43/22/13)/PD		
1998	†Cle A	88	226	31	64	14	0	6	29	29-0	5	60	.283	.372	.425	103	2	2-1	1.000	-0	77	238	O7(5/2/0)	79	
1999	Cle A	8	25	2	4	1	0	0	4	3-0		4	.160	.250	.320	42	-2	0-0	1.000	-0	77	238	O7(5/2/0)		

YEAR	TM LG	G	AB	R	H	2B	3B	HR	RBI	BB-IB	HP	SO	AVG	OBP	SLG	AOPS	ABR	SB-CS	FA	FR	RNG	THR	GAMES AT POSITION	DL	BFW
2000	Cle A	6	7	2	2	1	0	0	1	3-0	0	2	.286	.500	.429	134	1	0-0	1.000	-0	64	0	O5C		0.0
Total	11	940	3104	465	804	129	20	105	423	378-42	17	712	.259	.341	.415	101	7	78-40	.970	32	106	132	O867(131/67/696),D19/P	114	0.7

WHITESIDE, ELI Dustin Eli B10.22.1979 New Albany MS BR/TR/6-2/210 d7.5 Col Delta St.

YEAR	TM LG	G	AB	R	H	2B	3B	HR	RBI	BB-IB	HP	SO	AVG	OBP	SLG	AOPS	ABR	SB-CS	FA	FR	RNG	THR	GAMES AT POSITION	DL	BFW
2005	Bal A	9	12	1	3	0	0	1	0	0-0	0	2	.250	.250	.250	34	-1	0-0	.926	-0	66	119	C9		-0.1

WHITFIELD, FRED Fred Dwight B1.7.1938 Vandiver AL BL/TL/6-1/190* d5.27

YEAR	TM LG	G	AB	R	H	2B	3B	HR	RBI	BB-IB	HP	SO	AVG	OBP	SLG	AOPS	ABR	SB-CS	FA	FR	RNG	THR	GAMES AT POSITION	DL	BFW
1962	StL N	73	158	20	42	7	1	8	34	7-1	1	30	.266	.299	.475	95	-2	1-0	.987	1	119	133	1b38		-0.2
1963	Cle A	109	346	44	87	17	3	21	54	24-5	4	61	.251	.302	.500	123	9	0-1	.987	-4	83	97	1b92		-0.1
1964	Cle A	101	293	29	79	13	1	10	29	12-3	2	58	.270	.301	.423	100	-1	0-5	.992	-3	81	111	1b79		-1.0
1965	Cle A	132	468	49	137	23	1	26	90	16-7	2	42	.293	.316	.513	131	16	2-2	.993	4	107	94	1b122		1.4
1966	Cle A	137	502	59	121	15	2	27	78	27-9	4	76	.241	.283	.440	105	1	1-2	.991	-4	85	98	1b132		-1.3
1967	Cle A	100	257	24	56	10	0	9	31	25-8	1	45	.218	.290	.362	91	-3	3-3	.993	4	120	119	1b66		-0.3
1968	Cin N	87	171	15	44	8	0	6	32	9-1	2	29	.257	.302	.409	105	1	0-3	.981	-1	102	111	1b41		-0.3
1969	Cin N	74	74	2	11	0	0	1	8	18-0	0	27	.149	.315	.189	42	-5	0-0	.985	1	181	82	1b14		-0.5
1970	Mon N	4	15	0	1	0	0	0	0	1-0	0	3	.067	.125	.067	-47	-3	0-0	.976	2	253	89	1b4		-0.2
Total	9	817	2284	242	578	93	8	108	356	139-34	16	371	.253	.298	.443	107	13	7-16	.990	1	98	103	1b588		-2.5

WHITFIELD, TERRY Terry Bertland B1.12.1953 Blythe CA BL/TR/6-1/197* [NYA71 1/19] d9.29

YEAR	TM LG	G	AB	R	H	2B	3B	HR	RBI	BB-IB	HP	SO	AVG	OBP	SLG	AOPS	ABR	SB-CS	FA	FR	RNG	THR	GAMES AT POSITION	DL	BFW
1974	NY A	2	5	1	1	0	0	0	0	0-0	0	1	.200	.200	.200	15	-1	0-0	—	-1	0	0	/OC		-0.1
1975	NY A	28	81	9	22	1	1	0	7	1-0	0	17	.272	.274	.309	67	-4	1-0	.978	1	101	173	O25(2/0/23)/D		-0.4
1976	NY A	1	0	0	0	0	0	0	0	0-0	0	0	—	—	—	—	0	0-0	—	0	0	0	/OL		0.0
1977	SF N	114	326	41	93	21	3	7	36	20-1	2	46	.285	.329	.433	103	1	2-3	.972	0	107	72	O84(22/22/49)		-0.3
1978	SF N	149	488	70	141	20	2	10	32	33-5	2	69	.289	.335	.400	108	4	5-11	.988	-1	103	66	O140(138/5/0)		-0.5
1979	SF N	133	394	52	113	20	4	6	36	36-6	4	47	.287	.349	.396	112	7	5-4	.957	0	95	138	O106(105/1/0)		0.2
1980	SF N	118	321	38	95	16	2	4	26	20-3	1	44	.296	.337	.396	108	3	4-2	.987	2	94	188	O95L		0.2
1984	LA N	87	180	15	44	8	0	4	18	17-2	1	35	.244	.313	.356	88	-3	1-4	.988	-1	91	130	O58(23/2/37)		-0.7
1985	†LA N	79	104	8	27	7	0	3	16	6-1	0	27	.260	.300	.413	100	0	0-0	.926	-1	83	188	O28(21/1/7)	15	-0.2
1986	LA N	19	14	0	1	0	0	0	0	5-2	0	2	.071	.316	.071	14	-1	0-0	1.000	0	159	0	/OL		-0.1
Total	10	730	1913	233	537	93	12	33	179	128-20	10	328	.281	.330	.394	103	6	18-24	.976	1	98	118	O539(408/32/116)/D	15	-1.9

WHITING, ED Edward C. (aka Harry Zieber) B1860 Philadelphia PA BL/TR/?/188 d5.2

YEAR	TM LG	G	AB	R	H	2B	3B	HR	RBI	BB-IB	HP	SO	AVG	OBP	SLG	AOPS	ABR	SB-CS	FA	FR	RNG	THR	GAMES AT POSITION	DL	BFW
1882	Bal AA	74	308	43	80	14	5	0		7				.260	.276	.338	115	6		.834	-6			C72,1b3,O2(1/0/1)		0.4
1883	Lou AA	58	240	35	70	16	4	2		9				.292	.317	.417	145	13		.884	-9			C50,O6(3/3/0),2b2/31		0.7
1884	Lou AA	42	157	16	35	7	3	0	18	9	2			.223	.274	.306	93	-1		.891	-6			C40,O2(1/0/1),1b2		-0.3
1886	Was N	6	21	0	0	0	0	0	1				12	.000	.045	.000	-92	-5	0	.919	-2			C6		0.2
Total	4	180	726	94	185	37	12	2	18	26			12	.255	.282	.347	114	13	0	.866	-24			C168,O10(5/3/2),1b6,2b2/3		0.2

WHITMAN, DICK Dick Corwin B11.9.1920 Woodburn OR D2.12.2003 Peoria AZ BL/TL/5-11/170* d4.16 Col Oregon

YEAR	TM LG	G	AB	R	H	2B	3B	HR	RBI	BB-IB	HP	SO	AVG	OBP	SLG	AOPS	ABR	SB-CS	FA	FR	RNG	THR	GAMES AT POSITION	DL	BFW
1946	Bro N	104	265	39	69	15	3	2	31	22	0	19	.260	.317	.362	92	-3	5	1.000	3	110	83	O85(30/54/1)		-0.4
1947	Bro N	4	10	1	4	0	0	0	2	1	0	0	.400	.455	.400	124	0	0	1.000	0	114	0	O3(2/0/1)		0.0
1948	Bro N	60	165	24	48	13	0	0	20	14	0	12	.291	.346	.370	91	-2	4	.990	1	108	95	O48(12/4/34)		-0.2
1949	†Bro N	23	49	8	9	2	0	0	2	4	0	4	.184	.245	.224	26	-5	0	.952	-1	98	0	O11(10/0/1)		-0.7
1950	†Phi N	75	132	21	33	7	0	0	12	10	0	3	.250	.317	.303	65	-6	1	.983	0	101	101	O32(7/13/15)		-0.7
1951	Phi N	19	17	0	2	0	0	0	0	1	0	1	.118	.118	.118	-37	-3	0	—	-0	0	0	O6(5/1/0)		-0.3
Total	6	285	638	93	165	37	3	2	67	51	0	46	.259	.316	.335	78	-19	10-0	.992	3	107	82	O185(66/72/52)		-2.3

WHITMAN, FRANK Walter Franklin "Hooker" B8.15.1924 Marengo IN D2.6.1994 Maryville IL BR/TR/6-2/175 d6.30

YEAR	TM LG	G	AB	R	H	2B	3B	HR	RBI	BB-IB	HP	SO	AVG	OBP	SLG	AOPS	ABR	SB-CS	FA	FR	RNG	THR	GAMES AT POSITION	DL	BFW
1946	Chi A	17	16	7	1	0	0	0	1	2	1	6	.063	.211	.063	-22	-3	0-1	1.000	1	153	0	S6/12		-0.2
1948	Chi A	3	6	0	0	0	0	0	1	0	0	3	.000	.000	.000	-99	-2	0-0	.500	-1	63	124	/S		-0.3
Total	2	20	22	7	1	0	0	0	1	2	1	9	.045	.160	.045	-43	-5	0-1	.885	-0	128	35	S7/21		-0.5

WHITMER, DAN Daniel Charles B11.23.1955 Redlands CA BR/TR/6-3/195* [AnaA78 14/352] d7.20 C3 Col Cal St.-Fullerton

YEAR	TM LG	G	AB	R	H	2B	3B	HR	RBI	BB-IB	HP	SO	AVG	OBP	SLG	AOPS	ABR	SB-CS	FA	FR	RNG	THR	GAMES AT POSITION	DL	BFW
1980	Cal A	48	87	8	21	3	0	0	7	4-0	0	21	.241	.269	.276	52	-6	1-0	1.000	3	106	72	C48		-0.2
1981	Tor A	7	9	0	1	0	0	0	0	1-0	0	2	.111	.200	.222	20	-1	0-0	1.000	1	95	0	C7		0.0
Total	2	55	96	8	22	3	0	0	7	5-0	0	23	.229	.262	.271	49	-7	1-0	1.000	3	105	66	C55		-0.2

WHITMORE, DARRELL Darrell Lamont B11.18.1968 Front Royal VA BL/TR/6-1/210* [CleA90 2/46] d6.25 Col West Virginia

YEAR	TM LG	G	AB	R	H	2B	3B	HR	RBI	BB-IB	HP	SO	AVG	OBP	SLG	AOPS	ABR	SB-CS	FA	FR	RNG	THR	GAMES AT POSITION	DL	BFW
1993	Fla N	76	250	24	51	8	2	4	19	10-0	5	72	.204	.249	.300	44	-21	4-2	.979	0	108	60	O69(1/0/69)		-2.4
1994	Fla N	9	22	1	5	1	0	0	3	3-0	0	5	.227	.320	.273	54	-1	0-1	1.000	0	125	0	O6(5/0/1)		-0.2
1995	Fla N	27	58	6	11	2	0	1	2	5-0	0	15	.190	.250	.276	39	-5	0-0	.960	-2	85	0	O16(0/14/3)		-0.7
Total	3	112	330	31	67	11	2	5	21	18-0	5	92	.203	.254	.294	44	-27	4-3	.978	-1	106	47	O91(6/14/73)	120	-3.3

WHITNEY, PINKY Arthur Carter B1.2.1905 San Antonio TX D9.1.1987 Center TX BR/TR/5-10/165 d4.11

YEAR	TM LG	G	AB	R	H	2B	3B	HR	RBI	BB-IB	HP	SO	AVG	OBP	SLG	AOPS	ABR	SB-CS	FA	FR	RNG	THR	GAMES AT POSITION	DL	BFW
1928	Phi N	151	585	73	176	35	4	10	103	36		1	30	.301	.342	.426	96	-4	3	.955	5	99	83	3b149		1.0
1929	Phi N	154	612	89	200	43	14	8	115	61	2	35	.327	.390	.482	108	8	7	.967	23	116	113	3b154		3.7
1930	Phi N	149	606	87	207	41	5	8	117	40	1	38	.342	.383	.465	97	-2	3	.965	21	113	91	3b148		2.5
1931	Phi N	130	501	64	144	36	5	9	74	30	3	38	.287	.331	.433	96	-3	6	.948	-6	91	84	3b128		-0.4
1932	Phi N	154	624	93	186	33	11	13	124	35	0	66	.298	.335	.449	97	-3	6	.960	3	97	110	3b151,2b5		0.6
1933	Phi N	31	121	12	32	4	0	3	19	8	0		.264	.310	.372	83	-3	1	.963	-1	91	144	3b30		-0.3
	Bos N	100	382	42	94	17	2	8	49	25	2	23	.246	.296	.364	95	-3	2	.971	2	110	134	3b85,2b18		0.0
	Year	131	503	54	126	21	2	11	68	33	2	31	.250	.299	.366	92	-6	3	.969	1	105	136	3b115,2b18		0.0
1934	Bos N	146	563	58	146	26	2	12	79	25	3	54	.259	.294	.377	85	-14	7	.968	2	107	72	3b111,2b36,S2		-0.6
1935	Bos N	126	458	41	125	23	4	4	60	24	2	36	.273	.312	.367	89	-8	2	.958	3	110	65	3b74,2b49		0.1
1936	Bos N	10	40	1	7	0	0	0	5	2	1		.175	.233	.175	12	-5	0	.971	1	98	144	3b10		-0.4
	Phi N★	114	411	44	121	17	3	6	59	37	1	33	.294	.354	.394	92	-4	2	.955	8	120	100	3b111/2		1.2
	Year	124	451	45	128	17	3	6	64	39	2	36	.284	.343	.375	86	-9	2	.956	13	118	104	3b121/2		0.8
1937	Phi N	138	487	56	166	19	4	8	79	43	1	44	.341	.395	.446	118	13	6	.982	3	103	93	3b130		2.1
1938	Phi N	102	300	27	83	9	1	3	38	27	0	22	.277	.336	.343	90	-4	0	.934	-4	95	60	3b75,1b4,2b2		-0.6
1939	Phi N	34	75	9	14	0	1	1	9	8	0	4	.187	.256	.253	38	-7	0	.991	1	131	98	1b12,2b8,3b2		-0.6
Total	12	1539	5765	696	1701	303	56	93	927	400	17	438	.295	.343	.415	96	-39	45	.961	67	105	95	3b1358,2b119,1b16,S2		8.6

WHITNEY, ART Arthur Wilson B1.16.1858 Brockton MA D8.15.1943 Lowell MA BR/TR/5-8/155 d5.1 b-Frank ▲

YEAR	TM LG	G	AB	R	H	2B	3B	HR	RBI	BB-IB	HP	SO	AVG	OBP	SLG	AOPS	ABR	SB-CS	FA	FR	RNG	THR	GAMES AT POSITION	DL	BFW
1880	Wor N	76	302	38	67	13	5	1	36	9			15	.222	.244	.308	79	-7		.860	-2	103	78	3b76		-0.6
1881	Det N	58	214	23	39	7	0	0	9	7			15	.182	.208	.262	45	-14		.849	7	121	111	3b58		-0.4
1882	Pro N	11	40	2	3	0	0	0	1	2			11	.075	.119	.075	-36	-6		.784	-3	97	75	S11		-0.8
	Det N	31	115	10	21	0	0	0	4	1			12	.183	.190	.183	20	-10		.854	-5	82	97	3b22,S8,P3		-1.0
	Year	42	155	12	24	0	0	0	5	3			23	.155	.171	.155	5	-16		.854	-5	82	97	3b22,S19,P3		-1.8
1884	Pit AA	23	94	10	28	4	0	0		1	0			.298	.305	.340	112	1		.916	3	121	37	3b21/OCS		0.4
1885	Pit AA	90	373	53	87	10	4	0	28	16		6		.233	.267	.282	74	-11		.918	-15	85	101	S75,3b8,2b4,O3L		-2.1
1886	Pit AA	136	511	70	122	13	4	0	55	51		6		.239	.315	.280	87	-5	15	.906	12	108	139	3b95,S42/P		0.8
1887	Pit N	119	431	57	112	11	4	0	51	55		2	18	.260	.346	.304	89	-2	10	.924	-8	96	68	3b119		-0.7
1888	†NY N	90	328	28	72	1	4	0	28	8		1	22	.220	.240	.256	59	-16	7	.887	5	103	104	3b90		-1.0
1889	†NY N	129	473	71	103	12	2	1	59	56		3	39	.218	.303	.258	57	-27	19	.882	2	98	120	3b129/P		-2.0
1890	NY P	119	442	71	97	12	3	0	45	64		3	20	.219	.320	.262	52	-31	8	.865	-12	89	74	3b88,S31		-3.2
1891	Cin AA	93	347	42	69	6	1	0	33	31		3	20	.199	.270	.248	45	-27	8	.903	-6	95	74	3b93		-2.7
	StL AA	3	11	0	0	0	0	0	0	1		0	2	.000	.083	.000	-66	-2	0	.867	1	170	0	3b3		-0.1
	Year	96	358	42	69	6	1	0	33	32		3	22	.193	.265	.240	41	-29	8	.902	-5	98	71	3b96		-2.8
Total	11	978	3681	475	820	89	32	6	349	302		18	173	.223	.285	.269	64	-157	67	.888	-18	101	94	3b802,S168,P5,2b4,O4(3/1/0)		-13.4

WHITNEY, FRANK Frank Thomas "Jumbo" B2.18.1856 Brockton MA D10.30.1943 Baltimore MD BR/TR/5-7.5/152 d5.17 b-Art

YEAR	TM LG	G	AB	R	H	2B	3B	HR	RBI	BB-IB	HP	SO	AVG	OBP	SLG	AOPS	ABR	SB-CS	FA	FR	RNG	THR	GAMES AT POSITION	DL	BFW
1876	Bos N	34	139	27	33	7	1	0	15	1			3	.237	.243	.302	79	-3		.818	1	129	278	O34(24/0/10)/2		-0.3

WHITT, ERNIE Leo Ernest B6.13.1952 Detroit MI BL/TR/6-2/200* [BosA72 15/352] d9.12 C1 Col Macomb (MI) CC

YEAR	TM LG	G	AB	R	H	2B	3B	HR	RBI	BB-IB	HP	SO	AVG	OBP	SLG	AOPS	ABR	SB-CS	FA	FR	RNG	THR	GAMES AT POSITION	DL	BFW
1976	Bos A	8	18	4	4	2	0	0	1	0	0	2	.222	.300	.500	118	0	0-0	1.000	-1	264	38	C8		0.0
1977	Tor A	23	41	4	7	3	0	0	6	2-0	0	12	.171	.200	.244	23	-4	0-0	1.000	1	94	96	C14		0.0
1978	Tor A	2	4	0	0	0	0	0	0	1-0	0	1	.000	.200	.000	-38	-1	0-0	1.000	1	0	279	/C	41	-0.3
																									0.0

YEAR	TM LG	G	AB	R	H	2B	3B	HR	RBI	BB-IB	HP	SO	AVG	OBP	SLG	AOPS	ABR	SB-CS	FA	FR	RNG	THR	GAMES AT POSITION	DL	BFV
1980	Tor A	106	295	23	70	12	6	6	34	22-0	0	30	.237	.287	.353	72	-12	1-3	.986	6	87	107	C105		-0.
1981	Tor A	74	195	16	46	9	0	1	16	20-3	0	30	.236	.307	.297	71	-7	5-2	.991	13	129	105	C72		0.
1982	Tor A	105	284	28	74	14	2	11	42	26-5	0	34	.261	.346	.440	98	-1	3-1	.982	4	105	81	C98/D		0.
1983	Tor A	123	344	53	88	15	2	17	56	50-5	1	55	.256	.346	.459	113	7	1-1	.992	14	118	108	C119		0.
1984	Tor A	124	315	35	75	12	1	15	46	43-7	1	59	.238	.327	.425	104	2	0-3	.994	13	108	83	C118	15	2.
1985	†Tor A★	139	412	55	101	21	2	19	64	47-9	1	39	.245	.326	.444	105	3	3-6	.988	13	121	80	C134	15	0.
1986	Tor A	131	395	48	106	19	2	16	56	35-3	0	39	.268	.326	.448	106	3	0-1	.991	-1	114	89	C129		2.
1987	Tor A	135	446	57	120	24	1	19	75	44-4	1	50	.269	.334	.455	105	3	0-1	.994	17	107	116	C131		1.
1988	Tor A	127	398	63	100	11	2	16	70	61-4	1	38	.251	.348	.410	112	7	4-2	.994	-3	82	99	C123		1.
1989	†Tor N	129	385	42	101	24	1	11	53	52-2	0	53	.262	.349	.416	117	10	5-4	.992	1	112	87	C115,D8	57	-1.
1990	Atl N	67	180	14	31	8	0	2	10	23-1	0	27	.172	.265	.250	41	-14	0-2	1.000	-1	80	133	C20,D2		-0.
1991	Bal A	35	62	5	15	2	0	0	3	8-0	0	12	.242	.329	.274	71	-2	0-0	.991	72	106	90	C1246,D11	128	11.
Total	15	1328	3774	447	938	176	15	134	534	436-43	4	491	.249	.324	.410	98	-6	22-26							

WHITTED, POSSUM George Bostic B2.4.1890 Durham NC D10.16.1962 Wilmington NC BR/TR/5-8.5/168 d9.16 OF(442/94/117)

YEAR	TM LG	G	AB	R	H	2B	3B	HR	RBI	BB-IB	HP	SO	AVG	OBP	SLG	AOPS	ABR	SB-CS	FA	FR	RNG	THR	GAMES AT POSITION	DL	BFV
1912	StL N	12	46	7	12	3	0	0	7	3-0	1		.261	.306	.326	75	-1	2	.857	-3	71	56	3b12		-2.
1913	StL N	123	404	44	89	10	5	3	38	31	4	44	.220	.282	.270	59	-22	9-16	.989	3	106	90	O41(20/3/18),S38,3b22,2b7,1b2		-0.
1914	StL N	20	31	3	4	1	0	0	1	0	0	9	.129	.129	.161	-14	-4	1	.889	-2	97	148	3b5,O3(2/0/2)/2		-0.
	†Bos N	66	218	36	57	11	4	2	31	18	3	18	.261	.326	.376	109	2	10	.967	-2	100	76	O38(4/25/12),2b16,1b4,3b4,S3		0.
	Year	86	249	39	61	12	4	2	32	18	3	21	.245	.304	.349	95	-2	11	.957	-3	97	14	O41(6/25/12),2b16,3b9,1b4,S3		
1915	†Phi N	128	448	46	126	17	3	1	43	29	7		.281	.331	.339	101	0	24-15	.978	-1	100	48	O119(53/66/0),1b7		0
1916	Phi N	147	526	68	148	20	12	6	68	19	2	46	.281	.309	.399	113	5	29-17	.964	3	110	92	O136L,1b16		0
1917	Phi N	149	553	69	155	24	9	3	70	30	5	56	.280	.317	.373	107	3	10	.977	4	102	114	O141L,1b10,3b7/2		0
1918	Phi N	24	86	7	21	4	0	0	3	4	0	10	.244	.278	.291	69	-3	4	.982	1	104	112	O22L/1		0
1919	Phi N	78	289	32	72	14	1	3	32	14	1	20	.249	.284	.336	80	-7	5	.955	-1	96	138	O47L,2b26,1b2		0
	Pit N	35	131	15	51	7	7	0	21	6	1	4	.389	.420	.550	183	12	7	.955	2	96	137	O48L,1b35,2b26,3b2		0
	Year	113	420	47	123	21	8	3	53	20	2	24	.293	.327	.402	112	5	12	.961	1	96	135	3b125,1b10/OL		-1
1920	Pit N	134	494	53	129	11	12	1	74	35	3	36	.261	.314	.338	85	-10	11-11	.988	6	118	62	O102(15/0/87),1b7		-0
1921	Pit N	108	403	60	114	23	7	7	63	26	1	21	.283	.328	.427	96	-3	5-10	.988	3	125	1b10/OL		-0
1922	Bro N	1	1	0	0	0	0	0	0	0	0	0	.000	.000	.000	-99	-1	0-0	—	0			/H		-6
Total	11	1025	3630	440	978	145	60	23	451	215	16	310	.269	.313	.361	95	-29	116-69	.975	5	105	87	O651L,3b177,1b92,2b50,S41		

WICKER, FLOYD Floyd Euliss B9.12.1943 Burlington NC BL/TR/6-2/175* d6.23 Col East Carolina

YEAR	TM LG	G	AB	R	H	2B	3B	HR	RBI	BB-IB	HP	SO	AVG	OBP	SLG	AOPS	ABR	SB-CS	FA	FR	RNG	THR	GAMES AT POSITION	DL	BFV
1968	StL N	5	4	2	2	0	0	0	0	0-0	0	1	.500	.500	.500	204	0	0-0	—	0		149	O11(2/7/2)		-0
1969	Mon N	41	39	2	4	0	0	0	2	2-0	0	20	.103	.146	.103	-29	-7	0-0	1.000	1		103	O12(8/0/4)		-0
1970	Mil A	15	41	3	8	1	0	1	3	1-0	0	8	.195	.214	.293	38	-4	0-0	1.000	-0		103	/H	24	-0
1971	Mil A	11	8	0	1	0	0	0	0	2-0	0	1	.125	.300	.125	24	-1	0-0	—	0			/H		-0
	SF N	9	21	3	3	0	0	0	1	1-0	0	5	.143	.250	.143	14	-2	0-0	1.000	1	108	253	O7L	24	-0
Total	4	81	113	10	18	1	0	1	6	7-0	0	33	.159	.215	.195	15	-14	0-0	1.000	1	114	83	O30(17/7/6)		

WICKLAND, AL Albert B1.27.1888 Chicago IL D3.14.1980 Port Washington WI BL/TL/5-7/155 d8.21

YEAR	TM LG	G	AB	R	H	2B	3B	HR	RBI	BB-IB	HP	SO	AVG	OBP	SLG	AOPS	ABR	SB-CS	FA	FR	RNG	THR	GAMES AT POSITION	DL	BFV
1913	Cin N	26	79	7	17	5	0	0	6	2-0	1	19	.215	.279	.405	94	-1	3-4	.983	1	111	66	O24C		-0
1914	Chi F	157	536	74	148	31	10	6	68	81	4	58	.276	.375	.405	119	9	17	.962	-2	101	88	O157(30/1/129)		-0
1915	Chi F	30	86	11	21	2	2	1	5	13	0	11	.244	.343	.349	101	-1	3	.946	-0	92	111	O24(5/0/20)		-0
	Pit F	110	389	63	117	12	8	1	30	52	2	47	.301	.386	.380	117	5	23	.968	4	116	77	O109(109/0/1)		0
	Year	140	475	74	138	14	10	2	35	65	2	58	.291	.378	.375	114	4	26	.966	3	112	82	O133(114/0/21)		0
1918	Bos N	95	332	55	87	7	13	4	32	53	2	39	.262	.367	.398	139	17	12	.975	-0	109	71	O95(1/0/94)		-0
1919	NY A	26	46	2	7	1	0	0	1	2	0	15	.152	.188	.174	-2	-6	0	1.000	-1	95	0	O15R		0
Total	5	444	1468	212	397	58	38	12	144	207	9	184	.270	.364	.386	117	23	58-4	.968	1	107	79	O424(145/25/259)		

WIDGER, CHRIS Christopher Jon B5.21.1971 Wilmington DE BR/TR/6-3/210(195-215) [SeaA92 3/82] d6.23 Col George Mason [DL 2001 Sea A 190]

YEAR	TM LG	G	AB	R	H	2B	3B	HR	RBI	BB-IB	HP	SO	AVG	OBP	SLG	AOPS	ABR	SB-CS	FA	FR	RNG	THR	GAMES AT POSITION	DL	BFV
1995	†Sea A	23	45	2	9	0	0	1	3-0		1	11	.200	.245	.267	34	-3	0-0	1.000	-6	88	0	C19,O3(2/0/1)/D		
1996	Sea A	8	11	1	2	0	0	0	0	0-0	1	5	.182	.250	.182	12	-2	0-0	.905	-2	224	0	C7		
1997	Mon N	91	278	30	65	20	3	7	37	22-1	1	59	.234	.290	.403	81	-9	2-0	.981	4	88	143	C123		
1998	Mon N	125	417	36	97	18	1	15	53	29-2	7	86	.233	.281	.388	85	-16	6-1	.983	4	88	143	C118		
1999	Mon N	124	383	42	101	24	1	14	56	28-0	7	86	.264	.325	.441	95	-4	1-4	.992	-5	77	94	C85	14	
2000	Mon N	86	281	31	67	17	2	12	34	29-3	1	61	.238	.311	.441	87	-7	1-2	.985	0	90	93	C85		
	Sea A	10	11	1	1	0	0	0	1	1-0	0	2	.091	.167	.364	30	-1	0-0	1.000	-1	0	0	C6,1b2/OR		
2002	NY A	21	64	4	19	5	0	1	5	2-0	1	9	.297	.338	.375	90	-1	0-0	.983	-3	120	66	C21	23	
2003	StL N	44	102	9	24	9	0	2	14	6-1	1	20	.235	.279	.324	59	-6	0-0	.995	-3	131	84	C41/1OR		
2005	†Chi A	45	141	18	34	8	0	4	15	10-0	1	21	.241	.296	.383	75	-5	0-2	.981	-2	82	24	C42/13D	227	
Total	9	577	1733	174	419	101	7	54	213	130-7	14	360	.242	.299	.402	80	-56	10-9	.985	-41	85	93	C547,O5(2/0/3),1b4,D2/3		

WIEDENBAUER, TOM Thomas John B11.5.1958 Menomonie WI BR/TR/6-1/180 [HouN76 7/145] d9.14

YEAR	TM LG	G	AB	R	H	2B	3B	HR	RBI	BB-IB	HP	SO	AVG	OBP	SLG	AOPS	ABR	SB-CS	FA	FR	RNG	THR	GAMES AT POSITION	DL	BFV
1979	Hou N	4	6	0	4	1	0	0	0	2-0	0	2	.667	.667	.833	326	2	0-0	1.000	-0	97	0	O3(1/1/1)		

WIEDMAN, STUMP George Edward B2.17.1861 Rochester NY D3.2.1905 New York NY BR/TR/5-7.5/165 d8.26 U1 ▲

YEAR	TM LG	G	AB	R	H	2B	3B	HR	RBI	BB-IB	HP	SO	AVG	OBP	SLG	AOPS	ABR	SB-CS	FA	FR	RNG	THR	GAMES AT POSITION	DL	BFV
1880	Buf N	23	78	8	8	1	0	0		3	2		11	.103	.125	.115	-18	-9		.893	-1	79	0	P17,O13(1/11/1)		
1881	Det N	13	47	9	12	1	0	0		3	2		2	.255	.286	.277	75	-0		.906	-2	68	0	P13		
1882	Det N	50	193	20	42	7	1	0	20	2			19	.218	.226	.264	57	-9		.909	-4	91	43	P46,O6(1/2/2)/S		
1883	Det N	79	313	34	58	6	1	1	24	4			38	.185	.196	.220	27	-27		.846	-5	101	95	P52,O35(1/5/29),2b4		
1884	Det N	81	300	24	49	6	4	0	26	13			41	.163	.198	.183	22	-26		.867	-6	78	0	P38,O7(6/1/0)/2		
1885	Det N	44	153	7	24	2	1	0	14	8			32	.157	.199	.203	30	-4		.936	3	120	155	P51,O3(1/2/0)		
1886	KC N	51	179	13	30	2	0	1	9	3			46	.168	.190	.179	12	-19	3	.837	-1	102	0	P21,O2L		
1887	Det N	21	82	12	17	2	0	1	11	3	0		3	.207	.235	.268	38	-7	6	.882	2	106	0	P12,O1(1/0/2)		
	NY AA	14	46	5	7	1	1	0	1	4				.152	.220	.217	23	-5	2	.500	-0	67	0	/P		
	NY N	1	3	0	1	0	0	0	0	0				.333	.333	.333	90	0		.714	-0	51	0	P2		
1888	NY N	2	7	1	0	0	0	0	1	2				.000	.222	.000	-24	-0		—	0		0	/P		
Total	9	379	1401	133	248	28	4	3	142	45	0		193	.177	.203	.209	28	-114	11	.885	-12	95	57	P279,O122(13/21/87),2b6,S2		

WIEGHAUS, TOM Thomas Robert B2.1.1957 Chicago Heights IL BR/TR/6-0/195* [MonN78 10/243] d10.4 Col Illinois St.

YEAR	TM LG	G	AB	R	H	2B	3B	HR	RBI	BB-IB	HP	SO	AVG	OBP	SLG	AOPS	ABR	SB-CS	FA	FR	RNG	THR	GAMES AT POSITION	DL	BFV
1981	Mon N	1	1	0	0	0	0	0	0	0-0	0		.000	.000	.000	-97	-0	0-0	1.000	0	9	0	/C		
1983	Mon N	1	0	0	0	0	0	0	0	0-0	0		—	—	—	—	0	0-0	1.000	0	0	0	/P		
1984	Hou N	6	10	0	0	0	0	0	1	1-0	0	3	.000	.083	.000	-77	-2	0-0	1.000	-0	55	118	C6		
Total	3	8	11	0	0	0	0	0	1	1-0	0	3	.000	.077	.000	-79	-2	0-0	1.000	-0	50	107	C8		

WIETELMANN, WHITEY William Frederick B3.15.1919 Zanesville OH D3.26.2002 San Diego CA BB/TR (BR 1939-41)/6-0/170 d9.6 C13

YEAR	TM LG	G	AB	R	H	2B	3B	HR	RBI	BB-IB	HP	SO	AVG	OBP	SLG	AOPS	ABR	SB-CS	FA	FR	RNG	THR	GAMES AT POSITION	DL	BFV
1939	Bos N	23	69	2	14	1	0	0	5	2	0	9	.203	.225	.217	21	-8	1	.953	1	111	81	S22/2		
1940	Bos N	35	41	3	8	1	0	0	1	5		2	.195	.283	.220	43	-3	0	.962	2	84	175	2b15,3b9,S3		
1941	Bos N	16	33	1	3	0	0	0	0	1		2	.091	.118	.091	-43	-6	0	1.000	1	110	0	2b10,S5,3b2		
1942	Bos N	13	34	4	7	2	0	0	0	4		5	.206	.289	.265	64	-1	0	.941	-1	101	107	S11/2		
1943	Bos N	153	534	33	115	14	1	0	39	46	3	40	.215	.281	.245	53	-32	9	.957	18	115	101	S153		
1944	Bos N	125	417	46	100	18	1	2	32	33	3	25	.240	.300	.302	60	-18	0	.954	-2	96	108	S103,2b23/3		
1945	Bos N	123	428	53	116	15	3	4	33	39	2	27	.271	.335	.348	89	-6	4	.972	-5	94	124	2b87,S39,3b2/P		
1946	Bos N	44	78	7	16	0	0	0	5	14	0	4	.205	.326	.205	52	-4	1	.885	-12	77	59	S22,2b14,3b6/1		
1947	Pit N	48	128	21	30	4	1	6	7	12	0	20	.234	.300	.359	64	-3	0	.952	-2	104	100	S374,2b155,3b28,P4/1		
Total	9	580	1762	170	409	55	6	7	122	156	8	131	.232	.298	.282	63	-86	14							

WIGGINS, ALAN Alan Anthony B2.17.1958 Los Angeles CA D1.6.1991 Los Angeles CA BB/TR/6-2/164* [AnaA77*1/7] d9.4 Col Pasadena (CA) City

YEAR	TM LG	G	AB	R	H	2B	3B	HR	RBI	BB-IB	HP	SO	AVG	OBP	SLG	AOPS	ABR	SB-CS	FA	FR	RNG	THR	GAMES AT POSITION	DL	BFV
1981	SD N	15	14	4	5	0	0	0		1-0	0	1	.357	.400	.357	127	0	2-0	.750	-4	115	0	O4L		60
1982	SD N	72	254	40	65	3	3	1	15	20-0	1	26	.256	.299	.303	72	-11	33-6	.967	4	104	167	O68(51/19/6)/2		
1983	SD N	144	503	83	139	20	2	3	22	65-3	1	43	.276	.360	.324	94	2	66-13	.992	7	115	100	O105(63/48/14),1b45		
1984	†SD N	158	596	106	154	19	7	3	34	75-1	1	57	.258	.342	.329	89	-6	70-21	.988	-20	92	108	2b157		
1985	SD N	10	37	3	4	2	0	0	0	4-0	0	3	.108	.103	.081	-48	-7	0-1	1.000	-4	74	67	2b9		
	Bal A	76	298	43	85	11	4	0	21	29-0	2	16	.285	.353	.349	95	-1	30-13	.960	-19	82	109	2b76		
1986	Bal A	71	239	30	60	3	1	0	11	22-0	0	20	.251	.309	.272	62	-13	21-7	.978	-5	90	105	2b66/D		

YEAR	TM LG	G	AB	R	H	2B	3B	HR	RBI	BB-IB	HP	SO	AVG	OBP	SLG	AOPS	ABR	SB-CS	FA	FR	RNG	THR	GAMES AT POSITION	DL	BFW
1987	Bal A	85	306	37	71	4	2	1	15	28-0	1	34	.232	.298	.268	53	-21	20-7	.983	1	102	95	D44,2b33,O5L		-1.7
Total	7	631	2247	346	581	61	19	5	118	235-4	8	193	.259	.330	.309	79	-61	242-68	.967	-37	90	101	2b342,O182(123/67/20),D45,1b45	60	-5.9

WIGGINTON, TY Ty Allen B10.11.1977 San Diego CA BR/TR/6-0/200(200-225) [NYN98 17/514] d5.16 Col North Carolina-Asheville

YEAR	TM LG	G	AB	R	H	2B	3B	HR	RBI	BB-IB	HP	SO	AVG	OBP	SLG	AOPS	ABR	SB-CS	FA	FR	RNG	THR	GAMES AT POSITION	DL	BFW
2002	NY N	46	116	18	35	8	0	6	18	8-0	2	19	.302	.354	.526	140	6	2-1	.900	2	87	133	3b14,1b13,2b12,O2(1/0/1)		0.7
2003	NY N	156	573	73	146	36	6	11	71	46-2	9	124	.255	.318	.396	89	-10	12-2	.962	-10	93	91	3b155		-1.7
2004	NY N	86	312	46	89	23	2	12	42	23-4	1	48	.285	.334	.487	112	5	6-1	.924	-3	102	76	3b66,2b25,1b5		0.3
	Pit N	58	182	17	40	7	0	5	24	22-2	1	34	.220	.306	.341	67	-9	1-0	.955	-4	91	83	3b56	16	-1.2
	Year	144	494	63	129	30	2	17	66	45-6	2	82	.261	.324	.433	95	-4	7-1	.938	-7	97	79	3b122,2b25,1b5		-0.9
2005	Pit N	57	155	20	40	9	1	7	25	14-0	1	30	.258	.324	.465	104	0	1-0	.894	-10	78	72	3b40,1b3/2		-1.0
Total	4	403	1338	174	350	83	9	41	180	113-8	14	255	.262	.324	.429	97	-8	21-5	.945	-25	92	86	3b331,2b38,1b21,O2(1/0/1)	16	-2.9

WILBER, DEL Delbert Quentin "Babe" B2.24.1919 Lincoln Park MI D7.18.2002 St.Petersburg FL BR/TR/6-3/200* d4.21 M1/C4

YEAR	TM LG	G	AB	R	H	2B	3B	HR	RBI	BB-IB	HP	SO	AVG	OBP	SLG	AOPS	ABR	SB-CS	FA	FR	RNG	THR	GAMES AT POSITION	DL	BFW
1946	StL N	4	4	0	0	0	0	0	0	1	0	0	.000	.200	.000	-39	-1	0	1.000	1	0	0	C4		0.0
1947	StL N	51	99	7	23	8	1	0	12	5	0	13	.232	.269	.333	57	-6	0	.983	0	115	73	C34		-0.5
1948	StL N	27	58	5	11	2	0	0	10	4	0	9	.190	.242	.224	25	-6	0	.949	-1	301	75	C26		-0.7
1949	StL N	2	4	0	1	0	0	0	0	0	0	0	.250	.250	.250	33	0	0	1.000	0	0	0	C2		-0.0
1951	Phi N	84	245	30	68	7	3	8	34	17	0	26	.278	.324	.429	102	0	0-1	.978	2	119	68	C73		0.5
1952	Phi N	2	2	0	0	0	0	0	0	0	0	1	.000	.000	.000	-99	-1	0-0	—	0			/H		-0.1
	Bos A	47	135	7	36	10	1	3	23	7	1	20	.267	.308	.422	94	-1	1-0	.995	2	122	106	C39		0.3
1953	Bos A	58	112	16	27	6	1	7	29	6	1	21	.241	.286	.500	103	0	1-0	.980	-1	103	66	C28,1b2		-0.1
1954	Bos A	24	61	2	8	2	1	1	7	4	0	6	.131	.179	.246	15	-7	0-0	.950	-3	70	102	C18		-0.1
Total	8	299	720	67	174	35	7	19	115	44	2	96	.242	.286	.389	79	-22	1-1	.978	-0	128	78	C224,1b2		-1.6

WILBORN, CLAUDE Claude Edward B9.1.1912 Woodsdale NC D11.13.1992 Roxboro NC BL/TR/6-1/180 d9.8

YEAR	TM LG	G	AB	R	H	2B	3B	HR	RBI	BB-IB	HP	SO	AVG	OBP	SLG	AOPS	ABR	SB-CS	FA	FR	RNG	THR	GAMES AT POSITION	DL	BFW
1940	Bos N	5	7	0	0	0	0	0	0	0	0	1	.000	.000	.000	-99	-2	0	.500	-1	46	0	O3R		-0.3

WILBORN, TED Thaddeaus Iglehart B12.16.1958 Waco TX BB/TR/6-0/165* [NYA76 4/88] d4.5

YEAR	TM LG	G	AB	R	H	2B	3B	HR	RBI	BB-IB	HP	SO	AVG	OBP	SLG	AOPS	ABR	SB-CS	FA	FR	RNG	THR	GAMES AT POSITION	DL	BFW
1979	Tor A	22	13	3	0	0	0	0	0	1-0	0	7	.000	.077	.000	-76	-3	0-1	.875	-1	73	0	O7(4/1/2),D4		-0.4
1980	NY A	8	8	2	2	0	0	0	1	0-0	0	1	.250	.250	.250	38	-1	0-0	1.000	1	129	720	O3(1/1/1)		0.0
Total	2	30	20	5	2	0	0	0	1	1-0	0	8	.100	.143	.100	-33	-4	0-1	.933	0	91	227	O10(5/2/3),D4		-0.4

WILEY, JOHN John d6.23

YEAR	TM LG	G	AB	R	H	2B	3B	HR	RBI	BB-IB	HP	SO	AVG	OBP	SLG	AOPS	ABR	SB-CS	FA	FR	RNG	THR	GAMES AT POSITION	DL	BFW
1884	Was U	1	4	0	0	0	0	0	0	0			.000	.000	.000	-99	-1		.333	-1	61	0	/3		-0.2

WILFONG, ROB Robert Donald B9.1.1953 Pasadena CA BL/TR/6-1/185(160-185) [MinA71 13/314] d4.10

YEAR	TM LG	G	AB	R	H	2B	3B	HR	RBI	BB-IB	HP	SO	AVG	OBP	SLG	AOPS	ABR	SB-CS	FA	FR	RNG	THR	GAMES AT POSITION	DL	BFW
1977	Min A	73	171	22	42	1	1	3	13	17-0	1	26	.246	.321	.281	66	-8	10-4	.959	-1	102	112	2b66/D		-0.5
1978	Min A	92	199	23	53	8	0	1	11	19-1	2	27	.266	.336	.322	84	-4	8-4	.986	-8	94	82	2b80,D5		-0.7
1979	Min A	140	419	71	131	22	6	9	59	29-3	2	54	.313	.352	.458	114	8	11-4	.979	19	111	111	2b133,O3(1/1/1)	15	3.3
1980	Min A	131	416	55	103	16	5	8	45	34-3	3	61	.248	.308	.368	79	-13	10-6	.995	4	104	110	2b120,O6C		-0.2
1981	Min A	93	305	32	75	11	3	3	19	29-1	0	43	.246	.311	.331	80	-1	4-1	.980	0	102	82	2b93		-0.4
1982	Min A	25	81	7	13	1	0	0	5	7-0	1	13	.160	.236	.173	14	-10	0-2	.980	1	110	125	2b22		-0.9
	†Cal A	55	102	17	25	4	2	1	11	7-1	0	17	.245	.294	.353	76	-4	4-0	.982	6	133	106	2b28,3b5,O3(1/2/0),S2/D		-0.1
	Year	80	183	24	38	5	2	1	16	14-1	1	30	.208	.268	.273	48	-13	4-2	.981	6	121	116	2b50,3b5,O3(1/2/0),S2/D		-0.5
1983	Cal A	65	177	17	45	7	1	2	17	10-1	0	25	.254	.293	.339	74	-7	0-2	.995	8	111	100	2b39,3b13,S6/D		0.3
1984	Cal A	108	307	31	76	13	2	6	33	20-0	2	53	.248	.296	.362	82	-8	3-2	.975	6	112	94	2b97,S4/D		0.2
1985	Cal A	83	217	16	41	3	0	4	13	16-1	0	32	.189	.243	.258	38	-19	1-4	.986	13	119	116	2b69,D2		-0.2
1986	†Cal A	92	288	25	63	11	3	3	33	16-2	2	34	.219	.263	.309	56	-18	1-4	.982	4	109	102	2b90		-1.1
1987	SF N	2	8	2	1	0	0	1	2	1-0	0	2	.125	.222	.500	89	0	0-0	.833	-1	55	177	2b2		-0.1
Total	11	959	2690	318	668	97	23	39	261	205-13	14	387	.248	.303	.345	77	-91	54-33	.982	51	108	102	2b839,3b18,S12,O12(2/9/1),D11	15	0.1

WILHELM, SPIDER Charles Ernest B5.23.1929 Baltimore MD D10.20.1992 Venice FL BR/TR/5-9/170 d9.6

YEAR	TM LG	G	AB	R	H	2B	3B	HR	RBI	BB-IB	HP	SO	AVG	OBP	SLG	AOPS	ABR	SB-CS	FA	FR	RNG	THR	GAMES AT POSITION	DL	BFW
1953	Phi A	7	7	1	2	1	0	0	0	0	0	3	.286	.286	.429	87	0	0-0	.875	-0	108	0	S6		0.0

WILHELM, JIM James Webster B9.20.1952 San Rafael CA BR/TR/6-3/190* [SDN74 7/145] d9.4 Col Santa Clara

YEAR	TM LG	G	AB	R	H	2B	3B	HR	RBI	BB-IB	HP	SO	AVG	OBP	SLG	AOPS	ABR	SB-CS	FA	FR	RNG	THR	GAMES AT POSITION	DL	BFW
1978	SD N	10	19	2	7	2	0	0	4	0-0	1	2	.368	.381	.474	154	1	1-0	1.000	-1	59	0	O10(3/7/0)		0.0
1979	SD N	39	103	8	25	4	3	0	8	2-0	1	12	.243	.255	.340	65	-6	1-1	.985	0	90	200	O40(4/25/1)		-0.6
Total	2	49	122	10	32	6	3	0	12	2-0	1	14	.262	.276	.361	79	-5	2-1	.987	-1	84	164	O40(7/32/1)		-0.6

WILHOIT, JOE Joseph William B12.20.1885 Hiawatha KS D9.25.1930 Santa Barbara CA BL/TR/6-2/175 d4.12 Col DePaul

YEAR	TM LG	G	AB	R	H	2B	3B	HR	RBI	BB-IB	HP	SO	AVG	OBP	SLG	AOPS	ABR	SB-CS	FA	FR	RNG	THR	GAMES AT POSITION	DL	BFW
1916	Bos N	116	383	44	88	13	4	2	38	27	1	45	.230	.282	.300	82	-8	18	.979	3	109	98	O108(1/1/106)		-1.2
1917	Bos N	54	186	20	51	5	0	1	10	17	0	15	.274	.335	.317	107	2	5	.928	-2	86	112	O52R		-0.3
	Pit N	9	10	0	2	0	0	0	1	1	0	1	.200	.273	.200	45	-1	0	1.000	1	49	686	O3(1/0/2)/1		0.0
	†NY N	34	50	9	17	2	0	0	8	8	0	5	.340	.431	.460	179	5	0	1.000	0	104	97	O11(0/2/10)		0.5
	Year	97	246	29	70	7	2	1	18	26	0	21	.285	.353	.341	118	6	5	.941	-2	88	121	O66(1/2/64)/1		0.2
1918	NY N	64	135	13	37	3	3	0	15	17	0	14	.274	.355	.341	115	3	4	.975	-1	85	137	O55(3/34/15)		0.0
1919	Bos A	6	18	7	6	0	0	0	2	5	0	2	.333	.478	.333	138	1	1	1.000	0	81	0	O5R		0.0
Total	4	283	782	93	201	23	9	3	73	75	1	82	.257	.323	.321	101	2	28	.969	1	98	109	O234(5/37/190)/1		-1.0

WILIE, DENNEY Dennis Ernest B9.22.1890 Mt.Calm TX D6.20.1966 Hayward CA BL/TL/5-8/155 d7.27 Col Baylor

YEAR	TM LG	G	AB	R	H	2B	3B	HR	RBI	BB-IB	HP	SO	AVG	OBP	SLG	AOPS	ABR	SB-CS	FA	FR	RNG	THR	GAMES AT POSITION	DL	BFW
1911	StL N	28	51	10	12	3	1	0	3	8	2	11	.235	.361	.333	97	0	3	1.000	0	90	140	O15(11/3/2)		0.0
1912	StL N	30	48	2	11	0	1	0	6	7	2	9	.229	.351	.271	73	-1	0	.917	-1	101	58	O16(3/1/12)		-0.3
1915	Cle A	45	131	14	33	4	1	2	10	26	2	18	.252	.384	.344	115	4	2-6	.910	-3	104	21	O35(11/24/0)		-0.3
Total	3	103	230	26	56	7	3	2	19	41	6	38	.243	.372	.326	102	3	5-6	.925	-4	101	49	O66(25/28/14)		-0.6

WILKE, HARRY Henry Joseph B12.14.1900 Cincinnati OH D6.21.1991 Hamilton OH BR/TR/5-10.5/171 d5.12

YEAR	TM LG	G	AB	R	H	2B	3B	HR	RBI	BB-IB	HP	SO	AVG	OBP	SLG	AOPS	ABR	SB-CS	FA	FR	RNG	THR	GAMES AT POSITION	DL	BFW
1927	Chi N	3	9	0	0	0	0	0	0	0	0	1	.000	.000	.000	-99	-3	0	1.000	0	124	0	3b3		-0.2

WILKERSON, CURTIS Curtis Vernon B4.26.1961 Petersburg VA BB/TR/5-9/158(158-175) [TexA80 4/92] d9.10

YEAR	TM LG	G	AB	R	H	2B	3B	HR	RBI	BB-IB	HP	SO	AVG	OBP	SLG	AOPS	ABR	SB-CS	FA	FR	RNG	THR	GAMES AT POSITION	DL	BFW
1983	Tex A	16	35	7	6	0	1	0	2	1-0	0	5	.171	.216	.229	23	-4	3-0	1.000	1	111	70	S9,2b2,3b2		-0.1
1984	Tex A	153	484	47	120	12	0	1	26	22-0	1	72	.248	.282	.279	54	-30	12-10	.944	-25	92	79	S116,2b47		-4.4
1985	Tex A	129	360	35	88	11	6	0	22	22-0	4	63	.244	.293	.308	64	-18	14-7	.957	0	103	84	S110,2b19,D2		-0.6
1986	Tex A	110	236	27	56	10	3	0	15	11-0	1	42	.237	.273	.305	56	-15	9-7	.968	-1	99	110	2b60,S56,D2		-1.1
1987	Tex A	85	138	28	37	5	3	2	14	6-0	1	24	.268	.308	.391	83	-4	6-3	.946	-2	89	67	S33,2b28,3b18,D4		-0.3
1988	Tex A	117	338	41	99	12	5	0	28	26-3	2	43	.293	.345	.358	95	-2	9-4	.970	5	106	98	2b87,S24,3b11/D		0.7
1989	†Chi N	77	160	18	39	4	2	1	10	8-0	0	33	.244	.278	.313	65	-8	4-2	.881	4	103	63	3b26,2b15,S7/OL		-0.3
1990	Chi N	77	186	21	41	6	1	1	16	7-2	0	36	.220	.249	.258	37	-16	2-2	.888	-3	95	71	3b52,2b14/SOL		-2.0
1991	†Pit N	85	191	20	36	9	1	2	18	15-0	0	40	.188	.243	.277	48	-14	2-1	.992	7	121	124	2b30,S15,3b14		-0.5
1992	KC A	111	296	27	74	10	1	2	29	18-3	1	47	.250	.292	.311	68	-13	18-7	.969	-13	99	92	S69,2b39,3b5/D		-1.1
1993	KC A	12	28	1	4	0	0	0	1	0-0	0	6	.143	.172	.143	-13	-5	2-0	1.000	-1	120	104	S6,2b10,S4		-0.4
Total	11	972	2452	272	600	78	23	8	179	138-8	12	403	.245	.284	.296	59	-129	81-43	.957	-19	95	84	S444,2b351,3b128,D10,O2L	140	-10.1

WILKERSON, BRAD Stephen Bradley B6.1.1977 Owensboro KY BL/TL/6-0/200* [MonN98 1/33] d7.12 Col Florida

YEAR	TM LG	G	AB	R	H	2B	3B	HR	RBI	BB-IB	HP	SO	AVG	OBP	SLG	AOPS	ABR	SB-CS	FA	FR	RNG	THR	GAMES AT POSITION	DL	BFW
2001	Mon N	47	117	11	24	7	2	1	5	17-1	0	41	.205	.304	.325	64	-6	2-1	.970	-0	97	88	O38L		-0.8
2002	Mon N	153	507	92	135	27	8	20	59	81-7	5	161	.266	.370	.469	117	12	7-8	.972	-0	88	188	O129(72/73/3),1b23		0.6
2003	Mon N	146	504	78	135	34	4	19	77	89-0	4	155	.268	.380	.464	117	15	13-10	.982	3	101	145	O135(95/42/16),1b27		1.3
2004	Mon N	160	572	112	146	39	2	32	67	106-8	4	152	.255	.374	.498	118	18	13-6	.995	10	119	101	1b86,O80(59/18/10)		1.9
2005	Was N	148	565	76	140	42	7	11	57	54-9	9	147	.248	.351	.405	105	6	8-10	.985	3	107	87	O129(38/92/6),1b25		0.5
Total	5	654	2265	369	580	149	23	83	265	377-25	20	656	.256	.365	.452	112	45	43-35	.980	16	100	144	O511(302/225/35),1b161		3.5

WILKINS, RICK Richard David B6.4.1967 Jacksonville FL BL/TR/6-2/215* [ChiN86 23/582] d6.6 Col Furman

YEAR	TM LG	G	AB	R	H	2B	3B	HR	RBI	BB-IB	HP	SO	AVG	OBP	SLG	AOPS	ABR	SB-CS	FA	FR	RNG	THR	GAMES AT POSITION	DL	BFW
1991	Chi N	86	203	21	45	9	0	6	22	19-2	1	56	.222	.307	.355	82	-5	3-3	.993	5	112	119	C82		0.4
1992	Chi N	83	244	20	66	9	1	8	22	19-0	0	53	.270	.344	.414	111	4	0-2	.993	11	117	113	C73		2.0
1993	Chi N	136	446	78	135	23	1	30	73	50-13	3	99	.303	.376	.561	148	30	2-1	.996	16	140	131	C133		5.3
1994	Chi N	100	313	44	71	25	2	7	39	40-5	2	86	.227	.317	.387	83	-7	4-3	.993	0	119	111	C95,1b2		-0.2
1995	Chi N	50	162	24	31	2	0	6	14	36-1	1	51	.191	.340	.315	75	-0	0-0	.988	-1	113	130	C49,1b2		-0.3
	Hou N	15	40	6	10	1	0	1	5	10-1	0	10	.250	.392	.350	107	1	0-0	1.000	-1	112	78	C13	65	0.1
	Year	65	202	30	41	3	0	7	19	46-2	1	61	.203	.351	.322	84	-4	0-0	.990	-2	103	119	C62,1b2		-0.2

YEAR TM LG	G	AB	R	H	2B	3B	HR	RBI	BB-IB	HP	SO	AVG	OBP	SLG	AOPS	ABR	SB-CS	FA	FR	RNG	THR	GAMES AT POSITION	DL
1996 Hou N	84	254	34	54	8	2	6	23	46-10	1	81	.213	.330	.331	83	-5	0-1	.990	-1	101	98	C82	
SF N	52	157	19	46	10	0	8	21	21-3	0	40	.293	.366	.510	134	8	0-2	.991	-5	85	164	C42,1b7	
Year	136	411	53	100	18	2	14	59	67-13	1	121	.243	.344	.399	103	3	0-3	.990	-6	96	119	C124,1b7	
1997 SF N	66	190	18	37	5	0	6	23	17-0	0	65	.195	.257	.316	51	-15	0-0	1.000	-1	31	167	C3,D2	19
†Sea A	5	12	2	3	1	0	1	4	1-0	0	2	.250	.286	.583	126	0	0-0	1.000	-1	171	63	C6,1b6,D2	
1998 Sea A	19	41	5	8	1	1	1	4	4-0	0	14	.195	.261	.341	56	-3	0-0	.957	-2	82	90	C4	
NY N	5	15	3	2	0	0	0	1	2-0	0	2	.133	.235	.133	0	-2	0-0	1.000	0	0	0	/C	
1999 LA N	3	4	0	0	0	0	0	0	0-0	0	2	.000	.000	.000	-99	-1	0-0	1.000	0	0		C3	
2000 †StL N	4	11	3	3	0	0	0	1	2-0	0	2	.273	.385	.273	69	0	0-0	1.000	3	0	125	C3	
2001 SD N	12	22	3	4	1	0	1	4	2-0	0	8	.182	.250	.364	60	-1	0-0	1.000	1	104	0	C7/1	
Total 11	720	2114	280	515	95	7	81	275	278-42	13	571	.244	.332	.410	99	-1	9-12	.992	26	116	122	C650,1b18,D4	84

WILKINS, BOBBY Robert Linwood B8.11.1922 Denton NC BR/TR/5-9/165 d4.18 Col Catawba   .943 2 128 96 S9

YEAR TM LG	G	AB	R	H	2B	3B	HR	RBI	BB-IB	HP	SO	AVG	OBP	SLG	AOPS	ABR	SB-CS	FA	FR	RNG	THR	GAMES AT POSITION	DL
1944 Phi A	24	25	7	6	0	0	0	3	1	1	4	.240	.296	.240	55	-1	0-0	.923	-1	102	96	S40,O4L	
1945 Phi A	62	154	22	40	6	0	0	4	10	1	17	.260	.305	.299	76	-5	2-4	.926	1	105	96	S49,O4L	
Total 2	86	179	29	46	6	0	0	7	11	1	21	.257	.304	.291	73	-6	2-4				96		

WILKINSON, ED Edward Henry B6.20.1890 Jacksonville OR D4.9.1918 Tucson AZ BR/TR/6-0/170 d7.4 Col St. Marys (CA)

YEAR TM LG	G	AB	R	H	2B	3B	HR	RBI	BB-IB	HP	SO	AVG	OBP	SLG	AOPS	ABR	SB-CS	FA	FR	RNG	THR	GAMES AT POSITION	DL
1911 NY A	10	13	2	3	0	0	0	1	0	0		.231	.231	.231	27	-1	0	.800	-0	104	0	O3L/2	

WILL, BOB Robert Lee "Butch" B7.15.1931 Berwyn IL BL/TL/5-10.5/175* d4.16 Col Mankato St.

YEAR TM LG	G	AB	R	H	2B	3B	HR	RBI	BB-IB	HP	SO	AVG	OBP	SLG	AOPS	ABR	SB-CS	FA	FR	RNG	THR	GAMES AT POSITION	DL
1957 Chi N	70	112	13	25	3	0	1	10	5-0	0	21	.223	.254	.277	44	-9	1-0	.963	-2	94	67	O30C	
1958 Chi N	6	4	1	1	0	0	0	0	2-0	0	0	.250	.500	.250	108		0-0	—	-0	0	0	/OR	
1960 Chi N	138	475	58	121	20	9	6	53	47-3	0	54	.255	.321	.373	91	-6	1-5	.992	1	103	91	O121(4/0/117)	
1961 Chi N	86	113	9	29	9	0	0	8	15-0	0	19	.257	.341	.336	80	-2	0-1	1.000	-1	109	0	O30(9/0/22)/1	
1962 Chi N	87	92	6	22	3	0	2	15	13-2	0	22	.239	.327	.337	78	-3	0-0	1.000	-0	107	0	O9R	
1963 Chi N	23	23	0	4	0	0	0	1	1-0	0	3	.174	.208	.174	11	-3	0-0	1.000	0	170		/1	
Total 6	410	819	87	202	35	9	9	87	83-5	0	119	.247	.314	.344	80	-23	2-6	.988	-2	103	74	O191(13/30/149),1b2	

WILLARD, JERRY Gerald Duane B3.14.1960 Oxnard CA BL/TR/6-2/195* d4.11 Col Oxnard (CA) JC

YEAR TM LG	G	AB	R	H	2B	3B	HR	RBI	BB-IB	HP	SO	AVG	OBP	SLG	AOPS	ABR	SB-CS	FA	FR	RNG	THR	GAMES AT POSITION	DL
1984 Cle A	87	246	21	55	8	1	10	37	26-0	0	55	.224	.295	.386	86	-5	1-0	.981	-5	85	109	C76/D	
1985 Cle A	104	300	39	81	13	0	7	36	28-1	1	59	.270	.333	.383	96	-1	0-1	.990	3	76	109	C96/D	
1986 Oak A	75	161	17	43	7	0	4	26	22-0	1	28	.267	.354	.385	111	4	0-1	.994	-9	76	67	C71/D	49
1987 Oak A	7	6	1	1	0	0	0	0	2-0	0	1	.167	.375	.167	54	0	0-0	1.000	-0	0	0	/13D	
1990 Chi A	3	3	0	0	0	0	0	0	0-0	0	0	.000	.000	.000	-99	-1	0-0	—	-0	0	0	/C	
1991 †Atl N	17	14	1	3	0	0	1	4	2-0	0	5	.214	.313	.429	100	0	0-0	1.000	0	0		/C	
1992 Atl N	26	23	2	8	1	0	2	7	1-1	0	3	.348	.375	.652	175	2	0-0	1.000	0	0		/C	
Mon N	21	25	0	3	0	0	0	1	1-0	0	7	.120	.154	.120	-22	-4	0-0	.952	0	139		1b5	
Year	47	48	2	11	1	0	2	8	2-1	0	10	.229	.260	.375	75	-2	0-0	.952	0	139		1b5/C	
1994 Sea A	6	5	1	1	0	0	1	3	1-0	0	1	.200	.333	.800	176	0	0-0					/CD	49
Total 8	346	783	82	195	29	1	25	114	83-2	3	161	.249	.320	.384	94	-5	1-1	.988	-11	79	98	C247,D7,1b6/3	

WILLIAMS, RIP Alva Mitchel "Buff" B1.31.1882 Carthage IL D7.23.1933 Keokuk IA BR/TR/6-0.5/187 d4.12

YEAR TM LG	G	AB	R	H	2B	3B	HR	RBI	BB-IB	HP	SO	AVG	OBP	SLG	AOPS	ABR	SB-CS	FA	FR	RNG	THR	GAMES AT POSITION	DL
1911 Bos A	95	284	36	68	8	5	0	31	24	7		.239	.314	.303	73	-10	9	.975	-0	86	111	1b57,C38	
1912 Was A	60	157	14	50	11	4	0	22	7	1		.318	.352	.439	125	4	2	.978	8	131	106	C48	
1913 Was A	66	106	9	30	6	2	1	12	9	0	16	.283	.339	.406	115	2	3	.985	-0	100	95	C18,1b9,O5(0/1/4)	
1914 Was A	81	169	17	47	8	4	1	22	13	3	19	.278	.341	.379	112	2	2-2	.975	-3	99	108	C44,1b8/OR	
1915 Was A	91	197	14	48	8	4	0	31	18	4	20	.244	.320	.325	91	-2	4-3	.967	7	117	90	C40,1b15/3	
1916 Was A	76	202	16	54	10	2	0	20	15	2	19	.267	.324	.337	100	0	5	.982	-6	60	108	1b34,C23/3	
1918 Cle A	28	71	5	17	2	2	0	7	9	0	6	.239	.325	.324	87	-1	2	.980	-1	81	99	1b21/C	
Total 7	497	1186	111	314	51	23	2	145	95	17	80	.265	.328	.352	97	-5	27-5	.977	5	110	94	C212,1b144,O6(0/1/5),3b2	

WILLIAMS, ART Arthur Franklin B8.26.1877 Somerville MA D5.16.1941 Arlington VA BL/TR d5.7 Col Tufts

YEAR TM LG	G	AB	R	H	2B	3B	HR	RBI	BB-IB	HP	SO	AVG	OBP	SLG	AOPS	ABR	SB-CS	FA	FR	RNG	THR	GAMES AT POSITION	DL
1902 Chi N	49	167	20	38	3	0	0	14	17	3		.228	.310	.246	74	-4	9	.921	-2	33	0	O26(4/0/22),1b19	

WILLIAMS, GUS August Joseph "Gloomy Gus" B5.7.1888 Omaha NE D4.16.1964 Sterling IL BL/TL/6-0/185 d4.12 b-Harry

YEAR TM LG	G	AB	R	H	2B	3B	HR	RBI	BB-IB	HP	SO	AVG	OBP	SLG	AOPS	ABR	SB-CS	FA	FR	RNG	THR	GAMES AT POSITION	DL
1911 StL A	9	26	1	7	3	0	0	4	0	1		.269	.296	.385	93	0	0	.867	-2	106	0	O7L	
1912 StL A	64	216	32	63	13	7	2	32	27	0		.292	.370	.444	138	11	18	.930	2	101	136	O62R	
1913 StL A	148	538	72	147	21	16	5	53	57	3	87	.273	.346	.400	121	13	31	.933	4	102	118	O143R	
1914 StL A	144	499	51	126	19	6	4	47	36	4	120	.253	.308	.339	98	-3	35-20	.933	1	97	131	O142(1/0/141)	
1915 StL A	45	119	15	24	2	2	1	11	6	1	16	.202	.246	.277	59	-7	11-1	.949	-2	92	66	O35R	
Total 5	410	1398	171	367	58	31	12	147	126	9	223	.263	.327	.374	110	14	95-21	.939	5	99	120	O389(8/0/381)	

WILLIAMS, BERNIE Bernabe (Figueroa) B9.13.1968 San Juan, PR BB/TR/6-2/205(180-205) d7.7

YEAR TM LG	G	AB	R	H	2B	3B	HR	RBI	BB-IB	HP	SO	AVG	OBP	SLG	AOPS	ABR	SB-CS	FA	FR	RNG	THR	GAMES AT POSITION	DL
1991 NY A	85	320	43	76	19	4	3	34	48-0	1	57	.237	.336	.350	90	-3	10-5	.979	-1	104	68	O85C	
1992 NY A	62	261	39	73	14	2	5	26	29-1	1	36	.280	.354	.406	113	5	7-6	.995	5	109	135	O62(4/55/4)	25
1993 NY A	139	567	67	152	31	4	12	68	53-4	4	106	.268	.333	.400	99	-1	9-9	.989	-4	98	64	O139C	
1994 NY A	108	408	80	118	29	1	12	57	61-2	0	54	.289	.384	.453	120	14	16-9	.990	-2	95	119	O107C	
1995 †NY A	144	563	93	173	29	9	18	82	75-1	5	98	.307	.392	.487	129	25	8-6	.982	5	117	14	O140C,D2	15
1996 NY A	143	551	108	168	26	7	29	102	82-8	0	72	.305	.391	.535	132	28	17-4	.986	-4	96	121	O128C	35
1997 †NY A★	129	509	107	167	35	6	21	100	73-7	1	80	.328	.408	.544	149	39	15-8	.993	-15	85	31	O123C,D5	37
1998 †NY A★	128	499	101	169	30	5	26	97	74-9	1	81	.339	.422	.575	164	49	15-9	.980	-3	63	51	O123C,D2	
1999 †NY A★	158	591	116	202	28	6	25	115	100-17	1	95	.342	.435	.536	149	48	9-10	.987	-2	100	96	O155C,D2	
2000 †NY A★	141	537	108	165	37	6	30	121	71-11	5	84	.307	.391	.566	141	34	13-5	1.000		-14	30	O137C,D4	
2001 †NY A★	146	540	102	166	38	0	26	94	78-11	6	67	.307	.395	.522	139	34	11-5	.994	-5	101	39	O144C/D	
2002 †NY A	154	612	102	204	37	2	19	102	83-7	3	97	.333	.415	.493	142	41	8-4	.986	-12	91	26	O147C,D7	
2003 †NY A	119	445	77	117	19	1	15	64	71-8	3	61	.263	.367	.411	107	7	5-0	.997	-3	99	109	O115C,D4	47
2004 †NY A	148	561	105	147	29	1	22	70	85-5	2	95	.262	.360	.435	106	7	1-5	.995	-7	90	43	O97C,D50	
2005 †NY A	141	485	53	121	19	1	12	64	53-1	1	75	.249	.321	.367	83	-11	1-2	.991	-4	91	124	O112C,D23	
Total 15	1945	7449	1301	2218	420	55	275	1196	1036-92	37	1159	.298	.384	.480	126	316	145-87	.990	-58	98	64	O1835(4/1828/4),D98	159

WILLIAMS, BERNIE Bernard B10.8.1948 Alameda CA BR/TR/6-1/175* [SFN66 11/217] d9.7

YEAR TM LG	G	AB	R	H	2B	3B	HR	RBI	BB-IB	HP	SO	AVG	OBP	SLG	AOPS	ABR	SB-CS	FA	FR	RNG	THR	GAMES AT POSITION	DL
1970 SF N	7	16	2	5	2	0	0	1	2-0	0	1	.313	.389	.438	122	1	1-1	1.000	1	122	326	O6L	
1971 SF N	35	73	8	13	1	0	1	5	12-2	0	24	.178	.294	.233	52	-4	1-1	.933	-3	75	0	O27(22/0/5)	
1972 SF N	46	68	12	13	3	1	3	9	7-0	0	22	.191	.267	.397	85	-2	0-0	1.000	2	121	100	O15(14/1/0)	
1974 SD N	14	15	1	2	0	0	0	0	0-0	0	6	.133	.133	.133	-27	-3	0-0	1.000	-1	48	0	O3(1/2/0)	
Total 4	102	172	23	33	6	1	4	15	21-2	0	53	.192	.280	.308	66	-8	2-2	.974	-1	95	70	O51(43/3/5)	

WILLIAMS, BILLY Billy Leo B6.15.1938 Whistler AL BL/TR/6-1/175* d8.6 C18 HF1987

YEAR TM LG	G	AB	R	H	2B	3B	HR	RBI	BB-IB	HP	SO	AVG	OBP	SLG	AOPS	ABR	SB-CS	FA	FR	RNG	THR	GAMES AT POSITION	DL
1959 Chi N	18	33	0	5	0	1	0	2	1-0	0	7	.152	.176	.212	3	-5	0-0	1.000	0	123	0	O10L	
1960 Chi N	12	47	4	13	0	2	2	7	5-0	0	12	.277	.346	.489	127	1	0-0	.962	-1	103	0	O12L	
1961 Chi N	146	529	75	147	20	7	25	86	45-11	5	70	.278	.338	.484	114	9	6-0	.954	-6	89	80	O135(110/0/27)	
1962 Chi N★	159	618	94	184	22	8	22	91	70-3	4	72	.298	.369	.466	119	17	9-9	.967	4	93	156	O160L	
1963 Chi N	161	612	87	175	36	9	25	95	68-9	2	78	.286	.358	.497	136	30	7-6	.987	6	102	120	O162(162/2/0)	
1964 Chi N★	162	645	100	201	39	2	33	98	59-8	2	84	.312	.370	.532	144	39	10-7	.950	-6	93	91	O164(34/28/106)	
1965 Chi N★	164	645	115	203	39	6	34	108	65-7	3	76	.315	.377	.552	155	48	10-1	.976	1	108	77	O162(11/0/152)	
1966 Chi N	162	648	100	179	23	5	29	91	69-16	2	61	.276	.347	.461	122	19	6-3	.989	-6	97	29	O162(161/0/6)	
1967 Chi N	162	634	92	176	21	12	28	84	68-8	7	67	.278	.346	.481	129	23	6-4	.967	-9	94	35	O163(137/0/47)	
1968 Chi N★	163	642	91	185	30	8	30	98	48-10	2	53	.288	.336	.500	140	30	4-1	.957	1	92	163	O159(153/0/28)	
1969 Chi N★	163	642	103	188	33	10	21	95	59-15	2	70	.293	.355	.474	116	13	3-2	.989	2	98	118	O160(155/0/9)	
1970 Chi N	161	636	137	205	34	4	42	129	72-9	2	65	.322	.391	.586	141	37	7-1	.977	-1	101	81	O154(151/0/4)	
1971 Chi N	157	594	86	179	27	5	28	93	77-18	3	44	.301	.383	.505	131	26	7-5	.984	-6	83	91	O144L,1b5	
1972 Chi N★	150	574	95	191	34	6	37	122	62-26	4	59	.333	.398	.606	165	50	3-1	.985	9	94	158	O138L,1b19	
1973 Chi N	156	576	72	166	22	2	20	86	76-14	1	72	.288	.369	.438	128	17	4-5	.986	3	116	84	1b65,O43(41/0/4)	
1974 Chi N	117	404	55	113	22	0	16	68	67-12	1	44	.280	.382	.453	128	17	4-5						1
1975 †Oak A	155	520	68	127	20	1	23	81	76-7	1	68	.244	.341	.419	117	12	0-0	.971	0	115	158	D145,1b7	

AR	TM LG	G	AB	R	H	2B	3B	HR	RBI	BB-IB	HP	SO	AVG	OBP	SLG	AOPS	ABR	SB-CS	FA	FR	RNG	THR	GAMES AT POSITION	DL	BFW
76	Oak A	120	351	36	74	12	0	11	41	58-15	0	44	.211	.320	.339	98	1	4-2	—	-0	0	0	D106/OL		-0.2
al	18	2488	9350	1410	2711	434	88	426	1475	1045-182	43	1046	.290	.361	.492	130	380	90-49	.973	-13	94	101	O2088(1738/30/384),D251,1b96	15	24.6

WILLIAMS, DALLAS Dallas McKinley B2.28.1958 Brooklyn NY BL/TL/5-11/165* [BalA76 1/20] d9.19 C4

81	Bal A	2	2	1	0	0	0	0	0	0-0	0	0	.500	.500	.500	190	0	0-0	1.000	0	399	0	/OL		0.0
83	Cin N	18	36	2	2	0	0	1	3-0		0	6	.056	.128	.056	-46	-7	0-0	1.000	0	111	0	O12(6/3/3)		-0.8
al	2	20	38	2	3	0	0	1	3-0		0	6	.079	.146	.079	-35	-7	0-0	1.000	0	115	0	O13(7/3/3)		-0.8

WILLIAMS, DANA Dana Lamont B3.20.1963 Weirton WV BR/TR/5-10/170 d6.19 Col Enterprise St. (AL) JC

89	Bos A	8	5	1	1	0	0	0	1	1-0	1	1	.200	.333	.400	99	0	0-0	1.000	1	0	7581	/OLD		0.1

WILLIAMS, DAVEY David Carlous B11.2.1927 Dallas TX BR/TR/5-10/160* d9.16 C2

49	NY N	13	50	7	12	1	1	5	7	0	4	.240	.333	.360	86	-1	0	.953	-5	76	73	2b13		-0.6
51	†NY N	30	64	17	17	1	0	2	8	0	8	.266	.319	.375	85	-2	1-1	1.000	1	104	71	2b22		0.0
52	NY N★	138	540	70	137	26	3	13	55	48	8	63	.254	.324	.385	95	-4	2-3	.973	-10	98	114	2b138		-0.7
53	NY N	112	340	51	101	11	2	3	34	44	3	19	.297	.382	.368	95	-4	2-5	.982	-2	100	87	2b95		0.2
54	†NY N	142	544	65	121	18	3	9	46	43	5	33	.222	.284	.316	56	-36	1-1	.982	-4	97	109	2b142		-3.0
55	NY N	82	247	25	62	4	1	4	15	17-2	2	17	.251	.303	.324	67	-12	0-2	.968	-3	99	94	2b71		-1.2
al	6	517	1785	235	450	61	10	32	163	164-2	18	144	.252	.320	.351	79	-55	6-12	.978	-24	98	102	2b481		-5.3

WILLIAMS, KEITH David Keith B4.21.1972 Bedford PA BR/TR/6-0/190 [SFN93 7/190] d6.7 Col Clemson

96	SF N	9	20	0	5	0	0	0	0	0	6	.250	.250	.250	33	-2	0-0	1.000	-0	107		O4(1/0/3)		-0.2

WILLIAMS, DEWEY Dewey Edgar "Dee" B2.5.1916 Durham NC D3.19.2000 Williston ND BR/TR/6-0/160 d6.28

44	Chi N	79	262	23	63	7	2	0	27	23	0	18	.240	.302	.282	65	-12	0	.981	2	95	136	C77		-0.6
45	†Chi N	59	100	16	28	2	2	5	13	0	13	.280	.363	.400	114	2	0	.978	3	147	116	C54		0.7
46	Chi N	4	5	0	1	0	0	0	0	0	2	.200	.200	.200	14	-1	0	1.000	0	0	0	C2		0.0
47	Chi N	3	2	0	0	0	0	0	0	0	1	.000	.000	.000	-99	-1	0	—	0	0	0	/C		-0.1
48	Cin N	48	95	9	16	2	0	1	5	10	0	18	.168	.248	.221	29	-10	0	.961	-4	71	56	C47		-1.2
al	5	193	464	48	108	11	4	3	37	46	0	52	.233	.302	.293	67	-22	0	.976	1	100	114	C181		-1.2

WILLIAMS, EARL Earl Baxter B1.27.1903 Cumberland Gap TN D3.10.1958 Knoxville TN BR/TR/6-0.5/185 d5.27 Col Maryville

28	Bos N	3	2	0	0	0	0	0	0	0	1	.000	.000	.000	-99	-1	0	1.000	0	0	0	/C		0.0

WILLIAMS, EARL Earl Craig B7.14.1948 Newark NJ BR/TR/6-3/220(195-220) d9.13 [DL 1978 Oak A 42]

70	Atl N	10	19	4	7	0	0	4	7	1-0	0	5	.368	.417	.579	165	2	0-0	1.000	2	56	51	1b4,3b3		0.3
71	Atl N	145	497	64	129	14	1	33	87	42-5	7	80	.260	.324	.491	121	12	0-1	.981	-10	68	107	C72,3b42,1b31		0.3
72	Atl N	151	565	72	146	24	2	28	87	62-6	6	118	.258	.336	.457	114	11	0-0	.980	-19	74	77	C116,3b21,1b20		-0.5
73	†Bal A	132	459	58	109	18	1	22	83	66-8	3	107	.237	.333	.425	113	8	0-2	.987	-1	116	115	C95,1b42,D2		0.8
74	†Bal A	118	413	47	105	16	0	14	52	40-3	7	79	.254	.327	.395	110	6	0-2	.983	-9	96	104	C75,1b47/D		-0.4
75	Atl N	111	383	42	92	13	0	11	50	34-2	3	63	.240	.305	.360	82	-10	0-0	.989	5	83	98	1b90,C11		-2.3
76	Mon N	61	184	18	39	3	0	9	26	19-2	1	33	.212	.286	.375	83	-5	0-0	.995	-7	95	25	C38,1b17		-1.3
	Year	61	190	17	45	10	2	8	29	14-2	0	32	.237	.285	.437	99	-1	0-0	.981	4	150	100	1b47,C13		0.0
77	Oak A	100	348	39	84	13	0	13	38	18-3	1	58	.241	.288	.391	84	-9	2-0	.989	-2	71	165	D45,C36,1b29		-1.3
al	8	889	3058	361	756	115	6	138	457	298-31	32	574	.247	.318	.424	105	14	2-5	.984	-47	86	98	C456,1b327,3b66,D48	72	-4.2

WILLIAMS, EDDIE Edward Laquan B11.1.1964 Shreveport LA BR/TR/6-0/185(175-210) [NYN83 1/4] d4.18

86	Cle A	5	7	2	1	0	0	0	0	0	1	.143	.143	.143	-22	-1	0-0	—	-0	0	0	O4L		-0.2
87	Cle A	22	64	9	11	4	0	1	4	9-0	0	19	.172	.280	.281	50	-4	0-0	.982	2	103	155	3b22		-0.3
88	Cle A	10	21	3	4	0	0	0	1	0	3	.190	.227	.190	18	-2	0-0	1.000	1	123	0	3b10		-0.2
89	Chi A	66	201	25	55	8	0	3	10	18-3	4	31	.274	.341	.358	100	1	1-2	.909	-0	103	193	3b65		0.0
90	SD N	14	42	5	12	3	0	3	4	5-2	0	6	.286	.362	.571	151	3	0-1	.897	-2	92	118	3b13		0.1
91	SD N	49	175	32	58	11	1	11	42	15-1	5	26	.331	.392	.594	158	15	0-1	.988	-2	89	83	1b46/3		0.9
92	Det A	77	296	35	77	11	1	12	47	23-0	4	47	.260	.320	.426	96	-2	0-0	.989	-1	94	97	1b81		-0.9
93	Det A	77	215	22	43	5	0	6	26	18-0	2	50	.200	.267	.307	45	-19	0-2	1.000	-1	49	228	D52,1b7,3b3,O2R		-2.2
94	LA N	8	7	0	1	0	0	0	1	1-1	0	1	.143	.250	.143	7	-1	0-0	—	0			/H		-0.1
95	Pit N	30	89	12	22	5	0	3	11	10-1	2	24	.247	.333	.404	91	-1	1-0	.991	-3	57	101	1b26		-0.6
	Year	38	96	12	23	5	0	3	12	11-2	2	25	.240	.327	.385	87	-2	1-0	.991	-3	57	101	1b26		-0.7
96	SD N	17	28	1	4	0	0	3	2-0		0	6	.143	.194	.143	-8	-5	0-0	1.000	-0	81	80	1b7		-0.5
al	10	395	1145	146	288	47	2	39	150	101-8	17	216	.252	.319	.398	90	-16	2-6	.989	-7	85	96	1b167,3b114,D52,O6(4/0/2)		-4.0

WILLIAMS, DIB Edwin Dibrell B1.19.1910 Greenbrier AR D4.2.1992 Searcy AR BR/TR/5-11.5/175 d4.27 Col Hendrix

30	Phi A	67	191	24	50	10	3	3	22	15	2	19	.262	.322	.393	77	-7	2-1	.951	3	103	77	2b39,S19/3		-0.4
31	†Phi A	86	294	41	79	12	2	6	40	19	2	35	.269	.313	.384	78	-11	2-0	.931	2	93	158	S72,2b10/OL		-0.4
32	Phi A	62	215	30	54	10	1	4	24	22	3	23	.251	.329	.363	76	-8	0-1	.952	1	105	96	2b53,S3		-0.3
33	Phi A	115	408	52	118	20	5	11	73	32	1	35	.289	.342	.444	106	2	1-0	.921	-11	90	64	S84,2b29,1b2		-0.2
34	Phi A	66	205	25	56	10	1	2	17	21	0	18	.273	.341	.361	84	-1	0-1	.956	1	109	88	2b53,S2		-0.1
35	Phi A	4	10	0	1	0	0	0	0	1	.100	.100	.100	-49	-2	0-0	1.000	1	111	0	2b2		-0.3
	Bos A	75	251	26	63	12	0	3	25	24	1	23	.251	.319	.335	65	-13	2-0	.952	-3	115	126	3b30,2b29,S15/1		-1.1
	Year	79	261	26	64	12	0	3	25	24	1	24	.245	.311	.326	61	-15	2-0	.973	-3	91	62	2b31,3b30,S15/1		-1.4
6		475	1574	198	421	74	12	29	201	133	7	140	.267	.327	.385	82	-44	7-3	.955	-11	105	89	2b215,S195,3b31,1b3/OL		-2.6

WILLIAMS, DENNY Evon Daniel B12.13.1899 Portland OR D3.23.1929 San Clemente CA BL/TR/5-8.5/150 d4.15

	Cin N	10	7	0	0	0	0	0	2	.000	.000	.000	-99	-2	0-1	1.000	0	138	0	/OL		-0.2
	Bos A	25	85	17	31	3	0	4	10	1	5	.365	.438	.400	117	3	3-3	.972	-1	89	54	O19L		0.0
	Bos A	69	218	28	50	1	3	0	13	17	0	11	.229	.285	.261	39	-21	3-3	.953	-2	99	69	O52(42/11/0)		-2.7
	Bos A	16	18	1	4	0	0	0	1	1	.222	.263	.222	29	-2	0-0	1.000	-0	97	0	O6(0/5/1)		-0.2
4		120	328	46	85	4	3	0	18	28	1	19	.259	.319	.290	56	-22	5-5	.959	-3	97	63	O78(62/16/1)		-3.1

WILLIAMS, CY Fred B12.21.1887 Wadena IN D4.23.1974 Eagle River WI BL/TL/6-2/180 d7.18 Col Notre Dame

	Chi N	28	62	3	15	1	0	1	6	0	14	.242	.309	.290	65	-3	2	1.000	1	101	126	O22(5/17/0)		-0.3
	Chi N	49	156	17	35	3	3	4	32	5	2	26	.224	.262	.359	76	-6	5-10	.976	-2	95	77	O44(36/9/0)		-1.2
	Chi N	55	94	12	19	2	2	0	5	13	3	13	.202	.312	.266	73	-3	2	.941	-0	105	74	O27(22/7/0)		-0.5
	Chi N	151	518	59	133	22	6	13	64	26	10	49	.257	.305	.398	112	5	15-10	.968	2	106	83	O149C		-0.3
	Chi N	118	405	55	113	19	9	**12**	66	51	4	64	.279	.372	.459	140	21	6	.989	-8	95	49	O116(0/115/1)		0.5
	Chi N	138	468	53	113	22	4	6	42	38	7	78	.241	.308	.338	91	-4	8	.960	11	113	135	O136C		-0.3
	Phi N	94	351	49	97	14	1	6	39	27	5	30	.276	.337	.373	109	4	10	.968	2	106	88	O91C		0.1
	Phi N	109	435	54	121	21	1	9	39	30	7	28	.278	.335	.393	111	6	9	.970	-2	99	89	O108C		-0.4
	Phi N	148	590	88	192	36	10	**15**	72	32	4	45	.325	.364	.497	139	28	18-12	.972	10	110	110	O147C		3.0
	Phi N	146	562	67	180	26	6	18	75	30	9	39	.320	.357	.488	120	9	5-15	.979	-9	102	137	O146C		0.8
	Phi N	151	584	98	180	30	4	26	92	74	6	49	.308	.392	.514	120	18	11-14	.981	-5	93	102	O150C		0.5
	Phi N	136	535	98	157	22	3	**41**	114	59	7	57	.293	.371	.576	131	22	10-11	.981	-5	100	135	O135C		1.0
	Phi N	148	558	101	183	31	11	24	93	67	3	49	.328	.403	.552	137	30	7-12	.962	-6	95	85	O135C		1.5
	Phi N	107	314	78	104	11	5	13	60	53	5	34	.331	.435	.522	132	17	4-9	.989	3	104	104	O96R		1.1
	Phi N	107	336	63	116	13	4	18	53	38	4	35	.345	.418	**.568**	155	26	2	.963	-2	85	125	O93R		1.7
	Phi N	131	492	86	135	18	2	**30**	98	61	**9**	57	.274	.365	.528	128	19	0	.970	1	90	141	O130R		1.0
	Phi N	99	238	31	61	9	0	12	37	54	2	34	.256	.400	.445	117	1	0	1.000	2	92	165	O69(20/9/40)		0.5
	Phi N	66	65	11	19	2	0	3	21	22	0	6	.292	.471	.544	144	6	0	.966	1	119	122	O11(1/9/1)		0.6
	Phi N	21	17	1	8	2	0	2	4	1	3	.471	.571	.588	169	2	0	1.000	0	376	0	O3(1/1/1)		0.2
19		2002	6780	1024	1981	306	74	251	1005	690	86	721	.292	.365	.470	123	205	115-92	.973	11	100	102	O1818(85/1374/362)		9.5

WILLIAMS, PAPA Fred B7.17.1913 Meridian MS D11.2.1993 Meridian MS BR/TR/6-1/200 d4.19

	Cle A	16	19	0	4	0	0	0	0	2	.211	.250	.211	36	-2	0-0	1.000	0	164	149	1b3		-0.1

WILLIAMS, GEORGE George B10.23.1939 Detroit MI BR/TR/5-11/165* d7.16

	Phi N	17	36	4	9	0	0	1	4-0		0	7	.250	.325	.250	56	-2	0-0	.967	2	117	115	2b15		0.0
	Hou N	5	8	1	3	1	0	0	2	0-0		1	.375	.375	.500	143	0	0-0	1.000	-0	117	105	2b3		0.1

YEAR	TM LG	G	AB	R	H	2B	3B	HR	RBI	BB-IB	HP	SO	AVG	OBP	SLG	AOPS	ABR	SB-CS	FA	FR	RNG	THR	GAMES AT POSITION	DL	BFW
1964	KC A	37	91	10	19	6	0	0	5	6-2	1	12	.209	.265	.275	49	-6	0-0	.970	-0	114	138	2b20,S2,3b2,O2L		-0.5
Total	3	59	135	15	31	7	0	0	5	10-2	1	17	.230	.288	.281	56	-8	0-0	.970	1	115	128	2b38,O2L,3b2,S2		-0.4

WILLIAMS, GEORGE   George Erik   B4.22.1969 LaCrosse WI   BB/TR/5-10/190(190-214)   [OakA91 24/645]   d7.14   Col Texas-Pan American   [DL 1998 Oak A 181]

1995	Oak A	29	79	13	23	5	1	3	14	11-2	2	21	.291	.383	.494	135	4	0-0	.956	-2	59	134	C13,D10		0.2
1996	Oak A	56	132	17	20	5	0	3	10	28-1	2	32	.152	.311	.258	47	-10	0-0	.982	-6	78	84	C43,D11		-1.4
1997	Oak A	76	201	30	58	9	1	3	22	35-0	2	46	.289	.397	.388	107	4	0-1	.984	-8	95	80	C67/D	53	0.0
2000	SD N	11	16	2	3	0	0	1	2	0-0	1	4	.188	.235	.375	54	-1	0-1	1.000	-1	58		C6		-0.2
Total	4	172	428	62	104	19	2	10	48	74-3	8	103	.243	.362	.367	91	-3	0-1	.981	-17	85	85	C129,D22	234	-1.4

WILLIAMS, GERALD   Gerald Floyd   B8.10.1966 New Orleans LA   BR/TR/6-2/190*   [NYA87 14/367]   d9.15   Col Grambling St.

1992	NY A	15	27	7	8	2	0	3	6	0-0	0	3	.296	.296	.704	173	2	2-0	.913	1	125	190	O12R		0.3
1993	NY A	42	67	11	10	2	3	0	6	1-0	2	14	.149	.183	.269	21	-8	2-0	.956	-1	87	162	O37(10/17/12)/D		-0.9
1994	NY A	57	86	19	25	8	0	4	13	4-0	0	17	.291	.319	.523	117	2	1-3	.957	-2	82	112	O43(26/8/12),D2		-0.2
1995	†NY A	100	182	33	45	18	2	6	28	22-1	1	34	.247	.327	.467	106	2	4-7	.993	8	124	162	O92(70/2/26),D2		-1.1
1996	NY A	99	233	37	63	15	4	5	30	15-2	1	39	.270	.319	.433	90	-4	7-8	.978	-3	99	23	O92(70/14/10),D2		-0.6
	Mil A	26	92	6	19	4	0	4	4	4-1	1	18	.207	.247	.250	25	-11	3-1	.981	-1	102	67	O118(70/39/11),D2		-1.1
	Year	125	325	43	82	19	4	9	34	19-3	2	57	.252	.299	.382	71	-15	10-9	.981	-4	99	137	O154(39/129/0)/D		
1997	Mil A	155	566	73	143	32	2	10	41	19-1	6	90	.253	.282	.369	68	-28	23-9	.992	1	98	137	O154(39/129/0)/D		-0.1
1998	†Atl N	129	266	46	81	19	2	10	44	17-1	3	67	.305	.352	.504	123	8	11-5	.970	5	125		O139(120/1/32)		-0.2
1999	†Atl N	143	422	76	116	24	1	17	68	33-1	6	97	.275	.335	.457	99	-2	19-11	.985	9	93	136	O138C,D7		-2.1
2000	TB A	146	632	87	173	30	4	21	89	34-0	3	103	.274	.312	.427	86	-16	12-12	.983	-6	96	85	O59C		-0.5
2001	TB A	62	232	30	48	17	0	4	17	13-0	2	42	.207	.261	.332	56	-15	10-4	.989	9	127	159	O26(6/11/12),D7		-0.7
	NY A	38	47	12	8	1	0	2	2	5-0	1	13	.170	.264	.191	23	-5	3-1	.967	-3	116	0	O85(6/70/12),D7		-1.1
	Year	100	279	42	56	18	0	6	19	18-0	3	55	.201	.262	.308	50	-20	13-5	.986	9	125	131	O30(7/6/17)		
2002	NY A	33	17	6	0	0	0	0	0	2-0	0	4	.000	.105	.000	-69	-4	2-0	1.000	-0	66	211	O16(11/2/3)		-0.2
2003	Fla N	27	31	5	4	1	0	0	3	2-0	0	11	.129	.182	.161	-10	-4	3-0	.941	-0	110		O45(21/20/7)		-0.4
2004	NY N	57	129	17	30	8	2	4	11	8-1	0	26	.233	.277	.419	78	-5	2-1	.982	-2	74	176	O27(10/10/7)		-0.3
2005	NY N	39	30	9	7	2	0	1	3	1-0	0	5	.233	.258	.400	71	-1	2-0	1.000	-0	80	207	O1056(446/453/212),D22		-0.1
Total	14	1168	3059	474	780	183	18	85	365	180-8	31	530	.255	.301	.410	82	-90	106-57	.983	11	102	115	O1056(446/453/212),D22		

WILLIAMS, GLENN   Glenn David   B7.18.1977 Gosford, New South Wales, Australia   BB/TR/6-2/195   d6.7

2005	Min A	13	40	3	17	1	0	0	3	2-0	0	7	.425	.452	.450	138	2	1-2	.929	0	105	136	3b12	96	0.

WILLIAMS, HARRY   Harry Peter   B6.23.1890 Omaha NE   D12.21.1963 Huntington Park CA   BR/TR/6-1.5/200   d8.7   b-Gus

1913	NY A	27	82	18	21	3	1	1	12	15	1	10	.256	.378	.354	114	2	6	.981	-2	79	51	1b27		0.
1914	NY A	59	178	9	29	3	1	1	17	26	5	26	.163	.287	.230	56	-9	3-6	.976	-6	69	74	1b58		-2
Total	2	86	260	27	50	8	3	2	29	41	6	36	.192	.316	.269	75	-7	9-6	.977	-8	72	67	1b85		-2

WILLIAMS, JIM   James Alfred   B4.29.1947 Zachary LA   BR/TR/6-2/190*   [ChiN65 12/391]   d9.8

1969	SD N	13	25	4	7	1	0	0	2	3-0	1	11	.280	.345	.320	94	0	0-0	.900	-1	91	0	O6L		-0.
1970	SD N	11	14	4	4	0	0	0	0	1-0	1	3	.286	.333	.286	70	-1	1-0	1.000	-0	88	0	O6(1/0/5)		-0
Total	2	24	39	8	11	1	0	0	2	4-0	2	14	.282	.341	.308	85	-1	1-0	.938	-1	90	0	O12(7/0/5)		-0

WILLIAMS, JIMY   James Francis   B10.4.1943 Santa Maria CA   BR/TR/5-10/170*   d4.26   Mil 1966   M12/C13   Col Cal St.-Fresno

1966	StL N	13	11	1	3	0	0	0	1	1-0	0	5	.273	.333	.273	71	0	1-0	1.000	-3	51	57	S7,2b3		-0
1967	StL N	1	2	0	0	0	0	0	0	0-0	1		1.000	.000	.000	-99	-0	0-0	1.000	0	39	0	/S		-0
Total	2	14	13	1	3	0	0	0	1	1-0	1	6	.231	.286	.231	46	-1	0-0	1.000	-3	49	45	S8,2b3		-0

WILLIAMS, JIMMY   James Thomas   B12.20.1876 St.Louis MO   D1.16.1965 St.Petersburg FL   BR/TR/5-9/175   d4.15

1899	Pit N	153	621	126	220	28	**27**	9	116	60	6		.354	.416	.530	159	49	26	.900	-2	101	62	3b153		4
1900	†Pit N	106	416	73	110	15	11	5	68	32	4		.264	.323	.389	95	-4	18	.889	5	101	164	3b103,S4		
1901	Bal A	130	501	113	159	26	**21**	7	96	52	4		.317	.388	.495	138	25	21	.935	-1	101	81	2b130		C
1902	Bal A	125	498	83	156	27	**21**	8	83	36	1		.313	.361	.500	131	18	14	.945	1	107	93	2b104,3b19/1		C
1903	NY A	132	502	60	134	30	12	3	82	39	5		.267	.326	.392	108	5	9	**.957**	16	112	130	2b132		C
1904	NY A	146	559	62	147	31	7	7	74	62	5		.263	.314	.354	106	5	14	.951	15	106	131	2b146		C
1905	NY A	129	470	54	107	20	8	6	62	50	3		.228	.306	.343	95	-3	14	**.964**	3	92	149	2b129		C
1906	NY A	139	501	61	139	25	7	3	77	44	5		.277	.342	.373	112	8	8	.958	14	107	78	2b139		
1907	NY A	139	504	53	136	17	11	3	63	35	1		.270	.319	.359	107	4	14	.963	3	99	114	2b148		-1
1908	StL A	148	539	63	127	20	7	4	53	55	3		.236	.310	.321	104	4	7	.962	-1	94	112	2b109		-1
1909	StL A	110	374	32	73	3	6	0	22	29	2		.195	.257	.235	60	-18	14	.962	-5	101	109	2b176,3b275,S4/1		
Total	11	1457	5485	780	1508	242	138	49	796	474	36		.275	.337	.396	114	92	151	.955	52	101	109	2b1176,3b275,S4/1		

WILLIAMS, KEN   Kenneth Roy   B6.28.1890 Grants Pass OR   D1.22.1959 Grants Pass OR   BL/TR/6-0/170   d7.14   Mil 1918

1915	Cin N	71	219	22	53	10	4	0	16	15	2	20	.242	.297	.324	86	-4	4-3	.948	-3	97	156	O62(54/8/0)		-8
1916	Cin N	10	27	1	3	0	0	0	1	2	0	5	.111	.172	.111	-12	-4	1-0	.955	1	108	210	O10(8/1/0)		-C
1918	StL A	2	1	0	0	0	0	0	0	0	0	0	.000	.000	.000	53	0		—	0			/H		-0
1919	StL A	65	227	32	68	10	5	6	35	26	4	25	.300	.376	.467	133	10	7	.937	-2	106	110	O63C		-0
1920	StL A	141	521	90	160	34	13	10	72	41	4	26	.307	.362	.480	118	12	18-8	.961	4	107	92	O138(104/34/0)		-0
1921	StL A	146	547	115	190	31	7	24	117	74	4	42	.347	.429	.561	142	36	20-17	.932	4	103	129	O145L		
1922	StL A	153	585	128	194	34	11	**39**	**155**	74	7	31	.332	.413	**.627**	163	52	37-20	.970	2	105	98	O145L		
1923	StL A	147	555	106	198	37	12	29	91	79	4	32	.357	.439	.623	168	55	18-17	.967	8	106	128	O145L		
1924	StL A	114	398	78	129	21	4	18	84	69	3	17	.324	.425	.533	138	24	20-11	.968	3	108	113	O109L		
1925	StL A	102	411	83	136	31	5	25	105	37	3	14	.331	.390	**.613**	144	25	10-5	.955	-2	105	92	O102L		
1926	StL A	108	347	55	97	15	7	17	74	39	1	23	.280	.354	.510	118	7	5-4	.948	2	101	136	O92(91/1/0)/2		
1927	StL A	131	423	70	136	23	6	17	74	57	1	30	.322	.403	.525	135	22	9-7	.965	1	105	124	O113(110/4/0)		
1928	Bos A	133	462	59	140	25	1	8	67	37	3	15	.303	.356	.413	104	2	4-9	.963	0	103	99	O39(0/30/10),1b2		
1929	Bos A	74	139	21	48	14	2	3	21	15	0	7	.345	.409	.540	146	10	1-5	.958	1	106	128	O30(15/9/8),D9		1
Total	14	1397	4862	860	1552	285	77	196	913	566	28	287	.319	.393	.530	136	247	154-106	.958	38	104	111	O1298(1132/158/10),1b2/2		

WILLIAMS, KENNY   Kenneth Royal   B4.6.1964 Berkeley CA   BR/TR/6-2/187(184-195)   [ChiA82 3/68]   d9.2

1986	Chi A	15	31	2	4	0	0	1	1-0	1	11		.129	.182	.226	10	-4	1-1	1.000	0	93	189	O10(1/4/5)/D		
1987	Chi A	116	391	48	110	18	2	11	50	10-0	9	83	.281	.314	.422	90	-6	21-10	.981	1	102	95	O115(0/111/4)		36
1988	Chi A	73	220	18	35	4	2	8	28	10-0	1	64	.159	.221	.305	46	-17	6-5	.959	0	92	108	O38(0/12/29),3b32,D3		36
1989	Det A	94	258	29	53	5	1	6	23	18-0	1	24	.205	.269	.302	62	-14	9-4	.979	9	110	257	O87(28/35/27)/1D		
1990	Det A	57	83	10	11	2	0	0	5	3-0	1	24	.133	.170	.157	-7	-12	2-2	1.000	5	109	299	O47(17/13/19),D6		
	Tor A	49	72	13	14	6	1	0	13	7-0	1	18	.194	.272	.306	61	-4	7-2	1.000	-0	95	0	O30(15/9/8),D9		
	Year	106	155	23	25	8	1	0	18	10-0	2	42	.161	.226	.232	25	-16	9-4	1.000	4	104	183	O77(32/22/27),D15		
1991	Tor A	13	29	5	6	2	0	1	3	4-0	1	5	.207	.314	.379	90	-1	1-0	.957	2	116	257	O24(9/4/11)		15
	Mon N	34	70	11	19	5	2	0	11	3-0	1	22	.271	.311	.400	100	-3	2-1	.981	17	103	164	O360(71/189/111),3b32,D22/1		87
Total	6	451	1154	136	252	42	8	27	128	56-0	17	290	.218	.268	.339	66	-57	49-25	.981	17	103	164	O360(71/189/111),3b32,D22/1		

WILLIAMS, MARK   Mark Westley   B7.28.1953 Elmira NY   BL/TL/6-0/180   d5.20   Col Manatee (FL) CC

1977	Oak A	3	2	0	0	0	0	0	0	1-0	0	1	.000	.333	.000		0-0	1.000	0	220		0	/OR		0.

WILLIAMS, MATT   Matthew Derrick   B11.28.1965 Bishop CA   BR/TR/6-2/210(205-219)   [SFN86 1/3]   d4.11   gf-Bert Griffith   Col Nevada-Las Vegas

1987	SF N	84	245	28	46	9	2	8	21	16-4	1	68	.188	.240	.339	54	-18	4-3	.975	15	114	141	S70,3b17		
1988	SF N	52	156	17	32	6	1	8	19	8-0	2	41	.205	.251	.410	91	-3	0-1	.967	2	94	142	3b43,S14		
1989	†SF N	84	292	31	59	18	1	18	50	14-1	2	72	.202	.242	.455	98	-3	1-2	.961	4	114	112	3b73,S30		
1990	SF N★	159	617	87	171	27	2	33	**122**	33-9	7	138	.277	.319	.488	123	16	7-4	.959	9	107	139	3b159		
1991	SF N	157	589	72	158	24	5	34	98	33-6	6	128	.268	.310	.499	129	18	5-5	.964	3	99	122	3b155,S4		
1992	SF N	146	529	58	120	13	5	20	66	39-11	6	109	.227	.286	.384	93	-3	7-3	.970	1	95	160	3b144		
1993	SF N	145	579	105	170	33	4	38	110	27-4	2	80	.294	.325	.561	138	27	1-3	.963	12	115	130	3b110		16
1994	SF N★	112	445	74	119	16	3	**43**	96	33-8	2	87	.267	.319	.607	140	22	1-0	.958	7	119	80	3b74		76
1995	SF N★	76	283	53	95	17	1	23	65	30-8	2	58	.336	.399	.647	175	30	2-0	.958	7	99	117	3b92,1b13/S		56
1996	SF N★	105	404	69	122	16	1	22	85	33-9	6	91	.302	.367	.510	133	19	1-2	.951	2	99	117	3b151		
1997	†Cle A	151	596	86	157	32	3	32	105	34-4	4	108	.263	.307	.488	100	-3	12-4	.970	13	114	82	3b151		

YEAR	TM LG	G	AB	R	H	2B	3B	HR	RBI	BB-IB	HP	SO	AVG	OBP	SLG	AOPS	ABR	SB-CS	FA	FR	RNG	THR	GAMES AT POSITION	DL	BFW
1998	Ari N	135	510	72	136	26	1	20	71	43-8	3	102	.267	.327	.439	99	-2	5-1	.972	7	110	82	3b134		0.7
1999	†Ari N★	154	627	98	190	37	2	35	142	41-9	2	93	.303	.344	.536	118	15	2-0	.977	3	95	128	3b153	16	1.8
2000	Ari N	96	371	43	102	18	2	12	47	20-1	3	51	.275	.315	.431	83	-11	1-2	.964	1	92	123	3b94/D		-0.9
2001	†Ari N	106	408	58	112	30	1	16	65	22-3	3	70	.275	.314	.466	92	-5	1-0	.963	-0	94	115	3b102,S2	66	-0.4
2002	Ari N	60	215	29	56	7	2	12	40	21-1	0	41	.260	.324	.479	102	-1	3-1	.969	-4	87	75	3b56	55	-0.4
2003	Ari N	44	134	17	33	9	0	4	16	16-1	1	26	.246	.327	.403	84	-3	0-0	.959	1	100	76	3b42	102	-0.1
Total	17	1866	7000	997	1878	338	35	378	1218	469-86	55	1363	.268	.317	.489	112	90	53-35	.963	86	104	118	3b1743,S121,1b13/D	387	18.8

WILLIAMS, OTTO Otto George B11.2.1877 Newark NJ D3.19.1937 Omaha NE BR/TR/5-8/165 d10.5 C4

YEAR	TM LG	G	AB	R	H	2B	3B	HR	RBI	BB-IB	HP	SO	AVG	OBP	SLG	AOPS	ABR	SB-CS	FA	FR	RNG	THR	GAMES AT POSITION	DL	BFW
1902	StL N	2	5	0	2	0	0	0	2	1	0		.400	.500	.400	186	-1	1	.813	0	119		S2		0.1
1903	StL N	53	187	10	38	4	2	0	9	9	0		.203	.240	.246	40	-15	6	.885	-4	103	86	S52/2		-1.7
	Chi N	38	130	14	29	5	0	0	13	4	0		.223	.246	.262	46	-9	8	.937	3	111	111	S26,2b7,1b3/3		-0.6
	Year	91	317	24	67	9	2	0	22	13	0		.211	.242	.252	42	-25	14	.904	-1	106	94	S78,2b8,1b3/3		-2.3
1904	Chi N	57	185	21	37	4	1	0	8	13	1		.200	.256	.232	51	-11	9	.973	-0	110	139	O21(0/8/13),1b11,S10,2b6,3b6		-1.2
1906	Was A	20	51	3	7	0	0	0	2	2	1		.137	.185	.137	1	-6	0	.897	-0	100	42	S8,2b6,1b2/3		-0.7
Total	4	170	558	48	113	13	3	0	34	29	2		.203	.244	.237	43	-40	24	.905	-1	106	80	S98,O21(0/8/13),2b20,1b16,3b8		-4.1

WILLIAMS, REGGIE Reginald Bernard B5.5.1966 Laurens SC BB/TR/6-1/180* [SFN88 25/646] d9.8 Col South Carolina-Aiken

YEAR	TM LG	G	AB	R	H	2B	3B	HR	RBI	BB-IB	HP	SO	AVG	OBP	SLG	AOPS	ABR	SB-CS	FA	FR	RNG	THR	GAMES AT POSITION	DL	BFW
1992	Cal A	14	26	5	6	1	0	0	1	1-0	0	10	.231	.259	.346	67	-1	0-2	1.000	-1	110		O12C,D2		-0.2
1995	LA N	15	11	2	1	0	0	0	1	2-0	0	3	.091	.231	.091	-12	-2	0-0	1.000	-1	79		O14(10/1/4)		-0.2
1998	Ana A	29	36	7	13	1	0	1	5	7-0	1	11	.361	.477	.472	146	3	3-3	1.000	-0	106	0	O24(19/5/2),D2		0.2
1999	Ana A	30	63	8	14	1	2	1	8	4-0	0	21	.222	.286	.349	62	-4	2-1	.974	2	94	251	O24(4/3/18),D3	17	-0.3
Total	4	88	136	22	34	3	3	2	14	15-0	1	45	.250	.331	.360	81	-4	5-6	.989	1	99	104	O74(33/21/24),D7	17	-0.5

WILLIAMS, REGGIE Reginald Dewayne B8.29.1960 Memphis TN BR/TR/5-11/185(180-193) [LAN82 13/333] d9.2 Col Southern A&M

YEAR	TM LG	G	AB	R	H	2B	3B	HR	RBI	BB-IB	HP	SO	AVG	OBP	SLG	AOPS	ABR	SB-CS	FA	FR	RNG	THR	GAMES AT POSITION	DL	BFW
1985	LA N	22	9	4	3	0	0	0	0	0-0	0	4	.333	.333	.333	89	0	1-0	.900	1	115	383	O15(12/2/1)		0.1
1986	LA N	128	303	35	84	14	2	4	32	23-9	2	57	.277	.331	.376	102	-0	9-3	.984	-4	90	87	O124(26/79/35)		-0.6
1987	LA N	39	36	6	4	0	0	0	4	5-0	0	9	.111	.214	.111	-9	-6	1-1	.913	-1	95	0	O30(16/6/9)		-0.7
1988	Cle A	11	31	7	7	2	0	1	3	0-0	0	6	.226	.226	.387	66	-2	0-0	1.000	0	78	212	O11(10/0/3)		-0.2
Total	4	200	379	52	98	16	2	5	39	28-9	2	76	.259	.311	.351	87	-8	11-4	.974	-5	90	97	O180(64/87/48)		-1.4

WILLIAMS, DICK Richard Hirschfeld B5.7.1929 St.Louis MO BR/TR/6-0/190* d6.10 M21/C1 OF(283/156/64)

YEAR	TM LG	G	AB	R	H	2B	3B	HR	RBI	BB-IB	HP	SO	AVG	OBP	SLG	AOPS	ABR	SB-CS	FA	FR	RNG	THR	GAMES AT POSITION	DL	BFW
1951	Bro N	23	60	5	12	3	1	1	5	2	0	10	.200	.250	.333	54	-4	0-0	1.000	-1	84	97	O15L		-0.6
1952	Bro N	36	68	13	21	4	1	0	11	2	0	10	.309	.329	.397	99	0	0-0	1.000	1	117	76	O25(19/6/0)/13		-0.5
1953	†Bro N	30	55	4	12	2	0	2	5	3	1	10	.218	.271	.364	62	-3	0-0	.923	-1	96	0	O24(17/2/9)		-0.5
1954	Bro N	16	34	5	5	0	0	1	2	2	0	7	.147	.189	.235	11	-5	0-0	1.000	-1	80	0	O14(13/2/0)		-0.6
1956	Bro N	7	7	0	2	0	0	0	0	0	0	0	.286	.286	.286	50	0	0-0	—	0			/H		-0.1
	Bal A	87	353	45	101	18	4	11	37	30-1	0	40	.286	.342	.453	117	7	5-5	.990	-1	104	35	O81(9/66/19),1b10,2b10,3b4		0.1
1957	Bal A	47	167	16	39	2	1	1	17	14-3	0	21	.234	.293	.335	76	-6	0-1	1.000	3	102	237	O26(15/14/2),3b15,1b12		-0.6
	Cle A	67	205	33	58	7	0	6	17	12-0	1	19	.283	.324	.405	99	-1	3-4	.973	-2	103	53	O37(18/20/0),3b19		-0.5
	Year	114	372	49	97	17	2	7	34	26-3	1	40	.261	.310	.374	89	-7	3-5	.984	1	103	125	O63(33/34/2),3b34,1b12		-1.1
1958	Bal A	128	409	36	113	17	0	4	32	37-4	2	47	.276	.336	.347	94	-2	0-6	1.000	-3	103	144	O70(34/41/15),3b45,1b26,2b7		-1.2
1959	KC A	130	488	72	130	33	1	16	75	28-1	5	60	.266	.309	.436	102	0	4-1	.957	-2	98	65	3b80,1b32,O23(13/2/8),2b3		-0.4
1960	KC A	127	420	47	121	31	0	12	65	39-3	1	68	.288	.346	.448	113	8	0-0	.951	6	101	109	3b57,1b34,O25L		1.1
1961	Bal A	103	310	37	64	15	2	8	24	20-0	0	38	.206	.251	.345	61	-19	0-4	.968	-5	73	89	O75(73/2/2),1b20,3b2		-2.9
1962	Bal A	82	178	20	44	7	1	1	18	14-1	1	26	.247	.305	.315	72	-7	0-0	1.000	0	108	0	O29(21/0/9),1b21,3b4		-0.9
1963	Bos A	79	136	15	35	8	0	2	12	15-0	1	25	.257	.329	.360	91	-1	0-0	.976	-2	94	38	3b17,1b11,O7L		-0.4
1964	Bos A	61	69	10	11	4	1	1	7	7-0	1	16	.159	.247	.406	74	-3	0-0	1.000	3	137	54	1b21,3b13,O5(4/1/0)		0.0
Total	13	1023	2959	358	768	157	12	70	331	227-12	12	392	.260	.312	.392	92	-36	12-21	.989	-5	100	81	O456L,3b257,1b188,2b20		-7.5

WILLIAMS, RINALDO Rinaldo Lewis B12.18.1893 Santa Cruz CA D4.24.1966 Cottonwood AZ BL/TR d10.8

YEAR	TM LG	G	AB	R	H	2B	3B	HR	RBI	BB-IB	HP	SO	AVG	OBP	SLG	AOPS	ABR	SB-CS	FA	FR	RNG	THR	GAMES AT POSITION	DL	BFW
1914	Bro F	4	15	1	4	2	0	0	0	0	0	0	.267	.267	.400	81	-1	0-0	.923	0	111	0	3b4		-0.1

WILLIAMS, BOB Robert Elias B4.27.1884 Monday OH D8.6.1962 Nelsonville OH BR/TR/6-0/190 d7.3

YEAR	TM LG	G	AB	R	H	2B	3B	HR	RBI	BB-IB	HP	SO	AVG	OBP	SLG	AOPS	ABR	SB-CS	FA	FR	RNG	THR	GAMES AT POSITION	DL	BFW
1911	NY A	20	47	3	9	2	0	0	8	5	0		.191	.269	.234	38	-4	1	.942	-1	95	123	C20		-0.4
1912	NY A	20	44	7	6	1	0	0	3	9	0		.136	.283	.159	26	-4	0	.930	-2	90	69	C20		-0.5
1913	NY A	6	19	0	3	0	0	0	0	1	0	3	.158	.200	.158	5	-2	0	.971	-1	72	120	C6		-0.3
Total	3	46	110	10	18	3	0	0	11	15	0	3	.164	.264	.191	28	-8	1	.941	-4	89	99	C46		-1.2

WILLIAMS, TED Theodore Samuel "The Kid","The Thumper","The Splendid Splinter" B8.30.1918 San Diego CA D7.5.2002 Inverness FL BL/TR/6-3/205(190-205) d4.20 Mil 1943-45, 1952-53
HF1966

YEAR	TM LG	G	AB	R	H	2B	3B	HR	RBI	BB-IB	HP	SO	AVG	OBP	SLG	AOPS	ABR	SB-CS	FA	FR	RNG	THR	GAMES AT POSITION	DL	BFW
1939	Bos A	149	565	131	185	44	11	31	**145**	107	2	64	.327	.436	.609	158	53	2-1	.945	1	106	94	O149R		4.1
1940	Bos A★	144	561	**134**	193	43	14	23	113	96	3	54	.344	**.442**	.594	159	53	4-4	.960	-1	96	119	O143(128/0/16)/P		4.0
1941	Bos A★	143	456	**135**	185	33	3	**37**	120	**147**	3	27	**.406**	**.553**	**.735**	232	102	2-4	.961	-3	95	100	O133(130/0/4)		8.5
1942	Bos A★	150	522	**141**	186	34	5	**36**	**137**	**145**	4	51	.356	**.499**	**.648**	214	90	3-2	.988	4	100	130	O150L		8.5
1946	†Bos A★	150	514	**142**	176	37	8	38	123	156	2	44	.342	**.497**	**.667**	211	88	0-0	.971	2	106	73	O150L		8.1
1947	Bos A★	156	528	**125**	181	40	9	**32**	**114**	**162**	2	47	.343	**.499**	.634	199	83	0-1	.975	1	100	94	O134L		7.2
1948	Bos A★	137	509	124	188	**44**	3	25	127	126	3	41	**.369**	**.497**	.615	185	71	4-0	.983	-0	99	92	O134L		5.9
1949	Bos A★	**155**	566	**150**	194	**39**	3	**43**	**159**	**162**	2	48	.343	**.490**	**.650**	187	80	1-1	.983	-0	98	103	O155L		6.4
1950	Bos A★	89	334	82	106	24	1	28	97	82	2	21	.317	.452	.647	163	34	3-0	.956	-5	87	106	O86L		2.2
1951	Bos A★	148	531	109	169	28	4	30	126	**144**	0	45	.318	**.464**	**.556**	159	52	1-1	.988	2	97	105	O147L		4.1
1952	Bos A★	6	10	2	4	0	1	1	3	2	0	2	.400	.500	.900	264		0-0	1.000	0	103	0	O2L		0.2
1954	Bos A★	37	91	17	37	6	0	13	34	19	0	10	.407	.509	.901	261	21	0-1	.970	-2	77	69	O26L		1.7
1955	Bos A★	117	386	93	133	23	4	1	29	89	**136**	1	32	.345	**.513**	.635	193	61	0-1	.982	-4	93	71	O115L		5.1
1956	Bos A★	98	320	71	114	21	3	28	83	91-**17**	2	24	.356	.496	.703	203	52	2-0	.989	-4	92	68	O93L		4.3
1957	Bos A★	132	420	96	163	28	1	38	87	119-**33**	5	43	**.388**	**.526**	**.731**	227	84	0-1	.995	-6	90	32	O125L		2.9
1958	Bos A★	129	411	81	135	23	2	26	85	98-12	4	49	**.328**	**.458**	.584	174	48	1-0	.957	-11	78	49	O114L		7.1
1959	Bos A★	103	272	32	69	15	0	10	43	52-6	2	27	.254	.372	.419	113	7	0-0	.970	-5	77	103	O76L		3.2
1960	Bos A★	113	310	56	98	15	0	29	72	75-7	3	41	.316	.451	.645	187	42	1-1	.993	-3	81	112	O87L		3.4
Total	19	2292	7706	1798	2654	525	71	521	1839	2021-**86**	39	709	.344	.482	.634	186	1067	24-17	.974	-39	95	92	O2151(1984/0/169)/P		86.8

WILLIAMS, WALT Walter Allen "No-Neck" B12.19.1943 Brownwood TX BR/TR/5-6/185* d4.21 C1 Col San Francisco (CA) City

YEAR	TM LG	G	AB	R	H	2B	3B	HR	RBI	BB-IB	HP	SO	AVG	OBP	SLG	AOPS	ABR	SB-CS	FA	FR	RNG	THR	GAMES AT POSITION	DL	BFW
1964	Hou N	10	9	1	0	0	0	0	0	0-0	0	4	.000	.000	.000	-99	-2	1-0	1.000	-0	84	0	O5L		-0.3
1967	Chi A	104	275	35	66	16	3	3	15	17-0	2	20	.240	.289	.353	92	-3	3-2	.983	1	97	136	O73(59/0/21)		-0.3
1968	Chi A	63	133	6	32	6	0	1	8	4-1	0	17	.241	.271	.308	75	-4	0-1	1.000	-0	94	119	O34(9/0/28)	24	-0.5
1969	Chi A	135	471	59	143	22	1	3	32	26-1	3	33	.304	.343	.374	96	-2	6-2	.985	3	94	156	O111(34/0/83)		-0.7
1970	Chi A	110	315	43	79	18	1	3	15	19-0	2	30	.251	.296	.343	73	-11	3-3	.949	3	92	260	O79(13/3/64)		-1.3
1971	Chi A	114	361	43	106	17	3	8	35	24-1	5	27	.294	.344	.424	114	6	5-5	1.000	1	102	76	O90(35/0/62)/3		0.2
1972	Chi A	77	221	22	55	7	2	11	13-1	0	20	.249	.289	.317	79	-6	6-1	.990	-4	102	175	O57(5/0/53)/3	16	-0.1
1973	Cle A	104	350	43	101	15	1	8	38	14-2	1	29	.289	.316	.406	100	-1	9-4	.970	-4	100	167	O61L,D26		-0.1
1974	NY A	43	53	5	6	0	0	0	3	1-0	0	10	.113	.127	.113	-30	-9	1-0	.955	-1	88	119	O24(13/0/13),D3		-1.1
1975	NY A	82	185	27	52	5	1	5	16	4-0	3	23	.281	.320	.400	104	0	0-1	.982	-2	102	53	O31(8/10/14),D17,2b6	40	-0.4
Total	10	842	2373	284	640	106	11	33	173	126-7	18	211	.270	.310	.365	91	-32	34-19	.981	13	97	149	O565(242/13/338),D46,2b6,3b2	40	-5.3

WILLIAMS, WASH Washington J. B Philadelphia PA D1.1890 Philadelphia PA 5-11/180 d8.5

YEAR	TM LG	G	AB	R	H	2B	3B	HR	RBI	BB-IB	HP	SO	AVG	OBP	SLG	AOPS	ABR	SB-CS	FA	FR	RNG	THR	GAMES AT POSITION	DL	BFW
1884	Ric AA	2	8	0	2	0	0	0		0	0		.250	.250	.250	64	0		.500	-1	0	0	O2R		-0.1
1885	Chi N	1	4	0	1	0	0	0	0	0	0		.250	.250	.250	54	0		.500	-0	0	0	/ORP		-0.1
Total	2	3	12	0	3	0	0	0	0	0	0		.250	.250	.250	61	0		.500	-1	0	0	O3R/P		-0.2

WILLIAMS, BILLY William B6.13.1933 Newberry SC BL/TR/6-3/195 d8.15

YEAR	TM LG	G	AB	R	H	2B	3B	HR	RBI	BB-IB	HP	SO	AVG	OBP	SLG	AOPS	ABR	SB-CS	FA	FR	RNG	THR	GAMES AT POSITION	DL	BFW
1959	Sea A	4	10	1	0	0	0	0	1	1-0	1	9	.000	.167	.000	-50	-2	0-0	1.000	1	19	884	O3R		-0.2

WILLIAMS, WOODY Woodrow Wilson B8.21.1912 Pamplin VA D2.24.1995 Appomattox VA BR/TR/5-11/175 d9.5

YEAR	TM LG	G	AB	R	H	2B	3B	HR	RBI	BB-IB	HP	SO	AVG	OBP	SLG	AOPS	ABR	SB-CS	FA	FR	RNG	THR	GAMES AT POSITION	DL	BFW
1938	Bro N	20	51	6	17	1	1	0	6	3	1	1	.333	.389	.392	111	1	1	.931	-5	74	52	S18/3		-0.3
1943	Cin N	30	69	8	26	2	1	0	11	1	0	5	.377	.386	.435	139	3	0	.986	-0	110	71	2b12,3b7,S5		0.4
1944	Cin N	**155**	653	73	157	33	1	3	35	44	2	24	.240	.290	.289	66	-30	7	**.971**	16	**116**	119	2b155		-0.6

YEAR	TM LG	G	AB	R	H	2B	3B	HR	RBI	BB-IB	HP	SO	AVG	OBP	SLG	AOPS	ABR	SB-CS	FA	FR	RNG	THR	GAMES AT POSITION	DL	BFW
1945	Cin N	133	482	46	114	14	0	0	27	39	2	24	.237	.296	.266	58	-27	6	.969	-8	102	85	2b133		-2.8
Total	4	338	1255	133	314	40	5	1	79	88	4	52	.250	.301	.292	69	-53	14	.971	3	110	103	2b300,S23,3b8		-3.3

WILLIAMSON, ANTONE Anthony Joseph B7.18.1973 Harbor City CA BL/TR/6-1/195 [MilA94 1/4] d5.31 Col Arizona St.   -0.8

YEAR	TM LG	G	AB	R	H	2B	3B	HR	RBI	BB-IB	HP	SO	AVG	OBP	SLG	AOPS	ABR	SB-CS	FA	FR	RNG	THR	GAMES AT POSITION	DL	BFW
1997	Mil A	24	54	2	11	3	0	0	6	4-0	0	8	.204	.254	.259	35	-5	0-1	.977	-2	56	69	1b14,D4		-0.

WILLIAMSON, ED Edward Nagle B10.24.1857 Philadelphia PA D3.3.1894 Mountain Valley Springs AR BR/TR/5-11/210 d5.1 ▲

YEAR	TM LG	G	AB	R	H	2B	3B	HR	RBI	BB-IB	HP	SO	AVG	OBP	SLG	AOPS	ABR	SB-CS	FA	FR	RNG	THR	GAMES AT POSITION	DL	BFW
1878	Ind N	63	250	31	58	10	2	1	19	5		15	.232	.247	.300	91	-1		.867	-5	93	77	3b63		-0.4
1879	Chi N	80	320	66	94	20	13	1	36	24		31	.294	.343	.447	149	17		.871	18	131	158	3b70,1b6,C4		3.3
1880	Chi N	75	311	65	78	20	2	0	31	15		26	.251	.285	.328	101	1		.893	11	113	88	3b63,C11,2b3		1.3
1881	Chi N	82	343	56	92	12	6	1	48	19		19	.268	.307	.347	100	0		.909	21	128	94	3b76,2b4,P3,S2/C		2.6
1882	Chi N	83	348	66	98	27	4	3	60	27		21	.282	.333	.408	130	13		.881	15	120	171	3b83/P		2.4
1883	Chi N	98	402	83	111	49	5	2	59	22		48	.276	.314	.438	116	8		.807	18	133	155	3b97,C3/P		2.4
1884	Chi N	107	417	84	116	18	8	27	84	42		56	.278	.344	.554	164	29		.861	22	131	202	3b99,C10,P2		4.7
1885	†Chi N	113	407	87	97	16	5	3	65	75		60	.238	.357	.324	107	5		.892	9	115	140	3b113,P2/C		-0.
1886	†Chi N	121	430	69	93	17	8	6	58	80		71	.216	.339	.335	92	-3	13	.869	-5	94	117	S121,C4,P2		-2.
1887	Chi N	127	439	77	117	20	14	9	78	73	5	57	.267	.377	.437	111	6	45	.890	-33	84	78	S127/P		0.
1888	Chi N	132	452	75	113	9	14	8	73	65	6	71	.250	.317	.385	126	14	25	.884	-13	96	126	S132		-2.
1889	Chi N	47	173	16	41	3	1	1	20	23	4	22	.237	.340	.283	71	-6	2	.809	-11	85	77	3b52,S21		-2.
1890	Chi P	73	261	34	51	7	3	2	26	36	8	35	.195	.311	.268	53	-17	3					3b		
Total	13	1201	4553	809	1159	228	85	64	667	506	23	532	.255	.332	.384	112	66	88	.866	20	119	137	3b716,S450,C34,P12,2b7,1b6		10.

WILLIAMSON, HOWIE Nathaniel Howard B12.23.1904 Little Rock AR D8.15.1969 Texarkana AR BL/TL/6-0/170 d7.7 Col Texas

YEAR	TM LG	G	AB	R	H	2B	3B	HR	RBI	BB-IB	HP	SO	AVG	OBP	SLG	AOPS	ABR	SB-CS	FA	FR	RNG	THR	GAMES AT POSITION	DL	BFW
1928	StL N	10	9	0	2	0	0	0	0	4		4	.222	.300	.222	38	-1	0	—		0		/H		-0.

WILLIGROD, JULIUS Julius B10.27.1857 Marshalltown IA D11.27.1906 San Francisco CA BL d7.15

YEAR	TM LG	G	AB	R	H	2B	3B	HR	RBI	BB-IB	HP	SO	AVG	OBP	SLG	AOPS	ABR	SB-CS	FA	FR	RNG	THR	GAMES AT POSITION	DL	BFW
1882	Det N	1	3	0	1	0	0	0	0	0			.333	.333	.333	115	0		1.000	-0	80	0	/S		0.
	Cle N	9	36	5	5	1	1	0	2	3		7	.139	.205	.222	38	0		.813	-2	0	0	O9(0/9/1)		-0.
	Year	10	39	5	6	1	1	0	2	3		8	.154	.214	.231	44	-2		.813	-2	0	0	O9(0/9/1)/S		-0.

WILLINGHAM, JOSH Joshua David B2.17.1979 Florence AL BR/TR/6-1/200* [FlaN00 17/491] d7.6 Col North Alabama

YEAR	TM LG	G	AB	R	H	2B	3B	HR	RBI	BB-IB	HP	SO	AVG	OBP	SLG	AOPS	ABR	SB-CS	FA	FR	RNG	THR	GAMES AT POSITION	DL	BFW
2004	Fla N	12	25	2	5	0	0	1	1	4-0	0	8	.200	.310	.320	72	-1	0-0	.938	-2	35	187	C5,O3L	64	-0.
2005	Fla N	16	23	3	7	1	0	1	4	2-0	2	5	.304	.407	.348	107	0	0-0	1.000	-2	62	0	C8/OLD	64	-0.
Total	2	28	48	5	12	1	0	1	5	6-0	2	13	.250	.357	.333	86	-1	0-0	.974	-4	51	78	C13,O4L/D		-0.

WILLINGHAM, HUGH Thomas Hugh B5.30.1906 Dalhart TX D6.15.1988 El Reno OK BR/TR/6-0/180 d9.13

YEAR	TM LG	G	AB	R	H	2B	3B	HR	RBI	BB-IB	HP	SO	AVG	OBP	SLG	AOPS	ABR	SB-CS	FA	FR	RNG	THR	GAMES AT POSITION	DL	BFW
1930	Chi A	3	4	2	1	0	0	0	0	2		1	.250	.500	.250	100	-1		1.000	-0	112	0	/2		0
1931	Phi N	23	35	5	9	2	1	1	3	2		9	.257	.297	.457	93	-1		.875	-1	77	94	S8,3b2/OL		-0.
1932	Phi N	4	2	0	0	0	0	0	0	0			.000	.000	.000	-89	-1		—		0		/H		-0.
1933	Phi N	1	1	0	0	0	0	0	0	0			.000	.000	.000	-89	-0		—		0		/H		0
Total	4	31	42	7	10	2	1	1	3	4		10	.238	.304	.405	82	-2		.875	-2	77	94	S8,3b2/OL2		-0.

WILLS d5.14

YEAR	TM LG	G	AB	R	H	2B	3B	HR	RBI	BB-IB	HP	SO	AVG	OBP	SLG	AOPS	ABR	SB-CS	FA	FR	RNG	THR	GAMES AT POSITION	DL	BFW
1884	Was AA	4	15	1	2	2	0	0	0	0			.133	.133	.267	31	-1		.889	2	401	0	O4(1/3/0)		0
	KC U	5	21	2	3	1	0	0	0	0			.143	.143	.190	0	-3		1.000	1	208	0	O5C		-0
Total	1	9	36	3	5	3	0	0	0	0			.139	.139	.222	13	-4		.938	3	305	0	O9(1/8/0)		0

WILLS, DAVE Davis Bowles B1.26.1877 Charlottesville VA D10.13.1959 Washington DC BL/TL d6.8 Col Virginia

YEAR	TM LG	G	AB	R	H	2B	3B	HR	RBI	BB-IB	HP	SO	AVG	OBP	SLG	AOPS	ABR	SB-CS	FA	FR	RNG	THR	GAMES AT POSITION	DL	BFW
1899	Lou N	24	94	15	21	3	1	0	12	2	0		.223	.240	.277	41	-8	1	.957	-3	67	65	1b24		-1

WILLS, BUMP Elliott Taylor B7.27.1952 Washington DC BB/TR/5-9/177* [TexA75*S1/6] d4.7 f-Maury Col Arizona St.

YEAR	TM LG	G	AB	R	H	2B	3B	HR	RBI	BB-IB	HP	SO	AVG	OBP	SLG	AOPS	ABR	SB-CS	FA	FR	RNG	THR	GAMES AT POSITION	DL	BFW
1977	Tex A	152	541	87	155	28	6	9	62	65-7	0	96	.287	.361	.410	109	8	28-12	.982	6	104	98	2b150,S2/1D		2
1978	Tex A	157	539	78	135	17	4	9	57	63-3	4	91	.250	.331	.347	91	-5	52-14	.981	22	111	88	2b156		
1979	Tex A	146	543	90	148	21	3	5	46	53-4	2	58	.273	.340	.350	88	-8	35-11	.976	12	104	96	2b146	14	2
1980	Tex A	146	578	102	152	31	5	5	58	51-1	3	71	.263	.322	.360	90	-7	34-9	.984	20	102	100	2b144	16	2
1981	Tex A	102	410	51	103	13	2	2	41	32-2	1	49	.251	.304	.307	81	-10	12-9	.983	11	101	103	2b101/D		
1982	Chi N	128	419	64	114	18	4	6	38	46-3	5	76	.272	.347	.377	100	1	35-10	.963	-11	97	77	2b103	30	1
Total	6	831	3030	472	807	128	24	36	302	310-20	17	441	.266	.335	.360	94	-21	196-65	.979	60	104	94	2b800,D2,S2/1		

WILLS, MAURY Maurice Morning B10.2.1932 Washington DC BB/TR/5-11/170* d6.6 M2 s-Bump

YEAR	TM LG	G	AB	R	H	2B	3B	HR	RBI	BB-IB	HP	SO	AVG	OBP	SLG	AOPS	ABR	SB-CS	FA	FR	RNG	THR	GAMES AT POSITION	DL	BFW
1959	†LA N	83	242	27	63	5	2	0	7	13-5	0	27	.260	.298	.298	55	-15	7-3	.966	0	97	88	S82		-0
1960	LA N	148	516	75	152	15	2	0	27	35-8	3	50	.295	.342	.331	80	-13	50-12	.945	26	105	103	S145		-1
1961	LA N	148	613	105	173	12	10	1	31	59-2	1	50	.282	.346	.339	76	-20	35-15	.959	10	95	108	S148		
1962	LA N★	165	695	130	208	13	10	6	48	51-1	2	50	.299	.347	.373	100	-2	104-13	.956	-4	95	83	S165		
1963	†LA N☆	134	527	83	159	19	3	0	34	44-0	1	48	.302	.355	.349	112	9	40-19	.959	10	105	84	S109,3b33		-0
1964	LA N	158	630	81	173	15	5	2	34	41-0	4	73	.275	.318	.324	88	-11	53-17	.963	-13	91	94	S155		
1965	LA N★	158	650	92	186	14	7	0	33	40-2	4	64	.286	.330	.329	93	-7	94-31	.970	18	105	107	S139,3b4		-1
1966	†LA N★	143	594	60	162	14	2	1	39	34-0	2	60	.273	.314	.308	80	-17	29-10	.948	9	117	122	3b144,S2		
1967	Pit N	149	616	92	186	12	9	3	45	31-1	1	44	.302	.334	.365	100	-2	29-10	.957	-10	98	102	3b141,S10		
1968	Pit N	153	627	76	174	12	6	0	31	45-1	1	57	.278	.326	.316	95	-4	52-21	.950	-2	98	102	S46/2		
1969	Mon N	47	189	23	42	3	0	4	39	39-2	1	40	.222	.295	.238	51	-12	15-6	.950	-2	98	109	S104		
	LA N	104	434	57	129	7	9	0	47	59-2	0	61	.297	.356	.378	113	6	25-15	.969	11	109	109	S150/2		
	Year	151	623	80	171	10	9	4	47	59-2	1	61	.274	.337	.335	91	-9	28-13	.959	-17	101	104	S126,3b4		
1970	LA N	132	522	77	141	19	3	0	34	58-2	0	34	.270	.333	.318	78	-15	28-13	.978	6	104	105	S144,3b4		
1971	LA N	149	601	73	169	14	3	3	44	40-2	1	40	.281	.323	.329	91	-9	15-8	.984	-6	94	115	S31,3b26		-0
1972	LA N	71	132	16	17	3	1	0	4	4-0	0	20	.129	.190	.167	2	-17	1-1	.984	-6	101	98	S24,3b26		-1
Total	14	1942	7588	1067	2134	177	71	20	458	552-26	16	684	.281	.330	.331	88	-129	586-208	.963	52	100	98	S1555,3b362/2		1

WILLSON, KID Frank Hoxie B11.3.1895 Bloomington NE D4.17.1964 Union Gap WA BL/TL/6-1/190 d7.2

YEAR	TM LG	G	AB	R	H	2B	3B	HR	RBI	BB-IB	HP	SO	AVG	OBP	SLG	AOPS	ABR	SB-CS	FA	FR	RNG	THR	GAMES AT POSITION	DL	BFW
1918	Chi A	1	1	0	1	0	0	0	0	1	0	1	1.000	.500	.000	50	0		—		0		/H		
1927	Chi A	7	10	1	1	0	0	0	1	1	0	3	.091	.167	.091	-49	-2	0-0	1.000	0	143	0	O2(1/1/0)		
Total	2	11	11	1	3	1	0	0	1	1	0	3	.091	.167	.091	-31	-2	0-0	1.000	0	143	0	O2(1/1/0)		

WILMOT, WALT Walter Robert B10.18.1863 Plover WI D2.1.1929 Chicago IL BB/TR/5-9/165 d4.20

YEAR	TM LG	G	AB	R	H	2B	3B	HR	RBI	BB-IB	HP	SO	AVG	OBP	SLG	AOPS	ABR	SB-CS	FA	FR	RNG	THR	GAMES AT POSITION	DL	BFW
1888	Was N	119	473	61	106	16	9	4	43	23	2	55	.224	.263	.321	92	-5	46	.872	12	96	96	O119L		-0.
1889	Was N	108	432	88	125	19	19	9	57	51	2	32	.289	.367	.484	146	25	40	.927	14	106	92	O108(107/1/0)		0.
1890	Chi N	139	571	114	159	15	13	13	99	64	2	44	.278	.353	.419	120	12	76	.938	11	110	90	O139(27/112/0)		-0.
1891	Chi N	121	498	102	137	14	10	11	71	55	1	21	.275	.353	.410	122	13	42	.922	-4	83	0	O121(62/60/0)		-0.
1892	Chi N	92	380	47	82	7	7	3	36	40	1	20	.216	.297	.287	76	-11	31	.903	-1	50	27	O92L		-0.
1893	Chi N	94	392	69	118	14	14	3	61	40	1	8	.301	.367	.431	114	6	39	.870	-7	71	84	O135L		-0.
1894	Chi N	135	604	136	199	45	12	6	130	36	1	27	.329	.368	.469	95	-7	74	.914	3	114	130	O108L		-0.
1895	Chi N	108	466	86	132	16	6	8	72	30	1	23	.283	.327	.395	80	-17	28	.938	0	159	0	O9(5/1/3)		-0.
1897	NY N	11	34	8	9	2	0	1	4	2			.265	.306	.412	91	-1	1	.886	-4	89	0	O34(6/0/29)		-0.
1898	NY N	35	138	16	33	4	3	0	17	7	0	14	.239	.286	.341	58	-2	16	.903	-8	92	64	O35L		-0.
Total	10	962	3988	727	1100	152	92	58	594	350	17	226	.276	.337	.404	105	11	383	.903	23	92	64	O958(745/184/32)		

WILSON, ARCHIE Archie Clifton B11.25.1923 Los Angeles CA BR/TR/6-0/175* d9.18 Col USC

YEAR	TM LG	G	AB	R	H	2B	3B	HR	RBI	BB-IB	HP	SO	AVG	OBP	SLG	AOPS	ABR	SB-CS	FA	FR	RNG	THR	GAMES AT POSITION	DL	BFW
1951	NY A	4	4	0	0	0	0	0	1	0	0	1	.000	.200	.000	-44	-1	0-0	1.000	0	139	0	O2R		
1952	NY A	3	2	1	1	1	0	0	0	0	0	0	.500	.500	1.000	190	0	0-0	—		0		/H		
	Was A	26	96	8	20	2	0	1	9	14	5	11	.208	.255	.292	54	-7	0-0	.971	0	110	0	O24(14/10/0)		
	Bos A	18	38	1	10	3	0	0	8	3	1		.263	.300	.342	73	-1	0-0	.944	0	95	152	O13(2/2/9)		
	Year	47	136	9	31	5	0	1	17	17	6	14	.228	.271	.309	61	-8	0-0	.966	-0	106	39	O37(16/12/9)		
Total	2	51	140	9	31	5	3	0	17	17	7	14	.221	.268	.300	58	-9	0-0	.967	0	107	38	O39(16/12/11)		

WILSON, ART Arthur Earl "Dutch" B12.11.1885 Macon IL D6.12.1960 Chicago IL BR/TR/5-8/170 d9.29

YEAR	TM LG	G	AB	R	H	2B	3B	HR	RBI	BB-IB	HP	SO	AVG	OBP	SLG	AOPS	ABR	SB-CS	FA	FR	RNG	THR	GAMES AT POSITION	DL	BFW
1908	NY N	1	0	0	0	0	0	0	0	0	0	0					0		—		0		/R		
1909	NY N	19	42	4	10	2	1	0	9	5			.238	.304	.333	96	0	0	.985	-2	97	86	C19		
1910	NY N	26	52	10	14	4	1	0	5	9	1	6	.269	.387	.385	125	2	2	.975	-0	96	93	C25/1		

YEAR	TM LG	G	AB	R	H	2B	3B	HR	RBI	BB-IB	HP	SO	AVG	OBP	SLG	AOPS	ABR	SB-CS	FA	FR	RNG	THR	GAMES AT POSITION	DL	BFW
1911	†NY N	66	109	17	33	9	1	1	17	19	1	12	.303	.411	.431	132	6	6	.963	-1	125	82	C64		0.8
1912	†NY N	65	121	17	35	6	0	3	19	13	0	14	.289	.358	.413	107	1	2	.960	3	132	68	C61		0.8
1913	†NY N	54	79	5	15	0	1	0	8	11	0	11	.190	.289	.215	45	-5	1-5	.965	6	127	79	C49		0.1
1914	Chi F	137	440	78	128	31	8	10	64	70	5	80	.291	.394	.466	142	21	13	.974	21	143	94	C132		0.1
1915	Chi F	96	269	44	82	11	2	7	31	65	1	38	.305	.442	.439	157	22	8	.980	-5	116	79	C87		5.4
1916	Pit N	53	128	11	33	5	2	1	12	13	1	27	.258	.331	.352	109	2	4	.981	-7	81	92	C39		2.6
	Chi N	36	114	5	22	3	1	0	5	6	0	14	.193	.233	.237	40	-8	1	.953	-4	96	107	C34		-0.2
	Year	89	242	16	55	8	3	1	17	19	1	41	.227	.286	.298	76	-7	5	.967	-11	88	99	C73		-1.1
1917	Chi N	81	211	17	45	9	2	2	25	32	2	36	.213	.322	.303	85	-2	6	.968	6	101	105	C75		-1.3
1918	Bos N	89	280	15	69	8	2	0	19	24	2	31	.246	.310	.289	87	-4	5	.977	-11	89	100	C85		1.1
1919	Bos N	71	191	14	49	8	1	0	16	25	1	19	.257	.346	.309	102	2	2	.977	-2	99	98	C64/1		-0.9
1920	Bos N	16	19	0	1	0	0	0	0	1	1	1	.053	.143	.053	-44	-4	0-0	1.000	-1	81	0	3b6,C2		0.6
1921	Cle A	2	1	0	0	0	0	0	0	0	0	0	.000	.000	.000	-99	0	0-0	1.000	0	0	0	C2		-0.5
Total 14		812	2056	237	536	96	22	24	226	292	15	289	.261	.357	.364	120	10	50-5	.972	4	113	92	C738,3b6,1b2		9.0

WILSON, ARTIE
Arthur Lee B10.28.1920 Springville AL BL/TR/5-10/162 d4.18 Negro Lg 1944-48

YEAR	TM LG	G	AB	R	H	2B	3B	HR	RBI	BB-IB	HP	SO	AVG	OBP	SLG	AOPS	ABR	SB-CS	FA	FR	RNG	THR	GAMES AT POSITION	DL	BFW
1951	NY N	19	22	2	4	0	0	0	1	2	0	1	.182	.250	.182	18	-3	2-0	1.000	1	94	235	2b3,S3,1b2		-0.1

WILSON, CHARLIE
Charles Woodrow "Swamp Baby" B1.13.1905 Clinton SC D12.19.1970 Rochester NY BB/TR/5-10.5/178 d4.14 Col Presbyterian

YEAR	TM LG	G	AB	R	H	2B	3B	HR	RBI	BB-IB	HP	SO	AVG	OBP	SLG	AOPS	ABR	SB-CS	FA	FR	RNG	THR	GAMES AT POSITION	DL	BFW
1931	Bos N	16	58	7	11	4	0	1	11	3	0	5	.190	.230	.310	45	-5	0	.917	-1	100		3b14		-0.6
1932	StL N	24	96	7	19	3	3	1	2	3	0	8	.198	.222	.323	43	-8	0	.935	-3	97	98	S24		-0.9
1933	StL N	1	1	0	0	0	0	0	0	0	0	1	.000	.000	.000	-95		0	—	-0	0		/S		0.0
1935	StL N	16	31	1	10	0	0	0	1	2	0	2	.323	.364	.323	83	-1	0	.933	-1	81	129	3b8		-0.1
Total 4		57	186	15	40	7	3	2	14	8	0	16	.215	.247	.317	50	-14	0	.935	-5	97	98	S25,3b22		-1.6

WILSON, CRAIG
Craig B11.28.1964 Annapolis MD BR/TR/5-11/175(175-210) [StLN84 20/503] d9.6 Col Anne Arundel (MD) CC

YEAR	TM LG	G	AB	R	H	2B	3B	HR	RBI	BB-IB	HP	SO	AVG	OBP	SLG	AOPS	ABR	SB-CS	FA	FR	RNG	THR	GAMES AT POSITION	DL	BFW
1989	StL N	6	4	1	1	0	0	0	1	1-0	0	2	.250	.400	.250	87	0	0-0	.500	-0	0	0	3b2		0.0
1990	StL N	55	121	13	30	2	0	0	7	8-0	0	14	.248	.290	.264	55	-8	0-2	.971	-0	92	61	3b13,O13(7/0/7),2b9/1		-0.8
1991	StL N	60	82	5	14	2	0	0	13	6-2	0	15	.171	.222	.195	20	-9	0-0	.905	-2	77	242	3b12,O5L,1b4,2b3		-1.0
1992	StL N	61	106	6	33	6	0	0	13	10-2	0	18	.311	.368	.368	112	2	1-2	.970	-3	75	82	3b18,2b11,O3R		-1.0
1993	KC A	21	49	6	13	1	0	1	3	7-0	0	6	.265	.357	.347	84	-1	1-1	1.000	-0	91	204	3b15,2OL		-0.1
Total 5		203	362	31	91	11	0	1	37	32-4	0	50	.251	.306	.290	68	-16	2-5	.957	-3	83	133	3b60,2b24,O22(13/0/10),1b5		-2.0

WILSON, CRAIG
Craig Alan B11.30.1976 Fountain Valley CA BR/TR/6-2/217* [TorA95 2/47] d4.22

YEAR	TM LG	G	AB	R	H	2B	3B	HR	RBI	BB-IB	HP	SO	AVG	OBP	SLG	AOPS	ABR	SB-CS	FA	FR	RNG	THR	GAMES AT POSITION	DL	BFW
2001	Pit N	88	158	27	49	7	1	13	32	15-1	7	53	.310	.390	.589	145	10	3-1	.994	-3	123	114	1b26,O14(1/0/13),C10,D2		0.7
2002	Pit N	131	368	48	97	16	1	16	57	32-0	21	116	.264	.355	.443	110	4	2-3	.982	-1	85	142	O75(1/0/74),1b42,C5,D3		-0.4
2003	Pit N	116	309	49	81	18	4	18	48	35-4	13	89	.262	.360	.511	123	10	3-1	.978	3	124	126	O46(7/0/40),1b36,C21,D3		1.1
2004	Pit N	155	561	97	148	35	5	29	82	50-3	30	169	.264	.354	.499	118	15	2-2	.977	-5	100	38	O100(19/0/89),1b65,C4,D2		0.1
2005	Pit N	59	197	23	52	14	1	5	22	30-0	10	69	.264	.347	.421	113	6	3-0	.988	0	92	159	O47(19/0/30),1b15	105	0.3
Total 5		549	1593	244	427	83	12	81	241	162-10	81	496	.268	.363	.488	119	45	13-7	.979	-5	98	105	O282(47/0/246),1b184,C40,D10	105	1.8

WILSON, CRAIG
Craig Franklin B9.3.1970 Chicago IL BR/TR/6-0/185* [ChiA92 13/372] d9.5 Col Kansas St.

YEAR	TM LG	G	AB	R	H	2B	3B	HR	RBI	BB-IB	HP	SO	AVG	OBP	SLG	AOPS	ABR	SB-CS	FA	FR	RNG	THR	GAMES AT POSITION	DL	BFW
1998	Chi A	13	47	14	22	5	0	3	10	3-0	0	6	.468	.490	.766	227	9	1-0	1.000	-3	67	72	S8,2b4,3b2		0.6
1999	Chi A	98	252	28	60	8	1	4	26	23-0	0	22	.238	.301	.325	59	-16	1-1	.969	-0	110	112	3b72,S22,2b7/1D		-1.4
2000	Chi A	28	73	12	19	3	0	0	4	5-0	1	11	.260	.316	.301	56	-5	1-0	.938	6	137	124	3b15,S10,2b4		0.2
Total 3		139	372	54	101	16	1	7	40	31-0	1	39	.272	.328	.376	78	-12	3-1	.964	2	114	112	3b89,S40,2b15/D1	36	-0.6

WILSON, DAN
Daniel Allen B3.25.1969 Arlington Heights IL BR/TR/6-3/202(190-215) [CinN90 1/7] d9.7 Col Minnesota

YEAR	TM LG	G	AB	R	H	2B	3B	HR	RBI	BB-IB	HP	SO	AVG	OBP	SLG	AOPS	ABR	SB-CS	FA	FR	RNG	THR	GAMES AT POSITION	DL	BFW
1992	Cin N	12	25	2	9	1	0	0	3	3-0	0	8	.360	.429	.400	132	1	0-0	1.000	1	127	125	C9		0.2
1993	Cin N	36	76	6	17	3	0	0	8	9-4	0	16	.224	.302	.263	54	-5	0-0	.994	-4	68	38	C35		-0.8
1994	Sea A	91	282	24	61	14	2	3	27	10-0	1	57	.216	.244	.312	42	-26	1-2	.986	12	124	110	C91		-0.8
1995	†Sea A	119	399	40	111	22	3	9	51	33-1	2	63	.278	.336	.416	93	-4	2-1	.995	14	124	117	C119		1.6
1996	Sea A★	138	491	51	140	24	0	18	83	32-2	3	85	.285	.330	.444	94	-6	1-2	.995	10	134	109	C135		1.1
1997	†Sea A	146	508	66	137	31	1	15	74	39-1	5	72	.270	.326	.423	94	-5	7-2	.995	12	125	125	C144		1.7
1998	Sea A	96	325	39	82	17	1	9	44	24-0	5	56	.252	.308	.394	82	-9	2-1	.994	-3	90	93	C94		-0.7
1999	Sea A	123	414	46	110	23	2	7	38	29-4	3	78	.266	.315	.382	78	-14	5-0	.995	-2	91	70	C121,1b5	43	-0.5
2000	Sea A	90	268	31	63	12	0	5	27	22-0	0	51	.235	.291	.336	60	-17	1-2	.990	2	142	105	C88/13		-0.7
2001	†Sea A	123	377	44	100	20	1	10	42	20-0	2	69	.265	.305	.403	89	-7	3-2	.990	2	142	105	C122,1b2	28	-1.0
2002	Sea A	115	359	35	106	16	1	6	44	18-1	2	81	.295	.326	.396	96	-3	1-0	.997	-2	124	67	C113,1b4		0.4
2003	Sea A	96	316	32	76	16	3	4	43	15-0	5	52	.241	.273	.339	64	-17	0-0	.998	1	180	54	C96		0.2
2004	Sea A	103	319	23	80	13	0	2	33	26-0	1	57	.251	.305	.310	65	-16	0-1	.997	-3	107	98	C103	7	-1.0
2005	Sea A	11	27	2	5	0	0	0	2	0-0	1	10	.185	.214	.185	8	-4	0-1	.975	-2	106	167	C11		-1.3
Total 14		1299	4186	441	1097	211	13	88	519	280-13	24	763	.262	.309	.382	80	-132	23-14	.995	38	125	92	C1281,1b12/3	147	-0.6
																								225	-1.5

WILSON, DESI
Desi Bernard B5.9.1969 Glen Cove NY BL/TL/6-7/230 [TexA91 30/794] d8.7 Col Fairleigh Dickinson [DL 1997 SF N 5]

YEAR	TM LG	G	AB	R	H	2B	3B	HR	RBI	BB-IB	HP	SO	AVG	OBP	SLG	AOPS	ABR	SB-CS	FA	FR	RNG	THR	GAMES AT POSITION	DL	BFW
1996	SF N	41	118	10	32	2	0	2	12	12-2	0	27	.271	.338	.339	81	-3	0-2	.984	-2	89	84	1b33		-0.8

WILSON, EDDIE
Edward Francis B9.7.1909 Hamden CT D4.11.1979 Hamden CT BL/TL/5-11/165 d6.21 Col Holy Cross

YEAR	TM LG	G	AB	R	H	2B	3B	HR	RBI	BB-IB	HP	SO	AVG	OBP	SLG	AOPS	ABR	SB-CS	FA	FR	RNG	THR	GAMES AT POSITION	DL	BFW
1936	Bro N	52	173	28	60	8	1	3	25	14	2	25	.347	.402	.457	129	8	3	.926	-3	92	68	O47R		0.2
1937	Bro N	36	54	11	12	4	1	1	8	17	0	14	.222	.408	.389	124	2	1	.966	-0	102	71	O21(0/1/20)		0.1
Total 2		88	227	39	72	12	2	4	33	31	2	39	.317	.404	.441	126	10	4	.936	-4	95	69	O68(0/1/67)		0.3

WILSON, ENRIQUE
Enrique (Martes) B7.27.1973 Santo Domingo, D.R. BB/TR/5-11/160(160-195) d9.24

YEAR	TM LG	G	AB	R	H	2B	3B	HR	RBI	BB-IB	HP	SO	AVG	OBP	SLG	AOPS	ABR	SB-CS	FA	FR	RNG	THR	GAMES AT POSITION	DL	BFW
1997	Cle A	5	15	2	5	0	0	0	1	0-0	0	2	.333	.333	.333	72	-1	0-0	.941	1	120	205	S4/2		0.0
1998	†Cle A	32	90	13	29	6	0	2	12	4-0	1	8	.322	.354	.456	106	1	2-4	.989	1	107	58	2b22,S10,3b2	72	0.2
1999	†Cle A	113	332	41	87	22	1	6	24	25-1	1	41	.262	.310	.352	67	-17	5-4	.965	-12	98	17	3b61,S35,2b21/D		-2.5
2000	Cle A	40	117	16	38	9	0	2	12	7-0	0	11	.325	.360	.453	101	0	2-1	.950	-3	107	0	3b12,2b7,S7,D8	14	-0.1
	Pit N	40	122	11	32	6	1	3	15	11-2	0	13	.262	.321	.402	81	-0	0-1	.925	-0	110	34	3b16,2b11,S8	3	-0.3
2001	†NY A	48	99	10	24	5	1	1	12	6-0	0	14	.242	.283	.343	64	-5	0-2	.952	4	99	71	S28,2b10,3b2		-1.2
2002	†NY A	60	105	17	19	2	2	2	11	8-0	0	22	.181	.239	.295	41	-9	1-1	.932	1	99	47	S20,3b19,2b7/D		-0.1
2003	†NY A	63	135	18	31	9	0	3	15	7-0	0	14	.230	.276	.363	68	-6	3-1	.987	-4	78	65	3b26,S14,2b7/ORD		-0.8
2004	NY A	93	240	19	51	9	0	6	31	15-0	0	20	.213	.254	.325	51	-18	1-2	.977	-6	92	57	S33,3b17,2b10/D		-0.8
2005	Chi N	15	22	1	3	2	0	0	3	0-0	1	8	.136	.240	.227	23	-2	0-0	.929	2	143	365	2b80,S16		-2.0
Total 9		555	1406	155	343	73	5	22	141	89-3	4	169	.244	.288	.350	63	-78	14-19	.983	-13	95	72	2b181,S178,3b156,D13,1b3/OR	89	-7.7

WILSON, FRANK
Francis Edward "Squash" B4.20.1901 Malden MA D11.25.1974 Leicester MA BL/TR/6-0/185 d6.20 Col Boston College

YEAR	TM LG	G	AB	R	H	2B	3B	HR	RBI	BB-IB	HP	SO	AVG	OBP	SLG	AOPS	ABR	SB-CS	FA	FR	RNG	THR	GAMES AT POSITION	DL	BFW
1924	Bos N	61	215	20	51	7	0	1	15	23	0	22	.237	.311	.284	63	-11	3-4	.973	2	108	86	O55(35/20/0)		-1.3
1925	Bos N	12	31	3	13	1	0	0	4	3	0	1	.419	.486	.516	171	4	2-1	1.000	1	121	114	O10(9/0/1)		0.4
1926	Bos N	87	236	22	56	11	3	0	23	20	1	21	.237	.300	.309	70	-10	3	.934	1	107	109	O56(50/1/6)		-1.3
1928	Cle A	2	1	0	0	0	0	0	0	1	0	0	.000	.500	.000	41	0	0-0	—		0		/H		-1.3
	StL A	6	5	1	0	0	0	0	0	0	0	0	.000	.000	.000	-97	-1	0-0	—		0		/OR		-0.1
	Year	8	6	1	0	0	0	0	0	1	0	0	.000	.143	.000	-58	-1	0-0	—	-0	0	0	/OR		-0.1
Total 4		168	488	46	120	19	4	1	38	48	1	44	.246	.313	.307	72	-18	8-5	.958	4	108	99	O122(94/21/8)		-2.3

WILSON, TUG
George Archer B1860 Brooklyn NY D11.28.1914 New York NY 5-8/175 d5.9

YEAR	TM LG	G	AB	R	H	2B	3B	HR	RBI	BB-IB	HP	SO	AVG	OBP	SLG	AOPS	ABR	SB-CS	FA	FR	RNG	THR	GAMES AT POSITION	DL	BFW
1884	Bro AA	24	82	13	19	4	0	0		5				.232	.276	.280	81	-1		.826	-3	93	284	O12(5/6/1),C10,1b3/2		-0.4

WILSON, SQUANTO
George Francis B3.29.1889 Old Town ME D3.26.1967 Winthrop ME BB/TR/5-9.5/170 d10.2 Col Bowdoin

YEAR	TM LG	G	AB	R	H	2B	3B	HR	RBI	BB-IB	HP	SO	AVG	OBP	SLG	AOPS	ABR	SB-CS	FA	FR	RNG	THR	GAMES AT POSITION	DL	BFW
1911	Det A	5	16	3	3	0	0	0	0	2			.188	.278	.188	29	-1	0	.900	-1	106	97	C5		-0.2
1914	Bos A	1	0	0	0	0	0	0	0	0			—	—	—	0	0	0-0	—	0	0		/1		0.0
Total 2		6	16	3	3	0	0	0	0	2			.188	.278	.188	29	-1	0	.900	-1	106	97	C5/1		-0.2

WILSON, ICEHOUSE
George Peacock B9.14.1912 Maricopa CA D10.13.1973 Moraga CA BR/TR/6-0/186 d5.31 Col St. Marys (CA)

YEAR	TM LG	G	AB	R	H	2B	3B	HR	RBI	BB-IB	HP	SO	AVG	OBP	SLG	AOPS	ABR	SB-CS	FA	FR	RNG	THR	GAMES AT POSITION	DL	BFW
1934	Det A	1	1	0	0	0	0	0	0	0	0	0	.000	.000	.000	-99	0	0-0	—				/H		0.0

YEAR	TM LG	G	AB	R	H	2B	3B	HR	RBI	BB-IB	HP	SO	AVG	OBP	SLG	AOPS	ABR	SB-CS	FA	FR	RNG	THR	GAMES AT POSITION	DL	BFW

WILSON, GEORGE George Washington "Teddy" B8.30.1925 Cherryville NC D10.29.1974 Gastonia NC BL/TR/6-1.5/185* d4.15

1952	Chi A	8	9	0	1	0	0	0	1	1	0	.111	.200	.111	-12	-1	0-0	1.000	0	109	0	/OR		-0.2
	NY N	62	112	9	27	7	0	2	16	3	0	14	.241	.261	.357	69	-5	0-0	.923	-2	100	0	O21(16/1/4),1b2		-0.9
1953	NY N	11	8	0	1	0	0	0	2	1	1	2	.125	.364	.125	34	-1	0-0	—	0			/H		-0.1
1956	NY N	53	68	5	9	1	0	1	2	5-1	0	14	.132	.192	.191	3	-9	0-0	1.000	0	91	159	O8(2/0/6)		-1.0
	†NY A	11	12	1	2	0	0	0	0	3-0	0	1	.167	.333	.167	37	-1	0-0	.750	-1			O6(1/0/5)		-0.2
Total	3	145	209	15	40	8	0	3	19	14-1	1	32	.191	.246	.273	41	-17	0-0	.932	-3	96	42	O36(19/1/16),1b2		-2.4

WILSON, GLENN Glenn Dwight B12.22.1958 Baytown TX BR/TR/6-1/190* [DetA80 1/18] d4.15 Col Sam Houston St. OF(118/90/941)

1982	Det A	84	322	39	94	15	1	12	34	15-0	0	51	.292	.322	.457	111	4	2-3	.987	3	102	150	O80(2/71/8),D4		-0.5
1983	Det A	144	503	55	135	25	6	11	65	25-1	3	79	.268	.306	.408	97	-4	1-1	.988	-7	86	122	O143(0/8/140)		-1.8
1984	Phi N	132	341	28	82	21	3	6	31	17-1	1	56	.240	.276	.372	80	-10	7-1	.968	-5	91	60	O109(92/3/18),3b4		-1.9
1985	Phi N★	161	608	73	167	39	5	14	102	35-1	0	117	.275	.311	.424	102	0	7-4	.968	16	117	170	O158(2/0/157)		0.8
1986	Phi N	155	584	70	158	30	4	15	84	42-1	4	91	.271	.319	.413	98	-3	5-1	.989	15	112	156	O154(1/0/153)		0.5
1987	Phi N	154	569	55	150	21	2	14	54	38-2	1	82	.264	.308	.381	79	-18	3-6	.980	8	106	169	O154R/P		-1.7
1988	Sea A	78	284	28	71	10	1	3	17	15-0	0	52	.250	.286	.324	68	-13	1-1	.980	-2	93	92	O75R,D2		-1.7
	Pit N	37	126	11	34	8	0	2	15	3-1	1	18	.270	.286	.381	93	-2	0-0	.985	-1	96	59	O35(0/4/32)	15	-0.4
1989	Pit N	100	330	42	93	20	4	9	49	32-5	1	39	.282	.342	.448	130	13	1-4	.977	2	97	86	O85(0/1/85),1b10		0.7
	Hou N	28	102	8	22	6	0	2	15	5-0	0	14	.216	.250	.333	68	-5	0-1	.966	4	99	426	O25R		-0.2
	Year	128	432	50	115	26	4	11	64	37-5	1	53	.266	.321	.421	116	8	1-5	.974	2	97	167	O110(0/1/110),1b10		0.5
1990	Hou N	118	368	42	90	14	0	10	55	26-1	1	64	.245	.293	.364	83	-10	0-3	.975	10	112	172	O108(21/0/92)/1		-0.4
1993	Pit N	10	14	0	2	0	0	0	0	0-0	0	9	.143	.143	.143	-23	-2	0-0	.875	1	76	1203	O5(0/3/2)		-0.2
Total	10	1201	4151	451	1098	209	26	98	521	253-13	12	672	.265	.306	.398	93	-50	27-25	.977	42	103	145	O1131R,1b11,D6,3b4/P	15	-5.8

WILSON, GRADY Grady Herbert B11.23.1922 Columbus GA D7.23.2003 Columbus GA BR/TR/6-0.5/170 d5.15 Col Troy St.

| 1948 | Pit N | 12 | 10 | 1 | 1 | 0 | 0 | 0 | 0 | 3 | 0 | .100 | .100 | .200 | -20 | -2 | 0 | .846 | -0 | 68 | 185 | S7 | | -0.2 |

WILSON, HENRY Henry C. B4.8.1877 Baltimore MD d10.12

| 1898 | Bal N | 1 | 2 | 0 | 0 | 0 | 0 | 0 | 0 | 1 | 0 | .000 | .333 | .000 | -2 | 0 | 0 | 1.000 | 0 | 87 | 287 | /C | | 0.0 |

WILSON, JACK Jack Eugene B12.29.1977 Westlake Village CA BR/TR/6-0/175(175-190) [StLN98 9/258] d4.3 Col Oxnard (CA) JC

2001	Pit N	108	390	44	87	17	1	3	25	16-2	1	70	.223	.255	.295	41	-35	1-3	.968	9	115	101	S107		-1.9
2002	Pit N	147	527	77	133	22	4	4	47	37-2	4	74	.252	.306	.332	70	-26	1-3	.977	20	118	104	S143		0.4
2003	Pit N	150	558	58	143	21	3	9	62	36-3	4	74	.256	.303	.353	70	-25	5-5	.975	4	108	109	S149		-1.0
2004	Pit N★	157	652	82	201	41	12	11	59	26-0	3	71	.308	.335	.459	103	1	8-4	.977	27	109	129	S156		3.9
2005	Pit N	158	587	60	151	24	7	8	52	31-6	6	58	.257	.299	.363	74	-25	7-3	.982	27	113	120	S157		1.4
Total	5	720	2714	321	715	125	27	35	245	146-13	18	347	.263	.304	.368	74	-110	26-17	.977	87	112	113	S712		2.8

WILSON, JIMMIE James "Ace" B7.23.1900 Philadelphia PA D5.31.1947 Bradenton FL BR/TR/6-1.5/200 d4.17 M9/C5

1923	Phi N	85	252	27	66	9	0	1	25	4	1	17	.262	.276	.310	49	-19	4-2	.960	-9	83	91	C69,O2(1/1/0)		-2.2
1924	Phi N	95	280	32	78	16	3	6	39	17	1	12	.279	.322	.421	87	-5	5-4	.968	1	92	131	C82,1b2/OR		0.1
1925	Phi N	108	335	42	110	19	3	3	54	32	2	25	.328	.390	.430	100	2	5-3	.982	-7	97	71	C89/O		0.0
1926	Phi N	90	279	40	85	10	2	4	32	25	0	20	.305	.362	.398	99	0	3	.950	-4	83	132	C79		0.1
1927	Phi N	128	443	50	122	15	2	2	45	34	2	15	.275	.330	.332	77	-14	13	.975	-21	82	80	C124		-2.7
1928	Phi N	21	70	11	21	4	1	0	13	9	0	8	.300	.380	.386	97	0	3	.990	-0	74	142	C20		0.1
	†StL N	120	411	45	106	26	2	2	50	45	1	24	.258	.333	.345	76	-13	9	.983	4	130	102	C120		-0.1
	Year	141	481	56	127	30	3	2	63	54	1	32	.264	.340	.351	79	-13	12	.985	4	122	108	C140		0.0
1929	StL N	120	394	59	128	27	8	4	71	43	2	19	.325	.394	.464	111	8	4	.972	6	115	106	C119		1.9
1930	†StL N	107	362	54	115	25	7	1	58	28	1	17	.318	.368	.434	90	-5	8	.987	10	113	121	C99		1.0
1931	†StL N	115	383	45	105	20	2	0	51	28	5	15	.274	.332	.337	77	-11	5	.985	10	100	128	C110		0.5
1932	StL N	92	274	32	68	16	2	2	28	15	1	18	.248	.290	.343	67	-13	9	.982	2	76	164	C75,1b3/2		-0.6
1933	StL N★	113	369	34	94	17	0	1	45	23	1	33	.255	.300	.309	71	-13	6	.982	0	87	122	C107		-0.7
1934	Phi N	91	277	25	81	11	0	3	35	14	0	11	.292	.326	.365	75	-10	1	.987	4	118	117	C77/12M		-0.1
1935	Phi N★	93	290	38	81	20	0	1	37	19	1	19	.279	.326	.359	76	-9	4	.982	4	99	92	C78/2M		0.0
1936	Phi N	85	230	25	64	12	0	1	27	12	0	21	.278	.314	.343	70	-9	5	.960	-5	96	84	C63/1M		-1.1
1937	Phi N	39	87	15	24	3	0	1	8	6	0	4	.276	.323	.345	75	-3	1	.978	-1	127	91	C22,1b2,M		-0.3
1938	Phi N	3	2	0	0	0	0	0	0	0	0	1	.000	.000	.000	-99	-1	0	1.000	0	0	0	/CM		0.0
1939	Cin N	4	3	0	1	0	0	0	0	0	0	0	.333	.333	.333	79	0	0	—	-0	0	0	/C		0.0
1940	†Cin N	16	37	2	9	2	0	0	3	2	0	1	.243	.282	.297	59	-2	1	.982	1	101	122	C16		0.0
Total	18	1525	4778	580	1358	252	32	32	621	356	18	280	.284	.336	.370	82	-117	86-9	.977	-4	99	110	C1351,1b9,O4(1/1/1),2b3		-4.1

WILSON, GARY James Garrett B1.12.1879 Baltimore MD D5.1.1969 Randallstown MD BR/TR/5-7/168 d9.27

| 1902 | Bos A | 2 | 8 | 0 | 1 | 0 | 0 | 0 | 0 | 0 | 0 | .125 | .125 | .125 | -30 | -1 | 0 | .800 | -0 | 88 | 233 | 2b2 | | -0.2 |

WILSON, JIM James George B12.29.1960 Corvallis OR BR/TR/6-3/225* [CleA82 2/40] d9.13 Col Oregon St.

1985	Cle A	4	14	2	5	0	0	0	4	1-0	0	3	.357	.400	.357	110	-0	0-0	1.000	-0	0	67	1b2,D2		0.0
1989	Sea A	5	8	0	0	0	0	0	0	0-0	0	3	.000	.000	.000	-97	-2	0-0	—	0			D5		-0.2
Total	2	9	22	2	5	0	0	0	4	1-0	0	6	.227	.261	.227	36	-2	0-0	1.000	-0	0	67	D7,1b2		-0.2

WILSON, CHIEF John Owen B8.21.1883 Austin TX D2.22.1954 Bertram TX BL/TR/6-2/185 d4.15

1908	Pit N	144	529	47	120	8	7	3	43	22	2		.227	.260	.285	74	-18	12	.955	-1	108	72	O144(1/34/109)		-3.0
1909	†Pit N	154	569	64	155	22	12	4	59	19	6		.272	.303	.374	102	-2	17	.957	4	86	161	O154R		-0.6
1910	Pit N	146	536	59	148	14	13	4	50	21	7	68	.276	.312	.373	94	-8	8	.972	4	103	112	O146(1/7/138)		-1.1
1911	Pit N	148	544	72	163	34	12	12	107	41	4	55	.300	.353	.472	125	16	10	.977	5	110	98	O146(0/2/145)		1.2
1912	Pit N	152	583	80	175	19	36	11	95	35	2	67	.300	.342	.513	134	20	16	.961	-0	104	87	O152(0/87/69)		1.6
1913	Pit N	155	580	71	154	12	14	10	73	32	4	52	.266	.307	.386	102	-3	9-10	.969	-2	115	69	O155(0/3/153)		-1.4
1914	StL N	154	580	64	150	27	12	9	73	32	4	66	.259	.302	.393	107	2	14	.983	12	107	126	O154(0/9/148)		0.3
1915	StL N	107	348	33	96	13	6	3	39	19	4	43	.276	.321	.374	110	3	8-15	.984	11	107	164	O105(3/70/33)		0.3
1916	StL N	120	355	30	85	8	2	3	32	20	5	46	.239	.289	.299	81	-8	4	.955	-4	93	61	O113(0/58/61)		-2.5
Total	9	1280	4624	520	1246	157	114	59	571	241	37	407	.269	.311	.391	105	2	98-25	.968	32	104	108	O1269(5/270/1010)		-4.6

WILSON, JOSH Joshua Aaron B3.26.1981 Pittsburgh PA BR/TR/6-1/180 d9.7

| 2005 | Fla N | 11 | 10 | 2 | 1 | 1 | 0 | 0 | 0 | 0-0 | 1 | 4 | .100 | .182 | .200 | 0 | -1 | 0-0 | 1.000 | -1 | 100 | 145 | S6,2b4 | | -0.2 |

WILSON, LES Lester Wilbur "Tug" B7.17.1885 St.Louis MI D4.4.1969 Edmonds WA BL/TR/5-11/170 d7.15

| 1911 | Bos A | 5 | 7 | 0 | 0 | 0 | 0 | 0 | 0 | 0 | 0 | .000 | .222 | .000 | -36 | -1 | 0 | 1.000 | -0 | 122 | 0 | O3(2/0/1) | | -0.2 |

WILSON, HACK Lewis Robert B4.26.1900 Ellwood City PA D11.23.1948 Baltimore MD BR/TR/5-6/190 d9.29 HF1979

1923	NY N	3	10	2	0	0	0	0	0	0	0	1	.200	.200	.200	6	-1	0	.857	-1	88	0	O3(1/2/0)		-0.2
1924	†NY N	107	383	62	113	19	12	10	57	44	1	46	.295	.369	.486	131	16	4-3	.967	-6	92	78	O103(14/90/1)		-0.2
1925	NY N	62	180	28	43	7	4	6	30	21	1	33	.239	.322	.422	92	-3	5-2	.975	-5	77	76	O50(27/23/4)		-0.6
1926	Chi N	142	529	97	170	36	8	21	109	69	6	61	.321	.406	.539	150	39	10	.973	-5	95	85	O140C		2.0
1927	Chi N	146	551	119	175	30	12	30	129	71	6	70	.318	.401	.579	160	46	13	.967	-7	95	88	O146C		3.3
1928	Chi N	145	520	89	163	32	9	31	120	77	2	94	.313	.404	.588	159	45	4	.960	-13	87	90	O143C		2.1
1929	†Chi N	150	574	135	198	30	5	39	159	78	2	83	.345	.425	.618	155	49	3	.970	-3	97	101	O150C		3.5
1930	Chi N	155	585	146	208	35	6	56	191	105	1	84	.356	.454	.723	177	76	3	.951	-15	77	75	O155C		5.6
1931	Chi N	112	395	66	103	22	4	13	61	63	0	69	.261	.362	.435	112	8	1	.978	-4	88	129	O103(40/60/3)		0.0
1932	Bro N	135	481	77	143	37	5	23	123	51	1	85	.297	.366	.538	142	29	2	.955	-6	86	120	O125(1/8/116)		0.3
1933	Bro N	117	360	41	96	13	4	9	54	50	2	50	.267	.359	.389	119	10	7	.963	-5	99	46	O90(75/8/7),2b5		0.8
1934	Bro N	67	172	24	45	5	0	6	27	40	0	33	.262	.401	.395	120	7	0	.974	-1	89	101	O43(27/0/16)		0.0
	Phi N	7	20	0	2	0	0	0	3	3	0	4	.100	.217	.100	-11	-3	0	1.000	0	0	0	O6(5/0/1)		0.0
	Year	74	192	24	47	5	0	6	30	43	0	37	.245	.383	.365	116	5	0	.977	-1	91	90	O49(32/0/17)		0.0
Total	12	1348	4760	884	1461	266	67	244	1063	674	20	713	.307	.395	.545	145	318	52-5	.965	-70	91	88	O1257(190/925/148),2b5		18

YEAR	TM LG	G	AB	R	H	2B	3B	HR	RBI	BB-IB	HP	SO	AVG	OBP	SLG	AOPS	ABR	SB-CS	FA	FR	RNG	THR	GAMES AT POSITION	DL	BFW

WILSON, TACK Michael B5.16.1955 Shreveport LA BR/TR/5-10/185* d4.9 Col Laney (CA) JC

1983	Min A	5	4	1	1	0	0	0	0	1-0	0	0	.250	.250	.500	96	0	0-0	1.000	-0	39	0	/OCD		0.0
1987	Cal A	7	2	5	1	0	0	0	0	0	0	0	.500	.667	.500	223	1	0-0	1.000	-0	47	0	O4L,D2		0.0
Total	2	12	6	9	2	1	0	0	1	1-0	0	0	.333	.429	.500	150	1	0-0	1.000	-1	43	0	O5(4/1/0),D4		0.0

WILSON, NIGEL Nigel Edward B1.12.1970 Oshawa ON, Can. BL/TL/6-1/185* d9.8

1993	Fla N	7	16	0	0	0	0	0	0	0	0	11	.000	.000	.000	-94	-4	0-0	1.000	-0	75	0	O3L		-0.5
1995	Cin N	5	7	0	0	0	0	0	0	0	0	4	.000	.000	.000	-99	-2	0-0	1.000	-0	91	0	O2L		-0.2
1996	†Cle A	10	12	2	3	0	0	2	5	1-0	0	6	.250	.308	.750	156	1	0-0	—	-1	0	0	/OLD		0.0
Total	3	22	35	2	3	0	0	2	5	1-0	0	21	.086	.111	.257	-7	-5	0-0	1.000	-5	63	0	O6L,D3.		-0.7

WILSON, PARKE Parke Asel B10.26.1867 Keithsburg IL D12.20.1934 Hermosa Beach CA BR/TR/5-11/166 d7.19

1893	NY N	31	114	16	28	4	1	2	21	7	0	9	.246	.289	.351	69	-6	5	.969	-3	99	74	C31		-0.5
1894	NY N	51	181	35	59	5	5	1	34	15		6	.326	.384	.425	95	-2	9	.841	-5	108	64	C35,1b16		-0.3
1895	NY N	67	238	32	56	9	0	0	30	14	1	16	.235	.281	.273	44	-20	11	.938	-1	96	117	C53,1b11,3b3		-1.3
1896	NY N	75	253	30	60	2	0	0	23	13	1	14	.237	.277	.245	39	-22	9	.936	-6	94	95	C71,1b2		-1.9
1897	NY N	47	158	29	47	9	3	0	23	15	1		.297	.362	.392	102	1	6	.929	2	171	75	C30,1b11,O4C/2		0.4
1898	NY N	1	4	0	0	0	0	0	0	0	0		.000	.000	.000	-99	-1		—	-0	0	0	/OL		-0.1
1899	NY N	98	332	49	89	8	6	0	42	43	4		.268	.359	.328	92	-2	16	.925	-6	87	85	C31,1b29,S19,3b15,O7(3/0/4)		-0.1
Total	7	370	1280	194	339	37	15	3	173	107	9	45	.265	.326	.324	72	-52	56	.925	-19	105	90	C251,1b69,S19,3b18,O12(4/4/4)/2		-4.1

WILSON, PRESTON Preston James Richard B7.19.1974 Bamberg SC BR/TR/6-2/193(193-215) [NYN92 1/9] d5.7 f-Mookie

1998	NY N	8	20	3	6	2	0	0	2	2-0	0	8	.300	.364	.400	104	0	1-1	.909	-1	93	0	O7(4/2/1)		-0.1
	Fla N	14	31	4	2	0	0	1	4	4-0	1	13	.065	.194	.161	-5	-5	0-0	1.000	-1	79	0	O11(3/7/1)		-0.5
	Year	22	51	7	8	2	0	1	3	6-0	1	21	.157	.259	.255	38	-5	1-1	.958	-2	85	0	O18(7/9/2)		-0.7
1999	Fla N	149	482	67	135	21	4	26	71	46-3	9	156	.280	.350	.502	120	13	11-4	.973	3	103	136	O136(23/111/15)		1.5
2000	Fla N	**161**	605	94	160	35	3	31	121	55-1	8	187	.264	.331	.486	109	6	36-14	.988	3	101	94	O158C		0.8
2001	Fla N	123	468	70	128	30	2	23	71	36-2	6	107	.274	.331	.494	113	8	20-8	.993	3	100	183	O121C		1.3
2002	Fla N	141	510	80	124	22	2	23	65	58-3	9	140	.243	.329	.429	105	1	20-11	.981	-6	93	107	O138C		-0.4
2003	Col N★	155	600	94	169	43	1	36	**141**	54-1	4	139	.282	.343	.537	110	9	14-7	.980	-10	90	94	O155C		0.2
2004	Col N	58	202	24	50	11	0	6	29	17-2	3	49	.248	.315	.391	72	-8	2-1	.953	-2	97	117	O52C	110	-0.9
2005	Col N	71	267	39	69	15	1	15	47	25-0	1	77	.258	.322	.491	96	-2	3-2	.979	-8	88	58	O69C		-0.7
	Was N	68	253	34	66	14	1	10	43	20-0	6	71	.261	.329	.443	107	2	3-4	1.000	-3	91	80	O68(11/55/2)		-0.2
	Year	139	520	73	135	29	2	25	90	45-0	7	148	.260	.325	.467	101	0	6-6	.990	-9	90	69	O137(11/124/2)		-0.9
Total	8	948	3438	509	909	193	14	171	591	317-12	47	947	.264	.333	.478	106	24	110-52	.982	-26	110	110	O915(41/868/19)	149	0.9

WILSON, BOB Robert B2.22.1925 Dallas TX D4.23.1985 Dallas TX BR/TR/5-11/197 d5.17 Negro Lg 1947-50

| 1958 | LA N | 3 | 5 | 0 | 1 | 0 | 0 | 0 | 0 | 0-0 | 0 | 1 | .200 | .200 | .200 | 6 | -1 | 0-0 | 1.000 | -0 | 81 | 0 | /OR | | -0.1 |

WILSON, RED Robert James B3.7.1929 Milwaukee WI BR/TR/6-0/200(190-205) d9.22 Col Wisconsin-Madison

1951	Chi A	4	11	1	3	1	0	0	0	1	0	2	.273	.333	.364	90	-0	0-0	1.000	-0	78	167	C4		0.0
1952	Chi A	2	3	0	0	0	0	0	0	0	0	0	.000	.000	.000	-99	-1	0-0	1.000	1	0	0	C2		0.0
1953	Chi A	71	164	21	41	6	1	0	10	26	0	12	.250	.353	.299	75	-5	2-3	.981	5	98	95	C63		0.3
1954	Chi A	8	20	2	4	0	0	1	1	1	0	2	.200	.238	.350	58	-1	0-0	1.000	3	158	72	C8		0.2
	Det A	54	170	22	48	11	1	2	22	27	0	12	.282	.379	.394	115	5	3-1	.996	3	134	104	C53		1.0
	Year	62	190	24	52	11	1	3	23	28	0	14	.274	.365	.389	108	3	3-1	.997	.5	137	100	C61		1.2
1955	Det A	78	241	26	53	9	0	2	17	26-3	0	23	.220	.296	.282	57	-14	1-2	.984	-5	94	113	C72		-1.7
1956	Det A	78	228	32	66	12	2	7	38	42-7	0	18	.289	.393	.452	124	10	2-1	.991	2	136	127	C78		1.5
1957	Det A	60	180	21	43	8	1	3	29	35-5	2	19	.239	.341	.344	86	-3	2-3	1.000	2	144	82	C60		0.2
1958	Det A	103	298	31	89	13	1	3	29	35-5	2	30	.299	.373	.379	101	2	10-0	.992	7	109	80	C101		1.7
1959	Det A	67	228	28	60	17	2	4	35	10-1	2	23	.263	.295	.408	88	-4	2-2	.988	0	125	98	C64		-0.1
1960	Det A	45	134	17	29	4	0	1	14	16-1	0	14	.216	.298	.269	54	-8	3-0	.980	1	90	56	C45		-0.5
	Cle A	32	88	5	19	3	0	1	10	6-1	1	7	.216	.268	.284	53	-6	0-0	.989	4	90	110	C30		-0.1
	Year	77	222	22	48	7	0	2	24	22-2	1	21	.216	.286	.275	53	-14	3-0	.984	4	90	78	C75		-0.6
Total	10	602	1765	206	455	84	8	24	189	215-20	8	163	.258	.338	.355	87	-25	25-12	.990	23	115	96	C580		2.5

WILSON, MIKE Samuel Marshall B12.2.1896 Edge Hill PA D5.16.1978 Boynton Beach FL BR/TR/5-10.5/160 d6.4 Col Lehigh

| 1921 | Pit N | 5 | 4 | 0 | 0 | 0 | 0 | 0 | 0 | 0 | 0 | 0 | .000 | .000 | .000 | -97 | -1 | 0-0 | .833 | -0 | 0 | 141 | C5 | | -0.1 |

WILSON, NEIL Samuel O'Neil B6.14.1935 Lexington TN BL/TR/6-1/175 d4.17

| 1960 | SF N | 6 | 10 | 0 | 1 | 0 | 0 | 0 | 0 | 1-1 | 0 | 2 | .100 | .091 | .000 | -77 | -3 | 0-0 | .958 | -1 | 64 | 0 | C6 | | -0.3 |

WILSON, TOM Thomas G. "Slats" B6.3.1890 Fleming KS D3.7.1953 San Pedro CA BB/TR/6-1.5/160 d9.8

| 1914 | Was A | 1 | 1 | 0 | 0 | 0 | 0 | 0 | 0 | 0 | 0 | 0 | .000 | .000 | .000 | -96 | 0 | 0-0 | — | -0 | 0 | 0 | /C | | -0.1 |

WILSON, TOM Thomas Leroy B12.19.1970 Fullerton CA BR/TR/6-3/220* [NYA90 23/620] d5.19 Col Fullerton (CA) JC

2001	Oak A	9	21	4	4	0	0	2	4	1-0	1	5	.190	.250	.476	88	-1	0-0	.974	-3	74	0	C9		-0.3
2002	Tor A	96	265	33	68	10	0	8	37	28-0	5	79	.257	.334	.385	89	-4	0-0	.988	-10	66	93	C65,D12,1b11		-1.1
2003	Tor A	96	256	37	66	19	0	8	35	28-0	1	80	.258	.331	.391	87	-4	0-0	.991	-3	63	93	C76,1b14,O2(1/0/1)/D		-0.3
2004	†LA N	9	8	1	1	0	0	0	0	0-0	0	3	.125	.125	.125	-35	-2	0-0	1.000	-1	0	252	C7		-0.2
	NY N	4	4	0	1	0	0	0	0	1-0	0	2	.250	.400	.250	75	0	0-0	1.000	-0	24	0	C3		0.0
	Year	13	12	1	2	0	0	0	0	1-0	0	5	.167	.231	.167	5	-2	0-0	1.000	-1	10	148	C10		-0.2
Total	4	214	554	75	140	29	0	18	76	58-0	7	169	.253	.327	.386	86	-11	0-0	.989	-16	63	89	C160,1b25,D13,O2(1/0/1)		-1.9

WILSON, VANCE Vance Allen B3.17.1973 Mesa AZ BR/TR/5-11/190* [NYN93 44/1226] d4.24 Col Mesa (AZ) CC [DL 1998 NY N 20]

1999	NY N	1	0	0	0	0	0	0	0	0-0	0	0					0	0-0	—	-0	0	0	/C	38	0.0
2000	NY N	4	4	0	0	0	0	0	0	0-0	0	2	.000	.000	.000	-99	-1	0-0	1.000	1	85	0	C3		-0.1
2001	NY N	32	57	3	17	3	0	6	20	2-0	2	16	.298	.339	.351	86	-1	0-1	.993	2	187	132	C27		0.2
2002	NY N	74	163	19	40	7	0	5	26	5-0	2	32	.245	.301	.380	86	-5	0-1	.983	6	101	206	C66/1		0.4
2003	NY N	96	268	28	65	9	1	8	39	15-1	5	56	.243	.293	.399	76	-11	1-2	.990	6	119	150	C89		0.0
2004	NY N	79	157	18	43	10	1	4	21	11-2	5	24	.274	.335	.427	99	0	1-0	.993	-1	109	119	C69	41	0.2
2005	Det A	61	152	18	30	4	0	3	19	11-0	6	26	.197	.275	.283	51	-11	0-0	.989	-3	91	133	C60	99	-1.1
Total	7	347	801	86	195	33	2	20	111	44-3	26	156	.243	.301	.365	78	-29	2-4	.989	11	113	150	C315/1	99	-0.4

WILSON, BILL William Donald B11.6.1928 Central City NE BR/TR/6-2/200* d9.24 Mil 1951-52

1950	Chi A	3	6	0	0	0	0	0	0	0	0	2	.000	.000	.000	-33	-1	0-0	1.000	-0	80	0	O2C		-0.1
1953	Chi A	9	17	1	1	0	0	0	1	0	0	7	.059	.111	.059	-51	-4	0-0	1.000	-0	103	0	O3C		-0.4
1954	Chi A	20	35	4	6	1	0	2	5	7	0	5	.171	.310	.371	83	-1	0-1	.943	1	127	82	O19(15/0/4)		-0.1
	Phi A	94	323	43	77	10	1	15	33	39		59	.238	.334	.415	104	1	1-2	.989	4	110	82	O91C		0.0
	Year	114	358	47	83	11	1	17	38	46	8	64	.232	.332	.411	102	1	1-3	.984	5	112	72	O110(15/91/4)		0.0
1955	KC A	98	273	39	61	12	0	15	38	24-0	1	63	.223	.288	.432	91	-5	1-1	.969	-1	101	80	O82(23/57/4)/P		-1.0
Total	4	224	654	87	145	23	1	32	77	72-0	10	136	.222	.308	.407	92	-10	2-4	.979	3	107	73	O197(38/153/8)/P		-1.5

WILSON, BILL William G. B10.28.1867 Hannibal MO D5.9.1924 St.Paul MN TR d4.30

1890	Pit N	83	304	30	65	11	3	0	21	22	2	50	.214	.271	.270	65	-13	5	.875	-16	65	137	C38,O25(4/8/13),1b18/S		-2.5
1897	Lou N	107	389	44	83	12	4	1	41	18	5		.213	.257	.272	41	-34	9	.940	-4	92	111	C105/3		-2.5
1898	Lou N	29	102	5	17	1	2	1	13	5	1		.167	.213	.245	32	-10	3	.895	-7	83	119	C28/1		-1.3
Total	3	219	795	79	165	24	9	2	75	58-0	7		.208	.257	.268	48	-57	17	.913	-27	84	119	C171,O25(4/8/13),1b19/3S		-6.3

WILSON, MOOKIE William Hayward B2.9.1956 Bamberg SC BB/TR/5-10/170* [NYN77 2/42] d9.2 C6 s-Preston Col South Carolina-Aiken

1980	NY N	27	105	16	26	5	3	0	4	12-0	0	19	.248	.325	.352	92	0	7-7	.973	-0	106	57	O26(1/26/0)		-0.3
1981	NY N	92	328	49	89	8	8	3	14	20-3	1	59	.271	.317	.372	95	-4	24-12	.983	5	118	56	O80(6/68/10)		0.1
1982	NY N	159	639	90	178	25	9	5	55	32-4	2	102	.279	.314	.369	90	-10	58-16	.988	8	110	131	O159C		0.4
1983	NY N	152	638	91	176	25	6	7	51	18-3	4	103	.276	.300	.367	84	-16	54-16	.984	7	106	66	O148C		-1.1
1984	NY N	154	587	88	162	28	10	10	54	26-2	2	90	.276	.308	.409	101	-2	46-9	.990	10	114	104	O146C		1.4
1985	NY N	93	337	56	93	16	8	6	26	28-6	0	52	.276	.331	.430	112	4	24-9	.964	-1	112	0	O83(4/83/0)	61	0.4
1986	†NY N	123	381	61	110	17	5	9	45	32-5	1	72	.289	.345	.430	115	7	25-7	.979	9	**119**	126	O114(78/65/3)	32	1.7

YEAR	TM LG	G	AB	R	H	2B	3B	HR	RBI	BB-IB	HP	SO	AVG	OBP	SLG	AOPS	ABR	SB-CS	FA	FR	RNG	THR	GAMES AT POSITION	
1987	NY N	124	385	58	115	19	7	9	34	35-8	2	85	.299	.359	.455	119	10	21-6	.963	0	108	61	O109(20/88/14)	
1988	†NY N	112	378	61	112	17	5	8	41	27-2	2	63	.296	.345	.431	127	12	15-4	.976	0	102	60	O104(16/83/18)	
1989	NY N	80	249	22	51	10	1	3	18	10-3	1	47	.205	.237	.289	52	-16	7-4	.975	5	124	70	O71(13/44/25)	
	†Tor A	54	238	32	71	9	4	2	17	3-0	2	37	.298	.311	.370	93	-3	12-1	.991	-6	83	54	O54(16/22/20)	
1990	Tor A	147	588	81	156	36	4	3	51	31-0	5	102	.265	.300	.355	81	-15	23-4	.992	-2	100	67	O141(8/133/0),D6	
1991	†Tor A	86	241	26	58	12	4	2	28	8-0	5	35	.241	.277	.349	70	-11	11-3	.973	-2	88	95	O41(36/5/0),D34	
Total	12	1403	5094	731	1397	227	71	67	438	282-36	23	866	.274	.314	.386	96	-45	327-98	.982	25	108	81	O1273(198/1067/90),D40	93

WILSON, WILLIE Willie James B7.9.1955 Montgomery AL BB/TR (BR 1976)/6-3/195(187-200) [KCA74 1/18] d9.4

YEAR	TM LG	G	AB	R	H	2B	3B	HR	RBI	BB-IB	HP	SO	AVG	OBP	SLG	AOPS	ABR	SB-CS	FA	FR	RNG	THR	GAMES AT POSITION	
1976	KC A	12	6	0	1	0	0	0	1	0-0	0	2	.167	.167	.167	-2	-1	2-1	.875	1	103	637	O6C	
1977	KC A	13	34	10	11	2	0	0	1	1-0	0	8	.324	.343	.382	96	0	6-3	.960	-0	109	0	O9C,D2	
1978	†KC A	127	198	43	43	8	2	0	16	16-0	0	33	.217	.280	.278	56	-11	46-12	.978	7	119	143	O112(82/35/0),D6	
1979	KC A	154	588	113	185	18	13	6	49	28-3	7	92	.315	.351	.420	105	2	83-12	.985	13	120	109	O152(130/23/5),D2	
1980	KC A	161	705	133	230	28	15	3	49	28-3	6	81	.326	.357	.421	111	8	79-10	.988	14	121	73	O159(102/62/0)	
1981	†KC A	102	439	54	133	10	7	1	32	18-3	4	42	.303	.335	.364	102	0	34-8	.987	18	127	190	O101(83/19/0)	
1982	KC A★	136	585	87	194	19	15	3	46	26-2	6	81	.332	.365	.431	117	12	37-11	.987	11	127	47	O135(119/19/0)	
1983	KC A★	137	576	90	159	22	8	2	33	33-2	1	75	.276	.316	.352	83	-14	59-8	.975	-4	104	31	O136(63/75/0)	16
1984	†KC A	128	541	81	163	24	9	2	44	39-2	3	56	.301	.350	.390	104	3	47-5	.990	-2	102	67	O128C	
1985	†KC A	141	605	87	168	25	21	4	43	29-3	5	94	.278	.316	.408	96	-6	43-11	.995	-9	96	43	O140C	
1986	KC A	156	631	77	170	20	7	9	44	31-1	9	97	.269	.313	.366	82	-17	34-8	.993	-3	101	49	O155C	
1987	KC A	146	610	97	170	18	15	4	30	32-2	6	88	.279	.320	.377	82	-18	59-11	.997	-5	95	48	O143C,D2	
1988	KC A	147	591	61	155	17	11	1	37	22-1	2	106	.262	.289	.333	73	-23	35-7	.989	-8	97	16	O142C	
1989	KC A	112	383	58	97	17	7	3	43	27-0	1	78	.253	.300	.358	86	-8	24-6	.977	-3	102	40	O108C/D	21
1990	KC A	115	307	49	89	13	3	2	42	30-1	2	57	.290	.354	.371	105	3	24-6	1.000	-1	99	43	O106(54/48/4)/D	
1991	Oak A	113	294	38	70	14	4	0	28	18-1	4	43	.238	.290	.313	71	-12	20-5	.983	3	114	50	O87(40/33/19),D9	17
1992	†Oak A	132	396	38	107	15	5	0	37	35-2	1	65	.270	.329	.333	91	-5	28-8	.981	8	121	33	O120(0/118/3),D5	15
1993	Chi N	105	221	29	57	11	3	1	11	11-1	1	40	.258	.301	.348	74	-9	7-2	.991	-5	88	40	O82C	
1994	Chi N	17	21	4	5	0	2	0	1	0-0	0	6	.238	.273	.429	79	-1	1-0	1.000	-1	78	0	O10C	16
Total	19	2154	7731	1169	2207	281	147	41	585	425-27	62	1144	.285	.326	.376	93	-97	668-134	.987	34	109	62	O2031(673/1356/31),D28	85

WINCENIAK, ED Edward Joseph B4.16.1929 Chicago IL BR/TR/5-9/165* d4.25

YEAR	TM LG	G	AB	R	H	2B	3B	HR	RBI	BB-IB	HP	SO	AVG	OBP	SLG	AOPS	ABR	SB-CS	FA	FR	RNG	THR	GAMES AT POSITION	
1956	Chi N	15	17	1	2	0	0	0	1	1-0	0	3	.118	.167	.118	-22	-3	0-0	.889	-1	64	0	3b4/2	
1957	Chi N	17	50	5	12	3	0	1	8	2-0	0	9	.240	.269	.360	68	-2	0-0	1.000	-2	68	73	S5,3b4,2b3	
Total	2	32	67	6	14	3	0	1	8	3-0	0	12	.209	.243	.299	45	-5	0-0	.955	-3	93	221	3b8,S5,2b4	

WINDHORN, GORDIE Gordon Ray B12.19.1933 Watseka IL BR/TR/6-1/185* d9.10

YEAR	TM LG	G	AB	R	H	2B	3B	HR	RBI	BB-IB	HP	SO	AVG	OBP	SLG	AOPS	ABR	SB-CS	FA	FR	RNG	THR	GAMES AT POSITION	
1959	NY A	7	11	0	0	0	0	0	0	0-0	0	3	.000	.000	.000	-99	-3	0-0	1.000	-1	98	0	O4L	
1961	LA N	34	33	10	8	2	1	2	6	4-1	0	3	.242	.324	.545	115	1	0-1	.944	1	113	160	O17(5/3/9)	
1962	KC A	14	19	1	3	1	0	0	1	0-0	0	5	.158	.158	.211	-2	-3	0-0	1.000	-0	78	0	O7L	
	LA A	40	45	9	8	6	0	0	1	7-1	0	10	.178	.288	.311	63	-2	1-1	1.000	-1	90	0	O27(22/3/5)	
	Year	54	64	10	11	7	0	0	2	7-1	0	13	.172	.254	.281	44	-5	1-1	1.000	-1	87	0	O34(29/3/5)	
Total	3	95	108	20	19	9	1	2	8	11-2	0	19	.176	.252	.333	55	-7	1-2	.981	-1	96	47	O55(38/6/14)	

WINDLE, BILL Willis Brewer B12.13.1904 Galena KS D12.8.1981 Corpus Christi TX BL/TL/5-11.5/170 d9.27 Col Missouri

YEAR	TM LG	G	AB	R	H	2B	3B	HR	RBI	BB-IB	HP	SO	AVG	OBP	SLG	AOPS	ABR	SB-CS	FA	FR	RNG	THR	GAMES AT POSITION	
1928	Pit N	1	1	1	1	0	0	0	0	0-0	0	0	1.000	1.000	2.000	641	1	0	1.000	0	0	0	/1	0.
1929	Pit N	2	1	0	0	0	0	0	0	0-0	0	1	.000	.000	.000	-98	0	0	1.000	0	0	383	1b2	0.
Total	2	3	2	1	1	0	0	0	0	0-0	0	1	.500	.500	.500	264	1	0	1.000	0	0	230	1b3	0.

WINE, ROBBIE Robert Paul Jr. B7.13.1962 Norristown PA BR/TR/6-2/200* [HouN83 1/8] d9.2 f-Bobby Col Oklahoma St.

YEAR	TM LG	G	AB	R	H	2B	3B	HR	RBI	BB-IB	HP	SO	AVG	OBP	SLG	AOPS	ABR	SB-CS	FA	FR	RNG	THR	GAMES AT POSITION	
1986	Hou N	9	12	2	3	0	0	0	1	1-0	0	4	.250	.308	.333	79	0	0-0	1.000	1	69	62	C8	0.1
1987	Hou N	14	29	1	3	1	0	0	0	1-0	0	10	.103	.133	.138	-29	-5	0-0	.979	-4	64	92	C12	-0.9
Total	2	23	41	3	6	2	0	0	1	2-0	0	14	.146	.186	.195	2	-5	0-0	.988	-3	66	83	C20	-0.8

WINE, BOBBY Robert Paul Sr. B9.17.1938 New York NY BR/TR/6-1/187* d9.20 M1/C20 s-Robbie

YEAR	TM LG	G	AB	R	H	2B	3B	HR	RBI	BB-IB	HP	SO	AVG	OBP	SLG	AOPS	ABR	SB-CS	FA	FR	RNG	THR	GAMES AT POSITION	
1960	Phi N	4	14	1	2	0	0	0	0	0-0	0	2	.143	.143	.143	-22	-2	0-0	1.000	1	93	181	S4	-0.2
1962	Phi N	112	311	30	76	15	0	4	25	11-3	0	49	.244	.268	.331	62	-17	2-0	.979	-0	101	101	S89,3b20	-1.1
1963	Phi N	142	418	29	90	14	3	6	44	14-5	1	83	.215	.241	.306	58	-24	1-3	.971	14	102	105	S132,3b8	-0.1
1964	Phi N	126	283	28	60	8	3	4	34	25-6	0	37	.212	.274	.304	64	-14	0-0	.965	1	97	110	S108,3b16	-0.5
1965	Phi N	139	394	31	90	8	1	5	33	31-9	0	69	.228	.284	.292	64	-19	0-0	.967	17	105	112	S135,1b4	0.8
1966	Phi N	46	89	8	21	5	0	0	6	6-3	1	13	.236	.292	.292	63	-4	0-1	.974	5	107	118	S40,O2L	44	0.3
1967	Phi N	135	363	27	69	12	5	2	28	29-10	0	77	.190	.249	.267	48	-25	3-2	.980	18	105	134	S134,1b2	0.3
1968	Phi N	27	71	5	12	3	0	2	7	6-1	0	17	.169	.234	.296	58	-4	0-0	.972	3	94	82	S25/3	124	-0.5
1969	Mon N	121	370	23	74	8	1	3	25	28-6	0	49	.200	.256	.251	42	-29	0-0	.949	20	107	128	S118/13	0.4
1970	Mon N	159	501	40	116	21	3	3	51	39-5	1	94	.232	.287	.303	59	-30	0-1	.976	19	103	138	S159	0.6
1971	Mon N	119	340	25	68	9	0	1	16	25-5	0	46	.200	.253	.235	39	-27	0-0	.982	5	96	103	S119	-1.0
1972	Mon N	34	18	2	4	1	0	0	0	0-0	0	2	.222	.222	.278	41	-1	0-0	1.000	2	88	0	3b21,S4/2	0.1
Total	12	1164	3172	249	682	104	16	30	268	214-53	3	538	.215	.264	.286	54	-196	7-7	.971	98	102	118	S1067,3b67,1b7,O2L/2	190	-0.9

WINFIELD, DAVE David Mark B10.3.1951 St.Paul MN BR/TR/6-6/220(220-249) [SDN73 1/4] d6.19 HF2001 Col Minnesota OF(466/219/1879) [DL 1989 NY A 182]

YEAR	TM LG	G	AB	R	H	2B	3B	HR	RBI	BB-IB	HP	SO	AVG	OBP	SLG	AOPS	ABR	SB-CS	FA	FR	RNG	THR	GAMES AT POSITION	
1973	SD N	56	141	9	39	4	1	3	12	12-1	0	19	.277	.331	.383	107	1	0-0	.956	-2	92	42	O36(34/2/1)/1	-0.3
1974	SD N	145	498	57	132	18	4	20	75	40-2	1	96	.265	.318	.438	116	8	9-7	.960	6	108	129	O131(81/25/34)	0.7
1975	SD N	143	509	74	136	20	2	15	76	69-14	3	82	.267	.354	.403	119	14	23-4	.972	3	106	90	O138R	1.3
1976	SD N	137	492	81	139	26	4	13	69	65-8	3	78	.283	.366	.431	137	25	26-7	.982	8	106	132	O134(0/10/127)	3.1
1977	SD N★	157	615	104	169	29	7	25	92	58-10	0	75	.275	.335	.467	125	19	16-7	.972	12	115	120	O156R	2.3
1978	SD N★	158	587	88	181	30	5	24	97	55-20	2	81	.308	.367	.499	152	39	21-9	.979	-9	92	64	O154(1/84/112),1b2	2.7
1979	SD N★	159	597	97	184	27	10	34	118	85-24	2	71	.308	.395	.558	168	56	15-9	.986	4	105	103	O157R	5.2
1980	SD N★	162	558	89	154	25	6	20	87	79-14	2	83	.276	.365	.450	136	28	23-7	.987	-1	89	153	O159(0/20/154)	2.4
1981	†NY A★	105	388	52	114	25	1	13	68	43-3	1	41	.294	.360	.464	139	20	11-1	.985	-10	92	15	O102(80/23/0)/D	1.0
1982	NY A★	140	539	84	151	24	8	37	106	45-7	0	64	.280	.331	.560	143	28	5-3	.974	6	102	208	O135L,D4	15	2.8
1983	NY A★	152	598	99	169	26	8	32	116	58-2	2	77	.283	.345	.513	138	29	15-6	.978	-10	94	44	O151(122/39/9)	1.4
1984	NY A★	141	567	106	193	34	4	19	100	53-9	0	71	.340	.393	.515	155	43	6-4	.994	-2	102	35	O140(1/16/127)	15	3.4
1985	NY A★	155	633	105	174	34	6	26	114	52-8	0	96	.275	.328	.471	118	14	19-7	.991	4	101	126	O152R,D2	1.2
1986	NY A★	154	565	90	148	31	5	24	104	77-9	2	106	.262	.349	.462	120	17	6-5	.984	-1	98	88	O145R,3b2,D6	0.8
1987	NY A★	156	575	83	158	22	1	27	97	76-5	0	96	.275	.358	.457	115	14	5-6	.989	-11	85	57	O145R,D8	-0.6
1988	NY A★	149	559	96	180	37	2	25	107	69-10	2	88	.322	.398	.530	158	45	9-4	.989	-11	87	33	O141R,D4	3.0
1990	NY A	20	61	7	13	3	0	2	6	4-0	1	13	.213	.269	.361	75	-2	0-0	1.000	0	62	0	O12L,D7	-0.5
	Cal A	112	414	63	114	18	2	19	72	48-3	1	68	.275	.348	.466	129	16	0-1	.989	-11	74	91	O108R,D3	0.1
	Year	132	475	70	127	21	2	21	78	52-3	2	81	.267	.338	.453	122	13	0-1	.989	-13	73	84	O120(12/0/108),D10	-0.4
1991	Cal A	150	568	75	149	27	4	28	86	56-4	1	109	.262	.326	.472	119	13	7-2	.990	-6	86	87	O115R,D34	0.3
1992	†Tor A	156	583	92	169	33	3	26	108	82-10	1	89	.290	.377	.491	135	29	2-3	1.000	-0	103	60	D130,O26R	2.3
1993	Min A	143	547	72	148	27	2	21	76	45-2	0	106	.271	.325	.442	103	1	2-3	1.000	-0	102	91	D105,O31R,1b5	-0.7
1994	Min A	77	294	35	74	15	3	10	43	31-5	0	51	.252	.321	.425	90	-5	2-1	1.000	0	139	0	D76/OR	16	-0.8
1995	Cle A	46	115	11	22	5	0	2	4	14-2	1	26	.191	.285	.287	48	-9	1-0					D39	56	0.2
Total	22	2973	11003	1669	3110	540	88	465	1833	1216-172	25	1686	.283	.353	.475	130	443	223-96	.982	-33	97	92	O2469R,D419,1b8,3b2	284	30.1

WINGO, AL Absalom Holbrook "Red" B5.6.1898 Norcross GA D10.9.1964 Detroit MI BL/TR/5-11/180 d9.9 b-Ivey Col Oglethorpe

YEAR	TM LG	G	AB	R	H	2B	3B	HR	RBI	BB-IB	HP	SO	AVG	OBP	SLG	AOPS	ABR	SB-CS	FA	FR	RNG	THR	GAMES AT POSITION	
1919	Phi A	15	59	9	18	1	3	0	2	4	0	12	.305	.344	.424	115	1	0	.815	-2	77	72	O15L	-0.2
1924	Det A	78	150	21	43	12	2	1	26	21	0	13	.287	.374	.413	105	2	2-5	.925	-2	87	58	O43(30/7/6)	-0.4
1925	Det A	130	440	104	163	34	10	5	68	69	0	31	.370	.456	.527	151	38	14-13	.971	9	110	120	O122(120/2/0)	3.3
1926	Det A	108	298	45	84	19	0	1	45	52	0	32	.282	.389	.356	94	0	4-2	.923	2	97	166	O74(61/0/14),3b2	-0.4
1927	Det A	75	137	15	32	8	0	0	20	25	0	14	.234	.352	.321	74	-2	1-0	.891	-1	75	201	O34(9/4/21)	-0.7
1928	Det A	87	242	30	69	17	3	2	30	40	0	17	.285	.389	.380	101	2	2-2	.968	-2	97	77	O71(35/28/6)	-0.4
Total	6	493	1326	224	409	87	15	9	191	211	0	119	.308	.404	.423	114	39	23-22	.944	3	99	125	O359(270/41/47),3b2	1.2

WINGO, ED Edmond Armand (b Edmond Armand La Riviere) B10.8.1895 St.Anne de Bellevue QC, Can. D12.5.1964 Lachine QC, Can. BR/TR/5-6/145 d10.2

YEAR	TM LG	G	AB	R	H	2B	3B	HR	RBI	BB-IB	HP	SO	AVG	OBP	SLG	AOPS	ABR	SB-CS	FA	FR	RNG	THR	GAMES AT POSITION	
1920	Phi A	1	4	0	1	0	0	0	1	0	0	0	.250	.250	.250	32	0	1	1.000	0	87	125	/C	0.0

TM LG	G	AB	R	H	2B	3B	HR	RBI	BB-IB	HP	SO	AVG	OBP	SLG	AOPS	ABR	SB-CS	FA	FR	RNG	THR	GAMES AT POSITION	DL	BFW
O, IVEY		Ivey Brown	B7.8.1890	Gainesville GA	D3.1.1941	Waycross GA		BL/TR/5-10/160	d4.20		M1/C3	b-AI											
StL N	25	57	4	12	2	0	0	3	3	0	7	.211	.250	.246	40	-5	0	.916	-2	82	114	C18		-0.6
StL N	100	310	38	82	18	3	2	44	23	1	45	.265	.317	.394	96	-3	8	.957	-7	74	127	C92		-0.2
StL N	112	307	25	78	5	8	2	35	17	1	41	.254	.295	.342	83	-9	18-11	.945	-10	79	117	C98,1b5/O(1/1/0)		-1.1
StL N	80	237	24	71	8	5	4	26	18	1	17	.300	.352	.426	132	8	15	.958	-2	102	99	C70,O4R		1.3
Cin N	119	339	26	75	11	6	3	29	13	0	33	.221	.250	.316	69	-14	10-11	.966	-0	96	110	C98/OL		-0.9
Cin N	119	347	30	85	8	11	2	40	25	1	27	.245	.298	.349	100	-1	4	.958	-7	82	138	C107,M		0.1
Cin N	121	399	37	106	16	11	2	39	25	1	13	.266	.311	.376	115	5	9	.967	-7	88	109	C120		1.0
Cin N	100	323	35	82	15	6	0	31	19	0	18	.254	.297	.337	95	-3	6	.973	0	106	101	C93,O5(3/0/1)		0.6
†Cin N	76	245	30	67	12	6	0	27	23	0	19	.273	.346	.371	115	5	4	.969	5	110	113	C75		1.8
Cin N	108	364	32	96	11	5	2	38	19	0	13	.264	.300	.338	84	-8	6-4	.958	-5	105	101	C107,2b2		-0.5
Cin N	97	295	20	79	7	6	3	38	21	1	14	.268	.319	.363	84	-3	3-2	.959	7	114	100	C92/OL		0.5
Cin N	80	260	24	74	13	3	3	45	23	0	11	.285	.343	.392	91	-4	1-1	.964	5	119	120	C78		0.5
Cin N	61	171	10	45	9	2	1	24	9	1	11	.263	.304	.357	75	-6	1-1	.969	2	110	124	C57		-0.1
Cin N	66	192	21	55	5	4	1	23	14	1	8	.286	.338	.370	91	-3	1-1	.989	3	99	100	C65/1		0.4
Cin N	55	146	6	30	7	0	0	12	11	0	9	.205	.261	.253	33	-15	1-2	.965	1	79	116	C55		-1.1
Cin N	7	10	0	2	0	0	0	1	1	0	0	.200	.333	.200	48	-1	0	1.000	0	156	0	C7		0.0
Cin N	1	1	0	0	0	0	0	0	0	0	0	.000	.000	.000	-99	-0	0	—	-0	0	0	/C		0.0
17	1327	4003	362	1039	147	81	25	455	264	10	285	.260	.307	.355	91	-62	87-36	.962	-17	97	112	C1233,O12(7/1/5),1b6,2b2		1.7

NKELMAN, GEORGE		George	B1859 OH	D1.1.1921	New York NY		d8.4																	
3 Lou AA	4	13	2	0	0	0	0		1			.000	.071	.000	-81	-3		.625	-0	185	0	O4(3/1/0)		-0.3

NKELMAN, GEORGE		George Edward	B2.18.1865	Washington DC	D5.19.1960	Washington DC		BL/TL/5-9/140	d8.2															
6 Was N	1	5	0	1	0	0	0	0		0	1	.200	.200	.200	24	0		—	-0	0	0	/ORP		0.0

NN, RANDY		Dwight Randolph	B6.9.1974	Los Angeles CA	BB/TR (BR 2000p)/6-2/193(175-195)		[FlaN95 3/65]	d5.11		Col Santa Clara														
98 TB A	109	338	51	94	9	1	9	17	29-0	1	69	.278	.337	.367	81	-10	26-12	.980	-1	95	134	O96(16/70/12),D4		-0.9
99 TB A	79	303	44	81	16	4	2	24	17-0	1	63	.267	.307	.366	70	-14	9-9	.995	-0	101	92	O77C		-1.4
00 TB A	51	159	28	40	5	0	1	16	26-0	2	35	.252	.362	.302	72	-6	6-7	.990	0	93	166	O47(29/18/0)/D		-0.7
01 TB A	128	429	54	117	25	6	6	50	38-0	6	81	.273	.339	.401	96	-2	12-10	.981	5	103	180	O117(9/48/62),D3		-0.1
02 TB A★	152	607	87	181	39	9	14	75	55-3	6	109	.298	.360	.461	119	17	27-8	.993	5	102	162	O146(0/138/8),D4		2.6
03 Sea A	157	600	103	177	37	4	11	75	41-0	8	108	.295	.346	.425	108	7	23-5	.992	3	110	33	O157(139/20/4)		0.8
04 Sea A	157	626	84	179	34	4	6	81	53-1	8	98	.286	.346	.427	106	5	21-7	.991	6	111	63	O154(40/128/0),D2		1.2
05 Sea A	102	386	46	106	25	1	6	37	37-3	4	53	.275	.342	.391	102	2	12-6	1.000	8	124	57	O96(92/6/0),D2		0.7
SF N	58	231	39	83	22	5	14	26	11-1	1	38	.359	.391	.680	167	21	7-5	.994	4	121	34	O55C		2.5
Total 8	993	3679	536	1058	212	44	69	401	307-8	37	644	.288	.346	.425	104	20	143-69	.991	30	107	99	O945(325/560/86),D16		4.7

NINNINGHAM, HERM		Herman Son	B12.1.1961	Orangeburg SC	BL/TR/5-11/185(170-190)		[NYN81*S1/9]	d9.1		Col Georgia Perimeter JC														
1984 NY N	14	27	5	11	1	0	5	1-0	0	7	.407	.429	.519	167		2	2-1	1.000	-1	55	0	O10(1/9/1)		0.1
1985 Mon N	125	312	30	74	6	5	3	21	28-3	0	72	.237	.297	.317	77	-11	20-9	.983	0	102	108	O116(1/115/0)	19	-1.1
1986 Mon N	90	185	23	40	4	1	4	18	18-3	0	51	.216	.286	.346	74	-7	12-7	.980	-4	92	72	O66(3/56/7)/S		-1.2
1987 Mon N	137	347	34	83	20	3	4	41	34-7	0	68	.239	.304	.349	71	-14	29-10	.975	-3	98	92	O131C		-1.6
1988 Mon N	47	90	10	21	2	1	0	6	12-1	0	18	.233	.320	.278	70		4-5	.982	-1	98	0	O30(0/29/1)		-0.6
Cin N	53	113	6	26	1	3	0	15	5-0	0	27	.230	.261	.292	57	-7	8-3	1.000	1	110	68	O42(14/21/8)		-0.6
Year	100	203	16	47	3	4	0	21	17-1	0	45	.232	.288	.286	63	-10	12-8	.992	-0	105	38	O72(14/50/9)		-1.2
1989 Cin N	115	251	40	63	11	3	3	13	24-1	0	50	.251	.316	.355	89	-4	14-5	.980	1	106	92	O85(34/41/13)	15	-0.3
1990 †Cin N	84	160	20	41	8	5	3	17	14-1	0	31	.256	.314	.425	98	-1	6-4	1.000	-2	90	139	O64(5/58/1)		-0.3
1991 Cin N	98	169	17	38	6	1	1	4	11-1	0	40	.225	.272	.290	56	-10	4-4	.953	-0	99	66	O66(12/55/1)		-1.1
1992 Bos A	105	234	27	55	8	1	1	14	10-0	0	53	.235	.266	.291	52	-15	6-5	.975	1	91	220	O67(36/32/0),D6		-1.7
Total 9	868	1888	212	452	69	26	19	147	157-17	0	417	.239	.296	.334	73	-70	105-53	.980	-8	99	104	O677(106/547/32),D6/S	34	-8.4

WINSETT, TOM		John Thomas "Long Tom"	B11.24.1909	McKenzie TN	D7.20.1987	Memphis TN		BL/TR/6-2/190	d4.20		Col Bethel													
1930 Bos A	1	1	0	0	0	0	0	0	0	1	.000	.000	.000	-99		-0	0-0	—	0		/H		0.0
1931 Bos A	64	76	6	15	1	0	1	7	4	1	21	.197	.247	.250	33	-8	0-0	1.000	1	96	214	O8L		-0.7
1933 Bos A	6	12	1	1	0	0	0	1	0	6	.083	.154	.083	-36	-2	0-0	1.000	-1	28	0	O4(2/0/2)		-0.3
1935 StL A	7	12	2	6	1	0	0	2	2	0	3	.500	.571	.583	203	2	0	—	-0	0	0	O2R		0.2
1936 Bro N	22	85	13	20	7	0	1	18	11	1	14	.235	.330	.353	83	-3	0	1.000	1	97	193	O21L		-0.2
1937 Bro N	118	350	32	83	15	5	5	42	45	3	64	.237	.329	.351	84	-7	3	.960	2	109	88	O101(100/1/0)/P		-1.1
1938 Bro N	12	30	6	9	1	0	1	7	6	0	4	.300	.417	.433	131	2	0	.882	-1	96	0	O9(5/0/4)		0.0
Total 7	230	566	60	134	25	5	8	76	69	5	113	.237	.325	.341	79	-15	3-0	.963	2	105	104	O145(136/1/8)/P		-2.1

WINTERS, MATT		Matthew Littleton	B3.18.1960	Buffalo NY	BL/TR/6-3/215		[NYA78 1/24]	d5.30																
1989 KC A	42	107	14	25	6	0	2	14	10	0	23	.234	.320	.346	88	-1	0-0	.939	-2	89	54	O31R,D3		-0.4

WIRTS, KETTLE		Elwood Vernon	B10.31.1897	Consumne CA	D7.12.1968	Sacramento CA		BR/TR/5-11/170	d7.20		Col St. Marys (CA)													
1921 Chi A	7	11	0	2	0	0	0	3		0	3	.182	.182	.182	-3	-2	0-0	1.000	1	92	119	C5		-0.1
1922 Chi A	31	58	7	10	2	0	1	6	12	0	15	.172	.314	.259	48	-4	0-0	.968	-3	112	56	C27		-0.5
1923 Chi N	5	5	2	1	0	0	0	1	2	0	0	.200	.429	.200	71	0	0-0	1.000	0	100	0	C3		0.1
1924 Chi A	6	12	0	1	0	0	0	0	2	0	2	.083	.214	.083	-22	-2	1-0	1.000	0	96	255	C5		-0.1
Total 4	49	86	9	14	2	0	1	8	16	0	20	.163	.294	.221	35	-8	1-0	.981	-1	106	89	C40		-0.6

WISE, HUGHIE		Hugh Edward	B3.9.1906	Campbellsville KY	D7.21.1987	Plantation FL		BB/TR/6-0/178	d9.26		Col Purdue													
1930 Det A	2	6	0	2	0	0	0			0	0	.333	.333	.333	68	0	0	1.000	0	89	159	C2		0.0

WISE, CASEY		Kendall Cole	B9.8.1932	Lafayette IN	BB/TR/6-0/170*		d4.16		Col Florida															
1957 Chi N	43	106	12	19	3	1	0	7	11-0	0	14	.179	.256	.226	32	-10	0-0	.940	1	103	100	2b31,S5		-0.8
1958 †Mil N	31	71	8	14	1	0	0	4	4-0	0	8	.197	.240	.211	23	-8	1-1	1.000	1	122	72	2b10,S7/3		-0.6
1959 Mil N	22	76	11	13	2	0	1	5	5-0	0	5	.171	.267	.237	39	-7	0-0	.989	-5	79	114	2b20,S5		-1.0
1960 Det A	30	68	6	10	0	2	2	5	4-0	0	9	.147	.194	.294	29	-7	1-0	.983	0	109	92	2b17,S10/3		-0.6
Total 4	126	321	37	56	6	3	3	17	29-0	0	36	.174	.243	.240	31	-32	2-1	.968	-3	100	99	2b78,S27,3b2		-3.0

WISE, DEWAYNE		Larry Dewayne	B2.24.1978	Columbia SC	BL/TL/6-1/180*		[CinN97 5/158]	d4.6																
2000 Tor A	28	22	3	3	0	0	0	1-0	1	5	.136	.208	.136	-10	-4	1-0	1.000	1	144	0	O18(14/1/3)	86	-0.3
2002 Tor A	42	112	14	20	4	1	3	13	4-0	0	15	.179	.207	.313	34	-11	5-0	1.000	7	132	276	O33(6/3/26),D3		-0.4
2004 †Atl N	77	162	24	37	9	4	6	17	9-1	1	28	.228	.272	.444	81	-6	6-1	1.000	-2	86	96	O56(34/7/15)	22	-0.8
Total 3	147	296	41	60	13	5	9	30	14-1	2	48	.203	.243	.372	56	-21	12-1	1.000	6	110	161	O107(54/11/44),D3	108	-1.5

WISE, NICK		Nicholas Joseph	B6.15.1866	Boston MA	D1.25.1923	Boston MA		BR/TR/5-11/194	d6.20															
1888 Bos N	1	3	0	0	0	0	0	0		0	0	.000	.000	.000	-97	-1	0	—	-0	0	0	/ORC		-0.1

WISE, SAM		Samuel Washington "Modoc"	B8.18.1857	Akron OH	D1.22.1910	Akron OH		BL/TR/5-10.5/170	d7.30		OF(12/0/36)													
1881 Det N	1	4	0	2	0	0	0	0		0	2	.500	.500	.500	207	0		.571	-1	111	0	/3		0.0
1882 Bos N	78	298	44	66	11	4	6	34	5		45	.221	.234	.326	77	-8		.852	-13	86	70	S72,3b6		-1.7
1883 Bos N	96	406	73	110	25	7	4	58	13		74	.271	.294	.397	105	2		.823	-1	93	92	S96		0.3
1884 Bos N	114	426	60	91	15	9	4	41	25		104	.214	.257	.319	81	-10		.884	2	92	81	S107,2b7		-0.4
1885 Bos N	107	424	71	120	20	10	4	46	25		61	.283	.323	.406	139	18		.858	6	101	112	S79,2b22,O6(4/0/2)		2.5
1886 Bos N	96	387	71	112	19	12	4	72	33		61	.289	.345	.432	139	18	31	.956	-21	78	75	1b57,2b20,S18/OR		-0.6
1887 Bos N	113	467	103	164	17	9	7	92	36	7	44	.334	.390	.522	150	31	43	.883	-1	105	98	S72,O27(4/0/23),2b16		2.7
1888 Bos N	105	417	66	100	19	12	4	40	34	6	66	.240	.306	.372	112	6	33	.888	3	98	131	S89,3b6,1b5,O4L,2b2		1.1
1889 Was N	121	472	79	118	15	9	4	62	61	4	62	.250	.341	.341	91	-1	24	.916	-16	98	77	2b72,S26,3b13,O10R		-1.2
1890 Buf P	119	505	95	148	29	11	5	102	46	6	45	.293	.359	.424	119	14	19	.906	8	104	87	2b119		2.1
1891 Bal AA	103	388	70	96	14	5	1	48	62	9	52	.247	.364	.317	94	0	33	.888	-9	103	76	2b99,S4		-0.5
1893 Was N	122	521	102	162	27	17	5	77	49	2	27	.311	.375	.457	124	16	20	.924	16	104	91	2b91,3b31		2.9
Total 12	1175	4715	834	1281	221	112	48	672	389	36	643	.272	.334	.397	114	86	203	.859	-26	95	96	S563,2b448,1b62,3b57,O48R		7.2

YEAR	TM LG	G	AB	R	H	2B	3B	HR	RBI	BB-IB	HP	SO	AVG	OBP	SLG	AOPS	ABR	SB-CS	FA	FR	RNG	THR	GAMES AT POSITION	DL

WISNER, PHIL Philip N. B7.1869 Washington DC D7.5.1936 Washington DC TR d8.30

| 1895 | Was N | 1 | 0 | 0 | 0 | 0 | 0 | 0 | 0 | 0-0 | | — | — | — | — | — | 0 | 0 | .250 | -1 | 63 | 0 | /S | |

WISSMAN, DAVE David Alvin B2.17.1941 Greenfield MA BL/TR/6-2/178 d9.15 Col Bridgeport

| 1964 | Pit N | 16 | 27 | 2 | 4 | 0 | 0 | 0 | 0 | 1-0 | | 9 | .148 | .179 | .148 | -7 | -4 | 0-0 | 1.000 | -0 | 101 | 0 | O10(7/3/0) | |

WISTERZIL, TEX George John B3.7.1888 Detroit MI D6.27.1964 San Antonio TX BR/TR/5-9.5/150 d4.14

1914	Bro F	149	534	54	137	18	10	0	66	34	11	47	.257	.314	.328	76	-27	17	.956	16	107	101	3b149	
1915	Bro F	36	106	13	33	3	3	0	21	21	3	7	.311	.438	.396	137	5	8	.949	4	112	148	3b31	
	Chi F	7	20	3	4	1	0	0	0	3	0	2	.200	.304	.250	60	-1	0	.955	0	106	0	3b6	
	StL F	8	24	1	5	1	0	0	4	2	1	2	.208	.296	.250	52	-2	2	.939	2	116	0	3b8	
	Chi F	42	144	12	36	3	1	0	14	5	1	10	.250	.280	.285	63	-10	2	.968	5	106	0	3b42	
	Year	93	294	29	78	8	4	0	39	31	5	21	.265	.345	.320	90	-7	12	.958	10	112	103	3b87	
Total	2	242	828	83	215	26	14	0	105	65	16	68	.260	.326	.325	81	-35	29	.957	26	109	102	3b236	

WITEK, MICKEY Nicholas Joseph B12.19.1915 Luzerne PA D8.24.1990 Kingston PA BR/TR/5-10/170 d4.16 Mil 1944-45

1940	NY N	119	433	34	111	7	0	3	31	24		17	.256	.295	.293	62	-23	2	.958	16	105	86	S89,2b32	
1941	NY N	26	94	11	34	5	0	1	16	4		17	.362	.388	.447	132	4	0	.933	0	98	113	2b23	
1942	NY N	148	553	72	144	19	6	5	48	36		20	.260	.306	.344	89	-9	2	.978	8	105	86	2b147	
1943	NY N	153	622	68	195	17	6	5	55	41		23	.314	.356	.370	109	6	1	.967	15	106	83	2b153	
1946	NY N	82	284	32	75	13	2	4	29	28		10	.264	.330	.366	97	-1	1	.962	-8	91	81	2b42,3b35	
1947	NY N	51	160	22	35	4	1	3	17	15		12	.219	.286	.313	58	-10	1	.983	9	120	108	2b40,3b3	
1949	NY A	2	1	0	1	0	0	0	0	0		0	1.000	1.000	1.000	430	0	0-0		0			/H	
Total	7	581	2147	239	595	65	9	22	196	148		84	.277	.324	.347	90	-33	7-0	.969	40	106	88	2b437,S89,3b38	

WITHROW, FRANK Frank Blaine "Kid" B6.14.1891 Greenwood MO D9.5.1966 Omaha NE BR/TR/5-11.5/187 d4.15

1920	Phi N	48	132	8	24	4	1	0	12	8		26	.182	.239	.227	33	-11	0-0	.973	1	85	94	C48	
1922	Phi N	10	21	3	7	2	0	0	3	3		5	.333	.417	.429	108	0	0-0	.909	0	102	90	C8	
Total	2	58	153	11	31	6	1	0	15	11		31	.203	.265	.255	45	-11	0-0	.965	1	87	93	C56	

WITHROW, CORKY Raymond Wallace B11.28.1937 High Coal WV BR/TR/6-3.5/200 d9.6 Col Georgetown

| 1963 | StL N | 6 | 9 | 0 | 0 | 0 | 0 | 0 | 0 | 1-0 | | 2 | .000 | .000 | .000 | -91 | -2 | 0-0 | 1.000 | 0 | 128 | 0 | O2(1/0/1) | |

WITMEYER, RON Ronald Herman B6.28.1967 West Islip NY BL/TL/6-3/215 [OakA88 7/177] d8.25 Col Stanford

| 1991 | Oak A | 11 | 19 | 0 | 1 | 0 | 0 | 0 | 0 | 0-0 | | 5 | .053 | .053 | .053 | -75 | -1 | 0-0 | 1.000 | 0 | 103 | 58 | 1b8 | |

WITT, KEVIN Kevin Joseph B1.5.1976 High Point NC BL/TR/6-4/195(185-210) [TorA94 1/28] d9.15

1998	Tor A	5	7	0	1	0	0	0	0	0-0		3	.143	.143	.143	-25	-1	0-0	1.000	0	150	0	/1	
1999	Tor A	15	34	3	7	1	0	1	5	2-0		9	.206	.250	.324	44	-3	0-0		0	D11			
2001	SD N	14	27	5	5	0	0	2	5	2-0		7	.185	.233	.407	68	-2	0-0	1.000	-0	66	76	1b9	
2003	Det A	93	270	25	71	9	0	10	26	15-0	1	68	.263	.301	.407	89	-5	1-1	1.000	1	118	135	D36,1b27,O13L,3b5	
Total	4	127	338	33	84	10	0	13	36	19-0	1	87	.249	.287	.393	80	-11	1-1	1.000	1	108	119	D47,1b37,O13L,3b5	

WITT, WHITEY Lawton Walter (b Ladislaw Waldemar Wittkowski) B9.28.1895 Orange MA D7.14.1988 Salem Co. NJ BL/TR/5-7/150 d4.12 Mil 1918 Col Bowdoin

1916	Phi A	143	563	64	138	16	15	2	36	55	2	71	.245	.315	.337	101	-2	19	.902	5	99	96	S142	1
1917	Phi A	128	452	62	114	13	4	0	28	65	0	45	.252	.346	.299	98	2	12	.935	8	108	80	S111,O7L,3b6	1
1919	Phi A	122	460	56	123	15	6	0	33	46	0	26	.267	.334	.326	85	-9	11	.972	4	103	43	O59(40/19/0),2b56,3b2	-0.
1920	Phi A	65	218	29	70	11	3	1	25	27		16	.321	.396	.413	113	5	2-3	.960	-5	88	34	O50(0/5/45),2b10,S2	-0.
1921	Phi A	154	629	100	198	31	11	4	45	77	1	52	.315	.390	.418	106	8	16-15	.959	-3	105	72	O154R	-0.
1922	†NY A	140	528	98	157	11	6	4	40	89	1	29	.297	.400	.364	98	3	5-8	.976	7	96	62	O139(0/109/30)	-1.
1923	†NY A	146	596	113	187	18	10	6	56	67	3	42	.314	.386	.408	107	7	2-7	.979	-4	96	85	O144C	-0.
1924	NY A	147	600	88	178	26	5	1	36	45		20	.297	.346	.362	83	-16	9-7	.976	-4	97	83	O144C	-0.
1925	NY A	31	40	9	8	2	1	0	6	6		2	.200	.304	.300	55	-3	1-1	1.000	1	111	144	O10(0/9/1)	-0.
1926	Bro N	63	85	13	22	1	1	0	3	12		6	.259	.351	.294	76	-2	1	.920	1	108	126	O22(3/17/2)	-0.
Total	10	1139	4171	632	1195	144	62	18	302	489	7	309	.287	.362	.364	97	-7	78-41	.971	-13	99	73	O729(50/447/232),S255,2b66,3b8	-4.

WITTE, JERRY Jerome Charles B7.30.1915 St.Louis MO D4.27.2002 Houston TX BR/TR/6-1/190 d9.10

1946	StL A	18	73	7	14	2	0	2	4	0		18	.192	.192	.301	35	-7	0-0	.967	-2	70	95	1b18	-1.
1947	StL A	34	99	4	14	2	1	2	12	11		22	.141	.227	.242	30	-10	0-0	.983	-1	86	86	1b27	-1.
Total	2	52	172	11	28	4	1	4	16	11		40	.163	.213	.267	32	-17	0-0	.977	-4	80	94	1b45	-2.

WOCKENFUSS, JOHN Johnny Bilton B2.27.1949 Welch WV BR/TR/6-0/190(170-190) [TexA67 42/761] d8.11 OF(42/0/69)

1974	Det A	13	29	1	4	1	0	0	2	3-0		2	.138	.212	.172	13	-3	0-0	.932	-2	112	145	C13	-0.8
1975	Det A	35	118	15	27	6	3	4	13	10-0	1	15	.229	.287	.432	97	-1	0-0	.982	3	91	107	C34	0.4
1976	Det A	60	144	18	32	7	2	3	10	17-0	1	14	.222	.309	.361	92	-1	0-3	.941	-6	102	93	C59	-0.
1977	Det A	53	164	26	45	8	1	9	25	14-0		18	.274	.331	.500	117	3	0-0	.985	-1	111	85	C37,O9(6/0/3),D3	0.
1978	Det A	71	187	23	53	5	0	7	22	21-4	1	14	.283	.357	.422	115	4	0-1	.978	-6	82	52	O60(6/0/55),D2	-0.5
1979	Det A	87	231	27	61	9	1	15	46	18-0	2	40	.264	.320	.506	116	4	2-2	.996	5	111	102	1b31,C20,D18,O6(5/0/1)	0.4
1980	Det A	126	372	56	102	13	2	16	65	68-4	3	64	.274	.390	.449	126	16	1-4	.983	0	112	95	1b52,D28,C25,O23(21/0/2)	1.
1981	Det A	70	172	20	37	4	0	9	25	28-1		22	.215	.322	.395	103	1	0-0	.984	-3	37	172	D39,1b25,C5/OL	1.
1982	Det A	70	193	28	58	9	0	8	32	29-2		21	.301	.388	.472	135	10	1-1	.981	-4	66	105	C24,1b17,D17,O10(2/0/8)/3	0.
1983	Det A	92	245	32	66	8	1	9	44	31-1	3	37	.269	.349	.420	114	5	1-1	1.000	5	112	114	D39,C29,1b13/3OL	0.
1984	Phi N	86	180	20	52	3	1	6	24	30-1	1	24	.289	.390	.417	125	7	1-0	.996	-7	79	98	1b39,C21,3b2	-0.
1985	Phi N	32	37	1	6	0	0	0	2	8-1		8	.162	.311	.162	35	-3	0-0	1.000	-0	33	126	1b7,C2	-0.
Total	12	795	2072	267	543	73	11	86	310	277-14	7	278	.262	.349	.432	114	42	5-11	.972	-20	90	93	C269,1b184,D146,O110R,3b4	1.0

WOEHR, ANDY Andrew Emil B2.4.1896 Fort Wayne IN D7.24.1990 Fort Wayne IN BR/TR/5-11/165 d9.15

1923	Phi N	13	41	3	14	2	0	0	3	1		1	.341	.357	.390	87	-1	0-0	.975	2	112	173	3b13	0.2
1924	Phi N	50	152	11	33	4	5	0	17	5	2	8	.217	.252	.309	44	-13	2-2	.920	-5	85	113	3b44/2	-1.6
Total	2	63	193	14	47	6	5	0	20	6	2	9	.244	.274	.326	53	-14	2-2	.935	-3	91	127	3b57/2	-1.4

WOERLIN, JOE Joseph B10.9.1864 Trenheim, France D6.22.1919 St.Louis MO d7.21

| 1895 | Was N | 1 | 3 | 1 | 1 | 0 | 0 | 0 | 0 | 0 | | 0 | .333 | .333 | .333 | 73 | 0 | 0 | 1.000 | 0 | 125 | 0 | /S | 0.0 |

WOHLFORD, JIM James Eugene B2.28.1951 Visalia CA BR/TR/5-11/175(167-180) [KCA70*S3/61] d9.1 Col Sequoias (CA) [JC]

1972	KC A	15	25	3	6	1	0	0	6	2-0	1	6	.240	.321	.280	80	0	0-0	.950	-3	79	28	2b8	-0.4
1973	KC A	45	109	21	29	1	0	2	10	11-0	1	12	.266	.333	.385	95	-1	1-1	1.000	3	132	241	D19,O13(12/0/1)	0.0
1974	KC A	143	501	55	136	16	7	2	44	39-3	3	74	.271	.327	.343	88	-8	16-13	.982	-1	97	71	O138(126/0/16)/D	-1.8
1975	KC A	116	353	45	90	10	5	0	30	34-2	1	37	.255	.317	.312	78	-10	12-7	.953	-1	96	123	O102(43/0/66),D4	-1.6
1976	†KC A	107	293	47	73	9	2	1	24	29-0	1	24	.249	.314	.307	83	-6	22-16	.975	6	118	107	O93(84/2/8)/2D	-1.
1977	Mil A	129	391	44	97	16	3	2	36	21-1	1	49	.248	.285	.320	65	-19	17-16	.981	4	112	74	O125(97/4/33)/2D	-2.2
1978	Mil A	46	118	16	35	7	2	1	19	6-0		10	.297	.325	.415	108	1	3-2	.982	-3	85	101	O35(21/4/12),D4	-0.2
1979	Mil A	63	175	19	46	13	1	1	17	8-0		28	.263	.290	.366	77	-6	6-2	.969	-1	112	4	O55(35/14/8),3	-0.8
1980	SF N	91	193	17	54	6	4	1	24	13-0	1	23	.280	.324	.368	97	-1	1-4	.989	2	119	69	O49(40/4/8)/3	-0.3
1981	SF N	50	68	4	11	3	0	1	7	4-0		9	.162	.205	.250	30	-6	0-0	1.000	-2	21	152	O10L	-0.9
1982	SF N	97	250	37	64	12	1	2	25	30-4		36	.256	.331	.336	89	-3	8-3	.992	1	103	82	O72(68/0/6)	-0.4
1983	Mon N	83	141	7	39	8	0	1	14	5-0		19	.277	.297	.355	81	-4	0-0	.988	2	125	85	O61(8/6/48)	-0.3
1984	Mon N	95	213	20	64	13	2	6	29	14-0		19	.300	.342	.451	127	7	3-0	.989	-0	94	84	O59(44/1/14),3b2	0.6
1985	Mon N	70	125	7	24	5	1	1	15	16-5		18	.192	.284	.272	59	-7	0-2	1.000	-1	98	46	O43(8/0/36)	-1.1
1986	Mon N	70	94	10	25	4	0	1	11	9-3		25	.266	.327	.383	96	-1	0-2	1.000	4	98		O22(10/0/12),3b9	-0.3
Total	15	1220	3049	349	793	125	33	21	305	241-18	8	376	.260	.313	.343	85	-64	89-68	.980	6	105	84	O877(606/35/268),D37,2b10,3b9	-10.2

WOJCIK, JOHN John Joseph B4.6.1942 Olean NY BL/TR/6-0/175* d9.9

1962	KC A	16	43	8	13	4	0	0	9	13-0	1	4	.302	.474	.395	131	4	3-0	1.000	-0	85	138	O12(10/0/5)	0.3
1963	KC A	19	59	7	11	0	0	0	8	8-2		6	.186	.284	.186	33	-5	2-0	1.000	0	105	89	O17(10/2/6)	-0.6
1964	KC A	6	22	1	3	0	0	0	0	0		8	.136	.208	.136	-2	-3	0-0	1.000	-0	100	0	O6L	-0.4
Total	3	41	124	16	27	4	0	0	11	23-2	1	20	.218	.345	.250	64	-5	5-0	1.000	0	97	92	O35(26/2/11)	-0.7

R	TM LG	G	AB	R	H	2B	3B	HR	RBI	BB-IB	HP	SO	AVG	OBP	SLG	AOPS	ABR	SB-CS	FA	FR	RNG	THR	GAMES AT POSITION	DL	BFW

WOLF, RAY   Raymond Bernard "Grandpa" B7.15.1904 Chicago IL   D10.6.1979 Fort Worth TX   BR/TR/5-11/175   d7.27   Col TCU

7	Cin N	1	1	0	0	0	0	0	0	0	0	0	.000	.000	.000	-99	0	0	1.000	-0	0	0	/1		0.0

WOLF, JIMMY   William Van Winkle "Chicken" B5.12.1862 Louisville KY   D5.16.1903 Louisville KY   BR/TR/5-9/190   d5.2   M1   OF(17/3/1024) ▲

2 Lou AA		78	318	46	95	11	8	0		9				.299	.318	.384	144	14		.902	-2	**132**	134	O70(3/0/67),S9/1P	1.1
3 Lou AA		**98**	389	59	102	17	9	1		5				.262	.272	.360	110	5		.890	14	**186**	325	O78(0/1/77),C20,S5/2	1.7
4 Lou AA		110	486	79	146	24	11	3	73	4	3			.300	.310	.414	140	20		.884	-2	131	157	O101(0/1/101),C11,S31	1.7
5 Lou AA		112	483	79	141	23	17	1	52	11	1			.292	.309	.416	128	13		.917	-1	100	117	O111R,C2/3P	1.0
6 Lou AA		130	545	93	148	17	12	3	61	27	3			.272	.310	.363	105	-1	23	.934	7	132	130	O122(5/0/119),1b8,C3/2P	0.4
7 Lou AA		**137**	569	103	160	27	13	2	102	34				.281	.331	.385	97	-4	45	.940	8	128	116	O128(8/1/120),1b11	0.1
8 Lou AA		128	538	80	154	28	11	0	67	25	2			.286	.320	.379	126	15	41	.886	3	135	124	O85(1/0/84),S39,3b4,C3/1	1.7
9 Lou AA		130	546	72	159	20	9	3	57	29	5	34		.291	.333	.377	104	1	18	.946	1	94	46	O88R,1b16,2b13,S10,3b7,M	0.1
0 †Lou AA		**134**	543	100	**197**	29	11	4	98	43	12			**.363**	.421	.479	169	47	46	.939	-4	72	123	O123R,3b12	3.6
1 Lou AA		136	528	67	135	16	8	1	81	42	8	36		.256	.320	.322	85	-11	13	.922	3	117	101	O131R,1b5/3	-0.9
2 StL N		3	14	1	2	0	0	0		1				.143	.143	.143	-14	-2	0	1.000	-1	0	0	O3R	-0.3
al 11		1196	4959	779	1439	212	109	18	592	229	42	71		.290	.327	.388	118	97	186	.918	26	120	133	O1040R,S64,1b43,C39,3b26,2b15,P3	10.2

WOLFE, HARRY   Harold "Whitey" B11.24.1890 MA   D7.28.1971 Fort Wayne IN   BR/TR/5-8/160   d4.15

7 Chi N		9	5	1	2	0	0	0		1	1	1		.400	.500	.400	164	0	0	1.000	0	115	0	O2L/S	0.1
Pit N		3	5	0	0	0	0	0		1			4	.000	.167	.000	-45	-1	0	.875	0	81	343	/2S	-0.1
Year		12	10	1	2	0	0	0	1	2			5	.200	.333	.200	61	0	0	1.000	0	115	0	O2L,S2/2	0.0

WOLFE, LARRY   Laurence Marcy B3.2.1953 Melbourne FL   BR/TR/5-11/170*   [MinA73 9/203]   d9.16   Col Sacramento (CA) City

77 Min A		8	25	3	6	1	0	0	6	1-1	0		.240	.269	.280	51	-2	0-0	1.000	1	110	88	3b8	-0.1
78 Min A		88	235	25	55	10	1	3	25	36-0	1		27	.234	.332	.323	84	-4	0-1	.953	3	104	69	3b81,S7	-0.4
79 Bos A		47	78	12	19	4	0	3	15	17-0	1		21	.244	.378	.410	109	-2	0-0	.963	3	104	104	2b7,3b9,S2/C1D	0.5
80 Bos A		18	23	3	3	1	0	1	4	0-0	0		5	.130	.125	.304	15	-3	0-0	1.000	0	69	161	3b14,D4	-0.4
tal 4		161	361	43	83	16	1	7	50	54-1	1		53	.230	.327	.338	84	-7	0-1	.957	3	105	90	3b112,2b27,S9,D5/1C	-0.4

WOLFE, POLLY   Roy Chamberlain B9.1.1888 Knoxville IL   D11.21.1938 Morris IL   BL/TR/5-10/170   d9.22

12 Chi A		1	1	0	0	0	0	0	0	0	0		.000	.000	.000	-99	0	0	—	0			/H	0.0
14 Chi A		8	28	0	6	0	0	0	3	0	0	6	.214	.290	.214	53	-2	1-1	.875	-1	81	0	O7R	-0.4
tal 2		9	29	0	6	0	0	0	3	0	0	6	.207	.281	.207	47	-2	1-1	.875	-1	81	0	O7R	-0.4

WOLSTENHOLME, ABE   Abraham Lincoln B3.4.1861 Philadelphia PA   D3.4.1916 Philadelphia PA   d6.4

83 Phi N		3	11	0	1	1	0	0	0	0			.091	.091	.182	-22	-1		.727	-2			C2/OL	-0.3

WOLTER, HARRY   Harry Meiggs B7.11.1884 Monterey CA   D7.6.1970 Palo Alto CA   BL/TL/5-10/175   d5.14   Col Santa Clara ▲

07 Cin N		4	15	1	2	0	0	0	1	0	0		.133	.133	.133	-16	-0	0	1.000	-0	0	0	O4R	-0.3
Pit N		1	1	0	0	0	0	0	0	0	0		.000	.000	.000	-99	0	0	—	-0	-0	0	/P	0.0
StL N		16	47	4	16	0	0	0	6	3	0		.340	.380	.340	130	2	1	.962	1	304	236	O9(1/6/2),P3	0.3
Year		21	63	5	18	0	0	0	7	3	0		.286	.318	.286	91	-1	1	.969	1	241	187	O13(1/6/6),P4	0.0
09 Bos A		54	121	14	29	2	4	2	10	9	0		.240	.292	.372	107	0	2	.978	-2	120	63	1b17,P11,O9R	-0.2
10 NY A		135	479	84	128	15	9	4	42	66	7		.267	.364	.361	120	14	39	.940	-2	112	65	O129(1/0/128),1b2	0.7
11 NY A		122	434	78	132	17	15	4	36	62	4		.304	.396	.440	125	15	28	.951	5	114	100	O113(0/7/106),1b2	1.4
12 NY A		12	32	8	11	2	1	0	1	10	1		.344	.512	.469	171	4	5	.923	-1	76	91	O9(0/5/4)	0.3
13 NY A		127	425	53	108	18	6	2	43	80	4	50	.254	.377	.339	109	10	13	.946	-7	92	82	O121(0/106/15)	-0.6
17 Chi N		117	353	44	88	15	7	0	28	38	1	40	.249	.324	.331	94	-2	7	.942	1	93	132	O97(3/2/94)/1	-0.6
tal 7		588	1907	286	514	69	42	12	167	268	17	90	.270	.365	.369	114	41	95	.941	-5	106	92	O491(5/126/362),1b22,P15	1.0

WOLVERTON, HARRY   Harry Sterling "Fighting Harry" B12.6.1873 Mt.Vernon OH   D2.4.1937 Oakland CA   BL/TR/5-11/205   d9.25   M1   Col Kenyon

98 Chi N		13	49	4	16	1	0	0	7				.327	.353	.347	101	0	1	.848	0	113	51	3b13	0.0
99 Chi N		99	389	50	111	14	11	1	49	30	9		.285	.350	.386	105	2	14	.860	-7	102	85	3b98/S	-0.3
00 Chi N		3	11	2	2	0	0	0	2	0			.182	.308	.182	38	-1	1	.875	-1	82	0	3b3	-0.1
Phi N		101	383	42	108	10	8	3	58	20	3		.282	.323	.373	92	-6	-4	.881	-10	98	109	3b101	-1.3
Year		104	394	44	110	10	8	3	58	22	3		.279	.322	.368	91	-6	5	.881	-11	98	106	3b104	-1.4
01 Phi N		93	379	42	117	15	4	0	43	22	6		.309	.356	.369	108	4	13	.921	3	104	100	3b93	1.0
02 Was A		59	249	35	62	8	3	1	23	13	2		.249	.292	.317	68	-11	8	.904	3	106	90	3b59	-0.6
Phi N		34	136	12	40	3	2	0	16	9	2		.294	.347	.346	114	3	5	.931	-1	118	214	3b34	0.8
03 Phi N		123	494	72	152	13	12	0	53	18	8		.308	.342	.383	110	4	10	.941	1	99	59	3b123	0.5
04 Phi N		102	398	43	106	15	5	0	49	26	6		.266	.321	.329	105	2	18	.925	-1	93	117	3b102	-0.9
05 Bos N		122	463	38	104	15	7	2	55	23	10		.225	.276	.300	73	-16	10	.934	4	109	81	3b122	-0.2
12 NY A		34	50	6	15	1	1	0	4	2	1		.300	.340	.360	94	-1	1	.821	-2	69	95	3b8,M	-0.1
tal 9		783	3001	346	833	95	53	7	352	166	48		.278	.326	.352	96	-21	83	.909	-2	102	95	3b756/S	-0.1

WOMACK, TONY   Anthony Darrell B9.25.1969 Chatham VA   BL/TR/5-9/155(150-170)   [PitN91 7/201]   d9.10   Col Guilford

93 Pit N		15	24	5	2	0	0	0		3-0	0	3	.083	.185	.083	-25	-4	2-0	.971	3	134	183	S6	-0.1
94 Pit N		5	12	4	4	0	0	0	1	0-0	0		.333	.429	.333	100	0	0-0	.750	-2	44	62	2b3,S2	-0.2
96 Pit N		17	30	11	10	3	1	0	7	6-1	1	1	.333	.459	.500	148	3	2-0	1.000	-1	71	0	O6(0/5/1),2b4	0.2
97 Pit N★		155	641	85	178	26	9	6	50	43-2	3	109	.278	.326	.374	81	-19	60-7	.974	4	101	86	2b152,S4	0.3
98 Pit N		159	655	85	185	26	7	3	45	38-1	0	94	.282	.319	.357	78	-22	58-8	.978	9	105	109	2b152,O5C,S2	0.3
99 †Ari N		144	614	111	170	25	10	4	41	52-0	2	68	.277	.332	.370	78	-22	72-13	.992	-3	109	123	O123(0/6/122),2b19,S19	7	-1.7
00 Ari N		146	617	95	167	21	**14**	7	57	30-0	5	74	.271	.307	.384	71	-30	45-11	.970	-12	88	89	S143,O2R		-2.4
01 Ari N		125	481	66	128	19	5	3	30	23-2	6	54	.266	.307	.345	64	-26	28-7	.955	-7	92	**118**	S118/OC	15	-2.0
02 Ari N		153	590	90	160	23	5	5	57	46-2	4	80	.271	.325	.353	75	-23	29-12	.964	-22	85	87	S149/OR	19	-3.3
03 Ari N		61	219	30	52	10	3	2	15	8-0	2	27	.237	.270	.338	53	-16	8-3	.966	-5	87	89	S58		-1.6
Col N		21	79	5	15	2	0	0	5	0-0	1	9	.190	.200	.215	7	-11	3-1	.959	-4	90	60	S14,2b7/OC		-1.3
Chi N		21	51	4	12	2	1	0	2	1-0	1	11	.235	.250	.314	45	-4	2-1	1.000	-1	81	58	2b14/S		-0.5
Year		103	349	43	79	14	4	2	22	9-0	4	47	.226	.251	.307	41	-31	13-5	.965	-10	88	65	S73,2b21/OC		-3.4
04 †StL N		145	553	91	170	22	5	3	38	36-1	3	60	.307	.349	.385	90	-8	26-5	.976	-1	105	111	2b133		0.1
05 †NY A		108	329	46	82	8	1	0	15	12-0	1	49	.249	.276	.280	49	-25	27-5	.983	7	35	89	S516,2b508,O205(40/40/130),D11	41	-13.6
Total 12		1275	4895	732	1335	187	59	35	363	300-8	28	642	.273	.316	.356	72	-207	362-73	.964	-35	89	93			

WOMACK, SID   Sidney Kirk "Tex" B10.2.1896 Greensburg LA   D8.28.1958 Jackson MS   BR/TR/5-10.5/185   d8.15   Col Mississippi St.

1926 Bos N		1	3	0	0	0	0	0	1	0		0	.000	.000	.000	-99	-1	0	1.000	-0	44	0	/C	-0.1

WOOD   d9.30

1874 Bal NA		1	5	0	0	0	0	0	0	0			1	.000	.000	.000	-99	-1	0-0	.000	-1	0	0	/2	-0.2

WOOD, DOC   Charles Spencer B2.28.1900 Batesville MS   D11.3.1974 New Orleans LA   BR/TR/5-10/150   d7.21   Col U. of Mississippi

1923 Phi A		3	3	0	1	0	0	0	0	0		0	.333	.333	.333	75	0	0-0	.833	0	161	191	S3	0.0

WOOD, TED   Edward Robert B1.4.1967 Mansfield OH   BL/TL/6-2/178*   [SFN88 1/29]   d9.4   Col New Orleans

1991 SF N		10	25	0	3	0	0	0	1	2-0	0	11	.120	.185	.120	-13	-4	0-0	.909	-1	80	0	O8R	-0.5
1992 SF N		24	58	5	12	2	0	1	3	6-0	1	15	.207	.292	.293	70	-2	0-0	.972	1	126	0	O16(6/0/10)	23	-0.2
1993 Mon N		13	26	4	5	1	0	0	3	3-1	0	3	.192	.276	.231	36	-2	0-0	1.000	0	117	0	O8(8/0/1)	-0.3
Total 3		47	109	9	20	3	0	1	7	11-1	1	29	.183	.264	.239	42	-8	0-0	.968	-0	113	0	O32(14/0/19)	23	-1.0

WOOD, FRED   Frederick Llewellyn B7.21.1863 Dundas ON, Can.   BR/5-5/150   d5.14   b-Pete

1884 Det N		12	42	4	3	0	0	0	1	3		18	.048	.111	.048	-51	-7		.889	-2			C7,O6R/S	-0.8
1885 Buf N		1	4	0	1	0	0	0	0				.250	.250	.250	60	0		.833	-0			/C	0.0
Total 2		13	46	4	3	0	0	0	1	3		18	.065	.122	.065	-41	-7		.883	-2			C8,O6R/S	-0.8

WOOD, GEORGE   George A. "Dandy" B11.9.1858 Boston MA   D4.4.1924 Harrisburg PA   BL/TR/5-10.5/175   d5.1   M1/U1   OF(1192/5/36) ▲

1880 Wor N		81	327	37	80	16	5	0	28	10		37	.245	.267	.324	91	-4		.887	-2	57	53	O80L,3b2/1	-1.5
1881 Det N		80	337	54	100	18	9	2	32	19		32	.297	.334	.421	131	11		.862	-2	85	124	O80L	0.4
1882 Det N		84	375	69	101	12	12	**7**	29	14		30	.269	.296	.421	127	10		.884	2	73	199	O84L	0.9
1883 Det N		99	441	81	133	26	11	5	47	25		37	.302	.339	.444	142	23		.876	7	65	76	O99(96/3/0)/P	2.3

YEAR	TM LG	G	AB	R	H	2B	3B	HR	RBI	BB-IB	HP	SO	AVG	OBP	SLG	AOPS	ABR	SB-CS	FA	FR	RNG	THR	GAMES AT POSITION	DL	BR
1884	Det N	114	473	79	119	16	10	8	29	39		75	.252	.309	.378	122	14		.896	4	75	25	O114(114/0/1)/3		1
1885	Det N	82	362	62	105	19	8	5	28	13		19	.290	.335	.428	138	14		.885	2	79	51	O70L,3b12/SP		1
1886	Phi N	106	450	81	123	18	15	4	50	23		75	.273	.308	.407	115	6	9	.904	-4	67	77	O97(96/1/0),S6,3b3		
1887	Phi N	113	491	118	142	22	19	14	66	40	6	51	.289	.350	.497	125	14	19	.873	-10	54	63	O104L,S3,3b3,2b3		
1888	Phi N	106	433	67	99	19	6	6	51	39	7	44	.229	.303	.342	100	1	20	.905	-1	84	90	O104L,3b2,P2		-0
1889	Phi N	97	422	77	106	21	4	5	53	53	1	33	.251	.336	.355	86	-9	17	.915	-2	52	31	O92L,S6/P		-0
	Bal AA	3	10	1	2	0	0	0	1	0	0	2	.200	.200	.200	14	-1	1	1.000	-0	0	0	O3R		-1
1890	Phi P	132	539	115	156	20	14	9	102	51	8	35	.289	.360	.429	108	3	20	.895	14	142	180	O132(128/0/4)/3		-0
1891	Phi AA	132	528	105	163	18	14	3	61	72	7	52	.309	.399	.413	132	23	22	.939	7	115	222	O122L,3b6,S5,M		1
1892	Bal N	21	76	9	17	1	1	0	10	10	2	8	.224	.330	.263	78	-2	1	.911	2	174	116	O21L		-0
	Cin N	30	107	10	21	2	4	0	10	10	1	17	.196	.271	.290	71	-4	4	.863	-1	113	109	O30(1/1/28)		-0
	Year	51	183	19	38	3	5	0	20	20*	3	25	.208	.296	.279	74	-6	5	.885	1	140	112	O51(22/1/28)		-0
Total	13	1280	5371	965	1467	228	132	68	601	418	32	547	.273	.329	.403	116	99	113	.895	11	84	100	O1232L,3b30,S21,P5,2b3/1		6

WOOD, HARRY Harold Austin B2.10.1881 Waterville ME D5.18.1955 Bethesda MD BL/TR/5-10/155 d4.19 Col Maryland-Baltimore Co.

YEAR	TM LG	G	AB	R	H	2B	3B	HR	RBI	BB-IB	HP	SO	AVG	OBP	SLG	AOPS	ABR	SB-CS	FA	FR	RNG	THR	GAMES AT POSITION	DL	BR
1903	Cin N	2	3	0	0	0	0	0	0	0				.000	.250	.000	-24	0	0	—	-0	0	0	O2(1/0/1)		-0

WOOD, JAKE Jacob B6.22.1937 Elizabeth NJ BR/TR/6-1/170* d4.11 Col Delaware St.

1961	Det A	162	663	96	171	17	14	11	69	58-2	-4	141	.258	.320	.376	83	-18	30-9	.969	-26	91	81	2b162		-2
1962	Det A	111	367	68	83	10	5	8	30	33-0	1	59	.226	.291	.346	68	-17	24-3	.950	-24	85	59	2b90		-3
1963	Det A	85	351	50	95	11	2	11	27	24-0	7	61	.271	.330	.407	102	1	18-5	.958	-8	93	97	2b81/3		-0
1964	Det A	64	125	11	29	2	2	1	7	4-0	0	24	.232	.254	.304	54	-8	0-0	.989	-3	114	80	1b11,2b10,3b6/OL		-1
1965	Det A	58	104	12	30	3	0	2	7	10-0	1	19	.288	.357	.375	107	1	3-3	.977	-2	83	104	2b20/1S3		-0
1966	Det A	98	230	39	58	9	3	2	27	28-0	1	48	.252	.336	.343	94	-1	4-3	.968	-9	81	87	2b52,3b4,1b2		-0
1967	Det A	14	20	2	1	1	0	0	1	1-0	0	7	.050	.095	.100	-41	-4	0-0	1.000	0	0	261	1b2,2b2		-0
	Cin N	16	17	1	2	0	0	0	1	1-0	1	3	.118	.167	.118	-15	-3	0-0	1.000	0	88	0	O2R		-0
Total	7	608	1877	279	469	53	26	35	168	159-2	14	362	.250	.312	.362	82	-49	79-23	.963	-70	88	82	2b417,1b16,3b12,O3(1/0/2)/S	58	-7.

WOOD, JIMMY James Leon B12.1.1843, Can D11.30.1886 TR/5-8.5/150 d5.8 M4

1871	Chi NA	28	135	45	51	10	6	1	29	11		3	.378	.425	.563	163	10	18-2	.887	8	107	131	2b28,M		1.
1872	Tro NA	25	113	40	38	11	4	2	26	2		1	.336	.348	.558	172	9	1-0	.886	-1	82	54	2b25,M		0.
	Eck NA	7	31	10	6	1	1	0	0	4		1	.194	.286	.290	91	1	1-0	.840	-0	95	30	2b7,M		0.
	Year	32	144	50	44	12	5	2	26	6		2	.306	.333	.500	156	10	1-0	.875	-1	85	49	2b32		0.
1873	Phi NA	42	209	67	67	11	1	0	27	8		1	.321	.346	.383	112	3	9-3	.856	1	93	151	2b42		0.
Total	3 NA	102	488	162	162	33	12	3	82	25		6	.332	.365	.467	140	23	28-5	.871	9	94	114	2b102		1.

WOOD, JASON Jason William B12.16.1969 San Bernardino CA BR/TR/6-1/170(170-190) [OakA91 11/307] d4.1 Col Cal St.-Fresno

1998	Oak A	3	1	1	0	0	0	0	0	0-0	0	1	1.000	.000	.000	-99	0	0-0	1.000	1	198	446	S2/3		0.
	Det A	10	23	5	8	2	0	1	1	3-0	0	4	.348	.423	.565	152	2	0-1	1.000	-1	74	120	1b6/SD		0.
	Year	13	24	6	8	2	0	1	1	3-0	0	5	.333	.407	.542	143	2	0-1	1.000	-0	74	120	1b6,S3,D3/3		0.
1999	Det A	27	44	5	7	1	0	1	8	2-0	0	13	.159	.196	.250	12	-6	0-0	.909	-4	59	0	3b9,S9,1b5/2D		-1.0
Total	2	40	68	11	15	3	0	2	9	5-0	0	18	.221	.274	.353	59	-4	0-1	.875	-5	69	66	S12,1b11,3b10,D4/2	36	-0.9

WOOD, JOE Joe "Smokey Joe" (b Howard Ellsworth Wood) B10.25.1889 Kansas City MO D7.27.1985 West Haven CT BR/TR/5-11/180 d8.24 s-Joe ▲

1908	Bos A	6	7	1	0	0	0	0	0	0	0		.000	.000	.000	-97	-1	0	.889	-0	71	531	P6		0.0
1909	Bos A	24	55	4	9	0	1	0	3	2	0		.164	.207	.200	28	0	0	.971	-4	55	0	P24		0.0
1910	Bos A	35	69	9	18	2	1	1	5	5	0		.261	.311	.362	108	5	0	.975	2	98	188	P35		0.0
1911	Bos A	44	88	15	23	4	2	2	11	10	1		.261	.343	.420	114	8	1	.947	2	88	143	P44		0.0
1912	†Bos A	43	124	16	36	13	1	1	13	11		7	.290	.348	.435	118	11	0	.974	8	110	79	P43		0.0
1913	Bos A	25	56	10	15	5	0	0	10	4		14	.268	.317	.357	95	4	1	.955	4	128	73	P23		0.0
1914	Bos A	21	43	2	6	1	0	1	5	3		14	.140	.213	.163	13	0	1	1.000	0	86	0	P18		0.0
1915	Bos A	29	54	6	14	1	1	1	7	5	0	10	.259	.322	.370	111	4	1-1	.982	1	103	411	P25		0.0
1917	Cle A	10	6	1	0	0	0	0	0	0	0	3	.000	.000	.000	-93	-1	0	1.000	0	108	0	P5		0.0
1918	Cle A	119	422	41	125	22	4	5	66	36		38	.296	.356	.403	118	9	8	.962	-2	101	79	O95(84/1/10),2b19,1b4		0.0
1919	Cle A	72	192	30	49	10	6	0	27	32	2	21	.255	.367	.370	101	1	3	.932	-4	88	85	O64(15/6/43)/P		0.3
1920	†Cle A	61	137	25	37	11	2	1	30	25	2	16	.270	.390	.401	107	3	1-1	.987	0	99	95	O55(5/2/48)/P		0.1
1921	Cle A	66	194	32	71	16	5	4	60	25		17	.366	.438	.562	151	16	2-0	.973	-3	102	43	O64(0/21/56)		0.1
1922	Cle A	142	505	74	150	33	8	8	92	56		63	.297	.367	.442	109	7	5-1	.960	3	102	119	O141(2/1/138)		0.9
Total	14	697	1952	266	553	118	31	23	325	208		16	189	.283	.357	.411	110	66	23-3	.962	8	99	91	O419(106/31/295),P225,2b19,1b4		0.7

WOOD, JOE Joseph Perry "J.P.","Little Joe" B10.3.1919 Houston TX D3.25.1985 Houston TX BR/TR/5-9.5/160 d5.2 Mil 1944-45 Col Rice

| 1943 | Det A | 60 | 164 | 22 | 53 | 4 | 4 | 1 | 17 | 6 | 0 | 13 | .323 | .347 | .415 | 114 | 2 | 2-2 | .896 | -11 | 70 | 45 | 2b22,3b18 | | -0.9 |

WOOD, KEN Kenneth Lanier B7.1.1924 Lincolnton NC BR/TR/6-0/200* d4.28

1948	StL A	10	24	2	2	0	1	0	2	1	0	4	.083	.120	.167	-24	-5	0-0	1.000	1	97	275	O5R		-0.4
1949	StL A	7	4	0	0	0	0	0	0	1	0	2	.000	.143	.000	-58	-1	0-0	—	-0	0	0	O3(2/0/1)		-0.1
1950	StL A	128	369	42	83	24	0	13	62	38	1	58	.225	.299	.396	74	-16	0-4	.952	4	95	223	O94(7/0/88)		-1.6
1951	StL A	109	333	40	79	19	0	15	44	27	1	49	.237	.296	.429	92	-6	1-2	.959	0	101	111	O100(29/4/69)		-1.0
1952	Bos A	15	20	0	2	0	0	0	3	0	0	4	.100	.217	.100	-9	-3	0-0	.889	-1	93	0	O13(1/0/12)		-0.4
	Was A	61	210	26	50	8	6	6	32	30	0	21	.238	.333	.419	112	3	0-1	.954	4	111	144	O56(54/3/1)		0.2
	Year	76	230	26	52	8	6	6	32	33	0	25	.226	.323	.391	99	-1	0-1	.951	4	110	134	O69(55/3/13)		-0.2
1953	Was A	12	33	0	7	1	0	0	3	2	0	9	.212	.257	.242	36	-3	0-0	1.000	1	94	204	O7L		-0.2
Total	6	342	995	110	223	52	7	34	143	102	2	141	.224	.298	.393	81	-31	1-7	.956	8	101	160	O278(100/7/176)		-3.6

WOOD, BOB Robert Lynn B7.28.1865 Thorn Hill (now part of Youngstown) OH D5.22.1943 Churchill OH BR/TR/5-8.5/153 d5.2

1898	Cin N	39	109	14	30	6	0	0	16	9	0		.275	.331	.330	84	-2	1	.943	3	168	78	C29/OL1		0.4
1899	Cin N	63	195	34	61	11	7	0	24	25	5		.313	.404	.441	129	9	3	.937	-3	129	83	C53,O2(1/1/0),3b2/1		0.9
1900	Cin N	45	139	17	37	8	1	0	22	10	1		.266	.320	.338	84	-3	3	.967	-3	118	106	C18,3b15/OC		-0.4
1901	Cle A	98	346	45	101	23	3	1	49	12	6		.292	.327	.384	101	-3	6	.952	-3	93	97	C84,3b4,O3(1/0/2)/12S		0.5
1902	Cle A	81	258	23	76	18	2	0	40	27	6		.295	.375	.380	114	7	1	.941	-6	87	91	C52,1b16,O2R/23		0.5
1904	Det A	49	175	15	43	6	2	1	17	5	1		.246	.271	.320	89	-3	1	.974	4	90	119	C47		0.7
1905	Det A	8	24	1	2	1	0	0	0	1	0		.083	.120	.125	-22	-3	0	.886	-2	75	165	C7		-0.5
Total	7	383	1246	149	350	73	15	2	168	89	19		.281	.338	.368	101	6	15	.951	-9	107	98	C290,3b22,1b19,O9(3/2/4),2b2/S		2.1

WOOD, ROY Roy Winton "Woody" B8.29.1892 Monticello AR D4.6.1974 Fayetteville AR BR/TR/6-0/175 d6.16 Col Arkansas-Monticello

1913	Pit N	14	35	4	10	4	0	0	2	1	0		.286	.306	.400	105	0	3	.895	2	85	401	O8L/1		0.2
1914	Cle A	72	220	24	52	6	3	1	15	13	7	26	.236	.300	.305	79	-6	6-9	.946	1	102	128	O54(5/13/23),1b20		-1.1
1915	Cle A	33	78	5	15	2	1	0	3	2	2	13	.192	.232	.244	41	-6	1-2	.990	-1	77	77	1b21,O2(1/0/1)		-1.1
Total	3	119	333	33	77	12	4	1	20	16	9	47	.231	.285	.300	73	-12	7-11	.936	1	98	169	O50(14/13/24),1b42		-1.8

WOODALL, LARRY Charles Lawrence B7.26.1894 Staunton VA D5.16.1963 Cambridge MA BR/TR/5-9/165 d5.20 C7 Col North Carolina-Asheville

1920	Det A	18	49	4	12	1	0	0	6	2			.245	.277	.265	45	-4	0-0	.988	1	99	130	C15		-0.2
1921	Det A	46	80	10	29	4	1	0	14	6	0	7	.363	.407	.438	117	2	1-0	.966	-5	72	63	C25		-0.1
1922	Det A	50	125	19	43	2	2	0	18	8	1	11	.344	.388	.392	107	1	1-0	.977	-8	75	39	C40		-0.5
1923	Det A	71	148	20	41	12	2	1	19	22	0	9	.277	.371	.405	106	2	2-1	.983	-2	103	106	C60		0.3
1924	Det A	67	165	23	51	9	0	0	25	21	0	5	.309	.387	.388	102	1	0-0	.986	-1	96	100	C62		0.3
1925	Det A	75	171	20	35	4	1	0	13	24	0	8	.205	.303	.240	39	-16	1-0	.967	-7	86	85	C75		-1.8
1926	Det A	67	146	18	34	5	0	0	15	15	0	2	.233	.304	.267	49	-11	0-0	.979	-4	83	112	C59		-1.1
1927	Det A	88	246	28	69	8	0	0	39	37	0	9	.280	.375	.362	90	-3	9-1	.997	3	93	106	C86		0.7
1928	Det A	65	186	19	39	7	1	0	13	24	0	10	.210	.300	.258	49	-14	0-1	.992	2	101	142	C62		-0.8
1929	Det A	1	1	0	0	0	0	0	0	0	0		.000	.000	.000	-99	-0	0-0	—	0		0	/H		-0.8
Total	10	548	1317	161	353	52	7	1	161	159	1	67	.268	.347	.333	77	-42	16-4	.984	-21	91	102	C484		-3.2

WOODARD, DARRELL Darrell Lee B12.10.1956 Wilmar AR [OakA74 12/286] d8.6

| 1978 | Oak A | 33 | 9 | 10 | 0 | 0 | 0 | 0 | 0 | 1-0 | 0 | 1 | .000 | .100 | .000 | -73 | -2 | 3-4 | .964 | 2 | 114 | 112 | 2b14/3D | | -0.1 |

AR TM LG	G	AB	R	H	2B	3B	HR	RBI	BB-IB	HP	SO	AVG	OBP	SLG	AOPS	ABR	SB-CS	FA	FR	RNG	THR	GAMES AT POSITION	DL	BFW

WOODARD, MIKE Michael Cary B3.2.1960 Melrose Park IL BL/TR/5-9/155* [OakA78 4/82] d9.11

																							-0.6
85 SF N	24	82	12	20	1	0	0	9	5-0	0	3	.244	.287	.256	56	-5	6-1	.990	-2	81	107	2b23	-0.2
86 SF N	48	79	14	20	2	1	1	5	10-0	0	9	.253	.337	.342	92	-1	7-2	.986	-3	89	147	2b23,S2,3b2	0.1
87 SF N	10	19	0	4	1	0	0	1	0-0	0	5	.211	.263	.263	26	-2	0-0	1.000	2	123	158	2b8	-0.2
88 Chi A	18	45	3	6	1	0	4	1-0	1	.133	.170	.178	-2	-6	1-1	.975	4	111	99	2b14,D2	-0.9
Total 4	100	225	29	50	4	2	1	19	16-0	1	18	.222	.277	.271	54	-14	14-4	.985	1	94	121	2b68,D2,3b2,S2	

WOODHEAD, RED James B7.9.1851 Chelsea MA D9.7.1881 Boston MA 5-6/160 d4.15

																							0.0
73 Mar NA	1	5	0	0	0	0	0	0	0-0	.000	.000	.000	-99	-1	0-0	.900	1	179	0	/S	-1.9
79 Syr N	34	131	6	21	1	0	0	2	0	23	.160	.160	.168	9	-12	.792	-9	72	86	3b34	

WOODLING, GENE Eugene Richard B8.16.1922 Akron OH D6.2.2001 Barberton OH BL/TR/5-9.5/195(175-200) d9.23 Mil 1943-45 C4

																							0.2
43 Cle A	8	25	1	2	1	1	5	1	.320	.346	.600	186	2	0-0	1.000	-0	72	267	O6(0/1/5)	-1.2
46 Cle A	61	133	8	25	1	4	0	9	16	1	13	.188	.280	.256	-54	-9	1-2	1.000	-1	105	0	O37(6/31/0)	-0.3
47 Pit N	22	79	7	21	2	2	0	10	7	0	5	.266	.326	.342	75	-3	0	.968	1	111	70	O21(1/20/0)	-0.3
49 †NY A	112	296	60	80	13	7	5	44	52	1	21	.270	.381	.412	110	5	2-2	.982	-2	95	190	O118(117/2/0)	0.8
50 †NY A	122	449	81	127	20	10	6	60	70	1	37	.283	.381	.412	106	5	5-3	.993	12	109	56	O116(101/17/0)	0.7
51 †NY A	120	420	65	118	15	8	15	71	62	0	31	.281	.373	.462	130	17	0-4	.993	6	99	169	O118(112/6/0)	2.6
52 †NY A	122	408	58	126	19	6	12	63	59	1	31	.309	.397	.473	151	29	1-4	.996	9	99	71	O119L	2.4
53 †NY A	125	395	64	121	26	4	10	58	82	3	29	.306	**.429**	.468	147	32	2-7	.996	1	102	71	O89L	-0.6
54 NY A	97	304	33	76	12	5	3	40	53	36	.250	.358	.352	99	1	3-4	.983	-1	95	94	O89L	-0.5
55 Bal A	47	145	22	32	6	2	3	18	24-4	1	18	.221	.329	.352	91	-2	1-1	1.000	-2	96	33	O44(26/4/25)	-0.3
Cle A	79	259	33	72	15	1	5	35	36-2	3	15	.278	.368	.402	104	3	2-4	.993	-3	97	59	O114(90/4/41)	-0.8
Year	126	404	55	104	21	3	8	53	60-6	4	33	.257	.354	.384	100	2	3-5	.995	-3	97	50	O85(85/0/2)	32	-0.3
56 Cle A	100	317	56	83	17	0	8	38	69-2	3	29	.262	.395	.391	107	7	2-6	.981	-3	97	94	O113L	3.4
57 Cle A	133	430	74	138	25	2	19	78	64-2	5	49	.321	.408	.521	155	35	0-5	.992	7	105	96	O116(61/0/68)	1.2
58 Bal A	133	413	57	114	16	1	15	65	66-3	2	49	.276	.378	.429	128	18	4-2	.981	-5	96	29	O124(85/0/57)	1.6
59 Bal A★	140	440	63	132	22	2	14	77	78-4	0	35	.300	.402	.455	139	27	1-1	.981	-5	91	94	O124(124/0/1)	1.2
60 Bal A	140	435	68	123	18	3	11	62	84-7	4	40	.283	.401	.414	123	19	3-0	.995	-1	91	122	O90(15/0/77)	1.2
61 Was A	110	342	39	107	16	4	10	57	50-3	2	24	.313	.403	.471	135	19	1-0	.988	-1	91	0	O30(3/0/27)	0.2
62 Was A	44	107	19	30	4	0	5	16	24-4	2	5	.280	.421	.458	138	7	1-0	.953	-4	81	0	O48(27/0/21)	-0.3
NY N	81	190	18	52	8	1	5	24	24-3	1	22	.274	.353	.405	103	1	0-0	.986	-2	99	94	O1566(1230/93/304)	32	-0.3
Total 17	1796	5587	830	1585	257	63	147	830	921-34	28	477	.284	.386	.431	123	213	29-45	.989	2	98	94	O1566(1230/93/304)		11.7

WOODRUFF, PETE Franklin B6.1873 NY BR/TR d9.19

| | | | | | | | | | | | | | | | | | | | | | | | -0.1 |
| 899 NY N | 20 | 61 | 11 | 15 | 1 | 2 | 0 | 7 | 0 | .246 | .343 | .393 | 105 | 0 | 3 | 1.000 | -1 | 111 | 0 | O19R/1 | |

WOODRUFF, SAM Orville Francis B12.27.1876 Chilo OH D7.22.1937 Cincinnati OH BR/TR/5-9/160 d4.14

																							-2.1
904 Cin N	87	306	20	58	14	3	0	20	19	3	.190	.244	.255	50	-18	9	.932	-3	100	67	3b61,2b17,S8/OR	-0.8
910 Cin N	21	61	6	9	1	0	0	2	7	0	8	.148	.235	.164	18	-6	2	.933	-1	92	127	3b17,2b4	-2.9
Total 2	108	367	26	67	15	3	0	22	26	3	.183	.242	.240	45	-24	11	.932	-5	98	80	3b78,2b21,S8/OR	

WOODS, AL Alvis B8.8.1953 Oakland CA BL/TL/6-3/195* [MinA72 S2/35] d4.7 Col Laney (CA) JC

																							-1.0
1977 Tor A	122	440	58	125	17	4	6	35	36-3	0	38	.284	.336	.382	95	-3	8-7	.969	-1	100	75	O115(106/0/15),D4	-1.1
1978 Tor A	62	220	19	53	12	3	3	23	11-1	1	23	.241	.278	.364	78	-7	1-2	.978	0	107	50	O60L	-0.9
1979 Tor A	132	436	57	121	24	4	5	36	40-0	1	28	.278	.337	.385	94	-3	6-4	.991	2	104	74	O88L,D13	1.0
1980 Tor A	109	373	54	112	18	2	15	47	37-3	1	35	.300	.364	.480	124	13	4-4	.973	-0	101	71	O77L,D2	-1.6
1981 Tor A	85	288	20	71	15	0	1	19	19-5	0	31	.247	.291	.309	69	-11	3-4	.973	-6	90	68	O64L,D10	-1.3
1982 Tor A	85	201	20	47	11	1	3	24	21-4	0	20	.234	.302	.343	72	-7	1-3	.970	0			D7	16	0.2
1986 Min A	23	28	5	9	1	0	2	3	0	5	.321	.375	.571	152	2	0-0		0			D38	16	-4.7
Total 7	618	1986	233	538	98	14	35	196	167-16	3	180	.271	.326	.387	93	-16	23-24	.974	-2	100	78	O531(522/0/15),D38	

WOODS, GARY Gary Lee B7.20.1954 Santa Barbara CA BR/TR/6-2/190* d9.14 Col Santa Barbara (CA) City

																							-0.1
1976 Oak A	6	8	0	1	0	0	0	0	0-0	0	3	.125	.125	.125	-28	-1	0-0	1.000	0	162	0	O4(1/2/1)/D	-2.1
1977 Tor A	60	227	31	49	9	1	0	17	7-0	2	38	.216	.246	.264	39	-20	5-4	.994	0	102	97	O60C	-0.2
1978 Tor A	8	19	1	3	1	0	0	1	0-0	0	1	.158	.200	.211	15	-2	1-0	1.000	0	111	0	O6(0/1/5)	0.5
1980 †Hou N	19	53	8	20	5	0	2	15	2-0	0	9	.377	.400	.585	187	6	1-0	1.000	-1	80	93	O14(4/0/12)	-0.8
1981 †Hou N	54	110	10	23	4	0	1	12	11-4	0	22	.209	.276	.264	58	-6	2-1	.984	-2	112	45	O40(2/3/35)	0.1
1982 Chi N	117	245	28	66	15	1	4	30	21-2	0	48	.269	.327	.388	96	-1	3-3	.971	3	101	141	O73(40/27/13)/2	-0.6
1983 Chi N	93	190	25	46	9	0	4	22	15-2	0	27	.242	.296	.353	76	-6	5-3	1.000	1	110	124	O62(36/11/18),2b3	0.0
1984 Chi N	87	98	13	23	4	1	3	10	15-0	0	21	.235	.333	.388	95	0	2-1	1.000	1	105	68	O56(44/4/11)	-0.3
1985 Chi N	81	82	11	20	3	0	0	4	14-0	0	18	.244	.354	.280	72	-2	0-1	1.000	0	105	107	O418(164/175/107),2b4/D	30	-3.5
Total 9	525	1032	117	251	50	4	13	110	86-8	2	187	.243	.302	.337	76	-32	19-13	.992	7	104	107	O418(164/175/107),2b4/D	

WOODS, JIM James Jerome "Woody" B9.17.1939 Chicago IL BR/TR/6-0/175* d9.27

																							0.0
1957 Chi N	2	0	1	0	0	0	0	0	0-0	0	0					0	0-0	—	0			/R	-0.3
1960 Phi N	11	34	4	6	0	0	1	3	3-1	0	13	.176	.243	.265	39	-3	0-0	.939	-1	116	55	3b11	-0.3
1961 Phi N	23	48	6	11	3	0	2	9	4-2	1	15	.229	.296	.417	89	-1	0-0	.968	-2	77	122	3b15	-0.6
Total 3	36	82	11	17	3	0	3	12	7-3	1	28	.207	.275	.354	69	-4	0-0	.953	-2	95	91	3b26	

WOODS, RON Ronald Lawrence B2.1.1943 Hamilton OH BR/TR/5-10/173* d4.22

																							0.0
1969 Det A	17	15	3	4	0	0	1	3	2-0	0	3	.267	.353	.467	123	0	0-0	1.000	-0	103	0	O7(7/1/0)	-1.3
NY A	72	171	18	30	5	2	1	7	22-1	1	29	.175	.273	.246	48	-12	2-0	1.000	0	108	62	O67(1/66/0)	-1.3
Year	89	186	21	34	5	2	2	10	24-1	1	32	.183	.283	.263	54	-12	2-0	1.000	0	108	59	O74(8/67/0)	-0.6
1970 NY A	95	225	30	51	5	3	8	27	33-3	0	35	.227	.324	.382	99	-1	4-2	.974	-3	86	136	O78(2/9/70)	21	0.0
1971 NY A	25	32	4	8	1	0	1	2	4-0	0	6	.250	.333	.375	105	0	0-0	.989	6	114	239	O45(32/23/0)	0.9
Mon N	51	138	26	41	7	3	1	17	19-0	0	18	.297	.382	.413	124	5	0-2	.991	4	84	57	O73(8/58/10)	-0.4
1972 Mon N	97	221	21	57	5	1	10	31	22-2	0	33	.258	.321	.425	110	2	3-3	.977	3	101	126	O114(29/91/4)	-0.7
1973 Mon N	135	318	45	73	11	3	3	31	56-3	0	34	.230	.344	.311	80	-7	6-5	.987	0	108	0	O61(40/20/5)	-1.1
1974 Mon N	90	127	15	26	0	0	1	9	17-1	1	17	.205	.299	.228	49	-4	1-0	.984	3	99	103	O454(122/268/95)	21	-3.2
Total 6	582	1247	162	290	34	12	26	130	175-10	2	171	.233	.326	.342	87	-22	27-18	.984	3	99	103	O454(122/268/95)	

WOODSON, TRACY Tracy Michael B10.5.1962 Richmond VA BR/TR/6-3/215 [LAN84 3/77] d4.7 Col North Carolina St.

																							-1.1
																								-1.3
1987 LA N	53	136	14	31	8	1	1	9-2	2	21	.228	.284	.324	63	-7	1-1	.958	-3	79	67	3b45,1b7	-0.2
1988 †LA N	65	173	15	43	4	1	3	15	7-1	1	32	.249	.279	.359	79	-6	1-2	.938	-5	86	59	3b41,1b25	-0.6
1989 LA N	4	6	0	0	0	0	0	0-0	0	1	.000	.000	.000	-99	-2	0-0	1.000	-0	68	0	/3	-0.9
1992 StL N	31	114	9	35	8	0	1	22	3-0	1	10	.307	.331	.404	109	1	0-0	.945	-6	71	103	3b26,1b3	-4.1
1993 StL N	62	77	4	16	2	0	0	2	1-0	0	14	.208	.215	.234	21	-9	0-0	.909	-0	117	195	3b28,1b11	15	
Total 5	215	506	42	125	22	2	5	50	20-3	4	78	.247	.279	.328	70	-23	2-3	.943	-14	83	85	3b141,1b46	

WOODWARD, CHRIS Christopher Michael B6.27.1976 Covina CA BR/TR/6-0/185(165-190) [TorA94 54/1438] d6.7 Col Mt. San Antonio (CA) JC OF(13/5/6)

																							-0.1
1999 Tor A	14	26	1	6	1	0	0	2	2-0	0	6	.231	.276	.269	42	-2	0-0	.939	0	111	41	S10,3b2	-0.6
2000 Tor A	37	104	16	19	7	0	3	14	10-3	0	28	.183	.254	.337	46	-9	1-0	.955	1	103	68	S22,3b9,1b3,2b3	0.5
2001 Tor A	37	63	9	12	3	2	2	5	1-0	0	14	.190	.203	.397	52	-5	0-1	.959	10	153	142	2b17,3b10,S4,1b2/D	26	1.9
2002 Tor A	90	312	48	86	13	4	13	45	26-0	3	72	.276	.330	.468	107	2	3-0	.965	11	107	120	S79,2b6,1b3,3b2,D2	20	0.7
2003 Tor A	104	349	49	91	22	2	7	45	28-0	6	72	.261	.316	.395	84	-8	1-2	.981	1	103	107	S64,D2	27	-0.7
2004 Tor A	69	213	21	50	13	4	1	24	14-0	1	46	.235	.283	.347	60	-13	1-2	.991	-2	70	85	1b34,O23(13/5/6),S7,3b6,2b5/D	-0.6
2005 NY N	81	173	16	49	10	0	3	18	13-0	2	46	.283	.337	.393	94	-1	0-0	.967	31	106	105	S289,1b42,2b31,3b29,O23L,D6	73	1.2
Total 7	432	1240	160	313	69	12	29	153	94-3	9	284	.252	.305	.398	81	-36	6-5	.967	31	106	105	S289,1b42,2b31,3b29,O23L,D6	

WOODWARD, WOODY William Frederick B9.23.1942 Miami FL BR/TR/6-2/185* d9.9 Col Florida St.

																							0.1
1963 Mil N	10	2	1	0	0	0	0	0	0-0	0	0	.000	.000	.000	-99	-1	0-0	1.000	1	219	0	S5	-0.5
1964 Mil N	77	115	18	24	2	1	0	11	6-1	2	28	.209	.260	.243	43	-9	0-1	.958	2	93	139	2b40,S18,3b7/1	-1.2
1965 Mil N	112	265	17	55	7	4	0	11	10-3	1	50	.208	.235	.264	41	-22	2-2	.973	-5	106	103	2b79,S73	-0.5
1966 Atl N	144	455	46	120	23	3	0	43	37-5	4	54	.264	.323	.327	81	-10	2-2	**.982**	10	107	115	2b120,S16	-0.2
1967 Atl N	136	429	30	97	15	2	0	25	37-5	1	51	.226	.287	.270	62	-21	0-6	.973	1	123	97	S6,3b2/2	-0.1
1968 Atl N	12	24	2	4	1	0	0	1	1-0	0	6	.167	.200	.208	23	-2	1-0	.973	1	123	97	S6,3b2/2	

YEAR	TM LG	G	AB	R	H	2B	3B	HR	RBI	BB-IB	HP	SO	AVG	OBP	SLG	AOPS	ABR	SB-CS	FA	FR	RNG	THR	GAMES AT POSITION	DL	B
	Cin N	56	119	13	29	2	0	0	10	7-3	2	23	.244	.297	.261	64	-5	1-0	.968	-9	87	77	S41,2b9/1		
	Year	68	143	15	33	3	0	0	11	8-3	2	29	.231	.281	.252	58	-7	2-0	.969	-8	92	80	S47,2b10,3b2/1		
1969	Cin N	97	241	36	63	12	0	0	15	24-3	2	40	.261	.333	.311	77	-6	3-2	.966	-7	101	71	S93,2b2		
1970	†Cin N	100	264	23	59	8	3	1	14	20-6	2	21	.223	.280	.288	53	-18	1-2	.973	4	109	120	S77,3b20,2b10,1b2		
1971	Cin N	136	273	22	66	9	1	0	18	27-4	1	28	.242	.309	.282	69	-10	4-0	.987	-1	109	109	S85,3b63,2b9		
Total	9	880	2187	208	517	79	14	1	148	169-34	13	301	.236	.294	.287	64	-104	14-15	.974	-9	99	98	S521,2b278,3b92,1b4		

WOOTEN, JUNIOR Earl Hazwell B1.16.1924 Pelzer SC BR/TL/5-11/160 d9.16

YEAR	TM LG	G	AB	R	H	2B	3B	HR	RBI	BB-IB	HP	SO	AVG	OBP	SLG	AOPS	ABR	SB-CS	FA	FR	RNG	THR	GAMES AT POSITION	DL	B
1947	Was A	6	24	0	2	0	0	0	1	0	0	4	.083	.083	.083	-55	-5	1-0	.905	-0	113	0	O6(1/6/0)		
1948	Was A	88	258	34	66	8	3	1	23	24	0	21	.256	.324	.322	74	-10	2-1	.979	6	102	168	O73(0/55/22),1b6/P		
Total	2	94	282	34	68	8	3	1	24	24	0	25	.241	.305	.301	64	-15	3-1	.972	5	103	154	O79(1/61/22),1b6/P		

WOOTEN, SHAWN William Shawn B7.24.1972 Glendora CA BR/TR/5-10/205(205-230) [DetA93 18/501] d8.19 Col Mt. San Antonio (CA) JC

YEAR	TM LG	G	AB	R	H	2B	3B	HR	RBI	BB-IB	HP	SO	AVG	OBP	SLG	AOPS	ABR	SB-CS	FA	FR	RNG	THR	GAMES AT POSITION	DL	B
2000	Ana A	7	9	2	5	1	0	0	1	0-0	0	1	.556	.556	.667	202	1	0-0	1.000	-1	93	0	C4,1b3		
2001	Ana A	79	221	24	69	8	1	8	32	5-0	3	42	.312	.332	.466	106	1	2-0	1.000	-1	174	140	D27,C25,1b21/3		
2002	†Ana A	49	113	13	33	8	0	3	19	6-1	1	24	.292	.331	.442	105	1	2-0	1.000	-2	80	52	D26,1b16,C2/3		
2003	Ana A	98	272	25	66	8	0	7	32	24-5	1	45	.243	.303	.349	75	-10	0-4	.995	-3	82	107	1b32,D28,C19,3b17		
2004	Phi N	33	53	2	9	3	0	0	2	2-0	2	9	.170	.200	.226	18	-7	0-0	1.000	-2	66	108	1b11,3b4	102	
2005	Bos A	1	0	0	0	0	0	0	0	0-0	0	0	.000	.000	.000	-95	-0	0-0	—	-0	0	0	/C		
Total	6	267	669	66	182	28	1	18	86	37-6	7	120	.272	.314	.398	88	-14	4-4	.994	-8	91	116	1b83,D81,C51,3b23	102	

WORDSWORTH, FAVEL Favel Perry B11.22.1850 New York NY D8.12.1888 New York NY d4.28

YEAR	TM LG	G	AB	R	H	2B	3B	HR	RBI	BB-IB	HP	SO	AVG	OBP	SLG	AOPS	ABR	SB-CS	FA	FR	RNG	THR	GAMES AT POSITION	DL	B
1873	Res NA	12	40	5	10	0	0	0		3	2	1	.250	.286	.250	66	-1	1-0	.662	-4	97	35	S11/OR		

WORKMAN, CHUCK Charles Thomas B1.6.1915 Leeton MO D1.3.1953 Kansas City MO BL/TR/6-0/175 d9.18

YEAR	TM LG	G	AB	R	H	2B	3B	HR	RBI	BB-IB	HP	SO	AVG	OBP	SLG	AOPS	ABR	SB-CS	FA	FR	RNG	THR	GAMES AT POSITION	DL	B
1938	Cle A	2	5	1	2	0	0	0	0	0	0	0	.400	.400	.400	103	-0	0-0	.500	0	57	0	/OR		C
1941	Cle A	9	4	2	0	0	0	0	1	0	0	1	.000	.200	.000	-45	-1	0-0	—	0			/H		-C
1943	Bos N	153	615	71	153	17	1	10	67	53	3	72	.249	.311	.328	86	-12	12	.988	2	95	130	O149(16/0/133),1b3/3		-C
1944	Bos N	140	418	46	87	18	3	11	53	42	4	51	.208	.287	.344	74	-15	1	.983	4	91	167	O103R,3b19		-C
1945	Bos N	139	514	77	141	16	2	25	87	51	6	58	.274	.347	.459	122	13	9	.910	-15	97	91	3b107,O24(5/0/19)		-C
1946	Bos N	25	48	5	8	0	2	7	3	1	11	.167	.231	.333	58	-3	0	.920	-1	94	114	O12(3/8/1)		-C
	Pit N	58	145	11	32	4	1	2	16	11	1	19	.221	.280	.303	64	-7	2	1.000	5	131	94	O40(3/0/38)/3		-C
	Year	83	193	16	40	4	3	9	23	14	2	30	.207	.268	.311	63	-10	2	.986	3	124	98	O52(6/8/39)/3		-C
Total	6	526	1749	213	423	57	7	50	230	161	15	202	.242	.311	.368	91	-25	24-0	.985	-4	99	125	O329(27/8/295),3b128,1b3		-4

WORKMAN, HANK Henry Kilgariff B2.5.1926 Los Angeles CA BL/TR/6-1/185 d9.4 Col USC

YEAR	TM LG	G	AB	R	H	2B	3B	HR	RBI	BB-IB	HP	SO	AVG	OBP	SLG	AOPS	ABR	SB-CS	FA	FR	RNG	THR	GAMES AT POSITION	DL	B
1950	NY A	2	5	1	1	0	0	0	0	0	0	1	.200	.200	.200	3	-1	0-0	1.000	-0	0	126	/1		

WORTH, HERB Herbert B5.2.1847 Brooklyn NY D4.27.1914 Brooklyn NY d7.29

YEAR	TM LG	G	AB	R	H	2B	3B	HR	RBI	BB-IB	HP	SO	AVG	OBP	SLG	AOPS	ABR	SB-CS	FA	FR	RNG	THR	GAMES AT POSITION	DL	B
1872	Atl NA	1	5	1	1	1	0	0		0	0		.200	.200	.400	68	0	0-0	1.000	0	0	0	/OR		

WORTHINGTON, CRAIG Craig Richard B4.17.1965 Los Angeles CA BR/TR/6-0/200(190-202) [BalA85 S1/11] d4.26 Col Cerritos (CA) JC

YEAR	TM LG	G	AB	R	H	2B	3B	HR	RBI	BB-IB	HP	SO	AVG	OBP	SLG	AOPS	ABR	SB-CS	FA	FR	RNG	THR	GAMES AT POSITION	DL	B
1988	Bal A	26	81	5	15	2	0	2	4	9-0	0	24	.185	.267	.284	56	-5	1-0	.961	2	116	89	3b26		-0
1989	Bal A	145	497	57	123	23	0	15	70	61-2	4	114	.247	.334	.384	105	4	1-2	.951	-6	101	89	3b145		-0
1990	Bal A	133	425	46	96	17	0	8	44	63-2	3	96	.226	.328	.322	85	-6	1-2	.945	-7	96	128	3b131,D2		-0
1991	Bal A	31	102	11	23	3	0	4	12	12-0	1	14	.225	.313	.373	92	-1	0-1	.975	-2	89	54	3b30		-0
1992	Cle A	9	24	0	4	0	0	0	4	.167	.231	.167	13	-3	0-1	.857	1	123	155	3b9		-0
1995	Cin N	10	18	1	5	1	0	1	2	2-0	0	1	.278	.350	.500	120	-1	0-0	1.000	1	92	126	1b4,3b2		-0
	Tex A	26	68	4	15	4	0	7	0	8	.221	.293	.368	68	-3	0-0	.980	-2	90	79	3b26		-0
1996	Tex A	13	19	2	3	0	0	1	6-0	0	6	.158	.333	.316	69	-1	0-0	.917	0	89	96	3b7,1b6		-0
Total	7	393	1234	126	284	50	0	33	144	162-4	8	264	.230	.322	.351	90	-15	3-6	.950	-13	99	100	3b376,1b10,D2	39	-2

WORTHINGTON, RED Robert Lee B4.24.1906 Alhambra CA D12.8.1963 Sepulveda CA BR/TR/5-11/170 d4.14

YEAR	TM LG	G	AB	R	H	2B	3B	HR	RBI	BB-IB	HP	SO	AVG	OBP	SLG	AOPS	ABR	SB-CS	FA	FR	RNG	THR	GAMES AT POSITION	DL	B
1931	Bos N	128	491	47	143	25	10	4	44	26	1	38	.291	.328	.407	100	-2	1	.988	-2	95	113	O124(114/0/10)		-1
1932	Bos N	105	435	62	132	35	8	8	61	15	2	34	.303	.330	.476	118	10	1	.987	-2	92	120	O104L		0
1933	Bos N	17	45	3	7	4	0	0	1	0	3	.156	.174	.244	20	-5	0	.900	-1	86	119	O10(3/0/7)		-0
1934	Bos N	41	65	6	16	5	0	0	6	6	1	9	.246	.319	.323	78	-2	0	.920	-1	110	0	O11R		-0
	StL N	1	1	0	0	0	0	0	0	0	1	.000	.000	.000	-94	-0	0	—	0			/H		-0
	Year	42	66	6	16	5	0	0	6	6	1	10	.242	.315	.318	75	-2	0	.920	-1	110	0	O11R		-1
Total	4	292	1037	118	298	69	18	12	111	48	4	71	.287	.321	.423	103	1	2	.981	-5	94	112	O249(221/0/28)		-1

WORTMAN, CHUCK William Lewis B1.5.1892 Baltimore MD D8.19.1977 Las Vegas NV BR/TR/5-7/150 d7.20

YEAR	TM LG	G	AB	R	H	2B	3B	HR	RBI	BB-IB	HP	SO	AVG	OBP	SLG	AOPS	ABR	SB-CS	FA	FR	RNG	THR	GAMES AT POSITION	DL	B
1916	Chi N	69	234	17	47	2	2	16	18	0	22	.201	.258	.261	54	-13	4	.908	-15	90	88	S69		-2
1917	Chi N	75	190	24	33	4	1	0	9	18	0	23	.174	.245	.205	36	-14	6	.918	-11	88	104	S65/23		-2
1918	†Chi N	17	17	4	2	0	0	1	3	1	0	2	.118	.167	.294	39	-1	3	.864	-0	107	76	2b8,S4		-0
Total	3	161	441	45	82	8	3	3	28	37	0	47	.186	.249	.238	46	-28	13	.913	-25	89	95	S138,2b9/3		-5

WOTUS, RON Ronald Allan B3.3.1961 Colchester CT BR/TR/6-1/164(164-180) [PitN79 16/406] d9.3 C8 [DL 1985 Pit N 95]

YEAR	TM LG	G	AB	R	H	2B	3B	HR	RBI	BB-IB	HP	SO	AVG	OBP	SLG	AOPS	ABR	SB-CS	FA	FR	RNG	THR	GAMES AT POSITION	DL	B
1983	Pit N	5	3	0	0	0	0	0	0-0	0	1	.000	.000	.000	-97	-1	0-0	1.000	0	71	0	S2/2		
1984	Pit N	27	55	4	12	6	0	0	2	6-2	0	8	.218	.290	.327	74	-2	0-0	.976	8	138	153	S17,2b7		
Total	2	32	58	4	12	6	0	0	2	6-2	0	9	.207	.277	.310	66	-3	0-0	.976	8	136	148	S19,2b8	95	

WOULFE, JIMMY James Joseph B11.25.1859 New Orleans LA D12.20.1924 New Orleans LA TR/5-11/? d5.16

YEAR	TM LG	G	AB	R	H	2B	3B	HR	RBI	BB-IB	HP	SO	AVG	OBP	SLG	AOPS	ABR	SB-CS	FA	FR	RNG	THR	GAMES AT POSITION	DL	B
1884	Cin AA	8	34	3	5	0	1	0	2	1	0		.147	.171	.206	22	-3		.625	-3	0		O7(1/0/6)/3		-0
	Pit AA	15	53	7	6	1	0	1	0				.113	.113	.132	-20	-7		.893	1	119	439	O15(0/14/1)		-0
	Year	23	87	10	11	1	1	0	3	1	0		.126	.136	.161	-3	-10		.795	-2	76	279	O22(1/14/7)/3		-1

WRIGHT, AL Albert Edgar "A-1" B11.11.1912 San Francisco CA D11.13.1998 Oakland CA BR/TR/6-1.5/170 d4.25

YEAR	TM LG	G	AB	R	H	2B	3B	HR	RBI	BB-IB	HP	SO	AVG	OBP	SLG	AOPS	ABR	SB-CS	FA	FR	RNG	THR	GAMES AT POSITION	DL	B
1933	Bos N	4	1	0	1	0	0	0					1.000	1.000	1.000	515	1	0	.500	-1	0	0	2b3		0

WRIGHT, AB Albert Owen B11.16.1906 Terlton OK D5.23.1995 Muskogee OK BR/TR/6-3/200 d4.20 Col Oklahoma St.

YEAR	TM LG	G	AB	R	H	2B	3B	HR	RBI	BB-IB	HP	SO	AVG	OBP	SLG	AOPS	ABR	SB-CS	FA	FR	RNG	THR	GAMES AT POSITION	DL	B
1935	Cle A	67	160	17	38	11	1	2	18	10	2	17	.237	.291	.356	65	-9	2-1	.984	-2	80	141	O47(5/5/38)		-1
1944	Bos N	71	195	20	50	9	0	7	35	18	2	31	.256	.326	.410	102	0	0-0	.968	-3	91	53	O47(35/0/12)		-0
Total	2	138	355	37	88	20	1	9	53	28	4	48	.248	.310	.386	85	-9	2-1	.974	-5	86	91	O94(40/5/50)		-1

WRIGHT, CY Ceylon B8.16.1893 Minneapolis MN D11.7.1947 Hines IL BL/TR/5-9/150 d6.30

YEAR	TM LG	G	AB	R	H	2B	3B	HR	RBI	BB-IB	HP	SO	AVG	OBP	SLG	AOPS	ABR	SB-CS	FA	FR	RNG	THR	GAMES AT POSITION	DL	B
1916	Chi A	8	18	0	0	0	0	0		1		7	.000	.053	.000	-83	-4	0	.844	-1	103	102	S8		

WRIGHT, DAVID David Allen B12.20.1982 Norfolk VA BR/TR/6-0/200* [NYN01 1/38] d7.21

YEAR	TM LG	G	AB	R	H	2B	3B	HR	RBI	BB-IB	HP	SO	AVG	OBP	SLG	AOPS	ABR	SB-CS	FA	FR	RNG	THR	GAMES AT POSITION	DL	B
2004	NY N	69	263	41	77	17	1	14	40	14-0	3	40	.293	.332	.525	120	7	6-0	.942	-6	100	77	3b69		0.3
2005	NY N	160	575	99	176	42	1	27	102	72-2	7	113	.306	.388	.523	140	36	17-1	.948	2	107	79	3b160		4.0
Total	2	229	838	140	253	59	2	41	142	86-2	10	153	.302	.371	.524	134	43	23-7	.948	-3	105	78	3b229		4.3

WRIGHT, GLENN Forest Glenn "Buckshot" B2.6.1901 Archie MO D4.6.1984 Olathe KS BR/TR/5-11/170 d4.15 Col Missouri

YEAR	TM LG	G	AB	R	H	2B	3B	HR	RBI	BB-IB	HP	SO	AVG	OBP	SLG	AOPS	ABR	SB-CS	FA	FR	RNG	THR	GAMES AT POSITION	DL	B
1924	Pit N	153	616	80	177	28	18	7	111	27	1	52	.287	.318	.425	96	-6	14-6	.946	9	110	112	S153		2.8
1925	†Pit N	153	614	97	189	32	10	18	121	31	0	32	.308	.341	.480	100	-2	3-7	.939	2	102	116	S153/3		1.4
1926	Pit N	119	458	73	141	15	15	8	77	19	0	26	.308	.335	.459	106	1	6	.927	-8	99	116	S116		0.6
1927	†Pit N	143	570	78	160	26	4	9	105	39	1	46	.281	.328	.388	85	-12	4	.942	-14	94	103	S143		-1.1
1928	Pit N	108	407	63	126	20	8	8	66	21	0	53	.310	.343	.457	103	0	3	.927	-20	92	93	S101/1OR		-0.9
1929	Bro N	24	25	4	5	0	0	1	6	3	0	6	.200	.286	.320	51	-2	0	.667	-2	37	0	S3		-0.4
1930	Bro N	135	532	83	171	28	12	22	126	32	0	70	.321	.360	.543	116	11	3	.964	5	99	113	S134		2.6
1931	Bro N	77	268	36	76	9	4	9	52	24	2	35	.284	.324	.448	106	1	1	.942	8	107	109	S75		1.4
1932	Bro N	127	446	50	122	31	5	11	60	12	0	57	.274	.293	.439	96	-4	4	.939	8	103	119	S122,1b2		1.1
1933	Bro N	71	192	19	49	13	0	1	18	11	1	24	.255	.299	.339	85	-3	1	.936	-4	92	107	S51,1b9,3b2		-0.5
1935	Chi A	9	25	1	3	1	0	0	1	0	6	.120	.120	.160	-27	-5	0	.943	-0	105	92	3b9		-0.5
Total	11	1119	4153	584	1219	203	76	94	723	209	5	407	.294	.330	.447	99	-21	38-13	.941	-17	100	110	S1051,1b12,2b7,3b3/OR		5.7

R TM LG	G	AB	R	H	2B	3B	HR	RBI	BB-IB	HP	SO	AVG	OBP	SLG	AOPS	ABR	SB-CS	FA	FR	RNG	THR	GAMES AT POSITION	DL	BFW

RIGHT, GEORGE George B1.28.1847 Yonkers NY D8.21.1937 Boston MA BR/TR/5-9.5/150 d5.5 M1 HF1937 b-Sam b-Harry

'1 Bos NA	16	80	33	33	7	5	0	11	6		1	.412	.453	.625	200	10	9-1	.816	6	111	243	S15/1		1.1
'2 Bos NA	48	255	87	86	16	6	2	35	3		1	.337	.345	.471	141	10	14-4	.836	22	119	324	S48		2.2
'3 Bos NA	59	323	99	125	17	7	3	43	9		2	.387	.404	.511	157	20	9-9	.826	20	116	133	S59		2.6
'4 Bos NA	60	313	76	103	10	15	0	44	5		6	.329	.340	.476	150	15	2-0	.821	6	97	218	S60/3		1.5
'5 Bos NA	79	408	106	136	20	7	2	61	2		6	.333	.337	.431	159	22	13-6	.861	4	96	153	S79,P2		2.1
'6 Bos N	70	335	72	100	18	6	1	34	8		9	.299	.315	.397	134	12		.888	14	114	109	S68,2b2/P		2.5
'7 Bos N	61	290	58	80	15	1	0	35	9		15	.276	.298	.334	95	-1		.878	10	105	147	2b58,S3		1.0
'8 Bos N	59	267	35	60	5	1	0	12	6		22	.225	.242	.251	58	-13		.947	10	103	188	S59		0.0
'9 Pro N	85	388	79	107	15	10	1	42	13		20	.276	.299	.374	122	9		.924	20	112	95	S85,M		2.9
'80 Bos N	1	4	2	1	0	0	0	0	0		0	.250	.250	.250	72	0		1.000	0	118	0	/S		0.0
'81 Bos N	7	25	4	5	0	0	0	0	3		1	.200	.286	.200	58	-1		.963	-1	88	144	S7		-0.1
'82 Pro N	46	185	14	30	1	2	0	9	4		36	.162	.180	.189	19	-17		.873	-6	92	140	S46		-2.0
al 5 NA	262	1379	401	483	70	40	9	194	25		16	.350	.362	.479	156	77	47-20	.835	57	106	200	S261,P2/31		9.5
al 7	329	1494	264	383	54	20	2	132	43		93	.256	.277	.323	93	-11		.911	48	106	128	S269,2b60/P		4.3

RIGHT, GEORGE George De Witt B12.22.1958 Oklahoma City OK BB/TR/5-11/180* [TexA77 4/87] d4.10

'82 Tex A	150	557	69	147	20	5	11	50	30-4	3	78	.264	.305	.377	90	-9	3-7	.981	6	104	147	O149(0/147/3)		-0.7
'83 Tex A	162	634	79	175	28	6	18	80	41-9	2	82	.276	.321	.424	105	2	8-7	.985	-4	100	58	O161C		-0.4
'84 Tex A	101	383	40	93	19	4	9	48	15-2	2	54	.243	.273	.384	77	-13	0-2	.983	-8	86	58	O80(0/54/26),D18	30	-2.5
'85 Tex A	109	363	21	69	13	0	2	18	25-5	1	49	.190	.241	.242	33	-34	4-7	.991	0	98	131	O102(0/53/55),D4		-3.9
'86 Tex A	49	106	10	23	3	1	2	7	4-1	1	23	.217	.246	.321	53	-7	3-5	.969	1	104	113	O42(10/8/27)		-0.9
Mon N	56	117	12	22	5	2	0	5	11-0	1	28	.188	.258	.265	46	-9	1-1	1.000	-2	84	124	O32(10/21/3)		-1.2
al 5	627	2160	231	529	88	18	42	208	126-21	9	314	.245	.288	.361	78	-70	19-29	.984	-7	98	100	O566(20/444/114),D22	30	-9.6

RIGHT, JOE Joseph S. B1873 Pittsburgh PA BL/TL/5-8/175 d7.14

'95 Lou N	60	228	30	63	10	4	1	30	12		1	28	.276	.315	.368	81	-7	7	.963	-1	49	47	O60(0/43/17)	-0.9
'96 Lou N	2	7	0	2	0	0	0	0	0		0	2	.286	.286	.286	53	-1	-1	1.000	-0	0	0	O2R	-0.1
Pit N	15	52	5	16	2	1	0	6	1		0	2	.308	.321	.385	89	-1	1	.958	-2	0	0	O12C/3	-0.3
Year	17	59	5	18	2	1	0	6	1		0	3	.305	.317	.373	85	-2	1	.962	-2	0	0	O14(0/12/2)/3	-0.4
al 2	77	287	35	81	12	5	1	36	13		1	31	.282	.316	.369	82	-9	8	.963	-3	40	38	O74(0/55/19)/3	-1.3

RIGHT, PAT Patrick Francis B7.5.1865 Pottsville PA D5.29.1943 Springfield IL BB/TR/6-2/190 d7.11

'90 Chi N	1	2	0	0	0	0	0	0	0		0	.000	.333	.000	-1	0	0	1.000	0	122	0	/2		0.0

RIGHT, RON Ronald Wade B1.21.1976 Delta UT BR/TR/6-1/230 [AtlN94 7/202] d4.14

'02 Sea A	1	3	0	0	0	0	0	0	0		1	.000	.000	.000	-99	-1	0-0	—	0			/D		-0.1

RIGHT, SAM Samuel B11.25.1848 New York NY D5.6.1928 Boston MA BR/TR/5-7.5/146 d4.19 b-George b-Harry

'75 NH NA	33	127	10	24	4	0	0	5	1		1	.189	.195	.220	51	-5	1-0	.807	11	138	76	S33		0.5
'76 Bos N	2	8	0	1	0	0	0	0	0		0	.125	.125	.125	-16	-1		.778	-0	111	0	S2		-0.1
'80 Cin N	9	34	0	3	0	0	0	0	0		5	.088	.088	.088	-4	-5		.889	-1	105	0	S9		-0.5
'81 Bos N	1	4	0	1	0	0	0	0	0		0	.250	.250	.250	60	0		.667	-1	80	0	/S		-0.1
total 3	12	46	0	5	0	0	0	5	0		5	.109	.109	.109	-27	-6		.843	-2	103	0	S12		-0.7

RIGHT, TAFFY Taft Shedron B8.10.1911 Tabor City NC D10.22.1981 Orlando FL BL/TR/5-10/180 d4.18 Mil 1943-45

'38 Was A	100	263	37	92	18	10	2	36	13	4	17	.350	.389	.517	134	12	1-2	.982	-2	97	63	O60(14/1/45)		0.7
'39 Was A	129	499	77	154	29	11	4	93	38	1	19	.309	.359	.435	110	6	1-2	.950	-0	98	115	O123(39/0/84)		-0.1
'40 Chi A	147	581	79	196	31	9	5	88	43	2	25	.337	.385	.448	114	12	4-4	.963	-6	92	90	O144R		-0.4
'41 Chi A	136	513	71	165	35	5	10	97	60	6	27	.322	.399	.468	130	24	5-4	.973	-6	97	59	O134R		0.9
'42 Chi A	85	300	43	100	13	5	0	47	48	4	9	.333	.432	.410	141	19	1-8	.968	-2	98	89	O81(0/0/81)		1.1
'46 Chi A	115	422	46	116	19	4	7	52	42	1	17	.275	.342	.389	108	4	10-3	.991	-5	98	51	O107(8/0/99)		-0.4
'47 Chi A	124	401	48	130	13	4	4	54	48	1	17	.324	.398	.387	123	9	8-6	.971	-5	92	81	O100(35/0/66)		0.4
'48 Chi A	134	455	50	127	15	6	1	49	61	5	18	.279	.341	.365	91	-7	2-1	.987	-1	95	107	O114(6/0/108)		-1.2
'49 Phi A	59	149	14	35	7	2	5	25	16	3	9	.235	.321	.356	82	-5	0-0	.970	-0	90	157	O35R		-0.6
total	1029	3583	465	1115	175	55	38	553	346	27	155	.311	.376	.423	116	79	32-33	.972	-27	95	86	O898(183/1/716)		0.4

RIGHT, TOM Thomas Everette B9.22.1923 Shelby NC BL/TR/5-11.5/180* d9.15

'48 Bos A	3	2	1	1	0	1	0	0	0		0	.500	.500	1.500	400	1	0-0	—	0			/H		0.1
'49 Bos A	5	4	1	1	0	0	1	1	1		1	.250	.400	.500	128	0	0-0	—	0			/H		0.0
'50 Bos A	54	107	17	34	7	0	0	20	6		1	18	.318	.360	.383	82	-3	0-0	.953	-1	97	60	O24(5/0/19)		-0.4
'51 Bos A	28	63	8	14	1	1	1	9	11		1	8	.222	.347	.317	73	-2	0-0	.950	-2	74	0	O18(1/0/17)		-0.5
'52 StL A	29	66	6	16	0	1	0	6	12		0	20	.242	.359	.288	79	-1	1-1	.976	1	106	188	O18L		-0.2
Chi A	60	132	15	34	10	1	2	21	16		1	16	.258	.342	.386	102	1	1-0	.969	-0	99	95	O34(22/0/13)		-0.1
Year	89	198	21	50	10	2	2	27	28		1	36	.253	.348	.354	94	-1	2-1	.971	1	101	128	O52(40/0/13)		-0.3
'53 Chi A	77	132	14	33	5	3	2	25	12		2	21	.250	.322	.379	86	-3	0-0	.978	-2	90	46	O33(10/0/24)		-0.6
'54 Was A	76	171	13	42	4	4	1	17	18		2	38	.246	.323	.333	85	-4	0-0	1.000	-1	104	0	O43(15/0/28)		-0.7
'55 Was A	7	7	0	0	0	0	0	0	0-0		0	1	.000	.000	.000	-99	-2	0-0	—	0			/H		0.0
'56 Was A	2	1	0	0	0	0	0	0	0-0		0	1	.000	.000	.000	-99	-1	0-0	—	0			/H		0.0
total 9	341	685	75	175	28	11	6	99	76-0		7	123	.255	.336	.355	85	-13	2-1	.977	-6	97	58	O170(71/0/101)		-2.6

WRIGHT, DICK Willard James B5.5.1890 Worcester NY D1.24.1952 Bethlehem PA BR/TR/5-10/170 d6.30 Col Lafayette

'915 Bro F	4	5	0	0	0	0	0	0	0		0	.000	.000	.000	-99	-1		.833	-1	113	0	C3		-0.2

WRIGHT, HARRY William Henry B1.10.1835 Sheffield, England D10.3.1895 Atlantic City NJ BR/TR/5-9.5/157 d5.5 M23 HF1953 b-George b-Sam ▲

'871 Bos NA	31	147	42	44	5	2	0	26	13		1	.299	.356	.361	103	1	7-1	.855	-1	146	166	O30C,P9/SM		0.0
'872 Bos NA	48	208	39	53	5	1	0	24	9		2	.255	.286	.288	73	-7	0-0	.866	-5	78	121	O48C,P7,M		-0.8
'873 Bos NA	58	263	57	68	7	3	2	36	11		4	.259	.288	.331	77	-9	3-2	.819	-6	104	71	O58C,P14,M		-1.1
'874 Bos NA	40	184	44	58	4	2	2	27	4		3	.315	.330	.391	123	4	1-0	.827	-1	103	367	O40C,P6,M		0.2
'875 Bos NA	1	4	1	1	0	0	0	0	0		1	.250	.250	.250	72	0	0-0	1.000	0	0	0	/ORM		0.0
'876 Bos N	1	1	0	0	0	0	0	0	0		0	.000	.000	.000	-98	-1		—	0	0	0	/ORM		-0.1
'877 Bos N	1	4	0	0	0	0	0	0	0		0	.000	.000	.000	-97	-1		.667	0	398	2718	/OCM		0.0
Total 5 NA	178	806	183	224	21	8	4	113	37		12	.278	.310	.339	91	-11	11-3	.841	-13	103	162	O177(0/176/1),P36/S		-1.7
Total 2	2	7	0	0	0	0	0	0	0		0	.000	.000	.000	-97	-2		.667	0	367	2509	O2(0/1/1)		-0.1

WRIGHT, BILL William Hiram d9.16

'887 Was N	1	3	0	2	0	0	0	0	0		0	.667	.667	.667	290	-1		.778	-1			/C		0.0

WRIGHT, RASTY William Smith B1.31.1863 Birmingham MI D10.14.1922 Duluth MN BL/6-1/185 d4.17

'890 Syr AA	88	348	82	106	10	6	0	27	69	6		.305	.428	.368	150	30	30	.907	2	102	187	O88(0/70/18)		2.5
Cle N	13	45	7	5	1	0	0	2	12		4	.111	.298	.133	27	-3	3	.917	-1	46	0	O13R		-0.4
Total 1	101	393	89	111	11	6	0	29	81	6	4	.282	.412	.341	135	27	33	.908	1	95	164	O101(0/70/31)		2.1

WRIGHTSTONE, RUSS Russell Guy B3.18.1893 Bowmansdale PA D2.25.1969 Harrisburg PA BL/TR/5-10.5/176 d4.19 OF(85/0/33)

'920 Phi N	76	206	23	54	6	1	3	17	10	2	25	.262	.303	.345	82	-5	3-2	.934	3	106	71	3b56,S2/2		0.0
'921 Phi N	109	372	59	110	13	4	9	51	10	2	20	.296	.332	.425	92	-5	4-4	.922	5	111	60	3b54,O37(34/0/3),2b4		0.0
'922 Phi N	99	331	56	101	18	6	5	33	28	3	17	.305	.365	.441	98	-1	4-5	.973	10	120	66	3b40,S35,1b2		1.3
'923 Phi N	119	392	59	107	21	7	7	57	21	3	19	.273	.315	.416	82	-11	5-2	.942	-0	96	81	3b72,S21,2b9		-0.4
'924 Phi N	118	388	55	119	24	4	7	58	20	7	15	.307	.363	.443	102	2	5-4	.944	-9	91	108	3b97,2b9,S5/OR		0.0
'925 Phi N	92	286	48	99	18	5	14	61	19	1	18	.346	.389	.591	135	14	0-3	.937	-10	94	53	O45(37/0/10),S12,3b11,2b10,1b6		0.1
'926 Phi N	112	368	55	113	23	1	9	57	27	3	5	.307	.356	.432	106	3	5	.977	-2	104	0	1b53,3b37,2b13,O5L		0.4
'927 Phi N	141	533	62	163	24	5	6	75	48	3	20	.306	.365	.403	104	4	9	.989	2	107	94	1b136		-0.3
'928 Phi N	33	91	7	19	5	1	1	11	14	1	7	.209	.321	.319	65	-4	0	.936	-2	91	48	O26(9/0/19),1b4		-0.2
NY N	30	25	3	4	0	0	1	5	3	0	2	.160	.250	.280	38	-2	0	1.000	-0	0	0	1b2		-0.2
Year	63	116	10	23	5	1	2	16	17	1	7	.198	.306	.310	60	-7	0	.936	-2	91	48	O26(9/0/19),1b6		-1.0
Total 9	929	2992	427	889	152	34	60	425	215	22	152	.297	.349	.431	99	-5	35-20	.942	3	103	87	3b368,1b203,O114L,S75,2b47		0.1

YEAR	TM LG	G	AB	R	H	2B	3B	HR	RBI	BB-IB	HP	SO	AVG	OBP	SLG	AOPS	ABR	SB-CS	FA	FR	RNG	THR	GAMES AT POSITION	DL	B

WRIGLEY, ZEKE George Watson B1.18.1874 Philadelphia PA D9.28.1952 Philadelphia PA 5-8.5/150 d8.31

1896	Was N	5	9	1	1	0	0	0	2	1	0	1	.111	.200	.111	-17	-2	0	.909	2	172	0	2b3/S		
1897	Was N	104	388	65	110	14	8	3	64	21	0		.284	.320	.384	86	-10	5	.885	4	231	455	O36(4/13/19),S33,3b30,2b9		
1898	Was N	111	400	50	98	9	10	2	39	20	1		.245	.283	.333	76	-15	10	.895	11	102	94	S97,2b11,O3(0/2/1)/3		
1899	NY N	4	15	1	3	0	0	0	1	1	0		.200	.250	.200	-25	-2	1	.818	-1	103	0	3b4		
	Bro N	15	49	4	10	2	2	0	11	3	0		.204	.250	.327	56	-3	2	.870	4	78	84	S14/3		
	Year	19	64	5	13	2	2	0	12	4	0		.203	.250	.297	49	-5	3	.870	-5	78	84	S14,3b5		
Total	4	239	861	121	222	25	20	5	117	46	1	1	.258	.296	.351	78	-32	18	.892	12	101	85	S145,O39(4/15/20),3b36,2b23		

WRONA, RICK Richard James B12.10.1963 Tulsa OK BR/TR/6-1/185* [ChiN85 5/130] d9.3 Col Wichita St.

1988	Chi N	4	6	0	0	0	0	0	0	0-0	0	1	.000	.000	.000	-96	-2	0-0	1.000	1	135	181	C2		
1989	†Chi N	38	92	11	26	2	1	2	14	2-1	0	21	.283	.299	.391	91	-1	0-0	.983	1	163	60	C37		
1990	Chi N	16	29	3	5	0	0	0	2	2-1	0	11	.172	.226	.172	4	-4	1-0	.970	2	221	109	C16		
1992	Cin N	11	23	0	4	0	0	0	0	0-0	0	3	.174	.174	.174	-1	-3	0-0	.965	2	259	82	C10/1		
1993	Chi A	4	8	0	1	0	0	0	1	0-0	0	1	.125	.125	.125	-33	-2	0-0	1.000	-2	48	0	C4		
1994	Mil A	6	10	2	5	4	0	1	3	1-0	0	5	.500	.545	1.200	317	3	0-0	.923	-1	216	0	C5/1		
Total	6	79	168	16	41	6	1	3	18	5-2	0	41	.244	.267	.345	68	-9	1-0	.976	3	182	69	C74,1b2		

WUESTLING, YATS George B10.18.1903 St.Louis MO D4.26.1970 St.Louis MO BR/TR/5-11/167 d6.15

1929	Det A	54	150	13	30	4	1	0	16	9	1	24	.200	.250	.240	27	-17	1-3	.943	-4	104	62	S52/23		
1930	Det A	4	9	0	0	0	0	0	0	2	0	3	.000	.182	.000	-48	-2	0-0	.842	-0	105	101	S4		
	NY A	25	58	5	11	0	1	0	3	4	0	14	.190	.242	.224	20	-7	0-1	.918	1	104	100	S21,3b3		
	Year	29	67	5	11	0	1	0	3	6	0	17	.164	.233	.194	10	-10	0-1	.904	1	104	100	S25,3b3		
Total	2	83	217	18	41	4	2	0	19	15	1	41	.189	.245	.226	21	-26	1-4	.931	-3	104	73	S77,3b4/2		

WYATT, JOE Loral John B4.6.1900 Petersburg IN D12.5.1970 Oblong IL BR/TR/6-1/175 d9.11 Col Wabash

| 1924 | Cle A | 4 | 12 | 1 | 2 | 0 | 0 | 0 | 1 | 0 | 0 | 1 | .167 | .286 | .167 | 18 | -1 | 0 | .833 | -1 | 83 | 0 | O4R | | |

WYLIE, REN James Renwick B12.14.1861 Elizabeth PA D8.17.1951 Wilkinsburg PA BR/TR/5-11/155 d8.11 Col Geneva

| 1882 | Pit AA | 1 | 3 | 0 | 0 | 0 | 0 | 0 | | 0 | | | .000 | .000 | .000 | -99 | -1 | | 1.000 | 1 | 745 | 0 | /OC | | |

WYMAN, FRANK Frank H. B5.10.1862 Haverhill MA D2.4.1916 Everett MA d6.10 ▲

1884	KC U	30	124	16	27	4	0	0		3			.218	.236	.250	55	-10		.743	2	158	231	O25(13/11/0),P3,1b3,3b3		
	CP U	2	8	1	3	0	0	0		0			.375	.375	.375	129	0		.846	-0	155	0	1b2		
	Year	32	132	17	30	4	0	0		3			.227	.244	.258	60	-11		.743	2	158	231	O25(13/11/0),1b5,P3,3b3		

WYNEGAR, BUTCH Harold Delano B3.14.1956 York PA BB/TR/6-0/194(185-200) [MinA74 2/38] d4.9 C3

1976	Min A★	149	534	58	139	21	2	10	69	79-7	2	63	.260	.356	.363	109	9	0-0	.978	-7	101	106	C137,D15		
1977	Min A★	144	532	76	139	22	3	10	79	68-5	2	61	.261	.344	.370	97	-1	2-3	.993	-6	111	104	C142/3		
1978	Min A	135	454	36	104	22	1	4	45	47-2	6	42	.229	.307	.308	72	-15	1-0	.988	2	114	115	C131/3		
1979	Min A	149	504	74	136	20	0	7	57	74-5	2	36	.270	.363	.351	90	-4	2-2	.992	6	167	122	C146,D2		
1980	Min A	146	486	61	124	18	3	5	57	63-6	2	36	.255	.339	.335	81	-11	3-1	.988	14	146	105	C142/D		
1981	Min A	47	150	11	37	5	0	0	10	17-2	1	9	.247	.322	.280	72	-5	0-1	.995	-0	75	145	C37,D9	54	
1982	Min A	24	86	9	18	4	0	1	8	10-1	0	12	.209	.292	.291	59	-5	0-0	.986	-2	75	71	C24		
	NY A	63	191	27	56	8	1	3	20	40-1	1	21	.293	.413	.393	126	10	0-1	.993	1	105	89	C62	38	
	Year	87	277	36	74	12	1	4	28	50-2	1	33	.267	.378	.361	105	5	0-1	.991	-1	97	84	C86		
1983	NY A	94	301	40	89	18	2	6	42	52-1	1	29	.296	.399	.429	132	16	1-1	.985	-9	102	128	C93	15	
1984	NY A	129	442	48	118	13	1	6	45	65-6	0	35	.267	.360	.342	99	2	1-4	.993	-1	101	103	C126		
1985	NY A	102	309	27	69	15	0	5	32	64-2	0	43	.223	.356	.320	89	-2	0-0	.990	2	109	111	C96	15	
1986	NY A	61	194	19	40	4	0	7	29	30-2	1	21	.206	.310	.345	79	-6	0-0	.994	2	98	84	C57	15	
1987	Cal A	31	92	4	19	2	0	0	5	9-0	0	13	.207	.277	.228	37	-8	0-0	.994	4	107	110	C28/D	114	
1988	Cal A	27	55	8	14	4	1	1	8	8-1	0	7	.255	.338	.418	117	1	0-0	.981	2	123	162	C26	130	
Total	13	1301	4330	498	1102	176	15	65	506	626-41	17	428	.255	.348	.347	93	-19	10-13	.989	7	116	110	C1247,D28,3b2	381	4

WYNN, JIMMY James Sherman "The Toy Cannon" B3.12.1942 Hamilton OH BR/TR/5-9/170(159-170) d7.10 Col Central St. OF(298/1181/355)

1963	Hou N	70	250	31	61	10	5	4	27	30-4	0	53	.244	.319	.372	107	2	4-2	.963	-7	104	153	O53(43/10/0),S21,3b2		
1964	Hou N	67	219	19	49	7	0	5	18	24-2	1	45	.224	.301	.324	81	-5	5-5	.958	2	99	200	O64(13/51/0)		
1965	Hou N	157	564	90	155	30	7	22	73	84-3	5	126	.275	.371	.470	146	37	43-4	.978	9	111	147	O155C		
1966	Hou N	105	418	62	107	21	1	18	62	41-4	1	81	.256	.321	.440	118	10	13-10	.978	4	112	85	O104C		
1967	Hou N★	158	594	102	148	29	3	37	107	74-7	2	137	.249	.331	.495	139	16	16-4	.968	1	109	48	O157C	59	
1968	Hou N	156	542	85	146	23	5	26	67	90-9	5	131	.269	.376	.474	158	41	11-17	.988	11	100	212	O153(56/93/7)		
1969	Hou N	149	495	113	133	17	1	33	87	148-14	3	142	.269	.436	.507	167	55	23-7	.985	3	106	109	O149C		
1970	Hou N	157	554	82	156	32	2	27	88	106-12	1	96	.282	.394	.493	143	28	24-5	.987	3	98	149	O151(66/87/0)		
1971	Hou N	123	404	38	82	16	0	7	45	56-6	2	63	.203	.302	.295	72	-14	10-5	.988	2	96	118	O116(1/48/72)		
1972	Hou N	145	542	117	148	29	3	24	90	103-6	2	99	.273	.389	.470	148	39	17-7	.983	-1	102	75	O144(0/12/132)		
1973	Hou N	139	481	90	106	14	5	20	55	91-9	4	102	.220	.347	.395	107	6	14-11	.986	2	108	79	O133(2/10/125)		
1974	†LA N★	150	535	104	145	17	4	32	108	108-4	0	104	.271	.387	.497	153	41	18-15	.992	0	101	113	O148C		
1975	LA N★	130	412	80	102	16	0	18	58	110-2	1	77	.248	.403	.417	135	26	7-3	.983	-3	99	79	O120(21/107/0)		
1976	Atl N	148	449	75	93	19	4	17	66	127-1	0	111	.207	.377	.367	107	11	16-6	.971	7	99	196	O138(90/50/0)		
1977	NY N	30	77	7	11	2	1	1	3	15-1	0	16	.143	.283	.234	43	-6	1-0	1.000	1	121	157	D15,O8(5/0/3)		
	Mil A	36	117	10	23	3	1	0	10	17-0	0	31	.197	.294	.239	49	-8	3-0	.967	-2	91	0	O17(1/0/16),D15		
	Year	66	194	17	34	5	2	1	13	32-1	0	47	.175	.289	.237	46	-14	4-0	.981	-0	102	55	D30,O25(6/0/19)		
Total	15	1920	6653	1105	1665	285	39	291	964	1224-84	27	1427	.250	.366	.436	129	302	225-101	.981	33	103	122	O1810C,D30,S21,3b2	59	29

WYNNE, MARVELL Marvell B12.17.1959 Chicago IL BL/TL/5-11/185(169-185) d6.15

1983	Pit N	103	366	66	89	16	2	7	26	38-0	3	52	.243	.319	.355	84	-8	12-10	.983	-5	93	66	O102C		
1984	Pit N	154	653	77	174	24	11	0	39	42-0	0	81	.266	.310	.337	82	-17	24-19	.990	-7	93	91	O154C		
1985	Pit N	103	337	21	69	6	3	2	18	18-2	1	45	.205	.247	.258	42	-27	10-5	.986	3	107	132	O99C		
1986	SD N	137	288	34	76	19	2	7	37	15-2	1	45	.264	.300	.417	99	2	11-11	.986	2	113	67	O125C	30	
1987	SD N	98	188	17	47	8	2	2	24	20-1	0	37	.250	.321	.346	80	-5	11-6	.981	-1	100	71	O71(33/40/5)	15	
1988	SD N	128	333	37	88	13	4	11	42	31-2	0	62	.264	.325	.426	117	6	3-4	.987	4	105	124	O113(37/84/10)		
1989	SD N	105	294	19	74	11	1	6	35	12-1	1	41	.252	.282	.357	82	-5	4-1	.971	0	92	169	O96(39/41/25)		
	†Chi N	20	48	8	9	2	1	1	4	1-1	1	7	.188	.220	.333	52	-3	2-0	.944	-3	64	0	O13(4/6/3)		
	Year	125	342	27	83	13	2	7	39	13-2	2	48	.243	.274	.354	77	-11	6-1	.968	-3	88	147	O109(43/47/28)		
1990	Chi N	92	186	21	38	8	2	4	19	14-3	1	25	.204	.264	.333	59	-11	3-2	.991	-0	97	116	O66(13/54/4)	45	
Total	8	940	2693	300	664	107	28	40	244	191-12	8	398	.247	.297	.352	81	-75	80-58	.985	-5	101	106	O839(126/706/47)		

WYROSTEK, JOHNNY John Barney B7.12.1919 Fairmont City IL D12.12.1986 St.Louis MO BL/TR/6-2/180* d9.10 Mil 1944-45

1942	Pit N	9	35	4	4	0	1	0	3	3	0	2	.114	.184	.171	4	-4	0	1.000	1	100	177	O8L		
1943	Pit N	51	79	7	12	3	2	0	1	3	0	15	.152	.183	.190	7	-10	0	.919	-2	112	0	O20(5/6/9),3b2/12		
1946	Phi N	145	545	73	153	30	4	6	45	70	3	42	.281	.366	.383	116	13	7	.981	5	102	135	O142(6/138/0)		
1947	Phi N	128	454	68	124	24	7	5	51	61	0	45	.273	.364	.390	104	4	7	.971	0	100	109	O126(0/27/100)		
1948	Cin N	136	512	74	140	24	9	17	76	52	3	63	.273	.344	.455	119	12	7	.977	-5	96	85	O130C		
1949	Cin N	134	474	54	118	20	4	9	46	58	2	63	.249	.333	.365	86	-9	7	.971	-2	99	95	O129(2/60/67)		
1950	Cin N★	131	509	50	145	34	5	8	76	52	5	38	.285	.357	.418	103	3	1	.980	1	106	89	O129(11/9/115),1b4		
1951	Cin N	142	537	52	167	31	3	2	61	54	2	46	.311	.376	.391	105	6	2-1	.970	-9	93	62	O139(1/0/139)		
1952	Cin N	30	106	12	25	1	3	0	10	18	0	7	.236	.347	.330	89	-1	1-2	1.000	1	93	203	O29(0/25/6)/1		
	Phi N	98	321	45	88	16	3	1	37	44	1	26	.274	.363	.352	100	2	1-7	.972	5	115	116	O88(2/1/87)		
	Year	128	427	57	113	17	6	2	47	62	1	33	.265	.359	.347	97	1	2-9	.980	7	110	138	O117(2/26/93)/1		
1953	Phi N	125	409	42	111	14	2	6	47	38	1	43	.271	.339	.359	83	-10	0-3	.962	1	97	141	O110(8/0/102)		
1954	Phi N	92	259	28	62	12	3	2	19	39	1	34	.239	.334	.351	74	-10	0-0	.990	-1	105	129	O55(6/0/49),1b22		
Total	11	1221	4240	525	1149	209	45	58	481	482	25	437	.271	.349	.383	98	-4	33-13	.975	-5	101	106	O1105(49/396/674),1b28,3b2/2		

YAIK, HENRY Henry B3.1.1864 Detroit MI D9.21.1935 Detroit MI BL/5-11/185 d10.3

| 1888 | Pit N | 2 | 6 | 0 | 2 | 0 | 0 | 0 | 0 | 0 | 0 | 1 | .333 | .429 | .333 | 159 | 1 | 0 | .625 | 0 | 436 | 1104 | /OLC | | |

R	TM LG	G	AB	R	H	2B	3B	HR	RBI	BB-IB	HP	SO	AVG	OBP	SLG	AOPS	ABR	SB-CS	FA	FR	RNG	THR	GAMES AT POSITION	DL	BFW

LE, AD William M. B4.17.1870 Bristol CT D4.27.1948 Bridgeport CT BR d9.18

| '5 | Bro N | 4 | 13 | 1 | 1 | 0 | 0 | 0 | 1 | 1 | 0 | | .077 | .143 | .077 | -37 | -2 | 0 | 1.000 | -0 | 43 | 190 | 1b4 | | -0.3 |

NCY, HUGH Hugh B10.16.1949 Sarasota FL BR/TR/5-11/170* [ChiA68 2/34] d7.5

'2	Chi A	3	9	0	1	0	0	0	0	0-0	0	0	.111	.111	.111	-33	-1	0-1	1.000	1	122	0	3b3		-0.2
'4	Chi A	1	0	0	0	0	0	0	0	0-0	0	0	—	—	—	—	0	0-0	—	0			/D		0.0
'6	Chi A	3	10	0	1	1	0	0	0	0-0	0	3	.100	.100	.200	-14	-1	0-0	1.000	-1	50	157	2b3		-0.2
al	3	7	19	0	2	1	0	0	0	0-0	0	3	.105	.105	.158	-23	-2	0-1	1.000	-0	50	157	2b3,3b3/D		-0.4

NKOWSKI, GEORGE George Edward B11.19.1922 Cambridge MA BR/TR/6-0/180 d8.17 Mil 1943-46 Col Northeastern

42	Phi A	6	13	0	2	1	0	0	2	0	0	2	.154	.154	.231	7	-2	0-0	1.000	0	75	191	C6		-0.1
49	Chi A	12	18	0	3	1	0	0	2	0	0	2	.167	.167	.222	3	-3	0-0	1.000	1	96	131	C6		-0.2
al	2	18	31	0	5	2	0	0	4	0	0	4	.161	.161	.226	5	-5	0-0	1.000	1	86	160	C12		-0.3

ANTZ, GEORGE George Webb B7.27.1886 Louisville KY D2.26.1967 Louisville KY BR/TR/5-6.5/168 d9.30

| 42 | Chi N | 1 | 1 | 0 | 1 | 0 | 0 | 0 | 0 | 0 | 0 | 0 | 1.000 | 1.000 | 1.000 | 450 | 0 | 0 | — | 0 | 0 | 0 | /C | | 0.0 |

ARYAN, YAM Clarence Everett B11.5.1892 Knowlton IA D11.16.1964 Birmingham AL BR/TR/5-10.5/180 d4.23

21	Chi A	45	102	11	31	8	0	0	15	9		16	.304	.366	.422	102	0	1-0	.933	-5	77	125	C34		-0.2
22	Chi A	36	71	9	14	2	0	2	9	6		10	.197	.269	.310	51	-5	1-0	.966	0	115	84	C26		-0.4
al	2	81	173	20	45	10	2	2	24	15		26	.260	.326	.376	81	-5	1-0	.948	-5	93	108	C60		-0.6

ASTRZEMSKI, CARL Carl Michael "Yaz" B8.22.1939 Southampton NY BL/TR/5-11/182(170-185) d4.11 HF1989 Col Notre Dame OF(1917/159/7)

61	Bos A	148	583	71	155	31	6	11	80	50-3	3	96	.266	.324	.396	90	-9	6-5	.963	-5	87	111	O147L		-2.2
62	Bos A	160	646	99	191	43	6	19	94	66-7	3	82	.296	.363	.469	118	18	7-4	.969	8	100	161	O161L		1.7
63	Bos A★	151	570	91	183	40	3	14	68	95-6	1	72	.321	.418	.475	145	41	8-5	.980	9	98	173	O151(151/1/0)		4.2
64	Bos A	151	567	77	164	29	9	15	67	75-6	2	90	.289	.374	.451	122	19	6-5	.973	20	122	207	O148(18/131/0),3b2		3.5
65	Bos A★	133	494	78	154	45	3	20	72	70-8	1	58	.312	.395	.536	154	38	7-6	.987	3	95	147	O130(125/7/1)		3.5
66	Bos A☆	160	594	81	165	39	2	16	80	84-10	1	60	.278	.368	.431	117	17	8-9	.985	10	106	151	O158(157/1/0)		1.7
67	†Bos A★	161	579	112	189	31	4	44	121	91-11	4	69	.326	.418	.622	189	67	10-8	.978	6	102	120	O161(161/1/0)		6.9
68	Bos A★	157	539	90	162	32	2	23	74	119-13	2	90	.301	.426	.495	169	53	13-6	.991	6	112	124	O155(154/1/0),1b3		6.3
69	Bos A★	162	603	96	154	28	2	40	111	101-9	1	91	.255	.362	.507	135	29	15-7	.985	6	90	154	O143(140/3/0),1b22		2.7
70	Bos A★	161	566	125	186	29	0	40	102	128-12	1	66	.329	.452	.592	174	65	23-15	.990	1	104	83	1b94,O69(67/3/0)		5.5
71	Bos A★	148	508	75	129	21	2	15	70	106-12	1	60	.254	.381	.392	112	13	8-7	.993	1	106	181	O146L		1.6
72	Bos A★	125	455	70	120	18	2	12	68	67-3	4	44	.264	.357	.391	117	12	5-4	.974	6	95	163	O83L,1b42	30	1.1
73	Bos A★	152	540	82	160	25	4	19	95	105-13	0	58	.296	.407	.463	137	32	9-7	.994	-4	94	100	1b107,3b31,O14L		1.8
74	Bos A★	148	515	93	155	25	2	15	79	104-16	2	48	.301	.414	.445	139	33	12-7	.997	-8	90	96	1b84,O63L,D4		1.5
75	†Bos A★	149	543	91	146	30	1	14	60	87-12	2	67	.269	.371	.405	110	11	8-4	.996	-1	94	93	1b140,O8L,D2		-0.1
76	Bos A★	155	546	71	146	23	2	21	102	80-6	1	67	.267	.357	.432	118	4	5-6	.998	-9	76	105	1b94,O51L,D10		-0.7
77	Bos A★	150	558	99	165	27	3	28	102	73-6	1	40	.296	.372	.505	124	20	11-1	1.000	11	103	159	O140(138/0/2),1b7,D6		2.6
78	Bos A★	144	523	70	145	21	2	17	81	76-8	3	44	.277	.367	.423	111	10	4-5	.986	2	86	161	O71(63/8/0),1b50,D27		0.5
79	Bos A★	147	518	69	140	28	1	21	87	62-8	5	46	.270	.346	.450	108	7	3-3	.996	4	142	94	D56,1b51,O36L		0.3
80	Bos A	105	364	49	100	21	4	15	50	44-5	0	38	.275	.350	.462	115	8	0-2	1.000	-2	83	111	D49,O39(34/1/4),1b16		0.1
81	Bos A	91	338	36	83	14	1	7	53	49-4	0	28	.246	.338	.355	96	-1	0-1	.992	3	136	77	D48,1b39		-0.2
82	Bos A★	131	459	53	126	22	1	16	72	59-1	2	50	.275	.358	.431	109	7	0-1	1.000	1	130	116	D102,1b14,O2C		0.4
83	Bos A★	119	380	38	101	24	0	10	56	54-11	2	29	.266	.359	.408	103	4	0-0	1.000	-1	80	56	D107,1b2/OL	30	0.2
	23	3308	11988	1816	3419	646	59	452	1844	1845-190	40	1393	.285	.379	.462	128	508	168-116	.981	80	99	142	O2076L,1b765,D411,3b33	30	42.7

ATES, AL Albert Arthur B5.26.1945 Jersey City NJ BR/TR/6-2/210 d5.13

| 71 | Mil A | 24 | 47 | 5 | 13 | 2 | 0 | 1 | 4 | 3-0 | 0 | 7 | .277 | .308 | .383 | 99 | 0 | 1-0 | 1.000 | 1 | 104 | 317 | O12(3/0/9) | | 0.1 |

EABSLEY, BERT Robert Watkins B12.17.1893 Philadelphia PA D2.8.1961 Philadelphia PA BR/TR/5-9.5/175 d5.28

| 19 | Phi N | 3 | 0 | 0 | 0 | 0 | 0 | 0 | 0 | 1 | 0 | 0 | — | 1.000 | — | 200 | 0 | 0 | — | 0 | | | /H | | 0.0 |

EAGER, GEORGE George J. "Doc" B6.5.1874 Cincinnati OH D7.5.1940 Cincinnati OH BR/TR/5-10/190 d9.25 OF(8/5/13)

96	Bos N	2	5	1	1	0	0	0	0	0	0	0	.200	.200	.200	-5	-0	0	1.000	-0	0	411	1b2		-0.1
97	†Bos N	30	95	20	23	3	2	2	15	7		0	.242	.294	.389	75	-4	2	.970	1	153	78	C13,O10(2/1/7),2b4/3		-0.2
98	Bos N	68	221	37	59	13	1	3	24	16		4	.267	.328	.376	96	-1	1	.951	-2	117	86	C37,1b17,O9(6/3/1),S2		-0.1
99	Bos N	3	8	1	1	0	0	0	1	0		1	.125	.222	.125	-3	-1	0	1.000	0	0	0	O2(0/1/1)/C		-0.1
01	Cle A	39	139	13	31	5	0	0	14	4		1	.223	.250	.259	43	-11	2	.964	0	97	130	C25,1b5,O3R,2b2		-0.7
	Pit N	26	91	9	24	2	1	0	10	4		1	.264	.302	.308	75	-3	1	.971	0	128	92	C20,3b4/1		-0.5
02	NY N	39	108	6	22	2	1	0	9	11		0	.204	.277	.241	61	-5	1	.946	-1	96	100	C27,1b3/OR		-0.3
	Bal A	11	38	3	7	1	0	1	2	1		0	.184	.225	.211	20	-4	0	.930	-1	94	124	C11		-0.3
otal	6	218	705	90	168	26	5	6	73	45		6	1	.238	.290	.312	69	-30	7	.953	-2	112	100	C134,1b28,O25R,2b6,3b5,S2		-1.9

EAGER, JOE Joseph F. "Little Joe" B8.28.1875 Philadelphia PA D7.2.1937 Detroit MI BR/TR/5-10/160 d4.22 ▲

98	Bro N	43	134	12	23	5	1	0	15	7		1	.172	.218	.224	27	-13	4	.908	5	137	125	P36,O4(2/1/1),S2/2		0.1
99	Bro N	23	47	12	9	0	1	0	4	6		4	.191	.333	.234	55	-3	0	.914	3	117	232	S11,P10/OL3		0.1
00	Bro N	3	9	0	3	0	0	0	0	0		0	.333	.333	.333	79	0	0	1.000	-1	70	0	P2/3		0.0
01	Det A	41	125	18	37	7	1	2	17	4		5	.296	.343	.416	105	1	3	.919	5	115	209	P26,S12/2		0.4
02	Det A	50	161	17	39	6	5	1	23	5		4	.242	.282	.360	76	-6	0	.957	1	127	67	P19,O13(7/0/6),2b12,S3/3		-0.4
03	Det A	109	402	36	103	16	9	0	43	18		9	.256	.303	.323	91	-5	9	.921	-9	86	78	3b107/PS		-1.1
05	NY A	115	401	54	107	16	7	0	42	25		13	.267	.330	.342	102	1	8	.923	1	99	78	3b91,S21		0.6
06	NY A	57	123	20	37	6	1	0	12	13		9	.301	.407	.366	129	6	3	.905	0	93	133	S22,2b13,3b3		0.7
07	StL A	123	436	32	104	21	7	1	44	31		11	.239	.294	.326	98	-1	11	.938	5	104	129	3b91,2b17,S10		0.7
08	StL A	10	15	3	5	0	1	0	1	1		3	.333	.474	.400	183	2	2	1.000	0	114	0	2b4/S		1.3
otal	10	574	1853	204	467	77	29	4	201	110	51	.252	.312	.331	92	-18	37	.927	10	96	93	3b295,P94,S83,2b48,O18(10/1/7)		1.3

EAGER, STEVE Stephen Wayne B11.24.1948 Huntington WV BR/TR/6-0/190(190-205) [LAN67 4/80] d8.2

72	LA N	35	106	18	29	4	1	4	15	16-2	1	26	.274	.374	.406	123	4	0-0	.984	5	86	77	C35		1.1
73	LA N	54	134	18	34	5	0	2	10	15-1	3	33	.254	.340	.336	91	-1	1-0	.981	-2	97	71	C50		-0.1
74	†LA N	94	316	41	84	16	1	12	41	32-5	2	77	.266	.334	.437	120	8	2-2	.992	9	139	87	C93		2.1
75	LA N	135	452	34	103	16	1	12	54	40-7	8	75	.228	.298	.347	83	-11	2-5	.992	13	151	56	C135		0.7
76	LA N	117	359	42	77	11	3	11	35	30-3	7	84	.214	.286	.354	82	-10	3-1	.985	13	137	98	C115		0.9
77	†LA N	125	387	53	99	21	2	16	55	43-11	4	84	.256	.334	.444	107	4	1-3	.977	18	163	73	C123		2.6
78	†LA N	94	228	19	44	7	0	4	23	36-11	0	41	.193	.301	.276	63	-11	0-0	.988	11	138	132	C91	17	0.4
79	†LA N	105	310	33	67	9	2	13	41	29-8	0	68	.216	.282	.384	82	-9	1-0	.984	7	126	105	C103		0.2
80	LA N	96	227	20	48	8	0	2	20	20-6	0	54	.211	.274	.273	55	-14	2-3	.984	-1	119	62	C95		-1.1
81	†LA N	42	86	5	18	3	0	3	7	6-0	1	14	.209	.261	.337	72	-4	0-0	.994	-0	149	84	C40		-0.3
82	LA N	82	196	13	48	5	2	2	18	13-3	1	28	.245	.294	.321	75	-7	0-0	.990	5	144	112	C76	28	0.0
83	†LA N	113	335	31	68	8	3	15	41	23-4	1	57	.203	.256	.379	74	-14	1-1	.985	1	139	114	C112	22	-1.0
84	LA N	74	197	16	45	4	1	4	29	20-1	0	38	.228	.295	.310	72	-8	1-2	.994	-5	106	87	C65		-1.1
85	†LA N	53	121	4	25	4	1	0	9	7-2	0	24	.207	.246	.256	43	-10	0-1	.992	7	135	185	C48		-1.0
86	Sea A	50	130	10	27	2	0	2	12	12-0	0	23	.208	.273	.269	48	-10	0-0	1.000	-3	113	104	C49	15	-1.0
otal	15	1269	3584	357	816	118	16	102	410	342-64	27	726	.228	.298	.355	82	-93	14-18	.987	79	135	92	C1230	82	3.3

EATMAN, BILL William Suter B3.1839 Alexandria VA D4.20.1901 York PA d4.20

| 72 | Nat NA | 1 | 4 | 0 | 0 | 0 | 0 | 0 | 0 | 0 | | | 1 | .000 | .000 | .000 | -86 | -1 | 0-0 | .000 | -0 | 0 | 0 | /OR | | -0.1 |

YELDING, ERIC Eric Girard B2.22.1965 Montrose AL BR/TR/5-11/165* [TorA84*1/19] d4.9 Col Chipola (FL) JC

89	Hou N	70	90	19	21	2	0	0	9	7-0	1	19	.233	.290	.256	61	-5	11-5	1.000	2	102	87	S15,2b13,O8(1/4/3)		-0.1
90	Hou N	142	511	69	130	9	5	1	28	39-1	0	87	.254	.305	.297	69	-23	64-25	.971	-4	109	106	O94(11/83/6),S40,2b10,3b3		-2.0
91	Hou N	78	276	19	67	11	1	1	20	13-3	0	46	.243	.276	.301	65	-13	11-9	.939	-10	87	88	S72,O4(0/3/1)		-1.1
92	Hou N	9	8	1	2	0	0	0	0	0-0	0	3	.250	.250	.250	44	-1	0-0	—	-1	0	0	S2,O2(2/1/0)		-0.1
93	Chi N	69	108	14	22	5	1	0	10	11-2	0	22	.204	.277	.296	54	-7	3-2	.984	-5	120	106	2b32,3b7/SOC		-0.1
Total	5	368	993	122	242	27	7	3	67	70-6	1	177	.244	.292	.294	66	-49	89-41	.948	-8	89	85	S130,O109(14/92/10),2b55,3b10		-4.3

YELLE, ARCHIE   Archie Joseph   B6.11.1892 Saginaw MI   D5.2.1983 Woodland CA   BR/TR/5-10.5/170   d5.12

YEAR	TM LG	G	AB	R	H	2B	3B	HR	RBI	BB-IB	HP	SO	AVG	OBP	SLG	AOPS	ABR	SB-CS	FA	FR	RNG	THR	GAMES AT POSITION	DL
1917	Det A	25	51	4	7	1	0	0	0	5	0	4	.137	.214	.157	13	-5	2	.975	-2	85	94	C24	
1918	Det A	56	144	7	25	3	0	0	7	9	1	15	.174	.227	.194	28	-13	0	.948	-1	85	142	C52	
1919	Det A	6	4	1	0	0	0	0	0	1	0	0	.000	.200	.000	-97	-1	0	.833	-1	99	125	C6	
Total	3	87	199	12	32	4	0	0	7	15	1	19	.161	.223	.181	23	-19	2	.952	-4	85	130	C82	

YERKES, STEVE   Stephen Douglas   B5.15.1888 Hatboro PA   D1.31.1971 Lansdale PA   BR/TR/5-9/165   d9.29 Col Penn

YEAR	TM LG	G	AB	R	H	2B	3B	HR	RBI	BB-IB	HP	SO	AVG	OBP	SLG	AOPS	ABR	SB-CS	FA	FR	RNG	THR	GAMES AT POSITION	DL
1909	Bos A	5	7	0	2	0	0	0	0	0		0	.286	.286	.286	79	0	0	1.000	-0	77	0	S2	
1911	Bos A	142	502	70	140	24	3	1	57	52	6		.279	.354	.345	96	-1	14	.927	-14	91	92	S116,2b14,3b11	
1912	†Bos A	131	523	73	132	22	6	0	42	41	4		.252	.312	.317	76	-17	4	.943	-15	92	101	2b131	
1913	Bos A	137	483	67	129	29	6	1	48	50	2	32	.267	.338	.358	101	1	11	.957	-21	91	67	2b129	
1914	Bos A	92	293	23	64	17	2	1	23	14	2	23	.218	.259	.300	68	-12	5-6	.972	-1	98	154	2b91	
	Pit F	39	142	18	48	9	5	1	25	11	0	13	.338	.386	.493	139	5	2	.974	7	115	86	S39	
1915	Pit F	121	434	44	125	17	8	1	49	30	2	27	.288	.337	.371	100	-7	17	.967	-1	101	92	2b114,S8	
1916	Chi N	44	137	12	36	6	2	1	10	9	0	7	.263	.308	.358	94	-1	1	.919	-1	102	95	2b41	
Total	7	711	2521	307	676	124	32	6	254	207	16	102	.268	.328	.350	93	-32	54-6	.956	-46	95	97	2b520,S165,3b11	

YEWCIC, TOM   Thomas "Kibby"   B5.9.1932 Conemaugh PA   BR/TR/5-11/180   d6.27 Col Michigan St.

YEAR	TM LG	G	AB	R	H	2B	3B	HR	RBI	BB-IB	HP	SO	AVG	OBP	SLG	AOPS	ABR	SB-CS	FA	FR	RNG	THR	GAMES AT POSITION	DL
1957	Det A	1	0	0	0	0	0	0	0	0	0	0	.000	.000	.000	-97	0	0-0	.833	0	0	0	/C	

YEWELL, ED   Edwin Leonard   B8.22.1862 Washington DC   D9.15.1940 Washington DC   d5.12

YEAR	TM LG	G	AB	R	H	2B	3B	HR	RBI	BB-IB	HP	SO	AVG	OBP	SLG	AOPS	ABR	SB-CS	FA	FR	RNG	THR	GAMES AT POSITION	DL
1884	Was AA	27	93	14	23	3	1	0		1			.247	.263	.301	95	0		.885	0	112	103	2b11,O8(1/2/5),3b7,S2	
	Was U	1	4	0	0	0	0	0		0			.000	.000	.000	-99	-1		.571	-1	76	0	/3	
Total	1	28	97	14	23	3	1	0		1			.237	.253	.289	85	-1		.885	-1	112	103	2b11,3b8,O8(1/2/5),S2	

YINGLING, CHARLIE   Charles Christian   B12.7.1865 Baltimore MD   D4.13.1897 Baltimore MD   d6.22 b-Joe

YEAR	TM LG	G	AB	R	H	2B	3B	HR	RBI	BB-IB	HP	SO	AVG	OBP	SLG	AOPS	ABR	SB-CS	FA	FR	RNG	THR	GAMES AT POSITION	DL
1894	Phi N	1	4	0	1	0	0	0		1	0	1	.250	.250	.250	21	-1	0	1.000	-0	83	0	/S	

YOHE, BILL   William Clyde   B9.2.1878 Mt.Erie IL   D12.24.1938 Bremerton WA   BR/TR/5-8/180   d8.30

YEAR	TM LG	G	AB	R	H	2B	3B	HR	RBI	BB-IB	HP	SO	AVG	OBP	SLG	AOPS	ABR	SB-CS	FA	FR	RNG	THR	GAMES AT POSITION	DL
1909	Was A	21	72	6	15	2	0	0	4	3	0		.208	.240	.236	53	-4	2	.921	2	115	39	3b19	

YORK, RUDY   Preston Rudolph   B8.17.1913 Ragland AL   D2.5.1970 Rome GA   BR/TR/6-1/209   d8.22 M1/C4

YEAR	TM LG	G	AB	R	H	2B	3B	HR	RBI	BB-IB	HP	SO	AVG	OBP	SLG	AOPS	ABR	SB-CS	FA	FR	RNG	THR	GAMES AT POSITION	DL
1934	Det A	3	6	0	1	0	0	0	0	3	0	3	.167	.286	.167	19	-1	0	1.000	0	0	332	C2	
1937	Det A	104	375	72	115	18	3	35	103	41	0	52	.307	.375	.651	150	25	3-2	.960	-16	86	79	C54,3b41,1b2	
1938	Det A★	135	463	85	138	27	2	33	127	92	2	74	.298	.417	.579	139	29	1-2	.990	4	141	89	C116,O14L/1	
1939	Det A	102	329	66	101	16	2	20	68	41	2	50	.307	.387	.544	126	12	5-0	.985	-3	104	111	C67,1b19	
1940	†Det A	155	588	105	186	46	6	33	134	89	4	88	.316	.410	.583	141	37	3-2	.990	4	105	76	1b155	
1941	Det A★	155	590	91	153	29	4	27	111	92	1	88	.259	.360	.456	104	4	3-1	.986	-2	91	81	1b155	
1942	Det A★	153	577	81	150	26	4	21	90	73	0	71	.260	.343	.428	107	5	3-3	.988	15	133	90	1b152	
1943	Det A★	155	571	90	155	22	11	34	118	84	1	88	.271	.366	.527	148	33	5-5	.990	19	141	81	1b155	
1944	Det A☆	151	583	77	161	27	7	18	98	68	1	73	.276	.353	.439	119	14	5-3	.989	7	120	124	1b151	
1945	†Det A	155	595	71	157	25	5	18	87	60	0	85	.264	.331	.413	109	5	6-6	.988	-1	98	109	1b155	
1946	†Bos A★	154	579	78	160	30	6	17	119	86	1	93	.276	.371	.437	118	16	3-2	.994	6	111	118	1b154	
1947	Bos A	48	184	16	39	7	0	6	27	22	0	32	.212	.296	.348	73	-7	0-0	.995	2	108	106	1b48	
	Chi A☆	102	400	40	97	18	4	15	64	36	0	55	.243	.305	.420	104	-1	1-0	.995	1	103	111	1b102	
	Year	150	584	56	136	25	4	21	91	58	0	87	.233	.302	.397	94	-8	1-0	.995	3	105	109	1b150	
1948	Phi A	31	51	5	8	0	0	0	6	7	0	15	.157	.259	.157	12	-6	0-0	.988	-1	83	116	1b14	
Total	13	1603	5891	876	1621	291	52	277	1152	792	12	867	.275	.362	.483	121	165	38-26	.990	35	112	99	1b1263,C239,3b41,O14L	

YORK, TOM   Thomas Jefferson   B7.13.1851 Brooklyn NY   D2.17.1936 New York NY   BL/5-9/165   d5.9 M2/U2

YEAR	TM LG	G	AB	R	H	2B	3B	HR	RBI	BB-IB	HP	SO	AVG	OBP	SLG	AOPS	ABR	SB-CS	FA	FR	RNG	THR	GAMES AT POSITION	DL
1871	Tro NA	29	145	36	37	5	7	2	23	9		1	.255	.299	.428	104	0	2-2	.855	3	152	278	O29C	
1872	Bal NA	51	250	66	66	10	4	0	40	3		1	.264	.273	.336	82	-6	6-1	.916	10	120	185	O51(51/0/1)	
1873	Bal NA	57	278	70	84	11	7	2	50	3		4	.302	.310	.414	114	4	4-1	.872	11	123	71	O57(56/1/0)	
1874	Phi NA	50	224	36	56	4	7	0	37	5		4	.250	.266	.330	87	-4	1-0	.861	8	80	0	O50(49/1/0)	
1875	Har NA	86	375	68	111	14	7	0	37	3		4	.296	.302	.371	126	8	7-3	.868	4	50	48	O86L	
1876	Har N	67	263	47	68	12	7	1	39	10		4	.259	.286	.369	108	1		.899	3	71	52	O67(66/1/0)	
1877	Har N	56	237	43	67	16	7	1	37	3		11	.283	.292	.422	137	11		.865	3	46	58	O56L	
1878	Pro N	62	269	56	83	19	10	1	26	8		19	.309	.329	.465	159	16		.873	4	87	118	O62L,M	
1879	Pro N	81	342	69	106	25	5	1	50	19		28	.310	.346	.421	154	21		.898	-4	49	106	O81L	
1880	Pro N	53	203	21	43	9	2	0	18	8		29	.212	.242	.276	78	-4		.934	-2	41	55	O53(50/1/2)	
1881	Pro N	85	316	57	96	23	5	2	47	29		26	.304	.362	.427	150	20		.859	-2	75	29	O85L,M	
1882	Pro N	81	321	48	86	23	7	1	40	19		14	.268	.309	.393	124	9		.876	-2	59	88	O81L	
1883	Cle N	100	381	56	99	29	5	2	46	37		55	.260	.325	.378	114	9		.864	-1	66	89	O100L	
1884	Bal AA	83	314	64	70	14	7	1		34	10		.223	.318	.322	105	3		.843	-5	44	42	O83(68/0/15)	
1885	Bal AA	22	87	6	23	2	0	0	12	8		2	.264	.326	.356	117	2		.938	1	103	128	O22(2/1/19)	
Total	5 NA	273	1272	276	354	44	32	4	187	23		16	.278	.291	.393	105	2	20-7	.875	35	95	93	O273(242/31/1)	
Total	10	690	2733	467	741	174	57	10	315	175	10	186	.271	.317	.387	126	88		.879	-8	62	73	O690(651/3/36)	

YORK, TONY   Tony Batton   B11.27.1912 Irene TX   D4.18.1970 Hillsboro TX   BR/TR/5-10/165   d4.18 Mil 1945

YEAR	TM LG	G	AB	R	H	2B	3B	HR	RBI	BB-IB	HP	SO	AVG	OBP	SLG	AOPS	ABR	SB-CS	FA	FR	RNG	THR	GAMES AT POSITION	DL
1944	Chi N	28	85	4	20	1	0	0	7	4	0	11	.235	.270	.247	46	-6	0	.940	7	121	64	S15,3b12	

YOST, NED   Edgar Frederick   B8.19.1954 Eureka CA   BR/TR/6-1/185*   [NYN74 S1/7] d4.12 M3/C12 Col Chabot (CA) JC

YEAR	TM LG	G	AB	R	H	2B	3B	HR	RBI	BB-IB	HP	SO	AVG	OBP	SLG	AOPS	ABR	SB-CS	FA	FR	RNG	THR	GAMES AT POSITION	DL
1980	Mil A	15	31	0	5	0	0	0	0	0-0	0	6	.161	.161	.161	-12	-9	0-0	1.000	1	108	86	C15	
1981	Mil A	18	27	4	6	0	0	3	3	3-0	0	6	.222	.300	.556	148	1	0-0	.956	-1	112	120	C16	
1982	†Mil A	40	98	13	27	6	3	1	8	7-0	0	20	.276	.324	.429	110	1	3-1	.977	-8	96	19	C39/D	
1983	Mil A	61	196	21	44	5	1	6	28	5-0	0	36	.224	.243	.352	66	-10	1-0	.971	-13	68	43	C61	
1984	Tex A	80	242	15	44	4	0	6	25	6-0	0	47	.182	.201	.273	29	-24	1-2	.995	-12	61	59	C78	35
1985	Mon N	5	11	1	2	0	0	0	0	0-0	0	2	.182	.182	.182	2	-1	0-0	.962	-2	27	0	C5	
Total	6	219	605	54	128	15	4	16	64	21-0	0	117	.212	.237	.329	56	-38	5-3	.982	-36	74	51	C214/D	35

YOST, EDDIE   Edward Frederick Joseph "The Walking Man"   B10.13.1926 Brooklyn NY   BR/TR/5-10/170(170-185)   d8.16 Mil 1945-46 M1/C23 Col NYU

YEAR	TM LG	G	AB	R	H	2B	3B	HR	RBI	BB-IB	HP	SO	AVG	OBP	SLG	AOPS	ABR	SB-CS	FA	FR	RNG	THR	GAMES AT POSITION	DL
1944	Was A	7	14	3	2	0	0	0	0	1	0	2	.143	.200	.143	-1	-2	0-0	.917	-1	74	0	3b3,S2	
1946	Was A	8	25	2	2	1	0	0	1	5	0	5	.080	.233	.120	1	-3	2-1	1.000	1	115	60	3b7	
1947	Was A	115	428	52	102	17	3	0	14	45	2	57	.238	.314	.292	71	-16	3-5	.958	-8	91	52	3b114	
1948	Was A	145	555	74	138	32	11	2	50	82	4	51	.249	.349	.357	91	-6	4-3	.966	-11	88	71	3b145	
1949	Was A	124	435	57	110	19	7	9	45	91	1	41	.253	.383	.391	107	7	3-3	.954	1	100	75	3b122	
1950	Was A	155	573	114	169	26	2	11	58	141	8	63	.295	.440	.405	123	32	6-6	.945	-2	96	131	3b155	
1951	Was A	154	568	109	161	36	4	12	65	126	11	55	.283	.423	.424	132	34	6-4	.954	-21	80	67	3b152,O3L	
1952	Was A☆	157	587	92	137	32	3	12	49	129	8	73	.233	.378	.359	110	15	4-3	.962	-30	68	68	3b157	
1953	Was A	152	577	107	157	30	7	9	45	123	4	59	.272	.400	.395	119	23	7-3	.965	-11	91	90	3b152	
1954	Was A	155	539	101	138	26	4	11	49	131	5	71	.256	.405	.380	123	26	7-3	.968	-4	98	95	3b155	
1955	Was A	122	375	64	91	17	5	7	48	95-0	11	54	.243	.407	.371	117	16	4-3	.943	-4	96	95	3b107	
1956	Was A	152	515	94	119	17	2	11	53	151-9	8	82	.231	.412	.336	100	10	8-3	.963	8	104	96	3b135,O8R	
1957	Was A	110	414	47	104	13	5	9	38	73-2	5	49	.251	.370	.372	94	5	1-11	.952	-8	93	79	3b107	
1958	Was A	134	406	55	91	16	4	8	37	81-2	9	43	.224	.361	.323	93	1	3-6	.964	-12	85	83	3b114,O4L,1b2	
1959	Det A	148	547	115	145	19	0	21	61	135-1	12	77	.278	.435	.436	133	34	9-2	.962	-8	85	85	3b146/2	
1960	Det A	143	497	78	129	23	2	14	47	125-1	8	69	.260	.414	.398	118	21	5-4	.933	-26	67	67	3b142	
1961	LA A	76	213	29	43	4	0	3	15	50-0	2	48	.202	.358	.263	62	-10	0-1	.964	1	94	83	3b67	
1962	LA A	52	104	22	25	9	1	0	10	30-0	1	21	.240	.412	.346	111	4	0-2	.950	-3	91	40	3b28,1b7	
Total	18	2109	7346	1215	1863	337	56	139	683	1614-15	99	920	.254	.394	.371	109	191	72-66	.957	-148	90	81	3b2008,O15(7/0/8),1b9,S2/2	

YOTER, ELMER   Elmer Elsworth   B6.26.1900 Plainfield PA   D7.26.1966 Camp Hill PA   BR/TR/5-7/155   d9.9

YEAR	TM LG	G	AB	R	H	2B	3B	HR	RBI	BB-IB	HP	SO	AVG	OBP	SLG	AOPS	ABR	SB-CS	FA	FR	RNG	THR	GAMES AT POSITION	DL
1921	Phi A	3	3	0	0	0	0	0	0	0	0	0	.000	.000	.000	-99	-1	0-0	---		-0		/H	
1924	Cle A	19	66	3	18	1	0	0	7	5	0	8	.273	.324	.318	65	-4	0-0	.905	-1	108	33	3b19	
1927	Chi N	13	27	2	6	1	0	0	5	4	0	4	.222	.323	.333	76	-1	0-0	.947	0	118	6	3b11	
1928	Chi N	1	0	0	0	0	0	0	0	0	0	0	.—	.—	.—	—	0	0-0	---		-0		/3	
Total	4	36	96	5	24	2	2	0	12	9	0	12	.250	.314	.313	63	-6	0-0	.915	-1	110	24	3b31	

TM LG	G	AB	R	H	2B	3B	HR	RBI	BB-IB	HP	SO	AVG	OBP	SLG	AOPS	ABR	SB-CS	FA	FR	RNG	THR	GAMES AT POSITION	DL	BFW

KILIS, KEVIN   Kevin Edmund B3.15.1979 Cincinnati OH   BR/TR/6-1/220* [BosA01 8/243] d5.15 Col Cincinnati

TM LG	G	AB	R	H	2B	3B	HR	RBI	BB-IB	HP	SO	AVG	OBP	SLG	AOPS	ABR	SB-CS	FA	FR	RNG	THR	GAMES AT POSITION	DL	BFW
†Bos A	72	208	38	54	11	0	7	35	33-0	4	45	.260	.367	.413	98	1	0-1	.968	5	108	78	3b65,D2	16	0.5
Bos A	44	79	11	22	7	0	1	9	14-0	2	19	.278	.400	.405	109	2		1.000	-2	95	102	3b24,1b9,2b2		-0.1
2	116	287	49	76	18	0	8	44	47-0	6	64	.265	.376	.411	101	3	0-2	.975	-3	105	83	3b89,1b9,2b2,D2	16	0.4

NG, DEL   Delmer Edward B5.11.1912 Cleveland OH   D12.8.1979 San Francisco CA   BB/TR/5-11/168 d4.19 f-Del

TM LG	G	AB	R	H	2B	3B	HR	RBI	BB-IB	HP	SO	AVG	OBP	SLG	AOPS	ABR	SB-CS	FA	FR	RNG	THR	GAMES AT POSITION	DL	BFW
Phi N	109	360	36	70	9	2	0	24	18	1	55	.194	.235	.231	25	-38	6	.950	7	111	103	2b108		-2.5
Phi N	108	340	27	78	13	2	0	31	20	1	35	.229	.276	.279	55	-21	0	.933	-1	104	78	S87,2b17		-1.6
Phi N	77	217	22	57	9	2	3	20	8	0	24	.263	.289	.364	77	-8	1	.946	-12	88	59	S55,2b17		-1.7
Phi N	15	33	2	8	0	1	0	1	2	0	1	.242	.286	.303	65	-2	0	.962	-1	84	107	S6,2b5		-0.2
4	309	950	87	213	31	7	3	76	48	3	115	.224	.264	.281	48	-69	7	.938	-7	98	73	S148,2b147		-6.0

NG, DEL   Delmer John B10.24.1885 Macon MO   D12.17.1959 Cleveland OH   BL/TR/5-11/195 d9.24 s-Del

TM LG	G	AB	R	H	2B	3B	HR	RBI	BB-IB	HP	SO	AVG	OBP	SLG	AOPS	ABR	SB-CS	FA	FR	RNG	THR	GAMES AT POSITION	DL	BFW
Cin N	2	7	0	2	0	0	0	1	1	0		.286	.375	.286	106	0	0	1.000	0	371	0	O2(1/0/1)		0.0
Buf F	80	174	17	48	5	5	4	22	3	0	13	.276	.288	.431	92	-6	0	.944	-3	98	39	O41(7/2/32)		-1.1
Buf F	12	15	0	2	0	0	0	1	0	0		.133	.188	.133	-9	-2	1	.667	-1	70	0	O3(0/1/2)		-0.3
3	94	196	17	52	5	5	4	23	5	0	13	.265	.284	.403	85	-8	1	.933	-3	112	35	O46(8/3/35)		-1.4

NG, DMITRI   Dmitri Dell B10.11.1973 Vicksburg MS   BB/TR/6-2/235* [StLN91 1/4] d8.29 OF(403/0/102)

TM LG	G	AB	R	H	2B	3B	HR	RBI	BB-IB	HP	SO	AVG	OBP	SLG	AOPS	ABR	SB-CS	FA	FR	RNG	THR	GAMES AT POSITION	DL	BFW
†StL N	16	29	3	7	0	0	0	2	4-0	1	5	.241	.353	.241	60	-1	0-1	.976	-2	22	103	1b10		-0.4
StL N	110	333	38	86	14	3	5	34	38-3	2	63	.258	.335	.363	83	-8	6-5	.985	-2	88	95	1b74,O17(9/0/10)/D	18	-1.7
Cin N	144	536	81	166	48	1	14	83	47-4	2	94	.310	.364	.481	120	17	2-4	.940	-8	89	49	O105(91/0/14),1b44		0.0
Cin N	127	373	63	112	30	2	14	56	30-1	2	71	.300	.352	.504	111	6	3-1	.976	0	107	81	O91(23/0/75),1b9/D		0.2
Cin N	152	548	68	166	37	6	18	88	36-6	3	80	.303	.346	.491	106	4	0-3	.978	-5	91	65	O111(111/0/1),1b36,D4		-0.8
Cin N	142	540	68	163	28	3	21	69	37-10	5	77	.302	.346	.481	107	5	8-5	.957	0	96	147	O87(86/0/1),1b38,3b36		0.0
Det A	54	201	25	57	14	0	7	27	12-5	2	39	.284	.329	.458	111	3	2-0	.971	2	179	40	D35,1b15/3OL	107	0.2
Det A☆	155	562	78	167	34	7	29	85	58-16	11	130	.297	.372	.537	143	35	2-1	.985	3	99	131	D75,O61L,3b16/1		3.0
Det A	104	389	72	106	23	2	18	60	33-4	6	71	.272	.336	.481	115	8	0-1	1.000	1	114	73	D74,1b25,O2L/3	54	0.2
Det A	126	469	61	127	25	3	21	72	29-7	9	100	.271	.325	.471	111	6	1-0	.990	2	123	100	D71,1b30,O20(19/0/1)		0.1
10	1130	3980	557	1157	253	27	147	576	324-56	43	730	.291	.348	.479	113	75	24-21	.966	-9	97	93	O495L,1b282,D261,3b54	179	0.8

NG, DON   Donald Wayne B10.18.1945 Houston TX   BR/TR/6-2/185* d9.9

TM LG	G	AB	R	H	2B	3B	HR	RBI	BB-IB	HP	SO	AVG	OBP	SLG	AOPS	ABR	SB-CS	FA	FR	RNG	THR	GAMES AT POSITION	DL	BFW
Chi N	11	35	1	2	0	1	0	2	0-0	0	11	.057	.056	.143	-45	-7	0-0	.933	-1	80	0	O11C		-0.9
Chi N	101	272	36	65	12	3	7	29	38-5	5	74	.239	.343	.371	89	-3	1-5	.975	-2	100	75	O100(3/94/8)		-1.0
2	112	307	37	67	12	3	7	29	38-5	5	85	.218	.313	.345	76	-10	1-5	.972	-3	98	69	O111(3/105/8)		-1.9

NG, ERIC   Eric Orlando B5.18.1967 New Brunswick NJ   BR/TR/5-9/170(170-185) [LAN89 43/1123] d7.30 Col Rutgers

TM LG	G	AB	R	H	2B	3B	HR	RBI	BB-IB	HP	SO	AVG	OBP	SLG	AOPS	ABR	SB-CS	FA	FR	RNG	THR	GAMES AT POSITION	DL	BFW
LA N	49	132	9	34	1	0	1	11	8-0	0	9	.258	.300	.288	68	-6	6-1	.957	4	104	84	2b43		0.1
Col N	144	490	82	132	16	8	3	42	63-3	4	41	.269	.355	.353	78	-14	42-19	.962	-1	104	82	2b79,O52(46/10/0)		-1.0
Col N	90	228	37	62	13	4	7	30	38-1	2	17	.272	.378	.430	95	0	18-7	.981	-0	95	123	O60L/2		-0.1
†Col N	120	366	68	116	21	9	6	36	49-3	5	29	.317	.404	.473	102	3	35-12	.973	8	107	112	2b77,O19L		1.6
Col N★	141	568	113	184	23	4	8	74	47-1	21	31	.324	.393	.421	94	-3	53-19	.985	27	111	114	2b139	21	3.5
Col N	118	468	78	132	29	6	6	45	57-0	5	37	.282	.363	.408	83	-9	32-12	.978	26	120	117	2b117		2.4
LA N	37	154	28	42	4	2	2	16	14-1	4	17	.273	.347	.364	93	-2	13-2	.979	-16	70	82	2b37		-1.4
Year	155	622	106	174	33	8	8	61	71-1	9	54	.280	.359	.397	85	-11	45-14	.978	10	107	108	2b154		1.0
LA N	117	452	78	129	24	1	8	43	45-0	5	32	.285	.355	.396	103	3	42-13	.976	-3	96	113/D	18	1.0
LA N	119	456	73	128	24	2	4	41	63-0	5	26	.281	.371	.355	90	-4	51-22	.984	-5	101	88	2b116	20	0.0
Chi N	153	607	98	180	40	2	6	47	63-1	6	39	.297	.367	.399	96	-2	54-7	.979	-1	98	90	2b150		1.3
Chi N	149	603	98	168	43	4	6	42	42-1	9	45	.279	.333	.390	90	-8	31-14	.981	-3	91	80	2b147		-0.3
Mil N	138	496	57	139	29	3	3	28	39-0	6	38	.280	.338	.369	99	-9	31-11	.979	-2	99	95	2b123,O2(1/0/1),D2		-0.2
Mil N	109	404	71	105	18	1	15	31	48-2	4	34	.260	.344	.421	99	-1	25-7	.968	-14	94	81	2b99		-0.7
SF N	26	71	9	14	2	0	0	3	9-0	1	10	.197	.293	.225	38	-6	3-0	.989	2	112	109	2b18,O2C/D		-0.4
Year	135	475	80	119	20	1	15	34	57-2	5	44	.251	.336	.392	89	-7	28-12	.971	-12	97	85	2b117,O2C/D		-1.1
Tex A	104	344	55	99	25	2	1	27	43-0	8	28	.288	.377	.381	95	0	14-9	.976	-5	80	158	O53(47/9/0),D23,2b20,S8/3		-0.6
†SD N	56	142	22	39	9	0	2	12	18-0	0	12	.275	.356	.380	98	0	7-6	1.000	1	126	0	O25(21/4/0),2b14	85	0.1
14	1670	5981	976	1703	321	45	76	528	646-13	87	445	.285	.361	.392	91	-58	457-166	.976	19	101	95	2b1293,O213(194/25/1),D27,S8/3	144	5.2

NG, ERNIE   Ernest Wesley B7.8.1969 Chicago IL   BR/TR/6-1/214(190-234) [OakA90 10/289] d5.17 Col Lewis

TM LG	G	AB	R	H	2B	3B	HR	RBI	BB-IB	HP	SO	AVG	OBP	SLG	AOPS	ABR	SB-CS	FA	FR	RNG	THR	GAMES AT POSITION	DL	BFW
Oak A	11	30	2	2	1	0	0	3	1-0	0	8	.067	.097	.100	-53	-7	0-0	.958	1	123	179	O10(7/3/1)/D		-0.6
Oak A	26	50	9	10	3	0	2	5	8-0	0	12	.200	.310	.380	82	-1	0-0	.946	-1	103	0	O24(7/7/10)		-0.2
Oak A	141	462	72	112	19	4	19	64	52-1	7	118	.242	.326	.424	89	-9	7-5	.997	3	104	97	O140(8/133/17)		-0.5
Oak A	71	175	22	39	7	0	5	15	19-0	2	57	.223	.303	.349	70	-8	1-3	.980	2	102	169	O62(2/59/12)/D		-0.7
KC A	25	53	2	10	3	0	1	3	2-0	1	9	.189	.232	.302	36	-5	2-1	1.000	3	130	183	O24(1/5/19)	23	-0.3
Ari N	6	11	1	2	0	0	0	0	3-0	1	2	.182	.400	.182	54	-1	0-0	1.000	2	158	480	O4(1/0/3)		0.1
Det A	5	11	0	2	0	0	0	0	4-0	0	5	.182	.400	.182	64	0	0-2	—	0			D4		-0.1
Cle A	3	4	0	2	0	0	0	0	1-0	0	2	.500	.600	.500	199	1	0-0	—	0			D2		0.1
8	288	796	108	179	33	4	27	90	90-1	11	213	.225	.310	.378	76	-30	10-11	.989	9	107	122	O268(26/207/62),D8	23	-2.2

NG, GEORGE   George Joseph B4.1.1890 Brooklyn NY   D3.13.1950 Brightwaters NY   BL/TR/6-0/185 d8.10

TM LG	G	AB	R	H	2B	3B	HR	RBI	BB-IB	HP	SO	AVG	OBP	SLG	AOPS	ABR	SB-CS	FA	FR	RNG	THR	GAMES AT POSITION	DL	BFW
Cle A	3	2	0	0	0	0	0	0	0-0	0	0	.000	.000	.000	-97	-1	0		0			/H		-0.1

NG, GERALD   Gerald Anthony B10.22.1964 Tela, Honduras   BB/TR/6-2/185* [NYN82 5/111] d7.8

TM LG	G	AB	R	H	2B	3B	HR	RBI	BB-IB	HP	SO	AVG	OBP	SLG	AOPS	ABR	SB-CS	FA	FR	RNG	THR	GAMES AT POSITION	DL	BFW
Hou N	71	274	44	88	9	2	1	15	26-0	1	27	.321	.380	.380	107	3	26-9	.980	-1	98	144	O67C		0.5
Hou N	149	576	79	148	21	9	0	37	66-1	3	66	.257	.334	.325	94	-3	65-27	.992	1	99	156	O145C		0.2
Hou N	146	533	71	124	17	3	0	38	74-4	2	60	.233	.326	.276	77	-14	34-25	.998	14	111	197	O143C		-0.2
Hou N	57	154	15	27	4	1	1	9	20-0	0	23	.175	.269	.234	41	-12	6-3	.990	-1	94	197	O50C		-1.4
Hou N	108	142	26	31	3	1	1	11	24-0	0	17	.218	.327	.275	76	-4	16-5	1.000	2	107	188	O84(6/76/5)		-0.5
Hou N	74	76	14	14	1	1	0	4	10-0	0	11	.184	.279	.224	46	-5	6-2	.964	1	114	0	O57(6/14/43)	80	-0.5
Col N	19	19	5	1	0	0	0	1	4-0	0	4	.053	.197	.053	-20	-3	0-1	.882	9	137	0	O11(4/3/5)		-0.4
StL N	16	41	5	13	3	2	0	3	3-0	0	8	.317	.364	.488	119	1	2-1	1.000	-1	94	0	O11(3/6/2)		0.0
8	640	1815	259	446	58	19	3	113	227-5	6	213	.246	.329	.304	82	-37	155-73	.990	17	104	160	O568(19/504/55)	80	-1.8

NG, HERMAN   Herman John B4.14.1886 Boston MA   D12.13.1966 Ipswich MA   BR/TR/5-8/155 d6.11

TM LG	G	AB	R	H	2B	3B	HR	RBI	BB-IB	HP	SO	AVG	OBP	SLG	AOPS	ABR	SB-CS	FA	FR	RNG	THR	GAMES AT POSITION	DL	BFW
Bos N	9	25	2	6	0	0	0	3				.240	.269	.240	40	-2	0	.905	2	122	111	3b5,S3		0.0

NG, JOHN   John Thomas B2.9.1949 Los Angeles CA   BL/TL/6-3/210 d9.9 Col Chapman

TM LG	G	AB	R	H	2B	3B	HR	RBI	BB-IB	HP	SO	AVG	OBP	SLG	AOPS	ABR	SB-CS	FA	FR	RNG	THR	GAMES AT POSITION	DL	BFW
Det A	2	4	1	2	0	0	0	0	1-0	0	0	.500	.500	.750	240	1	0-0	1.000	-0	0	0	/1		0.1

NG, KEVIN   Kevin Stacey B6.16.1969 Alpena MI   BR/TR/6-3/221(210-225) [PitN90 7/187] d7.12 Col Southern Mississippi

TM LG	G	AB	R	H	2B	3B	HR	RBI	BB-IB	HP	SO	AVG	OBP	SLG	AOPS	ABR	SB-CS	FA	FR	RNG	THR	GAMES AT POSITION	DL	BFW
Pit N	10	7	2	4	0	0	0	4	2-0	1	5	.571	.667	.571	255	2	1-0	.750	-2	22	0	3b7/1		0.0
Pit N	141	449	38	106	24	3	6	47	36-3	9	82	.236	.300	.343	74	-17	2-2	.998	10	124	112	1b135,3b6		-1.8
Pit N	59	122	15	25	7	0	2	11	8-2	1	34	.205	.258	.320	49	-9	0-2	1.000	-0	66	138	1b37,3b17/O(1/0/1)		-1.2
Pit N	56	181	13	42	9	0	6	22	8-0	2	53	.232	.268	.381	68	-9	1-3	.919	5	120	89	3b48,1b6	15	-0.5
KC A	55	132	20	32	6	0	8	23	10-0	0	32	.242	.301	.470	90	-3	3-3	1.000	-1	114	142	1b27,O17(2/0/15),3b7,D3		-0.6
Pit N	97	333	59	100	18	3	18	74	16-1	4	89	.300	.332	.535	122	9	11-2	.997	3	106	86	1b77,3b12,O11(10/0/1)	40	0.7
Pit N	159	592	98	160	40	2	27	108	44-1	12	124	.270	.328	.481	110	7	15-7	.994	-13	70	112	1b157		-1.9
Pit N	156	584	103	174	41	6	26	106	75-5	12	124	.298	.387	.522	127	26	22-10	.985	-4	96	116	1b155		0.9
Pit N	132	496	77	128	27	0	20	88	32-1	9	96	.258	.311	.433	86	-12	8-3	.986	-11	73	110	1b129/D		-3.2
Pit N	142	449	52	104	33	0	14	65	42-3	11	119	.232	.310	.399	80	-13	15-11	.994	-2	96	113	1b137		-2.6
Pit N	146	468	60	115	26	1	16	51	50-2	4	101	.246	.322	.408	92	-7	4-6	.991	2	110	106	1b144		-1.9
Pit N	52	84	17	17	2	0	2	7	6-0	2	25	.202	.252	.321	62	-1	0-1	.995	-0	113	128	1b44/OR		-0.2
12	1205	3897	536	1007	235	17	144	606	336-18	62	882	.258	.324	.438	96	-31	83-49	.992	-13	95	111	1b1049,3b97,O30(13/0/18),D4	55	-12.7

NG, PEP   Lemuel Floyd B8.29.1907 Jamestown NC   D1.14.1962 Jamestown NC   BR/TR/5-9/162 d4.25

TM LG	G	AB	R	H	2B	3B	HR	RBI	BB-IB	HP	SO	AVG	OBP	SLG	AOPS	ABR	SB-CS	FA	FR	RNG	THR	GAMES AT POSITION	DL	BFW
Pit N	25	20	3	6	1	0	0	0	5	0		.300	.300	.450	112	0	1-0	1.000	-0	93	0	/2S		0.0
Pit N	19	17	3	4	0	0	0	0	2	0		.235	.235	.235	26	-2	0	1.000	1	203	189	2b2,S2		0.0
Pit N	128	494	60	131	25	10	7	82	21	0	8	.265	.298	.399	83	-14	2	.952	-16	89	86	2b107,3b6,O6(1/0/5),S4		-2.2

YEAR	TM·LG	G	AB	R	H	2B	3B	HR	RBI	BB-IB	HP	SO	AVG	OBP	SLG	AOPS	ABR	SB-CS	FA	FR	RNG	THR	GAMES AT POSITION	DL	B
1936	Pit N	125	475	47	118	23	10	6	77	29	1	52	.248	.293	.377	77	-17	3	.966	-22	88	57	2b123		-C
1937	Pit N	113	408	43	106	20	3	9	54	26		63	.260	.306	.390	88	-8	4	.942	13	116	133	S45,3b39,2b30		-C
1938	Pit N	149	562	58	156	36	5	4	79	40	3	64	.278	.329	.381	94	-4	7	.973	25	110	130	2b149		-C
1939	Pit N	84	293	34	81	14	3	3	29	23	2	29	.276	.333	.375	92	-4	1	.967	3	103	108	2b84		-C
1940	Pit N	54	136	19	34	8	2	2	20	12	2	23	.250	.320	.382	94	-1	1	.909	-4	100	51	2b33,S7,3b5		-C
1941	Cin N	4	12	2	2	0	0	0	0	0	1	1	.167	.231	.167	13	-1	0	.923	0	97	164	3b3		-C
	StL N	2	2	0	0	0	0	0	0	0	0	2	.000	.000	.000	-94	-1	0			0		/H		-C
	Year	6	14	2	2	0	0	0	0	0	1	3	.143	.200	.143	-2	-2	0	.923	0	97	164	3b3		-C
1945	StL N	27	47	5	7	1	0	1	4	1	0	8	.149	.167	.234	10	-6	0	.978	-1	80	72	S11,3b9,2b3		-C
Total	10	730	2466	274	645	128	34	32	347	152	12	312	.262	.308	.380	85	-58	18	.964	-1	98	94	2b532,S70,3b62,O6(1/0/5)		-C

YOUNG, MICHAEL Michael Brian B10.19.1976 Covina CA BR/TR/6-0/185(175-190) [TorA97 5/149] d9.29 Col California-Santa Barbara

YEAR	TM·LG	G	AB	R	H	2B	3B	HR	RBI	BB-IB	HP	SO	AVG	OBP	SLG	AOPS	ABR	SB-CS	FA	FR	RNG	THR	GAMES AT POSITION	DL	B
2000	Tex A	2	2	0	0	0	0	0	0	0-0		1	.000	.000	.000	-99	-1	0-0	—	-1	0	0	/2		-C
2001	Tex A	106	386	57	96	18	4	11	49	26-0	1	91	.249	.298	.402	81	-17	0-0	.984	-1	99	107	2b104		-C
2002	Tex A	156	573	77	150	26	8	9	62	41-1	0	112	.262	.308	.382	81	-17	6-7	.988	14	104	95	2b152,S11,3b4		-C
2003	Tex A	160	666	106	204	33	9	14	72	36-1	1	103	.306	.339	.446	99	-2	13-2	.987	8	100	102	2b159,S7		-C
2004	Tex A★	160	690	114	216	33	9	22	99	44-1	3	89	.313	.353	.483	111	10	12-3	.972	-21	93	93	S158,D2		2
2005	Tex A★	159	668	114	221	40	5	24	91	58-0	3	91	.331	.385	.513	132	31	5-2	.974	-15	96	88	S155,D4		2
Total	6	743	2985	468	887	150	35	80	373	205-3	8	487	.297	.341	.451	103	9	39-15	.987	-15	101	101	2b416,S331,D6,3b4		

YOUNG, MIKE Michael Darren B3.20.1960 Oakland CA BB/TR/6-2/195(194-206) [BalA80*S1/11] d9.14 Col St. Marys (CA)

YEAR	TM·LG	G	AB	R	H	2B	3B	HR	RBI	BB-IB	HP	SO	AVG	OBP	SLG	AOPS	ABR	SB-CS	FA	FR	RNG	THR	GAMES AT POSITION	DL	B
1982	Bal A	6	2	2	0	0	0	0	2	0-0			.000	.000	.000	-99	-1	0-0	1.000	0	399	0	/OLD		-C
1983	Bal A	25	36	5	6	2	1	0	2	2-0	1	8	.167	.231	.278	40	-3	1-0	.929	0	100	108	O22(14/0/8),D3		-C
1984	Bal A	123	401	59	101	17	2	17	52	58-2	7	110	.252	.355	.431	119	12	6-2	.982	-7	92	55	O115(40/1/85)/D		C
1985	Bal A	139	450	72	123	22	1	28	81	48-5	4	104	.273	.348	.513	135	11	1-5	.975	2	104	106	O90(83/0/20),D37		C
1986	Bal A	117	369	43	93	15	1	9	42	49-2	3	90	.252	.342	.371	96	-1	3-1	.962	0	113	24	O69L,D38		C
1987	Bal A	110	363	46	87	10	1	16	39	46-2	2	91	.240	.328	.405	95	-3	10-7	.975	-3	102		O60(54/7/0),D47	37	-C
1988	Phi N	75	146	13	33	14	0	1	14	26-1	1	43	.226	.343	.342	96	1	1-0	.938	1	126		O42(3/0/39)		-C
	Mil A	8	14	2	0	0	0	0	0	2-1	1	5	.000	.176	.000	-45	-3	0-0	—	-0	0		O2(1/0/1),D5		-C
1989	Cle A	32	59	2	11	0	0	1	5	6-1	1	13	.186	.273	.237	44	-4	1-2	1.000	-0	61		D15/OL		-C
Total	8	635	1840	244	454	80	6	72	235	237-14	20	465	.247	.338	.414	106	19	22-17	.969	-6	103	50	O402(266/8/153),D148	37	-C

YOUNG, BABE Norman Robert B7.1.1915 Astoria NY D12.25.1983 Everett MA BL/TL/6-2.5/185 d9.26 Mil 1943-45 Col Fordham

YEAR	TM·LG	G	AB	R	H	2B	3B	HR	RBI	BB-IB	HP	SO	AVG	OBP	SLG	AOPS	ABR	SB-CS	FA	FR	RNG	THR	GAMES AT POSITION	DL	B
1936	NY N	1	1	0	0	0	0	0	0	0-0	0	0	.000	.000	.000	-99	-0	0			0		/H		0
1939	NY N	22	75	8	23	0	0	3	14	5	3	6	.307	.373	.480	127	3	0	.982	-2	70	101	1b22		0
1940	NY N	149	556	75	159	27	4	17	101	69	2	28	.286	.367	.441	121	17	4	.992	-1	93	96	1b147		0
1941	NY N	152	574	90	152	28	5	25	104	66	5	39	.265	.346	.462	124	17	1	.986	-3	94	98	1b150		0
1942	NY N	101	287	37	80	17	1	11	59	34	5	22	.279	.365	.460	140	15	1	.972	-2	90	93	O54C,1b18		0
1946	NY N	104	291	30	81	11	0	7	33	30	1	21	.278	.346	.388	107	3	3	.988	-5	74	64	1b49,O24(0/17/7)		0
1947	NY N	14	14	0	1	1	0	0	0	0	0	1	.071	.071	.143	-44	-3	0			0		/H		0
	Cin N	95	364	55	103	21	3	14	79	35	2	26	.283	.349	.473	117	8	0	.990	-1	96	86	1b93		0
	Year	109	378	55	104	22	3	14	79	35	2	27	.275	.342	.460	111	5	0	.990	-1	96	86	1b93		0
1948	Cin N	49	130	11	30	7	2	1	12	19	0	12	.231	.329	.338	84	-3	0	.993	1	106	128	1b31/OR		-0
	StL N	41	111	14	27	5	2	1	13	16	0	6	.243	.339	.351	82	-2	0	.996	-4	43	110	1b35		-0
	Year	90	241	25	57	12	4	2	25	35	0	18	.237	.333	.344	83	-5	0	.995	-3	75	119	1b66/OR		-1
Total	8	728	2403	320	656	121	17	79	415	274	17	161	.273	.352	.436	117	55	9	.989	-18	90	94	1b545,O79(0/71/8)		-1

YOUNG, RALPH Ralph Stuart B9.19.1889 Philadelphia PA D1.24.1965 Philadelphia PA BB/TR/5-5/165 d4.10 Col Washington College

YEAR	TM·LG	G	AB	R	H	2B	3B	HR	RBI	BB-IB	HP	SO	AVG	OBP	SLG	AOPS	ABR	SB-CS	FA	FR	RNG	THR	GAMES AT POSITION	DL	B
1913	NY A	7	15	2	1	0	0	0	0	3	0	3	.067	.222	.067	-15	-2	2	.857	0	110	134	S7		-0
1915	Det A	123	378	44	92	6	1	0	31	53	2	31	.243	.339	.286	83	-7	12-11	.950	-1	107	101	2b119		-0
1916	Det A	153	528	60	139	16	6	1	45	62	1	43	.263	.342	.322	96	-2	20-20	.966	-6	97	87	2b146,S6/3		-0
1917	Det A	141	503	64	116	18	2	1	35	61	3	35	.231	.317	.280	83	-8	8	.958	5	107	77	2b141		-0
1918	Det A	91	298	31	56	7	1	0	21	54	0	17	.188	.313	.212	63	-11	15	.939	-1	94	67	2b91		-1
1919	Det A	125	456	63	96	13	5	1	25	53	1	32	.211	.294	.268	60	-24	8	.970	11	108	78	2b120,S5		-1
1920	Det A	150	594	84	173	21	6	0	33	85	2	30	.291	.382	.347	96	1	8-13	.969	-11	93	64	2b150		-1
1921	Det A	107	401	70	120	8	3	0	29	69	3	23	.299	.406	.334	91	-1	11-9	.947	-21	84	78	2b106		-1
1922	Phi A	125	470	62	105	19	2	1	35	55	3	21	.223	.309	.279	53	-32	8-6	.960	-7	97	81	2b120		-3
Total	9	1022	3643	480	898	108	30	4	254	495	15	235	.247	.339	.296	79	-86	92-59	.959	-42	99	79	2b993,S18/3		-11

YOUNG, DICK Richard Ennis B6.3.1928 Seattle WA BL/TR (BB 1952)/5-11/175* d9.11

YEAR	TM·LG	G	AB	R	H	2B	3B	HR	RBI	BB-IB	HP	SO	AVG	OBP	SLG	AOPS	ABR	SB-CS	FA	FR	RNG	THR	GAMES AT POSITION	DL	B
1951	Phi N	15	68	7	16	5	0	0	2	3	0	6	.235	.268	.309	55	-4	0-1	.922	-6	83	77	2b15		-1.
1952	Phi N	5	9	3	2	1	0	0	1	0	0	3	.222	.300	.333	76	0	1-0	.900	-1	80	96	2b2		0
Total	2	20	77	10	18	6	0	0	2	4	0	9	.234	.272	.312	58	-4	1-1	.919	-7	83	79	2b17		-1.

YOUNG, BOBBY Robert George B1.22.1925 Granite MD D1.28.1985 Baltimore MD BL/TR/6-1/175* d8.30

YEAR	TM·LG	G	AB	R	H	2B	3B	HR	RBI	BB-IB	HP	SO	AVG	OBP	SLG	AOPS	ABR	SB-CS	FA	FR	RNG	THR	GAMES AT POSITION	DL	B
1948	StL N	3	1	0	0	0	0	0	0	0-0	0	1	.000	.000	.000	-95	-0		1.000	-0	0	0	/3		0.
1951	StL A	147	611	75	159	13	9	1	31	44	0	51	.260	.310	.316	67	-30	8-7	.980	-4	102	88	2b147		-2.
1952	StL A	149	575	59	142	15	9	4	39	56	0	48	.247	.314	.325	76	-20	3-3	.984	-7	97	112	2b149		-3.
1953	StL A	148	537	48	137	22	2	4	25	41	1	40	.255	.309	.326	70	-23	2-1	.977	-19	87	97	2b148		-1.
1954	Bal A	130	432	43	106	13	6	4	24	54	1	42	.245	.329	.331	88	-7	4-4	.976	-14	92	82	2b127		-1.
1955	Bal A	59	186	15	37	3	0	1	8	11-1	0	23	.199	.244	.231	30	-19	1-4	.985	-1	104	100	2b58		-1.
	Cle A	18	45	7	14	1	1	0	6	1-0	0	2	.311	.326	.378	86	-1	0-0	.983	4	121	192	2b11/3		0.
	Year	77	231	12	51	4	1	1	14	12-1	0	25	.221	.259	.260	42	-20	1-4	.985	3	107	115	2b69/3		-1.
1956	Cle A	1	0	0	0	0	0	0	0	0-0	0	0	—	—	—		0	0-0	—	0			/R		0.
1958	Phi N	32	60	7	14	1	1	1	4	1-0	0	5	.233	.246	.333	52	-4	0-0	.968	-3	90	65	2b21		-0.
Total	8	687	2447	244	609	68	28	15	137	208-1	2	212	.249	.308	.318	71	-104	18-19	.980	-44	96	97	2b661,3b2		-10

YOUNG, RUSS Russell Charles B9.15.1902 Bryan OH D5.13.1984 Roseville CA BB/TR/6-0/175 d4.16

YEAR	TM·LG	G	AB	R	H	2B	3B	HR	RBI	BB-IB	HP	SO	AVG	OBP	SLG	AOPS	ABR	SB-CS	FA	FR	RNG	THR	GAMES AT POSITION	DL	B
1931	StL A	16	34	2	4	0	0	1	2	4		4	.118	.167	.206	-3	-5	0-0	1.000	2	124	90	C16		-0.

YOUNG, WALTER Walter Ernest B2.18.1980 Hattiesburg MS BL/TR/6-5/320 d9.6

YEAR	TM·LG	G	AB	R	H	2B	3B	HR	RBI	BB-IB	HP	SO	AVG	OBP	SLG	AOPS	ABR	SB-CS	FA	FR	RNG	THR	GAMES AT POSITION	DL	B
2005	Bal A	14	33	2	11	3	0	3	4-1		0	7	.333	.378	.424	113	1	0-0	1.000	1	156	163	1b10,D3		0.

YOUNGBLOOD, JOEL Joel Randolph B8.28.1951 Houston TX BR/TR/6-0/180(160-180) [CinN70*2/40] d4.13 C5 OF(233/107/454)

YEAR	TM·LG	G	AB	R	H	2B	3B	HR	RBI	BB-IB	HP	SO	AVG	OBP	SLG	AOPS	ABR	SB-CS	FA	FR	RNG	THR	GAMES AT POSITION	DL	B
1976	Cin N	55	57	8	11	1	0	1	1	2-0	1	8	.193	.233	.246	35	-5	1-0	.938	-0	112	241	O9(3/3/3),3b6/C2		-0.
1977	StL N	25	27	1	5	2	0	0	1	3-0	0	5	.185	.267	.259	42	-2	0-2	1.000	-0	76		O11(10/0/1),3b6		-0.
	NY N	70	182	16	46	11	1	0	11	13-1	0	40	.253	.301	.324	71	-8	1-3	.954	7	107	140	2b33,O22(4/7/13),3b10		-0.
	Year	95	209	17	51	13	1	0	12	16-1	0	45	.244	.296	.316	67	-10	1-5	1.000	7	110	224	O33(14/7/14),2b33,3b16		-0.
1978	NY N	113	266	40	67	12	8	7	30	16-1	1	39	.252	.294	.436	105	-0	4-0	.989	6	116	303	O50(7/14/33),2b39,3b9/S		0.
1979	NY N	158	590	90	162	37	5	16	60	60-7	0	84	.275	.346	.436	115	13	18-13	.985	9	107	155	O147(70/5/87),2b13,3b12		-0.
1980	NY N	146	514	58	142	26	2	8	69	52-10	2	69	.276	.340	.381	104	4	14-11	.984	21	126	200	O121(0/39/96),3b21,2b6		2.
1981	NY N★	43	143	16	50	10	2	4	25	12-1	2	19	.350	.398	.531	165	12	2-5	.962	2	101	202	O41(4/2/36)	86	1.
1982	NY N	80	202	21	52	12	0	3	21	8-1	1	37	.257	.302	.361	85	-4	0-4	.969	-1	99	156	O63(15/8/43),2b8/S3		-0.
	Mon N	40	90	16	18	2	0	0	8	9-1	2	21	.200	.291	.222	45	-6	2-1	1.000	-0	106	57	O35(0/2/33)		-0.
	Year	120	292	37	70	14	0	3	29	17-2	3	58	.240	.299	.318	72	-11	2-5	.979	-1	102	120	O98(15/10/76),2b8/S3		-1.
1983	SF N	124	373	59	109	20	3	17	53	33-4	1	59	.292	.356	.499	139	19	7-4	.948	-14	94	79	2b64,3b28,O22(14/0/8)		-2.
1984	SF N	134	469	50	119	17	1	10	51	48-1	4	86	.254	.328	.358	95	-3	5-6	.887	-22	85	74	3b117,O11(4/0/8),2b5		-2.
1985	SF N	95	230	24	62	6	0	4	24	30-1	1	37	.270	.355	.348	102	1	3-2	.955	-0	100	121	O56(7/17/34)/3		-0.
1986	SF N	97	184	20	47	12	0	5	28	18-0	1	34	.255	.320	.402	104	1	1-1	1.000	6	87	94	O45(29/0/17),1b7,3b5,2b4/S		-0.
1987	SF N	69	91	9	23	4	0	1	11	6-0	1	13	.253	.306	.330	83	-3	1-1	1.000	1	96	220	O22(9/1/14),3b2		-0.
1988	SF N	83	123	12	31	4	0	0	16	10-0	1	17	.252	.307	.285	76	-4	1-1	.980	-1	100	93	O45(22/9/18)		-0.
1989	Cin N	76	118	13	25	9	0	3	13	13-2	1	21	.212	.299	.331	78	-3	0-1	.970	-3	65	75	O45(35/0/10)		-0.
Total	14	1408	3659	463	969	180	23	80	422	293-30	20	586	.265	.329	.392	103	12	60-55	.981	3	106	159	O745R,3b218,2b173,1b7,S3/C	86	-1.4

YOUNGMAN, HENRY Henry B1865 Indiana PA D1.24.1936 Pittsburgh PA TR/5-9/175 d4.19

YEAR	TM·LG	G	AB	R	H	2B	3B	HR	RBI	BB-IB	HP	SO	AVG	OBP	SLG	AOPS	ABR	SB-CS	FA	FR	RNG	THR	GAMES AT POSITION	DL	B
1890	Pit N	13	47	6	6	1	1	0	4	6		9	.128	.226	.191	25	-4	1	.750	-3	101	198	3b7,2b6		-0.

R TM LG	G	AB	R	H	2B	3B	HR	RBI	BB-IB	HP	SO	AVG	OBP	SLG	AOPS	ABR	SB-CS	FA	FR	RNG	THR	GAMES AT POSITION	DL	BFW

YOUNGS, ROSS Ross Middlebrook "Pep" (b Royce Middlebrook Youngs) B4.10.1897 Shiner TX D10.22.1927 San Antonio TX BL/TR/5-8/162 d9.25 HF1972

17 NY N	7	26	5	9	2	3	0	1	1	0	5	.346	.370	.654	218	3	1	1.000	5	93	202	O7(1/6/0)		0.4
18 NY N	121	474	70	143	16	8	1	25	44	6	49	.302	.368	.376	129	18	10	.950	-4	99	89	O120R,2b7		0.8
19 NY N	130	489	73	152	31	7	2	43	51	7	47	.311	.384	.415	142	28	24	.942	1	96	117	O130R		2.3
20 NY N	153	581	92	204	27	14	6	78	75	2	55	.351	.427	.477	161	49	18-18	.935	0	96	129	O153R		4.1
21 †NY N	141	504	90	.165	24	16	3	102	71	1	47	.327	.411	.456	129	24	21-17	.978	-3	96	87	O137R		0.9
22 †NY N	149	559	105	185	34	10	7	86	55	7	50	.331	.398	.465	121	19	17-9	.942	3	94	144	O147R		1.0
23 †NY N	152	596	121	200	33	12	3	87	73	5	36	.336	.412	.446	128	28	13-19	.959	-2	90	123	O152R		0.9
24 †NY N	133	526	112	187	33	12	10	74	77	3	31	.356	.441	.521	161	50	11-9	.955	-3	93	110	O132R,2b2		3.5
25 NY N	130	500	82	132	24	6	6	53	66	4	51	.264	.354	.372	89	-6	17-11	.952	-10	80	123	O127R,2b3		-2.5
26 NY N	95	372	62	114	12	5	4	43	37	2	19	.306	.372	.398	109	5	21	.974	0	87	138	O94R		-0.2
al 10	1211	4627	812	1491	236	93	42	592	550	37	390	.322	.399	.441	131	218	153-83	.953	-17	92	119	O1199(1/6/1192),2b12		11.2

OUNT, EDDIE Floyd Edwin B12.19.1915 Newton NC D10.26.1973 Newton NC BR/TR/6-1/185 d9.9 Col Wake Forest

37 Phi A	4	7	1	2	0	0	0	1	0	0	1	.286	.286	.286	45	-1	0-0	1.000	-0	91		O2(1/1/0)		-0.1
39 Pit N	2	2	0	0	0	0	0	0	0	0	2	.000	.000	.000	-99	-1		—	0			/H		-0.1
al 2	6	9	1	2	0	0	0	1	0	0	3	.222	.222	.222	14	-2	0-0	1.000	-0	91	0	O2(1/1/0)		-0.2

OUNT, ROBIN Robin R B9.16.1955 Danville IL BR/TR/6-0/170(160-180) [MilA73 1/3] d4.5 C3 HF1999 b-Larry OF(69/1150/0)

74 Mil A	107	344	48	86	14	5	3	26	12-0	1	46	.250	.276	.346	79	-11	7-7	.962	-9	103	91	S107		-0.9
75 Mil A	147	558	67	149	28	2	8	52	33-3	1	69	.267	.307	.367	90	-8	12-4	.939	-13	96	86	S145		-0.3
76 Mil A	161	638	59	161	19	3	2	54	38-3	0	69	.252	.292	.301	76	-21	16-11	.963	-3	99	102	S161/OC		-0.4
77 Mil A	154	605	66	174	34	4	4	49	41-1	2	80	.288	.333	.377	93	-5	16-7	.964	-3	99	102	S153		0.8
78 Mil A	127	502	66	147	23	9	9	71	24-1	1	43	.293	.323	.428	110	4	16-5	.959	21	114	106	S125	28	4.0
79 Mil A	149	577	72	154	26	5	8	51	35-3	1	52	.267	.308	.371	83	-15	11-8	.969	4	107	100	S149		0.4
80 Mil A★	143	611	121	179	49	10	23	87	26-1	1	67	.293	.321	.519	130	22	20-5	.961	3	106	101	S133,D9		4.0
81 †Mil A	96	377	50	103	15	5	10	49	22-1	2	37	.273	.312	.419	115	6	4-1	.985	30	124	132	S93,D3		4.7
82 †Mil A★	156	635	129	210	46	12	29	114	54-2	1	63	.331	.379	.578	168	58	14-3	.969	-4	101	102	S154/D		7.1
83 Mil A★	149	578	102	178	42	10	17	80	72-6	1	58	.308	.383	.503	153	44	12-5	.973	3	98	105	S139,D8		5.6
84 Mil A	160	624	105	186	27	7	16	80	67-7	1	67	.298	.362	.441	127	23	14-4	.971	17	111	104	S120,D39		5.2
85 Mil A	122	466	76	129	26	3	15	68	49-3	2	56	.277	.342	.442	115	10	10-4	.970	-3	108	56	O108(69/40/0),D12,1b2		0.4
86 Mil A	140	522	82	163	31	7	9	46	62-7	4	73	.312	.388	.450	124	19	14-5	.997	3	103	130	O131C,1b3,D6		2.2
87 Mil A	158	635	99	198	25	9	21	103	76-10	1	94	.312	.384	.479	124	23	19-9	.987	-2	99	75	O150C,D8		1.9
88 Mil A	162	621	92	190	38	11	13	91	63-10	3	63	.306	.369	.465	132	27	22-4	.996	3	99	157	O158C,D4		3.2
89 Mil A	160	614	101	195	38	9	21	103	63-9	6	71	.318	.384	.511	152	43	19-3	.981	-4	96	104	O143C,D17		4.0
90 Mil A	158	587	98	145	17	5	17	77	78-6	6	89	.247	.337	.380	102	2	15-8	.991	-6	100	36	O157C/D		-0.4
91 Mil A	130	503	66	131	20	4	10	77	54-8	4	79	.260	.332	.376	99	0	6-4	.994	-5	101	16	O117C,D13	24	-0.7
92 Mil A	150	557	71	147	40	3	8	77	53-9	3	81	.264	.325	.390	103	3	15-6	.995	-6	95	75	O139C,D11		-0.4
93 Mil A	127	454	62	117	25	3	8	51	44-5	5	93	.258	.326	.379	91	-6	9-2	.997	-1	100	96	O114C,1b7,D6	17	-0.5
al 20	2856	11008	1632	3142	583	126	251	1406	966-95	48	1350	.285	.342	.430	115	218	271-105	.964	20	104	102	S1479,O1218C,D138,1b12	69	39.9

URAK, JEFF Jeffrey Lynn B2.26.1954 Pasadena CA BB/TR/6-3/195 [SFN74 24/536] d9.15 Col Citrus (CA) JC

78 Mil A	5	5	0	0	0	0	0	0	1-0	0	1	.000	.167	.000	-49	-1	0-0	1.000	1	332	0	/OL		-0.1

VARS, SAL Salvador Anthony B2.20.1924 New York NY BR/TR/5-10/187* d9.27

47 NY N	1	5	0	1	0	0	0	0	0	0	2	.200	.200	.200	6	-1	0	1.000	-0	0	0	/C		-0.1
48 NY N	15	38	4	8	1	0	1	6	3	1	1	.211	.286	.316	62	-2	0	1.000	2	104	109	C15		0.0
49 NY N	3	8	0	0	0	0	0	0	1	0	1	.000	.111	.000	-68	-2	0	.963	1	137	185	C9		-0.2
50 NY N	9	14	0	2	0	0	0	0	1	0	2	.143	.200	.143	-8	-2	0	.963	1	137	185	C9		-0.1
51 †NY N	25	41	9	13	2	0	2	3	5	2	7	.317	.417	.512	147	3	0-0	.942	-2	131	78	C23		0.2
52 NY N	66	151	15	37	3	0	4	18	10	1	16	.245	.296	.344	77	-5	0-0	.988	6	205	138	C59		0.3
53 NY N	23	47	1	13	0	0	1	7	0	1	0	.277	.370	.277	71	-2	0-0	1.000	1	134	118	C20		0.0
StL N	30	57	4	14	2	0	1	6	4	1	6	.246	.306	.333	67	-3	0-1	.989	1	91	146	C26		-0.1
Year	53	104	5	27	2	0	1	7	11	1	7	.260	.336	.308	69	-4	0-1	.994	3	112	133	C46		-0.1
54 StL N	38	57	8	14	4	0	2	8	6	1	5	.246	.328	.421	93	-1	0-0	1.000	-1	140	154	C21		-0.1
otal 8	210	418	41	102	12	0	10	42	37	6	41	.244	.315	.344	76	-15	1-1	.987	9	150	127	C176		-0.1

ACHER, ELMER Elmer Henry "Silver" B9.17.1883 Buffalo NY D12.20.1944 Buffalo NY BR/TR/5-9/190 d4.30

10 NY N	1	0	0	0	0	0	0	0	0	0	—	—	—	—	—	0	0	1.000	0	132	0	/OC		0.0
StL N	47	132	7	28	5	1	0	10	10	2	19	.212	.278	.265	61	-7	3	.966	2	107	143	O36(11/12/13)/2		-0.6
Year	48	132	7	28	5	1	0	10	10	2	19	.212	.278	.265	61	-7	3	.966	2	107	142	O37(11/13/13)/2		-0.6

AHNER, FRED Frederick Joseph B6.5.1870 Louisville KY D7.24.1900 Louisville KY d7.23

94 Lou N	14	49	7	10	1	0	4	3	0	0	6	.204	.250	.245	21	-7	2	.778	-3	102	60	C10,O2R/1S		-0.7
95 Lou N	21	49	7	11	1	1	0	6	6	1	4	.224	.321	.286	61	-3	0	.824	-5	90	114	C21		-0.6
otal 2	35	98	14	21	2	1	2	0	10	9	1	10	.214	.287	.265	41	-10	2	.805	-8	94	C31,O2R/S1		-1.3

AK, FRANKIE Frank Thomas B2.22.1922 Passaic NJ D2.6.1972 Passaic NJ BR/TR/5-10/150 d4.21

44 Pit N☆	87	160	33	48	3	1	0	11	22	0	18	.300	.385	.331	99	1	6	.948	-1	104	88	S67		0.3
45 Pit N	15	28	2	4	2	0	0	3	3	0	5	.143	.226	.214	22	-3	0	.971	1	117	83	S10/2		-0.2
46 Pit N	21	20	8	4	0	0	0	3	1	0	0	.200	.238	.200	24	-2	0	.929	4	159	148	S10		0.3
otal 3	123	208	43	56	5	1	0	14	26	0	23	.269	.350	.303	82	-4	6	.948	4	110	93	S87/2		0.4

ALUSKY, JACK John Francis B6.22.1879 Minneapolis MN D8.11.1935 Minneapolis MN BR/TR/5-11.5/172 d9.4

03 NY A	7	16	2	5	0	0	0	1	1	0	0	.313	.353	.313	95	0	0	1.000	-1	100	63	C6/1		-0.1

AMBRANO, EDDIE Eduardo Jose (Guerra) B2.1.1966 Maracaibo, Venez BR/TR/6-2/175(175-200) d9.19

93 Chi N	8	17	1	5	0	0	0	2	1-0	0	3	.294	.333	.294	70	-1	0-0	1.000	-1	24	0	O4(1/0/3),1b2		-0.2
94 Chi N	67	116	17	30	7	0	6	18	16-0	1	29	.259	.353	.474	113	2	2-1	.944	-3	85	71	O27(9/0/18),1b9,3b4		-0.2
otal 2	75	133	18	35	7	0	6	20	17-0	1	32	.263	.351	.451	108	1	2-1	.946	-4	79	64	O31(10/0/21),1b11,3b4		-0.4

APUSTAS, JOE Joseph John B7.25.1907 Boston MA D1.14.2001 Brockton MA BR/TR/6-1/185 d9.28 Col Fordham

33 Phi A	2	5	0	1	0	0	0	0	0	0	0	.200	.200	.200	6	-1	0-0	1.000	-0	83	0	O2(1/1/0)		-0.1

ARDON, JOSE Jose Antonio (Sanchez) "Guineo" B5.20.1923 Havana, Cuba BR/TR/6-0/150 d4.18

45 Was A	54	131	13	38	5	3	0	13	7	0	11	.290	.326	.374	112	1	3-1	.972	2	121	64	O43(16/25/3)		0.2

ARILLA, AL Allen Lee "Zeke" B5.1.1919 Los Angeles CA D8. 28 1996 Honolulu HI BL/TR/5-11/180* d6.30 Mil 1945 C1

43 StL A	70	228	27	58	7	1	2	17	17	1	20	.254	.309	.320	82	-5	1-1	.962	-9	104	123	O60(0/6/56)		-0.8
44 †StL A	100	288	43	86	13	6	6	45	29	1	33	.299	.375	.448	127	10	1-1	.977	-0	104	65	O79(74/2/4)		0.6
46 StL A	125	371	46	96	14	9	4	43	27	1	37	.259	.311	.377	87	-8	3-5	.973	10	111	169	O107(46/17/51)		-0.4
47 StL A	127	380	34	85	15	6	3	38	40	3	45	.224	.303	.318	71	-15	3-6	.986	-2	97	86	O110(23/22/72)		-2.4
48 StL A★	144	529	77	174	39	3	12	74	48	4	48	.329	.389	.482	128	21	11-6	.962	-9	96	47	O136(26/58/61)		0.7
49 StL A	15	56	10	14	1	0	1	6	8	1	2	.250	.354	.321	76	-2	1-1	1.000	-5	74	0	O15(10/1/8)		-0.5
Bos A	124	474	68	133	32	4	9	71	48	4	51	.281	.352	.422	97	-3	4-4	.984	-9	98	52	O122(2/2/119)		-1.2
Year	139	530	78	147	33	4	10	77	56	5	53	.277	.352	.411	95	-4	5-5	.985	-7	96	47	O137(12/3/127)		-1.7
50 Bos A	130	471	92	153	32	10	9	74	76	4	47	.325	.423	.493	122	18	2-3	.976	-4	92	124	O128R		0.9
51 Chi A	120	382	56	98	21	2	10	60	60	4	57	.257	.363	.401	109	6	2-4	.983	-9	80	94	O117(7/0/112)		-0.7
52 Chi A	39	99	14	23	4	1	2	7	14	1	6	.232	.333	.354	90	-1	1-0	.974	-2	80	123	O32(17/0/18)		-0.4
StL A	48	130	20	31	6	0	1	9	27	1	15	.238	.373	.308	88	0	2	.976	2	101	205	O35(21/10/8)		0.0
Bos A	21	60	9	11	0	1	2	8	7	0	8	.183	.269	.317	58	-4	2-0	.941	-1	92	247	O19(0/6/14)		-0.3
Year	108	289	43	65	10	2	5	24	48	2	29	.225	.339	.325	83	-5	5-1	.968	1	92	188	O86(38/16/40)		-0.7
53 Bos A	57	67	11	13	2	0	4	14	10	0	13	.194	.333	.224	50	-4	0-1	.947	-1	85	130	O18(3/7/9)		-0.5
Total 10	1120	3535	507	975	186	43	61	456	415	30	382	.276	.357	.405	102	13	33-33	.974	-19	96	97	O978(229/131/660)		-5.0

YEAR	TM LG	G	AB	R	H	2B	3B	HR	RBI	BB-IB	HP	SO	AVG	OBP	SLG	AOPS	ABR	SB-CS	FA	FR	RNG	THR	GAMES AT POSITION	DL	B

ZAUCHIN, NORM   Norbert Henry   B11.17.1929 Royal Oak MI   D1.31.1999 Birmingham AL   BR/TR/6-4.5/220*   d9.23   Mil 1952-53

1951	Bos A	5	12	0	2	0	0	0	4	.167			.167	.167	.250	11	-2	0-1	.957	0	121	327	1b4		-0
1955	Bos A	130	477	65	114	10	0	27	93	69-1	3	105	.239	.335	.430	97	-3	3-0	.995	0	98	95	1b126		-0
1956	Bos A	44	84	12	18	2	0	2	11	14-0	1	22	.214	.333	.310	63	-4	0-0	.990	-1	75	95	1b31		-0
1957	Bos A	52	91	11	24	3	0	3	14	9-0	2	13	.264	.343	.396	96	0	0-0	.972	0	113	147	1b36		-0
1958	Was A	96	303	35	69	8	2	15	37	38-1	1	68	.228	.310	.416	101	0	0-0	.995	1	101	86	1b91		-0
1959	Was A	19	71	11	15	4	0	3	4	7-0	1	14	.211	.291	.394	87	-1	2-0	.995	-2	48	104	1b19		-0
Total	6	346	1038	134	242	28	2	50	159	137-2	8	226	.233	.324	.408	93	-10	5-1	.993	-3	95	99	1b307		-3

ZAUN, GREGG   Gregory Owen   B4.14.1971 Glendale CA   BB/TR/5-10/190(170-190)   [BalA89 17/427]   d6.24

1995	Bal A	40	104	18	27	5	0	3	14	16-0	0	14	.260	.358	.394	94	-1	1-1	.987	3	117	98	C39/D		-0
1996	Bal A	50	108	16	25	8	1	1	13	11-2	2	15	.231	.309	.352	68	-5	0-0	.987	-5	72	65	C49		-0
	Fla N	10	31	4	9	1	0	1	2	3-1	0	5	.290	.353	.419	105	0	1-0	1.000	2	336	38	C10		-0
1997	†Fla N	58	143	21	43	10	2	2	20	26-4	2	18	.301	.415	.441	130	8	1-0	.978	5	95	97	C50/1		1
1998	Fla N	106	298	19	56	12	2	5	29	35-2	1	52	.188	.274	.292	53	-21	5-2	.986	-3	96	114	C88/2		1
1999	Tex A	43	93	12	23	2	1	1	12	10-0	0	7	.247	.314	.323	61	-6	1-0	.984	2	127	136	C37,D2		-0
2000	KC A	83	234	36	64	11	0	7	33	43-3	3	34	.274	.390	.410	98	1	7-3	.988	-9	66	76	C76/12	43	-0
2001	KC A	39	125	15	40	9	0	6	18	12-0	0	16	.320	.377	.536	125	5	1-2	.975	-2	104	84	C35,D2	113	-0
2002	Hou N	76	185	18	41	7	1	3	24	12-1	2	36	.222	.275	.319	54	-13	1-0	.985	-4	60	46	C44		-0
2003	Hou N	59	120	9	26	7	0	1	13	14-0	1	14	.217	.299	.300	55	-8	1-0	.976	-6	76	145	C31		-1
	Col N	15	46	6	12	1	0	3	8	5-0	0	7	.261	.333	.478	95	0	0-1	.973	-2	87	112	C14		-1
	Year	74	166	15	38	8	0	4	21	19-0	1	21	.229	.309	.349	67	-8	1-1	.975	-7	80	134	C45		-1
2004	Tor A	107	338	46	91	24	0	6	36	47-3	6	61	.269	.367	.393	93	-1	0-2	.987	1	79	105	C97,D6		1
2005	Tor A	133	434	61	109	18	1	11	61	73-2	0	70	.251	.355	.373	90	-4	2-3	.990	6	92	75	C132	15	1
Total	11	819	2259	281	566	115	8	50	283	307-18	17	349	.251	.342	.375	85	-45	21-14	.985	-12	91	91	C702,D11,2b2,1b2	171	-1

ZDEB, JOE   Joseph Edmund   B6.27.1953 Compton IL   BR/TR/5-11/185*   [KCA71 4/76]   d4.7

1977	†KC A	105	195	26	58	5	2	2	23	16-3	0	23	.297	.346	.374	97	-1	6-5	.970	-2	93	106	O93(88/1/8)/3D		-0
1978	KC A	60	127	18	32	2	3	0	11	7-0	0	18	.252	.287	.315	68	-6	3-0	.957	-1	95	88	O52(43/0/12)/23D		-0
1979	KC A	15	23	3	4	1	1	0	0	2-0	0	4	.174	.240	.304	45	-2	1-0	1.000	-0	108	0	O9(6/0/3)		-0
Total	3	180	345	47	94	8	6	2	34	25-3	0	45	.272	.317	.348	83	-9	10-5	.967	-3	94	96	O154(137/1/23),D5,3b2/2		-1

ZEARFOSS, DAVE   David William Tilden   B1.1.1868 Schenectady NY   D9.12.1945 Wilmington DE   TR/5-9/174   d4.17   Col Washington College

1896	NY N	19	60	5	13	1	0	0	6	5-1	1		.217	.288	.267	48	-5	2	.893	-3	93	91	C19		-0
1897	NY N	5	10	1	3	0	1	0	0	0-0	0		.300	.300	.500	112	0	0	.880	2	173	198	C5		0
1898	NY N	1	1	0	1	0	0	0	0	0-0	0		1.000	1.000	1.000	489	0	0	1.000	0	327	/C		0
1904	StL N	27	80	7	17	2	0	0	9	10	0		.213	.300	.237	70	-2	0	.966	-3	85	86	C25		-0
1905	StL N	20	51	2	8	0	1	0	2	4	0		.157	.218	.196	24	-5	0	.966	-1	88	109	C19		-0
Total	5	72	202	15	42	3	3	0	17	19	1	5	.208	.279	.252	56	-12	2	.943	-6	92	101	C69		-1

ZEBER, GEORGE   George William   B8.29.1950 Ellwood City PA   BB/TR/5-11/180(170-181)   [NYA68 5/88]   d5.7

1977	†NY A	25	65	8	21	0	3	0	10	9-1	0	11	.323	.405	.508	148	-0	0-0	.961	-0	107	102	2b21,S2,3b2/D		0
1978	NY A	3	6	0	0	0	0	0	0	0-0	0	0	.000	.000	.000	-99	-2	0-0	.750	1	57	0	/2		0
Total	2	28	71	8	21	0	3	0	10	9-1	0	11	.296	.375	.465	129	-3	0-0	.953	-1	104	96	2b22,3b2,S2/D		0

ZEIDER, ROLLIE   Rollie Hubert "Bunions"   B11.16.1883 Auburn IN   D9.12.1967 Garrett IN   BR/TR/5-10/162   d4.14   OF(6/1/1)

1910	Chi A	136	498	57	108	9	2	0	31	62	1		.217	.305	.243	75	-12	49	.931	-6	96	108	2b87,S45,3b4		-1
1911	Chi A	73	217	39	55	3	0	2	21	29	2		.253	.347	.295	82	-4	28	.997	-4	115	80	1b29,S17,3b10,2b9		-0
1912	Chi A	130	420	57	103	12	10	1	42	50	2		.245	.330	.329	91	-4	48	.979	4	136	91	1b66,3b56/S		-0
1913	Chi A	16	20	4	7	0	0	0	2	4	0	1	.350	.458	.350	139	1	3	1.000	1	95	0	3b6,1b3/2		0
	NY A	50	159	15	37	2	0	0	12	25	1	9	.233	.341	.245	72	-4	3	.901	-9	78	104	S24,2b19,1b4,3b2		-0
	Year	66	179	19	44	2	0	0	14	29	1	10	.246	.354	.257	79	-3	6	.901	-8	78	104	S24,2b20,3b8,1b7		-0
1914	Chi F	119	452	60	124	13	2	1	36	44	4	28	.274	.344	.319	86	-15	35	.936	-5	94	170	3b117/S		-1
1915	Chi F	129	494	65	112	22	2	0	34	43	6	30	.227	.297	.279	66	-30	16	.941	-3	97	125	2b83,3b30,S21		-3
1916	Chi N	98	345	29	81	11	2	1	22	26	3	26	.235	.294	.287	71	-11	9	.928	-2	105	138	3b55,2b33,O7(6/0/1),S5,1b2		-1
1917	Chi N	108	354	36	86	14	2	0	27	28	2	30	.243	.302	.294	77	-9	17	.901	-14	66	82	S48,3b26,2b24/1OC		-2
1918	†Chi N	82	251	31	56	3	2	0	26	23	0	21	.223	.288	.251	63	-11	16	.956	-7	95	80	2b79/13		-1
Total	9	941	3210	393	769	89	22	5	253	334	22	138	.240	.315	.286	77	-99	224	.945	-45	95	97	2b335,3b307,S162,1b106,O8L		-13

ZEILE, TODD   Todd Edward   B9.9.1965 Van Nuys CA   BR/TR/6-1/200(190-205)   [StLN86 2/55]   d8.18   Col UCLA

1989	StL N	28	82	7	21	3	1	1	8	9-1	0	14	.256	.326	.354	92	-1	0-0	.971	1	94	26	C23		0
1990	StL N	144	495	62	121	25	3	15	57	67-3	2	77	.244	.333	.398	101	1	2-4	.988	-5	93	119	C105,3b24,1b11/OL		0
1991	StL N	155	565	76	158	36	3	11	81	62-3	5	94	.280	.353	.412	114	12	17-11	.943	3	106	76	3b154		1
1992	StL N	126	439	51	113	18	4	7	48	68-4	0	70	.257	.352	.364	107	6	7-10	.960	-5	100	102	3b124		-0
1993	StL N	157	571	82	158	36	1	17	103	70-5	3	76	.277	.352	.433	110	-3	5-4	.923	-10	103	110	3b153		-0
1994	StL N	113	415	62	111	25	1	19	75	52-3	3	56	.267	.348	.470	112	8	1-3	.960	1	104	141	3b112		0
1995	StL N	34	127	16	37	6	0	5	22	18-1	1	23	.291	.378	.457	118	4	1-0	.980	2	129	118	1b34	14	0
	Chi N	79	299	34	68	16	0	9	30	16-0	3	53	.227	.271	.371	68	-15	0-0	.939	-6	95	107	3b75,O2L/1		-2
	Year	113	426	50	105	22	0	14	52	34-1	4	76	.246	.305	.397	84	-11	1-0	.939	-7	95	107	3b75,1b35,O2L		-2
1996	Phi N	134	500	61	134	24	0	20	80	67-4	1	88	.268	.353	.436	107	6	1-1	.962	-14	77	77	3b106,1b28		0
	†Bal A	29	117	17	28	8	0	5	19	15-0	1	16	.239	.326	.436	91	-2	0-0	.964	2	102	170	3b29		0
1997	LA N	160	575	89	154	17	0	31	90	85-7	6	112	.268	.365	.459	123	20	8-7	.931	-18	83	105	3b160		0
1998	LA N	40	158	22	40	7	1	7	27	10-0	1	24	.253	.300	.437	96	-2	1-1	.929	-11	68	28	3b40/1		-1
	Fla N	66	234	37	68	12	1	6	39	31-2	2	34	.291	.374	.427	119	7	2-3	.971	-4	96	83	3b65		0
	Year	106	392	59	108	18	2	13	66	41-2	3	58	.276	.345	.431	110	5	3-4	.957	-15	103	86	3b105/1		-0
	†Tex A	52	180	26	47	14	1	6	28	28-0	1	32	.261	.358	.450	104	2	1-0	.915	0	103	86	3b52		0
1999	†Tex A	156	588	80	172	41	1	24	98	56-3	4	94	.293	.354	.488	107	6	1-2	.941	6	108	90	3b155/1D		1
2000	†NY N	153	544	67	146	36	3	22	79	74-4	2	95	.268	.356	.467	112	11	3-4	.992	4	111	78	1b151		0
2001	NY N	151	531	66	141	25	1	10	62	73-3	6	102	.266	.359	.373	97	0	1-0	.992	10	129	100	1b149		0
2002	Col N	144	506	61	138	23	0	18	87	66-3	1	92	.273	.353	.425	96	-4	1-1	.942	-11	96	82	3b139/P		-1
2003	NY A	66	186	29	39	8	0	6	23	24-0	3	36	.210	.294	.349	72	-8	0-0	.917	2	101	199	3b30,1b23,D		0
	Mon N	34	113	11	29	2	2	5	19	10-0	3	18	.257	.331	.442	98	-1	1-0	.947	3	115	72	3b34		0
2004	NY N	137	348	30	81	16	0	9	35	44-1	1	83	.233	.319	.356	77	-12	0-0	.995	-4	87	99	1b67,3b46,C2/P		-1
Total	16	2158	7573	986	2004	397	23	253	1109	945-47	42	1279	.265	.346	.423	104	48	53-51	.942	-57	97	97	3b1498,1b466,C130,D9,O3L,P2	14	-3

ZELLER, BART   Barton Wallace   B7.22.1941 Chicago Heights IL   BR/TR/6-1/185   d5.21   C1   Col Arizona

| 1970 | StL N | 1 | 0 | 0 | 0 | 0 | 0 | 0 | 0 | 0-0 | 0 | | — | — | — | | 0 | 0-0 | 1.000 | 0 | 0 | 0 | /C | | 0 |

ZERNIAL, GUS   Gus Edward "Ozark Ike"   B6.27.1923 Beaumont TX   BR/TR/6-2.5/210*   d4.19

1949	Chi A	73	198	29	63	17	2	5	38	15	0	26	.318	.366	.500	132	8	0-1	1.000	-1	88	142	O46L	60	0.4
1950	Chi A	143	543	75	152	16	4	29	93	38	3	110	.280	.330	.484	110	2	0-2	.969	1	103	86	O137L		-0.7
1951	Chi A	4	19	2	2	0	0	0	4	2	0	2	.105	.190	.105	-19	-3	0-0	.933	1	107	241	O4L		-0.3
	Phi A	139	552	90	151	30	5	33	125	61	4	99	.274	.350	.525	132	21	2-2	.974	8	103	155	O138L		1.8
	Year	143	571	92	153	30	5	33	129	63	4	101	.268	.345	.511	127	18	2-2	.972	8	103	158	O142L		1.5
1952	Phi A	145	549	76	144	15	4	29	100	70	1	87	.262	.347	.452	114	6	5-1	.972	-3	98	65	O141L		-0.4
1953	Phi A★	147	556	85	158	21	3	42	108	57	4	79	.284	.355	.559	138	27	4-0	.972	5	99	156	O141L		2.4
1954	Phi A	97	336	42	84	8	2	14	62	30	4	60	.250	.316	.411	98	-2	0-0	.953	-1	102	74	O90L,1b2		-0.9
1955	KC A	120	413	62	105	9	3	30	84	30-1	3	90	.254	.304	.508	116	5	1-0	.964	5	110	106	O103L		-0.9
1956	KC A	109	272	36	61	12	0	16	44	33-2	4	65	.224	.315	.445	99	2	1-0	.984	3	93	201	O90L		-0.7
1957	KC A	131	437	58	103	20	1	27	69	34-0	1	84	.236	.290	.471	104	0	1-1	.952	-1	99	70	O113L/1		-0.8
1958	Det A	66	124	8	40	7	1	5	23	6-0	0	25	.323	.351	.516	127	4	0-0	.939	-2	82	89	O24L		0.0
1959	Det A	60	132	11	30	4	0	7	26	7-0	5	27	.227	.292	.417	80	-4	0-0	.972	-3	65	103	1b32/OR		0.0
Total	11	1234	4131	572	1093	159	22	237	776	383-3	24	755	.265	.326	.486	115	65	15-7	.968	12	100	112	O1007(1006/0/1),1b35	60	1.0

R TM LG	G	AB	R	H	2B	3B	HR	RBI	BB-IB	HP	SO	AVG	OBP	SLG	AOPS	ABR	SB-CS	FA	FR	RNG	THR	GAMES AT POSITION	DL	BFW

ZIEGLER, CHARLIE Charles Wallace B1.13.1875 Canton OH D4.18.1904 Canton OH TR d9.23

R TM LG	G	AB	R	H	2B	3B	HR	RBI	BB-IB	HP	SO	AVG	OBP	SLG	AOPS	ABR	SB-CS	FA	FR	RNG	THR	GAMES AT POSITION	DL	BFW
99 Cle N	2	8	2	2	0	0	0	0	0	0		.250	.250	.250	40	-1	0	.750	-1	72	0	/S2		-0.1
00 Phi N	3	11	0	3	0	0	0	1	0	0		.273	.273	.273	51	-1	0	.889	-1	69	0	3b3		-0.1
al 2	5	19	2	5	0	0	0	1	0	0		.263	.263	.263	47	-2	0	.889	-1	69	0	3b3/2S		-0.2

ENTARA, BENNY Benedict Joseph B2.14.1918 Chicago IL D4.16.1985 Lake Elsinore CA BR/TR/5-9/165 d9.11 Mil 1942-45

R TM LG	G	AB	R	H	2B	3B	HR	RBI	BB-IB	HP	SO	AVG	OBP	SLG	AOPS	ABR	SB-CS	FA	FR	RNG	THR	GAMES AT POSITION	DL	BFW
5 Cin N	9	21	3	6	0	0	0	2	1	0	3	.286	.318	.286	71	-1	0	.914	-0	105	91	2b6		-0.1
6 Cin N	78	280	26	81	10	2	0	16	14	0	11	.289	.323	.339	91	-4	3	.970	18	136	151	2b39,3b36		1.6
7 Cin N	117	418	60	108	18	1	2	24	23	0	23	.258	.297	.321	64	-22	2	.976	-10	92	81	2b100,3b13		-2.7
8 Cin N	74	187	17	35	1	2	0	7	12	0	11	.187	.236	.214	23	-21	0	.990	7	103	103	2b60,3b3,S2		-1.1
al 4	278	906	106	230	29	5	2	49	50	0	48	.254	.293	.304	64	-48	5	.976	15	103	100	2b205,3b52,S2		-2.3

ES, BILL William B6.16.1867 Rock Island IL D4.16.1907 Beardstown IL BL d8.9

R TM LG	G	AB	R	H	2B	3B	HR	RBI	BB-IB	HP	SO	AVG	OBP	SLG	AOPS	ABR	SB-CS	FA	FR	RNG	THR	GAMES AT POSITION	DL	BFW
91 StL AA	2	3	1	1	0	0	0			0		.333	.333	.333	79	0	0	1.000	0	155	106	C2		0.0

MMER, CHIEF Charles Louis B11.23.1860 Marietta OH D8.22.1949 Cleveland OH BR/TR/6-0/190 d7.18 M1/U1

R TM LG	G	AB	R	H	2B	3B	HR	RBI	BB-IB	HP	SO	AVG	OBP	SLG	AOPS	ABR	SB-CS	FA	FR	RNG	THR	GAMES AT POSITION	DL	BFW
34 Det N	8	29	0	2	1	0	0				14	.069	.100	.103	-38	-4		.830	-1			C6,O2R		-0.5
36 NY AA	6	19	1	3	0	0	0	1	1	1		.158	.238	.158	27	-1	0	.893	2			C6		0.1
37 Cle AA	14	52	9	12	5	0	0	4	4	1		.231	.298	.327	77	-1	1	.923	-2			C12,1b2		-0.2
38 Cle AA	65	212	27	51	11	4	0	22	18	4		.241	.312	.330	109	3	15	.917	9			C59,O3(0/1/2),1b3/S		1.5
39 Cle N	84	259	47	67	9	9	1	21	44	1	35	.259	.368	.375	110	4	14	.931	11			C81,1b3		1.8
90 Cle N	125	444	54	95	16	6	3	57	46	11	54	.214	.303	.291	75	-13	15	.937	21	117	114	C125		1.6
91 Cle N	116	440	55	112	21	4	3	69	33	4	49	.255	.312	.341	87	-8	15	.936	14	92	138	C116/3		1.4
92 †Cle N	111	413	63	109	29	13	1	64	32	7	47	.264	.327	.404	116	7	18	.938	21	130	82	C111		3.4
93 Cle N	57	227	27	70	13	7	2	41	16	1	15	.308	.357	.454	108	1	4	.968	11	113	129	C56/3		1.3
94 Cle N	90	341	55	97	20	5	4	65	17	5	31	.284	.328	.408	73	-17	14	.963	27	161	110	C89		1.4
95 †Cle N	88	315	60	107	21	2	5	56	33	9	30	.340	.417	.467	121	11	14	.975	10	120	88	C84,1b3		2.3
96 †Cle N	91	336	46	93	18	3	3	46	31	9	48	.277	.354	.375	87	-6	4	.972	17	150	83	C91/3		1.6
97 Cle N	80	294	50	93	22	3	0	40	25	4		.316	.378	.412	103	2	8	.976	11	113	96	C80		1.7
98 Cle N	20	63	5	15	2	0	0	4	5	1		.238	.304	.270	66	-3	2	.970	4	113	87	C19		0.3
99 Cle N	20	73	9	25	2	1	2	14	5	3		.342	.407	.479	154	6	1	.957	-5	59	120	C20		0.2
Lou N	75	262	43	78	11	3	2	29	22	8		.298	.370	.385	107	3	9	.985	5	115	102	C62,1b11		1.2
Year	95	335	52	103	13	4	4	43	27	11		.307	.378	.406	117	9	10	.978	-0	102	106	C82,1b2		1.4
00 †Pit N	82	271	27	80	7	10	0	35	17	11		.295	.361	.395	108	2	4	.961	6	129		C78,1b2		-0.4
01 Pit N	69	236	17	52	7	3	0	21	20	4		.220	.292	.275	63	-11	6	.975	-0	126	91	C68		0.7
02 Pit N	42	142	13	38	4	2	0	17	11	4		.268	.338	.324	101	0	4	.969	2	144	91	C41/1		-0.1
03 Phi N	37	118	9	26	3	1	1	19	9	3		.220	.292	.288	68	-5	3	.968	1	90	94	C35,M		-0.2
total 19	1280	4546	617	1225	222	76	26	625	390	91	323	.269	.339	.369	95	-30	151	.952	161	122	102	C1239,1b25,O5(0/1/4),3b3/S		20.7

MMER, DON Donald William B1.17.1931 Cincinnati OH BR/TR/5-9/177(165-187) d7.2 M14/C22

R TM LG	G	AB	R	H	2B	3B	HR	RBI	BB-IB	HP	SO	AVG	OBP	SLG	AOPS	ABR	SB-CS	FA	FR	RNG	THR	GAMES AT POSITION	DL	BFW
54 Bro N	24	33	3	6	0	1	0	3	1	1	8	.182	.270	.242	34	-3	2-0	.939	2	120	107	S13		-0.1
55 †Bro N	88	280	38	67	10	1	6	15	50	19-5	1	66	.239	.289	.443	89	-6	5-3	.976	3	97	138	2b62,S21,3b8		0.3
56 Bro N	17	20	4	6	1	0	0	2	0-0	1	7	.300	.333	.350	78	-1	0-1	.944	1	94	160	S8,3b3/2	68	0.0
57 Bro N	84	269	23	59	9	1	6	19	16-5	0	63	.219	.262	.327	52	-18	1-3	.957	4	99	51	3b39,S37,2b5		-1.2
58 LA N	127	455	52	119	15	4	17	60	28-1	1	92	.262	.305	.415	86	-11	14-2	.965	24	104	118	S114,3b12/2OL		2.6
59 †LA N	97	249	21	41	7	1	4	28	37-7	1	56	.165	.274	.249	38	-22	3-1	.972	2	98	96	S88,3b5/2		-1.4
60 Chi N	132	368	37	95	16	7	6	35	27-4	0	56	.258	.307	.389	90	-6	8-6	.980	8	119	60	2b75,3b45,S5,O2L		0.7
61 Chi N★	128	477	57	120	25	4	13	40	25-1	2	70	.252	.291	.403	81	-14	5-1	.973	6	102	121	2b116,3b5/OR		0.1
62 NY N	14	52	3	4	1	0	0	1	3-0	0	10	.077	.127	.096	-38	-10	0-1	.961	4	144	111	3b14		-0.7
Cin N	63	192	16	48	11	2	2	16	14-1	1	30	.250	.304	.359	75	-7	1-2	.949	-5	90	87	3b43,2b17/S		-1.2
Year	77	244	19	52	12	2	2	17	17-1	1	40	.213	.267	.303	51	-17	1-3	.952	-1	104	93	3b57,2b17/S		-1.9
63 LA N	22	23	4	5	1	0	1	2	3-0	0	10	.217	.308	.391	107	0	0-0	.933	1	125	0	3b10/2S		0.1
Was A	83	298	37	74	12	1	13	44	18-2	2	57	.248	.296	.426	100	-1	3-2	.935	5	111	110	3b78,2b2		0.3
64 Was A	121	341	38	84	16	2	12	38	27-0	0	94	.246	.302	.411	96	-2	1-3	.955	-7	99	46	3b87,O4(2/0/3),C2/2		-1.1
65 Was A	95	226	20	45	6	2	0	17	26-1	2	59	.199	.284	.252	56	-13	2-0	.966	-5	125	158	C33,3b26,2b12		-1.6
total 12	1095	3283	353	773	130	22	91	352	246-27	13	678	.235	.290	.372	76	-114	45-25	.941	41	103	76	3b375,2b294,S288,C35,O8(5/0/4)	68	-3.2

MMERMAN, EDDIE Edward Desmond B1.4.1883 Oceanic NJ D5.6.1945 Emmaus PA BR/TR/5-9/160 d9.29 Col Manhattan

R TM LG	G	AB	R	H	2B	3B	HR	RBI	BB-IB	HP	SO	AVG	OBP	SLG	AOPS	ABR	SB-CS	FA	FR	RNG	THR	GAMES AT POSITION	DL	BFW
06 StL N	5	14	0	3	0	0	0	1	0	0	2	.214	.214	.214	35	-1	0	.929	-0	78	0	3b5		-0.2
11 Bro N	122	417	31	77	10	7	3	36	34	2	37	.185	.249	.264	46	-33	9	.961	3	99	136	3b122		-2.7
total 2	127	431	31	80	10	7	3	37	34	2	37	.186	.248	.262	45	-34	9	.960	2	98	132	3b127		-2.9

MMERMAN, JERRY Gerald Robert B9.21.1934 Omaha NE D9.9.1998 Neskowin OR BR/TR/6-2/185* d4.14 C13

R TM LG	G	AB	R	H	2B	3B	HR	RBI	BB-IB	HP	SO	AVG	OBP	SLG	AOPS	ABR	SB-CS	FA	FR	RNG	THR	GAMES AT POSITION	DL	BFW
61 †Cin N	76	204	8	42	5	0	0	10	11-0	2	21	.206	.252	.230	29	-21	1-1	.975	1	94	82	C76		-1.7
62 Min N	34	62	8	17	4	0	0	7	3-0	1	5	.274	.318	.339	74	-2	0-0	.992	-1	139	126	C34		-0.2
63 Min A	39	56	3	13	1	0	0	3	2-0	0	8	.232	.259	.250	43	-4	0-0	1.000	1	165	62	C39		-0.3
64 Min A	63	120	6	24	3	0	0	12	10-0	3	15	.200	.278	.225	42	-9	0-0	.993	1	105	159	C63		-0.7
65 †Min A	83	154	8	33	1	1	1	11	12-3	1	23	.214	.275	.253	49	-10	0-0	.997	1	115	69	C82		-0.7
66 Min A	60	119	11	30	4	1	1	15	15-4	1	25	.252	.338	.328	88	-1	0-0	.996	7	148	102	C59		0.8
67 Min A	104	234	13	39	3	0	1	12	22-5	2	49	.167	.243	.192	28	-21	0-1	.992	9	113	114	C104		-0.9
68 Min A	24	45	3	5	1	0	0	2	3-0	1	10	.111	.180	.133	-3	-6	0-0	.991	1	131	108	C24		-0.5
total 8	483	994	60	203	22	3	4	72	78-12	11	154	.204	.269	.239	43	-74	1-2	.991	19	118	102	C481		-4.2

MMERMAN, HEINIE Henry B2.9.1887 New York NY D3.14.1969 New York NY BR/TR/5-11.5/176 d9.8 OF(3/8/2)

R TM LG	G	AB	R	H	2B	3B	HR	RBI	BB-IB	HP	SO	AVG	OBP	SLG	AOPS	ABR	SB-CS	FA	FR	RNG	THR	GAMES AT POSITION	DL	BFW
07 †Chi N	5	9	0	2	1	0	0	1	0	0		.222	.222	.333	70	0	0	.789	0	114	274	2b4/SOL		0.0
08 Chi N	46	113	17	33	4	1	0	9	9	0		.292	.298	.345	101	0	2	.923	-7	76	40	2b20,O8(2/4/2)/S3		-0.8
09 Chi N	65	183	23	50	9	2	0	21	3	0		.273	.285	.344	93	-3	7	.945	-7	77	94	2b31,S12,3b4		-0.9
10 †Chi N	99	335	35	95	16	6	3	38	20	1	36	.284	.326	.394	111	3	7	.948	-8	89	128	2b32,S26,3b23,O4C/1		-0.4
11 Chi N	143	535	80	164	22	17	9	85	25	5	50	.307	.343	.462	124	13	23	.946	-5	98	96	2b108,3b20,1b11		1.0
12 Chi N	145	557	95	207	41	14	14	99	38	6	60	.372	.418	.571	170	51	23	.916	1	106	103	3b121,1b22		5.3
13 Chi N	127	447	69	140	28	12	9	95	41	6	40	.313	.379	.490	147	27	18-19	.912	5	107	115	3b125		3.3
14 Chi N	146	564	75	167	36	12	4	87	31	5	46	.296	.326	.424	123	13	17	.897	-19	85	83	3b118,S15,2b12		-0.2
15 Chi N	139	520	65	138	28	11	3	62	21	5	33	.265	.300	.379	105	1	19-13	.943	-6	97	75	2b100,3b36,S4		-0.3
16 Chi N	107	398	54	116	25	5	6	64	16	1	33	.291	.324	.425	116	7	15-12	.932	8	116	92	3b85,2b14,S4		2.0
NY N	40	151	22	41	4	0	0	19	7	0	10	.272	.304	.298	90	-2	9-8	.943	-1	98	94	3b40/2		-0.3
Year	147	549	76	157	29	5	6	83	23	3	43	.286	.318	.390	110	6	24-20	.935	7	110	93	3b125,2b15,S4		1.7
17 †NY N	150	585	61	174	22	9	5	102	16	1	43	.297	.317	.391	121	11	13	.947	14	115	101	3b149,2b5		3.2
18 NY N	121	463	43	126	19	10	1	56	13	5	23	.272	.294	.363	102	-2	14	.955	-4	95	53	3b100,1b19		-0.4
19 NY N	123	444	56	113	20	6	1	58	21	5	30	.255	.296	.354	96	-3	8	.940	-0	107	93	3b123		0.0
total 13	1456	5304	695	1566	275	105	58	796	242	38	404	.295	.331	.419	121	116	175-52	.928	-29	103	92	3b945,2b327,S63,1b53,O13C		11.6

ZIMMERMAN, ROY Roy Franklin B9.13.1916 Pine Grove PA D11.22.1991 Pine Grove PA BL/TR/6-2/187 d8.27

R TM LG	G	AB	R	H	2B	3B	HR	RBI	BB-IB	HP	SO	AVG	OBP	SLG	AOPS	ABR	SB-CS	FA	FR	RNG	THR	GAMES AT POSITION	DL	BFW
45 NY N	27	98	14	27	7	1	1	16	3	1	16	.276	.330	.439	111	1	1	.988	-2	76	73	1b25/OR		-0.2

ZIMMERMAN, RYAN Ryan Wallace B9.28.1984 Washington NC BR/TR/6-3/220 d9.1 Col Virginia

R TM LG	G	AB	R	H	2B	3B	HR	RBI	BB-IB	HP	SO	AVG	OBP	SLG	AOPS	ABR	SB-CS	FA	FR	RNG	THR	GAMES AT POSITION	DL	BFW
2005 Was N	20	58	6	23	10	0	0	6	3-0	1	12	.397	.419	.569	169	6	0-0	1.000	1	112	208	3b14/S		0.7

ZIMMERMAN, BILL William Frederick B1.20.1887 Kengen, Germany D10.4.1952 Newark NJ BR/TR/5-8.5/172 d4.14

R TM LG	G	AB	R	H	2B	3B	HR	RBI	BB-IB	HP	SO	AVG	OBP	SLG	AOPS	ABR	SB-CS	FA	FR	RNG	THR	GAMES AT POSITION	DL	BFW
1915 Bro N	22	57	3	16	2	0	0	8	2	0	1	.281	.328	.316	93	0	1	.864	-2	86	0	O18R		-0.4

ZINN, FRANK Frank Patrick B12.21.1865 Phoenixville PA D5.12.1936 Philadelphia PA 5-8/150 d4.18

R TM LG	G	AB	R	H	2B	3B	HR	RBI	BB-IB	HP	SO	AVG	OBP	SLG	AOPS	ABR	SB-CS	FA	FR	RNG	THR	GAMES AT POSITION	DL	BFW
1888 Phi AA	2	7	0	0	0	0	0		1	0		.000	.125	.000	-2	-1	0	.938	-0			C2		-0.1

ZINN, GUY Guy B2.13.1887 Holbrook WV D10.6.1949 Park WV BL/TR/5-10.5/170 d9.11

R TM LG	G	AB	R	H	2B	3B	HR	RBI	BB-IB	HP	SO	AVG	OBP	SLG	AOPS	ABR	SB-CS	FA	FR	RNG	THR	GAMES AT POSITION	DL	BFW
1911 NY A	9	27	5	4	0	2	0	1	4	1		.148	.281	.296	57	-2	0	.923	0	77	180	O8(2/4/2)		-0.2
1912 NY A	106	401	56	105	15	10	6	55	50	1		.262	.343	.394	105	2	17	.893	-9	92	65	O106(13/31/61)		-1.3
1913 Bos A	36	138	16	41	8	2	1	15	4	1	23	.297	.322	.406	105	-3	3-4	.948	2	99	161	O35(1/34/0)		-0.1

YEAR	TM LG	G	AB	R	H	2B	3B	HR	RBI	BB-IB	HP	SO	AVG	OBP	SLG	AOPS	ABR	SB-CS	FA	FR	RNG	THR	GAMES AT POSITION	DL	BF
1914	Bal F	61	225	30	63	10	6	3	25	16	3	26	.280	.336	.418	101	-4	6	.935	-4	92	65	O57(31/12/14)		-1
1915	Bal F	102	312	30	84	18	3	5	43	35	0	28	.269	.343	.394	104	-2	2	.949	-1	94	107	O88(63/17/8)		-0
Total	5	314	1103	136	297	51	23	15	139	109	6	77	.269	.338	.398	103	-6	28-4	.927	-12	93	93	O294(110/98/85)		-3

ZINTER, ALAN Alan Michael B5.19.1968 El Paso TX BB/TR/6-2/200* [NYN89 1/24] d6.18 Col Arizona

YEAR	TM LG	G	AB	R	H	2B	3B	HR	RBI	BB-IB	HP	SO	AVG	OBP	SLG	AOPS	ABR	SB-CS	FA	FR	RNG	THR	GAMES AT POSITION	DL	BF
2002	Hou N	39	44	5	6	2	0	2	3	6-0	0	19	.136	.136	.318	15	-6	0-0	1.000	0	98	117	1b8/C		-0
2004	Ari N	28	34	2	7	2	0	1	6	5-0	0	15	.206	.300	.353	66	-2	0-0	.978	0	107	25	1b8,D2	60	-0
Total	2	67	78	7	13	4	0	3	9	5-0	0	34	.167	.214	.333	39	-8	0-0	.986	0	103	63	1b16,D2/C	60	-0

ZIPFEL, BUD Marion Sylvester B11.18.1938 Belleville IL BL/TR/6-3/200* d7.26

YEAR	TM LG	G	AB	R	H	2B	3B	HR	RBI	BB-IB	HP	SO	AVG	OBP	SLG	AOPS	ABR	SB-CS	FA	FR	RNG	THR	GAMES AT POSITION	DL	BF
1961	Was A	50	170	17	34	7	5	4	18	15-0	0	49	.200	.262	.371	69	-9	1-1	.983	-5	75	102	1b44		-1
1962	Was A	68	184	21	44	4	1	6	21	17-1	1	43	.239	.307	.370	82	-5	1-2	.976	-2	109	69	1b26,O23L		-1
Total	2	118	354	38	78	11	6	10	39	32-1	1	92	.220	.285	.370	76	-14	2-3	.981	-6	87	91	1b70,O23L		-2

ZISK, RICHIE Richard Walter B2.6.1949 Brooklyn NY BR/TR/6-1/208(200-220) [PitN67 3/56] d9.8 [DL 1984 Sea A 181]

YEAR	TM LG	G	AB	R	H	2B	3B	HR	RBI	BB-IB	HP	SO	AVG	OBP	SLG	AOPS	ABR	SB-CS	FA	FR	RNG	THR	GAMES AT POSITION	DL	BF
1971	Pit N	7	15	2	3	1	0	1	2	4-0	0	7	.200	.368	.467	134	1	0-0	1.000	0	91	0	O6(3/0/3)		0
1972	Pit N	17	37	4	7	3	0	0	4	7-0	0	10	.189	.318	.270	70	-1	0-0	.938	-1	73	148	O12(12/0/1)		-0
1973	Pit N	103	333	44	108	23	7	10	54	21-0	0	63	.324	.364	.526	147	19	0-0	.987	2	90	175	O84(22/0/65)		3
1974	†Pit N	149	536	75	168	30	3	17	100	65-7	0	91	.313	.386	.476	144	33	1-1	.985	7	113	90	O141(9/0/135)		3
1975	†Pit N	147	504	69	146	27	3	20	75	68-9	2	109	.290	.374	.474	134	24	0-1	.975	-5	99	64	O140L		
1976	Pit N	155	581	91	168	35	2	21	89	52-3	0	96	.289	.343	.465	127	20	1-0	.987	2	100	102	O152L		
1977	Chi A★	141	531	78	154	17	6	30	101	55-7	3	98	.290	.355	.514	135	25	0-4	.982	3	101	120	O109(10/0/100),D28		
1978	Tex A★	140	511	68	134	19	4	22	85	58-7	3	76	.262	.338	.432	115	10	3-3	.988	-6	83	94	O90(48/0/42),D49	15	
1979	Tex A	144	503	69	132	21	1	18	64	57-4	0	75	.262	.336	.416	103	2	1-1	.972	-6	88	103	O134(15/0/126),D3		-1
1980	Tex A	135	448	48	130	17	1	19	77	39-5	0	72	.290	.344	.460	122	13	0-2	.980	-3	73	129	D86,O37(2/0/35)		0
1981	Sea A	94	357	42	111	12	1	16	43	28-3	3	63	.311	.366	.485	137	16	0-2	—	0	0	0	D93		1
1982	Sea A	131	503	61	147	28	1	21	62	49-4	1	89	.292	.354	.477	122	16	2-1	—	0	0	0	D130		1
1983	Sea A	90	285	30	69	12	0	12	36	30-3	0	61	.242	.311	.411	94	-3	0-0	—	0	0	0	D84	20	
Total	13	1453	5144	681	1477	245	26	207	792	533-52	12	910	.287	.353	.466	125	175	8-15	.981	-7	96	103	O905(413/0/507),D473	216	10

ZITZMANN, BILLY William Arthur B11.19.1895 Long Island City NY D5.29.1985 Passaic NJ BR/TR/5-10.5/175 d4.17

YEAR	TM LG	G	AB	R	H	2B	3B	HR	RBI	BB-IB	HP	SO	AVG	OBP	SLG	AOPS	ABR	SB-CS	FA	FR	RNG	THR	GAMES AT POSITION	DL	BF
1919	Pit N	11	26	5	5	1	0	0	2	0	0	6	.192	.192	.231	26	-2	0-0	.917	-1	103	0	O8L		-0
	Cin N	2	1	0	0	0	0	0	0	0	0	0	.000	.000	.000	-99	-2	0-0	—	-0	0	0	/OL		0.
	Year	13	27	5	5	1	0	0	2	0	0	6	.185	.185	.222	22	-3	0-2	.917	-1	101	0	O9L		-0.
1925	Cin N	104	301	53	76	13	3	0	21	35	6	22	.252	.342	.316	71	-12	11-11	.959	-6	88	72	O89(80/4/7)/S		-2.
1926	Cin N	53	94	21	23	2	1	0	3	6	2	7	.245	.304	.287	61	-5	3	.965	-1	111	0	O31(22/5/2)		-0.
1927	Cin N	88	232	47	66	10	4	0	24	20	4	18	.284	.352	.362	94	-1	9	.958	-7	98	35	O60(17/36/7),S8,3b3		-1.
1928	Cin N	101	266	53	79	9	3	3	33	13	3	9	.297	.337	.387	90	-5	13	.958	-1	104	68	O78(46/12/23)/3		-1.
1929	Cin N	47	84	18	19	3	0	0	6	9	1	10	.226	.309	.262	45	-7	4	.940	-1	119	0	O22(15/0/7),1b5		-0.
Total	6	406	1004	197	268	38	11	3	89	83	16	85	.267	.333	.336	77	-32	42-11	.956	-16	100	48	O289(189/57/46),S9,1b5,3b4		-6.

ZOCCOLILLO, PETE Peter Jude B2.6.1977 Bronx NY BL/TR/6-2/200 [ChiN99 23/710] d9.5 Col Rutgers

YEAR	TM LG	G	AB	R	H	2B	3B	HR	RBI	BB-IB	HP	SO	AVG	OBP	SLG	AOPS	ABR	SB-CS	FA	FR	RNG	THR	GAMES AT POSITION	DL	BF
2003	Mil N	20	37	4	4	0	0	3	2-0	0	13	.108	.154	.135	-24	-7	0-0	1.000	0	128	0	O7(3/0/4)			

ZOSKY, EDDIE Edward James B2.10.1968 Whittier CA BR/TR/6-0/175* [TorA89 1/19] d9.2 Col Cal St.-Fresno [DL 1993 Tor A 128]

YEAR	TM LG	G	AB	R	H	2B	3B	HR	RBI	BB-IB	HP	SO	AVG	OBP	SLG	AOPS	ABR	SB-CS	FA	FR	RNG	THR	GAMES AT POSITION	DL	BF
1991	Tor A	18	27	2	4	1	0	0	2	0-0	0	8	.148	.148	.259	10	-2	0-0	1.000	-2	89	89	S18		-0.
1992	Tor A	8	7	1	2	0	1	0	1	0-0	0	2	.286	.286	.571	128	0	0-0	.923	1	126	124	S8		-0.
1995	Fla N	6	5	0	1	0	0	0	0	0-0	0	2	.200	.200	.200	6	-1	0-0	.667	-2	23	0	S4/2		-0.
1999	Mil N	8	7	1	1	0	0	0	1	1-0	0	2	.143	.250	.143	3	-1	0-0	1.000	0	90	0	3b4,2b2		-0.
2000	Hou N	4	4	0	0	0	0	0	0	0-0	0	1	.000	.000	.000	-93	-1	0-0	—	0			/H		-0.
Total	5	44	50	4	8	1	2	0	3	1-0	0	13	.160	.173	.260	16	-6	0-0	.963	-3	89	86	S30,3b4,2b3	128	

ZUBER, JON Jon Edward B12.10.1969 Encino CA BL/TL/6-0/190* [PhiN92 12/333] d4.19 Col California-Davis

YEAR	TM LG	G	AB	R	H	2B	3B	HR	RBI	BB-IB	HP	SO	AVG	OBP	SLG	AOPS	ABR	SB-CS	FA	FR	RNG	THR	GAMES AT POSITION	DL	BF
1996	Phi N	30	91	7	23	4	0	1	10	6-1	0	11	.253	.296	.330	65	-5	1-0	.987	-1	77	61	1b22		-0.
1998	Phi N	38	45	6	11	3	1	2	6	6-0	1	9	.244	.346	.489	146	1	0-0	1.000	0	83	0	O5L,1b4		0.
Total	2	68	136	13	34	7	1	3	16	12-1	1	20	.250	.313	.382	82	-4	1-0	.989	-2	77	62	1b26,O5L		-0.

ZULETA, JULIO Julio Ernesto (Tapia) B3.28.1975 Panama City, Pan BR/TR/6-6/230* d4.6

YEAR	TM LG	G	AB	R	H	2B	3B	HR	RBI	BB-IB	HP	SO	AVG	OBP	SLG	AOPS	ABR	SB-CS	FA	FR	RNG	THR	GAMES AT POSITION	DL	BF
2000	Chi N	30	68	13	20	8	0	3	12	2-0	3	19	.294	.342	.544	121	2	0-1	.966	-0	113	106	1b14,O6L		0.0
2001	Chi N	49	106	11	23	3	0	6	24	8-1	3	32	.217	.288	.415	82	-3	0-1	.991	-4	42	58	1b35		-0.9
Total	2	79	174	24	43	11	0	9	36	10-1	6	51	.247	.309	.466	97	-1	0-2	.984	-4	63	72	1b49,O6L		-0.9

ZUPCIC, BOB Robert B8.18.1966 Pittsburgh PA BR/TR/6-4/220* [BosA87 1/32] d9.7 Col Oral Roberts

YEAR	TM LG	G	AB	R	H	2B	3B	HR	RBI	BB-IB	HP	SO	AVG	OBP	SLG	AOPS	ABR	SB-CS	FA	FR	RNG	THR	GAMES AT POSITION	DL	BF
1991	Bos A	18	25	3	4	0	1	3	1-0	0	6	.160	.192	.280	27	-3	0-0	.875	-2	76	0	O16(3/7/6)		-0.4		
1992	Bos A	124	392	46	108	19	1	3	43	25-1	4	60	.276	.322	.352	84	-8	2-2	.977	1	94	176	O114(32/68/22),D5		-1.
1993	Bos A	141	286	40	69	24	2	2	26	27-2	2	54	.241	.308	.360	75	-10	5-2	.979	-0	95	129	O122(48/37/54),D5		-1.2
1994	Bos A	4	4	0	0	0	0	0	0	0-0	0	1	.000	.000	.000	-96	-1	0-1	1.000	-0	72	0	O2L/D		-0.2
	Chi A	32	88	10	18	4	1	1	8	4-0	0	16	.205	.237	.307	40	-8	0-1	1.000	1	107	128	O28(15/0/14),3b2/1		-0.8
	Year	36	92	10	18	4	1	1	8	4-0	0	17	.196	.227	.293	34	-10	0-1	1.000	0	105	121	O30(17/0/14),3b2/D1		-1.0
Total	4	319	795	99	199	47	4	7	80	57-3	6	137	.250	.303	.346	73	-30	7-5	.977	-1	95	146	O282(100/112/96),D11,3b2/1		-3.6

ZUPO, FRANK Frank Joseph "Noodles" B8.29.1939 San Francisco CA D3.25.2005 Burlingame CA BL/TR/5-11/182* d7.1

YEAR	TM LG	G	AB	R	H	2B	3B	HR	RBI	BB-IB	HP	SO	AVG	OBP	SLG	AOPS	ABR	SB-CS	FA	FR	RNG	THR	GAMES AT POSITION	DL	BF
1957	Bal A	10	12	2	1	0	0	0	1-0	0	4	.083	.154	.083	-36	-2	0-0	.913	-0	93	126	C8		-0.3		
1958	Bal A	1	2	0	0	0	0	0	0	1-0	0	1	.000	.000	.000	-99	-1	0-0	1.000	0	0	0	/C		0.0
1961	Bal A	5	4	1	2	1	0	0	0	1-0	0	1	.500	.600	.750	268	1	0-0	1.000	0	0	0	C4		0.1
Total	3	16	18	3	3	1	0	0	0	2-0	0	6	.167	.250	.222	31	-2	0-0	.941	0	64	87	C13		-0.2

ZUVELLA, PAUL Paul B10.31.1958 San Mateo CA BR/TR/6-0/178* [AtlN80 15/367] d9.4 C1 Col Stanford

YEAR	TM LG	G	AB	R	H	2B	3B	HR	RBI	BB-IB	HP	SO	AVG	OBP	SLG	AOPS	ABR	SB-CS	FA	FR	RNG	THR	GAMES AT POSITION	DL	BF
1982	Atl N	2	1	0	0	0	0	0	0	0-0	0	0	.000	.000	.000	-98	0	0-0	.800	0	225	0	/S		0.0
1983	Atl N	3	5	0	0	0	0	0	0	2-0	1	0	.000	.375	.000	11	0	0-0	.750	-2	39	0	S2		-0.2
1984	Atl N	11	25	2	5	1	0	0	1	0-0	0	3	.200	.259	.240	38	-2	0-0	1.000	-0	114	143	2b6,S6		-0.2
1985	Atl N	81	190	16	48	8	1	0	4	16-1	0	14	.253	.311	.305	69	-8	2-0	.986	1	110	79	2b42,S33,3b5		-0.4
1986	NY A	21	48	4	12	1	0	0	5	5-0	0	4	.083	.170	.104	-23	-8	0-0	.966	2	109	115	S21		-0.4
1987	NY A	14	34	2	6	0	0	0	0	0-0	0	5	.176	.176	.176	-6	-5	0-0	1.000	0	102	120	2b7,S6/3		-0.5
1988	Cle A	51	130	9	30	5	1	0	7	8-0	0	13	.231	.275	.285	55	-8	0-0	.959	-8	87	74	S49		-1.3
1989	Cle A	24	58	10	16	2	0	2	6	1-0	1	11	.276	.300	.414	97	0	0-0	.963	-4	79	25	S15,3b5,D3		-0.4
1991	KC A	2	0	0	0	0	0	0	0	0-0	0	0	—	—	—		0	0-0	—	0			3b2		0.0
Total	9	209	491	41	109	17	2	2	20	34-1	2	50	.222	.275	.277	52	-31	2-0	.959	-11	93	91	S133,2b55,3b13,D3		-3.2

ZWILLING, DUTCH Edward Harrison B11.2.1888 St.Louis MO D3.27.1978 LaCrescenta CA BL/TL/5-6.5/160 d8.14 C1

YEAR	TM LG	G	AB	R	H	2B	3B	HR	RBI	BB-IB	HP	SO	AVG	OBP	SLG	AOPS	ABR	SB-CS	FA	FR	RNG	THR	GAMES AT POSITION	DL	BF
1910	Chi A	27	87	7	16	5	0	0	5	11	1		.184	.241	.241	67	-3	1	.940	-2	90	56	O27C		-0.7
1914	Chi F	154	592	91	185	38	8	**16**	95	46	1	68	.313	.363	.485	138	19	21	.962	-6	99	66	O154(0/153/1)		0.2
1915	Chi F	150	548	65	157	32	7	13	**94**	67	2	65	.286	.366	.442	135	17	24	.979	3	105	91	O148C,1b3		1.0
1916	Chi N	35	53	4	6	1	0	1	8	4	0	6	.113	.175	.189	11	-6	0	1.000	-1	79	0	O10(0/5/4)		-0.8
Total	4	366	1280	167	364	76	15	30	202	128	4	139	.284	.351	.438	127	27	46	.969	-7	101	75	O339(0/333/5),1b3		-0.3

THE ART OF PITCHING: THE PITCHER REGISTER

Pitching has always been thought of as an *art,* in contrast to tting, which has generally been considered a *science.* Perhaps is is because the pitcher starts the action and controls the tempo the game. Perhaps this is because good pitching is seen as gressive, while hitting seems reactive. "Going after a hitter" is a gn of strength, and giving in to a hitter is a sign of weakness.

Good pitchers are creative, adjusting to the situation while venting new ways to confound enemy batters. Pitchers who mply rock back and hurl the ball as hard as they can are derid-d as "throwers" and not "pitchers"—most throwers don't last ng unless they can master the art of pitching. Pitchers of odest talent can fashion successful careers if they learn the t. Pitchers blessed with *a lot* of talent can achieve greatness if ey combine their physical gifts with the art.

Two of the greatest books ever written on the subject of tching show how similar the approach of the great pitchers has een over time, even under very different playing conditions. hristy Mathewson's *Pitching in a Pinch* and Tom Seaver's *The rt of Pitching* are both classics of baseball literature. Matty's ook (with ghostwriter John Wheeler) was first published in 912; it was reprinted by the University of Nebraska Press in 993. Tom Terrific's book, co-authored with Lee Lowenfish, was rst published in 1984 and remains in-print today.

During Mathewson's day, each at bat was a game of cat-nd-mouse between and the man on the mound and the man at e plate. It was mostly a contest of deception, especially from e pitcher's end. It was not a power game—pitchers didn't have throw that hard, but they were expected to start 35–40 games nd complete almost all of them. If he remained healthy, a star itcher could expect to log 350 or more innings, and pitch in elief 5–10 times in key games since the failed starters in the ullpen were relegated to mop-up and emergency duty.

What is now called "little ball" was the way of the day in e early twentieth century. Mathewson knew that the secret to eing a successful pitcher was letting hitters get themselves out. All batters who are good waiters, and will not hit at bad balls, re hard to deceive, because it means a twirler has to lay the all over, and then the hitter always has the better chance," he aid. "A pitcher will try to get a man to hit at a bad ball before e will put it near the plate."

What the "Big Six" didn't say—but what he understood and what he presumed the reader would understand as well—was hat a *good* pitcher tries to get the batter to swing at *bad* pitches.

Mathewson also understood the critical nature of pacing imself. In his day, a batted ball wouldn't travel nearly as far as t would today, and the fences were usually farther away. Therefore, he could save his very best stuff, especially his dev-astating screwball (then called a "fadeaway") for when he need-ed it most: The term *pinches* refers to what would be called *clutch* situations today.

"Many persons have asked me why I do not use my 'fade-away' oftener when it is so effective," he wrote, "and the only answer is that every time I throw the 'fade-away' it takes so much out of my arm. It is a very hard ball to deliver. Pitching it ten or twelve times a game kills my arm, so I save it for the pinches."

Decades later, another dominant NL right-hander named Tom Seaver also talked about a pitcher pacing himself. Seaver wrote about pacing himself *during the at bat* as well as during the game in order to get the job done. In the 1970s Seaver knew that batters could connect for a long ball at almost any time, so he had to be able to reach back and strike a hitter out if necessary.

"If he is thinking ahead," Seaver wrote, "[a pitcher] will select pitches in sequence—for instance, throwing a sinking fastball in spot A in order to get the batter out with a slider in Spot B."

Seaver was the archetype of the modern power pitcher. He made his big league debut immediately after Sandy Koufax retired, and within three years he had joined the corps of great power pitchers of the 1960s like Don Drysdale, Bob Gibson, Jim Maloney, Jim Bunning, Juan Marichal, Bob Veale, and Sam McDowell. Seaver had better control than all of them except

Marichal, and he clearly thought about the art of pitching in a very rigorous way.

The game in which Mathewson and Seaver pitched was fundamentally different. Scoring was much higher in Seaver's era, and the bullpens of the 1970s and 1980s were certainly more important than before World War II, so Seaver might expect to finish only about half the games he started.

As Seaver said, "You always have to throw more pitches when you walk batters. Even if they don't score, you are making pitches that you could save for key situations late in the ballgame."

While the game of 1970 was very different than the game of 1910, there is very little difference between Mathewson's "pitching in a pinch" and the following quote from Seaver:

"A game may ride on just three or four pitches that the pitcher must choose carefully and throw with accuracy . . . [Y]ou can train yourself to identify the outs that you *must* get, and within the bounds of sportsmanship, go about getting them." Sage advice, indeed.

This Pitcher Register chronicles the changes in pitching throughout baseball history, as shown by the records of the practitioners of the art. It allows for meaningful comparisons between Mathewson and Seaver, between Walter Johnson and Roger Clemens—the kind of reflection and analysis that adds so much to our understanding of the National Pastime.

BIOGRAPHICAL INFORMATION

There are 7,469 pitchers in this Pitcher Register, of which 311 are also in the Batter Register. In order for a pitcher to be included in the batter register, he must have one season of 10 or more games where pitcher was not his prime position, or he must have 150 more career games played than games pitched. In order for a batter to be shown in the pitcher register, he must have at least 9 career innings pitched (as well as more games at another position than pitcher).

More details on many of the statistics and formulas shown in this register can be found in the glossary at the end of the encyclopedia.

Every pitcher has (at least) a last name and a debut date. If an Hispanic pitcher has a matronymic name, it is placed in parentheses—for example, Marichal, Juan Antonio (Sanchez). Commonly used nicknames are also included on the biograph-ical line; if a player was primarily known by his nickname dur-ing his career, it will be part of his listed name—such as Waddell, Rube. Other features and abbreviations for biograph-ical information follow.

B (mm.dd.yyyy) is the place and date of birth.

D (mm.dd.yyyy) is the date and place of death.

The arm a pitcher threw with is expressed *TR* (throws right) or *TL* (throws left). The side of the plate a pitcher bats from is expressed *BR* (bats right), *BL* (bats left), or *BB* (bats both sides). In rare cases when a pitcher throws with both hands during a season, *TB* (throws both) is used and the sea-son is included in parentheses. (The only pitcher to do this since 1901 is Greg A. Harris, who threw with both hands in one game in 1995.)

Height is shown by feet followed by inches. Weight is expressed in pounds. Many pitchers after 1950 now have expan-ded information about their playing weights; see page 6 in the Batter Register introduction for details.

Pitchers selected in the annual amateur/first-year player drafts since 1965 now have their draft information shown in their biographical line. See page 6 in the Batter Register intro-duction for complete details.

Debuts are marked *d,* followed by the date the pitcher made his first major league appearance. The debut year is the first year listed in the register, so it is not included in the biog-raphical line.

Besides these basic pieces of information available in the biographical line, there are several other designations for play-ers whose career, family, or duty took them beyond the norm.

If a pitcher on a major league roster missed significant parts of any season serving the United States during wartime, the following abbreviations are used to identify how the player served:

Mil indicates military service in the army, navy, air force, or marines;

Mer indicates the merchant marine;

Def indicates defense plant work.

The seasons the pitcher missed at least a part of are listed after the abbreviation for duty. At least one major leaguer missed time during the seasons below as a result of the following wars (dates include post-war service by some veterans):

Spanish-American War, 1898;

World War I, 1917–19;

World War II, 1941–46;

Korean War 1951–59;

Vietnam War 1962–72.

Negro Lg indicates years spent playing in big-league caliber Negro Leagues prior to playing in the major leagues. If a former Negro League player also served in the military during wartime, his military service will be shown even if it predates his major league debut.

If the pitcher spent time as a coach, manager, or umpire, that is indicated by the following symbols, which are followed by the number of seasons during which he performed those jobs. Abbreviations are:

C: Coach;

M: Manager;

U: Umpire.

HF indicates that the player is a member of the Hall of Fame; the year of election follows *HF*.

If the player had a close family member in the major leagues, the relative's relationship is identified by the codes listed below followed by the relative's first name (and, if it is different, the last name):

b: brother;

twb: twin brother;

f: father;

s: son;

gf: grandfather;

gs: grandson;

ggf: great grandfather;

ggs: great grandson.

Col indicates that the player played collegiate baseball at the university, college, or junior college shown. (See Batter Register introduction for full explanation.)

▲ at the end of the biographical information indicates that the pitcher is also listed in the Batter Register.

STATISTICAL INFORMATION

Symbols for the first two columns:

† before the team name means the pitcher participated in postseason play that season;

★ after team name means that the pitcher participated in the All-Star Game;

☆ after team name means that the pitcher was selected to the All-Star team that season but did not play;

✳ after team name means that the pitcher was selected to the All-Star team but replaced due to injury.

Boldface statistics in any category indicates a league-leading total or average.

The columns that appear in the pitcher register after **Year**:

TM: Team. Each team is identified by a three-letter code that is usually the first three letters of the city, state, or area where the team is located.

LG: League. The leagues in this book include the National League (N), the American League (A), the Federal League (F), the Players League (P), the Union Association (U), the National Association (NA) and the American Association (AA).

W: Wins.

L: Losses.

PCT: Winning Percentage. This is calculated by dividi wins by (wins plus losses).

G: Games.

GS: Games Started.

CG: Complete Games.

SHO: Shutouts.

SV: Saves. This became an official statistic in 1969. Sav are calculated based on the official definition of saves at t time. Saves before 1969 are based on how many winning gam a relief pitcher finished for his team without getting a win.

BS: Blown Saves. From 1969–present, the number of tim a pitcher entered the game in a save situation and allowed t opposing team to tie the game or take the lead.

IP: Innings Pitched. Exact innings pitched, including thir of an inning, are available for all of baseball history, but thir were not included in official innings pitched totals until 1982.

H: Hits Allowed.

R: Runs Allowed. This includes unearned runs.

HR: Home Runs Allowed.

HB: Hit Batsmen. The rule awarding first base to batte hit by pitches was instituted in 1884 by the American Associ tion. It was adopted in 1887 by the National League.

BB: Bases On Balls Allowed. Generally referred to toda as walks.

IB: Intentional Walks Allowed. Walking an opponent o purpose was first counted as a distinct category in 1955.

SO: Strikeouts. Unlike batter strikeouts, these are avai able for all pitchers in all seasons.

ERA: Earned Run Average. ERA is calculated by dividin earned runs by innings pitched and multiplying by 9.

AERA: Adjusted Earned Run Average. AERA is calculate by normalizing ERA for the context of the offensive level o the league and the player's home park(s) and converting to scale in which 100 is average.

OAV: Opponents Batting Average. Hits allowed divided b opponent at bats.

OOB: Opponents On-Base Percentage.

AB: At Bats. At Bats by the pitcher as a batter.

HR: Home Runs. Home runs hit by the pitcher while battin

SH: Sacrifice Hits. Sacrifice hits by the pitcher. (Sacrific flies were counted as sacrifice hits from 1908–30 and in 1939.

AVG: Average. The pitcher's batting average. No average listed if he did not have an official at bat for a season or a caree

PB: Pitcher Batting Runs. Pitcher batting runs are calcu lated exactly the same way as adjusted batting runs except tha the pitcher's offense is compared to the average offensive leve of a pitcher, not an everyday player. The symbol * appear after pitcher batting if the pitcher played in games in additio to the ones in which he pitched.

SUP: Run Support. This is calculated by dividing the tota number of runs scored for the pitcher's team(s) in his starts b the pitcher's total Games Started, normalizing the product fo the context of the offensive level of the league and the player home park(s), and converting to a scale in which 100 is average

APR: Adjusted Pitching Runs. How many runs the pitche allowed compared to the average pitcher. APR leaders ar bolded for both starters and relievers.

DL: Disabled List. Days spent on the DL during the regu lar season. (See the introduction to the Batter Register for fu explanation.)

PW: Pitcher Wins. This adds the pitcher's adjusted pitch ing wins, batting wins, and fielding wins to calculate how man wins the pitcher added to or subtracted from his team com pared to what the average pitcher would have done.

AR TM LG	W	L	PCT	G	GS	CG-SHO	SV-BS	IP	H	R	HR	HB	BB-IB	SO	ERA	AERA	OAV	OOB	AB-HR-SH	AVG	PB	SUP	APR	DL	PW

AARDSMA, DAVID David Allan B12.27.1981 Denver CO BR/TR/6-5/200 d4.6 Col Rice

AR TM LG	W	L	PCT	G	GS	CG-SHO	SV-BS	IP	H	R	HR	HB	BB-IB	SO	ERA	AERA	OAV	OOB	AB-HR-SH	AVG	PB	SUP	APR	DL	PW
04 SF N	1	0	1.000	11	0	0	0-1	10.2	20	8	1	2	10-0	5	6.75	64	.417	.525	0	—	0		-3		-0.2

ASE, DON Donald William B9.8.1954 Orange CA BR/TR/6-3/210(185-222) [BosA72 6/136] d7.26 [DL 1983 Cal A 182]

AR TM LG	W	L	PCT	G	GS	CG-SHO	SV-BS	IP	H	R	HR	HB	BB-IB	SO	ERA	AERA	OAV	OOB	AB-HR-SH	AVG	PB	SUP	APR	DL	PW
77 Bos A	6	2	.750	13	13	4-2	0-0	92.1	85	36	6	1	19-1	49	3.12	144	.244	.283	0	—	0	80	12		1.0
78 Cal A	11	8	.579	29	29	6-1	0-0	178.2	185	88	14	2	80-4	93	4.03	90	.270	.348	0	—	0	125	-7		-0.7
†79 Cal A	9	10	.474	37	28	7-1	2-1	185.1	200	104	19	1	77-7	96	4.81	85	.277	.344	0	—	0	121	-13		-1.3
80 Cal A	8	13	.381	40	21	5-1	2-2	175	193	83	13	1	66-3	74	4.06	97	.287	.347	0	—	0	69	0		-0.1
81 Cal A	4	4	.500	39	0	0	11-0	65.1	56	17	4	0	24-2	38	2.34	157	.234	.303	0	—	0	11			1.7
82 Cal A	3	3	.500	24	0	0	4-4	52	45	20	5	0	23-2	40	3.46	118	.243	.327	0	—	0	4		73	0.5
84 Cal A	4	1	.800	23	0	0	8-5	39	30	7	1	0	19-5	28	1.62	247	.221	.312	0	—	0	11		72	1.7
85 Bal A	10	6	.625	54	0	0	14-5	88	83	44	6	1	35-7	67	3.78	107	.258	.330	0	—	0	11			1.0
86 Bal A★	6	7	.462	66	0	0	34-9	81.2	71	29	6	1	28-2	67	2.98	140	.234	.296	0	—	0	11			2.3
87 Bal A	1	0	1.000	7	0	0	2-0	8	8	2	1	0	4-0	3	2.25	197	.276	.364	0	—	0	2		159	0.3
88 Bal A	0	0	—	35	0	0	0-1	46.2	40	22	4	0	37-5	28	4.05	97	.240	.374	0	—	0	0		36	0.0
89 NY N	1	5	.167	49	0	0	2-1	59.1	56	27	5	1	26-3	34	3.94	84	.245	.320	5	.000	-1		-4		-0.4
90 LA N	3	1	.750	32	0	0	3-1	31	34	24	5	0	19-4	24	4.97	74	.232	.323	0	—	0		-6	47	-0.7
total 13	66	60	.524	448	91	22-5	82-29	1109.1	1085	503	89	7	457-45	641	3.80	104	.259	.331	5	.000	-1	104	22	569	4.5

BBEY, BERT Bert Wood B11.29.1869 Essex VT D6.11.1962 Essex Junction VT BR/TR/5-11/175 d6.14 Col Vermont

AR TM LG	W	L	PCT	G	GS	CG-SHO	SV-BS	IP	H	R	HR	HB	BB-IB	SO	ERA	AERA	OAV	OOB	AB-HR-SH	AVG	PB	SUP	APR	DL	PW
92 Was N	5	18	.217	27	22	19	1	195.2	207	139	7	6	76	77	3.45	94	.261	.330	75	.120	-3	88	-7		-0.9
93 Chi N	2	4	.333	7	7	5	0	56	74	52	1	4	20	6	5.46	85	.308	.371	26	.231	-0	97	-6		-0.5
94 Chi N	2	7	.222	11	11	10	0	92	119	74	3	3	37	24	5.18	109	.310	.375	39-0-2	.128	-5	75	5		-0.1
95 Chi N	0	1	.000	1	1	1	0	8	10	8	0	1	2	3	4.50	113	.303	.361	3	.333		42	0		0.0
Bro N	5	2	.714	8	6	5	0	52	66	34	0	3	9	14	4.33	102	.304	.341	19	.263	1	111	0		0.1
Year	5	3	.625	9	7	6	0	60	76	42	0	4	11	17	4.35	103	.304	.343	22	.273	1	100	1		0.1
96 Bro N	8	8	.500	25	18	12	0	164.1	210	135	7	9	48	37	5.15	80	.308	.361	63-0-4	.190	-1	109	-21		-1.6
total 5	22	40	.355	79	65	52	1	568	686	442	18	26	192	161	4.52	92	.292	.352	225-0-6	.169	-8	94	-29		-3.0

BBOTT, JIM James Anthony B9.19.1967 Flint MI BL/TL/6-3/210* [CalA88 1/8] d4.8 Col Michigan

AR TM LG	W	L	PCT	G	GS	CG-SHO	SV-BS	IP	H	R	HR	HB	BB-IB	SO	ERA	AERA	OAV	OOB	AB-HR-SH	AVG	PB	SUP	APR	DL	PW
89 Cal A	12	12	.500	29	29	4-2	0-0	181.1	190	95	13	4	74-3	115	3.92	98	.274	.345	0	—	0	98	-6		-0.7
90 Cal A	10	14	.417	33	33	4-1	0-0	211.2	246	116	16	5	72-6	105	4.51	85	.295	.353	0	—	0	94	-13		-1.3
91 Cal A	18	11	.621	34	34	5-1	0-0	243	222	85	14	5	73-6	158	2.89	143	.244	.302	0	—	0	93	33		4.0
92 Cal A	7	15	.318	29	29	7	0-0	211	208	73	12	4	68-3	130	2.77	145	.263	.323	0	—	0	58	28	27	2.9
93 NY A	11	14	.440	32	32	4-1	0-0	214	221	115	22	3	73-4	95	4.37	96	.271	.332	0	—	0	103	-5	15	-0.5
94 NY A	9	8	.529	24	24	2	0-0	160.1	167	88	24	2	64-1	90	4.55	101	.273	.341	0	—	0	101	1		0.1
95 Chi A	6	4	.600	17	17	3	0-0	112.1	116	50	10	1	35-1	45	3.36	133	.269	.324	0	—	0	116	13		1.0
Cal A	5	4	.556	13	13	1-1	0-0	84.2	93	43	4	1	29-0	41	4.15	114	.280	.337	0	—	0	84	5		0.5
Year	11	8	.579	30	30	4-1	0-0	197	209	93	14	2	64-1	86	3.70	124	.274	.330	0	—	0	102	16		1.5
96 Cal A	2	18	.100	27	23	1	0-0	142	171	128	23	4	78-3	58	7.48	68	.306	.389	0	—	0	65	-36		-3.9
98 Chi A	5	0	1.000	5	5	0	0-0	31.2	35	16	2	1	12-0	14	4.55	101	.292	.358	0	—	0	166	1		0.2
99 Mil N	2	8	.200	20	15	0	0-0	82	110	71	14	2	42-3	37	6.91	67	.317	.389	21-0-3	.095	-1	95	-22		-2.2
total 10	87	108	.446	263	254	31-6	0-0	1674	1779	880	154	32	620-30	888	4.25	100	.276	.340	21-0-3	.095	-1	92	-1	42	0.1

BBOTT, KYLE Lawrence Kyle B2.18.1968 Newburyport MA BL/TL/6-4/200(195-215) [CalA89 1/9] d9.10 Col Cal St.-Long Beach

AR TM LG	W	L	PCT	G	GS	CG-SHO	SV-BS	IP	H	R	HR	HB	BB-IB	SO	ERA	AERA	OAV	OOB	AB-HR-SH	AVG	PB	SUP	APR	DL	PW
91 Cal A	1	2	.333	5	4	0	0-0	19.2	22	11	4	1	13-0	12	4.58	90	.301	.414	0	—	0	52	-1		-0.1
92 Phi N	1	14	.067	31	19	0	0-0	133.1	147	80	20	1	45-0	88	5.13	68	.283	.338	29-0-6	.069	-1	83	-22		-2.5
95 Phi N	2	0	1.000	18	0	0	0-0	28.1	28	12	3	0	16-0	21	3.81	111	.267	.361	2	.500	0	2		70	0.2
96 Cal A	0	1	.000	3	0	0	0-1	4	10	9	1	0	5-0	3	20.25	25	.500	.600	0	—	0		-6		-1.0
total 4	4	17	.190	57	22	0	0-1	185.1	207	112	28	2	79-0	124	5.20	72	.288	.358	31-0-6	.097	-1	75	-27	70	-3.4

BBOTT, DAN Leander Franklin "Big Dan" B3.16.1862 Portage OH D2.13.1930 Ottawa Lake MI BR/TR/5-11/190 d4.19

AR TM LG	W	L	PCT	G	GS	CG-SHO	SV-BS	IP	H	R	HR	HB	BB-IB	SO	ERA	AERA	OAV	OOB	AB-HR-SH	AVG	PB	SUP	APR	DL	PW
90 Tol AA	0	2	.000	3	1	1	0	13	19	14	0	1	8	1	6.23	63	.328	.418	7	.143	0	102	-9		-0.4

BBOTT, PAUL Paul David B9.15.1967 Van Nuys CA BR/TR/6-3/195(185-205) [MinA85 3/67] d8.21

AR TM LG	W	L	PCT	G	GS	CG-SHO	SV-BS	IP	H	R	HR	HB	BB-IB	SO	ERA	AERA	OAV	OOB	AB-HR-SH	AVG	PB	SUP	APR	DL	PW
90 Min A	0	5	.000	7	7	0	0-0	34.2	37	24	0	1	28-0	25	5.97	70	.282	.410	0	—	0	75	-6		-0.8
91 Min A	3	1	.750	15	3	0	0-0	47.1	38	27	5	0	36-1	43	4.75	90	.232	.365	0	—	0	85	-2		-0.2
92 Min A	0	0	—	6	0	0	0-0	11	12	4	1	1	5-0	13	3.27	125	.279	.360	0	—	0	1		78	0.1
93 Cle A	0	1	.000	5	5	0	0-0	18.1	19	15	5	0	11-1	7	6.38	69	.260	.357	0	—	0	92	-4		-0.2
98 Sea A	3	1	.750	4	4	0	0-0	24.2	24	11	2	0	10-0	22	4.01	117	.255	.324	0	—	0	164	2		0.3
99 Sea A	6	2	.750	25	7	0	0-2	72.2	50	31	9	0	32-3	68	3.10	155	.193	.278	0	—	0	100	12		1.1
00 †Sea A	9	7	.563	35	27	0	0-0	179	164	89	23	5	80-4	100	4.22	114	.243	.325	5-0-1	.400	1	95	13		1.0
01 †Sea A	17	4	.810	28	27	1	0-0	163	145	79	21	7	87-5	118	4.25	100	.238	.338	4-0-1	.250	0	155	2	27	0.2
02 Sea A	1	3	.250	7	5	0	0-0	26.1	40	36	5	4	20-0	22	11.96	36	.351	.449	0	—	0	116	-23	147	-2.4
03 KC A	1	2	.333	10	8	0	0-0	47.2	47	29	8	2	26-2	32	5.29	91	.257	.354	0	—	0	105	-2		-0.1
04 TB A	2	5	.286	10	9	0	0-0	47	49	39	8	3	27-0	25	6.70	70	.257	.356	0	—	0	66	-11		-1.3
Phi N	1	6	.143	10	10	0	0-0	49	57	37	14	1	31-1	21	6.24	71	.291	.390	11-0-3	.182	-0	54	-10		-1.2
total 11	43	37	.538	162	112	1	0-2	720.2	682	421	101	21	393-17	496	4.92	92	.250	.346	20-0-5	.250	1	106	-28	252	-3.5

BBOTT, GLENN William Glenn B2.16.1951 Little Rock AR BR/TR/6-6/200(195-210) [OakA69 8/175] d7.29 Col Central Arkansas [DL 1982 Sea A 182]

AR TM LG	W	L	PCT	G	GS	CG-SHO	SV-BS	IP	H	R	HR	HB	BB-IB	SO	ERA	AERA	OAV	OOB	AB-HR-SH	AVG	PB	SUP	APR	DL	PW
973 Oak A	1	0	1.000	5	3	1	0-0	18.2	16	8	3	0	7-0	6	3.86	92	.225	.291	0	—	0	159	0		0.0
974 Oak A	5	7	.417	19	17	3	0-0	96	89	38	4	3	34-3	38	3.00	111	.247	.316	0	—	0	90	4		0.4
975 †Oak A	5	5	.500	30	15	3-1	0-0	114.1	109	61	12	2	50-7	51	4.25	86	.253	.330	0	—	0	129	-8		-0.6
976 Oak A	2	4	.333	19	10	0	0-0	62.1	87	41	6	1	16-0	27	5.49	61	.333	.371	0	—	0	93	-6		-0.7
977 Sea A	12	13	.480	36	34	7	0-0	204.1	212	111	32	12	56-2	100	4.45	93	.270	.327	0	—	0	93	-6		-0.7
978 Sea A	7	15	.318	29	28	8-1	0-0	155.1	191	99	22	2	44-5	67	5.27	73	.303	.349	0	—	0	83	-23	20	-2.8
979 Sea A	4	10	.286	23	19	3	0-0	116.2	138	78	19	3	38-2	25	5.17	85	.301	.351	0	—	0	90	-11	20	-1.2
980 Sea A	12	12	.500	31	31	7-2	0-0	215	228	110	27	3	49-4	78	4.10	102	.272	.314	0	—	0	96	1		0.2
981 Sea A	4	9	.308	22	20	1	0-0	130.1	127	64	14	0	28-1	35	3.94	99	.258	.296	0	—	0	88	-1		-0.1
983 Sea A	5	3	.625	14	14	2	0-0	82.1	103	46	9	4	15-2	38	4.59	93	.311	.347	0	—	0	103	-2	66	-0.2
Det A	2	1	.667	7	7	1	1-1	46.2	43	12	5	0	7-1	11	1.93	205	.244	.272	0	—	0	69	10		0.6
Year	7	4	.636	21	21	3-1	0-0	129	146	58	14	4	22-3	49	3.63	115	.288	.321	0	—	0	92	8		0.4
984 Det A	3	4	.429	13	8	1	0-0	44	62	39	9	2	15-0	8	5.93	67	.326	.356	0	—	0	111	-12		-1.7
total 11	62	83	.428	248	206	37-5	0-0	1286	1405	707	162	32	352-28	484	4.39	90	.280	.328	0	—	0	96	-62	288	-7.4

ABER, AL Albert Julius "Lefty" B7.31.1927 Cleveland OH D5.20.1993 Garfield Heights OH BL/TL/6-2/195* d9.15 Mil 1951-52

AR TM LG	W	L	PCT	G	GS	CG-SHO	SV-BS	IP	H	R	HR	HB	BB-IB	SO	ERA	AERA	OAV	OOB	AB-HR-SH	AVG	PB	SUP	APR	DL	PW
950 Cle A	1	0	1.000	1	1	1	0	7	5	2	0	0	4	2	2.00	217	.167	.265	2	.000	0	83	3		0.3
953 Cle A	1	1	.500	6	0	0	0	6	6	6	0	0	9	4	7.50	50	.240	.441	0	—	1		-3		-0.5
Det A	4	3	.571	17	10	1	0	66.2	63	35	3	0	41	34	4.45	91	.260	.367	23-0-1	.130	-1	122	-2		-0.3
Year	5	4	.556	23	10	2	0	72.2	69	41	3	0	50	38	4.71	86	.258	.375	23-0-1	.130	-1	123	-5		-0.8
954 Det A	5	11	.313	32	18	4	3	124.2	121	63	8	3	40	54	3.97	93	.257	.318	39-0-3	.128	0	86	-4		-0.6
955 Det A	6	3	.667	39	1	0	3	80	86	32	9	0	28-1	37	3.37	114	.275	.334	17-0-2	.059	-2	116	5		0.4
956 Det A	4	4	.500	42	0	0	7	63	65	30	1	2	25-6	21	3.43	120	.270	.341	10-0-2	.300	1		4		0.5
957 Det A	3	3	.500	28	0	0	1	37	46	33	6	1	11-3	15	6.81	57	.315	.363	8	.125	-0		-13		-1.9
KC A	0	0	—	3	0	0	0	3	6	4	0	0	2-0	0	12.00	33	.400	.471	1	1.000	0		-2		-0.1
Year	3	3	.500	31	0	0	1	40	52	37	8	1	13-3	15	7.20	54	.323	.373	9	.222	0		-16		-2.0
Total 6	24	25	.490	168	30	7	14	389.1	398	205	29	6	160-10	169	4.18	93	.269	.341	100-0-8	.140	-3	99	-12		-2.2

ABERNATHIE, BILL William Edward B1.30.1929 Torrance CA BR/TR/5-10/190 d9.27

AR TM LG	W	L	PCT	G	GS	CG-SHO	SV-BS	IP	H	R	HR	HB	BB-IB	SO	ERA	AERA	OAV	OOB	AB-HR-SH	AVG	PB	SUP	APR	DL	PW
1952 Cle A	0	0	—	1	0	0	0	2	4	3	1	0	1	0	13.50	25	.444	.500	1	.000	-0		-2		-0.2

ABERNATHY, TED Talmadge Lafayette B10.30.1921 Mebane NC D11.16.2001 Charlotte NC BR/TL/6-2/210 d9.19 Col Elon

AR TM LG	W	L	PCT	G	GS	CG-SHO	SV-BS	IP	H	R	HR	HB	BB-IB	SO	ERA	AERA	OAV	OOB	AB-HR-SH	AVG	PB	SUP	APR	DL	PW
1942 Phi A	0	0	—	1	0	0	0	2.2	3	2	0	0	3	1	10.13	37	.222	.417	0	—	0		-2		0.0
1943 Phi A	0	3	.000	5	2	1	0	14.2	24	22	0	0	13	10	12.89	26	.353	.457	4	.250	0	62	-14		-2.2
1944 Phi A	0	0	—	1	0	0	0	3	5	1	0	0	1	2	3.00	116	.417	.462	1	.000	0		0		0.0
Total 3	0	3	.000	7	2	1	0	20.1	31	26	0	0	17	13	11.07	31	.348	.453	5	.200	0	62	-16		-2.2

YEAR	TM LG	W	L	PCT	G	GS	CG-SHO	SV-BS	IP	H	R	HR	HB	BB-IB	SO	ERA	AERA	OAV	OOB	AB-HR-SH	AVG	PB	SUP	APR	DL	Pl

ABERNATHY, TED Theodore Wade B3.6.1933 Stanley NC D12.16.2004 Gastonia NC BR/TR/6-4/215* d4.13

1955	Was A	5	9	.357	40	14	3-2	0	119.1	136	87	9	7	67-1	79	5.96	64	.294	.386	26-0-4	.154	-1	78	-28		-2.1
1956	Was A	1	3	.250	5	4	2	0	30.1	35	16	2	1	10-0	18	4.15	104	.292	.348	11	.182	-0	57	1		0.
1957	Was A	2	10	.167	26	16	2	0	85	100	65	9	4	65-1	50	6.78	57	.314	.433	24-0-2	.167	0	69	-24		-2.
1960	Was A	0	0	—	2	0	0	0	3	4	4	0	0	4-0	1	12.00	32	.308	.471	1	1.000	0		-2		-0.
1963	Cle A	7	2	.778	43	0	0	12	59.1	54	25	3	0	29-6	31	2.88	126	.251	.339	5-0-1	.400	1		3		0.9
1964	Cle A	2	6	.250	53	0	0	11	72.2	66	40	5	2	46-5	57	4.33	83	.247	.360	6-0-1	.000	-1		-6		-0.8
1965	Chi N	4	6	.400	84	0	0	31	136.1	113	49	7	5	56-13	104	2.57	143	.227	.309	18-0-3	.167	0		15		2.
1966	Chi N	1	3	.250	20	0	0	4	27.2	26	19	4	2	17-1	18	6.18	60	.255	.372	4	.000	-0		-6		-1.0
	Atl N	4	4	.500	38	0	0	4	65.1	58	34	5	0	36-10	42	3.86	94	.247	.343	8	.250	1		-3		-0.2
	Year	5	7	.417	58	0	0	8	93	84	53	9	2	53-11	60	4.55	80	.249	.352	12	.167	0		-10		-1.2
1967	Cin N	6	3	.667	70	0	0	28	106.1	63	19	1	5	41-5	88	1.27	295	.170	.261	17	.059	-1		26		3.8
1968	Cin N	10	7	.588	78	0	0	13	135.1	111	43	9	4	55-15	64	2.46	128	.228	.307	17	.000	-1		10		1.6
1969	Chi N	4	3	.571	56	0	0	3-3	85.1	75	38	7	1	42-11	55	3.16	127	.234	.322	8	.250	-1		6		0.6
1970	Chi N	0	0	—	11	0	0	1-0	9	9	2	0	1	5-1	2	2.00	225	.281	.395	0	—	0		2		0.1
	StL N	1	0	1.000	11	0	0	1-2	18.1	15	6	0	3	12-4	8	2.95	141	.246	.353	3	.000	-0		3		0.2
	Year	1	0	1.000	22	0	0	2-2	27.1	24	8	0	4	17-5	10	2.63	162	.258	.388	3	.000	-0		5		0.3
	KC A	3	1	.750	36	0	0	12-3	55.2	41	23	3	1	38-0	49	2.59	144	.209	.340	14-0-3	.214	0		5		1.1
1971	KC A	4	6	.400	63	0	0	23-4	81	60	28	3	6	50-4	55	2.56	135	.210	.336	13-0-1	.077	-1		7		1.3
1972	KC A	3	4	.429	45	0	0	5-5	58.1	44	15	2	3	19-3	28	1.70	179	.210	.282	6	.000	-1		7		1.1
Total	14	63	69	.477	681	34	7-2	148-17	1148.1	1010	513	70	45	592-80	765	3.46	106	.241	.338	181-0-15	.138	-4	75	16		5.0

ABERNATHY, WOODY Virgil Woodrow B2.1.1915 Forest City NC D12.5.1994 Louisville KY BL/TL/6-0/170 d7.28

1946	NY N	1	1	.500	15	1	0	1	40	32	16	5	0	10	6	3.37	102	.232	.284	8	.000	-1	100	1		-0.1
1947	NY N	0	0		1	0	0	0	2	4	3	0	0	1	0	9.00	45	.400	.455	0		0		-1		0.0
Total	2	1	1	.500	16	1	0	1	42	36	19	5	0	11	6	3.64	95	.243	.296	8	.000	-1	100	0		-0.2

ABLES, HARRY Harry Terrell "Hans" B10.4.1884 Terrell TX D2.8.1951 San Antonio TX BR/TL/6-2.5/200 d9.4 Col Southwestern (TX)

1905	StL A	0	3	.000	6	3	1	0	30.2	37	22	0	0	13	11	3.82	67	.301	.368	10	.000	-1	37	-6		-0.7
1909	Cle A	1	1	.500	5	3	3	0	29.2	26	14	1	1	10	24	2.12	120	.226	.294	12	.000	-1	119	0		-0.2
1911	NY A	0	1	.000	3	2	0	0	11	16	15	1	0	7	6	9.82	37	.333	.418	4	.000	-1	140	-7		-0.6
Total	3	1	5	.167	14	8	4	0	71.1	79	51	2	1	30	41	4.04	67	.276	.347	26	.000	-4	102	-13		-1.5

ABRAMS, GEORGE George Allen B11.9.1899 Seattle WA D12.5.1986 Clearwater FL BR/TR/5-9/170 d4.19

| 1923 | Cin N | 0 | 0 | — | 3 | 0 | 0 | 0 | 4.2 | 10 | 5 | 0 | 1 | 3 | 1 | 9.64 | 40 | .500 | .583 | 1 | 1.000 | 0 | | -3 | | -0.1 |

ABREGO, JOHNNY Johnny Ray B7.4.1962 Corpus Christi TX BR/TR/6-0/185 [PhiN81 1/20] d9.4

| 1985 | Chi N | 1 | 1 | .500 | 6 | 5 | 0 | 0-0 | 24 | 32 | 18 | 3 | 0 | 12-1 | 13 | 6.38 | 63 | .352 | .423 | 1 | .000 | -1 | 133 | -5 | | -0.5 |

ACCARDO, JEREMY Jeremy Lee B12.8.1981 Phoenix AZ BR/TR/6-2/190 d5.4 Col Illinois St.

| 2005 | SF N | 1 | 5 | .167 | 28 | 0 | 0 | 0-0 | 26 | 13 | 2 | 1 | 9-1 | 16 | 3.94 | 108 | .232 | .293 | 2 | .500 | 0 | | 1 | | 0.2 |

ACEVEDO, JOSE Jose Omar B12.18.1977 Santo Domingo, D.R. BR/TR/6-0/185* d6.19

2001	Cin N	5	7	.417	18	18	0	0-0	96	101	61	17	3	34-2	68	5.44	84	.272	.336	34-0-2	.118	-1	113	-7		-0.9
2002	Cin N	4	2	.667	6	5	0	0-0	23.2	28	21	8	2	12-0	14	7.23	59	.292	.382	7-0-2	.143	0	82	-7		-1.3
2003	Cin N	2	0	1.000	5	4	1	0-0	27	17	8	3	1	6-1	23	2.67	156	.183	.235	9-0-2	.000	-1	141	5	53	0.2
2004	Cin N	5	12	.294	39	27	0	0-0	157.2	188	108	30	5	45-8	117	5.94	72	.292	.340	43-0-5	.047	-3	102	-27		-2.8
2005	Col N	2	4	.333	36	5	0	1-1	64	86	48	13	1	16-3	31	6.47	74	.321	.355	8-0-1	.125	1	70	-10	49	-0.9
Total	5	18	25	.419	104	59	1	1-1	368.1	420	246	71	12	113-14	253	5.74	77	.285	.338	101-0-12	.079	-4	103	-46	102	-5.7

ACEVEDO, JUAN Juan Carlos (Lara) B5.5.1970 Ciudad Juarez, Chihuahua, Mexico BR/TR/6-2/228(195-243) [ColN92 14/403] d4.30 Col Parkland (IL) JC [DL 1996 NY N 38]

1995	Col N	4	6	.400	17	11	0	0-0	65.2	82	53	15	6	20-2	40	6.44	83	.317	.376	18	.056	-2	84	-7		-1.0
1997	NY N	3	1	.750	25	2	0	0-4	47.2	52	24	6	4	22-2	33	3.59	112	.286	.366	6-0-1	.000	-1	184	1		0.0
1998	StL N	8	3	.727	50	9	0	15-1	98.1	83	30	7	4	29-2	56	2.56	164	.236	.301	17-0-2	.176	-3	90	19	29	2.5
1999	StL N	6	8	.429	50	12	0	4-2	102.1	115	71	17	4	48-3	52	5.89	78	.291	.369	20-0-2	.050	-2	115	-13		-1.9
2000	Mil N	3	7	.300	62	0	0	0-2	82.2	77	38	11	1	31-9	51	3.81	121	.246	.315	1	.000	0		8	22	0.8
2001	Col N	2	0	.000	39	0	0	0-5	32	37	24	4	1	19-6	26	5.63	95	.285	.377	0	—	0		-2	40	-0.1
	Fla N	2	3	.400	20	0	0	0-0	28.1	31	11	2	1	16-3	21	2.54	164	.284	.375	3-0-1	.333	1		4		0.7
	Year	2	5	.286	59	0	0	0-5	60.1	68	35	6	2	35-9	47	4.18	115	.285	.376	3-0-1	.333	1		2		0.6
2002	Det A	1	5	.167	65	0	0	28-7	74.2	68	33	4	5	23-3	43	2.65	165	.246	.311	0	—	0		11		1.5
2003	NY A	0	3	.000	25	0	0	6-1	25.2	34	24	5	2	10-3	19	7.71	57	.315	.374	0	—	0		-10		-1.4
	Tor A	1	2	.333	14	0	0	0-1	12.2	18	8	1	0	8-1	9	4.26	111	.327	.413	0	—	0		0		0.0
	Year	1	5	.167	39	0	0	6-2	38.1	52	32	6	2	18-4	28	6.57	69	.319	.387	0	—	0		-9		-1.4
Total	8	28	40	.412	367	34	0	53-23	570	597	316	72	28	226-34	350	4.33	106	.274	.346	65-0-6	.092	-3	105	11	129	1.1

ACKER, JIM James Justin B9.24.1958 Freer TX BR/TR/6-2/212* [AtlN80 1/21] d4.7 Col Texas

1983	Tor A	5	1	.833	38	5	0	1-1	97.2	103	52	7	8	38-1	44	4.33	101	.273	.351	0	—	0	205	0		0.1
1984	Tor A	3	5	.375	32	3	0	1-2	72	79	39	6	4	25-3	33	4.38	95	.286	.357	0	—	0	73	-2	16	-0.2
1985	†Tor A	7	2	.778	61	0	0	10-3	86.1	86	35	7	3	43-1	42	3.23	131	.268	.358	0	—	0		9		1.1
1986	Tor A	2	4	.333	23	5	0	0-2	60	63	34	6	2	22-3	32	4.35	98	.281	.344	0	—	0	68	-2		-0.1
	Atl N	3	8	.273	21	14	0	0-1	95	100	47	7	4	26-3	37	3.79	105	.274	.321	28	.107	-1	58	1		0.5
1987	Atl N	4	9	.308	68	0	0	14-2	114.2	109	57	11	4	51-4	68	4.16	104	.253	.336	14	.214	0		3		0.5
1988	Atl N	0	4	.000	21	0	0	0-0	42	45	26	6	1	14-3	25	4.71	78	.280	.335	4	.400	1		-5	102	-0.4
1989	Atl N	0	6	.000	59	0	0	2-3	97.2	84	29	5	1	20-8	68	2.67	137	.237	.278	7	.143	-0		12		0.8
	†Tor A	2	1	.667	14	0	0	0-0	28.1	24	7	1	1	12-3	24	1.59	239	.235	.322	0	—	0		6		0.7
1990	Tor A	4	4	.500	59	0	0	1-1	91.2	103	49	9	3	30-5	54	3.83	103	.281	.340	0	—	0		-2		-0.7
1991	†Tor A	3	5	.375	54	0	0	1-2	88.1	77	53	16	2	36-5	44	5.20	81	.238	.313	0	—	0	114	-8		-0.7
1992	Sea A	0	0	—	17	0	0	0-0	32	45	19	4	0	12-1	11	5.28	76	.338	.388	0	—	0		-4	36	-0.2
Total	10	33	49	.402	467	32	0	30-17	904.1	918	447	82	32	329-40	482	3.97	103	.267	.334	54	.167	0	91	8	154	1.5

ACKER, TOM Thomas James B3.7.1930 Paterson NJ BR/TR/6-4/215* d4.20

1956	Cin N	4	3	.571	29	7	1-1	1	83.2	60	23	7	2	29-1	54	2.37	168	.201	.272	19	.053	-1	139	15		1.1
1957	Cin N	10	5	.667	49	6	1	4	108.2	122	63	16	8	41-8	67	4.97	83	.293	.361	19-0-2	.053	-1	111	-9		-1.2
1958	Cin N	4	5	.571	38	10	3	1	124.2	126	64	10	4	43-6	90	4.55	91	.266	.328	30-0-2	.067	-1	139	-3		-0.2
1959	Cin N	1	2	.333	37	0	0	2	63.1	57	31	10	4	37-5	45	4.12	98	.246	.356	9-0-2	.111	-0		0		-0.1
Total	4	19	15	.594	153	23	5-1	8	380.1	365	181	43	17	150-20	256	4.22	99	.257	.331	77-0-6	.065	-3	132	3		-0.6

ACKLEY, FRITZ Florian Frederick B4.10.1937 Hayward WI D5.22.2002 Duluth MN BL/TR/6-1.5/193* d9.21

1963	Chi A	1	0	1.000	2	2	0	0	13	7	2	0	0	7-0	11	2.08	169	.167	.280	5	.200	1	127	2		0.2
1964	Chi A	0	0	—	3	0	0	0	6.1	10	6	2	0	4-0	6	8.53	41	.345	.424	1	1.000	1	154	-3		0.0
Total	2	1	0	1.000	5	2	0	0	19.1	17	8	2	0	11-0	17	4.19	83	.239	.337	6	.333	1	140	-1		0.2

ACOSTA, CY Cecilio (Miranda) B11.22.1946 ElSabino, Sinaloa, Mexico BR/TR/5-10/165* d6.4

1972	Chi A	2	0	1.000	26	0	0	5-0	34.2	25	6	2	0	17-3	28	1.56	201	.210	.309	4	.000	-0		6		0.7
1973	Chi A	10	6	.625	48	0	0	18-4	97	66	30	8	7	39-3	60	2.23	178	.193	.287	0	.000	-0		17		3.3
1974	Chi A	0	3	.000	27	0	0	3-4	45.2	43	22	3	5	18-2	19	3.74	100	.256	.338	2	.000	0		0	44	0.1
1975	Phi N	0	0	—	6	0	0	1-0	8.2	9	7	2	0	3-0	2	6.23	140	.265	.333	1	—	0		-2		-0.1
Total	4	13	9	.591	107	0	0	27-8	186	143	65	15	12	77-8	109	2.66	141	.216	.306	7	.000	-1		21	44	3.9

ACOSTA, ED Eduardo Elixbet B3.9.1944 Boquete, Pan BB/TR/6-5/215* d9.7

1970	Pit N	0	0	—	3	0	0	1-0	2.2	5	4	1	0	2-0	1	13.50	29	.417	.500	0	—	0		-3		-0.2
1971	SD N	3	3	.500	8	6	3-1	0-0	46	43	18	4	0	7-1	16	2.74	121	.246	.272	17	.000	-2	80	2		0.1
1972	SD N	3	6	.333	46	2	0	0-1	89	105	49	7	3	30-7	53	4.45	74	.302	.358	12	.083	-0	147	-11		-1.2
Total	3	6	9	.400	57	8	3-1	1-1	137.2	153	71	12	4	39-8	70	4.05	82	.286	.334	29	.034	-2	96	-12		-1.3

YEAR	TM LG	W	L	PCT	G	GS	CG-SHO	SV-BS	IP	H	R	HR	HB	BB-IB	SO	ERA	AERA	OAV	OOB	AB-HR-SH	AVG	PB	SUP	APR	DL	PW

ACOSTA, JOSE Jose "Acostica" B3.4.1891 Havana, Cuba D11.16.1977 Havana, Cuba BR/TR/5-6/134 d7.28 b-Merito

1920	Was A	5	4	.556	17	5	4-1	1	82.2	92	40	1	0	26	9	4.03	93	.290	.344	25-0-2	.240	1	89	0		0.0
1921	Was A	5	4	.556	33	7		3	115.2	148	65	4	0	36	30	4.36	94	.317	.366	30-0-1	.067	-2	96	-2		-0.4
1922	Chi A	0	2	.000	5	1	0	0	15	25	14	4	0	6	6	8.40	48	.417	.470	5	.200	0	146	-6		-0.7
Total	3	10	10	.500	55	13	6-1	4	213.1	265	119	9	0	68	45	4.51	88	.314	.365	60-0-3	.150	-1	97	-8		-1.1

ACRE, MARK Mark Robert B9.16.1968 Concord CA BR/TR/6-8/240(235-246) d5.13 Col New Mexico St.

1994	Oak A	5	1	.833	34	0	0	0-1	34.1	24	13	4	1	23-3	21	3.41	132	.202	.333	0	—	0		5		0.7
1995	Oak A	1	2	.333	43	0	0	0-4	52	52	35	7	2	28-2	47	5.71	79	.256	.349	0	—	0		-7	22	-0.4
1996	Oak A	1	3	.250	22	0	0	2-1	25	38	17	4	0	9-4	18	6.12	81	.339	.398	0	—	0		-3		-0.4
1997	Oak A	2	0	1.000	15	0	0	0-2	15.2	21	10	1	0	8-0	12	5.74	80	.318	.387	0	—	0		-2		-0.2
Total	4	9	6	.600	114	0	0	2-8	135	135	75	16	5	68-9	98	5.17	89	.270	.360	0	—	0		-7	22	-0.3

ADAMS, ACE Ace Townsend B3.2.1912 Willows CA BR/TR/5-10.5/182 d4.15

1941	NY N	4	1	.800	38	0	0	1	71	84	43	3	1	35	18	4.82	77	.304	.385	12	.083	-1		-8		-0.7
1942	NY N	7	4	.636	61	0	0	11	88	69	23	1	0	31	33	1.84	183	.223	.293	10	.100	-1		14		2.1
1943	NY N☆	11	7	.611	70	3	1	9	140.1	121	50	5	1	55	46	2.82	122	.236	.311	32-0-2	.125	-1	189	9		1.1
1944	NY N	8	11	.421	65	4	1	13	137.2	149	71	8	4	58	32	4.25	86	.279	.354	29-0-4	.103	-2	63	-6		-1.2
1945	NY N	11	9	.550	65	0	0	15	113	109	55	7	2	44	39	3.42	114	.252	.324	16-0-2	.188	0		3		0.7
1946	NY N	0	0	—	3	0	0	0	2.2	9	5	2	0	1	3	16.88	20	.500	.526	0	—	0		-4		-0.7
Total	6	41	33	.554	302	7	2	49	552.2	541	247	26	8	224	171	3.47	104	.260	.334	99-0-8	.121	-4	114	8		1.3

ADAMS, BABE Charles Benjamin B5.18.1882 Tipton IN D7.27.1968 Silver Spring MD BL/TR/5-11.5/185 d4.18

1906	StL N	0	1	.000	1	1	0	0	4	9	8	0	0	2	0	13.50	19	.474	.524	1	.000	-0	28	-5		-0.7
1907	Pit N	0	2	.000	4	3	1	0	22	40	25	1	3	3	11	6.95	35	.408	.442	7	.286	0	68	-11		-0.9
1909	†Pit N	12	3	.800	25	12	7-3	2	130	88	25	0	3	23	65	1.11	246	.196	.240	39-0-5	.051	-3	88	21		2.3
1910	Pit N	18	9	.667	34	30	16-3	0	245	217	95	4	6	60	101	2.24	138	.240	.291	83-0-5	.193	1	126	18		1.7
1911	Pit N	22	12	.647	40	37	24-6	0	293.1	253	97	5	8	42	133	2.33	147	.237	.271	103-0-1	.252	4	103	35		3.9
1912	Pit N	11	8	.579	28	20	11-2	0	170.1	169	73	4	3	35	63	2.91	112	.262	.303	53-0-1	.226	4	104	6		0.9
1913	Pit N	21	10	.677	43	37	24-4	0	313.2	271	94	8	0	49	144	2.15	140	.235	.267	114-0-3	.289	9	113	33		4.1
1914	Pit N	13	16	.448	40	35	19-3	1	283	253	97	5	7	39	91	2.51	105	.244	.276	97-1-2	.165	1	96	6		0.5
1915	Pit N	14	14	.500	40	30	17-2	2	245	229	90	6	2	34	62	2.87	95	.252	.280	85-0-2	.141	-2	103	1		-0.2
1916	Pit N	2	9	.182	16	10	4-1	0	72.1	91	51	2	3	12	22	5.72	47	.320	.355	22-0-1	.273	2	64	-20		-2.6
1918	Pit N	1	1	.500	3	3	2	0	22.2	15	4	0	0	4	6	1.19	241	.197	.237	9	.333	1	61	4		0.5
1919	Pit N	17	10	.630	34	29	23-6	1	263.1	213	66	1	3	23	92	1.98	152	.220	.241	92-0-3	.185	-0	83	30		3.0
1920	Pit N	17	13	.567	35	33	19-8	2	263	240	83	6	1	18	84	2.16	149	.244	.259	89-1-2	.146	-5	74	28		2.5
1921	Pit N	14	5	.737	26	20	11-2	0	160	155	57	4	0	18	55	2.64	145	.272	.254	63-0-2	.254	3	122	20		2.5
1922	Pit N	8	11	.421	27	19	12-4	0	171.1	191	77	1	4	15	39	3.57	114	.287	.307	56-1-5	.286	4	102	12		1.5
1923	Pit N	13	7	.650	26	22	11	1	158.2	196	83	8	1	25	38	4.42	91	.309	.336	55-0-1	.273	5	112	-4		-0.1
1924	Pit N	3	1	.750	9	3	2	0	39.2	31	9	1	0	3	5	1.13	338	.209	.225	11-0-1	.182	-0	74	11		0.9
1925	†Pit N	6	5	.545	33	10	3	3	101.1	129	67	7	3	17	18	5.42	82	.306	.338	31-0-1	.226	0	104	-7		-0.8
1926	Pit N	2	3	.400	19	0	0	3	32	52	32	5	0	8	7	6.14	64	.347	.381	9	.222	-0		-9		-1.3
Total	19	194	140	.581	482	354	206-44	15	2995.1	2841	1133	68	47	430	1036	2.76	118	.253	.284	1019-3-35	.212	24	101	169		17.7

ADAMS, RED Charles Dwight B10.7.1921 Parlier CA BR/TR/6-0/185 d5.5 C12

| 1946 | Chi N | 0 | 1 | .000 | 8 | 0 | 0 | 0 | 12 | 18 | 12 | 1 | 0 | 7 | 8 | 8.25 | 40 | .353 | .431 | 1 | .000 | -0 | | -6 | | -0.5 |

ADAMS, DAN Daniel Leslie "Rube" B6.19.1887 St.Louis MO D10.6.1964 St.Louis MO BR/TR/5-11.5/165 d5.22

1914	KC F	4	9	.308	36	14	6	3	136	141	67	3	7	52	38	3.51	79	.273	.347	46-1-1	.152	-2	85	-10		-1.2
1915	KC F	0	2	.000	11	2	0	0	35	41	20	2	1	13	16	4.63	57	.301	.367	9	.111	-1	27	-7		-0.4
Total	2	4	11	.267	47	16	6	3	171	182	87	5	8	65	54	3.74	74	.279	.351	55-1-1	.145	-2	78	-17		-1.6

ADAMS, WILLIE James Irvin B9.27.1890 Clearfield PA D6.18.1937 Albany NY BR/TR/6-4/180 d6.30 Col Albright

1912	StL A	2	3	.400	13	5	0	0	46.1	50	32	0	2	19	16	3.88	85	.284	.360	13	.000	-2	67	-5		-0.7
1913	StL A	0	0	—	4	0	0	0	9	12	14	1	3	4	5	10.00	29	.293	.396	1	.000	0		-7		-0.4
1914	Pit F	1	1	.500	15	2	1	2	55.1	70	29	4	1	22	14	3.74	77	.326	.391	15	.067	-1	120	-5		-0.5
1918	Phi A	5	12	.294	32	14	7	0	169	164	95	2	12	97	39	4.42	66	.272	.383	57-0-1	.140	-3	57	-22		-2.4
1919	Phi A	0	0	—	1	0	0	0	4.2	7	2	1	1	2	0	3.86	89	.389	.476	2	.000	-0		0		0.0
Total	5	8	16	.333	65	21	8	2	284.1	303	172	8	19	144	74	4.37	69	.287	.383	88-0-1	.102	-6	66	-39		-4.0

ADAMS, MIKE Jon Michael B7.29.1978 Corpus Christi TX BR/TR/6-5/190* d5.18 Col Texas A&M-Kingsville

2004	Mil N	2	3	.400	46	0	0	0-5	53	50	21	5	2	14-2	39	3.40	129	.248	.300	0	—	0		6		0.5
2005	Mil N	0	1	.000	13	0	0	1-1	13.1	12	4	2	0	10-1	14	2.70	159	.235	.361	0	—	0		2		0.2
Total	2	4	.333	59	0	0	1-6	66.1	62	25	7	2	24-3	53	3.26	134	.245	.313	0	—	0		8		0.7

ADAMS, JOE Joseph Edward B10.28.1877 Cowden IL D10.8.1952 Montgomery City MO BR/TL/6-0/190 d4.26

| 1902 | StL N | 0 | 0 | — | 1 | 0 | 0 | 0 | 4 | 9 | 6 | 0 | 1 | 2 | 0 | 9.00 | 30 | .450 | .522 | 2 | .000 | -0 | | -3 | | -0.1 |

ADAMS, KARL Karl Tutwiler "Rebel" B8.11.1891 Columbus GA D9.17.1967 Everett WA BR/TR/6-2/170 d4.19

1914	Cin N	0	0	—	4	0	0	0	8	14	10	1	0	5	5	9.00	33	.424	.500	2	.500	0		-5		-0.2
1915	Chi N	1	9	.100	26	12	3	0	107	105	62	5	2	43	57	4.71	59	.267	.342	30-0-1	.000	-4	65	-19		-2.1
Total	2	1	9	.100	30	12	3	0	115	119	72	6	2	48	62	5.01	56	.279	.355	32-0-1	.031	-4	65	-24		-2.3

ADAMS, RICK Reuben Alexander B12.23.1878 Paris TX D3.10.1955 Paris TX BL/TL/6-0/165 d7.13

| 1905 | Was A | 2 | 5 | .286 | 11 | 6 | 3-1 | 0 | 62.2 | 63 | 30 | 1 | 8 | 24 | 25 | 3.59 | 74 | .264 | .351 | 23 | .174 | 0 | 71 | -5 | | -0.4 |

ADAMS, BOB Robert Andrew B1.20.1907 Birmingham AL D3.6.1970 Jacksonville FL BR/TR/6-0.5/165 d9.27

1931	Phi N	0	1	.000	1	1	0	0	6	14	10	0	1	3	3	9.00	47	.424	.441	3	.000	-0	40	-4		-0.5
1932	Phi N	0	0	—	4	0	0	0	6	7	1	0	0	2	2	1.50	294	.318	.375	0	—	0		2		0.1
Total	2	0	1	.000	5	1	0	0	12	21	11	0	1	5	5	5.25	82	.382	.414	3	.000	-0	40	-2		-0.4

ADAMS, BOB Robert Burdette B7.24.1901 Holyoke MA D10.17.1996 Lemoyne PA BR/TR/5-11/168 d9.22 Col Lehigh

| 1925 | Bos A | 0 | 0 | — | 2 | 0 | 0 | 0 | 5.2 | 10 | 5 | 1 | 0 | 3 | 1 | 7.94 | 57 | .417 | .481 | 3 | .333 | 0 | | -2 | | 0.0 |

ADAMS, TERRY Terry Wayne B3.6.1973 Mobile AL BR/TR/6-3/205(205-225) [ChiN91 4/111] d8.10

1995	Chi N	1	1	.500	18	0	0	1-0	18	22	15	0	0	10-1	15	6.50	64	.289	.372	0	—	0		-5		-0.5
1996	Chi N	3	6	.333	69	0	0	4-4	101	84	36	6	1	49-6	78	2.94	149	.231	.322	6	.000	-0	16			1.3
1997	Chi N	2	9	.182	74	0	0	18-4	74	91	43	3	1	40-6	64	4.62	94	.306	.388	2	.000	-0		-3		-0.6
1998	Chi N	7	7	.500	63	0	0	1-6	72.2	72	39	7	1	41-3	73	4.33	102	.255	.349	1	.000	-0		0		0.0
1999	Chi N	3	6	.667	52	0	0	13-5	65	60	33	9	0	28-2	57	4.02	114	.245	.319	2	.000	-0		4	48	0.5
2000	LA N	6	9	.400	66	0	0	2-5	84.1	80	42	6	0	39-0	56	3.52	126	.245	.325	2-0-1	.000	-0		6		1.1
2001	LA N	12	8	.600	43	22	0	0-1	166.1	172	84	9	3	54-1	141	4.33	95	.267	.326	39-0-5	.051	-2	103	-3		-0.3
2002	Phi N	7	9	.438	46	19	0	0-1	136.2	132	76	9	3	58-5	96	4.35	88	.255	.333	25-0-6	.080	-1	112	-11		-1.1
2003	Phi N	1	4	.200	66	0	0	0-0	68	68	22	1	2	23-4	51	2.65	150	.268	.331	1	.000	-0		11	15	0.7
2004	Tor A	4	4	.500	42	0	0	3-3	43	49	24	4	1	22-2	35	3.98	123	.290	.371	0	—	0		4		0.7
	Bos A	2	0	1.000	19	0	0	0-0	27	35	19	6	1	6-1	21	6.00	81	.321	.353	0	—	0		-3		-0.2
	Year	6	4	.600	61	0	0	3-3	70	84	39	10	2	28-3	56	4.76	103	.302	.364	0	—	0		2		0.5
2005	Phi N	0	2	.000	16	0	0	0-1	13.1	25	19	4	3	10-2	4	12.83	34	.403	.513	0	—	0		-12		-1.5
Total	11	51	62	.451	574	41	0	42-30	869.1	890	448	63	17	380-33	691	4.17	102	.266	.342	78-0-12	.051	-3	100	4	63	0.1

ADAMS, WILLIE William Edward B10.8.1972 Gallup NM BR/TR/6-7/215* [OakA93 1/36] d6.11 Col Stanford [DL 1998 Oak A 181]

1996	Oak A	3	4	.429	12	11	1-1	0-0	76.1	76	39	11	5	23-3	68	4.01	124	.257	.319	0	—	0	85	7		0.5
1997	Oak A	3	5	.375	13	13	0	0-0	58.1	73	53	9	4	32-2	37	8.18	56	.307	.391	0	—	0	98	-21		-2.3
Total	2	6	9	.400	25	24	1-1	0-0	134.2	149	92	20	9	55-5	105	5.81	83	.279	.352	0	—	0	91	-14	181	-1.8

ADAMSON, JOEL Joel Lee B7.2.1971 Lakewood CA BL/TL/6-4/185* [PhiN90 7/185] d4.10 Col Cerritos (CA) JC

| 1996 | Fla N | 0 | 0 | — | 9 | 0 | 0 | 0-0 | 11 | 18 | 9 | 1 | 1 | 7-0 | 7 | 7.36 | 56 | .400 | .481 | 0 | — | 0 | | -4 | | -0.2 |
| 1997 | Mil A | 5 | 3 | .625 | 30 | 6 | 0 | 0-0 | 76.1 | 78 | 36 | 9 | 5 | 19-1 | 56 | 3.54 | 131 | .265 | .319 | 3 | .000 | -0 | 86 | 8 | | 0.7 |

YEAR	TM LG	W	L	PCT	G	GS	CG-SHO	SV-BS	IP	H	R	HR	HB	BB-IB	SO	ERA	AERA	OAV	OOB	AB-HR-SH	AVG	PB	SUP	APR	DL	PW
1998	Ari N	0	3	.000	5	5	0	0-0	23	25	21	5	3	11-0	14	8.22	52	.284	.379	7-0-1	.429	1	120	-9	154	-0.8
Total 3		5	6	.455	44	11	0	0-0	110.1	121	66	19	9	37-0	77	4.89	92	.283	.350	10-0-1	.300	1	100	-5	154	-0.3

ADAMSON, MIKE John Michael B9.13.1947 San Diego CA BR/TR/6-2/190* [BalA67 S1/1] d7.1 Col USC

YEAR	TM LG	W	L	PCT	G	GS	CG-SHO	SV-BS	IP	H	R	HR	HB	BB-IB	SO	ERA	AERA	OAV	OOB	AB-HR-SH	AVG	PB	SUP	APR	DL	PW
1967	Bal A	0	1	.000	3	2	0	0	9.2	9	9	1	0	12-0	8	8.38	.38	.257	.438	2	.500	1	97	-5		-0.4
1968	Bal A	0	2	.000	2	2	0	0	7.2	9	9	2	0	4-0	4	9.39	31	.281	.361	3	.333	0	89	-5		-0.9
1969	Bal A	0	1	.000	6	0	0	0-0	8	10	4	0	0	6-2	2	4.50	80	.357	.444	1-0-1	.000	-0		-1		-0.1
Total 3		0	4	.000	11	4	0	0-0	25.1	28	22	3	0	22-2	14	7.46	43	.295	.417	6-0-1	.333	1	88	-11		-1.4

ADKINS, GRADY Grady Emmett "Butcher Boy" B6.29.1897 Jacksonville AR D3.31.1966 Little Rock AR BR/TR/5-11/175 d4.13

YEAR	TM LG	W	L	PCT	G	GS	CG-SHO	SV-BS	IP	H	R	HR	HB	BB-IB	SO	ERA	AERA	OAV	OOB	AB-HR-SH	AVG	PB	SUP	APR	DL	PW
1928	Chi A	10	16	.385	36	27	14	1	224.2	235	113	12	6	89	54	3.73	109	.278	.351	70-0-9	.143	-3*	74	7		0.3
1929	Chi A	2	11	.154	31	15	5	1	138.1	168	98	12	1	67	24	5.33	80	.303	.379	46-0-1	.239	3*	64	-16		-0.9
Total 2		12	27	.308	67	42	19	1	363	403	211	24	7	156	78	4.34	95	.288	.363	116-0-10	.181	-1	70	-9		-0.6

ADKINS, DEWEY John Dewey B5.11.1918 Norcatur KS D12.26.1998 Santa Monica CA BR/TR/6-2/195 d9.19

YEAR	TM LG	W	L	PCT	G	GS	CG-SHO	SV-BS	IP	H	R	HR	HB	BB-IB	SO	ERA	AERA	OAV	OOB	AB-HR-SH	AVG	PB	SUP	APR	DL	PW
1942	Was A	0	0	—	1	1	0	0	6.1	7	8	0	0	6	3	9.95	37	.259	.394	2-0-1	.500	0	257	-4		-0.2
1943	Was A	0	0	—	7	0	0	0	10.1	9	3	0	0	5	1	2.61	123	.250	.341	0	—	0		1		0.0
1949	Chi N	2	4	.333	30	5	1	0	82.1	98	58	11	0	39	43	5.68	71	.298	.372	20-1-0	.200	1	96	-15		-0.8
Total 3		2	4	.333	38	6	1	0	99	114	69	11	0	50	47	5.64	70	.291	.371	22-1-1	.227	1	123	-18		-1.0

ADKINS, JON Jonathan Scott B8.30.1977 Huntington WV BL/TR/6-0/200(200-215) [OakA98 9/255] d8.14 Col Oklahoma St.

YEAR	TM LG	W	L	PCT	G	GS	CG-SHO	SV-BS	IP	H	R	HR	HB	BB-IB	SO	ERA	AERA	OAV	OOB	AB-HR-SH	AVG	PB	SUP	APR	DL	PW
2003	Chi A	0	0	—	4	0	0	0-0	9.1	8	5	1	1	7-0	4	4.82	95	.250	.390	0	—	0		0		0.0
2004	Chi A	2	3	.400	50	0	0	0-0	62	75	35	13	1	20-3	44	4.65	101	.305	.358	0	—	0		0		0.0
2005	Chi A	0	1	.000	5	0	0	0-0	8.1	13	8	0	1	4-2	1	8.64	52	.351	.429	0	—	0		-3		-0.3
Total 3		2	4	.333	59	0	0	0-0	79.2	96	48	14	3	31-5	48	5.08	92	.305	.370	0	—	0		-3		-0.3

ADKINS, DOC Merle Theron B8.5.1872 Troy WI D2.21.1934 Durham NC BR/TR/5-10.5/220 d6.24 Col Beloit

YEAR	TM LG	W	L	PCT	G	GS	CG-SHO	SV-BS	IP	H	R	HR	HB	BB-IB	SO	ERA	AERA	OAV	OOB	AB-HR-SH	AVG	PB	SUP	APR	DL	PW
1902	Bos A	1	1	.500	4	2	1	0	20	30	20	2	0	7	3	4.05	88	.345	.394	9	.222	-0	70	-3		-0.3
1903	NY A	0	0	—	2	1	0	1	7	10	8	0	1	5	0	7.71	40	.333	.444	3	.000	-0	183	-3		-0.3
Total 2		1	1	.500	6	3	1	1	27	40	28	2	1	12	3	5.00	69	.342	.408	12	.167	-0	104	-6		-0.5

ADKINS, STEVE Steven Thomas B10.26.1964 Chicago IL BR/TL/6-6/210 [NYA86 15/392] d9.12 Col Penn

YEAR	TM LG	W	L	PCT	G	GS	CG-SHO	SV-BS	IP	H	R	HR	HB	BB-IB	SO	ERA	AERA	OAV	OOB	AB-HR-SH	AVG	PB	SUP	APR	DL	PW
1990	NY A	1	2	.333	5	5	0	0-0	24	19	18	4	0	29-0	14	6.38	63	.226	.421	0	—	0	105	-6		-0.6

AFFELDT, JEREMY Jeremy David B6.6.1979 Phoenix AZ BL/TL/6-4/185(185-220) [KCA97 3/91] d4.6

YEAR	TM LG	W	L	PCT	G	GS	CG-SHO	SV-BS	IP	H	R	HR	HB	BB-IB	SO	ERA	AERA	OAV	OOB	AB-HR-SH	AVG	PB	SUP	APR	DL	PW
2002	KC A	3	4	.429	34	7	0	0-1	77.2	85	41	8	3	37-4	67	4.64	108	.274	.356	0	—	0	40	3	53	0.3
2003	KC A	7	6	.538	36	18	0	4-0	126	126	58	12	5	38-1	98	3.93	123	.261	.318	6	.333	1	109	12	16	1.3
2004	KC A	3	4	.429	38	8	0	13-4	76.1	91	49	6	3	32-2	49	4.95	94	.302	.371	0	—	0	87	-3	55	-0.4
2005	KC A	2	2	.000	49	0	0	0-0	49.2	56	35	3	0	29-2	39	5.26	80	.277	.366	0	—	0	-8	67		-0.4
Total 4		13	16	.448	157	33	0	17-5	329.2	358	183	29	11	136-9	253	4.53	104	.276	.347	6	.333	1	91	4	191	0.8

AGOSTO, JUAN Juan Roberto (Gonzalez) B2.23.1958 Rio Piedras, PR BL/TL/6-2/190(175-190) d9.7

YEAR	TM LG	W	L	PCT	G	GS	CG-SHO	SV-BS	IP	H	R	HR	HB	BB-IB	SO	ERA	AERA	OAV	OOB	AB-HR-SH	AVG	PB	SUP	APR	DL	PW
1981	Chi A	0	0	—	2	0	0	0-0	5.2	5	3	1	1	0-0	3	4.76	76	.238	.273	0	—	0		-1		0.0
1982	Chi A	0	0	—	1	0	0	0-0	2	7	4	0	0	0-0	1	18.00	23	.538	.538	0	—	0		-3		-0.1
1983	†Chi A	2	2	.500	39	0	0	7-1	41.2	41	20	2	1	11-1	29	4.10	103	.283	.329	0	—	0		1		0.1
1984	Chi A	2	1	.667	49	0	0	7-3	55.1	54	20	2	3	34-7	26	3.09	135	.270	.382	0	—	0		5		0.6
1985	Chi A	4	3	.571	54	0	0	1-3	60.1	45	27	3	3	23-1	39	3.58	121	.210	.292	0	—	0		5		0.6
1986	Chi A	0	2	.000	9	0	0	0-0	4.2	6	5	0	0	4-0	3	7.71	56	.300	.417	0	—	0		-2		-0.4
	Min A	1	2	.333	17	1	0	1-1	20.1	43	25	1	2	14-0	9	8.85	49	.443	.522	0	—	0	21	-11		-1.5
	Year	1	4	.200	26	1	0	1-1	25	49	30	1	2	18-0	12	8.64	50	.419	.504	0	—	0	21	-13		-1.9
1987	Hou N	1	1	.500	27	0	0	2-2	27.1	26	12	1	0	10-1	6	2.63	149	.248	.313	1	.000	-0		3		0.3
1988	Hou N	10	2	.833	75	0	0	4-6	91.2	74	27	6	0	30-13	33	2.26	147	.226	.287	5	.000	-0		11		1.7
1989	Hou N	4	5	.444	71	0	0	1-4	83	81	32	3	2	32-10	46	2.93	116	.256	.323	5	.200	0		4		-0.3
1990	Hou N	9	8	.529	82	0	0	4-4	92.1	91	46	4	7	39-8	50	4.29	87	.261	.345	2	.000	-0		-4		-0.7
1991	StL N	5	3	.625	72	0	0	2-5	86	92	52	4	8	39-4	34	4.81	78	.291	.380	3	.333	1		-11		-0.9
1992	StL N	2	4	.333	22	0	0	0-1	31.2	39	24	2	3	9-2	13	6.25	55	.312	.364	4	.000	-0		-10		-1.8
	Sea A	0	0	—	17	1	0	0-1	18.1	27	12	0	0	3-0	12	5.89	68	.346	.366	0	—	0	114	-3		-0.2
1993	Hou N	0	0	—	6	0	0	0-0	6	8	4	1	0	0-0	3	6.00	65	.308	.308	0	—	0		-1		-0.1
Total 13		40	33	.548	543	2	0	29-31	626.1	639	313	30	30	248-47	307	4.01	94	.272	.345	20-0-1	.100	-1	71	-15		-1.9

AGUILERA, RICK Richard Warren B12.31.1961 San Gabriel CA BR/TR/6-5/205(193-210) [NYN83 3/58] d6.12 Col Brigham Young

YEAR	TM LG	W	L	PCT	G	GS	CG-SHO	SV-BS	IP	H	R	HR	HB	BB-IB	SO	ERA	AERA	OAV	OOB	AB-HR-SH	AVG	PB	SUP	APR	DL	PW
1985	NY N	10	7	.588	21	19	2	0-0	122.1	118	49	8	2	37-2	74	3.24	108	.258	.314	36-0-7	.278	3*	88	3		0.8
1986	†NY N	10	7	.588	28	20	2	0-1	141.2	145	70	15	7	36-1	104	3.88	93	.263	.314	51-2-3	.157	2*	124	5		-0.1
1987	NY N	11	3	.786	18	17	1	0-0	115	124	53	12	3	33-2	77	3.60	106	.276	.329	40-1-6	.225	3	131	3	93	0.7
1988	†NY N	0	4	.000	11	3	0	0-0	24.2	29	20	2	1	10-2	16	6.93	47	.296	.367	4	.250	0	136	-10	118	-1.4
1989	NY N	6	6	.500	36	0	0	7-4	69.1	59	19	3	2	21-3	80	2.34	141	.231	.294	7	.000	0		8		1.5
	Min A	3	5	.375	11	11	3	0-0	75.2	71	32	5	1	17-1	57	3.21	129	.245	.289	0	—	0	93	6		0.7
1990	Min A	5	3	.625	56	0	0	32-7	65.1	55	27	5	4	19-6	61	2.76	151	.224	.291	0	—	0		8		1.4
1991	†Min A★	4	5	.444	63	0	0	42-9	69	44	20	3	1	30-6	61	2.35	182	.183	.274	0	—	0		14		2.9
1992	Min A★	2	6	.250	64	0	0	41-7	66.2	60	24	7	1	17-4	52	2.84	144	.238	.287	0	—	0		7		1.3
1993	Min A★	4	3	.571	65	0	0	34-6	72.1	60	25	9	1	14-3	59	3.11	142	.223	.263	0	—	0		11		1.9
1994	Min A	1	4	.200	44	0	0	23-6	44.2	57	23	7	0	10-3	46	3.63	136	.306	.340	0	—	0		5		0.9
1995	Min A	1	1	.500	22	0	0	12-3	25	20	7	2	1	6-1	29	2.52	191	.222	.273	0	—	0		7		1.0
	†Bos A	2	2	.500	30	0	0	20-1	30.1	26	9	4	0	7-0	23	2.67	182	.228	.268	0	—	0		8		1.5
	Year	3	3	.500	52	0	0	32-4	55.1	46	16	6	1	13-1	52	2.60	186	.225	.270	0	—	0		14		2.5
1996	Min A	8	6	.571	19	19	2	0-0	111.1	124	69	20	3	27-1	83	5.42	95	.276	.319	0	—	0	108	-2	71	-0.3
1997	Min A	5	4	.556	61	0	0	26-7	68.1	65	29	9	2	22-3	68	3.82	122	.257	.318	0	—	0		7		1.4
1998	Min A	4	9	.308	68	0	0	38-11	74.1	75	35	8	1	15-1	57	4.24	113	.262	.299	0	—	0		6		1.1
1999	Min A	3	1	.750	17	0	0	6-2	21.1	10	3	2	0	2-0	13	1.27	409	.135	.158	0	—	0		4		0.8
	Chi N	6	3	.667	44	0	0	8-5	46.1	44	22	6	2	10-1	32	3.69	124	.254	.299	1	.000	—		4	24	0.8
2000	Chi N	1	2	.333	54	0	0	29-8	47.2	47	28	11	4	18-2	38	4.91	93	.251	.330	0	—	0		-2	13	-0.3
Total 16		86	81	.515	732	89	10	318-77	1291.1	1233	568	138	36	351-42	1030	3.57	104	.251	.303	139-3-16	.201	8	106	87	319	17.3

AGUIRRE, HANK Henry John B1.31.1931 Azusa CA D9.5.1994 Bloomfield Hills MI BR/TL/6-4/205(195-210) d9.10 C3

YEAR	TM LG	W	L	PCT	G	GS	CG-SHO	SV-BS	IP	H	R	HR	HB	BB-IB	SO	ERA	AERA	OAV	OOB	AB-HR-SH	AVG	PB	SUP	APR	DL	PW
1955	Cle A	0	1	.000	4	1	0	0	12.2	6	3	1	0	3-0	4	1.42	281	.143	.333	0	.000	-1	156	3		0.4
1956	Cle A	3	5	.375	16	9	2-1	1	65.1	63	35	7	1	27-1	31	3.72	113	.253	.326	18-0-3	.111	-2	73	2		0.0
1957	Cle A	1	1	.500	10	1	0	0	20.1	26	15	0	0	13-3	9	5.75	65	.317	.394	4	.000	-1	96	-5		-0.5
1958	Det A	3	4	.429	44	3	0	5	69.2	67	31	5	1	27-2	38	3.75	108	.255	.322	14	.214	0	67	3		0.4
1959	Det A	0	0	—	3	0	0	0	2.2	4	1	0	0	3-0	3	3.38	120	.364	.500	0	—	0		0		0.0
1960	Det A	5	3	.625	37	6	1	10	94.2	75	31	7	3	30-1	80	2.85	139	.217	.283	28-0-2	.036	-3	115	13		0.9
1961	Det A	4	4	.500	45	0	0	0	55.1	44	22	5	2	38-3	32	3.25	126	.224	.354	9-0-3	.000	-1		6		0.8
1962	Det A★	16	8	.667	42	22	11-2	3	216	162	67	14	5	65-7	156	**2.21**	**184**	**.205**	**.267**	75-0-4	.027	-8	80	**41**		3.4
1963	Det A	14	15	.483	38	33	14-3	0	225.2	222	96	25	8	68-3	134	3.67	102	.256	.314	76-0-2	.132	-2	102	5		-0.8
1964	Det A	5	10	.333	32	27	8	1	161.2	134	76	15	8	59-4	88	3.79	97	.223	.300	53-0-4	.057	-1	92	-3		-0.8
1965	Det A	14	10	.583	32	32	10-2	0	208.1	185	89	24	10	60-2	141	3.59	97	.236	.295	70-0-4	.086	-2	116	-1		-0.4
1966	Det A	3	9	.250	30	14	2	0	103.2	104	50	14	3	26-2	50	3.82	91	.260	.310	25-0-2	.120	-1	89	-4		-0.5
1967	Det A	0	1	.000	31	0	0	0	41.1	34	17	2	0	17-2	33	2.40	136	.219	.295	2	.500	1	294	3		0.3
1968	LA N	1	3	.250	25	0	0	0	39	32	7	3	0	13-3	25	0.69	400	.227	.298	3	.000	-0		8		0.5
1969	Chi N	1	0	1.000	41	0	0	1-1	45	45	13	2	2	12-1	19	2.60	155	.269	.324	5	.400	0		7		0.5
1970	Chi N	3	0	1.000	17	0	0	1-1	14	13	10	3	1	9-1	11	4.50	100	.250	.371	2	.000	-0		-1		-0.2
Total 16		75	72	.510	447	149	44-9	33-2	1375.1	1216	562	123	47	479-35	856	3.25	116	.236	.305	388-0-24	.085	-21	97	77		5.3

AHEARNE, PAT Patrick Howard B12.10.1969 San Francisco CA BR/TR/6-3/195 [DetA92 7/196] d6.14 Col Pepperdine

YEAR	TM LG	W	L	PCT	G	GS	CG-SHO	SV-BS	IP	H	R	HR	HB	BB-IB	SO	ERA	AERA	OAV	OOB	AB-HR-SH	AVG	PB	SUP	APR	DL	PW
1995	Det A	0	2	.000	4	3	0	0-0	10	20	13	2	0	5-1	4	11.70	41	.400	.455	0	—	0	90	-7		-1.0

YEAR	TM LG	W	L	PCT	G	GS	CG-SHO	SV-BS	IP	H	R	HR	HB	BB-IB	SO	ERA	AERA	OAV	OOB	AB-HR-SH	AVG	PB	SUP	APR	DL	PW

AINSWORTH, KURT Kurt Harold B9.9.1978 Baton Rouge LA BR/TR/6-3/192(192-210) [SFN99 1/24] d9.5 Col Louisiana St. [DL 2005 Bal A 183]

2001	SF N	0	0	—	2	0	0	0-0	2	3	3	1	1	2-0	3	13.50	30	.333	.500	0	—	0		-2		-0.1
2002	SF N	1	2	.333	6	4	0	0-0	25.2	22	7	1	1	12-0	15	2.10	188	.237	.330	6-0-1	.167	0	76	5		0.7
2003	SF N	5	4	.556	11	11	0	0-0	66	66	31	7	1	26-0	48	3.82	111	.262	.331	22-0-4	.045	-2*	94	3	61	0.1
	Bal A	0	1	.000	3	0	0	0-0	2.1	6	3	1	0	1-0	4	11.57	40	.429	.467	0	—	0		-2	50	-0.3
2004	Bal A	0	1	.000	7	7	0	0-0	30.2	39	34	6	5	20-0	20	9.68	48	.320	.430	0	—	0	117	-16		-0.7
Total	4	6	8	.429	29	22	0	0-0	126.2	136	78	16	8	61-0	90	5.19	83	.278	.364	28-0-5	.071	-2	100	-12	294	-0.3

AITCHISON, RALEIGH Raleigh Leonidas B12.5.1887 Tyndall SD D9.26.1958 Columbus KS BR/TL/5-11.5/175 d4.19

1911	Bro N	0	1	.000	1	0	0		1.1	1	2	0	1	0	1	0.00	—	.200	.333	0	—	0		0		-0.1
1914	Bro N	12	7	.632	26	17	8-3	0	172.1	156	71	4	3	60	87	2.66	107	.244	.312	51-0-3	.196	1	112	4		0.5
1915	Bro N	0	4	.000	7	5	2	0	32.2	36	25	3	2	6	14	4.96	56	.267	.308	8	.000	-0	84	-8		-0.9
Total	3	12	12	.500	34	22	10-3	0	206.1	193	98	7	5	67	101	3.01	95	.247	.311	59-0-3	.169	1	104	-4		-0.5

AKER, JACK Jackie Delane B7.13.1940 Tulare CA BR/TR/6-2/190(190-202) d5.3 C3 Col Sequoias (CA) [JC]

1964	KC A	0	1	.000	9	0	0	0	16.1	17	18	6	6	10-1	7	8.82	43	.266	.412	3	.000	-0*		-9		-0.5
1965	KC A	4	3	.571	34	0	0	3	51.1	45	18	3	3	18-6	26	3.16	111	.242	.317	8-0-1	.000	-1		3		0.3
1966	KC A	8	4	.667	66	0	0	**32**	113	81	27	6	3	28-10	68	1.99	171	.201	.256	21-0-1	.095	-1		**19**		3.2
1967	KC A	3	8	.273	57	0	0	12	88	87	44	9	3	32-8	65	4.30	74	.264	.334	8-0-3	.125	-0		-9		-1.4
1968	Oak A	4	4	.500	54	0	0	11	74.2	72	39	6	6	33-6	44	4.10	69	.258	.344	7-0-1	.143	-0		-11		-1.6
1969	Sea A	0	2	.000	15	0	0	3-1	16.2	25	15	4	1	13-4	7	7.56	48	.357	.464	1	.000			-7		-1.0
	NY A	8	4	.667	38	0	0	11-4	65.2	51	17	4	4	22-5	40	2.06	171	.217	.294	9	.111	-0		11		2.4
	Year	8	6	.571	53	0	0	14-5	82.1	76	32	8	5	35-9	47	3.17	112	.249	.335	10	.100	-0		4		1.4
1970	NY A	4	2	.667	41	0	0	16-4	70	57	19	3	4	20-5	36	2.06	174	.226	.291	16-0-1	.063	-1		12		1.4
1971	NY A	4	4	.500	41	0	0	4-8	55.2	48	20	3	0	26-9	24	2.59	127	.238	.320	3-0-3	.000	-0		4		0.6
1972	NY A	0	0	—	4	0	0	0-0	6	5	2	0	1	3-0	1	3.00	100	.238	.360	0	—	0		0		0.0
	Chi N	6	6	.500	48	0	0	17-3	67	65	31	4	5	23-5	36	2.96	129	.259	.330	6	.000	-0		3		0.8
1973	Chi N	4	5	.444	47	0	0	12-3	63.2	76	33	8	2	23-6	25	4.10	96	.308	.370	7	.000	-1		-1		-0.2
1974	Atl N	0	1	.000	17	0	0	0-1	16.2	17	11	3	0	9-2	7	3.78	100	.298	.382	1	.000	-0		-1		-0.1
	NY N	2	1	.667	24	0	0	2-0	41.1	33	18	4	2	14-1	18	3.48	104	.213	.285	2	.500	1		1	21	0.1
	Year	2	2	.500	41	0	0	2-1	58	50	29	7	2	23-3	25	3.57	103	.236	.313	3	.333	1		-1		0.0
Total	11	47	45	.511	495	0	0	123-24	746	679	312	63	40	274-68	404	3.28	105	.247	.322	92-0-10	.076	-5		15	21	4.0

AKERFELDS, DARREL Darrel Wayne B6.12.1962 Denver CO BR/TR/6-2/210* [SeaA83 1/7] d8.1 C5 Col Mesa St.

1986	Oak A	0	0	—	2	0	0	0-0	5.1	7	5	2	0	3-1	5	6.75	58	.304	.385	0	—	0		-2		-0.1
1987	Cle A	2	6	.250	16	13	1	0-0	74.2	84	60	18	7	38-1	42	6.75	68	.284	.374	0	—	0	91	-16		-1.4
1989	Tex A	0	1	.000	6	0	0	0-1	11	11	6	1	0	5-2	9	3.27	122	.250	.320	0	—	0		0		0.0
1990	Phi N	5	2	.714	71	0	0	3-0	93	65	45	10	3	54-8	42	3.77	102	.201	.316	6	.167	-0		0		0.0
1991	Phi N	2	1	.667	30	0	0	0-0	49.2	49	30	5	3	27-4	31	5.26	70	.257	.354	3	.000	-0		-8		-0.4
Total	5	9	10	.474	125	13	1	3-2	233.2	216	146	36	13	127-16	129	5.08	80	.246	.346	9	.111	-0	91	-26		-1.9

AKERS, JERRY Albert Earl B11.1.1887 Shelbyville IN D5.15.1979 Bay Pines FL BR/TR/5-11/175 d5.4

| 1912 | Was A | 1 | 1 | .500 | 5 | 1 | 0 | | 20.1 | 24 | 17 | 1 | 2 | 15 | 11 | 4.87 | 68 | .300 | .423 | 6 | .333 | 0 | 22 | -4 | | -0.4 |

ALBA, GIBSON Gibson Alberto (Rosado) B1.18.1960 Santiago, D.R. BL/TL/6-2/160 d5.3

| 1988 | StL N | 0 | 0 | — | 3 | 0 | 0 | 0-0 | 3.1 | 1 | 2 | 0 | 0 | 2-0 | 3 | 2.70 | 130 | .091 | .214 | 0 | — | 0 | | 0 | | 0.0 |

ALBANESE, JOE Joseph Peter B6.26.1933 New York NY D6.17.2000 New York NY BR/TR/6-3/215 d7.18

| 1958 | Was A | 0 | 0 | — | 6 | 0 | 0 | | 6 | 8 | 3 | 1 | 0 | 2-0 | 3 | 4.50 | 85 | .348 | .370 | 0 | — | 0 | | 0 | | 0.0 |

ALBERRO, JOSE Jose Edgardo B6.29.1969 San Juan, PR BR/TR/6-2/190* d4.27

1995	Tex A	0	0	—	12	0	0	0-0	20.2	26	18	2	1	12-1	10	7.40	65	.299	.386	0	—	0		-6		-0.2
1996	Tex A	0	1	.000	5	1	0	0-0	9.1	14	6	1	0	7-1	2	5.79	91	.368	.457	0	—	0	35	0		0.0
1997	Tex A	0	3	.000	10	4	0	0-0	28.1	37	33	4	1	17-1	11	7.94	61	.303	.390	0	—	0	85	-11		-1.0
Total	3	0	4	.000	27	5	0	0-0	58.1	77	57	7	2	36-3	23	7.41	66	.312	.399	0	—	0	75	-17		-1.2

ALBERTS, CY Frederick Joseph B1.14.1882 Grand Rapids MI D8.27.1917 Fort Wayne IN BR/TR/6-0/230 d9.17

| 1910 | StL N | 1 | 2 | .333 | 4 | 3 | 2 | 0 | 27.2 | 35 | 22 | 1 | 0 | 20 | 10 | 6.18 | 48 | .330 | .437 | 7-0-1 | .000 | -0 | 83 | -9 | | -0.9 |

ALBOSTA, ED Edward John "Rube" B10.27.1918 Saginaw MI D1.7.2003 Saginaw MI BR/TR/6-1/175 d9.3 Mil 1943-45

1941	Bro N	0	2	.000	2	0	0	0	13	11	9	1	0	8	5	6.23	59	.239	.352	4	.000	-1	46	-3		-0.4
1946	Pit N	0	6	.000	17	6	0	0	39.2	41	34	3	1	35	19	6.13	58	.266	.405	8	.125	-0	40	-12		-1.7
Total	2	0	8	.000	19	6	0	0	52.2	52	43	4	1	43	24	6.15	58	.260	.393	12	.083	-1	42	-15		-2.1

ALBRECHT, ED Edward Arthur B2.28.1929 Affton MO D12.29.1979 Cahokia IL BR/TR/5-10.5/165* d10.2

1949	StL A	1	0	1.000	1	1	1	2	9	5	3	0	0	4	1	5.40	84	.063	.250	2	.000	-0	99	0		0.0
1950	StL A	0	1	.000	2	1	0	0	6.2	6	7	0	0	7	1	5.40	92	.250	.419	1	.000	-0	109	-1		-0.2
Total	2	1	1	.500	3	2	1	2	11.2	7	10	0	0	11	2	5.40	88	.175	.353	3	.000	-0	104	-1		-0.2

ALBURY, VIC Victor B5.12.1947 Key West FL BL/TL/6-0/183* [CleA65 8/173] d8.7

1973	Min A	1	0	1.000	14	0	0	0-0	23.1	13	7	1	0	19-2	13	2.70	147	.169	.333	0	—	0		4		0.1
1974	Min A	8	9	.471	32	22	4-1	0-0	164	159	83	19	6	80-1	85	4.12	91	.259	.348	0	—	0	102	-6		-0.6
1975	Min A	6	7	.462	32	15	2	1-0	135	115	82	16	4	97-1	72	4.53	85	.237	.364	1	.000	-0*	98	-12		-1.1
1976	Min A	3	1	.750	23	0	0	0-0	50.1	51	22	0	2	24-3	23	3.58	100	.271	.352	0	—	0		1	24	0.0
Total	4	18	17	.514	101	37	6-1	1-0	372.2	308	194	36	12	220-7	193	4.12	92	.247	.353	1	.000	-0	101	-13	24	-1.6

ALCALA, SANTO Santo (b Santo Anibal (Alcala)) B12.23.1952 San Pedro de Macoris, D.R. BR/TR/6-5/185* d4.10 [DL 1978 Sea A 24]

1976	Cin N	11	4	.733	30	21	3-1	0-1	132	131	72	12	3	67-3	67	4.70	74	.261	.348	43-0-5	.140	-0	155	-16		-1.8
1977	Cin N	1	1	.500	7	2	0	0-0	15.2	22	11	1	1	7-1	9	5.74	69	.349	.417	3	.000	-0	79	-3		-0.4
	Mon N	2	6	.250	31	10	0	2-1	101.2	104	55	12	2	47-5	64	4.69	82	.263	.343	25-1-2	.080	-1	65	-8		-0.7
	Year	3	7	.300	38	12	0	2-1	117.1	126	66	13	3	54-6	73	4.83	80	.275	.353	28-1-2	.071	-1	67	-11		-1.1
Total	2	14	11	.560	68	33	3-1	2-2	249.1	257	138	25	6	121-9	140	4.76	77	.268	.351	71-1-7	.113	-2	120	-27	24	-2.9

ALDERSON, DALE Dale Leonard B3.9.1918 Belden NE D2.12.1982 Garden Grove CA BR/TR/5-10/190 d9.18 Mil 1944-45 Col Upper Iowa

1943	Chi N	0	1	.000	4	2	0	0	14	21	12	2	0	3	4	6.43	52	.356	.387	3	.000	-0	127	-5		-0.4
1944	Chi N	0	0	—	12	1	0	0	21.2	31	18	2	0	9	7	6.65	53	.344	.404	4	.000	-1	166	-7		-0.4
Total	2	0	1	.000	16	3	0	0	35.2	52	30	4	0	12	11	6.56	53	.349	.398	7	.000	-1	138	-12		-0.8

ALDRED, SCOTT Scott Phillip B6.12.1968 Flint MI BL/TL/6-4/215(195-228) [DetA86 16/411] d9.9

1990	Det A	1	2	.333	3	3	0	0-0	14.1	13	6	0	1	10-1	7	3.77	106	.265	.393	0	—	0	53	1		0.1
1991	Det A	2	4	.333	11	11	0	0-0	57.1	58	37	9	0	30-2	35	5.18	81	.266	.352	0	—	0	115	-7		-0.6
1992	Det A	3	8	.273	16	13	0	0-0	65	80	51	12	3	33-4	34	6.78	56	.307	.387	0	—	0	97	-19		-2.7
1993	Col N	0	0	—	5	0	0	0	6.2	10	10	1	1	9-1	5	10.80	44	.357	.526	0	—	0		-4		-0.2
	Mon N	1	0	1.000	3	0	0	0-1	5.1	9	4	1	0	1-0	4	6.75	62	.375	.400	0	—	0		-1	119	-0.2
	Year	1	0	1.000	8	0	0	0-1	12	19	14	2	1	10-1	9	9.00	50	.365	.476	0	—	0		-6		-0.4
1996	Det A	0	4	.000	11	8	0	0-0	43.1	60	52	9	3	26-3	36	9.35	54	.328	.416	0	—	0	89	-21		-1.5
	Min A	6	5	.545	25	17	0	0-0	122	134	73	20	3	42-1	75	5.09	101	.281	.340	0	—	0	127	-1		0.0
	Year	6	9	.400	36	25	0	0-0	165.1	194	125	29	6	68-4	111	6.21	83	.294	.362	0	—	0	115	-21		-1.5
1997	Min A	2	10	.167	17	15	0	0-0	77.1	102	66	20	4	28-2	33	7.68	61	.323	.382	0	—	0	102	-23		-2.8
1998	TB A	0	0	—	48	0	0	0-0	31.1	33	13	1	2	12-3	21	3.73	128	.280	.356	0	—	0		4		0.2
1999	TB A	3	2	.600	37	0	0	0-0	24.1	26	15	1	2	14-0	22	5.18	96	.274	.375	0	—	0		0		0.2
	Phi N	1	1	.500	29	0	0	1-3	32.1	33	15	1	0	15-3	19	3.90	120	.277	.345	0	—	0		3		0.2
2000	Phi N	1	3	.250	23	0	0	0-1	20.1	23	14	3	1	10-0	21	5.75	80	.284	.362	1	.000	-0		-3	124	-0.2
Total	9	20	39	.339	229	67	1	1-5	499.2	581	356	78	19	230-20	312	6.02	78	.295	.371	1	.000	-0	105	-69	243	-7.9

ALDRICH, JAY Jay Robert B4.14.1961 Alexandria LA BR/TR/6-3/210* [MilA82 10/261] d6.5 Col Montclair St.

| 1987 | Mil A | 3 | 1 | .750 | 31 | 0 | 0 | 0-0 | 58.1 | 71 | 33 | 8 | 2 | 13-3 | 22 | 4.94 | 93 | .306 | .344 | 0 | — | 0 | | -1 | | -0.1 |
| 1989 | Mil A | 1 | 0 | 1.000 | 16 | 0 | 0 | 1-1 | 26 | 24 | 11 | 3 | 1 | 13-2 | 12 | 3.81 | 101 | .253 | .349 | 0 | — | 0 | | 1 | | 0.1 |

YEAR	TM LG	W	L	PCT	G	GS	CG-SHO	SV-BS	IP	H	R	HR	HB	BB-IB	SO	ERA	AERA	OAV	OOB	AB-HR-SH	AVG	PB	SUP	APR	DL	PW
	Atl N	1	2	.333	8	0	0	0-1	12.1	7	5	0	0	6-1	7	2.19	167	.167	.265	1	.000	-0		1		0.2
1990	Bal A	1	2	.333	7	0	0	1-2	12	17	13	1	0	7-3	5	8.25	46	.327	.407	0	—	-0		-7		-1.2
Total	3	6	5	.545	62	0	0	2-4	108.2	119	62	12	3	39-9	46	4.72	90	.283	.345	1	.000	-0		-6		-1.0

ALDRIDGE, VIC Victor Eddington B10.25.1893 Indian Springs IN D4.17.1973 Terre Haute IN BR/TR/5-9.5/175 d4.15 Mil 1918

YEAR	TM LG	W	L	PCT	G	GS	CG-SHO	SV-BS	IP	H	R	HR	HB	BB-IB	SO	ERA	AERA	OAV	OOB	AB-HR-SH	AVG	PB	SUP	APR	DL	PW
1917	Chi N	6	6	.500	30	6	1-1	2	106.2	100	52	1	2	37		44	3.12	93	.252	.319	29-0-1	.138	-2	69	-3		-0.4
1918	Chi N	0	0	.000	3	0	0		12.1	11	3	0	0	6		10	1.46	191	.275	.370	3-0-1	.333	0		2		0.2
1922	Chi N	16	15	.516	36	34	20-2	0	258.1	287	129	14	12	56	66	3.52	119	.286	.332	100-0-7	.260	3	96	16		2.0
1923	Chi N	16	9	.640	30	30	15-2	0	217	209	101	17	1	67	64	3.48	125	.251	.307	71-0-5	.268	3	101	13		1.6
1924	Chi N	15	12	.556	32	32	20	0	244.1	261	110	10	7	80	74	3.50	112	.279	.341	85-0-7	.176	-3	107	12		0.9
1925	†Pit N	15	7	.682	30	26	14-1	0	213.1	218	99	15	5	74	88	3.63	123	.269	.334	86-1-2	.233	-1	119	21		1.6
1926	Pit N	10	13	.435	30	26	12-1	1	190	204	100	7	4	73	61	4.07	97	.279	.348	71-0-4	.225	-1	98	-1		-0.3
1927	†Pit N	15	10	.600	35	34	17-1	1	239.1	248	123	16	5	74	86	4.25	97	.270	.328	96-0-3	.219	-0	112	0		-0.2
1928	NY N	4	7	.364	22	16	3	2	119.1	133	68	7	3	45	33	4.83	81	.285	.352	40-1-2	.275	2	112	-10		-0.7
Total	9	97	80	.548	248	204	102-8	6	1600.2	1671	785	87	39	512	526	3.76	107	.273	.333	581-2-32	.229	2	106	50		4.7

ALEXANDER, DOYLE Doyle Lafayette B9.4.1950 Cordova AL BR/TR/6-3/205(190-205) [LAN68 9/185] d6.26

YEAR	TM LG	W	L	PCT	G	GS	CG-SHO	SV-BS	IP	H	R	HR	HB	BB-IB	SO	ERA	AERA	OAV	OOB	AB-HR-SH	AVG	PB	SUP	APR	DL	PW
1971	LA N	6	6	.500	17	12	4	0-0	92.1	105	45	6	1	18-0	30	3.80	86	.282	.316	33-0-1	.273	3	107	-7		-0.6
1972	Bal A	6	8	.429	35	9	2-2	2-1	106.1	78	36	5	1	30-8	49	2.45	127	.203	.261	25-0-3	.080	-1	92	6		0.8
1973	†Bal A	12	8	.600	29	26	10	0-0	174.2	169	85	19	7	52-5	63	3.86	98	.258	.317	0	—	0	147	-2	27	-0.2
1974	Bal A	6	9	.400	30	12	2	0-2	114.1	127	65	7	4	43-4	40	4.01	87	.290	.356	0	—	0	97	-10		-1.1
1975	Bal A	8	8	.500	32	11	3-1	1-3	133.1	127	47	7	1	47-7	46	3.04	117	.251	.316	0	—	0	111	9		1.1
1976	Bal A	3	4	.429	11	6	2-1	0-0	64.1	58	27	3	0	24-2	17	3.50	94	.247	.312	0	—	0	98	-1		-0.1
	†NY A	10	5	.667	19	19	5-2	0-0	136.2	114	54	9	3	39-0	41	3.29	104	.229	.287	0	—	0	110	3		0.2
	Year	13	9	.591	30	25	7-3	0-0	201	172	81	12	3	63-2	58	3.36	101	.235	.295	0	—	0	107	2		0.1
1977	Tex A	17	11	.607	34	34	12-1	0-0	237	221	103	24	2	82-2	82	3.65	112	.246	.309	0	—	0	99	14		1.5
1978	Tex A	9	10	.474	31	28	7-1	0-0	191	198	84	18	1	71-1	81	3.86	97	.270	.333	0	—	0	97	2		0.2
1979	Tex A	5	7	.417	23	18	0	0-0	113.1	114	65	3	1	69-3	50	4.45	93	.268	.366	0	—	0	89	-5	25	-0.3
1980	Atl N	14	11	.560	35	35	7-1	0-0	231.2	227	120	20	4	74-5	114	4.20	88	.256	.315	83-0-3	.181	1	118	-13		-1.1
1981	SF N	11	7	.611	24	24	1-1	0-0	152.1	156	51	11	2	44-2	77	2.89	118	.263	.315	51-0-4	.176	1	115	11		1.1
1982	NY A	1	7	.125	16	11	0	0-0	66.2	81	52	14	0	14-2	26	6.08	66	.298	.329	0	—	0	70	-16	89	-1.7
1983	NY A	0	2	.000	8	5	0	0-0	28.1	31	21	6	0	7-0	17	6.35	62	.277	.317	0	—	0	111	-7		-0.5
	Tor A	7	6	.538	17	15	5	0-0	116.2	126	55	14	1	26-1	46	3.93	111	.279	.317	0	—	0	85	5		0.6
	Year	7	8	.467	25	20	5	0-0	145	157	76	20	1	33-1	63	4.41	97	.278	.317	0	—	0	90	-1		0.1
1984	Tor A	17	6	.739	36	35	11-2	0-0	261.2	238	99	21	3	59-1	139	3.13	132	.242	.284	0	—	0	102	29		2.4
1985	†Tor A	17	10	.630	36	36	6-1	0-0	260.2	268	105	28	4	67-0	142	3.45	123	.266	.315	0	—	0	91	25		2.4
1986	Tor A	5	4	.556	17	17	3	0-0	111	120	56	14	2	20-1	65	4.46	95	.273	.308	0	—	0	122	-1		-0.1
	Atl N	6	6	.500	17	17	2	0-0	117.1	135	58	9	0	17-1	74	3.84	103	.287	.311	38-0-6	.211	1*	95	1		0.1
1987	Atl N	5	10	.333	16	16	3	0-0	117.2	115	57	21	1	27-5	64	4.13	105	.257	.300	35-0-6	.029	-3	74	4		0.1
	†Det A	9	0	1.000	11	11	3-3		88.1	63	16	3	0	26-0	44	1.53	279	.201	.263	0	—	0	125	29		2.9
1988	Det A☆	14	11	.560	34	34	5-1	0-0	229	260	122	30	5	46-7	126	4.32	89	.282	.317	0	—	0	112	-13		-1.4
1989	Det A	6	18	.250	33	33	5-1	0-0	223	245	118	28	5	76-3	95	4.44	86	.280	.337	0	—	0	77	-12		-1.2
Total	19	194	174	.527	561	464	98-18	3-6	3367.2	3376	1541	324	53	978-60	1528	3.76	103	.261	.314	265-0-23	.166	1	103	51	141	5.4

ALEXANDER, GERALD Gerald Paul B3.26.1968 Baton Rouge LA BR/TR/5-11/190* [TexA89 21/535] d9.9 Col Tulane

YEAR	TM LG	W	L	PCT	G	GS	CG-SHO	SV-BS	IP	H	R	HR	HB	BB-IB	SO	ERA	AERA	OAV	OOB	AB-HR-SH	AVG	PB	SUP	APR	DL	PW
1990	Tex A	3	2	0	—	3	2	0	0-0	14	6	9	1	5-0	8	7.71	51	.438	.513	0		0	139	-3		-0.1
1991	Tex A	5	3	.625	30	9	0	0-0	89.1	93	56	11	3	48-7	50	5.24	77	.272	.364	0	—	0	130	-11	28	-0.9
1992	Tex A	1	0	1.000	3	0	0	0-0	1.2	5	5	1	0	1-0	1	27.00	14	.500	.500	0	—	0		-4		-0.7
Total	3	6	3	.667	36	11	0	0-0	98	112	67	12	4	54-7	59	5.79	70	.292	.380	0	—	0	132	-18	28	-1.7

ALEXANDER, GROVER Grover Cleveland "Old Pete" B2.26.1887 Elba NE D11.4.1950 St.Paul NE BR/TR/6-1/185 d4.15 Mil 1918 HF1938

YEAR	TM LG	W	L	PCT	G	GS	CG-SHO	SV-BS	IP	H	R	HR	HB	BB-IB	SO	ERA	AERA	OAV	OOB	AB-HR-SH	AVG	PB	SUP	APR	DL	PW
1911	Phi N	28	13	.683	48	37	31-7	3	367	285	133	5	8	129	227	2.57	134	**.219**	.293	138	.174	-2*	101	37		3.7
1912	Phi N	19	17	.528	46	34	25-3	3	310.1	289	133	11	6	105	195	2.81	129	.251	.317	102-2-9	.186	0	90	27		3.0
1913	Phi N	22	8	.733	47	36	23-9	2	306.1	288	106	9	3	75	159	2.79	120	.254	.302	103-0-3	.126	-4	95	22		1.8
1914	Phi N	27	15	.643	46	39	32-6	1	355	327	133	8	11	76	214	2.38	123	.244	.290	137-0-2	.234	2*	105	22		3.1
1915	†Phi N	31	10	.756	49	42	36-12	3	376.1	253	86	3	10	64	241	1.22	225	**.191**	.234	130-1-5	.169	0	116	58		7.5
1916	Phi N	33	12	.733	48	45	38-16	3	389	323	90	6	10	50	167	1.55	171	.230	.262	138-0-3	.239	8*	96	47		7.2
1917	Phi N	30	13	.698	45	44	34-8	0	388	336	107	4	6	56	200	1.83	153	.234	.266	139-1-7	.216	4*	101	39		5.4
1918	Chi N	2	1	.667	3	3	3	0	26	19	7	0	1	3	15	1.73	161	.207	.240	10	.100	1	127	3		0.3
1919	Chi N	16	11	.593	30	27	20-9	1	235	180	51	3	0	38	121	1.72	167	**.211**	.245	70-0-4	.171	1	92	34		4.6
1920	Chi N	27	14	.659	46	40	33-7	5	363.1	335	96	8	1	69	173	1.91	168	.248	.285	118-1-6	.229	4	83	52		6.9
1921	Chi N	15	13	.536	31	30	21-3	1	252	286	110	10	1	33	77	3.39	113	.296	.320	95-1-5	.305	6	100	12		1.8
1922	Chi N	16	13	.552	33	31	20-1	1	245.2	283	111	8	3	34	48	3.63	116	.295	.321	85-0-4	.176	-2	84	18		1.9
1923	Chi N	22	12	.647	39	36	26-3	2	305	308	128	17	0	30	72	3.19	126	.259	.277	111-1-7	.216	0	112	29		3.1
1924	Chi N	12	5	.706	21	20	12	0	169.1	183	82	9	1	25	33	3.03	129	.272	.299	65-1-4	.231	1	115	10		1.1
1925	Chi N	15	11	.577	32	30	20-1	0	236	270	106	14	3	29	63	3.39	127	.288	.312	79-2-9	.241	3	94	23		2.3
1926	Chi N	3	3	.500	7	7	4	0	52	55	26	0	0	7	12	3.46	111	.270	.294	15-0-3	.467	3	87	1		0.5
	†StL N	9	7	.563	23	16	11-2	2	148.1	136	57	8	2	24	35	2.91	134	.242	.276	50-0-3	.120	-4	79	16		1.3
	Year	12	10	.545	30	23	15-2	2	200.1	191	83	8	2	31	47	3.05	127	.250	**.281**	65-0-6	.200	-1	81	18		1.8
1927	StL N	21	10	.677	37	30	22-3	3	268	261	94	11	1	38	48	2.52	157	.258	**.286**	94-0-3	.245	3	109	41		5.0
1928	†StL N	16	9	.640	34	31	18-1	0	243.2	262	107	15	2	37	59	3.36	119	.277	.308	86-1-8	.291	6	122	18		2.2
1929	StL N	9	8	.529	22	19	9	0	132	149	65	10	1	23	33	3.89	120	.285	.317	41-0-3	.049	-0	103	12		1.0
1930	Phi N	0	3	.000	9	3	0	0	21.2	40	24	5	0	6	6	9.14	60	.396	.430	4	.000	-0	64	-7		-0.8
Total	20	373	208	.642	696	600	437-90	32	5190	4868	1852	164	70	951	2198	2.56	135	.250	.288	1810-11-88	.209	24	100	514		62.9

ALEXANDER, BOB Robert Somerville B8.7.1922 Vancouver BC, Can. D4.7.1993 Oceanside CA BR/TR/6-2.5/205* d4.11 Col Bethany

YEAR	TM LG	W	L	PCT	G	GS	CG-SHO	SV-BS	IP	H	R	HR	HB	BB-IB	SO	ERA	AERA	OAV	OOB	AB-HR-SH	AVG	PB	SUP	APR	DL	PW
1955	Bal A	1	0	1.000	4	0	0	0	4	8	6	0	1	2-0	1	13.50	28	.444	.500	0	—	0		-4		-0.7
1957	Cle A	0	1	.000	5	0	0	0	7	10	7	0	1	5-2	1	9.00	41	.357	.457	0	.000	-0		-4		-0.5
Total	2	1	1	.500	9	0	0	0	11	18	13	0	2	7-2	2	10.64	35	.391	.474	1	.000	-0		-8		-1.2

ALFONSECA, ANTONIO Antonio B4.16.1972 LaRomana, D.R. BR/TR/6-5/235(225-250) d6.17

YEAR	TM LG	W	L	PCT	G	GS	CG-SHO	SV-BS	IP	H	R	HR	HB	BB-IB	SO	ERA	AERA	OAV	OOB	AB-HR-SH	AVG	PB	SUP	APR	DL	PW
1997	†Fla N	1	3	.250	17	0	0	0-2	25.2	36	16	3	1	10-3	19	4.91	83	.324	.385	3	.000	-0		-3		-0.4
1998	Fla N	4	6	.400	58	0	0	8-6	70.2	75	36	10	3	33-9	46	4.08	100	.281	.359	4	.000	-0		0	17	-0.2
1999	Fla N	4	5	.444	73	0	0	21-4	77.2	79	28	4	4	29-6	46	3.24	135	.274	.348	2	.000	-0		-11		1.7
2000	Fla N	5	6	.455	68	0	0	45-4	70	82	35	7	1	24-3	47	4.24	103	.291	.347	0	—	0		2		0.3
2001	Fla N	4	4	.500	58	0	0	28-6	61.2	68	24	6	5	15-3	40	3.06	136	.281	.335	0	—	0		7		1.4
2002	Chi N	2	5	.286	66	0	0	19-9	74.1	73	34	5	1	26-3	61	4.00	101	.257	.344	3	.667	1		2		0.3
2003	†Chi N	3	1	.750	60	0	0	0-4	66.1	76	43	7	2	27-3	51	5.83	74	.290	.360	0-0-1	.000	-0		-9	36	-0.5
2004	†Atl N	6	4	.600	79	0	0	0-1	73.2	71	24	5	0	28-5	45	2.57	168	.255	.322	1	.000	-0		14		1.6
2005	Fla N	1	1	.500	33	0	0	0-2	27.1	29	15	2	2	14-4	16	4.94	81	.299	.391	0	—	0		-2	95	-0.1
Total	9	30	35	.462	512	0	0	121-38	547.1	589	255	49	21	216-39	371	3.95	107	.279	.349	13-0-1	.154	-0		22	148	4.1

ALLARD, BRIAN Brian Marshall B1.3.1958 Spring Valley IL BR/TR/6-1/175* [TexA76 4/84] d8.8 [DL 1982 Sea A 182]

YEAR	TM LG	W	L	PCT	G	GS	CG-SHO	SV-BS	IP	H	R	HR	HB	BB-IB	SO	ERA	AERA	OAV	OOB	AB-HR-SH	AVG	PB	SUP	APR	DL	PW
1979	Tex A	1	3	.250	7	4	2	0-0	33.1	36	17	4	0	13-2	14	4.32	96	.283	.348	0	—	0	44	0		-0.0
1980	Tex A	0	1	.000	5	2	0	0-0	14.1	13	13	0	1	10-1	10	5.65	69	.236	.358	0	—	0	115	-4		-0.3
1981	Sea A	3	6	.600	7	7	1	0-0	48	48	22	5	0	8-0	20	3.75	104	.265	.296	0	—	0	102	1	60	0.1
Total	3	4	6	.400	19	13	3	0-0	95.2	97	52	9	1	31-3	44	4.52	88	.266	.325	0	—	0	85	-3	242	-0.2

ALLEN, FRANK Frank Leon B8.26.1889 Newbern AL D7.30.1933 Gainesville AL BR/TL/5-9/175 d4.24 Col Rhodes

YEAR	TM LG	W	L	PCT	G	GS	CG-SHO	SV-BS	IP	H	R	HR	HB	BB-IB	SO	ERA	AERA	OAV	OOB	AB-HR-SH	AVG	PB	SUP	APR	DL	PW
1912	Bro N	3	9	.250	20	15	5-1	0	109	119	70	1	1	57	58	3.63	92	.285	.373	36-1-2	.167	2	83	-8		-0.5
1913	Bro N	4	18	.182	34	25	11	2	174.2	144	75	6	10	81	82	2.83	116	.231	.339	51-1-2	.137	-1	74	7		0.6
1914	Bro N	8	14	.364	36	21	10-1	0	171.1	165	79	6	3	57	68	3.10	92	.265	.330	47-0-3	.128	0*	85	-2		-0.3
	Pit F	1	0	1.000	1	1	1	0	7	9	4	0	0	4	3	5.14	56	.321	.321	2	.500	1	191	-1		-0.1
1915	Pit F	23	13	.639	41	37	24-6	0	283.1	230	90	9	11	100	127	2.51	108	.227	.304	89-0-4	.079	-6	87	9		0.4
1916	Bos N	8	2	.800	19	14	7-2	0	113	102	32	1	4	31	63	2.07	120	.244	.302	34-0-3	.206	3	122	6		0.9

YEAR	TM LG	W	L	PCT	G	GS	CG-SHO	SV-BS	IP	H	R	HR	HB	BB-IB	SO	ERA	AERA	OAV	OOB	AB-HR-SH	AVG	PB	SUP	APR	DL	PW
1917	Bos N	3	10	.231	29	14	2	0	112	124	61	3	6	47	56	3.94	65	.297	.376	29	.172	2	89	-18		-2.0
Total	6	50	66	.431	180	127	60-10	0	970.1	893	411	26	35	373	457	2.93	98	.252	.330	288-2-14	.135	1	88	-7		-1.0

ALLEN, JOHN   John Marshall   B10.27.1890 Berkeley Springs WV   D9.24.1967 Hagerstown MD   BR/TR/6-1/170   d6.2

YEAR	TM LG	W	L	PCT	G	GS	CG-SHO	SV-BS	IP	H	R	HR	HB	BB-IB	SO	ERA	AERA	OAV	OOB	AB-HR-SH	AVG	PB	SUP	APR	DL	PW
1914	Bal F	0	0	—	1	0	0	0	2	4	0	1	2	2	18.00	-17	.286	.500	0	—	0		-3		-0.1

ALLEN, JOHNNY   John Thomas   B9.30.1905 Lenoir NC   D3.29.1959 St.Petersburg FL   BR/TR/6-0/180   d4.19

YEAR	TM LG	W	L	PCT	G	GS	CG-SHO	SV-BS	IP	H	R	HR	HB	BB-IB	SO	ERA	AERA	OAV	OOB	AB-HR-SH	AVG	PB	SUP	APR	DL	PW
1932	†NY A	17	4	.810	33	21	13-3	4	192	162	86	10	5	76	109	3.70	110	.228	.306	73-1-3	.123	-2	119	11		0.9
1933	NY A	15	7	.682	25	24	10-1	1	184.2	171	96	9	4	87	119	4.39	89	.242	.328	72-0-2	.181	0	131	-7		-0.8
1934	NY A	5	2	.714	13	10	4	0	71.2	62	30	3	2	32	54	2.89	141	.227	.313	26-0-2	.192	1	120	9		0.8
1935	NY A	13	6	.684	23	23	12-2	0	167	149	76	11	4	58	113	3.61	112	.238	.307	67-1-3	.224	1	133	11		1.2
1936	Cle A	20	10	.667	36	31	19-4	1	243	234	108	7	1	97	165	3.44	146	.256	.328	87-0-8	.161	-3*	116	43		4.3
1937	Cle A	15	1	.938	24	20	14	0	173	157	55	4	5	60	87	2.55	181	.244	.313	67-0-4	.090	-7	139	40		2.7
1938	Cle A★	14	8	.636	30	27	13	0	200	189	107	15	3	81	112	4.18	111	.246	.321	79-1-3	.253	4	122	10		1.4
1939	Cle A	9	7	.563	28	26	9-2	0	175	199	96	9	3	56	79	4.58	96	.291	.347	71-0-2	.225	1*	118	-1		0.1
1940	Cle A	9	8	.529	32	17	5-3	5	138.2	126	61	3	3	48	62	3.44	123	.243	.311	48	.208	0	66	12		1.4
1941	StL A	2	5	.286	12	9	2	1	67	89	53	4	2	29	27	6.58	65	.319	.387	22-1-1	.136	0	119	-15		-1.4
	†Bro N	3	0	1.000	11	4	1	0	57.1	38	18	6	0	12	21	2.51	146	.188	.234	20-0-1	.050	-0	145	8		0.2
1942	Bro N	10	6	.625	27	15	5-1	0	118	106	53	11	2	39	50	3.20	102	.238	.302	39-0-4	.179	-0	105	-1		-0.2
1943	Bro N	5	1	.833	17	1	0	1	38	42	21	3	2	25	15	4.26	79	.280	.390	7-0-2	.429	2	227	-4		-0.4
	NY N	1	3	.250	15	0	0	2	41	37	16	4	0	14	24	3.07	112	.245	.309	14-0-1	.000	-2		2		0.0
	Year	6	4	.600	32	1	0	3	79	79	37	7	2	39	39	3.65	93	.262	.351	21-0-3	.143	-0	224	-2		-0.4
1944	NY N	4	7	.364	18	13	2-1	0	84	88	48	7	2	24	33	4.07	90	.260	.313	24	.083	-2*	86	-5		-0.9
Total	13	142	75	.654	352	241	109-17	18	1950.1	1849	924	104	38	738	1070	3.75	113	.249	.321	716-4-36	.173	-8	119	113		9.3

ALLEN, LLOYD   Lloyd Cecil   B5.8.1950 Merced CA   BR/TR/6-1/185*   [AnaA68 1/12]   d9.1

YEAR	TM LG	W	L	PCT	G	GS	CG-SHO	SV-BS	IP	H	R	HR	HB	BB-IB	SO	ERA	AERA	OAV	OOB	AB-HR-SH	AVG	PB	SUP	APR	DL	PW
1969	Cal A	0	1	.000	4	1	0	0-0	5	5	7	1	0	10-0	5	5.40	65	.147	.341	2	.500	1	0	-2		-0.1
1970	Cal A	1	1	.500	8	2	0	0-0	24	23	9	0	1	10-2	12	2.63	138	.261	.347	4	.000	-0	74	3		0.2
1971	Cal A	4	6	.400	54	1	0	15-3	94	75	29	4	0	40-8	72	2.49	131	.221	.302	17-1-0	.294	2	55	9		1.5
1972	Cal A	3	7	.300	42	6	0	5-3	85.1	76	38	7	3	55-5	53	3.48	84	.240	.356	17-0-3	.118	-1	50	-6		-0.9
1973	Cal A	0	0	—	5	0	0	1-0	8.2	15	10	0	0	5-0	4	10.38	34	.417	.465	0	—	0		-6		-0.3
	Tex A	0	6	.000	23	5	0	1-0	41	58	59	3	5	39-2	25	9.22	41	.326	.453	0	—	0	119	-30		-3.8
	Year	0	6	.000	28	5	0	2-0	49.2	73	69	3	5	44-2	29	9.42	40	.341	.455	0	—	0	120	-38		-4.1
1974	Tex A	0	1	.000	14	0	0	0-0	22	24	17	2	1	18-0	18	6.55	55	.276	.398	0	—	0		-7		-0.4
	Chi A	0	1	.000	6	2	0	0-0	7	7	9	0	1	12-1	3	10.29	36	.259	.500	0	—	0	176	-5		-0.6
	Year	0	2	.000	20	2	0	0-0	29	31	26	2	2	30-1	21	7.45	49	.272	.426	0	—	0	182	-12		-1.0
1975	Chi A	0	2	.000	3	2	0	0-0	5.1	8	7	2	0	6-0	2	11.81	33	.348	.467	0	—	0	11	-4		-0.7
Total	7	8	25	.242	159	19	0	22-6	297.1	291	183	19	11	196-18	194	4.69	71	.258	.369	40-1-3	.200	2	83	-48		-5.1

ALLEN, MYRON   Myron Smith "Zeke"   B3.22.1854 Kingston NY   D3.8.1924 Kingston NY   BR/TR/5-8/150   d7.19 ▲

YEAR	TM LG	W	L	PCT	G	GS	CG-SHO	SV-BS	IP	H	R	HR	HB	BB-IB	SO	ERA	AERA	OAV	OOB	AB-HR-SH	AVG	PB	SUP	APR	DL	PW
1883	NY N	0	1	.000	1	1	1	0	8	8	5	0	1	3	3	1.13	275	.276	.344	4	.000	-1	69	1		0.0
1887	Cle AA	1	0	1.000	2	0	0	0	9.2	9	4	0	1	3	1	0.93	466	.243	.317	463-4	.276	0*		3		0.2
1888	KC AA	0	2	.000	2	2	2	0	18	17	7	0	2	1	2	2.50	137	.239	.270	136	.213	0*	34	2		0.2
Total	3	1	3	.250	5	3	3	0	35.2	34	16	0	3	7	3	1.77	205	.248	.299	603-4	.260	-0	43	6		0.4

ALLEN, NEIL   Neil Patrick   B1.24.1958 Kansas City KS   BR/TR/6-2/190*   [NYN76 11/253]   d4.15

YEAR	TM LG	W	L	PCT	G	GS	CG-SHO	SV-BS	IP	H	R	HR	HB	BB-IB	SO	ERA	AERA	OAV	OOB	AB-HR-SH	AVG	PB	SUP	APR	DL	PW
1979	NY N	6	10	.375	50	5	0	8-1	99	100	46	4	0	47-13	65	3.55	105	.268	.345	14	.000	-2	52	1	24	0.0
1980	NY N	7	10	.412	59	0	0	22-5	97.1	87	43	7	0	40-9	79	3.70	98	.244	.317	14-0-1	.143	-0	0			-0.1
1981	NY N	7	6	.538	43	0	0	18-9	66.2	64	26	4	0	26-8	50	2.97	119	.259	.326	5-0-2	.200	1	4			1.0
1982	NY N	3	7	.300	50	0	0	19-5	64.2	65	22	5	1	30-5	59	3.06	120	.266	.348	6-0-1	.167	0	6			1.2
1983	NY N	2	7	.222	21	4	1-1	2-2	54	57	29	6	0	36-5	32	4.50	82	.278	.384	10-0-1	.000	-1	96	-4		-0.8
	StL N	10	6	.625	25	18	4-2	0-1	121.2	122	55	6	1	48-4	74	3.70	99	.265	.335	39-0-6	.128	-1	105	0		-0.1
	Year	12	13	.480	46	22	5-3	2-3	175.2	179	84	12	1	84-9	106	3.94	93	.269	.351	49-0-7	.102	-2	103	-6		-0.9
1984	StL N	9	6	.600	57	1	0	3-1	119	105	54	6	0	49-9	66	3.55	99	.239	.314	25	.240	1	50	-1		-0.9
1985	StL N	1	4	.200	23	1	0	2-1	29	32	22	3	1	17-6	10	5.59	64	.283	.373	2	.000	-0	49	-7		-1.3
	NY A	1	0	1.000	17	0	0	1-0	29.1	26	9	1	0	13-0	16	2.76	146	.234	.315	0	—	0		5		0.2
1986	Chi A	7	2	.778	22	17	2-2	0-0	113	101	50	8	2	38-1	57	3.82	114	.244	.306	0	—	0	114	8	35	0.5
1987	Chi A	0	7	.000	15	10	0	0-0	49.2	74	40	6	2	26-0	26	7.07	66	.365	.438	0	—	0	55	-12	70	-1.4
	NY A	0	1	.000	8	1	0	0-0	24.2	23	12	2	0	10-1	16	3.65	122	.242	.314	0	—	0	62	2		0.1
	Year	0	8	.000	23	11	0	0-0	74.1	97	52	8	2	36-1	42	5.93	77	.326	.399	0	—	0	56	-11		-1.3
1988	NY A	5	3	.625	41	0	0-1	0-2	117.1	121	51	14	2	37-7	61	3.84	104	.268	.322	0	—	0	57	3	36	0.1
1989	Cle A	0	1	.000	3	0	0	0-0	3	8	5	1	0	0-0	0	15.00	27	.500	.471	0	—	0		-3	65	-0.6
Total	11	58	70	.453	434	59	7-6	75-27	908.1	985	464	73	9	417-68	611	3.88	99	.264	.336	115-0-11	.130	-1	94	2	230	-1.2

ALLEN, BOB   Robert Earl "Thin Man"   B7.2.1914 Smithville TN   D10.30.2005 Chesapeake VA   BR/TR/6-1/165   d9.19

YEAR	TM LG	W	L	PCT	G	GS	CG-SHO	SV-BS	IP	H	R	HR	HB	BB-IB	SO	ERA	AERA	OAV	OOB	AB-HR-SH	AVG	PB	SUP	APR	DL	PW
1937	Phi N	0	1	.000	3	1	0	0	12	18	12	2	0	8	8	6.75	64	.321	.406	3	.333	0	20	-4		-0.3

ALLEN, BOB   Robert Gray   B10.23.1937 Tatum TX   BL/TL/6-2/190(185-198)   d4.14

YEAR	TM LG	W	L	PCT	G	GS	CG-SHO	SV-BS	IP	H	R	HR	HB	BB-IB	SO	ERA	AERA	OAV	OOB	AB-HR-SH	AVG	PB	SUP	APR	DL	PW
1961	Cle A	3	2	.600	48	0	0	3	81.2	96	42	7	1	40-5	42	3.75	105	.294	.373	12-0-1	.167	0		0		0.0
1962	Cle A	1	1	.500	30	0	0	4	30.2	29	24	5	0	25-5	23	5.87	66	.250	.378	5	.000	-1		-8		-0.7
1963	Cle A	1	2	.333	43	0	0	2	56	58	37	5	1	29-6	51	4.66	78	.266	.352	5	.200	-0		-8		-0.5
1966	Cle A	2	2	.500	36	0	0	5	51.1	56	27	2	2	13-6	33	4.21	82	.273	.318	9-0-1	.111	-0		-4		-0.4
1967	Cle A	0	5	.000	47	0	0	5	54.1	49	22	4	1	25-7	50	2.98	110	.243	.329	0	—	0	1			0.2
Total	5	7	12	.368	204	0	0	19	274	288	152	23	5	132-27	199	4.11	89	.270	.351	31-0-2	.129	-1		-19		-1.4

ALLISON, DANA   Dana Eric   B8.14.1966 Front Royal VA   BR/TL/6-3/215   [OakA89 21/556]   d4.12   Col James Madison

YEAR	TM LG	W	L	PCT	G	GS	CG-SHO	SV-BS	IP	H	R	HR	HB	BB-IB	SO	ERA	AERA	OAV	OOB	AB-HR-SH	AVG	PB	SUP	APR	DL	PW
1991	Oak A	1	1	.500	11	0	0	0-0	11	16	9	0	0	5-1	4	7.36	52	.381	.438	0	—	0		-4		-0.7

ALLISON, MACK   Mack Pendleton   B1.23.1887 Owensboro KY   D3.13.1964 Mount Vernon MO   BR/TR/6-1/185   d9.13

YEAR	TM LG	W	L	PCT	G	GS	CG-SHO	SV-BS	IP	H	R	HR	HB	BB-IB	SO	ERA	AERA	OAV	OOB	AB-HR-SH	AVG	PB	SUP	APR	DL	PW
1911	StL A	2	1	.667	3	3	3	0	26.1	24	9	0	2	5	2	2.05	165	.253	.304	10	.200	-0	93	4		0.3
1912	StL A	6	17	.261	31	20	11-1	1	169	171	102	4	6	49	43	3.62	92	.269	.327	52-0-1	.135	-3	58	-9		-1.5
1913	StL A	1	3	.250	11	4	3	0	51.1	52	24	0	3	13	12	2.28	129	.291	.349	14	.000	-2	19	1		-0.2
Total	3	9	21	.300	45	27	17-1	1	246.2	247	135	4	11	67	57	3.17	102	.271	.329	76-0-1	.118	-6	57	-4		-1.4

ALMANZA, ARMANDO   Armando   B10.26.1972 ElPaso TX   BL/TL/6-3/220(205-240)   [StLN93 21/592]   d7.29   Col New Mexico JC

YEAR	TM LG	W	L	PCT	G	GS	CG-SHO	SV-BS	IP	H	R	HR	HB	BB-IB	SO	ERA	AERA	OAV	OOB	AB-HR-SH	AVG	PB	SUP	APR	DL	PW
1999	Fla N	0	1	.000	14	0	0	0-0	15.2	8	4	1	1	9-1	20	1.72	254	.154	.286	3	.000	-0		4		0.2
2000	Fla N	4	2	.667	60	0	0	0-4	46.1	38	27	3	2	43-6	46	4.86	90	.228	.388	1-0-1	.000	-0		-3		-0.3
2001	Fla N	2	2	.500	52	0	0	0-2	41	34	24	8	0	26-1	45	4.83	86	.230	.339	0	—	0		-3		-0.3
2002	Fla N	3	2	.600	51	0	0	0-2	45.2	36	22	6	3	23-1	57	4.34	91	.224	.316	0	—	0		-1	51	-0.1
2003	Fla N	4	5	.444	51	0	0	0-2	50.1	59	37	10	2	25-2	49	6.08	67	.296	.376	0	—	0		-12	40	-1.9
2004	Atl N	1	1	.500	13	0	0	0-0	11.2	9	8	3	1	7-2	13	6.17	70	.200	.315	0-0-1	—	0		-2	37	-0.3
2005	Ari N	0	0	—	6	0	0	0-1	4	5	1	1	2	3-0	2	2.25	195	.313	.421	0	—	0		1		0.1
Total	7	14	13	.519	254	0	0	2-11	214.2	189	123	34	6	136-13	232	4.82	87	.240	.351	4-0-2	.000	-0		-15	128	-2.6

ALMANZAR, CARLOS   Carlos Manuel (Giron)   B11.6.1973 Santiago, D.R.   BR/TR/6-2/200(166-200)   d9.4

YEAR	TM LG	W	L	PCT	G	GS	CG-SHO	SV-BS	IP	H	R	HR	HB	BB-IB	SO	ERA	AERA	OAV	OOB	AB-HR-SH	AVG	PB	SUP	APR	DL	PW
1997	Tor A	0	1	.000	4	0	0	0-0	3.1	1	1	1	0	1-0	4	2.70	170	.091	.167	0	—	0		1		0.1
1998	Tor A	2	2	.500	25	0	0	0-3	28.2	34	18	4	1	8-2	20	5.34	87	.286	.336	0	—	0		-2		-0.2
1999	SD N	0	0	—	28	0	0	0-0	37.1	48	32	6	3	15-2	30	7.47	57	.316	.386	1	.000	-0		-13	33	-0.6
2000	SD N	4	5	.444	62	0	0	0-3	69.2	73	35	12	4	25-2	56	4.39	101	.266	.333	3	.000	-0		2		0.2
2001	NY A	0	0	—	10	0	0	0-2	15	14	4	2	0	2-1	6	3.38	132	.333	.356	0	—	0		1		0.1
2002	Cin N	0	1	.000	7	0	0	0-0	11.2	6	4	0	0	5-1	7	2.31	184	.158	.244	0	—	0	43	2	111	0.2
2004	Tex A	7	3	.700	67	0	0	0-2	72.2	66	32	8	4	19-4	44	3.72	133	.244	.301	0	—	0		10		1.1
2005	Tex A	0	0	—	6	0	0	0-0	5	10	8	2	1	7-0	3	14.40	32	.435	.545	0	—	0		-5	155	-0.2
Total	8	13	13	.500	210	0	0	0-10	239	252	134	35	13	82-12	170	4.82	95	.271	.335	4	.000	-0	43	-4	299	0.7

ALMONTE, ED   Edwin   B12.17.1976 Santiago, D.R.   BR/TR/6-3/200   [ChiA98 26/779]   d7.7   Col St. Francis (NY)

YEAR	TM LG	W	L	PCT	G	GS	CG-SHO	SV-BS	IP	H	R	HR	HB	BB-IB	SO	ERA	AERA	OAV	OOB	AB-HR-SH	AVG	PB	SUP	APR	DL	PW
2003	NY. N	0	0	—	12	0	0	0-0	11.1	21	15	3	0	7	7	11.12	38	.412	.464	1	.000	-0		-9		-0.4

YEAR	TM LG	W	L	PCT	G	GS	CG-SHO	SV-BS	IP	H	R	HR	HB	BB-IB	SO	ERA	AERA	OAV	OOB	AB-HR-SH	AVG	PB	SUP	APR	DL	PV
ALMONTE, HECTOR Hector Radhames (Moreta) B10.17.1975 Santo Domingo, D.R. BR/TR/6-2/190* d7.26																										
1999	Fla N	0	2	.000	15	0	0	0-0	15	20	7	1	0	6-2	8	4.20	104	.339	.394	0	—	0	1			0.
2003	Bos A	0	1	.000	7	0	0	0-0	7.2	9	7	1	0	7-1	6	8.22	57	.310	.421	0	—	0	-3			-0.
	Mon N	1	1	.500	28	0	0	0-1	29	34	22	4	2	17-2	26	6.83	65	.291	.390	1	.000	-0	-6			-0.
Total	2	1	4	.200	50	0	0	0-1	51.2	63	36	6	2	30-5	40	6.27	71	.307	.396	1	.000	0	-8			-0.
ALOMA, LUIS Luis (Barba) "Witto" B6.19.1923 Havana, Cuba D4.7.1997 Park Ridge IL BR/TR/6-2/195(180-195) d4.19																										
1950	Chi A	7	2	.778	42	0	0	4	87.2	77	44	6	1	53	49	3.80	118	.234	.342	15-0-1	.067	-2	6			0.
1951	Chi A	6	0	1.000	25	1	1-1	3	69.1	52	14	3	2	24	25	1.82	222	.215	.291	20-0-1	.350	2	198	18	35	1.
1952	Chi A	3	1	.750	25	0	0	6	40	42	20	5	1	11	18	4.27	85	.278	.331	7	.000	-1	-2		40	-0.
1953	Chi A	2	0	1.000	24	0	0	2	38.1	41	20	7	0	23	23	4.70	86	.283	.381	6	.000	-1	-2			-0.
Total	4	18	3	.857	116	1	1-1	15	235.1	212	98	21	4	111	115	3.44	120	.245	.333	48-0-2	.167	-2	198	20	75	1.
ALSTON, GARVIN Garvin James B12.8.1971 Mt.Vernon NY BR/TR/6-2/185 [ColN92 10/291] d6.6 Col Florida International [DL 1997 Col N 181]																										
1996	Col N	1	0	1.000	6	0	0	0-0	6	9	6	1	1	3-0	5	9.00	58	.375	.433	1	.000	-0	-2			-0.
ALTAMIRANO, PORFI Porfirio (Ramirez) B5.17.1952 Darillo, Nicaragua BR/TR/6-0/175* d5,9																										
1982	Phi N	5	1	.833	29	0	0	2-1	39	41	19	2	1	14-3	26	4.15	89	.281	.339	4	.250	-1	-1	23		-0.2
1983	Phi N	2	3	.400	31	0	0	0-0	41.1	38	18	9	2	15-3	24	3.70	97	.255	.329	2	.000	-0	0			0.
1984	Chi N	0	0	—	5	0	0	0-0	11.1	8	6	2	0	1-0	7	4.76	82	.195	.209	2	.000	-0	-1			0:
Total	3	7	4	.636	65	0	0	2-1	91.2	87	43	13	3	30-6	57	4.03	91	.259	.320	8	.125	-2	-2	23		-0..
ALTEN, ERNIE Ernest Matthias "Lefty" B12.1.1894 Avon OH D9.9.1981 Napa CA BR/TL/6-0/175 d4.17																										
1920	Det A	0	1	.000	14	1	0	0	23	40	27	2	1	9	4	9.00	41	.392	.446	3	.000	-1	213	-12		-0.•
ALTROCK, NICK Nicholas B9.15.1876 Cincinnati OH D1.20.1965 Washington DC BB/TL/5-10/197 d7.14 C42																										
1898	Lou N	3	3	.500	11	7	6	0	70	89	54	2	3	21	13	4.50	80	.307	.360	29	.241	0	127	-10		0.•
1902	Bos A	0	2	.000	3	2	1	1	18	19	13	0	1	7	5	2.00	179	.271	.346	8	.000	-1	70	1		0.•
1903	Bos A	0	1	.000	1	1	1	0	8	13	10	0	4	0	4	9.00	34	.361	.425	3	.667	1	71	-5		-0.
	Chi A	4	3	.571	12	8	6-1	0	71	59	35	3	3	19	19	2.15	104	.226	.286	30	.300	2*	130	2		0.•
	Year	4	4	.500	13	9	7-1	0	79	72	45	3	3	23	22	2.85	99	.242	.303	33	.333	4	123	-4		-0.
1904	Chi A	19	14	.576	38	36	31-6	1	307	274	117	2	3	48	87	2.96	83	.240	.272	111-1-6	.198	1*	126	-10		-0.
1905	Chi A	23	12	.657	38	34	31-3	0	315.2	274	89	3	2	63	97	1.88	131	.236	.276	112-0-5	.125	-3*	122	24		1.
1906	†Chi A	20	13	.606	38	30	25-4	0	287.2	269	95	0	3	42	99	2.06	123	.250	.281	100-0-2	.160	1	105	15		1.
1907	Chi A	7	13	.350	30	21	15-1	2	213.2	210	76	3	2	31	61	2.57	93	.259	.288	72	.181	1	67	-2		-0.
1908	Chi A	5	7	.417	23	13	8-1	2	136	127	55	2	2	18	21	2.71	85	.248	.276	49-0-1	.204	1	111	-6		-0.
1909	Chi A	0	1	.000	1	1	1	0	9	16	6	0	1	4	2	5.00	47	.485	.500	3	.000	-0	60	-2		-0.
	Was A	1	3	.250	9	5	2	0	38	55	23	0	1	5	9	5.45	45	.333	.357	19	.053	-1*	70	-10		-1.
	Year	1	4	.200	10	6	3	0	47	71	29	0	1	9	11	5.36	45	.359	.380	22	.045	0	68	-12		-1.
1912	Was A	0	1	.000	1	0	0	0	1	1	2	0	0	2	0	18.00	19	.200	.429	1	.000	-0	-1			-0.
1913	Was A	0	0	—	4	0	0	0	9	7	5	0	1	4	2	5.00	59	.194	.293	1	.000	-0	-1			-0.
1914	Was A	0	0	—	1	0	0	0	1	3	0	0	0	0	0	0.00	—	.750	.750	0	—	0	-2			-0.
1915	Was A	0	0	—	1	0	0	0	3	7	4	0	0	1	2	9.00	33	.438	.471	1	.000	-0	-2			-0.
1918	Was A	1	2	.333	5	3	1	0	24	24	11	1	1	6	5	3.00	91	.279	.333	8-1-1	.125	0	55	-1		0.
1919	Was A	0	0	—	1	0	0	0	0	4	4	0	0	0	0	∞	—	1.000	1.000	0	—	0	-4			0.
1924	Was A	0	0	—	1	0	0	0	2	4	1	0	0	0	0	0.00	—	.500	.500	1	1.000	1	1			0.
Total	16	83	75	.525	218	161	128-16	7	1514	1455	600	16	22	272	425	2.67	95	.255	.291	548-2-15	.175	1	108	-11		1.
ALVAREZ, ABE Abraham B10.17.1982 Los Angeles CA BL/TL/6-2/190* d7.22 Col Cal St.-Long Beach																										
2004	Bos A	0	1	.000	1	1	0	0-0	5	8	5	2	0	5-0	2	9.00	54	.400	.520	0	—	0	57	-2		-0.
2005	Bos A	0	0	—	2	0	0	0-0	2.1	6	4	1	0	0-0	1	15.43	30	.462	.462	0	—	0	-3			-0.
Total	2	0	1	.000	3	1	0	0-0	7.1	14	9	3	0	5-0	3	11.05	43	.424	.500	0	—	0	57	-5		-0.
ALVAREZ, TAVO Cesar Octavio B11.25.1971 Ciudad Obregon, Sonora, Mexico BR/TR/6-3/245* [MonN90 2/50] d8.21																										
1995	Mon N	1	5	.167	8	8	0	0-0	37.1	46	30	2	3	14-0	17	6.75	64	.297	.366	12-0-2	.000	-1	95	-10		-1.
1996	Mon N	2	1	.667	11	5	0	0-0	21	19	10	0	1	12-1	9	3.00	144	.235	.340	4-0-1	.500	1	100	2	16	0.
Total	2	3	6	.333	19	13	0	0-0	58.1	65	40	2	4	26-1	26	5.40	80	.275	.357	16-0-3	.125	-1	97	-8	16	-1.
ALVAREZ, JOSE Jose Lino B4.12.1956 Tampa FL BR/TR/5-10/170* [AtlN78 8/183] d10.1 Col Louisiana-Lafayette [DL 1990 SF N 178]																										
1981	Atl N	0	0	—	2	0	0	0-0	2	0	0	0	0	0-0	2	0.00	—	.000	.000	0	—	0	1			0.
1982	Atl N	0	0	—	7	0	0	0-0	7.2	8	4	1	0	2-1	6	4.70	79	.308	.357	0	—	-0	-1			0.
1988	Atl N	5	6	.455	60	0	0	3-1	102.1	88	34	7	6	53-12	81	2.99	123	.240	.343	8-0-1	.375	1*	9			1.
1989	Atl N	3	3	.500	30	0	0	2-3	50.1	44	18	4	1	24-2	45	2.86	128	.237	.325	3-0-2	.000	-0	4	99		0.
Total	4	8	9	.471	98	0	0	5-4	162.1	140	56	12	7	79-15	134	2.99	122	.240	.335	11-0-3	.273	1	13	277		1.
ALVAREZ, JUAN Juan M. B8.9.1973 Coral Gables FL BL/TL/6-1/175* d9.1 Col St. Thomas (FL)																										
1999	Ana A	0	1	.000	6	0	0	0-0	3	1	1	0	0	4-0	4	3.00	163	.111	.385	0	—	0	1			0.
2000	Ana A	0	0	—	11	0	0	0-0	6	14	9	3	0	7-1	2	13.50	38	.467	.553	0	—	0	-5			-0.
2002	Tex A	0	4	.000	52	0	0	0-3	39.2	35	22	7	3	21-0	30	4.76	101	.241	.345	0	—	0	2			0.
2003	Fla N	0	0	—	9	0	0	0-0	11.2	8	4	2	1	8-1	6	3.09	133	.216	.370	0	—	0	2			0.
Total	4	0	5	.000	80	0	0	0-3	60.1	58	36	12	4	40-2	42	5.22	90	.262	.381	0	—	0	-2			0.
ALVAREZ, VICTOR Victor Aurelio B11.8.1976 Culiacan, Sinaloa, Mexico BL/TL/5-10/150* d7.30																										
2002	LA N	0	1	.000	4	1	0	0-0	10.1	9	5	1	0	2-0	7	4.35	90	.237	.275	2	.000	-0	0			-0.
2003	LA N	0	1	.000	5	0	0	0-0	5.2	9	8	1	1	6-0	3	12.71	32	.391	.533	0	—	0	-5			-0.
Total	2	0	2	.000	9	1	0	0-0	16	18	13	2	1	8-0	10	7.31	54	.295	.386	2	.000	-0	0	-5		-0.
ALVAREZ, WILSON Wilson Eduardo (Fuenmayor) B3.24.1970 Maracaibo, Venez BL/TL/6-1/235(175-255) d7.24 [DL 2001 TB A 190]																										
1989	Tex A	0	1	.000	1	1	0	0-0	0	3	3	2	0	2-0	0	∞	—	1.000	1.000	0	—	0	68	-3		-0.
1991	Chi A	3	2	.600	10	9	2-1	0-0	56.1	47	26	9	0	29-0	32	3.51	114	.230	.325	0	—	0	127	2		0.
1992	Chi A	5	3	.625	34	9	0	1-0	100.1	103	64	12	4	65-2	66	5.20	75	.272	.381	0	—	0	149	-15		-1.
1993	†Chi A	15	8	.652	31	31	1-1	0-0	207.2	168	78	14	7	122-8	155	2.95	143	.230	.344	0	—	0	100	29		2.
1994	Chi A★	12	8	.600	24	24	2-1	0-0	161.2	147	72	16	0	62-1	108	3.45	136	.241	.309	0	—	0	102	22		2.
1995	Chi A	8	11	.421	29	29	3	0-0	175	171	96	21	4	93-4	118	4.32	104	.258	.349	0	—	0	101	1		0.
1996	Chi A	15	10	.600	35	35	0	0-0	217.1	216	106	21	4	97-3	181	4.22	113	.258	.337	0	—	0	119	16		1.
1997	Chi A	9	8	.529	22	22	2-1	0-0	145.2	126	61	9	3	55-1	110	3.03	146	.232	.303	3	.000	0	80	20		2.
	†SF N	4	3	.571	11	11	0	0-0	66.1	56	36	9	1	36-3	69	4.48	92	.224	.326	23-0-1	.130	0	130	-2		-0.
1998	TB A	6	14	.300	25	25	0	0-0	142.2	130	78	18	9	68-0	107	4.73	101	.239	.332	0	—	0	65	2	46	0.
1999	TB A	9	9	.500	28	28	1	0-0	160	159	92	22	6	79-1	128	4.22	118	.260	.349	3	.000	0	100	10	38	0.
2002	TB A	2	3	.400	23	10	0	1-0	75	80	47	14	4	36-3	56	5.28	86	.272	.356	4	.000	-0	111	-6	67	0.
2003	LA N	6	2	.750	21	12	1-1	1-0	95	80	27	5	5	23-1	82	2.37	174	.231	.288	29-0-1	.172	0	103	19		1.
2004	†LA N	7	6	.538	40	15	0	1-1	120.2	109	56	12	5	31-2	102	4.03	103	.244	.297	31-0-2	.161	-0	100	2		1.
2005	LA N	1	4	.200	21	2	0	1-0	24	31	17	7	0	7-0	16	5.63	73	.316	.355	2-0-1	.000	-0	57	-4	123	-0.
Total	14	102	92	.526	355	263	12-5	4-1	1747.2	1624	857	190	50	805-29	1330	3.96	113	.248	.333	95-0-5	.137	-1	102	93	464	9.
AMES, RED Leon Kessling B8.2.1882 Warren OH D10.8.1936 Warren OH BB/TR/5-10.5/185 d9.14																										
1903	NY N	2	0	1.000	2	2	2-1	0	14	5	4	0	0	8	14	1.29	260	.114	.250	6	.000	-1	121	3		0.
1904	NY N	4	6	.400	16	13	11-1	0	115	94	44	2	3	38	93	2.27	120	.222	.291	40	.125	-1	76	5		0.
1905	†NY N	22	8	.733	34	31	21-2	0	262.2	220	113	2	3	105	198	2.74	107	.230	.308	97-0-6	.144	-1	140	5		0.
1906	NY N	12	10	.545	31	25	15-1	1	203.1	166	79	3	9	93	156	2.66	98	.223	.312	61-0-1	.066	-3	109	0		0.
1907	NY N	10	12	.455	30	26	17-2	1	233.1	184	93	4	10	108	146	2.16	115	.219	.315	69-1-4	.174	-2	113	2		0.
1908	NY N	7	4	.636	18	15	5	1	114.1	96	35	0	4	27	81	1.81	133	.232	.281	36-0-4	.194	-0	132	6		0.
1909	NY N	15	10	.600	34	27	20-2	1	244	217	109	2	4	81	156	2.69	95	.241	.306	81-0-3	.074	-5	118	-4		0.
1910	NY N	12	11	.522	33	23	13-3	0	190.1	161	78	3	6	63	94	2.22	133	.237	.308	62-1-2	.177	-1	96	11		1.
1911	†NY N	11	10	.524	34	23	13-1	2	205	170	80	0	4	54	118	2.68	126	.223	.277	64-0-3	.094	-3	87	16		1.
1912	†NY N	11	5	.688	33	22	9-2	1	179	194	82	2	4	35	83	2.46	137	.281	.320	58-0-1	.224	-1	109	14		76
1913	NY N	2	1	.667	8	5	2	0	41.2	35	11	0	1	8	30	2.16	144	.241	.286	13-0-1	.154	-1				0

YEAR	TM LG	W	L	PCT	G	GS	CG-SHO	SV-BS	IP	H	R	HR	HB	BB-IB	SO	ERA	AERA	OAV	OOB	AB-HR-SH	AVG	PB	SUP	APR	DL	PW
	Cin N	11	13	.458	31	24	12-1	2	187.1	185	82	7	5	70	80	2.88	113	.265	.336	59-0-4	.102	-4	86	7		0.4
	Year	13	14	.481	39	29	14-1	3	229	220	93	7	6	78	110	2.75	117	.261	.328	72-0-5	.111	-5	92	14		0.9
1914	Cin N	15	23	.395	47	37	18-4	6	297	274	125	7	6	94	128	2.64	111	.248	.311	94-1-5	.128	-4	78	9		1.0
1915	Cin N	2	4	.333	17	7	4-1	1	68	82	39	2	0	24	26	4.50	64	.311	.368	20	.050	-1	82	-10		-1.0
	StL N	9	3	.750	15	14	8-2	1	113.1	93	35	1	0	32	48	2.46	113	.226	.282	35-0-3	.114	-2	116	6		0.6
	Year	11	7	.611	32	21	12-3	2	181.1	175	74	3	0	56	74	3.23	87	.259	.316	55-0-3	.091	-3	104	-3		-0.4
1916	StL N	11	16	.407	45	25	10-2	8	228	225	100	3	5	57	98	2.64	100	.263	.313	68-0-2	.176	-0	90	-4		-0.6
1917	StL N	15	10	.600	43	19	10-2	3	209	189	75	2	3	57	62	2.71	99	.249	.304	64-0-3	.188	2	93	0		0.5
1918	StL N	9	14	.391	27	25	17	1	206.2	192	75	1	5	52	68	2.31	117	.252	.304	64-0-4	.156	-1	81	8		0.8
1919	StL N	3	5	.375	23	6	1	1	70	88	44	1	1	25	19	4.89	57	.314	.373	18-0-1	.222	-0	123	-15		-1.8
	Phi N	0	2	.000	3	2	1	1	16	26	12	0	0	3	4	6.19	52	.400	.426	5	.400	1	37	-4		-0.4
	Year	3	7	.300	26	8	2	2	86	114	56	1	1	28	23	5.13	56	.330	.382	23-0-1	.261	1	100	-19		-2.2
Total	17	183	167	.523	533	371	209-27	36	3198	2896	1313	41	64	1034	1702	2.63	108	.245	.310	1014-3-47	.141	-21	101	60		5.5

AMOLE, DOC Morris George B7.5.1878 Coatesville PA D3.7.1912 Wilmington DE BR/TL/5-9/165 d8.19

YEAR	TM LG	W	L	PCT	G	GS	CG-SHO	SV-BS	IP	H	R	HR	HB	BB-IB	SO	ERA	AERA	OAV	OOB	AB-HR-SH	AVG	PB	SUP	APR	DL	PW
1897	Bal N	4	4	.500	11	7	6	0	70	67	34	0	6	17	19	2.57	162	.250	.309	28	.107	-3	73	11		0.8
1898	Was N	0	6	.000	7	5	4	0	49.1	83	57	0	6	22	11	7.84	47	.369	.439	20	.100	-2	93	-21		-2.0
Total	2	4	10	.286	18	12	10	0	119.1	150	91	0	12	39	30	4.75	83	.304	.369	48	.104	-4	81	-10		-1.2

AMOR, VICENTE Vicente (Alvarez) B8.8.1932 Havana, Cuba BR/TR/6-3/182* d4.16

YEAR	TM LG	W	L	PCT	G	GS	CG-SHO	SV-BS	IP	H	R	HR	HB	BB-IB	SO	ERA	AERA	OAV	OOB	AB-HR-SH	AVG	PB	SUP	APR	DL	PW
1955	Chi N	0	1	.000	4	0	0	0	6	11	3	0	0	3-1	3	4.50	91	.407	.467	0	—	0	0	0		0.0
1957	Cin N	1	2	.333	9	4	1	0	27.1	39	19	2	2	10-1	9	5.93	69	.345	.402	6	.167	-0	112	-5		-0.5
Total	2	1	3	.250	13	4	1	0	33.1	50	22	2	2	13-2	12	5.67	72	.357	.414	6	.167	-0	112	-5		-0.5

ANCKER, WALTER Walter B4.10.1893 New York NY D2.13.1954 Englewood NJ BR/TR/6-1/190 d9.3

YEAR	TM LG	W	L	PCT	G	GS	CG-SHO	SV-BS	IP	H	R	HR	HB	BB-IB	SO	ERA	AERA	OAV	OOB	AB-HR-SH	AVG	PB	SUP	APR	DL	PW
1915	Phi A	0	0	—	4	1	0	0	17.2	19	10	1	3	17	4	3.57	82	.279	.443	6	.000	-1	150	-1		-0.2

ANDERSEN, LARRY Larry Eugene B5.6.1953 Portland OR BR/TR/6-3/205(180-205) [CleA71 7/155] d9.5

YEAR	TM LG	W	L	PCT	G	GS	CG-SHO	SV-BS	IP	H	R	HR	HB	BB-IB	SO	ERA	AERA	OAV	OOB	AB-HR-SH	AVG	PB	SUP	APR	DL	PW
1975	Cle A	0	0	—	3	0	0	0-0	5.2	4	3	0	0	2-0	4	4.76	80	.200	.261	0	—	0	0	0		0.0
1977	Cle A	0	1	.000	11	0	0	0-0	14.1	10	7	1	0	9-3	8	3.14	127	.200	.322	0	—	0		1		0.1
1979	Cle A	0	0	—	8	0	0	0-0	16.2	15	14	3	0	4-0	7	7.56	57	.357	.382	0	—	0		-5		-0.2
1981	Sea A	3	3	.500	41	0	0	5-3	67.2	57	27	4	2	18-2	40	2.66	146	.228	.282	0	—	0		7		0.7
1982	Sea A	0	0	—	40	0	0	1-0	79.2	100	56	16	4	23-1	32	5.99	72	.311	.361	0	—	0	106	-13	21	-0.6
1983	†Phi N	1	0	1.000	17	0	0	0-1	26.1	19	7	0	0	9-1	14	2.39	151	.200	.267	2	.000	-0		4		0.2
1984	Phi N	3	7	.300	64	0	0	4-6	90.2	85	32	5	0	25-6	54	2.38	154	.248	.296	4	.000	-0		11		1.2
1985	Phi N	3	3	.500	57	0	0	3-6	73	78	41	5	3	26-4	50	4.32	86	.274	.340	4-0-1	.000	-0		-5		-0.4
1986	Phi N	0	0	—	10	0	0	0-0	12.2	19	8	0	0	3-0	9	4.26	92	.388	.415	0-0-1	—	0		-1		0.0
	†Hou N	2	1	.667	38	0	0	1-3	64.2	64	22	2	1	23-10	33	2.78	130	.276	.338	6	.000	-1		6		0.3
	Year	2	1	.667	48	0	0	1-3	77.1	83	30	2	1	26-10	42	3.03	121	.301	.351	6-0-1	.000	-1		5		0.3
1987	Hou N	9	5	.643	67	0	0	5-4	101.2	95	46	7	2	41-10	94	3.45	114	.246	.319	6	.167	0		4		0.6
1988	Hou N	2	4	.333	53	0	0	5-4	82.2	82	29	3	1	20-8	66	2.94	113	.254	.297	6	.333	1		4	15	0.4
1989	Hou N	4	4	.500	60	0	0	3-3	87.2	63	19	2	0	24-4	85	1.54	221	.198	.251	3-0-1	.333	0		18	30	1.7
1990	Hou N	5	2	.714	50	0	0	6-1	73.2	61	19	2	1	24-5	68	1.95	191	.229	.291	3-0-1	.000	-0		14		1.5
	†Bos A	0	0	—	15	0	0	1-3	22	18	3	0	1	3-0	25	1.23	334	.220	.256	0	—	0		7		0.3
1991	SD N	3	4	.429	38	0	0	13-3	47	39	13	0	0	13-3	40	2.30	166	.231	.283	2	.000	-0		8	41	1.5
1992	SD N	1	1	.500	34	0	0	2-0	35	26	14	2	1	8-2	35	3.34	108	.202	.252	1	.000	0		1	63	0.1
1993	†Phi N	3	2	.600	64	0	0	0-4	61.2	54	22	4	1	21-2	67	2.92	136	.233	.299	1	1.000	0		8	19	0.6
1994	Phi N	1	2	.333	29	0	0	0-0	32.2	33	20	2	0	15-3	27	4.41	97	.256	.333	0	—	0		-1	49	-0.1
Total	17	40	39	.506	699	1	0	49-41	995.1	932	402	58	17	311-64	758	3.15	120	.249	.306	38-0-4	.132	-0	106	68	238	7.9

ANDERSON, ALLAN Allan Lee B1.7.1964 Lancaster OH BL/TL/6-0/186(180-201) [MinA82 2/32] d6.11

YEAR	TM LG	W	L	PCT	G	GS	CG-SHO	SV-BS	IP	H	R	HR	HB	BB-IB	SO	ERA	AERA	OAV	OOB	AB-HR-SH	AVG	PB	SUP	APR	DL	PW
1986	Min A	3	6	.333	21	10	1	0-0	84.1	106	54	11	1	30-3	51	5.55	78	.316	.371	0	—	0*	77	-9		-0.9
1987	Min A	1	0	1.000	4	2	0	0-0	12.1	20	15	3	0	10-2	3	10.95	42	.392	.492	0	—	0	177	-8		-0.5
1988	Min A	16	9	.640	30	30	3-1	0-0	202.1	199	70	14	7	37-1	83	2.45	167	.261	.299	0	—	0	87	31		3.8
1989	Min A	17	10	.630	33	33	4-1	0-0	196.2	214	97	15	7	53-1	69	3.80	109	.275	.325	1	.000	-0*	125	4		0.5
1990	Min A	7	18	.280	31	31	5-1	0-0	188.2	214	106	20	4	39-1	82	4.53	92	.289	.325	0	—	0	70	-8		-0.8
1991	Min A	5	11	.313	29	22	2	0-0	134.1	148	82	24	5	42-4	51	4.96	86	.281	.336	0	—	0	79	-10		-1.1
Total	6	49	54	.476	148	128	15-3	0-0	818.2	901	424	87	25	211-12	339	4.11	102	.282	.329	1	.000	-0	92	0		1.0

ANDERSON, RED Arnold Revola B6.19.1912 Lawton IA D8.7.1972 Sioux City IA BR/TR/6-3/210 d9.19 Mil 1942

YEAR	TM LG	W	L	PCT	G	GS	CG-SHO	SV-BS	IP	H	R	HR	HB	BB-IB	SO	ERA	AERA	OAV	OOB	AB-HR-SH	AVG	PB	SUP	APR	DL	PW
1937	Was A	0	1	.000	2	1	0	0	10.2	11	9	0	1	9-1	3	6.75	66	.282	.451	3	.000	-0	20	-3		-0.2
1940	Was A	1	1	.500	2	2	2	0	14	12	6	0	0	5	3	3.86	108	.245	.315	5	.600	1	74	1		0.3
1941	Was A	4	6	.400	32	6	1	0	112	127	69	7	3	53	34	4.18	97	.296	.377	31-0-2	.258	2	100	-5		-0.2
Total	3	5	8	.385	36	9	3	0	136.2	150	84	7	4	69	40	4.35	94	.290	.378	39-0-2	.282	3	85	-7		-0.1

ANDERSON, BRIAN Brian James B4.26.1972 Portsmouth VA BL/TL/6-1/190* [CalA93 1/3] d9.10 Col Wright St.

YEAR	TM LG	W	L	PCT	G	GS	CG-SHO	SV-BS	IP	H	R	HR	HB	BB-IB	SO	ERA	AERA	OAV	OOB	AB-HR-SH	AVG	PB	SUP	APR	DL	PW
1993	Cal A	0	0	—	4	1	0	0-0	11.1	11	5	1	0	2-0	4	3.97	114	.256	.289	0	—	0	61	1		0.0
1994	Cal A	7	5	.583	18	18	0	0-0	101.2	120	63	13	5	27-0	47	5.22	94	.300	.347	0	—	0	115	-4	31	-0.4
1995	Cal A	6	8	.429	18	17	1	0-0	99.2	110	66	24	3	30-2	45	5.87	80	.282	.334	0	—	0	*108	-11	45	-1.2
1996	Cle A	3	1	.750	9	6	0	0-0	51.1	58	29	9	0	14-1	21	4.91	100	.296	.338	0	—	0	137	1		0.1
1997	†Cle A	4	2	.667	8	8	0	0-0	48	55	28	7	0	11-0	22	4.69	100	.301	.332	0	—	0	112	0	38	0.0
1998	Ari N	12	13	.480	32	32	2-1	0-0	208	221	109	39	4	24-2	95	4.33	99	.274	.297	66-0-6	.106	-3*	95	-1		-0.2
1999	†Ari N	8	2	.800	31	19	2-1	1-1	130	144	69	18	1	28-3	75	4.57	101	.279	.317	38-1-1	.132	1*	118	2		0.4
2000	Ari N	11	7	.611	33	32	2	0-0	213.1	226	101	38	3	39-7	104	4.05	118	.275	.308	69-0-9	.188	1*	97	18		1.6
2001	Ari N	4	9	.308	29	22	1	0-1	133.1	156	93	25	1	30-2	55	5.20	89	.295	.332	37	.135	-0*	103	-12	48	-1.0
2002	Ari N	6	11	.353	35	24	0	0-0	156	174	86	23	1	32-3	81	4.79	94	.284	.317	43-0-5	.116	-1*	87	-4		-0.4
2003	Cle A	9	10	.474	25	24	0	0-0	148	162	88	21	4	32-3	72	3.71	119	.282	.319	1	.000	0*	101	4		0.5
	KC A	5	1	.833	7	7	2-1	0-0	49.2	50	22	6	0	11-0	15	3.99	121	.272	.310	0	—	0	139	5		0.5
	Year	14	11	.560	32	31	2-1	0-0	197.2	212	110	27	4	43-3	87	3.78	120	.279	.317	1	.000	0	110	8		1.0
2004	KC A	6	12	.333	35	26	2-1	0-0	166	217	123	33	1	53-4	70	5.64	83	.320	.366	1-0-1	.000	-0	112	-21		-1.9
2005	KC A	1	2	.333	6	6	0	0-0	30.2	39	24	7	0	4-1	17	6.75	62	.305	.323	0	—	0	134	-9	147	-0.7
Total	13	82	83	.497	291	245	12-4	1-2	1547	1743	906	264	23	337-28	723	4.74	97	.287	.324	255-1-22	.137	-3	106	-31	309	-2.7

ANDERSON, DAVE David S. B10.10.1868 Chester PA D3.22.1897 Chester PA TL d8.24

YEAR	TM LG	W	L	PCT	G	GS	CG-SHO	SV-BS	IP	H	R	HR	HB	BB-IB	SO	ERA	AERA	OAV	OOB	AB-HR-SH	AVG	PB	SUP	APR	DL	PW
1889	Phi N	0	1	.000	5	2	1	0	23	30	21	2	0	14	8	7.43	59	.306	.393	11	.182	-0	93	-5		-0.2
1890	Phi N	1	1	.500	3	2	1	0	19.1	31	25	0	1	11	7	7.45	49	.352	.430	9	.111	-1	112	-8		-0.6
	Pit N	2	11	.154	13	13	13	0	108	116	84	2	7	49	41	4.67	71	.265	.349	42	.071	-5	65	-16		-1.7
	Year	3	12	.200	16	15	14	0	127.1	147	109	2	8	60	48	5.09	66	.280	.363	51	.078	-6	72	-26		-2.3
Total	2	3	13	.188	21	17	15	0	150.1	177	130	4	8	74	56	5.45	64	.284	.367	62	.097	-6	74	-29		-2.5

ANDERSON, JIMMY James Drew B1.22.1976 Portsmouth VA BL/TL/6-1/215(190-215) [PitN94 9/242] d7.4

YEAR	TM LG	W	L	PCT	G	GS	CG-SHO	SV-BS	IP	H	R	HR	HB	BB-IB	SO	ERA	AERA	OAV	OOB	AB-HR-SH	AVG	PB	SUP	APR	DL	PW
1999	Pit N	2	1	.667	13	4	0	0-0	29.1	25	15	2	1	16-2	13	3.99	115	.234	.336	9	.333	1	120	2		0.3
2000	Pit N	5	11	.313	27	26	1	0-0	144	169	94	13	7	58-2	73	5.25	88	.294	.366	50-0-4	.140	-1	93	-10		-1.0
2001	Pit N	9	17	.346	34	34	1	0-0	206.1	232	123	15	11	83-14	89	5.10	88	.287	.358	59-0-6	.119	-1	78	-13		-1.4
2002	Pit N	8	13	.381	28	25	1	0-0	140.2	167	91	20	5	63-5	47	5.44	77	.299	.372	42-0-3	.119	-1	96	-18		-2.3
2003	Cin N	1	5	.167	8	7	0	0-0	38.2	60	39	8	0	14-1	13	8.84	47	.359	.402	9-0-2	.111	0	119	-20		-2.3
2004	Chi N	0	0	—	7	0	0	1-0	9.2	9	5	0	2	3-0	3	4.66	95	.243	.333	1	.000	-0		0		-0.1
	Bos A	0	0	—	5	0	0	0-0	6	10	4	0	0	3-0	3	6.00	81	.400	.464	0	—	0		0		0.0
Total	6	25	47	.347	122	96	3	1-0	574.2	672	371	58	26	240-24	241	5.42	82	.295	.366	170-0-15	.135	-2	91	-59		-6.7

ANDERSON, JASON Jason R. B6.9.1979 Danville IL BL/TR/6-0/170(170-190) [NYA00 10/308] d3.31 Col Illinois

YEAR	TM LG	W	L	PCT	G	GS	CG-SHO	SV-BS	IP	H	R	HR	HB	BB-IB	SO	ERA	AERA	OAV	OOB	AB-HR-SH	AVG	PB	SUP	APR	DL	PW
2003	NY A	1	0	1.000	22	0	0	0-0	20.2	23	13	3	2	14-4	9	4.79	92	.280	.390	0	—	0		-1		-0.1
	NY N	0	0	—	6	0	0	0-0	10.2	10	6	2	1	5-1	7	5.06	83	.256	.340	0	—	0		0		0.0
2004	Cle A	0	0	—	1	0	0	0-0	1	1	5	1	0	4-1	1	45.00	10	.250	.625	0	—	0		-5		-0.2
2005	NY A	1	0	1.000	3	0	0	0-0	5.2	4	5	0	0	7-1	2	7.94	55	.200	.407	0	—	0		-2		-0.3
Total	3	2	0	1.000	32	0	0	0-0	38	38	29	6	3	30-7	19	6.39	68	.262	.390	0	—	0		-9		-0.6

YEAR	TM LG	W	L	PCT	G	GS	CG-SHO	SV-BS	IP	H	R	HR	HB	BB-IB	SO	ERA	AERA	OAV	OOB	AB-HR-SH	AVG	PB	SUP	APR	DL	PV

ANDERSON, JOHN   John Charles   B11.23.1929 St.Paul MN   D12.20.1998 Houston TX   BR/TR/6-1/190*   d8.17

YEAR	TM LG	W	L	PCT	G	GS	CG-SHO	SV-BS	IP	H	R	HR	HB	BB-IB	SO	ERA	AERA	OAV	OOB	AB-HR-SH	AVG	PB	SUP	APR	DL	PV
1958	Phi N	0	0	—	5	1	0	0	16	26	17	5	1	4-0	9	7.88	50	.361	.403	3	.000	-0	113	-7		-0.
1960	Bal A	0	0	—	4	0	0	0	4.2	8	7	0	0	4-0	1	13.50	28	.444	.522	0	—	0		-5		-0.2
1962	StL N	0	0	—	5	0	0	1	6.1	4	1	0	0	3-2	3	1.42	300	.182	.269	0		0		2		0.
	Hou N	0	0	—	10	0	0	0	17.2	26	12	1	0	3-1	6	5.09	73	.338	.363	2	.000	-0		-3		0.
	Year	0	0	—	15	0	0	1	24	30	13	1	0	6-3	9	4.13	94	.303	.340	2	.000	-0		-1		0.
Total	3	0	0	—	24	1	0	1	44.2	64	37	6	1	14-3	19	6.45	60	.339	.383	5	.000	-0	113	-13		-0.

ANDERSON, FRED   John Frederick   B12.11.1885 Calahaln NC   D11.8.1957 Winston-Salem NC   BR/TR/6-2/180   d9.25   Mil 1918   Col Maryland-Baltimore Co.

YEAR	TM LG	W	L	PCT	G	GS	CG-SHO	SV-BS	IP	H	R	HR	HB	BB-IB	SO	ERA	AERA	OAV	OOB	AB-HR-SH	AVG	PB	SUP	APR	DL	PV
1909	Bos A	0	0	—	1	1	0	0	8	3	3	0	0	1	5	1.13	222	.115	.148	3	.000	-0	113	1		0.
1913	Bos A	0	6	.000	10	8	4	0	57.1	84	51	0	1	21	32	5.97	49	.353	.408	20	.050	-2	104	-19		-1.1
1914	Buf F	13	15	.464	37	28	21-2	0	260.1	243	115	8	2	64	144	3.08	96	.249	.297	90	.189	-3*	79	-5		-0.
1915	Buf F	19	13	.594	36	28	14-5	0	240	192	80	5	3	72	142	2.51	111	.222	.285	80-0-1	.150	-5	88	9		0.
1916	NY N	9	13	.409	38	27	13-2	2	188	206	99	7	5	38	98	3.40	72	.277	.316	58-0-4	.138	-0	130	-26		-3.
1917	†NY N	8	8	.500	38	18	8-1	3	162	122	40	1	2	34	69	1.44	177	.209	.255	42-0-5	.071	-3	100	18		1.
1918	NY N	4	2	.667	18	4	2-1	3	70.2	62	27	1	2	17	24	2.67	98	.246	.299	19-0-3	.000	-3	151	0		-0.
Total	7	53	57	.482	178	114	62-11	8	986.1	912	415	22	15	247	514	2.86	95	.248	.298	312-0-13	.131	-16	99	-22		-4.

ANDERSON, BUD   Karl Adam   B5.27.1956 Westbury NY   BR/TR/6-3/210*   [SeaA77 3/78]   d6.11   Col Rutgers

YEAR	TM LG	W	L	PCT	G	GS	CG-SHO	SV-BS	IP	H	R	HR	HB	BB-IB	SO	ERA	AERA	OAV	OOB	AB-HR-SH	AVG	PB	SUP	APR	DL	PV
1982	Cle A	3	4	.429	25	5	1	0-1	80.2	84	37	4	1	30-2	44	3.35	124	.268	.330	0	—	0	57	5		0.
1983	Cle A	1	6	.143	39	1	0	7-3	68.1	64	34	8	0	32-6	32	4.08	105	.255	.337	0	—	0	21	2		0.
Total	2	4	10	.286	64	6	1	7-4	149	148	71	12	1	62-8	76	3.68	114	.262	.333	0	—	0	50	7		0.

ANDERSON, LARRY   Lawrence Dennis   B12.3.1952 Maywood CA   BR/TR/6-3/190*   [MilA71 2/27]   d9.25

YEAR	TM LG	W	L	PCT	G	GS	CG-SHO	SV-BS	IP	H	R	HR	HB	BB-IB	SO	ERA	AERA	OAV	OOB	AB-HR-SH	AVG	PB	SUP	APR	DL	PV
1974	Mil A	0	0	—	2	0	0	0-0	2.1	2	0	0	0	3-0	3	0.00	—	.250	.333	0	—	0		1		0.
1975	Mil A	1	0	1.000	8	1	0	1-1	30.1	36	18	3	0	6-0	13	5.04	76	.298	.328	0	—	0	160	-3		-0.
1977	Chi A	1	3	.250	6	0	0	0-1	8.2	10	10	1	0	15-4	7	9.35	44	.286	.490	0	—	0		-5		-0.
Total	3	2	3	.400	16	1	0	1-1	41.1	48	28	4	0	22-4	23	5.66	69	.293	.372	0	—	0	160	-7		-1.

ANDERSON, MATT   Matthew Jason   B8.17.1976 Louisville KY   BR/TR/6-4/200*   [DetA97 1/1]   d6.25   Col Rice

YEAR	TM LG	W	L	PCT	G	GS	CG-SHO	SV-BS	IP	H	R	HR	HB	BB-IB	SO	ERA	AERA	OAV	OOB	AB-HR-SH	AVG	PB	SUP	APR	DL	PV
1998	Det A	5	1	.833	42	0	0	0-4	44	38	16	3	2	31-4	44	3.27	145	.250	.378	0	—	0		8		0.
1999	Det A	2	1	.667	37	0	0	0-2	38	33	27	8	1	35-1	32	5.68	88	.232	.383	0	—	0		-3		-0.
2000	Det A	3	2	.600	69	0	0	1-0	74.1	61	44	8	3	45-4	71	4.72	104	.228	.339	0	—	0		1		0.
2001	Det A	3	1	.750	62	0	0	22-2	56	56	33	2	0	18-4	52	4.82	92	.257	.311	0	—	0		-2		-0.
2002	Det A	2	1	.667	12	0	0	0-2	11	17	13	1	2	8-1	8	9.00	49	.378	.474	0	—	0		-6	145	-1.
2003	Det A	0	1	.000	23	0	0	3-1	23.1	25	17	5	1	9-1	13	5.40	81	.272	.340	0	—	0		-4		-0.
2005	Col N	0	0	—	12	0	0	0-0	10	19	17	3	2	11-0	4	12.60	38	.404	.525	0	—	0		-9		-0.
Total	7	15	7	.682	257	0	0	26-11	256.2	249	167	30	11	157-15	224	5.19	91	.258	.363	0	—	0		-15	145	-1.

ANDERSON, MIKE   Michael James   B7.30.1966 Austin TX   BR/TR/6-3/205   d9.7   Col Southwestern (TX)

YEAR	TM LG	W	L	PCT	G	GS	CG-SHO	SV-BS	IP	H	R	HR	HB	BB-IB	SO	ERA	AERA	OAV	OOB	AB-HR-SH	AVG	PB	SUP	APR	DL	PV
1993	Cin N	0	0	—	3	0	0	0-0	5	12	11	3	0	3-0	3	18.56	22	.444	.500	1	.000	-0		-8		-0.

ANDERSON, CRAIG   Norman Craig   B7.1.1938 Washington DC   BR/TR/6-2/205*   d6.23   Col Lehigh

YEAR	TM LG	W	L	PCT	G	GS	CG-SHO	SV-BS	IP	H	R	HR	HB	BB-IB	SO	ERA	AERA	OAV	OOB	AB-HR-SH	AVG	PB	SUP	APR	DL	PV
1961	StL N	4	3	.571	25	0	0	1	38.2	38	15	3	1	12-0	21	3.26	135	.255	.313	9	.333	1		5		0.
1962	NY N	3	17	.150	50	14	2	4	131.1	150	108	18	5	63-2	62	5.35	78	.278	.357	32-0-3	.094	-2	79	-22		-3.
1963	NY N	0	2	.000	3	2	0	0	9.1	17	15	0	0	3-0	6	8.68	40	.362	.400	3	.333	-0	25	-7		-1.
1964	NY N	0	1	.000	4	1	0	0	13	21	9	0	0	3-0	5	5.54	65	.382	.407	3	.000	-0	0	-3		-0.
Total	4	7	23	.233	82	17	2	5	192.1	226	147	21	6	81-2	94	5.51	81	.286	.355	47-0-3	.149	-1	69	-27		-3.

ANDERSON, RICK   Richard Arlen   B11.29.1956 Everett WA   BR/TR/6-0/175*   [NYN78 24/580]   d6.9   C4   Col Washington

YEAR	TM LG	W	L	PCT	G	GS	CG-SHO	SV-BS	IP	H	R	HR	HB	BB-IB	SO	ERA	AERA	OAV	OOB	AB-HR-SH	AVG	PB	SUP	APR	DL	PV
1986	NY N	2	1	.667	15	5	0	1-0	49.2	45	17	3	0	11-3	21	2.72	132	.245	.281	11-0-1	.091	-1	80	5		0.
1987	KC A	0	2	.000	6	2	0	0-0	13	26	22	3	2	9-1	12	13.85	33	.394	.481	0	—	0	10	-13		-1.
1988	KC A	2	1	.667	7	3	0	0-0	34	41	17	3	1	9-2	9	4.24	95	.308	.349	0	—	0	61	0	16	-1.
Total	3	4	4	.500	28	10	0	1-0	96.2	112	56	9	3	29-6	42	4.75	81	.292	.341	11-0-1	.091	-1	58	-8	16	-1.

ANDERSON, RICK   Richard Lee   B12.25.1953 Inglewood CA   D6.23.1989 Wilmington CA   BR/TR/6-2/210*   [NYA72*S1/5]   d9.18   Col Los Angeles Valley (CA) JC   [DL 1981 Sea A 49]

YEAR	TM LG	W	L	PCT	G	GS	CG-SHO	SV-BS	IP	H	R	HR	HB	BB-IB	SO	ERA	AERA	OAV	OOB	AB-HR-SH	AVG	PB	SUP	APR	DL	PV
1979	NY A	0	0	—	1	0	0	0-0	2.1	1	1	0	0	4-0	0	3.86	107	.167	.500	0	—	0		0		0.
1980	Sea A	0	0	—	5	2	0	0-0	9.2	8	5	1	0	10-2	7	3.72	112	.229	.400	0	—	0	150	0		0.
Total	2	0	0	—	6	2	0	0-0	12	9	6	1	0	14-2	7	3.75	111	.220	.418	0	—	0	150	0	49	0.

ANDERSON, BOB   Robert Carl   B9.29.1935 E.Chicago IN   BR/TR/6-4.5/210*   d7.31   Col Western Michigan

YEAR	TM LG	W	L	PCT	G	GS	CG-SHO	SV-BS	IP	H	R	HR	HB	BB-IB	SO	ERA	AERA	OAV	OOB	AB-HR-SH	AVG	PB	SUP	APR	DL	PV
1957	Chi N	0	1	.000	8	0	0	0	16.1	20	16	2	1	8-1	7	7.71	50	.317	.397	4	.000	-1		-7		-0.
1958	Chi N	3	3	.500	17	8	2	0	65.2	61	29	3	1	29-1	51	3.97	99	.255	.335	17	.118	-1	109	1		0.
1959	Chi N	12	13	.480	37	36	7-1	0	235.1	245	117	21	5	77-3	113	4.13	96	.272	.329	80-0-6	.075	-4	96	-4		-0.
1960	Chi N	9	11	.450	38	30	5	1	203.2	201	105	26	7	68-8	115	4.11	92	.255	.320	71-0-5	.169	0*	90	-7		-0.
1961	Chi N	7	10	.412	57	12	1	8	152	162	85	14	2	56-11	96	4.26	98	.275	.338	42-2-2	.143	0	81	-2		-0.
1962	Chi N	2	7	.222	57	4	0	4	107.2	111	70	9	5	60-5	82	5.02	83	.266	.361	23-0-2	.130	0	79	-11		-0.
1963	Det A	3	1	.750	32	3	0	0	60	58	28	5	6	21-2	38	3.30	113	.258	.335	9	.444	2	87	1		0.
Total	7	36	46	.439	246	93	15-1	13	840.2	858	450	80	27	319-31	502	4.26	93	.266	.335	246-2-15	.134	-4	91	-29		-2.

ANDERSON, SCOTT   Scott Richard   B8.1.1962 Corvallis OR   BR/TR/6-6/190(185-200)   [TexA84 7/170]   d4.8   Col Oregon St.

YEAR	TM LG	W	L	PCT	G	GS	CG-SHO	SV-BS	IP	H	R	HR	HB	BB-IB	SO	ERA	AERA	OAV	OOB	AB-HR-SH	AVG	PB	SUP	APR	DL	PV
1987	Tex A	0	1	.000	8	0	0	0-1	11.1	17	12	0	1	8-2	6	9.53	47	.347	.448	0	—	0		-6		-0.
1990	Mon N	0	1	.000	4	3	0	0-0	18	12	6	1	0	5-0	16	3.00	123	.188	.243	4-0-1	.000	-0	123	2		-0.
1995	KC A	1	0	1.000	6	4	0	0-0	25.1	29	15	3	1	8-0	6	5.33	90	.290	.349	0	—	0	116	-1		-0.
Total	3	1	2	.333	18	7	0	0-1	54.2	58	33	4	2	21-2	28	5.43	80	.272	.342	4-0-1	.000	-0	117	-5		-0.

ANDERSON, VARNEY   Varney Samuel "Varn"   B6.18.1866 Geneva IL   D11.5.1941 Rockford IL   BR/TR/5-10/165   d8.1

YEAR	TM LG	W	L	PCT	G	GS	CG-SHO	SV-BS	IP	H	R	HR	HB	BB-IB	SO	ERA	AERA	OAV	OOB	AB-HR-SH	AVG	PB	SUP	APR	DL	PV
1889	Ind N	0	1	.000	2	1	1	0	12	13	10	0	3	9	3	4.50	93	.265	.410	5	.000	-1	161	-1		-0.
1894	Was N	0	2	.000	2	2	2	0	14	15	12	0	1	6	3	7.07	75	.273	.355	7	.429	0	60	-1		-0.
1895	Was N	9	16	.360	29	25	18	0	204.2	288	199	13	10	97	35	5.89	82	.327	.400	97-0-2	.289	3*	104	-19		-1.
1896	Was N	0	1	.000	2	2	1	0	9	23	16	0	0	3	0	13.00	34	.469	.500	5	.600	1	129	-7		-0.
Total	4	9	20	.310	35	30	22	0	239	339	237	13	14	115	41	6.16	78	.328	.402	114-0-2	.298	4	104	-28		-1.

ANDERSON, WALTER   Walter Carl "Lefty"   B9.25.1897 Grand Rapids MI   D1.6.1990 Battle Creek MI   BL/TL/6-2/160   d5.14   Mil 1918   Col Western Michigan

YEAR	TM LG	W	L	PCT	G	GS	CG-SHO	SV-BS	IP	H	R	HR	HB	BB-IB	SO	ERA	AERA	OAV	OOB	AB-HR-SH	AVG	PB	SUP	APR	DL	PV
1917	Phi A	0	0	—	14	2	0	0	38.2	32	16	0	1	21	10	3.03	91	.246	.355	7	.429	1	78	0		0.
1919	Phi A	1	0	1.000	3	0	0	0	14	13	8	0	1	8	10	3.86	89	.245	.355	4-0-1	.000	-1		-1		-0.
Total	2	1	0	1.000	17	2	0	0	52.2	45	24	0	2	29	20	3.25	90	.246	.355	11-0-1	.273	0	78	-1		0.

ANDERSON, BILL   William   B1.19.1865 Spencer Co. KY   D5.5.1936 Taylorsville KY   d8.12

YEAR	TM LG	W	L	PCT	G	GS	CG-SHO	SV-BS	IP	H	R	HR	HB	BB-IB	SO	ERA	AERA	OAV	OOB	AB-HR-SH	AVG	PB	SUP	APR	DL	PV
1889	Lou AA	0	1	.000	1	1	1	0	8	10	10	2	0	6	2	10.13	38	.294	.400	3	.333	0	80	-4		-0.

ANDERSON, BILL   William Edward "Lefty"   B11.28.1895 Boston MA   D3.13.1983 Medford MA   BR/TL/6-1/165   d9.10

YEAR	TM LG	W	L	PCT	G	GS	CG-SHO	SV-BS	IP	H	R	HR	HB	BB-IB	SO	ERA	AERA	OAV	OOB	AB-HR-SH	AVG	PB	SUP	APR	DL	PV
1925	Bos N	0	0	—	2	0	0	0	2.2	5	3	0	2	1	10.13	40	.500	.583	1	.000	-0		-2		-0.

ANDERSON, WINGO   Wingo Charlie   B8.13.1886 Alvarado TX   D12.19.1950 Fort Worth TX   BL/TL/5-10.5/150   d4.16

YEAR	TM LG	W	L	PCT	G	GS	CG-SHO	SV-BS	IP	H	R	HR	HB	BB-IB	SO	ERA	AERA	OAV	OOB	AB-HR-SH	AVG	PB	SUP	APR	DL	PV
1910	Cin N	0	0	—	7	0	0	0	17.1	16	15	0	1	17	11	4.67	62	.258	.425	5	.200	0	153	-4		-0.

ANDRE, JOHN   John Edward   B1.3.1923 Brockton MA   D11.25.1976 Barnstable MA   BL/TR/6-4/200   d4.16

YEAR	TM LG	W	L	PCT	G	GS	CG-SHO	SV-BS	IP	H	R	HR	HB	BB-IB	SO	ERA	AERA	OAV	OOB	AB-HR-SH	AVG	PB	SUP	APR	DL	PV
1955	Chi N	0	1	.000	22	3	0	1	45	45	34	7	1	28-4	19	5.80	70	.259	.361	9	.111	-1	153	-9		-0.

ANDREWS, CLAYTON   Clayton John   B5.15.1978 Dunedin FL   BR/TL/6-0/180   [TorA96 3/74]   d4.16

YEAR	TM LG	W	L	PCT	G	GS	CG-SHO	SV-BS	IP	H	R	HR	HB	BB-IB	SO	ERA	AERA	OAV	OOB	AB-HR-SH	AVG	PB	SUP	APR	DL	PV
2000	Tor A	1	2	.333	8	2	0	0-0	20.2	34	23	6	0	9-0	12	10.02	50	.374	.426	3	.000	0	140	-10		-1.

ANDREWS, ELBERT   Elbert De Vore   B12.11.1901 Greenwood SC   D11.25.1979 Greenwood SC   BL/TR/6-0/175   d5.1   Col Furman

YEAR	TM LG	W	L	PCT	G	GS	CG-SHO	SV-BS	IP	H	R	HR	HB	BB-IB	SO	ERA	AERA	OAV	OOB	AB-HR-SH	AVG	PB	SUP	APR	DL	PV
1925	Phi A	0	0	—	6	0	0	0	8	9	8	0	0	11	0	10.13	46	.375	.535	0	—	0		-5		-0.

ANDREWS, HUB   Herbert Carl   B8.31.1922 Burbank OK   BR/TR/6-0/170   d4.20

YEAR	TM LG	W	L	PCT	G	GS	CG-SHO	SV-BS	IP	H	R	HR	HB	BB-IB	SO	ERA	AERA	OAV	OOB	AB-HR-SH	AVG	PB	SUP	APR	DL	PV
1947	NY N	0	0	—	7	0	0	0	8.2	14	7	1	0	4	2	6.23	65	.368	.429	0	—	0		-2		-0.
1948	NY N	0	0	—	1	0	0	0	3	3	1	0	0	0	0	0.00	—	.300	.300	0	—	0		1		0.
Total	2	0	0	—	8	0	0	0	11.2	17	8	1	0	4	2	4.63	87	.354	.404	0	—	0		-1		-0.

YEAR	TM LG	W	L	PCT	G	GS	CG-SHO	SV-BS	IP	H	R	HR	HB	BB-IB	SO	ERA	AERA	OAV	OOB	AB-HR-SH	AVG	PB	SUP	APR	DL	PW

ANDREWS, IVY Ivy Paul "Poison" B5.6.1907 Dora AL D11.24.1970 Birmingham AL BR/TR/6-1/200 d8.15

1931	NY A	2	0	1.000	7	3	1	0	34.1	36	17	3	0	8	10	4.19	95	.273	.314	11	.182	0	248	6		0.0
1932	NY A	2	1	.667	4	1	1	0	24.2	20	8	0	0	9	7	1.82	223	.215	.284	9-0-1	.222	1	167	6		0.8
	Bos A	8	6	.571	25	19	8	0	141.2	144	76	4	2	53	30	3.81	118	.262	.329	51-0-2	.137	-3*	96	9		0.4
	Year	10	7	.588	29	20	9	0	166.1	164	84	4	2	62	37	3.52	126	.255	.322	60-0-3	.150	-2	100	15		1.2
1933	Bos A	7	13	.350	34	17	5	1	140	157	96	8	1	61	37	4.95	88	.279	.350	42-0-4	.214	-0*	87	-11		-1.4
1934	StL A	4	11	.267	43	13	2	3	139	166	84	7	0	65	51	4.66	107	.301	.375	40-0-1	.350	3	102	5		0.7
1935	StL A	13	7	.650	50	20	10	1	213.1	231	95	10	1	53	43	3.54	135	.273	.317	68-0-4	.132	-5	81	28		1.7
1936	StL A	7	12	.368	36	25	11	1	191.1	221	109	19	0	50	33	4.84	111	.286	.330	59-0-2	.169	-1	74	14		1.0
1937	Cle A	3	4	.429	20	4	1-1	0	59.2	76	33	3	0	9	16	4.37	105	.311	.336	12-0-1	.250	1	66	2		0.2
	†NY A	3	2	.600	11	5	3-1	1	49	49	19	2	0	17	17	3.12	142	.259	.320	15-0-2	.067	-1	67	8		0.6
	Year	6	6	.500	31	9	4-2	1	108.2	125	52	5	0	26	33	3.81	119	.289	.329	27-0-3	.148	-1	66	10		0.8
1938	NY A	1	3	.250	19	1	1	1	48	51	25	3	0	17	13	3.00	151	.268	.329	12	.167	-0	19	6		0.4
Total 8		50	59	.459	249	108	43-2	8	1041	1151	562	59	4	342	257	4.14	115	.279	.335	319-0-17	.185	-6	89	67		4.4

ANDREWS, JOHN John Richard B2.9.1949 Monterey Park CA BL/TL/5-10/180 d4.8 Col San Diego St.

| 1973 | StL N | 1 | 1 | .500 | 16 | 0 | 0 | 0-0 | 18.1 | 16 | 10 | 3 | 0 | 11-1 | 5 | 4.42 | 83 | .235 | .342 | 2 | .500 | 0 | | -1 | | -0.1 |

ANDREWS, NATE Nathan Hardy B9.30.1913 Pembroke NC D4.26.1991 Winston-Salem NC BR/TR/6-0/195 d5.1 Col North Carolina-Asheville

1937	StL N	0	0		4	0	0	0	9	12	4	1	0	3	6	4.00	100	.324	.375	0	—	0		1		0.1
1939	StL N	1	2	.333	11	1	0	0	16	24	14	0	0	12	6	6.75	61	.343	.439	0	.000	-0	106	-5		-0.8
1940	Cle A	0	1	.000	6	0	0	0	12	16	9	1	0	6	3	6.00	70	.327	.400	0	—	0		-2		-0.1
1941	Cle A	0	0		2	0	0	0	2.1	3	4	0	0	2	1	11.57	34	.300	.417	1	.000	-0		-2		-0.1
1943	Bos N	14	20	.412	36	34	23-3	0	283.2	253	100	11	6	75	80	2.57	133	.238	.291	90-0-6	.156	-0	72	26		3.2
1944	Bos N☆	16	15	.516	37	34	16-2	0	257.1	263	106	14	0	74	76	3.22	119	.261	.312	88-0-3	.114	-4	85	18		1.7
1945	Bos N	7	12	.368	21	19	8	0	137.2	160	75	9	0	52	26	4.58	84	.295	.356	43-0-7	.209	0*	78	-8		-1.0
1946	Cin N	2	4	.333	7	7	3	0	43.1	50	29	2	1	8	13	3.95	85	.281	.316	14-0-3	.071	-1	113	-6		-0.8
	NY N	1	0	1.000	3	2	0	0	12	17	9	2	0	4	5	6.00	57	.362	.412	2	.500	1	236	-3		-0.2
	Year	3	4	.429	10	9	3	0	55.1	67	38	4	1	12	18	4.39	77	.298	.336	16-0-3	.125	-0	141	-9		-1.0
Total 8		41	54	.432	127	97	50-5	2	773.1	798	350	40	9	236	216	3.46	106	.265	.321	240-0-19	.146	-4	84	18		2.0

ANDRUS, FRED Frederick Hotham B8.23.1850 Washington MI D11.10.1937 Detroit MI BR/TR/6-2/185 d7.25.1876 ▲

| 1884 | Chi N | 1 | 0 | 1.000 | 1 | 1 | 1 | 0 | 9 | 11 | 3 | 1 | | 2 | 2 | 2.00 | 157 | .297 | .333 | 5 | .200 | 0 | 372 | 1 | | 0.1 |

ANDUJAR, JOAQUIN Joaquin B12.21.1952 San Pedro de Macoris, D.R. BB/TR/6-0/180(170-190) d4.8

1976	Hou N	9	10	.474	28	25	9-4	0-0	172.1	163	74	8	1	75-2	59	3.60	90	.255	.332	57-0-4	.140	-0	84	-5		-0.6
1977	Hou N☆	11	8	.579	26	25	4-1	0-0	158.2	149	80	11	4	64-3	69	3.69	98	.251	.325	53-0-4	.189	2	108	-5		-0.2
1978	Hou N	5	7	.417	35	13	2	1-0	110.2	88	45	3	4	58-6	55	3.42	98	.224	.327	23-0-4	.130	-0*	89	-1	22	0.0
1979	Hou N★	12	12	.500	46	23	8	4-3	194	168	86	7	2	88-6	77	3.43	102	.233	.316	57-2-5	.088	0	82	1		0.3
1980	†Hou N	3	8	.273	35	14	0	2-2	122	132	59	8	0	43-2	75	3.91	84	.277	.335	29-1-5	.172	2	95	-8		-0.4
1981	Hou N	2	3	.400	9	4	0	0-1	23.2	29	17	2	0	12-0	18	4.94	66	.296	.366	4-0-1	.000	-0	108	-6		-1.1
	StL N	6	1	.857	11	8	1	0-1	55.1	56	24	4	0	11-1	19	3.74	97	.265	.302	19-0-1	.000	-2*	110	0		-0.2
	Year	8	4	.667	20	11	1	0-2	79	85	41	6	0	23-1	37	4.10	86	.275	.323	23-0-2	.000	-2	110	-4		-1.3
1982	†StL N	15	10	.600	38	37	9-5	0-0	265.2	237	85	11	7	50-7	137	2.47	149	.240	.281	95-0-9	.158	-1	95	33		3.0
1983	StL N	6	16	.273	39	34	5-2	1-0	225	215	112	23	8	75-7	125	4.16	88	.253	.315	73-0-5	.082	-4	97	-10		-1.0
1984	StL N✱	20	14	.588	36	36	12-4	0-0	261.1	218	104	20	7	70-13	147	3.34	105	.229	.284	84-2-7	.131	3	111	7		1.3
1985	†StL N✱	21	12	.636	38	38	10-2	0-0	269.2	265	113	15	11	82-12	112	3.40	105	.260	.321	94-0-7	.106	-2	121	6		0.5
1986	Oak A	12	7	.632	28	26	7-1	1-0	155.1	139	70	23	4	56-1	72	3.82	102	.239	.308	0	—	0	99	3	41	0.3
1987	Oak A	3	5	.375	13	13	1	0-0	60.2	63	43	11	3	26-0	32	6.08	68	.269	.348	0	—	-0	120	-13	125	-1.4
1988	Hou N	2	5	.286	23	10	0	0-1	78.2	94	43	9	5	21-5	35	4.00	83	.297	.346	19-0-1	.211	2	128	-8	36	-0.4
Total 13		127	118	.518	405	305	68-19	9-8	2153	2016	955	155	51	731-65	1032	3.58	99	.250	.314	607-5-51	.127	-2	103	-6	224	0.1

ANDUJAR, LUIS Luis (Sanchez) B11.22.1972 Bani, D.R. BR/TR/6-2/175(175-215) d9.8

1995	Chi A	2	1	.667	5	5	0	0-0	30.1	26	12	4	1	14-2	9	3.26	137	.230	.320	0	—	0	92	4		0.3
1996	Chi A	0	2	.000	5	5	0	0-0	23	32	22	4	0	15-0	6	8.22	58	.337	.420	0	—	0	117	-9		-0.6
	Tor A	1	1	.500	3	2	0	0-0	14.1	14	8	4	1	1-0	5	5.02	100	.264	.281	0	—	0	74	0		0.0
	Year	1	3	.250	8	7	0	0-0	37.1	46	30	8	1	16-0	11	6.99	69	.311	.373	0	—	0	104	-9		-0.6
1997	Tor A	0	6	.000	17	8	0	0-0	50	76	45	9	0	21-1	28	6.48	71	.352	.402	0	—	0	95	-13	25	-1.3
1998	Tor A	0	0	—	5	2	0	0-0	5.2	12	6	0	0	2-0	1	9.53	49	.429	.467	0	—	0		-3		-0.1
Total 4		3	10	.231	35	20	0	0-0	123.1	160	93	21	2	53-3	49	5.98	78	.317	.379	0	—	0	98	-21	25	-1.7

ANGELINI, NORM Norman Stanley B9.24.1947 San Francisco CA BL/TL/5-11/175* d7.22 Col Washington St.

1972	KC A	2	1	.667	21	0	0	2-1	16	13	4	1	1	12-1	16	2.25	135	.228	.371	2	.000	-0		2		0.3
1973	KC A	0	0		7	0	0	1-0	3.2	2	2	0	0	7-0	3	4.91	84	.200	.500	0	—	0		0		0.0
Total 2		2	1	.667	28	0	0	3-1	19.2	15	6	1	1	19-1	19	2.75	118	.224	.398	2	.000	-0		2		0.3

ANKIEL, RICK Richard Alexander B7.19.1979 Fort Pierce FL BL/TL/6-1/210* [StLN97 2/72] d8.23 [DL 2002 StL N 66]

1999	StL N	0	1	.000	9	5	0	0-0	33	26	12	2	1	14-1	39	3.27	141	.215	.301	10-0-1	.100	-1	76	5		0.2
2000	†StL N	11	7	.611	31	30	0	0-0	175	137	80	21	6	90-2	194	3.50	133	.219	.320	68-2-1	.250	6*	104	20		2.3
2001	StL N	1	2	.333	6	6	0	0-0	24	25	21	7	3	25-0	27	7.13	61	.275	.434	8-0-1	.000	-1	117	-8		-0.8
2004	StL N	1	0	1.000	5	0	0	0-0	10	10	6	2	2	1-0	9	5.40	79	.256	.310	1	.000	0		-1	150	-0.1
Total 4		13	10	.565	51	41	0	1-0	242	198	119	32	12	130-2	269	3.90	118	.226	.331	87-2-3	.207	5	103	16	216	1.6

ANTONELLI, JOHNNY John August B4.12.1930 Rochester NY BL/TL/6-0/190* d7.4 Mil 1951-52

1948	Bos N	0	0	—	4	0	0	1	4	3	2	1	0	3	2	2.25	170	.143	.294	0	—	0		1		0.1
1949	Bos N	3	7	.300	22	10	3-1	0	96	99	49	6	2	42	48	3.56	106	.273	.351	25-0-5	.120	-1	51	0		-0.1
1950	Bos N	2	3	.400	20	6	2-1	0	57.2	81	46	3	4	22	33	5.93	65	.335	.399	16	.125	-1	84	-15		-1.2
1953	Mil N	12	12	.500	31	26	11-2	1	175.1	167	83	15	1	71	131	3.18	123	.242	.314	62-0-4	.177	0	118	11		1.4
1954	†NY N★	21	7	.750	39	37	18-6	2	258.2	209	78	22	5	94	152	2.30	176	.219	.292	98-2-4	.163	0	109	50		5.3
1955	NY N	14	16	.467	38	34	14-2	1	235.1	206	105	24	11	82-5	143	3.33	121	.234	.306	82-4-3	.207	3	94	16		2.3
1956	NY N★	20	13	.606	41	36	15-5	1	258.1	225	93	20	3	75-10	145	2.86	132	.234	.287	89-3-6	.157	1*	76	26		3.5
1957	NY N☆	12	18	.400	40	30	8-3	0	212.1	228	98	19	3	67-7	114	3.77	104	.276	.330	72-3-1	.153	3*	66	5		0.9
1958	SF N☆	16	13	.552	40	34	13-2	3	241.2	216	101	31	3	87-7	143	3.28	116	.239	.306	84-1-5	.226	4*	110	14		1.9
1959	SF N★	19	10	.655	40	38	17-4	1	282	247	107	29	3	76-6	165	3.10	123	.233	.285	101-2-5	.158	1*	110	25		2.6
1960	SF N	6	7	.462	41	10	1-1	11	112.1	106	51	7	2	47-10	57	3.77	92	.253	.326	34-0-1	.235	2*	71	-2		0.0
1961	Cle A	0	4	.000	11	7	0	0	48	68	39	8	1	18-0	21	6.56	60	.338	.390	15-0-1	.267	1*	83	-14		-0.9
	Mil N	1	0	1.000	9	0	0	0	10.2	16	9	2	0	3-0	8	7.59	49	.340	.373	1	.000	-0		-5		-0.4
Total 12		126	110	.534	377	268	102-25	21	1992.1	1870	860	186	38	687-45	1162	3.34	116	.247	.312	679-15-35	.178	15	95	112		15.4

APODACA, BOB Robert John B1.31.1950 Los Angeles CA BR/TR/5-11/170* d9.18 C9 Col Cal St.-Los Angeles [DL 1978 NY N 155, 1979 NY N 127]

1973	NY N	0	0	—	1	0	0	0	1	0	0	0	0	2-0	0	∞	—	1.000	0	—	0		-1		-0.1
1974	NY N	6	6	.500	35	8	1	3-2	103	92	47	7	2	42-9	54	3.50	103	.241	.318	25-0-1	.120	0	112	1		0.1
1975	NY N	3	4	.429	46	0	0	13-1	84.2	66	18	4	0	28-9	45	1.49	236	.222	.286	11	.364	1	19		39	2.5
1976	NY N	3	7	.300	43	3	0	5-2	89.2	71	34	4	3	29-12	45	2.81	119	.223	.291	16-0-1	.125	0	88	5		0.6
1977	NY N	4	8	.333	59	0	0	5-5	84	83	38	7	1	30-11	53	3.43	111	.255	.318	6-0-1	.167	-0		2		0.4
Total 5		16	25	.390	184	11	1	26-10	462	312	175	22	6	131-41	197	2.86	124	.236	.305	58-0-3	.172	1	106	26	321	3.5

APONTE, LUIS Luis Eduardo (Yuripe) B6.14.1953 ElTigre, Venez BR/TR/6-0/165(165-185) d9.4

1980	Bos A	0	0	—	4	0	0	0	7	6	1	0	0	2-1	1	1.29	332	.250	.308	0	—	0		0		0.1
1981	Bos A	1	0	1.000	7	0	0	1-0	15.2	11	1	0	0	3-0	11	0.57	682	.208	.250	0	—	0		6		0.5
1982	Bos A	2	2	.500	40	0	0	3-0	85	78	31	5	0	25-3	44	3.18	137	.246	.299	0	—	0		11		0.6
1983	Bos A	5	4	.556	34	0	0	3-1	62	74	28	7	2	23-3	32	3.63	121	.301	.364	0	—	0		1		0.7
1984	Cle A	1	0	1.000	25	0	0	0-0	50.1	53	25	5	1	15-0	25	4.11	100	.269	.322	0	—	0		0		0.0
Total 5		9	6	.600	110	0	0	7-1	220	222	86	17	3	68-7	113	3.27	131	.265	.321	0	—	0		24		1.9

YEAR	TM LG	W	L	PCT	G	GS	CG-SHO	SV-BS	IP	H	R	HR	HB	BB-IB	SO	ERA	AERA	OAV	OOB	AB-HR-SH	AVG	PB	SUP	APR	DL	PW
APPIER, KEVIN	Robert Kevin	B12.6.1967 Lancaster CA			BR/TR/6-2/195(180-215)			[KCA87 1/9]	d6.4	Col Antelope Valley (CA) JC																
1989	KC A	1	4	.200	6	5	0	0-0	21.2	34	22	3	0	12-1	10	9.14	42	.374	.434	0	—	0	70	-12		-2.0
1990	KC A	12	8	.600	32	24	3-3	0-0	185.2	179	67	13	6	54-2	127	2.76	140	.252	.307	0	—	0	99	22		2.3
1991	KC A	13	10	.565	34	31	6-3	0-0	207.2	205	97	13	2	61-3	158	3.42	121	.255	.307	0	—	0	104	13		1.4
1992	KC A	15	8	.652	30	30	3	0-0	208.1	167	59	10	2	68-5	150	2.46	166	.217	.281	0	—	0	77	38		4.1
1993	KC A	18	8	.692	34	34	5-1	0-0	238.2	183	74	8	1	81-3	186	**2.56**	180	.212	.279	0	—	0	89	51		5.1
1994	KC A	7	6	.538	23	23	1	0-0	155	137	68	11	4	63-7	145	3.83	131	.240	.317	0	—	0	96	21		1.5
1995	KC A★	15	10	.600	31	31	4-1	0-0	201.1	163	90	14	8	80-1	185	3.89	123	.221	.303	0	—	0	95	22	17	2.4
1996	KC A	14	11	.560	32	32	5-1	0-0	211.1	192	87	17	5	75-2	207	3.62	139	.245	.314	0	—	0	87	35		3.5
1997	KC A	9	13	.409	34	34	4-1	0-0	235.2	215	96	24	4	74-2	196	3.40	140	.243	.303	6	.000	-1	76	34		2.7
1998	KC A	1	2	.333	3	3	0	0-0	15	21	13	3	1	5-1	9	7.80	62	.339	.391	0	—	0	64	-4	154	-0.6
1999	KC A	9	9	.500	22	22	1	0-0	140.1	153	81	18	6	51-3	78	4.87	104	.279	.345	2	.000	-0	97	4		0.4
	Oak A	7	5	.583	12	12	0	0-0	68.2	77	50	9	1	33-1	53	5.77	82	.280	.357	0	—	0	110	-9		-1.2
	Year	16	14	.533	34	34	1	0-0	209	230	131	27	7	84-4	131	5.17	96	.279	.349	2	.000	-0	101	-5		-0.8
2000	†Oak A	11	8	.579	31	31	1-1	0-0	195.1	200	109	23	9	102-10	129	4.52	108	.262	.354	6	.167	-0	120	7	17	0.9
2001	NY N	11	10	.524	33	33	1-1	0-0	206.2	181	89	22	15	60-4	172	3.57	113	.237	.306	62-0-3	.113	-2	91	12		0.8
2002	†Ana A	14	12	.538	32	32	0	0-0	188.1	191	89	23	7	64-2	132	3.92	114	.267	.330	2-0-2	.000	-0	93	12		1.3
2003	Ana A	7	7	.500	19	19	0	0-0	92.2	105	60	17	8	36-4	50	5.63	78	.279	.353	5	.000	-0	101	-12	17	-1.6
	KC A	1	2	.333	4	4	0	0-0	19	15	9	4	0	7-0	5	4.26	113	.217	.289	0	—	0	72	1	35	0.2
	Year	8	9	.471	23	23	0	0-0	111.2	120	69	21	8	43-4	55	5.40	82	.269	.343	5	.000	-0	95	-10		-1.4
2004	KC A	0	1	.000	2	2	0	0-0	4	7	8	0	0	3-0	2	13.50	35	.368	.455	0	—	0	90	-5	176	-0.7
Total	16	169	137	.552	414	402	34-12	0-0	2595.1	2425	1168	232	79	933-51	1994	3.74	122	.247	.316	83-0-5	.096	-3	93	230	416	20.3
APPLEGATE, FRED	Frederick Romaine	B5.9.1879 Williamsport PA		D4.21.1968 Williamsport PA		BR/TR/6-2/180	d9.30																			
1904	Phi A	1	2	.333	3	3	0	0-0	21	29	18	1	8	12	6.43	42	.330	.392	7-0-1	.286	0	115	-7		-0.9
APPLETON, ED	Edward Samuel "Whitey"	B2.29.1892 Arlington TX		D1.27.1932 Arlington TX		BR/TR/6-0.5/173	d4.16																			
1915	Bro N	4	10	.286	34	10	5	0	138.1	133	71	3	8	66	50	3.32	84	.263	.357	44	.159	-0	86	-9		-1.0
1916	Bro N	1	2	.333	14	3	1	1	47	49	25	1	1	18	14	3.06	88	.278	.349	12	.167	-0	102	-3		-0.3
Total	2	5	12	.294	48	13	6	1	185.1	182	96	4	9	84	64	3.25	85	.267	.355	56	.161	-1	89	-12		-1.3
APPLETON, PETE	Peter William "Jake" (aka Jablonowski in 1927-33)	B5.20.1904 Terryville CT		D1.18.1974 Trenton NJ		BR/TR/5-11/180	d9.14	Mil 1943-45	Col Michigan																	
1927	Cin N	2	1	.667	6	2	2-1	0	29.2	29	7	0	0	19	3	1.82	208	.261	.359	11	.545	2	45	7		0.9
1928	Cin N	3	4	.429	31	3	0	0	82.2	101	50	7	2	22	20	4.68	85	.311	.358	31-0-2	.323	3*	128	-7		-0.1
1930	Cle A	8	7	.533	39	7	2	1	118.2	122	71	8	5	53	45	4.02	120	.274	.357	40-0-1	.200	-0	84	8		0.8
1931	Cle A	4	4	.500	29	4	3	0	79.2	100	51	2	1	29	25	4.63	100	.293	.350	24-0-1	.208	0*	87	-1		-0.1
1932	Cle A	0	0	—	4	0	0	0	5	11	11	1	0	3	1	16.20	29	.407	.467	0	—	0		-6		-0.3
	Bos A	0	3	.000	11	3	0	0	46	49	35	2	2	26	15	4.11	109	.265	.362	17	.176	0	51	-2		0.0
	Year	0	3	.000	15	3	0	0	51	60	46	3	2	29	16	5.29	85	.283	.374	17	.176	0	50	-8		-0.3
1933	NY A	0	0	—	1	0	0	0	2	3	0	0	0	1	0	0.00	—	.375	.444	0	—	0		1		0.1
1936	Was A	14	9	.609	38	20	12-1	3	201.2	199	94	7	3	77	77	3.53	135	.254	.324	76-0-1	.250	2	88	29		3.0
1937	Was A	8	15	.348	35	18	7-4	2	168	167	103	16	5	72	62	4.39	101	.260	.339	59-0-1	.186	-2	66	-2		-0.1
1938	Was A	7	9	.438	43	10	5	5	164.1	175	99	12	1	61	62	4.60	98	.270	.333	59-0-2	.254	3	103	-2		0.1
1939	Was A	5	10	.333	40	4	2	6	102.2	104	62	7	4	48	50	4.56	95	.265	.351	25-0-3	.160	-1	71	-4		-0.5
1940	Chi A	4	0	1.000	25	0	0	5	57.2	54	39	8	1	28	21	5.62	79	.248	.336	17-0-1	.176	-0		-6		-0.5
1941	Chi A	0	3	.000	13	0	0	1	27.1	27	21	4	2	17	12	5.27	78	.257	.371	4	.250	-0		-5		-0.5
1942	Chi A	0	0	—	4	0	0	0	4.2	2	7	2	0	3	1	3.86	93	.133	.278	0	—	0		0		0.1
	StL A	1	1	.500	14	0	0	2	27.1	25	9	1	0	11	12	2.96	125	.243	.316	6	.167	1		3		0.4
	Year	1	1	.500	18	0	0	2	32	27	11	1	0	14	14	3.09	119	.229	.311	6	.167	1		3		0.4
1945	StL A	0	0	—	2	0	0	0	2.1	3	5	0	0	7	1	15.43	23	.273	.556	0	—	0		-3		-0.1
	Was A	1	0	1.000	6	2	1	1	21.1	16	8	1	0	11	12	3.38	92	.211	.310	5	.200	-0	137	0		0.0
	Year	1	0	1.000	8	2	1	1	23.2	19	13	1	0	18	13	4.56	69	.218	.352	5	.200	-0	135	-4		-0.1
Total	14	57	66	.463	341	73	34-6	26	1141	1187	667	76	26	486	420	4.30	104	.268	.343	374-0-12	.233	7	84	10		2.9
AQUINO, GREG	Gregori Emilio	B1.11.1978 Palenque, D.R.		BR/TR/6-1/190*	d7.2																					
2004	Ari N	0	2	.000	34	0	0	16-3	35.1	24	15	4	2	17-2	26	3.06	149	.194	.297	1	.000	-0		5		0.6
2005	Ari N	0	1	.000	35	0	0	1-2	31.1	42	29	7	4	17-1	34	7.76	57	.318	.409	0	—	0		-11	68	-0.5
Total	2	0	3	.000	69	0	0	17-5	66.2	66	44	11	6	34-3	60	5.26	85	.258	.355	1	.000	-0		-6	68	0.1
AQUINO, LUIS	Luis Antonio (Colon)	B5.19.1964 Santurce, PR		BR/TR/6-1/195(155-195)	d8.8																					
1986	Tor A	1	1	.500	7	0	0-1	0	11.1	14	8	2	0	3-1	5	6.35	67	.304	.340	0	—	0		-2		-0.3
1988	KC A	1	0	1.000	7	5	1-1	0-0	29	33	15	1	1	17-0	11	2.79	144	.282	.375	0	—	0	168	2		0.5
1989	KC A	6	8	.429	34	16	2-1	0-0	141.1	148	62	6	4	35-4	68	3.50	111	.271	.317	0	—	0	99	5	15	0.5
1990	KC A	4	1	.800	20	3	1	0-0	68.1	59	26	6	4	27-6	28	3.16	122	.237	.319	0	—	0	141	6	65	0.4
1991	KC A	8	4	.667	38	18	1-1	3-1	157	152	67	10	4	47-5	80	3.44	121	.253	.308	0	—	0	104	13		-0.2
1992	KC A	3	6	.333	15	13	0	0-1	67.2	81	35	5	1	20-1	11	4.52	90	.303	.351	0	—	0	60	-2	99	-0.9
1993	Fla N	6	8	.429	38	13	0	0-1	110.2	115	43	6	5	40-1	67	3.42	128	.276	.345	25-0-4	.080	-2	68	12	30	1.4
1994	Fla N	2	1	.667	29	1	0	0-0	50.2	39	22	3	3	22-4	22	3.73	119	.210	.300	6-0-1	.167	-0	61	5	38	0.2
1995	Mon N	0	2	.000	29	0	0	2-2	37.1	47	24	4	3	11-1	22	3.86	112	.301	.357	3	.333	1		-1		0.0
	SF N	0	1	.000	5	0	0	0-0	5	10	10	2	0	2-1	4	14.40	29	.400	.444	1	.000	0		-6	35	-1.0
	Year	0	3	.000	34	0	0	2-2	42.1	57	34	6	3	13-2	26	5.10	84	.315	.369	4	.250	0		-7		-1.0
Total	9	31	32	.492	222	69	5-3	5-6	678.1	698	311	45	25	224-24	318	3.68	112	.267	.329	35-0-5	.114	-1	92	32	282	2.1
ARCHER, FRED	Frederick Marvin "Lefty"	B3.7.1910 Johnson City TN		D10.31.1981 Charlotte NC		BL/TL/6-0/193	d9.5																			
1936	Phi A	2	3	.400	6	5	2	0	36.2	41	28	3	3	15	9	6.38	84	.289	.369	15	.267	0	86	-4		-0.4
1937	Phi A	0	0	—	1	0	0	0	3	4	2	0	0	0	2	6.00	79	.333	.333	0	—	0		0		0.0
Total	2	2	3	.400	7	5	2	0	39.2	45	30	3	3	15	11	6.35	80	.292	.366	15	.267	1	86	-4		-0.4
ARCHER, JIM	James William	B5.25.1932 Max Meadows VA		BR/TL/6-0/190*	d4.30																					
1961	KC A	9	15	.375	39	27	9-2	5	205.1	204	99	11	5	60-6	110	3.20	131	.257	.309	63-0-6	.063	-5	80	16		1.3
1962	KC A	0	1	.000	18	1	0	0	27.2	40	30	8	0	10-0	12	9.43	45	.342	.394	1	1.000	0	106	-14		-0.7
Total	2	9	16	.360	57	28	9-2	5	233	244	129	19	5	70-6	122	3.94	106	.268	.320	64-0-6	.078	-4	81	2		0.6
ARDIZOIA, RUGGER	Rinaldo Joseph	B11.20.1919 Oleggio, Italy		BR/TR/5-11/180	d4.30																					
1947	NY A	0	0	—	1	0	0	0	2	3	2	0	0	1	0	9.00	39	.500	.556	0	—	0		-1		-0.1
ARELLANES, FRANK	Frank Julian	B1.28.1882 Santa Cruz CA		D12.13.1918 San Jose CA		BR/TR/6-0/180	d7.28	Col Santa Clara																		
1908	Bos A	4	3	.571	11	8	6-1	0	79	60	26	1	3	18	33	1.82	135	.205	.259	30	.167	0*	97	3		0.1
1909	Bos A	16	12	.571	45	28	17-1	**8**	230.2	192	80	3	5	43	82	2.18	114	.229	.270	78-0-6	.167	-1*	114	7		0.8
1910	Bos A	4	7	.364	18	13	2	0	100	106	41	1	3	24	33	2.88	89	.283	.332	34-1-1	.176	0	93	-2		-0.2
Total	3	24	22	.522	74	49	25-2	0	409.2	358	147	5	11	85	148	2.28	110	.238	.283	142-1-7	.169	-1	105	10		0.9
ARIAS, RUDY	Rodolfo (Martinez)	B6.6.1931 Las Villas, Cuba		BL/TL/5-10/165	d4.10																					
1959	Chi A	2	0	1.000	34	0	0	2	44	49	23	7	1	20-7	28	4.09	92	.277	.354	4	.000	-1		-2		-0.1
ARLICH, DON	Donald Louis	B2.15.1943 Wayne MI		BL/TL/6-2/185*	d10.2																					
1965	Hou N	0	0	—	1	1	0	0	6	5	2	0	0	1-0	0	3.00	112	.227	.261	2	.000	-0	78	0		0.0
1966	Hou N	0	1	.000	7	0	0	0	4	11	9	0	9	4-0	1	15.75	22	.478	.571	1	.000	-0		-6		-1.2
Total	2	0	1	.000	8	1	0	0	10	16	11	0	9	5-0	1	8.10	42	.356	.431	3	.000	-0	78	-6		-1.2
ARLIN, STEVE	Stephen Ralph	B9.25.1945 Seattle WA		BR/TR/6-3.5/195*	d6.17	Col Ohio St.																				
1969	SD N	0	1	.000	9	5	0	0-0	10.2	13	11	2	0	9-1	9	9.28	39	.289	.407	2	.000	-0	0	-6		-0.4
1970	SD N	1	0	1.000	2	2	1-1	0-0	12.2	11	4	0	0	8-0	9	2.84	141	.244	.352	5	.000	-1	101	2		0.1
1971	SD N	9	19	.321	36	34	10-4	0-0	227.2	211	114	9	8	103-10	156	3.48	96	.244	.327	73-0-6	.123	-1	92	-8		-1.2
1972	SD N	10	21	.323	38	37	12-3	0-0	250	217	116	19	9	122-15	159	3.60	92	.237	.329	72-0-4	.153	3	74	-9		-0.8
1973	SD N	11	14	.440	34	27	7-3	0-1	180	196	107	26	1	72-7	98	5.10	69	.278	.343	60-0-2	.167	1	80	-28		-3.3
1974	SD N	1	7	.125	16	12	1	1-0	64	85	46	12	3	37-4	23	5.91	61	.326	.408	18-0-1	.111	-1	81	-16		-1.5

YEAR	TM LG	W	L	PCT	G	GS	CG-SHO	SV-BS	IP	H	R	HR	HB	BB-IB	SO	ERA	AERA	OAV	OOB	AB-HR-SH	AVG	PB	SUP	APR	DL	PW
	Cle A	2	5	.286	11	10	1	0-0	43.2	59	34	-1	0	22-4	20	6.60	55	.333	.405	0	—	0	94	-13		-1.9
Total	6	34	67	.337	141	123	32-11	1-1	788.2	792	431	61	18	373-41	463	4.33	79	.263	.345	230-0-13	.139	1	83	-78		-9.5

ARMAS, TONY Antonio Jose B4.29.1978 Puerto Piritu, Venez BR/TR/6-4/215(205-225) d8.16 f-Tony

YEAR	TM LG	W	L	PCT	G	GS	CG-SHO	SV-BS	IP	H	R	HR	HB	BB-IB	SO	ERA	AERA	OAV	OOB	AB-HR-SH	AVG	PB	SUP	APR	DL	PW
1999	Mon N	0	1	.000	1	1	0	0-0	6	8	4	0	0	2-1	2	1.50	297	.320	.357	2	.000	-0	82	1		0.1
2000	Mon N	7	9	.438	17	17	0	0-0	95	74	49	10	3	50-2	59	4.36	108	.218	.321	26-0-3	.038	-2	88	5	71	0.4
2001	Mon N	9	14	.391	34	34	0	0-0	196.2	180	101	18	10	91-6	176	4.03	107	.247	.336	53-0-6	.151	-1	85	4		0.3
2002	Mon N	12	12	.500	29	29	0	0-0	164.1	149	87	22	4	78-12	131	4.44	99	.243	.335	50-0-5	.100	-2	89	1	23	-0.1
2003	Mon N	2	1	.667	5	5	0	0-0	31	25	9	4	1	8-0	23	2.61	170	.225	.279	10	.200	0	102	7	161	0.6
2004	Mon N	2	4	.333	16	16	0	0-0	72	66	41	13	4	45-6	54	4.88	94	.247	.362	16-0-5	.000	-2*	88	-1	57	-0.2
2005	Was N	7	7	.500	19	19	0	0-0	101.1	100	57	16	5	54-4	59	4.97	81	.258	.355	32-0-1	.125	-1	80	-9	52	-1.2
Total	7	39	48	.448	121	121	0	0-0	666.1	602	348	83	30	328-31	504	4.32	102	.244	.337	189-0-20	.106	-8	87	8	364	-0.1

ARMBRUST, ORVILLE Orville Martin B3.2.1910 Beirne AR D10.2.1967 Mobile AL BR/TR/5-10/195 d9.18

YEAR	TM LG	W	L	PCT	G	GS	CG-SHO	SV-BS	IP	H	R	HR	HB	BB-IB	SO	ERA	AERA	OAV	OOB	AB-HR-SH	AVG	PB	SUP	APR	DL	PW
1934	Was A	1	0	1.000	3	2	0		12.2	10	3	1	0	3	3	2.13	203	.208	.255	4	.000	-1	50	3		0.2

ARMSTRONG, HOWARD Howard Elmer B12.2.1889 E.Claridon OH D3.8.1926 Canisteo NY BR/TR/5-9/165 d9.30

YEAR	TM LG	W	L	PCT	G	GS	CG-SHO	SV-BS	IP	H	R	HR	HB	BB-IB	SO	ERA	AERA	OAV	OOB	AB-HR-SH	AVG	PB	SUP	APR	DL	PW
1911	Phi A	0	1	.000	1	0	0	0	3	3	2	0	0	1	0	0.00	—	.273	.333	1	.000	-0		0		0.1

ARMSTRONG, JACK Jack William B3.7.1965 Englewood NJ BR/TR/6-5/215* [CinN87 1/18] d6.21 Col Oklahoma

YEAR	TM LG	W	L	PCT	G	GS	CG-SHO	SV-BS	IP	H	R	HR	HB	BB-IB	SO	ERA	AERA	OAV	OOB	AB-HR-SH	AVG	PB	SUP	APR	DL	PW
1988	Cin N	4	7	.364	14	13	0	0-0	65.1	63	44	8	0	38-2	45	5.79	62	.256	.349	21-0-1	.095	-1	77	-15		-2.2
1989	Cin N	2	3	.400	9	8	0	0-0	42.2	40	24	5	0	21-4	23	4.64	78	.245	.330	8-0-3	.000	-1*	92	-4		-0.5
1990	†Cin N★	12	9	.571	29	27	2-1	0-0	166	151	72	9	6	59-7	110	3.42	116	.241	.310	47-0-13	.106	-2	97	8	15	0.8
1991	†Cin N	7	13	.350	27	24	1	0-0	139.2	158	90	25	2	54-2	93	5.48	69	.293	.354	43-0-5	.093	-2	92	-23		-3.0
1992	Cle A	6	15	.286	35	23	1	0-0	166.2	176	100	23	3	67-0	114	4.64	85	.269	.337	66-0-4	.152	0	89	-15		-1.7
1993	Fla N	9	17	.346	36	33	0	0-0	196.1	210	105	29	7	78-6	118	4.49	97	.271	.339			-2	65	-2		-0.4
1994	Tex A	0	1	.000	2	2	0	0-0	10	9	4	3	0	2-0	7	3.60	134	.231	.268			0	114	2	116	0.1
Total	7	40	65	.381	152	130	4-1	0-0	786.2	807	439	102	18	319-21	510	4.58	87	.265	.335	185-0-26	.114	-6	84	-49	131	-6.9

ARMSTRONG, MIKE Michael Dennis B3.7.1954 Glen Cove NY BR/TR/6-3/206(193-206) [CinN74*1/24] d8.12 Col Miami

YEAR	TM LG	W	L	PCT	G	GS	CG-SHO	SV-BS	IP	H	R	HR	HB	BB-IB	SO	ERA	AERA	OAV	OOB	AB-HR-SH	AVG	PB	SUP	APR	DL	PW
1980	SD N	0	0	—	11	0	0	0-0	14.1	16	10	3	0	13-5	14	5.65	61	.296	.433	3	.000	-0		-4		-0.3
1981	SD N	0	2	.000	10	0	0	0-0	12	14	9	1	0	11-3	9	6.00	54	.311	.446	0	—	-0		-4		-0.7
1982	KC A	5	5	.500	52	0	0	6-2	112.2	88	45	9	3	43-4	75	3.20	128	.215	.290	0	—	0		11		0.9
1983	KC A	10	7	.588	58	0	0	3-3	102.2	86	53	11	3	45-3	52	3.86	107	.228	.312	0	—	0*		1		0.2
1984	NY A	3	2	.600	36	0	0	1-3	54.1	47	21	6	0	26-4	43	3.48	110	.239	.322	0	—	0		3	75	0.3
1985	NY A	0	0	—	9	0	0	0-0	14.2	9	5	4	0	2-0	11	3.07	132	.173	.204	0	—	0		2		0.1
1986	NY A	0	1	.000	7	1	0	0-0	8.2	13	9	4	0	5-1	8	9.35	44	.351	.429	0	—	0	176	-5		-0.5
1987	Cle A	1	0	1.000	14	0	0	1-0	18.2	27	18	4	0	10-0	9	8.68	53	.333	.407	0	—	0		-7		-0.4
Total	8	19	17	.528	197	1	0	11-8	338	300	170	42	6	155-20	221	4.10	98	.240	.323	3	.000	-0	176	-3	75	-0.4

ARNOLD, JAMIE James Lee B3.24.1974 Dearborn MI BR/TR/6-2/188* [AtlN92 1/21] d4.20

YEAR	TM LG	W	L	PCT	G	GS	CG-SHO	SV-BS	IP	H	R	HR	HB	BB-IB	SO	ERA	AERA	OAV	OOB	AB-HR-SH	AVG	PB	SUP	APR	DL	PW
1999	LA N	2	4	.333	36	3	0	1-2	69	81	50	6	6	34-2	26	5.48	80	.300	.390	10-0-1	.200	0	183	-11		-0.7
2000	Chi N	0	3	.000	12	4	0	1-0	32.2	34	28	1	3	19-0	13	6.61	69	.274	.376	9	.111	0	70	-9		-0.7
	LA N	0	0	—	2	0	0	0-0	6.2	4	3	0	1	5-0	3	4.05	110	.174	.333	0	—	0		0		0.0
	Year	0	3	.000	14	4	0	1-0	39.1	38	31	1	4	24-0	16	6.18	74	.259	.369		.111	0	71	-8		-0.7
Total	2	2	7	.222	50	7	0	2-2	108.1	119	81	7	10	58-2	42	5.73	77	.285	.382	19-0-1	.158	0	119	-20		-1.4

ARNOLD, SCOTT Scott Gentry B8.18.1962 Lexington KY BR/TR/6-2/210 [StLN84 5/113] d4.7 Col Miami-Ohio

YEAR	TM LG	W	L	PCT	G	GS	CG-SHO	SV-BS	IP	H	R	HR	HB	BB-IB	SO	ERA	AERA	OAV	OOB	AB-HR-SH	AVG	PB	SUP	APR	DL	PW
1988	StL N	0	0	—	6	0	0	0-0	6.2	9	4	0	0	4-1	8	5.40	65	.321	.406	0	—	0		-1		-0.1

ARNOLD, TONY Tony Dale B5.3.1959 ElPaso TX BR/TR/5-11/170(170-185) [BalA81 10/258] d8.9 Col Texas

YEAR	TM LG	W	L	PCT	G	GS	CG-SHO	SV-BS	IP	H	R	HR	HB	BB-IB	SO	ERA	AERA	OAV	OOB	AB-HR-SH	AVG	PB	SUP	APR	DL	PW
1986	Bal A	0	2	.000	11	0	0	0-0	25.1	25	15	0	0	11-3	7	3.55	117	.278	.356	0	—	0		0		0.1
1987	Bal A	0	0	—	27	0	0	0-0	53	71	35	8	2	17-5	18	5.77	77	.330	.383	0	—	0		-7	54	-0.2
Total	2	0	2	.000	38	0	0	0-0	78.1	96	50	8	2	28-8	25	5.06	86	.315	.375	0	—	0		-7	54	-0.1

ARNSBERG, BRAD Bradley James B8.20.1963 Seattle WA BR/TR/6-4/215* [NYA83 S1/9] d9.6 C5 Col Merced (CA) JC [DL 1988 Tex A 150]

YEAR	TM LG	W	L	PCT	G	GS	CG-SHO	SV-BS	IP	H	R	HR	HB	BB-IB	SO	ERA	AERA	OAV	OOB	AB-HR-SH	AVG	PB	SUP	APR	DL	PW
1986	NY A	0	0	—	2	1	0	0-0	8	13	3	1	0	1-0	3	3.38	123	.342	.359	0	—	0	110	1		0.0
1987	NY A	1	3	.250	6	2	0	0-0	19.1	22	12	5	0	13-3	14	5.59	79	.289	.385	0	—	0	62	-2	22	-0.3
1989	Tex A	2	1	.667	16	1	0	1-0	48	45	27	6	3	22-0	26	4.13	97	.247	.337	0	—	0	68	-1		0.0
1990	Tex A	6	1	.857	53	0	0	5-1	62.2	56	20	4	2	33-1	44	2.15	183	.235	.331	0	—	0		11		1.3
1991	Tex A	0	1	.000	9	0	0	0-0	9.2	10	9	5	0	5-0	8	8.38	48	.256	.341	0	—	0		-4	148	-0.4
1992	Cle A	0	0	—	8	0	0	0-0	10.2	13	14	6	2	11-0	5	11.81	33	.317	.481	0	—	0		-9		-0.4
Total	6	9	6	.600	94	4	0	6-1	158.1	159	85	27	7	85-4	100	4.26	95	.259	.353	0	—	0	79	-4	320	0.2

ARNTZEN, ORIE Orie Edgar "Old Folks" B10.18.1909 Beverly IL D1.28.1970 Cedar Rapids IA BR/TR/6-1/200 d4.20

YEAR	TM LG	W	L	PCT	G	GS	CG-SHO	SV-BS	IP	H	R	HR	HB	BB-IB	SO	ERA	AERA	OAV	OOB	AB-HR-SH	AVG	PB	SUP	APR	DL	PW
1943	Phi A	4	13	.235	32	20	9	4	164.1	172	85	5	6	69	66	4.22	81	.277	.354	50-0-2	.160	-1	66	-13		-1.6

AROCHA, RENE Rene (Magaly) B2.24.1966 Havana, Cuba BR/TR/6-0/180(180-205) d4.9

YEAR	TM LG	W	L	PCT	G	GS	CG-SHO	SV-BS	IP	H	R	HR	HB	BB-IB	SO	ERA	AERA	OAV	OOB	AB-HR-SH	AVG	PB	SUP	APR	DL	PW
1993	StL N	11	8	.579	32	29	1	0-0	188	197	89	20	3	31-2	96	3.78	107	.271	.302	58-0-7	.103	-2	102	5	22	0.2
1994	StL N	4	4	.500	45	7	1-1	11-1	83	94	42	9	4	21-4	62	4.01	106	.286	.335	9-0-3	.111	0	101	1		0.1
1995	StL N	3	5	.375	41	0	0	0-7	49.2	55	24	6	3	18-4	25	3.99	107	.297	.365	1	.000	-0		2	63	0.3
1997	SF N	0	0	—	6	0	0	0-1	10.1	17	14	2	1	5-2	7	11.32	36	.370	.434	1	.000	-0		-8		-0.4
Total	4	18	17	.514	124	36	2-1	11-9	331	363	169	37	11	75-12	190	4.11	100	.282	.325	69-0-10	.101	-2	101	0	85	0.2

ARRIGO, GERRY Gerald William B6.12.1941 Chicago IL BL/TL/6-1/195(175-195) d6.12

YEAR	TM LG	W	L	PCT	G	GS	CG-SHO	SV-BS	IP	H	R	HR	HB	BB-IB	SO	ERA	AERA	OAV	OOB	AB-HR-SH	AVG	PB	SUP	APR	DL	PW
1961	Min A	0	1	.000	7	2	0	0	9.2	9	12	0	2	10-0	6	10.24	41	.265	.429	2	.500	0	198	-6		-0.5
1962	Min A	0	0	—	1	0	0	0	3	3	3	0	0	1-0	1	18.00	23	.600	.667	—		0		-2		-0.1
1963	Min A	1	2	.333	5	1	0	0	15.2	12	5	2	0	4-0	13	2.87	127	.211	.262	4	.000	-0	24	2		0.3
1964	Min A	7	4	.636	41	12	2-1	1	105.1	97	48	11	2	45-3	96	3.84	93	.244	.323	29-0-1	.172	1	122	-1		-0.1
1965	Cin N	2	4	.333	27	5	0	2	54	75	38	4	2	30-5	43	6.17	61	.342	.420	12-1-0	.167	1*	103	-12		-1.4
1966	Cin N	0	3	—	3	0	0	0	7.1	7	4	2	0	3-0	3	4.91	79	.250	.323	1	.000	-0		-1		-0.1
	NY N	3	3	.500	17	5	0	0	43.1	47	20	5	0	16-2	28	3.74	97	.276	.337	10	.500	3	73	0	18	0.4
	Year	3	3	.500	20	5	0	0	50.2	54	24	7	0	19-2	31	3.91	94	.273	.335	11	.455	3	72	-1		0.3
1967	Cin N	6	6	.500	32	5	1-1	1	74	74	31	6	4	35-5	56	3.16	119	.232	.326	19-0-2	.211	1	61	4		0.6
1968	Cin N	12	10	.545	36	31	5-1	0	205.1	181	84	13	4	77-7	140	3.33	95	.237	.309	67-0-3	.075	-2	107	-3		-0.4
1969	Cin N	4	7	.364	20	16	1	0-0	91	89	50	9	8	61-3	35	4.15	91	.256	.376	31-0-1	.161	-0	79	-5		-0.6
1970	Chi A	0	3	.000	9	1	0	0-0	13.1	24	20	4	0	9-1	12	12.83	30	.393	.465	4-0-1	.000	-0	38	-12		-2.0
Total	10	35	40	.467	194	80	9-3	4-0	620	605	315	56	22	291-26	433	4.14	85	.258	.342	179-1-8	.151	2	96	-36	18	-3.9

ARROJO, ROLANDO Luis Rolando B7.18.1968 Santa Clara, Cuba BR/TR/6-4/215* d4.1

YEAR	TM LG	W	L	PCT	G	GS	CG-SHO	SV-BS	IP	H	R	HR	HB	BB-IB	SO	ERA	AERA	OAV	OOB	AB-HR-SH	AVG	PB	SUP	APR	DL	PW
1998	TB A★	14	12	.538	32	32	2-2	0-0	202	195	84	21	19	65-2	152	3.56	135	.256	.329	3	.000	-0	84	28	7	3.3
1999	TB A	7	12	.368	24	24	2	0-0	140.2	162	84	23	14	60-2	107	5.18	96	.296	.378	0	—	0	84	0	51	0.1
2000	Col N	5	9	.357	19	19	0	0-0	101.1	120	77	14	12	46-6	80	6.04	96	.299	.381	28-0-3	.107	-2	86	-4	14	-0.5
	Bos A	5	2	.714	13	13	0	0-0	71.1	67	41	10	4	22-0	44	5.05	99	.245	.310	0	—	0	108	1		0.1
2001	Bos A	5	4	.556	41	9	0	5-2	103.1	88	44	8	12	35-4	78	3.48	127	.230	.313	4	.000	-0	104	11	20	1.0
2002	Bos A	4	3	.571	29	8	0	1-3	81.1	83	47	7	6	27-1	51	4.98	90	.269	.337	2-0-1	.000	-0	78	-3	58	-0.3
Total	5	40	42	.488	158	105	4-2	6-5	700	715	377	83	67	255-15	512	4.55	108	.267	.344	37-0-4	.081	-3	90	33	150	3.7

ARROYO, BRONSON Bronson Anthony B2.24.1977 Key West FL BR/TR/6-5/180* [PitN95 3/69] d6.12

YEAR	TM LG	W	L	PCT	G	GS	CG-SHO	SV-BS	IP	H	R	HR	HB	BB-IB	SO	ERA	AERA	OAV	OOB	AB-HR-SH	AVG	PB	SUP	APR	DL	PW
2000	Pit N	2	6	.250	20	12	0	0-0	71.2	88	61	10	4	28-0	50	6.40	72	.302	.384	21-0-2	.143	-0*	109	-16		-1.5
2001	Pit N	5	7	.417	24	13	1	0-0	88.1	99	54	12	4	34-6	39	5.09	88	.289	.355	21	.048	-1	97	-6		-0.8
2002	Pit N	2	1	.667	9	3	0	0-0	27	30	14	1	0	15-3	22	4.00	105	.283	.369	6	.000	-1	94	0		0.0
2003	†Bos A	0	0	—	6	0	0	1-0	17.1	10	5	0	1	4-2	14	2.08	224	.164	.227	0	—	0		5		0.2
2004	†Bos A	10	9	.526	32	29	0	0-0	178.2	171	99	17	20	47-3	142	4.03	121	.249	.314	6-0-1	.000	-1	106	13		1.1
2005	†Bos A	14	10	.583	35	32	1	0-0	205.1	213	116	22	14	54-3	100	4.51	102	.266	.322	1	.000	-0	107	-1		-0.1
Total	6	33	33	.500	126	90	1	1-0	588.1	611	349	62	43	190-23	367	4.59	101	.267	.332	55-0-3	.073	-3	105	-5		-1.1

ARROYO, FERNANDO
Fernando B3.21.1952 Sacramento CA BR/TR/6-3/195(180-195) [DetA70 10/243] d6.28

YEAR	TM LG	W	L	PCT	G	GS	CG-SHO	SV-BS	IP	H	R	HR	HB	BB-IB	SO	ERA	AERA	OAV	OOB	AB-HR-SH	AVG	PB	SUP	APR	DL
1975	Det A	2	1	.667	14	8	1	0-0	53.1	56	28	5	1	22-2	25	4.56	89	.272	.343	0	—	0	76	-1	
1977	Det A	8	18	.308	38	28	8-1	0-0	209.1	227	102	23	4	52-5	60	4.17	103	.278	.319	0	—	0	74	6	
1978	Det A	0	0	—	2	0	0	0-0	4.1	8	4	1	0	0-0	1	8.31	47	.400	.429	0	—	0		-2	28
1979	Det A	1	1	.500	6	0	0	0-0	12	17	11	3	0	4-2	7	8.25	53	.340	.382	0	—	0		-5	
1980	Min A	6	6	.500	21	11	1-1	0-0	92.1	97	55	7	2	32-2	27	4.68	93	.273	.332	0	—	0	89	-3	
1981	Min A	7	10	.412	23	19	2	0-0	128.1	144	66	11	5	34-1	39	3.93	101	.290	.341	0	—	0	86	-1	
1982	Min A	0	1	.000	6	0	0	0-0	13.2	17	8	2	0	6-1	4	5.27	81	.321	.383	0	—	0*		-1	
	Oak A	0	0	—	10	0	0	0-1	22.1	23	14	4	1	7-0	9	5.24	76	.271	.330	0	—	0		-3	
	Year	0	1	.000	16	0	0	0-1	36	40	22	6	1	13-1	13	5.25	78	.290	.351	0	—	0		-4	
1986	Oak A	0	0	—	1	0	0	0-0						3-0	0	—	—	—	1.000	0	—	0		0	
Total	8	24	37	.393	121	60	12-2	0-1	535.2	589	288	56	11	160-13	172	4.44	95	.283	.335	0	—	0	81	-10	28

ARROYO, LUIS
Luis Enrique B2.18.1927 Penuelas, PR BL/TL/5-8/190(175-190) d4.20

YEAR	TM LG	W	L	PCT	G	GS	CG-SHO	SV-BS	IP	H	R	HR	HB	BB-IB	SO	ERA	AERA	OAV	OOB	AB-HR-SH	AVG	PB	SUP	APR	DL
1955	StL N☆	11	8	.579	35	24	9-1	0	159	162	80	22	2	63-6	68	4.19	97	.261	.329	56-1-4	.232	1	99	-2	
1956	Pit N	3	3	.500	18	2	1	0	28.2	36	17	5	0	12-1	17	4.71	80	.298	.361	4-0-2	.500	1	163	-3	
1957	Pit N	3	11	.214	54	10	0	1	130.2	151	76	19	7	31-9	101	4.68	81	.282	.329	32-0-1	.156	-1*	67	-12	
1959	Cin N	1	0	1.000	10	0	0	0	13.2	17	11	0	0	11-3	8	3.95	103	.321	.418	2	.000	-0		-2	
1960	†NY A	5	1	.833	29	0	0	7	40.2	30	14	2	0	22-3	29	2.88	125	.207	.311	5	.000	-0		4	
1961	†NY A☆	15	5	.750	65	0	0	29	119	83	34	5	3	49-8	87	2.19	169	.199	.284	25-0-3	.280	2		21	
1962	NY A	1	3	.250	27	0	0	7	33.2	33	20	5	1	17-2	21	4.81	78	.262	.352	4	.500	1		-4	34
1963	NY A	1	1	.500	6	0	0	0	6	12	9	0	0	3-1	5	13.50	26	.444	.484	0-0-1		1		-4	34
Total	8	40	32	.556	244	36	10-1	44	531.1	524	261	58	13	208-33	336	3.93	98	.256	.326	128-1-11	.227	3	97	-4	34

ARROYO, RUDY
Rudolph B6.19.1950 New York NY BL/TL/6-2/195 [StLN70*S4/79] d6.1 Col Foothill (CA) JC

YEAR	TM LG	W	L	PCT	G	GS	CG-SHO	SV-BS	IP	H	R	HR	HB	BB-IB	SO	ERA	AERA	OAV	OOB	AB-HR-SH	AVG	PB	SUP	APR	DL
1971	StL N	0	1	.000	9	0	0	0-0	11.2	18	8	2	0	5-1	5	5.40	67	.375	.426	1	.000	-0		-2	

ARUNDEL, HARRY
Harry B2.1855 Philadelphia PA D3.25.1904 Cleveland OH TR/5-6/145 d7.19

YEAR	TM LG	W	L	PCT	G	GS	CG-SHO	SV-BS	IP	H	R	HR	HB	BB-IB	SO	ERA	AERA	OAV	OOB	AB-HR-SH	AVG	PB	SUP	APR	DL
1875	Atl NA	0	1	.000	1	1	0	0	2.1	6	6	0	0	0	0	7.71	27	.400	.400	4	.000	-1	51	-2	
1882	Pit AA	4	10	.286	14	14	13	0	120	155	112	3		23	47	4.65	56	.294	.323	53	.189	0	105	-26	
1884	Pro N	1	0	1.000	1	1	1	0	9	8	2	0	4	4	1.00	285	.250	.333	3	.333	0	205	2	
Total	2	5	10	.333	15	15	14	0	129	163	114	3		27	51	4.40	60	.291	.324	56	.196	0	112	-24	

ASENCIO, MIGUEL
Miguel (Depaula) B9.29.1980 Villa Mella, D.R. BR/TR/6-2/190* d4.6 [DL 2004 KC A 183, 2005 SD N 68]

YEAR	TM LG	W	L	PCT	G	GS	CG-SHO	SV-BS	IP	H	R	HR	HB	BB-IB	SO	ERA	AERA	OAV	OOB	AB-HR-SH	AVG	PB	SUP	APR	DL
2002	KC A	4	7	.364	31	21	0	0-0	123.1	136	73	17	3	64-2	58	5.11	98	.282	.366	2	.000	-0	91	-1	
2003	KC A	2	1	.667	8	8	1	0-0	48.1	54	29	4	3	21-0	27	5.21	92	.295	.368	0	—	0	134	-2	
Total	2	6	8	.429	39	29	1	0-0	171.2	190	102	21	6	85-2	85	5.14	96	.286	.366	2	.000	-0	103	-3	251

ASH, KEN
Kenneth Lowther B9.16.1901 Anmoore WV D11.15.1979 Clarksburg WV BR/TR/5-11/165 d4.17 Col West Virginia Wesleyan

YEAR	TM LG	W	L	PCT	G	GS	CG-SHO	SV-BS	IP	H	R	HR	HB	BB-IB	SO	ERA	AERA	OAV	OOB	AB-HR-SH	AVG	PB	SUP	APR	DL
1925	Chi A	0	0	—	2	0	0	0	4	7	4	2	0	0	0	9.00	46	.389	.389	0		0		-2	
1928	Cin N	3	3	.500	8	5	2	0	36	43	26	1	1	13	6	6.50	61	.314	.377	14-0-1	.071	-1*	98	-9	
1929	Cin N	1	5	.167	29	7	2	2	82	91	57	2	5	30	26	4.83	95	.292	.363	21	.143	-1*	79	-6	
1930	Cin N	2	0	1.000	16	1	1	0	39.1	37	22	1	0	16	15	3.43	141	.268	.344	11	.182	-1*	90	4	
Total	4	6	8	.429	55	13	5	2	161.1	178	109	6	6	59	47	4.96	90	.292	.363	46-0-1	.130	-3	85	-13	

ASHBY, ANDY
Andrew Jason B7.11.1967 Kansas City MO BR/TR/6-1/190(180-202) d6.10 Col Crowder (MO) CC

YEAR	TM LG	W	L	PCT	G	GS	CG-SHO	SV-BS	IP	H	R	HR	HB	BB-IB	SO	ERA	AERA	OAV	OOB	AB-HR-SH	AVG	PB	SUP	APR	DL
1991	Phi N	1	5	.167	8	8	0	0-0	42	41	28	5	3	19-0	26	6.00	62	.256	.341	12-0-1	.083	-1	73	-10	
1992	Phi N	1	3	.250	10	8	0	0-0	37	42	31	6	1	21-0	24	7.54	47	.290	.379	11-0-2	.091	-0	113	-15	106
1993	Col N	0	4	.000	20	9	0	1-0	54	89	54	5	3	32-4	33	8.50	56	.377	.453	15	.267	0	117	-18	
	SD N	3	6	.333	12	12	0	0-0	69	79	46	14	1	24-1	44	5.48	75	.295	.350	21-0-2	.048	-1	105	-9	
	Year	3	10	.231	32	21	0	1-0	123	168	100	19	4	56-5	77	6.80	65	.333	.399	36-0-2	.139	-1	111	-28	
1994	SD N	6	11	.353	24	24	4	0-0	164.1	145	75	16	3	43-12	121	3.40	122	.233	.285	49-0-9	.163	-0	70	11	
1995	SD N	12	10	.545	31	31	2-2	0-0	192.2	180	79	17	11	62-3	150	2.94	138	.252	.320	49-0-17	.163	-0	105	21	
1996	†SD N	9	5	.643	24	24	1	0-0	150.2	147	60	17	3	34-1	85	3.23	125	.259	.304	45-0-9	.244	3*	104	14	68
1997	SD N	9	11	.450	30	30	2	0-0	200.2	207	108	17	5	49-2	144	4.13	95	.266	.311	60-0-7	.067	-3*	120	-8	26
1998	†SD N★	17	9	.654	33	33	5-1	0-0	226.2	223	90	23	7	58-8	151	3.34	119	.259	.309	72-0-9	.111	-2	113	17	
1999	SD N★	14	10	.583	31	31	4-3	0-0	206	204	95	26	7	54-4	132	3.80	112	.258	.311	62-0-7	.129	-0	92	12	17
2000	Phi N	4	7	.364	16	16	1	0-0	101.1	113	75	17	5	38-5	51	5.68	81	.288	.351	28-0-5	.179	-0	90	-15	14
	†Atl N	8	6	.571	15	15	2-1	0-0	98	103	49	12	1	23-4	55	4.13	109	.271	.314	33-0-4	.121	-1*	95	4	
	Year	12	13	.480	31	31	3-1	0-0	199.1	216	124	29	6	61-9	106	4.92	92	.280	.333	61-0-9	.148	-1	92	-12	
2001	LA N	2	0	1.000	2	2	0	0-0	11.2	14	5	2	0	1-0	7	3.86	107	.292	.306	2-0-2	.500	1*	134	1	175
2002	LA N	9	13	.409	30	30	0	0-0	181.2	179	85	20	8	65-3	107	3.91	106	.261	.330	48-1-6	.125	-0	92	0	
2003	LA N	3	10	.231	21	12	0	0-0	73	90	42	8	3	17-2	41	5.18	80	.311	.354	14-0-3	.000	-2	53	-7	
2004	SD N	0	0	—	2	0	0	0-0	2	1	0	0	0	0-0	2	0.00	—	.143	.143	0	—	0	1		
Total	14	98	110	.471	309	285	21-7	1-0	1810.2	1857	922	205	61	540-49	1173	4.12	100	.268	.324	521-1-83	.134	-6	98	-1	406

ASSENMACHER, PAUL
Paul Andre B12.10.1960 Detroit MI BL/TL/6-3/200* d4.12 Col Aquinas

YEAR	TM LG	W	L	PCT	G	GS	CG-SHO	SV-BS	IP	H	R	HR	HB	BB-IB	SO	ERA	AERA	OAV	OOB	AB-HR-SH	AVG	PB	SUP	APR	DL
1986	Atl N	7	3	.700	61	0	0	7-4	68.1	61	23	5	0	26-4	56	2.50	158	.241	.311	6	.000	-0		10	
1987	Atl N	1	1	.500	52	0	0	2-4	54.2	58	41	8	1	24-4	39	5.10	85	.260	.333	4-0-2	.000	-0		-7	10
1988	Atl N	8	7	.533	64	0	0	5-6	79.1	72	28	4	1	32-11	71	3.06	120	.251	.327	3-0-1	.333	1		6	15
1989	Atl N	1	3	.250	49	0	0	0-2	57.2	55	26	2	1	16-7	64	3.59	102	.249	.300	2	.000	-0		1	
	†Chi N	2	1	.667	14	0	0	0-1	19	19	11	1	0	12-1	15	5.21	72	.275	.378	3	.000	-0		-2	
	Year	3	4	.429	63	0	0	0-3	76.2	74	37	3	1	28-8	79	3.99	92	.255	.320	5	.000	-1		-2	
1990	Chi N	7	2	.778	74	1	0	10-10	103	90	33	10	1	36-8	95	2.80	146	.239	.305	8-0-2	.000	-1	111	15	
1991	Chi N	7	8	.467	75	0	0	15-9	102.2	85	41	10	3	31-6	117	3.24	120	.223	.284	4	.250	-0		7	
1992	Chi N	4	4	.500	70	0	0	8-5	68	72	32	6	4	26-5	67	4.10	88	.271	.340	4-0-2	.000	-0		-2	16
1993	Chi N	2	1	.667	46	0	0	0-4	38.2	44	15	5	0	13-3	34	3.49	116	.288	.343	2	.500	0		3	
	NY A	2	2	.500	26	0	0	0-1	17.1	10	6	0	1	9-3	11	3.12	134	.175	.299	0		0		2	
1994	Chi A	1	2	.333	44	0	0	1-2	33	26	13	2	1	13-2	29	3.55	132	.224	.301	0	—	0		5	
1995	†Cle A	6	2	.750	47	0	0	0-1	38.1	32	13	3	3	12-3	40	2.82	168	.225	.296	0	—	0		8	
1996	†Cle A	4	2	.667	63	0	0	1-2	46.2	46	18	1	4	14-5	44	3.09	158	.260	.325	0	—	0		6	
1997	†Cle A	5	0	1.000	75	0	0	4-1	49	43	17	5	1	15-5	53	2.94	160	.231	.289	0	—	0		10	
1998	†Cle A	2	5	.286	69	0	0	3-5	47	54	22	5	1	19-6	43	3.26	147	.286	.351	0	—	0		6	
1999	†Cle A	2	1	.667	55	0	0	0-2	33	50	32	6	1	17-5	29	8.18	62	.347	.415	0	—	0		-11	
Total	14	61	44	.581	884	1	0	56-59	855.2	817	371	73	22	315-78	807	3.53	118	.252	.320	36-0-7	.083	-0	111	60	41

ASTACIO, EZEQUIEL
Ezequiel F. B11.4.1979 Hato Mayor, D.R. BR/TR/6-3/150 d5.3

YEAR	TM LG	W	L	PCT	G	GS	CG-SHO	SV-BS	IP	H	R	HR	HB	BB-IB	SO	ERA	AERA	OAV	OOB	AB-HR-SH	AVG	PB	SUP	APR	DL
2005	†Hou N	3	6	.333	22	14	0	0-0	81	100	56	23	1	25-2	66	5.67	74	.301	.346	21-0-2	.143	-1	98	-14	

ASTACIO, PEDRO
Pedro Julio (Pura) B11.28.1969 Hato Mayor, D.R. BR/TR/6-2/195(174-210) d7.3

YEAR	TM LG	W	L	PCT	G	GS	CG-SHO	SV-BS	IP	H	R	HR	HB	BB-IB	SO	ERA	AERA	OAV	OOB	AB-HR-SH	AVG	PB	SUP	APR	DL
1992	LA N	5	5	.500	11	11	4-4	0-0	82	80	23	1	2	20-4	43	1.98	176	.255	.302	24-0-5	.125	-1	88	13	
1993	LA N	14	9	.609	31	31	3-2	0-0	186.1	165	80	14	5	68-5	122	3.57	108	.239	.309	62-0-7	.161	-1	99	9	
1994	LA N	6	8	.429	23	23	3-1	0-0	149	142	77	16	4	47-4	108	4.29	93	.252	.312	47-0-4	.064	-3	102	-5	
1995	†LA N	7	8	.467	48	11	1-1	0-1	104	103	53	12	4	29-5	80	4.24	91	.261	.316	24-0-2	.125	-0	100	-3	
1996	†LA N	9	8	.529	35	32	0	0-0	211.2	207	86	18	9	67-9	130	3.44	114	.261	.324	68-0-8	.088	-4	93	15	
1997	LA N	7	9	.438	26	24	2-1	0-0	153.2	151	75	15	4	47-0	115	4.10	95	.256	.313	41-0-10	.146	-0	93	-3	
	Col N	5	1	.833	7	7	0	0-0	48.2	49	23	9	5	14-0	51	4.25	121	.262	.327	13-0-1	.077	-1	112	5	
	Year	12	10	.545	33	31	2-1	0-0	202.1	200	98	24	9	61-0	166	4.14	102	.258	.317	54-0-11	.130	-1	98	4	
1998	Col N	13	14	.481	35	34	0	0-0	209.1	245	160	39	17	74-0	170	6.23	83	.294	.363	62-0-11	.129	-3	97	-22	
1999	Col N	17	11	.607	34	34	7	0-0	232	258	140	38	11	75-6	210	5.04	115	.285	.343	86-0-7	.233	-0*	96	15	
2000	Col N	12	9	.571	32	32	3	0-0	196.1	217	119	32	15	77-5	193	5.27	110	.281	.356	82-0-1	.098	-6	96	11	
2001	Col N	6	13	.316	22	22	4-1	0-0	141	151	91	21	10	50-3	125	5.49	97	.276	.345	42-0-10	.091	-1	94	-1	
	Hou N	2	1	.667	4	4	0	0-0	28.2	30	10	1	3	4-0	19	3.14	146	.280	.322	11-0-1	.091	-1	101	5	47
	Year	8	14	.364	26	26	4-1	0-0	169.2	181	101	22	13	54-3	144	5.09	102	.276	.341	53-0-11	.094	-4	95	3	
2002	NY N	12	11	.522	31	31	3-1	0-0	191.2	192	106	32	16	63-5	152	4.79	83	.263	.330	62-0-6	.161	-0	106	-15	
2003	NY N	3	6	.600	7	7	0	0-0	36.2	47	30	8	3	18-1	20	7.36	57	.311	.393	11-0-3	.091	-1	99	-12	148

AR	TM LG	W	L	PCT	G	GS	CG-SHO	SV-BS	IP	H	R	HR	HB	BB-IB	SO	ERA	AERA	OAV	OOB	AB-HR-SH	AVG	PB	SUP	APR	DL	PW
04	Bos A	0	0	—	5	1	0	0-0	8.2	13	10	2	0	5-0	6	10.38	47	.342	.419	0	—	0	133	-4		-0.2
05	Tex A	2	8	.200	12	12	0	0-0	67	79	45	13	1	11-1	45	6.04	76	.292	.319	1	.000	0	77	-9	6	-1.1
	†SD N	4	2	.667	12	10	0	0-0	59.2	54	21	4	1	26-3	33	3.17	122	.247	.327	16-0-5	.063	-1	99	6	15	0.4
tal	14	124	119	.510	375	326		0-1	2106.1	2183	1149	277	110	695-51	1622	4.61	99	.269	.333	652-0-81	.130	-24	97	5	216	-2.3

TCHISON, SCOTT Scott Barham B3.29.1976 Denton TX BR/TR/6-2/180(180-195) [SeaA98 49/1423] d7.31 Col TCU

04	Sea A	2	3	.400	25	0	0	0-0	30.2	29	12	4	0	14-2	36	3.52	127	.250	.328	0	—	0	4			0.6
05	Sea A	0	0	—	6	0	0	0-0	6.2	7	5	1	0	1-0	9	6.75	62	.269	.296	0	—	0	-2	153		-0.1
tal	2	2	3	.400	31	0	0	0-0	37.1	36	17	5	0	15-2	45	4.10	108	.254	.323	0	—	0	2	153		0.5

TCHLEY, JUSTIN Justin Scott B9.5.1973 Sedro-Woolley WA BL/TL/6-3/215 [CinN95 12/335] d4.7 Col Texas A&M-Commerce

| 01 | Cin N | 0 | 0 | — | 15 | 0 | 0 | 0-2 | 10.1 | 12 | 7 | 4 | 1 | 5-2 | 8 | 6.10 | 75 | .286 | .375 | 1 | .000 | -0 | -1 | 87 | | -0.1 |

THERTON, KEITH Keith Rowe B2.19.1959 Newport News VA BR/TR/6-4/200* [OakA78 2/30] d7.14

83	Oak A	2	5	.286	29	0	0	4-4	68.1	53	22	7	1	23-4	40	2.77	141	.215	.280	1	.000	-0	10			1.0
84	Oak A	7	6	.538	57	0	0	2-3	104	110	51	13	2	39-8	58	4.33	87	.274	.336	0	—	0	-4			-0.6
85	Oak A	4	7	.364	56	0	0	3-2	104.2	89	51	17	0	42-8	77	4.30	90	.231	.303	0	—	0	-3	15		-0.4
86	Oak A	1	2	.333	13	0	0	0-0	15.1	18	10	2	0	11-1	8	5.87	66	.295	.392	0	—	0*	-3			-0.5
	Min A	5	8	.385	47	0	0	10-4	81.2	82	37	9	1	35-3	59	3.75	116	.264	.336	0	—	0	5			0.9
	Year	6	10	.375	60	0	0	10-4	97	100	47	11	1	46-4	67	4.08	105	.269	.346	0	—	0	3			0.4
87	†Min A	7	5	.583	59	0	0	2-4	79.1	81	46	10	4	30-4	51	4.54	102	.262	.332	0	—	0	0			0.0
88	Min A	7	5	.583	49	0	0	3-4	74	65	29	10	2	22-4	43	3.41	120	.235	.293	0	—	0	6			0.9
89	Cle A	0	0	—	32	0	0	2-0	39	48	22	7	0	13-4	13	4.15	96	.293	.345	0	—	0	-2			-0.2
tal	7	33	41	.446	342	0	0	26-21	566.1	546	268	75	10	215-36	349	3.99	102	.253	.320	1	.000	-0	9	15		1.1

TKINS, TOMMY Francis Montgomery B12.9.1887 Ponca NE D5.7.1956 Cleveland OH BL/TL/5-10.5/165 d10.2

09	Phi A	0	0	—	1	1	0		6	6	4	0	0	5	4	4.50	53	.261	.393	2	.000	-0	176	-1		-0.1
10	Phi A	3	2	.600	15	3	2	2	57	53	33	0	1	23	29	2.68	88	.254	.330	17	.118	-1	113	-4		-0.5
tal	3	2	.600	16	4	2	2	63	59	37	0	1	28	33	2.86	83	.254	.337	19	.105	-1	128	-5		-0.6

TKINS, JAMES James Curtis B3.10.1921 Birmingham AL BL/TR/6-3/205* d9.29

50	Bos A	0	0	—	1	0	0		4.2	4	2	1	1	4	0	3.86	127	.235	.409	2	.000	-0	1			0.0
52	Bos A	0	1	.000	3	1	0		10.1	11	6	0	0	7	2	3.48	113	.275	.383	3	.667	1	44	0		0.1
tal	2	0	1	.000	4	1	0		15	15	8	1	1	11	2	3.60	118	.263	.391	5	.400	0	44	1		0.1

TKINSON, AL Albert Wright B3.9.1861 Clinton IL D6.17.1952 Elkhorn Twp. MO BR/TR/5-11.5/165 d5.1

84	Phi AA	11	11	.500	22	22	20-1	0	184.1	186	130	3	10	21	93	4.20	81	.244	.274	83	.193	-1	104	-16		-1.6
	CP U	6	10	.375	16	16	16-1	0	140	127	83	1		21	104	2.76	88	.226	.253	68	.206	-5*	66	-5		-0.9
	Bal U	3	5	.375	8	8	8-1	0	69.1	60	34	4		12	50	2.34	114	.217	.250	29	.138	-4	66	3		-0.1
	Year	9	15	.375	24	24	24-1	0	209.1	187	117	5		33	154	2.62	96	.223	.252	97	.186	-9	66	-3		-1.0
86	Phi AA	25	17	.595	45	45	44-1	0	396.2	414	288	11	22	101	154	3.95	89	.256	.308	148	.122	-6	114	-15		-1.9
87	Phi AA	6	8	.429	15	15	11	0	124.2	156	121	2	6	54	34	5.92	72	.292	.364	59-1	.203	-1*	120	-23		-1.8
tal	3	51	51	.500	106	106	99-3	0	915	943	656	21	38	209	435	3.96	85	.251	.297	387-1	.165	-16	102	-56		-6.3

TKINSON, BILL William Cecil Glenn B10.4.1954 Chatham ON, Can. BL/TR/5-7/165* d9.18

76	Mon N	0	0	—	4	0	0	0-0	5	3	0	0	1	1-1	4	0.00	—	.176	.222	0	—	0	2			0.1
77	Mon N	7	2	.778	55	0	0	7-1	83.1	72	33	12	0	29-11	56	3.35	115	.234	.296	5-0-1	.200	-0*	6			0.7
78	Mon N	2	2	.500	29	0	0	3-1	45.1	45	23	5	1	28-4	32	4.37	82	.268	.370	4	.500	1	-3			-0.2
79	Mon N	2	0	1.000	10	0	0	1-0	13.2	9	4	0	0	4-1	7	1.98	188	.170	.228	1	.000	-0	2			0.3
tal	4	11	4	.733	98	0	0	11-2	147.1	129	60	17	1	62-17	99	3.42	110	.236	.312	10-0-1	.300	1	7			0.9

UCOIN, DEREK Derek Alfred B3.27.1970 Lachine QC, Can. BR/TR/6-7/245 d5.21

| 96 | Mon N | 0 | 1 | .000 | 2 | 0 | 0 | 0-0 | 2.2 | 2 | 1 | 0 | 0 | 1-0 | 1 | 3.38 | 128 | .300 | .364 | 0 | — | 0 | 0 | | | 0.1 |

UGUST, DON Donald Glenn B7.3.1963 Inglewood CA BR/TR/6-3/190* [HouN84 1/17] d6.2 Col Chapman

88	Mil A	13	7	.650	24	22	6-1	0-0	148.1	137	55	12	0	48-6	66	3.09	129	.245	.303	0	—	0	98	16		2.1
89	Mil A	12	12	.500	31	25	2-1	0-0	142.1	175	93	17	2	58-2	51	5.31	73	.302	.364	0	—	0	91	-23		-3.2
90	Mil A	0	3	.000	5	0	0	0-1	11	13	10	0	0	5-0	2	6.55	59	.295	.367	0	—	0	-4			-0.7
91	Mil A	9	8	.529	28	23	1-1	0-0	138.1	166	87	18	3	47-2	62	5.47	73	.301	.358	0	—	0	121	-21		-2.2
tal	4	34	30	.531	88	70	9-3	0-1	440	491	245	47	5	158-10	181	4.64	85	.283	.343	0	—	0	103	-32		-4.0

UGUSTINE, JERRY Gerald Lee B7.24.1952 Kewaunee WI BL/TL/6-0/185* [MilA74 15/342] d9.9 Col Wisconsin-La Crosse

75	Mil A	2	0	1.000	5	3	1		26.2	26	9	4	1	12-1	9	3.04	127	.274	.355	0	—	0	122	3		0.6
76	Mil A	9	12	.429	39	24	5-3	0-3	171.2	167	69	9	4	56-4	59	3.30	106	.261	.321	0	—	0	94	5		0.5
77	Mil A	12	18	.400	33	33	10-1	0-0	209	222	119	23	3	72-3	68	4.48	92	.277	.334	0	—	0	88	-10		-1.2
78	Mil A	13	12	.520	35	30	9-2	0-0	188.1	204	100	14	4	61-2	59	4.54	84	.280	.335	0	—	0	127	-13		-1.4
79	Mil A	9	6	.600	43	2	0	5-2	85.2	95	38	6	1	30-4	41	3.47	121	.284	.341	0	—	0	129	7		1.0
80	Mil A	4	3	.571	39	1	0	2-1	69.2	83	37	5	2	36-5	22	4.52	87	.301	.382	0	—	0	46	-4		-0.3
81	Mil A	2	2	.500	27	2	0	2-1	61.1	75	30	4	1	18-3	26	4.26	82	.300	.348	0	—	0	194	-5		-0.3
82	Mil A	1	3	.250	20	2	1	0-0	62	63	43	13	2	26-2	22	5.08	76	.267	.340	0	—	0	83	-11		-0.7
83	Mil A	3	3	.500	34	7	1	0-0	64.1	89	45	11	1	25-4	40	5.74	66	.328	.383	0	—	0	134	-15	22	-1.3
84	Mil A	0	0	—	5	0	0	0-0	5.1	4	1	0	1	4-0	3	0.00	—	.211	.375	0	—	0	2			0.1
tal	10	55	59	.482	279	104	27-6	11-7	944	1028	491	87	20	340-28	348	4.23	91	.281	.342	0	—	0	106	-41	22	-3.4

UKER, ELDEN Elden Le Roy "Submarine" B9.21.1910 Norcatur KS BR/TR/6-2/194 d8.10 Col Kansas St.

33	Det A	3	3	.500	15	6	2-1	0	55	63	34	3	2	25	17	5.24	82	.285	.363	17-0-1	.118	-1	109	-4		-0.5
34	†Det A	15	7	.682	43	18	10-2	1	205	234	103	9	3	56	86	3.42	128	.288	.336	74-0-7	.149	-2	113	16		1.4
35	†Det A	18	7	.720	36	25	13-2	0	195	213	86	13	9	61	63	3.83	109	.279	.340	74-0-4	.216	1	122	12		1.5
36	Det A	13	16	.448	35	31	14-2	0	215.1	263	140	11	3	83	66	4.89	101	.302	.365	78-0-7	.308	7	100	-1		0.7
37	Det A	17	9	.654	39	32	19-1	1	252.2	250	127	13	6	97	73	3.88	120	.260	.331	91-3-6	.198	4*	107	20		2.4
38	Det A	11	10	.524	27	24	12-1	0	160.2	184	97	14	5	56	46	5.27	95	.284	.346	57-0-7	.088	-4	114	-1		-0.4
39	Bos A	9	10	.474	31	25	6-1	0	151	183	108	11	3	61	43	5.36	88	.294	.358	53-2-3	.226	2	114	-12		-1.0
40	StL A	16	11	.593	38	35	20-2	0	263.2	299	129	17	3	96	78	3.96	116	.281	.342	89-1-1	.213	3	105	18		2.0
41	StL A	14	15	.483	34	31	13	0	216	268	150	20	1	85	60	5.50	78	.303	.365	80-0-3	.125	-3*	110	-28		-3.3
42	StL A	14	13	.519	35	34	17-2	0	249	273	132	16	3	86	62	4.08	91	.277	.337	87-0-6	.161	-1*	111	-10		-1.1
tal	10	130	101	.563	333	261	126-14	2	1963.1	2230	1106	129	36	706	594	4.42	101	.285	.347	700-6-41	.187	6	110	10		1.7

USANIO, JOE Joseph John B12.9.1965 Kingston NY BR/TR/6-1/205* [PitN88 11/278] d7.14 Col Jacksonville

94	NY A	2	1	.667	13	0	0	0-0	15.2	16	9	3	0	6-0	15	5.17	89	.254	.319	0	—	0	-1			-0.1
95	NY A	2	0	1.000	28	0	0	1-2	37.2	42	24	9	0	23-0	36	5.73	81	.286	.378	0	—	0	-4			-0.2
tal	2	4	1	.800	41	0	0	1-2	53.1	58	33	12	0	29-0	51	5.57	83	.276	.361	0	—	0	-5			-0.3

UST, DENNIS Dennis Kay B11.25.1940 Tecumseh NE BR/TR/5-11/180* d9.6 Col Florida

65	StL N	0	0	—	6	0	0	1	7.1	6	4	0	0	2-1	7	4.91	78	.214	.267	1	.000	-0	-1			0.0
66	StL N	0	1	.000	9	0	0	1	9.2	12	7	1	0	6-2	7	6.52	55	.308	.391	1	.000	-0	-3			-0.3
tal	2	0	1	.000	15	0	0	2	17	18	11	1	0	8-3	14	5.82	64	.269	.342	2	.000	-0	-4			-0.3

USTIN, JIM James Parker B12.7.1963 Farmville VA BR/TR/6-2/200* [SDN86 6/144] d7.4 Col Virginia Commonwealth

91	Mil A	0	0	—	5	0	0	0-0	8.2	8	8	1	3	11-1	3	8.31	48	.276	.500	0	—	0	-4	41		-0.2
92	Mil A	5	2	.714	47	0	0	0-1	58.1	38	13	2	2	32-6	30	1.85	209	.191	.308	0	—	0	13			1.4
93	Mil A	1	2	.333	31	0	0	0-2	33	28	15	3	1	13-1	15	3.82	113	.230	.309	0	—	0	2	15		0.2
tal	3	6	4	.600	83	0	0	0-3	100	74	36	6	6	56-8	48	3.06	132	.211	.329	0	—	0	11	56		1.3

USTIN, JEFF Jeffrey Wellington B10.19.1976 San Bernardino CA BR/TR/6-0/185* [KCA98 1/4] d6.26 Col Stanford

01	KC A	0	0	—	21	0	0	0-0	26	27	17	4	1	14-2	27	5.54	90	.273	.362	0	—	0	-1			-0.1
02	KC A	0	0	—	10	0	0	0-0	11	14	6	0	0	6-1	6	4.91	102	.318	.385	0	—	0	0			0.0
03	Cin N	2	3	.400	7	7	0	0-0	28.1	28	27	9	0	21-0	22	8.58	49	.255	.374	8-0-2	.125	-0	116	-13		-1.8
tal	3	2	3	.400	38	7	0	0-0	65.1	69	50	13	1	41-3	55	6.75	68	.273	.371	8-0-2	.125	-0	116	-14		-1.9

YEAR	TM LG	W	L	PCT	G	GS	CG-SHO	SV-BS	IP	H	R	HR	HB	BB-IB	SO	ERA	AERA	OAV	OOB	AB-HR-SH	AVG	PB	SUP	APR	DL	PW

AUSTIN, RICK   Rick Gerald   B10.27.1946 Seattle WA   BR/TL/6-4/190*   [CleA68 S1/6]   d6.21 Col Washington St.

1970	Cle A	2	5	.286	31	8	1-1	3-0	67.2	74	36	10	3	26-6	53	4.79	84	.281	.352	18	.111	0	83	-4		-0.4
1971	Cle A	0	0	—	23	0	0	1-1	23	25	15	3	2	20-4	20	5.09	76	.291	.429	1	.000	-0		-3		-0.2
1975	Mil A	2	3	.400	32	0	0	2-2	40	32	19	3	1	32-5	30	4.05	95	.222	.367	0	—	0		0		0.0
1976	Mil A	0	0	—	3	0	0	0-0	5.1	10	3	1	1	0-0	3	5.06	69	.435	.423	0	—	0		-1		0.0
Total	4	4	8	.333	89	8	1-1	6-3	136	141	73	17	8	78-15	106	4.63*	85	.273	.373	19	.105	0	83	-8		-0.6

AUTRY, AL   Albert   B2.29.1952 Modesto CA   BR/TR/6-5/225   [KCA69 4/93]   d9.14

| 1976 | Atl N | 1 | 0 | 1.000 | 2 | 1 | 0 | 0-0 | 5 | 4 | 3 | 2 | 3 | 3-0 | 3 | 5.40 | 70 | .222 | .333 | 2 | .000 | -0 | 93 | -1 | | -0.1 |

AVERY, STEVE   Steven Thomas   B4.14.1970 Trenton MI   BL/TL/6-4/190(180-205)   [AtlN88 1/3]   d6.13

1990	Atl N	3	11	.214	21	20	1-1	0-0	99	121	79	7	2	45-2	75	5.64	72	.302	.372	30-0-2	.133	-1	92	-20		-2.5
1991	†Atl N	18	8	.692	35	35	3-1	0-0	210.1	189	89	21	3	65-0	137	3.38	115	.240	.299	79-0-5	.215	3*	122	12		1.7
1992	†Atl N	11	11	.500	35	35	2-2	0-0	233.2	216	95	14	0	71-3	129	3.20	115	.246	.300	76-0-9	.171	2	98	11		1.7
1993	†Atl N★	18	6	.750	35	35	3-1	0-0	223.1	216	81	14	0	43-5	125	2.94	138	.261	.295	75-0-8	.160	1	105	27		2.1
1994	Atl N	8	3	.727	24	24	1-	0-0	151.2	127	71	15	4	55-4	122	4.04	107	.227	.298	49-0-6	.102	-2	122	6		0.3
1995	†Atl N	7	13	.350	29	29	3-1	0-0	173.1	165	92	22	6	52-4	141	4.67	93	.252	.311	53-2-8	.208	3	89	-4		-0.1
1996	†Atl N	7	10	.412	24	23	1	0-0	131	146	70	10	4	40-8	86	4.47	100	.285	.339	46-2-1	.239	5	102	1	51	0.2
1997	Bos A	6	7	.462	22	18	0	0-0	96.2	127	76	15	2	49-0	51	6.42	72	.322	.394	1	.000	-0*	124	-19	62	-2.4
1998	Bos A	10	7	.588	34	23	0	0-1	123.2	128	74	14	4	64-0	57	5.02	94	.269	.361	1	.000	-0*	115	-3		-0.2
1999	Cin N	6	7	.462	19	19	0	0-0	96	75	62	11	1	78-0	51	5.16	91	.222	.364	26-0-2	.077	-2	92	-6	71	-0.4
2003	Det A	2	0	1.000	19	0	0	0-0	16	19	11	5	0	7-1	6	5.63	78	.302	.371	1	1.000	0		-2		-0.1
Total	11	96	83	.536	297	261	14-6	0-2	1554.2	1529	800	148	26	569-27	980	4.19	100	.259	.325	437-4-41	.174	9	107	3	184	1.5

AVREA, JAY   James Epherium   B7.6.1920 Cleburne TX   D6.26.1987 Dallas TX   BR/TR/6-1.5/175   d4.22

| 1950 | Cin N | 0 | 0 | — | 2 | 0 | 0 | 0-0 | 5.1 | 6 | 2 | 0 | 0 | 3-0 | 2 | 3.38 | 125 | .273 | .360 | 2 | .000 | -0 | | 1 | | 0.4 |

AYALA, LUIS   Luis Ignacio   B1.12.1978 Los Mochis, Sinaloa, Mexico   BR/TR/6-2/170(170-185)   d3.31

2003	Mon N	10	3	.769	65	0	0	5-3	71	65	27	8	5	13-3	46	2.92	152	.244	.291	1	.000	-0		11	29	2.1
2004	Mon N	6	12	.333	81	0	0	2-5	90.1	92	30	6	5	15-2	63	2.69	171	.268	.307	9-0-1	.333	1		18		3.3
2005	Was N	8	7	.533	68	0	0	1-2	71	75	23	7	6	14-4	40	2.66	152	.286	.333	3-0-1	.333	1		11	2	2.2
Total	3	24	22	.522	214	0	0	8-10	232.1	232	80	21	16	42-9	149	2.75	159	.266	.310	13-0-2	.308	1		40	29	7.5

AYALA, BOBBY   Robert Joseph   B7.8.1969 Ventura CA   BR/TR/6-3/200(190-210)   d9.5

1992	Cin N	2	1	.667	5	5	0	0-0	29	33	15	1	1	13-2	23	4.34	83	.297	.376	9-0-1	.000	-1	131	-2		-0.3
1993	Cin N	7	10	.412	43	9	0	3-2	98	106	72	16	7	45-4	65	5.60	72	.274	.358	21-0-2	.095	-1	82	-20		-3.1
1994	Sea A	4	3	.571	46	0	0	18-6	56.2	42	25	2	0	26-0	76	2.86	172	.203	.289	0	—	0		11		1.7
1995	†Sea A	6	5	.545	63	0	0	19-8	71	73	42	9	0	30-4	77	4.44	108	.262	.343	0	—	0		1		0.1
1996	†Sea A	6	3	.667	50	0	0	3-3	67.1	65	45	10	2	25-3	61	5.88	85	.256	.325	0	—	0		-6	58	-1.1
1997	†Sea A	10	5	.667	71	0	0	8-4	96.2	91	45	14	3	41-3	92	3.82	119	.260	.338	0	—	0		7		1.5
1998	Sea A	1	10	.091	62	0	0	8-9	75.1	100	66	9	1	26-4	68	7.29	64	.338	.370	0	—	0		-21		-3.3
1999	Mon N	1	6	.143	53	0	0	0-1	66	60	36	6	4	34-1	64	3.68	121	.235	.331	0	.000	-0		3		0.1
	Chi N	0	1	.000	13	0	0	0-0	16	11	7	4	2	5-1	15	2.81	163	.193	.281	0	—	0		2		0.5
	Year	1	7	.125	66	0	0	0-1	82	71	43	10	6	39-2	79	3.51	128	.228	.322	1	.000	-0		5		0.5
Total	8	37	44	.457	406	14	0	59-33	576	581	353	71	26	245-22	541	4.78	95	.263	.340	31-0-3	.065	-2	85	-25	58	-3.5

AYBAR, MANNY   Manuel Antonio   B5.4.1972 Bani, D.R.   BR/TR/6-1/177(165-177)   d8.4

1997	StL N	2	4	.333	12	12	0	0-0	68	66	33	8	4	29-0	41	4.24	99	.263	.344	21	.143	-1	92	1		0.1
1998	StL N	6	6	.500	20	14	0	0-0	81.1	90	58	6	2	42-1	57	5.98	70	.281	.367	27-1-1	.222	1	118	-15		-1.2
1999	StL N	4	5	.444	65	1	0	3-2	97	104	67	13	4	36-3	74	5.47	84	.272	.338	12-0-1	.083	-1*	180	-10		-1.4
2000	Col N	0	1	.000	1	0	0	0-0	1.2	5	3	1	0	0-0	0	16.20	36	.500	.500	0	—	-0		-1		-0.2
	Cin N	1	1	.500	32	0	0	0-0	50.1	51	31	7	2	22-2	31	4.83	99	.262	.338	6-0-1	.000	-0		6	21	0.4
	Fla N	1	0	1.000	21	0	0	0-1	27.1	18	8	3	0	13-1	14	2.63	166	.184	.277	0	—	0		6		1.0
	Year	2	2	.500	54	0	0	0-1	79.1	74	42	11	2	35-3	45	4.31	108	.244	.323	6-0-1	.000	-0		2		0.0
2001	Chi N	2	1	.667	17	1	0	0-0	22.2	28	19	5	2	17-0	16	6.35	66	.304	.420	3-0-1	1.000	1	243	-6		-0.6
2002	†SF N	1	0	1.000	15	0	0	0-0	14.1	16	6	1	1	3-2	11	2.51	157	.271	.317	1	.000	-0		2	17	0.5
2003	SF N	0	0	—	3	0	0	0-0	3	4	2	1	0	3-0	2	6.00	71	.333	.438	0	—	0		-1		-0.1
2005	NY N	0	0	—	22	0	0	0-1	25.1	31	17	4	1	7-1	27	6.04	69	.301	.345	0	—	0		-5		-0.6
Total	8	17	18	.486	208	28	0	3-4	391	413	244	49	16	172-10	273	5.11	86	.271	.348	70-1-4	.186	1	109	-30	38	-3.1

AYDELOTT, JAKE   Jacob Stuart   B7.6.1861 N.Manchester IN   D10.22.1926 Detroit MI   BL/TR/6-0/180   d5.15

1884	Ind AA	5	7	.417	12	12	11	0	106	129	100	0	0	29	30	4.92	67	.282	.324	44	.114	-3	93	-19		-1.6
1886	Phi AA	0	2	.000	2	2	2	0	18	21	11	0	0	12	5	4.00	88	.304	.407	6	.000	-1	34	0		-0.1
Total	2	5	9	.357	14	14	13	0	124	150	111	0	0	41	35	4.79	69	.285	.336	50	.100	-4	84	-19		-2.2

AYERS, BILL   William Oscar   B9.27.1919 Newnan GA   D9.24.1980 Newnan GA   BR/TR/6-3/185   d4.17

| 1947 | NY N | 0 | 3 | .000 | 13 | 4 | 0 | 1 | 35.1 | 46 | 35 | 7 | 1 | 14 | 22 | 8.15 | 50 | .322 | .386 | 8-0-2 | .250 | 0 | 87 | -15 | | -1.8 |

AYERS, DOC   Yancy Wyatt   B5.20.1890 Fancy Gap VA   D5.26.1968 Pulaski VA   BR/TR/6-1/185   d9.9 Col Roanoke

1913	Was A	1	1	.500	4	2	1-1	1	17.2	12	7	0	1	4	17	1.53	193	.188	.246	7	.000	-1	100	2		0.1
1914	Was A	11	15	.423	49	32	8-3	3	265.1	221	106	5	8	54	148	2.54	111	.238	.286	83-0-2	.169	-1	91	4		0.4
1915	Was A	14	9	.609	40	16	8-2	3	211.1	178	66	1	7	38	96	2.21	134	.234	.276	63-0-1	.190	-1	95	19		1.8
1916	Was A	5	8	.385	43	17	7	2	157	173	89	4	4	52	69	3.78	74	.285	.346	43-0-2	.140	-2	86	-19		-2.3
1917	Was A	11	10	.524	40	15	12-3	1	207.2	192	67	3	8	59	78	2.47	121	.256	.317	63-0-3	.206	-0	89	10		1.0
1918	Was A	10	12	.455	40	24	11-4	3	219.2	215	91	2	7	63	67	2.83	96	.261	.319	66-0-5	.152	-2	102	0		-0.1
1919	Was A	0	6	.000	11	5	0	1	43.2	52	27	0	4	17	12	2.89	111	.317	.395	12	.417	2	49	-2		-0.2
	Det A	5	3	.625	24	5	3-1	0	93.2	88	34	2	3	31	32	2.69	119	.254	.320	24-0-2	.125	-1	113	6		0.6
	Year	5	9	.357	35	10	3-1	1	137.1	140	61	2	7	48	44	2.75	116	.274	.345	36-0-2	.222	0	81	4		0.4
1920	Det A	7	14	.333	46	23	8-3	1	208.2	217	115	6	8	62	103	3.88	96	.280	.340	59-0-2	.153	-2	86	-2		-0.2
1921	Det A	0	0	—	2	1	0	0	4	9	6	0	2	2	0	9.00	47	.450	.500	0	—	0	117	-2		-0.2
Total	9	64	78	.451	299	140	58-17	15	1428.2	1357	608	27	50	382	622	2.84	105	.259	.315	420-0-17	.171	-8	91	16		0.9

AYRAULT, BOB   Robert Cunningham   B4.27.1966 South Lake Tahoe CA   BR/TR/6-4/230*   d6.7 Col Nevada-Las Vegas

1992	Phi N	2	2	.500	30	0	0	0-0	43.1	32	16	0	1	17-1	27	3.12	113	.209	.287	0	—	0		2		-0.1
1993	Phi N	2	0	1.000	10	0	0	0-1	10.1	18	11	1	1	10-1	8	9.58	41	.375	.492	0	.000	-0		-6		-1.1
	Sea A	1	1	.500	14	0	0	0-1	19.2	18	8	1	0	6-1	7	3.20	140	.254	.304	2	.000	-0		-2		-0.1
Total	2	5	3	.625	54	0	0	0-2	73.1	68	35	2	2	33-3	42	4.05	95	.250	.330	2	.000	-0		-6		-1.3

BABCOCK, BOB   Robert Ernest   B8.25.1949 New Castle PA   BR/TR/6-5/210(190-210)   d7.22   [DL 1982 Tex A 110]

1979	Tex A	0	0	—	4	0	0	0-0	5.1	7	7	1	0	7-0	6	10.13	41	.318	.452	0	—	0		-4		-0.7
1980	Tex A	1	2	.333	19	0	0	0-1	23.1	20	13	3	2	8-1	15	4.63	84	.238	.309	0	—	0		-2		-0.2
1981	Tex A	1	1	.500	16	0	0	0-2	28.2	21	7	2	1	16-1	18	2.20	158	.219	.333	0	—	0		5	110	0.7
Total	3	2	3	.400	39	0	0	0-3	57.1	48	27	6	3	31-2	39	3.92	94	.238	.339	0	—	0		-1	110	-0.2

BABICH, JOHNNY   John Charles   B5.14.1913 Albion CA   D1.19.2001 Richmond CA   BR/TR/6-1.5/185   d6.19

1934	Bro N	7	11	.389	25	18	7	1	135	148	76	5	2	51	62	4.20	93	.281	.347	50-0-1	.140	-3	98	-5		-0.5
1935	Bro N	7	14	.333	37	24	7-2	0	143.1	191	124	7	2	52	55	6.66	60	.317	.373	49-0-2	.184	-0	102	-42		-4.6
1936	Bos N	0	0	—	3	0	0	0	6	11	8	1	0	6	1	10.50	37	.440	.563	1	.000	-0		-5		-0.5
1940	Phi A	14	13	.519	31	30	16-1	0	229.1	222	111	16	1	80	94	3.73	119	.248	.310	86-0-2	.116	-6	98	19		1.8
1941	Phi A	2	7	.222	16	14	4	0	78.1	85	57	9	3	31	19	6.09	69	.281	.353	25-0-2	.400	4	106	-15		-1.5
Total	5	30	45	.400	112	86	34-3	1	592	657	376	38	9	220	231	4.93	85	.279	.343	211-0-7	.171	-5	100	-48		-5.3

BACKE, BRANDON   Brandon Allen   B4.5.1978 Galveston TX   BR/TR/6-0/182*   [TBA98 18/552]   d7.19 Col Galveston (TX) CC

2002	TB A	0	0	—	9	0	0	0-0	13	15	10	3	2	7-0	6	6.92	65	.288	.393	0	—	0		-3		-0.3
2003	TB A	1	1	.500	28	0	0	0-0	44.2	40	28	6	2	25-1	36	5.44	84	.247	.353	0	—	0*		-4		-0.5
2004	†Hou N	5	3	.625	33	9	0	0-0	67	75	33	10	1	27-4	54	4.30	102	.290	.358	16-1-3	.313	3*	118	1		0.1

YEAR	TM LG	W	L	PCT	G	GS	CG-SHO	SV-BS	IP	H	R	HR	HB	BB-IB	SO	ERA	AERA	OAV	OOB	AB-HR-SH	AVG	PB	SUP	APR	DL	PW
2005	†Hou N	10	8	.556	26	25	1-1	0-0	149.1	151	82	19	4	67-1	97	4.76	88	.263	.344	45-0-5	.222	4*	105	-8	40	-0.5
Total	4	16	12	.571	96	34	1-1	0-0	274	281	153	38	9	126-6	193	4.86	89	.268	.351	61-1-8	.246	6	106	-14	40	-0.5

BACKMAN, LES Lester John B3.20.1888 Cleves OH D11.8.1975 Cincinnati OH BR/TR/6-0.5/195 d7.3 Col Rose-Hulman Tech

YEAR	TM LG	W	L	PCT	G	GS	CG-SHO	SV-BS	IP	H	R	HR	HB	BB-IB	SO	ERA	AERA	OAV	OOB	AB-HR-SH	AVG	PB	SUP	APR	DL	PW
1909	StL N	3	11	.214	21	15	8	0	128.1	146	69	1	3	39	35	4.14	61	.302	.357	39-0-1	.103	-1	81	-19		-2.1
1910	StL N	6	7	.462	26	11	4	2	116	117	55	4	2	53	41	3.03	98	.265	.346	35	.114	0	89	-3		-0.3
Total	2	9	18	.333	47	26	12	2	244.1	263	124	5	5	92	76	3.61	76	.284	.352	74-0-1	.108	-1	84	-22		-2.4

BACSIK, MIKE Michael James B4.1.1952 Dallas TX BR/TR/6-1/185(180-195) d6.15 s-Mike Col Trinity (TX)

YEAR	TM LG	W	L	PCT	G	GS	CG-SHO	SV-BS	IP	H	R	HR	HB	BB-IB	SO	ERA	AERA	OAV	OOB	AB-HR-SH	AVG	PB	SUP	APR	DL	PW
1975	Tex A	1	2	.333	7	3	0	0-0	26.2	28	17	1	1	9-1	13	3.71	102	.275	.336	0	—	0	86	-2		-0.2
1976	Tex A	3	2	.600	23	0	0	0-2	55	66	31	3	2	26-4	21	4.25	84	.308	.385	0	—	0		-4		-0.4
1977	Tex A	0	0	—	2	0	0	0-0	2.1	9	5	1	0	0-0	1	19.29	21	.563	.563	0	—	0		-4		-0.2
1979	Min A	4	2	.667	31	0	0	0-1	65.2	61	39	6	0	29-4	33	4.39	100	.249	.325	0	—	0		-2		-0.2
1980	Min A	0	0	—	10	0	0	0-0	23	26	12	1	0	11-0	9	4.30	102	.286	.359	0	—	0		0		0.0
Total	5	8	6	.571	73	3	0	0-3	172.2	190	104	12	3	75-9	77	4.43	91	.284	.356	0	—	0	86	-12		-1.0

BACSIK, MIKE Michael Joseph B11.11.1977 Dallas TX BL/TL/6-3/190* [CleA96 18/543] d8.5 f-Mike

YEAR	TM LG	W	L	PCT	G	GS	CG-SHO	SV-BS	IP	H	R	HR	HB	BB-IB	SO	ERA	AERA	OAV	OOB	AB-HR-SH	AVG	PB	SUP	APR	DL	PW
2001	Cle A	0	0	—	3	0	0	0-0	9	13	10	0	1	3-1	4	9.00	51	.325	.378	0	—	0		-4		-0.2
2002	NY N	3	2	.600	11	9	1	0-0	55.2	63	29	8	4	19-3	30	4.37	91	.289	.355	18-0-3	.111	-0	125	-2		-0.1
2003	NY N	1	2	.333	5	3	0	0-0	17.2	28	21	5	0	9-1	12	10.19	41	.368	.424	3	.000	-0	60	-12		-1.5
2004	Tex A	1	1	.500	3	3	0	0-0	15.2	16	8	2	2	1-0	6	4.60	107	.267	.302	0	—	0	107	1		0.1
Total	4	5	5	.500	22	15	1	0-0	98	120	68	15	7	31-4	52	5.88	72	.305	.363	21-0-3	.095	-1	107	-17		-1.7

BACZEWSKI, FRED Frederic John "Lefty" B5.15.1926 St.Paul MN D11.14.1976 Culver City CA BL/TL/6-2.5/185(185-208) d4.26

YEAR	TM LG	W	L	PCT	G	GS	CG-SHO	SV-BS	IP	H	R	HR	HB	BB-IB	SO	ERA	AERA	OAV	OOB	AB-HR-SH	AVG	PB	SUP	APR	DL	PW
1953	Chi N	0	0	—	9	0	0	0	10	20	9	1	1	6	3	6.30	71	.435	.509	2-0-1	.500	0		-2		-0.1
	Cin N	11	4	.733	24	18	10-1		138.1	125	56	13	1	52	58	3.45	126	.244	.315	45-1-3	.178	-0	96	15		1.3
	Year	11	4	.733	33	18	10-1	1	148.1	145	65	14	2	58	61	3.64	120	.260	.332	47-1-4	.191	-0	96	12		1.2
1954	Cin N	6	6	.500	29	22	4-1	0	130	159	82	22	1	53	43	5.26	80	.305	.368	42-0-6	.071	-3	107	-14		-1.5
1955	Cin N	0	0	—	1	0	0	0	1	2	2	2	0	0-0	0	18.00	24	.400	.400	0	—	0		-1		-0.1
Total	3	17	10	.630	63	40	14-2	1	279.1	306	149	38	3	111-0	104	4.45	96	.282	.349	89-1-10	.135	-3	102	-2		-0.4

BADER, LORE Lore Verne "King" B4.27.1888 Bader IL D6.2.1973 LeRoy KS BL/TR/6-0/175 d9.30 C1

YEAR	TM LG	W	L	PCT	G	GS	CG-SHO	SV-BS	IP	H	R	HR	HB	BB-IB	SO	ERA	AERA	OAV	OOB	AB-HR-SH	AVG	PB	SUP	APR	DL	PW
1912	NY N	2	0	1.000	2	1	1	0	10	9	2	0	1	6	0.90	376	.250	.372		.000	-0	87	3		0.5
1917	Bos A	2	0	1.000	15	1	0	1	38.1	48	15	1	1	18	14	2.35	110	.306	.381	10-0-1	.300	1	84	0		0.1
1918	Bos A	1	3	.250	5	4	2-1	0	27	26	13	1	3	12	10	3.33	81	.271	.369	9	.111	-1	42	-2		-0.4
Total	3	5	3	.625	22	6	3-1	1	75.1	83	30	2	5	36	27	2.51	109	.287	.376	22-0-1	.182	-0	58	1		0.1

BAECHT, ED Edward Joseph B5.15.1907 Paden OK D8.15.1957 Grafton IL BR/TR/6-3/195 d4.24

YEAR	TM LG	W	L	PCT	G	GS	CG-SHO	SV-BS	IP	H	R	HR	HB	BB-IB	SO	ERA	AERA	OAV	OOB	AB-HR-SH	AVG	PB	SUP	APR	DL	PW
1926	Phi N	2	0	1.000	28	1	1	0	56	73	43	4	1	26	14	6.11	68	.324	.402	14	.143	-1	101	-10		-0.5
1927	Phi N	0	1	.000	1	1	0	1	6	12	8	0	0	2	0	12.00	34	.429	.467	2	.000	-0	185	-5		-0.5
1928	Phi N	1	1	.500	9	1	0	0	24	37	16	1	0	9	10	6.00	71	.385	.438	7	.143	-0	59	-3		-0.3
1931	Chi N	2	4	.333	22	6	2	0	67	64	34	1	8	32	34	3.76	103	.250	.351	18-0-3	.278	1	119	0		0.1
1932	Chi N	0	0	—	1	0	0	0	1	1	0	0	1	1	0.00	—	.333	.500	1	.000	0	0	0		0.0
1937	StL A	0	0	—	3	0	0	0	6.1	13	15	3	2	6	3	12.79	38	.419	.538	1	.000	-0		-7		-0.3
Total	6	5	6	.455	64	9	3	0	160.1	200	116	9	11	78	61	5.56	73	.313	.397	42-0-3	.190	-1	113	-25		-1.5

BAEK, CHA SEUNG Cha Seung B5.29.1980 Pusan, South Korea BR/TR/6-4/190 d8.8

YEAR	TM LG	W	L	PCT	G	GS	CG-SHO	SV-BS	IP	H	R	HR	HB	BB-IB	SO	ERA	AERA	OAV	OOB	AB-HR-SH	AVG	PB	SUP	APR	DL	PW
2004	Sea A	3	4	.333	7	5	0	0-0	31	35	23	5	3	11-1	20	5.52	81	.278	.345	0	—	0	104	-5		-0.8

BAEZ, BENITO Benito (Ceri) B5.6.1977 Bonao, D.R. BL/TL/6-0/160 d8.25 [DL 2002 Fla N 111]

YEAR	TM LG	W	L	PCT	G	GS	CG-SHO	SV-BS	IP	H	R	HR	HB	BB-IB	SO	ERA	AERA	OAV	OOB	AB-HR-SH	AVG	PB	SUP	APR	DL	PW
2001	Fla N	0	0	—	8	0	0	0-0	9.1	22	14	3	0	6-0	14	13.50	31	.449	.509	1	.000	-0		-10		-0.5

BAEZ, DANYS Danys B9.10.1977 Pinar Del Rio, Cuba BR/TR/6-3/225* d5.13

YEAR	TM LG	W	L	PCT	G	GS	CG-SHO	SV-BS	IP	H	R	HR	HB	BB-IB	SO	ERA	AERA	OAV	OOB	AB-HR-SH	AVG	PB	SUP	APR	DL	PW
2001	†Cle A	5	3	.625	43	0	0	0-1	50.1	34	22	5	3	20-4	52	2.50	183	.191	.282	0	—	0		8		1.1
2002	Cle A	10	11	.476	39	26	0	6-2	165.1	160	84	14	9	82-5	130	4.41	101	.256	.347	2	.000	-0	89	2		0.2
2003	Cle A	2	9	.182	73	0	0	25-10	75.2	65	36	9	4	23-0	66	3.81	116	.229	.295	1	.000	-0		6		1.0
2004	TB A	4	4	.500	62	0	0	30-3	68	60	31	6	7	29-4	52	3.57	131	.237	.331	0	—	0		8		1.4
2005	TB A☆	5	4	.556	67	0	0	41-8	72.1	66	27	7	2	30-0	51	2.86	153	.244	.322	0	—	0		11		2.3
Total	5	26	31	.456	284	26	0	102-24	431.2	385	200	41	25	184-13	351	3.69	121	.239	.324	3	.000	-0	89	35		6.0

BAGBY, JIM James Charles Jacob Jr. B9.8.1916 Cleveland OH D9.2.1988 Marietta GA BR/TR/6-2/170 d4.18 Def 1944 f-Jim

YEAR	TM LG	W	L	PCT	G	GS	CG-SHO	SV-BS	IP	H	R	HR	HB	BB-IB	SO	ERA	AERA	OAV	OOB	AB-HR-SH	AVG	PB	SUP	APR	DL	PW
1938	Bos A	15	11	.577	43	25	10-1	2	198.2	218	110	9	3	90	73	4.21	117	.283	.360	68-0-8	.191	-1*	119	14		1.6
1939	Bos A	5	5	.500	21	11	3	0	80	119	66	7	2	36	35	7.09	67	.347	.412	34-1-2	.294	3	117	-17		-1.5
1940	Cle A	10	16	.385	36	21	6-1	2	182.2	217	104	15	1	83	57	4.73	95	.296	.368	74-0-6	.203	-0*	93	-4		-0.5
1941	Cle A	9	15	.375	33	27	12	2	200.2	214	104	10	6	76	53	4.04	98	.273	.341	74-0-4	.243	2*	90	-4		-0.1
1942	Cle A☆	17	9	.654	38	35	16-4	1	270.2	267	105	9	1	64	54	2.96	117	.258	.302	95-1-7	.189	1*	109	15		1.5
1943	Cle A☆	17	14	.548	36	33	16-3	1	273	248	112	15	3	80	70	3.10	100	.240	.296	112-0-1	.268	4*	102	-1		0.6
1944	Cle A	4	5	.444	13	10	2	0	79	101	48	2	4	34	12	4.33	76	.312	.384	31-1-0	.226	1*	104	-11		-1.0
1945	Cle A	8	11	.421	25	19	11-3	1	159.1	171	70	3	2	59	38	3.73	87	.279	.344	58-0-1	.293	3	101	-6		-0.2
1946	†Bos A	7	6	.538	21	11	6-1	0	106.2	117	55	4	1	49	16	3.71	99	.279	.356	42	.119	-2	87	-3		-0.5
1947	Pit N	5	4	.556	37	6	2	0	115.2	143	75	14	5	37	23	4.67	90	.304	.361	32-0-3	.219	1	106	-8		-0.5
Total	10	97	96	.503	303	198	84-13	9	1666.1	1815	849	98	28	608	431	3.96	97	.278	.342	620-3-32	.226	12	104	-25		-0.5

BAGBY, JIM James Charles Jacob Sr. "Sarge" B10.5.1889 Barnett GA D7.28.1954 Marietta GA BB/TR/6-0/170 d4.22 s-Jim

YEAR	TM LG	W	L	PCT	G	GS	CG-SHO	SV-BS	IP	H	R	HR	HB	BB-IB	SO	ERA	AERA	OAV	OOB	AB-HR-SH	AVG	PB	SUP	APR	DL	PW
1912	Cin N	2	1	.667	5	1	0	0	17.1	17	6	2	0	9	10	3.12	108	.270	.361	5	.000	-1	87	1		0.1
1916	Cle A	16	17	.485	48	27	14-3	5	272.2	253	109	2	8	67	88	2.61	115	.251	.303	90-0-9	.167	-1*	116	10		1.0
1917	Cle A	23	13	.639	49	37	26-8	7	320.2	277	91	6	6	73	83	1.99	142	.235	.283	108-0-3	.231	2	102	30		3.9
1918	Cle A	17	16	.515	45	31	23-2	6	271.1	274	107	0	2	78	57	2.69	112	.276	.330	99-0-3	.212	-0*	92	8		1.0
1919	Cle A	17	11	.607	35	32	21	3	241.1	258	96	3	4	44	60	2.80	120	.275	.310	89-1-4	.258	5*	121	15		2.2
1920	†Cle A	31	12	.721	48	38	30-3	0	339.2	338	122	9	5	79	73	2.89	132	.266	.311	131-1-7	.252	6*	133	39		4.7
1921	Cle A	14	12	.538	40	26	13	1	191.2	238	112	14	4	44	37	4.70	91	.308	.348	76-0-2	.197	-1*	108	-6		-0.9
1922	Cle A	4	5	.444	25	10	4	1	98.1	134	77	7	3	39	25	6.32	63	.340	.404	42	.262	3	136	-24		-1.6
1923	Pit N	3	2	.600	21	6	2	3	62	95	49	6	1	25	16	5.24	78	.336	.392	20-0-2	.050	-2	126	-10		-0.9
Total	9	127	89	.588	316	208	133-16	29	1821.2	1884	769	47	33	458	450	3.11	110	.273	.321	660-2-30	.218	11	114	63		9.5

BAHNSEN, STAN Stanley Raymond B12.15.1944 Council Bluffs IA BR/TR/6-2/198(185-203) [NYA65 4/68] d9.9 Col Nebraska

YEAR	TM LG	W	L	PCT	G	GS	CG-SHO	SV-BS	IP	H	R	HR	HB	BB-IB	SO	ERA	AERA	OAV	OOB	AB-HR-SH	AVG	PB	SUP	APR	DL	PW
1966	NY A	1	1	.500	4	3	1	1	23	16	9	3	0	7-0	16	3.52	94	.181	.244	7	.143	-0	141	0		0.0
1968	NY A	17	12	.586	37	34	10-1	3	267.1	216	72	14	2	68-6	162	2.05	142	.221	.271	81-0-10	.049	-4	97	26		2.4
1969	NY A	9	16	.360	40	33	5-2	1-0	220.2	222	102	28	0	90-9	130	3.83	92	.260	.330	60-0-9	.083	-0	87	-6		-0.9
1970	NY A	14	11	.560	36	35	6-2	0-0	232.2	227	100	23	2	75-4	116	3.33	107	.256	.312	74-0-8	.149	-1	102	6		0.6
1971	NY A	14	12	.538	36	34	14-3	0-0	242	221	99	20	6	72-8	110	3.35	98	.248	.304	79-0-8	.152	0	121	0		0.2
1972	Chi A	21	16	.568	43	41	5-1	0-0	252.1	263	107	22	4	73-1	157	3.60	87	.268	.321	92-0-3	.152	-1*	103	-10		-1.5
1973	Chi A	18	21	.462	42	42	14-4	0-0	282.1	290	128	20	5	117-2	120	3.57	111	.269	.341	0	—	0	93	11		1.5
1974	Chi A	12	15	.444	38	35	10-1	0-0	216.1	230	128	17	4	110-6	102	4.70	80	.277	.362	0	—	0	96	-22		-2.5
1975	Chi A	4	6	.400	12	12	2	0-0	67.1	78	49	9	3	40-0	31	6.01	65	.291	.389	0	—	0	106	-15		-1.9
	Oak A	6	7	.462	21	16	2	0-1	100	88	42	2	3	37-1	49	3.24	113	.238	.350	1	.000	-0	101	4		0.5
	Year	10	13	.435	33	28	4	0-1	167.1	166	91	11	6	77-1	80	4.36	86	.261	.344	1	.000	-0	103	-11		-1.4
1976	Oak A	8	7	.533	35	14	1-1	0-2	143	124	55	13	2	43-3	82	3.34	101	.232	.290	0	—	0	110	3		0.3
1977	Oak A	1	2	.333	11	2	0	1-1	22	24	16	5	1	13-5	21	6.14	66	.286	.380	0	—	0	89	-5		-0.5
	Mon N	8	9	.471	23	22	3-1	0	127.1	142	76	14	0	38-2	59	4.81	80	.283	.332	42-0-4	.119	-1	103	-14		-1.7
1978	Mon N	1	5	.167	44	1	0	7-2	75	74	35	9	3	31-2	44	3.84	93	.261	.333	11-0-1	.091	-1	151	-2		-0.3
1979	Mon N	3	1	.750	55	0	0	5-2	94.1	80	34	10	0	42-4	71	3.15	118	.236	.319	14-1-0	.071	-0		-2	22	0.1
1980	Mon N	7	6	.538	57	0	0	4-3	91.1	80	40	7	0	33-4	48	3.05	119	.235	.300	9	.111	1		3		0.4
1981	†Mon N	2	1	.667	25	3	0	1-1	49	45	27	7	1	24-0	28	4.96	72	.247	.338	9	.111	1		3		0.6
1982	Cal A	0	1	.000	7	0	0	0-0	9.2	13	6	0	0	8-1	5	4.66	88	.310	.420	0	—	0		-1		-0.5
	Phi N	0	0	—	3	0	0	3-1	13.1	9	2	0	0	3-1	9	1.35	274	.182	.229	0	—	0		3		0.2
Total	16	146	149	.495	574	327	73-16	20-12	2529	2440	1127	223	34	924-59	1359	3.60	97	.255	.321	479-1-43	.117	-9	100	-17	22	-3.3

YEAR	TM	LG	W	L	PCT	G	GS	CG-SHO	SV-BS	IP	H	R	HR	HB	BB-IB	SO	ERA	AERA	OAV	OOB	AB-HR-SH	AVG	PB	SUP	APR	DL	P

BAHR, ED Edson Garfield B10.16.1919 Rouleau SK, Can. BR/TR/6-1.5/172 d5.1

1946	Pit	N	8	6	.571	27	14	7	0	136.2	128	57	8	5	52	44	2.63	134	.254	.330	45-0-1	.178	-1*	116	9		0
1947	Pit	N	3	5	.375	19	11	1	0	82.1	82	45	5	3	43	25	4.59	92	.263	.358	23-0-3	.087	-2*	74	-2		-0
Total	2		11	11	.500	46	25	8	0	219	210	102	13	8	95	69	3.37	112	.257	.341	68-0-4	.147	-3	97	7		0

BAICHLEY, GROVER Grover Cleveland B12.10.1889 Toledo IL D6.28.1956 San Jose CA BR/TR/5-8/165 d8.24 Col Valparaiso

| 1914 | StL | A | 0 | 0 | — | 4 | 0 | 0 | 0 | 7 | 9 | 5 | 0 | 0 | 3 | 3 | 5.14 | 53 | .346 | .414 | 1 | | .000 | -0 | | -2 | -0 |

BAILES, SCOTT Scott Alan B12.18.1961 Chillicothe OH BL/TL/6-2/184(171-184) [PitN82 S4/71] d4.9 Col Missouri St.

1986	Cle	A	10	10	.500	62	10	0	7-6	112.2	123	70	12	1	43-5	60	4.95	85	.276	.339	0	—	0	115	-10		-1
1987	Cle	A	7	8	.467	39	17	0	6-2	120.1	145	75	21	4	47-1	65	4.64	98	.296	.358	0	—	0	100	-3		-0
1988	Cle	A	9	14	.391	37	21	5-2	0-2	145	149	89	22	2	46-0	53	4.90	84	.266	.322	0	—	0	90	-13		-1
1989	Cle	A	5	9	.357	34	11	0	0-1	113.2	116	57	7	3	29-4	47	4.28	93	.269	.316	0	—	0	66	-2	24	-0
1990	Cal	A	2	0	1.000	27	0	0	0-0	35.1	46	30	8	1	20-0	16	6.37	60	.315	.390	0	—	0		-11		-0
1991	Cal	A	1	2	.333	42	0	0	0-1	51.2	41	26	5	4	22-5	25	4.18	99	.218	.310	0	—	0	0	-14	15	0
1992	Cal	A	3	1	.750	32	0	0	0-0	38.2	59	34	7	1	28-4	25	7.45	54	.351	.442	0	—	0	4		15	0
1997	Tex	A	1	0	1.000	24	0	0	0-0	22	19	8	2	0	10-2	14	2.86	170	.231	.315	0	—	0	-7		31	0
1998	Tex	A	1	0	1.000	46	0	0	0-0	40.1	61	33	5	0	11-0	30	6.47	76	.351	.385	0	—	0	93	-56	85	-6
Total	9		39	44	.470	343	59	5-2	13-12	679.2	758	423	89	16	256-21	351	4.95	86	.283	.345	0	—	0	93	-56	85	-6

BAILEY, SWEETBREADS Abraham Lincoln B2.12.1895 Joliet IL D9.27.1939 Joliet IL BR/TR/6-0/184 d5.23

1919	Chi	N	3	5	.375	21	5	0	0	71.1	75	30	2	3	20	19	3.15	91	.288	.346	18	.389	3	77	-1		0
1920	Chi	N	1	2	.333	21	1	0	0	36.2	55	38	1	2	11	8	7.12	45	.359	.410	7-0-1	.143	-0	25	-16		0
1921	Chi	N	0	0	—	3	0	0	0	5	6	2	0	1	2	2	3.60	106	.300	.391	0		-0	0			0
	Bro	N	0	0	—	7	0	0	0	24.1	35	15	1	1	7	6	5.18	75	.368	.417	5	.000	-0	-3			-0
	Year		0	0	—	10	0	0	0	29.1	41	17	1	2	9	8	4.91	79	.357	.413	5	.000	-0	-2			-1
Total	3		4	7	.364	52	6	0	0	137.1	171	85	4	7	40	35	4.59	69	.324	.379	30-0-1	.267	2	63	-20		-1

BAILEY, ROGER Charles Roger B10.3.1970 Chattahoochee FL BR/TR/6-1/180* [ColN92 3/95] d4.27 Col Florida St. [DL 1998 Col N 181]

1995	Col	N	7	6	.538	39	6	0	0-0	81.1	88	49	9	1	39-3	33	4.98	108	.283	.363	16-0-3	.125	-1	140	3		0
1996	Col	N	2	3	.400	24	11	0	1-0	83.2	94	64	7	1	52-0	45	6.24	84	.288	.384	19-1-3	.263	2	91	-8	23	0
1997	Col	N	9	10	.474	29	29	5-2	0-0	191	210	103	27	13	70-2	84	4.29	120	.283	.354	62-0-5	.210	-0*	111	14	15	0
Total	3		18	19	.486	92	46	5-2	1-0	356	392	216	43	15	161-5	162	4.90	107	.284	.363	97-1-11	.206	1	110	9	219	0

BAILEY, HARVEY Harvey Francis B11.24.1876 Adrian MI D7.10.1922 Toledo OH TL/6-0/160 d6.30

1899	Bos	N	6	4	.600	12	11	8	0	86.2	83	42	7	6	35	26	3.95	105	.252	.334	34	.235	0	85	5		0
1900	Bos	N	0	0	—	4	1	0	0	20	24	16	0	2	11	9	4.95	83	.296	.394	9	.222	0	167	-2		0
Total	2		6	4	.600	16	12	8	0	106.2	107	58	7	8	46	35	4.13	100	.260	.346	43	.233	0	92	3		0

BAILEY, HOWARD Howard L B7.31.1957 Grand Haven MI BR/TL/6-0/195* d4.12 Col Grand Valley St.

1981	Det	A	1	4	.200	9	5	0	0-0	36.2	45	31	4	3	13-2	17	7.36	51	.308	.372	0	—	0	66	-14		-1
1982	Det	A	0	0	—	8	0	0	1-0	10	6	0	0	2	2-1	3	0.00	—	.182	.222	0	—	0	5			-0
1983	Det	A	5	5	.500	33	3	0	0-1	72	69	45	11	5	25-3	21	4.88	81	.255	.321	0	—	0	100	-9		-1
Total	3		6	9	.400	50	8	0	1-1	118.2	120	76	15	5	40-6	41	5.23	75	.267	.331	0	—	0	78	-18		-2

BAILEY, JIM James Hopkins B12.16.1934 Strawberry Plains TN BB/TL/6-2.5/210 d9.10 b-Ed Col Lincoln Memorial

| 1959 | Cin | N | 0 | 1 | .000 | 3 | 1 | 0 | 0 | 11.2 | 17 | 8 | 1 | 1 | 6-1 | 7 | 6.17 | 66 | .333 | .414 | 3 | .000 | -0 | 66 | -2 | | -0 |

BAILEY, KING Linwood C. B11.1870 VA D11.19.1917 Macon GA BL/TL/6-0/185 d9.21

| 1895 | Cin | N | 1 | 0 | 1.000 | 1 | 1 | 1 | 0 | 8 | 13 | 8 | 1 | 0 | 0 | 0 | 5.63 | 88 | .361 | .378 | 4 | .500 | 1 | 273 | -1 | | 0 |

BAILEY, CORY Phillip Cory B1.24.1971 Marion IL BR/TR/6-1/202(195-210) [BosA91 15/408] d9.1 Col Southeastern Illinois JC

1993	Bos	A	0	1	.000	11	0	0	0-0	15.2	12	7	0	0	12-3	11	3.45	134	.231	.369	0	—	0	2			0
1994	Bos	A	0	1	.000	5	0	0	0-1	4.1	10	6	2	0	3-1	4	12.46	40	.476	.542	0	—	0	-3			-1
1995	StL	N	0	0	—	3	0	0	0-0	3.2	2	3	0	0	2-1	5	7.36	58	.154	.267	0	—	0	-1			0
1996	StL	N	5	2	.714	51	0	0	0-1	57	57	21	1	9	30-3	38	3.00	141	.263	.353	1-0-1	.000	1	8			-1
1997	SF	N	0	1	.000	7	0	0	0-0	9.2	15	9	1	0	4-0	5	8.38	49	.375	.422	1	1.000	0	-4			0
1998	SF	N	0	0	—	5	0	0	0-0	3.1	2	1	1	0	1-0	2	2.70	149	.167	.231	0	—	0	1			0
2001	KC	A	1	1	.500	53	0	0	0-1	67.1	57	28	3	0	33-2	61	3.48	143	.234	.321	0	—	0	10			0
2002	KC	A	3	4	.429	37	0	0	1-6	46	53	24	5	2	31-7	24	4.11	121	.306	.413	0	—	0	3			0
Total	8		9	10	.474	172	0	0	1-9	207	208	99	13	3	116-17	150	3.96	118	.269	.364	2-0-1	.500	1	16			0

BAILEY, STEVE Steven John B2.12.1942 Bronx NY BR/TR/6-1/194* d4.14

1967	Cle	A	2	5	.286	32	1	0	2	64.2	62	31	5	3	42-4	46	3.90	84	.259	.372	10	.000	-1	53	-4		0
1968	Cle	A	0	1	.000	2	1	0	0	5	4	3	1	0	2-0	1	3.60	83	.235	.300	0	—	0	88	-1		0
Total	2		2	6	.250	34	2	0	2	69.2	66	34	6	3	44-4	47	3.88	84	.258	.367	10	.000	-1	67	-5		0

BAILEY, BILL William F. B4.12.1889 Ft.Smith AR D11.2.1926 Houston TX BL/TL/5-11/165 d9.17

1907	StL	A	4	1	.800	6	5	3	0	48.1	39	16	0	4	15	17	2.42	104	.223	.299	20-0-1	.150	-1	102	1		0
1908	StL	A	3	5	.375	22	12	7	0	106.2	85	53	2	3	50	42	3.04	79	.220	.314	34-0-2	.088	-2*	109	-8		0
1909	StL	A	9	10	.474	32	20	17-1	0	199	174	71	2	6	75	114	2.44	99	.248	.325	77-0-2	.286	5*	79	0		0
1910	StL	A	3	18	.143	34	20	13	0	192.1	186	133	2	10	97	90	3.32	74	.262	.359	63-0-1	.206	-0	64	-26		0
1911	StL	A	0	3	.000	7	2	2	0	31.2	42	26	1	2	16	8	4.55	74	.339	.423	11	.000	-2	43	-5		0
1912	StL	A	0	1	.000	3	2	0	0	10.2	15	12	0	0	10	2	9.28	36	.341	.463	2	.500	1	78	-6		0
1914	Bal	F	7	9	.438	19	18	10-1	0	128.2	106	58	2	7	68	131	3.08	99	.230	.338	43-0-1	.163	-1	78	-1		0
1915	Bal	F	6	19	.240	36	23	11-2	0	190.1	179	118	8	9	115	98	4.63	62	.255	.366	65-0-7	.231	-0	103	-33		0
	Chi	F	3	1	.750	5	5	3-3	0	33.1	23	9	1	0	10	24	2.16	116	.202	.266	9	.222	0	117	2		0
	Year		9	20	.310	41	28	14-5	0	223.2	202	127	9	9	125	122	4.27	66	.247	.353	74-0-7	.230	-0	105	-30		0
1918	Det	A	1	2	.333	8	4	1	0	37.2	53	34	0	1	26	13	5.97	45	.368	.468	13	.077	-1	85	-15		0
1921	StL	N	2	5	.286	19	6	3-1	0	74	95	41	1	2	22	20	4.26	86	.330	.381	22	.091	-2	60	-4		0
1922	StL	N	0	2	.000	12	0	0	0	31.2	38	22	1	0	23	11	5.40	72	.325	.436	7	.286	0	-5			0
Total	11		38	76	.333	203	117	70-8	0	1084.1	1035	593	20	44	527	570	3.57	77	.261	.354	366-0-14	.194	-8	84	-100		0

BAIN, LOREN Herbert Loren B7.4.1922 Staples MN D11.24.1996 Chetek WI BR/TR/6-0/190 d6.23

| 1945 | NY | N | 0 | 0 | — | 8 | 0 | 0 | 0 | 10 | 7 | 1 | 1 | 4 | 7 | 1 | 7.88 | 50 | .323 | .417 | 3 | .333 | 0 | -3 | | | 0 |

BAIR, DOUG Charles Douglas B8.22.1949 Defiance OH BR/TR/6-0/180(165-185) [PitN71 2/46] d9.13 Col Bowling Green

1976	Pit	N	0	0	—	4	0	0	0-0	6.1	4	4	0	0	5-1	4	5.68	62	.174	.321	0	—	0	-1			0
1977	Oak	A	4	6	.400	45	0	0	8-6	83.1	78	39	11	0	57-9	68	3.46	117	.253	.364	0	—	0	5			0
1978	Cin	N	7	6	.538	70	0	0	28-5	100.1	87	23	6	0	38-3	91	1.97	180	.236	.305	14-0-1	.143	-0	18			0
1979	†Cin	N	11	7	.611	65	0	0	16-7	94.1	93	47	7	3	51-12	86	4.29	86	.256	.350	0	.000	-1	-5			0
1980	Cin	N	3	6	.333	61	0	0	6-0	85	91	42	7	1	39-10	62	4.24	83	.277	.351	2	.000	-0	-6			0
1981	Cin	N	2	2	.500	24	0	0	0-2	39	42	28	5	0	17-4	16	5.77	61	.271	.343	3-1-0	.333	1	-10			0
	StL	N	2	0	1.000	11	0	0	1-0	15.2	13	6	0	0	2-0	14	3.45	105	.224	.250	3	.000	-0	1			0
	Year		4	2	.667	35	0	0	1-2	54.2	55	34	5	0	19-4	30	5.10	69	.258	.319	6-1-0	.167	1	-8			0
1982	†StL	N	5	3	.625	63	0	0	8-1	91.2	69	27	7	1	36-13	68	2.55	144	.211	.288	13-0-2	.077	-1	12			0
1983	StL	N	1	1	.500	26	0	0	1-2	29.2	24	11	4	0	13-3	21	3.03	121	.224	.306	2	.000	-0	2			0
	Det	A	7	3	.700	27	1	0	4-4	55.2	51	27	8	1	19-4	39	3.88	102	.242	.307	0	—	0	46	0		0
1984	†Det	A	5	3	.625	47	1	0	4-3	93.2	82	42	10	0	36-2	57	3.75	106	.238	.306	0	—	0	170	-12		0
1985	Det	A	2	0	1.000	21	3	0	0-0	49	54	38	3	1	25-5	30	6.24	66	.281	.360	0	—	0	1			0
	StL	N	0	0	—	2	0	0	0-0	2	1	0	0	0	2-0	0	0.00	—	.167	.375	0	—	0	6			0
1986	Oak	A	2	3	.400	31	0	0	4-4	45	37	15	5	0	18-0	40	3.00	130	.224	.296	1-0-1	.000	0	-2			0
1987	Phi	N	0	1	.000	11	0	0	0-1	13.1	17	9	4	0	5-0	10	5.93	72	.309	.361	0	—	0	9			0
1988	Tor	A	0	0	—	10	0	0	0-0	13.1	14	6	1	0	3-0	8	4.05	98	.280	.321	0	—	0	9			0
1989	Pit	N	2	3	.400	44	0	0	1-1	67.1	52	19	4	0	28-10	56	2.27	149	.211	.291	5	.200	-0	-3			0
1990	Pit	N	0	0	—	22	0	0	0-0	24.1	30	15	0	2	11-1	19	4.81	76	.306	.376	1	.000	-0	9			0
Total	15		55	43	.561	584	5	0	81-36	909.1	839	398	86	7	405-77	689	3.63	103	.246	.325	52-1-4	.096	-2	153	18		0

YEAR	TM LG	W	L	PCT	G	GS	CG-SHO	SV-BS	IP	H	R	HR	HB	BB-IB	SO	ERA	AERA	OAV	OOB	AB-HR-SH	AVG	PB	SUP	APR	DL	PW

BAIRD, BOB   Robert Allen   B1.16.1940 Knoxville TN   D4.11.1974 Chattanooga TN   BL/TL/6-4/195*   d9.3   Col Carson-Newman

1962	Was A	0	1	.000	3	3	0	0	10.2	13	8	0	0	8-0	3	6.75	60	.310	.412	3	.000	-0	66	-3		-0.3
1963	Was A	0	3	.000	5	3	0	0	11.2	12	15	1	1	7-0	7	7.71	48	.261	.364	3	.333	0	112	-7		-1.2
total	2	0	4	.000	8	6	0	0	22.1	25	23	1	1	15-0	10	7.25	53	.284	.387	6	.167	-0	88	-10		-1.5

BAJENARU, JEFF   Jeffrey Michael   B3.21.1978 Pomona CA   BR/TR/6-1/190*   [ChiA99 36/1089]   d9.4   Col Oklahoma

2004	Chi A	0	1	.000	9	0	0	0-0	8.1	15	10	0	0	6-1	8	10.80	44	.405	.488	0	—	0		-5		-0.5
2005	Chi A	0	—		4	0	0	0-0	4.1	4	3	2	0	6-0	3	6.23	73	.222	.222	0	—	0		-1		0.0
total	2	0	1	.000	13	0	0	0-0	12.2	19	13	2	0	6-1	11	9.24	50	.345	.410	0	—	0		-6		-0.5

BAKELY, JERSEY   Edward Enoch (b Edward Enoch Bakley)   B4.17.1864 Blackwood NJ   D2.17.1915 Philadelphia PA   BR/TR/5-8/170   d5.11

1883	Phi AA	5	3	.625	8	8	7	0	61.1	65	47	0		12	14	3.23	110	.255	.288	26	.192	1	112	1		0.2
1884	Phi U	14	25	.359	39	38	38-1	0	344.2	390	305	0		76	204	4.47	52	.267	.303	167	.132	-16*	99	-87		-8.4
	Wil U	0	2	.000	2	2	2	0	17	24	17	0		1	9	4.24	63	.312	.321	5	.000	-1	32	-2		-0.3
	KC U	2	3	.400	5	5	3	0	33	29	16	0		4	13	2.45	91	.220	.243	20	.150	-2*	76	0		-0.2
	Year	16	30	.348	46	45	43-1	0	394.2	443	338	0		81	226	4.29	54	.265	.299	192	.130	-18	93	-87		-8.9
1888	Cle AA	25	33	.431	61	61	60-4	0	532.2	518	321	14	15	128	212	2.97	104	.246	.294	194-1	.134	-6	86	2		-0.3
1889	Cle N	12	22	.353	36	34	33-2	0	304.1	296	169	9	8	106	105	2.96	136	.247	.313	111-1	.135	-1	65	29		2.6
1890	Cle P	12	25	.324	43	38	32	0	326.1	412	307	13	7	147	67	4.47	89	.295	.365	138	.203	-2	95	-18		-1.7
1891	Was AA	2	10	.167	13	12	11	0	104.1	127	107	6	6	60	32	5.35	70	.291	.384	45	.222	-0	76	-19		-1.7
	Bal AA	4	2	.667	8	6	5	0	59	48	32	1	1	30	13	2.29	163	.214	.310	21	.095	0	103	8		0.6
	Year	6	12	.333	21	18	16	0	163.1	175	139	7	7	90	45	4.24	88	.265	.359	66	.182	-0	85	-12		-1.1
total	6	76	125	.378	215	204	191-7	0	1782.2	1909	1321	43	37	564	669	3.66	91	.262	.318	727-2	.153	-26	87	-86		-9.2

BAKENHASTER, DAVE   David Lee   B3.5.1945 Columbus OH   BR/TR/5-10/168   d6.20

| 1964 | StL N | 0 | 0 | — | 2 | 0 | 0 | 0 | 3 | 9 | 6 | 1 | 0 | 1-0 | 0 | 6.00 | 63 | .474 | .500 | 0 | — | 0 | | -2 | | -0.1 |

BAKER, AL   Albert Jones   B2.28.1906 Batesville MS   D11.6.1982 Kenedy TX   BR/TR/5-11/170   d8.20

| 1938 | Bos N | 0 | 0 | — | 3 | 0 | 0 | 0 | 7.2 | 14 | 8 | 2 | 1 | 2 | 2 | 9.39 | 53 | .371 | .421 | 4 | .000 | -1 | | -3 | | -0.2 |

BAKER, BOCK   Charles "Smiling Bock"   B7.17.1878 Troy NY   D8.17.1940 New York NY   TL/5-9/181   d4.28

1901	Cle A	0	1	.000	1	1	1	0	8	23	13	0	1	6	0	5.63	63	.500	.566	4	.000	-1	19	-4		-0.4
	Phi A	0	1	.000	1	1	0	0	6	6	11	0	0	6	1	10.50	36	.261	.414	3	.333	0	90	-5		-0.5
	Year	0	2	.000	2	2	1	0	14	29	24	0	1	12	1	7.71	47	.420	.512	7	.143	-1	56	-8		-0.9

BAKER, ERNIE   Earnest Gould   B8.8.1875 Concord MI   D10.25.1945 Homer MI   BR/TR/5-10/160   d8.18

| 1905 | Cin N | 0 | 0 | — | 1 | 0 | 0 | 0 | 4 | 7 | 4 | 1 | 0 | 1 | 0 | 4.50 | 73 | .412 | .444 | 2 | .000 | -0 | | -1 | | -0.1 |

BAKER, JESSE   Jesse Ormond   B6.3.1888 Anderson Island WA   D9.26.1972 Tacoma WA   BL/TL/5-11/188   d4.23

| 1911 | Chi A | 2 | 7 | .222 | 22 | 8 | 3 | 1 | 94 | 101 | 52 | 3 | 4 | 30 | 51 | 3.93 | 82 | .288 | .351 | 29 | .103 | -2 | 70 | -6 | | -0.6 |

BAKER, KIRTLEY   Kirtley "Whitey"   B6.24.1869 Aurora IN   D4.15.1927 Covington KY   BR/TR/5-9/160   d5.7

1890	Pit N	3	19	.136	25	21	19-2	0	178.1	209	176	11	20	86	76	5.60	59	.283	.373	68	.147	-1*	63	-50		-4.6
1893	Bal N	3	8	.273	15	12	8	0	91.2	138	111	5	5	58	26	8.44	56	.337	.426	57	.298	2*	114	-33		-2.4
1894	Bal N	0	1	.000	1	0	0	0	0	1	5	0	0	2	0	∞	—	1.000	1.000	4	.000	-0*		-4		-0.3
1898	Was N	2	3	.400	6	5	4	0	47	56	31	1	0	18	7	3.06	120	.293	.354	18	.278	2	101	0		0.1
1899	Was N	1	7	.125	11	6	3	0	54	79	65	3	6	22	6	6.83	57	.339	.410	19	.158	-1*	89	-20		-2.2
total	5	9	38	.191	58	44	34-2	0	371	483	388	20	31	186	115	6.28	60	.307	.391	166	.211	1	88	-107		-9.4

BAKER, NEAL   Neal Vernon   B4.30.1904 Harlingen TX   D1.5.1982 Houston TX   BR/TR/6-1/175   d6.26   Col Texas

| 1927 | Phi A | 0 | 0 | — | 5 | 2 | 0 | 0 | 17.1 | 27 | 17 | 2 | 0 | 7 | 3 | 5.71 | 75 | .365 | .420 | 6 | .167 | 0 | 98 | -4 | | -0.2 |

BAKER, NORM   Norman Leslie   B10.14.1863 Philadelphia PA   D2.20.1949 Hurffville NJ   d5.21

1883	Pit AA	0	2	.000	3	3	2	0	19	24	16	0		11	5	3.32	98	.289	.372	12	.000	-2*	106	-2		-0.3
1885	Lou AA	13	12	.520	25	24	24-1	0	217	210	142	3	10	69	79	3.40	95	.241	.304	87	.207	-1	88	1		0.0
1890	Bal AA	1	1	.500	2	2	2	0	17	16	9	0	0	6	10	3.71	109	.242	.306	7	.000	-1	83	1		0.0
total	3	14	15	.483	30	29	28-1	0	253	250	167	3	10	86	94	3.42	96	.245	.309	106	.170	-3	90	0		-0.3

BAKER, SCOTT   Scott   B5.18.1970 San Jose CA   BL/TL/6-2/175   [StLN90 7/195]   d7.17   Col Taft (CA) JC

| 1995 | Oak A | 0 | 0 | — | 1 | 0 | 0 | 5-0 | 3.2 | 5 | 4 | 0 | 0 | 3 | 3 | 9.82 | 46 | .333 | .500 | 0 | — | 0 | | -2 | | -0.1 |

BAKER, STEVE   Steven Byrne   B8.30.1956 Eugene OR   BR/TR/6-0/185(185-200)   d5.25   Col Oregon

1978	Det A	2	4	.333	15	10	0	0-1	63.1	66	37	6	0	42-0	39	4.55	86	.276	.379	0	—	0	76	-5		-0.5
1979	Det A	1	7	.125	21	12	0	1-1	84	97	63	13	6	51-2	54	6.64	66	.296	.396	0	—	0	106	-19		-1.6
1982	Oak A	1	1	.500	5	3	0	0	25.2	30	14	3	0	4-0	14	4.56	87	.288	.312	0	—	0	84	-2		-0.1
1983	Oak A	3	3	.500	35	1	0	5-6	54	59	32	4	2	26-4	23	4.33	90	.282	.363	0	—	0	140	4		-0.5
	StL N	1	1	.500	8	0	0	0	10	10	4	0	1	4-1	1	1.80	203	.286	.366	0	—	0		1		0.1
total	4	7	16	.304	84	26	0	6-8	237	262	150	26	9	127-7	131	5.13	79	.286	.374	0	—	0	95	-29		-2.6

BAKER, TOM   Thomas Calvin "Rattlesnake"   B6.11.1913 Nursery TX   D1.3.1991 Fort Worth TX   BR/TR/6-1.5/180   d8.15

1935	Bro N	1	0	1.000	11	1	0	0	42	48	25	2	0	20	10	4.29	93	.277	.352	19	.474	4	85	-2		0.2
1936	Bro N	1	8	.111	35	8	2	2	87.2	98	56	3	2	48	35	4.72	88	.288	.379	30	.233	1*	85	-6		-0.4
1937	Bro N	0	1	.000	7	0	0	0	8.1	14	10	1	1	5	2	8.64	47	.378	.465	0	—	0		-4		-0.4
	NY N	1	0	1.000	13	0	0	0	31	30	15	0	0	16	11	4.06	96	.268	.359	9	.222	0		0		0.0
	Year	1	1	.500	20	0	0	0	39.1	44	25	1	1	21	13	5.03	78	.295	.386	9	.222	-0		-4		-0.4
1938	NY N	0	0	—	2	0	0	0	4	5	3	0	0	3	0	6.75	56	.313	.421	0	—	0		-1		0.0
total	4	3	9	.250	68	9	2	2	173	195	109	6	3	92	58	4.73	85	.288	.375	58	.310	5	87	-13		-0.6

BAKER, TOM   Thomas Henry   B5.6.1934 Port Townsend WA   D3.9.1980 Port Townsend WA   BL/TL/6-0/195   d8.2

| 1963 | Chi N | 0 | 0 | — | 12 | 0 | 0 | 0 | 18 | 20 | 12 | 2 | 1 | 7-0 | 13 | 3.00 | 117 | .282 | .346 | 3 | .000 | -0 | 25 | -1 | | -0.1 |

BAKER, SCOTT   Timothy Scott   B9.19.1981 Shreveport LA   BR/TR/6-4/215   d5.7   Col Oklahoma St.

| 2005 | Min A | 3 | 3 | .500 | 10 | 9 | 0 | 0-0 | 53.2 | 48 | 21 | 5 | 0 | 14-0 | 32 | 3.35 | 131 | .241 | .288 | 0 | — | 0 | 83 | 7 | | 0.6 |

BALAS, MIKE   Mitchell Francis (b Mitchell Francis Balaski)   B5.9.1910 Lowell MA   D10.15.1996 Westford MA   BR/TR/6-0/195   d4.27

| 1938 | Bos N | 0 | 0 | — | 1 | 0 | 0 | 0 | 1.1 | 3 | 3 | 0 | 0 | 0 | 0 | 6.75 | 51 | .375 | .375 | 0 | — | 0 | | -1 | | -0.1 |

BALDSCHUN, JACK   Jack Edward   B10.16.1936 Greenville OH   BR/TR/6-0/190(175-195)   d4.28   Col Miami-Ohio

1961	Phi N	5	3	.625	65	0	0	3	99.2	90	53	7	5	49-11	85	3.88	105	.243	.337	11-1	.000	-1		0		-0.1
1962	Phi N	12	7	.632	67	0	0	13	112.2	95	41	6	2	58-9	95	2.96	131	.231	.326	16-0-2	.063	-1		12		2.1
1963	Phi N	11	7	.611	65	0	0	16	113.2	99	37	7	3	42-10	89	2.30	141	.232	.304	20-0-1	.000	-0		10		1.9
1964	Phi N	6	9	.400	71	0	0	21	118.1	111	50	8	3	40-7	96	3.12	111	.246	.310	16-0-2	.250	-2		10		0.8
1965	Phi N	5	8	.385	65	0	0	6	99	102	53	4	4	42-12	81	3.82	91	.273	.347	7-0-2	.250	-1		-6		-0.9
1966	Cin N	1	5	.167	42	0	0	0	57.1	71	35	4	4	25-8	44	5.49	71	.318	.395	3	.333	0		-8		-0.8
1967	Cin N	0	0	—	9	0	0	0	13	15	6	0	0	9-3	12	4.15	90	.283	.387	1	.000	-0		-8		0.0
1969	SD N	7	2	.778	61	0	0	0	77	80	45	7	4	29-6	67	4.79	75	.264	.331	4	.250	0		-10		-1.1
1970	SD N	1	0	1.000	12	0	0	0-1	13.1	24	15	2	4	9-3	14	12.03	40	.375	.406	0	—	0		-8		-0.6
total	9	48	41	.539	457	0	0	60-2	704	687	335	45	23	298-67	555	3.69	99	.257	.334	78-0-8	.090	-3		8		1.3

BALDWIN, LADY   Charles B.   B4.8.1859 Oramel NY   D3.7.1937 Hastings MI   BR/TL/5-11/160   d9.30

1884	Mil U	1	1	.500	2	2	2	0	17	7	5	0		1	21	2.65	50	.117	.131	27	.222	-0*	128	-3		-0.3
1885	Det N	11	9	.550	21	20	19-1	0	179.1	137	84	2		28	135	1.86	153	**.197**	**.228**	42	.242	3*	112	16		1.9
1886	Det N	**42**	13	.764	56	56	55-7	0	487	371	194	11		100	323	2.24	149	**.202**	**.243**	204	.201	3*	124	55		5.7
1887	†Det N	13	10	.565	24	24	24-1	0	211	225	136	8	5	61	60	3.84	106	.269	.323	85	.271	3	102	3		0.5
1888	Det N	3	3	.500	6	6	5	0	53	76	50	5	1	15	26	5.43	51	.322	.365	23	.261	2	172	-14		-1.2
1890	Bro N	1	0	1.000	2	1	0	0	7.2	15	6	0	4	0	1	7.04	49	.395	.452	3	.000	-0	312	-2		-0.2
	Buf P	2	5	.286	7	7	7	1	62	90	72	5	9	24	13	4.50	91	.325	.385	28	.286	1	85	-11		-0.7
total	9	73	41	.640	118	116	112-9	1	1017	921	547	36	9	233	582	2.85	119	.232	.276	494	.231	11	117	44		5.7

YEAR	TM LG	W	L	PCT	G	GS	CG-SHO	SV-BS	IP	H	R	HR	HB	BB-IB	SO	ERA	AERA	OAV	OOB	AB-HR-SH	AVG	PB	SUP	APR	DL	PW

BALDWIN, DAVE   David George   B3.30.1938 Tucson AZ   BR/TR/6-2/200(175-205)   d9.6   Col Arizona

1966	Was A	0	0	—	4	0	0	0	7	8	3	0	1	1-0	4	3.86	90	.267	.290	0	—	0	0	0		0.0
1967	Was A	2	4	.333	58	0	0	12	68.2	53	19	2	4	20-4	52	1.70	186	.215	.282	4	.000	-0	10			1.2
1968	Was A	0	2	.000	40	0	0	5	42	40	19	7	0	12-0	30	4.07	72	.260	.310	2	.000	0	-4			-0.3
1969	Was A	2	4	.333	43	0	0	4-0	66.2	57	31	4	5	34-2	51	4.05	87	.236	.337	7	.000	-1	-3			-0.4
1970	Mil A	2	1	.667	28	0	0	1-2	35.1	25	11	4	0	18-6	26	2.55	148	.205	.307	2	.500	0	5	25		0.6
1973	Chi A	0	0	—	3	0	0	0-0	5	7	2	0	0	4-1	1	3.60	110	.368	.478	0	—	0	0			0.0
Total	6	6	11	.353	176	0	0	22-2	224.2	190	85	17	9	89-13	164	3.08	108	.234	.313	15	.067	-1	8	25		1.1

BALDWIN, HARRY   Howard Edward   B6.3.1900 Baltimore MD   D1.23.1958 Baltimore MD   BR/TR/5-11/160   d5.4

1924	†NY N	3	1	.750	10	2	1	0	33.2	42	18	5	0	11	5	4.28	86	.309	.361	11-0-1	.364	1*	104	-2		-0.2
1925	NY N	0	0	—	1	0	0	0	1	3	2	0	0	1	0	9.00	45	.500	.571	0	—	0	1			0.0
Total	2	3	1	.750	11	2	1	0	34.2	45	20	5	0	12	5	4.41	83	.317	.370	11-0-1	.364	1	104	-2			-0.2

BALDWIN, JAMES   James   B7.15.1971 Pinehurst NC   BR/TR/6-3/235(210-265)   [ChiA90 4/105]   d4.30

1995	Chi A	0	1	.000	6	4	0	0-0	14.2	32	22	6	0	9-1	10	12.89	35	.444	.506	0	—	0	213	-14		-0.8
1996	Chi A	11	6	.647	28	28	0	0-0	169	168	88	24	6	57-3	127	4.42	108	.257	.319	0	—	0	100	7		0.6
1997	Chi A	12	15	.444	32	32	1	0-0	200	205	128	19	5	83-3	140	5.27	84	.262	.334	3-0-1	.000	-0	116	-19		-2.1
1998	Chi A	13	6	.684	37	24	1	0-1	159	176	103	18	10	60-2	108	5.32	86	.278	.347	2	.000	-0	102	-13		-1.4
1999	Chi A	12	13	.480	35	33	1	0-0	199.1	219	119	34	7	81-1	123	5.10	97	.278	.348	2	.500	1	89	-1		-0.1
2000	†Chi A★	14	7	.667	29	28	2-1	0-0	178	185	96	34	8	59-3	116	4.65	109	.272	.335	4-0-1	.000	-0	103	11	20	1.
2001	Chi A	7	5	.583	17	16	2-1	0-0	95.2	109	56	15	4	38-0	42	4.61	101	.286	.353	2	.000	-0	77	0	20	0.0
	LA N	3	6	.333	12	12	0	0-0	79.1	82	39	10	2	25-1	53	4.20	98	.274	.334	26-0-1	.077	-1	77	0		-0.2
2002	Sea A	7	10	.412	30	23	0	0-0	150	179	95	26	7	49-2	88	5.28	82	.298	.357	2	.500	0	111	-17		-1.1
2003	Min A	0	1	.000	10	0	0	1-1	15	21	10	6	0	4-1	7	5.40	83	.333	.362	0	—	0	-2			-0.1
2004	NY N	0	2	.000	2	2	0	0-0	6	13	10	3	1	5-1	1	15.00	29	.448	.543	2	.000	-0	129	-7		-0.1
2005	Bal A	0	0	—	12	0	0	1-0	22.1	17	4	2	1	3-0	12	1.61	275	.218	.253	1	.000	-0	7			0.3
	Tex A	0	2	.000	8	0	0	0-0	17.1	18	10	3	1	7-1	9	5.19	88	.273	.342	0	—	0	-1			-0.2
	Bal A	0	0	—	8	0	0	1-0	17	19	14	3	1	6-0	8	5.29	84	.275	.333	0	—	0	3			0.0
	Year	0	2	.000	28	0	0	1-0	56.2	54	28	8	3	16-1	29	3.81	118	.254	.308	1	.000	-0	104	-52	20	0.0
Total	11	79	74	.516	266	202	7-2	2-2	1322.2	1443	794	203	52	486-19	844	5.01	92	.278	.343	44-0-3	.091	-1	104	-52	20	-5.

BALDWIN, MARK   Marcus Elmore "Fido"   B10.29.1863 Pittsburgh PA   D11.10.1929 Pittsburgh PA   BR/TR/6-0/170   d5.2   Col Penn St.

1887	Chi N	18	17	.514	40	39	35-1	1	334	329	218	22	17	122	164	3.40	132	.248	.319	139-4	.187	-4*	83	33		2.
1888	Chi N	13	15	.464	30	30	27-2	0	251	241	137	13	13	99	157	2.76	110	.249	.327	106-1	.151	-1	100	5		0.
1889	Col AA	27	34	.443	63	59	54-6	1	513.2	458	358	9	20	274	368	3.61	130	.231	.331	208-2	.188	1*	92	-10		4.
1890	Chi P	33	24	.579	58	56	53-1	0	492	494	321	10	16	249	206	3.35	130	.250	.339	212-1	.212	-1	94	21		1.0
1891	Pit N	21	28	.429	53	51	48-2	1	437.2	385	278	10	23	227	197	2.76	119	.227	.327	177-1	.101	-3	91	-3		-1.8
1892	Pit N	26	27	.491	56	53	45	0	440.1	447	272	11	22	194	157	3.47	95	.253	.334	178-1	.121	-12	91	-2		-0.
1893	Pit N	0	1	.000	1	1	0	0	2.1	6	4	0	1	1	0	11.57	39	.462	.500	1	.000	-0	61	-2		-0.
	NY N	16	20	.444	45	39	33-2	2	331.1	335	228	6	12	141	100	4.10	114	.255	.332	134	.127	-11	87	18		0.
	Year	16	20	.444	46	40	33-2	2	333.2	341	232	6	12	142	100	4.15	112	.257	.334	135	.126	-11	87	22		0.
Total	7	154	165	.483	346	328	295-14	5	2802.1	2695	1816	81	123	1307	1349	3.37	113	.244	.331	1155-10	.163	-31	91	111		6.

BALDWIN, O. F.   Orson F.   B11.3.1881 Carson City MI   D2.16.1942 Los Angeles CA   TR/?/185   d9.6

1908	StL N	1	3	.250	4	4	0	0	14.2	16	10	0	3	11	5	6.14	38	.302	.448	6	.000	-1	52	-4		-1.

BALDWIN, RICK   Rickey Alan   B6.1.1953 Fresno CA   BL/TR/6-3/175*   [NYN71 9/210]   d4.10

1975	NY N	3	5	.375	54	0	0	6-5	97.1	97	39	4	4	34-4	54	3.33	106	.263	.329	15-0-2	.200	0	3			0.
1976	NY N	0	0	—	11	0	0	0-0	22.2	14	6	0	2	10-1	9	2.38	141	.189	.292	3	.333	0	3			0.
1977	NY N	1	2	.333	40	0	0	1-1	62.2	62	32	6	5	31-9	23	4.45	85	.256	.360	4	.500	1	-4			0.
Total	4	7	.364	105	0	0	7-6	182.2	173	77	10	11	75-14	86	3.60	100	.256	.336	22-0-2	.273	1	2			0.

BALE, JOHN   John Robert   B5.22.1974 Cheverly MD   BL/TL/6-4/195(195-210)   [TorA96 5/129]   d9.30   Col Southern Mississippi

1999	Tor A	0	0	—	1	0	0	0-0	2	2	3	1	0	2-0	4	13.50	36	.250	.400	—		0	-2			-0.
2000	Tor A	0	0	—	2	0	0	0-0	3.2	5	7	1	2	3-0	21	14.73	34	.313	.455	0	—	0	-4			-0.
2001	Bal A	1	0	1.000	14	0	0	0-0	26.2	18	14	2	1	17-0	21	3.04	142	.194	.319	0	—	0	2			-0.
2003	Cin N	1	2	.333	10	9	0	0-0	46.1	50	24	7	2	12-2	37	4.47	93	.281	.330	17	.118	-1	65	-1		-0.
Total	4	2	2	.500	27	9	0	0-0	78.2	75	48	11	5	34-2	68	4.69	91	.254	.336	17	.118	-1	65	-5		-0.

BALFOUR, GRANT   Grant Robert   B12.30.1977 Sydney, New South Wales, Australia   BR/TR/6-2/170(170-190)   d7.22   [DL 2005 Min A 183]

2001	Min A	0	0	—	2	0	0	0-0	2.2	3	4	2	0	3-0	2	13.50	35	.333	.462	—		0	-2			-0
2003	Min A	1	0	1.000	17	1	0	0-1	26	23	12	4	0	14-2	30	4.15	108	.235	.327	0	—	0	123	1		0
2004	†Min A	4	1	.800	36	0	0	0-1	39.1	35	19	4	2	21-1	42	4.35	106	.238	.341	0	—	0	2	55		0
Total	3	5	1	.833	55	1	0	0-2	68	61	35	10	2	38-3	74	4.63	99	.240	.341	0	—	0	123	1	238	0

BALLARD, JEFF   Jeffrey Scott   B8.13.1963 Billings MT   BL/TL/6-2/198(198-210)   [BalA85 7/177]   d5.9   Col Stanford

1987	Bal A	2	8	.200	14	14	0	0-0	69.2	100	60	15	0	35-1	27	6.59	67	.344	.413	0	—	0	117	-19		-2
1988	Bal A	8	12	.400	25	25	6-1	0-0	153.1	167	83	15	6	42-2	41	4.40	89	.278	.330	0	—	0	134	6		-1
1989	Bal A	18	8	.692	35	35	4-1	0-0	215.1	240	95	16	4	57-5	62	3.43	111	.287	.334	0	—	0	94	-17		0
1990	Bal A	2	11	.154	44	17	0	0-0	133.1	152	79	22	3	42-6	37	4.93	78	.289	.344	0	—	0	88	-27		-3
1991	Bal A	6	12	.333	26	22	0	0-0	123.2	153	91	16	2	28-2	37	5.60	71	.302	.340	11-0-1	.364	1	128	-5		-0
1993	Pit N	4	1	.800	25	5	0	0-0	53.2	70	31	3	2	15-3	16	4.86	84	.332	.380	2	.500	1	-5			-0
1994	Pit N	1	1	.500	28	0	0	2-3	24.1	32	19	5	1	10-3	11	6.66	66	.323	.387	0	—	0	-5			-0
Total	7	41	53	.436	197	118	10-2	2-3	773.1	914	458	92	18	229-22	244	4.71	84	.298	.348	13-0-1	.385	2	109	-75		-7

BALLER, JAY   Jay Scot   B10.6.1960 Stayton OR   BR/TR/6-7/225*   [PhiN79 4/98]   d9.19

1982	Phi N	0	0	—	4	0	0	0-0	8	7	4	1	1	2-0	7	3.38	109	.226	.294	0	—	0	119	0		-0
1985	Chi N	2	3	.400	20	4	0	1-0	52	52	21	8	1	17-7	31	3.46	116	.260	.320	8-0-1	.000	-1	50	3		-0
1986	Chi N	2	4	.333	36	0	0	5-5	53.2	58	37	7	2	28-4	42	5.37	76	.275	.361	5-0-1	.000	-1	-8			-1
1987	Chi N	0	1	.000	23	0	0	0-1	29.1	38	22	4	0	20-2	27	6.75	64	.325	.423	1	1.000	0	-7			-0
1990	KC A	0	1	.000	3	0	0	0-1	2.1	4	4	1	1	2-1	1	15.43	25	.364	.500	0	—	0	-3			-0
1992	Phi N	0	0	—	8	0	0	0-0	11	10	10	5	0	10-0	9	8.18	43	.250	.392	0	—	0	-5			-0
Total	6	4	9	.308	94	5	0	6-7	156.1	169	98	26	5	79-14	117	5.24	77	.277	.362	14-0-2	.071	-1	62	-20		-2

BALLINGER, MARK   Mark Alan   B1.31.1949 Glendale CA   BR/TR/6-6/205   [CleA67 2/31]   d8.6

1971	Cle A	2	3	.333	18	0	0	0	34.2	30	21	3	1	13-1	25	4.67	83	.233	.303	5	.200	-0	-3			-0

BALLOU, WIN   Noble Winfield   B11.30.1897 Mount Morgan KY   D1.29.1963 San Francisco CA   BR/TL/5-10.5/170   d8.24   Col Eastern Kentucky

1925	†Was A	1	1	.500	10	1	1	0	27.2	38	17	1	0	13	13	4.55	93	.342	.411	7	.143	-0	80	-1		-1
1926	StL A	11	10	.524	43	19	9	2	154	186	99	12	4	71	59	4.79	90	.311	.387	42-1-4	.048	-3	83	-9		-1
1927	StL A	5	6	.455	21	11	4	0	90.1	105	56	4	1	46	17	4.78	91	.309	.393	28-0-1	.036	-4	66	-3		-0
1929	Bro N	2	3	.400	25	2	0	0	57.2	69	52	5	0	38	20	6.71	69	.304	.404	16	.063	-2	76	-14		-1
Total	4	19	20	.487	99	28	10	2	329.2	398	224	22	5	168	109	5.11	86	.312	.394	93-1-5	.054	-9	75	-27		-1

BALSAMO, TONY   Anthony Fred   B11.21.1937 Brooklyn NY   BR/TR/6-2/185   d4.14   Col Fordham

1962	Chi N	1	1	.000	18	0	0	1	29.1	34	22	1	0	20-2	27	6.44	64	.293	.396	5	.200	0	-6			-0

BAMBERGER, GEORGE   George Irvin   B8.1.1923 Staten Island NY   D4.4.2004 North Redington Beach FL   BR/TR/6-0/175*   d4.19   M7/C10

1951	NY N	0	0	—	2	0	0	0	2	4	4	2	0	2	1	18.00	22	.444	.545	0	—	0	-3			-0
1952	NY N	0	0	—	5	0	0	0	4	6	4	1	0	6	0	9.00	41	.353	.522	0	—	0*	-2			-0
1959	Bal A	0	0	—	3	1	0	1	8.1	15	7	1	0	2-0	2	7.56	50	.405	.436	2	.000	-0	163	-3		-1
Total	3	0	0	—	10	1	0	1	14.1	25	15	4	0	10	3	9.42	40	.397	.479	2	.000	-0	163	-8		-1

BANE, EDDIE   Edward Norman   B3.22.1952 Chicago IL   BR/TL/5-9/160*   [MinA73 1/11]   d7.4   Col Arizona St.

1973	Min A	0	5	.000	23	6	0	2-2	60.1	60	40	5	2	30-0	42	4.92	81	.270	.353	0	—	0	79	-7		
1975	Min A	3	1	.750	4	4	0	0-0	28.1	28	11	2	1	15-0	14	2.86	134	.262	.355	0	—	0	81	3		

YEAR	TM LG	W	L	PCT	G	GS	CG-SHO	SV-BS	IP	H	R	HR	HB	BB-IB	SO	ERA	AERA	OAV	OOB	AB-HR-SH	AVG	PB	SUP	APR	DL	PW
1976	Min A	4	7	.364	17	15	1	0-0	79.1	92	52	6	0	39-2	24	5.11	70	.290	.367	0	—	0*	134	-13		-1.7
Total	3	7	13	.350	44	25	1	2-2	168	182	103	13	3	84-2	80	4.66	81	.278	.360	0	—	0	110	-17		-1.9

BANEY, DICK   Richard Lee   B11.1.1946 Fullerton CA   BR/TR/6-0/185(185-200)   [BosA66*S1/9]   d7.11

1969	Sea A	1	0	1.000	9	1	0	0-0	18.2	21	8	2	0	7-1	9	3.86	94	.292	.346	2-0-1	.000	-0	97	0		0.0
1973	Cin N	2	1	.667	11	1	0	2-0	30.2	26	10	1	4	6-1	17	2.93	118	.234	.298	9-0-1	.222	4	51	2		0.3
1974	Cin N	1	0	1.000	22	1	0	1-0	41	51	27	4	0	17-2	12	5.49	64	.305	.366	5-0-1	.000	-1	175	-9		-0.6
Total	3	4	1	.800	42	3	0	3-0	90.1	98	45	7	4	30-4	38	4.28	82	.280	.340	16-0-3	.125	-0	108	-7		-0.3

BANKHEAD, DAN   Daniel Robert   B5.3.1920 Empire AL   D5.2.1976 Houston TX   BR/TR/6-1/184*   d8.26   Negro Lg 1941-48   Mil 1943-45

1947	†Bro N	0	0	—	4	0	0	1	10	15	8	1	1	8	6	7.20	57	.341	.453	4-1-0	.250	1*		-3		0.0
1950	Bro N	9	4	.692	41	12	2-1	3	129.1	119	84	16	2	88	96	5.50	75	.252	.371	39	.231	1	128	-19		-1.7
1951	Bro N	0	1	.000	7	1	0	0	14	27	24	5	0	14	9	15.43	25	.422	.526	2	.000	-0*	157	-17		-1.0
Total	3	9	5	.643	52	13	2-1	4	153.1	161	116	22	3	110	111	6.52	63	.277	.395	45-1-0	.222	2	130	-39		-2.7

BANKHEAD, SCOTT   Michael Scott   B7.31.1963 Raleigh NC   BR/TR/5-10/185*   [KCA84 1/16]   d5.25   Col North Carolina-Asheville

1986	KC A	8	9	.471	24	17	0	0-0	121	121	66	14	3	37-7	94	4.61	93	.259	.314	0	—	0	96	-3		-0.5
1987	Sea A	9	8	.529	27	25	2	0-0	149.1	168	96	35	3	37-0	95	5.42	87	.283	.326	0	—	0	98	-9	19	-1.0
1988	Sea A	7	9	.438	21	21	2-1	0-0	135	115	53	8	1	38-5	102	3.07	136	.224	.278	0	—	0	66	15	40	1.7
1989	Sea A	14	6	.700	33	33	3-2	0-0	210.1	187	84	19	3	63-1	140	3.34	121	.239	.295	0	—	0	101	18		1.5
1990	Sea A	0	2	.000	4	4	0	0-0	13	18	16	2	0	7-0	10	11.08	36	.333	.397	0	—	0	132	-9	155	-1.1
1991	Sea A	3	6	.333	17	9	0	0-0	60.2	73	35	8	2	21-2	28	4.90	85	.297	.354	0	—	0	74	-5	101	-0.6
1992	Cin N	10	4	.714	54	0	0	1-4	70.2	57	26	4	3	29-5	53	2.93	123	.218	.301	9-0-2	.222	0		8		0.9
1993	Bos A	2	1	.667	40	0	0	0-2	64.1	59	28	7	0	29-3	47	3.50	133	.250	.327	0	—	0		8		0.3
1994	Bos A	3	2	.600	27	0	0	0-0	37.2	34	21	5	0	12-3	25	4.54	111	.239	.295	0	—	0		2	53	0.2
1995	NY A	1	1	.500	20	1	0	0-0	39	44	26	9	0	16-0	20	6.00	77	.278	.343	0	—	0	141	-5		-0.3
Total	10	57	48	.543	267	110	7-3	1-6	901	876	451	111	15	289-26	614	4.18	103	.254	.311	9-0-2	.222	0	92	17	368	1.1

BANKS, BILL   William John (b William John Yerrick)   B2.26.1874 Danville PA   D9.8.1936 Danville PA   BR/TR/5-11/150   d9.27

1895	Bos N	1	0	1.000	1	1	1	0	7	7	2	0	4	4	0.00	—	.259	.355	3	.000	-1	196	3		0.3
1896	Bos N	0	3	.000	4	3	2	0	23	42	31	2	0	13	6	10.57	43	.389	.463	11	.273	-1	73	-11		-1.0
Total	2	1	3	.250	5	4	3	0	30	49	33	2	2	17	10	8.10	58	.363	.442	14	.214	-1	107	-8		-0.7

BANKS, WILLIE   Willie Anthony   B2.27.1969 Jersey City NJ   BR/TR/6-1/202(190-202)   [MinA87 1/3]   d7.31

1991	Min A	1	1	.500	5	3	0	0-0	17.1	21	15	1	0	12-0	16	5.71	75	.288	.388	0	—	0	114	-4		-0.4
1992	Min A	4	4	.500	16	12	0	0-0	71	80	46	6	2	37-0	37	5.70	72	.288	.370	0	—	0	86	-11		-1.1
1993	Min A	11	12	.478	31	30	0	0-0	171.1	186	91	17	3	78-2	138	4.04	109	.280	.356	0	—	0	97	4		0.4
1994	Chi N	8	12	.400	23	23	1-1	0-0	138.1	139	88	16	2	56-3	91	5.40	78	.252	.332	41-0-7	.122	-1	79	-17		-2.3
1995	Chi N	0	1	.000	10	0	0	0-1	11.2	27	23	5	0	12-4	9	15.43	27	.458	.542	1	.000	-0		-15		-1.1
	LA N	0	2	.000	6	0	0	0-0	29	36	21	2	1	16-2	23	4.03	96	.300	.387	8-0-1	.125	-0	136	-3		-0.2
	Fla N	2	3	.400	9	9	0	0-0	50	43	27	7	1	30-1	30	4.32	99	.235	.344	17	.353	2*	65	0		0.1
	Year	2	6	.250	25	15	0	0-1	90.2	106	71	14	2	58-7	62	5.66	73	.294	.392	26-0-1	.269	2	92	-19		-1.2
1997	NY A	3	0	1.000	15	0	0	0-1	14	9	3	0	1	6-0	8	1.93	231	.188	.291	0	—	0	83	4		0.9
1998	NY A	1	1	.500	9	0	0	0-0	14.1	20	16	4	1	12-2	8	10.05	44	.323	.440	0	—	0		-9		-1.0
	Ari N	1	2	.333	14	0	0	1-1	43.2	34	21	2	1	25-2	32	3.09	138	.217	.326	1	.000	-0		4		0.2
2001	Bos A	0	0	—	5	0	0	0-0	10.2	5	4	0	0	4-0	10	0.84	526	.132	.214	0	—	0		3		0.1
2002	Bos A	2	1	.667	29	0	0	1-0	39	32	15	5	3	14-0	26	3.23	139	.222	.302	0	—	0		6		0.4
Total	9	33	39	.458	181	84	1-1	2-3	610.1	632	370	65	15	302-16	428	4.75	90	.268	.353	68-0-8	.176	1	90	-38		-4.0

BANNISTER, FLOYD   Floyd Franklin   B6.10.1955 Pierre SD   BL/TL/6-1/195*   [HouN76 1/1]   d4.19   Col Arizona St.

1977	Hou N	8	9	.471	24	23	4-1	0-0	142.2	138	70	11	4	45-6	112	4.04	90	.254	.339	48-0-6	.188	0	143	-6	27	-0.7
1978	Hou N	3	9	.250	28	16	2-2	0-0	110.1	120	59	13	1	63-4	94	4.81	69	.280	.372	31-0-5	.161	0	79	-17		-1.7
1979	Sea A	10	15	.400	30	30	6-2	0-0	182.1	185	92	25	4	68-4	115	4.05	108	.260	.327	0	—	0	81	6		0.7
1980	Sea A	9	13	.409	32	32	8	0-0	217.2	200	96	24	2	66-6	155	3.47	120	.239	.295	0	—	0	72	15		1.4
1981	Sea A	9	9	.500	21	20	5-2	0-0	121.1	128	62	14	3	39-0	85	4.45	87	.268	.327	0	—	0	80	-5	21	-0.7
1982	Sea A★	12	13	.480	35	35	5-3	0-0	247	225	112	32	4	77-0	209	3.43	125	.243	.301	0	—	0	98	19		1.8
1983	†Chi A	16	10	.615	34	34	5-2	0-0	217.1	191	88	19	2	71-3	193	3.35	126	.233	.294	0	—	0	102	21		2.3
1984	Chi A	14	11	.560	34	33	4	0-0	218	211	127	30	6	80-2	152	4.83	87	.252	.318	0	—	0	95	-10		-1.0
1985	Chi A	10	14	.417	34	34	4-1	0-0	210.2	211	121	30	4	100-5	198	4.87	89	.261	.343	0	.000	-0	100	-14		-1.5
1986	Chi A	10	14	.417	28	27	6-1	0-0	165.1	162	81	17	2	48-0	92	3.54	123	.259	.311	0	—	0	95	-10		-1.0
1987	Chi A	16	11	.593	34	34	11-2	0-0	228.2	216	100	38	0	49-0	124	3.58	129	.246	.285	0	—	0	89	25	29	2.5
1988	KC A	12	13	.480	31	31	2	0-0	189.1	182	102	22	5	68-6	113	4.33	93	.248	.316	0	—	0	92	-7		-0.8
1989	KC A	4	1	.800	14	14	0	0-0	75.1	87	40	8	1	18-1	35	4.66	83	.290	.330	0	—	0	92	-3		-0.8
1991	Cal A	0	0	—	16	0	0	0-0	25	25	12	5	0	10-1	16	3.96	104	.266	.337	0	—	0	0	0	112	-0.3
1992	Tex A	1	1	.500	30	0	0	1-0	37	39	27	3	3	21-6	30	6.32	60	.281	.371	0	—	0	0	-9	31	-0.5
Total	15	134	143	.484	431	363	62-16	0-1	2388	2320	1189	291	40	846-39	1723	4.06	102	.253	.317	80-0-11	.175	0	92	23	220	2.8

BANNON, JIMMY   James Henry "Foxy Grandpa"   B5.5.1871 Amesbury MA   D3.24.1948 Glen Rock NJ   BR/TR/5-5/160   d6.15   b-Tom   Col Holy Cross ▲

1893	StL N	0	1	.000	2	1	0	0	4	10	18	1	2	5	4	22.50	21	.455	.586	107	.336	0*	370	-9		-0.9
1894	Bos N	0	0	—	1	0	0	0	2	4	3	1	0	1	0	0.00	—	.400	.455	494-13-6	.336	0*				0.0
1895	Bos N	0	0	—	1	0	0	0	3	4	2	0	0	2	1	6.00	85	.308	.400	493-6-12	.347	0*		0		0.0
Total	3	0	1	.000	3	1	0	0	9	18	23	2	2	8	2	12.00	42	.400	.509	1094-19-18	.341	1	370	0		-0.9

BANTA, JACK   Jackie Kay   B6.24.1925 Hutchinson KS   BL/TR/6-2.5/175*   d9.18

1947	Bro N	0	1	.000	3	1	0	0	7.2	7	6	1	1	4	3	7.04	59	.226	.333	2	.000	-0	149	-2		-0.2
1948	Bro N	0	1	.000	2	1	0	0	3.1	5	4	0	1	4	1	8.10	49	.385	.556	1	.000	-0	0	-3		-0.5
1949	†Bro N	10	6	.625	48	12	2-1	3	152.1	125	63	12	6	68	97	3.37	122	.223	.314	46-0-1	.109	-2	102	12		1.0
1950	Bro N	4	4	.500	16	5	1	2	41.1	39	22	2	3	36	15	4.35	94	.252	.402	12	.167	-0	134	-1		-0.3
Total	4	14	12	.538	69	19	3-1	5	204.2	176	97	15	10	113	116	3.78	108	.232	.339	61-0-1	.115	-2	108	6		-0.3

BAPTIST, TRAVIS   Travis Steven   B12.30.1971 Forest Grove OR   BL/TL/6-0/195   [TorA90 45/1175]   d8.1

1998	Min A	1	0	1.000	13	0	0	0-0	27	34	18	5	0	11-1	11	5.67	85	.321	.366	0	—	0		-2		-0.1

BARBER, BRIAN   Brian Scott   B3.4.1973 Hamilton OH   BR/TR/6-1/175(170-190)   [StLN91 1/22]   d8.12   [DL 1997 StL N 63]

1995	StL N	2	1	.667	9	4	0	0-0	29.1	31	17	4	0	16-0	27	5.22	82	.279	.362	8	.125	-0	137	-2		-0.2
1996	StL N	0	0	—	1	1	0	0-0	3	4	5	0	1	6-0	1	15.00	28	.364	.550	0	—	0	128	-3		-0.2
1998	KC A	2	4	.333	8	8	0	0-0	42	45	28	5	1	13-1	24	6.00	81	.276	.328	0	—	0	67	-4		-0.5
1999	KC A	1	3	.250	8	3	0	1-0	18.2	31	20	6	2	10-1	7	9.64	53	.383	.457	0-0-1	—	0	122	-8		-1.4
Total	4	5	8	.385	26	16	0	1-0	93	111	70	15	4	45-3	59	6.77	69	.303	.377	8-0-1	.125	0	98	-17	63	-2.3

BARBER, STEVE   Stephen David   B2.22.1938 Takoma Park MD   BL/TL/6-0/200*   d4.21

1960	Bal A	10	7	.588	36	27	6-1	2	181.2	148	78	10	3	113-1	112	3.22	118	.226	.340	54-0-4	.056	-4	90	10		0.5
1961	Bal A	18	12	.600	37	34	14-8	1	248.1	194	102	13	2	130-4	150	3.33	115	.218	.331	80-2-0	.162	2	95	15		2.2
1962	Bal A	9	6	.600	28	19	5-2	0	140.1	145	66	9	1	61-2	91	3.46	107	.262	.335	42-0-5	.071	-0	107	-2	33	0.0
1963	Bal A★	20	13	.606	39	36	11-2	0	258.2	253	99	12	4	92-10	180	2.75	126	.258	.303	87-1-5	.138	-0	92	17		2.2
1964	Bal A	9	13	.409	36	26	4	1	157	144	72	15	7	81-5	118	3.84	93	.248	.345	47-1-1	.149	1	80	-4		-0.3
1965	Bal A	15	10	.600	31	32	7-2	0	220.2	177	79	16	2	81-5	130	2.69	129	.224	.294	65-1-6	.077	-2	83	19		2.0
1966	Bal A☆	10	5	.667	25	22	5-3	0	133.1	104	39	13	6	49-1	91	2.30	145	.218	.294	44-0-7	.068	-3	124	16	19	1.5
1967	Bal A	4	9	.308	15	15	1-1	0	74.2	47	39	5	4	49-1	71	4.10	77	.185	.351	22-0-1	.091	-2	83	-9		-1.5
	NY A	6	9	.400	17	17	3-1	0	97.2	103	47	4	3	54-3	70	4.05	77	.278	.371	29-0-2	.172	1	75	-9		-1.2
	Year	10	18	.357	32	32	4-2	0	172.1	150	86	9	7	103-4	141	4.07	77	.240	.363	51-0-3	.137	1	79	-16		-2.7
1968	NY A	6	5	.545	20	15	3-1	0	128.1	127	63	7	3	64-4	87	3.23	90	.256	.342	39-0-2	.051	-1	116	-9		-0.8
1969	Sea A	4	7	.364	25	16	0	0	86.1	99	51	9	1	44-0	56	4.76	86	.292	.349	25-0-0	.200	1	100	-11	37	-1.1
1970	Chi N	0	0	—	5	0	0	0	5.2	10	6	0	0	6-3	3	9.53	47	.417	.533	0	—	0		-1		-0.1
	Atl N	0	1	.000	5	0	0	0	14.2	17	10	3	1	5-0	11	4.91	87	.288	.354	4	.250	0	115	-3		-0.1
	Year	0	2	.000	10	2	0	0	20.1	27	16	3	1	11-3	14	6.20	70	.325	.411	4	.250	0	113	-4		-0.5
1971	Atl N	6	1	.750	39	3	0	2-0	75	92	42	6	2	25-2	40	4.80	78	.301	.356	13	.154	2	127	-7		-0.4

YEAR	TM LG	W	L	PCT	G	GS	CG-SHO	SV-BS	IP	H	R	HR	HB	BB-IB	SO	ERA	AERA	OAV	OOB	AB-HR-SH	AVG	PB	SUP	APR	DL	PV
1972	Atl N	0	0	—	5	0	0	0-0	15.2	18	10	1	1	6-0	6	5.74	66	.290	.357	5	.200	-0		-3		-0.
	Cal A	4	4	.500	34	3	0	2-2	58	37	16	4	1	30-11	34	2.02	146	.188	.297	7-0-2	.143	1	60	6		0.
1973	Cal A	3	2	.600	50	1	0	4-2	89.1	90	40	5	3	32-3	58	3.53	102	.265	.332	0	—	0	75	1		0.
1974	SF N	0	1	.000	13	0	0	1-0	13.2	13	12	0	0	12-1	13	5.27	72	.255	.391	4	—	-3		-0.
Total	15	121	106	.533	466	272	59-21	13-4	1999	1818	870	125	42	950-59	1309	3.36	105	.245	.332	563-5-45	.115	-6	94	27	89	3.

BARBER, STEVE   Steven Lee   B3.13.1948 Grand Rapids MI   BR/TR/6-1/190*   d4.9   Col La Verne

1970	Min A	0	0	—	18	0	0	2-0	27.1	26	14	1	2	18-2	14	4.61	80	.263	.377	2-0-1	.000	-0*		-2		-0.
1971	Min A	1	0	1.000	4	2	0	0-0	11.2	8	9	2	0	13-1	4	6.17	57	.190	.382	5	.000	-1*	139	-3		-0.
Total	2	1	0	1.000	22	2	0	2-0	39	34	23	3	2	31-3	18	5.08	72	.241	.379	7-0-1	.000	-1	139	-5		-0.

BARBERICH, FRANK   Frank Frederick   B2.3.1882 Newtown NY   D5.1.1965 Ocala FL   BB/TR/5-10.5/175   d9.17

1907	Bos N	1	1	.500	2	2	1	0	12.1	19	10	0	0	5	1	5.84	44	.358	.414	4-0-1	.000	-0	167	-4		-0.
1910	Bos A	0	0	—	2	0	0	0	5	7	6	0	0	2	0	7.20	35	.350	.409	1	.000		-3		-0.
Total	2	1	1	.500	4	2	1	0	17.1	26	16	0	0	7	1	6.23	41	.356	.412	5-0-1	.000	-1	167	-7		-0.

BARCELO, LORENZO   Lorenzo Antonio   B8.10.1977 San Pedro de Macoris, D.R.   BR/TR/6-4/220*   d7.22

2000	†Chi A	4	2	.667	22	1	0	0-1	39	34	17	5	0	9-1	26	3.69	137	.231	.274	0	—	0	93	6		0.
2001	Chi A	1	0	1.000	17	0	0	0-0	21	24	13	1	0	8-2	15	4.71	99	.282	.347	0	—	0		-1	126	0.
2002	Chi A	0	1	.000	4	0	0	0-0	6	9	6	1	0	1-0	1	9.00	50	.333	.357	0	—	0		-3		-0.
Total	3	5	3	.625	43	1	0	0-1	66	67	36	7	1	18-3	42	4.50	109	.259	.307	0	—	0	93	2	126	0.

BARCLAY, CURT   Curtis Cordell   B8.22.1931 Chicago IL   D3.25.1985 Missoula MT   BR/TR/6-3/210*   d4.21   Col Oregon

1957	NY N	9	9	.500	37	28	5-2	0	183	196	85	21	2	48-4	67	3.44	114	.274	.319	58-0-1	.190	0	94	7		0.
1958	SF N	1	0	1.000	6	1	0	0	16	16	5	3	3	5-3	6	2.81	136	.258	.343	6	.667	0	188	2		0.
1959	SF N	0	0	—	1	0	0	0	0.1	2	5	0	0	2-0	0	54.00	1	.500	.667	0	—	0		-3		-0.
Total	3	10	9	.526	44	29	5-2	0	199.1	214	95	24	5	55-7	73	3.48	113	.274	.323	64-0-1	.234	2	97	6		1.

BARE, RAY   Raymond Douglas   B4.15.1949 Miami FL   D3.29.1994 Miami FL   BR/TR/6-2/195*   d7.30   Col Miami-Dade North (FL) CC

1972	StL N	0	1	.000	14	0	0	1-1	16.2	18	2	0	0	6-2	5	0.54	635	.281	.343	0	—	0		5		0
1974	StL N	1	2	.333	14	3	0	0-0	24.1	25	17	2	0	9-0	6	5.92	61	.281	.343	5	.200	-0	81	-6		-0
1975	Det A	8	13	.381	29	21	6-1	0-0	150.2	174	81	10	1	47-5	71	4.48	90	.293	.343	0	—	0	106	-15		-1
1976	Det A	7	8	.467	30	21	3-2	0-0	134	157	85	13	0	51-6	59	4.63	80	.293	.353	0	—	0	94	-12		-1
1977	Det A	0	2	.000	5	4	0	0-0	14.1	24	21	3	0	7-1	4	12.56	34	.381	.443	0	—	0	91	-32		-3
Total	5	16	26	.381	88	49	9-3	1-1	340	398	206	28	1	120-14	145	4.79	81	.296	.351	5	.200	-0	91	-32		-3

BARFIELD, JOHN   John David   B10.15.1964 Pine Bluff AR   BL/TL/6-1/185*   [TexA86 11/267]   d9.7   Col Oklahoma City   [DL 1992 Tex A 28]

1989	Tex A	0	1	.000	4	2	0	0-0	11.2	15	10	0	0	4-0	9	6.17	65	.319	.373	0	—	0	102	-3		-0
1990	Tex A	4	3	.571	33	0	0	1-0	44.1	42	25	2	1	13-3	17	4.67	84	.268	.320	0	—	0		-3		-0
1991	Tex A	4	4	.500	28	9	0	1-0	83.1	96	51	11	0	22-3	27	4.54	89	.288	.330	0	—	0	133	-7	66	-0
Total	3	8	8	.500	65	11	0	2-0	139.1	153	86	13	1	39-6	53	4.72	85	.285	.330	0	—	0	128	-13	94	-1

BARFOOT, CLYDE   Clyde Raymond "Foots"   B7.8.1891 Richmond VA   D3.11.1971 Highland Park CA   BR/TR/6-0/170   d4.13

1922	StL N	4	5	.444	42	2	1	2	117.2	139	75	2	10	30	19	4.21	92	.307	.363	34	.353	5	148	-8		-0
1923	StL N	3	3	.500	33	2	1-1	1	101.1	112	49	7	1	27	23	3.73	105	.289	.337	37-0-1	.189	-1*	168	3		-0
1926	Det A	1	2	.333	11	1	0	2	31.1	42	27	4	0	9	7	4.88	83	.318	.362	5	.200	4	104	-5		-0
Total	3	8	10	.444	86	5	2-1	5	250.1	293	151	13	11	66	49	4.10	95	.301	.353	76-0-1	.263	4	147	-10		-0

BARGAR, GREG   Greg Robert   B1.27.1959 Inglewood CA   BR/TR/6-2/185*   [MonN80 3/73]   d7.17   Col Arizona

1983	Mon N	2	0	1.000	8	3	0	0-0	20	23	15	6	1	8-0	9	6.75	54	.271	.340	6	.167	-0	138	-6		-0
1984	Mon N	0	1	.000	3	1	0	0-0	8	8	7	1	0	7-1	2	7.88	44	.286	.417	1	.000	-0	26	-4		-0
1986	StL N	0	2	.000	22	0	0	0-0	27.1	36	19	3	3	10-1	12	5.60	66	.330	.395	2	.000	-0		-6		-0
Total	3	2	3	.400	33	4	0	0-0	55.1	67	41	10	4	25-2	23	6.34	57	.302	.378	9	.111	-0	110	-16		-1

BARGER, CY   Eros Bolivar   B5.18.1885 Jamestown KY   D9.23.1964 Columbia KY   BL/TR/6-0/160   d8.30   Col Transylvania

1906	NY A	0	0	—	2	1	0	1	5.1	7	8	0	3	3	3	10.13	29	.318	.400	3	.333	0	218	-4		-0
1907	NY A	0	0	—	1	0	0	0	6	10	2	0	1	1	0	3.00	93	.370	.414	2	.000	-0		0		-0
1910	Bro N	15	15	.500	35	30	25-2	1	271.2	267	105	2	6	107	87	2.88	105	.275	.351	104-0-3	.231	3*	78	7		-0
1911	Bro N	11	15	.423	30	30	21-1	0	217.1	224	112	4	7	71	60	3.52	95	.279	.342	145-0-5	.228	1*	82	-6		-0
1912	Bro N	1	9	.100	16	11	6	0	94	120	78	4	7	63	30	5.46	61	.326	.401	37	.189	-0*	76	-23		-3
1914	Pit F	10	16	.385	34	26	18-1	1	228.1	252	125	7	4	63	70	4.34	66	.290	.342	83-0-1	.205	-1*	78	-31		-3
1915	Pit F	9	8	.529	34	13	8-1	6	153	130	49	1	4	47	47	2.29	118	.238	.303	54	.278	2*	83	7		0
Total	7	46	63	.422	151	111	78-5	9	975.2	1010	479	18	28	334	297	3.56	85	.280	.346	428-0-9	.227	5	81	-50		-0

BARK, BRIAN   Brian Stuart   B8.26.1968 Baltimore MD   BL/TL/5-9/170   [AtlN90 12/318]   d7.6   Col North Carolina St.

1995	Bos A	0	0	—	3	0	0	0-0	4	3	1	0	0	1-0	0	0.00	—	.286	.375	0	—	0		1		-0

BARKER, LEN   Leonard Harold   B7.7.1955 Fort Knox KY   BR/TR/6-5/225(215-235)   [TexA73 3/49]   d9.14

1976	Tex A	1	0	1.000	2	1	2-1	0-0	15	7	4	0	2	4	7	2.40	150	.149	.273	0	—	0	86	2		-0
1977	Tex A	4	1	.800	15	3	0	1-1	47.1	36	15	1	1	24-3	51	2.66	153	.217	.318	0	—	0	169	8		-0
1978	Tex A	1	5	.167	29	0	0	4-2	52.1	63	31	6	2	29-2	33	4.82	78	.304	.395	0	—	0	95	-8		-0
1979	Cle A	6	6	.500	29	19	2	0-0	137.1	146	79	6	2	70-1	93	4.17	99	.252	.318	0	—	0	99	-2		-0
1980	Cle A	19	12	.613	36	36	8-1	0-0	246.1	237	127	17	3	92-3	187	4.17	99	.249	.301	0	—	0	130	-3		-0
1981	Cle A★	8	7	.533	22	22	9-3	0-0	154.1	150	72	7	1	46-0	127	3.91	94	.249	.301	0	—	0	102	7		-0
1982	Cle A	15	11	.577	33	33	10-1	0-0	244.2	211	117	17	3	88-2	187	3.90	106	.232	.299	0	—	0	94	-12		-0
1983	Cle A	8	13	.381	24	24	4-1	0-0	149.2	150	92	16	2	52-3	105	5.11	84	.266	.327	8-0-2	.125	-0	80	-1		-0
	Atl N	1	3	.250	6	6	0	0-0	33	31	17	0	0	14-2	21	3.82	101	.248	.321	38-0-4	.053	-1	102	1	58	
1984	Atl N	7	8	.467	21	20	1	0-0	126.1	120	59	10	2	38-2	95	3.85	100	.254	.309	17	.000	-2	66	-17	42	
1985	Atl N	2	9	.182	20	18	0	0-0	73.2	84	55	10	1	37-1	47	6.35	61	.288	.369	0	—	0	97	-3	49	
1987	Mil A	2	1	.667	11	11	0	0-0	43.2	54	27	6	2	17-1	22	4.34	94	.256	.325	63-0-6	.048	-3	100	-34	149	
Total	11	74	76	.493	248	194	35-7	5-3	1323.2	1289	695	96	21	513-20	975	4.34	94	.256	.323							

BARKER, RICHIE   Richard Frank   B10.29.1972 Revere MA   BR/TR/6-2/220   [ChiN94 37/1030]   d4.25   Col Quinsigamond (MA) CC

1999	Chi N	0	0	—	5	0	0	0-0	5	6	4	1	0	1-0	1	7.20	63	.300	.400	0	—	0		-1		

BARKLEY, BRIAN   Brian Edward   B12.8.1975 Conroe TX   BL/TL/6-2/180   [BosA94 5/131]   d5.28   gf-Red   Col Okaloosa-Walton (FL) CC   [DL 1999 Bos A 73]

1998	Bos A	0	0	—	6	0	0	0-0	11	16	13	2	1	9-1	2	9.82	48	.340	.441	0	—	0		-6		

BARKLEY, JEFF   Jeffrey Carver   B11.21.1959 Hickory NC   BB/TR/6-3/178*   [CleA82 13/326]   d9.16   Col The Citadel

1984	Cle A	0	0	—	3	0	0	0-0	4	6	3	0	0	1-0	4	6.75	107	.353	.368	0	—	0		-1		
1985	Cle A	0	3	.000	21	0	0	1-3	41	37	26	5	0	15-3	30	5.27	79	.243	.308	0	—	0		-5		
Total	2	0	3	.000	24	0	0	1-3	45	43	29	5	0	16-3	34	5.40	77	.254	.314	0	—	0		-6		

BARLOW, MIKE   Michael Roswell   B4.30.1948 Stamford NY   BL/TR/6-6/215(200-220)   d6.18   Col Syracuse

1975	StL N	0	0	—	9	0	0	0-0	7.2	11	6	0	1	3-1	2	4.70	81	.355	.405	0	—	0		-1		
1976	Hou N	2	2	.500	16	0	0	0-1	22	27	13	0	0	17-1	11	4.50	72	.318	.431	3	.000	-0	92	-4		
1977	Cal A	4	2	.667	20	1	0	1-0	59	53	33	3	4	27-6	25	4.58	86	.249	.343	0	—	0		0		
1978	Cal A	0	0	—	1	0	0	0-0	2	3	1	0	0	0-1	1	4.50	81	.375	.375	0	—	0		0		
1979	†Cal A	1	1	.500	35	0	0	5-2	86	106	54	8	4	30-2	33	5.13	80	.314	.373	0	—	0	83	-10	24	
1980	Tor A	3	1	.750	40	1	0	5-2	55	57	29	4	2	21-4	19	4.09	106	.273	.343	0	—	0		1		
1981	Tor A	0	0	—	12	0	0	6-1	15	22	11	1	4	6-1	5	4.20	94	.338	.416	0	—	-0	90	-20	24	
Total	7	10	6	.625	133	2	0	6-4	246.2	279	147	16	15	104-15	96	4.63	86	.294	.370	3	.000	-0	90	-20	24	

BARNABE, CHUCK   Charles Edward   B6.12.1900 Russell Gulch CO   D8.16.1977 Waco TX   BL/TL/5-11.5/164   d4.14

1927	Chi A	0	5	.000	17	4	1	0	61	86	46	2	5	20	5	5.31	76	.351	.411	19-0-1	.158	1*	72	-10		
1928	Chi A	0	2	.000	7	2	0	0	9.2	17	9	0	1	6	3	6.52	62	.395	.409	8-1-0	.500	2*	52	-3		
Total	2	0	7	.000	24	6	1	0	70.2	103	55	2	6	20	8	5.48	74	.358	.411	27-1-1	.259	3	65	-13		

YEAR	TM LG	W	L	PCT	G	GS	CG-SHO	SV-BS	IP	H	R	HR	HB	BB-IB	SO	ERA	AERA	OAV	OOB	AB-HR-SH	AVG	PB	SUP	APR	DL	PW
BARNES, BRIAN	Brian Keith B3.25.1967 Roanoke Rapids NC BL/TL/5-9/170* [MonN89 4/97] d9.14 Col Clemson																									
1990	Mon N	1	1	.500	4	4	1	0-0	28	25	10	2	0	7-0	23	2.89	127	.236	.283	9	.000	-1	92	2		0.1
1991	Mon N	5	8	.385	28	27	1	0-0	160	135	82	16	6	84-2	117	4.22	86	.233	.333	49-0-3	.082	-1	85	-9	27	-0.7
1992	Mon N	6	6	.500	21	17	0	0-0	100	77	34	9	3	46-1	65	2.97	117	.213	.306	29-0-6	.276	2	107	7		1.1
1993	Mon N	2	6	.250	52	8	0	3-2	100	105	53	9	0	48-2	60	4.41	95	.274	.353	20-0-2	.150	-0	84	0		-0.1
1994	Cle A	0	1	.000	6	0	0	0-0	13.1	12	10	2	0	15-2	5	5.40	88	.235	.403		—	0		-1		-0.1
	LA N	0	0	—	5	0	0	0-0	5	10	4	1	0	4-1	5	7.20	55	.400	.483		—	0		-2		-0.1
Total	5	14	22	.389	116	56	2	3-2	406.1	364	193	39	9	204-8	275	3.94	96	.242	.334	107-0-11	.140	1	89	-3	27	0.2
BARNES, FRANK	Frank B8.26.1926 Longwood MS BR/TR/6-0/170* d9.22 Negro Lg 1949-50																									
1957	StL N	0	1	.000	3	1	0	0	10	13	5	0	0	9-1	5	4.50	88	.317	.440	2	.000	-0*	67	0		-0.1
1958	StL N	1	1	.500	8	1	0	1	19	19	16	3	2	16-0	17	7.58	54	.260	.402	6	.167	-0*	131	-6		-0.6
1960	StL N	0	1	.000	4	1	0	1	7.2	8	5	1	0	9-0	8	3.52	116	.267	.450	2	.000	-0	0	0		-0.1
Total	3	1	3	.250	15	3	0	2	36.2	40	26	4	2	34-1	30	5.89	69	.278	.423	10	.100	-1	65	-6		-0.8
BARNES, FRANK	Frank Samuel "Lefty" B1.9.1900 Dallas TX D9.27.1967 Houston TX BL/TL/6-2.5/195 d4.18																									
1929	Det A	0	1	.000	4	1	0	0	5	13	7	0	0	3	0	7.20	60	.400	.483	1		-0	59	-5		-0.5
1930	NY A	0	1	.000	2	2	0	0	12.1	13	11	0	1	13	2	8.03	54	.283	.450	6	.333	1*	130	-4		-0.1
Total	2	0	2	.000	6	3	0	0	17.1	23	19	0	2	16	2	7.79	55	.324	.461	7	.286	1	106	-7		-0.6
BARNES, JESSE	Jesse Lawrence "Nubby" B8.26.1892 Perkins OK D9.9.1961 Santa Rosa NM BL/TR/6-0/170 d7.30 Mil 1918 b-Virgil																									
1915	Bos N	3	0	1.000	9	3	2	0	45.1	41	14	1	4	10	16	1.39	186	.244	.302	17-0-1	.176	0	124	5		0.3
1916	Bos N	6	15	.286	33	18	9-3	1	163	154	63	3	5	37	55	2.37	105	.254	.302	48-0-2	.188	0	97	-1		0.2
1917	Bos N	13	21	.382	50	33	26-2	1	295	261	115	3	3	50	107	2.68	95	.241	.277	101-0-1	.238	4*	83	-7		-0.1
1918	NY N	6	1	.857	9	9	4-2	0	54.2	53	15	0	0	12	12	1.81	145	.255	.299	18-0-3	.222	0	141	5		0.7
1919	NY N	25	9	.735	38	34	23-4	1	295.2	263	98	8	2	35	92	2.40	117	.236	.260	120-0-7	.267	5*	127	14		2.4
1920	NY N	20	15	.571	43	34	23-1	0	292.2	271	108	9	2	56	63	2.64	113	.250	.288	108-0-4	.204	-2*	109	11		1.2
1921	†NY N	15	9	.625	42	31	15-1	6	258.2	298	108	3	3	44	56	3.10	118	.299	.331	92-0-4	.207	-1	125	15		1.3
1922	†NY N	13	8	.619	37	29	14-2	0	212.2	236	108	10	3	38	52	3.51	114	.278	.311	77-0-4	.182	-1	127	9		0.8
1923	NY N	3	1	.750	12	4	1	1	36	48	25	1	0	13	12	6.25	61	.329	.384	11	.273	-4	161	-9		-0.8
	Bos N	10	14	.417	31	23	12-5	2	195.1	204	86	8	0	43	41	2.76	144	.270	.310	68-0-1	.147	-4	81	21		2.2
	Year	13	15	.464	43	27	13-5	3	231.1	252	111	9	0	56	53	3.31	120	.280	.322	79-0-1	.165	-4	92	10		1.4
1924	Bos N	15	20	.429	37	32	21-4	0	267.2	292	115	7	0	53	49	3.23	118	.284	.319	90-0-9	.222	-1	76	16		1.9
1925	Bos N	11	16	.407	32	28	17	0	216.1	255	127	14	1	63	55	4.53	88	.297	.346	81-1-3	.198	-1	95	-12		-1.3
1926	Bro N	10	11	.476	31	24	10-1	0	158	204	104	6	1	35	29	5.24	73	.321	.358	59-0-1	.237	-0	108	-22		-2.5
1927	Bro N	2	10	.167	18	10	2	0	78.2	106	64	5	0	25	14	5.72	69	.331	.380	23-0-1	.217	-0	67	-17		-2.2
Total	13	152	150	.503	422	312	179-26	13	2569.2	2686	1150	88	25	515	653	3.22	104	.273	.310	913-1-41	.214	1	105	28		4.1
BARNES, JUNIE	Junie Shoaf "Lefty" B12.1.1911 Linwood NC D12.31.1963 Jacksonville NC BL/TL/5-11.5/170 d9.12 Col Wake Forest																									
1934	Cin N	0	0	—	2	0	0	0	0.1	0	0	0	1	0	0.00	—	.000	.500		—	0	0	0		0.0
BARNES, RICH	Richard Monroe B7.21.1959 Palm Beach FL BR/TL/6-4/186* [ChiA77 2/27] d7.18																									
1982	Chi A	0	2	.000	6	2	0	1-0	17	21	15	1	2	4-0	6	4.76	86	.292	.342	0	—	0	45	-3		-0.4
1983	Cle A	1	1	.500	4	2	0	0-0	11.2	18	10	0	0	10-2	2	6.94	62	.375	.475	0	—	0	127	-3		-0.5
Total	2	1	3	.250	10	4	0	1-0	28.2	39	25	1	2	14-2	8	5.65	74	.325	.399	0	—	0	88	-6		-0.9
BARNES, BOB	Robert Avery "Lefty" B1.6.1902 Washburn IL D12.8.1993 Peoria IL BL/TL/5-11.5/150 d7.8 Col Illinois																									
1924	Chi A	0	0	—	2	0	0	0	4.2	14	11	1	0	1	0	19.29	21	.519	.519	2	.000	-0		-8		-0.4
BARNES, VIRGIL	Virgil Jennings "Zeke" B3.5.1897 Ontario KS D7.24.1958 Wichita KS BR/TR/6-0/165 d9.25 b-Jesse																									
1919	NY N	0	0	—	1	0	0	0	2	6	4	0	0	1	1	18.00	16	.545	.583	0		-0		-3		-0.2
1920	NY N	0	1	.000	1	1	0	0	7	9	3	0	0	1	3	3.86	78	.310	.333	1-0-1	.000	-0	52	0		-0.1
1922	NY N	1	0	1.000	22	1	2	1	51.2	46	27	1	0	11	16	3.48	115	.243	.285	12-0-1	.167	-1	214	2		0.1
1923	†NY N	2	3	.400	22	2	0	1	53	59	31	2	0	19	6	3.91	98	.285	.345	14	.000	-2	86	-3		-0.4
1924	†NY N	16	10	.615	35	29	15-1	3	229.1	239	87	10	0	57	59	3.06	120	.270	.314	77-0-4	.182	-2	139	18		1.8
1925	NY N	15	11	.577	32	27	17-1	2	221.2	242	110	9	1	53	53	3.53	114	.281	.323	89-0-2	.101	-9	114	10		0.1
1926	NY N	8	13	.381	31	25	9-2	1	185	183	73	4	3	56	54	2.87	131	.261	.318	56-0-1	.054	-7	78	17		1.0
1927	NY N	14	11	.560	35	29	12-2	2	228.2	251	116	14	4	51	66	3.98	97	.283	.325	83-0-4	.108	-7	110	-2		-0.9
1928	NY N	3	3	.500	10	9	3-1	0	55.1	71	32	3	0	18	11	5.04	78	.330	.382	22	.091	-2	127	-5		-0.7
	Bos N	2	7	.222	16	10	1	0	60.1	86	42	3	0	26	11	5.82	67	.344	.406	17-0-2	.059	-2	87	-11		-1.5
	Year	5	10	.333	26	19	4-1	0	115.2	157	74	6	0	44	18	5.45	72	.338	.395	39-0-2	.077	-3	106	-17		-2.2
Total	9	61	59	.508	205	134	58-7	11	1094	1192	525	46	8	293	275	3.66	105	.282	.329	371-0-15	.108	-31	111	23		-0.8
BARNEY, REX	Rex Edward B12.19.1924 Omaha NE D8.12.1997 Baltimore MD BR/TR/6-3/185* d8.18 Mil 1944-45																									
1943	Bro N	2	2	.500	9	8	1	0	45.1	36	32	4	2	41	23	6.35	53	.217	.378	18	.056	-2	139	-13		-1.2
1946	Bro N	2	5	.286	16	9	1	0	53.2	46	42	2	0	51	36	5.87	58	.240	.399	17	.235	1	93	-15		-1.7
1947	†Bro N	5	2	.714	28	9	0	0	77.2	66	52	4	2	59	36	4.75	87	.240	.378	27	.111	-1	159	-7		-0.8
1948	Bro N	15	13	.536	44	34	12-4	0	246.2	193	101	17	6	122	138	3.10	129	.217	.315	84-0-4	.167	-2	102	23		1.9
1949	†Bro N	9	8	.529	38	20	6-2	1	140.2	108	75	15	3	89	80	4.41	93	.216	.338	47-0-3	.213	0	128	-5		-0.6
1950	Bro N	2	1	.667	20	1	0	0	33.2	25	26	6	2	48	23	6.42	64	.214	.449	8	.125	0	151	-9		-0.7
Total	6	35	31	.530	155	81	20-6	1	597.2	474	328	48	15	410	336	4.31	91	.221	.350	201-0-7	.164	-4	117	-26		-3.1
ARNHART, EDGAR	Edgar Vernon B9.16.1904 Providence MO D9.14.1984 Columbia MO BL/TR/5-10/160 d9.23																									
1924	StL A	0	0	—	1	0	0	0	2	2	1	0	0	0	0		—	.000	.400	0		0		0		0.0
ARNHART, LES	Leslie Earl "Barney" B2.23.1905 Hoxie KS D10.7.1971 Scottsdale AZ BR/TR/6-0/180 d9.22																									
1928	Cle A	0	1	.000	2	1	0	0	9	13	7	1	0	4	1	7.00	59	.325	.386	2	.500	0	41	-2		-0.2
1930	Cle A	1	0	1.000	1	1	0	0	8.1	12	7	0	0	4	1	6.48	74	.364	.432	3-0-1	.000	-1	160	-1		-0.2
Total	2	1	1	.500	3	2	0	0	17.1	25	14	1	0	8	2	6.75	66	.342	.407	5-0-1	.200	-0	105	-3		-0.4
ARNICLE, GEORGE	George Bernard "Barney" B8.26.1917 Fitchburg MA D10.10.1990 Largo FL BR/TR/6-2/175 d9.6																									
1939	Bos N	2	2	.500	6	1	0	0	18.1	16	11	1	0	8	15	4.91	75	.235	.316	5	.000	-1	0	-2		-0.5
1940	Bos N	0	1	.000	13	2	1	0	32.2	28	28	1	6	31	11	7.44	50	.233	.414	11	.000	-1	152	-13		-0.7
1941	Bos N	0	1	.000	1	1	0	0	6.2	5	5	0	1	4	2	6.75	53	.238	.385	2	.000	-0	0	-2		-0.3
Total	3	2	4	.333	20	4	1	0	57.2	49	44	2	7	43	28	6.55	56	.234	.382	18	.000	-2	76	-17		-1.5
ARNOWSKI, ED	Edward Anthony B8.23.1943 Scranton PA BR/TR/6-2/195* d9.8 Col Syracuse																									
1965	Bal A	0	0	—	4	0	0	0	4.1	3	1	0	0	7	6	2.08	167	.200	.455	0		0		1		0.0
1966	Bal A	0	0	—	2	0	0	0	3	4	1	0	0	1-0	2	3.00	111	.364	.417	0		0		0		0.0
Total	2	0	0	—	6	0	0	0	7.1	7	2	0	0	8-0	8	2.45	139	.269	.441	0		0		1		0.0
AROJAS, SALOME	Salome (Romero) B6.16.1957 Cordoba, Veracruz, Mexico BR/TR/5-9/188(160-188) d4.11																									
1982	Chi A	6	6	.500	61	0	0	21-6	106.2	96	43	9	1	46-6	56	3.54	115	.244	.322	—		0		9		1.4
1983	†Chi A	3	3	.500	52	0	0	12-4	87.1	70	24	4	5	32-2	38	2.47	171	.224	.304	—		0		17		1.6
1984	Chi A	3	2	.600	24	0	0	1-4	39.1	48	24	3	0	19-1	36	4.58	91	.310	.385	—		0		-3		-0.3
	Sea A	6	5	.545	19	14	0	1-0	95.1	88	46	12	3	41-1	37	3.97	101	.249	.331	—		0	125	0		0.1
	Year	9	7	.563	43	14	0	2-4	134.2	136	70	15	3	60-2	55	4.14	98	.268	.347	—		0	124	-2		-0.2
1985	Sea A	4	5	.000	17	0	0	0-0	52.2	65	40	6	0	33-5	27	5.98	71	.305	.395	—		0		-3		-0.9
1988	Phi N	0	0	—	6	0	0	0-0	8.2	7	7	2	0	8-0	1	8.31	43	.250	.395	—		0	38	-19	24	-0.2
Total	5	18	21	.462	179	18	0	35-14	390	374	186	33	9	179-15	177	3.95	104	.257	.340	—		0	104	9	24	1.7
ARR, JIM	James Leland B2.10.1948 Lynwood CA BR/TR/6-3/205* [SFN70 S3/49] d7.31 Col USC																									
1971	†SF N	1	1	.500	17	0	0	0-0	35.1	33	15	3	1	5-1	15	3.57	96	.254	.281	4-0-1	.000	-0		-1		0.0
1972	SF N	8	10	.444	44	18	8-2	2-1	179	166	66	13	3	41-8	86	2.87	122	.246	.290	49-0-4	.184	1	88	12		1.3
1973	SF N	11	17	.393	41	33	8-3	2-0	231.1	240	105	24	5	49-7	86	3.81	101	.268	.307	66-0-12	.152	-1	95	4		0.3
1974	SF N	13	9	.591	44	27	11-5	2-1	239.2	223	81	17	2	47-10	84	2.74	139	.251	.288	71-1-6	.254	4*	82	30		3.2
1975	SF N	13	14	.481	35	33	12-2	0-0	244	244	94	17	3	58-10	77	3.06	124	.265	.309	76-0-12	.118	-3*	93	19		1.9
1976	SF N	15	12	.556	37	37	8-3	0-0	252.1	260	96	17	2	60-7	75	2.89	126	.266	.308	74-0-12	.162	2*	102	18		2.2

YEAR	TM LG	W	L	PCT	G	GS	CG-SHO	SV-BS	IP	H	R	HR	HB	BB-IB	SO	ERA	AERA	OAV	OOB	AB-HR-SH	AVG	PB	SUP	APR	DL	PW
1977	SF N	12	16	.429	38	38	6-2	0-0	234.1	286	130	18	3	56-4	97	4.76	83	.306	.345	76-0-13	.132	-2*	91	-15		-1.6
1978	SF N	8	11	.421	32	25	5-2	1-0	163	180	69	7	0	35-6	44	3.53	98	.281	.315	50-0-5	.100	-3*	87	0		-0.3
1979	Cal A	10	12	.455	36	25	5	0-1	197	217	100	22	3	55-5	69	4.20	97	.287	.335	0	—	0	100	-2		-0.1
1980	Cal A	1	4	.200	24	7	0	1-0	68	90	43	12	3	23-2	22	5.56	71	.323	.373	0	—	0	103	-11	40	0.4
1982	SF N	4	3	.571	53	9	1-1	2-2	128.2	125	54	9	4	20-5	36	3.29	109	.262	.291	32-0-2	.250	1	120	4		0.4
1983	SF N	5	3	.625	53	0	0	2-3	92.2	106	47	7	1	20-9	47	3.98	89	.294	.325	15-0-1	.133	-0		-4		-0.4
Total	12	101	112	.474	454	252	64-20	12-8	2065.1	2170	908	161	30	469-74	741	3.56	106	.273	.313	513-1-68	.162		95	55	40	6.2

BARR, BOB Robert Alexander B3.12.1908 Newton MA D7.25.2002 Dover NH BR/TR/6-0/175 d9.11

YEAR	TM LG	W	L	PCT	G	GS	CG-SHO	SV-BS	IP	H	R	HR	HB	BB-IB	SO	ERA	AERA	OAV	OOB	AB-HR-SH	AVG	PB	SUP	APR	DL	PW
1935	Bro N	0	0	—	2	0	0	0-0	2.1	5	3	0	0	2	0	3.86	103	.385	.467	0		0		-1		0.0

BARR, BOB Robert McClelland B12.1856 Washington DC D3.11.1930 Washington DC BR/TR/6-1/192 d6.23

YEAR	TM LG	W	L	PCT	G	GS	CG-SHO	SV-BS	IP	H	R	HR	HB	BB-IB	SO	ERA	AERA	OAV	OOB	AB-HR-SH	AVG	PB	SUP	APR	DL	PW
1883	Pit AA	6	18	.250	26	23	19	1	203.1	263	166	5		28	81	4.38	74	.294	.316	142	.246	3*	86	-27		-2.2
1884	Was AA	9	23	.281	32	32	32-2	0	281.1	312	210	9	13	31	138	3.45	88	.259	.285	135-2	.148	-2*	67	-13		-1.4
	Ind AA	3	11	.214	16	16	15	0	131.2	159	117	2	5	19	69	4.99	66	.274	.302	65	.185	0*	76	-22		-1.8
	Year	12	34	.261	48	48	47-2	0	413	471	327	11	18	50	207	3.94	79	.264	.291	200-2	.160	-2	72	-27		-3.2
1886	Was N	3	18	.143	23	23	21-1	0	191.2	221	153	7		54	80	4.41	73	.280	.326	79	.165	-2	72	-27		-2.5
1890	Roc AA	28	24	.538	57	54	52-3	0	493.1	458	267	7	14	219	209	3.25	110	.239	.321	201-2	.179	-1	107	21		1.8
1891	NY N	0	4	.000	5	4	2	0	27	47	25	1	3	12	11	5.33	60	.367	.434	11	.091	-0	103	-6		-0.7
Total	5	49	98	.333	159	152	141-6	1	1328.1	1460	938	31	35	363	588	3.85	86	.265	.314	633-4	.185	-3	89	-74		-6.8

BARR, STEVE Steven Charles B9.8.1951 St.Louis MO BL/TL/6-4/200* [BosA69 7/155] d10.1

YEAR	TM LG	W	L	PCT	G	GS	CG-SHO	SV-BS	IP	H	R	HR	HB	BB-IB	SO	ERA	AERA	OAV	OOB	AB-HR-SH	AVG	PB	SUP	APR	DL	PW
1974	Bos A	1	0	1.000	1	1	1	0-0	9	7	4	0	0	6-0	3	4.00	96	.212	.333	0		0	160	0		0.0
1975	Bos A	0	1	.000	3	2	0	0-0	7	11	9	1	0	7-0	2	2.57	158	.367	.474	0		0	108	-2		-0.2
1976	Tex A	2	6	.250	20	10	3	0-0	67.2	70	51	10	0	44-1	27	5.59	64	.269	.373	0		0	113	-16	23	-1.7
Total	3	3	7	.300	24	13	4	0-0	83.2	88	64	11	0	57-1	32	5.16	71	.272	.379	0		0	117	-18	23	-1.9

BARRETT, RED Charles Henry B2.14.1915 Santa Barbara CA D7.28.1990 Wilson NC BR/TR/5-11/183 d9.15

YEAR	TM LG	W	L	PCT	G	GS	CG-SHO	SV-BS	IP	H	R	HR	HB	BB-IB	SO	ERA	AERA	OAV	OOB	AB-HR-SH	AVG	PB	SUP	APR	DL	PW
1937	Cin N	0	0	—	1	0	0	0	6.1	7	1	0	0	1	1	1.42	263	.227	.292	3	.000	-0		2		0.0
1938	Cin N	2	0	1.000	6	2	2	0	28.2	28	13	2	0	15	5	3.14	116	.257	.347	7-0-4	.143	-0	151	1		0.0
1939	Cin N	0	0	—	2	0	0	0	5.1	5	1	0	0	1	1	1.69	227	.263	.300	1	.000	-0		1		0.0
1940	Cin N	1	0	1.000	3	0	0	0	2.2	5	2	0	0	1	0	6.75	56	.455	.500	0	—	0		-1		-0.1
1943	Bos N	12	18	.400	38	31	14-3	0	255	240	107	11	2	63	64	3.18	107	.250	.298	81-0-8	.136	-4	71	8		-0.6
1944	Bos N	9	16	.360	42	30	11-1	2	230.1	257	124	13	2	63	54	4.06	90	.279	.327	75-0-12	.173	-1	97	-6		-0.4
1945	Bos N	2	3	.400	9	5	2	0	38	43	22	6	1	16	13	4.74	81	.281	.353	9-0-4	.222	-1	137	-3		-0.2
	StL N*	21	9	.700	36	29	22-3	2	246.2	244	84	12	1	38	63	2.74	137	.256	.285	89-0-11	.112	-5	129	29		2.2
	Year	23	12	.657	45	34	24-3	2	284.2	287	106	18	2	54	76	3.00	125	.259	.295	98-0-15	.122	-5	130	25		2.0
1946	StL N	3	2	.600	23	9	1-1	2	67	75	35	6	2	24	22	4.03	86	.282	.346	17-0-2	.059	-1	94	-4		-0.4
1947	Bos N	11	12	.478	36	30	12-3	1	210.2	200	102	16	2	53	53	3.55	110	.244	.292	72-0-7	.111	-1	84	4		0.0
1948	†Bos N	7	8	.467	34	13	3	0	128.1	132	56	9	0	26	40	3.65	105	.268	.305	39-0-4	.179	-1	84	4		0.0
1949	Bos N	1	1	.500	23	0	0	0	44.1	58	32	4	2	10	17	5.68	66	.318	.368	5	.200	-0		-10		-0.4
Total	11	69	69	.500	253	149	67-11	7	1263.1	1292	579	78	12	312	312	3.53	105	.264	.309	398-0-52	.136	-16	102	26		0.4

BARRETT, FRANK Francis Joseph "Red" B7.1.1913 Ft.Lauderdale FL D3.6.1998 Leesburg FL BR/TR/6-2/173* d10.1 Col St.Leo

YEAR	TM LG	W	L	PCT	G	GS	CG-SHO	SV-BS	IP	H	R	HR	HB	BB-IB	SO	ERA	AERA	OAV	OOB	AB-HR-SH	AVG	PB	SUP	APR	DL	PW
1939	StL N	0	1	.000	1	0	0	0	1.2	1	1	0	0	3	3	5.40	76	.167	.286	—		0		0		0.0
1944	Bos A	8	7	.533	38	2	0	8	90.1	93	45	5	1	42	40	3.69	92	.271	.352	28-0-1	.143	-1	160	-4		-0.2
1945	Bos A	4	3	.571	37	0	0	3	86	77	30	0	0	29	35	2.62	130	.249	.314	20	.250	1		7		0.1
1946	Bos N	2	4	.333	23	0	0	1	35.1	35	21	2	1	17	12	5.09	67	.252	.338	6	.000	-0		-6		-0.2
1950	Pit N	1	2	.333	5	0	0	0	4.1	5	3	1	0	1	0	4.15	106	.357	.400	0	—	0		0		0.0
Total	5	15	17	.469	104	2	0	12	217.2	211	100	8	2	90	90	3.51	98	.260	.336	54-0-1	.167	-1	160	-3		-1.0

BARRETT, TIM Timothy Wayne B1.24.1961 Huntingburg IN BL/TR/6-1/185 d7.18 Col Indiana St.

YEAR	TM LG	W	L	PCT	G	GS	CG-SHO	SV-BS	IP	H	R	HR	HB	BB-IB	SO	ERA	AERA	OAV	OOB	AB-HR-SH	AVG	PB	SUP	APR	DL	PW
1988	Mon N	0	0	—	4	0	0	1-0	9.1	10	6	2	0	2-0	5	5.79	63	.270	.308	2	.000	-0		-2		-0.1

BARRETT, DICK Tracy Souter "Kewpie Dick" (aka Richard Oliver 1933 and Richard Oliver Barrett 1934-43) B9.28.1906 Montoursville PA D10.30.1966 Seattle WA BR/TR/5-9/175 d6.27 Col

YEAR	TM LG	W	L	PCT	G	GS	CG-SHO	SV-BS	IP	H	R	HR	HB	BB-IB	SO	ERA	AERA	OAV	OOB	AB-HR-SH	AVG	PB	SUP	APR	DL	PW
	Illinois																									
1933	Phi A	4	4	.500	15	7	3	0	70.1	74	51	2	1	49	26	5.76	74	.272	.385	21-0-2	.286	2	113	-10		-0.8
1934	Bos N	1	3	.250	15	3	0	0	32.1	50	27	2	0	12	14	6.68	57	.365	.416	7	.143	-0	83	-11		-1.1
1943	Chi N	0	4	.000	15	4	0	0	45	52	28	2	1	28	20	4.80	70	.291	.389	9-0-1	.111	-1	51	-7		-0.8
	Phi N	10	9	.526	23	20	10-2	1	169.1	137	53	5	2	51	65	2.39	141	.221	.282	49-0-6	.143	-0	80	18		2.2
	Year	10	13	.435	38	24	10-2	1	214.1	189	81	7	3	79	85	2.90	116	.237	.308	58-0-7	.138	-1	76	11		1.4
1944	Phi N	12	18	.400	37	28	11-1	0	221.1	223	110	7	3	88	74	3.86	94	.262	.333	74-0-6	.216	2	89	-6		-0.3
1945	Phi N	8	20	.286	36	30	8	1	190.2	217	129	11	7	92	72	5.38	71	.281	.363	62-0-2	.145	-1	83	-28		-3.0
Total	5	35	58	.376	141	92	32-3	2	729	753	398	29	14	320	271	4.28	86	.266	.343	222-0-17	.180	1	86	-44		-4.1

BARRIOS, FRANCISCO Francisco Javier (Jimenez) B6.10.1953 Hermosillo, Sonora, Mexico D4.9.1982 Hermosillo, Sonora, Mexico BR/TR/6-3/195(154-207) d8.18

YEAR	TM LG	W	L	PCT	G	GS	CG-SHO	SV-BS	IP	H	R	HR	HB	BB-IB	SO	ERA	AERA	OAV	OOB	AB-HR-SH	AVG	PB	SUP	APR	DL	PW
1974	Chi A	0	0	—	2	0	0	0-0	2	7	6	0	0	2-0	2	27.00	14	.538	.600	0	—	0		-5		-0.2
1976	Chi A	5	9	.357	35	14	6	3-1	141.2	136	72	13	4	46-3	81	4.32	83	.255	.314	0	—	0	127	-11		-1.6
1977	Chi A	14	7	.667	33	31	9	0-0	231.1	241	117	22	5	58-1	119	4.12	99	.267	.313	0	—	0	123	0		0.0
1978	Chi A	9	15	.375	33	32	9-2	0-0	195.2	180	93	13	7	85-2	79	4.05	94	.246	.327	0	—	0	83	-3		-0.3
1979	Chi A	8	3	.727	15	15	2	0-0	94.2	88	49	9	1	33-1	28	3.61	118	.242	.311	0	—	0	114	5	50	0.4
1980	Chi A	1	1	.500	3	3	0	0-0	16.1	21	9	4	1	8-0	12	4.96	82	.323	.400	0	—	0	110	-1	34	0.0
1981	Chi A	1	3	.250	8	7	1	0-0	36.1	45	23	3	1	14-1	12	3.96	91	.292	.355	0	—	0	99	-3	89	-0.1
Total	7	38	38	.500	129	102	27-2	3-1	718	718	369	64	23	246-8	323	4.15	94	.260	.323	0	—	0	108	-18	173	-1.8

BARRIOS, MANUEL Manuel Antonio B9.21.1974 Cabecera, Pan BR/TR/6-0/170(170-185) d9.16

YEAR	TM LG	W	L	PCT	G	GS	CG-SHO	SV-BS	IP	H	R	HR	HB	BB-IB	SO	ERA	AERA	OAV	OOB	AB-HR-SH	AVG	PB	SUP	APR	DL	PW
1997	Hou N	0	0	—	2	0	0	0-0	3	6	4	0	0	3-0	3	12.00	33	.400	.500	0		0		-3		0.0
1998	Fla N	0	0	—	2	0	0	0-0	2.2	4	1	1	0	2-0	1	3.38	120	.364	.462	0		0		0		0.0
	LA N	0	0	—	1	0	0	0-0	1	0	0	0	0	2-0	0	0.00	—	.000	.500	0		0		1		0.0
	Year	0	0	—	3	0	0	0-0	3.2	4	1	1	0	4-0	1	2.45	165	.308	.471	0		0		1		0.0
Total	2	0	0	—	5	0	0	0-0	6.2	10	5	1	0	7-0	4	6.75	60	.357	.486	0		0		-3		0.0

BARRON, FRANK Frank John B8.6.1890 St.Marys WV D9.18.1964 St.Marys WV BL/TL/6-1/175 d8.19 Col West Virginia

YEAR	TM LG	W	L	PCT	G	GS	CG-SHO	SV-BS	IP	H	R	HR	HB	BB-IB	SO	ERA	AERA	OAV	OOB	AB-HR-SH	AVG	PB	SUP	APR	DL	PW
1914	Was A	0	0	—	1	0	0	0	1	1	0	0	0	1	1	0.00	—	.333	.333	0		0		0		0.0

BARRY, ED Edward "Jumbo" B10.2.1882 Madison WI D6.19.1920 Montague MA BR/TL/6-3/185 d8.21

YEAR	TM LG	W	L	PCT	G	GS	CG-SHO	SV-BS	IP	H	R	HR	HB	BB-IB	SO	ERA	AERA	OAV	OOB	AB-HR-SH	AVG	PB	SUP	APR	DL	PW
1905	Bos A	1	2	.333	7	5	2	0	40.2	38	19	2	4	15	18	2.88	94	.248	.331	11-0-1	.091	-0	131	-2		-0.2
1906	Bos A	0	3	.000	3	3	3	0	21	23	22	2	3	5	10	6.00	46	.280	.344	9	.111	-0	44	-9		-1.0
1907	Bos A	0	1	.000	2	1	1	0	17.1	13	6	1	1	5	6	2.08	124	.210	.279	3-0-1	.000	-0	52	1		0.0
Total	3	1	6	.143	12	10	6	0	79	74	47	5	8	25	34	3.53	76	.249	.324	23-0-2	.087	-1	89	-10		-1.0

BARRY, HARDIN Hardin "Finn" B3.26.1891 Susanville CA D11.5.1969 Carson City NV BR/TR/6-0/185 d6.21 Col Santa Clara

YEAR	TM LG	W	L	PCT	G	GS	CG-SHO	SV-BS	IP	H	R	HR	HB	BB-IB	SO	ERA	AERA	OAV	OOB	AB-HR-SH	AVG	PB	SUP	APR	DL	PW
1912	Phi N	0	0	—	3	0	0	0	13	18	11	0	1	4	3	7.62	40	.360	.418	4	.000	-0		-6		0.0

BARRY, TOM Thomas Arthur B4.10.1879 St.Louis MO D6.4.1946 St.Louis MO TR/5-9/155 d4.15

YEAR	TM LG	W	L	PCT	G	GS	CG-SHO	SV-BS	IP	H	R	HR	HB	BB-IB	SO	ERA	AERA	OAV	OOB	AB-HR-SH	AVG	PB	SUP	APR	DL	PW
1904	Phi N	0	1	.000	1	1	0	0	0.2	6	5	0	0	1	1	40.50	7	.667	.700	0		0		0		0.0

BARTHELSON, BOB Robert Edward B7.15.1924 New Haven CT D4.14.2000 Branford CT BR/TR/6-0/185 d7.4

YEAR	TM LG	W	L	PCT	G	GS	CG-SHO	SV-BS	IP	H	R	HR	HB	BB-IB	SO	ERA	AERA	OAV	OOB	AB-HR-SH	AVG	PB	SUP	APR	DL	PW
1944	NY N	1	1	.500	7	1	0	0	9.2	13	9	2	3	8	4	4.66	79	.310	.383	0		0		0	-2		0.0

BARTHOLD, JOHN John Francis "Hans" B4.14.1882 Philadelphia PA D11.4.1946 Fairview Village PA BB/TL/5-11/180 d5.17

YEAR	TM LG	W	L	PCT	G	GS	CG-SHO	SV-BS	IP	H	R	HR	HB	BB-IB	SO	ERA	AERA	OAV	OOB	AB-HR-SH	AVG	PB	SUP	APR	DL	PW
1904	Phi N	0	0	—	4	0	0	0	10.2	12	9	0	1	8	5	5.06	53	.286	.412	3	.333	1		-3		0.0

BARTHOLOMEW, LES Lester Justin B4.4.1903 Madison WI D9.19.1972 Barrington IL BR/TL/5-11.5/195 d4.11

YEAR	TM LG	W	L	PCT	G	GS	CG-SHO	SV-BS	IP	H	R	HR	HB	BB-IB	SO	ERA	AERA	OAV	OOB	AB-HR-SH	AVG	PB	SUP	APR	DL	PW
1928	Pit N	0	0	—	6	0	0	0	22.2	31	18	2	0	9	6	7.15	57	.356	.417	7	.143	-0		-6		0.0
1932	Chi A	0	0	—	3	0	0	0	5.1	5	3	0	2	6	1	5.06	75	.250	.423	1	.000	-0		0		0.0
Total	2	0	0	—	9	0	0	0	28	36	21	2	2	15	7	6.75	61	.336	.418	8	.125	-0		-6		0.0

BARTLEY, BILL   William Jackson   B1.8.1885 Cincinnati OH   D5.17.1965 Cincinnati OH   BR/TR/5-11.5/190   d9.15

YEAR	TM LG	W	L	PCT	G	GS	CG-SHO	SV-BS	IP	H	R	HR	HB	BB-IB	SO	ERA	AERA	OAV	OOB	AB-HR-SH	AVG	PB	SUP	APR	DL	PW
1903	NY N	0	0	—	1	0	0	0	3	3	4	0	0	4	2	0.00	—	.273	.467	1	.000	-0	0			0.0
1906	Phi A	0	0	—	3	0	0	1	8.2	10	9	0	0	6	6	9.35	29	.294	.400	3	.333	1		-5		-0.2
1907	Phi A	0	1	.000	15	3	2	0	56.1	44	22	0	0	19	16	2.24	116	.218	.285	21	.095	-2	130	2		-0.1
Total 3		0	1	.000	19	3	2	1	68	57	35	0	0	29	24	3.04	87	.231	.312	25	.120	-1	130	-3		-0.3

BARTON, SHAWN   Shawn Edward   B5.14.1963 Los Angeles CA   BR/TL/6-3/195*   [PhiN84 21/542]   d8.6   Col Nevada-Reno

YEAR	TM LG	W	L	PCT	G	GS	CG-SHO	SV-BS	IP	H	R	HR	HB	BB-IB	SO	ERA	AERA	OAV	OOB	AB-HR-SH	AVG	PB	SUP	APR	DL	PW
1992	Sea A	0	1	.000	14	0	0	0-1	12.1	10	5	1	0	7-2	4	2.92	137	.238	.347	0	—	0		1		0.1
1995	SF N	4	1	.800	52	0	0	1-3	44.1	37	22	3	2	19-1	22	4.26	97	.237	.322	0-0-1	—	0		0		0.0
1996	SF N	0	0	—	7	0	0	0-0	8.1	19	12	2	0	1-0	3	9.72	43	.442	.455	0-0-1	—	0		-6		-0.3
Total 3		4	2	.667	73	0	0	1-4	65	66	39	6	2	27-3	29	4.71	87	.274	.348	0-0-1	—	0		-5		-0.2

BARTOSH, CLIFF   Clifford Paul   B9.5.1979 West TX   BL/TL/6-2/180*   [SDN98 29/862]   d5.15

YEAR	TM LG	W	L	PCT	G	GS	CG-SHO	SV-BS	IP	H	R	HR	HB	BB-IB	SO	ERA	AERA	OAV	OOB	AB-HR-SH	AVG	PB	SUP	APR	DL	PW
2004	Cle A	1	0	1.000	34	0	0	0-2	19.1	20	10	4	0	11-0	25	4.66	93	.275	.363	0	—	0		0		0.0
2005	Chi N	0	2	.000	19	0	0	0-0	19.2	23	13	7	2	11-0	15	5.49	80	.307	.404	1	1.000	0		-2		-0.2
Total 2		1	2	.333	53	0	0	0-2	39	45	23	11	2	22-0	40	5.08	86	.290	.383	1	1.000	0		-2		-0.2

BARTSON, CHARLIE   Charles Franklin   B3.13.1865 Peoria IL   D6.9.1936 Peoria IL   6-0/170   d5.14

YEAR	TM LG	W	L	PCT	G	GS	CG-SHO	SV-BS	IP	H	R	HR	HB	BB-IB	SO	ERA	AERA	OAV	OOB	AB-HR-SH	AVG	PB	SUP	APR	DL	PW
1890	Chi P	9	10	.474	26	20	17	1	197	226	145	8	13	66	52	4.11	106	.276	.339	78	.167	-3	92	7		0.5

BASKETTE, JIM   James Blaine "Big Jim"   B12.10.1887 Athens TN   D7.30.1942 Athens TN   BR/TR/6-2/185   d9.22

YEAR	TM LG	W	L	PCT	G	GS	CG-SHO	SV-BS	IP	H	R	HR	HB	BB-IB	SO	ERA	AERA	OAV	OOB	AB-HR-SH	AVG	PB	SUP	APR	DL	PW
1911	Cle A	1	2	.333	4	2	2	0	21.1	21	8	0	1	9	8	3.38	101	.273	.356	6	.333	1	74	1		0.2
1912	Cle A	8	4	.667	29	11	7-1	1	116	109	50	2	7	46	51	3.18	107	.252	.334	40-0-1	.125	-1	114	5		0.3
1913	Cle A	0	0	—	2	1	0	0	4.2	8	3	1	0	2	0	5.79	52	.400	.455	1	1.000	1	268	-1		0.1
Total 3		9	6	.600	35	14	9-1	1	142	138	61	3	8	57	59	3.30	103	.261	.342	47-0-1	.170	1	118	5		0.6

BASS, NORM   Norman Delaney   B1.21.1939 Laurel MS   BR/TR/6-3/205*   d4.23   Col Pacific (CA)

YEAR	TM LG	W	L	PCT	G	GS	CG-SHO	SV-BS	IP	H	R	HR	HB	BB-IB	SO	ERA	AERA	OAV	OOB	AB-HR-SH	AVG	PB	SUP	APR	DL	PW
1961	KC A	11	11	.500	40	23	6-2	0	170.2	164	98	17	4	82-0	74	4.69	89	.255	.340	59-1-3	.119	-2*	116	-7		-1.2
1962	KC A	2	6	.250	22	10	0	0	75.1	96	55	7	0	46-2	33	6.09	69	.317	.402	22-0-1	.045	-2	97	-14		-1.4
1963	KC A	0	0	—	3	1	0	0	7.2	11	11	2	0	9-0	4	11.74	33	.333	.465	1	.000	-0	137	-6		-0.3
Total 3		13	17	.433	65	34	6-2	0	253.2	271	164	26	4	137-2	111	5.32	79	.277	.364	82-1-4	.098	-4	111	-27		-2.9

BASS, DICK   Richard William   B7.7.1906 Rogersville TN   D2.3.1989 Graceville FL   BR/TR/6-2/175   d9.21   Col Miami-Ohio

YEAR	TM LG	W	L	PCT	G	GS	CG-SHO	SV-BS	IP	H	R	HR	HB	BB-IB	SO	ERA	AERA	OAV	OOB	AB-HR-SH	AVG	PB	SUP	APR	DL	PW
1939	Was A	0	1	.000	1	1	0	0	8	7	6	1	0	1	6	6.75	64	.241	.389	2	.000	-0	61	-2		-0.2

BATCHELDER, JOE   Joseph Edmund "Win"   B7.11.1898 Wenham MA   D5.5.1989 Beverly MA   BR/TL/5-7/165   d9.29

YEAR	TM LG	W	L	PCT	G	GS	CG-SHO	SV-BS	IP	H	R	HR	HB	BB-IB	SO	ERA	AERA	OAV	OOB	AB-HR-SH	AVG	PB	SUP	APR	DL	PW
1923	Bos N	1	0	1.000	4	1	1	0	9	12	7	2	1	1	2	7.00	57	.353	.389	1	.000	0	83	-2		-0.2
1924	Bos N	0	0	—	3	0	0	0	4.2	4	2	0	2	2	2	3.86	99	.235	.316	1	.000	0		0		0.0
1925	Bos N	0	0	—	4	0	0	0	7	10	5	0	0	1	2	5.14	78	.357	.379	1	.000	-0		-1		0.0
Total 3		1	0	1.000	11	1	1	0	20.2	26	14	2	1	4	6	5.66	70	.329	.369	3	.000	-0	83	-2		-0.2

BATCHELOR, RICHARD   Richard Anthony   B4.8.1967 Florence SC   BR/TR/6-1/195*   d9.3   Col South Carolina-Aiken

YEAR	TM LG	W	L	PCT	G	GS	CG-SHO	SV-BS	IP	H	R	HR	HB	BB-IB	SO	ERA	AERA	OAV	OOB	AB-HR-SH	AVG	PB	SUP	APR	DL	PW
1993	StL N	0	0	—	9	0	0	0-0	10	14	12	1	0	3-1	4	8.10	50	.359	.386	1	.000	-0		-5		-0.3
1996	StL N	2	0	1.000	11	0	0	0-0	15	9	2	0	0	1-0	11	1.20	353	.173	.189	1	.000	-0		5		0.6
1997	StL N	1	1	.500	10	0	0	0-1	16	21	12	0	2	7-1	8	4.50	93	.323	.405	0	—	0		-2		-0.2
	SD N	2	0	1.000	13	0	0	0-1	12.2	19	11	2	1	7-1	10	7.82	50	.358	.443	0	—	0		-5		-0.7
	Year	3	1	.750	23	0	0	0-2	28.2	40	23	2	3	14-2	18	5.97	68	.339	.422	0	—	0		-7		-0.9
Total 3		5	1	.833	43	0	0	0-2	53.2	63	37	3	3	18-3	33	5.03	82	.301	.362	2	.000	-0		-7		-0.6

BATES, DICK   Charles Richard   B10.7.1945 McArthur OH   BL/TR/6-0/190   d4.27

YEAR	TM LG	W	L	PCT	G	GS	CG-SHO	SV-BS	IP	H	R	HR	HB	BB-IB	SO	ERA	AERA	OAV	OOB	AB-HR-SH	AVG	PB	SUP	APR	DL	PW
1969	Sea A	0	0	—	1	0	0	0-0	1.2	3	5	1	0	3-0	0	27.00	13	.375	.545	0	—	0		-4		-0.2

BATES, FRANK   Creed Frank   B Chattanooga TN   d10.7

YEAR	TM LG	W	L	PCT	G	GS	CG-SHO	SV-BS	IP	H	R	HR	HB	BB-IB	SO	ERA	AERA	OAV	OOB	AB-HR-SH	AVG	PB	SUP	APR	DL	PW
1898	Cle N	2	1	.667	4	4	4	0	29	30	15	0	1	11	5	3.10	117	.265	.336	9-0-1	.111	0	73	1		0.1
1899	StL N	0	0	—	2	0	0	0	8.2	7	2	0	0	5	0	1.04	383	.219	.324	3	.333	1		3		0.2
	Cle N	1	18	.053	20	19	17	0	153	239	181	6	23	105	13	7.24	55	.355	.458	65	.215	1*	58	-67		-5.7
	Year	1	18	.053	22	19	17	0	161.2	246	183	6	23	110	13	6.90	54	.348	.452	68	.221	2	57	-59		-5.5
Total 2		3	19	.136	26	23	21	0	190.2	276	198	6	24	121	18	6.33	58	.337	.437	77-0-1	.208	2	60	-63		-5.4

BATES, JOHN   John William   B5.28.1868 OH   D3.24.1919 Oakland CA   d8.25

YEAR	TM LG	W	L	PCT	G	GS	CG-SHO	SV-BS	IP	H	R	HR	HB	BB-IB	SO	ERA	AERA	OAV	OOB	AB-HR-SH	AVG	PB	SUP	APR	DL	PW
1889	KC AA	0	1	.000					8	15	14	0	0	5	3	13.50	31	.385	.455	4	.000	-1	44	-6		-0.5

BATISTA, MIGUEL   Miguel Jerez (Decartes)   B2.19.1971 Santo Domingo, D.R.   BR/TR/6-0/190(160-195)   d4.11

YEAR	TM LG	W	L	PCT	G	GS	CG-SHO	SV-BS	IP	H	R	HR	HB	BB-IB	SO	ERA	AERA	OAV	OOB	AB-HR-SH	AVG	PB	SUP	APR	DL	PW
1992	Pit N	0	0	—	1	0	0	0-0	2	4	2	1	0	3-0	1	9.00	39	.400	.538	0	—	0		-1		-0.1
1996	Fla N	0	0	—	9	0	0	0-0	11.1	9	8	0	0	7-2	6	5.56	74	.231	.348	0	—	0		-2		-0.1
1997	Chi N	0	5	.000	11	6	0	0-0	36.1	36	24	4	1	24-2	27	5.70	76	.267	.372	8	.000	-1	82	-5		-0.7
1998	Mon N	3	4	.375	56	13	0	0-0	135	141	66	12	6	65-7	92	3.80	111	.274	.359	32-0-2	.000	-4	82	5		-0.1
1999	Mon N	8	7	.533	39	17	2-1	1-0	134.2	146	88	10	7	58-2	95	4.88	91	.280	.353	35-1-4	.200	2	120	-9	25	-0.6
2000	Mon N	0	1	.000	4	0	0	0-2	8.1	19	14	2	2	3-0	7	14.04	34	.452	.500	1	.000	0		-8		-0.8
	KC A	2	6	.250	14	9	0	0-0	57	66	54	17	0	34-2	30	7.74	68	.292	.383	3	.000	-0	84	-16		-1.8
2001	†Ari N	11	8	.579	48	18	0	0-0	139.1	113	57	13	10	60-2	90	3.36	138	.226	.320	32-0-2	.063	-2	83	18		2.0
2002	†Ari N	8	9	.471	36	29	0	0-0	184.2	172	99	12	6	70-3	112	4.29	105	.245	.316	51-1-2	.157	1	97	2		0.2
2003	Ari N	10	9	.526	36	29	2-1	0-0	193.1	197	85	13	8	60-3	142	3.54	131	.267	.326	57-0-4	.070	-4	99	21		1.5
2004	Tor A	10	13	.435	38	31	2-1	5-0	198.2	206	115	22	9	96-1	104	4.80	102	.273	.355	5	.000	-1	89	1		0.1
2005	Tor A	5	8	.385	71	0	0	31-8	74.2	80	39	9	2	27-5	54	4.10	113	.268	.331	0	—	-1		3		0.6
Total 11		57	71	.445	363	152	7-3	37-10	1175.1	1189	651	115	45	507-29	760	4.44	104	.265	.343	224-2-14	.094	-8	95	9	25	0.2

BATTON, CHRIS   Christopher Sean   B8.24.1954 Los Angeles CA   BR/TR/6-4/195   [OakA72 12/286]   d9.19

YEAR	TM LG	W	L	PCT	G	GS	CG-SHO	SV-BS	IP	H	R	HR	HB	BB-IB	SO	ERA	AERA	OAV	OOB	AB-HR-SH	AVG	PB	SUP	APR	DL	PW
1976	Oak A	0	0	—	2	1	0	0-0	4	9	4	0	0	3-0	1	9.00	37	.313	.421	0	—	0	235	-2		-0.1

BAUER, ALBERT   Albert   B8.7.1859 Columbus OH   D2.23.1944 Columbus OH   TL/5-9/190   d9.22   U1

YEAR	TM LG	W	L	PCT	G	GS	CG-SHO	SV-BS	IP	H	R	HR	HB	BB-IB	SO	ERA	AERA	OAV	OOB	AB-HR-SH	AVG	PB	SUP	APR	DL	PW
1884	Col AA	1	2	.333	3	3	3	0	25	22	21	1	0	14	13	4.68	65	.224	.321	11	.273	0	47	-5		-0.4
1886	StL N	0	4	.000	4	4	3	0	28.2	31	27	1	0	27	13	5.97	54	.267	.406	12	.167	-1	86	-7		-0.8
Total 2		1	6	.143	7	7	6	0	53.2	53	48	2	0	41	26	5.37	58	.248	.369	23	.217	-0	69	-12		-1.2

BAUER, LOU   Louis Walter   B11.30.1898 Egg Harbor City NJ   D2.4.1979 Pomona NJ   BR/TR/6-0/175   d8.13

YEAR	TM LG	W	L	PCT	G	GS	CG-SHO	SV-BS	IP	H	R	HR	HB	BB-IB	SO	ERA	AERA	OAV	OOB	AB-HR-SH	AVG	PB	SUP	APR	DL	PW
1918	Phi A	0	0	—	1	0	0	0	2	0	2	0	0	2	0	∞	—		1.000	0	—	0		-1		-0.1

BAUER, RICK   Richard Edward   B1.10.1977 Garden Grove CA   BR/TR/6-6/212(212-225)   [BalA97 5/165]   d9.2   Col Treasure Valley (OR) CC

YEAR	TM LG	W	L	PCT	G	GS	CG-SHO	SV-BS	IP	H	R	HR	HB	BB-IB	SO	ERA	AERA	OAV	OOB	AB-HR-SH	AVG	PB	SUP	APR	DL	PW
2001	Bal A	0	5	.000	6	6	0	0-0	33	35	22	7	1	9-0	16	4.64	93	.265	.315	0	—	0	54	-3		-0.4
2002	Bal A	6	7	.462	56	1	0	1-4	83.2	84	41	12	4	36-4	45	3.98	109	.268	.348	0	—	0	64	3		0.4
2003	Bal A	0	0	—	35	0	0	0-1	61.1	58	36	5	4	24-3	43	4.55	101	.256	.333	0	—	0		-1		0.0
2004	Bal A	2	1	.667	23	2	0	0-1	53.2	49	31	4	4	20-0	37	4.70	99	.238	.317	0	—	0	70	0		0.0
2005	Bal A	0	0	—	5	0	0	0-0	8.1	13	9	2	0	4-1	5	9.72	46	.361	.425	0	—	0		-4	15	-0.2
Total 5		8	13	.381	125	9	0	1-6	240	239	139	30	13	93-7	146	4.58	98	.261	.336	0	—	0	57	-5	15	-0.2

BAUERS, RUSS   Russell Lee   B5.10.1914 Townsend WI   D1.1.1995 Hines IL   BL/TR/6-3/195*   d8.20   Mil 1944-45

YEAR	TM LG	W	L	PCT	G	GS	CG-SHO	SV-BS	IP	H	R	HR	HB	BB-IB	SO	ERA	AERA	OAV	OOB	AB-HR-SH	AVG	PB	SUP	APR	DL	PW
1936	Pit N	0	0	—	1	1	0	0	1.1	2	5	0	1	4	0	33.75	12	.500	.778	0	—	0	167	-4		-0.2
1937	Pit N	13	6	.684	34	19	11-2	0	187.2	174	70	2	4	80	118	2.88	134	.245	.325	69-0-1	.217	1	115	21		2.2
1938	Pit N	13	14	.481	40	34	12-2	3	243	207	102	7	6	99	117	3.07	124	.233	.314	88-0-3	.239	4	89	18		2.1
1939	Pit N	2	4	.333	15	8	1	1	53.2	46	27	4	1	25	12	3.35	114	.240	.330	19-0-1	.211	-0	94	1		0.1
1940	Pit N	0	2	.000	15	2	0	0	30.2	42	29	2	2	18	11	7.63	50	.323	.413	7	.286	-2	80	-13		-0.7
1941	Pit N	1	3	.250	8	5	1	0	37.1	40	28	1	0	25	20	5.54	65	.267	.371	14	.357	1	136	-8		-0.7
1943	Chi N	2	1	.667	15	2	2	0	43.1	45	17	1	1	19	22	3.53	94	.273	.351	10	.300	1	90	0		0.2
1950	StL A	0	0	—	1	0	0	0	2	6	4	0	0	1	0	4.50	110	.600	.636	0	—	1		-1		0.0
Total 8		31	30	.508	129	71	27-4	6	599	562	282	17	15	271	300	3.53	107	.250	.334	207-0-5	.242	7	101	14		3.0

YEAR	TM LG	W	L	PCT	G	GS	CG-SHO	SV-BS	IP	H	R	HR	HB	BB-IB	SO	ERA	AERA	OAV	OOB	AB-HR-SH	AVG	PB	SUP	APR	DL

BAUMANN, FRANK Frank Matt "The Beau" B7.1.1933 St.Louis MO BL/TL/6-1/210* d7.31

1955	Bos A	2	1	.667	7	5	0		34	38	28	2	1	17-0	27	5.82	74	.281	.361	13	.231	-0	108	-7	-0
1956	Bos A	2	1	.667	7	1	0	0	24.2	22	11	3	0	14-0	18	3.28	141	.234	.333	9-0-1	.333	1	231	3	-0
1957	Bos A	1	0	1.000	4	1	0	0	12	13	5	1	1	3-0	7	3.75	106	.277	.333	2-0-1	.500	0	67	1	-0
1958	Bos A	2	2	.500	10	7	2	0	52.1	56	27	4	4	27-2	31	4.47	90	.276	.370	14-0-1	.214	1	77	-1	-0
1959	Bos A	6	4	.600	26	10	2	1	95.2	96	47	11	1	55-3	48	4.05	100	.259	.356	29-0-1	.207	1	104	0	-0
1960	Chi A	13	6	.684	47	20	7-2	3	185.1	169	67	11	1	53-8	71	**2.67**	142	.247	.300	52	.154	1	122	21	-2
1961	Chi A	10	13	.435	53	23	5-1	3	187.2	249	128	22	2	59-4	75	5.61	70	.318	.366	61-2-1	.262	6*	124	-35	-3
1962	Chi A	7	6	.538	40	10	3-1	4	119.2	117	46	10	2	36-5	55	3.38	115	.258	.314	30-0-1	.267	4	101	9	
1963	Chi A	2	1	.667	24	1	0	1	50.1	52	22	2	0	17-2	31	3.04	115	.265	.322	11	.091	-0	25	1	31
1964	Chi A	0	3	.000	22	0	0	1	32	40	22	4	0	16-8	19	6.19	56	.320	.392	4-0-1	.000	0		-9	-0
1965	Chi N	0	1	.000	4	0	0	0	3.2	4	3	0	0	3-0	1	7.36	50	.286	.412	0	—	0		-1	-0
Total 11		45	38	.542	244	78	19-4	13	797.1	856	406	70	12	300-32	384	4.11	95	.276	.340	225-2-7	.218	14	113	-18	31

BAUMGARDNER, GEORGE George Washington B7.22.1891 Barboursville WV D12.13.1970 Barboursville WV BL/TR/5-11/178 d4.14

1912	StL A	11	13	.458	30	27	18-2	0	218.1	222	101	1	11	79	102	3.38	98	.274	.346	76-0-1	.145	-0	91	3	-0
1913	StL A	10	20	.333	38	31	23-2	1	253.1	267	119	0	11	84	78	3.13	94	.286	.351	78	.167	2	86	-5	-0
1914	StL A	16	14	.533	45	18	9-3	1	183.2	152	72	3	8	84	93	2.79	97	.229	.323	53-0-4	.132	-1	109	0	-0
1915	StL A	0	2	.000	7	1	1	0	22.1	29	15	0	0	11	6	4.43	65	.358	.435	6	.000	-1	0	-4	-0
1916	StL A	1	0	1.000	4	2	0	0	8	12	8	0	0	5	4	7.88	35	.364	.447	2	.000	0	96	-4	-0
Total 5		38	49	.437	124	79	51-7	2	685.2	682	315	10	29	263	283	3.22	93	.270	.346	215-0-5	.144	-0	93	-10	

BAUMGARTEN, ROSS Ross B5.27.1955 Highland Park IL BL/TL/6-1/180* [ChiA77 20/491] d8.16 Col Florida

1978	Chi A	2	2	.500	7	4	1-1	0-0	23	29	15	3	1	9-0	15	5.87	65	.315	.375	0	—	0	106	-5	
1979	Chi A	13	8	.619	28	28	4-3	0-0	190.2	175	82	18	1	83-1	72	3.54	120	.243	.319	0	—	0	104	17	
1980	Chi A	2	12	.143	24	23	3-1	0-0	136	127	60	10	1	52-0	66	3.44	118	.256	.324	0	—	0*	118	-6	31
1981	Chi A	5	9	.357	19	19	2-1	0-0	101.2	101	56	9	1	40-3	52	4.07	89	.260	.329	12	.083	-1	99	-12	69
1982	Pit N	0	5	.000	12	10	0	0-0	44	60	33	3	0	27-1	17	6.55	57	.347	.429	12	.083	-1	89	3	100
Total 5		22	36	.379	90	84	10-6	0-0	495.1	492	246	43	4	211-5	222	4.00	100	.263	.336	12	.083	-1	89	3	100

BAUMGARTNER, HARRY Harry E. B10.8.1892 S.Pittsburg TN D12.3.1930 Augusta GA BR/TR/5-11/175 d9.6

| 1920 | Det A | 0 | 1 | .000 | 9 | 0 | 0 | 0 | 18 | 18 | 10 | 1 | 0 | 6 | 4 | 4.00 | 93 | .273 | .333 | 4 | .250 | 0 | | 0 | |

BAUMGARTNER, STAN Stanwood Fulton B12.14.1894 Houston TX D10.4.1955 Philadelphia PA BL/TL/6-0/175 d6.26 Col Chicago

1914	Phi N	2	2	.500	15	4	2-1	0	60.1	60	29	0	2	16	24	3.28	90	.270	.325	19	.053	-1	105	-1	
1915	Phi N	0	2	.000	16	1	0	0	48.1	38	22	2	1	23	27	2.42	113	.226	.323	12	.083	-1*	81	0	
1916	Phi N	0	0	—	1	0	0	0	4	5	2	0	0	1	0	2.25	118	.333	.375	1	.000	-0		0	
1921	Phi N	3	6	.333	22	7	2	0	66.2	103	72	8	2	22	13	7.02	60	.355	.404	30	.200	0*	72	-19	
1922	Phi N	1	1	.500	7	1	0	0	9.2	18	9	1	0	5	2	6.52	72	.409	.469	3	.333	0	105	-2	
1924	Phi A	13	6	.684	36	16	12-1	4	181	181	72	6	4	73	45	2.88	**149**	.271	.347	60-0-5	.217	-0	91	26	
1925	Phi A	6	3	.667	37	12	2-1	3	113.1	120	55	2	7	35	18	3.57	130	.275	.338	30-0-1	.233	-0	101	12	
1926	Phi A	1	1	.500	10	1	0	0	22.1	28	10	0	0	10	0	4.03	103	.326	.396	3-0-1	.333	0	182	1	
Total 8		26	21	.553	143	42	18-3	7	505.2	553	271	19	16	185	129	3.70	109	.287	.354	158-0-7	.190	-2	98	17	

BAUSEWINE, GEORGE George W. B3.22.1869 Philadelphia PA D7.29.1947 Norristown PA 6-2/207 d9.14 U1

| 1889 | Phi AA | 4 | 4 | .200 | 7 | 6 | 6 | 0 | 55.1 | 66 | 41 | 1 | 9 | 33 | 18 | 3.90 | 97 | .281 | .393 | 21 | .048 | -2 | 85 | -3 | |

BAUTA, ED Eduardo (Galvez) B1.6.1935 Florida, Cuba BR/TR/6-3/200* d7.6

1960	StL N	0	0	—	9	0	0	1	15.2	14	11	4	1	11-1	6	6.32	65	.237	.366	1	.000	-0		-3	
1961	StL N	2	0	1.000	13	0	0	5	19.1	12	5	2	0	5-1	12	1.40	315	.171	.224	4	.500	1		5	
1962	StL N	1	0	1.000	20	0	0	1	32.1	28	18	5	1	21-1	25	5.01	85	.239	.357	4	.250	0		-1	
1963	StL N	3	4	.429	38	0	0	3	52.2	55	26	2	2	21-4	30	3.93	90	.279	.351	5-0-1	.000	-1		-2	
	NY N	0	0	—	9	0	0	0	19	22	11	0	0	9-0	13	5.21	67	.289	.360	3	.000	-0		-3	
	Year	3	4	.429	47	0	0	3	71.2	77	37	2	2	30-4	43	4.27	83	.282	.354	8-0-1	.000	-1		-4	
1964	NY N	0	2	.000	8	0	0	0	10	17	6	1	0	3-1	3	5.40	66	.395	.435	0	—	0		-2	
Total 5		5	6	.500	97	0	0	11	149	148	77	14	4	70-8	89	4.35	89	.263	.346	17-0-1	.176	-0		-6	

BAUTISTA, DENNY Denny M. (German) B8.23.1980 Sanchez Ramirez, D.R. BR/TR/6-5/170* d5.25

2004	Bal A	0	0	—	2	0	0	0-0	2	6	8	1	1	2-0	1	36.00	13	.545	.600	0	—	0		-7	
	KC A	0	4	.000	5	5	0	0-0	27.2	38	20	2	2	11-1	18	6.51	72	.333	.402	0	—	0	44	-5	
	Year	0	4	.000	7	5	0	0-0	29.2	44	28	3	3	13-1	19	8.49	55	.352	.423	0	—	0	44	-11	
2005	KC A	2	2	.500	7	7	0	0-0	35.2	36	23	2	2	17-0	23	5.80	73	.259	.346	0	—	0	112	-6	144
Total 2		2	6	.250	14	12	0	0-0	65.1	80	51	5	5	30-1	42	7.03	63	.303	.382	0	—	0	81	-18	144

BAUTISTA, JOSE Jose Joaquin (Arias) B7.25.1964 Bani, D.R. BR/TR/6-2/205(195-210) d4.9

1988	Bal A	6	15	.286	33	25	3	0-0	171.2	171	86	21	7	45-3	76	4.30	92	.258	.310	0	—	0	63	-5	
1989	Bal A	3	4	.429	15	10	0	0-0	78	84	46	17	1	15-0	30	5.31	72	.274	.309	0	—	0	83	-12	22
1990	Bal A	1	0	1.000	22	0	0	0-0	26.2	28	15	4	0	7-3	15	4.05	94	.272	.315	0	—	0		-2	
1991	Bal A	0	1	.000	5	0	0	0-0	5.1	13	10	1	1	5-0	3	16.88	24	.464	.559	0	—	0		-8	
1993	Chi N	10	3	.769	58	7	1	2-0	111.2	105	38	11	5	27-3	63	2.82	143	.250	.301	21-0-2	.190	0*	153	4	6
1994	Chi N	4	5	.444	58	0	0	1-3	69.1	75	30	10	3	17-7	45	3.89	108	.284	.330	2	.000	-0	77	-25	
1995	SF N	3	8	.273	52	6	0	0-0	100.2	120	77	24	5	26-3	45	6.44	64	.295	.341	18-0-1	.000	-2	44	5	17
1996	SF N	3	4	.429	37	1	0	0-1	69.2	66	32	10	2	15-5	28	3.36	123	.249	.291	9-0-1	.111	0	44	9	
1997	Det A	2	2	.500	21	0	0	0-0	40.1	55	32	6	2	12-3	19	6.69	69	.324	.375	0	—	0		-9	
	StL N	0	0	—	11	0	0	0-0	12.1	15	10	2	1	2-1	4	6.57	64	.300	.340	0	—	0		-3	
Total 9		32	42	.432	312	49	4	3-4	685.2	732	376	106	27	171-28	328	4.62	88	.273	.321	50-0-4	.100	-2	79	-40	45

BAYLISS, JONAH Jonah James B8.13.1980 North Adams MA BR/TR/6-2/210 d6.21 Col Trinity (CT)

| 2005 | KC A | 0 | 0 | — | 11 | 0 | 0 | 0-0 | 11.2 | 7 | 6 | 2 | 2 | 4-0 | 10 | 4.63 | 91 | .167 | .271 | 0 | — | 0 | | 0 | |

BAYNE, BILL William Lear "Beverly" B4.18.1899 Pittsburgh PA D5.22.1981 St.Louis MO BL/TL/5-9/160 d9.20

1919	StL A	1	1	.500	2	1	0	0	12	16	8	0	0	6	0	5.25	63	.320	.393	5	.400	0	118	-2	
1920	StL A	5	6	.455	18	13	6-1	0	99.2	102	51	3	7	41	38	3.70	106	.279	.363	35-0-1	.171	-2	89	2	
1921	StL A	11	5	.688	47	14	6-1	3	164	167	103	8	5	80	82	4.72	95	.270	.348	60-1-0	.300	5	121	-4	
1922	StL A	4	5	.444	26	9	3	2	92.2	86	49	5	9	37	38	4.56	91	.249	.338	30	.233	-1	87	-1	
1923	StL A	2	2	.500	19	2	0	0	46	49	25	4	3	31	15	4.50	93	.287	.405	13-0-2	.231	-0	79	-1	
1924	StL A	1	3	.250	22	5	0	0	50.2	47	31	4	8	29	20	4.44	102	.250	.373	14	.429	2	118	0	
1928	Cle A	2	5	.286	37	6	3	3	108.2	128	68	3	10	43	39	5.13	81	.309	.388	30	.367	3	119	0	
1929	Bos A	5	5	.500	27	6	2	0	84.1	111	72	9	8	29	26	6.72	64	.326	.392	25-0-1	.320	2	63	-21	
1930	Bos A	0	0	—	1	0	0	0	4	5	2	1	0	1	1	4.50	102	.294	.333	2	.500	0		0	
Total 9		31	32	.492	199	55	21-2	8	662	711	409	37	50	297	259	4.84	87	.283	.370	214-1-4	.290	10	99	-36	

BAZARDO, YORMAN Yorman Michael (Osorio) B7.11.1984 Maracay, Venez BR/TR/6-2/170 d5.26

| 2005 | Fla N | 0 | 0 | — | 1 | 0 | 0 | 0 | 1.2 | 5 | 5 | 0 | 0 | 2-0 | 2 | 21.60 | 18 | .500 | .583 | 1 | .000 | -0 | | -4 | |

BEALL, WALTER Walter Esau B7.29.1899 Washington DC D1.28.1959 Suitland MD BR/TR/5-10/178 d9.3

1924	NY A	2	0	1.000	4	2	0	0	23	19	11	2	0	17	18	3.52	118	.237	.371	7	.143	-1	152	1	
1925	NY A	1	1	.000	8	1	0	0	11.1	11	17	0	3	19	8	12.71	34	.282	.541	3	.000	-1	39	-10	
1926	NY A	2	4	.333	20	9	1	1	81.2	71	46	2	6	68	56	3.53	109	.240	.392	22-0-1	.136	0	124	0	
1927	NY A	0	0	—	1	0	0	0	1	1	1	0	0	0	0	9.00	43	.333	.333	0	—	0		-1	
1929	Was A	1	0	1.000	3	0	0	0	7	8	4	0	0	7	3	3.86	110	.348	.500	3	.000	-1		0	
Total 5		5	5	.500	36	12	1	1	124	110	79	4	9	111	85	4.43	90	.249	.410	35-0-1	.114	-1	120	-10	

BEAM, ALEX Alexander Rodger B11.21.1869 Johnstown PA D4.17.1938 Nogales AZ d5.25

| 1889 | Pit N | | | | | | | | | | | | | 0 | 15 | 1 | 6.50 | 58 | .172 | .329 | 6 | .167 | 0 | 63 | -5 |

BEAM, ERNIE Ernest Joseph B3.17.1867 Mansfield OH D9.12.1918 Mansfield OH TR/6-0.5/185 d5.2

| 1895 | Phi N | 0 | 2 | .000 | 1 | 1 | **3** | | 24.2 | 33 | 33 | 1 | 1 | 25 | 3 | 11.31 | 42 | .317 | .454 | 11 | .182 | -1* | 179 | -15 | |

AR TM LG	W	L	PCT	G	GS	CG-SHO	SV-BS	IP	H	R	HR	HB	BB-IB	SO	ERA	AERA	OAV	OOB	AB-HR-SH	AVG	PB	SUP	APR	DL	PW

BEAMON, CHARLIE Charles Alfonzo Sr. B12.25.1934 Oakland CA BR/TR/5-11/195* d9.26 s-Charlie

'56 Bal A	2	0	1.000	2	1	1-1	0	13	9	2	0	0	8-0	14	1.38	283	.191	.309	5	.000	-1	23	4		0.6
'57 Bal A	0	0	—	4	1	0	0	8.2	8	6	1	1	7-0	5	5.19	69	.229	.372	2	.000	-0	273	-2		-0.1
'58 Bal A	1	3	.250	21	3	0	0	49.2	47	27	3	6	21-1	26	4.35	83	.266	.361	10-0-1	.000	-1*	108	-5		-0.3
tal 3	3	3	.500	27	5	1-1	0	71.1	64	35	4	7	36-1	45	3.91	93	.247	.353	17-0-1	.000	-2	123	-3		0.2

EAN, BELVE Beveric Benton "Bill" B4.23.1905 Mullin TX D6.1.1988 Comanche TX BR/TR/6-1.5/197 d5.30

'30 Cle A	3	3	.500	23	3	1	2	74.1	99	58	7	0	32	19	5.45	89	.331	.396	26	.346	2	107	-6		-0.2
'31 Cle A	0	1	.000	4	0	0	0	7	11	5	0	1	4	3	6.43	72	.379	.471	1	.000	-0		-1		-0.1
'33 Cle A	1	2	.333	27	2	0	0	70.1	80	43	6	1	20	41	5.25	85	.300	.351	22	.182	-1	105	-4		-0.2
'34 Cle A	5	1	.833	21	1	0	0	51.1	53	25	2	3	21	20	3.86	118	.265	.344	15-0-1	.200	0	96	4		0.5
'35 Cle A	0	0	—	1	0	0	0	1	2	1	1	0	0	0	9.00	50	.400	.400	0		0		0		0.0
Was A	2	0	1.000	10	2	0	0	31	43	28	5	0	19	6	7.26	60	.339	.425	8-1-0	.375	3	181	-10		-0.3
Year	2	0	1.000	11	2	0	0	32	45	29	6	0	19	6	7.31	59	.341	.424	8-1-0	.375	3	181	-11		-0.3
tal 5	11	7	.611	86	8	1	2	235	288	160	21	5	96	89	5.32	86	.311	.378	72-1-1	.264	4	122	-17		-0.3

EAN, COLTER Randall Colter B1.16.1977 Anniston AL BL/TR/6-6/255 d4.26 Col Auburn

| '05 NY A | 0 | 0 | — | 1 | 0 | 0 | 0-0 | 2 | 1 | 1 | 0 | 0 | 2-0 | 2 | 4.50 | 97 | .143 | .333 | 0 | — | 0 | | 0 | | 0.0 |

EARD, DAVE Charles David B10.2.1959 Atlanta GA BL/TR/6-5/215(190-215) [OakA77 6/147] d7.16

'80 Oak A	0	1	.000	13	0	0	1-0	16	12	6	0	1	7-1	12	3.38	113	.218	.313	0	—	0		1		0.1
'81 †Oak A	1	1	.500	8	0	0	3-1	13	9	5	1	1	4-1	15	2.77	127	.191	.264	0	—	0		1		0.2
'82 Oak A	10	9	.526	54	2	0	11-8	91.2	85	41	9	1	35-6	73	3.44	115	.244	.308	0	—	0	58	5		0.9
'83 Oak A	5	5	.500	43	0	0	10-3	61	55	39	8	2	36-4	40	5.61	69	.246	.351	0	—	0	-16	34	-1.1
'84 Sea A	3	2	.600	43	0	0	5-3	76	88	56	15	4	33-5	40	5.80	69	.291	.362	0	—	0	-11	22	-1.9
'85 Chi N	0	0	—	9	0	0	0-0	12.2	16	9	2	0	7-2	4	6.39	63	.314	.397	0	—	0	-16	34	-1.1
'89 Det A	0	2	.000	2	1	0	0-0	5.1	9	7	2	1	2-0	1	5.06	76	.375	.444	0	—	0	-3		-0.1
tal 7	19	20	.487	172	3	0	30-15	275.2	274	163	37	10	124-19	185	4.70	84	.261	.339	0	—	0	54	-25	126	-2.3

EARD, MIKE Michael Richard B6.21.1950 Little Rock AR BL/TR/6-1/185* [AtlN71 D1/18] d9.7 Col Texas

'74 Atl N	0	0	—	6	0	0	0-0	9.1	5	3	1	1	1-0	7	2.89	131	.156	.206	0	—	0		1		0.1
'75 Atl N	4	0	1.000	34	2	0	0-3	70.1	71	31	4	2	28-5	27	3.20	118	.265	.333	9-0-1	.111	-0	105	4		0.2
'76 Atl N	0	2	.000	30	0	0	1-2	33.2	38	18	1	0	14-3	8	4.28	89	.299	.364	1	.000	-0	-2		-0.1
'77 Atl N	0	0	—	4	0	0	0-0	4.2	14	11	3	0	2-0	1	9.64	46	.452	.485	0	—	0	-4		-0.1
tal 4	4	2	.667	74	2	0	1-5	118	128	63	9	3	45-8	43	3.74	102	.279	.343	10-0-1	.100	-0	105	-1		0.0

EARD, RALPH Ralph William B2.11.1929 Cincinnati OH D2.10.2003 West Palm Beach FL BR/TR/6-5/200 d6.29 Col Cincinnati

| '54 StL N | 0 | 4 | .000 | 13 | 10 | 0 | 0 | 58 | 62 | 32 | 2 | 2 | 28 | 17 | 3.72 | 110 | .278 | .357 | 17 | .059 | -1 | 69 | 0 | | -0.2 |

EARDEN, GENE Henry Eugene B9.5.1920 Lexa AR D3.18.2004 Alexander City AL BL/TL/6-3/204* d5.10

'47 Cle A	0	0	—	1	0	0	0	1	2	3	0	1	0	81.00	4	.667	.750	0	—	0		-3		-0.1
'48 †Cle A	20	7	.741	37	29	15-6	1	229.2	187	72	9	3	106	80	2.43	167	.229	.320	90-2-2	.256	5	145	43		5.5
'49 Cle A	8	8	.500	32	19	5	0	127	140	77	6	2	92	41	5.10	78	.286	.401	45-0-2	.111	-3	99	-15		-1.7
'50 Cle A	1	3	.250	14	3	0	0	45.1	57	32	5	0	32	10	6.15	70	.328	.432	13	.154	1	111	-8		-0.6
Was A	3	5	.375	12	9	4	0	68.1	81	35	1	2	33	20	4.21	107	.297	.377	22-0-1	.227	1*	74	3		0.4
Year	4	8	.333	26	12	4	0	113.2	138	67	6	2	65	30	4.99	89	.309	.399	35-0-1	.200	2	83	-5		-0.2
'51 Was A	0	0	—	1	1	0	0	2.2	6	5	0	0	2	1	16.88	24	.429	.500	0	—	0	152	-4		-0.2
Det A	3	4	.429	37	4	2-1	0	106	112	58	6	1	58	38	4.33	96	.275	.366	32-2-1	.188	1	101	-2		0.0
Year	3	4	.429	38	5	2-1	0	108.2	118	63	6	1	60	39	4.64	90	.280	.371	32-2-1	.188	1	111	-5		-0.2
'52 StL A	7	8	.467	34	16	3	0	150.2	158	89	13	1	78	45	4.30	91	.270	.357	65-0-1	.354	6*	81	-9		-0.1
'53 Chi A	3	3	.500	25	3	0	0	58.1	48	27	8	0	33	24	2.93	137	.223	.327	21-0-2	.190	-1*	169	4		0.3
tal 7	45	38	.542	193	84	29-7	1	788.1	791	398	48	9	435	259	3.96	103	.266	.361	288-4-9	.236	10	111	9		3.5

EARE, GARY Gary Ray B8.22.1952 San Diego CA BR/TR/6-4/200* [MilA74 5/102] d9.7 Col Cal St.-Long Beach

'76 Mil A	2	3	.400	6	5	2	0-0	41	43	16	4	0	15-0	32	3.29	107	.274	.335	0	—	0	125	1		0.2
'77 Mil A	3	3	.500	17	6	0	0-0	58.2	63	46	6	1	38-3	32	6.44	64	.276	.378	0	—	0	124	-15		-1.2
tal 2	5	6	.455	23	11	2	0-0	99.2	106	62	10	1	53-3	64	5.15	75	.275	.361	0	—	0	124	-14		-1.0

EARNARTH, LARRY Lawrence Donald B9.11.1941 New York NY D12.31.1999 Seminole FL BR/TR/6-2/203* d4.16 C11 Col St. Johns

'63 NY N	3	8	.273	58	2	0	4	126.1	127	61	7	5	47-9	48	3.42	102	.268	.338	30	.200	1	111	-1		0.2
'64 NY N	5	5	.500	44	1	0	1	78	79	38	6	2	38-1	31	4.15	86	.271	.358	14	.143	-0	123	-4		-0.4
'65 NY N	3	5	.375	40	3	0	1	60.2	75	43	6	4	28-2	16	4.60	77	.304	.381	9	.111	0	49	-11		-1.3
'66 NY N	2	3	.400	29	1	0	0	54.2	59	31	11	1	20-6	27	4.45	82	.281	.342	9	.111	-0	0	-5		-0.4
'71 Mil A	0	0	—	2	0	0	0-0	3	10	6	1	0	2-0	2	18.00	19	.556	.600	0	—	0		-4		-0.2
tal 5	13	21	.382	173	7	0	8-0	322.2	350	179	31	12	135-18	124	4.13	86	.282	.356	62	.161	1	70	-25		-2.1

EARSE, KEVIN Kevin Gerard B11.7.1965 Jersey City NJ BL/TL/6-2/195 [CleA87 22/567] d4.15 Col Old Dominion

| '90 Cle A | 0 | 2 | .000 | 1 | 1 | 0 | 0-0 | 7.2 | 16 | 11 | 2 | 0 | 5-0 | 2 | 12.91 | 31 | .421 | .511 | 0 | — | 0 | 62 | -7 | | -1.2 |

EASLEY, CHRIS Christopher Charles B6.23.1962 Jackson TN BR/TR/6-2/190 [CleA84 9/214] d7.20 Col Arizona St.

| '91 Cal A | 0 | 1 | .000 | 22 | 0 | 0 | 0-0 | 26.2 | 26 | 14 | 2 | 1 | 10-1 | 14 | 3.38 | 122 | .257 | .327 | 0 | — | 0 | | 1 | | 0.1 |

EATIN, ED Ebenezer Ambrose B8.10.1866 Baltimore MD D5.9.1925 Baltimore MD BR/TL/5-9/162 d8.2

'87 Det N	1	1	.500	2	2	2	0	18	13	11	2	1	8	6	4.00	102	.203	.301	7	.000	-1	103	0		-0.1
'88 Det N	5	7	.417	12	12	12-1	0	107	111	60	6	2	16	44	2.86	98	.251	.280	56-2	.250	5*	84	-1		0.3
'89 Cle N	20	15	.571	36	36	35-3	0	317.2	316	179	12	6	141	126	3.57	113	.251	.330	121-1	.116	5*	86	19		1.1
'90 Cle N	22	30	.423	54	54	53-1	0	474.1	518	300	11	15	186	155	3.83	94	.269	.338	191-1	.141	-9	80	-11		-1.6
'91 Cle N	0	3	.000	5	4	2	0	29	39	44	1	6	21	4	5.28	66	.310	.431	13	.077	-1	86	-9		-0.8
tal 5	48	56	.462	109	108	104-5	0	946	997	594	32	30	372	335	3.68	99	.261	.332	388-4	.144	-13	83	-2		-1.1

EATTIE, JIM James Louis B7.4.1954 Hampton VA BR/TR/6-6/220(205-225) [NYA75 4/91] d4.25 Col Dartmouth

'78 †NY A	6	9	.400	25	22	0	0-0	128	123	60	8	8	51-2	65	3.73	98	.255	.335	0	—	0	102	-1		-0.1
'79 NY A	3	6	.333	15	13	1-1	0-0	76	85	45	5	0	41-0	32	5.21	79	.294	.375	0	—	0	90	-8	27	-0.7
'80 Sea A	5	15	.250	33	29	3	0-0	187.1	205	115	19	4	98-9	67	4.85	86	.286	.372	0	—	0	93	-15		-1.4
'81 Sea A	3	2	.600	13	9	0	1-0	66.2	59	24	2	2	18-0	36	2.97	131	.232	.288	0	—	0	80	7		0.5
'82 Sea A	8	12	.400	28	26	6-1	0-0	172.1	149	73	13	1	65-0	140	3.34	128	.232	.303	0	—	0	81	16		1.8
'83 Sea A	10	15	.400	30	29	8-2	0-0	196.2	197	89	12	3	66-6	132	3.84	112	.259	.320	0	—	0	72	11	23	1.5
'84 Sea A	12	16	.429	32	32	12-2	0-0	211	206	86	15	5	75-6	135	3.41	118	.260	.326	0	—	0	91	16		2.0
'85 Sea A	5	6	.455	18	15	1-1	0-0	70.1	93	61	9	3	33-0	45	7.29	58	.316	.385	0	—	0	131	-23	84	-2.9
'86 Sea A	0	6	.000	9	7	0	0-0	40.1	57	28	7	3	14-2	24	6.02	71	.341	.398	0	—	0	73	-7	125	-0.8
tal 9	52	87	.374	203	182	31-7	1-0	1148.2	1194	581	88	29	461-25	660	4.17	99	.267	.338	0	—	0	90	-4	259	-0.1

EATTY, BLAINE Gordon Blaine B4.25.1964 Victoria TX BL/TL/6-2/185* [BalA86 9/227] d9.16 Col Baylor [DL 1990 NY N 178]

'89 NY N	0	0	—	2	1	0	0-0	6	5	1	1	0	2-0	3	1.50	220	.217	.280	2	.500	0	188	1		0.1
'91 NY N	0	0	—	5	0	0	0-0	9.2	9	3	0	0	4-1	7	2.79	131	.250	.317	0	—	0		1		0.1
tal 2	0	0	—	7	1	0	0-0	15.2	14	4	1	0	6-1	10	2.30	153	.237	.303	2	.500	0	188	2	178	0.2

EAZLEY, JOHNNY John Andrew "Nig" B5.25.1918 Nashville TN D4.21.1990 Nashville TN BR/TR/6-1.5/190 d9.28 Mil 1943-45

'41 StL N	1	0	1.000	1	1	0	0	9	10	1	0	0	3	1	1.00	394	.351	.351	3	.000	-0	68	3		0.3
'42 †StL N	21	6	.778	43	23	13-3	3	215.1	181	67	4	3	73	91	2.13	161	.226	.293	73-0-9	.137	-1	120	28		3.5
'46 †StL N	7	5	.583	19	15	2	0	103	109	55	6	4	55	36	4.46	77	.275	.368	33-0-3	.242	1	114	-9		-0.9
'47 Bos N	2	0	1.000	9	2	0	0	28.2	30	15	1	0	19	12	4.40	89	.273	.380	7-0-2	.000	0	193	-1		-0.2
'48 Bos N	0	1	.000	3	1	0	0	16	19	13	2	0	7	4	4.50	85	.284	.351	4-0-1	.000	-1	127	-3	94	-0.2
'49 Bos N	0	0	—	1	0	0	0	2							0.00	—	.000	.000	0	—	0		0		0.0
tal 6	31	12	.721	76	46	21-3	3	374	349	151	13	7	157	147	3.01	116	.247	.325	120-0-15	.150	-1	120	19	94	2.5

YEAR	TM LG	W	L	PCT	G	GS	CG-SHO	SV-BS	IP	H	R	HR	HB	BB-IB	SO	ERA	AERA	OAV	OOB	AB-HR-SH	AVG	PB	SUP	APR	DL	PW

BECANNON, BUCK James Melvin B8.22.1859 New York NY D11.5.1923 New York NY 5-10/165 d10.15

1884	†NY AA	1	0	1.000	1	1	1	0	6	2	4	0		2	2	1.50	208	.091	.167	3	.000	-0	251	1		0.
1885	NY AA	2	8	.200	10	10	10	0	85	108	84	5	5	24	13	6.25	50	.296	.348	33	.303	2	108	-28		-2.2
Total	2	3	8	.273	11	11	11	0	91	110	86	5	5	26	15	5.93	53	.284	.337	36	.278	1	121	-27		-2.

BECHLER, STEVE Steven Scott B11.18.1979 Medford OR D2.17.2003 Ft.Lauderdale FL BR/TR/6-2/207 [BalA98 3/99] d9.6

| 2002 | Bal A | 0 | 0 | — | 3 | 0 | 0 | 0-0 | 4.2 | 6 | 7 | 3 | 1 | 4-0 | 2 | 13.50 | 32 | .300 | .440 | 0 | — | 0 | | -5 | | -0. |

BECHTEL, GEORGE George A. B1848 Philadelphia PA 5-11/165 d5.20 ▲

1871	Ath NA	1	2	.333	3	3	2	0	26	43	42	0		11	1	7.96	51	.319	.370	94-1	.351	1*	99	-11		-0.
1873	Phi NA	0	2	.000	3	2	1	0	16	27	24	0		2	0	4.50	73	.318	.333	258-1	.244	0*	103	-3		-0.
1874	Phi NA	1	3	.250	6	4	4	0	39	57	42	0		1	0	1.62	137	.297	.301	151-1	.278	1*	85	1		-0.
1875	Cen NA	2	12	.143	14	14	14	0	126	169	138	0		5	6	2.71	80	.274	.280	61	.279	3	81	-8		-0.
	Ath NA	3	1	.750	4	4	4	0	36	41	19	0		3	3	2.50	96	.279	.293	164	.280	0*	158	0		0.
	Year	5	13	.278	18	18	18	0	162	210	157	0		8	9	2.67	83	.275	.283	225	.280	4	99	-15		-1.
Total	4 NA	7	20	.259	30	27	25	0	243	337	265	0		22	10	3.19	78	.287	.300	728-3	.276	6	98	-21		-1.

BECK, GEORGE Ernest George B. B2.21.1890 South Bend IN D10.29.1973 South Bend IN BR/TR/5-11/165 d5.15

| 1914 | Cle A | 0 | 0 | — | 1 | 0 | 0 | 0 | 1 | 0 | 1 | 0 | 0 | 0 | 0 | 0.00 | — | .250 | .400 | 0 | — | 0 | | 0 | | 0. |

BECK, FRANK Frank J. (b Frank J. Hengstebeck) B11.1858 TR/5-9/141 d5.2

1884	Pit AA	0	3	.000	3	3	3	0	25	33	29	0	5	6	11	6.12	54	.306	.370	12	.333	1	79	-8		-0.
	Bal U	0	2	.000	2	2	1	0	9	17	13	0		4	7	8.00	33	.378	.429	20	.100	-1*	112	-4		-0.
Total	1	0	5	.000	5	5	4	0	34	50	42	0	5	10	18	6.62	48	.327	.387	32	.188	-0	95	-12		-1.

BECK, RICH Richard Henry B1.21.1941 Pasco WA BB/TR/6-3/190 d9.14 Mil 1966-67 Col Gonzaga

| 1965 | NY A | 2 | 1 | .667 | 3 | 3 | 1-1 | 0 | 21 | 22 | 6 | 1 | 0 | 7-1 | 10 | 2.14 | 159 | .275 | .333 | 7 | .000 | -0 | 77 | 3 | | 0. |

BECK, ROD Rodney Roy B8.3.1968 Burbank CA BR/TR/6-1/236(215-236) [OakA86 13/327] d5.6

1991	SF N	1	1	.500	31	0	0	1-0	52.1	53	22	4	1	13-2	38	3.78	95	.273	.319	2	.500	0	0			0.
1992	SF N	3	3	.500	65	0	0	17-6	92	62	20	4	2	15-2	87	1.76	189	.190	.228	2	.500	-0	17			1.
1993	SF N★	3	1	.750	76	0	0	48-4	79.1	57	20	11	3	13-4	86	2.16	182	.201	.241	4-0-1	.000	-0	16			2.
1994	SF N★	2	4	.333	48	0	0	28-0	48.2	49	17	10	0	13-2	39	2.77	146	.261	.304	3	.000	-0	7		24	1.
1995	SF N	5	6	.455	60	0	0	33-10	58.2	60	31	7	2	21-3	42	4.45	93	.267	.331	3	.333	0	7			1
1996	SF N	0	9	.000	63	0	0	35-7	62	56	23	9	1	10-2	48	3.34	124	.238	.270	0	.333	0	5			0
1997	†SF N☆	7	4	.636	73	0	0	37-8	70	67	31	7	2	8-2	53	3.47	119	.248	.275	0		0	10			1
1998	†Chi N	3	4	.429	81	0	0	51-7	80.1	86	33	11	2	20-4	81	7.80	59	.331	.388	1	.000	-0	-10		65	-1
1999	Chi N	4	3	.333	31	0	0	7-4	30	41	26	5	0	13-3	31	3.10	162	.222	.287	0	—	0	5			0
	†Bos A	0	1	.000	12	0	0	3-1	14	9	3	0	1	5-0	12	1.93	258	.184	.273	0	—	0	9		94	0
2000	Bos A	3	0	1.000	34	0	0	0-3	40.2	34	15	3	0	28-6	63	3.90	114	.252	.319	1	.000	-0	3			0
2001	Bos A	6	4	.600	68	0	0	6-5	80.2	77	42	15	3	28-6	63	1.78	225	.197	.266	0		0	10			2
2003	SD N	3	2	.600	36	0	0	20-0	35.1	25	7	4	1	11-2	32	6.38	62	.278	.333	0		0	-7			-0
2004	SD N	0	2	.000	26	0	0		24	27	18	8	0	9-0	15	6.38	62	.278	.333	0		0	-7			-0
Total		38	45	.458	704	0	0	286-55	768	703	308	97	20	191-33	644	3.30	124	.242	.291	19-0-1	.211	0	70	183		10

BECK, BOOM-BOOM Walter William B10.16.1904 Decatur IL D5.7.1987 Champaign IL BR/TR/6-2/200 d9.22 C3

1924	StL A	0	0	—	1	0	0	0	1	2	0	0	1	0	0	0.00	—	.667	.750	0		0	0			-0
1927	StL A	1	0	1.000	3	1	1	0	11.1	15	8	0	1	5	6	5.56	78	.333	.412	4	.250	-0	153	-1		-0
1928	StL A	2	3	.400	16	4	2	0	49	52	29	4	4	20	17	4.41	95	.289	.373	14	.429	1	96	-2		-0
1933	Bro N	12	20	.375	43	35	15-3	1	257	270	128	9	11	69	89	3.54	91	.267	.321	95-0-2	.189	-0	111	-12		-1
1934	Bro N	2	6	.250	22	9	2	0	57	72	50	6	5	32	24	7.42	53	.301	.395	17-0-1	.235	1	118	-21		-1
1939	Phi N	7	14	.333	34	16	12	3	182.2	203	104	11	3	64	77	4.73	85	.284	.345	68-0-4	.132	-3	68	-13		-1
1940	Phi N	4	9	.308	29	15	4	0	129.1	147	69	13	9	41	38	4.31	90	.286	.349	36-0-3	.056	-3	58	-5		-C
1941	Phi N	1	9	.100	34	7	2	0	95.1	104	52	8	2	35	34	4.75	70	.325	.378	25-0-1	.120	-2	62	-8		-C
1942	Phi N	0	1	.000	26	1	0	0	53	69	30	4	1	17	10	9.88	34	.393	.456	4	.500	1	-9			-C
1943	Phi N	0	0	—	4	0	0	0	13.2	24	15	1	2	5	3	3.89	92	.243	.317	22-0-1	.318	2	105	-1		C
1944	Det A	1	2	.333	28	2	0	1	74	67	36	5	3	27	25	3.40	111	.236	.288	14-0-2	.214	-0	68	2		C
1945	Cin N	2	4	.333	11	6	2	1	47.2	42	21	0	1	12	9	2.14	184	.234	.278	16-0-5	.125	-1	94	12		-C
	Pit N	6	1	.857	14	5	4	0	63	54	19	2	0	14	20	2.68	144	.235	.282	30-0-7	.167	-1	81	13		-C
	Year	8	5	.615	25	11	6	1	110.2	96	40	2	1	26	29	4.30	86	.277	.340	327-0-19	.187	-2	89	-66		-C
Total	12	38	69	.355	265	101	44-3	6	1034	1121	561	63	42	342	352	4.30	86	.277	.340	327-0-19	.187	-2	89	-66		-C

BECKER, CHARLIE Charles Schlagel "Buck" B10.14.1890 Washington DC D7.30.1928 Washington DC BL/TL/6-2/180 d8.2

1911	Was A	3	5	.375	11	5	5-1	0	71.1	80	44	2	7	23	31	4.04	81	.268	.335	22-0-1	.227	-0	48	-5		-C
1912	Was A	0	0	—	4	0	0	0	9	8	6	0	0	6	5	3.00	111	.258	.378	2	.500	0	0			C
Total	2	3	5	.375	15	5	5-1	0	80.1	88	50	2	7	29	36	3.92	84	.267	.340	24-0-1	.250	-0	48	-5		-C

BECKER, BOB Robert Charles B8.15.1875 Syracuse NY D10.11.1951 Syracuse NY TL d9.6

1897	Phi N	0	2	.000	5	2	2	0	24	32	18	0	1	9	10	5.63	75	.317	.367	9	.111	-0	85	-3		-C
1898	Phi N	0	0	—	1	0	0	0	5	6	3	0	0	5	0	10.80	32	.300	.440	1	.000	-0	-3			-C
Total	2	0	2	.000	6	2	2	0	29	38	24	0	1	14	10	6.52	62	.314	.381	10	.100	-0	85	-6		-C

BECKETT, JOSH Joshua Patrick B5.15.1980 Spring TX BR/TR/6-4/190(190-220) [FlaN99 1/2] d9.4

2001	Fla N	2	2	.500	4	4	0	0-0	24	14	9	3	1	11-0	24	1.50	278	.161	.263	7-0-2	.286	1	116	5		-0
2002	Fla N	6	7	.462	23	21	0	0-0	107.2	93	56	9	4	44-2	113	4.10	96	.232	.307	31-0-5	.032	-3	109	-4	75	-0
2003	†Fla N	9	8	.529	24	23	0	0-0	142	132	54	9	2	56-4	152	3.04	135	.246	.319	46-0-5	.152	0	121	16	54	
2004	Fla N	9	9	.500	26	26	1-1	0-0	156.2	137	72	16	6	54-3	152	3.79	108	.235	.305	44-0-9	.159	0	88	5	58	
2005	Fla N	15	8	.652	29	29	2-1	0-0	178.2	153	75	14	7	58-2	166	3.38	118	.234	.303	59-1-4	.153	3	120	12	32	
Total	5	41	34	.547	106	103	3-2	0-0	609	529	266	55	17	223-11	607	3.46	117	.234	.306	187-1-25	.139	2	109	34	219	

BECKETT, ROBBIE Robert Joseph B7.16.1972 Austin TX BR/TL/6-5/235(225-240) [SDN90 1/25] d9.12

1996	Col N	0	0	—	5	0	0	0-1	5.1	8	6	3	0	9-0	6	13.50	39	.286	.484	0	—	0		-4		
1997	Col N	0	0	—	2	0	0	0-0	1.2	1	1	0	0	1-1	2	5.40	96	.167	.286	0	—	0		-4		
Total	2	0	0	—	7	0	0	0-1	7	7	9	3	0	10-1	8	11.57	45	.259	.447	0	—	0		-4		

BECKMAN, JIM James Joseph (b Reinhardt Boeckman) B3.1.1905 Cincinnati OH D12.5.1974 Montgomery OH BR/TR/5-10/172 d7.27

1927	Cin N	0	1	.000	4	1	0	0	12.1	18	10	2	1	6	0	5.84	65	.340	.417	1	.000	0	67	-3		-0
1928	Cin N	0	1	.000	6	0	0	0	15.1	19	12	1	0	9	4	5.87	65	.306	.394	3	.000	-0		-4		
Total	2	0	2	.000	10	1	0	0	27.2	37	22	3	1	15	4	5.86	66	.322	.405	4	.000	-0	67	-7		

BECKMANN, BILL William Aloysius B12.8.1907 Clayton MO D1.2.1990 Florissant MO BR/TR/6-0/175 d5.2 Col Washington-St. Louis

1939	Phi A	7	11	.389	27	19	7-2	0	155.1	198	104	15	1	41	20	5.39	87	.312	.355	52-0-6	.250	0	98	-9		
1940	Phi A	8	4	.667	34	9	6-2	1	127.1	132	68	11	1	35	47	4.17	107	.265	.314	39-0-3	.205	-1	81	5		
1941	Phi A	5	9	.357	22	15	4	0	130	141	76	11	2	33	28	4.57	92	.270	.315	47-0-4	.191	0	92	-6		
1942	Phi A	0	1	.000	5	1	0	0	20.1	24	17	1	0	9	10	7.08	53	.289	.359	4-0-1	.500	-0		3		
	StL N	1	0	1.000	2	0	0	0	7	4	0	0	0	1	3	0.00	—	.200	.238	1	.000	-0				
Total	4	21	25	.457	90	44	17-4	2	440	499	265	38	4	119	108	4.79	92	.284	.330	143-0-14	.224	1	94	-13		

BECKWITH, JOE Thomas Joseph B1.28.1955 Opelika AL BL/TR/6-3/200(185-200) [LAN77 2/46] d7.21 Col Auburn-Montgomery [DL 1981 LA N 180]

1979	LA N	1	2	.333	17	0	0	2-0	37.1	42	18	4	0	15-1	28	4.34	83	.284	.350	5-0-1	.000	-1		-2		
1980	LA N	3	3	.500	38	0	0	1-0	59.2	60	17	1	1	23-4	40	1.96	177	.263	.331	2	.000	-1	229	9		3
1982	LA N	2	1	.667	19	1	0	1-0	40	38	14	2	0	14-5	33	2.70	129	.252	.311	7-0-1	.000	0	49	-2		
1983	†LA N	3	4	.429	42	3	0	0	71	73	40	5	1	35-11	50	3.55	102	.264	.347	5	.200	-0	0	8		
1984	KC A	8	6	.667	49	1	0	2-1	100.2	92	39	13	2	25-1	75	3.40	119	.247	.293	0	—	0				
1985	†KC A	1	5	.167	49	0	0	1-2	95	99	45	9	3	32-8	80	4.07	103	.269	.350	0	—	0		-8		
1986	LA N	0	0	—	15	0	0	0-1	18.1	28	16	5	0	6-0	13	6.87	50	.350	.395	0	—	0	71	11	180	
Total	7	18	19	.486	229	5	0	7-4	422	432	189	39	7	150-30	319	3.54	107	.266	.328	19-0-2	.053	-1	71	11	180	

YEAR	TM LG	W	L	PCT	G	GS	CG-SHO	SV-BS	IP	H	R	HR	HB	BB-IB	SO	ERA	AERA	OAV	OOB	AB-HR-SH	AVG	PB	SUP	APR	DL	PW

BEDARD, ERIK Erik Joseph B3.5.1979 Navan ON, Can. BL/TL/6-1/180(180-195) [BalA99 6/187] d4.17 Col Norwalk (CT) CC [DL 2003 Bal A 183]

2002	Bal A	0	0	—	2	1	0	0-0	0.2	1	2	1	0	0	1	13.50	32	.500	.500	0	—	0	-1			0.0
2004	Bal A	6	10	.375	27	26	0	0-0	137.1	149	83	13	7	71-1	121	4.59	102	.270	.359	4	.000	-0	105	-2			-0.2
2005	Bal A	6	8	.429	24	24	0	0-0	141.2	139	66	10	5	57-1	125	4.00	111	.260	.333	0	—	-0	84	8	57	0.8
Total	3	12	18	.400	53	50	0	0-0	279.2	290	150	23	12	128-2	247	4.31	105	.266	.347	4	.000	-0	95	5	240	0.6

BEDGOOD, PHIL Phillip Burlette B3.8.1898 Harrison GA D11.8.1927 Fort Pierce FL BR/TR/6-3/218 d9.20

1922	Cle A	1	0	1.000	1	1	1	0	9	7	4	0	3	4	5	4.00	100	.233	.378	2-0-1	.000	-0	106	0			0.0
1923	Cle A	0	2	.000	9	2	0	0	18.2	16	13	0	2	14	7	5.30	75	.246	.395	4	.250	0	167	-3			-0.2
Total	2	1	2	.333	10	3	1	0	27.2	23	17	0	5	18	12	4.88	82	.242	.390	6-0-1	.167	0	147	-3			-0.2

BEDIENT, HUGH Hugh Carpenter B10.23.1889 Gerry NY D7.21.1965 Jamestown NY BR/TR/6-0/185 d4.26

1912	†Bos A	20	9	.690	41	28	19	2	231	206	93	6	3	55	122	2.92	116	.240	.288	73-0-6	.192	1	102	14			1.7
1913	Bos A	15	14	.517	43	28	15-1	5	259	255	104	6	6	67	122	2.78	106	.263	.314	80-0-5	.125	-3	80	7			0.2
1914	Bos A	8	12	.400	42	16	7-1	2	177.1	187	97	4	5	45	70	3.60	75	.281	.331	50-0-1	.100	-2	129	-19			-2.3
1915	Buf F	16	18	.471	53	30	16-2	10	269.1	284	131	5	3	69	106	3.17	88	.274	.321	83-0-5	.108	-5	92	-16			-2.7
Total	4	59	53	.527	179	102	57-4	19	936.2	932	425	15	17	236	420	3.08	96	.264	.313	286-0-17	.133	-9	98	-14			-3.1

BEDNAR, ANDY Andrew Jackson B8.16.1908 Streator IL D11.26.1937 Graham TX BR/TR/5-10.5/180 d9.6

1930	Pit N	0	0	—	2	0	0	0	1.1	4	4	0	0	1	1	27.00	18	.500	.556	0	—	0		-3			-0.1
1931	Pit N	0	0	—	3	0	0	0	4	10	5	1	0	0	2	11.25	34	.476	.476	0	—	0		-3			-0.1
Total	2	0	0	—	5	0	0	0	5.1	14	9	1	0	1	3	15.19	27	.483	.500	0	—	0		-6			-0.2

BEDROSIAN, STEVE Stephen Wayne B12.6.1957 Methuen MA BR/TR/6-3/200* [AtlN78 3/53] d8.14 Col New Haven

1981	Atl N	1	2	.333	15	1	0	0-1	24.1	15	14	2	1	15-2	9	4.44	79	.169	.292	2	.000	-0	101	-3			-0.4
1982	†Atl N	8	6	.571	64	3	0	11-6	137.2	102	39	7	4	57-5	123	2.42	152	.206	.292	26-0-4	.038	-2	80	20			2.1
1983	Atl N	9	10	.474	70	1	0	19-7	120	100	50	11	4	51-8	114	3.60	107	.229	.313	19-0-1	.105	-1	69	4			0.7
1984	Atl N	9	6	.600	40	4	0	11-2	83.2	65	23	5	1	33-5	81	2.37	163	.210	.288	17-0-1	.118	-1	109	14	15	2.6
1985	Atl N	7	15	.318	37	37	0	0-0	206.2	198	101	17	5	111-6	134	3.83	101	.254	.349	64-0-6	.078	-4	86	0			-0.5
1986	Phi N	8	6	.571	68	0	0	29-9	90.1	79	39	2	0	34-10	82	3.39	115	.232	.299	5	.200		0	5			1.0
1987	Phi N★	5	3	.625	65	0	0	40-8	89	79	31	11	1	28-5	74	2.83	152	.237	.297	4	.000	-0	0	14			2.1
1988	Phi N	6	6	.500	57	0	0	28-6	74.1	75	34	6	0	27-5	61	3.75	96	.257	.317	2	.000	-0		-1	46		-0.2
1989	Phi N	2	3	.400	28	0	0	6-3	33.2	21	13	7	1	17-1	24	3.21	112	.183	.289	0	—	0		2			0.3
	†SF N	1	4	.200	40	0	0	17-5	51	35	18	5	0	22-4	34	2.65	128	.192	.277	6	.167	-0		4			0.5
	Year	3	7	.300	68	0	0	23-8	84.2	56	31	12	1	39-5	58	2.87	121	.189	.282	6	.167	-0		5			0.8
1990	SF N	9	9	.500	68	0	0	17-5	79.1	72	40	6	2	44-9	43	4.20	87	.241	.341	4	.500	1		-5			-0.9
1991	†Min A	5	3	.625	56	0	0	6-1	77.1	70	42	11	3	35-6	44	4.42	97	.243	.327	0	—	0		-1			-0.2
1993	Atl N	5	2	.714	49	0	0	0-0	49.2	34	11	4	2	14-2	33	1.63	248	.194	.256	2	.000	-0		-13			1.6
1994	Atl N	0	2	.000	46	0	0	0-2	46	41	20	4	2	18-5	43	3.33	130	.243	.319	2	.500	0		4			0.2
1995	Atl N	1	2	.333	29	0	0	0-2	28	40	21	6	1	12-2	22	6.11	71	.354	.414	0	—	0		-5			-0.5
Total	14	76	79	.490	732	46	0	184-57	1191	1026	496	114	27	518-75	921	3.38	115	.232	.314	153-0-12	.098	-7	87	65	61	8.4

BEEBE, FRED Frederick Leonard B12.31.1880 Lincoln NE D10.30.1957 Elgin IL BR/TR/6-1/190 d4.17 Col Illinois

1906	Chi N	6	1	.857	14	6	4	1	70	56	27	1	5	32	55	2.70	98	.210	.306	29	.103	-1	170	0			-0.2
	StL N	9	9	.500	20	19	16-1	0	160.2	115	65	1	9	68	116	3.02	87	.208	.305	58-0-3	.172	0	88	-5			-0.5
	Year	15	10	.600	34	25	20-1	1	230.2	171	92	2	14	100	171	2.93	90	.209	.305	87-0-3	.149	-1	107	-5			-0.7
1907	StL N	5	13	.278	29	19	12	0	238.1	192	95	1	10	109	141	2.72	92	.230	.326	86-0-3	.128	-3	62	-2			-0.5
1908	StL N	15	21	.417	44	34	18-1	1	287.2	256	142	5	7	104	105	2.82	90	.229	.299	108-0-3	.167	-2	114	-16			-2.1
1909	Cin N	12	14	.462	35	26	11-2	1	214.1	193	101	3	7	94	93	3.07	95	.246	.333	73-0-1	.164	-2	89	-2			-0.4
1911	Phi N	3	3	.500	9	8	3	0	48.1	52	26	2	3	24	20	4.47	77	.297	.391	19	.263	2*	104	-3			-0.1
1916	Cle A	5	3	.625	20	12	5-1	2	100.2	92	43	1	1	37	32	2.41	125	.251	.325	28-0-3	.214	1	88	4			0.3
Total	7	62	83	.428	202	153	93-9	4	1294.1	1090	587	17	46	534	634	2.86	93	.227	.311	457-0-16	.158	-8	93	-32			-4.5

BEECH, MATT Lucas Matthew B1.20.1972 Oakland CA BL/TL/6-2/190(190-205) [PhiN94 7/198] d8.8 Col Houston [DL 1999 Phi N 176]

1996	Phi N	1	4	.200	8	8	0	0-0	41.1	49	32	8	3	11-0	33	6.97	62	.306	.350	14	.071	-1	94	-10			-1.1
1997	Phi N	4	9	.308	24	24	0	0-0	136.2	147	81	25	5	57-9	120	5.07	83	.279	.351	30-0-11	.167	-0	94	-11	16	-0.9
1998	Phi N	3	9	.250	21	21	0	0-0	117	126	78	19	4	63-2	113	5.15	84	.275	.366	33-0-6	.152	-1	83	-13	49	-1.3
Total	3	8	22	.267	53	53	0	0-0	295	322	191	52	12	131-11	266	5.37	80	.281	.357	77-0-17	.143	-2	90	-34	241	-3.3

BEECHER, ROY Leroy "Colonel" B5.10.1884 Swanton OH D10.11.1952 Toledo OH BL/TR/6-2/180 d9.29

1907	NY N	0	2	.000	2	2	2	1	14	17	8	0	0	6	5	2.57	96	.293	.359	5	.000	-1	43	-1			-0.2
1908	NY N	0	0	—	2	0	0	1	5.2	11	5	0	0	3	5	7.94	30	.440	.500	3	.333	1*		-3			-0.1
Total	2	0	2	.000	4	2	2	1	19.2	28	13	0	0	9	10	4.12	60	.337	.402	8	.125	-0	43	-4			-0.3

BEENE, FRED Freddy Ray B11.24.1942 Angleton TX BB/TR/5-9/160* d9.18 Col Sam Houston St.

1968	Bal A	0	0	—	1	0	0	1	2	1	1	0	0	1-0	1	9.00	33	.500	.500	0	—	0		-1			0.0
1969	Bal A	0	0	—	2	0	0	0-0	2.2	2	0	0	0	1-0	0	0.00	—	.200	.273	0	—	0		1			0.1
1970	Bal A	0	0	—	4	0	0	0-0	6	8	5	1	0	5-4	4	6.00	61	.320	.433	0	—	0		-2			-0.1
1972	NY A	1	3	.250	29	1	0	3-0	57.2	55	21	3	1	24-5	37	2.34	128	.256	.332	1	—	-1*	533	-2			1.4
1973	NY A	6	0	1.000	19	4	0	1-0	91	67	21	5	1	27-5	49	1.68	221	.209	.271	0	.000	0	108	21			1.4
1974	NY A	0	0	—	6	0	0	1-0	10	9	4	1	1	2-0	10	2.70	131	.231	.286	0	—	0		1			0.1
	Cle A	4	4	.500	32	0	0	2-3	73	68	44	7	1	26-2	35	4.93	74	.246	.310	0	—	0*		-10			-1.0
	Year	4	4	.500	38	0	0	3-3	83	77	48	8	2	28-2	45	4.66	78	.244	.307	0	—	0		-10			-0.9
1975	Cle A	1	0	1.000	19	1	0	1-1	46.2	63	42	4	3	25-3	20	6.94	55	.323	.406	0	—	0*	254	-16	62	-0.8
Total	7	12	7	.632	112	6	0	8-4	288	274	138	21	7	111-19	156	3.63	98	.253	.324	9	.000	-1	195	-4	62	-0.2

BEENE, ANDY Ramon Andrew B10.13.1956 Freeport TX BR/TR/6-3/205* [MilA79 5/127] d9.22 Col Baylor

1983	Mil A	0	0	—	1	0	0	0-0	2	3	3	0	0	1-1	0	4.50	84	.333	.400	0	—	0		-1			-0.1
1984	Mil A	0	2	.000	5	3	0	0-0	18.2	28	23	1	2	9-0	11	11.09	35	.350	.424	0	—	0	101	-14			-1.2
Total	2	0	2	.000	6	3	0	0-0	20.2	31	26	1	2	10-1	11	10.45	37	.348	.422	0	—	0	101	-15			-1.3

BEERS, CLARENCE Clarence Scott B12.9.1918 ElDorado KS D12.6.2002 Tucson AZ BR/TR/6-0/175 d5.2

| 1948 | StL N | 0 | 0 | — | 1 | 0 | 0 | 0 | 0.2 | 3 | 1 | 0 | 0 | 0 | 0 | 13.50 | 30 | .500 | .571 | 0 | — | 0 | | -2 | | | -0.1 |

BEGGS, JOE Joseph Stanley "Fireman" B11.4.1910 Rankin PA D7.19.1983 Indianapolis IN BR/TR/6-1/182 d4.19 Mil 1944-45 Col Geneva

1938	NY A	3	2	.600	14	9	4	0	58.1	69	41	7	0	20	8	5.40	84	.299	.355	20	.250	1	95	-6			-0.3
1940	†Cin N	12	3	.800	37	1	0	7	76.2	68	19	1	1	21	25	2.00	190	.243	.298	21-0-1	.190	-0	275	15			3.2
1941	Cin N	4	3	.571	37	0	0	0	57	57	29	2	0	27	19	3.79	95	.313	.402	10	.300	1		-2			-0.2
1942	Cin N	6	5	.545	38	0	0	8	88.2	65	28	4	1	33	24	2.13	154	.206	.283	21-0-1	.000	-3		11			1.4
1943	Cin N	7	5	.538	39	4	4-2	6	115.1	121	38	0	0	25	28	2.34	142	.276	.315	35-0-2	.143	-1	58	11			1.2
1944	Cin N	1	0	1.000	1	1	1	0	9	8	2	0	0	4	2	2.00	174	.222	.222	4	.000	-1	96	2			0.1
1946	Cin N	12	10	.545	28	22	14-2	1	190	175	63	15	1	39	38	2.32	144	.247	.287	63-0-7	.222	2	97	20			2.6
1947	Cin N	0	3	.000	11	4	0	0	32.1	42	26	4	1	13	6	5.29	78	.316	.345	11-0-1	.091	-1	118	-6			-0.6
	NY N	3	3	.500	32	0	0	2	66	81	38	6	1	18	11	5.29	78	.316	.345	13-0-2	.077	-1		-2			-0.3
	Year	3	6	.333	43	4	0	2	98.1	123	64	10	1	24	34	4.58	89	.305	.346	24-0-3	.083	-2	119	-9			-0.9
1948	NY N	0	0	—	1	0	0	0	0.1	2	0	0	0	0	0	0.00	—	.667	.667	0	—	0		0			0.0
Total	9	48	35	.578	238	41	23-4	29	693.2	688	284	39	4	189	178	2.96	122	.265	.316	198-0-14	.167	-3	101	43			7.1

BEGLEY, ED Edward N. (b Edward N. Bagley) B10.1863 New York NY D7.24.1919 Waterbury CT d5.3

1884	NY N	12	18	.400	31	30	30	0	266	296	209	9		99	104	4.16	72	.263	.323	121	.182	-3*	93	-33			-3.2
1885	NY AA	4	9	.308	15	14	10	0	115	131	102	5	8	48	44	4.93	63	.278	.355	52-1	.173	-3	91	-25			-2.1
Total	2	16	27	.372	46	44	40	0	381	427	311	14	8	147	148	4.39	69	.268	.333	173-1	.179	-3	92	-58			-5.3

BEHAN, PETIE Charles Frederick B12.11.1887 Dallas City PA D1.22.1957 Bradford PA BR/TR/5-10/160 d9.16

| 1921 | Phi N | 0 | 1 | .000 | 7 | 2 | 0 | 0 | 10.2 | 17 | 8 | 0 | 1 | 9 | 3 | 5.91 | 72 | .354 | .367 | 4 | .000 | -1 | 68 | -1 | | | -0.2 |
| 1922 | Phi N | 4 | 2 | .667 | 7 | 5 | 3-1 | 0 | 47.1 | 49 | 27 | 3 | 1 | 14 | 13 | 2.47 | 189 | .259 | .314 | 20 | .250 | -0 | 112 | 7 | | | 0.7 |

YEAR	TM LG	W	L	PCT	G	GS	CG-SHO	SV-BS	IP	H	R	HR	HB	BB-IB	SO	ERA	AERA	OAV	OOB	AB-HR-SH	AVG	PB	SUP	APR	DL	PV
1923	Phi N	3	12	.200	31	17	5	2	131	182	102	11	1	57	27	5.50	84	.336	.401	43-0-4	.186	-2*	88	-13		-1.
Total	3	7	15	.318	40	24	9-1	2	189	248	137	14	2	72	43	4.76	97	.319	.378	67-0-4	.194	-3	91	-7		-1.

BEHENNA, RICK Richard Kipp B3.6.1960 Miami FL BR/TR/6-2/170* [AtlN78 4/79] d4.12

YEAR	TM LG	W	L	PCT	G	GS	CG-SHO	SV-BS	IP	H	R	HR	HB	BB-IB	SO	ERA	AERA	OAV	OOB	AB-HR-SH	AVG	PB	SUP	APR	DL	PV
1983	Atl N	3	3	.500	14	6	0	0-0	37.1	37	20	7	1	12-2	17	4.58	84	.255	.314	12-1-0	.333	2	91	-2		-0.
	Cle A	0	2	.000	5	4	0	0-0	26	22	13	0	1	14-1	9	4.15	103	.232	.336	0	—	0	69	0		0.
1984	Cle A	0	3	.000	3	3	0	0-0	9.2	17	15	5	1	8-0	6	13.97	30	.386	.491	0	—	0	37	-10	139	-1.
1985	Cle A	0	2	.000	4	4	0	0-0	19.2	29	17	3	0	8-0	4	7.78	54	.354	.407	0	—	0	93	-7	139	-0.
Total	3	3	10	.231	26	17	0	0-0	92.2	105	65	15	3	42-3	36	6.12	67	.287	.363	12-1-0	.333	2	77	-19	278	-2.

BEHNEY, MEL Melvin Brian B9.2.1947 Newark NJ BL/TL/6-2/180 [CinN68 S1/5] d8.14 Mil 1970 Col Michigan St.

YEAR	TM LG	W	L	PCT	G	GS	CG-SHO	SV-BS	IP	H	R	HR	HB	BB-IB	SO	ERA	AERA	OAV	OOB	AB-HR-SH	AVG	PB	SUP	APR	DL	PV
1970	Cin N	0	2	.000	5	1	0	0-0	10	15	11	1	0	8-2	2	4.50	90	.341	.442	1	.000	-0	89	-3		-0.

BEHRMAN, HANK Henry Bernard B6.27.1921 Brooklyn NY D1.20.1987 New York NY BR/TR/5-11/174 d4.17

YEAR	TM LG	W	L	PCT	G	GS	CG-SHO	SV-BS	IP	H	R	HR	HB	BB-IB	SO	ERA	AERA	OAV	OOB	AB-HR-SH	AVG	PB	SUP	APR	DL	PV
1946	Bro N	11	5	.688	47	11	2	4	150.2	138	63	3	2	69	78	2.93	115	.241	.325	42-0-4	.095	-3	134	6		0.
1947	†Bro N	0	0	—	2	0	0	0	3.2	3	4	1	0	4	2	9.82	42	.231	.412	0	—	0		-2		-0.
	Pit N	0	2	.000	10	2	0	0	24.2	33	26	6	2	17	11	9.12	46	.347	.456	6-0-1	.000	-1	125	-12		-1.
	†Bro N	5	3	.625	38	6	0	8	88.1	94	60	9	0	44	31	5.30	78	.274	.357	26-0-4	.231	1	164	-11		-1.
	Year	5	5	.500	50	8	0	8	116.2	130	90	16	2	65	44	6.25	66	.288	.380	32-0-5	.188	-0	154	-26		-2.
1948	Bro N	5	4	.556	34	4	2-1	7	91	95	51	7	3	42	42	4.05	99	.268	.350	28-0-4	.107	-2	128	-2		-0
1949	NY N	3	3	.500	43	4	1-1	0	71.1	64	46	5	0	52	25	4.92	81	.239	.363	13	.077	-1	100	-7		-2
Total	4	24	17	.585	174	27	5-2	19	429.2	427	250	31	7	228	189	4.40	87	.259	.352	115-0-13	.122	-5	133	-28		-2

BEIMEL, JOE Joseph Ronald B4.19.1977 St.Marys PA BL/TL/6-3/205* [PitN98 18/538] d4.8 Col Duquesne

YEAR	TM LG	W	L	PCT	G	GS	CG-SHO	SV-BS	IP	H	R	HR	HB	BB-IB	SO	ERA	AERA	OAV	OOB	AB-HR-SH	AVG	PB	SUP	APR	DL	PV
2001	Pit N	7	11	.389	42	15	0	0-0	115.1	131	72	12	6	49-4	58	5.23	86	.290	.366	26-0-4	.269	1	88	-9		-1
2002	Pit N	2	5	.286	53	8	0	0-1	85.1	88	49	9	4	45-12	53	4.64	90	.267	.359	10-0-2	.300	1	110	-4		-0
2003	Pit N	1	3	.250	69	0	0	0-5	62.1	69	35	7	4	33-6	42	5.05	86	.299	.388	5	.000	-1*		-4		-0.
2004	Min A	0	0	—	3	0	0	0-0	1.2	8	8	1	0	2-0	2	43.20	11	.615	.667	0	—	0		-7		-0.
2005	TB A	0	0	—	7	0	0	0-0	11	15	4	1	0	4-1	3	3.27	133	.319	.373	0	—	0		2		0
Total	5	10	19	.345	174	23	0	0-6	275.2	311	168	30	14	133-23	158	5.16	84	.290	.373	41-0-6	.244	2	97	-22		-0

BEIRNE, KEVIN Kevin Patrick B1.1.1974 Houston TX BL/TR/6-4/210* [ChiA95 11/308] d5.17 Col Texas A&M-Commerce

YEAR	TM LG	W	L	PCT	G	GS	CG-SHO	SV-BS	IP	H	R	HR	HB	BB-IB	SO	ERA	AERA	OAV	OOB	AB-HR-SH	AVG	PB	SUP	APR	DL	PV
2000	Chi A	1	3	.250	29	1	0	0-1	49.2	50	41	9	4	20-1	41	6.70	75	.263	.338	0	—	0	56	-9		-0
2001	Tor A	0	0	—	5	0	0	0-0	7	13	10	1	0	6-1	5	12.86	36	.394	.487	0	—	0		-6		-0
2002	LA N	2	0	1.000	12	3	0	0-1	29	26	11	4	2	17-2	17	3.41	114	.245	.357	5-0-1	.400	1	174	2		-0
Total	3	3	3	.500	46	4	0	0-2	85.2	89	62	14	6	43-4	63	6.09	76	.271	.359	5-0-1	.400	1	126	-13		-0

BELCHER, TIM Timothy Wayne B10.19.1961 Mount Gilead OH BR/TR/6-3/220(210-235) [NYA84*S1/1] d9.6 Col Mount Vernon Nazarene

YEAR	TM LG	W	L	PCT	G	GS	CG-SHO	SV-BS	IP	H	R	HR	HB	BB-IB	SO	ERA	AERA	OAV	OOB	AB-HR-SH	AVG	PB	SUP	APR	DL	PV
1987	LA N	4	2	.667	6	5	0	0-0	34	30	11	2	0	7-0	23	2.38	167	.240	.278	10	.200	0	64	6		1
1988	†LA N	12	6	.667	36	27	4-1	4	179.2	143	65	8	2	51-7	152	2.91	115	.217	.275	56-1-5	.071	-2	110	9		1
1989	LA N	15	12	.556	39	30	**10-8**	1-0	230	182	81	20	7	80-5	200	2.82	122	.217	.289	70-0-10	.100	-2	92	16		1
1990	LA N	9	9	.500	24	24	5-2	0-0	153	136	76	17	2	48-0	102	4.00	92	.240	.299	43-0-9	.163	1	93	-5	48	-0
1991	LA N	10	9	.526	33	33	2-1	0-0	209.1	189	76	10	2	75-3	156	2.62	138	.240	.306	67-0-7	.119	-2	93	20		1
1992	Cin N	15	14	.517	35	34	2-1	0-0	227.2	201	104	17	3	80-2	149	3.91	92	.238	.303	76-1-7	.105	-2	118	-6		-1
1993	Cin N	9	6	.600	22	22	4-2	0-0	137	134	72	11	7	47-4	101	4.47	90	.254	.322	50-0-3	.200	1	77	0		-C
	†Chi A	3	5	.375	12	11	1-1	0-0	71.2	64	36	8	1	27-0	34	4.40	96	.242	.313	0	—	0	103	-20		-2
1994	Det A	7	15	.318	25	25	3	0-0	162	192	124	21	4	78-10	76	5.89	84	.300	.367	0	—	0	92	4		-C
1995	†Sea A	10	12	.455	28	28	1	0-0	179.1	188	101	19	5	88-5	96	4.52	106	.269	.352	0	—	0	92	27		2
1996	KC A	15	11	.577	35	35	4-1	0-0	238.2	262	117	28	6	68-4	113	3.92	128	.281	.331	6	.000	-1	109	-6		2
1997	KC A	13	12	.520	32	32	3-1	0-0	213.1	242	128	31	5	70-2	130	5.02	95	.288	.345	6	.000	0	92	12		-C
1998	KC A	14	14	.500	34	34	2	0-0	234	247	127	37	7	73-0	130	4.27	114	.272	.328	5-0-1	.200	0	95	-25	41	-0
1999	Ana A	6	8	.429	24	24	0	0-0	132.1	168	104	27	5	46-0	52	6.73	73	.315	.369	5	.200	0	87	-6	139	-0
2000	Ana A	4	5	.444	9	9	1	0-0	40.2	45	31	8	2	22-1	22	6.86	75	.281	.373	0	—	0	98	20	228	C
Total	14	146	140	.510	394	373	42-18	5-1	2442.2	2423	1253	264	58	860-43	1519	4.16	102	.259	.323	388-2-42	.124	-6	98	20	228	C

BELINDA, STAN Stanley Peter B8.6.1966 Huntingdon PA BR/TR/6-3/187(187-215) [PitN86 10/238] d9.8 Col Allegany (MD) CC

YEAR	TM LG	W	L	PCT	G	GS	CG-SHO	SV-BS	IP	H	R	HR	HB	BB-IB	SO	ERA	AERA	OAV	OOB	AB-HR-SH	AVG	PB	SUP	APR	DL	PV
1989	Pit N	0	1	.000	8	0	0	0-0	10.1	13	8	0	0	2-0	10	6.10	56	.295	.326	0	—	0		-3		-C
1990	†Pit N	3	4	.429	55	0	0	8-5	58.1	48	23	4	1	29-3	55	3.55	103	.227	.321	5-0-1	.000	-1		2		-C
1991	†Pit N	7	5	.583	60	0	0	16-4	78.1	50	30	10	4	35-4	71	3.45	104	.184	.283	7-0-2	.000	-0		3		C
1992	†Pit N	6	4	.600	59	0	0	18-6	71.1	58	26	8	0	29-5	57	3.61	113	.224	.276	1	.000	-0		2		C
1993	Pit N	3	1	.750	40	0	0	19-3	42.1	35	18	4	1	11-4	30	4.28	108	.280	.325	0	—	0		1		C
	KC A	1	1	.500	23	0	0	0-1	27.1	30	13	2	1	6-0	25	5.14	98	.250	.345	0	—	0		-3		C
1994	KC A	2	2	.500	37	0	0	1-1	49	47	36	6	5	24-3	37	5.14	98	.250	.345	0	—	0	14	11		C
1995	†Bos A	8	1	.889	63	0	0	10-4	69.2	51	25	5	4	28-3	57	3.10	157	.205	.291	0	—	0	14	113		C
1996	Bos A	2	1	.667	31	0	0	2-2	28.2	31	22	9	4	20-1	18	6.59	77	.272	.399	0	—	0	7			C
1997	Cin N	1	5	.167	84	0	0	1-4	99.1	84	42	11*	9	33-6	114	3.71	115	.229	.304	1	.333	0	7	85		C
1998	Cin N	4	8	.333	40	0	0	1-1	61.1	46	23	7	1	28-6	40	3.23	133	.212	.304	4	.250	-0	-2	81		C
1999	Cin N	3	1	.750	29	0	0	2-0	42.2	42	26	11	1	18-3	40	5.27	89	.258	.333	4	.000	-0*	-5			C
2000	Col N	1	3	.250	46	0	0	1-6	35.2	39	32	9	1	17-4	40	7.07	82	.277	.358	1	.000	0	-6			C
	Atl N	0	0	—	10	0	0	0-0	11	16	12	4	1	5-1	11	9.82	46	.348	.407	0	—	0	-10			C
	Year	1	3	.250	56	0	0	1-6	46.2	55	44	13	2	22-5	51	7.71	71	.294	.370	1	.000	0	16	290		C
Total	12	41	37	.526	585	0	0	79-37	685.1	590	336	85	34	285-43	622	4.15	103	.233	.315	25-0-3	.160	1	16	290		C

BELINSKY, BO Robert B12.7.1936 New York NY D11.23.2001 Las Vegas NV BL/TL/6-2/191* d4.18

YEAR	TM LG	W	L	PCT	G	GS	CG-SHO	SV-BS	IP	H	R	HR	HB	BB-IB	SO	ERA	AERA	OAV	OOB	AB-HR-SH	AVG	PB	SUP	APR	DL	PV
1962	LA A	10	11	.476	33	31	5-3	1	187.1	149	86	12	13	122-3	145	3.56	109	.216	.343	60-0-2	.167	1*	81	7		1
1963	LA A	2	9	.182	13	13	2	0	76.2	78	54	12	4	35-2	60	5.75	60	.262	.345	27	.074	-2	88	-20		-1
1964	LA A	9	8	.529	23	22	4-1	0	135.1	120	45	8	6	49-5	91	2.86	115	.240	.314	42-0-5	.095	-1	95	10		-C
1965	Phi N	4	9	.308	30	14	3	1	109.2	103	72	13	6	48-5	71	4.84	71	.248	.331	32-0-1	.188	1*	105	-19		-C
1966	Phi N	0	2	.000	9	1	0	0	15.1	14	5	3	1	5-1	8	2.93	123	.250	.344	3	.333	0	147	1		-C
1967	Hou N	3	9	.250	27	18	0	0	115.1	112	74	12	8	54-0	80	4.68	71	.255	.345	39-0-1	.077	-2	103	-20		-C
1969	Pit N	0	3	.000	8	3	0	0-0	17.2	17	10	1	2	14-2	15	4.58	76	.266	.412	2	.000	-0	42	-2		-C
1970	Cin N	0	0	—	3	0	0	0-0	8	10	6	0	0	6-0	6	4.50	90	.294	.400	1	1.000	1		-1		-C
Total	8	28	51	.354	146	102	14-4	2-0	665.1	603	352	61	42	333-18	476	4.10	86	.241	.339	206-0-9	.131	-2	91	-44		C

BELISLE, MATT Matthew Thomas B6.6.1980 Austin TX BR/TR/6-3/190* [AtlN98 2/52] d9.7

YEAR	TM LG	W	L	PCT	G	GS	CG-SHO	SV-BS	IP	H	R	HR	HB	BB-IB	SO	ERA	AERA	OAV	OOB	AB-HR-SH	AVG	PB	SUP	APR	DL	PV
2003	Cin N	1	1	.500	6	0	0	0-1	8.2	10	5	1	1	2-0	6	5.19	80	.303	.351	1	.000	-0		-1		C
2005	Cin N	4	8	.333	60	5	0	1-3	85.2	101	49	11	6	26-6	59	4.41	95	.294	.352	7-0-1	.143	-0*	134	-4		C
Total	2	5	9	.357	66	5	0	1-4	94.1	111	54	12	7	28-6	65	4.48	93	.294	.352	8-0-1	.125	-0	134	-5		C

BELITZ, TODD Todd Stephen B10.23.1975 Des Moines IA BL/TL/6-1/200(200-220) [TBA97 4/144] d9.4 Col Washington St.

YEAR	TM LG	W	L	PCT	G	GS	CG-SHO	SV-BS	IP	H	R	HR	HB	BB-IB	SO	ERA	AERA	OAV	OOB	AB-HR-SH	AVG	PB	SUP	APR	DL	PV
2000	Oak A	0	0	—	5	0	0	0-0	3.1	4	2	0	0	4-0	3	2.70	148	.308	.421	0	—	0		0		C
2001	Col N	1	1	.500	8	0	0	0-0	9.1	9	8	2	0	3-0	5	7.71	69	.250	.308	1	.000	-0		-2		C
Total	2	1	1	.500	13	0	0	0-0	12.2	13	10	2	0	7-0	8	6.39	82	.255	.345	1	.000	-0		-2		C

BELL, CHARLIE Charles C. B8.12.1868 Cincinnati OH D2.7.1937 Cincinnati OH TR d10.13 b-Frank

YEAR	TM LG	W	L	PCT	G	GS	CG-SHO	SV-BS	IP	H	R	HR	HB	BB-IB	SO	ERA	AERA	OAV	OOB	AB-HR-SH	AVG	PB	SUP	APR	DL	PV
1889	KC AA	1	0	1.000	1	1	1	0	9	4	5	0	1	3	3	1.00	425	.129	.229	6	.167	0*	87	2		
1891	Lou AA	2	6	.250	10	9	8	0	77	93	65	4	8	20	16	4.68	78	.289	.346	28	.036	-2	64	-10		
	Cin AA	1	0	1.000	1	1	1	0	9	2	2	0	1	3	1	1.00	—	.069	.182	4	.500	0	121	3		
	Year	3	6	.333	11	10	9	0	86	95	67	4	9	23	17	4.19	88	.271	.332	32	.094	-2	70	-4		
Total	2	4	6	.400	12	11	10	0	95	99	72	4	10	26	20	3.88	97	.259	.323	38	.105	-2	72	-5		

BELL, ERIC Eric Alvin B10.27.1963 Modesto CA BL/TL/6-0/165* [BalA82 9/234] d9.24

YEAR	TM LG	W	L	PCT	G	GS	CG-SHO	SV-BS	IP	H	R	HR	HB	BB-IB	SO	ERA	AERA	OAV	OOB	AB-HR-SH	AVG	PB	SUP	APR	DL	PV
1985	Bal A	0	0	—	4	0	0	0-0	5.2	4	3	1	0	4-0	4	4.76	85	.200	.333			0		0		
1986	Bal A	1	2	.333	4	4	0	0-0	23.1	23	14	4	0	14-0	18	5.01	83	.258	.356			0	93	-2		
1987	Bal A	10	13	.435	33	29	2	0-0	165	174	113	32	2	78-0	111	5.45	81	.271	.365			0	86	-20		
1991	Cle A	4	0	1.000	10	0	0	0-0	18	15	1	1	1	9-0	10	0.50	835	.091	.180			0	23	-6		
1992	Cle A	0	2	.000	7	1	0	0-0	15.1	22	13	1	1	9-0	7	7.63	52	.349	.432			0				

YEAR	TM LG	W	L	PCT	G	GS	CG-SHO	SV-BS	IP	H	R	HR	HB	BB-IB	SO	ERA	AERA	OAV	OOB	AB-HR-SH	AVG	PB	SUP	APR	DL	PW
1993	Hou N	0	1	.000	10	0	0	0-0	7.1	10	5	0	0	2-0	2	6.14	63	.313	.353	0	—	0		-2		-0.2
Total 6		15	18	.455	68	34	2	0-0	234.2	238	150	38	4	112-0	152	5.18	84	.264	.346	0	—	0	86	-23		-2.0

BELL, GARY — Gary B11.17.1936 San Antonio TX BR/TR/6-1/198* d6.1 Col San Antonio (TX) JC

YEAR	TM LG	W	L	PCT	G	GS	CG-SHO	SV-BS	IP	H	R	HR	HB	BB-IB	SO	ERA	AERA	OAV	OOB	AB-HR-SH	AVG	PB	SUP	APR	DL	PW
1958	Cle A	12	10	.545	33	23	10	1	182	141	70	18	5	73-0	110	3.31	110	.213	.294	56-0-5	.196	2	112	9		1.1
1959	Cle A	16	11	.593	44	28	12-1	5	234	208	107	28	5	105-4	136	4.04	91	.238	.321	75-0-8	.240	3	113	-5		-0.3
1960	Cle A★	9	10	.474	28	23	6-2	1	154.2	139	78	15	7	82-2	109	4.13	90	.242	.340	47-0-8	.149	-0*	94	-6		-0.6
1961	Cle A	12	16	.429	34	34	11-2	0	228.1	214	125	32	6	100-2	163	4.10	96	.245	.324	81-0-9	.198	1	116	-8		-0.8
1962	Cle A	10	9	.526	57	6	1	12	107.2	104	56	14	3	52-8	80	4.26	91	.264	.349	24	.208	1	100	-4		-0.7
1963	Cle A	8	5	.615	58	7	0	5	119	91	48	13	4	52-10	98	2.95	123	.208	.298	26-0-2	.115	-1	67	7		0.7
1964	Cle A	8	6	.571	56	2	0	4	106	106	56	15	4	53-5	89	4.33	83	.260	.349	16-0-3	.375	2	136	-8		-0.9
1965	Cle A☆	6	5	.545	60	0	0	17	103.2	86	43	7	2	50-10	86	3.04	115	.226	.318	16-1-1	.063	-0				0.4
1966	Cle A☆	14	15	.483	40	37	12	0	254.1	211	102	21	4	79-3	194	3.22	107	.228	.289	76-0-15	.132	-1	77	6		0.7
1967	Cle A	1	5	.167	9	9	1	0	60.2	50	28	7	1	24-1	39	3.71	88	.234	.311	15-0-5	.000	-2	89	-3		-0.4
	†Bos A	12	8	.600	29	24	8	3	165.1	143	70	16	4	47-3	115	3.16	110	.231	.288	59-0-2	.203	1	115	4		0.6
	Year	13	8	.500	38	33	9	3	226	193	98	23	5	71-4	154	3.31	104	.232	.294	74-0-7	.162	-1	108	2		0.2
1968	Bos A☆	11	11	.500	35	27	9-3	1	199.1	177	82	7	5	68-6	103	3.12	101	.239	.306	59-0-5	.220	2	101	-1		0.2
1969	Sea A	2	6	.250	13	11	1-1	2-0	61.1	76	40	8	2	34-8	30	4.70	78	.305	.389	14-0-5	.214	1	80	-9		-0.9
	Chi A	0	0	—	23	2	0	0-0	38.2	40	27	8	2	23-2	26	6.28	61	.308	.403	5	.000	-0				-0.5
	Year	2	6	.250	36	13	1-1	2-0	100	124	67	16	4	57-10	56	5.31	70	.306	.394	19-0-5	.158	1	91	-17		-1.4
Total 12		121	117	.508	519	233	71-9	51-0	2015	1794	932	207	54	842-64	1378	3.68	98	.239	.318	569-1-61	.185	9	101	-23		-1.4

BELL, GEORGE — George Glenn "Farmer" B11.2.1874 Greenwood NY D12.25.1941 New York NY BR/TR/6-0/195 d4.17

YEAR	TM LG	W	L	PCT	G	GS	CG-SHO	SV-BS	IP	H	R	HR	HB	BB-IB	SO	ERA	AERA	OAV	OOB	AB-HR-SH	AVG	PB	SUP	APR	DL	PW
1907	Bro N	8	16	.333	35	27	20-3	1	263.2	222	102	1	6	77	88	2.25	104	.238	.300	84-0-2	.095	-2	99	0		-0.1
1908	Bro N	4	15	.211	29	19	12-2	1	155.1	162	80	3	2	45	63	3.59	65	.270	.324	47-0-5	.170	1	70	-20		-2.3
1909	Bro N	16	15	.516	33	30	29-6	1	256	236	103	5	4	73	95	2.71	96	.251	.307	90-0-2	.167	1	85	-4		-0.3
1910	Bro N	10	27	.270	44	36	25-4	1	310	267	127	4	4	82	102	2.64	115	.241	.296	97-0-2	.134	-4	69	9		0.5
1911	Bro N	5	6	.455	19	12	6-2	1	101	123	59	2	2	28	28	4.28	78	.315	.364	33-0-1	.121	-1	88	-10		-1.0
Total 5		43	79	.352	160	124	92-17	4	1086	1010	471	15	18	305	376	2.85	94	.254	.310	351-0-12	.137	-6	81	-25		-3.2

BELL, HEATH — Heath Justin B9.29.1977 Oceanside CA BR/TR/6-3/230* d8.24 Col Santa Ana (CA) JC

YEAR	TM LG	W	L	PCT	G	GS	CG-SHO	SV-BS	IP	H	R	HR	HB	BB-IB	SO	ERA	AERA	OAV	OOB	AB-HR-SH	AVG	PB	SUP	APR	DL	PW
2004	NY N	0	2	.000	17	0	0	0-1	24.1	22	9	5	0	6-0	27	3.33	129	.253	.301	1	.000	-0		3		0.2
2005	NY N	1	3	.250	42	0	0	0-0	46.2	56	30	3	1	13-3	43	5.59	74	.298	.347	3	.000	-0		-7		-0.5
Total 2		1	5	.167	59	0	0	0-1	71	78	39	8	1	19-3	70	4.82	87	.284	.332	4	.000	-0		-4		-0.3

BELL, HI — Herman S B7.16.1897 Mt.Sherman KY D6.7.1949 Glendale CA BR/TR/6-0/185 d4.16

YEAR	TM LG	W	L	PCT	G	GS	CG-SHO	SV-BS	IP	H	R	HR	HB	BB-IB	SO	ERA	AERA	OAV	OOB	AB-HR-SH	AVG	PB	SUP	APR	DL	PW
1924	StL N	3	8	.273	28	10	3	1	113.1	124	68	5	5	29	29	4.92	77	.292	.344	31	.065	-2	83	-12		-1.3
1926	†StL N	6	6	.500	27	8	3	2	85	82	41	1	2	17	27	3.18	123	.255	.296	25-0-1	.120	-1	67	5		0.4
1927	StL N	1	3	.250	25	1	0	0	57.1	71	37	5	1	22	31	3.92	101	.317	.381	11	.091	-1	172	-2		-0.3
1929	StL N	0	2	.000	7	0	0	0	13	19	15	1	0	4	4	6.92	67	.339	.383	3	.000	-0		-5		-0.6
1931	†StL N	4	3	.571	39	9	2	8	115.1	143	65	4	2	23	42	3.90	129	.299	.334	26-0-3	.077	-3	108	11		0.5
1932	NY N	8	4	.667	35	10	3	2	120	132	58	12	2	16	25	3.68	101	.280	.307	34-0-1	.088	-2	129	1		-0.2
1933	†NY N	6	5	.545	38	7	1-1	5	105.1	100	31	4	2	16	24	2.05	157	.246	.285	29-0-1	.138	-1	104	13		1.4
1934	NY N	4	3	.571	22	2	0	6	54	72	25	2	2	12	9	3.67	105	.319	.358	19-0-1	.105	-1	268	2		0.1
Total 8		32	34	.485	221	47	14-1	24	663.1	743	340	34	16	143	191	3.69	107	.285	.326	178-0-7	.096	-12	108	13		-0.0

BELL, JERRY — Jerry Houston B10.6.1947 Madison TN BB/TR/6-4/190* d9.6 Col Rhodes

YEAR	TM LG	W	L	PCT	G	GS	CG-SHO	SV-BS	IP	H	R	HR	HB	BB-IB	SO	ERA	AERA	OAV	OOB	AB-HR-SH	AVG	PB	SUP	APR	DL	PW
1971	Mil A	2	1	.667	8	0	0	0-0	14.2	10	5	0	0	6-1	8	3.07	114	.200	.281	0	—	0		1		0.2
1972	Mil A	5	1	.833	25	3	0	0-0	70.2	50	15	1	3	33-4	20	1.66	185	.209	.310	14-0-1	.071	-1	135	11	20	0.9
1973	Mil A	9	9	.500	31	25	8	1-3	183.2	185	95	14	5	70-5	57	3.97	96	.263	.332	0	—	0	126	-5		-0.4
1974	Mil A	1	0	1.000	5	0	0	0-0	14	9	6	2	0	5-0	4	2.57	142	.315	.373	0	—	0		1		0.1
Total 4		17	11	.607	69	28	8	1-3	283	262	121	17	8	114-10	89	3.28	110	.250	.327	14-0-1	.071	-1	131	8	20	0.8

BELL, RALPH — Ralph Albert "Lefty" B11.6.1890 Kahoka MO D10.18.1959 Burlington IA BL/TL/5-11.5/170 d7.16

YEAR	TM LG	W	L	PCT	G	GS	CG-SHO	SV-BS	IP	H	R	HR	HB	BB-IB	SO	ERA	AERA	OAV	OOB	AB-HR-SH	AVG	PB	SUP	APR	DL	PW
1912	Chi A	0	0	—	3	0	0	0	6	8	7	1	0	8	5	9.00	36	.333	.500	2	.000	-0		-4		-0.2

BELL, ROB — Robert Allen B1.17.1977 Newburgh NY BR/TR/6-5/225* (AtlN95 3/85) d4.8

YEAR	TM LG	W	L	PCT	G	GS	CG-SHO	SV-BS	IP	H	R	HR	HB	BB-IB	SO	ERA	AERA	OAV	OOB	AB-HR-SH	AVG	PB	SUP	APR	DL	PW
2000	Cin N	7	8	.467	26	26	1	0-0	140.1	130	84	32	1	73-6	112	5.00	95	.243	.334	45-0-3	.067	-3	105	-3		-0.6
2001	Cin N	0	5	.000	9	9	0	0-0	44.1	46	28	9	3	17-1	33	5.48	84	.275	.351	7-0-2	.143	0	65	-3		-0.3
	Tex A	5	5	.500	18	18	0	0-0	105.1	130	87	23	4	47-0	64	7.18	67	.310	.378	0	—	0	125	-25		-2.0
2002	Tex A	4	3	.571	17	15	0	0-0	94	113	69	16	1	35-0	70	6.22	77	.296	.351	1	.000	0	124	-14		-0.8
2003	TB A	8	8	.500	24	19	1	0-0	101	103	64	15	5	39-1	44	5.52	83	.263	.336	2	.000	-0	106	-9		-0.7
2004	TB A	5	4	.556	19	18	1	0-0	123	121	71	16	5	41-0	57	4.46	105	.253	.317	0	—	-0	165	-11	56	-0.7
2005	TB A	1	1	.500	8	3	0	0-0	25	41	25	7	2	12-0	13	8.28	53	.360	.426	5	.200	-0	104	1		0.2
Total 6		30	34	.469	121	108	2	0-0	633	684	428	118	21	264-8	393	5.69	83	.275	.347	60-0-5	.083	-2	109	-64	56	-4.9

BELL, BILL — William Samuel "Ding Dong" B10.24.1933 Goldsboro NC D10.11.1962 Durham NC BR/TR/6-3/200(200-218) d9.5 Mil 1953-54

YEAR	TM LG	W	L	PCT	G	GS	CG-SHO	SV-BS	IP	H	R	HR	HB	BB-IB	SO	ERA	AERA	OAV	OOB	AB-HR-SH	AVG	PB	SUP	APR	DL	PW
1952	Pit N	0	1	.000	4	1	0	0	15.2	16	11	3	0	13	4	4.60	87	.254	.382	4	.000	-0	0	-2		-0.1
1955	Pit N	0	0	—	1	0	0	0	1	0	0	0	0	1-0	0	0.00	—	.000	.250	0		-0	0	0		0.0
Total 2		0	1	.000	5	1	0	0	16.2	16	11	3	0	14-0	4	4.32	93	.242	.375	4	.000	-0	0	-2		-0.1

BELTRAN, FRANCIS — Francis Lebron B7.25.1979 Santo Domingo, D.R. BR/TR/6-5/220* d6.28 [DL 2005 Was N 183]

YEAR	TM LG	W	L	PCT	G	GS	CG-SHO	SV-BS	IP	H	R	HR	HB	BB-IB	SO	ERA	AERA	OAV	OOB	AB-HR-SH	AVG	PB	SUP	APR	DL	PW
2002	Chi N	0	0	—	11	0	0	0-0	12	14	11	2	0	16-1	11	7.50	54	.311	.484	1	.000	-0		-5		-0.2
2004	Chi N	2	2	.500	34	0	0	0-0	35	27	19	8	0	22-0	40	4.63	96	.214	.329	1	.000	-0		-1		-0.1
	Mon N	0	0	—	11	0	0	1-0	14.1	20	12	3	2	5-1	8	7.53	61	.333	.397	2	.500	0		-1	15	-0.1
	Year	2	2	.500	45	0	0	1-0	49.1	47	31	11	2	27-1	48	5.47	82	.253	.350	3	.333	0		-4	15	-0.3
Total 2		2	2	.500	56	0	0	1-0	61.1	61	42	13	2	43-2	59	5.87	75	.264	.380	4	.250	0		-10	198	-0.5

BELTRAN, RIGO — Rigoberto B11.13.1969 Tijuana, Baja California, Mexico BL/TL/5-11/185(185-215) [StLN91 26/675] d6.2 Col Wyoming

YEAR	TM LG	W	L	PCT	G	GS	CG-SHO	SV-BS	IP	H	R	HR	HB	BB-IB	SO	ERA	AERA	OAV	OOB	AB-HR-SH	AVG	PB	SUP	APR	DL	PW
1997	StL N	1	2	.333	35	4	0	1-0	54.1	47	25	3	0	17-0	50	3.48	120	.237	.294	7	.143	0	88	0		0.2
1998	NY N	0	0	—	7	0	0	0-0	8	6	3	1	0	4-0	5	3.38	121	.214	.303	1	.000	-0		1		0.0
1999	NY N	1	0	.500	21	0	0	0-0	31	30	15	6	0	12-2	35	3.48	125	.250	.318	1	.000	-0		2		0.1
	Col N	0	0	—	12	0	0	0-0	11	20	9	2	1	7-1	15	7.36	79	.385	.467	2	.500	-0		0		0.0
	Year	1	0	.500	33	0	0	0-0	42	50	24	7	1	19-3	50	4.50	105	.291	.365	3	.333	0		0		0.1
2000	Col N	0	0	—	1	1	0	0-0	1.1	6	6	4	0	3-0	1	40.50	14	.600	.692	0	—	0	158	-4		0.1
2004	Mon N	0	0	—	2	0	0	0-0	0.2	1	1	0	0	0-0	1	13.50	34	.333	.333	0	—	0		-1		0.0
Total 5		2	3	.400	78	5	0	1-0	106.1	110	59	13	1	43-3	106	4.40	100	.268	.333	11	.182	0	108	-1	37	0.1

BENDER, CHIEF — Charles Albert B5.5.1884 Crow Wing Co. MN D5.22.1954 Philadelphia PA BR/TR/6-2/185 d4.20 C6 HF1953 Col Dickinson

YEAR	TM LG	W	L	PCT	G	GS	CG-SHO	SV-BS	IP	H	R	HR	HB	BB-IB	SO	ERA	AERA	OAV	OOB	AB-HR-SH	AVG	PB	SUP	APR	DL	PW
1903	Phi A	17	14	.548	36	33	29-2	0	270	239	115	6	25	65	127	3.07	100	.237	.299	120-0-4	.183	-1*	114	1		0.0
1904	Phi A	10	11	.476	29	20	18-4	0	203.2	167	90	1	4	59	149	2.87	93	.225	.285	79-0-2	.228	3*	78	-4		-0.2
1905	†Phi A	18	11	.621	35	23	18-4	0	229	193	103	5	11	90	142	2.83	94	.230	.313	92-0-2	.217	2*	111	-4		-0.2
1906	Phi A	15	10	.600	36	27	24	3	238.1	208	98	5	8	48	159	2.53	108	.238	.284	99-3-2	.253	7*	116	4		1.2
1907	Phi A	16	8	.667	33	24	20-4	1	219.1	185	67	1	3	34	112	2.05	127	.231	.265	100-0-4	.230	3*	112	15		2.0
1908	Phi A	8	9	.471	18	17	14-2	1	138.2	121	48	1	3	21	85	1.75	146	.236	.270	50-0-1	.220	3*	85	8		1.3
1909	Phi A	18	8	.692	34	29	24-5	1	250	196	68	1	8	45	161	1.66	145	.214	.254	93-0-5	.215	2*	130	20		2.7
1910	†Phi A	23	5	.821	30	28	25-3	0	250	182	63	1	10	47	155	1.58	150	.207	.255	93-0-4	.269	8*	130	25		4.1
1911	†Phi A	17	5	.773	31	24	16-2	3	216.1	198	66	2	4	58	114	2.16	146	.252	.307	79-0-5	.165	-3	117	26		2.2
1912	Phi A	13	8	.619	27	19	12-1	2	171	169	63	1	1	33	90	2.74	113	.277	.315	60-0-3	.150	-1	115	10		0.9
1913	†Phi A	21	10	.677	48	21	14-2	13	236.2	208	78	2	3	63	135	2.21	125	.236	.291	78-0-5	.154	0	154	13		1.7
1914	†Phi A	17	3	.850	28	23	14-7	2	179	159	49	4	1	55	107	2.26	115	.240	.299	62-1-4	.145	-1	152	10		1.2
1915	Bal F	4	16	.200	26	23	15	1	178.1	198	103	5	7	37	89	3.99	72	.298	.342	60-1-0	.267	3	81	-22		-2.0
1916	Phi N	7	7	.500	27	15	3	4	122.2	137	71	3	10	34	43	3.74	71	.287	.347	43-0-1	.279	4*	143	-16		-1.4
1917	Phi N	8	2	.800	20	10	8-4	2	113	84	24	1	7	26	43	1.67	168	.215	.277	39-1-0	.205	1	113	15		1.5
1925	Chi A	0	0	—	1	0	0	0	1	1	2	1	0	1	0	18.00	23	.333	.500					-1		-0.1
Total 16		212	127	.625	459	334	255-40	34	3017	2645	1108	40	102	712	1711	2.46	111	.239	.292	1147-6-42	.212	33	117	100		14.9

YEAR	TM LG	W	L	PCT	G	GS	CG-SHO	SV-BS	IP	H	R	HR	HB	BB-IB	SO	ERA	AERA	OAV	OOB	AB-HR-SH	AVG	PB	SUP	APR	DL	PW
BENES, ALAN	Alan Paul B1.21.1972 Evansville IN BR/TR/6-5/235(215-235) [StLN93 1/16] d9.19 b-Andy Col Creighton [DL 1998 StL N 181]																									
1995	StL N	1	2	.333	3	3	0	0-0	16	24	15	2	1	4-0	20	8.44	51	.343	.387	6	.000	-1	42	-6		-1.0
1996	†StL N	13	10	.565	34	32	3-1	0-0	191	192	120	27	7	87-3	131	4.90	87	.266	.347	61-0-7	.148	-0	108	-17	60	-1.8
1997	StL N	9	9	.500	23	23	2	0-0	161.2	128	60	13	4	68-3	160	2.89	145	.219	.303	52-0-2	.173	0	74	23	153	2.3
1999	StL N	0	0	—	2	0	0	0-0	2	2	0	0	0	0-0	2	0.00	—	.286	.286	0	—	0	1			0.1
2000	StL N	2	2	.500	30	0	0	0-1	46	54	33	7	2	23-2	26	5.67	82	.290	.373	4	.500	1		-6		-0.4
2001	StL N	2	0	1.000	9	1	0	0-0	14.2	14	12	5	0	5-0	10	7.36	59	.250	.382	2	.500	0	128	-5		-0.5
2002	Chi N	2	2	.500	7	7	0	0-0	39.1	42	22	3	0	12-1	32	4.35	93	.276	.325	13	.077	-1	94	-2		-0.2
2003	Chi N	0	0	—	3	0	0	1-0	8.1	8	2	0	0	6-0	9	2.16	201	.267	.389	1	.000	-0	2			0.1
	Tex A	0	3	.000	4	4	0	0-0	15	29	20	2	0	8-0	11	11.40	44	.414	.468	0	—	0	88	-10		-1.4
Total	8	29	28	.509	115	70	5-1	1-1	494	493	284	59	14	220-9	401	4.59	93	.263	.341	139-0-9	.158	0	92	-20	394	-2.8
BENES, ANDY	Andrew Charles B8.20.1967 Evansville IN BR/TR/6-6/240* [SDN88 1/1] d8.11 b-Alan Col Evansville																									
1989	SD N	6	3	.667	10	10	0	0-0	66.2	51	28	7	1	31-0	66	3.51	100	.213	.303	24-1-1	.250	2	111	1		0.3
1990	SD N	10	11	.476	32	31	2	0-0	192.1	177	87	18	1	69-5	140	3.60	107	.242	.306	60-0-5	.100	-2	92	5		0.1
1991	SD N	15	11	.577	33	33	4-1	0-0	223	194	76	23	4	59-7	167	3.03	126	.232	.285	62-1-7	.032	-2	77	22		2.3
1992	SD N	13	14	.481	34	34	2-2	0-0	231.1	230	90	14	5	61-6	169	3.35	107	.264	.314	67-1-5	.149	2	71	8		1.1
1993	SD N★	15	15	.500	34	34	4-2	0-0	230.2	200	111	23	4	86-7	179	3.78	109	.232	.303	72-1-14	.125	-0	85	9		0.9
1994	SD N	6	14	.300	25	25	2-2	0-0	172.1	155	82	20	1	51-2	126	4.17	98	.237	.293	49-0-13	.163	-0	102	-3		-0.3
1995	SD N	4	7	.364	19	19	1-1	0-0	118.2	121	65	10	4	45-3	126	4.17	98	.262	.330	40-0-3	.150	-0	138	-6		-0.7
	†Sea A	7	2	.778	12	12	0	0-0	63	72	42	8	2	33-2	45	5.86	81	.287	.369	0	—	0	108	11		1.0
1996	†StL N	18	10	.643	36	34	3-1	1-0	230.1	215	107	28	6	77-7	160	3.83	112	.247	.310	73-0-9	.151	-0	108	11		1.0
1997	StL N	10	7	.588	26	26	0	0-0	177	149	64	9	5	61-4	175	3.10	135	.230	.298	55-0-8	.218	3*	96	24	27	1.2
1998	Ari N	14	13	.519	34	34	1	0-0	231.1	221	111	25	4	74-3	164	3.97	108	.251	.311	65-1-10	.169	3*	98	8		1.2
1999	Ari N	13	12	.520	33	32	0	0-0	198.1	216	117	34	4	82-3	141	4.81	96	.273	.342	58-1-10	.155	1	110	-4	18	-0.5
2000	†StL N	12	9	.571	30	27	1	0-0	166	174	95	30	1	68-0	137	4.88	95	.275	.342	50-1-6	.080	-1	114	-2		-3.7
2001	StL N	7	7	.500	27	19	0	0-1	107.1	122	92	30	6	61-0	78	7.38	59	.286	.380	32-0-2	.156	1	124	-35		-3.7
2002	†StL N	5	4	.556	18	17	1	0-0	97	80	39	7	5	51-3	64	2.78	145	.228	.330	34-1-2	.206	2*	116	11	91	1.2
Total	14	155	139	.527	403	387	21-9	1-1	2505.1	2377	1206	289	55	909-52	2000	3.97	104	.250	.317	741-8-95	.143	6	99	55	136	5.1
BENGE, RAY	Raymond Adelphia B4.22.1902 Jacksonville TX D6.27.1997 Centerville TX BR/TR/5-9.5/160 d9.26 Col Sam Houston St.																									
1925	Cle A	1	0	1.000	2	2	1-1	0	11.2	9	2	0	0	3	3	1.54	286	.205	.255	5	.400	0	133	4		0.3
1926	Cle A	1	0	1.000	8	0	0	0	11.2	15	11	0	0	4	3	3.86	105	.313	.365	3	.333	1	0	-2		-0.1
1928	Phi N	8	18	.308	40	28	12-1	1	201.2	219	117	15	5	88	68	4.55	94	.286	.363	58-0-7	.207	-0*	80	-6		-0.8
1929	Phi N	11	15	.423	38	26	9-2	4	199	255	147	24	4	77	78	6.29	83	.322	.385	74-0-3	.203	-3*	91	-18		-2.2
1930	Phi N	11	15	.423	38	29	14	1	225.2	305	178	22	1	81	70	5.70	96	.328	.382	88-0-3	.205	-2	108	-10		-1.4
1931	Phi N	14	18	.438	38	31	16-2	2	247	251	107	12	5	61	117	3.17	134	.262	.310	88-0-6	.205	-2	81	26		2.8
1932	Phi N	13	12	.520	41	28	13-2	6	222.1	247	119	16	4	58	89	4.05	109	.281	.329	75-0-2	.173	-3	102	7		0.4
1933	Bro N	10	17	.370	37	30	16-2	1	228.2	238	104	11	6	65	74	3.42	94	.268	.315	76-0-6	.184	-1	103	-5		-0.7
1934	Bro N	14	12	.538	36	32	14-1	0	227	252	124	11	3	61	64	4.48	89	.272	.319	89-0-2	.169	-2	117	-9		-1.1
1935	Bro N	9	9	.500	23	17	5-1	1	124.2	142	77	12	1	47	39	4.48	90	.289	.353	47-0-1	.191	-1	93	-8		-1.2
1936	Bos N	7	9	.438	21	19	2	0	115	161	79	6	1	38	32	5.79	66	.333	.382	43-0-4	.140	-3	91	-23		-3.0
	Phi N	1	4	.200	15	6	0	1	45.2	70	35	3	0	19	13	4.73	96	.350	.406	10	.000	-1	56	-3		-3.8
	Year	8	13	.381	36	25	2	1	160.2	231	114	9	1	57	45	5.49	73	.338	.389	53-0-4	.113	-4	81	-23		-3.8
1938	Cin N	1	1	.500	9	0	0	2	15.1	13	8	1	0	6	5	4.11	89	.228	.302	3	.333	0	-1			-0.3
Total	12	101	130	.437	346	248	102-12	19	1875.1	2177	1108	132	30	598	655	4.52	95	.292	.347	659-0-34	.188	-17	96	-48		-7.2
BENITEZ, ARMANDO	Armando German B11.3.1972 Ramon Santana, D.R. BR/TR/6-4/225(180-230) d7.28																									
1994	Bal A	0	0	—	3	0	0	0-0	10	8	1	0	1	4-0	14	0.90	562	.216	.310	0	—	0	4			0.2
1995	Bal A	1	5	.167	44	0	0	2-3	47.2	37	33	8	5	37-2	56	5.66	84	.213	.361	0	—	0	-5			-0.4
1996	†Bal A	1	0	1.000	18	0	0	4-1	14.1	7	6	2	0	6-0	20	3.77	131	.143	.232	0	—	0	2		128	2.5
1997	†Bal A	4	5	.444	71	0	0	9-1	73.1	49	22	7	1	43-5	106	2.45	180	.191	.305	0	—	0	16			2.1
1998	Bal A	5	6	.455	71	0	0	22-4	68.1	48	29	10	4	39-2	87	3.82	119	.199	.318	0	—	0	6			1.3
1999	†NY N	4	3	.571	77	0	0	22-6	78	40	17	4	0	41-4	128	1.85	235	.148	.260	5	.000	-1	22			2.7
2000	†NY N	4	4	.500	76	0	0	41-5	76	39	24	10	0	38-2	106	2.61	168	.148	.255	0	—	0	4			2.4
2001	NY N	6	4	.600	73	0	0	43-3	76.1	59	32	12	1	40-6	93	3.77	107	.214	.314	0	—	0	13			1.1
2002	NY N	1	0	1.000	62	0	0	33-4	67.1	46	20	8	3	25-0	79	2.27	174	.190	.272	0	—	0	13			1.8
2003	NY N☆	3	3	.500	45	0	0	21-7	49.1	41	18	5	0	24-1	50	3.10	135	.223	.311	1	.000	-0	2			1.1
	NY A	1	1	.500	9	0	0	0-0	9.1	8	4	0	0	6-1	10	1.93	228	.235	.350	0	—	0	2			0.5
	Sea A	0	0	—	15	0	0	0-1	14.1	10	5	1	1	11-1	15	3.14	138	.189	.328	0	—	0	4			0.1
	Year	1	1	.500	24	0	0	0-1	23.2	18	9	1	1	17-2	25	2.66	164	.207	.337	0	—	0	6			0.6
2004	Fla N☆	2	2	.500	64	0	0	47-4	69.2	36	11	6	0	21-4	62	1.29	318	.152	.220	1	.000	-0	23	20		3.1
2005	SF N	2	3	.400	30	0	0	19-4	30	25	17	5	0	16-0	23	4.50	95	.229	.323	0	—	0	-1	110		-0.2
Total	12	34	36	.486	658	0	0	263-43	684	453	239	78	15	351-28	849	2.92	148	.187	.291	8	.000	-1	110	258		15.4
BENN, HENRY	Henry Omer B1.25.1890 Viola WI D6.4.1967 Madison WI BR/TR/6-0/190 d9.24																									
1914	Cle A	0	0	—	1	0	0	1	0	0	0	0	0	1	0.00	—	.000	.000	0	—	0	0			0
BENNETT, DAVE	David Hans B11.7.1945 Berkeley CA BR/TR/6-5/205 d6.12 b-Dennis																									
1964	Phi N	0	0	—	1	0	0	1	2	1	0	0	0-0	1	9.00	39	.400	.400	0	—	0	-1			0
BENNETT, JEFF	David Jeffrey B6.10.1980 Donelson TN BR/TR/6-3/206 [PitN98 19/568] d4.6																									
2004	Mil N	1	5	.167	60	0	0	0-1	71.1	79	43	12	2	26-2	45	4.79	92	.278	.338	2	.000	-0	-4			-0.2
BENNETT, DENNIS	Dennis John B10.5.1939 Oakland CA BL/TL/6-5/205(185-205) d5.12 b-Dave Col Shasta (CA) JC																									
1962	Phi N	9	9	.500	31	24	7-2	3	174.2	144	78	17	6	68-3	149	3.81	102	.224	.302	63-1-3	.127	-1	98	3		0.4
1963	Phi N	9	5	.643	23	16	6-1	1	119.1	102	44	12	4	33-5	82	2.64	124	.231	.287	40-1-1	.225	3	123	6	74	1.4
1964	Phi N	12	14	.462	41	32	7-2	1	208	222	92	23	5	58-8	125	3.68	94	.280	.331	66-0-2	.197	3	84	-2		-0.2
1965	Bos A	5	7	.417	34	18	3	0	141.2	152	76	15	6	53-6	85	4.38	85	.279	.346	39-0-2	.179	2	98	-8		-0.8
1966	Bos A	3	3	.500	16	13	0	0	75	75	30	9	1	23-2	47	3.24	117	.261	.316	23-1-2	.130	1	82	5	80	0.4
1967	Bos A	4	3	.571	13	11	4-1	0	69.2	72	32	12	2	22-2	34	3.88	90	.268	.327	25-1-1	.100	-0	141	-2		-0.2
	NY N	1	1	.500	8	6	0	0	26.1	37	15	4	1	7-1	14	5.13	66	.336	.378	8	.250	0	91	-4		-0.4
1968	Cal A	0	5	.000	16	7	1	1	48.1	46	22	6	4	17-0	36	3.54	82	.250	.324	13-0-2	.077	-1	97	-6	154	-0.6
Total	7	43	47	.478	182	127	28-6	6	863	850	389	98	29	281-27	572	3.69	96	.260	.322	277-4-13	.166	7	97	-6	154	-0.1
BENNETT, ERIK	Erik Hans B9.13.1968 Yreka CA BR/TR/6-2/205* [CalA89 4/96] d5.15 Col Cal St.-Sacramento																									
1995	Cal A	0	0	—	1	0	0	0-0	0.1	0	0	0	0	0-0	0	0.00	—	.000	.000	0	—	0	0			0
1996	Min A	2	0	1.000	24	0	0	1-0	27.1	33	24	7	2	16-1	13	7.90	65	.306	.402	0	—	0	-8			-0.4
Total	2	2	0	1.000	25	0	0	1-0	27.2	33	24	7	2	16-1	13	7.81	66	.303	.398	0	—	0	-8			-0.4
BENNETT, FRANK	Francis Allen "Chip" B10.27.1904 Mardela Springs MD D3.18.1966 Wilmington DE BR/TR/5-10.5/163 d9.17																									
1927	Bos A	0	1	.000	4	1	0	0	12.1	15	4	0	0	6	1	2.92	145	.333	.412	3	.000	-1	40	2		0
1928	Bos A	0	0	—	1	0	0	0	1	1	0	0	0	0	0	0.00	—	.250	.250	0	—	0	0			0
Total	2	0	1	.000	5	1	0	0	13.1	16	4	0	0	6	1	2.70	156	.327	.400	3	.000	-1	40	2		0
BENNETT, JOEL	Joel Todd B1.31.1970 Binghamton NY BR/TR/6-1/160(160-171) [BosA91 21/564] d7.15 Col East Stroudsburg																									
1998	Bal A	0	0	—	2	0	0	0-0	2	2	1	0	0	3-0	5	4.50	101	.250	.455	0	—	0	0			-0.1
1999	Phi N	2	1	.667	5	3	0	0-1	17	26	17	10	0	7-0	13	9.00	52	.351	.407	4-0-1	.000	-0	105	-7		-1.0
Total	2	2	1	.667	7	3	0	0-1	19	28	18	10	0	10-0	13	8.53	55	.341	.413	4-0-1	.000	-0	105	-7		-1.1
BENNETT, SHAYNE	Shayne Anthony B4.10.1972 Adelaide, South Australia, Australia BR/TR/6-5/200(200-220) [BosA93 25/695] d8.22 Col Du Page (IL) [JC]																									
1997	Mon N	0	1	.000	16	0	0	0-0	22.2	21	9	2	0	9-3	8	3.18	132	.247	.309	1	.000	-0	3			0
1998	Mon N	5	5	.500	62	0	0	1-1	91.2	97	61	6	8	45-3	59	5.50	77	.276	.363	6-0-1	.000	-0		-12		-1.0
1999	Mon N	0	1	.000	5	1	0	0-0	11.1	24	18	4	1	3-0	4	14.29	31	.444	.475	2	.000	-0	82	-12		-1.3
Total	3	5	7	.417	83	1	0	1-1	125.2	142	88	14	7	57-6	71	5.87	72	.290	.365	9-0-1	.000	-0	82	-21		-1.3

YEAR	TM LG	W	L	PCT	G	GS	CG-SHO	SV-BS	IP	H	R	HR	HB	BB-IB	SO	ERA	AERA	OAV	OOB	AB-HR-SH	AVG	PB	SUP	APR	DL	PW

BENOIT, JOAQUIN Joaquin Antonio (Pena) B7.26.1977 Santiago, D.R. BR/TR/6-3/205(205-220) d8.8

YEAR	TM LG	W	L	PCT	G	GS	CG-SHO	SV-BS	IP	H	R	HR	HB	BB-IB	SO	ERA	AERA	OAV	OOB	AB-HR-SH	AVG	PB	SUP	APR	DL	PW
2001	Tex A	0	0	—	1	1	0	0-0	5	5	3	4	0	3-0	4	10.80	44	.364	.423	0	—	0	116	-3		-0.1
2002	Tex A	4	5	.444	17	13	0	1-0	84.2	91	51	6	5	58-2	59	5.31	90	.272	.384	0	—	0	90	-4		-0.4
2003	Tex A	8	5	.615	25	17	0	0-0	105	99	67	23	3	51-0	87	5.49	91	.246	.332	0	—	0	91	-5	21	-0.5
2004	Tex A	3	5	.375	28	15	0	0-0	103	113	67	19	8	31-0	95	5.68	87	.279	.335	2	.000	-0	91	-5		-0.5
2005	Tex A	4	4	.500	32	9	0	0-0	87	69	39	9	2	38-0	78	3.72	123	.212	.297	6	.000	-0	112	-6	15	-0.5
Total	5	19	19	.500	103	55	0	1-0	384.2	380	230	60	18	181-2	323	5.17	93	.255	.339	1	.000	-0*	105	8	48	0.6

BENSON, ALLEN Allen Wilbert "Bullet Ben" B7.12.1908 Hurley SD D11.16.1999 Viborg SD BR/TR/6-1/185 d8.19

YEAR	TM LG	W	L	PCT	G	GS	CG-SHO	SV-BS	IP	H	R	HR	HB	BB-IB	SO	ERA	AERA	OAV	OOB	AB-HR-SH	AVG	PB	SUP	APR	DL	PW
1934	Was A	0	1	.000	2	2	0	0-0	9.2	19	14	0	2	5	4	12.10	36	.413	.491	3-0-2	.000	-0	131	-8		-0.7

BENSON, KRIS Kristen James B11.7.1974 Kennesaw GA BR/TR/6-4/190* [PitN96 1/1] d4.9 Col Clemson [DL 2001 Pit N 190]

YEAR	TM LG	W	L	PCT	G	GS	CG-SHO	SV-BS	IP	H	R	HR	HB	BB-IB	SO	ERA	AERA	OAV	OOB	AB-HR-SH	AVG	PB	SUP	APR	DL	PW
1999	Pit N	11	14	.440	31	31	2	0-0	196.2	184	105	16	6	83-5	139	4.07	113	.249	.327	65-0-6	.154	0	90	9		1.1
2000	Pit N	10	12	.455	32	32	2-1	0-0	217.2	206	104	24	10	86-5	184	3.85	121	.249	.325	65-0-9	.092	-2	88	19		1.5
2002	Pit N	9	6	.600	25	25	0	0-0	130.1	152	76	18	3	50-8	79	4.70	89	.295	.359	40-0-4	.175	-0*	108	-8	43	-0.9
2003	Pit N	5	9	.357	18	18	0	0-0	105	127	67	14	1	36-4	68	4.97	87	.295	.347	30-0-6	.000	-3	89	-10	73	-1.4
2004	Pit N	8	8	.500	20	20	0	0-0	132.1	137	69	7	6	44-5	83	4.22	103	.272	.336	39-0-10	.179	-0	97	1		0.1
	NY N	4	4	.500	11	11	1-1	0-0	68	65	37	8	4	17-3	51	4.50	95	.244	.298	19-0-5	.053	-1	76	-1		-0.3
	Year	12	12	.500	31	31	1-1	0-0	200.1	202	106	15	10	61-8	134	4.31	100	.263	.323	58-0-15	.138	-1	90	1		-0.2
2005	NY N	10	8	.556	28	28	0	0-0	174.1	171	86	24	4	49-5	95	4.13	101	.253	.306	49-0-6	.184	2	115	1	32	0.3
Total	6	57	61	.483	165	165	5-2	0-0	1024.1	1042	544	111	34	365-35	699	4.25	103	.263	.329	307-0-46	.130	-4	96	11	338	0.7

BENTLEY, CY Clytus G. B11.23.1850 East Haven CT D2.26.1873 Middletown CT d4.26

YEAR	TM LG	W	L	PCT	G	GS	CG-SHO	SV-BS	IP	H	R	HR	HB	BB-IB	SO	ERA	AERA	OAV	OOB	AB-HR-SH	AVG	PB	SUP	APR	DL	PW
1872	Man NA	2	15	.118	18	17	14	0	144	259	253	4		12	5	6.06	59	.331	.341	114-1	.219	-0*	74	-39		-2.6

BENTLEY, JACK John Needles B3.8.1895 Sandy Spring MD D10.24.1969 Olney MD BL/TL/5-11.5/200 d9.6 ▲

YEAR	TM LG	W	L	PCT	G	GS	CG-SHO	SV-BS	IP	H	R	HR	HB	BB-IB	SO	ERA	AERA	OAV	OOB	AB-HR-SH	AVG	PB	SUP	APR	DL	PW
1913	Was A	1	0	1.000	3	1	0	1	11	5	0	0	0	2	5	0.00	—	.152	.200	3	.000	-0	25	4		0.4
1914	Was A	5	7	.417	30	11	3-2	4	125.1	110	49	3	3	53	55	2.37	119	.249	.334	40	.275	2	89	4		0.6
1915	Was A	0	0	.000	4	2	0	0	11.1	8	4	0	0	3	0	0.79	374	.200	.256	2	.000	-0	12	2		0.3
1916	Was A	0	0		2	0	0	0	1.1	0	0	0	0	1	0	0.00	—	.000	.250	0	—	-0	0	0		0.0
1923	†NY N	13	8	.619	31	26	12-1	3	183	198	102	10	5	67	80	4.48	85	.277	.343	89-1-2	.427	16*	118	-13		0.1
1924	†NY N	16	5	.762	28	24	13-1	1	188	196	85	11	4	56	60	3.78	97	.273	.329	98-0-1	.265	4*	134	0		0.4
1925	NY N	11	9	.550	28	22	11	0	157	200	90	10	1	59	47	5.04	80	.323	.383	99-3-1	.303	6*	111	-12		-0.3
1926	Phi N	2	5	.000	7	3	0	0	25.1	37	28	2	0	10	7	8.17	51	.327	.382	240-2-7	.258	1*	107	-11		-0.7
	NY N	0	0		1	0	0	0	2	0	0	0	0	2	1	0.00	—	.000	.250	4	.250	-0*		1		0.0
	Year	0	2	.000	8	3	0	0	27.1	37	28	2	0	12	8	7.57	54	.311	.374	244-2-7	.258	1*	108	-10		-0.7
1927	NY N	0	0	—	4	0	0	0	9.2	7	7	1	1	10	3	2.79	138	.206	.400	9-1-0	.222	1*	0			0.0
Total	9	46	33	.582	138	89	39-4	9	714	761	365	37	14	263	259	4.01	91	.280	.346	584-7-11	.291	28	115	-25		0.8

BENTON, AL John Alton B3.18.1911 Noble OK D4.14.1968 Lynwood CA BR/TR/6-4/215* d4.18 Mil 1943-44

YEAR	TM LG	W	L	PCT	G	GS	CG-SHO	SV-BS	IP	H	R	HR	HB	BB-IB	SO	ERA	AERA	OAV	OOB	AB-HR-SH	AVG	PB	SUP	APR	DL	PW
1934	Phi A	7	9	.438	32	21	7	4	155	145	98	7	2	88	58	4.88	90	.249	.349	55-0-2	.109	-4	109	-10		-1.3
1935	Phi A	3	4	.429	27	9	0	0	78.1	110	81	7	1	47	42	7.70	59	.328	.413	25-0-1	.040	-3	127	-29		-2.4
1938	Det A	5	3	.625	19	10	6	0	95.1	93	40	10	1	39	33	3.30	151	.259	.333	33-0-2	.121	-3	95	17		1.0
1939	Det A	6	8	.429	37	16	3	5	150	182	94	11	1	58	67	4.56	107	.294	.355	44-0-7	.091	-4	101	3		-0.1
1940	Det A	6	10	.375	42	0	0	17	79.1	93	44	5	0	36	50	4.42	107	.294	.366	17-0-4	.000	-3		3		0.4
1941	Det A☆	15	6	.714	38	14	7-1	7	157.2	130	63	11	3	65	63	2.97	153	.221	.302	50-0-9	.060	-5	103	24		2.6
1942	Det A★	7	13	.350	35	30	9-1	2	226.2	210	87	9	4	84	110	2.90	136	.246	.314	67-0-9	.075	-5	65	25		1.5
1945	†Det A	13	8	.619	31	27	12-5	3	191.2	175	68	7	2	63	76	2.02	174	.241	.303	63-0-8	.063	-6	91	24		2.2
1946	Det A	11	7	.611	28	15	6-1	1	140.2	132	69	9	1	58	60	3.65	100	.245	.319	49-0-5	.184	-1	101	-10		-0.3
1947	Det A	6	7	.462	36	14	4	7	133	147	77	11	1	61	33	4.40	86	.288	.365	39-0-3	.154	-2	101	-10		-1.2
1948	Det A	2	2	.500	30	0	0	3	44.1	45	34	4	1	36	18	5.68	77	.273	.406	11-0-2	.182	-0		-7		-0.7
1949	Cle A	9	6	.600	40	11	4-2	10	135.2	116	33	7	1	51	41	2.12	188	.238	.312	38-0-3	.132	-2	65	31		3.3
1950	Cle A	3	4	.667	36	0	0	4	63	57	32	7	1	30	26	3.57	121	.243	.331	12-0-2	.083	-1		4		0.3
1952	Bos A	4	3	.571	24	0	0	6	37.2	37	11	1	0	17	20	2.39	165	.268	.348	9-0-2	.000	-1		6		1.2
Total	14	98	88	.527	455	167	58-10	66	1688.1	1672	831	106	15	733	697	3.66	115	.259	.336	512-0-59	.098	-39	94	79		6.5

BENTON, RUBE John Clebon B6.27.1887 Clinton NC D12.12.1937 Dothan AL BL/TL/6-1/190 d6.28 Mil 1918

YEAR	TM LG	W	L	PCT	G	GS	CG-SHO	SV-BS	IP	H	R	HR	HB	BB-IB	SO	ERA	AERA	OAV	OOB	AB-HR-SH	AVG	PB	SUP	APR	DL	PW
1910	Cin N	0	1	.000	12	2	0	0	38	44	34	1	1	23	15	4.74	62	.282	.378	11	.091	-1	64	-10		-0.6
1911	Cin N	3	3	.500	6	6	5	0	44.2	44	18	0	3	23	28	2.01	164	.270	.370	14-0-2	.143	-0	57	5		0.5
1912	Cin N	18	20	.474	50	39	22-2	2	302	316	143	2	18	118	162	3.10	108	.278	.356	104-0-3	.135	-6	88	9		0.5
1913	Cin N	11	7	.611	23	22	9-1	0	144.1	140	76	4	9	60	68	3.49	93	.265	.350	48-0-2	.208	1	108	-4		-0.4
1914	Cin N	16	18	.471	41	35	16-4	2	271	223	124	3	11	95	121	2.96	99	.228	.303	91-0-3	.143	-3	75	0		-0.3
1915	Cin N	6	13	.316	35	21	6-2	4	176.1	165	79	2	14	67	83	3.32	86	.257	.340	53-0-2	.208	-0	73	-7		-0.7
	NY N	3	5	.375	10	6	3	1	60.2	57	26	0	5	9	26	2.82	91	.253	.297	23-0-1	.217	1	131	-2		-0.2
	Year	9	18	.333	45	27	9-2	5	237	222	105	2	19	76	109	3.19	87	.256	.329	76-0-3	.211	1	85	-7		-0.9
1916	NY N	16	8	.667	38	29	15-3	2	238.2	210	84	5	10	58	115	2.87	85	.241	.296	78-0-4	.090	-4	109	-8		-1.4
1917	†NY N	15	9	.625	35	25	14-3	3	215	190	78	5	7	41	70	2.72	94	.238	.281	72-0-5	.167	-1	115	-3		-0.5
1918	NY N	1	2	.333	3	3	2	0	24	17	8	0	3	9	9	1.88	140	.202	.230	7	.143	1	86	1		0.3
1919	NY N	17	11	.607	35	28	11-1	2	209	181	71	5	4	52	53	2.63	107	.237	.289	67-1-3	.194	-1	120	6		0.7
1920	NY N	9	16	.360	33	25	12-4	2	193.1	222	82	8	3	31	52	3.03	99	.291	.321	65-0-4	.092	-7	96	-1		-0.6
1921	NY N	5	2	.714	18	9	3-1	0	72	72	28	2	0	17	11	2.88	128	.266	.309	21-0-2	.143	-1	139	6		1.2
1923	Cin N	14	10	.583	33	26	15	1	219	243	106	10	5	57	59	3.66	106	.284	.333	80-0-3	.287	4	123	8		1.2
1924	Cin N	7	9	.438	32	19	6-1	1	162.2	166	70	2	4	42	42	2.77	136	.266	.297	46	.261	2	85	15		1.6
1925	Cin N	9	10	.474	33	16	6-1	1	146.2	182	88	3	1	34	36	4.05	102	.301	.340	45-0-4	.200	1	94	-1		-0.2
Total	15	150	144	.510	437	311	145-23	21	2517.1	2472	1115	52	95	712	950	3.09	102	.261	.319	825-1-38	.172	-14	99	14		0.3

BENTON, LARRY Lawrence James B11.20.1897 St.Louis MO D4.3.1953 Amberley OH BR/TR/5-11/165 d4.25

YEAR	TM LG	W	L	PCT	G	GS	CG-SHO	SV-BS	IP	H	R	HR	HB	BB-IB	SO	ERA	AERA	OAV	OOB	AB-HR-SH	AVG	PB	SUP	APR	DL	PW
1923	Bos N	5	9	.357	35	9	2	1	128	141	78	4	4	90	41	4.99	80	.293	.373	31-0-4	.161	-1	53	-11		-1.0
1924	Bos N	5	7	.417	30	13	4	1	128	129	63	4	3	64	41	4.15	92	.274	.365	33-0-2	.091	-3	77	-2		-0.5
1925	Bos N	14	7	.667	31	21	16-2	1	183.1	170	72	24	6	70	49	3.09	130	.249	.320	58-0-8	.241	2*	96	21		2.3
1926	Bos N	14	14	.500	43	27	12-1	1	231.2	244	113	10	7	81	103	3.85	92	.280	.346	78-0-6	.154	-4*	81	-7		-1.2
1927	Bos N	4	2	.667	11	10	3	0	60.1	72	33	3	2	27	25	4.48	83	.310	.387	18-0-3	.222	1	142	-4		-0.3
	NY N	13	5	.722	29	23	8-1	2	173	183	83	9	2	54	65	3.95	98	.275	.331	50-0-8	.160	-2*	106	1		-0.1
	Year	17	7	.708	40	33	11-1	2	233.1	255	116	12	4	81	90	4.09	93	.284	.346	68-0-11	.176	-1	116	-2		-0.4
1928	NY N	25	9	.735	42	36	28-2	4	310.1	299	106	14	4	71	90	2.73	144	.258	.300	112-0-6	.143	-3	124	43		4.1
1929	NY N	11	17	.393	39	31	14-3	3	237	276	129	16	0	61	63	4.14	111	.297	.340	86-1-1	.105	-6*	82	11		0.6
1930	NY N	1	3	.250	8	4	1	1	30	42	31	8	0	14	16	7.80	61	.323	.389	10-1-1	.300	-2	166	-11		-1.1
	Cin N	7	12	.368	35	22	9	1	177.2	246	124	7	0	45	47	5.12	94	.337	.375	62-0-2	.177	-2	78	-10		-1.1
	Year	8	15	.348	43	26	10	2	207.2	288	155	15	0	59	63	5.50	87	.334	.377	72-1-3	.194	-0	91	-22		-2.2
1931	Cin N	10	15	.400	38	23	12-2	2	204.1	240	98	6	1	53	35	3.35	112	.299	.343	66-0-2	.167	-1	80	5		0.6
1932	Cin N	6	13	.316	35	22	7	2	179.2	201	104	0	0	27	35	4.31	90	.285	.311	54-0-5	.204	-0	89	-9		-0.8
1933	Cin N	10	11	.476	34	19	7-2	2	152.2	160	70	5	3	36	33	3.71	91	.271	.331	53-0-2	.170	-1	92	-2		-0.5
1934	Cin N	0	1	.000	16	1	0	2	29	53	25	1	0	7	5	6.52	63	.393	.423	7	.286	-0	85	-8		-0.3
1935	Bos N	2	3	.400	29	0	0	0	72	103	61	4	1	24	21	6.88	55	.338	.388	20-0-2	.200	0		-25		-1.4
Total	13	127	128	.498	455	261	123-13	22	2297	2559	1190	109	25	691	670	4.03	98	.288	.341	738-2-52	.165	-17	94	-8		-0.7

BENTON, SID Sidney Wright B8.4.1895 Buckner AR D3.8.1977 Fayetteville AR BR/TR/6-1/170 d4.18 Col Arkansas-Monticello

YEAR	TM LG	W	L	PCT	G	GS	CG-SHO	SV-BS	IP	H	R	HR	HB	BB-IB	SO	ERA	AERA	OAV	OOB	AB-HR-SH	AVG	PB	SUP	APR	DL	PW
1922	StL N	0	0		1	0	0	0	4							—	—		1.000	0	—	0		0		0.0

BENTZ, CHAD Chad Robert B5.5.1980 Seward AK BR/TL/6-2/215* [MonN01 7/202] d4.7 Col Cal St.-Long Beach

YEAR	TM LG	W	L	PCT	G	GS	CG-SHO	SV-BS	IP	H	R	HR	HB	BB-IB	SO	ERA	AERA	OAV	OOB	AB-HR-SH	AVG	PB	SUP	APR	DL	PW
2004	Mon N	0	3	.000	36	0	0	0-0	27.2	23	19	5	2	23-3	18	5.86	78	.228	.381	2	.500	0		-3		-0.3
2005	Fla N	0	0		4	0	0	0-0	2	8	7	2	0	0-0	0	31.50	13	.571	.571	0	—	0		-6		-0.3
Total	2	0	3	.000	40	0	0	0-0	29.2	31	26	7	2	23-3	18	7.58	60	.270	.400	2	.500	0		-9		-0.6

BENZ, JOE
Joseph Louis "Blitzen","Butcher Boy" B1.21.1886 New Alsace IN D4.22.1957 Chicago IL BR/TR/6-1.5/196 d8.16

YEAR	TM LG	W	L	PCT	G	GS	CG-SHO	SV-BS	IP	H	R	HR	HB	BB-IB	SO	ERA	AERA	OAV	OOB	AB-HR-SH	AVG	PB	SUP	APR	DL	PW
1911	Chi A	3	2	.600	12	6		0	55.2	52	23	0	2	13	28	2.26	142	.251	.302	17	.059	-2	101	5		0.2
1912	Chi A	13	17	.433	42	31	12-3	0	238.2	231	107	5	8	70	97	2.90	110	.259	.319	76-0-8	.132	-5	89	7		0.3
1913	Chi A	7	10	.412	33	17	6-1	1	151	146	64	1	2	59	79	2.74	107	.257	.329	50-0-2	.180	-1	106	3		0.5
1914	Chi A	15	19	.441	48	35	16-4	2	283.1	245	103	4	2	66	142	2.26	119	.236	.282	92-0-4	.130	-3	78	14		1.7
1915	Chi A	15	11	.577	39	28	17-2	0	238.1	209	78	4	3	43	81	2.11	141	.238	.276	79-0-4	.127	-5	113	21		1.9
1916	Chi A	9	5	.643	28	16	6-4	0	142	108	40	0	3	32	57	2.03	136	.214	.265	46-0-2	.065	-4	103	13		0.9
1917	Chi A	7	3	.700	19	13	7-2	0	94.2	76	36	1	2	23	25	2.47	108	.220	.272	30-0-3	.167	-1	150	2		0.1
1918	Chi A	8	8	.500	29	17	10-1	0	154	156	57	1	2	28	30	2.63	104	.269	.304	51-0-4	.216	-1	110	2		0.4
1919	Chi A	0	0	—	1	0	0	0	2	2	1	0	0	0	0	0.00	—	.250	.250	0	—	0	0	0		0.0
Total 9		77	75	.507	251	163	75-17	3	1359.2	1225	509	16	24	334	539	2.43	119	.244	.294	441-0-27	.138	-21	101	67		6.0

BERE, JASON
Jason Phillip B5.26.1971 Cambridge MA BR/TR/6-3/215(185-225) [ChiA90 36/952] d5.27 Col Middlesex (MA) CC

YEAR	TM LG	W	L	PCT	G	GS	CG-SHO	SV-BS	IP	H	R	HR	HB	BB-IB	SO	ERA	AERA	OAV	OOB	AB-HR-SH	AVG	PB	SUP	APR	DL	PW
1993 †Chi A		12	5	.706	24	24	1	0-0	142.2	109	60	12	5	81-0	129	3.47	122	.210	.322	0	—	0	126	13		1.3
1994 Chi A★		12	2	.857	24	24	1	0-0	141.2	119	65	17	1	80-0	127	3.81	123	.229	.331	0	—	0	120	15		1.2
1995	Chi A	8	15	.348	27	27	1	0-0	137.2	151	120	21	6	106-6	110	7.19	62	.277	.396	0	—	0	99	-44	15	-5.5
1996	Chi A	0	1	.000	5	5	0	0-0	16.2	26	19	3	0	18-1	19	10.26	46	.356	.478	0	—	0	117	-10	150	-0.1
1997	Chi A	4	2	.667	6	6	0	0-0	28.2	20	15	4	3	17-0	21	4.71	94	.198	.328	0	—	0	96	-20	140	-1.9
1998	Chi A	3	7	.300	18	15	0	0-0	83.2	98	71	14	2	58-0	53	6.45	71	.293	.395	0	—	0	96	-20		0.0
	Cin N	3	2	.600	9	7	0	0-0	43.2	39	20	3	1	20-0	31	4.12	104	.242	.326	14	.000	-1	122	1		0.0
1999	Cin N	3	0	1.000	12	10	0	0-0	43.1	56	37	6	2	40-3	28	6.85	68	.326	.456	14-0-2	.286	1	125	-10	48	-0.5
	Mil N	2	0	1.000	5	4	0	0-0	23.1	23	15	3	0	10-0	19	4.63	99	.256	.327	8	.375	1	175	-1		-0.5
	Year	5	0	1.000	17	14	0	0-0	66.2	79	52	9	2	50-3	47	6.08	77	.302	.415	22-0-2	.318	2	139	-12		-0.5
2000	Mil N	6	7	.462	20	20	0	0-0	115	115	66	19	1	63-7	98	4.93	94	.264	.304	39-0-1	.205	1	94	-3		-0.1
	Cle A	6	3	.667	11	11	0	0-0	54.1	65	41	6	4	26-0	44	6.63	76	.297	.377	0	—	0	126	-9		-1.2
2001	Chi N	11	11	.500	32	32	2	0-0	188	171	99	24	1	77-7	175	4.31	97	.241	.314	62-0-7	.194	2	103	-3		-0.2
2002	Chi N	1	10	.091	16	16	0	0-0	85.2	98	63	13	3	28-1	65	5.67	71	.290	.343	24-0-7	.125	-0	90	-17	177	-1.0
2003	Cle A	0	0	—	2	2	0	0-0	6.2	5	3	0	0	2-0	1	4.05	109	.208	.259	0	—	0	73	0		-0.0
Total 11		71	65	.522	211	203	4	0-0	1111	1095	694	145	29	626-25	920	5.14	87	.258	.354	161-0-17	.186	3	109	-88	619	-9.4

BERENGUER, JUAN
Juan Bautista B11.30.1954 Aguadulce, Pan BR/TR/5-11/215(186-225) d8.17

YEAR	TM LG	W	L	PCT	G	GS	CG-SHO	SV-BS	IP	H	R	HR	HB	BB-IB	SO	ERA	AERA	OAV	OOB	AB-HR-SH	AVG	PB	SUP	APR	DL	PW
1978	NY N	0	2	.000	5	3	0	0-0	13	17	12	1	1	11-0	8	8.31	43	.327	.446	3	.000	-0	59	-6		-0.9
1979	NY N	1	1	.500	5	5	0	0-0	30.2	28	13	2	1	12-0	25	2.93	127	.252	.328	7-0-1	.143	-0	81	2		0.9
1980	NY N	0	1	.000	6	0	0	0-0	9.1	9	9	1	0	10-2	7	5.79	62	.250	.413	0	—	0	83	-11		-1.9
1981	KC A	0	4	.000	8	3	0	0-0	19.2	22	21	4	2	16-0	20	8.69	42	.289	.412	0	—	0	56	-3		-0.8
	Tor A	2	9	.182	12	11	1	0-0	71	62	41	7	3	35-1	29	4.31	92	.235	.327	0	—	0	61	-14		-2.4
	Year	2	13	.133	20	14	1	0-0	90.2	84	62	11	5	51-1	49	5.26	74	.247	.347	0	—	0	134	-2		-0.0
1982	Det A	0	0	—	2	1	0	0-0	6.2	5	5	0	0	9-1	8	6.75	61	.200	.412	0	—	0	119	16		1.
1983	Det A	9	5	.643	37	19	2-1	1-1	157.2	110	58	19	6	71-3	129	3.14	126	.193	.288	0	—	0	108	8		1.
1984	Det A	11	10	.524	31	27	2-1	0-0	168.1	146	75	14	5	79-2	118	3.48	114	.232	.320	0	—	0	111	-16		-1.6
1985	Det A	5	6	.455	31	13	0	0-0	95	96	67	12	1	48-3	82	5.59	73	.259	.343	0	—	0	114	8	21	0.
1986	SF N	3	4	.400	46	4	0	4-4	73.1	64	23	4	2	44-3	72	2.70	131	.242	.353	7-0-3	.143	-0	124	10	19	0.
1987 †Min A		8	1	.889	47	6	0	4-5	112	100	51	10	0	47-7	110	3.94	118	.238	.312	0	—	0	178	3		0.
1988	Min A	8	4	.667	57	1	0	2-3	100	74	44	7	1	61-7	99	3.96	103	.207	.322	0	—	0		8		0.
1989	Min A	9	3	.750	56	0	0	3-4	106	96	44	11	2	47-0	93	3.48	119	.246	.326	0	—	0		7		0.
1990	Min A	8	5	.615	51	0	0	0-2	100.1	85	43	9	2	58-4	77	3.41	122	.232	.338	0	—	0		11		1.
1991	Atl N	0	3	.000	49	0	0	17-1	64.1	43	18	5	3	20-2	53	2.24	173	.189	.261	5	.000	-1		11	19	1.
1992	Atl N	3	1	.750	28	0	0	1-2	33.1	35	22	7	1	16-4	19	5.13	71	.269	.354	2	.000	-0		-6		-0.
	KC A	1	4	.200	19	2	0	0-0	44.2	42	30	3	1	20-3	26	5.64	72	.247	.325	0	—	0	22	-7		-0.
Total 15		67	62	.519	490	95	5-2	32-23	1205.1	1034	576	116	31	604-42	975	3.90	103	.232	.325	24-0-4	.083	-1	100	19	59	-0.

BERENYI, BRUCE
Bruce Michael B8.21.1954 Bryan OH BR/TR/6-3/215* [CinN76 S1/3] d7.5 Col Truman St.

YEAR	TM LG	W	L	PCT	G	GS	CG-SHO	SV-BS	IP	H	R	HR	HB	BB-IB	SO	ERA	AERA	OAV	OOB	AB-HR-SH	AVG	PB	SUP	APR	DL	PW
1980	Cin N	2	2	.500	6	6	0	0-0	27.2	24	26	1	0	23-0	19	7.81	45	.318	.438	7-0-4	.000	-1	135	-14		-1.
1981	Cin N	9	6	.600	21	20	5-3	0-0	126	97	55	3	0	77-0	106	3.50	100	.211	.322	42-0-3	.190	1	111	0		0.
1982	Cin N	9	18	.333	34	34	4-1	0-0	222.1	208	90	8	2	96-5	157	3.36	109	.255	.332	62-0-12	.242	3	62	9		1.
1983	Cin N	9	14	.391	32	31	4-1	0-0	186.1	173	92	9	2	102-3	151	3.86	99	.247	.343	55-0-10	.218	2	99	-2		0.
1984	Cin N	3	7	.300	13	11	0	0-0	51	63	35	0	0	42-2	53	6.00	63	.306	.422	16-0-2	.063	1	78	-11		-1.
	NY N	9	6	.600	19	19	0	0-0	115	100	58	6	1	53-2	81	3.76	95	.238	.324	53-0-7	.243	2	109	-3		-0.
	Year	12	13	.480	32	30	0	0-0	166	163	93	6	1	95-4	134	4.45	82	.260	.357	53-0-7	.189	0	98	-14		-2.
1985	NY N	1	0	1.000	3	3	0	0-0	13.2	8	6	0	1	10-0	10	2.63	133	.170	.328	4-0-2	.250	0	118	1	130	0.
1986	NY N	2	2	.500	14	7	0	0-0	39.2	47	30	5	1	22-0	30	6.35	56	.299	.383	11-0-1	.000	-1	114	-12		-3.
Total 7		44	55	.444	142	131	13-5	0-0	781.2	700	392	32	7	425-12	607	4.03	91	.251	.345	234-0-39	.197	5	94	-32	130	-3.

BERGER, HEINIE
Charles B1.7.1882 LaSalle IL D2.10.1954 Lakewood OH TR/5-9/? d5.6

YEAR	TM LG	W	L	PCT	G	GS	CG-SHO	SV-BS	IP	H	R	HR	HB	BB-IB	SO	ERA	AERA	OAV	OOB	AB-HR-SH	AVG	PB	SUP	APR	DL	PW
1907	Cle A	3	3	.500	14	7	5-1	0	87.1	74	35	0	1	20	50	2.99	84	.232	.279	28-0-3	.179	0	81	-2		-0.
1908	Cle A	13	8	.619	29	24	16	0	199.1	152	60	1	4	66	101	2.12	113	.219	.290	74-0-5	.108	-4	134	8		-0.
1909	Cle A	13	14	.481	34	29	19-4	1	247	221	95	2	12	58	162	2.73	94	.256	.312	83-0-2	.133	-1	78	0		-0.
1910	Cle A	3	4	.429	13	8	2	0	65.1	57	25	0	3	32	24	3.03	85	.243	.341	21-0-3	.143	-1	88	-1		-0.
Total 4		32	29	.525	90	68	42-5	1	599	504	215	3	20	176	337	2.60	96	.239	.303	206-0-13	.131	-6	98	5		-0.

BERGMAN, DUSTY
Dustin Michael B2.1.1978 Carson City NV BL/TL/6-5/200 [AnaA99 6/191] d6.9 Col Hawaii

YEAR	TM LG	W	L	PCT	G	GS	CG-SHO	SV-BS	IP	H	R	HR	HB	BB-IB	SO	ERA	AERA	OAV	OOB	AB-HR-SH	AVG	PB	SUP	APR	DL	PW
2004	Ana N	0	1	.000			1		0						1	13.50	33	.444	.455	0	—	0		-2		-0.

BERGMAN, SEAN
Sean Frederick B4.11.1970 Joliet IL BR/TR/6-4/225(205-225) [DetA91 4/114] d7.7 Col Southern Illinois

YEAR	TM LG	W	L	PCT	G	GS	CG-SHO	SV-BS	IP	H	R	HR	HB	BB-IB	SO	ERA	AERA	OAV	OOB	AB-HR-SH	AVG	PB	SUP	APR	DL	PW
1993	Det A	1	4	.200	9	6	1	0-0	39.2	47	29	6	1	23-3	19	5.67	77	.294	.382	0	—	0	109	-6		-0
1994	Det A	2	1	.667	3	3	0	0-0	17.2	22	11	2	1	7-0	12	5.60	88	.301	.366	0	—	-0	149	-1		-0
1995	Det A	7	10	.412	28	28	1-1	0-0	135.1	169	95	19	4	67-8	86	5.12	94	.307	.384	30-1-0	.100	-1*	115	-6	21	-1
1996	SD N	6	8	.429	41	14	0	0-0	113.1	119	63	14	2	33-3	85	4.37	92	.274	.325	13-0-3	.231	1	141	-24		-1
1997	SD N	2	4	.333	44	9	0	0-2	99	126	72	11	3	38-4	74	6.09	64	.316	.376							
1998	Hou N	12	9	.571	31	27	1	0-0	172	183	81	20	5	42-3	100	3.72	109	.268	.315	60-0-8	.083	-3	134	5		0
1999	Hou N	4	6	.400	19	16	2-1	0-0	99	130	60	9	3	26-1	38	5.36	82	.332	.374	28-2-1	.107	1	90	-9	40	0
	Atl N	1	0	1.000	6	0	0	0-1	6.1	5	2	0	0	3-0	6	2.84	157	.217	.308	0	—	0		1		0
	Year	5		.455	25	16	2-1	0-1	105.1	135	62	9	3	29-1	44	5.21	85	.325	.370	28-2-1	.107	1	108	-30		-0
2000	Min A	4	5	.444	47	1	0	0-3	68	111	76	18	2	33-1	35	9.66	55	.374	.436	2	.500	1	113	-80	61	-7
Total 8		39	47	.453	196	117	5-2	0-3	750.1	912	489	99	21	272-23	455	5.28	83	.303	.362	133-3-12	.113	-2	113	-80	61	-7

BERGMANN, JASON
Jason Chris B9.25.1981 Neptune NJ BR/TR/6-4/205 d8.28 Col Rutgers

YEAR	TM LG	W	L	PCT	G	GS	CG-SHO	SV-BS	IP	H	R	HR	HB	BB-IB	SO	ERA	AERA	OAV	OOB	AB-HR-SH	AVG	PB	SUP	APR	DL	PW
2005	Was N	2	0	1.000	15	1	0	0-0	19.2	14	6	1	2	11-1	21	2.75	147	.200	.321	3	.333	1	161	3		0

BERLY, JACK
John Chambers B5.24.1903 Natchitoches LA D6.26.1977 Houston TX BR/TR/5-11.5/190 d4.22

YEAR	TM LG	W	L	PCT	G	GS	CG-SHO	SV-BS	IP	H	R	HR	HB	BB-IB	SO	ERA	AERA	OAV	OOB	AB-HR-SH	AVG	PB	SUP	APR	DL	PW
1924	StL N	0	0	—	4	0	0	0	8	12	8	2	0	4	2	5.63	67	.267	.353	2	.000	0		-1		-0
1931	NY N	7	8	.467	27	11	4-1	0	111.1	114	55	6	4	51	45	3.88	95	.270	.354	35	.171	-1	122	-1		-1
1932	Phi N	1	2	.333	21	1	0	2	46	61	42	4	1	21	15	7.63	58	.333	.405	10	.000	-1	76	-13		-1
1933	Phi N	2	3	.400	13	6	1-1	0	50	62	30	5	2	22	4	5.04	76	.307	.381	13-0-1	.308	0	87	-5		-1
Total 4		10	13	.435	65	18	6-2	2	215.1	245	132	17	7	98	66	5.02	78	.292	.371	60-0-1	.167	-2	104	-20		-1

BERNAL, VICTOR
Victor Hugo B10.6.1953 Los Angeles CA BR/TR/6-1/175 [SDN75 6/122] d4.6 Col Cal Poly-Pomona

YEAR	TM LG	W	L	PCT	G	GS	CG-SHO	SV-BS	IP	H	R	HR	HB	BB-IB	SO	ERA	AERA	OAV	OOB	AB-HR-SH	AVG	PB	SUP	APR	DL	PW
1977	SD N	1	1	.500	15	0	0	0-0	20.1	23	13	4	0	9-2	6	5.31	67	.287	.360	1	.000	0		-4		-0

BERNARD, DWIGHT
Dwight Vern B5.31.1952 Mt.Vernon IL BR/TR/6-2/170* [NYN74 2/41] d6.29 Col Belmont

YEAR	TM LG	W	L	PCT	G	GS	CG-SHO	SV-BS	IP	H	R	HR	HB	BB-IB	SO	ERA	AERA	OAV	OOB	AB-HR-SH	AVG	PB	SUP	APR	DL	PW
1978	NY N	1	4	.200	30	1	0	0-2	48	54	25	4	0	27-3	26	4.31	82	.297	.386	5	.200	0	127	-4		-0
1979	NY N	0	3	.000	32	1	0	0-0	44	59	26	2	0	26-4	20	4.70	79	.331	.411	0-0-2	—	0	119	-5		-0
1981 †Mil A		0	0	—	6	0	0	0-0	5	5	3	0	0	6-1	1	3.60	96	.263	.407	0	—	0		0		0
1982 †Mil A		3	1	.750	47	0	0	6-3	79	78	39	4	1	27-0	45	3.76	102	.263	.321	0	—	0		0		-0
Total 4		4	8	.333	115	2	0	6-5	176	196	93	10	1	86-8	92	4.14	90	.290	.366	5-0-2	.200	1	121	-9		-0

YEAR	TM LG	W	L	PCT	G	GS	CG-SHO	SV-BS	IP	H	R	HR	HB	BB-IB	SO	ERA	AERA	OAV	OOB	AB-HR-SH	AVG	PB	SUP	APR	DL	PW

BERNARD, JOE   Joseph Carl "J.C." B3.24.1882 Brighton IL D9.22.1960 Springfield IL BR/TR/6-1/175 d9.23

| 1909 | StL N | 0 | 0 | — | 1 | 0 | 0 | 0 | 1 | 1 | 1 | 0 | 0 | 2 | 2 | 0.00 | — | .250 | .500 | 0 | | 0 | 0 | | | 0.0 |

BERNERO, ADAM   Adam Gino B11.28.1976 San Jose CA BR/TR/6-4/205* d8.1 Col Armstrong Atlantic

2000	Det A	0	1	.000	12	4	0	0-0	34.1	33	18	3	1	13-1	20	4.19	117	.270	.338	0	—	0	96	2		0.1
2001	Det A	0	0	—	5	0	0	0-0	12.1	13	13	4	1	4-0	8	7.30	61	.260	.321	0	—	0		-5		-0.2
2002	Det A	4	7	.364	28	11	0	0-0	101.2	128	74	17	6	31-1	69	6.20	71	.309	.362	4-0-1	.000	-0	98	-19		-1.8
2003	Det A	1	12	.077	18	17	0	0-0	100.2	104	68	14	7	41-0	54	6.08	72	.267	.342	4	.000	-0*	56	-17		-1.8
	Col N	0	2	.000	31	0	0	0-2	32.2	33	22	5	1	13-1	26	5.23	94	.266	.336	2	.000	-0		-2		-0.1
2004	Col N	1	1	.500	16	2	0	0-1	32.1	36	20	7	0	17-2	21	5.57	85	.283	.361	5-0-1	.000	-1	136	-2	87	-0.2
2005	Atl N	4	3	.571	36	0	0	0-1	47	61	35	5	4	12-3	37	6.51	66	.313	.360	1-0-1	1.000	0		-11		-1.4
Total	6		10	26	.278	146	34	0	0-4	361	408	250	55	20	131-8	235	5.91	76	.287	.350	16-0-3	.063	-1	79	-54	87	-5.4

BERNHARD, BILL   William Henry "Strawberry Bill" B3.16.1871 Clarence NY D3.30.1949 San Diego CA BB/TR/6-1/205 d4.24

1899	Phi N	6	6	.500	21	12	10-1	0	132.1	120	66	3	6	36	23	2.65	139	.242	.301	54		.241	0	109	12		0.9
1900	Phi N	15	10	.600	32	27	20	2	218.2	284	151	3	5	74	49	4.77	76	.313	.368	91		.154	-5	131	-25		-2.8
1901	Phi A	17	10	.630	31	27	26-1	0	257	328	169	6	2	50	58	4.52	84	.307	.339	107-0-3	.187	-1*	97	-16		-1.3
1902	Phi A	1	0	1.000	1	1	1	0	9	7	1	0	0	3	1	1.00	367	.212	.278	4	.000	-1	157	3		0.2
	Cle A	17	5	.773	27	24	22-3	1	217	169	78	4	5	34	57	2.20	157	.216	.253	90	.200	-1	120	32		2.9
	Year	18	5	.783	28	25	23-3	1	226	176	79	4	5	37	58	2.15	161	.215	.254	94	.191	-2	122	33		3.1
1903	Cle A	14	5	.737	20	19	18-3	0	165.2	151	62	1	0	21	60	2.12	135	.242	.267	65	.185	-1	121	13		1.5
1904	Cle A	23	13	.639	38	37	35-4	0	320.2	323	107	3	4	55	137	2.13	119	.263	.296	124-0-3	.177	-1	127	15		1.6
1905	Cle A	7	13	.350	22	19	17	0	174.1	185	93	5	1	34	56	3.36	78	.274	.309	69	.087	-6	72	-16		-2.3
1906	Cle A	16	15	.516	31	30	23-2	0	255.1	235	99	1	5	47	85	2.54	103	.248	.287	99-0-2	.212	2	123	5		0.9
1907	Cle A	0	4	.000	8	4	3	0	42	58	32	0	0	11	19	3.21	78	.330	.369	15	.200	0	74	-7		-0.6
Total	9		116	81	.589	231	200	175-14	3	1792	1860	858	26	28	365	545	3.04	102	.268	.307	718-0-8	.180	-13	114	16		1.0

BERNHARDT, WALTER   Walter Jacob B5.20.1893 Pleasant Valley Twp. PA D7.26.1958 Watertown NY BR/TR/6-2/175 d7.16 Col Penn

| 1918 | NY A | 0 | 0 | — | 1 | 0 | 0 | 0 | 0.2 | 0 | 1 | 0 | 0 | 0 | 1 | 0.00 | — | .000 | .000 | 0 | | — | 0 | | 0 | | 0.0 |

BERRY, JOE   Jonas Arthur "Jittery Joe" B12.16.1904 Huntsville AR D9.27.1958 Anaheim CA BL/TR/5-10.5/145 d9.6

1942	Chi N	0	0	—	2	0	0	0	2	7	4	0	0	2	1	18.00	18	.538	.600	0	—	0		-3		-0.2
1944	Phi A	10	8	.556	53	0	0	12	111.1	78	32	4	2	23	44	1.94	179	.192	.238	25-0-3	.120	-1	17			3.2
1945	Phi A	8	7	.533	52	0	0	5	130.1	114	40	5	0	38	51	2.35	146	.232	.287	35-0-2	.143	-1	15			1.8
1946	Phi A	0	1	.000	5	0	0	0	13	15	5	1	1	3	5	2.77	128	.288	.339	3-0-1	.333	0	1			0.1
	Cle A	3	6	.333	21	0	0	1	37.1	32	18	4	0	21	16	3.38	98	.235	.338	7-0-1	.286	0		-1		-0.3
	Year	3	7	.300	26	0	0	1	50.1	47	23	5	1	24	21	3.22	105	.250	.338	10-0-2	.300	1		0		-0.2
Total	4		21	22	.488	133	0	0	18	294	246	99	14	3	87	117	2.45	140	.224	.282	70-0-7	.157	-2		29		4.6

BERTAINA, FRANK   Frank Louis B4.14.1944 San Francisco CA BL/TL/5-11/180* d8.1

1964	Bal A	1	0	1.000	6	4	1-1	0	26	18	8	3	0	13-1	18	2.77	129	.198	.298	5-0-2	.000	-1	93	3		0.1
1965	Bal A	0	0	—	2	1	0	0	6	9	4	0	0	4-0	5	6.00	58	.360	.433	1	.000	-0	152	-1		-0.1
1966	Bal A	2	5	.286	16	8	0	0	63.1	52	29	3	4	36-2	46	3.13	107	.226	.338	19	.105	-1	120	-1		-0.2
1967	Bal A	1	1	.500	5	2	0	0	21.2	17	9	4	0	14-0	19	3.32	95	.224	.341	9	.111	-0	14	-1		-0.1
	Was A	6	5	.545	18	17	4-4	0	95.2	90	36	8	0	37-1	67	2.92	108	.251	.320	35-0-2	.057	-3*	102	3		0.0
	Year	7	6	.538	23	19	4-4	0	117.1	107	45	12	0	51-1	86	2.99	106	.247	.324	44-0-2	.068	-3	93	2		-0.1
1968	Was A	7	13	.350	27	23	1	0	127.1	133	76	15	6	69-1	81	4.66	63	.273	.366	38-0-1	.132	-0	101	-25		-3.8
1969	Was A	1	3	.250	14	5	0	0-0	35.2	43	30	4	0	23-0	25	6.56	53	.291	.384	11-1-1	.364	2	131	-13		-1.0
	Bal A	0	0	—	3	0	0	0-0	6	1	0	0	0	3-0	5	0.00	—	.063	.200	1	1.000	1		2		0.2
	Year	1	3	.250	17	5	0	0-0	41.2	44	30	8	0	26-0	30	5.62	63	.268	.365	12-1-1	.417	3	131	-10		-0.8
1970	StL N	1	2	.333	8	5	0	0-1	31.1	36	16	1	0	15-3	14	3.16	131	.293	.367	7	.143	-0	87	2		0.2
Total	7		19	29	.396	99	66	6-5	0-1	413	399	208	42	10	214-8	280	3.84	85	.257	.347	126-1-6	.127	-1	102	-31		-4.7

BERTOTTI, MIKE   Michael David B1.18.1970 Jersey City NJ BL/TL/6-1/185* [ChiA91 31/826] d7.29 Col Iona

1995	Chi A	1	1	.500	4	4	0	0-0	14.1	23	20	6	3	11-0	15	12.56	36	.365	.463	0	—	0	135	-13		-1.3
1996	Chi A	2	0	1.000	15	2	0	0-1	28	28	18	5	0	20-3	19	5.14	93	.257	.369	0	—	0	117	-2		-0.1
1997	Chi A	0	0	—	9	0	0	0-0	3.2	9	3	0	0	2-0	4	7.36	60	.450	.478	0	—	0		-1		-0.1
Total	3		3	1	.750	28	6	0	0-1	46	60	41	11	3	33-3	38	7.63	61	.313	.412	0	—	0	127	-16		-1.5

BERTRAND, LEFTY   Roman Mathias B2.28.1909 Cobden MN D3.17.2002 The Dalles OR BR/TL/6-0/180 d4.15 Col St. Marys (MN)

| 1936 | Phi N | 0 | 0 | — | 1 | 0 | 0 | 0 | 2 | 3 | 2 | 1 | 0 | 2 | 1 | 9.00 | 50 | .333 | .455 | 0 | — | 0 | | -1 | | 0.0 |

BERUMEN, ANDRES   Andres B4.5.1971 Tijuana, Baja California, Mexico BR/TR/6-2/210* [KCA89 27/699] d4.27

1995	SD N	2	3	.400	37	0	0	1-3	44.1	37	29	3	3	36-3	42	5.68	72	.226	.369	1	.000	-0		-7	21	-0.8
1996	SD N	0	0	—	3	0	0	0-0	3.1	3	2	1	1	2-1	4	5.40	75*	.231	.375	0		0		0		0.0
Total	2		2	3	.400	40	0	0	1-3	47.2	40	31	4	4	38-4	46	5.66	72	.226	.369	1	.000	-0		-7	21	-0.8

BESANA, FRED   Frederick Cyril B4.5.1931 Lincoln CA BR/TL/6-3.5/200 d4.18 Col Cal St.-Sacramento

| 1956 | Bal A | 1 | 0 | 1.000 | 7 | 2 | 0 | 0 | 17.2 | 22 | 12 | 0 | 2 | 14-0 | 7 | 5.60 | 70 | .310 | .427 | 4 | .000 | -0 | 136 | -3 | | -0.2 |

BESSE, HERMAN   Herman A. B8.16.1911 St.Louis MO D8.13.1972 Los Angeles CA BL/TL/6-2/190 d4.19 Mil 1944-45

1940	Phi A	0	3	.000	17	5	0	0	53	70	56	10	3	34	19	8.83	50	.315	.413	19	.263	2	130	-23		-0.9
1941	Phi A	2	0	1.000	6	2	1	0	19.2	28	22	4	0	12	8	10.07	42	.329	.412	5	.200	-0	103	-11		-0.9
1942	Phi A	2	9	.182	30	14	4	1	133	163	99	7	4	69	78	6.16	61	.300	.383	53	.226	2*	110	-31		-2.2
1943	Phi A	1	1	.500	5	1	0	0	16.1	18	6	2	1	4	3	3.31	103	.295	.348	8	.000	-1*	199	1		-0.1
1946	Phi A	0	2	.000	7	3	0	1	20.2	19	12	1	0	9	10	5.23	68	.247	.326	5	.000	0	81	-3		-0.3
Total	5		5	15	.250	65	25	5	2	242.2	298	195	24	8	128	118	6.79	58	.302	.386	90	.200	2	114	-67		-4.4

BESSENT, DON   Fred Donald B3.13.1931 Jacksonville FL D7.7.1990 Jacksonville FL BR/TR/6-0/175* d7.17

1955	†Bro N	8	1	.889	24	2	1	3	63.1	51	19	7	0	21-2	29	2.70	150	.220	.283	20-0-3	.100	-2	132	11		1.3
1956	†Bro N	4	3	.571	38	2	0	9	79.1	63	23	5	0	31-6	52	2.50	159	.221	.295	18-0-1	.111	-1		13		1.2
1957	Bro N	1	3	.250	27	0	0	0	44.2	58	28	5	0	19-3	24	5.73	73	.328	.387	4	.250	0		-6		-0.5
1958	LA N	1	0	1.000	19	0	0	0	24.1	24	14	3	1	17-0	13	3.33	123	.270	.303	2-0-1	.000	-0		0	77	0.0
Total	4		14	7	.667	108	2	1	12	211	196	84	20	1	88-11	118	3.33	122	.250	.324	44-0-5	.114	-3	132	18	77	2.0

BEST, KARL   Karl Jon B3.6.1959 Aberdeen WA BR/TR/6-4/210(190-210) [SeaA77 12/312] d8.19 [DL 1989 SF N 182]

1983	Sea A	0	1	.000	4	0	0	0-0	5.1	14	9	2	2	5-0	3	13.50	32	.483	.583	0	—	0		-5		-0.8
1984	Sea A	1	1	.500	9	0	0	0-0	6	7	2	0	0	4-0	6	3.00	134	.292	.280	0	—	0		1		0.2
1985	Sea A	2	1	.667	15	0	0	4-0	32.1	25	9	1	1	6-0	32	1.95	217	.207	.250	0	—	0		7	105	0.8
1986	Sea A	2	3	.400	26	0	0	1-2	35.2	35	19	3	1	21-2	23	4.04	106	.255	.354	0	—	0		0	11	0.0
1988	Min A	0	0	—	11	0	0	0-0	12	15	9	1	0	7-1	9	6.00	68	.306	.379	0	—	0		-3		-0.1
Total	5		5	6	.455	61	0	0	5-2	91.1	96	48	7	4	39-3	73	4.04	104	.267	.341	0	—	0		0	298	-0.1

BETANCOURT, RAFAEL   Rafael Jose B4.29.1975 Cumana, Venez BR/TR/6-2/170(170-200) d7.13

2003	Cle A	2	2	.500	33	0	0	1-2	38	27	11	5	1	13-2	36	2.13	208	.196	.268	0		0		10		0.9
2004	Cle A	5	6	.455	68	0	0	4-7	66.2	71	32	9	0	18-6	76	3.92	111	.268	.312	0		0		3	15	0.4
2005	Cle A	4	3	.571	54	0	0	1-2	67.2	57	23	3	0	17-2	73	2.79	147	.224	.273	0		0		11	18	0.9
Total		11	11	.500	155	0	0	6-11	172.1	155	66	17	1	48-10	185	3.08	139	.236	.288	0		0		24	33	2.2

BETHKE, JIM   James Charles B11.5.1946 Falls City NE BR/TR/6-3/185 d4.12

| 1965 | NY N | 2 | 0 | 1.000 | 25 | 0 | 0 | 0 | 40 | 41 | 24 | 3 | 6 | 22-2 | 19 | 4.27 | 83 | .266 | .377 | 4 | .000 | -0 | | -4 | | -0.2 |

BETTENDORF, JEFF   Jeffrey Allen B12.10.1960 Lompoc CA BR/TR/6-3/190 [NYN79 2/28] d4.8

| 1984 | Oak A | 0 | 0 | — | 2 | 0 | 0 | 1-0 | 9.2 | 9 | 5 | 3 | 0 | 5-0 | 5 | 4.66 | 81 | .243 | .333 | 0 | — | 0 | | -1 | | -0.1 |

YEAR	TM LG	W	L	PCT	G	GS	CG-SHO	SV-BS	IP	H	R	HR	HB	BB-IB	SO	ERA	AERA	OAV	OOB	AB-HR-SH	AVG	PB	SUP	APR	DL	Pl
BETTS, HARRY	Harold Matthew "Chubby","Ginger" B6.19.1881 Alliance OH D5.22.1946 San Antonio TX BR/TR/5-10/200 d9.22																									
1903	StL N	0	1	.000	1	1	1	0	9	11	10	0	2	2	2	10.00	33	.297	.409	3	.000	-0	21	-5		-0.
1913	Cin N	0	0	—	1	0	0	0	3.1	1	1	0	1	3	0	2.70	120	.143	.455	1	.000	-0	0			0.
Total	2	0	1	.000	2	1	1	0	12.1	12	11	0	3	8	2	8.03	41	.273	.418	4	.000	-1	21	-5		-0.
BETTS, HUCK	Walter McKinley B2.18.1897 Millsboro DE D6.13.1987 Millsboro DE BR/TR/5-11/170 d4.26																									
1920	Phi N	1	1	.500	27	4	1	0	88.1	86	48	3	2	33	18	3.57	96	.261	.332	25	.080	-2	115	-2		-0.
1921	Phi N	3	7	.300	32	2	1	4	100.2	141	65	8	4	14	28	4.47	95	.337	.365	30	.267	0	10	-1		-0.
1922	Phi N	1	0	1.000	7	0	0	0	15	23	17	3	0	8	4	9.60	49	.348	.419	4	.000	-0		-6		-0.
1923	Phi N	2	4	.333	19	4	3	1	84.1	100	38	7	4	14	18	3.09	149	.314	.351	31-0-1	.097	-3*	45	11		0.
1924	Phi N	7	10	.412	37	9	2	2	144.1	160	76	8	5	42	46	4.30	104	.286	.341	45-0-6	.156	-2*	93	4		-0.
1925	Phi N	4	5	.444	35	7	1	1	97.1	146	86	10	3	38	28	5.55	86	.342	.400	34	.294	2*	121	-12		-0.
1932	Bos N	13	11	.542	31	27	16-3	1	221.2	229	84	9	0	35	32	2.80	134	.267	.295	79-0-1	.241	2	94	23		2.
1933	Bos N	11	11	.500	35	26	17-2	1	242	225	79	9	0	55	40	2.79	114	.248	.290	76-0-9	.224	2	93	11		1.
1934	Bos N	17	10	.630	40	27	10-2	3	213	258	105	17	3	42	69	4.06	94	.296	.296	69-0-6	.188	1	107	-3		-0.
1935	Bos N	2	9	.182	44	19	2-1	0	159.2	213	118	9	2	40	40	5.47	69	.321	.362	44-0-2	.159	-0	85	-34		-2.
Total	10	61	68	.473	307	125	53-8	16	1366.1	1581	716	83	23	321	323	3.93	98	.292	.334	437-0-25	.197	-2	91	-9		-0.
BEVENS, BILL	Floyd Clifford B10.21.1916 Hubbard OR D10.26.1991 Salem OR BR/TR/6-3.5/210 d5.12 [DL 1948 NY A 63]																									
1944	NY A	4	1	.800	8	5	3	0	43.2	44	18	4	1	13	16	2.68	130	.273	.331	16-0-1	.063	-2	163	3		0.
1945	NY A	13	9	.591	29	25	14-2	0	184	174	83	12	1	68	76	3.67	94	.254	.322	63-1-4	.111	-4	118	-2		-0.
1946	NY A	16	13	.552	31	31	18-3	0	249.2	213	73	11	1	78	120	2.23	154	.232	.293	84-2-8	.083	-4	88	34		3.
1947	†NY A	7	13	.350	28	23	11-1	0	165	167	79	13	1	77	77	3.82	93	.264	.345	58-0-3	.121	-3	104	-7		-1
Total	4	40	36	.526	96	84	46-6	0	642.1	598	253	40	4	236	289	3.08	113	.250	.318	221-3-16	.100	-13	106	28	63	1
BEVERLIN, JASON	Jason Robert B11.27.1973 Ashtabula OH BL/TR/6-5/220 [OakA94 4/93] d7.29 Col Western Carolina																									
2002	Cle A	0	0	—	4	0	0	0-0	7.1	9	7	1	0	4-0	9	7.36	60	.290	.371	0	—	0		-3		-0
	Det A	0	3	.000	3	3	0	0-0	12.1	18	15	2	0	5-0	7	9.49	46	.327	.383	0	—	0	50	-7		-1
	Year	0	3	.000	7	3	0	0-0	19.2	27	22	3	0	9-0	16	8.69	51	.314	.379	0	—	0	49	-10		-1.
BEVIL, BRIAN	Brian Scott B9.5.1971 Houston TX BR/TR/6-3/190(190-225) [KCA90 30/817] d6.17 Col Angelina (TX) JC																									
1996	KC A	1	0	1.000	3	1	0	0-0	11	9	7	2	0	5-0	7	5.73	88	.237	.318	0	—	0	111	-1		0.
1997	KC A	1	2	.333	18	0	0	1-4	16.1	16	13	1	1	9-2	13	6.61	72	.267	.361	0	—	0		-3		-0
1998	KC A	3	1	.750	39	0	0	0-2	40	47	29	4	3	22-1	47	6.30	77	.283	.373	0	—	0		-5	67	-0
Total	3	5	3	.625	60	1	0	1-6	67.1	72	49	7	4	36-3	67	6.28	77	.273	.362	0	—	0	111	-9	67	-1
BEVIL, LOU	Louis Eugene (b Louis Eugene Bevilacqua) B11.27.1922 Nelson IL D2.1.1973 Dixon IL BB/TR/5-11.5/190 d9.2 Mil 1943-45 Col Notre Dame																									
1942	Was A	1	4	.000	4	1	0	0	9.2	9	7	0	1	11	2	6.52	56	.265	.457	3	.000	-0	140	-3		-0
BEVILLE, BEN	Clarence Benjamin B8.28.1877 Colusa CA D1.5.1937 Yountville CA BR/TR/5-9/190 d5.24																									
1901	Bos A	0	2	.000	2	2	1	0	9	8	7	0	1	9	1	4.00	88	.235	.409	7	.286	0*	29	-1		-0
BIBBY, JIM	James Blair B10.29.1944 Franklinton NC BR/TR/6-5/235(230-250) d9.4 Col Fayetteville St. [DL 1982 Pit N 182]																									
1972	StL N	1	3	.250	6	6	0	0-0	40.1	29	18	4	1	19-4	28	3.35	102	.206	.302	8-0-2	.125	0	103	0		0
1973	StL N	0	2	.000	6	3	0	0-0	16	19	17	2	2	17-2	12	9.56	38	.306	.463	2	.000	0	80	-9		-1
	Tex A	9	10	.474	26	23	11-2	1-0	180.1	121	73	14	6	106-4	155	3.24	116	.192	.312	0	—	0*	81	11		1
1974	Tex A	19	19	.500	41	41	11-5	0-0	264	255	146	25	9	113-4	149	4.74	76	.255	.334	0	—	0	119	-29		-3
1975	Tex A	2	6	.250	12	12	4-1	0-0	68.1	73	41	2	2	28-0	31	5.00	75	.274	.342	0	—	0	115	-8		-0
	Cle A	5	9	.357	24	12	2	1-2	112.2	99	48	4	0	50-3	62	3.20	119	.235	.313	0	—	0	100	-1		-0
	Year	7	15	.318	36	24	6-1	1-2	181	172	89	9	2	78-3	93	3.88	98	.250	.324	0	—	0	96	-1		-0
1976	Cle A	13	7	.650	34	21	4-3	1-0	163.1	162	61	6	1	56-1	84	3.20	110	.266	.325	0	—	0	96	6		-0
1977	Cle A	12	13	.480	37	30	9-2	2-0	206.2	197	100	17	6	73-2	141	3.57	112	.250	.315	0	—	0	95	1		C
1978	Pit N	8	7	.533	34	14	3-2	1-2	107	110	52	10	2	39-7	72	3.53	106	.246	.314	31-1-0	.129	1	95	1		C
1979	†Pit N	12	4	.750	34	17	4-1	0-1	137.2	110	51	9	4	47-6	103	2.81	139	.218	.289	45-2-6	.178	2	117	15		0
1980	Pit N★	19	6	.760	35	34	6-1	0-0	238.1	210	95	20	6	88-3	144	3.32	111	.238	.311	77-1-10	.156	2	126	11		1
1981	Pit N	6	3	.667	14	14	2-2	0-0	93.2	79	30	4	2	26-1	48	2.50	146	.225	.279	28-1-4	.143	1	103	11		-4
1983	Pit N	5	12	.294	29	12	0	2-1	78	92	60	10	1	51-0	44	6.69	56	.297	.393	18-0-2	.111	-1	89	-23		-4
1984	Tex A	0	0	—	8	0	0	0-0	16.1	19	8	1	0	10-1	6	4.41	95	.297	.392	0	—	0		0		-0
Total	12	111	101	.524	340	239	56-19	8-6	1722.2	1565	800	131	40	723-38	1079	3.76	99	.243	.321	209-5-24	.148	5	104	0	182	-2
BICKFORD, VERN	Vernon Edgell B8.17.1920 Hellier KY D5.6.1960 Concord VA BR/TR/6-0/185* d4.24																									
1948	†Bos N	11	5	.688	33	22	10-1	1	146	125	59	9	3	63	60	3.27	117	.226	.309	49-0-6	.204	1	131	10		1
1949	Bos N★	16	11	.593	37	36	15-2	0	230.2	246	125	20	6	106	101	4.25	89	.273	.354	81-0-10	.185	-1	123	-12		-C
1950	Bos N	19	14	.576	40	**39**	27-2	0	**311.2**	293	135	25	6	122	126	3.47	111	.248	.321	116-0-9	.138	-4	122	16		-C
1951	Bos N	11	9	.550	25	20	12-3	0	164.2	146	68	7	4	76	76	3.12	118	.240	.330	52-0-6	.115	-2	125	10		-C
1952	Bos N	7	12	.368	26	22	7-1	0	161.1	165	73	7	2	64	62	3.74	97	.269	.340	51-0-5	.176	-0	58	-2		-C
1953	Mil N	2	5	.286	20	9	2	1	58	60	35	8	2	35	25	5.28	74	.279	.385	15-0-1	.067	-1	114	-7		-C
1954	Bal A	0	1	.000	1	1	0	0	4	5	5	0	0	1	0	9.00	40	.333	.316	1	.000	-0	98	-3		-C
Total	7	66	57	.537	182	149	73-9	2	1076.1	1040	500	76	25	467	450	3.71	102	.254	.334	365-0-37	.156	-7	114	12		-C
BICKHAM, DAN	Daniel Denison B10.31.1864 Dayton OH D3.3.1951 Dayton OH BR/TR/5-10/160 d8.13 Col Princeton																									
1886	Cin AA	0	1	0	1.000	1	1	0	9	13	11	0	0	3	3.00	117	.351	.400	3	.333	0	202	-2		-C
BICKNELL, CHARLIE	Charles Stephen "Bud" B7.27.1928 Plainfield NJ BR/TR/5-11/170 d4.22																									
1948	Phi N	0	1	.000	17	1	0	0	25.2	29	20	5	0	17	5	5.96	66	.287	.390	5	.000	-1	67	-6		-C
1949	Phi N	0	0	—	13	0	0	0	28.1	32	24	3	2	17	4	7.62	52	.291	.395	1	.000	1		-11		-C
Total	2	0	1	.000	30	1	0	0	54	61	44	8	2	34	9	6.83	58	.289	.393	6	.000	-0	67	-17		-C
BIDDLE, ROCKY	Lee Francis B5.21.1976 Las Vegas NV BR/TR/6-3/230* [ChiA97 1/51] d8.10 Col Cal St.-Long Beach																									
2000	Chi A	1	2	.333	4	4	0	0-0	22.2	31	25	6	0	8-0	7	8.34	61	.326	.371	0	—	0	153	-9		-0
2001	Chi A	7	8	.467	30	21	0	0-3	128.2	137	87	16	8	52-3	85	5.39	87	.272	.347	1-0-1	.000	-0	104	-11	17	-
2002	Chi A	3	4	.429	44	7	0	1-2	77.2	72	42	13	5	39-4	64	4.06	111	.245	.342	0	—	0	112	2	33	C
2003	Mon N	5	8	.385	73	0	0	34-7	71.2	71	43	10	6	40-5	54	4.65	95	.254	.359	1	.000	-0		-2		-
2004	Mon N	4	8	.333	47	9	0	11-4	78	98	69	15	8	31-3	51	6.92	66	.307	.380	11-0-3	.000	-1	76	-20		-C
Total	5	20	30	.400	198	41	0	46-16	378.2	409	266	59	27	170-15	261	5.47	84	.274	.357	13-0-4	.000	-1	106	-40	50	-C
BIELECKI, MIKE	Michael Joseph B7.31.1959 Baltimore MD BR/TR/6-3/195* [PitN79 S1/8] d9.14 Col Valencia (FL) CC																									
1984	Pit N	0	0	—	4	0	0	0-0	4.1	4	0	0	0	1	0	0.00	—	.250	.250	0	—	0		2		-
1985	Pit N	2	3	.400	12	7	0	0-0	45.2	45	26	5	1	31-1	22	4.53	80	.257	.372	10-0-1	.000	-1*	63	-5		-
1986	Pit N	6	11	.353	31	27	0	0-0	148.2	149	87	10	2	83-3	83	4.66	83	.262	.355	48-0-4	.063	-3	102	-13		-
1987	Pit N	2	3	.400	8	8	2	0-0	45.2	43	25	6	1	12-0	25	4.73	88	.250	.299	16-0-2	.063	-0	103	-2		-
1988	Chi N	2	2	.500	19	5	0	0-0	48.1	55	22	4	0	16-1	33	3.35	109	.284	.332	10	.100	-0	97	1		-
1989	†Chi N	18	7	**.720**	33	33	4-3	0-0	212.1	187	82	16	0	81-8	147	3.14	120	.237	.307	70-0-9	.043	-5	105	14		-
1990	Chi N	8	11	.421	36	29	0	1-0	168	188	101	13	9	70-11	103	4.93	83	.287	.359	43-0-10	.163	-0	95	-14		-
1991	Chi N	13	11	.542	39	25	0	0-1	172	169	91	18	2	54-6	72	4.50	87	.262	.318	46-0-4	.065	-2	110	-9		-
	Atl N	0	0	—	2	0	0	0-0	1.2	2	0	0	0	2-0	3	0.00	—	.286	.444	0	—	0		-9		-
	Year	13	11	.542	41	25	0	0-1	173.2	171	91	18	2	56-6	75	4.46	86	.262	.319	46-0-4	.065	-2	110	-9		-
1992	Atl N	2	4	.333	19	14	1-1	0-0	80.2	77	27	2	1	27-1	62	2.57	143	.254	.315	24-0-4	.125	-1	90	9	68	-
1993	Cle A	4	5	.444	13	13	0	0-0	68.2	90	47	8	2	23-3	38	5.90	74	.310	.363	0	—	0	110	-10		-
1994	Atl N	0	1	.000	19	0	0	0-0	27	28	12	2	1	18-4	18	4.00	108	.277	.360	3-0-1	.000	-0	148	1		-
1995	Cal A	4	6	.400	22	11	0	0-0	75.1	80	56	15	3	31-1	45	5.97	79	.273	.343	0	—	0	106	-11	46	-
1996	†Atl N	4	3	.571	40	5	0	2-0	75.1	63	24	8	0	33-6	71	2.63	169	.224	.303	10	.000	0		-1	43	-
1997	Atl N	3	7	.300	50	1	0	0-0	57.1	70	33	4	2	21-3	60	4.08	103	.250	.316	2	.000	0	101	-22	157	-
Total	14	70	73	.490	347	178	7-4	5-5	1231	1236	633	116	19	496-45	783	4.16	96	.262	.332	282-0-35	.078	-14	101	-22	157	-

YEAR	TM LG	W	L	PCT	G	GS	CG-SHO	SV-BS	IP	H	R	HR	HB	BB-IB	SO	ERA	AERA	OAV	OOB	AB-HR-SH	AVG	PB	SUP	APR	DL	PW
BIEMILLER, HARRY	Harry Lee B10.9.1897 Baltimore MD D5.25.1965 Orlando FL BR/TR/6-1/171 d8.26																									
1920	Was A	1	0	1.000	5	2	1	0	17	21	13	1	0	13	10	4.76	78	.318	.430	4-0-1	.000	-1	128	-3		-0.2
1925	Cin N	0	1	.000	23	1	0	2	47	45	28	2	7	21	9	4.02	102	.280	.386	9	.000	-0	103	0		0.0
otal	2	1	1	.500	28	3	1	2	64	66	41	3	7	34	19	4.22	95	.291	.399	13-0-1	.000	-1	117	-3		-0.2
BIERBAUER, LOU	Louis W. B9.28.1865 Erie PA D1.31.1926 Erie PA BL/TR/5-8/140 d4.17 ▲																									
1886	Phi AA	0	0	—	2	0	0	0	10.2	8	9	0	0	5	1	4.22	83	.178	.260	522-2	.226	-0*		-1		-0.1
1887	Phi AA	0	0	—	1	0	0	0	1	1	0	0	0	0	1	0.00	—	.000	.000	530-1	.272	0*		0		0.1
1888	Phi AA	0	0	—	1	0	0	0	3	5	1	0	0	0	3	0.00	—	.357	.357	535	.267	0*		1		0.0
otal	3	0	0	—	4	0	0	1	14.2	13	10	0	0	5	5	3.07	112	.210	.269	1587-3	.255	0		0		0.0
BIERBRODT, NICK	Nicholas Raymond B5.16.1978 Tarzana CA BL/TL/6-5/190(185-215) [AriN96 1/30] d6.7																									
2001	Ari N	2	2	.500	5	5	0	0-0	23	29	21	6	0	12-0	17	8.22	56	.305	.380	6-0-2	.667	2*	195	-8	18	-0.8
	TB A	3	4	.429	11	11	0	0-0	61.1	71	38	11	4	27-1	56	4.55	99	.285	.363	0	—	0	92	-2		-0.2
2003	TB A	0	2	.000	13	5	0	0-0	35.1	59	41	9	5	23-3	20	9.68	47	.376	.463	0	—	0	116	-20		-0.9
	Cle A	0	0	—	5	0	0	0-0	8	5	6	0	0	4-0	9	6.75	66	.185	.273	0	—	0		-2		-0.1
	Year	0	2	.000	18	5	0	0-0	43.1	64	47	9	5	27-3	29	9.14	50	.348	.434	0	—	0	117	-21		-1.0
2004	Tex A	1	1	.500	4	4	0	0-0	17	14	11	4	2	19-0	10	5.82	85	.246	.443	2-0-1	.000	0	90	-1		-0.1
otal	3	6	9	.400	38	25	0	0-0	144.2	178	117	30	11	85-4	112	6.66	69	.304	.398	8-0-3	.500	2	118	-33	18	-2.1
BIGBEE, LYLE	Lyle Randolph "Al" B8.22.1893 Sweet Home OR D8.5.1942 Portland OR BL/TR/6-0/180 d4.15 b-Carson Col Oregon ▲																									
1920	Phi A	0	3	.000	12	2	0	0	45	66	42	5	0	25	12	8.00	50	.369	.446	75-1-1	.187	0*	128	-14		-0.8
1921	Pit N	0	0	—	5	0	0	0	8	4	1	0	4	4	1.13	341	.154	.267	2	.000	-0		2		0.1
otal	2	0	3	.000	17	2	0	0	53	70	43	5	0	29	13	6.96	57	.341	.423	77-1-1	.182	-0	128	-12		-0.7
BIGGS, CHARLIE	Charles Orval B9.15.1906 French Lick IN D5.24.1954 French Lick IN BR/TR/6-1/185 d9.3																									
1932	Chi A	1	1	.500	6	4	0	0	24.2	32	22	2	3	12	1	6.93	62	.314	.402	9	.111	-0	138	-7		-0.5
BILBREY, JIM	James Melvin B4.20.1924 Rickman TN D12.26.1985 Toledo OH BR/TR/6-2.5/205 d5.17																									
1949	StL A	0	0	—	1	0	0	0	1	1	2	0	0	3	1	18.00	25	.250	.571	0	—	0		-1		-0.1
BILDILLI, EMIL	Emil "Hill Billy" B9.16.1912 Diamond IN D9.16.1946 Hartford City IN BR/TL/5-10/170 d8.24																									
1937	StL A	0	1	.000	4	1	0	0	8	12	9	1	0	3	2	10.13	48	.353	.405	2	.000	-0	108	-4		-0.4
1938	StL A	1	2	.333	5	3	2	0	21.2	33	18	3	0	11	11	7.06	70	.359	.427	8	.250	-0	53	-4		-0.5
1939	StL A	1	1	.500	2	2	2	0	19	21	8	0	0	8	8	3.32	147	.266	.318	5-0-1	.000	-0	72	3		0.2
1940	StL A	2	4	.333	28	11	3	1	97	113	68	12	2	52	32	5.57	82	.298	.386	30-0-1	.200	-1*	105	-10		-0.5
1941	StL A	0	0	—	2	0	0	0	2.1	5	3	0	0	1	2	11.57	37	.417	.533	0	—	0		-2		-0.1
total	5	4	8	.333	41	17	7	1	148	184	106	16	2	75	55	5.84	80	.309	.388	45-0-2	.178	-2	92	-13		-1.3
BILLIARD, HARRY	Harry Pree "Pree" B11.11.1883 Monroe IN D6.3.1923 Wooster OH BR/TR/6-0/190 d7.31																									
1908	NY A	0	0	—	6	0	0	0	17	15	15	1	5	14	10	2.65	94	.234	.410	0	.167	-0		-3		-0.2
1914	Ind F	8	7	.533	32	16	3	2	125.2	117	71	4	7	63	45	3.72	84	.257	.356	38	.184	-1	111	-9		-1.2
1915	New F	0	1	.000	14	2	0	1	28.1	32	23	0	3	28	7	5.72	45	.291	.447	6-0-1	.333	0	82	-10		-0.5
otal	3	8	8	.500	52	18	5	3	171	164	109	5	15	105	62	3.95	75	.260	.379	50-0-1	.200	-1	112	-22		-1.9
BILLINGHAM, JACK	John Eugene B2.21.1943 Orlando FL BR/TR/6-4/215(185-215) d4.11																									
1968	LA N	3	0	1.000	50	1	0	8	71.1	54	18	0	2	30-9	46	2.14	129	.215	.304	3-0-2	.000	0	31	6		0.5
1969	Hou N	6	7	.462	52	4	1	2-3	82.2	92	45	12	5	29-11	71	4.25	84	.290	.357	14-0-1	.071	0	81	-6		-1.0
1970	Hou N	13	9	.591	46	24	8-2	0-2	187.2	190	102	10	10	63-2	134	3.98	98	.259	.325	58-0-7	.103	-2	104	-6		-0.8
1971	Hou N	10	16	.385	33	33	8-3	0-0	228.1	205	98	9	16	68-8	139	3.39	99	.243	.310	73-0-6	.123	-3	85	-2		-0.5
1972	†Cin N	12	12	.500	36	31	8-4	1-0	217.2	197	83	18	7	64-8	137	3.18	102	.241	.300	71-0-5	.070	-4	120	3		-0.2
1973	†Cin N☆	19	10	.655	40	**40**	**16-7**	0-0	**293.1**	257	112	20	10	95-10	155	3.04	114	.236	.303	93-0-13	.065	-5	115	13		0.8
1974	†Cin N	19	11	.633	36	35	8-3	0-0	212.1	233	105	16	4	64-9	103	3.94	89	.288	.343	67-0-11	.075	-5	117	-11		-1.9
1975	†Cin N	15	10	.600	33	32	5	0-0	208	222	100	22	9	76-12	79	4.11	87	.279	.347	65-0-10	.108	-1	133	-11		-1.5
1976	†Cin N	12	10	.545	34	29	5-2	1-1	177	190	96	17	4	62-5	76	4.32	81	.279	.347	59-0-8	.237	3	147	-17		-1.7
1977	†Cin N	10	10	.500	36	23	3-2	0-2	161.2	195	105	14	10	56-9	76	5.23	75	.306	.368	56-0-6	.161	-1	146	-25		-2.7
1978	Det A	15	8	.652	30	30	10-4	0-0	201.2	218	95	16	8	65-2	59	3.88	100	.284	.341	0	—	0	114	1		0.0
1979	Det A	10	7	.588	35	19	2	3-0	158	163	74	13	7	60-11	59	3.30	132	.275	.347	0	—	0	96	13		1.3
1980	Det A	0	0	—	8	0	0	0-1	7.1	11	6	1	0	6-1	3	7.36	56	.355	.447	0	—	0		-2		-0.1
	Bos A	1	3	.250	7	4	0	0-0	24.1	45	30	6	4	12-0	4	11.10	38	.413	.484	0	—	0	73	-16		-2.1
	Year	1	3	.250	15	4	0	0-1	31.2	56	36	7	4	18-1	7	10.23	41	.400	.476	0	—	0	74	-18		-2.2
otal	13	145	113	.562	476	305	74-27	15-9	2231.1	2272	1069	176	98	750-97	1141	3.83	94	.268	.333	559-0-69	.111	-17	117	-60		-9.9
BILLINGS, JOSH	Haskell Clark B9.27.1907 New York NY D12.26.1983 Greenbrae CA BR/TR/5-11/180 d8.17 Col Brown																									
1927	Det A	5	4	.556	10	9	5	0	67	64	36	3	6	39	18	4.84	87	.259	.373	27	.259	0	123	-1		-0.1
1928	Det A	5	10	.333	21	16	3-1	0	110.2	118	83	4	5	59	46	5.12	80	.276	.371	35-0-4	.286	3	109	-15		-1.4
1929	Det A	0	1	.000	8	0	0	0	19.1	27	14	0	1	9	1	5.12	84	.365	.440	6	.000	-1		-2		-0.1
otal	3	10	15	.400	39	25	8-1	0	197	209	133	7	12	107	67	5.03	83	.279	.378	68-0-4	.250	2	114	-18		-1.6
BILLINGSLEY, BRENT	Brent Aaron B4.19.1975 Downey CA BL/TL/6-2/200 [FlaN96 5/134] d5.20 Col Cal St.-Fullerton																									
1999	Fla N	0	0	—	8	0	0	0-0	7.2	11	14	3	2	10-0	3	16.43	27	.379	.548	0	—	0		-10		-0.5
BIRD, DOUG	James Douglas B3.5.1950 Corona CA BR/TR/6-4/180(180-195) [KCA69 S3/60] d4.29 Col Mt. San Antonio (CA) JC																									
1973	KC A	4	4	.500	54	0	0	20-4	102.1	81	37	10	2	30-7	83	2.99	138	.217	.276	0	—	0		12		1.3
1974	KC A	7	6	.538	55	1	1	10-7	92.1	100	31	6	1	27-9	62	2.73	140	.286	.333	0	—	0	23	11		1.8
1975	KC A	9	6	.600	51	4	0	11-7	105.1	100	42	7	2	40-10	67	3.25	119	.258	.326	0	—	0	80	8		1.2
1976	†KC A	12	10	.545	39	27	2-1	2-1	197.2	191	90	17	3	31-3	107	3.37	104	.251	.279	0	—	0	104	1		0.1
1977	†KC A	11	4	.733	53	5	0	14-4	118.1	120	52	14	3	29-4	86	3.88	104	.270	.314	0	—	0	152	5		0.6
1978	†KC A	6	6	.500	40	6	0	1-4	98.2	110	63	8	2	31-5	48	5.29	72	.284	.336	0	—	0	117	-14		-1.6
1979	Phi N	2	0	1.000	32	1	1	0-0	61	73	35	7	2	16-4	33	5.16	75	.305	.349	6	.167	0	137	-7	21	-0.4
1980	NY A	3	0	1.000	22	1	0	1-1	50.2	47	16	3	1	14-1	19	2.66	149	.257	.307	0	—	0	294	8		0.5
1981	NY A	5	1	.833	17	4	0	0-1	53.1	58	19	5	0	16-3	28	2.70	134	.280	.326	0	—	0	68	5		0.6
	Chi N	4	5	.444	12	12	2-1	0-0	75.1	72	34	5	1	16-3	34	3.58	105	.254	.293	20-0-2	.100	-1	75	1		0.0
1982	Chi N	9	14	.391	35	33	2-1	0-0	191	230	119	26	3	30-3	71	5.14	74	.297	.324	56-0-4	.143	-2	103	-26		-3.1
	Bos A	1	4	.200	12	5	0	0-0	67.2	91	52	14	2	16-4	33	6.65	66	.324	.360	0	—	0	76	-14		-1.0
otal	11	73	60	.549	432	100	8-3	60-29	1213.2	1273	590	122	22	296-56	680	3.99	96	.272	.315	82-0-6	.134	-2	99	-10	21	0.0
BIRD, RED	James Edward B4.25.1890 Stephenville TX D3.23.1972 Murfreesboro AR BL/TL/5-11/170 d9.17																									
1921	Was A	0	0	—	1	0	0	0	5	5	3	0	1	1	2	5.40	76	.294	.368	1	.000	-0		-1		-0.1
BIRKBECK, MIKE	Michael Lawrence B3.10.1961 Orrville OH BR/TR/6-1/190* [MilA83 4/106] d8.17 Col Akron [DL 1990 Mil A 43]																									
1986	Mil A	1	1	.500	7	4	0	0-0	22	24	12	0	0	12-0	13	4.50	97	.282	.371	0	—	0	99	0		0.0
1987	Mil A	1	4	.200	10	10	1	0-0	45	63	33	8	0	19-0	25	6.20	74	.335	.392	0	—	0	103	-7	105	-0.6
1988	Mil A	10	8	.556	23	23	3	0-0	124	141	69	10	1	37-1	64	4.72	85	.285	.335	0	—	0	110	-8		-1.0
1989	Mil A	0	4	.000	9	9	1	0-0	44.2	57	32	4	3	22-2	31	5.44	71	.310	.387	0	—	0	94	-9	90	-0.7
1992	NY N	0	1	.000	1	1	0	0-0	7	12	7	3	0	1-1	7	9.00	39	.387	.406	2	.000	-0	129	-4		-0.4
1995	NY N	1	1	.500	4	4	0	0-0	27.2	22	5	2	0	2-0	14	1.63	248	.220	.235	6-0-1	.333	1	34	8		0.5
otal	6	12	19	.387	54	51	2	0-0	270.1	319	158	27	4	93-4	149	4.86	84	.295	.351	8-0-1	.250	1	100	-20	238	-2.2
BIRKOFER, RALPH	Ralph Joseph "Lefty" B11.5.1908 Cincinnati OH D3.16.1971 Cincinnati OH BL/TL/5-11/213 d4.25																									
1933	Pit N	4	2	.667	9	8	3-1	0	50.2	43	22	1	0	17	20	2.31	144	.229	.296	22	.318	1	135	3		0.5
1934	Pit N	11	12	.478	41	23	11	1	204	227	106	11	5	66	71	4.10	100	.277	.335	75-0-2	.227	1	90	1		0.5
1935	Pit N	7	5	.583	37	18	8-1	1	150.1	173	87	5	6	42	80	4.07	101	.283	.335	58	.241	2*	94	0		0.0
1936	Pit N	7	5	.583	34	13	2	0	109.1	130	73	4	5	41	44	4.69	86	.295	.362	41	.220	0	166	-10		-1.1
1937	Bro N	2	4	.333	11	1	0	0	29.2	45	28	3	0	9	9	6.67	60	.341	.383	11	.273	1*	43	-9		-0.5
otal	5	31	28	.525	132	63	24-2	2	544	618	316	24	17	175	224	4.19	96	.282	.340	207-0-2	.242	5	111	-15		-1.1

YEAR	TM LG	W	L	PCT	G	GS	CG-SHO	SV-BS	IP	H	R	HR	HB	BB-IB	SO	ERA	AERA	OAV	OOB	AB-HR-SH	AVG	PB	SUP	APR	DL	PW

BIRRER, BABE Werner Joseph B7.4.1929 Buffalo NY BR/TR/6-0/195* d6.5

YEAR	TM LG	W	L	PCT	G	GS	CG-SHO	SV-BS	IP	H	R	HR	HB	BB-IB	SO	ERA	AERA	OAV	OOB	AB-HR-SH	AVG	PB	SUP	APR	DL	PW
1955	Det A	4	3	.571	36	3	1	3	80.1	77	39	9	0	29-4	28	4.15	93	.248	.311	19-2-0	.158	2	85	-1		0.1
1956	Bal A	0	0	—	4	0	0	0	5.1	9	5	0	0	1-0	1	6.75	58	.360	.385	1	.000	-0		-2		-0.1
1958	LA N	0	0	—	16	0	0	1	34	43	20	4	1	7-3	16	4.50	91	.309	.342	7	.571	2		-2		0.1
Total	3	4	3	.571	56	3	1	4	119.2	129	64	13	1	37-7	45	4.36	90	.272	.324	27-2-0	.259	4	85	-5		0.1

BIRTSAS, TIM Timothy Dean B9.5.1960 Pontiac MI BL/TL/6-7/240(225-245) [NYA82 2/36] d5.3 Col Michigan St.

YEAR	TM LG	W	L	PCT	G	GS	CG-SHO	SV-BS	IP	H	R	HR	HB	BB-IB	SO	ERA	AERA	OAV	OOB	AB-HR-SH	AVG	PB	SUP	APR	DL	PW
1985	Oak A	10	6	.625	29	25	2	0-0	141.1	124	72	18	3	91-0	94	4.01	97	.238	.352	0	—	0	111	-3		-0.4
1986	Oak A	0	0	—	2	0	0	0-0	2	2	5	1	0	4-1	1	22.50	17	.286	.545	0	—	0		-4		-0.2
1988	Cin N	1	3	.250	36	4	0	0-0	64.1	61	34	6	3	24-5	38	4.20	85	.250	.321	10	.000	-1	56	-5		-0.4
1989	Cin N	2	2	.500	42	1	0	1-0	69.2	68	33	5	3	27-8	57	3.75	96	.261	.330	4-1-0	.250	1	74	-1		0.0
1990	Cin N	1	3	.250	29	0	0	0-0	51.1	69	24	7	1	24-6	41	3.86	102	.325	.395	4-0-3	.000	-0		0		0.0
Total	5	14	14	.500	138	30	2	1-0	328.2	324	168	37	10	170-20	231	4.08	93	.260	.350	18-1-3	.056	-0	103	-13		-1.0

BISCAN, FRANK Frank Stephen "Porky" B3.13.1920 Mt.Olive IL D5.22.1959 St.Louis MO BL/TL/5-11/190 d5.3 Mil 1942-45

YEAR	TM LG	W	L	PCT	G	GS	CG-SHO	SV-BS	IP	H	R	HR	HB	BB-IB	SO	ERA	AERA	OAV	OOB	AB-HR-SH	AVG	PB	SUP	APR	DL	PW
1942	StL A	0	1	.000	11	0	0	1	27	13	8	1	0	11	10	2.33	159	.143	.235	6	.000	-0		4		0.2
1946	StL A	1	1	.500	16	0	0	1	22.2	28	13	0	0	22	9	5.16	72	.318	.455	3	.000	-0		-2		-0.3
1948	StL A	6	7	.462	47	4	1	2	98.2	129	78	3	9	71	45	6.11	75	.322	.435	26	.192	1	79	-18		-2.0
Total	3	7	9	.438	74	4	1	4	148.1	170	99	4	9	104	64	5.28	81	.294	.409	35	.143	-0	79	-16		-2.1

BISHOP, CHARLIE Charles Tuller B1.1.1924 Atlanta GA D7.5.1993 Lawrenceville GA BR/TR/6-2/195* d8.22

YEAR	TM LG	W	L	PCT	G	GS	CG-SHO	SV-BS	IP	H	R	HR	HB	BB-IB	SO	ERA	AERA	OAV	OOB	AB-HR-SH	AVG	PB	SUP	APR	DL	PW
1952	Phi A	2	2	.500	6	5	1	0	30.2	29	24	2	0	24	17	6.46	61	.238	.363	9-0-1	.111	-0	110	-8		-0.9
1953	Phi A	3	14	.176	39	20	1-1	2	160.2	174	106	15	5	86	66	5.66	76	.282	.375	56	.089	-4*	81	-21		-2.3
1954	Phi A	4	6	.400	20	12	4	1	96	98	49	10	5	50	34	4.41	89	.275	.369	33-0-1	.121	-2*	88	-4		-0.6
1955	KC A	1	0	1.000	4	0	0	0	6.2	6	7	1	3	8-2	4	5.40	77	.261	.486	2	.500	0		-2		-0.2
Total	4	10	22	.313	69	37	6-1	3	294	307	186	28	13	168-2	121	5.33	77	.275	.375	100-0-2	.110	-6	87	-35		-4.0

BISHOP, JIM James Morton B1.28.1898 Montgomery City MO D9.20.1973 Montgomery City MO BR/TR/6-0/195 d4.26

YEAR	TM LG	W	L	PCT	G	GS	CG-SHO	SV-BS	IP	H	R	HR	HB	BB-IB	SO	ERA	AERA	OAV	OOB	AB-HR-SH	AVG	PB	SUP	APR	DL	PW
1923	Phi N	0	3	.000	15	0	0	1	32.2	48	31	2	3	11	5	6.34	73	.353	.413	10	.000	-2		-6		-0.7
1924	Phi N	0	1	.000	7	1	0	1	16.2	24	14	3	0	7	3	6.48	69	.348	.408	5	.200	-0	76	-3		-0.2
Total	2	0	4	.000	22	1	0	1	49.1	72	45	5	3	18	8	6.39	71	.351	.412	15	.067	-2	76	-9		-0.9

BISHOP, LLOYD Lloyd Clifton B4.25.1890 Conway Springs KS D6.18.1968 Wichita KS BR/TR/6-0/180 d9.5 Col Wichita St.

YEAR	TM LG	W	L	PCT	G	GS	CG-SHO	SV-BS	IP	H	R	HR	HB	BB-IB	SO	ERA	AERA	OAV	OOB	AB-HR-SH	AVG	PB	SUP	APR	DL	PW
1914	Cle A	0	1	.000	9	1	0	0	8	14	5	0	0	3	1	5.63	51	.389	.436	2	.000	-0	101	-2		-0.2

BISHOP, BILL William Henry "Lefty" B10.22.1900 Houtzdale PA D2.14.1956 St.Joseph MO BR/TR/5-8/170 d9.15

YEAR	TM LG	W	L	PCT	G	GS	CG-SHO	SV-BS	IP	H	R	HR	HB	BB-IB	SO	ERA	AERA	OAV	OOB	AB-HR-SH	AVG	PB	SUP	APR	DL	PW
1921	Phi A	0	0	—	2	0	0	0	7	8	9	0	0	10	4	9.00	50	.267	.450	3	.000	-1		-4		-0.2

BISHOP, BILL William Robinson B12.27.1869 Adamsburg PA D12.15.1932 Pittsburgh PA 5-8/187 d9.13

YEAR	TM LG	W	L	PCT	G	GS	CG-SHO	SV-BS	IP	H	R	HR	HB	BB-IB	SO	ERA	AERA	OAV	OOB	AB-HR-SH	AVG	PB	SUP	APR	DL	PW
1886	Pit AA	0	1	.000	2	2	2	0	17	17	14	0	1	11	4	3.18	107	.221	.326	7	.143	-1	105	-1		-0.1
1887	Pit N	0	3	.000	3	3	3	0	27	45	46	2	2	22	4	13.33	29	.354	.457	9	.000	-1	34	-26		-1.8
1889	Chi N	0	0	—	2	0	0	2	3	6	13	0	0	6	1	18.00	23	.400	.571	1	.000	0		-6		-0.6
Total	3	0	4	.000	7	5	5	2	47	68	73	2	3	39	9	9.96	35	.311	.421	17	.059	-2	61	-33		-2.5

BITHORN, HI Hiram Gabriel (Sosa) B3.18.1916 Santurce, PR D12.30.1951 Ciudad Victoria, Tamaulipas, Mexico BR/TR/6-1/200 d4.15 Mil 1944-45

YEAR	TM LG	W	L	PCT	G	GS	CG-SHO	SV-BS	IP	H	R	HR	HB	BB-IB	SO	ERA	AERA	OAV	OOB	AB-HR-SH	AVG	PB	SUP	APR	DL	PW
1942	Chi N	9	14	.391	38	16	9	2	171.1	191	93	8	0	81	65	3.68	87	.296	.374	57-0-1	.123	-1	95	-14		-1.9
1943	Chi N	18	12	.600	39	30	19-7	2	249.2	227	79	8	2	65	86	2.60	129	.244	.294	92-0-5	.174	-0	110	23		2.9
1946	Chi N	6	5	.545	26	7	2-1	1	86.2	97	42	5	0	25	34	3.84	86	.283	.332	28-0-2	.179	0	111	-5		-0.7
1947	Chi A	1	0	1.000	2	0	0	0	2	2	0	0	0	0	0	0.00	—	.286	.286	0	—	0		1		0.2
Total	4	34	31	.523	105	53	30-8	5	509.2	517	214	21	2	171	185	3.16	104	.268	.328	177-0-8	.158	-2	106	5		0.5

BITKER, JOE Joseph Anthony B2.12.1964 Glendale CA BR/TR/6-1/175* [SDN84 S2/32] d7.31 Col Sacramento (CA) City

YEAR	TM LG	W	L	PCT	G	GS	CG-SHO	SV-BS	IP	H	R	HR	HB	BB-IB	SO	ERA	AERA	OAV	OOB	AB-HR-SH	AVG	PB	SUP	APR	DL	PW
1990	Oak A	0	0	—	1	0	0	0-0	3	1	0	0	0	1-0	2	0.00	—	.111	.200	0	—	0		1		0.1
	Tex A	0	0	—	5	0	0	0-0	9	7	3	0	1	3-0	6	3.00	131	.212	.289	0	—	0		1		0.1
	Year	0	0	—	6	0	0	0-0	12	8	3	0	1	4-0	8	2.25	173	.190	.271	0	—	0		2		0.2
1991	Tex A	1	0	1.000	9	0	0	0-0	14.2	17	11	4	0	8-3	16	6.75	60	.274	.357	0	—	0		-4		-0.2
Total	2	1	0	1.000	15	0	0	0-0	26.2	25	14	4	1	12-3	24	4.73	84	.240	.322	0	—	0		-2		0.0

BITTIGER, JEFF Jeffrey Scott B4.13.1962 Jersey City NJ BR/TR/5-10/175* [NYN80 7/157] d9.2

YEAR	TM LG	W	L	PCT	G	GS	CG-SHO	SV-BS	IP	H	R	HR	HB	BB-IB	SO	ERA	AERA	OAV	OOB	AB-HR-SH	AVG	PB	SUP	APR	DL	PW
1986	Phi N	1	1	.500	3	3	0	0-0	14.2	16	10	2	1	7-1	8	5.52	71	.271	.358	3-1-1	.333	1	114	-2		-0.2
1987	Min A	1	0	1.000	3	1	0	0-0	8.1	11	5	2	1	0-0	5	5.40	86	.314	.333	0	—	0	157	0		0.0
1988	Chi A	2	4	.333	25	7	0	0-0	61.2	59	31	11	0	29-2	33	4.23	95	.255	.333	0	—	0	49	-1	20	-0.2
1989	Chi A	0	1	.000	2	1	0	0-0	9.2	9	7	2	0	6-0	7	6.52	59	.257	.366	0	—	0	71	-3	44	-0.2
Total	4	4	6	.400	33	12	0	0-0	94.1	95	53	17	2	42-3	53	4.77	84	.264	.341	3-1-1	.333	1	77	-6	64	-0.5

BIVIN, JIM James Nathaniel B12.11.1909 Jackson MS D11.7.1982 Pueblo CO BR/TR/6-0/155 d4.16

YEAR	TM LG	W	L	PCT	G	GS	CG-SHO	SV-BS	IP	H	R	HR	HB	BB-IB	SO	ERA	AERA	OAV	OOB	AB-HR-SH	AVG	PB	SUP	APR	DL	PW
1935	Phi N	2	9	.182	47	14	0	1	161.2	220	129	20	3	65	54	5.79	78	.316	.377	48	.146	-1	72	-22		-1.4

BLACK, DAVE David B4.19.1892 Chicago IL D10.27.1936 Pittsburgh PA BL/TR/6-2/175 d5.2

YEAR	TM LG	W	L	PCT	G	GS	CG-SHO	SV-BS	IP	H	R	HR	HB	BB-IB	SO	ERA	AERA	OAV	OOB	AB-HR-SH	AVG	PB	SUP	APR	DL	PW
1914	Chi F	1	0	1.000	8	1	1	0	25	28	19	1	0	4	19	6.12	43	.311	.340	6	.333	1	207	-9		-0.4
1915	Chi F	6	7	.462	25	10	2	0	121.1	104	46	4	6	33	43	2.45	103	.241	.304	37-0-4	.108	-3	123	0		-0.3
	Bal F	1	3	.250	8	4	1	0	34	32	18	2	2	15	10	3.71	77	.260	.350	12-0-2	.250	0	110	-3		-0.3
	Year	7	10	.412	33	14	3	0	155.1	136	64	6	8	48	53	2.72	95	.245	.315	49-0-6	.143	-3	120	-3		-0.6
1923	Bos A				2	0	0	0	1	2	0	0	0	0	0	0.00	—	.500	.500	0	—	0		0		0.0
Total	3	8	10	.444	43	15	4	0	181.1	166	83	7	8	52	72	3.18	82	.256	.319	55-0-6	.164	-2	125	-12		-1.0

BLACK, DON Donald Paul B7.20.1916 Salix IA D4.21.1959 Cuyahoga Falls OH BR/TR/6-0/185 d4.24

YEAR	TM LG	W	L	PCT	G	GS	CG-SHO	SV-BS	IP	H	R	HR	HB	BB-IB	SO	ERA	AERA	OAV	OOB	AB-HR-SH	AVG	PB	SUP	APR	DL	PW
1943	Phi A	6	16	.273	33	26	12-1	1	208	193	105	8	6	110	65	4.20	81	.247	.344	69-0-2	.188	-1	75	-15		-1.6
1944	Phi A	10	12	.455	29	27	8	0	177.1	177	94	6	4	75	78	4.06	86	.259	.336	59-0-3	.186	-1	100	-11		-1.3
1945	Phi A	5	11	.313	26	18	8	0	125.1	154	77	5	0	69	47	5.17	66	.307	.391	37-0-1	.162	-2	81	-21		-2.7
1946	Cle A	1	2	.333	18	4	0	0	43.2	45	26	5	1	21	15	4.53	73	.273	.358	10-0-1	.200	-1	110	-9		-1.1
1947	Cle A	10	12	.455	30	28	8-3	0	190.2	177	90	17	1	85	72	3.92	89	.249	.330	66-0-3	.182	-1	107	-7		-0.5
1948	Cle A	2	2	.500	18	10	1	1	52	57	33	5	1	40	16	5.37	76	.282	.403	15-0-1	.200	-0	107	-7		-0.9
Total	6	34	55	.382	154	113	37-4	1	797	803	425	46	13	400	293	4.35	80	.264	.352	256-0-11	.184	-4	95	-70		-7.6

BLACK, BUD Harry Ralston B6.30.1957 San Mateo CA BL/TL/6-2/180* [SeaA79 17/417] d9.5 C6 Col San Diego St.

YEAR	TM LG	W	L	PCT	G	GS	CG-SHO	SV-BS	IP	H	R	HR	HB	BB-IB	SO	ERA	AERA	OAV	OOB	AB-HR-SH	AVG	PB	SUP	APR	DL	PW
1981	Sea A	0	0	—	2	0	0	0-0	1	2	0	0	0	3-1	0	0.00	—	.500	.714	0	—	0*	78	-4		-0.4
1982	KC A	4	6	.400	22	14	0	0-0	88.1	92	48	10	3	34-6	40	4.58	89	.269	.338	0	—	0	120	6		0.2
1983	KC A	10	7	.588	24	24	3	0-0	161.1	159	75	19	2	43-1	58	3.79	108	.257	.305	0	—	0	85	25		2.8
1984	†KC A	17	12	.586	35	35	8-1	0-0	257	226	99	22	4	64-2	140	3.12	130	.233	**.283**	0	—	0	84	-3		-0.4
1985	†KC A	10	15	.400	33	33	5-2	0-0	205.2	216	111	17	8	59-4	122	4.33	96	.268	.323	0	—	0	80	13		1.2
1986	KC A	5	10	.333	56	4	0	9-2	121	100	49	14	7	43-5	68	3.20	134	.225	.300	0	—	0	108	10	26	1.0
1987	KC A	8	6	.571	29	18	0	1-1	122.1	126	63	16	5	35-2	61	3.60	127	.265	.320	0	—	0	91	-5	33	-0.2
1988	KC A	2	1	.667	17	0	0	0-1	22	23	12	2	0	11-2	19	4.91	82	.267	.351	0	—	0	92	-7		-0.2
	Cle A	2	3	.400	16	7	0	1-0	59	59	36	4	4	23-1	44	5.03	82	.262	.337	0	—	0	91	-5	33	-0.2
	Year	4	4	.500	33	7	0	1-1	81	82	47	8	4	34-3	63	5.00	82	.264	.341	0	—	0	87	14		0.2
1989	Cle A	12	11	.522	33	32	6-3	0-0	222.1	213	95	14	1	52-0	88	3.36	118	.252	.295	0	—	0	104	10		1.3
1990	Cle A	11	10	.524	29	29	5-2	0-0	191	171	79	14	4	58-1	103	3.53	112	.236	.294	0	—	0	69	0		0.1
	Tor A	2	1	.667	3	2	0	0-0	15.2	10	7	2	1	3-0	3	4.02	99	.189	.237	0	—	0	101	12		1.1
	Year	13	11	.542	32	31	5-2	0-1	206.2	181	86	19	5	61-1	106	3.57	110	.233	.290	0	—	0	87	14		1.2
1991	SF N	12	16	.429	34	34	3-3	0-0	214.1	201	104	25	4	71-8	104	3.99	90	.251	.313	71-0-9	.183	1*	93	-10	31	-1.1
1992	SF N	10	12	.455	28	28	2-1	0-0	177	178	88	23	1	59-11	82	3.97	94	.263	.321	54-0-10	.056	0	84	-14	99	-1.2
1993	SF N	8	2	.800	16	16	0	0-0	93.2	89	44	13	2	33-2	45	3.56	111	.256	.321	37-0-3	.243	-0	139	2		0.9
1994	SF N	4	2	.667	10	10	0	0-0	54.1	50	33	5	3	16-1	28	4.47	91	.245	.307	17-0-5	.059	-1	122	-12		-1.1
1995	Cle A	4	2	.667	11	10	0	0	47.1	63	42	8	0	16-2	34	6.85	69	.317	.362	0	—	0		-1		-1.2
Total	15	121	116	.511	398	296	32-12	11-5	2053.1	1978	982	217	49	623-49	1039	3.84	104	.253	.310	179-0-27	.145	-1	97	27	266	3.7

YEAR	TM LG	W	L	PCT	G	GS	CG-SHO	SV-BS	IP	H	R	HR	HB	BB-IB	SO	ERA	AERA	OAV	OOB	AB-HR-SH	AVG	PB	SUP	APR	DL	PW

BLACK, JOE Joseph B2.8.1924 Plainfield NJ D5.17.2002 Scottsdale AZ BR/TR/6-2/220(215-229) d5.1 Negro Lg 1943-50 Mil 1943-45 Col Morgan St.

YEAR	TM LG	W	L	PCT	G	GS	CG-SHO	SV-BS	IP	H	R	HR	HB	BB-IB	SO	ERA	AERA	OAV	OOB	AB-HR-SH	AVG	PB	SUP	APR	DL	PW
1952	†Bro N	15	4	.789	56	2	1	15	142.1	102	40	9	1	41	85	2.15	169	.201	.262	36-0-6	.139	-1*	135	23		3.3
1953	†Bro N	6	3	.667	34	3	0	5	72.2	74	46	12	1	27	42	5.33	80	.259	.325	17	.235	-0	56	-8		-1.0
1954	Bro N	0	0	—	5	0	0	0	7	11	9	3	0	5	3	11.57	35	.355	.432	0		-0		-5		-0.3
1955	Bro N	1	0	1.000	6	0	0	0	15.1	15	5	1	0	5-1	9	2.93	138	.273	.328	3	.333	-0		2		0.1
1955	Cin N	5	2	.714	32	11	1	3	102.1	106	63	13	0	25-3	54	4.22	100	.263	.303	30-0-3	.100	-2	134	-1		-0.3
	Year	6	2	.750	38	11	1	3	117.2	121	63	14	0	30-4	63	4.05	104	.264	.306	33-0-3	.121	-2	134	1		-0.2
1956	Cin N	3	2	.600	32	0	0	2	61.2	61	31	11	0	25-3	27	4.52	88	.256	.326	10	.000	-1*		-2		-0.3
1957	Was A	0	1	.000	7	0	0	0	12.2	12	11	4	0	1-0	2	7.11	55	.393	.397	0	—	0		-4		-0.3
Total 6		30	12	.714	172	16	2	25	414	391	200	53	2	129-7	222	3.91	102	.248	.304	96-0-9	.135	-5	124	5		1.2

BLACK, BOB Robert Benjamin B12.10.1862 Cincinnati OH D3.21.1933 Sioux City IA 5-5.5/155 d8.19 ▲

| 1884 | KC U | 4 | 9 | .308 | 16 | 15 | 13 | 0 | 123 | 127 | 79 | 1 | | 17 | 93 | 3.22 | 69 | .249 | .273 | 146-1 | .247 | 1* | 64 | -13 | | -0.8 |

BLACK, BUD William Carroll B7.9.1932 St.Louis MO D10.2.2005 St.Louis MO BR/TR/6-3/197* d9.13 Mil 1953-54

1952	Det A	0	1	.000	2	2	0	0	8	14	11	0	0	5	5	10.13	38	.389	.463	3	.000	-0	103	-6		-0.6
1955	Det A	1	1	.500	3	2	1-1	0	14	12	5	0	2	8-0	7	1.29	299	.231	.355	4-0-1	.250	-0	81	3		0.4
1956	Det A	1	1	.500	5	1	0	0	10	10	4	2	0	5-0	7	3.60	114	.256	.333	2	.000	-0	86	1		0.1
Total 3		2	3	.400	10	5	1-1	0	32	36	20	2	2	18-0	14	4.22	93	.283	.378	9-0-1	.111	-1	90	-2		-0.1

BLACKBURN, CHARLIE Foster Edwin B1.6.1895 Chicago IL D3.9.1984 New Port Richey FL BR/TR/6-1/165 d4.17 Col Chicago

1915	KC F	0	1	.000	7	2	0	0	15.2	19	15	2	0	13	7	8.62	31	.306	.427	4	.000	-1	160	-9		-0.6
1921	Chi N	0	0	—	1	0	0	0	1	0	0	0	0	1	0	0.00	—	.000	.333	0	—	0		0		0.0
Total 2		0	1	.000	8	2	0	0	16.2	19	15	2	0	14	7	8.10	34	.297	.423	4	.000	-1	160	-9		-0.6

BLACKBURN, GEORGE George W. "Smiling George" B9.21.1871 Ozark MO TR/5-11/184 d7.6

| 1897 | Bal N | 2 | 2 | .500 | 5 | 4 | 3 | 0 | 33 | 34 | 30 | 2 | 1 | 12 | 1 | 6.82 | 61 | .264 | .331 | 13 | .077 | -2 | 115 | -8 | | -0.9 |

BLACKBURN, JIM James Ray "Bones" B6.19.1924 Warsaw KY D10.26.1969 Cincinnati OH BR/TR/6-4/175* d7.24

1948	Cin N	0	2	.000	16	0	0	0	32.1	38	18	1	0	14	10	4.18	94	.302	.371	6	.000	-0		-1		-0.1
1951	Cin N	0	0	—	2	0	0	0	3.2	8	7	3	2	2	1	17.18	24	.444	.545	0	—	-0		-5		-0.2
Total 2		0	2	.000	18	0	0	0	36	46	25	4	2	16	11	5.50	71	.319	.395	6	.000	-0		-6		-0.3

BLACKBURN, RON Ronald Hamilton B4.23.1935 Mt.Airy NC D4.29.1998 Morganton NC BR/TR/6-0.5/160* d4.15 Mil 1959

1958	Pit N	2	1	.667	38	2	0	3	63.2	61	33	7	3	27-5	31	3.39	114	.261	.338	7-0-1	.286	1	58	1		0.2
1959	Pit N	1	1	.500	26	0	0	1	44.1	50	21	5	2	15-4	19	3.65	106	.286	.345	5-1-0	.200	1		1		0.1
Total 2		3	2	.600	64	2	0	4	108	111	54	12	5	42-9	50	3.50	110	.271	.341	12-1-1	.250	2	58	2		0.3

BLACKLEY, TRAVIS Travis Jarrod B11.4.1982 Melbourne, Victoria, Australia BL/TL/6-3/190 d7.1 [DL 2005 Sea A 183]

| 2004 | Sea A | 3 | 3 | .250 | 6 | 6 | 0 | 0-0 | 26 | 35 | 31 | 9 | 1 | 22-0 | 16 | 10.04 | 45 | .321 | .436 | 0 | | 0 | 128 | -17 | | -1.9 |

BLACKWELL, EWELL Ewell "The Whip" B10.23.1922 Fresno CA D10.29.1996 Hendersonville NC BR/TR/6-6/195* d4.21 Mil 1943-45 Col La Verne

1942	Cin N	0	0	—	2	0	0	0	3	3	4	0	0	3	1	6.00	55	.231	.375	1	.000	-0		-2		-0.1
1946	Cin N★	9	13	.409	33	25	10-5	0	194.1	.160	62	1	4	79	100	2.45	136	.226	.307	56-0-6	.107	-3	69	20		2.1
1947	Cin N★	22	8	.733	33	33	23-6	0	273	227	91	10	4	95	193	2.47	166	.234	.304	65-0-4	.123	-5	94	46		4.5
1948	Cin N★	7	9	.438	22	20	4-1	1	138.2	134	73	12	4	52	114	4.54	86	.251	.323	48-0-3	.229	-1	96	-7		-0.4
1949	Cin N★	5	5	.500	30	4	0	1	76.2	80	36	7	3	34	55	4.23	99	.271	.352	19-0-1	.211	-0	42	2		0.3
1950	Cin N★	17	15	.531	40	32	18-1	4	261	203	105	12	13	112	188	2.97	143	**.210**	.301	89-0-7	.146	-2	81	32		3.6
1951	Cin N★	16	15	.516	38	32	11-2	2	232.2	204	110	16	9	97	120	3.44	118	.233	.315	82-1-2	.293	7*	81	13		2.5
1952	Cin N	3	12	.200	23	17	3	0	102	107	66	6	5	60	48	5.38	70	.275	.379	32-0-1	.156	-0	71	-18		-2.4
	†NY A	1	0	1.000	5	2	0	1	16	12	2	0	2	12	7	0.56	591	.203	.338	5	.200	-0	105	5		0.4
1953	NY A	2	0	1.000	8	4	0	1	19.2	17	10	2	1	13	11	3.66	101	.233	.356	5	.000	-1	144	0		-0.1
1955	KC A	0	1	.000	2	0	0	0	4	3	3	1	1	5-0	2	6.75	62	.250	.500	0	—	0		-1		-0.2
Total 10		82	78	.512	236	169	69-15	11	1321	1150	562	67	44	562-0	839	3.30	120	.235	.319	443-1-28	.174	-3	83	90		10.2

BLAEHOLDER, GEORGE George Franklin B1.26.1904 Orange CA D12.29.1947 Garden Grove CA BR/TR/5-11/175 d4.20

1925	StL A	0	0	—	2	0	0	0	2	6	7	3	1	1	1	31.50	15	.600	.667	0	—	0		-5		-0.2
1927	StL A	0	1	.000	1	1	0	0	9	8	5	1	1	4	2	5.00	87	.258	.361	3	.333	0	77	0		0.0
1928	StL A	10	15	.400	38	26	9-1	3	214.1	235	123	23	2	52	87	4.37	96	.280	.324	71-2-1	.211	2	95	-5		-0.1
1929	StL A	14	15	.483	42	24	13-4	2	222	237	113	18	0	61	72	4.18	106	.275	.323	74-1-2	.122	-4	74	8		0.8
1930	StL A	11	13	.458	37	23	10-1	4	191.1	235	119	20	2	46	70	4.61	106	.303	.343	66-0-7	.185	-1	99	3		0.1
1931	StL A	11	15	.423	35	32	13-1	0	226.1	280	137	15	1	56	79	4.53	102	.295	.335	77-0-3	.143	-3	84	3		0.2
1932	StL A	14	14	.500	42	36	16-1	0	258.1	304	163	19	3	76	80	4.70	103	.290	.340	88-0-2	.136	-4	91	2		-0.1
1933	StL A	15	19	.441	38	36	14-3	0	255.2	283	146	24	0	69	63	4.72	99	.280	.326	77-0-7	.182	-1	71	0		0.1
1934	StL A	14	18	.438	39	33	14-1	1	234.1	276	130	16	0	68	66	4.22	118	.296	.343	75-0-10	.093	-5	75	18		1.7
1935	StL A	1	1	.500	6	2	0	0	17.2	25	15	3	0	6	4	7.13	67	.342	.392	1	.000	-1	109	-4		-0.4
	Phi A	6	10	.375	23	22	10-1	0	149	173	78	10	4	49	22	3.99	114	.289	.343	47-0-6	.043	-6	88	8		0.2
	Year	7	11	.389	29	24	10-1	0	166.2	198	93	13	0	55	22	4.32	106	.295	.348	50-0-7	.040	-7	89	4		-0.2
1936	Cle A	8	4	.667	35	16	6-1	0	134.1	158	83	21	3	47	30	5.09	99	.295	.356	50-0-7	.133	-3	126	1		-0.1
Total 11		104	125	.454	338	251	106-14	12	1914.1	2220	1119	173	13	535	572	4.54	103	.290	.337	626-3-39	.142	-25	87	29		2.2

BLAIR, DENNIS Dennis Herman B6.5.1954 Middletown OH BR/TR/6-5/182* [MonN72 5/101] d5.26

1974	Mon N	11	7	.611	22	22	4-1	0-0	146	113	61	7	5	72-4	76	3.27	118	.210	.307	51-0-6	.118	-2	127	9		1.0
1975	Mon N	8	15	.348	30	27	4-1	0-0	163.1	150	77	14	9	106-3	82	3.80	102	.251	.362	49-0-2	.143	-1	64	1		0.0
1976	Mon N	0	2	.000	5	4	1	0-0	15.2	21	11	1	2	11-0	9	4.02	93	.300	.405	4	.000	-0	76	-2		-0.2
1980	SD N	0	1	.000	5	1	0	0-0	14	18	10	3	0	3-0	11	6.43	53	.310	.344	5	.200	0	78	-4		-0.3
Total 4		19	25	.432	62	54	6-1	0-0	339	302	159	25	10	192-7	178	3.69	104	.239	.341	109-0-8	.128	-4	91	4		0.5

BLAIR, WILLIE William Allen B12.18.1965 Paintsville KY BR/TR/6-1/185* [TorA86 11/289] d4.11 Col Morehead St.

1990	Tor A	3	5	.375	27	6	0	0-0	68.2	66	33	4	1	28-4	43	4.06	97	.250	.320	0	—	0	80	-1		-0.1
1991	Cle A	2	3	.400	11	5	0	0-1	36	58	27	7	1	10-0	13	6.75	62	.377	.413	0	—	0	74	-9		-1.0
1992	Hou N	5	7	.417	29	8	0	0-0	78.2	74	47	5	2	25-2	48	4.00	85	.249	.309	17-0-1	.059	-1	83	-9		-1.5
1993	Col N	6	10	.375	46	18	1	0-0	146	184	90	20	3	42-4	84	4.75	101	.306	.350	36-0-3	.111	-2	60	-1		-0.3
1994	Col N	0	5	.000	47	1	0	3-3	77.2	98	57	9	4	39-3	68	5.79	86	.308	.390	6	.000	-1	37	-7		-0.6
1995	SD N	7	5	.583	40	12	0	0-0	114	112	60	11	2	45-3	83	4.34	94	.262	.333	24-0-4	.000	-2	81	-2		-0.5
1996	†SD N	2	6	.250	60	0	0	1-4	88	80	52	13	7	29-5	67	4.60	87	.240	.311	3	.000	-0		-7		-0.7
1997	Det A	16	8	.667	29	27	2	0-0	175	186	85	18	3	46-2	90	4.17	111	.273	.319	4		-0	101	10	29	1.0
1998	Ari N	4	15	.211	23	23	0	0-0	146.2	165	91	27	4	51-2	71	5.34	80	.292	.352	48-0-4	.083	-3	67	-15		-1.9
	NY N	1	1	.500	11	2	0	0-0	28.2	23	10	4	1	10-0	21	3.14	131	.228	.301	4	.250	1	11	3		0.3
	Year	5	16	.238	34	25	0	0-0	175.1	188	101	31	4	61-2	92	4.98	85	.282	.344	52-0-4	.096	-2	63	-13		-1.6
1999	Det A	3	11	.214	39	16	0	0-0	134	169	107	29	4	44-0	82	6.85	73	.308	.361	1	.000	-0	84	-26		-2.2
2000	Det A	10	6	.625	47	17	0	0-2	156.2	185	89	20	2	35-0	74	4.88	101	.296	.331	3	.333	-0	124	2		0.1
2001	Det A	4	4	.200	9	8	0	0-0	24	38	30	4	3	11-3	15	10.50	42	.369	.437	2	.000	-0	79	-16		-2.5
Total 12		60	86	.411	418	139	4	4-10	1348	778	170	36		415-28	759	5.04	89	.286	.342	148-0-12	.074	-8	85	-78	29	-9.9

BLAIR, BILL William Ellsworth B9.17.1863 Pittsburgh PA D2.22.1890 Pittsburgh PA BL/TL/5-8.5/172 d7.19

| 1888 | Phi AA | 1 | 3 | .250 | 4 | 4 | 3 | 0 | 31 | 29 | 21 | 0 | 1 | 8 | 17 | 2.61 | 114 | .238 | .290 | 13 | .308 | 1 | 44 | 6 | | 0.2 |

BLAISDELL, DICK Howard Carleton B6.18.1862 Bradford MA D8.20.1886 Malden MA d7.9

| 1884 | KC U | 0 | 3 | .000 | 3 | 3 | 3 | 0 | 26 | 49 | 39 | 0 | 0 | 16 | 8 | 8.65 | 26 | .377 | .396 | 16 | .313 | 0* | 70 | -17 | | -1.3 |

BLAKE, ED Edward James B12.23.1925 E.St.Louis IL BR/TR/5-11/175* d5.1

1951	Cin N	0	0	—	3	0	0	0	4	10	5	3	0	1	1	11.25	36	.476	.500	0	—	0		-3		-0.1
1952	Cin N	0	0	—	2	0	0	0	3	3	0	0	0	4	0	0.00	—	.250	.250	0	—	0		1		0.1
1953	Cin N	0	0	—	1	0	0	0	1	0	1	0	0	1	0	0.00	—	.250	.250	0	—	0		1		0.1
1957	KC A	0	0	—	2	0	0	0	1.2	2	2	0	1	2-1	0	∞	—	1.000	1.000	0	—	0		-2		-0.2
Total 4		0	0	—	8	0	0	0	8.2	15	8	4	1	4-1	1	8.31	48	.375	.432	0	—	0		-4		-0.2

YEAR	TM LG	W	L	PCT	G	GS	CG-SHO	SV-BS	IP	H	R	HR	HB	BB-IB	SO	ERA	AERA	OAV	OOB	AB-HR-SH	AVG	PB	SUP	APR	DL	PW
BLAKE, SHERIFF	John Frederick	B9.17.1899 Ansted WV		D10.31.1982 Beckley WV		BB/TR/6-0/180	d6.29	Col West Virginia Wesleyan																		
1920	Pit N	0	0	—	6	0	0	0	13.1	21	14	0	1	6	7	8.10	40	.368	.438	4	.250	-0		-7		-0.3
1924	Chi N	6	6	.500	29	11	4	1	106.1	123	58	3	2	44	42	4.57	85	.299	.370	31-0-1	.290	1	99	-5		-0.4
1925	Chi N	10	18	.357	36	31	14	2	231.1	260	144	17	5	114	93	4.86	89	.287	.370	79-0-3	.152	-4	78	-14		-1.8
1926	Chi N	11	12	.478	39	27	11-4	1	197.2	204	91	7	6	92	95	3.60	107	.280	.366	65-0-3	.215	-1	80	7		0.7
1927	Chi N	13	14	.481	32	27	13-2		224.1	238	101	3	4	82	64	3.29	117	.282	.348	83-0-4	.193	-2	104	12		1.3
1928	Chi N	17	11	.607	34	29	16-4	1	240.2	209	80	4	3	101	78	2.47	156	.240	.321	88-0-7	.216	0*	98	37		4.0
1929	†Chi N	14	13	.519	35	29	13-1	1	218.1	244	122	8	2	103	70	4.29	108	.291	.370	81-0-5	.173	-2*	123	8		0.6
1930	Chi N	10	14	.417	34	24	7	0	186.2	213	127	14	3	99	80	4.82	101	.291	.378	66-0-3	.227	-1*	95	-3		-0.4
1931	Chi N	0	4	.000	16	5	0	0	50	64	34	4	1	26	29	5.22	74	.312	.392	16	.500	3	124	-8		-0.2
	Phi N	4	5	.444	14	9	1	1	71	90	49	2	3	35	31	5.58	76	.305	.384	25	.240	-0	97	-8		-0.8
	Year	4	9	.308	30	14	1	1	121	154	83	6	4	61	60	5.43	75	.308	.388	41	.341	3	106	-17		-1.0
1937	StL A	2	2	.500	15	1	0	0	36.2	55	33	5	0	20	12	7.61	63	.350	.424	10-0-1	.100	-1	144	-10		0.1
	StL N	3	0	.000	14	2	2	0	43.2	45	23	1	0	18	20	3.71	107	.271	.342	10-0-1	.300	-0	65	1		0.1
Total	10	87	102	.460	304	195	81-11	8	1620	1766	876	68	30	740	621	4.13	101	.284	.363	558-0-28	.211	-6	97	10		1.8
BLANCHE, AL	Prosper Albert (b Prosper Bilangio)	B9.21.1909 Somerville MA		D4.2.1997 Melrose MA		BR/TR/6-0/178	d8.23	Col Providence																		
1935	Bos N	0	0	—	6	0	0	0	17.1	14	3	0	0	5	4	1.56	243	.230	.288	6	.167	-0		5		0.2
1936	Bos N	0	1	.000	11	0	0	1	16	20	15	1	1	8	4	6.19	62	.303	.387	4	.250	0		-5		-0.3
Total	2	0	1	.000	17	0	0	1	33.1	34	18	1	1	13	8	3.78	101	.268	.340	10	.200	-0		1		-0.1
BLANCO, GIL	Gilbert Henry	B12.15.1945 Phoenix AZ		BL/TL/6-5/205(205-217)	d4.24	Col Phoenix (AZ) JC																				
1965	NY A	1	1	.500	17	1	0	0	20.1	16	10	1	1	12-0	14	3.98	85	.232	.341	0	—	0	26	-1		-0.1
1966	KC A	2	4	.333	11	8	0	0	38.1	31	26	3	4	36-1	21	4.70	72	.237	.415	12-0-1	.167	-0	84	-7		-1.0
Total	2	3	5	.375	28	9	0	0	58.2	47	36	4	5	48-1	35	4.45	76	.235	.391	12-0-1	.167	-0	78	-8		-1.1
BLAND, NATE	Nathan Garrett	B12.27.1974 Birmingham AL		BL/TL/6-5/190	[LAN93 4/102]	d5.5																				
2003	Hou N	2	2	.333	12	0	0	0-1	20.1	13	3	2	12	12-2	18	5.75	77	.286	.391	0	—	0		-2		-0.3
BLANDING, FRED	Frederick James "Fritz"	B2.8.1886 Redlands CA		D7.16.1950 Salem VA		BR/TR/5-11/185	d9.15	Col Michigan																		
1910	Cle A	2	2	.500	6	5	4-1	0	45.1	43	19	0	4	12	25	2.78	93	.254	.319	18	.111	-1	99	-1		-0.2
1911	Cle A	7	11	.389	29	16	11	2	176	190	95	5	6	60	80	3.68	93	.283	.347	65-0-1	.262	2*	70	-4		-0.2
1912	Cle A	18	14	.563	39	31	23-1	1	262	259	117	6	3	79	75	2.92	117	.267	.324	93-1-9	.226	1	106	14		1.7
1913	Cle A	15	10	.600	41	22	14-3	0	215	234	79	4	3	72	63	2.55	119	.284	.324	86-0-2	.244	4	101	13		1.7
1914	Cle A	4	9	.308	29	12	5	0	116	133	82	0	1	54	35	3.96	73	.301	.378	39	.103	-2*	69	-16		-1.9
Total	5	46	46	.500	144	86	57-5	3	814.1	859	392	15	17	277	278	3.13	102	.279	.342	301-1-12	.216	4	92	6		1.1
BLANK, MATT	Clarence Matthew	B4.5.1976 Texarkana TX		BL/TL/6-2/195*	[MonN97 11/346]	d4.3	Col Texas A&M-Commerce																			
2000	Mon N	0	1	.000	13	0	0	0-1	14	12	8	1	1	5-1	4	5.14	92	.222	.295	1	.000	0		0	135	0.0
2001	Mon N	2	2	.500	5	4	0	0-0	22.2	23	14	5	2	13-1	11	5.16	84	.267	.369	8	.500	2	112	-2		-0.1
Total	2	2	3	.400	18	4	0	0-1	36.2	35	22	6	3	18-2	15	5.15	87	.250	.341	9	.444	2	112	-2	135	-0.1
BLANK, FRED	Frederick August	B6.18.1874 DeSoto MO		D2.5.1936 St.Louis MO		BL/TL/6-0.5/175	d6.20																			
1894	Cin N	0	1	.000	1	1	1	0	8	5	4	0	0	9	1	4.50	123	.179	.378	3	.000	-0		26	-1	0.1
BLANKENSHIP, HOMER	Homer "Si"	B8.4.1902 Bonham TX		D6.22.1974 Longview TX		BR/TR/6-0/185	d9.6	b-Ted																		
1922	Chi A	0	0	—	4	0	0	0	13	21	7	1	0	5	3	4.85	84	.389	.441	4	.000	-1		-1		-0.1
1923	Chi A	1	1	.500	4	0	0	1	5	9	5	0	0	1	1	3.60	110	.429	.455	0	—	0		-1		-0.2
1928	Pit N	0	2	.000	5	2	1	0	21.2	27	15	1	0	9	6	5.82	70	.321	.387	8	.375	-1	31	-3		-0.2
Total	3	1	3	.250	13	2	1	1	39.2	57	27	2	0	15	10	5.22	78	.358	.414	12	.250	0	31	-5		-0.5
BLANKENSHIP, KEVIN	Kevin De Wayne	B1.26.1963 Anaheim CA		BR/TR/6-0/180*	d9.20	Col Arizona																				
1988	Atl N	0	1	.000	2	2	0	0-0	10.2	7	4	0	1	7-0	5	3.38	109	.194	.341	3	.000	-0	61	1		0.0
	Chi N	1	0	1.000	1	1	0	0-0	5	7	4	2	0	1-0	4	7.20	51	.318	.348	3	.000	-0	219	-2		-0.3
	Year	1	1	.500	3	3	0	0-0	15.2	14	8	2	1	8-0	9	4.60	80	.241	.343	6	.000	-1	113	-1		-0.3
1989	Chi N	0	0	—	2	0	0	0-0	5.1	4	1	0	0	2-0	2	1.69	224	.200	.273	1	.000	-0		1		0.0
1990	Chi N	0	2	.000	3	2	0	0-0	12.1	13	10	1	0	6-0	5	5.84	70	.265	.333	4	.000	-0	66	-3		-0.4
Total	3	1	3	.250	8	5	0	0-0	33.1	31	19	3	1	16-0	16	4.59	84	.244	.329	11	.000	-1	93	-3		-0.7
BLANKENSHIP, TED	Theodore	B5.10.1901 Bonham TX		D1.14.1945 Atoka OK		BR/TR/6-1/170	d7.2	b-Homer																		
1922	Chi A	8	10	.444	24	15	7	1	127.2	124	58	4	2	47	42	3.81	107	.266	.335	41-0-3	.171	-1	78	5		0.8
1923	Chi A	9	14	.391	44	23	9-1	0	204.2	219	115	8	4	100	57	4.35	91	.287	.372	76-3-2	.211	2	88	-8		-0.4
1924	Chi A	7	6	.538	25	11	7	1	129.1	167	79	1	1	38	36	5.01	82	.317	.364	46-1-3	.326	6	140	-10		-1.4
1925	Chi A	17	8	.680	40	23	16-3	1	232	218	90	11	0	69	81	3.03	137	.253	.308	88-2-4	.132	-2	114	7		0.4
1926	Chi A	13	10	.565	29	26	15-1	1	209.1	217	96	13	4	65	66	3.61	107	.273	.328	76-0-6	.188	3*	93	-26		-2.5
1927	Chi A	12	17	.414	37	34	11-3	0	236.2	280	156	14	2	74	51	4.61	88	.306	.388	59-0-5	.169	-2	91	-8		-1.1
1928	Chi A	9	11	.450	27	22	8	0	158	186	92	9	2	80	36	4.61	88	.306	.388	4	.250	-0	20	-8		-0.7
1929	Chi A	0	2	.000	8	1	0	0	18.1	28	18	3	0	9	7	8.84	48	.359	.425	4	.250	-0	20	-8		-0.7
1930	Chi A	2	1	.667	7	1	0	0	14.2	13	15	0	1	7	2	9.20	50	.371	.443	5	.200	-0	74	-6		-1.0
Total	9	77	79	.494	241	156	73-8	4	1330.2	1462	719	63	13	489	378	4.29	94	.287	.351	475-9-22	.196	7	99	-23		-2.1
BLANTON, CY	Darrell Elijah	B7.6.1908 Waurika OK		D9.13.1945 Norman OK		BL/TR/5-11.5/180	d9.23																			
1934	Pit N	0	1	.000	1	1	0	0	8	5	3	1	4	4	5	3.38	122	.161	.278	1	.000	0	42	1		0.1
1935	Pit N	18	13	.581	35	30	23-4	1	254.1	220	93	3	2	55	142	2.58	159	.229	.272	97-0-3	.134	-4	91	41		4.4
1936	Pit N	13	15	.464	44	32	15-4	3	235.2	235	114	9	3	55	127	3.51	115	.257	.301	84-0-5	.155	-3	94	12		1.0
1937	Pit N★	14	12	.538	36	34	14-4	0	242.2	250	115	13	5	76	143	3.30	117	.266	.324	64-0-4	.203	-1	132	2		0.2
1938	Pit N	11	7	.611	29	26	10-1	0	172.2	190	84	13	2	46	80	3.70	103	.281	.329	14	.286	-1	102	-2		-0.1
1939	Pit N	2	3	.400	10	6	1	0	42	45	23	4	0	10	11	4.32	90	.272	.322	24-0-2	.083	-1	85	-4		-0.3
1940	Phi N	4	3	.571	13	10	5	0	77	82	43	7	1	21	24	4.51	82	.284	.344	51-0-4	.118	-2	82	-16		-2.0
1941	Phi N☆	6	13	.316	28	25	7-1	0	163.2	186	98	11	3	57	64	5.64	59	.345	.436	8	.125	-0	59	-5		-0.7
1942	Phi N	0	4	.000	6	3	0	0	22.1	30	15	3	1	13	15	3.55	110	.262	.314	428-0-22	.154	-11	98	41		3.
Total	9	68	71	.489	202	167	75-14	4	1218.1	1243	588	66	18	337	611											
BLANTON, JOE	Joseph Matthew	B12.11.1980 Nashville TN		BR/TR/6-3/225*	[OakA02 1/24]	d9.21	Col Kentucky																			
2004	Oak A	0	0	—	3	0	0	0-0	8	6	5	1	0	2-0	6	5.63	82	.214	.267	0	—	0		-1		0.
2005	Oak A	12	12	.500	33	33	2	0-0	201.1	178	86	23	5	67-3	116	3.53	126	.236	.300	3-0-1	.333	0	91	21		2.
Total	2	12	12	.500	36	33	2	0-0	209.1	184	91	24	5	69-3	122	3.61	124	.235	.299	3-0-1	.333	0	91	20		2.
BLASINGAME, WADE	Wade Allen	B11.22.1943 Deming NM		BL/TL/6-1/185*	d9.17																					
1963	Mil N	0	0	—	2	0	0	0	3	7	4	0	0	2-0	6	12.00	27	.467	.529	0	—	0		-3		-0.
1964	Mil N	9	5	.643	28	13	3-1	2	116.2	113	58	15	4	51-2	70	4.24	83	.257	.333	40-1-6	.175	3*	142	-7		-0.
1965	Mil N	16	10	.615	38	36	10-1	1	224.2	200	103	17	5	116-10	117	3.77	94	.244	.339	81-1-3	.185	3	119	-5		-0.
1966	Atl N	3	7	.300	16	12	0	0	67.2	71	42	5	2	25-2	34	5.32	68	.272	.340	23	.217	1*	75	-11	22	-1.
1967	Atl N	1	0	1.000	10	4	0	0	25.1	27	13	1	1	21-1	20	4.62	72	.287	.422	7	.143	0	165	-3		-0.
	Hou N	4	7	.364	15	14	0	0	77	91	57	9	2	27-2	46	5.96	56	.298	.357	22-0-2	.182	2*	140	-25		-2.
	Year	5	7	.417	25	18	0	0	102.1	118	70	10	3	48-3	66	5.63	59	.296	.374	29-0-2	.172	2	147	-7	51	-2.
1968	Hou N	1	2	.333	22	2	0	1	36	45	21	3	0	10-1	32	4.75	62	.308	.348	5	.000	-1*	50	-15		-1.
1969	Hou N	0	0	—	26	5	0	1-1	52	66	47	4	2	33-7	33	5.37	66	.306	.396	12	.000	-0	96	3		0.
1970	Hou N	3	3	.500	13	13	0	0-0	77.2	76	34	4	2	23-3	55	3.48	112	.261	.318	24	.083	-0	93	1		0.
1971	Hou N	9	11	.450	30	28	2	0-0	158.1	177	90	11	13	45-3	93	4.60	73	.285	.344	49-1-2	.204	4	119	-23		-2.
1972	Hou N	0	0	—	10	0	0	0-0	8.1	4	9	1	2	8-0	9	8.64	39	.148	.360	0	—	0		-5		-0.
	NY A	0	1	.000	12	1	0	0	17	14	8	1	1	11-1	7	4.24	71	.250	.382	2-0-1	.000	0	59	-2		-0.
Total	8	46	51	.474	243	122	18-3	5-1	863.2	891	486	75	30	372-32	512	4.52	77	.271	.348	265-3-8	.166	14	115-100	73		-9.
BLASS, STEVE	Stephen Robert	B4.18.1942 Canaan CT		BR/TR/6-0/165*	d5.10																					
1964	Pit N	5	8	.385	24	13	3-1	0	104.2	107	52	9	1	45-5	67	4.04	87	.266	.339	30-0-2	.067	-1	91	-6		-0.
1966	Pit N	11	7	.611	34	25	1	0	155.2	173	80	12	2	46-1	76	3.87	92	.284	.336	52-0-2	.231	1	109	-8		-0.

YEAR	TM LG	W	L	PCT	G	GS	CG-SHO	SV-BS	IP	H	R	HR	HB	BB-IB	SO	ERA	AERA	OAV	OOB	AB-HR-SH	AVG	PB	SUP	APR	DL	PW
1967	Pit N	6	8	.429	32	16	2	0	126.2	126	65	12	2	47-7	72	3.55	95	.261	.328	39-0-2	.128	-1	104	-6		-0.7
1968	Pit N	18	6	.750	33	31	12-7	0	220.1	191	64	13	4	57-5	132	2.12	138	.234	.287	80-0-4	.138	-1*	142	19		2.0
1969	Pit N	16	10	.615	38	32	9	2-0	210	207	119	21	6	86-3	147	4.46	78	.258	.333	84-1-2	.250	6*	146	-24		-2.1
1970	Pit N	10	12	.455	31	31	6-1	0-0	196.2	187	92	14	5	73-8	120	3.52	112	.254	.324	70-0-3	.114	-2*	106	7	29	0.4
1971	†Pit N	15	8	.652	33	33	12-5	0-0	240	226	81	16	2	68-8	136	2.85	119	.249	.302	83-0-8	.120	-3*	132	17		1.3
1972	†Pit N★	19	8	.704	33	32	11-2	0-0	249.2	227	80	18	4	84-8	117	2.49	134	.246	.311	82-0-12	.183	1*	115	24		2.9
1973	Pit N	3	9	.250	23	18	1	0-0	88.2	109	98	11	12	84-4	27	9.85	36	.313	.454	24-0-5	.417	4*	129	-59		-6.0
1974	Pit N	0	0	—	1	0	0	0-0	5	5	8	1	2	7-0	2	9.00	39	.238	.429	2	.000	-0		-4		-0.2
Total 10		103	76	.575	282	231	57-16	2-0	1597.1	1558	739	128	38	597-49	896	3.63	95	.258	.327	546-1-40	.172	4	122	-40	29	-4.0

BLATERIC, STEVE Stephen Lawrence B3.20.1944 Denver CO BR/TR/6-3/200* d9.17 Col Denver

YEAR	TM LG	W	L	PCT	G	GS	CG-SHO	SV-BS	IP	H	R	HR	HB	BB-IB	SO	ERA	AERA	OAV	OOB	AB-HR-SH	AVG	PB	SUP	APR	DL	PW
1971	Cin N	0	0	—	2	0	0	0-0	2.2	5	5	4	1	0-0	4	13.50	25	.385	.429	0	—	0		-3		-0.1
1972	NY A	0	0	—	1	0	0	0-0	4	2	0	0	0	0-0	4	0.00	—	.143	.143	1	.000	-0		1		0.1
1975	Cal A	0	0	—	2	0	0	0-0	4.1	9	5	0	0	1-0	5	6.23	57	.429	.435	1	.000	-0		-2		-0.1
Total 3		0	0	—	5	0	0	0-0	11	16	9	2	1	1-0	13	5.73	58	.333	.353	1	.000	-0		-4		-0.1

BLAUVELT, HENRY Henry Russell B4.8.1873 Nyack NY D12.28.1926 Portland OR d6.22

YEAR	TM LG	W	L	PCT	G	GS	CG-SHO	SV-BS	IP	H	R	HR	HB	BB-IB	SO	ERA	AERA	OAV	OOB	AB-HR-SH	AVG	PB	SUP	APR	DL	PW
1890	Roc AA	0	0	—	2	0	0	0	12.1	19	23	0	8		5	10.22	35	.339	.422	6	.500	1		-10		-0.3

BLAYLOCK, GARY Gary Nelson B10.11.1931 Clarkton MO BR/TR/6-0/198 d4.10 C4

YEAR	TM LG	W	L	PCT	G	GS	CG-SHO	SV-BS	IP	H	R	HR	HB	BB-IB	SO	ERA	AERA	OAV	OOB	AB-HR-SH	AVG	PB	SUP	APR	DL	PW
1959	StL N	4	5	.444	26	12	3	0	100	117	61	14	2	43-3	61	5.13	83	.298	.366	34-2-1	.118	0*	81	-8		-0.7
	NY A	0	1	.000	15	1	0	0	25.2	30	13	0	1	15-0	20	3.51	104	.306	.400	2	.500	1	48	0		0.0
Total 1		4	6	.400	41	13	3	0	125.2	147	74	14	3	58-3	81	4.80	86	.300	.373	36-2-1	.139	1	80	-8		-0.7

BLAYLOCK, BOB Robert Edward B6.28.1935 Chattanooga OK BR/TR/6-1/185(185-198) d7.22

YEAR	TM LG	W	L	PCT	G	GS	CG-SHO	SV-BS	IP	H	R	HR	HB	BB-IB	SO	ERA	AERA	OAV	OOB	AB-HR-SH	AVG	PB	SUP	APR	DL	PW
1956	StL N	1	6	.143	14	6	0	0	41	45	32	7	0	24-1	39	6.37	59	.276	.369	11	.091	-1	101	-11		-1.7
1959	StL N	0	1	.000	3	1	0	0	9	8	5	1	0	3-0	3	4.00	106	.229	.289	1	.000	-0	232	0		0.0
Total 2		1	7	.125	17	7	0	0	50	53	37	8	0	27-1	42	5.94	65	.268	.356	12	.083	-1	121	-11		-1.7

BLAZIER, RON Ronald Patrick B7.30.1971 Altoona PA BR/TR/6-6/215(205-248) d5.31 [DL 1998 Phi N 181]

YEAR	TM LG	W	L	PCT	G	GS	CG-SHO	SV-BS	IP	H	R	HR	HB	BB-IB	SO	ERA	AERA	OAV	OOB	AB-HR-SH	AVG	PB	SUP	APR	DL	PW
1996	Phi N	3	1	.750	27	0	0	0-0	38.1	49	30	6	0	10-3	25	5.87	73	.310	.347	1	1.000	0		-7		-0.7
1997	Phi N	1	1	.500	36	0	0	0-0	53.2	62	31	8	0	21-3	42	5.03	84	.290	.347	5-0-1	.400	1		-4		-0.2
Total 2		4	2	.667	63	0	0	0-0	92	111	61	14	0	31-6	67	5.38	79	.298	.347	6-0-1	.500	1		-11	181	-0.9

BLEMKER, RAY Raymond B8.9.1937 Huntingburg IN D2.15.1994 Evansville IN BR/TL/5-11/190 d7.3 Col Georgia Tech

YEAR	TM LG	W	L	PCT	G	GS	CG-SHO	SV-BS	IP	H	R	HR	HB	BB-IB	SO	ERA	AERA	OAV	OOB	AB-HR-SH	AVG	PB	SUP	APR	DL	PW
1960	KC A	0	0	—	1	0	0	0	1.2	3	5	1	1	2-0	0	27.00	15	.375	.545	0	—	0		-4		-0.2

BLETHEN, CLARENCE Clarence Waldo "Climax" B7.11.1893 Dover-Foxcroft ME D4.11.1973 Frederick MD BL/TR/5-11/165 d9.17 Col Maine

YEAR	TM LG	W	L	PCT	G	GS	CG-SHO	SV-BS	IP	H	R	HR	HB	BB-IB	SO	ERA	AERA	OAV	OOB	AB-HR-SH	AVG	PB	SUP	APR	DL	PW
1923	Bos A	0	0	—	5	0	0	0	17.2	29	15	0	7		2	7.13	58	.382	.434	6	.000	-1		-5		-0.4
1929	Bro N	0	0	—	2	0	0	0	2	4	2	0	0	3	0	9.00	51	.444	.583	0		0		-1		-0.0
Total 2		0	0	—	7	0	0	0	2	33	17	0	0	10	2	7.32	57	.388	.453	6	.000	-1		-6		-0.4

BLEWETT, BOB Robert Lawrence B6.28.1877 Fond Du Lac WI D3.17.1958 Sedro Woolley WA BL/TL/5-11/170 d6.17 Col Beloit

YEAR	TM LG	W	L	PCT	G	GS	CG-SHO	SV-BS	IP	H	R	HR	HB	BB-IB	SO	ERA	AERA	OAV	OOB	AB-HR-SH	AVG	PB	SUP	APR	DL	PW
1902	NY N	0	2	.000	5	3	2	0	28	39	26	0	1	7	8	4.82	58	.328	.370	10	.000	-1	81	-7		-0.6

BLISS, ELMER Elmer Ward B3.9.1875 Penfield PA D3.18.1962 Bradford PA BL/TR/6-0/180 d9.28

YEAR	TM LG	W	L	PCT	G	GS	CG-SHO	SV-BS	IP	H	R	HR	HB	BB-IB	SO	ERA	AERA	OAV	OOB	AB-HR-SH	AVG	PB	SUP	APR	DL	PW
1903	NY A	1	0	1.000	1	1	0	0	7	4	1	0	0	3		0.00	—	.167	.167	3	.000	-0		2		0.2

BLOMDAHL, BEN Benjamin Earl B12.30.1970 Long Beach CA BR/TR/6-2/185 [DetA90 14/373] d4.28 Col Riverside (CA) CC

YEAR	TM LG	W	L	PCT	G	GS	CG-SHO	SV-BS	IP	H	R	HR	HB	BB-IB	SO	ERA	AERA	OAV	OOB	AB-HR-SH	AVG	PB	SUP	APR	DL	PW
1995	Det A	0	0	—	14	0	0	0	24.1	36	21	5	0	13-0	15	7.77	62	.356	.430	0	—	0		-7		-0.3

BLONG, JOE Joseph Myles B9.17.1853 St.Louis MO D9.17.1892 St.Louis MO BR/TR d5.4 ▲

YEAR	TM LG	W	L	PCT	G	GS	CG-SHO	SV-BS	IP	H	R	HR	HB	BB-IB	SO	ERA	AERA	OAV	OOB	AB-HR-SH	AVG	PB	SUP	APR	DL	PW
1875	RS NA	3	12	.200	15	15	12-1	0	129	169	121	0	0	2	14	3.07	71	.284	.286	68	.147	-4*	47	-10		-0.9
1876	StL N	0	0	—	1	0	0	0	4	2	0	0	0	1	0	0.00	—	.154	.214	264	.235	-0*		1		0.1
1877	StL N	10	9	.526	25	21	17	0	187.1	203	121	0	0	38	51	2.74	95	.262	.296	218	.216	0*	106	-5		-0.5
Total 2		10	9	.526	26	21	17	0	191.1	205	121	0	0	39	51	2.68	97	.260	.295	482	.226	0*	106	-4		-0.4

BLUE, VIDA Vida Rochelle B7.28.1949 Mansfield LA BB/TL/6-0/189(182-200) [OakA67 2/27] d7.20

YEAR	TM LG	W	L	PCT	G	GS	CG-SHO	SV-BS	IP	H	R	HR	HB	BB-IB	SO	ERA	AERA	OAV	OOB	AB-HR-SH	AVG	PB	SUP	APR	DL	PW
1969	Oak A	1	1	.500	12	4	0	1-0	42	49	34	13	0	18-1	24	6.64	52	.290	.358	10	.000	-0	154	-16		-0.9
1970	Oak A	2	0	1.000	6	6	2-2	0-0	38.2	20	12	0	1	12-0	35	2.09	168	.152	.228	15-1-1	.200	2	131	6		0.5
1971	†Oak A★	24	8	.750	39	39	24-8	0-0	312	209	73	19	4	88-3	301	1.82	183	.189	.251	102-0-13	.118	-2	107	54		5.3
1972	†Oak A	6	10	.375	25	23	5-4	0-0	151	147	55	11	1	48-3	111	2.80	102	.215	.277	45-0-2	.044	-2*	92	0		-0.4
1973	Oak A	20	9	.690	37	37	13-4	0-0	263.2	214	108	26	4	105-2	158	3.28	109	.224	.300	1	.000	-0*	125	10		1.0
1974	†Oak A	17	15	.531	40	40	12-1	0-0	282.1	246	118	17	1	98-7	174	3.25	103	.236	.299	1	.000	-0*	122	4		0.1
1975	†Oak A★	22	11	.667	39	38	13-2	1-0	278	243	103	21	5	99-4	189	3.01	121	.236	.305	0	—	0	135	22		2.4
1976	Oak A	18	13	.581	37	37	20-6	0-0	298.1	268	90	9	1	63-3	166	2.35	143	.239	.279	0	—	0	92	34		3.5
1977	Oak A★	14	19	.424	38	38	16-1	0-0	279.2	284	138	23	1	86-5	157	3.83	105	.264	.317	1	.000	-0	70	6		0.6
1978	SF N★	18	10	.643	35	35	9-4	0-0	258	233	87	12	0	70-4	171	2.79	124	.246	.295	79-1-5	.076	2	101	21		2.4
1979	SF N	14	14	.500	34	34	10	0-0	237	246	143	23	1	111-11	138	5.01	70	.272	.348	83-1-8	.120	0*	124	-40		-4.0
1980	SF N★	14	10	.583	31	31	10-3	0-0	224	202	79	14	0	61-8	129	2.97	118	.242	.292	68-0-7	.074	-4	83	16	35	1.4
1981	SF N★	8	6	.571	18	18	1	0-0	124.2	97	40	7	1	54-3	63	2.45	139	.217	.302	35-0-5	.200	2	80	13		1.8
1982	KC A	.13	12	.520	31	31	6-2	0-0	181	163	80	20	0	80-3	103	3.78	108	.238	.316	0	—	0	97	8		1.0
1983	KC A	0	5	.000	19	14	1	0-0	85.1	96	62	12	2	63-3	50	6.01	68	.286	.352	0	—	0	101	-17		-0.9
1985	SF N	8	8	.500	33	20	1	0-0	131	115	70	17	1	80-1	103	4.47	78	.240	.348	30-0-8	.133	-0	122	-13		-1.3
1986	SF N	10	10	.500	28	28	0	0-0	156.2	137	70	17	1	77-3	100	3.27	108	.239	.326	43-1-4	.093	1	100	5	26	0.7
Total 17		209	161	.565	502	473	143-37	2-0	3343.1	2939	1357	263	23	1185-61	2175	3.27	108	.237	.303	512-4-53	.104	-2	106	113	61	13.2

BLUEJACKET, JIM James (b James Smith) B7.8.1887 Adair OK D3.26.1947 Pekin IL BR/TR/6-2.5/200 d8.6 ggs-Bill Wilkinson

YEAR	TM LG	W	L	PCT	G	GS	CG-SHO	SV-BS	IP	H	R	HR	HB	BB-IB	SO	ERA	AERA	OAV	OOB	AB-HR-SH	AVG	PB	SUP	APR	DL	PW
1914	Bro F	4	5	.444	17	7	3-1	0	67	77	34	2	0	19	29	3.76	76	.302	.350	22	.136	-1	89	-6		-0.7
1915	Bro F	10	11	.476	24	21	10-2	0	162.2	155	74	2	0	75	48	3.15	86	.258	.340	61-0-1	.131	-5	98	-7		-1.5
1916	Cin N	0	1	.000	3	2	0	0	7	12	6	0	0	3	1	7.71	34	.400	.455	2	.000	-0	144	-3		-0.5
Total 3		14	17	.452	44	30	13-3	0	236.2	244	114	4	0	97	78	3.46	80	.275	.347	85-0-1	.129	-6	98	-16		-2.7

BLUMA, JAIME James Andrew B5.18.1972 Beaufort SC BR/TR/5-11/195 [KCA94 3/79] d8.9 Col Wichita St. [DL 1997 KC A 181]

YEAR	TM LG	W	L	PCT	G	GS	CG-SHO	SV-BS	IP	H	R	HR	HB	BB-IB	SO	ERA	AERA	OAV	OOB	AB-HR-SH	AVG	PB	SUP	APR	DL	PW
1996	KC A	0	0	—	17	0	0	0	20	18	9	2	2	4-1	14	3.60	140	.247	.300	0	—	0		3		0.2

BLUME, CLINT Clinton Willis B10.17.1898 Brooklyn NY D6.12.1973 Islip NY BR/TR/5-11/175 d9.30 Col Colgate

YEAR	TM LG	W	L	PCT	G	GS	CG-SHO	SV-BS	IP	H	R	HR	HB	BB-IB	SO	ERA	AERA	OAV	OOB	AB-HR-SH	AVG	PB	SUP	APR	DL	PW
1922	NY N	1	0	1.000	1	1	1	0	9	7	3	0	0	1	2	1.00	400	.212	.235	1	1.000	1	102	2		0.4
1923	NY N	2	0	1.000	12	1	0	0	24	22	11	0	2	20	2	3.75	102	.265	.419	5	.000	-0	129	0		0.0
Total 2		3	0	1.000	13	2	1	0	33	29	14	0	2	21	4	3.00	129	.250	.374	6	.167	1	117	2		0.4

BLYLEVEN, BERT Rik Aalbert B4.6.1951 Zeist, Netherlands BR/TR/6-3/207(190-220) [MinA69 3/55] d6.5 [DL 1991 Cal A 182]

YEAR	TM LG	W	L	PCT	G	GS	CG-SHO	SV-BS	IP	H	R	HR	HB	BB-IB	SO	ERA	AERA	OAV	OOB	AB-HR-SH	AVG	PB	SUP	APR	DL	PW
1970	†Min A	10	9	.526	27	25	5-1	0-0	164	143	66	17	2	47-6	135	3.18	116	.232	.288	50-0-7	.140	-1	94	10		0.9
1971	Min A	16	15	.516	38	38	17-5	0-0	278.1	267	95	21	5	59-1	224	2.81	126	.255	.287	91-0-7	.132	-3	87	23		2.2
1972	Min A	17	17	.500	39	38	11-3	0-0	287.1	247	93	22	10	69-7	228	2.73	118	.233	.285	94-0-11	.160	-1	105	20		2.4
1973	Min A★	20	17	.541	40	40	25-9	0-0	325	296	109	16	9	67-4	258	2.52	158	.242	.284	0	—	0	93	48		5.3
1974	Min A	17	17	.500	37	37	19-3	0-0	281	244	99	14	9	77-3	249	2.66	141	.233	.290	0	—	0	96	31		3.7
1975	Min A	15	10	.600	35	35	20-3	0-0	275.2	219	104	24	4	84-2	233	3.00	128	.219	.281	0	—	0	110	26		2.3
1976	Min A	4	5	.444	12	12	4	0-0	95.1	101	39	3	4	35-5	75	3.12	115	.283	.351	0	—	0	74	5		0.4
	Tex A	9	11	.450	24	24	14-6	0-0	202.1	182	67	11	8	46-1	144	2.76	130	.242	.292	0	—	0	64	-20		2.1
	Year	13	16	.448	36	36	18-6	0-0	297.2	283	106	14	12	81-6	219	2.87	125	.255	.312	0	—	0	67	24		2.5
1977	Tex A	14	12	.538	30	30	15-5	0-0	234.2	181	81	20	7	69-1	182	2.72	150	.214	.278	0	—	0	107	35		3.7
1978	Pit N	14	10	.583	34	34	11-4	0-0	243.2	217	94	17	6	66-5	182	3.03	123	.235	.290	85-0-7	.129	-2*	103	19		1.6
1979	†Pit N	12	5	.706	37	37	4	0-0	237.1	238	102	21	6	92-8	172	3.60	109	.265	.335	70-0-15	.129	-3*	105	10		1.3
1980	Pit N	8	13	.381	34	34	5-2	0-2	216.2	219	102	20	9	59-5	168	3.82	97	.262	.310	61-0-9	.082	-4*	105	-7		-0.7
1981	Cle A	11	7	.611	20	20	9-1	0-0	159.1	145	52	9	5	40-1	107	2.88	128	.245	.296	0	—	0	99	16		1.7
1982	Cle A	2	2	.500	4	4	1	0-0	20.1	16	14	2	0	11-1	19	4.87	85	.211	.303	0	—	0	121	-2		-0.4
1983	Cle A	7	10	.412	24	24	5	0-0	156.1	160	74	10	8	44-4	123	3.91	109	.267	.325	0	—	0	81	6		0.7
1984	Cle A	19	7	.731	33	32	12-4	0-0	245	204	86	19	10	74-4	170	2.87	144	.224	.289	0	—	0	116	33	18	3.4

YEAR	TM LG	W	L	PCT	G	GS	CG-SHO	SV-BS	IP	H	R	HR	HB	BB-IB	SO	ERA	AERA	OAV	OOB	AB-HR-SH	AVG	PB	SUP	APR	DL	PW
1985	Cle A★	9	11	.450	23	23	15-4	0-0	179.2	163	76	14	7	49-1	129	3.26	128	.240	.296	0	—	0	92	16		1.6
	Min A	8	5	.615	14	14	9-1	0-0	114	101	45	9	2	26-0	77	3.00	148	.237	.281	0	—	0	78	16		1.7
	Year	17	16	.515	37	37	24-5	0-0	293.2	264	121	23	9	75-1	206	3.16	135	.239	.290	0	—	0	86	32		3.3
1986	Min A	17	14	.548	36	36	16-3	0-0	271.2	262	134	50	10	58-4	215	4.01	108	.250	.294	0	—	0	98	17		1.6
1987	†Min A	15	12	.556	37	37	8-1	0-0	267	249	132	46	9	101-4	196	4.01	116	.249	.321	0	—	0	93	-27	16	-3.1
1988	Min A	10	17	.370	33	33	7	0-0	207.1	240	128	21	16	51-1	145	5.43	75	.294	.345	0	—	0	114	32		0.8
1989	Cal A	17	5	.773	33	33	8-5	0-0	241	225	76	14	8	44-2	131	2.73	140	.248	.287	0	—	0	109	-19	54	-1.9
1990	Cal A	8	7	.533	23	23	2	0-0	134	163	85	15	7	25-0	69	5.24	73	.303	.339	0	—	0	72	-10		-1.4
1992	Cal A	8	12	.400	25	24	1	0-0	133	150	76	17	5	29-2	70	4.74	85	.285	.326	0	—	0	96	331	425	31.8
Total	22	287	250	.534	692	685	242-60	0-2	4970	4632	2029	430	155	1322-71	3701	3.31	118	.247	.301	451-0-56	.131	-14	96	331	425	31.8

BLYZKA, MIKE Michael John (b Michael John Bliska) B12.25.1928 Hamtramck MI D10.13.2004 Cheyenne WY BR/TR/5-11.5/190* d4.21

YEAR	TM LG	W	L	PCT	G	GS	CG-SHO	SV-BS	IP	H	R	HR	HB	BB-IB	SO	ERA	AERA	OAV	OOB	AB-HR-SH	AVG	PB	SUP	APR	DL	PW
1953	StL A	2	6	.250	33	9	2	0	94.1	110	78	6	0	56	23	6.39	66	.292	.383	23-0-2	.000	-3	73	-23		-2.0
1954	Bal A	1	5	.167	37	0	0	1	86.1	83	48	2	0	51	35	4.69	76	.254	.351	15-0-1	.133	-1		-10		-0.7
Total	2	3	11	.214	70	9	2	1	180.2	193	126	8	0	107	58	5.58	70	.274	.368	38-0-3*	.053	-4	73	-33		-2.7

BOARDMAN, CHARLIE Charles Louis B3.27.1893 Seneca Falls NY D8.10.1968 Sacramento CA BL/TR/6-2.5/194 d9.26

YEAR	TM LG	W	L	PCT	G	GS	CG-SHO	SV-BS	IP	H	R	HR	HB	BB-IB	SO	ERA	AERA	OAV	OOB	AB-HR-SH	AVG	PB	SUP	APR	DL	PW
1913	Phi A	0	2	.000	2	2	1	0	9	10	5	0	0	6	4	2.00	138	.323	.432	3	.000	-0	54	0		-0.1
1914	Phi A	0	0	—	2	0	0	0	7.1	10	5	0	0	4	2	4.91	53	.357	.438	2	.000	-0		-2		-0.1
1915	StL N	1	0	1.000	3	1	1	0	19	12	12	0	0	15	7	2.84	98	.188	.342	7	.286	0	160	-2		-0.1
Total	3	1	2	.333	7	3	2	0	35.1	32	22	0	0	25	13	3.06	90	.260	.385	12	.167	-0	90	-4		-0.3

BOCHTLER, DOUG Douglas Eugene B7.5.1970 W.Palm Beach FL BR/TR/6-3/200* [MonN89 9/228] d5.5 Col Indian River (FL) CC

YEAR	TM LG	W	L	PCT	G	GS	CG-SHO	SV-BS	IP	H	R	HR	HB	BB-IB	SO	ERA	AERA	OAV	OOB	AB-HR-SH	AVG	PB	SUP	APR	DL	PW
1995	SD N	4	4	.500	34	0	0	1-3	45.1	38	18	5	0	19-0	45	3.57	114	.239	.318	2	.000	—	0	4		0.6
1996	†SD N	2	4	.333	63	0	0	3-4	65.2	45	25	6	1	39-8	68	3.02	134	.195	.311	0	—	0	7			0.6
1997	SD N	3	6	.333	54	0	0	2-1	60.1	51	35	3	1	50-4	46	4.77	82	.229	.368	0	—	0	-6		15	-0.8
1998	Det A	0	2	.000	51	0	0	0-2	67.1	73	48	17	3	42-6	45	6.15	77	.279	.381	0	—	0	-9			-0.1
1999	LA N	0	0	—	12	0	0	0-0	13	11	8	4	1	6-1	9	5.54	79	.224	.316	0	—	0	-1			-0.1
2000	KC A	0	2	.000	6	0	0	0-0	8.1	13	6	2	0	10-4	2	6.48	81	.371	.511	0	—	-0	-1			-0.2
Total	6	9	18	.333	220	0	0	6-10	260	231	140	36	6	166-23	215	4.57	93	.241	.353	2	.000	-0	-6		15	0.0

BOCKUS, RANDY Randy Walter B10.5.1960 Canton OH BL/TR/6-2/195(190-205) [SFN82 34/796] d9.10 Col Kent St.

YEAR	TM LG	W	L	PCT	G	GS	CG-SHO	SV-BS	IP	H	R	HR	HB	BB-IB	SO	ERA	AERA	OAV	OOB	AB-HR-SH	AVG	PB	SUP	APR	DL	PW
1986	SF N	0	0	—	5	0	0	0	7	7	5	1	0	5-0	4	2.57	137	.241	.371	1	.000	-0*	0			0.0
1987	SF N	1	0	1.000	12	0	0	0-1	17.1	17	8	2	0	4-1	9	3.63	106	.266	.309	1	.000	-0	0			0.0
1988	SF N	1	1	.500	20	0	0	0-1	32	35	19	2	1	13-2	18	4.78	68	.297	.368	6	.167	0	-6			-0.3
1989	Det A	0	0	—	2	0	0	0-0	5.1	7	3	0	0	2-1	2	5.06	76	.333	.391	0	—	0	-1			0.0
Total	4	2	1	.667	39	0	0	0-3	61.2	66	35	5	1	25-5	33	4.23	83	.284	.355	8	.125	0	-7			-0.3

BODDICKER, MIKE Michael James B8.23.1957 Cedar Rapids IA BR/TR/5-11/172(172-190) [BalA78 6/152] d10.4 Col Iowa

YEAR	TM LG	W	L	PCT	G	GS	CG-SHO	SV-BS	IP	H	R	HR	HB	BB-IB	SO	ERA	AERA	OAV	OOB	AB-HR-SH	AVG	PB	SUP	APR	DL	PW
1980	Bal A	0	1	.000	1	1	0	0	7.1	6	6	1	0	5-0	4	6.14	65	.207	.324	0	—	0	90	-2		-0.2
1981	Bal A	0	0	—	2	0	0	0	5.2	6	4	1	0	2-0	2	4.76	77	.261	.320	0	—	0		-1		-0.1
1982	Bal A	1	0	1.000	7	0	0	0	25.2	25	10	2	0	12-2	20	3.51	116	.258	.339	0	—	0		2		0.1
1983	†Bal A	16	8	.667	27	26	10-5	0-0	179	141	65	13	0	52-1	120	2.77	145	.216	.273	0	—	0*	104	23		3.1
1984	Bal A☆	20	11	.645	34	34	16-4	0-0	261.1	218	95	23	5	81-1	128	2.79	140	.228	.290	0	—	0*	100	32		3.9
1985	Bal A	12	17	.414	32	32	9-2	0-0	203.1	227	104	13	5	89-7	135	4.07	100	.286	.361	0	—	0	99	-1		-1.1
1986	Bal A	14	12	.538	33	33	7	0-0	218.1	214	125	30	11	74-4	175	4.70	89	.255	.321	0	—	0*	87	7	20	1.6
1987	Bal A	10	12	.455	33	33	7-2	0-0	226	212	114	29	7	78-4	152	4.18	106	.248	.315	0	—	0	71	0		0.0
1988	Bal A	6	12	.333	21	21	4	0-0	147	149	72	14	11	51-5	100	3.86	102	.265	.333	0	—	0	121	14		1.6
	†Bos A	7	3	.700	15	14	1-1	0-0	89	85	30	3	3	26-1	56	2.63	157	.257	.313	0	—	0	92	14		1.6
	Year	13	15	.464	36	35	5-1	0-0	236	234	102	17	14	77-6	156	3.39	118	.262	.326	0	—	0	104	5		0.6
1989	Bos A	15	11	.577	34	34	3-2	0-0	211.2	217	101	19	10	71-4	145	4.00	103	.267	.330	0	—	0	111	19		2.0
1990	†Bos A	17	8	.680	34	34	4	0-0	228	225	92	16	10	69-6	143	3.36	122	.258	.319	0	—	0	94	3	16	0.4
1991	KC A	12	12	.500	30	29	1	0-0	180.2	188	89	13	13	59-0	79	4.08	101	.272	.340	0	—	0	61	-7	57	-0.4
1992	KC A	1	4	.200	29	8	0	3-0	86.2	92	50	5	3	37-3	47	4.98	82	.269	.351	0	—	0	96	-7	39	-0.6
1993	Mil A	3	5	.375	10	10	1	0-0	54	77	35	6	4	15-1	24	5.67	76	.338	.387	0	—	0	99	75	132	9.9
Total	14	134	116	.536	342	309	63-16	3-0	2123.2	2082	992	188	87	721-39	1330	3.80	108	.257	.323	0	—	0	99	75	132	9.9

BOEHLER, GEORGE George Henry B1.2.1892 Lawrenceburg IN D6.23.1958 Lawrenceburg IN BR/TR/6-2/180 d9.13

YEAR	TM LG	W	L	PCT	G	GS	CG-SHO	SV-BS	IP	H	R	HR	HB	BB-IB	SO	ERA	AERA	OAV	OOB	AB-HR-SH	AVG	PB	SUP	APR	DL	PW
1912	Det A	0	2	.000	5	4	2	0	32	50	31	0	2	14	15	6.47	50	.365	.431	10	.100	-1	108	-11		-0.6
1913	Det A	0	1	.000	1	1	1	0	8	11	9	0	2	6	2	6.75	43	.367	.500	3	.333	1	0	-4		-0.3
1914	Det A	2	3	.400	18	6	2	0	63	54	39	1	8	48	37	3.57	79	.242	.394	17	.176	1	121	-7		-0.5
1915	Det A	.1	1	.500	8	0	0	0	15	19	10	0	1	4	7	1.80	168	.328	.381	4	.750	2*		0		-0.3
1916	Det A	1	1	.500	5	2	1	0	13.1	12	8	0	2	9	8	4.73	61	.261	.404	3	.000	1	158	-2		-0.3
1920	StL A	0	1	.000	3	1	0	0	7	10	10	1	0	4	2	7.71	51	.303	.378	1	.000	1	162	-4		-0.4
1921	StL A	0	0	—	1	0	0	0	1	1	1	0	0	0	0	0.00	—	.500	.500	0	—	0		-1		0.0
1923	Pit N	1	3	.250	10	3	1	0	28.1	33	26	1	1	19	12	6.04	66	.314	.455	10	.300	1	103	-8		-0.9
1926	Bro N	1	0	1.000	10	1	0	0	34.2	42	23	1	3	23	10	4.41	87	.302	.412	12	.250	0*	65	-3		-0.2
Total	9	6	12	.333	61	18	7	0	202.1	232	156	4	19	134	93	4.71	70	.300	.416	60	.233	3	110	-39		-3.1

BOEHLING, JOE John Joseph B3.20.1891 Richmond VA D9.8.1941 Richmond VA BL/TL/5-11/168 d6.20

YEAR	TM LG	W	L	PCT	G	GS	CG-SHO	SV-BS	IP	H	R	HR	HB	BB-IB	SO	ERA	AERA	OAV	OOB	AB-HR-SH	AVG	PB	SUP	APR	DL	PW
1912	Was A	0	0	—	3	0	0	0	5	4	4	0	2	2	2	7.20	46	.235	.480		—	0		-2		-0.1
1913	Was A	17	7	.708	38	25	18-3	4	235.1	197	82	3	9	82	110	2.14	138	.236	.312	86-0-1	.221	1	106	18		2.2
1914	Was A	13	8	.619	37	24	14-2	0	196	180	76	3	9	76	91	3.03	93	.258	.339	71-0-2	.239	4	107	-1		-0.2
1915	Was A	14	13	.519	40	32	14-2	0	229.1	217	105	5	9	119	108	3.22	92	.255	.352	75-1-4	.173	0*	97	-4		-0.2
1916	Was A	9	11	.450	27	19	7-2	0	139.2	134	62	1	3	54	52	3.09	90	.260	.333	41-0-1	.171	1	66	-5		-0.4
	Cle A	2	4	.333	12	9	3	0	60.2	63	23	0	2	23	18	2.67	113	.281	.353	19	.263	1*	67	2		0.4
	Year	11	15	.423	39	28	10-2	0	200.1	197	85	1	5	77	70	2.97	96	.266	.339	60-0-1	.200	1	66	-3		-1.0
1917	Cle A	1	4	.143	12	7	1	0	46.1	50	27	1	3	16	11	4.66	61	.291	.361	16-0-1	.188	-0*	54	-7		-1.0
1920	Cle A	0	1	.000	3	2	0	0	13	16	10	0	0	10	4	4.85	78	.333	.448	4	.500	1	115	-2		0.0
Total	7	56	50	.528	162	118	57-9	4	925.1	861	389	13	37	386	396	2.97	99	.256	.340	312-1-9	.212	7	79	-2		1.2

BOEHRINGER, BRIAN Brian Edward B1.8.1969 St.Louis MO BB/TR/6-2/190* [ChiA91 4/124] d4.30 Col Nevada-Las Vegas

YEAR	TM LG	W	L	PCT	G	GS	CG-SHO	SV-BS	IP	H	R	HR	HB	BB-IB	SO	ERA	AERA	OAV	OOB	AB-HR-SH	AVG	PB	SUP	APR	DL	PW
1995	NY A	0	3	.000	7	3	0	0	17.2	24	27	5	1	22-1	10	13.75	34	.320	.475	0	—	0	74	-18		-2.2
1996	†NY A	2	4	.333	15	3	0	0-1	46.1	46	28	6	1	21-2	37	5.44	91	.260	.337	0	—	0	75	-2		-0.2
1997	†NY A	3	2	.600	34	0	0	0-3	48	39	16	4	0	32-6	53	2.63	170	.225	.343	0	—	0		10	87	0.3
1998	†SD N	5	2	.714	56	1	0	0-1	76.1	75	38	10	4	45-4	67	4.36	91	.257	.363	7	.000	-0	23	-3		-0.3
1999	SD N	6	5	.545	33	11	0	0-2	94.1	97	38	6	1	35-4	64	3.24	132	.267	.330	16-0-2	.063	-1	92	11	50	1.1
2000	SD N	0	3	.000	7	3	0	0	15.2	18	15	4	0	10-0	9	5.74	78	.286	.378	4-0-1	.250	-0	41	-4	152	-0.4
2001	NY A	0	1	.000	22	0	0	1-0	34.2	35	15	3	4	12-0	33	3.12	143	.255	.325	0	—	-0	-2			-0.2
	SF N	3	0	1.000	29	0	0	1-0	34.1	32	20	4	2	17-5	27	4.19	98	.239	.329	3	.000	-0	-4			-0.2
2002	Pit N	5	4	.556	70	0	0	1-5	79.2	65	30	5	2	33-6	65	3.39	124	.229	.311	0	—	-0	-7			-1.0
2003	Pit N	5	4	.556	62	0	0	0-3	62.1	64	39	11	3	30-3	47	5.49	79	.267	.353	0	—	-0	-1	124		-0.1
2004	Pit N	2	1	.500	21	0	0	0-1	25.1	27	14	2	1	17-3	20	4.62	94	.293	.398	1	.000	-0	78	-4	413	-0.1
Total	10	26	32	.448	356	21	0	3-19	534.2	522	280	64	18	274-34	432	4.36	99	.257	.347	31-0-3	.065	-1	78	-4	413	-1.7

BOERNER, LARRY Lawrence Hyer B1.21.1905 Staunton VA D10.16.1969 Staunton VA BR/TR/6-4.5/175 d6.30 Col McDaniel

YEAR	TM LG	W	L	PCT	G	GS	CG-SHO	SV-BS	IP	H	R	HR	HB	BB-IB	SO	ERA	AERA	OAV	OOB	AB-HR-SH	AVG	PB	SUP	APR	DL	PW
1932	Bos A	0	4	.000	21	5	0	0	61	71	41	2	3	37	19	5.02	90	.302	.404	17-0-1	.000	-3	61	-4		-0.4

BOEVER, JOE Joseph Martin B10.4.1960 Kirkwood MO BR/TR/6-1/200(200-215) d7.19 Col Nevada-Las Vegas

YEAR	TM LG	W	L	PCT	G	GS	CG-SHO	SV-BS	IP	H	R	HR	HB	BB-IB	SO	ERA	AERA	OAV	OOB	AB-HR-SH	AVG	PB	SUP	APR	DL	PW
1985	StL N	0	0	—	13	0	0	0-1	16.1	17	8	3	0	4-1	20	4.41	81	.270	.309	0	—	0		-1		-0.1
1986	StL N	0	1	.000	11	0	0	0-0	21.2	19	5	2	0	11-0	8	1.66	222	.232	.323	4	.500	0	5			0.3
1987	Atl N	1	0	1.000	14	0	0	0	18.1	29	15	4	0	12-1	18	7.36	59	.367	.446	0	—	0	-5			-0.4
1988	Atl N	0	2	.000	16	0	0	1-0	20.1	12	4	1	1	1-0	7	1.77	207	.182	.206	0	—	0	4			0.5
1989	Atl N	4	11	.267	66	0	0	21-9	82.1	78	37	6	1	34-5	68	3.94	93	.252	.328	1	.000	-0	-1			-0.3
1990	Atl N	1	3	.250	33	0	0	8-4	42.1	40	23	6	0	35-10	35	4.68	86	.252	.383	2	.000	-0	-2			-0.2
	Phi N	2	3	.400	34	0	0	6-1	46	37	12	0	0	16-2	40	2.15	179	.215	.282	1	.000	-0	9			1.1
	Year	3	6	.333	67	0	0	14-5	88.1	77	35	6	0	51-12	75	3.36	117	.233	.333	3	.000	-0	6			0.9

YEAR	TM LG	W	L	PCT	G	GS	CG-SHO	SV-BS	IP	H	R	HR	HB	BB-IB	SO	ERA	AERA	OAV	OOB	AB-HR-SH	AVG	PB	SUP	APR	DL	PW
1991	Phi N	3	5	.375	68	0	0	0-2	98.1	90	45	10	0	54-11	89	3.84	96	.245	.336	3	.333	0		-1		-0.1
1992	Hou N	3	6	.333	81	0	0	2-4	111.1	103	38	3	4	45-9	67	2.51	135	.248	.324	7	.000	-1		10		0.7
1993	Oak A	4	2	.667	42	0	0	0-1	79.1	87	40	8	4	33-4	49	3.86	107	.280	.353	0	—	0		1		0.1
	Det A	2	1	.667	19	0	0	3-1	23	14	10	1	0	11-3	14	2.74	159	.179	.269	0	—	0		2		0.1
	Year	6	3	.667	61	0	0	3-2	102.1	101	50	9	4	44-7	63	3.61	116	.260	.336	0	—	0		3		0.4
1994	Det A	9	2	.818	46	0	0	3-3	81.1	80	40	12	2	37-12	49	3.98	124	.263	.345	0	—	0		5		0.5
1995	Det A	5	7	.417	60	0	0	3-3	98.2	128	74	17	3	44-12	71	6.39	75	.319	.384	0	—	0		-16		-1.8
1996	Pit N	0	2	.000	13	0	0	2-1	15	17	11	2	1	6-0	6	5.40	81	.288	.364	1	.000	-0		-2		-0.3
Total	12	34	45	.430	516	0	0	49-30	754.1	751	362	75	16	343-70	541	3.93	103	.262	.341	17	.118	-1		12		1.1

BOGART, JOHN   John Renzie "Big John"   B9.21.1900 Bloomsburg PA   D12.7.1986 Clarence NY   BR/TR/6-2/195   d9.17

| 1920 | Det A | 2 | 1 | .667 | 4 | 0 | 0 | 0 | 23.2 | 16 | 12 | 0 | 0 | 18 | 5 | 3.04 | 122 | .195 | .340 | 8 | .250 | -0 | 149 | 1 | | 0.1 |

BOGGS, RAY   Raymond Joseph "Lefty"   B12.12.1904 Reamsville KS   D11.27.1989 Grand Junction CO   BL/TL/6-0.5/170   d9.1   Col Denver

| 1928 | Bos N | 0 | 0 | — | 5 | 2 | 0 | 0 | 5 | 3 | 3 | 0 | 7 | 3 | 0 | 5.40 | 72 | .167 | .545 | 0 | — | 0 | | -1 | | 0.0 |

BOGGS, TOMMY   Thomas Winton   B10.25.1955 Poughkeepsie NY   BR/TR/6-2/200*   [TexA74 1/2]   d7.19

1976	Tex A	1	7	.125	13	13	3	0-0	90.1	87	42	7	1	34-1	15	3.49	103	.257	.322	0	—	0	64	0		-0.5
1977	Tex A	0	3	.000	6	6	0	0-0	27.1	40	18	1	1	12-0	15	5.93	69	.351	.417	0	—	0	107	-5		-0.5
1978	Atl N	2	8	.200	16	12	1-1	0-0	59	80	46	8	1	26-3	21	6.71	60	.323	.386	18-1-1	.167	0	48	-14		-2.1
1979	Atl N	0	2	.000	3	3	0	0-0	12.2	21	11	0	1	4-0	1	6.39	63	.362	.413	4	.250	0	81	-3		-0.4
1980	Atl N	12	9	.571	32	26	4-3	0-0	192.1	180	80	14	4	46-0	84	3.42	108	.249	.295	63-0-6	.159	-2	97	6		0.3
1981	Atl N	3	13	.188	25	24	1	0-0	142.2	140	72	11	3	54-4	81	4.10	86	.265	.332	46-0-1	.152	-1	77	-9		-1.0
1982	Atl N	2	2	.500	10	10	0	0-0	46.1	43	22	2	2	22-1	29	3.30	112	.253	.345	17-0-1	.235	0	110	1	129	0.1
1983	Atl N	0	0	—	5	0	0	0-0	6.1	8	4	1	0	1-0	5	5.68	68	.320	.346	0	—	0		-1	151	0.0
1985	Tex A	0	0	—	4	0	0	0-1	7	13	9	3	0	2-0	6	11.57	37	.342	.417	0	—	0		-5		-0.2
Total	9	20	44	.313	114	94	10-4	0-1	584	612	304	47	13	201-9	278	4.22	88	.273	.334	148-1-9	.169	-2	83	-30	280	-3.8

BOGLE, WARREN   Warren Frederick   B10.19.1946 Passaic NJ   BL/TL/6-4/230   [OakA67 S4/73]   d7.31   Col Miami

| 1968 | Oak A | 0 | 0 | — | 16 | 1 | 0 | 0 | 26 | 26 | 12 | 3 | 1 | 26 | 26 | 4.30 | 66 | .283 | .337 | 5 | .000 | -1 | 185 | -4 | | -0.2 |

BOHANON, BRIAN   Brian Edward   B8.1.1968 Denton TX   BL/TL/6-2/220(210-250)   [TexA87 1/19]   d4.10

1990	Tex A	0	3	.000	11	6	0	0-0	34	40	30	6	2	18-0	15	6.62	60	.296	.380	0	—	0	77	-11		-0.8
1991	Tex A	4	3	.571	11	11	1	0-0	61.1	66	35	4	2	23-0	34	4.84	84	.274	.336	0	—	0	152	-5	84	-0.5
1992	Tex A	1	1	.500	18	7	0	0-0	45.2	57	38	7	1	25-0	29	6.31	61	.297	.377	0	—	0	130	-14	15	-0.7
1993	Tex A	4	4	.500	36	8	0	0-1	92.2	107	54	8	4	46-3	45	4.76	88	.296	.377	0	—	0	104	-6	21	-0.4
1994	Tex A	2	2	.500	11	5	0	0-0	37.1	51	31	7	1	8-1	26	7.23	67	.321	.357	0	—	0	91	-9		-0.7
1995	Det A	1	1	.500	52	0	0	1-0	105.2	121	68	10	4	41-5	63	5.54	87	.285	.350	0	—	0	139	-7		-0.3
1996	Tor A	0	1	.000	20	0	0	1-0	22	27	19	4	2	19-4	17	7.77	64	.303	.429	0	—	0		-6		-0.3
1997	NY N	6	4	.600	19	14	0	0-0	94.1	95	49	9	4	34-2	66	3.82	105	.258	.328	33-0-1	.182	0*	122	0		0.0
1998	NY N	2	4	.333	25	4	0	0-1	54.1	47	21	4	6	21-2	39	3.15	131	.234	.325	14	.429	2	84	6		0.9
	LA N	5	7	.417	14	14	2	0-0	97.1	74	35	9	5	36-0	72	2.40	168	.213	.294	29-0-4	.207	2	73	16		2.2
	Year	7	11	.389	39	18	2	0-1	151.2	121	56	13	11	57-2	111	2.67	152	.220	.305	43-0-4	.279	4	75	21		3.1
1999	Col N	12	12	.500	33	33	3-1	0-0	197.1	236	146	30	14	92-1	120	6.20	93	.304	.386	71-1-5	.197	-0*	92	-7		-0.7
2000	Col N	12	10	.545	34	26	2-1	0-0	177	181	101	24	6	79-4	98	4.68	124	.266	.346	53-2-11	.208	1*	104	17		1.9
2001	Col N	5	8	.385	20	19	0	0-0	97	127	79	20	7	47-3	47	7.14	75	.323	.404	31-0-1	.323	2*	104	-14	83	-1.4
Total	12	54	60	.474	304	157	8-2	2-2	1116	1229	706	142	58	489-25	671	5.19	93	.281	.359	231-3-22	.229	8	106	-40	203	-0.8

BOHEN, PAT   Leo Ignatius   B9.30.1890 Oakland IA   D4.8.1942 Napa CA   BR/TR/5-10.5/155   d10.1

1913	Phi A	0	1	.000	1	1	1	0	8	3	1	0	0	2	5	1.13	246	.120	.185	3	.000	-0	0	2		0.2
1914	Pit N	0	0	—	1	0	0	0	1	2	2	0	1	2	0	18.00	15	.500	.714	1	.000	-0		-2		-0.1
Total	2	0	1	.000	2	1	1	0	9	5	3	0	1	4	5	3.00	92	.172	.294	4	.000	-1	0	0		0.1

BOHN, CHARLIE   Charles   B5.1856 Cleveland OH   D8.1.1903 Cleveland OH   BR/TR/5-9/165   d6.20

| 1882 | Lou AA | 1 | 1 | .500 | 2 | 2 | 1 | 0 | 16 | 22 | 13 | 0 | 1 | 3 | 1 | 3.00 | 83 | .273 | .300 | 13 | .154 | -0* | 52 | 0 | | 0.0 |

BOHNET, JOHN   John Kelly   B1.18.1961 Pasadena CA   BB/TL/6-0/180   [CleA79 1/7]   d5.10

| 1982 | Cle A | 0 | 0 | — | 3 | 3 | 0 | 0-0 | 11.2 | 11 | 9 | 4 | 1 | 7-0 | 4 | 6.94 | 60 | .250 | .365 | 0 | — | 0 | 88 | -3 | | -0.1 |

BOITANO, DAN   Danny Jon   B3.22.1953 Sacramento CA   BR/TR/6-0/185*   [PhiN73 S1/11]   d10.1   Col Fresno (CA) City

1978	Phi N	0	0	—	1	0	0	0-0	1	0	0	0	0	0-0	0	0.00	—	.000	.250	0	—	0	0	0		0.0
1979	Mil A	0	0	—	5	0	0	0-0	6	6	1	1	0	3-0	5	1.50	280	.273	.360	0	—	0	0	2		0.1
1980	Mil A	0	1	.000	11	0	0	0-0	17.2	26	17	7	1	6-0	11	8.15	48	.342	.393	0	—	0	0	-8		-0.4
1981	NY N	2	1	.667	15	0	0	0-1	16.1	21	10	2	5	5-0	8	5.51	64	.309	.368	0	—	0*	0	-3		-0.5
1982	Tex A	0	0	—	19	0	0	0-1	30.1	33	19	5	2	13-2	28	5.34	73	.280	.356	0	—	0	0	-5		-0.2
Total	5	2	2	.500	51	0	0	0-2	71.1	86	47	15	8	28-2	52	5.68	68	.300	.367	0	—	0	0	-14		-1.0

BOKELMANN, DICK   Richard Werner   B10.26.1926 Arlington Heights IL   BR/TR/6-0.5/180*   d8.3   Col Northwestern

1951	StL N	3	3	.500	20	1	0	3	52.1	49	30	2	1	31	22	3.78	105	.245	.349	14-0-2	.000	-2	67	-2		-0.4
1952	StL N	0	1	.000	11	0	0	0	12.2	20	17	0	0	7	5	9.24	40	.357	.429	0	—	0		-9		-0.6
1953	StL N	0	0	—	3	0	0	0	3	4	2	0	0	0	0	6.00	71	.308	.308	0	—	0	0	0		0.0
Total	3	3	4	.429	34	1	0	3	68	73	49	2	1	38	27	4.90	80	.271	.364	14-0-2	.000	-2	67	-11		-1.0

BOKINA, JOE   Joseph   B4.4.1910 Northampton MA   D10.25.1991 Chattanooga TN   BR/TR/6-0/184   d4.16

| 1936 | Was A | 0 | 2 | .000 | 5 | 1 | 0 | 0 | 8.1 | 15 | 8 | 0 | 0 | 6 | 3 | 8.64 | 55 | .395 | .477 | 1 | .000 | -0 | 18 | -3 | | -0.5 |

BOLAND, BERNIE   Bernard Anthony   B1.21.1892 Rochester NY   D9.12.1973 Detroit MI   BR/TR/5-8.5/168   d4.14

1915	Det A	13	7	.650	45	18	8-1	3	202.2	167	86	2	6	75	72	3.11	98	.230	.307	63-0-1	.175	-1*	124	1		0.0
1916	Det A	10	3	.769	46	9	5-1	3	130.1	111	69	1	4	73	59	3.94	73	.240	.349	32-0-2	.250	2*	173	-14		-1.4
1917	Det A	16	11	.593	43	28	13-3	6	238	192	89	0	6	95	89	2.68	99	.226	.308	72-0-5	.056	-5*	111	4		-0.2
1918	Det A	14	10	.583	29	25	14-4	0	204	176	69	1	6	67	63	2.65	101	.236	.304	69	.174	-0	103	4		0.3
1919	Det A	14	16	.467	35	30	18-1	1	242.2	222	93	7	3	80	71	3.04	105	.253	.318	74-0-3	.108	-3	76	8		0.6
1920	Det A	0	2	.000	4	3	1	0	17.1	23	18	0	2	14	4	7.79	48	.348	.476	1	.143	-0	114	-7		-0.7
1921	StL A	1	4	.200	7	6	1	0	27	34	36	2	1	28	6	9.33	48	.309	.453	1	.100	-1	109	-15		-2.1
Total	7	68	53	.562	209	119	59-10	13	1062	925	460	13	28	432	364	3.25	91	.241	.322	327-0-11	.138	-8	108	-20		-3.5

BOLDEN, BILL   William Horace "Big Bill"   B5.9.1893 Dandridge TN   D12.8.1966 Jefferson City TN   BR/TR/6-4/200   d6.27

| 1919 | StL N | 0 | 1 | .000 | 3 | 1 | 0 | 0 | 12 | 17 | 7 | 0 | 1 | 4 | 4 | 5.25 | 53 | .340 | .400 | 3 | .333 | 0 | 57 | -3 | | -0.2 |

BOLEN, STEW   Stewart O'Neal   B10.12.1902 Jackson AL   D8.30.1969 Mobile AL   BL/TL/5-11/180   d4.15

1926	StL A	0	0	—	5	0	0	0	14.2	21	10	2	0	6	7	6.14	70	.356	.415	4	.500	1		-2		-0.1
1927	StL A	0	1	.000	3	1	1	0	9.2	14	9	0	0	5	7	8.38	52	.368	.442	3	.333	0	96	-3		-0.2
1931	Phi N	3	12	.200	28	16	2	0	98.2	117	75	5	4	63	55	6.39	66	.297	.399	32	.156	-1	82	-18		-2.4
1932	Phi N	0	0	—	5	0	0	0	16	18	8	0	2	10	3	2.81	157	.281	.395	7	.143	-0		2		0.0
Total	4	3	13	.188	41	17	3	0	139	170	102	7	6	84	72	6.09	70	.306	.403	46	.196	-0	82	-21		-2.7

BOLIN, BOBBY   Bobby Donald   B1.29.1939 Hickory Grove SC   BR/TR/6-4/200(200-212)   d4.18

1961	SF N	2	2	.500	37	1	0	5	48	37	20	6	3	37-8	48	3.19	120	.210	.352	7	.286	0	186	3		0.3
1962	†SF N	7	3	.700	41	5	2	5	92	84	41	10	5	35-5	74	3.62	105	.243	.320	23	.261	2	162	2		0.4
1963	SF N	10	6	.625	47	12	2	7	137.1	128	73	13	7	57-4	134	3.28	98	.242	.322	35-1-4	.143	1*	110	-7		-0.9
1964	SF N	6	9	.400	38	23	5-3	3	174.2	143	71	16	10	77-3	146	3.25	110	.220	.332	50-0-4	.100	0*	102	6		0.5
1965	SF N	14	6	.700	45	13	2	2	163	125	51	17	4	56-4	135	2.76	130	.214	.285	54-1-1	.167	1	103	14		1.5
1966	SF N	11	10	.524	35	34	10-4	1	224.1	174	85	25	10	70-10	143	2.89	127	.211	.280	76-2-1	.171	3	82	19	15	2.0
1967	SF N	6	8	.429	37	15	0	0	120	120	71	16	3	40-9	69	4.88	67	.258	.331	33-0-2	.242	2	116	-20		-2.0
1968	SF N	10	5	.667	34	19	6-3	0	176.2	128	44	9	4	46-9	126	1.99	148	.200	.258	55-0-1	.091	-1	101	20		1.7
1969	SF N	7	7	.500	30	22	2	0-0	146.1	149	86	17	7	49-3	102	4.43	79	.260	.323	41-0-2	.154	3	126	-15		-1.0
1970	Mil A	5	11	.313	32	20	3	1-0	132	131	84	20	4	67-7	85	4.91	77	.256	.343	36-1-6	.194	-2	86	-18		-1.9
	Bos A	2	0	1.000	6	0	0	2-0	8	2	0	0	1	5-2	8	0.00	—	.080	.250	1	.250	-2		3		0.7

YEAR	TM LG	W	L	PCT	G	GS	CG-SHO	SV-BS	IP	H	R	HR	HB	BB-IB	SO	ERA	AERA	OAV	OOB	AB-HR-SH	AVG	PB	SUP	APR	DL	PW
	Year	7	11	.389	38	20	3	3-0	140	133	84	20	5	72-9	89	4.63	82	.248	.338	37-1-6	.189	2	86	-13		-1.2
1971	Bos A	5	3	.625	52	0	0	6-3	69.2	74	34	7	0	24-4	51	4.26	87	.273	.329	12	.250	0		-3		-0.4
1972	Bos A	0	1	.000	21	0	0	5-1	30.2	24	11	3	1	11-1	27	2.93	110	.209	.283	2	.000	-0		1		0.1
1973	Bos A	3	4	.429	39	0	0	15-5	53.1	45	16	5	1	13-2	31	2.70	149	.232	.282	0	—	-0		8		1.6
Total	13	88	75	.540	495	164	32-10	50-9	1576	1364	687	164	60	597-71	1175	3.40	103	.231	.306	423-6-21	.163	15	103	16	15	3.3

BOLLO, GREG Gregory Gene B11.16.1943 Detroit MI BR/TR/6-4/183* d5.9 Col Western Michigan

YEAR	TM LG	W	L	PCT	G	GS	CG-SHO	SV-BS	IP	H	R	HR	HB	BB-IB	SO	ERA	AERA	OAV	OOB	AB-HR-SH	AVG	PB	SUP	APR	DL	PW
1965	Chi A	0	0	—	15	0	0	0	22.2	12	11	5	2	9-1	16	3.57	89	.152	.256	0	—	0		-1		-0.1
1966	Chi A	0	1	.000	3	1	0	0	7	7	2	0	1	3-0	4	2.57	123	.269	.367	1	.000	-0	0	1		0.1
Total	2	0	1	.000	18	1	0	0	29.2	19	13	5	3	12-1	20	3.34	96	.181	.283	1	.000	-0	0	0		0.0

BOLTON, ROD Rodney Earl B9.23.1968 Chattanooga TN BR/TR/6-2/190* [ChiA90 13/348] d4.10 Col Kentucky

YEAR	TM LG	W	L	PCT	G	GS	CG-SHO	SV-BS	IP	H	R	HR	HB	BB-IB	SO	ERA	AERA	OAV	OOB	AB-HR-SH	AVG	PB	SUP	APR	DL	PW
1993	Chi A	2	6	.250	9	8	0	0-0	42.1	55	40	4	1	16-0	17	7.44	57	.314	.367	0	—	0	76	-16		-2.3
1995	Chi A	0	2	.000	8	3	0	0-0	22	33	23	4	0	14-1	10	8.18	55	.351	.431	0	—	0	118	-10		-0.7
Total	2	2	8	.200	17	11	0	0-0	64.1	88	63	8	1	30-1	27	7.69	56	.327	.390	0	—	0	88	-26		-3.0

BOLTON, TOM Thomas Edward B5.6.1962 Nashville TN BL/TL/6-3/175* [BosA80 20/518] d5.17

YEAR	TM LG	W	L	PCT	G	GS	CG-SHO	SV-BS	IP	H	R	HR	HB	BB-IB	SO	ERA	AERA	OAV	OOB	AB-HR-SH	AVG	PB	SUP	APR	DL	PW
1987	Bos A	1	0	1.000	29	0	0	0-0	61.2	83	33	5	2	27-2	49	4.38	104	.329	.394	0	—	0		1		0.1
1988	Bos A	1	3	.250	28	0	0	1-0	30.1	35	17	1	0	14-1	21	4.75	87	.285	.355	0	—	0		-2		-0.2
1989	Bos A	0	4	.000	4	4	0	0-0	17.1	21	18	1	0	10-1	9	8.31	50	.292	.373	0	—	0	33	-8		-1.3
1990	†Bos A	10	5	.667	21	16	3	0-0	119.2	111	46	6	3	47-3	65	3.38	121	.251	.323	0	—	0	97	11		1.3
1991	Bos A	8	9	.471	25	19	0	0-0	110	136	72	16	1	51-2	64	5.24	83	.308	.378	0	—	0	87	-11	22	-1.5
1992	Bos A	1	2	.333	21	1	0	0-0	29	34	11	0	2	14-1	23	3.41	125	.286	.370	0	—	0	21	3		0.3
	Cin N	3	3	.500	16	8	0	0-0	46.1	52	28	9	2	23-2	27	5.24	69	.284	.368	14-0-1	.000	-1	113	-8		-1.0
1993	Det A	6	6	.500	43	8	0	0-0	102.2	113	57	5	7	45-10	66	4.47	97	.282	.363	0	—	0	127	-1		-0.1
1994	Bal A	1	2	.333	22	0	0	0-0	23.1	29	15	3	0	13-1	12	5.40	94	.309	.389	0	—	0		-1		-0.1
Total	8	31	34	.477	209	56	3	1-0	540.1	614	297	46	17	244-23	336	4.56	93	.289	.364	14-0-1	.000	-1	92	-16	22	-2.5

BOMBACK, MARK Mark Vincent B4.14.1953 Portsmouth VA BR/TR/5-11/170* [BosA71 25/584] d9.12

YEAR	TM LG	W	L	PCT	G	GS	CG-SHO	SV-BS	IP	H	R	HR	HB	BB-IB	SO	ERA	AERA	OAV	OOB	AB-HR-SH	AVG	PB	SUP	APR	DL	PW
1978	Mil A	0	0	—	2	1	0	0-0	1.2	5	3	1	0	1-0	1	16.20	23	.500	.545	0	—	0	118	-2		-0.1
1980	NY N	10	8	.556	36	25	2-1	0-0	162.2	191	80	17	4	49-3	68	4.09	88	.297	.347	43-0-5	.233	3	84	-7		-0.3
1981	Tor A	5	5	.500	20	11	0	0-1	90.1	84	42	6	1	35-2	33	3.89	102	.251	.321	0	—	0*	84	2		0.2
1982	Tor A	1	5	.167	16	8	0	0-0	59.2	87	44	10	3	25-0	22	6.03	75	.343	.405	0	—	0	73	-9		-0.8
Total	16	18	.471	74	45	2-1	0-1	314.1	367	169	34	8	110-5	124	4.47	87	.295	.353	43-0-5	.233	3	82	-16		-1.0

BOND, TOMMY Thomas Henry B4.2.1856 Granard, Ireland D1.24.1941 Boston MA BR/TR/5-7.5/160 d5.5 M1/U2

YEAR	TM LG	W	L	PCT	G	GS	CG-SHO	SV-BS	IP	H	R	HR	HB	BB-IB	SO	ERA	AERA	OAV	OOB	AB-HR-SH	AVG	PB	SUP	APR	DL	PW
1874	Atl NA	22	32	.407	55	55	55-1	0	497	606	440	15		8	42	2.03	102	.266	.268	245	.220	-0	76	1		0.6
1875	Har NA	19	16	.543	40	39	37-6	0	352	302	152	3		7	70	1.41	167	.216	.219	289	.266	3*	81	33		3.1
1876	Har N	31	13	.705	45	45	45-6	0	408	355	164	2		13	88	1.68	141	.220	.227	182	.275	1	97	32		3.1
1877	Bos N	**40**	17	**.702**	58	58	58-**6**	0	521	530	248	6		36	**170**	**2.11**	115	.269	**.261**	259	.228	-4*	115	40		3.3
1878	Bos N	**40**	19	**.678**	**59**	**59**	**57**-9	0	532.2	571	222	5		33	**182**	2.06	115	.269	.280	236	.212	-4	91	14		0.9
1879	Bos N	.43	19	.694	64	64	59-**11**	0	555.1	543	206	8		24	155	**1.96**	126	.251	.259	257	.241	2*	136	**39**		**4.1**
1880	Bos N	26	29	.473	63	57	49-3	0	493	559	298	1		45	118	2.67	85	.274	.290	282	.220	-2*	106	-33		-2.9
1881	Bos N	0	3	.000	3	3	2	0	25.1	40	17	3		2	2	4.26	62	.360	.372	10	.200	-0	27	-3		-0.3
1882	Wor N	0	1	.000	2	2	0	0	12.1	12	13	0		7	2	4.38	71	.218	.306	30	.133	-1*	60	-2		-0.2
1884	Bos U	13	9	.591	23	21	19	0	189	185	120	3		14	128	3.00	79	.239	.263	162	.296	-1*	117	-13		-1.1
	Ind AA	0	5	.000	5	5	5	0	43	62	51	5	2	4	15	5.65	58	.310	.330	23	.130	-1*	48	-12		-1.2
Total	2 NA	41	48	.461	95	94	92-7	0	849	908	592	18		15	112	1.77	123	.247	.250	534	.245	2	77	34		3.7
Total	193	115	.627	322	314	294-35	0	2779.2	2857	1339	32	2	178	860	2.25	110	.255	.267	1441	.236	-9	109	62		5.7

BONDERMAN, JEREMY Jeremy Allen B10.28.1982 Kennewick WA BR/TR/6-2/210* [OakA01 1/26] d4.2

YEAR	TM LG	W	L	PCT	G	GS	CG-SHO	SV-BS	IP	H	R	HR	HB	BB-IB	SO	ERA	AERA	OAV	OOB	AB-HR-SH	AVG	PB	SUP	APR	DL	PW
2003	Det A	6	19	.240	33	28	0	0-0	162	193	118	23	4	58-2	108	5.56	79	.294	.352	2	.000	-0	76	-26		-3.3
2004	Det A	11	13	.458	33	32	2-2	0-0	184	168	101	24	10	73-5	168	4.89	92	.242	.321	7	.000	-1	112	-6		-0.7
2005	Det A	14	13	.519	29	29	4	0-0	189	199	101	21	4	57-0	145	4.57	93	.271	.326	6	.000	-1	114	-6		-0.8
Total	3	31	45	.408	95	89	6-2	0-0	535	560	320	68	18	188-7	421	4.98	88	.269	.332	15	.000	-1	101	-38		-4.8

BONES, RICKY Ricardo Ricky B4.7.1969 Salinas, PR BR/TR/6-0/193(175-219) d8.11

YEAR	TM LG	W	L	PCT	G	GS	CG-SHO	SV-BS	IP	H	R	HR	HB	BB-IB	SO	ERA	AERA	OAV	OOB	AB-HR-SH	AVG	PB	SUP	APR	DL	PW
1991	SD N	4	6	.400	11	11	0	0-0	54	57	33	3	0	18-0	31	4.83	79	.269	.321	13-0-4	.077	-0	139	-6		-1.1
1992	Mil A	9	10	.474	31	28	0	0-0	163.1	169	90	27	9	48-0	65	4.57	85	.264	.321	0	—	0	99	-13		-1.4
1993	Mil A	11	11	.500	32	31	3	0-0	203.2	222	122	28	8	63-3	63	4.86	89	.278	.334	0	—	0*	113	-13		-1.2
1994	Mil A☆	10	9	.526	24	24	4-1	0-0	170.2	166	76	17	3	45-1	57	3.43	148	.253	.304	0	—	0	85	28		2.6
1995	Mil A	10	12	.455	32	31	3	0-0	200.1	218	108	26	4	83-2	77	4.63	108	.281	.349	0	—	0	104	10		1.0
1996	Mil A	7	14	.333	32	23	0	0-0	145	170	104	28	9	62-2	59	5.83	89	.294	.369	0	—	0	101	-11		-1.3
	NY A	0	0	—	4	1	0	0-0	7	14	11	2	1	6-0	4	14.14	35	.438	.525	0	—	0	94	-7		-0.3
	Year	7	14	.333	36	24	0	0-0	152	184	115	30	10	68-2	63	6.22	83	.301	.378	0	—	0	101	-18		-1.6
1997	Cin N	1	0	1.000	9	2	0	0-0	17.2	31	22	2	2	11-2	8	10.19	42	.378	.454	2	.000	-0	140	-12		-0.6
	KC A	4	7	.364	21	11	1	0-1	78.1	102	59	10	5	25-2	36	5.97	79	.325	.377	0	—	0*	107	-11		-1.3
1998	KC A	2	2	.500	32	0	0	1-1	53.1	49	18	4	1	24-5	38	3.04	160	.244	.327	1	.000	-0		11		0.8
1999	Bal A	0	3	.000	30	2	0	0-3	43.2	59	29	7	2	19-0	26	5.98	79	.322	.390	0	—	0*	40	-5	15	-0.1
2000	Fla N	2	3	.400	56	0	0	0-3	77.1	94	43	6	3	27-8	59	4.54	97	.303	.358	2	.000	0		-2	14	-0.7
2001	Fla N	4	4	.500	54	0	0	0-0	64	71	39	7	3	33-9	41	5.06	82	.286	.374	2	.500	0		-7		-0.6
Total	11	63	82	.434	375	164	11-1	1-8	1278.1	1422	754	167	50	464-34	564	4.85	95	.283	.346	20-0-4	.100	-0	103	-38	29	-3.8

BONETTI, JULIO Julio Giacomo B7.14.1911 Genoa, Italy D6.17.1952 Belmont CA BR/TR/6-0/180 d4.22

YEAR	TM LG	W	L	PCT	G	GS	CG-SHO	SV-BS	IP	H	R	HR	HB	BB-IB	SO	ERA	AERA	OAV	OOB	AB-HR-SH	AVG	PB	SUP	APR	DL	PW
1937	StL A	4	11	.267	28	16	7	1	143.1	190	103	13	2	60	43	5.84	83	.321	.385	47-0-2	.149	-2	77	-15		-1.3
1938	StL A	2	3	.400	17	0	0	0	28.1	41	21	1	0	13	7	6.35	78	.350	.415	8	.000	-1		-4		-0.6
1940	Chi N	0	0	—	1	0	0	0	1.1	3	3	0	0	4	0	20.25	19	.429	.636	0	—	-0		-2		-0.1
Total	3	6	14	.300	46	16	7	1	173	234	127	14	2	77	50	6.03	80	.327	.394	55-0-2	.127	-3	77	-21		-2.0

BONEY, HANK Henry Tate "Haney" B10.28.1903 Wallace NC D6.12.2002 Lake Worth FL BL/TR/5-11/176 d6.28 Col Florida

YEAR	TM LG	W	L	PCT	G	GS	CG-SHO	SV-BS	IP	H	R	HR	HB	BB-IB	SO	ERA	AERA	OAV	OOB	AB-HR-SH	AVG	PB	SUP	APR	DL	PW
1927	NY N	0	0	—	3	0	0	0	4	1	0	0	2		2	2.25	171	.267	.353	0	—	0		1		0.0

BONG, JUNG Jung Keun B7.15.1980 Seoul, South Korea BL/TL/6-3/175(175-215) d4.23 [DL 2005 Cin N 183]

YEAR	TM LG	W	L	PCT	G	GS	CG-SHO	SV-BS	IP	H	R	HR	HB	BB-IB	SO	ERA	AERA	OAV	OOB	AB-HR-SH	AVG	PB	SUP	APR	DL	PW
2002	Atl N	0	1	.000	1	1	0	0-0	6	9	5	2	0	2-0	4	7.50	54	.320	.370	2	.000	-0*	46	-2		-0.3
2003	Atl N	6	2	.750	44	0	0	1-2	57	56	32	8	2	31-6	47	5.05	83	.267	.365	5-0-1	.000	-0		-4		-0.4
2004	Cin N	1	1	.500	3	3	0	0-0	15.1	17	13	3	0	10-0	11	4.70	92	.270	.370	4	.000	0	122	-3		-0.3
Total	3	7	4	.636	48	4	0	1-2	78.1	81	50	11	2	43-6	62	5.17	81	.272	.366	11-0-1	.000	-1	106	-9	183	-1.0

BONHAM, TINY Ernest Edward B8.16.1913 Ione CA D9.15.1949 Pittsburgh PA BR/TR/6-2/215 d8.5

YEAR	TM LG	W	L	PCT	G	GS	CG-SHO	SV-BS	IP	H	R	HR	HB	BB-IB	SO	ERA	AERA	OAV	OOB	AB-HR-SH	AVG	PB	SUP	APR	DL	PW
1940	NY A	9	3	.750	12	12	10-3	0	99.1	83	24	4	0	13	37	1.90	212	.224	.250	37	.189	0	76	25		2.8
1941	†NY A	9	6	.600	23	14	7-1	2	126.2	118	44	12	1	31	43	2.98	132	.246	.294	50-0-1	.160	-1	116	16		1.5
1942	†NY A☆	21	5	**.808**	28	27	22-6	0	226	199	65	11	1	24	71	2.27	152	.237	**.259**	74-0-10	.122	-2	112	31		3.0
1943	†NY A☆	15	8	.652	28	26	17-4	1	225.2	197	63	13	1	52	71	2.27	142	.236	.282	76-0-5	.197	0	102	26		2.5
1944	NY A	12	9	.571	26	25	17-1	0	213.2	228	84	14	0	41	54	2.99	116	.273	.307	75-0-5	.133	-3	98	11		0.6
1945	NY A	8	11	.421	23	23	12	0	180.2	186	72	11	1	22	42	3.29	105	.265	.288	63-0-3	.238	3	79	5		0.7
1946	NY A	5	8	.385	18	14	6-2	0	104.2	97	47	6	0	23	30	3.90	93	.243	.284	31-0-1	.129	-0	85	-2		-0.3
1947	Pit N	11	8	.579	33	18	7-3	0	149.2	167	67	17	2	35	63	3.85	110	.277	.319	45-0-6	.156	-0	116	9		0.8
1948	Pit N	6	10	.375	22	20	7	0	135.2	145	71	18	3	23	42	4.31	94	.276	.310	49-0-1	.163	-2	94	-3		-0.7
1949	Pit N	7	4	.636	18	14	5-1	0	89	81	43	11	0	23	25	4.25	99	.246	.295	22-0-5	.045	-1	90	1		-0.1
Total	10	103	72	.589	231	193	110-21	3	1551	1501	580	117	9	287	478	3.06	120	.254	.289	522-0-37	.161	-7	98	119		10.8

BONHAM, BILL William Gordon B10.1.1948 Glendale CA BR/TR/6-3/195(190-210) d4.7 Col UCLA [DL 1981 Cin N 104]

YEAR	TM LG	W	L	PCT	G	GS	CG-SHO	SV-BS	IP	H	R	HR	HB	BB-IB	SO	ERA	AERA	OAV	OOB	AB-HR-SH	AVG	PB	SUP	APR	DL	PW
1971	Chi N	2	1	.667	33	2	0	0-0	60	63	38	6	5	36-5	41	4.65	85	.281	.390	12	.167	-0	56	-6		-0.3
1972	Chi N	1	1	.500	19	4	0	4-1	57.2	56	22	4	1	25-2	49	3.12	122	.260	.340	14-0-3	.286	1	116	4		0.4
1973	Chi N	7	5	.583	44	15	3	6-0	152	126	55	10	4	64-7	121	3.02	131	.230	.313	43-0-6	.093	-3	88	15		-0.8
1974	Chi N	11	22	.333	44	36	10-2	1-0	242.2	246	133	15	6	109-8	191	3.86	99	.263	.342	84-0-5	.183	-0*	113	-19		-2.0
1975	Chi N	13	15	.464	38	36	7-2	0-0	229.1	254	133	16	5	109-6	165	4.71	83	.281	.359	82-0-8	.183	-0*	113	-19		-2.0

YEAR	TM LG	W	L	PCT	G	GS	CG-SHO	SV-BS	IP	H	R	HR	HB	BB-IB	SO	ERA	AERA	OAV	OOB	AB-HR-SH	AVG	PB	SUP	APR	DL	PW
1976	Chi N	9	13	.409	32	31	3	0-0	196	215	102	11	2	96-2	110	4.27	91	.283	.361	65-0-7	.200	1	101	-6		-0.5
1977	Chi N	10	13	.435	34	34	1	0-0	214.2	207	111	15	3	82-16	134	4.36	101	.254	.324	65-0-7	.231	1*	91	3		0.6
1978	Cin N	11	5	.688	23	23	1	0-0	140.1	151	59	9	1	50-8	83	3.53	101	.276	.336	43-0-8	.186	2	132	2		0.6
1979	Cin N	9	7	.563	29	29	2	0-0	175.2	173	80	14	8	60-3	78	3.79	98	.261	.329	57-0-6	.140	-1	114	0		-0.1
1980	Cin N	2	1	.667	4	4	0	0-0	19	21	10	1	0	5-0	13	4.74	74	.276	.321	6	.000	-0	108	-2	91	-0.4
Total	10	75	83	.475	300	214	27-4	11-2	1487.1	1512	743	98	35	636-57	985	4.01	97	.266	.342	471-0-54	.172	-2	100	-14	195	-1.1

BONIKOWSKI, JOE   Joseph Peter   B1.16.1941 Philadelphia PA   BR/TR/6-0/176   d4.12

YEAR	TM LG	W	L	PCT	G	GS	CG-SHO	SV-BS	IP	H	R	HR	HB	BB-IB	SO	ERA	AERA	OAV	OOB	AB-HR-SH	AVG	PB	SUP	APR	DL	PW
1962	Min A	5	7	.417	30	13	3	2	99.2	95	47	6	1	38-2	45	3.88	105	.255	.323	27-0-2	.148	-1	106	3		0.3

BONNESS, BILL   William John "Lefty"   B12.15.1923 Cleveland OH   D12.3.1977 Detroit MI   BR/TL/6-4/200   d9.26

YEAR	TM LG	W	L	PCT	G	GS	CG-SHO	SV-BS	IP	H	R	HR	HB	BB-IB	SO	ERA	AERA	OAV	OOB	AB-HR-SH	AVG	PB	SUP	APR	DL	PW
1944	Cle A	0	1	.000	2	1	0		7	11	6	0	2	5	1	7.71	43	.367	.486	3	.000	-0	51	-3		-0.4

BONO, GUS   Adlai Wendell   B8.29.1894 Doe Run MO   D12.3.1948 Dearborn MI   BR/TR/5-11/175   d9.13

YEAR	TM LG	W	L	PCT	G	GS	CG-SHO	SV-BS	IP	H	R	HR	HB	BB-IB	SO	ERA	AERA	OAV	OOB	AB-HR-SH	AVG	PB	SUP	APR	DL	PW
1920	Was A	0	2	.000	4	1	0	0	12.1	17	13	0	0	6	4	8.76	43	.315	.383	3	.000	-0	149	-6		-0.8

BOOKER, CHRIS   Christopher Scott   B12.9.1976 Monroeville AL   BR/TR/6-3/235   d9.5

YEAR	TM LG	W	L	PCT	G	GS	CG-SHO	SV-BS	IP	H	R	HR	HB	BB-IB	SO	ERA	AERA	OAV	OOB	AB-HR-SH	AVG	PB	SUP	APR	DL	PW
2005		0	0	—	3	0	0	0	2	6	8	2	0	4-0	2	31.50	13	.545	.667	0	—	0		-6		-0.3

BOOKER, GREG   Gregory Scott   B6.22.1960 Lynchburg VA   BR/TR/6-6/233(230-245)   [SDN81 10/239]   d9.11   C7   Col Elon

YEAR	TM LG	W	L	PCT	G	GS	CG-SHO	SV-BS	IP	H	R	HR	HB	BB-IB	SO	ERA	AERA	OAV	OOB	AB-HR-SH	AVG	PB	SUP	APR	DL	PW
1983	SD N	0	1	.000	6	1	0	0-0	11.2	18	10	2	0	9-0	5	7.71	45	.375	.474	1	.000	-0	76	-5		-0.4
1984	†SD N	1	1	.500	32	1	0	0-1	57.1	67	27	4	0	27-4	28	3.30	109	.295	.367	7	.286	1	74	0		0.1
1985	SD N	0	1	.000	17	0	0	0-0	22.1	20	17	3	1	17-2	7	6.85	52	.247	.376	1	.000	-0		-7		-0.4
1986	SD N	1	0	1.000	9	0	0	0-0	11	10	5	0	0	4-2	7	1.64	224	.233	.298	0	—	0		1		0.1
1987	SD N	1	1	.500	44	0	0	1-0	68.1	62	29	5	3	30-1	17	3.16	126	.246	.332	6	.000	-1		5	9	0.2
1988	SD N	2	2	.500	34	2	0	0-0	63.2	68	31	5	1	19-2	43	3.39	100	.278	.327	8	.250	1	144	-2		0.0
1989	SD N	0	1	.000	11	0	0	0-0	19	15	10	2	0	10-1	8	4.26	82	.224	.325	0	—	0		-1		-0.1
	Min A	0	0	—	6	0	0	0-0	8.2	11	4	1	0	2-0	3	4.15	100	.306	.342	0	—	0		0		0.0
1990	SF N	0	0	—	2	0	0	0-0	2	7	3	0	0	0-0	1	13.50	27	.538	.538	0	—	0		-2		-0.1
Total	8	5	7	.417	161	4	0	1-1	264	278	136	22	5	118-12	119	3.89	94	.275	.351	23	.174	1	104	-11	9	-0.6

BOOLES, RED   Seabron Jesse   B7.14.1880 Bernice LA   D3.16.1955 Monroe LA   BL/TR/5-10/150   d7.30

YEAR	TM LG	W	L	PCT	G	GS	CG-SHO	SV-BS	IP	H	R	HR	HB	BB-IB	SO	ERA	AERA	OAV	OOB	AB-HR-SH	AVG	PB	SUP	APR	DL	PW
1909	Cle A	0	1	.000	4	1	0	0	22.2	20	12	0	1	8	6	1.99	129	.235	.309	6	.167	0	55	0		0.0

BOONE, DANNY   Daniel Hugh   B1.14.1954 Long Beach CA   BL/TL/5-8/140(131-150)   [CalA76 S2/33]   d4.11   Col St.-Fullerton

YEAR	TM LG	W	L	PCT	G	GS	CG-SHO	SV-BS	IP	H	R	HR	HB	BB-IB	SO	ERA	AERA	OAV	OOB	AB-HR-SH	AVG	PB	SUP	APR	DL	PW
1981	SD N	1	0	1.000	37	0	0	2-0	63.1	63	23	2	1	21-7	43	2.84	114	.267	.327	4-0-1	.500	1		3		0.3
1982	SD N	1	0	1.000	10	0	0	1-2	16	21	10	2	0	3-0	8	5.63	61	.323	.353	5	.200	0		-3		-0.2
	Hou N	0	1	.000	10	0	0	1-1	12.2	7	6	1	0	4-1	4	3.55	94	.171	.239	1	.000	-0		-1		-0.1
	Year	1	1	.500	20	0	0	2-3	28.2	28	16	3	0	7-1	12	4.71	72	.264	.307	6	.167	0		-4		-0.3
1990	Bal A	0	0	—	4	1	0	0-0	9.2	12	5	1	1	3-0	2	2.79	137	.308	.372	0	—	0	72	1		0.1
Total	3	2	1	.667	61	1	0	3-3	101.2	103	42	6	2	31-8	57	3.36	99	.270	.326	10-0-1	.300	1	72	0		0.1

BOONE, GEORGE   George Morris   B3.1.1871 Louisville KY   D9.24.1910 Louisville KY   d4.23

YEAR	TM LG	W	L	PCT	G	GS	CG-SHO	SV-BS	IP	H	R	HR	HB	BB-IB	SO	ERA	AERA	OAV	OOB	AB-HR-SH	AVG	PB	SUP	APR	DL	PW
1891	Lou AA	0	0	—	4	1	0		15	15	15	0	0	9	4	7.80	47	.250	.348	6	.333	0	68	-5		-0.2

BOONE, DAN   James Albert   B1.19.1895 Samantha AL   D5.11.1968 Tuscaloosa AL   BR/TR/6-2/190   d9.10   b-Ike   Col Alabama

YEAR	TM LG	W	L	PCT	G	GS	CG-SHO	SV-BS	IP	H	R	HR	HB	BB-IB	SO	ERA	AERA	OAV	OOB	AB-HR-SH	AVG	PB	SUP	APR	DL	PW
1919	Phi A	0	1	.000	3	2	0	0	14.2	24	14	0	0	10	6	6.75	51	.375	.459	4	.000	-1	91	-5		-0.3
1921	Det A	0	0	—	1	0	0	1	2	1	1	0	0	2	0	0.00	—	.200	.429	1	.000	-0		1		0.0
1922	Cle A	4	6	.400	11	10	4-2	0	75.1	87	39	3	1	19	9	4.06	99	.298	.343	26-0-1	.192	-1	72	0		-0.1
1923	Cle A	4	6	.400	27	4	2	0	70.1	93	56	3	3	31	15	6.01	66	.322	.393	19	.211	0	78	-15		-1.6
Total	4	8	13	.381	42	16	6-2	1	162.1	205	110	6	4	62	25	5.10	77	.315	.378	50-0-1	.180	-1	75	-19		-2.0

BOOTCHECK, CHRIS   Christopher Brandon   B10.24.1978 Laporte IN   BR/TR/6-5/200*   [AnaA00 1/20]   d9.9   Col Auburn

YEAR	TM LG	W	L	PCT	G	GS	CG-SHO	SV-BS	IP	H	R	HR	HB	BB-IB	SO	ERA	AERA	OAV	OOB	AB-HR-SH	AVG	PB	SUP	APR	DL	PW
2003	Ana A	0	1	.000	4	1	0	0-0	10.1	16	13	5	0	6-0	7	9.58	46	.340	.415	0	—	0	21	-7		-0.5
2005	LA A	0	1	.000	5	2	0	1-0	18.2	19	7	1	0	4-1	8	3.38	128	.257	.291	0	—	0	120	2		0.1
Total	2	0	2	.000	9	3	0	1-0	29	35	20	6	0	10-1	15	5.59	78	.289	.341	0	—	0	86	-5		-0.4

BOOTH, AMOS   Amos Smith "Darling"   B9.14.1848 Lebanon OH   D7.1.1921 Miamisburg OH   BR/TR/5-9/159   d4.25 ▲

YEAR	TM LG	W	L	PCT	G	GS	CG-SHO	SV-BS	IP	H	R	HR	HB	BB-IB	SO	ERA	AERA	OAV	OOB	AB-HR-SH	AVG	PB	SUP	APR	DL	PW
1876	Cin N	0	1	.000	3	1	0	0	9.2	22	18	0	0	0	0	9.31	24	.431	.431	272	.261	0*	264	-7		-0.5
1877	Cin N	1	7	.125	8	6	6	0	86	114	75	1	0	13	18	3.56	74	.296	.319	157	.172	-1*	74	-11		-0.9
Total	2	1	8	.111	15	9	6	0	95.2	136	93	1	0	13	18	4.14	63	.312	.332	429	.228	-1	96	-18		-1.4

BOOZER, JOHN   John Morgan   B7.6.1938 Columbia SC   D1.24.1986 Lexington SC   BR/TR/6-3/205*   d7.22   Col Wofford

YEAR	TM LG	W	L	PCT	G	GS	CG-SHO	SV-BS	IP	H	R	HR	HB	BB-IB	SO	ERA	AERA	OAV	OOB	AB-HR-SH	AVG	PB	SUP	APR	DL	PW
1962	Phi N	0	0	—	9	0	0	0	20.1	22	13	3	0	10-1	15	5.75	67	.282	.364	1	.000	-0		-4		-0.2
1963	Phi N	3	4	.429	26	8	2	1	83	67	31	11	1	33-5	69	2.93	110	.227	.303	21	.143	-0	70	3		0.1
1964	Phi N	3	4	.429	22	3	0	2	60.1	64	37	6	2	18-2	51	5.07	68	.271	.327	13	.077	-1*	51	-10		-1.2
1966	Phi N	0	0	—	2	2	0	0	5.1	8	5	0	0	3-0	5	6.75	53	.348	.423	2	.000	-0	135	-2		-0.1
1967	Phi N	5	4	.556	28	7	1	1	74.2	86	39	6	1	24-5	48	4.10	83	.292	.347	19	.211	1	129	-5		-0.6
1968	Phi N	2	2	.500	38	0	0	5	68.2	76	32	3	2	15-3	49	3.67	86	.279	.320	9-0-2	.111	-0		-5		-0.4
1969	Phi N	1	2	.333	46	2	0	3	82	91	46	12	0	36-5	47	4.28	83	.283	.354	9-0-2	.333	1	50	-8		-0.3
Total	7	14	16	.467	171	22	3	15-3	394.1	414	203	42	6	139-21	282	4.09	82	.272	.334	74-0-4	.162	-0	91	-31		-2.7

BORBON, PEDRO   Pedro (Rodriguez)   B12.2.1946 Mao, D.R.   BR/TR/6-2/185(185-200)   d4.9   s-Pedro

YEAR	TM LG	W	L	PCT	G	GS	CG-SHO	SV-BS	IP	H	R	HR	HB	BB-IB	SO	ERA	AERA	OAV	OOB	AB-HR-SH	AVG	PB	SUP	APR	DL	PW
1969	Cal A	2	3	.400	22	0	0	0-0	41	55	31	5	4	11-2	20	6.15	57	.324	.376	3	.000	-0		-12	29	-1.4
1970	Cin N	0	2	.000	12	1	0	0-0	17.1	21	15	2	0	6-1	6	6.75	60	.309	.390	3	.000	-0	22	-5		-0.5
1971	Cin N	0	0	—	3	0	0	0-0	4.1	3	3	1	0	1-0	4	4.15	81	.200	.250	0	—	0		-1		0.0
1972	†Cin N	8	3	.727	62	2	0	11-1	122	115	45	7	5	32-11	48	3.17	102	.254	.304	21	.048	-1	68	2		0.1
1973	†Cin N	11	4	.733	80	0	0	14-5	121	137	33	4	1	35-15	60	2.16	160	.298	.345	15	.333	1		18		2.7
1974	Cin N	10	7	.588	73	0	0	14-6	139	133	54	11	4	32-16	53	3.24	108	.255	.300	26-0-1	.192	-0		5		0.7
1975	†Cin N	9	5	.643	67	0	0	5-1	125	145	47	6	3	21-6	29	2.95	121	.301	.333	24-0-3	.292	2		7		1.0
1976	†Cin N	4	3	.571	69	1	0	8-3	121	135	49	4	4	31-11	53	3.35	105	.292	.338	18-0-2	.222	0	252	2		0.2
1977	Cin N	10	5	.667	73	0	0	18-5	127	131	48	7	3	24-4	48	3.19	124	.268	.304	22-0-2	.182	-0		11		1.4
1978	Cin N	8	2	.800	58	0	0	4-1	99.1	102	56	6	3	27-8	35	4.98	71	.274	.324	11-0-1	.182	-0		-13		-1.4
1979	Cin N	2	2	.500	30	0	0	2-2	44.2	48	17	2	0	8-4	23	3.43	108	.277	.303	6	.333	1		2		0.3
	SF N	4	3	.571	30	0	0	3-1	46	56	28	7	0	13-3	26	4.89	71	.303	.347	3	.333	0		-8		-1.2
	Year	6	5	.545	60	0	0	5-3	90.2	104	45	9	0	21-7	49	4.17	86	.291	.326	9	.333	1		-5		-0.9
1980	StL N	1	0	1.000	10	0	0	1-0	19	17	10	3	0	10-2	4	3.79	94	.250	.329	4	.250	0		-1		0.0
Total	12	69	39	.639	593	4	0	80-25	1026.2	1098	436	63	28	251-83	409	3.52	101	.280	.325	156-0-9	.205	2	100	7	29	1.9

BORBON, PEDRO   Pedro Felix (Marte)   B11.15.1967 Mao, D.R.   BR/TL/6-1/205(205-230)   d10.2   f-Pedro   Col Ranger (TX) JC   [DL 1998 Atl N 181]

YEAR	TM LG	W	L	PCT	G	GS	CG-SHO	SV-BS	IP	H	R	HR	HB	BB-IB	SO	ERA	AERA	OAV	OOB	AB-HR-SH	AVG	PB	SUP	APR	DL	PW
1992	Atl N	0	1	.000	2	0	0	0-0	1.1	2	1	0	0	1-1	1	6.75	54	.333	.429	0	—	0		0		-0.1
1993	Atl N	0	0	—	3	0	0	0-0	1.2	3	4	0	0	3-0	2	21.60	19	.429	.600	0	—	0		-3		-0.2
1995	†Atl N	2	2	.500	41	0	0	2-2	32	29	12	2	1	17-4	33	3.09	140	.240	.336	1	.000	-0		4		0.5
1996	Atl N	3	0	1.000	43	0	0	1-0	36	26	12	1	1	7-0	31	2.75	162	.203	.250	1	1.000	0		7		0.6
	LA N	4	3	.571	70	0	0	1-1	50.2	39	23	5	1	29-1	33	4.09	107	.209	.314	2-0-1	.000	-0		3	56	0.3
2000	Tor A	1	1	.500	59	0	0	1-0	41.2	45	37	5	4	38-5	29	6.48	78	.280	.417	0	—	0		-8		-0.3
2001	Tor A	2	4	.333	71	0	0	0-5	53.1	48	24	8	4	12-3	45	3.71	124	.244	.298	0	—	0		5		0.5
2002	Tor A	1	2	.333	16	0	0	0-2	12.2	12	8	1	1	6-3	11	4.97	93	.231	.317	0	—	0		-1		-0.3
	Hou N	3	2	.600	56	0	0	1-2	37.2	41	24	7	2	19-5	39	5.50	79	.287	.367	3	.000	0		-4		-0.6
2003	StL N	0	1	.000	4	0	0	0-0	4	14	9	2	1	5-1	0	20.25	20	.560	.607	0	—	0		-7		-1.3
Total	9	16	16	.500	368	0	0	6-12	271	259	154	33	16	134-24	224	4.68	96	.252	.342	7-0-1	.143	0		-4	237	-0.7

BORCHERS, GEORGE   George Benard "Chief"   B4.18.1869 Sacramento CA   D10.24.1938 Sacramento CA   BB/TR/5-10/180   d5.18

YEAR	TM LG	W	L	PCT	G	GS	CG-SHO	SV-BS	IP	H	R	HR	HB	BB-IB	SO	ERA	AERA	OAV	OOB	AB-HR-SH	AVG	PB	SUP	APR	DL	PW
1888	Chi N	4	4	.500	10	10	7-1		67	67	45	2	6	29	26	3.49	87	.251	.338	33	.061	-2	124	-4		-0.5
1895	Lou N	0	1	.000	1	1	0		0.2	1	2	0	0	3	0	27.00	17	.333	.667	0	—	0	0	-1		-0.2
Total	2	4	5	.444	11	11	7-1		67.2	68	47	2	6	32	26	3.72	82	.252	.344	33	.061	-2	112	-5		-0.7

YEAR	TM LG	W	L	PCT	G	GS	CG-SHO	SV-BS	IP	H	R	HR	HB	BB-IB	SO	ERA	AERA	OAV	OOB	AB-HR-SH	AVG	PB	SUP	APR	DL	PW

BORDEN, JOE   Joseph Emley (aka Joseph Emley Josephs in 1875)   B5.9.1854 Jacobstown NJ   D10.14.1929 Yeadon PA   BR/TR/5-9/140   d7.24

| 1875 | Phi NA | 2 | 4 | .333 | 7 | 7 | 7-2 | 0 | 66 | 47 | 30 | 0 | | 7 | 9 | 1.50 | 152 | .181 | .203 | 28 | .107 | -3 | 80 | 5 | | 0.1 |
| 1876 | Bos N | 11 | 12 | .478 | 29 | 24 | 16-2 | 1 | 218.1 | 257 | 155 | 4 | | 51 | 34 | 2.89 | 78 | .276 | .313 | 121 | .207 | -3* | 105 | -11 | | -1.3 |

BORDI, RICH   Richard Albert   B4.18.1959 San Francisco CA   BR/TR/6-7/220*   [OakA80 3/56]   d7.16   Col Cal St.-Fresno

1980	Oak A	0	0	—	1	0	0	0-0	2	4	1	0	0	0-0	0	4.50	85	.400	.400	0	—	0	0			0.0
1981	Oak A	0	0	—	1	0	0	0-0	2	1	0	0	0	1-0	0	0.00	—	.143	.250	0	—	0	1			0.0
1982	Sea A	0	2	.000	7	2	0	0-0	13	18	12	4	1	1-0	10	8.31	52	.310	.333	0	—	0	74	-5		-0.7
1983	Chi N	0	2	.000	11	1	0	1-0	25.1	34	15	2	0	12-1	21	4.97	77	.321	.390	4	.000	-0	23	-3		-0.3
1984	Chi N	5	2	.714	31	7	0	4-0	83.1	78	37	11	0	20-4	41	3.46	113	.242	.284	19	.053	-1	136	3	15	0.1
1985	NY A	6	8	.429	51	3	0	2-0	98	95	41	5	1	29-4	64	3.21	126	.253	.306	0	—	0	112	8	15	1.1
1986	Bal A	6	4	.600	52	1	0	3-2	107	105	56	13	4	41-5	83	4.46	94	.254	.325	0	—	0	0	-2		-0.2
1987	NY A	3	1	.750	16	1	0	0-1	33	42	28	7	0	12-0	23	7.64	58	.309	.365	0	—	0	82	-11		-1.1
1988	Oak A	0	1	.000	2	2	0	0-0	7.2	6	4	0	0	5-0	5	4.70	81	.214	.324	0	—	0	132	-2		-0.1
Total	9	20	20	.500	173	17	0	10-3	371.1	383	196	42	6	121-14	247	4.34	94	.263	.320	23	.043	-2	104	-11	30	-1.3

BORDLEY, BILL   William Clarke   B1.9.1958 Los Angeles CA   BR/TL/6-3/200   d6.30   Col USC   [DL 1982 SF N 49]

| 1980 | SF N | 2 | 3 | .400 | 8 | 6 | 0 | 0-0 | 30.2 | 34 | 19 | 3 | 0 | 21-1 | 11 | 4.70 | 75 | .288 | .396 | 6-0-2 | .167 | 0 | 119 | -4 | | -0.6 |

BORIS, PAUL   Paul Stanley   B12.13.1955 Irvington NJ   BR/TR/6-2/200   d5.21   Col Rutgers

| 1982 | Min A | 1 | 2 | .333 | 23 | 0 | 0 | | 49.2 | 46 | 24 | 8 | 2 | 19-3 | 30 | 3.99 | 107 | .246 | .318 | 0 | — | 0 | 1 | | | 0.0 |

BORK, FRANK   Frank Bernard   B7.13.1940 Buffalo NY   BR/TL/6-2/175   d4.15

| 1964 | Pit N | 2 | 2 | .500 | 33 | 2 | 0 | 2 | 42 | 51 | 22 | 6 | 1 | 11-3 | 31 | 4.07 | 86 | .295 | .341 | 5-0-1 | .200 | 0 | 138 | -3 | | -0.2 |

BORKOWSKI, DAVE   David Richard   B2.7.1977 Detroit MI   BR/TR/6-1/200(200-220)   [DetA95 11/294]   d7.17

1999	Det A	2	6	.250	17	12	0	0-0	76.2	86	58	10	4	40-0	50	6.10	82	.283	.371	3	.000	0	99	-10		-0.9
2000	Det A	0	1	.000	2	1	0	0-0	5.1	11	13	2	0	7-1	1	21.94	22	.423	.529	0	—	0	76	-10		-1.1
2001	Det A	0	2	.000	15	0	0	0-0	29.2	30	21	5	3	15-3	30	6.37	69	.261	.356	0	—	0		-6	93	-0.3
2004	Bal A	3	4	.429	17	8	0	0-1	56	65	37	6	3	15-1	45	5.14	91	.289	.339	0	—	0	80	-4		-0.5
Total	4	5	13	.278	51	21	0	0-1	167.2	192	129	23	10	77-5	126	6.33	75	.287	.365	3	.000	-0	93	-30	93	-2.8

BORLAND, TOM   Thomas Bruce "Spike"   B2.14.1933 ElDorado KS   BL/TL/6-3/175*   d5.15   Col Oklahoma St.

1960	Bos A	0	4	.000	26	4	0	3	51	67	40	4	0	23-4	32	6.53	62	.322	.388	13	.000	-2	125	-13		-1.2
1961	Bos A	0	0	—	1	0	0	0	1	3	2	0	0	0-0	0	18.00	23	.500	.500	0	—	0		-1		-0.1
Total	2	0	4	.000	27	4	0	3	52	70	42	4	0	23-4	32	6.75	60	.327	.391	13	.000	-2	125	-14		-1.3

BORLAND, TOBY   Toby Shawn   B5.29.1969 Ruston LA   BR/TR/6-6/193(186-215)   [PhiN87 27/702]   d5.27

1994	Phi N	1	0	1.000	24	0	0	1-0	34.1	31	10	1	4	14-3	26	2.36	181	.248	.343	3	.000	-0	7			0.3
1995	Phi N	1	3	.250	50	0	0	6-3	74	81	37	3	5	37-7	59	3.77	112	.277	.366	5	.200	-0	2		24	0.1
1996	Phi N	7	3	.700	69	0	0	0-2	90.2	83	51	9	3	43-3	76	4.07	106	.239	.327	4	.000	-0	0			-0.1
1997	NY N	0	1	.000	13	0	0	1-1	13.1	11	9	1	1	14-0	7	6.08	66	.220	.400	0-0-1	—	0	-3			-0.2
	Bos A	0	0	—	3	0	0	0-0	3.1	6	5	1	2	7-0	1	13.50	34	.400	.625	0	—	0	-3			-0.1
1998	Phi N	0	0	—	6	0	0	0-0	9	8	5	1	0	5-0	9	5.00	86	.242	.342	0	—	0	-1			0.0
2001	Ana A	0	1	.000	2	0	0	0-1	3.1	8	5	1	0	1-0	0	10.80	43	.471	.500	0	—	0	-2			-0.4
2002	Fla N	1	0	1.000	15	0	0	0-0	13.2	14	8	3	3	5-0	11	5.27	75	.269	.355	0	—	0	-2			-0.1
2003	Fla N	0	0	—	7	0	0	0-0	9.2	3	3	0	0	8-1	4	1.86	220	.097	.275	0	—	0	2		137	0.2
2004	Fla N	1	1	.500	18	0	0	0-1	18.1	18	11	3	0	12-5	18	5.40	76	.254	.357	0	—	0	-2			-0.2
Total	9	11	9	.550	207	0	0	8-8	269.2	263	144	23	18	146-19	211	4.17	102	.254	.354	12-0-1	.083	-1	-2		161	-0.6

BOROWSKI, JOE   Joseph Thomas   B5.4.1971 Bayonne NJ   BR/TR/6-2/225*   [ChiA89 32/823]   d7.9

1995	Bal A	0	0	—	6	0	0	0-0	7.1	5	1	0	0	4-0	3	1.23	390	.192	.300	0	—	0	3			0.1
1996	Atl N	2	4	.333	22	0	0	0-0	26	33	15	4	1	13-4	15	4.85	92	.324	.405	2-0-1	.000	-0	-1			-0.1
1997	Atl N	2	2	.500	20	0	0	0-0	24	27	11	2	0	16-4	6	3.75	112	.287	.391	0	—	0	1			0.2
	NY A	0	0	—	1	0	0	0-0	2	2	2	0	0	4-1	2	9.00	49	.250	.500	0	—	0	-1			-0.2
1998	NY A	1	0	1.000	8	0	0	0-0	9.2	11	7	0	0	3-0	7	6.52	67	.289	.357	0	—	0	-2		15	-0.2
2001	Chi N	0	1	.000	1	1	0	0-0	1.2	6	6	1	0	3-0	1	32.40	13	.667	.750	0	—	0	88	-5		-0.7
2002	Chi N	4	4	.500	73	0	0	2-4	95.2	84	31	10	1	29-6	97	2.73	149	.238	.295	7	.286	0	15			1.2
2003	†Chi N	2	2	.500	68	0	0	33-4	68.1	53	23	5	1	19-1	66	2.63	165	.207	.264	0	—	0	12		121	1.7
2004	Chi N	2	4	.333	22	0	0	9-2	21.1	27	19	3	0	15-2	17	8.02	55	.303	.400	0	—	0	-8		47	-0.5
2005	Chi N	0	0	—	11	0	0	0-0	11	12	8	5	0	1-0	11	6.55	67	.261	.277	0	—	0	-2			0.3
	TB A	1	5	.167	32	0	0	0-4	35.1	26	15	3	0	11-1	16	3.82	114	.208	.272	0	—	0				0.4
Total	9	14	23	.378	264	1	0	44-14	302.1	286	138	33	3	119-19	241	3.90	110	.250	.321	9-0-1	.222	0	88	15	183	0.8

BOROWY, HANK   Henry Ludwig   B5.12.1916 Bloomfield NJ   D8.23.2004 Brick NJ   BR/TR/6-0/175*   d4.18   Col Fordham

1942	†NY A	15	4	.789	25	21	13-4	1	178.1	157	56	6	0	66	85	2.52	136	.233	.301	70-0-4	.157	-1	132	20		2.0
1943	†NY A	14	9	.609	29	27	14-3	0	217.1	195	75	11	2	72	113	2.82	114	.241	.305	74-0-8	.203	3	106	12		1.6
1944	NY A★	17	12	.586	35	30	19-3	2	252.2	224	93	15	0	88	107	2.64	132	.236	.301	90-0-7	.133	-3	97	21		2.1
1945	NY A*	10	5	.667	18	18	7-1	0	132.1	107	61	6	1	58	35	3.13	111	.221	.305	50-0-3	.220	1	134	2		0.3
	†Chi N	11	2	.846	15	14	11-1	1	122.1	105	33	2	0	47	47	2.13	171	.231	.303	41-0-7	.171	0	137	22		2.3
1946	Chi N	12	10	.545	32	28	8-1	0	201	220	96	9	1	61	95	3.76	88	.274	.326	72-0-7	.181	1*	123	-10		-0.9
1947	Chi N	8	12	.400	40	25	7-1	2	183	190	99	19	1	63	75	4.38	90	.267	.328	56	.125	-1*	90	-6		-0.7
1948	Chi N	5	10	.333	39	17	2-1	1	127	156	80	9	0	49	50	4.89	80	.308	.369	36	.222	2	75	-14		-1.2
1949	Phi N	12	12	.500	28	28	12-1	0	193.1	188	99	19	0	63	43	4.19	94	.259	.319	61-0-5	.213	3	101	-5		-0.3
1950	Phi N	0	0	—	3	0	0	0	6.1	5	4	0	0	4	3	5.68	71	.250	.375	0-0-1	—	0	-1			-0.1
	Pit N	1	3	.250	11	3	0	0	25.1	32	19	6	1	9	9	6.39	69	.311	.372	6-0-2	.167	-0	94	-5		-0.7
	Year	1	3	.250	14	3	0	0	31.2	37	23	6	1	13	12	6.25	69	.301	.372	6-0-3	.167	-0	95	-6		-0.8
	Det A	1	1	.500	13	2	1	0	32.2	23	15	3	0	16	16	3.31	142	.205	.305	7-0-2	.143	-0	106	4		0.2
1951	Det A	2	2	.500	26	1	0	0	45.1	58	39	3	1	27	16	6.95	60	.314	.404	8	.000	-1	85	-14		-1.1
Total	10	108	82	.568	314	214	94-16	7	1717	1660	769	108	7	623	690	3.50	104	.254	.320	571-0-46	.173	3	108	26		3.5

BOSIO, CHRIS   Christopher Louis   B4.3.1963 Carmichael CA   BR/TR/6-3/225(220-235)   [MilA82*S2/44]   d8.3   C1   Col Sacramento (CA) City

1986	Mil A	0	4	.000	10	4	0	0	34.2	41	27	9	0	13-0	29	7.01	62	.293	.353	0	—	0	78	-8		-0.8
1987	Mil A	11	8	.579	46	19	2-1	2-2	170	187	102	18	1	50-3	150	5.24	88	.276	.326	0	—	0	103	-9		-0.8
1988	Mil A	7	15	.318	38	22	9-1	6-0	182	190	80	13	2	38-6	84	3.36	119	.268	.303	0	—	0	69	11		1.4
1989	Mil A	15	10	.600	33	33	8-2	0-0	234.2	225	90	16	6	48-1	173	2.95	131	.249	.289	0	—	0	123	22		2.3
1990	Mil A	4	9	.308	20	20	4-1	0-0	132.2	131	67	6	3	38-1	76	4.00	97	.258	.311	0	—	0	89	-1	79	0.0
1991	Mil A	14	10	.583	32	32	5-1	0-0	204.2	187	80	15	8	58-0	117	3.25	123	.244	.302	0	—	0	114	18	15	1.9
1992	Mil A	16	6	.727	33	33	4-2	0-0	231.1	223	100	21	4	44-1	120	3.62	107	.254	.291	0	—	0	121	7		0.6
1993	Sea A	9	9	.500	29	24	3-1	1-1	164.1	138	75	14	6	59-3	119	3.45	130	.229	.303	0	—	0*	79	15	48	1.3
1994	Sea A	4	10	.286	19	19	4	0-0	125	137	72	15	2	40-3	67	4.32	114	.277	.330	0	—	0	81	6	33	0.7
1995	†Sea A	10	8	.556	31	31	0	0-0	170	211	98	18	5	69-3	85	4.92	97	.312	.375	0	—	0	110	-1		-0.1
1996	Sea A	4	4	.500	18	9	0	0-1	60.2	72	44	8	4	24-1	39	5.93	84	.299	.364	0	—	0	151	-7	80	-0.7
Total	11	94	93	.503	309	246	39-9	9-3	1710	1742	835	162	41	481-22	1059	3.96	107	.264	.315	0	—	0	104	53	255	6.0

BOSKIE, SHAWN   Shawn Kealoha   B3.28.1967 Hawthorne NV   BR/TR/6-3/200*   [ChiN86*1/10]   d5.20   Col Modesto (CA) JC

1990	Chi N	5	6	.455	15	15	1	0-0	97.2	99	42	8	4	31-3	49	3.69	111	.265	.322	36-0-2	.222	1	83	5	52	0.7
1991	Chi N	4	9	.308	28	20	0	0-0	129	150	78	14	5	52-4	62	5.23	75	.294	.361	41-1-3	.171	2*	94	-15		-1.2
1992	Chi N	5	11	.313	23	18	0	0-0	91.2	96	55	14	4	36-3	39	5.01	72	.284	.354	27-0-3	.185	1	76	-13	36	-1.8
1993	Chi N	5	3	.625	39	2	0	0-3	65.2	63	30	7	7	21-2	39	3.43	118	.258	.330	11	.273	1	134	3		0.4
1994	Chi N	0	0	—	2	0	0	0-0	3.2	3	1	0	0	1-0	1	0.00	—	.214	.214	0	—	0	37	2		0.1
	Phi N	4	6	.400	18	14	1	0-1	84.1	85	56	14	3	29-2	59	5.23	82	.258	.321	26-0-1	.115	1*	93	-9		-0.8
	Year	4	6	.400	20	14	1	0-1	88	88	57	14	3	30-2	61	5.01	85	.256	.317	26-0-1	.115	1	93	-9		-0.7
	Sea A	0	1	.000	2	1	0	0-0	2.2	4	2	1	0	1-1	0	6.75	73	.333	.385	0	—	0	37	0	12	-0.1
1995	Cal A	7	7	.500	20	20	1	0-0	111.2	127	73	16	7	25-0	51	5.64	84	.281	.324	0	—	0	109	-10	57	-0.6
1996	Cal A	12	11	.522	37	28	1	1-0	189.1	226	126	40	13	67-7	133	5.32	95	.294	.358	0	—	0*	97	-17	16	-2.2
1997	Bal A	6	6	.500	28	9	0	1-0	77	95	57	14	7	26-1	50	6.43	69	.304	.359	0	—	0				

YEAR	TM LG	W	L	PCT	G	GS	CG-SHO	SV-BS	IP	H	R	HR	HB	BB-IB	SO	ERA	AERA	OAV	OOB	AB-HR-SH	AVG	PB	SUP	APR	DL	PW
1998	Mon N	1	3	.250	5	5	0	0-0	17.2	34	21	5	2	4-1	10	9.17	46	.415	.449	4	.000	-0	136	-10		-1.7
Total	9	49	63	.438	217	132	4	1-4	870.1	982	540	133	44	292-24	494	5.14	85	.286	.346	145-1-9	.179	5	95	-70	173	-8.3

BOSMAN, DICK   Richard Allen B2.17.1944 Kenosha WI   BR/TR/6-3/208*   d6.1 C11

YEAR	TM LG	W	L	PCT	G	GS	CG-SHO	SV-BS	IP	H	R	HR	HB	BB-IB	SO	ERA	AERA	OAV	OOB	AB-HR-SH	AVG	PB	SUP	APR	DL	PW
1966	Was A	2	6	.250	13	7	0	0	39	60	36	4	0	12-4	20	7.62	45	.361	.402	12-0-2	.250	0	98	-17		-3.0
1967	Was A	3	1	.750	7	7	2-1	0	51.1	38	12	3	0	15-0	25	1.75	180	.204	.242	15-0-2	.200	0*	98	8		0.7
1968	Was A	2	9	.182	46	10	0	1	139	139	63	9	4	35-5	63	3.69	79	.262	.310	30-0-1	.200	1	80	-11		0.4
1969	Was A	14	5	.737	31	26	5-2	1-0	193	156	59	11	4	39-0	99	2.19	160	.220	.260	64-0-5	.094	-1*	119	27		2.6
1970	Was A	16	12	.571	36	34	7-3	0-0	230.2	212	81	16	2	71-8	134	3.00	120	.245	.302	80-0-6	.138	-2	84	18		1.9
1971	Was A	12	16	.429	35	35	7-1	0-0	236.2	245	110	29	5	71-9	113	3.73	91	.272	.327	75-0-5	.093	-1	102	-9		-1.2
1972	Tex A	8	10	.444	29	29	1-1	0-0	173.1	183	87	11	6	48-6	105	3.63	84	.273	.326	53-0-13	.094	-2	122	-14	21	-1.6
1973	Tex A	2	5	.286	7	7	1-1	0-0	40.1	42	24	6	1	17-1	14	4.24	89	.268	.341	0	—	0	68	-3		-0.5
	Cle A	1	8	.111	22	17	2	0-0	97	130	74	19	6	29-5	41	6.22	64	.320	.373	0	—	0	96	-23		-1.9
	Year	3	13	.188	29	24	3-1	0-0	137.1	172	98	25	7	46-6	55	5.64	69	.306	.364	0	—	0	88	-27		-2.4
1974	Cle A	7	5	.583	25	18	2-1	0-0	127.1	126	69	13	1	29-3	56	4.10	89	.255	.297	0	—	0	112	-8		-0.8
1975	Cle A	0	2	.000	6	3	0	0-0	28.2	33	17	3	3	8-1	11	4.08	93	.292	.349	0	—	0	54	-2		-0.1
†Oak A	11	4	.733	22	21	2	0-0	122.2	112	50	12	3	24-3	42	3.52	104	.240	.280	0	—	0	115	4		0.4
	Year	11	6	.647	28	24	2	0-0	151.1	145	67	15	6	32-4	53	3.63	101	.250	.294	0	—	0	107	2		0.3
1976	Oak A	4	2	.667	27	15	0	0-0	112	118	54	13	1	19-1	34	4.10	82	.274	.305	0	—	0	136	-8		-0.4
Total	11	82	85	.491	306	229	29-10	2-0	1591	1594	736	149	34	412-48	757	3.67	94	.261	.310	329-0-34	.125	-5	105	-38	21	-4.7

BOSSER, MEL   Melvin Edward B2.8.1914 Johnstown PA D3.26.1986 Crossville TN   BR/TR/6-0/173   d4.29

YEAR	TM LG	W	L	PCT	G	GS	CG-SHO	SV-BS	IP	H	R	HR	HB	BB-IB	SO	ERA	AERA	OAV	OOB	AB-HR-SH	AVG	PB	SUP	APR	DL	PW
1945	Cin N	2	0	1.000	7	1	0	0	16	9	6	0	0	17	3	3.38	111	.158	.351	4	.000	-1	68	1		0.0

BOSWELL, ANDY   Andrew Cottrell B9.5.1874 New Greta NJ D2.3.1936 Ocean City NJ   TR/6-1/165   d5.10 Col Penn

YEAR	TM LG	W	L	PCT	G	GS	CG-SHO	SV-BS	IP	H	R	HR	HB	BB-IB	SO	ERA	AERA	OAV	OOB	AB-HR-SH	AVG	PB	SUP	APR	DL	PW
1895	NY N	2	2	.500	5	4	3	0	34	41	35	1	3	22	18	5.82	80	.293	.400	16	.188	-1	115	-6		-0.6
	Was N	1	2	.333	6	3	3	0	30	44	32	1	2	19	12	6.00	80	.336	.428	14	.286	0*	114	-4		-0.3
	Year	3	4	.429	11	7	6	0	64	85	67	2	5	41	30	5.91	80	.314	.413	30	.233	-1	114	-11		-0.9

BOSWELL, DAVE   David Wilson B1.20.1945 Baltimore MD   BR/TR/6-3/185(180-195)   d9.18

YEAR	TM LG	W	L	PCT	G	GS	CG-SHO	SV-BS	IP	H	R	HR	HB	BB-IB	SO	ERA	AERA	OAV	OOB	AB-HR-SH	AVG	PB	SUP	APR	DL	PW
1964	Min A	2	0	1.000	4	4	0	0	23.1	21	11	4	0	12-1	25	4.24	84	.236	.327	9-0-1	.222	0	118	-1		0.0
1965	†Min A	6	5	.545	27	12	1	0	106	77	43	20	5	46-0	85	3.40	105	.204	.298	38	.316	4*	117	4	30	0.7
1966	Min A	12	5	.706	28	21	8-1	0	169.1	120	66	19	5	65-2	173	3.14	115	.197	.279	63-0-2	.143	-1*	117	9		0.8
1967	Min A	14	12	.538	37	32	11-3	0	222.2	162	84	14	7	107-5	204	3.27	106	.202	.301	73-1-3	.219	4*	100	8		1.3
1968	Min A	10	13	.435	34	28	7-2	0	190	148	79	19	7	87-2	143	3.32	93	.213	.305	60-1-5	.233	5*	98	-3		0.5
1969	†Min A	20	12	.625	39	38	10	0-0	256.1	215	105	18	8	99-2	190	3.23	113	.226	.303	94-2-6	.170	3*	116	12		1.5
1970	Min A	3	7	.300	18	15	0	0-0	68.2	80	55	12	2	44-3	45	6.42	58	.292	.390	25	.160	-0*	128	-20	29	-2.6
1971	Det A	0	0	—	3	0	0	0-0	4.1	3	3	0	0	6-0	3	6.23	58	.200	.409	0	—	0		-1		-0.4
	Bal A	1	2	.333	15	1	0	0-0	24.2	32	16	4	0	15-1	14	4.38	78	.305	.388	5	.200	0	53	-4		-0.4
	Year	1	2	.333	18	1	0	0-0	29	35	19	4	0	21-1	17	4.66	74	.292	.392	5	.200	0	52	-5		-0.4
Total	8	68	56	.548	205	151	37-6	0-0	1065.1	858	462	110	34	481-16	882	3.52	99	.219	.309	367-4-17	.202	13	111	4	59	1.3

BOTELHO, DEREK   Derek Wayne B8.2.1956 Long Beach CA   BR/TR/6-2/180*   [PhiN76*2/42] d7.18 Col Miami-Dade Kendall (FL) CC

YEAR	TM LG	W	L	PCT	G	GS	CG-SHO	SV-BS	IP	H	R	HR	HB	BB-IB	SO	ERA	AERA	OAV	OOB	AB-HR-SH	AVG	PB	SUP	APR	DL	PW
1982	KC A	2	1	.667	8	4	0	0-0	24	25	11	4	0	8-0	12	4.13	99	.275	.330	0	—	0	145	0		0.0
1985	Chi N	1	3	.250	11	7	1	0-0	44	52	27	8	2	23-1	23	5.32	75	.299	.387	14	.143	-0	117	-5		-0.5
Total	2	3	4	.429	19	11	1	0-0	68	77	38	12	2	31-1	35	4.90	83	.291	.368	14	.143	-0	127	-5		-0.5

BOTTALICO, RICKY   Ricky Paul B8.26.1969 New Britain CT   BL/TR/6-2/217(200-217)   d7.29 Col Central Connecticut

YEAR	TM LG	W	L	PCT	G	GS	CG-SHO	SV-BS	IP	H	R	HR	HB	BB-IB	SO	ERA	AERA	OAV	OOB	AB-HR-SH	AVG	PB	SUP	APR	DL	PW
1994	Phi N	0	0	—	3	0	0	0-0	3	3	0	0	0	1-0	2	0.00	—	.250	.308	0	—	0		1		0.1
1995	Phi N	5	3	.625	62	0	0	1-4	87.2	50	25	4	4	42-3	87	2.46	171	.167	.277	5-0-1	.000	-1	17			1.4
1996	Phi N★	4	5	.444	61	0	0	34-4	67.2	47	24	6	2	23-2	74	3.19	135	.197	.272	3	.333	1	9			1.9
1997	Phi N	2	5	.286	69	0	0	34-7	74	68	31	7	2	42-4	89	3.65	116	.245	.347	1	.000	0	5			0.9
1998	Phi N	1	5	.167	39	0	0	6-1	43.1	54	31	7	1	25-5	27	6.44	67	.305	.390	0	—	0	-9	68		-1.3
1999	StL N	3	7	.300	68	0	0	20-8	73.1	83	45	8	3	49-1	66	4.91	94	.284	.392	3	.000	-0	-3			-0.5
2000	KC A	9	6	.600	62	0	0	16-7	72.2	65	40	12	2	41-3	56	4.83	108	.239	.342	0	—	0	4			0.7
2001	Phi N	3	4	.429	66	0	0	3-4	67	58	31	11	4	25-2	57	3.90	106	.241	.318	3	.333	1	2	21		0.4
2002	Phi N	0	3	.000	30	0	0	0-1	27.1	33	16	3	2	13-2	24	4.61	83	.300	.381	0	—	0	-3	99		-0.3
2003	Ari N	1	0	1.000	2	0	0	0-0	1.2	3	1	0	0	2-1	1	5.40	86	.375	.500	0	—	0	0			0.0
2004	NY N	3	2	.600	60	0	0	0-4	69.1	54	30	3	4	34-7	61	3.38	127	.215	.314	2	.000	-0	7			0.4
2005	Mil N	2	2	.500	40	0	0	2-4	41.2	43	24	7	3	19-0	29	4.54	94	.265	.349	0	—	0	-2			-0.2
Total	12	33	42	.440	562	0	0	116-44	628.2	561	298	71	27	316-30	575	3.99	110	.240	.335	17-0-1	.118	-0	28	188		3.3

BOTTENFIELD, KENT   Kent Dennis B11.14.1968 Portland OR   BR/TR/6-3/245(225-245)   [MonN86 4/96] d7.6

YEAR	TM LG	W	L	PCT	G	GS	CG-SHO	SV-BS	IP	H	R	HR	HB	BB-IB	SO	ERA	AERA	OAV	OOB	AB-HR-SH	AVG	PB	SUP	APR	DL	PW
1992	Mon N	1	2	.333	10	4	0	1-0	32.1	26	9	1	1	11-1	14	2.23	157	.217	.284	8-0-1	.375	1	58	4		0.5
1993	Mon N	2	5	.286	23	11	0	0-0	83	93	49	11	5	33-2	33	4.12	101	.288	.362	24-0-1	.167	-0	76	-1		-0.1
	Col N	3	5	.375	14	14	1	0-0	76.2	86	53	13	1	38-1	30	6.10	78	.302	.382	26-0-2	.269	1	89	-8		-0.5
	Year	5	10	.333	37	25	1	0-0	159.2	179	102	24	6	71-3	63	5.07	88	.294	.372	50-0-3	.220	1	85	-10		-0.6
1994	Col N	3	1	.750	15	1	0	1-0	24.2	28	16	1	2	10-0	15	5.84	85	.283	.360	1	.000	-0	55	-1	36	-0.3
	SF N	0	0	—	1	0	0	0-0	1.2	5	2	1	0	0-0	0	10.80	38	.556	.556	0	—	0		-1		-0.1
	Year	3	1	.750	16	1	0	1-0	26.1	33	18	2	2	10-0	15	6.15	80	.306	.375	1	.000	-0	56	-3		-0.4
1996	Chi N	3	5	.375	48	0	0	1-2	61.2	59	25	3	4	19-4	33	2.63	166	.255	.320	2-0-1	.500	0	9			1.2
1997	Chi N	2	3	.400	64	0	0	2-2	84	82	39	13	2	35-7	74	3.86	112	.259	.333	4-0-4	.000	-0	4			0.1
1998	StL N	4	6	.400	44	17	0	4-1	133.2	128	72	13	4	57-3	98	4.44	95	.254	.333	34-0-5	.088	-2	122	-3		-0.4
1999	StL N★	18	7	.720	31	31	0	0-0	190.1	197	91	21	5	89-5	124	3.97	116	.270	.350	61-0-8	.148	-1	105	14		1.6
2000	Ana N	7	8	.467	21	21	0	0-0	127.2	144	82	25	3	56-4	75	5.71	90	.285	.357	3	.667	1	99	-5	15	-0.4
	Phi N	1	2	.333	8	8	0	1-1	44	41	24	5	0	21-0	31	4.50	102	.240	.320	14-0-3	.000	-2	75	0		-0.1
2001	Hou N	2	5	.286	13	9	0	1-0	52	61	44	16	2	16-0	39	6.40	72	.288	.338	14-0-1	.143	0	83	-12	120	-1.4
Total	9	46	49	.484	292	116	2-1	10-5	911.2	950	506	123	28	385-27	566	4.54	100	.271	.345	191-0-26	.162	-3	97	0	171	0.1

BOTTING, RALPH   Ralph Wayne B5.12.1955 Houlton ME   BL/TL/6-0/195*   [AnaA74 7/154] d6.28

YEAR	TM LG	W	L	PCT	G	GS	CG-SHO	SV-BS	IP	H	R	HR	HB	BB-IB	SO	ERA	AERA	OAV	OOB	AB-HR-SH	AVG	PB	SUP	APR	DL	PW
1979	Cal A	2	0	1.000	12	1	0	0-0	29.2	46	30	6	1	15-1	22	8.80	46	.362	.428	0	—	0	111	-15		-0.9
1980	Cal A	0	3	.000	6	6	0	0-0	26.1	40	20	1	0	13-0	12	5.81	68	.348	.411	0	—	0	98	-6		-0.6
Total	2	2	3	.400	18	7	0	0-0	56	86	50	7	1	28-1	34	7.39	54	.355	.420	0	—	0	99	-21		-1.5

BOTZ, BOB   Robert Allen B4.28.1935 Milwaukee WI   BR/TR/5-11/170   d5.8

YEAR	TM LG	W	L	PCT	G	GS	CG-SHO	SV-BS	IP	H	R	HR	HB	BB-IB	SO	ERA	AERA	OAV	OOB	AB-HR-SH	AVG	PB	SUP	APR	DL	PW
1962	LA A	2	1	.667	35	0	0	2	63	71	30	7	2	11-0	24	3.43	113	.285	.319	9-0-1	.000	-1		2		-0.1

BOUCHER, DENIS   Denis B3.7.1968 Montreal QC, Can.   BR/TL/6-1/195*   d4.12

YEAR	TM LG	W	L	PCT	G	GS	CG-SHO	SV-BS	IP	H	R	HR	HB	BB-IB	SO	ERA	AERA	OAV	OOB	AB-HR-SH	AVG	PB	SUP	APR	DL	PW
1991	Tor A	0	3	.000	7	7	0	0-0	35.1	39	20	6	2	16-1	16	4.58	92	.279	.358	0	—	0	93	-2		-0.1
	Cle A	1	4	.200	5	5	0	0-0	22.2	35	21	6	0	8-0	13	8.34	50	.350	.398	0	—	0	53	-9		-1.5
	Year	1	7	.125	12	12	0	0-0	58	74	41	12	2	24-1	29	6.05	69	.308	.375	0	—	0	76	-10		-1.6
1992	Cle A	2	2	.500	8	7	0	0-0	41	48	29	9	1	20-0	17	6.37	62	.302	.377	0	—	0	129	-10		-0.8
1993	Mon N	3	1	.750	5	5	0	0-0	28.1	24	7	1	0	3-1	14	1.91	219	.229	.243	6-0-2	.167	1	82	7		1.0
1994	Mon N	0	1	.000	10	2	0	0-1	18.2	24	16	6	0	7-0	17	6.75	63	.324	.378	3-0-1	.333	1	54	-5		-0.2
Total	4	6	11	.353	35	26	0	0-1	146	170	93	28	3	54-2	77	5.42	76	.294	.353	9-0-3	.222	1	89	-19		-1.6

BOULDIN, CARL   Carl Edward B9.17.1939 Germantown KY   BB/TR/6-2/178*   d9.2 Col Cincinnati

YEAR	TM LG	W	L	PCT	G	GS	CG-SHO	SV-BS	IP	H	R	HR	HB	BB-IB	SO	ERA	AERA	OAV	OOB	AB-HR-SH	AVG	PB	SUP	APR	DL	PW
1961	Was A	0	1	.000	2	1	0	0	3.1	9	6	0	0	2-0	2	16.20	25	.500	.550	1	.000	-0	66	-4		-0.7
1962	Was A	1	2	.333	6	3	1	0	20	26	13	0	1	9-0	12	5.85	69	.321	.387	7	.000	-1*	81	-3		-0.5
1963	Was A	2	2	.500	10	3	0	0	23.1	31	18	3	0	8-1	10	5.79	64	.307	.355	7	.000	-1	88	-6		-0.9
1964	Was A	0	3	.000	9	3	0	0	25	30	20	2	2	11-2	12	5.40	69	.294	.368	6	.000	-0*	64	-6		-0.7
Total	4	3	8	.273	27	10	1	0	71.2	96	57	5	3	30-3	36	6.15	62	.318	.379	21	.000	-2	77	-19		-2.8

BOULTES, JAKE   Jacob John B8.6.1884 St.Louis MO D12.24.1955 St.Louis MO   BR/TR/6-3/?   d4.18

YEAR	TM LG	W	L	PCT	G	GS	CG-SHO	SV-BS	IP	H	R	HR	HB	BB-IB	SO	ERA	AERA	OAV	OOB	AB-HR-SH	AVG	PB	SUP	APR	DL	PW
1907	Bos N	5	9	.357	24	12	11	0	139.2	140	75	1	8	50	49	2.71	94	.266	.338	68	.132	-2*	86	-10		-0.9
1908	Bos N	3	5	.375	17	5	1	0	74.2	80	40	7	4	28	28	3.01	80	.274	.296	21-0-4	.143	-0*	134	-7		-0.8

YEAR	TM LG	W	L	PCT	G	GS	CG-SHO	SV-BS	IP	H	R	HR	HB	BB-IB	SO	ERA	AERA	OAV	OOB	AB-HR-SH	AVG	PB	SUP	APR	DL	PW
1909	Bos N	0	0	—	1	0	0	0	8	9	7	2	1	0	1	6.75	42	.290	.313	3	.333	0		-3		-0.1
Total	3	8	14	.364	42	17	12	0	222.1	229	122	10	10	58	78	2.96	85	.269	.324	92-0-4	.141	-2	100	-20		-1.8

BOURGEOIS, STEVE Steven James B8.4.1972 Lutcher LA BR/TR/6-1/220 [SFN93 21/582] d4.3 Col Louisiana-Monroe
| 1996 | SF N | 1 | 3 | .250 | 15 | 5 | 0 | 0-0 | 40 | 60 | 35 | 4 | 4 | 21-4 | 17 | 6.30 | 66 | .355 | .434 | 11-0-1 | .273 | 2 | 104 | -11 | | -0.7 |

BOUTON, JIM James Alan B3.8.1939 Newark NJ BR/TR/6-0/185(174-185) d4.22 Col Western Michigan
1962	NY A	7	7	.500	36	16	3-1	0	133	124	63	9	0	59-1	71	3.99	94	.254	.330	32-0-4	.063	-2*	122	-2		-0.4
1963	†NY A★	21	7	.750	40	30	12-6	1	249.1	191	79	18	3	87-2	148	2.53	139	.212	.282	83-0-11	.072	-6	111	27		2.3
1964	†NY A	18	13	.581	38	37	11-4	0	271.1	227	100	32	6	60-4	125	3.02	120	.225	.272	100-0-7	.130	-3	110	18		1.4
1965	NY A	4	15	.211	30	25	0	0	151.1	158	89	23	5	60-1	71	4.82	71	.269	.339	43-0-2	.093	-0*	97	-23		-2.7
1966	NY A	3	8	.273	24	19	3	1	120.1	117	49	13	1	38-5	65	2.69	123	.257	.313	38-0-3	.105	-2	91	5		0.3
1967	NY A	1	0	1.000	17	1	0	0	44.1	47	31	5	1	18-5	31	4.67	67	.275	.344	7-0-1	.000	-0	195	-10		-0.6
1968	NY A	1	1	.500	12	3	1	0	44	49	20	5	2	9-0	24	3.68	79	.287	.326	7	.000	-0	90	-3		-0.2
1969	Sea A	2	1	.667	57	1	0	1-0	92	77	48	12	2	38-4	68	3.91	93	.219	.298	9	.000	-1	170	-4		-0.3
	Hou N	0	2	.000	16	1	1	1-0	30.2	32	16	1	2	12-1	32	4.11	87	.267	.343	4	.000	-0	50	-2		-0.2
1970	Hou N	4	6	.400	29	6	1	0-0	73.1	84	53	5	1	33-3	49	5.40	72	.285	.357	17-0-1	.353	-2	154	-15		-1.5
1978	Atl N	1	3	.250	5	5	0	0	29	25	18	4	0	21-1	10	4.97	81	.234	.357	7	.000	-1	67	-3		-0.4
Total	10	62	63	.496	304	144	34-11	6-0	1238.2	1131	566	127	23	435-27	720	3.57	99	.243	.309	347-0-29	.101	-13	108	-12		-2.3

BOVEE, MIKE Michael Craig B8.21.1973 San Diego CA BR/TR/5-10/200 [KCA91 6/158] d9.13
| 1997 | Ana A | 0 | 0 | — | 3 | 0 | 0 | 0-0 | 3.1 | 3 | 2 | 1 | 0 | 1-0 | 5 | 5.40 | 85 | .231 | .286 | 0 | — | 0 | 0 | 0 | | 0* |

BOWEN, RYAN Ryan Eugene B2.10.1968 Hanford CA BR/TR/6-0/185* [HouN86 1/13] d7.22
1991	Hou N	6	4	.600	14	13	0	0-0	71.2	73	43	4	3	36-1	49	5.15	69	.268	.353	22-0-1	.182	1*	114	-12		-1.4
1992	Hou N	0	7	.000	11	9	0	0-0	33.2	48	43	8	2	30-3	22	10.96	31	.333	.455	9	.111	-0*	80	-28		-4.5
1993	Fla N	8	12	.400	27	27	2-1	0-0	156.2	156	83	11	3	87-7	98	4.42	99	.263	.358	51-0-3	.118	-1	86	-1		-0.2
1994	Fla N	1	5	.167	8	8	1	0-0	47.1	50	28	9	2	19-0	32	4.94	90	.273	.345	14-0-1	.357	-2	77	-2	89	0.0
1995	Fla N	2	0	1.000	4	3	0	0-0	16.2	23	11	3	0	12-2	15	3.78	114	.329	.417	6	.333	0	119	-1	131	0.0
Total	5	17	28	.378	64	60	3-1	0-0	326	350	208	35	10	184-13	216	5.30	77	.277	.370	102-0-5	.176	2	90	-44	220	-6.1

BOWEN, CY Sutherland McCoy B2.17.1871 Kingston IN D1.25.1925 Greensburg IN BR/TR/6-0/175 d4.28
| 1896 | NY N | 0 | 1 | .000 | 2 | 1 | 1 | 0 | 12 | 12 | 13 | 0 | 3 | 9 | 3 | 6.00 | 70 | .261 | .414 | 3-0-2 | .333 | 0 | 51 | -3 | | -0.1 |

BOWERS, SHANE Shane Patrick B7.27.1971 Glendora CA BR/TR/6-4/215 [MinA93 21/597] d7.26 Col Loyola Marymount
| 1997 | Min A | 0 | 3 | .000 | 5 | 5 | 0 | 0-0 | 19 | 27 | 20 | 2 | 1 | 8-0 | 7 | 8.05 | 58 | .329 | .391 | 0 | — | 0 | 67 | -8 | | -1.0* |

BOWERS, STEW Stewart Cole "Doc" B2.26.1915 New Freedom PA D12.4.2005 Havertown PA BB/TR/6-0/170 d8.5 Col Gettysburg
1935	Bos A	2	1	.667	10	2	1	0	23.2	26	14	1	0	17	5	3.42	139	.283	.394	5	.200	0*	46	2		0.2
1936	Bos A	0	0	—	5	0	0	0	5.2	10	7	1	0	2	0	9.53	56	.370	.414	0	—	0*		-3		-0.1
Total	2	2	1	.667	15	2	1	0	29.1	36	21	2	0	19	5	4.60	106	.303	.399	5	.200	0	46	-1		0.1

BOWIE, MICAH Micah Andrew B11.10.1974 Humble TX BL/TL/6-4/185(185-210) [AtlN93 8/236] d7.24
1999	Atl N	0	1	.000	3	0	0	0-0	4	8	6	1	0	4-0	2	13.50	33	.421	.522	0	—	0		-4		-0.6
	Chi N	2	6	.250	11	11	0	0-0	47	73	54	8	2	30-2	39	9.96	46	.358	.439	14	.214	0	101	-27		-3.3
	Year	2	7	.222	14	11	0	0-0	51	81	60	9	2	34-2	41	10.24	45	.363	.447	14	.214	0	101	-31		-3.9
2002	†Oak A	2	0	1.000	13	0	0	0-0	12	12	2	1	1	8-1	8	1.50	299	.261	.382	0	—	0		4		0.6
2003	Oak A	0	1	.000	6	0	0	0-0	8.1	13	7	1	0	2-0	4	7.56	61	.361	.395	0	—	0		-2	129	-0.2
Total	3	4	8	.333	33	11	0	0-0	71.1	106	69	11	3	44-3	53	8.45	54	.348	.431	14	.214	0	101	-29	129	-3.5

BOWLER, GRANT Grant Tierney "Moose" B10.24.1907 Denver CO D6.25.1968 Denver CO BR/TR/6-0/190 d8.21 Col DePaul
1931	Chi A	0	1	.000	13	3	1	0	35.1	40	26	1	0	24	15	5.35	80	.288	.393	10	.100	-0	106	-5		-0.3
1932	Chi A	0	0	—	4	0	0	0	6.1	15	12	1	0	3	2	15.63	28	.484	.529	2	.000	-0		-8		-0.4
Total	2	0	1	.000	17	3	1	0	41.2	55	38	2	0	27	17	6.91	62	.324	.416	12	.083	-1	106	-13		-0.7

BOWLES, BRIAN Brian Christopher B8.18.1976 Harbor City CA BR/TR/6-5/220* [TorA94 50/1361] d6.27
2001	Tor A	0	0	—	2	0	0	0-0	3.2	4	0	0	0	1-0	4	0.00	—	.286	.333	0	—	0		2		0.1
2002	Tor A	2	1	.667	17	0	0	0-1	20	13	11	0	3	14-1	19	4.05	114	.183	.337	0	—	0		1		0.1
2003	Tor A	0	0	—	5	0	0	0-0	7	8	4	1	2	2-0	2	2.57	185	.267	.353	0	—	0		1		0.0
Total	3	2	1	.667	24	0	0	0-1	30.2	25	15	1	5	17-1	25	3.23	144	.217	.341	0	—	0		4		0.2

BOWLES, CHARLIE Charles James B3.15.1917 Norwood MA D12.23.2003 Newton NC BR/TR/6-3/180 d9.25 Mil 1943-45
1943	Phi A	1	1	.500	2	2	2	0	18	17	10	0	0	4	6	3.00	113	.258	.300	8	.125	-1*	136	-1		-0.1
1945	Phi A	0	3	.000	8	4	1	0	33.1	35	19	3	0	23	11	5.13	67	.273	.384	21	.238	0*	93	-5		-0.4
Total	2	1	4	.200	10	6	3	0	51.1	52	29	3	0	27	17	4.38	78	.268	.357	29	.207	-0	108	-6		-0.5

BOWLES, EMMETT Emmett Jerome "Chief" B8.2.1898 Wanette OK D9.3.1959 Flagstaff AZ BR/TR/6-0/180 d9.12
| 1922 | Chi A | 0 | 0 | — | 1 | 0 | 0 | 0 | 1 | 2 | 3 | 0 | 0 | 1 | 0 | 27.00 | 15 | .500 | .600 | 0 | — | 0 | | -2 | | -0.1 |

BOWMAN, ABE Alvah Edson B1.25.1893 Greenup IL D10.11.1979 Longview TX BR/TR/6-1/190 d5.19
1914	Cle A	2	7	.222	22	10	2-1	0	72.2	74	45	0	4	45	27	4.46	65	.277	.389	21	.048	-2	78	-10		-1.4
1915	Cle A	0	1	.000	2	1	0	0	1.1	1	4	0	0	3	0	20.25	15	.250	.571	0	—	0	72	-2		-0.4
Total	2	2	8	.200	24	11	2-1	0	74	75	49	0	4	48	27	4.74	61	.277	.393	21	.048	-2	78	-12		-1.7

BOWMAN, JOE Joseph Emil B6.17.1910 Kansas City KS D11.22.1990 Kansas City MO BL/TR/6-2/190 d4.18
1932	Phi A	0	1	.000	7	0	0	0	11	14	10	2	3	6	4	8.18	55	.318	.434	1	1.000	0		-4		-0.2
1934	NY N	5	4	.556	30	10	3	3	107.1	119	52	9	2	36	36	3.61	107	.279	.338	29-0-1	.172	0*	125	3		0.2
1935	Phi N	7	10	.412	33	17	6-1	1	148.1	157	86	13	4	56	58	4.25	107	.269	.337	67-1-1	.194	0*	85	3		0.4
1936	Phi N	9	20	.310	40	28	12	1	203.2	243	140	14	7	53	80	5.04	90	.289	.336	77-0-1	.195	-1*	90	-10		-1.4
1937	Pit N	8	8	.500	30	19	7	1	128	161	78	11	1	35	38	4.57	85	.306	.340	21-0-2	.333	2*	134	-4		-0.3
1938	Pit N	3	4	.429	17	1	0	1	60	68	33	2	0	20	25	4.65	82	.285	.340	21-0-2	.333	2*	134	-4		-0.3
1939	Pit N	10	14	.417	37	27	10-1	1	184.2	217	105	15	7	66	58	4.48	86	.292	.336	96-0-4	.344	12*	109	-13		-0.5
1940	Pit N	9	10	.474	32	24	10	2	187.2	209	113	10	7	66	57	4.46	85	.274	.337	90-1-0	.244	9*	132	-16		-0.5
1941	Pit N	3	2	.600	18	7	1-1	1	69.1	77	24	3	1	28	22	2.99	121	.278	.346	31	.258	1*	121	6		0.4
1944	Bos A	12	8	.600	26	24	10-1	0	168.1	175	95	14	2	64	53	4.81	71	.269	.336	100	.200	3*	138	-23		-2.2
1945	Bos A	0	2	.000	3	3	0	0	11.2	16	12	1	0	9	0	9.26	37	.360	.468	9	.222	0*	92	-7		-0.9
	Cin N	11	13	.458	25	24	15-1	0	185.2	198	89	8	7	68	71	3.59	105	.270	.338	71-0-2	.070	-5*	88	2		-0.7
Total	11	77	96	.445	298	184	74-5	11	1465.2	1656	837	102	41	484	502	4.40	89	.282	.341	639-2-14	.221	24	108	-73		-6.1

BOWMAN, BOB Robert James B10.3.1910 Keystone WV D9.4.1972 Bluefield WV BR/TR/5-10.5/160 d4.21
1939	StL N	13	5	.722	51	15	4-2	9	169.1	141	54	8	1	60	78	2.60	158	.232	.302	47-0-5	.085	-3	108	28		2.1
1940	StL N	7	5	.583	28	17	7	0	114.1	118	66	9	4	43	43	4.33	92	.267	.337	33-0-2	.061	-2	121	-5		-0.5
1941	NY N	6	7	.462	29	6	2	1	80.1	100	55	10	1	36	25	5.71	65	.302	.337	21-1-3	.048	-1	119	-16		-2.0
1942	Chi N	0	0	—	1	0	0	0	1	1	0	0	0	0	0	0.00	—	.250	.250	0	—	0		0		0.0
Total	4	26	17	.605	109	38	13-2	10	365	360	175	27	6	139	146	3.82	104	.260	.330	101-1-10	.069	-5	115	7		-0.4

BOWMAN, ROGER Roger Clinton B8.18.1927 Amsterdam NY D7.21.1997 Los Angeles CA BR/TL/6-0/175* d9.22
1949	NY N	0	0	—	2	2	0	0	6.1	6	3	1	0	7	4	4.26	93	.261	.433	2	.000	-0	100	0		0.0
1951	NY N	2	4	.333	9	5	0	0	26.1	35	18	2	1	22	24	6.15	64	.297	.411	6-0-1	.000	-0	86	-5		-1.0
1952	NY N	0	0	—	2	1	0	0	3	6	4	1	0	3	3	12.00	31	.429	.556	1	.000	-0	216	-2		-0.2
1953	Pit N	0	4	.000	30	2	0	0	65.1	65	42	9	1	29	36	4.82	93	.261	.341	7	.286	0	20	-4		-0.4
1955	Pit N	0	3	.000	7	2	0	0	16.2	25	18	2	1	10-2	8	8.64	48	.347	.434	2-0-1	.500	-0	54	-8		-1.0
Total	5	2	11	.154	50	12	0	0	117.2	137	85	14	4	71-2	75	5.81	73	.288	.385	18-0-2	.167	-0	77	-19		-2.6

BOWMAN, SUMNER Sumner Sallade B2.9.1867 Millersburg PA D1.11.1954 Millersburg PA BL/TL/6-0/160 d6.11 Col Penn
1890	Phi N	0	0	—	1	1	0	0	8	11	7	0	1	2	2	7.88	46	.314	.368	4	.500	1	138	-2		-0.4
		2	5	.286	9	7	6	0	70.2	100	90	1	11	50	22	6.62	50	.323	.434	36	.278	2*	134	-31		-2.5
	Year	2	5	.286	10	8	6	0	78.2	111	97	1	12	52	24	6.75	49	.322	.428	40	.300	1	135	-34		-2.9

YEAR	TM LG	W	L	PCT	G	GS	CG-SHO	SV-BS	IP	H	R	HR	HB	BB-IB	SO	ERA	AERA	OAV	OOB	AB-HR-SH	AVG	PB	SUP	APR	DL	PW
1891	Phi AA	2	5	.286	8	8	8	0	68	73	54	0	5	37	22	3.44	110	.265	.363	54	.241	0*	82	-3		-0.2
Total	2	4	10	.286	18	16	14	0	146.2	184	151	1	17	89	46	5.22	68	.297	.399	94	.266	3	107	-36		-2.3

BOWSFIELD, TED   Edward Oliver   B1.10.1935 Vernon BC, Can.   BR/TL/6-1/190*   d7.20

YEAR	TM LG	W	L	PCT	G	GS	CG-SHO	SV-BS	IP	H	R	HR	HB	BB-IB	SO	ERA	AERA	OAV	OOB	AB-HR-SH	AVG	PB	SUP	APR	DL	PW
1958	Bos A	4	2	.667	16	10	2	0	65.2	58	32	3	1	36-1	38	3.84	104	.233	.331	26	.154	-1*	121	1		0.0
1959	Bos A	0	1	.000	5	2	0	0	9	16	15	2	0	9-0	4	15.00	27	.390	.500	1	.000	-0	152	-10		-0.9
1960	Bos A	1	2	.333	17	2	0	2	21	20	12	1	1	13-0	18	5.14	79	.260	.366	4-0-2	.250	0	163	-2		-0.2
	Cle A	3	4	.429	11	6	1-1	0	40.2	47	30	1	0	20-1	14	5.09	73	.296	.372	10-0-1	.100	-0	67	-8		-1.2
	Year	4	6	.400	28	8	1-1	2	61.2	67	42	2	1	33-1	32	5.11	75	.284	.370	14-0-3	.143	-0	92	-10		-1.4
1961	LA A	11	8	.579	41	21	4-1	0	157	154	75	18	1	63-3	88	3.73	121	.255	.323	51-0-2	.137	-1*	95	12		1.1
1962	LA A	9	8	.529	34	25	1	1	139	154	82	12	2	40-0	52	4.40	88	.277	.325	37-0-4	.162	1*	104	-10		-1.0
1963	KC A	5	7	.417	41	11	2-1	3	111.1	115	60	14	3	47-5	67	4.45	88	.269	.343	23-0-2	.043	-1*	83	-6		-0.6
1964	KC A	4	7	.364	50	9	2-1	0	118.2	135	63	12	4	31-4	45	4.10	93	.285	.331	21-0-2	.095	-1*	78	-5		-0.5
Total	7	37	39	.487	215	86	12-4	6	662.1	699	369	63	12	259-14	326	4.35	93	.270	.336	173-0-13	.127	-3	99	-28		-3.3

BOWYER, TRAVIS   Travis Charlton   B8.3.1981 Lynchburg VA   BR/TR/6-3/210   d9.10

YEAR	TM LG	W	L	PCT	G	GS	CG-SHO	SV-BS	IP	H	R	HR	HB	BB-IB	SO	ERA	AERA	OAV	OOB	AB-HR-SH	AVG	PB	SUP	APR	DL	PW
2005	Min A	0	1	.000	8	0	0	0-1	9.2	10	6	3	1	3-0	12	5.59	79	.270	.333	0	—	0		-1		-0.1

BOYD, OIL CAN   Dennis Ray   B10.6.1959 Meridian MS   BR/TR/6-1/155(144-160)   [BosA80 16/414]   d9.13   Col Jackson St.

YEAR	TM LG	W	L	PCT	G	GS	CG-SHO	SV-BS	IP	H	R	HR	HB	BB-IB	SO	ERA	AERA	OAV	OOB	AB-HR-SH	AVG	PB	SUP	APR	DL	PW
1982	Bos A	0	1	.000	3	1	0	0-1	8.1	11	5	2	0	2-0	2	5.40	81	.314	.351	0	—	0	21	-1		-0.1
1983	Bos A	4	8	.333	15	13	5	0-0	98.2	103	46	9	1	23-0	43	3.28	134	.269	.308	0	—	0	81	9		0.9
1984	Bos A	12	12	.500	29	26	10-3	0-0	197.2	207	109	18	1	53-5	134	4.37	96	.269	.314	0	—	0	108	-3		-0.3
1985	Bos A	15	13	.536	35	35	13-3	0-0	272.1	273	117	26	4	67-3	154	3.70	117	.261	.306	0	—	0	107	20		2.1
1986	†Bos A	16	10	.615	30	30	10	0-0	214.1	222	99	32	2	45-1	129	3.78	111	.265	.302	0	—	0	119	11		1.2
1987	Bos A	1	3	.250	7	7	0	0-0	36.2	47	31	6	2	9-1	12	5.89	78	.315	.356	0	—	0	108	-8	143	-0.6
1988	Bos A	9	7	.563	23	23	1	0-0	129.2	147	82	25	2	41-2	71	5.34	77	.289	.341	0	—	0	112	-16	57	-1.7
1989	Bos A	3	2	.600	10	10	0	0-0	59	57	31	8	0	19-0	26	4.42	93	.253	.309	0	—	0	128	-1	122	-0.1
1990	Mon N	10	6	.625	31	31	3-3	0-0	190.2	164	64	19	3	52-10	113	2.93	126	.233	.287	59-0-12	.051	-4	110	18		0.9
1991	Mon N	6	8	.429	19	19	1-1	0-0	120.1	115	49	9	0	40-2	82	3.52	104	.256	.314	36-0-3	.083	-1	94	3		0.2
	Tex A	2	7	.222	12	12	0	0-0	62	81	47	12	0	17-1	33	6.68	61	.314	.356	0	—	0	68	-16		-2.0
Total	10	78	77	.503	214	207	43-10	0-1	1389.2	1427	680	166	15	368-25	799	4.04	102	.266	.313	95-0-15	.063	-5	105	16	322	0.5

BOYD, GARY   Gary Lee   B8.22.1946 Pasadena CA   BR/TR/6-4/200   d8.1   Col El Camino (CA) JC

YEAR	TM LG	W	L	PCT	G	GS	CG-SHO	SV-BS	IP	H	R	HR	HB	BB-IB	SO	ERA	AERA	OAV	OOB	AB-HR-SH	AVG	PB	SUP	APR	DL	PW
1969	Cle A	0	2	.000	8	3	0	0-0	11	8	11	1	0	14-1	9	9.00	42	.205	.407	1	.000	-0	54	-5		-0.9

BOYD, JAKE   Jacob Henry   B1.19.1874 Martinsburg WV   D8.12.1932 Gettysburg PA   TL/?/160   d9.20 ▲

YEAR	TM LG	W	L	PCT	G	GS	CG-SHO	SV-BS	IP	H	R	HR	HB	BB-IB	SO	ERA	AERA	OAV	OOB	AB-HR-SH	AVG	PB	SUP	APR	DL	PW
1894	Was N	0	3	.000	3	3	3	0	19	37	35	1	1	14	3	8.53	62	.402	.486	21	.143	-1*	76	-9		-0.9
1895	Was N	2	11	.154	15	13	8	0	92.2	132	95	1	1	40	18	6.80	71	.329	.405	159-1-0	.270	2*	73	-15		-1.3
1896	Was N	1	2	.333	4	2	2	0	32	45	34	0	6	15	6	6.75	65	.328	.418	13	.077	-1	56	-7		-0.6
Total	3	3	16	.158	22	18	13	0	143.2	214	164	2	18	69	27	7.02	68	.340	.420	193-1-0	.244	-1	73	-31		-2.8

BOYD, JASON   Jason Pernell   B2.23.1973 St.Clair IL   BR/TR/6-3/170*   [PhiN94 8/226]   d9.10   Col John A. Logan (IL) CC

YEAR	TM LG	W	L	PCT	G	GS	CG-SHO	SV-BS	IP	H	R	HR	HB	BB-IB	SO	ERA	AERA	OAV	OOB	AB-HR-SH	AVG	PB	SUP	APR	DL	PW
1999	Pit N	0	0	—	4	0	0	0-0	5.1	5	2	1	0	2-0	4	3.38	136	.250	.333	1	.000	-0		1		0.0
2000	Phi N	0	1	.000	30	0	0	0-1	34.1	39	28	2	1	24-4	32	6.55	70	.293	.405	0	—	0		-8	90	-0.4
2002	SD N	1	0	1.000	23	0	0	0-3	28.1	33	29	6	0	15-1	18	7.94	49	.300	.375	0	—	0		-14		-0.7
2003	Cle A	3	1	.750	44	0	0	0-1	52.1	38	25	4	3	26-1	31	4.30	103	.200	.303	0	—	0		2	19	0.2
2004	Pit N	1	0	1.000	12	0	0	0-0	13	13	9	4	3	8-1	12	5.54	78	.260	.393	0	—	0		-2		-0.1
Total	5	5	2	.714	113	0	0	0-5	133.1	128	93	16	8	75-7	97	5.74	76	.254	.356	1	.000	0		-21	109	-1.0

BOYD, RAY   Raymond C.   B2.11.1887 Hortonville IN   D2.11.1920 Hortonville IN   BR/TR/5-10/160   d9.24

YEAR	TM LG	W	L	PCT	G	GS	CG-SHO	SV-BS	IP	H	R	HR	HB	BB-IB	SO	ERA	AERA	OAV	OOB	AB-HR-SH	AVG	PB	SUP	APR	DL	PW
1910	StL A	0	2	.000	3	2	1	0	14.1	16	10	0	1	5	6	4.40	56	.286	.355	5	.200	-0	41	-3		-0.4
1911	Cin N	2	2	.500	7	4	3	1	44	34	22	0	2	19	20	2.66	124	.206	.296	12-0-1	.083	-0	62	2		0.1
Total	2	2	4	.333	10	6	4	1	58.1	50	32	0	3	24	26	3.09	101	.226	.310	17-0-1	.118	-0	55	-1		-0.3

BOYER, BLAINE   Blaine Thomas   B7.11.1981 Atlanta GA   BR/TR/6-3/215   d6.12

YEAR	TM LG	W	L	PCT	G	GS	CG-SHO	SV-BS	IP	H	R	HR	HB	BB-IB	SO	ERA	AERA	OAV	OOB	AB-HR-SH	AVG	PB	SUP	APR	DL	PW
2005	Atl N	4	2	.667	43	0	0	0-2	37.2	32	13	1	2	17-0	33	3.11	138	.234	.325	0	—	0		5		0.7

BOYER, CLOYD   Cloyd Victor "Junior"   B9.1.1927 Alba MO   BR/TR/6-1/188*   d4.23   C8   b-Clete   b-Ken

YEAR	TM LG	W	L	PCT	G	GS	CG-SHO	SV-BS	IP	H	R	HR	HB	BB-IB	SO	ERA	AERA	OAV	OOB	AB-HR-SH	AVG	PB	SUP	APR	DL	PW
1949	StL N	0	0	—	3	1	0	0	3.1	5	4	0	0	7	0	10.80	39	.357	.571	0	—	0*	85	-2		-0.1
1950	StL N	7	7	.500	36	14	6-1	1	120.1	105	52	15	3	49	82	3.52	122	.233	.312	33-0-3	.182	0	123	10		1.1
1951	StL N	2	5	.286	19	8	1	1	63.1	68	42	9	3	46	40	5.26	75	.286	.408	20-0-1	.200	0	123	-10		-1.0
1952	StL N	6	6	.500	23	14	4-2	0	110.1	108	56	11	4	44	44	4.24	88	.258	.338	38	.211	2*	101	-5		-0.4
1955	KC A	5	5	.500	30	11	2	0	98.1	107	81	21	7	69-3	32	6.22	67	.282	.398	29-0-1	.069	-2	97	-24		-2.3
Total	5	20	23	.465	111	48	13-3	2	395.2	393	235	56	17	218-3	198	4.73	86	.262	.361	120-0-5	.167	1	110	-31		-2.7

BOYLE, HENRY   Henry J. "Handsome Henry"   B9.20.1860 Philadelphia PA   D5.25.1932 Philadelphia PA   BR/TR   d7.9 ▲

YEAR	TM LG	W	L	PCT	G	GS	CG-SHO	SV-BS	IP	H	R	HR	HB	BB-IB	SO	ERA	AERA	OAV	OOB	AB-HR-SH	AVG	PB	SUP	APR	DL	PW
1884	StL U	15	3	.833	19	16	16-2	1	150	118	63	3	0	10	88	1.74	137	.202	.215	262-4	.260	-1*	127	10		0.7
1885	StL N	16	24	.400	42	39	39-1	0	366.2	346	207	2	0	100	133	2.75	100	.239	.288	258-1	.202	1*	80	-7		-0.6
1886	StL N	9	15	.375	25	24	23-2	0	210	183	106	5	0	46	101	1.76	183	.220	.261	108-1	.250	4*	85	26		3.0
1887	Ind N	13	24	.351	38	38	37	0	328	356	204	11	12	69	85	3.65	114	.265	.307	141-2	.191	-1*	73	17		1.3
1888	Ind N	15	22	.405	37	37	36-3	0	323	315	179	11	10	58	98	3.26	91	.245	.283	125-1	.144	-3	108	-14		-1.5
1889	Ind N	21	23	.477	46	45	38-2	0	378.2	422	224	14	14	95	97	3.92	106	.273	.321	155-1	.245	5	84	14		1.6
Total	6	89	111	.445	207	199	189-10	1	1756.1	1740	983	46	36	378	602	3.06	110	.247	.289	1049-10	.219	5	89	46		4.5

BOYLES, HARRY   Harry "Stretch"   B11.29.1913 Granite City IL   D1.7.2005 McAllen TX   BR/TR/6-5/185   d8.3

YEAR	TM LG	W	L	PCT	G	GS	CG-SHO	SV-BS	IP	H	R	HR	HB	BB-IB	SO	ERA	AERA	OAV	OOB	AB-HR-SH	AVG	PB	SUP	APR	DL	PW
1938	Chi A	0	4	.000	9	2	1	1	29.1	31	27	2	2	25	18	5.22	94	.263	.400	8	.125	-1	36	-4		-0.5
1939	Chi A	0	0	—	2	0	0	0	3.1	4	4	0	0	6	1	10.80	44	.308	.526	1	.000	-0		-2		-0.1
Total	2	0	4	.000	11	2	1	1	32.2	35	31	2	2	31	19	5.79	84	.267	.415	9	.111	-1	36	-6		-0.6

BOZE, MARSHALL   Marshall Wayne   B5.23.1971 San Manuel AZ   BR/TR/6-1/214   [MilA90 12/331]   d4.28   Col Southwestern (CA) CC

YEAR	TM LG	W	L	PCT	G	GS	CG-SHO	SV-BS	IP	H	R	HR	HB	BB-IB	SO	ERA	AERA	OAV	OOB	AB-HR-SH	AVG	PB	SUP	APR	DL	PW
1996	Mil A	0	2	.000	25	0	0	1-1	32.1	47	29	5	6	25-4	19	7.79	67	.362	.481	0	—	0		-8		-0.4

BRABENDER, GENE   Eugene Mathew   B8.16.1941 Madison WI   D12.27.1996 Madison WI   BR/TR/6-5.5/220*   d5.11   Col Wisconsin-Whitewater

YEAR	TM LG	W	L	PCT	G	GS	CG-SHO	SV-BS	IP	H	R	HR	HB	BB-IB	SO	ERA	AERA	OAV	OOB	AB-HR-SH	AVG	PB	SUP	APR	DL	PW
1966	Bal A	4	3	.571	31	1	0	0	71	57	30	4	1	29-0	62	3.55	94	.229	.310	13	.077	-1	159	-1		-0.2
1967	Bal A	6	4	.600	14	14	3-1	0	94	77	38	6	1	29-1	71	3.35	94	.220	.269	28-0-1	.071	-1	109	-2		-0.3
1968	Bal A	6	7	.462	37	15	3-2	3	124.2	116	52	9	3	48-4	92	3.32	88	.248	.320	35-1-3	.086	-0	105	-5		-0.7
1969	Sea A	13	14	.481	40	29	7-1	0-1	202.1	193	111	26	13	103-7	139	4.36	84	.254	.350	70-1-2	.129	-1*	100	-16		-2.2
1970	Mil A	6	15	.286	29	21	2	1-0	128.2	127	94	9	2	79-7	76	6.02	63	.255	.357	41-0-3	.098	-2	82	-31		-4.5
Total	5	35	43	.449	151	80	15-4	6-1	620.2	570	325	54	20	282-19	440	4.25	80	.245	.330	187-2-9	.102	-5	99	-55		-7.9

BRACKEN, JACK   John James   B4.14.1881 Cleveland OH   D7.16.1954 Highland Park MI   BR/TR/5-11/175   d8.7

YEAR	TM LG	W	L	PCT	G	GS	CG-SHO	SV-BS	IP	H	R	HR	HB	BB-IB	SO	ERA	AERA	OAV	OOB	AB-HR-SH	AVG	PB	SUP	APR	DL	PW
1901	Cle A	4	8	.333	12	12	12	0	100	137	94	4	10	31	18	6.21	57	.322	.381	44	.227	0	87	-26		-2.4

BRACKENRIDGE, JOHN   John Givler   B12.24.1880 Harrisburg PA   D3.20.1953 Harrisburg PA   BR/TR/6-0/?   d4.15

YEAR	TM LG	W	L	PCT	G	GS	CG-SHO	SV-BS	IP	H	R	HR	HB	BB-IB	SO	ERA	AERA	OAV	OOB	AB-HR-SH	AVG	PB	SUP	APR	DL	PW
1904	Phi N	0	1	.000	7	1	0	0	34	37	32	4	4	16	11	5.56	48	.298	.396	13	.154	-0	77	-11		-0.5

BRADEY, DON   Donald Eugene   B10.4.1934 Charlotte NC   BR/TR/5-9/180   d9.25

YEAR	TM LG	W	L	PCT	G	GS	CG-SHO	SV-BS	IP	H	R	HR	HB	BB-IB	SO	ERA	AERA	OAV	OOB	AB-HR-SH	AVG	PB	SUP	APR	DL	PW
1964	Hou N	0	0	—	7	0	0	0	7	7	7	0		3-1	2	19.29	18	.429	.500	0	—	0		26	-5		-0.9

BRADFORD, CHAD   Chadwick Lee   B9.14.1974 Jackson MS   BR/TR/6-5/205*   [ChiA96 13/377]   d8.1   Col Southern Mississippi   [DL 2005 Oak A 86]

YEAR	TM LG	W	L	PCT	G	GS	CG-SHO	SV-BS	IP	H	R	HR	HB	BB-IB	SO	ERA	AERA	OAV	OOB	AB-HR-SH	AVG	PB	SUP	APR	DL	PW
1998	Chi A	2	1	.667	29	0	0	1-2	30.2	27	16	0	0	7-0	11	3.23	142	.229	.272	0	—	0		3		0.3
1999	Chi A	0	0	—	3	0	0	0-0	3.2	9	8	1	0	5-0	0	19.64	25	.474	.583	0	—	0		-6		-0.2
2000	†Chi A	1	0	1.000	12	0	0	0-0	13.2	13	4	0	0	1-1	9	1.98	256	.255	.269	0	—	0		4		0.3
2001	†Oak A	2	1	.667	35	0	0	1-3	36.2	41	12	6	1	6-0	34	2.70	169	.281	.314	0	—	0		8		0.6
2002	†Oak A	4	2	.667	75	0	0	2-3	75.1	79	29	5	5	14-5	56	3.11	144	.253	.298	0	—	0		11		0.9
2003	†Oak A	7	4	.636	72	0	0	2-3	77	67	28	7	7	30-9	62	3.04	151	.236	.324	0	—	0		13		1.8
2004	Oak A	5	7	.417	68	0	0	1-3	59	51	32	5	5	24-9	34	4.42	105	.234	.323	0	—	0		1		0.2
2005	†Bos A	2	1	.667	31	0	0	0-1	23.1	23	10	1	3	4-1	10	3.86	119	.312	.356	0	—	0		15		0.3
Total	8	23	16	.590	325	0	0	7-15	319.1	310	139	24	21	91-25	216	3.49	131	.255	.317	0	—	0		36	101	4.2

YEAR	TM LG	W	L	PCT	G	GS	CG-SHO	SV-BS	IP	H	R	HR	HB	BB-IB	SO	ERA	AERA	OAV	OOB	AB-HR-SH	AVG	PB	SUP	APR	DL	PW

BRADFORD, LARRY Larry B12.21.1949 Chicago IL D9.11.1998 Atlanta GA BR/TL/6-1/200* [AtlN73 19/442] d9.24

1977	Atl N	0	0	—	2	0	0	0-0	2.2	3	1	1	0	0-0	1	3.38	132	.273	.273	0	—	0		0		0.0
1979	Atl N	1	0	1.000	21	0	0	2-1	19	11	5	0	1	10-1	11	0.95	424	.172	.286	1	.000	-0		5		0.4
1980	Atl N	3	4	.429	56	0	0	4-3	55.1	49	20	3	1	22-8	32	2.44	151	.243	.317	3	.000	0		6		0.8
1981	Atl N	2	0	1.000	25	0	0	1-0	26.2	26	13	1	0	12-0	14	3.71	95	.268	.342	1	1.000	0		-1		0.0
Total	4	6	4	.600	104	0	0	7-4	103.2	89	39	5	2	44-9	58	2.52	148	.238	.317	5	.200	-0		10		1.2

BRADFORD, BILL William D B8.28.1921 Choctaw AR D8.22.2000 Fairfield Bay AR BR/TR/6-2/180 d4.24

1956	KC A	0	0	—	1	0	0	0	2	2	2	2	0	1-0	0	9.00	48	.250	.333	0	—	0		-1		0.0

BRADLEY, FRED Fred Langdon B7.31.1920 Parsons KS BR/TR/6-1/180 d5.1

1948	Chi A	0	0	—	8	0	0	0	15.2	11	12	2	1	4	2	4.60	93	.190	.254	1	.000	-0		-2	108	-0.1
1949	Chi A	0	0	—	1	1	0	0	2	4	3	0	0	3	0	13.50	31	.444	.583	1	.000	-0	300	-2		-0.1
Total	2	0	0	—	9	1	0	0	17.2	15	15	2	1	7	2	5.60	76	.224	.307	2	.000	-0	300	-4	108	-0.2

BRADLEY, FOGHORN George H. B7.1.1855 Milford MA D3.31.1900 Philadelphia PA BR/TR/6-0/175 d8.23 U6

1876	Bos N	9	10	.474	22	21	16-1	1	173.1	201	116	1		16	16	2.49	91	.263	.279	82	.232	-1	103	-3		-0.4

BRADLEY, GEORGE George Washington "Grin" B7.13.1852 Reading PA D10.2.1931 Philadelphia PA BR/TR/5-10.5/175 d5.4 ▲

1875	StL NA	33	26	.559	60	60	57-5	0	535.2	540	304	3		17	60	2.13	94	.241	.247	254	.244	7	93	-5		0.3
1876	StL N	45	19	.703	64	64	63-16	0	573	470	229	3		38	103	1.23	174	.211	.224	265	.249	4	109	63		6.2
1877	Chi N	18	23	.439	50	44	35-2	0	394	452	266	4		39	59	3.31	90	.269	.286	214	.243	0*	100	-13		-1.1
1879	Tro N	13	40	.245	54	54	53-3	0	487	590	361	0		26	133	2.85	88	.275	.284	251	.247	4*	82	-14		-0.4
1880	Pro N	13	8	.619	28	20	16-4	2	196	158	66	2		6	54	1.38	160	.210	.217	309	.227	1*	106	18		1.9
1881	Cle N	2	4	.333	6	6	5	0	51	70	36	2		3	6	3.88	67	.320	.329	241-2	.249	0*	69	-6		-0.6
1882	Cle N	6	9	.400	18	16	15	0	147	164	102	5		22	32	3.73	75	.264	.289	115	.183	-3*	84	-14		-1.2
1883	Phi AA	16	7	.696	26	23	22	0	214.1	215	129	7		22	56	3.15	112	.244	.263	312-1	.234	-0*	114	13		1.0
1884	Cin U	25	15	.625	41	38	36-3	0	342	350	203	7		23	168	2.71	94	.248	.260	226	.190	-12*	98	-7		-1.6
Total	8	138	125	.525	287	265	245-28	2	2404.1	2469	1392	42		179	611	2.50	103	.248	.262	1933-3	.231	-5	99	40		4.2

BRADLEY, HERB Herbert Theodore B1.3.1903 Agenda KS D10.16.1959 Clay Center KS BR/TR/6-0/170 d5.9 Col Kansas

1927	Bos A	1	1	.500	6	2	1	0	23	16	9	0	2	7	6	3.13	135	.198	.278	7	.429	1	69	3		0.3
1928	Bos A	0	3	.000	15	5	1-1	0	47.1	64	41	2	2	16	14	7.23	57	.339	.396	13-0-2	.154	-1	74	-15		-0.8
1929	Bos A	0	0	—	3	0	0	0	4	7	3	1	0	2	0	6.75	63	.438	.500	1	.000	-0		-1		0.0
Total	3	1	4	.200	24	7	3-1	0	74.1	87	53	3	4	25	20	5.93	70	.304	.368	21-0-2	.238	-0	72	-13		-0.5

BRADLEY, RYAN Ryan J. B10.26.1975 Covina CA BR/TR/6-4/226 [NYA97 1/40] d8.22 Col Arizona St.

1998	NY A	2	1	.667	5	1	0	0-0	12.2	12	9	2	1	9-0	13	5.68	77	.250	.373	0	—	0	85	-2		-0.4

BRADLEY, BERT Steven Bert B12.23.1956 Athens GA BB/TR/6-1/190 [OakA79 27/670] d9.3 Col Brigham Young

1983	Oak A	0	0	—	6	0	0	0-0	8.1	14	7	1	0	4-1	3	6.48	60	.400	.450	0	—	0		-3		-0.1

BRADLEY, TOM Thomas William B3.16.1947 Asheville NC BR/TR/6-3/185(173-195) [AnaA68 7/144] d9.9 Col Maryland-Baltimore Co.

1969	Cal A	0	1	.000	3	0	0	0-0	2	9	9	1	0	2	2	27.00	13	.600	.600	—	—	0		-6		-1.1
1970	Cal A	2	5	.286	17	11	1-1	0-0	69.2	71	38	3	1	33-6	53	4.13	88	.270	.350	18-0-3	.167	0	94	-5		-0.4
1971	Chi A	15	15	.500	45	39	7-6	2-2	285.2	273	111	16	2	74-5	206	2.96	120	.248	.295	96-1-7	.156	-1*	88	19		1.7
1972	Chi A	15	14	.517	40	40	11-2	0-0	260	225	94	19	2	65-4	209	2.98	105	.231	.280	91-0-9	.132	-2*	110	5		0.3
1973	SF N	13	12	.520	35	34	6-1	0-0	224	212	109	26	3	69-10	136	3.90	99	.246	.302	77-0-6	.195	1	113	0		0.0
1974	SF N	8	11	.421	30	21	2	0-0	134.1	152	90	15	1	52-4	72	5.16	74	.282	.342	40-0-6	.075	-2	105	-18		-2.6
1975	SF N	2	3	.400	13	6	0	0-0	42	57	33	6	1	18-4	13	6.21	61	.326	.390	10-0-1	.000	-1	108	-11		-1.2
Total	7	55	61	.474	183	151	27-10	2-2	1017.2	999	484	86	10	311-33	691	3.72	96	.254	.309	332-1-32	.145	-5	103	-16		-3.3

BRADSHAW, JOE Joe Siah B8.17.1897 RoEllen TN D1.30.1985 Tavares FL BR/TR/6-2.5/200 d5.9

1929	Bro N	0	0	—	2	0	0	0	4	3	3	0	2	4	1	4.50	103	.231	.474	0	—	0		0		0.0

BRADY, NEAL Cornelius Joseph B3.4.1897 Covington KY D6.19.1947 Fort Mitchell KY BR/TR/6-0.5/197 d9.25 Mil 1918

1915	NY A	0	0	—	2	1	0	0	8.2	9	3	0	0	7	6	3.12	94	.281	.410	4	.000	-1	99	0		-0.1
1917	NY A	1	0	1.000	2	1	0	0	9	6	2	0	0	5	4	2.00	134	.188	.297	2	.500	0	80	1		0.2
1925	Cin N	1	3	.250	20	3	2	1	63.2	73	44	4	4	20	12	4.66	88	.289	.350	25	.240	1	103	-5		-0.2
Total	3	2	3	.400	24	5	2	1	81.1	88	49	4	4	32	22	4.20	91	.278	.351	31	.226	1	94	-4		-0.1

BRADY, JIM James Joseph "Diamond Jim" B3.2.1936 Jersey City NJ BL/TL/6-2/185 d5.12 Col Notre Dame

1956	Det A	0	0	—	6	0	0	0	6.1	15	21	3	0	11-1	3	28.42	14	.484	.619	0	—	0		-17		-0.7

BRADY, KING James Ward B5.28.1881 Elmer NJ D8.21.1947 Albany NY BR/TR/6-0/190 d9.21

1905	Phi N	1	1	.500	2	2	2	0	13	19	7	0	0	2	3	3.46	84	.333	.356	5	.200	-0	86	-1		-0.1
1906	Pit N	1	1	.500	3	2	1	0	23	30	7	0	0	4	14	2.35	114	.313	.340	10	.100	-1	123	1		0.0
1907	Pit N	0	0	—	1	0	0	0	2	2	1	0	0	1	0	0.00	—	.286	.375	2	—	0		0		0.0
1908	Bos A	1	0	1.000	1	1	1-1	0	9	8	0	0	0	3	3	0.00	—	.242	.242	2	.000	-0	111	2		0.3
1912	Bos N	0	0	—	1	0	0	0	2.2	5	6	0	0	3	0	20.25	18	.313	.421	1	.000	-0		-4		-0.2
Total	5	3	2	.600	8	5	4-1	0	49.2	64	21	0	0	10	20	3.08	89	.306	.338	18	.111	-1	105	-2		0.0

BRADY, BILL William Aloysius "King" B8.18.1889 New York NY D4.10.1956 Brooklyn NY TR/6-2/? d7.9

1912	Bos N	0	0	—	1	0	0	0	1	2	0	0	0	0	0	0.00	—	.500	.500	0	—	0		0		0.0

BRAGGINS, DICK Richard Realf B12.25.1879 Mercer PA D8.16.1963 Lake Wales FL BR/TR/5-11/170 d5.16 Col Case Western Reserve

1901	Cle A	1	2	.333	4	3	2	0	32	44	28	1	1	15	1	4.78	74	.324	.395	13-0-1	.154	-1	82	-5		-0.5

BRAINARD, ASA Asahel "Count" B1841 Albany NY D12.29.1888 Denver CO TR/5-8.5/150 d5.5

1871	Oly NA	12	15	.444	30	30	30	0	264	361	292	4		37	13	4.50	93	.288	.308	134	.224	-6	89	-10		-0.9
1872	Oly NA	2	7	.222	9	9	9	0	79	148	140	1		5	1	6.38	56	.333	.341	43	.372	4	64	-25		-1.4
	Man NA	0	2	.000	2	2	1	0	8	13	17	1		0	0	5.63	64	.260	.260	25	.200	-0*	69	-2		-0.3
	Year	2	9	.182	11	11	10	0	87	161	157	1		5	1	6.31	57	.326	.333	68	.309	3	65	-26		-1.7
1873	Bal NA	5	7	.417	14	14	12	0	108.2	182	139	0		9	3	4.14	79	.326	.336	69	.261	0*	126	-11		-0.8
1874	Bal NA	5	22	.185	30	27	25	0	240	405	329	1		27	8	3.71	60	.327	.341	196	.240	-1*	73	-37		-3.0
Total	4 NA	24	53	.312	85	82	77	0	699.2	1109	917	6		78	25	4.40	75	.313	.327	467	.248	-4	88	-85		-6.4

BRAITHWOOD, AL Alfred B2.15.1892 Braceville IL D11.24.1960 Rowlesburg WV BR/TL/6-1.5/145 d9.1

1915	Pit F	0	0	—	2	0	0	0	3	0	0	0	0	0	2	0.00	—	.000	.000	0	—	0		1		0.0

BRAME, ERV Ervin Beckham B10.12.1901 Big Rock TN D11.22.1949 Hopkinsville KY BL/TR/6-2/190 d4.14

1928	Pit N	7	4	.636	24	11	6	0	95.2	110	62	5	1	44	22	5.08	80	.291	.366	49-1-1	.265	4*	138	-10		-0.6
1929	Pit N	16	11	.593	37	28	19-1	0	229.2	250	123	17	0	71	68	4.55	105	.278	.331	116-4-2	.310	12*	106	11		2.6
1930	Pit N	17	8	.680	32	28	22	1	235.2	291	153	21	5	56	55	4.70	106	.305	.346	116-3-5	.353	11*	113	4		1.1
1931	Pit N	9	13	.409	26	21	15-2	0	179.2	211	102	14	0	45	33	4.21	91	.295	.336	95	.274	6*	103	-7		-0.1
1932	Pit N	3	1	.750	23	3	0	0	51	84	52	6	0	16	10	7.41	51	.365	.407	20	.250	1*	154	-21		-1.1
Total	5	52	37	.584	142	91	62-3	1	791.2	946	492	63	6	232	188	4.76	94	.298	.347	396-8-8	.306	33	113	-23		0.4

BRANCA, RALPH Ralph Theodore Joseph "Hawk" B1.6.1926 Mt.Vernon NY BR/TR/6-3/220* d6.12

1944	Bro N	0	2	.000	21	1	0	1	44.2	46	36	2	5	32	16	7.05	50	.274	.405	6	.000	-1	94	-15		-0.9
1945	Bro N	5	6	.455	16	15	7	1	109.2	73	44	4	0	79	69	3.04	124	.189	.327	40-0-2	.100	-3	81	10		0.7
1946	Bro N	3	1	.750	24	10	2-2	3	67.1	62	34	4	0	41	42	3.88	87	.246	.352	18	.111	0	177	-4		-0.2
1947	†Bro N☆	21	12	.636	43	36	15-4	1	280	251	100	22	6	98	148	2.67	155	.240	.309	97-0-9	.124	-3	94	43		4.5
1948	Bro N★	14	9	.609	36	28	11-1	1	215.2	189	93	24	4	80	122	3.51	114	.232	.304	74-0-3	.203	1	101	13		1.3
1949	†Bro N☆	13	5	.722	34	27	9-2	1	186.2	181	100	21	2	71	109	4.39	93	.253	.339	62-0-8	.081	0	147	-6		-0.1
1950	Bro N	7	9	.438	43	15	5	7	142	152	80	24	0	55	100	4.69	87	.271	.336	34-2-7	.118	1	132	-9		-0.3
1951	Bro N	13	12	.520	42	27	13-3	3	204	180	81	19	3	85	118	3.26	120	.237	.316	63-0-6	.175	-0	136	15	37	-0.2
1952	Bro N	4	2	.667	16	7	2	0	61	52	29	8	4	21	26	3.84	95	.232	.309	19-0-1	.158	-0	136	-2		-0.1
1953	Bro N	0	0	—	7	0	0	0	11	15	14	4	2	5	5	9.82	43	.341	.431	0	—	0		-6		-0.1

YEAR	TM LG	W	L	PCT	G	GS	CG-SHO	SV-BS	IP	H	R	HR	HB	BB-IB	SO	ERA	AERA	OAV	OOB	AB-HR-SH	AVG	PB	SUP	APR	DL	PW
	Det A	4	7	.364	17	14	7	1	102	98	55	7	2	31	50	4.15	98	.253	.311	34-0-1	.118	-1	108	-2		-0.4
1954	Det A	3	3	.500	17	5	0	0	45.1	63	33	10	2	30	15	5.76	64	.330	.424	13	.308	2	115	-11		-1.1
	NY A	1	0	1.000	5	3	0	0	12.2	9	5	0	1	13	7	2.84	121	.209	.390	4	.500	1	77	1		0.1
	Year	4	3	.571	22	8	0	0	58	72	38	10	3	43	22	5.12	71	.308	.417	17	.353		100	-10		-1.0
1956	Bro N	0	0	—	1	0	0	0	1.0	1	0	0	0	2-0	2	0.00	—	.143	.333	0		0	1			0.1
Total	12	88	68	.564	322	188	71-12	19	1484	1372	702	149	31	663-0	829	3.79	104	.245	.328	464-2-37	.142	-6	111	28	37	2.8

BRANCH, HARVEY   Harvey Alfred   B2.8.1939 Memphis TN   BR/TL/6-0/175   d9.18   Col Alabama St.

| 1962 | StL N | 0 | 1 | .000 | 1 | 1 | 0 | 0 | 5 | 5 | 3 | 1 | 0 | 5-0 | 2 | 5.40 | 79 | .263 | .417 | 1 | .000 | -0 | 62 | 0 | | -0.1 |

BRANCH, NORM   Norman Downs "Red"   B3.22.1915 Spokane WA   D11.21.1971 Navasota TX   BR/TR/6-3/200   d5.5   Mil 1942-45   Col Texas

1941	NY A	5	1	.833	27	0	0	2	47	37	16	2	0	26	28	2.87	137	.224	.330	10	.000	-1		6		0.7
1942	NY A	0	1	.000	10	0	0	2	15.2	18	15	3	0	16	13	6.32	54	.290	.436	3	.333	0		-6		-0.5
Total	2	5	2	.714	37	0	0	4	62.2	55	31	5	0	42	41	3.73	102	.242	.361	13	.077	-1		0		0.2

BRANCH, ROY   Roy   B7.12.1953 St.Louis MO   BR/TR/6-0/175   [KCA71 1/5]   d9.11

| 1979 | Sea A | 0 | 1 | .000 | 2 | 2 | 0 | 0-0 | 11.1 | 12 | 11 | 2 | 0 | 7-1 | 6 | 7.94 | 55 | .273 | .365 | 0 | — | 0 | 83 | -4 | | -0.3 |

BRANDENBURG, MARK   Mark Clay   B7.14.1970 Houston TX   BR/TR/6-0/180*   [TexA92 26/734]   d7.20   Col Texas Tech   [DL 1998 Tex A 181]

1995	Tex A	0	1	.000	11	0	0	0-0	27.1	36	18	5	1	7-1	21	5.93	82	.316	.358	0	—	0		-3		-0.1
1996	Tex A	1	3	.250	26	0	0	0-1	47.2	48	22	3	2	25-1	37	3.21	164	.262	.354	0	—	0		9		0.6
	Bos A	4	2	.667	29	0	0	0-1	28.1	28	13	5	1	8-1	29	3.81	134	.250	.301	0	—	0		4		0.8
	Year	5	5	.500	55	0	0	0-2	76	76	35	8	3	33-2	66	3.43	151	.258	.334	0	—	0		13		1.4
1997	Bos A	0	2	.000	31	0	0	0-0	41	49	25	3	2	16-3	34	5.49	85	.299	.364	0	—	0		-3	62	-0.1
Total	3	5	8	.385	97	0	0	0-2	144.1	161	78	16	6	56-6	121	4.49	111	.281	.347	0	—	0		7	243	1.2

BRANDOM, CHICK   Chester Milton   B3.31.1887 Coldwater KS   D10.7.1958 Santa Ana CA   BR/TR/5-8/161   d9.3   Col Oklahoma

1908	Pit N	1	0	1.000	3	1	1	0	17	13	5	0	1	4	9	0.53	435	.228	.290	7	.143	-0	92	2		0.2
1909	Pit N	1	0	1.000	13	2	0	2	40.2	33	12	0	1	10	21	1.11	246	.239	.295	10	.100	-1	77	5		0.3
1915	New F	1	1	.500	16	1	1	0	50.1	55	36	0	1	15	15	3.40	75	.293	.348	10	.200	1	137	-9		-0.4
Total	3	3	1	.750	32	4	2	3	108	101	53	0	3	29	44	2.08	124	.264	.320	27	.148	-0	95	-2		0.1

BRANDON, BUCKY   Darrell G   B7.8.1940 Nacogdoches TX   BR/TR/6-2/200*   d4.19

1966	Bos A	8	8	.500	40	17	5-2	2	157.2	129	70	13	4	70-3	101	3.31	115	.222	.309	44-0-6	.182	1*	98	6		0.8
1967	Bos A	5	11	.313	39	19	2	3	157.2	147	86	21	4	59-7	96	4.17	84	.245	.318	43-0-5	.186	1	96	-13		-1.2
1968	Bos A	0	0	—	8	0	0	0	12.2	19	11	1	1	9-0	10	6.39	49	.333	.433	1	.000	-0		-5		-0.3
1969	Sea A	0	1	.000	8	0	0	0-0	15	15	15	4	2	16-1	10	8.40	43	.250	.423	0	—	0	170	-8		-0.5
	Min A	0	0	—	3	0	0	0-0	3.1	5	3	1	0	3-2	1	2.70	135	.357	.471	1	.000	0		0		0.0
	Year	0	1	.000	11	0	0	0-0	18.1	20	18	5	2	19-3	11	7.36	49	.290	.432	1	.000	0	170	-8		-0.5
1971	Phi N	6	6	.500	52	0	0	4-4	83	81	42	6	0	47-9	44	3.90	91	.264	.357	13-0-2	.154	-0		-4		-0.6
1972	Phi N	7	7	.500	42	6	0	2-2	104.1	106	49	9	4	46-8	67	3.45	105	.268	.352	15-0-4	.067	-1	98	0		-0.2
1973	Phi N	2	4	.333	36	0	0	2-0	56.1	54	35	5	3	25-7	25	5.43	70	.261	.343	5	.200	0		-9		-0.9
Total	7	28	37	.431	228	43	7-2	13-6	590	556	311	59	23	275-37	354	4.04	90	.250	.337	122-0-17	.164	1	99	-33		-2.9

BRANDT, ED   Edward Arthur "Big Ed"   B2.17.1905 Spokane WA   D11.1.1944 Spokane WA   BL/TL/6-1/190   d4.26

1928	Bos N	9	21	.300	38	32	12-1	0	225.1	234	141	22	7	109	84	5.07	77	.273	.359	70-0-3	.243	5*	80	-25		-2.2
1929	Bos N	8	13	.381	26	21	13	0	167.2	196	111	12	5	83	50	5.53	85	.302	.385	64-0-3	.234	2*	82	-13		-1.0
1930	Bos N	4	11	.267	41	13	4-1	1	147.1	168	88	15	0	59	65	5.01	99	.291	.356	50-0-1	.240	1	68	1		0.2
1931	Bos N	18	11	.621	33	29	23-3	2	250	228	94	11	4	77	112	2.92	130	.244	.304	82-0-7	.256	5*	90	24		3.4
1932	Bos N	16	16	.500	35	31	19-2	1	254	271	122	11	5	57	79	3.97	95	.275	.318	92-0-5	.207	-0	87	-2		-0.1
1933	Bos N	18	14	.563	41	32	23-4	4	287.2	256	85	10	3	77	104	2.60	118	.245	.298	97-0-4	.309	9*	93	21		3.5
1934	Bos N	16	14	.533	40	29	20-3	5	255	249	111	13	4	83	106	3.53	108	.254	.315	96-0-2	.240	4*	114	11		1.5
1935	Bos N	5	19	.208	29	25	12	0	174.2	224	110	12	1	66	61	5.00	76	.319	.378	62	.210	-0*	81	-23		-2.6
1936	Bro N	11	13	.458	38	29	12-1	2	234	246	105	14	4	65	104	3.50	118	.268	.319	84-0-2	.190	0*	93	18		1.6
1937	Pit N	11	10	.524	33	25	7-2	2	176.1	177	73	11	2	67	74	3.11	124	.263	.332	59-0-1	.169	1	96	15		1.8
1938	Pit N	5	4	.556	24	13	5-1	0	96.1	93	44	3	0	35	38	3.46	110	.250	.314	37-0-2	.297	2	91	4		0.5
Total	11	121	146	.453	378	279	150-18	17	2268.1	2342	1084	134	35	778	877	3.86	101	.269	.332	793-0-30	.236	30	89	31		6.6

BRANDT, BILL   William George   B3.21.1915 Aurora IN   D5.16.1968 Fort Wayne IN   BR/TR/5-8.5/170   d9.20   Mil 1944-45

1941	Pit N	0	1	.000	2	0	0	0	5	5	3	0	0	3	0	3.86	94	.200	.286	1	.000	-0	71	0		0.0
1942	Pit N	1	1	.500	3	3	1	0	16.1	23	10	1	0	5	4	4.96	68	.343	.389	7	.143	-0	108	-3		-0.3
1943	Pit N	4	1	.800	29	3	0	0	57.1	57	25	3	1	19	17	3.14	111	.248	.308	7-0-1	.143	-0	65	2		0.1
Total	3	5	3	.625	34	7	1	0	80.2	85	38	4	1	27	21	3.57	97	.264	.323	15-0-1	.133	-1	84	-1		-0.2

BRANTLEY, CLIFF   Clifford   B4.12.1968 Staten Island NY   BR/TR/6-1/190*   [PhiN86 2/35]   d9.3

1991	Phi N	2	2	.500	6	5	0	0-0	31.2	26	12	0	2	19-0	25	3.41	108	.228	.341	8-0-2	.000	-1	102	1		0.1
1992	Phi N	2	6	.250	28	9	0	0-0	76.1	71	45	6	4	58-4	32	4.60	76	.251	.382	14-0-7	.214	1	137	-10		-0.9
Total	2	4	8	.333	34	14	0	0-0	108	97	57	6	6	77-4	57	4.25	84	.244	.370	22-0-9	.136	0	125	-9		-0.8

BRANTLEY, JEFF   Jeffrey Hoke   B9.5.1963 Florence AL   BR/TR/5-11/190(180-197)   [SFN85 6/134]   d8.5   Col Mississippi St.

1988	SF N	0	1	.000	9	1	0	1-0	20.2	22	13	2	1	6-1	11	5.66	58	.275	.333	2	.500	0	27	-5		-0.2
1989	†SF N	7	1	.875	59	1	0	0-1	97.1	101	50	10	2	37-8	69	4.07	83	.271	.337	12-0-3	.083	-1	52	-8		-0.7
1990	SF N★	5	3	.625	55	0	0	19-5	86.2	77	18	3	3	33-6	61	1.56	235	.240	.315	7-0-4	.286	1		20		2.7
1991	SF N	5	2	.714	67	0	0	15-4	95.1	78	27	8	5	52-10	81	2.45	146	.225	.332	3-0-1	.000	-0		13		1.2
1992	SF N	7	7	.500	56	4	0	7-2	91.2	67	32	8	3	45-5	86	2.95	113	.207	.307	9	.111	0	102	5		0.7
1993	SF N	5	6	.455	53	12	0	0-3	113.2	112	60	19	7	46-2	76	4.28	92	.259	.336	28-0-1	.107	-1	114	-5		-0.7
1994	Cin N	6	6	.500	50	0	0	15-6	65.1	46	20	6	0	28-5	63	2.48	169	.202	.288	3	.000	-0		13		2.6
1995	†Cin N	3	2	.600	56	0	0	28-4	70.1	53	22	11	1	20-3	62	2.82	148	.206	.263	3	.000	-0		11		1.5
1996	Cin N	1	2	.333	66	0	0	44-5	71	54	21	7	0	28-6	76	2.41	178	.215	.289	1-0-1	.000	-0		15	5	2.1
1997	Cin N	1	1	.500	13	0	0	1-2	11.2	9	5	2	2	7-1	16	3.86	111	.205	.340	0	—	0		0	146	0.1
1998	StL N	0	5	.000	48	0	0	14-8	50.2	40	26	12	0	18-3	48	4.44	95	.220	.289	0-0-1	—	0		-1	9	-0.1
1999	Phi N	1	2	.333	10	0	0	5-1	8.2	5	6	0	0	4-1	9	5.19	90	.161	.325	0	—	0		-1	150	-0.1
2000	Phi N	2	7	.222	55	0	0	23-5	55.1	64	36	12	2	29-0	57	5.86	78	.288	.373	0	—	0		-6	30	-1.3
2001	Tex A	0	1	.000	8	0	0	0-0	21	26	12	5	0	9-1	16	5.14	93	.310	.372	0	—	0		0		-0.1
Total	14	43	46	.483	615	18	0	172-46	859.1	754	348	105	27	366-51	728	3.39	114	.237	.319	68-0-11	.118	-2	101	52	340	7.7

BRASHEAR, KITTY   Norman C.   B8.27.1877 Mansfield OH   D12.22.1934 Los Angeles CA   BR/TR   d6.25   b-Roy

| 1899 | Lou N | 1 | 0 | 1.000 | 3 | 0 | 0 | 0 | 8 | 8 | 7 | 0 | 1 | 2 | 0 | 4.50 | 86 | .258 | .324 | 2 | .500 | 0 | | -1 | | -0.1 |

BRAUN, JOHN   John Paul   B12.26.1939 Madison WI   BR/TR/6-5/218   d10.2

| 1964 | Mil N | 0 | 0 | — | 1 | 0 | 0 | 0 | 2 | 2 | 0 | 0 | 0 | 1-0 | 1 | 0.00 | — | .286 | .375 | 0 | — | 0 | | 1 | | 0.0 |

BRAXTON, GARLAND   Edgar Garland   B6.10.1900 Snow Camp NC   D2.25.1966 Norfolk VA   BB/TL/5-11/152   d5.27

1921	Bos N	1	3	.250	17	2	0	0	37.1	44	26	0	2	17	16	4.82	76	.310	.391	7	.000	-1	0	-6		-0.7
1922	Bos N	1	2	.333	25	5	2	0	66.2	75	37	3	4	24	15	3.38	118	.286	.355	16-0-3	.063	-2	102	2		-0.1
1925	NY A	1	1	.500	3	2	0	0	19.1	26	14	1	1	5	11	6.52	65	.338	.386	6	.333	0	69	-4		-0.3
1926	NY A	5	1	.833	37	1	0	2	67.1	71	28	1	0	19	30	2.67	144	.275	.325	20	.300	1	153	8		0.7
1927	Was A	10	9	.526	58	2	0	13	155.1	144	62	5	2	33	96	2.95	138	.246	.289	39-0-3	.231	-4	41	19		2.3
1928	Was A	13	11	.542	38	24	15-2	6	218.1	177	78	7	5	44	94	2.51	160	.222	.267	72-0-5	.125	-4	88	34		3.2
1929	Was A	12	10	.545	37	20	9	4	182	219	116	6	2	51	59	4.85	88	.299	.346	54-0-5	.148	1	97	-12		-1.4
1930	Was A	3	2	.600	19	1	0	5	27.1	22	11	3	0	9	7	3.29	140	.222	.287	5-0-1	.000	-1	4	0		0.7
	Chi A	4	10	.286	19	10	2	0	90.2	127	80	9	1	33	44	6.45	72	.333	.389	23-0-1	.087	-2	69	-18		-2.4
	Year	7	12	.368	34	10	2	6	118	149	91	12	1	42	51	5.72	81	.310	.367	28-0-2	.071	-2	69	-18		-1.7
1931	Chi A	0	3	.000	11	3	1	0	47.1	71	43	1	2	7	28	6.85	62	.338	.409	11	.091	-2	99	-14		-0.8
	StL A	0	0	—	11	1	1	0	18	27	24	2	1	10	7	10.50	44	.370	.452	3	.667	1	109	-11		-0.4
1933	StL A	0	1	.000	5	1	0	0	8.1	11	9	0	3	3	35	9.72	48	.289	.426	14	.214	1	146	-4		-0.4
Total	10	50	53	.485	282	71	28-2	32	938	1014	529	28	21	276	412	4.13	101	.278	.332	257-0-18	.156	-8	88	-2		0.4

BRAZELTON, DEWON Dewon Cortez B6.16.1980 Tullahoma TN BR/TR/6-4/215* [TBA01 1/3] d9.13 Col Middle Tennessee

YEAR	TM LG	W	L	PCT	G	GS	CG-SHO	SV-BS	IP	H	R	HR	HB	BB-IB	SO	ERA	AERA	OAV	OOB	AB-HR-SH	AVG	PB	SUP	APR	DL	PW
2002	TB A	0	1	.000	2	2	0	0-0	13	12	7	3	2	6-0	5	4.85	93	.279	.392	0	—	0	51	0		0.0
2003	TB A	1	6	.143	10	10	0	0-0	48.1	57	49	9	3	23-1	24	6.89	67	.292	.372	1	.000	-0	86	-16		-1.9
2004	TB A	6	8	.429	22	21	0	0-0	120.2	121	71	12	11	53-2	64	4.77	98	.346		1	.000	-0	79	-1		-0.2
2005	TB A	1	8	.111	20	8	0	0-1	71	87	65	12	4	60-3	43	7.61	57	.307	.431	0	—	0	54	-25		-2.6
Total 4		8	23	.258	54	41	0	0-1	253	277	192	36	20	142-6	136	5.98	76	.281	.379	2	.000	-0	75	-42		-4.7

BRAZLE, AL Alpha Eugene "Cotton" B10.19.1913 Loyal OK D10.24.1973 Grand Junction CO BL/TL/6-2/185* d7.25 Mil 1944-45

YEAR	TM LG	W	L	PCT	G	GS	CG-SHO	SV-BS	IP	H	R	HR	HB	BB-IB	SO	ERA	AERA	OAV	OOB	AB-HR-SH	AVG	PB	SUP	APR	DL	PW
1943	†StL N	8	2	.800	13	9	8-1	0	88	74	18	0	0	29	26	1.53	219	.231	.295	32	.281	2	106	18		2.4
1946	†StL N	11	10	.524	37	15	6-2	0	153.1	152	69	1	2	55	85	3.29	105	.261	.327	52-0-2	.212	-0	119	1		0.1
1947	StL N	14	8	.636	44	19	7	4	168	186	65	7	2	48	85	2.84	146	.284	.335	64-0-3	.219	1	113	22		3.0
1948	StL N	10	6	.625	42	23	6-2	1	156.1	171	77	8	0	50	55	3.80	108	.281	.335	55	.145	-2*	96	3		0.2
1949	StL N	14	8	.636	39	25	9-1	0	206.1	208	85	18	6	61	75	3.18	131	.263	.321	82-0-1	.134	-4	119	21		1.6
1950	StL N	11	9	.550	46	12	3	6	164.2	188	81	12	4	80	47	4.10	105	.296	.378	61	.213	-1*	91	5		0.5
1951	StL N	6	5	.545	56	8	5	7	154.1	139	61	13	5	60	66	3.09	128	.245	.322	46	.109	-3	81	14		0.6
1952	StL N	12	5	.706	46	6	3-1	16	109.1	75	38	2	1	42	55	2.72	137	.198	.280	32-0-1	.125	-1	88	12		2.0
1953	StL N	6	7	.462	60	0	0	18	92	101	47	8	2	43	57	4.21	101	.280	.360	15-0-2	.333	1		1		0.3
1954	StL N	5	4	.556	58	0	0	8	84.1	93	48	10	3	24	30	4.16	99	.288	.339	14	.000	-2		-2		-0.4
Total 10		97	64	.602	441	117	47-7	60	1376.2	1387	589	83	25	492	554	3.31	120	.266	.332	453-0-9	.177	-9	105	95		10.3

BRAZOBAN, YHENCY Yhency Jose B6.11.1980 Santo Domingo, D.R. BR/TR/6-1/170* d8.5

YEAR	TM LG	W	L	PCT	G	GS	CG-SHO	SV-BS	IP	H	R	HR	HB	BB-IB	SO	ERA	AERA	OAV	OOB	AB-HR-SH	AVG	PB	SUP	APR	DL	PW
2004	†LA N	6	2	.750	31	0	0	0-0	32.2	25	9	2	0	15-2	27	2.48	167	.219	.310	1	.000	-0		7		1.3
2005	LA N	4	10	.286	74	0	0	21-6	72.2	70	46	11	5	32-4	61	5.33	77	.258	.345	2	.000	-0		-10		-2.0
Total 2		10	12	.455	105	0	0	21-6	105.1	95	55	13	5	47-6	88	4.44	92	.247	.335	3	.000	-0		-3		-0.7

BREA, LESLI Lesli Guillermo B10.12.1973 San Pedro de Macoris, D.R. BR/TR/5-10/170* d8.13

YEAR	TM LG	W	L	PCT	G	GS	CG-SHO	SV-BS	IP	H	R	HR	HB	BB-IB	SO	ERA	AERA	OAV	OOB	AB-HR-SH	AVG	PB	SUP	APR	DL	PW
2000	Bal A	0	1	.000	6	1	0	0-0	9	12	11	1	1	10-0	5	11.00	43	.324	.469	0	—	0	100	-6		-0.6
2001	Bal A	0	0	—	2	0	0	0-0	2	6	4	2	0	3-0	0	18.00	24	.545	.643	0	—	0		-3		-0.1
Total 2		0	1	.000	8	1	0	0-0	11	18	15	3	1	13-0	5	12.27	38	.375	.508	0	—	0	100	-9		-0.7

BRECHEEN, HARRY Harry David "Harry the Cat" B10.14.1914 Broken Bow OK D1.17.2004 Bethany OK BL/TL/5-10/160* d4.22 C14 Col East Central

YEAR	TM LG	W	L	PCT	G	GS	CG-SHO	SV-BS	IP	H	R	HR	HB	BB-IB	SO	ERA	AERA	OAV	OOB	AB-HR-SH	AVG	PB	SUP	APR	DL	PW
1940	StL N	0	0	—	3	0	0	0	3.1	2	1	0	0	4	4	0.00	—	.167	.286	0	—	0		1		0.1
1943	†StL N	9	6	.600	29	13	8-1	4	135.1	98	41	4	3	39	68	2.26	149	.206	.270	42-0-4	.190	1	97	16		2.0
1944	†StL N	16	5	.762	30	22	13-3	0	189.1	174	67	8	3	46	88	2.85	124	.242	.290	68-0-4	.162	1*	125	16		1.7
1945	StL N	15	4	.789	24	18	13-3	2	157.1	136	48	5	5	44	63	2.52	149	.238	.298	57-0-2	.123	-1	97	23		2.5
1946	†StL N	15	15	.500	36	30	14-5	3	231.1	212	73	8	4	67	117	2.49	139	.244	.316	83-0-1	.133	-3*	78	25		3.1
1947	StL N★	16	11	.593	29	28	18-1	1	223.1	220	92	20	3	66	89	3.30	125	.260	.316	83-0-4	.241	-5	109	21		2.9
1948	StL N☆	20	7	.741	33	30	21-7	1	233.1	193	62	6	2	49	149	2.24	183	.222	.265	82-0-2	.146	-1	98	47		5.3
1949	StL N	14	11	.560	32	31	14-2	1	214.2	207	96	18	7	65	88	3.35	124	.252	.312	77-0-3	.273	5	94	17		2.3
1950	StL N	8	11	.421	27	23	12-2	1	163.1	151	77	18	3	45	80	3.80	113	.244	.298	58-1-0	.241	3	95	9		1.2
1951	StL N	8	4	.667	24	16	5	2	138.2	134	54	11	1	54	57	3.25	112	.256	.327	55-1-1	.218	2	97	12		1.1
1952	StL N	7	5	.583	25	13	4-1	2	100.1	82	39	12	3	28	54	3.32	112	.223	.283	29-0-1	.207	1	109	6		1.0
1953	StL A	5	13	.278	26	16	3	1	117.1	122	51	7	3	31	44	2.92	133	.269	.320	39-0-2	.179	-1*	41	12		1.7
Total 12		133	92	.591	318	240	125-25	18	1907.2	1731	701	117	37	536	901	2.92	133	.242	.298	673-2-24	.192	11	95	205		24.9

BRECKINRIDGE, BILL William Robertson B10.16.1907 Tulsa OK D8.23.1958 Tulsa OK BR/TR/5-11/175 d6.30 Col Dartmouth

YEAR	TM LG	W	L	PCT	G	GS	CG-SHO	SV-BS	IP	H	R	HR	HB	BB-IB	SO	ERA	AERA	OAV	OOB	AB-HR-SH	AVG	PB	SUP	APR	DL	PW
1929	Phi A	0	0	—	3	0	0	0	10	10	10	0	0	16	2	8.10	52	.270	.491	4	.000	-1	199	-4		-0.3

BREINING, FRED Fred Lawrence B11.15.1955 San Francisco CA BR/TR/6-4/185* [PitN74*3/57] d9.4 Col San Mateo (CA) [JC]

YEAR	TM LG	W	L	PCT	G	GS	CG-SHO	SV-BS	IP	H	R	HR	HB	BB-IB	SO	ERA	AERA	OAV	OOB	AB-HR-SH	AVG	PB	SUP	APR	DL	PW
1980	SF N	0	0	—	5	0	0	0-0	6.2	4	4	0	0	4-1	3	5.40	65	.333	.448	0	—	0		-1		-0.1
1981	SF N	5	2	.714	45	1	0	1-0	77.2	66	28	4	2	38-8	37	2.55	134	.243	.334	11-0-1	.000	-1	104	6		0.4
1982	SF N	11	6	.647	54	9	2	0-1	143.1	146	61	6	1	52-10	98	3.08	116	.269	.333	29-0-5	.207	1	109	6		0.9
1983	SF N	11	12	.478	32	32	6	0-0	202.2	202	97	15	5	60-11	117	3.82	93	.259	.322	67-0-5	.149	1	108	-5		-0.5
1984	Mon N	0	0	—	4	0	0	0-0	6.2	4	1	0	0	5-0	5	1.35	256	.190	.346	1	.000	-0	109	8	139	0.8
Total 5		27	20	.574	140	42	8	1-1	437	426	191	25	9	159-30	260	3.34	106	.260	.325	108-0-11	.148	1	109	8	139	0.8

BREITENSTEIN, ALONZO Alonzo B11.9.1857 Utica NY D6.19.1932 Utica NY d7.7

YEAR	TM LG	W	L	PCT	G	GS	CG-SHO	SV-BS	IP	H	R	HR	HB	BB-IB	SO	ERA	AERA	OAV	OOB	AB-HR-SH	AVG	PB	SUP	APR	DL	PW
1883	Phi N	0	1	.000	1	1	0	0	5	9	8	0	0	2	0	9.00	34	.320	.370	2	.000	-0	69	-3		-0.5

BREITENSTEIN, TED Theodore P. "Theo" B6.1.1869 St.Louis MO D5.3.1935 St.Louis MO BL/TL/5-9/167 d4.28

YEAR	TM LG	W	L	PCT	G	GS	CG-SHO	SV-BS	IP	H	R	HR	HB	BB-IB	SO	ERA	AERA	OAV	OOB	AB-HR-SH	AVG	PB	SUP	APR	DL	PW
1891	StL AA	2	0	1.000	6	1	1-1	1	28.2	15	14	2	0	14	13	2.20	191	.150	.254	12	.000	-2	118	5		0.2
1892	StL N	9	19	.321	39	32	28-1	0	282.1	280	192	8	6	148	126	4.69	68	.248	.339	131	.122	-3*	88	-40		-3.7
1893	StL N	19	24	.442	48	42	38-1	1	382.2	359	197	8	8	156	102	3.18	149	.241	.316	160-1	.181	-5*	78	68		5.6
1894	StL N	27	23	.540	56	50	46-1	0	447.1	497	320	21	11	191	140	4.79	113	.278	.352	182-0-9	.220	-1*	82	35		2.1
1895	StL N	19	30	.388	55	51	47-1	0	438.2	468	299	6	14	182	131	4.37	111	.269	.343	221-0-2	.190	-7*	92	22		1.2
1896	StL N	18	26	.409	44	43	37-1	0	339.2	376	236	12	5	138	114	4.48	97	.278	.341	162-0-7	.259	3*	81	-6		-0.2
1897	Cin N	23	12	.657	40	39	32-2	0	320.1	345	172	9	9	91	98	3.62	126	.273	.326	124-0-4	.266	1*	96	31		2.8
1898	Cin N	20	14	.588	39	37	32-3	0	315.2	313	170	2	11	123	68	3.42	112	.257	.330	121-0-5	.215	1*	98	12		1.1
1899	Cin N	13	9	.591	26	24	21	0	210.2	219	111	2	9	71	59	3.65	101	.272	.352	126-2-1	.190	-0*	106	-1		0.0
1900	Cin N	10	10	.500	24	20	18-1	0	192.1	205	111	4	14	79	39					6	.333	0	149	-10		-1.7
1901	StL N	0	3	.000	9	5	1	0	15	24	20	1	1	8	3	6.60	48	.358	.469				89	125		10.5
Total 11		160	170	.485	380	342	301-12	3	2973.1	3101	1848	79	87	1207	893	4.03	109	.265	.338	1350-4-32	.216	-4	89	125		10.5

BRENNAN, AD Addison Foster B7.18.1881 LaHarpe KS D1.7.1962 Kansas City MO BL/TL/5-11/170 d5.19

YEAR	TM LG	W	L	PCT	G	GS	CG-SHO	SV-BS	IP	H	R	HR	HB	BB-IB	SO	ERA	AERA	OAV	OOB	AB-HR-SH	AVG	PB	SUP	APR	DL	PW
1910	Phi N	2	0	1.000	19	5	2	0	73.1	72	36	2	3	28	28	2.33	134	.264	.339	25	.280	1*	162	2		0.2
1911	Phi N	2	1	.667	5	3	1	0	22.2	22	12	0	1	12	12	3.57	96	.259	.357	9-0-1	.222	-0	124	0		0.1
1912	Phi N	11	9	.550	27	19	13-1	2	174	185	88	4	3	49	78	2.39	139	.268	.314	59-1-2	.254	4	106	4		0.5
1913	Phi N	14	12	.538	40	24	12-1	1	207	204	76	5	6	46	94	3.57	74	.256	.305	32-0-2	.250	1	96	-9		-0.7
1914	Chi F	5	5	.500	16	11	5-1	0	85.2	84	44	7	2	21	31	3.74	67	.287	.346	27-0-3	.185	0*	86	-15		-1.1
1915	Chi F	3	9	.250	19	13	7-2	0	106	117	55	4	7	30	40	5.06	54	.241	.371	1	.000	-0	110	-1		-0.1
1918	Was A	0	0	—	2	1	0	0	5.1	7	4	0	1	5	0					1	.000	-0	0	0		0.0
	Cle A	0	0	—	1	0	0	0	3	3	1	0	0	3	0	3.00	100	.333	.500	1	.000	-0	107	-1		0.0
	Year	0	0	—	3	1	0	0	8.1	10	5	0	1	8	0	4.32	65	.263	.404	1	.000	-0	107	-1		0.0
Total 7		37	36	.507	129	76	40-5	3	677	694	316	22	23	194	283	3.11	102	.270	.327	220-1-11	.218	4	103	-1		0.0

BRENNAN, DON James Donald B12.2.1903 Augusta ME D4.26.1953 Boston MA BR/TR/6-0/210 d4.16 Col Georgetown

YEAR	TM LG	W	L	PCT	G	GS	CG-SHO	SV-BS	IP	H	R	HR	HB	BB-IB	SO	ERA	AERA	OAV	OOB	AB-HR-SH	AVG	PB	SUP	APR	DL	PW
1933	NY N	5	1	.833	18	10	3	3	85	92	56	4	0	46	46	4.98	78	.275	.365	27-0-3	.259	2	193	-12		-0.5
1934	Cin N	4	3	.571	28	7	2	2	78	89	51	3	1	35	31	3.81	107	.290	.364	22-0-1	.227	0	109	-2		-0.2
1935	Cin N	5	5	.500	38	5	2-1	5	114.1	101	43	4	4	44	48	3.15	126	.242	.320	30	.100	-1	115	13		0.9
1936	Cin N	5	2	.714	41	4	0	7	94.1	117	60	2	1	35	40	4.39	87	.305	.364	25-0-2	.080	-1	105	-9		-1.0
1937	Cin N	1	1	.500	10	0	0	0	16	25	14	1	0	10	6	6.75	55	.347	.427	5	.000	-0		-6		-0.5
	†NY N	1	0	1.000	6	0	0	0	9.1	12	8	0	1	9	1	6.75	58	.316	.458	1	.000	0		-3		
	Year	2	1	.667	16	0	0	0	25.1	37	22	1	1	19	7	6.75	56	.336	.438	6	.000	-1	142	-19		-1.1
Total 5		21	12	.636	141	26	7-1	19	397	436	232	14	7	180	172	4.19	94	.281	.358	110-0-6	.155	-0	142	-19		

BRENNAN, TOM Thomas Martin B10.30.1952 Chicago IL BR/TR/6-1/180* [CleA74 1/4] d9.5 Col Lewis

YEAR	TM LG	W	L	PCT	G	GS	CG-SHO	SV-BS	IP	H	R	HR	HB	BB-IB	SO	ERA	AERA	OAV	OOB	AB-HR-SH	AVG	PB	SUP	APR	DL	PW
1981	Cle A	2	2	.500	7	6	1	0-0	48.1	49	20	5	0	14-1	15	3.17	116	.259	.310	0	—	0	89	2		0.1
1982	Cle A	4	2	.667	30	4	1	2-2	92.2	112	51	9	2	10-1	46	4.27	97	.300	.317	0	—	0	66	-2		-0.2
1983	Cle A	2	2	.500	11	5	1-1	0-0	39.2	45	22	3	1	8-1	21	3.86	111	.288	.323	0	—	0	98	0		0.1
1984	Chi A	0	1	.000	4	1	0	0-0	6.2	8	5	1	0	3-0	3	4.05	103	.308	.379	0	—	0	22	-1		-0.1
1985	LA N	1	3	.250	12	4	0	2-1	31.2	41	26	2	2	11-4	17	7.39	47	.333	.374	8-0-1	.125	-0	69	-12		-0.8
Total 5		9	10	.474	64	20	2-1	2-1	219	255	124	20	3	46-7	102	4.40	90	.294	.327	8-0-1	.125	-0	78	-13		

BRENNAN, WILLIAM William Raymond B1.15.1963 Tampa FL BR/TR/6-3/185(185-200) d7.19 Col Mercer

YEAR	TM LG	W	L	PCT	G	GS	CG-SHO	SV-BS	IP	H	R	HR	HB	BB-IB	SO	ERA	AERA	OAV	OOB	AB-HR-SH	AVG	PB	SUP	APR	DL	PW
1988	LA N	0	1	.000	2	1	0	0-0	9.1	13	7	0	0	6-1	7	6.75	50	.342	.432	2	.000	-0	106	-3		-0.4
1993	Chi N	2	1	.667	8	1	0	0-0	15	16	8	2	1	8-1	11	4.20	96	.291	.385	1-0-1	.000	-0	0	0		0.1
Total 2		2	2	.500	12	3	0	0-0	24.1	29	15	2	1	14-2	18	5.18	73	.312	.404	3-0-1	.000	-0	63	-3		

YEAR TM LG	W	L	PCT	G	GS	CG-SHO	SV-BS	IP	H	R	HR	HB	BB-IB	SO	ERA	AERA	OAV	OOB	AB-HR-SH	AVG	PB	SUP	APR	DL	PW

BRENNEMAN, JIM James Leroy B2.13.1941 San Diego CA D3.10.1994 Pearl MS BR/TR/6-2/180 d7.9 Col Mesa St.

YEAR TM LG	W	L	PCT	G	GS	CG-SHO	SV-BS	IP	H	R	HR	HB	BB-IB	SO	ERA	AERA	OAV	OOB	AB-HR-SH	AVG	PB	SUP	APR	DL	PW
1965 NY A	0	0	—	3	0	0	0	2	5	5	1	0	3-0	2	18.00	19	.455	.571	0	—	0		-4		-0.2

BRENNER, BERT Delbert Henry "Dutch" B7.18.1887 Minneapolis MN D4.11.1971 St.Louis Park MN BR/TR/6-0/175 d9.21

YEAR TM LG	W	L	PCT	G	GS	CG-SHO	SV-BS	IP	H	R	HR	HB	BB-IB	SO	ERA	AERA	OAV	OOB	AB-HR-SH	AVG	PB	SUP	APR	DL	PW
1912 Cle A	1	0	1.000	2	1	1	0	13	14	8	0	0	4	3	2.77	123	.286	.340	5	.000	-1	108	0		-0.1

BRENTON, LYNN Lynn Davis "Buck","Herb" B10.7.1890 Peoria IL D10.14.1968 Los Angeles CA BR/TR/5-10/165 d8.10

YEAR TM LG	W	L	PCT	G	GS	CG-SHO	SV-BS	IP	H	R	HR	HB	BB-IB	SO	ERA	AERA	OAV	OOB	AB-HR-SH	AVG	PB	SUP	APR	DL	PW
1913 Cle A	0	0	—	1	0	0	0	4	2	0	0	0	0	2	9.00	34	.400	.400	0	—	0		-1		-0.1
1915 Cle A	2	3	.400	11	5	1-1	0	51	60	31	1	2	20	18	3.35	91	.308	.378	17	.118	-1	62	-3		-0.5
1920 Cin N	2	1	.667	5	1	1	1	18.1	17	14	0	0	4	13	4.91	62	.236	.276	8	.250	-0	181	-4		-0.6
1921 Cin N	1	8	.111	17	8	2	1	60	80	35	0	1	17	19	4.05	88	.342	.389	15-0-3	.133	-0	60	-4		-0.4
Total 4	5	12	.294	34	14	4-1	2	131.1	161	82	1	3	41	52	3.97	83	.315	.369	40-0-3	.150	-1	69	-12		-1.6

BRESLOW, CRAIG Craig Andrew B8.8.1980 New Haven CT BL/TL/6-1/180 d7.23 Col Yale

YEAR TM LG	W	L	PCT	G	GS	CG-SHO	SV-BS	IP	H	R	HR	HB	BB-IB	SO	ERA	AERA	OAV	OOB	AB-HR-SH	AVG	PB	SUP	APR	DL	PW
2005 SD N	0	0	—	14	0	0	0-0	16.1	15	6	1	1	13-0	14	2.20	175	.238	.372	1	.000	-0		2		0.1

BRESNAHAN, ROGER Roger Philip "The Duke of Tralee" B6.11.1879 Toledo OH D12.4.1944 Toledo OH BR/TR/5-9/200 d8.27 M5/C6 HF1945 ▲

YEAR TM LG	W	L	PCT	G	GS	CG-SHO	SV-BS	IP	H	R	HR	HB	BB-IB	SO	ERA	AERA	OAV	OOB	AB-HR-SH	AVG	PB	SUP	APR	DL	PW
1897 Was N	4	0	1.000	6	5	3-1	0	41	52	21	1	3	10	12	3.95	110	.306	.355	16	.375	1	112	4		0.4
1901 Bal A	1	0	1.000	2	1	0	0	6	10	8	0	0	4	3	6.00	64	.370	.452	295-1-4	.268	0*	105	-2		-0.2
1910 StL N	0	0	—	1	0	0	0	3.1	6	1	0	0	1	0	0.00	—	.400	.438	234-0-8	.278	0*				
Total 3	4	1	.800	9	6	3-1	0	50.1	68	30	1	3	15	15	3.93	107	.321	.374	545-1-12	.275	2	113	3		0.3

BRESSLER, RUBE Raymond Bloom B10.23.1894 Coder PA D11.7.1966 Cincinnati OH BR/TL/6-0/187 d4.24 Mil 1918 ▲

YEAR TM LG	W	L	PCT	G	GS	CG-SHO	SV-BS	IP	H	R	HR	HB	BB-IB	SO	ERA	AERA	OAV	OOB	AB-HR-SH	AVG	PB	SUP	APR	DL	PW
1914 Phi A	10	4	.714	29	10	8-1	2	147.2	112	37	1	4	56	96	1.77	148	.220	.302	51-0-2	.216	4	165	14		1.7
1915 Phi A	4	17	.190	32	20	7-1	0	178.1	183	133	3	7	118	69	5.20	56	.283	.399	55-1-3	.145	1*	87	-42		-4.2
1916 Phi A	0	2	.000	4	2	0	0	15	16	11	0	2	14	8	6.60	43	.296	.457	5-0-1	.200	1	79	-5		-0.6
1917 Cin N	0	0	—	2	1	0	0	9	15	11	0	0	5	2	6.00	44	.429	.500	5	.200	-0*	259	-4		-0.2
1918 Cin N	8	5	.615	17	13	10	0	128	124	48	3	1	39	37	2.46	108	.261	.318	62-0-1	.274	4*	129	2		0.9
1919 Cin N	2	4	.333	13	4	1	0	41.2	37	19	1	0	8	13	3.46	80	.248	.287	165-2-7	.206	2*	65	-3		-0.3
1920 Cin N	2	0	1.000	10	2	1-1	0	20.1	24	8	0	0	2	4	1.77	172	.300	.317	30-0-1	.267	0*	142	-2		0.2
Total 7	26	32	.448	107	52	27-3	2	540	511	267	8	14	242	229	3.40	81	.262	.348	373-3-15	.214	12	115	-36		-2.5

BRETT, HERB Herbert James "Duke" B5.23.1900 Lawrenceville VA D11.25.1974 St.Petersburg FL BR/TR/6-0/175 d8.8

YEAR TM LG	W	L	PCT	G	GS	CG-SHO	SV-BS	IP	H	R	HR	HB	BB-IB	SO	ERA	AERA	OAV	OOB	AB-HR-SH	AVG	PB	SUP	APR	DL	PW
1924 Chi N	0	0	—	1	1	0	0	5.1	6	4	0	0	7	1	5.06	77	.300	.481	2	.000	-0	217	-1		-0.1
1925 Chi N	1	1	.500	10	1	0	0	17.1	12	7	0	1	3	6	3.63	119	.194	.242	1	.000	-0	20	2		0.2
Total 2	1	1	.500	11	2	0	0	22.2	18	11	0	1	10	7	3.97	106	.220	.312	3	.000	-0	110	1		0.1

BRETT, KEN Kenneth Alven B9.18.1948 Brooklyn NY D11.18.2003 Spokane WA BL/TL/5-11/195(180-195) [BosA66 1/4] d9.27 b-George

YEAR TM LG	W	L	PCT	G	GS	CG-SHO	SV-BS	IP	H	R	HR	HB	BB-IB	SO	ERA	AERA	OAV	OOB	AB-HR-SH	AVG	PB	SUP	APR	DL	PW
1967 †Bos A	0	0	—	1	0	0	0	2	3	1	0	0	0-0	2	4.50	77	.375	.375	0	—	0		0		0.0
1969 Bos A	2	3	.400	8	8	0	0-0	39.1	41	24	6	3	22-1	23	5.26	73	.275	.377	10-1-2	.300	2	101	-5		-0.4
1970 Bos A	8	9	.471	41	14	1	2-0	139.1	118	71	17	3	79-6	155	4.07	98	.223	.327	41-2-1	.317	6	101	-1		0.6
1971 Bos A	0	3	.000	29	2	0	1-0	59	57	38	7	1	35-6	57	5.34	70	.253	.356	10-0-1	.200	-0	36	-10		-0.5
1972 Mil A	7	12	.368	26	22	2-1	0-0	133	121	76	13	1	49-9	74	4.53	68	.242	.310	44-0-1	.227	2*	93	-22	24	-2.9
1973 Phi N	13	9	.591	31	25	10-1	0-0	211.2	206	91	19	0	74-12	111	3.44	111	.259	.320	80-4-0	.250	8*	120	8		1.9
1974 †Pit N★	13	9	.591	27	27	10-3	0-0	191	192	81	9	2	52-9	96	3.30	106	.257	.306	87-2-3	.310	11*	142	4		1.6
1975 †Pit N	9	5	.643	23	16	4-1	0-0	118	110	47	10	2	43-5	47	3.36	107	.250	.318	52-1-1	.231	4*	101	5	30	1.0
1976 NY A	0	0	—	2	0	0	1-0	2.1	2	0	0	0	0-0	1	0.00	—	.222	.222	0	—	0		1		0.1
Chi A	10	12	.455	27	26	16-1	1-0	200.2	171	82	5	8	76-3	91	3.32	107	.234	.305	12	.083	-1*	85	5		0.5
Year	10	12	.455	29	26	16-1	2-0	203	173	82	5	8	76-3	92	3.28	109	.233	.304	12	.083	-1	85	7		0.6
1977 Chi A	6	4	.600	13	13	2	0-0	82.2	101	47	10	1	15-0	39	5.01	82	.305	.334	0	—	0	151	-6		-0.7
Cal A	7	10	.412	21	21	5	0-0	142	157	73	15	3	38-0	41	4.25	93	.287	.334	0	—	0	88	-3		-0.2
Year	13	14	.481	34	34	7	0-0	224.2	258	120	25	4	53-0	80	4.53	88	.294	.334	0	—	0*	113	-10		-0.9
1978 Cal A	3	5	.375	34	10	1-1	1-1	100	100	60	12	1	42-5	43	4.95	73	.262	.335	0	—	0	94	-14		-1.0
1979 Min A	0	0	—	9	0	0	0-1	12.2	16	7	1	0	6-0	3	4.97	88	.320	.393	0	—	0		-1		0.0
LA N	4	3	.571	30	0	0	2-1	47	52	20	1	1	12-2	13	3.45	105	.277	.322	11	.273	1		1		0.3
1980 KC A	0	0	—	5	0	0	1-0	13.1	8	0	0	1	5-0	4	0.00	—	.174	.269	0	—	0		6		0.3
1981 KC A	1	1	.500	22	0	0	2-0	32.1	35	16	2	1	14-4	7	4.18	87	.282	.355	0	—	0		-2		0.3
Total 14	83	85	.494	349	184	51-8	11-3	1526.1	1490	734	127	23	562-62	807	3.93	94	.257	.323	347-10-9	.262	32	107	-34	54	0.5

BREUER, MARV Marvin Howard "Baby Face" B4.29.1914 Rolla MO D1.17.1991 Rolla MO BR/TR/6-2/185 d5,4

YEAR TM LG	W	L	PCT	G	GS	CG-SHO	SV-BS	IP	H	R	HR	HB	BB-IB	SO	ERA	AERA	OAV	OOB	AB-HR-SH	AVG	PB	SUP	APR	DL	PW
1939 NY A	0	0	—	1	0	0	0	1	2	1	0	1	0	0	9.00	48	.667	.750	0	—	0		0		0.0
1940 NY A	8	9	.471	27	22	10	0	164	175	89	20	0	61	71	4.55	89	.267	.329	54-0-6	.037	-5	123	-8		-1.2
1941 †NY A	9	7	.563	26	18	7-1	2	141	131	73	10	2	49	77	4.09	96	.243	.308	46-0-4	.087	-3	99	-2		-0.6
1942 †NY A	8	9	.471	27	19	6	1	164.1	157	67	11	1	37	72	3.07	112	.252	.295	54-0-5	.056	-3	89	6		0.1
1943 NY A	0	1	.000	5	1	0	0	14	22	16	0	0	6	6	8.36	39	.349	.406	3	.333	1	79	-8		-0.5
Total 5	25	26	.490	86	60	23-1	3	484.1	487	246	41	3	154	226	4.03	94	.258	.315	157-0-15	.064	-11	105	-12		-2.2

BREWER, JACK Jack Herndon "Buddy" B7.21.1919 Los Angeles CA D11.30.2003 Sun City CA BR/TR/6-2/170 d7.15 Col USC

YEAR TM LG	W	L	PCT	G	GS	CG-SHO	SV-BS	IP	H	R	HR	HB	BB-IB	SO	ERA	AERA	OAV	OOB	AB-HR-SH	AVG	PB	SUP	APR	DL	PW
1944 NY N	1	4	.200	14	7	2	0	55	56	40	8	3	16	21	5.56	66	.288	.343	19	.211	-0	85	-11		-0.9
1945 NY N	8	6	.571	28	21	8	0	159.2	162	77	14	3	58	49	3.83	102	.260	.326	56-0-7	.179	-1	97	1		-0.1
1946 NY N	0	0	—	1	0	0	0	2	3	3	0	0	2	3	13.50	25	.333	.455	0	—	0		-2		-0.1
Total 3	9	10	.474	43	28	10	0	216.2	231	120	22	6	76	73	4.36	88	.268	.332	75-0-7	.187	-1	94	-12		-1.1

BREWER, JIM James Thomas B11.17.1937 Merced CA D11.16.1987 Tyler TX BL/TL/6-2/195* d7.17 C3

YEAR TM LG	W	L	PCT	G	GS	CG-SHO	SV-BS	IP	H	R	HR	HB	BB-IB	SO	ERA	AERA	OAV	OOB	AB-HR-SH	AVG	PB	SUP	APR	DL	PW
1960 Chi N	0	3	.000	9	4	0	0	21.2	25	14	2	1	6-2	7	5.82	65	.272	.323	6	.167	0*	47	-4	58	-0.5
1961 Chi N	1	7	.125	36	11	0	0	86.2	116	65	17	1	21-2	57	5.82	72	.321	.358	22-0-1	.182	0	114	-15		-1.3
1962 Chi N	0	1	.000	6	1	0	0	5.2	10	6	2	0	3-0	1	9.53	44	.435	.500	—		0	169	-3		-0.4
1963 Chi N	3	2	.600	29	1	0	0	49.2	59	32	10	0	15-0	35	4.89	72	.294	.339	6-0-1	.000	0	49	-7		-0.8
1964 LA N	3	4	.571	34	5	1-1	1	93	79	33	5	0	25-5	63	3.00	108	.232	.282	22	.273	1	130	4		0.4
1965 †LA N	3	2	.600	19	2	0	2	49.1	33	13	1	0	28-4	31	1.82	179	.196	.311	10	.000	-1*	80	8	43	0.8
1966 †LA N	0	2	.000	13	0	0	2	22	17	9	0	0	11-0	8	3.68	90	.221	.315	—		0		0		0.0
1967 LA N	5	4	.556	30	11	0	1	100.2	78	32	8	1	31-7	74	2.68	116	.218	.281	22-0-1	.045	-1	85	4		0.8
1968 LA N	8	3	.727	54	0	0	14	76	59	22	5	0	33-13	75	2.49	111	.219	.303	9-0-1	.222	0		4		0.8
1969 LA N	7	6	.538	59	0	0	20-10	88.1	71	30	5	4	41-6	92	2.55	132	.221	.316	11	.091	-0		4		1.5
1970 LA N	7	6	.538	58	0	0	24-5	89	66	36	10	0	33-9	91	3.13	123	.207	.280	12-0-1	.083	-1		7		1.2
1971 LA N	6	5	.545	55	0	0	22-5	81.1	55	17	4	0	24-5	66	1.88	173	.194	.254	4	.333	1		14		3.3
1972 LA N	8	7	.533	51	0	0	17-7	78.1	41	16	6	2	25-11	69	1.26	266	.157	.233	1	.000	0		18		4.0
1973 LA N★	6	8	.429	56	0	0	20-8	71.2	58	26	8	0	25-9	56	3.01	116	.229	.293	5-0-2	.400	1		5		1.0
1974 †LA N	4	4	.500	24	0	0	0-2	39.1	29	14	0	4	10-1	26	2.52	136	.207	.258	2	.000	-0		4	49	0.7
1975 LA N	3	1	.750	21	0	0	2-2	33	44	20	2	1	12-2	21	5.18	66	.333	.380	3	.000	-0		-6		-0.8
Cal A	1	0	1.000	21	0	0	5-1	34.2	38	9	2	0	11-1	22	1.82	197	.279	.325	0	—	0		7		0.4
1976 Cal A	3	1	.750	12	0	0	2-3	20	20	7	0	0	6-0	16	2.70	124	.256	.306	0	—	0		7		0.4
Total 17	69	65	.515	584	35	1-1	132-43	1509.1	898	401	92	0	360-77	810	3.07	111	.236	.300	140-0-7	.150	1	103	51	276	10.7

BREWER, TOM Thomas Austin B9.3.1931 Wadesboro NC BR/TR/6-1/175* d4.18 Col Elon

YEAR TM LG	W	L	PCT	G	GS	CG-SHO	SV-BS	IP	H	R	HR	HB	BB-IB	SO	ERA	AERA	OAV	OOB	AB-HR-SH	AVG	PB	SUP	APR	DL	PW
1954 Bos A	10	9	.526	33	23	7	0	162.2	152	90	15	7	95	69	4.65	88	.249	.355	60-0-2	.267	3*	123	-6		-0.5
1955 Bos A	11	10	.524	31	28	9-2	0	192.2	198	101	21	8	87-3	91	4.20	102	.263	.344	73-0-3	.151	-2*	121	2		0.2
1956 Bos A★	19	9	.679	32	32	15-4	0	244.1	200	103	14	5	112-6	127	3.50	132	.220	.307	94-1-1	.298	4*	98	30		3.9
1957 Bos A	16	13	.552	32	32	15-2	0	238.1	225	113	24	5	93-9	128	3.85	103	.250	.324	94-0-4	.202	-1*	119	4		0.3
1958 Bos A	12	12	.500	33	32	10-1	0	227.1	227	122	23	8	93-2	124	3.72	108	.259	.333	82-0-3	.195	-0*	111	1		0.3
1959 Bos A	10	12	.455	36	32	11-3	0	215.1	219	96	14	2	83-2	121	3.76	108	.265	.336	72-1-7	.111	-4*	103	8		0.6
1960 Bos A	10	15	.400	34	29	8-1	0	186.2	220	115	13	6	72-5	60	4.82	84	.301	.364	62-1-3	.194	0*	92	-17		-1.9
1961 Bos A	3	2	.600	10	9	0	0	42	37	21	4	0	29-0	13	3.43	122	.242	.357	14	.286	1*	85	2	90	0.4
Total 8	91	82	.526	241	217	75-13	0	1509.1	1478	761	126	43	669-30	733	4.00	104	.257	.337	551-3-23	.207	1	108	24	90	3.6

YEAR	TM LG	W	L	PCT	G	GS	CG-SHO	SV-BS	IP	H	R	HR	HB	BB-IB	SO	ERA	AERA	OAV	OOB	AB-HR-SH	AVG	PB	SUP	APR	DL	PW
BREWER, BILLY	William Robert B4.15.1968 Fort Worth TX BL/TL/6-1/175(175-200) [MonN90 28/751] d4.8 Col Dallas Baptist																								
1993	KC A	2	2	.500	46	0	0	0-2	39	31	16	6	0	20-4	28	3.46	133	.230	.327	0	—	0	5		0.4
1994	KC A	4	1	.800	50	0	0	3-4	38.2	28	11	4	2	16-1	25	2.56	196	.207	.297	0	—	0	11		1.3
1995	KC A	2	4	.333	48	0	0	0-4	45.1	54	28	9	2	20-1	31	5.56	86	.290	.365	0	—	0	-3		-0.3
1996	NY A	1	0	1.000	4	0	0	0-0	5.2	7	6	0	0	8-0	8	9.53	52	.292	.469	0	—	0	-3		-0.4
1997	Oak A	0	0	—	3	0	0	0-0	2	4	3	1	0	2-0	1	13.50	34	.444	.500	0	—	-0	-2	22	-0.1
	Phi N	1	2	.333	25	0	0	0-2	22	15	8	2	0	11-0	16	3.27	129	.188	.280	1	.000	-0	3	42	0.3
1998	Phi N	0	1	.000	2	0	0	0-0	0.1	3	4	0	0	2-0	0	108.00	4	.750	.833	0	—	0	-4	172	-0.6
1999	Phi N	1	1	.500	25	0	0	2-0	25.2	30	20	4	0	14-1	32	7.01	67	.294	.376	0	—	0	-6		-0.5
Total	7	11	11	.500	203	0	0	5-12	178.2	172	96	26	4	93-7	137	4.79	99	.255	.345	1	.000	-0	1	236	0.1
BREWINGTON, JAMIE	Jamie Chancellor B9.28.1971 Greenville NC BR/TR/6-4/180* [SFN92 10/271] d7.24 Col Virginia Commonwealth																								
1995	SF N	6	4	.600	13	13	0	0-0	75.1	68	38	8	4	45-6	45	4.54	91	.245	.355	23-0-4	.217	0*	101	-2		-0.2
2000	Cle A	3	0	1.000	26	0	0	0-0	45.1	56	28	3	2	19-0	34	5.36	93	.311	.379	1	.000	0	-2		-0.1
Total	2	9	4	.692	39	13	0	0-0	120.2	124	66	11	6	64-6	79	4.85	92	.271	.364	24-0-4	.208	1	101	-4		-0.3
BRICE, ALAN	Alan Healey B10.1.1937 New York NY BR/TR/6-5/215 d9.22																								
1961	Chi A	0	1	.000	3	0	0	0-0	3.1	2	2	0	0	3-0	3	0.00	—	.308	.438	0	—	0	1		0.1
BRICKNER, RALPH	Ralph Harold "Brick" B5.2.1925 Cincinnati OH D5.9.1994 Port Jefferson NY BR/TR/6-3.5/215 d5.4 Col Indiana																								
1952	Bos A	3	1	.750	14	1	0	0-0	33	32	8	1	0	11	9	2.18	181	.264	.326	8	.250	0	44	6		0.8
BRIDGES, MARSHALL	Marshall "Sheriff" B6.2.1931 Jackson MS D9.3.1990 Jackson MS BB/TL/6-1/180(165-190) d6.17																								
1959	StL N	6	3	.667	27	4	1	.1	76	67	38	10	0	37-8	76	4.26	99	.240	.324	23-1-2	.217	2	95	1		0.1
1960	StL N	2	2	.500	20	1	0	0	31.1	33	15	2	1	16-1	27	3.45	119	.266	.350	6	.000	-0	65	1		0.1
	Cin N	4	0	1.000	14	0	0	2	25.1	14	3	1	0	7-0	26	1.07	359	.161	.223	4-0-1	.250	0	8			1.4
	Year	6	2	.750	34	1	0	3	56.2	47	18	3	1	23-1	53	2.38	167	.223	.300	10-0-1	.100	-0	-8			1.5
1961	Cin N	0	1	.000	13	0	0	0	20.2	26	19	4	1	11-0	17	7.84	52	.317	.400	2	.000	-0	4			-0.4
1962	†NY A	8	4	.667	52	0	0	18	71.2	49	30	4	0	48-6	66	3.14	119	.194	.321	14-0-1	.000	-0	-2			-0.1
1963	NY A	2	0	1.000	23	0	0	1	33	27	18	2	1	30-2	35	3.82	92	.237	.392	0	—	0	-7			-0.7
1964	Was A	0	3	.000	17	0	0	2	30	37	22	3	0	17-2	16	5.70	65	.303	.383	3	.000	-0	2			0.2
1965	Was A	1	2	.333	40	0	0	0	57.1	62	26	3	0	25-4	39	2.67	130	.268	.340	7-0-1	.143	1	2			0.2
Total	7	23	15	.605	206	5	1	25	345.1	315	171	29	3	191-23	302	3.75	102	.244	.339	59-1-5	.119	-0	97	-1		1.4
BRIDGES, TOMMY	Thomas Jefferson Davis B12.28.1906 Gordonsville TN D4.19.1968 Nashville TN BR/TR/5-10.5/155 d8.13 Mil 1944-45 C2 Col Tennessee																								
1930	Det A	3	2	.600	8	5	2	0	37.2	28	18	4	0	23	17	4.06	118	.215	.333	10-0-2	.300	1	104	4		0.5
1931	Det A	8	16	.333	35	23	8-2	0	173	182	120	13	0	108	105	4.99	92	.263	.363	54-0-5	.148	-2	67	-10		-1.4
1932	Det A	14	12	.538	34	26	10-4	1	201	174	95	14	1	119	108	3.36	140	.233	.339	67-0-5	.164	-1	93	27		2.9
1933	Det A	14	12	.538	33	28	17-2	2	233	192	102	8	6	110	120	3.09	140	**.226**	.319	78-0-7	.205	2	71	29		3.2
1934	†Det A☆	22	11	.667	36	**35**	23-3	1	275	249	117	16	3	104	151	3.67	120	.241	.312	98-0-6	.122	-4	117	28		2.4
1935	†Det A☆	21	10	.677	36	34	23-4	1	274.1	277	129	22	3	113	**163**	3.51	119	.259	.332	109-0-4	.239	3	126	19		2.1
1936	Det A*	**23**	11	.676	39	**38**	26-5	0	294.2	289	141	21	5	115	**175**	3.60	137	.255	.326	118-0-6	.212	0	115	43		4.2
1937	Det A★	15	12	.556	34	31	18-3	0	245.1	267	129	15	3	91	138	4.07	115	.274	.338	96-0-3	.240	2	108	15		1.6
1938	Det A	13	9	.591	25	20	13	1	151	171	83	14	2	58	101	4.59	109	.287	.353	54-0-4	.130	-1	113	8		0.7
1939	Det A★	17	7	.708	29	26	16-2	2	198	186	87	11	6	61	129	3.50	140	.243	.304	71-0-8	.197	0	114	30		3.2
1940	†Det A☆	12	9	.571	29	28	12-2	0	197.2	171	89	11	0	88	133	3.41	133	.233	.320	47-0-4	.085	-3	65	17		1.9
1941	Det A	9	12	.429	25	22	10-1	0	147.2	128	66	10	1	70	90	2.74	144	.246	.313	63-0-1	.095	-2	84	21		1.6
1942	Det A	9	7	.563	23	22	11-2	1	174	164	66	6	4	61	97	2.39	147	.246	.287	64-0-4	.219	2	102	24		2.6
1943	Det A	12	7	.632	25	22	11-3	0	191.2	159	57	9	0	61	124	3.27	107	.226	.287	64-0-4	.180	-5	101	277		27.3
1945	†Det A	1	0	1.000	4	1	0	0	11	14	6	2	0	2	6	3.27	132	.311	.340	3	.000	-0	145	0		0.0
1946	Det A	1	1	.500	9	1	0	1	21.1	24	16	5	1	8	17	5.91	62	.279	.347	5	.000	-0	117	-5		-0.5
Total	16	194	138	.584	424	362	200-33	10	2826.1	2675	1321	181	35	1192	1674	3.57	126	.248	.325	1003-0-65	.180	-5	101	277		27.3
BRIGGS, BUTTONS	Herbert Theodore B7.8.1875 Poughkeepsie NY D2.18.1911 Cleveland OH BR/TR/6-1/180 d4.23																								
1896	Chi N	12	8	.600	26	21	19	6	194	202	129	6	15	108	84	4.31	105	.266	.368	78	.128	-6	97	5		-0.3
1897	Chi N	4	17	.190	22	22	21	0	186.2	246	166	6	9	85	60	5.26	85	.315	.388	81-0-2	.160	-6	90	-18		-2.0
1898	Chi N	1	3	.250	4	4	3	0	30	38	22	0	1	10	14	5.70	63	.306	.363	14	.429	2	119	-4		-0.3
1904	Chi N	19	11	.633	34	30	28-3	3	277	252	102	3	8	77	112	2.05	130	.246	.304	94-1-2	.170	-0	95	16		1.4
1905	Chi N	8	8	.500	20	20	13-5	0	168	141	58	1	6	52	68	2.14	139	.237	.304	57-0-3	.053	-4	91	15		0.7
Total	5	44	47	.484	106	97	84-8	4	855.2	879	477	16	39	332	338	3.41	104	.268	.342	324-1-7	.148	-15	95	14		-0.5
BRIGGS, JOHN	Jonathan Tift B1.24.1934 Natoma CA BR/TR/5-10/175* d4.17																								
1956	Chi N	0	0	—	3	0	0	0	5.1	5	1	1	3	4-1	1	1.69	223	.238	.429	—		0	1			0.1
1957	Chi N	0	1	.000	7	0	0	0	4.1	7	6	2	0	3-0	1	12.46	31	.368	.435	0	—	0	-4			-0.7
1958	Chi N	5	5	.500	20	17	3-1	0	95.2	99	52	12	1	45-1	46	4.52	87	.270	.351	35-0-1	.257	2	107	-5		-0.4
1959	Cle A	0	1	.000	4	1	0	0	12.2	12	5	1	0	3-0	5	2.13	173	.245	.283	2	.000	-0	96	2		0.1
1960	Cle A	4	2	.667	21	2	0	1	36.1	32	20	4	1	15-0	19	4.46	84	.250	.329	8-0-1	.125	-0	165	-3		-0.5
	KC A	0	2	.000	8	1	0	0	11.1	19	17	3	0	12-0	8	12.71	31	.380	.500	3	.000	-0	66	-10		-1.5
	Year	4	4	.500	29	3	0	1	47.2	51	37	7	1	27-0	27	6.42	59	.287	.380	11-0-1	.091	-1	132	-13		-2.0
Total	5	9	11	.450	59	21	3-1	1	165.2	174	101	23	5	82-2	80	5.00	77	.275	.360	48-0-2	.208	1	110	-19		-2.9
BRILES, NELSON	Nelson Kelley B8.5.1943 Dorris CA D2.13.2005 Orlando FL BR/TR/5-11/200* d4.19 Col Santa Clara																								
1965	StL N	3	3	.500	37	2	0	4	82.1	79	33	4	6	26-6	52	3.50	110	.258	.327	15	.133	-0	216	4		0.2
1966	StL N	4	15	.211	49	17	0	6	154	162	65	14	7	54-11	100	3.21	112	.279	.345	38-0-1	.079	-2	91	5		0.5
1967	†StL N	14	5	.737	49	14	4-2	0	155.1	139	45	8	5	40-8	94	2.43	135	.236	.289	40-0-5	.150	0	109	16		2.1
1968	†StL N	19	11	.633	33	33	13-4	0	243.2	251	90	18	7	55-12	141	2.81	103	.266	.310	80-0-9	.138	-1	128	1		0.1
1969	StL N	15	13	.536	36	33	10-3	0-0	227.2	218	104	17	2	63-7	126	3.52	102	.251	.301	76-1-5	.105	-1	103	0		-0.2
1970	StL N	6	7	.462	30	19	1-1	0-0	106.2	129	84	14	2	36-7	59	6.24	66	.297	.349	39-0-3	.179	1	154	-25	23	-2.6
1971	†Pit N	8	4	.667	37	14	4-2	1-1	136	131	51	12	3	35-12	76	3.04	112	.250	.301	39-1-3	.256	4	151	6		0.3
1972	†Pit N	14	11	.560	28	27	9-2	0-0	195.2	185	83	14	1	43-8	120	3.08	108	.249	.288	70-0-5	.157	-0	119	3		1.9
1973	Pit N	14	13	.519	33	33	7-1	0-0	218.2	201	87	19	1	51-3	94	2.84	124	.244	.287	72-1-6	.194	3	106	14		1.9
1974	KC A	5	7	.417	18	17	3	0-0	103	118	48	9	2	21-1	41	4.02	95	.293	.329	—		0	94	-4	73	0.0
1975	KC A	6	6	.500	24	16	3	2-0	112	127	60	19	5	25-1	73	4.26	91	.285	.329	0	—	0	103	8		0.0
1976	Tex A	11	9	.550	32	31	7-1	1-0	210	224	87	17	2	47-0	98	3.26	110	.273	.332	0	—	0	109	-2		-0.2
1977	Tex A	6	4	.600	28	15	2-1	0-0	108.1	114	58	13	6	30-1	57	4.24	96	.275	.332	0	—	0	109	-2		-0.2
	Bal A	0	0	—	2	0	0	0-0	4	5	3	2	0	0-0	2	6.75	57	.294	.294	0	—	0	-1			-0.3
	Year	6	4	.600	30	15	2-1	2-0	112.1	119	61	15	6	30-1	59	4.33	94	.276	.330	0	—	0	109	-3		-0.3
1978	Bal A	4	4	.500	16	8	1	0-0	54.1	58	31	6	2	21-2	30	4.64	76	.279	.345	0	—	0	124	-7	28	-1.0
Total	14	129	112	.535	452	279	64-17	22-1	2111.2	2141	929	186	51	547-79	1163	3.44	103	.264	.312	469-3-37	.154	5	113	18	124	2.1
BRILL, FRANK	Francis Hasbrouck (b Francis Hasbrouck Briell) B3.30.1864 Astoria NY D11.19.1944 Flushing NY BR/TR/5-8/155 d6.23																								
1884	Det N	2	10	.167	12	12	12-1	0	103	148	97	2		18	26	5.50	53	.312	.348	44	.136	-3*	79	-24		-2.3
BRILLHEART, JIM	James Benson B9.28.1903 Dublin VA D9.2.1972 Radford VA BR/TL/5-11/170 d4.17 Col Roanoke																								
1922	Was A	4	6	.400	31	10	3	1	119.2	120	58	3	8	72	47	3.61	107	.275	.388	36-0-1	.083	-4	114	4		-0.2
1923	Was A	0	4	.000	12	0	0	0	18	27	11	1	1	12	8	7.00	54	.360	.455	2	.000	-0	-6			-0.5
1927	Chi N	4	2	.667	32	12	4	0	128.2	140	67	4	4	38	36	4.13	94	.286	.343	44-0-6	.023	-5	123	-3		-0.5
1931	Bos A	0	0	—	11	1	0	0	19.2	27	16	2	0	15	7	5.49	78	.325	.429	4-1-0	.500	3	79	-4		-0.5
Total	4	8	9	.471	86	23	7	1	286	314	156	10	13	137	98	4.19	90	.290	.376	86-1-7	.070	-8	117	-9		-0.5
BRINK, BRAD	Bradford Albert B1.20.1965 Roseville CA BR/TR/6-2/195(195-208) [PhiN86 1/7] d5.17 Col USC																								
1992	Phi N	0	4	.000	8	7	0	0-0	41.1	53	27	7	1	13-2	16	4.14	85	.308	.360	12-0-1	.083	-0	63	-6		-0.4
1993	Phi N	0	0	—	2	0	0	0-0	6	3	2	1	0	4-3	8	3.00	132	.143	.250	1	.000	0	1			0.0
1994	SF N	0	0	—	4	0	0	0-0	8.1	4	1	0	0	4-1	3	1.08	376	.143	.250	1	.000	0	63	-2		-0.1
Total	3	0	4	.000	14	7	0	0-0	55.2	60	30	4	1	20-3	27	3.56	103	.271	.335	14-0-1	.071	0	63	-2		-0.1

YEAR	TM LG	W	L	PCT	G	GS	CG-SHO	SV-BS	IP	H	R	HR	HB	BB-IB	SO	ERA	AERA	OAV	OOB	AB-HR-SH	AVG	PB	SUP	APR	DL	PW

BRISCOE, JOHN John Eric B9.22.1967 LaGrange IL BR/TR/6-3/185* [OakA88 3/73] d4.18 Col TCU

1991	Oak A	0	0	—	11	0	0	0-0	14	12	11	3	0	10-0	9	7.07	55	.235	.355	0	—	0		-5		-0.3
1992	Oak A	0	1	.000	2	2	0	0-0	7	12	6	0	0	9-0	4	6.43	59	.400	.538	0	—	0	109	-2		-0.3
1993	Oak A	1	0	1.000	17	0	0	0-0	24.2	26	25	2	0	26-3	24	8.03	52	.277	.426	0	—	0		-12		-0.6
1994	Oak A	4	2	.667	37	0	0	1-1	49.1	31	24	7	1	39-2	45	4.01	112	.185	.340	0	—	0*	3		26	0.3
1995	Oak A	0	1	.000	16	0	0	0-0	18.1	25	17	4	2	21-1	19	8.35	54	.347	.495	0	—	0	-7		91	-0.3
1996	Oak A	0	1	.000	17	0	0	1-1	26.1	18	11	2	0	24-2	14	3.76	132	.205	.368	0	—	0	109	-19	117	0.2
Total	6	5	5	.500	100	2	0	2-2	139.2	124	94	18	3	129-8	115	5.67	78	.247	.398	0	—	0	109	-19	117	-1.0

BRISSIE, LOU Leland Victor B6.5.1924 Anderson SC BL/TL/6-4/215* d9.28 Col Presbyterian

1947	Phi A	0	1	.000	1	1	0	0	7	9	5	1	0	5	4	6.43	59	.310	.412	2	.000	-0	70	-2		-0.2
1948	Phi A	14	10	.583	39	25	11	5	194	202	100	6	2	95	127	4.13	104	.269	.352	76-0-5	.237	0	101	2		0.2
1949	Phi A★	16	11	.593	34	29	18	3	229.1	220	113	20	5	118	118	4.28	96	.251	.344	90-0-6	.267	3	107	0		0.1
1950	Phi A	7	19	.269	46	31	15-2	8	246	237	127	22	4	117	101	4.02	113	.253	.338	87-0-1	.172	-3	81	12		0.9
1951	Phi A	0	2	.000	2	2	0	0	13.1	20	10	0	0	8	3	6.75	63	.357	.438	5-0-1	.200	-0	83	-3		-0.4
	Cle A	4	3	.571	54	4	0	9	112.1	90	44	5	3	61	50	3.20	118	.223	.329	23-0-1	.261	0	135	9		0.6
	Year	4	5	.444	56	6	1	9	125.2	110	54	5	3	69	53	3.58	107	.239	.342	28-0-2	.250	0	120	5		0.2
1952	Cle A	3	2	.600	42	1	0	2	82.2	68	41	5	0	34	28	3.48	96	.221	.299	12-0-3	.250	1	52	-3		-0.1
1953	Cle A	0	0	—	16	0	0	2	13	21	11	2	0	13	5	7.62	49	.389	.507	0	—	0		-5		-0.3
Total	7	44	48	.478	234	93	45-2	29	897.2	867	451	61	14	451	436	4.07	102	.254	.343	295-0-17	.227	1	98	10		0.8

BRITO, EUDE Eude Ezequiel B8.19.1978 Saban de la Mar, D.R. BL/TL/5-11/160 d8.21

| 2005 | Phi N | 1 | 2 | .333 | 6 | 5 | 0 | 0-0 | 22 | 20 | 9 | 2 | 2 | 11-1 | 15 | 3.68 | 118 | .250 | .351 | 7 | .143 | -0 | 86 | 2 | | 0.3 |

BRITT, JIM James Edward B2.25.1856 Brooklyn NY D2.28.1923 San Francisco CA d5.2

1872	Atl NA	9	28	.243	37	37	37		336	568	473	6		21	13	4.53	100	.326	.334	155	.265	-7	54	0		-0.3
1873	Atl NA	17	36	.321	54	54	51-1	0	480.2	696	519	6		41	16	4.08	74	.301	.313	240	.196	-3	79	-52		-3.7
Total	2 NA	26	64	.289	91	91	88-1	0	816.2	1264	992	12		62	29	4.26	85	.312	.322	395	.223	-10	67	-52		-4.0

BRITTIN, JACK John Albert B3.4.1924 Athens IL D1.5.1994 Springfield IL BR/TR/5-11/175* d9.15 Col Illinois

1950	Phi N	0	0	—	3	0	0	0	4	2	1	0	0	3	3	4.50	90	.143	.294	0	—	0		0		0.0
1951	Phi N	0	0	—	3	0	0	0	4	5	5	0	0	6	3	9.00	43	.294	.478	0	—	0		-3		-0.1
Total	2	0	0	—	6	0	0	0	8	7	7	0	0	9	6	6.75	58	.226	.400	0	—	0		-3		-0.1

BRITTON, JIM James Allan B3.25.1944 N.Tonawanda NY BR/TR/6-5/225(215-230) d9.20 [DL 1970 Mon N 156]

1967	Atl N	0	2	.000	2	2	0	0	13.1	15	9	2	0	2-0	6	6.08	55	.278	.304	4	.000	-0	66	-4		-0.5
1968	Atl N	4	6	.400	34	9	2-2	3	90.1	81	35	1	2	34-5	61	3.09	97	.245	.318	21-0-2	.143	-0	106	-1		-0.1
1969	†Atl N	7	5	.583	24	13	2-1	1-0	88	69	38	10	0	49-1	60	3.78	96	.218	.322	21-0-4	.190	0	87	0		0.0
1971	Mon N	2	3	.400	16	6	0	0-0	45.2	49	33	10	2	27-1	23	5.72	62	.274	.375	9-0-1	.000	-1	54	-11	78	-1.3
Total	4	13	16	.448	76	30	4-3	4-0	237.1	214	115	23	4	112-7	148	4.23	83	.243	.331	55-0-7	.127	-2	85	-16	234	-1.9

BRIZZOLARA, TONY Anthony John B1.14.1957 Santa Monica CA BR/TR/6-5/215* [AtlN77 2/30] d5.19 Col Texas

1979	Atl N	6	9	.400	20	19	2	0	107.1	133	70	6	3	33-1	64	5.28	76	.303	.352	35-0-1	.029	-3	88	-13		-1.8
1983	Atl N	1	0	1.000	14	0	0	1-0	20.1	22	8	2	0	6-0	17	3.54	109	.278	.329	0	—	0	1			0.0
1984	Atl N	1	2	.333	10	4	0	0-0	29	33	22	4	0	13-1	17	5.28	73	.284	.351	7-0-2	.000	-1	115	-5		0.0
Total	3	8	11	.421	44	23	2	1-0	156.2	188	100	12	3	52-2	98	5.06	79	.297	.349	42-0-3	.024	-4	93	-17		-2.4

BROACA, JOHNNY John Joseph B10.3.1909 Lawrence MA D5.16.1985 Lawrence MA BR/TR/5-11/190 d6.2 Col Yale

1934	NY A	12	9	.571	26	24	13-1	0	177.1	203	94	9	1	65	74	4.16	98	.284	.344	66-0-4	.030	-7	120	-2		-0.9
1935	NY A	15	7	.682	29	27	14-2	0	201	199	96	16	0	79	78	3.58	113	.254	.323	80-0-5	.150	-4	133	11		0.5
1936	NY A	12	7	.632	37	27	12-1	3	206	235	110	16	0	66	84	4.24	110	.284	.337	82-0-3	.110	-6	115	10		0.0
1937	NY A	1	4	.200	7	6	3	0	44	58	27	5	0	17	9	4.70	94	.324	.383	14-0-1	.000	-2	72	-1		-0.4
1939	Cle A	4	2	.667	22	2	0	0	46	53	39	5	0	28	13	4.70	94	.288	.382	12	.000	-2	100	-7		-0.9
Total	5	44	29	.603	121	86	42-4	3	674.1	748	366	51	1	255	258	4.08	105	.278	.341	254-0-13	.091	-21	118	11		-1.7

BROBERG, PETE Peter Sven B3.2.1950 W.Palm Beach FL BR/TR/6-3/205* [TexA71 D1/1] d6.20 Col Dartmouth

1971	Was A	5	9	.357	18	18	7-1	0-0	124.2	104	57	10	10	53-2	89	3.47	97	.228	.319	44-1-3	.114	-0	100	-2		-0.3
1972	Tex A	5	12	.294	39	25	3-2	1-0	176.1	153	93	14	13	85-3	133	4.29	71	.237	.332	51-0-5	.078	-2	93	-22		-2.4
1973	Tex A	5	9	.357	22	20	6-1	0-0	118.2	130	77	8	5	66-3	57	5.61	57	.287	.375	0	—	0*	80	-21		-2.2
1974	Tex A	0	4	.000	12	2	0	0-0	29	29	29	7	1	13-0	15	8.07	44	.264	.344	0	—	0	74	-14		-1.7
1975	Mil A	14	16	.467	38	32	7-2	0-0	220.1	219	114	18	16	106-2	100	4.13	93	.263	.356	0	—	0	106	-6		-0.7
1976	Mil A	1	7	.125	20	11	1	0-0	92.1	99	59	5	4	72-6	28	4.97	71	.281	.403	0	—	0	86	-16		-1.3
1977	Chi N	1	2	.333	22	0	0	0-0	36	34	22	8	0	18-4	20	4.75	93	.256	.340	6	.000	-1	-1			-0.2
1978	Oak A	10	12	.455	35	26	2	2-0	165.2	174	101	16	3	85-6	94	4.62	79	.269	.336	0	—	0	90	-18		-2.1
Total	8	41	71	.366	206	134	26-6	1-0	963	942	552	86	52	478-25	536	4.06	78	.259	.350	101-1-8	.089	-5	93-100			-10.9

BROCAIL, DOUG Douglas Keith B5.16.1967 Clearfield PA BL/TR/6-5/235(220-235) [SDN86*1/12] d9.8 Col Lamar (CO) CC [DL 2002 Hou N 183]

1992	SD N	0	0	—	3	3	0	0-0	14	17	10	2	0	5-0	15	6.43	56	.298	.355	5	.200	0	118	-4		-0.2
1993	SD N	4	13	.235	24	24	0	0-0	128.1	143	75	16	4	42-4	70	4.56	91	.282	.337	33-0-11	.182	-0*	87	-6		-0.7
1994	SD N	0	0	—	12	0	0	0-1	17	21	13	1	2	5-3	11	5.82	71	.304	.364	2	.000	-0*	-4	86		-0.2
1995	Hou N	6	4	.600	36	7	0	1-0	77.1	87	40	10	4	22-2	39	4.19	92	.280	.334	16-0-4	.250	-1*	127	-3		-0.2
1996	Hou N	1	5	.167	23	4	0	0-0	53	58	31	7	2	23-1	34	4.58	85	.289	.364	11	.000	-1*	23	-5	96	-0.6
1997	Det A	3	4	.429	61	4	0	2-7	78	74	31	10	3	36-4	60	3.23	143	.256	.341	0	—	0	104	12		1.0
1998	Det A	5	2	.714	60	0	0	0-1	62.2	47	23	2	1	18-3	55	2.73	174	.211	.269	0	—	0	13	15		1.2
1999	Det A	4	4	.500	70	0	0	2-2	82	60	23	7	4	14-2	78	2.52	198	.206	.276	0	—	0	23			2.0
2000	Det A	5	4	.556	49	0	0	0-5	50.2	57	25	5	1	14-2	41	4.09	120	.285	.330	0	—	0	5	19		0.7
2004	Tex A	4	1	.800	43	0	0	1-0	52.1	54	29	2	5	20-1	43	4.13	119	.269	.346	0	—	0	3	44		0.3
2005	Tex A	5	3	.625	61	0	0	1-3	73.1	90	48	2	4	34-3	61	5.52	83	.301	.375	0	—	0	-7			-0.6
Total	11	37	40	.481	442	42	0	7-19	688.2	708	348	64	30	244-24	507	4.06	109	.267	.333	67-0-15	.164	-0	85	27	443	2.7

BROCK, CHRIS Terrence Christopher B2.5.1970 Orlando FL BR/TR/6-0/185* [AtlN92 12/341] d6.11 Col Florida St.

1997	Atl N	0	0	—	7	6	0	0-0	30.2	34	23	2	0	19-2	16	5.58	75	.288	.376	10	.100	-0	146	-5		-0.3
1998	SF N	0	0	—	13	0	0	0-0	27.2	31	13	3	0	7-1	19	3.90	103	.279	.322	4	.250	0		0		0.0
1999	SF N	6	8	.429	19	19	0	0-0	106.2	124	69	18	4	41-2	76	5.48	78	.291	.357	35-0-4	.200	1	118	-14	72	-1.4
2000	Phi N	7	8	.467	63	5	0	1-2	93.1	85	49	21	3	41-0	69	4.34	106	.239	.321	9-1-2	.222	1	52	3		0.5
2001	Phi N	3	0	1.000	24	0	0	0-1	32.2	35	16	6	2	15-2	26	4.13	100	.276	.359	3	.333	0		0		0.0
2002	Bal A	1	1	.667	22	0	0	0-0	44	52	24	6	1	14-1	21	4.70	92	.297	.349	2	.000	-0	-1	48		-0.1
Total	6	18	17	.514	148	30	0	1-3	335	361	193	56	10	137-8	227	4.81	90	.275	.345	63-1-6	.190	3	111	-17	120	-1.3

BROCKETT, LEW Lewis Albert "King" B7.23.1880 Brownsville IL D9.19.1960 Norris City IL BR/TR/5-10.5/168 d4.25

1907	NY A	1	2	.333	8	4	1	0	46.1	58	36	1	2	26	13	6.22	45	.309	.398	22	.182	-0*	73	-13		-0.9
1909	NY A	10	8	.556	26	18	10-3	1	170	148	68	3	6	59	70	2.12	119	.245	.318	60-0-3	.283	3	94	5		1.1
1911	NY A	4	4	.333	16	8	2	0	75.1	73	45	2	5	39	25	4.66	77	.256	.356	39	.308	2*	93	-6		-0.2
Total	3	13	14	.481	50	30	13-3	1	291.2	279	149	6	13	124	108	3.43	83	.259	.343	121-0-3	.273	5	91	-14		0.0

BRODOWSKI, DICK Richard Stanley B7.26.1932 Bayonne NJ BR/TR/6-2/190* d6.15 Mil 1953-54

1952	Bos A	5	5	.500	20	12	4	0	114.2	111	66	12	3	50	42	4.40	90	.252	.333	39-1-1	.205	1	124	-6		-0.4
1955	Bos A	1	0	1.000	32	0	0	0	32	36	25	5	1	25-2	10	5.63	76	.295	.416	10-1-0	.500	3	-5			0.0
1956	Was A	0	3	.000	7	3	1	0	17.2	31	18	5	0	12-0	8	9.17	47	.397	.473	5	.000	-0	48	-9		-1.2
1957	Was A	1	1	.500	11	0	0	0	11.1	10	5	1	1	6-0	4	11.12	36	.261	.404	1	.000	-0	-9			-0.7
1958	Cle A	1	1	.500	0	0	0	0	10	9	6	0	0	6-0	12	0.00	—	.100	.250	1	.000	-0	-4			0.0
1959	Cle A	1	1	.500	2	0	0	5	30	19	13	3	3	21-1	9	1.80	205	.181	.328	6-0-2	.333	0	4			0.6
Total	6	9	11	.450	72	15	5	5	215.2	212	137	27	8	124-3	85	4.76	84	.258	.359	62-2-3	.242	1	109	-20		-1.3

BROGLIO, ERNIE Ernest Gilbert B8.27.1935 Berkeley CA BR/TR/6-2/200* d4.11

| 1959 | StL N | 7 | 12 | .368 | 35 | 25 | 6-3 | 0 | 181.1 | 174 | 104 | 20 | 0 | 89-10 | 133 | 4.72 | 90 | .250 | .334 | 61-0-3 | .098 | -3 | 80 | -9 | | -1.0 |
| 1960 | StL N | **21** | 9 | **.700** | 52 | 24 | 9-3 | 0 | 226.1 | 172 | 76 | 18 | 2 | 100-5 | 188 | 2.74 | **149** | .213 | .299 | 68-0-4 | .206 | 2 | 87 | 32 | | 4.4 |

YEAR	TM LG	W	L	PCT	G	GS	CG-SHO	SV-BS	IP	H	R	HR	HB	BB-IB	SO	ERA	AERA	OAV	OOB	AB-HR-SH	AVG	PB	SUP	APR	DL	PW
1961	StL N	9	12	.429	29	26	7-2	0	174.2	166	97	19	1	75-5	113	4.12	107	.248	.322	62-0-4	.145	-2	88	4		0.1
1962	StL N	12	9	.571	34	30	11-4	0	222.1	193	80	22	2	93-5	132	3.00	143	.237	.316	72-0-6	.139	-2	83	31		2.5
1963	StL N	18	8	.692	39	35	11-5	0	250	202	97	24	4	90-4	145	2.99	119	.216	.286	89-0-10	.112	-3	128	14		1.2
1964	StL N	3	5	.375	11	11	3-1	0	69.1	65	33	7	1	26-2	36	3.50	109	.247	.317	21-0-2	.095	-0	86	2		0.1
	Chi N	4	7	.364	18	16	3	1	100.1	111	51	12	0	30-4	46	4.04	92	.281	.331	35-0-2	.286	3	81	-4		-0.1
	Year	7	12	.368	29	27	6-1	1	169.2	176	84	19	1	56-6	82	3.82	98	.267	.325	56-0-4	.214		83			-2.2
1965	Chi N	1	6	.143	26	6	0	0	50.1	63	44	7	0	46-8	22	6.93	53	.313	.440	.000	-0	111	-17		-2.2
1966	Chi N	2	6	.250	15	11	2	1	62.1	70	46	14	0	38-6	34	6.35	58	.290	.384	19-0-1	.368	3	104	-16		-1.5
Total	8	77	74	.510	259	184	52-18	2	1337.1	1216	628	143	10	587-49	849	3.74	107	.242	.321	431-0-33	.158	-2	94	37		3.4

BROHAWN, TROY   Michael Troy B1.14.1973 Cambridge MD BL/TL/6-1/190* [SFN94 4/116] d4.14 Col Nebraska [DL 1999 Ari N 34]

YEAR	TM LG	W	L	PCT	G	GS	CG-SHO	SV-BS	IP	H	R	HR	HB	BB-IB	SO	ERA	AERA	OAV	OOB	AB-HR-SH	AVG	PB	SUP	APR	DL	PW
2001	†Ari N	2	3	.400	59	0	0	1-2	49.1	55	27	5	1	23-2	30	4.93	94	.289	.362	1	.000	-0		-1		-0.2
2002	SF N	0	1	.000	11	0	0	0-0	5.2	5	4	1	2	1-0	3	6.35	62	.227	.320	1	—	0		-1	139	0.1
2003	LA N	2	0	1.000	12	0	0	0-0	11.2	10	6	2	0	4-0	13	3.86	107	.227	.292	1	1.000	0		0	173	-0.2
Total	3		4	4	.500	82	0	0	1-2	66.2	70	37	8	3	28-2	46	4.86	92	.273	.347	2	.500	0		-2		-0.2

BRONDELL, KEN   Kenneth Leroy B10.17.1921 Bradshaw NE D10.3.2004 Van Nuys CA BR/TR/6-1/195 d5.3

YEAR	TM LG	W	L	PCT	G	GS	CG-SHO	SV-BS	IP	H	R	HR	HB	BB-IB	SO	ERA	AERA	OAV	OOB	AB-HR-SH	AVG	PB	SUP	APR	DL	PW
1944	NY N	0	1	.000	7	2	1	0	19.1	27	18	3	0	8	1	8.38	44	.329	.389	4	.000	-1*	114	-9		-0.5

BRONKEY, JEFF   Jacob Jeffrey B9.18.1965 Kabul, Afghanistan BR/TR/6-3/215* [MinA86 2/38] d5.2 Col Oklahoma St.

YEAR	TM LG	W	L	PCT	G	GS	CG-SHO	SV-BS	IP	H	R	HR	HB	BB-IB	SO	ERA	AERA	OAV	OOB	AB-HR-SH	AVG	PB	SUP	APR	DL	PW
1993	Tex A	1	1	.500	21	0	0	1-2	36	39	20	4	1	11-4	18	4.00	105	.285	.338	1	.000	-0		0		0.0
1994	Mil A	1	1	.500	16	0	0	1-1	20.2	20	10	3	0	12-4	13	4.35	117	.247	.344	0	—	-0		2	79	0.2
1995	Mil A	0	0	—	8	0	0	0-0	12.1	15	6	0	0	6-0	5	3.65	137	.313	.389	0	—	-0		4	115	0.1
Total	3		2	2	.500	45	0	0	2-3	69	74	36	7	1	29-8	36	4.04	114	.278	.349	1	.000	-0		4	194	0.1

BRONSTAD, JIM   James Warren B6.22.1936 Ft.Worth TX BR/TR/6-3/196* d6.7

YEAR	TM LG	W	L	PCT	G	GS	CG-SHO	SV-BS	IP	H	R	HR	HB	BB-IB	SO	ERA	AERA	OAV	OOB	AB-HR-SH	AVG	PB	SUP	APR	DL	PW
1959	NY A	0	3	.000	16	3	0	2	29.1	34	19	2	1	13-0	14	5.22	70	.288	.361	5	.000	-0	73	-5		-0.6
1963	Was A	1	3	.250	25	0	0	1	57.1	66	38	9	1	22-2	22	5.65	66	.297	.359	12	.000	-1*		-11		-0.6
1964	Was A	0	1	.000	4	0	0	0	7	10	4	0	0	2-0	9	5.14	72	.345	.387	0		0		-1		-0.1
Total	3		1	7	.125	45	3	0	3	93.2	110	61	11	2	37-2	45	5.48	67	.298	.362	17	.000	-2	73	-17		-1.5

BROOKENS, IKE   Edward Dwain B1.3.1949 Chambersburg PA BR/TR/6-5/170 [TexA67 5/85] d6.17

YEAR	TM LG	W	L	PCT	G	GS	CG-SHO	SV-BS	IP	H	R	HR	HB	BB-IB	SO	ERA	AERA	OAV	OOB	AB-HR-SH	AVG	PB	SUP	APR	DL	PW
1975	Det A	0	0	—	3	0	0	0-0	10.1	11	6	3	1	5-0	8	5.23	77	.282	.378	0	—			-1		0.0

BROOKS, FRANK   Frank J. B9.6.1978 Brooklyn NY BL/TL/6-1/200* [PhiN99 13/396] d8.27 Col St. Peters

YEAR	TM LG	W	L	PCT	G	GS	CG-SHO	SV-BS	IP	H	R	HR	HB	BB-IB	SO	ERA	AERA	OAV	OOB	AB-HR-SH	AVG	PB	SUP	APR	DL	PW
2004	Pit N	0	1	.000	11	0	0	0-0	17.1	13	10	5	0	9-2	18	4.67	93	.203	.301	1	.000	-0	43	-1		-0.
2005	Atl N	0	0	—	1	0	0	0-0	0.1	1	0	0	0	0-0	0	0.00	—	1.000	1.000	0		0		0		0.
Total	2		0	1	.000	12	0	0	0-0	17.2	14	10	5	0	9-2	18	4.58	94	.215	.311	1	.000	-0	43	-1		-0.

BROOKS, HARRY   Harry Frank B11.30.1865 Philadelphia PA D12.5.1945 Philadelphia PA d7.24

YEAR	TM LG	W	L	PCT	G	GS	CG-SHO	SV-BS	IP	H	R	HR	HB	BB-IB	SO	ERA	AERA	OAV	OOB	AB-HR-SH	AVG	PB	SUP	APR	DL	PW
1886	NY AA	0	1	.000	1	1	0	0	2	9	13	0	0	2	0	36.00	9	.429	.478	1		-0	55	-8		-0.

BROSNAN, JIM   James Patrick B10.24.1929 Cincinnati OH BR/TR/6-4/210(197-250) d4.15

YEAR	TM LG	W	L	PCT	G	GS	CG-SHO	SV-BS	IP	H	R	HR	HB	BB-IB	SO	ERA	AERA	OAV	OOB	AB-HR-SH	AVG	PB	SUP	APR	DL	PW
1954	Chi N	1	0	1.000	18	0	0	0	33.1	44	35	9	1	18-0	17	9.45	44	.331	.409	8	.125	-0		-17		-0.
1956	Chi N	5	9	.357	30	10	1-1	1	95	95	44	9	0	45-8	51	3.79	100	.270	.349	22-0-2	.182	-0	98	1		0.
1957	Chi N	5	5	.500	41	5	1	0	98.2	79	38	11	1	46-4	73	3.38	115	.219	.308	20-0-2	.250	-1	96	7		0.
1958	Chi N	3	4	.429	8	8	2	0	51.2	41	20	3	0	29-3	24	3.14	125	.225	.327	19	.105	-1	111	10		1.
	StL N	8	4	.667	33	12	2	7	115	107	46	10	1	50-3	65	3.44	120	.243	.328	31-0-3	.097	-1	99	4		1.
	Year	11	8	.579	41	20	4	7	166.2	148	66	13	1	79-6	89	3.35	121	.243	.328	50-0-3	.100	-2	99	14		-0.
1959	StL N	1	3	.250	20	1	0	2	33	34	18	5	1	15-5	18	4.91	86	.276	.357	7	.286	1	190	-2		-0.
	Cin N	8	3	.727	26	9	1-1	2	83.1	79	35	7	5	26-2	56	3.35	121	.248	.313	23-0-1	.043	-2	98	6		0.
	Year	9	6	.600	46	10	1-1	4	116.1	113	53	12	6	41-7	74	3.79	108	.256	.325	30-0-1	.100	-1	107	5		0.
1960	Cin N	7	2	.778	57	0	0	12	99	79	31	6	0	22-5	62	2.36	162	.225	.269	15-1-1	.200	-0	8			1.
1961	†Cin N	10	4	.714	53	0	0	16	80	77	34	7	0	18-3	40	3.04	134	.249	.288	13-0-1	.154	-0	5			0.
1962	Cin N	4	4	.500	48	0	0	13	64.2	76	27	6	0	18-5	51	3.34	120	.292	.335	6-0-2	.000	-1	-2			0.
1963	Cin N	0	1	.000	6	0	0	0	4.2	8	4	2	0	3-1	4	7.71	43	.421	.500	0	—	1	6			1.
	Chi A	3	8	.273	45	0	0	14	73	71	24	7	0	22-5	47	2.84	124	.263	.315	13	.308	1	106	42		7
Total	9		55	47	.539	385	47	7-2	67	831.1	790	356	81	9	312-44	507	3.54	111	.254	.322	177-1-12	.153	1	106	42		7

BROSS, TERRY   Terrence Paul B3.30.1966 ElPaso TX BR/TR/6-9/230* [NYN87 13/342] d9.4 Col St. Johns

YEAR	TM LG	W	L	PCT	G	GS	CG-SHO	SV-BS	IP	H	R	HR	HB	BB-IB	SO	ERA	AERA	OAV	OOB	AB-HR-SH	AVG	PB	SUP	APR	DL	PW
1991	NY N	0	0	—	8	0	0	0-0	10	7	2	1	0	3-0	5	1.80	204	.200	.263	0	—	0		2		-0.
1993	SF N	0	0	—	2	0	0	0-0	2	3	2	1	0	1-0	1	9.00	44	.333	.400	0	—	0		1		-0.
Total	2		0	0	—	10	0	0	0-0	12	10	4	2	0	4-0	6	3.00	124	.227	.292	0	—	0		1		-0.

BROSSEAU, FRANK   Franklin Lee B7.31.1944 Drayton ND BR/TR/6-1/180* [PitN66 S1/19] d9.10 Col Minnesota

YEAR	TM LG	W	L	PCT	G	GS	CG-SHO	SV-BS	IP	H	R	HR	HB	BB-IB	SO	ERA	AERA	OAV	OOB	AB-HR-SH	AVG	PB	SUP	APR	DL	PW
1969	Pit N	0	0	—	2	0	0	0-0	1.2	2	2	0	0	2-1	2	10.80	32	.286	.444	0	—	0		-1		-0
1971	Pit N	0	0	—	1	0	0	0-0	2	1	0	0	0	0-0	0	4.50	—	.200	.200	0	—	0		1		0
Total	2		0	0	—	3	0	0	0-0	3.2	3	2	0	0	2-1	2	4.91	70	.250	.357	0	—	0		0		0

BROUTHERS, DAN   Dennis Joseph "Big Dan" B5.8.1858 Sylvan Lake NY D8.2.1932 E.Orange NJ BL/TL/6-2/207 d6.23 HF1945 ▲

YEAR	TM LG	W	L	PCT	G	GS	CG-SHO	SV-BS	IP	H	R	HR	HB	BB-IB	SO	ERA	AERA	OAV	OOB	AB-HR-SH	AVG	PB	SUP	APR	DL	PW
1879	Tro N	0	2	.000	3	2	2	0	21	35	30	0	0	6	6	5.57	45	.343	.391	168-4	.274	1*	0	-7		-0
1883	Buf N	0	0	—	1	0	0	0	2	9	7	0	0	3	2	31.50	10	.643	.706	425-3	.374	1*		-5		-0
Total		0	2	.000	4	2	2	0	23	44	37	0	0	11	8	7.83	33	.379	.433	593-7	.346	1	0	-12		-0

BROW, SCOTT   Scott John B3.17.1969 Butte MT BR/TR/6-3/200* [TorA90 7/204] d4.28 Col Washington

YEAR	TM LG	W	L	PCT	G	GS	CG-SHO	SV-BS	IP	H	R	HR	HB	BB-IB	SO	ERA	AERA	OAV	OOB	AB-HR-SH	AVG	PB	SUP	APR	DL	PW
1993	Tor A	1	1	.500	6	3	0	0-0	18	19	15	2	1	10-1	7	6.00	73	.275	.366	0	—	0	168	-4		-0
1994	Tor A	0	3	.000	18	0	0	2-0	29	34	27	4	1	19-2	15	5.90	83	.288	.386	0	—	0		-6		-0
1996	Tor A	1	0	1.000	18	1	0	0-1	38.2	45	25	5	0	25-1	23	5.59	90	.294	.391	0	—	0	111	-2		-0
1998	Ari N	1	0	1.000	17	0	0	0-0	21.1	22	17	2	0	14-2	13	7.17	60	.272	.375	1	.000	-0		-6		-0
Total	4		3	4	.429	59	4	0	2-1	107	120	84	13	2	68-6	58	6.06	78	.285	.382	1	.000	-0	146	-18		-0

BROWER, FRANK   Frank Willard "Turkeyfoot" B3.26.1893 Gainesville VA D11.20.1960 Baltimore MD BL/TR/6-2/180 d8.14.1920 Col Washington and Lee ▲

YEAR	TM LG	W	L	PCT	G	GS	CG-SHO	SV-BS	IP	H	R	HR	HB	BB-IB	SO	ERA	AERA	OAV	OOB	AB-HR-SH	AVG	PB	SUP	APR	DL	PW
1924	Cle A	0	0	—	4	0	0	0	9.2	7	2	0	1	4	0	0.93	459	.212	.316	107-3-0	.280	1*		3		

BROWER, JIM   James Robert B12.29.1972 Edina MN BR/TR/6-2/205* [TexA94 6/169] d9.5 Col Minnesota

YEAR	TM LG	W	L	PCT	G	GS	CG-SHO	SV-BS	IP	H	R	HR	HB	BB-IB	SO	ERA	AERA	OAV	OOB	AB-HR-SH	AVG	PB	SUP	APR	DL	PW
1999	Cle A	3	1	.750	9	2	0	0-0	25.2	27	13	8	1	10-1	18	4.56	112	.270	.339	0	—	0	229	2		
2000	Cle A	2	3	.400	17	11	0	0-0	62	80	45	11	2	31-1	32	6.24	80	.309	.387	3	.000	-0	90	-8		
2001	Cin N	7	10	.412	46	10	0	1-1	129.1	119	65	17	5	60-5	94	3.97	116	.247	.335	26-0-2	.308	2*	125	8		
2002	Cin N	2	0	1.000	22	0	0	0-0	39.1	38	18	2	0	10-1	24	3.89	110	.260	.306	4-0-1	.000	-0		2		
	Mon N	1	2	.333	30	0	0	0-1	41	39	22	4	4	22-1	33	4.83	91	.245	.351	5	.000	-1		-1		
	Year	3	2	.600	52	0	0	0-1	80.1	77	40	7	4	32-2	57	4.37	99	.252	.330	9-0-1	.176	0	119	3		
2003	†SF N	5	2	.615	51	5	0	2-1	100	90	48	8	1	39-2	65	3.29	132	.239	.318	2	.500	1		9		
2004	SF N	7	7	.500	89	0	0	1-4	93	90	42	6	4	36-2	63	3.87	111	.258	.332	2	.000	-0		-7		
2005	SF N	2	1	.667	32	0	0	1-2	30.1	40	22	5	2	15-0	28	6.53	65	.320	.399	2	.000	-0		1		
	†Atl N	1	2	.333	37	0	0	0-0	30	33	14	6	1	17-3	25	4.20	102	.282	.387	0	—	-0		-6		
	Year	3	3	.500	69	0	0	1-2	60.1	73	36	11	5	32-3	53	5.37	80	.302	.393	2	.000	0	124	9		
Total	7		33	34	.516	333	28	0	5-9	550.2	556	289	68	22	240-16	382	4.35	103	.265	.345	59-0-4	.203	1	124	9		

BROWN, ALTON   Alton Leo "Deacon" B4.16.1925 Norfolk VA BR/TR/6-2/195 d4.21

YEAR	TM LG	W	L	PCT	G	GS	CG-SHO	SV-BS	IP	H	R	HR	HB	BB-IB	SO	ERA	AERA	OAV	OOB	AB-HR-SH	AVG	PB	SUP	APR	DL	PW
1951	Was A	0	0	—	7	0	0	0	11.2	14	12	1	1	12	7	9.26	44	.298	.450	1	.000	-0		-6		

BROWN, BOARDWALK   Carroll William B2.20.1887 Woodbury NJ D2.8.1977 Burlington NJ BR/TR/6-1.5/178 d9.27

YEAR	TM LG	W	L	PCT	G	GS	CG-SHO	SV-BS	IP	H	R	HR	HB	BB-IB	SO	ERA	AERA	OAV	OOB	AB-HR-SH	AVG	PB	SUP	APR	DL	PW
1911	Phi A	0	1	.000	2	1	1	0	12	12	7	0	0	2	6	4.50	70	.267	.298	4	.000	-1	91	-2		
1912	Phi A	13	11	.542	34	24	15-3	0	199	204	115	2	9	87	64	3.66	84	.283	.367	76-0-4	.145	-3	142	-17		
1913	Phi A	17	11	.607	43	35	11-3	1	235.1	200	94	6	10	87	70	2.94	94	.233	.310	82-1-2	.159	-1	145	-5		
1914	Phi A	1	5	.167	19	15	7	0	66	64	34	1	0	26	20	4.09	64	.268	.340	20-0-1	.000	-2	96	-10		
	NY A	6	5	.545	20	14	8	0	122.1	123	57	2	1	42	57	3.24	85	.271	.334	44-0-2	.182	1	123	-7		
	Year	7	10	.412	35	21	10	0	188.1	187	91	3	1	68	77	3.54	77	.270	.336	64-0-3	.125	-1	114	-14		

YEAR	TM LG	W	L	PCT	G	GS	CG-SHO	SV-BS	IP	H	R	HR	HB	BB-IB	SO	ERA	AERA	OAV	OOB	AB-HR-SH	AVG	PB	SUP	APR	DL	PW
1915	NY A	3	6	.333	19	11	5	0	96.2	95	49	4	5	47	34	4.10	72	.275	.370	32	.188	-1*	66	-10		-1.0
Total	5	40	39	.506	133	92	42-6	1	731.1	698	356	15	25	291	251	3.47	83	.262	.340	258-1-9	.147	-6	126	-51		-5.4

BROWN, CHARLIE Charles Edward B8.17.1871 Bluffton IN D4.3.1938 Monclova OH TL/6-0/180 d8.4

1897	Cle N	1	2	.333	4	4	2	0	30	25	2	5	17		7	8	7.77	58	.300	.426	11	.273	0	91	-7		-0.6

BROWN, BUSTER Charles Edward "Yank" B8.31.1881 Boone IA D2.9.1914 Sioux City IA BR/TR/6-0/180 d6.22 Col Iowa St.

1905	StL N	8	11	.421	23	21	17-3	0	178.2	172	80	5	10	62	57	2.97	100	.260	.332	65	.092	-3	73	0		-0.2
1906	StL N	8	16	.333	32	27	21	0	238.1	208	98	2	11	112	109	2.64	99	.234	.327	85-1-6	.165	0	88	-3		-0.1
1907	StL N	1	6	.143	9	8	6	0	63.2	57	38	2	5	45	17	3.39	74	.263	.401	26-0-1	.269	2	107	-7		-0.4
	Phi N	9	6	.600	21	16	13-4	0	130	118	47	3	6	56	38	2.42	100	.246	.333	53	.189	2	120	0		0.1
	Year	10	12	.455	30	24	19-4	0	193.2	175	85	5	11	101	55	2.74	89	.251	.355	79-0-1	.215	3	115	-6		-0.3
1908	Phi N	0	0	—	3	0	0	0	7	9	6	0	1	5	3	2.57	94	.346	.469	5	.200	-0*		-1		0.0
1909	Phi N	0	0	—	7	1	0	0	25	22	10	1	4	16	10	3.24	80	.259	.382	9	.000	0	81	-1		-0.2
	Bos N	4	8	.333	18	17	8-2	0	123.1	108	45	1	7	56	32	3.14	90	.244	.339	48	.146	-2	64	1		-0.1
	Year	4	8	.333	25	18	8-2	0	148.1	130	55	2	8	72	42	3.16	88	.247	.346	57	.123	-3	66	0		-0.3
1910	Bos N	9	23	.281	46	29	16-1	2	263	251	113	4	4	94	88	2.67	125	.268	.337	81-1-5	.198	0	63	16		2.1
1911	Bos N	8	18	.308	42	25	13	2	241	258	161	11	10	116	76	4.29	89	.284	.371	84-1-3	.250	3	80	-15		-1.0
1912	Bos N	0	0	—	2	0	0	0	13.1	19	10	0	2	6	6	4.01	89	.239	.315	61-0-1	.213	1	98	-10		-0.8
Total	9	51	103	.331	234	165	106-10	4	1451.2	1368	715	36	59	631	501	3.21	96	.258	.343	522-3-16	.182	3	82	-22		-0.7

BROWN, CURLY Charles Roy "Lefty" B12.9.1888 Spring Hill KS D6.10.1968 Spring Hill KS BL/TL/5-10.5/165 d9.8

1911	StL A	1	2	.333	3	2	1	0	23	22	9	0	1	9	8	2.74	123	.247	.295	9	.000	-1	53	2		0.1
1912	StL A	1	3	.250	16	4	2-1	0	64.2	69	56	0	3	35	28	4.87	68	.277	.373	24	.208	-0*	78	-14		-0.9
1913	StL A	1	1	.500	2	2	2	0	14	12	5	0	0	4	3	2.57	114	.245	.302	5	.400	1	76	1		0.2
1915	Cin N	0	2	.000	7	3	0	0	27	26	20	2	2	4	13	4.67	61	.245	.298	11	.364	1*	147	-6		-0.4
Total	4	3	8	.273	28	11	6-1	0	128.2	129	90	2	6	52	52	4.20	76	.262	.337	49	.224	0	88	-17		-1.0

BROWN, CLINT Clinton Harold B7.8.1903 Blackash PA D12.31.1955 Rocky River OH BL/TR/6-1/190 d9.27

1928	Cle A	0	1	.000	2	1	1	0	11	14	6	0	0	2	2	4.91	84	.304	.333	5	.200	-0	102	0		0.0
1929	Cle A	0	2	.000	3	1	1	0	16.1	18	8	0	0	2	1	3.31	134	.286	.348	7	.000	-1	38	2		0.1
1930	Cle A	11	13	.458	35	31	16-3	1	213.2	271	138	14	4	51	54	4.97	97	.314	.356	73-0-3	.247	2	86	0		0.3
1931	Cle A	11	15	.423	39	33	12-2	0	233.1	284	143	10	1	55	50	4.71	98	.295	.333	87-0-3	.172	-2	104	-1		-0.1
1932	Cle A	15	12	.556	37	32	21-1	1	262.2	298	143	14	4	50	59	4.08	116	.279	.314	100-2-5	.250	6*	100	18		2.2
1933	Cle A	11	12	.478	33	23	10-2	1	185	202	83	10	2	34	47	3.41	130	.276	.310	62-0-3	.145	-3*	81	21		2.2
1934	Cle A	4	3	.571	17	2	1	0	50.1	83	42	3	0	14	15	5.90	77	.359	.396	17	.294	1	105	-9		-0.9
1935	Cle A	4	3	.571	23	5	1	2	49	61	34	3	1	14	20	5.14	88	.300	.349	10	.200	1	77	-4		-0.5
1936	Chi A	6	2	.750	38	2	0	5	83	106	50	5	3	24	19	4.99	104	.315	.366	25-0-2	.160	-0*	127	3		0.2
1937	Chi A	7	7	.500	53	0	0	18	100	92	47	7	1	36	51	3.42	135	.242	.309	18-0-1	.222	1		12		2.1
1938	Chi A	1	3	.250	9	0	0	0	13.2	16	8	0	0	9	2	4.61	106	.333	.439	2	.500	1		1		0.2
1939	Chi A	11	10	.524	61	0	0	18	118.1	127	58	8	0	27	41	3.88	122	.281	.322	19-0-4	.211	1		11		2.1
1940	Chi A	4	6	.400	37	0	0	10	66	75	30	5	2	16	23	3.68	120	.284	.330	14-0-3	.071	-1		6		0.9
1941	Cle A	3	3	.500	41	0	0	5	74.1	77	30	3	1	28	22	3.27	120	.279	.348	17	.118	0		6		0.7
1942	Cle A	1	1	.500	7	0	0	0	9	16	10	2	1	2	4	6.00	57	.356	.396	1	.000	-0		-4		-0.8
Total	15	89	93	.489	434	130	62-8	64	1485.2	1740	830	84	20	368	410	4.26	109	.291	.335	457-2-24	.199	5	95	62		8.7

BROWN, CURT Curtis Steven B1.15.1960 Ft.Lauderdale FL BR/TR/6-5/175(165-200) d6.10 Col Broward (FL) CC

1983	Cal A	1	1	.500	10	0	0	0-0	16	25	13	1	0	4-1	7	7.31	55	.368	.397	0	—	0		-5		-0.6
1984	NY A	1	1	.500	13	0	0	0-1	16.2	18	5	1	0	4-0	10	2.70	142	.281	.319	0	—	0		2		0.3
1986	Mon N	0	1	.000	6	0	0	0-0	12	15	6	0	0	2-2	4	3.00	125	.319	.340	1	.000	0		0		0.0
1987	Mon N	0	1	.000	5	0	0	0-0	7	10	7	2	0	4-1	6	7.71	55	.333	.412	0	—	0		0		-0.0
Total	4	2	4	.333	34	0	0	0-1	51.2	68	31	4	0	14-4	27	4.88	81	.325	.363	1	.000	-0		-6		-0.6

BROWN, ED Edward P. B Chicago IL TR/?/178 d8.19 ▲

1882	StL AA	0	1	.000	1	0	0	0	2	2	1	0	0	0	1	0.00	—	.250	.250	60	.183	-0*				0.0
1884	Tol AA	0	1	.000	1	1	1	0	9	19	16	0	1	4	1	9.00	38	.396	.453	153	.176	-0*	0	-5		-0.4
Total	2	0	1	.000	2	1	1	0	11	21	17	0	1	4	2	7.36	45	.375	.426	213	.178	-0	0	-5		-0.4

BROWN, ELMER Elmer Young "Shook" B8.25.1883 Southport IN D1.23.1955 Indianapolis IN BL/TR/5-11.5/172 d9.16

1911	StL A	1	1	.500	5	3	1-1	0	16.2	16	17	0	0	14	5	6.48	52	.242	.375	8	.125	-1	135	-6		-0.6
1912	StL A	5	8	.385	23	13	2-1	0	120.1	122	56	2	12	42	45	2.99	111	.280	.359	36-0-2	.167	-1	96	4		0.2
1913	Bro N	0	0	—	3	1	0	0	13	6	3	0	1	10	6	2.08	159	.158	.347	4	.000	0	91	2		0.0
1914	Bro N	1	2	.333	11	5	1	0	36.2	33	28	2	7	23	22	3.93	73	.402	.563	12-0-1	.083	-1	175	-6		-0.5
1915	Bro N	0	0	—	1	0	0	0	2	4	1	0	0	3	1	9.00	31	.500	.636	0	—	0		-2		-0.1
Total	5	7	11	.389	43	22	4-2	0	188.2	181	108	4	20	92	79	3.48	93	.287	.395	60-0-3	.133	-3	116	-8		-1.0

BROWN, HAL Hector Harold "Skinny" B12.11.1924 Greensboro NC BR/TR/6-2/182* d4.19 C1 Col North Carolina-Asheville

1951	Chi A	0	0	—	3	0	0	0	8.2	15	9	3	0	4	4	9.35	43	.385	.442	2	1.000	1*		-5		-0.3
1952	Chi A	2	3	.400	24	8	1	0	72.1	82	39	8	0	21	31	4.23	86	.284	.332	19-1-1	.158	1*	108	-5		-0.3
1953	Bos A	11	6	.647	30	25	6-1	0	166.1	177	94	16	0	57	62	4.65	90	.269	.327	58-1-4	.293	5	89	-6		-0.1
1954	Bos A	1	8	.111	40	5	1	0	118	126	64	6	3	41	66	4.12	100	.269	.329	24-0-1	.125	0	82	-1		-0.1
1955	Bos A	1	0	1.000	2	0	0	0	4	2	1	0	0	2-0	2	2.25	191	.143	.250	1	1.000	0		1		0.2
	Bal A	0	4	.000	15	5	1	0	57	51	30	5	0	26-1	26	4.11	93	.241	.322	16	.000	-1*	84	-2		-0.3
	Year	1	4	.200	17	5	1	0	61	53	31	5	0	28-1	28	3.98	97	.235	.318	17	.059	-1	83	-1		-0.1
1956	Bal A	9	7	.563	35	14	4-1	0	151.2	142	72	18	1	37-3	57	4.04	97	.247	.292	48-0-6	.190	1*	101	0		0.1
1957	Bal A	7	8	.467	25	20	7-2	1	150	132	68	17	2	37-3	62	3.90	92	.236	.283	48-0-6	.208	2*	86	-4		-0.2
1958	Bal A	7	5	.583	19	17	4-2	1	96.2	96	35	9	0	20-0	44	3.07	117	.259	.296	27-0-1	.148	-0*	88	7	45	0.8
1959	Bal A	11	9	.550	31	21	2	3	164	158	73	16	1	32-5	81	3.79	100	.252	.289	42-0-9	.048	-3	77	2		-0.1
1960	Bal A	12	5	.706	30	20	6-1	0	159	155	61	14	1	22-3	66	3.06	125	.258	.283	44-0-5	.182	3	135	13		1.6
1961	Bal A	10	6	.625	27	23	6-3	1	166.2	153	62	14	1	33-0	61	3.19	121	.247	.284	50-0-3	.140	-0	91	15		1.3
1962	Bal A	6	4	.600	22	11	0	1	85.2	88	41	12	3	21-2	25	4.10	90	.268	.317	28-0-2	.286	2	112	-3		-0.2
	NY A	0	1	.000	2	1	0	0	6.2	9	10	3	0	2-0	2	6.75	56	.333	.367	1	.000	0	71	-4		-0.5
	Year	6	5	.545	24	12	0	1	92.1	97	51	15	3	23-2	27	4.29	84	.273	.321	29-0-2	.276	1	109	-8		-0.7
1963	Hou N	5	11	.313	26	20	6-3	0	141.1	137	54	14	0	8-0	68	3.31	95	.255	.264	43-0-3	.093	-2	66	0		-0.3
1964	Hou N	3	15	.167	27	21	6-1	0	132	154	68	18	2	26-10	53	3.95	86	.292	.326	39-0-2	.128	-1	45	-16		-1.2
Total	14	85	92	.480	358	211	47-13	11	1680	1677	781	173	14	389-22	710	3.81	98	.260	.302	484-2-40	.169	8	88	0	45	0.6

BROWN, JACKIE Jackie Gene B5.31.1943 Holdenville OK BR/TR/6-1/195* d7.2 C9 b-Paul

1970	Was A	2	2	.500	24	5	1	0-0	57	49	28	8	0	37-1	47	3.95	91	.231	.344	13	.154	-0	94	-2		-0.2
1971	Was A	3	4	.429	14	9	0	0-0	47	60	34	9	1	27-2	21	5.94	57	.316	.404	15	.133	-1	91	-13		-1.8
1973	Tex A	5	5	.500	25	3	2-1	2-4	66.2	82	31	7	2	25-0	45	3.92	96	.309	.372	0	—	0	143	0		-0.1
1974	Tex A	13	12	.520	35	26	9-2	0-0	216.2	219	97	13	4	74-4	134	3.57	100	.265	.327	0	—	0	108	1		-0.1
1975	Tex A	5	5	.500	17	7	2-1	0-0	70.1	70	37	7	2	35-2	35	4.22	89	.266	.355	0	—	0	97	-3		-0.5
	Cle A	1	2	.333	25	3	1	1-2	69.1	72	40	9	0	29-6	41	4.28	89	.276	.342	0	—	0	121	-8		-0.8
	Year	6	7	.462	42	10	3-1	1-2	139.2	142	77	16	2	64-8	76	4.25	89	.271	.349	0	—	0	177	-5		-0.8
1976	Cle A	9	11	.450	32	27	5-2	0-0	180	193	94	14	7	55-4	104	4.25	83	.276	.332	0	—	0	107	-15		-1.5
1977	Mon N	9	12	.429	42	25	6-2	0-0	185.2	189	99	15	4	71-5	89	4.51	86	.264	.332	56-0-4	.125	-2	99	-11		-1.5
Total	7	47	53	.470	234	105	26-8	3-6	892.2	934	460	82	20	353-24	516	4.18	88	.272	.341	84-0-4	.131	-3	105	-48		-5.8

BROWN, KEVIN James Kevin B3.14.1965 Milledgeville GA BR/TR/6-4/195(188-220) [TexA86 1/4] d9.30 Col Georgia Tech

1986	Tex A	1	0	1.000	1	1	0	0-0	6	6	3	0	0	0-0	4	3.60	120	.316	.316	0	—	0	189	0		0.1
1988	Tex A	1	1	.500	4	4	1	0-0	23.1	33	15	2	1	8-0	12	4.24	97	.330	.385	0	—	0	156	-1		-0.1
1989	Tex A	12	9	.571	28	28	7	0-0	191	167	81	10	4	70-3	104	3.35	119	.234	.303	0	—	0	96	13		1.6
1990	Tex A	12	10	.545	26	26	6-2	0-0	180	175	84	13	3	60-3	88	3.60	109	.255	.315	0	—	0	96	13		1.5
1991	Tex A	9	12	.429	33	33	0	0-0	210.2	233	116	17	10	90-5	96	4.40	82	.284	.338	0	.000	-0*	108	6	15	0.6
																						0	111	-9		-0.8

YEAR	TM LG	W	L	PCT	G	GS	CG-SHO	SV-BS	IP	H	R	HR	HB	BB-IB	SO	ERA	AERA	OAV	OOB	AB-HR-SH	AVG	PB	SUP	APR	DL	PW
1992	Tex A★	21	11	.656	35	35	11-1	0-0	265.2	262	117	11	10	76-2	173	3.32	115	.260	.316	0	—	0	110	13		1.5
1993	Tex A	15	12	.556	34	34	12-3	0-0	233	228	105	14	15	74-5	142	3.59	100	.252	.318	0	—	0*	107	15	6	1.7
1994	Tex A	7	9	.438	26	25	3	0-0	170	218	109	18	6	50-3	123	4.82	100	.314	.361	0	—	0	93	-3		-0.1
1995	Bal A	10	9	.526	26	26	3-1	0-0	172.1	155	73	10	9	48-1	117	3.60	133	.241	.302	75-0-4	.120	-1*	66	57	15	6.9
1996	Fla N★	17	11	.607	32	32	5-3	0-0	233	187	60	8	16	33-2	159	1.89	218	.220	.262	72-0-6	.125	-0	95	37		3.8
1997	†Fla N★	16	8	.667	33	33	6-2	0-0	237.1	214	77	10	14	66-7	205	2.69	151	.240	.303	82-0-7	.207	4	101	47		4.9
1998	†SD N★	18	7	.720	36	35	7-3	0-0	257	225	77	8	10	49-4	257	2.38	167	.235	.279	78-0-13	.064	-5	93	37		3.2
1999	LA N	18	9	.667	35	35	5-1	0-0	252.1	210	99	19	7	59-1	221	3.00	145	.222	.273	66-0-14	.076	-3	95	48	15	3.4
2000	LA N★	13	6	.684	33	33	5-1	0-0	230	181	76	21	9	47-1	216	2.58	172	.213	.261	36-1-2	.083	2	99	18	77	2.1
2001	LA N	10	4	.714	20	19	1	0-0	115.2	94	41	8	2	38-2	104	2.65	156	.224	.291	20-1-2	.250	2	88	-7	96	-0.4
2002	LA N	3	4	.429	17	10	0	0-0	63.2	68	36	9	5	23-1	58	4.81	81	.274	.348	63-0-6	.159	0	85	39	15	0.7
2003	LA N✻	14	9	.609	32	32	0	0-0	211	184	67	11	5	56-2	185	2.39	173	.236	.290			0	103	7	50	0.7
2004	†NY A	10	6	.625	22	22	0	0-0	132	132	65	14	3	35-0	83	4.09	112	.262	.309	2	.500	1	119	-17	117	-2.0
2005	NY A	4	7	.364	13	13	0	0-0	73.1	107	57	5	7	19-1	50	6.50	67	.341	.388	0			97	-3	406	-2.0
Total	19	211	144	.594	486	476	72-17	0-0	3256.1	3079	1357	208	139	901-42	2397	3.28	128	.249	.306	495-2-54	.129	-3	97	322	406	33.8

BROWN, JIM   James W. H. B12.12.1860 Clinton Co. PA D4.6.1908 Williamsport PA d4.17 ▲

YEAR	TM LG	W	L	PCT	G	GS	CG-SHO	SV-BS	IP	H	R	HR	HB	BB-IB	SO	ERA	AERA	OAV	OOB	AB-HR-SH	AVG	PB	SUP	APR	DL	PW
1884	Alt U	1	9	.100	11	11	7	0	74	99	80	0	0	36	39	5.35	50	.301	.370	88-1	.250	-2*	58	-20		-2.0
	NY U	1	1	1.000	1	1	1	0	9	10	9	0	0	8	2	5.00	60	.263	.391	3	.000	-1	0	-2		-0.2
	StP U	1	4	.200	6	6	4-1	0	36	43	34	1	0	14	20	3.75	35	.277	.337	16	.313	-1	96	-18		-1.4
1886	Phi AA	1	1	1.000	1	1	1	0	8.1	9	5	0	0	3	4	3.24	108	.265	.324	3	.000	-1	68	0		0.0
Total	2	2	15	.118	19	19	13-1	0	127.1	161	128	1	0	61	65	4.74	50	.290	.360	110-1	.245	1	62	-40		-3.6

BROWN, JAMIE   Jamie Monroe B3.31.1977 Meridian MS BR/TR/6-2/200 [CleA96 21/633] d5.20 Col Meridian (MS) CC [DL 2000 Cle A 27]

YEAR	TM LG	W	L	PCT	G	GS	CG-SHO	SV-BS	IP	H	R	HR	HB	BB-IB	SO	ERA	AERA	OAV	OOB	AB-HR-SH	AVG	PB	SUP	APR	DL	PW
2004	Bos A	0	0	—	4	0	0	0-0	7.2	15	7	1	0	4-0	6	5.87	83	.417	.463	0	—	0		-1		-0.1

BROWN, JOHN   John J. "Ad" B Trenton NJ d8.11

YEAR	TM LG	W	L	PCT	G	GS	CG-SHO	SV-BS	IP	H	R	HR	HB	BB-IB	SO	ERA	AERA	OAV	OOB	AB-HR-SH	AVG	PB	SUP	APR	DL	PW
1897	Bro N	0	1	.000	1	1	0		5	7	8	0	3	4		7.20	57	.333	.500	2	.500	0	52	-3		-0.3

BROWN, JOPHERY   Jophery Clifford B1.22.1945 Grambling LA BL/TR/6-2/190 [ChiN66 S2/23] d9.21 Col Grambling St.

YEAR	TM LG	W	L	PCT	G	GS	CG-SHO	SV-BS	IP	H	R	HR	HB	BB-IB	SO	ERA	AERA	OAV	OOB	AB-HR-SH	AVG	PB	SUP	APR	DL	PW
1968	Chi N	0	0	—	1	0	0		2	2	1	0	0	1-1	0	4.50	70	.286	.375	0	—	0		0		0.0

BROWN, JOE   Joseph E. B4.4.1859 Warren PA D6.28.1888 Warren PA 5-10/162 d8.16 ▲

YEAR	TM LG	W	L	PCT	G	GS	CG-SHO	SV-BS	IP	H	R	HR	HB	BB-IB	SO	ERA	AERA	OAV	OOB	AB-HR-SH	AVG	PB	SUP	APR	DL	PW
1884	Chi N	4	2	.667	7	6	5	0	50	56	36	4	0	7	27	4.68	67	.258	.281	61	.213	-1*	155	-5		-0.5
1885	Bal AA	0	4	.000	4	4	4	0	38	52	33	0	0	4	9	5.68	57	.306	.322	19	.158	-1*	113	-8		-0.7
Total	2	4	6	.400	11	10	9	0	88	108	69	4	0	11	36	5.11	62	.279	.299	80	.200	-2	139	-13		-1.2

BROWN, JOE   Joseph Henry B7.3.1900 Little Rock AR D3.7.1950 Los Angeles CA BR/TR/6-0/176 d5.17

YEAR	TM LG	W	L	PCT	G	GS	CG-SHO	SV-BS	IP	H	R	HR	HB	BB-IB	SO	ERA	AERA	OAV	OOB	AB-HR-SH	AVG	PB	SUP	APR	DL	PW
1927	Chi A	0	0	—	1	1	0		1	1	1	0	0	0	6	∞	—	1.000	1.000	0	—	0	62	-3		-0.2

BROWN, KEITH   Keith Edward B2.14.1964 Flagstaff AZ BB/TR/6-4/215* [CinN86 21/540] d8.25 Col Cal St.-Sacramento

YEAR	TM LG	W	L	PCT	G	GS	CG-SHO	SV-BS	IP	H	R	HR	HB	BB-IB	SO	ERA	AERA	OAV	OOB	AB-HR-SH	AVG	PB	SUP	APR	DL	PW
1988	Cin N	2	1	.667	4	3	0	0-0	16.1	14	5	1	0	4-0	6	2.76	130	.237	.286	4-0-1	.000	-0	50	2		0.3
1990	Cin N	0	0	—	8	0	0	0-0	11.1	12	6	2	0	3-0	8	4.76	83	.286	.333	0	—	0		-1		0.0
1991	Cin N	0	0	—	11	0	0	0-0	12	15	4	0	0	6-1	4	2.25	169	.306	.382	0	—	0		2		0.1
1992	Cin N	0	1	.000	2	2	0	0-0	8	10	5	2	0	5-0	5	4.50	80	.313	.405	2-0-1	.000	-0	113	-1		0.1
Total	4	2	2	.500	25	5	0	0-0	47.2	51	20	5	0	18-1	23	3.40	110	.280	.345	6-0-2	.000	0	72	2		0.1

BROWN, KEVIN   Kevin Dewayne B3.5.1966 Oroville CA BL/TL/6-1/185* [AtlN86*S1/2] d7.27 Col Sacramento (CA) City

YEAR	TM LG	W	L	PCT	G	GS	CG-SHO	SV-BS	IP	H	R	HR	HB	BB-IB	SO	ERA	AERA	OAV	OOB	AB-HR-SH	AVG	PB	SUP	APR	DL	PW
1990	NY N	0	0	—	2	0	0	0-0	1	2	1	0	0	1-0	1	0.00	—	.250	.333	0	—	0		1		0.
	Mil A	1	1	.500	5	3	0	0-0	21	14	7	1	1	7-1	12	2.57	151	.182	.256	0	—	0	55	3		0.
1991	Mil A	2	4	.333	15	10	0	0-1	63.2	66	39	6	1	34-2	30	5.51	72	.270	.361	0	—	0	119	-9		-0.
1992	Sea A	0	0	—	2	0	0	0-1	3	3	1	0	0	3-0	2	9.00	45	.333	.467	0	—	0		-2		-0.
Total	3	3	5	.375	24	13	0	0-1	89.2	86	49	8	2	45-3	44	4.82	82	.252	.341	0	—	0	105	-7		-0.

BROWN, LLOYD   Lloyd Andrew "Gimpy" B12.25.1904 Beeville TX D1.14.1974 Opa-Locka FL BL/TL/5-9/170 d7.17

YEAR	TM LG	W	L	PCT	G	GS	CG-SHO	SV-BS	IP	H	R	HR	HB	BB-IB	SO	ERA	AERA	OAV	OOB	AB-HR-SH	AVG	PB	SUP	APR	DL	PW
1925	Bro N	0	3	.000	17	5	1	0	63.1	79	39	1	2	25	23	4.12	101	.319	.385	23-0-1	.087	-2	113	-1		-0.
1928	Was A	4	4	.500	27	10	2	0	107	112	62	7	2	40	38	4.04	99	.273	.341	13	.161	0	99	-3		0.
1929	Was A	8	7	.533	40	15	7-1	0	168	186	92	7	1	69	48	4.18	101	.297	.368	50-0-2	.220	3	101	1		0.
1930	Was A	16	12	.571	38	22	10-1	0	197	220	99	6	5	65	59	4.25	108	.293	.354	65-1-2	.215	2	79	11		1.
1931	Was A	15	14	.517	42	32	15-1	0	258.2	256	120	13	0	79	79	3.20	134	.257	.311	96-0-3	.229	3	100	27		3.
1932	Was A	15	12	.556	46	24	10-2	5	202.2	239	115	11	1	55	53	4.44	97	.296	.342	70-0-6	.100	-5	99	-4		-0.
1933	StL A	1	6	.143	8	6	0	0	39	57	35	1	0	17	7	7.15	65	.350	.411	11	.273	1	82	-10		-1.
	Bos A	8	11	.421	33	21	9-2	1	163.1	180	93	4	0	64	37	4.02	109	.281	.347	57-2-4	.281	6	85	4		1.
	Year	9	17	.346	41	27	9-2	1	202.1	237	128	5	0	81	44	4.63	96	.295	.360	68-2-4	.279	7	85	-6		-0.
1934	Cle A	5	10	.333	38	15	5	0	117	116	69	7	2	51	39	3.85	118	.263	.342	30-0-1	.233	1	61	6		0.
1935	Cle A	8	7	.533	42	8	4-2	4	122	123	52	6	3	37	45	3.61	125	.265	.323	37-0-2	.108	-2	75	14		1.
1936	Cle A	8	8	.444	24	16	12-1	1	140.1	166	78	7	13	45	34	4.17	121	.294	.349	45-1-4	.222	1	76	12		1.
1937	Cle A	2	6	.250	31	5	2	0	77	107	59	4	2	27	32	6.55	70	.329	.386	24	.167	-1	49	-14		-1.
1940	Phi N	1	3	.250	18	2	0	1	37.2	58	26	3	0	16	16	6.21	63	.354	.411	13-0-1	.077	-1	123	-8		-1.
Total	12	91	105	.464	404	181	77-10	21	1693	1899	937	83	22	590	510	4.20	105	.288	.348	552-4-26	.192	6	88	35		5.

BROWN, MACE   Mace Stanley B5.21.1909 North English IA D3.24.2002 Greensboro NC BR/TR/6-1/190 d5.21 Mil 1944-45 Col Iowa

YEAR	TM LG	W	L	PCT	G	GS	CG-SHO	SV-BS	IP	H	R	HR	HB	BB-IB	SO	ERA	AERA	OAV	OOB	AB-HR-SH	AVG	PB	SUP	APR	DL	PW
1935	Pit N	4	1	.800	18	5	2	0	72.2	84	41	5	0	22	28	3.59	114	.287	.337	60-0-3	.167	-0	141	2		0
1936	Pit N	10	11	.476	47	10	3	3	165	178	89	8	1	55	56	3.87	105	.275	.332	60-0-3	.167	-2	98	1		0
1937	Pit N	7	2	.778	50	2	0	7	107.2	109	59	2	1	45	60	4.18	92	.261	.334	38-0-5	.132	-2	123	-1		0
1938	Pit N★	15	9	.625	51	2	0	5	132.2	155	68	5	0	44	55	3.80	100	.294	.349	64-0-4	.109	-4	83	9		0
1939	Pit N	9	13	.409	47	19	8-1	7	200.1	232	90	8	2	52	71	3.37	114	.293	.338	52-0-5	.115	-1	129	6		0
1940	Pit N	10	9	.526	48	17	5-1	7	173	181	78	5	2	49	73	3.49	109	.267	.318	52-0-5	.115	-1		1		0
1941	Pit N	0	0	—	1	0	0	0	1.1	2	0	0	0	0	0	0.00	—	.333	.333	0	—	0		3		
	Bro N	3	2	.600	24	0	0	3	42.2	31	17	3	1	26	22	3.16	116	.208	.330	8	.000	-1		3		
	Year	3	2	.600	25	0	0	3	44	33	17	3	1	28	22	3.07	109	.213	.330	8	.000	-1		2		
1942	Bos A	9	3	.750	34	0	0	6	60.1	56	27	4	0	28	20	3.43	109	.255	.339	15-0-3	.059	-1		12		
1943	Bos A	6	6	.500	49	0	0	9	93.1	71	26	2	0	51	40	2.12	156	.222	.329	17-0-1	.000	-1		4		
1946	†Bos A	3	1	.750	18	0	0	1	26.1	26	7	2	0	16	10	2.05	179	.268	.372	5-0-1	.000	-1		4		
Total	10	76	57	.571	387	55	18-2	48	1075.1	1125	502	44	7	388	435	3.46	110	.271	.335	313-0-24	.137	-11	110	35		

BROWN, MARK   Mark Anthony B7.13.1959 Bellows Falls VT BB/TR/6-2/190* [BalA80 6/156] d8.9 Col Massachusetts

YEAR	TM LG	W	L	PCT	G	GS	CG-SHO	SV-BS	IP	H	R	HR	HB	BB-IB	SO	ERA	AERA	OAV	OOB	AB-HR-SH	AVG	PB	SUP	APR	DL	PW
1984	Bal A	1	2	.333	9	0	0	0-0	23	22	11	2	1	7-0	10	3.91	100	.256	.319	0	—	0		0		0
1985	Min A	0	0	—	6	0	0	0-0	15.2	21	13	1	0	7-0	5	6.89	64	.333	.384	0	—	0		-4		0
Total	2	1	2	.333	15	0	0	0-0	38.2	43	24	3	1	14-0	15	5.12	80	.289	.347	0	—	0		-4		0

BROWN, MIKE   Michael Gary B3.4.1959 Camden Co. NJ BR/TR/6-2/195* [BosA80 2/48] d9.16 C1 Col Clemson

YEAR	TM LG	W	L	PCT	G	GS	CG-SHO	SV-BS	IP	H	R	HR	HB	BB-IB	SO	ERA	AERA	OAV	OOB	AB-HR-SH	AVG	PB	SUP	APR	DL	PW
1982	Bos A	1	0	1.000	3	0	0	0-0	6	7	0	0	0	1-0	4	0.00	—	.304	.333			0		3		
1983	Bos A	6	6	.500	19	18	3-1	0-0	104	110	62	12	2	43-1	35	4.67	94	.276	.345			0	134	-4	22	
1984	Bos A	1	8	.111	15	11	0	0-0	67	104	63	9	3	19-1	32	6.85	61	.347	.388			0	76	-21		
1985	Bos A	0	0	—	2	1	0	0-0	3	9	8	0	0	2-1	2	21.60	20	.500	.545			0	126	-6		
1986	Bos A	4	4	.500	15	10	0	0-0	57.1	72	35	10	1	25-1	32	5.34	79	.316	.381			0	84	-6		
	Sea A	0	2	.000	7	3	0	0-0	15.2	19	14	4	0	11-0	9	7.47	57	.302	.405			0	70	-11		
	Year	4	6	.400	21	12	0	0-0	73	91	49	14	1	36-1	41	5.79	73	.313	.387			0				
1987	Sea A	0	0	—	1	0	0	0-0	0.1	3	2	0	0	0-0	0	54.00	—	.750	.750			0	101	-41	22	
Total	6	12	20	.375	61	42	3-1	0-0	253.2	324	184	35	6	102-3	115	5.75	75	.313	.374			0		3		

BROWN, MORDECAI   Mordecai Peter Centennial "Three Finger", "Miner" B10.19.1876 Nyesville IN D2.14.1948 Terre Haute IN BB/TR/5-10/175 d4.19 M1 HF1949

YEAR	TM LG	W	L	PCT	G	GS	CG-SHO	SV-BS	IP	H	R	HR	HB	BB-IB	SO	ERA	AERA	OAV	OOB	AB-HR-SH	AVG	PB	SUP	APR	DL	PW
1903	StL N	9	13	.409	26	26	21-4	0	201	231	105	7	6	59	83	2.60	126	.293	.347	77-0-2	.195	-0	77	11		
1904	Chi N	15	10	.600	26	23	21-4	1	212.1	155	74	1	6	50	81	1.86	143	.199	.253	89-0-1	.213	1*	100	16		
1905	Chi N	18	12	.600	30	24	24-4	0	249	219	89	3	1	44	89	2.17	138	.235	.271	93-1-7	.140	-1*	111	20		
1906	†Chi N	26	6	.813	36	32	27-9	3	277.1	198	56	1	4	61	144	1.04	254	.202	.252	98-0-5	.204	1	141	45		
1907	†Chi N	20	6	.769	34	27	20-6	3	233	180	51	2	4	40	107	1.39	179	.221	.262	85-1-5	.153	-0*	123	29		

YEAR	TM LG	W	L	PCT	G	GS	CG-SHO	SV-BS	IP	H	R	HR	HB	BB-IB	SO	ERA	AERA	OAV	OOB	AB-HR-SH	AVG	PB	SUP	APR	DL	PW
1908	†Chi N	29	9	.763	44	31	27-9	5	312.1	214	64	1	7	49	123	1.47	160	.195	.232	121-0-5	.207	1*	105	32		4.4
1909	Chi N	27	9	.750	50	34	32-8	7	342.2	246	78	1	7	53	172	1.31	193	.202	.239	125-0-5	.176	1	125	45		5.3
1910	†Chi N	25	14	.641	46	31	27-6	7	295.1	256	95	3	4	64	143	1.86	155	.232	.277	103-0-6	.175	-0	132	29		4.0
1911	Chi N	21	11	.656	53	27	21	13	270	267	110	5	6	55	129	2.80	118	.262	.303	103-0-6		-0	113	16		2.3
1912	Chi N	5	6	.455	15	8	5-2	0	88.2	92	35	2	1	20	34	2.64	126	.275	.317	31-0-1	.290	2*	113	6		0.8
1913	Cin N	11	12	.478	39	16	11-1	6	173.1	174	79	7	1	44	41	2.91	112	.277	.325	54-0-3	.204	-0	80	5		0.6
1914	StL F	12	6	.667	26	18	13-2	0	175	172	73	7	3	43	81	3.29	92	.254	.302	59-0-2	.254	1	101	-1		-0.1
	Bro F	2	5	.286	9	8	5	0	57.2	63	33	1	0	18	32	4.21	68	.276	.329	19	.211	-1	128	-8		-0.9
	Year	14	11	.560	35	26	18-2	0	232.2	235	106	8	3	61	113	3.52	85	.260	.309	78-0-2	.244	0	109	-7		-1.0
1915	Chi F	17	8	.680	35	25	17-3	4	236.1	189	75	2	7	64	95	2.09	120	.220	.279	82-0-4	.293	5*	125	11		1.8
1916	Chi N	2	3	.400	12	4	2	0	48.1	52	27	0	4	9	21	3.91	74	.289	.337	16	.250	-0	167	-5		-0.5
Total	14	239	130	.648	481	332	271-55	49	3172.1	2708	1044	43	61	673	1375	2.06	137	.233	.278	1143-2-49	.206	15	114	251		32.7

BROWN, MYRL Myrl Lincoln B10.10.1894 Waynesboro PA D2.23.1981 Harrisburg PA BR/TR/5-11/172 d8.19 Col Lebanon Valley

| 1922 | Pit N | 3 | 1 | .750 | 7 | 5 | 2 | 0 | 34.2 | 42 | 25 | 2 | 0 | 13 | 9 | 5.97 | 68 | .296 | .355 | 11-0-2 | .273 | 1 | 164 | -6 | | -0.5 |

BROWN, NORM Norman Ladelle B2.1.1919 Evergreen NC D5.31.1995 Bennettsville SC BB/TR/6-3/180 d10.3 Mil 1944-45

1943	Phi A	0	0	—	1	1	0	0	7	5	4	0	0	0	1	0.00	—	.185	.185	3	.000	-0	99	1		0.0
1946	Phi A	0	1	.000	4	0	0	0	7.1	8	8	2	0	6	3	6.14	58	.267	.389	0		0		-3		-0.4
Total	2	0	1	.000	5	1	0	0	14.1	13	12	2	0	6	4	3.14	111	.228	.302	3	.000	-0	99	-2		-0.4

BROWN, PAUL Paul Dwayne B6.18.1941 Ft.Smith AR BR/TR/6-1/190* d7.23 b-Jackie

1961	Phi N	0	1	.000	5	1	0	0	10	13	9	3	1	8-0	1	8.10	50	.325	.440	2	.500	-0	0	-4		-0.3
1962	Phi N	0	6	.000	23	9	0	1	63.2	74	45	9	3	33-0	29	5.94	65	.298	.385	13-0-1	.154	-0	93	-14	72	-1.2
1963	Phi N	0	1	.000	6	2	0	0	15.1	15	10	2	2	5-0	11	4.11	79	.238	.314	2	.500	0	173	-2		-0.1
1968	Phi N	0	0	—	2	0	0	0	4	6	4	0	0	1-0	4	9.00	33	.353	.389	0	—	0		-2		-0.1
Total	4	0	8	.000	36	12	0	1	93	108	68	14	6	47-0	45	6.00	63	.293	.380	17-0-1	.235	-0	97	-22	72	-1.7

BROWN, RAY Paul Percival B1.31.1889 Chicago IL D5.29.1955 Los Angeles CA BR/TR/6-1/172 d9.29

| 1909 | Chi N | 1 | 0 | 1.000 | 1 | 1 | 1 | 0 | 9 | 5 | 3 | 0 | 0 | 4 | 2 | 2.00 | 127 | .172 | .273 | 3 | .000 | -0 | 165 | 0 | | 0.0 |

BROWN, STUB Richard P. B8.3.1870 Baltimore MD D3.10.1948 Baltimore MD TL/6-2/220 d8.15

1893	Bal N	0	0	—	2	0	0	0	9	13	8	0	1	5	0	6.00	79	.325	.413	5	.200	-0		-1		-0.1
1894	Bal N	4	0	1.000	9	6	3	0	49.2	59	39	3	1	24	8	4.89	112	.292	.370	23-0-1	.087	-4	104	2		-0.2
1897	Cin N	0	1	.000	2	1	1	0	13	17	8	1	0	8	2	4.15	110	.315	.403	5	.000	-1	0	1		-0.1
Total	3	4	1	.800	13	7	4	0	71.2	89	55	4	2	37	10	4.90	106	.301	.382	33-0-1	.091	-5	93	2		-0.4

BROWN, BOB Robert Murray B4.1.1911 Dorchester MA D8.3.1990 Pembroke MA BR/TR/6-0.5/190 d4.21

1930	Bos N	0	0	—	3	0	0	0	6	10	7	0	0	8	1	10.50	47	.417	.563	2	.000	-0		-3		-0.2
1931	Bos N	1	0	1.000	3	1	0	0	6.1	9	7	0	0	3	2	8.53	44	.375	.444	2	.500	-0	45	-3		-0.4
1932	Bos N	14	7	.667	35	28	9	1	213	187	89	6	2	104	110	3.30	114	.238	.329	67-0-5	.194	-0	104	13		1.1
1933	Bos N	0	0	—	5	0	0	0	6.2	6	4	0	0	3	3	2.70	114	.250	.333	2	.000	-0*		-1		-0.1
1934	Bos N	1	3	.250	16	8	2-1	0	58.1	59	40	2	3	36	21	5.71	67	.262	.371	21	.238	-0	141	-12		-0.7
1935	Bos N	1	8	.111	15	10	2-1	0	65	79	55	2	0	36	17	6.37	59	.302	.386	19-0-1	.105	-1*	87	-20		-2.4
1936	Bos N	0	2	.000	2	2	0	0	8.1	10	6	1	0	3	5	5.40	71	.278	.333	2	.000	-0	55	-2		-0.3
Total	7	16	21	.432	79	49	13-2	1	363.2	360	208	11	5	193	159	4.48	84	.261	.354	115-0-6	.183	-2	103	-28		-3.0

BROWN, SCOTT Scott Edward B8.30.1956 DeQuincy LA BR/TR/6-2/220 [CinN75 4/94] d8.11 [DL 1982 KC A 181]

| 1981 | Cin N | 1 | 0 | 1.000 | 10 | 0 | 0 | 0-2 | 13 | 16 | 4 | 0 | 0 | 1-1 | 7 | 2.77 | 127 | .314 | .321 | 1 | .000 | -0 | | 1 | | 0.1 |

BROWN, STEVE Steven Elbert B2.12.1957 San Francisco CA BR/TR/6-5/200* d8.1 Col California-Davis

1983	Cal A	2	3	.400	12	4	2-1	0-0	46	45	19	4	0	16-1	23	3.52	115	.256	.314	0	—	0	34	3		0.3
1984	Cal A	0	1	.000	3	3	0	0-0	11	16	13	0	0	9-1	5	9.00	44	.340	.439	0	—	0	121	-7		-0.5
Total	2	2	4	.333	15	7	2-1	0-0	57	61	32	4	0	25-2	28	4.58	88	.274	.343	0	—	0	71	-4		-0.2

BROWN, TOM Thomas Dale B8.10.1949 Lafayette LA BR/TR/6-1/170 d9.14 Col Louisiana-Monroe

| 1978 | Sea A | 0 | 0 | — | 6 | 0 | 0 | 0-0 | 13 | 14 | 6 | 2 | 0 | 4-0 | 8 | 4.15 | 93 | .286 | .340 | 0 | — | 0 | 0 | 0 | | 0.0 |

BROWN, TOM Thomas Tarlton B9.21.1860 Liverpool, England D10.25.1927 Washington DC BL/TR/5-10/168 d7.6 M2/U4 ▲

1882	Bal A	0	0	—	2	0	0	0	8.1	13	7	0	0	6	2	1.08	255	.333	.422	181-1	.304	1*		0		0.0
1883	Col AA	0	1	.000	3	1	1	0	14	14	17	0	0	10	6	5.79	53	.246	.358	420-5	.274	1*	93	-5		-0.2
1884	Col AA	2	1	.667	4	0	0	0	19	27	24	0	0	7	5	7.11	43	.281	.330	451-5	.273	1*		-9		-1.0
1885	Pit AA	0	0	—	2	0	0	0	6	0	3	0	3	3	2	3.00	107	.000	.333	437-4	.307	1*		0		0.0
1886	Pit AA	0	0	—	1	0	0	0	2	2	4	0	0	5	1	9.00	38	.125	.333	460-1	.285	0*		-1		0.0
Total	5	2	2	.500	12	1	1	0	49.1	56	55	0	3	31	16	5.29	57	.242	.340	1949-16	.286	4	93	-15		-1.2

BROWN, JUMBO Walter George B4.30.1907 Greene RI D10.2.1966 Freeport NY BR/TR/6-4/295 d8.26

1925	Chi A	0	0	—	2	0	0	0	6	5	5	0	0	4	0	3.00	144	.217	.333	1	.000	-0	0		0.0
1927	Cle A	0	2	.000	8	0	0	0	18.2	19	14	3	1	26	8	6.27	67	.284	.489	3	.000	1		-4		-0.2
1928	Cle A	0	1	.000	5	0	0	0	14.2	19	15	0	0	15	12	6.75	61	.365	.507	3	.667	1		-5		-0.2
1932	NY A	5	2	.714	19	3	3-1	1	55.2	58	30	1	2	30	31	4.53	90	.270	.364	23-0-1	.174	-1	70	-2		-0.2
1933	NY A	7	5	.583	21	8	1	0	74	78	39	1	2	50	55	5.23	74	.269	.380	28-0-1	.179	-1	145	-11		-1.5
1935	NY A	6	5	.545	20	8	3-1	0	87.1	94	41	2	0	37	41	3.61	112	.279	.350	32	.313	3	102	5		0.8
1936	Cin N	1	4	.200	20	3	0	1	64	93	47	4	0	29	19	5.91	79	.352	.416	19	.000	-3	107	-9		-0.8
1937	Cin N	1	0	1.000	4	0	0	0	9.2	16	10	0	0	3	4	8.38	45	.390	.432	2	.000	-0	139	-5		-0.4
	NY N	1	0	1.000	4	0	0	0	8.2	5	2	0	0	5	4	1.04	374	.172	.294	0	—	0		2		0.3
	Year	2	0	1.000	8	1	0	0	18.1	21	12	0	0	8	8	4.91	78	.300	.372	2	.000	0	136	-2		-0.1
1938	NY N	5	3	.625	43	0	0	5	90	65	26	5	1	28	42	1.80	209	.204	.271	16	.188	1		18		1.7
1939	NY N	4	0	1.000	31	0	0	7	56.1	69	30	1	1	25	24	4.15	95	.304	.371	11	.364	1		-1		0.0
1940	NY N	2	4	.333	41	0	0	7	55.1	49	25	5	0	25	31	3.42	114	.232	.314	10	.100	-1		2		0.2
1941	NY N	1	5	.167	31	0	0	8	57	49	23	2	0	21	30	3.32	111	.238	.308	9	.111	-1		3		0.3
Total	12	33	31	.516	249	23	7-2	29	597.1	669	316	26	5	300	304	4.07	99	.271	.357	157-0-2	.204	2	116	-7		0.0

BROWN, WALTER Walter Irving B4.23.1915 Jamestown NY D2.3.1991 Westfield NY BR/TR/5-11/175 d5.16

| 1947 | StL A | 1 | 0 | 1.000 | 19 | 0 | 0 | 0 | 46 | 50 | 27 | 3 | 0 | 28 | 10 | 4.89 | 79 | .294 | .394 | 11 | .000 | -1 | | -4 | | -0.3 |

BROWNING, CAL Calvin Duane B3.16.1938 Burns Flat OK BL/TL/5-11/190 d6.12 Col Oklahoma St.

| 1960 | StL N | 0 | 0 | — | 1 | 0 | 0 | 0 | 0.2 | 5 | 3 | 1 | 0 | 1-0 | 0 | 40.50 | 10 | .714 | .750 | 0 | — | 0 | | -2 | | -0.1 |

BROWNING, FRANK Frank "Dutch" B10.29.1882 Falmouth KY D5.20.1948 San Antonio TX BR/TR/5-6/155 d4.16 Col Georgetown

| 1910 | Det A | 2 | 2 | .500 | 11 | 6 | 2 | 0 | 51 | 52 | 29 | 0 | 2 | 10 | 16 | 2.57 | 102 | .262 | .298 | 14-0-2 | .000 | -2 | 119 | -1 | | -0.2 |

BROWNING, TOM Thomas Leo B4.28.1960 Casper WY BL/TL/6-1/190(180-195) [CinN82 9/233] d9.9 Col Tennessee Wesleyan

1984	Cin N	1	0	1.000	3	3	0	0-0	23.1	27	4	0	0	5-0	14	1.54	246	.303	.340	7	.143	-0	70	6		0.3
1985	Cin N	20	9	.690	38	38	6-4	0-0	261.1	242	111	29	3	73-8	155	3.55	107	.245	.297	88-0-9	.193	2*	112	8		1.1
1986	Cin N	14	13	.519	39	39	4-0	0-0	243.1	225	123	26	1	70-6	147	3.81	101	.245	.295	86-0-7	.163	-1*	109	-2		-0.4
1987	Cin N	10	13	.435	32	31	2	0-0	183	201	107	27	5	61-7	117	5.02	84	.284	.342	52-0-6	.154	0*	92	-13		-1.5
1988	Cin N	18	5	.783	36	36	5-2	0-0	250.2	205	98	36	7	64-3	124	3.41	105	.224	.277	83-0-9	.145	1*	123	7		0.6
1989	Cin N	15	12	.556	37	37	9-2	0-0	249.2	241	109	31	3	64-10	118	3.39	106	.255	.302	78-0-14	.090	-3*	106	5		0.1
1990	†Cin N	15	9	.625	35	35	2-1	0-0	227.2	235	98	24	5	52-13	99	3.80	104	.266	.309	75-0-9	.093	-3*	93	7		0.3
1991	Cin N☆	14	14	.500	36	36	1	0-0	230.1	241	124	32	4	56-4	115	4.18	91	.266	.309	70-1-10	.171	2	114	-11		-1.2
1992	Cin N	6	5	.545	16	16	0	0-0	87	108	49	6	3	28-7	33	5.07	71	.311	.362	31-0-2	.226	1	99	-12	95	-1.2
1993	Cin N	7	7	.500	21	20	0	0-0	114	159	61	15	1	20-2	53	4.74	85	.333	.359	37-1-4	.216	2	102	-7	58	-0.4
1994	Cin N	3	1	.750	7	7	2-1	0-0	40.2	34	20	8	1	13-1	22	4.20	99	.222	.284	14-0-2	.143	-0	131	0	94	0.0
1995	KC A	0	2	.000	2	2	0	0-0	10	13	9	2	0	5-0	3	8.10	59	.302	.375	0	—	0	39	-3	135	-0.5
al	12	123	90	.577	302	300	31-12	0-0	1921	1931	913	236	32	511-61	1000	3.94	97	.262	.310	621-2-72	.153	2	106	-15	382	-2.8

YEAR	TM LG	W	L	PCT	G	GS	CG-SHO	SV-BS	IP	H	R	HR	HB	BB-IB	SO	ERA	AERA	OAV	OOB	AB-HR-SH	AVG	PB	SUP	APR	DL	PW

BROWNSON, MARK Mark Phillip B6.17.1975 Lake Worth FL BL/TR/6-2/185* [ColN93 30/856] d7.21 Col Palm Beach (FL) CC

																										0.0
1998	Col N	1	0	1.000	2	2	1-1	0-0	13.1	16	7	2	1	2-0	8	4.73	110	.296	.333	5	.000	-1	115	1		-0.3
1999	Col N	0	2	.000	7	7	0	0-0	29.2	42	26	8	1	8-0	21	7.89	73	.333	.378	9-0-2	.111	0	77	-5		-0.2
2000	Phi N	1	0	1.000	2	0	0	0-1	5	7	4	1	0	3-0	3	7.20	64	.333	.417	0	—	0		-1		-0.5
Total	3	2	2	.500	11	9	1-1	0-1	48	65	37	11	2	13-0	32	6.94	79	.323	.370	14-0-2	.071	-1	87	-5		

BROXTON, JONATHAN Jonathan Ray B6.16.1984 Augusta GA BR/TR/6-4/275 d7.29

2005	LA N	1	0	1.000	14	0	0	0-1	13.2	13	11	0	1	12-2	22	5.93	69	.245	.382	0		0		-3		-0.2

BRUBAKER, BRUCE Bruce Ellsworth B12.29.1941 Harrisburg PA BR/TR/6-1/198* d4.15

1967	LA N	0	0	—	1	0	0	0	1.1	3	3	1	0	0-0	2	20.25	15	.429	.429	0		0		-3		-0.1
1970	Mil A	0	0	—	1	0	0	0-0	2	2	2	1	0	1-0	0	9.00	42	.250	.333	0		0		-1		-0.1
Total	2	0	0	—	2	0	0	0-0	3.1	5	5	2	0	1-0	2	13.50	26	.333	.375	0		0		-4		-0.2

BRUCE, LOU Louis R. B1.16.1877 St.Regis NY D2.9.1968 Ilion NY BL/TR/5-5/145 d6.22 Col Syracuse ▲

1904	Phi A	0	0	—	2	0	0	0	11	11	7	1	0	2	4	4.91	55	.262	.295	101-0-6	.267	0*		-2		-0.1

BRUCE, BOB Robert James B5.16.1933 Detroit MI BR/TR/6-3/210* d9.14 Col Alma

1959	Det A	0	1	.000	2	1	0	0	2	2	1	0	1	3-0	1	9.00	45	.250	.455	0	—	0	87	-2		-0.4
1960	Det A	4	7	.364	34	15	1	0	130	127	68	16	5	56-1	76	3.74	106	.250	.331	39-0-2	.179	0	89	0		0.1
1961	Det A	1	2	.333	14	6	0	0	44.2	57	28	6	2	24-2	25	4.43	92	.320	.403	9-0-1	.111	0	129	-3		-0.2
1962	Hou N	10	9	.526	32	27	6	0	175	164	92	16	12	82-3	135	4.06	92	.248	.339	55-0-1	.200	5	112	-7		-0.1
1963	Hou N	5	9	.357	30	25	1-1	0	170.1	162	73	7	8	60-3	123	3.59	88	.250	.318	55-0-3	.127	2*	87	-6		-0.3
1964	Hou N	15	9	.625	35	29	9-4	0	202.1	191	70	8	3	33-4	135	3.72	90	.270	.305	74-0-4	.122	2*	82	16		2.2
1965	Hou N	9	18	.333	35	34	7-1	0	229.2	241	107	22	9	38-4	145	5.34	64	.301	.344	39-0-7	.077	-1	83	-9		-1.1
1966	Hou N	3	13	.188	25	23	1	0	129.2	160	83	16	8	29-4	71	4.89	68	.269	.337	12	.167	-2	91	-27	30	-3.1
1967	Atl N	2	3	.400	12	7	1	1	38.2	42	25	3	1	15-4	22	3.85	91	.263	.321	346-0-23	.150	0	94	-7	30	-0.9
Total	9	49	71	.408	219	167	26-6	1	1122.1	1146	551	96	48	340-25	733	3.85	91	.263	.321	346-0-23	.150	6	94	-45	30	

BRUCKBAUER, FRED Frederick John B5.27.1938 New Ulm MN BR/TR/6-1/185 d4.25 Col Minnesota

1961	Min A	0	0	—	1	0	0	0	0	3	3	0	0	1-0	0	∞	—	1.000	1.000	0		0		-3		-0.2

BRUCKMILLER, ANDY Andrew B1.1.1882 Pittsburgh PA D1.12.1970 McKeesport PA BR/TR/5-11/175 d6.26

1905	Det A	0	0	—	1	0	0	0	1	4	3	0	1	1	1	27.00	10	.571	.625	1	.000	-0		-2		-0.1

BRUHERT, MIKE Michael Edwin B6.24.1951 Jamaica NY BR/TR/6-6/220 d4.9

1978	NY N	4	11	.267	27	22	1-1	0	133.2	171	83	6	1	34-5	56	4.78	74	.317	.357	40-0-1	.075	-3	100	-21		-2.4

BRUMLEY, DUFF Duff Lechaun B8.25.1970 Cleveland TN BR/TR/6-4/220 [StLN90 24/649] d6.1 Col Cleveland St. (TN) CC

1994	Tex A	0	0	—	2	0	0	0-0	3.1	6	6	1	0	5-0	4	16.20	30	.400	.500	0		0		-4		-0.2

BRUMMETT, GREG Gregory Scott B4.20.1967 Wichita KS BR/TR/6-0/180 [SFN89 11/284] d5.29 Col Wichita St.

1993	SF N	2	3	.400	8	8	0	0-0	46	53	25	9	0	13-1	20	4.70	84	.294	.338	15-0-2	.000	-1	126	-4		-0.5
	Min A	2	1	.667	5	5	0	0-0	26.2	29	17	3	0	15-1	10	5.74	77	.299	.383	0	—	0	146	-3		-0.1
Total	1	4	4	.500	13	13	0	0-0	72.2	82	42	12	0	28-2	30	5.08	81	.296	.355	15-0-2	.000	-1	134	-7		

BRUNER, JACK Jack Raymond B7.1.1924 Waterloo IA D6.24.2003 Lincoln NE BL/TL/6-1/185* d9.16 Col Iowa

1949	Chi A	1	2	.333	4	2	0	0	7.2	10	7	0	0	8	4	8.22	51	.357	.500	1	.000	0	43	-3		-0.1
1950	Chi A	0	0	—	9	0	0	0	12.1	7	6	0	1	14	8	3.65	123	.184	.415	0	—	0	1			0.1
	StL A	1	2	.333	13	1	0	1	35	36	21	4	2	23	16	4.63	107	.267	.381	10	.000	-1	55	1		0.1
	Year	1	2	.333	22	1	0	1	47.1	43	27	4	3	37	24	4.37	110	.249	.390	10	.000	-1	56	2		0.2
Total	2	2	4	.333	26	3	0	1	55	53	34	4	3	45	28	4.91	96	.264	.406	11	.000	-1	44	-1		-0.1

BRUNER, ROY Walter Roy B2.10.1917 Cecilia KY D11.30.1986 St.Matthews KY BR/TR/6-0/165 d9.14 Mil 1941-45

1939	Phi N	0	4	.000	4	4	2	0	27	38	22	3	0	13	11	6.67	60	.339	.408	9-0-1	.111	-1	65	-8		-1.1
1940	Phi N	0	0	—	2	0	0	0	6.1	5	4	2	0	6	4	5.68	69	.227	.393	2	.500	0		-1		0.1
1941	Phi N	0	3	.000	13	1	0	0	29.1	37	17	1	0	25	13	4.91	75	.336	.459	6	.000	-0	23	-3		-0.1
Total	3	0	7	.000	19	5	2	0	62.2	80	43	6	0	44	28	5.74	67	.328	.431	17-0-1	.118	-1	58	-12		-1.1

BRUNET, GEORGE George Stuart "Lefty" B6.8.1935 Houghton MI D10.25.1991 Poza Rica, Veracruz, Mexico BR/TL/6-1/210(193-210) d9.14

1956	KC A	0	0	—	6	1	0	0	9	10	8	1	0	11-0	5	7.00	62	.286	.457	2	.000	-0	144	-3		-0.2
1957	KC A	0	1	.000	4	2	0	0	11.1	13	7	2	0	4-0	3	5.56	71	.277	.333	2	.000	0	68	-2		-0.2
1959	KC A	0	0	—	2	0	0	0	4.2	10	9	2	1	7-1	7	11.57	35	.435	.581	0	—	0		-5		-0.2
1960	KC A	0	2	.000	3	2	0	0	10.1	12	6	0	1	10-2	4	4.35	91	.308	.460	3	.000	-0	22	-1		-0.1
	Mil N	2	0	1.000	17	6	0	0	49.2	53	31	6	1	22-5	39	5.07	68	.275	.345	11	.091	-1	150	-10		-0.8
1961	Mil N	0	0	—	5	0	0	0	5	7	3	1	0	2-0	5	5.40	69	.412	.450	17-0-1	.059	-1	92	-5	30	-1.1
1962	Hou N	2	4	.333	17	11	2	0	54	62	31	2	0	21-1	36	4.50	83	.291	.353	0	—	0	55	-6		-1.0
1963	Hou N	0	3	.000	5	2	0	0	12.2	24	11	2	0	6-1	11	7.11	44	.393	.448	3	.000	-0		-5		-0.5
	Bal A	0	1	.000	16	0	0	0	20	25	15	3	1	9-0	13	5.40	44	.301	.372	1	.000	-0	77	0		-0.2
1964	LA A	2	2	.500	10	7	0	0	42.1	38	17	2	0	25-1	36	3.61	91	.237	.337	11-0-1	.182	0	77	0		-0.1
1965	Cal A	9	11	.450	41	26	8-3	2	197	149	96	9	3	69-8	141	2.56	133	.209	.280	56-0-6	.054	-2	78	18		1.9
1966	Cal A	13	13	.500	41	32	8-2	0	212	183	88	21	6	90-9	148	3.31	101	.234	.327	68-1-1	.103	-2	91	-2		-0.3
1967	Cal A	11	19	.367	40	37	7-2	1	250	203	99	19	4	90-9	165	3.31	95	.223	.293	74-0-4	.077	-4	91	4		-0.4
1968	Cal A	13	17	.433	39	36	8-5	0	245.1	191	83	23	2	68-3	132	2.86	102	.215	.270	74-0-4	.081	-3	78	4		-0.3
1969	Cal A	6	7	.462	23	19	2-2	0-1	100.2	98	51	15	1	39-4	56	5.37	68	.280	.353	20-1-0	.150	-1	97	-11		-1.0
	Sea A	2	5	.286	12	11	2	0-0	63.2	70	41	11	0	28-5	37	4.44	80	.265	.335	47-1-2	.085	-0	90	-16		-1.1
	Year	8	12	.400	35	30	4-2	0-1	164.1	168	92	26	1	67-9	93	4.42	82	.275	.345	38-1-4	.158	-1	117	-11		-1.1
1970	Was A	8	6	.571	24	20	2-1	0-0	118	124	64	10	1	48-4	67	4.42	82	.271	.408	0	.000	-0	45	3		0.0
	Pit N	1	1	.500	12	1	0	0-0	16.2	19	5	1	1	9-1	17	2.70	147	.311	.408	3	.333	0		-2		-0.1
1971	StL N	0	0	1.000	7	0	0	0-1	9.1	12	6	3	0	7-0	15	5.79	63	.316	.422	3	.333	0		-2	30	-0.2
Total	15	69	93	.426	324	213	39-15	4-2	1431.2	1303	639	133	21	581-53	921	3.62	92	.244	.318	418-3-23	.089	-14	91	-43	30	-5.0

BRUNETTE, JUSTIN Justin Thomas B10.7.1975 Los Alamitos CA BL/TL/6-1/200 [StLN97 20/614] d4.13 Col San Diego St.

2000	StL N	0	0	—	4	0	0	0-0	4.2	9	3	0	0	5-0	2	5.79	80	.364	.481	1	1.000	0		0		0.0

BRUNEY, BRIAN Brian Anthony B2.17.1982 Astoria OR BR/TR/6-3/225* [AriN00 12/369] d5.8

2004	Ari N	3	4	.429	30	0	0	0-1	31.1	20	16	2	1	27-5	34	4.31	106	.189	.358	0		0		1	40	0.0
2005	Ari N	1	3	.250	47	0	0	12-4	46	56	39	6	5	35-2	51	7.43	59	.299	.421	1	.000	-0		-14	40	-1.0
Total	2	4	7	.364	77	0	0	12-5	77.1	76	55	8	6	62-7	85	6.17	72	.259	.398	1	.000	-0		-13	40	-1.0

BRUNO, TOM Thomas Michael B1.26.1953 Chicago IL BR/TR/6-5/210* d8.1

1976	KC A	1	0	1.000	12	0	0	0-0	17.1	20	13	3	0	9-1	11	6.75	52	.290	.367	0	—	0		-5		-0.2
1977	Tor A	0	1	.000	12	0	0	0-0	18.1	30	18	4	1	13-1	9	7.85	54	.366	.444	0		0		-7		-0.4
1978	StL N	4	3	.571	18	13	0	1-2	49.2	38	12	3	0	17-1	33	1.99	179	.209	.275	12-0-2	.083	-1	92	9		0.5
1979	StL N	2	3	.400	27	1	0	0-1	38.1	37	18	1	2	22-5	27	4.23	90	.253	.355	5-0-1	.200	0	46	-1		-0.1
Total	4	7	7	.500	69	14	0	1-3	123.2	125	61	11	3	61-8	80	4.22	88	.261	.344	17-0-3	.118	-1	78	-4		-0.3

BRUNSON, WILL William Donald B3.20.1970 Irving TX BL/TL/6-4/185* [CinN92 21/577] d6.21 Col Southwest Texas

1998	LA N	0	1	.000	2	0	0	0-0	2.1	3	3	0	0	2-0	1	11.57	35	.333	.455	—		0		-2		-0.1
	Det A	0	0	—	3	0	0	0-0	3	2	0	0	0	1-0	1	0.00	—	.200	.273	—		0		-2		-0.1
1999	Det A	1	0	1.000	17	0	0	0-0	12	18	9	0	0	6-1	9	6.00	83	.367	.421	—		0		-2		-0.1
Total	2	1	1	.500	27	0	0	0-0	17.1	23	12	0	0	9-1	11	5.71	84	.338	.405	—		0		-2		-0.2

BRUSKE, JIM James Scott B10.7.1964 E.St.Louis IL BR/TR/6-1/185* [CleA86 S1/6] d8.25 Col Loyola Marymount

1995	LA N	0	0	—	9	0	0	1-0	10	12	7	0	1	4-0	5	4.50	86	.300	.378	—		0		-1		0.0
1996	LA N	0	0	—	11	0	0	0-0	12.2	17	8	2	1	3-1	12	5.68	69	.315	.362	6	.167	0*		1	19	0.1
1997	SD N	4	1	.800	28	0	0	0-1	44.2	37	22	4	1	25-1	32	3.63	108	.228	.330	—		0		3		0.2
1998	LA N	3	0	1.000	35	0	0	1-1	44	47	18	4	1	19-1	31	3.48	116	.272	.354	0	.000	-0		0		0.1
	SD N	0	0	—	4	0	0	0-0	7	10	14	1	0	4-2	4	3.86	103	.333	.412	—		0		0		0.0

YEAR	TM LG	W	L	PCT	G	GS	CG-SHO	SV-BS	IP	H	R	HR	HB	BB-IB	SO	ERA	AERA	OAV	OOB	AB-HR-SH	AVG	PB	SUP	APR	DL	PW
	Year	3	0	1.000	39	0	0	1-1	51	57	22	3	3	23-3	35	3.53	114	.281	.362	3	.000	-0		3		0.1
	NY A	1	0	1.000	3	1	0	0-0	9	9	3	2	0	1-0	3	3.00	146	.257	.278	0	—	0	170	2		0.2
2000	Mil N	1	0	1.000	15	0	0	0-0	16.2	22	15	5	2	12-1	8	6.48	71	.314	.424	1	.000	-0		-4	73	-0.2
Total	5	9	1	.900	105	1	0	2-2	144	154	77	16	8	68-6	95	4.13	98	.273	.357	10	.100	-0	170	-1	92	0.0

BRUSSTAR, WARREN   Warren Scott   B2.2.1952 Oakland CA   BR/TR/6-3/200*   [PhiN74*S4/67]   d5.6 Col Cal St.-Fresno

YEAR	TM LG	W	L	PCT	G	GS	CG-SHO	SV-BS	IP	H	R	HR	HB	BB-IB	SO	ERA	AERA	OAV	OOB	AB-HR-SH	AVG	PB	SUP	APR	DL	PW
1977	†Phi N	7	2	.778	46	0	0	3-1	71.1	64	26	7	1	24-3	46	2.65	152	.250	.316	6-0-1	.000	-1		9		1.2
1978	†Phi N	6	3	.667	58	0	0	0-3	88.2	74	25	0	3	30-7	60	2.33	155	.239	.310	7	.143	0		13		1.4
1979	Phi N	1	0	1.000	13	0	0	1-1	14.1	23	12	1	0	4-2	3	6.91	56	.383	.415	0	—	0		-5	84	-0.4
1980	†Phi N	2	2	.500	26	0	0	0-1	38.2	42	16	3	0	13-2	21	3.72	103	.286	.344	1	—	0		1	94	0.1
1981	†Phi N	0	1	.000	14	0	0	0-1	12.1	12	6	0	1	10-4	8	4.38	84	.250	.383	0	—	-0		-1		-0.1
1982	Phi N	2	3	.400	22	0	0	2-1	22.2	31	12	2	1	5-3	11	4.76	78	.348	.381	2	.000	0		-2		-0.4
	Chi A	2	0	1.000	10	0	0	0-0	18.1	19	7	2	1	3-0	8	3.44	119	.257	.295	0	—	0		2		0.2
1983	Chi A	3	1	.750	59	0	0	1-3	80.1	67	21	1	2	37-10	46	2.35	162	.234	.321	4-0-1	.000	-0		13		0.7
1984	†Chi N	1	1	.500	41	0	0	3-2	63.2	57	23	4	1	21-7	36	3.11	126	.247	.307	5-0-1	.200	-1		6	14	0.4
1985	Chi N	4	3	.571	51	0	0	4-1	74.1	87	55	8	3	36-11	34	6.05	66	.292	.368	8	.143	0		-15		-1.6
Total	9	28	16	.636	340	0	0	14-14	484.2	476	203	28	13	183-49	273	3.51	110	.265	.333	32-0-3	.094	-1		21	192	1.5

BRYANT, CLAY   Claiborne Henry   B11.16.1911 Madison Heights VA   D4.9.1999 Boca Raton FL   BR/TR/6-2.5/195   d4.19 C3

YEAR	TM LG	W	L	PCT	G	GS	CG-SHO	SV-BS	IP	H	R	HR	HB	BB-IB	SO	ERA	AERA	OAV	OOB	AB-HR-SH	AVG	PB	SUP	APR	DL	PW
1935	Chi N	1	2	.333	9	1	0	2	22.2	34	15	1	0	7	13	5.16	76	.358	.402	6-1-1	.333	2*	173	-3		-0.2
1936	Chi N	1	2	.333	26	0	0	0	57.1	57	25	0	2	24	35	3.30	121	.259	.337	12-0-1	.417	1*		4		0.3
1937	Chi N	9	3	.750	38	9	4-1	3	135.1	117	69	1	1	78	75	4.26	94	.232	.336	45-1-2	.311	5*	99	-3		0.1
1938	†Chi N	19	11	.633	44	30	17-3	2	270.1	235	105	6	1	125	135	3.10	124	.235	.321	106-3-1	.226	4*	97	22		2.6
1939	Chi N	2	1	.667	4	4	2	0	31.1	42	23	3	1	14	9	5.74	69	.307	.375	14	.214	0*	116	-6		-0.5
1940	Chi N	0	1	.000	8	0	0	0	26.1	26	17	2	0	14	5	4.78	78	.265	.357	9	.333	1*		-3		-0.1
Total	6	32	20	.615	129	44	23-4	7	543.1	511	254	13	5	262	272	3.73	104	.249	.335	192-5-5	.266	1*	101	11		2.2

BRYANT, RON   Ronald Raymond   B11.12.1947 Redlands CA   BB/TL/6-0/190*   [SFN65 12/422]   d9.29

YEAR	TM LG	W	L	PCT	G	GS	CG-SHO	SV-BS	IP	H	R	HR	HB	BB-IB	SO	ERA	AERA	OAV	OOB	AB-HR-SH	AVG	PB	SUP	APR	DL	PW
1967	SF N	0	0	—	1	0	0	0	4	3	2	1	0	0-0	2	4.50	73	.200	.250	1	.000	-0		0		0.0
1969	SF N	4	3	.571	16	8	0	1-0	57.2	60	29	8	2	25-1	30	4.37	80	.271	.349	16-0-3	.188	1	123	-4		-0.4
1970	SF N	5	8	.385	34	11	1	0-1	96	103	58	7	2	38-0	66	4.78	83	.274	.342	27-0-2	.111	-1	76	-9		-1.1
1971	†SF N	7	10	.412	27	22	3-2	0-0	140	146	69	9	3	49-3	79	3.79	90	.272	.333	50-0-1	.200	1	96	-5		-0.5
1972	SF N	14	7	.667	35	28	11-4	0-0	214	176	81	20	2	77-5	107	2.90	121	.224	.293	70-0-6	.171	1	125	13		1.1
1973	SF N	24	12	.667	41	39	8	0-0	270	240	125	23	9	115-12	143	3.53	109	.234	.315	95-0-3	.168	1*	103	8		1.1
1974	SF N	3	15	.167	41	23	0	0-1	126.2	142	92	11	4	68-9	75	5.61	68	.286	.372	31-0-4	.129	-1	76	-23	18	-3.1
1975	StL N	0	1	.000	10	1	0	0-0	8.2	20	17	2	0	7-1	7	16.62	23	.444	.519	1	.000	-0	93	-11		-1.1
Total	8	57	56	.504	205	132	23-6	1-2	917	890	473	80	23	379-26	509	4.02	92	.254	.329	291-0-19	.165	1	100	-31	18	-4.0

BRYDEN, T.R.   Thomas Ray   B1.17.1959 Moses Lake WA   BR/TR/6-4/190   d4.10 Col Gonzaga

YEAR	TM LG	W	L	PCT	G	GS	CG-SHO	SV-BS	IP	H	R	HR	HB	BB-IB	SO	ERA	AERA	OAV	OOB	AB-HR-SH	AVG	PB	SUP	APR	DL	PW
1986	Cal A	2	1	.667	16	0	0	0-1	34.1	38	25	4	2	21-0	25	6.55	63	.290	.386	0		0		-8		-0.6

BRYNAN, TOD   Charles Ruley   B7.1863 Philadelphia PA   D5.10.1925 Philadelphia PA   BR/TR/5-10/?   d6.22

YEAR	TM LG	W	L	PCT	G	GS	CG-SHO	SV-BS	IP	H	R	HR	HB	BB-IB	SO	ERA	AERA	OAV	OOB	AB-HR-SH	AVG	PB	SUP	APR	DL	PW
1888	Chi N	2	1	.667	3	3	2	0	25	29	26	2	2	7	11	6.48	47	.271	.328	11	.182	0	128	-8		-0.7
1891	Bos N	0	1	.000	1	1	0	0	1	4	6	0	3	3	0	54.00	7	.571	.700	0	—	0	163	-4		-0.5
Total	2	2	2	.500	4	4	2	0	26	33	32	2	2	10	11	8.31	37	.289	.357	11	.182	0	146	-12		-1.2

BUCHANAN, JIM   James Forrest   B7.1.1876 Chatham Hill VA   D6.15.1949 Norfolk NE   BL/TR/5-10/165   d4.16 Col Austin

YEAR	TM LG	W	L	PCT	G	GS	CG-SHO	SV-BS	IP	H	R	HR	HB	BB-IB	SO	ERA	AERA	OAV	OOB	AB-HR-SH	AVG	PB	SUP	APR	DL	PW
1905	StL A	5	9	.357	22	15	12-1	2	141.1	149	76	2	2	27	54	3.50	73	.272	.309	46-0-1	.152	-0	96	-15		-1.4

BUCHANAN, BOB   Robert Gordon   B5.3.1961 Ridley Park PA   BL/TL/6-1/185*   [CinN79 2/41]   d7.13

YEAR	TM LG	W	L	PCT	G	GS	CG-SHO	SV-BS	IP	H	R	HR	HB	BB-IB	SO	ERA	AERA	OAV	OOB	AB-HR-SH	AVG	PB	SUP	APR	DL	PW
1985	Cin N	1	0	1.000	14	0	0	0-0	16	25	15	4	0	9-1	3	8.44	45	.368	.442	1	.000	-0		-7	21	-0.4
1989	KC A	0	0	—	2	0	0	0-0	3.1	5	6	1	0	3-2	3	16.20	24	.333	.444	0	—	0		-4		-0.2
Total	2	1	0	1.000	16	0	0	0-0	19.1	30	21	5	0	12-3	6	9.78	39	.361	.442	1	.000	-0		-11	21	-0.6

BUCKELS, GARY   Gary Scott   B7.22.1965 LaMirada CA   BR/TR/6-0/185   d7.23 Col Cal St.-Fullerton

YEAR	TM LG	W	L	PCT	G	GS	CG-SHO	SV-BS	IP	H	R	HR	HB	BB-IB	SO	ERA	AERA	OAV	OOB	AB-HR-SH	AVG	PB	SUP	APR	DL	PW
1994	StL N	0	1	.000	10	0	0	0-0	12	8	5	2	0	7-1	9	2.25	189	.186	.300	1	.000	-0		2		0.1

BUCKEYE, GARLAND   Garland Maiers "Gob"   B10.16.1897 Heron Lake MN   D11.14.1975 Stone Lake WI   BB/TL/6-0/260   d6.19 Col Wabash

YEAR	TM LG	W	L	PCT	G	GS	CG-SHO	SV-BS	IP	H	R	HR	HB	BB-IB	SO	ERA	AERA	OAV	OOB	AB-HR-SH	AVG	PB	SUP	APR	DL	PW
1918	Was A	0	0	—	1	0	0	0	2	3	4	0	0	2	2	18.00	15	.333	.600	0	—	0		-3		-0.1
1925	Cle A	13	8	.619	30	18	11-1	0	153	161	74	3	6	58	49	3.65	121	.267	.338	62-3-3	.226	2	104	13		1.7
1926	Cle A	6	9	.400	32	18	5-1	0	165.2	160	79	3	6	69	36	3.10	131	.264	.345	60-2-2	.200	2	103	12		1.1
1927	Cle A	10	17	.370	35	25	13-2	1	204.2	231	106	6	5	74	38	3.96	106	.296	.360	71-0-2	.268	3	69	6		0.9
1928	Cle A	1	5	.167	9	6	0	0	35	58	32	2	2	5	6	6.69	62	.389	.417	9	.111	-1	95	-10		-1.4
	NY N	0	0	—	1	0	0	0	3.2	9	6	1	0	2	3	14.73	27	.409	.458	2	.500	1		-4		-0.1
Total	5	30	39	.435	108	67	29-4	1	564	622	301	15	19	214	134	3.91	108	.287	.356	204-5-7	.230	7	90	14		2.1

BUCKINGHAM, ED   Edward Taylor   B5.12.1874 Metuchen NJ   D7.30.1942 Bridgeport CT   d8.30 Col Yale

YEAR	TM LG	W	L	PCT	G	GS	CG-SHO	SV-BS	IP	H	R	HR	HB	BB-IB	SO	ERA	AERA	OAV	OOB	AB-HR-SH	AVG	PB	SUP	APR	DL	PW
1895	Was N	0	0	—	1	0	0	0	4	6	6	0	0	1	1	6.00	80	.400	.471	1	.000	-0	74	-1		-0.1

BUCKLES, JESS   Jesse Robert "Jim"   B5.20.1890 LaVerne CA   D8.2.1975 Westminster CA   BL/TL/6-2.5/205   d9.17

YEAR	TM LG	W	L	PCT	G	GS	CG-SHO	SV-BS	IP	H	R	HR	HB	BB-IB	SO	ERA	AERA	OAV	OOB	AB-HR-SH	AVG	PB	SUP	APR	DL	PW
1916	NY A	0	0	—	2	0	0	0	4	3	2	0	1	2	1	2.25	128	.188	.235	1	.000	-0		0		0.0

BUCKLEY, JOHN   John Edward   B3.20.1869 Marlborough MA   D5.3.1942 Westborough MA   BL/TR/6-1/200   d7.15

YEAR	TM LG	W	L	PCT	G	GS	CG-SHO	SV-BS	IP	H	R	HR	HB	BB-IB	SO	ERA	AERA	OAV	OOB	AB-HR-SH	AVG	PB	SUP	APR	DL	PW
1890	Buf P	1	3	.250	4	4	4	0	34	49	32	5	0	16	4	7.68	53	.325	.389	15	.000	-2	82	-10		-0.9

BUDDIE, MIKE   Michael Joseph   B12.12.1970 Berea OH   BR/TR/6-3/210*   [NYA92 4/102]   d4.6 Col Wake Forest

YEAR	TM LG	W	L	PCT	G	GS	CG-SHO	SV-BS	IP	H	R	HR	HB	BB-IB	SO	ERA	AERA	OAV	OOB	AB-HR-SH	AVG	PB	SUP	APR	DL	PW
1998	NY A	4	1	.800	24	2	0	0-0	41.2	46	29	5	3	13-1	20	5.62	78	.284	.346	0	—	0	149	-7		-0.7
1999	NY A	0	0	—	2	0	0	0-0	2	3	1	1	0	0-0	1	4.50	105	.333	.333	0	—	0		0		0.0
2000	Mil N	0	0	—	5	0	0	0-0	6	8	3	0	0	1-1	5	4.50	103	.320	.346	0	—	0		0		0.0
2001	Mil N	0	1	.000	31	0	0	2-0	41.2	34	20	2	4	17-2	22	3.89	110	.225	.316	4	.250	0		2	20	0.2
2002	Mil N	1	2	.333	25	0	0	0-2	39.2	46	23	4	1	21-7	28	4.54	91	.293	.378	2	.000	-0		-2		-0.1
Total	5	5	4	.556	87	2	0	2-2	131	137	76	13	8	52-11	76	4.67	92	.272	.347	6	.167	-0	149	-7	20	-0.6

BUDNICK, MIKE   Michael Joe   B9.15.1919 Astoria OR   D12.2.1999 Seattle WA   BR/TR/6-1/200   d4.18

YEAR	TM LG	W	L	PCT	G	GS	CG-SHO	SV-BS	IP	H	R	HR	HB	BB-IB	SO	ERA	AERA	OAV	OOB	AB-HR-SH	AVG	PB	SUP	APR	DL	PW
1946	NY N	2	3	.400	35	7	1-1	0	88.1	75	40	13	0	48	36	3.16	109	.231	.330	20-1-0	.300	3	107	1		0.4
1947	NY N	0	0	—	7	1	0	0	12	16	16	0	0	10	6	10.50	39	.314	.426	4*	.250	0	217	-9		-0.4
Total	2	2	3	.400	42	8	1-1	0	100.1	91	56	13	0	58	42	4.04	87	.242	.343	24-1-0	.292	3	122	-8		0.0

BUEHRLE, MARK   Mark Anthony   B3.23.1979 St.Charles MO   BL/TL/6-2/200(200-220)   [ChiA98 38/1139]   d7.16 Col Jefferson (MO) CC

YEAR	TM LG	W	L	PCT	G	GS	CG-SHO	SV-BS	IP	H	R	HR	HB	BB-IB	SO	ERA	AERA	OAV	OOB	AB-HR-SH	AVG	PB	SUP	APR	DL	PW
2000	†Chi A	4	1	.800	28	3	0	0-2	51.1	55	27	5	3	19-1	37	4.21	120	.272	.344	0	—	0	93	5		0.4
2001	Chi A	16	8	.667	32	32	4-2	0-0	221.1	188	89	24	8	48-2	126	3.29	142	.230	.279	3	.000	-0	104	32		3.4
2002	Chi A★	19	12	.613	34	34	5-2	0-0	239	236	102	25	3	61-7	134	3.58	126	.260	.308	6	.167	-0	127	26		3.2
2003	Chi A	14	14	.500	35	35	2	0-0	230.1	250	124	22	8	61-2	119	4.14	111	.278	.325	6	.167	-0	96	7		0.8
2004	Chi A	16	10	.615	35	35	4-1	0-0	245.1	257	119	33	8	51-2	165	3.89	121	.271	.312	3-0-2	.000	-0	120	19		1.9
2005	†Chi A★	16	8	.667	33	33	3-1	0-0	236.2	240	99	20	4	40-4	149	3.12	145	.262	.295	3	.000	-0	88	31		3.0
Total	6	85	53	.616	197	172	18-6	0-2	1224	1226	560	129	31	280-18	730	3.63	127	.262	.306	21-0-2	.095	-1	107	120		12.7

BUFFINTON, CHARLIE   Charles G.   B6.14.1861 Fall River MA   D9.23.1907 Fall River MA   BR/TR/6-1/180   d5.17 M1   ▲

YEAR	TM LG	W	L	PCT	G	GS	CG-SHO	SV-BS	IP	H	R	HR	HB	BB-IB	SO	ERA	AERA	OAV	OOB	AB-HR-SH	AVG	PB	SUP	APR	DL	PW
1882	Bos N	3	4	.400	5	4	4-1		42	53	34	2		14	17	4.07	70	.296	.347	50	.260	0*	111	-6		-0.5
1883	Bos N	25	14	.641	43	41	34-4	1	333	346	187	4		51	188	3.03	102	.254	.281	341-1	.238	0*	135	9		0.7
1884	Bos N	48	16	.750	67	67	63-8	0	587	506	225	15		76	417	2.15	135	.219	.244	352-1	.267	12*	116	51		5.8
1885	Bos N	22	27	.449	51	50	49-6	0	434.1	425	238	10		112	242	2.88	93	.246	.244	338-1	.240	5*	99	-7		0.0
1886	Bos N	7	10	.412	18	17	16	0	151	203	129	4		39	47	4.59	70	.308	.346	176-1	.290	4*	106	-22		-1.6
1887	Phi N	21	17	.553	40	38	35-1	0	332.1	352	216	4	4	92	160	3.66	116	.264	.313	269-1	.268	2*	102	18		2.0
1888	Phi N	28	17	.622	46	46	43-6	0	400.1	324	139	6	4	59	199	1.91	156	.213	.244	160	.181	1*	76	45		5.1
1889	Phi N	28	16	.636	47	43	37-2	0	380	390	196	10	6	121	153	3.24	134	.257	.315	154	.208	-3	89	45		4.0
1890	Phi P	19	15	.559	36	33	28	0	283.1	312	211	8	7	126	89	3.81	112	.268	.343	150-1	.273	4*	102	10		1.2
1891	Bos AA	29	9	.763	48	43	33-2	1	363.2	303	153	8	7	120	158	2.55	137	.219	.284	181-1	.188	-0*	112	45		4.0

YEAR	TM LG	W	L	PCT	G	GS	CG-SHO	SV-BS	IP	H	R	HR	HB	BB-IB	SO	ERA	AERA	OAV	OOB	AB-HR-SH	AVG	PB	SUP	APR	DL	PW
1892	Bal N	4	8	.333	13	13	9	0	97	130	88	4	3	46	30	4.92	70	.309	.381	43	.349	4	115	-16		-1.1
Total	11	233	152	.605	414	396	351-30	3	3404	3344	1824	87	31	856	1700	2.96	114	.246	.292	2214-7	.245	27	105	172		19.6

BUHL, BOB   Robert Ray   B8.12.1928 Saginaw MI   D2.16.2001 Titusville FL   BR/TR/6-2/190*   d4.17

YEAR	TM LG	W	L	PCT	G	GS	CG-SHO	SV-BS	IP	H	R	HR	HB	BB-IB	SO	ERA	AERA	OAV	OOB	AB-HR-SH	AVG	PB	SUP	APR	DL	PW
1953	Mil N	13	8	.619	30	18	8-3	0	154.1	133	59	9	3	73	83	2.97	132	.235	.326	53-0-5	.113	-3	101	18		1.9
1954	Mil N	2	7	.222	31	14	2-1	3	110.1	117	54	5	2	65	57	4.00	93	.277	.374	31	.032	-3	97	-3		-0.5
1955	Mil N	13	11	.542	38	27	11-1	0	201.2	168	85	13	1	109-5	117	3.21	117	.227	.324	57-0-7	.105	-4	105	11		0.8
1956	Mil N	18	8	.692	38	33	13-2	0	216.2	190	96	18	2	105-7	86	3.32	104	.236	.325	73-0-6	.096	-3	116	3		-0.1
1957	†Mil N	18	7	.720	34	31	14-2	0	216.2	191	77	15	0	121-4	117	2.74	128	.241	.338	73-0-3	.082	-3	123	19		1.6
1958	Mil N	5	2	.714	11	10	3	1	73	74	33	5	1	30-0	27	3.45	102	.260	.330	25-0-1	.200	-0	115	0	72	0.9
1959	Mil N	15	9	.625	31	25	12-4	0	198	181	76	19	2	74-3	105	2.86	124	.243	.312	70-0-2	.057	-5	124	15		1.3
1960	Mil N★	16	9	.640	36	33	11-2	0	238.2	202	89	23	3	103-7	121	3.09	111	.229	.310	89-0-3	.157	-2	115	12		-1.3
1961	Mil N	9	10	.474	32	28	9-1	0	188.1	180	99	23	5	98-4	77	4.11	91	.256	.350	60-0-2	.067	-4	123	-11		-0.6
1962	Mil N	0	1	.000	1	1	0	0	2	6	5	0	0	4-1	1	22.50	17	.545	.625	1	.000	-0	92	-4		0.0
	Chi N	12	13	.480	34	30	8-1	0	212	204	108	23	6	94-6	109	3.69	112	.255	.339	69-0-7	.000	-6	91	6		-0.6
	Year	12	14	.462	35	31	8-1	0	214	210	113	23	6	98-7	110	3.87	104	.259	.339	70-0-7	.000	-6	91	2		0.1
1963	Chi N	11	14	.440	37	34	6	0	226	219	96	24	3	62-1	108	3.38	104	.259	.310	74-0-7	.108	-3	94	4		0.1
1964	Chi N	15	14	.517	36	35	11-3	0	227.2	208	103	22	5	68-4	107	3.83	97	.244	.301	73-0-5	.096	-2	101	-1		-0.2
1965	Chi N	13	11	.542	32	31	2	0	184.1	207	100	26	0	57-4	92	4.39	84	.284	.333	67-0-2	.060	-4	101	-12		-1.8
1966	Chi N	0	0	—	1	1	0	0	2.1	4	4	1	0	1-0	1	15.43	24	.400	.417	1	.000	-0	215	-3		-1.1
	Phi N	6	8	.429	32	18	1	1	132	156	74	10	4	39-6	59	4.77	75	.298	.349	41-0-3	.098	-2	111	-16		-1.1
	Year	6	8	.429	33	19	1	1	134.1	160	78	11	4	40-6	60	4.96	73	.300	.351	42-0-3	.095	-2	117	-20		-1.1
1967	Phi N	0	0	—	3	0	0	0	3	6	4	2	0	2-0	1	12.00	28	.462	.533	—	—	0		-3		-0.1
Total	15	166	132	.557	457	369	111-20	6	2587	2446	1162	238	37	1105-52	1268	3.55	103	.251	.328	857-0-53	.089	-43	108	35	72	4.4

BUICE, DE WAYNE   De Wayne Allison   B8.20.1957 Lynwood CA   BR/TR/6-0/170(170-185)   d4.25   Col Cal St.-Dominguez Hills

YEAR	TM LG	W	L	PCT	G	GS	CG-SHO	SV-BS	IP	H	R	HR	HB	BB-IB	SO	ERA	AERA	OAV	OOB	AB-HR-SH	AVG	PB	SUP	APR	DL	PW
1987	Cal A	6	7	.462	57	0	0	17-4	114	87	45	12	2	40-3	109	3.39	128	.213	.285	0	—	0		14		1.8
1988	Cal A	2	4	.333	32	0	0	3-4	41.1	45	29	5	0	19-3	38	5.88	66	.287	.360	0	—	0	-9	50		-1.1
1989	Tor A	1	0	1.000	7	0	0	0-0	17	13	12	2	0	13-1	10	5.82	65	.220	.351	0	—	0	-4	15		0.1
Total	3	9	11	.450	96	0	0	20-8	172.1	145	86	19	2	72-7	157	4.23	99	.232	.311	0	—	0	1	65		0.8

BUKER, CY   Cyril Owen   B2.5.1919 Greenwood WI   BL/TR/5-11/190   d5.17   Col Wisconsin-Madison

| 1945 | Bro N | 7 | 2 | .778 | 42 | 4 | 0 | 5 | 87.1 | 90 | 41 | 2 | 1 | 45 | 48 | 3.30 | 114 | .268 | .356 | 16-0-3 | .188 | -0 | 147 | 4 | | 0.8 |

BUKVICH, RYAN   Ryan Adrien   B5.13.1978 Naperville IL   BR/TR/6-3/250*   [KCA00 11/314]   d7.12   Col U. of Mississippi

2002	KC A	1	0	1.000	26	0	0	0-1	25	26	19	2	1	19-3	20	6.12	82	.277	.393	0	—	0	-3			-0.5
2003	KC A	1	0	1.000	9	0	0	0-0	10.1	12	11	2	0	9-0	8	9.58	50	.293	.412	0	—	0	-5			-0.5
2004	KC A	0	0	—	9	0	0	1-0	7.1	4	3	0	0	7-0	7	3.68	127	.182	.379	0	—	0	1			-0.0
2005	Tex A	0	0	—	4	0	0	0-0	4	2	5	0	0	6-0	4	11.25	41	.167	.444	0	—	0	-3	169		-0.2
Total	4	2	0	1.000	48	0	0	1-1	46.2	44	38	4	1	41-3	39	6.94	70	.260	.400	0	—	0	-10	169		-0.2

BULGER, JASON   Jason Patrick   B12.6.1979 Atlanta GA   BR/TR/6-4/215   d8.26   Col Valdosta St.

| 2005 | Ari N | 1 | 0 | 1.000 | 9 | 0 | 0 | 0-0 | 10 | 14 | 6 | 1 | 0 | 5-1 | 9 | 5.40 | 81 | .333 | .404 | 0 | — | 0 | -1 | | | -0.2 |

BULLINGER, JIM   James Eric   B8.21.1965 New Orleans LA   BR/TR/6-2/185*   [ChiN86 9/220]   d5.27   b-Kirk   Col New Orleans

1992	Chi N	2	8	.200	39	9	1	7-0	85	72	49	9	4	54-6	36	4.66	78	.233	.350	20-1-1	.250	2	78	-9		-0.6
1993	Chi N	1	0	1.000	15	0	0	1-0	16.2	18	9	1	0	9-0	10	4.32	93	.277	.360	1	.000	-0		-1		0.0
1994	Chi N	6	2	.750	33	10	1	2-0	100	87	43	6	1	34-2	72	3.60	117	.235	.298	22-0-5	.136	1	97	7		0.5
1995	Chi N	12	8	.600	24	24	1-1	0-0	150	152	80	14	9	65-7	93	4.14	101	.265	.346	47-0-8	.128	1*	118	-1	32	-2.0
1996	Chi N	6	10	.375	37	20	1-1	1-0	129.1	144	101	15	8	68-5	90	6.54	67	.283	.373	32-2-3	.250	5*	105	-29		-2.7
1997	Mon N	7	12	.368	36	25	2-2	0-1	155.1	165	106	17	12	74-5	87	5.56	75	.276	.364	43-1-3	.209	2	91	-24		-2.2
1998	Sea A	0	1	.000	2	1	0	0-0	5.2	13	10	3	0	2-0	4	15.88	29	.433	.455	0	—	0	139	-7		-0.5
Total	7	34	41	.453	186	89	6-4	11-1	642	651	398	65	34	306-25	392	5.06	82	.265	.351	165-4-20	.188	10	102	-64	32	-5.4

BULLINGER, KIRK   Kirk Matthew   B10.28.1969 New Orleans LA   BR/TR/6-2/170*   [StLN92 32/895]   d8.30   b-Jim   Col Southeastern Louisiana

1998	Mon N	1	0	1.000	8	0	0	0-1	7	14	8	1	0	2-0	2	9.00	47	.400	.400	1	.000	-0		-4		-0.5
1999	Bos A	0	0	—	4	0	0	0-0	2	2	1	0	0	2-0	4	4.50	111	.286	.444	0	—	0	0	69		0.0
2000	Phi N	0	0	—	3	0	0	0-0	3.1	4	2	0	0	1-0	5	6.75	65	.219	.242	0	—	0	-2			-0.1
2003	Hou N	0	0	—	7	0	0	0-0	8	7	6	2	0	1-0	5	6.16	71	.286	.341	0	.000	-0	-6			-0.1
2004	Hou N	1	0	1.000	27	0	0	1-1	30.2	36	22	5	1	10-2	22	6.53	67	.296	.336	4	.000	-0	-12	69		-0.4
Total	5	2	0	1.000	49	0	0	1-2	51	63	39	8	1	13-2	22	6.53	67	.296	.336							

BULLINGTON, BRYAN   Bryan Paul   B9.30.1980 Indianapolis IN   BR/TR/6-4/220   d9.18   Col Ball St.

| 2005 | Pit N | 0 | 0 | — | 1 | 0 | 0 | 0-0 | 1.1 | 1 | 2 | 0 | 1 | 1-0 | 1 | 13.50 | 31 | .250 | .429 | 0 | — | 0 | | -1 | | -0.2 |

BULLOCK, RED   Malton Joseph   B10.12.1911 Biloxi MS   D6.27.1988 Pascagoula MS   BL/TL/6-1/192   d5.19   Col Millsaps

| 1936 | Phi A | 0 | 2 | .000 | 12 | 2 | 0 | 0 | 16.2 | 19 | 32 | 0 | 0 | 37 | 7 | 14.04 | 36 | .271 | .523 | | .000 | -1 | 52 | -17 | | -1.9 |

BUMP, NATE   Nathan Louis   B1.24.1976 Towanda PA   BL/TR/6-2/180(180-195)   [SFN98 1/25]   d6.28   Col Penn St.

2003	†Fla N	4	0	1.000	32	0	0	0-0	36.1	34	21	3	7	20-0	17	4.71	87	.246	.367	0-0-1	—	0		-3		-0.0
2004	Fla N	2	4	.333	50	2	0	1-3	73.2	86	46	7	3	32-8	44	5.01	82	.297	.370	5	.000	-1	146	-9		-0.6
2005	Fla N	0	3	.000	31	0	0	0-1	38	43	18	5	2	12-1	18	4.03	99	.289	.350	5-0-1	.200	-1		-0	78	0.0
Total	3	6	7	.462	113	2	0	1-4	148	163	85	15	12	64-9	79	4.68	87	.282	.364	10-0-2	.100	-1	146	-12	78	-0.6

BUNCH, MELVIN   Melvin Lynn   B11.4.1971 Texarkana TX   BR/TR/6-1/165*   [KCA92 15/414]   d5.6   Col Texarkana (TX) JC

1995	KC A	1	3	.250	13	5	0	0-0	40	42	25	11	0	14-1	19	5.62	85	.261	.320	0	—	0	89	-3		-0.0
1999	Sea A	0	0	—	5	1	0	0-0	10	20	13	3	0	7-0	4	11.70	41	.426	.491	0	—	0	117	-7		-0.6
Total	2	1	3	.250	18	6	0	0-0	50	62	38	14	0	21-1	23	6.84	70	.298	.361	0	—	0	94	-10		-0.6

BUNKER, WALLY   Wallace Edward   B1.25.1945 Seattle WA   BR/TR/6-2/197*   d9.29

1963	Bal A	0	1	.000	1	1	0	0	4	10	6	1	0	3-0	1	13.50	26	.476	.542	2	.500	0	77	-4		-0.4
1964	Bal A	19	5	.792	29	29	12-1	0	214	161	72	17	3	62-5	96	2.69	133	.207	.267	72-0-2	.069	-2	122	21		4.4
1965	Bal A	10	8	.556	34	27	4-1	2	189	170	79	16	4	58-2	84	3.38	103	.242	.301	55-0-3	.073	-1	133	4		0.6
1966	†Bal A	10	6	.625	29	24	3	0	142.2	151	74	16	2	48-2	89	4.29	78	.269	.327	48-0-3	.104	-0*	143	-15	20	0.0
1967	Bal A	3	7	.300	29	9	1	1	88	83	46	7	2	31-1	51	4.09	77	.254	.322	26-0-1	.077	-2	132	-10		-0.2
1968	Bal A	2	0	1.000	18	10	2-1	0	71	59	25	4	1	14-1	44	2.41	121	.226	.265	18-0-7	.111	0	158	3		0.7
1969	KC A	12	11	.522	35	31	10-1	2-0	222.2	198	89	29	4	62-3	130	3.23	114	.238	.293	70-0-7	.143	0	90	12	43	1.3
1970	KC A	2	11	.154	24	15	2-1	0-0	121.2	109	63	16	0	50-2	59	5.01	69	.271	.301	9	.000	-1	87	-5		-1.2
1971	KC A	2	3	.400	7	6	0	5-0	32.1	35	19	7	0	6-0	15	5.01	69	.271	.301			-5	114	1	63	-0.8
Total	9	60	52	.536	206	152	34-5	5-0	1085.1	976	473	113	16	334-16	569	3.51	99	.240	.299	331-0-19	.094	-5	114	1	63	4.4

BUNNING, JIM   James Paul David   B10.23.1931 Southgate KY   BR/TR/6-3/195(185-203)   d7.20   HF1996   Col Xavier

1955	Det A	3	5	.375	15	8	1	1	51	59	38	8	3	32-2	37	6.35	60	.291	.395	15-0-2	.200	-0	84	-13		-1.8
1956	Det A	5	1	.833	15	3	0	1	53.1	55	24	6	0	28-4	34	3.71	111	.257	.339	18-0-2	.333	2	137	3		0.3
1957	Det A★	20	8	.714	45	30	14-1	1	267.1	214	91	33	11	72-5	182	2.69	143	.218	.277	75-0-6	.187	-1*	105	12		5.4
1958	Det A	14	12	.538	35	34	10-3	0	219.2	188	96	28	10	79-4	177	3.52	115	.228	.302	75-0-6	.191	1	106	10		2.0
1959	Det A★	17	13	.567	40	35	14-1	1	249.2	220	111	37	11	75-0	201	3.89	104	.234	.297	81-0-8	.160	-2*	72	31		2.9
1960	Det A★	11	14	.440	36	34	10-3	0	252	217	92	20	11	64-7	201	2.79	142	.228	.292	81-0-8	.191	-4	103	26		4.9
1961	Det A★	17	11	.607	38	37	12-4	1	268	232	113	28	8	71-3	194	3.19	128	.229	.284	100-0-2	.130	-4	111	15		2.5
1962	Det A★	19	10	.655	41	35	12-2	6	258	262	112	28	13	74-3	184	3.59	113	.261	.319	95-1-4	.242	4*	111	-1		1.9
1963	Det A★	12	13	.480	39	35	6-2	1	248.1	245	119	38	5	69-3	196	3.88	97	.254	.306	84-0-6	.155	-1*	91	-4		0.4
1964	Phi N	19	8	.704	41	39	13-5	1	284.1	248	99	23	14	46-3	219	2.63	132	.233	.274	99-0-9	.121	-2	133	26		5.7
1965	Phi N	19	9	.679	39	39	15-7	0	291	253	92	21	26	62-10	268	2.60	133	.232	.279	103-1-4	.214	4	102	31		6.9
1966	Phi N★	19	14	.576	43	41	16-5	0	314	260	91	26	19	55-8	252	2.41	149	.223	.268	106-0-4	.179	1	97	42		7.5
1967	Phi N	17	15	.531	40	40	16-6	0	302.1	241	94	18	13	73-20	253	2.29	149	.217	.271	104-2-7	.163	2	100	35		6.7
1968	Pit N	4	14	.222	27	26	3-1	0	160	168	75	16	4	48-6	95	3.88	75	.272	.332	51-0-2	.098	-3	96	-15		-0.6
1969	Pit N	10	9	.526	25	25	4	0	156	147	74	10	6	49-4	124	3.81	91	.249	.311	47-0-7	.043	-3	103	-6		-0.3
	LA N	3	1	.750	9	9	1	0	56.1	65	24	10	0	10-0	33	3.36	100	.288	.321	18-0-3	.111	-1	106	0		0.1

YEAR	TM LG	W	L	PCT	G	GS	CG-SHO	SV-BS	IP	H	R	HR	HB	BB-IB	SO	ERA	AERA	OAV	OOB	AB-HR-SH	AVG	PB	SUP	APR	DL	PW
	Year	13	10	.565	34	34	5	0-0	212.1	212	97	15	7	59-4	157	3.69	93	.259	.314	65-0-10	.062	-4	104	-5		-1.2
1970	Phi N	10	15	.400	34	33	4	0-0	219	233	111	19	8	56-9	147	4.11	98	.274	.321	71-0-3	.127	-2*	85	-4		-0.7
1971	Phi N	5	12	.294	29	16	1	1-1	110	126	72	11	6	37-7	58	5.48	65	.297	.358	25-1-3	.120	0*	90	-21		-3.1
Total	17	224	184	.549	591	519	151-40	16-1	3760.1	3433	1527	372	160	1000-98	2855	3.27	114	.242	.297	1275-7-85	.167	-1	100	200		16.4

BURBA, DAVE David Allen B7.7.1966 Dayton OH BR/TR/6-4/240(220-255) [SeaA87 2/33] d9.8 Col Ohio St.

YEAR	TM LG	W	L	PCT	G	GS	CG-SHO	SV-BS	IP	H	R	HR	HB	BB-IB	SO	ERA	AERA	OAV	OOB	AB-HR-SH	AVG	PB	SUP	APR	DL	PW
1990	Sea A	0	0	—	6	0	0	0-0					1	2-0	4	4.50	88	.267	.333	0	—	0		-1		0.0
1991	Sea A	2	2	.500	22	2	0	1-0	36.2	34	16	6	0	14-3	16	3.68	112	.245	.314	0	—	0	88	2		0.2
1992	SF N	2	7	.222	23	11	0	0-0	70.2	80	43	4	2	31-2	47	4.97	67	.287	.358	15-0-3	.067	-1	76	-13		-1.7
1993	SF N	10	3	.769	54	5	0	0-0	95.1	95	49	14	3	37-5	88	4.25	93	.265	.336	17-0-3	.294	2	128	-4		-0.2
1994	SF N	3	6	.333	57	0	0	0-3	74	59	39	5	6	45-3	84	4.38	93	.221	.345	3	.000	-0		-2		-0.3
1995	SF N	4	2	.667	37	0	0	0-1	43.1	38	26	5	0	25-2	46	4.98	83	.235	.335	0	—	0		-4		-0.5
	†Cin N	6	2	.750	15	9	1-1	0-0	63.1	52	24	4	0	26-1	50	3.27	128	.223	.301	15-0-4	.067	-0	101	7		0.7
	Year	10	4	.714	52	9	1-1	0-1	106.2	90	50	9	0	51-3	96	3.97	105	.228	.315	15-0-4	.067	-0	101	3		0.2
1996	Cin N	11	13	.458	34	33	0	0-0	195	179	96	18	0	97-9	148	3.83	112	.244	.329	67-2-3	.104	-1	92	8		0.7
1997	Cin N	11	10	.524	30	27	2	0-0	160	157	88	22	9	73-10	131	4.72	91	.255	.341	46-0-4	.196	1	91	-7	20	-0.6
1998	†Cle A	15	10	.600	32	31	0	0-0	203.2	210	100	30	7	69-4	132	4.11	116	.269	.330	6-1-0	.167	1	104	15		1.7
1999	†Cle A	15	9	.625	34	34	1	0-0	220	211	113	30	4	96-3	174	4.25	120	.254	.336	3	.333	1	102	19		1.9
2000	Cle A	16	6	.727	32	32	0	0-0	191.1	199	99	19	2	91-2	180	4.47	112	.267	.346	1-0-2	.000	-0	109	12		1.2
2001	†Cle A	10	10	.500	32	27	1	0-0	150.2	188	112	16	2	54-2	118	6.21	74	.306	.361	2-0-2	.000	-0	129	-26		-2.8
2002	Tex A	4	5	.444	23	18	1	0-1	111.1	125	71	13	7	40-3	70	5.42	88	.279	.346	2-0-2	.000	-0	108	-7		-0.5
	Cle A	1	0	1.000	12	3	0	0-1	34	30	20	3	2	17-0	25	4.50	99	.236	.333	5	.200	0	139	-1		-0.1
	Year	5	5	.500	35	21	1	0-2	145.1	155	91	16	9	57-3	95	5.20	90	.270	.343	5	—	-0	139	-1		-0.1
2003	Mil N	1	1	.500	17	2	0	0-0	43.1	42	19	5	4	19-2	35	3.53	122	.250	.340		.200	-0	113	-7		-0.6
2004	Mil N	3	1	.750	45	0	0	2-2	70.2	63	36	6	2	24-2	47	4.08	108	.237	.302	10-0-1	.000	-1	87	3		0.1
	SF N	1	0	1.000	6	0	0	0-1	6.1	7	4	1	0	2-0	3	5.68	76	.280	.333	1	.000	-0		2		0.1
	Year	4	1	.800	51	0	0	2-3	77	70	40	7	2	26-2	50	4.21	104	.241	.304	4	.000	-0		2		0.0
Total	15	115	87	.569	511	234	6-1	3-9	1777.2	1777	961	201	58	762-53	1398	4.49	100	.260	.337	194-3-22	.134	-0	106	2	20	-0.2

BURBACH, BILL William David B8.22.1947 Dickeyville WI BR/TR/6-4/215* [NYA65 1/19] d4.11

YEAR	TM LG	W	L	PCT	G	GS	CG-SHO	SV-BS	IP	H	R	HR	HB	BB-IB	SO	ERA	AERA	OAV	OOB	AB-HR-SH	AVG	PB	SUP	APR	DL	PW
1969	NY A	6	8	.429	31	24	2-1	0-0	140.2	112	68	15	2	102-1	82	3.65	97	.219	.349	40-0-6	.100	-1	97	-3		-0.5
1970	NY A	0	2	.000	4	4	0	0-0	16.2	23	19	2	1	9-0	10	10.26	35	.324	.402	5	.000	-1	150	-12		-1.2
1971	NY A	0	1	.000	2	0	0	0-0	3.1	6	6	0	0	5-2	3	10.80	30	.400	.524	2	.000	-0		-4		-0.7
Total	3	6	11	.353	37	28	2-1	0-0	160.2	141	93	17	3	116-3	95	4.48	79	.236	.360	47-0-6	.085	-2	105	-19		-2.4

BURCHART, LARRY Larry Wayne B2.8.1946 Tulsa OK BR/TR/6-3/210 [LAN67 S3/54] d4.10 Col Oklahoma St.

YEAR	TM LG	W	L	PCT	G	GS	CG-SHO	SV-BS	IP	H	R	HR	HB	BB-IB	SO	ERA	AERA	OAV	OOB	AB-HR-SH	AVG	PB	SUP	APR	DL	PW
1969	Cle A	2	0	.000	29	0	0	0-0	42.1	42	28	7	3	24-2	26	4.25	89	.266	.358	0	—	0		-4	62	-0.3

BURCHELL, FRED Frederick Duff B7.14.1879 Perth Amboy NJ D11.20.1951 Jordan NY BL/TL/5-11/175 d4.17

YEAR	TM LG	W	L	PCT	G	GS	CG-SHO	SV-BS	IP	H	R	HR	HB	BB-IB	SO	ERA	AERA	OAV	OOB	AB-HR-SH	AVG	PB	SUP	APR	DL	PW
1903	Phi N	0	3	.000	6	3	2	0	44	48	28	0	2	14	12	2.86	114	.293	.356	16	.188	-1	7	-1		-0.1
1907	Bos A	0	1	.000	2	1	0	0	10	8	5	0	1	2	6	2.70	95	.222	.282	5	.200	-0	131	0		-0.1
1908	Bos A	10	8	.556	31	19	9	0	179.2	161	84	2	11	65	94	2.96	83	.247	.326	69-0-3	.246	1*	133	-9		-0.9
1909	Bos A	3	3	.500	10	5	1	0	52	51	22	1	2	11	12	2.94	85	.271	.318	19	.158	-0	102	-2		-0.2
Total	4	13	15	.464	49	28	12	0	285.2	268	139	3	16	92	124	2.93	89	.258	.328	109-0-3	.220	-0	108	-12		-1.3

BURDETTE, FREDDIE Freddie Thomason B9.15.1936 Moultrie GA BR/TR/6-1/170* d9.5

YEAR	TM LG	W	L	PCT	G	GS	CG-SHO	SV-BS	IP	H	R	HR	HB	BB-IB	SO	ERA	AERA	OAV	OOB	AB-HR-SH	AVG	PB	SUP	APR	DL	PW
1962	Chi N	0	0	—	8	0	0	1	9.2	5	4	2	0	8-3	8	3.72	111	.161	.325	1	.000	-0		1		0.0
1963	Chi N	0	0	—	4	0	0	1	4.2	5	2	1	0	2-0	1	3.86	91	.313	.389			-0		0		0.0
1964	Chi N	1	0	1.000	18	0	0	1	20	17	7	2	1	10-2	1	3.15	118	.243	.333	1	1.000	0		2		0.1
Total	3	1	0	1.000	30	0	0	0	34.1	27	13	5	1	20-5	10	3.41	112	.231	.338	2	.500	-0		3		0.1

BURDETTE, LEW Selva Lewis B11.22.1926 Nitro WV BR/TR/6-2/190(180-195) d9.26 C2 Col Richmond

YEAR	TM LG	W	L	PCT	G	GS	CG-SHO	SV-BS	IP	H	R	HR	HB	BB-IB	SO	ERA	AERA	OAV	OOB	AB-HR-SH	AVG	PB	SUP	APR	DL	PW
1950	NY A	0	0	—	2	0	0	0	1.1	3	1	0	0	0	0	6.75	64	.500	.500	0	—	0		0		0.0
1951	Bos N	0	0	—	3	0	0	0	4.1	6	4	0	1	5	1	6.23	59	.375	.545	1	.000	-0		-2		-0.1
1952	Mil N	6	11	.353	45	9	5	7	137	138	58	8	2	47	47	3.61	100	.265	.328	35-0-6	.114	-0	77	1		0.2
1953	Mil N	15	5	.750	46	13	6-1	8	175	177	73	7	5	56	58	3.24	121	.264	.326	53-0-5	.170	-1	100	15		1.5
1954	Mil N	15	14	.517	38	32	13-4	0	238	224	87	17	4	62	79	2.76	135	.251	.300	79-0-5	.089	-5*	84	26		2.5
1955	Mil N	13	8	.619	42	33	11-2	0	230	253	114	25	6	73-9	70	4.03	93	.280	.336	86-0-3	.233	3*	124	-6		-0.2
1956	Mil N	19	10	.655	39	35	16-6	1	256.1	234	92	23	3	52-7	110	2.70	128	.241	.281	86-0-11	.186	1*	125	23		2.6
1957	†Mil N★	17	9	.654	37	33	14-1	0	256.2	260	117	25	2	59-4	78	3.72	94	.264	.304	88-2-4	.148	1*	137	-6		-0.3
1958	†Mil N★	20	10	.667	40	36	19-3	0	275.1	279	102	18	5	50-7	113	2.91	121	.264	.300	99-3-5	.242	9*	123	19		2.9
1959	Mil N★	21	15	.583	41	39	20-4	1	289.2	312	144	38	1	38-3	105	4.07	87	.273	.295	104-0-5	.202	6*	126	-16		-1.2
1960	Mil N	19	13	.594	45	32	18-4	4	275.2	277	116	19	5	35-7	83	3.36	102	.260	.287	91-2-2	.176	5*	126	3		1.1
1961	Mil N	18	11	.621	40	36	14-3	0	272.1	295	131	31	2	33-3	92	4.00	94	.273	.295	103-3-3	.204	5*	114	-8		-0.2
1962	Mil N	10	9	.526	37	19	6-1	2	143.2	172	85	26	2	23-6	59	4.89	78	.298	.325	51-0-2	.176	0*	114	-16		-1.9
1963	Mil N	6	5	.545	15	13	4-1	0	84	71	40	15	1	24-4	28	3.64	88	.228	.284	26-0-4	.038	-0*	109	-5		-0.7
	StL N	3	8	.273	21	14	3	2	98	106	50	6	7	16-2	45	3.77	94	.278	.314	31-0-3	.097	-1	88	-3		-0.6
	Year	9	13	.409	36	27	7-1	2	182	177	90	21	8	40-6	73	3.71	92	.255	.300	57-0-7	.070	-2	98	-7		-1.3
1964	StL N	1	0	1.000	8	0	0	0	10	10	3	1	0	3-0	3	1.80	211	.256	.302	1	.000	-2		-7		-1.3
	Chi N	9	9	.500	28	17	8-2	0	131	152	74	15	1	19-2	40	4.88	76	.292	.317	43-2-3	.279	6	103	-14		-1.1
	Year	10	9	.526	36	17	8-2	0	141	162	77	16	1	22-2	43	4.66	80	.290	.316	44-2-3	.273	6	103	-11		-0.9
1965	Chi N	2	0	.000	7	3	0	0	20.1	26	17	3	1	4-1	5	5.31	69	.299	.337	6	.333	1*	95	-9		-0.3
	Phi N	3	3	.500	19	9	1-1	0	70.2	95	50	5	5	17-2	23	5.48	63	.329	.374	20-0-2	.300	1	107	-16		-1.1
	Year	3	5	.375	26	12	1-1	0	91	121	67	8	6	21-3	28	5.44	65	.322	.365	26-0-2	.308	2	104	-22		-1.4
1966	Cal A	7	2	.778	54	0	0	5	79.2	80	32	4	1	12-2	27	3.39	99	.268	.297	8	.125	-0		0		0.0
1967	Cal A	1	0	1.000	19	0	0	1	18.1	16	10	4	1	5-2	10	4.91	64	.232	.243			-0		-3		-0.2
Total	18	203	144	.585	626	373	158-33	31	3067.1	3186	1400	289	56	628-63	1074	3.66	99	.268	.306	1011-12-63	.183	30	115	-11		3.1

BURDICK, BILL William Byron B10.11.1859 Austin MN D10.23.1949 Spokane WA BR/TR d7.23

YEAR	TM LG	W	L	PCT	G	GS	CG-SHO	SV-BS	IP	H	R	HR	HB	BB-IB	SO	ERA	AERA	OAV	OOB	AB-HR-SH	AVG	PB	SUP	APR	DL	PW
1888	Ind N	10	10	.500	20	20	20	0	176	168	88	12	6	43	55	2.81	105	.242	.292	68	.147	-2*	82	0		-0.3
1889	Ind N	2	4	.333	10	4	2	1	45.2	58	42	7	0	13	16	4.53	92	.301	.345	17	.118	-0	141	-5		-0.5
Total	2	12	14	.462	30	24	22	1	221.2	226	130	19	6	56	71	3.17	101	.255	.304	85	.141	-3	93	-5		-0.8

BURGMEIER, TOM Thomas Henry B8.2.1943 St.Paul MN BL/TL/5-11/185* d4.10 C4

YEAR	TM LG	W	L	PCT	G	GS	CG-SHO	SV-BS	IP	H	R	HR	HB	BB-IB	SO	ERA	AERA	OAV	OOB	AB-HR-SH	AVG	PB	SUP	APR	DL	PW
1968	Cal A	1	4	.200	56	2	0	5	72.2	65	41	5	0	24-3	33	4.33	67	.250	.310	2	.000	0*	75	-12		-0.9
1969	KC A	3	1	.750	31	0	0	0-3	54	67	31	5	1	21-3	23	4.17	89	.316	.374	18	.167	-0*		-4		-0.2
1970	KC A	6	6	.500	41	0	0	1-1	68.1	59	31	6	0	23-1	43	3.16	118	.236	.297	14-0-1	.143	-0*		-4		0.6
1971	KC A	9	7	.563	67	0	0	17-4	88.1	71	23	7	2	33-4	44	1.73	199	.223	.303	20	.250	2*		15		3.7
1972	KC A	6	2	.750	51	0	0	9-3	55.1	67	32	0	1	33-6	11	4.23	72	.313	.401	12	.333	1		-9		-1.5
1973	KC A	0	0	—	6	0	0	1-0	10	13	6	2	1	4-0	6	5.40	76	.310	.383	0	—	-1		-1		-0.1
1974	Min A	5	3	.625	50	0	0	4-1	91.2	92	46	7	2	26-2	34	4.52	83	.270	.319	0	—	0*		-5		-0.3
1975	Min A	5	5	.385	46	0	0	11-4	75.2	76	32	7	1	23-2	45	3.09	124	.264	.318	0	—	0*		5		1.0
1976	Min A	8	1	.889	57	0	0	1-2	115.1	95	36	11	2	29-3	45	2.50	143	.226	.279	0	—	0*		14		1.2
1977	Min A	6	4	.600	61	0	0	7-4	97.1	113	56	15	2	33-0	35	5.09	78	.299	.354	0	—	-0		-10		-1.0
1978	Bos A	2	1	.667	35	1	0	4-2	61.1	74	33	7	3	23-1	41	4.40	94	.302	.368	0	—	-0	87	-2		-0.2
1979	Bos A	3	2	.600	44	0	0	4-3	88.2	89	32	8	4	16-4	60	2.74	163	.263	.302	0	—	0		15		0.9
1980	Bos A☆	5	4	.556	62	0	0	24-2	99	87	29	6	3	20-3	54	2.00	213	.241	.283	0	—	0		21		3.1
1981	Bos A	4	5	.444	32	0	0	6-1	59.2	61	23	4	4	17-4	35	2.87	137	.268	.329	0	—	0		6		1.1
1982	Bos A	0	1	1.000	18	0	0	2-2	102.1	98	30	6	2	22-7	44	2.29	191	.259	.300	0	—	0		23		1.6
1983	Oak A	6	7	.462	49	0	0	4-2	96	89	33	2	0	32-8	39	2.81	138	.244	.303	0	—	0		21		1.6
1984	Oak A	3	0	1.000	17	0	0	1-0	23	15	6	2	0	8-4	8	2.35	161	.190	.261	0	—	0		12		1.7
Total	17	79	55	.590	745	3	0	102-34	1258.2	1231	521	92	32	384-55	584	3.23	118	.261	.318	66-0-1	.212	2	70	74	97	11.5

BURGOS, AMBIORIX Ambiorix B4.19.1984 Nagua, D.R. BR/TR/6-3/235 d4.23

YEAR	TM LG	W	L	PCT	G	GS	CG-SHO	SV-BS	IP	H	R	HR	HB	BB-IB	SO	ERA	AERA	OAV	OOB	AB-HR-SH	AVG	PB	SUP	APR	DL	PW
2005	KC A	3	5	.375	59	0	0	2-4	63.1	60	29	6	5	31-1	65	3.98	106	.251	.348	0	—	0		2	24	0.2

YEAR	TM LG	W	L	PCT	G	GS	CG-SHO	SV-BS	IP	H	R	HR	HB	BB-IB	SO	ERA	AERA	OAV	OOB	AB-HR-SH	AVG	PB	SUP	APR	DL	PW

BURGOS, ENRIQUE   Enrique (Calles)   B10.7.1965 Chorrera, Pan   BL/TL/6-4/195(195-230)   d7.15

1993	KC A	0	1	.000	5	0	0	0-0	5	5	5	0	1	6-1	6	9.00	51	.238	.429	0	—	0		-2		-0.4
1995	SF N	0	0	—	5	0	0	0-0	8.1	14	8	1	1	6-0	12	8.64	48	.378	.477	0	—	0		-4		-0.2
Total	2	0	1	.000	10	0	0	0-0	13.1	19	13	1	2	12-1	18	8.78	49	.328	.458	0	—	0		-6		-0.6

BURK, SANDY   Charles Sanford   B4.22.1887 Columbus OH   D10.11.1934 Brooklyn NY   BR/TR/5-8/155   d9.12

1910	Bro N	0	3	.000	4	3	1	0	19.1	17	16	0	2	27	14	6.05	50	.258	.484	5	.000	-1	49	-6		-0.9
1911	Bro N	1	3	.250	13	7	1	0	58	54	36	1	3	47	15	5.12	65	.261	.405	19-0-1	.105	-1	103	-9		-0.7
1912	Bro N	0	0	—	2	0	0	0	8.1	9	3	0	0	3	2	3.24	103	.273	.333	4	.250	0		0		0.1
	StL N	1	3	.250	12	4	2	1	44.2	37	19	0	1	12	17	2.42	142	.236	.294	11	.000	-1	43	4		0.1
	Year	1	3	.250	14	4	2	1	53	46	22	0	1	15	19	2.55	134	.242	.301	15	.067	-1	43	4		0.2
1913	StL N	0	2	.000	19	7	0	1	70	81	45	1	6	33	29	5.14	63	.290	.377	22	.091	-2	113	-14		-0.9
1915	Pit F	2	0	1.000	2	2	1	0	18	8	3	0	0	11	9	1.00	271	.140	.279	6	.167	0	77	3		0.3
Total	5	4	11	.267	52	23	5	2	218.1	206	122	2	12	133	86	4.25	76	.258	.372	67-0-1	.090	-6	86	-22		-2.0

BURKART, ELMER   Elmer Robert "Swede"   B2.1.1917 Philadelphia PA   D2.6.1995 Baltimore MD   BR/TR/6-2/190   d9.14 Col Temple

1936	Phi N	0	0	—	2	0	0	0	7.2	9	3	0	0	12	2	3.52	129	.160	.432	2	.000	-0	65	1		0.0
1937	Phi N	0	0	—	7	0	0	0	16	20	11	0	0	9	4	6.19	70	.323	.408	6	.000	-1		-2		-0.2
1938	Phi N	1	0	1.000	2	1	1	0	10	12	5	0	1	3	1	4.50	86	.286	.348	3	.000	-0	22	0		-0.1
1939	Phi N	1	0	1.000	5	0	0	0	8.1	11	4	0	0	2	2	4.32	93	.344	.382	1	1.000	1		0		0.1
Total	4	1	1	.500	16	3	1	0	42	47	23	0	1	26	9	4.93	85	.292	.394	12	.083	-1	55	-1		-0.2

BURKE, JAMES   James B Attleboro MA   d6.10

1882	Buf N	0	1	.000	1	1	1	0	4	10	9	0		0	0	11.25	26	.435	.435	4	.000	-1	72	-4		-0.5
1883	Buf N	0	0	—	1	1	0	0	8	9	8	0		3	1	5.63	56	.243	.300	5	.200	-0	152	-1		-0.1
1884	Bos U	19	15	.559	38	36	34	0	322	326	201	10		31	255	2.85	83	.245	.263	184	.223	-7*	109	-18		-2.2
Total	3	19	16	.543	40	38	34	0	334	345	218	10		34	256	3.02	80	.249	.267	193	.218	-8	109	-24		-2.8

BURKE, JOHN   John C.   B2.9.1970 Durango CO   BB/TR/6-4/215*   [ColN92 1/27]   d8.13 Col Florida   [DL 1998 Col N 181]

1996	Col N	2	1	.667	11	0	0	0-0	15.2	21	13	3	1	7-0	19	7.47	70	.318	.387	1	.500	0		-3		-0.4
1997	Col N	2	5	.286	17	9	0	0-0	59	83	46	13	6	26-0	39	6.56	79	.329	.401	19-0-2	.158	-1*	58	-7		-0.8
Total	2	4	6	.400	28	9	0	0-0	74.2	104	59	16	7	33-0	58	6.75	77	.327	.398	21-0-2	.190	-1	58	-10	181	-1.2

BURKE, JOHN   John Patrick   B1.27.1877 Hazleton PA   D8.4.1950 Jersey City NJ   BR/TR   d6.27 Col St. Bonaventure

1902	NY N	0	1	.000	1	1	1	0	14	21	11	1	0	3	3	5.79	49	.344	.375	13	.154	-0*	24	-4		-0.3

BURKE, BOBBY   Robert James "Lefty"   B1.23.1907 Joliet IL   D2.8.1971 Joliet IL   BL/TL/6-0.5/150   d4.16

1927	Was A	3	2	.600	36	6	1	0	100	91	48	6	7	32	26	3.96	103	.245	.316	24-0-3	.125	-2	109	3		-0.1
1928	Was A	2	4	.333	26	7	2-1	0	85.1	87	44	1	2	18	27	3.90	103	.277	.320	20-0-1	.250	-1	69	1		0.1
1929	Was A	6	8	.429	37	17	4	0	141	154	91	6	4	51	51	4.79	89	.279	.349	43-0-7	.140	-3	81	-9		-1.1
1930	Was A	3	4	.429	24	4	2	3	74.1	62	41	2	3	29	35	3.63	127	.229	.310	23-0-1	.174	-1	168	5		0.3
1931	Was A	8	3	.727	30	13	3-1	0	128.2	124	67	6	2	50	38	4.27	101	.255	.327	47-0-2	.213	-0	97	-7		-0.6
1932	Was A	3	6	.333	22	10	2	0	91	98	55	4	1	44	32	3.23	129	.256	.343	17-0-2	.235	0*	88	6		0.6
1933	Was A	4	3	.571	25	6	4-1	0	64	64	29	1	2	31	28	3.21	134	.245	.323	57-0-3	.228	2*	75	22		2.0
1934	Was A	8	8	.500	37	15	7-1	0	168	155	67	2	1	72	52	7.46	58	.327	.391	22-0-1	.182	-0*	72	-24		-2.6
1935	Was A	1	8	.111	15	10	2	0	66.1	90	63	7	2	27	16		∞		.500	.750		—	0		-1		-0.1
1937	Phi N	0	0	—	2	0	0	0	1	1	0	0	1	2	0	4.29	99	.263	.336	278-0-21	.194	-3	97	-1		-1.3
Total	10	38	46	.452	254	88	27-4	5	918.2	926	506	35	24	360	299	4.29	99	.263	.336	278-0-21	.194	-3	97	-1		-1.3

BURKE, STEVE   Steven Michael   B3.5.1955 Stockton CA   BB/TR/6-2/200*   [BosA74*S2/31]   d9.10 Col Merritt (CA) JC

1977	Sea A	0	1	.000	6	0	0	0-0	15.2	12	6	0	0	7-1	6	2.87	144	.226	.311	0	—	0		2		0.1
1978	Sea A	0	1	.000	18	0	0	0-0	49	46	22	2	1	24-0	16	3.49	110	.258	.346	0	—	0		4		0.1
Total	2	0	2	.000	24	0	0	0-0	64.2	58	28	2	1	31-1	22	3.34	117	.251	.338	0	—	0		4		0.2

BURKE, TIM   Timothy Philip   B2.19.1959 Omaha NE   BR/TR/6-3/205*   [PitN80 2/49]   d4.8 Col Nebraska

1985	Mon N	9	4	.692	78	0	0	8-1	120.1	86	32	9	7	44-14	87	2.39	144	.204	.288	10	.100	-0		16		1.1
1986	Mon N	9	7	.563	68	2	0	4-6	101.1	103	37	7	4	46-13	82	2.93	128	.262	.344	7-0-1	.000	-1	83	9		1.1
1987	Mon N	7	0	1.000	55	0	0	18-4	91	64	18	3	0	17-6	58	1.19	359	.196	.234	10-0-2	.000	-1		28	16	2.1
1988	Mon N	3	5	.375	61	0	0	18-6	82	84	36	7	3	25-13	42	3.40	107	.272	.327	2	.000	-0		11		2.1
1989	Mon N★	9	3	.750	68	0	0	28-11	84.2	68	24	6	0	22-7	54	2.55	140	.225	.314	6	.167	-0		7	42	1.3
1990	Mon N	3	3	.500	58	0	0	20-5	75	71	29	6	2	21-6	47	2.52	146	.247	.300	6	.000	-0		-3		1.2
1991	Mon N	3	4	.429	37	0	0	5-7	46	44	23	4	3	14-6	25	4.11	89	.243	.314	1	.000	-0		5		0.1
	NY N	3	3	.500	35	0	0	1-3	55.2	55	22	5	0	12-2	34	2.75	133	.255	.291	5	.000	-0		1		0.1
	Year	6	7	.462	72	0	0	6-10	101.2	96	45	8	4	26-8	59	3.36	109	.249	.301	6	.000	-0		-6		-1.2
1992	NY N	1	2	.333	15	0	0	0-2	15.2	26	15	1	0	3-0	7	5.74	61	.366	.387	0	—	0		1	31	0.1
	NY A	2	2	.500	23	0	0	0-0	27.2	26	14	2	1	15-4	8	3.25	121	.250	.350	0	—	0		1	58	0.1
Total	8	49	33	.598	498	2	0	102-45	699.1	624	251	49	21	219-71	444	2.72	137	.240	.302	44-0-3	.045	-2	83	70	89	8.1

BURKE, BILLY   William Ignatius   B7.11.1889 Clinton MA   D2.9.1967 Worcester MA   BL/TL/5-10/165   d4.30 Col Notre Dame

1910	Bos N	1	0	1.000	19	1	1	0	64	68	32	1	2	29	22	4.08	82	.302	.387	21-0-1	.190	-1*	179	-2		-0.2
1911	Bos N	0	1	.000	2	1	0	0	3.1	6	7	0	0	5	1	18.90	20	.429	.579	1	1.000	0	39	-4		-0.2
Total	2	1	1	.500	21	2	1	0	67.1	74	39	1	2	34	23	4.81	70	.310	.400	22-0-1	.227	-0	111	-6		-0.3

BURKE, TURK   William R.   B11.1865 Cincinnati OH   D3.17.1939 Atchison KS   TR/6-0/200   d7.20

1887	Det N	0	1	.000	2	1	1	0	5	15	21	14	0	3	5	6.00	68	.318	.384	8	.250	-0	151	-3		-0.1

BURKETT, JESSE   Jesse Cail "Crab"   B12.4.1868 Wheeling WV   D5.27.1953 Worcester MA   BL/TL/5-8/155   d4.22 C1 HF1946 ▲

1890	NY N	3	10	.231	21	14	6	0	118	134	123	3	14	92	82	5.57	63	.277	.407	401-4	.309	8*	80	-26		-1.7
1894	Cle N	0	0	—	1	0	0	0	4	6	2	0	0	1	0	4.50	122	.333	.368	523-8-10	.358	0*		1		-0.2
1902	StL A	0	1	.000	1	0	0	0	1	4	4	0	0	1	2	9.00	39	.571	.625	553-5-7	.306	0*		-2		-0.1
Total	3	3	11	.214	23	14	6	0	123	144	129	3	14	94	84	5.56	64	.283	.408	1477-17-17	.325	9	80	-27		-2.1

BURKETT, JOHN   John David   B11.28.1964 New Brighton PA   BR/TR/6-2/211(175-215)   [SFN83 6/148]   d9.15

1987	SF N	0	0	—	3	0	0	0-0	6	7	4	2	1	3-0	5	4.50	86	.304	.407	1	.000	-0		-1		0.0
1990	SF N	14	7	.667	33	32	2	1-0	204	201	92	18	4	61-7	118	3.79	96	.257	.313	63-0-8	.048	-3	128	-3		-0.6
1991	SF N	12	11	.522	36	34	3-1	0-0	206.2	223	103	19	10	60-2	131	4.18	86	.277	.332	55-0-9	.091	-2	93	-14		-1.1
1992	SF N	13	9	.591	32	32	3-1	0-0	189.2	194	96	13	4	45-6	107	3.84	87	.264	.308	55-0-8	.018	-3	127	-14		-2.1
1993	SF N★	22	7	.759	34	34	2-1	0-0	231.2	224	100	18	11	40-4	145	3.65	108	.255	.294	76-0-12	.118	-1	125	8		0.7
1994	SF N	6	8	.429	25	25	0	0-0	159.1	176	72	14	7	36-7	85	3.62	112	.286	.330	51-0-3	.059	-4	87	7		0.3
1995	Fla N	14	14	.500	30	30	4	0-0	188.1	208	99	22	6	57-5	126	4.30	100	.282	.339	66-0-4	.106	-2*	89	2		0.2
1996	Fla N	6	10	.375	24	24	1	0-0	154	154	84	15	9	42-2	108	4.06	100	.280	.323	0	—	0	86	9		-0.0
	†Tex A	5	2	.714	10	10	1-1	0	68.2	75	33	4	2	16-2	47	4.06	113	.280	.323	5	.200	0	101	6	26	-0.0
1997	Tex A	9	12	.429	32	30	2	0-0	189.1	240	106	20	4	30-1	139	4.56	107	.307	.333	5	.200	0	82	-15		-0.3
1998	Tex A	9	13	.409	32	32	0	0-0	195	230	131	19	4	46-1	96	5.68	82	.307	.358	2	.000	-0	96	-6	18	-1.2
1999	Tex A	9	8	.529	30	25	0	0-0	147.1	184	95	18	4	46-1	110	4.89	92	.303	.365	42-0-6	.143	-0	118	-5		-0.4
2000	†Atl N	10	6	.625	31	22	0	0-1	134.1	162	79	13	4	51-2	110	3.04	142	.300	.294	65-0-7	.092	-3	98	31		2.4
2001	†Atl N★	12	12	.500	34	34	1-1	0-0	219.1	187	83	17	6	70-13	187	3.04	142	.231	.294	3-0-1	.000	-0	122	0	20	2.4
2002	Bos A	13	8	.619	29	29	1-1	0-0	173	199	93	25	8	50-5	124	4.53	99	.287	.340	3-0-1	.000	-0	109	-7		-0.4
2003	†Bos A	12	9	.571	32	30	1	0-0	181.2	202	108	20	9	47-1	107	4.31	99	.287	.326	540-0-62	.093	-19	104	-6	64	-2.7
Total	15	166	136	.550	445	423	21-6	1-1	2648.1	2866	1374	257	90	700-59	1766	4.31	99	.287	.326	540-0-62	.093	-19	104	-6	64	-2.7

BURKHART, KEN   Kenneth William (b Kenneth William Burkhardt)   B11.18.1916 Knoxville TN   D12.29.2004 Knoxville TN   BR/TR/6-1/190   d4.21 U17

1945	StL N	18	8	.692	42	22	12-4	2	217.1	206	76	9	3	66	66	2.90	129	.251	.309	72-0-4	.181	1	98	23		2.5
1946	StL N	6	3	.667	25	13	5-2	2	100	111	34	4	2	36	32	2.88	120	.282	.346	34	.147	-0	143	8		0.2
1947	StL N	3	6	.333	34	6	1	0	95	108	55	13	4	23	23	5.21	79	.292	.340	24-0-2	.125	-1	103	-8		-0.6
1948	StL N	0	0	—	7	0	0	0	37.1	50	24	4	2	14	16	5.54	74	.331	.395	4	.250	-1		-5		-0.2
	Cin N	0	3	.000	16	0	0	0	41.2	42	24	4	1	16	14	6.91	57	.255	.324	9-1-0	.333	2		-13		-0.5

YEAR	TM LG	W	L	PCT	G	GS	CG-SHO	SV-BS	IP	H	R	HR	HB	BB-IB	SO	ERA	AERA	OAV	OOB	AB-HR-SH	AVG	PB	SUP	APR	DL	PW
	Year	0	3	.000	36	0	0	1	79	92	58	7	3	30	30	6.27	64	.291	.358	13-1-0	.308	2		-18		-0.9
1949	Cin N	0	0	—	11	0	0	1	28.1	29	10	2	0	10	8	3.18	132	.282	.345	7	.286			4		0.2
Total	5	27	20	.574	148	41	18-6	7	519.2	546	233	35	12	165	181	3.84	99	.273	.332	150-1-6	.180	2	110	9		1.6

BURNETT, A.J. Allan James B1.3.1977 North Little Rock AR BR/TR/6-5/205(204-230) [NYN95 8/217] d8.17

YEAR	TM LG	W	L	PCT	G	GS	CG-SHO	SV-BS	IP	H	R	HR	HB	BB-IB	SO	ERA	AERA	OAV	OOB	AB-HR-SH	AVG	PB	SUP	APR	DL	PW
1999	Fla N	4	2	.667	7	7	0	0-0	41.1	37	23	3	0	25-2	33	3.48	126	.242	.343	17	.118	-1	102	2		0.1
2000	Fla N	3	7	.300	13	13	0	0-0	82.2	80	46	8	2	44-3	57	4.79	91	.259	.352	25-1-2	.280	4	85	-3	107	0.1
2001	Fla N	11	12	.478	27	27	2-1	0-0	173.1	145	82	20	7	83-3	128	4.05	103	.231	.323	50-0-7	.080	-2	80	3	36	0.2
2002	Fla N	12	9	.571	31	29	7-5	0-1	204.1	153	84	12	9	90-5	203	3.30	119	.209	.302	57-1-7	.105	1	91	13	26	1.3
2003	Fla N	0	2	.000	4	4	0	0-0	23	18	13	2	2	18-2	21	4.70	87	.217	.365	7	.143	0	74	-2	166	-0.1
2004	Fla N	7	6	.538	20	19	1	0-0	120	102	50	9	4	38-0	113	3.68	112	.231	.296	29-0-8	.138	0	109	7	60	0.7
2005	Fla N	12	12	.500	32	32	4-2	0-0	209	184	97	12	7	79-1	198	3.44	116	.237	.312	68-1-9	.147	2	99	9		1.0
Total	7	49	50	.495	134	131	14-8	0-1	853.2	719	395	66	31	377-16	753	3.73	110	.230	.317	253-3-33	.134	4	93	29	395	3.3

BURNETT, SEAN Sean Richard B9.17.1982 Dunedin FL BL/TL/5-11/190 [PitN00 1/19] d5.30 [DL 2005 Pit N 183]

| 2004 | Pit N | 5 | 5 | .500 | 13 | 13 | 1-1 | 0-0 | 71.2 | 86 | 41 | 9 | 1 | 28-2 | 30 | 5.02 | 86 | .301 | .364 | 23-0-2 | .000 | -2 | 94 | -4 | 43 | -0.7 |

BURNETTE, WALLY Wallace Harper B6.20.1929 Blairs VA D2.12.2003 Danville VA BR/TR/6-0.5/178(178-195) d7.15

1956	KC A	6	8	.429	18	14	4-1	0	121.1	115	48	13	2	39-3	54	2.89	150	.252	.312	39-0-5	.051	-4	79	17		1.3
1957	KC A	7	12	.368	38	14	1	1	113	115	62	8	1	44-3	57	4.30	92	.268	.333	32-0-3	.250	1	78	-5		-0.6
1958	KC A	1	1	.500	12	4	0	0	28.1	29	14	2	0	14-0	11	3.49	112	.264	.344	6-0-1	.167	-1	132	0		0.0
Total	3	14	21	.400	68	27	5-1	1	262.2	259	124	23	3	97-6	122	3.56	116	.260	.325	77-0-9	.143	-4	87	12		0.7

BURNS, DENNIS Dennis B5.24.1898 Tiff City MO D5.21.1969 Tulsa OK BR/TR/5-10/180 d9.22 Col Missouri

1923	Phi A	2	1	.667	4	3	0	1	27	21	9	1	0	7	8	2.00	205	.210	.262	9	.111	-1	81	5		0.5
1924	Phi A	6	8	.429	37	17	7	1	154	191	101	3	1	68	26	5.08	84	.314	.384	42-0-2	.143	-2	96	-13		-1.2
Total	2	8	9	.471	41	20	9	1	181	212	110	4	1	75	34	4.62	92	.299	.367	51-0-2	.137	-3	94	-8		-0.7

BURNS, FARMER James Joseph "Slab" B6.2.1876 Ashtabula OH TR/5-7/168 d7.6 Col Washington & Jefferson

| 1901 | StL N | 0 | 0 | — | 1 | 0 | 0 | | 2 | 1 | 1 | 0 | 0 | 1 | 0 | 9.00 | 35 | .400 | .571 | 0 | | 0 | | -1 | | 0.0 |

BURNS, MIKE Michael John B7.14.1978 Westminster CA BR/TR/6-0/205 d5.13 Col Cal St.-Los Angeles

| 2005 | Hou N | 0 | 0 | — | 27 | 0 | 0 | 0-0 | 31 | 29 | 18 | 6 | 5 | 8-1 | 20 | 4.94 | 85 | .238 | .311 | 0 | | 0 | | -2 | | -0.1 |

BURNS, DICK Richard Simon B12.26.1863 Holyoke MA D11.16.1937 Holyoke MA BL/TL/5-7/140 d5.3 ▲

1883	Det N	2	12	.143	17	13	13	0	127.2	172	122	8	0	33	30	4.51	69	.301	.339	140	.186	-2*	78	-21		-1.9
1884	Cin U	23	15	.605	40	40	34-1	0	329.2	298	179	7	0	47	167	2.46	104	.225	.252	350-4	.306	3*	113	2		0.4
1885	StL N	0	0	—	1	0	0	0	3	3	3	0	0	0	2	9.00	31	.250	.250	54	.222	0*		-2		0.0
Total	3	25	27	.481	58	53	47-1	0	460.1	473	304	15	0	80	199	3.07	89	.248	.278	544-4	.267	2	105	-21		-1.5

BURNS, BRITT Robert Britt B6.8.1959 Houston TX BL/TL/6-5/218(215-231) [ChiA78 3/70] d8.5 [DL 1986 NY A 182]

1978	Chi A	0	2	.000	2	2	0	0-0	7.2	14	14	4	0	3-0	3	12.91	29	.378	.425	0		0	35	-8		-1.1
1979	Chi A	0	0	—	2	0	0	0-1	5	10	5	1	0	1-0	2	5.40	79	.435	.423	0		0		-1		-0.1
1980	Chi A	15	13	.536	34	32	11-1	0-0	238	213	83	17	4	63-2	133	2.84	143	.241	.293	0		0	67	34		3.8
1981	Chi A☆	10	6	.625	24	23	5-1	0-0	156.2	139	52	14	6	49-1	108	2.64	137	.238	.300	0		0	102	18		1.6
1982	Chi A	13	5	.722	28	28	5-1	0-0	169.1	168	89	12	3	67-1	116	4.04	101	.257	.328	0		0	115	0		-0.1
1983	†Chi A	10	11	.476	29	26	8-4	0-0	173.2	165	79	14	5	55-2	115	3.58	118	.249	.310	0		0	91	-11		1.1
1984	Chi A	4	12	.250	34	16	2	3-2	117	130	74	7	4	45-1	85	5.00	84	.280	.347	0		0	77	11	35	-1.4
1985	Chi A	18	11	.621	36	34	8-4	0-0	227	206	105	26	2	79-1	172	3.96	110	.242	.306	0		0	78	-11	32	1.3
Total	8	70	60	.538	193	161	39-11	3-3	1094.1	1045	499	93	24	362-8	734	3.66	112	.251	.313	0		0	91	54	249	5.1

BURNS, TOMMY Thomas P. "Oyster" B9.6.1864 Philadelphia PA D11.11.1928 Brooklyn NY BL/TR/5-8/183 d8.18 ▲

1884	Bal AA	0	0	—	2	0	0	1	9	12	5	0	0	2	6	3.00	116	.343	.378	131-6	.298	1*		1		0.1
1885	Bal AA	7	4	.636	15	11	10-1	3	105.2	112	76	2	13	21	30	3.58	91	.266	.321	321-5	.231	3*	101	-6		-0.4
1887	Bal AA	1	0	1.000	3	0	0	0	11.1	16	16	0	3	4	2	9.53	43	.291	.371	551-9	.341	2*		-6		-0.3
1888	Bal AA	0	1	.000	5	0	0	0	12.2	12	8	0	0	3	2	4.26	70	.240	.283	325-4	.298	2*		-1		0.0
Total	4	8	5	.615	25	11	10-1	4	138.2	152	105	2	16	30	40	4.09	81	.271	.326	1328-24	.300	7	101	-12		-0.6

BURNS, TODD Todd Edward B7.6.1963 Maywood CA BR/TR/6-2/190* [OakA84 7/168] d5.31 Col Oral Roberts

1988	†Oak A	8	2	.800	17	14	2	1-0	102.2	93	38	8	1	34-1	57	3.16	121	.241	.303	0		0	125	8		0.7
1989	†Oak A	6	5	.545	50	2	0	8-3	96.1	66	27	3	1	28-5	49	2.24	165	.196	.259	0		0	86	17		2.0
1990	†Oak A	3	3	.500	43	2	0	3-1	78.2	78	28	8	0	32-4	43	2.97	126	.263	.331	0		0	97	7		0.5
1991	Oak A	1	0	1.000	9	0	0	0-0	13.1	10	5	2	0	8-1	3	3.38	114	.217	.321	0		0		1	61	0.1
1992	Tex A	3	5	.375	35	10	0	1-1	103	97	54	8	4	32-3	55	3.84	100	.248	.309	0		0	67	-2		-0.2
1993	Tex A	0	4	.000	25	5	0	0-3	65	63	36	6	2	32-3	35	4.57	92	.253	.339	0		0	57	-3		-0.2
	StL N	0	4	.000	24	0	0	1	30.2	32	21	8	0	9-6	10	6.16	65	.274	.320	3-0-1	.000	-0		-6		-0.0
Total	6	21	23	.477	203	33	2	13-10	489.2	439	209	43	8	175-21	252	3.47	111	.241	.307	3-0-1	.000	-0	93	22	61	2.1

BURNS, BILL William Thomas "Sleepy Bill" B1.29.1880 San Saba TX D6.6.1953 Ramona CA BB/TL/6-2/195 d4.18

1908	Was A	6	11	.353	23	19	11-2	0	164	135	58	3	4	18	55	1.70	134	.229	.257	54	.148	-1	71	7		0.8
1909	Was A	1	1	.500	6	4	1	0	29.1	25	7	0	3	7	13	1.23	198	.229	.294	11	.273	0	51	3		0.3
	Chi A	7	13	.350	23	19	10-3	0	168	161	64	2	8	34	50	2.04	115	.264	.312	59-0-1	.153	1	70	2		0.4
	Year	8	14	.364	29	23	11-3	0	197.1	186	71	2	11	41	63	1.92	123	.259	.309	70-0-1	.171	1	66	7		0.7
1910	Chi A	0	0	—	1	0	0	0	0.1	0	0	0	0	1	0	0.00	—	.000	.500	0	—	0				0.0
	Cin N	8	13	.381	31	21	13-2	0	178.2	183	103	3	12	49	57	3.48	84	.273	.333	61-0-1	.262	2*	100	-13		-1.1
1911	Cin N	1	0	1.000	6	3	0	1	17.2	17	11	1	3	6	5	3.06	108	.254	.315	7	.429	1	151	-1		0.2
	Phi N	6	10	.375	21	14	8-3	1	121	132	59	5	6	26	47	3.42	101	.287	.333	40	.150	-1	59	1		0.0
	Year	7	10	.412	27	17	8-3	2	138.2	149	70	6	9	29	52	3.38	102	.283	.331	47	.191	0	75	0		0.2
1912	Det A	1	4	.200	6	5	2	0	38.2	52	29	0	2	9	6	5.35	61	.338	.382	13	.231	1	104	-8		-0.8
Total	5	30	52	.366	117	85	45-10	2	717.2	705	331	14	38	147	233	2.72	100	.265	.313	245-0-2	.196	4	81	-9		-0.2

BURNSIDE, PETE Peter Willits B7.2.1930 Evanston IL BR/TL/6-2/190* d9.20

1955	NY N	1	0	1.000	2	2	1	0	12.2	10	9	1	0	9-0	2	2.84	142	.204	.328		.200	0	210	0		0.0
1957	NY N	0	4	.200	10	9	1-1	0	30.2	47	30	5	1	13-0	18	8.80	45	.356	.415	9-0-2	.000	-1	114	-15		-2.1
1958	SF N	0	0	—	6	1	0	0	10.2	20	10	3	0	5-0	4	6.75	56	.400	.455	0	—	-1	141	-4		-0.2
1959	Det A	1	3	.250	30	0	0	1	62	55	31	7	2	25-1	49	3.77	108	.237	.315	10-0-1	.000	-1		1		0.0
1960	Det A	7	7	.500	31	15	2	0	113.2	122	56	14	4	50-1	71	4.28	93	.277	.355	27-0-5	.148	-1	96	-2		-0.3
1961	Was A	4	9	.308	33	16	4-2	2	113.1	106	66	11	8	51-2	56	4.53	89	.251	.330	34-0-3	.059	-1	74	-6		-1.0
1962	Was A	5	11	.313	40	20	6	2	149.2	152	82	20	2	51-3	74	4.45	91	.263	.322	35-0-5	.057	-3	83*	-7		-1.0
1963	Bal A	0	1	.000	6	0	0	0	7.1	11	4	1	1	2-0	6	4.91	71	.344	.400	1	.000	-0		-1		-0.2
	Was A	0	0	—	38	1	0	0	67.1	84	49	12	0	24-1	23	6.15	60	.308	.359	11	.091	-0	48	-16		-0.9
	Year	0	2	.000	44	1	0	0	74.2	95	53	12	1	26-1	29	6.03	61	.311	.363	12	.083	-1	48	-17		-1.1
Total	8	19	36	.345	196	64	14-3	7	567.1	607	337	73	13	230-8	303	4.81	82	.275	.344	132-0-16	.076	-8	93	-50		-5.7

BURNSIDE, SHELDON Sheldon John B12.22.1954 South Bend IN BR/TL/6-5/200* d9.4

1978	Det A	0	0	—	2	0	0	0-0	4	4	4	0	0	2-0	3	9.00	43	.250	.333	0	—	0		-2		-0.1
1979	Det A	1	1	.500	10	0	0	0-0	21.1	28	16	2	1	9-0	13	6.33	69	.333	.394	0	—	0		-4		-0.3
1980	Cin N	1	0	1.000	7	0	0	0-0	4.2	6	1	1	0	1-0	2	1.93	183	.333	.368	1	.000	-0		1		0.2
Total	3	2	1	.667	19	0	0	0	30	38	21	3	1	12-0	18	6.00	69	.322	.382	1	.000	-0		-5		-0.2

BURPO, GEORGE George Harvie B6.19.1922 Jenkins KY BR/TL/6-0/195 d6.9

| 1946 | Cin N | 0 | 0 | — | 2 | 0 | 0 | 0 | 2.1 | 4 | 4 | 0 | 0 | 5 | 0 | 15.43 | 22 | .400 | .600 | | | 0 | | -3 | | -0.2 |

BURRELL, HARRY Harry J. B5.26.1869 Bethel VT D12.11.1914 Omaha NE BR/TL d9.13

| 1891 | StL AA | 4 | 2 | .667 | 7 | 4 | 3 | 1 | 43 | 51 | 36 | 4 | 2 | 21 | 19 | 4.81 | 87 | .285 | .366 | 20 | .200 | -1* | 52 | -2 | | -0.3 |

BURRIS, AL Alva Burton B1.28.1874 Warwick MD D3.25.1938 Salisbury MD BR/TR d6.22 Col Washington College

| 1894 | Phi N | 0 | 0 | — | 1 | 0 | 0 | 0 | 5 | 14 | 10 | 0 | 0 | 2 | 0 | 18.00 | 29 | .500 | .533 | 4 | .500 | 1 | | -6 | | -0.2 |

YEAR	TM LG	W	L	PCT	G	GS	CG-SHO	SV-BS	IP	H	R	HR	HB	BB-IB	SO	ERA	AERA	OAV	OOB	AB-HR-SH	AVG	PB	SUP	APR	DL	PW

BURRIS, RAY Bertram Ray B8.22.1950 Idabel OK BR/TR/6-5/200(192-210) [ChiN72 17/399] d4.8 C3 Col Southwestern Oklahoma

YEAR	TM LG	W	L	PCT	G	GS	CG-SHO	SV-BS	IP	H	R	HR	HB	BB-IB	SO	ERA	AERA	OAV	OOB	AB-HR-SH	AVG	PB	SUP	APR	DL	PW
1973	Chi N	1	1	.500	31	1	0	0-0	64.2	65	22	2	0	27-7	57	2.92	135	.261	.331	7-0-1	.143	0	22	7		0.
1974	Chi N	3	5	.375	40	5	0	1-1	75	91	61	8	4	26-6	40	6.60	58	.300	.359	13-0-1	.077	-1*	50	-20		-2.
1975	Chi N	15	10	.600	36	35	8-2	0-0	238.1	259	121	25	4	73-6	108	4.12	94	.281	.334	82-0-7	.183	1*	111	-5		-0.
1976	Chi N	15	13	.536	37	36	10-4	0-0	249	251	102	22	5	70-5	112	3.11	125	.263	.315	81-0-8	.111	-4*	81	17		1
1977	Chi N	14	16	.467	39	39	5-1	0-0	221	270	132	29	3	67-9	105	4.72	93	.305	.355	69-1-9	.174	1*	98	-7		-1.
1978	Chi N	7	13	.350	40	32	4-1	1-1	199	210	112	19	10	79-11	94	4.75	85	.274	.346	61-0-7	.115	-1*	96	-12		-1.
1979	Chi N	0	0	—	14	0	0	0-0	21.2	23	17	0	1	15-1	14	6.23	67	.284	.398	1	.000	0		-5		-0.
	NY A	1	3	.250	15	0	0	0-2	27.2	40	22	5	0	10-1	19	3.32	112	.247	.304	6-0-1	.167	-0	66	0	15	0
	NY N	0	2	.000	4	4	0	0-0	21.2	21	10	2	1	6-3	10	4.02	90	.277	.333	51-0-3	.098	-2	85	-8	32	-1.
1980	NY N	7	13	.350	29	29	1	0-0	170.1	181	86	20	4	54-5	83	3.05	117	.235	.294	37-0-4	.189	1	118	5		0
1981	†Mon N	9	7	.563	22	21	2	0-0	135.2	117	56	9	3	41-3	52	4.73	78	.297	.365	28-0-4	.179	1	76	-15		-2
1982	Mon N	4	14	.222	37	15	2	2-3	123.2	143	77	14	2	53-7	55	3.68	98	.244	.312	39-0-2	.231	3	83	0		0.
1983	Mon N	4	7	.364	40	17	2-1	0-0	154	139	68	13	2	56-4	100	3.15	120	.244	.325	0	—	0*	106	15		0.
1984	Oak A	13	10	.565	34	28	5-1	0-0	211.2	193	84	15	8	90-1	93	4.81	87	.272	.325	0	—	0	98	-8		-0
1985	Mil A	9	13	.409	29	28	6	0-0	170.1	182	95	25	3	53-0	81	5.60	66	.287	.359	27	.148	0	101	-15		-1
1986	StL N	4	5	.444	23	10	0	0-0	82	92	52	13	4	32-4	34	5.87	79	.351	.417	0	—	0	79	-3		-0
1987	Mil A	2	2	.500	10	2	0	0-0	23	33	16	4	0	12-3	8											
Total	15	108	134	.446	480	302	47-10	4-7	2188.2	2310	1133	221	54	764-76	1065	4.17	94	.274	.335	502-1-50	.151	-1	95	-61	47	-7

BURROWS, JOHN John B10.30.1913 Winnfield LA D4.27.1987 Coal Run OH BR/TL/5-10/200 d4.25

YEAR	TM LG	W	L	PCT	G	GS	CG-SHO	SV-BS	IP	H	R	HR	HB	BB-IB	SO	ERA	AERA	OAV	OOB	AB-HR-SH	AVG	PB	SUP	APR	DL	PW
1943	Phi A	0	1	.000	4	1	0		7.2	8	7	0	1	9	3	8.22	41	.276	.462	1	.000	-0		0	-4		-0
	Chi N	0	2	.000	23	1	0	2	32.2	25	17	0	2	16	18	3.86	87	.205	.307	2	.667	1	51	-2		0
1944	Chi N	0	0	—	3	0	0		3	7	7	0	0	3	1	18.00	20	.467	.556	0	—	0		-5		-0
Total	2	0	3	.000	30	2	0	2	43.1	40	31	0	3	28	22	5.61	60	.241	.360	4	.500	1	25	-11		-0

BURROWS, TERRY Terry Dale B11.28.1968 Lake Charles LA BL/TL/6-1/185* [TexA90 7/198] d6.12 Col McNeese St.

YEAR	TM LG	W	L	PCT	G	GS	CG-SHO	SV-BS	IP	H	R	HR	HB	BB-IB	SO	ERA	AERA	OAV	OOB	AB-HR-SH	AVG	PB	SUP	APR	DL	PW
1994	Tex A	0	0	—	1	0	0	0-0	1	1	1	1	0	1-0	1	9.00	54	.250	.400	0	—			0	0		-0
1995	Tex A	2	2	.500	28	0	0	1-2	44.2	60	37	11	2	19-0	22	6.45	75	.323	.391	0	—	0	96	-9		-0
1996	Mil A	2	0	1.000	8	0	0	0-0	12.2	12	4	2	1	10-0	5	2.84	183	.261	.404	0	—	0		3		-1
1997	SD N	0	2	.000	13	0	0	0-0	10.1	12	13	1	1	8-1	8	10.45	38	.286	.412	0	—	0		-8		-1
Total	4	4	4	.500	50	3	0	1-2	68.2	85	55	15	4	38-1	35	6.42	74	.306	.397	0	—	0	96	-14		-1

BURTON, JIM Jim Scott B10.27.1949 Royal Oak MI BR/TL/6-3/195* [BosA71 D1/5] d6.10 Col Michigan

YEAR	TM LG	W	L	PCT	G	GS	CG-SHO	SV-BS	IP	H	R	HR	HB	BB-IB	SO	ERA	AERA	OAV	OOB	AB-HR-SH	AVG	PB	SUP	APR	DL	PW
1975	†Bos A	1	2	.333	29	4	0	1-1	53	58	30	6	0	19-2	39	2.89	141	.276	.333	0	—	0	87	2		0
1977	Bos A	0	0	—	1	0	0		2.2	2	0	0	0	1-0	3	0.00	—	.200	.273	0	—	0		1		0
Total	2	1	2	.333	30	4	0	1-1	55.2	60	30	6	0	20-2	42	2.75	149	.273	.331	0	—	0	87	3		0

BURTSCHY, MOE Edward Frank B4.18.1922 Cincinnati OH D5.2.2004 Cincinnati OH BR/TR/6-3/208* d6.17

YEAR	TM LG	W	L	PCT	G	GS	CG-SHO	SV-BS	IP	H	R	HR	HB	BB-IB	SO	ERA	AERA	OAV	OOB	AB-HR-SH	AVG	PB	SUP	APR	DL	PW
1950	Phi A	0	1	.000	9	1	0		19	22	16	2	1	21	12	7.11	64	.289	.449	5	.000	-0	20	-5		-0
1951	Phi A	0	0	—	7	0	0		17	18	11	0	1	12	4	5.29	81	.277	.397	3	.333	0		-2	64	-0
1954	Phi A	5	4	.556	46	0	0	4	94.2	80	45	7	8	53	54	3.80	103	.234	.346	17	.118	-1		1		-
1955	KC A	2	0	1.000	7	0	0		11.1	17	13	0	1	10-1	9	10.32	40	.354	.467	3	.333	0		-7		-
1956	KC A	3	1	.750	21	0	0		43.1	41	22	6	3	30-4	18	3.95	110	.263	.389	8	.125	-1		1		-
Total	5	10	6	.625	90	1	0	4	185.1	178	107	15	14	126-5	97	4.71	88	.259	.381	36	.139	-1	20	-12	64	-

BURTT, DENNIS Dennis Allen B11.29.1957 San Diego CA BB/TR/6-0/187* [BosA76*2/45] d9.4 Col Santa Ana (CA) JC

YEAR	TM LG	W	L	PCT	G	GS	CG-SHO	SV-BS	IP	H	R	HR	HB	BB-IB	SO	ERA	AERA	OAV	OOB	AB-HR-SH	AVG	PB	SUP	APR	DL	PW
1985	Min A	2	2	.500	5	2	0	0-0	28.1	20	13	2	0	7-0	7	3.81	116	.200	.250	0	—	0	103	2		
1986	Min A	0	0	—	3	0	0	0-0	2	7	7	1	0	3-1	1	31.50	14	.538	.625	0	—	0		-6		
Total	2	2	2	.500	8	2	0	0-0	30.1	27	20	3	0	10-1	10	5.64	78	.239	.298	0	—	0	103	-4		

BURWELL, DICK Richard Matthew B1.23.1940 Alton IL BR/TR/6-1/190* d9.13 Col Illinois Wesleyan

YEAR	TM LG	W	L	PCT	G	GS	CG-SHO	SV-BS	IP	H	R	HR	HB	BB-IB	SO	ERA	AERA	OAV	OOB	AB-HR-SH	AVG	PB	SUP	APR	DL	PW
1960	Chi N	0	0	—	3	1	0	0	9.2	11	6	1	1	7-0	1	5.59	68	.306	.432	3	.333	0	140	-2		
1961	Chi N	0	0	—	2	0	0	0	3.2	6	4	0	0	4-0	0	9.00	46	.375	.476	1	.000	-0		-2		
Total	2	0	0	—	5	1	0	0	13.2	17	10	2	1	11-0	1	6.59	59	.327	.446	4	.250	0	140	-4		

BURWELL, BILL William Edwin B3.27.1895 Jarbalo KS D6.11.1973 Ormond Beach FL BL/TR/5-11/175 d5.1 M1/C8

YEAR	TM LG	W	L	PCT	G	GS	CG-SHO	SV-BS	IP	H	R	HR	HB	BB-IB	SO	ERA	AERA	OAV	OOB	AB-HR-SH	AVG	PB	SUP	APR	DL	PW
1920	StL A	6	4	.600	33	4	0	4	113.1	133	55	5	4	42	30	3.65	107	.303	.369	42-0-2	.167	-2*	91	4		
1921	StL A	2	4	.333	33	3	1	2	84.1	102	62	2	2	29	17	5.12	87	.309	.368	25	.240	-0	130	-8		
1928	Pit N	1	0	1.000	4	1	0	0	20.2	18	12	2	0	8	2	5.23	78	.234	.306	9-0-1	.222	-0	125	-2		
Total	3	9	8	.529	70	6	1	6	218.1	253	129	9	6	79	49	4.37	95	.299	.363	76-0-3	.197	-2	118	-6		

BUSBY, MIKE Michael James B12.27.1972 Lomita CA BR/TR/6-4/210(210-225) [StLN91 14/363] d4.7

YEAR	TM LG	W	L	PCT	G	GS	CG-SHO	SV-BS	IP	H	R	HR	HB	BB-IB	SO	ERA	AERA	OAV	OOB	AB-HR-SH	AVG	PB	SUP	APR	DL	PW
1996	StL N	0	1	.000	1	1	0	0-0	4	9	13	4	1	4-0	4	18.00	24	.409	.519	2	.500	0	64	-8		
1997	StL N	0	2	.000	3	3	0	0-0	14.1	24	14	2	0	4-0	5	8.79	48	.393	.424	4	.500	1	73	-7		
1998	StL N	5	2	.714	26	2	0	0-2	46	45	23	3	6	15-0	33	4.50	93	.254	.327	3	.000	0	98	0	101	
1999	StL N	1	1	1.000	15	0	0	0-0	17.2	21	15	2	2	14-0	7	7.13	66	.300	.430	0	—	0		-5		
Total	4	5	6	.455	45	6	0	0-2	82	99	65	11	8	37-0	50	6.48	66	.300	.381	9	.333	1	79	-20	101	

BUSBY, STEVE Steven Lee B9.29.1949 Burbank CA BR/TR/6-2/195(190-205) [KCA71 D2/39] d9.8 Col USC [DL 1977 KC A 28]

YEAR	TM LG	W	L	PCT	G	GS	CG-SHO	SV-BS	IP	H	R	HR	HB	BB-IB	SO	ERA	AERA	OAV	OOB	AB-HR-SH	AVG	PB	SUP	APR	DL	PW
1972	KC A	3	1	.750	5	5	3	0-0	40	28	9	4	0	14-0	31	1.57	193	.200	.238	15	.200	0	116	6		
1973	KC A	16	15	.516	37	37	7-1	0-0	238.1	246	125	18	6	105-7	174	4.23	97	.271	.347	0	—	0	119	17		
1974	KC A☆	22	14	.611	38	38	20-3	0-0	292.1	284	118	14	9	92-6	198	3.39	113	.258	.319	0	—	0	93	25		
1975	KC A★	18	12	.600	34	34	18-3	0-0	260.1	233	96	18	3	81-4	160	3.08	125	.242	.302	0	—	0	154	-8	95	
1976	KC A	3	3	.500	13	13	1	0-0	71.2	58	42	7	3	49-1	29	4.40	80	.218	.344	0	—	0	127	-9		
1978	KC A	1	0	1.000	7	5	0	0-0	21.1	24	18	2	2	15-1	10	7.59	50	.282	.402	0	—	0	87	6		
1979	KC A	6	6	.500	22	12	4	0-0	94.1	71	45	10	0	64-3	45	3.63	118	.220	.343	0	—	0	77	-9		
1980	KC A	1	3	.250	11	6	0	0-0	42.1	59	30	3	2	19-0	12	6.17	66	.335	.402	0	—	0	105	26	123	
Total	8	70	54	.565	167	150	53-7	0-0	1060.2	1003	483	73	25	433-22	659	3.72	105	.253	.328	15	.200	0	105	26	123	

BUSCHHORN, DON Donald Lee B4.29.1946 Independence MO BR/TR/6-0/170 d5.15

YEAR	TM LG	W	L	PCT	G	GS	CG-SHO	SV-BS	IP	H	R	HR	HB	BB-IB	SO	ERA	AERA	OAV	OOB	AB-HR-SH	AVG	PB	SUP	APR	DL	PW
1965	KC A	0							31	36	17	7	1	8-0	9	4.35	80	.295	.341	4	.500	1*	101	-3	32	

BUSH, DAVE David T. B11.9.1979 Pittsburgh PA BR/TR/6-2/212* [TorA02 2/55] d7.2 Col Wake Forest

YEAR	TM LG	W	L	PCT	G	GS	CG-SHO	SV-BS	IP	H	R	HR	HB	BB-IB	SO	ERA	AERA	OAV	OOB	AB-HR-SH	AVG	PB	SUP	APR	DL	PW
2004	Tor A	5	4	.556	16	16	1-1	0-0	97.2	95	47	11	6	25-2	64	3.69	133	.255	.309	2	.000	-0	85	10		
2005	Tor A	5	11	.313	25	24	2	0-0	136.1	142	73	20	13	29-3	75	4.49	103	.269	.322	0	—	-0	96	2		
Total	2	10	15	.400	41	40	3-1	0-0	234	237	120	31	19	54-5	139	4.15	114	.263	.316	2	.000	-0	92	12		

BUSH, GUY Guy Terrell "The Mississippi Mudcat" B8.23.1901 Aberdeen MS D7.2.1985 Shannon MS BR/TR/6-0/175 d9.17 Col Tupelo Mil. Inst. [JC]

YEAR	TM LG	W	L	PCT	G	GS	CG-SHO	SV-BS	IP	H	R	HR	HB	BB-IB	SO	ERA	AERA	OAV	OOB	AB-HR-SH	AVG	PB	SUP	APR	DL	PW
1923	Chi N	0	0	—	1	0	0		1	1	0	0	0	0	2	0.00	—	.250	.250	0	—	0		0		
1924	Chi N	2	5	.286	16	8	4		80.2	91	51	7	2	24	36	4.02	97	.285	.339	26	.154	-1	82	-4		
1925	Chi N	6	13	.316	42	15	5	4	182	213	102	15	3	52	76	4.30	101	.300	.350	48-0-3	.167	-2	83	0		
1926	Chi N	13	9	.591	35	15	7-2	2	157.1	149	58	3	3	42	32	2.86	134	.258	.331	48-0-3	.167	-2	94	18		
1927	Chi N	10	10	.500	36	22	9-1	2	193.1	177	76	3	6	79	62	3.03	128	.250	.330	65-0-5	.123	-4	86	18		
1928	Chi N	15	6	.714	42	24	9-2	2	204.1	229	104	10	5	86	61	3.83	100	.293	.367	73-0-4	.082	-6	112	0		
1929	†Chi N	18	7	.720	50	30	18-2	8	270.2	277	135	16	4	107	82	3.66	126	.265	.335	91-0-10	.165	-4	115	27		
1930	Chi N	15	10	.600	46	25	11	3	225	291	164	17	7	86	75	6.20	79	.316	.376	78-0-3	.282	3	121	-31		
1931	Chi N	16	8	.667	39	24	14-1	3	180.1	190	104	9	2	66	54	4.49	86	.268	.332	57-0-5	.123	-2	108	13		
1932	†Chi N	19	11	.633	40	30	15-1	3	238.2	262	106	13	7	70	73	3.21	118	.278	.332	88-0-5	.179	0	117	16		
1933	Chi N	20	12	.625	41	32	20-4	2	259	261	95	9	1	68	84	2.75	119	.257	.304	70-0-6	.229	1*	110	3		
1934	Chi N	18	10	.643	40	27	15-1	2	209.1	213	96	15	1	54	75	4.32	95	.285	.321	63-0-3	.127	-1	102	-2		
1935	Pit N	11	11	.500	44	25	8-1	2	204.1	237	115	16	5	40	10	5.97	68	.336	.382	9	.333	0		-8		
1936	Pit N	1	3	.250	16	0	0		34.2	49	34	3	0	11	10			.281	.320	25-0-6	.120	-1	86	5		
	Bos N	4	5	.444	15	11	5		90.1	98	38	2	0	20	28	3.89	113	.281	.338							
	Year	5	8	.385	31	11	5		125	147	66	5	0	31	38	4.10	95	.297	.338	34-0-6	.176	-0	85	-1		
1937	Bos N	8	15	.348	32	20	11-1	1	180.2	201	77	8	0	48	56	3.54	101	.282	.328	54-0-2	.111	-2*	71	3		
1938	StL N	0	1	.000	6	0	0		6	6	3	0	0	3	1	4.50	88	.286	.375	0	—	0		0		

YEAR	TM LG	W	L	PCT	G	GS	CG-SHO	SV-BS	IP	H	R	HR	HB	BB-IB	SO	ERA	AERA	OAV	OOB	AB-HR-SH	AVG	PB	SUP	APR	DL	PW
1945	Cin N	0	0	—	4	0	0	1	4.1	5	4	0	0	3	1	8.31	45	.278	.381	0		0		-2		-0.1
Total	17	176	136	.564	542	308	151-16	34	2722	2950	1366	152	41	859	850	3.86	103	.277	.334	888-0-61	.161	-22	105	43		3.4

BUSH, JOE   Leslie Ambrose "Bullet Joe"   B11.27.1892 Brainerd MN   D11.1.1974 Ft.Lauderdale FL   BR/TR/5-9/173   d9.30

YEAR	TM LG	W	L	PCT	G	GS	CG-SHO	SV-BS	IP	H	R	HR	HB	BB-IB	SO	ERA	AERA	OAV	OOB	AB-HR-SH	AVG	PB	SUP	APR	DL	PW
1912	Phi A	0	0	—	1	1	0	0	8	14	10	0	0	4	3	7.88	39	.368	.429	4	.500	1	264	-5		-0.1
1913	†Phi A	15	6	.714	39	16	6-1	3	200.1	199	95	3	5	66	81	3.82	72	.261	.324	70-0-2	.157	-0	126	-21		-1.9
1914	†Phi A	17	13	.567	38	23	14-2	2	206	184	84	2	8	81	109	3.06	85	.242	.322	74-1-4	.189	2	113	-10		-1.2
1915	Phi A	5	15	.250	25	18	8	0	145.2	137	86	3	4	89	89	4.14	71	.263	.375	49-0-2	.143	-3	78	-17		-2.4
1916	Phi A	15	24	.385	40	33	25-8	0	286.2	222	109	3	3	130	157	2.57	111	.219	.310	100-0-2	.140	-4*	69	9		1.1
1917	Phi A	11	17	.393	37	31	17-4	2	233.1	207	101	3	1	111	121	2.47	111	.241	.328	80	.200	1	75	3		0.5
1918	†Bos A	15	15	.500	36	31	26-7	2	272.2	241	88	3	3	91	125	2.11	127	.242	.307	98-0-1	.276	6	80	16		2.8
1919	Bos A	0	0	—	3	2	0	0	9	11	5	0	0	4	3	5.00	60	.324	.395	5	.400	1*	195	-2		0.0
1920	Bos A	15	15	.500	35	32	18	1	243.2	287	138	3	10	94	88	4.25	86	.300	.369	102-0-3	.245	2*	95	-18		-1.6
1921	Bos A	16	9	.640	37	32	21-3	1	254.1	244	111	10	6	93	96	3.50	121	.260	.330	120-0-3	.325	6*	107	22		2.8
1922	†NY A	26	7	**.788**	39	30	20	3	255.1	240	109	16	1	85	92	3.31	121	.252	.314	95-0-5	.326	8	118	20		3.2
1923	†NY A	19	15	.559	37	30	22-3	0	275.2	263	115	7	5	117	125	3.43	115	.260	.340	113-2-0	.274	7*	103	17		2.6
1924	NY A	17	16	.515	39	31	19-3	1	252	262	117	9	7	109	80	3.57	116	.273	.352	124-1-1	.339	14*	102	16		3.2
1925	StL A	14	14	.500	33	30	15-2	0	208.2	230	129	18	2	94	63	5.09	92	.284	.357	102-2-1	.255	3*	103	-4		0.2
1926	Was A	1	8	.111	12	11	3	0	71.1	83	54	6	5	35	27	6.69	58	.292	.380	30	.233	1*	87	-20		-1.9
	Pit N	6	6	.500	19	12	9-2	3	110.2	97	45	7	2	35	38	3.01	131	.236	.299	49-1-0	.265	2*	85	11		1.4
1927	Pit N	1	2	.333	5	3	0	0	6.2	14	14	1	0	5	1	13.50	30	.412	.487	5	.600	1*	76	-8		-1.2
	NY N	1	1	.500	3	2	1	0	12	18	10	1	0	5	6	7.50	51	.340	.397	4	.500	1	99	-4		-0.5
	Year	2	3	.400	8	5	1	0	18.2	32	24	2	0	10	7	9.64	41	.368	.433	9	.556	2	86	-12		-1.7
1928	Phi A	2	1	.667	11	2	1	1	35.1	39	21	1	1	18	5	5.09	79	.300	.389	15	.067	-1*	106	-3		-0.3
Total	17	196	184	.516	489	370	225-35	19	3087.1	2992	1441	96	63	1263	1319	3.51	99	.260	.336	1239-7-24	.253	49	98	2		6.7

BUSHELMAN, JACK   John Francis   B8.29.1885 Cincinnati OH   D10.26.1955 Roanoke VA   BR/TR/6-2/175   d10.5   Col Cincinnati

YEAR	TM LG	W	L	PCT	G	GS	CG-SHO	SV-BS	IP	H	R	HR	HB	BB-IB	SO	ERA	AERA	OAV	OOB	AB-HR-SH	AVG	PB	SUP	APR	DL	PW
1909	Cin N	0	1	.000	1	1	1	0	7	7	7	1	0	4	3	2.57	101	.241	.333	1	.000	-0	108	-1		-0.2
1911	Bos A	0	1	.000	3	1	1	0	12	8	9	0	1	10	5	3.00	109	.186	.352	3	.000	-0	22	-1		-0.1
1912	Bos A	1	0	1.000	3	0	0	0	7.2	9	4	0	0	5	5	4.70	72	.310	.412	3	.000	-0	-1	-1		-0.1
Total	3	1	2	.333	7	2	2	0	26.2	24	20	1	1	19	13	3.38	93	.238	.364	7	.000	-1	57	-3		-0.4

BUSHEY, FRANK   Francis Clyde   B8.1.1906 Wheaton KS   D3.18.1972 Topeka KS   BR/TR/6-0/180   d9.17

YEAR	TM LG	W	L	PCT	G	GS	CG-SHO	SV-BS	IP	H	R	HR	HB	BB-IB	SO	ERA	AERA	OAV	OOB	AB-HR-SH	AVG	PB	SUP	APR	DL	PW
1927	Bos A	0	0	—	1	0	0	0	1.1	2	1	0	0	2	0	6.75	63	.500	.667	0		0		0		0.0
1930	Bos A	0	1	.000	11	0	0	0	30	34	22	1	2	15	4	6.30	73	.306	.398	9	.111	-1		-5		-0.3
Total	2	0	1	.000	12	0	0	0	31.1	36	23	1	2	17	4	6.32	73	.313	.410	9	.111	-1		-5		-0.3

BUSHING, CHRIS   Christopher Shaun   B11.4.1967 Rockville Centre NY   BR/TR/6-0/190   d9.3   Col Broward (FL) CC

YEAR	TM LG	W	L	PCT	G	GS	CG-SHO	SV-BS	IP	H	R	HR	HB	BB-IB	SO	ERA	AERA	OAV	OOB	AB-HR-SH	AVG	PB	SUP	APR	DL	PW
1993	Cin N	0	0	—	6	0	0	0-0	4.1	9	7	1	0	4-0	3	12.46	32	.450	.520	0		0		-4		-0.2

BUSKEY, TOM   Thomas William   B2.20.1947 Harrisburg PA   D6.7.1998 Harrisburg PA   BR/TR/6-3/220(200-228)   d8.5   Col North Carolina-Asheville

YEAR	TM LG	W	L	PCT	G	GS	CG-SHO	SV-BS	IP	H	R	HR	HB	BB-IB	SO	ERA	AERA	OAV	OOB	AB-HR-SH	AVG	PB	SUP	APR	DL	PW
1973	NY A	0	1	.000	8	0	0	1-1	16.2	18	12	2	1	4-0	5	5.40	69	.286	.324	0		0		-3		-0.2
1974	NY A	0	1	.000	4	0	0	1-0	5.2	10	4	1	1	3-1	3	6.35	56	.400	.483	0		0		-2		-0.3
	Cle A	2	6	.250	51	0	0	17-7	93	93	36	10	1	33-8	40	3.19	114	.263	.322	0		0		-2		0.7
	Year	2	7	.222	55	0	0	18-7	98.2	103	40	11	2	36-9	43	3.38	108	.272	.333	0		0		5		0.7
1975	Cle A	5	3	.625	50	0	0	7-3	77	79	29	7	1	29-10	29	2.57	148	.252	.324	0		0		3		0.4
1976	Cle A	5	4	.556	39	0	0	1-2	94.1	88	42	9	3	34-8	32	3.63	97	.256	.326	0		0		10	38	1.2
1977	Cle A	0	0	—	21	0	0	0-0	34	45	24	6	1	8-1	15	5.29	75	.313	.348	0		0		-1		-0.1
1978	Tor A	0	1	.000	8	0	0	0-0	13.1	14	5	1	0	5-4	7	3.38	117	.275	.339	0		0		-6		-0.3
1979	Tor A	6	10	.375	44	0	0	7-4	78.2	74	33	10	1	25-7	44	3.43	128	.249	.310	0		0		1		0.1
1980	Tor A	3	1	.750	33	0	0	0-1	66.2	68	35	11	0	26-6	34	4.45	97	.278	.341	0		0		8	7	1.8
Total	8	21	27	.438	258	0	0	34-18	479.1	479	218	57	9	167-45	212	3.66	106	.267	.328	0		0		12	45	2.9

BUTCHER, MAX   Albert Maxwell   B9.21.1910 Holden WV   D9.15.1957 Man WV   BR/TR/6-2/220   d4.20

YEAR	TM LG	W	L	PCT	G	GS	CG-SHO	SV-BS	IP	H	R	HR	HB	BB-IB	SO	ERA	AERA	OAV	OOB	AB-HR-SH	AVG	PB	SUP	APR	DL	PW
1936	Bro N	6	6	.500	38	15	5	2	147.2	154	85	11	1	59	55	3.96	104	.268	.337	48	.125	-3*	89	0		-0.3
1937	Bro N	11	15	.423	39	24	8-1	0	191.2	203	106	12	7	75	57	4.27	94	.280	.354	62-0-1	.161	-1*	69	-2		-0.3
1938	Bro N	5	4	.556	24	8	3	2	72.2	104	66	9	1	39	21	6.56	59	.334	.410	25-1-2	.160	0*	141	-22		-2.4
	Phi N	4	8	.333	12	12	11	0	98.1	94	40	6	2	31	29	2.93	133	.253	.314	35	.257	1	42	9		1.1
	Year	9	12	.429	36	20	14	2	171	198	106	15	3	70	50	4.47	87	.290	.359	60-1-2	.217	1	82	-13		-1.3
1939	Phi N	2	13	.133	19	16	3	0	104.1	131	72	10	1	51	27	5.61	71	.308	.383	38-0-3	.184	-1	75	-18		-2.3
	Pit N	4	4	.500	14	12	5-2	0	86.2	104	37	2	0	23	21	3.43	112	.297	.340	31-0-3	.097	-2	70	5		0.3
	Year	6	17	.261	33	28	8-2	0	191	235	109	12	1	74	48	4.62	85	.303	.364	69-0-6	.145	-3	73	-13		-2.0
1940	Pit N	8	9	.471	35	24	6-2	2	136.1	161	99	13	1	46	61	6.01	63	.290	.346	50-0-1	.300	4*	120	-31		-3.0
1941	Pit N	17	12	.586	33	32	19	0	236	249	98	11	1	66	61	3.05	118	.265	.314	82-0-5	.183	-1	101	14		1.6
1942	Pit N	5	8	.385	24	18	9	1	150.2	144	59	7	2	44	49	2.93	116	.247	.303	49-0-2	.143	-2	90	7		0.4
1943	Pit N	10	8	.556	33	21	10	0	193.2	191	65	4	4	57	45	2.60	134	.262	.317	61-0-7	.164	-1	100	20		1.8
1944	Pit N	13	11	.542	35	27	13-5	0	199	216	83	8	1	46	43	3.12	119	.273	.314	63-0-5	.190	-1	104	13		1.6
1945	Pit N	10	8	.556	28	20	12-2	0	169.1	184	76	7	4	46	37	3.03	130	.277	.328	54-0-6	.222	-0*	104	13		1.6
Total	10	95	106	.473	334	229	104-14	9	1786.1	1935	886	100	23	583	485	3.73	101	.276	.333	598-1-35	.184	-6	93	8		1.3

BUTCHER, JOHN   John Daniel   B3.8.1957 Glendale CA   BR/TR/6-4/190*   [TexA77 S1/18]   d9.8   Col Yavapai (AZ) JC

YEAR	TM LG	W	L	PCT	G	GS	CG-SHO	SV-BS	IP	H	R	HR	HB	BB-IB	SO	ERA	AERA	OAV	OOB	AB-HR-SH	AVG	PB	SUP	APR	DL	PW
1980	Tex A	3	3	.500	6	6	1	0-0	35.1	34	19	2	0	13-0	27	4.08	95	.248	.313	0	—	0	100	-1		-0.1
1981	Tex A	1	2	.333	5	3	1-1	0-0	27.2	18	6	0	0	8-1	19	1.63	214	.186	.248	0	—	0	43	6		0.7
1982	Tex A	1	5	.167	18	13	2	1-0	94.1	102	53	10	2	34-4	39	4.87	80	.280	.342	0	—	0	94	-9		-0.5
1983	Tex A	6	6	.500	38	6	1-1	5-3	123	128	50	8	1	41-4	58	3.51	115	.270	.328	0	—	0	86	9		0.9
1984	Min A	13	11	.542	34	34	8-1	0-0	225	242	98	18	4	53-5	92	3.44	123	.276	.317	0	—	0	92	17		1.6
1985	Min A	11	14	.440	34	33	8-2	0-0	207.2	239	125	24	6	43-4	92	4.98	89	.289	.325	0	—	0	98	-11		-1.2
1986	Min A	0	3	.000	16	10	1	0-1	70	82	50	11	1	24-1	29	6.30	69	.294	.349	0	—	0	105	-13		-1.5
	Cle A	1	5	.167	13	8	1-1	0-0	50.2	86	43	6	3	13-0	16	6.93	60	.381	.416	0	—	0	103	-15	15	-1.5
	Year	1	8	.111	29	18	2-1	0-1	120.2	168	93	17	4	37-1	45	6.56	65	.333	.379	0	—	0	104	-28		-2.1
Total	7	36	49	.424	164	113	23-6	6-4	833.2	931	444	79	17	229-19	363	4.42	95	.284	.331	0	—	0	96	-17	15	-0.7

BUTCHER, MIKE   Michael Dana   B5.10.1965 Davenport IA   BR/TR/6-1/200*   [KCA86 S2/36]   d7.6   Col NE Oklahoma A&M JC

YEAR	TM LG	W	L	PCT	G	GS	CG-SHO	SV-BS	IP	H	R	HR	HB	BB-IB	SO	ERA	AERA	OAV	OOB	AB-HR-SH	AVG	PB	SUP	APR	DL	PW
1992	Cal A	2	2	.500	19	0	0	0-1	27.2	29	11	3	2	13-1	24	3.25	124	.264	.352	0	—	0	2			0.3
1993	Cal A	1	0	1.000	23	0	0	8-2	28.1	21	12	2	2	15-1	24	2.86	159	.204	.309	0	—	0	4	71		0.3
1994	Cal A	2	1	.667	33	0	0	1-2	29.2	31	24	2	2	23-5	19	6.67	74	.274	.406	0	—	0	-6			-0.5
1995	Cal A	6	1	.857	40	0	0	0-2	51.1	49	28	7	1	31-2	29	4.73	100	.257	.358	0	—	0	0			0.0
Total	4	11	4	.733	115	0	0	9-7	137	130	75	14	7	82-9	96	4.47	103	.257	.358	0	—	0	0	71		0.1

BUTLAND, BILL   Wilburn Rue   B3.22.1918 Terre Haute IN   D9.19.1997 Terre Haute IN   BR/TR/6-5/185   d5.29   Mil 1943-45

YEAR	TM LG	W	L	PCT	G	GS	CG-SHO	SV-BS	IP	H	R	HR	HB	BB-IB	SO	ERA	AERA	OAV	OOB	AB-HR-SH	AVG	PB	SUP	APR	DL	PW
1940	Bos A	1	2	.333	3	3	1	0	21	27	13	0	0	10	8	5.57	81	.307	.378	7-0-1	.000	-1	59	-2		-0.3
1942	Bos A	7	1	.875	23	10	6-2	1	111.1	85	35	8	3	33	46	2.51	149	.206	.270	28-0-2	.036	-1	126	15		1.0
1946	Bos A	1	0	1.000	5	2	0	0	16.1	23	20	3	0	13	10	11.02	33	.343	.450	4	.250	0	164	-12		-0.6
1947	Bos A	0	0	—	1	0	0	0	2	3	1	0	0	0	1	4.50	86	.333	.333	0		0		0		0.0
Total	4	9	3	.750	32	15	7-2	1	150.2	138	69	11	3	56	62	3.88	99	.240	.310	39-0-3	.051	-2	117	1		0.1

BUTLER, ADAM   Adam Christopher   B8.17.1973 Fairfax VA   BL/TL/6-2/225   d3.31   Col William and Mary

YEAR	TM LG	W	L	PCT	G	GS	CG-SHO	SV-BS	IP	H	R	HR	HB	BB-IB	SO	ERA	AERA	OAV	OOB	AB-HR-SH	AVG	PB	SUP	APR	DL	PW
1998	Atl N	0	1	.000	8	0	0	0-0	5	5	7	1	0	6-1	7	10.80	39	.278	.462	0		0		-4		-0.7

BUTLER, CECIL   Cecil Dean "Slewfoot"   B10.23.1937 Dallas GA   BR/TR/6-4/195*   d4.23

YEAR	TM LG	W	L	PCT	G	GS	CG-SHO	SV-BS	IP	H	R	HR	HB	BB-IB	SO	ERA	AERA	OAV	OOB	AB-HR-SH	AVG	PB	SUP	APR	DL	PW
1962	Mil N	2	0	1.000	9	2	1	0	31	26	13	4	0	9-1	22	2.61	145	.217	.271	8	.000	-1	92	3	65	0.1
1964	Mil N	0	0	—	2	0	0	0	4.1	7	4	2	0	0-0	2	8.31	42	.368	.368	0		0		-2		-0.1
Total	2	2	0	1.000	11	2	1	0	35.1	33	17	6	0	9-1	24	3.31	114	.237	.284	8	.000	-1	92	1	65	0.0

BUTLER, CHARLIE   Charles Thomas   B5.12.1906 Green Cove Springs FL   D5.10.1964 Brunswick GA   BR/TL/6-1.5/210   d5.1

YEAR	TM LG	W	L	PCT	G	GS	CG-SHO	SV-BS	IP	H	R	HR	HB	BB-IB	SO	ERA	AERA	OAV	OOB	AB-HR-SH	AVG	PB	SUP	APR	DL	PW
1933	Phi N	0	0	—	1	0	0	0	1	1	1	0	0	2	0	9.00	42	.250	.500	0		0		0		0.0

YEAR	TM LG	W	L	PCT	G	GS	CG-SHO	SV-BS	IP	H	R	HR	HB	BB-IB	SO	ERA	AERA	OAV	OOB	AB-HR-SH	AVG	PB	SUP	APR	DL	PW

BUTLER, IKE   Isaac Burr   B8.22.1873 Langston MI   D3.17.1948 Oakland CA   TR/6-0/175   d8.5

YEAR	TM LG	W	L	PCT	G	GS	CG-SHO	IP	H	R	HR	HB	BB-IB	SO	ERA	AERA	OAV	OOB	AB-HR-SH	AVG	PB	SUP	APR	PW
1902	Bal A	1	10	.091	16	14	12	116.1	168	103	1	2	45	13	5.34	71	.337	.394	53-0-2	.113	-3*	90	-20	-1.8

BUTLER, BILL   William Franklin   B3.12.1947 Hyattsville MD   BL/TL/6-2/210(185-210)   [DetA65 16/610]   d4.9

YEAR	TM LG	W	L	PCT	G	GS	CG-SHO	SV-BS	IP	H	R	HR	HB	BB-IB	SO	ERA	AERA	OAV	OOB	AB-HR-SH	AVG	PB	SUP	APR	PW
1969	KC A	9	10	.474	34	29	5-4	0-0	193.2	174	91	16	3	91-5	156	3.90	95	.240	.326	60-0-5	.050	-4	97	-2	-0.7
1970	KC A	4	12	.250	25	25	2-1	0-0	140.2	117	66	17	3	87-1	75	3.77	99	.229	.340	44-0-1	.045	-3	77	0	-0.4
1971	KC A	1	2	.333	14	6	0	0-0	44.1	45	19	6	0	18-0	32	3.45	100	.268	.339	12	.083	-1	122	0	-0.1
1972	Cle A	0	0	—	6	2	0	0-0	11.2	9	3	1	0	10-0	6	1.54	211	.220	.373	1	.000	0	90	-2	-0.3
1974	Min A	4	6	.400	26	12	2	1-0	98.2	91	47	9	1	56-2	79	4.10	91	.251	.350	0	—	0	152	-19	-1.8
1975	Min A	5	4	.556	23	8	1	0-0	81.2	100	61	12	0	35-0	55	5.95	64	.301	.363	0	—	0	203	-7	-0.?
1977	Min A	0	1	1.000	6	4	0	0-0	21	19	17	5	1	15-0	5	6.86	58	.244	.372	0	—	0	103	-28	-3.?
Total 7		23	35	.397	134	86	10-5	1-0	591.2	555	304	65	6	312-8	408	4.21	88	.250	.342	117-0-6	.051	-7	103	-28	-3.5

BUTTERS, TOM   Thomas Arden   B4.8.1938 Delaware OH   BR/TR/6-2/195*   d9.8   Col Ohio Wesleyan

YEAR	TM LG	W	L	PCT	G	GS	CG-SHO	SV-BS	IP	H	R	HR	HB	BB-IB	SO	ERA	AERA	OAV	OOB	AB-HR-SH	AVG	PB	SUP	APR	DL	PW
1962	Pit N	0	0	—	4	0	0	0	6	5	1	0	1	6-1	10	1.50	262	.238	.429	0	—	0		2		0.
1963	Pit N	0	0	—	6	1	0	0	16.1	15	8	1	2	8-0	11	4.41	75	.259	.352	3	.333	0	105	-1		-0.
1964	Pit N	2	2	.500	28	4	0	0	64.1	52	21	3	0	37-1	58	2.38	148	.221	.324	1	.000	-0	69	7		0.
1965	Pit N	0	1	.000	5	0	0	0	9	9	8	2	0	5-0	6	7.00	50	.250	.341	1	.000	-0		-3	38	-0.
Total 4		2	3	.400	43	5	0	0	95.2	81	38	6	3	56-2	85	3.10	113	.231	.337	15-0-2	.200	-0	75	5	38	-0.

BUTTERY, FRANK   Frank   B5.13.1851 Silvermine CT   D12.16.1902 Norwalk CT   d4.26 ▲

YEAR	TM LG	W	L	PCT	G	GS	CG-SHO	IP	H	R	HR	HB	BB-IB	SO	ERA	AERA	OAV	OOB	AB-HR-SH	AVG	PB	SUP	APR	PW
1872	Man NA	3	2	.600	8	5	5	59	94	78	1	3	5	5	4.27	84	.322	.329	93	.215	-2*	187	-5	-0.

BUXTON, RALPH   Ralph Stanley "Buck"   B6.7.1914 Rainton SK, Can.   D1.6.1988 San Leandro CA   BR/TR/5-11.5/163   d9.11

YEAR	TM LG	W	L	PCT	G	GS	CG-SHO	SV-BS	IP	H	R	HR	HB	BB-IB	SO	ERA	AERA	OAV	OOB	AB-HR-SH	AVG	PB	SUP	APR	PW
1938	Phi A	0	1	.000	5	0	0	0	9.1	12	7	1	0	5	9	4.82	100	.324	.405	1	.000	-0		0	-0.
1949	NY A	0	1	.000	14	0	0	2	26.2	22	13	3	0	16	14	4.05	100	.229	.339	3	.000	-0		0	-0.
Total 2		0	2	.000	19	0	0	2	36	34	20	4	0	21	23	4.25	100	.256	.357	4	.000	-1		0	-0.

BUZHARDT, JOHN   John William   B8.17.1936 Prosperity SC   BR/TR/6-2/198*   d9.10

YEAR	TM LG	W	L	PCT	G	GS	CG-SHO	SV-BS	IP	H	R	HR	HB	BB-IB	SO	ERA	AERA	OAV	OOB	AB-HR-SH	AVG	PB	SUP	APR	DL	PW
1958	Chi N	3	0	1.000	6	2	1	0	24.1	16	5	2	0	7-1	9	1.85	212	.184	.245	8	.125	-0	57	6		0.
1959	Chi N	4	5	.444	31	10	1-1	0	101.1	107	64	12	1	29-4	73	4.97	79	.271	.318	62-0-2	.069	-1	109	-12		-0.
1960	Phi N	5	16	.238	30	29	5	0	200.1	198	101	14	2	68-12	73	3.86	100	.259	.319	57-0-7	.105	-2	92	-6		-0.
1961	Phi N	6	18	.250	41	27	6-1	0	202.1	200	107	28	6	65-6	92	4.49	91	.263	.324	57-0-7	.118	-2	91	-4		-0
1962	Chi A	8	12	.400	28	25	8-2	0	152.1	156	75	16	4	59-3	64	4.19	93	.264	.332	48-0-1	.083	-3*	101	17	30	1
1963	Chi A	9	4	.692	19	18	6-3	0	126.1	100	35	8	5	31-5	59	2.42	145	.216	.272	51-0-4	.204	2	119	9		1
1964	Chi A	10	8	.556	31	25	8-3	0	160	150	60	13	4	35-4	97	3.01	106	.250	.291	56-0-9	.125	0*	114	5		0
1965	Chi A	13	8	.619	32	30	4-1	1	188.2	167	69	12	7	56-9	108	3.01	106	.242	.304	43-0-1	.116	-1*	104	-11		-1
1966	Chi A	6	11	.353	33	22	5-4	1	150.1	144	74	13	4	30-4	66	3.83	83	.248	.288	20-0-2	.200	0	104	-7		0
1967	Chi A	3	9	.250	28	7	0	0	88.2	100	44	11	6	37-5	33	3.96	78	.294	.370	1	.000	-0	111	-2		-0
	Bal A	0	1	.000	7	1	0	0	11.2	14	6	1	0	5-1	7	4.63	98	.298	.365	1	.000	-0	105	-10		-1
	Year	3	10	.231	35	8	0	0	100.1	114	50	12	6	42-6	40	4.04	77	.295	.370	21-0-2	.190	0		0		-0
1968	Hou N	0	0	—	1	0	0	0	0.2	0	0	0	0	0-0	0	0.00	—	.000	.000	0	—	0		0		-0
	Hou N	4	4	.500	39	4	0	5	83.2	73	35	0	4	35-13	37	3.12	95	.239	.319	16-0-1	.250	1	198	-3	30	-0
Total 11		71	96	.425	326	200	44-15	7	1490.2	1425	675	130	43	457-67	678	3.66	97	.253	.312	445-0-33	.135	-7	100	-9	30	-1

BYERLY, BUD   Eldred William   B10.26.1920 Webster Groves MO   BR/TR/6-2.5/185*   d9.26

YEAR	TM LG	W	L	PCT	G	GS	CG-SHO	SV-BS	IP	H	R	HR	HB	BB-IB	SO	ERA	AERA	OAV	OOB	AB-HR-SH	AVG	PB	SUP	APR	PW
1943	StL N	1	0	1.000	2	2	0	0	13	14	6	0	0	5	6	3.46	97	.280	.345	3	.000	-0	88	0	-0
1944	†StL N	2	2	.500	9	4	2	0	42.1	37	18	2	0	20	13	3.40	104	.228	.313	12	.167	-0	107	1	0
1945	StL N	4	5	.444	33	8	2	0	95	111	61	3	1	41	39	4.74	79	.288	.358	23-0-5	.217	1	158	-12	-0
1950	Cin N	0	1	.000	4	1	0	0	14.2	12	4	1	0	4	5	2.45	173	.218	.271	3	.000	-0	21	3	0
1951	Cin N	2	1	.667	40	0	0	0	66	69	33	6	2	25	28	3.27	125	.267	.337	6	.000	-0*		4	0
1952	Cin N	2	1	.000	12	0	0	0	24.2	29	15	0	0	7	14	5.11	74	.309	.356	5	.200	-1	24	-4	0
1956	Was A	4	4	.333	25	0	0	4	51.2	45	19	6	2	14-3	19	2.96	146	.243	.303	11	.091	-1		7	0
1957	Was A	6	6	.500	47	0	0	6	95	94	38	6	1	22-5	39	3.13	125	.247	.305	15	.067	-1		8	-0
1958	Was A	2	0	1.000	17	0	0	1	24	34	20	4	1	11-2	16	6.75	56	.347	.411	2	.000	-0		5	-0
	Bos A	1	2	.333	18	0	0	0	30.1	31	12	1	1	7-3	16	1.78	225	.272	.312	4	.000	-1		-3	-0
	Year	3	2	.600	35	0	0	1	54.1	65	32	5	2	18-5	29	3.98	99	.307	.359	6	—	-1		4	-0
1959	SF N	1	0	1.000	11	0	0	0	13	11	2	2	0	5-1	4	1.38	275	.234	.308	0	—	-0		-4	-
1960	SF N	1	1	.500	19	0	0	2	22	32	14	3	1	6-0	13	5.32	65	.340	.379	1-0-1	.000	-0	112	-4	-
Total 11		22	22	.500	237	17	4	14	491.2	519	242	34	9	167-14	209	3.70	105	.273	.333	85-0-6	.118	-4	112	0	

BYNUM, MIKE   Michael Alan   B3.20.1978 Tampa FL   BL/TL/6-4/200*   [SDN99 1/49]   d8.17   Col North Carolina-Asheville

YEAR	TM LG	W	L	PCT	G	GS	CG-SHO	SV-BS	IP	H	R	HR	HB	BB-IB	SO	ERA	AERA	OAV	OOB	AB-HR-SH	AVG	PB	SUP	APR	PW
2002	SD N	1	0	1.000	14	3	0	0-0	27.1	33	16	3	3	15-2	17	5.27	74	.308	.402	8	.000	-1	206	-4	-0
2003	SD N	1	4	.200	13	5	0	0-0	36	44	35	14	1	15-0	35	8.75	46	.297	.366	10-0-1	.300	1	103	-19	-0
2004	SD N	0	1	.000	2	0	0	0-0	0.2	1	4	0	0	3-0	1	54.00	7	.333	.667	0	—	-0		-4	-
Total 3		2	5	.286	29	8	0	0-0	64	78	55	17	4	33-2	52	7.73	51	.302	.387	18-0-1	.167	-0	142	-27	-0

BYRD, HARRY   Harry Gladwin   B2.3.1925 Darlington SC   D5.14.1985 Darlington SC   BR/TR(BB 1955)/6-1/188*   d4.21

YEAR	TM LG	W	L	PCT	G	GS	CG-SHO	SV-BS	IP	H	R	HR	HB	BB-IB	SO	ERA	AERA	OAV	OOB	AB-HR-SH	AVG	PB	SUP	APR	PW
1950	Phi A	0	0	—	6	0	0	0	10.2	25	20	3	2	9	2	16.88	27	.481	.571	2	.000	-0		-14	-
1952	Phi A	15	15	.500	37	28	15-3	2	228.1	244	106	17	12	98	122	3.31	120	.274	.351	75-0-6	.133	-3	83	13	-0
1953	Phi A	11	20	.355	40	37	11-2	0	236.2	279	155	23	14	115	122	5.51	78	.294	.379	81-0-3	.222	-1	82	-29	-0
1954	NY A	9	7	.563	25	21	5-1	0	132.1	131	56	10	7	43	52	2.99	115	.258	.321	46-0-3	.196	1	136	4	0
1955	Bal A	3	2	.600	14	8	1-1	1	65.1	64	33	7	7	28-1	27	4.55	84	.261	.350	19-0-5	.158	-0	125	-3	-0
	Chi A	4	6	.400	25	12	1-1	1	91	85	49	10	2	30-4	44	4.65	85	.251	.329	49-0-6	.102	-3	107	-8	-0
	Year	7	8	.467	39	20	2-2	2	156.1	149	82	17	9	58-5	69	4.61	85	.255	.329			-0	0	-3	
1956	Chi A	0	1	.000	3	1	0	0	4.1	9	6	0	0	4-0	1	10.38	39	.474	.542	1	.000	-0	208	4	-
1957	Det A	4	3	.571	37	1	0	5	59	53	23	6	2	28-4	20	3.36	115	.249	.339	8-0-2	.000	-1	96	-34	-
Total 7		46	54	.460	187	108	33-8	9	827.2	890	442	71	41	355-9	381	4.35	91	.277	.355	262-0-20	.160	-8	96	-34	-

BYRD, JEFF   Jeffrey Alan   B11.11.1956 LaMesa CA   BR/TR/6-3/195   d6.20

YEAR	TM LG	W	L	PCT	G	GS	CG-SHO	SV-BS	IP	H	R	HR	HB	BB-IB	SO	ERA	AERA	OAV	OOB	AB-HR-SH	AVG	PB	SUP	APR	PW
1977	Tor A	2	13	.133	17	17	1	0-0	87.1	98	68	5	0	68-1	40	6.18	69	.286	.399	0	—	0	76	-18	-

BYRD, PAUL   Paul Gregory   B12.3.1970 Louisville KY   BR/TR/6-1/185*   [CleA91 4/112]   d7.28   Col Louisiana St.   [DL 2003 Atl N 183]

YEAR	TM LG	W	L	PCT	G	GS	CG-SHO	SV-BS	IP	H	R	HR	HB	BB-IB	SO	ERA	AERA	OAV	OOB	AB-HR-SH	AVG	PB	SUP	APR	DL	PW
1995	NY N	2	0	1.000	17	0	0	0-0	22	18	6	1	1	7-1	26	2.05	197	.222	.286	1	1.000	-0		5		69
1996	NY N	1	2	.333	38	0	0	0-2	46.2	48	22	7	0	21-4	31	4.24	95	.265	.340	2	.000	-0	0	88	-6	
1997	Atl N	4	4	.500	31	4	0	*0-0	53	47	34	6	4	28-4	37	5.26	80	.235	.338	7-0-2	.143	-0	88	-2	
1998	Atl N	0	0	—	1	0	0	0-0	2	4	3	0	0	1-0	1	13.50	31	.400	.455	0	—	0		-2	
	Phi N	5	2	.714	8	8	2-1	0-0	55	41	16	6	0	17-1	38	2.29	189	.203	.264	18	.167	0	104	12	
	Year	5	2	.714	9	8	2-1	0-0	57	45	19	6	0	18-1	39	2.68	161	.212	.273	18	.167	0	117	-3	
1999	Phi N☆	15	11	.577	32	32	1	0-0	199.2	205	119	34	17	70-2	106	4.60	102	.265	.337	55-0-11	.127	-1	76	-19	66
2000	Phi N	2	9	.182	17	15	0	0-0	83	89	67	17	3	35-2	53	6.51	71	.271	.345	20-0-2	.150	0	76	-19	66
2001	Phi N	0	1	.000	3	1	0	0-0	10	10	9	1	1	4-0	3	8.10	51	.278	.345	2-0-1	.500	0*	67	-4	
	KC A	6	6	.500	16	15	1	0-0	93.1	110	45	11	1	22-1	49	4.05	123	.297	.335	4-0-1	.000	-0	92	22	
2002	KC A	17	11	.607	33	33	7-2	0-0	228.1	224	111	36	7	38-1	129	3.90	128	.256	.288	2	.000	2	113	4	76
2004	†Atl N	8	7	.533	19	19	0	0-0	114.1	123	57	18	2	19-0	79	3.94	109	.270	.301	30-0-8	.200	2	98	11	
2005	†LA A	12	11	.522	31	31	2-1	0-0	204.1	216	95	22	7	28-1	102	3.74	115	.272	.301	4	.250	1	100	29	410
Total 10		72	64	.529	246	158	13-4	0-2	1111.2	1135	584	159	43	290-17	654	4.23	108	.264	.314	145-0-25	.159	1	100	29	410

BYRDAK, TIM   Timothy Christopher   B10.31.1973 Oak Lawn IL   BL/TL/5-11/170(160-190)   [KCA94 5/135]   d8.7   Col Rice

YEAR	TM LG	W	L	PCT	G	GS	CG-SHO	SV-BS	IP	H	R	HR	HB	BB-IB	SO	ERA	AERA	OAV	OOB	AB-HR-SH	AVG	PB	SUP	APR	PW
1998	KC A	0	0	—	3	0	0	0-0	1.2	5	1	1	0	0-0	1	5.40	90	.556	.556	0	—	-0		0	-
1999	KC A	0	3	.000	33	0	0	1-3	24.2	32	24	5	1	20-2	17	7.66	66	.308	.424	2	.500	1		-7	-
2000	KC A	0	0	—	12	0	0	0-2	6.1	11	8	1	0	7-0	8	11.37	46	.367	.441	0	—	0		-4	-
2005	Bal A	0	2	.000	41	0	0	1-0	26.2	27	15	3	1	21-1	31	4.05	109	.255	.380	0	—	0		1	-
Total 4		0	5	.000	89	0	0	2-5	59.1	75	47	10	2	45-3	57	6.37	75	.301	.411	2	.500	1		-10	-

BYRNE, JERRY   Gerald Wilfred   B2.2.1907 Parnell MI   D8.11.1955 Lansing MI   BR/TR/6-0/170   d8.31   Col Michigan St.

YEAR	TM LG	W	L	PCT	G	GS	CG-SHO	SV-BS	IP	H	R	HR	HB	BB-IB	SO	ERA	AERA	OAV	OOB	AB-HR-SH	AVG	PB	SUP	APR	PW
1929	Chi A	0	1	.000	3	1	0	0	7.1	11	6	0	0	6	1	7.36	58	.379	.486	2	.000	-0	59	-2	

YEAR	TM LG	W	L	PCT	G	GS	CG-SHO	SV-BS	IP	H	R	HR	HB	BB-IB	SO	ERA	AERA	OAV	OOB	AB-HR-SH	AVG	PB	SUP	APR	DL	PW
BYRNE, TOMMY								Thomas Joseph B12.31.1919 Baltimore MD BL/TL/6-1/182* d4.27 Mil 1944-45 Col Wake Forest																	
1943	NY A	2	1	.667	11	2	0	0	31.2	28	26	1	3	35	22	6.54	49	.248	.437	11-0-1	.091	-0*	105	-11		-1.0
1946	NY A	0	1	.000	4	1	0	0	9.1	7	8	1	1	8	5	5.79	60	.194	.356	9	.222	0*	75	-3		-0.2
1947	NY A	0	0	—	4	1	0	0	4.1	5	2	0	0	6	2	4.15	85	.294	.478	0	—	0	225	0		0.0
1948	NY A	8	5	.615	31	11	5-1	2	133.2	79	55	8	9	101	93	3.30	124	.172	.332	46-1-4	.326	6	123	12		1.6
1949	†NY A	15	7	.682	32	30	12-3	0	196	125	84	11	11	179	129	3.72	109	.183	.362	83-0-1	.193	1*	140	11		1.0
1950	NY A☆	15	9	.625	31	31	10-2	0	203.1	188	115	23	11	160	118	4.74	91	.245	.387	81-2-0	.272	7*	140	-10		-0.8
1951	NY A	2	1	.667	9	3	0	0	21	16	17	0	3	36	14	6.86	56	.213	.482	9-1-0	.222	1	124	-7		1.2
	StL A	4	10	.286	19	17	7-2	0	122.2	104	56	5	12	114	57	3.82	115	.235	.404	57-1-2	.281	3*	64	8		0.4
	Year	6	11	.353	28	20	7-2	0	143.2	120	73	5	15	150	71	4.26	101	.232	.417	66-2-2	.273	4	72	3		-1.2
1952	StL A	7	14	.333	29	24	14	0	196	182	117	16	10	112	91	4.68	84	.247	.354	84-1-0	.250	5*	90	-16		-0.9
1953	Chi A	0	1	.000	6	6	0	0	16	18	18	0	0	26	4	10.13	40	.295	.506	18-1-0	.167	1*	158	-10		-0.2
	Was A	0	5	.000	6	5	2	0	33.2	35	17	3	1	22	22	4.28	91	.276	.387	17	.059	-1*	55	-1		-1.1
	Year	2	5	.286	12	11	2	0	49.2	53	35	3	1	48	26	6.16	64	.282	.430	35-1-0	.114	-0	113	-11		-1.1
1954	NY A	3	2	.600	5	5	4-1	0	40	36	13	1	0	19	24	2.70	127	.240	.325	19	.368	4*	149	4		1.0
1955	†NY A	16	5	**.762**	27	22	9-3	2	160	137	69	12	7	87-3	76	3.15	119	.237	.340	78-1-1	.205	4*	117	9		1.5
1956	†NY A	7	3	.700	37	8	1	6	109.2	108	50	9	2	72-5	52	3.36	115	.262	.372	52-3-2	.269	6*	129	5		1.0
1957	†NY A	4	6	.400	30	4	1	2	84.2	70	41	8	7	60-2	57	4.36	82	.227	.363	37-3-0	.189	4*	87	-5		-0.2
Total	13	85	69	.552	281	170	65-12	12	1362	1138	688	98	85	1037-10	766	4.11	97	.229	.370	601-14-11	.238	41	118	-14		2.4
BYSTROM, MARTY								Martin Eugene B7.26.1958 Coral Gables FL BR/TR/6-5/200* d9.7 Col Miami-Dade Kendall (FL) CC																	
1980	†Phi N	5	0	1.000	6	5	1-1	0-0	36	26	6	1	0	9-0	21	1.50	255	.195	.246	14	.071	-1	168	9		1.3
1981	Phi N	4	3	.571	9	9	1	0-0	53.2	55	21	3	1	16-1	24	3.35	109	.264	.319	17-0-1	.118	-1	105	2		0.2
1982	Phi N	5	6	.455	19	16	1	0-0	89	93	53	2	3	35-4	50	4.85	76	.277	.350	24-0-3	.125	-0	99	-11	64	-1.3
1983	†Phi N	6	9	.400	24	23	1-1	0-0	119.1	136	75	6	7	44-2	87	4.60	78	.285	.348	38-0-1	.237	2	107	-15	50	-1.6
1984	Phi N	4	4	.500	11	11	0	0-0	56.2	66	36	5	0	22-1	36	5.08	72	.283	.341	19-0-3	.158	-0	110	-8		-1.1
	NY A	2	2	.500	7	7	0	0-0	39.1	34	16	3	1	13-1	24	2.97	129	.230	.296	0	—	-0	77	3	33	0.3
1985	NY A	3	2	.600	8	8	0	0-0	41	44	29	8	1	19-0	16	5.71	71	.280	.360	0	—	0	107	-8	106	-0.8
Total	6	29	26	.527	84	79	4-2	0-0	435	454	236	28	15	158-9	258	4.26	87	.268	.333	112-0-8	.161	-0	107	-28	253	-3.0
CABRERA, DANIEL								Daniel Alberto B5.28.1981 San Pedro de Macoris, D.R. BR/TR/6-7/230(230-250) d5.13																	
2004	Bal A	12	8	.600	28	27	1-1	1-0	147.2	145	85	14	2	89-2	76	5.00	93	.259	.359	4	.000	-0	117	-3		-0.6
2005	Bal A	10	13	.435	29	29	0	0-0	161.1	144	92	14	11	87-2	157	4.52	98	.235	.339	1	.000	-0	80	-3	20	-0.4
Total	2	22	21	.512	57	56	1-1	1-0	309	289	177	28	13	176-4	233	4.75	96	.246	.348	5	.000	-1	98	-6	20	-1.0
CABRERA, FERNANDO								Fernando Jose B11.16.1981 Toa Baja, PR BR/TR/6-4/170(170-225) [CleA99 10/317] d8.20																	
2004	Cle A	0	0	—	4	0	0	0-0	5.1	3	3	0	0	1-0	6	3.38	129	.167	.200	0		0		0		0.0
2005	Cle A	2	1	.667	15	0	0	0-0	30.2	24	7	1	0	11-1	29	1.47	279	.212	.282	0		0		9		0.7
Total	2	2	1	.667	19	0	0	0-0	36	27	10	1	0	12-1	35	1.75	236	.206	.271	0		0		9		0.7
CABRERA, JOSE								Jose Alberto B3.24.1972 Santiago, D.R. BR/TR/6-0/180(160-180) d7.15																	
1997	Hou N	0	0	—	12	0	0	0-1	15.1	6	2	1	0	6-0	18	1.17	341	.125	.211	2	.000	-0		5		0.2
1998	Hou N	0	0	—	3	0	0	0-0	4.1	7	4	0	0	1-1	1	8.31	49	.389	.421	0	—	0		-2	176	-0.1
1999	†Hou N	4	0	1.000	26	0	0	0-1	29.1	21	7	3	0	9-2	28	2.15	206	.196	.252	0	—	0		8		0.9
2000	.Hou N	2	3	.400	52	0	0	2-1	59.1	74	40	10	3	17-2	41	5.92	83	.308	.357	1	.000	-0		-5		-0.4
2001	Atl N	7	4	.636	55	0	0	2-6	59.1	52	24	5	2	25-4	43	2.88	150	.239	.315	1	.000	-0		8		1.4
2002	Atl N	6	10	.375	50	11	0	0-1	103.1	131	84	23	9	36-9	61	6.79	61	.314	.378	19-0-1	.105	-1	106	-30		-4.2
Total	6	19	17	.528	198	11	0	4-10	271	291	161	42	14	94-18	192	4.95	88	.278	.340	23-0-1	.087	-1	106	-16	176	-2.2
CADARET, GREG								Gregory James B2.27.1962 Detroit MI BL/TL/6-3/214(205-230) [OakA83 11/267] d7.5 Col Grand Valley St.																	
1987	Oak A	6	2	.750	29	0	0	0-1	39.2	37	22	6	1	24-1	30	4.54	92	.252	.356	0	—	0		-2		-0.2
1988	†Oak A	5	2	.714	58	0	0	3-1	71.2	60	26	2	1	36-1	64	2.89	132	.226	.317	0	—	0		7		0.7
1989	Oak A	0	0	—	26	0	0	0-1	27.2	21	9	0	0	19-3	14	2.28	163	.214	.336	0	—	0		4		0.2
	NY A	5	5	.500	20	13	3-1	0-0	92.1	109	53	7	2	38-1	66	4.58	85	.298	.364	0	—	0	95	-7		-0.7
	Year	5	5	.500	46	13	3-1	0-2	120	130	62	7	2	57-4	80	4.05	95	.280	.358	0	—	0	96	-4		-0.5
1990	NY A	5	4	.556	54	6	0	3-1	121.1	120	62	8	1	64-5	80	4.15	96	.268	.359	0	—	0	84	-2		0.0
1991	NY A	8	6	.571	68	5	0	3-4	121.2	110	52	8	2	59-6	105	3.62	115	.246	.335	0	—	0	167	8		0.9
1992	NY A	4	8	.333	46	11	1-1	1-2	103.2	104	53	12	2	74-7	73	4.25	93	.267	.385	2	.000	-0	107	-3		-0.3
1993	Cin N	2	1	.667	34	0	0	1-0	32.2	40	19	3	1	23-5	23	4.96	81	.305	.413	2	.000	-0		-3		-0.3
	KC A	1	1	.500	13	0	0	0-0	15.1	14	5	0	1	7-0	7	2.93	157	.264	.361	0	—	0		-3		0.3
1994	Tor A	0	1	.000	21	0	0	0-0	20	24	15	4	0	17-2	15	5.85	83	.289	.410	0	—	0		-3		-0.1
	Det A	1	0	1.000	17	0	0	2-0	20	17	9	0	0	16-3	14	3.60	137	.227	.363	0	—	0		3		0.2
	Year	1	1	.500	38	0	0	2-0	40	41	24	4	0	33-5	29	4.72	104	.259	.387	0	—	0		1		0.1
1997	Ana A	0	0	—	15	0	0	0-0	13.2	11	5	1	2	8-2	11	3.29	140	.220	.350	0	—	0		1		0.1
1998	Ana A	1	2	.333	39	0	0	1-1	37	38	17	6	3	31-6	37	4.14	115	.257	.337	0	—	0		2		0.1
	Tex A	0	0	—	11	0	0	0-0	7.2	11	4	1	0	3-0	5	4.70	104	.355	.400	0	—	0		0		0.0
	Year	1	2	.333	50	0	0	1-1	44.2	49	21	7	3	18-0	42	4.23	113	.274	.348	0	—	0		4		0.2
Total	10	38	32	.543	451	35	4-2	14-12	724.1	716	351	56	16	403-36	539	3.99	103	.262	.358	2	.000	-0	104	10		1.0
CADORE, LEON								Leon Joseph "Caddy" B11.20.1890 Chicago IL D3.16.1958 Spokane WA BR/TR/6-1/190 d4.28 Mil 1918 Col Gonzaga																	
1915	Bro N	0	2	.000	7	0	0	0	21	28	15	0	2	8	12	5.57	50	.337	.409	6	.000	-1	40	-5		-0.6
1916	Bro N	0	0	—	1	0	0	0	6	10	4	0	0	2	8	4.50	60	.370	.370	3	.000	-0		-1		-0.1
1917	Bro N	13	13	.500	37	30	21-1	3	264	231	86	3	7	63	115	2.45	114	.241	.292	92-0-5	.261	5	92	12		1.7
1918	Bro N	1	0	1.000	2	2	1-1	0	17	6	1	0	1	7	5	0.53	526	.115	.164	4	.000	-0	54	4		0.2
1919	Bro N	14	12	.538	35	27	16-3	0	250.2	228	80	5	6	39	94	2.37	125	.245	.280	87	.161	-3	94	19		1.5
1920	†Bro N	15	14	.517	35	30	16-4	0	254.1	256	91	4	3	56	79	2.62	122	.270	.333	91-2-4	.220	2	106	17		2.3
1921	Bro N	13	14	.481	35	30	12-1	0	211.2	243	112	17	6	46	79	4.17	93	.292	.334	75-1-3	.187	-1	101	-4		-0.6
1922	Bro N	8	15	.348	29	21	13	0	190.1	224	115	13	1	57	49	4.35	94	.299	.349	71-2-3	.268	4	88	-8		-0.5
1923	Bro N	4	1	.800	8	4	3	0	36	39	14	2	0	13	5	3.25	119	.291	.354	13	.077	-1*	106	4		0.3
	Chi A	0	1	.000	1	1	0	0	2.1	6	2	0	0	3	2	23.14	17	.500	.571	0	—	0	42	-5		-0.7
1924	NY N	0	0	—	2	0	0	0	4	2	0	0	3	2	0.00	—	.154	.313	0	—	0		2		0.1
Total	10	68	72	.486	192	147	83-10	3	1257.1	1273	525	44	26	289	445	3.14	106	.269	.314	442-5-15	.208	5	96	35		3.6
CADY, CHARLIE								Charles B. B12.1865 Chicago IL D6.7.1909 Kankakee IL 5-11/180 d9.5 ▲																	
1883	Cle N	0	1	.000	1	1	1	0	8	13	13	0		4		7.88	40	.361	.425	11	.000	-1*	17	-4		-0.4
1884	CP U	3	1	.750	4	4	4	0	35	37	25	0		13	15	2.83	86	.253	.314	20	.100	-1*	158	-2		-0.3
Total	2	3	2	.600	5	5	5	0	43	50	38	0		17		3.77	68	.275	.337	31	.065	-2	129	-6		-0.7
CAHILL, JOHN								John Patrick Parnell "Patsy" B4.30.1865 San Francisco CA D10.31.1901 Pleasanton CA BR/TR/5-7.5/168 d5.31 ▲																	
1884	Col AA	1	0	1.000	2	1	1	0	16	15	15	0	3	4	1	5.06	60	.211	.282	210	.219	0*	299	-4		-0.2
1886	StL N	1	1	.500	2	0	0	0	12	11	5	0	1	3	2	3.00	107	.268	.318	463-1	.199	-0*	1	-1		0.1
1887	Ind N	0	2	.000	6	1	1	0	22	40	38	0	2	19	5	14.32	29	.430	.535	263	.205	-1*	47	-19		-1.3
Total	3	2	2	.500	10	2	2	0	373																	-1.4
CAIN, LES								Leslie B1.13.1948 San Luis Obispo CA BL/TL/6-1/200* [DetA66 4/74] d4.28																	
1968	Det A	1	0	1.000	8	4	0	0	24	25	9	4	0	20-1	13	3.00	100	.269	.398	7	.143	0	137	0		0.0
1970	Det A	12	7	.632	29	29	5	0-0	180.2	167	92	15	7	98-1	156	3.84	98	.247	.346	68-1-3	.162	0	115	-4		-0.4
1971	Det A	10	9	.526	26	26	3-1	0-0	144.2	121	77	14	6	91-1	118	4.35	83	.230	.347	55-1-2	.145	-0*	116	-12		-1.5
1972	Det A	0	3	.000	5	4	0	0-0	23.2	18	12	2	0	16-0	16	3.80	83	.209	.330	7-0-1	.143	-0	73	-2	29	-0.3
Total	4	23	19	.548	68	64	8-1	0-0	373	331	190	32	13	225-3	303	3.98	91	.239	.349	137-2-6	.153	-0	113	-18	29	-2.2
CAIN, MATT								Matthew Thomas B10.1.1984 Dothan AL BR/TR/6-3/230 d8.29																	
2005	SF N	2	1	.667	7	7	1	0-0	46.1	24	12	4	0	19-1	30	2.33	183	.151	.240	15-0-1	.067	-1	72	10		0.5
CAIN, SUGAR								Merritt Patrick B4.5.1907 Macon GA D4.3.1975 Atlanta GA BL/TR(BB 1932-33)/5-11/190 d4.15																	
1932	Phi A	3	4	.429	10	6	3	0	45	42	27	1	0	28	24	5.00	90	.256	.365	12	.250	1	75	-2		-0.2
1933	Phi A	13	12	.520	38	32	16-1	1	218	244	132	18	3	137	43	4.25	101	.280	.379	80-0-4	.200	-1*	109	-3		-0.4

YEAR	TM LG	W	L	PCT	G	GS	CG-SHO	SV-BS	IP	H	R	HR	HB	BB-IB	SO	ERA	AERA	OAV	OOB	AB-HR-SH	AVG	PB	SUP	APR	DL	PW
1934	Phi A	9	17	.346	36	32	15	0	230.2	235	128	15	3	128	66	4.41	99	.266	.360	82-0-5	.159	-3	97	-1		-0.4
1935	Phi A	0	5	.000	6	5	0	0	26	39	22	1	0	19	5	6.58	69	.382	.479	8	.000	-1	53	-6		-1.0
	StL A	9	8	.529	31	24	8	0	167.2	197	112	7	4	104	68	5.26	91	.290	.388	57-0-3	.193	-2	107	-8		-1.0
	Year	9	13	.409	37	29	8	0	193.2	236	134	8	4	123	73	5.44	88	.302	.400	65-0-3	.169	-4	98	-14		-2.0
									16.1	20	13	0	0	9	8	6.61	81	.286	.367	7	.286	0	147	-2		-0.2
1936	StL A	1	1	.500	4	3	1	0	195.1	228	112	18	5	75	42	4.75	110	.293	.359	68-0-4	.103	-4*	97	12		0.6
	Chi A	14	10	.583	30	26	14-1	0	211.2	248	125	18	5	84	50	4.89	107	.292	.360	75-0-4	.120	-4	102	11		0.4
	Year	15	11	.577	34	29	15-1	0	68.2	88	48	7	0	51	17	6.16	75	.325	.432	22-0-2	.182	-1	133	-9		-0.3
1937	Chi A	4	2	.667	18	6	1	0	19.2	26	17	0	0	18	6	4.58	107	.321	.444	8	.000	-1	78	-1		-0.2
1938	Chi A	0	1	.000	5	3	0	0																	
Total	7	53	60	.469	178	137	58-2	1	987.1	1119	611	67	15	569	279	4.83	96	.287	.380	344-0-18	.163	-13	101	-20		-3.5

CAIN, BOB Robert Max "Sugar" B10.16.1924 Longford KS D4.8.1997 Cleveland OH BL/TL/6-0/165* d9.18

YEAR	TM LG	W	L	PCT	G	GS	CG-SHO	SV-BS	IP	H	R	HR	HB	BB-IB	SO	ERA	AERA	OAV	OOB	AB-HR-SH	AVG	PB	SUP	APR	DL	PW
1949	Chi A	0	0		6	0	0	1	11	7	3	0	0	5	5	2.45	170	.179	.273	3	.000	-0		2		0.4
1950	Chi A	9	12	.429	34	23	11-1	2	171.2	153	80	12	5	109	77	3.93	114	.244	.361	61-0-3	.197	-0*	93	13		1.3
1951	Chi A	1	2	.333	4	4	1	0	26.1	25	14	3	3	13	3	3.76	107	.248	.350	9	.333	1	88	0		0.3
	Det A	11	10	.524	35	22	6-1	2	149.1	135	88	13	11	82	58	4.70	89	.239	.347	53-0-2	.245	2	120	-9		-0.6
	Year	12	12	.500	39	26	7-1	2	175.2	160	102	16	14	95	61	4.56	91	.241	.348	62-0-2	.258	3	115	-8		-0.3
1952	StL A	12	10	.545	29	27	8-1	2	170	169	79	15	2	62	70	4.13	95	.264	.331	58-0-5	.138	-1*	97	0		-0.1
1953	StL A	4	10	.286	32	13	1	1	99.2	129	74	8	1	45	36	6.23	67	.310	.379	30	.200	0*	106	-20		-2.3
Total	5	37	44	.457	140	89	27-3	8	628	618	338	51	22	316	249	4.50	93	.259	.351	214-0-10	.196	2	102	-14		-2.2

CAIRNCROSS, CAMERON Cameron B5.11.1972 Cairns, Queensland, Australia BL/TL/6-0/195 d7.20 [DL 2001 Cle A 190]

YEAR	TM LG	W	L	PCT	G	GS	CG-SHO	SV-BS	IP	H	R	HR	HB	BB-IB	SO	ERA	AERA	OAV	OOB	AB-HR-SH	AVG	PB	SUP	APR	DL	PW
2000	Cle A	1	0	1.000	15	0	0	0-0	9.1	11	4	1	0	3-1	8	3.86	130	.306	.350	0	—	0		0		0.1

CALDWELL, CHARLIE Charles William "Chuck" B8.2.1901 Bristol VA D11.1.1957 Princeton NJ BR/TR/5-10/180 d7.7 Col Princeton

YEAR	TM LG	W	L	PCT	G	GS	CG-SHO	SV-BS	IP	H	R	HR	HB	BB-IB	SO	ERA	AERA	OAV	OOB	AB-HR-SH	AVG	PB	SUP	APR	DL	PW
1925	NY A	0	0	—	3	0	0	0	2.2	7	6	0	0	3	1	16.88	25	.467	.556	1	.000	-0		-4		-0.3

CALDWELL, EARL Earl Welton "Teach" B4.9.1905 Sparks TX D9.15.1981 Mission TX BR/TR/6-1/178 d9.8

YEAR	TM LG	W	L	PCT	G	GS	CG-SHO	SV-BS	IP	H	R	HR	HB	BB-IB	SO	ERA	AERA	OAV	OOB	AB-HR-SH	AVG	PB	SUP	APR	DL	PW
1928	Phi N	1	4	.200	5	5	1-1	0	34.2	46	23	5	0	17	5	5.71	75	.348	.423	9-0-1	.111	-0	44	-4		-0.3
1935	StL A	3	2	.600	6	5	2-1	0	36.2	34	16	2	0	17	5	3.68	130	.245	.327	11-0-1	.182	-0	65	5		0.2
1936	StL A	7	16	.304	41	25	10-2	2	189	252	146	15	15	83	59	6.00	90	.319	.394	58-1-4	.190	-1	79	-13		-1.3
1937	StL A	0	0	—	9	2	0	0	29	39	22	3	2	13	8	6.83	71	.317	.391	9-0-1	.222	-0	99	-5		-0.4
1945	Chi A	6	7	.462	27	11	5-1	4	105.1	108	50	8	3	37	45	3.59	92	.265	.331	37-0-3	.216	-0	110	-4		0.3
1946	Chi A	13	4	.765	39	0	0	8	90.2	60	28	2	1	29	42	2.08	164	.186	.255	18-0-2	.167	1		13		2.6
1947	Chi A	1	4	.200	40	0	0	8	54.1	53	23	4	1	30	22	3.64	100	.261	.359	7-0-1	.000	-1		1		0.0
1948	Chi A	1	5	.167	25	1	0	3	39	53	25	3	2	22	10	5.31	80	.335	.423	5	.000	-0	42	-4		-0.5
	Bos A	1	1	.500	8	0	0	0	9	11	14	2	1	11	5	13.00	34	.333	.511	3	.333	0		-8		-1.0
	Year	2	6	.250	33	1	0	3	48	64	39	5	3	33	15	6.75	63	.335	.441	8	.125	-0	42	-12		-1.5
Total	8	33	43	.434	200	49	18-5	25	587.2	656	347	44	25	259	202	4.69	92	.284	.363	157-1-13	.178	-1	87	-19		-1.5

CALDWELL, RALPH Ralph Grant "Lefty" B1.18.1884 Philadelphia PA D8.5.1969 W.Trenton NJ BL/TL/5-9/155 d9.10 Col Penn

YEAR	TM LG	W	L	PCT	G	GS	CG-SHO	SV-BS	IP	H	R	HR	HB	BB-IB	SO	ERA	AERA	OAV	OOB	AB-HR-SH	AVG	PB	SUP	APR	DL	PW
1904	Phi N	2	2	.500	6	5	5	0	41	40	29	1	2	15	30	4.17	64	.242	.313	18	.444	3	154	-7		-0.6
1905	Phi N	1	3	.250	7	2	1	1	34	44	25	1	3	7	29	4.24	69	.321	.367	15	.000	-2	136	-6		-0.6
Total	2	3	5	.375	13	7	6	1	75	84	54	2	5	22	59	4.20	66	.278	.337	33	.242	1	148	-13		-1.2

CALDWELL, MIKE Ralph Michael B1.22.1949 Tarboro NC BR/TL/6-0/185* [SDN71 12/271] d9.4 Col North Carolina St.

YEAR	TM LG	W	L	PCT	G	GS	CG-SHO	SV-BS	IP	H	R	HR	HB	BB-IB	SO	ERA	AERA	OAV	OOB	AB-HR-SH	AVG	PB	SUP	APR	DL	PW
1971	SD N	1	0	1.000	6	0	0	0-0	6.2	4	0	0	0	3-3	5	0.00	—	.174	.269	1	1.000	1		3		0.4
1972	SD N	7	11	.389	42	20	4-2	2-3	163.2	183	92	10	4	49-14	102	4.01	83	.282	.335	50-0-4	.140	-1	108	-18		-1.2
1973	SD N	5	14	.263	55	13	3-1	10-2	149	146	77	8	2	53-10	86	3.74	94	.260	.325	35-0-3	.143	-1*	75	-6		-0.8
1974	SF N	14	5	.737	31	27	6-2	0-1	189.1	176	80	17	4	63-1	57	2.95	129	.249	.312	63-0-7	.143	-2	120	15		1.6
1975	SF N	7	13	.350	38	21	4	1-0	163.1	194	102	16	3	48-7	57	4.79	79	.296	.346	44-0-7	.159	-0	109	-19		-2.3
1976	SF N	1	7	.125	50	9	0	2-0	107.1	145	74	5	2	20-2	11	4.86	75	.324	.354	19-0-1	.158	-0	102	-16		-1.6
1977	Cin N	0	0	—	14	0	0	1-0	24.2	31	15	1	0	8-1	11	4.01	98	.260	.317	4	.500	2	88	-7		-0.6
	Mil A	5	8	.385	21	12	2	0-0	94.1	101	58	6	2	36-7	38	4.58	90	.271	.337	0	—	0	101	45		-0.1
1978	Mil A	22	9	.710	37	34	23-6	1-0	293.1	258	90	14	7	54-3	131	2.36	161	.234	.273	0	—	0	114	24		4.6
1979	Mil A	16	6	.727	30	30	16-4	0-0	235	252	96	18	4	39-2	89	3.29	128	.278	.309	0	—	0	133	-2		1.0
1980	Mil A	13	11	.542	34	33	11-2	1-0	225.1	248	112	29	2	56-2	74	3.93	88	.272	.317	0	—	0	120	-9		-0.6
1981	†Mil A	11	9	.550	24	23	3	0-0	144.1	151	70	18	1	38-4	41	3.93	88	.272	.317	0	—	0	114	0		0.0
1982	†Mil A	17	13	.567	35	34	12-3	0-1	258	269	119	30	1	58-3	75	4.53	84	.296	.332	0	—	0	119	-20		-0.5
1983	Mil A	12	11	.522	32	32	10-2	0-0	228.1	269	125	35	1	51-1	58	4.64	84	.314	.338	0	—	0	85	-12	27	-0.8
1984	Mil A	6	13	.316	26	19	4-1	0-0	126	160	76	11	1	21-2	34	4.64	84	.314	.338	216-0-22	.157	-2	111	-22	27	-1.4
Total	14	137	130	.513	475	307	98-23	18-7	2408.2	2581	1182	218	35	597-62	939	3.81	100	.276	.320	216-0-22	.157	-2	111	-22		-3.2

CALDWELL, RAY Raymond Benjamin "Rube","Sum" B4.26.1888 Corydon PA D8.17.1967 Salamanca NY BL/TR/6-2/190 d9.9 ▲

YEAR	TM LG	W	L	PCT	G	GS	CG-SHO	SV-BS	IP	H	R	HR	HB	BB-IB	SO	ERA	AERA	OAV	OOB	AB-HR-SH	AVG	PB	SUP	APR	DL	PW
1910	NY A	1	0	1.000	6	2	1	1	19.1	19	8	1	0	9	17	3.72	71	.260	.341	6	.000	-1	126	-1		0.1
1911	NY A	14	14	.500	41	26	19-1	1	255	240	115	7	13	79	145	3.35	107	.260	.327	147-0-1	.272	3*	83	11		1.6
1912	NY A	8	16	.333	30	26	13-3	0	183.1	196	111	1	6	67	95	4.47	80	.277	.344	76-0-1	.237	1*	92	-11		-1.2
1913	NY A	9	8	.529	27	16	15-2	1	164.1	131	59	5	9	60	87	2.41	124	.221	.303	97-0-2	.289	3*	113	11		1.4
1914	NY A	18	9	.667	31	23	22-5	0	213	153	53	5	4	51	92	1.94	142	.205	.260	113-0-5	.195	1*	99	21		2.3
1915	NY A	19	16	.543	36	35	31-3	0	305	266	115	6	5	107	130	2.89	101	.244	.315	144-4-2	.243	8*	108	4		0.7
1916	NY A	5	12	.294	21	18	14-1	0	165.2	142	62	6	4	65	76	2.86	94	.234	.302	124-2-0	.258	6*	93	-2		-0.3
1917	NY A	13	16	.448	32	29	21-1	0	236	199	92	8	6	76	102	2.86	94	.234	.302	151-1-4	.291	4*	114	-3		-0.2
1918	NY A	9	8	.529	24	21	14-1	1	176.2	173	69	2	1	62	59	3.06	93	.261	.325	48-0-3	.271	1*	115	-11		-1.1
1919	Bos A	7	4	.636	18	12	6-1	0	86.1	92	49	1	3	31	24	1.71	196	.181	.266	23	.348	2	105	9		0.9
	Cle A	5	1	.833	6	6	4-1	0	52.2	33	13	1	2	19	23	3.11	101	.244	.317	71-0-3	.296	4	111	0		0.0
	Year	12	5	.706	24	18	10-2	0	139	125	62	2	5	50	47	3.86	98	.303	.350	89-0-5	.213	1*	137	-6		-0.5
1920	†Cle A	20	10	.667	34	33	20-1	0	237.2	286	135	9	4	80	80	4.90	87	.275	.333	53-1-1	.208	0*	144	-9		-0.7
1921	Cle A	6	6	.500	37	12	4-1	4	147	159	91	7	2	49	76	3.22	99	.253	.319	1164-8-24	.248	31	105	14		-1.6
Total	12	134	120	.528	343	259	184-21	8	2242	2089	972	59	63	738	1006	3.22	99	.253	.319	1164-8-24	.248	31	105	14		9.3

CALERO, KIKO Enrique Nomar B1.9.1975 Santurce, PR BR/TR/6-1/180* [KCA96 27/799] d4.2 Col St. Thomas (FL)

YEAR	TM LG	W	L	PCT	G	GS	CG-SHO	SV-BS	IP	H	R	HR	HB	BB-IB	SO	ERA	AERA	OAV	OOB	AB-HR-SH	AVG	PB	SUP	APR	DL	PW
2003	StL N	1	1	.500	26	1	0	1-3	38.1	29	12	5	1	20-2	51	2.82	146	.212	.311	4	.250	0	91	6	92	0.6
2004	†StL N	3	1	.750	41	0	0	2-1	45.1	27	14	5	1	10-1	47	2.78	153	.176	.232	1	.000	-0		8	28	0.9
2005	Oak A	4	1	.800	58	0	0	1-1	55.2	45	20	6	1	18-2	52	3.23	138	.216	.281	1	.000	-0		8	27	0.9
Total	3	8	3	.727	125	1	0	4-5	139.1	101	46	16	3	48-5	150	2.97	145	.203	.275	6	.167	-0	91	22	147	2.4

CALHOUN, JEFF Jeffrey Wilton B4.11.1958 LaGrange GA BL/TL/6-2/190* [HouN80 3/69] d9.2 Col U. of Mississippi

YEAR	TM LG	W	L	PCT	G	GS	CG-SHO	SV-BS	IP	H	R	HR	HB	BB-IB	SO	ERA	AERA	OAV	OOB	AB-HR-SH	AVG	PB	SUP	APR	DL	PW
1984	Hou N	0	1	.000	9	0	0	0-0	15.1	5	3	0	0	2-2	11	1.17	285	.100	.135	0	—	0		4		0.5
1985	Hou N	2	5	.286	44	0	0	4-3	63.2	56	21	2	0	24-4	47	2.54	137	.243	.313	5	.000	-0		7	15	0.9
1986	†Hou N	1	0	1.000	20	0	0	0-0	26.2	28	16	3	0	12-1	14	3.71	97	.264	.339	0	—	0		-2		-0.2
1987	Phi N	3	1	.750	42	0	0	1-1	42.2	25	13	1	1	26-8	31	1.48	291	.168	.292	1	.000	-0		10	26	1.0
1988	Phi N	0	0	—	3	0	0	0-1	2.1	6	4	2	0	1-0	1	15.43	23	.462	.500	0	—	0		-3	62	-0.3
Total	5	6	7	.462	118	0	0	5-4	150.2	120	57	8	1	65-15	104	2.51	148	.219	.301	6	.000	-0		16	103	1.8

CALI, CARMEN Carmen S. B11.4.1978 Cleveland OH BL/TL/5-10/185* [StLN00 10/293] d9.8 Col Florida Atlantic

YEAR	TM LG	W	L	PCT	G	GS	CG-SHO	SV-BS	IP	H	R	HR	HB	BB-IB	SO	ERA	AERA	OAV	OOB	AB-HR-SH	AVG	PB	SUP	APR	DL	PW
2004	StL N	0	0	—	10	0	0	0-0	7.1	13	7	1	0	6-1	8	8.59	50	.394	.475	0		0		-3		-0.3
2005	StL N	0	0	—	6	0	0	0-0	6	10	8	3	0	6-1	5	10.50	40	.385	.485	0		0		-4		-0.4
Total	2	0	0	—	16	0	0	0-0	13.1	23	15	4	0	12-2	13	9.45	45	.390	.479	0		0		-7		-0.7

CALIGIURI, FRED Frederick John B10.22.1918 W.Hickory PA BR/TR/6-0/190 d9.3 Mil 1943-46

YEAR	TM LG	W	L	PCT	G	GS	CG-SHO	SV-BS	IP	H	R	HR	HB	BB-IB	SO	ERA	AERA	OAV	OOB	AB-HR-SH	AVG	PB	SUP	APR	DL	PW
1941	Phi A	2	2	.500	5	5	4	0	43	45	22	2	0	14	7	2.93	143	.257	.312	20-0-1	.200	1	107	3		0.2
1942	Phi A	0	3	.000	13	2	0	1	36.2	45	27	2	2	18	20	6.38	59	.300	.382	12	.083	-0	79	-9		-0.9
Total	2	2	5	.286	18	7	4	1	79.2	90	49	4	2	32	27	4.52	89	.277	.345	32-0-1	.156	1	101	-6		-0.7

YEAR	TM	LG	W	L	PCT	G	GS	CG-SHO	SV-BS	IP	H	R	HR	HB	BB-IB	SO	ERA	AERA	OAV	OOB	AB-HR-SH	AVG	PB	SUP	APR	DL	PW

CALIHAN, WILL William T. (b William T. Callahan) B5.1868 Oswego NY D12.20.1917 Rochester NY 5-8/150 d4.17

1890	Roc	AA	18	15	.545	37	36	31	0	296.1	276	170	4	16	.125	127	3.28	109	.239	.322	159-1	.145	-3*	97	9		0.6
1891	Phi	AA	6	6	.500	13	11	11	0	112	151	103	7	12	47	28	6.43	59	.312	.387	56	.196	-1*	97	-28		-2.2
Total	2		24	21	.533	50	47	42	0	408.1	427	273	11	28	172	155	4.14	88	.261	.341	215-1	.158	-4	96	-19		-1.6

CALLAHAN, BEN Benjamin Franklin B5.19.1957 Mt.Airy NC BR/TR/6-7/230 [NYA80 31/742] d6.22 Col Catawba

| 1983 | Oak | A | 1 | 2 | .333 | 4 | 2 | 0 | 0-0 | 9.1 | 18 | 16 | 0 | 0 | 5-1 | 2 | 12.54 | 31 | .400 | .451 | 0 | — | 0 | 140 | -10 | | -1.6 |

CALLAHAN, NIXEY James Joseph B3.18.1874 Fitchburg MA D10.4.1934 Boston MA BR/TR/5-10.5/180 d5.12 M7 ▲

1894	Phi	N		2	.333	9	2	1	2	33.2	64	52	3	5	17	9	9.89	52	.398	.470	21	.238	-1	76	-19		-1.3
1897	Chi	N	12	9	.571	23	22	21-1	0	189.2	221	111	6	8	55	52	4.03	111	.289	.343	360-3-8	.292	3*	108	13		1.5
1898	Chi	N	20	10	.667	31	31	30-2	0	274.1	267	137	2	10	71	73	2.46	146	.253	.307	164-0-4	.262	4*	119	29		3.3
1899	Chi	N	21	12	.636	35	34	33-3	0	294.1	327	155	5	24	76	77	3.06	123	.281	.353	150-0-5	.260	4*	92	22		2.8
1900	Chi	N	13	16	.448	32	32	32-2	0	285.1	347	195	5	22	74	77	3.82	94	.299	.353	115-0-5	.235	2	104	-6		0.0
1901	Chi	A	15	8	.652	27	22	20-1	0	215.1	195	94	4	9	50	70	2.42	144	.239	.290	118-1-4	.331	8*	100	25		3.7
1902	Chi	A	16	14	.533	35	31	29-2	0	282.1	287	150	4	11	89	75	3.60	94	.264	.326	218-0-13	.234	3*	114	-9		-0.2
1903	Chi	A	1	2	.333	3	3	3-0	0	28	40	24	0	1	5	12	4.50	62	.333	.365	28	.292	1*	161	-7		-0.5
Total	8		99	73	.576	195	177	169-11	2	1603	1748	918	33	90	437	445	3.39	109	.276	.332	1585-6-50	.276	25	106	48		9.3

CALLAHAN, JOHN John W. B Moberly MO d9.3

| 1898 | StL | N | 0 | 2 | .000 | 2 | 2 | 1 | 0 | 8.1 | 18 | 20 | 2 | 2 | 7 | 2 | 16.20 | 23 | .429 | .529 | 4 | .000 | -1 | 56 | -11 | | -1.4 |

CALLAHAN, JOE Joseph Thomas B10.8.1916 E.Boston MA D5.24.1949 S.Boston MA BR/TR/6-2/170 d9.13 Col Northeastern

1939	Bos	N	1	0	1.000	4	1	1	0	17.1	17	6	0	1	3	8	3.12	119	.250	.292	4	.000	-0	71	2		0.1
1940	Bos	N	0	2	.000	6	2	0	0	15	20	17	1	0	13	3	10.20	36	.351	.471	5	.000	-1	35	-10		-1.1
Total	2		1	2	.333	10	3	1	0	32.1	37	23	1	1	16	11	6.40	58	.296	.380	9	.000	-1	47	-8		-1.0

CALLAHAN, RAY Raymond James "Pat" B8.29.1891 Ashland WI D1.23.1973 Olympia WA BL/TL/5-10.5/170 d9.12

| 1915 | Cin | N | 0 | 0 | — | 3 | 0 | 0 | 0 | 6.1 | 12 | 7 | 1 | 0 | 1 | 4 | 8.53 | 34 | .364 | .382 | 3 | .333 | 0 | | -4 | | -0.2 |

CALLAWAY, MICKEY Michael Christopher B5.13.1975 Memphis TN BR/TR/6-2/190(190-215) [TBA96 7/214] d6.12 Col U. of Mississippi

1999	TB	A	1	2	.333	5	4	0	0-0	19.1	30	20	2	0	14-1	11	7.45	67	.357	.444	3	.667	1*	70	-6	17	-0.6
2001	TB	A	0	0	—	2	0	0	0-0	5	3	4	2	0	2-0	2	7.20	63	.167	.250	0	—	0		-1		-0.1
2002	Ana	A	2	1	.667	6	6	0	0-0	34.1	31	20	4	3	11-0	23	4.19	107	.235	.308	0	—	0	128	0		0.0
2003	Ana	A	1	4	.200	17	4	0	0-0	38.1	57	32	7	1	16-1	22	6.81	64	.345	.402	0	—	0	147	-11	47	-1.2
	Tex	A	0	3	.000	6	3	0	0-0	22.1	27	18	0	1	8-0	19	6.45	77	.314	.367	0	—	0	56	-4		-0.4
	Year		1	7	.125	23	7	0		60.2	84	50	7	2	24-1	41	6.68	69	.335	.390	0	—	0	106	-14		-1.6
2004	Tex	A	0	1	.000	4	3	0	0-0	11.1	18	10	2	1	7-0	9	7.94	62	.367	.448	0	—	0	119	-3	167	-0.2
Total	4		4	11	.267	40	20	0	0-0	130.2	166	104	17	6	58-2	86	6.27	74	.311	.380	3	.667	1	108	-25	231	-2.5

CALMUS, DICK Richard Lee B1.7.1944 Los Angeles CA BR/TR/6-4/187* d4.22

1963	LA	N	3	1	.750	21	1	0	0	44	32	14	3	0	16-1	25	2.66	114	.204	.277	4	.000	-1	29	3		0.1
1967	Chi	N	0	0	—	1	1	0	0	4.1	5	4	2	0	0-0	1	8.31	43	.278	.278	2	.500	-0	99	-2		-0.1
Total	2		3	1	.750	22	2	0	0	48.1	37	18	5	0	16-1	26	3.17	97	.211	.277	6	.125	-0	70	1		0.0

CALVERT, MARK Mark B9.29.1956 Tulsa OK BR/TR/6-1/195* [SFN78 21/521] d4.17 Col Tulsa

1983	SF	N	1	4	.200	18	4	0	0	37.1	46	33	2	3	34-4	14	6.27	57	.307	.441	8-0-1	.000	-1	150	-13		-1.6
	SF	N	2	4	.333	10	5	1	0	32	40	21	4	1	9-1	5	5.06	70	.303	.350	8	.000	-1	115	-6	15	-1.0
Total	2		3	8	.273	28	9	1	0	69.1	86	54	6	4	43-5	19	5.71	62	.305	.402	16-0-1	.000	-1	130	-19	15	-2.6

CALVERT, PAUL Paul Leo Emile B10.6.1917 Montreal QC, Can. D2.1.1999 Sherbrooke QC, Can. BR/TR/6-0/185* d9.24

1942	Cle	A	0	0	—	1	0	0	0	2	0	0	0	0	0	2	0.00		—	.000	.286	0		0		1		0.0
1943	Cle	A	0	0	—	5	0	0	0	8.1	6	4	0	1	6	2	4.32	72	.200	.351	1	.000	-0		-1		-0.1
1944	Cle	A	1	3	.250	35	4	0	0	77	89	48	4	0	38	31	4.56	72	.289	.367	15-0-1	.267	0	120	-12		-0.4
1945	Cle	A	0	0	—	1	0	0	0	1.1	3	2	0	0	1	1	13.50	24	.429	.500	0	—	0		-1		-0.1
1949	Was	A	6	17	.261	34	23	5	1	160.2	175	111	11	2	86	52	5.43	78	.279	.368	51-0-4	.137	-2*	91	-21		-2.6
1950	Det	A	2	2	.500	32	0	0	4	51.1	71	42	7	2	25	14	6.31	74	.324	.398	7	.000	-1		-10		-0.8
1951	Det	A	0	0	—	1	0	0	0	1	1	0	0	0	0	0	0.00		.250	.250	0	—	0		0		0.0
Total	7		9	22	.290	109	27*	5	5	301.2	345	207	22	5	158	102	5.31	76	.287	.373	74-0-5	.149	-2	95	-44		-4.0

CAMACHO, ERNIE Ernest Carlos B2.1.1955 Salinas CA BR/TR/6-1/180* [OakA76 S1/17] d5.22 Col Hartnell (CA) CC

1980	Oak	A	0	0	—	5	0	0	0-0	11.2	20	9	1	1	5-0	9	6.94	55	.364	.426	0	—	0		-4		-0.2
1981	Pit	N	0	1	.000	7	3	0	0	21.2	23	13	0	0	15-1	11	4.98	73	.295	.400	4-0-1	.000	-0	89	-3		-0.2
1983	Cle	A	1	0	1.000	4	0	0	0-0	5.1	5	3	1	1	2-0	5	5.06	84	.250	.348	0	—	0		0		-0.1
1984	Cle	A	5	9	.357	69	0	0	23-10	100	83	31	6	1	37-5	48	2.43	170	.229	.300	0	—	0		18		3.2
1985	Cle	A	1	0	1.000	9	0	0	0-2	3.1	4	3	1	1	1-0	2	8.10	51	.333	.333	0	—	0		-1	177	-0.1
1986	Cle	A	2	4	.333	51	0	0	20-10	57.1	60	26	1	3	31-6	36	4.08	103	.269	.355	0	—	0		2	15	-0.4
1987	Cle	A	0	1	.000	15	0	0	1-3	13.2	21	14	1	3	5-1	9	9.22	50	.350	.426	0	—	0		-6		-0.4
1988	Hou	N	0	0	—	13	0	0	1-0	17.2	25	15	1	0	12-2	13	7.64	44	.352	.446	1	.000	-0		-8		-1.3
1989	SF	N	3	0	1.000	13	0	0	0-0	16.1	10	5	1	0	11-2	14	2.76	123	.175	.309	1	.000	-0		1		0.3
1990	SF	N	0	0	—	8	0	0	0-0	10	10	4	1	0	3-0	8	3.60	102	.256	.310	0	—	0		1		0.3
	StL	N	0	0	—	6	0	0	0-1	5.2	7	6	2	0	6-1	7	7.94	48	.318	.433	0	—	0		-3		-0.1
	Year		0	0	—	14	0	0	0-1	15.2	17	10	3	0	9-1	15	5.17	72	.279	.361	0	—	0		-3		-0.1
Total	10		10	20	.333	193	3	0	45-26	262.2	268	129	16	8	128-18	159	4.21	95	.268	.351	6-0-1	.000	-1	89	-4	192	1.3

CAMBRIA, FRED Frederick Dennis B1.22.1948 Cambria Heights NY BR/TR/6-2/195 [PitN69 3/58] d8.26 Col St. Leo

| 1970 | Pit | N | 1 | 2 | .333 | 6 | 5 | 0 | 0 | 33.1 | 37 | 15 | 2 | 1 | 12-0 | 14 | 3.51 | 113 | .272 | .336 | 10-0-2 | .200 | 1 | 95 | 1 | | 0.2 |

CAMMACK, ERIC Eric Wade B8.14.1975 Nederland TX BR/TR/6-1/180 [NYN97 13/390] d4.28 Col Lamar [DL 2001 NY N 190]

| 2000 | NY | N | 0 | 0 | — | 8 | 0 | 0 | 0-0 | 10 | 7 | 7 | 1 | 0 | 10-1 | 9 | 6.30 | 69 | .194 | .375 | 1 | 1.000 | 1 | | -2 | | 0.0 |

CAMNITZ, HARRY Henry Richardson B10.26.1884 McKinney KY D1.6.1951 Louisville KY BR/TR/6-1/168 d9.29 b-Howie Col Centre

1909	Pit	N	0	0	—	1	0	0	0	4	6	2	0	0	1	1	4.50	60	.353	.389	2	.000	-0		0		-0.1
1911	StL	N	1	0	1.000	2	0	0	0	2	0	0	0	0	1	2	0.00		.143		0	—	0		1		0.2
Total	2		1	0	1.000	3	0	0	0	6	6	2	0	0	2	3	3.00	98	.261	.320	2	.000	-0		1		0.1

CAMNITZ, HOWIE Samuel Howard "Red" B8.22.1881 Covington KY D3.2.1960 Louisville KY BR/TR/5-9/169 d4.22 b-Harry Col Centre

1904	Pit	N	1	4	.200	10	2	2	0	49	48	39	0	3	20	21	4.22	65	.259	.341	16	.063	-1	50	-11		-1.2
1906	Pit	N	1	0	1.000	2	1	1-1	0	9	6	2	0	0	5	5	2.00	134	.188	.297	3	.000	-0	27	1		0.0
1908	Pit	N	13	8	.619	31	19	15-4	1	180	135	65	0	3	59	85	2.15	113	.211	.281	60-0-3	.050	-5	103	5		0.0
1908	Pit	N	16	9	.640	38	26	17-3	2	236.2	182	76	6	5	69	118	1.56	148	.210	.272	72-0-6	.083	-3	98	13		1.1
1909	†Pit	N	25	6	**.806**	41	30	20-6	3	283	207	75	0	4	77	133	1.62	168	.211	.267	87-0-9	.138	-0	120	31		3.5
1910	Pit	N	12	13	.480	38	31	16-1	2	260	246	110	1	12	61	120	3.22	96	.256	.308	88-1-7	.125	-3	97	1		-0.4
1911	Pit	N	20	15	.571	40	33	18-1	1	267.2	245	112	8	4	84	139	3.13	110	.248	.309	84-0-12	.143	-3	107	12		0.9
1912	Pit	N	22	12	.647	41	32	22-2	2	276.2	256	104	8	13	82	121	2.83	115	.251	.315	98-0-8	.235	1	119	17		1.8
1913	Pit	N	6	17	.261	36	22	5-1	2	192.1	203	106	7	8	84	64	3.74	81	.282	.363	59	.153	-1	80	-18		-2.1
	Phi	N	3	3	.500	9	5	1	1	49	49	25	1	2	23	21	3.67	91	.268	.356	16	.063	-1	81	-2		-0.4
	Year		9	20	.310	45	27	6-1	3	241.1	252	131	8	10	107	85	3.73	83	.279	.362	75	.133	-3	81	-14		-2.5
1914	Pit	F	14	19	.424	36	34	20-1	1	262	256	132	8	9	90	82	3.23	89	.258	.324	87-0-8	.161	-5	101	-15		-2.4
1915	Pit	F	0	0	—	3	0	0	0	20	19	11	1	0	11	6	4.50	60	.257	.353	1	.000	-1	77	-4		-0.3
Total	11		133	106	.556	326	237	137-20	15	2085.1	1832	957	41	65	656	915	2.75	106	.242	.307	677-1-53	.136	-24	103	30		0.5

CAMP, RICK Rick Lamar B6.10.1953 Trion GA BR/TR/6-0/198* [AtlN74 7/149] d9.15 Col West Georgia

1976	Atl	N	0	1	.000	7	0	0	0-0	11.1	14	9	1	0	2-0	5	6.35	60	.302	.326	2	.000	-0	70	-3		-0.2
1977	Atl	N	6	3	.667	54	0	0	10-4	78.2	89	47	6	1	47-13	51	4.00	111	.283	.373	6	.000	-1		1	35	-0.4
1980	Atl	N	2	4	.333	42	4	0	7-2	74.1	99	42	5	3	32-10	23	3.75	107	.329	.396	8-0-1	.000	-1		-1		-0.1
1980	Atl	N	6	4	.600	77	0	0	22-2	108.1	92	26	3	4	29-8	33	1.91	193	.235	.291	0	.111	-0	72	-1		2.9
1981	Atl	N	6	2	.750	48	0	0	17-5	76	68	19	7	5	12-3	47	1.78	199	.239	.271	12-0-1	.000	-1		21		2.9

YEAR	TM LG	W	L	PCT	G	GS	CG-SHO	SV-BS	IP	H	R	HR	HB	BB-IB	SO	ERA	AERA	OAV	OOB	AB-HR-SH	AVG	PB	SUP	APR	DL	PW
1982	†Atl N	11	13	.458	51	21	3	5-2	177.1	199	84	18	1	52-8	68	3.65	101	.291	.339	41-0-5	.024	-3	73	0		-0.4
1983	Atl N	10	9	.526	40	16	1	0-0	140	146	64	16	4	38-2	61	3.79	102	.270	.321	39-0-3	.077	-2	101	1		0.7
1984	Atl N	8	6	.571	31	21	1	0-0	148.2	134	59	11	2	63-3	69	3.27	118	.245	.324	45-0-3	.111	-2	86	10	15	0.3
1985	Atl N	4	6	.400	66	2	0	3-0	127.2	130	72	8	5	61-11	49	3.95	98	.263	.347	13-1-1	.231	1	92	4		-0.3
Total	9	56	49	.533	414	65	5	57-17	942.1	970	420	72	21	336-58	407	3.37	114	.269	.333	175-1-14	.074	-8	85	40	50	5.5

CAMP, SHAWN Shawn Anthony B11.18.1975 Fairfax VA BR/TR/6-1/200* [SDN97 16/500] d4.5 Col George Mason/North Alabama

YEAR	TM LG	W	L	PCT	G	GS	CG-SHO	SV-BS	IP	H	R	HR	HB	BB-IB	SO	ERA	AERA	OAV	OOB	AB-HR-SH	AVG	PB	SUP	APR	DL	PW
2004	KC A	2	2	.500	42	0	0	2-1	66.2	74	37	10	5	16-1	51	3.92	119	.285	.335	0	—	0	3			0.2
2005	KC A	1	4	.200	29	0	0	0-2	49	69	40	4	4	13-3	28	6.43	66	.332	.377	0	—	0	-14			-1.2
Total	2	3	6	.333	71	0	0	2-3	115.2	143	77	14	9	29-4	79	4.98	90	.306	.354	0	—	0	-11			-1.0

CAMP, KID Winfield Scott B12.8.1869 New Albany OH D3.2.1895 Omaha NE BB/TR/6-0/160 d5.3 b-Lew

YEAR	TM LG	W	L	PCT	G	GS	CG-SHO	SV-BS	IP	H	R	HR	HB	BB-IB	SO	ERA	AERA	OAV	OOB	AB-HR-SH	AVG	PB	SUP	APR	DL	PW
1892	Pit N	0	1	.000	4	1	1	0	23	31	23	4	1	9	6	6.26	53	.310	.373	11	.091	-1	77	-6		-0.4
1894	Chi N	0	1	.000	3	2	2	0	22	34	24	0	1	12	6	6.55	86	.351	.427	11-0-1	.000	-3	57	-2		-0.3
Total	2	0	2	.000	7	3	3	0	45	65	47	4	2	21	12	6.40	69	.330	.400	22-0-1	.045	-4	66	-8		-0.7

CAMPBELL, ARCHIE Archibald Stewart "Iron Man" B10.20.1903 Maplewood NJ D12.22.1989 Sparks NV BR/TR/6-0/180 d4.21

YEAR	TM LG	W	L	PCT	G	GS	CG-SHO	SV-BS	IP	H	R	HR	HB	BB-IB	SO	ERA	AERA	OAV	OOB	AB-HR-SH	AVG	PB	SUP	APR	DL	PW
1928	NY A	0	1	.000	13	1	0	2	24	30	22	0	0	11	9	5.25	72	.288	.357	4-0-2	.250	0	90	-7		-0.4
1929	Was A	0	1	.000	4	0	0	0	4	10	7	1	0	5	1	15.75	27	.500	.600	0	—	0	-5			-0.2
1930	Cin N	2	4	.333	23	3	1	4	58	71	38	2	1	31	19	5.43	89	.311	.396	15	.267	0	42	-9		-0.2
Total	3	2	6	.250	40	4	1	6	86	111	67	3	1	47	29	5.86	77	.315	.398	19-0-2	.263	0	53	-15		-1.-

CAMPBELL, DAVE David Alan B9.3.1951 Princeton IN BR/TR/6-3/210* d5.6 Col East Tennessee

YEAR	TM LG	W	L	PCT	G	GS	CG-SHO	SV-BS	IP	H	R	HR	HB	BB-IB	SO	ERA	AERA	OAV	OOB	AB-HR-SH	AVG	PB	SUP	APR	DL	PW
1977	Atl N	0	6	.000	65	0	0	13-0	88.2	78	32	7	3	33-6	42	3.05	146	.239	.311	12-0-2	.083	-1	13			1.0
1978	Atl N	4	4	.500	53	0	0	1-1	69.1	67	39	10	5	49-12	45	4.80	84	.258	.383	0	—	0	-4			-0.9
Total	2	4	10	.286	118	0	0	14-1	158	145	71	17	8	82-18	87	3.82	112	.247	.345	12-0-2	.083	-1	9			0.1

CAMPBELL, HUGH Hugh F. B1846, Ireland D3.1.1881 Newark NJ d4.28 b-Mat

YEAR	TM LG	W	L	PCT	G	GS	CG-SHO	SV-BS	IP	H	R	HR	HB	BB-IB	SO	ERA	AERA	OAV	OOB	AB-HR-SH	AVG	PB	SUP	APR	DL	PW
1873	Res NA	2	16	.111	19	18	18	0	165	251	213	6		8	7	2.95	114	.297	.304	86	.151	-5*	42	10		0.

CAMPBELL, JIM James Marcus B5.19.1966 Santa Maria CA BL/TL/5-11/175 [KCA87 32/821] d8.21 Col San Diego St.

YEAR	TM LG	W	L	PCT	G	GS	CG-SHO	SV-BS	IP	H	R	HR	HB	BB-IB	SO	ERA	AERA	OAV	OOB	AB-HR-SH	AVG	PB	SUP	APR	DL	PW
1990	KC A	1	0	1.000	2	2	0	0-0	9.2	15	9	1	0	2	8	8.38	46	.349	.364	0	—	0	189	-4		-0.

CAMPBELL, JOHN John Millard B9.13.1907 Washington DC D4.24.1995 Daytona Beach FL BR/TR/6-1.5/184 d7.23 Col Alabama

YEAR	TM LG	W	L	PCT	G	GS	CG-SHO	SV-BS	IP	H	R	HR	HB	BB-IB	SO	ERA	AERA	OAV	OOB	AB-HR-SH	AVG	PB	SUP	APR	DL	PW
1933	Was A	0	0	—	1	0	0	0	1	1	1	0	1	0	0	0.00	—	.200	.333	0	—	0	0	0		0.

CAMPBELL, KEVIN Kevin Wade B12.6.1964 Marianna AR BR/TR/6-2/225* [LAN86 5/126] d7.19 Col Arkansas-Monticello

YEAR	TM LG	W	L	PCT	G	GS	CG-SHO	SV-BS	IP	H	R	HR	HB	BB-IB	SO	ERA	AERA	OAV	OOB	AB-HR-SH	AVG	PB	SUP	APR	DL	PW
1991	Oak A	1	0	1.000	14	0	0	0-1	23	13	7	4	1	14-0	16	2.74	141	.167	.301	0	—	0	3			0.
1992	Oak A	2	3	.400	32	5	0	1-0	65	66	39	4	0	45-3	38	5.12	74	.267	.378	0	—	0	87	-9		-0.
1993	Oak A	0	0	—	11	0	0	0-0	16	20	13	1	1	11-1	9	7.31	57	.313	.416	0	—	0	-5			-0.
1994	Min A	1	0	1.000	14	0	0	0-0	24.2	20	8	2	1	5-0	15	2.92	169	.233	.274	0	—	0	6			0.
1995	Min A	0	0	—	6	0	0	0-0	9.2	8	5	0	0	5-0	5	4.66	103	.235	.333	0	—	0	87	-5			0.
Total	5	4	3	.571	77	5	0	1-1	138.1	127	72	11	3	80-4	83	4.55	90	.250	.351	0	—	0	3			0.

CAMPBELL, MIKE Michael Thomas B2.17.1964 Seattle WA BR/TR/6-3/210* [SeaA85 1/7] d7.4 Col Hawaii-Manoa [DL 1990 KC A 18]

YEAR	TM LG	W	L	PCT	G	GS	CG-SHO	SV-BS	IP	H	R	HR	HB	BB-IB	SO	ERA	AERA	OAV	OOB	AB-HR-SH	AVG	PB	SUP	APR	DL	PW
1987	Sea A	1	4	.200	9	9	1	0-0	49.1	41	29	9	2	25-2	35	4.74	100	.224	.319	0	—	0	77	0		0
1988	Sea A	6	10	.375	20	20	2	0-0	114.2	128	81	18	0	43-1	63	5.89	71	.280	.339	0	—	0	112	-19		-2
1989	Sea A	1	2	.333	5	5	0	0-0	21	28	22	4	0	10-0	6	7.29	55	.301	.369	0	—	0	121	-8		-1
1992	Tex A	0	1	.000	1	0	0	0-0	3.2	3	4	1	0	2-0	2	9.82	39	.231	.333	0	—	0	-2			-0
1994	SD N	1	1	.500	3	2	0	0-1	8.1	13	12	5	0	5-0	10	4.46	98	.361	.429	3	.333	2	165	0	63	-1
1996	Chi N	3	1	.750	13	5	0	0-0	36.1	29	19	7	0	10-0	19	5.86	74	.264	.331	14-0-1	.357	2	111	-37	81	-4
Total	6	12	19	.387	51	41	3	0-1	233.1	242	167	44	2	95-3	135	5.86	74	.264	.331	14-0-1	.357	2	111	-37	81	-4

CAMPBELL, BILLY William James B11.5.1873 Pittsburgh PA D10.6.1957 Cincinnati OH BL/TL/5-10/165 d4.17

YEAR	TM LG	W	L	PCT	G	GS	CG-SHO	SV-BS	IP	H	R	HR	HB	BB-IB	SO	ERA	AERA	OAV	OOB	AB-HR-SH	AVG	PB	SUP	APR	DL	PW
1905	StL N	1	1	.500	2	2	2	0	17	27	17	0	0	7	2	7.41	40	.365	.420	7-0-1	.143	0	133	-8		-0
1907	Cin N	3	0	1.000	3	3	3	0	21	19	5	0	0	3	4	2.14	121	.244	.272	8	.250	0	174	2		0
1908	Cin N	12	13	.480	35	24	19-2	2	221.1	203	99	3	10	44	73	2.60	89	.252	.299	72-0-6	.083	-3	93	-9		-1
1909	Cin N	7	11	.389	30	15	7	2	148.1	162	65	0	9	39	37	2.67	97	.288	.344	43-0-6	.140	-1	104	-1		-1
Total	4	23	25	.479	70	44	31-2	4	407.2	411	186	3	19	93	116	2.80	88	.270	.320	130-0-13	.115	-4	105	-16		-1

CAMPBELL, BILL William Richard B8.9.1948 Highland Park MI BR/TR/6-3/190* d7.14 C1 Col Mt. San Antonio (CA) JC

YEAR	TM LG	W	L	PCT	G	GS	CG-SHO	SV-BS	IP	H	R	HR	HB	BB-IB	SO	ERA	AERA	OAV	OOB	AB-HR-SH	AVG	PB	SUP	APR	DL	PW
1973	Min A	3	3	.500	28	2	0	7-2	51.2	44	20	5	1	20-1	42	3.14	127	.226	.301	0	—	0	45	5		0
1974	Min A	8	7	.533	63	0	0	19-8	120.1	109	37	4	2	55-4	89	2.62	143	.242	.326	0	—	-0	161	1		0
1975	Min A	4	6	.400	47	7	2-1	5-6	121	119	58	13	2	46-2	76	3.79	101	.262	.330	1	.000	-0	11	1		0
1976	Min A	17	5	.773	78	0	0	20-10	167.2	145	63	9	5	62-11	115	3.01	119	.234	.305	0	—	0	22	4		4
1977	Bos A★	13	9	.591	69	0	0	31-11	140	112	48	11	3	60-10	114	2.96	152	.224	.311	0	—	0	1			C
1978	Bos A	7	5	.583	29	0	0	4-11	50.2	62	25	9	0	17-3	47	3.91	105	.308	.362	0	—	0	1			C
1979	Bos A	3*	4	.429	41	0	0	9-8	54.2	55	28	5	1	23-6	25	4.79	89	.284	.367	0	—	0	-3	72	-C
1980	Bos A	4	0	1.000	23	0	0	0-0	41.1	44	26	1	0	22-0	17	3.17	124	.245	.316	0	—	0	2			-C
1981	Bos A	1	1	.500	30	0	0	7-0	48.1	45	23	5	0	20-4	37	3.69	102	.245	.314	7	.143	-0	2			-C
1982	Chi N	3	6	.333	62	0	0	8-5	100	89	44	6	1	40-13	71	4.49	85	.275	.342	10	.100	-1	-8			-C
1983	Chi N	8	6	.429	82	0	0	8-5	122.1	128	65	4	1	49-18	97	3.43	107	.222	.301	1	.000	-0	-1			-C
1984	Phi N	6	5	.545	57	0	0	1-4	81.1	68	43	2	0	35-13	52	3.50	102	.230	.294	6	.333	1	-1			-C
1985	†StL N	5	3	.625	50	0	0	4-1	64.1	55	32	5	2	21-9	41	3.08	112	.232	.309	0	—	0	2	32	-C
1986	Det A	3	6	.333	34	0	0	3-1	55.2	46	26	5	1	21-5	37	3.88	107	.230	.302	1	.000	0	-5			-C
1987	Mon N	0	0	—	7	0	0	0-0	10	18	12	0	4	4-1	4	8.10	53	.360	.400	1	.000	1	134	45	104	9
Total	15	83	68	.550	700	9	2-1	126-72	1229.1	1139	550	82	20	495-100	864	3.54	110	.248	.321	26	.154	-1	134	45	104	9

CAMPER, CARDELL Cardell B7.6.1952 Boley OK BR/TR/6-3/208 d9.11 Col Glendale (AZ) CC

YEAR	TM LG	W	L	PCT	G	GS	CG-SHO	SV-BS	IP	H	R	HR	HB	BB-IB	SO	ERA	AERA	OAV	OOB	AB-HR-SH	AVG	PB	SUP	APR	DL	PW
1977	Cle A	1	0	1.000	3	1	0	0-0	9.1	4	4	1	0	4-1	9	3.86	104	.200	.282	0	—	0	113	0		C

CAMPFIELD, SAL William Holton B2.19.1868 Meadville PA D5.16.1952 Meadville PA BR/TR/6-0.5/? d5.15

YEAR	TM LG	W	L	PCT	G	GS	CG-SHO	SV-BS	IP	H	R	HR	HB	BB-IB	SO	ERA	AERA	OAV	OOB	AB-HR-SH	AVG	PB	SUP	APR	DL	PW
1896	NY N	1	1	.500	6	2	1	0	27	31	15	1	2	6	6	4.00	105	.284	.333	12	.167	-0	127	1		C

CAMPILLO, JORGE Jorge Hidalgo B8.10.1978 Tijuana, Baja California, Mexico BR/TR/6-1/190 d5.20

YEAR	TM LG	W	L	PCT	G	GS	CG-SHO	SV-BS	IP	H	R	HR	HB	BB-IB	SO	ERA	AERA	OAV	OOB	AB-HR-SH	AVG	PB	SUP	APR	DL	PW
2005	Sea A	0	0	—	2	1	0	0-0	8	8	1	0	0	1	1	0.00	—	.125	.222	0	—	0	89	1	61	

CAMPISI, SAL Salvatore John B8.11.1942 Brooklyn NY BR/TR/6-2/210* d8.15 Col Long Island-Brooklyn

YEAR	TM LG	W	L	PCT	G	GS	CG-SHO	SV-BS	IP	H	R	HR	HB	BB-IB	SO	ERA	AERA	OAV	OOB	AB-HR-SH	AVG	PB	SUP	APR	DL	PW
1969	StL N	1	0	1.000	7	0	0	0-0	9.2	4	1	0	0	6-2	9	0.93	385	.121	.256	0	—	0	3			
1970	StL N	2	2	.500	37	0	0	4-0	49.1	53	19	2	3	37-11	26	2.92	142	.282	.406	1	.000	-0	6			
1971	Min A	0	0	—	6	0	0	0-1	4.1	5	2	1	0	4-0	0	4.15	85	.294	.429	1	.000	-0	9			
Total	3	3	2	.600	50	0	0	4-1	63.1	62	22	3	3	47-13	35	2.70	149	.261	.388	2	.000	-0	4			

CANAVAN, HUGH Hugh Edward "Hugo" B5.13.1897 Worcester MA D9.4.1967 Boston MA BL/TL/5-8/160 d4.23 Mil 1918

YEAR	TM LG	W	L	PCT	G	GS	CG-SHO	SV-BS	IP	H	R	HR	HB	BB-IB	SO	ERA	AERA	OAV	OOB	AB-HR-SH	AVG	PB	SUP	APR	DL	PW
1918	Bos N	0	4	.000	11	3	3	0	46.2	70	42	0	1	45-8	18	6.36	42	.336	.427	21	.095	-0*	94	-19		

CANDELARIA, JOHN John Robert "Candy Man" B11.6.1953 New York NY BL/TL/6-7/232(210-250) [PitN72 2/47] d6.8

YEAR	TM LG	W	L	PCT	G	GS	CG-SHO	SV-BS	IP	H	R	HR	HB	BB-IB	SO	ERA	AERA	OAV	OOB	AB-HR-SH	AVG	PB	SUP	APR	DL	PW
1975	†Pit N	8	6	.571	18	18	4-1	0-0	120.2	95	47	8	2	36-9	95	2.76	130	.212	.271	43	.140	-0	142	10		
1976	Pit N	16	7	.696	32	31	11-4	1-0	220	173	87	22	2	60-5	138	3.15	112	.216	.271	76-0-5	.211	3	123	10		
1977	Pit N☆	20	5	.800	33	33	6-1	0-0	230.2	197	64	29	2	50-2	133	2.34	172	.232	.274	80-0-4	.225	4	93	43		
1978	Pit N	12	11	.522	30	29	3-1	1-0	189	191	73	15	2	49-6	101	3.24	115	.261	.311	52-0-7	.173	-1	104	16		
1979	†Pit N	14	9	.609	33	30	8	0-0	207	201	83	25	3	50-4	97	4.01	92	.276	.313	77-0-3	.195	-2	100	-7		
1980	Pit N	11	14	.440	35	34	7	1-0	233.1	246	114	19	4	50-4	97	3.54	103	.271	.317	13-0-2	.281	0	126	1	147	
1981	Pit N	2	2	.500	6	6	0	0-0	40.2	42	17	3	0	11-1	14	2.94	128	.259	.296	54-0-3	.222	3*	94	16		
1982	Pit N	12	7	.632	31	30	1-0	1-0	174.2	166	62	13	4	37-3	133	3.23	116	.257	.300	65-0-5	.138	-0	94	14		
1983	Pit N	15	8	.652	33	32	2	0-0	197.2	191	73	15	2	45-3	157	2.72	134	.256	.289	62-1-4	.129	1	104	16		
1984	Pit N	12	11	.522	33	28	3-1	2-1	185.1	179	69	19	1	34-3	133	3.64	100	.256	.319	1-0-2	.000	-0	1			
1985	Pit N	2	4	.333	37	0	0	9-6	54.1	57	23	7	1	24-1	47	3.80	108	.262	.327	0	—	0	119	3		
	Cal A	7	3	.700	13	13	1-1	0-0	71	67	33	5	1	13-3	53	3.80	108	.262	.327	0	—	0	119	3		

YEAR	TM LG	W	L	PCT	G	GS	CG-SHO	SV-BS	IP	H	R	HR	HB	BB-IB	SO	ERA	AERA	OAV	OOB	AB-HR-SH	AVG	PB	SUP	APR	DL	PW
1986	†Cal A	10	2	.833	16	16	1-1	0-0	91.2	68	30	4	3	26-2	81	2.55	162	.206	.268	0	—	0	132	16	84	1.9
1987	Cal A	8	6	.571	20	20	0	0-0	116.2	127	70	17	1	20-0	74	4.71	92	.279	.308	0	—	0	111	-6	62	-0.5
	NY N	2	0	1.000	3	3	0	0-0	12.1	17	8	1	0	3-0	10	5.84	66	.333	.364	0	—	0	110	-2		-0.3
1988	NY A	13	7	.650	25	25	6-2	1-0	157	150	69	18	2	23-2	121	3.38	117	.248	.275	0	.200	0	112	8		1.0
1989	NY A	3	3	.500	10	6	1	0-0	49	49	28	8	0	12-1	37	5.14	76	.258	.299	0	—	0	101	-5	105	-0.6
	Mon N	0	2	.000	12	0	0	0-0	16.1	17	8	3	0	4-2	14	3.31	108	.283	.313	0	—	0	0			0.0
1990	Min A	7	3	.700	34	1	0	4-3	58.1	55	23	9	0	9-2	44	3.39	123	.244	.270	0	—	0	66	5		0.9
	Tor A	0	3	.000	13	2	0	1-0	21.1	32	13	2	2	11-3	19	5.48	72	.356	.425	0	—	0	57	-3		-0.4
	Year	7	6	.538	47	3	0	5-3	79.2	87	36	11	2	20-5	63	3.95	104	.276	.318	0	—	0	59	3		0.5
1991	LA N	1	1	.500	59	0	0	2-3	33.2	31	16	3	0	11-2	38	3.74	96	.252	.307	0	—	0		-1		-0.1
1992	LA N	2	5	.286	50	0	0	5-2	25.1	20	9	1	0	13-3	23	2.84	122	.220	.311	0	—	0		2		0.5
1993	Pit N	0	3	.000	24	0	0	1-2	19.2	25	19	2	1	9-1	17	8.24	50	.313	.385	0	—	0		-9	17	-1.3
Total 19		177	122	.592	600	356	54-13	29-17	2525.2	2399	1038	245	37	592-63	1673	3.33	115	.251	.295	596-1-43	.174	14	106	140	415	17.0

CANDINI, MILO Mario Cain B8.3.1917 Manteca CA D3.17.1998 Manteca CA BR/TR/6-0/187* d5.1 Mil 1945

YEAR	TM LG	W	L	PCT	G	GS	CG-SHO	SV-BS	IP	H	R	HR	HB	BB-IB	SO	ERA	AERA	OAV	OOB	AB-HR-SH	AVG	PB	SUP	APR	DL	PW
1943	Was A	11	7	.611	28	21	8-3	1	166	144	55	3	1	65	67	2.49	128	.238	.313	56-1-6	.161	-1	109	14		1.5
1944	Was A	6	7	.462	28	10	4-2	1	103	110	53	3	1	49	31	4.11	79	.276	.357	32-0-6	.313	3	118	-8		-0.6
1946	Was A	2	0	1.000	9	0	0	1	21.2	15	5	1	0	4	6	2.08	161	.192	.232	6	.333	1		4		0.4
1947	Was A	3	4	.429	38	2	0	1	87	96	53	5	0	35	31	5.17	72	.273	.339	18-0-2	.167	-0	83	-13		-0.9
1948	Was A	2	3	.400	35	4	1	3	94.1	96	56	1	1	63	23	5.15	84	.267	.378	22	.364	3	73	-6		0.0
1949	Was A	0	0	—	3	0	0	1	5.2	4	3	0	0	1	1	4.76	89	.200	.238	1	1.000	0		0		0.0
1950	Phi N	1	0	1.000	18	0	0	0	30	32	11	2	0	15	10	2.70	150	.281	.364	6	.167	-0		4		0.2
1951	Phi N	1	0	1.000	15	0	0	0	30	33	22	3	0	18	14	6.00	64	.275	.370	4	.333	1		-7		-0.3
Total 8		26	21	.553	174	37	13-5		537.2	530	258	18	3	250	183	3.92	92	.259	.341	144-1-14	.243	7	100	-12		0.3

CANDIOTTI, TOM Thomas Caesar B8.31.1957 Walnut Creek CA BR/TR/6-2/200(200-230) d8.8 Col St. Marys (CA)

YEAR	TM LG	W	L	PCT	G	GS	CG-SHO	SV-BS	IP	H	R	HR	HB	BB-IB	SO	ERA	AERA	OAV	OOB	AB-HR-SH	AVG	PB	SUP	APR	DL	PW
1983	Mil A	4	4	.500	10	8	2-1	0-0	55.2	62	21	4	2	16-0	21	3.23	117	.291	.343	0	—	0	78	4		0.5
1984	Mil A	2	2	.500	8	6	1	0-0	32.1	38	21	5	0	10-0	23	5.29	74	.277	.327	0	—	0	81	-5	30	-0.6
1986	Cle A	16	12	.571	36	34	**17**-3	0-0	252.1	234	112	18	8	106-0	167	3.57	117	.246	.324	0	—	0	113	18		1.9
1987	Cle A	7	18	.280	32	32	7-2	0-0	201.2	193	132	28	4	93-2	111	4.78	96	.250	.330	0	—	0	74	-9		-0.9
1988	Cle A	14	8	.636	31	31	11-1	0-0	216.2	225	86	15	6	53-3	137	3.28	126	.272	.319	0	—	0	99	20	15	2.0
1989	Cle A	13	10	.565	31	31	4	0-0	206	188	80	10	4	55-5	124	3.10	128	.242	.294	0	—	0	75	19	15	2.2
1990	Cle A	15	11	.577	31	29	3-1	0-0	202	207	92	23	6	55-1	128	3.65	108	.263	.315	0	—	0	108	5	15	0.8
1991	Cle A	7	6	.538	15	15	3	0-0	108.1	88	35	6	2	28-0	86	2.24	186	.218	.268	0	—	0	77	21		2.4
	†Tor A	6	7	.462	19	19	3	0-0	129.2	114	47	6	4	45-1	81	2.98	142	.236	.304	0	—	0	79	17		1.7
	Year	13	13	.500	34	34	6	0-0	238	202	82	12	6	73-1	167	2.65	159	.228	.288	0	—	0	78	39		4.1
1992	LA N	11	15	.423	32	30	6-2	0-0	203.2	177	78	13	3	63-5	152	3.00	116	.237	.297	56-0-12	.107	-1	82	11	15	1.3
1993	LA N	8	10	.444	33	32	2	0-0	213.2	192	86	12	6	71-1	155	3.12	124	.241	.305	60-0-9	.133	-1	68	18		1.3
1994	LA N	7	7	.500	23	22	5	0-0	153	149	77	9	5	54-2	102	4.12	97	.259	.323	50-0-7	.140	-1	112	-3		-0.3
1995	LA N	7	14	.333	30	30	1-1	0-0	190.1	187	93	18	9	58-2	141	3.50	111	.255	.316	55-0-5	.109	-2	79	5		0.3
1996	†LA N	9	11	.450	28	27	1	0-0	152.1	172	91	18	3	43-3	79	4.49	87	.288	.336	45-0-9	.089	-2	96	-12	24	-1.4
1997	LA N	10	7	.588	41	18	0	0-0	135	128	60	21	11	40-4	89	3.60	109	.248	.314	32-0-9	.094	-1*	119	5		0.4
1998	Oak A	11	16	.407	33	33	3	0-0	201	222	124	30	4	63-2	98	4.84	96	.281	.338	1-0-1	1.000	1	92	-6		-0.5
1999	Oak A	3	5	.375	11	11	0	0-0	56.2	67	46	11	2	23-0	30	6.35	75	.298	.362	0	—	0	98	-11		-1.3
	Cle A	1	1	.500	7	2	0	0-0	14.2	19	18	3	1	7-0	11	11.05	46	.306	.386	0	—	0	174	-9		-0.9
	Year	4	6	.400	18	13	0	0-0	71.1	86	64	14	3	30-0	41	7.32	66	.300	.367	0	—	0	110	-21		-2.2
Total 16		151	164	.479	451	410	68-11	0-0	2725	2662	1299	250	85	883-31	1735	3.73	109	.256	.317	299-0-52	.117	-7	91	88	114	8.9

CANEIRA, JOHN John Cascaes B10.7.1952 Waterbury CT BR/TR/6-3/200(180-200) [AnaA74 S1/2] d9.10 Col Eastern Connecticut

YEAR	TM LG	W	L	PCT	G	GS	CG-SHO	SV-BS	IP	H	R	HR	HB	BB-IB	SO	ERA	AERA	OAV	OOB	AB-HR-SH	AVG	PB	SUP	APR	DL	PW
1977	Cal A	2	2	.500	6	4	0	0-0	28.2	27	15	5	0	16-2	17	4.08	96	.252	.347	0	—	0	86	0		-0.1
1978	Cal A	0	0	—	2	2	0	0-0	7.2	8	6	2	0	3-0	0	7.04	52	.286	.344	0	—	0	74	-3		-0.2
Total 2		2	2	.500	8	6	0	0-0	36.1	35	21	7	0	19-2	17	4.71	82	.259	.346	0	—	0	81	-3		-0.3

CANO, JOSE Joselito (Soriano) B3.7.1962 Boca Del Soco, D.R. BR/TR/6-3/175 d8.28 s-Robinson [DL 1990 Hou N 63]

YEAR	TM LG	W	L	PCT	G	GS	CG-SHO	SV-BS	IP	H	R	HR	HB	BB-IB	SO	ERA	AERA	OAV	OOB	AB-HR-SH	AVG	PB	SUP	APR	DL	PW
1989	Hou N	1	1	.500	6	3	1	0-0	23	24	13	2	0	7-2	8	5.09	67	.267	.316	6	.000	-1	113	-4		-0.4

CANTRELL, GUY Guy Dewey "Gunner" B4.9.1904 Clarita OK D1.31.1961 McAlester OK BR/TR/6-0/190 d8.18

YEAR	TM LG	W	L	PCT	G	GS	CG-SHO	SV-BS	IP	H	R	HR	HB	BB-IB	SO	ERA	AERA	OAV	OOB	AB-HR-SH	AVG	PB	SUP	APR	DL	PW
1925	Bro N	1	0	1.000	14	3	1	0	36	42	27	0	1	14	13	3.00	139	.294	.361	9	.000	-1	121	0		-0.1
1927	Bro N	0	0	—	6	0	0	0	10	10	3	0	0	6	5	2.70	147	.250	.348	3	.333	0		2		0.1
	Phi A	0	2	.000	2	2	2	0	18	25	10	0	0	7	7	5.00	85	.338	.395	4	.167	-0	39	-1		-0.4
1930	Det A	1	5	.167	16	2	1	0	35	38	30	5	1	20	20	5.66	85	.271	.366	6	.167	-0	81	-5		-0.8
Total 3		2	7	.222	38	7	4	0	99	115	70	5	2	47	45	4.27	103	.291	.368	27	.074	-3	86	-4		-0.9

CANTWELL, BEN Benjamin Caldwell B4.13.1902 Milan TN D12.4.1962 Salem MO BR/TR/6-1/168 d8.19 Col Tennessee

YEAR	TM LG	W	L	PCT	G	GS	CG-SHO	SV-BS	IP	H	R	HR	HB	BB-IB	SO	ERA	AERA	OAV	OOB	AB-HR-SH	AVG	PB	SUP	APR	DL	PW
1927	NY N	1	1	.500	5	2	1	0	19.2	26	9	1	1	2	6	4.12	94	.313	.337	8	.250	0	99	0		0.0
1928	NY N	1	0	1.000	7	1	0	1	18.1	20	10	1	1	4	0	4.42	89	.282	.329	4	.500	1	173	-1		0.0
	Bos N	3	3	.500	22	10	3	0	90	112	63	7	2	36	18	5.10	77	.304	.369	29	.172	-1	115	-13		-0.8
	Year	4	3	.571	29	11	3	1	108.1	132	73	8	3	40	18	4.98	79	.301	.363	33	.212	-0	120	-15		-0.8
1929	Bos N	4	13	.235	27	20	8	2	157	171	98	11	2	52	25	4.47	105	.280	.338	50-0-3	.180	0	74	-1		0.2
1930	Bos N	9	15	.375	31	21	10	2	173.1	213	99	15	1	45	43	4.88	101	.312	.355	63-0-2	.302	2*	62	4		0.9
1931	Bos N	7	9	.438	33	16	9-2	2	156.1	160	73	4	0	34	32	3.63	104	.262	.301	57-0-2	.228	0*	83	2		0.4
1932	Bos N	13	11	.542	37	28	3-1	5	146	133	56	6	5	53	33	2.96	127	.247	.296	50	.280	2	99	14		2.6
1933	Bos N	20	10	**.667**	40	29	18-2	2	254.2	242	89	12	5	54	57	2.62	117	.249	.291	85-0-3	.141	-1*	97	12		1.5
1934	Bos N	5	11	.313	27	19	6-1	5	143.1	163	88	8	2	34	45	4.33	88	.285	.327	43-0-5	.279	1*	86	-13		-1.1
1935	Bos N	4	25	.138	39	24	13	0	210.2	235	117	15	7	44	34	4.61	82	.282	.320	67-0-5	.284	4*	54	-16		-1.5
1936	Bos N	9	9	.500	34	12	4	2	133.1	127	55	8	4	35	42	3.04	126	.252	.306	41-0-3	.195	-1*	82	11		1.4
1937	NY N	0	1	.000	1	1	0	0	4	6	4	1	0	1	1	9.00	43	.375	.412	0	—	0	44	-2		-0.3
	Bro N	0	0	—	13	0	0	0	27.1	32	17	1	0	8	12	4.61	88	.288	.336	6	.167	-0		-2		0.0
	Year	0	1	.000	14	1	0	0	31.1	38	21	2	0	9	13	5.17	78	.299	.346	6	.167	-0	43	-4		-0.3
Total 11		76	108	.413	316	164	75-6	21	1534	1640	778	90	23	382	348	3.91	100	.275	.321	503-0-23	.231	8	81	-5		3.3

CANTWELL, MIKE Michael Joseph B6.15.1894 Washington DC D1.5.1953 Oteen NC BL/TL/5-10/155 d8.17 b-Tom Col Georgetown

YEAR	TM LG	W	L	PCT	G	GS	CG-SHO	SV-BS	IP	H	R	HR	HB	BB-IB	SO	ERA	AERA	OAV	OOB	AB-HR-SH	AVG	PB	SUP	APR	DL	PW
1916	NY A	0	0	—	1	0	0	0	2	0	0	0	0	0	1	0.00	—	.000	.333		—	0		0		0.0
1919	Phi N	1	3	.250	5	3	2	0	27.1	36	19	1	2	9	6	5.60	58	.343	.405	9	.222	-0	107	-6		-0.8
1920	Phi N	0	3	.000	5	1	0	0	23.1	25	18	1	3	15	3	3.86	89	.284	.406	7-0-1	.143	-1	138	-3		-0.4
Total 3		1	6	.143	11	4	2	0	52.2	61	39	2	4	26	14	4.61	71	.310	.404	16-0-1	.188	-1	114	-9		-1.2

CANTWELL, TOM Thomas Aloysius B12.23.1888 Washington DC D4.1.1968 Washington DC BR/TR/6-0/170 d5.19 b-Mike Col Georgetown

YEAR	TM LG	W	L	PCT	G	GS	CG-SHO	SV-BS	IP	H	R	HR	HB	BB-IB	SO	ERA	AERA	OAV	OOB	AB-HR-SH	AVG	PB	SUP	APR	DL	PW
1909	Cin N	1	0	1.000	6	1	1	0	21.2	16	10	0	1	7	7	1.66	156	.205	.279	5	.600	1	81	1		0.2
1910	Cin N	0	0	—	2	0	0	0	1.1	2	2	0	0	3	0	13.50	22	.400	.625	0	—	0		-1		-0.1
Total 2		1	0	1.000	8	1	1	0	23	18	12	0	1	10	7	2.35	111	.217	.309	5	.600	1	81	0		0.1

CAPEL, MIKE Michael Lee B10.13.1961 Marshall TX BR/TR/6-1/175* [ChiN83 13/320] d5.7 Col Texas

YEAR	TM LG	W	L	PCT	G	GS	CG-SHO	SV-BS	IP	H	R	HR	HB	BB-IB	SO	ERA	AERA	OAV	OOB	AB-HR-SH	AVG	PB	SUP	APR	DL	PW
88	Chi N	2	1	.667	22	0	0	0-3	29.1	34	19	5	3	13-2	19	4.91	74	.293	.379	2	.000	-0		-5		-0.5
90	Mil A	0	0	—	2	0	0	0-0	0.1	6	6	0	1	1-0	1	135.00	3	.857	.889	0	—	0		-5		-0.2
91	Hou N	1	3	.250	25	0	0	3-1	32.2	33	14	3	0	15-1	23	3.03	117	.266	.343	0	—	0		1		0.1
Total 3		3	4	.429	49	0	0	3-4	62.1	73	39	8	4	29-3	43	4.62	78	.296	.377	2	.000	-0		-9		-0.6

CAPELLAN, JOSE Jose Francisco B1.13.1981 Cotui, D.R. BR/TR/6-4/235* d9.12

YEAR	TM LG	W	L	PCT	G	GS	CG-SHO	SV-BS	IP	H	R	HR	HB	BB-IB	SO	ERA	AERA	OAV	OOB	AB-HR-SH	AVG	PB	SUP	APR	DL	PW
04	Atl N	0	1	.000	3	2	0	0-0	8	14	10	2	0	5-0	4	11.25	38	.400	.463	0	—	0	140	-6		-0.6
05	Mil N	1	1	.500	17	0	0	0-0	15.2	17	6	1	0	5-0	14	2.87	149	.293	.338	0	—	0		2		0.2
Total 2		1	2	.333	20	2	0	0-0	23.2	31	16	3	0	10-0	18	5.70	75	.333	.387	0	.000	-0	140	-4		-0.4

CAPILLA, DOUG Douglas Edmund B1.7.1952 Honolulu HI BL/TL/5-8/175* [SFN70 25/600] d9.12

YEAR	TM LG	W	L	PCT	G	GS	CG-SHO	SV-BS	IP	H	R	HR	HB	BB-IB	SO	ERA	AERA	OAV	OOB	AB-HR-SH	AVG	PB	SUP	APR	DL	PW
76	StL N	1	0	1.000	7	0	0	0-1	8.1	8	5	4	0	4-0	5	5.40	66	.242	.324	0	—	0		-1		-0.1
77	StL N	0	0	—	2	1	0	0-0	2	3	3	1	0	3-0	0	15.43	25	.222	.364	0	—	0		-3		-0.1
	Cin N	7	8	.467	22	16	1	0-0	106.1	94	53	10	2	59-1	74	4.23	93	.237	.338	34-0-3	.059	-3	100	-3		-0.7

YEAR	TM LG	W	L	PCT	G	GS	CG-SHO	SV-BS	IP	H	R	HR	HB	BB-IB	SO	ERA	AERA	OAV	OOB	AB-HR-SH	AVG	PB	SUP	APR	DL	PW
	Year	7	8	.467	24	16	1	0-0	108.2	96	57	10	2	61-1	75	4.47	88	.236	.339	34-0-3	.059	-3	100	-5		-0.8
1978	Cin N	0	1	.000	6	3	0	0-0	11	14	12	1	0	11-0	9	9.82	36	.318	.439	2	.000	-0*	169	-7		-0.6
1979	Cin N	0	1	1.000	5	0	0	0-0	6.1	7	6	1	1	5-0	0	8.53	43	.269	.406	1	1.000	0		-3		-0.
	Chi N	0	1	1.000	13	1	0	0-0	17.1	14	6	1	0	7-0	10	2.60	160	.206	.280	0	—	0	64	3		0.2
	Year	1	1	.500	18	1	0	0-0	23.2	21	12	2	1	12-0	10	4.18	96	.223	.318	1	1.000	0*	66	0		-0.7
1980	Chi N	2	8	.200	39	11	0	0-1	89.2	82	46	7	3	51-5	51	4.12	96	.253	.355	21-0-1	.190	0*	39	-1		0.6
1981	Chi N	1	0	1.000	42	0	0	0-3	51	52	20	1	2	34-3	28	3.18	118	.284	.396	3	.000	-0		3		0.
Total	6	12	18	.400	136	31	1	0-5	292.1	273	152	21	8	173-9	178	4.34	90	.252	.356	61-0-4	.115	-3	83	-12		-1.0

CAPPS, MATT   Matthew Dicus   B9.3.1983 Douglasville GA   BR/TR/6-3/240   d9.16

YEAR	TM LG	W	L	PCT	G	GS	CG-SHO	SV-BS	IP	H	R	HR	HB	BB-IB	SO	ERA	AERA	OAV	OOB	AB-HR-SH	AVG	PB	SUP	APR	DL	PW
2005	Pit N	0	0	—	4	0	0	0-0	1	1	0	0	0	1-0	3	4.50	94	.333	.375	0		0		0		0.0

CAPPUZZELLO, GEORGE   George Angelo   B1.15.1954 Youngstown OH   BR/TL/6-0/175(175-195)   [DetA72 27/623]   d5.31

YEAR	TM LG	W	L	PCT	G	GS	CG-SHO	SV-BS	IP	H	R	HR	HB	BB-IB	SO	ERA	AERA	OAV	OOB	AB-HR-SH	AVG	PB	SUP	APR	DL	PW
1981	Det A	1	1	.500	18	3	0	1-0	33.2	28	14	2	2	18-2	19	3.48	109	.222	.329	0	—	0	111	1		0.
1982	Hou N	0	1	.000	17	0	0	0-2	19.1	16	6	2	3	7-1	13	2.79	119	.232	.321	1	.000	-0		2	59	0.
Total	2	1	2	.333	35	3	0	1-2	53	42	20	4	5	25-3	32	3.23	112	.226	.326	1	.000	-0	111	3	59	0.

CAPRA, BUZZ   Lee William   B10.1.1947 Chicago IL   BR/TR/5-10/168*   [NYN69 27/625]   d9.15 Col Illinois St.

YEAR	TM LG	W	L	PCT	G	GS	CG-SHO	SV-BS	IP	H	R	HR	HB	BB-IB	SO	ERA	AERA	OAV	OOB	AB-HR-SH	AVG	PB	SUP	APR	DL	PW
1971	NY N	0	1	.000	3	0	0	0-0	5.1	3	6	0	0	5-1	6	8.44	41	.167	.348	1	.000	-0		-3		-0.
1972	NY N	3	2	.600	14	6	0	0-0	53	50	27	7	0	27-1	45	4.58	74	.253	.341	12	.250	1	83	-6		-0.
1973	NY N	2	7	.222	24	0	0	4-3	42	35	18	4	2	28-9	35	3.86	95	.233	.357	2-0-1	.000	0	0	0		-0.
1974	Atl N☆	16	8	.667	39	27	11-5	1-0	217	163	67	13	3	84-6	137	**2.28**	**166**	**.208**	.286	67-0-7	.164	0	95	33		3.
1975	Atl N	4	7	.364	12	12	5	0-0	78.1	77	41	8	1	28-1	35	4.25	89	.257	.320	23-0-5	.043	-2	85	-3	111	-0.
1976	Atl N	0	1	.000	5	0	0	0-0	9.1	9	9	0	0	6-2	4	8.68	44	.265	.366	0	—	0		-4	82	-0.
1977	Atl N	6	11	.353	45	16	0	0-0	139.1	142	88	28	4	80-12	100	5.36	83	.263	.360	36-0-3	.111	-2	66	-10		-1.
Total	7	31	37	.456	142	61	16-5	5-3	544.1	479	256	60	10	258-32	362	3.87	101	.237	.324	141-0-16	.135	-2	84	7	193	0.

CAPUANO, CHRIS   Christopher Frank   B8.19.1978 Springfield MA   BL/TL/6-3/210*   [AriN99 8/238]   d5.4 Col Duke

YEAR	TM LG	W	L	PCT	G	GS	CG-SHO	SV-BS	IP	H	R	HR	HB	BB-IB	SO	ERA	AERA	OAV	OOB	AB-HR-SH	AVG	PB	SUP	APR	DL	PW
2003	Ari N	2	4	.333	9	4	0	0-0	33	27	19	3	6	11-1	23	4.64	100	.231	.326	8	.000	-1	81	0		-0.
2004	Mil N	6	8	.429	17	17	0	0-0	88.1	91	55	18	5	37-1	80	4.99	88	.269	.349	30	.200	1	84	-6	93	-0.
2005	Mil N	18	12	.600	35	35	0	0-0	219	212	105	31	12	91-6	176	3.99	107	.256	.337	71-0-5	.169	0	107	8		1.
Total	3	26	24	.520	61	57	0	0-0	340.1	330	179	52	23	139-8	279	4.31	101	.257	.339	109-0-5	.165	1	98	2	93	0.

CARAWAY, PAT   Cecil Bradford Patrick   B9.26.1905 Erath Co. TX   D6.9.1974 ElPaso TX   BL/TL/6-4/175   d4.19

YEAR	TM LG	W	L	PCT	G	GS	CG-SHO	SV-BS	IP	H	R	HR	HB	BB-IB	SO	ERA	AERA	OAV	OOB	AB-HR-SH	AVG	PB	SUP	APR	DL	PW
1930	Chi A	10	10	.500	38	21	9-1	0	193.1	194	96	11	3	57	83	3.86	120	.267	.323	64-0-3	.172	-1	93	19		1
1931	Chi A	10	24	.294	51	32	11-1	2	220	268	177	17	7	101	55	6.22	68	.295	.370	72-0-8	.194	-1*	79	-47		-5
1932	Chi A	2	6	.250	19	9	1	0	64.2	80	55	6	3	37	13	6.82	63	.304	.396	21-0-1	.143	-1	68	-16		-1
Total	3	22	40	.355	108	62	21-2	2	478	542	328	34	13	195	151	5.35	83	.286	.356	157-0-12	.178	-3	82	-44		-5

CARDEN, JOHN   John Bruton   B5.19.1921 Killeen TX   D2.8.1949 Mexia TX   BR/TR/6-5/210   d5.18   Col Texas A&M-Commerce

YEAR	TM LG	W	L	PCT	G	GS	CG-SHO	SV-BS	IP	H	R	HR	HB	BB-IB	SO	ERA	AERA	OAV	OOB	AB-HR-SH	AVG	PB	SUP	APR	DL	PW
1946	NY N	0	0	—	1	0	0	0	2	4	7	0	1	4	1	22.50	15	.400	.600	0	—	0		-5		-0

CARDINAL, CONRAD   Conrad Seth   B3.30.1942 Brooklyn NY   BR/TR/6-1/190   d4.11

YEAR	TM LG	W	L	PCT	G	GS	CG-SHO	SV-BS	IP	H	R	HR	HB	BB-IB	SO	ERA	AERA	OAV	OOB	AB-HR-SH	AVG	PB	SUP	APR	DL	PW
1963	Hou N	0	1	.000	6	1	0	0	13.1	15	14	0	0	7-0	7	6.08	52	.283	.355	2	.000	0	82	-6		-0

CARDONI, BEN   Armand Joseph "Big Ben"   B8.21.1920 Jessup PA   D4.2.1969 Jessup PA   BR/TR/6-3/195   d8.22

YEAR	TM LG	W	L	PCT	G	GS	CG-SHO	SV-BS	IP	H	R	HR	HB	BB-IB	SO	ERA	AERA	OAV	OOB	AB-HR-SH	AVG	PB	SUP	APR	DL	PW
1943	Bos N	0	0	—	11	0	0	1	28	38	20	1	1	14	5	6.43	53	.336	.414	7	.000	-1		-8		-0
1944	Bos N	0	6	.000	22	5	1	0	75.2	83	40	5	1	37	24	3.93	97	.284	.367	17-0-4	.235	-0*	48	-1		-0
1945	Bos N	0	0	—	3	0	0	0	4	6	5	0	1	3	5	9.00	43	.300	.417	0	—	0		-2		-0
Total	3	0	6	.000	36	5	1	1	107.2	127	65	6	3	54	34	4.76	78	.299	.382	24-0-4	.167	-1	48	-11		-0

CARDWELL, DON   Donald Eugene   B12.7.1935 Winston-Salem NC   BR/TR/6-4/210*   d4.21 Col Appalachian St.

YEAR	TM LG	W	L	PCT	G	GS	CG-SHO	SV-BS	IP	H	R	HR	HB	BB-IB	SO	ERA	AERA	OAV	OOB	AB-HR-SH	AVG	PB	SUP	APR	DL	PW
1957	Phi N	4	8	.333	30	19	5-1	0	128.1	122	71	17	4	42-1	92	4.91	78	.251	.313	35-1-3	.200	1	86	-13		-0
1958	Phi N	3	6	.333	16	14	3	0	107.2	99	55	16	2	37-4	77	4.51	88	.241	.306	38-0-1	.211	1	84	-4		-0
1959	Phi N	9	10	.474	35	22	5-1	0	153	135	77	22	4	65-5	106	4.06	87	.238	.317	55-1-5	.055	-3*	84	1		-0
1960	Phi N	1	2	.333	5	4	0	0	28.1	28	14	4	1	11-1	21	4.45	87	.262	.336	8-2-2	.250	2	119	-1		0
	Chi N	8	14	.364	31	26	6-1	0	177	166	101	19	5	68-10	129	4.37	86	.249	.320	69-3-0	.203	3*	97	-13		-1
	Year	9	16	.360	36	30	6-1	0	205.1	194	115	23	6	79-11	150	4.38	87	.251	.322	77-5-2	.208	5	100	-14		-1
1961	Chi N	15	14	.517	39	**38**	13-3	0	259.1	243	121	22	10	88-0	156	3.82	110	.246	.312	95-3-4	.105	-1*	97	13		-1
1962	Chi N	7	16	.304	41	29	6-1	4	195.2	205	116	27	9	60-7	104	4.92	84	.267	.326	61-0-4	.148	-2	91	3		-1
1963	Pit N	13	15	.464	33	32	7-2	0	213.2	195	92	21	16	52-10	112	3.07	107	.245	.303	71-0-3	.085	-2	113	8		-1
1964	Pit N	1	2	.333	4	4	1-1	0	19.1	15	9	1	3	7-1	10	2.79	126	.217	.313	7	.143	-0	88	1	35	-0
1965	Pit N	13	10	.565	37	34	12-2	0	240.1	214	101	21	4	59-1	107	3.18	110	.239	.294	74-2-10	.162	3	117	8		-1
1966	Pit N	6	6	.500	32	14	1	1	101.2	112	58	15	6	27-8	60	4.60	78	.282	.335	29-0-1	.103	-1	106	-12	44	-1
1967	NY N	5	9	.357	26	16	3-3	0	118.1	117	51	15	6	39-8	71	3.57	95	.249	.319	38-1-0	.158	2*	84	-3		-1
1968	NY N	7	13	.350	29	25	5-1	1	180	156	69	9	10	50-11	82	2.95	102	.233	.293	61-1-3	.049	-3*	75	0		-1
1969	†NY N	8	10	.444	30	21	4	0-0	152.1	145	63	15	5	47-10	60	3.01	122	.252	.313	47-1-2	.170	1	92	8		-1
1970	NY N	0	2	.000	16	1	0	0-0	25	31	19	3	3	6-1	16	6.48	63	.316	.364	5	.000	-1	44	-6		-0
	Atl N	2	1	.667	16	2	1-1	0-1	23	31	23	5	1	13-2	16	9.00	48	.326	.409	5	.400	1	115	-10		-0
	Year	2	3	.400	32	3	1-1	0-1	48	62	42	8	4	19-3	24	7.69	54	.321	.386	10	.200	-0	93	-16		-1
Total	14	102	138	.425	410	301	72-17	7-1	2123	2009	1044	225	98	671-80	1211	3.92	95	.250	.313	698-15-34	.135	2	92	-42	79	-1

CARLETON, TEX   James Otto   B8.19.1906 Comanche TX   D1.11.1977 Fort Worth TX   BB/TR/6-1.5/180   d4.17   Col TCU

YEAR	TM LG	W	L	PCT	G	GS	CG-SHO	SV-BS	IP	H	R	HR	HB	BB-IB	SO	ERA	AERA	OAV	OOB	AB-HR-SH	AVG	PB	SUP	APR	DL	PW
1932	StL N	10	13	.435	44	22	9-3	0	196.1	198	94	12	3	70	113	4.08	96	.261	.326	60-1-0	.150	-2	88	1		-1
1933	StL N	17	11	.607	44	33	15-4	3	277	263	117	15	4	97	147	3.38	103	.249	.315	91-1-8	.187	1*	130	5		-1
1934	†StL N	16	11	.593	40	31	16	2	240.2	260	126	14	7	52	103	4.26	99	.271	.314	88-1-3	.193	-3	116	3		-1
1935	†Chi N	11	8	.579	31	22	8	1	171	169	82	17	3	60	84	3.89	101	.257	.322	62-0-1	.129	-3	116	3		-1
1936	Chi N	14	10	.583	35	26	12-4	1	197.1	204	85	14	6	67	88	3.65	109	.268	.332	60-3-4	.233	6	115	9		-1
1937	Chi N	16	8	.667	32	27	18-4	0	208.1	183	80	10	4	94	105	3.15	126	.236	.321	71-0-6	.169	1*	117	19		-1
1938	†Chi N	10	9	.526	33	24	9	0	167.2	213	118	11	8	76	80	5.42	71	.307	.381	65	.231	3	125	-31		-1
1940	Bro N	6	6	.500	34	17	4-1	2	149	140	68	12	3	47	88	3.81	105	.245	.305	43-0-5	.186	-0	100	4		-1
Total	8	100	76	.568	293	202	91-16	9	1607.1	1630	770	105	38	561	808	3.91	100	.261	.326	540-6-27	.185	4	114	11		-1

CARLOS, CISCO   Francisco Manuel   B9.17.1940 Monrovia CA   BR/TR/6-3/205*   d8.25   Col Northern Colorado

YEAR	TM LG	W	L	PCT	G	GS	CG-SHO	SV-BS	IP	H	R	HR	HB	BB-IB	SO	ERA	AERA	OAV	OOB	AB-HR-SH	AVG	PB	SUP	APR	DL	PW
1967	Chi A	2	0	1.000	8	7	1-1	0	41.2	23	5	0	1	9-0	27	0.86	359	.161	.216	16	.063	-1	88	11		0
1968	Chi A	4	14	.222	29	21	0	0	122.1	121	64	13	10	37-5	57	3.90	78	.258	.324	31-0-4	.065	-1	67	-12		-0
1969	Chi A	4	3	.571	25	4	0	0-1	49.1	52	33	4	5	23-3	28	5.66	68	.274	.367	10-0-2	.065	-1	132	-9		-0
	Was A	1	1	.500	6	4	0	0	17.2	23	9	2	0	6-0	5	4.58	76	.348	.403	5	.200	-0	114	-2		-0
	Year	5	4	.556	31	8	0	0-1	67	75	42	6	5	29-3	33	5.37	70	.293	.376	15-0-2	.067	-0	121	-10		-0
1970	Was A	0	0	—	5	0	0	0-0	6	3	1	0	0	4-0	2	1.50	241	.150	.292	0	—	0		-1		-0
Total	4	11	18	.379	73	36	1-1	0-1	237	222	112	19	16	79-8	119	3.72	88	.250	.322	62-0-6	.065	-3	84	-10		-0

CARLSEN, DON   Donald Herbert   B10.15.1926 Chicago IL   D9.22.2002 Denver CO   BR/TR/6-1/175*   d4.28

YEAR	TM LG	W	L	PCT	G	GS	CG-SHO	SV-BS	IP	H	R	HR	HB	BB-IB	SO	ERA	AERA	OAV	OOB	AB-HR-SH	AVG	PB	SUP	APR	DL	PW
1948	Chi N	0	0	—	1	0	0	0	1	5	4	0	2	1	1	36.00	11	.625	.700	0	—	0		-3		-0
1951	Pit N	2	3	.400	7	6	2	0	43	50	22	4	1	14	20	4.19	101	.292	.349	16	.250	0	66	1		-0
1952	Pit N	0	1	.000	5	1	0	0	10	20	13	1	0	5	2	10.80	37	.417	.472	3	.333	0	0	-7		-0
Total	3	2	4	.333	13	7	2	0	54	75	39	5	1	21	23	6.00	70	.330	.390	19	.263	0	57	-9		-0

CARLSON, DAN   Daniel Steven   B1.26.1970 Portland OR   BR/TR/6-1/185(185-200)   [SFN89 33/856]   d9.13   Col Mt. Hood (OR) CC

YEAR	TM LG	W	L	PCT	G	GS	CG-SHO	SV-BS	IP	H	R	HR	HB	BB-IB	SO	ERA	AERA	OAV	OOB	AB-HR-SH	AVG	PB	SUP	APR	DL	PW
1996	SF N	1	0	1.000	5	0	0	0-0	10	13	6	2	0	2-0	4	2.70	153	.310	.326	1	.000	-0		0		-0
1997	SF N	0	0	—	6	0	0	0-0	15.1	20	14	5	0	8-1	14	7.63	54	.317	.389	3	.000	-0		-6	10	-0
1998	TB A	0	0	—	10	0	0	0-0	17.2	25	15	3	0	8-0	16	7.64	63	.347	.429	0	—	0		-5		-0
1999	Ari N	0	0	—	2	0	0	0-0	4	5	4	0	0	0	3	9.00	51	.278	.278	0	—	0		-2		-0
Total	4	1	0	1.000	23	0	0	0-0	47	63	39	10	0	18-1	37	6.70	66	.323	.382	4	.000	-0		-13	10	-0

CARLSON, HAL   Harold Gust   B5.17.1892 Rockford IL   D5.28.1930 Chicago IL   BR/TR/6-0/180   d4.13   Mil 1918

YEAR	TM LG	W	L	PCT	G	GS	CG-SHO	SV-BS	IP	H	R	HR	HB	BB-IB	SO	ERA	AERA	OAV	OOB	AB-HR-SH	AVG	PB	SUP	APR	DL	PW
1917	Pit N	7	11	.389	34	17	9-1	1	161.1	140	64	0	4	49	68	2.90	98	.241	.304	49-0-3	.122	-2	70	-1		1
1918	Pit N	0	1	.000	3	2	0	0	12	13	7	0	1	5	5	3.75	77	.286	.362	5	.200	-0	53	-1		

YEAR	TM LG	W	L	PCT	G	GS	CG-SHO	SV-BS	IP	H	R	HR	HB	BB-IB	SO	ERA	AERA	OAV	OOB	AB-HR-SH	AVG	PB	SUP	APR	DL	PW
1919	Pit N	8	10	.444	22	14	7-1	0	141	114	41	0	2	39	49	2.23	135	.243	.303	43-0-1	.163	-1	58	12		1.5
1920	Pit N	14	13	.519	39	31	16-3	3	246.2	262	102	4	8	63	62	3.36	96	.281	.331	85-0-2	.271	3	94	0		0.1
1921	Pit N	4	8	.333	31	10	3	4	109.2	121	59	6	2	23	37	4.27	90	.290	.330	34	.294	1	79	-4		-0.2
1922	Pit N	9	12	.429	39	18	6	2	145.1	193	106	10	4	58	64	5.70	72	.323	.386	56-1-4	.268	3	131	-25		-2.6
1923	Pit N	0	0	—	4	0	0		13.1	19	9	2	1	2	4	4.73	85	.358	.393	5	.000	-0		-1		-0.1
1924	Phi N	8	17	.320	38	23	12-1	2	203.2	267	122	9	3	55	66	4.86	92	.329	.374	76-2-2	.276	2*	78	-6		-0.4
1925	Phi N	13	14	.481	35	32	18-4	0	234	281	131	19	6	52	80	4.23	113	.298	.338	93-2-2	.183	-2*	101	14		1.2
1926	Phi N	17	12	.586	35	34	20-3	0	267.1	293	116	9	2	47	55	3.23	128	.281	.313	96-0-3	.240	2*	85	25		2.6
1927	Phi N	4	5	.444	11	9	4	1	63.2	80	41	7	0	18	13	5.23	79	.316	.362	25-0-1	.240	0*	149	-7		-0.9
	Chi N	12	8	.600	27	22	15-2	0	184.1	201	73	9	2	27	27	3.17	122	.280	.307	67-0-3	.164	-3	104	16		1.2
	Year	16	13	.552	38	31	19-2	1	248	281	114	16	2	45	40	3.70	106	.289	.322	92-0-4	.185	-3	118	10		0.3
1928	Chi N	3	2	.600	20	4	2	4	56.1	74	42	4	0	15	11	5.91	65	.329	.371	19	.263	0	77	-13		-1.1
1929	†Chi N	11	5	.688	31	13	6-2	2	111.2	131	71	8	1	31	35	5.16	90	.292	.340	39-0-3	.231	1	144	-5		-0.5
1930	Chi N	4	2	.667	39	1	0	2	51.2	68	31	5	1	14	14	5.05	97	.313	.358	20	.250	0	119	0		0.1
Total	14	114	120	.487	377	235	121-17	19	2002	2256	1013	93	36	498	590	3.99		.291	.337	712-5-24	.223	4	98	4		0.6

CARLSON, LEON Leon Alton "Swede" B2.17.1895 Jamestown NY D9.15.1961 Jamestown NY BR/TR/6-3/195 d5.31

| 1920 | Was A | 0 | 0 | — | 3 | 0 | 0 | | 12.1 | 14 | 7 | 1 | 0 | 2 | 3 | 3.65 | 102 | .292 | .320 | 6 | .167 | -0 | | -1 | | -0.1 |

CARLTON, STEVE Steven Norman "Lefty" B12.22.1944 Miami FL BL/TL/6-4/210(178-220) d4.12 HF1994

1965	StL N	0	0	—	15	2	0		25	27	7	3	1	8-1	21	2.52	153	.287	.350	2	.000	-0	148	4		0.2
1966	StL N	3	3	.500	9	9	2-1	0	52	56	22	2	0	8-1	25	3.12	115	.280	.335	15-0-2	.267	1	82	2		0.4
1967	†StL N	14	9	.609	30	28	11-2	1	193	173	71	10	2	62-1	168	2.98	110	.238	.299	72-0-1	.153	1	114	7		0.9
1968	†StL N★	13	11	.542	34	33	10-5	0	232	214	87	11	3	61-4	162	2.99	97	.246	.295	73-2-6	.164	1	107	-2		0.0
1969	StL N★	17	11	.607	31	31	12-2	0-0	236.1	185	66	15	4	93-6	210	2.17	165	.216	.294	80-1-4	.213	5*	81	37		5.0
1970	StL N	10	19	.345	34	33	13-2	0-0	253.2	239	123	25	2	109-16	193	3.73	111	.251	.326	80-0-3	.200	2	75	9		1.1
1971	StL N☆	20	9	.690	37	36	18-4	0-0	273.1	275	120	23	5	98-11	172	3.56	102	.262	.326	96-0-5	.177	1	122	2		0.3
1972	Phi N★	27	10	.730	41	41	30-8	0-0	346.1	257	84	17	1	87-8	310	1.97	183	.206	.257	117-1-7	.197	4	92	60		7.4
1973	Phi N	13	20	.394	40	40	18-3	0-0	293.1	293	146	29	3	113-12	223	3.90	98	.260	.329	100-2-4	.160	0	83	-5		-0.5
1974	Phi N☆	16	13	.552	39	39	17-1	0-0	291	249	118	21	5	136-8	240	3.22	118	.234	.321	102-0-7	.245	2	114	17		1.8
1975	Phi N	15	14	.517	37	37	14-3	0-0	255.1	217	116	24	2	104-5	192	3.56	106	.233	.308	90-0-7	.156	-0	106	5		0.4
1976	†Phi N	20	7	.741	35	35	13-2	0-0	252.2	224	94	19	1	72-4	195	3.13	114	.237	.290	92-0-7	.217	2	150	14		1.5
1977	†Phi N☆	23	10	.697	36	36	17-2	0-0	283	229	99	25	4	89-5	198	2.64	153	.223	.286	97-3-7	.268	8	107	40		5.5
1978	†Phi N	16	13	.552	34	34	12-3	0-0	247.1	228	91	30	3	63-7	161	2.84	127	.246	.295	86-0-3	.291	7	118	19		3.1
1979	Phi N★	18	11	.621	35	35	13-4	0-0	251	202	112	25	5	89-11	213	3.62	107	.219	.290	94-0-2	.223	3*	111	5		0.9
1980	†Phi N☆	24	9	.727	38	38	13-3	0-0	304	243	87	15	2	90-12	286	2.34	163	.218	.276	101-0-6	.188	-1	103	48		5.2
1981	†Phi N☆	13	4	.765	24	24	10-1	0-0	190	152	59	9	1	62-3	179	2.42	151	.222	.286	67-0-2	.134	-0	107	24		2.0
1982	Phi N★	23	11	.676	38	38	19-6	0-0	295.2	253	114	17	1	86-5	286	3.10	119	.232	.288	101-2-8	.218	4	104	19		2.5
1983	Phi N	15	16	.484	37	37	8-3	0-0	283.2	277	117	20	3	84-10	275	3.11	116	.258	.313	97-0-6	.196	3	92	15		1.8
1984	Phi N	13	7	.650	33	33	1	0-0	229	214	104	14	0	79-7	163	3.58	102	.246	.306	84-1-3	.190	2*	127	3		0.4
1985	Phi N	1	8	.111	16	16	0	0-0	92	84	43	6	0	53-4	48	3.33	112	.249	.349	28-0-1	.179	0	58	2		-0.2
1986	Phi N	4	8	.333	16	16	0	0-0	83	102	70	15	0	45-4	62	6.18	63	.297	.376	34-0-1	.206	1	111	-22		-2.7
	SF N	1	3	.250	6	6	0	0-0	30	36	20	4	1	16-0	18	5.10	69	.303	.303	11-0-0	.182	1	139	-6		-0.6
	Year	5	11	.313	22	22	0	0-0	113	138	90	19	1	61-4	80	5.89	65	.299	.380	45-1-1	.200	2	118	-28		-3.3
	Chi A	4	3	.571	10	10	0	0-0	63.1	58	30	6	0	25-0	40	3.69	118	.252	.323	0	—	0	84	4		0.4
1987	Cle A	5	9	.357	23	14	3	1-3	109	111	76	17	2	63-3	71	5.37	85	.266	.361	0	—	0	107	-10		-1.1
	Min A	1	5	.167	9	7	0		43	54	35	7	2	23-1	20	6.70	69	.310	.397	0	—	0	65	-9		-1.1
	Year	6	14	.300	32	21	3	1-3	152	165	111	24	4	86-4	91	5.74	80	.279	.372	0	—	0	93	-22		-2.2
1988	Min A	0	1	.000	4	1	0	0-0	9.2	20	19	5	0	5-1	5	16.76	24	.408	.463	0	—	0	45	-13		-1.1
Total	24	329	244	.574	741	709	254-55	2-3	5217.2	4672	2130	414	53	1833-150	4136	3.22	116	.240	.306	1719-13-94	.201	48	104	269	73	34.0

CARLYLE, BUDDY Earl L. B12.21.1977 Omaha NE BL/TR/6-3/175* [CinN96 2/38] d8.29

1999	SD N	1	3	.250	7	7	0	0-0	37.2	36	28	7	2	17-0	29	5.97	71	.257	.342	9	.222	1	111	-8		-0.6
2000	SD N	0	0	—	4	0	0	0-0	3	6	7	0	0	3-0	2	21.00	21	.400	.500	0	—	0		-5		-0.2
2005	LA N	0	0	—	10	0	0	0-1	14	16	13	4	1	4-0	13	8.36	49	.291	.350	0	—	0		-6		-0.3
Total	3	1	3	.250	21	7	0	0-1	54.2	58	48	11	3	24-0	44	7.41	57	.274	.356	9	.222	1	111	-19		-1.1

CARMAN, DON Donald Wayne B8.14.1959 Oklahoma City OK BL/TL/6-3/195(190-201) d10.1 Col Seminole St. (OK) JC

1983	Phi N	0	0	—	1	0	0	1-0	1	1	0	0	0	0-0	0	0.00	—	.000	.000	0		0	0	0		0.1
1984	Phi N	0	1	.000	11	0	0	0-0	13.1	14	9	2	0	4-0	16	5.40	68	.255	.328	1	.000	-0		-2		-0.2
1985	Phi N	9	4	.692	71	0	0	7-5	86.1	52	25	6	2	38-3	87	2.08	178	.178	.273	3-0-1	.000	-0		14		2.3
1986	Phi N	10	5	.667	50	14	2-1	1-6	134.1	113	50	11	3	52-11	98	3.22	121	.234	.311	31-0-2	.000	-3	78	12		1.0
1987	Phi N	13	11	.542	35	35	3-2	0-0	211	194	110	34	5	69-7	125	4.22	102	.244	.306	61-0-10	.082	-3	96	2		-0.3
1988	Phi N	10	14	.417	36	32	2	0-0	201.1	211	101	20	4	70-6	116	4.29	84	.270	.330	63-0-8	.048	-3	92	0		-0.3
1989	Phi N	5	15	.250	49	20	0	0-0	149.1	152	98	21	3	86-6	81	5.24	68	.260	.355	34-0-7	.029	-5	95	-12		-2.0
1990	Phi N	6	2	.750	59	1	0	1-1	86.2	69	43	13	4	38-7	58	4.15	93	.218	.301	0	—	-3	83	-26		-3.6
1991	Cin N	0	0	.000	28	0	0	1-0	36	40	23	8	1	19-1	15	5.25	72	.286	.373	5	.273	1	94	-2		-0.1
1992	Tex A	0	0	—	2	0	0	0-0	2.1	3	3	0	0	2-0	2	7.71	50	.364	.364	0	—	0		-5		-0.3
Total	10	53	54	.495	342	102	7-3	11-12	921.2	849	462	115	22	378-45	598	4.11	94	.245	.321	209-0-28	.057	-14	91	-20		-3.2

CARMICHAEL, CHET Chester Keller B1.9.1888 Muncie IN D8.22.1960 Rochester NY BR/TR/5-11.5/200 d9.5

| 1909 | Cin N | 0 | 0 | — | 2 | 0 | 0 | 0 | 7 | 9 | 6 | 0 | 2 | 3 | 2 | 0.00 | — | .321 | .424 | 2 | .000 | -0 | | 1 | | 0.0 |

CARMONA, RAFAEL Rafael B10.2.1972 Rio Piedras, PR BL/TR/6-2/185* [SeaA93 13/353] d5.18 Col Indian Hills (IA) CC [DL 1998 Sea A 181]

1995	Sea A	2	4	.333	15	3	0	1-1	47.2	55	31	9	2	34-1	28	5.66	84	.293	.397	0	—	0	124	-4		-0.4
1996	Sea A	8	3	.727	53	1	0	1-4	90.1	95	47	11	3	55-9	62	4.28	116	.273	.375	0	—	0	75	7		0.7
1997	Sea A	0	0	—	4	0	0	0-0	5.2	3	3	1	0	2-0	6	3.18	143	.150	.227	0	—	0		0		0.0
1999	Sea A	1	0	1.000	9	0	0	0-0	11.1	18	11	3	0	9-1	0	7.94	60	.409	.491	0	—	0		0		0.0
Total	4	11	7	.611	81	4	0	2-5	155	171	92	24	5	100-11	96	4.94	99	.285	.387	0	—	0	109	4	59	-0.3

CARNEY, PAT Patrick Joseph "Doc" B8.7.1876 Holyoke MA D1.9.1953 Worcester MA BL/TL/6-0/200 d9.20.1901 Col Holy Cross ▲

1902	Bos N	0	1	.000	2	1	0	0	5	6	5	1	1	3	3	9.00	31	.300	.417	522-2-4	.270	0*	48	-3		-0.4
1903	Bos N	5	4	.444	10	9	9	0	78	93	52	2	2	31	29	4.04	79	.284	.349	392-1-5	.240	2*	105	-7		-0.5
1904	Bos N	0	4	.000	4	3	1	0	26.1	40	27	1	1	12	5	5.81	47	.364	.431	279-0-8	.204	0*	62	-10		-1.2
Total	3	4	10	.286	16	13	10	0	109.1	139	84	4	4	46	37	4.69	66	.303	.372	1193-3-17	.245	2	95	-20		-2.1

CARPENTER, CHRIS Christopher John B4.27.1975 Exeter NH BR/TR/6-6/215(215-230) [TorA93 1/15] d5.12 [DL 2003 StL N 183]

1997	Tor A	3	7	.300	14	13	1-1	0-0	81.1	108	55	7	2	37-0	55	5.09	90	.325	.394	0		0	71	-6		-0.7
1998	Tor A	12	7	.632	33	24	1-1	0-0	175	177	97	18	5	61-1	136	4.37	107	.265	.329	1	.000	-0	114	4		0.3
1999	Tor A	9	8	.529	24	24	4-1	0-0	150	177	81	16	3	48-1	106	4.38	112	.294	.346	1	.000	0	104	8	25	0.8
2000	Tor A	10	12	.455	34	27	2	0-0	175.1	204	130	30	4	83-1	113	6.26	80	.290	.369	2	.000	0	94	-22		-2.3
2001	Tor A	11	11	.500	34	34	3-2	0-0	215.2	229	112	29	16	75-5	157	4.09	112	.274	.345	6-0-1	.167	-0	107	9		0.8
2002	Tor A	4	5	.444	13	13	1	0-0	73.1	85	45	11	4	27-0	45	5.28	88	.306	.368	1-0-1	1.000	0	85	-5	125	-0.5
2004	StL N	15	5	.750	28	28	1	0-0	182	169	75	20	8	38-2	152	3.46	123	.245	.291	62-0-4	.081	-4	90	17		1.4
2005	†StL N★	21	5	.808	33	33	7-3	0-0	241.2	204	82	18	3	51-0	213	2.83	148	.231	.273	77-0-10	.065	-4	116	39		3.7
Total	8	85	60	.586	213	196	20-9		1294.1	1357	677	153	46	420-10	977	4.26	107	.271	.331	150-0-16	.080	-7	101	44	333	3.5

CARPENTER, CRIS Cris Howell B4.5.1965 St.Augustine FL BR/TR/6-1/185* [StLN87 1/14] d5.14 Col Georgia

1988	StL N	2	3	.400	8	8	1	0-0	47.2	56	27	3	1	9-2	24	4.72	75	.298	.327	14-0-3	.143	-0	101	-6		-0.6
1989	StL N	4	4	.500	36	5	0	0-2	68	70	30	4	2	26-9	35	3.18	115	.262	.328	9-0-2	.444	1	101	2		0.4
1990	StL N	0	0	—	4	0	0	0-0	8	5	4	2	0	2-1	5	4.50	86	.167	.219	1	.000	0		0		0.0
1991	StL N	10	4	.714	59	0	0	0-0	66	53	31	6	4	20-9	47	4.23	89	.220	.278	3	.333	0		-2		-0.4
1992	StL N	5	4	.556	73	0	0	1-7	88	69	29	10	4	27-8	46	2.97	115	.212	.288	3-0-1	.333	0		6		0.6
1993	Fla N	0	1	.000	29	0	0	0-2	37.1	29	15	1	2	13-2	26	2.89	151	.212	.288	0-0-1		0		5		0.6
	Tex A	0	0	—	6	0	0	1-1	32	35	15	4	2	12-1	27	4.22	99	.289	.355	0	—	0		0		0.3
1994	Tex A	2	5	.286	47	0	0	5-6	59	69	34	9	4	20-7	39	5.03	96	.291	.342	0	—	0		0		0.0

YEAR	TM LG	W	L	PCT	G	GS	CG-SHO	SV-BS	IP	H	R	HR	HB	BB-IB	SO	ERA	AERA	OAV	OOB	AB-HR-SH	AVG	PB	SUP	APR	DL	PW
1996	Mil A	0	0	—	8	0	0	0-0	8.1	12	8	1	0	2-0	2	7.56	69	.333	.359	0	—	0		-2		-0.1
Total	8	27	22	.551	291	13	1	7-18	414.1	398	194	38	11	131-39	252	3.91	100	.254	.312	30-0-7	.267	1	94	4		0.3

CARPENTER, LEW Lewis Emmett B8.16.1913 Woodstock GA D4.25.1979 Marietta GA BR/TR/6-2/195 d5.1 Col Georgia Tech

YEAR	TM LG	W	L	PCT	G	GS	CG-SHO	SV-BS	IP	H	R	HR	HB	BB-IB	SO	ERA	AERA	OAV	OOB	AB-HR-SH	AVG	PB	SUP	APR	DL	PW
1943	Was A	0	0	—	4	0	0	0-0	3.1	1	0	0	1	4	1	0.00	—	.125	.462	0		0		1		0.1

CARPENTER, PAUL Paul Calvin B8.12.1894 Granville OH D3.14.1968 Newark OH BR/TR/5-11/165 d7.26

| 1916 | Pit N | 0 | 0 | — | 5 | 0 | 0 | 0-0 | 7.2 | 8 | 3 | 0 | 0 | 4 | 5 | 1.17 | 229 | .258 | .343 | 2 | .000 | -0 | | 1 | | 0.0 |

CARPENTER, BOB Robert Louis B12.12.1917 Chicago IL D10.19.2005 Evergreen Park IL BR/TR/6-3/195 d9.12 Mil 1943-45

YEAR	TM LG	W	L	PCT	G	GS	CG-SHO	SV-BS	IP	H	R	HR	HB	BB-IB	SO	ERA	AERA	OAV	OOB	AB-HR-SH	AVG	PB	SUP	APR	DL	PW
1940	NY N	2	0	1.000	5	3	2	0-0	33	29	11	2	0	14	25	2.73	142	.238	.316	10	.100	-0	127	4		0.2
1941	NY N	11	6	.647	29	19	8-1	2	131.2	138	71	15	2	42	42	3.83	97	.265	.323	45-0-2	.156	-0	128	-5		-0.7
1942	NY N	11	10	.524	28	25	12-2	0	185.2	192	73	13	1	51	53	3.15	107	.263	.312	65-0-6	.185	-1	117	6		-0.4
1946	NY N	1	3	.250	12	6	1-1	0	39	37	22	7	0	18	13	4.85	71	.245	.325	10-0-2	.100	-0	54	-5		-0.5
1947	NY N	0	0	—	2	0	0	0	3	5	5	0	0	3	0	12.00	34	.385	.500	0	—	0		-3		-0.1
	Chi N	0	1	.000	4	1	0	0	7.1	10	5	1	0	4	1	4.91	80	.323	.400	1	1.000	0	45	-1		-0.1
	Year	0	1	.000	6	1	0	0	10.1	15	10	1	0	7	1	6.97	57	.341	.431	1	1.000	0	44	-4		-0.2
Total	5	25	20	.556	80	54	23-4	2	399.2	411	187	38	3	132	134	3.60	98	.262	.321	131-0-10	.168	-1	113	-4		-0.8

CARPIN, FRANK Frank Dominic B9.14.1938 Brooklyn NY BL/TL/5-10/172* d5.25 Col Notre Dame

YEAR	TM LG	W	L	PCT	G	GS	CG-SHO	SV-BS	IP	H	R	HR	HB	BB-IB	SO	ERA	AERA	OAV	OOB	AB-HR-SH	AVG	PB	SUP	APR	DL	PW
1965	Pit N	3	1	.750	39	0	0	4	39.2	35	16	0	3	24-3	27	3.18	111	.243	.360	.000	-0		2		0.3
1966	Hou N	1	0	1.000	10	0	0	0	6	9	7	0	0	6-2	2	7.50	46	.346	.469	0	—	-0		-3		-0.5
Total	2	4	1	.800	49	0	0	4	45.2	44	23	0	3	30-3	29	3.74	93	.259	.377	1	.000	-0		-1		-0.2

CARRARA, GIOVANNI Giovanni (Jimenez) B3.4.1968 Edo Anzoategui, Venez BR/TR/6-2/210(210-235) d7.29

YEAR	TM LG	W	L	PCT	G	GS	CG-SHO	SV-BS	IP	H	R	HR	HB	BB-IB	SO	ERA	AERA	OAV	OOB	AB-HR-SH	AVG	PB	SUP	APR	DL	PW
1995	Tor A	2	4	.333	12	7	1	0-0	48.2	64	46	10	1	25-1	27	7.21	66	.320	.395	0		0	115	-14		-1.5
1996	Tor A	0	1	.000	11	0	0	0-1	15	23	19	5	0	12-2	10	11.40	44	.359	.461	0		0	160	-4		-0.5
	Cin N	1	0	1.000	8	5	0	0-0	23	31	17	6	2	13-1	13	5.87	73	.323	.414	7	.000	-1	65	-4		-0.3
1997	Cin N	0	0	—	2	2	0	0-0	10.1	14	9	4	0	6-1	5	7.84	55	.333	.417	2-0-2	.000	-0	65	-4		-0.3
2000	Col N	0	1	.000	8	0	0	0-1	13.1	21	19	5	1	11-2	15	12.83	45	.356	.458	1	.000	0		-8	32	-0.5
2001	LA N	6	1	.857	47	3	0	0-3	85.1	73	30	12	1	24-3	70	3.16	138	.231	.287	12	.250	1	134	11		0.8
2002	LA N	6	3	.667	63	1	0	1-5	90.2	83	34	14	6	32-4	56	3.28	119	.243	.318	6-0-1	.000	-0	71	-7	20	0.4
2003	Sea A	2	0	1.000	23	0	0	0-0	29	40	22	6	2	14-0	13	6.83	63	.333	.412	0		0		-8		-0.4
2004	†LA N	5	2	.714	42	0	0	2-1	53.2	46	15	1	1	20-3	48	2.18	190	.228	.300	2	.000	-0		12		1.5
2005	LA N	7	4	.636	72	0	0	0-2	75.2	65	35	6	6	38-5	56	3.93	104	.243	.344	1-0-1	.000	-0	128	-16	-52	-0.2
Total	9	29	17	.630	288	18	1	3-13	444.2	460	246	69	20	195-22	313	4.70	90	.269	.349	31-0-4	.097	-1	128	-16		

CARRASCO, D.J. Daniel B4.12.1977 Safford AZ BR/TR/6-1/210* [BalA97 26/795] d4.2 Col Pima (AZ) CC

YEAR	TM LG	W	L	PCT	G	GS	CG-SHO	SV-BS	IP	H	R	HR	HB	BB-IB	SO	ERA	AERA	OAV	OOB	AB-HR-SH	AVG	PB	SUP	APR	DL	PW
2003	KC A	6	5	.545	50	2	0	2-3	80.1	82	44	8	7	40-4	57	4.82	100	.271	.364	2	.000	-0	124	1		0.1
2004	KC A	2	2	.500	30	0	0	0-3	35.1	41	22	5	3	15-3	22	4.84	96	.287	.364	0	—	0		-1		-0.1
2005	KC A	6	8	.429	21	20	1	0-0	114.2	129	67	11	6	51-2	49	4.79	88	.289	.366	7-0-1	.000	-1	98	-8		-0.8
Total	3	14	15	.483	101	22	1	2-6	230.1	252	133	24	16	106-9	128	4.81	93	.283	.365	9-0-1	.000	-1	95	-8		-0.9

CARRASCO, HECTOR Hector (Pacheco) B10.22.1969 San Pedro de Macoris, D.R. BR/TR/6-2/220(175-220) d4.4

YEAR	TM LG	W	L	PCT	G	GS	CG-SHO	SV-BS	IP	H	R	HR	HB	BB-IB	SO	ERA	AERA	OAV	OOB	AB-HR-SH	AVG	PB	SUP	APR	DL	PW
1994	Cin N	5	6	.455	45	0	0	6-2	56.1	42	17	3	2	30-1	41	2.24	187	.210	.319	6	.000	-1		12	20	2.1
1995	†Cin N	2	7	.222	64	0	0	5-4	87.1	86	45	1	2	46-5	64	4.12	101	.257	.344	7	.000	-1		0		-0.1
1996	Cin N	4	3	.571	56	0	0	0-2	74.1	58	37	6	1	45-5	59	3.75	114	.214	.324	5	.200	0		3		0.3
1997	Cin N	1	2	.333	38	0	0	0-0	51.1	51	25	3	4	25-2	46	3.68	116	.250	.342	0	—	0		2		0.1
	KC A	1	6	.143	28	0	0	0-1	34.2	29	21	4	4	16-3	30	5.45	87	.227	.327	0	—	0		4		0.0
1998	Min A	4	2	.667	63	0	0	1-1	61.2	75	30	4	1	31-1	46	4.38	110	.304	.373	0	—	0		1	81	0.2
1999	Min A	2	3	.400	39	0	0	1-1	49	48	29	3	1	18-0	35	4.25	124	.270	.349	0	—	0		7		0.1
2000	Min A	4	3	.571	61	0	0	1-4	72	75	38	6	3	33-0	57	4.25	114	.270	.349	0	—	0	37	-3		-0.2
	Bos A	1	1	.500	8	1	0	0-1	6.2	15	8	2	1	5-1	7	9.45	53	.469	.553	0	—	0	36	0		-0.3
	Year	5	4	.556	69	1	0	1-5	78.2	90	46	8	4	38-1	64	4.69	112	.290	.371	0	—	0	54	-3		-0.5
2001	Min A	4	3	.571	56	0	0	1-1	73.2	77	40	8	0	30-3	70	4.64	101	.277	.344	0	—	0		-1		-0.1
2003	Bal A	2	6	.250	40	0	0	1-2	38.1	40	22	5	2	38-7	27	5.16	93	.270	.365	8-0-2	.000	-1	83	20		1.1
2005	Was N	5	4	.556	64	5	0	2-2	88.1	59	23	6	6	38-7	75	2.04	199	.193	.291	26-0-2	.038	-2	68	43	101	4.3
Total	10	35	46	.432	562	6	0	18-22	693.2	655	335	51	27	337-31	557	3.94	115	.251	.339	45-0-6	.040	-6	68			

CARRASQUEL, ALEX Alejandro Eloy (Aparicio) B7.24.1912 Caracas, Venez D8.19.1969 Caracas, Venez BR/TR/6-1/182 d4.23

YEAR	TM LG	W	L	PCT	G	GS	CG-SHO	SV-BS	IP	H	R	HR	HB	BB-IB	SO	ERA	AERA	OAV	OOB	AB-HR-SH	AVG	PB	SUP	APR	DL	PW
1939	Was A	5	9	.357	40	17	7	0	159.1	165	89	7	1	68	41	4.69	93	.266	.340	42-1-5	.167	1	91	-3		-0.2
1940	Was A	6	2	.750	28	0	0	0	48	42	26	4	0	29	19	4.88	86	.240	.348	7	.000	-1		-2		-0.1
1941	Was A	6	2	.750	35	5	4	2	96.2	103	44	7	1	49	30	3.44	117	.278	.364	21-0-2	.095	0	133	7		0.3
1942	Was A	7	7	.500	35	15	7-1	4	152.1	161	74	7	1	53	40	3.43	107	.267	.327	44-0-4	.136	-0	103	-2		0.0
1943	Was A	11	7	.611	39	13	4-1	5	144.1	140	76	3	1	54	48	3.68	87	.279	.342	43-0-4	.186	1	144	-10		-1.1
1944	Was A	8	7	.533	43	7	3	2	134	143	68	7	0	40	35	3.43	95	.273	.339	36	.194	1	110	-5		-0.3
1945	Was A	7	5	.583	35	7	5-2	1	122.2	105	43	5	0	40	38	2.71	114	.228	.289	36-0-1	.083	-1	145	7		0.6
1949	Chi A	0	0	—	3	0	0	0	3.2	8	6	1	0	4	1	14.73	28	.421	.522	0	—	0		-4		-0.2
Total	8	50	39	.562	258	64	30-4	16	861	887	426	42	6	347	252	3.73	98	.265	.335	229-1-16	.144	0	115	-8		-0.8

CARRENO, AMALIO Amalio Rafael (Adrian) B4.11.1964 Chacachacare, Venez BR/TR/6-0/170 d7.7

| 1991 | Phi N | 0 | 0 | — | 3 | 0 | 0 | 0 | 2 | 3 | 3 | 0 | 2 | 3-0 | 2 | 16.20 | 23 | .333 | .500 | 1 | .000 | | | -4 | | -0.1 |

CARRICK, BILL William Martin "Doughnut Bill" B9.5.1873 Erie PA D3.7.1932 Philadelphia PA TR/5-10/150 d7.30

YEAR	TM LG	W	L	PCT	G	GS	CG-SHO	SV-BS	IP	H	R	HR	HB	BB-IB	SO	ERA	AERA	OAV	OOB	AB-HR-SH	AVG	PB	SUP	APR	DL	PW
1898	NY N	3	1	.750	5	4	4	0	39.2	39	23	0	5	21	10	3.40	102	.255	.363	18	.167	-1	138	0		0.0
1899	NY N	16	27	.372	44	43	40-3	0	361.2	485	250	4	18	122	60	4.65	81	.320	.378	130-0-4	.138	-6	87	-32		-3.2
1900	NY N	19	22	.463	45	41	32-1	0	341.2	415	224	7	13	92	63	3.53	102	.299	.348	115-0-4	.174	-3	97	-2		-0.3
1901	Was A	14	22	.389	42	37	34	0	324	367	198	12	20	93	70	4.86	76	.320	.368	108-0-4	.185	-2*	100	-34		-3.0
1902	Was A	11	17	.393	31	30	28	0	257.2	344	194	10	9	72	36	4.86	76	.320	.368	126-0-3	.159	-5	76	-5		-0.3
Total	5	63	89	.414	167	155	138-4	0	1324.2	1650	889	33	65	400	239	4.14	89	.304	.359	497-0-15	.163	-16	90	-73		-8.9

CARRITHERS, DON Donald George B9.15.1949 Lynwood CA BR/TR/6-2/180* [SFN67 3/58] d8.1

YEAR	TM LG	W	L	PCT	G	GS	CG-SHO	SV-BS	IP	H	R	HR	HB	BB-IB	SO	ERA	AERA	OAV	OOB	AB-HR-SH	AVG	PB	SUP	APR	DL	PW
1970	SF N	2	1	.667	11	1	0	0-0	22	31	19	5	0	14-1	14	7.36	54	.333	.417	6	.000	-0	56	-8		-0.6
1971	†SF N	5	3	.625	22	12	2-1	1-0	80.1	77	48	6	2	37-1	41	4.03	85	.254	.331	17-0-4	.176	0	136	-8		-0.4
1972	SF N	4	8	.333	25	14	2	1-0	90	108	66	10	5	42-4	42	5.80	60	.296	.375	29-0-1	.207	1*	128	-23		-2.0
1973	SF N	1	3	.333	25	3	0	0-1	58	64	40	4	4	35-2	36	4.81	80	.278	.381	16-0-1	.250	0*	84	-8		-0.7
1974	Mon N	5	2	.714	22	3	0	1-1	60	56	22	6	3	17-4	31	3.30	117	.240	.316	14-0-1	.176	0	104	7	35	0.5
1975	Mon N	5	3	.625	19	14	5-2	0-0	101	90	39	7	4	38-1	37	4.43	85	.286	.381	37-0-3	.108	-1*	55	-12		-1.2
1976	Mon N	6	12	.333	34	19	2	0-0	140.1	153	84	9	7	78-13	71	6.91	58	.271	.348	37-0		0		-5	88	-0.5
1977	Min A	0	1	.000	7	1	0	0-0	14.1	16	13	2	1	6-1	5	8.16		.271							123	
Total	8	28	32	.467	165	67	11-3	3-2	566	595	331	47	26	267-27	275	4.45	84	.272	.355	153-0-11	.176	0	97	-51	123	-6.0

CARROLL, CLAY Clay Palmer "Hawk" B5.2.1941 Clanton AL BR/TR/6-1/200(178-205) d9.2

YEAR	TM LG	W	L	PCT	G	GS	CG-SHO	SV-BS	IP	H	R	HR	HB	BB-IB	SO	ERA	AERA	OAV	OOB	AB-HR-SH	AVG	PB	SUP	APR	DL	PW
1964	Mil N	2	0	1.000	11	1	0	1	20.1	15	4	1	0	3-1	17	1.77	199	.200	.231	2	.000	-0	200	4		-0.3
1965	Mil N	1	0	1.000	19	1	0	0	34.2	35	18	3	1	13-2	16	4.41	80	.269	.336	5-0-1	.000	-1	99	-3		-0.2
1966	Atl N	8	7	.533	73	3	0	11	144.1	127	45	8	4	29-4	67	2.37	154	.236	.277	30-0-8	.100	-2	201	19		1.0
1967	Atl N	6	12	.333	42	7	1	0	93	111	60	6	3	29-10	35	5.52	60	.304	.357	16-0-2	.063	-1	113	-22		-2.3
1968	Atl N	0	1	.000	10	0	0	0	22.1	26	15	1	0	6-2	11	4.84	62	.310	.348	5	.000	-0		-5		-0.4
	Cin N	7	7	.500	58	0	0	17	121.2	102	35	3	6	32-10	61	2.29	138	.230	.289	24-0-1	.250	1	27	11		0.3
	Year	7	8	.467	68	1	0	17	144	128	50	4	6	38-12	72	2.69	117	.242	.299	29-0-1	.207	1	28	6		-0.1
1969	Cin N	12	6	.667	71	4	0	7-10	150.1	149	70	9	7	78-18	90	3.52	111	.262	.356	29-1-5	.207	2	183	3		1.4
1970	†Cin N	9	4	.692	65	0	0	16-2	104.1	104	38	4	2	27-9	63	2.59	156	.259	.309	14	.071	-1		15		1.1
1971	Cin N☆	10	4	.714	61	0	0	15-3	93.2	78	26	5	2	42-9	64	2.50	135	.234	.303	11-0-1	.182	0		9		0.4
1972	†Cin N☆	6	4	.600	65	0	0	37-3	96	89	27	5	1	32-9	51	2.25	144	.256	.316	14-0-4	.214	0	87	-5		-0.7
1973	Cin N	8	8	.500	53	5	0	14-4	92.2	111	44	9	5	34-11	46	3.69	93	.307	.372	14-0-4	.167	-0	100	16		0.3
1974	Cin N	12	5	.706	57	3	0	6-3	100.2	96	27	3	0	30-9	46	2.62	137	.255	.315	19-0-2	.000	-0	147	11		1.0
1975	†Cin N	7	5	.583	56	0	0	7-6	96.1	79	30	2	9	32-8	44											

YEAR	TM LG	W	L	PCT	G	GS	CG-SHO	SV-BS	IP	H	R	HR	HB	BB-IB	SO	ERA	AERA	OAV	OOB	AB-HR-SH	AVG	PB	SUP	APR	DL	PW
1976	Chi A	4	4	.500	29	0	0	6-4	77.1	67	26	1	2	24-2	38	2.56	139	.242	.306	0	—	0	8		30	0.9
1977	StL N	4	2	.667	51	1	0	4-4	90	77	28	4	7	24-8	34	2.50	156	.238	.290	11-0-3	.091	-1	68	14		1.0
	Chi A	1	3	.250	7	0	0	1-0	11.1	14	7	3	0	4-0	4	4.76	86	.311	.367	0	—	0		-1		-0.2
1978	Pit N	0	0	—	4	0	0	0-0	4.2	2	1	0	0	3-0	0	2.25	166	.143	.294	0	—	0		1		0.0
Total	15	96	73	.568	731	28	1	143-39	1353.1	1296	506	67	37	442-112	681	2.94	121	.257	.319	208-1-30	.130	-5	127	87	30	12.2

CARROLL, ED Edgar Fleischer B7.27.1907 Baltimore MD D10.13.1984 Rossville MD BR/TR/6-3/185 d5.1

YEAR	TM LG	W	L	PCT	G	GS	CG-SHO	SV-BS	IP	H	R	HR	HB	BB-IB	SO	ERA	AERA	OAV	OOB	AB-HR-SH	AVG	PB	SUP	APR	DL	PW
1929	Bos A	1	0	1.000	24	1	0	0-0	67.1	77	46	4	2	20	13	5.61	76	.291	.349	16-0-3	.063	-2	99	-8		-0.6

CARROLL, OWNIE Owen Thomas B11.11.1902 Kearny NJ D6.8.1975 Orange NJ BR/TR/5-10.5/165 d6.20 Col Holy Cross

YEAR	TM LG	W	L	PCT	G	GS	CG-SHO	SV-BS	IP	H	R	HR	HB	BB-IB	SO	ERA	AERA	OAV	OOB	AB-HR-SH	AVG	PB	SUP	APR	DL	PW
1925	Det A	2	2	.500	10	4	1	0	40.2	46	30	1	2	28	12	3.76	114	.293	.406	16	.375	1*	112	-2		-0.1
1927	Det A	10	6	.625	31	15	8	0	172	186	99	5	6	73	41	3.98	106	.281	.358	69-0-1	.174	-2*	110	3		0.1
1928	Det A	16	12	.571	34	28	19-2	2	231	219	100	6	7	87	51	3.27	126	.262	.337	98-0-9	.194	-0*	95	22		2.5
1929	Det A	9	17	.346	34	26	12	1	202	249	133	10	8	86	54	4.63	93	.310	.383	74-0-2	.230	2*	94	-11		-0.9
1930	Det A	0	5	.000	6	3	0	0	20.1	30	24	3	0	9	4	10.62	45	.333	.394	7	.143	-1	66	-11		-1.8
	NY A	0	1	.000	10	1	0	0	32.2	49	32	2	4	18	8	6.61	65	.374	.464	10-0-1	.200	0*	140	-10		-0.4
	Year	0	6	.000	16	4	0	0	53	79	56	5	4	27	12	8.15	55	.357	.437	17-0-1	.176	-0	86	-21		-2.2
	Cin N	0	0	—	3	2	1	0	14	17	9	3	0	3	0	4.50	107	.309	.345	5	.200	-0	45	0		0.0
1931	Cin N	3	9	.250	29	12	4	0	107.1	135	76	6	4	51	24	5.53	67	.314	.392	34-0-1	.206	0*	86	-21		-2.0
1932	Cin N	10	19	.345	32	26	15	1	210	245	124	7	9	44	55	4.50	86	.286	.328	77-0-2	.208	2*	76	-14		-1.5
1933	Bro N	13	15	.464	33	31	11	0	226.1	248	117	9	7	54	45	3.78	85	.281	.327	74-0-4	.149	-1*	112	-16		-1.7
1934	Bro N	1	3	.250	26	5	0	1	74.1	108	64	9	1	33	17	6.42	61	.342	.406	25	.240	-1*	115	-22		-0.8
Total	9	64	90	.416	248	153	71-2	5	1330.2	1532	808	61	48	486	311	4.43	89	.294	.359	489-0-20	.200	2	95	-82		-6.6

CARROLL, DICK Richard Thomas "Shadow" B7.21.1884 Cleveland OH D11.22.1945 Cleveland OH BR/TR/6-2/? d9.25

YEAR	TM LG	W	L	PCT	G	GS	CG-SHO	SV-BS	IP	H	R	HR	HB	BB-IB	SO	ERA	AERA	OAV	OOB	AB-HR-SH	AVG	PB	SUP	APR	DL	PW
1909	NY A	0	0	—	2	1	0	0	5	7	6	1	0	1	1	3.60	70	.292	.320	2	.500		307	-2		-0.1

CARROLL, TOM Thomas Michael B11.5.1952 Utica NY BL/TR/6-3/190* [CinN70 6/138] d7.7

YEAR	TM LG	W	L	PCT	G	GS	CG-SHO	SV-BS	IP	H	R	HR	HB	BB-IB	SO	ERA	AERA	OAV	OOB	AB-HR-SH	AVG	PB	SUP	APR	DL	PW
1974	Cin N	4	3	.571	16	13	0	0-0	78.1	68	44	11	0	44-3	37	3.68	95	.231	.331	26-0-2	.154	-1	123	-5		-0.5
1975	Cin N	4	1	.800	12	7	0	0-0	47	52	28	1	2	26-0	14	4.98	72	.284	.379	14	.000	-2	116	-7		-0.9
Total	2	8	4	.667	28	20	0	0-0	125.1	120	72	12	2	70-3	51	4.16	85	.252	.350	40-0-2	.100	-4	120	-12		-1.4

CARSEY, KID Wilfred B10.22.1870 New York NY D3.29.1960 Miami FL BL/TR/5-7/168 d4.8

YEAR	TM LG	W	L	PCT	G	GS	CG-SHO	SV-BS	IP	H	R	HR	HB	BB-IB	SO	ERA	AERA	OAV	OOB	AB-HR-SH	AVG	PB	SUP	APR	DL	PW
1891	Was AA	14	37	.275	54	53	46-1	0	415	513	358	17	28	161	174	4.99	75	.293	.362	187	.150	-5*	79	-49		-4.7
1892	Phi N	19	16	.543	43	36	30-1	1	317.2	317	160	6	12	104	76	3.12	104	.250	.312	131-1	.153	-3*	109	7		0.4
1893	Phi N	20	15	.571	39	35	30-1	0	318.1	375	229	7	19	124	50	4.81	95	.285	.355	145	.186	-7	110	-7		-1.2
1894	Phi N	18	12	.600	37	32	26	0	288.1	366	241	22	18	106	43	5.52	93	.306	.371	129-0-1	.279	4	136	-12		-0.5
1895	Phi N	24	16	.600	44	40	35	1	342.1	460	274	14	21	118	64	4.92	97	.317	.376	141-0-11	.291	3	124	-13		-0.9
1896	Phi N	11	11	.500	27	21	18-1	1	187.1	273	164	4	9	72	36	5.62	77	.337	.397	81-0-3	.222	1	130	-29		-2.3
1897	Phi N	2	1	.667	4	4	3	0	28	35	20	0	1	16	1	5.14	82	.304	.394	13-0-1	.231	-1	153	-2		-0.3
	StL N	3	8	.273	12	11	11	0	99	133	81	5	4	31	14	6.00	73	.319	.372	43	.302	2*	74	-13		-0.9
	Year	5	9	.357	16	15	13	0	127	168	101	5	5	47	15	5.81	75	.316	.377	56-0-1	.286	2	94	-16		-1.2
1898	StL N	2	12	.143	20	13	10	0	123.2	177	112	2	10	37	10	6.33	60	.333	.387	105-1-4	.200	-0*	72	-30		-2.7
1899	Cle N	1	8	.111	10	9	8	0	77.2	109	66	2	2	24	11	5.68	65	.330	.379	36	.278	1*	89	-17		-1.3
	Was N	1	2	.333	4	3	2	0	29	27	14	0	1	4	3	3.72	105	.248	.281	11-0-1	.000	-2	92	1		0.0
	Year	2	10	.167	14	12	10	0	106.2	136	80	2	3	28	14	5.15	73	.310	.355	47-0-1	.213	-1	90	-13		-1.3
1901	Bro N	1	0	1.000	2	0	0	0	7	9	9	1	1	3	1	10.29	33	.310	.394	2	.000	-0		-5		-0.5
Total	10	116	138	.457	296	257	218-4	3	2233.1	2794	1728	80	126	800	486	4.95	85	.300	.363	1024-2-21	.212	-8	108-169		-14.9

CARSON, AL Albert James "Soldier" B8.22.1882 Chicago IL D11.26.1962 San Diego CA BR/TR/5-10.5/162 d5.6 Col Santa Clara

YEAR	TM LG	W	L	PCT	G	GS	CG-SHO	SV-BS	IP	H	R	HR	HB	BB-IB	SO	ERA	AERA	OAV	OOB	AB-HR-SH	AVG	PB	SUP	APR	DL	PW
1910	Chi N	0	0	—	2	0	0	0	6.2	6	5	0	0	1	2	4.05	71	.240	.269	1	.000	0		-1		-0.1

CARTER, ANDY Andrew Godfrey B11.9.1968 Philadelphia PA BL/TL/6-5/200(200-220) [PhiN87 37/952] d5.3

YEAR	TM LG	W	L	PCT	G	GS	CG-SHO	SV-BS	IP	H	R	HR	HB	BB-IB	SO	ERA	AERA	OAV	OOB	AB-HR-SH	AVG	PB	SUP	APR	DL	PW
1994	Phi N	0	2	.000	20	0	0	0-0	34.1	34	18	5	6	12-2	18	4.46	96	.268	.351	6	.000	-1	0			-0.1
1995	Phi N	0	0	—	4	0	0	0-0	7.1	4	5	3	1	2-1	6	6.14	69	.167	.250	1	1.000	0		-1		0.0
Total	2	0	2	.000	24	0	0	0-0	41.2	38	23	8	7	14-3	24	4.75	90	.252	.335	7	.143	-0		-1		-0.1

CARTER, ARNOLD Arnold Lee "Hook","Lefty" B3.14.1918 Rainelle WV D4.12.1989 Louisville KY BL/TL/5-10/170 d4.29

YEAR	TM LG	W	L	PCT	G	GS	CG-SHO	SV-BS	IP	H	R	HR	HB	BB-IB	SO	ERA	AERA	OAV	OOB	AB-HR-SH	AVG	PB	SUP	APR	DL	PW
1944	Cin N	11	7	.611	33	18	9-3	3	148.2	143	54	1	3	40	33	2.60	134	.256	.309	48-2-2	.250	5*	91	13		2.2
1945	Cin N	2	4	.333	13	6	2-1	0	46.2	54	21	2	2	13	4	3.09	122	.286	.338	17	.176	0*	38	2		0.3
Total	2	13	11	.542	46	24	11-4	3	195.1	197	75	3	5	53	37	2.72	131	.264	.317	65-2-2	.231	5	77	15		2.5

CARTER, NICK Conrad Powell B5.19.1879 Oatlands VA D11.23.1961 Grasonville MD BR/TR/5-8/140 d4.14 Col Virginia

YEAR	TM LG	W	L	PCT	G	GS	CG-SHO	SV-BS	IP	H	R	HR	HB	BB-IB	SO	ERA	AERA	OAV	OOB	AB-HR-SH	AVG	PB	SUP	APR	DL	PW
1908	Phi A	2	5	.286	14	4	2	0	60.2	58	26	1	2	17	17	2.97	86	.270	.329	20	.100	-2	40	-2		-0.3

CARTER, JEFF Jeffrey Allen B12.3.1964 Tampa FL BR/TR/6-3/195 [MonN87 19/486] d7.31 Col Tampa

YEAR	TM LG	W	L	PCT	G	GS	CG-SHO	SV-BS	IP	H	R	HR	HB	BB-IB	SO	ERA	AERA	OAV	OOB	AB-HR-SH	AVG	PB	SUP	APR	DL	PW
1991	Chi A	0	1	.000	5	2	0	0-0	12	8	8	1	0	5-0	2	5.25	76	.182	.265	0	—	0	160	-2		-0.2

CARTER, LANCE Lance David B12.18.1974 Bradenton FL BR/TR/6-1/190* [KCA94 21/583] d9.15 Col Manatee (FL) CC

YEAR	TM LG	W	L	PCT	G	GS	CG-SHO	SV-BS	IP	H	R	HR	HB	BB-IB	SO	ERA	AERA	OAV	OOB	AB-HR-SH	AVG	PB	SUP	APR	DL	PW
1999	KC A	0	1	.000	6	0	0	0-0	5.1	3	3	2	0	3-0	3	5.06	100	.167	.286	0	—	0		0		0.0
2002	TB A	2	0	1.000	8	0	0	2-0	20.1	15	3	2	0	5-1	14	1.33	340	.203	.253	0	—	0		7		0.8
2003	TB A☆	7	5	.583	62	0	0	26-7	79	72	39	12	4	19-6	47	4.33	106	.242	.291	0	—	0		3		0.5
2004	TB A	3	3	.500	56	0	0	0-1	80.1	77	32	12	1	23-2	36	3.47	134	.252	.301	0	—	0		12		0.7
2005	TB A	1	2	.333	39	0	0	1-3	57	61	31	9	1	15-1	22	4.89	89	.279	.324	0	—	0		-2		-0.1
Total	5	13	11	.542	171	0	0	29-11	242	228	108	37	6	65-10	122	3.94	116	.249	.299	0	—	0		20		1.9

CARTER, LARRY Larry Gene B5.22.1965 Charleston WV BR/TR/6-5/195 [StLN86 10/260] d9.6 Col West Virginia St.

YEAR	TM LG	W	L	PCT	G	GS	CG-SHO	SV-BS	IP	H	R	HR	HB	BB-IB	SO	ERA	AERA	OAV	OOB	AB-HR-SH	AVG	PB	SUP	APR	DL	PW
1992	SF N	1	5	.167	14	6	0	0-0	33	34	17	6	0	18-0	21	4.64	72	.270	.359	10-0-1	.200	1	68	-4		-0.7

CARTER, PAUL Paul Warren "Nick" B5.1.1894 Lake Park GA D9.11.1984 Lake Park GA BL/TR/6-3/175 d9.15 Col Rhodes

YEAR	TM LG	W	L	PCT	G	GS	CG-SHO	SV-BS	IP	H	R	HR	HB	BB-IB	SO	ERA	AERA	OAV	OOB	AB-HR-SH	AVG	PB	SUP	APR	DL	PW
1914	Cle A	1	3	.250	5	4	1	0	24.2	35	15	0	0	5	9	2.92	99	.340	.370	7	.000	-1	69	-1		-0.3
1915	Cle A	1	1	.500	11	2	2	0	42	44	22	1	0	18	14	3.21	95	.272	.344	14-0-1	.214	1*	72	-1		0.0
1916	Chi N	2	2	.500	8	5	2	0	36	26	16	1	0	17	14	2.75	106	.203	.297	12-0-1	.167	-0	98	0		0.0
1917	Chi N	5	8	.385	23	13	6	2	113.1	115	47	2	3	19	34	3.26	89	.276	.313	35-0-1	.171	-0	76	-1		-0.2
1918	Chi N	3	2	.600	21	4	1	2	73	78	29	2	1	19	13	2.71	103	.290	.339	25	.240	-1	129	1		0.2
1919	Chi N	5	4	.556	28	7	2	1	85	81	36	1	2	28	17	2.65	109	.252	.316	26	.269	1*	110	1		0.1
1920	Chi N	3	6	.333	31	8	2	2	106	131	68	3	5	36	14	4.67	69	.324	.387	35-0-1	.171	-1	101	-17		-1.7
Total	7	20	26	.435	127	43	16	7	480	510	233	10	11	142	115	3.32	89	.283	.339	154-0-4	.195	-1	144	-16		-1.5

CARTER, SOL Solomon Mobley "Buck" B12.23.1908 Picayune MS BR/TR/6-0/178 d4.15 Col Auburn-Montgomery

YEAR	TM LG	W	L	PCT	G	GS	CG-SHO	SV-BS	IP	H	R	HR	HB	BB-IB	SO	ERA	AERA	OAV	OOB	AB-HR-SH	AVG	PB	SUP	APR	DL	PW
1931	Phi A	0	0	—	2	0	0	0	4	8	9	1	0	4	1	19.29	23	.143	.455	0	—	0		-3		-0.1

CARUTHERS, BOB Robert Lee "Parisian Bob" B1.5.1864 Memphis TN D8.5.1911 Peoria IL BL/TR/5-7/138 d9.7 M1/U2 ▲

YEAR	TM LG	W	L	PCT	G	GS	CG-SHO	SV-BS	IP	H	R	HR	HB	BB-IB	SO	ERA	AERA	OAV	OOB	AB-HR-SH	AVG	PB	SUP	APR	DL	PW
1884	StL AA	7	2	.778	13	7	7	0	82.2	61	34	2	3	15	58	2.61	125	.189	.232	82-2	.268	2*	122	9		0.9
1885	†StL AA	40	13	.755	53	53	53-6	0	482.1	430	196	3	19	57	190	2.07	158	.230	.260	222-1	.225	6*	103	61		6.3
1886	†StL AA	30	14	.682	44	43	42-2	0	387.1	323	164	3	7	86	166	2.32	148	.217	.263	317-4	.334	26*	113	51		7.2
1887	†StL AA	29	9	.763	39	39	39-2	0	341	337	185	6	16	61	74	3.30	138	.247	.287	364-8	.357	20*	122	45		5.9
1888	Bro AA	29	15	.659	44	43	42-4	0	391.2	337	176	4	10	53	140	2.39	125	.224	.255	335-5	.230	10*	112	28		3.7
1889	†Bro AA	40	11	.784	56	50	46-7	1	445	444	215	16	13	104	118	3.13	119	.252	.298	172-2	.250	17*	123	33		4.6
1890	†Bro N	23	11	.676	37	33	30-1	0	300	292	163	9	12	87	64	3.09	112	.247	.305	238-1	.265	11*	100	12		2.2
1891	Bro N	18	14	.563	38	32	29-2	1	297	323	185	7	13	107	69	3.12	106	.267	.333	171-2	.281	11*	111	-1		1.0
1892	StL N	2	10	.167	16	10	10	1	101.2	131	75	1	6	27	21	5.84	55	.300	.350	513-3	.277	6*	55	-23		-1.8
Total	9	218	99	.688	340	310	298-24	3	2828.2	2678	1393	59	99	597	900	2.83	123	.240	.285	2414-28	.282	111	112	215		30.0

CARVAJAL, MARCOS Marcos Jose (Rendon) B8.19.1984 Ciudad Bolivar, Venez BR/TR/6-4/175 d4.6

YEAR	TM LG	W	L	PCT	G	GS	CG-SHO	SV-BS	IP	H	R	HR	HB	BB-IB	SO	ERA	AERA	OAV	OOB	AB-HR-SH	AVG	PB	SUP	APR	DL	PW
2005	Col N	0	2	.000	39	0	0	0-1	53	52	30	8	3	21-0	47	5.09	93	.259	.335	4	.250	0		-1		0.0

YEAR	TM LG	W	L	PCT	G	GS	CG-SHO	SV-BS	IP	H	R	HR	HB	BB-IB	SO	ERA	AERA	OAV	OOB	AB-HR-SH	AVG	PB	SUP	APR	DL	PV

CARY, CHUCK Charles Douglas B3.3.1960 Whittier CA BL/TL/6-4/210* [DetA81 7/172] d8.22 Col California-Davis

1985	Det A	0	1	.000	16	0	0	2-1	23.2	16	9	2	2	8-1	22	3.42	120	.190	.274	0	—	0	2			0.
1986	Det A	1	2	.333	22	0	0	0-1	31.2	33	18	3	0	15-4	21	3.41	122	.273	.348	0	—	-0	1			0.
1987	Atl N	1	1	.500	13	0	0	1-1	16.2	17	7	3	1	4-3	15	3.78	115	.266	.319	1	.000	0	-2	129		0.
1988	Atl N	0	0	—	7	0	0	0-0	8.1	8	6	1	1	4-0	7	6.48	57	.250	.351	0	—	0	-2			0.
1989	NY A	4	4	.500	22	11	2	0-0	99.1	78	42	13	0	29-6	79	3.26	119	.209	.266	0	—	0	99	6	26	-0.
1990	NY A	6	12	.333	28	27	2	0-0	156.2	155	77	21	4	55-1	134	4.19	95	.260	.321	0	—	0	76	-2	36	-0.
1991	NY A	1	6	.143	10	9	0	0-0	53.1	61	35	6	0	32-2	34	5.91	71	.285	.378	0	—	0	76	-9		-1.
1993	Chi A	1	0	1.000	16	0	0	0-0	20.2	22	12	1	3	11-0	10	5.23	81	.286	.379	0	—	0	-2	127		-0.
Total	8	14	26	.350	134	47	4	3-3	410.1	390	206	50	8	158-17	322	4.17	97	.250	.319	1	.000	-0	81	-5	318	-0.

CARY, SCOTT Scott Russell "Red" B4.11.1923 Kendallville IN BL/TL/5-11.5/168 d5.1

| 1947 | Was A | 3 | 1 | .750 | 23 | 3 | 1 | 0 | 54.2 | 73 | 38 | 5 | 1 | 20 | 25 | 5.93 | 63 | .312 | .369 | 13-0-1 | .077 | -1 | 119 | -12 | | -0. |

CASALE, JERRY Jerry Joseph B9.27.1933 Brooklyn NY BR/TR/6-2/200* d9.14

1958	Bos A	0	0	—	2	0	0	0	3	1	0	0	0	2-0	3	0.00	—	.111	.273	0	—	0	1			0.
1959	Bos A	13	8	.619	31	26	9-3	0	179.2	162	89	20	5	89-3	93	4.31	94	.238	.329	59-3-4	.169	3	110	-2		-0.
1960	Bos A	2	9	.182	29	14	1	0	96.1	113	78	14	1	67-5	54	6.17	66	.294	.394	33	.273	3	87	-24		-2.
1961	LA A	1	5	.167	13	7	0	1	42.2	52	34	9	1	25-0	35	6.54	69	.297	.386	13-1-0	.462	3	56	-8		-0.
	Det A	0	0	—	3	1	0	0	12	15	8	3	0	3-0	6	5.25	78	.313	.353	3	.000	-0	108	-1		-0.
	Year	1	5	.167	16	8	0	1	54.2	67	42	12	1	28-0	41	6.26	71	.300	.379	16-1-0	.375	3	63	-10		-0.
1962	Det A	1	2	.333	18	1	0	0	36.2	33	19	5	0	18-1	16	4.66	87	.236	.321	8	.222	-1	88	-1		-0.
Total	5	17	24	.415	96	49	10-3	1	370.1	376	228	51	7	204-9	207	5.08	81	.262	.354	116-4-4	.216	7	95	-35		-3.

CASCARELLA, JOE Joseph Thomas "Crooning Joe" B6.28.1907 Philadelphia PA D5.22.2002 Baltimore MD BR/TR/5-10.5/175 d4.17

1934	Phi A	12	15	.444	42	22	9-2	1	194.1	214	111	8	3	104	71	4.68	94	.288	.377	64-0-3	.094	-4	86	-5		-0.
1935	Phi A	1	6	.143	9	3	1	0	32.1	29	21	1	0	22	15	5.29	86	.252	.372	8-0-2	.125	-3	32	-2		-0.
	Bos A	0	3	.000	6	4	0	0	17	25	17	3	0	11	9	6.88	69	.329	.414	2-0-1	.000	-0	78	-4		-0.
	Year	1	9	.100	15	7	1	0	49.1	54	38	4	0	33	24	5.84	79	.283	.388	10-0-3	.100	-1	59	-7		-1.
1936	Bos A	0	2	.000	10	1	0	0	20.2	27	16	0	0	9	7	6.97	76	.329	.396	4	.000	-1	265	-3		1
	Was A	9	8	.529	22	16	7-1	1	139.1	147	66	7	6	54	34	4.07	117	.276	.349	49-0-4	.143	-2	113	15		1
	Year	9	10	.474	32	17	7-1	1	160	174	82	7	6	63	41	4.44	109	.283	.355	53-0-4	.132	-3	122	12		0
1937	Was A	0	5	.000	10	4	1	1	32.1	50	41	3	1	23	10	8.07	55	.347	.440	9	.222	-1	59	-17		-0
	Cin N	1	2	.333	11	3	2	1	43.2	44	24	1	0	22	16	3.92	95	.263	.349	11	.091	-1	116	-5		-1
1938	Cin N	4	7	.364	33	1	0	8	61	66	33	2	0	30	30	4.57	80	.275	.336	18	.167	-1	54	-2		-0
Total	5	27	48	.360	143	54	20-3	8	540.2	602	329	25	10	267	192	4.84	91	.287	.370	165-0-10	.121	-9	93	-23		-4

CASE, CHARLIE Charles Emmett B9.7.1879 Smith Landing OH D4.16.1964 Batavia OH BR/TR/6-0/170 d7.5

1901	Cin N	1	2	.333	3	3	3	0	27	34	21	0	0	4	5	4.67	69	.306	.342	10	.100	-1	66	-5		-0
1904	Pit N	10	5	.667	18	17	14-3	0	141	129	56	0	4	31	57	2.94	93	.243	.290	53	.170	1	118	-1		0
1905	Pit N	11	11	.500	31	24	18-3	1	217	202	81	2	15	66	57	2.57	117	.251	.319	68-0-1	.103	-2	79	10		0
1906	Pit N	1	1	.500	2	2	1	0	11	8	9	0	1	5	3	5.73	47	.190	.292	2	.500	1	95	1		-0
Total	4	23	19	.548	54	46	36-6	1	396	373	167	2	20	108	114	2.93	99	.251	.310	133-0-1	.135	-1	95	1		

CASEY, DAN Daniel Maurice B11.20.1862 Binghamton NY D2.8.1943 Washington DC BR/TR/6-0/180 d8.18 b-Dennis

1884	Wil U	1	1	.500	2	2	2	0	18	23	17	0		4	10	1.00	267	.291	.325	6	.167	-1	32	1		0
1885	Det N	4	8	.333	12	12	12-1	0	104	105	61	1		35	79	3.29	86	.256	.315	43	.116	-3	90	-2		-0
1886	Phi N	24	18	.571	44	44	39-4	0	369	326	169	9		104	193	2.41	136	.223	.275	151	.152	-5	95	37		3
1887	Phi N	28	13	.683	45	45	43-4	0	390.1	377	199	15	14	115	119	3.15	94	.259	.291	118	.153	-4	76	-3		-0
1888	Phi N	14	18	.438	33	33	31-2	0	285.2	298	156	6	5	48	65	3.77	115	.273	.356	68	.221	-2	74	10		-1
1889	Phi N	6	10	.375	20	20	15-1	0	152.2	170	92	4	8	72	65	4.14	85	.255	.337	68	.162	-4*	98	-35		-3
1890	Syr AA	19	22	.463	45	42	40-2	0	360.2	365	249	8	14	165	169	3.18	113	.249	.309	160	.162	-4*	98	-35		-3
Total	7	96	90	.516	201	198	182-14	0	1680.1	1664	943	43	41	543	743	3.18	113	.249	.309	710-1	.162	-28	88	65		

CASEY, HUGH Hugh Thomas B10.14.1913 Atlanta GA D7.3.1951 Atlanta GA BR/TR/6-1/207 d4.29 Mil 1943-45

1935	Chi N	0	0	—	13	0	0	0	25.2	29	13	2	0	14	9	3.86	102	.279	.364	6	.167	-0	0			0
1939	Bro N	15	10	.600	40	25	15	1	227.1	228	88	13	11	54	79	2.93	137	.260	.311	74-0-10	.203	1	101	25		-0
1940	Bro N	11	8	.579	44	10	5-2	5	154	136	63	13	6	51	53	3.62	110	.237	.306	36-0-8	.250	2*	130	9		
1941	†Bro N	14	11	.560	45	18	4-1	7	162	155	81	8	1	57	61	3.89	94	.251	.316	50-0-5	.120	-1	96	-4		-0
1942	Bro N	6	3	.667	50	2	0	13	112	91	32	3	2	44	54	2.25	145	.221	.300	27-0-4	.148	-0	51	13		
1946	Bro N	11	5	.688	46	1	0	5	99.2	101	31	2	2	33	31	1.99	170	.267	.329	22-0-5	.136	-1	101	14		
1947	†Bro N	10	4	.714	46	0	0	18	76.2	75	36	7	2	29	40	3.99	104	.260	.331	18-0-2	.056	-1	2			
1948	Pit N	3	0	1.000	22	0	0	4	36	59	36	6	2	17	7	8.00	50	.391	.459	7-0-1	.000	-1	-16	60		
1949	Bro N	4	1	.800	33	0	0	5	38.2	50	24	4	1	14	14	4.66	90	.314	.374	3-0-1	.333	-0	-3			
	NY A	1	0	1.000	4	0	0	0	7.2	11	10	0	0	8	5	8.22	49	.324	.452	1	.000	-0	-5			
Total	9	75	42	.641	343	56	24-3	55	939.2	935	414	58	27	321	349	3.45	110	.260	.325	244-0-36	.164	-2	105	35	60	

CASEY, BILL William B. B St.Louis MO d8.17

| 1887 | Phi AA | 0 | 1 | .000 | 1 | 0 | 0 | 0 | 1 | 4 | 3 | 0 | 0 | 1 | 0 | 18.00 | 24 | .667 | .714 | 0 | — | 0 | -2 | | | |

CASHION, CARL Jay Carl B6.6.1891 Mecklenburg Co. NC D11.17.1935 Lake Millicent WI BL/TR/6-2/200 d8.4 Col Erskine

1911	Was A	1	5	.167	11	9	5	0	71.1	67	45	4	7	47	26	4.16	79	.220	.338	37-0-1	.324	2*	51	-6		-0
1912	Was A	10	6	.625	26	17	13-1	1	170.1	150	84	4	5	103	84	3.17	105	.250	.365	103-2-1	.214	2*	109	4		-0
1913	Was A	1	1	.500	4	3	0	0	9	7	11	0	3	14	7	6.00	49	.333	.632	12	.250	0*	134	-4		-0
1914	Was A	0	1	.000	2	1	0	0	5	4	7	0	1	6	1	10.80	26	.250	.478	1	.000	-0	52	-4		-0
Total	4	12	13	.480	43	30	18-1	1	255.2	228	147	8	16	170	114	3.70	89	.243	.368	153-2-2	.242	5	91	-10		-0

CASIAN, LARRY Lawrence Paul B10.28.1965 Lynwood CA BR/TL/6-0/170* [MinA87 6/139] d9.9 Col Cal St.-Fullerton

1990	Min A	2	1	.667	5	3	0	0-0	22.1	26	14	4	0	4-0	11	3.22	129	.306	.333	0	—	0	95	2		0
1991	Min A	0	0	—	15	0	0	0-0	18.1	28	16	4	1	7-2	6	7.36	58	.354	.414	0	—	0	-6			
1992	Min A	1	0	1.000	6	0	0	0-0	6.2	7	2	0	0	1-0	2	2.70	151	.259	.286	0	—	0	1			
1993	Min A	5	3	.625	54	0	0	1-2	56.2	59	23	1	1	14-2	31	3.02	146	.268	.311	0	—	0	8	44		
1994	Min A	1	3	.250	33	0	0	1-0	40.2	57	34	11	2	12-2	18	7.08	70	.343	.390	0	—	0	-4			
	Cle A	0	2	.000	7	0	0	0-0	8.1	16	9	1	0	4-1	2	8.64	55	.421	.476	0	—	0	-12			
	Year	1	5	.167	40	0	0	1-0	49	73	43	12	2	16-3	20	7.35	67	.358	.406	2	.000	-0	6	48		
1995	Chi N	1	0	1.000	42	0	0	0-3	23.1	23	6	1	0	15-6	11	1.93	216	.258	.358	0	—	0	7			
1996	Chi N	0	1	.000	35	0	0	0-1	24	14	5	2	1	11-3	15	1.88	233	.187	.295	1	.000	-0	-3	15		
1997	Chi N	0	1	.000	12	0	0	0-0	9.2	16	9	3	1	2-1	7	7.45	58	.364	.388	1	—	0	0			
	KC A	0	2	.000	32	0	0	0-2	26.2	32	15	5	0	6-1	16	5.06	94	.299	.333	0	—	0	-3			
1998	Chi A	0	0	—	4	0	0	0-0	4	8	5	0	2	1-0	6	11.25	41	.400	.478	0	.000	-0	95	-1	107	
Total	9	11	13	.458	245	3	0	2-8	240.2	286	133	30	8	77-18	125	4.56	98	.301	.354	0	.000	-0	95	-1	107	

CASKEY, CRAIG Craig Douglas B12.11.1949 Visalia CA BB/TL/5-11/185 [MonN72 S1/12] d7.19 Col Puget Sound

| 1973 | Mon N | 0 | 0 | — | 9 | 0 | 0 | 0-0 | 14.1 | 11 | 13 | 1 | 1 | 14-3 | 6 | 5.65 | 80 | .278 | .339 | 1-0-1 | .000 | -0 | 139 | -3 | | |

CASSIAN, ED Edward T. B11.28.1867 Wilbraham MA D9.10.1918 Meriden CT TR/5-8/160 d6.26

1891	Phi N	1	3	.250	6	4	3	0	38	40	20	0	3	16	10	2.84	120	.260	.341	17	.118	-1	57	2		
	Was AA	2	4	.333	7	5	5	0	53	73	63	4	5	35	14	5.60	67	.316	.417	26	.346	2	133	-13		
Total	3	7	7	.300	13	9	8	0	91	113	83	4	8	51	24	4.45	81	.294	.387	43	.256	1	100	-11		

CASSIDY, JOHN John P. B1857 Brooklyn NY D7.2.1891 Brooklyn NY BR/TL/5-8/168 d4.24 ▲

| 1875 | Atl NA | 1 | 21 | .045 | 30 | 22 | 18 | 0 | 213.2 | 284 | 242 | 3 | | 11 | 9 | 3.03 | 69 | .277 | .285 | 166-1 | .175 | -3* | 47 | -27 | | |
| 1877 | Har N | 1 | 1 | .500 | 2 | 2 | 2 | 0 | 18 | 24 | 11 | 0 | | 3 | 5.00 | 49 | .320 | .329 | 251 | .378 | 1* | 170 | -3 | | |

CASSIDY, SCOTT Scott Robert B10.3.1975 Syracuse NY BR/TR/6-2/175* d4.1 Col LeMoyne (NY)

| 2002 | Tor A | 1 | 4 | .200 | 58 | 0 | 0 | 0-7 | 66 | 52 | 42 | 12 | 7 | 32-3 | 48 | 5.73 | 81 | .222 | .327 | 0 | — | 0 | -6 | | | |
| 2005 | Bos A | 0 | 0 | — | 1 | 0 | 0 | 0-0 | 0.2 | 4 | 3 | 0 | 0 | 0-0 | 0 | 40.50 | 11 | .667 | .667 | 0 | — | 0 | -2 | | | |

YEAR	TM LG	W	L	PCT	G	GS	CG-SHO	SV-BS	IP	H	R	HR	HB	BB-IB	SO	ERA	AERA	OAV	OOB	AB-HR-SH	AVG	PB	SUP	APR	DL	PW
	SD N	1	1	.500	10	0	0	0-0	12.1	15	10	3	0	3-0	12	6.57	59	.306	.346	1	.000	0		-4		-0.5
Total 2		2	5	.286	69	0	0	0-7	79	71	55	15	7	35-3	60	6.15	73	.246	.336	1	.000	0		-12		-1.0

CASTER, GEORGE George Jasper "Ug" B8.4.1907 Colton CA D12.18.1955 Lakewood CA BR/TR/6-1.5/180 d9.10 Col San Bernardino Valley (CA) JC

YEAR	TM LG	W	L	PCT	G	GS	CG-SHO	SV-BS	IP	H	R	HR	HB	BB-IB	SO	ERA	AERA	OAV	OOB	AB-HR-SH	AVG	PB	SUP	APR	DL	PW
1934	Phi A	3	2	.600	5	3	2	0	37	32	16	3	3	14	15	3.41	129	.235	.320	15	.267	0	106	4		0.5
1935	Phi A	1	4	.200	25	1	0	1	63.1	86	59	8	2	37	24	6.25	73	.322	.408	22	.227	0*	0	-15		-1.0
1937	Phi A	12	19	.387	34	33	19-3	0	231.2	227	141	23	2	107	100	4.43	106	.258	.339	90-0-1	.211	-1*	85	5		0.5
1938	Phi A	16	20	.444	42	40	20-2	1	281.1	310	156	26	3	117	112	4.35	111	.277	.347	101-0-2	.198	1	84	17		2.0
1939	Phi A	9	9	.500	28	17	7-1	0	136	144	82	16	3	45	59	4.90	96	.276	.337	43-0-2	.209	-1	78	-1		-0.1
1940	Phi A	4	19	.174	36	24	11	2	178.1	234	160	18	3	69	75	6.56	68	.312	.372	62-0-2	.129	-3	82	-43		-4.8
1941	StL A	3	7	.300	32	9	3	3	104.1	105	66	12	2	37	36	5.00	86	.259	.324	29-0-1	.103	-2	74	-8		-0.9
1942	StL A	8	2	.800	39	0	0	5	80	62	30	3	3	39	34	2.81	132	.217	.317	15	.067	-1		8		0.9
1943	StL A	6	8	.429	38	0	0	8	76.1	69	22	4	1	41	46	2.12	157	.284	.345	22	.136	-1		10		2.0
1944	StL A	6	6	.500	42	0	0	12	81	91	37	5	0	33	46	2.44	147	.284	.351	20	.250	-1		6		1.0
1945	StL A	1	2	.333	10	0	0	1	15.2	20	13	0	0	7	9	6.89	51	.308	.375	3	.333	0		-5		-1.0
	†Det A	5	1	.833	22	0	0	2	51.1	47	25	3	2	27	23	3.86	91	.250	.350	11-0-2	.182	0		-1		-0.1
	Year	6	3	.667	32	0	0	3	67	67	38	3	2	34	32	4.57	77	.265	.356	14-0-2	.214	0		-7		-1.1
1946	Det A	1	2	.667	10	0	0	4	41.1	42	26	1	1	24	19	5.66	65	.264	.364	7-0-1	.143	-0		-7		-0.7
Total 12		76	100	.432	376	127	62-6	39	1377.2	1469	833	121	25	597	595	4.54	96	.273	.349	440-0-11	.184	-7	87	-30		-1.7

CASTILLO, TONY Antonio Jose (Jimenez) B3.1.1963 Quibor, Venez BL/TL/5-10/188(177-190) d8.14

YEAR	TM LG	W	L	PCT	G	GS	CG-SHO	SV-BS	IP	H	R	HR	HB	BB-IB	SO	ERA	AERA	OAV	OOB	AB-HR-SH	AVG	PB	SUP	APR	DL	PW
1988	Tor A	1	0	1.000	14	0	0	0-0	15	10	5	2	0	2-0	14	3.00	132	.200	.222	0	—	0		2		0.1
1989	Tor A	1	1	.500	17	0	0	1-0	17.2	23	14	0	1	10-5	10	6.11	62	.333	.405	0	—	0		-5		-0.6
	Atl N	0	1	.000	12	0	0	0-0	9.1	8	5	0	0	4-1	9	4.82	76	.222	.300	0	—	-0		-1		-0.1
1990	Atl N	5	1	.833	52	3	0	1-1	76.2	93	41	5	1	20-3	64	4.23	95	.302	.342	1	.000	-0		-1		-0.1
1991	Atl N	1	1	.500	7	0	0	0-0	8.2	13	9	3	0	5-0	8	7.27	53	.342	.419	0	—	0	142	-2		-0.1
	NY N	1	0	1.000	10	3	0	0-0	23.2	27	7	1	0	6-1	10	1.90	193	.281	.320	4-0-2	.000	0	74	4		-0.7
	Year	2	1	.667	17	3	0	0-0	32.1	40	16	4	0	11-1	18	3.34	112	.299	.349	4-0-2	.000	-0	72	4		0.2
1993	†Tor A	3	2	.600	51	0	0	0-1	50.2	44	19	4	0	22-5	28	3.38	130	.242	.320	0	—	0		6		-0.5
1994	Tor A	5	2	.714	41	0	0	1-3	68	66	22	7	3	28-1	43	2.51	194	.260	.337	0	—	0		17		0.6
1995	Tor A	1	5	.167	55	0	0	13-8	72.2	64	27	7	3	24-1	38	3.22	148	.243	.308	0	—	0		13		1.6
1996	Tor A	2	5	.400	40	0	0	1-1	72.1	72	38	9	2	20-1	48	4.23	118	.260	.312	0	—	0		6		1.3
	Chi A	3	1	.750	15	0	0	1-3	22.2	23	7	1	1	4-1	9	1.59	300	.267	.298	0	—	0		7		0.4
	Year	5	4	.556	55	0	0	2-4	95	95	45	10	3	24-2	57	3.60	138	.262	.309	0	—	0		12		1.1
1997	Chi A	4	4	.500	64	0	0	4-5	62.1	74	48	6	1	23-7	42	4.91	90	.296	.358	1	.000	0		12		1.5
1998	Chi A	1	2	.333	25	0	0	0-0	27	38	25	7	2	11-0	14	8.00	57	.328	.395	0	—	-0		-8	15	-0.9
Total 10		28	23	.549	403	6	0	22-22	526.2	555	267	52	14	179-26	333	3.93	114	.274	.333	13-0-4	.077	-1	96	25	15	2.1

CASTILLO, CARLOS Carlos B4.21.1975 Boston MA BR/TR/6-2/240* [ChiA94 3/89] d4.2

YEAR	TM LG	W	L	PCT	G	GS	CG-SHO	SV-BS	IP	H	R	HR	HB	BB-IB	SO	ERA	AERA	OAV	OOB	AB-HR-SH	AVG	PB	SUP	APR	DL	PW
1997	Chi A	2	1	.667	37	0	0	1-0	66.1	68	35	9	1	33-3	43	4.48	99	.265	.346	1	1.000	0	135	0		0.0
1998	Chi A	6	4	.600	54	0	0	0-2	100.1	94	61	17	5	35-1	64	5.11	90	.246	.312	1	.000	-0	81	-5		-0.4
1999	Chi A	2	2	.500	18	0	0	0-0	41	45	26	10	0	14-1	23	5.71	87	.274	.331	0	—	0	113	-5		-0.2
2001	Bos A	0	0	—	2	0	0	0-0	3	3	2	1	0	0-0	0	6.00	74	.273	.250	0	—	0		0		-0.2
Total 4		10	7	.588	111	6	0	1-2	210.2	210	124	37	6	82-5	130	5.04	91	.258	.326	2	.500	0	111	-7		-0.6

CASTILLO, FRANK Frank Anthony B4.1.1969 ElPaso TX BR/TR/6-1/200(180-200) [ChiN87 6/140] d6.27

YEAR	TM LG	W	L	PCT	G	GS	CG-SHO	SV-BS	IP	H	R	HR	HB	BB-IB	SO	ERA	AERA	OAV	OOB	AB-HR-SH	AVG	PB	SUP	APR	DL	PW
1991	Chi N	6	7	.462	18	18	4	0-0	111.2	107	56	5	0	33-2	73	4.35	90	.252	.304	35-0-6	.143	-0	88	-3	16	-0.5
1992	Chi N	10	11	.476	33	33	0	0-0	205.1	179	91	19	6	63-6	135	3.46	105	.232	.293	65-0-5	.092	-2	86	3		0.0
1993	Chi N	5	8	.385	29	25	2	0-0	141.1	162	83	20	9	39-4	84	4.84	83	.293	.348	43-0-8	.163	-0	96	-12		-0.9
1994	Chi N	2	1	.667	4	4	1	0-0	23	25	13	3	0	5-0	19	4.30	98	.278	.316	4	.000	-1	151	-1	39	-0.2
1995	Chi N	11	10	.524	29	29	2-2	0-0	188	179	75	22	6	52-4	135	3.21	130	.248	.302	59-0-7	.102	-2	83	20		1.8
1996	Chi N	7	16	.304	33	33	1-1	0-0	182.1	209	112	28	8	46-4	139	5.28	88	.288	.335	57-0-4	.088	-3	87	-16		-2.0
1997	Chi N	6	9	.400	20	19	0	0-0	98	113	64	9	4	44-1	67	5.42	80	.292	.360	33-0-4	.152	-1	92	-12		-1.6
	Col N	6	3	.667	14	14	0	0-0	86.1	107	57	16	4	25-3	59	5.42	95	.308	.360	25-0-6	.080	-2	121	-2		-0.4
	Year	12	12	.500	34	33	0	0-0	184.1	220	121	25	8	69-4	126	5.42	87	.300	.365	58-0-10	.121	-2	105	-13		-2.0
1998	Det A	3	9	.250	27	19	0	1-0	116	150	91	17	5	44-0	81	6.83	70	.316	.376	1	.000	-0	99	-24	28	-2.1
2000	Tor A	10	5	.667	25	24	0	0-0	138	112	58	18	5	56-0	104	3.59	140	.220	.303	7	.143	-0	106	23	32	2.2
2001	Bos A	10	9	.526	26	26	0	0-0	136.2	138	72	14	5	35-2	89	4.21	105	.260	.308	2-0-1	.000	-0	95	3	40	0.3
2002	Bos A	6	15	.286	36	23	0	1-1	163.1	174	101	19	7	58-6	112	5.07	88	.274	.337	1-0-1	.000	-0	82	-11		-1.2
2004	Bos A	0	0	—	2	0	0	0-0	1	1	0	0	0	1-0	0	0.00	—	.333	.500	0	—	0		1		0.0
2005	Fla N	0	0	1.000	1	1	0	0-0	4.1	4	5	0	0	5-0	4	10.38	38	.235	.409	1	.000	-0	93	-3		-0.5
Total 13		82	104	.441	297	268	10-3	2-1	1595.1	1660	878	190	59	506-32	1101	4.56	95	.268	.327	338-0-42	.109	-12	94	-34	155	-5.1

CASTILLO, JUAN Juan Francisco (Azdura) B6.23.1970 Caracas, Venez BR/TR/6-5/205 d7.26

YEAR	TM LG	W	L	PCT	G	GS	CG-SHO	SV-BS	IP	H	R	HR	HB	BB-IB	SO	ERA	AERA	OAV	OOB	AB-HR-SH	AVG	PB	SUP	APR	DL	PW
1994	NY N	0	0	—	2	0	0	0-0	11.2	17	9	2	0	5-0	1	6.94	60	.362	.423	5	.200	0	175			-0.1

CASTILLO, BOBBY Robert Ernie B4.18.1955 Los Angeles CA BR/TR/5-10/170* d9.10 Col Los Angeles Valley (CA) JC

YEAR	TM LG	W	L	PCT	G	GS	CG-SHO	SV-BS	IP	H	R	HR	HB	BB-IB	SO	ERA	AERA	OAV	OOB	AB-HR-SH	AVG	PB	SUP	APR	DL	PW
1977	LA N	1	0	1.000	6	1	0	0-0	11.1	12	5	2	0	2-0	7	3.97	97	.279	.304	1	.000	-0	69	0		0.0
1978	LA N	0	4	.000	18	0	0	1-1	34	28	19	2	0	33-7	30	3.97	88	.239	.399	7	.000	-1		-3		-0.4
1979	LA N	2	0	1.000	19	0	0	7-1	24.1	26	5	0	1	13-1	25	1.11	326	.277	.364	3	.000	-0		6		0.9
1980	LA N	8	6	.571	61	0	0	5-1	98.1	70	31	4	1	45-5	60	2.75	127	.206	.297	9-0-1	.111	-0*		9		1.4
1981	†LA N	2	4	.333	34	1	0	5-2	50.2	50	31	5	0	24-4	35	5.33	62	.262	.341	9	.444	2	81	-12		-1.3
1982	Min A	13	11	.542	40	25	6-1	0-0	218.2	194	96	26	0	85-7	123	3.66	117	.241	.310	0	—	0	81	14		-1.3
1983	Min A	8	12	.400	27	25	3	0-0	158.1	170	91	17	1	65-4	90	4.77	90	.278	.347	0	—	0	89	-8		-0.8
1984	Min A	2	1	.667	10	2	0	0-0	25.1	14	7	2	0	19-2	7	1.78	238	.177	.327	0	—	0	83			0.6
1985	†LA N	2	2	.500	35	5	0	0-0	68	59	42	9	1	41-6	57	5.43	65	.230	.337	10-0-2	.100	-0*	131	-12	11	-0.7
Total 9		38	40	.487	250	59	9-1	18-5	689	623	327	72	4	327-36	434	3.94	100	.246	.329	39-0-3	.154	0	92	0	105	1.0

CASTLEMAN, SLICK Clydell B9.8.1913 Donelson TN D3.2.1998 Nashville TN BR/TR/6-0/185 d5.9

YEAR	TM LG	W	L	PCT	G	GS	CG-SHO	SV-BS	IP	H	R	HR	HB	BB-IB	SO	ERA	AERA	OAV	OOB	AB-HR-SH	AVG	PB	SUP	APR	DL	PW
1934	NY N	1	0	1.000	7	0	0	0	16.2	18	11	1	0	10	5	5.40	72	.277	.373	4	.250	1		-3		0.0
1935	NY N	15	6	.714	29	25	9-1	0	173.2	186	93	14	1	64	64	4.09	94	.268	.330	67-1-0	.179	-0	110	-6		-0.6
1936	†NY N	4	7	.364	29	12	2-1	1	111.2	148	80	6	5	56	54	5.64	69	.323	.403	39-1-0	.128	-1*	94	-22		-1.9
1937	NY N	11	6	.647	23	23	10-2	0	160.1	148	66	19	0	33	78	3.31	117	.247	.287	57-0-3	.070	-5	109	11		0.5
1938	NY N	4	5	.444	21	14	4	0	90.2	108	55	4	3	37	18	4.17	90	.296	.365	31-0-3	.097	-2*	130	-7		-0.8
1939	NY N	1	2	.333	12	4	0	0	33.2	36	18	1	0	23	16	4.54	86	.286	.366	9-0-1	.333	1	106	-2		-0.1
Total 6		36	26	.581	121	78	25-4	1	586.2	644	323	45	9	223	225	4.25	91	.279	.345	207-2-7	.135	-0	110	-29		-2.9

ASTLETON, ROY Royal Eugene B7.26.1885 Salt Lake City UT D6.24.1967 Los Angeles CA BR/TL/5-11/167 d4.16

YEAR	TM LG	W	L	PCT	G	GS	CG-SHO	SV-BS	IP	H	R	HR	HB	BB-IB	SO	ERA	AERA	OAV	OOB	AB-HR-SH	AVG	PB	SUP	APR	DL	PW
1907	NY A	1	1	.500	3	2	1	0	16	11	6	1	0	3	3	2.81	99	.196	.237	5	.000	-1	60			0.0
1909	Cin N	1	1	.500	4	1	1	0	14	14	6	2	0	2	4	1.93	135	.275	.373	5	.000	1	350	1		0.2
1910	Cin N	1	2	.333	4	2	1	0	13.2	15	5	0	1	6	5	3.29	89	.288	.373	5	.667	1	128	1		0.2
Total 3		3	4	.429	11	5	3	0	43.2	40	17	1	3	15	13	2.68	104	.252	.328	13	.154	-0	142	1		0.2

ASTNER, PAUL Paul Henry "Lefty" B2.16.1897 St.Paul MN D3.3.1986 St.Paul MN BL/TL/5-11/187 d8.6 Col Notre Dame

YEAR	TM LG	W	L	PCT	G	GS	CG-SHO	SV-BS	IP	H	R	HR	HB	BB-IB	SO	ERA	AERA	OAV	OOB	AB-HR-SH	AVG	PB	SUP	APR	DL	PW
1923	Chi A	0	0	—	6	0	0		10	14	9	0	0	5		6.30	63	.326	.396	3-0-2	.000	-0		-3		-0.2

ASTRO, BILL William Radhames (Checo) B12.13.1953 Santiago, D.R. BR/TR/5-11/170* d8.20 C14

YEAR	TM LG	W	L	PCT	G	GS	CG-SHO	SV-BS	IP	H	R	HR	HB	BB-IB	SO	ERA	AERA	OAV	OOB	AB-HR-SH	AVG	PB	SUP	APR	DL	PW
1974	Mil A	0	0	—	8	0	0	0-0	18	19	10	2	0	5-0	10	4.50	81	.264	.308	0	—	0		-2		-0.1
1975	Mil A	3	2	.600	18	5	0	1-0	75	78	28	3	2	17-5	25	2.52	153	.271	.313	0	—	0	119	9	40	0.6
1976	Mil A	4	6	.400	39	0	0	8-2	70.1	70	29	4	2	19-5	33	3.45	102	.265	.322	0	—	0	1	21		0.2
1977	Mil A	6	6	.571	51	0	0	13-6	69.1	76	34	7	2	23-10	28	4.15	99	.293	.347	0	—	0		0		0.1
1978	Mil A	5	4	.556	42	0	0	8-5	49.2	43	14	2	6	14-5	17	1.81	209	.244	.296	0	—	0		19		2.0
1979	Mil A	3	1	.750	39	0	0	6-6	44.1	40	14	2	0	13-5	10	2.03	207	.244	.296	0	—	0		9		1.0
1980	Mil A	3	3	.500	56	0	0	8-4	84.1	89	35	2	7	17-6	32	2.77	141	.274	.311	0	—	0	32	6	94	0.8
1981	NY A	1	1	.500	11	0	0	0-0	19	26	13	2	0	5-1	4	3.79	95	.329	.369	0	—	0		9		0.5
1982	KC A	2	3	.600	21	4	0	1-0	75.2	72	34	8	2	20-4	37	3.45	118	.243	.352	0	—	0	139	4		0.2

YEAR	TM LG	W	L	PCT	G	GS	CG-SHO	SV-BS	IP	H	R	HR	HB	BB-IB	SO	ERA	AERA	OAV	OOB	AB-HR-SH	AVG	PB	SUP	APR	DL	PW
1983	KC A	2	0	1.000	18	0	0	0-0	40.2	51	34	4	5	12-1	17	6.64	62	.300	.358	0	—	0		-11		-0.6
Total 10		31	26	.544	303	9	0	45-23	546.1	564	245	36	22	145-42	203	3.33	118	.268	.319	0	—	0	130	27	61	4.0

CATES, ELI Eli Eldo B1.26.1877 Greens Fork IN D5.29.1964 Anderson IN BR/TR/5-9.5/175 d4.20 ▲

YEAR	TM LG	W	L	PCT	G	GS	CG-SHO	SV-BS	IP	H	R	HR	HB	BB-IB	SO	ERA	AERA	OAV	OOB	AB-HR-SH	AVG	PB	SUP	APR	DL	PW
1908	Was A	4	8	.333	19	10	7	0	113.2	112	46	3	1	32	33	2.53	90	.261	.314	59-0-5	.186	1*	90	-3		0.0

CATHER, MIKE Michael Peter B12.17.1970 San Diego CA BR/TR/6-2/195* [TexA93 41/1151] d7.13 Col California-Davis

YEAR	TM LG	W	L	PCT	G	GS	CG-SHO	SV-BS	IP	H	R	HR	HB	BB-IB	SO	ERA	AERA	OAV	OOB	AB-HR-SH	AVG	PB	SUP	APR	DL	PW
1997	†Atl N	2	4	.333	35	0	0	0-3	37.2	23	12	1	2	19-4	29	2.39	176	.174	.288	1	.000	-0		7		1.0
1998	Atl N	2	2	.500	36	0	0	0-3	41.1	39	21	7	2	12-1	33	3.92	106	.255	.314	0	—	0		1	28	0.1
1999	Atl N	1	0	1.000	4	0	0	0-1	2.2	5	3	2	0	1-0	3	10.13	44	.417	.462	0	—	0		-2		-0.3
Total .3		5	6	.455	75	0	0	0-7	81.2	67	36	10	4	32-5	62	3.42	123	.226	.307	1	.000	-0		6	28	0.8

CATHEY, HARDIN Hardin Abner "Lil Abner" B7.6.1919 Burns TN D7.27.1997 Nashville TN BR/TR/6-4/190 d4.16

YEAR	TM LG	W	L	PCT	G	GS	CG-SHO	SV-BS	IP	H	R	HR	HB	BB-IB	SO	ERA	AERA	OAV	OOB	AB-HR-SH	AVG	PB	SUP	APR	DL	PW
1942	Was A	1	1	.500	12	1	0	0	30.1	44	26	1	0	16	8	7.42	49	.341	.414	8-0-1	.375	1	187	-11		-0.6

CATO, KEEFE John Keefe B5.6.1958 Yonkers NY BR/TR/6-1/185* [CinN79 2/30] d6.13 Col Fairfield

YEAR	TM LG	W	L	PCT	G	GS	CG-SHO	SV-BS	IP	H	R	HR	HB	BB-IB	SO	ERA	AERA	OAV	OOB	AB-HR-SH	AVG	PB	SUP	APR	DL	PW
1983	Cin N	1	0	1.000	2	1	0	0-0	3.2	2	1	0	0	1-0	3	2.45	156	.154	.214	0-0-1	—	0		1		0.1
1984	Cin N	0	1	.000	8	0	0	1-0	15.2	22	14	5	0	4-0	12	8.04	47	.344	.371	4	.500	1		-6		-0.4
Total 2		1	1	.500	12	0	0	1-0	19.1	24	15	5	0	5-0	15	6.98	54	.312	.345	4-0-1	.500	1		-5		-0.3

CATTANACH, JOHN John Leckie B5.10.1863 Providence RI D11.10.1926 Providence RI 5-10/190 d6.5

YEAR	TM LG	W	L	PCT	G	GS	CG-SHO	SV-BS	IP	H	R	HR	HB	BB-IB	SO	ERA	AERA	OAV	OOB	AB-HR-SH	AVG	PB	SUP	APR	DL	PW
1884	Pro N	0	0	—	1	1	0	0	5	2	7	0	0	4	2	9.00	32	.100	.250	4	.000	-1	149	-3		-0.2
	StL U	1	1	.500	2	2	2	0	17	12	10	0	0	4	13	2.12	113	.185	.232	7	.000	-2	80	0		-0.1
Total 1		1	1	.500	3	3	2	0	22	14	17	0	0	8	15	3.68	68	.165	.237	11	.000	-2	102	-3		-0.3

CAUDILL, BILL William Holland B7.13.1956 Santa Monica CA BR/TR/6-1/210(175-225) [StLN74 8/181] d5.12

YEAR	TM LG	W	L	PCT	G	GS	CG-SHO	SV-BS	IP	H	R	HR	HB	BB-IB	SO	ERA	AERA	OAV	OOB	AB-HR-SH	AVG	PB	SUP	APR	DL	PW
1979	Chi N	1	7	.125	29	12	0	0-0	90	89	57	16	4	41-5	104	4.80	87	.255	.337	17-0-4	.059	-1	76	-7		-0.7
1980	Chi N	4	6	.400	72	2	0	1-3	127.2	100	37	10	1	59-12	112	2.19	181	.223	.309	9-0-1	.222	0	68	22		1.7
1981	Chi N	1	5	.167	30	10	0	0-2	71	87	50	9	2	31-2	45	5.83	64	.301	.368	14-0-1	.143	0	97	-14		-1.2
1982	Sea A	12	9	.571	70	0	0	26-6	95.2	65	25	9	1	35-4	111	2.35	182	.192	.269	0	—	0		21		4.2
1983	Sea A	2	8	.200	63	0	0	26-3	72.2	70	39	10	2	38-6	73	4.71	91	.257	.348	0	—	0		-2	18	-0.4
1984	Oak A★	9	7	.563	68	0	0	36-8	96.1	77	30	9	0	31-4	89	2.71	139	.218	.278	1	.000	-0		13		2.6
1985	Tor A	4	6	.400	67	0	0	14-5	69.1	53	26	9	2	35-6	46	2.99	142	.209	.306	0	—	0		9		1.5
1986	Tor A	2	4	.333	40	0	0	2-2	36.1	36	25	6	2	17-1	32	6.19	69	.254	.342	0	—	0		-7	15	-1.1
1987	Oak A	0	0	—	6	0	0	1-0	8	10	8	3	0	1-0	4	9.00	46	.294	.314	0	—	0		-4	31	-0.2
Total 9		35	52	.402	445	24	0	106-29	667	587	297	81	14	288-40	620	3.68	111	.237	.316	41-0-6	.122	-1	83	31	64	6.4

CAUSEY, RED Cecil Algernon B8.11.1893 Georgetown FL D11.11.1960 Avon Park FL BR/TR/6-1/160 d4.26

YEAR	TM LG	W	L	PCT	G	GS	CG-SHO	SV-BS	IP	H	R	HR	HB	BB-IB	SO	ERA	AERA	OAV	OOB	AB-HR-SH	AVG	PB	SUP	APR	DL	PW
1918	NY N	11	6	.647	29	18	10-2	2	158.1	143	58	2	7	42	48	2.79	94	.245	.304	48-0-1	.125	-3	126	-1		-0.5
1919	NY N	9	3	.750	19	16	6	0	105	99	52	5	2	38	25	3.69	76	.251	.320	38-0-1	.132	-2*	160	-10		-1.3
	Bos N	4	5	.444	10	10	3	0	69	81	38	1	1	20	14	4.57	63	.308	.359	21-0-2	.095	-3	131	-21		-2.8
	Year	13	8	.619	29	26	9	0	174	180	90	6	3	58	39	4.32	79	.299	.376	59-0-3	.119	-2*	104	-16		-2.1
1920	Phi N	7	14	.333	35	26	11-1	3	181.1	203	109	4	5	79	30	2.84	149	.294	.335	20	.150	-1*	83	7		0.7
1921	Phi N	3	3	.500	7	7	4	0	50.2	58	22	4	1	11	8	2.45	149	.228	.302	3	.333	0*	67	1		0.1
	NY N	1	1	.500	7	1	0	0	14.2	13	8	0	0	6	1	2.76	149	.280	.327	23	.174	-1	83	7		0.8
	Year	4	4	.500	14	8	4	0	65.1	71	30	4	1	17	9	3.18	126	.262	.347	21-0-1	.238	-0*	214	5		0.5
1922	NY N	4	3	.571	24	2	1	1	70.2	69	34	2	0	34	13											
Total 5		39	35	.527	131	80	35-3	6	649.2	666	321	18	16	230	139	3.59	89	.273	.340	210-0-7	.157	-9	115	-25		-4.1

CAVET, PUG Tillar H. B12.26.1889 McGregor TX D8.4.1966 San Luis Obispo CA BL/TL/6-3/176 d4.25

YEAR	TM LG	W	L	PCT	G	GS	CG-SHO	SV-BS	IP	H	R	HR	HB	BB-IB	SO	ERA	AERA	OAV	OOB	AB-HR-SH	AVG	PB	SUP	APR	DL	PW
1911	Det A	0	0	—	1	1	0	0	6	5	0	0	1	4		4.50	77	.316	.350	1	.000	-0	229	-1		-0.1
1914	Det A	7	7	.500	31	14	6-1	2	151.1	129	61	2	9	44	51	2.44	115	.238	.306	47-0-2	.106	-2	102	4		0.3
1915	Det A	4	2	.667	17	7	2	1	71	83	39	2	2	22	26	4.06	75	.300	.355	24-0-1	.250	1	131	-7		-0.4
Total 3		11	9	.550	49	22	8-1	3	226.1	218	105	4	11	67	78	2.98	97	.260	.323	72-0-3	.153	-0	119	-4		-0.2

CECCARELLI, ART Arthur Edward "Chic" B4.2.1930 New Haven CT BR/TL(BB 1957)/6-0/190* d5.3

YEAR	TM LG	W	L	PCT	G	GS	CG-SHO	SV-BS	IP	H	R	HR	HB	BB-IB	SO	ERA	AERA	OAV	OOB	AB-HR-SH	AVG	PB	SUP	APR	DL	PW
1955	KC A	4	7	.364	31	16	3-1	0	123.2	123	81	20	0	71-2	68	5.31	79	.258	.351	38-0-3	.079	-3	84	-15		-1.5
1956	KC A	0	1	.000	3	2	0	0	10	13	13	3	1	4-1	2	7.20	60	.317	.391	3	.000	-0	123	-5		-0.4
1957	Bal A	5	0	.000	20	8	1	0	58	62	34	3	2	31-3	30	4.50	80	.278	.371	14	.000	-2	62	-7		-0.8
1959	Chi N	5	5	.500	18	15	4-2	0	102	95	58	19	1	37-6	56	4.76	83	.245	.369	33-0-2	.091	-1	110	-8		-0.9
1960	Chi N	0	0	—	7	1	0	0	13	16	12	1	0	4-0	10	5.54	68	.296	.339	0-0-1	—	-0	210	-4		-0.2
Total 5		9	18	.333	79	42	8-3	0	306.2	309	198	46	4	147-12*	166	5.05	79	.261	.342	88-0-6	.068	-6	94	-39		-3.8

CECENA, JOSE Jose Isabel (Lugo) B8.20.1963 Ciudad Obregon, Sonora, Mexico BR/TR/5-11/180 d4.6

YEAR	TM LG	W	L	PCT	G	GS	CG-SHO	SV-BS	IP	H	R	HR	HB	BB-IB	SO	ERA	AERA	OAV	OOB	AB-HR-SH	AVG	PB	SUP	APR	DL	PW
1988	Tex A	0	0	—	22	0	0	1-1	26.1	20	16	5	2	23-1	27	4.78	86	.213	.372	0	—	0		-2	74	-0.1

CECIL, REX Rex Rolston B10.8.1916 Lindsay OK D10.30.1966 Long Beach CA BL/TR/6-3/195 d8.13

YEAR	TM LG	W	L	PCT	G	GS	CG-SHO	SV-BS	IP	H	R	HR	HB	BB-IB	SO	ERA	AERA	OAV	OOB	AB-HR-SH	AVG	PB	SUP	APR	DL	PW
1944	Bos A	4	5	.444	11	9	4	0	61	72	44	5	1	33	33	5.16	66	.286	.371	18-0-2	.278	2	112	-14		-1.6
1945	Bos A	2	5	.286	7	7	1	0	45	46	37	4	0	27	30	5.20	66	.261	.366	20	.300	1	114	-12		-1.1
Total 2		6	10	.375	18	16	5	0	106	118	81	9	1	60	63	5.18	66	.276	.366	38-0-2	.289	2	113	-26		-3.7

CENTER, PETE Marvin Earl B4.22.1912 Hazel Green KY D8.8.2004 Campton KY BR/TR/6-4/190 d9.11 Mil 1943-44 Col Morehead St.

YEAR	TM LG	W	L	PCT	G	GS	CG-SHO	SV-BS	IP	H	R	HR	HB	BB-IB	SO	ERA	AERA	OAV	OOB	AB-HR-SH	AVG	PB	SUP	APR	DL	PW
1942	Cle A	0	0	—	3	0	0	0	3.1	7	6	0	1	4	0	16.20	21	.438	.571	1	.000	-0		-5		-0.2
1943	Cle A	1	2	.333	24	1	0	0	42.1	29	18	3	0	18	10	2.76	112	.201	.290	5	.000	-1	108	0		-0.1
1945	Cle A	6	3	.667	31	8	2	1	85.2	89	42	2	1	28	34	3.99	81	.270	.329	22	.091	-2	141	-7		-1.1
1946	Cle A	0	2	.000	21	0	0	1	29	29	16	2	1	20	6	4.97	67	.269	.388	3	.000	-0		-5		-0.2
Total 4		7	7	.500	77	9	2	3	160.1	154	82	7	3	70	50	4.10	79	.258	.338	31	.065	-3	138	-17		-1.5

CERDA, JAIME Jaime Magana B10.26.1978 Fresno CA BL/TL/6-0/175(175-200) [NYN98 23/694] d6.28 Col Fresno (CA) City

YEAR	TM LG	W	L	PCT	G	GS	CG-SHO	SV-BS	IP	H	R	HR	HB	BB-IB	SO	ERA	AERA	OAV	OOB	AB-HR-SH	AVG	PB	SUP	APR	DL	PW
2002	NY N	0	0	—	32	0	0	0-0	25.2	20	7	1	1	14-0	21	2.45	161	.232	.327	1	.000	-0		5		0.2
2003	NY N	1	1	.500	27	0	0	0-1	32.1	32	21	4	0	20-1	19	5.85	72	.267	.366	1	.000	-0		-5		-0.0
2004	KC A	1	4	.200	53	0	0	2-1	45.2	41	21	1	3	30-3	33	3.15	148	.244	.363	0	—	0		6		0.1
2005	KC A	1	4	.200	20	0	0	0-1	19	21	14	3	0	11-2	18	6.63	64	.284	.372	0	—	0		-5		-0.1
Total 4		3	9	.250	132	0	0	2-3	122.2	116	63	8	4	75-6	91	4.26	101	.254	.358	2	.000	-1		1		0.1

CERROS, JUAN R.Juan B9.25.1976 Monterrey, Nuevo Leon, Mexico BR/TR/6-1/200 d9.8

YEAR	TM LG	W	L	PCT	G	GS	CG-SHO	SV-BS	IP	H	R	HR	HB	BB-IB	SO	ERA	AERA	OAV	OOB	AB-HR-SH	AVG	PB	SUP	APR	DL	PW
2003	Cin N	0	0	—	11	0	0	0-0	9.1					5-2	9	4.85	86	.224	.316	0	—	0		-1		0.1

CERUTTI, JOHN John Joseph B4.28.1960 Albany NY D10.3.2004 Toronto ON, Can. BL/TL/6-2/200* [TorA81 1/21] d9.1 Col Amherst

YEAR	TM LG	W	L	PCT	G	GS	CG-SHO	SV-BS	IP	H	R	HR	HB	BB-IB	SO	ERA	AERA	OAV	OOB	AB-HR-SH	AVG	PB	SUP	APR	DL	PW
1985	Tor A	0	2	.000	4	1	0	0	6.2	10	7	1	1	4	5	5.40	79	.323	.417	0	—	0		0	-2	-0.0
1986	Tor A	9	4	.692	34	20	2-1	1-0	145.1	150	73	25	1	47-2	89	4.15	102	.268	.324	0	—	0		122	2	0.0
1987	Tor A	11	4	.733	44	21	2	0	151.1	144	75	30	1	59-5	92	4.40	103	.251	.321	0	—	0		104	8	0.0
1988	Tor A	6	7	.462	46	12	0	1-1	123.2	120	56	12	3	42-6	65	3.13	127	.256	.320	0	—	0		109	11	1.0
1989	†Tor A	11	11	.500	33	31	3-1	0-0	205.1	214	90	19	6	53-2	69	3.07	124	.273	.322	0	—	0		112	-11	-1.1
1990	Tor A	9	9	.500	30	23	0	0-0	140	162	77	23	4	49-3	49	4.76	83	.297	.356	0	—	0		93	-4	-0.1
1991	Det A	3	6	.333	38	8	1	2-3	88.2	94	49	9	2	37-9	29	4.57	91	.276	.348	0	—	0		111	9	0.0
Total 7		49	43	.533	229	116	8-2	4-4	861	894	427	119	18	291-27	398	3.94	104	.271	.331	0	—	0		111	9	0.0

CHACIN, GUSTAVO Gustavo G. (Adolfo) B12.4.1980 Maracaibo, Venez BL/TL/5-11/193* d9.20

YEAR	TM LG	W	L	PCT	G	GS	CG-SHO	SV-BS	IP	H	R	HR	HB	BB-IB	SO	ERA	AERA	OAV	OOB	AB-HR-SH	AVG	PB	SUP	APR	DL	PW
2004	Tor A	1	1	.500	2	2	0	0-0	14	8	4	0	1	3-0	6	2.57	190	.167	.231	0	—	0		57	4	0.0
2005	Tor A	13	9	.591	34	34	0	0-0	203	213	93	20	8	70-3	121	3.72	124	.274	.337	7-0-1	.000	-1	103	18		1.2
Total 2		14	10	.583	36	36	0	0-0	217	221	97	20	9	73-3	127	3.65	127	.268	.331	7-0-1	.000	-0	100	22		2.2

CHACON, SHAWN Shawn Anthony B12.23.1977 Anchorage AK BR/TR/6-3/212* [ColN96 3/86] d4.29

YEAR	TM LG	W	L	PCT	G	GS	CG-SHO	SV-BS	IP	H	R	HR	HB	BB-IB	SO	ERA	AERA	OAV	OOB	AB-HR-SH	AVG	PB	SUP	APR	DL	PW
2001	Col N	6	10	.375	27	27	0	0-0	160	157	96	26	10	87-10	134	5.06	105	.260	.360	47-0-7	.043	-4	86	4		-1.5
2002	Col N	5	11	.313	21	21	0	0-0	119.1	122	84	25	7	60-3	67	5.73	83	.263	.355	35-0-2	.257	1	68	-12	28	-1.1
2003	Col N★	11	8	.579	23	23	0	0-0	137	124	73	12	12	58-4	93	4.60	106	.243	.331	46-1-2	.196	1	98	5	62	0.0
2004	Col N	1	9	.100	66	0	0	35-9	63.1	71	52	12	5	52-7	52	7.11	67	.282	.414	20-0-3	.150	-0		-15		-2.2
2005	Col N	1	7	.125	13	12	0	0-0	72.2	69	38	6	4	36-4	39	4.09	116	.260	.361				55	6	33	0

YEAR	TM LG	W	L	PCT	G	GS	CG-SHO	SV-BS	IP	H	R	HR	HB	BB-IB	SO	ERA	AERA	OAV	OOB	AB-HR-SH	AVG	PB	SUP	APR	DL	PW
	†NY A	7	3	.700	14	12	0	0-0	79	66	26	7	6	30-0	40	2.85	154	.225	.309	0	—	0	97	14		1.6
Total	5	31	48	.392	164	95	0	35-9	631.1	609	364	89	48	323-28	425	4.90	100	.255	.353	148-1-14	.155	-3	83	2	123	-1.4

CHADWICK, RAY Ray Charles B11.17.1962 Durham NC BB/TR/6-2/180 [AnaA83 16/415] d7.29 Col Winston-Salem St.

YEAR	TM LG	W	L	PCT	G	GS	CG-SHO	SV-BS	IP	H	R	HR	HB	BB-IB	SO	ERA	AERA	OAV	OOB	AB-HR-SH	AVG	PB	SUP	APR	DL	PW
1986	Cal A	0	5	.000	7	7	0	0-0	27.1	39	26	5	1	15-0	9	7.24	57	.336	.417	0	—	0	75	-10		-1.5

CHAGNON, LEON Leon Wilbur "Shag" B9.28.1902 Pittsfield NH D7.30.1953 Amesbury MA BR/TR/6-0/182 d10.5

YEAR	TM LG	W	L	PCT	G	GS	CG-SHO	SV-BS	IP	H	R	HR	HB	BB-IB	SO	ERA	AERA	OAV	OOB	AB-HR-SH	AVG	PB	SUP	APR	DL	PW
1929	Pit N	0	0	—	1	1	0	0	7	11	7	1	0	1	4	9.00	53	.333	.353	2		-0	146	-3		-0.1
1930	Pit N	0	3	.000	18	4	3	0	62	92	52	9	5	23	27	6.82	73	.355	.418	20	.200	-1	118	-11		-0.5
1932	Pit N	9	6	.600	30	10	4-1	0	128	140	62	10	2	34	52	3.94	97	.276	.324	40-0-1	.225	2	88	1		0.2
1933	Pit N	6	4	.600	39	5	1	1	100	100	48	2	3	17	35	3.69	90	.259	.296	21-0-2	.048	-2	156	-3		-0.5
1934	Pit N	4	1	.800	33	0	0	1	58	68	32	5	1	24	19	4.81	86	.288	.356	13	.231	0		-3		-0.1
1935	NY N	0	2	.000	14	1	0	1	38.1	32	17	7	0	5	16	3.52	109	.232	.259	9	.000	-1	0	2		0.0
Total	6	19	16	.543	135	21	8-1	3	393.1	443	218	34	11	104	153	4.51	87	.284	.333	105-0-3	.162	-1	109	-17		-1.0

CHAKALES, BOB Robert Edward "Chick" B8.10.1927 Asheville NC BR/TR/6-1/185* d4.21

YEAR	TM LG	W	L	PCT	G	GS	CG-SHO	SV-BS	IP	H	R	HR	HB	BB-IB	SO	ERA	AERA	OAV	OOB	AB-HR-SH	AVG	PB	SUP	APR	DL	PW
1951	Cle A	3	4	.429	17	10	2-1	0	68.1	80	40	3	0	43	32	4.74	80	.292	.388	20-1-1	.350	2	82	-7		-0.5
1952	Cle A	1	2	.333	5	1	0	0	12	19	13	2	0	8	7	9.75	34	.388	.474	4	.500	1	287	-8		-1.4
1953	Cle A	0	2	.000	7	3	1	0	27	28	13	2	1	10	6	2.67	141	.283	.355	7	.286	0	32	2		0.1
1954	Cle A	2	0	1.000	5	0	0	0	10.1	4	1	0	0	12	3	0.87	422	.114	.340	3-0-1	.333	1		3		0.7
	Bal A	3	7	.300	38	6	0	3	89.1	81	43	8	1	43	44	3.73	96	.245	.331	22-0-2	.364	2	131	-2		0.0
	Year	5	7	.417	41	6	0	3	99.2	85	44	8	1	55	47	3.43	105	.232	.332	25-0-3	.360	3	131	1		0.7
1955	Chi A	0	0	—	7	0	0	0	12.1	11	2	2	0	6-1	11	1.46	271	.256	.347	2	.000	-0		3		0.2
	Was A	2	3	.400	29	0	0	0	54.2	55	38	4	1	25-3	28	5.27	73	.263	.342	8	.000	-1		-10		-0.9
	Year	2	3	.400	36	0	0	0	67	66	40	6	1	31-4	34	4.57	84	.262	.343	10	.000	-1		-6		-0.7
1956	Was A	4	4	.500	43	1	0	4	96	94	53	3	3	57-7	33	4.03	107	.268	.369	20-0-3	.150	-1	123	1		0.1
1957	Was A	0	1	.000	4	2	0	0	18.1	20	13	2	0	10-1	12	5.40	72	.274	.357	7	.143	0	172	-3		-1.0
	Bos A	0	2	.000	18	0	0	1	32	53	30	5	1	11-0	16	8.16	49	.379	.425	3-0-1	.667	1		-13		-1.0
	Year	0	3	.000	22	2	0	1	50.1	73	43	7	1	21-1	28	7.15	55	.343	.401	10-0-1	.300	1	169	-17		-1.1
Total	7	15	25	.375	171	23	3-1	10	420.1	445	246	31	7	225-12	187	4.54	85	.277	.366	96-1-8	.271	5	102	-34		-2.8

CHALMERS, GEORGE George W. "Dut" B6.7.1888 Aberdeen, Scotland D8.5.1960 Bronx NY BR/TR/6-1/189 d9.21 Col Manhattan

YEAR	TM LG	W	L	PCT	G	GS	CG-SHO	SV-BS	IP	H	R	HR	HB	BB-IB	SO	ERA	AERA	OAV	OOB	AB-HR-SH	AVG	PB	SUP	APR	DL	PW
1910	Phi N	1	1	.500	4	3	2	0	22	21	17	0	1	11	12	5.32	59	.280	.379	7	.143	-0	151	-5		-0.4
1911	Phi N	13	10	.565	38	22	11-3	0	208.2	196	107	5	4	101	101	3.11	111	.256	.346	73-0-2	.178	-1	96	3		0.2
1912	Phi N	3	4	.429	12	8	3	0	57.2	64	34	4	2	37	22	3.28	111	.296	.404	16-0-1	.188	-0	111	1		0.0
1913	Phi N	3	10	.231	26	15	4	1	116	133	75	3	5	51	46	4.81	69	.296	.374	33-0-1	.212	-1	83	-17		-1.8
1914	Phi N	0	3	.000	3	2	1	0	18	23	17	0	1	15	6	5.50	53	.324	.448	6	.000	-1	73	-5		-0.8
1915	†Phi N	8	9	.471	26	20	13-1	1	170.1	159	58	3	0	45	82	2.48	110	.255	.305	59-0-2	.169	-0	89	8		0.7
1916	Phi N	1	4	.200	12	8	2	0	53.2	49	31	2	2	19	21	3.19	83	.248	.315	15-0-3	.000	-2	106	-5		-0.7
Total	7	29	41	.414	121	78	36-4	6	646.1	645	339	17	15	279	290	3.41	93	.269	.348	209-0-9	.163	-5	96	-20		-2.8

CHAMBERLAIN, CRAIG Craig Philip B2.2.1957 Hollywood CA BR/TR/6-1/190* [KCA78 S1/2] d8.12 Col Arizona

YEAR	TM LG	W	L	PCT	G	GS	CG-SHO	SV-BS	IP	H	R	HR	HB	BB-IB	SO	ERA	AERA	OAV	OOB	AB-HR-SH	AVG	PB	SUP	APR	DL	PW
1979	KC A	4	4	.500	10	10	4	0-0	69.2	68	31	7	1	18-0	30	3.75	114	.261	.306	0	—	0	102	5		0.4
1980	KC A	0	1	.000	5	0	0	0-1	9.1	10	8	3	0	5-2	3	6.75	60	.270	.349	0	—	0		-3		-0.3
Total	2	4	5	.444	15	10	4	0-1	79	78	39	10	1	23-2	33	4.10	103	.262	.312	0	—	0	102	2		0.1

CHAMBERLAIN, ELTON Elton P. "Icebox" B11.5.1867 Buffalo NY D9.22.1929 Baltimore MD BR/TR(TB 1888p)/5-9/168 d9.13

YEAR	TM LG	W	L	PCT	G	GS	CG-SHO	SV-BS	IP	H	R	HR	HB	BB-IB	SO	ERA	AERA	OAV	OOB	AB-HR-SH	AVG	PB	SUP	APR	DL	PW
1886	Lou AA	0	3	.000	4	4	4	0	31.1	39	43	0	0	17	18	6.61	55	.287	.366	19	.158	-0*	57	-9		-0.7
1887	Lou AA	18	16	.529	36	36	35-1	0	309	340	226	0	14	117	118	3.79	116	.274	.343	131-1	.198	-3*	97	17		1.2
1888	Lou AA	14	9	.609	24	24	21-1	0	196	178	123	2	11	59	119	2.53	122	.233	.298	94	.191	0*	131	8		0.9
	†StL AA	11	2	.846	14	14	13-1	0	112	61	34	1	6	27	57	1.61	203	.154	.220	50-1	.100	-3	128	20		1.7
	Year	25	11	.694	38	38	34-2	0	308	239	157	3	17	86	176	2.19	143	.206	.271	144-1	.160	-3	130	26		2.6
1889	StL AA	32	15	.681	53	51	44-3	1	421.2	376	220	18	17	165	202	2.97	142	.231	.309	171-2	.199	-2	94	56		4.6
1890	StL AA	3	1	.750	5	5	3	0	35	47	37	1	0	26	14	5.91	73	.311	.412	15	.133	-1	125	-6		-0.7
	Col AA	12	6	.667	25	21	19-6	0	175	128	69	2	8	70	114	2.21	162	.198	.285	65	.231	3	87	28		2.6
	Year	15	7	.682	30	26	22-6	0	210	175	106	3	8	96	128	2.83	131	.220	.310	80	.213	1	96	16		1.9
1891	Phi AA	22	23	.489	49	46	44	0	405.2	397	263	10	12	206	204	4.22	90	.248	.338	176-2	.188	2*	86	-15		-1.1
1892	Cin N	19	23	.452	52	49	43-2	0	406.1	391	230	8	17	170	169	3.39	96	.243	.322	160-2	.225	2*	88	-5		-0.5
1893	Cin N	16	12	.571	34	27	19-1	0	241	248	148	3	15	112	59	3.73	128	.258	.345	97	.196	-3	95	24		1.7
1894	Cin N	10	9	.526	23	22	18-1	0	177.2	220	155	10	12	91	57	5.77	96	.301	.387	70-1-3	.314	4	91	-2		-0.2
1896	Cle N	0	1	.000	2	2	1	0	11	21	12	0	1	5	2	7.36	62	.396	.458	3	.000	-0	180	-3		-0.2
Total	10	157	120	.567	321	301	264-16	1	2521.2	2446	1560	63	113	1065	1133	3.57	112	.247	.327	1051-9-3	.203	-2	97	113		9.7

CHAMBERLAIN, BILL William Vincent B4.21.1909 Stoughton MA D2.6.1994 Brockton MA BR/TL/5-10.5/173 d8.2 Col St. Anselm

YEAR	TM LG	W	L	PCT	G	GS	CG-SHO	SV-BS	IP	H	R	HR	HB	BB-IB	SO	ERA	AERA	OAV	OOB	AB-HR-SH	AVG	PB	SUP	APR	DL	PW
1932	Chi A	0	5	.000	12	5	0	0	41.1	39	30	3	0	25	11	4.57	95	.250	.354	10	.100	-1	32	-3		-0.4

CHAMBERS, CLIFF Clifford Day "Lefty" B1.10.1922 Portland OR BL/TL/6-3/208* d4.24 Col Washington St.

YEAR	TM LG	W	L	PCT	G	GS	CG-SHO	SV-BS	IP	H	R	HR	HB	BB-IB	SO	ERA	AERA	OAV	OOB	AB-HR-SH	AVG	PB	SUP	APR	DL	PW
1948	Chi N	2	9	.182	29	12	3-1	0	103.2	100	57	4	3	48	51	4.43	88	.254	.339	30-0-3	.133	-1	74	-5		-0.6
1949	Pit N	13	7	.650	34	21	10-1	0	177.1	186	89	15	5	58	93	3.96	106	.268	.329	55-0-6	.236	3	99	3		0.7
1950	Pit N	12	15	.444	37	33	11-2	0	249.1	262	138	18	6	92	93	4.30	102	.265	.332	90-2-2	.289	7	92	1		0.7
1951	Pit N	3	6	.333	10	10	2-1	0	59.2	64	38	5	4	31	19	5.58	76	.273	.371	21-1-1	.333	2	67	-7		-0.7
	StL N	11	6	.647	21	16	9-1	0	129.1	120	59	13	0	56	45	3.83	104	.251	.329	49-0-1	.163	0	129	3		0.3
	Year	14	12	.538	31	26	11-2	0	189	184	97	18	4	87	64	4.38	92	.259	.343	70-1-2	.214	2	105	-2		-0.4
1952	StL N	4	4	.500	26	13	2-1	1	98.1	110	60	4	6	33	47	4.12	90	.285	.344	32-0-1	.281	3	105	-4		0.1
1953	StL N	3	6	.333	32	8	0	1	79.2	82	50	7	1	43	26	4.86	88	.266	.358	17	.118	-1	76	-7	30	-0.7
Total	6	48	53	.475	189	113	37-7	1	897.1	924	482	70	21	361	374	4.29	96	.266	.338	294-3-14	.235	13	95	-16	30	-0.2

CHAMBERS, JOHNNIE Johnnie Monroe B9.10.1911 Copperhill TN D5.11.1977 Palatka FL BL/TR/6-0/185 d5.4

YEAR	TM LG	W	L	PCT	G	GS	CG-SHO	SV-BS	IP	H	R	HR	HB	BB-IB	SO	ERA	AERA	OAV	OOB	AB-HR-SH	AVG	PB	SUP	APR	DL	PW
1937	StL N	0	0	—	2	0	0	0	2	5	4	0	0	2	1	18.00	22	.455	.538	0	—	0		-3		-0.1

CHAMBERS, ROME Richard Jerome B8.31.1875 Weaverville NC D8.30.1902 Weaverville NC BL/TL/6-2/173 d5.7

YEAR	TM LG	W	L	PCT	G	GS	CG-SHO	SV-BS	IP	H	R	HR	HB	BB-IB	SO	ERA	AERA	OAV	OOB	AB-HR-SH	AVG	PB	SUP	APR	DL	PW
1900	Bos N	0	0	—	1	0	0	1	4	5	6	0	0	5	2	11.25	37	.313	.476	1	.000	-0		-2		-0.1

CHAMBERS, BILL William Christopher B9.13.1889 Cameron WV D3.27.1962 Fort Wayne IN BR/TR/5-9/185 d7.11

YEAR	TM LG	W	L	PCT	G	GS	CG-SHO	SV-BS	IP	H	R	HR	HB	BB-IB	SO	ERA	AERA	OAV	OOB	AB-HR-SH	AVG	PB	SUP	APR	DL	PW
1910	StL N	0	0	—	1	0	0	0	2	0	0	0	0	1	0	0.00	—	.250	.250	0		0	0	0		0.0

CHAMPION, BILL Buford Billy B9.18.1947 Shelby NC BR/TR/6-4/188(178-200) [PhiN65 3/58] d6.4

YEAR	TM LG	W	L	PCT	G	GS	CG-SHO	SV-BS	IP	H	R	HR	HB	BB-IB	SO	ERA	AERA	OAV	OOB	AB-HR-SH	AVG	PB	SUP	APR	DL	PW
1969	Phi N	5	10	.333	23	20	4-2	1-0	116.2	130	68	7	3	63-4	70	5.01	71	.286	.373	35-0-3	.171	0	114	-17		-1.9
1970	Phi N	0	2	.000	7	1	0	0-0	14	21	14	3	1	10-2	12	9.00	45	.375	.471	3	.000	-0	67	-7		-0.9
1971	Phi N	3	5	.375	37	9	0	0-0	108.2	100	61	10	3	48-4	49	4.39	81	.249	.329	27	.111	-1	61	-10		-0.8
1972	Phi N	4	14	.222	30	22	2	0-0	132.2	155	80	7	4	54-8	49	5.09	71	.301	.366	34-1-5	.147	-1*	73	-19		-2.4
1973	Mil A	5	8	.385	37	11	2	1-1	136.1	139	58	10	4	62-4	67	3.70	103	.267	.349	0	—	0	90	4		0.5
1974	Mil A	11	4	.733	31	23	2	0-0	161.2	168	72	10	0	49-3	60	3.62	101	.270	.321	0	—	0	99	0		-0.1
1975	Mil A	6	6	.500	27	13	3-1	0-0	110	125	77	11	0	55-8	40	5.89	65	.290	.367	0	—	0	97	-22	56	-2.1
1976	Mil A	0	1	.000	10	3	0	0-0	24.1	35	20	0	1	13-2	8	7.03	50	.361	.430	0	—	0	100	-9		-0.4
Total	8	34	50	.405	202	102	13-3	2-1	804.1	873	450	64	13	354-35	360	4.69	78	.282	.355	99-1-8	.141	-1	91	-80	56	-8.1

CHANCE, DEAN Wilmer Dean B6.1.1941 Plain Twp. OH BR/TR/6-3/200* d9.11

YEAR	TM LG	W	L	PCT	G	GS	CG-SHO	SV-BS	IP	H	R	HR	HB	BB-IB	SO	ERA	AERA	OAV	OOB	AB-HR-SH	AVG	PB	SUP	APR	DL	PW
1961	LA A	0	2	.000	5	4	0	0	18.1	33	15	0	1	5-1	11	6.87	66	.412	.443	5	.000	-1	69	-4		-0.4
1962	LA A	14	10	.583	50	24	6-2	8	206.2	195	83	14	5	66-5	127	2.96	130	.250	.311	65-0-7	.062	-5	109	20		1.8
1963	LA A	13	18	.419	45	35	6-2	3	248	229	109	10	10	90-7	168	3.19	107	.243	.315	80-0-7	.150	-1	89	4		0.4
1964	LA A★	20	9	.690	46	35	15-11	4	278.1	194	56	7	2	86-9	207	1.65	199	.195	.260	89-0-8	.079	-5	80	58		5.6
1965	Cal A	15	10	.600	36	33	11-1	0	225.2	197	86	12	9	101-10	196	3.15	108	.238	.327	75-0-5	.093	-2	104	7		0.8
1966	Cal A	12	17	.414	41	37	11-2	1	259.2	206	113	18	7	114-9	180	3.08	109	.222	.310	76-0-8	.026	-6	103	2		-0.4
1967	Min A★	20	14	.588	41	39	18-5	1	283.2	244	109	17	7	68-7	220	2.73	127	.229	.278	92-0-7	.033	-6	107	18		1.6
1968	Min A	16	16	.500	43	39	15-6	0	292	224	96	15	10	63-8	234	2.53	122	.211	.260	93-0-9	.054	-6	94	18		1.6
1969	†Min A	5	4	.556	20	15	1	0	88.1	76	39	6	4	35-3	50	2.95	123	.233	.314	24-0-5	.042	-1	118	4	54	0.2
1970	Cle A	9	8	.529	45	19	1-1	4-0	155	172	80	14	8	59-11	109	4.24	95	.287	.355	42-0-4	.071	-3	92	-4		-0.8

YEAR	TM LG	W	L	PCT	G	GS	CG-SHO	SV-BS	IP	H	R	HR	HB	BB-IB	SO	ERA	AERA	OAV	OOB	AB-HR-SH	AVG	PB	SUP	APR	DL	PW
	NY N	0	1	.000	3	0	0	1-0	2	3	3	0	0	2-1	0	13.50	30	.500	.625	0	—	0		-2		-0.4
1971	Det A	4	6	.400	31	14	0	0-0	89.2	91	43	5	4	50-4	64	3.51	103	.265	.363	21-0-1	.000	-2	76	-1	21	-0.4
Total	11	128	115	.527	406	294	83-33	23-0	2147.1	1864	832	122	65	739-75	1534	2.92	119	.234	.303	662-0-61	.066	-37	97	120	75	9.6

CHANDLER, ED Edward Oliver B2.17.1922 Pinson AL D7.6.2003 Las Vegas NV BR/TR/6-2/190 d4.18

YEAR	TM LG	W	L	PCT	G	GS	CG-SHO	SV-BS	IP	H	R	HR	HB	BB-IB	SO	ERA	AERA	OAV	OOB	AB-HR-SH	AVG	PB	SUP	APR	DL	PW
1947	Bro N	0	1	.000	15	1	0	1	29.2	31	23	7	0	12	8	6.37	65	.263	.331	2-0-1	.000	0	85	-7		-0.3

CHANDLER, SPUD Spurgeon Ferdinand B9.12.1907 Commerce GA D1.9.1990 S.Pasadena FL BR/TR/6-0/181 d5.6 Mil 1944-45 C2 Col Georgia

YEAR	TM LG	W	L	PCT	G	GS	CG-SHO	SV-BS	IP	H	R	HR	HB	BB-IB	SO	ERA	AERA	OAV	OOB	AB-HR-SH	AVG	PB	SUP	APR	DL	PW
1937	NY A	7	4	.636	12	10	6-2	0	82.1	79	31	8	1	20	31	2.84	156	.253	.300	30-0-5	.133	-2	129	15		1.7
1938	NY A	14	5	.737	23	23	14-2	0	172	183	86	7	2	47	36	4.03	113	.271	.320	69-3-3	.203	2	128	12		1.5
1939	NY A	3	0	1.000	11	0	0	0	19	26	7	0	0	9	4	2.84	153	.329	.398	5	.400	1		3		0.6
1940	NY A	8	7	.533	27	24	6-1	0	172	184	100	12	6	60	60	4.60	88	.275	.341	60-2-4	.150	1	141	-12		-0.7
1941	†NY A	10	4	.714	28	20	11-4	4	163.2	146	68	9	0	60	60	3.19	123	.239	.307	60-0-3	.183	-1	120	14		1.2
1942	†NY A★	16	5	.762	24	24	17-3	0	200.2	176	64	13	4	74	74	2.38	145	.237	.309	71-0-6	.211	4	138	24		3.0
1943	†NY A☆	20	4	.833	30	30	20-5	0	253	197	62	5	4	54	134	1.64	197	.215	.261	97-2-3	.258	7	110	42		5.3
1944	NY A	0	0	—	1	1	1-0	0	6	6	3	1	1	1	1	4.50	77	.300	.364	1-0-1	.000	-0	144	0		0.0
1945	NY A	2	1	.667	4	4	2-1	0	31	30	16	2	0	7	12	4.65	75	.250	.291	12	.333	1	111	-3		-0.2
1946	NY A☆	20	8	.714	34	32	20-6	2	257.1	200	71	7	1	90	138	2.10	164	.218	.288	94-0-5	.149	-0	119	38		4.5
1947	†NY A☆	9	5	.643	17	16	13-2	0	128	100	41	4	0	41	68	2.46	144	.214	.277	49-2-3	.245	4	106	15		2.2
Total	11	109	43	.717	211	184	109-26	6	1485	1327	549	64	19	463	614	2.84	132	.240	.301	548-9-33	.201	17	124	148		19.1

CHANEY, ESTY Esty Clyon B1.29.1891 Hadley PA D2.5.1952 Cleveland OH BR/TR/5-11/170 d8.2

YEAR	TM LG	W	L	PCT	G	GS	CG-SHO	SV-BS	IP	H	R	HR	HB	BB-IB	SO	ERA	AERA	OAV	OOB	AB-HR-SH	AVG	PB	SUP	APR	DL	PW
1913	Bos A	0	0	—	1	0	0	0	1	1	1	0	0	2	0	9.00	33	.200	.429	0	—	0		-1		0.0
1914	Bro F	0	0	—	1	0	0	0	4	7	3	0	0	2	1	6.75	43	.389	.450	1	.000	-0		-1		-0.1
Total	2	0	0	—	2	0	0	0	5	8	4	0	0	2	1	7.20	40	.348	.444	1	.000	-0		-2		-0.1

CHAPIN, DARRIN Darrin John B2.1.1966 Warren OH BR/TR/6-0/170* [NYA86*6/155] d9.21 Col Cleveland St.

YEAR	TM LG	W	L	PCT	G	GS	CG-SHO	SV-BS	IP	H	R	HR	HB	BB-IB	SO	ERA	AERA	OAV	OOB	AB-HR-SH	AVG	PB	SUP	APR	DL	PW
1991	NY A	0	1	.000				0-0	5.1	5	4	1	0	6-0	5	5.06	82	.158	.360	0	—	0		-1		-0.1
1992	Phi N	0	0	—	1	0	0	0-0	2	2	2	1	0	0-0	1	9.00	39	.250	.250	0	—	0		-1		-0.1
Total	2	0	1	.000	4	0	0	0-0	7.1	5	5	1	0	6-0	6	6.14	65	.185	.333	0	—	0		-1		-0.2

CHAPLIN, TINY James Bailey B7.13.1905 Los Angeles CA D3.25.1939 National City CA BR/TR/6-1/195 d4.13 Col Florida

YEAR	TM LG	W	L	PCT	G	GS	CG-SHO	SV-BS	IP	H	R	HR	HB	BB-IB	SO	ERA	AERA	OAV	OOB	AB-HR-SH	AVG	PB	SUP	APR	DL	PW
1928	NY N	0	2	.000	12	1	0	0	24	27	15	0	0	8	5	4.50	87	.284	.340	5	.000	-1	152	-2		-0.2
1930	NY N	2	6	.250	19	8	3	1	73	89	45	8	4	16	20	5.18	91	.305	.349	19-1-1	.105	-0	62	-2		-0.2
1931	NY N	3	0	1.000	16	3	1	1	42.1	39	17	2	2	16	7	3.19	116	.242	.318	11-0-1	.182	0	155	3		0.2
1936	Bos N	10	15	.400	40	31	14	2	231.2	273	131	21	3	62	86	4.12	93	.294	.340	84-0-5	.202	-0	113	-12		-1.1
Total	4	15	23	.395	87	43	18	4	371	428	208	31	9	102	118	4.25	94	.290	.340	119-1-7	.176	-1	105	-13		-1.3

CHAPMAN, ED Edwin Volney B11.28.1905 Courtland MS D5.3.2000 Clarksdale MS BB/TR/6-1/185 d8.6 b-Calvin Col Mississippi St.

YEAR	TM LG	W	L	PCT	G	GS	CG-SHO	SV-BS	IP	H	R	HR	HB	BB-IB	SO	ERA	AERA	OAV	OOB	AB-HR-SH	AVG	PB	SUP	APR	DL	PW
1933	Was A	0	0	—	6	1	0	0	9	10	9	2	0	2	4	8.00	52	.270	.308	3	.000	-0	163	-4		-0.2

CHAPMAN, FRED Frederick Joseph B11.24.1872 Little Cooley PA D12.14.1957 Union City PA BR/TR/5-8/165 d7.22

YEAR	TM LG	W	L	PCT	G	GS	CG-SHO	SV-BS	IP	H	R	HR	HB	BB-IB	SO	ERA	AERA	OAV	OOB	AB-HR-SH	AVG	PB	SUP	APR	DL	PW
1887	Phi AA	0	0	—	1	1	1	0	7	8	6	0	0	4	0	7.20	60	.364	.417	2	—	-0	59	-2		-0.1

CHAPMAN, BEN William Benjamin B12.25.1908 Nashville TN D7.7.1993 Hoover AL BR/TR/6-0/190 M4/C1 ▲

YEAR	TM LG	W	L	PCT	G	GS	CG-SHO	SV-BS	IP	H	R	HR	HB	BB-IB	SO	ERA	AERA	OAV	OOB	AB-HR-SH	AVG	PB	SUP	APR	DL	PW
1944	Bro N	5	3	.625	11	9	6	0	79.1	75	36	4	3	33	37	3.40	104	.242	.321	38-0-1	.368	6*	157	1		0.7
1945	Bro N	3	3	.500	10	7	2	0	53.2	64	33	3	3	32	23	5.53	68	.296	.394	22	.136	-1*	110	-7		-0.7
	Phi N	0	0	—	3	0	0	0	7	7	8	0	0	6	4	7.71	50	.259	.394	51	.314	0*		-3		-0.8
	Year	3	3	.500	13	7	2	0	60.2	71	41	3	3	38	27	5.79	65	.292	.394	73	.260	-0	109	-12		-0.8
1946	Phi N	0	0	—	2	0	0	0	1	1	0	0	0	0	1	0.00	—	.200	.200	1	.000	-0		0		0.0
Total	3	8	6	.571	26	16	8	0	141	147	77	7	6	71	65	4.40	83	.263	.353	112-0-1	.295	6	136	-9		-0.1

CHAPPELLE, BILL William Hogan "Big Bill" B3.22.1881 Waterloo NY D12.31.1944 Mineola NY BR/TR/6-2/206 d8.20

YEAR	TM LG	W	L	PCT	G	GS	CG-SHO	SV-BS	IP	H	R	HR	HB	BB-IB	SO	ERA	AERA	OAV	OOB	AB-HR-SH	AVG	PB	SUP	APR	DL	PW
1908	Bos N	2	4	.333	13	6	3-1	0	70.1	60	28	0	4	17	23	1.79	135	.233	.290	21-0-2	.048	-1	54	2		0.7
1909	Bos N	1	1	.500	5	3	2	0	29	31	13	0	1	11	8	1.86	151	.279	.350	11-1-0	.364	2	107	1		0.4
	Cin N	0	0	—	1	0	0	0	4	5	2	0	1	2	0	2.25	115	.278	.381	1	.000	-0		0		0.0
	Year	1	1	.500	6	3	2	1	33	36	15	0	2	13	8	1.91	146	.279	.354	12-1-0	.333	2	108	1		0.4
1914	Bro F	4	2	.667	16	6	4	0	74.1	71	43	1	3	29	31	3.15	91	.255	.332	23-0-1	.000	-4	119	-6		-0.8
Total	3	7	7	.500	35	15	9-1	1	177.2	167	86	1	9	59	62	2.38	113	.251	.321	56-1-3	.089	-3	91	-3		-0.4

CHARLTON, NORM Norman Wood B1.6.1963 Fort Polk LA BB/TL/6-3/205(195-210) [MonN84 1/28] d8.19 Col Rice [DL 1987 Cin N 81, 1994 Phi N 131, 2002 Sea A 138]

YEAR	TM LG	W	L	PCT	G	GS	CG-SHO	SV-BS	IP	H	R	HR	HB	BB-IB	SO	ERA	AERA	OAV	OOB	AB-HR-SH	AVG	PB	SUP	APR	DL	PW
1988	Cin N	4	5	.444	10	10	0	0-0	61.1	60	29	7	2	20-2	39	3.96	90	.256	.318	15-0-4	.000	-1	72	-1		-0.3
1989	Cin N	8	3	.727	69	0	0	0-1	95.1	67	38	5	2	40-7	98	2.93	123	.197	.284	5	.000	-1		6		0.6
1990	†Cin N	12	9	.571	56	16	1-1	2-1	154.1	131	53	10	4	70-4	117	2.74	144	.231	.319	37	.135	0*	77	19	48	2.4
1991	Cin N	3	5	.375	39	11	0	1-3	108.1	92	37	6	6	34-4	77	2.91	131	.236	.306	23-0-4	.043	-2*	64	12		0.9
1992	Cin N★	4	2	.667	64	0	0	26-8	81.1	79	34	9	7	26-4	90	2.99	121	.262	.323	5-0-2	.200	-0		1	72	0.6
1993	Sea A	1	3	.250	34	0	0	18-3	34.2	22	14	2	4	17-0	48	2.34	191	.179	.277	0	—	0		7		1.1
1995	Phi N	2	5	.286	25	0	0	0-1	22	23	19	2	3	15-3	12	7.36	57	.280	.406	1	1.000	0		-1		-1.4
	†Sea A	2	1	.667	30	0	0	14-1	47.2	23	12	2	1	16-0	58	1.51	316	.143	.223	0	—	0		16		1.1
1996	Sea A	4	7	.364	70	0	0	20-7	75.2	68	37	7	1	38-1	73	4.04	123	.244	.334	0	—	0		-8		-0.3
1997	†Sea A	3	8	.273	71	0	0	14-11	69.1	89	59	7	4	47-2	55	7.27	62	.312	.417	0	—	0		-21		-3.5
1998	Bal A	2	1	.667	36	0	0	0-1	35	46	27	5	0	25-0	41	6.94	66	.305	.401	0	—	0		-9		-0.6
	Atl N	0	0	—	13	0	0	1-0	13	7	2	0	1	8-0	6	1.38	301	.167	.308	1	.000	-0		4		0.3
1999	TB A	2	3	.400	42	0	0	0-1	50.2	49	29	4	1	36-0	45	4.44	112	.257	.372	0	—	0		-7		-0.5
2000	Cin N	0	0	—	2	0	0	0-0	3	6	4	0	1	6-0	1	27.00	18	.429	.600	0	—	0		-7		-0.2
2001	†Sea A	4	1	.800	47	0	0	1-1	47.2	36	19	4	4	16-0	48	3.02	141	.212	.274	0	—	0		6	48	0.3
Total	13	51	54	.486	605	37	1-1	79-39	899.1	798	419	70	32	409-27	808	3.71	112	.240	.327	87-0-10	.092	-2	67	37	518	3.1

CHARTON, PETE Frank Lane B12.21.1942 Jackson TN BL/TR/6-2/190 d4.19 Col Baylor

YEAR	TM LG	W	L	PCT	G	GS	CG-SHO	SV-BS	IP	H	R	HR	HB	BB-IB	SO	ERA	AERA	OAV	OOB	AB-HR-SH	AVG	PB	SUP	APR	DL	PW
1964	Bos A	0	2	.000	25	5	0	0	65	67	39	12	1	24-1	37	5.26	73	.275	.342	10	.100	-0	55	-8		-0.4

CHASE, KEN Kendall Fay "Lefty" B10.6.1913 Oneonta NY D1.16.1985 Oneonta NY BL/TL/6-2/210 d4.23

YEAR	TM LG	W	L	PCT	G	GS	CG-SHO	SV-BS	IP	H	R	HR	HB	BB-IB	SO	ERA	AERA	OAV	OOB	AB-HR-SH	AVG	PB	SUP	APR	DL	PW
1936	Was A	0	0	—	1	0	0	0	2.1	2	3	0	0	4	1	11.57	41	.250	.500	1	1.000	1		-2		0.0
1937	Was A	4	3	.571	14	9	4	0	76.1	74	41	4	0	60	43	4.13	107	.257	.385	29-0-1	.034	-4	79	3		-0.1
1938	Was A	9	10	.474	32	21	7	1	150	151	99	4	4	113	64	5.58	81	.268	.394	48-0-4	.208	1	91	-14		-1.3
1939	Was A	10	19	.345	32	31	15-1	0	232	215	116	10	1	114	118	3.80	114	.243	.330	89	.169	-3	78	13		1.3
1940	Was A	15	17	.469	35	34	20-1	0	261.2	260	120	14	5	143	129	3.23	129	.261	.357	92-1-5	.163	-1	81	24		2.1
1941	Was A	6	18	.250	33	30	8-1	0	205.2	228	136	11	3	115	98	5.08	80	.280	.371	74-0-1	.149	-2	90	-23		0.4
1942	Bos A	5	1	.833	10	4	0	0	80.1	82	37	5	0	41	34	3.81	98	.263	.348	33-0-3	.182	1	154	0		0.3
1943	Bos A	0	4	.000	7	5	0	0	27.1	36	25	0	0	30	9	6.91	48	.316	.458	11	.091	-1	66	-12		-1.2
	NY N	4	12	.250	21	20	6-1	0	129.1	140	70	7	2	74	86	4.11	84	.275	.369	42-0-3	.214	0*	76	-11		-1.1
Total	8	53	84	.387	188	160	62-4	1	1165	1188	647	55	15	694	582	4.27	97	.265	.365	419-1-17	.165	-8	86	-22		-3.1

CHAVEZ, ANTHONY Anthony Francisco B10.22.1970 Turlock CA BR/TR/5-11/180 [AnaA92 50/1392] d9.2 Col San Jose St.

YEAR	TM LG	W	L	PCT	G	GS	CG-SHO	SV-BS	IP	H	R	HR	HB	BB-IB	SO	ERA	AERA	OAV	OOB	AB-HR-SH	AVG	PB	SUP	APR	DL	PW
1997	Ana A	0	0	—	7	0	0	0-0	9.2	7	1	1	0	5-1	10	0.93	495	.206	.300	0	—	0		1		0.0

CHAVEZ, NESTOR Nestor Isais (Silva) B7.6.1947 Chacao, Venez D3.16.1969 Maracaibo, Venez BR/TR/6-0/170 d9.9

YEAR	TM LG	W	L	PCT	G	GS	CG-SHO	SV-BS	IP	H	R	HR	HB	BB-IB	SO	ERA	AERA	OAV	OOB	AB-HR-SH	AVG	PB	SUP	APR	DL	PW
1967	SF N	1	0	1.000	2	0	0	0	3	3	1	0	0	3	3	0.00	—	.211	.318	1	.000	-0		1		0.0

CHEADLE, DAVE David Baird B2.19.1952 Greensboro NC BL/TL/6-2/203 [NYA70 1/12] d9.16

YEAR	TM LG	W	L	PCT	G	GS	CG-SHO	SV-BS	IP	H	R	HR	HB	BB-IB	SO	ERA	AERA	OAV	OOB	AB-HR-SH	AVG	PB	SUP	APR	DL	PW
1973	Atl N	0	0	—	2	1	0	0	2	4	4	2	0	3-2	2	18.00	22	.250	.455	0	—	0		-3		-0.1

CHECH, CHARLIE Charles William B4.27.1878 Madison WI D1.31.1938 Los Angeles CA BR/TR/5-11.5/190 d4.14 Col Wisconsin-Madison

YEAR	TM LG	W	L	PCT	G	GS	CG-SHO	SV-BS	IP	H	R	HR	HB	BB-IB	SO	ERA	AERA	OAV	OOB	AB-HR-SH	AVG	PB	SUP	APR	DL	PW
1905	Cin N	14	14	.500	39	25	20-1	0	267.2	300	139	4	11	77	79	2.89	114	.288	.344	89-0-8	.191	1	113	9		0
1906	Cin N	1	4	.200	11	5	5	0	66	59	32	1	6	24	17	2.32	119	.243	.326	25	.200	1	74	0		0
1908	Cle A	11	7	.611	27	20	14-4	0	165.1	136	51	2	7	34	51	1.74	137	.229	.279	48-0-3	.104	-1	92	10		1
1909	Bos A	7	5	.583	17	13	6-1	0	106.2	107	51	3	6	27	40	2.95	85	.260	.314	36	.083	-2	115	-6		-1
Total	4	33	30	.524	94	63	45-6	3	606	602	273	10	29	162	187	2.52	113	.263	.320	198-0-11	.152	-1	103	13		1

YEAR	TM LG	W	L	PCT	G	GS	CG-SHO	SV-BS	IP	H	R	HR	HB	BB-IB	SO	ERA	AERA	OAV	OOB	AB-HR-SH	AVG	PB	SUP	APR	DL	PW

CHECO, ROBINSON Robinson (Perez) B9.9.1971 Santo Domingo, D.R. BR/TR/6-1/185* d9.16

1997	Bos A	1	1	.500	5	2	0	0-0	13.1	12	5	0	0	3-0	14	3.38	138	.235	.278	0	—	0	49	2	42	0.3
1998	Bos A	0	2	.000	5	2	0	0-0	7.2	11	8	3	0	5-0	5	9.39	50	.379	.471	0	—	0	89	-4		-0.6
1999	LA N	2	2	.500	9	2	0	0-0	15.2	24	20	5	0	13-1	11	10.34	42	.333	.435	3-0-1	.333	0	137	-11	45	-1.9
Total	3	3	5	.375	16	6	0	0-0	36.2	47	33	8	0	21-1	30	7.61	60	.309	.393	3-0-1	.333	0	91	-13	87	-2.2

CHEEVES, VIRGIL Virgil Earl "Chief" B2.12.1901 Oklahoma City OK D5.5.1979 Dallas TX BR/TR/6-0/195 d9.7

1920	Chi N	0	0	—	5	2	0	0	18	16	7	0	0	7	3	3.50	92	.250	.324	4	.000	-0	61	0		-0.1
1921	Chi N	11	12	.478	37	22	9-1	0	163	192	97	8	9	47	39	4.64	82	.309	.366	48-0-4	.167	-2	85	-14		-2.1
1922	Chi N	12	11	.522	39	22	9-1	2	182.2	195	99	9	10	76	40	4.09	103	.281	.360	62-1-2	.210	1	88	2		0.3
1923	Chi N	3	4	.429	19	8	0	0	71.1	89	54	8	3	37	13	6.18	65	.314	.399	23	.174	-1	121	-15		-1.3
1924	Cle A	0	0	—	8	1	0	0	17.1	26	17	2	1	17	2	7.79	55	.388	.518	4	.250	-1	138	-6		-0.3
1927	NY N	0	0	—	3	0	0	0	6.1	8	3	1	0	4	1	4.26	90	.333	.429	0-0-1	—	0		0		0.0
Total	6	26	27	.491	111	55	18-2	2	458.2	526	277	28	23	188	98	4.73	84	.300	.375	141-1-7	.184	-1	92	-33		-3.5

CHELINI, ITALO Italo Vincent "Chilly", "Lefty" B10.10.1914 San Francisco CA D8.25.1972 San Francisco CA BL/TL/5-10.5/175 d9.12

1935	Chi A	0	0	—	2	0	0	0	5	7	7	1	1	4	1	12.60	37	.350	.480	2	.500	0				-0.2
1936	Chi A	4	3	.571	18	6	5	0	83.2	100	51	8	0	30	16	4.95	105	.291	.348	32	.156	-1	110	3		-0.2
1937	Chi A	0	1	.000	4	0	0	0	8.2	15	10	2	1	0	3	10.38	44	.405	.421	1	.000	0		-5		-0.4
Total	3	4	4	.500	24	6	5	0	97.1	122	68	11	2	34	20	5.83	88	.304	.362	35	.171	-1	110	-6		-0.6

CHEN, BRUCE Bruce Kastulo B6.19.1977 Panama City, Pan BL/TL/6-2/210(150-214) d9.7

1998	Atl N	2	0	1.000	4	4	0	0-0	20.1	23	9	3	1	9-1	17	3.98	105	.287	.367	7-0-2	.143	-0	149	1		0.0
1999	Atl N	2	2	.500	16	7	0	0-0	51	38	32	11	2	27-3	45	5.47	82	.208	.315	11-0-1	.000	-1	73	-5		-0.5
2000	Atl N	4	0	1.000	22	0	0	0-0	39.2	35	15	4	1	19-2	32	2.50	181	.232	.318	5-0-2	.000	-1	8			0.6
	Phi N	3	4	.429	15	15	0	0-0	94.1	81	39	14	1	27-2	80	3.63	127	.232	.288	25-0-5	.040	-1	91	11		0.5
	Year	7	4	.636	37	15	0	0-0	134	116	54	18	2	46-4	112	3.29	139	.232	.298	30-0-7	.033	-3	91	18		1.1
2001	Phi N	4	5	.444	16	16	0	0-0	86.1	90	53	19	1	31-4	79	5.00	82	.262	.322	28-0-3	.107	-1	122	-10		-1.0
	NY N	3	2	.600	11	11	0	0-0	59.2	56	37	10	0	28-0	47	4.68	86	.255	.335	19-0-2	.158	-0	131	-6		-0.4
	Year	7	7	.500	27	27	0	0-0	146	146	90	29	1	59-4	126	4.87	84	.259	.327	47-0-5	.128	-1	126	-15		-1.4
2002	NY N	0	0	—	1	0	0	0-0	0.2	1	0	0	0	0-0	0	0.00	—	.333	.333	0	—	0		0		0.0
	Mon N	2	3	.400	15	5	0	0-0	37.1	47	29	9	1	23-3	43	6.99	63	.303	.397	12-0-1	.417	2	59	-9		-0.9
	Cin N	0	2	.000	39	1	0	0-0	39.2	37	24	7	1	20-2	37	4.31	99	.243	.330	3-0-1	.000	-0	65	-1		-0.1
	Year	2	5	.286	55	6	0	0-0	77.2	85	53	16	2	43-5	80	5.56	78	.274	.363	15-0-2	.333	1	61	-11		-1.0
2003	Hou N	0	0	—	11	0	0	0-0	12	14	8	2	2	8-1	8	6.00	74	.311	.421	1	.000	0	128	-1		-0.1
	Bos A	0	1	.000	5	2	0	0-0	12.1	12	8	4	0	2-0	12	5.11	91	.255	.280	0	—	0		-2		-0.1
2004	Bal A	2	1	.667	8	7	1	0-0	47.2	39	19	7	0	16-0	32	3.02	154	.220	.284	0	—	0	105	8		0.5
2005	Bal A	13	10	.565	34	32	1	0-0	197.1	187	94	33	9	63-0	133	3.83	116	.248	.312	3	.333	1	109	12		1.4
Total	8	35	30	.538	197	100	2	0-0	698.1	660	367	123	19	273-18	565	4.27	103	.248	.320	114-0-17	.123	-4	106	6		-0.1

CHENEY, LARRY Laurance Russell B5.2.1886 Belleville KS D1.6.1969 Daytona Beach FL BR/TR/6-1.5/185 d9.9

1911	Chi N	1	0	1.000	3	1	0	0	10	8	0	0	3	11	0.00	—	.229	.289	4	.250	0	113	4		0.4
1912	Chi N	**26**	10	.722	42	37	28-4	0	303.1	262	122	5	7	111	140	2.85	117	.234	.307	106-1-10	.226	5	119	17		2.2
1913	Chi N	21	14	.600	54	36	25-2	**11**	305	271	117	7	8	98	136	2.57	124	.241	.306	104-0-6	.192	2*	108	20		2.6
1914	Chi N	20	18	.526	**50**	40	21-6	5	311.1	239	136	9	10	140	157	2.54	109	.215	.308	100-0-5	.180	3	100	8		1.3
1915	Chi N	8	9	.471	25	18	6-2	0	131.1	120	69	1	4	55	68	3.56	78	.246	.327	40-0-2	.150	-1	107	-12		-1.6
	Bro N	0	2	.000	5	4	1	0	27	16	10	0	2	17	11	1.67	167	.174	.315	7	.143	0	94	2		0.2
	Year	8	11	.421	30	22	7-2	0	158.1	136	79	1	6	72	79	3.24	86	.234	.325	47-0-2	.149	-1	105	-9		-1.4
1916	†Bro N	18	12	.600	41	32	15-5	2	253	178	91	5	10	105	166	1.92	140	**.198**	.289	79-0-4	.114	-3	105	15		1.6
1917	Bro N	8	12	.400	35	24	14-1	2	210.1	185	80	4	5	73	102	2.35	119	.239	.309	68-0-1	.206	2	88	6		0.8
1918	Bro N	11	13	.458	32	21	15	1	200.2	177	84	2	10	74	83	3.00	93	.241	.319	66-0-3	.242	2*	71	-3		-0.1
1919	Bro N	1	3	.250	9	4	2	0	39	45	21	1	2	14	14	4.15	72	.300	.367	11	.182	-0	80	-4		-0.5
	Bos N	2	2	.000	8	2	0	0	33	35	20	0	0	15	13	3.55	81	.294	.373	11	.182	0	125	-4		-0.2
	Phi N	3	5	.286	9	6	5	0	57.1	69	34	2	1	28	25	4.55	71	.315	.395	21	.095	-2	82	-7		-1.1
	Year	3	10	.231	26	12	7	0	129.1	149	75	3	3	57	52	4.18	73	.305	.381	43	.140	-2	89	-15		-1.8
Total	9	116	100	.537	313	225	132-20	19	1881.1	1605	784	36	59	733	926	2.70	109	.234	.313	617-1-31	.186	9	102	42		5.6

CHENEY, TOM Thomas Edgar B10.14.1934 Morgan GA D11.1.2001 Rome GA BR/TR/6-0/180* d4.21

1957	StL N	0	1	.000	4	3	0	0	9	6	6	0	0	15-0	10	5.00	79	.207	.477	2-0-1	.000	-0	126	-1		-0.1
1959	StL N	0	1	.000	11	2	0	0	11.2	9	7	9	2	11-2	8	6.94	61	.354	.484	0	—	0	105	-3		-0.2
1960	†Pit N	2	2	.500	11	8	1-1	0	52	44	25	5	0	33-0	35	3.98	94	.238	.352	17-0-1	.176	0	103	-1		-0.1
1961	Pit N	0	0	—	1	0	0	0	0	1	5	1	0	4-0	0	∞	—	.500	.833	0	—	0		-4		-0.3
	Was A	1	3	.250	10	7	0	0	29.2	32	30	8	0	26-0	20	8.80	46	.283	.408	8-0-1	.500	2*	91	-14	38	-1.4
1962	Was A	7	9	.438	37	23	4-3	1	173.1	134	68	12	8	97-0	147	3.17	127	.213	.318	48-0-6	.063	-3	79	16		1.1
1963	Was A	8	9	.471	23	21	7-4	0	136.1	99	51	14	1	40-3	97	2.71	137	.202	.262	46-0-2	.109	-3*	75	13		1.2
1964	Was A	1	3	.250	15	6	1	1	48.2	45	26	10	0	13-1	25	3.70	100	.245	.293	12-0-4	.250	-1	84	-1	101	-0.1
1966	Was A	0	1	.000	3	1	0	0	5.1	4	4	1	1	6-0	3	5.06	68	.222	.440	0	—	0	178	-1		-0.2
Total	8	19	29	.396	115	71	13-8	2	466	382	224	55	3	145-6	345	3.77	103	.222	.322	133-0-15	.135	-8	86	4	139	-0.1

CHESBRO, JACK John Dwight "Happy Jack" B6.5.1874 N.Adams MA D11.6.1931 Conway MA BR/TR/5-9/180 d7.12 C1 HF1946

1899	Pit N	6	9	.400	19	17	15	0	149	165	99	3	11	59	28	4.11	99	.280	.357	58-0-2	.155	-3	88	-6		-0.9
1900	Pit N	15	13	.536	32	26	20-3	1	215.2	220	123	4	12	79	56	3.67	99	.264	.336	85	.176	-1	112	1		-0.1
1901	Pit N	21	10	**.677**	36	28	26-6	1	287.2	261	104	4	14	52	129	2.38	137	.240	.284	116-1-4	.216	3	108	32		3.3
1902	Pit N	**28**	6	**.824**	35	33	31-8	1	286.1	242	81	1	21	62	136	2.17	126	.229	.285	112-0-4	.179	-2	147	23		2.3
1903	NY A	21	15	.583	40	36	33-1	0	324.2	300	140	7	9	74	147	2.77	113	.245	.293	124-2-3	.185	-1	93	12		1.2
1904	NY A	**41**	12	**.774**	55	51	48-6	0	454.2	338	128	4	7	88	239	1.82	149	**.208**	.252	174-1-3	.236	6*	113	**41**		6.1
1905	NY A	19	15	.559	41	38	24-3	1	303.1	262	125	5	6	71	156	2.20	134	.235	.284	112-0-2	.188	0	98	16		1.8
1906	NY A	23	17	.575	**49**	**42**	24-4	1	325	314	138	2	10	75	152	2.96	100	.257	.305	125-1-0	.208	-1	103	0		-0.1
1907	NY A	10	10	.500	30	25	17-1	0	206	192	83	0	6	46	78	2.53	110	.249	.297	76	.197	-1	82	6		0.6
1908	NY A	14	20	.412	45	31	20-3	1	288.2	276	134	6	14	67	124	2.93	85	.256	.307	102-0-3	.176	-2	80	-12		-1.6
1909	NY A	0	4	.000	9	4	2	0	49.2	76	47	2	3	13	17	6.34	40	.347	.394	17	.176	-0	77	-19		-1.4
	Bos A	0	1	.000	1	1	0	0	6	7	4	1	0	4	3	4.50	56	.318	.423	2	.500	0	141	-1		-0.2
	Year	0	5	.000	10	5	2	0	55.2	77	51	3	3	17	20	6.14	41	.344	.398	19	.211	0	89	-20		-1.6
Total	11	198	132	.600	392	332	260-35	5	2896.2	2647	1206	39	113	690	1265	2.68	111	.244	.297	1103-5-21	.197	-2	103	93		11.0

CHESNES, BOB Robert Vincent B5.6.1921 Oakland CA D5.23.1979 Everett WA BB/TR/6-0/180* d5.6

1948	Pit N	14	6	.700	25	23	15	0	194.1	180	92	13	4	90	69	3.57	114	.247	.333	91-1-0	.275	7*	134	8		1.6
1949	Pit N	7	13	.350	27	25	8-1	1	145.1	153	104	16	5	82	49	5.88	71	.276	.384	68-1-0	.250	6*	98	-26		-2.3
1950	Pit N	3	3	.500	9	7	2	0	39	44	26	7	3	17	12	5.54	79	.293	.376	13	.154	-1	118	-4		-0.5
Total	3	24	22	.522	61	55	25-1	1	378.2	377	222	36	12	189	130	4.66	89	.263	.354	172-2-0	.256	12	116	-22		-1.2

CHETKOVICH, MITCH Mitchell B7.21.1917 Fairpoint OH D8.24.1971 Grass Valley CA BR/TR/6-3.5/208 d4.19

| 1945 | Phi N | 0 | 0 | — | 4 | 0 | 0 | 0 | 4 | 4 | 1 | 0 | 0 | 5-0 | 1 | 2.25 | 193 | — | .182 | .357 | — | 0 | 0 | | | 0.0 |

CHEVEZ, TONY Silvio Antonio (b Silvio Antonio Aguilera (Chevez)) B6.20.1954 Telica, Nicaragua BR/TR/5-11/177 d5.31

| 1977 | Bal A | 0 | 0 | — | 4 | 0 | 0 | 0-0 | 8 | 10 | 13 | 3 | 2 | 8-1 | 7 | 12.38 | 31 | .294 | .435 | 0 | — | 0 | | -9 | | -0.4 |

CHIAMPARINO, SCOTT Scott Michael B8.22.1966 San Mateo CA BR/TR/6-2/190(190-205) [OakA87 4/95] d9.5 Col Santa Clara [DL 1993 Fla N 182]

1990	Tex A	1	2	.333	6	6	0	0-0	37.2	36	14	1	2	12-0	19	2.63	150	.250	.314	0	—	0	69	5		0.3
1991	Tex A	1	0	1.000	4	4	0	0-0	22.1	26	11	1	0	12-0	8	4.03	101	.295	.380	0	—	0	122	0	134	0.0
1992	Tex A	0	4	.000	4	4	0	0-0	25.1	25	11	0	0	5-0	13	3.55	108	.260	.294	0	—	0	48	1	112	0.1
Total	3	2	6	.250	14	14	0	0-0	85.1	87	36	4	2	29-0	40	3.27	120	.265	.327	0	—	0	82	6	428	0.4

CHIASSON, SCOTT Scott Christopher B8.14.1977 Norwich CT BR/TR/6-3/200* [KCA98 5/137] d9.19 Col Eastern Connecticut [DL 2003 Chi N 183]

2001	Chi N	1	1	.500	6	0	0	0-0	6.2	5	2	1	0	2-0	6	2.70	155	.200	.286	0	—	0	1	1		0.3
2002	Chi N	0	0	—	4	0	0	0-0	4.2	11	14	2	0	6-1	3	23.14	18	.440	.548	0	—	0		-9		-0.4
Total	2	1	1	.500	10	0	0	0-0	11.1	16	16	3	0	8-1	9	11.12	37	.320	.424	0	—	0		-8	183	-0.1

YEAR	TM	LG	W	L	PCT	G	GS	CG-SHO	SV-BS	IP	H	R	HR	HB	BB-IB	SO	ERA	AERA	OAV	OOB	AB-HR-SH	AVG	PB	SUP	APR	DL	PW

CHIFFER, FLOYD   Floyd John   B4.20.1956 Glen Cove NY   BR/TR/6-2/180*   [SDN78 5/109]   d4.7   Col UCLA

1982	SD	N	4	3	.571	51	0	0	4-7	79.1	73	33	9	4	34-1	48	2.95	116	.247	.330	8	.000	-1		3		0.1
1983	SD	N	0	2	.000	15	0	0	1-0	22.2	17	10	0	0	10-1	15	3.18	110	.210	.297	1		-0		0		0.0
1984	SD	N	1	0	1.000	15	1	0	0-0	28	42	24	1	0	16-2	20	7.71	47	.347	.417	3	.000	-0	197	-12		-0.7
Total	3		5	5	.500	81	1	0	5-7	130	132	67	10	4	60-4	83	4.02	87	.266	.346	12	.000	-1	197	-9		-0.6

CHILD, HARRY   Harry Stephen Patrick (b Harry Stephen Patrick Chesley)   B5.23.1905 Baltimore MD   D11.8.1972 Alexandria VA   BB/TR/5-11/187   d7.16   Col Loyola-Maryland

| 1930 | Was | A | 0 | 0 | — | 6 | 0 | 0 | 0-0 | 10 | 10 | 7 | 1 | 0 | 5 | 5 | 6.30 | 73 | .263 | .349 | 4 | .250 | -0 | | -1 | | -0.1 |

CHILDERS, MATT   Matthew Wilkie   B12.3.1978 Douglas GA   BR/TR/6-5/215*   [MilA97 9/277]   d8.3

2002	Mil	N	0	0	—	8	0	0	0-0	9	13	12	2	1	8-1	6	12.00	34	.342	.468	1	.000	-0		-7		-0.4
2005	Atl	N	0	0	—	3	0	0	0-0	4	5	2	1	1	3-0	2	4.50	96	.294	.429	0	—	0		0		0.0
Total	2		0	0	—	11	0	0	0-0	13	18	14	3	2	11-1	8	9.69	43	.327	.456	1	.000	-0		-7		-0.4

CHILDERS, BILL   William   B St.Louis MO   d7.27

| 1895 | Lou | N | 0 | 0 | — | 1 | 0 | 0 | 0 | 0 | 2 | 6 | 0 | 0 | 5 | 0 | ∞ | — | 1.000 | 1.000 | 0 | — | 0 | | -5 | | -0.4 |

CHILDRESS, ROCKY   Rodney Osborne   B2.18.1962 Santa Rosa CA   BR/TR/6-2/195*   [PhiN80 21/532]   d5.17

1985	Phi	N	0	1	.000	16	1	0	0-0	33.1	45	23	3	0	9-3	14	6.21	60	.326	.362	6-0-2	.167	-0	0	-8		-0.4
1986	Phi	N	0	0	—	2	0	0	0-0	2.2	4	3	0	0	1-0	1	6.75	58	.364	.417	0		0		6		0.3
1987	Hou	N	1	2	.333	32	0	0	0-4	48.1	46	17	4	0	18-6	26	2.98	132	.260	.323	2	.000	-0		-7		-0.4
1988	Hou	N	1	0	1.000	11	0	0	0-0	23.1	26	17	3	1	9-2	24	6.17	54	.280	.350	4	.250	-0		-7		-0.4
Total	4		2	3	.400	61	1	0	0-4	107.2	121	60	10	1	37-11	65	4.76	78	.289	.344	12-0-2	.167	-0	0	-10		-0.6

CHIPMAN, BOB   Robert Howard "Mr. Chips"   B10.11.1918 Brooklyn NY   D11.8.1973 Huntington NY   BL/TL/6-2/190*   d9.28

1941	Bro	N	1	0	1.000	1	0	0	0	5	3	0	0	0	1	3	0.00	—	.150	.190	3	.000	-0		2		0.4
1942	Bro	N	0	0	—	2	0	0	0	1.1	1	0	0	0	2	1	0.00	—	.250	.500	0	—	0		0		0.0
1943	Bro	N	0	0	—	1	0	0	0	1.2	2	0	0	0	0	2	0.00	—	.400	.571	0	—	0		1		0.0
1944	Bro	N	3	1	.750	11	3	1	0	36.1	38	19	1	0	24	20	4.21	84	.270	.376	11-0-2	.182	-0	197	-2		-0.2
	Chi	N	9	9	.500	26	21	8-1	2	129	147	62	9	0	40	41	3.49	101	.288	.340	48	.104	-3	122	0		-0.3
	Year		12	10	.545	37	24	9-1	2	165.1	185	81	10	0	64	61	3.65	97	.284	.348	59-0-2	.119	-3	131	-2		-0.5
1945	†Chi	N	4	5	.444	25	10	3-1	0	72	63	37	4	1	34	29	3.50	104	.230	.317	17-0-3	.176	-1	100	-1		0.0
1946	Chi	N	6	5	.545	34	10	5-3	2	109.1	103	44	8	1	54	42	3.13	106	.255	.344	33-0-1	.061	-3	80	2		-0.1
1947	Chi	N	7	6	.538	32	17	5-1	0	134.2	135	58	6	0	66	51	3.68	107	.264	.348	44-0-3	.091	-3*	80	7		0.4
1948	Chi	N	2	1	.667	34	3	0	4	60.1	73	34	5	0	24	16	3.58	109	.293	.355	16	.250	-0	129	0		0.1
1949	Chi	N	7	8	.467	38	11	3-1	1	113.1	110	65	9	2	63	46	3.97	102	.248	.344	24-0-3	.125	-0	83	-3		-0.4
1950	Bos	N	7	7	.500	27	12	4	1	124	127	75	10	4	37	40	4.43	87	.262	.319	39-0-1	.154	-1	94	-11		-1.2
1951	Bos	N	4	3	.571	33	0	0	4	52	59	29	5	2	19	17	4.85	76	.284	.349	10	.100	-1		-6		-0.9
1952	Bos	N	1	1	.500	29	0	0	0	41.2	28	15	1	0	20	16	2.81	129	.188	.284	5	.400	1		4		0.3
Total	12		51	46	.526	293	87	29-7	14	880.2	889	438	61	10	386	322	3.72	100	.261	.338	250-0-13	.128	-8	101	-7		-1.9

CHITREN, STEVE   Stephen Vincent   B6.8.1967 Tokyo, Japan   BR/TR/6-0/180*   [OakA89 6/166]   d9.5   Col Stanford

1990	Oak	A	1	0	1.000	8	0	0	4-0	17.2	7	2	0	0	4-0	19	1.02	367	.117	.172	0	—	0		6		0.3
1991	Oak	A	1	4	.200	56	0	0	4-3	60.1	59	31	8	4	32-4	47	4.33	89	.258	.356	0	—	0		-4		-0.3
Total	2		2	4	.333	64	0	0	4-3	78	66	33	8	4	36-4	66	3.58	107	.228	.320	0	—	0		2		0.0

CHITTUM, NELSON   Nelson Boyd   B3.25.1933 Harrisonburg VA   BR/TR/6-1/180*   d8.17   Col Elizabethtown

1958	StL	N	0	1	.000	13	2	0	0	29.1	31	21	5	1	7-0	13	6.44	64	.265	.310	4	.250	0	141	-6		-0.3
1959	Bos	A	3	0	1.000	21	0	0	0	30.1	29	9	0	0	11-2	12	1.19	342	.266	.333	5-0-1	.200	0		7		0.1
1960	Bos	A	0	0	—	6	0	0	0	8.1	8	4	0	0	6-1	5	4.32	94	.242	.359	1	.000	-0		-1		0.0
Total	3		3	1	.750	40	2	0	0	68	68	34	5	1	24-3	30	3.84	106	.263	.326	10-0-1	.200	0	141	1		0.4

CHLUPSA, BOB   Robert Joseph   B9.16.1945 New York NY   BR/TR/6-7/215*   [StLN67 S590/90]   d7.16   Col Manhattan

1970	StL	N	0	2	.000	14	0	0	0-0	16.1	26	16	2	0	9-3	10	8.82	47	.366	.432	0	—	0		-7		-0.8
1971	StL	N	0	0	—	1	0	0	0-0	2	3	2	0	0	0-0	1	9.00	40	.333	.333	0	—	0		-1		0.0
Total	2		0	2	.000	15	0	0	0-0	18.1	29	18	2	0	9-3	11	8.84	46	.363	.422	0	—	0		-8		-0.8

CHO, JIN HO   Jin Ho   B8.16.1975 Jun Ju City, South Korea   BR/TR/6-0/207(175-220)   d7.4   [DL 2000 Bos A 24]

1998	Bos	A	0	3	.000	4	4	0	0-0	18.2	28	17	4	1	3-0	15	8.20	58	.341	.368		—	0	93	-6		-0.8
1999	Bos	A	2	3	.400	9	7	0	0-0	39.1	45	26	7	2	8-0	16	5.72	87	.287	.324	1	.000	-0	72	-2		-0.3
Total	2		2	6	.250	13	11	0	0-0	58	73	43	11	3	11-0	31	6.52	75	.305	.339	1	.000	-0	80	-8	24	-1.

CHOATE, DON   Donald Leon   B7.2.1938 Potosi MO   BR/TR/6-0/185   d9.12

| 1960 | SF | N | 0 | 0 | — | 4 | 0 | 0 | 0 | 8 | 7 | 4 | 0 | 0 | 4-0 | 7 | 2.25 | 155 | .233 | .324 | | — | 0 | | 0 | | 0. |

CHOATE, RANDY   Randol Doyle   B9.5.1975 San Antonio TX   BL/TL/6-3/180(180-195)   [NYA97 5/169]   d7.1   Col Florida St.

2000	†NY	A	0	1	.000	22	0	0	0-0	17	14	10	3	1	8-0	12	4.76	100	.215	.307	0	—	0		0		0.
2001	†NY	A	3	1	.750	37	0	0	0-0	48.1	34	21	0	9	27-2	35	3.35	133	.202	.341	3	.000	-0		5		0.
2002	NY	A	0	0	—	18	0	0	0-0	22.1	18	18	1	3	15-0	17	6.04	72	.217	.356	1	.000	-0		-5		-0.
2003	NY	A	0	0	—	5	0	0	0-0	3.2	7	3	0	0	1-0	0	7.36	60	.467	.500	0	—	0		-1		-0.
2004	Ari	N	2	4	.333	74	0	0	0-2	50.2	52	26	1	5	28-11	44	4.62	99	.267	.366	1	.000	-0		1		0.
2005	Ari	N	0	0	—	8	0	0	0-0	7.2	8	7	0	1	5-1	4	9.00	49	.276	.400	0	—	0		-3		-0.
Total	6		5	6	.455	164	0	0	0-2	149	133	85	5	19	84-14	117	4.71	96	.240	.355	5	.000	-1		-3		-0.

CHOUINARD, BOBBY   Robert William   B5.1.1972 Manila, Philippines   BR/TR/6-1/190(170-190)   [BalA90 5/148]   d5.26

1996	Oak	A	4	2	.667	13	11	0	0-0	59	75	41	10	3	32-3	32	6.10	82	.316	.400	0	—	0	127	-7		-0.
1998	Mil	N	0	0	—	1	0	0	0-0	3	5	1	0	0	0-0	1	3.00	145	.455	.417	0	—	0		0		0.
	Ari	N	0	2	.000	26	2	0	0-1	38.1	41	23	5	0	11-2	26	4.23	101	.268	.315	2	.000	-0	172	-1	17	-0.
	Year		0	2	.000	27	2	0	0-1	41.1	46	24	5	0	11-2	27	4.14	104	.280	.322	2	.000	-0	172	-1		-0.
1999	†Ari	N	5	2	.714	32	0	0	1-1	40.1	31	16	3	0	12-2	23	2.68	172	.220	.274	3-0-1	.000	-0		7		1.
2000	Col	N	2	2	.500	31	0	0	0-2	32.2	35	17	4	1	9-2	23	3.86	99	.280	.273	3	.333	0		5	49	-0.
2001	Col	N	0	0	—	8	0	0	0-0	7.2	10	7	4	0	1-1	5	8.22	65	.303	.324	0	—	0	132	2	66	-0.
Total	5		11	8	.579	111	13	0	1-4	181	197	105	26	4	65-10	110	4.57	107	.280	.340	8-0-1	.125	-0	132	2	66	-0.

CHOUNEAU, CHIEF   William (b William Cadreau)   B9.2.1888 Cloquet MN   D9.17.1946 Cloquet MN   BR/TR/5-9/150   d10.9

| 1910 | Chi | A | 0 | 1 | .000 | 1 | 1 | 0 | 0 | 5.1 | 7 | 2 | 0 | 0 | 0 | 1 | 3.38 | 71 | .292 | .292 | 1 | .000 | 0 | 28 | 0 | | 0. |

CHRIS, MIKE   Michael   B10.8.1957 Santa Monica CA   BL/TL/6-3/180*   [DetA77*S1/10]   d7.31   Col Los Angeles Pierce (CA) JC

1979	Det	A	3	3	.500	13	8	0	0-0	39	46	30	3	0	21-0	31	6.92	63	.297	.376	0	—	0	68	-10		-1
1982	SF	N	0	2	.000	9	6	0	0-0	26	23	16	2	1	26-2	10	4.85	74	.245	.410	7	.143	-0	107	-4		-0
1983	SF	N	0	0	—	7	0	0	0-0	13.1	16	14	1	2	16-2	5	8.10	44	.308	.479	2	.000	-0		-7		-0
Total	3		3	5	.375	29	14	0	0-0	78.1	85	60	6	3	63-4	46	6.43	61	.282	.407	9	.111	-0	84	-21		-1

CHRISTENSON, GARY   Gary Richard   B5.5.1953 Mineola NY   BL/TL/6-5/200(200-212)   [DetA71 13/304]   d9.1

1979	KC	A	0	0	—	6	0	0	0-1	10.2	10	5	1	0	2-0	4	3.38	126	.250	.279	0	—	0		1		0
1980	KC	A	3	0	1.000	24	0	0	1-2	31.1	35	23	4	2	18-1	16	5.17	78	.278	.372	0	—	0		-5		-0
Total	2		3	0	1.000	30	0	0	1-3	42	45	28	5	2	20-1	20	4.71	87	.271	.351	0	—	0		-4		-0

CHRISTENSON, LARRY   Larry Richard   B11.10.1953 Everett WA   BR/TR/6-4/215*   [PhiN72 1/3]   d4.13

1973	Phi	N	1	4	.200	10	9	0	0-0	34.1	53	25	3	1	20-1	11	6.55	58	.366	.443	10	.000	-1	72	-9		-1
1974	Phi	N	1	1	.500	10	1	0	2-0	23	20	11	2	0	15-3	18	4.30	88	.241	.357	4-0-1	.000	-1	46	-1		-0
1975	Phi	N	11	6	.647	29	26	5-2	1-0	171.2	149	73	12	1	45-2	88	3.67	103	.236	.286	57-2-8	.246	1	108	4		-0
1976	Phi	N	13	8	.619	32	29	2	0-0	168.2	199	77	8	1	42-4	54	3.68	97	.297	.338	51-2-6	.196	4	122	-2		0
1977	Phi	N	19	6	.760	34	34	5-1	0-0	219.1	229	113	21	7	69-1	118	4.06	99	.268	.324	74-3-10	.135	-0	140	-2		-0
1978	†Phi	N	13	14	.481	33	33	9-3	0-0	228	209	90	16	1	47-7	131	3.24	112	.244	.282	67-1-7	.075	-2	85	10		0
1979	†Phi	N	5	10	.333	19	17	2	0-0	106	118	56	7	6	20-3	53	4.50	86	.291	.339	31-1-3	.290	5	67	-7	67	-0
1980	†Phi	N	5	1	.833	14	14	0	0-0	73.2	62	35	4	3	27-4	49	4.03	95	.227	.303	19-1-3	.368	3	117	-1	77	-0
1981	†Phi	N	4	7	.364	20	15	0	1-0	106.2	108	43	7	0	30-3	70	3.54	103	.267	.313	30-0-3	.100	-1	95	0	21	-0

YEAR	TM LG	W	L	PCT	G	GS	CG-SHO	SV-BS	IP	H	R	HR	HB	BB-IB	SO	ERA	AERA	OAV	OOB	AB-HR-SH	AVG	PB	SUP	APR	DL	PW
1982	Phi N	9	10	.474	33	33	3	0-0	223	212	95	15	3	53-5	145	3.47	106	.253	.297	67-1-12	.075	-3	98	6		0.2
1983	Phi N	2	4	.333	9	9	0	0-0	48.1	42	25	2	1	17-1	44	3.91	92	.233	.297	17-0-1	.059	-1	87	-2	118	-0.3
Total	11	83	71	.539	243	220	27-6	4-0	1402.2	1401	648	100	21	395-34	781	3.79	99	.262	.313	427-11-54	.150	9	104	-4	283	-0.4

CHRISTIANSEN, CLAY   Clay C.   B6.28.1958 Wichita KS   BR/TR/6-5/205   [NYA80 15/386]   d5.10   Col Kansas

YEAR	TM LG	W	L	PCT	G	GS	CG-SHO	SV-BS	IP	H	R	HR	HB	BB-IB	SO	ERA	AERA	OAV	OOB	AB-HR-SH	AVG	PB	SUP	APR	DL	PW
1984	NY A	2	4	.333	24	1	0	2-2	38.2	50	28	4	1	12-0	27	6.05	63	.309	.356	0	—	0	0	-10		-1.4

CHRISTIANSEN, JASON   Jason Samuel   B9.21.1969 Omaha NE   BR/TL/6-5/242(230-246)   d4.26   Col Cameron

YEAR	TM LG	W	L	PCT	G	GS	CG-SHO	SV-BS	IP	H	R	HR	HB	BB-IB	SO	ERA	AERA	OAV	OOB	AB-HR-SH	AVG	PB	SUP	APR	DL	PW
1995	Pit N	1	3	.250	63	0	0	0-4	56.1	49	28	5	3	34-9	53	4.15	105	.234	.345	1	.000	-0	1			0.1
1996	Pit N	3	3	.500	33	0	0	0-2	44.1	56	34	7	1	19-2	38	6.70	66	.311	.374	4-0-1	.000	-0	-10			-1.2
1997	Pit N	3	0	1.000	39	0	0	0-2	33.2	37	11	2	2	17-3	37	2.94	146	.274	.364	0	—	0	5	78		0.4
1998	Pit N	3	3	.500	60	0	0	6-4	64.2	51	22	2	0	27-7	71	2.51	171	.216	.295	4	.250	0	12			1.2
1999	Pit N	2	3	.400	39	0	0	3-2	37.2	26	17	2	2	22-4	35	4.06	113	.198	.321	1	.000	-0*	3	75		0.4
2000	Pit N	2	8	.200	44	0	0	1-2	38	28	22	2	0	25-4	41	4.97	93	.207	.329	0	—	0	-1			-0.1
	†StL N	1	0	1.000	21	0	0	0-1	10	13	7	1	2	2-1	12	5.40	86	.317	.378	0	—	0	-1			-0.1
	Year	3	8	.273	65	0	0	1-3	48	41	29	3	2	27-5	53	5.06	92	.233	.340	0	—	0	-2			-0.2
2001	StL N	1	1	.500	30	0	0	3-0	19.1	15	10	4	1	10-1	19	4.66	93	.211	.313	0	—	0	0	36		0.0
	SF N	1	0	1.000	25	0	0	0-1	17	14	3	1	0	5-0	12	1.59	258	.241	.292	0	—	0	5			0.3
	Year	2	1	.667	55	0	0	3-1	36.1	29	13	5	1	15-1	31	3.22	131	.225	.304	0	—	0	5			0.3
2002	SF N	0	1	.000	6	0	0	0-0	5	6	3	1	0	2-0	1	5.40	73	.316	.381	0	—	0	-1	165		-0.1
2003	†SF N	0	0	—	40	0	0	0-1	26	25	15	3	1	11-0	22	5.19	82	.243	.322	0	—	0	-2	65		-0.1
2004	SF N	4	3	.571	60	0	0	3-3	36	34	20	3	3	26-1	22	4.50	96	.250	.377	0	—	0	-1	17		-0.2
2005	SF N	6	1	.857	56	0	0	0-2	42	48	27	4	0	15-2	17	5.36	80	.286	.337	0	—	0	-5			-0.8
	LA A	0	0	—	12	0	0	0-0	3.2	7	1	0	0	2-0	4	2.45	176	.389	.450	0	—	0	1			0.0
Total	11	27	26	.509	528	0	0	16-24	433.2	409	220	37	15	217-34	384	4.30	102	.249	.339	10-0-1	.100	-1	6	436		-0.2

CHRISTMAN, TIM   Timothy Arthur   B3.31.1975 Oneonta NY   BL/TL/6-0/195   [ColN96 11/326]   d4.21   Col Siena

YEAR	TM LG	W	L	PCT	G	GS	CG-SHO	SV-BS	IP	H	R	HR	HB	BB-IB	SO	ERA	AERA	OAV	OOB	AB-HR-SH	AVG	PB	SUP	APR	DL	PW
2001	Col N	0	0	—	1	0	0	0-0	2	1	1	1	0	0-0	2	4.50	119	.143	.143	0	—	0	0			0.0

CHRISTOPHER, MIKE   Michael Wayne   B11.3.1963 Petersburg VA   BR/TR/6-5/205*   [NYA85 7/181]   d9.10   Col East Carolina

YEAR	TM LG	W	L	PCT	G	GS	CG-SHO	SV-BS	IP	H	R	HR	HB	BB-IB	SO	ERA	AERA	OAV	OOB	AB-HR-SH	AVG	PB	SUP	APR	DL	PW
1991	LA N	0	0	—	3	0	0	0-0	4	2	0	0	0	3-0	2	0.00	—	.167	.333	0	—	0	2			0.1
1992	Cle A	0	0	—	10	0	0	0-0	18	17	8	2	0	10-1	13	3.00	131	.254	.346	0	—	0	1			0.1
1993	Cle A	0	0	—	9	0	0	0-0	11.2	14	6	3	0	2-1	8	3.86	114	.286	.314	0	—	0	0			0.0
1995	Det A	4	0	1.000	36	0	0	1-1	61.1	71	28	8	2	14-2	34	3.82	126	.292	.333	0	—	0	7			0.4
1996	Det A	1	1	.500	13	0	0	0-0	30	47	36	12	0	11-2	19	9.30	55	.351	.389	0	—	0	-15			-0.8
Total	5	5	1	.833	71	0	0	1-1	125	151	78	25	2	40-6	76	4.90	95	.299	.348	0	—	0	-5			-0.2

CHRISTOPHER, RUSS   Russell Ormand   B9.12.1917 Richmond CA   D12.5.1954 Richmond CA   BR/TR/6-3/180   d4.14   b-Loyd

YEAR	TM LG	W	L	PCT	G	GS	CG-SHO	SV-BS	IP	H	R	HR	HB	BB-IB	SO	ERA	AERA	OAV	OOB	AB-HR-SH	AVG	PB	SUP	APR	DL	PW
1942	Phi A	4	13	.235	30	18	10	1	165	154	78	8	3	99	58	3.82	99	.254	.362	56-0-3	.089	-3	78	1		0.1
1943	Phi A	5	8	.385	24	15	5	2	133	120	58	3	3	58	56	3.45	98	.242	.325	45-0-1	.156	-1	93	-1		0.2
1944	Phi A	14	14	.500	35	24	13-1	1	215.1	200	91	6	9	63	84	2.97	117	.245	.306	81-1-1	.222	3	68	9		1.8
1945	Phi A*	13	13	.500	33	27	17-2	2	227.1	213	92	9	9	75	100	3.17	108	.251	.319	76-1-6	.171	-1*	80	6		1.1
1946	Phi A	5	7	.417	30	13	1	0	119.1	119	71	5	3	44	79	4.30	82	.254	.322	36-0-1	.139	-0	112	-12		-0.9
1947	Phi A	10	7	.588	44	0	0	12	80.2	70	30	4	0	33	33	2.90	131	.236	.313	16-0-2	.125	-0	8			1.6
1948	†Cle A	3	2	.600	45	0	0	17	59	55	21	3	0	27	14	2.90	140	.247	.328	6-0-2	.000	-0	8			1.1
Total	7	54	64	.458	241	97	46-3	35	999.2	931	441	38	27	399	424	3.37	106	.248	.325	316-2-16	.158	-3	82	19		5.0

CHULK, VINNIE   Charles Vincent   B12.19.1978 Miami FL   BR/TR/6-2/180(180-195)   [TorA00 12/358]   d9.8   Col St. Thomas (FL)

YEAR	TM LG	W	L	PCT	G	GS	CG-SHO	SV-BS	IP	H	R	HR	HB	BB-IB	SO	ERA	AERA	OAV	OOB	AB-HR-SH	AVG	PB	SUP	APR	DL	PW
2003	Tor A	0	0	—	3	0	0	0-1	5.1	4	3	0	0	3-0	2	5.06	94	.273	.360	0	—	0	0			0.0
2004	Tor A	1	3	.250	47	0	0	2-3	56	59	30	6	1	27-1	44	4.66	105	.271	.352	0	—	0	2			0.1
2005	Tor A	0	1	.000	62	0	0	0-1	72	68	33	9	1	26-3	39	3.88	119	.255	.319	0	—	0	6			0.3
Total	3	1	4	.200	112	0	0	2-5	133.1	133	66	15	2	56-4	85	4.25	112	.262	.335	0	—	0	8			0.4

CHURCH, BUBBA   Emory Nicholas   B9.12.1924 Birmingham AL   D9.17.2001 Birmingham AL   BR/TR/6-0/180*   d4.30

YEAR	TM LG	W	L	PCT	G	GS	CG-SHO	SV-BS	IP	H	R	HR	HB	BB-IB	SO	ERA	AERA	OAV	OOB	AB-HR-SH	AVG	PB	SUP	APR	DL	PW
1950	Phi N	8	6	.571	31	18	8-2	1	142	113	50	12	0	56	50	2.73	149	.225	.303	44-0-3	.182	0*	84	21		1.9
1951	Phi N	15	11	.577	38	33	15-4	1	247	246	107	17	1	90	104	3.53	109	.261	.326	86-1-7	.256	5*	99	9		1.2
1952	Phi N	0	0	—	2	1	0	0	5	11	6	0	1	1	3	10.80	34	.440	.481	1	.000	-0	195	-4		-0.2
	Cin N	5	9	.357	29	22	5-1	0	153.1	173	85	21	3	48	47	4.34	87	.301	.358	50-1-1	.240	-0	98	-12		-0.7
	Year	5	9	.357	31	23	5-1	0	158.1	184	91	21	4	49	50	4.55	83	.307	.363	51-1-1	.235	3	102	-13		-0.9
1953	Cin N	3	3	.500	11	7	2	0	43.2	55	32	9	2	14	12	5.98	73	.318	.392	15	.267	1*	129	-8		-0.8
	Chi N	4	5	.444	27	11	1	1	104.1	115	67	16	2	49	47	5.00	89	.276	.355	33-1-1	.212	1	97	-6		-0.4
	Year	7	8	.467	38	18	3	1	148	170	99	25	4	68	59	5.29	84	.289	.366	48-1-1	.229	2	108	-16		-1.2
1954	Chi N	1	3	.250	7	3	1	0	14.2	21	18	8	0	13	8	9.82	43	.350	.459	5	.000	-1*	156	-9		-1.6
1955	Chi N	0	0	—	2	0	0	1	3.1	4	2	1	0	1-0	3	5.40	76	.286	.333	1	.000	-0*	0			0.0
Total	6	36	37	.493	147	95	32-7	4	713.1	738	367	84	9	277-0	274	4.10	97	.272	.342	235-3-12	.226	9	100	-9		-0.6

CHURCH, LEN   Leonard   B3.21.1942 Chicago IL   D4.22.1988 Richardson TX   BB/TR/6-0/190   d8.27   Col Wilbur Wright (IL) JC

YEAR	TM LG	W	L	PCT	G	GS	CG-SHO	SV-BS	IP	H	R	HR	HB	BB-IB	SO	ERA	AERA	OAV	OOB	AB-HR-SH	AVG	PB	SUP	APR	DL	PW
1966	Chi N	0	1	.000	4	0	0	0	6	10	6	1	0	7-2	3	7.50	49	.400	.515	1	.000	-0	-3			-0.4

CHURN, CHUCK   Clarence Nottingham   B2.1.1930 Bridgetown VA   BR/TR/6-3/205*   d4.18

YEAR	TM LG	W	L	PCT	G	GS	CG-SHO	SV-BS	IP	H	R	HR	HB	BB-IB	SO	ERA	AERA	OAV	OOB	AB-HR-SH	AVG	PB	SUP	APR	DL	PW
1957	Pit N	0	0	—	5	0	0	0	8.1	9	4	1	0	4-1	4	4.32	88	.333	.406	1	.000	-0	0			0.0
1958	Cle A	0	0	—	6	0	0	0	8.2	12	7	1	0	5-0	4	6.23	59	.343	.425	0	—	0	-3			-0.2
1959	†LA N	3	2	.600	14	0	0	1	30.2	28	17	2	1	10-4	24	4.99	85	.255	.315	6	.167	0	-2			-0.1
Total	3	3	2	.600	25	0	0	1	47.2	49	28	4	1	19-5	32	5.10	79	.285	.352	7	.143	0	-5			-0.3

CIARDI, MARK   Mark Thomas   B8.19.1961 New Brunswick NJ   BR/TR/6-0/180   [MilA83 15/392]   d4.9   Col Maryland-Baltimore Co.

YEAR	TM LG	W	L	PCT	G	GS	CG-SHO	SV-BS	IP	H	R	HR	HB	BB-IB	SO	ERA	AERA	OAV	OOB	AB-HR-SH	AVG	PB	SUP	APR	DL	PW
1987	Mil A	1	1	.500	4	3	0	0-0	16.1	26	17	5	0	9-0	8	9.37	49	.361	.432	0	—	0	86	-8		-0.7

CICOTTE, AL   Alva Warren "Bozo"   B12.23.1929 Melvindale MI   D11.29.1982 Westland MI   BR/TR/6-3/185*   d4.22

YEAR	TM LG	W	L	PCT	G	GS	CG-SHO	SV-BS	IP	H	R	HR	HB	BB-IB	SO	ERA	AERA	OAV	OOB	AB-HR-SH	AVG	PB	SUP	APR	DL	PW
1957	NY A	2	2	.500	20	2	0	2	65.1	57	25	5	1	30-1	36	3.03	118	.237	.324	20	.150	-0	50	4		0.2
1958	Was A	0	3	.000	8	4	0	0	28	36	18	3	0	14-0	14	4.82	79	.316	.388	10	.200	-0*	59	-4		-0.4
	Det A	3	1	.750	14	2	0	0	43	50	19	7	0	15-1	21	3.56	113	.307	.359	17	.176	-1*	134	2		0.2
	Year	3	4	.429	22	6	0	0	71	86	37	4	0	29-1	35	4.06	97	.310	.371	27	.185	-1	83	-1		-0.2
1959	Cle A	3	1	.750	26	1	0	1	44	46	29	4	2	25-3	23	5.32	69	.299	.395	3-0-1	.333	1	192	-8		-0.7
1961	StL N	2	6	.250	29	7	0	1	75	83	47	16	2	34-2	51	5.28	83	.283	.362	21	.286	1	72	-5		-0.4
1962	Hou N	0	0	—	4	0	0	0	4.2	8	4	1	0	1-0	4	3.86	97	.381	.409	0	—	0	-1			0.0
Total	5	10	13	.435	102	16	0	4	260	280	142	30	5	119-7	149	4.36	90	.284	.361	71-0-1	.211	0	83	-12		-1.1

CICOTTE, EDDIE   Edward Victor "Knuckles"   B6.19.1884 Springwells MI   D5.5.1969 Detroit MI   BB/TR/5-9/175   d9.3

YEAR	TM LG	W	L	PCT	G	GS	CG-SHO	SV-BS	IP	H	R	HR	HB	BB-IB	SO	ERA	AERA	OAV	OOB	AB-HR-SH	AVG	PB	SUP	APR	DL	PW
1905	Det A	1	1	.500	3	1	1	0	18	25	8	0	5	6	3.50	78	.329	.370	7	.429	1	78	-1		0.0
1908	Bos A	11	12	.478	39	24	17-2	2	207.1	198	77	0	11	59	95	2.43	101	.256	.318	72	.236	2*	109	2		0.5
1909	Bos A	14	5	.737	27	17	10-1	5	162.1	117	63	3	1	56	82	1.94	129	.207	.280	51-0-3	.235	3	134	5		0.9
1910	Bos A	15	11	.577	36	30	20-3	0	250	213	94	4	13	86	104	2.74	93	.233	.308	85-0-4	.141	-1	116	0		0.1
1911	Bos A	11	15	.423	35	25	16-1	0	220	236	121	2	4	73	106	2.82	116	.282	.342	71-0-5	.141	-2	99	7		0.5
1912	Bos A	1	3	.250	9	6	2	0	46	58	34	0	1	15	20	5.67	60	.319	.374	13	.154	0	137	-10		-0.7
	Chi A	9	7	.563	20	18	13-1	0	152	159	63	3	0	37	70	2.84	113	.277	.320	53-0-3	.245	1	97	7		0.9
	Year	10	10	.500	29	24	15-1	0	198	217	97	3	1	52	90	3.50	93	.287	.333	66-0-3	.227	1	108	-2		0.2
1913	Chi A	18	11	.621	41	30	18-3	1	268	224	77	3	3	73	121	1.58	185	.227	.283	91-0-4	.143	-3	93	36		4.1
1914	Chi A	11	16	.407	45	30	15-6	3	269.1	220	96	0	3	72	122	2.04	132	.232	.288	86-0-6	.163	-1	79	17		2.1
1915	Chi A	13	12	.520	39	26	15-1	3	223.1	216	89	2	6	48	106	3.02	99	.261	.306	67-0-10	.209	1*	116	3		0.4
1916	Chi A	15	7	**.682**	44	19	11-2	5	187	138	56	1	4	70	91	1.78	155	.218	.296	57-0-8	.211	2	143	18		2.6
1917	†Chi A	**28**	12	.700	49	35	29-7	4	346.2	246	76	2	3	70	150	**1.53**	**174**	.203	**.248**	112-0-8	.179	1	105	**45**		**5.7**
1918	Chi A	12	19	.387	38	30	24-1	2	266	275	102	2	2	40	104	2.77	99	.271	.300	86-0-1	.163	2	84	1		0.2
1919	†Chi A	**29**	7	**.806**	40	35	30-5	1	306.2	256	77	5	2	49	110	1.82	175	.228	.261	99-0-11	.202	1	108	47		5.5
1920	Chi A	21	10	.677	37	35	28-0	0	303.1	316	128	6	2	74	87	3.26	115	.275	.320	112-0-4	.186	-3	121	19		1.5
Total	14	209	148	.585	502	361	249-35	24	3226	2897	1161	32	52	827	1374	2.38	123	.245	.297	1062-0-67	.186	4	108	196		24.3

YEAR	TM LG	W	L	PCT	G	GS	CG-SHO	SV-BS	IP	H	R	HR	HB	BB-IB	SO	ERA	AERA	OAV	OOB	AB-HR-SH	AVG	PB	SUP	APR	DL	PW

CIMINO, PETE   Peter William   B10.17.1942 Philadelphia PA   BR/TR/6-2/195(195-213)   d9.22

1965	Min A	0	0	—	0	0	0	0	1	0	0	0	0	0-0	0	0.00	—	.000	.000	0		0		0		0.0
1966	Min A	2	5	.286	35	0	0	4	64.2	53	40	5	1	30-3	57	2.92	123	.222	.310	6-0-1	.000	-0		4		0.3
1967	Cal A	3	3	.500	46	1	0	1	88.1	73	38	12	2	31-4	80	3.26	96	.229	.297	12	.417	2	111	-2		0.0
1968	Cal A	0	0	—	4	0	0	5	7	7	5	0	0	4-0	2	2.57	113	.259	.355	0		0		-1		-0.1
Total	4	5	8	.385	86	1	0	5	161	133	70	16	3	65-7	139	3.07	108	.226	.304	18-0-1	.278	1	111	1		0.2

CIMORELLI, FRANK   Frank Thomas   B8.2.1968 Poughkeepsie NY   BR/TR/6-0/175   [StLN89 37/952]   d4.30   Col Dominican

1994	StL N	0	0	—	11	0	0	1-0	13.1	20	14	0	2	10-2	1	8.78	48	.345	.444	2	.000	-0		-7		-0.4

CIOLA, LOU   Louis Alexander   B9.6.1922 Norfolk VA   D10.18.1981 Austin MN   BR/TR/5-9/165   d7.25   Mil 1944-46   Col Richmond

1943	Phi A	1	3	.250	12	3	2	0	43.2	48	33	2	1	22	7	5.56	61	.273	.357	18	.167	-1	157	-11		-1.0

CISCO, GALEN   Galen Bernard   B3.7.1936 St.Marys OH   BR/TR/5-11/215(200-215)   d6.11   C28   Col Ohio St.

1961	Bos A	2	4	.333	17	8	0	0	52.1	67	40	5	0	28-0	26	6.71	62	.325	.397	10-0-3	.100	-0*	72	-12		-1.2
1962	Bos A	4	7	.364	23	9	1	0	83	95	66	11	3	50-1	43	6.72	61	.292	.387	25	.080	-1	77	-21		-2.4
	NY N	1	1	.500	4	2	1	0	19.1	15	7	0	3	11-2	13	3.26	128	.208	.337	7	.000	-1	63	2		0.1
1963	NY N	7	15	.318	51	17	1	0	155.2	165	88	15	7	64-1	81	4.34	80	.273	.348	38-0-2	.132	-0	62	-14		-1.8
1964	NY N	6	19	.240	36	25	5-2	0	191.2	182	85	17	6	54-4	78	3.62	99	.256	.311	54-0-6	.111	-0	83	0		0.1
1965	NY N	4	8	.333	35	17	1-1	0	112.1	119	63	12	1	51-2	58	3.63	96	.266	.326	27-0-4	.259	2	102	-11		-1.0
1967	Bos A	0	1	.000	11	0	0	0	22.1	21	10	4	0	8-0	8	3.63	102	.215	.340	3	.000	0		0		-0.1
1969	KC A	1	1	.500	15	0	0	1-0	22.1	17	11	4	0	15-0	18	3.63	102	.215	.340	0	—	0	80	-56		0.0
Total	7	25	56	.309	192	78	9-3	2-0	659	681	370	68	20	281-10	325	4.56	81	.271	.346	164-0-15	.128	0	80	-56		-6.3

CITARELLA, RALPH   Ralph Alexander   B2.7.1958 East Orange NJ   BR/TR/6-0/180*   [StLN79 S1/12]   d9.13   Col Florida Southern

1983	StL N	0	0	—	6	0	0	0-0	11	8	2	0	0	3-1	4	1.64	224	.205	.262	1	.000	-0		3		0.1
1984	StL N	0	1	.000	10	2	0	0-0	22.1	20	9	0	3	7-2	15	3.63	97	.238	.319	4	.250	0	164	0	15	0.0
1987	Chi A	0	0	—	5	0	0	0-0	11	13	9	4	2	4-0	9	7.36	63	.302	.388	0	—	0		-3		-0.1
Total	3	0	1	.000	21	2	0	0-0	44.1	41	20	4	5	14-3	28	4.06	94	.247	.324	5	.200	0	164	0	15	0.0

CLANCY, JIM   James   B12.18.1955 Chicago IL   BR/TR/6-4/220(185-220)   [TexA74 4/74]   d7.26

1977	Tor A	4	9	.308	13	13	4-1	0-0	76.2	80	47	7	0	47-1	44	5.05	84	.280	.374	0	—	0	81	-6		-0.8
1978	Tor A	10	12	.455	31	30	7	0-0	193.2	199	96	10	1	91-1	106	4.09	97	.270	.347	0	—	0	76	-3		-0.3
1979	Tor A	2	7	.222	12	11	2	0-0	63.2	65	44	8	0	31-0	33	5.51	80	.272	.349	0	—	0	68	24		2.6
1980	Tor A	13	16	.448	34	34	15-2	0-0	250.2	217	108	19	2	128-4	152	3.30	131	.233	.326	0	—	0	82	-11		-1.6
1981	Tor A	6	12	.333	22	22	4	0-0	125	126	77	12	5	64-0	56	4.90	81	.262	.352	0	—	0	87	21		2.1
1982	Tor A★	16	14	.533	40	40	11-3	0-0	266.2	251	122	26	2	77-1	139	3.71	121	.248	.301	0	—	0	101	6		0.6
1983	Tor A	15	11	.577	34	34	11-1	0-0	223	238	115	29	1	61-0	99	3.91	111	.271	.315	0	—	0	92	-21		-2.3
1984	Tor A	13	15	.464	36	36	5	0-0	219.2	249	132	25	3	88-2	118	5.12	81	.287	.353	0	—	0	112	9	59	0.9
1985	†Tor A	9	6	.600	23	23	1	0-0	128.2	117	54	15	0	37-0	66	3.78	112	.241	.292	0	—	0	100	10		1.1
1986	Tor A	14	14	.500	34	34	6-3	0-0	219.1	202	100	24	4	63-0	126	3.94	108	.243	.296	0	—	0	104	26		2.6
1987	Tor A	15	11	.577	37	37	5-1	0-0	241.1	234	103	24	1	80-5	180	3.54	128	.255	.314	0	—	0	101	-10		-1.2
1988	Tor A	11	13	.458	36	31	4	1-0	196.1	207	106	26	9	47-3	118	4.49	88	.272	.321	41-0-7	.146	-0	84	-32		-4.2
1989	Hou N	7	14	.333	33	26	1	0-0	147	155	100	13	0	66-15	91	5.08	67	.269	.342	14-0-2	.214	-0	63	-22		-2.6
1990	Hou N	2	8	.200	33	10	0	1-1	76	100	58	4	3	33-9	44	6.51	57	.322	.387	3-0-1	.000	-0		5		0.2
1991	Hou N	0	3	.000	30	0	0	5-1	55	37	19	5	0	20-3	33	2.78	127	.193	.266	3	.000	-0		-6		-0.9
	†Atl N	3	2	.600	24	0	0	3-2	34.2	36	23	3	1	14-1	17	5.71	68	.267	.336	3	.000	-1		-2		-0.7
	Year	3	5	.375	54	0	0	8-3	89.2	73	42	8	1	34-4	50	3.91	94	.223	.295	6-0-1	.000	-1		-2		
Total	15	140	167	.456	472	381	74-11	10-4	2517.1	2513	1304	244	32	947-45	1422	4.23	99	.261	.326	61-0-10	.148	-1	90	-18	169	-4.7

CLARK, BRYAN   Bryan Donald   B7.12.1956 Madera CA   BL/TL/6-2/185(185-200)   [PitN74 10/227]   d4.11

1981	Sea A	2	5	.286	29	9	1	2-3	93.1	92	54	3	1	55-4	52	4.34	89	.261	.359	0	—	0*	87	-6		-0.4
1982	Sea A	5	2	.714	37	5	1-1	0-0	114.2	104	44	6	0	58-2	70	2.75	156	.241	.330	0	—	0	98	16		1.0
1983	Sea A	7	10	.412	41	17	2	0-0	162.1	160	82	14	3	72-6	76	3.94	109	.261	.340	0	—	0	77	5		0.6
1984	Tor A	1	2	.333	20	3	0	0-0	45.2	66	33	6	1	22-2	21	5.91	70	.342	.410	0	—	0	109	-9		-0.5
1985	Cle A	3	4	.429	31	3	0	2-2	62.2	78	47	8	0	34-2	24	6.32	66	.311	.390	0	—	0	80	-14		-1.4
1986	Chi A	0	0	—	5	0	0	0-0	8	8	4	0	0	2-0	5	4.50	97	.276	.323	0	—	0		0		0.0
1987	Chi A	0	0	—	11	0	0	0-0	18.2	19	5	1	0	8-0	8	2.41	197	.297	.365	0	—	0		5		0.2
1990	Sea A	2	0	1.000	12	0	0	0-0	11	9	4	0	0	10-0	3	3.27	122	.237	.396	0	—	0		1		0.2
Total	8	20	23	.465	186	37	4-1	4-5	516.1	536	273	38	5	261-16	259	4.15	101	.272	.356	0	—	0	85	-2		-0.3

CLARK, ED   Edward C.   B Cincinnati OH   d7.4

1886	Phi AA	0	1	.000	1	1	1	0	8	10	8	2	2	2-0	2	6.75	52	.294	.368	2	.000	-0	0	-2		-0.2
1891	Col AA	0	0	—	1	0	0	0	2	2	0	0	0	0-0	1	0.00	—	.250	.250	1	.000	-0		1		0.0
Total	2	0	1	.000	2	1	1	0	10	12	8	2	2	2-0	3	5.40	65	.286	.348	3	.000	-0		-1		-0.2

CLARK, GEORGE   George Myron   B5.19.1891 Smithland IA   D11.14.1940 Sioux City IA   BR/TL/6-0/190   d5.16   Col Iowa St.

1913	NY A	0	1	.000	11	1	0	0	19	22	23	1	3	19	5	9.00	33	.278	.436	4	.500	1	50	-11		-0.5

CLARK, GINGER   Harvey Daniel   B3.7.1879 Wooster OH   D5.10.1943 Lake Charles LA   BR/TR/5-11/165   d8.11

1902	Cle A	0	1	0.000	1	1	0	0	6	10	6	1	0	4	1	6.00	57	.370	.452	4	.500	1		-2		-0.2

CLARK, MARK   Mark Willard   B5.12.1968 Bath IL   BR/TR/6-5/225*   [StLN88 9/236]   d9.6   Col MacMurray

1991	StL N	1	1	.500	7	2	0	0-0	22.1	17	10	3	0	11-0	13	4.03	93	.215	.301	7-0-1	.000	-1	84	0		-0.1
1992	StL N	3	10	.231	20	20	1-1	0-0	113.1	117	59	12	0	36-2	44	4.45	77	.265	.318	36-0-4	.139	-1	95	-12		-1.5
1993	Cle A	7	5	.583	26	15	1	0-0	109.1	119	55	18	1	25-1	57	4.28	102	.279	.320	0	—	0	126	13	22	1.3
1994	Cle A	11	3	.786	20	20	4-1	0-0	127.1	133	61	14	4	40-0	60	3.82	125	.273	.329	0	—	0	100	-6		-0.7
1995	Cle A	9	7	.563	22	21	2	0-0	124.2	143	77	13	4	42-0	68	5.27	90	.288	.344	0	—	0	110	13		0.7
1996	NY N	14	11	.560	32	32	2	0-0	212.1	217	98	20	3	48-8	142	3.43	117	.265	.306	69-0-10	.043	-5	110	13		0.7
1997	NY N	8	7	.533	23	22	0	0-0	142	158	74	18	3	47-2	72	4.25	94	.289	.347	43-1-4	.047	-2	111	10		-0.6
	Chi N	6	1	.857	9	9	2	0-0	63	55	22	6	1	12-1	51	2.86	151	.226	.264	23-0-2	.000	-2	111	10		0.2
	Year	14	8	.636	32	31	3	0-0	205	213	96	24	4	59-3	123	3.82	107	.270	.322	66-1-6	.030	-4	103	6		0.2
1998	†Chi N	9	14	.391	33	33	2-1	0-0	213.2	236	116	23	4	48-4	161	4.84	91	.278	.318	62-0-8	.065	-3	87	-7		-1.1
1999	Tex A	3	7	.300	15	15	0	0-0	74.1	103	73	17	1	34-1	44	8.60	60	.329	.392	2	.000	0	106	-13	106	-2.2
2000	Tex A	3	5	.375	12	8	0	0-0	44	66	42	10	3	24-2	16	7.98	64	.347	.425	0	—	0	101	-26	182	-1.8
Total	10	74	71	.510	219	197	15-3	0-0	1246.1	1364	687	154	24	367-21	728	4.61	94	.279	.330	242-1-29	.058	-14	103	-30	182	-5.1

CLARK, MIKE   Michael John   B2.12.1922 Camden NJ   D1.25.1996 Camden NJ   BR/TR/6-4/190*   d7.27

1952	StL N	2	0	1.000	12	4	0	0	25.1	32	18	2	0	14	10	6.04	61	.311	.393	5	.000	-1	150	-6		-0.5
1953	StL N	1	0	1.000	23	2	0	1	35.2	46	21	2	2	21	17	4.79	89	.315	.408	6	.000	-1	115	-2		-0.5
Total	2	3	0	1.000	35	6	0	1	61	78	39	4	2	35	27	5.31	76	.313	.402	11	.000	-1	133	-8		-0.5

CLARK, PHIL   Philip James   B10.3.1932 Albany GA   BR/TR/6-3/210(190-210)   d4.15

1958	StL N	0	1	.000	7	0	0	1	7.2	11	5	2	0	3-0	1	3.52	117	.355	.412	1	.000	-0*		0		-0.1
1959	StL N	0	1	.000	7	0	0	0	7	8	11	0	0	8-1	5	12.86	33	.286	.444	0	—	0		-6		-0.1
Total	2	0	2	.000	14	0	0	1	14.2	19	16	2	0	11-1	6	7.98	52	.322	.429	1	.000	-0		-6		-0.1

CLARK, RICKEY   Rickey Charles   B3.21.1946 Mt.Clemens MI   BR/TR/6-2/170*   d4.22

1967	Cal A	12	11	.522	32	26	3	1-1	0	174	144	69	15	6	69-0	81	2.59	121	.224	.303	50-0-9	.040	-4	100	6		0.2
1968	Cal A	1	11	.083	21	17	0	0	94.1	74	51	4	1	54-1	60	3.53	83	.217	.323	28-0-3	.107	-1	91	-11		-1.0
1969	Cal A	0	0	—	6	1	0	0-0	9.2	12	6	2	0	7-1	6	5.59	63	.300	.404	2	.500	0	25	-2		-0.1
1971	Cal A	2	1	.667	11	7	1-1	1-0	44	36	15	6	2	28-2	28	2.86	113	.220	.340	15-0-1	.267	1	122	2		0.2
1972	Cal A	4	9	.308	26	15	2	1-1	109.2	105	59	10	2	55-2	61	4.51	65	.261	.345	31-0-1	.097	-1*	72	-19		-2.1
Total	5	19	32	.373	96	70	4-2	2-1	431.2	371	200	37	11	213-6	236	3.38	91	.233	.325	126-0-14	.103	-5	93	-24		-3.1

CLARK, BOB Robert William B8.22.1897 Newport PA D5.18.1944 Carlsbad NM BR/TR/6-3/188 d5.26 Col Susquehanna

YEAR	TM LG	W	L	PCT	G	GS	CG-SHO	SV-BS	IP	H	R	HR	HB	BB-IB	SO	ERA	AERA	OAV	OOB	AB-HR-SH	AVG	PB	SUP	APR	DL	PW
1920	Cle A	1	2	.333	11	2	2-1	0	42	59	19	0	1	13	8	3.43	111	.383	.435	10		.200	-0	73	2		0.1
1921	Cle A	0	0	—	5	0	0	0	9.1	23	17	2	1	6	2	14.46	29	.511	.577	3		.000	-1		-10		-0.5
Total	2	1	2	.333	16	2	2-1	0	51.1	82	36	2	2	19	10	5.44	71	.412	.468	13		.154	-1	73	-8		-0.4

CLARK, TERRY Terry Lee B10.18.1960 Los Angeles CA BR/TR/6-2/196* [StLN79 23/575] d7.7 Col Mt. San Antonio (CA) JC

YEAR	TM LG	W	L	PCT	G	GS	CG-SHO	SV-BS	IP	H	R	HR	HB	BB-IB	SO	ERA	AERA	OAV	OOB	AB-HR-SH	AVG	PB	SUP	APR	DL	PW
1988	Cal A	6	6	.500	15	15	2-1	0-0	94	120	54	8	0	31-6	39	5.07	77	.323	.370	0	—	0	122	-11		-1.2
1989	Cal A	0	2	.000	4	2	0	0-0	11	13	8	0	0	3-0	7	4.91	78	.310	.348	0	—	0	83	-2	30	-0.3
1990	Hou N	0	0	—	1	1	0	0-0	4	9	7	0	0	3-0	2	13.50	28	.429	.500	2	.500	0	193	-5		-0.2
1995	Atl N	0	0	—	3	0	0	0-0	3.2	3	2	0	0	5-0	2	4.91	88	.231	.444	0	—	0		6		0.0
	Bal A	2	5	.286	38	0	0	1-0	39	40	15	3	1	15-5	18	3.46	138	.276	.346	0	—	0		-5		0.9
1996	KC A	1	1	.500	12	0	0	0-0	17.1	28	15	3	0	7-1	12	7.79	65	.350	.402	0	—	0		-5		-0.5
	Hou N	0	2	.000	5	0	0	0-0	6.1	16	10	1	1	2-1	5	11.37	34	.471	.514	0	—	0		-6	53	-1.1
1997	Cle A	0	3	.000	4	4	0	0-0	26.1	29	21	3	0	13-1	13	6.15	76	.284	.359	0	—	0	44	-5		-0.4
	Tex A	1	4	.200	9	5	0	0-0	30.2	41	20	3	2	10-0	11	5.87	83	.325	.384	1	1.000	0	42	-2		-0.2
	Year	1	7	.125	13	9	0	0-0	57	70	41	6	2	23-1	24	6.00	80	.307	.373	1	1.000	0	43	-7		-0.6
Total	6	10	23	.303	91	27	2-1	1-0	232.1	299	152	21	4	89-14	109	5.54	78	.320	.378	3	.667	0	89	-30	83	-3.0

CLARK, OTEY William Otis B5.22.1915 Boscobel WI BR/TR/6-1.5/190 d4.17

YEAR	TM LG	W	L	PCT	G	GS	CG-SHO	SV-BS	IP	H	R	HR	HB	BB-IB	SO	ERA	AERA	OAV	OOB	AB-HR-SH	AVG	PB	SUP	APR	DL	PW
1945	Bos A	4	4	.500	12	9	4-1	0	82	86	33	6	1	19	20	3.07	111	.268	.311	24-0-3		.208	0	75	3		0.1

CLARK, WATTY William Watson "Lefty" B5.16.1902 St.Joseph LA D3.4.1972 Clearwater FL BL/TL/6-0.5/175 d5.28 Col Mississippi College

YEAR	TM LG	W	L	PCT	G	GS	CG-SHO	SV-BS	IP	H	R	HR	HB	BB-IB	SO	ERA	AERA	OAV	OOB	AB-HR-SH	AVG	PB	SUP	APR	DL	PW
1924	Cle A	1	3	.250	12	1	0	0	25.2	38	27	0	2	14	6	7.01	61	.345	.429	9		.222	1	20	-9		-1.0
1927	Bro N	7	2	.778	27	3	1	2	73.2	74	23	2	0	19	32	2.32	171	.265	.312	21-0-1		.143	-1	86	13		1.5
1928	Bro N	12	9	.571	40	19	10-2	3	194.2	193	75	4	1	50	85	2.68	148	.259	.306	66-0-6		.152	-2	105	28		2.6
1929	Bro N	16	19	.457	41	39	19-3	1	279	295	136	14	3	71	140	3.74	123	.270	.316	97-0-4		.165	-3*	96	29		2.7
1930	Bro N	13	13	.500	44	29	9-1	6	200	209	110	20	0	38	81	4.18	117	.271	.306	68-1-1		.206	0	87	17		2.0
1931	Bro N	14	10	.583	34	28	16-3	1	233.1	243	86	4	1	52	96	3.20	119	.267	.308	84-0-3		.250	4	93	21		2.3
1932	Bro N	20	12	.625	40	36	19-2	0	273	282	122	10	4	49	99	3.49	109	.264	.299	97-0-4		.216	1	105	9		1.2
1933	Bro N	2	4	.333	11	8	4-1	1	50.2	61	29	2	3	6	14	4.80	67	.303	.333	13-0-2		.154	-0	68	-8		-0.9
	NY N	3	4	.429	16	5	0	0	44	58	25	3	1	11	11	4.70	68	.317	.359	11		.273	1	161	-6		-0.8
	Year	5	8	.385	27	13	4-1	1	94.2	119	54	5	4	17	25	4.75	68	.310	.346	24-0-2		.208	1	104	-15		-1.7
1934	NY N	1	2	.333	5	4	1	0	18.2	23	15	5	0	5	6	6.75	57	.295	.337	6-0-1		.167	-0	78	-5		-0.7
	Bro N	2	0	1.000	17	1	0	0	25.1	40	19	0	1	9	10	5.33	73	.345	.397	8		.125	-1	111	-5		-0.4
	Year	3	2	.600	22	5	1	0	44	63	34	5	1	14	16	5.93	66	.325	.373	14-0-1		.143	-0	84	-10		-1.1
1935	Bro N	13	8	.619	33	25	11-1	0	207	215	93	11	1	28	35	3.30	120	.264	.289	79-0-3		.177	-0*	97	15		1.4
1936	Bro N	7	11	.389	34	16	1-1	2	120	162	73	11	0	28	28	4.43	93	.316	.351	39		.231	0	63	-4		-0.6
1937	Bro N	0	0	—	2	0	0	0	2.1	5	4	0	0	3	0	7.71	52	.308	.438	0		—	0		-1		0.0
Total	12	111	97	.534	355	209	91-14	16	1747.1	1897	836	86	17	383	643	3.66	112	.275	.315	598-1-25		.196	1	94	94		9.3

CLARKE, LEFTY Alan Thomas B3.8.1896 Clarksville MD D3.11.1975 Cheverly MD BB/TL/5-11/180 d10.2

YEAR	TM LG	W	L	PCT	G	GS	CG-SHO	SV-BS	IP	H	R	HR	HB	BB-IB	SO	ERA	AERA	OAV	OOB	AB-HR-SH	AVG	PB	SUP	APR	DL	PW
1921	Cin N	0	1	.000	1	1	1	0	5	7	7	0	0	2	1	5.40	66	.304	.360	1		.000	-0	0	-2		-0.4

CLARKE, HENRY Henry Tefft B8.28.1875 Bellevue NE D3.28.1950 Colorado Springs CO BR/TR d6.26 Col Chicago

YEAR	TM LG	W	L	PCT	G	GS	CG-SHO	SV-BS	IP	H	R	HR	HB	BB-IB	SO	ERA	AERA	OAV	OOB	AB-HR-SH	AVG	PB	SUP	APR	DL	PW
1897	Cle N	0	4	.000	4	3	0	0	30.2	32	29	4	3	12	3	5.87	76	.267	.348	25		.280	0*	83	-5		-0.5
1898	Chi N	1	0	1.000	2	1	0	0	9	8	4	0	1	5	1	2.00	179	.235	.350	4		.250	0*	99	1		0.1
Total	2	1	4	.200	6	4	0	0	39.2	40	33	4	4	17	4	4.99	86	.260	.349	29		.276	0	86	-4		-0.4

CLARKE, RUFE Rufus Rivers B4.13.1900 Estill SC D2.8.1983 Columbia SC BR/TR/6-1/203 d9.3 b-Sumpter Col Davidson

YEAR	TM LG	W	L	PCT	G	GS	CG-SHO	SV-BS	IP	H	R	HR	HB	BB-IB	SO	ERA	AERA	OAV	OOB	AB-HR-SH	AVG	PB	SUP	APR	DL	PW
1923	Det A	1	1	.500	5	0	0	0	6	6	3	0	1	6	2	4.50	86	.300	.481	0			0		0		0.0
1924	Det A	0	0	—	2	0	0	0	5.1	6	3	0	1	5	1	3.38	122	.158	.360	1		.000	-0		1		0.0
Total	2	1	1	.500	7	0	0	0	11.1	9	5	0	2	11	3	3.97	100	.231	.423	1		.000	-0		1		0.0

CLARKE, STAN Stanley Martin B8.9.1960 Toledo OH BL/TL/6-1/180* [TorA81 6/134] d6.7 Col Toledo

YEAR	TM LG	W	L	PCT	G	GS	CG-SHO	SV-BS	IP	H	R	HR	HB	BB-IB	SO	ERA	AERA	OAV	OOB	AB-HR-SH	AVG	PB	SUP	APR	DL	PW
1983	Tor A	1	1	.500	10	0	0	0-1	11	10	4	2	0	5-0	7	3.27	133	.256	.333	0	—	0		1		0.2
1985	Tor A	0	0	—	4	0	0	0-1	4	3	2	1	0	2-0	2	4.50	94	.214	.313	0	—	0		0		0.0
1986	Tor A	0	1	.000	10	0	0	0-0	12.2	18	13	4	0	10-1	9	9.24	46	.375	.475	0	—	0		-6		-0.4
1987	Sea A	2	2	.500	22	0	0	0-0	23	31	14	7	0	10-1	13	5.48	87	.333	.387	0	—	0		-1		-0.4
1989	KC A	0	2	.000	2	2	0	0-0	7	14	12	2	0	4-0	2	15.43	25	.438	.500	0	—	0	35	-8		-1.2
1990	StL N	0	0	—	2	0	0	0-0	3.1	2	1	0	0	0-0	3	2.70	143	.167	.167	0	—	0		0		0.0
Total	6	3	6	.333	50	2	0	0-2	61	78	46	16	0	31-2	36	6.79	65	.328	.398	0	—	0	35	-14		-1.6

CLARKE, WEBBO Vibert Ernesto B6.8.1928 Colon, Pan D6.14.1970 Cristobal, Canal Zone BL/TL/6-0/165 d9.4

YEAR	TM LG	W	L	PCT	G	GS	CG-SHO	SV-BS	IP	H	R	HR	HB	BB-IB	SO	ERA	AERA	OAV	OOB	AB-HR-SH	AVG	PB	SUP	APR	DL	PW
1955	Was A	0	0	—	7	2	0	0	21.1	17	11	2	0	14-0	9	4.64	83	.221	.341	6		.167	-0	151	-1		-0.1

CLARKE, DAD William H. B1.7.1865 Oswego NY D6.3.1911 Lorain OH BB/TR/5-7/160 d4.23

YEAR	TM LG	W	L	PCT	G	GS	CG-SHO	SV-BS	IP	H	R	HR	HB	BB-IB	SO	ERA	AERA	OAV	OOB	AB-HR-SH	AVG	PB	SUP	APR	DL	PW
1888	Chi N	1	0	1.000	2	2	1	0	16	23	17	2	2	6	6	5.06	60	.315	.383	7-1		.286	2	223	-4		0.0
1891	Col AA	1	2	.333	4	3	2	0	21	30	21	0	1	16	2	6.86	50	.326	.431	9		.111	0	150	-7		-0.7
1894	NY N	3	4	.429	15	6	5	1	84	114	76	3	3	26	15	4.93	107	.320	.371	37		.216	-0*	108	1		0.0
1895	NY N	18	15	.545	37	30	27-1	1	281.2	336	174	5	11	60	67	3.39	137	.292	.333	121		.240	-2	105	33		2.6
1896	NY N	17	24	.415	48	40	33-1	1	351	431	246	9	11	60	66	4.26	99	.300	.332	147-0-1		.204	-4*	89	-5		-1.0
1897	NY N	2	1	.667	6	4	2	0	31	43	34	1	2	11	10	6.10	68	.326	.386	18		.167	-1*	137	-8		-0.6
	Lou N	2	4	.333	7	6	6	0	54.2	74	33	3	2	10	7	3.95	108	.320	.354	22		.227	-1	56	3		0.2
	Year	4	5	.444	13	10	8	0	85.2	117	67	4	4	21	17	4.73	89	.322	.366	40		.200	-2	88	-7		-0.4
1898	Lou N	0	1	.000	1	1	0	0	9	10	7	1	2	2	1	5.00	72	.278	.350	3		.000	-1	139	-2		-0.2
Total	7	44	51	.463	120	92	77-2	3	848.1	1061	608	24	34	191	174	4.90	99	.302	.344	364-1-1		.214	-6	100	11		0.3

CLARKSON, DAD Arthur Hamilton B8.31.1866 Cambridge MA D2.5.1911 Somerville MA BR/TR/5-10/165 d8.20 b-John b-Walter

YEAR	TM LG	W	L	PCT	G	GS	CG-SHO	SV-BS	IP	H	R	HR	HB	BB-IB	SO	ERA	AERA	OAV	OOB	AB-HR-SH	AVG	PB	SUP	APR	DL	PW
1891	NY N	1	2	.333	5	2	1	0	28	24	23	0	3	18	11	2.89	111	.222	.349	9		.444	2	121	-1		0.1
1892	Bos N	1	0	1.000	1	1	1	0	7	5	1	0	0	3	0	1.29	273	.192	.276	3		.000	-0	54	2		0.2
1893	StL N	12	9	.571	24	21	17-1	0	186.1	194	116	4	14	79	37	3.48	136	.260	.342	75		.133	-5*	82	23		1.6
1894	StL N	8	17	.320	32	32	24-1	0	233.1	318	236	9	11	117	46	6.36	85	.321	.399	88		.182	-4*	74	-26		-2.1
1895	StL N	1	6	.143	7	7	7	0	61	91	66	7	2	26	9	7.38	65	.340	.402	23		.043	-3	53	-16		-1.5
	Bal N	12	3	.800	20	14	10	0	142	169	84	5	4	64	23	3.87	123	.291	.365	57-1-3		.140	-4	119	13		0.8
	Year	13	9	.591	27	21	17	0	203	260	150	12	6	90	32	4.92	97	.306	.377	80-1-3		.112	-7	96	0		-0.7
1896	Bal N	4	2	.667	7	4	3	0	47	72	40	1	2	18	7	4.98	86	.348	.405	18-0-1		.278	0	116	-5		-0.5
Total	6	39	39	.500	96	81	63-2	0	704.2	873	566	26	36	325	133	4.90	99	.298	.376	273-1-4		.161	-14	85	-10		-1.4

CLARKSON, JOHN John Gibson B7.1.1861 Cambridge MA D2.4.1909 Belmont MA BR/TR/5-10/155 d5.2 HF1963 b-Dad b-Walter

YEAR	TM LG	W	L	PCT	G	GS	CG-SHO	SV-BS	IP	H	R	HR	HB	BB-IB	SO	ERA	AERA	OAV	OOB	AB-HR-SH	AVG	PB	SUP	APR	DL	PW
1882	Wor N	1	2	.333	3	2	2	0	24	49	31	0		2	3	4.50	69	.392	.402	11		.364	1	74	-5		-0.4
1884	Chi N	10	3	.769	14	13	12	0	118	94	64	10		25	102	2.14	147	.208	.249	84-3		.262	4*	168	10		1.4
1885	†Chi N	53	16	.768	70	70	68-10	0	623	497	255	21		97	308	1.85	163	.208	.239	283-4		.216	2*	131	71		7.3
1886	†Chi N	36	17	.679	55	55	50-3	0	466.2	419	248	19		86	313	2.41	150	.229	.264	210-3		.233	1	110	50		5.0
1887	Chi N	38	21	.644	60	59	56-2	0	523	513	283	19	8	92	237	3.08	146	.246	.281	215-6		.242	2*	101	76		7.5
1888	Bos N	33	20	.623	54	54	53-3	0	483.1	448	247	17	10	119	223	2.76	104	.236	.284	205-1		.195	2*	129	9		1.2
1889	Bos N	49	19	.721	73	72	68-8	1	620	589	280	16	17	203	284	2.73	153	.243	.306	262-2		.206	0	85	93		8.9
1890	Bos N	26	18	.591	44	44	43-2	0	383	370	186	14	16	140	138	3.27	115	.246	.316	173-2		.249	3*	91	28		2.8
1891	Bos N	33	19	.635	55	51	47-3	3	460.2	435	244	18	15	154	141	2.79	131	.240	.305	187		.225	3	84	41		4.4
1892	Bos N	8	6	.571	16	16	15-4	0	145.2	115	64	5	4	49	48	2.35	150	.208	.292	57-1		.228	1	107	15		1.4
	†Cle N	17	10	.630	29	28	27-1	0	243.1	235	132	4	4	72	91	2.55	133	.244	.299	101		.139	-5	118	18		1.1
	Year	25	16	.610	45	44	42-5	0	389	350	197	9	8	132	139	2.48	139	.231	.296	158-1		.171	-4*	114	30		2.5
1893	Cle N	16	17	.485	36	35	31	0	295	358	240	11	5	95	62	4.45	110	.291	.344	131-1		.206	-4*	110	10		0.7
1894	Cle N	8	10	.444	22	18	13-1	0	150.2	173	109	6	0	46	28	4.42	124	.285	.335	55-1-4		.219	-0	93	16		1.2
Total	12	328	178	.648	531	518	485-37	5	4536.1	4295	2384	159	80	1191	1978	2.81	134	.240	.291	1974-24-4		.219	-3	106	432		42.5

YEAR TM LG	W	L	PCT	G	GS	CG-SHO	SV-BS	IP	H	R	HR	HB	BB-IB	SO	ERA	AERA	OAV	OOB	AB-HR-SH	AVG	PB	SUP	APR	DL	PW

CLARKSON, WALTER
Walter Hamilton B11.3.1878 Cambridge MA D10.10.1946 Cambridge MA BR/TR/5-10/150 d7.2 b-Dad b-John Col Harvard

YEAR TM LG	W	L	PCT	G	GS	CG-SHO	SV-BS	IP	H	R	HR	HB	BB-IB	SO	ERA	AERA	OAV	OOB	AB-HR-SH	AVG	PB	SUP	APR	DL	PW
1904 NY A	1	2	.333	13	4	2	1	66.1	63	42	3	10	25	43	5.02	54	.251	.343	26	.269	2	105	-14		-0.6
1905 NY A	3	3	.500	9	4	3	0	46	40	26	1	2	13	35	3.91	75	.235	.297	19	.053	-2	72	-4		-0.7
1906 NY A	9	4	.692	32	16	9-3	0	151	135	59	6	5	55	64	2.32	128	.242	.316	51-0-3	.157	-1	106	7		0.4
1907 NY A	1	1	.500	5	2	0	1	17.1	19	12	1	2	8	3	6.23	45	.279	.372	7	.286	0	145	-4		-0.5
Cle A	4	6	.400	17	10	9-1	0	90.2	77	40	1	3	29	32	1.99	126	.232	.299	28-0-1	.036	-3	75	2		-0.2
Year	5	7	.417	22	12	9-1	1	108	96	52	2	5	37	35	2.67	96	.240	.312	35-0-1	.086	-3	88	-3		-0.7
1908 Cle A	0	0	—	2	1	0	0	3.1	6	4	0	2	2	1	10.80	22	.400	.526	1	1.000	0	315	-3		-0.1
Total 5	18	16	.529	78	37	23-4	2	374.2	340	183	12	24	132	178	3.17	88	.244	.320	132-0-4	.152	-4	102	-16		-1.7

CLARKSON, BILL
William Henry "Blackie" B9.27.1898 Portsmouth VA D8.27.1971 Raleigh NC BR/TR/5-11/160 d5.2

YEAR TM LG	W	L	PCT	G	GS	CG-SHO	SV-BS	IP	H	R	HR	HB	BB-IB	SO	ERA	AERA	OAV	OOB	AB-HR-SH	AVG	PB	SUP	APR	DL	PW
1927 NY N	3	9	.250	26	7	2	2	86.2	92	50	3	1	52	28	4.36	88	.280	.380	20	.050	-1*	44	-5		-0.8
1928 NY N	0	0	—	4	0	0	0	5.2	10	6	0	1	3	3	7.94	48	.455	.478	0	—	0		-3		-0.1
Bos N	0	2	.000	19	2	0	0	34.2	53	29	2	1	22	8	6.75	58	.349	.434	3	.000	-0	0	-10		-0.5
Year	0	2	.000	23	2	0	0	40.1	63	35	2	1	23	11	6.92	57	.362	.439	3	.000	-0	0	-14		-0.6
1929 Bos N	0	1	.000	2	1	0	0	7	16	10	0	0	4	0	10.29	45	.485	.541	2	.500	1	112	-5		-0.5
Total 3	3	12	.200	51	10	2	2	134	171	95	5	2	79	39	5.44	72	.319	.408	25	.080	-1	48	-23		-1.9

CLARY, MARTY
Martin Keith B4.3.1962 Detroit MI BR/TR/6-4/190* [AtlN83 3/74] d9.5 Col Northwestern

YEAR TM LG	W	L	PCT	G	GS	CG-SHO	SV-BS	IP	H	R	HR	HB	BB-IB	SO	ERA	AERA	OAV	OOB	AB-HR-SH	AVG	PB	SUP	APR	DL	PW
1987 Atl N	0	1	.000	7	1	0	0-0	14.2	20	13	2	1	4-0	7	6.14	71	.328	.373	1	.000	-0	63	-3		-0.2
1989 Atl N	4	3	.571	18	17	2-1	0-0	108.2	103	47	6	1	31-3	30	3.15	116	.249	.301	31-0-5	.161	0	88	4		0.3
1990 Atl N	1	10	.091	33	14	0	0-0	101.2	128	72	9	1	39-4	44	5.67	71	.308	.364	28-0-2	.000	-3	82	-17		-1.9
Total 3	5	14	.263	58	32	2-1	0-0	225	251	132	17	3	74-7	81	4.48	86	.282	.336	60-0-7	.083	-2	84	-16		-1.8

CLASET, GOWELL
Gowell Sylvester "Lefty" B11.26.1907 Battle Creek MI D3.8.1981 St.Petersburg FL BB/TL/6-3.5/210 d4.12

YEAR TM LG	W	L	PCT	G	GS	CG-SHO	SV-BS	IP	H	R	HR	HB	BB-IB	SO	ERA	AERA	OAV	OOB	AB-HR-SH	AVG	PB	SUP	APR	DL	PW
1933 Phi A	2	0	1.000						23	15	1	0	13	1	9.53	45	.426	.523	2		.500	1	258	-7	-0.9

CLAUSEN, FRITZ
Frederick William B4.26.1869 New York NY D2.11.1960 Memphis TN BR/TL/5-11/190 d7.23

YEAR TM LG	W	L	PCT	G	GS	CG-SHO	SV-BS	IP	H	R	HR	HB	BB-IB	SO	ERA	AERA	OAV	OOB	AB-HR-SH	AVG	PB	SUP	APR	DL	PW
1892 Lou N	9	13	.409	24	24	24-2	0	200	181	120	3	3	87	94	3.06	100	.232	.311	84	.155	-3	87	-3		-0.6
1893 Lou N	1	4	.200	5	5	3	0	33	41	25	2	1	22	4	6.00	73	.295	.395	14	.214	-1	89	-5		-0.5
Chi N	6	2	.750	10	9	8	1	76	71	46	1	5	39	31	3.08	150	.240	.338	33	.121	-3	96	10		0.6
Year	7	6	.538	15	14	11	1	109	112	71	3	6	61	35	3.96	115	.257	.357	47	.149	-4	93	9		0.1
1894 Chi N	0	1	.000	2	2	0	0	4.1	7	5	0	0	5	1	14.54	39	.294	.455	1	.000	-0	75	-3		-0.4
1896 Lou N	0	2	.000	2	2	1	0	11	17	13	1	3	6	4	6.55	66	.347	.448	4	.000	-1	123	-3		-0.4
Total 4	16	22	.421	43	42	36-2	1	324.1	315	211	7	12	159	134	3.64	100	.246	.334	136	.147	-8	93	-4		-1.3

CLAUSS, AL
Albert Stanley "Lefty" B6.24.1891 New Haven CT D9.13.1952 New Haven CT BR/TL/5-10.5/178 d4.22

YEAR TM LG	W	L	PCT	G	GS	CG-SHO	SV-BS	IP	H	R	HR	HB	BB-IB	SO	ERA	AERA	OAV	OOB	AB-HR-SH	AVG	PB	SUP	APR	DL	PW
1913 Det A	0	1	.000	5	1	0	0	13.1	11	9	0	1	9	2	4.73	62	.224	.397	4	.000	-1	0	-4		-0.2

CLAUSSEN, BRANDON
Brandon Allen Falker B5.1.1979 Rapid City SD BR/TL/6-2/200* [NYA98 34/1027] d6.28 Col Howard (TX) JC

YEAR TM LG	W	L	PCT	G	GS	CG-SHO	SV-BS	IP	H	R	HR	HB	BB-IB	SO	ERA	AERA	OAV	OOB	AB-HR-SH	AVG	PB	SUP	APR	DL	PW
2003 NY A	1	0	1.000	1	1	0	0-0	6.1	8	2	1	0	1-0	5	1.42	309	.296	.321	4	.250	0	188	2		0.3
2004 Cin N	2	8	.200	14	14	0	0-0	66	80	50	9	2	35-2	45	6.14	70	.299	.380	19-0-2	.105	-1	75	-14		-1.9
2005 Cin N	10	11	.476	29	29	0	0-0	166.2	178	89	24	7	57-5	121	4.21	90	.273	.335	55-0-6	.091	-2	116	-15		-0.6
Total 3	13	19	.406	44	44	0	0-0	239	266	141	34	9	93-7	171	4.67	90	.281	.347	78-0-8	.103	-3	105	-15		-2.2

CLAY, DANNY
Danny Bruce B10.24.1961 Sun Valley CA BR/TR/6-1/200 d5.1 Col Loyola Marymount

YEAR TM LG	W	L	PCT	G	GS	CG-SHO	SV-BS	IP	H	R	HR	HB	BB-IB	SO	ERA	AERA	OAV	OOB	AB-HR-SH	AVG	PB	SUP	APR	DL	PW
1988 Phi N	0	1	.000	17	0	0	0-0	24	27	17	5	0	21-2	12	6.00	60	.303	.432	2-0-1	.000	-0		-6		-0.

CLAY, KEN
Kenneth Earl B4.6.1954 Lynchburg VA BR/TR/6-3/195* [NYA72 2/38] d6.7

YEAR TM LG	W	L	PCT	G	GS	CG-SHO	SV-BS	IP	H	R	HR	HB	BB-IB	SO	ERA	AERA	OAV	OOB	AB-HR-SH	AVG	PB	SUP	APR	DL	PW
1977 †NY A	2	3	.400	21	3	0	1-1	55.2	53	32	6	1	24-3	20	4.37	91	.251	.329	0	—	0	128	-3		-0.3
1978 †NY A	3	4	.429	28	6	0	0-0	75.2	89	41	3	2	21-3	32	4.28	85	.291	.338	0	—	0	131	-6	21	-0.8
1979 NY A	1	7	.125	32	5	0	2-2	78.1	88	49	12	2	25-1	28	5.40	76	.291	.346	0	—	0	57	-10		-1.1
1980 Tex A	2	3	.400	8	8	0	0-0	43	43	24	4	3	29-2	17	4.60	84	.256	.373	0	—	0	109	-3	66	-0.7
1981 Sea A	2	7	.222	22	14	0	0-0	101	116	62	10	3	42-3	32	4.63	84	.294	.363	0	—	0	91	-32	87	-3.1
Total 5	10	24	.294	111	36	0	3-3	353.2	389	208	35	11	141-12	129	4.68	83	.281	.350	0	—	0	91	-32	87	-3.1

CLEAR, MARK
Mark Alan B5.27.1956 Los Angeles CA BR/TR/6-4/215(200-215) [PhiN74 8/171] d4.4

YEAR TM LG	W	L	PCT	G	GS	CG-SHO	SV-BS	IP	H	R	HR	HB	BB-IB	SO	ERA	AERA	OAV	OOB	AB-HR-SH	AVG	PB	SUP	APR	DL	PW
1979 †Cal A★	11	5	.688	52	0	0	14-7	109	82	46	3	8	68-5	98	3.63	112	.219	.333	0	—	0		6		0.
1980 Cal A	11	11	.500	58	0	0	9-6	106.1	82	51	2	5	65-9	105	3.30	120	.216	.336	0	—	0		4		0.
1981 Bos A	8	3	.727	34	0	0	9-5	76.2	69	36	11	2	51-2	82	4.11	95	.239	.357	0	—	0		15		3.
1982 Bos A☆	14	9	.609	55	0	0	14-9	105	92	39	11	7	61-6	109	6.28	70	.273	.385	0	—	0		-17		-1.
1983 Bos A	4	5	.444	48	0	0	4-1	96	101	71	10	3	70-3	76	4.03	104	.198	.378	0	—	0		3		-0.
1984 Bos A	8	3	.727	47	0	0	8-2	67	47	38	2	7	70-3	76	3.72	116	.225	.389	0	—	0		3		0.
1985 Bos A	1	3	.250	41	0	0	3-3	55.2	45	26	1	5	50-10	55	3.72	116	.225	.389	0	—	0		16		2.
1986 Mil A	5	5	.500	59	0	0	16-3	73.2	53	23	4	1	36-2	63	2.20	198	.201	.295	0	—	0	99	-1		2.
1987 Mil A	8	5	.615	58	1	0	6-3	78.1	70	52	9	5	55-3	81	4.48	103	.239	.363	0	—	0		3	63	0.
1988 Mil A	1	0	1.000	25	0	0	0-0	29	23	12	4	0	21-0	26	2.79	143	.215	.338	0	—	0		-2		-0.
1990 Cal A	0	0	—	4	0	0	0-0	7.2	5	7	1	0	6-0	6	5.87	65	.200	.421	0	—	0		99		5.
Total 11	71	49	.592	481	1	0	83-39	804.1	674	397	60	35	554-45	804	3.85	110	.228	.353	0	—	0	99	27	63	5.

CLEARY, JOE
Joseph Christopher "Fire" B12.3.1918 Cork, Ireland D6.3.2004 Yonkers NY BR/TR/5-9/150 d8.4

YEAR TM LG	W	L	PCT	G	GS	CG-SHO	SV-BS	IP	H	R	HR	HB	BB-IB	SO	ERA	AERA	OAV	OOB	AB-HR-SH	AVG	PB	SUP	APR	DL	PW
1945 Was A	0	0	—	1	0	0	0	0.1	5	7	0	0	3	1	189.00	2	.833	.889	0	—	0		-7		-0.

CLEMENS, ROGER
William Roger "Rocket" B8.4.1962 Dayton OH BR/TR/6-4/220(205-235) [BosA83 1/19] d5.15 Col Texas

YEAR TM LG	W	L	PCT	G	GS	CG-SHO	SV-BS	IP	H	R	HR	HB	BB-IB	SO	ERA	AERA	OAV	OOB	AB-HR-SH	AVG	PB	SUP	APR	DL	PW
1984 Bos A	9	4	.692	21	20	5-1	0-0	133.1	146	67	13	2	29-3	126	4.32	97	.271	.309	0	—	0	132	1		0.
1985 Bos A	7	5	.583	15	15	3-1	0-0	98.1	83	38	5	3	37-0	74	3.29	131	.228	.303	0	—	0	86	11	73	1.
1986 †Bos A★	24	4	.857	33	33	10-1	0-0	254	179	77	21	4	67-0	238	2.48	169	.195	.252	0	—	0	132	49		5.
1987 †Bos A★	20	9	.690	36	36	18-7	0-0	281.2	248	100	19	9	83-4	256	2.97	154	.235	.295	0	—	0	97	34		3.
1988 †Bos A★	18	12	.600	35	35	14-8	0-0	264	217	93	17	6	62-4	291	2.93	141	.220	.270	0	—	0	100	26		3.
1989 Bos A	17	11	.607	35	35	8-3	0-0	253.1	215	101	20	8	93-5	230	3.13	132	.231	.305	0	—	0	94	51		6.
1990 †Bos A☆	21	6	.778	31	31	7-4	0-0	228.1	193	59	7	7	54-3	209	1.93	212	.228	.278	0	—	0	95	47		4.
1991 Bos A★	18	10	.643	35	35	13-4	0-0	271.1	219	93	15	5	65-12	241	2.62	165	.224	.270	0	—	0	86	45		5.
1992 Bos A★	18	11	.621	32	32	11-5	0-0	246.2	203	80	11	9	62-5	208	2.41	177	.224	.278	0	—	0	64	7	27	3.
1993 Bos A	11	14	.440	29	29	2-1	0-0	191.2	175	99	17	11	67-4	160	4.46	104	.244	.315	0	—	0	71	38		3.
1994 Bos A	9	7	.563	24	24	3-1	0-0	170.2	124	62	15	4	71-1	168	2.85	177	.203	.288	0	—	0	108	11	38	1.
1995 Bos A	10	5	.667	23	23	0	0-0	140	141	70	15	14	60-0	132	4.18	116	.259	.346	0	—	0	80	41		3.
1996 Bos A	10	13	.435	34	34	6-2	0-0	242.2	216	106	19	4	106-2	257	3.63	140	.237	.317	1	1.000	1	91	75		7.
1997 Tor A★	21	7	.750	34	34	9-3	0-0	264	204	65	9	12	68-1	292	2.05	224	.213	.273	1	.500	1	91	52		5.
1998 Tor A★	20	6	.769	33	33	5-3	0-0	234.2	169	78	11	7	88-0	271	2.65	176	.197	.277	4-0-1	.000	-0	88	5	23	0.
1999 †NY A	14	10	.583	30	30	1-1	0-0	187.2	185	101	20	9	90-0	163	4.60	103	.261	.350	3	.000	0	95	23	16	2.
2000 †NY A	13	8	.619	32	32	1	0-0	204.1	184	96	26	10	84-0	188	3.70	129	.236	.317	3	.000	0	123	23		2.
2001 †NY A★	20	3	.870	33	33	0	0-0	220.1	205	94	19	9	72-1	213	3.51	126	.246	.309	2	.000	0	116	1	25	1.
2002 †NY A★	13	6	.684	29	29	0	0-0	180	172	94	18	9	63-0	192	4.35	100	.253	.317	3	.667	1	107	12		1.
2003 †NY A★	17	9	.654	33	33	1-1	0-0	211.2	199	99	24	5	58-1	190	3.91	112	.247	.299	1-0-1	.000	0	100	33		1.
2004 †Hou N★	18	4	.818	33	33	0	0-0	214.1	169	76	15	9	79-5	218	2.98	147	.217	.292	72-0-3	.167	3	75	53		3.
2005 †Hou N★	13	8	.619	32	32	1	0-0	211.1	151	51	11	8	62-5	185	1.87	224	.198	.261	68-0-5	.207	3	77	53		5.
Total 22	341	172	.665	672	671	118-46	0-0	4704.1	3997	1799	347	150	1520-62	4502	3.12	143	.229	.294	150-0-11	.187	5	97	687	202	70

CLEMENSEN, BILL
William Melville B6.20.1919 New Brunswick NJ D2.18.1994 Alta CA BR/TR/6-1/193 d5.22 Mil 1942-45 Col San Jose St.

YEAR TM LG	W	L	PCT	G	GS	CG-SHO	SV-BS	IP	H	R	HR	HB	BB-IB	SO	ERA	AERA	OAV	OOB	AB-HR-SH	AVG	PB	SUP	APR	DL	PW
1939 Pit N	0	1	.000	12	1	0	0	27	32	26	0	3	20	13	7.33	52	.311	.437	6	.333	1	23	-11		-0.
1941 Pit N	1	0	1.000	1	1	0	0	13	7	5	0	0	4	2	2.77	130	.159	.275	4	.000	-1	71	1		0.
1946 Pit N	0	0	—	2	0	0	0	2	0	0	0	0	3	4	0.00		.000	.000	0	—	0		1		-0.
Total 3	1	1	.500	15	2	0	0	42	39	31	0	3	27	19	5.57	67	.255	.377	10	.200	0	46	-9		-0.

CLEMENT, MATT
Matthew Paul B8.12.1974 McCandless Twp. PA BR/TR/6-3/195(180-210) [SDN93 3/86] d9.6

YEAR TM LG	W	L	PCT	G	GS	CG-SHO	SV-BS	IP	H	R	HR	HB	BB-IB	SO	ERA	AERA	OAV	OOB	AB-HR-SH	AVG	PB	SUP	APR	DL	PW
1998 SD N	2	0	1.000	4	2	0	0-0	13.2	16	9	0	0	7-1	13	4.61	86	.283	.367	2-0-2	.000	-0	93	-1		-0.
1999 SD N	10	12	.455	31	31	0	0-0	180.2	190	106	18	9	86-2	135	4.48	95	.273	.358	52-0-6	.077	-2	101	-8		-1.

YEAR TM LG	W	L	PCT	G	GS	CG-SHO	SV-BS	IP	H	R	HR	HB	BB-IB	SO	ERA	AERA	OAV	OOB	AB-HR-SH	AVG	PB	SUP	APR	DL	PW
2000 SD N	13	17	.433	34	34	0	0-0	205	194	131	22	16	125-4	170	5.14	87	.248	.361	60-0-5	.067	-3	94	-17		-2.2
2001 Fla N	9	10	.474	31	31	0	0-0	169.1	172	102	15	15	85-2	134	5.05	83	.267	.365	50-0-8	.080	-2*	114	-17		-1.9
2002 Chi N	12	11	.522	32	32	3-2	0-0	205	162	84	18	6	85-7	215	3.60	113	.215	.299	61-0-10	.049	-3	110	13		1.0
2003 †Chi N	14	12	.538	32	32	2-1	0-0	201.2	169	100	22	14	79-2	171	4.11	106	.227	.312	62-0-8	.145	-1	88	6		0.6
2004 Chi N	9	13	.409	30	30	0	0-0	181	155	79	23	12	77-4	190	3.68	121	.229	.317	55-0-4	.145	-0	83	15		1.5
2005 †Bos A★	13	6	.684	32	32	1	0-0	191	192	102	18	16	68-1	146	4.57	101	.260	.333	3	.000	-0	121	1		0.1
Total 8	82	81	.503	226	224	6-3	0-0	1347.1	1249	712	136	88	612-23	1174	4.37	99	.246	.335	345-0-43	.093	-12	101	-8		-2.2

CLEMENTS, PAT Patrick Brian B2.2.1962 McCloud CA BR/TL/6-0/180* [CalA83 4/103] d4.9 Col UCLA

YEAR TM LG	W	L	PCT	G	GS	CG-SHO	SV-BS	IP	H	R	HR	HB	BB-IB	SO	ERA	AERA	OAV	OOB	AB-HR-SH	AVG	PB	SUP	APR	DL	PW
1985 Cal A	5	0	1.000	41	0	0	1-1	62	47	23	4	2	25-2	19	3.34	124	.218	.305	0	—	0		7		0.6
Pit N	0	2	.000	27	0	0	2-4	34.1	39	14	2	0	15-3	17	3.67	99	.289	.358	3-0-1	.333	0		1		0.0
1986 Pit N	0	4	.000	65	0	0	2-3	61	53	20	1	2	32-6	31	2.80	139	.251	.349	6	.000	-1		8		0.5
1987 NY A	3	3	.500	55	0	0	7-3	80	91	45	4	3	30-2	36	4.95	90	.299	.364	0	—	0		-4		-0.2
1988 NY A	0	0	—	6	0	0	0-1	8.1	12	8	1	0	4-0	5	6.48	61	.343	.390	0	—	0		-4		-0.2
1989 SD N	4	1	.800	23	0	0	0-1	39	39	17	4	0	15-5	18	3.92	89	.267	.333	6	.000	0	69	-3		-0.1
1990 SD N	0	0	—	9	0	0	0-0	13	20	9	1	0	7-1	6	4.15	92	.357	.429	0	—	0	76	-1		-0.1
1991 SD N	1	0	1.000	12	0	0	0-0	14.1	13	8	0	0	9-4	8	3.77	101	.255	.349	1	.000	-0		0		-0.1
1992 SD N	2	1	.667	27	0	0	0-1	23.2	25	9	0	2	12-4	11	2.66	135	.281	.379	1	.000	-0		0	131	0.0
Bal A	2	0	1.000	23	0	0	0-0	24.2	23	10	0	2	11-0	9	3.28	124	.235	.350	0	—	0		2		0.2
Total 8	17	11	.607	288	0	0	12-14	360.1	362	163	17	11	160-27	158	3.77	106	.272	.351	17-0-1	.059	-1	68	11	131	1.0

CLEMONS, CHRIS Christopher Hale B10.31.1972 Baytown TX BR/TR/6-4/225 [ChiA94 S1/33] d7.23 Col Texas A&M-Commerce

YEAR TM LG	W	L	PCT	G	GS	CG-SHO	SV-BS	IP	H	R	HR	HB	BB-IB	SO	ERA	AERA	OAV	OOB	AB-HR-SH	AVG	PB	SUP	APR	DL	PW
1997 Chi A	0	2	.000	9	0	0	0-0	12.2	19	13	4	1	11-0	8	8.53	52	.345	.463	0	—	0	21	-6		-0.7

CLEMONS, LANCE Lance Levis B7.6.1947 Philadelphia PA BL/TL/6-2/205* [KCA68 7/156] d8.12 Col West Chester

YEAR TM LG	W	L	PCT	G	GS	CG-SHO	SV-BS	IP	H	R	HR	HB	BB-IB	SO	ERA	AERA	OAV	OOB	AB-HR-SH	AVG	PB	SUP	APR	DL	PW
1971 KC A	1	0	1.000	10	3	0	0-0	24	26	16	2	1	12-0	20	4.13	83	.263	.345	7-1-1	.286	2	122	-4		0.0
1972 Stl N	0	1	.000	3	1	0	0-0	5.1	8	7	1	1	5-0	2	10.13	34	.364	.500	1	.000	-0	52	-4		-0.7
1974 Bos A	1	0	1.000	6	0	0	0-0	6.1	8	8	1	1	4-3	1	9.95	39	.296	.406	0	—	0		-4		-0.6
Total 3	2	1	.667	19	4	0	0-0	35.2	42	31	4	3	21-3	23	6.06	58	.284	.382	8-1-1	.250	2	102	-12		-1.3

CLEVELAND, REGGIE Reginald Leslie B5.23.1948 Swift Current SK, Can. BR/TR/6-1/195(185-205) d10.1

YEAR TM LG	W	L	PCT	G	GS	CG-SHO	SV-BS	IP	H	R	HR	HB	BB-IB	SO	ERA	AERA	OAV	OOB	AB-HR-SH	AVG	PB	SUP	APR	DL	PW
1969 Stl N	0	0	—	1	1	0	0-0	4	7	4	0	0	1-0	3	9.00	40	.368	.400	1-0-1	.000	-0	148	-2		-0.1
1970 Stl N	0	4	.000	16	1	0	0-0	26	31	27	3	0	18-6	22	7.62	54	.298	.392	4	.250	0	152	-11		-1.4
1971 Stl N	12	12	.500	34	34	10-2	0-0	222	238	107	20	6	53-12	148	4.01	91	.271	.315	82-0-4	.171	-1	100	-8		-0.9
1972 Stl N	14	15	.483	34	33	11-3	0-0	230.2	229	120	21	5	60-12	153	3.94	87	.258	.306	71-0-11	.239	3	102	-16		-1.7
1973 Stl N	14	10	.583	32	32	6-3	0-0	224	211	88	13	4	61-12	122	3.01	122	.246	.298	74-0-9	.230	4	101	15		1.9
1974 Bos A	12	14	.462	41	27	10	0-0	221.1	234	121	25	9	69-5	103	4.31	89	.271	.329	0	—	0	115	-13		-1.3
1975 †Bos A	13	9	.591	31	20	3-1	0-1	170.2	173	90	19	3	52-1	78	4.43	92	.263	.317	0	—	0	104	-5		-0.6
1976 Bos A	10	9	.526	41	14	3	2-2	170	159	73	7	4	61-4	76	3.07	127	.246	.314	0	—	0	82	12		1.3
1977 Bos A	11	8	.579	36	27	9-1	2-1	190.1	211	97	20	4	43-2	85	4.26	105	.281	.320	0	—	0	108	5		0.3
1978 Bos A	0	1	.000	1	0	0	0-0	0.1	1	1	0	0	0-0	0	0.00	—	.333	.333	0	—	0		4		-0.1
Tex A	5	7	.417	53	0	0	12-7	75.2	65	33	5	3	23-6	46	3.09	121	.236	.295	0	—	0		4		0.8
Year	5	8	.385	54	0	0	12-7	76	66	34	5	3	23-6	46	3.08	122	.237	.296	0	—	0		4		0.7
1979 Mil A	1	5	.167	29	1	0	4-2	55	77	44	9	0	23-4	22	6.71	63	.344	.394	0	—	0	129	-15		-1.6
1980 Mil A	11	9	.550	45	13	5-2	4-2	154.1	150	73	9	5	49-2	54	3.73	105	.254	.312	0	—	0	109	3		0.3
1981 Mil A	2	3	.400	35	0	0	1-0	64.2	57	41	5	1	30-2	18	5.15	67	.239	.326	0	—	0		-13		-1.1
Total 13	105	106	.498	428	203	57-12	25-15	1809	1843	919	152	44	543-68	930	4.01	96	.264	.318	232-0-25	.211	6	104	-44		-4.2

CLEVENGER, TEX Truman Eugene B7.9.1932 Visalia CA BR/TR/6-1/180* d4.18 Col Cal St.-Fresno

YEAR TM LG	W	L	PCT	G	GS	CG-SHO	SV-BS	IP	H	R	HR	HB	BB-IB	SO	ERA	AERA	OAV	OOB	AB-HR-SH	AVG	PB	SUP	APR	DL	PW
1954 Bos A	2	4	.333	23	8	1	0	67.2	67	42	9	2	29	43	4.79	86	.262	.337	14	.214	0*	70	-5		-0.4
1956 Was A	0	0	—	20	0	1	0	31.2	33	22	4	0	21-0	17	5.40	80	.264	.365	2	.000	-0	144	-4		-0.2
1957 Was A	7	6	.538	52	9	2	8	139.2	139	69	11	4	47-4	75	4.19	93	.261	.322	33-0-4	.212	1	87	-4		-0.1
1958 Was A	9	9	.500	55	4	0	6	124	119	65	12	1	50-6	70	4.35	88	.251	.321	22-0-2	.136	0	59	-8		-1.0
1959 Was A	8	5	.615	50	7	2-2	8	117.1	114	56	8	2	51-3	71	3.91	100	.256	.332	23-0-4	.174	1	84	1		0.5
1960 Was A	5	11	.313	53	11	1	7	128.2	150	77	10	3	49-10	49	4.20	93	.298	.358	22-0-4	.091	-1	70	-7		-1.0
1961 LA A	2	1	.667	12	0	0	0	16	13	5	1	0	13-1	11	1.69	267	.220	.361	3	.000	-0		4		0.7
NY A	1	1	.500	21	0	0	0	31.2	35	20	3	1	21-1	14	4.83	77	.287	.396	4	.250	0		-5		-0.2
Year	3	2	.600	33	0	0	1	47.2	48	25	4	1	34-2	25	3.78	105	.265	.384	7	.143	0		4		0.5
1962 NY A	2	0	1.000	21	0	0	0	38	36	14	3	1	17-5	11	2.84	132	.248	.329	4	.000	-0*		4		0.1
Total 8	36	37	.493	307	40	6-2	30	694.2	706	370	61	14	298-30	361	4.18	94	.265	.339	127-0-14	.157	1	78	-24		-1.6

CLIBURN, STEW Stewart Walker B12.19.1956 Jackson MS BR/TR/6-0/195* [PitN77 4/96] d9.17 twb-Stan Col Delta St.

YEAR TM LG	W	L	PCT	G	GS	CG-SHO	SV-BS	IP	H	R	HR	HB	BB-IB	SO	ERA	AERA	OAV	OOB	AB-HR-SH	AVG	PB	SUP	APR	DL	PW
1984 Cal A	0	0	—	2	3	3	0-0	2	3	3	0	1	1-1	1	13.50	30	.333	.400	0	—	0		-2		-0.1
1985 Cal A	9	3	.750	44	0	0	6-1	99	87	25	5	1	26-6	48	2.09	197	.241	.292	0	—	0		23		2.9
1988 Cal A	4	2	.667	40	1	0	0-4	84	83	45	11	6	32-6	42	4.07	95	.266	.342	0	—	0	47	-3		-0.2
Total 3	13	5	.722	85	1	0	6-5	185	173	73	16	7	59-13	91	3.11	129	.254	.317	0	—	0*	47	18		2.6

CLINTON, JIM James Lawrence "Big Jim" B8.10.1850 New York NY D9.3.1921 Brooklyn NY BR/TR/5-8.5/174 d5.18 U1 ▲

YEAR TM LG	W	L	PCT	G	GS	CG-SHO	SV-BS	IP	H	R	HR	HB	BB-IB	SO	ERA	AERA	OAV	OOB	AB-HR-SH	AVG	PB	SUP	APR	DL	PW
1872 Eck NA	0	1	.000	1	1	1	0	9	25	36	1	0	—	7	7.00	48	.373	.382	98	.245	0*	0	-8		-0.4
1875 Atl NA	1	13	.071	17	14	9	0	123	141	104	0	0	5	7	2.41	86	.262	.268	81	.123	-5*	40	-5		-0.7
1876 Lou N	0	1	.000	1	1	1	0	9	12	11	0	0	1	1	6.00	45	.279	.279	65	.338	0*	28	-2		-0.1
Total 2 NA	1	14	.067	18	15	10	0	132	166	140	1	0	6	8	2.73	80	.274	.281	179	.190	-5	36	-13		-1.1

CLONINGER, TONY Tony Lee B8.13.1940 Lincoln Co. NC BR/TR/6-0/210(200-215) d6.15 C12

YEAR TM LG	W	L	PCT	G	GS	CG-SHO	SV-BS	IP	H	R	HR	HB	BB-IB	SO	ERA	AERA	OAV	OOB	AB-HR-SH	AVG	PB	SUP	APR	DL	PW
1961 Mil N	7	2	.778	19	10	3	0	84	84	49	16	1	33-1	51	5.25	71	.258	.326	30-0-2	.167	-0	154	-13		-1.2
1962 Mil N	8	3	.727	24	15	4-1	0	111	113	61	10	1	46-1	69	4.30	88	.264	.335	39-0-2	.103	-2	123	-7		-0.8
1963 Mil N	9	11	.450	41	18	4-2	1	145.1	131	68	17	2	63-12	100	3.78	85	.239	.318	37-0-5	.135	-0	125	-9		-1.3
1964 Mil N	19	14	.576	38	34	15-3	2	242.2	206	112	20	3	82-9	163	3.56	99	.231	.294	87-0-11	.241	3	112	-2		0.0
1965 Mil N	24	11	.686	40	38	16-1	1	279	247	115	20	3	119-5	211	3.29	107	.236	.315	105-1-7	.162	2*	133	7		0.9
1966 Atl N	14	11	.560	39	38	11-1	1	257.2	253	134	29	6	116-9	178	4.12	88	.258	.336	111-5-2	.234	10*	129	-14		-0.3
1967 Atl N	4	7	.364	16	16	1	0	76.2	85	50	11	0	31-4	55	5.17	64	.285	.348	25	.200	1	111	-16	51	-2.0
1968 Atl N	1	3	.250	8	1	0	0	19	15	9	0	0	11-2	7	4.26	70	.227	.329	4	.000	0	58	-2		-0.5
Cin N	4	3	.571	17	17	2-2	0	91.1	81	49	7	3	48-6	65	4.04	78	.233	.330	34-2-3	.206	3*	156	-9		-0.4
Year	5	6	.455	25	18	2-2	0	110.1	96	58	7	3	59-8	72	4.08	77	.232	.330	38-2-3	.184	3	152	-12		-0.9
1969 Cin N	11	17	.393	35	34	6-2	0-0	189.2	184	123	24	5	103-4	103	5.03	75	.250	.344	72-1-3	.167	1*	118	-26		-3.5
1970 †Cin N	9	7	.563	30	18	0	1-1	148	136	69	10	4	78-6	56	3.83	106	.249	.346	47-2-2	.213	3	97	5		0.9
1971 Cin N	3	6	.333	28	8	1-1	0-0	97.1	79	42	12	4	49-3	51	3.88	87	.230	.328	27-0-2	.259	1	128	-4		0.9
1972 Stl N	0	2	.000	9	2	0	0-1	26	29	17	2	1	19-5	11	5.19	66	.293	.405	3	.000	-0		-5		-0.4
Total 12	113	97	.538	352	247	63-13	6-2	1767.2	1643	898	180	33	798-65	1120	4.07	88	.247	.328	621-11-39	.192	21	124	-95	51	-8.8

CLONTZ, BRAD John Bradley B4.25.1971 Stuart VA BR/TR/6-1/180(180-203) [AtlN92 10/285] d4.26 Col VPI

YEAR TM LG	W	L	PCT	G	GS	CG-SHO	SV-BS	IP	H	R	HR	HB	BB-IB	SO	ERA	AERA	OAV	OOB	AB-HR-SH	AVG	PB	SUP	APR	DL	PW
1995 †Atl N	8	1	.889	59	0	0	4-2	69	71	29	6	4	22-4	55	3.65	118	.269	.332	2	.000	-0		6		0.7
1996 †Atl N	6	3	.667	81	0	0	1-5	80.2	78	53	11	2	33-8	49	5.69	78	.255	.328	2-0-1	.000	0		-9		-0.8
1997 Atl N	5	1	.833	51	0	0	1-1	48	52	24	3	1	18-3	42	3.75	112	.286	.350	1	.000	0		-3		-0.2
1998 LA N	2	0	1.000	18	0	0	0-1	20.2	15	13	3	2	10-4	14	5.66	71	.200	.310	1	.000	-0		-3		-0.3
NY N	0	0	—	2	0	0	0	3	4	3	1	0	2-0	2	9.00	46	.333	.429	1	.000	-0		-3		0.0
Year	2	0	1.000	20	0	0	0-1	23.2	19	16	4	2	12-4	16	6.08	66	.218	.327	2	.000	-0		-6	18	-0.1
1999 Pit N	1	3	.250	56	0	0	2-1	49.1	49	21	6	3	24-5	40	2.74	168	.254	.344	3	.000	-0		-5		-0.4
2000 Pit N	0	0	—	5	0	0	0-0	7	7	4	1	0	11-2	8	5.14	90	.269	.486	0	—	0			153	0.2
Total 6	22	8	.733	272	0	0	8-10	277.2	276	147	30	12	120-26	210	4.34	101	.261	.340	10-0-1	.000	0		2	171	0.2

CLOSTER, AL Alan Edward B6.15.1943 Creighton NE BL/TL/6-2/190(190-212) d4.19 Col Iowa St.

YEAR TM LG	W	L	PCT	G	GS	CG-SHO	SV-BS	IP	H	R	HR	HB	BB-IB	SO	ERA	AERA	OAV	OOB	AB-HR-SH	AVG	PB	SUP	APR	DL	PW
1966 Was A	0	0	—	1	0	0	0-0	0.1	1	0	0	0	0-0	0	0.00	—	.500	.750	0	—	0				0.0
1971 NY A	2	0	.500	14	1	0	0-0	28.1	33	22	4	2	13-7	22	5.08	65	.289	.364	6-0-1	.000	0	27	-8		-1.0
1972 NY A	0	0	—	2	0	0	0-0	2.1	2	3	1	0	4-0	2	11.57	26	.250	.500	1	.000	-0		-2		-0.1
1973 Atl N	0	0	—	4	0	0	0-1	4.1	7	7	2	0	6-1	2	14.54	27	.389	.500	0	—	0		-2		-0.2
Total 4	2	2	.500	21	1	0	0-1	35.1	43	32	6	2	23-8	26	6.62	51	.303	.402	7-0-1	.000	0	27	-14		-1.3

YEAR	TM LG	W	L	PCT	G	GS	CG-SHO	SV-BS	IP	H	R	HR	HB	BB-IB	SO	ERA	AERA	OAV	OOB	AB-HR-SH	AVG	PB	SUP	APR	DL	PW
CLOUDE, KEN	Kenneth Brian B1.9.1975 Baltimore MD BR/TR/6-1/180(180-200) [SeaA93 6/157] d8.9 [DL 2000 Sea A 31]																								
1997	Sea A	4	2	.667	10	9	0	0-0	51	41	32	8	3	26-0	46	5.12	89	.218	.321	2	.000	-0	122	-4		-0.4
1998	Sea A	8	10	.444	30	30	0	0-0	155.1	187	116	29	3	80-4	114	6.37	73	.296	.376	3	.000	-0	109	-27		-2.6
1999	Sea A	4	4	.500	31	6	0	1-2	72.1	106	67	10	5	46-5	35	7.96	60	.346	.435	2	.000	-0	156	-25		-2.3
Total	3	16	16	.500	71	45	0	1-2	278.2	334	215	47	11	152-9	195	6.56	71	.297	.383	7	.000	-1	117	-56	31	-5.3
CLOUGH, ED	Edgar George "Big Ed","Spec" B10.28.1906 Wiconisco PA D1.30.1944 Harrisburg PA BL/TL/6-0/188 d8.28.1924 ▲																								
1925	StL N	0	1	.000	3	1	0	0	10	11	9	1	1	5	3	8.10	53	.289	.386	4	.250	-0	59	-3		-0.3
1926	StL N	0	0	—	1	0	0	0	2	5	6	0	1	3	0	22.50	17	.556	.692	1	.000	-0		-4		-0.2
Total	2	0	1	.000	4	1	0	0	12	16	15	1	2	8	3	10.50	40	.340	.456	5	.200	-0	59	-7		-0.5
CLOWERS, BILL	William Perry B8.14.1898 San Marcos TX D1.13.1978 Sweeny TX BL/TL/5-11/175 d7.20																								
1926	Bos A	0	0	—	2	0	0	0	1.2	2	1	0	0	0	0	0.00	—	.333	.333	0	—	0		0		0.0
CLUTTERBUCK, BRYAN	Bryan Richard B12.17.1959 Detroit MI BR/TR/6-4/225* [MilA81 7/176] d7.18 Col Eastern Michigan																								
1986	Mil A	1	1	.000	20	0	0	0-0	56.2	68	32	8	2	16-2	38	4.29	102	.296	.345	0	—	0	94	-4	86	-0.5
1989	Mil A	2	5	.286	14	11	1	0-0	67.1	73	39	11	0	16-1	29	4.14	93	.269	.306	0	—	0	94	-4	86	-0.5
Total	2	2	6	.250	34	11	1	0-0	124	141	71	19	2	32-3	67	4.21	97	.281	.324	0	—	0	94	-4	86	-0.5
CLYDE, DAVID	David Eugene B4.22.1955 Kansas City KS BL/TL/6-1/185* [TexA73 1/1] d6.27																								
1973	Tex A	4	8	.333	18	18	0	0-0	93.1	106	63	8	4	54-1	74	5.01	75	.293	.388	0	—	0	102	-15		-1.7
1974	Tex A	3	9	.250	28	21	4	0-0	117	129	64	14	4	47-0	52	4.38	82	.286	.355	0	—	0	96	-10		-1.0
1975	Tex A	0	1	.000	1	1	0	0-0	7	6	3	0	0	6-0	2	2.57	147	.273	.429	0	—	0	47	1		0.1
1978	Cle A	8	11	.421	28	25	5	0-0	153.1	166	80	14	3	60-3	83	4.28	88	.280	.345	0	—	0*	92	-8		-0.9
1979	Cle A	3	4	.429	9	8	1	0-0	45.2	50	33	7	1	13-0	17	5.91	73	.279	.330	0	—	0	95	-8	82	-1.0
Total	5	18	33	.353	84	73	10	0-0	416.1	457	243	33	12	180-4	228	4.63	82	.285	.358	0	—	0	95	-40	82	-4.5
CLYDE, TOM	Thomas Knox B8.17.1923 Wachapreague VA D10.1.2005 Dallas TX BR/TR/6-3/195 d5.31 Mil 1944-46 Col Presbyterian																								
1943	Phi A	0	0	—	4	0	0	0	6	7	8	1	1	4	0	9.00	38	.304	.429	2	.000	-0		-4		-0.3
COAKLEY, ANDY	Andrew James (aka Jack McAllister in 1902) B11.20.1882 Providence RI D9.27.1963 New York NY BL/TR/6-0/165 d9.17 Col Holy Cross																								
1902	Phi A	2	1	.667	3	3	3	0	27	25	15	0	2	9	9	2.67	138	.245	.319	3	.375	1	92	2		0.3
1903	Phi A	0	3	.000	6	3	2	0	37.2	48	31	2	2	11	20	5.50	56	.310	.363	15	.200	-0	70	-10		-0.8
1904	Phi A	4	3	.571	8	8	7-2	0	62	48	19	1	2	23	33	1.89	142	.215	.294	23-0-1	.087	-2	63	5		0.3
1905	†Phi A	18	8	.692	36	31	21-3	0	255	227	93	2	6	73	145	1.84	145	.240	.299	94-0-4	.138	-3	123	17		1.3
1906	Phi A	7	8	.467	22	16	10	0	149	144	78	0	3	44	59	3.14	87	.257	.314	49-0-2	.143	-2	115	-8		-1.1
1907	Cin N	17	16	.515	37	30	21-1	1	265.1	269	97	1	7	79	89	2.34	111	.274	.332	84-0-6	.071	-6	91	8		0.2
1908	Cin N	8	18	.308	32	28	20-4	2	242.1	219	79	3	4	64	61	1.86	124	.249	.303	76-0-5	.092	-4	66	10		0.4
	Chi N	2	0	1.000	4	3	2-1	0	20.1	14	4	0	0	6	7	0.89	266	.192	.253	6	.000	-0	140	3		0.2
	Year	10	18	.357	36	31	22-5	2	262.2	233	83	3	4	70	68	1.78	130	.245	.299	82-0-5	.085	-5	74	10		0.6
1909	Chi N	0	1	.000	2	1	0	0	2	7	7	0	0	3	1	18.00	14	.583	.667	—	0		55	-4		-0.6
1911	NY A	0	1	.000	5	1	0	0	11.2	20	13	0	0	2	4	5.40	67	.377	.400	4	.250	-0	60	-3		-0.2
Total	9	58	59	.496	150	124	87-11	3	1072.1	1021	436	9	26	314	428	2.35	111	.256	.315	359-0-18	.117	-16	95	20		-0.0
COATES, JIM	James Alton B8.4.1932 Farnham VA BR/TR/6-4/192(180-192) d9.21																								
1956	NY A	0	0	—	2	1	0	1	2	1	3	0	1	4-0	0	13.50	29	.167	.545	0	—	0		-2		-0.1
1959	NY A	6	1	.857	37	4	2	3	100.1	89	39	10	3	36-4	64	2.87	127	.234	.305	21	.095	-1	133	8		0.4
1960	†NY A★	13	3	.813	35	18	6-2	1	149.1	139	78	16	2	66-4	73	4.28	84	.248	.327	48-0-8	.250	4	189	-11		-0.8
1961	†NY A	11	5	.688	43	11	4-1	5	141.1	128	60	15	7	53-0	80	4.44	84	.263	.339	35-0-8	.029	-3	104	4		0.1
1962	†NY A	7	6	.538	50	6	0	6	117.2	119	62	9	5	50-5	67	5.28	70	.297	.377	6	.000	-1	144	-7		-1.0
1963	Was A	2	4	.333	20	2	0	0	44.1	51	29	4	3	21-4	31	5.51	61	.313	.378	3	.000	-0		-3		-0.2
	Cin N	0	0	—	9	0	0	0	16.1	21	10	2	0	7-1	11	5.51	61	.313	.378	3	.000	-0		-1		-0.1
1965	Cal A	2	0	1.000	17	0	0	3	28	23	13	1	0	16-2	15	3.54	96	.228	.325	1	.000	-0	118	-2		-0.2
1966	Cal A	1	1	.500	9	4	1-1	0	31.2	32	16	3	0	10-0	16	3.98	84	.258	.311	11	.091	-1	28	-6		-0.2
1967	Cal A	1	2	.333	25	1	0	0	52.1	47	26	5	4	23-5	39	4.30	73	.244	.336	3	.333	1	142	-6		-0.2
Total	9	43	22	.662	247	46	13-4	18	683.1	650	336	65	25	286-25	396	4.00	90	.252	.330	160-0-19	.131	-3	142	-28		-3.2
COBB, GEORGE	George Woodworth B9.25.1865 Independence IA D8.19.1926 Pomona CA 6-0/168 d4.15																								
1892	Bal N	10	37	.213	53	47	42	0	394.1	495	333	21	19	140	159	4.86	71	.295	.356	172-1	.209	5*	93	-55		-4.6
COBB, HERB	Herbert Edward B8.6.1904 Pinetops NC D1.8.1980 Tarboro NC BR/TR/5-11/150 d4.21																								
1929	StL A	0	0	—	1	0	0	0	1	3	4	0	0	1	0	36.00	12	.600	.667	—	0		-3		-0.1
COCANOWER, JAIME	James Stanley B2.14.1957 San Juan, PR BR/TR/6-4/200* d9.7 Col Baylor																								
1983	Mil A	2	0	1.000	5	3	1	0-0	30	21	8	1	1	12-0	8	1.80	211	.200	.288	0	—	0	192	6		0.4
1984	Mil A	8	16	.333	33	27	1	0-1	174.2	188	99	13	9	78-3	65	4.02	97	.279	.359	0	—	0	83	-7		-0.8
1985	Mil A	6	8	.429	24	15	3-1	0-0	116.1	122	72	6	8	73-2	44	4.33	97	.274	.383	0	—	0	97	-5		-0.6
1986	Mil A	0	1	.000	17	2	0	0-0	44.2	40	29	1	2	38-0	22	4.43	98	.248	.396	0	—	0	94	-2		0.0
Total	4	16	25	.390	79	47	5-1	0-1	365.2	371	208	21	20	201-5	139	3.99	101	.268	.366	0	—	0	94	-8		-1.0
COCHRAN, GOAT	Alvah Jackson "Al","Goat" B1.31.1891 Concord GA D5.23.1947 Atlanta GA BR/TR/5-10/175 d8.25																								
1915	Cin N	0	0	—	1	0	0	0	1	0	0	0	1	0	1	9.00	32	.455	.455	0	—	0		-1		-0.1
COCO, PASQUAL	Pasqual (Reynoso) B9.8.1977 Santo Domingo, D.R. BR/TR/6-1/185* d7.17																								
2000	Tor A	0	0	—	2	0	0	0-0	4	5	4	1	1	5-0	2	9.00	56	.294	.478	0	—	0	93	-2		-0.1
2001	Tor A	1	0	1.000	7	1	0	0-0	14.1	12	8	0	2	6-0	9	4.40	104	.226	.323	0	—	0	141	0		0.0
2002	Tor A	0	1	.000	2	0	0	0-0	1	4	2	0	0	3-1	0	18.00	26	.571	.700	0	—	0		-1		-0.2
Total	3	1	1	.500	10	2	0	0-0	19.1	21	14	1	3	14-1	11	6.05	77	.273	.400	0	—	0	119	-3		-0.3
COCREHAM, GENE	Eugene B11.14.1884 Luling TX D12.27.1945 Luling TX BR/TR/6-3.5/192 d9.25																								
1913	Bos N	0	1	.000	1	1	0	0	8.1	13	7	0	1	4	3	7.56	43	.371	.450	4	.000	-1	138	-3		-0.3
1914	Bos N	3	4	.429	15	3	1	0	44.2	48	30	2	0	27	15	4.84	57	.296	.397	10-0-1	.100	-0	112	-10		-1.6
1915	Bos N	0	0	—	1	0	0	0	1.2	3	2	0	0	0	0	5.40	48	.429	.429	0	—	-1		-1		-0.1
Total	3	3	5	.375	17	4	1	0	54.2	64	39	2	1	31	18	5.27	54	.314	.407	14-0-1	.071	-1	121	-14		-2.0
CODIROLI, CHRIS	Christopher Allen B3.26.1958 Oxnard CA BR/TR/6-1/160* [DetA78*1/11] d9.11 Col San Jose St.																								
1982	Oak A	1	2	.333	3	3	0	0-0	16.2	16	8	1	0	4-0	5	4.32	92	.246	.290	0	—	0	46	0		0.0
1983	Oak A	12	12	.500	37	31	7-2	1-0	205.2	208	115	17	7	72-4	85	4.46	87	.264	.328	0	—	0	109	-14		-1.6
1984	Oak A	6	4	.600	28	14	1	1-1	89.1	111	67	16	3	34-4	44	5.84	65	.304	.366	0	—	0	112	-16		-2.3
1985	Oak A	14	14	.500	37	37	4	0-0	226	228	125	23	3	78-2	111	4.46	87	.259	.318	0	—	0	112	-6	100	-0.7
1986	Oak A	5	8	.385	16	16	1	0-0	92.1	91	54	15	2	38-2	43	4.03	97	.250	.323	0	—	0	95	-6		-0.7
1987	Oak A	0	3	.000	3	3	0	0-0	11.1	12	11	1	1	8-0	4	8.74	48	.273	.396	0	—	0	55	-11		-2.0
1988	Cle A	0	4	.000	14	2	0	1-1	19.1	32	22	2	3	10-2	12	9.31	44	.372	.455	0	—	0	12	-6		-0.5
1990	KC A	0	0	—	6	2	0	0-0	10.1	13	11	1	4	17-1	8	9.58	40	.325	.557	0	—	0	106	-82	100	-9.6
Total	8	38	47	.447	144	108	13-2	3-2	670.1	711	413	76	23	261-15	312	4.87	80	.270	.339	0	—	0	106	-82	100	-9.6
COFFEY, TODD	Justin Todd B9.9.1980 Shelby NC BR/TR/6-5/230 d4.19																								
2005	Cin N	4	1	.800	57	0	0	1-1	58	84	33	5	5	11-2	26	4.50	93	.344	.382	3	.000	-0		-3		-0.3
COFFMAN, SLICK	George David B12.11.1910 Veto AL D5.8.2003 Birmingham AL BR/TR/6-0/155 d5.21 b-Dick																								
1937	Det A	7	5	.583	28	5	1	0	101	121	61	8	3	39	22	4.37	107	.295	.361	29-0-4	.172	0	116	1		0.1
1938	Det A	4	4	.500	39	6	1	2	95.2	120	70	6	4	48	31	6.02	83	.310	.386	24-0-1	.167	-0	103	-10		-0.8
1939	Det A	2	1	.667	23	1	0	0	42.1	51	36	4	1	22	10	6.38	77	.295	.378	5	.000	0	126	-7		-0.5
1940	StL A	2	2	.500	31	4	1	1	74.2	108	62	5	0	23	26	6.27	73	.334	.379	15-0-2	.200	-0*	101	-15		-0.7
Total	4	15	12	.556	121	16	3	3	313.2	400	229	23	4	132	89	5.60	85	.309	.375	73-0-7	.164	-0	108	-31		-2.1
COFFMAN, KEVIN	Kevin Reese B1.19.1965 Austin TX BR/TR/6-2/175(175-206) [AtlN83 11/282] d9.5																								
1987	Atl N	2	3	.400	5	5	0	0-0	25.1	31	14	2	3	22-0	11	4.62	94	.313	.448	10	.100	-0	63	0		-0.1
1988	Atl N	2	6	.250	18	11	0	0-0	67	62	52	3	4	54-2	24	5.78	63	.251	.390	22-0-1	.227	2*	90	-16		-1.6

YEAR	TM LG	W	L	PCT	G	GS	CG-SHO	SV-BS	IP	H	R	HR	HB	BB-IB	SO	ERA	AERA	OAV	OOB	AB-HR-SH	AVG	PB	SUP	APR	DL	PW
1990	Chi N	0	2	.000	8	2	0	0-0	18.1	26	24	0	0	19-0	9	11.29	36	.333	.459	5	.200	0	99	-13		-1.2
Total	3	4	11	.267	31	18	0	0-0	110.2	119	90	5	7	95-2	47	6.42	60	.281	.416	37-0-1	.189	1	83	-29		-2.9

COFFMAN, DICK Samuel Richard B12.18.1906 Veto AL D3.24.1972 Athens AL BR/TR/6-2/195 d4.28 b-Slick

YEAR	TM LG	W	L	PCT	G	GS	CG-SHO	SV-BS	IP	H	R	HR	HB	BB-IB	SO	ERA	AERA	OAV	OOB	AB-HR-SH	AVG	PB	SUP	APR	DL	PW
1927	Was A	0	1	.000	5	2	0	0	16	20	9	0	2	2	5	3.38	120	.313	.353	3-0-1	.333	0	62	0		0.1
1928	StL A	4	5	.444	29	7	3	1	85.2	122	68	7	1	37	25	6.09	69	.359	.423	23-0-2	.043	-3	95	-18		-1.9
1929	StL A	1	1	.500	27	3	1-1	1	52.2	61	40	3	3	14	11	5.98	74	.295	.348	7	.000	-1	70	-9		-0.5
1930	StL A	8	18	.308	38	30	12-1	1	196	250	134	14	5	69	54	5.14	95	.311	.369	66-0-2	.136	-5	78	-8		-1.3
1931	StL A	9	13	.409	32	17	11-2	1	169.1	159	81	10	2	51	39	3.88	119	.241	.298	51-0-6	.078	-5	72	16		1.3
1932	StL A	5	3	.625	9	6	3-1	0	61	66	24	3	2	21	14	3.10	157	.277	.341	22	.045	-5	72	16		1.3
	Was A	1	6	.143	22	9	2	0	76.1	92	45	2	1	31	17	4.83	89	.307	.373	22	.091	-1	88	-4		-0.4
	Year	6	9	.400	31	15	5-1	0	137.1	158	69	5	3	52	31	4.06	112	.294	.359	44	.068	-3	86	10		0.7
1933	StL A	3	7	.300	21	13	3-1	1	81	114	57	9	2	39	19	5.89	79	.329	.399	27	.037	-3	86	-9		-1.2
1934	StL A	9	10	.474	40	21	6-1	3	173	212	112	11	1	59	55	4.53	110	.303	.358	51-0-5	.216	-1	71	5		0.4
1935	StL A	5	11	.313	41	18	5	2	143.2	206	116	14	2	46	34	6.14	78	.335	.383	41-0-4	.146	-1	87	-21		-2.1
1936	†NY N	7	5	.583	42	2	0	7	101.2	119	53	7	2	23	26	3.90	100	.296	.337	20-0-1	.200	-0	0	-1		-0.1
1937	†NY N	8	3	.727	42	1	0	3	80	93	36	4	4	31	30	3.04	128	.289	.359	19	.368	2	222	6		1.0
1938	NY N	8	4	.667	51	3	1-1	12	111.1	116	50	5	3	21	21	3.48	108	.268	.306	28	.071	-3	67	4		0.1
1939	NY N	1	2	.333	28	0	0	3	38	50	18	1	3	6	9	3.08	128	.316	.353	4	.000	-1	2	0		0.1
1940	Bos N	1	5	.167	31	0	0	3	48.1	63	33	4	2	11	11	5.40	69	.323	.365	12	.083	-1		-9		-1.3
1945	Phi N	2	1	.667	14	0	0	0	26.1	39	19	0	2	2	2	5.13	75	.351	.363	4	.250	0		-4		-0.3
Total	15	72	95	.431	472	132	47-8	38	1460.1	1782	894	92	35	463	372	4.65	96	.302	.357	400-0-21	.127	-22	83	-39		-5.0

COGAN, TONY Anthony Michael B12.21.1976 Chicago IL BL/TL/6-2/205 [KCA99 12/361] d4.2 Col Stanford

YEAR	TM LG	W	L	PCT	G	GS	CG-SHO	SV-BS	IP	H	R	HR	HB	BB-IB	SO	ERA	AERA	OAV	OOB	AB-HR-SH	AVG	PB	SUP	APR	DL	PW
2001	KC A	0	4	.000	39	0	0	0-2	24.2	32	17	7	5	13-0	17	5.84	85	.320	.420	0	—	0		-2		-0.3

COGAN, DICK Richard Henry B12.5.1871 Paterson NJ D5.2.1948 Paterson NJ BR/TR/5-7/150 d5.10

YEAR	TM LG	W	L	PCT	G	GS	CG-SHO	SV-BS	IP	H	R	HR	HB	BB-IB	SO	ERA	AERA	OAV	OOB	AB-HR-SH	AVG	PB	SUP	APR	DL	PW
1897	Bal N	0	0	—	1	0	0	0	2	4	3	0	1	2	0	13.50	31	.400	.538	1	.000	-0		-2		-0.1
1899	Chi N	2	3	.400	5	5	5	0	44	54	32	1	4	24	9	4.30	87	.302	.396	25-0-1	.200	1*	92	-3		-0.2
1900	NY N	0	0	—	2	0	0	0	8	10	6	0	0	6	1	6.75	54	.303	.410	8	.125	-0*		-2		-0.1
Total	3	2	3	.400	8	5	5	0	54	68	41	1	5	32	10	5.00	75	.306	.405	34-0-1	.176	0	92	-7		-0.4

COGGIN, DAVID David Raymond B10.30.1976 Covina CA BR/TR/6-4/205* [PhiN95 1/30] d6.23 [DL 2003 Phi N 183]

YEAR	TM LG	W	L	PCT	G	GS	CG-SHO	SV-BS	IP	H	R	HR	HB	BB-IB	SO	ERA	AERA	OAV	OOB	AB-HR-SH	AVG	PB	SUP	APR	DL	PW
2000	Phi N	2	0	1.000	5	5	0	0-0	27	35	20	2	1	12-0	17	5.33	86	.315	.387	7-0-1	.000	-1	160	-4		-0.3
2001	Phi N	6	7	.462	17	17	0	0-0	95	99	46	7	5	39-6	62	4.17	99	.272	.348	33-0-1	.061	-1	78	0		-0.1
2002	Phi N	2	5	.286	38	7	0	0-0	77	65	42	4	4	51-3	64	4.68	82	.231	.355	8-0-2	.000	-1	86	-7		-0.7
Total	3	10	12	.455	60	29	0	0-0	199	199	108	13	10	102-9	143	4.52	90	.263	.356	48-0-4	.042	-3	97	-11	183	-1.1

COHEN, HY Hyman B1.29.1931 Brooklyn NY BR/TR/6-5/220 d4.17

YEAR	TM LG	W	L	PCT	G	GS	CG-SHO	SV-BS	IP	H	R	HR	HB	BB-IB	SO	ERA	AERA	OAV	OOB	AB-HR-SH	AVG	PB	SUP	APR	DL	PW
1955	Chi N	0	0	—	7	1	0	0	17	28	17	2	1	10-0	4	7.94	51	.378	.459	3	.000	-0	174	-7		-0.4

COHEN, SYD Sydney Harry B5.7.1906 Baltimore MD D4.9.1988 ElPaso TX BB/TL/5-11/180 d9.18 b-Andy Col SMU

YEAR	TM LG	W	L	PCT	G	GS	CG-SHO	SV-BS	IP	H	R	HR	HB	BB-IB	SO	ERA	AERA	OAV	OOB	AB-HR-SH	AVG	PB	SUP	APR	DL	PW
1934	Was A	1	1	.500	7	3	2	1	18	25	15	2	0	6	6	7.50	58	.333	.383	11	.273	0*	91	-6		-0.4
1936	Was A	0	2	.000	19	1	0	1	36	44	27	4	3	14	21	5.25	91	.303	.377	8	.000	-1	111	-3		-0.2
1937	Was A	2	4	.333	33	0	0	4	55	64	30	1	0	17	22	3.11	142	.299	.351	14	.143	-1		5		0.6
Total	3	3	7	.300	55	3	2	5	109	133	72	7	3	37	49	4.54	100	.306	.365	33	.152	-2	97	-4		0.0

COLBERT, VINCE Vincent Norman B12.20.1945 Washington DC BR/TR/6-4/200* [CleA68 11/234] d5.19 Col East Carolina

YEAR	TM LG	W	L	PCT	G	GS	CG-SHO	SV-BS	IP	H	R	HR	HB	BB-IB	SO	ERA	AERA	OAV	OOB	AB-HR-SH	AVG	PB	SUP	APR	DL	PW
1970	Cle A	1	1	.500	23	0	0	2-1	31	37	25	4	1	16-2	17	7.26	55	.298	.380	2	.000	-0		-10		-0.7
1971	Cle A	7	6	.538	50	10	2	2-1	142.2	140	71	11	6	71-9	74	3.97	97	.265	.355	29-0-2	.138	-0*	63	-2		-0.2
1972	Cle A	1	7	.125	22	11	1-1	0-0	74.2	74	42	8	7	38-5	36	4.58	71	.267	.365	20-0-1	.200	1*	77	-10		-1.0
Total	3	9	14	.391	95	21	3-1	4-2	248.1	251	138	23	14	125-16	127	4.57	81	.270	.361	51-0-3	.157	0	67	-22		-1.9

COLBORN, JIM James William B5.22.1946 Santa Paula CA BR/TR/6-0/191* d7.13 C5 Col Whittier

YEAR	TM LG	W	L	PCT	G	GS	CG-SHO	SV-BS	IP	H	R	HR	HB	BB-IB	SO	ERA	AERA	OAV	OOB	AB-HR-SH	AVG	PB	SUP	APR	DL	PW
1969	Chi N	1	0	1.000	6	2	0	0-0	14.2	15	6	4	0	9-1	4	3.07	131	.283	.397	3	.000	-0	88	1		0.1
1970	Chi N	3	1	.750	34	5	0	4-3	72.2	88	37	3	1	23-6	50	3.59	125	.298	.347	15-0-1	.067	-1	147	5		0.2
1971	Chi N	0	1	.000	14	0	0	0-0	10.1	18	8	1	0	3-0	2	6.97	56	.383	.420	0	—	0		-3		-0.2
1972	Mil A	7	7	.500	39	12	4-1	0-0	147.2	135	53	14	2	43-7	97	3.11	99	.245	.300	37-0-2	.081	-1	99	-1		-0.1
1973	Mil A☆	20	12	.625	43	36	22-4	1-0	314.1	297	133	21	3	87-5	135	3.18	120	.251	.302	0	—	0	109	19		1.9
1974	Mil A	10	13	.435	33	31	10-1	0-0	224	230	104	27	6	60-4	83	4.06	90	.268	.319	0	—	0	93	-8		-0.8
1975	Mil A	11	13	.458	36	29	8-1	2-0	206.1	215	111	18	5	65-5	79	4.27	90	.270	.327	0	—	0	109	-9		-0.9
1976	Mil A	9	15	.375	32	32	7	0-0	225.2	232	97	20	2	54-9	101	3.71	95	.268	.310	0	—	0	87	-1		-0.2
1977	KC A	18	14	.563	36	35	6-1	0-0	239	233	106	22	13	81-2	103	3.62	112	.255	.323	0	—	0*	109	12		1.6
1978	KC A	1	2	.333	8	3	0	0-0	28.1	31	18	4	2	12-1	8	4.76	80	.282	.363	0	—	0	86	-3		-0.3
	Sea A	3	10	.231	20	19	3	0-0	114.1	125	77	21	6	38-1	26	5.35	72	.279	.341	0	—	0	85	-19		-1.8
	Year	4	12	.250	28	22	3	0-0	142.2	156	95	25	8	50-2	34	5.24	73	.280	.345	0	—	0	85	-22		-2.1
Total	10	83	88	.485	301	204	60-8	7-3	1597.1	1619	750	153	41	475-41	688	3.80	99	.265	.320	55-0-3	.073	-3	102	-5		-0.5

COLCOLOUGH, TOM Thomas Bernard B10.8.1870 Charleston SC D12.10.1919 Charleston SC BR/TR/5-10.5/180 d8.1

YEAR	TM LG	W	L	PCT	G	GS	CG-SHO	SV-BS	IP	H	R	HR	HB	BB-IB	SO	ERA	AERA	OAV	OOB	AB-HR-SH	AVG	PB	SUP	APR	DL	PW
1893	Pit N	1	0	1.000	8	3	1	2	43.2	45	30	1	0	32	7	4.12	110	.259	.374	14	.143	0	113	2		0.1
1894	Pit N	8	5	.615	23	14	11	0	150.2	213	147	5	5	32	29	7.23	73	.329	.401	70-0-1	.200	-3	129	-28		-1.8
1895	Pit N	1	1	.500	7	6	3	0	43.1	54	49	3	5	21	16	6.65	68	.300	.388	17-0-1	.294	3*	140	-11		-0.3
1899	NY N	4	5	.444	11	8	7	0	81.2	85	49	1	3	41	14	3.97	95	.268	.357	37	.270	1*	101	-1		0.0
Total	4	14	11	.560	49	31	22	2	319.1	397	275	10	13	166	66	5.89	79	.301	.385	138-0-2	.225	1	123	-38		-2.0

COLE, BERT Albert George B7.1.1896 San Francisco CA D5.30.1975 San Mateo CA BL/TL/6-1/180 d4.19

YEAR	TM LG	W	L	PCT	G	GS	CG-SHO	SV-BS	IP	H	R	HR	HB	BB-IB	SO	ERA	AERA	OAV	OOB	AB-HR-SH	AVG	PB	SUP	APR	DL	PW
1921	Det A	7	4	.636	20	11	7-1	1	109.2	134	66	3	4	36	22	4.27	100	.305	.363	46-0-3	.283	3*	115	0		0.2
1922	Det A	1	6	.143	23	5	2-1	0	79.1	105	60	4	4	39	21	4.88	80	.313	.387	25	.160	-1*	92	-13		-1.0
1923	Det A	13	5	.722	52	13	6-1	5	163	183	95	9	6	61	32	4.14	93	.284	.351	55-1-1	.255	2*	161	-8		-0.6
1924	Det A	3	9	.250	28	12	2-1	2	109.1	135	69	4	5	61	16	4.69	88	.314	.371	37-0-2	.270	1*	82	-7		-0.5
1925	Det A	2	3	.400	14	2	1	1	33.2	44	27	2	1	15	7	5.88	73	.336	.408	11	.273	0	146	-7		-0.8
	Cle A	1	1	.500	13	2	0	1	44	55	33	1	1	25	9	6.14	72	.322	.411	13	.154	-0	95	-7		-0.3
	Year	3	4	.429	27	4	1	2	77.2	99	60	3	2	40	16	6.03	73	.328	.410	24	.208	-0	120	-12		-1.1
1927	Chi A	4	4	.200	27	2	0	0	66.2	79	43	3	3	19	12	4.72	86	.309	.363	18-0-2	.167	-1	93	-6		-0.4
Total	6	28	32	.467	177	47	18-4	10	605.2	735	393	26	19	230	119	4.67	87	.305	.370	205-1-8	.239	5	116	-48		-3.4

COLE, DAVE David Bruce B8.29.1930 Williamsport MD BR/TR/6-2/175* d9.9

YEAR	TM LG	W	L	PCT	G	GS	CG-SHO	SV-BS	IP	H	R	HR	HB	BB-IB	SO	ERA	AERA	OAV	OOB	AB-HR-SH	AVG	PB	SUP	APR	DL	PW
1950	Bos N	0	1	.000	4	0	0	0	8	7	2	0	1	3	8	1.13	342	.259	.355	1	.000	-0		2		0.2
1951	Bos N	2	4	.333	23	7	1	0	67.2	64	43	3	2	64	33	4.26	86	.254	.409	17-1-0	.353	4	117	-8		-0.2
1952	Bos N	1	1	.500	22	3	1	0	44.2	38	21	2	3	42	22	4.03	90	.241	.409	8	.000	0	132	-2		-0.2
1953	Mil N	0	1	.000	10	0	0	0	14.2	17	14	1	0	14	13	8.59	46	.279	.413	2-1-0	.500	1		-7		-0.3
1954	Chi N	3	8	.273	18	14	2-1	0	84	74	56	7	1	62	37	5.36	78	.241	.365	28-1-1	.214	1*	85	-11	49	-1.1
1955	Phi N	0	3	.000	7	3	0	0	18.1	21	15	3	0	14-0	6	6.38	62	.304	.412	5	.200	-0	82	-5		-0.7
Total	6	6	18	.250	84	27	3-1	0	237.1	221	151	16	7	199-0	119	4.93	79	.253	.393	61-3-1	.230	5	99	-31	49	-2.3

COLE, ED Edward William (b Edward William Kisleauskas) B3.22.1909 Wilkes-Barre PA D7.28.1999 Nashville TN BR/TR/5-11/170 d4.22

YEAR	TM LG	W	L	PCT	G	GS	CG-SHO	SV-BS	IP	H	R	HR	HB	BB-IB	SO	ERA	AERA	OAV	OOB	AB-HR-SH	AVG	PB	SUP	APR	DL	PW
1938	StL A	1	5	.167	36	6	1	3	88.2	116	69	8	5	48	26	5.18	96	.313	.399	21	.143	-1	97	-7		-0.6
1939	StL A	0	2	.000	6	0	0	0	6.1	8	7	1	0	6	5	7.11	68	.308	.438	1	.000	-0		-2		-0.4
Total	2	1	7	.125	42	6	1	3	95	124	76	9	5	54	31	5.31	94	.312	.401	22	.136	-2	97	-9		-1.0

COLE, KING Leonard Leslie B4.15.1886 Toledo IA D1.6.1916 Bay City MI BR/TR/6-1/170 d10.6

YEAR	TM LG	W	L	PCT	G	GS	CG-SHO	SV-BS	IP	H	R	HR	HB	BB-IB	SO	ERA	AERA	OAV	OOB	AB-HR-SH	AVG	PB	SUP	APR	DL	PW
1909	Chi N	1	0	1.000	1	1	1-1	0	9	6	0	1	0	0	1	0.00	—	.194	.265	4	.750	2	220	3		0.7
1910	†Chi N	20	4	.833	33	29	21-4	1	239.2	174	64	2	9	130	114	1.80	160	.211	.325	91-0-5	.231	2*	138	29		3.1
1911	Chi N	18	7	.720	32	27	13-2	1	221.1	188	87	3	9	99	101	3.13	106	.236	.328	79-0-3	.152	-2	120	10		0.8
1912	Chi N	2	3	.333	8	3	0	0	19	36	26	2	2	8	5	10.89	31	.409	.469	5	.400	-1	147	-15		-1.8
	Pit N	2	1	.667	12	5	2	0	49	61	42	1	4	18	11	6.43	51	.330	.395	15-0-1	.133	-1	180	-17		-1.2
	Year	4	4	.429	20	8	2	0	68	97	68	3	6	26	16	7.68	43	.355	.419	20-0-1	.200	-1	168	-32		-3.0
1914	NY A	10	9	.526	33	15	8-2	0	141.2	151	63	3	1	51	43	3.30	84	.288	.352	42-0-2	.048	-3	90	-8		-1.5

YEAR	TM LG	W	L	PCT	G	GS	CG-SHO	SV-BS	IP	H	R	HR	HB	BB-IB	SO	ERA	AERA	OAV	OOB	AB-HR-SH	AVG	PB	SUP	APR	DL	PW
1915	NY A	2	3	.400	10	6	2	1	51	41	17	2	3	22	19	3.18	92	.224	.317	13-0-2	.077	-1	87	-3		-0.4
Total	6	54	27	.667	129	86	47-9	2	730.2	657	309	13	26	331	298	3.12	97	.250	.340	249-0-13	.173	-2	125	-1		-0.3

COLE, VICTOR Victor Alexander B1.23.1968 Leningrad, USSR BB/TR/5-10/160 [KCA88 14/361] d6.6 Col Santa Clara

YEAR	TM LG	W	L	PCT	G	GS	CG-SHO	SV-BS	IP	H	R	HR	HB	BB-IB	SO	ERA	AERA	OAV	OOB	AB-HR-SH	AVG	PB	SUP	APR	DL	PW
1992	Pit N	0	2	.000	8	4	0	0-0	23	23	14	1	0	14-0	12	5.48	63	.261	.359	4-0-1	.000	-0	72	-5		-0.4

COLEMAN, JOHN John Francis B3.6.1863 Saratoga Springs NY D5.31.1922 Detroit MI BL/TR(BB 1887)/5-9.5/170 d5.1 Col Syracuse ▲

YEAR	TM LG	W	L	PCT	G	GS	CG-SHO	SV-BS	IP	H	R	HR	HB	BB-IB	SO	ERA	AERA	OAV	OOB	AB-HR-SH	AVG	PB	SUP	APR	DL	PW
1883	Phi N	12	48	.200	65	61	59-3	0	538.1	772	510	17		48	159	4.87	63	.309	.322	354	.234	4*	82	-110		-8.5
1884	Phi N	5	15	.250	21	19	14-1	0	154.1	216	147	9		22	37	4.90	61	.308	.329	171	.246	2*	78	-29		-2.6
	Phi AA	0	2	.000	3	2	2	0	21	28	14	0	4	2	5	3.43	99	.304	.347	107-2	.206	0*	36	-1		0.0
1885	Phi AA	2	2	.500	8	3	3	0	60.1	82	46	0	0	5	12	3.43	100	.366	.380	398-3	.299	0*	92	0		0.2
1886	Phi AA	1	1	.500	3	1	1	0	20.2	18	9	1	1	5	2	2.61	134	.225	.279	492	.246	0*	85	2		0.2
1889	Phi AA	3	2	.600	5	5	4	0	34	38	23	2	1	14	6	2.91	130	.273	.344	19	.053	-2*	144	2		0.0
1890	Pit N	0	2	.000	2	2	1	0	14	28	23	1	0	6	3	9.64	34	.400	.447	11	.182	0*	105	-10		-0.9
Total	6	23	72	.242	107	93	84-4	0	842.2	1182	772	30	6	102	224	4.68	67	.311	.330	1552-5	.251	7	84	-146		-11.6

COLEMAN, JOHN John W. B1.29.1860 Philadelphia PA D1.27.1915 Bristol PA TR d6.23

YEAR	TM LG	W	L	PCT	G	GS	CG-SHO	SV-BS	IP	H	R	HR	HB	BB-IB	SO	ERA	AERA	OAV	OOB	AB-HR-SH	AVG	PB	SUP	APR	DL	PW
1890	Phi N														2	21.60	17	.444	.583	0	—	0	207	-4		-0.5

COLEMAN, JOE Joseph Howard B2.3.1947 Boston MA BR/TR/6-3/195(170-195) [TexA65 1/3] d9.28 C11 f-Joe

YEAR	TM LG	W	L	PCT	G	GS	CG-SHO	SV-BS	IP	H	R	HR	HB	BB-IB	SO	ERA	AERA	OAV	OOB	AB-HR-SH	AVG	PB	SUP	APR	DL	PW
1965	Was A	2	0	1.000	2	2	2	0	18	9	3	0	0	8-0	13	1.50	232	.153	.254	6-0-1	.000	-1	114	4		0.5
1966	Was A	1	0	1.000	1	1	1	0	9	6	2	0	0	2-0	4	2.00	173	.188	.235	3	.000	-0	76	2		0.2
1967	Was A	8	9	.471	28	22	3	0	134	154	78	6	9	47-4	77	4.63	68	.291	.355	36-0-5	.056	-1	120	-22		-2.8
1968	Was A	12	16	.429	33	33	12-2	0	223	212	98	18	8	51-3	139	3.27	89	.250	.299	70-0-6	.129	-1*	92	-11		-1.6
1969	Was A	12	13	.480	40	36	12-4	1-2	247.2	222	102	26	6	100-7	182	3.27	107	.243	.320	84-0-4	.107	-3	100	7		0.5
1970	Was A	8	12	.400	39	29	6-1	0-1	218.2	190	98	25	4	89-6	152	3.58	101	.233	.309	67-0-4	.119	-2	95	0		0.3
1971	Det A	20	9	.690	39	38	16-3	0-0	286	241	106	17	7	96-3	236	3.15	115	.229	.296	96-0-9	.094	-3	108	16	15	1.1
1972	†Det A*	19	14	.576	40	39	9-3	0-0	280	216	99	23	9	110-7	222	2.80	113	.214	.296	82-0-15	.110	-3	106	11		0.9
1973	Det A	23	15	.605	40	40	13-2	0-0	288.1	283	125	32	10	93-2	202	3.53	116	.258	.321	0	—	0	87	16		1.9
1974	Det A	14	12	.538	41	41	11-2	0-0	285.2	272	160	30	12	158-13	177	4.32	89	.254	.355	0	—	0	100	-16		-1.3
1975	Det A	10	18	.357	31	31	6-1	0-0	201	234	137	27	9	85-6	125	5.55	73	.291	.363	0	—	0	87	-28		-3.4
1976	Det A	2	5	.286	12	12	1	0-0	66.2	80	44	1	5	34-0	38	4.86	77	.308	.395	0	—	0	100	-9		-0.8
	Chi N	2	8	.200	39	4	0	4-4	79	72	43	9	2	35-8	66	4.10	95	.246	.327	13	.154	-0	51	-3		-0.4
1977	Oak A	4	4	.500	43	12	2	2-2	127.2	114	51	11	2	49-2	55	2.96	136	.241	.313	0	—	0	124	14		0.8
1978	Oak A	3	0	1.000	10	0	0	0-0	19.2	12	3	1	0	5-0	4	1.37	267	.185	.239	0	—	0		-4		-0.3
	Tor A	2	0	1.000	31	0	0	0-1	60.2	67	34	6	1	30-3	28	4.60	86	.286	.364	0	—	0		1		0.5
	Year	5	0	1.000	41	0	0	0-1	80.1	79	37	7	1	35-3	32	3.81	102	.264	.338	0	—	0		1		0.0
1979	SF N	0	0	—	5	0	0	0-0	3.2	3	2	0	1	2-0	0	0.00	—	.231	.353	0	—	0		-5		-0.3
	Pit N	0	0	—	10	0	0	0-0	20.2	29	17	1	1	9-1	14	6.10	64	.326	.390	5	.200	-0		-5		-0.3
	Year	0	0	—	15	0	0	0-0	24.1	32	19	1	2	11-1	14	5.18	74	.314	.385	5	.200	-0		-5		-0.3
Total	15	142	135	.513	484	340	94-18	7-10	2569.1	2416	1202	233	90	1003-65	1728	3.55	98	.250	.324	462-0-44	.106	-10	98	-22	15	-3.9

COLEMAN, JOE Joseph Patrick B7.30.1922 Medford MA D4.9.1997 Ft.Myers FL BR/TR/6-2.5/200* d9.19 Mil 1943-45 s-Joe Col Boston College

YEAR	TM LG	W	L	PCT	G	GS	CG-SHO	SV-BS	IP	H	R	HR	HB	BB-IB	SO	ERA	AERA	OAV	OOB	AB-HR-SH	AVG	PB	SUP	APR	DL	PW
1942	Phi A	0	1	.000	1	0	0	0	6	8	5	0	1	3	3	3.00	126	.308	.333	4	.000	-1		-1		-0.1
1946	Phi A	0	2	.000	4	2	0	0	13	19	8	1	0	8	8	5.54	64	.345	.429	5	.400	1	97	-2		-0.3
1947	Phi A	6	12	.333	32	21	9-2	1	160.1	171	84	17	0	62	65	4.32	88	.275	.341	48-0-3	.146	-4	65	-8		-1.0
1948	Phi A*	14	13	.519	33	29	13-3	0	215.2	224	105	11	4	90	86	4.09	105	.269	.341	74-0-6	.122	0	80	6		0.4
1949	Phi A	13	14	.481	33	30	18-1	1	240.1	249	119	12	3	127	109	3.86	107	.271	.361	79-1-7	.177	0	83	-23		-1.8
1950	Phi A	0	5	.000	15	6	2	0	54	74	54	9	0	50	12	8.50	54	.332	.454	17-1-0	.059	1	108	-17		-1.0
1951	Phi A	1	6	.143	28	9	1	0	96.1	117	69	12	3	59	34	5.98	72	.305	.402	27-0-1	.259	1	78	2		0.2
1953	Phi A	3	4	.429	21	9	2-1	0	90	85	46	8	1	49	18	4.00	107	.254	.352	28	.286	1	75	0		0.3
1954	Bal A	13	17	.433	33	32	15-4	0	221.1	184	102	16	3	96	103	3.50	102	.232	.315	74-2-4	.176	2	75	0		0.3
1955	Bal A	0	1	.000	6	2	0	0	11.2	19	15	5	1	10-0	4	10.80	35	.373	.469	3	.667	1	116	-9	32	-0.5
	Det A	2	1	.667	17	0	0	3	25.1	22	9	1	1	14-0	5	3.20	120	.239	.346	4-0-1	.750	1		2		0.0
	Year	2	2	.500	23	2	0	3	37	41	24	6	2	24-0	9	5.59	69	.287	.392	7-0-1	.714	3	116	-6		0.0
Total	10	52	76	.406	223	140	60-11	6	1134	1172	616	92	13	566-0	444	4.38	92	.271	.356	363-4-22	.182	2	82	-44	32	-3.1

COLEMAN, PERCY Pierce Devon B10.15.1876 Mason OH D2.16.1948 Van Nuys CA TR d7.2

YEAR	TM LG	W	L	PCT	G	GS	CG-SHO	SV-BS	IP	H	R	HR	HB	BB-IB	SO	ERA	AERA	OAV	OOB	AB-HR-SH	AVG	PB	SUP	APR	DL	PW
1897	StL N	1	2	.333	13	5	3	0	66.1	108	76	0	8	33	10	7.19	61	.362	.440	31	.226	-1	133	-21		-0.9
1898	Cin N	0	1	1.000	1	1	1	0	9	13	7	0	1	3	2	3.00	128	.333	.395	3	.000	-1	56	0		-0.1
Total	2	1	3	.250	14	6	4	0	75.1	121	83	0	9	36	12	6.69	65	.359	.435	34	.206	-1	120	-21		-1.0

COLEMAN, RIP Walter Gary B7.31.1931 Troy NY D5.14.2004 Wolfeboro NH BL/TL/6-2/185* d8.15 Col Syracuse

YEAR	TM LG	W	L	PCT	G	GS	CG-SHO	SV-BS	IP	H	R	HR	HB	BB-IB	SO	ERA	AERA	OAV	OOB	AB-HR-SH	AVG	PB	SUP	APR	DL	PW
1955	†NY A	2	1	.667	10	6	0	1	29	40	19	2	1	16-0	15	5.28	71	.331	.413	10-0-1	.200	1	135	-5		-0.4
1956	NY A	0	3	.375	29	9	0	2	88.1	97	42	6	1	42-1	42	3.67	105	.285	.363	24-0-2	.042	-3	153	2		-0.7
1957	KC A	0	7	.000	19	6	1-1	0	41	53	32	5	0	25-5	15	5.93	67	.325	.408	9-0-1	.000	-1	64	-9		-1.3
1959	KC A	2	10	.167	29	11	2	2	81	85	46	8	4	34-0	54	4.56	88	.273	.345	25-0-1	.080	-2	78	-4		-0.8
	Bal A	0	0	—	3	0	0	0	4	4	0	0	1	2-0	4	0.00	—	.267	.353	0	—	0		2		0.1
	Year	2	10	.167	32	11	2	2	85	89	46	8	1	36-0	58	4.34	92	.273	.345	25-0-1	.080	-2	78	-3		-0.7
1960	Bal A	0	2	.000	5	1	0	0	4	8	5	0	1	5-1	0	11.25	34	.444	.583	1	.000	-0	46	-3		-0.6
Total	5	7	25	.219	95	33	3-1	5	247.1	287	144	21	4	124-2	130	4.58	85	.296	.376	69-0-5	.072	-5	104	-17		-3.1

COLEMAN, WALTER Walter L. B6.13.1873 Lees Summit MO D11.20.1925 Bunceton MO TL/5-10/174 d9.25

YEAR	TM LG	W	L	PCT	G	GS	CG-SHO	SV-BS	IP	H	R	HR	HB	BB-IB	SO	ERA	AERA	OAV	OOB	AB-HR-SH	AVG	PB	SUP	APR	DL	PW
1895	StL N	0	1	1.000	1	1	1	0							5	13.50	36	.343	.477	5	.200	-0	118	-7		-0.5

COLLAMORE, ALLAN Allan Edward B6.5.1887 Worcester MA D8.8.1980 Battle Creek MI BR/TR/6-0/170 d4.15

YEAR	TM LG	W	L	PCT	G	GS	CG-SHO	SV-BS	IP	H	R	HR	HB	BB-IB	SO	ERA	AERA	OAV	OOB	AB-HR-SH	AVG	PB	SUP	APR	DL	PW
1911	Phi A	0	1	.000	2	0	0	0	2	6	9	0	2	3	1	36.00	9	.600	.733	0	—	0		-7		-1.1
1914	Cle A	3	7	.300	27	8	3	0	105.1	100	52	3	6	49	32	3.25	89	.264	.357	32-0-1	.094	-2	73	-3		0.4
1915	Cle A	2	5	.286	11	6	5-2	0	64.1	52	22	1	0	22	15	2.38	128	.235	.305	23	.174	0*	72	5		0.4
Total	3	5	13	.278	40	14	8-2	0	171.2	158	83	4	8	74	48	3.30	89	.259	.347	55-0-1	.127	-2	72	-5		-1.1

COLLARD, HAP Earl Clinton B8.29.1898 Williams AZ D7.9.1968 Jamestown CA BR/TR/6-0/170 d4.23

YEAR	TM LG	W	L	PCT	G	GS	CG-SHO	SV-BS	IP	H	R	HR	HB	BB-IB	SO	ERA	AERA	OAV	OOB	AB-HR-SH	AVG	PB	SUP	APR	DL	PW
1927	Cle A	0	0	—	4	0	0	0	5.1	8	7	0	0	3	2	5.06	83	.333	.407	0	—	0		-2		-0.1
1928	Cle A	0	0	—	1	0	0	0	4	4	3	0	0	4	1	2.25	184	.250	.400	1	1.000	0		-0		0.0
1930	Phi N	6	12	.333	30	15	4	0	127	188	106	15	3	39	25	6.80	80	.350	.397	44	.205	-2*	88	-15		-1.1
Total	3	6	12	.333	35	15	4	0	136.1	200	116	15	3	46	28	6.60	81	.347	.398	45	.222	-1	88	-17		-1.2

COLLIER, ORLIN Orlin Edward B2.17.1907 E.Prairie MO D9.9.1944 Memphis TN BR/TR/5-11.5/180 d9.11 Col U. of Mississippi

YEAR	TM LG	W	L	PCT	G	GS	CG-SHO	SV-BS	IP	H	R	HR	HB	BB-IB	SO	ERA	AERA	OAV	OOB	AB-HR-SH	AVG	PB	SUP	APR	DL	PW
1931	Det A	0	1	.000	2	2	0	0	10.1	17	12	0	0	7	3	7.84	59	.362	.444	3	.000	-0	83	-4		-0.4

COLLIFLOWER, HARRY James Harry "Collie" B3.11.1869 Petersville MD D8.12.1961 Washington DC BL/TL/5-11.5/175 d7.21 U1

YEAR	TM LG	W	L	PCT	G	GS	CG-SHO	SV-BS	IP	H	R	HR	HB	BB-IB	SO	ERA	AERA	OAV	OOB	AB-HR-SH	AVG	PB	SUP	APR	DL	PW
1899	Cle N	1	11	.083	14	12	11	0	98	152	122	6	11	41	8	8.17	45	.353	.422	76	.303	2*	85	-50		-4.

COLLINS, DAN Daniel Thomas B7.12.1854 St.Louis MO D9.21.1883 New Orleans LA d6.8 ▲

YEAR	TM LG	W	L	PCT	G	GS	CG-SHO	SV-BS	IP	H	R	HR	HB	BB-IB	SO	ERA	AERA	OAV	OOB	AB-HR-SH	AVG	PB	SUP	APR	DL	PW
1874	Chi NA	1	1	.500	2			0							2	4.91	45	.386	.407	12	.083	-1*	59	-3		-0.

COLLINS, DON Donald Edward B9.15.1952 Lyons GA BR/TL/6-2/195* [AtlN72 S2/30] d5.4 Col South Georgia JC

YEAR	TM LG	W	L	PCT	G	GS	CG-SHO	SV-BS	IP	H	R	HR	HB	BB-IB	SO	ERA	AERA	OAV	OOB	AB-HR-SH	AVG	PB	SUP	APR	DL	PW
1977	Atl N	3	9	.250	40	6	0	2-1	70.2	82	43	8	1	41-8	27	5.09	87	.299	.389	11-0-1	.000	-1	47	-3		-0.
1980	Cle A	0	0	—	4	0	0	0-0	6	9	5	0	0	7-1	0	7.50	56	.346	.485	0	—	0		-2		-0.
Total	2	3	9	.250	44	6	0	2-1	76.2	91	48	8	1	48-9	27	5.28	84	.303	.398	11-0-1	.000	-1	47	-5		-0.

COLLINS, RIP Harry Warren B2.26.1896 Weatherford TX D5.27.1968 Bryan TX BR/TR(BB 1920-23)/6-1/205 d4.19 Col Texas A&M-Commerce

YEAR	TM LG	W	L	PCT	G	GS	CG-SHO	SV-BS	IP	H	R	HR	HB	BB-IB	SO	ERA	AERA	OAV	OOB	AB-HR-SH	AVG	PB	SUP	APR	DL	PW
1920	NY A	14	8	.636	36	18	10-2	1	187.1	171	83	6	14	79	66	3.22	119	.247	.337	62-0-8	.129	-4	109	12		0.
1921	†NY A	11	5	.688	28	16	7-2	0	137.1	158	103	6	10	78	64	5.44	78	.293	.392	66-0-6	.196	-1	128	-19		-2.
1922	Bos A	14	11	.560	32	29	15-3	0	210.2	219	101	4	10	103	69	3.76	109	.274	.364	76-0-1	.158	-3*	86	9		0.
1923	Det A	3	7	.300	17	14	3-1	0	92.1	104	61	3	10	42	25	4.87	79	.284	.342	27-0-2	.111	-2	99	-11		1.
1924	Det A	14	7	.667	34	30	11-1	0	216	199	99	6	4	93	75	3.21	128	.249	.307	76-0-5	.145	-5*	117	20		1.
1925	Det A	6	11	.353	26	20	5	0	140	149	86	7	6	52	33	4.56	94	.281	.352	42-0-2	.119	-4	88	-5		-0.

YEAR	TM LG	W	L	PCT	G	GS	CG-SHO	SV-BS	IP	H	R	HR	HB	BB-IB	SO	ERA	AERA	OAV	OOB	AB-HR-SH	AVG	PB	SUP	APR	DL	PW
926	Det A	8	8	.500	30	13	5-3	1	122	128	53	4	7	44	44	2.73	149	.278	.350	39-0-1	.154	-1*	105	15		1.7
927	Det A	13	7	.650	30	25	10-1	0	172.2	207	116	5	8	59	37	4.69	90	.312	.375	54-0-7	.204	0	126	-10		-0.8
929	StL A	11	6	.647	26	20	10-1	1	155.1	162	79	16	6	73	47	4.00	111	.270	.355	62-1-1	.274	4	120	7		1.1
930	StL A	9	7	.563	35	20	6-1	2	171.2	168	90	11	5	63	75	4.35	112	.259	.330	54-0-4	.130	-2	89	12		0.7
931	StL A	5	5	.500	17	14	2	0	107	130	55	5	1	38	34	3.79	122	.307	.366	34-0-2	.147	-1	82	9		0.8
Total	11	108	82	.568	311	219	84-15	5	1712.1	1795	926	73	81	674	569	3.99	106	.275	.351	582-1-35	.165	-18	105	39		2.3

COLLINS, PHIL   Philip Eugene "Fidgety Phil" B8.27.1901 Chicago IL D8.14.1948 Chicago IL BR/TR/5-11/175 d10.7

YEAR	TM LG	W	L	PCT	G	GS	CG-SHO	SV-BS	IP	H	R	HR	HB	BB-IB	SO	ERA	AERA	OAV	OOB	AB-HR-SH	AVG	PB	SUP	APR	DL	PW
923	Chi N	1	0	1.000	1	1	0	0	5	8	2	0	0	1	2	3.60	111	.400	.429	2	.000	-0	205	0		0.1
929	Phi N	9	7	.563	43	11	3	5	153.1	172	106	18	4	83	61	5.75	90	.284	.374	58-1-0	.190	-0*	125	-7		-0.7
930	Phi N	16	11	.593	47	25	17-1	3	239	287	148	22	10	86	87	4.78	114	.299	.363	87-3-2	.253	3*	101	17		1.8
931	Phi N	12	16	.429	42	27	16-2	4	240.1	268	126	14	5	83	73	3.86	110	.283	.344	95	.168	-4*	92	8		0.6
932	Phi N	14	12	.538	43	21	6	3	184.1	231	117	21	6	65	66	5.27	84	.314	.375	68	.265	2	123	-12		-1.4
933	Phi N	8	13	.381	42	13	5-1	6	151	178	79	9	6	57	40	4.11	93	.293	.360	53-0-1	.132	-2*	57	-4		-0.8
934	Phi N	13	18	.419	45	32	15	1	254	277	138	30	3	87	72	4.18	113	.273	.333	88-0-7	.170	-5*	83	13		0.8
935	Phi N	0	2	.000	3	3	0	0	14.2	24	20	5	0	9	4	11.66	39	.348	.423	6	.000	-1	94	-9		-1.0
	StL N	7	6	.538	26	9	2	2	82.2	96	48	6	3	26	18	4.57	90	.290	.347	25-0-4	.160	-1	129	-4		-0.7
	Year	7	8	.467	29	12	2	2	97.1	120	68	11	3	35	22	5.64	74	.300	.361	31-0-4	.129	-2	120	-13		-1.7
Total	8	80	85	.485	292	142	64-4	24	1324.1	1541	784	125	37	497	423	4.66	100	.291	.356	482-4-14	.193	-8	99	2		-1.3

COLLINS, RAY   Ray Williston B2.11.1887 Colchester VT D1.9.1970 Burlington VT BL/TL/6-1/185 d7.19 Col Vermont

YEAR	TM LG	W	L	PCT	G	GS	CG-SHO	SV-BS	IP	H	R	HR	HB	BB-IB	SO	ERA	AERA	OAV	OOB	AB-HR-SH	AVG	PB	SUP	APR	DL	PW
909	Bos A	4	3	.571	12	8	4-2	0	73.2	70	29	2	0	18	31	2.81	89	.269	.317	23-0-1	.130	-0	120	-1		-0.1
910	Bos A	13	11	.542	35	26	18-4	1	244.2	205	73	1	1	41	109	1.62	158	.229	.264	84-0-4	.179	-1	90	22		1.9
911	Bos A	11	12	.478	31	24	14	1	194.2	184	81	1	4	44	86	2.40	136	.256	.302	60-0-3	.150	0	76	19		2.0
912	†Bos A	13	8	.619	27	24	17-4	1	199.1	192	65	4	2	42	82	2.53	135	.256	.297	65-0-3	.169	-1	118	22		2.1
913	Bos A	19	8	.704	30	30	19-3	0	246.2	242	88	3	2	37	88	2.63	112	.264	.294	80-1-7	.150	2	108	12		1.3
914	Bos A	20	13	.606	39	30	16-6	0	272.1	252	95	3	0	56	72	2.51	107	.258	.298	79-0-9	.139	-0	91	8		0.7
915	Bos A	4	7	.364	25	9	2	2	104.2	101	62	1	1	31	43	4.30	65	.261	.317	28-0-1	.286	5	122	-17		-1.4
Total	7	84	62	.575	199	151	90-19	4	1336	1246	493	15	10	269	511	2.51	115	.254	.294	419-1-28	.165	6	100	65		6.5

COLLUM, JACKIE   Jack Dean B6.21.1927 Victor IA BL/TL/5-7/163* d9.21

YEAR	TM LG	W	L	PCT	G	GS	CG-SHO	SV-BS	IP	H	R	HR	HB	BB-IB	SO	ERA	AERA	OAV	OOB	AB-HR-SH	AVG	PB	SUP	APR	DL	PW
951	StL N	2	1	.667	3	2	1-1	0	17	11	3	0	0	10	5	1.59	250	.204	.328	7	.429	1	111	5		1.0
952	StL N	0	0	—	2	0	0	0	3	2	1	0	0	1	0	0.00	—	.200	.273	0	—	0		1		0.1
953	StL N	0	0	—	7	0	0	0	11.1	15	10	1	0	4	5	6.35	67	.326	.380	3	.000	-0		-3		-0.1
	Cin N	7	11	.389	30	12	4-1	3	124.2	123	57	8	6	39	51	3.75	116	.263	.328	36-0-3	.278	3	92	9		1.5
	Year	7	11	.389	37	12	4-1	3	136	138	67	9	6	43	56	3.97	109	.269	.333	39-0-3	.256	2	92	5		1.4
954	Cin N	7	3	.700	36	2	0	1	79	86	43	8	5	32	28	3.76	112	.283	.359	13-1-2	.231	2	106	1		0.4
955	Cin N	9	8	.529	32	17	5	1	134	128	65	17	2	37-4	49	3.63	117	.254	.306	40-0-5	.250	2	131	7		1.1
956	StL N	6	2	.750	38	1	0	7	60	63	29	6	2	27-6	17	4.20	90	.281	.358	14	.214	1	140	-1		-0.1
957	Chi N	1	1	.500	9	0	0	1	10.2	8	8	0	1	9-1	7	6.75	57	.211	.367	0	—	0		-3		-0.6
	Bro N	0	0	—	3	0	0	0	4.1	7	4	1	0	1-0	3	8.31	50	.368	.381	0	—	0		-2		-0.1
	Year	1	1	.500	12	0	0	1	15	15	12	1	1	10-1	10	7.20	55	.263	.371	0	—	0		-5		-0.7
958	LA N	0	0	—	2	0	0	0	3.1	4	3	2	0	2-0	0	8.10	51	.308	.400	1	.000	-0		-1		-0.1
962	Min A	0	2	.000	8	3	0	0	15.1	29	22	1	0	11-0	5	11.15	37	.414	.482	4	.000	-0	95	-12		-1.3
	Cle A	0	0	—	1	0	0	0	1.1	4	2	0	0	0-0	1	13.50	29	.571	.571	0	—	0		-1		-0.1
	Year	0	2	.000	9	3	0	0	16.2	33	24	1	0	11-0	6	11.34	36	.429	.489	4	.000	-0	95	-13		-1.4
Total	9	32	28	.533	171	37	11-2	12	464	480	247	44	16	173-11	171	4.15	100	.273	.342	118-1-10	.246	8	115	0		1.7

COLOME, JESUS   Jesus (De La Cruz) B12.23.1977 San Pedro de Macoris, D.R. BR/TR/6-2/170(170-205) d6.21

YEAR	TM LG	W	L	PCT	G	GS	CG-SHO	SV-BS	IP	H	R	HR	HB	BB-IB	SO	ERA	AERA	OAV	OOB	AB-HR-SH	AVG	PB	SUP	APR	DL	PW
001	TB A	2	3	.400	30	0	0	0-0	48.2	37	22	8	2	25-4	31	3.33	135	.208	.309	0		0		6		0.4
002	TB A	2	7	.222	32	0	0	0-5	41.1	56	41	6	2	33-5	33	8.27	55	.341	.455	0		0		-17		-3.0
003	TB A	3	7	.300	54	0	0	2-6	74	69	37	9	3	46-5	69	4.50	102	.247	.355	0		0		2		0.3
004	TB A	2	2	.500	33	0	0	3-1	41.1	28	16	4	1	18-1	40	3.27	143	.193	.287	1-0-1	.000	-0		7	20	0.7
005	TB A	2	3	.400	36	0	0	1-1	45.1	54	29	7	2	18-3	28	4.57	96	.283	.351	0		0		-3	68	-0.3
Total	5	11	22	.333	185	0	0	5-13	250.2	244	145	34	10	140-18	201	4.70	96	.255	.354	1-0-1	.000	-0		-5	88	-1.9

COLON, BARTOLO   Bartolo B5.24.1973 Altamira, D.R. BR/TR/6-0/225(185-240) d4.4

YEAR	TM LG	W	L	PCT	G	GS	CG-SHO	SV-BS	IP	H	R	HR	HB	BB-IB	SO	ERA	AERA	OAV	OOB	AB-HR-SH	AVG	PB	SUP	APR	DL	PW
997	Cle A	4	7	.364	19	17	1	0-0	94	107	66	12	3	45-1	66	5.65	83	.286	.366	1	.000	-0	103	-10		-1.0
998	†Cle A★	14	9	.609	31	31	6-2	0-0	204	205	91	15	3	79-5	158	3.71	129	.260	.329	2	.500	0	101	24		2.4
999	†Cle A	18	5	.783	32	32	1-1	0-0	205	185	97	24	7	76-5	161	3.95	129	.242	.314	7-0-1	.143	0	120	25		2.5
000	Cle A	15	8	.652	30	30	2-1	0-0	188	163	86	21	4	98-4	212	3.88	129	.233	.329	5	.000	-1	100	23	25	2.4
001	Cle A	14	12	.538	34	34	1	0-0	222.1	220	106	26	2	90-2	201	4.09	112	.261	.332	7	.143	-0	100	14		1.5
002	Cle A	10	4	.714	16	16	4-2	0-0	116.1	104	37	11	2	31-1	75	2.55	174	.245	.297	6	.167	-0	81	24		2.7
	Mon N	10	4	.714	17	17	4-1	0-0	117	115	48	9	0	39-0	74	3.31	132	.259	.317	39-0-2	.128	-1	110	13		1.3
003	Chi A	15	13	.536	34	34	9	0-0	242	223	107	30	5	67-3	173	3.87	119	.248	.301	6-0-1	.000	-1	103	22		2.2
004	†Ana N	18	12	.600	34	34	0	0-0	208.1	215	122	38	3	71-1	158	5.01	89	.265	.324	3	.000	-0	118	-12		-1.5
005	†LA A★	21	8	.724	33	33	2	0-0	222.2	215	93	26	3	43-0	157	3.48	124	.254	.291	3	.333	0	119	21		2.3
Total	9	139	82	.629	280	278	30-7	0-0	1819.2	1752	853	212	32	639-26	1435	3.94	118	.254	.318	79-0-4	.127	-3	107	144	25	14.6

COLON, ROMAN   Roman Benedicto B8.13.1979 Monte Cristi, D.R. BR/TR/6-6/225* d8.21

YEAR	TM LG	W	L	PCT	G	GS	CG-SHO	SV-BS	IP	H	R	HR	HB	BB-IB	SO	ERA	AERA	OAV	OOB	AB-HR-SH	AVG	PB	SUP	APR	DL	PW
004	Atl N	2	1	.667	18	0	0	0-1	19	18	9	0	0	8-1	15	3.32	130	.254	.321	0		0		2		0.2
005	Atl N	1	5	.167	23	4	0	0-0	44.1	47	28	10	0	14-1	30	5.28	81	.272	.323	7-0-1	.000	-1	86	-5		-0.7
	Det A	1	1	.500	12	3	0	0-1	25	35	17	7	0	7-0	17	6.12	69	.327	.365	0		-1	22	-5		-0.3
Total	2	4	7	.364	53	7	0	0-1	88.1	100	54	17	0	29-2	62	5.09	84	.285	.335	7-0-1	.000	-1	59	-8		-0.8

COLPAERT, DICK   Richard Charles B1.3.1944 Fraser MI BR/TR/5-10/182 d7.21

YEAR	TM LG	W	L	PCT	G	GS	CG-SHO	SV-BS	IP	H	R	HR	HB	BB-IB	SO	ERA	AERA	OAV	OOB	AB-HR-SH	AVG	PB	SUP	APR	DL	PW
970	Pit N	1	0	1.000	8	0	0	0-0	10.2	9	7	3	0	8-2	9	5.91	67	.237	.370	0		0		-2		-0.2

COLSON, LOYD   Loyd Albert B11.4.1947 Wellington TX BR/TR/6-1/195 [NYA67 28/530] d9.25 Col Bacone

YEAR	TM LG	W	L	PCT	G	GS	CG-SHO	SV-BS	IP	H	R	HR	HB	BB-IB	SO	ERA	AERA	OAV	OOB	AB-HR-SH	AVG	PB	SUP	APR	DL	PW
970	NY A	0	0	—	1	0	0	0-0	2	3	1	0	0	0-0	3	4.50	79	.333	.333	0		0		0		0.0

COLTON, LARRY   Lawrence Robert B6.8.1942 Los Angeles CA BL/TR/6-3/200 d5.6 Col California-Davis

YEAR	TM LG	W	L	PCT	G	GS	CG-SHO	SV-BS	IP	H	R	HR	HB	BB-IB	SO	ERA	AERA	OAV	OOB	AB-HR-SH	AVG	PB	SUP	APR	DL	PW
968	Phi N	0	0	—	1	0	0	0-0	2	2	1	0	0	2	2	4.50	67	.333	.333	0		0		0	30	0.0

COLYER, STEVE   Stephen Edward B2.22.1979 St.Louis MO BL/TL/6-4/200* [LAN97 2/83] d4.3 Col St. Louis-Meramec (MO) CC

YEAR	TM LG	W	L	PCT	G	GS	CG-SHO	SV-BS	IP	H	R	HR	HB	BB-IB	SO	ERA	AERA	OAV	OOB	AB-HR-SH	AVG	PB	SUP	APR	DL	PW
003	LA N	0	0	—	13	0	0	0-0	19.2	22	6	4	0	16	16	2.75	150	.297	.373	0		0		3		0.2
004	Det A	1	0	1.000	41	0	0	0-0	32	33	24	8	1	24-1	31	6.47	69	.270	.395	0		0		-7		-0.3
Total	2	1	0	1.000	54	0	0	0-0	51.2	55	30	8	1	33-1	47	5.05	86	.281	.387	0		0		-4		-0.1

COMBE, GEOFF   Geoffrey Wade B2.1.1956 Melrose MA BR/TR/6-2/185* d9.2

YEAR	TM LG	W	L	PCT	G	GS	CG-SHO	SV-BS	IP	H	R	HR	HB	BB-IB	SO	ERA	AERA	OAV	OOB	AB-HR-SH	AVG	PB	SUP	APR	DL	PW
980	Cin N	0	0	—	4	0	0	0-0	6.2	9	8	0	0	4-1	10	10.80	33	.346	.433	0		0		-5		-0.3
981	Cin N	1	0	1.000	14	0	0	0-0	17.2	27	15	3	0	10-1	9	7.64	46	.370	.440	0		0		-7		-0.4
Total	2	1	0	1.000	18	0	0	0-0	24.1	36	23	3	0	14-2	19	8.51	41	.364	.439	0		0		-12		-0.7

COMBS, PAT   Patrick Dennis B10.29.1966 Newport RI BL/TL/6-3/200* [PhiN88 1/11] d9.5 Col Baylor

YEAR	TM LG	W	L	PCT	G	GS	CG-SHO	SV-BS	IP	H	R	HR	HB	BB-IB	SO	ERA	AERA	OAV	OOB	AB-HR-SH	AVG	PB	SUP	APR	DL	PW
989	Phi N	4	0	1.000	6	6	1-1	0-0	38.2	36	10	2	0	6-1	30	2.09	171	.248	.278	12-0-1	.167	0	103	6		0.7
990	Phi N	10	10	.500	32	31	3-2	0-0	183.1	179	90	12	4	86-7	108	4.07	95	.257	.336	60-0-4	.150	0	91	-4		-0.3
991	Phi N	2	6	.250	14	13	1	0-0	64.1	64	41	7	2	43-1	41	4.90	76	.254	.365	15-0-2	.133	-1	100	-10	102	-1.1
992	Phi N	1	1	.500	4	4	0	0-0	18.2	20	16	0	0	12-0	11	7.71	46	.278	.376	8-0-1	.125	1	101	-10	102	-1.0
Total	4	17	17	.500	56	54	5-3	0-0	305	299	157	21	6	147-9	190	4.22	89	.257	.340	95-0-8	.147	1	98	-16	102	-1.4

COMELLAS, JORGE   Jorge (Pous) "Pancho" B12.7.1916 Havana, Cuba D9.13.2001 Miami FL BR/TR/6-0/190 d4.19

YEAR	TM LG	W	L	PCT	G	GS	CG-SHO	SV-BS	IP	H	R	HR	HB	BB-IB	SO	ERA	AERA	OAV	OOB	AB-HR-SH	AVG	PB	SUP	APR	DL	PW
945	Chi N	0	2	.000	7	1	0	0	12	11	7	1	0	6	6	4.50	81	.244	.333	3	.000	-0	93	-1		-0.1

COMER, STEVE   Steven Michael B1.13.1954 Minneapolis MN BB/TR/6-3/205(195-207) d4.15 C1 Col Minnesota

YEAR	TM LG	W	L	PCT	G	GS	CG-SHO	SV-BS	IP	H	R	HR	HB	BB-IB	SO	ERA	AERA	OAV	OOB	AB-HR-SH	AVG	PB	SUP	APR	DL	PW
978	Tex A	11	5	.688	30	11	3-2	1-2	117.1	107	36	5	1	37-3	65	2.30	163	.249	.309	0	—	0	137	18		2.5
979	Tex A	17	12	.586	36	36	6-1	0-0	242.1	230	114	24	8	84-4	86	3.68	113	.252	.319	0	—	0	94	12		1.3
980	Tex A	2	4	.333	12	11	0	0-0	41.2	65	41	5	2	22-0	9	7.99	49	.367	.441	0	—	0	151	-19	61	-2.2

YEAR	TM LG	W	L	PCT	G	GS	CG-SHO	SV-BS	IP	H	R	HR	HB	BB-IB	SO	ERA	AERA	OAV	OOB	AB-HR-SH	AVG	PB	SUP	APR	DL	PW
1981	Tex A	8	2	.800	36	1	0	6-3	77.1	70	25	1	1	31-8	22	2.56	136	.241	.313	0	—	0	0	8		1.2
1982	Tex A	1	6	.143	37	3	1	6-2	97	133	64	11	2	36-9	23	5.10	76	.342	.395	0	—	0	78	-16	27	-1.2
1983	Phi N	1	0	1.000	3	1	0	0-0	8.2	11	6	0	0	3-2	1	5.19	69	.314	.360	1-0-1	.000	-0	196	-2		-0.2
1984	Cle A	4	8	.333	22	20	1	0-0	117.1	146	80	11	4	39-2	39	5.68	73	.309	.360	1-0-1	.000	-0	83	-19		-1.7
Total	7	44	37	.543	176	83	11-3	13-7	701.2	762	366	57	18	252-26	245	4.13	96	.281	.344	1-0-1	.000	-0	106	-18	88	-0.3

COMISKEY, CHARLIE Charles Albert "Commy","The Old Roman" B8.15.1859 Chicago IL D10.26.1931 Eagle River WI BR/TR/6-0/180 d5.2 M12 HF1939 ▲

YEAR	TM LG	W	L	PCT	G	GS	CG-SHO	SV-BS	IP	H	R	HR	HB	BB-IB	SO	ERA	AERA	OAV	OOB	AB-HR-SH	AVG	PB	SUP	APR	DL	PW
1882	StL AA	0	1	.000	2	1	1	0	8	12	8	0		3	2	0.00	—	.324	.375	329-1	.243	0*	55	1		0.1
1884	StL AA	0	0	—	1	0	0	0	4	1	1	0	0	0	4	2.25	145	.059	.059	460-2	.237	0*		1		0.0
1889	StL AA	0	0	—	1	0	0	0	0.1	0	0	0	0	0	0	0.00	—	.000	.000	587-3	.286	0*		0		0.0
Total	3	0	1	.000	4	1	1	0	12.1	13	9	0	3	6	0.73	410	.236	.276	1376-6	.259	2	55	2		0.1

COMPTON, JACK Harry Leroy B3.9.1882 Lancaster OH D7.4.1974 Lancaster OH BR/TR/5-9/157 d9.7

| 1911 | Cin N | 1 | 1 | .000 | 9 | 8 | 3 | 0 | 1 | 25.1 | 19 | 11 | 0 | 1 | 15 | | 6 | 3.91 | 85 | .204 | .321 | 6 | | .333 | 0 | 129 | 0 | | 0.0 |

COMPTON, CLINT Robert Clinton B11.1.1950 Montgomery AL BL/TL/5-11/185 d10.3

| 1972 | Chi N | 0 | 0 | — | 1 | 0 | 0 | 0-0 | 2 | 2 | 2 | 0 | 0 | 2-0 | 0 | 9.00 | 42 | .286 | .444 | 0 | — | 0 | -1 | | -0.1 |

COMSTOCK, KEITH Keith Martin B12.23.1955 San Francisco CA BL/TL/6-0/175* [CalA76*5/93] d4.3 Col Canada (CA) JC

1984	Min A	0	0	—	4	0	0	0-0	6.1	6	6	2	0	4-0	2	8.53	50	.261	.370	0	—	0	-3		-0.1
1987	SF N	2	0	1.000	15	0	0	1-1	20.2	19	8	1	0	10-2	21	3.05	126	.253	.337	1	.000	-0	2		0.2
	SD N	0	1	.000	26	0	0	0-0	36	33	22	4	0	21-3	38	5.50	72	.252	.348	1	.000	-0	-5		-0.3
	Year	2	1	.667	41	0	0	1-1	56.2	52	30	5	0	31-5	59	4.61	85	.252	.344	2	.000	-0	-3		-0.1
1988	SD N	0	0	—	7	0	0	0-1	8	8	6	1	0	3-1	9	6.75	50	.250	.314	0	—	0	-3		-0.1
1989	Sea A	1	2	.333	31	0	0	0-1	25.2	26	8	2	0	10-2	22	2.81	144	.268	.330	0	—	0	4		0.4
1990	Sea A	7	4	.636	60	0	0	2-5	56	40	22	4	0	26-5	50	2.89	138	.206	.296	0	—	0	6		1.2
1991	Sea A	0	0	—	1	0	0	0-0	0.1	2	2	0	0	1-0	0	54.00	8	.667	.750	0	—	0	-2	62	-0.1
Total	6	10	7	.588	144	0	0	3-8	153	134	74	14	0	75-13	142	4.06	97	.241	.327	2	.000	-1	-1	62	1.2

COMSTOCK, RALPH Ralph Remick "Commy" B11.24.1890 Sylvania OH D9.13.1966 Toledo OH BR/TR/5-10/168 d8.26

1913	Det A	2	5	.286	10	7	1	1	60.1	90	55	0	1	16	37	5.37	54	.346	.386	22	.227	1	112	-18		-1.8
1915	Bos A	1	0	1.000	3	0	0	0	9	10	3	0	0	2	1	2.00	139	.294	.333	2	.000	0		1		0.1
	Pit F	3	3	.500	12	7	3	0	52.2	44	25	2	1	7	18	3.25	83	.237	.268	16-0-1	.000	-2	103	-4		-0.7
1918	Pit N	5	6	.455	15	8	6	1	81	78	33	0	2	14	44	3.00	96	.259	.297	26	.192	-0	69	0		-0.1
Total	3	11	14	.440	40	22	10	4	203	222	116	4	4	39	100	3.72	76	.284	.322	66-0-1	.152	-2	94	-21		-2.5

CONDREY, CLAY Clayton Lee B11.19.1975 Beaumont TX BR/TR/6-3/195* d8.28 Col McNeese St.

2002	SD N	1	2	.333	9	3	0	0-0	26.2	20	7	1	2	8-1	16	1.69	230	.217	.288	6	.000	-1	32	6		0.6
2003	SD N	1	2	.333	9	6	0	0-0	34	43	32	7	3	21-4	25	8.47	47	.305	.406	10	.200	0	133	-17	55	-1.2
Total	2	2	4	.333	18	9	0	0-0	60.2	63	39	8	5	29-5	41	5.49	72	.270	.361	16	.125	-1	100	-11	55	-0.6

CONE, DAVID David Brian B1.2.1963 Kansas City MO BL/TR/6-1/190(180-200) [KCA81 3/74] d6.8

1986	KC A	0	0	—	11	0	0	1-0	22.2	29	14	2	1	13-1	21	5.56	77	.309	.398	0	—	0	-3		-0.1
1987	NY N	5	6	.455	21	13	1	1-0	99.1	87	46	11	4	44-1	68	3.71	103	.239	.327	31-0-3	.065	-1	89	1	78	0.0
1988	†NY N★	20	3	.870	35	28	8-4	0-0	231.1	178	67	10	4	80-7	213	2.22	147	.213	.283	80-0-5	.150	1	126	28		2.8
1989	NY N	14	8	.636	34	33	7-2	0-0	219.2	183	92	20	4	74-6	190	3.52	94	.223	.289	77-0-6	.234	4	122	-4		-0.1
1990	NY N	14	10	.583	31	30	6-2	0-0	211.2	177	84	21	1	65-1	**233**	3.23	117	.226	.284	70-0-9	.200	3*	118	13		1.7
1991	NY N	14	14	.500	34	34	5-2	0-0	232.2	204	95	13	5	73-2	**241**	3.29	112	.235	.296	72-0-6	.125	1	94	11		1.1
1992	NY N★	13	7	.650	27	27	7-5	0-0	196.2	162	75	12	9	82-5	214	2.88	122	.223	.307	65-0-7	.092	-2	111	11		0.9
	†Tor A	4	3	.571	8	7	0	0-0	53	39	16	3	1	29-2	47	2.55	161	.206	.317	0	—	0	76	9		1.1
1993	KC A	11	14	.440	34	34	6-1	0-0	254	205	102	20	10	114-2	191	3.33	139	.223	.312	0	—	0	59	33		3.0
1994	KC A★	16	5	.762	23	23	4-3	0-0	171.2	130	60	15	7	54-0	132	2.94	171	.209	.277	0	—	0	90	**39**		4.3
1995	Tor A	9	6	.600	17	17	5-2	0-0	130.1	113	53	12	5	41-2	102	3.38	140	.232	.297	0	—	0	103	20		2.1
	†NY A	9	2	.818	13	13	1	0-0	99	82	42	12	1	47-0	89	3.82	121	.223	.312	0	—	0	128	10		1.0
	Year	18	8	.692	30	30	6-2	0-0	**229.1**	195	95	24	6	88-2	191	3.57	132	.228	.304	0	—	0	114	29		3.1
1996	†NY A	7	2	.778	11	11	1	0-0	72	50	25	3	2	34-0	71	2.88	172	.198	.293	0	—	-0	126	16	122	1.1
1997	†NY A★	12	6	.667	29	29	1	0-0	195	155	67	17	4	86-2	222	2.82	158	.218	.305	3	.000	-0	134	19	33	2.2
1998	†NY A	**20**	7	.741	31	31	3	0-0	207.2	186	89	20	15	59-1	209	3.55	123	.237	.302	3-0-1	.000	1	109	27		2.5
1999	†NY A★	12	9	.571	31	31	1-1	0-0	193.1	164	84	21	11	90-2	177	3.44	137	.229	.322	3	.333	1	109	27		2.5
2000	†NY A	4	14	.222	30	29	0	0-0	155	192	124	25	9	82-3	120	6.91	69	.306	.389	3	.333	0	93	-36		-3.2
2001	Bos A	9	7	.563	25	25	0	0-0	135.2	148	74	17	10	57-4	115	4.31	103	.275	.351	0	.000	-0	96	1	43	0.0
2003	NY N	1	3	.250	5	4	0	0-0	18	20	13	4	0	13-1	13	6.50	65	.282	.393	4	.250	0	50	-4	34	-0.8
Total	17	194	126	.606	450	419	56-22	1-0	2898.2	2504	1222	258	106	1137-42	2668	3.46	120	.232	.309	412-0-38	.155	5	103	227	310	23.2

CONE, BOB Robert Earl B2.27.1894 Galveston TX D5.24.1955 Galveston TX BR/TR/6-2/172 d7.25 Col Texas

| 1915 | Phi A | 0 | 0 | — | 1 | 1 | 0 | 0 | 0.2 | 5 | 3 | 0 | 0 | 0 | 0 | 40.50 | 7 | .714 | .714 | 0 | — | 0 | 100 | -2 | | -0.1 |

CONGER, DICK Richard B4.3.1921 Los Angeles CA D2.16.1970 Los Angeles CA BR/TR/6-0/185 d4.22 Mil 1944-46 Col UCLA

1940	Det A	1	0	1.000	2	0	0	0	3	2	1	0	3	1	3.00	159	.200	.385	0	—	0		1		0.1
1941	Pit N	0	0	—	2	1	0	0	4	3	0	0	0	3	2	0.00	—	.214	.353	0	—	0	24	2		0.1
1942	Pit N	0	0	—	2	1	0	0	8.1	9	3	0	0	5	3	2.16	157	.290	.389	3	.000	-0*	74	1		0.0
1943	Phi N	2	7	.222	13	10	2	0	54.2	72	46	3	5	24	18	6.09	55	.327	.406	16	.063	-1	91	-18		-2.6
Total	4	3	7	.300	19	12	2	0	70	86	50	3	5	35	24	5.14	67	.313	.400	19	.053	-1	82	-14		-2.4

CONKWRIGHT, ALLEN Allen Howard "Red" B12.4.1896 Sedalia MO D7.30.1991 LaMesa CA BR/TR/5-10/170 d9.16 Col Utah St.

| 1920 | Det A | 2 | 1 | .667 | 5 | 3 | 0 | 1 | 19.1 | 29 | 16 | 0 | 16 | 4 | 6.98 | 53 | .397 | .506 | 5 | .200 | 1 | 164 | -6 | | -0.7 |

CONLEY, GENE Donald Eugene B11.10.1930 Muskogee OK BR/TR/6-8/225* d4.17 Col Washington St.

1952	Bos N	0	3	.000	4	3	0	0	12.2	23	16	4	2	9	6	7.82	46	.397	.493	5	.400	1	66	-8		-1.3
1954	Mil N★	14	9	.609	28	27	12-2	0	194.1	171	73	17	7	79	113	2.96	126	.240	.320	77-0-3	.156	-2	100	18		1.6
1955	Mil N★	11	7	.611	22	21	10	0	158	152	81	23	1	52-9	107	4.16	90	.254	.313	54-0-8	.204	-1	122	-7		-0.8
1956	Mil N	8	9	.471	31	19	5-1	3	158.1	169	74	13	2	52-10	68	3.13	111	.276	.333	45-0-8	.156	-1	106	2	30	0.1
1957	†Mil N	9	9	.500	35	18	6-1	1	148	133	63	9	2	64-5	61	3.16	111	.244	.323	46-0-2	.196	1	94	4		0.6
1958	Mil N	0	6	.000	26	7	0	2	72	89	44	8	4	17-1	53	4.88	72	.309	.353	16-1-0	.188	1	106	-13		-0.9
1959	Phi N★	12	7	.632	25	22	12-3	1	180	159	68	13	2	42-6	102	3.00	**137**	.235	.280	67-0-4	.239	2	119	21	39	2.4
1960	Phi N	8	14	.364	29	25	9-2	0	183.1	192	85	10	2	42-6	117	3.68	105	.272	.311	63-1-2	.127	-1	77	4		-0.7
1961	Bos A	11	14	.440	33	30	6-2	1	199.2	229	116	33	3	65-2	113	4.91	85	.287	.343	73-2-2	.219	4	94	-11		-1.0
1962	Bos A	15	14	.517	34	33	9-2	1	241.2	238	116	28	5	68-5	134	3.95	105	.256	.308	87-1-1	.207	3	98	6	66	1.0
1963	Bos A	3	4	.429	9	9	0	0	40.2	51	31	4	1	21-2	14	6.64	57	.305	.386	15-0-1	.200	1	128	-11	66	-1.7
Total	11	91	96	.487	276	214	69-13	9	1588.2	1606	767	162	31	511-42	888	3.82	101	.264	.322	548-5-31	.192	8	101	4	135	0.2

CONLEY, ED Edward J. B7.10.1864 Sandwich MA D10.16.1894 Cumberland RI 5-8/142 d7.20 Col Holy Cross

| 1884 | Pro N | 4 | 4 | .500 | 8 | 8 | 8-1 | 0 | 71 | 63 | 47 | 4 | | 22 | 33 | 2.15 | 132 | .223 | .280 | 28 | .143 | -2 | 88 | 3 | | 0.0 |

CONLEY, SNIPE James Patrick B4.25.1894 Cressona PA D1.7.1978 DeSoto TX BR/TR/5-11.5/179 d5.20

1914	Bal F	4	6	.400	35	11	4-2	1	125	112	49	2	6	47	86	2.52	120	.259	.340	35	.114	-3	84	5		0.0
1915	Bal F	1	4	.200	25	6	4	0	86	97	48	5	4	32	40	4.29	67	.314	.386	24	.250	1	69	-11		-0.8
1918	Cin N	2	0	1.000	5	0	0	1	13.2	17	10	2	0	5	2	5.27	51	.321	.379	4-0-1	.250	0		-4		-0.6
Total	3	7	10	.412	65	17	8-2	2	224.2	226	107	9	10	84	128	3.36	88	.284	.360	63-0-1	.175	-2	80	-10		-1.1

CONLEY, BOB Robert Burns B2.1.1934 Mousie KY BR/TR/6-1/188 d9.11

| 1958 | Phi N | 0 | 0 | — | 2 | 2 | 0 | 0 | 8.1 | 9 | 7 | 0 | 0 | 1-0 | 0 | 7.56 | 52 | .273 | .278 | 1-0-1 | .000 | -0 | 136 | -3 | | -0.2 |

CONN, BERT Albert Thomas B9.22.1879 Philadelphia PA D11.2.1944 Philadelphia PA TR/6-0/178 d9.16 ▲

1898	Phi N	0	1	.000	1	1	0	0	7	13	9	1	0	2	3	6.43	53	.394	.429	3	.333	1	103	-3		-0.3
1900	Phi N	0	2	.000	4	1	1	0	17.1	29	29	0	6	16	2	8.31	44	.372	.510	9	.333	1*	76	-12		-1.0
Total	2	0	3	.000	5	2	1	0	24.1	42	38	1	6	18	5	7.77	46	.378	.489	12	.333	2	88	-15		-1.3

YEAR	TM LG	W	L	PCT	G	GS	CG-SHO	SV-BS	IP	H	R	HR	HB	BB-IB	SO	ERA	AERA	OAV	OOB	AB-HR-SH	AVG	PB	SUP	APR	DL	.PW

CONNALLY, SARGE George Walter B8.31.1898 McGregor TX D1.27.1978 Houston TX BR/TR/5-11/170 d9.10 Col Meridian (TX) JC

1921	Chi A	0	1	.000	5	2	0	0	22.1	29	16	0	1	10	6	6.45	66	.330	.404		.500	2	59	-5		-0.1
1923	Chi A	0	0	—	3	0	0	0	8.2	7	6	0	1	12	3	6.23	64	.241	.476	3-0-1	.333	0		-2		-0.1
1924	Chi A	7	13	.350	44	13	6	6	160	177	95	4	9	68	55	4.05	102	.290	.369	50-0-1	.220	1	82	-3		-0.3
1925	Chi A	6	7	.462	40	2	0	8	104.2	122	66	2	2	58	45	4.64	89	.310	.402	28-0-4	.250	1	91	-7		-0.6
1926	Chi A	6	5	.545	31	8	5	3	108.1	128	51	0	2	35	47	3.16	122	.300	.356	32-0-4	.156	-1	117	6		0.5
1927	Chi A	10	15	.400	43	18	11-1	5	198.1	217	108	8	9	83	58	4.08	99	.292	.370	67-0-7	.328	1	77	-1		0.3
1928	Chi A	2	5	.286	28	5	1	2	74.1	89	52	1	4	29	28	4.84	84	.313	.385	19-0-1	.105	-1	67	-8		-0.9
1929	Chi A	0	0	—	11	0	0	1	11.1	13	6	0	0	8	4	4.76	90	.317	.429	0		0		0		0.0
1931	Cle A	5	5	.500	17	9	5	1	85.2	87	56	7	6	50	37	4.20	110	.256	.361	27-0-4	.185	-0	73	1		0.1
1932	Cle A	8	6	.571	35	7	4-1	3	112.1	119	59	6	3	42	32	4.33	110	.266	.333	40-1-2	.175	-0	126	7		0.7
1933	Cle A	5	3	.625	41	3	1	1	103	112	60	4	3	49	30	4.89	91	.271	.353	26-0-3	.231	1	83	-2		-0.2
1934	Cle A	0	0	—	5	0	0	1	5.1	4	3	0	0	5	1	5.06	90	.222	.391	1	.000	-0		0		0.0
Total	12	49	60	.450	303	67	33-2	31	994.1	1104	578	32	40	449	345	4.30	98	.288	.368	301-1-27	.233	5	87	-14		-0.6

CONNELLY, STEVE Steven Lee B4.27.1974 Long Beach CA BR/TR/6-4/210 [OakA95 24/652] d6.28 Col Oklahoma

| 1998 | Oak A | 0 | 0 | — | 3 | 0 | 0 | 0-0 | 4.2 | 10 | 1 | 0 | 1 | 1 | 1 | 1.93 | 240 | .435 | .536 | 0 | | 0 | | 1 | | 0.1 |

CONNELLY, BILL William Wirt "Wild Bill" B6.29.1925 Alberta VA D11.27.1980 Richmond VA BL/TR/6-0/175* d8.22

1945	Phi A	1	1	.500	2	1	0	0	8	7	4	0	0	8	0	4.50	76	.259	.429	1	.000	0	25	-1		-0.1
1950	Chi A	0	0	—	2	0	0	0	2.1	5	3	1	0	1	0	11.57	39	.455	.500	0		0	-2		-0.1
	Det A	0	0	—	2	0	0	0	4	4	3	1	0	2	1	6.75	69	.250	.333	1	.000	0	-1		0.0
	Year	0	0	—	4	0	0	0	6.1	9	6	2	0	3	1	8.53	54	.333	.400	1	.000	0	-2		-0.1
1952	NY N	5	0	1.000	11	4	0	0	31.2	22	18	4	0	25	22	4.55	81	.208	.359	11	.364	3	150	-3		-0.1
1953	NY N	0	1	.000	8	2	0	0	20.1	33	26	4	0	17	11	11.07	39	.371	.472	6	.000	-1	73	-14		-0.7
Total	4	6	2	.750	25	7	0	0	66.1	71	54	10	0	53	34	6.92	57	.285	.411	19	.211	3	106	-21		-1.0

CONNELLY, ED Edward Joseph Jr. B12.3.1939 Brooklyn NY D7.1.1998 New Canaan CT BL/TL/6-1/190* d4.19 f-Ed Col Massachusetts

1964	Bos A	4	11	.267	27	15	1-1	0	80.2	80	50	3	6	64-2	73	4.91	79	.261	.395	18-0-2	.167	0	57	-9		-1.6
1967	Cle A	2	1	.667	15	4	0	0	49.1	63	46	6	1	34-2	45	7.48	44	.315	.414	11-0-1	.182	0	133	-22		-1.3
Total	2	6	12	.333	42	19	1-1	0	130	143	96	9	7	98-4	118	5.88	62	.282	.402	29-0-3	.172	0	73	-31		-2.9

CONNOR, JOHN John B7.1861 Nashua NH D11.14.1905 Nashua NH d7.26

1884	Bos N	1	4	.200	7	7	7	0	60	70	44	1		18	29	3.15	92	.275	.322	25	.080	-3	79	-5		-0.5
1885	Buf N	0	1	.000	1	1	1	0	9	14	9	1		2	0	4.00	75	.378	.410	3	.000	-0	76	-2		-0.2
	Lou AA	1	3	.250	4	4	4	0	35	43	27	0	2	12	19	4.89	66	.295	.356	14	.143	-1	69	-4		-0.5
Total	2	2	8	.200	12	12	12	0	104	127	80	1	2	32	48	3.81	79	.290	.341	42	.095	-4	75	-11		-1.2

CONNORS, JOE Joseph C. (b Joseph C. O'Connor) B1862 Paterson NJ D1.13.1891 Denver CO d5.3

1884	Alt U	0	1	.000	1	1	1	0	9	18	14	0		5	0	7.00	38	.391	.451	11	.091	-1*	80	-4		-0.3
	KC U	0	1	.000	2	1	1	0	12	24	14	1	0	0	1	4.50	50	.393	.393	11	.091	-1*	57	-4		-0.3
	Year	0	2	.000	3	2	2	0	21	42	28	1		5	1	5.57	43	.393	.420	22	.091	-2	71	-8		-0.6

CONNORS, BILL William Joseph B11.2.1941 Schenectady NY BR/TR/6-1/180* d5.3 C17 Col Syracuse

1966	Chi N	0	1	.000	11	0	0	0	16	20	13	4	0	7-1	3	7.31	50	.308	.370	0		0		-5		-0.3
1967	NY N	0	0	—	6	1	0	0	13	8	9	3	1	5-0	13	6.23	54	.170	.264	1	.000	-0	130	-4		-0.2
1968	NY N	0	1	.000	9	0	0	0	14	21	14	0	1	7-1	8	9.00	34	.339	.414	1-0-1	1.000	1		-8		-0.5
Total	3	0	2	.000	26	1	0	0	43	49	36	7	2	19-2	24	7.53	45	.282	.357	2-0-1	.500	1	130	-17		-1.0

CONOVAR, TED Theodore "Huck" B3.10.1868 Lexington KY D7.27.1910 Paris KY BR/TR/5-10.5/165 d5.26

| 1889 | Cin AA | 0 | 0 | — | 1 | 0 | 0 | 0 | 4 | 4 | 4 | 0 | 0 | 2 | 1 | 13.50 | 29 | .400 | .500 | 0 | | 0 | | -2 | | -0.2 |

CONROY, TIM Timothy James B4.3.1960 McKeesport PA BL/TL/5-11/185* [OakA78 1/20] d6.23

1978	Oak A	0	0	—	2	0	0	0-0	4.2	3	6	0	1	9-0	0	7.71	47	.188	.481	0		0	160	-3		-0.1
1982	Oak A	2	2	.500	5	5	1	0-0	25.1	20	13	1	0	18-0	17	3.55	111	.222	.349	0		0	111	0		0.0
1983	Oak A	7	10	.412	39	18	3-1	0-0	162.1	141	89	17	2	98-2	112	3.94	99	.232	.338	0		0	83	-6		-0.6
1984	Oak A	1	6	.143	38	14	0	0-1	93	82	58	11	2	63-0	69	5.23	72	.236	.353	0		0	84	-15		-1.0
1985	Oak A	1	0	1.000	16	2	0	0-1	25.1	22	15	3	1	15-1	8	4.26	91	.237	.345	0		0	70	-2		-0.1
1986	StL N	5	11	.313	25	21	1	0-0	115.1	122	72	15	3	56-7	79	5.23	71	.275	.353	29-0-8	.138	1*	90	-19	53	-2.3
1987	StL N	3	2	.600	10	9	0	0-0	40.2	48	26	0	1	25-3	22	5.53	76	.306	.400	15-0-2	.200	-2	148	-5	109	-0.7
Total	7	18	32	.360	135	71	5-1	0-2	466.2	438	279	47	10	284-13	307	4.69	82	.249	.353	44-0-10	.091	-1	98	-50	162	-4.8

CONSTABLE, JIM Jimmy Lee "Sheriff" B6.14.1933 Jonesborough TN D9.4.2002 Johnson City TN BB/TL/6-1/185* d6.24

1956	NY N	0	0	—	3	0	0	0	4.1	9	7	0	1	7-0	1	14.54	26	.429	.586	0		0		-5		-0.2
1957	NY N	1	1	.500	16	0	0	0	28.1	27	10	2	4	7-0	13	2.86	138	.262	.333	5	.000	-0		3		0.2
1958	SF N	1	0	1.000	9	0	0	1	8	10	6	1	0	3-0	4	5.63	68	.323	.382	1	1.000	1		-2		-0.1
	Cle A	0	1	.000	6	2	0	0	9.1	17	13	2	1	4-0	5	11.57	32	.415	.478	2	1.000	1	74	-8		-0.7
	Was A	0	1	.000	15	2	0	0	27.2	29	15	3	1	15-0	25	4.88	78	.271	.360	4	.250	1	71	-3		-0.1
	Year	0	2	.000	21	4	0	0	37	46	28	5	2	19-0	28	6.57	57	.311	.392	6	.500	1	71	-11		-0.8
1962	Mil N	1	1	.500	3	2	1-1	1	18	14	4	1	0	4-0	12	2.00	190	.222	.265	5-0-1	.000	0		0		0.4
1963	SF N	0	0	—	4	0	0	0	2.1	3	1	0	0	1-0	1	3.86	83	.333	.400	0		0	46	4		0.0
Total	5	3	4	.429	56	6	1-1	2	98	109	56	9	7	41-0	59	5.14	78	.291	.369	17-0-1	.235	2	62	-11		-0.5

CONSUEGRA, SANDY Sandalio Simeon (Castello) B9.3.1920 Potrerillos, Cuba D11.16.2005 Miami FL BR/TR/5-10/165(150-165) d6.10

1950	Was A	7	8	.467	21	18	8-2	2	124.2	132	71	6	1	57	38	4.40	102	.270	.347	40-0-4	.175	-1*	102	1		0.0
1951	Was A	7	8	.467	40	12	5	3	146	140	71	10	0	68	31	4.01	102	.251	.327	43-0-3	.233	-0	112	2		0.2
1952	Was A	6	0	1.000	30	2	0	5	73.2	80	30	2	0	27	19	3.05	116	.276	.338	17-0-2	.176	-0	368	4		0.3
1953	Was A	0	0	—	4	0	0	0	5	9	6	0	0	4	0	10.80	36	.391	.481	0		0		-4		-0.2
	Chi A	7	5	.583	29	13	5-1	3	124	122	39	9	2	28	30	2.54	158	.258	.302	35-0-6	.057	-4	65	20		1.7
	Year	7	5	.583	33	13	5-1	3	129	131	45	9	2	32	30	2.86	141	.264	.311	35-0-6	.057	-4	65	16		1.5
1954	Chi A★	16	3	.842	39	17	3-2	3	154	142	52	7	0	35	31	2.69	139	.248	.289	48-0-4	.229	1	107	17		2.3
1955	Chi A	6	5	.545	44	7	3	7	126.1	120	42	4	2	18-7	35	2.64	150	.256	.283	29-0-3	.103	-2	125	18		1.4
1956	Chi A	1	2	.333	28	1	0	0	38.1	45	25	0	1	11-3	7	5.17	79	.296	.345	4	.000	-1	22	-5		-0.5
	Bal A	1	1	.500	4	1	0	0	8.2	10	4	2	0	2-0	1	4.15	94	.294	.324	2	.500	0	91	0		0.0
	Year	2	3	.400	32	2	0	3	47	55	29	2	1	13-3	8	4.98	80	.296	.342	6	.167	-0	55	-5		-0.5
1957	Bal A	0	0	—	5	0	0	0	5	4	1	0	0	0-0	1	1.80	200	.211	.200	0		0		1		0.1
	NY N	0	0	—	3	0	0	0	3.2	7	5	1	0	1-1	1	2.45	160	.389	.400	—		0		-1		0.0
Total	8	51	32	.614	248	71	24-5	26	809.1	811	346	43	6	246-11	193	3.37	119	.262	.316	218-0-22	.170	-5	107	53		5.3

CONTRERAS, NARDI Arnaldo Juan B9.19.1951 Tampa FL BB/TR/6-2/193 [CinN69 12/276] d5.23 C7

| 1980 | Chi A | 0 | 0 | — | 8 | 0 | 0 | 0-0 | 13.2 | 18 | 10 | 1 | 2 | 7-2 | 8 | 5.93 | 69 | .333 | .422 | 0 | | 0 | | -3 | | -0.1 |

CONTRERAS, JOSE Jose Ariel B12.6.1971 Las Martinas, Cuba BR/TR/6-4/230(230-245) d3.31

2003	†NY A	7	2	.778	18	9	0	0-1	71	52	27	4	5	30-1	72	3.30	133	.202	.297	3	.000	-0	107	10	78	1.0
2004	NY A	8	5	.615	18	18	0	0-0	95.2	93	66	22	6	42-1	82	5.64	81	.250	.333	8	.000	-1	126	-12		-1.5
	Chi A	5	4	.556	13	13	0	0-0	74.2	73	48	9	2	42-0	68	5.30	89	.256	.353	—		0	102	-6		-0.6
	Year	13	9	.591	31	31	0	0-0	170.1	166	114	31	8	84-1	150	5.50	84	.253	.342	8	.000	-1	116	-17		-2.1
2005	†Chi A	15	7	.682	32	32	1	0-0	204.2	177	91	23	9	75-2	154	3.61	125	.232	.307	3	.000	-0	84	19		1.8
Total	3	35	18	.660	81	72	1	0-1	446	395	232	58	22	189-4	376	4.28	106	.235	.319	14	.000	-1	101	11	78	0.7

CONVERSE, JIM James Daniel B8.17.1971 San Francisco CA BL/TR/5-9/180* [SeaA90 16/431] d5.22 [DL 1996 KC A 182]

1993	Sea A	1	3	.250	4	4	0	0-0	20.1	23	12	0	0	14-2	10	5.31	84	.295	.398	0		0	52	-1		-0.2
1994	Sea A	0	5	.000	13	8	0	0-0	48.2	73	49	5	1	40-4	39	8.69	51	.353	.454	0		0	56	-18		-1.5
1995	Sea A	0	3	.000	6	1	0	1-0	11	16	9	2	0	8-0	9	7.36	65	.348	.444	0		0	39	-3		-0.5
	KC A	1	0	1.000	9	0	0	0-0	12.1	12	8	0	2	8-2	5	5.84	82	.267	.377	0		0		-1		-0.1
	Year	1	3	.250	15	1	0	1-0	23.1	28	17	2	2	16-2	14	6.56	73	.308	.411	0		0	39	-4		-0.6

YEAR	TM LG	W	L	PCT	G	GS	CG-SHO	SV-BS	IP	H	R	HR	HB	BB-IB	SO	ERA	AERA	OAV	OOB	AB-HR-SH	AVG	PB	SUP	APR	DL	PW
1997	KC A	0	0	—	3	0	0	0-0	5	4	2	2	0	5-0	5	3.60	132	.222	.391	0	—	0	1			0.0
Total	4	2	11	.154	35	13	0	1-0	97.1	128	80	9	1	75-8	66	7.21	66	.325	.430			0	53	-22	182	-2.3

CONWAY, JIM   James P.   B10.8.1858 Clifton PA   TR   d5.5   b-Pete

1884	Bro AA	3	9	.250	13	13	10	0	105.1	132	84	4	3	15	25	4.44	75	.289	.316	47	.128	-4*	110	-13		-1.5
1885	Phi AA	0	1	.000	2	2	1	0	12.1	19	16	0	0	2	0	7.30	47	.358	.382	6	.000	-0*	154	-4		-0.3
1889	KC AA	19	19	.500	41	37	33	0	335	334	232	12	14	90	115	3.25	131	.252	.306	149	.208	-6	91	29		2.1
Total	3	22	29	.431	56	52	44	0	452.2	485	332	16	17	107	140	3.64	110	.264	.311	202	.183	-10	97	12		0.3

CONWAY, JERRY   Jerome Patrick   B6.7.1901 Holyoke MA   D4.16.1980 Holyoke MA   BL/TL/6-2/190   d8.31 Col St. Anselm

1920	Was A	0	0	—	1	0	0	0	2	1	0	0	1	0	0	0.00	—	.167	.286	0	—	0	1			0.0

CONWAY, PETE   Peter J.   B10.30.1866 Burmont PA   D1.13.1903 Clifton Heights PA   BR/TR/5-10.5/162   d8.10   b-Jim ▲

1885	Buf N	10	17	.370	27	27	26-1	0	210	256	173	10		44	94	4.67	64	.287	.320	90-1	.111	-4*	71	-35		-3.8
1886	KC N	5	15	.250	23	20	19	0	180	236	185	6		61	81	5.75	65	.294	.343	194-1	.242	0*	76	-38		-3.2
	Det N	6	5	.545	11	11	11	0	91	93	55	1		25	35	3.36	99	.255	.303	43-2	.186	1*	127	-1		-0.1
	Year	11	20	.355	34	31	30	0	271	329	240	7		86	116	4.95	73	.282	.331	237-3	.232	1	93	-38		-3.3
1887	†Det N	8	9	.471	17	17	16	0	146	132	95	3	5	47	40	2.90	141	.235	.300	95-1	.232	0*	95	9		0.9
1888	Det N	30	14	.682	45	45	43-4	0	391	315	170	11	13	57	176	2.26	124	.208	.243	167-3	.275	14	131	23		3.9
1889	Pit N	2	1	.667	3	3	2	0	22	26	16	1	0	16	2	4.91	76	.286	.393	10-1	.100	1	113	-3		-0.2
Total	5	61	61	.500	126	123	117-5	0	1040	1058	694	32	18	250	428	3.59	100	.250	.295	599-9	.224	12	101	-45		-2.5

CONWAY, DICK   Richard Butler   B4.25.1865 Lowell MA   D9.9.1926 Lowell MA   BL/TR/5-7.5/140   d7.22   b-Bill

1886	Bal AA	2	7	.222	9	9	8	0	76.2	106	91	6	3	43	64	6.81	50	.312	.394	34	.206	0	121	-28		-2.3
1887	Bos N	9	15	.375	26	26	25	0	222.1	249	161	10	7	86	45	4.66	88	.276	.343	145	.248	2*	81	-12		-0.8
1888	Bos N	4	2	.667	6	6	6	0	53	49	31	2	4	8	12	2.38	121	.240	.282	25	.160	-1*	117	1		0.0
Total	3	15	24	.385	41	41	39	0	352	404	283	18	14	137	121	4.78	79	.279	.347	204	.230	1	94	-39		-3.1

CONZELMAN, JOE   Joseph Harrison   B7.14.1885 Bristol CT   D4.17.1979 Mountain Brook AL   BR/TR/6-0/170   d5.1 Col Brown

1913	Pit N	1	1	.000	3	2	1	0	15	13	4	0	1	5	5	1.20	252	.245	.322	4	.000	-1	37	3		0.1
1914	Pit N	5	6	.455	33	9	4-1	2	101	88	39	2	3	40	39	2.94	90	.254	.337	27	.111	-2	66	-2		-0.3
1915	Pit N	1	1	.500	18	1	0	0	47.1	41	18	0	3	20	22	3.42	80	.248	.340	11	.091	-1	82	-2		-0.2
Total	3	6	8	.429	54	12	5-1	2	163.1	142	61	2	7	65	70	2.92	93	.252	.336	42	.095	-3	63	-1		-0.4

COOK, AARON   Aaron Lane   B2.8.1979 Fort Campbell KY   BR/TR/6-3/175(175-205)   [ColN97 2/70]   d8.10

2002	Col N	2	1	.667	9	5	0	0-0	35.2	41	18	4	2	13-0	14	4.54	104	.295	.364	11-0-1	.091	-1	86	1		0.1
2003	Col N	4	6	.400	43	16	1	0-0	124	160	89	8	8	57-7	43	6.02	81	.317	.391	29-0-6	.172	-0	106	-13		-0.9
2004	Col N	6	4	.600	16	16	1	0-0	96.2	112	47	7	7	39-5	40	4.28	111	.294	.369	34-0-2	.118	-1	97	5	57	0.8
2005	Col N	7	2	.778	13	13	2	0-0	83.1	101	38	2	2	16-2	24	3.67	130	.301	.334	30-0-5	.167	-0	117	8	118	0.8
Total	4	19	13	.594	81	50	4	0-0	339.2	414	192	21	19	125-14	121	4.80	100	.305	.369	104-0-14	.144	-3	104	1	175	0.4

COOK, ANDY   Andrew Bernard   B8.30.1967 Memphis TN   BR/TR/6-5/215   [NYA88 11/287]   d5.9 Col Memphis

1993	NY A	1	0	1.000	4	0	0	0-0	5.1	4	3	1	0	2-0	4	5.06	83	.200	.407	0	—	0	0			-0.1

COOK, DENNIS   Dennis Bryan   B10.4.1962 LaMarque TX   BL/TL/6-3/185*   [SFN85 18/446]   d9.12 Col Texas

1988	SF N	2	1	.667	4	4	1-1	0-0	22	9	8	1	0	11-1	13	2.86	114	.125	.233	4-0-1	.000	1	116	1		0.2
1989	SF N	1	0	1.000	2	2	1	0-0	15	13	3	1	0	5-0	9	1.80	188	.245	.310	6	.167	1	131	3		0.3
	Phi N	6	8	.429	21	16	1-1	0-0	106	97	56	17	2	33-6	58	3.99	90	.243	.303	36-0-2	.222	1*	97	-6		-0.7
	Year	7	8	.467	23	18	2-1	0-0	121	110	59	18	2	38-6	67	3.72	96	.243	.304	42-0-2	.214	2	101	-4		-0.4
1990	Phi N	8	3	.727	42	13	2-1	1-1	141.2	132	61	13	2	54-9	58	3.56	108	.250	.319	42-1-4	.310	4*	126	5		0.8
	LA N	1	1	.500	5	3	0	0-0	14.1	23	13	7	0	2-0	6	7.53	49	.365	.373	7	.286	1	123	-6		-0.6
	Year	9	4	.692	47	16	2-1	1-1	156	155	74	20	2	56-9	64	3.92	98	.262	.325	49-1-4	.306	5	125	0		0.3
1991	LA N	1	0	1.000	20	1	0	0-1	17.2	12	3	0	0	7-1	6	0.51	709	.203	.279	1-0-1	.000	1	50	5		0.3
1992	Cle A	5	7	.417	32	25	1	0-0	158	156	79	29	2	50-2	96	3.82	103	.255	.312	0	—	0	88	-7		-1.1
1993	Cle A	5	5	.500	25	6	0	0-2	54	62	36	9	2	16-1	34	5.67	77	.295	.348	0	—	0		3		0.3
1994	Chi A	3	1	.750	38	0	0	0-1	33	29	17	4	0	14-3	26	3.55	132	.230	.307	0	—	0		3		-0.1
1995	Cle A	0	0	—	11	0	0	0-0	12.2	16	9	3	1	10-2	13	6.39	74	.320	.443	0	—	0	115	-3		0.1
	Tex A	0	2	.000	35	1	0	2-0	45	47	23	6	1	16-1	40	4.00	121	.280	.337	0	—	0	116	1		0.0
	Year	0	2	.000	46	1	0	2-0	57.2	63	32	9	2	26-3	53	4.53	106	.289	.363	0	—	0		0		0.7
1996	†Tex A	5	2	.714	60	0	0	0-2	70.1	53	34	2	7	35-7	64	3.90	104	.214	.322	0	—	0		2		0.4
1997	†Fla N	1	2	.333	59	0	0	0-2	62.1	64	28	4	2	28-4	63	2.38	173	.240	.318	9-1-0	.556	3*	2			2.0
1998	NY N	8	4	.667	73	0	0	1-4	68	60	21	5	3	27-4	79	3.86	113	.216	.299	3	.000	-0	13			0.8
1999	†NY N	10	5	.667	71	0	0	3-3	63	50	27	11	1	27-1	68	3.86	113	.216	.299	1	.000	-0	-5			-0.6
2000	†NY N	6	3	.667	68	0	0	2-6	59	63	35	8	5	31-4	53	5.34	82	.270	.368	0-0-1	—	0	-1			-0.1
2001	NY N	1	1	.500	43	0	0	0-2	36	28	18	6	1	10-1	34	4.25	95	.207	.265	1	.000	-0	-1			-0.1
	Phi N	0	0	—	19	0	0	0-1	9.2	15	6	2	1	4-2	4	5.59	74	.385	.455	0	—	-0	-2			-0.2
	Year	1	1	.500	62	0	0	0-3	45.2	43	24	8	2	14-3	38	4.53	90	.247	.309	1	.000	-0	-2			-0.2
2002	Ana A	1	1	.500	37	0	0	0-1	24	21	9	2	1	10-1	13	3.38	133	.241	.320	0	—	0		3	68	0.3
Total	15	64	46	.582	665	71	6-3	9-26	1011.2	950	486	130	31	390-49	739	3.91	106	.250	.322	110-2-9	.264	9	100	23	84	2.7

COOK, EARL   Earl Davis   B12.10.1908 Stouffville ON, Can.   D11.21.1996 Markham ON, Can.   BR/TR/6-0/195   d9.12

1941	Det A	0	0	—	1	0	0	0	2	4	1	0	0	1	1	4.50	101	.400	.400	0	—	0	0			0.0

COOK, GLEN   Glen Patrick   B9.8.1959 Buffalo NY   BR/TR/5-11/180   [TexA81 24/604]   d6.23 Col Ithaca

1985	Tex A	2	3	.400	9	7	0	0	40	53	42	12	3	18-1	19	9.45	45	.327	.396	0	—	0	107	-21			-2.1

COOK, MIKE   Michael Horace   B8.14.1963 Charleston SC   BR/TR/6-3/200(200-225)   [CalA85 1/19]   d7.1 Col South Carolina-Aiken

1986	Cal A	0	2	.000	4	1	0	0-1	9	13	12	3	0	7-1	6	9.00	46	.333	.435	0	—	0	66	-6			-1.0
1987	Cal A	1	1	.333	16	1	0	0-1	34.1	34	21	7	0	18-0	27	5.50	79	.264	.354	0	—	0	0	-3			-0.2
1988	Cal A	0	1	.000	3	0	0	0-0	3.2	4	2	0	1	1-0	2	4.91	79	.308	.400	0	—	0		0			-0.1
1989	Min A	0	1	.000	15	0	0	0-0	21.1	22	12	1	1	17-1	15	5.06	82	.268	.392	0	—	0		-2			-0.1
1993	Bal A	0	1	.000	3	0	0	0-0	3	1	0	0	0	2-1	3	0.00	—	.091	.231	0	—	0		0			0.1
Total	5	1	6	.143	41	2	0	0-2	71.1	74	47	11	2	45-3	53	5.55	76	.270	.375	0	—	0	32	-10			-1.3

COOK, ROLLIN   Rollin Edward   B10.5.1890 Toledo OH   D8.11.1975 Toledo OH   BR/TR/5-9/152   d7.6 Col Ohio St.

1915	StL A	0	0	—	5	0	0	0	13.2	16	14	0	1	9	7	7.24	40	.276	.382	4	.250	0	-6			-0.3

COOK, RON   Ronald Wayne   B7.11.1947 Jefferson TX   BL/TL/6-1/175*   d4.10 Col Kilgore (TX) JC

1970	Hou N	4	4	.500	41	7	0	2-0	82.1	80	37	4	3	42-4	50	3.72	105	.274	.367	17-0-1	.235	2*	102	2			0.4
1971	Hou N	0	4	.000	5	0	0	0-0	25.2	23	14	2	1	8-1	10	4.91	69	.237	.299	8	.250	0*	26	-4	9		-0.5
Total	2	4	8	.333	46	11	0	2-0	108	103	51	6	4	50-5	60	4.00	94	.265	.350	25-0-1	.240	2	76	-2	9		-0.1

COOKE, STEVE   Steven Montague   B1.14.1970 Lihue HI   BR/TL/6-6/229(220-240)   [PitN89 35/912]   d7.28 Col Southern Idaho [JC]   [DL 1995 Pit N 160]

1992	Pit N	2	0	1.000	11	0	0	1-0	23	22	9	2	0	4-1	10	3.52	99	.253	.286	3-0-2	.333	1	0	0			0.0
1993	Pit N	10	10	.500	32	32	3-1	0-0	210.2	207	101	23	9	59-4	132	3.89	105	.258	.310	71-0-6	.155	-1	103	2			-0.8
1994	Pit N	4	11	.267	25	23	2	0-0	134.1	157	79	21	5	46-7	74	5.02	87	.298	.358	42-0-5	.190	0	83	-7			-0.8
1996	Pit N	0	0	—	3	0	0	0-0	8.1	11	7	1	0	5-0	7	7.56	58	.314	.390	1	.000	-0		-2	79		-0.1
1997	Pit N	9	15	.375	32	32	0	0-0	167.1	184	95	15	9	77-11	109	4.30	100	.284	.366	52-0-7	.058	-4	76	-3			-0.7
1998	Cin N	1	0	1.000	1	1	0	0-0	6	4	1	0	1	0-0	3	1.50	286	.182	.217	2	.500	0	107	2	177		0.2
Total	6	26	36	.419	104	88	5-1	1-0	549.2	585	292	61	18	191-23	335	4.31	97	.276	.339	171-0-20	.140	-4	89	-8	416		-1.2

COOMBS, DANNY   Daniel Bernard   B3.23.1942 Lincoln ME   BR/TL/6-5/210*   d9.27 Mil 1964 Col Seton Hall

1963	Hou N	0	0	—	1	0	0	0	0.1	1	1	0	0	0-0	0	27.00	12	.750	.750	0	—	0	-1			-0.3
1964	Hou N	1	1	.500	9	2	0	0	18	21	10	1	1	10-0	14	5.00	68	.300	.395	4	.000	-0	154	-3			-0.3
1965	Hou N	0	2	.000	26	3	0	0	47	54	26	3	3	23-1	35	4.79	70	.292	.374	9	.111	0	35	-7			-0.3
1966	Hou N	0	0	—	2	0	0	0	2.2	4	1	0	0	3-0	3	3.38	101	.333	.333	1	.000	-0		0			0.0
1967	Hou N	0	1	.000	9	0	0	0	24.1	21	9	0	1	9-4	23	3.33	94	.233	.300	8	.125	0	80	1			0.1
1968	Hou N	3	4	.571	40	2	0	2	46.2	52	21	3	4	17-4	29	3.28	90	.286	.345	10	.400	0	88	-3			-0.2

YEAR	TM LG	W	L	PCT	G	GS	CG-SHO	SV-BS	IP	H	R	HR	HB	BB-IB	SO	ERA	AERA	OAV	OOB	AB-HR-SH	AVG	PB	SUP	APR	DL	PW
1969	Hou N	0	1	.000	8	0	0	0-0	8	12	6	0	1	2-1	3	6.75	53	.364	.417	2	.000	-0		-2		-0.3
1970	SD N	10	14	.417	35	27	5-1	0-0	188.1	185	83	12	2	76-14	105	3.30	122	.256	.326	52-0-7	.096	-2	80	13		1.3
1971	SD N	1	6	.143	19	7	0	0-1	57.2	81	52	10	0	25-5	37	6.24	53	.327	.387	14-0-2	.214	1	130	-22		-2.2
Total 9		19	27	.413	144	42	5-1	2-1	393	433	209	26	8	162-29	249	4.08	89	.280	.349	100-0-9	.140	-0	89	-24		-1.9

COOMBS, JACK John Wesley "Colby Jack" B11.18.1882 LeGrand IA D4.15.1957 Palestine TX BB/TR/6-0/185 d7.5 M1/C1 Col Colby ▲

YEAR	TM LG	W	L	PCT	G	GS	CG-SHO	SV-BS	IP	H	R	HR	HB	BB-IB	SO	ERA	AERA	OAV	OOB	AB-HR-SH	AVG	PB	SUP	APR	DL	PW
1906	Phi A	10	10	.500	23	18	13-1	0	173	144	65	0	7	68	90	2.50	109	.229	.312	67-0-1	.239	1*	81	5		0.7
1907	Phi A	6	9	.400	23	17	10-2	2	132.2	109	58	2	9	64	73	3.12	83	.227	.329	48-1-2	.167	-1*	93	-5		-0.7
1908	Phi A	7	5	.583	26	18	10-4	0	153	130	63	1	4	64	80	2.00	128	.233	.316	220-1-9	.255	4*	104	4		0.7
1909	Phi A	12	11	.522	30	24	18-6	1	205.2	156	63	1	6	73	97	2.32	104	.213	.289	83-0-2	.169	1*	104	6		0.8
1910	†Phi A	31	9	.775	45	38	35-13	1	353	248	74	0	7	115	224	1.30	183	.201	.273	132-0-1	.220	4*	110	47		5.8
1911	†Phi A	28	12	.700	47	40	26-1	1	336.2	360	166	8	16	119	185	3.53	89	.280	.348	141-2-3	.319	14*	150	-12		-0.2
1912	Phi A	21	10	.677	40	32	23-1	0	262.1	227	120	2	10	94	120	3.29	93	.241	.316	110-0-2	.255	6*	121	-4		0.2
1913	Phi A	0	0	—	2	2	0	0	5.1	5	9	0	1	6	0	10.13	27	.313	.522	3	.333	1	201	-5		-0.2
1914	Phi A	0	1	.000	2	2	0	0	8	8	4	0	1	3	1	4.50	58	.267	.353	11	.273	0*	56	-1		-0.1
1915	Bro N	15	10	.600	29	24	17-2	0	195.2	166	71	1	16	91	56	2.58	108	.236	.337	75-0-1	.280	4	88	6		1.0
1916	†Bro N	13	8	.619	27	19	10-3	0	159	136	54	3	2	44	47	2.66	101	.239	.296	61	.180	-0	94	4		0.3
1917	Bro N	7	11	.389	31	14	9	0	141	147	76	7	3	49	34	3.96	71	.284	.355	44-0-1	.227	2*	79	-17		-2.1
1918	Bro N	8	14	.364	27	20	16-2	0	189	191	97	10	2	49	44	3.81	73	.266	.315	113-0-1	.168	-0*	74	-18		-2.2
1920	Det A	0	0	—	2	0	0	0	5.2	7	5	0	0	2	1	3.18	117	.318	.375	2	.000	-0		-1		-0.1
Total 14		158	110	.590	354	268	187-35	8	2320	2034	925	38	88	841	1052	2.78	99	.241	.316	1110-4-23	.235	36	107	9		3.9

COOMBS, BOBBY Raymond Franklin B2.2.1908 Goodwins Mills ME D10.21.1991 Ogunquit ME BR/TR/5-9.5/160 d6.8 Col Duke

YEAR	TM LG	W	L	PCT	G	GS	CG-SHO	SV-BS	IP	H	R	HR	HB	BB-IB	SO	ERA	AERA	OAV	OOB	AB-HR-SH	AVG	PB	SUP	APR	DL	PW
1933	Phi A	0	1	.000	21	0	0	2	31.1	47	30	4	0	20	8	7.47	57	.348	.432	5	.400	1		-11		-0.4
1943	NY N	0	1	.000	9	0	0	0	16	33	26	1	0	8	5	12.94	27	.423	.477	2	.000	-0		-17		-0.9
Total 2		0	2	.000	30	0	0	2	47.1	80	56	5	0	28	13	9.32	43	.376	.448	7	.286	1		-28		-1.3

COONEY, JOHNNY John Walter B3.18.1901 Cranston RI D7.8.1986 Sarasota FL BR/TL/5-10/165 d4.19 M1/C21 f-Jimmy b-Jimmy ▲

YEAR	TM LG	W	L	PCT	G	GS	CG-SHO	SV-BS	IP	H	R	HR	HB	BB-IB	SO	ERA	AERA	OAV	OOB	AB-HR-SH	AVG	PB	SUP	APR	DL	PW
1921	Bos N	0	1	.000	6	1	0	0	20.2	19	12	3	0	10	9	3.92	93	.241	.326	5	.200	-0	113	-1		-0.1
1922	Bos N	1	2	.333	4	3	1	0	25	19	10	1	0	6	7	2.16	185	.224	.283	8	.000	-1	41	4		0.3
1923	Bos N	3	5	.375	23	8	5-2	0	98	92	43	3	3	22	23	3.31	121	.246	.293	66-0-3	.379	4*	64	8		0.9
1924	Bos N	8	9	.471	34	19	12-2	2	181	176	79	4	4	50	67	3.18	120	.260	.314	130-0-5	.254	2*	64	11		1.1
1925	Bos N	14	14	.500	31	29	20-2	0	245.2	267	123	18	3	65	65	3.48	115	.274	.312	103-0-5	.320	5*	95	11		2.1
1926	Bos N	3	3	.500	19	8	3-1	0	83.1	106	52	0	7	29	23	4.00	89	.320	.387	126-0-8	.302	3*	132	-8		-0.2
1928	Bos N	3	7	.300	24	5	2	1	89.2	106	47	7	0	31	18	4.32	91	.303	.360	41-0-1	.171	-0*	105	-2		-0.1
1929	Bos N	2	3	.400	14	2	1	3	45	57	29	4	0	22	11	5.00	94	.315	.389	72	.319	2*	56	-2		0.0
1930	Bos N	0	0	—	2	0	0	0	7	16	14	2	1	3	1	18.00	27	.471	.526	3	.000	-1*		-9		-0.4
Total 9		34	44	.436	159	75	44-7	6	795.1	858	409	41	19	223	224	3.72	106	.278	.331	554-0-22	.289	15	85	12		3.6

COONEY, BOB Robert Daniel B7.12.1907 Glens Falls NY D5.4.1976 Glens Falls NY BR/TR/5-11/160 d9.6 Col Fordham

YEAR	TM LG	W	L	PCT	G	GS	CG-SHO	SV-BS	IP	H	R	HR	HB	BB-IB	SO	ERA	AERA	OAV	OOB	AB-HR-SH	AVG	PB	SUP	APR	DL	PW
1931	StL A	0	3	.000	5	4	1	0	39.1	46	21	1	1	20	13	4.12	113	.291	.374	13	.385	1	64	2		0.3
1932	StL A	1	2	.333	23	3	1	1	71	94	61	8	2	36	23	6.97	70	.324	.402	22	.000	-3*	82	-14		-1.0
Total 2		1	5	.167	28	7	2	1	110.1	140	82	9	3	56	36	5.95	80	.313	.393	35	.143	-2	71	-12		-0.7

COOPER, WILBUR Arley Wilbur B2.24.1892 Bearsville WV D8.7.1973 Encino CA BR/TL/5-11/175 d8.29

YEAR	TM LG	W	L	PCT	G	GS	CG-SHO	SV-BS	IP	H	R	HR	HB	BB-IB	SO	ERA	AERA	OAV	OOB	AB-HR-SH	AVG	PB	SUP	APR	DL	PW
1912	Pit N	3	0	1.000	6	4	3-2	0	38	32	7	1	0	15	30	1.66	197	.227	.301	13-0-3	.154	-0	129	8		0.5
1913	Pit N	5	3	.625	30	9	3-1	0	93	98	52	0	2	45	39	3.29	92	.276	.361	26-0-1	.077	-1	166	-6		-0.7
1914	Pit N	16	15	.516	40	34	19	0	266.2	246	99	4	5	79	102	2.13	125	.254	.313	92-0-3	.207	1	100	9		1.1
1915	Pit N	5	16	.238	38	20	11-1	4	185.2	180	92	4	9	52	71	3.30	83	.262	.323	60-0-2	.117	-3	101	-13		-1.8
1916	Pit N	12	11	.522	42	23	16-2	2	246	189	72	4	4	74	111	1.87	144	.215	.279	79-0-7	.215	0*	73	20		2.1
1917	Pit N	17	11	.607	40	34	23-7	1	297.2	276	96	4	4	54	99	2.36	120	.258	.297	103-0-2	.204	2*	100	16		2.1
1918	Pit N	19	14	.576	38	29	26-2	3	273.1	219	86	2	10	65	117	2.11	136	.223	.279	95-0-5	.242	3	84	22		3.0
1919	Pit N	19	13	.594	35	32	27-4	1	286.2	229	97	10	15	74	106	2.67	113	.225	.287	101-0-1	.287	6*	90	11		1.7
1920	Pit N	24	15	.615	44	37	28-3	2	327	307	113	4	11	52	114	2.39	134	.253	.290	113-0-2	.221	1	85	26		3.0
1921	Pit N	22	14	.611	38	38	29-2	0	327	341	145	9	10	80	134	3.25	118	.272	.320	122-0-4	.254	4	95	19		3.0
1922	Pit N	23	14	.622	41	36	27-4	0	294.2	330	130	13	7	61	129	3.18	128	.286	.326	108-4-3	.269	4	110	27		3.9
1923	Pit N	17	19	.472	39	38	26-1	0	294.2	331	136	11	11	71	77	3.57	112	.288	.335	107-0-3	.262	4	90	15		1.8
1924	Pit N	20	14	.588	38	35	25-4	1	268.2	296	116	13	5	40	62	3.28	117	.283	.313	104-0-1	.346	10	122	16		2.7
1925	Chi N	12	14	.462	32	26	13	0	212.1	249	115	18	4	61	41	4.28	101	.291	.341	82-2-1	.207	1	100	2		0.1
1926	Chi N	2	1	.667	8	3	3-2	0	55	66	32	6	0	21	18	4.42	87	.311	.374	18	.389	3	168	-3		0.1
	Det A	0	4	.000	8	3	0	0	13.2	27	18	0	3	9	2	11.20	36	.443	.534	4-0-1	.000	-1	83	-10		-1.7
Total 15		216	178	.548	517	406	279-35	14	3480	3415	1406	103	100	853	1252	2.89	116	.262	.312	1227-6-38	.239	39	101	159		19.7

COOPER, BRIAN Brian John B8.19.1974 Hollywood CA BR/TR/6-1/180(175-195) [AnaA95 4/88] d9.7 Col USC

YEAR	TM LG	W	L	PCT	G	GS	CG-SHO	SV-BS	IP	H	R	HR	HB	BB-IB	SO	ERA	AERA	OAV	OOB	AB-HR-SH	AVG	PB	SUP	APR	DL	PW
1999	Ana A	1	1	.500	5	5	0	0-0	27.2	29	15	3	4	8-0	15	4.88	100	.228	.363	0	—	0	126	1		0.1
2000	Ana A	4	8	.333	15	15	1-1	0-0	87	105	66	18	2	35-1	36	5.90	88	.299	.362	4	.000	-0	75	-9		-1.0
2001	Ana A	0	1	.000	7	1	0	0-0	13.2	10	5	2	0	4-0	7	2.63	177	.200	.255	0	—	-0	40	3		0.2
2002	Tor A	0	1	.000	2	2	0	0-0	8.1	14	13	5	0	4-0	3	14.04	30	.400	.450	0	—	0	201	-4		-0.7
2004	SF N	0	2	.000	5	2	0	0-0	13.1	15	13	4	1	5-1	7	8.78	49	.288	.356	3	.000	-0	0	-6		-0.8
2005	SF N	0	1	.000	8	1	0	0-0	17.2	15	6	0	0	8-0	7	3.06	139	.234	.319	2	.500	0	22	3		0.1
Total 6		5	14	.263	42	26	1-1	0-0	167.2	182	118	32	7	74-2	75	5.80	84	.279	.354	9	.111	-0	87	-16		-2.1

COOPER, CAL Calvin Asa B8.11.1922 Great Falls SC D7.4.1994 Clinton SC BR/TR/6-2.5/180 d9.14 Col Newberry

YEAR	TM LG	W	L	PCT	G	GS	CG-SHO	SV-BS	IP	H	R	HR	HB	BB-IB	SO	ERA	AERA	OAV	OOB	AB-HR-SH	AVG	PB	SUP	APR	DL	PW
1948	Was A	0	0	—	1	0	0	0	1	5	5	1	0	1	0	45.00	10	.625	.667	0	—	0		-4		-0.2

COOPER, DON Donald James B1.15.1957 New York NY BR/TR/6-1/185* [NYA78 17/442] d4.9 C4 Col New York Tech

YEAR	TM LG	W	L	PCT	G	GS	CG-SHO	SV-BS	IP	H	R	HR	HB	BB-IB	SO	ERA	AERA	OAV	OOB	AB-HR-SH	AVG	PB	SUP	APR	DL	PW
1981	Min A	1	5	.167	27	2	0	0-0	58.2	61	33	9	1	32-4	33	4.30	92	.274	.364	0	—	0	91	-3		-0.3
1982	Min A	0	1	.000	6	0	0	0-0	11.1	14	12	0	1	11-2	5	9.53	45	.311	.439	0	—	0	149	-6		-0.5
1983	Tor A	0	0	—	4	0	0	0-0	5.1	8	4	3	0	4-0	5	6.75	65	.348	.348	0	—	0		-1		-0.1
1985	NY A	0	0	—	7	0	0	0-0	10	12	6	2	0	3-0	4	5.40	75	.300	.341	0	—	0		-1		-0.1
Total 4		1	6	.143	44	3	0	0-0	85.1	95	55	14	1	46-6	47	5.27	77	.287	.372	0	—	0	112	-11		-1.0

COOPER, GUY Guy Evans "Rebel" B1.28.1893 Rome GA D8.2.1951 Santa Monica CA BB/TR/6-1/185 d5.2

YEAR	TM LG	W	L	PCT	G	GS	CG-SHO	SV-BS	IP	H	R	HR	HB	BB-IB	SO	ERA	AERA	OAV	OOB	AB-HR-SH	AVG	PB	SUP	APR	DL	PW
1914	NY A	0	0	—	1	0	0	0	3	3	3	0	0	2	3	9.00	31	.273	.385	1	.000	-0		-2		-0.1
	Bos A	1	0	1.000	9	1	0	0	22	23	15	1	3	9	5	5.32	51	.299	.393		.000	-1*	244	-6		-0.4
	Year	1	0	1.000	10	1	0	0	25	26	18	1	3	11	8	5.76	47	.295	.392	8	.000	-1*	243	-7		-0.5
1915	Bos A	0	0	—	1	0	0	0	2	3	0	0	0	2	3	0.00	—	.000	.286	0			1			0.0
Total 2		1	0	1.000	11	1	0	0	27	26	18	1	3	13	8	5.33	51	.280	.385	8	.000	-1	242	-7		-0.5

COOPER, MORT Morton Cecil B3.2.1913 Atherton MO D11.17.1958 Little Rock AR BR/TR/6-2/210 d9.14 b-Walker

YEAR	TM LG	W	L	PCT	G	GS	CG-SHO	SV-BS	IP	H	R	HR	HB	BB-IB	SO	ERA	AERA	OAV	OOB	AB-HR-SH	AVG	PB	SUP	APR	DL	PW
1938	StL N	2	1	.667	4	3	1	1	23.2	17	11	1	1	12	12	3.04	130	.195	.300	9-0-1	.222	0	86	2		0.3
1939	StL N	12	6	.667	45	26	7-2	4	210.2	208	94	6	2	97	130	3.25	127	.260	.342	69-2-6	.232	3*	96	16		1.5
1940	StL N	11	12	.478	38	29	16-3	3	230.2	225	103	12	3	86	95	3.63	110	.253	.321	83-0-7	.157	-0	97	11		0.7
1941	StL N	13	9	.591	29	25	12	0	186.2	175	88	15	3	69	118	3.91	96	.244	.313	70-0-1	.186	-0	92	0		-0.1
1942	†StL N★	22	7	.759	37	35	22-10	0	278.2	207	73	9	5	68	152	1.78	193	.204	.258	103-0-7	.184	-1	106	47		4.7
1943	†StL N★	21	8	.724	37	32	24-6	0	274	228	81	5	5	79	141	2.30	146	.226	.286	100-1-5	.170	-1	117	33		3.3
1944	†StL N	22	7	.759	34	33	22-7	0	252.1	227	74	6	5	60	97	2.46	143	.239	.288	94-0-4	.202	2	146	33		3.7
1945	StL N	2	0	1.000	4	3	1	0	23.2	20	7	1	1	7	14	1.52	246	.227	.292	6-0-1	.333	1	143	5		0.5
	Bos N★	7	4	.636	20	14	4-1	0	78	77	35	4	1	27	45	3.35	115	.257	.320	26-1-0	.231	-1	135	4		0.6
	Year	9	4	.692	24	14	5-1	0	101.2	97	42	5	2	34	59	2.92	130	.250	.314	32-1-1	.250	2	136	8		1.1
1946	Bos N☆	13	11	.542	28	27	15-4	0	199	181	76	16	0	39	83	3.12	110	.239	.276	67-1-8	.209	1	107	9		1.0
1947	Bos N	2	5	.286	10	7	2	0	46.2	48	26	2	1	13	15	4.05	96	.271	.328	13-0-1	.000	1	71	-2		-0.4
	NY N	1	5	.167	9	8	2	0	36.2	51	32	7	0	13	12	7.12	57	.323	.350	14-1-2	.429	4	89	-12		-1.3
	Year	3	10	.231	18	15	4	0	83.1	99	58	9	1	26	27	5.40	74	.296	.350	27-1-3	.222	4	81	-14		-1.7
1949	Chi N	0	0	—	2	1	0	0	2	3	1	0	1	2	1	∞	—	1.000	1.000	0	—	0		-3		-0.2
Total 11		128	75	.631	295	239	128-33	14	1840.2	1666	703	85	28	571	913	2.97	123	.240	.300	654-6-43	.194	6	109	143		14.3

YEAR	TM LG	W	L	PCT	G	GS	CG-SHO	SV-BS	IP	H	R	HR	HB	BB-IB	SO	ERA	AERA	OAV	OOB	AB-HR-SH	AVG	PB	SUP	APR	DL	PW
COPELAND, MAYS	Mays B8.31.1913 Mountain View AR						D11.29.1982 Indio CA	BR/TR/6-0/180	d4.27																	
1935	StL N	0	0	—	1	0	0	0	0.2	2	1	0	0	2-0	0	13.50	30	.667	.667	0	—	0		-1		0.0
COPPINGER, ROCKY	John Thomas B3.19.1974 ElPaso TX				BR/TR/6-5/245(225-250)			[BalA93 19/539]	d6.11	Col Hill (TX) JC			[DL 2000 Mil N 181]													
1996	†Bal A*	10	6	.625	23	22	0	0-0	125	126	76	25	2	60-1	104	5.18	95	.263	.344	0	—	0	123	-3		-0.4
1997	Bal A	1	1	.500	5	4	0	0-0	20	21	14	2	1	16-1	22	6.30	70	.273	.400	0	—	0	146	-4	156	-0.3
1998	Bal A	0	0	—	6	1	0	0-0	15.2	16	9	3	0	7-1	13	5.17	88	.246	.319	0	—	0	119	-9		-0.4
1999	Bal A	0	1	.000	11	2	0	0-0	21.2	25	21	8	0	19-0	17	8.31	57	.294	.419	1	1.000	0	119	-9		-0.4
	Mil N	5	3	.625	29	0	0	0-2	36.2	35	16	5	0	23-3	39	3.68	125	.250	.354	2	.000	-0	4			0.7
2001	Mil N	1	0	1.000	8	3	0	0-0	22.2	24	17	5	1	15-0	15	6.75	64	.282	.392	5-0-1	.000	-1	143	-6		-0.3
Total 5		17	11	.607	82	32	0	0-2	241.2	247	153	48	4	140-6	210	5.47	87	.265	.361	8-0-1	.125	-0	132	-19	337	-0.8
COPPOLA, HENRY	Henry Peter B8.4.1912 E.Douglas MA				D7.10.1990 Norfolk MA	BR/TR/5-11/175	d4.19																			
1935	Was A	3	4	.429	19	5	2-1	0	59.1	72	40	6	1	29	19	5.92	73	.300	.378	14	.071	-0	88	-9		-0.9
1936	Was A	0	0	—	6	0	0	1	14	17	9	1	0	12	2	4.50	106	.315	.439	3	.333	1	0			0.1
Total 2		3	4	.429	25	5	2-1	1	73.1	89	49	7	1	41	21	5.65	78	.303	.390	17	.118	0	88	-9		-0.8
CORBETT, DOUG	Douglas Mitchell B11.4.1952 Sarasota FL				BR/TR/6-1/185*	d4.10	Col Florida																			
1980	Min A	8	6	.571	73	0	0	23-7	136.1	102	31	7	1	42-8	89	1.98	221	.213	.277	0	—	0		35		4.8
1981	Min A☆	2	6	.250	**54**	0	0	17-8	87.2	80	29	5	0	34-13	60	2.57	154	.239	.305	0	—	0		12		1.7
1982	Min A	0	2	.000	10	0	0	3-3	22	27	13	3	0	10-1	15	5.32	80	.300	.370	0	—	0		-2		-0.2
	Cal A	1	7	.125	33	0	0	8-4	57	46	32	8	0	25-5	37	5.05	81	.223	.307	0	—	0		-5		-0.7
	Year	1	9	.100	43	0	0	11-7	79	73	45	11	0	35-6	52	5.13	81	.247	.326	0	—	0		-6		-0.9
1983	Cal A	1	1	.500	11	0	0	0-1	17.1	26	10	1	1	4-2	18	3.63	111	.351	.392	0	—	0				0.0
1984	Cal A	5	1	.833	45	1	0	4-3	85	76	22	2	2	30-12	48	2.12	189	.244	.310	0	—	0	136	18		1.3
1985	Cal A	3	3	.500	30	0	0	0-1	46	49	33	7	1	20-3	24	4.89	84	.274	.348	0	—	0		-6	35	-0.7
1986	†Cal A	4	2	.667	46	0	0	10-0	78.2	66	36	11	4	22-2	36	3.66	113	.231	.286	0	—	0		4		0.4
1987	Bal A	0	2	.000	11	0	0	1-1	23	25	20	1	0	13-3	16	7.83	57	.281	.369	0	—	0		-8	21	-0.6
Total 8		24	30	.444	313	1	0	66-28	553	497	226	49	6	200-49	343	3.32	125	.242	.310	0	—	0	136	48	56	6.0
CORBETT, JOE	Joseph A. B12.4.1875 San Francisco CA				D5.2.1945 San Francisco CA	BR/TR/5-10/175	d8.23	Col St. Marys (CA)																		
1895	Was N	0	2	.000	3	3	3	0	19	26	22	3	2	9	3	5.68	84	.321	.402	15	.133	-1*	69	-3		-0.3
1896	†Bal N	3	0	1.000	8	3	3	1	41	31	17	0	5	17	28	2.20	195	.208	.310	22	.273	1*	116	9		0.5
1897	†Bal N	24	8	.750	37	37	34-1	0	313	330	173	2	21	115	149	3.11	134	.269	.341	150-0-1	.247	-0*	147	31		2.5
1904	StL N	5	8	.385	14	14	12	0	108.2	110	75	2	8	51	68	4.39	61	.240	.327	43	.209	1	118	-20		-1.9
Total 4		32	18	.640	62	57	52-1	1	481.2	497	287	7	36	192	248	3.42	113	.259	.338	230-0-1	.235	1	134	17		0.8
CORBETT, SHERMAN	Sherman Stanley B11.3.1962 New Braunfels TX				BL/TL/6-4/205*	[CalA84 3/60]	d5.29	Col Texas A&M-Commerce																		
1988	Cal A	2	1	.667	34	0	0	1-1	45.2	47	23	2	0	23-3	28	4.14	94	.273	.350	0	—	0		-1		-0.1
1989	Cal A	0	0	—	4	0	0	0-0	5.1	3	2	1	0	1-0	3	3.38	113	.158	.200	0	—	0		0		0.0
1990	Cal A	0	0	—	4	0	0	0-0	5	8	5	0	0	3-0	2	9.00	43	.364	.423	0	—	0		-3		-0.1
Total 3		2	1	.667	42	0	0	1-1	56	58	30	3	0	27-3	33	4.50	86	.272	.346	0	—	0		-4		-0.2
CORBIN, RAY	Alton Ray B2.12.1949 Live Oak FL				BR/TR/6-2/190*	d4.6	Col Lake City (FL) JC/North Florida CC																			
1971	Min A	8	11	.421	52	11	2	3-1	140.1	141	74	19	3	70-11	83	4.10	86	.265	.351	34-0-4	.206	1	87	-10		-1.2
1972	Min A	8	9	.471	31	19	5-3	0	161.2	135	56	12	6	53-3	83	2.62	123	.230	.299	49-0-2	.082	-2*	97	10		0.8
1973	Min A	8	5	.615	51	7	1	14-2	148.1	124	58	7	5	60-4	52	3.03	131	.229	.308	0	—	0	129	14		1.4
1974	Min A	7	6	.538	29	15	1	0-1	112.1	133	78	8	3	40-4	50	5.29	71	.294	.352	0	—	0	110	-20		-2.0
1975	Min A	5	7	.417	18	11	3	0-0	89.2	105	59	13	2	38-5	49	5.12	75	.295	.363	0	—	0	86	-13	49	-1.5
Total 5		36	38	.486	181	63	12-3	17-4	652.1	638	325	59	19	261-27	348	3.84	95	.258	.331	83-0-6	.133	-2	99	-19	49	-2.5
CORBIN, ARCHIE	Archie Ray B12.30.1967 Beaumont TX				BR/TR/6-4/190(190-230)		[NYN86 16/414]	d9.10																		
1991	KC A	0	0	—	2	0	0	0-0	2.1	3	1	0	0	2-0	1	3.86	107	.300	.417	0	—	0	0			0.0
1996	Bal A	2	0	1.000	18	0	0	0-0	27.1	22	7	2	1	22-0	20	2.30	215	.222	.366	0	—	0		8		0.5
1999	Fla N	0	1	.000	17	0	0	0-0	21	25	20	2	1	15-0	30	7.29	60	.291	.398	1	.000	-0		-8	36	-0.4
Total 3		2	1	.667	37	0	0	0-0	50.2	50	28	4	2	39-0	51	4.44	105	.256	.382	1	.000	-0		0	36	0.1
CORCORAN, LARRY	Lawrence J. B8.10.1859 Brooklyn NY				D10.14.1891 Newark NJ	BL/TR(TB 1884p)/?/120	d5.1	b-Mike ▲																		
1880	Chi N	43	14	.754	63	60	57-4	2	536.1	404	218	6		99	**268**	1.95	124	.199	.236	286	.231	-0*	128	29		2.9
1881	Chi N	**31**	14	.689	45	44	43-4	0	396.2	380	205	10		78	150	2.31	118	.242	.278	189	.222	-1*	128	16		1.2
1882	Chi N	27	12	**.692**	39	39	38-3	0	355.2	281	153	5		63	170	**1.95**	**148**	**.200**	**.234**	169-1	.207	-2*	136	34		2.9
1883	Chi N	34	20	.630	56	53	51-3	0	473.2	483	281	7		82	216	2.49	132	.247	.277	263	.209	-2*	116	37		3.2
1884	Chi N	35	23	.603	60	59	57-7	0	516.2	473	286	35		116	272	2.40	130	.229	.270	251-1	.243	2*	118	35		3.5
1885	Chi N	5	2	.714	7	7	6-1	0	59.1	63	38	2		24	10	3.64	83	.259	.326	22	.273	2	156	-2		-0.1
	NY N	2	1	.667	3	3	2	0	25	24	12	1		11	10	2.88	93	.245	.321	14	.357	1	191	0		0.2
	Year	7	3	.700	10	10	8-1	0	84.1	87	50	3		35	20	3.42	85	.255	.324	36	.306	3	165	-4		0.1
1886	Was N	0	1	.000	2	1	1	0	14	16	11	0		4	3	5.79	56	.271	.317	81	.185	0*	76	-3		-0.2
1887	Ind N	0	2	.000	2	2	1	0	15	23	31	2	2	19	4	12.60	33	.338	.494	10	.200	-0	94	-14		-1.1
Total 8		177	89	.665	277	268	256-22	2	2392.1	2147	1235	68	2	496	1103	2.36	123	.226	.264	1285-2	.223	-1	125	132		12.5
CORCORAN, MIKE	Michael B Brooklyn NY				d7.15	b-Larry																				
1884	Chi N	0	1	.000	1	1	1	0	9	16	14	1	0	7	2	4.00	78	.372	.460	3	.000	-0	0	-2		-0.2
CORCORAN, ROY	Roy Elliot B5.11.1980 Baton Rouge LA				BR/TR/5-10/170*	d7.30	Col Louisiana St.																			
2003	Mon N	0	0	—	5	0	0	0-0	7.1	7	2	0	0	3-0	2	1.23	362	.250	.323	1	.000	-0		2		0.1
2004	Mon N	0	0	—	5	0	0	0-0	5.1	7	4	0	0	5-0	4	6.75	68	.304	.429	0	—	0		-1		-0.1
Total 2		0	0	—	10	0	0	0-0	12.2	14	6	0	0	8-0	6	3.55	127	.275	.373	1	.000	-0		1		-0.0
CORCORAN, TIM	Timothy Hugh B4.15.1978 Baton Rouge LA				BR/TR/6-2/205	d6.14	Col Gulf Coast (FL) CC																			
2005	TB A	0	2	.000	12	0	0	0-0	22.2	19	15	1	1	12-0	13	5.96	73	.226	.330	0	—	0	43	-3		-0.2
CORDERO, CHAD	Chad Patrick B4.18.1982 Upland CA				BR/TR/6-0/190*	d8.30	Col Cal St.-Fullerton																			
2003	Mon N	1	0	1.000	12	0	0	1-0	11	4	2	1	0	3-1	12	1.64	271	.111	.179	0-0-1	—	0		3		0.1
2004	Mon N	7	3	.700	69	0	0	14-4	82.2	68	28	8	1	43-4	83	2.94	156	.221	.315	2-0-1	.000	-0		15		2.1
2005	Was N★	2	4	.333	74	0	0	47-7	74.1	55	24	9	2	17-2	61	1.82	223	.198	.248	0	—	0		15		2.8
Total 3		10	7	.588	155	0	0	62-11	168	127	54	18	3	63-7	156	2.36	184	.205	.279	2-0-2	.000	-0		33		5.1
CORDERO, FRANCISCO	Francisco Javier B5.11.1975 Santo Domingo, D.R.				BR/TR/6-2/200(200-235)		d8.2																			
1999	Det A	2	2	.500	20	0	0	0-0	19	19	7	2	0	18-2	19	3.32	151	.284	.416	0	—	0		4		0.1
2000	Tex A	1	2	.333	56	0	0	0-3	77.1	87	51	11	4	48-3	49	5.35	95	.285	.383	0	—	0		-2		-0.4
2001	Tex A	0	1	.000	3	0	0	0-0	2.1	3	1	0	0	2-1	1	3.86	124	.300	.417	0	—	0		0	186	0.1
2002	Tex A	2	0	1.000	39	0	0	10-2	45.1	33	12	2	2	13-1	41	1.79	268	.204	.271	1	.000	0		13	32	1.2
2003	Tex A	5	8	.385	73	0	0	15-10	82.2	70	33	4	2	38-6	90	2.94	169	.230	.315	0	—	0		15		2.4
2004	Tex A☆	3	4	.429	67	0	0	49-5	71.2	60	19	1	1	32-2	79	2.13	231	.226	.311	0	—	0		21		4.3
2005	Tex A	3	1	.750	69	0	0	37-8	69	61	28	5	3	32-2	79	3.39	135	.234	.319	0	—	0		9		1.7
Total 7		16	18	.471	327	0	0	111-28	367.1	333	151	25	13	181-17	358	3.26	150	.242	.332	1	.000	-0		60	218	9.4
CORDOVA, FRANCISCO	Francisco B4.26.1972 Cerro Azul, Veracruz, Mexico				BR/TR/6-1/183(163-197)		d4.2	[DL 2001 Pit N 190]																		
1996	Pit N	4	7	.364	59	6	0	12-6	99	103	49	11	2	20-6	95	4.09	107	.263	.303	16-0-2	.125	-1	127	4		0.1
1997	Pit N	11	8	.579	29	29	2-2	0-0	178.2	175	80	14	9	49-4	121	3.63	118	.259	.334	56-0-8	.089	-2	111	13	15	1.1
1998	Pit N	13	14	.481	33	33	3-2	0-0	220.1	204	91	22	3	69-5	157	3.31	129	.245	.303	75-0-2	.120	-2	95	6	38	2.2
1999	Pit N	8	10	.444	27	27	0	0-0	160.2	166	83	16	4	59-6	98	4.43	104	.273	.339	49-0-5	.163	-0	95	6	90	0.2
2000	Pit N	6	8	.429	18	17	0	0-0	95	107	63	6	2	38-4	66	5.21	89	.285	.352	35	.114	-1	98	-1		-0.1
Total 5		42	47	.472	166	112	7-4	12-6	753.2	755	366	69	20	235-25	537	3.96	111	.262	.320	231-0-17	.121	-6	98	40	333	3.5

YEAR	TM LG	W	L	PCT	G	GS	CG-SHO	SV-BS	IP	H	R	HR	HB	BB-IB	SO	ERA	AERA	OAV	OOB	AB-HR-SH	AVG	PB	SUP	APR	DL	PW

COREY, BRYAN Bryan Scott B10.21.1973 Thousand Oaks CA BR/TR/6-1/170* [DetA93 12/333] d5.13 Col Los Angeles Pierce (CA) JC

1998	Ari N	0	0	—	3	0	0	0-0	4	6	4	1	1	2-0	1	9.00	48	.375	.474	0	—	0	-2			-0.1
2002	LA N	0	0	—	1	0	0	0-0	1	0	0	0	0	0-0	0	0.00	—	.000	.000	0	—	0	0	15		0.0
Total	2	0	0	—	4	0	0	0-0	5	6	4	1	1	2-0	1	7.20	58	.316	.409	0	—	0	-2	15		-0.1

COREY, ED Edward Norman "Ike" (b Abraham Simon Cohen) B7.13.1899 Chicago IL D9.17.1970 Kenosha WI BR/TR/6-0/170 d7.2

| 1918 | Chi A | 0 | 0 | — | 1 | 0 | 0 | | 2 | 2 | 1 | 0 | 0 | 1 | 0 | 4.50 | 61 | .333 | .429 | 1 | .000 | -0 | 0 | | | 0.0 |

COREY, FRED Frederick Harrison B1855 Coventry RI D11.27.1912 Providence RI BR/TR/5-7/160 d5.1 ▲

1878	Pro N	1	2	.333	5	5	2	0	23	22	10	0		7	7	2.35	94	.250	.305	21	.143	-1*	146	0		0.0
1880	Wor N	8	9	.471	25	17	9-2	2	148.1	131	72	6		16	47	2.43	107	.219	.239	138	.174	-3*	77	4		0.0
1881	Wor N	6	15	.286	23	21	20-1	0	188.2	231	127	3		31	33	3.72	81	.299	.326	203	.222	-1*	79	-12		-1.2
1882	Wor N	1	13	.071	21	14	12	0	139	180	132	5		19	36	3.56	87	.286	.307	255	.247	0*	83	-10		-0.7
1883	Phi AA	10	7	.588	18	16	15	0	148.1	182	106	3		24	42	3.40	104	.283	.309	298-1	.258	2*	123	3		0.4
1885	Phi AA	1	0	1.000	1	1	1	0	9	18	9	2	0	1	3	7.00	49	.419	.432	384-1	.245	0*	257	-2		-0.2
Total	6	27	46	.370	93	74	59-3	2	656.1	764	456	19	0	98	168	3.32	92	.276	.300	1299-2	.236	-3	96	-17		-1.7

COREY, MARK Mark Franklin B11.16.1974 Coudersport PA BR/TR/6-2/220(210-225) [CinN95 4/111] d10.2 Col Edinboro

2001	NY N	0	0	—	2	0	0	0-0	1.2	5	3	0	3	3-1	3	16.20	25	.500	.615	0	—	0	-2			-0.1
2002	NY N	0	3	.000	12	0	0	0-0	10	10	7	2	1	8-1	9	4.50	88	.250	.388	0	.000	-0*	-1	15		-0.3
	Col N	0	0	—	14	0	0	0-0	12	22	16	7	2	8-1	12	12.00	39	.400	.492	0	.000	-0	-8			-0.4
	Year	0	3	.000	26	0	0	0-0	22	32	23	9	3	16-2	21	8.59	51	.337	.447	0	.000	-0	-8			-0.7
2003	Pit N	1	2	.333	22	0	0	0-0	30.1	29	19	2	1	11-1	27	5.34	81	.252	.315	2	.000	0	-10			-0.3
2004	Pit N	1	2	.333	31	0	0	0-1	35.2	39	20	3	2	19-3	28	4.54	95	.275	.366	1	.000	-0	-3			-0.1
Total	4	2	7	.222	81	0	0	0-1	89.2	105	65	14	6	49-7	79	6.02	72	.290	.380	3	.000	-0	-15	15		-1.2

CORKHILL, POP John Stewart B4.11.1858 Parkesburg PA D4.3.1921 Pennsauken NJ BL/TR/5-10/180 d5.1.1883 ▲

1884	Cin AA	1	0	1.000	1	0	0	0	5	1	1	0		2	4	1.80	185	.063	.167	452-4	.274	0*	1			0.2
1885	Cin AA	1	4	.200	8	1	0	1	37	36	25	2	1	10	12	3.65	89	.243	.296	440-1	.252	1*	18	-2		-0.2
1886	Cin AA	0	0	—	1	0	0	0	0.2	1	1	0	0	0	1	13.50	26	.333	.333	540-5	.265	0*	-1			0.0
1887	Cin AA	1	0	1.000	5	0	0	0	14.2	22	15	0	0	5	3	5.52	79	.324	.370	541-5	.311	1*	-2			-0.1
1888	Cin AA	0	0	—	2	0	0	1	5	8	6	1	0	0	1	10.80	29	.348	.348	490-1	.271	0*	-3			-0.1
Total	5	3	4	.429	17	1	0	2	62.1	68	48	3	1	17	21	4.62	76	.264	.312	2463-16	.276	-0*	18	-7		-0.2

CORKINS, MIKE Michael Patrick B5.25.1946 Riverside CA BR/TR/6-1/200* d9.8

1969	SD N	1	3	.250	6	4	0	0-0	17	27	17	3	0	8-1	13	8.47	42	.370	.427	3	.000	0	74	-9		-1.6
1970	SD N	5	6	.455	24	18	1	0-1	111	109	62	11	4	79-10	75	4.62	87	.258	.377	37-1-5	.216	2*	113	-7		-0.4
1971	SD N	0	0	—	8	0	0	0-0	13	14	6	1	0	6-0	16	3.46	96	.280	.357	0	—	0	0			0.0
1972	SD N	6	9	.400	47	9	2-1	6-4	140	125	61	14	4	62-9	108	3.54	94	.240	.322	38-1-4	.237	2	65	-3		0.0
1973	SD N	5	8	.385	47	11	2	3-2	122	130	79	12	11	61-10	82	4.50	78	.274	.367	33-3-1	.212	4*	114	-17		-1.4
1974	SD N	2	2	.500	25	2	0	0-0	56.1	53	32	5	1	32-4	41	4.79	75	.255	.354	8-0-1	.000	-0*	122	-7		-0.5
Total	6	19	28	.404	157	44	5-1	9-7	459.1	458	257	46	20	248-34	335	4.39	82	.262	.357	119-5-11	.202	9	104	-43		-3.9

CORMIER, LANCE Lance Robert B8.19.1980 Lafayette LA BR/TR/6-1/190* [AriN02 4/129] d6.19 Col Alabama

2004	Ari N	1	4	.200	17	5	0	0-0	45.1	62	42	13	2	25-2	24	8.14	56	.333	.412	8-0-1	.250	1	89	-15		-1.4
2005	Ari N	7	3	.700	67	0	0	0-1	79.1	86	50	7	5	43-5	63	5.11	86	.284	.381	6-0-1	.333	0	-7			-0.7
Total	2	8	7	.533	84	5	0	0-1	124.2	148	92	20	7	68-7	87	6.21	72	.303	.393	14-0-2	.286	1	89	-22		-2.1

CORMIER, RHEAL Rheal Paul B4.23.1967 Moncton NB, Can. BL/TL/5-10/187* [StLN88 6/158] d8.15 Col CC of Rhode Island

1991	StL N	4	5	.444	11	10	2	0-0	67.2	74	35	5	2	8-1	38	4.12	91	.277	.300	21-0-1	.238	1	77	-3		-0.3
1992	StL N	10	10	.500	31	30	3	0-0	186	194	83	15	5	33-2	117	3.68	93	.269	.305	59-0-10	.102	-2	105	-6		-0.7
1993	StL N	7	6	.538	38	21	1	0-0	145.1	163	80	18	4	27-3	75	4.33	93	.284	.319	47-0-6	.234	2	113	-6		-0.2
1994	StL N	3	2	.600	7	7	0	0-0	39.2	40	24	6	3	7-0	26	5.45	78	.256	.298	14	.286	1*	104	-5	26	-0.2
1995	†Bos A	7	5	.583	48	12	0	0-2	115	131	60	12	3	31-2	69	4.07	119	.294	.342	0	—	0	97	9	89	0.8
1996	Mon N	7	10	.412	33	27	1	1-1	159.2	165	80	16	9	41-3	100	4.17	104	.270	.321	43-0-11	.186	0	79	4	15	0.6
1997	Mon N	0	1	.000	1	1	0	0-0	1.1	4	5	1	0	1-0	0	33.75	12	.500	.556	0	—	0	66	-4	176	-0.6
1999	†Bos A	2	0	1.000	60	0	0	0-3	63.1	61	34	4	5	18-2	39	3.69	135	.246	.307	0	—	1	7			0.3
2000	Bos A	3	3	.500	64	0	0	0-2	68.1	74	40	7	0	17-2	43	4.61	109	.275	.316	0	—	0	2			0.2
2001	Phi N	5	6	.455	60	0	0	1-5	51.1	49	26	5	4	17-4	37	4.21	98	.247	.320	1	.000	-0	-1	19		-0.1
2002	Phi N	5	6	.455	54	0	0	0-3	60	61	38	6	4	22-6	49	5.25	73	.265	.362	3	.333	1	-10			-1.5
2003	Phi N	8	0	1.000	65	0	0	1-3	84.2	54	18	4	1	25-6	67	1.70	234	.182	.248	2	.500	1	23			2.2
2004	Phi N	4	5	.444	84	0	0	0-7	81	70	32	7	5	26-6	46	3.56	125	.237	.309	1	.000	1	9			0.9
2005	Phi N	4	2	.667	57	0	0	0-2	47.1	56	33	9	2	16-1	34	5.89	74	.296	.354	1-0-2	.188	-0	-8			-0.8
Total	14	69	61	.531	613	108	7-1	2-27	1170.2	1196	588	115	47	299-34	740	4.08	102	.265	.316	192-0-30	.188	4	93	11	325	0.4

CORNEJO, NATE Nathan J. B9.24.1979 Wellington KS BR/TR/6-5/200(200-245) [DetA98 1/34] d8.8 f-Mardie

2001	Det A	4	4	.500	10	10	0	0-0	42.2	63	38	10	3	28-4	22	7.38	60	.342	.437	0	—	0	124	-14		-2.0
2002	Det A	1	5	.167	9	9	1	0-0	50	63	33	6	2	18-0	23	5.04	87	.303	.362	0	—	0	73	-5		-0.5
2003	Det A	6	17	.261	32	32	2	0-0	194.2	236	111	18	3	58-8	46	4.67	94	.307	.356	4-0-1	.000	-0	66	-7		-0.7
2004	Det A	1	3	.250	5	5	0	0-0	25.2	42	25	4	1	11-1	12	8.42	53	.375	.435	0	—	0	124	-11	154	-1.3
Total	4	12	29	.293	56	56	3	0-0	313	404	207	38	9	115-13	103	5.41	81	.318	.376	4-0-1	.000	-0	83	-37	154	-4.5

CORNEJO, MARDIE Nieves Mardie B8.5.1951 Wellington KS BR/TR/6-3/200 [NYN73 21/493] d4.8 s-Nate Col Tulsa

| 1978 | NY N | 4 | 2 | .667 | 25 | 0 | 0 | 3-0 | 36.2 | 37 | 12 | 1 | 3 | 14-5 | 17 | 2.45 | 144 | .285 | .358 | 0 | — | 0 | 4 | | | 0.7 |

CORNELIUS, REID Jonathan Reid B6.2.1970 Thomasville AL BR/TR/6-0/200* [MonN88 11/284] d4.29

1995	Mon N	0	0	—	4	0	0	0-0	9	11	8	3	2	5-0	4	8.00	54	.306	.419	0	—	0	-3			-0.2
	NY N	3	7	.300	10	10	0	0-0	57.2	64	36	8	1	25-5	35	5.15	78	.284	.354	20	.100	-1	101	-7		-1.1
	Year	3	7	.300	18	10	0	0-0	66.2	75	44	11	3	30-5	39	5.54	74	.287	.364	20	.100	-1	100	-11		-1.3
1999	Fla N	1	0	1.000	5	2	0	0-0	19.1	16	7	0	0	5-1	12	3.26	134	.229	.280	5-0-1	.200	0	84	3		0.2
2000	Fla N	4	10	.286	22	21	0	0-0	125	135	74	19	4	50-4	50	4.82	91	.282	.351	37-0-4	.135	-1*	76	-7		-0.6
Total	3	8	17	.320	45	33	0	0-0	211	226	125	30	7	85-10	101	4.91	87	.279	.349	62-0-5	.129	-2	83	-14		-1.7

CORNELL, JEFF Jeffery Ray B2.10.1957 Kansas City MO BB/TR/5-11/170 [KCA78 8/207] d6.2 Col Missouri

| 1984 | SF N | 1 | 3 | .250 | 23 | 0 | 0 | 0-1 | 38.1 | 51 | 30 | 4 | 1 | 16-2 | 19 | 6.10 | 58 | .340 | .423 | 4 | .000 | -0 | -11 | | | -1.2 |

CORNETT, BRAD Brad Byron B2.4.1969 Lamesa TX BR/TR/6-3/190* d6.8 Col Lubbock Christian

1994	Tor A	1	3	.250	9	4	0	0-0	31	40	25	6	1	11-2	22	6.68	73	.331	.394	0	—	0	52	-6		-0.6
1995	Tor A	0	0	—	5	0	0	0-0	5	9	6	1	3	3-0	4	9.00	53	.429	.520	0	—	0	-3	30		-0.1
Total	2	1	3	.250	14	4	0	0-0	36	49	31	2	4	14-2	26	7.00	69	.345	.414	0	—	0	52	-9	30	-0.7

CORNUTT, TERRY Terry Stanton B10.2.1952 Roseburg OR BR/TR/6-2/195* [SFN72 S4/49] d4.9 Col Linn-Benton (OR) CC

1977	SF N	1	2	.333	28	1	0	0-0	44.1	38	24	4	0	22-5	23	3.86	102	.229	.316	1-0-1	.000	-0	0	0		-0.1
1978	SF N	0	0	—	1	0	0	0-0	3	1	0	0	0	0-0	0	0.00	—	.100	.100	0	—	-0	1			0.1
Total	2	1	2	.333	29	1	0	0-0	47.1	39	24	4	0	22-5	23	3.61	108	.222	.305	1-0-1	.000	-0	0	1		0.1

CORREA, ED Edwin Josue (Andino) B4.29.1966 Hato Rey, PR BR/TR/6-2/192(192-205) d9.18 [DL 1988 Tex A 150, 1989 Tex A 151]

1985	Chi A	1	0	1.000	5	1	0	0-0	10.1	11	9	2	0	11-0	10	6.97	62	.275	.431	0	—	0	63	-3		-0.3
1986	Tex A	12	14	.462	32	32	4-2	0-0	202.1	167	102	15	3	126-2	189	4.23	102	.223	.336	0	—	0	82	4		0.6
1987	Tex A	3	5	.375	15	15	0	0-0	70	83	63	17	4	52-2	61	7.59	60	.296	.411	0	—	0	110	-22	63	-2.0
Total	3	16	19	.457	52	48	4-2	0-0	282.2	261	174	34	7	189-4	260	5.16	85	.244	.360	0	—	0	91	-21	364	-1.7

CORREIA, KEVIN Kevin John B8.24.1980 San Diego CA BR/TR/6-3/200* [SFN02 4/127] d7.10 Col Cal Poly-San Luis Obispo

2003	SF N	3	1	.750	9	8	0	0-0	39.1	41	16	4	4	18-1	28	3.66	116	.275	.366	13-0-1	.154	-0	120	3		0.2
2004	SF N	0	1	.000	12	1	0	0-0	19	25	20	3	1	10-0	15	8.05	54	.333	.404	3	.333	1	256	-8		-0.3
2005	SF N	2	5	.286	16	11	0	0-0	58.1	61	31	12	4	31-2	44	4.63	92	.274	.371	14-0-1	.071	-0	79	-2		-0.3
Total	3	5	7	.417	38	19	0	0-0	116.2	127	67	21	9	59-3	86	4.86	88	.284	.375	30-0-2	.133	1	103	-7		-0.4

YEAR	TM LG	W	L	PCT	G	GS	CG-SHO	SV-BS	IP	H	R	HR	HB	BB-IB	SO	ERA	AERA	OAV	OOB	AB-HR-SH	AVG	PB	SUP	APR	DL	PW

CORRIDON, FRANK   Francis Joseph "Fiddler"   B11.25.1880 Newport RI   D2.21.1941 Syracuse NY   BB/TR/6-0/170   d4.15

YEAR	TM LG	W	L	PCT	G	GS	CG-SHO	SV-BS	IP	H	R	HR	HB	BB-IB	SO	ERA	AERA	OAV	OOB	AB-HR-SH	AVG	PB	SUP	APR	DL	PW
1904	Chi N	5	5	.500	12	10	9	0	100.1	88	43	2	7	37	34	3.05	87	.240	.321	58-0-1	.224	0*	72	-2		0.0
	Phi N	6	5	.545	12	11	11-1	0	94.1	88	33	2	8	28	44	2.19	122	.250	.320	35	.171	-0	65	6		0.8
	Year	11	10	.524	24	21	20-1	0	194.2	176	76	4	15	65	78	2.64	101	.245	.320	93-0-1	.204	0	69	4		0.8
1905	Phi N	10	12	.455	35	26	18-1	1	212	203	109	2	16	57	79	3.48	84	.257	.319	72-1-2	.208	4	101	-12		-0.6
1907	Phi N	18	14	.563	37	32	23-3	2	274	228	107	0	9	89	131	2.46	98	.230	.299	97	.165	0*	112	-4		-0.2
1908	Phi N	14	10	.583	27	24	18-2	1	208.1	178	69	0	6	48	50	2.51	97	.239	.290	73-0-3	.123	-2	109	1		0.2
1909	Phi N	11	7	.611	27	19	11-3	0	171	147	61	0	6	61	69	2.11	123	.242	.318	59-0-3	.186	0	119	7		1.0
1910	StL N	6	14	.300	30	18	9	3	156	168	88	1	9	55	51	3.81	78	.283	.353	51-0-1	.196	0	83	-16		-1.8
Total	6	70	67	.511	180	140	99-10	7	1216	1100	510	7	61	375	458	2.80	95	.247	.315	445-1-10	.180	3	99	-20		-0.6

CORSI, JIM   James Bernard   B9.9.1961 Newton MA   BR/TR/6-1/220(210-230)   [NYA82 25/642]   d6.28   Col St. Leo   [DL 1990 Oak A 178]

YEAR	TM LG	W	L	PCT	G	GS	CG-SHO	SV-BS	IP	H	R	HR	HB	BB-IB	SO	ERA	AERA	OAV	OOB	AB-HR-SH	AVG	PB	SUP	APR	DL	PW
1988	Oak A	0	1	.000	11	1	0	0-0	21.1	20	10	1	0	6-1	10	3.80	100	.260	.302	0		-0	168			0.0
1989	Oak A	1	2	.333	22	0	0	0-0	38.1	26	8	2	1	10-0	21	1.88	197	.194	.252	0		-0	9			0.6
1991	Hou N	0	5	.000	47	0	0	0-3	77.2	76	37	6	0	23-5	53	3.71	95	.259	.310	1	.000	-0	-2			-0.1
1992	†Oak A	4	2	.667	32	0	0	0-0	44	44	12	2	0	18-2	19	1.43	264	.273	.343	0		0	10			1.3
1993	Fla N	0	2	.000	15	0	0	0-0	20.1	28	15	1	0	10-3	7	6.64	66	.337	.404	0		-0	-4	115		1.4
1995	Oak A	2	4	.333	38	0	0	2-2	45	31	14	2	2	26-1	26	2.20	206	.203	.324	0		0	9	21		0.7
1996	Oak A	6	0	1.000	56	0	0	3-3	73.2	71	33	6	3	34-4	43	4.03	123	.269	.356	0		0	7	29		0.9
1997	Bos A	5	3	.625	52	0	0	2-7	57.2	56	26	1	4	21-7	40	3.43	136	.255	.327	0		0	14	19		1.0
1998	†Bos A	3	2	.600	59	0	0	0-3	66	58	23	6	1	23-2	49	2.59	182	.235	.301	1	.000	-0	0			1.0
1999	Bos A	1	2	.333	23	0	0	0-3	24	25	15	4	2	19-3	14	5.25	95	.284	.418	0		0	3	15		0.2
	Bal A	0	1	.000	13	0	0	0-1	13.1	15	4	2	0	1-0	8	2.70	174	.294	.308	0		0	2			0.2
	Year	1	3	.250	36	0	0	0-4	37.1	40	19	6	2	20-3	22	4.34	113	.288	.383	0		0	2			0.2
Total	10	22	14	.478	368	1	0	7-22	481.1	450	197	33	13	191-28	290	3.25	133	.254	.328	2	.000	-0	168	57	424	5.6

CORT, BARRY   Barry Lee   B4.15.1956 Toronto ON, Can.   BR/TR/6-5/210   [MilA74 4/78]   d4.22

YEAR	TM LG	W	L	PCT	G	GS	CG-SHO	SV-BS	IP	H	R	HR	HB	BB-IB	SO	ERA	AERA	OAV	OOB	AB-HR-SH	AVG	PB	SUP	APR	DL	PW
1977	Mil A	1	1	.500	7	3	1	0-0	24.1	25	9	1	1	9-1	17	3.33	123	.281	.350	0		0	80	3	22	0.2

CORTES, DAVID   David C.   B10.15.1973 Mexicali, Baja California, Mexico   BR/TR/5-11/195(195-220)   d8.30   [DL 2000 Atl N 181]

YEAR	TM LG	W	L	PCT	G	GS	CG-SHO	SV-BS	IP	H	R	HR	HB	BB-IB	SO	ERA	AERA	OAV	OOB	AB-HR-SH	AVG	PB	SUP	APR	DL	PW
1999	Atl N	0	0	—	4	0	0	0-0	3.2	3	3	0	0	4-0	2	4.91	91	.214	.389	0		0	-1			0.0
2003	Cle A	0	0	—	2	0	0	0-0	3	8	5	1	0	0-0	1	12.00	37	.471	.444	0		0	-3			-0.1
2005	Col N	2	0	1.000	50	0	0	2-1	52.2	50	24	9	1	10-2	36	4.10	116	.251	.288	2	.000	-0	4		181	0.2
Total	3	2	0	1.000	56	0	0	2-1	59.1	61	32	10	1	14-2	39	4.55	104	.265	.306	2	.000	-0	0	181		0.1

CORWIN, AL   Elmer Nathan   B12.3.1926 Newburgh NY   D10.23.2003 Geneva IL   BR/TR/6-1/170*   d7.25

YEAR	TM LG	W	L	PCT	G	GS	CG-SHO	SV-BS	IP	H	R	HR	HB	BB-IB	SO	ERA	AERA	OAV	OOB	AB-HR-SH	AVG	PB	SUP	APR	DL	PW
1951	†NY N	5	1	.833	15	8	3-1	1	59	49	27	7	0	21	30	3.66	107	.222	.289	20-0-2	.050	-2	110	2		-0.1
1952	NY N	6	1	.857	21	7	1	2	67.2	58	23	5	0	36	36	2.66	139	.237	.335	21-0-1	.095	-1*	117	8		0.7
1953	NY N	6	4	.600	48	7	2-1	2	106.2	122	65	17	3	68	49	4.98	86	.290	.393	32-2-2	.281	4*	110	-1		-0.7
1954	NY N	1	3	.250	20	0	0	0	31.1	35	19	4	0	14	14	4.02	100	.297	.363	3	.000	-0*	-1			-0.2
1955	NY N	0	1	.000	13	0	0	0	24.2	25	11	3	0	17-2	13	4.01	100	.263	.372	3	.000	-0	1			0.1
Total	5	18	10	.643	117	22	6-2	5	289.1	289	145	36	3	156-2	142	3.98	101	.263	.355	79-2-5	.152	0	111	3		0.1

COSGROVE, MIKE   Michael John   B2.17.1951 Phoenix AZ   BL/TL/6-1/170*   [HouN70*S2/38]   d9.10   Col Phoenix (AZ) JC

YEAR	TM LG	W	L	PCT	G	GS	CG-SHO	SV-BS	IP	H	R	HR	HB	BB-IB	SO	ERA	AERA	OAV	OOB	AB-HR-SH	AVG	PB	SUP	APR	DL	PW
1972	Hou N	1	0	1.000	7	1	0	1-0	13.2	16	8	4	0	3-0	7	4.61	73	.286	.317	2-0-1	.000	-0	53	-2		-0.2
1973	Hou N	1	1	.500	13	0	0	0-1	10	11	2	1	0	8-2	8	1.80	203	.282	.396	0		0	2			0.1
1974	Hou N	7	3	.700	45	0	0	2-3	90	76	35	2	1	39-3	47	3.50	100	.232	.313	18-0-2	.056	-1	95	4		0.3
1975	Hou N	1	2	.333	32	3	1	5-3	71.1	62	24	2	0	37-1	32	3.03	112	.245	.338	13-0-2	.154	0	95	4		0.1
1976	Hou N	3	4	.429	22	16	1-1	0-0	89.2	106	63	6	2	58-2	34	5.52	58	.303	.399	23-0-5	.087	-1	126	-25		-1.8
Total	5	12	11	.522	119	20	2-1	8-7	274.2	271	132	13	3	145-8	122	4.03	84	.264	.353	56-0-10	.089	-2	113	-19		-1.2

COSMAN, JIM   James Henry   B2.19.1943 Brockport NY   BR/TR/6-4.5/211*   d10.2   Col Middle Tennessee

YEAR	TM LG	W	L	PCT	G	GS	CG-SHO	SV-BS	IP	H	R	HR	HB	BB-IB	SO	ERA	AERA	OAV	OOB	AB-HR-SH	AVG	PB	SUP	APR	DL	PW
1966	StL N	1	0	1.000	1	1	1-1	0	9	2	0	0	1	2-0	5	0.00	—	.074	.167	3	.000	-0	49	4		0.4
1967	StL N	1	0	1.000	10	5	0	0	31.1	21	12	2	5	24-2	11	3.16	104	.198	.368	8-0-1	.125	-0	112	1		0.0
1970	Chi N	0	0	—	1	0	0	0-0	1	3	3	1	0	1-1	0	27.00	17	.600	.667	0		-0	-2			-0.1
Total	3	2	0	1.000	12	6	1-1	0-0	41.1	26	15	3	6	27-3	16	3.05	111	.188	.343	11-0-1	.091	-0	100	3		0.3

COSTELLO, JOHN   John Reilly   B12.24.1960 Bronx NY   BR/TR/6-1/190*   [StLN83 24/612]   d6.2   Col Mercyhurst

YEAR	TM LG	W	L	PCT	G	GS	CG-SHO	SV-BS	IP	H	R	HR	HB	BB-IB	SO	ERA	AERA	OAV	OOB	AB-HR-SH	AVG	PB	SUP	APR	DL	PW
1988	StL N	5	2	.714	36	0	0	1-1	49.2	44	15	3	0	25-4	38	1.81	194	.235	.324	5	.000	-0	8			1.0
1989	StL N	5	4	.556	48	0	0	3-3	62.1	48	24	5	2	20-7	40	3.32	110	.213	.278	6-0-2	.000	-1	3	21		0.3
1990	StL N	0	0	—	4	0	0	0-0	4.1	7	3	1	1	1-1	1	6.23	62	.368	.429	0		-0	-1	6		-0.1
	Mon N	0	0	—	4	0	0	0-1	6.1	5	5	2	0	1-0	1	5.68	65	.208	.231	0		0	-2	46		-0.1
	SD N	0	0	—	8	0	0	0-1	10.2	12	8	3	1	2-1	2	5.91	63	.279	.319	0		0	-3			0.0
	Year	0	0	—	8	0	0	0-1	35	37	15	2	0	17-3	24	3.09	123	.276	.353	1-0-1	.000	-0	2			0.0
1991	SD N	1	0	1.000	27	0	0	4-6	35	37	15	2	0	17-3	24	3.09	123	.276	.353	1-0-1	.000	-0	2			0.0
Total	4	11	6	.647	119	0	0	4-6	157.2	141	62	13	3	64-15	104	2.97	123	.239	.313	12-0-3	.000	-1	10	73		1.2

COTTER, DAN   Daniel Joseph   B4.14.1867 Boston MA   D9.4.1935 Boston MA   BR/TR   d7.16

YEAR	TM LG	W	L	PCT	G	GS	CG-SHO	SV-BS	IP	H	R	HR	HB	BB-IB	SO	ERA	AERA	OAV	OOB	AB-HR-SH	AVG	PB	SUP	APR	DL	PW
1890	Buf P	0	1	.000	1	1	1	0	9	18	19	1	0	7	0	14.00	29	.400	.481	4	.000	-1	0	-9		-0.1

COTTRELL, ENSIGN   Ensign Stover   B8.29.1888 Hoosick Falls NY   D2.27.1947 Syracuse NY   BL/TL/5-9.5/173   d6.21   Col Syracuse

YEAR	TM LG	W	L	PCT	G	GS	CG-SHO	SV-BS	IP	H	R	HR	HB	BB-IB	SO	ERA	AERA	OAV	OOB	AB-HR-SH	AVG	PB	SUP	APR	DL	PW
1911	Pit N	0	0	—	1	0	0	0	1	4	4	0	0	1	1	9.00	38	.667	.714	0		0	-2			-0.1
1912	Chi N	0	0	—	1	0	0	0	4	8	4	0	0	1	1	9.00	37	.444	.474	1	.000	-0	-2			-0.1
1913	Phi A	1	0	1.000	2	1	1	0	10	15	7	0	0	2	1	5.40	51	.333	.362	1	.250	1	268	-3		-0.1
1914	Bos N	0	1	.000	7	0	0	0	2	2	2	0	0	3	1	9.00	31	.333	.556	0		-1	26	-1		-0.1
1915	NY A	0	0	—	7	0	0	0	21.1	29	12	2	1	7	7	3.38	87	.330	.385	1	.000	-1	137	-10		-0.1
Total	5	1	2	.333	12	2	2	0	37.1	58	29	2	1	14	12	4.82	61	.356	.410	12	.083	-0	137	-10		-0.4

COTTS, NEAL   Neal James   B3.25.1980 Belleville IL   BL/TL/6-2/200*   [OakA01 2/69]   d8.12   Col Illinois St.

YEAR	TM LG	W	L	PCT	G	GS	CG-SHO	SV-BS	IP	H	R	HR	HB	BB-IB	SO	ERA	AERA	OAV	OOB	AB-HR-SH	AVG	PB	SUP	APR	DL	PW
2003	Chi A	1	1	.500	4	4	0	0-0	13.1	15	12	1	0	17-0	10	8.10	57	.294	.471	0		0	130	-5		-0.4
2004	Chi A	4	4	.500	56	0	0	0-2	65.1	61	45	13	3	30-2	58	5.65	83	.247	.335	1	1.000	0	20	-7		-0.1
2005	†Chi A	4	0	1.000	69	0	0	0-2	60.1	38	15	1	4	29-5	58	1.94	233	.179	.286	0		0	109	4		1.2
Total	3	9	5	.643	129	5	0	0-4	139	114	72	15	7	76-7	126	4.27	108	.224	.330	1	1.000	-0	109	4		-0.3

COUCH, JOHNNY   John Daniel   B3.31.1891 Vaughn MT   D12.8.1975 Palo Alto CA   BL/TR/6-0/180   d4.11   Mil 1918   Col Stanford

YEAR	TM LG	W	L	PCT	G	GS	CG-SHO	SV-BS	IP	H	R	HR	HB	BB-IB	SO	ERA	AERA	OAV	OOB	AB-HR-SH	AVG	PB	SUP	APR	DL	PW
1917	Det A	0	0	—	3	0	0	0	13.1	13	6	0	1	1	5	2.70	98	.255	.269	4	.000	-0	0			0.0
1922	Cin N	16	9	.640	43	33	18-2	1	264	301	132	13	5	56	45	3.89	103	.289	.328	91-0-3	.132	-3	105	7		0.4
1923	Cin N	2	7	.222	19	8	3	0	69.1	98	60	2	0	15	14	5.97	65	.344	.377	23-0-1	.174	-1	85	-18		-2.2
	Phi N	2	4	.333	11	7	2	0	65	91	45	4	3	21	18	5.26	87	.335	.389	24	.250	0*	105	-4		-2.3
	Year	4	11	.267	30	15	3	0	134.1	189	105	6	3	36	32	5.63	75	.339	.383	47-0-1	.213	-1	95	-24		-2.2
1924	Phi N	4	8	.333	37	7	3	0	137	170	97	13	1	39	23	4.73	94	.306	.352	49-2-2	.204	-1	65	-9		-0.5
1925	Phi N	5	6	.455	34	7	2-1	2	94.1	112	71	9	1	39	11	5.44	88	.298	.365	31-1-1	.161	-1	76	-7		-0.5
Total	5	29	34	.460	147	62	26-3	6	643	785	411	41	10	171	112	4.63	91	.304	.350	222-3-7	.167	-6	93	-31		-3.3

COUCHEE, MIKE   Michael Eugene   B12.4.1957 San Jose CA   BR/TR/6-0/190   [SDN80 19/473]   d4.5   C1   Col USC

YEAR	TM LG	W	L	PCT	G	GS	CG-SHO	SV-BS	IP	H	R	HR	HB	BB-IB	SO	ERA	AERA	OAV	OOB	AB-HR-SH	AVG	PB	SUP	APR	DL	PW
1983	SD N	0	1	.000	8	0	0	0-0	14	12	8	1	0	6-1	12	5.14	68	.214	.286	2	.500	0	-2	36		-0.1

COUGHLIN, ROSCOE   William Edward   B3.15.1868 Walpole MA   D3.20.1951 Chelsea MA   TR/5-10/160   d4.22

YEAR	TM LG	W	L	PCT	G	GS	CG-SHO	SV-BS	IP	H	R	HR	HB	BB-IB	SO	ERA	AERA	OAV	OOB	AB-HR-SH	AVG	PB	SUP	APR	DL	PW
1890	Chi N	4	6	.400	11	10	10	0	95	102	60	3	4	40	29	4.26	86	.266	.341	39	.256	1	84	-3		-0.5
1891	NY N	3	4	.429	7	7	6	0	61	74	50	5	3	23	22	3.84	83	.289	.355	23	.130	1	115	-6		-0.6
Total	2	7	10	.412	18	17	16	0	156	176	110	8	7	63	51	4.10	85	.275	.348	62	.210	2	96	-9		-0.5

COUMBE, FRITZ   Frederick Nicholas   B12.13.1889 Antrim PA   D3.21.1978 Paradise CA   BL/TL/6-0/152   d4.22

YEAR	TM LG	W	L	PCT	G	GS	CG-SHO	SV-BS	IP	H	R	HR	HB	BB-IB	SO	ERA	AERA	OAV	OOB	AB-HR-SH	AVG	PB	SUP	APR	DL	PW
1914	Bos A	1	2	.333	17	5	1	0	62.1	49	20	0	0	16	17	1.44	186	.222	.274	18	.111	-1	97	6		0.7
	Cle A	1	5	.167	14	5	2	0	55.1	59	31	0	4	16	22	3.25	89	.288	.351	23	.261	1	71	-3		0.0
	Year	2	7	.222	31	10	3	0	117.2	108	51	0	4	32	39	2.29	121	.254	.312	41	.195	0	84	3		0.7
1915	Cle A	4	7	.364	30	12	4-1	0	114	123	63	3	3	37	37	3.47	88	.294	.355	37-0-3	.270	1*	74	6		1.1
1916	Cle A	7	5	.583	29	13	7-2	0	120.1	121	36	1	1	27	39	2.02	149	.251	.307	39-0-2	.154	-1*	109	6		1.8
1917	Cle A	8	6	.571	34	10	4-1	5	134.1	119	50	1	3	35	30	2.14	132	.236	.307							

YEAR	TM LG	W	L	PCT	G	GS	CG-SHO	SV-BS	IP	H	R	HR	HB	BB-IB	SO	ERA	AERA	OAV	OOB	AB-HR-SH	AVG	PB	SUP	APR	DL	PW
1918	Cle A	13	7	.650	30	17	9	3	150	164	61	4	1	52	41	3.06	98	.286	.347	56-0-5	.214	-1*	131	1		0.3
1919	Cle A	1	1	.500	8	2	0	1	23.2	32	15	2	0	9	7	5.32	63	.348	.406	6-0-1	.500	1	129	-4		-0.2
1920	Cin N	0	1	.000	3	0	0	0	14.2	17	13	0	0	4	7	4.91	62	.304	.350	13-1-0	.231	1*		-4		-0.2
1921	Cin N	3	4	.429	28	6	3	1	86.2	89	42	2	1	21	12	3.22	111	.280	.326	25-0-1	.320	1*	80	2		0.4
Total	8	38	38	.500	193	70	30-4	13	761.1	773	335	10	13	217	212	2.80	108	.277	.332	252-1-14	.206	-1	98	10		2.0

COURTNEY, HARRY Henry Seymour B11.19.1898 Asheville NC D12.11.1954 Lyme CT BL/TL/6-4/185 d9.13

YEAR	TM LG	W	L	PCT	G	GS	CG-SHO	SV-BS	IP	H	R	HR	HB	BB-IB	SO	ERA	AERA	OAV	OOB	AB-HR-SH	AVG	PB	SUP	APR	DL	PW
1919	Was A	3	0	1.000	4	3	2-1	0	26.1	25	9	0	0	19	6	2.73	117	.269	.393	10-0-1	.200	-0	163	2		0.1
1920	Was A	8	11	.421	37	24	10-1	0	188	223	128	6	9	77	48	4.74	79	.298	.371	69-1-3	.232	4	99	-23		-1.7
1921	Was A	6	9	.400	30	15	3	1	132.2	159	103	7	8	71	26	5.63	73	.305	.397	47-0-1	.298	2*	95	-24		-2.1
1922	Was A	0	1	.000	5	0	0	0	10	11	4	0	0	9	4	3.60	107	.306	.444	4	.000	-1		1		0.0
	Chi A	5	6	.455	18	11	5	0	86.2	100	52	5	1	37	28	4.98	82	.299	.371	33	.273	3	82	-8		-0.6
	Year	5	7	.417	23	11	5	0	96.2	111	56	5	1	46	32	4.84	84	.300	.379	37	.243	2	82	-5		-0.6
Total	4	22	27	.449	94	53	20-2	1	443.2	518	296	18	18	213	112	4.91	79	.299	.382	163-1-5	.252	7	97	-52		-4.3

COURTRIGHT, JOHN John Charles B5.30.1970 Marion OH BL/TL/6-2/185 [CinN91 8/223] d5.6 Col Duke

| 1995 | Cin N | 0 | 0 | — | 1 | 0 | 0 | 0-0 | 1 | 2 | 1 | 0 | 0 | 0 | 0 | 9.00 | 46 | .500 | .500 | 0 | — | 0 | | -1 | | 0.0 |

COVELESKI, HARRY Harry Frank "The Giant Killer" (b Harry Frank Kowalewski) B4.23.1886 Shamokin PA D8.4.1950 Shamokin PA BB/TL/6-0/180 d9.10 b-Stan

YEAR	TM LG	W	L	PCT	G	GS	CG-SHO	SV-BS	IP	H	R	HR	HB	BB-IB	SO	ERA	AERA	OAV	OOB	AB-HR-SH	AVG	PB	SUP	APR	DL	PW
1907	Phi N	1	0	1.000	4	0	0	0	20	10	2	0	1	3	6	0.00	—	.147	.194	8	.000	-0		5		0.2
1908	Phi N	4	1	.800	6	5	5-2	0	43.2	29	7	0	2	12	22	1.24	196	.196	.265	15-0-2	.133	-0	99	6		0.8
1909	Phi N	6	10	.375	24	17	8-2	1	121.2	109	51	0	5	49	56	2.74	95	.247	.329	37-0-3	.108	-2	63	-2		-0.5
1910	Cin N	1	1	.500	7	4	2	0	39.1	35	14	1	4	42	27	5.26	55	.246	.431	16-0-1	.063	-1	172	-14		-0.8
1914	Det A	22	12	.647	44	36	23-5	2	303.1	251	109	4	4	100	124	2.49	153	.227	.298	95-0-6	.242	5	97	13		2.3
1915	Det A	22	13	.629	50	38	20-1	4	312.2	271	123	2	20	87	150	2.45	124	.233	.298	103-0-8	.175	-2	114	16		1.7
1916	Det A	21	11	.656	44	39	22-3	2	324.1	278	105	6	11	63	108	1.97	145	.237	.282	118-0-1	.212	1	100	26		3.1
1917	Det A	4	6	.400	16	11	2	0	69	70	39	0	7	14	15	2.61	101	.265	.307	22-0-1	.227	-0	146	-3		-0.4
1918	Det A	0	1	.000	3	1	1	0	14	17	9	0	0	6	3	3.86	93	.315	.383	4	.250	0	57	-3		-0.1
Total	9	81	55	.596	198	151	83-13	9	1248	1070	486	13	57	376	511	2.39	118	.235	.301	418-0-22	.189	-0	104	44		6.3

COVELESKI, STAN Stanley Anthony (b Stanislaus Kowalewski) B7.13.1889 Shamokin PA D3.20.1984 South Bend IN BR/TR/5-11/166 d9.10 HF1969 b-Harry

YEAR	TM LG	W	L	PCT	G	GS	CG-SHO	SV-BS	IP	H	R	HR	HB	BB-IB	SO	ERA	AERA	OAV	OOB	AB-HR-SH	AVG	PB	SUP	APR	DL	PW
1912	Phi A	2	1	.667	5	2	2-1	0	21	19	9	0	1	4	9	3.43	90	.231	.277	7	.143	-0	48	0		-0.1
1916	Cle A	15	13	.536	45	27	11-1	3	232	247	100	6	1	58	76	3.41	88	.278	.323	75-1-4	.173	-0	115	-4		-0.4
1917	Cle A	19	14	.576	45	36	24-9	1	298.1	202	78	3	1	94	133	1.81	157	.194	.261	90-7	.134	-4*	77	33		3.2
1918	Cle A	22	13	.629	38	33	25-2	1	311	261	90	2	4	76	87	1.82	165	.229	.279	110-0-5	.191	-3	87	35		3.9
1919	Cle A	24	12	.667	43	34	24-4	4	286	286	99	2	5	60	118	2.61	128	.267	.308	94-0-3	.213	4	98	26		3.9
1920	†Cle A	24	14	.632	41	38	26-3	2	315	284	110	6	4	65	133	2.49	153	.243	.285	111-0-9	.225	3	105	44		5.5
1921	Cle A	23	13	.639	43	40	28-2	2	315	341	137	6	3	84	99	3.37	126	.280	.329	116-0-11	.155	-6	116	33		3.0
1922	Cle A	17	14	.548	35	33	21-3	2	276.2	292	120	14	2	64	98	3.32	121	.274	.316	99-0-2	.101	-7	96	20		1.4
1923	Cle A	13	14	.481	33	31	17-5	2	228	251	98	8	2	42	54	2.76	143	.282	.316	79-0-9	.089	-8	98	26		2.2
1924	Cle A	15	16	.484	37	33	18-2	0	240.1	286	140	6	4	73	58	4.04	106	.294	.346	82-0-1	.134	-5	96	3		-0.1
1925	†Was A	20	5	.800	32	32	15-3	0	241	230	86	7	2	73	58	2.84	149	.255	.312	81-0-11	.111	-8	107	41		2.9
1926	Was A	14	11	.560	36	34	11-3	1	245.1	272	112	1	0	81	50	3.12	124	.286	.342	82-0-3	.207	1	108	16		1.6
1927	Was A	2	1	.667	5	4	0	0	14.1	13	7	0	0	8	3	3.14	129	.250	.350	6	.333	0	113	1		0.2
1928	NY A	5	1	.833	12	8	2	0	58	72	41	5	0	20	5	5.74	66	.323	.379	19-0-4	.053	-2	158	-12		-1.2
Total	14	215	142	.602	450	385	224-38	21	3082	3055	1227	66	30	802	981	2.89	128	.262	.311	1058-0-72	.159	-34	102	262		26.0

COVINGTON, CHET Chester Rogers "Chesty" B11.6.1910 Cairo IL D6.11.1976 Pembroke Park FL BB/TL/6-2/195 d4.23

| 1944 | Phi N | 1 | 1 | .500 | 19 | 0 | 0 | 0 | 38.2 | 46 | 22 | 2 | 0 | 8 | 13 | 4.66 | 78 | .297 | .331 | 6 | .000 | -1 | | -4 | | -0.3 |

COVINGTON, TEX William Wilkes B3.19.1887 Henryville TN D12.10.1931 Denison TX BL/TR/6-1/175 d4.25 b-Sam

1911	Det A	7	1	.875	17	6	5	0	83.2	94	43	2	10	33	29	4.09	85	.297	.381	32	.188	-1	160	-3		-0.4
1912	Det A	3	4	.429	14	9	2-1	0	63.1	58	33	0	3	30	19	4.12	79	.253	.347	15	.133	0	75	-4		-0.4
Total	2	10	5	.667	31	15	7-1	0	147	152	76	2	13	63	48	4.10	82	.278	.367	47	.170	-1	109	-7		-0.8

COWLEY, JOE Joseph Alan B8.15.1958 Lexington KY BR/TR/6-5/210(207-220) d4.13

1982	Atl N	1	2	.333	17	8	0	0-0	52.1	53	27	6	1	16-2	27	4.47	82	.265	.321	15-0-1	.200	0	96	-3	33	-0.2
1984	NY A	9	2	.818	16	11	3-1	0-0	83.1	75	34	12	2	31-1	71	3.56	108	.234	.303	0	—	0	163	4		0.5
1985	NY A	12	6	.667	30	26	1	0-0	159.2	132	75	29	6	85-2	97	3.95	103	.224	.327	0	—	0	116	3		0.3
1986	Chi A	11	11	.500	27	27	4	0-0	162.1	133	81	20	3	83-1	132	3.88	112	.223	.319	0	—	0*	97	7		0.8
1987	Phi N	0	4	.000	5	4	0	0-0	11.2	21	26	2	2	17-1	5	15.43	28	.389	.548	3	.333	1	42	-15		-2.3
Total	5	33	25	.569	95	76	8-1	0-0	469.1	414	243	69	14	232-7	332	4.20	97	.235	.327	18-0-1	.222	1	110	-4	33	-0.9

COX, DANNY Danny Bradford B9.21.1959 Northampton, England BR/TR/6-4/235(225-250) [StLN81 13/319] d8.6 Col Troy St. [DL 1990 StL N 178]

1983	StL N	3	6	.333	12	12	0	0-0	83	92	38	6	0	23-2	36	3.25	112	.286	.332	27-0-3	.074	-2	68	2		0.1
1984	StL N	9	11	.450	29	27	1-1	0-0	156.1	171	81	9	7	54-6	70	4.03	87	.289	.353	53-0-1	.132	0*	96	-11		-1.2
1985	†StL N	18	9	.667	35	35	10-4	0-0	241	226	91	19	3	64-5	131	2.88	124	.251	.300	79-0-8	.152	0	106	17		1.9
1986	StL N	12	13	.480	32	32	8	0-0	220	189	85	14	2	60-6	108	2.90	127	.234	.288	65-0-16	.077	-3	83	17	17	1.2
1987	†StL N	11	9	.550	31	31	2	0-0	199.1	224	99	17	3	71-6	101	3.88	108	.280	.290	69-0-4	.116	-2*	105	4	29	0.1
1991	Phi N	4	6	.400	23	17	0	0-0	102.1	98	57	14	3	25-7	47	3.98	89	.272	.323	23-0-5	.043	-2	70	-3	115	-0.6
1992	Phi N	2	2	.500	9	7	0	0-0	38.1	46	28	3	0	19-1	30	5.40	65	.299	.371	11	.091	-1	119	-10	29	-1.0
	†Pit N	3	1	.750	16	0	0	3-2	24.1	20	9	2	0	8-1	18	3.33	104	.225	.286	3	.000	-1	114	-9		-0.9
	Year	5	3	.625	25	7	0	3-2	62.2	66	37	5	0	27-2	48	4.60	76	.272	.341	14	.071	-1	115	-9		-0.8
1993	†Tor A	7	6	.538	44	0	0	2-4	83.2	73	31	8	0	29-5	84	3.12	140	.230	.293	0	—	0	12	14		1.6
1994	Tor A	1	1	.500	10	0	0	3-0	18.2	7	3	0	1	7-1	14	1.45	337	.113	.211	0	—	0		7	97	0.9
1995	Tor A	1	3	.250	24	0	0	0-2	45	57	40	4	5	33-4	38	7.40	64	.317	.419	0	—	-9	95	14	504	1:3
Total	11	74	75	.497	278	174	21-5	8-8	1298	1292	602	102	19	432-46	723	3.64	104	.263	.323	359-0-41	.109	-9		-13	39	-0.9

COX, ERNIE Ernest Thompson B2.19.1894 Birmingham AL D4.29.1974 Birmingham AL BL/TR/6-1/180 d5.5

| 1922 | Chi A | 0 | 0 | — | 1 | 0 | 0 | 0 | 1 | 1 | 2 | 0 | 0 | 2 | 0 | 18.00 | 23 | .250 | .500 | 0 | — | 0 | | -1 | | -0.1 |

COX, GEORGE George Melvin B11.15.1904 Sherman TX D12.17.1995 Bedford TX BR/TR/6-1/170 d4.12

| 1928 | Chi A | 1 | 2 | .333 | 26 | 2 | 0 | 0 | 89 | 110 | 58 | 6 | 2 | 39 | 22 | 5.26 | 77 | .313 | .385 | 26-0-1 | .077 | -2 | 94 | -10 | | -0.6 |

COX, GLENN Glenn Melvin B2.3.1931 Montebello CA BR/TR/6-2/210* d9.20

1955	KC A	0	2	.000	2	2	0	0	2.1	11	8	0	0	1-0	2	30.86	14	.611	.632	1	.000	0	32	-6		-1.0
1956	KC A	0	0	.000	3	3	1	0	23.1	15	11	2	0	22-0	6	4.24	102	.203	.381	7	.000	-1	34	1		-0.1
1957	KC A	1	0	1.000	10	0	0	0	14.1	18	9	1	0	9-1	8	5.02	79	.321	.415	2	.000	0	-2			-0.1
1958	KC A	0	0	—	2	0	0	0	3.2	6	4	1	0	3-0	1	9.82	40	.400	.500	0	—	0	-2			-0.1
Total	4	1	2	.200	17	5	1	0	43.2	50	32	4	0	35-1	17	6.39	65	.307	.427	10	.000	-1	34	-9		-1.3

COX, CASEY Joseph Casey B7.3.1941 Long Beach CA BR/TR/6-5/200(200-215) d4.15 Col Cal St.-Los Angeles

1966	Was A	4	5	.444	66	0	0	7	113	104	53	6	4	35-15	46	3.50	99	.250	.310	8-0-1	.000	-1		-2		-0.3
1967	Was A	7	4	.636	54	0	0	1	73	67	33	2	4	21-7	32	2.96	107	.250	.311	3	.000	-0		-1		-0.1
1968	Was A	0	1	.000	9	0	0	0	7.2	7	2	0	0	4-0	4	2.35	124	.250	.241	0	—	0		1		0.1
1969	Was A	12	7	.632	52	13	4	0-2	171.2	161	62	15	1	64-7	73	2.78	126	.251	.318	47-0-6	.106	-2	120	14		1.2
1970	Was A	8	12	.400	37	30	1	1-1	192.1	211	108	27	4	44-4	68	4.45	81	.285	.324	58-0-7	.121	-2	97	-19		-2.1
1971	Was A	5	7	.417	54	11	0	7-3	124.1	131	69	9	7	46-8	43	3.98	85	.273	.335	26-0-1	.077	-1	99	-12		-1.4
1972	Tex A	3	5	.375	35	4	0	4-3	65.1	73	41	7	1	26-7	27	4.41	69	.277	.341	9	.111	-1	99	-12		-1.4
	NY A	0	1	.000	5	1	0	0-0	11.2	13	6	2	0	3-1	4	4.63	65	.289	.353	0	—	0	36	-12	22	-0.2
	Year	3	6	.333	40	5	0	4-3	77	86	47	9	1	29-8	31	4.44	68	.278	.343	9-0-1	.111	1	29	-14		-1.7
1973	NY A	0	0	—	2	0	0	0-0	3	5	5	1	0	1-0	0	6.00	62	.357	.444	0	—	0		-1		-0.1
Total	8	39	42	.481	308	59	5	20-9	762	772	374	66	25	234-49	297	3.70	93	.266	.323	151-0-16	.099	-6	99	-34	22	-4.4

COX, LES Leslie Warren B8.14.1905 Junction TX D10.14.1934 San Angelo TX BR/TR/6-0/164 d9.11 Col Texas

| 1926 | Chi A | 0 | 1 | .000 | 2 | 0 | 0 | 0 | 5 | 6 | 10 | 2 | 0 | 5 | 3 | 5.40 | 72 | .261 | .393 | 1 | .500 | 0 | | -4 | | -0.6 |

YEAR	TM LG	W	L	PCT	G	GS	CG-SHO	SV-BS	IP	H	R	HR	HB	BB-IB	SO	ERA	AERA	OAV	OOB	AB-HR-SH	AVG	PB	SUP	APR	DL	PW
COX, RED	Plateau Rex B2.16.1895 Laurel Springs NC D10.15.1984 Roanoke VA BL/TR/6-2/190 d4.17																									
1920	Det A	0	0	—	3	0	0	0	5	9	4	0	0	3	1	5.40	69	.375	.444	1	.000	-0		-1		-0.1
COX, TERRY	Terry Lee B3.30.1949 Odessa TX BR/TR/6-5/215 d9.7																									
1970	Cal A	0	0	—	3	0	0	0-0	2.1	4	1	0	0	0-0	3	3.86	94	.400	.400	0	—	0		0		0.0
COX, BILL	William Donald B6.23.1913 Ashmore IL D2.16.1988 Charleston IL BR/TR/6-1/185 d6.6																									
1936	StL N	0	0	—	2	0	0	0	2.2	4	5	0	0	1	1	6.75	58	.333	.385	0	—	0		-2		-0.1
1937	Chi N	1	0	1.000	3	2	1-1	0	12.2	9	1	0	0	5	8	0.71	648	.200	.280	4	.250	0	47	6		0.4
1938	Chi A	0	2	.000	7	1	0	0	11.2	11	14	0	0	13	5	6.94	70	.244	.414	2	.000	-0	18	-4		-0.6
	StL A	1	4	.200	22	7	1	0	63	81	53	8	0	35	16	7.00	71	.315	.397	17	.059	-1*	81	-13		-0.9
	Year	1	6	.143	29	8	1	0	74.2	92	67	8	0	48	21	6.99	71	.305	.400	19	.053	-2	73	-17		-1.5
1939	StL A	0	2	.000	4	2	1	0	9.1	10	10	0	0	8	7	9.64	50	.256	.383	1	.000	-0*		-5		-0.3
1940	StL A	0	1	.000	12	0	0	0	17.1	23	17	3	0	12	7	7.27	63	.333	.432	1	.000	-0	63	-4		-0.7
Total	5	2	9	.182	50	12	3-1	0	116.2	138	100	11	0	74	45	6.56	74	.296	.392	25	.080	-2	68	-22		-2.2
COYLE, BILL	William Claude B9.20.1871 KY D6.4.1941 San Francisco CA TR d7.7																									
1893	Bos N	0	1	.000	1	1	0	0	3	10	3			2	9.00	55	.368	.415	4	.000	-1	184	-3		-0.3
COZART, CHARLIE	Charles Rhubin B10.17.1919 Lenoir NC D12.31.2004 Lenoir NC BR/TL/6-0/190 d4.17																									
1945	Bos N	1	0	1.000	5	0	0	0	8	10	11	2	0	15	4	10.13	38	.303	.521	2	.000	-0		-6		-0.6
CRABB, ROY	James Roy B8.23.1890 Monticello IA D3.30.1940 Lewistown MT BR/TR/5-11/160 d8.10																									
1912	Chi A	0	1	.000	2	1	0	0	8.2	6	2	0	0	4	3	1.04	308	.214	.313	3	.000	-0	23	2		0.2
	Phi A	2	4	.333	7	7	3	0	43.1	48	22	0	4	17	12	3.74	82	.287	.367	16-0-1	.000	-3	103	-3		-0.6
	Year	2	5	.286	9	8	3	0	52	54	24	0	4	21	15	3.29	94	.277	.359	19-0-1	.000	-3	92	0		-0.4
CRABLE, GEORGE	George Elmer B1.9.1885 NE BL/TL/6-1/190 d8.3																									
1910	Bro N	0	0	—	2	1	1	0	7.1	5	4	0	2	5	3	4.91	62	.217	.400	2	.000	0	123	-1		-0.1
CRABTREE, TIM	Timothy Lyle B10.13.1969 Jackson MI BR/TR/6-4/205(195-225) [TorA92 2/63] d6.23 Col Michigan St.																									
1995	Tor A	0	2	.000	31	0	0	0-2	32	30	16	1	2	13-0	21	3.09	154	.240	.319	0	—	0	4			0.3
1996	Tor A	5	3	.625	53	0	0	1-4	67.1	59	26	4	3	22-4	57	2.54	197	.231	.298	0	—	0	16	21		1.7
1997	Tor A	3	3	.500	37	0	0	2-3	40.2	65	32	7	2	17-3	26	7.08	65	.374	.431	0	—	0	-10	61		-1.3
1998	†Tex A	6	1	.857	64	0	0	0-1	85.1	86	40	3	3	35-2	60	3.59	136	.264	.335	1	.000	-0	11			0.7
1999	†Tex A	5	1	.833	68	0	0	0-3	65	71	26	4	1	18-1	54	3.46	149	.280	.328	0	—	0	12			0.9
2000	Tex A	2	7	.222	68	0	0	2-7	80.1	86	52	7	2	31-6	54	5.15	99	.274	.339	0	—	0	-1			-0.1
2001	Tex A	0	5	.000	21	0	0	4-2	23.1	37	18	3	1	14-2	16	6.56	73	.385	.456	0	—	-0	28	127		-0.8
Total	7	21	22	.488	342	0	0	9-22	394	434	210	29	14	150-18	288	4.20	118	.281	.346	1	.000	-0	28	209		1.4
CRADDOCK, WALT	Walter Anderson B3.25.1932 Pax WV D7.6.1980 Parma Heights OH BR/TL/5-11.5/176* d9.3 Col Syracuse																									
1955	KC A	0	2	.000	4	2	0	0	15	18	14	3	0	10-0	9	7.80	54	.300	.400	5	.000	-1	43	-6		-0.7
1956	KC A	0	2	.000	2	2	0	0	9.1	9	7	1	0	10-0	8	6.75	64	.265	.432	2	.000	-0	21	-2		-0.4
1958	KC A	0	3	.000	23	1	0	0	36.2	41	25	4	1	20-0	22	5.89	66	.289	.376	2	.000	-0	69	-7		-0.5
Total	3	0	7	.000	29	5	0	0	61	68	46	8	1	40-0	39	6.49	62	.288	.391	9	.000	-1	40	-15		-1.6
CRAFT, MOLLY	Maurice Montague B11.28.1895 Portsmouth VA D10.25.1978 Los Angeles CA BR/TR/6-2/165 d8.8 Mil 1918																									
1916	Was A	0	1	.000	1	1	1	0	11	12	5	0	0	9	9	3.27	85	.316	.409	4	.000	-0*	27	-1		0.0
1917	Was A	0	0	—	8	0	0	1	14	17	10	0	0	3	2	3.86	68	.315	.403	2	.500	-0	-3			-0.1
1918	Was A	0	0	—	3	0	0	0	7	5	1	0	0	1	5	1.29	212	.208	.240	2	.000	-0	1			0.0
1919	Was A	0	3	.000	16	2	0	1	48.2	59	28	2	2	18	17	3.88	83	.309	.374	18-0-1	.111	-2	98	-4		-0.4
Total	4	0	4	.000	29	3	1	2	80.2	93	44	2	2	33	33	3.57	84	.303	.374	26-0-1	.115	-2	77	-7		-0.5
CRAGHEAD, HOWARD	Howard Oliver "Judge" B5.25.1908 Selma CA D7.14.1962 San Diego CA BR/TR/6-2/200 d4.30																									
1931	Cle A	0	0	—	4	0	0	0	5.2	8	14	3	0	10	2	6.35	73	.320	.370	0	—	0	-1			0.0
1933	Cle A	0	0	—	11	0	0	0	17.1	19	13	1	1	10	2	6.23	71	.292	.395	3	.000	-0	-3			-0.2
Total	2	0	0	—	15	0	0	0	23	27	17	1	1	12	4	6.26	72	.300	.388	3	.000	-0	-4			-0.2
CRAIG, GEORGE	George McCarthy "Lefty" B11.15.1887 Philadelphia PA D4.23.1911 Indianapolis IN TL d7.19																									
1907	Phi A	0	0	—	2	0	0	0	1.2	2	3	0	2	3		10.80	24	.286	.583	1	.000	-0		-2		-0.1
CRAIG, PETE	Peter Joel B7.10.1940 LaSalle ON, Can. BL/TR/6-5/220* d9.6 Col Detroit Mercy																									
1964	Was A	0	0	—	2	1	0	0	1.2	8	9	1	0	4-1	0	48.60	8	.667	.750	0	—	0	192	-8		-0.4
1965	Was A	0	3	.000	3	3	0	0	14.1	18	15	1	0	8-1	2	8.16	43	.321	.394	3	.667	1	101	-7		-1.1
1966	Was A	0	0	—	1	0	0	0	2	2	2	0	0	1-1	1	4.50	77	.250	.333	0	—	0	-1			0.0
Total	3	0	3	.000	6	4	0	0	18	28	26	2	0	13-3	3	11.50	30	.368	.451	3	.667	1	126	-16		-1.5
CRAIG, ROGER	Roger Lee B2.17.1930 Durham NC BR/TR/6-4/191(180-200) d7.17 M10/C13 Col North Carolina St.																									
1955	†Bro N	5	3	.625	21	10	3	2	90.2	81	37	8	1	43-6	48	2.78	146	.238	.323	26-0-1	.077	-2	132	11		0.6
1956	†Bro N	12	11	.522	35	32	8-2	1	199	169	90	25	4	47-5	109	3.71	107	.231	.313	61-0-5	.016	-5	104	6		-0.1
1957	Bro N	6	9	.400	32	13	1	0	111.1	102	58	18	2	41-5	69	4.61	90	.249	.328	29-0-2	.138	-1	67	-2		-0.4
1958	LA N	2	1	.667	9	2	1	0	32	30	20	3	0	12-1	16	4.50	91	.242	.309	9	.000	-1	121	-2		-0.2
1959	†LA N	11	5	.688	29	17	7-4	0	152.2	122	49	13	1	45-3	76	2.06	205	.217	.275	52-0-4	.058	-2	88	30		2.6
1960	LA N	8	3	.727	21	15	6-1	0	115.2	99	48	8	3	43-4	69	3.27	121	.230	.304	36-0-3	.056	-2	117	8	44	0.5
1961	LA N	5	6	.455	40	14	2	2	112.2	130	87	22	4	52-7	63	6.15	71	.288	.365	27-0-3	.148	-0	104	-21		-2.0
1962	NY N	10	24	.294	42	33	13	3	233.1	261	133	35	7	70-3	118	4.51	93	.288	.341	69-0-3	.087	-2	57	-7		-0.9
1963	NY N	5	22	.185	46	31	14	2	236	249	117	28	6	58-2	108	3.25	117	.276	.316	48-0-1	.208	2	80	7		1.1
1964	†StL N	7	9	.438	39	19	3	5	166	180	76	16	4	35-4	84	3.25	117	.276	.316	11-0-2	.182	-0	-1			-0.7
1965	Cin N	1	4	.200	40	0	0	3	64.1	74	33	6	3	25-7	30	3.64	103	.289	.355	4	.000	-0	-5	15		-0.3
1966	Phi N	2	1	.667	14	0	0	1	22.2	31	15	4	0	5-2	13	5.56	65	.326	.393	4			-6	59		-0.4
Total	12	74	98	.430	368	186	58-7	19	1536.1	1528	763	186	35	522-48	803	3.83	104	.259	.321	448-0-28	.085	-22	89	18	59	-0.7
CRAIN, JESSE	Jesse Alan B7.5.1981 Toronto ON, Can. BR/TR/6-1/205* [MinA02 2/61] d8.5 Col Houston																									
2004	†Min A	3	0	1.000	22	0	0	0-1	27	17	6	2	1	12-1	14	2.00	231	.179	.278	0	—	0	8			2.
2005	Min A	12	5	.706	75	0	0	1-3	79.2	61	28	6	5	29-7	25	2.71	162	.218	.300	0	—	0	14			3.
Total	2	15	5	.750	97	0	0	1-4	106.2	78	34	8	6	41-8	39	2.53	176	.208	.294	0	—	0	22			3.
CRAM, JERRY	Gerald Allen B12.9.1947 Los Angeles CA BR/TR/6-0/180* d9.3 Col Riverside (CA) CC																									
1969	KC A	0	1	.000	6	0	0	0-0	16.2	15	8	0	0	6-1	10	3.24	114	.231	.296	3	.000	-0	108	0		0.
1974	NY N	0	1	.000	10	0	0	0-0	22.1	22	4	1	0	4-3	8	1.61	224	.275	.310	3	.333	0	5			0.
1975	NY N	0	1	.000	4	0	0	0-0	5	7	3	2	0	2-0	2	5.40	65	.333	.391	0	—	0	-1			0.
1976	KC A	0	0	—	4	0	0	0-0	4.1	8	1	0	1	1-0	2	6.23	56	.421	.450	0	—	0	-1			0.
Total	4	0	3	.000	23	2	0	0-0	48.1	52	16	3	1	13-4	22	2.98	121	.281	.328	6	.167	-0	108	3		0.
CRAMER, BILL	William Wendell B5.22.1891 Bedford IN D9.11.1966 Fort Wayne IN BR/TR/6-0/175 d6.25																									
1912	Cin N	0	0	—	2	0	0	0	2.1	6	6	0	0	0	1	0.00	—	.500	.500	1	.000	-0		-0.
CRANDALL, DOC	James Otis B10.8.1887 Wadena IN D8.17.1951 Bell CA BR/TR/5-10.5/180 d4.24 C4 ▲																									
1908	NY N	12	12	.500	32	24	13	0	214.2	198	83	3	9	59	77	2.93	82	.248	.307	72-2-6	.222	5*	125	-8		-0.
1909	NY N	6	4	.600	30	8	4	6	122	117	58	5	3	33	55	2.88	89	.252	.305	41-1-2	.244	3	150	-4		0.
1910	NY N	17	4	.810	42	18	13-2	5	207.2	194	86	10	4	43	73	2.63	116	.246	.289	73-1-3	.342	10*	157	8		1.
1911	†NY N	15	5	.750	41	15	9-2	5	198.2	199	82	10	6	51	94	2.63	128	.256	.307	113-2-5	.239	6*	138	14		2.
1912	†NY N	13	7	.650	37	11	7	3	162	181	85	7	2	35	60	3.61	94	.286	.326	80-0-3	.313	6*	167	-1		0.
1913	†NY N	2	4	.333	24	1	1	1	55.1	61	24	3	1	11	28	3.09	101	.293	.338	25	.280	2*	0	1		0.
	†NY N	2	0	1.000	11	1	1	2	42.1	41	17	1	0	11	14	2.55	122	.248	.295	22	.364	3*	289	2		0.
	Year	4	4	.500	35	2	2	6	97.2	102	45	3	1	24	42	2.86	109	.273	.319	47	.319	5	145	**2**		0.
1914	StL F	13	9	.591	27	21	18-1	0	196	194	94	8	2	52	84	3.54	86	.256	.305	278-2-5	.309	7*	102	-9		2.
1915	StL F	21	15	.583	51	33	22-4	1	312.2	307	116	9	1	60	117	2.59	111	.263	.314	141-1-0	.284	12*	103	7		2.
1916	StL A	0	0	—	2	0	0	0	1.1	7	9	0	1	0	0	27.00	10	.636	.692	12	.083	-0*	-5			-0.

YEAR	TM LG	W	L	PCT	G	GS	CG-SHO	SV-BS	IP	H	R	HR	HB	BB-IB	SO	ERA	AERA	OAV	OOB	AB-HR-SH	AVG	PB	SUP	APR	DL	PW
1918	Bos N	1	2	.333	5	3	3	0	34	39	11	1	1	4	4	2.38	113	.307	.333	28	.286	1*	56	1		0.3
Total	10	102	62	.622	302	134	91-9	25	1546.2	1538	669	52	39	379	606	2.92	101	.310	.310	885-9-24	.286	54	124	4		6.8

CRANE, ED Edward Nicholas "Cannon-Ball" B5.27.1862 Boston MA D9.20.1896 Rochester NY BR/TR/5-10.5/204 d4.17 ▲

YEAR	TM LG	W	L	PCT	G	GS	CG-SHO	SV-BS	IP	H	R	HR	HB	BB-IB	SO	ERA	AERA	OAV	OOB	AB-HR-SH	AVG	PB	SUP	APR	DL	PW
1884	Bos U	0	2	.000	4	2	1	0	18	17	14	1		6	13	4.00	59	.233	.291	428-12	.285	0*	36	-3		-0.2
1886	Was N	1	7	.125	10	8	7-1	0	70	91	85	4		53	39	7.20	45	.313	.419	292	.171	-1*	38	-30		-2.5
1888	†NY N	5	6	.455	12	11	11-2	1	92.2	70	51	3	2	40	58	2.43	113	.193	.277	37-1	.162	1	75	2		0.3
1889	†NY N	14	11	.560	29	25	23	0	230.2	221	159	10	10	136	130	3.63	109	.244	.350	103-2	.204	3	112	5		0.5
1890	NY P	16	19	.457	43	35	28	0	330.1	323	280	12	10	208	116	4.63	98	.245	.352	146	.315	7	108	-5		0.0
1891	Cin AA	14	14	.500	32	31	25-1	0	250	216	151	3	14	139	122	**2.45**	**167**	.225	.332	110-1	.155	-6*	76	35		2.6
	Cin N	4	8	.333	15	13	11-1	0	116.2	134	91	3		64	51	4.09	83	.277	.365	46	.109	-3	90	-10		-1.1
1892	NY N	16	24	.400	47	42	35-2	1	364.1	350	276	10	12	189	174	3.80	85	.243	.335	163	.245	4*	112	-28		-2.3
1893	NY N	2	4	.333	10	7	4	0	68.1	84	62	2	6	41	11	5.93	79	.294	.393	26	.462	4*	144	-8		-0.1
	Bro N	0	2	.000	2	2	1	0	10	19	19	2	1	9	5	13.50	33	.388	.492	5	.400	0*	79	-10		-1.1
	Year	2	6	.250	12	9	5	0	78.1	103	81	4	7	50	16	6.89	67	.307	.408	31	.452	5	129	-16		-1.2
Total	8	72	97	.426	204	176	146-7	2	1551	1525	1188	50	58	885	719	3.99	95	.247	.347	1356-16	.237	11	98	-52		-3.9

CRAWFORD, CARLOS Carlos Lamonte B10.4.1971 Charlotte NC BR/TR/6-1/190 [CleA90 51/1279] d6.7 Col Montreal

| 1996 | Phi N | 0 | 1 | .000 | 1 | 1 | 0 | 0-0 | 3.2 | 7 | 10 | 1 | 1 | 2-0 | 4 | 4.91 | 88 | .389 | .476 | 1 | .000 | -0 | 105 | -4 | | -0.5 |

CRAWFORD, LARRY Charles Lowrie B4.27.1914 Swissvale PA D12.20.1994 Hanover PA BL/TL/6-1/165 d7.21

| 1937 | Phi N | 0 | 0 | — | 6 | 0 | 0 | 0 | 6 | 12 | 10 | 2 | 0 | 1 | 2 | 15.00 | 29 | .387 | .406 | 0 | | 0 | | -6 | | -0.3 |

CRAWFORD, JIM James Frederick "Catfish" B9.29.1950 Chicago IL BL/TL/6-3/200* [HouN72 14/321] d4.6 Col Arizona St.

1973	Hou N	2	4	.333	48	0	0	6-4	70	69	41	7	2	33-8	56	4.50	81	.256	.338	13	.231	1		-8		-0.6
1975	Hou N	3	5	.375	44	0	0	4-3	86.2	92	40	7	2	37-4	37	3.63	93	.280	.354	17-0-1	.294	2	91	-3		-0.1
1976	Det A	1	8	.111	32	5	1	2-1	109.1	115	65	4	0	43-4	68	4.53	82	.275	.335	0	—	0	57	-10		-0.6
1977	Det A	7	8	.467	37	7	0	1-2	126	156	82	13	1	50-5	91	4.79	90	.310	.369	0	—	0	77	-9		-0.9
1978	Det A	2	3	.400	20	0	0	0-0	39.1	45	24	3	2	19-3	24	4.35	90	.292	.371	0	—	0		-3		-0.4
Total	5	15	28	.349	181	14	1	13-10	431.1	477	252	27	7	182-24	276	4.40	87	.285	.353	30-0-1	.267	3	74	-33		-2.6

CRAWFORD, JOE Joseph Randal B5.2.1970 Gainesville FL BL/TL/6-3/225 [NYN91 17/459] d4.7 Col Kent St.

| 1997 | NY N | 4 | 3 | .571 | 19 | 2 | 0 | 0 | 46.1 | 36 | 18 | 7 | 0 | 13-1 | 25 | 3.30 | 121 | .216 | .272 | 11 | .000 | -1 | 46 | 4 | | 0.5 |

CRAWFORD, PAXTON Paxton Keith B8.4.1977 Little Rock AR BR/TR/6-3/205* [BosA95 9/242] d7.1 [DL 2002 Bos A 82]

2000	Bos A	2	1	.667	7	4	0	0-0	29	25	15	0	2	13-2	17	3.41	147	.240	.325	0		0	75	4		0.3
2001	Bos A	3	0	1.000	8	7	0	0-0	36	40	19	3	2	13-0	25	4.75	93	.276	.342	0	—	0	143	0		0.0
Total	2	5	1	.833	15	11	0	0-0	65	65	34	3	4	26-2	42	4.15	113	.261	.335	0	—	0	115	4	82	0.3

CRAWFORD, STEVE Steven Ray B4.29.1958 Pryor OK BR/TR/6-5/225(220-240) d9.2

1980	Bos A	2	0	1.000	6	4	2	0-0	32.1	41	14	3	0	8-2	10	3.62	118	.306	.345	0		0	142	2		0.1
1981	Bos A	0	5	.000	14	11	0	0-0	57.2	69	38	10	3	18-0	29	4.99	78	.301	.354	0	—	0	106	-7		-0.6
1982	Bos A	1	0	1.000	5	0	0	0-0	9	14	3	0	0	0-0	2	2.00	218	.341	.341	0	—	0	2	129		0.2
1984	Bos A	5	0	1.000	35	0	0	1-3	62	69	31	6	1	21-5	21	3.34	126	.286	.341	0	—	0	4			0.3
1985	Bos A	6	5	.545	44	1	0	12-4	91	103	47	5	0	28-8	58	3.76	115	.289	.338	0	—	0	105	3	30	0.4
1986	†Bos A	0	2	.000	40	0	0	4-4	57.1	69	29	5	0	19-7	32	3.92	107	.308	.359	0	—	0	1	45		0.1
1987	Bos A	5	4	.556	29	0	0	0-0	72.2	91	48	13	2	32-2	43	5.33	86	.314	.386	0	—	0	-7	15		-0.7
1989	KC A	3	1	.750	25	0	0	0-1	54	48	19	2	3	19-3	33	2.83	137	.242	.317	0	—	0	6			0.5
1990	KC A	5	4	.556	46	0	0	1-1	80	79	38	7	3	23-3	54	4.16	93	.254	.310	0	—	0	-1	29		0.0
1991	KC A	3	2	.600	33	0	0	1-0	46.2	60	31	3	1	17-5	38	5.98	69	.311	.367	0	—	0	-8	72		-0.8
Total	10	30	23	.566	277	16	2	19-13	562.2	643	298	54	13	186-35	320	4.17	100	.290	.346	0	—	0	113	-5	320	-0.5

CREEK, DOUG Paul Douglas B3.1.1969 Winchester VA BL/TL/6-0/200(200-225) [StLN91 7/181] d9.17 Col Georgia Tech

1995	StL N	0	0	—	6	0	0	0-0	6.2	2	0	0	3	3-0	10	0.00	—	.095	.208	0		0	3			0.1
1996	SF N	0	2	.000	63	0	0	0-1	48.1	45	41	11	2	32-2	38	6.52	64	.243	.361	0	—	0	-14			-0.7
1997	SF N	1	2	.333	3	3	0	0-0	13.1	12	12	1	0	14-0	14	6.75	61	.240	.406	1-0-1	.000	-0	89	-4		-0.7
1999	Chi N	0	0	—	3	0	0	0-0	6	6	7	1	0	8-1	6	10.50	44	.261	.438	3-0-2	.333	0		-4		-0.2
2000	TB A	1	3	.250	45	0	0	1-2	60.2	49	33	10	2	39-3	73	4.60	107	.224	.342	0	—	0	2			0.2
2001	TB A	2	5	.286	66	0	0	0-3	62.2	51	34	7	4	49-5	66	4.31	105	.230	.374	0	—	0	1			0.1
2002	TB A	2	1	.667	29	0	0	0-2	37.1	39	27	8	3	21-1	37	6.27	72	.264	.366	1	.000	-0	-7			-0.5
	Sea A	1	1	.500	23	0	0	0-0	18.1	18	10	2	4	14-1	19	4.91	88	.257	.404	0	—	0	-1			-0.1
	Year	3	2	.600	52	0	0	0-2	55.2	57	37	10	7	35-2	56	5.82	76	.261	.379	1	.000	-0	-7			-0.6
2003	Tor A	0	0	—	21	0	0	0-1	13.2	16	6	2	2	12-3	11	3.29	144	.264	.406	0	—	-0	2	135		0.1
2005	Det A	0	0	—	20	0	0	0-0	22.1	27	18	7	0	7-0	18	6.85	62	.293	.340	0	—	0	-6			-0.3
Total	9	7	14	.333	279	3	0	1-9	289.1	263	188	49	17	199-16	292	5.32	84	.243	.366	5-0-3	.200	0	89	-28	135	-2.0

CREEL, JACK Jack Dalton "Tex" B4.23.1916 Kyle TX D8.13.2002 Houston TX BR/TR/6-0/165 d4.22

| 1945 | StL N | 5 | 4 | .556 | 26 | 8 | 2 | 2 | 87 | 78 | 41 | 5 | 6 | 45 | 34 | 4.14 | 90 | .245 | .349 | 26-0-4 | .077 | -2* | 116 | -2 | | -0.3 |

CREEL, KEITH Steven Keith B2.4.1959 Dallas TX BR/TR/6-2/180* [KCA80 S1/4] d5.25 Col Texas

1982	KC A	1	4	.200	9	6	0	0-0	41.2	43	28	8	0	25-0	13	5.40	76	.267	.362	0		0	74	-6		-0.6
1983	KC A	2	5	.286	25	10	1	0-0	89.1	116	66	17	2	35-0	31	6.35	65	.320	.380	0	—	0	86	-20		-1.4
1985	Cle A	2	5	.286	15	8	0	0-0	62	73	35	7	2	23-2	31	4.79	87	.296	.354	0	—	0	109	-4		-0.4
1987	Tex A	0	0	—	6	0	0	0-0	9.2	12	5	2	0	5-0	5	4.66	97	.293	.370	0	—	0	0			0.0
Total	4	5	14	.263	55	24	1	0-0	202.2	244	134	34	4	88-2	80	5.60	74	.300	.368	0	—	0	91	-30		-2.4

CREMINS, BOB Robert Anthony "Lefty","Crooked Arm" B2.15.1906 Pelham Manor NY D3.27.2004 Pelham NY BL/TL/5-11/178 d8.17

| 1927 | Bos A | 0 | 0 | — | 4 | 0 | 0 | 0 | 5.1 | 5 | 4 | 0 | 3 | 0 | 5.06 | 83 | .250 | .348 | 0 | | 0 | | -1 | | 0.0 |

CRESS, WALKER Walker James "Foots" B3.6.1917 Ben Hur VA D4.21.1996 Baton Rouge LA BR/TR/6-5/205 d4.27 Col Louisiana St.

1948	Cin N	0	1	.000	30	2	1	0	60	60	32	2	1	42	33	4.50	87	.271	.390	8-0-1	.500	2*	79	-3		0.0
1949	Cin N	0	0	—	3	0	0	0	2	2	0	0	1	3	0.00	—	.286	.500	0	—	0*	1			0.0
Total	2	0	1	.000	33	2	1	0	62	62	32	2	1	45	33	4.35	90	.272	.394	8-0-1	.500	2	79	-2		0.0

CRESSEND, JACK John Baptiste B5.13.1975 New Orleans LA BR/TR/6-1/185* d8.26 Col Tulane

2000	Min A	0	0	—	11	0	0	0-0	13.2	20	8	0	0	6-0	6	5.27	100	.364	.426	0		0	0			0.0
2001	Min A	3	2	.600	44	0	0	0-2	56.1	50	24	6	1	19-2	40	3.67	127	.237	.291	0	—	0	-6	114		0.6
2002	Min A	0	1	.000	23	0	0	0-0	32	40	25	6	1	14-0	22	5.91	76	.305	.392	0	—	0	-6	114		-0.3
2003	Cle A	2	1	.667	33	0	0	0-1	43	40	12	1	2	9-1	28	2.51	176	.252	.300	0	—	0	10			0.5
2004	Cle A	0	1	.000	11	0	0	0-0	15.2	22	11	4	0	10-2	8	6.32	69	.333	.416	0	—	0	-3			-0.2
Total	5	5	5	.500	122	0	0	0-3	160.2	172	80	17	4	60-7	104	4.20	109	.277	.342	0	—	0	7	114		0.6

CREWS, TIM Stanley Timothy B4.3.1961 Tampa FL D3.23.1993 Orlando FL BR/TR/6-0/192(180-195) [MilA81*2/48] d7.27 Col Valencia (FL) CC

1987	LA N	1	1	.500	20	0	0	3-3	29	30	9	2	2	8-1	20	2.48	160	.268	.325	2	.000	-0		5		0.4
1988	LA N	4	0	1.000	42	0	0	0-1	71.2	77	29	3	0	16-7	45	3.14	107	.278	.312	5-0-1	.200	0	1			0.0
1989	LA N	0	1	.000	44	0	0	1-2	61.2	69	27	7	2	23-9	56	3.21	107	.284	.351	0	—	0	1			0.0
1990	LA N	4	5	.444	66	2	0	5-4	107.1	98	40	9	1	24-6	76	2.77	133	.238	.280	7	.000	-1	98	10		0.7
1991	LA N	2	3	.400	60	0	0	6-2	76	75	30	7	0	19-11	53	3.43	105	.256	.299	1	.000	0		3		0.7
1992	LA N	0	3	.000	49	2	0	0-1	78	95	46	6	2	20-9	43	5.19	67	.310	.351	0	—	0		-1		-0.6
Total	6	11	13	.458	281	4	0	15-13	423.2	444	181	34	7	110-43	293	3.44	103	.270	.316	22-0-1	.136	-0	82	7		0.2

CRIDER, JERRY Jerry Stephen B9.2.1941 Sioux Falls SD BR/TR/6-2/200* d5.21

1969	Min A	1	0	1.000	21	1	0	1-1	28.2	31	15	3	2	15-6	16	4.71	77	.284	.378	9	.444	2	267	-2		0.1
1970	Chi A	4	7	.364	32	8	0	4-0	91	101	49	13	2	34-2	40	4.45	87	.288	.350	24-0-2	.083	-1	83	-5		-0.8
Total	2	5	7	.417	53	9	0	5-1	119.2	132	64	16	4	49-8	56	4.51	85	.287	.357	33-0-2	.182	-1	103	-7		-0.7

CRIM, CHUCK Charles Robert B7.23.1961 Van Nuys CA BR/TR/6-0/185(170-190) [MilA82 17/443] d4.8 Col Hawaii-Manoa

| 1987 | Mil A | 6 | 8 | .429 | 53 | 0 | 0 | 12-5 | 130 | 133 | 60 | 15 | 3 | 39-5 | 56 | 3.67 | 126 | .266 | .322 | 0 | | 0 | 115 | 12 | | 1.3 |
| 1988 | Mil A | 7 | 6 | .538 | **70** | 0 | 0 | 9-2 | 105 | 95 | 38 | 11 | 4 | 28-3 | 52 | 2.91 | 137 | .247 | .298 | 0 | — | 0 | | 13 | | 1.6 |

YEAR TM LG	W	L	PCT	G	GS	CG-SHO	SV-BS	IP	H	R	HR	HB	BB-IB	SO	ERA	AERA	OAV	OOB	AB-HR-SH	AVG	PB	SUP	APR	DL	PW
1989 Mil A	9	7	.563	76	0	0	7-7	117.2	114	42	7	2	36-9	59	2.83	136	.259	.314	0	—	0		13		1.8
1990 Mil A	3	5	.375	67	0	0	11-5	85.2	88	39	7	2	23-4	39	3.47	112	.261	.309	0	—	0		4	19	0.4
1991 Mil A	8	5	.615	66	0	0	3-2	91.1	115	52	9	2	25-9	39	4.63	86	.305	.351	0	—	0		-7		-0.9
1992 Cal A	7	6	.538	57	0	0	1-2	87	100	56	11	6	29-6	30	5.17	78	.293	.355	0	—	0		-12		-1.6
1993 Cal A	2	2	.500	11	0	0	0-0	15.1	17	11	2	2	5-1	10	5.87	77	.298	.369	0	—	0		-2		-0.4
1994 Chi N	5	4	.556	49	1	0	2-3	64.1	69	36	9	1	24-6	43	4.48	94	.271	.336	2	.000	-0	173	-2		-0.3
Total 8	47	43	.522	449	6	0	45-26	696.1	731	334	71	20	209-43	334	3.83	107	.272	.326	2	.000	-0	137	19	19	1.9
CRIMIAN, JACK John Melvin B2.17.1926 Philadelphia PA BR/TR/5-10/180* d7.3																									
1951 StL N	1	0	1.000	11	0	0	1	17	24	17	3	0	8	5	9.00	44	.338	.405	3	.333	0		-9		-0.6
1952 StL N	0	0	—	5	0	0	1	8.1	15	9	4	0	4	4	9.72	38	.417	.475	1	.000	0		-5		-0.2
1956 KC A	4	8	.333	54	7	0	3	129	129	87	19	5	49-2	59	5.51	79	.265	.334	22-0-5	.227	1*	94	-16		-1.3
1957 Det A	0	1	.000	4	0	0		5.2	9	8	1	0	4-2	1	12.71	30	.375	.448	0	—	0		-5		-0.8
Total 4	5	9	.357	74	7	0	4	160	177	121	27	5	65-4	69	6.36	67	.287	.355	26-0-5	.231	1	94	-35		-2.9
CRISS, DODE Dode B3.12.1885 Sherman MS D9.8.1955 Sherman MS BL/TR/6-2/200 d4.20 ▲																									
1908 StL A	0	1	.000	9	1	0	0	18	15	14	1	3	13	9	3.42	71	.262	.369	48	.292	5*	78	-8		-0.3
1909 StL A	1	5	.167	11	6	3	0	55.1	53	33	0	2	32	43	1.40	177	.176	.309	91-1-0	.231	1*		2		0.4
1910 StL A	2	1	.667	6	0	0	0	19.1	12	7	0	4	9	9	8.35	40	.333	.429	83-2-1	.253	0*	43	-9		-0.7
1911 StL A	0	2	.000	4	2	0	0	18.1	24	21	0	2	10	9	4.38	59	.259	.375	304-3-1	.276	8	96	-22		-0.8
Total 4	3	9	.250	30	9	3	0	111	104	75	1	11	64	70	6.50	37	.250	.408	82	.341	1*	343	-7		-0.2
CRISTALL, BILL William Arthur "Lefty" B9.12.1878 Odessa, Russia D1.28.1939 Buffalo NY BL/TL/5-7/145 d9.3																									
1901 Cle A	1	5	.167	6	6	5-1	0	48.1	54	42	1	4	30	12	4.84	73	.280	.388	20-0-1	.350	2	111	-8		-0.5
CRISTANTE, LEO Dante Leo B12.10.1926 Detroit MI D8.24.1977 Dearborn MI BR/TR/6-1/195* d4.21																									
1951 Phi N	1	1	.500	10	1	0	0	22	28	13	3	1	9	6	4.91	78	.318	.388	6-0-1	.167	-0	206	-3		-0.2
1955 Det A	0	1	.000	20	1	0	0	36.2	37	15	1	0	14-2	9	3.19	120	.261	.325	7	.000	-1	162	3		0.0
Total 2	1	2	.333	30	2	0	0	58.2	65	28	4	1	23-2	15	3.84	100	.283	.349	13-0-1	.077	-1	184	0		-0.2
CRITCHLEY, MORRIE Morris Arthur B3.26.1850 New London CT D3.6.1910 Pittsburgh PA 6-1/190 d5.8																									
1882 Pit AA	1	0	1.000	1	1	1-1	0	9	7	0	0	0	1	3	—		.200	.222	5	.000	-1	39	3		0.2
StL AA	0	4		4	4	4	0	34	43	31	3		7	2	4.24	66	.289	.321	14	.214	-0	87	-4		-0.5
Year	1	4	.200	5	5	5-1	0	43	50	31	3		8	5	3.35	83	.272	.302	19	.158	-1	78	-3		-0.3
CROCKER, CLAUDE Claude Arthur B7.20.1924 Caroleen NC D12.19.2002 Clinton SC BR/TR/6-2/185 d8.1 Col North Carolina-Asheville																									
1944 Bro N	0	0	—	2	0	0	0	3.1	6	4	0	0	5	1	10.80	33	.400	.550	1	1.000	0		-2		-0.
1945 Bro N	0	0	—	1	0	0	0	2	2	0	0	0	1	1	0.00	—	.286	.375	0	—	0		1		0.
Total 2	0	0	—	3	0	0	0	5.1	8	4	0	0	6	2	6.75	54	.364	.500	1	1.000	0		-1		0.
CRONE, RAY Raymond Hayes B8.7.1931 Memphis TN BR/TR/6-2/185(165-190) d4.13																									
1954 Mil N	1	0	1.000	19	2	1	1	49	44	11	6	1	19	33	2.02	184	.247	.322	10	.200	-0	48	11		0.
1955 Mil N	10	9	.526	33	15	6-1	0	140.1	117	63	11	0	42-7	76	3.46	108	.227	.285	44-0-3	.159	-1	90	4		-1.
1956 Mil N	11	10	.524	35	21	6	2	169.2	173	92	19	1	44-3	73	3.87	89	.263	.307	49-0-5	.122	1	122	-11		-1.
1957 Mil N	3	1	.750	11	5	2	0	42.1	54	23	8	0	15-2	15	4.46	78	.312	.365	11-0-1	.182	1	161	-5		-0.
NY N	4	8	.333	25	17	2	1	120.2	131	68	11	3	40-1	56	4.33	91	.272	.330	40-0-1	.025	-4	113	-6		-1.
Year	7	9	.438	36	22	4	1	163	185	91	19	3	55-3	71	4.36	88	.282	.339	51-0-2	.059	-3	124	-11		-1.
1958 SF N	1	2	.333	14	1	0	0	24	35	18	5	0	13-0	7	6.75	56	.354	.421	2	.000	-0	94	-7		-0.
Total 5	30	30	.500	137	61	17-1	0	546	554	275	60	5	173-13	260	3.87	95	.263	.319	156-0-10	.115	-3	112	-14		-2.
CRONIN, JACK John J. B5.26.1874 Staten Island NY D7.12.1929 Middletown NY BR/TR/6-0/200 d8.24																									
1895 Bro N	0	0	—	2	0	0	2	10	10	8	0	0	3	1	10.80	41	.417	.481	2	.500	1	140	-4		-0.
1898 Pit N	2	2	.500	4	4	2-1	0	28	35	14	0	0	8	9	3.54	101	.304	.350	10	.100	-0	136	-7		-0.
1899 Cin N	2	2	.500	5	5	5	0	41	56	35	2	5	16	9	5.49	71	.324	.397	17	.118	-1	83	1		-0.
1901 Det A	13	16	.448	30	28	21-1	0	219.2	261	145	6	11	42	62	3.89	99	.292	.331	85-0-4	.247	2*		1		1
1902 Det A	0	0	—	4	0	0	0	17.1	26	21	1	3	6	5	9.35	39	.347	.430	7	.000	-1		-10		-0.
Bal A	3	5	.375	10	8	8	0	75.2	66	29	1	0	24	20	2.62	144	.236	.296	27-0-2	.148	-1	69	10		1
Year	3	5	.375	14	8	8	0	93	92	52	2	3	32	25	3.87	97	.259	.326	34-0-2	.118	-2	70	1		0
NY N	5	6	.455	13	12	11	0	114	105	49	3	0	18	52	2.45	115	.245	.275	65-0-2	.169	-1*	73	4		0
1903 NY N	6	4	.600	13	12	11	1	115.2	130	67	5	6	37	50	3.81	88	.284	.345	46-0-2	.196	-3	80	4		-0.
1904 Bro N	12	23	.343	40	34	33-4	3	307	284	132	10	12	79	110	2.70	102	.245	.300	108-0-3	.157	-3	89	-7		-0
Total 7	43	58	.426	128	102	88-6	3	923.1	973	502	28	37	235	318	3.40	96	.270	.321	367-0-13	.180	-5	89	-4		0
CROSBY, GEORGE George Washington B1860 IA D1.9.1913 San Francisco CA d5.22																									
1884 Chi N	2	2	.333	3	3	3	0	28	27	21	3	3	12	11	3.54	89	.227	.298	13-1	.308	1	85	-1		0
CROSBY, KEN Kenneth Stewart B12.15.1947 New Denver BC, Can. BR/TR/6-2/179* [NYA69 10/225] d8.5 Col Brigham Young																									
1975 Chi N	1	0	1.000	9	0	0	0-0	8.1	10	5	0	0	7-0	6	3.24	120	.294	.415	0	—	0		1		-0
1976 Chi N	0	0	—	7	1	0	0-0	12	20	16	3	0	8-0	5	12.00	32	.377	.459	2	.500	0	113	-9		-0
Total 2	1	0	1.000	16	1	0	0-0	20.1	30	19	3	0	15-0	11	8.41	46	.345	.441	2	.500	1	113	-8		-0
CROSS, LEM George Lewis B1.9.1872 Sanbornton NH D10.9.1930 Manchester NH TR/5-9/155 d8.6																									
1893 Cin N	0	2	.000	3	3	2	0	21	24	16	3	0	9	7	5.57	86	.279	.347	6	.333	1	54	-1		0
1894 Cin N	3	4	.429	8	7	3	0	53	94	73	9	5	21	11	8.49	65	.381	.440	26	.231	-1*	111	-17		-1
Total 2	3	6	.333	11	10	5	0	74	118	89	12	5	30	18	7.66	69	.354	.416	32	.250	-0	95	-18		-1
CROTHERS, DOUG Douglas B11.16.1859 Natchez MS D3.29.1907 St.Louis MO BR/TR d8.3																									
1884 KC U	1	2	.333	3	3	3	0	25	26	15	0	0	6	11	1.80	124	.250	.291	15	.133	-2*	114	0		-0
1885 NY AA	7	11	.389	18	18	18-1	0	154	192	135	4	2	49	40	5.08	61	.293	.344	51	.157	-2	117	-34		-2
Total 2	8	13	.381	21	21	21-1	0	179	218	150	4	2	55	51	4.63	65	.287	.337	66	.152	-2	116	-34		-3
CROUCH, BILL William Henry "Skip" B12.3.1886 Marshallton DE D12.22.1945 Highland Park MI BL/TL/6-1/210 d7.12 s-Bill																									
1910 StL A	0	0	—	1	1	1	0	8	6	4	0	0	7	1	3.38	73	.231	.394	3	.000	-0	108	-1		-0
CROUCH, BILL Wilmer Elmer B8.20.1910 Wilmington DE D12.26.1980 Howell MI BB/TR/6-1/180 d5.9 f-Bill Col Eastern Michigan																									
1939 Bro N	4	0	1.000	6	3	3	0	38.1	37	14	3	0	14	10	2.58	156	.255	.321	15-0-1	.133	-1	224	5		-0
1941 Phi N	2	3	.400	20	5	1	1	59	65	31	4	0	17	26	4.42	84	.286	.336	11-0-3	.091	-0	83	-4		-0
StL N	1	2	.333	18	4	0	6	45	45	16	2	0	14	15	3.00	125	.271	.328	13-0-1	.000	-1	39	4		-0
Year	3	5	.375	38	9	1	7	104	110	47	6	0	31	41	3.81	98	.280	.333	24-0-4	.042	-2	63	1		-0
1945 StL N	1	0	1.000	6	0	0	0	13.1	12	5	1	1	7	4	3.38	111	.255	.364	2	.000	-0	105	6		
Total 3	8	5	.615	50	12	4	7	155.2	159	66	10	1	52	55	3.47	110	.272	.332	41-0-5	.073	-3	105	6		
CROUCH, ZACH Zachary Quinn B10.26.1965 Folsom CA BL/TL/6-3/190 [BosA84 13/328] d6.4																									
1988 Bos A	0	0	—	3	0	0	0-0	1.1	4	1	0	0	2-0	0	6.75	61	.571	.667	0	—	0		0		
CROUSHORE, RICH Richard Steven B8.7.1970 Lakehurst NJ BR/TR/6-4/210* d5.18 Col James Madison [DL 2001 NY N 17]																									
1998 StL N	0	3	.000	41	0	0	8-3	54.1	44	31	6	4	29-2	47	4.97	85	.213	.320	0-0-2		0		-4		
1999 StL N	3	7	.300	59	0	0	3-7	71.2	68	42	9	3	43-4	88	4.14	111	.247	.354	3	.333	1		1		
2000 Col N	2	0	1.000	9	0	0	0-0	11.1	15	11	1	0	6-1	11	8.74	66	.313	.393	1-0-1	1.000	0		-3		
Bos A	0	1	.000	5	0	0	0-0	4.2	4	3	0	2	5-1	3	5.79	87	.250	.435	0	—	0		0		
Total 3	5	11	.313	111	0	0	11-10	142	131	87	16	9	83-8	149	4.88	93	.240	.347	4-0-3	.500	1		-6	17	
CROW, DEAN Paul Dean B8.21.1972 Garland TX BL/TR/6-4/215 [SeaA93 10/269] d5.29 Col Baylor																									
1998 Det A	2	2	.500	32	0	0	0-0	45.2	55	22	6	2	16-6	18	3.94	121	.313	.374	0	—	0		4		
CROWDER, ALVIN Alvin Floyd "General" B1.11.1899 Winston-Salem NC D4.3.1972 Winston-Salem NC BL/TR/5-10/170 d7.24																									
1926 Was A	7	4	.636	19	12	6	1	100	97	52	3	2	26	26	3.96	98	.261	.367	38-0-2	.237	1	122	-1		
1927 Was A	4	7	.364	15	11	4-2	0	67.1	58	44	3	2	42	22	4.54	89	.232	.347	22-0-1	.136	-1	95	-5		
StL A	3	5	.375	21	8	2-1	3	73.2	71	44	3	1	42	30	5.01	87	.260	.361	23-0-1	.261	1	103	-3		

YEAR	TM LG	W	L	PCT	G	GS	CG-SHO	SV-BS	IP	H	R	HR	HB	BB-IB	SO	ERA	AERA	OAV	OOB	AB-HR-SH	AVG	PB	SUP	APR	DL	PW
	Year	7	12	.368	36	19	6-3	3	141	129	88	6	3	84	52	4.79	88	.247	.354	45-0-2	.200	-1	98	-9		-1.2
1928	StL A	21	5	.808	41	31	19-1	2	244	238	113	11	1	91	99	3.69	114	.258	.325	80-0-9	.188	-2	114	15		1.0
1929	StL A	17	15	.531	40	34	19-4	4	266.2	272	133	22	0	93	79	3.92	113	.271	.332	96-0-1	.188	-3	89	14		1.1
1930	StL A	3	7	.300	13	10	5-1	0	77.1	85	43	11	1	27	42	4.66	105	.283	.345	25	.160	-2	78	3		0.2
	Was A	15	9	.625	27	25	20	1	202.1	191	90	6	1	69	65	3.60	128	.249	.312	76-0-6	.171	-2	111	24		2.0
	Year	18	16	.529	40	35	25-1	2	279.2	276	133	17	2	96	107	3.89	120	.259	.321	101-0-6	.168	-4	101	30		2.2
1931	Was A	18	11	.621	44	26	13-1	2	234.1	255	117	13	1	72	85	3.88	111	.275	.328	88-0-3	.216	-1	99	12		1.0
1932	Was A	26	13	.667	50	39	21-3	1	327	319	136	17	0	77	103	3.33	130	.252	.295	122-0-5	.221	2*	98	37		3.8
1933	†Was A★	24	15	.615	52	35	17	4	299.1	311	140	14	3	81	110	3.97	105	.267	.316	102-0-8	.186	1	110	11		1.2
1934	Was A	4	10	.286	29	13	4	3	100.2	142	88	9	0	38	39	6.79	64	.326	.380	32-0-2	.219	1	116	-30		-3.4
	†Det A	5	1	.833	9	9	3-1	0	66.2	81	35	3	2	20	30	4.18	105	.295	.342	30	.133	-2	117	2		-0.1
	Year	9	11	.450	38	22	7-1	3	167.1	223	123	12	0	58	69	5.75	76	.314	.365	62-0-2	.177	-1	116	-27		-3.5
1935	†Det A	16	10	.615	33	32	16-2	0	241	269	127	16	4	67	59	4.26	98	.285	.335	93-0-5	.183	-2	118	-1		-0.5
1936	Det A	4	3	.571	9	7	1	0	44	64	42	5	0	21	10	8.39	59	.342	.409	20-0-1	.150	-1	135	-15		-1.8
Total	11	167	115	.592	402	292	150-16	22	2344.1	2453	1204	136	16	800	799	4.12	105	.270	.330	847-0-44	.194	-12	106	63		3.3

CROWELL, JIM James Everette B5.14.1974 Minneapolis MN BL/TL/6-4/225* d9.12 Col Indianapolis

1997	Cin N	0	1	.000	2	1	0	0-0	6.1	12	7	2	0	5-0	5	9.95	43	.414	.500	2	.000	-0	108	-4		-0.5
2004	Phi N	0	0	—	4	0	0	0-0	3	6	2	0	0	0-0	1	3.00	148	.333	.333	0	—	0	0	0		0.0
2005	Fla N	0	0	—	4	0	0	0-0	3.1	10	8	1	2	0-0	0	21.60	18	.526	.545	0	—	0		-7		-0.3
Total	3	0	1	.000	10	1	0	0-0	12.2	28	17	3	2	5-0	6	11.37	37	.424	.473	2	.000	-0	108	-11		-0.8

CROWELL, CAP Minot Joy B9.5.1892 Roxbury MA D9.30.1962 Central Falls RI BR/TR/6-1/178 d6.23 Col Brown

1915	Phi A	2	6	.250	10	8	4	0	54.1	56	53	1	5	47	15	5.47	54	.292	.443	22	.227	-0	78	-18		-2.3
1916	Phi A	0	5	.000	9	6	1	0	39.2	43	33	0	2	34	15	4.99	57	.289	.427	12	.000	-2	57	-11		-1.4
Total	2	2	11	.154	19	14	5	0	94	99	86	1	7	81	30	5.27	55	.290	.436	34	.147	-2	69	-29		-3.7

CROWELL, BILLY William Theodore B11.6.1865 Cincinnati OH D7.24.1935 Ft.Worth TX BR/TR/5-8.5/160 d4.20

1887	Cle AA	14	31	.311	45	45	45-1	0	389.1	541	350	9	20	138	72	4.88	89	.327	.386	156	.141	-13	71	-17		-2.5
1888	Cle AA	5	13	.278	18	18	16	0	150.2	212	148	8	9	61	61	5.79	53	.320	.385	58	.086	-5	93	-39		-3.9
	Lou AA	0	1	.000	1	1	1	0	9	12	14	1	1	6	5	6.00	51	.308	.413	3	.000	-0	57	-3		-0.3
	Year	5	14	.263	19	19	17	0	159.2	224	162	9	10	67	66	5.81	53	.320	.387	61	.082	-5	91	-41		-4.2
Total	2	19	45	.297	64	64	62-1	0	549	765	512	18	30	205	138	5.15	77	.325	.386	217	.124	-18	76	-59		-6.7

CROWSON, WOODY Thomas Woodrow B9.9.1918 Fuquay Sprgs. (now Fuquay-Varina) NC D8.14.1947 Mayodan NC BR/TR/6-2/185 d4.17

| 1945 | Phi A | 0 | 0 | — | 1 | 0 | 0 | 0 | 3 | 2 | 2 | 0 | 3 | 2 | 6.00 | 57 | .200 | .385 | 1 | .000 | -0 | | -1 | | 0.0 |

CRUCETA, FRANCISCO Francisco Alberto B7.4.1981 LaVega, D.R. BR/TR/6-2/180 d9.21

| 2004 | Cle A | 0 | 1 | .000 | 2 | 2 | 0 | 0-0 | 7.2 | 10 | 9 | 1 | 1 | 4-0 | 9 | 9.39 | 46 | .303 | .385 | 0 | — | 0 | 107 | -5 | | -0.5 |

CRUDALE, MIKE Michael Christopher B1.3.1977 San Diego CA BR/TR/6-0/205* [StLN99 24/732] d4.10 Col Santa Clara

2002	†StL N	3	0	1.000	49	1	0	0-1	52.2	43	11	3	1	14-2	47	1.88	215	.228	.276	2	.000	-0	115	13		0.6
2003	StL N	0	1	.000	13	0	0	0-1	11.1	11	5	1	1	12-1	6	2.38	173	.250	.414	0	—	0		1		0.1
	Mil N	0	0	—	9	0	0	0-0	9.1	1	3	0	0	6-0	7	2.89	149	.036	.206	0	—	0		2		0.1
	Year	0	1	.000	22	0	0	0-1	20.2	12	8	1	1	18-1	13	2.61	161	.167	.337	0	—	0		3		0.2
Total	2	3	1	.750	71	1	0	0-2	73.1	55	19	4	2	32-3	60	2.09	196	.211	.295	2	.000	-0	115	16		0.8

CRUM, CAL Calvin N. B7.27.1890 Cooks Mills IL D12.7.1945 Tulsa OK BR/TR/6-1/175 d5.4

1917	Bos N	0	0	—	1	0	0	0	1	1	0	0	0	1	0	0.00	—	.250	.400	0	—	0		0		0.0
1918	Bos N	0	1	.000	1	1	0	0	2.1	6	4	0	1	3	0	15.43	17	.600	.714	1	.000	-0	56	-3		-0.5
Total	2	0	1	.000	2	1	0	0	3.1	7	4	0	1	4	0	10.80	24	.500	.632	1	.000	-0	56	-3		-0.5

CRUMPLER, ROY Roy Maxton B7.8.1896 Clinton NC D10.6.1969 Fayetteville NC BL/TL/6-1/195 d9.16

1920	Det A	1	0	1.000	2	2	1	0	13	17	13	2	1	11	2	5.54	67	.315	.439	9	.333	1*	245	-4		-0.1
1925	Phi N	0	0	—	3	1	0	0	4.2	8	4	0	0	2	1	7.71	62	.381	.435	2	.000	-0	124	-1		-0.1
Total	2	1	0	1.000	5	3	1	0	17.2	25	17	2	1	13	3	6.11	65	.333	.438	11	.273	1	203	-5		-0.2

CRUTCHER, DICK Richard Louis B11.25.1889 Frankfort KY D6.19.1952 Frankfort KY BR/TR/5-9/148 d4.14

1914	Bos N	5	7	.417	33	15	5-1	0	158.2	169	73	4	6	66	48	3.46	80	.293	.371	54-0-1	.148	-1	100	-11		-0.8
1915	Bos N	2	2	.500	14	4	1	2	43.2	50	28	1	2	16	17	4.33	60	.309	.378	13-0-1	.231	1	115	-9		-0.8
Total	2	7	9	.438	47	19	6-1	2	202.1	219	101	5	8	82	65	3.65	75	.296	.373	67-0-2	.164	-0	103	-20		-1.6

CRUZ, JUAN Juan Carlos B10.15.1978 Bonao, D.R. BR/TR/6-2/155* d8.21

2001	Chi N	3	1	.750	8	8	0	0-0	44.2	40	16	4	2	17-1	39	3.22	130	.244	.322	16-0-2	.125	-1*	132	6		0.4
2002	Chi N	3	11	.214	45	24	0	1-3	97.1	84	56	11	8	59-4	81	3.98	102	.241	.356	14-0-2	.143	-0	76	-3	15	-0.5
2003	†Chi N	2	7	.222	25	6	0	0-1	61	66	44	7	7	28-0	65	6.05	72	.275	.365	12-0-1	.250	1	87	-11		-1.3
2004	†Atl N	6	2	.750	50	0	0	0-0	72	59	24	7	2	30-1	70	2.75	157	.224	.307	5	.200	1		13	1.3
2005	Oak A	0	3	.000	28	0	0	0-0	32.2	38	33	5	4	22-4	34	7.44	60	.290	.403	0	—	0		-12		-1.1
Total	5	14	24	.368	156	23	0	1-4	307.2	287	173	34	23	156-10	289	4.36	97	.250	.348	47-0-5	.170	1	97	-7	15	-1.1

CRUZ, NELSON Nelson B9.13.1972 Puerto Plata, D.R. BR/TR/6-1/185* d8.1

1997	Chi A	0	2	.000	19	0	0	0-0	26.1	29	19	6	0	9-1	23	6.49	68	.274	.330	0	—	0		-5		-0.4
1999	Det A	2	5	.286	29	6	0	0-0	66.2	74	44	11	3	23-1	46	5.67	88	.281	.341	0	—	0	90	-4		-0.3
2000	Det A	5	2	.714	27	0	0	0-1	41	39	14	4	3	13-3	34	3.07	160	.253	.320	1	.000	-0		9		1.3
2001	†Hou N	3	3	.500	66	0	0	2-2	82.1	72	41	11	9	24-4	75	4.15	111	.237	.310	6	.167	-0		4		0.3
2002	Hou N	2	6	.250	43	5	0	0-2	78.1	90	44	12	6	29-4	61	4.48	97	.284	.352	13-0-2	.000	-1	124	-2	15	-0.3
2003	Col N	3	5	.375	20	7	0	0-1	53.2	65	43	15	3	11-2	38	7.21	68	.301	.341	13-0-2	.154	-0	134	-11	77	-1.4
Total	6	15	23	.395	204	18	0	2-6	348.1	369	205	59	24	109-15	277	5.04	93	.271	.333	33-0-4	.091	-2	118	-9	92	-0.8

CRUZ, VICTOR Victor Manuel (b Victor Manuel De La Cruz (Gil)) B12.24.1957 Rancho Viejo, D.R. D9.26.2004 Santo Domingo, D.R. BR/TR/5-9/200(175-215) d6.24

1978	Tor A	7	3	.700	32	0	0	9-3	47.1	28	10	0	1	35-4	51	1.71	231	.179	.330	0	—	0		11		2.4
1979	Cle A	3	9	.250	61	0	0	10-5	78.2	70	41	10	1	44-4	63	4.23	102	.244	.341	0	—	0		0		0.0
1980	Cle A	6	7	.462	55	0	0	12-8	86	71	36	10	3	27-8	88	3.45	120	.229	.289	0	—	0		6		1.0
1981	Pit N	1	1	.500	22	0	0	1-3	34	33	10	6	1	15-4	28	2.65	138	.264	.348	4-0-1	.000	0		4		0.2
1983	Tex A	1	3	.250	17	0	0	5-2	25	16	7	2	1	10-3	18	1.44	281	.184	.270	0	—	0		6		1.2
Total	5	18	23	.439	187	0	0	37-21	271	218	104	28	7	131-23	248	3.09	132	.226	.317	4-0-1	.000	-0		27		4.8

CUBILLAN, DARWIN Darwin Harrikson (Salom) B11.15.1972 Bobures, Venez BR/TR/6-2/170* d5.20

2000	Tor A	1	0	1.000	7	0	0	0-0	15.2	20	14	5	1	11-0	14	8.04	63	.317	.427	1	.000	-0		-5		-0.2
	Tex A	0	0	—	13	0	0	0-0	17.2	32	22	4	0	14-0	13	10.70	48	.400	.474	0	—	0		-10		-0.5
	Year	1	0	1.000	20	0	0	0-0	33.1	52	36	9	1	25-0	27	9.45	54	.364	.453	1	.000	-0		-14		-0.7
2001	Mon N	0	0	—	29	0	0	0-0	26.1	31	13	1	0	12-1	19	4.10	105	.295	.358	0	—	0		1		0.0
2004	Bal A	0	0	—	7	0	0	0-1	10	13	7	3	0	7-0	8	5.40	86	.302	.400	0	—	0		-1		-0.1
Total	3	1	0	1.000	56	0	0	0-1	69.2	96	56	13	1	44-1	54	6.85	69	.330	.412	1	.000	-0		-15		-0.8

CUCCURULLO, COOKIE Arthur Joseph B2.8.1918 Asbury Park NJ D1.23.1983 W.Orange NJ BL/TL/5-10/168 d10.3

1943	Pit N	0	1	.000	10	0	0	1	19	10	7	0	0	3	3	6.43	54	.357	.419	0	—	1	73	-3		-0.2
1944	Pit N	2	1	.667	32	4	0	4	106.1	110	65	5	9	44	31	4.06	91	.270	.346	38	.368	5*	152	-6		0.2
1945	Pit N	1	3	.250	29	4	0	1	56.2	68	41	2	1	34	17	5.24	75	.305	.399	14	.214	-0	70	-9		-0.6
Total	3	3	5	.375	62	9	0	6	170	188	113	7	4	81	51	4.55	83	.286	.367	52	.327	5	106	-18		-0.6

CUDWORTH, JIM James Alaric "Cuddy" B8.22.1858 Fairhaven MA D12.21.1943 Middleboro MA BR/TR/6-0/165 d7.27 ▲

| 1884 | KC U | 0 | 0 | — | 2 | 1 | 1 | 0 | 17 | 19 | 14 | 0 | 0 | 3 | 0 | 4.24 | 53 | .264 | .293 | 116 | .147 | -1* | 153 | -4 | | -0.3 |

CUELLAR, CHARLIE Jesus Patracis B8.23.1917 Ybor City FL D10.11.1994 Tampa FL BR/TR/5-11/183 d7.2

| 1950 | Chi A | 0 | 0 | — | 2 | 0 | 0 | 0 | 1.1 | 6 | 4 | 0 | 0 | 3 | 1 | 33.75 | 13 | .600 | .692 | 0 | — | 0 | | -5 | | -0.2 |

YEAR	TM LG	W	L	PCT	G	GS	CG-SHO	SV-BS	IP	H	R	HR	HB	BB-IB	SO	ERA	AERA	OAV	OOB	AB-HR-SH	AVG	PB	SUP	APR	DL	PW

CUELLAR, MIKE Miguel Angel (Santana) B5.8.1937 Santa Clara, Cuba BL/TL/5-11/175* d4.18

YEAR	TM LG	W	L	PCT	G	GS	CG-SHO	SV-BS	IP	H	R	HR	HB	BB-IB	SO	ERA	AERA	OAV	OOB	AB-HR-SH	AVG	PB	SUP	APR	DL	PW
1959	Cin N	0	0	—	2	0	0		4	7	8	5	1	4-1	5	15.75	26	.368	.458	1	.000	-0		-5		-0.3
1964	StL N	5	5	.500	32	7	1	4	72	80	43	8	1	33-4	56	4.50	85	.288	.362	18	.000	-1	102	-5		-0.9
1965	Hou N	1	4	.200	25	4	0	2	56	55	24	2	1	21-4	46	3.54	95	.262	.330	12-0-1	.000	-1	52	-1		-0.1
1966	Hou N	12	10	.545	38	28	11-1	2	227.1	193	79	10	2	52-8	175	2.22	54	.229	.273	71-1-4	.113	-1	106	25		2.4
1967	Hou N★	16	11	.593	36	32	16-3	1	246.1	233	99	16	1	63-3	203	3.03	109	.248	.295	93-0-3	.140	1*	97	6		0.8
1968	Hou N	8	11	.421	28	24	11-2	1	170.2	152	60	8	1	45-7	133	2.74	108	.237	.286	57-1-3	.193	2	97	3	21	0.7
1969	†Bal A	23	11	.676	39	39	18-5	0-0	290.2	213	94	18	1	79-7	182	2.38	151	.204	.260	103-0-8	.117	-3	105	36		3.8
1970	†Bal A☆	24	8	.750	40	40	21-4	0-0	297.2	273	126	34	1	69-5	190	3.48	106	.242	.284	112-2-9	.089	-4*	127	11		0.2
1971	†Bal A★	20	9	.690	38	38	21-4	0-0	292.1	250	111	30	1	78-1	124	3.08	111	.234	.285	107-1-8	.103	-4	109	11		0.7
1972	Bal A	18	12	.600	35	35	17-4	0-0	248.1	197	78	21	0	71-4	132	2.57	121	.220	.276	87-2-7	.126	-1	105	15		1.1
1973	Bal A	18	13	.581	38	38	17-2	0-0	267	265	120	29	0	84-2	140	3.27	115	.258	.313	0	—	0	111	10		1.2
1974	†Bal A☆	22	10	.688	38	38	20-5	0-0	269.1	253	106	17	2	86-4	106	3.66	97	.249	.310	0	—	0	99	-3		-0.2
1975	Bal A	14	12	.538	36	36	17-5	0-0	256	229	112	17	1	84-5	105	4.96	66	.307	.379	0	—	0	84	-20		-2.9
1976	Bal A	4	13	.235	26	19	2-1	1-0	107	129	63	8	2	50-5	32	18.90	21	.500	.571	0	—	0	23	-5		-0.8
1977	Cal A	0	0	1.000	2	1	0	0-1	3.1	9	7	2	0	3-1	5	18.90	21	.500	.571	0	—	0	23	-5		-0.8
Total	15	185	130	.587	453	379	172-36	11-1	2808	2538	1130	222	12	822-61	1632	3.14	110	.243	.297	661-7-43	.115	-14	105	87	21	7.5

CUELLAR, BOBBY Robert B8.20.1952 Alice TX BR/TR/5-11/190 [TexA74 29/594] d9.9 C7 Col Texas

| 1977 | Tex A | 0 | 0 | — | 4 | 0 | 0 | 0-0 | 6.2 | 4 | 1 | 0 | 0 | 2-0 | 3 | 1.35 | 302 | .182 | .250 | 0 | — | 0 | | 2 | | 0.1 |

CUETO, BERT Dagoberto (Concepcion) B8.14.1937 San Luis, Cuba BR/TR/6-4/170 d6.18

| 1961 | Min A | 1 | 3 | .250 | 7 | 5 | 0 | 0 | 21.1 | 27 | 24 | 7 | 1 | 10-0 | 5 | 7.17 | 59 | .300 | .376 | 5-0-2 | .000 | -0 | 138 | -8 | | -1.3 |

CULLEN, JACK John Patrick B10.6.1939 Newark NJ BR/TR/5-11/170* d9.9

1962	NY A	0	0	—	2	0	0	1	3	2	0	0	0	2-0	2	0.00	—	.182	.308	0		0		1		0.1
1965	NY A	3	4	.429	12	9	2-1	0	59	59	22	2	0	21-2	25	3.05	112	.262	.324	20	.150	-0	72	3		0.3
1966	NY A	1	0	1.000	5	0	0	0	11.1	11	5	0	0	5-2	7	3.97	84	.256	.327	3	.000	-0		-1		-0.1
Total	3	4	4	.500	19	9	2-1	1	73.1	72	27	2	0	28-4	34	3.07	111	.258	.324	23	.130	-1	72	3		0.3

CULLOP, NICK Norman Andrew B9.17.1887 Chilhowie VA D4.15.1961 Tazewell VA BL/TL/5-11.5/172 d5.20

1913	Cle A	3	6	.333	23	8	4	0	97.2	105	58	3	3	35	30	4.42	69	.294	.362	31-0-3	.129	-1	98	-12		-1.1
1914	Cle A	1	0	1.000	1	0	0	0	3.1	4	3	0	0	1	3	2.70	107	.364	.417	1	.000	-0	0			-0.1
	KC F	14	19	.424	44	36	22-4	1	295.2	256	116	6	12	87	149	2.34	119	.235	.299	99-0-4	.141	-5	84	9		0.5
1915	KC F	22	11	.667	44	36	22-3	2	302.1	278	105	8	9	67	111	2.44	108	.249	.297	96-0-9	.188	-1	108	7		1.0
1916	NY A	13	6	.684	28	22	9	1	167	151	60	4	3	32	77	3.32	81	.307	.348	44-0-2	.159	-1	88	-9		-1.0
1917	NY A	5	9	.357	30	18	5-2	1	146.1	161	70	2	2	31	27	3.32	81	.307	.348							
1921	StL A	0	2	.000	4	1	0	0	11.2	18	12	1	0	6	3	8.49	53	.340	.407	3	.000	-0	93	-5		-0.1
Total	6	57	54	.514	174	121	62-9	5	1024	973	424	24	29	259	400	2.73	102	.258	.311	329-0-19	.149	-12	97	1		-0.1

CULLOTON, BUD Bernard Aloysius B5.19.1897 Kingston NY D11.9.1976 Kingston NY BR/TR/5-11/180 d4.16 Col Fordham

1925	Pit N	0	1	.000	9	1	0	0	21	19	8	1	0	1	3	2.57	173	.241	.250	3-0-1	.000	-0	19	4		0.
1926	Pit N	0	0	—	4	0	0	0	3.2	3	4	0	0	6	1	7.36	53	.214	.450	0	—	0		-1		-0.
Total	2	0	1	.000	13	1	0	0	24.2	22	12	1	0	7	4	3.28	133	.237	.290	3-0-1	.000	-0	19	3		-0.

CULP, RAY Raymond Leonard B8.6.1941 Elgin TX BR/TR/6-0/200* d4.10

1963	Phi N★	14	11	.560	34	30	10-5	0	203.1	148	76	15	6	102-8	176	2.97	109	.206	.308	66-0-7	.136	-0	106	7		0.*
1964	Phi N	8	7	.533	30	19	3-1	0	135	139	77	15	5	56-4	96	4.13	84	.263	.337	44	.114	-1	112	-12		-1.
1965	Phi N	14	10	.583	33	30	11-2	0	204.1	188	89	14	12	78-9	134	3.22	108	.243	.321	68-0-8	.088	-2	114	4		0.
1966	Phi N	7	4	.636	34	12	1	1	110.2	106	66	19	7	53-4	100	5.04	71	.246	.337	26-0-5	.077	-2	100	-17		-1.
1967	Chi N	8	11	.421	30	22	4-1	0	152.2	138	69	22	2	59-4	111	2.91	108	.240	.291	70-0-7	.114	-1	109	6		0.
1968	Bos A	16	6	.727	35	30	11-6	0	216.1	166	79	18	9	82-8	190	2.91	108	.210	.291	79-1-6	.152	1	124	3		0.
1969	Bos A★	17	8	.680	32	32	9-2	0-0	227	195	103	25	6	79-6	172	3.81	100	.231	.299	90-0-5	.124	-3	104	22		2.
1970	Bos A	17	14	.548	33	33	15-1	0-0	251.1	211	104	22	11	91-8	197	3.04	131	.224	.299	68-0-17	.118	-2	85	2		-0.
1971	Bos A	14	16	.467	35	35	12-3	0-0	242.1	236	108	21	5	67-4	151	3.60	103	.253	.305	68-0-15	.212	1	128	-13	48	-1.
1972	Bos A	5	8	.385	16	16	4-1	0-0	105	104	60	8	3	53-3	52	4.46	73	.260	.347	33-0-4	.123	0	76	-4	31	-0.
1973	Bos A	2	6	.250	10	9	0	0-0	50.1	46	32	9	4	32-0	22	4.47	90	.247	.366	0	—	0	107	-6	79	-2.
Total	11	122	101	.547	322	268	80-22	1-0	1898.1	1677	863	188	70	752-58	1411	3.58	100	.235	.313	602-1-67	.123	-11	107	-6	79	-2.

CULP, BILL William Edward B6.11.1887 Bellaire OH D9.3.1969 Arnold PA BB/TR/6-1.5/165 d9.8

| 1910 | Phi N | 0 | 0 | — | 4 | 0 | 0 | 0 | 6.2 | 8 | 6 | 0 | 0 | 4 | 4 | 8.10 | 39 | .333 | .429 | 2 | .000 | -0 | | -3 | | -0. |

CULVER, GEORGE George Raymond B7.8.1943 Salinas CA BR/TR/6-2/185* d9.7 Col Bakersfield (CA) JC

1966	Cle A	0	2	.000	5	1	0	1	9.2	15	9	1	1	7-0	6	8.38	41	.357	.460	2	.000	-0	103	-5		-0.*
1967	Cle A	7	3	.700	53	1	0	3	75	71	40	2	6	31-9	41	3.96	82	.258	.344	4	.250	-1*	101	-3		-0.
1968	Cin N	11	16	.407	42	35	5-2	2	226	229	95	8	14	84-7	114	3.23	98	.264	.336	66-0-11	.121	-2	91	-5	49	-0.
1969	Cin N	5	7	.417	32	13	0	4-0	101.1	117	55	8	9	52-6	58	4.26	88	.291	.383	17-0-1	.176	-0	111	-2		-0.
1970	StL N	3	3	.500	11	7	2	0-0	56.2	64	31	6	1	21-2	31	3.20	122	.254	.343	4-0-1	.250	-0		4		-0.
	Hou N	3	3	.500	32	0	0	3-0	45	44	17	1	3	45-6	54	3.98	104	.271	.350	21-0-2	.190	0	114	2		1
	Year	6	6	.500	43	7	2	3-0	101.2	108	48	7	4	66-8	85	3.53										
1971	Hou N	5	8	.385	59	0	0	7-2	95.1	89	33	4	2	38-10	57	2.64	127	.257	.331	11-0-3	.091	-1		7		1
1972	Hou N	6	2	.750	45	0	0	2-1	97.1	73	33	7	5	43-3	82	3.05	110	.212	.306	19-0-2	.158	-0		3		0
1973	LA N	4	4	.500	28	0	0	2-2	42	45	15	4	1	21-6	23	3.00	116	.292	.376	4	.000	-0		3		-0
	Phi N	3	1	.750	14	0	0	0-1	18.2	26	10	0	0	15-6	7	4.82	79	.342	.451	0	—	-0		-2		-0
	Year	7	5	.583	42	0	0	2-3	60.2	71	25	4	1	36-12	30	3.56	101	.309	.401	4	.000	-0		-6		-0
1974	Phi N	1	0	1.000	14	0	0	0-0	21.2	20	16	1	5	16-1	16	6.65	57	.267	.394	3	.000	-0		-6		-0
Total	9	48	49	.495	335	57	7-2	23-6	788.2	793	354	42	43	352-54	451	3.62	96	.266	.350	161-0-20	.124	-4	99	-11	49	-1

CUMBERLAND, JOHN John Sheldon B5.10.1947 Westbrook ME BR/TL/6-0/190* d9.27 C7 Col Maine

1968	NY A	0	0	—	1	0	0	0	2	3	4	1	0	1-0	1	9.00	32	.333	.400	0	—	0		-2		-0
1969	NY A	0	0	—	2	0	0	0-0	4	3	2	0	0	4-1	0	4.50	78	.231	.389	0	—	0		0		-0
1970	NY A	3	4	.429	15	8	1	0-0	64	62	31	9	0	15-3	38	3.94	91	.252	.292	17-0-3	.059	-1	78	-2		-0
	SF N	2	0	1.000	7	0	0	0-0	11	6	3	0	0	4-0	6	0.82	486	.158	.233	1	.000	-0		3		0
1971	†SF N	9	6	.600	45	21	5-2	2-1	185	153	66	22	0	55-6	65	2.92	117	.223	.280	59-0-1	.119	-2	103	13		0
1972	SF N	0	4	.000	9	6	0	0-0	25	38	29	6	0	7-0	8	8.64	41	.336	.372	9	.111	-0	114	-15		0
	StL N	1	1	.500	14	1	0	0-0	21.2	23	17	6	0	7-0	7	6.65	52	.291	.341	5-0-1	.000	-1	77	-7		-2
	Year	1	5	.167	23	7	0	0-0	46.2	61	46	12	0	14-0	15	7.71	45	.318	.359	14-0-1	.071	-1	109	-22		-2
1974	Cal A	0	1	.000	17	0	0	0-1	21.2	24	9	2	0	10-2	12	3.74	93	.289	.362	0	—	-5	98	-10		-2
Total	6	15	16	.484	110	36	6-2	2-2	334.1	312	161	46	0	103-12	137	4.28	91	.246	.301	91-0-5	.099	-10	98	-10		-1

CUMMINGS, JOHN John Russell B5.10.1969 Torrance CA BL/TL/6-3/200* [SeaA90 8/215] d4.10 Col USC

1993	Sea A	0	6	.000	10	8	1	0-0	46.1	59	34	6	2	16-2	19	6.02	74	.316	.372	0	—	0	62	-8	17	-0
1994	Sea A	2	4	.333	17	8	1	0-0	64	66	43	7	0	37-2	33	5.63	88	.270	.363	0	—	0	84	-4	17	-4
1995	Sea A	0	0	—	4	0	0	0-0	5.1	8	8	0	0	7-2	6	11.81	40	.400	.517	0	—	-0		4		4
	†LA N	3	1	.750	35	0	0	0-0	39	38	16	3	0	10-4	21	3.00	129	.250	.294	.000	—	-0		-3		-0
1996	LA N	0	1	.000	9	0	0	0-0	5.1	12	7	1	0	2-1	5	6.75	58	.462	.483	0	—	0		0		-0
	Det A	3	3	.500	21	0	0	0-0	31.2	36	20	3	2	20-3	24	5.12	100	.283	.387	0	—	-0		-5		-0
1997	Det A	2	0	1.000	14	0	0	0-0	24.2	32	22	3	0	14-1	6	5.47	84	.311	.393	0	—	0	75	-20	17	-0
Total	5	10	15	.400	110	16	1	0-1	216.1	251	150	23	4	106-15	114	5.33	86	.292	.369	3	.000	-0	75	-20	17	-0

CUMMINGS, STEVE Steven Brent B7.15.1964 Houston TX BB/TR/6-2/200* [TorA86 2/54] d6.24 Col Houston

1989	Tor A	2	0	1.000	5	2	0	0-0	21	18	9	1	1	11-0	8	3.00	126	.231	.333	0	—	0	191	1		-0
1990	Tor A	0	0	—	6	2	0	0-0	12.1	22	7	4	1	5-0	4	5.11	78	.431	.491	0	—	0	80	-1		-0
Total	2	2	0	1.000	11	4	0	0-0	33.1	40	16	5	2	16-0	12	3.78	102	.310	.395	0	—	0	135	0		-0

YEAR	TM LG	W	L	PCT	G	GS	CG-SHO	SV-BS	IP	H	R	HR	HB	BB-IB	SO	ERA	AERA	OAV	OOB	AB-HR-SH	AVG	PB	SUP	APR	DL	PW

CUMMINGS, CANDY William Arthur B10.18.1848 Ware MA D5.16.1924 Toledo OH BR/TR/5-9/120 d4.22 HF1939

1872	Mut NA	33	20	.623	55	55	53-3	0	497	604	347	2		31	45	3.01	112	.272	.282	249	.209	-3	106	23		1.1
1873	Bal NA	28	14	.667	42	42	42-1	0	382	475	292	4		33	34	2.80	116	.274	.287	192	.250	2	123	28		2.1
1874	Phi NA	28	26	.519	54	54	52-3	0	483	616	386	4		18	61	1.96	113	.276	.282	231	.225	-4	110	16		0.7
1875	Har NA	35	12	.745	48	47	46-7	0	416	397	184	0		4	82	1.60	146	.235	.236	221	.199	-5*	111	34		2.7
1876	Har N	16	8	.667	24	24	24-5	0	216	215	97	0		14	26	1.67	142	.239	.251	105	.162	-8	109	15		0.5
1877	Cin N	5	14	.263	19	19	16	0	155.2	219	144	2		13	11	4.34	61	.315	.327	70	.200	0	106	-29		-2.6
Total	4 NA	124	72	.633	199	198	193-14	0	1778	2092	1209	10		86	222	2.35	120	.266	.274	893	.219	-10	111	101		6.6
Total	2	21	22	.488	43	43	40-5	0	371.2	434	241	2		27	37	2.78	90	.272	.284	175	.177	-7	107	-14		-2.1

CUNNANE, WILL William Joseph B4.24.1974 Suffern NY BR/TR/6-2/200(175-200) d4.3

1997	SD N	6	3	.667	54	0	0	0-2	91.1	114	69	11	5	49-3	79	5.81	68	.305	.392	14-0-1	.357	3*	158	-22		-1.7
1998	SD N	0	0	—	3	0	0	0-0	3	4	2	1	0	1-1	1	6.00	66	.308	.357	0	—	0		-1		0.0
1999	SD N	2	1	.667	24	0	0	0-0	31	34	19	8	0	12-3	22	5.23	82	.293	.359	3	.000	-0		-3	82	0.0
2000	Mil N	1	1	.500	27	3	0	0-0	38.1	35	21	2	1	21-0	34	4.23	105	.241	.339	7	.143	0	138	1		-0.3
2001	Mil N	0	3	.000	31	1	0	0-0	51.2	66	34	6	2	22-6	37	5.40	79	.320	.390	7	.000	-1*	65	-7		-0.4
2002	Chi N	1	1	.500	16	0	0	0-1	26.1	27	16	5	1	13-1	30	5.47	74	.270	.360	4	.250	0		-3		-0.2
2003	†Atl N	2	2	.500	20	0	0	3-0	20	14	6	2	0	6-2	20	2.70	156	.189	.250	4	.250	0		-3		-0.2
2004	Atl N	1	1	.500	9	0	0	0-1	12.1	18	10	3	1	4-1	11	7.30	59	.346	.390	0	—	0		4		0.7
Total	8	13	12	.520	184	12	0	3-4	274	312	177	38	10	128-17	234	5.26	79	.289	.368	35-0-1	.200	2	142	-35	82	-2.4

CUNNINGHAM, BRUCE Bruce Lee B9.29.1905 San Francisco CA D3.8.1984 Hayward CA BR/TR/5-10.5/165 d5.7

1929	Bos N	4	6	.400	17	8	4	1	91.2	100	52	7	2	32	22	4.52	104	.282	.344	27-0-2	.148	-0*	58	2		0.2
1930	Bos N	5	6	.455	36	6	2	0	106.2	121	73	7	0	41	28	5.48	90	.289	.352	31	.194	0*	53	-7		-0.4
1931	Bos N	3	12	.200	33	16	6-1	0	136.2	157	74	7	7	54	32	4.48	85	.296	.363	42	.071	-4*	74	-9		-1.1
1932	Bos N	1	0	1.000	18	3	0	1	47	50	21	1	4	19	21	3.45	109	.281	.363	9	.222	2	157	2		0.3
Total	4	13	24	.351	104	33	12-1	2	382	428	220	22	8	146	103	4.64	93	.289	.356	109-0-2	.138	-2	70	-12		-1.0

CUNNINGHAM, BERT Ellsworth Elmer B11.25.1865 Wilmington DE D5.14.1952 Cragmere DE BR/TR/5-6/187 d9.15 U1

1887	Bro AA	0	2	.000	3	3	3	0	23	26	22	0	4	13	8	5.09	85	.263	.371	8	.000	-1	44	-3		-0.2
1888	Bal AA	22	29	.431	51	51	50	0	453.1	412	275	8	30	157	186	3.39	88	.233	.307	171-1	.186	-2	88	-25		-2.5
1889	Bal AA	16	19	.457	39	33	29	1	279.1	306	245	11	15	141	140	4.87	81	.270	.358	131	.206	-3*	88	-25		-2.6
1890	Phi P	3	9	.250	14	11	11	0	108.2	133	103	0	7	67	33	5.22	82	.289	.387	52	.115	-4*	96	-25		-2.6
	Buf P	9	15	.375	25	25	24-2	0	211	251	190	8	6	134	78	5.84	70	.283	.381	101	.228	1*	79	-35		-2.6
	Year	12	24	.333	39	36	35-2	0	319.2	384	293	8	13	201	111	5.63	74	.285	.383	153	.190	-4	80	-42		-3.7
1891	Bal AA	11	14	.440	30	25	21	0	237.2	241	181	8	11	138	59	4.01	93	.254	.356	100-1	.150	-2*	115	-7		-0.7
1895	Lou N	11	16	.407	31	28	24-1	0	231	299	185	6	5	104	49	4.75	97	.309	.378	100	.300	6*	79	-5		0.2
1896	Lou N	7	14	.333	27	20	17	1	189.1	242	168	6	17	74	37	5.09	85	.308	.380	88-2-1	.250	3*	89	-18		-1.2
1897	Lou N	14	13	.519	30	28	26	0	242.2	294	152	3	14	72	49	4.15	103	.297	.353	97-2-5	.227	-1*	83	9		0.8
1898	Lou N	28	15	.651	44	42	41	0	362	387	174	8	20	65	34	3.16	114	.272	.313	140-1-0	.229	2	109	15		1.6
1899	Lou N	17	17	.500	39	37	33-1	0	323.2	385	188	4	15	75	36	3.84	100	.295	.340	154-2-4	.260	3*	108	7		1.1
1900	Chi N	4	3	.571	8	7	7	0	64	84	53	0	3	21	7	4.36	83	.316	.375	27	.148	-1	131	-6		-0.7
1901	Chi N	0	1	.000	2	1	1	0	9	11	6	0	0	3	2	5.00	65	.297	.350	1-0-2	.000	0	88	-1		-0.1
Total	12	142	167	.460	342	311	287-4	2	2734.2	3063	1942	62	148	1064	718	4.22	91	.277	.349	1176-9-12	.216	1	94	-105		-8.0

CUNNINGHAM, GEORGE George Harold B7.13.1894 Sturgeon Lake MN D3.10.1972 Chattanooga TN BR/TR/5-11/185 d4.14

1916	Det A	7	10	.412	35	14	5	2	150.1	146	71	0	3	74	68	2.75	104	.269	.360	41-0-1	.268	5	126	-3		0.3
1917	Det A	2	7	.222	44	8	4	4	139	113	72	2	4	51	49	2.91	91	.227	.304	34-1-2	.176	-1	150	-7		-0.4
1918	Det A	6	7	.462	27	14	10	1	140	131	68	0	5	38	39	3.15	84	.255	.312	112-0-4	.223	3*	97	-10		-0.5
1919	Det A	1	1	.500	17	0	0	1	47.2	54	36	0	5	15	11	4.91	65	.292	.361	23	.217	2*		-11		-0.3
Total	4	16	25	.390	123	36	19	8	477	444	247	2	17	178	167	3.13	89	.255	.330	210-1-7	.224	11	119	-31		-0.9

CUNNINGHAM, MIKE Mody B6.14.1882 Lancaster SC D12.10.1969 Lancaster SC BR/TR/5-10.5/175 d8.31 Col South Carolina-Aiken

| 1906 | Phi A | 1 | 0 | 1.000 | 5 | 1 | 1 | 0 | 28 | 31 | 15 | 1 | 1 | 9 | 3 | 3.21 | 85 | .271 | .333 | 12 | .333 | 1* | 132 | -2 | | 0.0 |

CUPPY, NIG George Joseph (b George Koppe) B7.3.1869 Logansport IN D7.27.1922 Elkhart IN BR/TR/5-7/160 d4.16

1892	†Cle N	28	13	.683	47	42	38-1	0	376	333	175	9	10	121	103	2.51	135	.228	.292	168	.214	0*	113	37		3.7
1893	Cle N	17	10	.630	31	30	24	0	243.2	316	200	6	10	75	39	4.47	109	.305	.357	109	.248	1*	106	8		0.6
1894	Cle N	24	15	.615	43	33	29-3	0	316	381	246	11	10	128	65	4.56	120	.295	.363	135-0-1	.259	1*	91	26		2.4
1895	†Cle N	26	14	.650	47	40	36-1	2	353	384	210	9	8	95	91	3.54	141	.273	.323	140-0-4	.286	7	101	51		5.2
1896	Cle N	25	14	.641	46	40	35-1	1	358	388	173	8	7	75	86	3.12	146	.274	.314	141-1-4	.270	6*	90	55		5.5
1897	Cle N	10	6	.625	19	17	13-1	0	138	150	69	3	5	62	23	3.20	140	.275	.314	55-0-1	.145	-4*	77	19		1.3
1898	Cle N	9	8	.529	18	15	13-1	0	128	147	62	4	6	25	25	3.30	110	.286	.327	48-0-2	.104	-4	76	6		0.2
1899	StL N	11	8	.579	21	21	18-1	0	171.2	203	89	3	5	26	27	3.15	127	.294	.324	70-0-2	.186	-3	104	15		1.2
1900	Bos N	8	4	.667	17	13	9	1	105.1	107	64	8	6	24	25	3.08	134	.263	.314	42	.262	1	117	7		0.8
1901	Bos A	4	6	.400	13	11	9	0	93.1	111	58	1	2	14	22	4.15	85	.292	.321	49-0-1	.204	0*	106	-5		-0.5
Total	10	162	98	.623	302	262	224-9	5	2283	2520	1346	62	69	609	504	3.48	127	.275	.325	957-1-15	.233	6	98	219		20.4

CURRAN, SAMMY Simon Francis B10.30.1874 Dorchester MA D5.19.1936 Dorchester MA TL d8.1 Col Tufts

| 1902 | Bos N | 0 | 0 | — | 1 | 0 | 0 | 0 | 6.2 | 6 | 1 | 0 | 0 | 3 | 3 | 1.35 | 209 | .240 | .240 | 2 | .000 | -0 | | 1 | | 0.0 |

CURRENCE, LAFAYETTE Delancy Lafayette B12.3.1951 Rock Hill SC BB/TL/5-11/175 d7.24

| 1975 | Mil A | 0 | 2 | .000 | 8 | 1 | 0 | 0 | 18.2 | 25 | 17 | 5 | 0 | 14-1 | 7 | 7.71 | 50 | .316 | .415 | 0 | — | 0 | 114 | -7 | | -0.7 |

CURRIE, MURPHY Archibald Murphy B8.31.1893 Fayetteville NC D6.22.1939 Asheboro NC BR/TR/5-11.5/185 d8.31

| 1916 | StL N | 0 | 0 | — | 6 | 0 | 0 | 0 | 14.1 | 7 | 4 | 0 | 9 | 10 | 8 | 1.88 | 140 | .149 | .286 | 3 | .000 | -0 | | 1 | | 0.0 |

CURRIE, CLARENCE Clarence Franklin B12.30.1878 Windsor ON, Can. D7.15.1941 Little Chute WI BR/TR/5-10/170 d4.25

1902	Cin N	3	4	.429	10	7	6-1	0	65.1	70	37	1	2	17	20	3.72	81	.273	.324	24-0-1	.083	-2	68	-4		-0.5
	StL N	7	5	.583	15	12	10-2	0	124.2	125	54	0	6	35	30	2.60	106	.261	.319	46-0-1	.196	-0*	81	2		0.3
	Year	10	9	.526	25	19	16-3	0	190	195	91	1	8	52	50	2.98	95	.265	.321	70-0-2	.157	-2	76	-5		-0.2
1903	StL N	4	12	.250	22	16	13-1	1	148	155	93	7	10	60	52	4.01	81	.281	.362	47-0-2	.085	-3	63	-8		-0.9
	Chi N	1	2	.333	6	3	2	1	33.1	35	25	1	3	9	9	2.97	106	.254	.313	12	.417	2	79	-2		0.0
	Year	5	14	.263	28	19	15-1	2	181.1	190	118	8	13	69	61	3.82	85	.275	.352	59-0-2	.153	-1	66	-16		-0.9
Total	2	15	23	.395	53	38	31-4	2	371.1	385	209	9	21	121	111	3.39	89	.270	.336	129-0-4	.155	-4	70	-12		-1.1

CURRIE, BILL William Cleveland B11.29.1928 Leary GA BR/TR/6-0/175 d4.13

| 1955 | Was A | 0 | 0 | — | 3 | 0 | 0 | 0 | 4.1 | 7 | 3 | 1 | 2-0 | 2 | 12.46 | 31 | .350 | .435 | 0 | — | 0 | | -4 | | -0.2 |

CURRY, GEORGE George James "Soldier Boy" B12.21.1888 Bridgeport CT D10.5.1963 West Haven CT BR/TR/6-0/185 d7.16

| 1911 | StL A | 0 | 3 | .000 | 3 | 3 | 0 | 0 | 15.2 | 19 | 15 | 0 | 0 | 24 | 2 | 7.47 | 45 | .339 | .538 | 5 | .000 | -1 | 78 | -6 | | -0.9 |

CURRY, STEVE Stephen Thomas B9.13.1965 Winter Park FL BR/TR/6-6/217 [BosA84 7/172] d7.10 Col Manatee (FL) CC

| 1988 | Bos A | 0 | 1 | .000 | 4 | 2 | 0 | 0 | 11 | 15 | 10 | 1 | 0 | 14-2 | 4 | 8.18 | 50 | .357 | .500 | 0 | — | 0 | 133 | -4 | | -0.3 |

CURRY, WES Wesley B4.1.1860 Wilmington DE D5.19.1933 Philadelphia PA d8.6 U6

| 1884 | Ric AA | 0 | 2 | .000 | 2 | 2 | 2 | 0 | 16 | 15 | 14 | 2 | 1 | 3 | 1 | 5.06 | 66 | .221 | .264 | 8 | .250 | -0 | 55 | -3 | | -0.3 |

CURTIS, CLIFF Clifton Garfield B7.3.1881 Delaware OH D4.23.1943 Utica OH BR/TR/6-2/180 d8.23

1909	Bos N	4	5	.444	10	9	8-2	0	83	53	17	1	2	30	22	1.41	200	.191	.275	29	.034	-3	47	12		1.2
1910	Bos N	6	24	.200	43	37	12-2	2	251	251	154	9	12	124	75	3.55	94	.277	.371	82-0-2	.146	-4	68	-11		-1.3
1911	Bos N	1	8	.111	12	9	5	0	77	79	50	4	2	34	12	4.44	86	.265	.344	28-0-1	.250	-0	72	-5		-0.2
	Chi N	2	1	.333	4	1	0	0	7	7	4	0	3	5	4	3.86	86	.241	.405	2	.500	0	0	0		-0.1
	Year	2	1	.667	8	5	3-1	0	45	45	19	0	1	15	13	2.60	132	.260	.323	15-0-1	.267	0	87	3		0.2
1912	Phi N	4	11	.267	24	15	8-1	1	129	131	73	4	6	54	40	3.77	97	.262	.341	45-0-2	.267	0	72	-3		-0.4
	Bro N	2	5	.286	10	8	2	0	50	55	30	3	4	20	20	3.24	112	.286	.357	15	.000	-2	78	0		-0.1
	Year	6	16	.333	34	23	10-1	1	179	186	103	7	10	74	60	3.57	103	.270	.345	60-0-2	.205	-2	74	-3		-0.5

YEAR	TM LG	W	L	PCT	G	GS	CG-SHO	SV-BS	IP	H	R	HR	HB	BB-IB	SO	ERA	AERA	OAV	OOB	AB-HR-SH	AVG	PB	SUP	APR	DL	PW
1913	Bro N	8	9	.471	30	16	6	2	151.2	145	75	1	7	55	57	3.26	101	.255	.328	49-0-5	.122	-3	93	-1		-0.4
Total	5	28	61	.315	136	94	39-5	6	744.2	707	393	22	37	317	236	3.31	101	.259	.344	246-0-11	.159	-10	76	-6		-1.4

CURTIS, JACK   Jack Patrick   B1.11.1937 Rhodhiss NC   BL/TL/5-10/175*   d4.22

YEAR	TM LG	W	L	PCT	G	GS	CG-SHO	SV-BS	IP	H	R	HR	HB	BB-IB	SO	ERA	AERA	OAV	OOB	AB-HR-SH	AVG	PB	SUP	APR	DL	PW
1961	Chi N	10	13	.435	31	27	6	0	180.1	220	117	21	3	51-6	57	4.89	85	.303	.346	60-2-2	.167	3	90	-15		-1.3
1962	Chi N	0	2	.000	4	3	0	0	18	18	8	2	0	6-1	8	3.50	118	.277	.333	4	.250	0	42	1		0.1
	Mil N	4	4	.500	30	5	0	1	75.2	82	39	8	2	27-3	40	4.16	91	.282	.345	18	.222	2	120	-3		-0.1
	Year	4	6	.400	34	8	0	1	93.2	100	47	10	2	33-4	48	4.04	96	.281	.343	22	.227	2	91	-2		0.0
1963	Cle A	0	0	—	4	0	0	0	5	8	10	0	1	5-1	3	18.00	20	.348	.483	0	—	0		-7		-0.4
Total	3	14	19	.424	69	35	6	1	279	328	174	33	4	89-11	108	4.84	84	.297	.349	82-2-2	.183	5	91	-24		-1.7

CURTIS, JOHN   John Duffield   B3.9.1948 Newton MA   BL/TL/6-2/185(175-190)   [BosA68 S1/10]   d8.13   Col Clemson

YEAR	TM LG	W	L	PCT	G	GS	CG-SHO	SV-BS	IP	H	R	HR	HB	BB-IB	SO	ERA	AERA	OAV	OOB	AB-HR-SH	AVG	PB	SUP	APR	DL	PW
1970	Bos A	0	0	—	1	0	0	0-0	2.1	4	4	1	0	1-0	1	11.57	34	.333	.385	0		0		-2		-0.1
1971	Bos A	2	2	.500	5	3	1	0-1	26	30	9	4	0	6-1	19	3.12	120	.291	.330	9	.111	-0	64	2		0.2
1972	Bos A	11	8	.579	26	21	8-3	0-0	154.1	161	69	8	0	50-6	106	3.73	87	.271	.327	53-0-3	.094	-3*	100	-6		-1.0
1973	Bos A	13	13	.500	35	30	10-4	0-0	221.1	225	103	24	2	83-10	101	3.58	113	.264	.330	0		0	91	8		0.9
1974	StL N	10	14	.417	33	29	5-2	1-0	195	199	91	15	2	83-6	67	3.44	111	.268	.342	38-0-5	.211	2	90	-3		0.8
1975	StL N	8	9	.471	39	18	4	1-0	146.2	151	70	13	2	65-6	52	4.50	80	.276	.357	35-0-5	.200	2*	74	-9		-1.0
1976	StL N	6	11	.353	37	15	3-1	1-0	134	139	68	11	0	48-9	47	5.49	72	.314	.406	13-0-3	.231	1*	120	-10		-0.6
1977	SF N	3	3	.500	43	9	1-1	1-2	77	95	48	5	1	48-9	38	3.71	93	.262	.336	2-0-1	.000	-0		-3		-0.3
1978	SF N	4	3	.571	46	0	0	1-2	63	60	31	1	0	29-8	85	4.18	84	.257	.316	34-0-6	.147	1*	89	-9		-1.3
1979	SF N	10	9	.526	27	18	3-2	0-0	120.2	121	62	15	0	42-7	71	3.51	97	.262	.328	62-0-5	.194	1*	98	-4		-0.2
1980	SD N	10	8	.556	30	27	6	0-0	187	184	84	9	2	67-13	71	5.13	63	.275	.349	13-0-1	.077	-1	127	-15		-1.7
1981	SD N	2	6	.250	28	8	0	0-1	66.2	70	41	11	1	30-2	31	4.10	84	.271	.340	37-0-4	.297	3	123	-10		-0.2
1982	SD N	8	6	.571	26	18	1-1	0-0	116.1	121	62	15	1	46-0	54	6.00	68	.320	.358	0	—	0		-2		-0.2
	Cal A	0	1	.000	8	0	0	1-1	12	16	8	0	0	3-2	10	3.80	107	.258	.334	0	—	0	75	1		-0.1
1983	Cal A	1	2	.333	37	3	0	5-3	90	89	44	5	2	40-11	36	4.40	91	.263	.325	0	—	0		-2	82	-0.1
1984	Cal A	1	2	.333	12	1	0	0	28.2	30	16	4	0	11-1	11	4.40	91	.270	.339	0	—	0	97	-60	82	-5.8
Total	15	89	97	.478	438	199	42-14	11-10	1641	1695	810	140	13	669-92	825	3.96	92	.270	.339	359-0-39	.175	4	97	-60		-5.8

CURTIS, VERN   Vernon Eugene "Turk"   B5.24.1920 Cairo IL   D6.24.1992 Cairo IL   BR/TR/6-0/170   d9.6   Mil 1944-45

YEAR	TM LG	W	L	PCT	G	GS	CG-SHO	SV-BS	IP	H	R	HR	HB	BB-IB	SO	ERA	AERA	OAV	OOB	AB-HR-SH	AVG	PB	SUP	APR	DL	PW
1943	Was A	0	0	—	2	0	0	0	4	3	3	0	0	6	1	6.75	47	.200	.429	—		0		-1		-0.1
1944	Was A	0	1	.000	3	1	0	0	9.2	8	3	0	0	3	2	2.79	117	.235	.297	2	.000	-0	0	1		0.8
1946	Was A	0	0	—	11	0	0	0	16.1	19	13	1	0	10	7	7.16	47	.297	.392	2	.000	-0		-6		-0.3
Total	3	0	1	.000	16	1	0	0	30	30	19	1	0	19	10	5.70	58	.265	.371	4	.000	-1	0	-6		-0.7

CUSHMAN, ED   Edgar Leander   B3.27.1852 Eagleville OH   D9.26.1915 Erie PA   BR/TL/6-0/177   d7.6

YEAR	TM LG	W	L	PCT	G	GS	CG-SHO	SV-BS	IP	H	R	HR	HB	BB-IB	SO	ERA	AERA	OAV	OOB	AB-HR-SH	AVG	PB	SUP	APR	DL	PW
1883	Buf N	3	3	.500	7	7	5	0	50.1	61	41	0		17	34	3.93	81	.285	.338	23	.217	-0	130	-4		-0.6
1884	Mil U	4	0	1.000	4	4	4-2	0	36	10	4	0		3	47	1.00	133	.082	.104	11	.091	-1	144	3		0.5
1885	Phi AA	3	7	.300	10	10	10	0	87	101	77	1	3	17	37	3.52	98	.269	.306	37	.189	-1	127	-4		-0.1
	NY AA	8	14	.364	22	22	22	0	191	158	105	2	3	33	133	2.78	112	.210	.246	69	.145	-1	72	4		0.5
	Year	11	21	.344	32	32	32	0	278	259	182	3	6	50	170	3.01	107	.229	.266	106	.160	-2	91	-3		0.1
1886	NY AA	17	21	.447	38	38	37-2	0	325.2	278	180	6	1	99	167	3.12	105	.220	.277	126	.151	-6	82	7		0.4
1887	NY AA	10	15	.400	26	26	25	0	220	310	232	9	9	83	64	5.97	71	.325	.384	93	.247	3	97	-43		-3.6
1890	Tol AA	21	21	.447	40	38	34	1	315.2	346	208	5	10	107	125	4.19	94	.270	.331	130	.100	-9	101	-4		-1.2
Total	6	62	81	.434	147	145	137-4	1	1225.2	1264	847	23	26	359	607	3.86	92	.254	.308	489	.160	-16	96	-41		-5.0

CUSHMAN, HARVEY   Harvey Barnes   B7.10.1877 Rockland ME   D12.27.1920 Emsworth PA   d8.24   Col Maine

YEAR	TM LG	W	L	PCT	G	GS	CG-SHO	SV-BS	IP	H	R	HR	HB	BB-IB	SO	ERA	AERA	OAV	OOB	AB-HR-SH	AVG	PB	SUP	APR	DL	PW
1902	Pit N	0	4	.000	4	4	3	0	25.2	30	31	0	2	31	12	7.36	37	.291	.463	10	.200	-0	50	-14		-1.1

CVENGROS, MIKE   Michael John   B12.1.1901 Pana IL   D8.2.1970 Hot Springs AR   BL/TL/5-8/159   d9.30

YEAR	TM LG	W	L	PCT	G	GS	CG-SHO	SV-BS	IP	H	R	HR	HB	BB-IB	SO	ERA	AERA	OAV	OOB	AB-HR-SH	AVG	PB	SUP	APR	DL	PW
1922	NY N	0	1	.000	1	1	1	0	6	5	1	1	3	3	3	4.00	100	.194	.286	3	.000	-0	20	0		0.0
1923	Chi A	12	13	.480	40	26	14	3	214.1	216	110	6	13	107	86	4.41	90	.269	.364	74-0-4	.203	-1*	98	-5		-0.4
1924	Chi A	3	12	.200	26	15	2	0	105.2	119	80	7	3	67	36	5.88	70	.300	.405	30-0-1	.200	2	93	-20		-2.0
1925	Chi A	3	9	.250	22	11	4	0	104.2	109	56	7	5	36	32	4.30	97	.278	.371	33-0-3	.152	-1	105	-1		-0.2
1927	†Pit N	2	1	.667	23	4	0	1	53.2	55	25	3	1	24	21	3.35	123	.271	.351	19-0-1	.158	-0	114	4		0.4
1929	Chi N	5	4	.556	32	4	0	2	64	82	39	2	1	29	23	4.64	99	.319	.390	15	.400	2*	109	0		0.0
Total	6	25	40	.385	144	61	21	6	551.1	587	315	24	22	285	201	4.59	90	.282	.374	174-0-9	.201	1	98	-22		-2.2

CYR, ERIC   Eric   B2.11.1979 Montreal QC, Can.   BR/TL/6-4/200   [SDN97 30/892]   d6.23   Col Seminole St. (OK) JC

YEAR	TM LG	W	L	PCT	G	GS	CG-SHO	SV-BS	IP	H	R	HR	HB	BB-IB	SO	ERA	AERA	OAV	OOB	AB-HR-SH	AVG	PB	SUP	APR	DL	PW
2002	SD N	0	1	.000	5	0	0	0	6	8	7	0	0	6-1	4	10.50	37	.286	.429	1	.000	-0		-4	31	-0.6

CZAJKOWSKI, JIM   James Mark   B12.18.1963 Parma OH   BB/TR/6-4/215   [AtlN86 29/711]   d7.29   Col North Alabama

YEAR	TM LG	W	L	PCT	G	GS	CG-SHO	SV-BS	IP	H	R	HR	HB	BB-IB	SO	ERA	AERA	OAV	OOB	AB-HR-SH	AVG	PB	SUP	APR	DL	PW
1994	Col N	0	0	—	5	0	0	0-0	8.2	9	4	2	3	6-1	2	4.15	120	.281	.439	0		0	1			0.0

DAAL, OMAR   Omar Jesus (Cordero)   B3.1.1972 Maracaibo, Venez   BL/TL/6-3/185(160-204)   d4.23   [DL 2004 Bal A 183]

YEAR	TM LG	W	L	PCT	G	GS	CG-SHO	SV-BS	IP	H	R	HR	HB	BB-IB	SO	ERA	AERA	OAV	OOB	AB-HR-SH	AVG	PB	SUP	APR	DL	PW
1993	LA N	2	3	.400	47	0	0	0-1	35.1	36	20	5	0	21-3	19	5.09	76	.277	.373	0	—	0		-4		-0.0
1994	LA N	0	0	—	24	0	0	0-0	13.2	12	5	1	0	5-0	11	3.29	121	.245	.315	0	—	0		1		0.0
1995	LA N	4	0	1.000	28	0	0	0-1	20	29	16	1	1	15-4	11	7.20	54	.354	.455	0	—	0		-7		-0.0
1996	Mon N	4	5	.444	64	6	0	0-4	87.1	74	40	10	1	37-3	82	4.02	108	.228	.308	11	.000	-1	87	4		0.3
1997	Mon N	1	2	.333	33	0	0	1-2	30.1	48	35	4	2	15-3	16	9.79	43	.378	.448	5	.200	0	80	2		0.1
	Tor A	1	1	.500	9	5	0	0-0	27	34	13	3	0	6-0	28	4.00	115	.304	.339	0	—	0	68	24	19	2.0
1998	Ari N	8	12	.400	33	23	3-1	0-0	162.2	146	60	12	1	51-3	132	2.88	149	.245	.305	46-0-5	.109	-1	106	25		2.5
1999	†Ari N	16	9	.640	32	32	2-1	0-0	214.2	188	92	21	7	79-3	148	3.65	127	.236	.308	69-0-6	.232	3	89	27		2.7
2000	Ari N	2	10	.167	20	16	0	0-0	96	127	88	17	7	42-11	45	7.22	66	.315	.385	27-1-3	.259	2	89	-27		-2.7
	Phi N	2	9	.182	12	12	0	0-0	71	81	40	9	2	30-0	51	4.69	98	.290	.362	18-0-2	.278	2	73	-1		0.0
	Year	4	19	.174	32	28	0	0-0	167	208	128	26	9	72-11	96	6.14	77	.305	.376	45-1-5	.267	5	82	-29		-2.9
2001	Phi N	13	7	.650	32	32	0	0-0	185.2	199	100	26	5	56-3	107	4.46	92	.273	.327	55-0-7	.236	3	116	-8		-0.7
2002	LA N	11	9	.550	39	23	0	0-0	161.1	142	73	20	2	54-3	105	3.90	100	.239	.304	39-1-8	.154	1	95	1	74	0.1
2003	Bal A	4	11	.267	19	17	0	0-0	93.2	134	69	11	2	32-0	51	6.34	73	.343	.390	0	—	0	83	-17	276	-1.7
Total	11	68	78	.466	392	164	5-2	1-8	1198.2	1250	651	140	34	441-37	806	4.55	95	.271	.337	270-2-31	.196	10	94	-25		-1.4

D'ACQUISTO, JOHN   John Francis   B12.24.1951 San Diego CA   BR/TR/6-2/200*   [SFN70 1/17]   d9.2

YEAR	TM LG	W	L	PCT	G	GS	CG-SHO	SV-BS	IP	H	R	HR	HB	BB-IB	SO	ERA	AERA	OAV	OOB	AB-HR-SH	AVG	PB	SUP	APR	DL	PW
1973	SF N	1	1	.500	7	3	1	0-0	27.2	23	14	4	0	19-0	29	3.58	108	.219	.336	9	.000	-1	145	0		0.0
1974	SF N	12	14	.462	38	36	5-1	0-0	215	182	101	13	6	124-7	167	3.77	101	.237	.334	71-1-2	.113	-1*	81	3		0.5
1975	SF N	2	4	.333	10	6	0	0-0	28	29	35	5	2	34-0	22	10.29	37	.264	.445	7	.000	-0	115	-19	100	-1.9
1976	SF N	3	8	.273	28	19	0	0-0	106	93	69	9	3	102-1	53	5.35	68	.243	.401	26-0-4	.269	2	94	-17		-1.7
1977	StL N	0	0	—	3	2	0	0-0	8.1	5	4	0	1	10-0	9	4.32	90	.185	.410	2	.000	-0	137	0	21	0.0
	SD N	1	2	.333	17	12	0	0-0	44	49	41	9	1	47-0	45	6.95	51	.297	.451	6-0-2	.000	-0	116	-19		-1.9
	Year	1	2	.333	20	14	0	0-0	52.1	54	45	9	2	57-0	54	6.54	56	.281	.445	8-0-2	.000	1	119	-20		-2.0
1978	SD N	4	3	.571	45	3	0	10-0	93	60	24	2	3	56-2	104	2.13	157	.185	.305	21	.190	1	54	14		1.4
1979	SD N	9	13	.409	51	11	1-1	2-4	133.2	140	83	15	3	86-6	97	4.92	72	.275	.380	31-0-3	.129	1	96	-22		-2.2
1980	SD N	2	3	.400	39	0	0	1-1	67	67	29	2	1	36-9	44	3.76	91	.270	.359	8-0-2	.000	-1		-2		-0.0
	Mon N	2	0	1.000	11	0	0	2-1	20.2	14	7	0	0	9-0	15	2.18	167	.206	.295	0		0		1		0.1
	Year	2	5	.286	50	0	0	3-2	87.2	81	36	2	1	45-9	59	3.39	102	.256	.345	8-0-2	.000	-1		-14		-0.1
1981	Cal A	0	0	—	6	0	0	0-0	19.1	26	24	2	1	12-0	8	10.71	34	.338	.415	0		0		-3		-0.0
1982	Oak A	1	0	1.000	11	0	0	0-0	17	20	11	1	0	9-0	7	5.29	75	.290	.372	0		0	97	-76	121	-7.6
Total	10	34	51	.400	266	92	7-2	15-6	779.2	708	442	52	19	544-25	600	4.56	80	.245	.365	181-1-13	.127	0	97	-76		-7.6

DAGENHARD, JOHN   John Douglas   B4.25.1917 Magnolia OH   D7.16.2001 Bolivar OH   BR/TR/6-2/195   d9.28   Col Ohio St.

YEAR	TM LG	W	L	PCT	G	GS	CG-SHO	SV-BS	IP	H	R	HR	HB	BB-IB	SO	ERA	AERA	OAV	OOB	AB-HR-SH	AVG	PB	SUP	APR	DL	PW
1943	Bos N	1	0	1.000	2	1	1	0	9	7	2	0	1	5-0	2	2.00	—	.225	.326	3-0-1	.000	-0	124	3		0.3

DAGLIA, PETE   Peter George   B2.28.1907 Napa CA   D3.11.1952 Willits CA   BR/TR/6-3/210   d6.8

YEAR	TM LG	W	L	PCT	G	GS	CG-SHO	SV-BS	IP	H	R	HR	HB	BB-IB	SO	ERA	AERA	OAV	OOB	AB-HR-SH	AVG	PB	SUP	APR	DL	PW
1932	Chi A	4	4	.333	12	5	2	0	50	67	35	4	4	20	16	5.76	75	.324	.394	13-0-2	.077	-1	83	-6		-0.6

DAHL, JAY   Jay Steven   B12.6.1945 San Bernardino CA   D6.20.1965 Salisbury NC   BB/TL/5-10/183   d9.27

YEAR	TM LG	W	L	PCT	G	GS	CG-SHO	SV-BS	IP	H	R	HR	HB	BB-IB	SO	ERA	AERA	OAV	OOB	AB-HR-SH	AVG	PB	SUP	APR	DL	PW
1963	Hou N	0	1	.000	1	1	0	0	2.2	7	7	0	0	0-0	0	16.88	19	.438	.438	0		0	82	-5		-0.5

YEAR	TM LG	W	L	PCT	G	GS	CG-SHO	SV-BS	IP	H	R	HR	HB	BB-IB	SO	ERA	AERA	OAV	OOB	AB-HR-SH	AVG	PB	SUP	APR	DL	PW

DAHLKE, JERRY Jerome Alexander "Joe" B6.8.1930 Marathon WI BR/TR/6-0/180 d5.6
| 1956 | Chi A | 0 | 0 | — | 5 | 0 | 0 | 0 | 2.1 | 5 | 5 | 0 | 0 | 6-0 | 1 | 19.29 | 21 | .455 | .647 | 0 | — | 0 | | -4 | | -0.2 |

DAIGLE, CASEY Sean Casey B4.4.1981 Lake Charles LA BR/TR/6-5/215 [AriN99 1/31] d4.9
| 2004 | Ari N | 2 | 3 | .400 | 10 | 10 | 0 | 0-0 | 49 | 63 | 41 | 9 | 2 | 27-3 | 17 | 7.16 | 64 | .320 | .405 | 17-0-1 | .118 | -0* | 104 | -12 | | -1.1 |

DAILEY, SAM Samuel Laurence B3.31.1904 Oakford IL D12.2.1979 Columbia MO BL/TR/5-11/168 d7.4
| 1929 | Phi N | 2 | 2 | .500 | 20 | 4 | 0 | 0 | 51.1 | 74 | 48 | 5 | 1 | 23 | 18 | 7.54 | 69 | .349 | .415 | 17 | .059 | -2 | 80 | -12 | | -1.0 |

DAILEY, BILL William Garland B5.13.1935 Arlington VA BR/TR/6-3/185* d8.17
1961	Cle A	1	0	1.000	12	0	0	0	19	16	4	0	0	6-1	7	0.95	415	.232	.289	2	.000	-0		6		0.3
1962	Cle A	2	2	.500	27	0	0	1	42.2	43	18	0	2	17-4	24	3.59	108	.270	.341	3	.000	-0		2		0.1
1963	Min A	6	3	.667	66	0	0	21	108.2	80	26	9	0	19-5	72	1.99	183	.208	.244	21-1-1	.238	-2		21		2.9
1964	Min A	1	2	.333	14	0	0	0	15.1	23	16	3	4	17-2	6	8.22	44	.377	.537	0	—	0		-8		-1.4
Total	4	10	7	.588	119	0	0	22	185.2	162	64	12	6	59-12	109	2.76	135	.241	.304	26-1-1	.192	1		21		1.9

DAILY, ED Edward M. B9.7.1862 Providence RI D10.21.1891 Washington DC BR/TR/5-10.5/174 d5.4 b-Con ▲
1885	Phi N	26	23	.531	50	50	49-4	0	440	370	212	12		90	140	2.21	126	.217	.256	184-1	.207	-0	82	29		2.6
1886	Phi N	16	9	.640	27	23	22-1	0	218	211	123	7		59	95	3.06	108	.242	.290	309-4	.227	3*	104	7		0.9
1887	Phi N	0	4	.000	6	5	4	0	41.1	52	52	2	0	25	7	7.19	59	.376	.376		.283	1*	101	-13		-0.8
	Was N	0	1	.000	1	1	1	0	7	5	6	0	0	6	3	7.71	52	.208	.367	311-2	.251	0*	48	-2		-0.2
	Year	0	5	.000	7	6	5	0	48.1	57	58	2	0	31	10	7.26	58	.279	.374	417-3	.259	1	92	-14		-1.0
1888	Was N	2	7	.222	9	8	8	0	73.2	88	69	7	3	19	20	4.89	57	.278	.325	453-7	.225	1*	77	-20		-1.8
1889	Col AA	0	0	—	2	0	0	0	1.2	1	7	0	0	4	2	21.60	17	.167	.500	578-3	.256	0*		-4		-0.4
1890	Bro AA	10	14	.417	27	27	27	0	235.2	252	161	3	18	93	82	4.05	96	.265	.342	394-1	.239	3*	95	-2		0.3
	NY N	2	0	1.000	2	1	1	0	16	9	6	0	4	6	0	2.25	156	.113	.254	15	.133	-1*	72	3		0.2
†Lou AA		6	3	.667	12	10	9-1	0	93	83	35	2	4	30	31	1.94	199	.232	.298	80	.250	2*	107	20		2.0
1891	Lou AA	4	8	.333	15	14	11	0	111.1	149	109	6	8	48	27	5.74	64	.310	.382	64	.250	2*	101	-26		-1.9
Total	7	66	69	.489	151	139	132-6	1	1237.2	1217	780	39	37	380	407	3.39	98	.246	.305	2494-19	.240	12	93	-8		0.9

DAILY, HUGH Hugh Ignatius "One Arm" (b Harry Criss) B1848 , Ireland BR/TR/6-2/180 d5.1
1882	Buf N	15	14	.517	29	29	29	0	255.2	246	165	7		70	116	2.99	98	.234	.282	110	.164	-6	103	-7		-1.4
1883	Cle N	23	19	.548	45	43	40-4	1	378.2	360	193	5		99	171	2.42	130	.243	.291	142	.127	-10	72	34		2.1
1884	CP U	27	27	.500	56	56	54-5	0	484.2	430	257	11		71-	469	2.43	100	.222	.249	196		-11	89	-1		-0.2
	Was U	1	1	.500	2	2	2	0	16	16	11	0		1	14	2.25	107	.242	.254	5	.000	-11*	78	0		-0.9
	Year	28	28	.500	58	58	56-5	0	500.2	446	268	11		72	483	2.43	100	.223	.250	201	.214	-12	79	-4		-1.1
1885	StL N	3	8	.273	11	11	10-1	0	91.1	92	72	5		44	31	3.94	70	.252	.333	35	.086	-3	71	-14		-1.6
1886	Was N	0	6	.000	6	6	6	0	49	69	60	2		40	15	7.35	44	.332	.440	16	.125	-1	69	-22		-1.9
1887	Cle AA	4	12	.250	16	16	16	0	139.2	181	108	1	3	44	30	3.67	118	.311	.362	58	.069	-8	77	8		0.0
Total	6	73	87	.456	165	163	157-10	1	1415	1394	866	31	3	369	846	2.92	101	.245	.291	562	.157	-39	80	-2		-3.9

DalCANTON, BRUCE John Bruce B6.15.1942 California PA BR/TR/6-2/205(205-230) d9.3 C5 Col California (PA)
1967	Pit N	2	1	.667	8	2	1	0	24	19	5	1	1	10-3	13	1.88	179	.211	.297	6	.333	1	65	4		0.6
1968	Pit N	1	1	.500	7	0	0	2	17	7	4	0	1	6-2	8	2.12	138	.127	.234	3-0-1	.000	-0		2		0.2
1969	Pit N	8	2	.800	57	0	0	5-1	86.1	79	34	3	0	49-12	56	3.34	104	.252	.351	10	.300	2		2		0.5
1970	Pit N	9	4	.692	41	6	1	1-3	84.2	94	48	7	1	39-8	53	4.57	87	.282	.356	16-0-1	.000	-1	178	-6		-1.0
1971	KC A	8	6	.571	25	22	2	0-0	141.1	144	63	8	0	44-0	58	3.44	100	.262	.315	46-0-6	.087	-3	105	-1	28	-0.5
1972	KC A	6	6	.500	35	16	1	2-0	132.1	135	64	7	1	29-6	75	3.40	90	.265	.304	41-0-5	.098	-2	124	-5		-0.7
1973	KC A	4	3	.571	32	3	1	3-3	97.1	108	60	8	4	46-12	38	4.81	86	.284	.367	0	—	0	43	-8		-0.6
1974	KC A	8	10	.444	31	22	9-2	0-0	175.1	135	71	5	5	82-3	96	3.13	122	.211	.304	0	—	0				
1975	KC A	0	2	.000	4	2	0	0-0	8.2	13	18	0	1	7-0	5	15.58	25	.479	.554	0	—	0	110	13		1.3
	Atl N	2	7	.222	26	9	0	3-3	67	63	33	2	6	24-1	38	3.36	113	.248	.321	19	.105	-1	103	-11		-1.8
1976	Atl N	3	5	.375	42	1	0	1-0	73.1	67	41	6	2	42-8	36	3.56	107	.244	.344	9-0-1	.222	-1	77	2		0.1
1977	Chi A	0	2	.000	8	0	0	0-0	24	20	11	1	0	13-0	9	3.75	109	.230	.330	0	—	0	70	-2		-0.1
Total	11	51	49	.510	316	83	15-2	19-10	931.1	894	442	48	23	391-55	485	3.67	99	.253	.329	150-0-14	.113	-3	106	-9	117	-1.9

DALE, GENE Emmett Eugene B6.16.1889 St.Louis MO D3.20.1958 St.Louis MO BR/TR/6-3/179 d9.19
1911	StL N	0	2	.000	5	2	0	0	14.2	13	12	0	2	16	13	6.75	50	.250	.443	5	.400	1	100	-5		-0.5
1912	StL N	0	5	.000	19	3	1	0	61.2	76	58	4	3	51	37	6.57	52	.311	.436	22	.273	1*	43	-19		-1.3
1915	Cin N	18	17	.514	49	35	20-4	3	296.2	256	115	6	6	107	104	2.46	116	.243	.316	91-0-8	.220	2	90	9		0.1
1916	Cin N	3	4	.429	17	5	2	0	69.2	80	44	3	2	33	23	5.17	50	.304	.386	21	.143	-0	98	-17		-1.7
Total	4	21	28	.429	90	45	23-4	3	442.2	425	229	13	13	207	177	3.60	81	.263	.352	139-0-8	.223	3	87	-32		-2.3

DALE, CARL James Carl B12.7.1972 Indianapolis IN BR/TR/6-2/215 [StLN94 2/53] d9.7 Col Winthrop
| 1999 | Mil N | 0 | 1 | .000 | 4 | 0 | 0 | 0-0 | 4 | 9 | 9 | 2 | 1 | 6-0 | 4 | 20.25 | 23 | .400 | .556 | 0 | — | 0 | | -7 | | -1.1 |

DALEY, BUD Leavitt Leo B10.7.1932 Orange CA BL/TL/6-1/185* d9.10
1955	Cle A	0	1	.000	2	1	0	0	7	10	5	1	0	1-0	2	6.43	62	.333	.355	2	.000	-0	45	-2		-0.2
1956	Cle A	1	0	1.000	14	0	0	0	20.1	21	15	2	5	1-0	13	6.20	68	.273	.408	2-0-1	.000	-0		-4		-0.2
1957	Cle A	2	8	.200	34	10	1	2	87.1	99	59	6	10	40-4	54	4.43	84	.279	.367	20-0-2	.200	0	79	-11		-1.1
1958	KC A	3	2	.600	26	5	1	0	70.2	67	29	5	6	19-1	39	3.31	118	.249	.312	16-0-1	.125	-1	78	4		0.3
1959	KC A★	16	13	.552	39	29	12-2	0	216.1	212	90	24	11	62-2	125	3.16	127	.257	.317	78-0-5	.295	4	100	19		2.9
1960	KC A★	16	16	.500	37	35	13-1	0	231	234	129	27	10	96-3	126	4.56	87	.263	.339	75-0-6	.160	-1	114	-13		-1.4
1961	KC A	4	8	.333	16	10	2	1	63.2	84	46	6	5	22-2	36	4.95	84	.319	.378	18-0-1	.111	-1	87	-8		-1.3
	†NY A	8	9	.471	23	17	7	0	129.2	127	63	17	4	51-6	83	3.96	104	.257	.347	45-0-2	.133	-1	119	-4		-0.6
	Year	12	17	.414	39	27	9	1	193.1	211	109	23	9	73-8	119	4.28	90	.278	.347	63-0-3	.127	-2	107	-12		-1.9
1962	†NY A	7	5	.583	43	6	0	4	105.1	105	47	8	5	21-0	55	3.59	104	.258	.301	27-0-1	.185	-0	147	2		0.2
1963	NY A	0	0	—	1	0	0	0	1	2	0	0	0	0-0	0	0.00	—	.667	.667	0	—	0		0	149	0.1
1964	NY A	3	2	.600	13	3	0	1	35	37	19	3	4	25-1	16	4.63	78	.274	.400	8-0-1	.250	1	147	-4		-0.4
Total	10	60	64	.484	248	116	36-3	10	967.1	992	502	99	60	351-20	549	4.03	97	.266	.337	291-0-20	.192	3	107	-21	149	-1.7

DALEY, BILL William B6.27.1868 Poughkeepsie NY D5.4.1922 Poughkeepsie NY TL/5-7/140 d7.17
1889	Bos N	3	3	.500	9	7	4	0	48	34	29	1	2	43	40	4.31	97	.193	.357	20	.150	-1	94	1		0.1
1890	Bos P	18	7	.720	34	25	19-2	2	235	246	178	7	9	167	110	3.60	122	.258	.373	110-2	.155	-5*	113	12		0.5
1891	Bos AA	8	6	.571	19	11	10	2	126.2	119	76	6	7	81	68	2.98	117	.240	.354	59	.169	-3*	169	5		0.2
Total	3	29	16	.644	62	43	33-2	4	409.2	399	283	14	18	291	218	3.49	117	.245	.356	189-2	.159	-8	123	18		0.8

DALTON, MIKE Michael Edward B3.27.1963 Palo Alto CA BR/TL/6-0/215 [BosA83 15/385] d5.31 Col De Anza (CA) JC
| 1991 | Det N | 0 | 0 | — | 8 | 0 | 0 | 0 | 8 | 12 | 3 | 1 | 0 | 2-0 | 4 | 3.38 | 124 | .333 | .368 | 0 | — | 0 | | 1 | | 0.0 |

DALY, GEORGE George Josephs "Pecks" B7.28.1887 Buffalo NY D12.12.1957 Buffalo NY BR/TR/5-10.5/175 d9.26 Col St. Bonaventure
| 1909 | NY N | 0 | 3 | .000 | 3 | 3 | 3 | 0 | 21 | 31 | 19 | 0 | 5 | 8 | 6 | 8.14 | 43 | .341 | .400 | 9 | .111 | -1 | 55 | -7 | | -1.0 |

D'AMICO, JEFF Jeffrey Charles B12.27.1975 St.Petersburg FL BR/TR/6-7/250* [MilA93 1/23] d6.28 [DL 1998 Mil N 181]
1996	Mil A	6	6	.500	17	17	0	0-0	86	88	53	21	0	31-0	75	5.44	95	.267	.327	0	—	0	101	-1		-0.1
1997	Mil A	9	7	.563	23	23	1-1	0-0	135.2	139	81	25	8	43-2	94	4.71	98	.264	.327	4-0-1	.000	-0	92	-2	45	-0.3
1999	Mil N	0	0	—	1	0	0	0	1	1	0	0	0	0-0	0	0.00	—	.250	.250	0	—	0		172		0.0
2000	Mil N	12	7	.632	23	23	1-1	0-0	162.1	143	55	14	0	46-5	101	2.66	174	.238	.297	44-1-6	.091	-1	76	34	24	3.5
2001	Mil N	4	3	.333	10	10	0	0-0	47.1	60	42	11	1	16-4	32	6.08	71	.306	.360	15	.067	-0	110	-13	131	-1.3
2002	NY N	6	10	.375	29	29	1-1	0-0	145.2	152	84	20	3	37-8	100	4.94	80	.267	.313	37-0-5	.108	-1	105	-14		-1.5
2003	Pit N	9	16	.360	29	29	2-1	0-0	175.1	204	104	23	7	42-6	100	4.77	91	.291	.336	48-1-9	.125	-1	94	-11		-1.3
2004	Cle A	1	2	.333	7	7	0	0-0	30.2	25	26	5	2	6-0	16	7.63	57	.333	.361	0	—	0	144	-12	46	-0.9
Total	8	45	52	.464	139	131	5-4	0-0	784	832	448	120	26	221-25	498	4.61	97	.272	.324	148-2-21	.101	-1	97	-18	599	-1.9

D'AMICO, JEFF Jeffrey Michael B11.9.1974 Inglewood CA BR/TR/6-3/200 [OakA93 2/67] d6.3
| 2000 | KC A | 0 | 1 | .000 | 7 | 1 | 0 | 0-0 | 13.2 | 19 | 14 | 2 | 0 | 15-1 | 9 | 9.22 | 57 | .345 | .486 | 0 | — | 0 | 54 | -5 | | -0.3 |

YEAR	TM	LG	W	L	PCT	G	GS	CG-SHO	SV-BS	IP	H	R	HR	HB	BB-IB	SO	ERA	AERA	OAV	OOB	AB-HR-SH	AVG	PB	SUP	APR	DL	PW

DAMMANN, BILL   William Henry "Wee Willie"   B8.9.1872 Chicago IL   D12.6.1948 Lynnhaven VA   BL/TL/5-7/155   d4.24

																											-0.1
1897	Cin	N	6	4	.600	16	11	7-1		95	122	65	2	5	37	21	4.74	96	.309	.375	31	.161	-1	100	-1		0.1
1898	Cin	N	16	10	.615	35	22	16-2	2	224.2	277	132	3	7	67	51	3.61	106	.301	.353	82-0-1	.195	1	101	2		-0.3
1899	Cin	N	2	1	.667	9	5	3-1	1	48	74	30	0	1	11	2	4.88	80	.351	.386	18	.056	-2	143	-3		-0.3
Total	3		24	15	.615	60	38	26-4	3	367.2	473	227	5	13	115	74	4.06	99	.310	.363	131-0-1	.168	-1	106	-2		-2.8

DANEKER, PAT   Patrick Rees   B1.14.1976 Williamsport PA   BR/TR/6-3/195   [ChiA97 5/159]   d7.2   Col Virginia

| 1999 | Chi | A | 0 | 0 | — | 3 | 2 | 0 | | 6.1 | 15 | 14 | 8 | 1 | 6-0 | 5 | 4.20 | 118 | .255 | .323 | 2 | .000 | -0 | 151 | 1 | | 0.0 |

DANEY, ART   Arthur Lee   B7.9.1904 Talihina OK   D3.11.1988 Phoenix AZ   BR/TR/5-11/165   d5.25

| 1928 | Phi | A | 0 | 0 | — | 1 | 0 | 0 | 0 | 1 | 1 | 0 | 0 | 0 | 0 | 0 | 0.00 | — | .250 | .250 | 0 | | | 0 | | | 0.0 |

DANFORTH, DAVE   David Charles "Dauntless Dave"   B3.7.1890 Granger TX   D9.19.1970 Baltimore MD   BL/TL/6-0/167   d8.1   Col Baylor

																											-0.3
1911	Phi	A	4	1	.800	14	2	1	1	33.2	29	18	1	3	17	21	3.74	84	.240	.348	6-0-1	.167	0	126	-2		-0.1
1912	Phi	A	0	0	—	3	0	0	0	20.1	26	14	0	0	12	8	3.98	77	.338	.427	8	.250	0		-3		-0.6
1916	Chi	A	6	5	.545	28	8	1	2	93.2	87	43	1	3	37	49	3.27	85	.259	.338	23-0-2	.087	-1	82	-4		0.4
1917	†Chi	A	11	6	.647	50	9	1-1	9	173	155	56	1	3	74	79	2.65	100	.244	.325	42-0-2	.143	-2	68	-13		-2.1
1918	Chi	A	6	15	.286	39	11	5	2	139	148	73	1	5	40	48	3.43	117	.288	.345	42-0-2	.143	-2	49	-21		-1.5
1919	Chi	A	1	2	.333	15	1	0	1	41.2	58	44	1	1	20	17	7.78	41	.333	.405	9-0-1	.111	-0	49	-21		0.3
1922	StL	A	5	2	.714	20	10	3	1	79.2	93	37	1	1	38	48	3.28	127	.304	.383	23	.087	-2	113	7		1.3
1923	StL	A	16	14	.533	38	29	16	1	226.1	221	111	4	12	87	96	3.94	106	.262	.340	71-0-8	.211	2	100	9		-0.2
1924	StL	A	15	12	.556	41	27	12-1	4	219.2	246	126	16	3	69	65	4.51	100	.292	.348	76-0-6	.171	-2	91	1		0.0
1925	StL	A	7	9	.438	38	15	5	2	159	172	96	19	3	61	53	4.36	107	.284	.353	46-0-5	.174	-2	115	4		-2.8
Total	10		71	66	.518	286	112	44-2	23	1186	1235	618	45	34	455	484	3.89	95	.277	.349	350-0-30	.160	-6	102	-17		

DANIEL, CHUCK   Charles Edward   B9.17.1933 Bluffton AR   BR/TR/6-2/195   d9.21   Col Ozarks

| 1957 | Det | A | 0 | 0 | — | 1 | 0 | 0 | 0 | 2.1 | 3 | 2 | 1 | 0 | 0-0 | 2 | 7.71 | 50 | .333 | .333 | 0 | — | 0 | | -1 | | 0.0 |

DANIELS, BENNIE   Bennie   B6.17.1932 Tuscaloosa AL   BL/TR/6-1.5/193(190-214)   d9.24   Col Compton (CA) CC

1957	Pit	N	0	1	.000	1	1	0	0	7	5	2	0	0	3-0	2	1.29	295	.208	.296	2	.000	-0	0	2		0.
1958	Pit	N	0	3	.000	8	5	1	0	27.2	31	19	3	1	15-1	7	5.53	70	.290	.379	8	.125	-0	56	-5		-0.
1959	Pit	N	7	9	.438	34	12	0	1	100.2	115	69	9	2	39-6	67	5.45	71	.287	.351	29-1-0	.310	6*	83	-18		-2.
1960	Pit	N	1	3	.250	10	6	0	0	40.1	52	35	4	0	17-1	16	7.81	48	.311	.371	16	.188	-0	122	-17		-1.
1961	Was	A	12	11	.522	32	28	12-1	0	212	184	90	14	3	80-8	110	3.44	117	.237	.309	76-2-3	.197	3	78	15		-1.
1962	Was	A	7	16	.304	44	21	3-1	2	161.1	172	98	14	2	68-5	66	4.85	83	.280	.351	46-1-4	.130	-1	78	-15		-1.
1963	Was	A	5	10	.333	35	24	6-1	1	168.2	163	90	19	1	58-9	88	3.70	100	.250	.314	47-1-4	.128	1*	93	-11		0.
1964	Was	A	8	10	.444	33	24	3-2	0	163	147	75	20	0	64-8	73	3.70	100	.245	.314	47-1-4	.128	0	82	1		0.
1965	Was	A	5	13	.278	33	18	1	1	116.1	135	75	16	0	39-7	42	4.72	74	.290	.343	30-0-3	.133	-1	70	-18		-2.
Total	9		45	76	.372	230	139	26-5	5	997	1004	553	99	9	383-45	471	4.44	86	.264	.330	300-5-20	.170	9	85	-66		-6.

DANIELS, CHARLIE   Charles L.   B7.1.1861 Roxbury MA   D2.9.1938 Boston MA   d4.18

| 1884 | Bos | U | 0 | 2 | .000 | 2 | 2 | 2 | 0 | 16.2 | 20 | 14 | 1 | | 2 | 12 | 4.32 | 55 | .278 | .297 | 11 | .273 | 0* | 108 | -3 | | -0. |

DANIELS, PETE   Peter J. "Smiling Pete"   B4.8.1864 Co. Cavan, Ireland   D2.13.1928 Indianapolis IN   BL/TL   d4.19

1890	Pit	N	1	2	.333	4	4	3	0	28	40	29	1	3	12	8	7.07	47	.325	.399	12	.333	1	153	-11		-0.
1898	StL	N	1	6	.143	10	6	3	0	54.2	62	41	0	3	14	13	3.62	105	.283	.335	17	.176	0	62	-3		-0.
Total	2		2	8	.200	14	10	6	0	82.2	102	70	1	6	26	21	4.79	76	.298	.358	29	.241	1	98	-14		-1

DARBY, GEORGE   George William "Deacon"   B2.6.1869 Kansas City MO   D2.25.1937 Sacramento CA   BR/TR/5-10.5/160   d4.28

| 1893 | Cin | N | 1 | 1 | .500 | 4 | 3 | 2 | 0 | 29 | 41 | 32 | 2 | 3 | 18 | 6 | 7.76 | 62 | .323 | .419 | 10 | .300 | 0 | 83 | -9 | | -0 |

DARCY, PAT   Patrick Leonard   B5.12.1950 Troy OH   BL/TR/6-3/175*   d9.12   Col Mesa (AZ) CC

1974	Cin	N	1	0	1.000	6	2	0	0-0	17	17	7	2	0	8-1	14	3.71	94	.262	.342	3-0-1	.333	0	125	0		0
1975	†Cin	N	11	5	.688	27	22	1	1-1	130.2	134	54	4	0	59-9	46	3.58	100	.269	.344	47-0-2	.085	-3	114	1		-0
1976	Cin	N	2	3	.400	11	4	0	2-0	39	41	27	2	0	22-2	15	6.23	56	.279	.368	11-0-1	.182	1	164	-11		-1
Total	3		14	8	.636	44	28	1	3-1	186.2	192	88	8	0	89-12	75	4.15	86	.270	.349	61-0-4	.115	-2	122	-10		-1

DARENSBOURG, VIC   Victor Anthony   B11.13.1970 Los Angeles CA   BL/TL/5-10/165(165-180)   d4.1   Col Lewis-Clark St.   [DL 1995 Fla N 17]

1998	Fla	N	0	7	.000	59	0	0	1-1	71	52	29	5	0	30-6	74	3.68	110	.207	.289	0	.000	-1*	5			0
1999	Fla	N	0	1	.000	56	0	0	0-1	34.2	50	36	3	6	21-1	16	8.83	50	.340	.434	0		0	-17			-0
2000	Fla	N	5	3	.625	56	0	0	0-1	62	61	32	7	2	28-1	59	4.06	108	.260	.336	8	.250	0	2			-0
2001	Fla	N	1	2	.333	58	0	0	1-2	48.2	52	24	4	1	10-6	33	4.25	98	.277	.313	0	—	0*	0		28	0
2002	Fla	N	1	2	.333	42	0	0	0-0	48.1	61	34	10	2	26-4	33	6.14	64	.305	.385	1-0-1	.000	-0*	-12			-0
2003	Col	N	0	0	—	3	0	0	0-0	2.1	4	1	0	0	1-0	4	0.00		.333	.333	0	—	-0*	1			-0
	Mon	N	0	0	—	6	0	0	0-0	6.2	13	8	2	0	1-0	4	10.80	41	.406	.424	1	.000	-0*	-4			-0
	Year		0	0	—	9	0	0	0-0	9	17	9	2	0	2-0	8	8.00	57	.386	.400	1	.000	-0	-3			-0
2004	NY	N	0	1	.000	5	0	0	0-0	5.2	10	5	1	0	2-0	1	7.94	84	.435	.444	0	—	0	1			-0
	Chi	A	0	0	—	2	0	0	0-0	1.1	1	0	0	0	0-0	1	0.00	—	.333	.500	0	—	0	4			-0
2005	Det	A	1	1	.500	22	0	0	0-0	22.1	24	7	2	0	7-2	9	2.82	150	.282	.330	0	—	-0	-22		45	-1
Total	8		8	17	.320	309	0	0	2-5	303	328	176	34	10	126-20	229	4.96	85	.279	.348	18-0-1	.111	-0				

DARLING, RON   Ronald Maurice   B8.19.1960 Honolulu HI   BR/TR/6-3/195*   [TexA81 1/9]   d9.6   Col Yale

1983	NY	N	1	3	.250	5	5	0	0-0	35.1	31	11	0	3	17-1	23	2.80	131	.248	.352	10-0-1	.100	-1	63	4		0
1984	NY	N	12	9	.571	33	33	2-2	0-0	205.2	179	97	17	5	104-2	136	3.81	94	.235	.328	67-0-6	.149	-1*	109	-4		-0
1985	NY	N☆	16	6	.727	36	35	4-2	0-0	248	214	93	21	4	114-1	167	2.90	121	.235	.321	76-0-13	.171	-2*	104	15		-0
1986	†NY	N	15	6	.714	34	34	4-2	0-0	237	203	84	21	3	81-2	184	2.81	128	.234	.300	81-0-10	.099	-2	122	21	23	-0
1987	NY	N	12	8	.600	32	32	2	0-0	207.2	183	111	24	3	96-3	167	4.29	89	.233	.318	65-0-10	.123	0	119	-11		-0
1988	†NY	N	17	9	.654	34	34	7-4	0-0	240.2	218	97	24	0	60-7	161	3.25	100	.258	.314	73-2-5	.123	1*	105	-8		-0
1989	NY	N	14	14	.500	33	33	4	0-0	217.1	214	100	19	3	70-7	153	3.52	94	.258	.314	73-2-5	.123	1*	105	-8		-0
1990	NY	N	7	9	.438	33	18	1	0-0	126	135	73	20	6	44-4	99	4.50	84	.273	.336	31-0-5	.129	0*	97	-2		-0
1991	NY	N	5	6	.455	17	17	0	0-0	102.1	96	59	17	6	28-1	58	3.87	95	.251	.310	34-0-5	.118	-0	90	-7		-0
	Mon	N	0	2	.000	3	3	0	0-0	17	25	16	6	1	5-0	11	7.41	49	.333	.383	6-0-1	.167	-0	96	-10		-0
	Year		5	8	.385	20	20	0	0-0	119.1	121	66	9	2	33-1	69	4.37	84	.265	.321	40-0-6	.125	-0	61	-1		-0
	Oak	A	3	7	.300	12	12	0	0-0	75	64	34	7	2	38-2	64	4.08	94	.237	.331	0	—	0*	103	1		-0
1992	†Oak	A	15	10	.600	33	33	4-3	0-0	206.1	198	98	15	4	72-5	99	3.66	103	.253	.318	0	—	0*	116	-20		-0
1993	Oak	A	5	9	.357	31	29	3	0-0	178	198	107	22	6	72-5	95	5.16	80	.281	.349	0	—	0*	89	-1		-0
1994	Oak	A	10	11	.476	33	25	1	0-0	160	162	89	18	7	59-3	69	4.50	100	.267	.337	1	.000	-0*	119	-21		-0
1995	Oak	A	4	7	.364	21	21	1	0-0	104	124	79	16	4	46-2	69	6.23	73	.296	.365	0	—	5	107	-44	23	-0
Total	13		136	116	.540	382	364	37-13	0-0	2360.1	2244	1139	239	59	906-40	1590	3.87	96	.252	.323	526-2-65	.144	5	107	-44	23	

DARNELL, BOB   Robert Jack   B11.6.1930 Wewoka OK   D1.3.1995 Fredericksburg TX   BR/TR/5-10/175*   d8.10

1954	Bro	N	0	0	—	6	1	0	0	14.1	15	7	2	0	7	5	3.14	130	.278	.361	2-0-1	.000	-0	131	1		
1956	Bro	N	0	0	—	1	0	0	0	1.1	1	0	0	0	0-0	0	0.00	—	.200	.200	0		0		1		
Total	2		0	0	—	7	1	0	0	15.2	16	7	2	0	7-0	5	2.87	142	.271	.348	2-0-1	.000	-0	131	2		

DARR, MIKE   Michael Edward   B3.23.1956 Pomona CA   BR/TR/6-4/190   [BalA74 4/96]   d9.6

| 1977 | Tor | A | 0 | 0 | 1.000 | 1 | 1 | 0 | 0 | 1.1 | 3 | 5 | 1 | 1 | 4-0 | 1 | 33.75 | 13 | .429 | .667 | 0 | — | 0 | 42 | -4 | | |

DARROW, GEORGE   George Oliver   B7.12.1903 Beloit KS   D3.24.1983 Sun City AZ   BL/TL/6-0/180   d4.22   Col Washburn Topeka

| 1934 | Phi | N | 2 | 6 | .250 | 17 | 8 | 2 | 1 | 49 | 57 | 37 | 4 | 4 | 28 | 14 | 5.51 | 86 | .302 | .403 | 15 | .133 | 0 | 103 | -5 | | |

DARWIN, DANNY   Daniel Wayne   B10.25.1955 Bonham TX   BR/TR/6-3/190(185-202)   d9.8   b-Jeff   Col Grayson Co. (TX) JC

1978	Tex	A	1	0	1.000	3	1	0	0-0	8.2	11	4	0	0	4-0	8	4.15	90	.324	.333	0	—	0	96	0		
1979	Tex	A	4	4	.500	20	6	1	0-0	78	50	36	5	5	30-2	58	4.04	103	.186	.274	0	—	0	138	3		
1980	Tex	A	13	4	.765	53	2	0	8-6	109.2	98	37	4	2	50-7	104	2.63	148	.243	.324	0	—	0	150	16	21	
1981	Tex	A	9	9	.500	22	22	6-2	0-0	146	115	67	12	6	57-5	98	3.64	96	.218	.300	0	—	0	121	-4		
1982	Tex	A	10	8	.556	56	1	0	7-7	89	95	38	6	4	37-8	61	3.44	113	.279	.349	0	—	0	88	9	29	
1983	Tex	A	8	13	.381	28	26	9-2	0-0	183	175	86	9	6	62-3	92	3.49	116	.250	.310	0						

YEAR	TM LG	W	L	PCT	G	GS	CG-SHO	SV-BS	IP	H	R	HR	HB	BB-IB	SO	ERA	AERA	OAV	OOB	AB-HR-SH	AVG	PB	SUP	APR	DL	PW
1984	Tex A	8	12	.400	35	32	5-1	0-0	223.2	249	110	19	4	54-2	123	3.94	106	.279	.322	0	—	0	89	6		0.4
1985	Mil A	8	18	.308	39	29	11-1	2-0	217.2	212	112	34	4	65-4	125	3.80	110	.254	.308	0	—	0	73	6		0.5
1986	Mil A	6	8	.429	27	14	5-1	0-1	130.1	120	62	13	3	35-1	80	3.52	124	.246	.297	0	—	0	70	10		1.0
	Hou N	5	2	.714	12	8	1	0-0	54.1	50	19	3	0	9-0	40	2.32	156	.239	.267	16-0-2	.063	-1	114	6		0.7
1987	Hou N	9	10	.474	33	30	3-1	0-0	195.2	184	87	17	5	69-12	134	3.59	110	.246	.313	66-0-1	.182	2*	102	7		0.7
1988	Hou N	8	13	.381	44	20	3	3-0	192	189	86	20	7	48-9	129	3.84	87	.259	.307	56-1-2	.071	-1	99	-8		-0.9
1989	Hou N	11	4	.733	68	0	0	7-4	122	92	34	8	2	33-9	104	2.36	144	.212	.268	17	.118	-1		15		1.9
1990	Hou N	11	4	.733	48	17	3	2-2	162.2	136	42	11	4	31-4	109	2.21	169	.225	.266	38-0-3	.132	1*	97	29		2.6
1991	Bos A	3	6	.333	12	12	0	0-0	68	71	39	15	4	15-1	42	5.16	84	.263	.309	0	—	0	74	-4	123	-0.5
1992	Bos A	9	9	.500	51	15	2	3-3	161.1	159	76	11	5	53-9	124	3.96	107	.257	.319	0	—	0	79	7		0.7
1993	Bos A	15	11	.577	34	34	2-1	0-0	229.1	196	93	31	3	49-8	130	3.26	142	.230	.272	0	—	0	87	33		3.5
1994	Bos A	7	5	.583	13	13	0	0-0	75.2	101	54	13	1	24-6	54	6.30	80	.317	.361	0	—	0	119	-8	57	-1.1
1995	Tor A	1	8	.111	13	11	1	0-0	65	91	60	13	3	24-2	36	7.62	62	.340	.393	0	—	0	64	-20		-2.2
	Tex A	2	2	.500	7	4	0	0-0	34	40	27	12	1	7-1	22	7.15	68	.292	.331	0	—	0	135	-7		-0.7
	Year	3	10	.231	20	15	1	0-0	99	131	87	25	4	31-3	58	7.45	64	.323	.373	0	—	0	83	-29		-2.9
1996	Pit N	7	9	.438	19	19	0	0-0	122.1	117	48	9	6	16-0	69	3.02	145	.253	.285	39-1-5	.205	2	80	17		2.4
	Hou N	3	2	.600	15	6	0	0-2	42.1	43	31	7	6	11-3	27	5.95	65	.267	.331	0	—	0	105	-10		-1.1
	Year	10	11	.476	34	25	0	0-2	164.2	160	79	16	12	27-3	96	3.77	113	.257	.297	49-1-7	.184	2	86	8		1.3
1997	Chi A	4	8	.333	21	17	1	0-0	113.1	130	60	21	1	31-1	62	4.13	107	.257	.329	3-0-1	.000	-0	92	3		0.3
	SF N	1	3	.250	10	7	0	0-0	44	51	26	5	1	14-0	30	4.91	84	.288	.342	0	.133	-0	118	-4		-0.0
1998	SF N	8	10	.444	33	25	0	0-0	176	176	97	23	8	49-4	81	5.51	73	.297	.352	45-0-4	.089	-2	115	-25		-2.8
Total	21	171	182	.484	716	371	53-9	32-25	3016.2	2951	1431	321	81	874-101	1942	3.84	106	.276	.310	305-2-20	.128	-0	95	81	230	9.2

DARWIN, JEFF   Jeffrey Scott   B7.6.1969 Sherman TX   BR/TR/6-3/180*   [SeaA88 13/331]   d6.13   b-Danny   Col Alvin (TX) CC

YEAR	TM LG	W	L	PCT	G	GS	CG-SHO	SV-BS	IP	H	R	HR	HB	BB-IB	SO	ERA	AERA	OAV	OOB	AB-HR-SH	AVG	PB	SUP	APR	DL	PW
1994	Sea A	0	0	—	2	0	0	0-0	4	7	6	1	1	3-1	4	13.50	37	.389	.500	0	—	0		-3		-0.2
1996	Chi A	0	1	.000	22	0	0	0-1	30.2	26	10	5	2	9-1	15	2.93	162	.232	.301	0	—	0		7		0.3
1997	Chi A	0	1	.000	14	0	0	0-0	13.2	17	8	1	0	7-0	9	5.27	84	.298	.369	0	—	0		-1		-0.1
Total	3	0	2	.000	38	0	0	0-1	48.1	50	24	7	3	19-2	25	4.47	105	.267	.343	0	—	0		3		0.0

DASHNER, LEE   Lee Claire "Lefty"   B4.25.1887 Renault IL   D12.16.1959 ElDorado KS   BB/TL/5-11.5/192   d8.4

| 1913 | Cle A | 0 | 0 | — | 1 | 0 | 0 | 0 | 1.2 | 1 | 1 | 0 | 0 | 2-0 | 1 | 5.40 | 56 | .000 | .000 | 0 | — | 0 | | | | 0.0 |

DASSO, FRANK   Francis Joseph Nicholas   B8.31.1917 Chicago IL   BR/TR/5-11.5/185   d4.22   Col American International

1945	Cin N	4	5	.444	16	12	6	0	95.2	89	50	9	0	53	39	3.67	102	.253	.351	31-0-4	.161	-1	99	-1		-0.2
1946	Cin N	0	0	—	2	0	0	0	1	2	3	0	0	2	1	27.00	12	.400	.571	0	—	0		-2		-0.1
Total	2	4	5	.444	18	12	6	0	96.2	91	53	9	0	55	40	3.91	96	.255	.354	31-0-4	.161	-1	99	-3		-0.3

DAUB, DAN   Daniel William "Mickey"   B1.12.1868 Middletown OH   D3.25.1951 Bradenton FL   BR/TR/5-10/160   d8.31   Col Denison

1892	Cin N	1	2	.333	4	3	2	0	25	23	10	0	2	13	7	2.88	113	.235	.336	7	.000	-1	39	2		0.1
1893	Bro N	6	6	.500	12	12	12	0	103	104	64	3	5	61	25	3.84	115	.254	.358	42	.190	-2	91	7		0.6
1894	Bro N	10	12	.455	34	27	15	0	224	291	209	7	18	91	45	6.11	81	.311	.383	95-0-4	.189	-6	103	-29		-2.4
1895	Bro N	10	10	.500	25	21	16	0	184.2	212	134	5	11	51	36	4.29	103	.284	.339	71	.197	-2	100	-5		-0.5
1896	Bro N	12	11	.522	32	24	18	0	225	255	120	4	8	63	53	3.60	115	.283	.335	84	.226	2	95	16		1.6
1897	Bro N	6	11	.353	19	16	11	0	137.2	180	117	8	10	48	19	6.08	67	.313	.376	49-0-2	.224	2	105	-28		-2.3
Total	6	45	52	.464	126	103	74	0	899.1	1065	654	27	54	327	185	4.75	93	.291	.357	348-0-6	.201	-6	98	-37		-2.9

DAUSS, HOOKS   George August (b George August Daus)   B9.22.1889 Indianapolis IN   D7.27.1963 St.Louis MO   BR/TR/5-10.5/168   d9.28

1912	Det A	1	1	.500	2	1	1	0	17	11	7	0	3	9	7	3.18	103	.186	.324	4	.250	1	68	1		0.2
1913	Det A	13	12	.520	33	29	22-2	1	225	188	96	4	13	82	107	2.48	118	.231	.311	79-0-1	.177	3*	113	8		1.1
1914	Det A	19	15	.559	45	35	22-3	3	302	286	126	3	18	87	150	2.86	98	.257	.321	97-1-5	.216	6*	102	0		0.7
1915	Det A	24	13	.649	46	35	27-1	2	309.2	261	115	1	11	115	132	2.50	121	.235	.313	103-0-5	.146	0	125	17		2.6
1916	Det A	19	12	.613	39	29	18-1	4	238.2	220	102	2	16	90	95	3.21	89	.257	.339	72-1-4	.222	8	117	-6		0.1
1917	Det A	17	14	.548	37	31	22-6	2	270.2	243	105	3	7	87	102	2.43	109	.245	.311	87-0-3	.126	-1*	105	7		1.0
1918	Det A	12	16	.429	33	26	21-1	2	249.2	243	105	3	9	58	73	2.99	89	.263	.313	77-0-4	.182	3	103	-10		-0.6
1919	Det A	21	9	.700	34	32	22-2	0	256.1	262	125	9	5	73	73	3.55	90	.267	.315	97-0-5	.144	-3	146	-9		-1.0
1920	Det A	13	21	.382	38	32	18	0	270.1	308	158	11	8	84	82	3.56	105	.289	.345	83-0-3	.169	1	88	-1		0.5
1921	Det A	10	15	.400	32	28	16	1	233	275	141	11	13	81	68	4.33	99	.297	.362	88-1-2	.261	2	106	-2		0.3
1922	Det A	13	13	.500	39	25	12-1	4	218.2	251	123	7	6	59	78	4.20	92	.289	.339	72-1-3	.208	3	110	-9		-0.6
1923	Det A	21	13	.618	50	39	22-4	3	316	331	140	10	7	78	105	3.62	107	.272	.319	104-0-6	.231	5	117	18		1.9
1924	Det A	12	11	.522	40	10	5	6	131.1	155	78	7	4	40	44	4.59	90	.302	.354	38-0-2	.132	-2	109	-6		-1.0
1925	Det A	16	11	.593	35	30	16-1	1	228	238	110	11	4	85	58	3.16	136	.272	.339	81-1-0	.185	1	114	23		2.4
1926	Det A	12	6	.667	35	5	0	5	124.1	135	63	6	0	49	27	4.20	97	.287	.354	42-1-2	.238	4	112	1		0.5
Total	15	223	182	.551	538	388	245-22	35	3390.2	3407	1594	87	121	1067	1201	3.30	103	.266	.329	1124-6-45	.189	32	112	28		8.1

DAVENPORT, CLAUDE   Claude Edwin "Big Dave"   B5.28.1898 Runge TX   D6.13.1976 Corpus Christi TX   BR/TR/6-6/193   d10.2   b-Dave

| 1920 | NY N | 0 | 0 | — | 1 | 0 | 0 | 0 | 1 | 4 | 1 | 0 | 1 | 0-1 | 0 | 4.50 | 67 | .250 | .333 | 1 | .000 | -0 | | 0 | | 0.0 |

DAVENPORT, DAVE   David W.   B2.20.1890 DeRidder LA   D10.16.1954 ElDorado AR   BR/TR/6-6/220   d4.17   b-Claude

1914	Cin N	2	2	.500	10	6	3-1	2	54	38	18	1	3	30	22	2.50	117	.202	.321	18-0-1	.111	-1	106	4		0.2
	StL F	8	13	.381	33	26	13-2	4	215.2	204	100	3	7	80	142	3.46	88	.251	.324	68-0-3	.088	-6	79	-7		-1.3
1915	StL F	22	18	.550	55	46	30-10	4	392.2	300	116	5	9	96	229	2.20	131	.215	.268	130-0-7	.092	-11	101	28		1.2
1916	StL A	12	11	.522	59	31	13-1	2	290.2	267	112	4	8	100	129	2.85	96	.256	.326	73-0-5	.137	3	105	0		0.2
1917	StL A	17	17	.500	47	39	20-2	2	280.2	273	137	5	8	105	100	3.08	84	.260	.331	92-0-4	.098	-6	107	-17		-2.7
1918	StL A	10	11	.476	31	22	12-2	1	180	182	84	0	7	69	60	3.25	84	.273	.347	52-1-5	.135	1	96	-10		-0.9
1919	StL A	2	11	.154	24	16	5	0	123.1	135	74	4	2	41	37	3.94	84	.280	.339	39-0-3	.077	-24	97	-12		-1.3
Total	6	73	83	.468	259	186	96-18	12	1537	1399	641	22	40	521	719	2.93	97	.248	.316	472-1-28	.104	-24	97	-12		-4.6

DAVENPORT, JOE   Joseph Jonathan   B3.24.1976 Chicago IL   BR/TR/6-5/225*   [TorA94 13/371]   d7.20

1999	Chi A	0	0	—	3	0	0	0-0	1.2	0	0	0	0	2-0	0	0.00	—	.000	.429	0	—	0		1		0.0
2001	Col N	0	0	—	7	0	0	0-0	10.1	9	7	1	0	7-0	8	3.48	153	.222	.349	1	1.000	0		1		0.0
Total	2	0	0	—	10	0	0	0-0	12	9	7	1	0	9-0	8	3.00	170	.220	.360	1	1.000	0		2		0.1

DAVENPORT, LUM   Joubert Lum   B6.26.1900 Tucson AZ   D4.21.1961 Dallas TX   BL/TL/6-1/165   d5.2   Col Arizona

1921	Chi A	0	3	.000	13	2	0	0	35.1	41	35	1	1	32	9	6.88	62	.318	.457	17	.412	2*	158	-12		-0.7
1922	Chi A	1	1	.500	9	1	0	0	16.2	14	21	2	0	13	9	10.80	38	.233	.370	3	.000	-0*	188	-12		-1.2
1923	Chi A	0	0	—	2	0	0	0	4.1	7	4	0	0	4	1	6.23	64	.438	.550	1-0-1	1.000	0		-1		0.0
1924	Chi A	0	0	—	1	0	0	0	2	1	1	0	0	2	1	0.00	—	.125	.300	0	—	0		1		0.0
Total	4	1	4	.200	25	3	0	0	58.1	63	61	3	1	51	20	7.71	54	.296	.434	21-0-1	.381	2	168	-24		-1.9

DAVEY, MIKE   Michael Gerard   B6.2.1952 Spokane WA   BR/TL/6-2/190*   [AtlN74*S2/32]   d8.13   Col Gonzaga

1977	Atl N	0	0	—	16	0	0	2-0	16	19	9	1	0	9-4	7	5.06	88	.302	.389	1	.000	-0		0		0.0
1978	Atl N	0	0	—	3	0	0	0-0	2.2	1	0	0	0	1-0	0	0.00	—	.125	.222	1	.000	-0		1		0.0
Total	2	0	0	—	19	0	0	2-0	18.2	20	9	1	0	10-4	7	4.34	101	.282	.370	1	.000	-0		1		0.0

DAVEY, TOM   Thomas Joseph   B9.11.1973 Garden City MI   BR/TR/6-7/230(215-230)   [TorA94 5/147]   d4.6   Col Henry Ford (MI) CC

1999	Tor A	1	1	.500	29	0	0	1-0	44	40	28	5	3	26-0	42	4.70	105	.241	.350	0	—	0		0		0.0
	Sea A	1	0	1.000	16	0	0	0-0	21	22	13	0	4	14-1	17	4.71	102	.268	.400	0	—	0		0		0.0
	Year	2	1	.667	45	0	0	1-0	65	62	41	5	7	40-1	59	4.71	104	.250	.367	0	—	0		0		0.0
2000	SD N	2	1	.667	11	0	0	0-1	12.2	12	1	0	0	2-0	9	0.71	627	.250	.280	0	—	0		6		1.1
2001	SD N	2	4	.333	39	0	0	0-4	38	41	22	3	1	17-3	37	4.50	94	.275	.349	0	—	0		-2	72	-0.2
2002	SD N	1	0	1.000	19	0	0	0-1	21	23	14	2	3	11-1	21	5.57	70	.287	.381	0	—	0		4	45	-0.2
Total	4	7	6	.538	114	0	0	1-6	136.2	138	78	10	11	70-5	123	4.41	101	.262	.357	0	—	0		0	117	0.7

DAVIAULT, RAY   Raymond Joseph Robert   B5.27.1934 Montreal QC, Can.   BR/TR/6-1/170   d4.13

| 1962 | NY N | 1 | 5 | .167 | 36 | 3 | 0 | 1-0 | 81 | 92 | 64 | 14 | 4 | 48-1 | 51 | 6.22 | 67 | .288 | .384 | 15 | .067 | -1 | 91 | -16 | | -1.2 |

DAVIDSON, BOB   Robert Banks   B1.6.1963 Bad Kurznach, W.Germany   BR/TR/6-0/185   [NYA84 24/615]   d7.15   Col East Carolina

| 1989 | NY A | 0 | 0 | — | 1 | 0 | 0 | 0-0 | 1 | 1 | 2 | 1 | 0 | 1-0 | 0 | 18.00 | 22 | .250 | .400 | 0 | — | 0 | | -1 | | -0.1 |

YEAR	TM LG	W	L	PCT	G	GS	CG-SHO	SV-BS	IP	H	R	HR	HB	BB-IB	SO	ERA	AERA	OAV	OOB	AB-HR-SH	AVG	PB	SUP	APR	DL	PW

DAVIDSON, TED　Thomas Eugene　B10.4.1939 Las Vegas NV　BR/TL/6-0/192(180-192)　d7.24　Col Hancock (CA) JC

																				17-0-2	.000	-2	140	10		0.9
1965	Cin N	4	3	.571	24	1	0	1	68.2	57	21	5	2	17-4	54	2.23	168	.233	.285							-0.2
1966	Cin N	5	4	.556	54	0	0	4	85.1	82	41	11	1	23-2	54	3.90	100	.253	.302	12	.000	0	0	0	62	0.0
1967	Cin N	1	0	1.000	9	0	0	0	13	13	6	0	0	3-1	6	4.15	90	.250	.291	0	—	0		-6		-0.4
1968	Cin N	1	0	1.000	23	0	0	0	21.2	27	15	3	0	7-0	7	6.23	60	.307	.358	2	.000	-0		-6		-0.1
	Atl N	0	0	—	4	0	0	0	6.2	10	5	2	0	4-1	3	6.75	44	.345	.424	0	—	0		-9		-0.5
	Year	1	0	1.000	27	0	0	0	28.1	37	20	5	0	11-1	10	6.35	49	.316	.375	2	.000	-0		-9		-0.1
Total	4	11	7	.611	114	1	0	5	195.1	189	88	21	3	54-8	124	3.69	101	.256	.307	31-0-2	.000	-3	140	2	62	0.2

DAVIE, JERRY　Gerald Lee　B2.10.1933 Detroit MI　BR/TR/6-0/185　d4.14

| 1959 | Det A | 2 | 2 | .500 | 11 | 5 | 1 | 0 | 36.2 | 40 | 25 | 8 | 4 | 17-1 | 20 | 4.17 | 97 | .265 | .351 | 10 | .400 | 2 | 100 | -3 | | -0.1 |

DAVIES, GEORGE　George Washington　B2.22.1868 Portage WI　D9.22.1906 Waterloo WI　?/180　d8.18　Col Wisconsin-Madison

1891	Mil AA	7	5	.583	12	12	12-1	0	102	94	48	2	3	35	61	2.65	166	.237	.303	37	.243	1	67	18		1.8
1892	Cle N	10	16	.385	26	26	23	0	215.2	201	112	4	6	69	95	2.59	131	.237	.299	87	.138	-5	69	17		1.3
1893	Cle N	0	2	.000	3	3	1	0	15	28	25	1	0	10	3	11.40	43	.389	.463	6	.333	0	110	-9		-0.8
	NY N	1	1	.500	5	1	1	0	36.1	41	31	1	0	13	7	6.19	75	.275	.333	12	.333	2	120	-4		0.0
	Year	1	3	.250	8	4	2	0	51.1	69	56	2	0	23	10	7.71	61	.312	.377	18	.333	2	115	-13		-0.8
Total	3	18	24	.429	46	42	37-1	0	369	364	216	8	9	127	166	3.32	116	.248	.312	142	.190	-3	73	22		2.3

DAVIES, KYLE　Hiram Kyle　B9.9.1983 Decatur GA　BR/TR/6-2/205　d5.21

| 2005 | Atl N | 7 | 6 | .538 | 21 | 14 | 0 | 0-1 | 87.2 | 98 | 51 | 8 | 1 | 49-5 | 62 | 4.93 | 87 | .280 | .370 | 15-0-10 | .200 | 1 | 113 | -6 | | -0.8 |

DAVIES, CHICK　Lloyd Garrison　B3.6.1892 Peabody MA　D9.5.1973 Middletown CT　BL/TL/5-8/145　d7.11　Col Massachusetts ▲

																	0	.261	.258	.324	46-0-3	.239	0*	167	0		0.1
1914	Phi A	1	0	1.000	1	1	1	0	9	8	4	0	0	3	4	1.00	261	.258	.324	132-0-5	.182	0*	125	-8		-1.3
1915	Phi A	1	2	.333	4	2	0	0	15.1	20	16	0	1	12	2	8.80	33	.339	.458	6	.000	-0*	188	-3		-0.1
1925	NY N	0	0	—	2	1	0	0	7.1	13	8	0	0	4	5	6.14	66	.361	.425	18	.222	1	44	-8		-0.5
1926	NY N	2	4	.333	38	1	0	6	89	96	60	3	0	35	27	3.94	95	.277	.344	202-0-8	.193	1	123	-19		-1.8
Total	4	4	6	.400	45	5	1	6	120.2	137	88	3	1	54	38	4.48	80	.290	.364							

DAVIS, CURT　Curtis Benton "Coonskin"　B9.7.1903 Greenfield MO　D10.12.1965 Covina CA　BR/TR/6-2/185　d4.21

1934	Phi N	19	17	.528	51	31	18-3	5	274.1	283	114	14	7	60	99	2.95	164	.269	.313	95-1-7	.211	-2	71	43		5.7
1935	Phi N	16	14	.533	44	27	19-3	2	231	264	103	14	7	47	74	3.66	124	.285	.324	75-1-4	.173	-1*	70	23		2.8
1936	Phi N	2	4	.333	10	8	3	0	60.1	71	37	6	1	19	18	4.62	98	.291	.345	26	.154	-1*	94	0		-0.1
	Chi N★	11	9	.550	24	20	10	1	153	146	60	11	1	31	52	3.00	133	.251	.290	53-0-6	.151	-2	102	15		1.8
	Year	13	13	.500	34	28	13	1	213.1	217	97	17	2	50	70	3.46	120	.263	.307	79-0-6	.152	-3	99	17		1.7
1937	Chi N	10	5	.667	28	14	8	1	123.2	138	64	7	5	30	32	4.08	98	.286	.336	40-1-5	.300	4	122	-2		1.1
1938	StL N	12	8	.600	40	21	8-2	3	173.1	187	80	9	1	27	36	3.63	109	.272	.301	57-3-4	.228	2	99	8		1.1
1939	StL N☆	22	16	.579	49	31	13-3	7	248	279	121	8	3	48	70	5.17	77	.327	.383	105-1-7	.381	12*	108	10		2.8
1940	StL N	0	4	.000	14	7	0	1	54	73	34	4	1	19	12	5.17	77	.327	.383	19-0-1	.000	-2	65	-6		-0.1
	Bro N	8	7	.533	22	18	9	2	137	135	62	13	1	19	46	3.81	105	.256	.283	47-1-4	.128	-1	110	4		0.4
	Year	8	11	.421	36	25	9	3	191	208	96	17	2	38	58	4.19	95	.277	.304	66-1-5	.091	-3	97	-1		-0.1
1941	†Bro N	13	7	.650	28	16	10-5	2	154.1	141	58	6	2	27	50	2.97	123	.244	.280	59-2-5	.186	2*	137	12		1.9
1942	Bro N	15	6	.714	32	26	13-5	2	206	179	62	10	7	51	60	2.36	138	.233	.287	68-0-8	.176	-0	129	21		2.1
1943	Bro N	10	13	.435	31	21	8-2	3	164.1	182	85	8	2	39	49	3.34	106	.270	.310	63-0-6	.159	-2	90	5		0.1
1944	Bro N	10	11	.476	31	23	12-1	4	194	207	84	12	5	39	39	3.25	116	.280	.308	51-1-2	.137	-1	101	9		1.1
1945	Bro N	10	10	.500	24	18	10	0	149.2	171	66	9	3	21	39					2		-0		-2		-0.1
1946	Bro N	0	0	—	1	0	0	0	2	3	3	1	1	2	3	13.50	25	.375	.545	0	—	0		-2		-0.1
Total	13	158	131	.547	429	281	141-24	33	2325	2459	1033	142	47	479	684	3.42	116	.270	.310	813-11-63	.203	7	100	129		18.

DAVIS, DOUG　Douglas　B9.21.1975 Sacramento CA　BR/TL/6-4/190(185-215)　[TexA96 10/293]　d8.9　Col San Francisco (CA) City

1999	Tex A	0	0	—	2	2	0	0-0	12	12	10	3	0	0-0	3	33.75	15	.600	.600	0	—	0		-8		-0.
2000	Tex A	7	6	.538	30	13	1	0-3	98.2	109	61	14	3	58-3	66	5.38	95	.288	.383	0	—	-0	108	-1		-0.
2001	Tex A	11	10	.524	30	30	1	0-0	186	220	103	14	3	69-1	115	4.45	107	.295	.354	3-0-1	.000	-0	89	-2		-0.
2002	Tex A	3	5	.375	10	10	0	0-0	59.2	67	36	7	3	22-0	28	4.98	96	.290	.355	0	—	0	93	-2		-0.
2003	Tex A	0	0	—	1	1	0	0-0	3	4	4	2	0	4-0	2	12.00	41	.308	.471	1	.000	-0	109	-1		-0.
	Tor A	4	6	.400	12	11	0	0-0	54	70	33	6	1	26-1	25	5.00	95	.318	.393			-0	108	-3		-0.
	Year	4	6	.400	13	12	0	0-0	57	74	37	8	1	30-1	27	5.37	89	.318	.398	1	.000	-0	82	9		0.
	Mil N	3	2	.600	8	8	1	0-0	52.1	49	18	8	0	21-0	35	2.58	167	.247	.317	20-0-1	.100	-6	84	24		1.
2004	Mil N	12	12	.500	34	34	0	0-0	207.1	192	84	14	7	79-3	166	3.39	130	.247	.320	64-0-6	.016	-6	103	11		1.
2005	Mil N	11	11	.500	35	35	2-1	0-3	222.2	196	103	26	4	93-5	208	3.84	111	.235	.314	73-0-2	.137	-1	97	34		3
Total	7	51	52	.495	162	142	6-2	0-3	886.1	919	452	94	21	372-13	648	4.22	108	.269	.342	161-0-10	.081	-8	97	34		

DAVIS, DIXIE　Frank Talmadge　B10.12.1890 Wilsons Mills NC　D2.4.1944 Raleigh NC　BR/TR/5-11/155　d7.12　Mil 1918

1912	Cin N	0	1	.000	7	0	0	0	26.2	25	17	0	1	16	12	2.70	124	.258	.368	10	.200	-0	0	0		-0
1915	Chi A	0	0	—	2	0	0	0	3	2	0	0	1	2	2	0.00	—	.250	.455	0	—	1		0		-0
1918	Phi N	0	2	.000	17	2	1	0	47	43	25	1	0	30	18	3.06	98	.247	.358	9	.000	-0*	101	-9		-0
1920	StL A	18	12	.600	38	31	22	0	269.1	250	117	10	7	149	85	3.17	123	.256	.359	94-0-7	.266	3	110	22		2
1921	StL A	16	16	.500	40	36	20-2	0	265.1	279	150	12	10	123	100	4.44	101	.281	.366	95-0-4	.211	-3	111	3		0
1922	StL A	11	6	.647	25	25	7-2	0	174.1	162	91	10	8	87	65	3.62	115	.259	.365	40-0-1	.250	-0	77	3		0
1923	StL A	4	6	.400	19	17	5-1	0	109.1	106	61	4	5	63	36	3.62	115	.259	.365	46-0-7	.152	-2	85	8		0
1924	StL A	11	13	.458	29	24	11-5	0	160.1	159	84	9	6	72	45	4.10	110	.263	.347	64-0-5	.172	-4	108	-3		-0
1925	StL A	12	7	.632	35	22	9	1	180.1	192	121	10	6	106	58	4.59	102	.279	.380	24	.167	-0	76	-5		-0
1926	StL A	3	8	.273	27	7	2	1	83	93	56	7	1	40	39	4.66	92	.292	.372	441-0-30	.197	-10	99	31		0
Total	10	75	71	.514	239	164	77-10	2	1318.2	1311	722	63	45	688	460	3.97	107	.267	.362							

DAVIS, GEORGE　George Allen "Iron"　B3.9.1890 Lancaster NY　D6.4.1961 Buffalo NY　BB/TR/5-10.5/175　d7.16　Col Williams

1912	NY A	1	4	.200	10	7	5	0	54	67	43	3	3	28	22	6.50	55	.293	.385	18	.111	-1	111	-12		-1
1913	Bos N	0	0	—	2	0	0	0	8	7	5	1	0	5	3	4.50	73	.241	.353	2	.000	-0	117	-3		-0
1914	Bos N	3	3	.500	9	6	4-1	0	55.2	42	25	1	3	26	26	3.40	81	.215	.317	18	.167	0	134	-12		-0
1915	Bos N	3	3	.500	15	9	4	0	73.1	85	45	2	4	19	26	3.80	68	.304	.356	23-0-1	.261	1	134	-1		-0
Total	4	7	10	.412	36	22	13-1	0	191	195	118	7	10	78	77	4.48	66	.274	.354	61-0-1	.180	-0	122	-28		-2

DAVIS, STORM　George Earl　B12.26.1961 Dallas TX　BR/TR/6-4/207(194-225)　[BalA79 7/175]　d4.29

1982	Bal A	8	4	.667	29	8	1	0-1	100.2	96	40	4	0	28-4	67	3.49	117	.257	.304	0	—	0	121	7		0
1983	†Bal A	13	7	.650	34	29	6-1	0-0	200.1	180	90	14	2	64-4	125	3.59	111	.238	.298	0	—	0	121	9		0
1984	Bal A	14	9	.609	35	31	10-2	1-1	225	205	86	7	5	71-6	105	3.12	125	.247	.307	0	—	0	98	21		0
1985	Bal A	10	8	.556	31	28	8-1	0-0	175	172	92	11	1	70-5	93	4.53	90	.256	.325	0	—	0	121	-7		
1986	Bal A	9	12	.429	25	25	2	0-0	154	166	70	16	2	36-6	96	3.62	115	.275	.329	16-0-1	.063	-1	71	-16	18	
1987	SD N	2	7	.222	21	10	0	0-0	62.2	70	48	7	3	26-6	37	6.18	64	.280	.372	0	—	0	140	3	48	
	Oak A	1	1	.500	5	5	0	0-0	30.1	28	13	3	0	11-0	28	3.26	127	.241	.305	0	—	0	127	4		
1988	†Oak A	16	7	.696	33	33	1	0-0	201.2	211	86	16	1	91-2	127	3.70	103	.274	.349	0	—	0	137	-12	23	
1989	†Oak A	19	7	.731	31	31	1	0-0	169.1	187	91	19	2	68-1	91	4.36	85	.281	.330	0	—	0	110	-10	37	
1990	KC A	7	10	.412	21	20	0	0-0	112	129	66	9	0	35-1	62	4.74	81	.281	.330	0	—	0	81	-9		
1991	KC A	3	9	.250	51	9	1	1-1	114.1	140	69	11	1	46-9	53	4.96	84	.306	.367	0	—	0	56	7	15	
1992	Bal A	7	3	.700	48	2	0	4-3	89.1	79	35	5	2	33-2	37	6.18	67	.276	.364	0	—	0	92	-14		
1993	Oak A	6	2	.250	19	8	0	0-0	62.2	68	45	5	6	33-2	36	3.06	143	.198	.287	0	—	0	90	-7		
	Det A	2	6	.000	24	0	0	4-1	35.1	25	12	4	1	15-4	35	5.05	84	.250	.338	0	—	0		-6		
	Year	2	8	.200	43	8	0	4-1	98	93	57	9	7	48-6	73	3.56	138	.207	.335	0	—	0	110	4	141	
Total	13	113	96	.541	442	239	30-5	11-8	1780.2	1792	866	136	20	687-59	1048	4.02	100	.263	.330	16-0-1	.063	-1	110	4	141	

DAVIS, JIM　James Bennett　B9.15.1924 Red Bluff CA　D11.30.1995 San Mateo CA　BB/TL/6-0/180*　d4.18

																3.52	119	.247	.321	32	.063	-1	99	9		
1954	Chi N	11	7	.611	46	12	2	4	127.2	114	57	12	3	51	58	3.52	119	.247	.321	37-0-3	.027	-4	63	-8		
1955	Chi N	7	11	.389	42	16	0	3	133.2	122	79	16	2	58-5	62	4.44	92	.246	.323	28-0-3	.179	0	68	2		
1956	Chi N	5	7	.417	46	11	2-1	2	120.1	116	56	10	4	59-4	66	3.66	103	.256	.347							

YEAR	TM LG	W	L	PCT	G	GS	CG-SHO	SV-BS	IP	H	R	HR	HB	BB-IB	SO	ERA	AERA	OAV	OOB	AB-HR-SH	AVG	PB	SUP	APR	DL	PW
1957	StL N	0	1	.000	10	0	0	1	13.2	18	8	1	0	6-0	5	5.27	75	.340	.400			-0		-2		-0.1
	NY N	1	0	1.000	10	0	0	0	11	13	9	2	0	5-1	6	6.55	60	.283	.353	1	.000	-0		-3		-0.2
	Year	1	1	.500	20	0	0	1	24.2	31	17	3	0	11-1	11	5.84	68	.313	.378	2	1.000	-0		-5		-0.3
Total	4	24	26	.480	154	39	4-1	10	406.1	383	209	42	11	179-10	197	4.01	100	.253	.333	99-0-6	.091	-5	76	-2		-0.4

DAVIS, JASON Jason Thomas B5.8.1980 Chattanooga TN BR/TR/6-6/195(195-230) [CleA99 21/647] d9.9 Col Cleveland St. (TN) CC

YEAR	TM LG	W	L	PCT	G	GS	CG-SHO	SV-BS	IP	H	R	HR	HB	BB-IB	SO	ERA	AERA	OAV	OOB	AB-HR-SH	AVG	PB	SUP	APR	DL	PW
2002	Cle A	1	0	1.000	3	2	0	0-0	14.2	12	3	1	0	4-0	11	1.84	241	.218	.271		—	0	84	4		0.3
2003	Cle A	8	11	.421	27	27	1	0-0	165.1	172	101	25	4	47-4	85	4.68	95	.273	.329	2-0-1	—	-0*	89	-6		-0.6
2004	Cle A	2	7	.222	26	19	0	0-0	114.1	148	81	13	4	51-1	72	5.51	79	.311	.381	5-1-0	.200	-1	109	-18		-1.0
2005	Cle A	4	2	.667	11	4	0	0-0	40.1	44	22	4	3	20-0	32	4.69	88	.282	.368	2-0-1	.000	-0	143	-2		-0.3
Total	4	15	20	.429	67	52	1	0-0	334.2	376	207	43	15	122-5	200	4.84	90	.285	.351	9-1-2	.111	1	100	-22		-1.6

DAVIS, JOEL Joel Clark B1.30.1965 Jacksonville FL BL/TR/6-5/205* [ChiA83 1/13] d8.11

YEAR	TM LG	W	L	PCT	G	GS	CG-SHO	SV-BS	IP	H	R	HR	HB	BB-IB	SO	ERA	AERA	OAV	OOB	AB-HR-SH	AVG	PB	SUP	APR	DL	PW
1985	Chi A	3	3	.500	12	11	1	0-0	71.1	71	34	6	1	26-0	37	4.16	104	.256	.320	0	—	0	103	2		0.1
1986	Chi A	4	5	.444	19	19	1	0-0	105.1	115	64	9	1	51-0	54	4.70	92	.280	.359	0	—	0	87	-5		-0.4
1987	Chi A	1	5	.167	13	9	1	0-1	55	56	35	7	0	29-1	25	5.73	81	.264	.351	0	—	0	72	-5		-0.5
1988	Chi A	0	1	.000	5	2	0	0-0	16	21	12	4	0	5-0	10	6.75	59	.328	.371	0	—	0	68	-4		-0.2
Total	4	8	14	.364	49	41	3	0-1	247.2	263	145	26	2	111-1	126	4.91	89	.273	.347	0		0	87	-12		-1.0

DAVIS, DAISY John Henry Albert B11.28.1858 Boston MA D11.5.1902 Lynn MA TR/5-6.5/150 d5.6

YEAR	TM LG	W	L	PCT	G	GS	CG-SHO	SV-BS	IP	H	R	HR	HB	BB-IB	SO	ERA	AERA	OAV	OOB	AB-HR-SH	AVG	PB	SUP	APR	DL	PW
1884	StL AA	10	12	.455	25	24	20-1	0	198.1	196	113	1	14	35	143	2.90	112	.249	.293	87	.172	-2	85	9		0.5
	Bos N	1	3	.250	4	4	3	0	31	50	36	2	0	8	13	7.84	37	.355	.389	16	.000	-3	87	-15		-1.5
1885	Bos N	5	6	.455	11	11	10-1	0	94.1	110	58	2	0	28	30	4.29	63	.280	.328	37	.189	-0	90	-11		-1.1
Total	2	16	21	.432	40	39	33-2	0	323.2	356	207	5	14	71	186	3.78	81	.269	.313	140	.157	-5	87	-17		-2.1

DAVIS, JOHN John Kirk B1.5.1963 Chicago IL BR/TR/6-7/215* [KCA81 7/178] d7.24

YEAR	TM LG	W	L	PCT	G	GS	CG-SHO	SV-BS	IP	H	R	HR	HB	BB-IB	SO	ERA	AERA	OAV	OOB	AB-HR-SH	AVG	PB	SUP	APR	DL	PW
1987	KC A	5	2	.714	27	0	0	2-1	43.2	29	13	0	2	26-4	24	2.27	203	.195	.315	0	—	0		11		1.6
1988	Chi A	2	5	.286	34	1	0	1-3	63.2	77	58	5	4	50-10	37	6.64	60	.297	.413	0	—	0	46	-20		-2.0
1989	Chi A	0	1	.000	4	0	0	1-0	6	5	4	2	0	2-0	5	4.50	85	.217	.280	0	—	0		-1		-0.1
1990	SD N	0	1	.000	6	0	0	0-0	9.1	9	7	1	0	4-0	7	5.79	66	.257	.333	1	.000	-0		-2		-0.2
Total	4	7	9	.438	71	1	0	4-4	122.2	120	82	8	6	82-14	73	4.92	85	.258	.370	1	.000	-0	46	-12		-0.7

DAVIS, BUD John Wilbur "Country" B12.7.1896 Merry Point VA D5.26.1967 Williamsburg VA BL/TR/6-0/207 d4.19

YEAR	TM LG	W	L	PCT	G	GS	CG-SHO	SV-BS	IP	H	R	HR	HB	BB-IB	SO	ERA	AERA	OAV	OOB	AB-HR-SH	AVG	PB	SUP	APR	DL	PW
1915	Phi A	0	2	.000	18	2	2	0	66.2	65	53	1	6	59	18	4.05	72	.273	.429	26	.308	2*	62	-13		-0.4

DAVIS, LANCE Johnny Lance B9.1.1976 Winter Haven FL BR/TL/6-0/170 [CinN95 16/447] d6.16 [DL 2002 Cin N 26]

YEAR	TM LG	W	L	PCT	G	GS	CG-SHO	SV-BS	IP	H	R	HR	HB	BB-IB	SO	ERA	AERA	OAV	OOB	AB-HR-SH	AVG	PB	SUP	APR	DL	PW
2001	Cin N	8	4	.667	20	20	1	0-0	106.1	124	60	12	1	34-0	53	4.74	97	.294	.348	33-0-4	.121	-1*	106	-1		-0.1

DAVIS, KANE Kane Thomas B6.25.1975 Ripley WV BR/TR/6-3/194* [PitN93 13/374] d6.12 [DL 1998 Pit N 31]

YEAR	TM LG	W	L	PCT	G	GS	CG-SHO	SV-BS	IP	H	R	HR	HB	BB-IB	SO	ERA	AERA	OAV	OOB	AB-HR-SH	AVG	PB	SUP	APR	DL	PW
2000	Cle A	0	3	.000	5	2	0	0-0	11	20	21	3	1	8-0	2	14.73	34	.385	.475	1	.000	-0	56	-13		-1.9
	Mil N	0	0	—	3	0	0	0-0	4	7	3	1	1	5-0	2	6.75	68	.389	.542	0	—	0		-1		0.0
2001	Col N	2	4	.333	57	0	0	0-5	68.1	66	36	11	4	32-4	47	4.35	123	.252	.331	5	.000	-1	6	29		0.4
2002	NY N	1	1	.500	16	0	0	0-0	14	15	11	2	1	11-2	24	7.07	56	.273	.397	0	—	0		-4	140	-0.6
2005	Mil N	1	1	.500	15	0	0	0-2	16.2	10	6	2	0	11-2	11	2.70	159	.167	.286	0	—	0	3			0.3
Total	4	4	9	.308	96	2	0	0-7	114	118	77	19	4	66-6	86	5.53	90	.264	.360	6	.000	-1	56	-9	200	-1.8

DAVIS, MARK Mark William B10.19.1960 Livermore CA BL/TL/6-4/205(180-215) [PhiN79*S1/1] d9.12 C3 Col Chabot (CA) JC

YEAR	TM LG	W	L	PCT	G	GS	CG-SHO	SV-BS	IP	H	R	HR	HB	BB-IB	SO	ERA	AERA	OAV	OOB	AB-HR-SH	AVG	PB	SUP	APR	DL	PW
1980	Phi N	0	0	—	2	1	0	0-0	7	4	2	0	0	5-0	5	2.57	149	.160	.300	2	.500	0	164	1		0.1
1981	Phi N	1	4	.200	9	9	0	0-0	43	49	37	7	0	24-0	29	7.74	47	.299	.380	11-0-1	.091	-0	92	-17		-1.7
1983	SF N	6	4	.600	20	20	2-2	0-0	111	93	51	14	3	50-4	83	3.49	102	.227	.313	30-0-9	.133	0	125	0		0.1
1984	SF N	5	17	.227	46	27	1	0-2	174.2	201	113	25	5	54-12	124	5.36	66	.293	.344	46-0-6	.130	1	100	-34		-3.9
1985	SF N	5	12	.294	77	1	0	7-9	114.1	89	49	13	4	41-7	131	3.54	98	.219	.294	12-0-4	.250	1	51	0		0.1
1986	SF N	5	7	.417	67	2	0	4-3	84.1	63	33	6	1	34-7	90	2.99	118	.212	.291	8	.125	0	50	5		0.7
1987	SF N	4	5	.444	20	11	0	0-1	70.2	72	38	9	4	28-1	51	4.71	82	.273	.349							
	SD N	5	3	.625	43	0	0	2-1	62.1	51	26	5	2	31-7	47	3.18	125	.224	.322	23-0-2	.217	2*	120	-6		-0.5
	Year	9	8	.529	63	11	0	2-2	133	123	64	14	6	59-8	98	3.99	98	.250	.336	7	.286	0	5			0.7
1988	SD N★	5	10	.333	62	0	0	28-6	98.1	70	24	2	0	42-11	102	2.01	169	.199	.284	30-0-2	.233	2	118	0		0.2
1989	SD N★	4	3	.571	70	0	0	44-4	92.2	66	21	6	2	31-1	92	1.85	190	.200	.270	10-1-1	.200	1	16			3.6
1990	KC A	2	7	.222	53	3	0	6-4	68.2	71	43	9	4	52-3	73	5.11	76	.259	.383	0	.000	-1		17		2.7
1991	KC A	6	3	.667	29	5	0	1-1	62.2	55	36	6	4	39-0	47	4.45	93	.240	.347	0	—	0	118	-9	26	-1.2
1992	KC A	1	3	.250	13	6	0	0-0	36.1	42	31	6	0	28-0	19	7.18	57	.294	.400	0	—	0	93	-3	63	-0.3
	Atl N	1	0	1.000	14	0	0	0-0	16.2	22	13	3	1	13-2	15	7.02	52	.314	.424	1	.000	-0	112	-12		-1.1
1993	Phi N	1	2	.333	25	0	0	0-1	31.1	35	22	4	1	24-1	28	5.17	77	.273	.392	3	.333	0	-5			-0.4
	SD N	0	3	.000	35	0	0	4-2	38.1	44	15	6	0	20-6	42	3.52	117	.295	.376	1-0-1	.000	-0	3			0.3
	Year	1	5	.167	60	0	0	4-3	69.2	79	37	10	1	44-7	70	4.26	95	.285	.384	4-0-1	.250	0				-0.1
1994	SD N	0	1	.000	20	0	0	0-0	16.1	20	18	4	1	13-1	15	8.82	47	.299	.412	0		0	-9			-0.5
1997	Mil A	0	0	—	19	0	0	0-1	16.1	21	10	4	1	5-0	14	5.51	84	.323	.380	0		0	-1			0.0
Total	15	51	84	.378	624	85	4-2	96-35	1145	1068	582	129	28	534-63	1007	4.17	89	.249	.333	167-1-24	.156	4	107	-54	89	-1.6

DAVIS, BOB Robert Edward B9.11.1933 New York NY D12.22.2001 New York NY BR/TR/6-0/170* d7.26 Col Yale

YEAR	TM LG	W	L	PCT	G	GS	CG-SHO	SV-BS	IP	H	R	HR	HB	BB-IB	SO	ERA	AERA	OAV	OOB	AB-HR-SH	AVG	PB	SUP	APR	DL	PW
1958	KC A	0	4	.000	8	4	0	0	31	45	28	5	2	12-0	22	7.84	50	.346	.410	6-0-1	.167	-0	75	-12		-1.3
1960	KC A	0	0	—	21	0	0	1	32	31	15	1	1	22-1	28	3.66	109	.263	.383	4	.250	0		1		0.1
Total	2	0	4	.000	29	4	0	1	63	76	43	6	3	34-1	50	5.71	69	.306	.396	10-0-1	.200	-0	75	-11		-1.2

DAVIS, RON Ronald Gene B8.6.1955 Houston TX BR/TR/6-4/207(196-207) [ChiN76*3/56] d7.29 Col Blinn (TX) JC

YEAR	TM LG	W	L	PCT	G	GS	CG-SHO	SV-BS	IP	H	R	HR	HB	BB-IB	SO	ERA	AERA	OAV	OOB	AB-HR-SH	AVG	PB	SUP	APR	DL	PW
1978	NY A	0	0	—	4	0	0	0-0	2.1	3	4	0	0	3-0	0	11.57	32	.333	.500	0	—	0		-2		-0.1
1979	NY A	14	2	.875	44	0	0	9-10	85.1	84	29	5	3	28-9	43	2.85	145	.262	.320	1	.000	-0	13			2.5
1980	†NY A	9	3	.750	53	0	0	7-2	131	121	50	9	5	32-3	65	2.95	134	.246	.296	1	.000	-0	14			1.4
1981	†NY A★	4	5	.444	43	0	0	6-2	73	47	22	6	0	25-3	83	2.71	133	.186	.256	0	—	0	9			1.2
1982	Min A	3	9	.250	63	0	0	22-5	106	106	53	16	4	47-12	89	4.42	97	.261	.338	0	—	0	9			-0.1
1983	Min A	5	8	.385	66	0	0	30-3	89	89	34	6	3	33-3	84	3.34	128	.266	.332	0	—	0	10			1.9
1984	Min A	7	11	.389	64	0	0	29-14	83	79	44	14	2	41-9	74	4.55	93	.253	.338	0	—	0	-2			-0.4
1985	Min A	2	6	.250	57	0	0	25-3	64.2	55	28	7	4	35-6	72	3.48	127	.230	.333	0	—	0	6			1.1
1986	Min A	2	6	.250	36	0	0	2-4	38.2	55	42	7	4	29-8	30	9.08	48	.340	.449	0	—	0	-19			-3.5
	Chi N	0	2	.000	17	0	0	0-0	20	31	18	3	0	3-0	15	7.65	53	.356	.374	2	.000	-0	-7			-0.7
1987	Chi N	0	0	—	21	0	0	0-0	32.1	43	23	8	0	12-1	31	5.85	74	.328	.382	0	—	0	-5	21		-0.3
	LA N	0	0	—	4	0	0	0-0	4	7	4	0	1	6-2	1	6.75	59	.412	.560	0	—	0	-2			-0.1
	Year	0	0	—	25	0	0	0-0	36.1	50	27	8	1	18-3	32	5.94	72	.338	.408	0		0	-6			-0.4
1988	SF N	1	1	.500	29	0	0	1-1	17.1	15	10	4	1	6-2	6	4.67	70	.234	.310	2	.000	-0	12	21		2.6
Total	11	47	53	.470	481	0	0	130-43	746.2	735	361	82	22	300-56	597	4.05	102	.260	.332	6	.000	-1	12	21		2.6

DAVIS, PEACHES Roy Thomas B5.31.1905 Glen Rose TX D4.28.1995 Duncan OK BL/TR/6-3.5/190 d7.11

YEAR	TM LG	W	L	PCT	G	GS	CG-SHO	SV-BS	IP	H	R	HR	HB	BB-IB	SO	ERA	AERA	OAV	OOB	AB-HR-SH	AVG	PB	SUP	APR	DL	PW
1936	Cin N	8	8	.500	26	15	5	5	125.2	139	62	7	2	36	32	3.58	107	.280	.331	43-0-1	.163	-1	101	2		0.2
1937	Cin N	11	13	.458	42	24	11-1	3	218	252	105	5	2	51	59	3.59	104	.295	.337	78-0-3	.128	-4	105	3		-0.3
1938	Cin N	7	12	.368	29	19	11-1	1	167.2	193	86	9	1	40	27	3.97	92	.290	.331	61-0-3	.246	-1	98	-7		-0.7
1939	Cin N	1	0	1.000	20	0	0	2	30.2	43	24	5	1	11	4	6.46	59	.341	.399	3	.333	1		-8		-0.4
Total	4	27	33	.450	117	58	27-2	11	542	627	277	26	6	138	123	3.87	96	.297	.337	185-0-7	.178	-4	101	-10		-1.2

DAVIS, STEVE Steven Kennon B8.4.1960 San Antonio TX BL/TL/6-1/185(170-195) [TorA82 21/523] d8.25 Col Texas A&M-Commerce

YEAR	TM LG	W	L	PCT	G	GS	CG-SHO	SV-BS	IP	H	R	HR	HB	BB-IB	SO	ERA	AERA	OAV	OOB	AB-HR-SH	AVG	PB	SUP	APR	DL	PW
1985	Tor A	2	1	.667	10	5	0	0-0	28	23	14	5	0	13-0	22	3.54	120	.223	.308	—		0	133	1		0.1
1986	Tor A	0	0	—	3	0	0	0-0	3.2	8	7	2	0	5-1	5	17.18	25	.471	.591	—		0		-5		-0.2
1989	Cle A	1	1	.500	12	2	0	0-0	25.2	34	24	2	0	14-1	12	8.06	49	.318	.420	0	—	0	102	-11		-0.7
Total	3	3	2	.600	25	7	0	0-0	57.1	65	45	9	0	32-2	39	6.44	64	.286	.373	0		0	126	-15		-0.8

DAVIS, TIM Timothy Howard B7.14.1970 Marianna FL BL/TL/5-11/165* [SeaA92 6/166] d4.4 Col Florida St. [DL 1998 Sea A 181]

YEAR	TM LG	W	L	PCT	G	GS	CG-SHO	SV-BS	IP	H	R	HR	HB	BB-IB	SO	ERA	AERA	OAV	OOB	AB-HR-SH	AVG	PB	SUP	APR	DL	PW
1994	Sea A	2	2	.500	42	1	0	2-2	49.1	57	25	4	1	25-5	28	4.01	123	.295	.374	0	—	0	205	5		0.4
1995	Sea A	2	1	.667	5	5	0	0-0	24	30	21	4	2	18-2	19	6.38	75	.306	.410	0	—	0	141	6		-0.5
1996	Sea A	2	2	.500	40	0	0	0-0	42.2	43	21	4	2	17-1	34	4.01	124	.259	.333	0	—	0	-5	24		0.3

YEAR	TM LG	W	L	PCT	G	GS	CG-SHO	SV-BS	IP	H	R	HR	HB	BB-IB	SO	ERA	AERA	OAV	OOB	AB-HR-SH	AVG	PB	SUP	APR	DL	PW
1997	Sea A	0	0	—	2	0	0	0-0	6.2	6	5	1	1	4-0	10	6.75	67	.231	.355	0	—	0		-1	158	-0.
Total	4	6	5	.545	89	6	0	2-2	122.2	136	72	11	4	64-8	91	4.62	106	.282	.367	0	—	0	148	3	408	0.

DAVIS, WILEY Wiley Anderson B8.1.1875 Seymour TN D9.22.1942 Detroit MI BR/TR/5-10/165 d4.18

YEAR	TM LG	W	L	PCT	G	GS	CG-SHO	SV-BS	IP	H	R	HR	HB	BB-IB	SO	ERA	AERA	OAV	OOB	AB-HR-SH	AVG	PB	SUP	APR	DL	PW
1896	Cin N	1	1	.500	2	0	0		4.1	8	4	0	2	1		8.31	56	.400	.455	1	.000	0		-1		-0.

DAVIS, WOODY Woodrow Wilson "Babe" B4.25.1913 Nicholls GA D7.18.1999 Jesup GA BL/TR/6-1/200 d5.2 Col Brewton-Parker

| 1938 | Det A | 0 | 0 | — | 2 | 0 | 0 | | 6 | 3 | 1 | 0 | 0 | 4 | 1 | 1.50 | 333 | .158 | .304 | 1 | .000 | -0 | | 2 | | 0 |

DAVISON, MIKE Michael Lynn B8.4.1945 Galesburg IL BL/TL/6-1/170* d10.1 Col Augsburg

1969	SF N	0	0	—	1	0	0	0-0	2	2	1	0	0	0-0	2	4.50	78	.250	.250	0	—	0		0		0
1970	SF N	3	5	.375	31	0	0	1-2	36	46	29	4	0	22-4	21	6.50	61	.324	.410	1	.000	0		-10		-1
Total	2	3	5	.375	32	0	0	1-2	38	48	30	4	0	22-4	23	6.39	62	.320	.402	1	.000	0		-10		-1

DAVISON, SCOTT Scotty Ray B10.16.1970 Inglewood CA BR/TR/6-0/190* [MonN88 4/102] d9.4

1995	Sea A	0	0	—	3	0	0	0-0	4.1	7	3	1	0	1-0	3	6.23	77	.350	.381	0	—	0		-1		0
1996	Sea A	0	0	—	5	0	0	0-0	9	11	9	6	0	3-0	9	9.00	55	.297	.350	0	—	0		-4	27	-0.
Total	2	0	0	—	8	0	0	0-0	13.1	18	12	7	0	4-0	12	8.10	61	.316	.361	0	—	0		-5	27	-0.

DAWLEY, JOEY Joseph Thomas B9.19.1971 Riverside CA BR/TR/6-4/205* [BalA92 28/772] d9.29 Col Riverside (CA) CC

2002	Atl N	0	0	—	1	0	0	0-0	0.1	0	0	0	0	0-0	1	—	.000	.000	1	.000	-0		-10		C
2003	Atl N	0	0	—	5	0	0	0-0	7	15	14	3	1	3-0	8	18.00	23	.405	.463	1	.000	0	118	-1	120	C
2004	Cle A	0	0	—	2	2	0	0-0	8.1	7	5	1	0	7-0	8	5.40	80	.233	.378	0		-0	118	-11	120	C
Total	3	0	0	—	8	2	0	0-0	15.2	22	19	4	1	10-0	17	10.91	39	.324	.418	1	.000	-0	118	-11	120	C

DAWLEY, BILL William Chester B2.6.1958 Norwich CT BR/TR/6-4/240* [CinN76 7/167] d4.15

1983	Hou N★	6	6	.500	48	0	0	14-2	79.2	51	26	9	1	22-4	60	2.82	121	.185	.247	9	.222	0		7		1
1984	Hou N	11	4	.733	60	0	0	5-5	98	82	24	5	0	35-9	47	1.93	173	.234	.298	9-0-2	.333	2		17		1
1985	Hou N	5	3	.625	49	0	0	2-1	81	76	35	7	0	37-7	48	3.56	98	.259	.337	10	.200	0		0	18	C
1986	Chi A	0	7	.000	46	0	0	2-2	97.2	91	38	10	1	28-3	66	4.47	94	.259	.330	2	.000	-0		-2		-C
1987	StL N	5	8	.385	60	0	0	2-5	96.2	93	51	15	1	38-11	65	4.47	94	.259	.330	12-0-1	.167	0		-9	100	-C
1988	Phi N	0	2	.000	8	0	0	0-0	8.2	16	13	3	0	4-1	3	13.50	27	.381	.426	0	—	0		-1		-C
1989	Oak A	0	0	—	4	0	0	0-0	9	11	5	0	1	2-0	3	4.00	93	.297	.341	0	—	0		-9		3
Total	7	27	30	.474	275	0	0	25-15	470.2	420	192	49	4	166-35	292	3.42	110	.243	.308	42-0-3	.214	2		24	118	3

DAWSON, JOE Ralph Fenton B3.9.1897 Bow WA D1.4.1978 Longview TX BR/TR/5-11/182 d7.4

1924	Cle A	1	2	.333	4	4	0	0	20.1	24	17	0	1	21	7	6.64	64	.300	.451	7-0-1	.286	0	64	-5		-.
1927	†Pit N	3	7	.300	20	7	4	0	80.2	80	47	2	0	32	17	4.46	92	.268	.338	25-0-1	.200	-1	80	-3		-.
1928	Pit N	7	7	.500	31	7	1	3	128.2	116	54	5	1	56	36	3.29	124	.242	.322	43-0-1	.279	3	51	12		-.
1929	Pit N	0	1	.000	4	0	0	0	8.2	13	9	2	0	3	2	8.31	57	.342	.390	2	.500	1		-3		-.
Total	4	11	17	.393	59	18	5	3	238.1	233	127	9	2	112	62	4.15	99	.260	.343	77-0-3	.260	3	65	1		-.

DAWSON, REX Rexford Paul B2.10.1889 Skagit Co. WA D10.20.1958 Indianapolis IN BL/TR/6-0/185 d10.3

| 1913 | Was A | 0 | 0 | — | 1 | 0 | 0 | 0 | 1 | 0 | 0 | 0 | 0 | 1 | 0 | 0.00 | — | .250 | .250 | 0 | — | 0 | | 0 | | -. |

DAY, PEA RIDGE Clyde Henry B8.26.1899 Pea Ridge AR D3.21.1934 Kansas City MO BR/TR/6-0/190 d9.19

1924	StL N	1	1	.500	3	3	1	0	17.2	22	11	0	0	6	3	4.58	82	.306	.359	8	.125	-1	105	-2		-.
1925	StL N	2	4	.333	17	4	1	1	40	53	31	5	3	7	13	6.30	69	.325	.364	13	.154	-1	142	-8		-.
1926	Cin N	0	0	—	4	0	0	0	7.1	13	13	1	0	2	2	7.36	50	.406	.441	2	.000	-0	56	-7		-.
1931	Bro N	2	2	.500	22	2	1	1	57.1	75	38	5	0	13	30	4.55	84	.315	.351	18	.222	0	114	-23		-.
Total	4	5	7	.417	46	9	3	2	122.1	163	93	11	3	28	48	5.30	75	.323	.362	41	.171	-2	114	-23		-.

DAY, ZACH Stephen Zachary B6.15.1978 Cincinnati OH BR/TR/6-4/185(185-215) [NYA96 5/149] d6.15

2002	Mon N	4	1	.800	19	2	0	1-1	37.1	28	18	3	1	15-2	25	3.62	121	.207	.289	6-0-2	.167	0	116	2		
2003	Mon N	9	8	.529	23	23	1-1	0-0	131.1	132	64	8	10	59-3	61	4.18	106	.262	.348	47-0-1	.043	-4	97	5	58	
2004	Mon N	5	10	.333	19	19	1-1	0-0	116.2	117	53	13	4	45-7	61	3.93	117	.265	.337	29-1-3	.034	-2	55	9	79	
2005	Was N	1	2	.333	12	5	0	0-0	36	41	29	4	1	25-3	16	6.75	60	.289	.396	8-0-1	.125	-0	78	-11	48	
	Col N	0	1	.000	5	3	0	0-1	11.1	20	11	2	0	7-1	7	7.15	67	.385	.458	3	.333	-0	96	-15	16	
	Year	1	3	.250	17	8	0	0-1	47.1	61	40	6	1	32-4	23	6.85	62	.314	.412	11-0-1	.182	-0	82			
Total	4	19	22	.463	78	52	2-2	1-2	332.2	338	175	30	16	151-16	170	4.41	101	.265	.348	93-1-7	.065	-6	82	2	201	

DAY, BILL William M. B7.28.1867 Marcus Hook PA D8.16.1923 Wilmington DE TR/5-8/150 d8.20

1889	Phi N	0	3	.000	4	3	2	0	19	16	24	0	0	23	20	5.21	83	.222	.411	10	.000	-2	77	-4		-.
1890	Phi N	1	1	.500	4	2	2	0	23.2	26	16	0	0	12	9	3.04	120	.271	.352	10	.100	-1	78	1		-.
	Pit N	0	6	.000	6	6	6	0	50	66	50	1	1	24	10	5.22	63	.308	.381	23	.043	-4	73	-13		-.
	Year	1	7	.125	10	8	8	0	73.2	92	66	1	1	36	19	4.52	76	.297	.372	33	.061	-5	74	-13		-.
Total	2	1	10	.091	14	11	10	0	92.2	108	90	1	1	59	39	4.77	83	.283	.380	43	.047	-6	76	-16		-.

DAYLEY, KEN Kenneth Grant B2.25.1959 Jerome ID BL/TL/6-0/175* [AtlN80 1/3] d5.13 Col Portland [DL 1992 Tor A 182]

1982	Atl N	5	6	.455	20	11	0	0-0	71.1	79	39	9	0	25-2	34	4.54	81	.286	.340	20-0-1	.250	1	115	-6		
1983	Atl N	5	8	.385	24	16	0	0-0	104.2	100	59	12	2	39-2	70	4.30	90	.257	.326	32-0-5	.219	1*	97	-7		
1984	Atl N	0	3	.000	4	4	0	0-0	18.2	28	18	5	1	6-1	10	5.30	73	.341	.393	4	.500	1*	76	-8		
	StL N	0	2	.000	3	2	0	0-0	5	16	10	1	0	5-0	0	18.00	19	.615	.677	0-0-1	—	1*	90	-12		
	Year	0	5	.000	7	6	0	0-0	23.2	44	28	6	1	11-1	10	7.99	47	.407	.467	4-0-1	.500	1	4			
1985	†StL N	4	4	.500	57	0	0	11-5	65.1	65	24	2	0	18-9	62	2.76	130	.263	.311	5	.200	0*	0	85		
1986	StL N	0	3	.000	31	0	0	5-2	38.2	42	19	1	1	11-3	33	3.26	113	.275	.325	5	—	-0	10	45		
1987	†StL N	9	5	.643	53	0	0	4-6	61	52	21	2	2	33-8	63	2.66	158	.234	.337	4	.000	-0	4	35		
1988	StL N	2	7	.222	54	0	0	5-3	55.1	48	20	2	1	19-7	38	2.77	127	.239	.306	4	.000	-1	7			
1989	StL N	4	3	.571	71	0	0	12-5	75.1	63	26	3	0	30-7	51	3.56	108	.233	.305	6	.000	-1	3			
1990	StL N	4	4	.500	58	0	0	2-5	73.1	63	32	5	0	30-7	51	6.23	68	.368	.500	0	—	0	-1	163		
1991	Tor A	0	0	—	8	0	0	0-0	4.1	7	3	0	1	5-0	3	0.00	—	.333	.714	0	—	0				
1993	Tor A	0	0	—	2	0	0	0-0	0.2	1	2	0	0	2-0	2	4.66	77	.333	.500	0	—	0	-1	510		
Total	11	33	45	.423	385	33	0	39-26	573.2	564	273	42	8	225-49	406	3.64	104	.261	.330	81-0-7	.210	3	112	1	510	

DEAGLE, REN Lorenzo Burroughs B6.26.1858 New York NY D12.24.1936 Kansas City MO BR/TR/5-9/190 d5.17

1883	Cin AA	10	8	.556	18	18	17-1	0	148	136	78	0		34	48	2.31	141	.229	.270	70	.129	-5*	91	14		-.
1884	Cin AA	3	1	.750	4	4	4-1	0	34	38	26	0	1	9	12	5.03	66	.314	.366	13	.000	-2	86	-6		-.
	Lou AA	4	6	.400	12	12	8	0	87.1	81	43	0	7	13	23	2.58	120	.241	.284	45	.133	-3	83	6		-.
	Year	7	7	.500	16	16	12-1	0	121.1	119	69	0	8	22	35	3.26	97	.260	.306	58	.103	-5	84	1		-.
Total	2	17	15	.531	34	34	29-2	0	269.1	255	147	0	8	56	83	2.74	117	.242	.286	128	.117	-9	87	14		-.

DEAGO, ROGER Roger I. (Villarreal) B6.21.1977 Monagrillo, Pan BR/TR/5-10/180 d5.10

| 2003 | SD N | 0 | 1 | .000 | 2 | 2 | 0 | 0-0 | 10.1 | 11 | 9 | 0 | 0 | 8-0 | 10 | 7.84 | 51 | .282 | .396 | 4 | .000 | -0 | 94 | -4 | | |

DEAL, COT Ellis Fergason B1.23.1923 Arapaho OK BB/TR(BL 1947-48)/5-10.5/185* d9.11 C15

1947	Bos A	1	0	1.000	5	2	0	0	12.2	20	14	0	0	7	6	9.24	42	.364	.435	4	.500	1*	125	-6		-.
1948	Bos A	1	0	1.000	4	0	0	0	3	3	0	0	0	3	2	0.00	—	.200	.333	0	—	0		-3		-.
1950	StL N	0	0	—	3	0	0	0	1	3	5	0	0	2	1	18.00	24	.500	.625	0	—	0		-17		-.
1954	StL N	2	3	.400	33	0	0	0	71.2	85	56	14	4	36	25	6.28	68	.297	.379	20-1-0	.100	0				-.
Total	4	3	4	.429	45	2	0	0	89.1	111	74	14	4	48	34	6.55	63	.307	.390	24-1-0	.167	1	125	-24		-.

DEAN, CHUBBY Alfred Lovell B8.24.1915 Mt.Airy NC D12.21.1970 Riverside NJ BL/TL/5-11/181 d4.14.1936 Mil 1943-46 ▲

1937	Phi A	1	0	1.000	9	1	0	0	6	6	4	0	0	6	4	4.00	118	.219	.342	309-2-7	.262	0*	148	1		-.
1938	Phi A	2	1	.667	6	1	0	0	21	22	10	3	0	15	3	3.52	137	.250	.359	20	.300	2*	91	4		-.
1939	Phi A	5	8	.385	54	1	0	0	116.2	132	93	8	0	80	39	5.25	90	.289	.395	77-0-3	.351	8*	37	-12		-.
1940	Phi A	6	13	.316	30	19	8-1	0	159.1	220	136	21	0	63	22	6.19	68	.294	.367	37-0-1	.243	2*	71	-14		-.
1941	Phi A	2	4	.333	18	7	2	0	75.2	90	50	9	0	35	14	4.39	90	.282	.358	25-0-1	.160	0*	77	-4		-.
	Cle A	1	4	.200	8	8	2	0	53.1	57	31	3	0	24	22	5.23	—	—	—	—	—					-.
	Year	3	8	.273	26	15	4	0	129	147	81	12	0	59	36	5.44	75	.289	.363	62-0-2	.210	4	73	-16		-.

YEAR	TM LG	W	L	PCT	G	GS	CG-SHO	SV-BS	IP	H	R	HR	HB	BB-IB	SO	ERA	AERA	OAV	OOB	AB-HR-SH	AVG	PB	SUP	APR	DL	PW
1942	Cle A	8	11	.421	27	22	8	1	172.2	170	83	7	0	66	46	3.81	91	.261	.329	101	.267	8*	87	-6		0.1
1943	Cle A	5	5	.500	17	9	3	0	76	83	46	1	1	34	29	4.50	69	.281	.358	46-0-1	.196	1*	157	-13		-1.5
Total 7		30	46	.395	162	68	23-1	9	685.2	781	456	52	1	323	195	5.08	79	.288	.364	705-2-15	.268	25	89	-80		-4.7

DEAN, DORY   Charles Wilson   B11.6.1852 Cincinnati OH   D5.4.1935 Nashville TN   BR/TR   d6.22

| 1876 | Cin N | 4 | 26 | .133 | 30 | 30 | 26 | 0 | 262.2 | 397 | 268 | 1 | | 24 | 22 | 3.73 | 59 | .322 | .335 | 138 | .261 | 1* | 70 | -48 | | -3.8 |

DEAN, HARRY   James Harry   B5.12.1915 Rockmart GA   D6.1.1960 Rockmart GA   BR/TR/6-4/185   d4.16   Col Oglethorpe

| 1941 | Was A | 0 | 0 | — | 2 | 0 | 0 | 0 | 2 | 3 | 2 | 0 | 1 | 3 | 0 | 4.50 | 90 | .250 | .500 | 0 | — | 0 | | -1 | | -0.1 |

DEAN, DIZZY   Jay Hanna   B1.16.1910 Lucas AR   D7.17.1974 Reno NV   BR/TR/6-2/182   d9.28   C1   HF1953   b-Paul

1930	StL N	1	0	1.000	1	1	1	0	9	3	1	0	0	3	5	1.00	502	.103	.188	3	.333	0	52	4		0.5
1932	StL N	18	15	.545	46	33	16-4	2	286	280	122	14	5	102	191	3.30	119	.260	.327	97-2-8	.258	5*	91	20		2.5
1933	StL N	20	18	.526	48	34	26-3	4	293	279	113	11	5	64	199	3.04	114	.250	.293	105-1-3	.181	1*	107	15		1.7
1934	†StL N★	30	7	.811	50	33	24-7	7	311.2	288	110	14	6	75	195	2.66	159	.241	.289	118-2-7	.246	4*	119	51		6.1
1935	StL N	28	12	.700	50	36	29-3	5	325.1	324	126	16	4	77	190	3.04	135	.256	.300	128-2-4	.234	4*	124	38		4.5
1936	StL N★	24	13	.649	51	34	28-2	11	315	310	128	21	3	53	195	3.17	124	.253	.285	121-0-3	.223	1	118	27*		3.0
1937	StL N★	13	10	.565	27	25	17-4	1	197.1	200	76	9	2	33	120	2.69	148	.259	.291	66-1-9	.227	2	100	25		2.8
1938	†Chi N	7	1	.875	13	10	3-1	0	74.2	63	20	2	1	8	22	1.81	212	.226	.250	26-0-1	.192	-0	113	15		1.5
1939	Chi N	6	4	.600	19	13	7-2	0	96.1	98	40	4	1	17	27	3.36	117	.261	.294	34-0-2	.147	-1	119	7		0.5
1940	Chi N	3	3	.500	10	9	3	0	54	68	35	4	0	20	18	5.17	73	.306	.364	18-0-2	.222	0	93	-8		-0.8
1941	Chi N	0	0	—	1	1	0	0	3	3	3	0	0	1	0	18.00	19	.429	.429	0	—	0	193	-2		-0.1
1947	StL A	0	0	—	1	1	0	0	4	3	0	0	0	1	0	0.00	—	.231	.286	1	1.000	0	46	2		0.1
Total 12		150	83	.644	317	230	154-26	30	1967.1	1919	774	95	27	453	1163	3.02	130	.253	.298	717-8-39	.225	15	110	194		22.3

DEAN, PAUL   Paul Dee "Daffy"   B8.14.1913 Lucas AR   D3.17.1981 Springdale AR   BR/TR/6-0/175   d4.18   b-Dizzy

1934	†StL N	19	11	.633	39	26	16-5	2	233.1	225	96	19	5	52	150	3.43	123	.248	.292	83-0-3	.241	1	101	23		2.5
1935	StL N	19	12	.613	46	33	19-2	5	269.2	261	109	16	9	55	143	3.37	122	.249	.292	90-0-4	.133	-5	102	25		1.8
1936	StL N	5	5	.500	17	14	5	1	92	113	57	3	1	20	28	4.60	86	.300	.337	34-0-3	.059	-4	105	-8		-1.3
1937	StL N	0	0	—	1	0	0	0	0	1	3	0	0	2	0	∞	—	1.000	1.000	0	—	0		-3		-0.2
1938	StL N	3	1	.750	5	4	2-1	0	31	37	13	3	0	7	14	2.61	151	.298	.326	11	.182	-0	96	4		0.4
1939	StL N	0	1	.000	16	2	0	0	43	54	30	4	1	10	16	6.07	68	.310	.351	9-0-1	.111	-1	74	4		-0.5
1940	NY N	4	4	.500	27	7	2	0	99.1	110	50	8	0	29	32	3.90	100	.281	.330	26-0-5	.115	-2	90	1		-0.3
1941	NY N	0	0	—	5	0	0	1	5.2	8	2	0	0	3	3	3.18	116	.320	.393	0	—	0	0	0		0.0
1943	StL A	0	0	—	3	1	0	0	13.1	16	5	0	1	3	3	3.38	99	.296	.345	3	.000	-0	152	0		0.0
Total 9		50	34	.595	159	87	44-8	8	787.1	825	364	53	17	179	387	3.75	109	.266	.309	256-0-16	.156	-10	101	33		2.4

DEAN, WAYLAND   Wayland Ogden   B6.20.1902 Richwood WV   D4.11.1930 Huntington WV   BB/TR/6-1/178   d4.17

1924	†NY N	6	12	.333	26	20	6	0	125.2	139	80	9	5	45	39	5.01	73	.280	.346	40-2-1	.200	1	106	-19		-2.2
1925	NY N	10	7	.588	33	14	6-1	1	151.1	169	98	13	4	50	53	4.64	82	.282	.342	51-1-0	.235	3	85	-13		-1.3
1926	Phi N	8	16	.333	33	26	15-1	0	203.2	245	136	9	3	89	52	4.91	84	.307	.379	102-3-3	.265	5*	84	-17		-1.3
1927	Phi N	0	1	.000	2	0	0	0	3	6	4	0	0	2	1	12.00	34	.500	.571	3	.667	1*		-2		-0.3
	Chi N	0	0	—	2	0	0	0	2	0	0	0	1	2	2	0.00	—	.000	.429	0	—	0		1		0.1
	Year	0	1	.000	4	0	0	0	5	6	4	0	1	4	3	7.20	56	.375	.524	3	.667	1		-1		-0.2
Total 4		24	36	.400	96	60	27-2	1	485.2	559	318	31	13	188	147	4.87	82	.293	.360	196-6-4	.250	10	90	-50		-4.7

DeBARR, DENNIS   Dennis Lee   B1.16.1953 Cheyenne WY   BL/TL/6-2/190   [DetA71 2/35]   d5.14

| 1977 | Tor A | 0 | 1 | .000 | 14 | 0 | 0 | 0-1 | 21.1 | 29 | 14 | 1 | 0 | 8-0 | 10 | 5.91 | 72 | .337 | .385 | 0 | — | 0 | | -3 | | -0.1 |

DeBERRY, JOE   Joseph Gaddy   B11.29.1896 Mt.Gilead NC   D10.9.1944 Southern Pines NC   BL/TR/6-1/175   d8.24   Col North Carolina St.

1920	StL A	2	4	.333	10	7	3-1	0	54.2	65	35	2	2	20	12	4.94	79	.307	.372	18-0-2	.167	-1	87	-5		-0.5
1921	StL A	0	1	.000	10	1	0	0	12.1	15	9	0	0	10	1	6.57	68	.300	.417	2	.000	-0	75	-2		-0.2
Total 2		2	5	.286	20	8	3-1	0	67	80	44	2	2	30	13	5.24	77	.305	.381	20-0-2	.150	-1	85	-7		-0.7

DeBUSSCHERE, DAVE   David Albert   B10.16.1940 Detroit MI   D5.14.2003 New York NY   BR/TR/6-6/225*   d4.22   Mil 1964   Col Detroit Mercy

1962	Chi A	0	0	—	12	0	0	0	18	5	7	1	1	23-1	8	2.00	195	.089	.358	0	—	0		3		0.1
1963	Chi A	3	4	.429	24	10	1-1	0	84.1	80	35	9	4	34-1	53	3.09	113	.249	.327	22-0-2	.045	-2	89	3		0.1
Total 2		3	4	.429	36	10	1-1	0	102.1	85	42	10	5	57-2	61	2.90	123	.225	.333	22-0-2	.045	-2	89	6		0.2

DECATUR, ART   Arthur Rue   B1.14.1894 Cleveland OH   D4.25.1966 Talladega AL   BR/TR/6-1/190   d4.15

1922	Bro N	3	4	.429	27	8	2	3	87.2	87	31	3	1	29	31	2.77	147	.265	.327	25-0-1	.080	-2	67	13		0.7
1923	Bro N	3	3	.500	36	5	2	3	97.2	101	44	3	2	32	25	2.58	150	.264	.325	21-0-1	.000	-3	64	11		0.3
1924	Bro N	10	9	.526	31	10	3	1	126.1	156	74	12	4	27	38	4.13	91	.308	.348	44	.114	-4	68	-7		-1.4
1925	Bro N	0	0	—	1	0	0	0	1	3	2	0	0	0	0	18.00	23	.600	.600	0	—	0		-1		-0.1
	Phi N	4	13	.235	25	15	4	2	128	170	87	13	2	35	31	5.27	91	.316	.360	41-0-4	.049	-5	71	-4		-1.0
	Year	4	13	.235	26	15	4	2	129	173	89	13	2	35	31	5.37	89	.319	.362	41-0-4	.049	-5	71	-5		-1.1
1926	Phi N	0	0	—	2	0	0	0	3	6	3	0	0	2	0	6.00	69	.375	.444	1	.000	-0	40	-1		-0.1
1927	Phi N	3	5	.375	29	3	0	0	94.2	130	78	11	4	20	27	7.42	56	.334	.373	27-0-3	.222	-0	48	-29		-2.2
Total 6		23	34	.404	153	37	10	7	538.1	653	310	42	13	145	152	4.51	92	.302	.349	159-0-9	.094	-14	68	-18		-3.8

DECKER, MARTY   Dee Martin   B6.7.1957 Upland CA   BR/TR/5-10/168   [PhiN80 23/582]   d9.20   Col Point Loma Nazarene

| 1983 | SD N | 0 | 0 | — | 4 | 0 | 0 | 0-0 | 8.2 | 5 | 2 | 1 | 1 | 3-0 | 9 | 2.08 | 169 | .167 | .265 | 0 | — | 0 | | 2 | | 0.1 |

DECKER, JOE   George Henry   B6.16.1947 Storm Lake IA   D3.2.2003 Fraser MI   BR/TR/6-0/180*   [ChiN65 8/148]   d9.18

1969	Chi N	1	0	1.000	4	1	0	0-0	12.1	10	4	0	0	6-0	13	2.92	138	.222	.314	2	.000	-0	66	2		0.1
1970	Chi N	2	7	.222	24	17	1	0-1	108.2	108	64	12	4	56-3	79	4.64	97	.263	.354	34-1-2	.176	1	76	-2		-0.1
1971	Chi N	3	2	.600	21	4	0	0-0	45.2	62	24	2	0	25-3	37	4.73	83	.343	.418	8-0-1	.250	1*	62	-2		-0.1
1972	Chi N	1	0	1.000	5	1	0	0-0	12.2	9	3	1	0	4-0	7	2.13	179	.188	.250	2-0-3	.000	-0	348	2		0.1
1973	Min A	10	10	.500	29	24	6-3	0-0	170.1	167	87	12	4	88-0	109	4.17	95	.260	.350	0	—	0	101	-2		-0.3
1974	Min A	16	14	.533	37	37	11-1	0-0	248.2	234	105	24	2	97-1	158	3.29	114	.252	.321	0	—	0	89	11		1.2
1975	Min A	1	3	.250	10	7	1	0-0	26.1	25	25	2	0	36-0	8	8.54	45	.260	.462	0	—	0	108	-12	49	-1.6
1976	Min A	2	7	.222	13	12	0	0-0	58	60	37	3	0	51-0	35	5.28	68	.273	.404	0	—	0	105	-10		-1.3
1979	Sea A	0	1	.000	9	0	0	0-0	27.1	27	14	2	1	14-1	12	4.28	102	.255	.339	0	—	0	83	0		0.1
Total 9		36	44	.450	152	105	19-4	0-1	710	702	363	58	11	377-8	458	4.17	95	.262	.353	46-1-6	.174	-0	93	-13	49	-1.9

DEDMON, JEFF   Jeffrey Linden   B3.4.1960 Torrance CA   BL/TR/6-2/200*   [AtlN80 S1/5]   d9.2   Col West Los Angeles (CA) CC

1983	Atl N	0	0	—	5	0	0	0-2						0-0	3	13.50	29	.455	.455	0	—	0		-4		-0.2
1984	Atl N	4	3	.571	54	0	0	4-2	81	86	39	5	2	35-9	51	3.78	102	.277	.352	6-0-1	.000	-1		1		0.1
1985	Atl N	6	3	.667	60	0	0	0-4	86	84	52	5	1	49-14	41	4.08	94	.264	.363	9-0-1	.111	-0		-5		-0.3
1986	Atl N	6	6	.500	57	0	0	3-6	99.2	90	43	8	4	39-5	58	2.98	133	.242	.319	16-0-1	.125	-1		8		1.0
1987	Atl N	3	4	.429	53	0	0	4-5	89.2	82	46	8	5	42-1	40	3.91	111	.246	.327	16-0-3	.250	1	153	3		0.4
1988	Cle A	1	0	1.000	21	0	0	1-0	33.2	35	20	3	0	21-1	17	4.54	91	.276	.383	0	—	0		0		0.0
Total 6		20	16	.556	250	0	0	12-19	394	387	206	30	11	186-30	210	3.84	105	.261	.345	47-0-6	.149	-0	153	1		1.0

DEDRICK, JIM   James Michael   B4.4.1968 Los Angeles CA   BB/TR/6-0/185   [BalA90 33/890]   d8.12   Col Vanguard

| 1995 | Bal A | 0 | 0 | — | 6 | 0 | 0 | 0 | 7.2 | 8 | 2 | 1 | 1 | 6-0 | 3 | 2.35 | 204 | .308 | .429 | 0 | — | 0 | | 2 | | 0.1 |

DEEGAN, DUMMY   William John   B11.16.1874 Bronx NY   D5.17.1957 Bronx NY   d8.3

| 1901 | NY N | 0 | 1 | .000 | 2 | 1 | 1 | 0 | 17 | 27 | 17 | 0 | 0 | 6 | 8 | 6.35 | 52 | .355 | .402 | 5 | .000 | -1 | 43 | -6 | | -0.3 |

DEERING, JOHN   John Thomas   B6.25.1879 Lynn MA   D2.15.1943 Beverly MA   BR/TR/6-0/180   d5.12

1903	Det A	3	4	.429	10	8	5	0	60.2	77	38	3	1	24	14	3.86	75	.308	.371	24-0-1	.333	2	83	-6		-0.5
1903	NY A	4	3	.571	9	7	6-1	0	60	59	33	0	1	18	14	3.75	83	.257	.313	23	.043	-3	92	-3		-0.7
	Year	7	7	.500	19	15	11-1	0	120.2	136	71	3	2	42	28	3.80	79	.283	.344	47-0-1	.191	-1	87	-10		-1.2

DEGERICK, MIKE   Michael Arthur   B4.1.1943 New York NY   BR/TR/6-2/180*   d9.4   [DL 1963 Chi A 128]

1961	Chi A	0	0	—	1	0	0	0	1.2	1	1	0	0	1-0	0	5.40	72	.400	.429	0	—	0		0		0.0
1962	Chi A	0	0	—	1	0	0	0	1	2	0	0	0	1-0	0	0.00	—	.250	.400	0	—	0		0		0.0
Total 2		0	0	—	2	0	0	0	2.2	3	1	0	0	2-0	0	3.38	116	.333	.417	0	—	0		0	128	0.0

YEAR	TM LG	W	L	PCT	G	GS	CG-SHO	SV-BS	IP	H	R	HR	HB	BB-IB	SO	ERA	AERA	OAV	OOB	AB-HR-SH	AVG	PB	SUP	APR	DL	PW
DeHART, RICK Rick Allen B3.21.1970 Topeka KS BL/TL/6-1/180* d7.16 Col Washburn Topeka																										
1997	Mon N	2	1	.667	23	0	0	0-1	29.1	33	21	7	0	14-4	29	5.52	76	.292	.364	2	.000	-0		-5		-0.4
1998	Mon N	0	0	—	26	0	0	1-1	28	34	22	3	0	13-1	14	4.82	87	.291	.359	0	—	-0		-3		-0.2
1999	Mon N	0	0		3	0	0	0-0	1.2	6	4	2	0	3-1	1	21.60	21	.545	.643	0		-0		-3		-0.1
2003	KC A	0	2	.000	4	0	0	0-0	4	8	6	1	0	2-0	1	13.50	36	.421	.476	1	.000	-0		-3		-0.6
Total 4		2	3	.400	56	0	0	1-2	63	81	53	13	0	32-6	45	6.14	69	.312	.383	3	.000	-0		-15		-1.3
DEININGER, PEP Otto Charles B10.10.1877 Wasseralfingen, Germany D9.25.1950 Boston MA BL/TL/5-8.5/180 d4.26 ▲																										
1902	Bos A	0	0	—	2	1	0		12	19	16	3	2	9	2	9.75	37	.358	.469	6	.333	1	101	-7		-0.2
DeJEAN, MIKE Michel Dwain B9.28.1970 Baton Rouge LA BR/TR/6-2/212(205-220) [NYA92 24/662] d5.2 Col West Alabama																										
1997	Col N	5	0	1.000	55	0	0	2-2	67.2	74	34	4	3	24-2	38	3.99	129	.280	.346	3-0-1	.333	0*		7	21	0.5
1998	Col N	3	1	.750	59	1	0	2-1	74.1	78	29	4	1	24-1	27	3.03	171	.285	.340	5	.000	-1	124	14	26	0.6
1999	Col N	2	4	.333	56	0	0	0-4	61	83	61	14	2	32-8	31	8.41	69	.335	.411	2	.000	-0*		-14	18	-1.1
2000	Col N	4	4	.500	54	0	0	0-4	53.1	54	31	9	0	30-6	34	4.89	118	.269	.362	3	.000	-0		13		0.9
2001	Mil N	4	2	.667	75	0	0	2-2	84.1	75	31	4	9	39-7	68	2.77	155	.236	.332	1	.000	0		-8		1.1
2002	Mil N	1	5	.167	68	0	0	27-3	75	66	28	7	2	39-8	65	4.87	89	.271	.339	0	—	0		-4		-0.7
2003	Mil N	4	7	.364	58	0	0	18-8	64.2	69	38	12	1	27-7	58	4.00	103	.262	.385	0	—	0		0		0.1
	StL N	1	1	.500	18	0	0	1-0	18	17	8	1	1	12-0	13	4.68	91	.269	.349	0	—	0		-4		-0.6
	Year	5	8	.385	76	0	0	19-8	82.2	86	46	13	2	39-7	71	4.68	91	.308	.426	1	.000	-0		-6		-0.7
2004	Bal A	0	5	.000	37	0	0	0-0	39.2	49	29	2	6	28-6	36	6.13	76	.308	.426	1	.000	-0		-6	37	-0.7
	NY N	0	0	—	17	0	0	0-0	21.1	21	5	0	2	5-2	24	1.69	255	.256	.315	0	—	0*		-6		-0.8
2005	NY N	3	1	.750	28	0	0	0-0	25.2	36	19	3	1	18-2	17	6.31	66	.327	.423	0	—	0		6		0.7
	Col N	2	3	.400	38	0	0	0-3	36.2	26	14	0	2	12-1	35	3.19	149	.195	.268	0	—	0		6		-0.1
	Year	5	4	.556	66	0	0	0-3	62.1	62	33	3	3	30-3	52	4.48	101	.255	.341	0	—	0		6		
Total 9		29	33	.468	563	1	0	52-27	621.2	648	327	59	30	290-50	446	4.31	111	.271	.354	17-0-1	.059	-1	124	28	146	1.4
DeJESUS, JOSE Jose Luis B1.6.1965 Brooklyn NY BR/TR/6-5/195(175-223) d9.9 [DL 1993 Phi N 120]																										
1988	KC A	0	1	.000	2	1	0	0-0	5	5	5	0	0	5-1	2	27.00	15	.429	.579	0	—	0	136	-7		-1.1
1989	KC A	0	0	—	3	1	0	0-0	8	7	4	1	0	8-0	2	4.50	86	.241	.405	2	—	0	70	0		-0.1
1990	Phi N	7	8	.467	22	22	3-1	0-0	130	97	63	10	2	73-3	87	3.74	103	.210	.321	38-0-4	.079	-1	91	6		-0.1
1991	Phi N	10	9	.526	31	29	3	1-0	181.2	147	74	7	4	128-4	118	3.42	106	.224	.353	62-0-4	.129	-1	91	6		0.1
1994	KC A	3	1	.750	5	4	0	0-0	26.2	27	14	2	0	13-0	12	4.73	106	.276	.360	4	—	0	96	1		0.1
Total 5		20	19	.513	63	57	6-1	1-0	349	284	165	20	6	227-8	221	3.84	100	.226	.346	100-0-8	.110	-2	90	0	120	-0.1
DE LA CRUZ, TOMMY Tomas (Rivero) B9.18.1911 Marianao, Cuba D9.6.1958 Havana, Cuba BR/TR/6-2/168 d4.20																										
1944	Cin N	9	9	.500	34	20	9	1	191.1	170	73	9	1	45	65	3.25	108	.238	.284	58-0-4	.155	-0*		89	9	0.1
DE LA MAZA, ROLAND Roland Robert (Suastegui) B11.11.1971 Granada Hills CA BR/TR/6-2/195 [CleA93 15/419] d9.26 Col Cal St.-Sacramento																										
1997	KC A	0	0	—	1	1	0	1-0	1	1	1	1	0	1-0	1	4.50	105	.125	.222	0		0		0		0.1
DELANEY, ART Arthur Dewey "Swede" (b.Arthur Dewey Helenius) B1.5.1895 Chicago IL D5.2.1970 Hayward CA BR/TR/5-10.5/178 d4.16																										
1924	StL N	1	0	1.000	8	1	1	0	20	19	4	0	0	6	2	1.80	210	.250	.305		.286	0		157	5	0.1
1928	Bos N	9	17	.346	39	22	8	2	192.1	197	100	11	1	56	45	3.79	103	.267	.319	63-0-1	.143	-3		80	2	-1.1
1929	Bos N	3	5	.375	20	8	3-1	0	75	103	59	6	1	35	17	6.12	76	.336	.405	21-1-2	.143	-1		86	-13	-0.1
Total 3		13	22	.371	67	31	12-1	2	287.1	319	163	17	2	97	64	4.26	96	.285	.343	91-1-3	.154	-2		84	-6	
DE LA ROSA, FRANCISCO Francisco (Jimenez) B3.3.1966 LaRomana, D.R. BB/TR/5-11/185 d9.7																										
1991	Bal A	0	0	—	2	0	0	0-0	4	4	2	0	0	4-0	1	4.50	88	.353	.400	0	—			-1		0
DE LA ROSA, JORGE Jorge Alberto (Gonzalez) B4.5.1981 Monterrey, Nuevo Leon, Mexico BL/TL/6-1/190* d8.14																										
2004	Mil N	0	3	.000	5	5	0	0-0	22.2	29	20	1	1	14-0	6	6.35	69	.309	.393	6-0-1	.000	-1		80	-6	-0
2005	Mil N	2	2	.500	38	0	0	0-2	42.1	48	23	1	0	38-4	42	4.46	96	.289	.417	0	—	0		-1		-0
Total 2		2	5	.286	43	5	0	0-2	65	77	43	2	1	52-4	47	5.12	84	.296	.409	6-0-1	.000	-1		80	-7	-0
DELCARMEN, MANNY Manuel B2.16.1982 Boston MA BR/TR/6-2/190 d7.26																										
2005	Bos A	0	0	—	10	0	0	0-0	9	8	3	0	1	7-0	9	3.00	153	.242	.390	0		0		2		0
DeLEON, JOSE Jose (Chestaro) B12.20.1960 Rancho Viejo, D.R. BR/TR/6-3/215(210-226) [PitN79 3/62] d7.23																										
1983	Pit N	7	3	.700	15	15	3-2	0-0	108	75	36	5	1	47-2	118	2.83	132	.196	.283	34-0-3	.059	-1		102	12	0
1984	Pit N	7	13	.350	30	28	5-1	0-1	192.1	147	86	10	3	92-5	153	3.74	97	.214	.307	59-0-4	.085	-2		57	-19	-0
1985	Pit N	2	19	.095	31	25	3-0	1-0	162.2	138	93	15	3	89-3	149	4.70	77	.231	.332	36-0-7	.056	-2		92	-7	-1
1986	Pit N	1	3	.250	9	1	0	1-0	16.1	17	16	2	1	17-3	11	8.27	47	.266	.427	1	—	0		72	11	1
	Chi A	4	5	.444	13	13	1	0-0	79	49	30	7	4	42-0	68	2.96	147	.179	.296	0	—	0		90	10	
1987	Chi A	11	12	.478	33	31	0	0-0	206	177	106	24	10	97-4	153	4.02	115	.230	.322	0	—	0		96	0	-0
1988	StL N	13	10	.565	34	34	3-1	0-0	225.1	190	95	13	2	86-7	208	3.67	96	.237	.308	72-0-12	.139	-1*		96	0	-0
1989	StL N	16	12	.571	36	36	5-3	0-0	244.2	173	96	16	6	86-9	201	3.05	120	**.197**	.268	83-0-9	.096	-4		80	14	-1
1990	StL N	7	19	.269	32	32	0	0-0	182.2	168	96	15	5	86-9	164	4.43	87	.246	.331	56-0-5	.107	-1		73	-9	-1
1991	StL N	5	9	.357	28	28	1	0-0	162.2	144	57	16	5	61-1	118	2.71	138	.239	.313	46-0-5	.043	-4		96	17	-1
1992	StL N	2	7	.222	29	15	0	0-0	102.1	95	56	7	2	43-1	72	4.57	75	.245	.320	21-0-4	.048	-1		95	-13	-1
	Phi N	0	1	.000	3	3	0	0-0	15	16	7	0	0	5-0	7	3.00	117	.281	.339	5-0-1	.400	1		103	0	-1
	Year	2	8	.200	32	18	0	0-1	117.1	111	63	7	2	48-1	79	4.37	79	.250	.322	26-0-5	.115	-1		91	1	-1
1993	Phi N	3	0	1.000	24	3	0	0-1	47	39	25	5	5	27-3	34	3.26	122	.229	.348	6-0-1	.000	-1		3		0
	†Chi A	0	0	—	11	0	0	0-1	10.1	5	2	2	1	2-1	8	1.74	242	.152	.243	0	—	0		10		0
1994	Chi A	3	2	.600	42	0	0	2-2	67	48	28	6	2	31-5	67	3.36	140	.200	.301	0	—	0		-5		-0
1995	Chi A	5	3	.625	38	0	0	0-0	67.2	60	41	10	6	28-2	53	5.19	86	.238	.323	0-0-1	—	0		-3		-0
	Mon N	0	1	.000	7	0	0	0-0	8.1	7	7	2	1	7-0	12	7.56	57	.233	.375	0	—	0		-3		-0
Total 13		86	119	.420	415	264	21-7	6-10	1897.1	1556	877	153	62	841-50	1594	3.76	103	.224	.311	419-0-52	.091	-16		83	21	-2
DeLEON, LUIS Luis Antonio (Tricoche) B8.19.1958 Ponce, PR BR/TR/6-1/153* d9.6																										
1981	StL N	0	1	.000	10	0	0	0-0	15.1	11	4	4	1	3-2	8	2.35	154	.200	.241	1	.000	-0		2		0
1982	SD N	9	5	.643	61	0	0	15-8	102	77	25	10	1	16-9	60	2.03	169	.212	.246	11-0-1	.091	0*		17		0
1983	SD N	6	6	.500	63	0	0	13-6	111	89	34	8	1	27-7	90	2.68	131	.224	.269	14-0-3	.143	-0		12		-.
1984	SD N	2	2	.500	32	0	0	0-3	42.2	44	34	4	2	12-2	44	5.48	65	.256	.317	4-0-1	.000	-0		-11	95	
1985	SD N	0	3	.000	29	0	0	3-2	38.2	39	18	6	2	10-4	31	4.79	93	.267	.325	5	.200	-0		-2		-.
1987	Bal A	0	2	.000	11	0	0	1-1	20.2	19	15	1	2	9-1	13	4.79	93	.253	.326	0	—	-0		157	-1	
1989	Sea A	0	0	—	1	1	0	0-0	4	5	1	1	1	1-0	5	2.25	180	.313	.389	0	—	-0		157	17	95
Total 7		17	19	.472	207	1	0	32-20	334.1	284	131	39	12	77-26	248	3.12	114	.232	.280	35-0-5	.114	-0		157	17	95
DELHI, FLAME Lee William B11.5.1892 Harqua Hala AZ D5.9.1966 Greenbrae CA BR/TR/6-2.5/198 d4.16																										
1912	Chi A	0	0	—	1	0	0	0-0	3	7	6	0	3	4	0	9.00	36	.412	.500	0	—	0		-3		
DELL, WHEEZER William George B6.11.1886 Tuscarora NV D8.24.1966 Lone Pine CA BR/TR/6-4/210 d4.22																										
1912	StL N	0	0	—	3	0	0	0	2.1	3	3	0	0	3	0	11.57	30	.188	.316	0	—	0		-2		
1915	Bro N	11	10	.524	40	24	12-4	1	215	166	80	5	8	100	94	2.34	119	.215	.315	66-0-2	.152	-0		91	9	
1916	†Bro N	8	9	.471	32	16	9-2	1	155	143	62	4	4	43	76	2.26	118	.256	.314	44-0-2	.091	-2		77	8	
1917	Bro N	0	4	.000	17	4	0	1	58	55	35	3	2	25	28	3.72	75	.263	.347	16	.063	-2		108	-8	
Total 4		19	23	.452	92	44	21-6	3	430.1	367	170	10	14	171	198	2.55	108	.237	.319	126-0-4	.119	-5		88	7	
DELOCK, IKE Ivan Martin B11.11.1929 Highland Park MI BR/TR/5-11/175* d4.17																										
1952	Bos A	4	9	.308	39	7	1-1	5	95	88	50	9	2	50	46	4.26	92	.245	.341	22-0-1	.045	-1		89	-3	
1953	Bos A	3	1	.750	23	1	0	4	48.2	60	27	2	2	20	22	4.44	95	.308	.308	10	.100	-1		42	-1	
1955	Bos A	3	7	.563	29	18	6	9	143.2	136	67	17	4	61-2	88	3.76	114	.247	.325	49-0-4	.143	-1		91	8	
1956	Bos A	13	7	.650	48	9	0	9	128.1	122	65	12	5	80-3	105	4.21	110	.252	.359	29-0-7	.103	-2		67	7	
1957	Bos A	9	8	.529	49	2	0	11	94	80	40	11	4	45-7	62	3.83	104	.230	.322	21	.048	-1		34	4	
1958	Bos A	14	8	.636	31	19	9-1	2	160	155	66	13	2	45-5	82	3.37	119	.252	.314	48-0-5	.063	-4		90	12	
1959	Bos A	11	6	.647	28	17	4	2	134.1	120	53	12	2	62-1	55	2.95	138	.236	.318	47-1-5	.064	-3		116	14	
1960	Bos A	9	10	.474	24	23	3-1	0	129.1	145	77	24	4	52-3	49	4.73	85	.283	.353	43-0-6	.116	-0		104	-10	

YEAR	TM LG	W	L	PCT	G	GS	CG-SHO	SV-BS	IP	H	R	HR	HB	BB-IB	SO	ERA	AERA	OAV	OOB	AB-HR-SH	AVG	PB	SUP	APR	DL	PW
1961	Bos A	6	9	.400	28	28	3-1	0	156	185	110	24	2	52-2	80	4.90	85	.293	.346	48-0-5	.104	-1	111	-17		-1.7
1962	Bos A	4	5	.444	17	13	4-2	0	86.1	89	39	10	0	24-2	49	3.75	110	.268	.315	23-0-4	.087	-1	73	4		0.2
1963	Bos A	1	2	.333	6	6	1	0	32	31	18	4	0	12-0	23	4.50	84	.246	.309	12	.000	-1	98	-3	39	-0.4
	Bal A	1	3	.250	7	5	0	0	30.1	25	17	4	0	16-1	11	5.04	69	.236	.336	9	.000	-1	56	-5		-0.7
	Year	2	5	.286	13	11	1	0	62.1	56	35	8	0	28-1	34	4.76	76	.241	.322	21	.000	-3	80	-7		-1.1
Total	11	84	75	.528	329	147	32-6	31	1238	1236	629	142	24	530-27	672	4.03	102	.259	.335	361-1-35	.086	-20	94	10	39	-0.3

DE LOS SANTOS, LUIS   Luis B11.1.1977 Santo Domingo, D.R. BR/TR/6-2/216 d7.20 [DL 2000 NY A 181]

YEAR	TM LG	W	L	PCT	G	GS	CG-SHO	SV-BS	IP	H	R	HR	HB	BB-IB	SO	ERA	AERA	OAV	OOB	AB-HR-SH	AVG	PB	SUP	APR	DL	PW
2002	TB A	0	3	.000	3	3	0	0-0	14	24	19	5	3	4-0	7	11.57	39	.387	.437	0	—	0	82	-11		-1.5

DE LOS SANTOS, RAMON   Ramon (Genero) B1.19.1949 Santo Domingo, D.R. BL/TL/6-1/175 d8.21

YEAR	TM LG	W	L	PCT	G	GS	CG-SHO	SV-BS	IP	H	R	HR	HB	BB-IB	SO	ERA	AERA	OAV	OOB	AB-HR-SH	AVG	PB	SUP	APR	DL	PW
1974	Hou N	1	1	.500	12	0	0	0-0	37	33	12	0	0	9-4	7	2.19	159	.234	.351	0	—	0		1		0.1

DE LOS SANTOS, VALERIO   Valerio Lorenzo B10.6.1972 Las Matas de Farfan, D.R. BL/TL/6-2/180(180-210) d7.31

YEAR	TM LG	W	L	PCT	G	GS	CG-SHO	SV-BS	IP	H	R	HR	HB	BB-IB	SO	ERA	AERA	OAV	OOB	AB-HR-SH	AVG	PB	SUP	APR	DL	PW
1998	Mil N	0	0		13	0	0	0-0	21.2	11	4	0	0	2-0	18	2.91	149	.151	.173	0	—	0		4		0.2
1999	Mil N	0	1	.000	7	0	0	0-0	8.1	12	6	1	1	7-0	15	6.48	71	.343	.465	0	—	0		-1	156	-0.1
2000	Mil N	2	3	.400	66	2	0	0-1	73.2	72	43	15	1	33-7	70	5.13	90	.254	.333	6	.000	-1	70	-3		-0.2
2001	Mil N	0	0		1	0	0	0-0	1	1	1	0	0	1-0	1	9.00	48	.250	.400	0		-1	70	-3		-0.1
2002	Mil N	2	3	.400	51	0	0	0-0	57.2	42	21	4	2	26-3	38	3.12	132	.211	.299	0		0		7	187	0.5
2003	Mil N	3	3	.500	45	0	0	1-3	48	38	24	8	4	22-0	35	4.13	105	.225	.322	2-0-2	.000	-0		7		0.1
	Phi N	1	0	1.000	6	0	0	0-0	4	7	7	0	1	3-0	4	9.00	44	.389	.500	1	.000	-0		1	30	0.1
	Year	4	3	.571	51	0	0	1-3	52	45	31	8	5	25-0	39	4.50	95	.241	.339	1	.000	-0		-4		-0.7
2004	Tor A	0	0		17	0	0	0-1	11.2	11	8	4	0	10-2	10	6.17	79	.250	.382	0	—	0		-3		-0.6
2005	Fla A	1	2	.333	27	0	0	0-1	22	25	15	4	2	12-3	16	6.14	65	.281	.379	0	—	0		-1	120	-0.6
Total	8	9	12	.429	233	2	0	1-6	248	219	132	36	11	116-15	197	4.54	96	.240	.328	9-0-2	.000	-1	70	-2	493	-0.9

DeLTORO, MIGUEL   Miguel B6.22.1972 San Ignacio, Sonora, Mexico D10.6.2001 Obregon, Sonora, Mexico BR/TR/6-1/160(160-180) d4.6

YEAR	TM LG	W	L	PCT	G	GS	CG-SHO	SV-BS	IP	H	R	HR	HB	BB-IB	SO	ERA	AERA	OAV	OOB	AB-HR-SH	AVG	PB	SUP	APR	DL	PW
1999	SF N	0	0		14	0	0	0-0	23.2	24	11	6	0	11-0	20	4.18	102	.264	.343	4-0-1	.000	-0		1		0.0
2000	†SF N	2	0	1.000	9	1	0	0-0	17.1	17	10	3	2	6-2	16	5.19	84	.250	.329	2	.500	0	190	-1		-0.1
Total	2	2	0	1.000	23	1	0	0-0	41	41	21	8	2	17-2	36	4.61	93	.258	.337	6-0-1	.167	-0	190	0		-0.1

DeLUCIA, RICH   Richard Anthony B10.7.1964 Reading PA BR/TR/6-0/185* [SeaA86 6/141] d9.8 Col Tennessee

YEAR	TM LG	W	L	PCT	G	GS	CG-SHO	SV-BS	IP	H	R	HR	HB	BB-IB	SO	ERA	AERA	OAV	OOB	AB-HR-SH	AVG	PB	SUP	APR	DL	PW
1990	Sea A	1	2	.333	5	5	1	0-0	36	30	9	0	0	9-0	20	2.00	199	.226	.275	0	—	0	55	8		0.6
1991	Sea A	12	13	.480	32	31	0	0-0	182	176	107	31	4	78-4	98	5.09	81	.260	.333	0	—	0	110	-17		-2.1
1992	Sea A	3	6	.333	30	11	0	1-2	83.2	100	55	13	2	35-1	66	5.49	73	.293	.361	0	—	0	114	-13	27	-1.3
1993	Sea A	3	6	.333	30	1	0	0-4	42.2	46	24	5	1	23-3	48	4.64	96	.272	.361	0	—	0	82	-1	24	-0.2
1994	Cin N	0	0		8	0	0	0-0	10.2	9	6	4	0	5-0	15	4.22	99	.214	.298	0	—	0		0		0.0
1995	StL N	8	7	.533	56	1	0	0-1	82.1	63	38	9	3	36-2	76	3.39	126	.213	.303	10-0-1	.200	0	84	7		1.2
1996	SF N	3	6	.333	56	0	0	0-2	61.2	62	44	8	4	31-6	55	5.84	71	.259	.349	4	.250	0		-11	58	-1.3
1997	SF N	0	0		3	0	0	0-0	1.2	6	3	0	0	0-0	2	10.80	38	.500	.500		—	0		-2		-0.1
	Ana A	6	4	.600	33	0	0	3-4	42.1	29	18	5	1	27-2	42	3.61	128	.204	.331	0	—	0		5	49	0.9
1998	Ana A	2	6	.250	61	0	0	3-3	71.2	56	36	10	3	46-5	73	4.27	111	.221	.340	0	—	0		4		0.4
1999	Cle A	0	1	.000	6	0	0	0-0	9.1	13	7	4	0	9-2	7	6.75	75	.317	.440	0	—	0		-1		-0.1
Total	10	38	51	.427	320	49	1	7-16	624	590	347	91	17	299-25	502	4.62	93	.251	.337	14-0-1	.214	1	100	-21	158	-2.0

DEMARAIS, FRED   Frederick B11.1.1866 Montreal QC, Can. D3.6.1919 Stamford CT TR/5-9/168 d7.26

YEAR	TM LG	W	L	PCT	G	GS	CG-SHO	SV-BS	IP	H	R	HR	HB	BB-IB	SO	ERA	AERA	OAV	OOB	AB-HR-SH	AVG	PB	SUP	APR	DL	PW
1890	Chi N	0	0		1	0	0		2	1	0	0	0	1	1	0.00	—	.143	.250	2	.000	-0		1		0.0

DEMAREE, AL   Albert Wentworth B9.8.1884 Quincy IL D4.30.1962 Los Angeles CA BL/TR/6-0/170 d9.26

YEAR	TM LG	W	L	PCT	G	GS	CG-SHO	SV-BS	IP	H	R	HR	HB	BB-IB	SO	ERA	AERA	OAV	OOB	AB-HR-SH	AVG	PB	SUP	APR	DL	PW
1912	NY N	1	0	1.000	2	2	1-1	0	16	17	3	0	0	2	11	1.69	200	.288	.311	5	.000	-1	87	3		0.1
1913	†NY N	13	4	.765	31	25	11-2	2	199.2	176	65	4	5	38	76	2.21	141	.243	.286	66-0-1	.106	-3	106	21		1.2
1914	NY N	10	17	.370	38	29	13-2	0	224	219	97	3	8	77	89	3.09	86	.263	.331	68-0-2	.132	-2	116	-11		-1.6
1915	Phi N	14	11	.560	32	26	13-3	1	209.2	201	84	4	3	58	69	3.05	90	.260	.314	68-0-3	.176	0	112	-2		-0.5
1916	Phi N	19	14	.576	39	35	25-4	1	285	252	99	4	4	48	130	2.62	101	.242	.281	101-0-1	.109	-4	105	6		-0.2
1917	Chi N	5	9	.357	24	18	6-1	1	141.1	125	53	5	2	37	43	2.55	114	.242	.297	41-0-1	.122	-1	84	6		0.5
	NY N	4	5	.444	15	11	1	0	78.1	70	33	1	1	17	23	2.64	97	.239	.283	18-0-3	.111	-1	67	-3		-0.4
	Year	9	14	.391	39	29	7-1	1	219.2	195	86	6	3	54	66	2.58	108	.242	.292	59-0-4	.119	-2	78	2		0.1
1918	NY N	8	6	.571	26	14	8-2	1	142	143	56	5	2	25	39	2.47	106	.262	.297	47-0-4	.128	-3	152	0		-0.3
1919	Bos N	6	6	.500	25	13	6	3	128	147	66	8	4	35	34	3.80	75	.300	.348	42	.048	-5	111	-13		-1.8
Total	8	80	72	.526	232	173	84-15	9	1424	1350	556	34	30	337	514	2.77	100	.256	.304	456-0-15	.118	-20	107	7		-3.0

DEMARIA, CHRIS   Chris Neil B9.28.1980 Torrance CA BB/TR/6-3/210 d9.9 Col Cal St.-Long Beach

YEAR	TM LG	W	L	PCT	G	GS	CG-SHO	SV-BS	IP	H	R	HR	HB	BB-IB	SO	ERA	AERA	OAV	OOB	AB-HR-SH	AVG	PB	SUP	APR	DL	PW
2005	KC A	1	0	1.000	8	0	0	0-0	9	14	10	3	0	5-0	11	9.00	47	.359	.432	0	—	0		-5		-0.5

DEMERY, LARRY   Lawrence Calvin B6.4.1953 Bakersfield CA BR/TR/6-0/170* [PitN72*S7/107] d6.2 Col Los Angeles (CA) City [DL 1978 Pit N 58]

YEAR	TM LG	W	L	PCT	G	GS	CG-SHO	SV-BS	IP	H	R	HR	HB	BB-IB	SO	ERA	AERA	OAV	OOB	AB-HR-SH	AVG	PB	SUP	APR	DL	PW
1974	†Pit N	6	6	.500	19	15	2	0-0	95.1	95	47	12	0	51-5	51	4.25	82	.262	.351	33-0-3	.152	0*	132	-6		-0.7
1975	†Pit N	7	5	.583	45	8	1	4-1	114.2	95	40	7	3	43-6	59	2.90	123	.230	.305	24-0-2	.125	1*	166	10		1.1
1976	Pit N	10	7	.588	36	15	4-1	2-1	145	123	56	8	2	58-8	72	3.17	111	.234	.309	40-0-4	.125	-1*	92	7		0.7
1977	Pit N	6	5	.545	39	8	0	1-1	90.1	100	59	13	0	47-3	35	5.08	79	.279	.360	20	.150	0	94	-11		-1.3
Total	4	29	23	.558	139	46	7-1	7-3	445.1	413	202	40	5	199-22	217	3.72	98	.249	.328	117-0-9	.137	0	117	0	58	-0.2

DeMILLER, HARRY   Harry B11.12.1867 Wooster OH D10.19.1928 Santa Ana CA BR/TL d8.20

YEAR	TM LG	W	L	PCT	G	GS	CG-SHO	SV-BS	IP	H	R	HR	HB	BB-IB	SO	ERA	AERA	OAV	OOB	AB-HR-SH	AVG	PB	SUP	APR	DL	PW
1892	Chi N	1	1	.500	4	2	2	0	24	29	22	1	1	16	15	6.38	52	.287	.390	10	.300	1	105	-6		-0.3

DeMOLA, DON   Donald John B7.5.1952 Glen Cove NY BR/TR/6-2/180* [NYA70 7/160] d4.13 [DL 1976 Mon N 157]

YEAR	TM LG	W	L	PCT	G	GS	CG-SHO	SV-BS	IP	H	R	HR	HB	BB-IB	SO	ERA	AERA	OAV	OOB	AB-HR-SH	AVG	PB	SUP	APR	DL	PW
1974	Mon N	1	0	1.000	25	1	0	0-0	57.2	46	21	7	0	21-1	47	3.12	123	.223	.295	4	.000	-1	23	5		0.2
1975	Mon N	4	7	.364	60	0	0	1-1	97.2	92	47	8	4	42-4	63	4.15	93	.251	.333	8	.000	-1		-1		-0.4
Total	2	5	7	.417	85	1	0	1-1	155.1	138	68	15	4	63-5	110	3.77	103	.241	.320	12	.000	-1	23	4	157	-0.2

DeMOTT, BEN   Benyew Harrison B4.2.1889 Green Village NJ D7.5.1963 Somerville NJ BR/TR/6-0/192 d8.12 Col Lafayette

YEAR	TM LG	W	L	PCT	G	GS	CG-SHO	SV-BS	IP	H	R	HR	HB	BB-IB	SO	ERA	AERA	OAV	OOB	AB-HR-SH	AVG	PB	SUP	APR	DL	PW
1910	Cle A	0	3	.000	6	4	1	0	28.1	45	25	0	1	8	13	5.40	48	.388	.432	18	.167	-0*	58	-9		-0.9
1911	Cle A	0	1	.000	1	1	0	0	3.2	10	5	0	0	2	2	12.27	28	.588	.632	4	.000	-0*	21	-3		-0.4
Total	2	0	4	.000	7	5	1	0	32	55	30	0	1	10	15	6.19	43	.414	.458	22	.136	-0	51	-12		-1.3

DEMPSEY, CON   Cornelius Francis B9.16.1923 San Francisco CA BR/TR/6-4/190 d4.28 Col San Francisco

YEAR	TM LG	W	L	PCT	G	GS	CG-SHO	SV-BS	IP	H	R	HR	HB	BB-IB	SO	ERA	AERA	OAV	OOB	AB-HR-SH	AVG	PB	SUP	APR	DL	PW
1951	Pit N	0	2	.000	3	2	0	0	7	7	4	0	1	4	3	9.00	47	.393	.469	1	.000	-0	31	-3		-0.6

DEMPSEY, MARK   Mark Steven B12.17.1957 Dayton OH BR/TR/6-6/220 [SFN80 26/646] d9.4 Col Ohio St.

YEAR	TM LG	W	L	PCT	G	GS	CG-SHO	SV-BS	IP	H	R	HR	HB	BB-IB	SO	ERA	AERA	OAV	OOB	AB-HR-SH	AVG	PB	SUP	APR	DL	PW
1982	SF N	0	0		3	1	0	0-0	5.2	11	5	1	0	2-0	4	7.94	45	.440	.464	0	—	-0	123	-2		-0.1

DEMPSTER, RYAN   Ryan Scott B5.3.1977 Sechelt BC, Can. BR/TR/6-1/201(195-215) [TexA95 3/66] d5.23

YEAR	TM LG	W	L	PCT	G	GS	CG-SHO	SV-BS	IP	H	R	HR	HB	BB-IB	SO	ERA	AERA	OAV	OOB	AB-HR-SH	AVG	PB	SUP	APR	DL	PW
1998	Fla N	1	5	.167	14	11	0	0-1	54.2	72	47	6	9	38-1	35	7.08	57	.336	.446	13-0-1	.000	-1	78	-19		-1.8
1999	Fla N	7	8	.467	25	25	0	0-0	147	146	77	21	6	93-2	126	4.71	93	.262	.370	49-0-1	.102	-2*	96	-2		-0.4
2000	Fla N☆	14	10	.583	33	33	2-1	0-0	226.1	210	102	30	21	97-7	209	3.66	120	.243	.322	77-0-4	.078	-4	90	19		1.3
2001	Fla N	15	12	.556	34	34	2-1	0-0	211.1	218	123	21	10	112-5	171	4.94	84	.269	.362	61-0-16	.049	-4	117	-18		-2.2
2002	Fla N	5	8	.385	18	18	3	0-0	120.1	126	66	12	7	55-1	87	4.79	82	.281	.366	34-0-4	.059	-2	121	-10		-1.1
	Cin N	5	5	.500	15	15	1	0-0	88.2	102	61	16	3	38-1	66	6.19	69	.293	.365	29-0-5	.207	1*	124	-15		-1.4
	Year	10	13	.435	33	33	4	0-0	209	228	127	28	10	93-2	153	5.38	76	.286	.365	63-0-9	.127	-1	123	-27		-2.5
2003	Cin N	3	7	.300	22	20	0	0-0	115.2	134	89	14	5	70-4	84	6.54	64	.293	.390	33-0-1	.030	-3*	100	-30	77	-2.5
2004	Chi N	1	1	.500	23	0	0	2-0	20.2	16	9	1	2	13-0	18	3.92	113	.208	.337	1	.000	-0		1	119	0.1
2005	Chi N	5	3	.625	63	6	0	33-2	92	83	35	4	4	49-7	89	3.13	140	.242	.343	14	.071	-1	64	12		1.6
Total	8	56	59	.487	247	162	8-2	35-3	1076.2	1107	609	125	51	565-28	885	4.83	86	.269	.361	311-0-32	.077	-16	102	-62	196	-6.4

DENEHY, BILL   William Francis B3.31.1946 Middletown CT BB/TR/6-3/200* d4.16

YEAR	TM LG	W	L	PCT	G	GS	CG-SHO	SV-BS	IP	H	R	HR	HB	BB-IB	SO	ERA	AERA	OAV	OOB	AB-HR-SH	AVG	PB	SUP	APR	DL	PW
1967	NY N	1	7	.125	15	8	0	0	53.2	51	38	8	0	29-2	35	4.70	72	.248	.338	9-0-2	.000	-1	26	-11		-1.5
1968	Was A	0	0		3	0	0	0	2	4	3	0	0	4-0	1	9.00	32	.444	.615	0	—	0		-2		-0.1
1971	Det A	0	3	.000	31	1	0	1-0	49	47	25	4	4	28-0	27	4.22	86	.250	.357	2-0-1	.000	0		-3		-0.1
Total	3	1	10	.091	49	9	0	1-0	104.2	102	66	12	4	61-3	63	4.56	77	.253	.355	11-0-3	.000	-1	25	-16		-1.7

YEAR	TM LG	W	L	PCT	G	GS	CG-SHO	SV-BS	IP	H	R	HR	HB	BB-IB	SO	ERA	AERA	OAV	OOB	AB-HR-SH	AVG	PB	SUP	APR	DL	PW

DENMAN, BRIAN Brian John B2.12.1956 Minneapolis MN BR/TR/6-4/205 [BosA78*S1/13] d8.22 Col Minnesota

																										-0.5
1982	Bos A	3	4	.429	9	9	2-1	0-0	49	55	32	6	0	9-3	9	4.78	91	.282	.312	0	—	0	95	-4		

DENNEY, KYLE Kyle Dean B7.27.1977 Prague OK BR/TR/6-2/190 [CleA99 26/797] d9.14 Col Oklahoma [DL 2005 Cle A 35]

2004	Cle A	1	2	.333	4	4	0	0-0	16	17	17	3	0	13-0	13	9.56	45	.421	.471	0	—	0	96	-9		-1.2

DENNIS, DON Donald Ray B3.3.1942 Uniontown KS BR/TR/6-2/190* d6.18 Col Emporia St.

1965	StL N	2	3	.400	41	0	0	6	55	47	17	3	1	16-11	29	2.29	168	.236	.294	5	.400	1	221	8		1.
1966	StL N	4	2	.667	38	1	0	0	59.2	73	36	8	1	17-10	25	4.98	72	.302	.346	12	.083	-1	221	-9		-0.
Total	2	6	5	.545	79	1	0	6	114.2	120	53	11	2	33-21	54	3.69	101	.272	.322	17	.176	-0	221	-1		

DENNY, JOHN John Allen B11.8.1952 Prescott AZ BR/TR/6-3/190* [StLN70 29/679] d9.12

1974	StL N	0	0	—	2	0	0-0		2	3	1	0	0	1-1	1	0.00	—	.273	.273	0	—	0	0	0		0.
1974	StL N	0	0	—	2	0	0-0		2	3	1	0	0	1-1	1	0.00	—	.273	.273	0	—	0	0	0		0.0
1974	StL N	0	0	—	2	0	0-0		2	3	1	0	0	1-1	1	0.00	—	.273	.273	0	—	0	0	0		-0.2
1975	StL N	10	7	.588	25	24	3-2	0-0	136	149	73	5	3	51-6	72	3.97	96	.280	.344	44-0-6	.227	1*	95	-3		2.
1976	StL N	11	9	.550	30	30	8-3	0-0	207	189	71	11	8	74-3	74	**2.52**	**142**	.246	.318	67-0-7	.224	-1	103	22		2.
1977	StL N	8	8	.500	26	26	3-1	0-0	149.2	165	85	9	6	62-0	60	4.51	87	.281	.353	51-0-5	.098	-3	138	-10	37	-1.
1978	StL N	14	11	.560	33	33	11-2	0-0	234	200	81	13	6	74-4	103	2.96	120	.238	.302	73-0-7	.178	1	105	19		2.
1979	StL N	8	11	.421	31	31	5-2	0-0	206	206	116	24	4	100-7	99	4.85	79	.264	.349	70-0-8	.129	-1	104	-20		-1.
1980	Cle A	8	6	.571	16	16	4-1	0-0	108.2	116	54	4	5	47-2	59	4.39	94	.284	.363	0	—	0	89	-1		-0.
1981	Cle A	10	6	.625	19	19	6-3	0-0	145.2	139	62	9	3	66-3	94	3.15	117	.254	.335	0	—	0	103	6		-1.
1982	Cle A	6	11	.353	21	21	5	0-0	138.1	126	80	11	6	73-2	94	5.01	83	.240	.338	0	—	0	95	-10		-1.
	Phi N	0	2	.000	4	4	0	0-0	22.1	18	12	1	0	10-1	19	4.03	92	.217	.301	6	.167	0	30	-1		3.
1983	†Phi N	**19**	6	**.760**	36	36	7-1	0-0	242.2	229	77	9	4	53-5	139	2.37	152	.250	.293	77-0-17	.169	0	112	**32**	60	6.
1984	Phi N	7	7	.500	22	22	2	0-0	154.1	122	53	11	4	29-2	94	2.45	149	.214	.256	47-0-5	.191	0	103	19		-0.
1985	Phi N	11	14	.440	33	33	6-2	0-0	230.2	252	112	15	3	83-5	123	3.82	97	.282	.342	81-0-3	.123	-2	103	-3		-0.
1986	Cin N	11	10	.524	27	27	2-1	0-0	171.1	179	89	15	4	56-9	115	4.20	92	.272	.331	54-0-5	.222	0	104	44	152	6.
Total	13	123	108	.532	325	322	62-18	0-0	2148.2	2093	967	137	54	778-49	1146	3.59	105	.258	.325	570-0-63	.170	2	104	44		

DENT, EDDIE Elliott Estill B12.8.1887 Baltimore MD D11.25.1974 Birmingham AL BR/TR/6-1/190 d8.31

1909	Bro N	2	4	.333	6	5	4	0	42	47	23	2	0	15	17	4.29	60	.307	.369	15	.067	-1	119	-7		-1.
1911	Bro N	2	1	.667	3	1	0	0	31.2	30	15	0	2	10	3	3.69	90	.256	.326	10	.100	-0	158	-1		-0.
1912	Bro N	0	0	—	1	0	0	0	1	4	4	0	0	1	1	36.00	9	.571	.625	1	.000	-0		-3		-0.
Total	3	4	5	.444	12	8	5	0	74.2	81	42	2	2	26	21	4.46	65	.292	.357	26	.077	-2	133	-11		-1

DENZER, ROGER Roger "Peaceful Valley" B10.5.1871 LeSueur MN D9.18.1949 LeSueur MN BL/TR/6-0/180 d4.24

1897	Chi N	2	8	.200	12	10	8	0	94.2	125	91	4	2	34	17	5.13	87	.315	.372	39	.154	-3	85	-10		-1
1901	NY N	2	6	.250	11	9	3-1	0	61.2	69	30	2	2	5	22	3.36	98	.280	.300	22	.091	-1	52	1		-0
Total	2	4	14	.222	23	19	11-1	0	156.1	194	121	6	4	39	39	4.43	90	.302	.345	61	.131	-4	70	-9		-1

DePAULA, JORGE Jorge B11.10.1978 Sabana Grande, D.R. BR/TR/6-1/160* d9.5

2003	NY A	0	0	—	4	1	0	0-0	11.1	3	1	1	1	1-0	7	0.79	553	.083	.132	0	—	0	42	5		0.
2004	NY A	0	1	.000	3	1	0	0-0	9	9	6	2	0	4-0	2	5.00	92	.281	.342	0	—	0	61	-1	170	-0
2005	NY A	0	0	—	3	0	0	0-0	6.2	8	6	2	0	3-0	3	8.10	54	.296	.367	0	—	0		-2		-0
Total	3	0	1	.000	10	2	0	0-0	27	20	13	5	1	8-0	12	4.00	111	.211	.274	0	—	0	52	2	170	0

DePAULA, SEAN Sean Michael B11.7.1973 Newton MA BR/TR/6-4/215* [CleA96 9/273] d8.31 Col Wake Forest

1999	†Cle A	0	0	—	11	0	0	0-0	11.2	8	6	0	0	4-0	18	4.63	110	.200	.256	0	—	0	1			0.
2000	Cle A	0	0	—	13	0	0	0-2	16.2	20	11	3	0	14-2	16	5.94	84	.294	.410	0	—	0	-1		65	-1
2002	Cle A	1	1	.500	5	0	0	0-2	6.1	11	9	3	0	3-0	8	12.79	35	.367	.424	0	—	0	-6			-1
Total	3	1	1	.500	29	0	0	0-4	34.2	39	26	6	0	20-2	42	6.75	73	.283	.371	0	—	0	-6		65	-1

DERBY, GEORGE George H. "Jonah" B7.6.1857 Webster MA D7.4.1925 Philadelphia PA BL/TR/6-0/175 d5.2

1881	Det N	29	26	.527	56	55	55-9	0	494.2	505	252	3		86	**212**	2.20	132	.251	.281	236	.186	-10*	99	**34**		2
1882	Det N	17	20	.459	40	39	38-3	0	362	386	267	8		81	182	3.26	90	.256	.294	149	.195	-6	84	-20		-2
1883	Buf N	2	10	.167	14	13	12	1	107.2	173	120	3		15	34	5.85	54	.334	.353	59	.237	-1*	92	-30		-2
Total	3	48	56	.462	110	107	105-12	1	964.1	1064	639	14		182	428	3.01	98	.263	.295	444	.196	-17	92	-16		-2

DERRINGER, PAUL Samuel Paul "Duke" B10.17.1906 Springfield KY D11.17.1987 Sarasota FL BR/TR/6-3.5/205 Col Georgetown

1931	†StL N	18	8	**.692**	35	23	15-4	2	211.2	225	89	9	4	65	134	3.36	117	.274	.330	72-0-6	.097	-6	99	15		2.
1932	StL N	11	14	.440	39	30	14-1	0	233.1	296	133	6	2	67	78	4.05	97	.310	.356	73-0-3	.178	-0	92	-8		-2.
1933	StL N	0	2	.000	3	2	1	0	17	24	11	0	1	9	3	4.24	82	.353	.436	5	.000	-1	12	-2		-0.
	Cin N	7	25	.219	33	31	16-2	1	231	240	106	4	5	51	86	3.23	105	.271	.315	76-0-2	.184	-1	55	3		-3.
	Year	7	27	.206	36	33	17-2	1	248	264	117	4	6	60	89	3.30	103	.277	.324	81-0-2	.173	-2	53	-3		
1934	Cin N	15	21	.417	47	31	18-1	4	261	297	129	8	4	59	122	3.59	114	.283	.323	92-0-3	.196	0	79	14		-1.
1935	Cin N★	22	13	.629	45	33	20-3	2	276.2	295	132	13	4	49	120	3.51	113	.271	.305	93-0-6	.140	-5	90	13		2.
1936	Cin N	19	19	.500	**51**	**37**	13-2	5	282.1	331	147	11	4	42	94	4.04	92	.271	.313	80-0-2	.200	1	116	-5		-0.
1937	Cin N	10	14	.417	43	26	12-1	1	222.2	240	112	7	0	55	132	2.93	124	.262	.291	119-2-4	.176	-0	114	28		1.
1938	Cin N☆	21	14	.600	41	**37**	26-4	3	**307**	315	110	20	0	49	128	2.93	131	.272	.295	110-0-17	.209	0	134	30		4.
1939	†Cin N★	25	7	**.781**	38	35	28-5	0	301	321	115	15	3	35	115	3.06	124	.246	**.276**	108-0-4	.167	-2	97	25		2.
1940	Cin N★	20	12	.625	37	**37**	26-3	0	296.2	280	110	17	0	48	115	3.06	124	.246	.309	84-0-2	.155	-3	78	10		3.
1941	Cin N★	12	14	.462	29	29	17-2	1	228.1	233	91	16	0	54	76	3.31	109	.266	.296	68-0-6	.132	-2	81	7		-0.
1942	Cin N*	10	11	.476	29	27	13-1	0	208.2	203	83	4	4	49	68	3.06	107	.250	.296	58-0-4	.224	1	99	-8		-1.
1943	Chi N	10	14	.417	32	22	10-2	3	174	184	90	7	0	39	75	3.57	93	.264	.303	57-0-2	.158	-2	104	-11		-1.
1944	Chi N	7	13	.350	42	16	7	3	180	205	96	13	0	39	86	3.45	106	.265	.308	75-0-9	.200	0	97	4		1.
1945	†Chi N	16	11	.593	35	30	15-1	4	213.2	223	99	8	1	51	86	3.45	106	.265	.308	75-0-9	.175	-20	96	110		-0.
Total	15	223	212	.513	579	445	251-32	29	3645	3912	1652	158	32	761	1507	3.46	108	.272	.310	1260-2-77	.175	-20	96	110		

DERRINGTON, JIM Charles James "Blackie" B11.29.1939 Compton CA BL/TL/6-3/190* d9.30

1956	Chi A	0	1	.000	1	1	0	0	6	9	6	2	0	6-0	3	7.50	55	.375	.500	2	.500	0	130	-3		-0
1957	Chi A	0	1	.000	20	5	0	0	37	29	21	4	1	29-0	14	4.86	77	.216	.358	4-0-2	.000	-0	158	-4		-0
Total	2	0	2	.000	21	6	0	0	43	38	27	6	1	35-0	17	5.23	72	.241	.379	6-0-2	.167	0	153	-7		-0

DESHAIES, JIM James Joseph B6.23.1960 Massena NY BL/TL/6-4/220* [NYA82 21/542] d8.7 Col LeMoyne (NY)

1984	NY A	0	1	.000	2	2	0	0-0	7	14	9	1	0	7-0	5	11.57	37	.438	.525	0	—	0	94	-6		
1985	Hou N	0	0	—	2	0	0	0-0	3	1	0	0	0	0-0	5	0.00	—	.100	.100	0	—	0	105	6	16	
1986	Hou N	12	5	.706	26	26	1-1	0-0	144	124	58	16	2	59-2	128	3.25	114	.231	.311	43-0-4	.047	-0	107	-10	21	
1987	Hou N	11	6	.647	26	25	1	0-0	152	149	81	22	0	57-7	104	4.62	85	.257	.322	53-0-4	.094	-4	77	8		
1988	Hou N	11	14	.440	31	31	3-2	0-0	207	164	77	20	2	72-5	127	3.00	111	.218	.284	63-0-6	.048	-4	108	13		
1989	Hou N	15	10	.600	34	34	6-3	0-0	225.2	180	80	15	4	79-8	153	2.91	117	.217	.287	75-0-9	.120	-4	108	13		
1990	Hou N	7	12	.368	34	34	2	0-0	209.1	186	93	21	8	84-9	119	3.78	99	.245	.322	63-0-7	.063	-4	95	2		
1991	Hou N	5	12	.294	28	28	1	0-0	161	156	90	24	0	72-5	98	4.98	71	.259	.336	45-0-8	.098	-1	86	-23		
1992	SD N	4	7	.364	15	15	0	0-0	96	92	46	9	2	33-2	46	3.28	110	.258	.321	29-0-5	.207	-1	84	2		
1993	Min A	11	13	.458	27	27	1	0-0	167.1	159	85	24	9	51-1	80	4.41	100	.254	.313	0	—	-1	103	-1		
	SF N	2	2	.500	5	4	0	0-0	17	24	9	2	1	6-0	5	4.24	93	.348	.408	5-0-1	.000	-1	103	-32		
1994	Min A	6	12	.333	25	**25**	0	0-0	130.1	170	90	30	2	54-0	78	7.39	67	.321	.382	0	—	-0.	75	-9		
1995	Phi N	0	1	.000	2	2	0	0-0	5.1	15	12	3	0	1-0	6	20.25	21	.484	.500	1	.000	-0.	91	-37	37	
Total	12	84	95	.469	257	253	15-6	0-0	1525	1434	743	179	27	575-39	951	4.29	91	.255	.319	373-0-44	.088	-12	95	-47		

DeSHONG, JIMMIE James Brooklyn B11.30.1909 Harrisburg PA D10.16.1993 Lower Paxton Twp. PA BR/TR/5-11/165 d4.12

1932	Phi A	0	0	—	6	0	0	0	10	17	14	3	1	9	5	11.70	39	.378	.491	3	.000	-0		-8		
1934	NY A	6	7	.462	31	12	6	3	133.2	126	71	6	2	56	40	4.11	99	.243	.319	42-0-4	.190	-2	103	-7		
1935	NY A	4	1	.800	29	3	0	1	69	64	30	6	3	33	30	3.26	124	.242	.331	14-0-2	.071	-1	121	6		
1936	Was A	18	10	.643	34	31	16-2	1	223.2	255	135	11	3	96	86	4.90	90	.280	.359	94-0-4	.202	2	111	-10		
1937	Was A	14	15	.483	37	34	20	0	264.1	290	161	16	3	124	41	6.58	69	.310	.407	46-0-1	.261	3	106	-28		
1938	Was A	5	8	.385	31	0	0	1	131.1	160	104	11	1	92	26	8.63	50	.337	.442	15	.200	0	128	-21		
1939	Was A	0	0	—	7	6	1	0	40.2	56	45	7	0	31	12	8.63	50	.337	.442	15	.200	0	117	-58		
Total	7	47	44	.516	175	100	44-2	9	872.2	968	560	59	12	432	273	5.08	87	.281	.363	293-0-19	.198	-0				

YEAR	TM LG	W	L	PCT	G	GS	CG-SHO	SV-BS	IP	H	R	HR	HB	BB-IB	SO	ERA	AERA	OAV	OOB	AB-HR-SH	AVG	PB	SUP	APR	DL	PW

DeSILVA, JOHN   John Reed B9.30.1967 Fort Bragg CA   BR/TR/6-0/193*   [DetA89 8/213]   d8.15   Col Brigham Young

YEAR	TM LG	W	L	PCT	G	GS	CG-SHO	SV-BS	IP	H	R	HR	HB	BB-IB	SO	ERA	AERA	OAV	OOB	AB-HR-SH	AVG	PB	SUP	APR	DL	PW
1993	Det A	0	0	—	1	0	0	0-0	1	2	1	1	0	0-0	0	9.00	48	.667	.500	0	—	0		0		0.0
	LA N	0	0	—	3	0	0	0-0	5.1	6	4	0	0	1-0	6	6.75	57	.273	.304	0	—	0		-2		-0.1
1995	Bal A	1	0	1.000	2	2	0	0-0	8.2	8	7	3	1	7-0	1	7.27	66	.258	.400	0	—	0	195	-2		-0.2
Total 2		1	0	1.000	6	2	0	0-0	15	16	12	3	1	8-0	7	7.20	61	.286	.373	0	—	0	195	-4		-0.3

DesJARDIEN, SHORTY   Paul Raymond B8.24.1893 Coffeyville KS D3.7.1956 Monrovia CA   BR/TR/6-4.5/205   d5.20   Col Chicago

YEAR	TM LG	W	L	PCT	G	GS	CG-SHO	SV-BS	IP	H	R	HR	HB	BB-IB	SO	ERA	AERA	OAV	OOB	AB-HR-SH	AVG	PB	SUP	APR	DL	PW
1916	Cle A	0	0	—	1	0	0	0	1	2	2	0	1	2-0	0	18.00	17	.200	.333	0	—	0		-1		-0.1

DESSAU, RUBE   Frank Rolland B3.29.1883 New Galilee PA D5.6.1952 York PA   BB/TR/5-11/175   d9.22

YEAR	TM LG	W	L	PCT	G	GS	CG-SHO	SV-BS	IP	H	R	HR	HB	BB-IB	SO	ERA	AERA	OAV	OOB	AB-HR-SH	AVG	PB	SUP	APR	DL	PW
1907	Bos N	0	1	.000	3	2	1	0	9.1	13	11	0	1	10	1	10.61	24	.394	.545	4	.000	-0	167	-7		-0.6
1910	Bro N	2	3	.400	19	0	1	0	51.1	67	48	0	5	29	24	5.79	52	.328	.424	15-0-1	.067	-1		-18		-1.8
Total 2		4	.333	21	2	1	1		60.2	80	59	0	6	39	25	6.53	45	.338	.443	19-0-1	.053	-1	167	-25		-2.4

DESSENS, ELMER   Elmer (Jusaino) B1.13.1971 Hermosillo, Sonora, Mexico   BR/TR/6-0/187(178-200)   d6.24

YEAR	TM LG	W	L	PCT	G	GS	CG-SHO	SV-BS	IP	H	R	HR	HB	BB-IB	SO	ERA	AERA	OAV	OOB	AB-HR-SH	AVG	PB	SUP	APR	DL	PW
1996	Pit N	0	2	.000	15	3	0	0-0	25	40	23	2	0	4-0	13	8.28	53	.385	.404	5	.400	1	62	-9	41	-0.6
1997	Pit N	0	0	—	3	0	0	0-0	3.1	2	0	0	1	0-0	2	0.00	—	.167	.231	0	—	0		2		0.1
1998	Pit N	2	6	.250	43	5	0	0-1	74.2	90	50	10	0	25-2	43	5.67	75	.300	.351	0	—	0	52	-10	16	-1.0
2000	Cin N	11	5	.688	40	16	1	1-0	147.1	170	73	10	3	43-7	85	4.28	112	.296	.344	40-0-1	.100	-1	118	9		0.9
2001	Cin N	10	14	.417	34	34	1	0-0	205	221	103	32	1	56-1	128	4.48	102	.279	.325	57-0-10	.193	1*	86	7		0.7
2002	Cin N	7	8	.467	30	30	0	0-0	178	173	70	24	7	49-8	93	3.03	141	.257	.325	45-0-9	.200	1*	85	22	25	1.8
2003	Ari N	8	8	.500	34	30	0	0-0	175.2	212	107	22	4	57-6	113	5.07	91	.299	.354	46-0-10	.196	1*	104	-7		-0.5
2004	Ari N	1	6	.143	38	5	0	2-2	85.1	107	54	11	1	23-4	55	4.75	96	.301	.343	18-0-4	.167	1	106	-3		-0.1
	†LA N	1	0	1.000	12	1	0	0-1	19.2	16	7	4	0	8-0	18	3.20	129	.216	.293	4	.250	0	156	2		0.1
	Year	2	6	.250	50	10	0	2-3	105	123	61	15	1	31-4	73	4.46	101	.287	.334	22-0-4	.182	1	112	-1		0.0
2005	LA N	1	2	.333	28	7	0	0-0	65.2	63	30	6	1	19-2	37	3.56	115	.249	.301	10	.000	-1	97	-3		0.1
Total 9		41	51	.446	277	135	2-1	3-4	979.2	1094	517	121	18	284-30	587	4.40	102	.285	.334	233-0-37	.167	3	95	16	138	1.5

DETTMER, JOHN   John Franklin B3.4.1970 Centreville IL   BR/TR/6-0/185*   [TexA92 11/314]   d6.16   Col Missouri

YEAR	TM LG	W	L	PCT	G	GS	CG-SHO	SV-BS	IP	H	R	HR	HB	BB-IB	SO	ERA	AERA	OAV	OOB	AB-HR-SH	AVG	PB	SUP	APR	DL	PW
1994	Tex A	0	6	.000	11	9	0	0-0	54	63	42	10	3	20-3	27	4.33	112	.286	.347	0	—	0	95	-3		-0.2
1995	Tex A	0	0	—	1	0	0	0-0	0.1	2	1	0	0	0-0	0	27.00	18	.667	.500	0	—	0		-1		0.0
Total 2		0	6	.000	12	9	0	0-0	54.1	65	43	10	3	20-3	27	4.47	108	.291	.349	0	—	0	95	-4		-0.2

DETTORE, TOM   Thomas Anthony B11.17.1947 Canonsburg PA   BL/TR/6-4/200*   [PitN68*S3/58]   d6.11

YEAR	TM LG	W	L	PCT	G	GS	CG-SHO	SV-BS	IP	H	R	HR	HB	BB-IB	SO	ERA	AERA	OAV	OOB	AB-HR-SH	AVG	PB	SUP	APR	DL	PW
1973	Pit N	0	1	.000	12	1	0	0-0	22.2	33	19	1	3	14-4	13	5.96	59	.340	.435	4-0-1	.000	-0	25	-7		-0.4
1974	Chi N	3	5	.375	16	9	0	0-1	64.2	64	39	4	4	31-3	43	4.18	92	.255	.348	20-0-1	.250	1	152	-4		-0.2
1975	Chi N	5	4	.556	36	5	0	0-2	85.1	88	57	8	9	31-4	46	5.38	72	.270	.348	24	.250	1	68	-13		-1.2
1976	Chi N	0	1	.000	4	0	0	0-1	7	11	8	3	0	2-0	4	10.29	38	.355	.394	0	—	0		-4		-0.5
Total 4		8	11	.421	68	15	0	0-4	179.2	196	123	16	18	78-11	106	5.21	73	.278	.362	48-0-2	.229	2	116	-28		-2.3

DEUTSCH, MEL   Melvin Elliott B7.26.1915 Caldwell TX D11.18.2001 Austin TX   BR/TR/6-4/215   d4.21   Col Texas

YEAR	TM LG	W	L	PCT	G	GS	CG-SHO	SV-BS	IP	H	R	HR	HB	BB-IB	SO	ERA	AERA	OAV	OOB	AB-HR-SH	AVG	PB	SUP	APR	DL	PW
1946	Bos A	0	0	—	3	0	0	0	6.1	7	5	1	0	3	2	5.68	64	.280	.357	2	.000	-0		-2		-0.1

DEVENS, CHARLIE   Charles B1.1.1910 Milton MA D8.13.2003 Scarborough ME   BR/TR/6-1/180   d9.24   Col Harvard

YEAR	TM LG	W	L	PCT	G	GS	CG-SHO	SV-BS	IP	H	R	HR	HB	BB-IB	SO	ERA	AERA	OAV	OOB	AB-HR-SH	AVG	PB	SUP	APR	DL	PW
1932	NY A	1	0	1.000	1	1	1	0	9	6	2	0	0	7	4	2.00	204	.200	.351	2-0-1	.000	0	167	2		0.2
1933	NY A	3	3	.500	14	8	2	0	62	59	39	1	0	50	23	4.35	89	.250	.381	21-0-1	.095	-1	148	-5		-0.6
1934	NY A	1	0	1.000	1	1	1	0	11	9	3	0	0	5	4	1.64	248	.225	.311	2	.500	1	86	3		0.5
Total 3		5	3	.625	16	10	4	0	82	74	44	1	0	62	31	3.73	105	.242	.370	25-0-2	.120	0	143	0		0.1

DEVINE, JOEY   Joseph Neal B9.19.1983 Junction City KS   BR/TR/6-0/210   d8.20   Col North Carolina St.

YEAR	TM LG	W	L	PCT	G	GS	CG-SHO	SV-BS	IP	H	R	HR	HB	BB-IB	SO	ERA	AERA	OAV	OOB	AB-HR-SH	AVG	PB	SUP	APR	DL	PW
2005	†Atl N	0	1	.000	5	0	0	0-0	5	6	7	2	0	5-1	3	12.60	34	.286	.423	1	.000	-0		-4		-0.7

DEVINE, ADRIAN   Paul Adrian B12.2.1951 Galveston TX   BR/TR/6-4/205(185-205)   [AtlN70 2/45]   d6.27   [DL 1981 Tex A 32]

YEAR	TM LG	W	L	PCT	G	GS	CG-SHO	SV-BS	IP	H	R	HR	HB	BB-IB	SO	ERA	AERA	OAV	OOB	AB-HR-SH	AVG	PB	SUP	APR	DL	PW
1973	Atl N	2	3	.400	24	1	0	4-1	32.1	45	24	6	2	12-3	15	6.40	62	.338	.399	4	.250	0	111	-7		-1.2
1975	Atl N	1	0	1.000	5	2	0	0-0	16.1	19	8	2	1	7-1	8	4.41	86	.284	.360	5	.000	-1	151	0		-0.1
1976	Atl N	5	6	.455	48	1	0	9-2	73	72	30	4	4	26-7	48	3.21	118	.255	.316	14-0-2	.000	-2	139	4	35	0.5
1977	Tex A	11	6	.647	56	2	0	15-4	105.2	102	43	8	4	31-11	67	3.58	114	.259	.316	0	—	-2	121	8		1.5
1978	Atl N	5	4	.556	31	6	0	3-1	65.1	84	45	3	0	25-5	26	5.92	68	.323	.380	11-0-1	.091	-1	108	-11	57	-1.5
1979	Atl N	1	2	.333	40	0	0	0-2	66.2	84	28	8	2	25-5	22	3.24	124	.311	.372	7	.000	-1		-5		0.5
1980	Tex A	1	1	.500	13	0	0	0-0	28	49	22	4	1	9-1	8	4.82	81	.377	.415	0	—	0		-5	86	-0.3
Total 7		26	22	.542	217	12	0	31-10	387.1	455	200	34	11	135-33	194	4.21	95	.296	.354	41-0-3	.049	-3	119	-6	210	-0.9

DEVINEY, HAL   Harold John B4.11.1893 Newton MA D1.4.1933 Westwood MA   BR/TR   d7.30

YEAR	TM LG	W	L	PCT	G	GS	CG-SHO	SV-BS	IP	H	R	HR	HB	BB-IB	SO	ERA	AERA	OAV	OOB	AB-HR-SH	AVG	PB	SUP	APR	DL	PW
1920	Bos A	0	0	—	3	0	0	0	3	7	5	0	0	2	0	15.00	24	.500	.563	2	1.000	2		-4		0.0

DEVLIN, JIM   James Alexander B6.6.1849 Philadelphia PA D10.10.1883 Philadelphia PA   BR/TR/5-11/175   d4.21.1873 ▲

YEAR	TM LG	W	L	PCT	G	GS	CG-SHO	SV-BS	IP	H	R	HR	HB	BB-IB	SO	ERA	AERA	OAV	OOB	AB-HR-SH	AVG	PB	SUP	APR	DL	PW
1875	Chi NA	7	16	.304	28	24	24	0	224	254	179	0	12	23		1.93	118	.256	.265	318	.289	7*	81	8		1.2
1876	Lou N	30	35	.462	68	68	66-5	0	622	566	309	3	37		122	1.56	174	.224	.235	298	.315	2	58	67		6.2
1877	Lou N	35	25	.583	61	61	64-4	0	559	617	288	4	41		141	2.25	147	.270	.283	268-1	.269	-2	82	56		5.0
Total 2		65	60	.520	129	129	127-9	0	1181	1183	597	7	78		263	1.89	159	.246	.258	566-1	.293	1	69	123		11.2

DEVLIN, JIM   James H. B4.16.1866 Troy NY D12.14.1900 Troy NY   TL/5-7/135   d6.28

YEAR	TM LG	W	L	PCT	G	GS	CG-SHO	SV-BS	IP	H	R	HR	HB	BB-IB	SO	ERA	AERA	OAV	OOB	AB-HR-SH	AVG	PB	SUP	APR	DL	PW
1886	NY N	0	0	—	1	1	0	0	2	3	5	0	4	2		18.00	18	.250	.438	1	.000	-0		-3		-0.3
1887	Phi N	0	2	.000	2	2	2	0	18	20	19	0	3	10	6	6.00	71	.267	.375	6	.333	0	122	-3		-0.2
1888	†StL AA	6	5	.545	11	11	10	0	90.1	82	54	3	8	20	45	3.19	102	.233	.289	37	.297	2	103	1		0.3
1889	StL AA	5	3	.625	9	8	5	0	60	56	38	0	7	24	37	2.40	176	.239	.328	26	.192	-2	101	8		0.7
Total 4		11	10	.524	23	21	17	1	170.1	161	116	3	18	58	90	3.38	109	.239	.316	70	.257	1	105	3		0.5

DEWALD, CHARLIE   Charles H. B9.22.1867 Newark NJ D8.22.1904 Cleveland OH   TL   d9.2

YEAR	TM LG	W	L	PCT	G	GS	CG-SHO	SV-BS	IP	H	R	HR	HB	BB-IB	SO	ERA	AERA	OAV	OOB	AB-HR-SH	AVG	PB	SUP	APR	DL	PW
1890	Cle P	2	0	1.000	2	2	0	0	14	13	7	0	0	5	6	0.64	618	.236	.300	8	.375	1	108	4		0.5

DEWEY, MARK   Mark Alan B1.3.1965 Grand Rapids MI   BR/TR/6-0/207(185-216)   [SFN87 23/594]   d8.24   Col Grand Valley St.

YEAR	TM LG	W	L	PCT	G	GS	CG-SHO	SV-BS	IP	H	R	HR	HB	BB-IB	SO	ERA	AERA	OAV	OOB	AB-HR-SH	AVG	PB	SUP	APR	DL	PW
1990	SF N	1	1	.500	14	0	0	0-1	22.2	22	7	1	0	5-1	11	2.78	132	.259	.300	1	.000	0		3		-0.2
1992	NY N	1	0	1.000	2	0	0	0-0	33.1	37	16	0	2	10-2	24	4.32	81	.280	.331	1	.000	-0		-2		-0.1
1993	Pit N	1	2	.333	21	0	0	7-5	26.2	14	8	0	3	10-1	14	2.36	173	.157	.257	0	—	0		5		0.8
1994	Pit N	1	0	.667	45	0	0	1-1	51.1	61	24	4	3	19-3	30	3.68	119	.303	.371	1	1.000	0		4	15	0.3
1995	SF N	1	0	1.000	27	0	0	0-0	31.2	30	12	2	0	17-6	22	3.13	132	.254	.346	1	.000	0		4	89	0.2
1996	SF N	6	3	.667	78	0	0	0-5	83.1	79	40	9	5	41-9	57	4.21	98	.257	.350	7	.000	-0		1		0.1
Total 6		12	7	.632	205	0	0	8-12	249	243	108	16	11	102-22	168	3.65	111	.261	.338	11	.091	0	15	104		1.5

DEWITT, MATT   Matthew Brian B9.4.1977 San Bernardino CA   BR/TR/6-4/220*   [StLN95 10/267]   d6.20

YEAR	TM LG	W	L	PCT	G	GS	CG-SHO	SV-BS	IP	H	R	HR	HB	BB-IB	SO	ERA	AERA	OAV	OOB	AB-HR-SH	AVG	PB	SUP	APR	DL	PW
2000	Tor A	1	0	1.000	1	1	0	0-0	13.2	20	13	4	2	9-0	6	8.56	59	.351	.456	0	—	0		-5	39	-0.3
2001	Tor A	0	2	.000	16	0	0	0-0	19	22	8	2	1	10-5	13	3.79	121	.293	.384	0	—	0		2		0.2
2002	SD N	0	1	.000	12	0	0	0-0	7.1	6	3	1	0	3-0	5	1.23	317	.231	.300	0	—	0		2	150	0.2
Total 3		1	3	.250	29	0	0	0-0	40	48	23	7	3	22-5	24	4.95	93	.304	.397	0	—	0		-1	189	0.2

DIAZ, CARLOS   Carlos Antonio B1.7.1958 Kaneohe HI   BR/TL/6-0/170*   [SeaA79 S1/15]   d6.30   Col Hancock (CA) JC

YEAR	TM LG	W	L	PCT	G	GS	CG-SHO	SV-BS	IP	H	R	HR	HB	BB-IB	SO	ERA	AERA	OAV	OOB	AB-HR-SH	AVG	PB	SUP	APR	DL	PW
1982	Atl N	3	2	.600	19	0	0	1-0	25.1	31	15	3	0	9-2	16	4.62	80	.307	.360	3	.000	-0		-3		-0.5
	NY N	0	0	—	4	0	0	0-0	3.2	6	2	0	0	4-1	0	0.00	—	.353	.476	0	.000	-0		1		0.0
	Year	3	2	.600	23	0	0	1-0	29	37	17	3	0	13-3	16	4.03	91	.314	.379	3	.000	-0		-2		-0.5
1983	NY N	3	1	.750	54	0	0	2-1	83.1	62	22	1	1	35-13	64	2.05	179	.211	.294	5-0-1	.000	0		15		0.8
1984	†LA N	1	0	1.000	37	0	0	1-1	41	47	26	4	0	24-5	36	5.49	65	.285	.374	1-0-1	.000	-0		-8		-0.4
1985	LA N	6	3	.667	46	0	0	0-1	79.1	70	28	7	0	18-6	73	2.61	134	.230	.272	4	.000	0		8		0.3
Total 5		13	6	.684	179	0	0	4-4	258	249	107	17	1	97-29	207	3.21	112	.253	.318	14-0-2	.000	0		16		0.6

DIAZ, FELIX   Felix Antonio B7.27.1980 Las Matas de Farfan, D.R.   BR/TR/6-1/180   d5.13   [DL 2005 Chi A 32]

YEAR	TM LG	W	L	PCT	G	GS	CG-SHO	SV-BS	IP	H	R	HR	HB	BB-IB	SO	ERA	AERA	OAV	OOB	AB-HR-SH	AVG	PB	SUP	APR	DL	PW
2004	Chi A	2	5	.286	18	7	0	0-0	49.1	62	38	13	3	16-1	33	6.75	70	.307	.362	1	.000	-0	99	-10		-1.2

YEAR	TM LG	W	L	PCT	G	GS	CG-SHO	SV-BS	IP	H	R	HR	HB	BB-IB	SO	ERA	AERA	OAV	OOB	AB-HR-SH	AVG	PB	SUP	APR	DL	PW

DIBBLE, ROB   Robert Keith   B1.24.1964 Bridgeport CT   BL/TR/6-4/230(220-235)   [CinN83 S1/20]   d6.29   Col Florida Southern   [DL 1994 Cin N 130]

YEAR	TM LG	W	L	PCT	G	GS	CG-SHO	SV-BS	IP	H	R	HR	HB	BB-IB	SO	ERA	AERA	OAV	OOB	AB-HR-SH	AVG	PB	SUP	APR	DL	PW
1988	Cin N	1	1	.500	37	0	0	0-1	59.1	43	12	2	1	21-5	59	1.82	196	.207	.279	2-0-2	.000	-0	12			0.5
1989	Cin N	10	5	.667	74	0	0	2-6	99	62	23	4	3	39-11	141	2.09	172	.176	.261	8	.000	-1	17	15		2.5
1990	†Cin N★	8	3	.727	68	0	0	11-6	98	62	22	0	1	34-3	136	1.74	226	.183	.255	7-0-3	.000	-0	6			2.8
1991	Cin N★	3	5	.375	67	0	0	31-5	82.1	67	32	5	0	25-2	124	3.17	120	.223	.280	2-0-1	.000	-0	4	10		0.9
1992	Cin N	3	5	.375	63	0	0	25-5	70.1	48	26	3	2	31-2	110	3.07	117	.193	.285	5	.400	0	-12	48		0.8
1993	Cin N	1	4	.200	45	0	0	19-9	41.2	34	33	4	2	42-0	49	6.48	62	.225	.400	1	1.000	0	-3			-2.0
1995	Chi A	0	1	.000	16	0	0	1-0	14.1	7	10	1	3	27-2	16	6.28	71	.156	.481	0	—	0	-3			-0.2
	Mil A	1	1	.500	15	0	0	0-1	12	9	11	1	0	19-0	10	8.25	61	.225	.444	0	—	0	-7			-0.7
	Year	1	2	.333	31	0	0	1-1	26.1	16	21	2	3	46-2	26	7.18	66	.188	.464	0	—	-1	42	203		-4.8
Total	7	27	25	.519	385	0	0	89-33	477	332	169	27	12	238-25	645	2.98	128	.197	.297	25-0-6	.120	-1	42	203		

DIBUT, PEDRO   Pedro (Villafana)   B11.18.1892 Cienfuegos, Cuba   D12.4.1979 Hialeah FL   BR/TR/5-8/190   d5.1

1924	Cin N	3	0	1.000	7	2	2	0	36.2	12	9	0	0	12	15	2.21	170	.188	.257	11-0-1	.273	1	203	7		0.7
1925	Cin N				1	0	0	0	0	3	2	0	0	0	0	∞	—	1.000	1.000		—	0	-2			-0.2
Total	2	3	0	1.000	8	2	2	0	36.2	27	11	1	0	12	15	2.70	139	.206	.273	11-0-1	.273	1	203	5		0.5

DICKERMAN, LEO   Leo Louis   B10.31.1896 DeSoto MO   D4.30.1982 Atkins AR   BR/TR/6-4/192   d4.21

1923	Bro N	8	12	.400	35	20	7-1	0	159.2	180	95	4	2	72	58	3.72	104	.283	.357	52-2-4	.250	3	112	-2		0.2
1924	Bro N				7	2	0	0	19.2	20	16	0	2	16	9	5.49	68	.263	.404	6	.167	-0	181	-5		-0.2
	StL N	7	4	.636	18	13	8-1	0	119.2	108	43	6	0	51	28	2.41	157	.249	.328	39-0-3	.231	1	135	11		1.
	Year	7	4	.636	25	15	8-1	0	139.1	128	59	6	2	67	37	2.84	133	.251	.346	45-0-3	.222	1	135	11		1.
1925	StL N	4	11	.267	29	18	7-2	1	130.2	135	95	10	2	79	40	5.58	77	.273	.376	44-0-3	.114	-3	92	-18		-1.1
Total	3	19	27	.413	89	53	22-4	1	429.2	443	249	20	6	218	135	4.00	99	.270	.358	141-2-10	.199	1	112	-8		-0.3

DICKERSON, GEORGE   George Clark   B12.1.1892 Renner TX   D7.9.1938 Los Angeles CA   BR/TR/6-1/170   d8.2

1917	Cle A				1	0	0	0	1	0	0	0	0	0	0	0.00	—	.000	.000	0	—	0	0			0.

DICKEY, R.A.   Robert Alan   B10.29.1974 Nashville TN   BR/TR/6-3/205(200-220)   [TexA96 1/18]   d4.22   Col Tennessee

2001	Tex A	0	1	.000	4	0	0	0-0	12	13	9	3	0	7-1	4	6.75	71	.283	.377	0	—	0	88	0		-0.
2003	Tex A	9	8	.529	38	13	1-1	1-0	116.2	135	68	16	5	38-5	94	5.09	98	.292	.350	1	1.000	0	101	-10	48	-1.
2004	Tex A	6	7	.462	25	15	0	1-0	104.1	136	77	17	4	33-1	57	5.61	88	.311	.363	0	—	0	92	-6	42	-0.
2005	Tex A	1	2	.333	9	4	0	0-0	29.2	29	23	4	2	17-0	15	6.67	69	.254	.358	0	—	0	94	-18	90	-1.
Total	4	16	18	.471	76	32	1-1	2-0	262.2	313	177	40	11	95-7	170	5.55	88	.295	.357	1	1.000	0	94	-18	90	-1.

DICKMAN, EMERSON   George Emerson   B11.12.1914 Buffalo NY   D4.27.1981 New York NY   BR/TR/6-2/175   d6.27   Mil 1941-42   Col Washington and Lee

1936	Bos A	0	0		1	0	0	0	1	2	2	0	1	2	2	9.00	59	.400	.500		—	0	-1			0.
1938	Bos A	5	5	.500	32	11	3-1	0	104	117	74	9	4	54	22	5.28	93	.288	.377	35-1-2	.286	4	104	-5		-0.
1939	Bos A	8	3	.727	48	1	0	5	113.2	126	70	10	3	43	46	4.43	107	.282	.349	36	.056	-4	317	2		-0.
1940	Bos A	8	6	.571	35	9	2	3	100	121	74	15	4	38	40	6.03	75	.291	.356	28-0-2	.107	-2	109	-17		-2.
1941	Bos A	1	1	.500	9	3	1	0	31	37	23	4	0	17	16	6.39	65	.301	.386	11	.091	-1	138	-6		-0.
Total	5	22	15	.595	125	24	6-1	8	349.2	403	243	38	11	153	126	5.33	88	.288	.363	110-1-4	.145	-2	118	-27		-2.

DICKSON, JIM   James Edward   B4.20.1938 Portland OR   BL/TR/6-1/185*   d7.2   Col Clark (WA) CC

1963	Hou N	0	1	.000	13	0	0	2	14.2	22	13	0	0	2-0	6	6.14	51	.344	.353	1	.000	-0	-6			-0
1964	Cin N	1	0	1.000	4	0	0	0	5	8	4	0	0	5-1	6	7.20	50	.444	.542	0	—	0	-2			-0
1965	KC A	3	2	.600	68	0	0	6	85.2	68	40	6	2	47-7	54	3.47	101	.220	.324	2	.250	0	104	-9		-0
1966	KC A	1	0	1.000	24	1	0	1	37	37	28	4	0	23-2	20	5.35	63	.264	.366	4	.143	0	104	-18		-0
Total	4	5	3	.625	109	1	0	9	142.1	135	85	10	2	77-10	86	4.36	79	.254	.347	7	.143	0	104	-18		-0

DICKSON, JASON   Jason Royce   B3.30.1973 London ON, Can.   BL/TR/6-0/190(190-202)   [CalA94 6/153]   d8.21   Col NE Oklahoma A&M JC   [DL 1999 Ana A 182]

1996	Cal A	1	4	.200	7	7	0	0-0	43.1	52	22	6	1	18-1	20	4.57	111	.306	.374	0	—	0	63	3		0
1997	Ana A☆	13	9	.591	33	32	2-1	0-0	203.2	236	111	32	7	56-3	115	4.29	108	.289	.338	4	.000	0	105	5		0
1998	Ana A	10	10	.500	27	18	0	0-0	122	147	89	17	4	41-1	65	6.05	78	.303	.359	4	.000	0	98	-17		-2
2000	Ana A	2	2	.500	6	6	0	0-0	28	39	20	5	1	7-0	18	6.11	85	.336	.379	0	—	0	103	-3	153	-2
Total	4	26	25	.510	73	63	2-1	0-0	397	474	242	60	15	122-5	214	4.99	95	.299	.351	6	.000	0	98	-12	335	-2

DICKSON, LANCE   Lance Michael   B10.19.1969 Fullerton CA   BR/TL/6-0/185   [ChiN90 1/23]   d8.9   Col Arizona

1990	Chi N	0	3	.000	3	3	0	0-0	13.2	20	12	2	0	4-1	4	7.24	56	.370	.407	3	.000	-0	66	-4	23	-0

DICKSON, MURRY   Murry Monroe   B8.21.1916 Tracy MO   D9.21.1989 Kansas City KS   BR/TR/5-10.5/157*   d9.30   Mil 1944-45

1939	StL N	0	0	—	1	0	0	0	3.2	1	0	0	1	1	2	0.00		.091	.167	1	.000	-0	2			C
1940	StL N	0	0	—	1	1	0	0	1.2	5	4	0	0	1	1	16.20	25	.500	.545		—	0	174	-2		C
1942	StL N	6	3	.667	36	7	2	2	120.2	91	41	1	1	61	66	2.91	118	.216	.316	42-0-1	.190	-0*	137	9		C
1943	†StL N	8	2	.800	31	7	2	0	115.2	119	51	4	1	49	44	3.58	94	.269	.343	34-0-3	.265	-2	101	-2		C
1946	†StL N	15	6	.714	47	19	12-2	1	184.1	160	71	4	0	88	82	3.07	135	.243	.315	80-0-2	.213	1	87	23		2
1947	StL N	13	16	.448	47	25	11-4	3	231.2	211	101	16	2	88	111	3.07	134	.245	.324	96-0-4	.281	4*	107	1		2
1948	StL N	12	16	.429	42	29	11-1	1	252.1	257	121	39	0	85	113	4.14	99	.265	.325	84-0-1	.202	0	94	19		2
1949	Pit N	12	14	.462	44	20	11-2	0	224.1	216	97	17	6	80	76	3.80	115	.260	.326	82	.256	3*	75	15		-C
1950	Pit N	10	15	.400	51	22	8	3	225	227	104	20	2	83	76	4.02	105	.262	.327	110-1-4	.273	5*	101	5		-C
1951	Pit N	20	16	.556	45	35	19-3	2	288.2	294	151	32	6	101	112	3.57	112	.261	.311	107-0-2	.224	2*	88	11		-C
1952	Pit N	14	21	.400	43	34	21-2	2	277.2	278	128	26	1	76	112	3.57	107	.266	.311	61-0-4	.115	-4	64	-4		-C
1953	Pit N★	10	19	.345	45	26	10-1	4	200.2	240	121	27	2	58	64	3.78	107	.298	.348	79-0-4	.190	0	77	7		-C
1954	Phi N	10	20	.333	40	31	12-4	3	226.1	256	107	31	2	73	92	3.50	113	.238	.309	82-1-3	.220	1	98	10		-C
1955	Phi N	12	11	.522	36	28	12-4	0	216	190	84	17	4	82-8	92	3.50	113	.238	.309	71-0-3	.333	1	71	-4		-C
1956	Phi N	0	3	.000	3	3	0	0	23	20	15	1	4	12-1	1	5.09	73	.241	.337	9	.333	1	71	-4		-C
	StL N	13	8	.619	28	27	12-3	0	196.1	175	75	20	1	57-4	110	3.07	123	.240	.295	77-0-2	.247	4*	122	16		-C
	Year	13	11	.542	31	30	12-3	0	219.1	195	90	21	1	69-5	110	3.28	115	.240	.300	86-0-2	.256	4*	117	11		-C
1957	StL N	5	3	.625	14	13	3-1	0	74	87	41	8	1	25-0	29	4.14	96	.296	.350	27	.222	1	135	-3	33	-C
1958	KC A	9	5	.643	27	9	3	1	99	99	42	12	1	31-4	46	3.27	119	.258	.317	35-1-2	.257	2*	102	6		-C
	†NY A	1	2	.333	14	2	0	1	20.1	18	17	4	1	12-0	9	5.75	61	.237	.348	7	.286	-0	106	0		-C
	Year	10	7	.588	33	11	3	2	119.1	117	59	16	2	43-4	55	3.70	104	.255	.322	42-1-2	.262	2	106	0		-C
1959	KC A	2	1	.667	38	0	0	0	71	85	46	9	0	27-1	36	4.94	81	.290	.349	17	.176	-1	-8			-C
Total	18	172	181	.487	625	338	149-27	23	3052.1	3029	1431	302	37	1058-18	1281	3.66	110	.260	.323	1095-3-33	.231	25	97	106	33	1

DICKSON, WALT   Walter R. "Hickory"   B12.3.1878 New Summerfield TX   D12.9.1918 Ardmore OK   BR/TR/5-11.5/175   d4.26

1910	NY N	1	0	1.000	12	1	0	1	29.2	31	19	1	0	9	9	5.46	54	.272	.325	4	.250	0	176	-6		C
1912	Bos N	3	19	.136	36	20	9-1	1	189	233	123	2	3	61	47	3.86	93	.320	.375	60-0-3	.167	-1	85	-11		C
1913	Bos N	6	7	.462	19	15	8	0	128	118	71	4	1	45	47	3.23	102	.249	.316	45-0-1	.178	-1	134	-1		C
1914	Pit F	9	19	.321	40	32	19-3	1	256.2	262	117	5	2	74	63	3.16	91	.273	.327	83-0-5	.084	-9	82	-9		C
1915	Pit F	7	5	.583	27	11	4	0	96.2	115	51	5	2	33	36	4.19	65	.316	.376	31-0-3	.129	-1	152	-14		C
Total	5	26	50	.342	134	79	40-4	2	700	759	381	17	8	222	202	3.60	86	.288	.345	223-0-12	.135	-12	103	-41		C

DIEHL, GEORGE   George Krause   B2.25.1918 Emmaus PA   D8.24.1986 Kingsport TN   BR/TR/6-2/196   d4.19

1942	Bos N	0	0	—	1	0	0	0	3.2	2	2	0	1	2	0	2.45	136	.167	.333	1	.000	-0	0			C
1943	Bos N	0	0	—	1	0	0	0	4	4	2	0	0	3	0	4.50	76	.267	.389	1	.000	-0	0			C
Total	2	0	0	—	2	0	0	0	7.2	6	4	0	1	5	1	3.52	96	.222	.364	2	.000	-0	0			C

DIERKER, LARRY   Lawrence Edward   B9.22.1946 Hollywood CA   BR/TR/6-4/210(190-215)   d9.22   Mil 1967   M5

1964	Hou N	0	1	.000	3	1	0	0	9	7	4	1	0	3	5	2.00	171	.219	.278	3	.000	-0	26	1		C
1965	Hou N	7	8	.467	26	19	1	0	146.2	135	69	16	3	37-4	109	3.50	96	.240	.288	50-1-4	.100	-1	88	-4		C
1966	Hou N	10	8	.556	29	28	8-2	0	187	173	73	14	4	45-0	108	3.18	109	.249	.284	67-1-2	.149	1	95	7	17	C
1967	Hou N	6	5	.545	15	15	4	0	99	95	44	4	1	25-0	68	3.36	98	.252	.300	31-0-1	.226	2	95	-1		C
1968	Hou N	12	15	.444	32	32	10-1	0	233.2	206	95	14	8	89-12	161	3.31	99	.240	.314	118-1-7	.144	1	102	40		C
1969	Hou N★	20	13	.606	39	37	20-4	0	305.1	240	97	18	1	72-6	232	2.33	153	.214	.261	92-0-9	.174	-0	113	3		C
1970	Hou N	16	12	.571	37	36	17-2	1-0	269.2	263	124	31	6	82-4	191	3.87	101	.254	.311	54-0-3	.074	-3	111	13		
1971	Hou N*	12	6	.667	24	23	6-2	0-1	159	150	50	14	3	33-1	91	2.72	124	.248	.287							

YEAR	TM LG	W	L	PCT	G	GS	CG-SHO	SV-BS	IP	H	R	HR	HB	BB-IB	SO	ERA	AERA	OAV	OOB	AB-HR-SH	AVG	PB	SUP	APR	DL	PW
1972	Hou N	15	8	.652	31	31	12-5	0-0	214.2	209	87	14	5	51-0	115	3.40	99	.256	.301	78-0-6	.167	-0	140	0		-0.2
1973	Hou N	1	1	.500	4	3	0	0-1	27	27	14	3	2	13-0	18	4.33	84	.265	.356	4	.000	-0	73	-2	74	-0.2
1974	Hou N	11	10	.524	33	33	7-3	0-0	223.2	189	76	18	6	82-4	150	2.90	120	.238	.306	71-0-11	.197	-0	90	18		1.7
1975	Hou N	14	16	.467	34	34	14-2	0-0	232	225	109	24	7	91-6	127	4.00	85	.260	.331	76-0-13	.092	-4	104	-15		-2.3
1976	Hou N	13	14	.481	28	28	7-4	0-0	187.2	171	85	9	6	72-6	112	3.69	87	.243	.317	64-1-3	.141	-1	109	-9		-1.3
1977	StL N	2	6	.250	11	9	0	0-0	39.1	40	21	7	2	16-0	6	4.58	85	.243	.343	6-2-0	.136	-1	48	-2	83	-0.5
Total 14		139	123	.531	356	329	106-25	1-2	2333.2	2130	948	184	50	711-43	1493	3.31	104	.243	.302	789-4-70	.136	-12	102	40	174	1.4

DIETRICH, BILL William John "Bullfrog" B3.29.1910 Philadelphia PA D6.20.1978 Philadelphia PA BR/TR/6-0/185 d4.13 Col Villanova

YEAR	TM LG	W	L	PCT	G	GS	CG-SHO	SV-BS	IP	H	R	HR	HB	BB-IB	SO	ERA	AERA	OAV	OOB	AB-HR-SH	AVG	PB	SUP	APR	DL	PW
1933	Phi A	0	1	.000	8	1	0	0	17	13	11	1	0	19	4	5.82	74	.236	.432	3	.333	1	20	-2		0.0
1934	Phi A	11	12	.478	39	23	14-4	3	207.2	201	121	12	3	114	88	4.68	94	.255	.351	72-1-4	.208	3*	81	-7		-0.4
1935	Phi A	7	13	.350	43	15	8-1	3	185.1	203	128	7	1	101	59	5.39	84	.276	.364	60-0-3	.083	-6*	82	-17		-2.2
1936	Phi A	4	6	.400	21	4	0	3	71.2	91	55	4	0	40	34	6.53	78	.305	.388	27-0-1	.111	-2	60	-9		-1.2
	Was A	0	1	.000	5	0	0	0	8.1	13	11	0	0	6	4	9.72	49	.351	.442	0	—	0		-5		-0.5
	Chi A	4	4	.500	14	11	6-1	0	82.2	93	50	8	1	36	39	4.68	111	.284	.356	30-0-2	.267	1	97	4		0.3
	Year	8	11	.421	40	15	6-1	3	162.2	197	116	12	1	82	77	5.75	89	.297	.375	57-0-3	.193	-1	88	-9		-1.4
1937	Chi A	8	10	.444	29	20	7-1	1	143.1	162	93	15	0	72	62	4.90	94	.285	.366	44-0-3	.182	1	90	-6		-0.5
1938	Chi A	2	4	.333	7	1	0	0	48	48	33	7	0	31	11	5.44	90	.259	.364	16	.063	-1	67	-2		-0.4
1939	Chi A	7	8	.467	25	19	2,	0	127.2	134	81	14	2	56	43	5.22	91	.272	.349	37-1-2	.216	2	88	-6		-0.4
1940	Chi A	10	6	.625	23	17	6-1	0	149.2	154	78	10	0	65	43	4.03	110	.266	.340	50-1-3	.240	3	89	7		0.8
1941	Chi A	5	8	.385	19	15	4-1	0	109.1	114	73	7	4	50	26	5.35	77	.263	.345	48-0-1	.088	0	92	-14		-1.4
1942	Chi A	6	11	.353	26	23	6	0	160	173	92	16	5	70	39	4.89	74	.277	.355	48-0-7	.104	-1	93	-19		-1.9
1943	Chi A	12	10	.545	26	26	12-2	0	186.2	180	72	4	2	53	52	2.80	119	.253	.307	56-1-6	.143	0	82	10		1.3
1944	Chi A	16	17	.485	36	36	15-2	0	246	269	132	15	2	68	70	3.62	95	.279	.328	77-1-8	.117	-3	90	-11		-1.7
1945	Chi A	7	10	.412	18	16	6-3	0	122.1	136	61	4	0	36	43	4.19	79	.279	.329	36-0-3	.167	0	109	-10		-1.2
1946	Chi A	3	3	.500	11	9	3	1	62	63	21	4	0	24	20	2.61	131	.267	.335	19	.053	-2	84	6	76	0.5
1947	Phi A	5	2	.714	11	9	2-1	0	60.2	48	24	0	2	40	18	3.12	122	.223	.350	16-0-4	.063	-2	116	4		0.3
1948	Phi A	1	2	.333	4	2	0	0	15.1	21	10	0	0	9	5	5.87	73	.356	.441	2	.000	-0	42	-2		-0.4
Total 16		108	128	.458	366	253	92-17	11	2003.2	2117	1146	128	22	890	660	4.48	92	.271	.348	627-5-47	.150	-5	87	-79	76	-9.0

DIETZ, DUTCH Lloyd Arthur B2.9.1912 Cincinnati OH D10.29.1972 Beaumont TX BR/TR/5-11.5/180 d4.26 Mil 1944-45 Col Western Michigan

YEAR	TM LG	W	L	PCT	G	GS	CG-SHO	SV-BS	IP	H	R	HR	HB	BB-IB	SO	ERA	AERA	OAV	OOB	AB-HR-SH	AVG	PB	SUP	APR	DL	PW
1940	Pit N	0	1	.000	4	2	0	0	15.1	22	11	2	0	4	8	5.87	65	.355	.394		.143	-0*	148	-3		-0.2
1941	Pit N	7	2	.778	33	6	4-1	1	100.1	88	28	6	2	33	22	2.33	155	.233	.298	25-0-1	.160	-1	67	16		1.3
1942	Pit N	6	9	.400	40	13	3	3	134.1	139	67	8	1	57	35	3.95	86	.268	.342	35-0-2	.200	1	84	-7		-0.9
1943	Pit N	0	3	.000	8	0	0	0	9	12	6	0	1	4	4	6.00	58	.324	.405	0	—	0*		-2		-0.3
	Phi N	1	1	.500	21	0	0	2	36	42	29	2	0	15	10	6.50	52	.292	.358	6	.167	0		-12		-0.8
	Year	1	4	.200	29	0	0	2	45	54	35	2	1	19	14	6.40	53	.298	.368	6	.167	0		-14		-1.1
Total 4		14	16	.467	106	21	7-1	6	295	303	141	18	4	113	79	3.87	90	.266	.334	73-0-3	.178	-0	85	-9		-0.9

DIGGINS, BEN Benjamin Howard B6.13.1979 Leoti KS BR/TR/6-7/230 [LAN00 1/17] d9.2 Col Arizona

YEAR	TM LG	W	L	PCT	G	GS	CG-SHO	SV-BS	IP	H	R	HR	HB	BB-IB	SO	ERA	AERA	OAV	OOB	AB-HR-SH	AVG	PB	SUP	APR	DL	PW
2002	Mil N	0	4	.000	5	5	0	0-0	24	28	24	4	1	18-1	15	8.63	48	.298	.409	7-0-1	.143	-0	49	-12		-1.5

DIGGS, REESE Reese Wilson "Diggsy" B9.22.1915 Mathews VA D10.30.1978 Baltimore MD BB/TR/6-2/180 d9.15

YEAR	TM LG	W	L	PCT	G	GS	CG-SHO	SV-BS	IP	H	R	HR	HB	BB-IB	SO	ERA	AERA	OAV	OOB	AB-HR-SH	AVG	PB	SUP	APR	DL	PW
1934	Was A	1	2	.333	4	3	2	0	21.1	26	17	3	0	15	2	6.75	64	.313	.418	8-0-2	.250	0	155	-6		-0.6

DiLAURO, JACK Jack Edward B5.3.1943 Akron OH BB/TL/6-2/185* d5.15 Col Akron

YEAR	TM LG	W	L	PCT	G	GS	CG-SHO	SV-BS	IP	H	R	HR	HB	BB-IB	SO	ERA	AERA	OAV	OOB	AB-HR-SH	AVG	PB	SUP	APR	DL	PW
1969	NY N	1	4	.200	23	4	0	1-1	63.2	50	19	4	0	18-5	27	2.40	152	.216	.269	12	.000	-1	67	9		0.5
1970	Hou N	1	3	.250	42	0	0	3-6	33.2	34	23	4	0	17-2	23	4.28	91	.262	.340	2	.000	-0*		-4		-0.5
Total 2		2	7	.222	65	4	0	4-7	97.1	84	42	8	0	35-7	50	3.05	123	.232	.295	14	.000	-2	67	5		0.0

DILLARD, GORDON Gordon Lee B5.20.1964 Salinas CA BL/TL/6-1/190* [BalA86 14/357] d8.12 Col Oklahoma St.

YEAR	TM LG	W	L	PCT	G	GS	CG-SHO	SV-BS	IP	H	R	HR	HB	BB-IB	SO	ERA	AERA	OAV	OOB	AB-HR-SH	AVG	PB	SUP	APR	DL	PW
1988	Bal A	0	0	—	2	1	0	0-0	3	3	2	1	0	4-0	2	6.00	66	.273	.467	0	—	0	93	-1		0.0
1989	Phi N	0	0	—	5	0	0	0-0	4	7	3	0	0	4-0	2	6.75	53	.368	.368	0	—	0		-1		-0.1
Total 2		0	0	—	7	1	0	0-0	7	10	5	1	0	4-0	6	6.43	58	.333	.412	0	—	0	93	-2		-0.1

DILLINGER, HARLEY Harley Hugh "Hoke","Lefty" B10.30.1894 Pomeroy OH D1.8.1959 Cleveland OH BR/TL/5-11/175 d8.16 Col Rio Grande

YEAR	TM LG	W	L	PCT	G	GS	CG-SHO	SV-BS	IP	H	R	HR	HB	BB-IB	SO	ERA	AERA	OAV	OOB	AB-HR-SH	AVG	PB	SUP	APR	DL	PW
1914	Cle A	0	1	.000	11	2	1	0	33.2	41	23	0	1	25	11	4.54	64	.325	.441	10	.000	-1	189	-7		-0.6

DILLMAN, BILL William Howard B5.25.1945 Trenton NJ BR/TR/6-2/180* [BalA65 6/118] d4.14 Col Wake Forest

YEAR	TM LG	W	L	PCT	G	GS	CG-SHO	SV-BS	IP	H	R	HR	HB	BB-IB	SO	ERA	AERA	OAV	OOB	AB-HR-SH	AVG	PB	SUP	APR	DL	PW
1967	Bal A	5	9	.357	32	15	2-1	0	124	115	61	13	3	33-2	69	4.43	72	.249	.301	31-0-4	.161	-0*	87	-15		-1.8
1970	Mon N	2	3	.400	18	0	0	0-0	30.2	28	18	4	1	18-4	17	5.28	79	.255	.356	2	.000	0		-3		-0.4
Total 2		7	12	.368	50	15	2-1	3-0	154.2	143	79	17	4	51-6	86	4.54	74	.250	.313	33-0-4	.152	-1	87	-18		-2.2

DILLON, STEVE Stephen Edward B3.20.1943 Yonkers NY BL/TL/5-10/160* d9.5

YEAR	TM LG	W	L	PCT	G	GS	CG-SHO	SV-BS	IP	H	R	HR	HB	BB-IB	SO	ERA	AERA	OAV	OOB	AB-HR-SH	AVG	PB	SUP	APR	DL	PW
1963	NY N	0	0	—	1	0	0	0	1.2	3	2	0	0	0-0	1	10.80	32	.429	.429	0	—	0		-1		-0.1
1964	NY N	0	0	—	2	0	0	0	3	4	3	1	0	2-0	2	9.00	40	.333	.400	0	—	0		-2		-0.1
Total 2		0	0	—	3	0	0	0	4.2	7	5	1	0	2-0	3	9.64	37	.368	.409	0	—	0		-3		-0.2

DiMICHELE, FRANK Frank Lawrence B2.16.1965 Philadelphia PA BR/TL/6-3/205 [CalA85 15/381] d4.8 Col CC of Philadelphia (PA)

YEAR	TM LG	W	L	PCT	G	GS	CG-SHO	SV-BS	IP	H	R	HR	HB	BB-IB	SO	ERA	AERA	OAV	OOB	AB-HR-SH	AVG	PB	SUP	APR	DL	PW
1988	Cal A	0	0	—	4	0	0	0	4.2	5	5	2	0	2-0	1	9.64	40	.263	.333	0	—	0		-3		-0.1

DiNARDO, LENNY Leonard Edward B9.19.1979 Miami FL BL/TL/6-4/195* [NYN01 3/102] d4.23 Col Stetson

YEAR	TM LG	W	L	PCT	G	GS	CG-SHO	SV-BS	IP	H	R	HR	HB	BB-IB	SO	ERA	AERA	OAV	OOB	AB-HR-SH	AVG	PB	SUP	APR	DL	PW
2004	Bos A	0	0	—	22	0	0	0-0	27.2	34	17	1	2	12-1	21	4.23	115	.298	.372	0	—	0	1		106	0.0
2005	Bos A	0	1	.000	8	1	0	0-0	14.2	13	6	1	0	5-1	15	1.84	250	.236	.295	0	—	0	61	3		0.2
Total 2		0	1	.000	30	1	0	0-0	42.1	47	23	2	2	17-2	36	3.40	141	.278	.347	0	—	0	61	4	106	0.2

DINGMAN, CRAIG Craig Allen B3.12.1974 Wichita KS BR/TR/6-4/215(195-230) [NYA93 36/1009] d6.30 Col Hutchinson (KS) CC

YEAR	TM LG	W	L	PCT	G	GS	CG-SHO	SV-BS	IP	H	R	HR	HB	BB-IB	SO	ERA	AERA	OAV	OOB	AB-HR-SH	AVG	PB	SUP	APR	DL	PW
2000	NY A	0	0	—	10	0	0	0-0	11	18	8	1	0	3-0	8	6.55	73	.375	.412	0	—	0		-2		-0.1
2001	Col N	0	0	—	7	0	0	1-0	7.1	11	11	4	2	3-2	5	13.50	40	.355	.444	0	—	0		-5	15	-0.2
2004	Det A	2	2	.500	24	0	0	0-2	29.1	33	22	3	4	22-3	16	6.75	66	.295	.421	0	—	0		-7		-0.8
2005	Det A	2	3	.400	34	0	0	4-1	32	30	14	5	1	9-0	24	3.66	116	.259	.317	0	—	0		2		0.3
Total 4		4	5	.444	75	0	0	5-3	79.2	92	55	13	7	37-5	50	6.10	74	.300	.385	0	—	0		-12	15	-0.8

DINNEEN, BILL William Henry "Big Bill" (b William Henry Dineen) B4.5.1876 Syracuse NY D1.13.1955 Syracuse NY BR/TR/6-1/190 d4.22 U29

YEAR	TM LG	W	L	PCT	G	GS	CG-SHO	SV-BS	IP	H	R	HR	HB	BB-IB	SO	ERA	AERA	OAV	OOB	AB-HR-SH	AVG	PB	SUP	APR	DL	PW
1898	Was N	9	16	.360	29	27	22	0	218.1	238	140	6	16	88	83	4.00	92	.275	.353	80-0-1	.100	-4*	89	-9		-1.2
1899	Was N	14	14	.412	37	35	30	0	291	350	191	6	11	106	91	3.93	100	.297	.361	119-0-2	.303	5	94	-6		0.1
1900	Bos N	20	14	.588	40	37	33-1	0	320.2	304	161	9	9	105	107	3.12	133	.250	.314	125-0-6	.280	2*	98	32		3.1
1901	Bos N	15	18	.455	37	34	31	0	309.1	295	136	8	6	77	141	2.94	123	.250	.299	147-1-4	.211	0*	70	22		2.3
1902	Bos A	21	21	.500	42	42	39-2	0	371.1	348	155	9	8	99	136	2.93	122	.248	.302	141-0-2	.128	-6*	95	33		2.3
1903	†Bos A	21	13	.618	37	34	32-6	2	299	255	98	6	4	66	148	2.26	134	.230	.276	106-0-5	.160	-1	103	28		2.9
1904	Bos A	23	14	.622	37	37	37-5	0	335.2	283	115	8	2	63	153	2.20	122	.230	.268	120-0-4	.208	-0	105	17		1.7
1905	Bos A	12	14	.462	31	29	23-2	1	243.2	235	117	7	7	50	97	3.73	72	.255	.299	88-0-4	.148	-3	100	-22		-2.6
1906	Bos A	8	19	.296	28	27	22-1	0	218.2	209	101	4	1	52	60	2.92	94	.255	.300	63-0-3	.111	-1	67	-6		-1.0
1907	Bos A	0	4	.000	5	5	3	0	32.2	42	25	5	2	8	7	5.23	49	.313	.361	10	.000	-1	63	-9		-1.1
	StL A	7	10	.412	24	16	15-2	4	155.1	153	67	3	5	33	38	2.43	103	.260	.305	49-0-3	.204	-2	97	-2		-0.2
	Year	7	14	.333	29	21	18-2	4	188	195	92	8	7	41	46	2.92	86	.270	.315	59-0-3	.169	1	89	-10		-1.3
1908	StL A	14	7	.667	27	16	11-2	0	167	133	52	2	4	43	43	2.10	114	.231	.300	59-0-1	.203	0	89	7		0.8
1909	StL A	6	7	.462	17	13	8-3	0	112	112	53	3	1	29	26	3.46	70	.267	.316	36-0-1	.194	2	90	-12		-1.1
Total 12		170	177	.490	391	352	306-24	7	3074.2	2957	1411	78	76	829	1127	3.01	107	.254	.308	1143-1-36	.192	-6	92	73		5.8

DiORIO, RON Ronald Michael B7.15.1946 Waterbury CT BR/TR/6-6/212* d8.9 Col New Haven

YEAR	TM LG	W	L	PCT	G	GS	CG-SHO	SV-BS	IP	H	R	HR	HB	BB-IB	SO	ERA	AERA	OAV	OOB	AB-HR-SH	AVG	PB	SUP	APR	DL	PW
1973	Phi N	0	0	—	23	0	0	1-0	19.1	18	5	1	0	6-4	11	2.33	164	.257	.312	0	—	0		3		0.2
1974	Phi N	0	0	—	2	0	0	0-0	1	2	1	0	0	1-0	0	18.00	21	.400	.500	0	—	0		-1		-0.1
Total 2		0	0	—	25	0	0	1-0	20.1	20	7	2	0	7-4	11	4.43	123	.267	.325	0	—	0		2		0.1

DiPINO, FRANK Frank Michael B10.22.1956 Syracuse NY BL/TL/6-0/180(175-195) d9.14 Col St. Leo [DL 1991 StL N 182]

YEAR	TM LG	W	L	PCT	G	GS	CG-SHO	SV-BS	IP	H	R	HR	HB	BB-IB	SO	ERA	AERA	OAV	OOB	AB-HR-SH	AVG	PB	SUP	APR	DL	PW
1981	Mil A	0	0	—	2	0	0	0-0	2.1	0	0	0	0	3-0	5	0.00	—	.000	.300	0	—	0		0		0.0
1982	Hou N	2	2	.500	26	0	0	0-0	28.1	32	20	1	0	11-1	25	6.04	55	.302	.361	8-0-1	.000	-1	102	-9		-1.1

YEAR	TM LG	W	L	PCT	G	GS	CG-SHO	SV-BS	IP	H	R	HR	HB	BB-IB	SO	ERA	AERA	OAV	OOB	AB-HR-SH	AVG	PB	SUP	APR	DL	PW
1983	Hou N	3	4	.429	53	0	0	20-9	71.1	52	21	2	1	20-5	67	2.65	129	.205	.263	6	.167	1		8		1.3
1984	Hou N	4	9	.308	57	0	0	14-4	75.1	74	32	3	1	36-11	65	3.35	100	.260	.343	10	.000	-1		0		0.0
1985	Hou N	3	7	.300	54	0	0	6-2	76	69	44	7	2	43-6	49	4.03	87	.248	.350	12	.167	-0		-7		-1.0
1986	Hou N	1	3	.250	31	0	0	3-3	40.1	27	18	5	2	16-1	27	3.57	101	.189	.278	5	.200	0		0		-0.7
	Chi N	2	4	.333	30	0	0	0-2	40	47	27	6	0	14-5	43	5.17	79	.297	.351	1	.000	-0		-5		-0.7
	Year	3	7	.300	61	0	0	3-5	80.1	74	45	11	2	30-6	70	4.37	88	.246	.315	6	.167	-0		-5		0.8
1987	Chi N	3	3	.500	69	0	0	4-1	80	75	31	7	1	34-2	61	3.15	137	.252	.326	2-0-1	.500	-1		10		-0.9
1988	Chi N	2	3	.400	63	0	0	6-2	90.1	102	54	6	0	32-7	69	4.98	73	.285	.338	10-0-1	.100	-1		-12		1.1
1989	StL N	9	0	1.000	67	0	0	0-3	88.1	73	26	6	0	20-7	44	2.45	150	.227	.269	13-0-1	.077	-1		12		-0.4
1990	StL N	5	2	.714	62	0	0	3-2	81	92	45	8	1	31-12	49	4.56	85	.294	.352	4-0-1	.250	0		-6		-0.4
1992	StL N	0	0	—	9	0	0	0-0	11	9	2	0	0	3-0	8	1.64	209	.220	.273	1	1.000	0	131	2		0.2
1993	KC A	1	1	.500	11	0	0	0-0	15.2	21	12	2	2	6-0	5	6.89	67	.328	.392	0		-2	31	-3		-0.4
Total	12	35	38	.479	514	6	0	56-28	700	673	332	53	10	269-57	515	3.83	97	.256	.324	72-0-5	.125	-2	102	-9	344	-1.1

DIPOTO, JERRY   Gerard Peter   B5.24.1968 Jersey City NJ   BR/TR/6-2/200*   [CleA89 3/71]   d5.11   Col Virginia Commonwealth   [DL 2001 Col N 151]

YEAR	TM LG	W	L	PCT	G	GS	CG-SHO	SV-BS	IP	H	R	HR	HB	BB-IB	SO	ERA	AERA	OAV	OOB	AB-HR-SH	AVG	PB	SUP	APR	DL	PW
																								10		1.7
1993	Cle A	4	4	.500	46	0	0	11-6	56.1	57	21	0	1	30-7	41	2.40	183	.270	.361	0		0		-5	70	-0.2
1994	Cle A	0	0	—	7	0	0	1-0	15.2	26	14	1	1	10-0	9	8.04	59	.406	.468	0		-1		0		0.0
1995	NY N	4	6	.400	58	0	0	2-4	78.2	77	41	2	4	29-8	49	3.78	107	.267	.340	5-0-1	.000	-1		-3		-0.3
1996	NY N	7	2	.778	57	0	0	0-5	77.1	91	44	5	3	45-8	52	4.19	96	.298	.389	1	.000	-0		3		0.3
1997	Col N	5	3	.625	74	0	0	16-5	95.2	108	56	6	4	33-5	74	4.70	110	.288	.346	9	.111	-1		10		1.4
1998	Col N	3	4	.429	68	0	0	19-4	71.1	61	31	8	3	25-3	49	3.53	147	.232	.304	1	.000	-0		12		1.6
1999	Col N	4	5	.444	63	0	0	1-0	86.2	91	44	10	3	44-4	69	4.26	136	.279	.365	5	.000	-0		2	138	0.7
2000	Col N	0	0	—	17	0	0	0-1	13.2	16	6	1	0	5-2	9	3.95	147	.314	.362	1	.000	-0				4.8
Total	8	27	24	.529	390	0	0	49-25	495.1	527	257	33	19	221-37	352	4.05	119	.280	.356	22-0-1	.045	-2		29	359	

DISCH, GEORGE   George Charles   B3.15.1879 Lincoln MO   D8.25.1950 Rapid City SD   TR/5-11/?   d8.8

YEAR	TM LG	W	L	PCT	G	GS	CG-SHO	SV-BS	IP	H	R	HR	HB	BB-IB	SO	ERA	AERA	OAV	OOB	AB-HR-SH	AVG	PB	SUP	APR	DL	PW
1905	Det A	0	2	.000	8	3	1	0	47.2	43	19	1	2	8	14	2.64	103	.243	.283	19	.105	-1	52	1		-0.

DISHMAN, GLENN   Glenelg Edward   B11.5.1970 Baltimore MD   BR/TL/6-1/195*   d6.22   Col TCU

YEAR	TM LG	W	L	PCT	G	GS	CG-SHO	SV-BS	IP	H	R	HR	HB	BB-IB	SO	ERA	AERA	OAV	OOB	AB-HR-SH	AVG	PB	SUP	APR	DL	PW
1995	SD N	4	8	.333	19	16	0	0-0	97	104	60	11	4	34-1	43	5.01	81	.278	.342	30-0-2	.200	0	108	-10		-1.
1996	SD N	0	0	—	3	0	0	0-0	2.1	3	2	0	0	1-0	3	7.71	52	.300	.364	0		0		-1		-0.
	Phi N	0	0	—	4	1	0	0-0	7	9	6	2	0	2-0	0	7.71	56	.321	.355	0-0-2	—	0	188	-2		-0.
	Year	0	0	—	7	1	0	0-0	9.1	12	8	2	0	3-0	3	7.71	55	.316	.357	0-0-2	—	0	191	-3		-0.
1997	Det A	1	2	.333	7	4	0	0-0	29	30	18	4	2	8-0	20	5.28	88	.268	.323	0		0	114	-2		-0.
Total	3	5	10	.333	33	21	0	0-0	135.1	146	86	17	6	45-1	66	5.25	80	.279	.339	30-0-4	.200	0	113	-15		-1.

DISTASO, ALEC   Alec John   B12.23.1948 Los Angeles CA   BR/TR/6-2/200   [ChiN67*1/1]   d4.20

YEAR	TM LG	W	L	PCT	G	GS	CG-SHO	SV-BS	IP	H	R	HR	HB	BB-IB	SO	ERA	AERA	OAV	OOB	AB-HR-SH	AVG	PB	SUP	APR	DL	PW
1969	Chi N	0	0	—	2	0	0	0-0	4.2	6	2	0	0	1-0	1	3.86	104	.316	.350	0		0				

DITMAR, ART   Arthur John   B4.3.1929 Winthrop MA   BR/TR/6-2/196(185-197)   d4.19

YEAR	TM LG	W	L	PCT	G	GS	CG-SHO	SV-BS	IP	H	R	HR	HB	BB-IB	SO	ERA	AERA	OAV	OOB	AB-HR-SH	AVG	PB	SUP	APR	DL	PW
1954	Phi A	1	4	.200	14	5	0.	0	39.1	50	35	4	1	36	14	6.41	61	.314	.442	8-0-1	.125	0	131	-12		-1
1955	KC A	12	12	.500	35	22	7-1	1	175.1	180	109	23	7	86-5	79	5.03	83	.270	.358	62-0-4	.210	-0	107	-16		-1
1956	KC A	12	22	.353	44	34	14-2	1	254.1	254	141	30	7	108-6	126	4.42	98	.262	.338	35-0-1	.200	-0	115	4		-0
1957	†NY A	8	3	.727	46	11.	0	6	127.1	128	55	9	2	35-1	64	3.25	110	.261	.312	44-0-2	.250	2	143	-2		-0
1958	†NY A	9	8	.529	38	13	4	4	139.2	124	71	14	5	38-2	52	2.90	126	.211	.268	76-1-1	.197	2	118	18		1
1959	NY A	13	9	.591	38	25	7-1	1	202	156	75	17	8	52-2	96	3.06	117	.256	.308	69-0-3	.159	0*	117	13		1
1960	†NY A	15	9	.625	34	28	8-1	0	200	195	77	25	1	56-1	65	3.46	104	.257	.318	88-0-8	.140	-2	128	-7		-0
1961	NY A	2	3	.400	12	8	1	0	54.1	59	33	9	2	14-0	24	4.64	80	.285	.329	19	.053	-2	55	-6		0
	KC A	0	5	.000	20	5	0	1	54	60	34	6	2	23-1	19	5.67	74	.286	.359	12-0-1	.167	-0	96	-14		-1
	Year	2	8	.200	32	13	1	1	108.1	119	67	15	4	37-1	43	5.15	77	.285	.344	31-0-1	.097	-2	97	-6		-0
1962	KC A	0	2	.000	6	5	0	0	21.2	31	19	1	2	13-1	13	6.65	64	.323	.411	6	.167	-0	110	-17		-2
Total	9	72	77	.483	287	156	41-5	14	1268	1237	649	138	37	461-19	552	3.98	97	.256	.324	422-2-17	.178	-3	110	-17		

DIVEN, FRANK   Frank Robert   B8.29.1859   D5.30.1914 Nutley NJ   TL   d5.9

YEAR	TM LG	W	L	PCT	G	GS	CG-SHO	SV-BS	IP	H	R	HR	HB	BB-IB	SO	ERA	AERA	OAV	OOB	AB-HR-SH	AVG	PB	SUP	APR	DL	PW
1883	Bal AA	1	1	.500	2	1	1	0	15	11	15	15	0	1	3	7.36	47	.306	.320	9	.222	-0	174	-4		-0

DIXON, SONNY   John Craig   B11.5.1924 Charlotte NC   BB/TR/6-2.5/205*   d4.20

YEAR	TM LG	W	L	PCT	G	GS	CG-SHO	SV-BS	IP	H	R	HR	HB	BB-IB	SO	ERA	AERA	OAV	OOB	AB-HR-SH	AVG	PB	SUP	APR	DL	PW
1953	Was A	5	8	.385	43	6	3	3	120	123	57	13	2	31	40	3.75	104	.267	.316	26-0-2	.154	0	99	2		0
1954	Was A	1	2	.333	16	0	0	1	29.2	26	15	3	0	12	7	3.03	117	.236	.309	6	.000	-1	0			-0
	Phi A	5	7	.417	38	6	1	4	107.1	136	63	8	3	27	42	4.86	80	.308	.349	28	.250	2	75	-10		-0
	Year	6	9	.400	54	6	1	5	137	162	78	11	3	39	49	4.47	86	.293	.341	34	.206	1	77	-10		-0
1955	KC A	0	0	—	2	0	0	0	1.2	6	3	1	0	0-0	0	16.20	16	.545	.545	0	—	-0		-2		-0
1956	NY A	0	1	.000	3	0	1	1	4.1	5	3	0	0	5-1	1	2.08	186	.294	.455	1	.000	-0	0			-0
Total	4	11	18	.379	102	12	4	9	263	296	141	25	5	75-1	90	4.17	93	.284	.334	61-0-2	.180	0	88	-10		-0

DIXON, KEN   Kenneth John   B10.17.1960 Monroe VA   BB/TR/5-11/166(166-192)   [BalA80 3/61]   d9.22

YEAR	TM LG	W	L	PCT	G	GS	CG-SHO	SV-BS	IP	H	R	HR	HB	BB-IB	SO	ERA	AERA	OAV	OOB	AB-HR-SH	AVG	PB	SUP	APR	DL	PW
1984	Bal A	0	1	.000	2	2	0	0-0	13	14	6	1	0	4-0	8	4.15	94	.269	.321	0	—	0*	58	0		-0
1985	Bal A	8	4	.667	34	18	3-1	1-0	162	144	68	20	2	64-7	108	3.67	111	.237	.311	0	—	0	94	-8		-0
1986	Bal A	11	13	.458	35	33	2	0-0	202.1	194	111	33	1	83-6	170	4.58	91	.249	.320	0	—	0	108	-23		-3
1987	Bal A	7	10	.412	34	15	0	5-4	105	128	81	31	1	27-4	91	6.43	69	.292	.333	0	—	0	102	-22		-3
Total	4	26	28	.481	105	68	5-1	6-4	482.1	480	266	85	4	178-17	377	4.66	90	.256	.320	0	—	0	102	-22		-3

DIXON, STEVE   Steven Ross   B8.3.1969 Cincinnati OH   BL/TL/6-0/190*   [StLN89 31/796]   d9.7   Col Kentucky

YEAR	TM LG	W	L	PCT	G	GS	CG-SHO	SV-BS	IP	H	R	HR	HB	BB-IB	SO	ERA	AERA	OAV	OOB	AB-HR-SH	AVG	PB	SUP	APR	DL	PW
1993	StL N	0	0	—	4	0	0	0-0	2.2	7	10	1	0	5-0	2	33.75	12	.538	.667	0	—	0		-8		-0
1994	StL N	0	0	—	2	0	0	0-0	2.1	3	6	0	0	8-0	1	23.14	18	.333	.611	0	—	0		-5		-0
Total	2	0	0	—	6	0	0	0-0	5	10	16	1	0	13-0	3	28.80	14	.455	.639	0	—	0		-13		-0

DIXON, TOM   Thomas Earl   B4.23.1955 Orlando FL   BR/TR/5-11/175*   d7.30

YEAR	TM LG	W	L	PCT	G	GS	CG-SHO	SV-BS	IP	H	R	HR	HB	BB-IB	SO	ERA	AERA	OAV	OOB	AB-HR-SH	AVG	PB	SUP	APR	DL	PW
																				7-0-3	.000	-1	154	1		
1977	Hou N	1	0	1.000	9	4	1	0-0	30.1	40	12	0	1	7-0	15	3.26	111	.320	.361	40-0-3	.100	-2	91	-12		
1978	Hou N	7	11	.389	30	19	3-2	1-0	140	140	70	8	1	40-3	66	3.99	84	.265	.312	1	1.000	1	126	-10	71	
1979	Hou N	1	2	.333	19	1	0	0-1	25.2	39	23	2	0	15-1	9	6.66	53	.348	.425	0		0		-2		
1983	Mon N	0	1	.000	4	0	0	0-0	3.2	6	4	1	1	1-0	4	9.82	37	.375	.421	0		0		-2		
Total	4	9	14	.391	62	24	4-2	1-1	199.2	225	109	11	3	63-4	94	4.33	79	.288	.338	48-0-6	.104	-2	103	-23	71	

DOAK, BILL   William Leopold "Spittin' Bill"   B1.28.1891 Pittsburgh PA   D11.26.1954 Bradenton FL   BR/TR/6-0.5/165   d9.1

YEAR	TM LG	W	L	PCT	G	GS	CG-SHO	SV-BS	IP	H	R	HR	HB	BB-IB	SO	ERA	AERA	OAV	OOB	AB-HR-SH	AVG	PB	SUP	APR	DL	PW
1912	Cin N	0	0	—	1	1	0	0	2	4	2	0	0	1	0	4.50	75	.444	.500	0	—	0	240	0		
1913	StL N	2	8	.200	15	12	5-1	1	93	79	42	4	5	39	51	3.10	104	.236	.325	31	.032	-3	39	0		
1914	StL N	19	6	.760	36	33	16-7	1	256	193	79	2	7	87	118	1.72	162	.216	.290	85-0-3	.118	-3	94	27		
1915	StL N	16	18	.471	38	36	19-3	1	276	263	103	4	8	85	124	2.64	106	.261	.323	86-0-10	.174	1	102	6		
1916	StL N	12	8	.600	29	26	11-2	0	192	177	76	5	3	69	82	2.63	101	.251	.308	62-0-4	.129	-2	114	0		
1917	StL N	16	20	.444	44	37	16-3	2	281.1	257	123	6	9	85	111	3.10	87	.250	.312	95-0-2	.126	-4	94	-16		
1918	StL N	9	15	.375	31	23	16-1	1	211	191	76	3	4	60	74	2.43	111	.249	.306	66-0-7	.182	1	87	7		
1919	StL N	13	14	.481	31	29	13-3	0	202.2	182	87	5	2	55	69	3.11	90	.246	.299	64-0-5	.109	-4	93	-7		
1920	StL N	20	12	.625	39	37	20-5	1	270	256	94	7	6	80	90	2.53	118	.253	.312	88-0-8	.114	-6	105	15		
1921	StL N	15	6	.714	32	29	13-1	1	208.2	224	85	3	4	37	83	2.59	142	.278	.313	70-0-10	.143	-3	118	21		
1922	StL N	11	13	.458	37	29	8-2	2	180.1	222	107	12	6	69	73	5.54	70	.311	.374	54-0-7	.130	-3	125	-32		
1923	StL N	8	13	.381	30	26	7-2	0	185	199	85	4	3	69	53	3.26	120	.279	.346	67-0-3	.045	-9	96	12		
1924	StL N	2	1	.667	11	1	0	3	22	25	8	0	0	14	7	3.27	116	.313	.415	5	.200	-0	67	2		
	Bro N	11	5	.688	21	16	8-2	3	149.1	130	58	3	4	49	32	3.07	122	.239	.289	56-1-2	.179	-0	105	13		
	Year	13	6	.684	32	17	8-2	6	171.1	155	66	3	4	63	39	3.10	121	.249	.307	61-1-2	.180	-1	94	14		
1927	Bro N	11	8	.579	27	20	6-1	0	145	153	73	6	4	40	32	3.10	121	.271	.322	47-0-8	.128	-3	85	5		
1928	Bro N	3	8	.273	28	12	4-1	3	99.1	104	51	1	5	40	12	3.26	122	.271	.340	27-0-1	.111	-2	50	6		
1929	Bro N	2	2	.333	3	2	0	0	9	17	15	1	0	5	3	12.00	39	.415	.478	2-0-1	.000	-2	103	-8		
Total	16	169	157	.518	453	369	162-34	16	2782.2	2676	1184	71	65	851	1014	2.98	107	.259	.319	905-1-71	.127	-42	99	51		

YEAR	TM LG	W	L	PCT	G	GS	CG-SHO	SV-BS	IP	H	R	HR	HB	BB-IB	SO	ERA	AERA	OAV	OOB	AB-HR-SH	AVG	PB	SUP	APR	DL	PW

DOANE, WALT Walter Rudolph B3.12.1887 Bellevue ID D10.19.1935 Coatesville PA BL/TR/6-0/165 d9.20

YEAR	TM LG	W	L	PCT	G	GS	CG-SHO	SV-BS	IP	H	R	HR	HB	BB-IB	SO	ERA	AERA	OAV	OOB	AB-HR-SH	AVG	PB	SUP	APR	DL	PW
1909	Cle A	0	1	.000	1	1	0	0	5	10	7	0	0	1	2	5.40	47	.400	.423	9	.111	-0*	110	-2		-0.4
1910	Cle A	0	0	—	6	0	0	0	17.2	31	21	1	1	8	7	5.60	46	.413	.476	7	.286	1		-8		-0.4
Total 2		0	1	.000	7	1	0	0	22.2	41	28	1	1	9	9	5.56	46	.410	.464	16	.188	1	110	-10		-0.8

DOBB, JOHN John Kenneth "Lefty" B11.15.1901 Muskegon MI D7.31.1991 Muskegon MI BR/TL/6-2/180 d8.13 Col Central Michigan

YEAR	TM LG	W	L	PCT	G	GS	CG-SHO	SV-BS	IP	H	R	HR	HB	BB-IB	SO	ERA	AERA	OAV	OOB	AB-HR-SH	AVG	PB	SUP	APR	DL	PW
1924	Chi A	0	0	—	2	0	0	0	2	4	2	0	0	1	2	9.00	46	.400	.455	0	—	0		-1		0.0

DOBENS, RAY Raymond Joseph "Lefty" B7.28.1906 Nashua NH D4.21.1980 Stuart FL BL/TL/5-8/175 d7.7 Col Holy Cross

YEAR	TM LG	W	L	PCT	G	GS	CG-SHO	SV-BS	IP	H	R	HR	HB	BB-IB	SO	ERA	AERA	OAV	OOB	AB-HR-SH	AVG	PB	SUP	APR	DL	PW
1929	Bos A	0	0	—	11	1	0	0	28.1	32	12	0	1	9	4	3.81	112	.302	.362	8-0-1	.375	1	197	2		0.1

DOBERNIC, JESS Andrew Joseph B11.20.1917 Mt.Olive IL D7.16.1998 St.Louis MO BR/TR/5-10/170 d7.2

YEAR	TM LG	W	L	PCT	G	GS	CG-SHO	SV-BS	IP	H	R	HR	HB	BB-IB	SO	ERA	AERA	OAV	OOB	AB-HR-SH	AVG	PB	SUP	APR	DL	PW
1939	Chi A	0	1	.000	4	0	0	0	3.1	3	6	0	1	6	1	13.50	35	.231	.500	1	.000	-0		-3		-0.6
1948	Chi A	7	2	.778	54	0	0	1	85.2	67	33	8	1	40	48	3.15	124	.213	.303	10	.200	-0		8		0.7
1949	Chi N	0	0	—	4	0	0	0	4	9	9	2	0	4	0	20.25	20	.450	.542	0	—	0		-7		-0.3
	Cin N	0	0	—	14	0	0	0	19.1	28	22	7	0	16	6	9.78	43	.329	.436	2	.000	0		-11		-0.5
	Year	0	0	—	18	0	0	0	23.1	37	31	9	0	20	6	11.57	36	.352	.456	2	.000	0		-17		-0.8
Total 3		7	3	.700	76	0	0	1	112.1	107	70	17	2	66	55	5.21	76	.247	.349	13	.154	0		-13		-0.7

DOBSON, CHUCK Charles Thomas B1.10.1944 Kansas City MO BR/TR/6-4/200* d4.19 Col Kansas [DL 1972 Oak A 17]

YEAR	TM LG	W	L	PCT	G	GS	CG-SHO	SV-BS	IP	H	R	HR	HB	BB-IB	SO	ERA	AERA	OAV	OOB	AB-HR-SH	AVG	PB	SUP	APR	DL	PW
1966	KC A	4	6	.400	14	14	1	0	83.2	71				50-0	61	4.09	83	.234	.345	26-0-2	.115	-1	69	-5	63	-0.7
1967	KC A	10	10	.500	32	29	4-1	0	197.2	172	83	17	3	75-6	110	3.69	86	.233	.305	72-0-3	.181	0*	102	-7		-0.7
1968	Oak A	12	14	.462	35	34	11-3	0	225.1	197	91	20	4	80-10	168	3.00	94	.234	.302	72-0-3	.200	2	99	-7		-0.5
1969	Oak A	15	13	.536	35	35	11-1	0-0	235.1	244	111	16	1	80-2	137	3.86	89	.270	.328	79-0-9	.101	-3	113	-11		-1.7
1970	Oak A	16	15	.516	41	40	13-5	0-0	267	230	122	32	5	92-7	149	3.74	94	.229	.296	93-0-5	.118	-3	115	-6		-1.1
1971	Oak A	15	5	.750	30	30	7-1	0-0	189	185	84	24	1	71-6	100	3.81	87	.259	.326	66-0-5	.197	3	165	-8	27	-0.5
1973	Oak A	0	1	.000	1	1	0	0-0	2.1	6	4	1	0	2	3	7.71	46	.429	.500	0	—	0	100	-2		-0.3
1974	Cal A	2	3	.400	5	5	2	0-0	30	39	19	3	0	13-1	16	5.70	61	.315	.380	0	—	0	46	-6		-0.9
1975	Cal A	2	2	.000	9	2	0	0-0	28	30	26	5	2	13-1	14	6.75	53	.275	.349	0	—	0	74	-11		-0.7
Total 9		74	69	.517	202	190	49-11	0-0	1258.1	1174	581	125	18	476-33	758	3.78	87	.247	.316	411-0-30	.153	-2	112	-63	107	-7.1

DOBSON, JOE Joseph Gordon "Burrhead" B1.20.1917 Durant OK D6.23.1994 Jacksonville FL BR/TR/6-2/197* d4.26 Mil 1944-45

YEAR	TM LG	W	L	PCT	G	GS	CG-SHO	SV-BS	IP	H	R	HR	HB	BB-IB	SO	ERA	AERA	OAV	OOB	AB-HR-SH	AVG	PB	SUP	APR	DL	PW
1939	Cle A	2	3	.400	35	3	0	1	78	87	56	3	1	51	27	5.88	75	.290	.395	18-0-1	.056	-2	87	-13		-0.9
1940	Cle A	3	7	.300	40	7	2-1	3	100	101	60	3	0	51	57	4.95	85	.268	.351	24	.125	-1	71	-7		-0.7
1941	Bos A	12	5	.706	27	18	7-1	0	134.1	136	70	8	2	67	48	4.49	93	.262	.349	47-1-3	.149	0	119	-1		-0.2
1942	Bos A	11	9	.550	30	23	10-3	0	182.2	155	73	9	2	68	72	3.30	113	.231	.303	69-0-5	.145	0	92	10		1.0
1943	Bos A	7	11	.389	25	20	9-3	0	164.1	144	63	4	0	57	63	3.12	106	.239	.305	52-0-3	.096	-3	98	4		-0.1
1946	†Bos A	13	7	.650	32	24	9-1	0	166.2	148	72	11	1	68	91	3.24	113	.234	.300	50-0-6	.100	-2	119	6		0.5
1947	Bos A	18	8	.692	33	31	15-1	0	228.2	203	84	15	1	73	110	2.95	132	.238	.299	77-0-7	.208	1	110	23		2.6
1948	Bos A☆	16	10	.615	38	32	16-5	2	245.1	237	115	14	1	92	116	3.56	123	.253	.320	84-1-8	.202	1	124	19		1.8
1949	Bos A	14	12	.538	33	27	12-2	2	212.2	219	103	12	2	97	87	3.85	113	.269	.348	68-0-5	.147	-1	94	10		0.9
1950	Bos A	15	10	.600	39	27	12-1	4	206.2	217	103	15	0	81	81	4.18	117	.275	.343	70-0-8	.214	1	115	16		1.9
1951	Chi A	7	6	.538	28	21	6	3	146.2	136	68	17	0	51	67	3.62	111	.248	.312	46-0-7	.065	-6	131	7		0.0
1952	Chi A	14	10	.583	29	25	11-3	1	200.2	164	66	11	0	60	101	2.51	145	.222	.280	63-0-10	.190	0	90	24		2.7
1953	Bos A	5	5	.500	23	15	3-1	1	100.2	96	46	10	0	37	50	3.67	110	.249	.314	29-0-1	.069	-2	85	4		0.1
1954	Bos A	0	0	—	2	0	0	0	2.2	5	2	0	0	1	1	6.75	61	.385	.429	0	—	0		-1		0.0
Total 14		137	103	.571	414	273	112-22	18	2170	2048	981	137	10	851	992	3.62	112	.250	.322	697-2-64	.152	-15	107	103		9.6

DOBSON, PAT Patrick Edward B2.12.1942 Depew NY BR/TR/6-3/190* d5.31 C8

YEAR	TM LG	W	L	PCT	G	GS	CG-SHO	SV-BS	IP	H	R	HR	HB	BB-IB	SO	ERA	AERA	OAV	OOB	AB-HR-SH	AVG	PB	SUP	APR	DL	PW
1967	Det A	1	2	.333	28	1	0	0	49.1	38	20	6	2	27-1	34	2.92	112	.216	.324	5	.000	-1	80	1		0.0
1968	†Det A	5	8	.385	47	10	2-1	7	125	89	39	13	2	48-6	93	2.66	113	.200	.280	28-0-2	.143	0	90	5		0.7
1969	Det A	5	10	.333	49	9	1	9-4	105	100	48	10	1	39-5	64	3.60	105	.253	.316	22-0-2	.091	-1	118	1		0.1
1970	SD N	14	15	.483	40	34	8-1	1-0	251	257	126	28	4	78-13	185	3.76	107	.265	.320	71-0-19	.141	-0	110	4		0.3
1971	†Bal A	20	8	.714	38	37	18-4	1-0	282.1	248	104	24	2	63-2	187	2.90	118	.235	.278	91-0-13	.110	-3	132	15		1.0
1972	Bal A	16	18	.471	38	36	13-3	0-0	268.1	220	89	13	4	69-7	161	2.65	118	.224	.277	85-0-8	.141	-2	81	13		1.4
1973	Atl N	3	7	.300	12	10	1-1	0-0	57.2	73	33	1	1	19-5	23	4.99	79	.315	.362	15-0-3	.067	-1	60	-5		-0.9
	NY A	9	8	.529	22	21	6-1	0-0	142.1	150	72	22	2	34-8	70	4.17	89	.266	.309	0	—	-1	60	-5		-0.9
1974	NY A	19	15	.559	39	39	12-2	0-0	281	282	111	23	4	75-5	157	3.07	115	.262	.311	0	—	0	119	-6		1.7
1975	NY A	11	14	.440	33	30	7-1	0-0	207.2	205	105	21	1	83-10	129	4.07	91	.261	.330	0	—	0	90	15		-0.9
1976	Cle A	16	12	.571	35	35	6	0-0	217.1	226	98	24	2	65-7	117	3.48	101	.272	.323	0	—	0	97	-8		-0.2
1977	Cle A	3	12	.200	33	17	0	1-0	133.1	155	94	21	1	65-7	61	6.14	65	.299	.376	0	—	0	85	-29		-2.8
Total 11		122	129	.486	414	279	74-14	19-4	2120.1	2043	939	197	26	665-76	1301	3.54	101	.255	.312	317-0-47	.123	-8	99	5		-0.2

DOCKINS, GEORGE George Woodrow "Lefty" B5.5.1917 Clyde KS D1.22.1997 Clyde KS BL/TL/6-0/175 d5.5

YEAR	TM LG	W	L	PCT	G	GS	CG-SHO	SV-BS	IP	H	R	HR	HB	BB-IB	SO	ERA	AERA	OAV	OOB	AB-HR-SH	AVG	PB	SUP	APR	DL	PW
1945	StL N	8	6	.571	31	12	5-2	0	126.1	132	53	4	0	38	33	3.21	117	.269	.321	34-0-4	.176	1	106	7		0.8
1947	Bro N	0	0	—	4	0	0	0	5.1	10	7	2	0	2	1	11.81	35	.400	.444	1	.000	-0		-4		-0.2
Total 2		8	6	.571	35	12	5-2	0	131.2	142	60	6	0	40	34	3.55	106	.275	.327	35-0-4	.171	1	106	3		0.6

DODD, ROBERT Robert Wayne B3.14.1973 Kansas City KS BL/TL/6-3/195 [PhiN94 14/394] d5.28 Col Florida

YEAR	TM LG	W	L	PCT	G	GS	CG-SHO	SV-BS	IP	H	R	HR	HB	BB-IB	SO	ERA	AERA	OAV	OOB	AB-HR-SH	AVG	PB	SUP	APR	DL	PW
1998	Phi N	1	0	1.000	4	0	0	0-0	5	7	6	1	1	4	0	7.20	60	.333	.360		—	0		-2		-0.4

DODGE, SAM Samuel Edward B12.9.1889 Neath PA D4.5.1966 Utica NY BR/TR/6-1/170 d9.24

YEAR	TM LG	W	L	PCT	G	GS	CG-SHO	SV-BS	IP	H	R	HR	HB	BB-IB	SO	ERA	AERA	OAV	OOB	AB-HR-SH	AVG	PB	SUP	APR	DL	PW
1921	Bos A	0	0	—	1	0	0	0	1	1	1	0	0	1	0	9.00	47	.500	.667	0	—	0		0		0.0
1922	Bos A	0	0	—	3	0	0	0	6	11	6	0	0	3	3	4.50	91	.379	.438	2	.000	-0		-1		-0.1
Total 2		0	0	—	4	0	0	0	7	12	7	0	0	4	3	5.14	80	.387	.457	2	.000	-0		-1		-0.1

DOE, FRED Alfred George "Count" B4.18.1864 Rockport MA D10.4.1938 Quincy MA BR/TR/5-10/165 d8.23

YEAR	TM LG	W	L	PCT	G	GS	CG-SHO	SV-BS	IP	H	R	HR	HB	BB-IB	SO	ERA	AERA	OAV	OOB	AB-HR-SH	AVG	PB	SUP	APR	DL	PW
1890	Buf P	0	1	.000	1	1	0	0	6	10	10	0	0	7	2	12.00	34	.357	.486	2	.000	-0	0	-5		-0.5
	Pit P	0	0	—	1	0	0	0	4	4	2	0	0	2	2	4.50	87	.250	.333	2	.500	0	0			0.0
	Year	0	1	.000	2	1	0	0	10	14	12	0	0	9	4	9.00	45	.318	.434	4	.250	-0	0	-4		-0.5

DOHENY, ED Edwin Richard B11.24.1873 Northfield VT D12.29.1916 Medfield MA BL/TL/5-10.5/165 d9.16

YEAR	TM LG	W	L	PCT	G	GS	CG-SHO	SV-BS	IP	H	R	HR	HB	BB-IB	SO	ERA	AERA	OAV	OOB	AB-HR-SH	AVG	PB	SUP	APR	DL	PW
1895	NY N	0	3	.000	3	3	3	0	25.2	37	29	2	3	19	9	6.66	70	.333	.444	10	.100	-1	82	-6		-0.6
1896	NY N	6	7	.462	17	15	9	0	108.1	112	78	3	6	59	39	4.49	94	.265	.363	40	.150	-2	119	-4		-0.5
1897	NY N	7	4	.500	10	10	10	0	85	69	45	0	8	45	37	2.12	196	.220	.333	35	.200	-1	79	15		1.1
1898	NY N	7	19	.269	28	27	23	0	213	238	164	1	20	101	96	3.68	95	.280	.370	86-2-0	.163	-1	108	-15		-1.5
1899	NY N	14	17	.452	36	34	31-1	0	277.2	291	207	2	37	158	120	4.41	85	.269	.381	116	.233	-1	99	-26		-2.1
1900	NY N	4	14	.222	20	18	12	0	133.2	148	134	2	22	66	44	5.45	66	.280	.411	54	.222	-0	103	-31		-3.1
1901	NY N	2	5	.286	10	6	6	0	74	88	53	1	6	17	36	4.50	73	.293	.344	29-0-1	.345	3*	104	-10		-0.5
	Pit	6	2	.750	11	10	6-1	0	76.2	68	36	1	5	22	28	2.00	164	.236	.302	26	.115	0	135	7		0.7
	Year	8	7	.533	21	16	12-1	0	150.2	156	89	2	11	39	64	3.23	102	.265	.323	55-0-1	.236	4	123	-2		0.2
1902	Pit N	16	4	.800	22	21	19-2	0	188.1	161	68	0	15	61	88	2.53	108	.231	.307	77-1-1	.156	-2	141	6		0.3
1903	Pit N	16	8	.667	27	25	22-2	0	222.2	209	91	1	19	89	75	3.19	101	.252	.338	91-0-1	.209	-0	125	9		0.2
Total 9		75	83	.475	184	169	141-6	2	1405	1421	936	13	141	667	572	3.73	94	.262	.358	564-3-3	.197	-4	112	-64		-6.0

DOHERTY, JOHN John Harold B6.11.1967 New York NY BR/TR/6-4/210(200-215) [DetA89 19/499] d4.8 Col Concordia (NY)

YEAR	TM LG	W	L	PCT	G	GS	CG-SHO	SV-BS	IP	H	R	HR	HB	BB-IB	SO	ERA	AERA	OAV	OOB	AB-HR-SH	AVG	PB	SUP	APR	DL	PW
1992	Det A	7	4	.636	47	11	0	3-1	116	131	61	4	4	25-5	37	3.88	103	.287	.328	0	—	0	129	-2	19	-0.1
1993	Det A	14	11	.560	32	31	3-2	0-0	184.2	205	104	19	5	48-7	63	4.44	98	.286	.333	0	—	0	114	-3	15	-0.4
1994	Det A	6	7	.462	18	17	2	0-0	101.1	139	75	13	9	26-6	28	6.48	76	.337	.374	0	—	0	104	-15	33	-1.4
1995	Det A	5	9	.357	48	2	0	6-3	113	130	66	10	6	37-10	46	5.10	94	.288	.349	0	—	0	87	-2		-0.2
1996	Bos A	0	0	—	3	0	0	0	6.1	10	4	1	1	6	1	5.68	90	.370	.382	0	—	0		-5		-0.1
Total 5		32	31	.508	148	61	5-2	9-4	521.1	613	316	47	19	140-28	177	4.87	92	.296	.344	0	—	0	112	-23	67	-2.2

DOHMANN, SCOTT Christopher Scott B2.13.1978 New Orleans LA BR/TR/6-1/180* [ColN00 6/167] d5.15 Col Louisiana-Lafayette

YEAR	TM LG	W	L	PCT	G	GS	CG-SHO	SV-BS	IP	H	R	HR	HB	BB-IB	SO	ERA	AERA	OAV	OOB	AB-HR-SH	AVG	PB	SUP	APR	DL	PW
2004	Col N	0	3	.000	41	0	0	0-4	46	41	22	8	0	19-0	49	4.11	116	.236	.306	1-0-1	.000	0		3		0.2
2005	Col N	2	1	.667	32	0	0	0-3	31	33	21	6	0	19-1	35	6.10	78	.266	.364	1-0-0	.000	0		-4		-0.4
Total 2		2	4	.333	73	0	0	0-7	77	74	43	14	0	38-1	84	4.91	97	.248	.330	2-0-1	.000	0		-1		-0.2

YEAR	TM LG	W	L	PCT	G	GS	CG-SHO	SV-BS	IP	H	R	HR	HB	BB-IB	SO	ERA	AERA	OAV	OOB	AB-HR-SH	AVG	PB	SUP	APR	DL	PW
DOLAN, JOHN	John B9.12.1867 Newport KY D5.8.1948 Springfield OH TR/5-10/170 d9.5																									
1890	Cin N	1	1	.500	2	2	2	0	18	17	13	3	1	10	9	4.50	79	.243	.346	8	.125	-1	80	-1		-0.2
1891	Col AA	12	11	.522	27	24	19	0	203.1	216	131	8	0	84	68	4.16	83	.263	.331	78-1	.090	-4*	92	-13		-1.5
1892	Was N	2	2	.500	5	4	3	0	37	39	26	0	1	15	8	4.38	74	.260	.331	13	.231	0	112	-3		-0.3
1893	StL N	0	1	.000	3	1	1	1	17.1	26	22	2	1	7	1	4.15	114	.338	.400	7-1	.143	-1	74	-2		-0.1
1895	Chi N	0	1	.000	2	2	1	0	11	16	12	0	1	6	1	6.55	78	.333	.418	3	.000	-0	77	-2		-0.1
Total	5	15	16	.484	39	33	26	1	286.2	314	204	13	4	122	87	4.30	83	.269	.341	109-2	.110	-5	92	-21		-2.2
DOLAN, COZY	Patrick Henry B12.3.1872 Cambridge MA D3.29.1907 Louisville KY BL/TL/5-10/160 d4.26 ▲																									
1895	Bos N	11	7	.611	25	21	18-3	1	198.1	215	142	11	14	67	47	4.27	119	.272	.340	83-0-1	.241	-1*	90	16		1.1
1896	Bos N	1	4	.200	6	5	3	0	41	55	44	1	3	27	14	4.83	94	.318	.419	14-0-2	.143	-1	122	-4		-0.5
1905	Bos N	0	1	.000	2	0	0	0	4	7	5	2	0	1	1	9.00	34	.368	.400	433-3-9	.275	1*		-2		-0.4
1906	Bos N	0	1	.000	2	0	0	0	12	12	6	1	0	6	7	4.50	60	.300	.391	549-0-13	.248	0*		-2		-0.1
Total	4	12	13	.480	35	26	21-3	1	255.1	289	197	15	17	101	69	4.44	109	.283	.357	1079-3-25	.257	-2	98	8		0.1
DOLL, ART	Arthur James "Moose" B5.7.1913 Chicago IL D4.28.1978 Calumet City IL BR/TR/6-1/190 d9.21.1935																									
1936	Bos N	0	1	.000	1	1	0	0	8	11	4	1	1	2	2	3.38	114	.355	.412	2	.000	-0	44	1		0.0
1938	Bos N	0	0	—	3	0	0	0	4	4	1	0	0	3	1	2.25	153	.286	.412	1	1.000	-0		1		0.1
Total	2	0	1	.000	4	1	0	0	12	15	5	1	1	5	3	3.00	123	.333	.412	3	.333	0	44	2		0.1
DOMINGUEZ, JUAN	Juan Ramon B5.18.1980 Sanchez Ramirez, D.R. BR/TR/6-2/180(180-195) d8.12																									
															13	7.16	69	.271	.389	0	—	0	68	-4		-0.4
2003	Tex A	0	2	.000	6	3	0-0		16.1	16	14	5	0	12-0	13	7.16	69	.271	.389	0	—	0	68	-4		-0.4
2004	Tex A	1	2	.333	4	4	0	0	23	25	11	2	2	5-0	14	3.91	126	.281	.330	0	—	0	108	2	93	0.3
2005	Tex A	4	6	.400	22	10	0-1	0	70.1	78	37	11	2	25-0	45	4.22	109	.277	.338	0	—	0	111	2		0.2
Total	3	5	10	.333	32	17	0-1	0	109.2	119	62	18	4	42-0	72	4.60	103	.277	.344	0	—	0	103	0	93	0.2
DONAHUE, RED	Francis Rostell B1.23.1873 Waterbury CT D8.25.1913 Philadelphia PA BR/TR/6-0/187 d5.6 Col Villanova																									
1893	NY N	0	0	—	2	0	0	1	5	8	10	1	2	3	1	9.00	52	.348	.464	2	.000	-0		-3		-0.2
1895	StL N	0	1	.000	1	1	1	0	8	9	6	2	1	3	2	6.75	72	.281	.361	3	.000	-1	0	-1		-0.1
1896	StL N	7	24	.226	32	32	28	0	267	376	235	6	13	98	70	5.80	75	.329	.389	107-0-3	.159	-8*	78	-42		-4.2
1897	StL N	10	35	.222	46	42	**38**-1	0	348	485	306	16	22	106	64	6.13	72	.327	.380	155-1-4	.213	-3*	72	-57		-5.5
1898	Phi N	16	17	.485	35	35	33-1	0	284.1	327	165	7	14	80	57	3.55	97	.286	.316	112-0-7	.143	-7	105	-4		-0.9
1899	Phi N	21	8	.724	35	31	27-4	0	279	292	147	6	11	63	51	3.39	100	.269	.316	111-0-5	.180	-5	136	11		0.9
1900	Phi N	15	10	.600	32	24	21-2	0	240	299	144	6	9	50	41	3.60	100	.304	.344	90-0-5	.222	-1	123	-4		0.1
1901	Phi N	20	13	.606	34	33	33-1	1	295.1	299	111	2	9	59	88	2.59	131	.261	.302	113-0-3	.097	-9	88	28		1.1
1902	StL A	22	11	.667	35	34	33-2	0	316.1	322	134	7	8	65	63	2.76	128	.264	.306	118-0-5	.093	-9	91	25		1.1
1903	StL A	8	7	.533	16	15	14	0	131	145	59	0	4	22	51	2.75	106	.279	.309	50-1-0	.157	-2	126	1		-0.1
	Cle A	7	9	.438	16	15	14-4	0	136.2	142	61	3	6	12	45	2.44	117	.267	.291	53-0-1	.151	-1	112	5		0.1
	Year	15	16	.484	32	30	28-4	0	267.2	287	120	3	6	34	96	2.59	111	.273	.300	104-0-3	.154	-3	119	4		0.1
1904	Cle A	19	14	.576	35	32	30-6	0	277	281	96	2	5	49	127	2.40	105	.264	.295	101-0-5	.168	-1	118	8		0.5
1905	Cle A	6	12	.333	20	18	14-1	0	137.2	132	68	2	5	25	45	3.40	77	.254	.295	53-0-3	.075	-5	93	-11		-1.1
1906	Det A	3	14	.481	28	28	26-3	0	241	260	96	1	8	54	82	2.73	101	.278	.323	81-0-5	.123	-4*	86	1		-0.0
Total	13	164	175	.484	367	340	312-25	3	2966.1	3377	1638	61	113	689	787	3.61	96	.286	.331	1150-1-48	.152	-56	97	-43		-8.
DONAHUE, DEACON	John Stephen Michael B6.23.1920 Chicago IL BR/TR/6-0/180 d9.16																									
1943	Phi N	0	0	—	2	0	0	0	4	4	3	0	1	1	1	4.50	75	.235	.316	0	—	0		-1		0
1944	Phi N	0	2	.000	6	0	0	0	9.1	18	8	0	0	2	2	7.71	47	.429	.455	1	.000	-0		-4		-0.
Total	2	0	2	.000	8	0	0	0	13.1	22	11	0	1	3	2	6.75	52	.373	.413	1	.000	-0		-5		-0.
DONALD, ATLEY	Richard Atley "Swampy" B8.19.1910 Morton MS D10.19.1992 West Monroe LA BL/TR/6-1/186 d4.21 Col Louisiana Tech																									
1938	NY A	0	1	.000	2	2	0	0	12	7	8	0	1	14	6	5.25	86	.175	.400	6	.167	-0	78	-1		-0
1939	NY A	13	3	.813	24	20	11-2	1	153	144	74	12	0	60	55	3.71	118	.247	.317	60	.250	3	138	10		1
1940	NY A	8	3	.727	24	11	6-1	0	118.2	113	49	11	2	59	60	3.03	133	.249	.339	41-0-5	.146	-2	111	13		0
1941	†NY A	9	5	.643	22	20	10	0	159	141	69	11	3	69	71	3.57	110	.237	.320	62	.081	-4	117	6		0
1942	†NY A	11	3	.786	20	19	10-1	0	147.2	133	58	6	0	45	57	4.60	70	.276	.329	47-0-4	.128	-2	159	-18		-1
1943	NY A	6	4	.600	22	15	2	0	119.1	134	69	10	0	38	57	3.34	104	.280	.345	55-0-1	.182	-0	138	-1		-0
1944	NY A	13	10	.565	30	19	9	0	159	173	77	13	2	59	48	2.97	117	.248	.316	24-1-2	.208	-0	126	2		-0
1945	NY A	5	4	.556	9	9	6-2	0	63.2	62	29	3	0	25	19	3.52	107	.253	.325	356-1-14	.160	-7	132	19		0
Total	8	65	33	.663	153	115	54-6	1	932.1	907	433	66	8	369	369	3.52	107	.253	.325	356-1-14	.160	-7	132	19		0
DONALDS, ED	Edward Alexander "Erston" B6.22.1885 Bidwell OH D7.3.1950 Columbus OH BR/TR/5-11/180 d9.1																									
1912	Cin N	0	1	.000	1	0	0	0	4	7	2	0	0	1	1	4.50	75	.438	.438	1	.000	-0		0		-0
DONLIN, MIKE	Michael Joseph "Turkey Mike" B5.30.1878 Peoria IL D9.24.1933 Hollywood CA BL/TL/5-9/170 d7.19 ▲																									
1899	StL N	0	1	.000	3	1	0	0	15.1	15	15	1	1	14	6	7.63	52	.254	.405	266-6-3	.323	1*	126	-5		-0
1902	Cin N	0	0	—	1	0	0	0	1	1	0	0	0	0	0	0.00	—	.250	.250	143	.287	0*		0		0
Total	2	0	1	.000	4	1	0	0	16.1	16	15	1	1	14	6	7.16	55	.254	.397	409-6-3	.311	1	126	-5		-0
DONNELLY, BRENDAN	Brendan Kevin B7.4.1971 Washington DC BR/TR/6-3/205(205-240) [ChiA92 27/764] d4.9 Col Mesa St.																									
																					—	0	13		0
2002	†Ana A	1	1	.500	46	0	0	1-2	49.2	32	13	2	2	19-3	54	2.17	206	.184	.270	0	—	0	24			1
2003	Ana A★	2	2	.500	63	0	0	3-2	74	55	14	2	4	24-1	79	1.58	277	.200	.273	0	—	0	8	74		3
2004	†Ana A	5	2	.714	40	0	0	0-0	42	34	14	5	1	15-0	56	3.00	149	.224	.294	0	—	-0*	4			1
2005	†LA A	9	3	.750	65	0	0	0-5	65.1	60	30	9	2	19-3	53	3.72	116	.244	.302	1	.000	0	49	74		3
Total	4	17	8	.680	214	0	0	4-9	231	181	71	18	9	77-7	242	2.57	171	.214	.285	1	.000	0				
DONNELLY, ED	Edward "Big Ed","Ned" (b Edward O'Donnell) B7.29.1880 Hampton NY D11.28.1957 Rutland VT BR/TR/6-1/205 d9.19																									
															16	2.45	156	.236	.291	14	.071	-1	98	4		-0
1911	Bos N	3	2	.600	5	4	4-1	0	36.2	33	15	0	2	9	16	2.45	156	.236	.291	14	.071	-1	98	4		-0
1912	Bos N	5	10	.333	37	18	10	0	184.1	225	127	10	5	72	67	4.35	82	.304	.370	69-0-4	.275	3*	83	-18		-0
Total	2	8	12	.400	42	22	14-1	0	221	258	142	10	7	81	83	4.03	90	.294	.358	83-0-4	.241	1	86	-14		-0
DONNELLY, ED	Edward Vincent B12.10.1932 Allen MI D12.25.1997 Houston TX BR/TR/6-0/175 d8.1																									
1959	Chi N	1	1	.500	9	0	0	0	14.1	18	7	1	0	9-1	6	3.14	126	.305	.397	0	—	0		1		
DONNELLY, FRANK	Franklin Marion B10.7.1869 Tamaroa IL D2.3.1953 Canton IL 5-6/180 d8.15																									
1893	Chi N	3	1	.750	7	5	3	2	42	51	42	1	4	17	6	5.36	86	.291	.367	18	.444	4	124	-5		
1894	Chi N	0	0	—	1	0	0	0	4.2	6	15	0	0	2	1	15.43	37	.316	.519	1	.000	-0		-4		
Total	2	3	1	.750	8	5	3	2	46.2	57	57	1	4	19	7	6.36	74	.294	.386	19	.421	4	124	-9		
DONNELLY, BLIX	Sylvester Urban B1.21.1914 Olivia MN D6.20.1976 Olivia MN BR/TR/5-10/178* d5.6																									
1944	†StL N	2	1	.667	27	4	2-1	2	76.1	61	26	2	2	34	45	2.12	166	.218	.307	16-0-2	.063	-1	119	10		
1945	StL N	8	10	.444	31	23	9-4	2	166.1	157	79	10	4	87	76	3.52	106	.250	.346	54-0-6	.130	-2	101	2		
1946	StL N	1	2	.333	13	0	0	1	13.2	17	7	1	1	10	11	3.95	87	.347	.467	0	—	-0		-1		
	Phi N	3	4	.429	12	8	2	1	76.1	64	31	7	2	24	38	2.95	116	.220	.284	25	.280	2	90	3		
	Year	4	6	.400	25	8	2	2	90	81	38	8	3	34	49	3.10	111	.238	.313	25	.280	2	90	3		
1947	Phi N	4	6	.400	18	10	5-1	5	120.1	113	44	6	4	46	31	2.98	134	.265	.340	32-0-5	.063	-2	97	15		
1948	Phi N	5	7	.417	26	19	8-1	2	131.2	125	65	13	0	49	46	5.06	78	.294	.382	23-0-1	.222	1	123	-10		
1949	Phi N	2	1	.667	23	10	1	0	78.1	84	50	7	1	40	36	4.29	94	.330	.396	5	.200	-0	65	-1		
1950	Phi N	4	3	.333	14	1	0	0	21	30	13	5	0	10	10	7.36	50	.286	.429	1	.000	-0		-3		
1951	Bos N	0	1	.000	14	0	0	1	7.1	8	5	0	0	6	3	3.49	50	.286	.429				104			
Total	8	27	36	.429	190	75	27-7	12	691.2	659	321	52	16	306	296	3.49	109	.257	.340	201-0-15	.159	-1	104	18		
DONOHUE, JIM	James Thomas B10.31.1938 St.Louis MO BR/TR/6-4/190* d4.11																									
1961	Det A	1	1	.500	14	0	1	0	20.1	23	10	2	0	15-2	20	3.54	116	.287	.400	1	.000	-0		1		
	LA A	4	6	.400	38	7	0	5	100.1	93	48	16	0	50-4	79	4.31	105	.246	.332	27	.148	-1	84	5		
	Year	5	7	.417	52	7	1	5	120.2	116	58	18	0	65-6	99	4.18	106	.253	.344	28	.143	-1	85	5		
1962	LA A	1	0	1.000	12	1	0	0	24.1	24	14	4	2	11-0	14	3.70	104	.258	.349	4-0-1	.250	-2	46	-1		
	Min A	0	1	.000	16	0	0	1	10.1	12	11	3	0	6-0	3	6.97	59	.324	.419	0	—	0	109	-3		

YEAR	TM LG	W	L	PCT	G	GS	CG-SHO	SV-BS	IP	H	R	HR	HB	BB-IB	SO	ERA	AERA	OAV	OOB	AB-HR-SH	AVG	PB	SUP	APR	DL	PW
	Year	1	1	.500	18	2	0	1	34.2	36	22	6	2	17-0	17	4.67	84	.277	.369	6-0-1	.167	0	80	-4		-0.3
Total	2	6	8	.429	70	9	0	7	155.1	152	80	24	2	82-6	116	4.29	101	.259	.350	34-0-1	.147	-1	84	2		0.1

DONOHUE, PETE Peter Joseph B11.5.1900 Athens TX D2.23.1988 Ft.Worth TX BR/TR/6-2/185 d7.1 Col TCU

YEAR	TM LG	W	L	PCT	G	GS	CG-SHO	SV-BS	IP	H	R	HR	HB	BB-IB	SO	ERA	AERA	OAV	OOB	AB-HR-SH	AVG	PB	SUP	APR	DL	PW
1921	Cin N	7	6	.538	21	11	7	1	118.1	117	48	5	0	26	44	3.35	107	.263	.304	38-1-4	.211	1	98	6		0.8
1922	Cin N	18	9	.667	33	30	18-2	1	242	257	110	7	5	43	66	3.12	128	.276	.312	88-0-5	.182	-3	117	22		1.9
1923	Cin N	21	15	.583	42	36	19-2	3	274.1	304	138	3	10	68	84	3.38	114	.278	.326	96-1-4	.250	3	87	12		1.7
1924	Cin N	16	9	.640	35	31	16-3	0	222.1	248	100	9	9	36	72	3.60	105	.285	.321	73-1-4	.192	-0*	100	8		0.7
1925	Cin N	21	14	.600	42	38	27-3	2	301	310	122	3	2	49	78	3.08	133	.268	.299	109-1-7	.294	7*	97	38		4.6
1926	Cin N	20	14	.588	47	36	17-5	2	285.2	298	133	6	9	39	73	3.37	109	.268	.298	106-0-5	.311	9	112	9		1.7
1927	Cin N	6	16	.273	33	24	12-1	1	190.2	253	111	3	1	32	48	4.11	92	.328	.356	48-0-3	.250	1	91	-9		-0.8
1928	Cin N	7	11	.389	23	18	8	0	150	180	84	10	3	32	37	4.74	83	.309	.348	48-1-3	.146	-0	96	-10		-1.0
1929	Cin N	10	13	.435	32	24	7	0	177.2	243	123	12	4	51	30	5.42	84	.331	.377	60-0-4	.333	4	93	-18		-1.5
1930	Cin N	1	3	.250	8	5	2	1	34.1	53	24	0	1	13	4	6.29	77	.363	.419	10-0-1	.100	-1	76	-4		-0.5
	NY N	7	6	.538	18	11	4	1	86.2	135	65	6	2	18	26	6.13	77	.360	.392	33-1-2	.273	1	129	-12		-1.4
	Year	8	9	.471	26	16	6	2	121	188	89	6	3	31	30	6.17	77	.361	.400	43-1-3	.233	0	112	-18		-1.9
1931	NY N	0	1	.000	4	1	0	0	11.1	14	7	1	0	4	4	5.56	66	.311	.367	2	.000	-0	23	-2		-0.2
	Cle A	0	0	—	2	0	0	0	5.1	9	6	1	0	5	4	8.44	55	.429	.538	2	.000	-0		-2		-0.1
1932	Bos A	0	1	.000	4	2	0	0	12.2	18	11	2	0	6	4	7.82	57	.340	.407	3	.000	-0	66	-4		-0.3
Total	12	134	118	.532	344	267	137-16	12	2112.1	2439	1082	68	46	422	571	3.87	103	.293	.330	732-6-42	.246	21	100	34		5.6

DONOSO, LINO Lino (Galata) B9.23.1922 Havana, Cuba D10.13.1990 Veracruz, Veracruz, Mexico BL/TL/5-11/160* d6.18 Negro Lg 1947-49

YEAR	TM LG	W	L	PCT	G	GS	CG-SHO	SV-BS	IP	H	R	HR	HB	BB-IB	SO	ERA	AERA	OAV	OOB	AB-HR-SH	AVG	PB	SUP	APR	DL	PW
1955	Pit N	4	6	.400	25	9	3	1	95	106	58	16	1	35-3	38	5.31	78	.287	.345	27-0-3	.185	-1	108	-10		-1.0
1956	Pit N	0	0	—	3	0	0	0	1.2	2	0	0	0	1-0	1	0.00	—	.250	.333	0		0	1			0.0
Total	2	4	6	.400	28	9	3	1	96.2	108	58	16	1	36-3	39	5.21	79	.286	.345	27-0-3	.185	-1	108	-9		-1.0

DONOVAN, DICK Richard Edward B12.7.1927 Boston MA D1.6.1997 Weymouth MA BL/TR/6-3/205(190-215) d4.24

YEAR	TM LG	W	L	PCT	G	GS	CG-SHO	SV-BS	IP	H	R	HR	HB	BB-IB	SO	ERA	AERA	OAV	OOB	AB-HR-SH	AVG	PB	SUP	APR	DL	PW
1950	Bos N	0	2	.000	10	3	0	0	29.2	28	28	4	2	34	9	8.19	47	.255	.438	6	.167	1	115	-14		-0.7
1951	Bos N	0	0	—	8	2	0	0	13.2	17	11	0	0	11	4	5.27	70	.298	.412	3	.333	1	264	-3		0.0
1952	Bos N	0	2	.000	7	2	0	1	13	18	10	1	0	12	6	5.54	65	.346	.485	3	.000	-0	25	-3		-0.5
1954	Det A	0	0	—	2	0	0	0	6	9	7	1	0	5	2	10.50	35	.360	.438	1	.000	-0		-4		-0.2
1955	Chi A☆	15	9	.625	29	24	11-5	0	187	186	77	17	3	48-5	88	3.32	119	.261	.310	76-1-1	.224	5*	94	12		1.9
1956	Chi A	12	10	.545	34	31	14-3	0	234.2	212	99	22	6	59-6	120	3.64	113	.240	.290	90-3-1	.222	8*	117	15		2.1
1957	Chi A	16	6	.727	28	28	16-2	0	220.2	203	76	17	8	45-8	88	2.77	135	.247	.291	83-3-1	.145	2*	118	23		2.4
1958	Chi A	15	14	.517	34	34	16-4	0	248	240	92	23	7	53-5	127	3.01	121	.251	.295	80-0-2	.112	-1	81	18		1.8
1959	†Chi A	9	10	.474	31	29	5-1	0	179.2	171	84	15	5	58-3	71	3.66	103	.247	.308	61-1-3	.131	1	86	1		0.1
1960	Chi A	6	1	.857	33	8	0	3	78.2	87	49	13	0	25-3	30	5.38	70	.283	.333	23	.130	-0	114	-13		-1.1
1961	Was A★	10	10	.500	23	22	11-2	0	168.2	138	60	14	0	35-3	62	2.40	167	.224	.267	56-1-1	.179	2*	86	27		3.3
1962	Cle A★	20	10	.667	34	34	16-5	0	250.2	255	109	23	2	47-5	94	3.59	108	.263	.297	89-4-2	.180	6	107	10		1.6
1963	Cle A	11	13	.458	30	30	7-3	0	206	211	106	27	5	28-5	84	4.24	85	.265	.292	69-1-3	.130	-1*	102	-12		-1.5
1964	Cle A	7	9	.438	30	23	5	1	158.1	181	86	19	2	29-6	83	4.55	79	.290	.321	48-1-4	.146	3*	117	-15		-1.1
1965	Cle A	1	3	.250	12	3	0	0	22.2	32	15	6	0	6-0	12	5.96	58	.333	.373	6	.000	-1	76	-5		-0.9
Total	15	122	99	.552	345	273	101-25	5	2017.1	1988	909	198	45	495-49	880	3.67	104	.258	.305	694-15-18	.163	24	100	5		7.2

DONOVAN, BILL Willard Earl B7.6.1916 Maywood IL D9.25.1997 Maywood IL BB/TL/6-2/198 d4.19 Mil 1943-45

YEAR	TM LG	W	L	PCT	G	GS	CG-SHO	SV-BS	IP	H	R	HR	HB	BB-IB	SO	ERA	AERA	OAV	OOB	AB-HR-SH	AVG	PB	SUP	APR	DL	PW
1942	Bos N	3	6	.333	31	10	2	0	89.1	97	43	2	0	32	23	3.43	97	.283	.344	25-0-2	.240	1	75	-2		0.0
1943	Bos N	1	0	1.000	7	0	0	0	14.2	17	4	0	0	9	1	1.84	185	.304	.400	3	.333	0	2			0.2
Total	2	4	6	.400	38	10	2	0	104	114	47	2	0	41	24	3.20	105	.286	.352	28-0-2	.250	1	75	0		0.2

DONOVAN, BILL William Edward "Wild Bill" B10.13.1876 Lawrence MA D12.9.1923 Forsyth NY BR/TR/5-11/190 d4.22 M4/C1 ▲

YEAR	TM LG	W	L	PCT	G	GS	CG-SHO	SV-BS	IP	H	R	HR	HB	BB-IB	SO	ERA	AERA	OAV	OOB	AB-HR-SH	AVG	PB	SUP	APR	DL	PW
1898	Was N	1	6	.143	17	7	6	0	88	88	74	0	7	69	36	4.30	85	.259	.394	103-2-1	.165	-1*	41	-11		-0.8
1899	Bro N	1	2	.333	5	2	2	1	25	35	22	0	0	9	11	4.32	91	.330	.403	13	.231	-0	110	-3		-0.3
1900	Bro N	1	2	.333	5	4	2	0	31	36	23	0	3	18	13	6.68	57	.290	.393	13	.000	-2	104	-7		-0.6
1901	Bro N	25	15	.625	45	38	36-2	3	351	324	151	1	8	152	226	2.77	121	.244	.325	135-2-8	.170	-1*	117	23		2.2
1902	Bro N	17	15	.531	35	33	30-4	1	297.2	250	122	1	7	111	170	2.78	99	.228	.303	161-1-2	.174	-0*	98	1		0.1
1903	Det A	17	16	.515	35	34	34-4	0	307	247	104	5	10	95	187	2.29	127	.220	.284	124-0-9	.242	4*	106	25		3.0
1904	Det A	16	16	.500	34	34	30-3	0	293	251	111	5	10	94	137	2.46	104	.232	.300	140-1-5	.271	5*	100	4		1.1
1905	Det A	18	15	.545	34	32	27-5	0	280.2	236	111	2	10	101	135	2.60	105	.230	.305	130-0-13	.192	1*	100	5		0.7
1906	Det A	9	15	.375	25	25	22	0	211.2	221	92	4	8	72	85	3.15	88	.272	.337	91-0-4	.121	-5*	76	-7		-1.3
1907	†Det A	25	4	.862	32	28	27-3	1	271	222	96	3	8	82	123	2.19	119	.226	.291	109-0-4	.266	7*	156	13		1.9
1908	†Det A	18	7	.720	29	28	25-6	0	242.2	210	78	2	6	53	141	2.08	116	.231	.278	82-0-1	.159	0*	122	11		0.8
1909	†Det A	8	7	.533	21	17	13-4	2	140.1	121	50	0	6	60	76	2.31	109	.235	.322	45-0-5	.200	1*	97	3		0.3
1910	Det A	17	7	.708	26	23	20-3	0	206.2	184	74	4	7	61	107	2.44	108	.243	.305	69-0-2	.145	-2*	101	5		0.4
1911	Det A	10	9	.526	20	19	15-1	0	168.1	160	83	4	3	64	81	3.31	104	.250	.321	60-1-1	.200	3*	133	3		0.4
1912	Det A	1	0	1.000	3	0	0	0	10	5	2	0	1	2	6	0.90	362	.147	.216	13	.077	-1*	226	2		0.1
1915	NY A	0	3	.000	9	1	0	0	33.2	35	18	1	1	10	17	4.81	61	.278	.336	12	.083	-1*	99	-5		-0.6
1916	NY A	0	0	—	1	0	0	0	1	1	0	0	0	1	0	0.00	—	.250	.400	0	—	-1*	0			0.0
1918	Det A	1	0	1.000	2	1	0	0	6	5	1	0	0	1	1	1.50	177	.227	.261	2	.500	0	198	1		0.2
Total	18	185	139	.571	378	327	289-35	8	2964.2	2631	1212	30	90	1059	1552	2.69	106	.239	.310	1302-7-55	.193	8	108	63		7.2

DOPSON, JOHN John Robert B7.14.1963 Baltimore MD BL/TR/6-4/225(205-235) [MonN82 2/45] d9.4

YEAR	TM LG	W	L	PCT	G	GS	CG-SHO	SV-BS	IP	H	R	HR	HB	BB-IB	SO	ERA	AERA	OAV	OOB	AB-HR-SH	AVG	PB	SUP	APR	DL	PW
1985	Mon N	0	2	.000	4	3	0	0-0	13	25	17	4	0	4-0	4	11.08	31	.379	.414	4	.000	0	51	-11		-1.3
1988	Mon N	3	11	.214	26	26	1	0-0	168.2	150	69	15	1	58-3	101	3.04	120	.235	.299	51-0-4	.059	-3	80	9		0.3
1989	Bos A	12	8	.600	29	28	2	0-0	169.1	166	84	14	2	69-0	95	3.99	103	.257	.328	0	—	0	102	9	26	0.2
1990	Bos A	0	0	—	4	4	0	0-0	17.2	13	7	2	0	9-0	9	2.04	201	.200	.293	0	—	0	94	3	151	0.2
1991	Bos A	0	0	—	1	0	0	0-0	1	2	2	0	0	1-0	0	18.00	24	.500	.500	0	—	0		-1	148	-0.1
1992	Bos A	7	11	.389	25	25	0	0-0	141.1	159	78	17	2	38-2	55	4.08	104	.287	.334	0	—	0	80	1	41	0.1
1993	Bos A	7	11	.389	34	28	1-1	0	155.2	170*	93	16	2	59-12	89	4.97	93	.281	.343	0	—	0	98	-4		-0.3
1994	Cal A	1	4	.200	21	5	0	1-1	58.2	67	41	6	3	26-3	33	6.14	80	.288	.365	0	—	-1	71	-7	50	-0.5
Total	8	30	47	.390	144	119	4-1	1-1	725.1	752	391	74	10	264-20	386	4.27	98	.268	.331	55-0-4	.055	-3	89	-7	416	-1.2

DORAN, JOHN John F. B1867 Chicago IL TL/5-11/175 d4.11

YEAR	TM LG	W	L	PCT	G	GS	CG-SHO	SV-BS	IP	H	R	HR	HB	BB-IB	SO	ERA	AERA	OAV	OOB	AB-HR-SH	AVG	PB	SUP	APR	DL	PW
1891	Lou AA	5	10	.333	15	14	12-1	0	126	160	111	3	13	75	55	5.43	67	.299	.398	53	.189	-2	78	-23		-2.2

DORGAN, MIKE Michael Cornelius B10.2.1853 Middletown CT D4.26.1909 Hartford CT BR/TR/5-9/180 d5.8.1877 M3 b-Jerry ▲

YEAR	TM LG	W	L	PCT	G	GS	CG-SHO	SV-BS	IP	H	R	HR	HB	BB-IB	SO	ERA	AERA	OAV	OOB	AB-HR-SH	AVG	PB	SUP	APR	DL	PW
1879	Syr N	0	0	—	2	0	0	0	12	13	6	0		0	8	2.25	105	.260	.288	270-1	.267	0*		1		0.1
1880	Pro N	0	0	—	1	0	0	0	8	4	3	0		0	2	1.13	196	.138	.138	321	.246	0*		0		0.1
1883	NY N	0	1	.000	1	1	1	0	7	8	7	0		0	6	3.86	80	.286	.412	261	.234	0*	35	-1		-0.1
1884	NY N	8	6	.571	14	14	12	0	113	98	84	5		51	90	3.50	85	.215	.294	341-1	.276	2*	130	-8		-0.6
Total	4	8	7	.533	18	15	13	0	140	123	100	5		51	103	3.28	88	.218	.293	1193-2	.256	3	126	-8		-0.6

DORISH, HARRY Harry "Fritz" B7.13.1921 Swoyersville PA D12.31.2000 Wilkes-Barre PA BR/TR/5-11/206* d4.15 C5

YEAR	TM LG	W	L	PCT	G	GS	CG-SHO	SV-BS	IP	H	R	HR	HB	BB-IB	SO	ERA	AERA	OAV	OOB	AB-HR-SH	AVG	PB	SUP	APR	DL	PW
1947	Bos A	7	8	.467	41	19	7	2	136	149	80	6	1	54	50	4.70	83	.283	.351	35-0-4	.143	-1	94	-11		-1.3
1948	Bos A	1	1	.000	9	0	0	0	14.1	18	13	1	0	6	5	5.65	78	.281	.343	4	.250	-0		-3		-0.2
1949	Bos A	0	0	—	5	0	0	0	7.2	7	2	1	0	4	1	2.35	186	.241	.267	0	—	0		2		0.1
1950	StL A	4	9	.308	29	13	4	0	109	162	90	13	0	36	36	6.44	77	.337	.394	31-0-1	.161	0*	91	-16		-1.6
1951	Chi A	5	6	.455	32	4	2-1	0	96.2	101	50	6	0	31	29	3.54	114	.272	.328	31	.258	0	88	3		0.4
1952	Chi A	8	4	.667	39	1	0	11	91	96	28	4	1	42	47	2.47	148	.208	.303	22-0-2	.091	-1	72	12		1.8
1953	Chi A	10	6	.625	55	6	2	18	145.2	140	59	6	6	52	69	3.40	118	.254	.325	41-0-3	.171	-2	92	11		1.3
1954	Chi A	4	6	.400	35	2	2-1	6	109	88	35	9	1	29	48	2.72	137	.228	.282	27-0-2	.111	-2	106	13		1.0
1955	Bal A	2	0	1.000	13	0	0	1	17	16	4	0	0	9-1	6	1.59	249	.256	.352	3	.333	0		6		0.5
	Bal A	3	3	.500	35	1	0	6	65.2	58	25	1	1	28-2	22	3.15	121	.238	.318	10-0-1	.000	-1	0	6		0.5
	Year	5	3	.625	48	1	0	7	82.2	74	29	5	1	37-3	28	2.83	136	.242	.325	13-0-1	.077	-1	0	10		1.0
1956	Bal A	0	0	—	13	0	0	1	19.2	22	10	3	0	3-0	5	4.12	95	.282	.316	0	—	0	0			0.0
	Bos A	0	2	.000	15	0	0	0	22.2	23	10	1	0	10-1	11	3.57	129	.277	.351	0	—	0	3			0.3

YEAR	TM LG	W	L	PCT	G	GS	CG-SHO	SV-BS	IP	H	R	HR	HB	BB-IB	SO	ERA	AERA	OAV	OOB	AB-HR-SH	AVG	PB	SUP	APR	DL	PV
	Year	0	2	.000	28	0	0	0	42.1	45	20	4	0	13-1	15	3.83	112	.287	.335	0	—	0	2			0.3
Total	10	45	43	.511	323	40	13-2	44	834.1	850	406	58	19	301-4	332	3.83	106	.267	.333	204-0-13	.157	-6	95	24		2.4

DORNER, GUS　Augustus　B8.18.1876 Chambersburg PA　D5.4.1956 Chambersburg PA　BR/TR/5-10/176　d9.17

YEAR	TM LG	W	L	PCT	G	GS	CG-SHO	SV-BS	IP	H	R	HR	HB	BB-IB	SO	ERA	AERA	OAV	OOB	AB-HR-SH	AVG	PB	SUP	APR	DL	PV
															5	1.25	275	.244	.315	13-0-1	.385	2	63	7		1.1
1902	Cle A	3	1	.750	4	4	4-1	0	36	33	13	1	1	13	5											
1903	Cle A	3	5	.375	12	8	4-2	0	73.2	83	51	4	1	24	28	4.52	63	.283	.340	25-0-3	.080	-2	106	-12		-1.1
1906	Cin N	0	1	.000	2	1	1	0	15	16	5	0	1	4	5	1.20	230	.276	.333	5	.000	-1	26	2		0.5
	Bos N	8	25	.242	34	32	29	0	273.1	264	152	5	16	103	104	3.65	74	.260	.338	100-0-5	.140	-4	68	-28		-3.5
	Year	8	26	.235	36	33	30	0	288.1	280	157	5	17	107	109	3.53	76	.261	.338	105-0-5	.133	-5	66	-29		-3.1
1907	Bos N	12	16	.429	36	31	24-2	0	271.1	253	120	4	15	92	85	3.12	82	.255	.327	92-0-7	.130	-3	81	-15		-2.2
1908	Bos N	8	19	.296	38	28	14-3	0	216.1	176	120	4	15	77	41	3.54	68	.224	.305	67-0-5	.179	-1	103	-27		-3.3
1909	Bos N	1	2	.333	5	2	0	1	24.2	17	11	1	2	17	7	2.55	110	.198	.343	6-0-1	.167	-0	37	0		0.1
Total	6	35	69	.337	131	106	76-8	1	910.1	842	472	18	51	330	275	3.37	78	.250	.326	308-0-22	.149	-9	82	-73		-9.9

DORR, BERT　Charles Albert　B2.2.1862 NY　D6.16.1914 Dickinson NY　d8.24

YEAR	TM LG	W	L	PCT	G	GS	CG-SHO	SV-BS	IP	H	R	HR	HB	BB-IB	SO	ERA	AERA	OAV	OOB	AB-HR-SH	AVG	PB	SUP	APR	DL	PV
1882	StL AA	2	6	.250	8	8	8	0	66	53	39	0		1	34	2.59	108	.205	.208	26	.154	-2	64	2		0.4

DORSETT, CAL　Calvin Leavelle "Preacher"　B6.10.1913 Lone Oak TX　D10.22.1970 Elk City OK　BR/TR/6-0/180　d8.19　Mil 1942-45

YEAR	TM LG	W	L	PCT	G	GS	CG-SHO	SV-BS	IP	H	R	HR	HB	BB-IB	SO	ERA	AERA	OAV	OOB	AB-HR-SH	AVG	PB	SUP	APR	DL	PV
1940	Cle A	0	0	—	1	0	0	0	1	1	1	1	0	0	0	9.00	47	.250	.250			-0				0.0
1941	Cle A	0	1	.000	5	2	0	0	11.1	21	15	0	0	10	5	10.32	38	.382	.477	2	.000	-0	88	-9		-0.7
1947	Cle A	0	0	—	2	0	0	0	1.1	3	4	1	0	3	1	27.00	13	.500	.667	0-0-1	—	-0		-4		-0.4
Total	3	0	1	.000	8	2	0	0	13.2	25	20	2	0	13	6	11.85	33	.385	.487	2-0-1	.000	-0	88	-13		-0.9

DORSEY, JIM　James Edward　B8.2.1955 Oak Park IL　BR/TR/6-2/190*　[AnaA75*2/26]　d9.2　Col Los Angeles Valley (CA) JC

YEAR	TM LG	W	L	PCT	G	GS	CG-SHO	SV-BS	IP	H	R	HR	HB	BB-IB	SO	ERA	AERA	OAV	OOB	AB-HR-SH	AVG	PB	SUP	APR	DL	PV
1980	Cal A	1	2	.333	4	4	0	0-0	15.2	25	16	2	1	8-0	4	9.19	43	.368	.436	0	—	0	96	-8		-1.7
1984	Bos A	0	0	—	2	0	0	0-0	2.2	6	3	0	0	2-0	4	10.13	42	.462	.533	0	—	0	63	-9		-1.0
1985	Bos A	0	1	.000	2	1	0	0-0	5.1	12	12	2	0	10-1	6	20.25	21	.444	.595	0	—	0	88	-18		-2.1
Total	3	1	3	.250	8	5	0	0-0	23.2	43	31	4	1	20-1	14	11.79	34	.398	.492	0	—	0	88	-35		-4.8

DORSEY, JERRY　Michael Jeremiah　B1.1856 , Can　D11.3.1938 Auburn NY　BL　d7.9

YEAR	TM LG	W	L	PCT	G	GS	CG-SHO	SV-BS	IP	H	R	HR	HB	BB-IB	SO	ERA	AERA	OAV	OOB	AB-HR-SH	AVG	PB	SUP	APR	DL	PV
1884	Bal U	0	1	.000	1	1	0	0	4	7	8	1		0	3	9.00	30	.368	.368	3	.000	-1	32	-3		-0.6

DOSCHER, JACK　John Henry Jr.　B7.27.1880 Troy NY　D5.27.1971 Park Ridge NJ　BL/TL/6-1/205　d7.2　f-Herm　Col Fordham

YEAR	TM LG	W	L	PCT	G	GS	CG-SHO	SV-BS	IP	H	R	HR	HB	BB-IB	SO	ERA	AERA	OAV	OOB	AB-HR-SH	AVG	PB	SUP	APR	DL	PV
1903	Chi N	0	1	.000	1	1	0	0	3	6	5	0	1	2	5	12.00	26	.429	.529	1	.000	-0	43	-3		-0.6
	Bro N	0	0	—	3	0	0	0	7	8	8	1	1	9	4	7.71	41	.296	.486	3	.000	-0		-3		-0.3
	Year	0	1	.000	4	1	0	0	10	14	13	1	2	11	9	9.00	35	.341	.500	4	.000	-1	42	-6		-0.9
1904	Bro N	0	0	—	2	0	0	0	6.1	1	1	0	0	1	2	0.00	—	.053	.100	2	.500	0		2		0.2
1905	Bro N	1	5	.167	12	7	6	0	71	60	34	1	3	30	33	3.17	91	.232	.318	24-0-1	.083	-2	78	-2		-0.6
1906	Bro N	0	1	.000	2	1	0	0	14	12	3	0	0	4	10	1.29	196	.250	.308	5	.000	-1	0	2		0.3
1908	Cin N	1	3	.250	7	4	3	0	44.1	31	19	1	3	22	7	1.83	126	.196	.306	15	.133	-3	53	0		0.5
Total	5	2	10	.167	27	13	10	0	145.2	118	70	3	8	68	61	2.84	95	.225	.323	50-0-1	.100	-3	63	-4		-0.7

DOTEL, OCTAVIO　Octavio Eduardo (Diaz)　B11.25.1973 Santo Domingo, D.R.　BR/TR/6-0/175(175-210)　d6.26

YEAR	TM LG	W	L	PCT	G	GS	CG-SHO	SV-BS	IP	H	R	HR	HB	BB-IB	SO	ERA	AERA	OAV	OOB	AB-HR-SH	AVG	PB	SUP	APR	DL	PV
1999	†NY N	8	3	.727	19	14	0	0-0	85.1	69	52	12	6	49-1	85	5.38	81	.226	.340	24-0-1	.125	1	122	-10		-1.2
2000	Hou N	3	7	.300	50	16	0	16-7	125	127	80	26	6	61-3	142	5.40	91	.265	.351	32-0-7	.031	-3	92	-6		-0.7
2001	†Hou N	7	5	.583	61	4	0	2-2	105	79	35	5	2	47-2	145	2.66	173	.205	.294	11-0-1	.091	-1	101	21		2.7
2002	Hou N	6	4	.600	83	0	0	6-4	97.1	58	21	7	4	27-2	118	1.85	234	.173	.239	1	.000	-0		26		2.9
2003	Hou N	6	4	.600	76	0	0	4-2	87	53	25	9	3	31-2	97	2.48	178	.172	.253	6	.000	-1		19		2.4
2004	Hou N	2	4	.000	32	0	0	14-3	34.2	27	15	4	1	15-4	50	3.12	140	.213	.299	0	—	0		4		0.7
	Oak A	6	2	.750	45	0	0	22-6	50.2	41	23	9	3	18-3	72	4.09	113	.220	.298	0	—	0		2	137	0.8
2005	Oak A	1	2	.333	15	0	0	7-4	15.1	10	6	2	0	11-2	16	3.52	127	.185	.323	0	—	-4	108	60	137	0.3
Total	7	37	31	.544	381	34	0	71-28	600.1	464	257	74	26	259-19	725	3.13	150	.213	.301	74-0-9	.068	-4	108	60	137	7.8

DOTSON, RICHARD　Richard Elliott　B1.10.1959 Cincinnati OH　BR/TR/6-0/204(185-205)　[CalA77 1/7]　d9.4

YEAR	TM LG	W	L	PCT	G	GS	CG-SHO	SV-BS	IP	H	R	HR	HB	BB-IB	SO	ERA	AERA	OAV	OOB	AB-HR-SH	AVG	PB	SUP	APR	DL	PV
1979	Chi A	2	0	1.000	5	5	1-1	0-0	24.1	28	13	0	0	6-0	13	3.70	115	.286	.321	0	—	0	128	1		0.4
1980	Chi A	12	10	.545	33	32	8	0-0	198	185	105	20	4	87-2	109	4.27	95	.247	.328	0	—	0*	99	-3		-0.7
1981	Chi A	9	8	.529	24	24	5-4	0-0	141	145	67	13	4	49-0	73	3.77	96	.270	.333	0	—	0	92	5		0.4
1982	Chi A	11	15	.423	34	31	3-1	0-0	196.2	219	97	19	8	73-4	109	3.84	106	.282	.345	0	—	0	127	27		2.1
1983	†Chi A	22	7	.759	35	35	8-1	0-0	240	209	92	19	8	106-1	120	3.23	131	.240	.325	0	—	0*	92	14		1.5
1984	Chi A★	14	15	.483	32	32	14-1	0-0	245.2	216	110	24	7	103-5	120	3.59	117	.238	.317	0	—	0	65	-1	132	-0.0
1985	Chi A	3	4	.429	9	9	0	0-0	52.1	53	30	4	1	17-1	33	4.47	97	.261	.324	0	—	0	81	-21		-1.9
1986	Chi A	10	17	.370	34	34	3-1	0-0	197	226	125	24	2	69-2	110	5.48	79	.289	.347	0	—	0	78	9		0.6
1987	Chi A	11	12	.478	31	31	7-2	0-0	211.1	201	109	24	0	86-2	114	4.17	111	.249	.320	0	—	0	130	-20	17	-1.8
1988	NY A	12	9	.571	32	29	4	0-0	171	178	103	27	4	72-3	77	5.00	79	.266	.338	0	—	0	101	-9		-0.9
1989	NY A	2	5	.286	11	9	1	0-0	51.2	69	33	8	1	17-0	14	5.57	70	.317	.366	0	—	0	99	-2		-0.5
	Chi A	3	7	.300	17	17	1	0-0	99.2	112	51	8	0	41-3	55	3.88	99	.282	.348	0	—	0	99	-11		-0.9
	Year	5	12	.294	28	26	2	0-0	151.1	181	84	16	1	58-3	69	4.46	86	.294	.354	0	—	0	94	-14		-1.4
1990	KC A	0	4	.000	8	7	0	0-0	28.2	43	29	3	0	14-1	9	8.48	46	.355	.410	0	—	0	101	-16	149	-1.5
Total	12	111	113	.496	305	295	55-11	0-0	1857.1	1884	964	194	40	740-24	973	4.23	98	.264	.334	0	—	0				-4.4

DOTTER, GARY　Gary Richard　B8.7.1942 St.Louis MO　BL/TL/6-1/180*　d9.10

YEAR	TM LG	W	L	PCT	G	GS	CG-SHO	SV-BS	IP	H	R	HR	HB	BB-IB	SO	ERA	AERA	OAV	OOB	AB-HR-SH	AVG	PB	SUP	APR	DL	PV
1961	Min A	0	0	—	2	0	0	0	6	6	6	0	0	4-1	2	9.00	47	.273	.357	1	.000	-0		-3		-0.3
1963	Min A	0	0	—	2	0	0	0	2	0	0	0	0	0-0	2	0.00	—	.000	.000	0	—	0		1		0.1
1964	Min A	0	0	—	4	0	0	0	4.1	3	2	1	0	3-0	6	2.08	172	.188	.316	0	—	-0		0		0.2
Total	3	0	0	—	8	0	0	0	12.1	9	8	1	0	7-1	10	5.11	76	.205	.302	1	.000	-0		-2		-0.1

DOTY, BABE　Elmer L.　B12.17.1867 Lyons NY　D11.20.1929 Toledo OH　BL/TR/6-0/160　d8.18

YEAR	TM LG	W	L	PCT	G	GS	CG-SHO	SV-BS	IP	H	R	HR	HB	BB-IB	SO	ERA	AERA	OAV	OOB	AB-HR-SH	AVG	PB	SUP	APR	DL	PV
1890	Tol AA	1	0	1.000	1	1	1	0	9	9	1	0	0	1	4	1.00	395	.250	.270	3	.000	-0	85	3		0.4

DOUGHERTY, JIM　James E.　B3.8.1968 Brentwood NY　BR/TR/6-0/210(210-225)　[HouN90 26/703]　d4.27　Col North Carolina-Asheville

YEAR	TM LG	W	L	PCT	G	GS	CG-SHO	SV-BS	IP	H	R	HR	HB	BB-IB	SO	ERA	AERA	OAV	OOB	AB-HR-SH	AVG	PB	SUP	APR	DL	PV
1995	Hou N	8	4	.667	56	0	0	0-2	67.2	76	37	7	3	25-1	49	4.92	78	.292	.357	8-0-1	.125	—		-6		-0.6
1996	Hou N	0	2	.000	12	0	0	0-1	13	14	14	2	1	11-1	6	9.00	43	.280	.413	0	—	0		-8		-0.8
1998	Oak A	0	2	.000	9	0	0	0-1	12	17	11	2	1	7-0	3	8.25	56	.340	.431	0	—	0		-4		-0.4
1999	Pit N	0	0	—	2	0	0	0-0	2	3	3	0	0	3-0	1	9.00	51	.333	.500	0	—	0		-1		-0.1
Total	4	8	8	.500	79	0	0	0-4	94.2	110	65	11	5	46-2	59	5.99	66	.298	.380	8-0-1	.125	0		-19		-1.9

DOUGHERTY, TOM　Thomas James "Sugar Boy"　B5.30.1881 Chicago IL　D11.6.1953 Milwaukee WI　BL/TR/5-11.5/195　d4.24

YEAR	TM LG	W	L	PCT	G	GS	CG-SHO	SV-BS	IP	H	R	HR	HB	BB-IB	SO	ERA	AERA	OAV	OOB	AB-HR-SH	AVG	PB	SUP	APR	DL	PV
1904	Chi A	1	0	1.000	1	0	0	0	2	0	0	0	1	0	0	0.00	—	.000	.000	1	.000	-0		1		0.1

DOUGLAS, WHAMMY　Charles William　B2.17.1935 Carrboro NC　BR/TR/6-2/185　d7.29

YEAR	TM LG	W	L	PCT	G	GS	CG-SHO	SV-BS	IP	H	R	HR	HB	BB-IB	SO	ERA	AERA	OAV	OOB	AB-HR-SH	AVG	PB	SUP	APR	DL	PV
1957	Pit N	3	3	.500	11	8	0	0	47	48	23	5	3	30-2	28	3.26	116	.270	.384	16	.063	-1	93	1		0.1

DOUGLAS, LARRY　Lawrence Howard　B6.5.1890 Jellico TN　D11.4.1949 Jellico TN　6-3/175　d6.17

YEAR	TM LG	W	L	PCT	G	GS	CG-SHO	SV-BS	IP	H	R	HR	HB	BB-IB	SO	ERA	AERA	OAV	OOB	AB-HR-SH	AVG	PB	SUP	APR	DL	PV
1915	Bal F	0	1	.000	2	0	0	0	3	1	1	0	0	2	1	3.00	96	.273	.385	0	—	0	0	0		0.0

DOUGLAS, PHIL　Phillip Brooks "Shufflin' Phil"　B6.17.1890 Cedartown GA　D8.1.1952 Sequatchie TN　BR/TR/6-3/190　d8.30

YEAR	TM LG	W	L	PCT	G	GS	CG-SHO	SV-BS	IP	H	R	HR	HB	BB-IB	SO	ERA	AERA	OAV	OOB	AB-HR-SH	AVG	PB	SUP	APR	DL	PV
1912	Chi A	0	1	.000	3	1	0	0	12.1	21	17	0	0	6	7	7.30	44	.382	.443	2-0-1	.000	-0	46	-7		-0.7
1914	Cin N	11	18	.379	45	25	13	1	239.1	186	111	7	11	92	121	2.56	115	.223	.308	73-0-4	.137	-2	91	5		0.6
1915	Cin N	1	5	.167	8	7	0	0	46.2	53	35	0	0	23	29	5.40	53	.299	.380	17	.118	-1	97	-12		-1.2
	Bro N	5	5	.500	20	13	5-1	0	116.2	104	45	1	5	17	63	2.62	106	.241	.278	39	.154	-1	101	2		0.2
	Chi N	1	1	.500	4	4	2-1	0	25	17	9	0	1	7	18	2.16	129	.187	.253	8	.000	-1	100	1		0.2
	Year	7	11	.389	32	24	7-2	0	188.1	174	89	1	6	47	110	2.55	114	.250	.287	64	.125	-3	100	-8		-0.8
1917	Chi N	14	20	.412	51	37	20-5	1	293.1	269	123	13	6	50	151	2.55	114	.246	.285	87-0-7	.255	1	90	9		1.2
1918	†Chi N	10	9	.526	25	19	11-2	1	156.2	145	57	2	1	31	51	2.13	131	.252	.285	51-0-3	.157	-2	93	14		1.4
1919	Chi N	10	6	.625	25	19	8-4	0	161.2	133	52	0	2	34	63	2.00	144	.230	.288	53-0-2	.208	-3	90	1		0.1
	NY N	2	4	.333	8	6	4-1	0	51.1	53	22	0	1	6	21	2.10	133	.264	.288	15-0-1	.000	-1	92	15		1.5
	Year	12	10	.545	33	25	12-4	0	213	186	74	0	3	40	84	2.03	141	.238	.278	66-0-4	.121	-4	92	15		1.5
1920	NY N	14	10	.583	46	21	10-3	2	226	225	74	6	2	55	71	2.71	111	.263	.309	73-0-2	.151	-4	125	8		0.8

YEAR	TM LG	W	L	PCT	G	GS	CG-SHO	SV-BS	IP	H	R	HR	HB	BB-IB	SO	ERA	AERA	OAV	OOB	AB-HR-SH	AVG	PB	SUP	APR	DL	PW
1921	†NY N	15	10	.600	40	27	13-3	2	221.2	266	119	17	2	55	55	4.22	87	.308	.351	81-1-5	.198	0	147	-13		-1.2
1922	NY N	11	4	.733	24	21	9-1	0	157.2	154	56	6	4	35	33	2.63	152	.257	.302	58-1-1	.207	1	115	25		2.1
Total	9	94	93	.503	299	200	95-20	8	1708.1	1626	730	52	35	411	683	2.80	111	.256	.305	559-2-26	.161	-16	105	41		3.1

DOUGLASS, SEAN　Sean Reed B4.28.1979 Lancaster CA　BR/TR/6-6/198(198-220)　[BalA97 2/73]　d7.18

YEAR	TM LG	W	L	PCT	G	GS	CG-SHO	SV-BS	IP	H	R	HR	HB	BB-IB	SO	ERA	AERA	OAV	OOB	AB-HR-SH	AVG	PB	SUP	APR	DL	PW
2001	Bal A	2	1	.667	4	4	0	0-0	20.1	21	12	3	1	11-0	17	5.31	81	.259	.351	0		0	124	-2		-0.2
2002	Bal A	0	5	.000	15	8	0	0-0	53.1	58	41	10	2	35-2	44	6.08	71	.283	.391	0	—	0	88	-12		-0.9
2003	Bal A	0	0	—	3	0	0	0-0	8	14	12	2	1	6-0	3	13.50	34	.378	.477	0	—	0		-7		-0.3
2004	Tor A	0	2	.000	14	3	0	0-0	38.2	37	27	6	2	28-4	36	6.28	78	.252	.374	0	—	0	76	-5		-0.3
2005	Det A	5	5	.500	18	16	0	0-0	87.1	92	57	13	2	33-2	55	5.56	76	.276	.340	0	—	0	110	-12		-1.2
Total	5	7	13	.350	54	31	0	0-0	207.2	222	149	34	8	113-8	155	6.11	72	.276	.368	2	.000	-0	100	-38		-2.9

DOWD, SKIP　James Joseph B2.16.1889 Holyoke MA D12.20.1960 Holyoke MA　BR/TR/5-10.5/160　d7.5　Col Holy Cross

YEAR	TM LG	W	L	PCT	G	GS	CG-SHO	SV-BS	IP	H	R	HR	HB	BB-IB	SO	ERA	AERA	OAV	OOB	AB-HR-SH	AVG	PB	SUP	APR	DL	PW
1910	Pit N	0	0	—	1	0	0		2	4	4	0	1	2	1	0.00	—	.400	.538	0		0		-1		0.0

DOWLING, DAVE　David Barclay B8.23.1942 Baton Rouge LA　BR/TL/6-2/182*　d10.3　Col California-Davis

YEAR	TM LG	W	L	PCT	G	GS	CG-SHO	SV-BS	IP	H	R	HR	HB	BB-IB	SO	ERA	AERA	OAV	OOB	AB-HR-SH	AVG	PB	SUP	APR	DL	PW
1964	StL N	0	0	—	1	0	0	0	.1	2	0	0	0	0-0	0	0.00	—	.400	.400	0		0		0		0.0
1966	Chi N	1	0	1.000	1	1	1	0	9	10	2	0	0	0-0	3	2.00	184	.270	.270	2-0-2	.000	-0	167	2		0.2
Total	2	1	0	1.000	2	1	1	0	10	12	2	0	0	0-0	3	1.80	205	.286	.286	2-0-2	.000	-0	167	2		0.2

DOWLING, PETE　Henry Peter B St.Louis MO D6.30.1905 Hot Lake OR　BL/TL/5-11/165　d7.17

YEAR	TM LG	W	L	PCT	G	GS	CG-SHO	SV-BS	IP	H	R	HR	HB	BB-IB	SO	ERA	AERA	OAV	OOB	AB-HR-SH	AVG	PB	SUP	APR	DL	PW
1897	Lou N	1	2	.333	4	4	2	0	26	39	30	0	6	8	3	5.88	72	.342	.414	10	.200	-0	121	-6		-0.5
1898	Lou N	13	20	.394	36	32	30	0	285.2	284	176	7	22	120	84	4.16	86	.257	.342	107-0-2	.196	1	85	-19		-1.7
1899	Lou N	13	17	.433	35	33	30	0	298.1	329	166	6	17	95	89	3.05	127	.279	.342	119-0-2	.227	-1	90	22		1.7
1901	Mil A	1	3	.250	10	4	3	1	49.2	71	49	1	4	14	25	5.62	64	.332	.384	19	.211	1	103	-12		-0.7
	Cle A	11	22	.333	33	30	28-2	0	256.1	269	160	1	15	104	99	3.86	92	.267	.344	99-1-1	.162	-4	71	-6		-1.0
	Year	12	25	.324	43	34	31-2	1	306	340	209	2	19	118	124	4.15	86	.278	.351	118-1-1	.169	-3	75	-21		-1.7
Total	4	39	64	.379	118	103	93-2	1	916	992	581	16	64	341	300	3.84	96	.274	.347	354-1-5	.198	-3	85	-21		-2.2

DOWNING, AL　Alphonso Erwin B6.28.1941 Trenton NJ　BR/TL/5-11/177*　d7.19　Col Rider

YEAR	TM LG	W	L	PCT	G	GS	CG-SHO	SV-BS	IP	H	R	HR	HB	BB-IB	SO	ERA	AERA	OAV	OOB	AB-HR-SH	AVG	PB	SUP	APR	DL	PW
1961	NY A	0	1	.000	5	2	0	0	23	7	8	0	.1	12-0	12	8.00	46	.212	.426	1	.000	-0	48	-4		-0.4
1962	NY A	0	0	—	1	0	0	0	1	0	0	0	0	0-0	1	0.00	—	.000	.000	0	—	0	0	0		0.0
1963	†NY A	13	5	.722	24	22	10-4	0	175.2	114	52	7	0	80-1	171	2.56	137	.184	.277	58-0-3	.103	-2	106	21		1.8
1964	†NY A	13	8	.619	37	35	11-1	2	244	201	104	18	0	120-5	217	3.47	104	.223	.312	85-0-4	.176	1*	107	4		0.4
1965	NY A	12	14	.462	35	32	8-2	0	212	185	92	16	2	105-2	179	3.40	100	.237	.326	74-1-6	.108	-1*	104	0		-0.1
1966	NY A	10	11	.476	30	30	1	0	200	178	90	23	1	79-3	152	3.56	94	.235	.307	70-0-5	.100	-2	109	-5		-0.9
1967	NY A★	14	10	.583	31	28	10-4	0	201.2	158	65	13	6	61-1	171	2.63	119	.217	.281	66-1-1	.121	1	88	13		1.7
1968	NY A	3	3	.500	15	12	1	0	61.1	54	24	7	1	20-2	40	3.52	83	.237	.299	17	.176	-0	65	-2	31	-0.2
1969	NY A	7	5	.583	30	15	5-1	0-0	130.2	117	57	12	0	49-6	85	3.38	104	.240	.306	44-0-2	.136	-0	112	2		0.0
1970	Oak A	3	3	.500	10	6	1	0-0	41	39	19	5	1	22-0	26	3.95	89	.252	.346	11-0-1	.182	-0	122	-1		-0.1
	Mil A	2	10	.167	17	16	1	0-0	94.1	79	47	8	3	59-2	53	3.34	113	.232	.346	24-0-7	.083	-2	58	1		0.0
	Year	5	13	.278	27	22	2	0-0	135.1	118	66	13	4	81-2	79	3.52	105	.238	.346	35-0-8	.114	-2	74	-1		-0.1
1971	LA N	20	9	.690	37	36	12-5	0	262.1	245	93	16	3	84-3	136	2.68	122	.247	.307	92-0-8	.174	2	126	15		1.9
1972	LA N	9	9	.500	31	30	7-4	0	202.2	196	81	13	7	67-2	117	2.98	113	.254	.317	66-0-6	.121	-1	116	9		0.9
1973	LA N	9	9	.500	30	28	5-2	0-0	193	155	87	19	1	68-3	124	3.31	105	.219	.288	57-0-7	.088	-1	110	1		0.9
1974	†LA N	5	6	.455	21	16	1-1	0-1	98.1	94	52	7	3	45-0	63	3.66	94	.255	.338	29-0-3	.172	-0	132	-5		-0.5
1975	LA N	2	1	.667	22	6	0	1-2	74.2	59	31	6	2	28-1	39	2.89	118	.215	.292	16	.000	-1	103	3		0.1
1976	LA N	1	2	.333	17	3	0	0-0	46.2	43	21	3	0	18-1	30	3.86	88	.250	.318	6	.000	-1	52	-2		-0.2
1977	LA N	0	1	.000	12	1	0	0-0	20	22	15	4	0	16-0	23	6.75	57	.278	.400	1	.000	-0	115	-6	21	-0.3
Total	17	123	107	.535	405	317	73-24	3-3	2268.1	1946	938	177	31	933-32	1639	3.22	106	.232	.309	717-2-53	.127	-7	105	44	52	4.1

DOWNS, DAVE　David Ralph B6.21.1952 Logan UT　BR/TR/6-5/220　[PhiN70 6/128]　d9.2　b-Kelly

YEAR	TM LG	W	L	PCT	G	GS	CG-SHO	SV-BS	IP	H	R	HR	HB	BB-IB	SO	ERA	AERA	OAV	OOB	AB-HR-SH	AVG	PB	SUP	APR	DL	PW
1972	Phi N	1	1	.500	4	4	1-1	0-0	23	20	7	1	1	3-0	9	2.74	132	.294	.326	8	.250	0	80	2		0.2

DOWNS, KELLY　Kelly Robert B10.25.1960 Ogden UT　BR/TR/6-4/200*　[PhiN79 26/661]　d7.29　b-Dave

YEAR	TM LG	W	L	PCT	G	GS	CG-SHO	SV-BS	IP	H	R	HR	HB	BB-IB	SO	ERA	AERA	OAV	OOB	AB-HR-SH	AVG	PB	SUP	APR	DL	PW
1986	SF N	4	4	.500	14	14	1	0-0	88.1	78	29	5	2	30-7	64	2.75	128	.236	.302	29	.172	0*	81	9		0.8
1987	†SF N	12	9	.571	41	28	4-3	1-0	186	185	83	14	4	67-11	137	3.63	106	.258	.324	56-0-7	.143	-0	94	5		0.2
1988	SF N	13	9	.591	27	26	6-3	0-0	168	140	67	11	3	47-8	118	3.32	98	.225	.279	54-0-4	.167	2	148	4	33	0.3
1989	†SF N	4	8	.333	18	15	0	0-0	82.2	82	47	7	1	26-4	49	4.79	71	.261	.316	22-0-3	.091	-1	80	-12	103	-1.8
1990	SF N	3	2	.600	13	9	0	0-0	63	56	26	2	2	20-4	31	3.43	107	.233	.297	13-0-3	.000	-1	93	2	123	0.0
1991	SF N	10	4	.714	45	11	0	0-2	111.2	99	59	12	3	53-9	62	4.19	86	.239	.297	23-0-2	.087	-1	73	-9	9	-1.1
1992	SF N	1	2	.333	19	7	0	0-0	62.1	65	27	4	3	24-0	33	3.47	96	.275	.347	14-0-2	.000	-1	97	-1		-0.3
	†Oak A	5	5	.500	18	13	0	0-0	82	72	36	4	4	46-0	38	3.29	115	.237	.341	0	—	0	97	4		0.4
1993	Oak A	5	10	.333	42	12	0	0-1	119.2	135	80	14	2	60-8	66	5.64	73	.287	.368	0	—	0	93	-21		-2.3
Total	8	57	53	.518	237	135	11-6	1-3	963.2	912	454	73	25	373-54	598	3.86	94	.250	.321	211-0-21	.123	-2	99	-23	268	-3.8

DOWNS, SCOTT　Scott Jeremy B3.17.1976 Louisville KY　BL/TL/6-2/190*　[ChiN97 3/94]　d4.9　Col Kentucky　[DL 2002 Mon N 71]

YEAR	TM LG	W	L	PCT	G	GS	CG-SHO	SV-BS	IP	H	R	HR	HB	BB-IB	SO	ERA	AERA	OAV	OOB	AB-HR-SH	AVG	PB	SUP	APR	DL	PW
2000	Chi N	4	3	.571	18	18	0	0-0	94	117	59	13	5	37-1	63	5.17	89	.310	.375	26-0-4	.077	-1	116	-7		-0.6
	Mon N	0	0	—	1	1	0	0-0	3	5	3	0	0	3-0	0	9.00	52	.385	.500	2	.000	-0	175	-1	53	-0.1
	Year	4	3	.571	19	19	0	0-0	97	122	62	13	5	40-1	63	5.29	87	.312	.380	28-0-4	.071	-1	119	-8		-0.7
2003	Mon N	1	0	1.000	1	1	0	0-0	3	5	5	2	0	3-2	4	15.00	30	.357	.471	1	.000	-0	42	-3		-0.5
2004	Mon N	3	6	.333	12	12	1-1	0-0	63	79	47	9	3	23-2	38	5.14	89	.310	.372	15-0-6	.067	-1	82	-7		-0.6
2005	Tor A	3	4	.571	26	13	0	0-0	94	93	49	12	5	34-0	75	4.31	107	.253	.324	0	—	0	98	3		0.3
Total	4	11	13	.458	58	45	1-1	0-0	257	299	163	36	13	100-5	180	5.08	92	.291	.360	44-0-10	.068	-2	102	-15	124	-1.8

DOYLE, JESS　Jesse Herbert B4.14.1898 Knoxville TN D4.15.1961 Belleville IL　BR/TR/5-11/175　d4.14

YEAR	TM LG	W	L	PCT	G	GS	CG-SHO	SV-BS	IP	H	R	HR	HB	BB-IB	SO	ERA	AERA	OAV	OOB	AB-HR-SH	AVG	PB	SUP	APR	DL	PW
1925	Det A	4	7	.364	45	3	0	8	118.1	158	83	6	5	50	31	5.93	73	.340	.410	33-2-0	.242	3	98	-18		-1.4
1926	Det A	0	0	—	2	0	0	1	4.1	6	3	0	0	1	2	4.15	98	.316	.350	1-0-1	1.000	0		0		0.0
1927	Det A	0	0	—	7	0	0	0	12.1	16	11	0	0	5	5	8.03	52	.314	.375	3	.333	0		-2		-0.2
1931	StL A	0	0	—	1	0	0	0	1	3	3	1	0	1	0	27.00	17	.500	.571	0	—	0		-2		-0.1
Total	4	4	7	.364	55	3	0	9	136	183	100	6	5	57	38	6.22	69	.338	.406	37-2-1	.270	4	98	-24		-1.7

DOYLE, JOHN　John Aloysius B1858 Halifax NS, Can. D12.24.1915 Providence RI　TR/5-10/160　d7.26　Col Fordham

YEAR	TM LG	W	L	PCT	G	GS	CG-SHO	SV-BS	IP	H	R	HR	HB	BB-IB	SO	ERA	AERA	OAV	OOB	AB-HR-SH	AVG	PB	SUP	APR	DL	PW
1882	StL AA	0	3	.000	3	3	3	0	24	41	33	0		3	5	2.63	107	.353	.370	11	.182	-0	24	-3		-0.4

DOYLE, SLOW JOE　Judd Bruce B9.15.1881 Clay Center KS D11.21.1947 Tannersville NY　BR/TR/5-8/150　d8.25

YEAR	TM LG	W	L	PCT	G	GS	CG-SHO	SV-BS	IP	H	R	HR	HB	BB-IB	SO	ERA	AERA	OAV	OOB	AB-HR-SH	AVG	PB	SUP	APR	DL	PW
1906	NY A	2	1	.667	9	6	3-2	0	45.1	34	15	1	1	13	28	2.38	124	.211	.274	14	.214	-0	81	3		0.2
1907	NY A	11	11	.500	29	23	15-1	1	193.2	169	86	2	6	67	94	2.65	105	.237	.308	58-0-4	.138	-1	92	2		0.0
1908	NY A	1	1	.500	12	4	2-1	0	48	42	24	1	2	14	20	2.63	94	.235	.297	14	.214	-0	110	-2		-0.1
1909	NY A	8	6	.571	17	15	8-3	0	125.2	103	49	3	2	37	57	2.58	98	.232	.294	42-0-2	.167	0	132	1		-0.1
1910	NY A	0	2	.000	3	2	1	0	12.1	19	13	0	1	5	4	8.03	33	.367	.431	4	.250	-0	38	-6		-0.8
	Cin N	0	0	—	5	0	0	0	11.1	16	19	0	0	11	6	6.35	46	.327	.450	3	.000	-0		-7		-0.2
Total	5	22	21	.512	75	50	29-7	1	436.1	383	206	7	12	147	209	2.85	95	.240	.308	135-0-6	.163	-1	101	-9		-1.2

DOYLE, PAUL　Paul Sinnott B10.2.1939 Philadelphia PA　BL/TL/5-11/172*　d5.28

YEAR	TM LG	W	L	PCT	G	GS	CG-SHO	SV-BS	IP	H	R	HR	HB	BB-IB	SO	ERA	AERA	OAV	OOB	AB-HR-SH	AVG	PB	SUP	APR	DL	PW
1969	†Atl N	2	0	1.000	36	0	0	4-3	39	31	9	4	0	16-3	25	2.08	174	.231	.307	3	.000	-0		6		0.5
1970	Cal A	3	1	.750	40	0	0	5-2	42	43	25	7	1	21-3	34	5.14	70	.267	.355	3	.000	-0		-6		-0.7
	SD N	0	2	.000	9	0	0	0-0	7	9	5	0	0	6-1	2	6.43	62	.360	.455	1	.000	-0		-2		-0.3
1972	Cal A	0	0	—	2	0	0	0-0	2.1	2	0	0	0	3-0	4	0.00	—	.250	.455	0	—	0		1		0.1
Total	3	5	3	.625	87	0	0	11-5	90.1	85	39	11	1	46-7	65	3.79	96	.259	.348	7	.000	-1		0		-0.4

DOYLE, CARL　William Carl B7.30.1912 Knoxville TN D9.4.1951 Knoxville TN　BR/TR/6-1/185　d8.5

YEAR	TM LG	W	L	PCT	G	GS	CG-SHO	SV-BS	IP	H	R	HR	HB	BB-IB	SO	ERA	AERA	OAV	OOB	AB-HR-SH	AVG	PB	SUP	APR	DL	PW
1935	Phi A	2	7	.222	14	9	3	0	79.2	86	63	3	2	72	34	5.99	76	.282	.422	30	.133	-2	85	-13		-1.4
1936	Phi A	0	3	.000	8	6	1	0	38.2	66	53	4	5	29	12	10.94	47	.369	.469	15	.267	-1	126	-24		-1.3
1939	Bro N	2	0	.333	5	1	1-1	1	17.2	18	5	1	0	7	7	1.02	395	.136	.227	6	.167	0	174	5		0.8
1940	Bro N	0	0	—	3	0	0	1	5.2	18	17	3	4	6	1	27.00	15	.545	.651	1	1.000	1		-13		-0.5
	StL N	3	3	.500	21	5	1	0	81	99	57	7	6	41	44	5.89	68	.294	.380	30-1-0	.200	-1	100	-14		-0.8

YEAR	TM LG	W	L	PCT	G	GS	CG-SHO	SV-BS	IP	H	R	HR	HB	BB-IB	SO	ERA	AERA	OAV	OOB	AB-HR-SH	AVG	PB	SUP	APR	DL	PW
	Year	3	3	.500	24	5	0	1	86.2	117	74	10	10	47	48	7.27	55	.316	.407	31-1-0	.226	2	100	-28		-1.3
Total	4	6	15	.286	51	21	6-1	2	222.2	277	195	18	17	155	101	6.95	63	.303	.414	82-1-0	.195	1	109	-59		-3.2

DOZIER, TOM   Thomas Dean   B9.5.1961 San Pablo CA   BR/TR/6-2/190   [StLN79 11/266]   d5.17

YEAR	TM LG	W	L	PCT	G	GS	CG-SHO	SV-BS	IP	H	R	HR	HB	BB-IB	SO	ERA	AERA	OAV	OOB	AB-HR-SH	AVG	PB	SUP	APR	DL	PW
1986	Oak A	0	0	—	4	0	0	0-0	6.1	6	6	1	0	5-1	4	5.68	69	.261	.367	0	—	0		-2		-0.1

DOZIER, BUZZ   William Joseph   B8.31.1928 Waco TX   BR/TR/6-3/185   d9.12   Col Baylor

YEAR	TM LG	W	L	PCT	G	GS	CG-SHO	SV-BS	IP	H	R	HR	HB	BB-IB	SO	ERA	AERA	OAV	OOB	AB-HR-SH	AVG	PB	SUP	APR	DL	PW
1947	Was A	0	0	—	2	0	0	0	4.2	2	0	0	0	1	2	0.00	—	.133	.188	1	.000	-0		2		0.1
1949	Was A	0	0	—	2	0	0	0	6.1	12	8	0	0	6	1	11.37	37	.429	.529	2	.000	-0		-4		-0.2
Total	2	0	0	—	4	0	0	0	11	14	8	0	0	7	3	6.55	62	.326	.420	3	.000	-0		-2		-0.1

DRABEK, DOUG   Douglas Dean   B7.25.1962 Victoria TX   BR/TR/6-1/185*   [ChiA83 11/279]   d5.30   Col Houston

YEAR	TM LG	W	L	PCT	G	GS	CG-SHO	SV-BS	IP	H	R	HR	HB	BB-IB	SO	ERA	AERA	OAV	OOB	AB-HR-SH	AVG	PB	SUP	APR	DL	PW
1986	NY A	7	8	.467	27	21	0	0-0	131.2	126	64	13	3	50-1	76	4.10	101	.251	.322	0	—	0	95	2		0.1
1987	Pit N	11	12	.478	29	28	1-1	0-0	176.1	165	86	22	6	46-2	120	3.88	107	.247	.294	59-0-7	.119	-1*	95	5	22	0.5
1988	Pit N	15	7	.682	33	32	3-1	0-0	219.1	194	83	21	6	50-4	127	3.08	121	.239	.286	76-0-5	.171	3	116	9		1.2
1989	Pit N	14	12	.538	35	34	8-5	0-0	244.1	215	83	21	3	69-3	123	2.80	121	.238	.293	77-0-6	.104	-2*	76	18		1.6
1990	†Pit N	**22**	6	**.786**	33	33	9-3	0-0	231.1	190	78	15	3	56-2	131	2.76	132	.225	.274	84-1-7	.214	5	133	25		3.6
1991	†Pit N	15	14	.517	35	35	5-2	0-0	234.2	245	92	16	3	62-6	142	3.07	117	.274	.321	84-0-4	.179	1*	109	14		1.8
1992	†Pit N	15	11	.577	34	34	10-4	0-0	256.2	218	84	17	6	54-8	177	2.77	125	.231	.274	89-0-8	.157	1*	103	21		2.2
1993	Hou N	9	18	.333	34	34	7-2	0-0	237.2	242	108	18	3	60-12	157	3.79	102	.267	.312	71-1-9	.085	-2	74	5		0.3
1994	Hou N★	12	6	.667	23	23	6-2	0-0	164.2	132	58	14	2	45-2	121	2.84	139	.220	.275	58-0-4	.241	3*	117	22		2.7
1995	Hou N	10	9	.526	31	**31**	2-1	0-0	185	205	104	18	8	54-4	143	4.77	81	.282	.337	60-0-8	.233	0*	118	-17		-1.1
1996	Hou N	7	9	.438	30	30	1	0-0	175.1	208	102	21	7	60-5	137	4.57	85	.298	.355	56-0-7	.179	-0*	103	-21		-2.4
1997	Chi A	12	11	.522	31	31	0	0-0	169.1	170	109	30	4	69-5	85	5.74	77	.261	.334	1-0-1	.000	-0	114	-33	31	-4.0
1998	Bal A	6	11	.353	23	21	1	0-0	108.2	138	90	20	5	29-2	55	7.29	62	.312	.355	1	.000	-0	105	34	69	5.3
Total	13	155	134	.536	398	387	53-21	0-0	2535	2448	1141	246	53	704-56	1594	3.73	102	.255	.308	716-2-66	.166	12	105	34	69	

DRABOWSKY, MOE   Myron Walter   B7.21.1935 Ozanna, Poland   BR/TR/6-2/200(190-212)   d8.7   C2   Col Trinity (CT)

YEAR	TM LG	W	L	PCT	G	GS	CG-SHO	SV-BS	IP	H	R	HR	HB	BB-IB	SO	ERA	AERA	OAV	OOB	AB-HR-SH	AVG	PB	SUP	APR	DL	PW
1956	Chi N	2	4	.333	9	7	3	0	51	37	19	1	2	39-3	36	2.47	153	.207	.353	16-0-2	.250	0	70	6		0.7
1957	Chi N	13	15	.464	36	33	12-2	0	239.2	214	103	22	10	94-6	170	3.53	110	.242	.319	82-1-3	.183	2	85	10		1.4
1958	Chi N	9	11	.450	22	20	4-1	0	125.2	118	73	19	5	73-4	77	4.51	87	.245	.349	45-0-3	.156	-1	110	-9		-1.4
1959	Chi N	5	10	.333	31	23	3-1	0	141.2	138	78	21	3	75-4	70	4.13	96	.251	.343	45	.111	-1	91	-6		-0.7
1960	Chi N	3	1	.750	32	7	0	1	50.1	71	44	3	1	23-0	26	6.44	59	.338	.397	6-0-1	.000	-1*	137	-16		-1.3
1961	Mil N	0	2	.000	16	0	0	2	25.1	26	15	4	1	18-3	5	4.62	81	.277	.391	4	.250	0		-3		-0.2
1962	Cin N	2	6	.250	23	10	1	1	83	84	49	13	6	31-0	56	4.99	81	.267	.340	17-0-1	.000	-2	74	-8		-0.5
	KC A	1	1	.500	10	3	0	0	28	29	20	8	1	10-0	19	5.14	82	.266	.328	6-0-1	.167	-0	120	-4		-0.3
1963	KC A	7	13	.350	26	22	9-2	0	174.1	135	62	16	8	64-2	109	3.05	128	.214	.294	62-2-3	.161	1	81	17		1.9
1964	KC A	5	13	.278	53	21	1	1	168.1	176	103	24	8	72-5	119	5.29	72	.273	.350	43-0-1	.023	-4*	84	-24		-2.8
1965	KC A	1	5	.167	14	5	0	0	38.2	44	22	5	3	18-2	25	4.42	79	.291	.367	11	.091	-1	96	-4		-0.7
1966	†Bal A	6	0	1.000	44	3	0	7	96	62	31	10	1	29-5	98	2.81	118	.181	.246	22-0-1	.364	4	106	7		0.9
1967	Bal A	7	5	.583	43	0	0	12	95.1	66	21	7	2	25-3	96	1.60	196	.194	.252	20-0-3	.350	2		16		2.8
1968	Bal A	4	4	.500	45	0	0	7	61.1	35	17	3	4	25-5	62	1.91	153	.166	.266	7	.286	0		6		1.7
1969	KC A	11	9	.550	52	0	0	11-5	98	68	33	10	2	30-2	76	2.94	126	.190	.255	17-0-2	.235	1		10		2.2
1970	KC A	1	2	.333	24	0	0	2-4	35.2	28	13	3	2	12-3	38	3.28	114	.217	.288	4	.250	0		3		0.2
	†Bal A	4	2	.667	21	0	0	1-1	33.1	30	17	7	1	15-3	21	3.78	97	.233	.317	5-0-1	.000	-1		2		-0.1
	Year	5	4	.556	45	0	0	3-5	69	58	30	10	3	27-6	59	3.52	105	.225	.302	9-0-1	.111	-0		2		0.1
1971	StL N	6	1	.857	51	0	0	8-2	60.1	45	23	2	2	33-8	49	3.43	106	.207	.315	6	.167	1		2		0.8
1972	StL N	1	1	.500	30	0	0	2-1	27.2	29	13	4	1	14-4	22	2.60	132	.259	.346	1	.000	-0		1		0.6
	Chi N	0	0	—	7	0	0	0-0	7.1	6	2	0	0	2-0	4	2.45	127	.240	.296	1	.000	0		1		0.0
Total	17	88	105	.456	589	154	33-6	55-13	1641	1441	758	182	63	702-62	1162	3.71	101	.236	.318	420-3-22	.162	-0	94	4		2.1

DRAGO, DICK   Richard Anthony   B6.25.1945 Toledo OH   BR/TR/6-1/190(186-200)   d4.11   Col Detroit Mercy

YEAR	TM LG	W	L	PCT	G	GS	CG-SHO	SV-BS	IP	H	R	HR	HB	BB-IB	SO	ERA	AERA	OAV	OOB	AB-HR-SH	AVG	PB	SUP	APR	DL	PW
1969	KC A	11	13	.458	41	26	10-2	1-0	200.2	190	95	19	2	65-6	108	3.77	98	.248	.306	52-0-9	.058	-3	74	-1		-0.5
1970	KC A	9	15	.375	35	34	7-1	0-0	240	239	110	20	7	72-5	127	3.75	100	.266	.322	76-0-9	.053	-6	88	2		-0.8
1971	KC A	17	11	.607	35	34	15-4	0-0	241.1	251	84	14	9	46-1	109	2.98	115	.276	.315	77-0-7	.130	1	95	14		1.8
1972	KC A	12	17	.414	34	33	11-2	0-0	239.1	230	88	22	6	51-4	135	3.01	101	.254	.297	68-0-7	.059	-2*	82	1		-0.5
1973	KC A	12	14	.462	37	33	10-1	0-0	212.2	252	116	16	7	76-10	98	4.23	97	.300	.360	0	—	0	105	-5		0.3
1974	Bos A	7	10	.412	33	18	8	3-1	175.2	165	71	17	5	56-9	90	3.48	106	.247	.321	0	—	0	69	8		0.3
1975	†Bos A	2	2	.500	40	2	0	15-3	72.2	69	31	5	0	31-3	43	3.84	106	.247	.321	0	—	0		-9		-1.0
1976	Cal A	7	8	.467	43	0	0	6-3	79.1	80	42	7	5	31-8	43	4.42	76	.264	.338	0	—	0		2		0.1
1977	Cal A	0	1	.000	13	0	0	2-1	21	22	8	3	0	3-2	15	3.00	131	.272	.291	0	—	0		2		0.1
	Bal A	6	3	.667	36	0	0	3-6	39.2	49	19	2	1	15-4	20	3.63	106	.308	.363	0	—	0		3		0.0
	Year	6	4	.600	49	0	0	5-7	60.2	71	27	5	1	18-6	35	3.41	113	.296	.340	0	—	0	218	8		1.2
1978	Bos A	4	4	.500	37	1	0	7-3	77.1	71	30	5	4	32-5	42	3.03	136	.246	.327	0	—	0	387	13		2.9
1979	Bos A	10	6	.625	53	1	0	13-4	89	85	33	6	3	21-6	67	4.14	103	.251	.316	1	.000	-0	81	2		0.1
1980	Bos A	7	7	.500	43	7	1	3-4	132.2	127	67	17	5	44-7	63	5.53	70	.324	.361	0	—	0		-8		-1.7
1981	Sea A	4	6	.400	39	0	0	5-3	53.2	71	33	4	0	15-5	27	3.62	103	.266	.321	274-0-32	.077	-11	89	30		1.6
Total	13	108	117	.480	519	189	62-10	58-28	1875	1901	827	157	54	558-75	987	3.62	103	.266	.321	274-0-32	.077	-11	89	30		1.6

DRAHMAN, BRIAN   Brian Stacy   B11.7.1966 Kenton KY   BR/TR/6-3/205(205-231)   [MilA86 S2/30]   d4.16   Col Miami-Dade Kendall (FL) CC

YEAR	TM LG	W	L	PCT	G	GS	CG-SHO	SV-BS	IP	H	R	HR	HB	BB-IB	SO	ERA	AERA	OAV	OOB	AB-HR-SH	AVG	PB	SUP	APR	DL	PW
1991	Chi A	3	2	.600	28	0	0	0-2	30.2	21	12	4	0	13-1	18	3.23	124	.193	.276	0	—	0		3		0.4
1992	Chi A	0	0	—	5	0	0	0-0	7	6	3	0	0	2-0	1	2.57	151	.222	.276	0	—	0		1		0.2
1993	Chi A	0	0	—	5	0	0	1-0	5.1	7	0	0	0	2-0	3	0.00	—	.333	.391	0	—	0		3		0.3
1994	Fla N	0	0	—	9	0	0	0-0	13	15	9	2	0	6-1	7	6.23	71	.300	.362	0	—	0		-2		0.2
Total	4	3	2	.600	47	0	0	1-2	56	49	24	6	0	23-2	29	3.54	116	.237	.309	0	—	0		5		0.4

DRAKE, LOGAN   Logan Gaffney "L.G."   B12.26.1900 Spartanburg SC   D6.1.1940 Columbia SC   BR/TR/5-10.5/165   d9.21

YEAR	TM LG	W	L	PCT	G	GS	CG-SHO	SV-BS	IP	H	R	HR	HB	BB-IB	SO	ERA	AERA	OAV	OOB	AB-HR-SH	AVG	PB	SUP	APR	DL	PW
1922	Cle A	0	0	—	1	0	0	0	3	4	1	0	0	2	1	3.00	134	.364	.462	1	.000	-0		0		-0.0
1923	Cle A	0	0	—	4	0	0	0	4.1	2	2	0	1	4	2	4.15	95	.133	.350	0	—	0		0		0.0
1924	Cle A	0	1	.000	5	1	0	0	11.1	18	15	0	1	10	8	10.32	41	.400	.518	1	.000	-0	138	-7		-0.4
Total	3	0	1	.000	10	1	0	0	18.2	24	18	0	2	16	11	7.71	54	.338	.472	2	.000	-0	138	-7		-0.4

DRAKE, TOM   Thomas Kendall   B8.7.1912 Birmingham AL   D7.2.1988 Birmingham AL   BR/TR/6-1/185   d4.24   Col Troy St.

YEAR	TM LG	W	L	PCT	G	GS	CG-SHO	SV-BS	IP	H	R	HR	HB	BB-IB	SO	ERA	AERA	OAV	OOB	AB-HR-SH	AVG	PB	SUP	APR	DL	PW
1939	Cle A	0	1	.000	8	1	0	0	15	23	14	2	2	19	11	9.00	49	.347	.537	2-0-1	.000	-0	160	-9		-0.7
1941	Bro N	1	1	.500	10	2	0	0	24.2	26	13	2	0	9	12	4.38	84	.280	.343	5	.400	0*	81	-1		-0.2
Total	2	1	2	.333	18	3	0	0	39.2	49	31	4	2	28	13	6.13	65	.318	.429	7-0-1	.286	0	109	-10		-0.9

DRAPER, MIKE   Michael Anthony   B9.14.1966 Hagerstown MD   BR/TR/6-2/180   [NYA88 26/677]   d4.10   Col George Mason

YEAR	TM LG	W	L	PCT	G	GS	CG-SHO	SV-BS	IP	H	R	HR	HB	BB-IB	SO	ERA	AERA	OAV	OOB	AB-HR-SH	AVG	PB	SUP	APR	DL	PW
1993	NY N	1	1	.500	29	1	0	0-2	42.1	53	22	5	3	14-6	24	4.25	94	.327	.370	3	.667	1	224	-1	52	0.4

DRAVECKY, DAVE   David Francis   B2.14.1956 Youngstown OH   BR/TL/6-1/195*   [PitN78 21/531]   d6.15   Col Youngstown St.

YEAR	TM LG	W	L	PCT	G	GS	CG-SHO	SV-BS	IP	H	R	HR	HB	BB-IB	SO	ERA	AERA	OAV	OOB	AB-HR-SH	AVG	PB	SUP	APR	DL	PW
1982	SD N	5	3	.625	31	10	0	2-0	105	86	37	8	1	33-3	59	2.57	133	.225	.288	23-0-4	.130	-0*	93	9		0.9
1983	SD N★	14	10	.583	28	28	9-1	0-0	183.2	181	78	18	3	44-4	74	3.58	98	.262	.307	61-0-6	.098	-1	100	0		0.0
1984	†SD N	9	8	.529	50	14	3-2	8-2	156.2	125	53	12	4	51-0	71	2.93	123	.222	.289	41-0-5	.098	-0	123	13		1.1
1985	SD N	13	11	.542	34	31	7-2	0-0	214.2	200	79	18	1	57-5	105	2.93	121	.249	.299	69-0-6	.116	-0	88	15		1.1
1986	SD N	9	11	.450	26	26	3-1	0-0	161.1	149	86	17	1	54-7	60	3.76	106	.240	.315	18-0-2	.167	0*	80	1		0.0
1987	SD N	3	7	.300	30	10	1	0-0	79	71	39	10	3	31-4	78	3.20	120	.272	.325	38-0-2	.132	0	111	9		1.1
	†SF N	7	5	.583	18	18	4-3	0-0	112.1	115	43	8	2	33-3	60	3.43	114	.259	.321	56-0-4	.143	1	99	11		1.0
	Year	10	12	.455	48	28	5-3	0-0	191.1	186	82	18	5	64-7	138	3.43	116	.264	.323	94-0-6	.138	1	101	-2	150	-0.1
1988	SF N	2	2	.500	7	7	1	0-0	37	33	19	4	0	8-0	19	3.16	103	.243	.279	10-0-3	.100	-0	92	0	176	0.2
1989	SF N	2	0	1.000	2	2	0	0-0	13	8	5	1	0	4-0	5	3.46	98	.182	.265	3	.333	1	92	0	326	0.4
Total	8	64	57	.529	226	146	28-9	10-2	1062.2	968	421	97	16	315-26	558	3.13	115	.245	.302	313-1-34	.121	-2	96	53	326	

DREES, TOM   Thomas Kent   B6.17.1963 Des Moines IA   BB/TL/6-6/210   [ChiA85 17/423]   d9.3   Col Creighton

YEAR	TM LG	W	L	PCT	G	GS	CG-SHO	SV-BS	IP	H	R	HR	HB	BB-IB	SO	ERA	AERA	OAV	OOB	AB-HR-SH	AVG	PB	SUP	APR	DL	PW
1991	Chi A	0	0	—	4	0	0	0-0	7.1	10	10	4	0	5-0	2	12.27	33	.345	.444	0	—	0		-6		-0.0

YEAR	TM LG	W	L	PCT	G	GS	CG-SHO	SV-BS	IP	H	R	HR	HB	BB-IB	SO	ERA	AERA	OAV	OOB	AB-HR-SH	AVG	PB	SUP	APR	DL	PW

DREIFORT, DARREN   Darren James B5.3.1972 Wichita KS BR/TR/6-2/211* [LAN93 1/2] d4.7 Col Wichita St. [DL 1995 LA N 160, 2002 LA N 183, 2005 LA N 183]

1994	LA N	0	5	.000	27	0	0	6-3	29	45	21	0	4	15-3	22	6.21	64	.357	.441	1-0-1	1.000	1*		-7		-1.3
1996	†LA N	1	4	.200	19	0	0	0-2	23.2	23	13	2	0	12-4	24	4.94	79	.256	.340	3	.000	-0*		-2	45	-0.4
1997	LA N	5	2	.714	48	0	0	4-3	63	45	21	3	1	34-2	63	2.86	137	.202	.308	7	.143	-0		8	36	1.0
1998	LA N	8	12	.400	32	26	1-1	0-0	180	171	84	12	10	57-2	168	4.00	101	.256	.321	49-1-5	.224	3*	91	3		0.8
1999	LA N	13	13	.500	30	29	1-1	0-0	178.2	177	105	20	7	76-2	140	4.79	91	.260	.340	62-1-4	.210	4	118	-9		-0.7
2000	LA N	12	9	.571	32	32	1-1	0-0	192.2	175	105	31	12	87-1	164	4.16	107	.238	.329	68-3-1	.162	3	117	3		0.8
2001	LA N	4	7	.364	16	16	0	0-0	94.2	89	62	11	6	47-0	91	5.13	80	.251	.347	33-1-3	.152	1	106	-13	100	-1.1
2003	LA N	4	4	.500	10	10	0	0-0	60.1	58	29	6	0	25-0	67	4.03	102	.250	.322	15-0-3	.133	0	59	1	123	0.2
2004	LA N	1	4	.200	60	0	0	1-3	50.2	43	25	5	0	36-2	63	4.44	93	.232	.354	1		-0		-1	48	-0.1
Total	9		48	60	.444	274	113	3-3	11-11	872.2	826	465	90	40	389-16	802	4.36	96	.251	.336	239-6-17	.184	12	107	-17	878	-0.2

DREISEWERD, CLEM   Clemens Johann "Steamboat" B1.24.1916 Old Monroe MO D9.11.2001 Ocean Springs MS BL/TL/6-1.5/195 d8.29 Mil 1945

1944	Bos A	2	4	.333	7	7	3	0	48.2	52	25	2	0	9	9	4.07	84	.268	.300	16-0-2	.188	0	95	-4		-0.4
1945	Bos A	0	1	.000	2	2	0	1	9.2	13	5	0	1	2	3	4.66	73	.325	.372	3	.000	-0	50	-1		-0.2
1946	†Bos A	4	1	.800	20	1	0	0	47.1	50	22	3	0	15	19	4.18	88	.276	.332	10-0-2	.000	-1	210	-1		-0.2
1948	StL A	0	2	.000	13	0	0	1	22.1	28	15	6	0	8	6	5.64	81	.318	.375	5	.000	-1		-2		-0.3
	NY N	0	0	—	4	0	0	1	12.2	17	8	3	0	5	2	5.68	69	.321	.379	4	.250	1		-2		0.0
Total	6		8	.429	46	10	3	2	140.2	160	75	14	1	39	39	4.54	82	.288	.336	38-0-4	.105	-1	93	-10		-1.1

DRESE, RYAN   Ryan Thomas B4.5.1976 San Francisco CA BR/TR/6-3/235(220-235) [CleA98 5/153] d7.29 Col California-Davis

2001	Cle A	1	2	.333	9	4	0	0-0	36.2	32	15	2	1	15-2	24	3.44	134	.242	.324	0		0	91	5		0.3
2002	Cle A	10	9	.526	26	26	1	0-0	137.1	176	104	15	6	62-1	102	6.55	68	.317	.386	3-0-1	.000	0	113	-31		-3.3
2003	Tex A	2	4	.333	11	8	0	0-0	46	61	42	8	5	24-1	26	6.85	73	.314	.404	0	—	0	123	-11		-1.2
2004	Tex A	14	10	.583	34	33	2	0-0	207.2	233	104	16	11	58-6	98	4.20	117	.285	.339	4	.500	1	97	17		1.8
2005	Tex A	4	6	.400	12	12	1	0-0	69.2	96	52	5	3	24-1	20	6.46	71	.334	.390	1	.000	-0	106	-13		-1.5
	Was N	3	6	.333	11	11	0	0-0	59.2	66	38	3	5	22-1	26	4.98	81	.283	.352	14-0-5	.071	-1*	79	-8	45	-1.1
Total	5		34	37	.479	103	94	4	0-0	557	664	355	49	31	205-12	296	5.32	87	.299	.364	22-0-6	.136	-0	103	-41	45	-5.0

DRESSENDORFER, KIRK   Kirk Richard B4.8.1969 Houston TX BR/TR/5-11/190 [OakA90 1/36] d4.13 Col Texas [DL 1992 Oak A 182]

| 1991 | Oak A | 3 | 3 | .500 | 7 | 7 | 0 | 0-0 | 34.2 | 33 | 28 | 5 | 0 | 21-0 | 17 | 5.45 | 71 | .244 | .344 | 0 | — | 0 | 156 | -9 | 41 | -1.3 |

DRESSER, BOB   Robert Nicholson B10.4.1878 Newton MA D7.27.1924 Duxbury MA BL/TL d8.13

| 1902 | Bos N | 0 | 1 | .000 | 1 | 1 | 1 | 0 | 6 | 9 | 12 | 6 | 0 | 0 | 0 | 8 | 3.00 | 94 | .316 | .316 | 4 | .250 | 0 | 24 | -1 | | -0.1 |

DRESSLER, ROB   Robert Alan B2.2.1954 Portland OR BR/TR/6-3/180(175-195) [SFN72 1/19] d9.7

1975	SF N	1	0	1.000	3	2	1	0-0	16.1	17	3	0	0	4-2	5	1.10	346	.274	.318	4	.000	-0	92	4		0.3
1976	SF N	3	10	.231	25	19	0	0-1	107.2	125	68	8	2	35-4	33	4.43	82	.291	.343	31-0-2	.129	-1	69	-11		-1.3
1978	StL N	0	1	.000	3	2	0	0-0	13	12	3	0	0	4-1	4	2.08	172	.267	.327	3-0-1	.000	-0	88	2		0.1
1979	Sea A	3	2	.600	21	11	2	0-0	104	134	61	11	0	22-3	36	4.93	89	.312	.344	0	—	0	88	-5		-0.3
1980	Sea A	4	10	.286	30	14	3	0-0	149.1	161	75	14	3	33-7	50	3.98	105	.280	.318	0	—	0	89	3		0.3
Total	5		11	23	.324	82	48	6	0-1	390.1	449	210	33	5	98-17	129	4.17	97	.291	.333	38-0-3	.105	-1	80	-7		-0.9

DREW, TIM   Timothy Andrew B8.31.1978 Valdosta GA BR/TR/6-1/195* [CleA97 1/28] d5.24 b-J.D.

2000	Cle A	1	0	1.000	3	3	0	0-0	9	17	12	1	1	8-0	5	10.00	50	.425	.510	0	—	0	144	-6		-0.5
2001	Cle A	0	2	.000	8	6	0	0-0	35	51	39	9	4	16-0	15	7.97	58	.340	.413	0	—	0	141	-15		-0.7
2002	Mon N	1	0	1.000	7	1	0	2-1	16	12	8	1	0	2-0	10	2.81	156	.200	.222	4	.000	-0	148	2		0.1
2003	Mon N	0	2	.000	6	1	0	0-0	8.2	12	12	3	0	8-1	5	12.46	36	.343	.444	1-0-1	.000	-0	106	-7		-1.2
2004	Atl N	0	0	—	11	0	0	0-0	16	21	11	2	1	5-0	7	4.50	96	.318	.375	2	.000	0*		-1	15	0.0
Total	5		2	4	.333	35	11	0	2-1	84.2	113	82	16	6	39-1	40	7.02	65	.322	.392	7-0-1	.000	-0	144	-27	15	-2.3

DREWS, KARL   Karl August B2.22.1920 Staten Island NY D8.15.1963 Dania FL BR/TR/6-4/198* d9.8

1946	NY A	0	1	.000	3	1	0	0	6.1	6	6	0	1	6	4	8.53	40	.250	.419	1	.000	-0	199	-3		-0.5
1947	†NY A	6	6	.500	30	10	0	1	91.2	92	57	6	5	55	45	4.91	72	.264	.373	27-0-1	.037	-2	105	-16		-2.1
1948	StL A	3	2	.600	20	2	0	2	38	35	17	3	0	31	11	3.79	108	.248	.384	7-0-2	.000	-1	55	2		0.2
	NY A	2	3	.400	19	2	0	1	38	43	35	3	0	38	11	8.05	57	.289	.433	8	.000	-1	59	-13		-1.6
	Year	5	5	.500	39	4	0	3	76	78	52	6	0	69	22	5.92	73	.269	.409	15-0-2	.000	-1	58	-12		-1.4
1949	StL A	4	12	.250	31	23	3-1	0	139.2	180	113	11	9	66	35	6.64	68	.317	.397	46-0-1	.000	0	75	-27		-3.1
1951	Phi N	1	0	1.000	8	3	0	0	23	29	16	2	4	7	13	6.26	61	.296	.367	8	.250	1	130	-6		-0.2
1952	Phi N	14	15	.483	33	30	15-5	0	228.2	213	79	13	4	52	96	2.72	135	.252	.298	82-0-2	.110	-2	76	25		2.9
1953	Phi N	9	10	.474	47	27	6	3	185.1	218	116	26	10	50	72	4.52	93	.293	.346	59-0-1	.119	-2	101	-10		-1.1
1954	Phi N	1	0	1.000	8	0	0	0	16	18	10	2	0	8	6	5.63	72	.300	.377	4	.000	-1		-2		-0.2
	Cin N	4	4	.500	22	9	1-1	0	60	79	44	6	2	19	29	6.00	70	.326	.376	12-0-1	.167	1	135	-11		-1.2
	Year	5	4	.556	30	9	1-1	0	76	97	54	8	2	27	35	5.92	70	.321	.376	16-0-1	.125	1	136	-14		-1.4
Total	8		44	53	.454	218	107	26-7	7	826.2	913	493	72	35	332	322	4.76	84	.284	.356	254-0-8	.083	-12	92	-61		-6.9

DREYER, STEVE   Steven William B11.19.1969 Ames IA BR/TR/6-3/180* [TexA90 8/225] d8.8 Col Northern Iowa [DL 1995 Tex A 61]

1993	Tex A	3	3	.500	10	6	0	0-0	41	48	26	7	1	20-1	23	5.71	74	.291	.371	0	—	0	143	-6		-0.7
1994	Tex A	1	1	.500	5	3	0	0-0	17.1	19	15	1	1	8-0	11	5.71	85	.271	.350	0	—	0	158	-3		-0.3
Total	2		4	4	.500	15	9	0	0-0	58.1	67	41	8	2	28-1	34	5.71	77	.285	.365	0	—	0	149	-9	61	-1.0

DRISCOLL, DENNY   John F. B11.19.1855 Lowell MA D7.11.1886 Lowell MA BL/TL/5-10.5/160 d7.1 ▲

1880	Buf N	1	3	.250	6	4	4	0	41.2	48	33	1		9	17	3.89	63	.270	.305	65	.154	-1*	95	-6		-0.6
1882	Pit AA	13	9	.591	23	23	23	0	201	162	73	0		12	59	1.21	216	.206	.218	80-1	.138	-2	101	27		2.1
1883	Pit AA	18	21	.462	41	40	35-1	0	336.1	427	239	3		39	79	3.99	82	.290	.309	148	.182	-5	111	-27		-2.5
1884	Lou AA	6	6	.500	13	13	10	0	102	110	69	3	2	7	16	3.44	90	.252	.267	48	.188	-1	126	-4		-0.4
Total	4		38	39	.494	83	80	72-1	0	681	747	414	7	2	67	171	3.08	97	.260	.277	341-1	.167	-9	110	-10		-1.4

DRISCOLL, MICHAEL   Michael Columbus B10.19.1892 N.Abington MA D3.22.1953 Foxboro MA BR/TR/5-11/160 d7.6 Col Maine

| 1916 | Phi A | 0 | 1 | .000 | 1 | 0 | 0 | 0 | 5 | 6 | 5 | 0 | 2 | 1 | 2 | 5.40 | 53 | .273 | .333 | 2 | .000 | -0* | | -2 | | -0.3 |

DRISKILL, TRAVIS   Travis Corey B8.1.1971 Omaha NE BR/TR/6-0/185(185-215) [CleA93 4/111] d4.26 Col Texas Tech

2002	Bal A	8	8	.500	29	19	0	0-0	132.2	150	78	21	8	48-1	78	4.95	88	.284	.351	3	.000	0	84	-9		-1.0
2003	Bal A	3	5	.375	20	0	0	1-0	48	62	35	8	1	9-2	33	6.00	77	.310	.340	1	.000	-0		-8		-1.1
2004	Col N	0	0	—	5	0	0	0-1	8.1	13	6	3	0	3-0	6	6.48	73	.361	.410	1	.000	-0		-1		-0.1
2005	Hou N	0	0	—	1	0	0	0-0	1	1	0	0	0	0-0	2	0.00	—	.250	.250	0		0	0	0		0.0
Total	4		11	13	.458	55	19	0	1-1	190	226	119	29	9	60-3	119	5.26	84	.294	.350	5	.000	-0	84	-18		-2.2

DROHAN, TOM   Thomas F. B8.26.1887 Fall River MA D9.17.1926 Kewanee IL BR/TR/5-10/175 d5.1

| 1913 | Was A | 0 | 0 | — | 2 | 0 | 0 | 0 | 2 | 5 | 2 | 1 | 0 | 2 | 1 | 9.00 | 33 | .500 | .500 | 0 | — | 0 | | -1 | | -0.1 |

DROTT, DICK   Richard Fred "Hummer" B7.1.1936 Cincinnati OH D8.16.1985 Glendale Heights IL BR/TR/6-0/185* d4.16

1957	Chi N	15	11	.577	38	32	7-3	0	229	200	107	22	7	129-2	170	3.58	108	.234	.337	80-0-3	.100	-5	107	5		0.0
1958	Chi N	7	11	.389	39	31	4	0	167.1	156	118	23	6	99-6	127	5.43	72	.245	.347	55-0-1	.273	3	121	-30		-2.5
1959	Chi N	1	2	.333	8	6	1-1	0	27.1	25	19	6	0	26-1	15	5.93	67	.245	.398	8	.125	-0	94	-6	31	-0.6
1960	Chi N	0	6	.000	23	9	0	0	55.1	63	49	7	3	42-0	32	7.16	53	.296	.409	10	.100	-1	83	-20		-2.0
1961	Chi N	1	4	.200	35	6	0	0	98	75	54	13	1	51-0	48	4.22	99	.215	.311	22	.273	1	69	-1		0.0
1962	Hou N	1	0	1.000	6	1	0	0	13	12	12	1	0	9-0	10	7.62	49	.240	.356	4	.000	-0	188	-6		-0.4
1963	Hou N	2	12	.143	27	14	2-1	0	97.2	95	61	13	6	49-2	58	4.98	63	.257	.349	23-0-1	.130	-1	49	-20		-2.8
Total	7		27	46	.370	176	101	14-5	0	687.2	626	420	84	23	405-11	460	4.78	80	.247	.347	202-0-5	.168	-2	99	-78	31	-8.3

DRUCKE, LOUIS   Louis Frank B12.3.1888 Waco TX D9.22.1955 Waco TX BR/TR/6-1/188 d9.25 Col TCU

1909	NY N	2	1	.667	3	3	2	0	24	20	9	0	0	13	8	2.25	114	.227	.327	8-0-2	.125	-0	146	1		0.0
1910	NY N	12	10	.545	34	27	15	0	215.1	174	73	3	11	82	151	2.47	120	.228	.312	70-1-9	.214	4	115	15		2.0
1911	NY N	4	4	.500	15	10	4	0	75.2	83	39	1	8	41	42	4.04	83	.281	.384	23-0-1	.087	-1*	121	-4		-0.4
1912	NY N	0	0	—	1	0	0	0	2	5	4	0	0	1	0	13.50	25	.417	.462	0	—	0		-2		-0.2
Total	4		18	15	.545	53	40	21	0	317	282	125	4	19	137	201	2.90	105	.243	.333	101-1-12	.178	2	119	10		1.4

YEAR	TM LG	W	L	PCT	G	GS	CG-SHO	SV-BS	IP	H	R	HR	HB	BB-IB	SO	ERA	AERA	OAV	OOB	AB-HR-SH	AVG	PB	SUP	APR	DL	PW

DRUHOT, CARL Carl A. "Collie" B9.1.1882 OH D2.5.1918 Portland OR BL/TL/5-7/150 d4.18
1906	Cin N	2	2	.500	4	3	1	0	25	27	17	0	2	7	14	4.32	64	.270	.330	9	.222	0	150	-4		-0.6
	StL N	6	7	.462	15	13	12-1	0	130.1	117	55	1	5	46	45	2.62	100	.238	.310	56-0-1	.232	1	105	-2		0.0
	Year	8	9	.471	19	16	13-1	0	155.1	144	72	1	7	53	59	2.90	91	.244	.313	65-0-1	.231	1	113	-7		-0.6
1907	StL N	0	1	1.000	1	1	0	0	2.1	3	5	0	1	4	1	15.43	16	.600	.800	0	—	0	57	-3		-0.5
Total	2	8	10	.444	20	17	13-1	0	157.2	147	77	1	8	57	60	3.08	86	.247	.321	65-0-1	.231	1	110	-9		-1.1

DRUMMOND, TIM Timothy Darnell B12.24.1964 LaPlata MD BR/TR/6-3/170(170-195) [PitN83*12/272] d9.12 Col CC of Southern Maryland
1987	Pit N	0	0	—	6	0	0	3-0	6	5	3	0	0	3-0	5	4.50	93	.227	.320	1	.000	-0	0			0.0
1989	Min A	0	0	—	8	0	0	1-0	16.1	16	7	0	2	8-1	9	3.86	108	.246	.347	0	—	0	1			0.0
1990	Min A	3	5	.375	35	4	0	1-1	91	104	46	8	1	36-1	49	4.35	96	.295	.357	0	—	0	38	-1		-0.1
Total	3	3	5	.375	49	4	0	2-1	113.1	125	56	8	3	47-2	63	4.29	97	.284	.354	1	.000	-0	38	0		-0.1

DRYSDALE, DON Donald Scott B7.23.1936 Van Nuys CA D7.3.1993 Montreal QC, Can. BR/TR/6-6/216(189-220) d4.17 HF1984
1956	†Bro N	5	5	.500	25	12	2	0	99	95	35	9	3	31-3	55	2.64	150	.255	.315	26-1-2	.192	1*	89	13		1.4
1957	Bro N	17	9	.654	34	29	9-4	0	221	197	76	17	7	61-3	148	2.69	155	.236	.293	73-2-3	.123	-0*	108	33		4.1
1958	LA N	12	13	.480	44	29	6-1	0	211.2	214	107	21	14	72-6	131	4.17	98	.263	.331	66-7-3	.227	8*	90	0		0.9
1959	†LA N★	17	13	.567	44	36	15-4	2	270.2	237	113	26	18	93-9	242	3.46	122	.233	.308	91-4-8	.165	3*	86	23		2.9
1960	LA N	15	14	.517	41	36	15-5	2	269	214	93	27	10	72-5	246	2.84	140	.215	.274	83-0-9	.157	2	88	33		4.0
1961	LA N☆	13	10	.565	40	37	10-3	0	244	236	111	29	20	83-15	182	3.69	118	.254	.326	83-5-5	.193	4	91	17		1.8
1962	LA N★	25	9	.735	43	41	19-2	1	314.1	272	122	21	11	78-12	232	2.83	128	.230	.282	111-0-8	.198	5	137	27		3.3
1963	†LA N★	19	17	.528	42	42	17-3	0	315.1	287	114	25	10	57-13	251	2.63	115	.242	.282	96-0-6	.167	4	116	41		5.0
1964	LA N★	18	16	.529	40	40	21-5	0	321.1	242	91	15	10	68-9	237	2.18	148	.207	.255	110-1-14	.173	4	114	16		4.2
1965	†LA N★	23	12	.657	44	42	20-7	1	308.1	270	113	30	8	66-11	210	2.77	118	.232	.279	130-7-2	.300	22*	97	-1		0.2
1966	†LA N	13	16	.448	40	40	11-3	0	273.2	279	114	21	17	45-8	177	3.42	96	.265	.304	106-2-2	.189	4*	97	-1		1.2
1967	LA N★	13	16	.448	38	38	9-3	0	282	269	101	19	8	60-19	196	2.74	116	.251	.296	93-0-2	.129	-0	81	10		2.3
1968	LA N★	14	12	.538	31	31	12-8	0	239	201	68	11	12	56-10	155	2.15	129	.231	.284	79-0-4	.177	1	91	17		
1969	LA N	5	4	.556	12	12	1-1	0-0	62.2	71	34	9	2	13-0	24	4.45	75	.291	.327	22-0-1	.136	0	121	-8	47	-1.0
Total	14	209	166	.557	518	465	167-49	6-0	3432	3084	1292	280	154	855-123	2486	2.95	121	.239	.293	1169-29-69	.186	60	101	234	47	32.4

DUBIEL, MONK Walter John B2.12.1918 Hartford CT D10.23.1969 Hartford CT BR/TR/6-0/190* d4.19
1944	NY A	13	13	.500	30	28	19-3	0	232	217	93	12	1	86	79	3.38	103	.248	.316	83-0-5	.181	-2*	93	7		0.5
1945	NY A	10	9	.526	26	20	9-1	0	151.1	157	88	9	0	62	45	4.64	75	.266	.335	58-1-4	.276	4	133	-18		-1.8
1948	Phi N	8	10	.444	37	17	6-2	4	150.1	139	84	13	1	58	42	3.89	101	.248	.320	42-0-4	.167	0*	93	-2		-0.3
1949	Chi N	6	9	.400	32	20	3-1	4	147.2	142	75	16	1	54	52	4.14	97	.250	.317	35-0-7	.286	3*	101	-1		0.3
1950	Chi N	6	10	.375	39	12	4-2	5	142.2	152	79	12	1	67	51	4.16	101	.270	.348	45-0-1	.200	1	96	0		0.2
1951	Chi N	2	2	.500	22	0	0	1	54.2	46	17	3	0	22	19	2.30	178	.232	.309	12	.000	-1		10		0.0
1952	Chi N	0	0	—	1	0	0	0	0.2	1	0	0	0	0	1	0.00	—	.333	.333	0	—	-0	0			0.0
Total	7	45	53	.459	187	97	41-9	11	879.1	854	436	65	4	349	289	3.87	98	.254	.325	275-1-21	.207	5	102	-4		-0.5

DuBOIS, BRIAN Brian Andrew B4.18.1967 Joliet IL BL/TL/5-10/170(165-195) [BalA85 4/99] d8.17 [DL 1991 Bal A 182]
1989	Det A	0	4	.000	6	5	0	1-0	36	29	14	2	2	13	13	1.75	219	.218	.314	0	—	0	38	6		0.8
1990	Det A	3	5	.375	12	11	0	0-0	58.1	70	37	9	1	22-1	34	5.09	78	.310	.368	0	—	0	117	-8		-1.0
Total	2	3	9	.250	18	16	0	1-0	94.1	99	51	11	3	39-4	47	3.82	103	.276	.347	0	—	0	93	-2	182	-0.2

DUBOSE, ERIC Eric Ladell B5.15.1976 Bradenton FL BL/TL/6-3/230(215-235) [OakA97 1/21] d9.19 Col Mississippi St.
2002	Bal A	0	0	—	4	0	0	0-0	6	7	2	1	1	1-0	4	3.00	145	.304	.360	0	—	0	1			0.0
2003	Bal A	3	6	.333	17	10	1	0-1	73.2	60	33	6	5	25-2	44	3.79	122	.222	.297	0	—	0	48	7		0.0
2004	Bal A	4	6	.400	14	14	0	0-0	74.2	76	55	12	3	44-0	48	6.39	80	.263	.365	2	.000	-0	120	-13	106	-1.2
2005	Bal A	2	3	.400	15	3	0	0-0	29.1	28	21	4	1	19-0	17	5.52	80	.243	.356	0	—	0	99	-4		-0.3
Total	4	9	15	.375	50	27	1	0-1	183.2	171	111	23	10	89-2	113	5.10	90	.245	.338	2	.000	-0	91	-9	106	-1.2

DUBUC, JEAN Jean Joseph Octave Arthur "Chauncey" B9.15.1888 St.Johnsbury VT D8.28.1958 Fort Myers FL BR/TR/5-10.5/185 d6.25 C2 Col Notre Dame
1908	Cin N	5	6	.455	15	9	7-1	0	85.1	62	34	2	5	41	32	2.74	84	.205	.309	29-0-2	.138	-1	75	-3		-0.4
1909	Cin N	2	5	.286	19	5	2	1	71.1	72	58	0	4	46	19	3.66	71	.269	.384	18-0-1	.167	0	70	-13		-1.2
1912	Det A	17	10	.630	37	26	23-2	3	250	217	107	2	7	109	97	2.77	101	.235	.321	108-1-3	.269	6*	128	13		2.2
1913	Det A	15	14	.517	36	28	22-1	2	242.2	228	113	1	8	91	73	2.89	101	.254	.324	135-2-4	.267	5*	111	-1		1.3
1914	Det A	12	14	.462	36	27	15-2	1	224	216	124	3	6	76	70	3.46	81	.257	.324	124-1-4	.226	7*	117	-18		-1.4
1915	Det A	17	12	.586	39	33	22-5	2	258	231	116	5	10	88	74	3.21	94	.245	.316	112-0-3	.205	0*	115	-3		0.1
1916	Det A	10	10	.500	36	16	8-1	1	170.1	134	66	1	5	84	40	2.96	97	.233	.316	78-0-2	.256	5*	106	0		0.2
1918	†Bos A	0	1	.000	2	1	1	0	10.2	11	5	1	0	5	1	4.22	64	.268	.348	6	.167	0*	84	-1		-0.2
1919	NY N	6	4	.600	36	5	1	3	132	119	49	4	2	37	32	2.66	105	.246	.303	42	.143	-1*	85	2		0.1
Total	9	84	76	.525	256	150	101-12	13	1444.1	1290	672	19	47	577	438	3.04	96	.245	.325	652-4-17	.230	21	113	-24		1.3

DUCHSCHERER, JUSTIN Justin Craig B11.19.1977 Aberdeen SD BR/TR/6-3/164(164-190) [BosA96 8/241] d7.25
2001	Tex A	1	1	.500	5	2	0	0-0	14.2	24	20	5	4	4-0	11	12.27	39	.353	.421	0	—	0	78	-11		-1.0
2003	Oak A	1	1	.500	4	3	0	0-0	16.1	17	7	1	2	3-0	15	3.31	139	.262	.314	0	—	0	114	2		0.5
2004	Oak A	7	6	.538	53	0	0	0-2	96.1	85	37	13	5	32-6	59	3.27	141	.241	.312	0	—	0	15			1.5
2005	Oak A☆	7	4	.636	65	0	0	5-2	85.2	67	25	7	2	19-3	85	2.21	202	.215	.263	0	—	0	20			3.0
Total	4	16	12	.571	127	5	0	5-4	213	193	89	26	13	58-9	170	3.46	132	.242	.303	0	—	0	102	26		3.5

DUCKWORTH, BRANDON Brandon J. B1.23.1976 Salt Lake City UT BB/TR/6-2/185* d8.7 Col Cal St.-Fullerton
2001	Phi N	3	2	.600	11	11	0	0-0	69	57	29	2	6	29-5	40	3.52	117	.234	.326	22-0-2	.227	2	88	5		0.5
2002	Phi N	8	9	.471	30	29	0	0-0	163	167	103	26	9	69-5	167	5.41	71	.261	.338	48-0-6	.188	2	113	-29		-2.2
2003	Phi N	4	7	.364	24	18	0	0-0	93	98	58	12	10	44-3	68	4.94	81	.272	.366	27-0-1	.185	1	104	-12	21	-1.0
2004	Hou N	1	2	.333	19	6	0	0-0	39.1	55	30	11	0	13-3	23	6.86	64	.337	.384	9	.222	0	141	-10		-0.9
2005	Hou N	0	1	.000	7	2	0	0-0	16.1	24	20	4	5	7-1	10	11.02	38	.348	.439	3	.667	1	133	-12		-0.6
Total	5	16	21	.432	91	66	0	0-0	380.2	401	240	55	28	162-17	308	5.34	75	.272	.353	109-0-9	.211	6	109	-58	21	-4.5

DUCKWORTH, JIM James Raymond B5.24.1939 National City CA BR/TR/6-4/194* d4.13
1963	Was A	4	12	.250	37	15	4	0	120.2	131	89	13	10	67-3	66	6.04	61	.278	.373	27-0-3	.000	-3	93	-29		-3.0
1964	Was A	1	6	.143	30	2	0	3	56	52	37	9	3	25-4	56	4.34	85	.244	.332	9	.222	0	60	-6	35	-0.7
1965	Was A	2	4	.500	17	8	0	0	64	45	30	11	2	36-4	74	3.94	88	.202	.314	18-0-1	.000	-2	88	-2		-0.2
1966	Was A	0	3	.000	5	4	0	0	14.1	14	12	2	1	10-1	14	5.02	69	.259	.379	3	.000	-0	76	-4	19	-0.3
	KC A	0	2	.000	8	0	0	0	12	14	12	2	1	10-0	10	9.00	38	.292	.424	2	.000	-0		-7		-1.0
	Year	0	5	.000	13	4	0	0	26.1	28	24	4	2	20-1	24	6.84	50	.275	.400	5	.000	-1	77	-10		-2.0
Total	4	7	25	.219	97	29	4	2	267	256	180	37	17	148-12	220	5.26	69	.253	.355	59-0-4	.034	-5	87	-48	54	-5.0

DUDLEY, CLISE Elzie Clise B8.8.1903 Graham NC D1.12.1989 Moncks Corner SC BL/TL/6-1/195 d4.18 Col South Carolina-Aiken
1929	Bro N	6	14	.300	35	20	8-1	0	156.2	202	130	9	10	64	33	5.69	81	.315	.385	51-2-3	.098	-1*	75	-24		-2.0
1930	Bro N	2	4	.333	21	7	2	1	66.2	103	62	3	2	27	18	6.35	77	.371	.430	24	.208	-0	104	-13		-1.0
1931	Phi N	8	14	.364	30	24	8	0	179	206	95	10	6	56	50	3.52	121	.287	.343	84-0-1	.214	-0*	82	9		1.0
1932	Phi N	1	1	.500	13	0	0	0	17.2	23	14	3	0	8	5	7.13	62	.329	.397	14-1-0	.286	3*		-4		-0.1
1933	Pit N	0	0	—	1	0	0	0	0.1	6	5	0	1	0	0	135.00	2	.857	.875	0	—	-0		-4		-0.2
Total	5	17	33	.340	100	51	18-1	2	420.1	540	306	25	18	156	106	5.03	90	.315	.378	173-3-4	.185	1	82	-36		-2.3

DUES, HAL Hal Joseph B9.22.1954 LaMarque TX BR/TR/6-3/185* d9.9 Col Mary Hardin-Baylor
1977	Mon N	1	1	.500	6	4	0	0-0	23	26	14	2	0	9-1	9	4.30	90	.265	.327	5-0-1	.000	-1	69	-2		-0.2
1978	Mon N	5	6	.455	25	12	1	1-0	99	85	29	5	4	42-4	36	2.36	151	.240	.326	31	.194	-0	76	13		1.1
1980	Mon N	0	1	.000	6	1	0	0-0	12.1	17	9	1	0	4-1	2	6.57	55	.333	.382	3	.000	-0	98	-4		-0.3
Total	3	6	8	.429	37	17	1	1-0	134.1	128	52	8	4	55-6	47	3.08	118	.254	.332	39-0-1	.154	-1	76	7		0.6

DUFF, LARRY Cecil Elba B11.20.1896 Radersburg MT D11.10.1969 Bend OR BL/TL/6-1/175 d9.5
| 1922 | Chi A | 1 | 1 | .500 | 3 | 1 | 0 | 0 | 12.2 | 16 | 7 | 1 | 0 | 7 | 7 | 4.97 | 82 | .340 | .380 | | .400 | | 42 | -1 | | -0.1 |

DUFF, MATT Matthew Clark B10.6.1974 Clarksdale MS BR/TR/6-1/192 d7.30 Col U. of Mississippi
| 2002 | StL N | 0 | 0 | — | 7 | 0 | 0 | 0-0 | 5.2 | 3 | 3 | 0 | 2 | 8-2 | 4 | 4.76 | 85 | .150 | .393 | 0 | — | 0 | 0 | 0 | | 0.0 |

YEAR	TM LG	W	L	PCT	G	GS	CG-SHO	SV-BS	IP	H	R	HR	HB	BB-IB	SO	ERA	AERA	OAV	OOB	AB-HR-SH	AVG	PB	SUP	APR	DL	PW

DUFFALO, JIM   James Francis   B11.25.1935 Helvetia PA   BR/TR/6-1/180*   d4.12

1961	SF N	5	1	.833	24	4	1	1	61.2	59	31	9	2	32-7	37	4.23	90	.257	.347	17-1-0	.294	3*	140	-2		0.0
1962	SF N	1	2	.333	24	2	0	0	42	42	27	3	0	23-3	29	3.64	104	.256	.344	6-0-1	.000	-0	104	-3		-0.3
1963	SF N	4	2	.667	34	5	0	2	75.1	56	26	3	2	37-6	55	2.87	112	.209	.307	18-0-1	.111	-1	81	4	31	0.3
1964	SF N	5	1	.833	35	3	1	3	74	57	25	9	2	31-4	55	2.92	122	.209	.293	14	.071	-1	82	6	31	0.4
1965	SF N	0	1	.000	2	0	0	0	0.1	1	1	0	0	2-0	0	27.00	13	.500	.750	0	—	0		-1		-0.2
	Cin N	0	1	.000	22	0	0	0	44.1	33	21	3	5	30-2	34	3.45	109	.212	.351	8	.000	-1		1		0.0
	Year	0	2	.000	24	0	0	0	44.2	34	22	3	5	32-2	34	3.63	102	.215	.359	8	.000	-1		0		-0.2
Total	5	15	8	.652	141	14	2	6	297.2	248	131	27	11	155-22	210	3.39	106	.227	.326	63-1-2	.127	1	101	5	62	0.2

DUFFIE, JOHN   John Brown   B10.4.1945 Greenwood SC   BR/TR/6-7/215   d9.18   Col Brewton-Parker

| 1967 | LA N | 0 | 2 | .000 | 2 | 2 | 0 | 0 | 9.2 | 11 | 6 | 1 | 0 | 4-1 | 6 | 2.79 | 111 | .282 | .341 | | .000 | -0 | 43 | -1 | | -0.2 |

DUFFY, BERNIE   Bernard Allen   B8.18.1893 Vinson OK   D2.9.1962 Abilene TX   BR/TR/5-11/180   d9.20

| 1913 | Pit N | 0 | 0 | — | 3 | 2 | 0 | 0 | 11.1 | 18 | 8 | 0 | 0 | 3 | 8 | 5.56 | 54 | .360 | .396 | 4 | .250 | 0 | 87 | -3 | | -0.1 |

DUGAN, DAN   Daniel Phillip   B2.22.1907 Plainfield NJ   D6.25.1968 Green Brook NJ   BL/TL/6-1.5/187   d9.5   Col St. Louis

1928	Chi A	0	0	—	1	0	0	0	0.1	0	0	0	0	0	0	0.00	—	.000	.000	0	—	0		0		0.0
1929	Chi A	1	4	.200	19	2	0	1	65	77	51	8	2	19	15	6.65	64	.300	.353	20-0-1	.150	-1	30	-14		-1.1
Total	2	1	4	.200	20	2	0	1	65.1	77	51	8	2	19	15	6.61	65	.298	.351	20-0-1	.150	-1	30	-14		-1.1

DUGAN, ED   Edward John   B1864 Brooklyn NY   TR   d8.5   b-Bill

| 1884 | Ric AA | 5 | 14 | .263 | 20 | 20 | 20 | 0 | 166.1 | 196 | 137 | 5 | 2 | 15 | 60 | 4.49 | 74 | .267 | .284 | 70 | .114 | -4* | 77 | -23 | | -2.5 |

DUGGLEBY, BILL   William James "Frosty Bill"   B3.16.1874 Utica NY   D8.30.1944 Redfield NY   TR   d4.21

1898	Phi N	3	3	.500	9	5	4	0	54	70	39	4	6	18	12	5.50	62	.311	.378	21-1-1	.238	2	149	-10		-0.6
1901	Phi N	20	12	.625	35	29	26-5	0	284.2	302	120	9	10	41	95	2.88	118	.270	.302	115-0-3	.165	-3	92	18		1.7
1902	Phi N	1	1	.500	2	2	2	0	17	19	9	0	0	4	4	3.18	116	.284	.324	7	.000	-1	78	1		0.0
	Phi N	11	17	.393	33	27	25	1	258.2	282	130	2	12	57	60	3.38	83	.277	.323	98-0-1	.173	-1	93	-15		-1.5
1903	Phi N	13	16	.448	34	30	28-3	2	264.1	318	162	4	12	79	57	3.75	87	.303	.358	104-0-3	.231	2	98	-18		-1.4
1904	Phi N	12	13	.480	32	27	22-2	1	223.2	265	138	3	11	53	55	3.78	71	.292	.338	82-2-2	.171	0	124	-26		-2.6
1905	Phi N	18	17	.514	38	36	27-1	0	289.1	270	116	10	13	83	75	2.46	119	.253	.315	101-1-3	.109	-2	102	12		1.2
1906	Phi N	13	19	.406	42	30	22-5	2	280.1	241	93	5	12	66	83	2.25	116	.227	.280	99-2-1	.141	-2*	80	14		1.5
1907	Phi N	0	2	.000	5	2	2	0	29	43	27	2	5	11	8	7.45	33	.371	.447	9	.111	0	103	-14		-0.8
	Pit N	2	2	.500	9	3	1-1	0	40.1	34	17	0	2	12	4	2.68	91	.239	.308	13	.154	-0	88	-1		0.0
	Year	2	4	.333	14	5	3-1	0	69.1	77	44	2	7	23	12	4.67	52	.298	.372	22	.136	0	94	-14		-0.8
Total	8	93	102	.477	241	191	159-17	6	1741.1	1844	851	39	83	424	453	3.18	93	.272	.323	649-6-14	.165	-4	99	-14		-2.5

DUKE, MARTIN   Martin F. "Duck" (b Martin F. Duck)   B1867 Zanesville OH   D12.31.1898 Minneapolis MN   TL/5-8/157   d8.24

| 1891 | Was AA | 0 | 3 | .000 | 4 | 3 | 2 | 0 | 23 | 36 | 33 | 0 | 0 | 19 | 5 | 7.43 | 50 | .346 | .447 | 9 | .111 | -1 | 44 | -10 | | -0.9 |

DUKE, ZACH   Zachary Thomas   B4.19.1983 Clifton TX   BL/TL/6-2/210   d7.2

| 2005 | Pit N | 8 | 2 | .800 | 14 | 14 | 2 | 0 | 84.2 | 79 | 20 | 3 | 2 | 23-2 | 58 | 1.81 | 235 | .253 | .308 | 28 | .143 | -0 | 96 | 22 | 23 | 2.6 |

DUKES, JAN   Noble Jan   B8.16.1945 Cheyenne WY   BL/TL/5-11/175*   [TexA67*S1/8]   d9.6   Col Santa Clara

1969	Was A	0	2	.000	8	0	0	0-0	11	8	3	0	0	4-1	3	2.45	143	.216	.293	1	.000	0		2		0.3
1970	Was A	0	0	—	5	0	0	0-0	6.2	6	3	0	1	1-0	4	2.70	134	.240	.286	1	.000	-0		0		0.0
1972	Tex A	0	0	—	3	0	0	0-0	2.1	1	2	0	0	5-1	0	3.86	79	.167	.500	0	—	0		-1		0.0
Total	3	0	2	.000	16	0	0	0-0	20	15	8	0	1	10-2	7	2.70	129	.221	.321	2	.000	0		1		0.3

DUKES, TOM   Thomas Earl   B8.31.1942 Knoxville TN   BR/TR/6-2/185(185-200)   d8.15

1967	Hou N	0	2	.000	17	0	0	1	23.2	25	14	2	2	11-1	23	5.32	62	.275	.362	2	.500	0		-4		-0.4
1968	Hou N	2	2	.500	43	0	0	4	52.2	62	31	3	2	28-12	37	4.27	69	.291	.376	4	.000	-0		-9		-0.9
1969	SD N	1	0	1.000	13	0	0	1-0	22.1	26	18	2	0	10-2	15	7.25	49	.295	.360	1	.000	-0		-8		-0.4
1970	SD N	1	6	.143	53	0	0	10-6	69	62	39	7	2	25-9	56	4.04	90	.246	.312	7	.000	-1		-2	32	-0.4
1971	†Bal A	1	5	.167	28	0	0	4-1	38.1	40	15	4	1	8-2	30	3.52	97	.263	.299	7	.143	0	21	0		0.1
1972	Cal A	0	1	.000	7	0	0	1-0	11	11	3	1	1	0-0	8	1.64	179	.262	.279	0	—	0		1	47	0.1
Total	6	5	16	.238	161	0	0	21-7	217	226	120	19	8	82-26	169	4.35	80	.270	.335	21	.095	-1	-22	100	-2.0

DULIBA, BOB   Robert John "Ach"   B1.9.1935 Glen Lyon PA   BR/TR/5-10/185*   d8.11

1959	StL N	0	1	.000	11	0	0	1	22.2	19	7	2	0	12-1	14	2.78	153	.237	.330	4	.000	-0		4		0.2
1960	StL N	4	4	.500	27	0	0	0	40.2	49	20	6	0	16-4	23	4.20	97	.310	.367	5	.200	-0		0	72	0.0
1962	StL N	2	0	1.000	28	0	0	2	39.1	33	11	3	0	17-0	22	2.06	207	.239	.321	4	.000	-0		9		0.5
1963	LA A	1	1	.500	6	0	0	1	7.2	3	1	0	0	6-0	4	1.17	292	.125	.290	1	.000	-0		2		0.4
1964	LA A	6	4	.600	58	0	0	0	72.2	80	35	5	1	22-3	33	3.59	91	.287	.339	5-0-1	.000	-1		-3		-0.5
1965	Bos A	4	2	.667	39	0	0	0	64.1	60	31	6	0	22-7	27	3.78	99	.248	.308	7	.000	-0		-3		-0.1
1967	KC A	0	0	—	7	0	0	0	9.2	13	7	3	0	1-0	6	6.52	49	.342	.359	0	—	0		-3		-0.2
Total	7	17	12	.586	176	0	0	14	257	257	112	25	1	96-15	129	3.47	108	.268	.332	26-0-1	.038	-2	9	72	0.3

DUMONT, GEORGE   George Henry "Pea Soup"   B11.13.1895 Minneapolis MN   D10.13.1956 Minneapolis MN   BR/TR/5-11/163   d9.14

1915	Was A	2	1	.667	6	4	3-2	0	40	23	17	0	2	12	18	2.02	147	.169	.247	12-0-2	.167	-0	80	2		0.1
1916	Was A	2	3	.400	17	5	2	1	53	37	25	0	1	17	21	3.06	91	.194	.263	14-0-1	.071	-0	125	-2		-0.3
1917	Was A	5	14	.263	37	23	8-2	2	204.2	171	76	3	6	76	65	2.55	103	.227	.303	58-0-2	.034	-5	89	-5		-0.7
1918	Was A	1	1	.500	4	1	1	0	14	18	12	0	0	6	12	5.14	53	.295	.358	3	.333	1	0	-4		-0.4
1919	Bos A	0	4	.000	13	2	0	0	35.1	45	21	1	1	19	12	4.33	70	.326	.411	7	.000	-0	52	-6		-0.6
Total	5	10	23	.303	77	35	14-4	3	347	294	151	4	10	130	128	2.85	96	.230	.306	94-0-5	.064	-5	74	-8		-1.8

DUMOULIN, DAN   Daniel Lynn   B8.20.1953 Kokomo IN   BR/TR/6-0/175*   d9.5

1977	Cin N	0	0	—	5	0	0	0-0	5.1	12	8	0	0	3-1	5	13.50	29	.462	.517	0	—	0		-5		-0.3
1978	Cin N	1	0	1.000	3	0	0	0-0	5	7	1	0	1	3-1	2	1.80	197	.368	.478	0	—	0		1		0.2
Total	2	1	0	1.000	8	0	0	0-0	10.1	19	9	0	1	6-2	7	7.84	48	.422	.500	0	—	0		-4		-0.1

DUMOVICH, NICK   Nicholas   B1.2.1902 Sacramento CA   D12.12.1978 Laguna Hills CA   BL/TL/6-0/170   d4.20

| 1923 | Chi N | 3 | 5 | .375 | 28 | 8 | 1 | 1 | 94 | 118 | 60 | 4 | 3 | 45 | 23 | 4.60 | 87 | .319 | .397 | 29 | .241 | 1 | 98 | -7 | | -0.4 |

DUNBAR, MATT   Matthew Marshall   B10.15.1968 Tallahassee FL   BL/TL/6-0/175   [NYA94 25/672]   d4.25   Col Florida St.

| 1995 | Fla N | 0 | 1 | .000 | 8 | 0 | 0 | 0-0 | 7 | 12 | 9 | 1 | 0 | 11-3 | 5 | 11.57 | 37 | .387 | .558 | 0 | — | 0 | | -5 | | -0.6 |

DUNCAN, COURTNEY   Courtney Demond   B10.9.1974 Mobile AL   BL/TR/6-0/185*   [ChiN96 20/592]   d4.2   Col Grambling St.

2001	Chi N	3	3	.500	36	0	0	0-2	42.2	42	24	5	2	25-3	49	5.06	83	.259	.359	3	.000	0		-3	50	-0.4
2002	Chi N	0	0	—	2	0	0	0-0	2.1	2	0	0	0	1-0	1	0.00	—	.222	.300	0	—	0		1		0.1
Total	2	3	3	.500	38	0	0	0-2	45	44	24	5	2	26-3	50	4.80	87	.257	.356	3	.000	0		-2	50	-0.3

DUNDON, ED   Edward Joseph "Dummy"   B7.10.1859 Columbus OH   D8.18.1893 Columbus OH   TR/6-0/170   d6.2 ▲

1883	Col AA	3	16	.158	20	19	16	0	166.2	213	153	7		38	31	4.48	69	.292	.327	93	.161	-3*	85	-30		-2.7
1884	Col AA	6	4	.600	11	9	7	0	81	85	55	9	0	15	37	3.78	80	.249	.281	86	.140	-1*	73	-8		-0.8
Total	2	9	20	.310	31	28	23	0	247.2	298	208	16	0	53	68	4.25	72	.278	.312	179	.151	-4	81	-38		-3.5

DUNEGAN, JIM   James William   B8.6.1947 Burlington IA   BR/TR/6-1/205   [ChiN67*2/21]   d5.28

| 1970 | Chi N | 0 | 0 | — | 7 | 0 | 0 | 0-0 | 13.1 | 13 | 7 | 2 | 0 | 12-1 | 3 | 4.73 | 95 | .277 | .417 | 4 | .250 | 0* | 0 | | | 0.1 |

DUNHAM, WILEY   Henry Huston   B1.30.1877 Piketon OH   D1.16.1934 Cleveland OH   6-1/180   d5.24

| 1902 | StL N | 2 | 3 | .400 | 7 | 5 | 3 | 1 | 38 | 47 | 31 | 1 | 3 | 15 | 15 | 5.68 | 48 | .303 | .368 | 12 | .083 | -1 | 55 | -11 | | -1.4 |

DUNKLE, DAVEY   Edward Perks   B8.30.1872 Philipsburg PA   D11.19.1941 Lock Haven PA   BB/TR/6-2/220   d8.28

1897	Phi N	5	2	.714	7	7	7	0	62	72	41	0	1	23	9	3.48	120	.288	.350	23-0-1	.174	-1	82	2		0.0
1898	Phi N	1	4	.200	12	7	6	0	68.1	83	70	1	9	38	21	6.98	49	.297	.399	28	.214	-0	133	-25		-1.5
1899	Was N	0	2	.000	4	2	2	0	26	46	34	3	1	14	9	10.04	39	.383	.452	11	.273	-0	15	-15		-0.9
1903	Chi A	4	4	.500	8	7	6	1	82	96	58	1	3	31	26	4.06	69	.291	.357	33	.303	2	98	-13		-1.1
	Was A	5	9	.357	14	13	10	0	108.1	111	60	4	4	33	51	4.24	74	.264	.324	41	.098	-4	58	-10		-1.6

YEAR	TM LG	W	L	PCT	G	GS	CG-SHO	SV-BS	IP	H	R	HR	HB	BB-IB	SO	ERA	AERA	OAV	OOB	AB-HR-SH	AVG	PB	SUP	APR	DL	PW
	Year	9	13	.409	26	20	16	1	190.1	207	118	5	7	64	77	4.16	72	.276	.339	74	.189	-2	72	-23		-2.7
1904	Was A	2	9	.182	12	11	7	0	74.1	95	56	5	4	23	23	4.96	54	.311	.366	28	.143	-2*	85	-19		-2.6
Total	5	17	30	.362	61	47	36	1	421	503	319	10	21	162	139	5.02	65	.295	.364	164-0-1	.189	-4	82	-80		-7.7

DUNLEAVY, JACK John Francis B9.14.1879 Harrison NJ D4.11.1944 S.Norwalk CT BL/TL/5-6/167 d5.30 Col Amherst ▲

YEAR	TM LG	W	L	PCT	G	GS	CG-SHO	SV-BS	IP	H	R	HR	HB	BB-IB	SO	ERA	AERA	OAV	OOB	AB-HR-SH	AVG	PB	SUP	APR	DL	PW
1903	StL N	6	8	.429	14	13	9	0	102	101	59	2	8	57	51	4.06	80	.264	.371	193-0-7	.249	2*	91	-4		-0.3
1904	StL N	1	4	.200	7	5	5	0	55	63	32	4	1	23	28	4.42	61	.275	.344	172-1-1	.233	2*	82	-8		-0.5
Total	2	7	12	.368	21	18	14	0	157	164	91	6	9	80	79	4.18	73	.268	.361	365-1-8	.241	4	90	-12		-0.8

DUNN, JIM James William "Bill" B2.25.1931 Valdosta GA D1.6.1999 Gadsden AL BR/TR/6-0.5/185 d8.26 Col Alabama

YEAR	TM LG	W	L	PCT	G	GS	CG-SHO	SV-BS	IP	H	R	HR	HB	BB-IB	SO	ERA	AERA	OAV	OOB	AB-HR-SH	AVG	PB	SUP	APR	DL	PW
1952	Pit N	0	0	—	3	0	0	0	5.1	4	2	0	0	3	2	3.38	118	.190	.292	1	.000	-0		0		0.0

DUNN, JACK John Joseph B10.6.1872 Meadville PA D10.22.1928 Towson MD BR/TR/5-9/? d5.6 ▲

YEAR	TM LG	W	L	PCT	G	GS	CG-SHO	SV-BS	IP	H	R	HR	HB	BB-IB	SO	ERA	AERA	OAV	OOB	AB-HR-SH	AVG	PB	SUP	APR	DL	PW
1897	Bro N	14	9	.609	25	21	21	0	216.2	251	147	6	9	66	26	4.57	90	.288	.344	131-0-4	.221	-2*	116	-10		-1.0
1898	Bro N	16	21	.432	41	37	31	0	322.2	352	180	10	15	82	66	3.60	100	.275	.327	167-0-1	.246	1*	82	0		-0.1
1899	Bro N	23	13	.639	41	34	29-2	2	299.1	323	161	8	18	86	48	3.70	106	.275	.334	122-0-2	.246	0*	108	12		1.3
1900	Bro N	3	4	.429	10	7	5	0	63	88	48	1	4	28	6	5.57	69	.330	.401	26	.231	0	93	-10		-0.9
	Phi N	5	5	.500	10	9	9-1	0	80	87	50	2	5	29	12	4.84	75	.276	.347	33	.303	1	59	-8		-0.7
	Year	8	9	.471	20	16	14-1	0	143	175	98	3	9	57	18	5.16	72	.301	.372	59	.271	1	74	-16		-1.6
1901	Phi N	0	1	.000	2	2	1	0	4.2	11	16	0	2	7	5	21.21	16	.458	.606	1	1.000	1	219	-9		-1.2
	Bal A	3	3	.500	9	6	6	0	59.2	74	45	2	1	21	6	3.62	107	.301	.358	362-0-14	.249	0*	102	-1		0.0
1902	NY N	0	3	.000	3	2	2	0	26.2	28	14	0	0	12	6	4.50	61	.167	.286	181-1-5	.309	0*		-1		0.0
1904	NY N	0	0	—	1	0	0	1				3	1	0	3					342-0-19	.211	0*	24	-2		-0.1
Total	7	64	59	.520	142	118	103-3	3	1076.2	1217	664	30	54	334	171	4.11	92	.283	.342	1365-1-45	.245	1	97	-29		-2.7

DUNN, SCOTT Scott Allen B5.23.1978 San Antonio TX BR/TR/6-3/200 [CinN99 10/308] d9.11

YEAR	TM LG	W	L	PCT	G	GS	CG-SHO	SV-BS	IP	H	R	HR	HB	BB-IB	SO	ERA	AERA	OAV	OOB	AB-HR-SH	AVG	PB	SUP	APR	DL	PW
2004	Ana A	0	0	—	3	0	0	0-0	3	7	3	0	0	1-0	2	9.00	50	.438	.471	0	—	0		-1		-0.1

DUNNE, MIKE Michael Dennis B10.27.1962 South Bend IN BR/TR/6-4/200(200-221) [StLN84 1/7] d6.5 Col Bradley [DL 1993 Chi A 107]

YEAR	TM LG	W	L	PCT	G	GS	CG-SHO	SV-BS	IP	H	R	HR	HB	BB-IB	SO	ERA	AERA	OAV	OOB	AB-HR-SH	AVG	PB	SUP	APR	DL	PW
1987	Pit N	13	6	.684	23	23	5-1	0-0	163.1	143	66	10	1	68-8	72	3.03	138	.240	.317	53-0-7	.094	-1	86	18		2.0
1988	Pit N	7	11	.389	30	28	1	0-0	170	163	88	15	5	88-3	70	3.92	88	.255	.345	46-0-7	.109	-1*	101	-11	22	-1.2
1989	Pit N	1	1	.500	3	3	0	0-0	14.1	21	12	1	1	9-1	4	7.53	45	.328	.419	4	.250	0	130	-6		-0.7
	Sea A	2	9	.182	15	15	1	0-0	85.1	104	61	7	2	37-1	38	5.27	77	.307	.373	6	.000	-1	90	-6	91	-0.6
1990	SD N	0	3	.000	10	6	0	0-0	28.2	28	21	4	0	17-0	15	5.65	68	.241	.338	6	—	0	94	-1		-0.1
1992	Chi A	2	0	1.000	4	1	0	0-1	12.2	12	7	0	1	6-1	6	4.26	91	.255	.352	0	—	0	92	-19		
Total	7	25	30	.455	85	76	7-1	0-1	474.1	471	255	37	10	225-14	205	4.08	94	.261	.344	109-0-14	.101	-1	92	-19	220	-2.0

DUNNING, ANDY Andrew Jackson B8.12.1871 New York NY D6.21.1952 New York NY BR/TR/6-0/175 d5.23

YEAR	TM LG	W	L	PCT	G	GS	CG-SHO	SV-BS	IP	H	R	HR	HB	BB-IB	SO	ERA	AERA	OAV	OOB	AB-HR-SH	AVG	PB	SUP	APR	DL	PW
1889	Pit N	0	2	.000	2	2	2	0	18	20	19	1	0	16	4	7.00	54	.274	.404	7	.000	-1	63	-7		-0.6
1891	NY N	0	1	.000	1	1	0	0	2	3	5	1	0	3	1	4.50	71	.333	.500	0	—	0	93	-1		-0.2
Total	2	0	3	.000	3	3	2	0	20	23	24	2	0	19	5	6.75	55	.280	.416	7	.000	-1	72	-8		-0.8

DUNNING, STEVE Steven John B5.15.1949 Denver CO BR/TR/6-2/205* [CleA70 1/2] d6.14 Col Stanford

YEAR	TM LG	W	L	PCT	G	GS	CG-SHO	SV-BS	IP	H	R	HR	HB	BB-IB	SO	ERA	AERA	OAV	OOB	AB-HR-SH	AVG	PB	SUP	APR	DL	PW
1970	Cle A	4	9	.308	19	17	0	0-1	94.1	93	55	16	4	54-3	77	4.96	81	.261	.362	31-0-3	.161	-1	86	-9		-1.1
1971	Cle A	8	14	.364	31	29	3-1	1-0	184	173	98	25	6	109-5	132	4.50	86	.254	.359	55-1-8	.182	1*	78	-10		-1.0
1972	Cle A	6	4	.600	16	16	1	0-0	105	98	39	16	0	43-8	52	3.26	100	.248	.321	33-3-3	.273	5*	88	1		0.7
1973	Cle A	0	2	.000	4	3	0	0-0	18	17	15	2	0	13-0	10	6.50	61	.250	.370	0	—	0*	83	-5		-0.5
	Tex A	2	6	.250	23	12	2	0-1	94.1	101	63	11	1	52-2	38	5.34	70	.275	.362	0	—	0	94	-23		-1.3
	Year	2	8	.200	27	15	2	0-1	112.1	118	78	13	1	65-2	48	5.53	69	.271	.364	0	—	0	94	-23		-1.8
1974	Tex A	0	0	—	1	0	0	0-0	2.1	3	5	2	0	3-1	1	19.29	19	.333	.500	0	—	0		-4		-0.2
1976	Cal A	0	0	—	4	0	0	0-0	6	9	9	4	2	6-1	4	7.50	45	.310	.417	0	—	0		-4		-0.3
	Mon N	2	6	.250	32	7	1	0-0	91.1	93	50	6	2	33-4	72	4.14	91	.274	.338	15-0-3	.133	-0	74	-4		0.0
1977	Oak A	1	0	1.000	6	0	0	0-0	18.1	17	8	2	0	10-1	4	3.93	103	.254	.351	0	—	0	84	1		-0.2
Total	7	23	41	.359	136	84	7-1	1-2	613.2	604	342	82	12	323-25	390	4.56	82	.261	.352	134-4-17	.194	6	84	-50		-3.9

DUPEE, FRANK Frank Oliver B4.29.1877 Monkton VT D8.14.1956 Portland ME TR/6-1/200 d8.24

YEAR	TM LG	W	L	PCT	G	GS	CG-SHO	SV-BS	IP	H	R	HR	HB	BB-IB	SO	ERA	AERA	OAV	OOB	AB-HR-SH	AVG	PB	SUP	APR	DL	PW
1901	Chi A	0	1	.000	1	0	0	0	3	3	3	0	0	3	0	∞	—	—	1.000	0	—	0	78	-3		-0.2

DUPREE, MIKE Michael Dennis B5.29.1953 Kansas City KS BR/TR/6-1/185 [SDN73*4/70] d4.13 Col Fresno (CA) City

YEAR	TM LG	W	L	PCT	G	GS	CG-SHO	SV-BS	IP	H	R	HR	HB	BB-IB	SO	ERA	AERA	OAV	OOB	AB-HR-SH	AVG	PB	SUP	APR	DL	PW
1976	SD N	0	0	—	12	0	0	0-0	15.2	18	17	4	0	7-0	5	9.19	36	.286	.352	1	1.000	1		-10		-0.5

DURAN, ROBERTO Roberto Alejandro B3.6.1973 Moca, D.R. BL/TL/6-0/190(167-205) d7.6

YEAR	TM LG	W	L	PCT	G	GS	CG-SHO	SV-BS	IP	H	R	HR	HB	BB-IB	SO	ERA	AERA	OAV	OOB	AB-HR-SH	AVG	PB	SUP	APR	DL	PW
1997	Det A	0	0	—	13	0	0	0-0	10.2	7	9	0	3	15-0	11	7.59	61	.189	.446	0	—	0		-3		-0.2
1998	Det A	0	1	.000	18	0	0	0-0	15.1	9	10	0	2	17-0	12	5.87	81	.170	.389	0	—	0		-1	122	-0.1
Total	2	0	1	.000	31	0	0	0-0	26	16	19	0	5	32-0	23	6.58	71	.178	.414	0	—	0		-4	122	-0.3

DURBIN, KID Blaine Alphonsus B9.10.1886 Lamar MO D9.11.1943 Kirkwood MO BL/TL/5-8/155 d4.24 ▲

YEAR	TM LG	W	L	PCT	G	GS	CG-SHO	SV-BS	IP	H	R	HR	HB	BB-IB	SO	ERA	AERA	OAV	OOB	AB-HR-SH	AVG	PB	SUP	APR	DL	PW
1907	Chi N	0	1	.000	5	1	1	1	16.2	14	13	0	1	10	5	5.40	46	.233	.352	18	.333	1*	57	-5		-0.1

DURBIN, CHAD Chad Griffin B12.3.1977 Spring Valley IL BB/TR/6-2/200(175-200) [KCA96 3/79] d9.26

YEAR	TM LG	W	L	PCT	G	GS	CG-SHO	SV-BS	IP	H	R	HR	HB	BB-IB	SO	ERA	AERA	OAV	OOB	AB-HR-SH	AVG	PB	SUP	APR	DL	PW
1999	KC A	0	0	—	1	0	0	0-0	2.1	1	0	0	0	0-0	2	0.00	—	.125	.222	0	—	0		1		0.0
2000	KC A	2	5	.286	16	16	0	0-0	72.1	91	71	14	0	43-1	37	8.21	64	.301	.385	0	—	0	106	-23		-1.2
2001	KC A	9	16	.360	29	29	2	0-0	179	201	109	26	11	58-0	95	4.93	101	.288	.348	1-0-1	.000	-0	69	0		-0.5
2002	KC A	0	1	.000	2	2	0	0-0	8.1	13	11	3	1	4-0	5	11.88	42	.342	.419	0	—	0	145	-5		-0.4
2003	Cle A	0	1	.000	3	1	0	0-0	8.2	18	12	2	0	3-0	9	7.27	61	.429	.467	0	—	0	99	-13		-2.2
2004	Cle A	5	6	.455	17	8	1	0-0	51.1	63	40	10	4	24-3	38	6.66	65	.301	.381	0	—	0		-4		-0.7
	Ari N	1	1	.500	7	0	0	0-0	9.1	10	9	0	1	11-0	10	8.68	53	.237	.420	1	.000	-0		-4		
Total	6	17	30	.362	75	56	3	0-0	331.1	396	253	56	17	144-4	196	6.22	79	.296	.369	2-0-1	.000	-0	86	-49		-5.

DURBIN, J.D. Joseph Adam B2.24.1982 Portland OR BR/TR/6-0/200 [MinA00 2/54] d9.8

YEAR	TM LG	W	L	PCT	G	GS	CG-SHO	SV-BS	IP	H	R	HR	HB	BB-IB	SO	ERA	AERA	OAV	OOB	AB-HR-SH	AVG	PB	SUP	APR	DL	PW
2004	Min A	0	0	—	2	2	0	0-0	7.1	12	6	2	0	6-0	6	7.36	63	.387	.474	0	—	0	141	-2		-0.2

DUREN, RYNE Rinold George B2.22.1929 Cazenovia WI BR/TR/6-1/195* d9.25

YEAR	TM LG	W	L	PCT	G	GS	CG-SHO	SV-BS	IP	H	R	HR	HB	BB-IB	SO	ERA	AERA	OAV	OOB	AB-HR-SH	AVG	PB	SUP	APR	DL	PW
1954	Bal A	0	0	—	1	0	0	0	2	3	3	0	0	1	2	9.00	40	.333	.400	0		0		-2		
1957	KC A	0	3	.000	14	6	0	0	42.2	37	26	4	2	30-1	37	5.27	75	.236	.359	14	.071	-1	53	-5		2.
1958	†NY A☆	6	4	.600	44	1	0	20	75.2	40	20	4	7	43-1	87	2.02	175	.157	.300	14-0-3	.000	-1		16		2.
1959	NY A★	3	6	.333	41	1	0	14	76.2	49	18	6	3	43-2	96	4.96	72	.160	.367	6-0-1	.000	0	123	-7		-1.
1960	†NY A	3	4	.429	42	1	0	9	49	27	29	3	7	49-1	67	5.40	69	.125	.300	0	—	0		-1		-0.
1961	NY A	0	1	.000	4	0	0	0	5	2	3	2	0	4-0	7	5.18	87	.233	.361	25-0-1	.040	-2	90	-9		-1.
	LA A☆	6	12	.333	40	14	1-1	2	99	87	70	13	3	75-1	108	5.19	86	.229	.358	25-0-1	.040	-2	90	-10		-1.
	Year	6	13	.316	44	14	1-1	2	104	89	73	15	3	79-1	115							-1	154	-3		-0.
1962	LA A	2	9	.182	42	3	0	1	71.1	53	38	1	6	57-2	74	4.42	87	.206	.361	15-0-1	.067	-1	118	1		1
1963	Phi N	6	2	.750	33	7	1	2	87.1	65	33	6	5	52-1	84	3.30	98	.210	.332	21	.143	1*	118	1		
1964	Phi N	0	0	—	2	0	0	0	3	3	0	1	1-0		5	6.00	58	.357	.438	0	—	0		-1		
	Cin N	0	2	.000	26	0	0	1	43.2	41	17	1	3	15-1	39	2.89	125	.248	.319	5	.000	-0		3		
	Year	0	2	.000	28	0	0	1	46.2	44	20	1	4	16-1	44	3.09	117	.257	.328	5	.000	-0		2		
1965	Phi N	0	0	—	6	0	0	0	11	10	7	0	1	4-1	6	3.27	106	.270	.349	1	.000	0		-1		-0.
	Was A	1	1	.500	23	0	0	0	23	24	17	0	3	18-4	18	6.65	52	.286	.421	0	—	0		-7		0.
Total	14	27	44	.380	311	32	2-1	57	589.1	443	284	40	41	392-15	630	3.83	98	.209	.341	114-0-10	.061	-5	100	-2		0.

DURHAM, DON Donald Gary B3.21.1949 Yosemite KY BR/TR/6-0/165* [StLN70 7/159] d7.16 Col Western Kentucky

YEAR	TM LG	W	L	PCT	G	GS	CG-SHO	SV-BS	IP	H	R	HR	HB	BB-IB	SO	ERA	AERA	OAV	OOB	AB-HR-SH	AVG	PB	SUP	APR	DL	PW
1972	StL N	2	7	.222	10	8	1	0-0	47.2	42	28	1	0	22-5	35	4.34	79	.240	.318	14-2-0	.500	4*	48	-6		-1.
1973	Tex A	0	4	.000	15	4	0	1-0	40.1	49	35	7	1	23-0	23	7.59	50	.304	.390	0	—	0*	77	-16		-2.
Total	2	2	11	.154	25	12	1	1-0	88	91	63	8	1	45-5	58	5.83	61	.271	.353	14-2-0	.500	4	58	-22		-2.

DURHAM, ED Edward Fant "Bull" B8.17.1907 Chester SC D4.27.1976 Chester SC BL/TR/5-11/170 d4.19

YEAR	TM LG	W	L	PCT	G	GS	CG-SHO	SV-BS	IP	H	R	HR	HB	BB-IB	SO	ERA	AERA	OAV	OOB	AB-HR-SH	AVG	PB	SUP	APR	DL	PW
1929	Bos A	1	0	1.000	14	0	0	0	22.1	34	24	2	0	14	6	9.27	46	.374	.457	4	.000	-0	39	-11		-0
1930	Bos A	4	15	.211	33	12	6-1	1	140	144	81	9	2	43	28	4.69	98	.270	.326	41-0-2	.098	-4	54	0		-0
1931	Bos A	8	10	.444	38	15	7-2	0	165.1	175	97	9	4	50	53	4.25	101	.266	.322	54-0-1	.056	-6*	64	0		-0

YEAR	TM LG	W	L	PCT	G	GS	CG-SHO	SV-BS	IP	H	R	HR	HB	BB-IB	SO	ERA	AERA	OAV	OOB	AB-HR-SH	AVG	PB	SUP	APR	DL	PW
1932	Bos A	6	13	.316	34	22	4	0	175.1	187	90	13	4	49	52	3.80	118	.274	.327	57-0-1	.123	-3*	71	13		0.9
1933	Chi A	10	6	.625	24	21	6	0	138.2	137	74	12	5	46	65	4.48	95	.256	.320	46-0-8	.217	0	118	0		0.0
Total	5	29	44	.397	143	71	23-3	1	641.2	677	360	45	15	202	204	4.45	99	.271	.329	202-0-12	.119	-14	79	2		-0.6

DURHAM, JIM　James Garfield　B10.7.1881 Douglass KS　D5.7.1949 Coffeyville KS　BR/TR/6-0/175　d9.15　Col Southwestern (KS)

YEAR	TM LG	W	L	PCT	G	GS	CG-SHO	SV-BS	IP	H	R	HR	HB	BB-IB	SO	ERA	AERA	OAV	OOB	AB-HR-SH	AVG	PB	SUP	APR	DL	PW
1902	Chi A	1	1	.500	3	3	3	0	20	21	15	0	0	16	3	5.85	58	.269	.394	15		.067	-1*	57	-5		-0.4

DURHAM, BULL　Louis Raphael (b Louis Raphael Staub)　B6.27.1877 New Oxford PA　D6.28.1960 Bentley KS　BR/TR/5-10/?　d9.15

YEAR	TM LG	W	L	PCT	G	GS	CG-SHO	SV-BS	IP	H	R	HR	HB	BB-IB	SO	ERA	AERA	OAV	OOB	AB-HR-SH	AVG	PB	SUP	APR	DL	PW
1904	Bro N	2	0	1.000	2	2	1	0	11	10	5	0	0	5	1	3.27	84	.250	.333	4	.250	0	213	0		-0.1
1907	Was A	0	0	—	2	0	0	0	5	10	9	0	1	4	1	12.60	19	.417	.517	1	.000	-0		-5		-0.3
1908	NY N	0	0	—	1	0	0	0	2	2	2	0	0	1	2	9.00	27	.250	.333	0	—	0		-1		-0.1
1909	NY N	0	0	—	4	0	0	1	11	15	8	0	0	2	2	3.27	78	.326	.354	2	.000	-0		-1		-0.1
Total	4	2	0	1.000	9	2	1	1	29	37	24	0	1	12	6	5.28	49	.314	.382	7	.143	-0	213	-8		-0.6

DURNING, RICH　Richard Knott　B10.10.1892 Louisville KY　D9.23.1948 Castle Point NY　BL/TL/6-2/178　d4.16

YEAR	TM LG	W	L	PCT	G	GS	CG-SHO	SV-BS	IP	H	R	HR	HB	BB-IB	SO	ERA	AERA	OAV	OOB	AB-HR-SH	AVG	PB	SUP	APR	DL	PW
1917	Bro N	0	0	—	1	0	0	0	1	0	0	0	0	0	0	.000	—	.000	.000	0	—	0		0		0.0
1918	Bro N	0	0	—	1	0	0	0	2	3	5	0	0	4	0	13.50	21	.375	.583	0	—	0		-3		-0.1
Total	2	0	0	—	2	0	0	0	3	3	5	0	0	4	0	9.00	31	.273	.467	0	—	0		-3		-0.1

DUROCHER, JAYSON　Jayson Paul　B8.18.1974 Hartford CT　BR/TR/6-3/195*　[MonN93 9/258]　d6.11

YEAR	TM LG	W	L	PCT	G	GS	CG-SHO	SV-BS	IP	H	R	HR	HB	BB-IB	SO	ERA	AERA	OAV	OOB	AB-HR-SH	AVG	PB	SUP	APR	DL	PW
2002	Mil N	1	1	.500	39	0	0	0-1	48	27	13	3	2	21-2	44	1.88	220	.164	.265	2	.000	-0		11		0.5
2003	Mil N	2	0	1.000	6	0	0	0-0	7.1	9	9	4	1	2-0	7	11.05	39	.300	.364	0	.000	-0		-5	165	-0.9
Total	2	3	1	.750	45	0	0	0-1	55.1	36	22	7	3	23-2	51	3.09	134	.185	.279	2	.000	-0		6	165	-0.4

DURYEA, JESSE　James Newton "Cyclone Jim"　B9.7.1859 Osage IA　D8.19.1942 Algona IA　BR/TR/5-10/175　d4.20

YEAR	TM LG	W	L	PCT	G	GS	CG-SHO	SV-BS	IP	H	R	HR	HB	BB-IB	SO	ERA	AERA	OAV	OOB	AB-HR-SH	AVG	PB	SUP	APR	DL	PW
1889	Cin AA	32	19	.627	53	48	38-2	1	401	372	208	9	16	127	183	2.56	153	.238	.302	162	.272	6*	114	51		5.7
1890	Cin N	16	12	.571	33	32	29-2	0	274	270	148	11	8	60	108	2.92	122	.249	.294	99-1	.152	1	93	21		1.8
1891	Cin N	1	9	.100	10	10	8	0	77	101	67	4	7	25	23	5.38	63	.305	.366	32	.031	-5	71	-14		-1.8
	StL AA	1	1	.500	3	3	2	0	24	19	13	0	0	10	13	3.38	124	.211	.290	11	.364	1	99	3		0.2
1892	Cin N	2	5	.286	9	7	5	0	68	55	37	3	3	26	21	3.57	91	.212	.292	27	.111	-1	94	-1		-0.1
	Was N	3	11	.214	18	15	13-1	2	127	102	59	6	9	45	48	2.41	135	.211	.291	50	.120	-2	64	12		1.1
	Year	5	16	.238	27	22	18-1	2	195	157	96	9	12	71	69	2.82	116	.212	.291	77	.117	-3	73	12		1.0
1893	Was N	1	4	.286	17	15	9	0	117	182	137	8	13	56	20	7.54	61	.345	.420	47	.277	2	118	-36		-2.8
Total	5	59	67	.468	143	130	104-5	3	1088	1101	669	41	56	349	416	3.45	109	.254	.318	428-1	.201	3	100	36		4.1

DOUSAK, ERV　Ervin Frank "Four Sack"　B7.29.1920 Chicago IL　D11.6.1994 Glendale Heights IL　BR/TR/6-2/185*　d9.18.1941　Mil 1943-45 ▲

YEAR	TM LG	W	L	PCT	G	GS	CG-SHO	SV-BS	IP	H	R	HR	HB	BB-IB	SO	ERA	AERA	OAV	OOB	AB-HR-SH	AVG	PB	SUP	APR	DL	PW
1948	StL N	0	0	—	1	0	0	0	1	0	0	0	0	1	0	0.00	—	.000	.250	311-6-5	.209	0*		0		0.0
1950	StL N	0	2	.000	14	1	0	1	36.1	27	17	2	1	27	16	3.72	116	.211	.353	12	.083	-0*	72	2		0.1
1951	StL N	0	0	—	5	0	0	0	10	14	8	0	0	7	8	7.20	55	.333	.429	2-1-0	.500	1		-3		0.0
	Pit N	0	1	.000	3	1	0	0	6.2	10	10	2	1	9	2	12.15	35	.357	.526	39-1-0	.308	1*	84	-5	70	-0.6
	Year	0	1	.000	8	1	0	0	16.2	24	18	2	1	16	10	9.18	44	.343	.471	41-2-0	.317	2	87	-8	70	-0.6
Total	3	0	3	.000	23	3	0	1	54	51	35	4	2	44	26	5.33	79	.254	.393	364-8-5	.217	2	77	-6	70	-0.5

DOUSER, CARL　Carl Robert　B7.22.1932 Hazleton PA　BL/TL/6-1/175*　d9.15

YEAR	TM LG	W	L	PCT	G	GS	CG-SHO	SV-BS	IP	H	R	HR	HB	BB-IB	SO	ERA	AERA	OAV	OOB	AB-HR-SH	AVG	PB	SUP	APR	DL	PW
1956	KC A	1	1	.500	2	2	0	0	6	14	6	0	0	2-0	5	9.00	48	.452	.485	3	.000	-0	134	-3		-0.5
1958	KC A	0	0	—	1	0	0	0	2	5	1	0	0	1-1	0	4.50	87	.500	.545	0	—	0		0		0.0
Total	2	1	1	.500	3	2	0	0	8	19	7	0	0	3-1	5	7.88	54	.463	.500	3	.000	-0	134	-3		-0.5

DUSTAL, BOB　Robert Andrew　B9.28.1935 Sayreville NJ　BR/TR/6-0/175　d4.9

YEAR	TM LG	W	L	PCT	G	GS	CG-SHO	SV-BS	IP	H	R	HR	HB	BB-IB	SO	ERA	AERA	OAV	OOB	AB-HR-SH	AVG	PB	SUP	APR	DL	PW
1963	Det A	0	1	.000	7	0	0	0	6	10	9	0	0	5-1	4	9.00	42	.357	.455	0	—	0		-4		-0.6

DUVALL, MIKE　Michael Alan　B10.11.1974 Warrenton VA　BR/TL/6-0/185(185-200)　[FlaN95 19/513]　d9.22　Col Potomac St. (WV) JC　[DL 2002 Min A 183]

YEAR	TM LG	W	L	PCT	G	GS	CG-SHO	SV-BS	IP	H	R	HR	HB	BB-IB	SO	ERA	AERA	OAV	OOB	AB-HR-SH	AVG	PB	SUP	APR	DL	PW
1998	TB A	0	0	—	3	0	0	0-0	4	4	3	0	0	2-0	1	6.75	71	.267	.353	0	—	0		-1		0.0
1999	TB A	1	1	.500	40	0	0	0-1	40	46	21	5	2	27-1	18	4.05	123	.293	.401	0	—	0		-1		0.0
2000	TB A	0	0	—	2	0	0	0-0	2.1	5	2	0	0	1-0	0	7.71	63	.455	.500	0	—	0		4	27	0.2
2001	Min A	0	0	—	8	0	0	0-1	4.2	7	4	1	0	2-0	4	7.71	61	.368	.409	0	—	0		-1		0.0
Total	4	1	1	.500	53	0	0	0-2	51	62	30	6	2	32-1	23	4.76	103	.307	.403	0	—	0		-1	210	0.1

DUZEN, BILL　William George　B2.21.1870 Buffalo NY　D3.11.1944 Buffalo NY　BR/TR/5-11/165　d9.21

YEAR	TM LG	W	L	PCT	G	GS	CG-SHO	SV-BS	IP	H	R	HR	HB	BB-IB	SO	ERA	AERA	OAV	OOB	AB-HR-SH	AVG	PB	SUP	APR	DL	PW
1890	Buf P	0	2	.000	2	2	1	0	13	20	24	2	0	14	5	13.85	30	.339	.466	4	.250	1	89	-12		-1.0

DWYER, FRANK　John Francis　B3.25.1868 Lee MA　D2.4.1943 Pittsfield MA　BR/TR/5-8/145　d9.20　M1　Col Hobart and William Smith

YEAR	TM LG	W	L	PCT	G	GS	CG-SHO	SV-BS	IP	H	R	HR	HB	BB-IB	SO	ERA	AERA	OAV	OOB	AB-HR-SH	AVG	PB	SUP	APR	DL	PW
1888	Chi N	4	1	.800	5	5	5-1	0	42	32	20	1	0	9	17	1.07	283	.198	.240	21	.190	-0	170	5		0.6
1889	Chi N	16	13	.552	32	30	27	0	276	307	177	14	7	72	63	3.59	116	.273	.321	135-1	.200	-2*	94	16		1.8
1890	Chi P	3	6	.333	12	6	6	1	69.1	98	71	4	0	25	17	6.23	70	.319	.370	53	.264	-0*	94	-11		-1.1
1891	Cin AA	13	19	.406	35	31	29-1	0	289	332	225	10	10	124	101	4.52	91	.279	.351	141	.284	3*	87	-1		0.2
	Mil AA	6	4	.600	10	10	10	0	86	92	41	2	4	21	27	2.20	199	.264	.314	40	.225	-1*	79	17		1.5
	Year	19	23	.452	45	41	39-1	0	375	424	266	12	14	145	128	3.98	104	.275	.343	181	.271	1	85	11		1.7
1892	StL N	2	8	.200	10	10	4	0	64	90	58	1	2	24	16	5.63	57	.319	.372	25	.080	-1	113	-18		-2.1
	Cin N	20	10	.667	34	28	25-3	1	268.1	262	101	6	5	49	47	2.31	141	.246	.282	132	.159	-4*	106	30		2.2
	Year	22	18	.550	44	38	31-3	1	332.1	352	159	7	7	73	63	2.95	110	.261	.302	157	.146	-6	107	19		0.1
1893	Cin N	18	15	.545	37	30	28-1	2	287.1	332	187	17	5	93	53	4.13	116	.281	.336	120-1	.200	-3*	96	18		1.4
1894	Cin N	19	21	.475	45	39	34-1	1	348	471	282	26	15	106	49	5.07	109	.320	.371	172-2-0	.267	1*	97	17		1.5
1895	Cin N	18	15	.545	37	31	23-2	0	280.1	355	191	10	14	74	46	4.24	107	.304	.353	113-1-1	.265	2	90	19		1.7
1896	Cin N	24	11	.686	36	34	30-3	1	288.2	321	144	8	11	60	57	3.15	147	.279	.321	110-0-3	.264	4	90	42		4.4
1897	Cin N	18	13	.581	37	31	22	0	247.1	315	142	5	11	56	41	3.78	120	.307	.350	94-0-7	.266	0	88	19		1.7
1898	Cin N	16	10	.615	31	28	24	0	240	257	117	3	16	42	29	3.04	126	.272	.314	85-0-1	.141	-4	86	18		1.2
1899	Cin N	0	0	—	5	5	0	0	32.2	48	26	1	4	9	2	5.51	71	.340	.384	11	.364	1	48	-5		-0.6
Total	12	177	151	.540	366	318	271-12	6	2819	3312	1782	108	101	764	565	3.84	115	.286	.336	1252-5-12	.229	-7	93	166		13.6

DYER, EDDIE　Edwin Hawley　B10.11.1899 Morgan City LA　D4.20.1964 Houston TX　BL/TL/5-11.5/168　d7.8　M5　Col Rice ▲

YEAR	TM LG	W	L	PCT	G	GS	CG-SHO	SV-BS	IP	H	R	HR	HB	BB-IB	SO	ERA	AERA	OAV	OOB	AB-HR-SH	AVG	PB	SUP	APR	DL	PW
1922	StL N	0	0	—	2	0	0	0	3.2	7	2	0	0	4	3	2.45	157	.412	.412	3	.333	1*		0		0.1
1923	StL N	2	1	.667	4	3	2-1	0	22	30	10	0	1	5	3	4.09	95	.333	.375	45-2-0	.267	0*	70	0		0.2
1924	StL N	8	11	.421	29	15	7-1	0	136.2	174	82	6	4	51	23	4.61	82	.331	.395	76-0-3	.237	1*	133	-12		-1.2
1925	StL N	4	3	.571	27	5	1	3	82.1	93	52	4	7	24	25	4.15	104	.278	.340	31-0-1	.097	-2*	137	-1		-0.3
1926	StL N	1	0	1.000	6	0	0	0	9.1	7	14	0	1	14	4	11.57	34	.219	.468	2	.500	0		-8		-0.7
1927	StL N	0	0	—	1	0	0	0	2	5	4	1	0	2	1	18.00	22	.500	.583	0	—	0		-3		-0.1
Total	6	15	15	.500	69	23	10-2	3	256	316	164	11	13	96	63	4.75	84	.313	.380	157-2-4	.223	1	124	-24		-2.0

DYER, MIKE　Michael Lawrence　B9.8.1966 Upland CA　BR/TR/6-3/195*　[MinA86*4/87]　d6.29　Col Citrus (CA) JC

YEAR	TM LG	W	L	PCT	G	GS	CG-SHO	SV-BS	IP	H	R	HR	HB	BB-IB	SO	ERA	AERA	OAV	OOB	AB-HR-SH	AVG	PB	SUP	APR	DL	PW
1989	Min A	4	7	.364	16	12	1	0-0	71	74	43	2	2	37-0	37	4.82	86	.273	.362	0	—	0	80	-6		-0.9
1994	Pit N	1	1	.500	14	0	0	4-2	15.1	15	12	1	3	12-1	13	5.87	75	.268	.411	1	.000	-0		-3		-0.5
1995	Pit N	4	5	.444	55	0	0	0-2	74.2	81	40	9	5	30-3	35	4.34	100	.281	.358	7-0-1	.571	1		0		-0.1
1996	Mon N	5	5	.500	70	1	0	2-4	75.2	79	40	7	5	34-4	51	4.40	98	.277	.360	7	.000	-1	62	0		-0.1
Total	4	14	18	.438	155	13	1	6-8	236.2	249	135	19	15	113-11	154	4.60	93	.277	.364	15-0-1	.267	1	76	-9		-1.3

DYGERT, JIMMY　James Henry "Sunny Jim"　B7.5.1884 Utica NY　D2.8.1936 New Orleans LA　BR/TR/5-10/158　d9.8

YEAR	TM LG	W	L	PCT	G	GS	CG-SHO	SV-BS	IP	H	R	HR	HB	BB-IB	SO	ERA	AERA	OAV	OOB	AB-HR-SH	AVG	PB	SUP	APR	DL	PW
1905	Phi A	1	4	.200	6	3	2	0	35.1	41	20	2	0	11	24	4.33	61	.291	.351	15	.267	-0	89	-5		-0.6
1906	Phi A	11	13	.458	35	25	15-4	0	213.2	175	88	1	10	91	106	2.70	101	.226	.316	74-1-2	.176	-0	95	2		0.1
1907	Phi A	21	8	.724	42	28	18-5	1	261.2	200	98	2	18	85	151	2.34	111	.214	.292	94-0-6	.128	-4	121	8		0.4
1908	Phi A	11	15	.423	41	28	15-5	1	238.2	194	95	3	11	97	164	2.87	89	.220	.309	75-0-5	.080	-6	77	-4		-1.0
1909	Phi A	9	5	.643	32	13	6	0	137.1	117	60	1	11	50	79	2.42	103	.231	.330	44-0-3	.205	0	156	-4		-0.4
1910	Phi A	4	4	.500	19	8	6-1	0	99.1	81	44	0	3	49	59	2.54	94	.231	.331	36	.083	-1	124	-2		-0.5
Total	6	57	49	.538	175	105	62-16	2	986	798	405	9	55	383	583	2.65	97	.227	.312	338-1-16	.139	-11	107	-5		-2.0

DYKHOFF, RADHAMES　Radhames Alviro　B9.27.1974 Paradera, Aruba　BL/TL/6-0/205　d6.7

YEAR	TM LG	W	L	PCT	G	GS	CG-SHO	SV-BS	IP	H	R	HR	HB	BB-IB	SO	ERA	AERA	OAV	OOB	AB-HR-SH	AVG	PB	SUP	APR	DL	PW
1998	Bal A	0	0	—	1	0	0	0-0	1	2	2	0	0	1-0	1	18.00	25	.400	.500	0	—	0		-1		-0.1

YEAR	TM LG	W	L	PCT	G	GS	CG-SHO	SV-BS	IP	H	R	HR	HB	BB-IB	SO	ERA	AERA	OAV	OOB	AB-HR-SH	AVG	PB	SUP	APR	DL	PW

EARLEY, ARNOLD   Arnold Carl   B6.4.1933 Lincoln Park MI   D9.29.1999 Flint MI   BL/TL/6-1/200*   d9.27

1960	Bos A	0	1	.000	4	0	0	0	4	9	8	1	0	4-0	5	15.75	26	.429	.520	1	.000	0		-5		-0.8
1961	Bos A	2	4	.333	33	0	0	7	49.2	42	31	3	0	34-3	44	3.99	105	.226	.345	6	.000	-1		-1		-0.3
1962	Bos A	4	5	.444	38	3	0	5	68.1	76	53	8	1	46-1	59	5.80	71	.281	.384	10	.200	0	58	-14		-1.8
1963	Bos A	3	7	.300	53	4	0	1	115.2	124	73	13	8	43-8	97	4.75	80	.270	.342	18	.278	1	112	-14		-1.1
1964	Bos A	1	1	.500	25	3	1	1	50.1	51	17	3	1	18-0	45	2.68	144	.266	.332	9-0-1	.111	-0	123	6	63	0.4
1965	Bos A	0	1	.000	57	0	0	0	74.1	79	42	5	3	29-8	12	3.63	103	.271	.338	6	.000	-0		-2		-0.1
1966	Chi N	2	1	.667	13	0	0	0	17.2	14	11	1	0	9-0	12	3.57	103	.226	.319	1-0-1*	.000	-0		-1		-0.2
1967	Hou N	0	0	—	2	0	0	0	1.1	5	5	1	0	1-0	1	27.00	12	.625	.667	0	—	0		-4		-0.2
Total	8	12	20	.375	223	10	1	14	381.1	400	240	35	13	184-20	310	4.48	87	.269	.352	51-0-2	.157	0	98	-35	63	-4.1

EARLEY, TOM   Thomas Francis Aloysius   B2.19.1917 Roxbury MA   D4.5.1988 Nantucket MA   BR/TR/6-0/180   d9.27   Mil 1943-44

1938	Bos N	1	0	1.000	2	1	1	0	11	8	9	2	1	4	4	3.27	105	.186	.222	4	.000	-1	99	-2		-0.2
1939	Bos N	1	4	.200	14	2	0	1	40	49	28	1	2	19	5	4.72	78	.304	.385	10	.300	1	59	-6		-0.7
1940	Bos N	2	0	1.000	4	1	1-1	0	16.1	16	7	1	2	3	5	3.86	96	.267	.323	5	.400	1	187	0		0.1
1941	Bos N	6	8	.429	33	13	6-1	3	138.2	120	52	9	3	46	54	2.53	141	.233	.300	47-0-2	.234	1*	93	14		1.5
1942	Bos N	6	11	.353	27	18	6	1	112.2	120	65	10	1	55	28	4.71	71	.276	.359	34-0-3	.118	-1	95	-16		-2.2
1945	Bos N	2	1	.667	11	2	1	0	41	36	22	4	0	19	4	4.61	83	.235	.320	14-0-1	.214	1*	166	-2		-0.1
Total	6		18	24	.429	91	37	15-2	5	359.2	349	183	27	9	143	104	3.78	94	.256	.330	114-0-6	.202	2	98	-12		-1.6

EARLEY, BILL   William Albert   B1.30.1956 Cincinnati OH   BR/TL/6-4/200   d9.22   Col Miami-Ohio

1986	StL N	0	0	—	3	0	0	0-0	3	0	0	0	0	2-0	2	0.00	—	.000	.182	0	—	0		1		0.1

EARNSHAW, GEORGE   George Livingston "Moose"   B2.15.1900 New York NY   D12.1.1976 Little Rock AR   BR/TR/6-4/210   d6.3   C2   Col Swarthmore

1928	Phi A	7	7	.500	26	22	7-3	1	158.1	143	81	7	1	100	117	3.81	105	.240	.351	57-0-5	.246	1	123	3		0.3
1929	†Phi A	24	8	.750	44	33	13-3	1	254.2	233	110	8	5	125	149	3.29	129	**.241**	.331	87-1-10	.172	-2	118	27		2.6
1930	†Phi A	22	13	.629	49	39	20-3	2	296	299	162	20	1	139	193	3.67	122	.266	.347	114-2-3	.228	1	118	10		1.0
1931	†Phi A	21	7	.750	43	30	23-3	6	281.2	255	130	16	3	75	152	3.67	122	.236	.288	114-2-3	.263	6	118	28		3.1
1932	Phi A	19	13	.594	36	33	21-1	0	245.1	262	147	28	4	94	109	4.77	95	.270	.336	91-0-11	.286	4	121	-9		-0.6
1933	Phi A	5	10	.333	21	18	4	0	117.2	153	93	8	1	58	37	5.97	72	.311	.385	44-0-2	.182	-0	133	-22		-2.3
1934	Chi A	14	11	.560	33	30	16-2	0	227	242	128	28	4	104	97	4.52	105	.270	.349	79-0-3	.203	0	82	7		0.6
1935	Chi A	1	2	.333	3	3	0	0	18	26	19	2	0	11	8	9.00	51	.342	.425	7-0-1	.286	0	110	-1		0.0
	Bro N	8	12	.400	25	22	6-2	0	166	175	87	14	0	53	72	4.12	96	.270	.325	60-0-1	.217	1	81	-11		-1.2
1936	Bro N	4	9	.308	19	13	4-1	1	93	113	63	7	3	30	40	6.40	62	.333	.392	18	.222	-0	122	-14		-0.7
	StL N	2	1	.667	20	6	1	1	57.2	80	43	4	3	20	28	5.73	71	.311	.368	51-0-1	.235	0	93	-23		-1.9
	Year	6	10	.375	39	19	5-1	2	150.2	193	106	11	6	50	68	5.73	71	.311	.368	51-0-1	.235	0	93	-23		-1.9
Total	9		127	93	.577	319	249	115-18	12	1915.1	1981	1063	142	25	809	1002	4.38	100	.265	.339	704-3-44	.230	9	113	10		1.9

EASLEY, LOGAN   Kenneth Logan   B11.4.1961 Salt Lake City UT   BR/TR/6-1/185*   [NYA81 20/519]   d4.9   Col Southern Idaho [JC]

1987	Pit N	1	1	.500	17	0	0	1-0	26.1	23	17	5	1	17-4	21	5.47	76	.242	.357	2	.000	-0		-3		-0.2
1989	Pit N	1	0	1.000	10	0	0	1-0	12.1	8	6	1	1	7-1	6	4.38	78	.190	.320	1	.000	-0		-1		-0.1
Total	2	1	1	.667	27	0	0	2-0	38.2	31	23	6	2	24-5	27	5.12	76	.226	.345	3	.000	-0		-4		-0.3

EASON, MAL   Malcolm Wayne "Kid"   B3.13.1879 Brookville PA   D4.16.1970 Douglas AZ   BR/TR/6-0/175   d10.1   U8   Col Grove City

1900	Chi N	1	0	1.000	1	1	1	0	9	9	2	0	0	3	3	1.00	361	.257	.316	3	.000	-1	77	3		0.2
1901	Chi N	8	17	.320	27	25	23-1	0	220.2	246	136	9	13	60	68	3.59	90	.280	.335	87-0-1	.138	-5	76	-10		-1.5
1902	Chi N	1	1	.500	2	2	2	0	18	21	7	0	0	2	4	1.00	271	.292	.311	5-0-1	.200	0	75	2		0.3
	Bos N	9	12	.429	27	27	20-2	0	213.1	249	100	4	12	61	51	2.91	97	.291	.347	72-0-6	.083	-6	94	-3		-1.0
	Year	10	13	.435	29	29	22-2	0	231.1	270	107	4	12	63	55	2.76	102	.291	.344	77-0-7	.091	-6	92	-2		-0.7
1903	Det A	2	5	.286	7	6	6-1	0	56.1	60	33	1	3	19	21	3.36	87	.271	.337	20	.100	-2	53	-4		-0.5
1905	Bro N	5	21	.192	27	27	20-3	0	207	230	128	5	5	72	64	4.30	67	.292	.355	81-0-2	.173	-1*	69	-29		-3.2
1906	Bro N	10	17	.370	34	26	18-3	1	227	212	109	1	9	74	64	3.25	78	.256	.323	88-0-1	.091	-4*	98	-19		-2.6
Total	6		36	73	.330	125	114	90-10	1	951.1	1027	515	20	42	291	274	3.42	84	.279	.339	356-0-11	.121	-19	82	-60		-8.3

EAST, HUGH   Gordon Hugh   B7.7.1919 Birmingham AL   D11.2.1981 Charleston SC   BR/TR/6-2/185   d9.13   Mil 1943-45

1941	NY N	1	1	.500	2	2	0	0	15.2	19	12	0	0	9	4	3.45	107	.297	.384	9	.222	0	138	-2		-0.2
1942	NY N	0	2	.000	4	1	0	0	7.1	15	16	1	0	7	2	9.82	34	.429	.524	2-1-0	.500	2	50	-8		-1.2
1943	NY N	1	3	.250	13	5	1	0	40.1	51	27	4	0	25	21	5.36	64	.298	.388	13	.077	-1*	64	-8		-0.9
Total	3		2	6	.250	19	8	1	0	63.1	85	55	5	0	41	27	5.40	65	.315	.405	24-1-0	.167	1	82	-18		-2.3

EASTERLY, JAMIE   James Morris   B2.17.1953 Houston TX   BL/TL/5-9/180*   [AtlN71 2/34]   d4.6

1974	Atl N	0	0	—	3	0	0	0-0	2.2	5	6	0	0	4-0	0	16.88	23	.400	.526	0		0		-4		-1.0
1975	Atl N	2	9	.182	21	13	0	0-0	68.2	73	47	5	2	42-2	34	4.98	76	.275	.375	18-0-3	.056	-2	91	-32		-1.6
1976	Atl N	1	1	.500	4	4	0	0-0	22	23	12	0	0	13-1	11	4.91	77	.280	.379	9	.111	-0	70	-2		-0.2
1977	Atl N	2	4	.333	22	5	0	1-0	58.2	72	46	5	3	30-4	37	6.14	72	.303	.386	15-0-2	.267	1*	92	-10	88	-1.7
1978	Atl N	3	6	.333	37	6	0	1-1	78	91	52	9	2	45-6	42	5.65	71	.299	.391	19-0-1	.211	0	85	-11		-0.2
1979	Atl N	0	0	—	4	0	0	0-0	2.2	4	6	0	0	3-0	3	13.50	30	.467	.556	0	—	0		-3		-0.2
1981	†Mil A	3	3	.500	44	0	0	4-3	62	46	23	0	0	34-4	31	3.19	109	.219	.321	0	—	0		2		0.3
1982	Mil A	0	0	—	28	0	0	2-1	30.2	39	19	6	0	15-0	16	4.70	82	.312	.380	0	—	-0*		~1	51	-0.2
1983	Mil A	0	1	.000	12	0	0	1-1	11.2	14	7	0	2	10-1	6	3.86	98	.350	.491	1-0-1	.000	-0*		4		0.0
	Cle A	4	2	.667	41	0	0	3-4	57	69	25	4	2	22-4	39	3.63	118	.309	.375	0	—	0		4		0.0
	Year	4	3	.571	53	0	0	4-5	68.2	83	32	4	4	32-5	45	3.67	114	.316	.395	1-0-1	.000	-0	88	5	74	0.0
1984	Cle A	3	1	.750	26	1	0	2-0	69.1	74	31	3	1	23-3	42	3.38	122	.273	.330	0	—	0	159	1		0.0
1985	Cle A	4	1	.800	50	7	0	0-0	98.2	96	52	9	4	53-4	58	3.92	106	.264	.356	0	—	0		-6	127	-0.4
1986	Cle A	0	2	.000	13	0	0	0-0	17.2	27	16	3	0	12-0	9	7.64	55	.365	.443	0	—	0		1	125	-0.6
1987	Cle A	1	1	.500	16	0	0	0-1	31.2	26	11	4	1	13-1	22	4.55	100	.218	.296	0	—	-1	101	-38	465	-4.1
Total	13		23	33	.411	321	36	0	14-11	611.1	663	360	48	17	319-30	350	4.62	88	.283	.368	62-0-7	.161	-1	101	-38	465	-4.1

EASTON, JACK   John S.   B2.28.1867 Bridgeport OH   D11.28.1903 Steubenville OH   d9.23

1889	Col AA	1	0	1.000	2	2	1	1	18	13	8	0	3	21	7	3.50	104	.197	.411	7	.000	-1	120	1		0.0
1890	Col AA	15	14	.517	37	29	23	1	255.2	213	148	4	20	125	147	3.52	102	.220	.321	107	.178	0*	109	4		0.0
1891	Col AA	5	10	.333	18	16	13	0	135.1	145	111	3	15	59	52	4.52	76	.265	.352	63	.238	2*	86	-20		-1.3
	StL AA	3	2	.600	7	6	4	0	47.2	48	38	3	4	23	22	5.10	82	.253	.346	28	.179	-1*	108	-2		-0.5
	Col AA	0	2	.000	2	2	2	0	15	15	8	2	2	4	13	3.60	98	.250	.318	11	.000	-1	18	0		-0.1
	Year	8	14	.364	27	24	19	0	198	208	157	8	21	86	87	4.59	79	.261	.348	102	.196	-1	88	-17		-1.3
1892	StL N	2	0	1.000	5	2	2	0	31	38	31	2	3	26	19	6.39	50	.290	.419	17	.176	-1	54	1		-0.0
1894	Pit N	0	1	.000	3	1	1	0	19.2	26	16	0	3	4	1	4.12	127	.313	.367	5-2-0	.000	-1	100	-27		-2.2
Total	5		26	29	.473	76	57	46	2	522.1	498	360	14	50	262	246	4.12	89	.243	.343	238-0-2	.176	-2	100	-27		-2.2

EASTWICK, RAWLY   Rawlins Jackson   B10.24.1950 Camden NJ   BR/TR/6-3/180*   [CinN69 3/62]   d9.12

1974	Cin N	0	0	—	8	0	0	2-0	17.2	12	5	1	0	5-0	14	2.04	172	.188	.243	1	.000	-0		3		0.0
1975	†Cin N	5	3	.625	58	0	0	22-3	90	77	26	6	2	25-4	61	2.60	138	.229	.287	15-0-1	.067	-1		11		1.0
1976	†Cin N	11	5	.688	71	0	0	26-9	107.2	93	30	3	2	27-3	70	2.09	167	.232	.282	17-0-2	.000	-2		16		2.0
1977	Cin N	2	2	.500	23	0	0	7-2	43.1	40	14	3	0	8-1	17	2.91	135	.244	.279	6-0-1	.167	0		5		0.0
	StL N	3	7	.300	41	0	0	4-2	53.2	74	34	6	0	21-3	30	4.70	83	.332	.385	5-0-0	.400	1	114	-6		-1.0
	Year	5	9	.357	64	0	0	11-4	97	114	48	9	0	29-4	47	3.90	101	.295	.341	11-0-1	.273	1	113	-1		-1.0
1978	NY A	2	1	.667	8	0	0	0-2	24.2	22	9	2	1	4-0	13	3.28	111	.232	.270	0	.000	-0		-2		-0.0
	†Phi N	2	1	.667	22	0	0	0-2	40.1	31	21	5	0	18-2	14	4.02	90	.209	.292	7	.000	-0		-8		-1.0
1979	Phi N	3	6	.333	51	0	0	6-3	82.2	90	46	8	1	25-3	47	4.90	79	.284	.336	7	—	0		-3		-0.0
1980	KC A	0	1	.000	5	0	0	0-1	6.2	7	6	0	0	3-0	2	8.10	47	.280	.348	0	—	0		5	21	0.0
1981	Chi N	0	1	.000	30	0	0	1-1	43.1	43	16	2	1	15-3	24	2.28	164	.264	.322	2	.000	-4	119	23	21	0.0
Total	8		28	27	.509	326	0	0	68-23	525.1	519	215	38	6	156-21	295	3.31	112	.258	.312	56-0-4	.071	-7	119	23	21	0.0

EATON, ADAM   Adam Thomas   B11.23.1977 Seattle WA   BR/TR/6-2/190*   [PhiN96 1/11]   d5.30

2000	SD N	7	4	.636	22	22	0	0-0	135	134	63	14	2	61-3	90	4.13	108	.260	.338	38	.289	5*	106	8		1
2001	SD N	8	5	.615	17	17	2	0-0	116.2	108	61	20	5	40-3	109	4.32	96	.241	.308	38-0-2	.105	-0*	114	-1	94	1

YEAR	TM LG	W	L	PCT	G	GS	CG-SHO	SV-BS	IP	H	R	HR	HB	BB-IB	SO	ERA	AERA	OAV	OOB	AB-HR-SH	AVG	PB	SUP	APR	DL	PW
2002	SD N	1	1	.500	6	6	0	0-0	33.1	28	20	5	2	17-0	25	5.40	72	.235	.336	9	.111	-0	91	-5	154	-0.3
2003	SD N	9	12	.429	31	31	1	0-0	183	173	91	20	7	68-6	146	4.08	98	.246	.316	56-2-7	.196	5*	99	-3	15	0.4
2004	SD N	11	14	.440	33	33	0	0-0	199.1	204	113	28	10	52-3	153	4.61	86	.266	.318	64-0-5	.203	6*	109	-17		-1.3
2005	SD N	11	5	.688	24	22	0	0-0	128.2	140	70	14	5	44-6	100	4.27	91	.275	.335	46-0-3	.174	2*	128	-8	67	-0.8
Total 6		47	41	.534	133	131	3	0-0	796	787	418	101	31	282-21	623	4.34	93	.257	.323	251-2-17	.191	18	109	-26	330	-0.9

EATON, CRAIG Craig B9.7.1954 Glendale OH BR/TR/5-11/175 d9.5 Col Florida St.

YEAR	TM LG	W	L	PCT	G	GS	CG-SHO	SV-BS	IP	H	R	HR	HB	BB-IB	SO	ERA	AERA	OAV	OOB	AB-HR-SH	AVG	PB	SUP	APR	DL	PW
1979	KC A	0	0	—	5	0	0	0-0	10	8	3	0	0	3-2	4	2.70	158	.222	.282	0	—	0		2		0.1

EATON, ZEB Zebulon Vance "Red" B2.2.1920 Cooleemee NC D12.17.1989 W.Palm Beach FL BR/TR/5-10/185 d4.18

YEAR	TM LG	W	L	PCT	G	GS	CG-SHO	SV-BS	IP	H	R	HR	HB	BB-IB	SO	ERA	AERA	OAV	OOB	AB-HR-SH	AVG	PB	SUP	APR	DL	PW
1944	Det A	0	0	—	6	0	0	0	15.2	19	12	2	0	8	4	5.74	62	.322	.403	10	.100	-1*		-4		-0.2
1945	†Det A	4	2	.667	17	3	0	0	53.1	48	28	0	3	40	15	4.05	87	.247	.384	32-2-0	.250	2*	40	-3		-0.1
Total 2		4	2	.667	23	3	0	0	69	67	40	2	3	48	19	4.43	80	.265	.388	42-2-0	.214	2	40	-7		-0.3

EAVE, GARY Gary Louis B7.22.1963 Monroe LA BR/TR/6-4/190* [AtlN85 12/302] d4.12 Col Grambling St.

YEAR	TM LG	W	L	PCT	G	GS	CG-SHO	SV-BS	IP	H	R	HR	HB	BB-IB	SO	ERA	AERA	OAV	OOB	AB-HR-SH	AVG	PB	SUP	APR	DL	PW
1988	Atl N	0	0	—	5	0	0	0-0	5	7	5	0	0	3-0	0	9.00	41	.333	.417	0	—	0		-3		-0.1
1989	Atl N	2	0	1.000	3	3	0	0-0	20.2	15	3	0	1	12-0	9	1.31	280	.200	.318	6-0-1	.000	-1	81	5		0.4
1990	Sea A	0	3	.000	8	5	0	0-0	30	27	16	5	2	20-1	16	4.20	95	.241	.366	0	—	0	87	-1		0.2
Total 3		2	3	.400	16	8	0	0-0	55.2	49	24	5	3	35-1	25	3.56	108	.236	.354	6-0-1	.000	-1	85	1		0.4

EAVES, VALLIE Vallie Ennis "Chief" B9.6.1911 Allen OK D4.19.1960 Norman OK BR/TR/6-2.5/180 d9.12

YEAR	TM LG	W	L	PCT	G	GS	CG-SHO	SV-BS	IP	H	R	HR	HB	BB-IB	SO	ERA	AERA	OAV	OOB	AB-HR-SH	AVG	PB	SUP	APR	DL	PW
1935	Phi A	1	2	.333	3	3	1	0	14	12	9	0	0	15	6	5.14	88	.240	.415	4	.000	-1	57	-1		-0.2
1939	Chi A	0	1	.000	2	1	1	0	11.2	11	7	1	1	8	5	4.63	102	.250	.377	6	.333	-1	56	0		0.0
1940	Chi A	0	2	.000	5	3	0	0	18.2	22	16	2	1	24	11	6.75	66	.301	.480	5-0-1	.000	-1	73	-5		-0.5
1941	Chi A	3	5	.500	12	7	4	0	58.2	56	27	4	3	21	24	3.53	99	.253	.327	20-0-1	.100	-1	100	0		-0.2
1942	Chi N	0	0	—	2	0	0	0	3	4	3	0	1	2	0	9.00	36	.308	.438	0	—	0		-2		-0.1
Total 5		4	8	.333	24	14	6	0	106	105	62	7	6	70	46	4.58	86	.262	.379	35-0-2	.114	-3	82	-1		-1.0

EAYRS, EDDIE Edwin B11.10.1890 Blackstone MA D11.30.1969 Warwick RI BL/TL/5-7/160 d6.30 Col Brown ▲

YEAR	TM LG	W	L	PCT	G	GS	CG-SHO	SV-BS	IP	H	R	HR	HB	BB-IB	SO	ERA	AERA	OAV	OOB	AB-HR-SH	AVG	PB	SUP	APR	DL	PW
1913	Pit N	0	0	—	2	0	0	0	8	6	6	0	0	6	5	2.25	134	.267	.389	1	.167	-0*		-1		-0.1
1920	Bos N	1	2	.333	7	3	0	0	26.1	36	18	1	2	12	7	5.47	56	.346	.424	244-1-6	.328	2*	69	-7		-0.5
1921	Bos N	0	0	—	2	0	0	0	4.2	9	10	0	0	9	1	17.36	21	.391	.563	15	.067	-2*		-7		-0.5
Total 3		1	2	.333	11	3	0	0	39	53	34	1	2	27	13	6.23	50	.338	.441	265-1-6	.309	0	69	-15		-1.1

EBERT, DERRIN Derrin Lee B8.21.1976 Anaheim CA BR/TL/6-3/200 [AtlN94 18/510] d4.6

YEAR	TM LG	W	L	PCT	G	GS	CG-SHO	SV-BS	IP	H	R	HR	HB	BB-IB	SO	ERA	AERA	OAV	OOB	AB-HR-SH	AVG	PB	SUP	APR	DL	PW
1999	Atl N	0	1	.000	5	0	0	1-0	8	9	5	2	0	5-1	4	5.63	79	.300	.400	1	.000	-0		-1		-0.1

ECCLES, HARRY Harry Josiah "Bugs" B7.9.1893 Kennedy NY D6.2.1955 Jamestown NY BL/TL/6-2/170 d9.13

YEAR	TM LG	W	L	PCT	G	GS	CG-SHO	SV-BS	IP	H	R	HR	HB	BB-IB	SO	ERA	AERA	OAV	OOB	AB-HR-SH	AVG	PB	SUP	APR	DL	PW
1915	Phi A	0	1	.000	5	1	0	1	21	18	16	2	0	6	13	4.71	62	.240	.296	6	.167	-0	125	-4		-0.3

ECKENSTAHLER, ERIC Eric Ryan B12.17.1976 Waukegan IL BL/TL/6-7/210* [DetA99 32/957] d9.9 Col Illinois St.

YEAR	TM LG	W	L	PCT	G	GS	CG-SHO	SV-BS	IP	H	R	HR	HB	BB-IB	SO	ERA	AERA	OAV	OOB	AB-HR-SH	AVG	PB	SUP	APR	DL	PW
2002	Det A	1	0	1.000	7	0	0	0-0	8	14	5	1	0	2-0	13	5.63	78	.378	.410	0	—	0		-1		-0.1
2003	Det A	0	0	—	20	0	0	0-0	15.2	9	6	0	2	15-1	12	2.87	153	.167	.366	0	—	0		2		0.1
Total 2		1	0	1.000	27	0	0	0-0	23.2	23	11	1	2	17-1	25	3.80	115	.253	.382	0	—	0		1		0.0

ECKERSLEY, DENNIS Dennis Lee B10.3.1954 Oakland CA BR/TR/6-2/190(175-195) [CleA72 3/50] d4.12 HF2004

YEAR	TM LG	W	L	PCT	G	GS	CG-SHO	SV-BS	IP	H	R	HR	HB	BB-IB	SO	ERA	AERA	OAV	OOB	AB-HR-SH	AVG	PB	SUP	APR	DL	PW
1975	Cle A	13	7	.650	34	24	6-2	2-1	186.2	147	61	16	7	90-8	152	2.60	146	.215	.310	0	—	0	110	25		2.5
1976	Cle A	13	12	.520	36	30	9-3	1-0	199.1	155	82	13	5	78-2	200	3.43	102	.214	.293	0	—	0	94	3		0.3
1977	Cle A★	14	13	.519	33	33	12-3	0-0	247.1	214	100	31	7	54-11	191	3.53	113	.231	.276	0	—	0*	91	17		1.5
1978	Bos A	20	8	.714	35	35	16-3	0-0	268.1	258	99	30	7	71-8	162	2.99	133	.251	.302	0	—	0	111	32		3.1
1979	Bos A	17	10	.630	33	33	17-2	0-0	246.2	234	89	29	6	59-4	150	2.99	149	.250	.297	0	—	0	105	39		4.0
1980	Bos A	12	14	.462	30	30	8	0-0	197.2	188	101	25	2	44-7	121	4.28	100	.248	.289	0	—	0	87	0		0.0
1981	Bos A	9	8	.529	23	23	8-2	0-0	154	160	82	9	3	35-2	79	4.27	92	.267	.308	0	—	0	111	-5		-0.6
1982	Bos A★	13	13	.500	33	33	11-3	0-0	224.1	228	101	31	2	43-3	127	3.73	117	.261	.296	0	—	0	79	15		1.5
1983	Bos A	9	13	.409	28	28	2	0-0	176.1	223	119	27	6	39-4	77	5.61	84	.303	.341	0	—	0	78	-21		-2.3
1984	Bos A	4	4	.500	9	9	2	0-0	64.2	71	38	10	1	13-2	33	5.01	84	.284	.318	0	—	0	119	-4		-0.4
	†Chi N	10	8	.556	24	24	2	0-0	160.1	152	59	11	4	36-7	81	3.03	129	.250	.294	55-0-1	.109	-3	99	15		1.3
1985	Chi N	11	7	.611	25	25	6-2	0-0	169.1	145	61	15	3	19-4	117	3.08	130	.229	.254	56-1-2	.125	0*	89	16	27	1.8
1986	Chi N	6	11	.353	33	32	1	0-0	201	226	109	21	3	43-3	137	4.57	89	.285	.320	69-2-2	.159	1	88	-10		-0.6
1987	Oak A	6	8	.429	54	2	0	16-4	115.2	99	41	11	3	17-3	113	3.03	137	.228	.260	0	—	0	77	17		2.2
1988	†Oak A★	4	2	.667	60	0	0	45-8	72.2	52	20	5	1	11-2	70	2.35	162	.198	.230	0	—	0	13			2.4
1989	†Oak A	4	0	1.000	51	0	0	33-6	57.2	32	10	5	1	3-0	55	1.56	237	.162	.175	0	—	0	15		45	2.5
1990	†Oak A★	4	2	.667	63	0	0	48-2	73.1	41	9	2	0	4-1	73	0.61	609	.160	.172	0	—	0	25			4.7
1991	Oak A★	5	4	.556	67	0	0	43-8	76	60	26	11	1	9-3	87	2.96	130	.208	.235	0	—	0	8			1.7
1992	†Oak A★	7	1	.875	69	0	0	51-3	80	62	17	5	1	11-6	93	1.91	197	.211	.242	0	—	0	18			3.8
1993	Oak A	2	4	.333	64	0	0	36-10	67	67	32	7	2	13-4	80	4.16	99	.261	.299	0	—	0	0			-0.1
1994	Oak A	5	4	.556	45	0	0	19-6	44.1	49	26	5	1	13-2	47	4.26	105	.275	.328	0	—	0	-2			-0.3
1995	Oak A	4	6	.400	52	0	0	29-9	50.1	53	29	5	1	11-0	40	4.83	94	.269	.308	0	—	0	-2			-0.3
1996	†StL N	0	6	.000	63	0	0	30-4	60	65	26	8	4	6-2	49	3.30	129	.274	.300	1	.000	-0	5		25	0.9
1997	StL N	1	5	.167	57	0	0	36-7	53	49	24	9	2	8-0	45	3.91	107	.238	.273	0	—	0	3			0.5
1998	†Bos A	4	1	.800	50	0	0	1-3	39.2	46	21	6	2	8-3	45	4.76	99	.291	.331	0	—	0	1		53	0.1
Total 24		197	171	.535	1071	361	100-20	390-71	3285.2	3076	1382	347	75	738-91	2401	3.50	117	.246	.290	181-3-5	.133	-1	96	225	150	30.5

ECKERT, AL Albert George "Obbie" B5.17.1906 Milwaukee WI D4.20.1974 Milwaukee WI BL/TL/5-10/174 d4.21

YEAR	TM LG	W	L	PCT	G	GS	CG-SHO	SV-BS	IP	H	R	HR	HB	BB-IB	SO	ERA	AERA	OAV	OOB	AB-HR-SH	AVG	PB	SUP	APR	DL	PW
1930	Cin N	0	1	.000	2	1	0	0	5	7	6	0	0	4	1	7.20	67	.304	.407	1	.000	-0	54	-2		-0.3
1931	Cin N	0	1	.000	14	1	0	0	18.2	26	20	3	0	9	5	9.16	41	.325	.393	3	.333	0	92	-11		-0.5
1935	StL N	0	0	—	2	0	0	0	3	7	4	0	0	1	1	12.00	34	.467	.500	0	—	0		-2		-0.1
Total 2		0	2	.000	18	2	0	0	26.2	40	30	3	0	14	7	9.11	44	.339	.409	4	.250	0	76	-15		-0.9

ECKERT, CHARLIE Charles William "Buzz" B8.8.1897 Philadelphia PA D8.22.1986 Trevose PA BR/TR/5-10.5/165 d9.18

YEAR	TM LG	W	L	PCT	G	GS	CG-SHO	SV-BS	IP	H	R	HR	HB	BB-IB	SO	ERA	AERA	OAV	OOB	AB-HR-SH	AVG	PB	SUP	APR	DL	PW
1919	Phi A	0	1	.000	4	0	0	0	16	17	9	1	0	3	6	3.94	87	.270	.303	6	.167	-0	23	-1		-0.1
1920	Phi A	0	0	—	2	0	0	0	5.2	8	3	0	1	1	1	4.76	84	.421	.476	1	.000	-0		0		0.0
1922	Phi A	0	2	.000	21	0	0	0	50	61	33	7	1	23	15	4.68	91	.319	.395	4	.091	-1		-3		-0.2
Total 3		0	3	.000	25	1	1	0	71.2	86	45	8	2	27	22	4.52	90	.315	.381	11	.111	-2	23	-4		-0.3

EDDY, CHRIS Christopher Mark B11.27.1969 Dallas TX BL/TL/6-3/200 [KCA92 3/78] d4.26 Col TCU

YEAR	TM LG	W	L	PCT	G	GS	CG-SHO	SV-BS	IP	H	R	HR	HB	BB-IB	SO	ERA	AERA	OAV	OOB	AB-HR-SH	AVG	PB	SUP	APR	DL	PW
1995	Oak A	0	0	—	6	0	0	0-0	3.2	7	3	0	2	2-0	2	7.36	62	.438	.550	0	—	0		-1		0.0

EDDY, DON Donald Eugene B10.25.1946 Mason City IA BR/TL/5-11/170* d9.7

YEAR	TM LG	W	L	PCT	G	GS	CG-SHO	SV-BS	IP	H	R	HR	HB	BB-IB	SO	ERA	AERA	OAV	OOB	AB-HR-SH	AVG	PB	SUP	APR	DL	PW
1970	Chi A	0	0	—	7	0	0	0-0	11.2	10	4	0	0	6-0	9	2.31	168	.244	.340	0	—	0		2		0.1
1971	Chi A	0	2	.000	22	0	0	0-1	22.2	19	6	1	0	19-2	14	2.38	150	.232	.373	1	1.000	0		1		0.4
Total 2		0	2	.000	29	0	0	0-1	34.1	29	10	1	0	25-2	23	2.36	156	.236	.362	1	1.000	1		3		0.5

EDDY, STEVE Steven Allen B8.21.1957 Sterling IL BR/TR/6-2/185 [AnaA75 19/433] d6.13

YEAR	TM LG	W	L	PCT	G	GS	CG-SHO	SV-BS	IP	H	R	HR	HB	BB-IB	SO	ERA	AERA	OAV	OOB	AB-HR-SH	AVG	PB	SUP	APR	DL	PW
1979	Cal A	1	1	.500	7	4	0	1-2	32.1	36	19	1	2	20-0	9	4.73	86	.290	.389	0	—	0	128	-2		-0.1

EDELEN, JOE Benny Joe B9.16.1955 Durant OK BR/TR/6-0/165(165-180) [StlN73 1/12] d4.18

YEAR	TM LG	W	L	PCT	G	GS	CG-SHO	SV-BS	IP	H	R	HR	HB	BB-IB	SO	ERA	AERA	OAV	OOB	AB-HR-SH	AVG	PB	SUP	APR	DL	PW
1981	StL N	1	0	1.000	13	0	0	0-0	17.1	29	18	2	1	3-1	10	9.35	39	.367	.393	3	.333	-0		-10		-0.5
	Cin N	1	0	1.000	5	0	0	0-0	12.2	5	1	0	0	3-1	5	0.71	493	.128	.128	2	.000	-0		4		0.3
Year		2	0	1.000	18	0	0	0-0	30	34	19	3	1	6-2	15	5.70	63	.288	.309	5	.200	-0		-6		-0.2
1982	Cin N	0	0	—	9	0	0	0-0	15.1	22	15	2	0	8-3	11	8.80	42	.344	.411	2	.500	0		-8		-0.4
Total 2		2	0	1.000	27	0	0	0-0	45.1	56	34	5	1	14-4	26	6.75	53	.308	.347	7	.286	0		-14		-0.6

EDELEN, ED Edward Joseph "Doc" B3.16.1912 Bryantown MD D2.1.1982 LaPlata MD BR/TR/6-0/191 d8.20 Col Mount St. Marys

YEAR	TM LG	W	L	PCT	G	GS	CG-SHO	SV-BS	IP	H	R	HR	HB	BB-IB	SO	ERA	AERA	OAV	OOB	AB-HR-SH	AVG	PB	SUP	APR	DL	PW
1932	Was A	0	0	—	2	0	0	0	3	3	0	0	0	6	2	0	27.00	16	.000	.600	0	—	0		-2		-0.1

EDELMAN, JOHN John Rogers B7.27.1935 Philadelphia PA BR/TR/6-3/185 d6.2 Col West Chester

YEAR	TM LG	W	L	PCT	G	GS	CG-SHO	SV-BS	IP	H	R	HR	HB	BB-IB	SO	ERA	AERA	OAV	OOB	AB-HR-SH	AVG	PB	SUP	APR	DL	PW
1955	Mil N	0	0	—	5	0	0	0-0	5.2	7	6	0	0	8-0	3	11.12	34	.304	.484	0	—	0		-5		-0.2

YEAR	TM LG	W	L	PCT	G	GS	CG-SHO	SV-BS	IP	H	R	HR	HB	BB-IB	SO	ERA	AERA	OAV	OOB	AB-HR-SH	AVG	PB	SUP	APR	DL	PW

EDEN, CHARLIE Charles M. B1.18.1855 Lexington KY D9.17.1920 Cincinnati OH BL/TL/?/168 d8.17.1877 ▲

1884	Pit AA	0	1	.000	2	1	1	0	12	12	9	1	1	3	3	6.00	55	.255	.314	122-1			.270	1*	91	-2		-0.1
1885	Pit AA	1	2	.333	4	1	0	0	15.2	22	13	0	0	5	5	5.17	62	.314	.342	405			.254	1*	92	-3		-0.4
Total	2	1	3	.250	6	2	1	0	27.2	34	22	1	1	6	8	5.53	59	.291	.331	527-1			.258	1	92	-5		-0.5

EDENFIELD, KEN Kenneth Edward B3.18.1967 Jesup GA BR/TR/6-1/165* [CalA90 21/582] d5.11 Col Western Kentucky

1995	Cal A	0	0	—	7	0	0	0-0	12.2	15	7	1	0	5-0	6	4.26	96	.300	.357	0	—	0		0			0.0
1996	Cal A	0	0	—	2	0	0	0-0	4.1	10	5	2	1	2-0	4	10.38	49	.435	.500	0	—	0		-2			-0.1
Total	2	0	0	—	9	0	0	0-0	17	25	12	3	1	7-0	10	5.82	82	.342	.402	0	—	0		-2			-0.1

EDENS, TOM Thomas Patrick B6.9.1961 Ontario OR BR/TR/6-2/188* [KCA83 14/361] d6.2 Col Lewis-Clark St.

1987	NY N	0	0	—	4	0	0	0-0	8	15	6	2	0	4-0	4	6.75	47	.417	.475	3	.000	-0	142	-2		-0.1
1990	Mil A	4	5	.444	35	6	0	2-0	89	89	52	8	4	33-3	40	4.45	87	.262	.331	0	—	0	102	-6		-0.6
1991	Min A	2	2	.500	8	6	0	0-0	33	34	15	2	0	10-1	19	4.09	105	.256	.308	0	—	0	107	1		0.2
1992	Min A	6	3	.667	52	0	0	3-2	76.1	65	26	1	2	36-3	57	2.83	144	.236	.329	0	—	0	10	1		1.2
1993	Hou N	1	1	.500	38	0	0	0-1	49	47	17	4	0	19-7	21	3.12	124	.263	.332	1	.000	-0	5	31	0.3
1994	Hou N	4	1	.800	39	0	0	1-2	50	55	25	3	2	17-4	38	4.50	88	.289	.349	2-0-1	.000	-0	1		-0.1
	Phi N	1	0	1.000	3	0	0	0-0	4	4	1	0	0	1-0	1	2.25	190	.267	.313	0	—	-0	-1		0.2
	Year	5	1	.833	42	0	0	1-2	54	59	26	3	2	18-4	39	4.33	92	.288	.346	2-0-1	.000	0	-1		0.1
1995	Chi N	1	0	1.000	5	0	0	0-0	3	6	3	0	0	3-0	2	6.00	70	.400	.500	0	—	0	-1		-0.2
Total	7	19	12	.613	182	14	0	6-5	312.1	315	145	20	8	123-18	182	3.86	103	.266	.337	6-0-1	.000	-1	111	6	31	0.9

EDGE, BUTCH Claude Lee B7.18.1956 Houston TX BR/TR/6-3/203 [MilA74 1/6] d8.13

| 1979 | Tor A | 3 | 4 | .429 | 9 | 9 | 1 | 0-0 | 51.2 | 60 | 32 | 6 | 1 | 24-1 | 19 | 5.23 | 84 | .283 | .357 | 0 | | 0 | 85 | -4 | | -0.5 |

EDGERTON, BILL William Albert B8.16.1941 South Bend IN BL/TL/6-2/185* d9.3

1966	KC A	0	1	.000	6	0	0	0	8.1	10	3	0	0	7-2	3	3.24	105	.303	.425	0-0-1	—	0	26	0		0.
1967	KC A	1	0	1.000	7	0	0	0	8.1	11	4	1	1	3-0	6	2.16	147	.324	.395	0	—	0	0		0.0
1969	Sea A	0	1	.000	4	0	0	0-0	4	10	7	1	1	0-0	2	13.50	27	.455	.478	0	—	0	-4		-0.8
Total	3	1	2	.333	17	1	0	0-0	20.2	31	14	2	2	10-2	11	4.79	70	.348	.426	0-0-1	—	0	26	-4		-0.7

EDMONDSON, BRIAN Brian Christopher B1.29.1973 Fontana CA BR/TR/6-2/175* [DetA91 3/78] d4.2 [DL 2000 Fla N 181]

1998	Atl N	0	1	.000	10	0	0	0-1	16.2	14	10	2	0	8-1	8	4.32	96	.215	.301	2	.000	-1		-1		0.0
	Fla N	4	3	.571	43	0	0	0-2	59.1	62	28	8	3	29-4	32	3.79	107	.281	.367	10-0-1	.000	-1		2		0.0
	Year	4	4	.500	53	0	0	0-3	76	76	38	10	3	37-5	40	3.91	104	.266	.353	12-0-1	.000	-1		0		0.0
1999	Fla N	5	8	.385	68	0	0	1-5	94	106	65	11	6	44-5	58	5.84	75	.290	.370	11	.364	2		-15		-1.1
Total	2	9	12	.429	121	0	0	1-8	170	182	103	21	9	81-10	98	4.98	85	.280	.362	23-0-1	.174	0		-14	181	-1.1

EDMONDSON, GEORGE George Henderson "Big Ed" B5.18.1896 Waxahachie TX D7.11.1973 Waco TX BR/TR/6-1/179 d8.15

1922	Cle A	0	0	—	2	0	0	0	2	4	2	0	0	0	0	9.00	45	.444	.444	0	—	-0		-1		0.
1923	Cle A	0	0	—	1	0	0	0	4	8	5	0	1	3	0	11.25	35	.444	.545	1	.000	-0		-3		-0.
1924	Cle A	0	0	—	5	1	0	0	8	10	8	1	0	5	3	9.00	47	.294	.385	4	.333	0	178	-3		-0.
Total	3	0	0	—	8	1	0	0	14	22	15	1	1	8	3	9.64	43	.361	.443	4	.250	0	178	-7		-0.

EDMONDSON, PAUL Paul Michael B2.12.1943 Kansas City KS D2.13.1970 Santa Barbara CA BR/TR/6-5/195 [ChiA65 12/421] d6.20 Col Cal St.-Northridge

| 1969 | Chi A | 1 | 6 | .143 | 14 | 13 | 1 | 0-1 | 87.2 | 72 | 36 | 5 | 4 | 39-4 | 46 | 3.70 | 104 | .227 | .316 | 29-0-1 | .172 | -1 | 62 | 3 | | 0. |

EDMONDSON, BOB Robert E. B4.30.1879 Paris KY D8.14.1931 Lawrence KS BR/TR/5-11/185 d9.15 ▲

| 1906 | Was A | 0 | 1 | .000 | 2 | 1 | 0 | 0 | 10 | 10 | 8 | 0 | 0 | 4 | 2 | 4.50 | 59 | .263 | .300 | 3 | .333 | 0* | 27 | -3 | | -0. |

EDMONSTON, SAM Samuel Sherwood "Big Sam" B8.30.1883 Washington DC D4.12.1979 Corpus Christi TX BL/TL/5-11.5/185 d6.24 Col Georgetown

| 1907 | Was A | 0 | 0 | — | 1 | 0 | 0 | 0 | 3 | 8 | 3 | 0 | 1 | 2 | 0 | 9.00 | 27 | .500 | .529 | 2 | .000 | -0 | | -2 | | -0. |

EDWARDS d9.11

| 1875 | Atl NA | 0 | 1 | .000 | 1 | 1 | 0 | 0 | 2 | 4 | 6 | 0 | | 0 | 0 | 4.50 | 46 | .308 | .308 | 5 | .200 | -0 | 102 | -1 | | -0. |

EDWARDS, FOSTER Foster Hamilton "Eddie" B9.1.1903 Holstein IA D1.4.1980 Orleans MA BR/TR/6-3/175 d7.2 Col Dartmouth

1925	Bos N	0	0	—	1	0	0	0	2	6	5	0	0	1	1	9.00	45	.545	.583	0	—	0		0		-0.
1926	Bos N	2	0	1.000	3	3	1	0	25	20	4	0	0	13	4	0.72	492	.230	.330	9	.000	-2	55	8		0.
1927	Bos N	2	8	.200	29	11	1	0	92	95	59	2	3	45	37	4.99	74	.274	.362	22-0-4	.045	-2*	85	-13		-1.
1928	Bos N	2	1	.667	21	3	2	0	49.1	67	36	2	2	23	17	5.66	69	.327	.400	11-0-2	.091	-1	108	-9		-0.
1930	NY A	0	0	—	2	0	0	0	1.2	5	4	0	0	2	1	21.60	20	.500	.583	0	—	0		-3		-0.
Total	5	6	9	.400	56	17	4	0	170	193	108	4	5	84	60	4.76	79	.292	.377	42-0-6	.048	-5	84	-19		-1

EDWARDS, JIM JOE James Corbette "Little Joe" B12.14.1894 Banner MS D1.19.1965 Sarepta MS BR/TL/6-2/185 d5.14 Col Mississippi College

1922	Cle A	3	8	.273	25	7	0	0	92.1	113	56	1	5	40	44	4.47	90	.313	.389	23	.087	-2	58	-6		-0
1923	Cle A	10	10	.500	38	21	7-1	0	179.1	200	101	5	5	75	68	3.71	107	.286	.359	59-0-2	.119	-5	110	1		-0
1924	Cle A	4	3	.571	10	7	5-1	0	57	64	29	3	0	34	15	2.84	150	.305	.402	20-0-2	.150	-1	101	-17		-1
1925	Cle A	0	3	.000	13	3	1	0	36	60	44	0	1	23	12	8.25	54	.382	.464	9	.111	-1	101	-17		-1
	Chi A	1	2	.333	9	4	1-1	0	45.1	46	25	4	1	23	20	3.97	105	.263	.352	17	.176	-1	101	0		-0
	Year	1	5	.167	22	7	2-1	0	81.1	106	69	4	2	46	32	5.86	73	.319	.405	26	.154	-2	101	-16		-1
1926	Chi A	6	9	.400	32	16	8-3	1	142	140	76	4	1	63	41	4.18	92	.264	.343	46-0-3	.109	-3	94	-5		-1
1928	Cin N	2	2	.500	18	1	0	2	32	43	29	1	0	20	11	7.59	52	.347	.438	10	.300	-1	43	-12		-1
Total	6	26	37	.413	145	59	22-6	4	584.1	666	360	18	13	278	211	4.37	92	.295	.376	184-0-7	.130	-13	94	-33		-4

EDWARDS, SHERMAN Sherman Stanley B7.25.1909 Mt.Ida AR D3.8.1992 ElDorado AR BR/TR/6-0/165 d9.21

| 1934 | Cin N | 0 | 0 | — | 1 | 0 | 0 | 0 | 3 | 4 | 1 | 0 | 1 | 2 | 1 | 3.00 | 136 | .333 | .385 | 1 | .000 | -0. | | 0 | | 0 |

EDWARDS, WAYNE Wayne Maurice B3.7.1964 Burbank CA BL/TL/6-5/185* [ChiA85 10/241] d9.11 Col Azusa Pacific

1989	Chi A	0	0	—	7	0	0	0-0	7.1	7	3	1	0	3-0	4	3.68	104	.269	.333	0	—	0	85	6		0
1990	Chi A	5	3	.625	42	5	0	2-0	95	81	39	6	3	41-2	63	3.22	119	.234	.319	0	—	0		-1		-0
1991	Chi A	0	2	.000	13	0	0	0-0	23.1	22	14	2	0	17-3	12	3.86	104	.259	.375	0	—	0	85	5		0
Total	3	5	5	.500	62	5	0	2-0	125.2	110	56	9	3	61-5	84	3.37	115	.241	.331	0	—	0		0		0

EELLS, HARRY Harry Archibald "Slippery" B2.14.1880 Danbury IA D12.7.1940 Los Angeles CA BR/TR/6-1/195 d4.22

| 1906 | Cle A | 4 | 5 | .444 | 14 | 8 | 6-1 | 0 | 86.1 | 77 | 39 | 1 | 3 | 48 | 35 | 2.61 | 100 | .242 | .347 | 32 | .188 | 1 | 124 | -1 | | 0 |

EGAN, WISH Aloysius Jerome B6.16.1881 Evart MI D4.13.1951 Detroit MI BR/TR/6-3/185 d9.3

1902	Det A	0	2	.000	3	2	0	0	22	23	12	0	0	6	9	2.86	127	.271	.319	8	.250	-0	92	1		0
1905	StL N	6	15	.286	23	19	18	0	171.1	189	93	2	9	39	29	3.57	83	.285	.333	59-0-2	.102	-3	74	-12		-1
1906	StL N	2	9	.182	16	12	7	0	86.1	97	45	2	4	27	23	4.59	57	.278	.333	29-0-1	.069	-2	76	-14		-1
Total	3	8	26	.235	42	34	27	0	279.2	309	150	4	13	72	52	3.83	76	.282	.332	96-0-3	.104	-5	76	-25		-3

EGAN, JIM James K. "Troy Terrier" B1858 Derby CT D9.26.1884 New Haven CT TL d5.15 ▲

| 1882 | Tro N | 4 | 6 | .400 | 12 | 10 | 10 | 0 | 100 | 133 | 79 | 2 | | 24 | 20 | 4.14 | 68 | .315 | .352 | 115 | .200 | -2* | 116 | -12 | | -1 |

EGAN, RIP John Joseph B7.9.1871 Philadelphia PA D12.22.1950 Cranston RI TR/5-11/168 d4.30 U9

| 1894 | Was N | 0 | 0 | — | 1 | 0 | 0 | 0 | 5 | 8 | 6 | 1 | 0 | 2 | 2 | 10.80 | 49 | .364 | .417 | 3 | .000 | -0 | | -2 | | -0 |

EGAN, DICK Richard Wallis B3.24.1937 Berkeley CA BL/TL/6-4/193* d4.9 C2 Col Diablo Valley (CA) JC

1963	Det A	0	1	.000	20	0	0	0	21	25	12	4	0	3-0	16	5.14	73	.287	.311	0	—	0		-3		-0
1964	Det A	0	0	—	23	0	0	2	34.1	33	22	4	1	17-1	21	4.46	82	.246	.333	3	.000	-0		-5		-0
1966	Cal A	0	0	—	11	0	0	0	14.1	17	7	1	1	6-2	11	4.40	76	.309	.365	1	.000	-0		-1		-0
1967	LA N	1	1	.500	20	0	0	2	31.2	34	25	4	1	15-4	20	6.25	50	.272	.368	1	.000	-0		-12		-0
Total	4	1	2	.333	74	0	0	2	101.1	109	66	13	3	41-7	68	5.15	67	.272	.344	5	.000	-1		-21		-0

EGLOFF, BRUCE Bruce Edward B4.10.1965 Denver CO BR/TR/6-2/215 [CleA86 5/109] d4.13 Col California-Santa Barbara [DL 1992 Cle A 136]

| 1991 | Cle A | 0 | 0 | — | 6 | 0 | 0 | 0-0 | 5.2 | 8 | 3 | 0 | 0 | 4-1 | 8 | 4.76 | 88 | .333 | .429 | 0 | | 0 | | 0 | | |

YEAR	TM LG	W	L	PCT	G	GS	CG-SHO	SV-BS	IP	H	R	HR	HB	BB-IB	SO	ERA	AERA	OAV	OOB	AB-HR-SH	AVG	PB	SUP	APR	DL	PW
EHMKE, HOWARD									Howard Jonathan "Bob" B4.24.1894 Silver Creek NY D3.17.1959 Philadelphia PA BR/TR/6-3/190 d4.12 Mil 1918																	
1915	Buf F	0	2	.000	18	2	0	0	53.2	69	46	2	3	25	18	5.53	51	.325	.409	12	.000	-2	100	-18		-1.1
1916	Det A	3	1	.750	5	4	4	0	37.1	34	16	0	0	15	15	3.13	91	.252	.327	14	.143	-1	152	-1		-0.1
1917	Det A	10	15	.400	35	25	13-4	2	206	174	84	3	5	88	90	2.97	89	.243	.330	69-0-1	.246	2	104	-2		0.1
1919	Det A	17	10	.630	33	31	20-2	0	248.2	255	114	5	6	107	79	3.18	100	.274	.353	91-0-3	.253	3	109	-1		0.4
1920	Det A	15	18	.455	38	33	23-2	3	268.1	250	132	8	13	124	98	3.25	115	.253	.344	105-0-2	.238	2	83	13		2.0
1921	Det A	13	14	.481	30	22	13-1	0	196.1	220	123	15	13	81	68	4.54	94	.286	.364	74-0-4	.284	2	114	-5		-0.4
1922	Det A	17	17	.500	45	29	16-1	1	279.2	299	146	12	23	101	108	4.22	92	.281	.356	102-0-4	.157	-4	95	-6		-1.0
1923	Bos A	20	17	.541	43	39	28-2	3	316.2	318	155	12	20	119	121	3.78	109	.272	.349	112-0-6	.223	-2	89	16		1.9
1924	Bos A	19	17	.528	45	36	26-4	4	**315**	324	139	9	11	81	119	3.46	126	.265	.316	126-0-4	.222	-2*	94	33		3.4
1925	Bos A	9	20	.310	34	31	**22**	1	260.2	285	141	8	11	85	95	3.73	122	.285	.348	88-0-6	.148	-5	61	21		1.7
1926	Bos A	3	10	.231	14	14	7-1	0	97.1	115	69	4	4	45	38	5.46	75	.303	.382	34-0-1	.147	-1	103	-15		-1.7
	Phi A	12	4	.750	20	18	10-1	0	147.1	125	54	1	4	50	55	2.81	148	.232	.302	46-0-9	.152	-2*	92	23		2.1
	Year	15	14	.517	34	32	17-2	0	244.2	240	123	4	8	95	93	3.86	107	.261	.336	80-0-10	.150	-3	97	7		0.4
1927	Phi A	12	10	.545	30	27	10-1	0	189.2	200	103	13	14	60	68	4.22	101	.281	.349	68-0-3	.206	-1	93	2		0.2
1928	Phi A	9	8	.529	23	18	5-1	0	139.1	135	65	6	4	44	34	3.62	111	.254	.316	46-0-10	.239	1	109	7		0.9
1929	†Phi A	7	2	.778	11	8	2	0	54.2	48	24	2	1	15	20	3.29	129	.233	.288	19	.105	-2	100	6		0.6
1930	Phi A	0	1	.000	3	1	0	0	10	22	13	4	3	2	4	11.70	40	.458	.509	3	.333	0	18	-7		-0.5
Total	15	166	166	.500	427	338	199-20	14	2820.2	2873	1424	103	137	1042	1030	3.75	104	.271	.343	1009-0-53	.208	-11	94	66		8.5
EHRET, RED									Philip Sydney B8.31.1868 Louisville KY D7.28.1940 Cincinnati OH BR/TR/6-0/175 d7.7 ▲																	
1888	KC AA	3	2	.600	7	6	5	0	52	58	30	1	3	22	12	3.98	86	.272	.349	63	.190	-1*	135	-1		-0.1
1889	Lou AA	10	29	.256	45	38	35-1	0	364	441	287	11	18	115	135	4.80	80	.290	.347	258-1	.252	2*	73	-28		-2.0
1890	†Lou AA	25	14	.641	43	38	35-4	2	359	351	182	5	17	79	174	2.53	152	.248	.296	146	.212	-3	99	50		4.1
1891	Lou AA	13	13	.500	26	24	23-2	0	220.2	225	150	2	11	70	76	3.47	105	.255	.318	91	.242	-1	100	-2		-0.1
1892	Pit N	16	20	.444	39	36	32	0	316	290	183	7	22	83	101	2.65	124	.234	.294	132	.258	3*	94	16		1.6
1893	Pit N	18	18	.500	39	35	32-4	0	314.1	322	203	9	23	115	70	3.44	132	.257	.331	136-1	.176	-6*	95	29		2.1
1894	Pit N	19	21	.475	46	38	31-1	0	346.2	441	269	12	10	128	102	5.14	102	.306	.367	135-0-10	.170	-11	87	3		-0.7
1895	StL N	6	19	.240	37	32	18	0	231.2	360	223	11	10	88	55	6.02	80	.349	.405	96-1-3	.219	-3	98	-32		-2.7
1896	Cin N	18	14	.563	34	33	29-2	0	276.2	298	147	5	9	74	60	3.42	135	.273	.324	102-1-5	.196	-3	91	34		2.8
1897	Cin N	8	10	.444	34	19	11	2	184.1	256	135	3	13	47	43	4.78	95	.326	.374	66-0-2	.197	-3	84	-6		-0.7
1898	Lou N	3	7	.300	12	10	9	0	89	130	72	3	3	20	20	5.76	62	.338	.375	40	.225	1*	89	-20		-1.8
Total	11	139	167	.454	362	309	260-14	4	2754.1	3172	1881	63	139	841	848	4.02	105	.282	.339	1265-4-20	.217	-22	92	43		2.5
EHRHARDT, RUBE									Welton Claude B11.20.1894 Beecher IL D4.27.1980 Chicago Heights IL BR/TR/6-2/190 d7.18																	
1924	Bro N	5	3	.625	15	9	6-2	0	83.2	71	27	5	1	17	13	2.26	166	.232	.275	29-0-1	.138	-2	103	14		0.9
1925	Bro N	10	14	.417	36	25	12	1	207.2	239	134	10	3	62	47	5.03	83	.293	.345	71-1-2	.211	2	113	-17		-1.3
1926	Bro N	2	5	.286	44	1	0	4	97	101	52	5	0	35	25	3.90	98	.275	.338	24-0-2	.250	0	109	-1		-0.1
1927	Bro N	3	7	.300	46	3	2	2	95.2	90	46	3	3	37	22	3.57	111	.264	.341	24	.250	1	86	4		0.6
1928	Bro N	1	3	.250	28	2	1	2	54	74	36	1	1	27	12	4.67	85	.352	.429	14	.286	0	64	-4		-0.2
1929	Cin N	1	2	.333	24	1	1-1	1	49.1	58	29	2	1	22	9	4.74	96	.305	.380	11	.182	-0	172	-1		-0.1
Total	6	22	34	.393	193	41	22-3	10	587.1	633	324	26	9	200	128	4.15	97	.284	.345	173-1-5	.214	1	109	-5		-0.2
EIBEL, HACK									Henry Hack B12.6.1893 Brooklyn NY D10.16.1945 Macon GA BL/TL/5-11/220 d6.13.1912 ▲																	
1920	Bos A	0	0	—	3	0	0	0	10.1	10	4	0	3	5	3.48	105	.270	.325	43-0-1	.186	-0*	0			0.0
EICHELBERGER, JUAN									Juan Tyrone B10.21.1953 St.Louis MO BR/TR/6-3/205* [SDN75*S1/19] d9.7 Col California-Davis																	
1978	SD N	0	0	—	3	0	0	0-0	3.1	4	4	0	0	2-0	2	10.80	31	.267	.353	0		0		-3		-0.1
1979	SD N	1	1	.500	3	3	0	0-0	21	15	10	1	0	11-1	12	3.43	103	.211	.193	5-0-1	.400	1	75	0		0.1
1980	SD N	4	2	.667	15	13	0	0-0	88.2	73	41	8	1	55-4	43	3.65	94	.233	.348	27-0-4	.111	-1	133	-3	21	-0.3
1981	SD N	8	8	.500	25	24	3-1	0-0	141.1	136	60	5	3	74-5	81	3.50	93	.259	.351	46-0-6	.087	-3	104	-4		-0.7
1982	SD N	7	14	.333	31	24	0	0-0	177.2	171	98	23	2	72-5	74	4.20	82	.251	.321	55-0-5	.091	-2	103	-18	21	-2.1
1983	Cle A	4	11	.267	28	15	2	0-1	134	132	80	10	2	59-3	56	4.90	87	.259	.336	0		0	85	-9		-0.9
1988	Atl N	2	0	1.000	20	0	0	0-0	37.1	44	19	3	0	10-2	13	3.86	95	.297	.333	3	.000	-0		-1		0.0
Total	7	26	36	.419	125	79	14-1	0-1	603.1	575	312	50	8	283-20	281	4.10	87	.254	.336	136-0-16	.103	-4	102	-38	42	-4.0
EICHHORN, MARK									Mark Anthony B11.21.1960 San Jose CA BR/TR/6-3/210(185-210) [TorA79*2/30] d8.30 Col Cabrillo (CA) JC [DL 1995 Bal A 160]																	
1982	Tor A	0	3	.000	7	7	0	0-0	38	40	28	4	0	14-1	16	5.45	83	.260	.318	0		0	78	-5		-0.4
1986	Tor A	14	6	.700	69	0	0	10-3	157	105	32	8	7	45-14	166	1.72	247	.191	.260	0		0		44	15	5.8
1987	Tor A	10	6	.625	**89**	0	0	4-2	127.2	110	47	14	6	52-13	96	3.17	143	.234	.315	0		0	20	2		2.4
1988	Tor A	0	3	.000	37	0	0	1-0	66.2	79	32	3	6	27-4	28	4.18	95	.304	.381	0		-0	-1		0.0
1989	Atl N	5	5	.500	45	0	0	0-2	68.1	70	36	6	1	19-8	49	4.35	84	.275	.323	2-0-1	.000	-0	-4		-0.5
1990	Cal A	2	5	.286	60	0	0	13-3	84.2	98	36	2	6	23-0	69	3.08	125	.289	.341	0		0	6		0.7
1991	Cal A	3	3	.500	70	0	0	1-3	81.2	63	21	2	2	13-1	49	1.98	208	.219	.255	0		0	19		1.4
1992	Cal A	2	4	.333	42	0	0	2-4	56.2	51	19	2	0	18-8	42	2.38	169	.238	.294	0		0	19		1.0
	†Tor A	2	0	1.000	23	0	0	0-0	31	35	15	1	2	7-0	19	4.35	94	.285	.328	0		0	9		1.0
	Year	4	4	.500	65	0	0	2-4	87.2	86	34	3	2	25-8	61	3.08	132	.255	.306	0		0	9		1.0
1993	†Tor A	3	1	.750	54	0	0	0-2	72.2	76	26	3	3	22-7	47	2.72	161	.272	.330	0		0	12		0.7
1994	Bal A	6	5	.545	43	0	0	1-4	71	62	19	1	5	19-4	35	2.15	235	.240	.301	0		0	21		3.0
1996	Cal A	1	2	.333	24	0	0	0-2	30.1	36	17	3	2	11-3	24	5.04	100	.308	.371	0		0		103		0.1
Total	11	48	43	.527	563	7	0	32-25	885.2	825	328	49	40	270-63	640	3.00	142	.249	.311	2-0-1	.000	0	78	122	278	14.2
EILAND, DAVE									David William B7.5.1966 Dade City FL BR/TR/6-3/205* [NYA87 7/185] d8.3 Col South Florida																	
1988	NY A	0	0	—	3	3	0	0-0	12.2	15	9	6	2	4-0	7	6.39	62	.294	.368	0		0	161	-3		-0.1
1989	NY A	1	3	.250	6	6	0	0-0	34.1	44	25	6	2	13-3	11	5.77	67	.328	.391	0		0	105	-7		-0.8
1990	NY A	2	1	.667	5	5	0	0-0	30.1	31	14	2	0	5-0	16	3.56	112	.254	.283	0		0	146	1		0.1
1991	NY A	2	5	.286	18	13	0	0-0	72.2	87	51	10	3	23-1	18	5.33	78	.302	.356	0		0	73	-11	45	-1.0
1992	SD N	0	2	.000	7	7	0	0-0	27	33	21	1	0	5-0	10	5.67	63	.287	.317	9-1-1	.111	1	101	-7	105	-0.4
1995	SD N	0	3	.000	10	9	0	0-0	48.1	58	33	5	1	17-1	14	5.21	79	.297	.353	12-0-3	.083	-1	94	-6		-0.4
1995	NY A	1	1	.500	4	1	0	0-0	10	16	10	4	1	3-1	6	6.30	73	.348	.392	0		0	161	-3		-0.5
1998	TB A	0	1	.000	1	1	0	0-0	2.2	6	4	0	0	3-0	1	20.25	24	.429	.529	0		0	19	-4		-0.6
1999	TB A	4	8	.333	21	15	0	0-1	80.1	98	59	8	3	27-1	53	5.60	89	.294	.349	1-0-1	.000	-0	85	-7	30	-0.8
2000	TB A	2	3	.400	17	10	0	0-1	54.2	77	46	8	4	18-0	17	7.24	68	.326	.381	0		0	82	-13	76	-0.9
Total	10	12	27	.308	92	70	0	0-1	373	465	274	46	16	118-7	153	5.74	76	.303	.356	22-1-5	.091	-0	93	-60	256	-5.4
EILERS, DAVE									David Louis B12.3.1936 Oldenburg TX BR/TR/5-11/188* d7.27																	
1964	Mil N	0	0	—	6	0	0	0	7.2	11	5	1	1	1-1	1	4.70	75	.333	.351	0		0	-1		-0.1
1965	Mil N	0	0	—	3	0	0	0	3.2	8	5	1	0	0-0	1	12.27	29	.421	.421	0		0	-3		-0.2
	NY N	1	1	.500	11	0	0	2	18	20	11	2	2	4-3	9	4.00	88	.274	.325	1	1.000	0	-3		-0.2
	Year	1	1	.500	17	0	0	2	21.2	28	16	3	2	4-3	10	5.40	65	.304	.343	1	1.000	0	-5		-0.4
1966	NY N	1	1	.500	23	0	0	0	34.2	39	18	4	1	7-2	14	4.67	78	.287	.326	1	.000	-0	-3		-0.1
1967	Hou N	6	4	.600	35	0	0	1	59.1	68	29	3	3	17-7	27	3.94	84	.296	.349	7-0-2	.000	-1	-4		-0.7
Total	4	8	6	.571	81	0	0	3	123.1	146	68	14	7	29-13	52	4.45	78	.297	.342	9-0-2	.111	-1	-13		-1.3
EINERTSON, DARRELL									Darrell Lee B9.4.1972 Rhinelander WI BR/TR/6-2/190 [NYA95 11/310] d4.15 Col Iowa Wesleyan [DL 1999 NY A 104, 2001 NY A 190]																	
2000	NY A	0	0	—	11	0	0	0-0	12.2	16	9	1	0	4-0	3	3.55	134	.302	.345	0		0		26		0.0
EISCHEN, JOEY									Joseph Raymond B5.25.1970 West Covina CA BL/TL/6-1/200(190-215) [TexA89 4/92] d6.19 Col Pasadena (CA) City																	
1994	Mon N	0	0	—	1	0	0	0-0	0.2	4	4	0	1	0-0	0	54.00	4	.667	.714	0		0	-3		-0.2
1995	LA N	0	0	—	17	0	0	0-0	20.1	19	9	3	2	11-1	15	3.10	125	.232	.337	1	.000	0	1		0.1
1996	LA N	1	1	.500	28	0	0	0-0	43.1	48	25	4	4	20-4	36	4.78	82	.282	.369	6	.000	-1	-4		-0.3
	Det A	1	1	.500	24	0	0	0-2	25	27	11	3	0	14-3	15	3.24	157	.284	.373	0		0	5		0.3
1997	Cin N	0	0	—	2	0	0	0-0	1.1	2	1	0	0	1-0	2	6.75	63	.333	.429	1	.000	0	-1	105	0.0
2001	Mon N	0	0	—	24	0	0	0-0	29.2	29	17	4	1	16-3	19	4.85	89	.257	.354	0		0	-2		-0.1
2002	Mon N	6	1	.857	59	0	0	2-1	53.2	43	11	1	2	18-5	51	1.34	326	.224	.294	8	.125	0	16		2.1
2003	Mon N	2	2	.500	70	0	0	1-3	53	57	27	7	3	13-1	40	3.06	145	.282	.335	4	.250	0*	5		0.4

YEAR	TM LG	W	L	PCT	G	GS	CG-SHO	SV-BS	IP	H	R	HR	HB	BB-IB	SO	ERA	AERA	OAV	OOB	AB-HR-SH	AVG	PB	SUP	APR	DL	PW
2004	Mon N	0	1	.000	21	0	0	0-1	18.1	16	10	2	1	8-2	17	3.93	117	.232	.316	3-0-1	.667	1*		1	120	0.1
2005	Was N	2	1	.667	57	0	0	0-1	36.1	34	14	1	6	19-7	30	3.22	126	.252	.364	3-0-1	.333	0*		3	60	0.3
Total	9	11	8	.579	302	0	0	3-10	281.2	279	130	23	20	120-24	226	3.42	126	.261	.344	26-0-2	.192	0		21	285	2.7

EISENHART, JAKE Jacob Henry B10.3.1922 Perkasie PA D12.20.1987 Huntingdon PA BL/TL/6-3.5/195 d6.10 Col Juniata

YEAR	TM LG	W	L	PCT	G	GS	CG-SHO	SV-BS	IP	H	R	HR	HB	BB-IB	SO	ERA	AERA	OAV	OOB	AB-HR-SH	AVG	PB	SUP	APR	DL	PW
1944	Cin N	0	0	—	1	0	0		0.1	0	0	0	0	1	0	0.00	—	.000	.500	0	—	0		0		0.0

EISENSTAT, HARRY Harry B10.10.1915 Brooklyn NY D3.21.2003 Beachwood OH BL/TL/5-11/185 d5.19 Mil 1943-46

YEAR	TM LG	W	L	PCT	G	GS	CG-SHO	SV-BS	IP	H	R	HR	HB	BB-IB	SO	ERA	AERA	OAV	OOB	AB-HR-SH	AVG	PB	SUP	APR	DL	PW
1935	Bro N	0	1	.000	2	0	0		4.2	9	8	0	0	2	2	13.50	29	.429	.478	1	.000	-0		-5		-0.7
1936	Bro N	1	2	.333	5	2	1	0	14.1	22	17	1	0	6	5	5.65	73	.344	.400	3	.333	0	72	-5		-0.8
1937	Bro N	3	3	.500	13	5	0	0	47.2	61	28	2	1	11	12	3.97	102	.308	.348	11-0-1	.000	-1	68	0		-0.1
1938	Det A	9	6	.600	32	9	5	4	125.1	131	60	7	1	29	37	3.73	134	.266	.308	36-0-5	.139	-1	78	16		1.6
1939	Det A	2	2	.500	10	2	1	0	29.2	39	24	3	0	9	6	6.98	70	.315	.361	8-0-1	.375	1	162	-5		-0.5
	Cle A	6	7	.462	26	11	4-1	2	103.2	109	45	8	0	23	38	3.30	133	.265	.304	32-0-2	.250	1	80	12		1.4
	Year	8	9	.471	36	13	5-1	2	133.1	148	69	11	0	32	44	4.12	110	.277	.317	40-0-3	.275	1	93	6		0.9
1940	Cle A	1	4	.200	27	3	0	4	71.2	78	25	6	0	12	27	3.14	134	.282	.311	22	.273	1	76	**11**		0.8
1941	Cle A	1	1	.500	21	0	0	2	34	43	16	2	2	16	11	4.24	93	.312	.391	6	.333	1		0		0.0
1942	Cle A	2	1	.667	29	1	0	2	47.2	58	19	1	0	6	19	2.45	140	.304	.325	4	.250	1	25	4		0.3
Total	8	25	27	.481	165	33	11-1	14	478.2	550	242	30	4	114	157	3.84	114	.287	.328	123-0-9	.211	1	83	28		2.0

EITELJORGE, ED Edward Henry B10.14.1871 Berlin, Germany D12.5.1942 Greencastle IN BR/TR/6-2/190 d5.2 Col DePauw

YEAR	TM LG	W	L	PCT	G	GS	CG-SHO	SV-BS	IP	H	R	HR	HB	BB-IB	SO	ERA	AERA	OAV	OOB	AB-HR-SH	AVG	PB	SUP	APR	DL	PW
1890	Chi N	0	1	.000	1	1	0	0	2	5	7	0	0	1	1	22.50	16	.455	.500	1	.000	-0	155	-4		-0.5
1891	Was AA	1	5	.167	8	7	6	0	61.1	79	67	3	9	41	23	6.16	61	.303	.415	26	.192	-1	86	-15		-1.1
Total	2	1	6	.143	9	8	6	0	63.1	84	74	3	9	42	24	6.68	56	.309	.418	27	.185	-1	94	-19		-1.6

ELARTON, SCOTT Vincent Scott B2.23.1976 Lamar CO BR/TR/6-7/240(240-260) [HouN94 1/25] d6.20 [DL 2002 N 183]

YEAR	TM LG	W	L	PCT	G	GS	CG-SHO	SV-BS	IP	H	R	HR	HB	BB-IB	SO	ERA	AERA	OAV	OOB	AB-HR-SH	AVG	PB	SUP	APR	DL	PW
1998	†Hou N	2	1	.667	28	2	0	2-1	57	40	21	5	1	20-0	55	3.32	122	.196	.270	7-0-3	.000	-1	159	6		0.2
1999	†Hou N	9	5	.643	42	15	0	1-3	124	111	55	8	4	43-0	121	3.48	127	.238	.306	26-0-7	.192	0*	108	12	19	1.1
2000	Hou N	17	7	.708	30	30	2	0-0	192.2	198	117	29	6	84-1	131	4.81	102	.263	.339	63-0-6	.159	-0	126	0	19	-0.1
2001	Hou N	4	8	.333	20	20	0	0-0	109.2	126	88	26	6	49-1	76	7.14	64	.290	.368	30-0-5	.067	-1	124	-27	14	-2.5
	Col N	0	2	.000	4	4	0	0-0	23	20	17	8	0	10-1	11	6.65	80	.233	.313	8	.125	-0	65	-2	35	-0.2
	Year	4	10	.286	24	24	0	0-0	132.2	146	105	34	6	59-2	87	7.06	67	.280	.359	38-0-5	.079	-1	117	-10	31	-2.7
2003	Col N	4	4	.500	11	10	0	0-0	51.2	73	46	13	4	20-3	20	6.27	78	.329	.388	14-0-1	.071	-1	100	-20		-1.3
2004	Col N	0	6	.000	8	8	0	0-0	41.1	57	45	8	0	20-1	23	9.80	49	.328	.391	9-0-4	.222	0	95	-1		-2.2
	Cle A	3	5	.375	21	21	1-1	0-0	117.1	107	62	25	4	42-2	80	4.53	96	.240	.309	3	.333	-0	107	-10		-1.1
2005	Cle A	11	9	.550	31	31	1	0-0	181.2	189	100	32	6	48-1	103	4.61	89	.267	.315	2	.000	-0	112	-52	282	-6.2
Total	7	50	47	.515	195	141	4-1	3-4	898.1	921	551	154	31	336-10	621	5.10	89	.264	.331	162-0-26	.136	-3	112	-52	282	-6.2

ELDER, DAVE David Matthew B9.23.1975 Atlanta GA BR/TR/6-0/180* [TexA97 4/137] d7.24 Col Georgia Tech

YEAR	TM LG	W	L	PCT	G	GS	CG-SHO	SV-BS	IP	H	R	HR	HB	BB-IB	SO	ERA	AERA	OAV	OOB	AB-HR-SH	AVG	PB	SUP	APR	DL	PW
2002	Cle A	0	2	.000	15	0	0	0-0	23	18	10	1	1	14-3	23	3.13	142	.220	.333	0	—	0		3		0.2
2003	Cle A	1	1	.500	4	0	0	0-1	2.1	5	5	2	0	4-0	3	19.29	23	.417	.563	0	—	0		-4	140	-0.6
Total	2	1	3	.250	19	0	0	0-1	25.1	23	15	3	1	18-3	26	4.62	96	.245	.365	0	—	0		-1	140	-0.4

ELDER, HEINIE Henry Knox B8.23.1890 Seattle WA D11.13.1958 Long Beach CA BL/TL/6-2/200 d7.7 Col Minnesota

YEAR	TM LG	W	L	PCT	G	GS	CG-SHO	SV-BS	IP	H	R	HR	HB	BB-IB	SO	ERA	AERA	OAV	OOB	AB-HR-SH	AVG	PB	SUP	APR	DL	PW
1913	Det A	0	0	—	1	0	0	0	3.1	4	3	0	0	5		8.10	36	.286	.474	1	.000	-0		-1		-0.1

ELDRED, CAL Calvin John B11.24.1967 Cedar Rapids IA BR/TR/6-4/235(215-240) [MilA89 1/17] d9.24 Col Iowa

YEAR	TM LG	W	L	PCT	G	GS	CG-SHO	SV-BS	IP	H	R	HR	HB	BB-IB	SO	ERA	AERA	OAV	OOB	AB-HR-SH	AVG	PB	SUP	APR	DL	PW
1991	Mil A	2	0	1.000	3	3	0	0-0	16	20	9	2	0	6-0	10	4.50	89	.299	.356	0	—	0	99	-1		-0.1
1992	Mil A	11	2	.846	14	14	2-1	0-0	100.1	76	21	4	2	23-0	62	1.79	216	.207	.257	0	—	0	133	24		3.2
1993	Mil A	16	16	.500	36	**36**	8-1	0-0	**258**	232	120	32	10	91-5	180	4.01	108	.239	.308	0	—	0	85	10		1.1
1994	Mil A	11	11	.500	25	**25**	6	0-0	179	158	96	23	4	84-0	98	4.68	109	.236	.322	0	—	0	97	4	140	0.3
1995	Mil A	1	1	.500	4	4	0	0-0	23.2	24	10	4	1	10-0	18	3.42	147	.261	.340	0	—	0	101	8	104	0.6
1996	Mil A	4	4	.500	15	15	0	0-0	84.2	82	43	8	4	38-0	50	4.46	116	.259	.342	3-0-1	.000	-0	93	-5		-0.8
1997	Mil A	13	15	.464	34	34	1-1	0-0	202	207	118	31	9	89-0	122	4.80	90	.266	.372	32-0-5	.125	-0*	109	-9	63	-0.8
1998	Mil N	4	8	.333	23	23	0	0-0	133	157	82	14	4	61-3	86	7.79	59	.297	.379	24-0-4	.083	-1*	108	-28	60	-2.8
1999	Mil N	2	8	.200	20	15	0	0-0	82	101	75	19	1	46-0	60	4.58	110	.243	.342	4	.250	0	122	7	73	0.7
2000	Chi A	10	2	.833	20	20	2-1	0-0	112	103	61	12	5	59-0	97	4.58	110	.243	.342	4	.250	0	109	-5	179	-0.6
2001	Chi A	0	1	.000	2	2	0	0-0	6	12	9	1	3	3-1	6	13.50	35	.429	.529	0	—	0*		2		0.3
2003	StL N	7	4	.636	62	0	0	8-6	67.1	62	32	9	4	31-4	67	3.74	110	.248	.337	2	.500	0		4		0.2
2004	†StL N	4	2	.667	52	0	0	1-2	67	71	31	11	3	18-3	29	4.16		.259	.353	2	.000	-0	133	9	62	0.4
2005	†StL N	1	0	1.000	31	1	0	0-1	37	35	9	3	2	18-3	29	2.19	192	.259	.353	2	.000	-0	104	32	681	3.0
Total	14	86	74	.538	341	192	19-4	9-9	1368	1340	716	173	50	576-17	939	4.42	103	.257	.334	72-0-11	.111	-1	104	32	681	3.0

ELLER, HOD Horace Owen B7.5.1894 Muncie IN D7.18.1961 Indianapolis IN BR/TR/5-11.5/185 d4.16

YEAR	TM LG	W	L	PCT	G	GS	CG-SHO	SV-BS	IP	H	R	HR	HB	BB-IB	SO	ERA	AERA	OAV	OOB	AB-HR-SH	AVG	PB	SUP	APR	DL	PW
1917	Cin N	10	5	.667	37	11	7-1	1	152.1	131	60	2	3	37	77	2.36	111	.239	.290	45-0-3	.133	-2	149	4		0.1
1918	Cin N	16	12	.571	37	22	14	1	217.2	205	71	1	6	59	84	2.36	113	.253	.309	70-0-5	.157	-2	82	9		0.7
1919	†Cin N	19	9	.679	38	30	16-7	2	248.1	216	80	7	4	50	137	2.39	116	.238	.281	93-1-1	.280	7	137	12		2.1
1920	Cin N	13	12	.520	35	23	15-1	0	210.1	208	79	6	5	52	76	2.95	103	.266	.315	87-0-2	.253	1*	93	6		0.7
1921	Cin N	2	2	.500	13	3	0	1	34.1	46	23	3	0	15	7	4.98	72	.322	.386	13	.231	0	138	-5		-0.6
Total	6	60	40	.600	160	89	52-9	5	863	806	313	19	18	213	381	2.62	108	.253	.303	308-1-11	.221	5	113	26		3.0

ELLINGSEN, BRUCE Harold Bruce B4.26.1949 Pocatello ID BL/TL/6-0/180 [LAN67 63/944] d7.4

YEAR	TM LG	W	L	PCT	G	GS	CG-SHO	SV-BS	IP	H	R	HR	HB	BB-IB	SO	ERA	AERA	OAV	OOB	AB-HR-SH	AVG	PB	SUP	APR	DL	PW
1974	Cle A	1	1	.500	16	2	0	0-1	42	45	21	5	0	17-4	16	3.21	113	.278	.339	0	—	0	97	0		0.0

ELLIOTT, CLAUD Claud Judson "Chaucer", "Old Pardee" B11.17.1876 Pardeeville WI D6.21.1923 Pardeeville WI BR/TR/6-0/190 d4.16

YEAR	TM LG	W	L	PCT	G	GS	CG-SHO	SV-BS	IP	H	R	HR	HB	BB-IB	SO	ERA	AERA	OAV	OOB	AB-HR-SH	AVG	PB	SUP	APR	DL	PW
1904	Cin N	3	1	.750	9	6	4-1	0	57.2	53	25	1	4	23	19	2.99	99	.247	.331	24-1-0	.208	1	131	1		0.1
	NY N	0	1	.000	3	1	1	0	15	21	14	2	0	3	8	3.00	91	.328	.358	5	.200	0	0	-3		-0.2
	Year	3	2	.600	12	7	5-1	0	72.2	74	39	3	4	26	27	2.97	97	.265	.337	29-1-0	.207	1	116	-2		-0.1
1905	NY N	0	1	.000	10	2	2	**6**	38	41	20	3	1	12	20	4.03	73	.270	.327	16	.188	0	62	-3		-0.2
Total	2	3	3	.500	22	9	7-1	6	110.2	115	59	6	5	38	47	3.33	87	.267	.333	45-1-0	.200	1	106	-5		-0.3

ELLIOTT, DONNIE Donald Glenn B9.20.1968 Pasadena TX BR/TR/6-4/225(190-225) [PhiN87 7/182] d4.23

YEAR	TM LG	W	L	PCT	G	GS	CG-SHO	SV-BS	IP	H	R	HR	HB	BB-IB	SO	ERA	AERA	OAV	OOB	AB-HR-SH	AVG	PB	SUP	APR	DL	PW
1994	SD N	0	1	.000	30	1	0	0-1	33	31	12	3	1	21-2	24	3.27	126	.250	.363	1-0-1	.000	-0	176	4	33	0.2
1995	SD N	0	0	—	1	0	0	0-0	2	2	0	0	0	1-0	3	0.00	—	.250	.333	0	—	0		1	146	0.0
Total	2	0	1	.000	31	1	0	0-1	35	33	12	3	1	22-2	27	3.09	134	.250	.361	1-0-1	.000	-0	176	5	179	0.2

ELLIOTT, HAL Harold William B5.29.1899 Mt.Clemens MI D4.25.1963 Honolulu HI BR/TR/6-1.5/170 d4.19 Col Michigan

YEAR	TM LG	W	L	PCT	G	GS	CG-SHO	SV-BS	IP	H	R	HR	HB	BB-IB	SO	ERA	AERA	OAV	OOB	AB-HR-SH	AVG	PB	SUP	APR	DL	PW
1929	Phi N	3	7	.300	40	8	2	2	114.1	146	94	5	0	59	32	6.06	86	.313	.390	30	.167	-1	84	-13		-1.0
1930	Phi N	6	11	.353	**48**	18	2	0	117.1	191	120	7	1	58	37	7.67	71	.382	.447	32-0-1	.094	-3	136	-15		-3.2
1931	Phi N	2	0	2.000	16	4	0	2	33	46	36	5	1	19	8	9.55	44	.338	.423	9	.111	-0	95	-8		-0.9
1932	Phi N	2	4	.333	16	7	0	0	57.2	70	45	5	1	38	13	6.95	73	.338	.415	89-0-1	.135	-5	88	-63		-6.1
Total	4	11	24	.314	120	30	4	4	322.1	453	295	22	2	174	90	6.95	73	.338	.415	89-0-1	.135	-5	88	-63		-6.1

ELLIOTT, GLENN Herbert Glenn "Lefty" B11.11.1919 Sapulpa OK D7.27.1969 Portland OR BB/TL/5-10/170 d4.17 Col Oregon St.

YEAR	TM LG	W	L	PCT	G	GS	CG-SHO	SV-BS	IP	H	R	HR	HB	BB-IB	SO	ERA	AERA	OAV	OOB	AB-HR-SH	AVG	PB	SUP	APR	DL	PW
1947	Bos N	0	1	.000	11	0	0	1	19	18	10	4	0	11	8	4.74	82	.269	.372	2-0-1	.500	0		-1		0.0
1948	Bos N	1	0	1.000	1	1	0	0	3	5	1	0	1	1	2	3.00	128	.357	.400	2	.000	-0	254	0		-0.2
1949	Bos N	3	4	.429	22	6	1	0	68.1	70	35	7	0	27	15	3.95	96	.269	.338	17-0-1	.059	-1	74	-2		-0.2
Total	3	4	5	.444	34	7	1	1	90.1	93	46	11	0	39	25	4.08	93	.273	.347	21-0-2	.095	-1	99	-3		-0.2

ELLIOTT, JUMBO James Thomas B10.22.1900 St.Louis MO D1.7.1970 Terre Haute IN BR/TL/6-3/235 d4.21

YEAR	TM LG	W	L	PCT	G	GS	CG-SHO	SV-BS	IP	H	R	HR	HB	BB-IB	SO	ERA	AERA	OAV	OOB	AB-HR-SH	AVG	PB	SUP	APR	DL	PW
1923	StL A	0	0	—	1	0	0	0	1	3	0	0	3	0	27.00	15	.333	.667	0	—	0		-2		-0.1
1925	Bro N	0	2	.000	3	1	0	0	10.2	17	14	0	1	9	3	8.44	50	.362	.474	4	.000	-1	61	-6		-0.9
1927	Bro N	6	13	.316	30	21	12-2	3	188.1	188	82	5	1	60	99	3.30	120	.269	.327	64-0-1	.141	-1	80	14		1.0
1928	Bro N	9	14	.391	41	21	7-2	1	192	194	106	8	6	64	74	3.89	102	.268	.332	68-3-0	.176	2	117	2		0.3
1929	Bro N	1	2	.333	6	3	0	0	19	21	17	2	1	16	7	6.63	70	.280	.413	4	.250	0	69	-4		-0.5
1930	Bro N	10	7	.588	35	21	6-2	1	198.1	204	100	15	5	70	59	3.95	124	.271	.337	68-1-1	.147	-2	101	23		1.4
1931	Phi N	**19**	14	.576	**52**	30	12-2	1	249	288	138	15	4	83	99	4.27	100	.287	.344	90-0-2	.122	-6	92	1		-0.8
1932	Phi N	11	10	.524	39	22	8	0	166	210	115	14	2	47	62	5.42	81	.300	.346	61	.197	-1	111	-16		-1.9

YEAR	TM LG	W	L	PCT	G	GS	CG-SHO	SV-BS	IP	H	R	HR	HB	BB-IB	SO	ERA	AERA	OAV	OOB	AB-HR-SH	AVG	PB	SUP	APR	DL	PW
1933	Phi N	6	10	.375	35	21	6		2	161.2	188	89	8	3	49	43	3.84	99	.295	.348	52-0-2	.231	0*	95	-3		-0.5
1934	Phi N	0	1	.000	3	1	0		0	5.1	8	7	0	1	4	1	10.13	47	.333	.448	1	.000	0	18	-3		-0.4
	Bos N	1	1	.500	7	3	0		0	15.1	19	16	2	1	9	6	5.87	65	.284	.377	4	.250	0	105	-6		-0.6
	Year	1	2	.333	10	4	0		0	20.2	27	23	2	2	13	7	6.97	58	.297	.396	5	.200	0	80	-8		-1.0
Total	10	63	74	.460	252	144	51-8		12	1206.2	1338	687	70	25	414	453	4.24	100	.283	.344	416-4-6	.163	-8	97	0		-3.0

ELLIS, DOCK Dock Phillip B3.11.1945 Los Angeles CA BB/TR/6-3/203(185-210) d6.18

YEAR	TM LG	W	L	PCT	G	GS	CG-SHO	SV-BS	IP	H	R	HR	HB	BB-IB	SO	ERA	AERA	OAV	OOB	AB-HR-SH	AVG	PB	SUP	APR	DL	PW
1968	Pit N	6	5	.545	26	10	2	0		104.1	82	35	4	1	38-4	52	2.50	117	.213	.285	29-0-3	.069	-1*	122	5		0.3
1969	Pit N	11	17	.393	35	33	8-2	0-0		218.2	206	101	14	4	76-7	173	3.58	97	.250	.314	68-0-7	.088	-3*	84	-4		0.9
1970	†Pit N	13	10	.565	30	30	9-4	0-0		201.2	194	81	9	10	87-11	128	3.21	123	.257	.340	70-0-4	.100	-3*	90	17	21	1.5
1971	†Pit N★	19	9	.679	31	31	11-2	0-0		226.2	207	93	15	2	63-5	137	3.06	111	.239	.290	79-0-10	.203	2*	150	6		0.9
1972	†Pit N	15	7	.682	25	25	4-1	0-0		163.1	156	60	6	3	33-4	96	2.70	123	.253	.292	59-0-1	.153	-1*	128	10		1.2
1973	Pit N	12	14	.462	28	28	3-1	0-0		192	186	77	6	7	55-7	122	3.05	116	.240	.297	65-0-6	.108	-3*	92	5		0.5
1974	Pit N	12	9	.571	26	26	9			176.2	163	71	13	7	41-5	91	3.16	110	.242	.291	56-0-5	.214	3*	110	7		1.0
1975	†Pit N	8	9	.471	27	24	5-2	0-0		140	163	69	9	3	43-9	69	3.79	95	.292	.342	36-0-7	.111	0*	93	-3		-0.4
1976	†NY A	17	8	.680	32	32	8-1	0-0		211.2	195	83	14	4	76-1	65	3.19	107	.247	.312	0	—	0	96	6		0.5
1977	NY A	1	1	.500	3	3	1			19.2	18	9	1	0	8-0	5	1.83	107	.237	.306	0	—	0	98	3		0.2
	Oak A	1	5	.167	7	7	0	0-0		26	35	33	5	1	14-0	11	9.69	42	.315	.394	0	—	0	83	-17		-2.7
	Tex A	10	6	.625	23	22	7-1	1-0		167.1	158	60	13	0	42-1	90	2.90	140	.254	.297	0	—	0	106	22		1.9
	Year	12	12	.500	33	32	8-1	1-0		213	211	102	19	1	64-1	106	3.63	112	.260	.312	0	—	0	100	8		-0.6
1978	Tex A	9	7	.563	22	22	3	0-0		141.1	131	81	15	2	46-0	45	4.20	89	.245	.305	0	—	0	120	-10		-1.0
1979	Tex A	1	5	.167	10	9	0	0-0		46.2	64	34	6	0	16-2	10	5.98	69	.323	.372	0	—	0	109	-9		-1.0
	NY N	3	7	.300	17	14	1	0-0		85	110	60	4	0	34-10	41	6.04	62	.320	.377	26-0-1	.077	-1	126	-20		-2.2
	Pit N	0	0	—	3	1	0			7	9	2	1	0	2-0	1	2.57	152	.360	.393	1	.000	0	136	†		0.0
	Year	3	7	.300	20	15	1	0-0		92	119	62	10	1	36-10	42	5.77	65	.322	.378	27-0-1	.074	-2	127	-19		-2.2
Total	12	138	119	.537	345	317	71-14	1-0		2128	2067	958	140	44	674-66	1136	3.46	104	.255	.313	489-0-44	.133	-7	107	19	21	-0.1

ELLIS, JIM James Russell B3.25.1945 Tulare CA BR/TL/6-2/185(170-185) d8.11

YEAR	TM LG	W	L	PCT	G	GS	CG-SHO	SV-BS	IP	H	R	HR	HB	BB-IB	SO	ERA	AERA	OAV	OOB	AB-HR-SH	AVG	PB	SUP	APR	DL	PW
1967	Chi N	1	1	.500	8	1	0	0		16.2	20	7	1	0	9-1	8	3.24	109	.313	.397	5-0-1	.200	0	74	0		0.1
1969	StL N	0	0	—	2	1	0	0-0		5.1	7	1	0	0	3-1	0	1.69	213	.318	.400	0-0-1	1	0	148	1		0.1
Total	2	1	1	.500	10	2	0	0-0		22	27	8	1	0	12-2	8	2.86	124	.314	.398	5-0-2	.200	0	111	1		0.2

ELLIS, ROBERT Robert Randolph B12.15.1970 Baton Rouge LA BR/TR/6-5/220* [ChiA90 3/77] d9.12 Col Northwestern Louisiana

YEAR	TM LG	W	L	PCT	G	GS	CG-SHO	SV-BS	IP	H	R	HR	HB	BB-IB	SO	ERA	AERA	OAV	OOB	AB-HR-SH	AVG	PB	SUP	APR	DL	PW
1996	Cal A	0	0	—	3	0	0			5	0	0	0	0	4-0	5	0.00	—	.000	.211	0		0	3			0.1
2001	Ari N	6	5	.545	19	17	0	0-0		92	106	61	12	4	34-2	41	5.77	80	.293	.354	26-0-1	.154	-0	108	-10	67	-1.1
2002	LA N	0	1	.000	3	0	0	0-0		2.2	6	3	1	0	0-0	0	10.13	38	.462	.462	0	—	0		-2		-0.4
2003	Tex A	1	1	.500	4	4	0	0-0		18.1	26	17	7	1	10-0	8	8.35	60	.342	.416	0	—	0	134	-6		-0.5
Total	4	7	7	.500	29	21	0	0-0		118	138	81	20	5	48-2	54	6.03	78	.296	.362	26-0-1	.154	-0	113	-15	67	-1.9

ELLIS, SAMMY Samuel Joseph B2.11.1941 Youngstown OH BL/TR/6-1/180* d4.14 C12 Col Mississippi St.

YEAR	TM LG	W	L	PCT	G	GS	CG-SHO	SV-BS	IP	H	R	HR	HB	BB-IB	SO	ERA	AERA	OAV	OOB	AB-HR-SH	AVG	PB	SUP	APR	DL	PW
1962	Cin N	2	2	.500	8	4	0	0		28	29	25	6	1	29-0	27	6.75	60	.269	.424	10	.200	-0	125	-9		-1.1
1964	Cin N	10	3	.769	52	5	2	14		122.1	101	38	9	1	28-2	125	2.57	140	.223	.269	24-0-3	.083	-0	165	14		1.9
1965	Cin N☆	22	10	.688	44	39	15-2	2		263.2	222	119	22	6	104-4	183	3.79	99	.226	.303	96-0-7	.125	-1	131	1		-0.2
1966	Cin N	12	19	.387	41	36	7	0		221	226	135	35	3	78-8	154	5.29	74	.264	.324	70-0-9	.114	-2*	98	-29		-4.1
1967	Cin N	8	11	.421	32	27	8-1	0		175.2	197	86	18	4	67-7	80	3.84	98	.286	.351	49-0-6	.082	-2	101	-2		-0.5
1968	Cal A	9	10	.474	42	24	3	2		164	160	80	22	6	56-4	93	3.95	74	.244	.310	44-0-7	.045	-3	116	-19		-2.7
1969	Chi A	0	3	.000	10	4	0	0-0		29.1	42	20	6	1	16-2	15	5.83	66	.336	.415	6-0-1	.167	0	106	-6		-0.5
Total	7	63	58	.521	229	140	35-3	18-0		1004	967	503	118	22	378-27	677	4.15	88	.253	.321	299-0-33	.104	-8	114	-50		-7.2

ELLISON, GEORGE George Russell B1.24.1897 San Francisco CA D1.20.1978 San Francisco CA BR/TR/6-3/185 d8.21 Col California-Davis

YEAR	TM LG	W	L	PCT	G	GS	CG-SHO	SV-BS	IP	H	R	HR	HB	BB-IB	SO	ERA	AERA	OAV	OOB	AB-HR-SH	AVG	PB	SUP	APR	DL	PW
1920	Cle A	0	0	—	1	0	0			1	1	0	0	0	0-0	0	.000	—	.400		0	—	0	0			0.0

ELLSWORTH, DICK Richard Clark B3.22.1940 Lusk WY BL/TL/6-4/195(180-200) d6.22 s-Steve Col Fresno (CA) City

YEAR	TM LG	W	L	PCT	G	GS	CG-SHO	SV-BS	IP	H	R	HR	HB	BB-IB	SO	ERA	AERA	OAV	OOB	AB-HR-SH	AVG	PB	SUP	APR	DL	PW
1958	Chi N	0	1	.000	1	1	0			2.1	4	4	0	1	3-0	0	15.43	25	.364	.533	1	.000	-0	46	-3		-0.4
1960	Chi N	7	13	.350	31	27	6	0		176.2	170	83	12	2	72-8	94	3.72	102	.257	.329	48-0-6	.042	-3	86	1		-0.1
1961	Chi N	10	11	.476	37	31	7-1	0		186.2	213	90	23	3	48-3	91	3.86	108	.292	.337	56-0-5	.036	-5	86	8		0.5
1962	Chi N	9	20	.310	37	33	6	1		208.2	241	131	23	4	77-6	113	5.09	81	.291	.354	62-0-2	.113	1	80	-19		-2.2
1963	Chi N☆	22	10	.688	37	37	19-4	0		290.2	223	75	14	2	75-7	185	2.11	167	.210	.262	94-0-8	.096	-2	98	44		5.0
1964	Chi N	14	18	.438	37	36	16-1	0		256.2	267	129	34	3	71-9	148	3.75	99	.266	.315	87-0-6	.046	-5	92	-6		-1.1
1965	Chi N	14	15	.483	36	34	8	1		222.1	227	108	22	4	57-7	130	3.81	97	.265	.312	73-0-6	.096	-2	92	-2		-0.3
1966	Chi N	8	22	.267	38	37	9	0		269.1	321	150	28	5	51-5	144	3.98	92	.294	.326	90-0-5	.156	-0	92	-14		-1.4
1967	Phi N	6	7	.462	32	21	3-1	0		125.1	152	75	6	5	36-10	45	4.38	78	.306	.357	37-0-4	.108	-1	126	-15		-1.5
1968	Bos A	16	7	.696	31	28	10-1	0		196	196	74	16	7	37-3	106	3.03	104	.260	.300	72-0-5	.056	-5	129	3		-0.2
1969	Bos A	0	0	—	2	2	0	0-0		12	16	5	1	0	4-0	6	3.75	102	.320	.370	3-0-1	.000	-0	81	0		0.0
	Cle A	6	9	.400	34	22	3-1			135	162	73	10	5	40-10	48	4.13	92	.301	.353	45-0-1	.133	-1	99	-6		-0.7
	Year	6	9	.400	36	24	3-1	0-0		147	178	78	11	5	44-10	52	4.10	93	.302	.354	48-0-2	.125	-2	98	-5		-0.7
1970	Cle A	3	3	.500	29	1	0	2-2		43.2	49	23	4	1	14-2	13	4.53	88	.299	.354	4	.000	-0	156	-2		-0.3
	Mil A	0	0	—	14	0	0	1-0		15.2	11	3	0	1	3-0	9	1.72	219	.196	.250	0-0-1	—	0		4		0.2
	Year	3	3	.500	43	1	0	3-2		59.1	60	26	4	2	17-2	22	3.79	104	.273	.328	4-0-1	.000	-0	158	2		-0.1
1971	Mil A	0	1	.000	11	0	0	0-0		14.2	22	10	1	1	7-1	10	4.91	71	.361	.423	1	.000	0		-3		-0.2
Total	13	115	137	.456	407	310	87-9	5-2		2155.2	2274	1033	194	45	595-71	1140	3.72	100	.272	.322	673-0-50	.088	-25	96	-10		-2.7

ELLSWORTH, STEVE Steven Clark B7.30.1960 Chicago IL BR/TR/6-8/220 [BosA81 S1/9] d4.7 f-Dick Col Cal St.-Northridge

YEAR	TM LG	W	L	PCT	G	GS	CG-SHO	SV-BS	IP	H	R	HR	HB	BB-IB	SO	ERA	AERA	OAV	OOB	AB-HR-SH	AVG	PB	SUP	APR	DL	PW
1988	Bos A	1	6	.143	8	7	0			36	47	27	6	3	16-1	16	6.75	61	.315	.383	0	—	0	117	-10		-1.6

ELSTON, DON Donald Ray B4.6.1929 Campbellstown OH D1.2.1995 Arlington Heights IL BR/TR/6-0/170* d9.17

YEAR	TM LG	W	L	PCT	G	GS	CG-SHO	SV-BS	IP	H	R	HR	HB	BB-IB	SO	ERA	AERA	OAV	OOB	AB-HR-SH	AVG	PB	SUP	APR	DL	PW
1953	Chi N	0	1	.000	2	1	0			5	11	8	1	0	2	2	14.40	31	.458	.458	1	.000	-0	80	-5		-0.7
1957	Bro N	0	0	—	1	0	0	0		1	1	0	0	0	0-0	1	0.00	—	.250	.250	0	—	0	0	0		0.0
	Chi N	6	7	.462	39	14	2	8		144	139	61	15	5	55-4	102	3.56	109	.259	.332	37-0-2	.108	-2	76	6		0.4
	Year	6	7	.462	40	14	2	8		145	140	61	15	5	55-4	103	3.54	109	.259	.331	37-0-2	.108	-2	76	7		0.4
1958	Chi N	9	8	.529	69	0	0	10		97	75	35	9	1	39-10	84	2.88	136	.214	.291	14-0-1	.357	1		11		2.3
1959	Chi N★	10	8	.556	65	0	0	13		97.2	77	40	11	9	46-7	82	3.32	119	.218	.310	19-0-3	.211	0		7		1.4
1960	Chi N	8	9	.471	60	0	0	11		127	109	57	17	4	55-8	85	3.40	111	.231	.312	24-0-2	.125	-1		4		0.4
1961	Chi N	7	7	.462	58	0	0	8		93.1	108	64	11	6	45-12	59	5.59	75	.297	.381	11-0-3	.182	-0		-13		-1.8
1962	Chi N	4	8	.333	57	0	0	8		66.1	57	25	6	1	32-7	37	2.44	170	.247	.338	8	.000	-0		10		1.9
1963	Chi N	4	1	.800	51	0	0	4		70	57	26	6	2	21-3	41	2.83	124	.226	.290	4-0-1	.000	-0		5		0.3
1964	Chi N	2	5	.286	48	0	0	1		54.1	68	38	4	3	34-12	26	5.30	70	.330	.422	6	.167	-0		-10		-1.2
Total	9	49	54	.476	450	15	2	63		755.2	702	354	80	25	327-63	519	3.69	106	.251	.332	124-0-12	.153	-3	77	15		3.0

ELVIRA, NARCISO Narciso Chicho (Delgado) B10.29.1967 Tlalixcoyan, Veracruz, Mexico BL/TL/5-10/160 d9.9

YEAR	TM LG	W	L	PCT	G	GS	CG-SHO	SV-BS	IP	H	R	HR	HB	BB-IB	SO	ERA	AERA	OAV	OOB	AB-HR-SH	AVG	PB	SUP	APR	DL	PW
1990	Mil A	0	0	—	4	0	0	0-0		5	6	3	0	0	5-0	6	5.40	72	.300	.440	0	—	0		-1		0.0

ELY, HARRY Harry d9.24

YEAR	TM LG	W	L	PCT	G	GS	CG-SHO	SV-BS	IP	H	R	HR	HB	BB-IB	SO	ERA	AERA	OAV	OOB	AB-HR-SH	AVG	PB	SUP	APR	DL	PW
1892	Bal N	0	1	.000	1	1	1			9	14	9	0	2	7		7.71	44	.400	.523	3	.000	0	0	-1		-0.3

ELY, BONES William Frederick B6.7.1863 N.Girard PA D1.10.1952 Berkeley CA BR/TR/6-1/155 d6.19 ▲

YEAR	TM LG	W	L	PCT	G	GS	CG-SHO	SV-BS	IP	H	R	HR	HB	BB-IB	SO	ERA	AERA	OAV	OOB	AB-HR-SH	AVG	PB	SUP	APR	DL	PW
1884	Buf N	0	1	.000	1	1	0			5	17	15	1	0	4		14.40	22	.500	.564	4	.000	-1	34	-6		-0.7
1886	Lou AA	0	4	.000	6	4	4	1		44	53	47	0	0	26	28	5.32	68	.280	.367	32	.156	-1*	94	-7		-0.6
1890	Syr AA	0	0	—	1	0	0			2	7	5	0	0	0	0	22.50	16	.538	.538	496	.262	0*		-4		-0.1
1894	StL N	0	0	—	1	0	0			1	0	0	0	0	0	0	0.00	—	.000	.500	510-12-13	.306	0*		1		0.0
Total	4	0	5	.000	9	5	4	1		52	77	67	1	0	34	32	11.65	54	.322	.407	1042-12-13	.279	-1	82	-16		-1.4

EMBREE, ALAN Alan Duane B1.23.1970 The Dalles OR BL/TL/6-2/190* [CleA89 5/125] d9.15 [DL 1993 Cle A 124]

YEAR	TM LG	W	L	PCT	G	GS	CG-SHO	SV-BS	IP	H	R	HR	HB	BB-IB	SO	ERA	AERA	OAV	OOB	AB-HR-SH	AVG	PB	SUP	APR	DL	PW
1992	Cle A	0	2	.000	4	4	0			18	19	14	3	1	8-0	12	7.00	56	.271	.346	0	—	0	87	-5		-0.5
1995	†Cle A	3	2	.600	23	0	0	1-0		24.2	23	16	2	0	16-0	23	5.11	92	.253	.358	0	—	0		-1		-0.2
1996	†Cle A	1	1	.500	24	0	0	0-0		31	30	26	10	0	23-2	33	6.39	77	.259	.364	0	—	0		-6		-0.3
1997	†Atl N	3	1	.750	66	0	0	0-0		46	36	13	1	2	20-2	45	2.54	165	.221	.312	0	—	0		9	37	0.7

YEAR	TM LG	W	L	PCT	G	GS	CG-SHO	SV-BS	IP	H	R	HR	HB	BB-IB	SO	ERA	AERA	OAV	OOB	AB-HR-SH	AVG	PB	SUP	APR	DL	PW
1998	Atl N	1	0	1.000	20	0	0	0-1	18.2	23	14	2	0	10-0	19	4.34	96	.307	.384	1	.000	-0		-2		-0.1
	Ari N	3	2	.600	35	0	0	1-1	35	33	18	5	1	13-0	24	4.11	104	.248	.320	0	—	0		0		0.1
	Year	4	2	.667	55	0	0	1-2	53.2	56	32	7	1	23-0	43	4.19	101	.269	.343	1	.000	0		-2		0.0
1999	SF N	3	2	.600	68	0	0	0-3	58.2	42	22	6	3	26-2	53	3.38	127	.200	.295	0	—	0		7		0.5
2000	†SF N	3	5	.375	63	0	0	2-3	60	62	34	4	3	25-2	49	4.95	88	.274	.347	0	—	0		-3		-0.4
2001	SF N	0	2	.000	22	0	0	0-1	20	34	26	7	2	10-2	25	11.25	36	.374	.434	1	.000	-0		-16	20	-1.4
	Chi A	1	2	.333	39	0	0	0-2	34	31	21	7	1	7-0	34	5.03	93	.242	.281	0	—	0		-1		-0.1
2002	SD N	3	4	.429	36	0	0	0-2	28.2	23	7	2	0	9-2	38	1.26	309	.211	.271	0	—	0		8		1.6
	Bos A	2	2	.333	32	0	0	2-3	33.1	24	12	4	1	11-1	43	2.97	151	.203	.273	0	—	0		6	15	0.3
2003	†Bos A	4	1	.800	65	0	0	1-1	55	49	26	5	0	16-3	66	4.25	110	.241	.294	0	—	0		4	20	0.3
2004	†Bos A	2	2	.500	71	0	0	0-1	52.1	49	28	7	1	11-1	37	4.13	118	.244	.284	0	—	0		4		0.3
2005	Bos A	1	4	.200	43	0	0	1-2	37.2	42	33	8	1	11-2	30	7.65	60	.284	.333	0	—	0		-12		-1.3
	NY A	1	1	.500	24	0	0	0-0	14.1	20	14	2	0	3-1	8	7.53	58	.328	.364	0	—	0		-5		-0.7
	Year	2	5	.286	67	0	0	1-2	52	62	47	10	2	14-3	38	7.62	60	.297	.342	0	—	0		-16		-1.0
Total	12	30	33	.476	635	4	0	8-20	567.1	540	324	75	17	217-21	518	4.70	95	.252	.321	2	.000	0		87	-13	216	-1.0

EMBREE, RED   Charles Willard   B8.30.1917 ElMonte CA   D9.24.1996 Eugene OR   BR/TR/6-0/165   d9.10   Def 1943   Col Citrus (CA) JC

YEAR	TM LG	W	L	PCT	G	GS	CG-SHO	SV-BS	IP	H	R	HR	HB	BB-IB	SO	ERA	AERA	OAV	OOB	AB-HR-SH	AVG	PB	SUP	APR	DL	PW
1941	Cle A	0	1	.000	1	1	0	0	4	7	3	0	1	3	4	6.75	58	.438	.550	1	.000	-0	88	-1		-0.2
1942	Cle A	3	4	.429	19	6	2	0	63	58	31	0	2	31	44	3.86	89	.242	.333	15-0-1	.133	-0	66	-3		-0.3
1944	Cle A	0	1	.000	3	1	0	0	3.1	2	5	0	0	5	4	13.50	24	.167	.412	0	—	0	25	-4		-0.7
1945	Cle A	4	4	.500	8	8	5-1	0	70	56	17	3	0	26	42	1.93	168	.215	.287	21-0-4	.143	-1	105	11		1.3
1946	Cle A	8	12	.400	28	26	8	0	200	170	86	15	2	79	87	3.47	95	.227	.302	70-0-7	.186	-1	100	-3		-0.2
1947	Cle A	8	10	.444	27	21	6	0	162.2	137	65	13	1	67	56	3.15	110	.233	.313	52-0-6	.173	-1*	116	5		0.4
1948	NY A	5	3	.625	20	8	4	0	76.2	77	37	6	1	30	25	3.76	109	.261	.331	27	.148	-1*	133	2		0.0
1949	StL A	3	13	.188	35	19	4	1	127.1	146	90	13	3	89	24	5.37	84	.294	.405	37-0-3	.162	-1*	89	-11		-1.4
Total	8	31	48	.392	141	90	29-1	1	707	653	334	50	10	330	286	3.72	98	.246	.331	223-0-21	.166	-4	102	-4		-1.1

EMBREY, SLIM   Charles Akin   B8.17.1901 Columbia TN   D10.10.1947 Nashville TN   BR/TR/6-2/184   d10.1   Col Vanderbilt

| 1923 | Chi A | 0 | 0 | — | 1 | 0 | 0 | 0 | 2.2 | 7 | 6 | 0 | 0 | 2 | 1 | 10.13 | 39 | .500 | .563 | 0 | | 0 | | -3 | | -0.1 |

EMIG, CHARLIE   Charles Henry   B4.5.1875 Cincinnati OH   D10.2.1975 Oklahoma City OK   TL   d9.4

| 1896 | Lou N | 0 | 1 | .000 | 1 | 1 | 1 | 0 | 8 | 12 | 17 | 1 | 3 | 7 | 1 | 7.88 | 55 | .343 | .489 | 3 | .000 | -1 | 49 | -5 | | -0.4 |

EMMERICH, SLIM   William Peter   B9.29.1919 Allentown PA   D9.17.1998 Allentown PA   BR/TR/6-1/170   d5.14

1945	NY N	4	4	.500	31	7	1	0	100	111	55	8	1	33	27	4.86	80	.278	.334	25-0-4	.120	-2	84	-8		-0.7
1946	NY N	0	0	—	2	0	0	0	4	6	2	1	0	0	1	4.50	76	.400	.400	0	—	0		0		0.0
Total	2	4	4	.500	33	7	1	0	104	117	57	9	1	33	28	4.85	80	.282	.336	25-0-4	.120	-2	84	-8		-0.7

EMSLIE, BOB   Robert Daniel   B1.27.1859 Guelph ON, Can.   D4.26.1943 St.Thomas ON, Can.   BR/TR/5-11/180   d7.25   U35

1883	Bal AA	9	13	.409	24	23	21-1	0	201.1	188	149	3		41	62	3.17	110	.231	.268	97	.165	-3*	78	4		0.1
1884	Bal AA	32	17	.653	50	50	50-4	0	455.1	419	241	5	14	88	264	2.75	126	.224	.264	195	.190	-5*	96	36		2.8
1885	Bal AA	3	10	.231	13	13	11	0	107	131	87	0	5	30	27	4.29	76	.298	.350	51	.235	0	112	-14		-1.3
	Phi AA	0	4	.000	4	4	3	0	28.2	37	30	1	0	6	9	6.28	55	.291	.323	12	.083	-1	107	-6		-0.7
	Year	3	14	.176	17	17	14	0	135.2	168	117	1	5	36	36	4.71	70	.297	.344	63	.206	-1	111	-22		-2.0
Total	3	44	44	.500	91	90	85-5	0	792.1	775	507	9	19	165	362	3.19	108	.239	.279	355	.186	-9	94	20		0.9

ENCARNACION, LUIS   Luis Martin Lora (b Luis Martin Lora (Encarcnacion))   B10.20.1963 Santo Domingo, D.R.   BR/TR/5-10/180   d7.27

| 1990 | KC A | 0 | 0 | — | 4 | 0 | 0 | 0-0 | 14 | 10 | 14 | 1 | 0 | 4-0 | 8 | 7.84 | 49 | .311 | .367 | 0 | | 0 | | -5 | | -0.2 |

ENDERS, TREVOR   Trevor Hale   B12.22.1974 Milwaukee WI   BR/TL/6-1/214   d9.2   Col Houston Baptist

| 2000 | TB A | 0 | 1 | .000 | 9 | 0 | 0 | 0-1 | 9.1 | 14 | 13 | 2 | 0 | 5-0 | 5 | 10.61 | 46 | .359 | .432 | 0 | — | 0 | | -6 | | -0.5 |

ENGEL, JOE   Joseph William   B3.12.1893 Washington DC   D6.12.1969 Chattanooga TN   BR/TL/6-1.5/183   d5.30   Col Mount St. Marys

1912	Was A	2	5	.286	17	10	2	1	75	70	41	2	4	50	29	3.96	84	.253	.375	17-0-1	.059	-1	102	-3		-0.3
1913	Was A	8	9	.471	36	24	6-2	0	164.2	124	75	2	11	85	70	3.06	97	.218	.331	49-0-1	.061	-5	93	-2		-0.8
1914	Was A	7	5	.583	35	15	1	3	124.1	108	53	2	5	75	41	2.97	95	.254	.372	28-0-2	.107	1	123	-2		-0.2
1915	Was A	0	3	.000	11	3	0	0	33.2	30	15	0	3	19	9	3.21	93	.261	.380	6	.000	-1	57	0		-0.1
1917	Cin N	0	1	.000	1	1	1	0	8	12	8	0	0	6	2	5.63	47	.353	.450	3	.000	-0	0	-3		-0.3
1919	Cle A	0	0	—	1	0	0	0	0	0	3	0	0	3	0	∞	—	—	1.000	0	—	0		-2		-0.2
1920	Was A	0	0	—	1	0	0	0	1.2	0	4	0	1	4	0	21.60	17	.000	.556	1	.000	-0*		-3		-0.2
Total	7	17	23	.425	102	53	10-2	4	407.1	344	199	6	24	242	151	3.38	88	.242	.361	104-0-4	.067	-6	99	-15		-2.1

ENGEL, STEVE   Steven Michael   B12.31.1961 Cincinnati OH   BR/TL/6-3/216   [ChiN83 5/112]   d7.30   Col Eastern Kentucky

| 1985 | Chi N | 1 | 5 | .167 | 11 | 8 | 1 | 1-0 | 51.2 | 61 | 36 | 10 | 0 | 26-1 | 29 | 5.57 | 72 | .298 | .375 | 16-1-0 | .188 | 1 | 91 | -9 | | -0.8 |

ENGLE, RICK   Richard Douglas   B4.7.1957 Corbin KY   BR/TL/5-11.5/181   d9.2

| 1981 | Mon N | 0 | 0 | — | 1 | 0 | 0 | 0-0 | 1 | 4 | 2 | 0 | 0 | 1-0 | 2 | 18.00 | 20 | .500 | .538 | 0 | | 0 | | -3 | | -0.1 |

ENNIS, JOHN   John Wayne   B10.17.1979 Montrose CO   BR/TR/6-5/220*   [AtlN98 14/431]   d4.10

2002	Atl N	0	0	—	1	0	0	0-0	4	4	2	0	0	3-0	1	4.50	90	.385	.471	1	.000	-0	114	0		0.0
2004	Det A	0	0	—	12	0	0	1-1	16	20	16	3	0	5-0	13	8.44	53	.290	.333	0	—	0		-7		-0.4
Total	2	0	0	—	13	1	0	1-1	20	25	18	3	0	8-0	14	7.65	57	.305	.359	1	.000	-0	114	-7		-0.4

ENRIGHT, JACK   Jackson Percy   B11.29.1895 Fort Worth TX   D8.18.1975 Pompano Beach FL   BR/TR/5-11/177   d9.26

| 1917 | NY A | 0 | 1 | .000 | 1 | 1 | 0 | 0 | 5 | 5 | 5 | 0 | 0 | 3 | 1 | 5.40 | 50 | .294 | .400 | 1 | .000 | -0 | 27 | -2 | | -0.3 |

ENYART, TERRY   Terry Gene   B10.10.1950 Ironton OH   BR/TL/6-2/190   d6.17   Col Chipola (FL) JC

| 1974 | Mon N | 0 | 0 | — | 2 | 0 | 0 | 0-0 | 1.2 | 4 | 6 | 0 | 0 | 4-0 | 1 | 16.20 | 24 | .444 | .615 | 0 | | 0 | | -3 | | -0.2 |

ENZMANN, JOHNNY   John "Gentleman John"   B3.4.1890 Brooklyn NY   D3.14.1984 Riverhead NY   BR/TR/5-10/165   d7.10

1914	Bro N	1	0	1.000	7	1	0	0	19	21	16	1	3	8	5	4.74	60	.300	.395	6	.000	-1	275	-4		-0.3
1918	Cle A	5	7	.417	30	14	8	2	136.2	130	44	2	5	29	38	2.37	127	.263	.310	47-0-2	.149	-2	86	10		0.7
1919	Cle A	3	2	.600	14	4	2	0	55.1	67	29	0	2	8	13	2.28	147	.312	.342	15-0-1	.133	-0	111	2		0.1
1920	Phi N	2	3	.400	16	2	1	0	58.2	79	40	1	5	16	35	3.84	89	.320	.373	24	.167	1*	115	-5		-0.4
Total	4	11	12	.478	67	21	11	2	269.2	297	129	4	15	61	91	2.84	111	.289	.338	92-0-3	.141	-3	102	3		0.1

EPPERLY, AL   Albert Paul "Tub","Pard"   B5.7.1918 Glidden IA   D4.14.2003 McFarland MI   BL/TR/6-2/194*   d4.25

1938	Chi N	2	0	1.000	9	4	1	0	27	28	11	1	0	15	10	3.67	104	.264	.355	8	.250	1	243	1		0.2
1950	Bro N	0	0	—	5	0	0	0	9	14	8	1	0	5	3	5.00	82	.378	.452	0	—	0		-2		-0.1
Total	2	2	0	1.000	14	4	1	0	36	42	19	2	0	20	13	4.00	97	.294	.380	8	.250	1	243	-1		0.1

ERARDI, GREG   Joseph Gregory   B5.31.1954 Syracuse NY   BR/TR/6-1/190   [MilA72 24/552]   d9.6

| 1977 | Sea A | 0 | 0 | — | 9 | 0 | 0 | 0-0 | 12 | 8 | 3 | 0 | 3 | 6-1 | 5 | 6.00 | 69 | .300 | .391 | 0 | | 0 | | -2 | | -0.2 |

ERAUTT, EDDIE   Edward Lorenz Sebastian   B9.26.1924 Portland OR   BR/TR/6-0/186*   d4.16   b-Joe

1947	Cin N	4	9	.308	36	10	2	0	119	146	78	6	2	53	43	5.07	81	.307	.379	29-0-3	.069	-1	77	-14		-1.4
1948	Cin N	0	0	—	2	0	0	0	3	3	2	0	0	1	0	6.00	65	.250	.308	0	—	0		-1		0.0
1949	Cin N	4	11	.267	39	9	1	0	112.2	99	53	9	3	61	43	3.36	125	.247	.351	23-0-1	.174	0	47	8		1.0
1950	Cin N	4	2	.667	33	2	1	1	65.1	82	48	9	6	22	35	5.65	75	.307	.373	13-0-1	.154	0	83	-11		-0.9
1951	Cin N	0	0	—	30	0	0	0	39.1	50	31	4	3	23	20	5.72	71	.314	.411	3	.000	-0		-8		-0.7
1953	Cin N	0	0	—	4	0	0	0	4.2	11	3	1	0	3	1	5.79	75	.500	.560	1		-0		-1		0.0
	StL N	3	1	.750	20	1	0	0	35.2	43	25	6	2	16	15	6.31	67	.299	.377	6-0-1	.167	-0	84	-7		-0.7
	Year	3	1	.750	24	1	0	0	40.1	54	28	7	2	19	16	6.25	68	.325	.401	7-0-1	.143	-0	84	-8		-0.7
Total	6	15	23	.395	164	22	4	2	379.2	434	240	34	16	179	157	4.86	86	.293	.376	75-0-6	.120	-2	66	-34		-2.4

ERDOS, TODD   Todd Michael   B11.21.1973 Washington PA   BR/TR/6-1/190(190-204)   [SDN92 9/253]   d6.8

1997	SD N	2	0	1.000	11	0	0	0-0	13.2	17	9	1	2	4-0	13	5.27	75	.293	.359	1	.000	-0		-2		-0.3
1998	NY A	0	0	—	2	0	0	0-0	2	4	2	0	0	1-1	2	9.00	49	.500	.545	0	—	0		-1		-0.1
1999	NY A	0	0	—	4	0	0	0-0	7	5	4	2	0	4-0	8	3.86	123	.192	.290	0		0		0		0.0

YEAR	TM LG	W	L	PCT	G	GS	CG-SHO	SV-BS	IP	H	R	HR	HB	BB-IB	SO	ERA	AERA	OAV	OOB	AB-HR-SH	AVG	PB	SUP	APR	DL	PW
2000	NY A	0	0	—	14	0	0	1-0	25	31	14	2	1	11-0	18	5.04	95	.304	.377	1	.000	-0	0			0.0
	SD N	0	0	—	22	0	0	1-1	29.2	32	24	5	6	17-1	16	6.67	67	.271	.379	1	.000	-0	-7			-0.4
2001	Bos A	0	0	—	10	0	0	0-0	16.1	15	9	2	3	8-1	7	4.96	89	.263	.366	0	—	0	-1			0.0
Total	5	2	0	1.000	63	0	0	2-1	93.2	105	62	12	12	45-3	58	5.57	80	.283	.372	3	.000	-0	-11			-0.8

ERICKS, JOHN   John Edward B6.16.1967 Tinley Park IL   BR/TR/6-7/250(220-255)   [StLN88 1/22]   d6.24   Col Illinois

1995	Pit N	3	9	.250	19	18	1	0-0	106	108	59	7	2	50-4	80	4.58	95	.263	.343	31-0-6	.097	-2	72	-2		-0.5
1996	Pit N	4	5	.444	28	4	0	8-2	46.2	56	35	11	0	19-2	46	5.79	76	.292	.354	5	.000	-1	72	-8		-1.6
1997	Pit N	1	0	1.000	10	0	0	6-1	9.1	7	3	1	0	4-0	6	1.93	222	.200	.282	0	—	0	2	153	0.4
Total	3	8	14	.364	57	22	1	14-3	162	171	97	19	2	73-6	132	4.78	91	.268	.343	36-0-6	.083	-2	72	-8	153	-1.7

ERICKSON, DON   Don Lee B12.13.1931 Springfield IL   BR/TR/6-0/175   d9.1   Col Western Illinois

1958	Phi N	0	1	.000	9	0	0	1	11.2	11	7	3	0	9-1	9	4.63	86	.244	.364	1	.000	-0	-1			-0.1

ERICKSON, ERIC   Eric George Adolph B3.13.1895 Goteborg, Sweden D5.19.1965 Jamestown NY   BR/TR/6-2/190   d10.6   Mil 1918

1914	NY N	0	1	.000	1	1	0	0	5	8	7	0	0	3	3	0.00	—	.364	.440	1	.000	-0	0	-1		-0.3
1916	Det A	0	0	—	8	0	0	0	16	13	6	0	1	8	7	2.81	102	.220	.324	4	.000	-1		0		-0.1
1918	Det A	4	5	.444	12	9	8	1	94.1	81	32	2	3	29	48	2.48	107	.240	.306	33-0-1	.121	-3	97	2		-0.2
1919	Det A	0	2	.000	3	2	0	0	14.2	17	17	0	1	10	4	6.75	47	.293	.406	5	.200	-0	123	-7		-0.8
	Was A	6	11	.353	20	15	7-1	0	132	130	69	7	7	63	86	3.95	81	.254	.344	48-0-4	.146	-1	111	-8		-1.2
	Year	6	13	.316	23	17	7-1	0	146.2	147	86	7	8	73	90	4.23	76	.258	.351	53-0-4	.151	-2	112	-16		-2.0
1920	Was A	12	16	.429	39	27	12	1	239.1	231	142	13	11	128	87	3.84	97	.264	.365	83-1-8	.277	4	107	-8		-0.6
1921	Was A	8	10	.444	32	22	9-3	0	179	181	90	7	9	65	71	3.62	114	.269	.341	60-0-3	.150	-3	71	9		0.3
1922	Was A	4	12	.250	30	17	6-2	2	141.2	144	95	8	3	73	61	4.96	78	.279	.372	45-0-1	.133	-2	80	-18		-2.1
Total	7	34	57	.374	145	93	42-6	4	822	805	458	37	35	379	367	3.85	93	.264	.352	279-1-17	.179	-6	92	-31		-5.0

ERICKSON, HAL   Harold James B7.17.1919 Portland OR   BR/TR/6-5/230   d4.14

1953	Det A	0	1	.000	18	0	0	0	32.1	43	23	4	2	10	19	4.73	86	.323	.379	4	.000	-1		-4		-0.3

ERICKSON, PAUL   Paul Walford "Li'L Abner" B12.14.1915 Zion IL   D4.5.2002 Fond Du Lac WI   BR/TR/6-2/200   d6.29

1941	Chi N	5	7	.417	32	15	7-1	1	141	126	70	2	2	64	85	3.70	95	.234	.318	46-1-1	.152	0	100	-4		-0.3
1942	Chi N	1	6	.143	18	7	1	0	63	70	40	4	0	41	26	5.43	59	.288	.391	21	.143	-1	60	-14		-1.5
1943	Chi N	1	3	.250	15	4	0	0	42.2	47	32	4	2	22	24	6.12	55	.280	.370	15	.200	0	172	-12		-1.1
1944	Chi N	5	9	.357	33	15	5-3	1	124.1	113	59	5	0	67	82	3.55	100	.243	.338	36-1-0	.056	-1	93	0		-0.1
1945	†Chi N	7	4	.636	28	9	3	3	108.1	94	41	5	7	48	53	3.32	110	.233	.325	32-0-4	.156	0	147	7		0.7
1946	Chi N	9	7	.563	32	14	5-1	0	137	199	46	2	3	65	70	2.43	137	.232	.321	40-0-6	.050	-4	105	13		0.9
1947	Chi N	7	12	.368	40	20	6	1	174	179	90	17	5	93	82	4.34	91	.268	.362	60-1-0	.250	3	85	-4		-0.1
1948	Chi N	0	0	—	3	0	0	0	5.2	7	5	0	0	6	4	6.35	61	.292	.433	1	.000	-0		-2		-0.1
	Phi N	2	0	1.000	4	2	0	0	17.1	19	10	2	0	17	5	5.19	76	.292	.439	7	.143	-0	112	-2		-0.2
	NY N	0	0	—	2	0	0	0	1	0	0	0	0	2	1	0.00	—	.000	.400	0	—	0		0		0.0
	Year	2	0	1.000	9	2	0	0	24	26	15	2	0	25	10	5.25	75	.283	.436	8	.125	-0	113	-3		-0.3
Total	8	37	48	.435	207	86	27-5	6	814.1	774	393	41	19	425	432	3.86	93	.250	.345	258-3-11	.147	-2	101	-18		-1.8

ERICKSON, RALPH   Ralph Lief B6.25.1902 Dubois ID   D6.27.2002 Chandler AZ   BL/TL/6-1/175   d9.11   Col Idaho St.

1929	Pit N	0	0	—	1	0	0	0	1	2	3	0	0	2	0	27.00	18	.500	.667	0	—	0		-2		-0.1
1930	Pit N	1	0	1.000	7	0	0	0	14	21	12	1	0	10	2	7.07	70	.375	.470	4	.250	-0		-3		-0.2
Total	2	1	0	1.000	8	0	0	0	15	23	15	1	0	12	2	8.40	59	.383	.486	4	.250	-0		-5		-0.3

ERICKSON, ROGER   Roger Farrell B8.30.1956 Springfield IL   BR/TR/6-3/190(180-199)   [MinA77 3/67]   d4.6   Col New Orleans

1978	Min A	14	13	.519	37	37	14	0-0	265.2	268	129	19	8	79-1	121	3.96	97	.263	.319	0	—	0	105	-2		-0.2
1979	Min A	3	10	.231	24	21	0	0-0	123	154	86	17	1	48-1	47	5.63	78	.310	.368	0	—	0	91	-17		-1.6
1980	Min A	7	13	.350	32	27	7	0-0	191.1	198	83	13	4	56-0	97	3.25	135	.268	.320	0	—	0*	70	20		2.0
1981	Min A	3	8	.273	14	14	1	0-0	91.1	93	48	7	0	31-4	44	3.84	103	.262	.316	0	—	0	63	-1	47	-0.1
1982	Min A	4	3	.571	7	7	2	0-0	40.2	56	29	6	1	12-1	12	4.87	88	.326	.369	0	—	0	119	-5		-0.7
	NY A	4	5	.444	16	11	0	1-0	70.2	86	36	5	0	17-1	37	4.46	90	.301	.334	0	—	0	78	-2	28	-0.3
	Year	8	8	.500	23	18	2	1-0	111.1	142	65	11	1	29-2	49	4.61	89	.310	.347	0	—	0	95	-7		-1.0
1983	NY A	0	1	.000	5	0	0	0-0	16.2	13	8	1	0	8-1	7	4.32	91	.213	.304	0	—	0		0		0.0
Total	6	35	53	.398	135	117	24	1-0	799.1	868	419	68	14	251-9	365	4.13	99	.277	.331	0	—	0	88	-7	75	-0.9

ERICKSON, SCOTT   Scott Gavin B2.2.1968 Long Beach CA   BR/TR/6-4/224(222-234)   [MinA89 4/112]   d6.25   Col Arizona   [DL 2001 Bal A 190, 2003 Bal A 183]

1990	Min A	8	4	.667	19	17	1	0-0	113	108	49	9	5	51-4	53	2.87	145	.256	.342	0	—	0	112	11		1.1
1991	†Min A	20	8	.714	32	32	5-3	0-0	204	189	80	13	6	71-3	108	3.18	135	.248	.314	0	—	0	115	24	15	3.1
1992	Min A	13	12	.520	32	32	5-3	0-0	212	197	86	18	8	83-3	101	3.40	120	.252	.328	0	—	0	87	16		1.9
1993	Min A	8	19	.296	34	34	1	0-0	218.2	266	138	17	10	71-1	116	5.19	85	.305	.359	0	—	0	91	-19	13	-1.9
1994	Min A	8	11	.421	23	23	2-1	0-0	144	173	95	15	9	59-0	104	5.44	91	.299	.370	0	—	0	85	-8	16	-0.8
1995	Min A	4	6	.400	15	15	0	0-0	87.2	102	61	11	4	32-0	45	5.95	81	.291	.356	0	—	0	101	-10		-0.9
	Bal A	9	4	.692	17	16	7-2	0-0	108.2	111	47	7	1	35-0	61	3.89	123	.273	.330	0	—	0	122	12		1.4
	Year	13	10	.565	32	31	7-2	0-0	196.1	213	108	18	5	67-0	106	4.81	100	.281	.342	0	—	0	111	1		0.5
1996	†Bal A	13	12	.520	34	34	6	0-0	222.1	262	137	21	11	66-4	100	5.02	99	.297	.352	0	—	0	103	-4		-0.2
1997	†Bal A	16	7	.696	34	33	3-2	0-0	221.2	218	100	16	5	61-5	131	3.69	120	.257	.309	2-0-2	.000	0	103	17		1.7
1998	Bal A	16	13	.552	36	36	11-2	0-0	251.1	284	125	23	13	69-4	186	4.01	114	.281	.334	2-0-1	.000	1	108	11		1.4
1999	Bal A	15	12	.556	34	34	6-3	0-0	230.1	244	127	27	11	99-4	106	4.81	98	.280	.358	6-0-1	.000	-1	96	0		0.0
2000	Bal A	5	8	.385	16	16	1	0-0	92.2	127	81	14	5	48-0	41	7.87	60	.330	.406	5	.400	1*	92	-31	97	-3.3
2002	Bal A	5	12	.294	29	28	3-1	0-0	160.2	192	109	20	8	68-2	74	5.55	78	.303	.374	4	.000	-0	95	-23		-2.1
2004	NY N	0	1	.000	2	2	0	0-0	8	15	9	1	0	4-0	3	7.88	55	.395	.452	3	.000	-0	162	-4	87	-0.4
	Tex A	1	3	.250	4	4	0	0-0	19	23	13	2	0	16-0	6	6.16	80	.307	.415	0	—	0	94	-2		-0.3
2005	LA N	1	4	.200	19	0	0	0-0	55.1	62	37	12	4	25-0	15	6.02	68	.288	.370	13-0-1	.154	-0	102	-11		-0.8
Total	14	142	136	.511	380	364	51-17	0-0	2349.1	2573	1294	226	100	858-30	1250	4.57	99	.282	.348	35-0-5	.114	0	100	-21	601	-0.1

ERRICKSON, DICK   Richard Merriwell "Lief" B3.5.1912 Vineland NJ   D11.28.1999 Vineland NJ   BL/TR/6-1/175   d4.27

1938	Bos N	9	7	.563	34	10	6-1	6	122.2	113	53	1	2	56	40	3.15	109	.246	.330	35-0-5	.114	-1	106	3		0.4
1939	Bos N	6	9	.400	28	11	3	1	128.1	143	63	6	1	54	33	4.00	92	.293	.365	44-0-2	.227	1	75	-3		-0.2
1940	Bos N	12	13	.480	34	29	17-3	4	236.1	241	91	8	1	90	34	3.16	118	.270	.338	80-2-5	.157	-2	87	16		1.5
1941	Bos N	6	12	.333	38	23	5-2	1	165.2	192	100	12	4	62	45	4.78	75	.287	.351	45-0-4	.178	-0	85	-21		-2.1
1942	Bos N	2	5	.286	21	4	0	1	59.1	76	34	8	0	20	15	5.01	67	.309	.361	16-0-1	.125	-1	82	-9		-1.2
	Chi N	1	1	.500	13	0	0	0	24	39	12	1	1	8	9	4.13	78	.411	.462	5	.000	-1		-2		-0.2
	Year	3	6	.333	34	4	0	1	83.1	115	46	9	1	28	24	4.75	69	.337	.389	21-0-1	.095	-1	83	-11		-1.4
Total	5	36	47	.434	168	77	31-6	13	736.1	804	353	36	9	290	176	3.85	93	.282	.350	228-0-17	.162	-5	87	-16		-1.8

ERSKINE, CARL   Carl Daniel "Oisk" B12.13.1926 Anderson IN   BR/TR/5-10/165*   d7.25

1948	Bro N	6	3	.667	17	9	3	0	64	51	28	5	1	35	29	3.23	124	.231	.339	21	.095	-2	109	5		0.4
1949	†Bro N	8	1	.889	22	3	2	0	79.2	68	44	6	2	51	49	4.63	89	.235	.354	26-0-2	.115	-2	179	-4		-0.6
1950	Bro N	7	6	.538	22	13	3	1	103	109	56	15	1	35	50	4.72	87	.273	.333	37-0-1	.243	2	121	-6		-0.6
1951	Bro N	16	12	.571	46	19	7	4	189.2	206	105	23	2	78	95	4.46	88	.280	.351	61-0-3	.131	-2	130	-12		-1.9
1952	†Bro N	14	6	.700	33	26	10-4	2	206.2	167	72	17	2	71	131	2.70	135	.220	.289	66-0-7	.152	-0*	116	20		2.0
1953	†Bro N	20	6	.769	39	33	16-4	3	246.2	213	106	21	3	95	187	3.54	120	.230	.304	93-0-7	.215	0*	138	20		1.8
1954	Bro N★	18	15	.545	38	37	12-2	1	260.1	239	128	31	4	92	166	4.15	98	.243	.310	88-0-5	.159	-1*	94	0		-0.1
1955	†Bro N	11	8	.579	31	29	7-2	1	194.2	185	89	29	0	64-3	84	3.79	107	.253	.312	74-1-0	.203	-0*	98	8		0.6
1956	†Bro N	13	11	.542	31	28	8-1	0	186.1	189	92	25	1	57-5	95	4.25	94	.264	.317	66-0-5	.121	-3*	95	-3		-0.7
1957	Bro N	5	3	.625	15	7	1	0	66	62	27	8	0	20-1	26	3.55	118	.248	.301	22	.091	-2*	88	5		0.4
1958	LA N	4	4	.500	31	9	2-1	0	98.1	115	61	14	0	35-3	54	5.13	80	.297	.353	27-0-1	.037	-3*	105	-10		-1.0
1959	LA N	0	3	.000	10	3	0	1	23.1	33	22	5	0	13-1	15	7.71	55	.320	.397	7	.000	-1	70	-8		-1.1
Total	12	122	78	.610	335	216	71-14	13	1718.2	1637	830	199	16	646-13	981	4.00	101	.252	.320	588-1-31	.156	-13	111	15		-0.8

ESCARREGA, CHICO   Ernesto (Acosta) B12.27.1949 Los Mochis, Sinaloa, Mexico   BR/TR/5-11/185   d4.26

1982	Chi A	1	3	.250	38	2	0	1-1	73.2	73	33	7	0	16-2	33	3.67	111	.263	.299	0	—	0	56	4		0.2

YEAR	TM LG	W	L	PCT	G	GS	CG-SHO	SV-BS	IP	H	R	HR	HB	BB-IB	SO	ERA	AERA	OAV	OOB	AB-HR-SH	AVG	PB	SUP	APR	DL	PW

ESCOBAR, KELVIM   Kelvim Jose (Bolivar)   B4.11.1976 LaGuaira, Venez   BR/TR/6-1/210(195-220)   d6.29

YEAR	TM LG	W	L	PCT	G	GS	CG-SHO	SV-BS	IP	H	R	HR	HB	BB-IB	SO	ERA	AERA	OAV	OOB	AB-HR-SH	AVG	PB	SUP	APR	DL	PW
1997	Tor A	3	2	.600	27	0	0	14-3	31	28	12	1	0	19-2	36	2.90	158	.237	.343	0	—	0		5		1.0
1998	Tor A	7	3	.700	22	10	0	0-1	79.2	72	37	5	0	35-0	72	3.73	125	.237	.313	0	—	0	124	8	20	0.8
1999	Tor A	14	11	.560	33	30	1	0-0	174	203	118	19	10	81-2	129	5.69	87	.293	.371	4	.000	-0	109	-14		-1.7
2000	Tor A	10	15	.400	43	24	3-1	2-1	180	186	118	26	3	85-3	142	5.35	94	.267	.347	7	.000	-1	78	-6		-0.8
2001	Tor A	6	8	.429	59	11	1-1	0-0	126	93	51	8	3	52-5	121	3.50	131	.204	.287	0	—	0	90	16		1.4
2002	Tor A	5	7	.417	76	0	0	38-8	78	75	39	10	5	44-6	85	4.27	108	.246	.350	0	—	0		3		0.6
2003	Tor A	13	9	.591	41	26	1-1	4-1	180.1	189	94	15	9	78-3	159	4.29	111	.270	.348	6	.167	-0	84	9		1.0
2004	†Ana A	11	12	.478	33	33	0	0-0	208.1	192	91	21	7	76-2	191	3.93	114	.244	.314	2	.000	-0	81	16		1.5
2005	†LA A	3	2	.600	16	7	0	1-0	59.2	45	21	4	2	21-1	63	3.02	143	.207	.283	1-0-1	.000	-0	112	9	126	0.7
Total	9	72	69	.511	350	141	6-3	59-14	1117	1083	581	109	39	491-24	998	4.38	108	.253	.333	17-0-1	.059	-1	93	46	146	4.5

ESHELMAN, VAUGHN   Vaughn Michael   B5.22.1969 Philadelphia PA   BL/TL/6-3/210*   [BalA91 4/108]   d5.2   Col Houston   [DL 1998 TB A 181]

YEAR	TM LG	W	L	PCT	G	GS	CG-SHO	SV-BS	IP	H	R	HR	HB	BB-IB	SO	ERA	AERA	OAV	OOB	AB-HR-SH	AVG	PB	SUP	APR	DL	PW
1995	Bos A	6	3	.667	23	14	0	0-0	81.2	86	47	3	1	36-0	41	4.85	100	.272	.346	0	—	0	107	1	52	0.0
1996	Bos A	6	3	.667	39	10	0	0-0	87.2	112	79	13	2	58-4	59	7.08	72	.311	.405	0	—	0	127	-19	26	-1.6
1997	Bos A	3	3	.500	21	6	0	0-1	42.2	58	32	3	2	17-5	18	6.33	74	.330	.391	4	.250	0	118	-7		-0.9
Total	3	15	9	.625	83	30	0	0-2	212	256	158	19	5	111-9	118	6.07	81	.300	.380	4	.250	0	116	-25	259	-2.5

ESPER, DUKE   Charles H. (b Charles Esbacher)   B7.28.1868 Salem NJ   D8.31.1910 Philadelphia PA   TL/5-11.5/185   d4.18

YEAR	TM LG	W	L	PCT	G	GS	CG-SHO	SV-BS	IP	H	R	HR	HB	BB-IB	SO	ERA	AERA	OAV	OOB	AB-HR-SH	AVG	PB	SUP	APR	DL	PW
1890	Phi AA	8	9	.471	18	16	14-1	0	143.2	176	99	1	5	67	61	4.89	79	.292	.368	61	.295	4	108	-12		-0.7
	Pit N	0	2	.000	2	2	2	0	17	18	16	0	1	10	9	5.29	62	.265	.367	7	.143	-1	10	-4		-0.4
	Phi N	5	0	1.000	5	5	4	0	41	40	22	1	0	16	18	3.07	119	.247	.315	19	.158	-1	131	3		0.2
	Year	5	2	.714	7	7	6	0	58	58	38	1	1	26	27	3.72	95	.252	.331	26	.154	-2	99	-2		-0.2
1891	Phi N	20	15	.571	39	36	25-1	1	296	302	185	8	7	121	108	3.56	96	.254*	.327	123	.220	1	102	-8		-0.6
1892	Phi N	11	6	.647	21	18	14	1	160.1	171	84	2	1	60	45	3.42	95	.262	.325	70-1	.243	2*	112	0		0.1
	Pit N	2	0	1.000	3	3	1	0	18.1	18	13	0	0	12	5	5.40	61	.247	.353	*9	.000	-1	179	-3		-0.4
	Year	13	6	.684	24	21	15	1	178.2	189	97	2	1	72	50	3.63	90	.261	.328	79-1	.215	0	121	0		-0.3
1893	Was N	12	28	.300	42	36	34	0	334.1	442	277	14	12	156	78	4.71	98	.309	.381	143	.287	7	87	-10		-0.2
1894	Was N	5	10	.333	18	14	7	0	116	177	132	8	2	39	24	7.45	71	.346	.395	54-1-0	.259	1*	98	-20		-1.6
	†Bal N	10	2	.833	16	9	8	2	101	107	56	1	1	36	25	3.92	139	.269	.331	45	.222	-1	117	18		1.5
	Year	15	12	.556	34	23	15	2	217	284	188	9	3	75	49	5.81	92	.312	.367	99-1-0	.242	0	105	-6		-0.1
1895	†Bal N	10	12	.455	34	25	16-1	1	218.1	248	132	2	0	79	39	3.92	122	.281	.341	90-0-2	.178	-6	98	19		0.8
1896	Bal N	14	5	.737	20	18	14-1	0	155.2	168	80	5	2	39	19	3.58	119	.273	.319	66-0-1	.197	-2	95	14		1.1
1897	StL N	1	6	.143	8	8	7	0	61.1	95	51	5	1	12	8	5.28	83	.351	.380	25	.320	1	63	-6		-0.4
1898	StL N	3	5	.375	10	8	6	0	64.2	86	49	1	0	22	14	5.98	63	.316	.367	27	.370	2*	66	-11		-1.0
Total	9	101	100	.502	236	198	152-4	5	1727.2	2048	1196	46	32	669	453	4.39	96	.288	.351	739-2-3	.241	0	97	-20		-1.6

ESPINOSA, NINO   Arnulfo Acevedo (b Arnulfo Acevedo (Espinosa))   B8.15.1953 Villa Altagracia, D.R.   D12.24.1987 Villa Altagracia, D.R.   BR/TR/6-1/186(165-192)   d9.13

YEAR	TM LG	W	L	PCT	G	GS	CG-SHO	SV-BS	IP	H	R	HR	HB	BB-IB	SO	ERA	AERA	OAV	OOB	AB-HR-SH	AVG	PB	SUP	APR	DL	PW
1974	NY N	0	0	—	2	1	0	0-0	9	12	5	1	0	0-0	2	5.00	72	.324	.324	2	.500	0	73	-1		0.0
1975	NY N	0	1	.000	2	0	0	0-0	3	8	6	0	0	1-0	2	18.00	20	.471	.500	0	—	0		-5		-0.8
1976	NY N	4	4	.500	12	5	0	0-0	41.2	41	21	3	0	13-3	30	3.67	91	.265	.316	9-0-1	.000	-1	63	-2		-0.5
1977	NY N	10	13	.435	32	29	7-1	0-0	200	188	82	17	5	55-5	105	3.42	111	.249	.304	62-0-7	.129	-2	86	9		0.8
1978	NY N	11	15	.423	32	32	6-1	0-0	203.2	230	117	24	3	75-10	76	4.73	75	.292	.352	67-0-7	.209	2	108	-22		-2.7
1979	Phi N	14	12	.538	33	33	8-3	0-0	212	211	94	20	3	65-8	88	3.65	106	.262	.318	72-0-4	.194	2*	82	5		0.6
1980	Phi N	3	5	.375	12	12	1	0-0	76.1	73	36	9	2	19-2	13	3.77	101	.250	.298	26-0-3	.115	-1*	82	0	83	-0.3
1981	Phi N	2	5	.286	14	14	2	0-0	73.2	98	52	11	1	24-2	22	6.11	60	.333	.378	20-0-3	.200	-0	113	-18		-1.6
	Tor A	0	0	—	1	0	0	0-0	1	4	1	0	0	0-0	0	9.00	44	.667	.667	0	—	0		0		0.0
Total	8	44	55	.444	140	126	24-5	0-0	820.1	865	414	85	14	252-30	338	4.17	89	.275	.329	258-0-25	.171	0	92	-39	83	-4.3

ESPOSITO, MIKE   Michael Anthony   B9.27.1981 Los Angeles CA   BR/TR/6-0/190   d9.21   Col Arizona St.

YEAR	TM LG	W	L	PCT	G	GS	CG-SHO	SV-BS	IP	H	R	HR	HB	BB-IB	SO	ERA	AERA	OAV	OOB	AB-HR-SH	AVG	PB	SUP	APR	DL	PW
2005	Col N	2	2	.000	3	2	0	0-0	14.2	21	11	3	0	9-1	9	6.75	71	.333	.417	5-0-1	.200	-0	59	-3		-0.3

ESSER, MARK   Mark Gerald   B4.1.1956 Erie PA   BR/TL/6-1/190   [ChiA77*8/160]   d4.22   Col Miami-Dade North (FL) CC

YEAR	TM LG	W	L	PCT	G	GS	CG-SHO	SV-BS	IP	H	R	HR	HB	BB-IB	SO	ERA	AERA	OAV	OOB	AB-HR-SH	AVG	PB	SUP	APR	DL	PW
1979	Chi A	0	0	—	2	0	0	0-0	1.2	3	3	0	0	4-0	1	16.20	26	.286	.545	0	—	0		-2		-0.1

ESSICK, BILL   William Earl "Vinegar Bill"   B12.18.1880 Grand Ridge IL   D10.12.1951 Los Angeles CA   TR/5-10/175   d9.12   Col Knox

YEAR	TM LG	W	L	PCT	G	GS	CG-SHO	SV-BS	IP	H	R	HR	HB	BB-IB	SO	ERA	AERA	OAV	OOB	AB-HR-SH	AVG	PB	SUP	APR	DL	PW
1906	Cin N	2	2	.500	6	4	3	0	39.1	39	18	1	2	16	16	2.97	93	.273	.354	13-0-2	.077	-1	106	-1		-0.2
1907	Cin N	0	2	.000	3	2	2	0	21.2	23	15	0	1	8	7	2.91	89	.274	.344	8	.000	-1	41	-2		-0.3
Total	2	2	4	.333	9	6	5	0	61	62	33	1	3	24	23	2.95	91	.273	.350	21-0-2	.048	-2	85	-3		-0.5

ESTELLE, DICK   Richard Henry   B1.18.1942 Lakewood NJ   BB/TL/6-2/187(170-187)   d9.4

YEAR	TM LG	W	L	PCT	G	GS	CG-SHO	SV-BS	IP	H	R	HR	HB	BB-IB	SO	ERA	AERA	OAV	OOB	AB-HR-SH	AVG	PB	SUP	APR	DL	PW
1964	SF N	1	2	.333	6	6	0	0	41.2	39	15	3	0	23-0	23	3.02	118	.247	.341	15-0-1	.067	-1	107	3		0.1
1965	SF N	0	0	—	6	1	0	0	11.1	12	6	0	1	8-1	6	3.97	91	.261	.375	1	.000	0	146	-1		0.0
Total	2	1	2	.333	12	7	0	0	53	51	21	3	1	31-1	29	3.23	111	.250	.349	16-0-1	.063	-0	112	2		0.1

ESTES, SHAWN   Aaron Shawn   B2.18.1973 San Bernardino CA   BR/TL/6-2/192(185-200)   [SeaA91 1/11]   d9.16

YEAR	TM LG	W	L	PCT	G	GS	CG-SHO	SV-BS	IP	H	R	HR	HB	BB-IB	SO	ERA	AERA	OAV	OOB	AB-HR-SH	AVG	PB	SUP	APR	DL	PW
1995	SF N	0	3	.000	3	3	0	0-0	17.1	16	14	2	1	5	14	6.75	61	.229	.289	5	.000	-1	36	-5		-0.7
1996	SF N	3	5	.375	11	11	0	0-0	70	63	30	3	2	39-3	60	3.60	115	.243	.347	19-0-6	.158	-0*	91	5		0.5
1997	†SF N★	19	5	.792	32	32	3-2	0-0	201	162	80	12	8	100-2	181	3.18	130	.223	.323	68-1-7	.147	1*	122	21	6	2.3
1998	SF N	7	12	.368	25	25	1-1	0-0	149.1	150	89	14	5	80-6	136	5.06	80	.269	.364	42-0-8	.190	1*	91	-17	55	-1.7
1999	SF N	11	11	.500	32	32	1-1	0-0	203	209	121	21	5	112-2	159	4.92	87	.268	.362	61-0-10	.164	2*	117	-16		-1.1
2000	†SF N	15	6	.714	30	30	4-2	0-0	190.1	194	99	11	3	108-1	136	4.26	102	.275	.371	68-1-11	.206	4*	156	2	13	0.8
2001	SF N	9	8	.529	27	27	0	0-0	159	151	78	11	5	77-7	109	4.02	102	.253	.339	42-0-6	.071	-2	96	1	30	0.0
2002	NY N	4	9	.308	23	23	1-1	0-0	132.2	133	70	9	2	66-9	92	4.55	87	.267	.356	35-1-5	.086	-1*	85	-7		-0.7
	Cin N	1	3	.250	6	6	0	0-0	28	38	24	4	4	17-0	17	7.71	55	.345	.444	8-0-2	.000	-1	119	-9		-1.1
	Year	5	12	.294	29	29	1-1	0-0	160.2	171	94	13	6	83-9	109	5.10	79	.281	.373	43-1-7	.070	-2	93	-18		-1.8
2003	Chi N	8	11	.421	29	28	1-1	0-0	152.1	182	113	20	1	83-1	103	5.73	76	.305	.387	39-1-9	.179	2*	104	-26		-2.5
2004	Col N	15	8	.652	34	34	1	0-0	202	223	133	30	11	105-5	117	5.84	82	.291	.380	72-0-7	.236	2*	105	-20		-1.8
2005	Ari N	7	8	.467	21	21	0	0-0	123.2	132	70	15	4	45-0	63	4.80	91	.280	.345	29-0-2	.069	-2	82	-5	65	-0.6
Total	11	99	89	.527	273	272	14-8	0-0	1628.2	1653	921	152	54	837-36	1187	4.71	91	.269	.359	488-4-73	.158	6	107	-76	169	-6.4

ESTOCK, GEORGE   George John   B11.2.1924 Stirling NJ   BR/TR/6-0/185   d4.21

YEAR	TM LG	W	L	PCT	G	GS	CG-SHO	SV-BS	IP	H	R	HR	HB	BB-IB	SO	ERA	AERA	OAV	OOB	AB-HR-SH	AVG	PB	SUP	APR	DL	PW
1951	Bos N	0	1	.000	37	1	0	3	60.1	56	33	2	0	37	11	4.33	85	.258	.366	7-0-1	.286	1	0	-5		-0.1

ESTRADA, CHUCK   Charles Leonard   B2.15.1938 San Luis Obispo CA   BR/TR/6-1/185*   d4.21   C6

YEAR	TM LG	W	L	PCT	G	GS	CG-SHO	SV-BS	IP	H	R	HR	HB	BB-IB	SO	ERA	AERA	OAV	OOB	AB-HR-SH	AVG	PB	SUP	APR	DL	PW
1960	Bal A★	**18**	11	.621	36	25	12-1	2	208.2	162	87	18	15	101-3	144	3.58	106	**.218**	.319	64-0-9	.141	-0	105	8		1.0
1961	Bal A	15	9	.625	33	31	6-1	0	212	159	91	19	10	132-0	160	3.69	104	**.207**	.329	70-0-9	.114	-3	116	7		0.3
1962	Bal A	9	17	.346	34	33	6	0	223.1	199	112	24	10	121-16	165	3.83	97	.240	.341	66-1-8	.152	-0*	81	-5		-0.7
1963	Bal A	3	2	.600	8	7	0	0	31.1	26	17	2	1	19-0	16	4.60	76	.226	.336	10-0-2	.100	-1	121	-4	100	-0.6
1964	Bal A	3	2	.600	20	17	6	0	54.2	62	34	8	2	21-5	32	5.27	68	.282	.348	14-0-2	.143	-0*	162	-10	41	-0.7
1966	Chi N	1	1	.500	9	1	0	0	12.1	16	12	2	1	5-0	3	7.30	50	.314	.379	3	.000	-0	167	-5		-0.8
1967	NY N	1	2	.333	9	2	0	0	22	28	24	1	1	17-1	15	9.41	36	.326	.442	5	.000	-1	0	-14		-1.7
Total	7	50	44	.532	146	105	24-2	2	764.1	652	377	78	40	416-25	535	4.07	92	.232	.336	232-1-30	.129	-5	103	-23	141	-3.4

ESTRADA, HORACIO   Horacio (Jimenez)   B10.19.1975 San Joaquin, Venez   BL/TL/6-1/185(160-192)   d5.4

YEAR	TM LG	W	L	PCT	G	GS	CG-SHO	SV-BS	IP	H	R	HR	HB	BB-IB	SO	ERA	AERA	OAV	OOB	AB-HR-SH	AVG	PB	SUP	APR	DL	PW
1999	Mil N	0	0	—	4	0	0	0-0	7.1	10	6	4	0	4-0	5	7.36	63	.313	.389	2	.000	-0		-2		-0.1
2000	Mil N	3	0	1.000	7	4	0	0-0	24.1	30	18	5	2	20-4	13	6.29	73	.300	.423	7-0-1	.143	-0	179	-4		-0.4
2001	Col N	1	1	.500	4	0	0	0-0	4.1	8	7	1	1	1-0	4	14.54	37	.400	.455	0	—	0		-3	90	-0.4
Total	3	4	1	.800	15	4	0	0-0	36	48	31	10	3	25-4	22	7.50	63	.316	.420	9-0-1	.111	-0	179	-9	90	-1.1

ESTRADA, OSCAR   Oscar   B2.15.1904 Havana, Cuba   D1.2.1978 Havana, Cuba   BL/TL/5-8/160   d4.21

YEAR	TM LG	W	L	PCT	G	GS	CG-SHO	SV-BS	IP	H	R	HR	HB	BB-IB	SO	ERA	AERA	OAV	OOB	AB-HR-SH	AVG	PB	SUP	APR	DL	PW
1929	StL A	0	0	—	1	0	0	0	1	1	0	0	0	1	0	0.00	—	.250	.400	0	—	0		0		0.0

ESTRELLA, LEO   Leoncio (Ramirez)   B2.20.1975 Puerto Plata, D.R.   BR/TR/6-1/185*   d7.18

YEAR	TM LG	W	L	PCT	G	GS	CG-SHO	SV-BS	IP	H	R	HR	HB	BB-IB	SO	ERA	AERA	OAV	OOB	AB-HR-SH	AVG	PB	SUP	APR	DL	PW
2000	Tor A	0	0	—	4	0	0	0-0	4.2	9	3	1	0	1-0	3	5.79	87	.450	.429	0	—	0		0		0.0
2003	Mil N	7	3	.700	58	0	0	3-5	66	75	32	10	3	21-5	25	4.36	99	.290	.346	0	—	0		1		0.2

YEAR	TM LG	W	L	PCT	G	GS	CG-SHO	SV-BS	IP	H	R	HR	HB	BB-IB	SO	ERA	AERA	OAV	OOB	AB-HR-SH	AVG	PB	SUP	APR	DL	PW
2004	SF N	0	0	—	2	0	0	0-0	1.1	8	4	0	0	1-0	0	27.00	16	.727	.692	0	—	0		-3		-0.2
Total	3	7	3	.700	62	0	0	3-5	72	92	39	11	3	22-5	64	4.88	90	.317	.366	0	—	0		-2		0.0

ETHERTON, SETH Seth Michael B10.17.1976 Laguna Beach CA BR/TR/6-1/200* [AnaA98 1/18] d5.26 Col USC [DL 2002 Cin N 69]

YEAR	TM LG	W	L	PCT	G	GS	CG-SHO	SV-BS	IP	H	R	HR	HB	BB-IB	SO	ERA	AERA	OAV	OOB	AB-HR-SH	AVG	PB	SUP	APR	DL	PW
2000	Ana A	5	1	.833	11	11	0	0-0	60.1	68	38	16	1	22-0	32	5.52	94	.278	.338	2	.000	0	114	-1	57	-0.1
2003	Cin N	2	4	.333	7	7	0	0-0	30	39	23	4	3	15-1	17	6.90	60	.322	.401	7-0-3	.143	-0	77	-8		-1.4
2005	Oak A	1	1	.500	3	3	0	0-0	17.2	16	13	4	0	5-0	10	6.62	67	.235	.284	0	—	-0	133	-4		-0.4
Total	3	8	6	.571	21	21	0	0-0	108	123	74	24	4	42-1	59	6.08	78	.283	.348	9-0-3	.111	-0	105	-13	126	-1.9

ETTLES, MARK Mark Edward B10.30.1966 Perth, Western Australia, Australia BR/TR/6-0/185 [DetA89 33/863] d6.5 Col West Florida

1993	SD N	1	0	1.000	14	0	0	0-0																		
									14	13	4	0	0	4-0	6	6.50	64	.307	.333	2	.000	-0		-5		-0.3

EUBANK, JOHN John Franklin "Honest John" B9.9.1872 Servia IN D11.3.1958 Bellevue MI BR/TR/6-2/215 d9.19

1905	Det A	1	0	1.000	3	2	0		17.1	13	12	0	1	3	1	2.08	132	.210	.258	14	.357	1*	194	-1		0.0
1906	Det A	4	10	.286	24	12	7-1	2	135	147	69	0	8	35	38	3.53	78	.280	.335	63-0-2	.206	0*	69	-11		-1.1
1907	Det A	3	3	.500	15	8	4-1		81	88	40	0	0	20	17	2.67	98	.279	.322	31	.129	-1	110	-2		-0.3
Total	3	8	13	.381	42	22	11-2	2	233.1	248	121	0	9	58	56	3.12	87	.275	.325	108-0-2	.204	-1	96	-14		-1.4

EUBANKS, UEL Uel Melvin "Poss" B2.14.1903 Quinlan TX D11.21.1954 Dallas TX BR/TR/6-3/175 d7.20

1922	Chi N	0	0	—	2	0	0		1	2	5	9	0	4	1	27.00	16	.556	.692	1	1.000	1		-5		-0.2

EUFEMIA, FRANK Frank Anthony B12.23.1959 Bronx NY BR/TR/5-11/185 [MinA82 18/448] d5.21 Col Ramapo

1985	Min A	4	2	.667	39	0	0	2-0	61.2	56	27	7	0	21-7	30	3.79	117	.250	.310	0	—	0		5		0.5

EVANS, BART Bart Steven B12.30.1970 Springfield MO BR/TR/6-2/210 [KCA92 9/246] d6.16 Col Missouri St.

1998	KC A	0	0	—	8	0	0	0-0	9	7	3	1	0	0-0	7	2.00	243	.206	.206	0	—	0		2	31	0.1

EVANS, CHICK Charles Franklin B10.15.1889 Arlington VT D9.2.1916 Schenectady NY BR/TR d9.19

1909	Bos N	0	3	.000	4	3	1		21.2	25	16	0	0	14	11	4.57	62	.305	.406	9	.000	-1	50	-4		-0.6
1910	Bos N	1	1	.500	13	1	0	2	31	28	20	1	3	27	12	5.23	64	.275	.439	10	.100	-1	22	-4		-0.4
Total	2	1	4	.200	17	4	1	2	52.2	53	36	1	3	41	23	4.96	63	.288	.425	19	.053	-2	41	-8		-1.0

EVANS, ROY Roy B3.19.1874 Knoxville TN D8.15.1915 Galveston TX BR/TR/6-0/180 d5.15 Col Emporia St.

1897	StL N	0	0	—	3	0	0	0	13	33	27	1	0	13	4	9.69	45	.471	.554	3	.000	0		-10		-0.4
	Lou N	5	4	.556	9	8	6	0	59.1	66	40	4	8	24	20	4.10	104	.280	.366	23	.130	-2	94	2		-0.1
	Year	5	4	.556	12	8	6	0	72.1	99	67	5	8	37	24	5.10	84	.324	.410	26	.115	-2	93	-10		-0.4
1898	Was N	3	3	.500	7	6	4	0	50.2	50	27	0	7	25	11	3.38	109	.256	.361	19	.053	-2	94	2		-0.1
1899	Was N	3	4	.429	7	7	6	0	54	60	40	1	0	25	27	5.67	69	.280	.356	20-0-2	.200	-1	100	-8		-0.8
1902	NY N	8	13	.381	23	17	17	0	176	186	87	2	9	58	48	3.17	89	.271	.336	54-0-4	.148	-1	54	-5		-0.5
	Bro N	5	6	.455	13	11	11-2	0	97.1	91	42	0	2	33	35	2.68	103	.247	.313	34	.265	2	58	0		0.1
	Year	13	19	.406	36	28	28-2	0	273.1	277	129	2	11	91	83	3.00	93	.263	.327	88-0-4	.193	1	56	-8		-0.4
1903	Bro N	5	9	.357	15	12	9	0	110	121	75	1	7	41	42	3.27	98	.297	.371	29-0-4	.172	0	58	-7		-0.8
	StL A	0	4	.000	7	7	4	0	54	66	30	1	3	14	24	4.17	70	.300	.350	19-0-1	.105	-1	60	-6		-0.5
Total	5	29	43	.403	84	68	57-2	0	614.1	673	368	10	35	233	211	3.66	88	.281	.353	201-0-11	.159	-4	72	-32		-3.0

EVANS, RED Russell Edison B11.12.1906 Chicago IL D6.14.1982 Lakeview AR BR/TR/5-11/168 d4.24

1936	Chi A	0	3	.000	17	0	0	1	47.1	70	46	4	0	22	19	7.61	68	.338	.402	15	.133	-1*		-12		-0.7
1939	Bro N	1	8	.111	24	6	0	1	64.1	74	43	4	0	26	28	5.18	78	.284	.348	13-0-2	.308	1	29	-9		-0.9
Total	2	1	11	.083	41	6	0	2	111.2	144	89	8	0	48	47	6.21	73	.308	.372	28-0-2	.214	-0	29	-21		-1.6

EVANS, JAKE Uriah L. P. "Bloody Jake" B9.1856 Baltimore MD D1.16.1907 Baltimore MD TR/5-8/154 d5.1.1879 ▲

1880	Tro N	0	0	—	1	0	0	0	4	11	8	0		0	3	13.50	19	.524	.524	180	.256	0*		-4		-0.1
1882	Wor N	0	1	.000	1	1	1	0	8	13	10	1		0	2	5.63	55	.317	.317	334	.213	-0*	119	-2		-0.2
1883	Cle N	0	0	—	1	0	0	0	3	0	0	0		0	1	0.00	—	.000	.000	332	.238	0*		1		0.1
Total	3	0	1	.000	3	1	1	0	15	24	18	1		0	3	6.60	45	.338	.338	846	.232	-0	119	-5		-0.2

EVANS, ART William Arthur B8.3.1911 Elvins MO D1.8.1952 Wichita KS BB/TL/6-1.5/181 d6.20

1932	Chi A	0	0	—	7	0	0	0	18	19	9	1	0	8	6	3.00	144	.257	.345	5	.000	-0		2		0.1

EVANS, BILL William James B2.10.1894 Reidsville NC D12.21.1946 Burlington NC BR/TR/6-0/175 d8.13 Mil 1918 Col North Carolina St.

1916	Pit N	2	5	.286	13	7	3	0	63	57	27	2	3	16	21	3.00	89	.249	.306	20-0-1	.150	-1	56	-2		-0.2
1917	Pit N	0	4	.000	8	2	1	0	26.2	24	14	0	1	14	5	3.38	84	.231	.328	9	.111	-0	27	-2		-0.3
1919	Pit N	0	4	.000	7	3	2	0	36.2	41	25	1	0	18	15	5.65	53	.297	.378	11-0-1	.000	-1	44	-10		-1.1
Total	3	2	13	.133	28	12	6	0	126.1	122	66	3	4	48	41	3.85	73	.259	.333	40-0-2	.100	-2	47	-14		-1.6

EVANS, BILL William Lawrence B3.25.1919 Quanah TX D11.30.1983 Grand Junction CO BR/TR/6-2/180* d4.21

1949	Chi A	0	1	.000	4	0	0	0	6.1	6	6	0	0	8	1	7.11	59	.261	.452	1	.000	-0		-2		-0.3
1951	Bos A	0	0	—	9	0	0	0	15.1	15	8	0	0	8	3	4.11	109	.268	.359	4	.000	-1		1		-0.1
Total	2	0	1	.000	13	0	0	0	21.2	21	14	0	0	16	4	4.98	88	.266	.389	5	.000	-1		-1		-0.4

EVELAND, DANA Dana James B10.29.1983 Olympia WA BL/TL/6-1/220 d7.16 Col Canyons (CA) [JC]

2005	Mil N	1	1	.500	27	0	0	1-1	31.2	40	21	2	1	18-3	23	5.97	72	.317	.404	1-0-1	.000	-0		-5		-0.3

EVERITT, LEON Edward Leon B1.12.1947 Marshall TX BL/TR/6-1.5/195 [LAN65 10/303] d4.21

1969	SD N	0	0	—	9	0	0	0	15.2	18	14	1	1	12-1	11	8.04	45	.300	.425	3	.000	-0*		-7		-0.4

EVERSGERD, BRYAN Bryan David B2.11.1969 Centralia IL BR/TL/6-1/190* d4.30 Col Kaskaskia (IL) CC

1994	StL N	2	3	.400	40	0	0	0-1	67.2	75	36	8	2	20-1	47	4.52	94	.295	.349	6-0-2	.000	-1	64	-2		-0.2
1995	Mon N	0	0	—	25	0	0	0-0	21	22	13	2	1	9-2	8	5.14	84	.268	.340	1	.000	-0		-2		-0.1
1997	Tex A	0	2	.000	3	0	0	0-0	1.1	5	3	0	0	3-0	2	20.25	24	.556	.667	0	—	-0		-2		-0.4
1998	StL N	0	0	—	8	0	0	0-0	6	9	7	1	1	2-0	4	9.00	47	.346	.387	0	—	0		-3		-0.2
Total	4	2	5	.286	76	1	0	0-2	96	111	59	11	4	34-3	61	5.16	83	.299	.359	7-0-2	.000	-1	64	-9		-0.9

EWING, BOB George Lemuel "Long Bob" B4.24.1873 New Hampshire OH D6.20.1947 Wapakoneta OH BR/TR/6-1.5/170 d4.19

1902	Cin N	5	6	.455	15	12	10	0	117.2	126	67	1	3	47	44	2.98	101	.274	.345	71	.169	-1*	125	-2		-0.4
1903	Cin N	14	13	.519	29	28	27-1	1	246.2	254	127	3	10	64	104	2.77	128	.265	.317	95-0-1	.253	4*	93	17		2.3
1904	Cin N	11	13	.458	26	24	22	0	212	198	85	3	4	58	99	2.46	119	.253	.308	97-1-0	.258	5*	92	11		1.7
1905	Cin N	20	11	.645	40	34	30-4	0	311.2	284	125	5	11	79	164	2.51	132	.246	.301	122-0-5	.262	4*	113	27		2.9
1906	Cin N	13	14	.481	33	32	26-2	0	287.2	248	98	4	2	60	145	2.38	116	.238	.281	101-1-1	.139	-3	87	15		1.0
1907	Cin N	17	19	.472	41	37	32-2	0	332.2	279	104	2	7	85	147	1.73	150	.231	.286	123-1-10	.154	-0	100	26		2.6
1908	Cin N	17	15	.531	37	32	23-4	3	293.2	247	105	4	5	57	95	2.21	105	.241	.284	94-0-4	.149	-0	100	3		0.2
1909	Cin N	11	12	.478	31	29	14-2	0	218.1	195	94	1	6	63	86	2.43	107	.238	.298	73-0-5	.110	-4	105	2		-0.4
1910	Phi N	16	14	.533	34	32	20-4	0	255.1	235	110	5	7	86	102	3.00	104	.251	.318	90-0-4	.222	2	106	5		0.6
1911	Phi N	0	1	.000	4	3	1	0	24	29	25	2	0	14	12	7.88	44	.309	.398	6-0-1	.333	0	138	-11		-0.5
1912	StL N	0	0	—	1	1	0	0	1.1	2	0	0	0	1	2	0.00	—	.333	.429	0	—	0	86	1		0.0
Total	11	124	118	.512	291	264	205-19	4	2301	2097	940	31	55	614	998	2.49	116	.247	.302	872-3-31	.195	7	102	94		10.0

EWING, JOHN John "Long John" B6.1.1863 Cincinnati OH D4.23.1895 Denver CO TR/6-1/168 d6.18.1883 b-Buck

1888	Lou AA	8	13	.381	21	21	21-2	0	191	175	105	3	8	34	87	2.83	109	.235	.276	79	.203	-2	78	8		0.6
1889	Lou AA	6	30	.167	40	39	37-1	0	331	407	296	6	14	147	155	4.87	79	.293	.367	134	.172	-6*	64	-37		-3.3
1890	NY P	18	12	.600	35	31	27-1	2	267.1	294	196	6	10	104	145	4.24	107	.267	.339	114-2	.211	-3	92	10		0.6
1891	NY N	21	8	.724	33	30	28-5	0	269.1	237	118	2	11	105	138	2.27	141	.237	.305	113	.204	-2	108	30		2.5
Total	4	53	63	.457	129	121	113-9	2	1058.2	1113	715	17	49	390	525	3.68	101	.260	.329	440-2	.195	-12	85	11		0.4

EWING, BUCK William B10.17.1859 Hoagland OH D10.20.1906 Cincinnati OH BR/TR/5-10/188 d9.9.1880 M7 HF1939 b-John ▲

1882	Tro N	0	0	—	1	0	0	0	1	2	1	0		1	0	9.00	31	.400	.500	328-2	.271	0*		0		0.0
1884	NY N	0	1	.000	1	1	1	0	8	7	3	0		4	3	3.13	265	.241	.333	382-3	.277	0*	36	1		0.2
1885	NY N	0	1	.000	1	1	0	0	2	4	4	0		3	0	4.50	59	.444	.583	342-6	.304	0*		-1		-0.2
1888	†NY N	0	0	—	2	0	0	0	7	8	9	1		4	6	2.57	107	.174	.255	415-6	.306	1*		1		0.0
1889	†NY N	2	0	1.000	3	2	2	0	20	23	14	0		8	12	4.05	97	.280	.344	407-4	.327	2*	136	0		0.1

YEAR	TM LG	W	L	PCT	G	GS	CG-SHO	SV-BS	IP	H	R	HR	HB	BB-IB	SO	ERA	AERA	OAV	OOB	AB-HR-SH	AVG	PB	SUP	APR	DL
1890	NY P	0	1	.000	1	1	1	0	9	11	5	1	0	3	2	4.00	114	.289	.341	352-8	.338	0*	27	1	0.1
Total	6	2	3	.400	9	4	4	0	47	55	36	2	1	23	23	3.45	105	.263	.339	2226-29	.305	4	86	0	0.2

EYRE, SCOTT   Scott Alan   B5.30.1972 Inglewood CA   BL/TL/6-1/200(190-210)   [TexA91 9/248]   d8.1 Col Southern Idaho [JC]

YEAR	TM LG	W	L	PCT	G	GS	CG-SHO	SV-BS	IP	H	R	HR	HB	BB-IB	SO	ERA	AERA	OAV	OOB	AB-HR-SH	AVG	PB	SUP	APR	DL
1997	Chi A	4	4	.500	11	11	0	0-0	60.2	62	36	11	1	31-1	36	5.04	87	.267	.353	2	.500	0	91	-4	-0.4
1998	Chi A	3	8	.273	33	17	0	0-0	107	114	78	24	2	64-0	73	5.38	85	.271	.368	3	.000	-0	100	-13	-1.1
1999	Chi A	1	1	.500	21	0	0	0-0	25	38	22	6	1	15-2	17	7.56	65	.339	.419	0	—	0	-7	26	-0.5
2000	Chi A	1	1	.500	13	1	0	0-0	19	29	15	3	1	12-0	16	6.63	76	.372	.452	0	—	0	93	-3	-0.3
2001	Tor A	1	2	.333	17	0	0	2-1	15.2	15	6	1	1	7-2	16	3.45	133	.263	.348	0	—	0	2	0.2
2002	Tor A	2	4	.333	49	3	0	0-1	63.1	69	37	4	0	29-7	51	4.97	93	.278	.349	0	—	0	127	-2	-0.4
	†SF N	0	0	—	21	0	0	0-0	11.1	11	4	0	1	7-1	7	1.59	249	.256	.360	0	—	0	2	0.1
2003	†SF N	2	1	.667	74	0	0	1-2	57	60	23	4	1	26-0	35	3.32	128	.268	.343	2	.500	0	6	0.3
2004	SF N	2	2	.500	83	0	0	1-4	52.2	43	26	8	0	27-3	49	4.10	106	.219	.310	2	.000	-0	1	18	0.1
2005	SF N	2	2	.500	86	0	0	0-2	68.1	48	21	3	4	26-0	65	2.63	162	.200	.286	2	.000	0	12	-0.6
Total	9	18	25	.419	408	32	0	4-10	480	489	268	64	11	244-16	365	4.52	99	.264	.350	11	.182	0	101	-6	44	-1.0

EYRICH, GEORGE   George Lincoln   B3.3.1925 Reading PA   BR/TR/5-11/175   d6.13 Mil 1943-46

YEAR	TM LG	W	L	PCT	G	GS	CG-SHO	SV-BS	IP	H	R	HR	HB	BB-IB	SO	ERA	AERA	OAV	OOB	AB-HR-SH	AVG	PB	SUP	APR	DL
1943	Phi N	0	0	—	9	0	0	0	18.2	27	11	4	0	9	5	3.38	100	.342	.409	2	.000	-0	0		0.0

FABER, RED   Urban Clarence   B9.6.1888 Cascade IA   D9.25.1976 Chicago IL   BB/TR/6-2/180   d4.17 Mil 1918 C3 HF1964 Col Loras

YEAR	TM LG	W	L	PCT	G	GS	CG-SHO	SV-BS	IP	H	R	HR	HB	BB-IB	SO	ERA	AERA	OAV	OOB	AB-HR-SH	AVG	PB	SUP	APR	DL
1914	Chi A	10	9	.526	40	19	11-2	4	181.1	154	77	3	12	64	88	2.68	100	.239	.319	55-0-2	.145	2	100	0	0.3
1915	Chi A	24	14	.632	50	32	21-2	1	299.2	264	118	3	11	99	182	2.55	117	.240	.309	84-0-12	.131	2	134	12	1.9
1916	Chi A	17	9	.654	35	25	15-3	1	205.1	167	67	1	5	61	87	2.02	137	.228	.292	63-0-4	.095	-3	102	15	1.7
1917	†Chi A	16	13	.552	41	29	16-3	3	248	224	92	1	10	85	84	1.92	138	.247	.319	69-0-8	.058	-4	113	11	1.2
1918	Chi A	4	1	.800	11	9	5-1	1	80.2	70	23	3	0	23	26	1.23	223	.245	.301	24-0-2	.042	-2	98	10	0.5
1919	Chi A	11	9	.550	25	20	9		162.1	185	92	7	8	45	45	3.83	83	.287	.341	54-0-3	.185	-0	112	-14	-1.6
1920	Chi A	23	13	.639	40	39	28-2	1	319	332	136	8	4	88	108	2.99	126	.277	.328	104-0-6	.106	-4	124	24	2.0
1921	Chi A	25	15	.625	43	39	32-4	1	330.2	293	107	10	7	87	124	2.48	171	.242	.297	108-0-8	.148	-4	84	64	6.8
1922	Chi A	21	17	.553	43	38	31-4	2	352	334	128	10	6	83	148	2.81	145	.252	.299	125-0-10	.200	-2	89	47	4.6
1923	Chi A	14	11	.560	32	31	15-2	0	232.1	233	114	6	4	62	91	3.41	116	.259	.311	69-1-8	.217	3*	100	10	1.4
1924	Chi A	9	11	.450	21	20	9		161.1	173	78	5	2	58	47	3.85	107	.282	.346	54-0-2	.148	-2	106	7	0.4
1925	Chi A	12	11	.522	34	32	16-1	0	238	266	117	8	2	59	71	3.78	110	.289	.333	77-0-6	.104	-4	106	10	0.5
1926	Chi A	15	9	.625	27	25	13-1	0	184.2	203	84	3	2	57	65	3.56	109	.281	.335	60-0-6	.150	-0	110	7	0.6
1927	Chi A	4	7	.364	18	15	6		110.2	131	64	2	5	41	39	4.55	89	.312	.380	37-0-5	.270	2	77	-5	-0.2
1928	Chi A	13	9	.591	27	27	16-2	0	201.1	223	98	11	4	68	43	3.75	108	.286	.347	70-1-4	.114	-3	94	7	0.4
1929	Chi A	13	13	.500	31	31	15-1	0	234	241	119	10	9	61	68	3.88	110	.273	.327	78-1-4	.128	-3	87	11	0.8
1930	Chi A	8	13	.381	29	26	10	1	169	188	101	7	5	49	62	4.21	110	.283	.337	49-0-5	.041	-5	83	7	0.3
1931	Chi A	10	14	.417	44	19	5-1	1	184	210	96	11	3	57	49	3.82	112	.285	.339	53-0-4	.075	-3	70	8	0.6
1932	Chi A	2	11	.154	42	5	0	6	106	123	61	0	1	38	26	3.74	116	.290	.350	18-0-4	.222	3	118	-5	0.7
1933	Chi A	3	4	.429	36	2	0	5	86.1	92	41	2	1	28	18	3.44	123	.275	.332	18-0-1	.000	-3	50	7	0.3
Total	20	254	213	.544	669	483	273-29	28	4086.2	4106	1813	111	103	1213	1471	3.15	119	.266	.323	1269-3-104	.134	-31	100	245	23.3

FACE, ROY   Elroy Leon   B2.20.1928 Stephentown NY   BR/TR/5-8/155*   d4.16

YEAR	TM LG	W	L	PCT	G	GS	CG-SHO	SV-BS	IP	H	R	HR	HB	BB-IB	SO	ERA	AERA	OAV	OOB	AB-HR-SH	AVG	PB	SUP	APR	DL
1953	Pit N	6	8	.429	41	13	2	0	119	145	90	19	2	30	56	6.58	68	.297	.340	30-0-4	.133	-1*	81	-23	-2.5
1955	Pit N	5	7	.417	42	10	4	5	125.2	128	58	10	0	40-4	84	3.58	115	.268	.323	26-0-3	.115	-1*	58	7	0.5
1956	Pit N	12	13	.480	68	3	0	6	135.1	131	57	16	1	42-15	96	3.52	107	.256	.313	26-0-1	.192	-0*	86	5	1.0
1957	Pit N	4	6	.400	59	1	0	10	93.2	97	41	9	1	24-5	53	3.07	123	.270	.311	16-0-1	.125	-1	70	6	0.6
1958	Pit N	5	2	.714	57	0	0	20	84	77	30	6	0	22-6	47	2.89	134	.244	.293	7-0-2	.000	-1	9	1.2
1959	Pit N★	18	1	.947	57	0	0	10	93.1	91	29	5	1	25-8	69	2.70	143	.266	.315	13-0-1	.231	0*	14	2.8
1960	†Pit N★	10	8	.556	68	0	0	24	114.2	93	39	11	0	29-9	72	2.90	129	.226	.274	17-0-2	.412	2	11	2.4
1961	Pit N★	6	12	.333	62	0	0	17	92	94	44	12	1	10-4	55	3.82	105	.267	.287	11	.273	0	2	0.5
1962	Pit N	8	7	.533	63	0	0	28	91	74	23	7	1	18-7	45	1.88	209	.231	.270	12-0-1	.083	-1	20	4.1
1963	Pit N	3	9	.250	56	0	0	16	69.2	75	33	6	3	19-11	41	3.23	102	.285	.338	8	.250	0	-1	-0.1
1964	Pit N	3	3	.500	55	0	0	4	79.2	82	48	11	1	27-10	63	5.20	68	.269	.324	4	.000	-0	-13	-1.1
1965	Pit N	5	2	.714	16	0	0	0	20.1	20	6	1	0	7-5	19	2.66	132	.263	.321	1	.000	-0	2	105	0.5
1966	Pit N	6	6	.500	54	0	0	18	70	68	24	9	1	24-5	67	2.70	132	.262	.325	11-0-1	.000	-1	7	1.3
1967	Pit N	7	5	.583	61	0	0	17	74.1	62	23	5	0	22-11	41	2.42	139	.230	.286	6	.000	-1	8	1.6
1968	Pit N	2	4	.333	43	0	0	13	52	46	17	3	2	7-2	34	2.60	113	.238	.271	4-0-1	.000	-0	3	0.3
	Det A	0	0	—	2	0	0	0	1	2	0	0	0	1-1	1	0.00	—	.500	.600	0	—	0	0	0.0
1969	Mon N	4	2	.667	44	0	0	5-1	59.1	62	29	11	0	15-3	34	3.94	94	.263	.307	2-0-1	.500	0	-1	-0.1
Total	16	104	95	.523	848	27	6	193-1	1375	1347	591	141	14	362-106	877	3.48	109	.260	.308	194-0-18	.160	-4	81	55	105	13.2

FAETH, TONY   Anthony Joseph   B7.9.1893 Aberdeen SD   D12.22.1982 St.Paul MN   BR/TR/6-0/180   d8.10

YEAR	TM LG	W	L	PCT	G	GS	CG-SHO	SV-BS	IP	H	R	HR	HB	BB-IB	SO	ERA	AERA	OAV	OOB	AB-HR-SH	AVG	PB	SUP	APR	DL
1919	Cle A	0	0	—	6	0	0	0	18.1	13	4	0	0	10	7	0.49	682	.224	.338	4	.000	-1	5	0.2
1920	Cle A	0	0	—	13	0	0	0	25	31	19	0	1	20	14	4.32	88	.333	.456	5	.000	-1	-3	-0.2
Total	2	0	0	—	19	0	0	0	43.1	44	23	0	1	30	21	2.70	134	.291	.412	9	.000	-1	2	0.0

FAGAN, EVERETT   Everett Joseph   B1.13.1918 Pottersville NJ   D2.16.1983 Morristown NJ   BR/TR/6-0/195   d4.24 Mil 1943-46

YEAR	TM LG	W	L	PCT	G	GS	CG-SHO	SV-BS	IP	H	R	HR	HB	BB-IB	SO	ERA	AERA	OAV	OOB	AB-HR-SH	AVG	PB	SUP	APR	DL
1943	Phi N	2	6	.250	18	2	0	3	37.1	41	28	4	2	14	9	6.27	54	.283	.354	7	.000	-0	124	-11	-2.2
1946	Phi N	0	1	.000	20	0	0	0	45	47	27	2	3	24	12	4.80	74	.264	.361	14	.286	1	-6	-0.2
Total	2	2	7	.222	38	2	0	3	82.1	88	55	6	5	38	21	5.47	64	.272	.358	21	.190	1	124	-17	-2.4

FAGAN, BILL   William A. "Clinkers"   B2.15.1869 Troy NY   D3.21.1930 Troy NY   TL/5-11/165   d9.15

YEAR	TM LG	W	L	PCT	G	GS	CG-SHO	SV-BS	IP	H	R	HR	HB	BB-IB	SO	ERA	AERA	OAV	OOB	AB-HR-SH	AVG	PB	SUP	APR	DL
1887	NY AA	1	4	.200	6	6	6	0	45	55	34	1	2	24	12	4.00	106	.306	.393	21	.143	-2	50	0	-0.1
1888	KC AA	5	11	.313	17	17	15	0	142.1	179	148	4	1	75	49	5.69	60	.296	.375	65	.215	-1*	91	-33	-2.8
Total	2	6	15	.286	23	23	21	0	187.1	234	182	5	3	99	61	5.28	69	.298	.379	86	.198	-3	79	-33	-2.9

FAHEY, FRANK   Francis Raymond   B1.22.1896 Milford MA   D3.19.1954 Boston MA   BB/TR/6-1/190   d4.25 Col Catholic America ▲

YEAR	TM LG	W	L	PCT	G	GS	CG-SHO	SV-BS	IP	H	R	HR	HB	BB-IB	SO	ERA	AERA	OAV	OOB	AB-HR-SH	AVG	PB	SUP	APR	DL
1918	Phi A	0	0	—	3	0	0	0	9	5	7	0	1	14	1	6.00	49	.200	.500	17-0-1	.176	-0*	-3	-0.2

FAHR, JERRY   Gerald Warren   B12.9.1924 Marmaduke AR   BR/TR/6-5/185   d4.29

YEAR	TM LG	W	L	PCT	G	GS	CG-SHO	SV-BS	IP	H	R	HR	HB	BB-IB	SO	ERA	AERA	OAV	OOB	AB-HR-SH	AVG	PB	SUP	APR	DL
1951	Cle A	0	0	—	5	0	0	0	5.2	11	3	0	0	2	0	4.76	80	.500	.542	—	0	0	0.0

FAHRER, PETE   Clarence Willie   B3.10.1890 Holgate OH   D6.10.1967 Fremont MI   BL/TR/6-0/190   d8.17

YEAR	TM LG	W	L	PCT	G	GS	CG-SHO	SV-BS	IP	H	R	HR	HB	BB-IB	SO	ERA	AERA	OAV	OOB	AB-HR-SH	AVG	PB	SUP	APR	DL
1914	Cin N	0	0	—	5	0	0	0	8	8	3	0	0	4	2	1.13	260	.308	.400	1	.000	-0	1	0.1

FAIRBANK, JIM   James Lee "Lee","Smoky"   B3.17.1881 Deansboro NY   D12.27.1955 Utica NY   BR/TR/5-9.5/175   d9.18

YEAR	TM LG	W	L	PCT	G	GS	CG-SHO	SV-BS	IP	H	R	HR	HB	BB-IB	SO	ERA	AERA	OAV	OOB	AB-HR-SH	AVG	PB	SUP	APR	DL
1903	Phi A	1	1	.500	4	1	1	0	24	33	14	1	0	12	10	4.88	63	.327	.398	10	.100	-1	164	-4	-0.3
1904	Phi A	0	1	.000	3	1	0	0	17	19	14	0	2	13	6	6.35	42	.284	.415	6	.000	-0	0	-6	-0.4
Total	2	1	2	.333	7	2	1	0	41	52	28	1	2	25	16	5.49	53	.310	.405	16	.063	-1	86	-10	-0.7

FAIRCLOTH, RAGS   James Lamar   B8.19.1892 Kenton TN   D10.5.1953 Tucson AZ   BR/TR/5-11/160   d5.6 Col Mississippi St.

YEAR	TM LG	W	L	PCT	G	GS	CG-SHO	SV-BS	IP	H	R	HR	HB	BB-IB	SO	ERA	AERA	OAV	OOB	AB-HR-SH	AVG	PB	SUP	APR	DL
1919	Phi N	0	0	—	3	0	0	0	9	9	9	0	0	5	0	9.00	36	.625	.625	0	—	0	-1	-0.1

FAJARDO, HECTOR   Hector (Nabaratte)   B11.16.1970 Sahuayo, Michoacan, Mexico   BR/TR/6-4/185(185-200)   d8.10 [DL 1992 Tex A 112]

YEAR	TM LG	W	L	PCT	G	GS	CG-SHO	SV-BS	IP	H	R	HR	HB	BB-IB	SO	ERA	AERA	OAV	OOB	AB-HR-SH	AVG	PB	SUP	APR	DL
1991	Pit N	0	0	—	2	0	0	0-0	6.1	10	7	0	0	7-0	3	9.95	36	.357	.486	3	.000	-0	187	-4	-0.2
	Tex A	0	2	.000	4	3	0	0-0	19	25	13	2	1	4-0	15	5.68	71	.329	.357	0	—	0	113	-3	-0.3
1993	Tex A	0	0	—	1	0	0	0-0	0.2	0	0	0	0	0-0	1	0.00	—	.000	.000	0	—	0	0	148	0.0
1994	Tex A	5	7	.417	18	12	0	0-0	83.1	95	67	15	2	26-0	45	6.91	70	.284	.336	0	—	0	76	-17	-1.9
1995	Tex A	0	0	—	5	0	0	0-0	15	19	13	2	1	5-0	9	7.80	62	.311	.373	0	—	0	-4	-0.2
Total	4	5	9	.357	30	17	0	0-0	124.1	149	100	19	4	42-0	78	6.95	67	.297	.352	3	.000	-0	91	-28	260	-2.6

FALCONE, PETE   Peter Frank   B10.1.1953 Brooklyn NY   BL/TL/6-2/185*   [SFN73 S1/4]   d4.13 Col Kingsborough (NY) CC

YEAR	TM LG	W	L	PCT	G	GS	CG-SHO	SV-BS	IP	H	R	HR	HB	BB-IB	SO	ERA	AERA	OAV	OOB	AB-HR-SH	AVG	PB	SUP	APR	DL
1975	SF N	12	11	.522	34	32	3-1	0-0	190	171	97	16	4	111-7	131	4.17	91	.244	.348	65-0-4	.062	-5	92	-6	-1.2
1976	StL N	12	16	.429	32	32	9-2	0-0	212	173	87	12	2	93-1	138	3.23	111	.222	.300	62-0-12	.129	-2	84	8	0.7
1977	StL N	4	8	.333	27	22	1-1	1-0	124	130	84	19	3	61-3	75	5.44	72	.273	.355	41-0-4	.244	-1	124	-19	-1.5
1978	StL N	2	7	.222	19	14	0	0-0	75	94	52	9	2	48-2	28	5.76	62	.319	.414	21-0-2	.238	1	86	-17	-1.8
1979	NY N	6	14	.300	33	31	1-1	0-0	184	194	91	24	1	76-10	113	4.16	89	.276	.343	52-0-5	.173	0	82	-7	-0.9

		PCT	G	GS	CG-SHO	SV-BS	IP	H	R	HR	HB	BB-IB	SO	ERA	AERA	OAV	OOB	AB-HR-SH	AVG	PB	SUP	APR	DL	PW
		.412	37	23	1	1-0	157.1	163	89	16	2	58-9	109	4.52	80	.269	.332	41-0-6	.146	-1	115	-16		-1.8
		.625	35	9	3-1	1-0	95.1	84	32	3	0	36-4	56	2.55	139	.241	.308	22-1-0	.182	1	117	10		0.9
		.444	40	23	3	2-1	171	159	82	24	3	71-4	101	3.84	96	.252	.326	53-0-2	.113	-2	85	-2		-0.6
	4	.692	33	15	2	0-0	106.2	102	47	14	1	60-2	59	3.63	107	.256	.352	26-0-5	.115	-1	120	3		0.1
	7	.417	35	16	2-1	2-1	120	115	61	15	0	57-3	55	4.13	93	.252	.333	33-0-3	.212	1	99	-3		-0.2
	90	.438	325	217	25-7	7-2	1435.1	1385	717	152	16	671-45	865	4.07	91	.257	.337	416-1-43	.149	-6	98	-49		-6.3

FALK, ...hester Emanuel "Spot" B5.15.1905 Austin TX D1.7.1982 Austin TX BL/TL/6-2/170 d4.20 b-Bibb Col Texas
1925	StL A	0	0	—	13	0	0		25	38	26	2	0	17		7	8.28	56	.362	.451	8		.625	2*		-9		-0.2
1926	StL A	4	4	.500	18	8	3	0	74	95	53	1	6	27	7	5.35	80	.338	.408	31	.194	-1*	115	-8		-0.9
1927	StL A	1	0	1.000	9	0	0		15.2	25	18	1	0	10	2	5.74	76	.352	.432	5	.200	-0		-5		-0.3
Total	3	5	4	.556	40	8	3	0	114.2	158	97	4	6	54	16	6.04	73	.346	.422	44	.273	1	115	-22		-1.4

FALKENBERG, CY Frederick Peter B12.17.1879 Chicago IL D4.15.1961 San Francisco CA BR/TR/6-5/180 d4.21 Col Illinois
1903	Pit N	1	5	.167	10	6	3	0	56	65	43	0	2	32	24	3.86	84	.295	.390	21-0-1	.190	-0	90	-6		-0.5
1905	Was A	7	2	.778	12	10	6-2	0	75.1	71	41	1	5	31	35	3.82	69	.251	.335	32	.125	-2	209	-8		-1.1
1906	Was A	14	20	.412	40	36	30-2	1	298.2	277	136	1	13	108	178	2.86	92	.249	.323	106-1-4	.170	1	118	-9		-0.8
1907	Was A	6	17	.261	32	24	17-1	1	233.2	195	105	0	8	77	108	2.35	103	.229	.299	86	.140	-3*	99	-3		-0.6
1908	Was A	6	2	.750	17	8	5-1	0	82.2	70	29	2	2	21	34	1.96	117	.236	.291	27-0-1	.222	0	150	2		0.3
	Cle A	2	4	.333	7	7	2	0	46.1	52	25	1	2	10	17	3.88	62	.284	.328	17	.118	-1	135	-6		-0.9
	Year	8	6	.571	25	15	7-1	0	129	122	54	3	4	31	51	2.65	88	.254	.305	44-0-1	.182	-1	143	-4		-0.6
1909	Cle A	10	9	.526	24	18	13-2	0	165	135	56	0	5	50	82	2.40	107	.231	.297	52-0-3	.173	-1	69	5		0.7
1910	Cle A	14	13	.519	37	29	18-3	1	256.2	246	114	3	8	75	107	2.95	88	.261	.320	82-0-3	.183	-0	85	-9		-0.8
1911	Cle A	8	5	.615	15	13	7	1	106.2	117	56	0	3	24	46	3.29	104	.282	.326	40-0-5	.175	-1*	102	0		-0.1
1913	Cle A	23	10	.697	39	36	23-6	0	276	238	85	2	5	88	166	2.22	137	.237	.302	84-0-6	.119	-2	97	27		2.9
1914	Ind F	25	16	.610	**49**	**43**	33-**9**	3	**377.1**	332	127	5	5	89	**236**	2.22	141	.236	.284	125-0-12	.168	-4	109	33		3.2
1915	New F	9	11	.450	25	21	14	1	172	175	78	6	9	47	76	3.24	79	.268	.326	57-0-5	.053	-7	105	-11		-1.9
	Bro F	3	3	.500	7	7	5-1	0	48	31	15	1	1	12	20	1.50	181	.189	.249	15-0-1	.067	-2	59	5		0.4
	Year	12	14	.462	32	28	19-1	1	220	206	93	7	10	59	96	2.86	91	.252	.311	72-0-6	.056	-9	93	-7		-1.5
1917	Phi A	2	6	.250	15	8	4	0	80.2	86	53	1	0	26	35	3.35	82	.293	.350	27-0-2	.185	-1	72	-9		-0.7
Total	12	130	123	.514	330	266	180-27	8	2275	2090	963	23	68	690	1164	2.68	103	.248	.311	771-1-43	.152	-23	104	11		0.1

FALKENBORG, BRIAN Brian Thomas B1.18.1978 Newport Beach CA BR/TR/6-6/190* [BalA96 2/51] d10.1 [DL 2000 Bal A 181]
1999	Bal A	0	0	—	2	0	0	0-0	3	2	0	1	0	2-0	1			—	.200	.333			—	0		2		0.1
2004	LA N	1	0	1.000	6	0	0	0-0	14.1	19	14	2	3	9-0	11	7.53	55	.322	.437	2	.000	0		-6	19	-0.4
2005	SD N	0	0	—	10	0	0	0-0	11	17	11	2	0	5-1	10	8.18	47	.347	.407	0	—	0		-6		-0.3
Total	3	1	0	1.000	18	0	0	0-0	28.1	38	25	4	3	16-1	22	6.99	59	.322	.416	2	.000	0		-10	200	-0.6

FALLENSTEIN, ED Edward Joseph "Jack" (b Edward Joseph Valestin) B12.22.1908 Newark NJ D11.24.1971 Orange NJ BR/TR/6-3/180 d4.16
1931	Phi N	0	0	—	24	0	0	0	41.2	56	37	2	0	26	15	7.13	60	.333	.423	5	.200	-0		-11		-0.5
1933	Bos N	2	1	.667	9	4	1-1	0	35	43	23	1	1	13	5	3.60	85	.305	.368	8-0-1	.375	1*	122	-6		-0.3
Total	2	2	1	.667	33	4	1-1	0	76.2	99	60	3	1	39	20	5.52	67	.320	.398	13-0-1	.308	1	122	-17		-0.8

FALLON, BOB Robert Joseph B2.18.1960 Bronx NY BL/TL/6-3/211(200-211) [ChiA79 S1/5] d4.26 Col Miami-Dade North (FL) CC
1984	Chi A	0	0	—	3	3	0	0-0	14.2	12	7	0	0	11-0	10	3.68	114	.235	.371	0	—	0	130	1		0.0
1985	Chi A	0	0	—	10	0	0	0-0	16	25	11	5	0	9-2	17	6.19	70	.362	.430	0	—	0		-3		-0.1
Total	2	0	0	—	13	3	0	0-0	30.2	37	18	5	0	20-2	27	4.99	86	.308	.404	0	—	0	130	-2		-0.1

FALTEISEK, STEVE Steven James B1.28.1972 Mineola NY BR/TR/6-2/200* [MonN92 10/267] d7.22 Col South Alabama
1997	Mon N	0	0	—	5	0	0	0-0	8	8	4	0	1	3-0	5	3.38	124	.286	.353	2-0-1	.000	-0		0		0.0
1999	Mil N	0	0	—	10	0	0	0-0	12	18	10	3	0	3-0	2	7.50	61	.375	.404	1	.000	0		-3		-0.2
Total	2	0	0	—	15	0	0	0-0	20	26	14	3	1	6-0	7	5.85	76	.342	.384	3-0-1	.000	0		-3		-0.2

FANNIN, CLIFF Clifford Bryson "Mule" B5.13.1924 Louisa KY D12.11.1966 Sandusky OH BL/TR/6-0/170* d9.2
1945	StL A	0	0	—	5	0	0	0	10.1	8	3	0	0	5	5	2.61	135	.222	.317	1	.000	-0		1		0.0
1946	StL A	5	2	.714	27	7	4-1	2	86.2	76	37	4	1	42	52	3.01	124	.236	.326	31	.161	-1	128	5		0.3
1947	StL A	6	8	.429	26	18	6-2	1	145.2	134	70	10	1	77	77	3.58	108	.245	.340	46-0-4	.196	-0	94	3		0.2
1948	StL A	10	14	.417	34	29	10-3	1	213.2	198	106	14	1	104	102	4.17	109	.245	.332	65-0-6	.169	-0*	94	10		0.9
1949	StL A	8	14	.364	30	25	5	1	143	177	106	15	0	93	57	6.17	73	.308	.404	55-0-1	.164	-2*	92	-21		-3.0
1950	StL A	5	9	.357	25	16	3	1	102	116	82	18	0	58	42	6.53	76	.280	.369	34	.176	-2*	87	-15		-1.9
1951	StL A	0	2	.000	7	1	0	0	15.1	20	16	7	0	5	11	6.46	68	.317	.368	4	.250	-0*	202	-5		-0.5
1952	StL A	0	2	.000	10	2	0	0	16.1	34	25	5	0	9	6	12.67	31	.453	.512	1	.000	0*	67	-14		-1.5
Total	8	34	51	.400	164	98	28-6	6	733	763	445	73	3	393	352	4.85	89	.269	.358	237-0-11	.173	-5	96	-36		-5.5

FANNING, JACK John Jacob B1863 S.Orange NJ D6.10.1917 Aberdeen WA TR/5-9/163 d9.20
1889	Ind N	0	1	.000	1	1	0	0	3	3	0	0	2		0	18.00	23	.500	.625	1	.000	-0	161	-2		-0.2
1894	Phi N	1	3	.250	6	4	2	0	34.1	54	52	4	2	22	7	8.91	58	.353	.441	14	.143	-1	100	-17		-1.3
Total	2	1	4	.200	7	5	2	0	35.1	57	55	4	2	24	7	9.17	56	.358	.449	15	.133	-1	108	-19		-1.5

FANOK, HARRY Harry Michael "The Flame Thrower" B5.11.1940 Whippany NJ BB/TR/6-0/180* d4.16
1963	StL N	2	1	.667	12	0	0	1	25.2	24	16	3	1	21-1	25	5.26	67	.255	.387	5	.400	1		-4		-0.4
1964	StL N	0	0	—	4	0	0	0	7.2	5	6	0	0	3-0	10	5.87	65	.179	.250	1	.000	-0		-2		-0.1
Total	2	2	1	.667	16	0	0	1	33.1	29	22	3	1	24-1	35	5.40	67	.238	.358	6	.333	1		-6		-0.5

FANOVICH, FRANK Frank Joseph "Lefty" B1.11.1922 New York NY BL/TL/5-11/185* d4.25
1949	Cin N	0	2	.000	29	1	0	0	43.1	44	31	2	2	28	27	5.40	77	.257	.368	4	.000	0	42	-6		-0.3
1953	Phi A	0	3	.000	26	3	0	0	61.2	62	41	5	6	37	37	5.55	77	.273	.389	11	.182	-1	69	-8		-0.5
Total	2	0	5	.000	55	4	0	0	105	106	72	7	8	65	64	5.49	77	.266	.380	15	.133	-1	63	-14		-0.8

FANSLER, STAN Stanley Robert B2.12.1965 Elkins WV BR/TR/5-11/185 [PitN83 2/36] d9.6
| 1986 | Pit N | 0 | 3 | .000 | 5 | 5 | 0 | 0-0 | 24 | 30 | 12 | 2 | 1 | 15-0 | 13 | 3.75 | 104 | .247 | .361 | 6-0-1 | .167 | 0 | 55 | 0 | | 0.0 |

FANWELL, HARRY Harry Clayton B10.16.1886 Patapsco MD D7.15.1965 Baltimore MD BR/TR/6-0/175 d7.23
| 1910 | Cle A | 2 | 9 | .182 | 17 | 11 | 5-1 | 0 | 92 | 87 | 52 | 0 | 6 | 38 | 30 | 3.62 | 71 | .260 | .347 | 30-0-1 | .033 | -3 | 47 | -10 | | -1.5 |

FARMER, ED Edward Joseph B10.18.1949 Evergreen Park IL BR/TR/6-5/210* [CleA67 5/91] d6.9
1971	Cle A	5	4	.556	43	4	0	4-1	78.2	77	42	9	3	41-3	48	4.35	89	.263	.356	14-0-1	.071	-1	64	-4		-0.6
1972	Cle A	2	5	.286	46	3	0	7-2	61.1	51	32	10	1	27-6	33	4.40	74	.231	.316	7-0-1	.143	-0	136	-7		-1.0
1973	Cle A	0	2	.000	16	0	0	1-1	17.1	25	12	4	0	5-0	10	4.67	85	.325	.361	0	—	0		-2		-0.3
	Det A	3	0	1.000	24	0	0	2-0	45	52	26	3	2	27-0	28	5.00	82	.292	.389	0	—	0		-4		-0.3
	Year	3	2	.600	40	0	0	3-1	62.1	77	38	7	2	32-0	38	4.91	83	.302	.381	0	—	0		-6		-0.6
1974	Phi N	2	1	.667	14	3	0	0-0	31	41	32	5	0	27-0	20	8.42	45	.323	.433	9	.111	-1	130	-15		-1.4
1977	Bal A	0	0	—	1	0	0	0-0	0	1	1	0	1	1-0	0	∞		1.000	1.000	0	—	0		-1		-0.1
1978	Mil A	1	0	1.000	3	0	0	1-0	11	7	1	1	0	4-0	6	0.82	464	.175	.250	0	—	0		4		0.4
1979	Tex A	2	0	1.000	11	2	0	0-1	33	30	21	2	2	19-2	25	4.36	95	.252	.359	0	—	0	164	-2		-0.1
	Chi A	3	7	.300	42	3	0	14-3	81.1	66	36	2	1	34-8	48	2.43	175	.219	.299	0	—	0	57	12		1.8
	Year	5	7	.417	53	5	0	14-4	114.1	96	57	4	3	53-10	73	2.99	141	.229	.317	0	—	0	99	10		1.7
1980	Chi A★	7	9	.438	64	0	0	30-11	99.2	92	37	6	1	56-11	54	3.34	122	.244	.343	0	—	0		10		2.2
1981	Chi A	3	3	.500	42	0	0	10-5	52.2	53	33	5	1	34-1	42	4.61	78	.262	.368	0	—	0		-7		-1.0
1982	Phi N	2	6	.250	47	0	0	6-3	76	66	44	2	0	50-11	58	4.86	76	.234	.347	11-0-2	.000	-1	107	-9		-1.1
1983	Phi N	0	6	.000	12	3	0	0-0	26.2	35	22	2	1	20-8	16	6.08	59	.307	.412	6-0-1	.167	-0	65	-8	41	-1.5
	Oak A	0	0	—	5	1	0	0-0	10.1	15	4	1	0	0-0	7	3.48	112	.366	.357	0	—	0	187	1		0.0
Total	11	30	43	.411	370	21	0	75-27	624	611	343	52	12	345-50	395	4.30	90	.257	.352	47-0-5	.085	-3	99	-32	41	-3.0

FARMER, HOWARD Howard Earl B11.18.1966 Gary IN BR/TR/6-3/190 [MonN87 7/174] d7.2 b-Mike Col Jackson St. [DL 1991 Mon N 44]
| 1990 | Mon N | 0 | 3 | .000 | 6 | 6 | 0 | 0-0 | 23 | 26 | 18 | 0 | 0 | 10-1 | 14 | 7.04 | 52 | .302 | .371 | 5-0-1 | .400 | 1 | 135 | -8 | | -0.8 |

YEAR	TM LG	W	L	PCT	G	GS	CG-SHO	SV-BS	IP	H	R	HR	HB	BB-IB	SO	ERA	AERA	OAV	OOB	AB-HR-SH	AVG	PB	SUP	APR	DL	PW
FARMER, MIKE Michael Anthony B7.3.1968 Gary IN BB/TL/6-1/193 d5.4 b-Howard Col Jackson St.																										
1996	Col N	0	0	1.000	7	4	0	0-0	28	32	25	8	0	13-0	16	7.71	68	.286	.360	10	.400	1	151	-6		-0.2
FARNSWORTH, JEFF Jeffrey Ellis B10.6.1975 Wichita KS BR/TR/6-2/190 [SeaA96 2/57] d4.3 Col Okaloosa-Walton (FL) CC																										
2002	Det A	2	3	.400	44	0	0	0-1	70	100	47	6	2	29-8	28	5.79	76	.338	.399	0	—	0		-10		-0.6
FARNSWORTH, KYLE Kyle Lynn B4.14.1976 Wichita KS BR/TR/6-4/220(215-240) [ChiN94 47/1290] d4.29 Col Abraham Baldwin (GA) JC																										
1999	Chi N	5	9	.357	27	21	1-1	0-0	130	140	80	28	3	52-1	70	5.05	90	.271	.340	35-0-6	.086	-1	111	-7		-0.8
2000	Chi N	2	9	.182	46	5	0	1-5	77	90	58	14	4	50-8	74	6.43	71	.291	.392	14-0-2	.071	-1	104	-16		-2.0
2001	Chi N	4	6	.400	76	0	0	2-1	82	65	26	8	1	29-2	107	2.74	153	.213	.282	1	.000	-0		14		1.5
2002	Chi N	4	6	.400	45	0	0	1-6	46.2	53	47	9	1	24-7	46	7.33	55	.293	.370	1	.000	-0		-20	55	-3.7
2003	†Chi N	3	2	.600	77	0	0	0-3	76.1	53	31	6	0	36-1	92	3.30	132	.196	.289	1	.000	-0		9		0.5
2004	Chi N	4	5	.444	72	0	0	0-4	66.2	67	39	10	2	33-1	78	4.72	94	.260	.348	1		-0		-3	15	-0.3
2005	Det A	1	1	.500	46	0	0	6-2	42.2	29	12	1	1	20-0	55	2.32	182	.192	.289	0	—	0		9		0.6
	†Atl N	0	0	—	26	0	0	10-0	27.1	15	6	4	2	7-0	32	1.98	218	.161	.235	0	—	0		7		0.5
Total	7	23	38	.377	415	26	1-1	20-21	548.2	512	299	80	14	251-20	554	4.45	99	.246	.329	54-0-8	.074	-3	115	-7	70	-3.7
FARR, JIM James Alfred B5.18.1956 Waverly NY BR/TR/6-1/195 [TexA78 29/675] d9.7 Col Penn St.																										
1982	Tex A	0	0	—	7	0	0	0-0	18	20	8	0	0	7-2	6	2.50	155	.278	.338	0	—	0		2		0.1
FARR, STEVE Steven Michael B12.12.1956 LaPlata MD BR/TR/5-11/200(190-206) d5.16 Col American																										
1984	Cle A	3	11	.214	31	16	0	1-1	116	106	61	14	4	46-3	83	4.58	90	.245	.323	0	—	0	68	-4	15	-0.4
1985	†KC A	2	1	.667	16	3	0	1-0	37.2	34	15	2	2	20-4	36	3.11	135	.243	.344	0	—	0	94	4		0.3
1986	KC A	8	4	.667	56	0	0	8-1	109.1	90	39	10	4	39-8	83	3.13	137	.228	.302	0	—	0		15		1.7
1987	KC A	4	3	.571	47	0	0	1-4	91	97	47	9	2	44-4	88	4.15	111	.270	.350	0	—	0		5		0.2
1988	KC A	5	4	.556	62	1	0	20-6	82.2	74	25	5	2	30-6	72	2.50	160	.240	.309	0	—	0	45	14		2.0
1989	KC A	2	5	.286	51	2	0	18-4	63.1	75	35	5	1	22-5	56	4.12	94	.296	.351	0	—	0	82	-3	23	-0.5
1990	KC A	13	7	.650	57	6	1-1	1-1	127	99	32	6	4	48-9	94	1.98	195	.220	.301	0	—	0	67	27		4.1
1991	NY A	5	5	.500	60	0	0	23-6	70	57	19	4	5	20-3	60	2.19	191	.219	.288	0	—	0		15		2.9
1992	NY A	2	2	.500	50	0	0	30-6	52	34	10	2	2	19-0	37	1.56	254	.186	.267	0	—	0		14	18	2.3
1993	NY A	2	2	.500	49	0	0	25-6	47	44	22	8	2	28-4	39	4.21	99	.253	.356	0	—	0	1	10		0.2
1994	Cle A	1	1	.500	19	0	0	4-2	15.1	17	12	3	2	15-1	12	5.28	90	.279	.430	0	—	0	-2	-6		-0.3
	Bos A	1	0	1.000	11	0	0	0-1	13	24	9	4	0	3-0	8	6.23	81	.407	.435	0	—	0	-1	9		-0.1
	Year	2	1	.667	30	0	0	4-3	28.1	41	21	5	2	18-1	20	5.72	85	.342	.433	0	—	0	-3			-0.4
Total	11	48	45	.516	509	28	1-1	132-38	824.1	751	326	70	32	334-47	668	3.25	128	.244	.322	0	—	0	70	85	88	12.4
FARRELL, JOHN John Edward B8.4.1962 Monmouth Beach NJ BR/TR/6-4/210* [CleA84 2/32] d8.18 Col Oklahoma St. [DL 1992 Cal A 182]																										
1987	Cle A	5	1	.833	10	9	1	0-0	69	68	29	7	5	22-1	28	3.39	135	.256	.323	0	—	0	131	9		0.7
1988	Cle A	14	10	.583	31	30	4	0-0	210.1	216	106	15	9	67-3	92	4.24	98	.269	.330	0	—	0	96	-1	23	-0.1
1989	Cle A	9	14	.391	31	31	7-2	0-0	208	196	97	14	7	71-4	132	3.63	110	.244	.309	0	—	0	84	6	13	0.5
1990	Cle A	4	5	.444	17	17	1	0-0	96.2	108	49	10	1	33-1	44	4.28	92	.286	.344	0	—	0	102	-3	88	-0.3
1993	Cal A	3	12	.200	21	17	0	0-0	90.2	110	74	22	7	44-3	45	7.35	62	.301	.385	0	—	0	78	-23		-3.2
1994	Cal A	1	2	.333	3	3	0	0-0	13	16	14	2	1	8-0	10	9.00	55	.308	.410	0	—	0	87	-6		-0.9
1995	Cal A	0	0	—	1	0	0	0-0	4.2	7	4	0	0	4-0	4	3.86	122	.368	.350	0	—	0	0	0		0.0
1996	Det A	0	2	.000	2	2	0	0-0	6.1	11	10	2	1	5-0	0	14.21	36	.407	.515	0	—	0	73	-6		-0.9
Total	8	36	46	.439	116	109	13-2	0-0	698.2	732	383	72	31	250-12	355	4.56	92	.270	.336	0	—	0	93	-24	306	-4.2
FARRELL, KERBY Major Kerby B9.3.1913 Leapwood TN D12.17.1975 Nashville TN BL/TL/5-11/172 d4.24 M1/C6 Col Freed-Hardeman ▲																										
1943	Bos N	0	1	.000	6	0	0	0-0	23	24	11	0	3	9-1	4	4.30	79	.275	.344	280-0-7	.268	1*		-1		0.0
FARRELL, TURK Richard Joseph B4.8.1934 Boston MA D6.10.1977 Great Yarmouth, England BR/TR/6-4/220(192-220) d9.21																										
1956	Phi N	0	1	.000	1	1	0	0-0	4.1	6	6	0	1	3-0	0	12.46	30	.353	.476	1-0-1	.000	-0	71	-4		-0.6
1957	Phi N	10	2	.833	52	0	0	10	83.1	74	29	2	2	36-9	54	2.38	160	.242	.323	9-1-0	.111	0		11		1.9
1958	Phi N★	8	9	.471	54	0	0	11	94	84	41	7	0	40-7	73	3.35	118	.244	.320	24	.208	0		6		1.0
1959	Phi N	1	6	.143	38	0	0	6	57	61	30	9	0	25-7	31	4.74	87	.288	.354	6-0-1	.167	-0		-2		-0.3
1960	Phi N	10	6	.625	59	0	0	11	103.1	88	36	3	4	29-6	70	2.70	144	.239	.298	15-0-2	.200	1		13		2.2
1961	Phi N	2	1	.667	5	0	0	0	9.2	10	8	3	1	6-1	10	6.52	63	.270	.386	2	.500	0		-3		-0.5
	LA N	6	6	.500	50	0	0	10	89	107	56	12	1	43-14	80	5.06	86	.296	.371	18-0-3	.000	-2	-6			-1.2
	Year	8	7	.533	55	0	0	10	98.2	117	64	15	2	49-15	90	5.20	83	.294	.373	20-0-3	.050	-2		-9		-1.7
1962	Hou N★	10	20	.333	43	29	11-2	4	241.2	210	91	21	5	55-2	203	3.02	124	.233	.279	78-2-3	.179	2	64	22		2.7
1963	Hou N	14	13	.519	34	26	12	1	202.1	161	76	12	2	35-2	141	3.02	104	.219	.255	63-0-3	.143	1	71	4		0.7
1964	Hou N★	11	10	.524	32	27	7	0	198.1	196	80	21	3	52-4	117	3.27	105	.261	.308	69-0-2	.072	-3	96	5		0.1
1965	Hou N★	11	11	.500	33	29	8-3	1	208.1	202	94	18	3	35-8	122	3.50	96	.252	.284	74-0-2	.135	-1	99	-4		-0.6
1966	Hou N	6	10	.375	32	21	3	2	152.2	167	84	23	0	28-4	101	4.60	74	.278	.307	48-1-1	.146	-0	87	-18		-1.9
1967	Hou N	1	0	1.000	7	0	0	0	11.2	11	7	0	1	7-1	10	4.63	72	.244	.358	1	.000	-0		-2		-0.2
	Phi N	9	6	.600	50	1	0	12	92	76	26	6	1	15-5	68	2.05	166	.228	.284	19-0-1	.105	-0	52	13		2.5
	Year	10	6	.625	57	1	0	12	103.2	87	33	6	2	22-6	78	2.34	145	.230	.271	20-0-1	.100	-0	52	11		2.3
1968	Phi N	4	6	.400	54	0	0	12	82.2	83	40	7	2	32-6	55	3.48	86	.271	.340	6	.167	-0		-6		-1.0
1969	Phi N	3	4	.429	46	0	0	3-3	74.1	92	33	8	1	27-6	40	4.00	89	.307	.364	3-0-1	.000	-0		-3		-0.3
Total	14	106	111	.488	590	134	41-5	88-3	1704.2	1628	737	152	27	468-82	1177	3.45	103	.254	.304	436-4-20	.135	-3	80	27		4.5
FASS, FRED Frederick Peter B10.30.1859 Milwaukee WI D7.5.1930 Burnt Mill CO d7.11																										
1887	Ind N	0	1	.000	4	2	1	**1**	15.2	25	22	1	2	8	0	10.34	40	.347	.427	11	.182	-1	94	-9		-0.5
FASSERO, JEFF Jeffrey Joseph B1.5.1963 Springfield IL BL/TL/6-1/195* [StLN84 22/554] d5.4 Col U. of Mississippi																										
1991	Mon N	2	5	.286	51	0	0	8-3	55.1	39	17	1	1	17-1	42	2.44	149	.196	.263	3-0-2	.000	0		7		1.1
1992	Mon N	8	7	.533	70	0	0	1-6	85.2	81	35	1	2	34-6	63	2.84	123	.249	.322	7-0-1	.143	0		4		0.7
1993	Mon N	12	5	.706	56	15	1	1-2	149.2	119	50	7	0	54-0	140	2.29	183	.216	.284	32-0-5	.063	-2	78	28		2.8
1994	Mon N	8	6	.571	21	21	1	0-0	138.2	119	54	13	1	40-4	119	2.99	142	.229	.285	44-0-0	.068	-2	92	18	18	1.6
1995	Mon N	13	14	.481	30	30	1	0-0	189	207	102	15	2	74-3	164	4.33	99	.283	.348	57-0-8	.070	-3	95	-2		-0.5
1996	Mon N	15	11	.577	34	34	5-1	0-0	231.2	217	95	20	3	55-3	222	3.30	131	.244	.289	64-0-14	.094	-1	89	25		2.7
1997	†Sea A	16	9	.640	35	**35**	2-1	0-0	234.1	226	108	21	3	84-6	189	3.61	126	.254	.312	.5	.200	0	113	21		2.1
1998	Sea A	13	12	.520	32	32	7	0-0	224.2	223	115	33	10	66-2	176	3.97	118	.259	.316	3	.000	-0	103	15	12	1.4
1999	Sea A	4	14	.222	30	24	0	0-0	139	188	133	34	4	73-3	101	7.38	65	.321	.397	7	.000	-1	106	-41		-4.1
	†Tex A	1	0	1.000	7	3	0	0-0	17.1	20	12	1	0	10-0	13	5.71	91	.286	.370	0	—	0	126	-1		-0.1
	Year	5	14	.263	37	27	0	0-0	156.1	208	135	35	4	83-3	114	7.20	67	.318	.394	7	.000	-1	109	-41		-4.2
2000	Bos A	8	8	.500	38	23	0	0-0	130	153	72	16	1	50-2	97	4.78	105	.296	.358	2-0-1	.000	-0	94	5	15	0.5
2001	Chi N	4	4	.500	82	0	0	12-5	73.2	66	31	6	1	23-5	79	3.42	122	.235	.293	2	.000	-0		6		0.8
2002	Chi N	5	6	.455	57	0	0	0-1	51	65	37	5	3	22-5	44	6.18	66	.313	.385	1	.333	0		-12		-2.2
	†StL N	3	0	1.000	16	0	0	0-2	18	16	6	4	0	5-0	12	3.00	134	.232	.284	0	—	0		2		0.4
	Year	8	6	.571	73	0	0	0-3	69	81	43	9	3	27-5	56	5.35	76	.292	.360	3	.333	0		-10		-1.8
2003	StL N	1	7	.125	62	6	0	3-3	77.2	93	51	17	2	34-4	55	5.68	73	.296	.368	9-0-1	.000	-0	129	-13		-1.4
2004	Col N	3	8	.273	40	12	0	0-0	111	136	73	17	4	44-5	59	5.51	86	.306	.368	21-0-2	.190	-0	107	-9		-0.7
	Ari N	0	0	—	1	0	0	0-0	1	0	0	0	0	0-0	1	0.00	—	.000	.000	0	—	0	0	0		0.0
	Year	3	8	.273	41	12	0	0-0	112	136	73	9	4	44-5	60	5.46	87	.304	.366	21-0-2	.190	-0	107	-6		-0.7
2005	SF N	4	7	.364	48	6	0	0-2	91	92	48	7	0	31-1	60	4.05	105	.268	.326	13-0-1	.000	-1	44	0		0.0
Total	15	120	123	.494	710	241	17-2	25-24	2018.2	2060	1029	210	37	716-50	1636	4.08	108	.264	.326	272-0-44	.081	-11	101	53	45	5.1
FAST, DARCY Darcy Rae B3.10.1947 Dallas OR BL/TL/6-3/195 d6.15 Mil 1969 Col Warner Pacific																										
1968	Chi N	0	1	.000	8	1	0	0-0	14	9	8	1	0	8-0	10	5.40	58	.216	.348	3	.000	0	110	-2		-0.2
FASZHOLZ, JACK John Edward "Preacher" B4.11.1927 St.Louis MO BR/TR/6-3/205 d4.25																										
1953	StL N	0	0	—	4	1	0	0-0	11.2	16	9	3	1	1	7	6.94	61	.327	.353	3	.000	-0	126	-3		-0.2
FAUL, BILL William Alvan B4.21.1940 Cincinnati OH D2.21.2002 Cincinnati OH BR/TR/5-10/190* d9.19 Col Cincinnati																										
1962	Det A	0	0	—	1	0	0	0-0	1.2	4	6	1	4	3-0	2	32.40	13	.444	.615	0	—	0		-5		-0.2
1963	Det A	5	6	.455	28	10	2	1	97	93	55	14	4	48-3	64	4.64	81	.251	.340	27-0-1	.148	0	93	-9		-1.0

YEAR	TM LG	W	L	PCT	G	GS	CG-SHO	SV-BS	IP	H	R	HR	HB	BB-IB	SO	ERA	AERA	OAV	OOB	AB-HR-SH	AVG	PB	SUP	APR	DL	PW
1964	Det A	0	0	—	1	1	0	0	5	5	6	2	0	2-0	1	10.80	34	.250	.318	2	.000	-0	146	-4		-0.2
1965	Chi N	6	6	.500	17	16	5-3	0	96.2	83	43	12	3	18-0	59	3.54	104	.232	.274	30	.100	-1	84	2		0.1
1966	Chi N	1	4	.200	17	6	1	0	51.1	47	31	12	4	18-1	32	5.08	72	.242	.318	13	.000	-2	44	-7		-0.8
1970	SF N	0	0	—	7	0	0	1-0	9.2	15	9	1	0	6-2	6	7.45	53	.357	.438	0	—	0		-4		-0.2
Total	6	12	16	.429	71	33	8-3	2-0	261.1	247	150	42	12	95-6	164	4.72	79	.249	.320	72-0-1	.097	-2	81	-27		-2.3

FAULKNER, JIM James Leroy "Lefty" B7.27.1899 Beatrice NE D6.1.1962 W.Palm Beach FL BB/TL(BL 1927)/6-3/190 d9.15

YEAR	TM LG	W	L	PCT	G	GS	CG-SHO	SV-BS	IP	H	R	HR	HB	BB-IB	SO	ERA	AERA	OAV	OOB	AB-HR-SH	AVG	PB	SUP	APR	DL	PW
1927	NY N	1	0	1.000	3	1	0	0	9.2	13	4	0	1	5	2	3.72	104	.317	.404	2	.500	1	243	0		0.1
1928	NY N	9	8	.529	38	8	3	2	117.1	131	61	5	3	41	32	3.53	111	.289	.351	39-0-2	.231	1	84	2		0.3
1930	Bro N	0	0	—	2	1	0	1	0.1	2	3	1	0	1	0	81.00	6	.667	.750	0	—	0	266	-3		-0.4
Total	3	10	8	.556	43	10	3	3	127.1	146	68	6	4	47	34	3.75	104	.293	.359	41-0-2	.244	2	124	-1		0.0

FAUSETT, BUCK Robert Shaw "Leaky" B4.8.1908 Sheridan AR D5.2.1994 College Station TX BL/TR/5-10/170 d4.18 Col Texas A&M-Commerce ▲

YEAR	TM LG	W	L	PCT	G	GS	CG-SHO	SV-BS	IP	H	R	HR	HB	BB-IB	SO	ERA	AERA	OAV	OOB	AB-HR-SH	AVG	PB	SUP	APR	DL	PW
1944	Cin N	0	0	—	2	2	0	0	10.2	13	8	0	2	1	5	5.91	59	.295	.415	31-0-1	.097	-0*		-3		-0.2

FAUST, CHARLIE Charles Victor "Victory" B10.9.1880 Marion KS D6.18.1915 Fort Steilacoom WA BR/TR/6-2/? d10.7

YEAR	TM LG	W	L	PCT	G	GS	CG-SHO	SV-BS	IP	H	R	HR	HB	BB-IB	SO	ERA	AERA	OAV	OOB	AB-HR-SH	AVG	PB	SUP	APR	DL	PW
1911	NY N	0	0	—	2	0	0	0	2	2	1	0	0	0	0	4.50	75	.250	.250	0		0		0		0.0

FAUVER, CLAY Clayton King "Cayt" B8.1.1872 N.Eaton OH D3.3.1942 Chatsworth GA BB/TR/5-10/? d9.7 Col Oberlin

YEAR	TM LG	W	L	PCT	G	GS	CG-SHO	SV-BS	IP	H	R	HR	HB	BB-IB	SO	ERA	AERA	OAV	OOB	AB-HR-SH	AVG	PB	SUP	APR	DL	PW
1899	Lou N	1	0	1.000	1	1	1	0	9	11	4	0	0	2	1	0.00	—	.297	.333	4	.000	-1	75	3		0.2

FEAR, VERN Luvern Carl B8.21.1924 Everly IA D9.6.1976 Spencer IA BB/TR/6-0/170 d8.3

YEAR	TM LG	W	L	PCT	G	GS	CG-SHO	SV-BS	IP	H	R	HR	HB	BB-IB	SO	ERA	AERA	OAV	OOB	AB-HR-SH	AVG	PB	SUP	APR	DL	PW
1952	Chi N	0	0	—	4	0	0	0	8	9	7	1	1	3	4	7.88	49	.290	.371	1	.000	-0		-3		-0.2

FEE, JACK John B12.23.1867 Carbondale PA D3.3.1913 Carbondale PA d9.14

YEAR	TM LG	W	L	PCT	G	GS	CG-SHO	SV-BS	IP	H	R	HR	HB	BB-IB	SO	ERA	AERA	OAV	OOB	AB-HR-SH	AVG	PB	SUP	APR	DL	PW
1889	Ind N	2	2	.500	7	3	2	0	40	39	29	2	6	31	10	4.27	98	.248	.392	21	.143	-2	96	-1		-0.2

FELDMAN, HARRY Harry B11.10.1919 New York NY D3.16.1962 Fort Smith AR BR/TR/6-0/175 d9.10

YEAR	TM LG	W	L	PCT	G	GS	CG-SHO	SV-BS	IP	H	R	HR	HB	BB-IB	SO	ERA	AERA	OAV	OOB	AB-HR-SH	AVG	PB	SUP	APR	DL	PW
1941	NY N	1	1	.500	3	3	1-1	0	20.1	21	10	0	0	6	9	3.98	93	.280	.333	6-0-1	.167	0	115	0		-0.1
1942	NY N	7	1	.875	31	6	2-1	0	114	100	46	5	1	73	49	3.16	106	.236	.350	39-1-1	.282	3	121	3		0.5
1943	NY N	4	5	.444	31	10	1	0	104.2	114	59	7	4	58	49	4.30	80	.279	.374	30	.133	-1*	79	-11		-1.0
1944	NY N	11	13	.458	40	27	8-1	2	205.1	214	120	18	2	91	70	4.16	88	.266	.342	73-0-3	.205	0*	110	-14		-1.6
1945	NY N	12	13	.480	35	30	10-3	1	217.2	213	92	14	1	69	74	3.27	120	.251	.308	72-1-0	.097	-3*	77	14		1.1
1946	NY N	0	2	.000	3	2	0	0	4	9	8	1	0	3	3	18.00	19	.474	.545	1	.000	-0	25	-6		-1.0
Total	6	35	35	.500	143	78	22-6	3	666	671	335	45	8	300	254	3.80	96	.260	.339	221-2-5	.172	-1	93	-14		-2.1

FELDMAN, SCOTT Scott Wayne B2.7.1983 Kailua HI BL/TR/6-5/210 d8.31 Col San Mateo (CA) JC

YEAR	TM LG	W	L	PCT	G	GS	CG-SHO	SV-BS	IP	H	R	HR	HB	BB-IB	SO	ERA	AERA	OAV	OOB	AB-HR-SH	AVG	PB	SUP	APR	DL	PW
2005	Tex A	0	1	.000	8	0	0	0-0	9.1	9	1	0	0	2-1	4	0.96	476	.257	.297	0	—	0		4		0.3

FELICIANO, PEDRO Pedro Juan (Molina) B8.25.1976 Rio Piedras, PR BL/TL/5-11/165(165-185) [LAN95 31/863] d9.4

YEAR	TM LG	W	L	PCT	G	GS	CG-SHO	SV-BS	IP	H	R	HR	HB	BB-IB	SO	ERA	AERA	OAV	OOB	AB-HR-SH	AVG	PB	SUP	APR	DL	PW
2002	NY N	0	0	—	6	0	0	0-0	6	9	5	0	0	1-0	4	7.50	53	.360	.385	0	—	0		-2		-0.1
2003	NY N	0	0	—	23	0	0	0-0	48.1	52	21	5	3	21-3	43	3.35	125	.269	.349	3-0-1	.000	-0		4		0.2
2004	NY N	1	1	.500	22	0	0	0-0	18.1	14	12	2	1	12-0	14	5.40	74	.209	.333	0	—	-0		-2		-0.2
Total	3	1	1	.500	51	0	0	0-0	72.2	75	38	7	4	34-3	61	4.21	100	.263	.348	3-0-1	.000	-0		0		-0.1

FELIX, HARRY Harry B1870 Brooklyn NY D10.17.1961 Miami FL BR/TR/5-7.5/160 d10.5

YEAR	TM LG	W	L	PCT	G	GS	CG-SHO	SV-BS	IP	H	R	HR	HB	BB-IB	SO	ERA	AERA	OAV	OOB	AB-HR-SH	AVG	PB	SUP	APR	DL	PW
1901	NY N	0	0	—	1	0	0	0	2	3	0	0	0	0	0	0.00	—	.333	.333	1	.000	-0		1		0.0
1902	Phi N	1	3	.250	9	5	3	0	45	61	37	1	0	11	10	5.60	50	.323	.360	37-0-3	.135	-1*	53	-13		-1.1
Total	2	1	3	.250	10	5	3	0	47	64	37	1	0	11	10	5.36	53	.323	.359	38-0-3	.132	-1	53	-12		-1.1

FELLER, BOB Robert William Andrew "Rapid Robert" (b Robert William Feller) B11.3.1918 Van Meter IA BR/TR/6-0/185* d7.19 Mil 1942-45 HF1962

YEAR	TM LG	W	L	PCT	G	GS	CG-SHO	SV-BS	IP	H	R	HR	HB	BB-IB	SO	ERA	AERA	OAV	OOB	AB-HR-SH	AVG	PB	SUP	APR	DL	PW
1936	Cle A	5	3	.625	14	8	5	1	62	52	29	1	4	47	76	3.34	151	.229	.371	22-0-1	.136	-2	109	11		1.0
1937	Cle A	9	7	.563	26	19	9	1	148.2	116	68	4	2	106	150	3.39	136	.218	.351	53	.170	-1	80	19		1.7
1938	Cle A☆	17	11	.607	39	36	20-2	1	277.2	225	136	13	7	208	240	4.08	114	.220	.356	94-0-9	.181	-2	104	21		1.8
1939	Cle A★	24	9	.727	39	35	24-4	1	296.2	227	105	13	3	142	246	2.85	154	.210	.303	99-0-6	.212	5	114	54		6.0
1940	Cle A★	27	11	.711	43	37	31-4	4	320.1	245	102	13	5	118	261	2.61	161	.210	.285	115-2-6	.157	1	99	61		6.8
1941	Cle A★	25	13	.658	44	40	28-6	4	343	284	129	15	5	194	260	3.15	125	.226	.332	120-1-10	.150	2	108	34		3.6
1945	Cle A	5	3	.625	9	9	7-1	0	72	50	21	4	1	35	59	2.50	130	.192	.293	25-0-1	.160	-0	111	7		0.7
1946	Cle A★	26	15	.634	48	42	36-10	4	371.1	277	101	11	3	153	348	2.18	152	.208	.291	124-0-8	.129	-2	80	50		5.4
1947	Cle A★	20	11	.645	42	37	20-5	3	299	230	97	17	4	127	196	2.68	130	.215	.300	98-0-8	.184	-3	105	29		3.2
1948	†Cle A❋	19	15	.559	44	38	18-2	3	280.1	255	123	20	2	116	164	3.56	114	.241	.317	95-0-9	.095	-8	109	17		1.0
1949	Cle A	15	14	.517	36	28	15	0	211	198	104	18	1	84	108	3.75	106	.248	.320	72-2-7	.236	4	95	3		0.5
1950	Cle A★	16	11	.593	35	34	16-3	0	247	230	105	20	5	103	119	3.43	126	.247	.325	83-2-8	.120	-2	99	27		2.1
1951	Cle A	22	8	.733	33	32	16-4	0	249.2	239	105	22	7	95	111	3.50	108	.253	.325	81-0-10	.123	-4	125	11		0.6
1952	Cle A	9	13	.409	30	30	11	0	191.2	219	124	24	3	83	81	4.74	71	.288	.360	60-1-1	.117	1	152	-36		-3.5
1953	Cle A	10	7	.588	25	25	10-1	0	175.2	163	78	24	3	60	60	3.59	105	.251	.317	56-0-8	.107	-2	124	4		0.2
1954	Cle A	13	3	.813	19	19	9-1	0	140	127	53	13	3	39	59	3.09	119	.239	.292	48-0-3	.188	1	128	10		1.1
1955	Cle A	4	4	.500	25	11	2-1	0	83	71	43	7	1	31-2	25	3.47	115	.235	.305	21-0-3	.048	0	93	2		-0.1
1956	Cle A	0	4	.000	19	5	0	0	58	63	34	7	0	23-4	18	4.97	85	.280	.344	16	.000	-2	69	-4		-0.5
Total	18	266	162	.621	570	484	279-44	21	3827	3271	1557	224	60	1764-6	2581	3.25	122	.231	.319	1282-8-100	.151	-7	107	320		31.6

FELTON, TERRY Terry Lane B10.29.1957 Texarkana AR BR/TR/6-1/180* [MinA76 2/34] d9.28

YEAR	TM LG	W	L	PCT	G	GS	CG-SHO	SV-BS	IP	H	R	HR	HB	BB-IB	SO	ERA	AERA	OAV	OOB	AB-HR-SH	AVG	PB	SUP	APR	DL	PW
1979	Min A	0	0	—	3	0	0	0-0	2	0	1	0	0	1	1	0.00	—	.000	.000	0	—	0		1		0.0
1980	Min A	0	3	.000	5	4	0	0-0	17.2	20	18	2	1	9-1	14	7.13	61	.286	.370	0	—	0	56	-6		-0.8
1981	Min A	0	0	—	1	0	0	0-0	1.1	4	6	1	0	2-0	1	40.50	10	.500	.600	0	—	0		-5		-0.2
1982	Min A	0	13	.000	48	6	0	3-3	117.1	99	71	18	4	76-8	92	4.99	86	.230	.348	0	—	0	50	-9		-1.1
Total	4	0	16	.000	55	10	0	3-3	138.1	123	95	21	5	87-9	108	5.53	77	.240	.352	0	—	0	53	-19		-2.1

FENNER, HOD Horace Alfred B7.12.1897 Martin MI D11.20.1954 Detroit MI BR/TR/5-10.5/165 d9.9 Col Kalamazoo

YEAR	TM LG	W	L	PCT	G	GS	CG-SHO	SV-BS	IP	H	R	HR	HB	BB-IB	SO	ERA	AERA	OAV	OOB	AB-HR-SH	AVG	PB	SUP	APR	DL	PW
1921	Chi A	0	0	—	2	1	0	0	7	14	6	0	3	1	1	7.71	55	.452	.500	2	.000	-0	394	-2		-0.2

FERENS, STAN Stanley "Lefty" B3.5.1915 Wendel PA D10.7.1994 Hempfield Twp. PA BB/TL/5-11/170 d6.10

YEAR	TM LG	W	L	PCT	G	GS	CG-SHO	SV-BS	IP	H	R	HR	HB	BB-IB	SO	ERA	AERA	OAV	OOB	AB-HR-SH	AVG	PB	SUP	APR	DL	PW
1942	StL A	3	4	.429	19	3	1	0	69	76	31	2	0	21	23	3.78	98	.279	.331	21-0-1	.143	-1	192	1		0.0
1946	StL A	2	9	.182	34	6	1	0	88	100	60	3	3	38	28	4.50	83	.293	.369	24-0-2	.167	-1	77	-10		-1.3
Total	2	5	13	.278	53	9	2	0	157	176	91	5	3	59	51	4.18	89	.287	.353	45-0-3	.156	-1	115	-9		-1.3

FERGUSON, CHARLIE Charles Augustus B5.10.1875 Okemos MI D5.17.1931 Sault Ste.Marie MI TR/5-11/? d9.20

YEAR	TM LG	W	L	PCT	G	GS	CG-SHO	SV-BS	IP	H	R	HR	HB	BB-IB	SO	ERA	AERA	OAV	OOB	AB-HR-SH	AVG	PB	SUP	APR	DL	PW
1901	Chi N	0	0	—	1	0	0	0	2	1	0	0	0	2	0	0.00	—	.143	.333	1	.000	-0		1		0.0

FERGUSON, CHARLIE Charles J. B4.17.1863 Charlottesville VA D4.29.1888 Philadelphia PA BB/TR/6-0/165 d5.1

YEAR	TM LG	W	L	PCT	G	GS	CG-SHO	SV-BS	IP	H	R	HR	HB	BB-IB	SO	ERA	AERA	OAV	OOB	AB-HR-SH	AVG	PB	SUP	APR	DL	PW
1884	Phi N	21	25	.457	50	47	46-2	1	416.2	443	297	13		93	194	3.54	84	.253	.291	203	.246	7*	98	-21		-1.2
1885	Phi N	26	20	.565	48	48	45-5	0	405	345	197	5		81	197	2.22	126	.219	.257	235-1	.306	17*	104	26		4.3
1886	Phi N	30	9	.769	48	45	43-4	2	395.2	317	145	11		69	212	1.98	166	.210	.244	261-2	.253	12*	101	59		6.5
1887	Phi N	22	10	.688	37	33	31-2	1	297.1	297	154	13	11	47	125	3.00	142	.254	.289	264-3	.337	14*	106	40		4.7
Total	4	99	64	.607	183	170	165-13	4	1514.2	1402	793	42	11	290	728	2.67	122	.233	.270	963-6	.288	49	102	104		14.3

FERGUSON, GEORGE George Cecil "Cecil" B8.19.1886 Ellsworth IN D9.5.1943 Orlando FL BR/TR/5-10/165 d4.19

YEAR	TM LG	W	L	PCT	G	GS	CG-SHO	SV-BS	IP	H	R	HR	HB	BB-IB	SO	ERA	AERA	OAV	OOB	AB-HR-SH	AVG	PB	SUP	APR	DL	PW
1906	NY N	2	0	1.000	22	1	1-1	7	52.1	43	22	1	2	24	32	2.58	101	.229	.322	15	.333	2	56	0		0.3
1907	NY N	3	2	.600	15	5	4	1	64	63	32	2	5	20	37	2.11	118	.266	.336	18-0-1	.056	-1	138	-2		-0.3
1908	Bos N	11	11	.500	37	21	13-3	0	208	168	72	7	8	84	98	2.47	98	.230	.316	65-0-3	.169	1*	113	2		0.1
1909	Bos N	5	23	.179	36	30	19-3	0	226.2	235	121	2	12	83	87	3.73	76	.282	.355	73-0-1	.205	1	65	-18		-1.9
1910	Bos N	7	7	.500	26	14	10-1	0	123	110	56	7	7	58	40	3.80	87	.254	.351	40-1-2	.175	-1	85	0		-0.1
1911	Bos N	1	3	.250	6	3	0	0	24	40	29	1	0	12	4	9.75	39	.388	.452	7	.286	1	52	-12		-1.5
Total	6	29	46	.387	142	74	47-8	8	698	659	332	12	34	281	298	3.26	86	.261	.343	218-1-7	.188	3	86	-30		-3.4

FERGUSON, ALEX James Alexander B2.16.1897 Montclair NJ D4.26.1976 Sepulveda CA BR/TR/6-0/180 d8.16 Mil 1918

YEAR	TM LG	W	L	PCT	G	GS	CG-SHO	SV-BS	IP	H	R	HR	HB	BB-IB	SO	ERA	AERA	OAV	OOB	AB-HR-SH	AVG	PB	SUP	APR	DL	PW
1918	NY A	0	0	—	1	0	0	0	1.2	2	1	0	0	1	0	0.00	—	.333	.500	1	.000	-0		1		0.0
1921	NY A	3	1	.750	17	4	1	2	56.1	64	40	4	2	27	9	5.91	72	.296	.385	19	.211	-1	118	-8		-0.6
1922	Bos A	9	16	.360	39	27	10-1	2	198.1	201	106	4	4	63	44	4.31	95	.265	.326	65-0-6	.092	-6	69	-3		-1.0

YEAR	TM LG	W	L	PCT	G	GS	CG-SHO	SV-BS	IP	H	R	HR	HB	BB-IB	SO	ERA	AERA	OAV	OOB	AB-HR-SH	AVG	PB	SUP	APR	DL	PW
1923	Bos A	9	13	.409	34	27	11	0	198.1	229	115	5	9	67	72	4.04	102	.297	.360	62-0-6	.097	-5	77	1		-0.6
1924	Bos A	14	17	.452	41	32	15	2	237.2	259	115	6	6	108	78	3.79	115	.286	.366	86-0-8	.140	-6	78	17		1.4
1925	Bos A	0	2	.000	5	4	0	1	15.2	22	22	6	1	5	5	10.91	42	.314	.368	4	.000	-8	88	-10		-1.1
	NY A	4	2	.667	21	6	0	1	54.1	83	57	3	2	42	20	7.79	55	.358	.460	15-0-2	.133	-1	135	-23		-2.1
	†Was A	5	1	.833	7	6	3	0	55.1	52	22	2	2	23	24	3.25	130	.256	.338	20-0-4	.050	-3	126	7		0.3
	Year	9	5	.643	33	16	3	2	125.1	157	101	11	5	70	49	6.18	69	.311	.400	39-0-6	.077	-4	120	-24		-2.9
1926	Was A	3	4	.429	19	4	0	1	47.2	69	51	4	3	18	16	7.74	50	.343	.405	11-0-1	.182	-0	136	-23		-2.8
1927	Phi N	8	16	.333	31	31	16	0	227	280	132	15	6	65	73	4.84	85	.313	.363	70-0-10	.100	-5	85	-15		-1.8
1928	Phi N	5	10	.333	34	19	5-1	2	134.2	168	91	14	6	52	51	5.88	73	.315	.382	39-0-2	.026	-1	118	-19		-2.2
1929	Phi N	1	2	.333	5	4	1	0	12.2	19	18	2	0	10	3	12.08	43	.345	.446	4	.000	-1	50	-8		-1.4
	Bro N	0	1	.000	3	2	0	0	2	7	7	2	0	1	1	22.50	21	.583	.615	1	1.000	-0	189	-4		-0.7
	Year	1	3	.250	8	6	1	0	14.2	26	25	4	0	11	4	13.50	38	.388	.474	5	.200	-0	91	-13		-2.1
Total	10	61	85	.418	257	166	62-2	10	1241.2	1455	778	68	45	482	397	4.93	85	.299	.368	397-0-39	.106	-33	90	-87		-12.6

FERGUSON, BOB   Robert Lester B4.18.1919 Birmingham AL BR/TR/6-1.5/180 d4.29

| 1944 | Cin N | 0 | 3 | .000 | 9 | 2 | 0 | 1 | 16 | 24 | 17 | 3 | 2 | 10 | 9 | 9.00 | 39 | .358 | .456 | 1 | .333 | 0 | 84 | -9 | | -1.6 |

FERGUSON, BOB   Robert Vavasour B1.31.1845 Brooklyn NY D5.3.1894 Brooklyn NY BB/TR/5-9.5/149 d5.18 M16/U10 ▲

1871	Mut NA	0	0	—	1	0	0	0	1	8	9	0	0	0	0	27.00	14	.571	.571	158	.241	-0*		-3		-0.1
1873	Atl NA	0	1	.000	4	1	1	0	19.1	41	30	2	0	2	0	5.59	54	.383	.394	228	.259	1*	47	-6		-0.2
1874	Atl NA	0	1	.000	1	1	1	0	9	12	10	0	0	3	0	4.00	51	.273	.319	245	.261	0*	99	-1		-0.1
1875	Har NA	0	0	—	1	0	0	0	2	9	7	1	0	0	0	22.50	10	.600	.600	366	.240	0*		-3		-0.1
1877	Har N	1	1	.500	3	2	2	0	25	38	15	0	0	2	1	3.96	61	.352	.364	254	.256	0*	140	-2		-0.1
1883	Phi N	0	0	—	1	0	0	0	1	2	2	0	0	0	0	9.00	34	.286	.286	329	.258	0*		-1		0.0
Total	4 NA	0	2	.000	7	2	2	0	31.1	70	56	3	0	5	0	6.89	40	.389	.405	997	.250	1	69	-13		-0.5
Total	2	1	1	.500	4	2	2	0	26	40	17	0	0	2	1	4.15	59	.348	.359	583	.257	0	139	-3		-0.1

FERMIN, RAMON   Ramon Antonio (Ventura) B11.25.1972 San Francisco de Macoris, D.R. BR/TR/6-3/180 d8.6

| 1995 | Oak A | 1 | 0 | 1.000 | 1 | 1 | 0 | 0 | 2 | 5 | 3 | 1 | 0 | 1 | 0 | 13.50 | 34 | .500 | .556 | 0 | — | 0 | | -1 | | -0.1 |

FERNANDEZ, ALEX   Alexander B8.13.1969 Miami Beach FL BR/TR/6-1/215(205-225) [ChiA90 1/4] d8.2 Col Miami [DL 1998 Fla N 181, 2001 Fla N 190]

1990	Chi A	5	5	.500	13	13	3	0-0	87.2	89	40	6	3	34-0	61	3.80	101	.265	.338	0	—	0	89	1		0.0
1991	Chi A	9	13	.409	34	32	2	0-0	191.2	186	100	16	2	88-2	145	4.51	89	.259	.337	0	—	0	83	-9		-0.9
1992	Chi A	8	11	.421	29	29	4-2	0-0	187.2	199	100	21	8	50-3	95	4.27	91	.270	.322	0	—	0	113	-9		-0.7
1993	†Chi A	18	9	.667	34	34	3-1	0-0	247.1	221	95	27	6	67-5	169	3.13	135	.240	.295	0	—	0	112	31		3.2
1994	Chi A	11	7	.611	24	24	4-3	0-0	170.1	163	83	25	1	50-4	122	3.86	122	.250	.302	0	—	0	118	16		1.6
1995	Chi A	12	8	.600	30	30	5-2	0-0	203.2	200	98	19	0	65-7	159	3.80	118	.255	.310	0	—	0	114	14		1.2
1996	Chi A	16	10	.615	35	35	6-1	0-0	258	248	110	34	7	72-4	200	3.45	138	.253	.299	66-0-7	.152	3*	102	13		2.1
1997	†Fla N	17	12	.586	32	32	5-1	0-0	220.2	193	93	25	4	69-2	183	3.59	113	.238	.299	43-3-3	.233	4*	86	15	57	2.0
1999	Fla N	7	8	.467	24	24	1	0-0	141	135	60	19	4	41-1	91	3.38	129	.252	.307	17	.118	1*	86	2	135	0.4
2000	Fla N	4	4	.500	8	8	0	0-0	52.1	59	25	7	0	15-3	36	4.13	106	.292	.342	17	.118	1*	92	3		-0.1
Total	10	107	87	.552	263	261	33-10	0-0	1760.1	1693	804	190	35	552-29	1252	3.74	115	.254	.312	126-3-10	.175	8	102	112	563	12.3

FERNANDEZ, SID   Charles Sidney B10.12.1962 Honolulu HI BL/TL/6-1/230(205-230) [LAN81 3/73] d9.20

1983	LA N	0	1	.000	2	1	0	0-0	6	7	4	0	1	7-0	9	6.00	60	.280	.455	1	1.000	0	73	-1		-0.1
1984	NY N	6	6	.500	15	15	0	0-0	90	74	40	8	0	34-3	62	3.50	102	.226	.295	28-0-3	.179	-0	109	1		0.0
1985	NY N	9	9	.500	26	26	3	0-0	170.1	108	56	14	2	80-3	180	2.80	125	.181	.279	52-0-7	.212	2	102	15		1.7
1986	†NY N★	16	6	.727	32	31	2-1	1-0	204.1	161	82	13	2	91-1	200	3.52	102	.216	.300	68-0-6	.162	1	128	5		0.6
1987	†NY N★	12	8	.600	28	27	3-1	0-0	156	130	75	16	8	67-8	134	3.81	101	.224	.310	43-0-10	.163	1*	123	9	18	-0.0
1988	†NY N	12	10	.545	31	31	1-1	0-0	187	127	69	21	6	70-1	189	3.03	108	.191	.271	56-0-7	.250	6	109	7		1.2
1989	NY N	14	5	.737	35	32	6-2	0-0	219.1	157	73	21	6	75-3	198	2.83	116	.198	.271	71-1-10	.211	4	126	14		1.5
1990	NY N	9	14	.391	30	30	2-1	0-0	179.1	130	79	18	5	67-4	181	3.46	109	.200	.277	58-0-5	.190	1	101	5		0.6
1991	NY N	1	3	.250	8	8	0	0-0	44	36	18	4	0	9-0	31	2.86	128	.222	.262	13-0-1	.154	0	92	3	101	0.3
1992	NY N	14	11	.560	32	32	5-2	0-0	214.2	162	67	12	4	67-4	193	2.73	129	.210	.273	74-0-7	.203	2	112	21		2.6
1993	NY N	5	6	.455	18	18	1-1	0-0	119.2	82	42	17	3	36-0	81	2.93	137	.192	.260	32-0-8	.094	-1	84	16	89	1.1
1994	Bal A	6	6	.500	19	19	2	0-0	115.1	109	66	27	2	46-2	95	5.15	98	.248	.320	0	—	0	101	0	29	-1.0
1995	Bal A	0	4	.000	8	7	0	0-0	28	36	26	9	0	17-2	31	7.39	65	.305	.390	0	—	0	100	-9	23	-1.0
	Phi N	6	1	.857	11	11	0	0-0	64.2	48	25	11	1	21-0	79	3.34	126	.200	.267	23-0-1	.043	-2	109	7		0.4
1996	Phi N	3	6	.333	11	11	0	0-0	63	50	25	5	1	26-2	77	3.43	126	.215	.294	19-0-2	.105	0	68	7	122	0.1
1997	Hou N	1	0	1.000	1	1	0	0-0	5	4	2	1	0	2-0	3	3.60	111	.211	.286	1	.000	0	138	0	109	0.1
Total	15	114	96	.543	307	300	25-9	1-0	1866.2	1421	749	191	41	715-33	1743	3.36	111	.209	.286	539-1-67	.182	14	109	91	491	9.8

FERNANDEZ, JARED   Jared Wade B2.2.1972 Salt Lake City UT BR/TR/6-2/223(223-235) d9.19 Col Cal St.-Fresno

2001	Cin N	0	1	.000	5	2	0	0-0	12.1	13	9	1	2	6-0	5	4.38	105	.265	.368	2	.000	-0	70	-1		-0.1
2002	Cin N	1	3	.250	14	8	0	0-0	50.2	59	31	5	3	24-1	36	4.44	96	.294	.374	10-0-2	.200	0	100	-2		-0.1
2003	Hou N	3	3	.500	12	6	0	0-0	38.1	37	17	2	2	12-2	19	3.99	111	.259	.323	9-0-1	.000	-1	74	2		0.3
2004	Hou N	0	0	—	2	1	0	0-0	1	6	6	0	0	5-0	0	54.00	8	.750	.786	0	—	0	212	-5		-0.2
Total	4	4	7	.364	33	17	0	0-0	102.1	115	63	8	7	47-3	60	4.75	92	.287	.368	21-0-3	.095	-1	94	-6		-0.1

FERNANDEZ, OSVALDO   Osvaldo B11.4.1968 Holguin, Cuba BR/TR/6-2/190* d4.5 [DL 1998 SF N 181]

1996	SF N	7	13	.350	30	28	2	0-0	171.2	193	95	20	10	57-4	106	4.61	90	.286	.348	57-0-5	.088	-3*	79	-7		-0.1
1997	SF N	3	4	.429	11	11	0	0-0	56.1	74	39	9	0	15-2	31	4.95	83	.314	.353	17-0-2	.000	-1*	102	-7	126	-0.9
2000	Cin N	4	3	.571	15	14	1	0-0	79.2	69	33	6	2	31-2	36	3.62	132	.238	.313	22-0-5	.091	-1	95	11	55	0.7
2001	Cin N	5	6	.455	20	14	0	0-1	79.1	103	62	8	0	33-3	35	6.92	66	.316	.376	19-0-3	.053	-1	88	-17		-2.0
Total	4	19	26	.422	76	67	3	0-1	387	439	229	43	12	136-11	208	4.93	88	.287	.348	115-0-15	.070	-7	88	-20	362	-3.2

FERRARESE, DON   Donald Hugh B6.19.1929 Oakland CA BR/TL/5-9/170* d4.11 Col St. Marys (CA)

1955	Bal A	0	0	—	6	0	0	0	9	8	3	0	6	11-0	5	3.00	127	.276	.463	1	.000	-0		1		0.0
1956	Bal A	4	10	.286	36	14	3-1	2	102	86	60	8	3	64-0	81	5.03	78	.229	.342	28	.036	-0	81	-12		-1.7
1957	Bal A	1	1	.500	8	2	0	1	19	14	13	1	0	12-1	13	4.74	76	.200	.317	3	.000	-0	137	-4		-0.4
1958	Cle A	3	4	.429	28	10	2	1	94.2	91	44	4	1	46-2	62	3.71	98	.254	.346	26	.115	1	91	-1		-0.3
1959	Cle A	5	3	.625	15	10	4	0	76	58	29	6	1	51-2	45	3.20	115	.219	.346	27-0-1	.259	2	105	5		0.7
1960	Chi A	0	1	.000	5	0	0	0	4	8	8	2	0	9-0	4	18.00	21	.400	.586	2	.500	0		-6		-1.1
1961	Phi N	5	12	.294	42	14	3-1	1	138.2	120	64	14	1	68-4	89	3.76	108	.234	.325	35-0-4	.171	-1*	72	5		0.4
1962	Phi N	0	1	.000	5	0	0	0	6.2	9	8	1	0	3-0	6	8.10	48	.310	.364	1	1.000	0		-4		-0.4
	StL N	1	4	.200	38	0	0	1	56.2	55	19	2	1	31-4	45	2.70	158	.270	.367	5-1-0	.200	1		9		0.9
	Year	1	5	.167	43	0	0	1	63.1	64	27	3	1	34-4	51	3.27	129	.275	.367	6-1-0	.333	1	6			0.5
Total	8	19	36	.345	183	50	12-2	5	506.2	449	249	38	7	295-13	350	4.00	98	.241	.345	128-1-5	.156	-2	86	-7		-1.9

FERRARI, ANTHONY   Anthony Michael B6.22.1978 San Francisco CA BL/TL/5-9/160 [MonN00 44/1300] d6.7 Col Lewis-Clark St.

| 2003 | Mon N | 0 | 0 | — | 4 | 0 | 0-0 | 4 | 4 | 3 | 1 | 1 | 5-1 | 1 | 6.75 | 66 | .267 | .476 | 0 | — | 0 | | -1 | | 0.0 |

FERRAZZI, BILL   William Joseph B4.19.1907 W.Quincy MA D8.10.1993 Gainesville FL BR/TR/6-2.5/200 d9.7 Col Florida

| 1935 | Phi A | 1 | 2 | .333 | 3 | 2 | 0 | 0 | 7 | 5 | 5 | 0 | 0 | 5-0 | 0 | 5.14 | 88 | .269 | .387 | 1 | .000 | 0 | 76 | -1 | | -0.1 |

FERREIRA, TONY   Anthony Ross B10.4.1962 Riverside CA BL/TL/6-1/160 [KCA81 2/49] d9.17

| 1985 | KC A | 0 | 0 | — | 2 | 0 | 0 | 0 | 5.2 | 6 | 5 | 0 | 0 | 2-0 | 5 | 7.94 | 53 | .273 | .333 | 0 | — | 0 | | -2 | | -0.1 |

FERRELL, WES   Wesley Cheek B2.2.1908 Greensboro NC D12.9.1976 Sarasota FL BR/TR/6-2/195 d9.9 b-Rick ▲

1927	Cle A	0	0	—	1	0	0	0	1	3	3	0	0	4-0	0	27.00	16	.600	.714	0	—	0		-2		-0.1
1928	Cle A	2	0	1.000	2	2	1	0	16	15	5	0	0	5	4	2.25	184	.242	.299	4	.250	1	0	3		0.5
1929	Cle A	21	10	.677	43	25	18-1	5	242.2	256	112	7	3	109	100	3.60	124	.279	.358	93-1-3	.237	4*	105	24		3.3
1930	Cle A	25	13	.658	43	35	25-1	3	296.2	299	141	14	0	106	143	3.31	146	.262	.325	118-0-3	.297	8*	113	46		5.9
1931	Cle A	22	12	.647	40	35	27-2	1	276.1	276	134	9	3	130	123	3.75	123	.255	.336	116-9-2	.319	17*	111	27		5.0
1932	Cle A	23	13	.639	38	34	26-3	1	287.2	299	141	17	0	104	105	3.66	130	.264	.326	128-2-6	.242	5*	90	32		4.0
1933	Cle A☆	11	12	.478	28	26	16-1	0	201	225	108	8	2	70	41	4.21	106	.282	.341	140-7-1	.271	7*	97	7		1.8
1934	Bos A	14	5	.737	26	23	17-3	1	181	205	87	4	0	49	67	3.63	132	.282	.327	78-4-3	.282	8*	106	22		2.8

YEAR	TM LG	W	L	PCT	G	GS	CG-SHO	SV-BS	IP	H	R	HR	HB	BB-IB	SO	ERA	AERA	OAV	OOB	AB-HR-SH	AVG	PB	SUP	APR	DL	PW
1935	Bos A	25	14	.641	41	38	31-3	0	322.1	336	149	16	3	108	110	3.52	135	.267	.326	150-7-8	.347	20*	101	41		6.8
1936	Bos A	20	15	.571	39	38	28-3	0	301	330	160	11	6	119	106	4.19	127	.274	.343	135-5-5	.267	11*	89	36		4.4
1937	Bos A	3	6	.333	12	11	5	0	73.1	111	66	14	1	34	31	7.61	62	.348	.412	33-1-1	.364	6*	134	-21		-1.4
	Was A☆	11	13	.458	25	24	21	0	207.2	214	111	11	2	88	92	3.94	112	.265	.339	106-0-2	.255	5*	87	10		1.5
	Year	14	19	.424	37	35	26	0	281	325	177	25	3	122	123	4.90	92	.289	.360	139-1-3	.281	11	103	-11		0.1
1938	Was A	13	8	.619	23	22	9	0	149	193	111	12	1	68	36	5.92	76	.311	.380	49-1-6	.224	7*	119	-23		-1.9
	NY A	2	2	.500	5	4	1	0	30	52	33	6	0	18	7	8.10	56	.388	.461	12	.167	0	121	-13		-1.2
	Year	15	10	.600	28	26	10	0	179	245	144	18	1	86	43	6.28	72	.325	.394	61-1-6	.213	7	119	-39		-3.1
1939	NY A	1	2	.333	3	3	1	0	19.1	14	10	2	0	17	6	4.66	94	.219	.383	8	.125	-0	47	0		0.0
1940	Bro N	0	0		1	0	0	0	4	4	3	0	1	4	4	6.75	59	.250	.429	2	.000	-0*		-1		-0.1
1941	Bos N	2	1	.667	4	3	1	0	14	13	8	1	1	9	10	5.14	69	.241	.359	4-1-0	.500	2	103	-2		-0.2
Total	15	193	128	.601	374	323	227-17	0	2623	2845	1382	132	23	1040	985	4.04	117	.275	.343	1176-38-40	.280	100	102	186		31.1

FERRICK, TOM Thomas Jerome B1.6.1915 New York NY D10.15.1996 Lima PA BR/TR/6-2.5/220* d4.19 Mil 1943-45 C12

YEAR	TM LG	W	L	PCT	G	GS	CG-SHO	SV-BS	IP	H	R	HR	HB	BB-IB	SO	ERA	AERA	OAV	OOB	AB-HR-SH	AVG	PB	SUP	APR	DL	PW
1941	Phi A	8	10	.444	36	4	2-1	7	119.1	130	61	8	0	33	30	3.77	111	.275	.322	44	.205	1	134	4		0.9
1942	Cle A	3	2	.600	31	2	2	3	81.1	56	20	3	0	32	28	1.99	173	.200	.282	19-0-1	.211	0	186	14		1.1
1946	Cle A	0	0		9	0	0	1	18	25	12	3	0	4	9	5.00	66	.321	.354	3	.667	1		-4		-0.1
	StL A	4	1	.800	25	1	0	5	32.1	26	13	1	0	5	13	2.78	134	.224	.256	4	.000	-1	69	3		0.5
	Year	4	1	.800	34	1	0	6	50.1	51	25	4	0	9	22	3.58	100	.263	.296	7	.286	1	72	-1		0.4
1947	Was A	1	7	.125	31	0	0	9	60	57	24	1	0	20	23	3.15	118	.256	.317	10	.100	-1		4		0.6
1948	Was A	2	5	.286	37	0	0	10	73.2	75	37	3	0	38	34	4.15	105	.261	.348	15	.067	-1		2		0.2
1949	StL A	6	4	.600	50	0	0	6	104.1	102	51	9	1	41	34	3.88	117	.258	.329	21-0-2	.143	-1*		8		0.7
1950	StL A	1	3	.250	16	0	0	2	24	24	14	2	0	7	6	4.13	120	.267	.320	4	.250	-0		1		0.2
	†NY A	8	4	.667	30	0	0	9	56.2	49	27	5	0	22	20	3.65	118	.233	.306	14-0-1	.143	0		4		0.8
	Year	9	7	.563	46	0	0	11	80.2	73	41	7	0	29	26	3.79	118	.243	.310	18-0-1	.167	0		5		1.0
1951	NY A	1	1	.500	9	0	0	1	12	21	12	4	0	7	3	7.50	51	.389	.459	1-0-1	1.000	1		-6		-0.8
	Was A	2	0	1.000	22	0	0	2	41.2	36	16	3	0	7	17	2.38	172	.234	.267	7-0-1	.286	1		6		0.4
	Year	3	1	.750	31	0	0	3	53.2	57	28	7	0	14	20	3.52	115	.274	.320	8-0-2	.375	1		1		-0.4
1952	Was A	4	3	.571	27	0	0	1	50.2	53	19	2	0	11	28	3.02	118	.273	.312	5-0-1	.200	1		3		0.6
Total	9	40	40	.500	323	7	4-1	56	674	654	306	44	1	227	245	3.47	117	.256	.317	147-0-7	.184	1	137	39		5.1

FERRIS, BOB Robert Eugene B5.7.1955 Arlington VA BR/TR/6-6/225* [AnaA76 2/30] d9.12 Col Maryland-Baltimore Co.

YEAR	TM LG	W	L	PCT	G	GS	CG-SHO	SV-BS	IP	H	R	HR	HB	BB-IB	SO	ERA	AERA	OAV	OOB	AB-HR-SH	AVG	PB	SUP	APR	DL	PW
1979	Cal A	0	0		2	0	0	0-0	6	5	2	1	0	3-1	2	1.50	272	.217	.308	0	—	0		1		0.1
1980	Cal A	0	2	.000	5	3	0	0-0	15.1	23	13	2	0	9-0	4	5.87	67	.354	.432	0	—	0	83	-4		-0.5
Total	2	0	2	.000	7	3	0	0-0	21.1	28	15	3	0	12-1	6	4.64	86	.318	.400	0	—	0	83	-3		-0.4

FERRISS, DAVE David Meadow "Boo" B12.5.1921 Shaw MS BL/TR/6-2/208* d4.29 C5 Col Mississippi St.

YEAR	TM LG	W	L	PCT	G	GS	CG-SHO	SV-BS	IP	H	R	HR	HB	BB-IB	SO	ERA	AERA	OAV	OOB	AB-HR-SH	AVG	PB	SUP	APR	DL	PW
1945	Bos A★	21	10	.677	35	31	26-5	2	264.2	263	101	6	7	85	94	2.96	115	.264	.327	120-1-1	.267	11*	118	13		3.0
1946	†Bos A☆	25	6	.806	40	35	26-6	3	274	274	109	14	3	71	106	3.25	113	.259	.308	115-0-2	.209	2*	144	13		1.8
1947	Bos A	12	11	.522	33	28	14-1	0	218.1	241	106	14	7	92	64	4.04	96	.287	.362	99	.273	7*	113	-1		0.5
1948	Bos A	7	3	.700	31	9	1	3	115.1	127	71	7	7	61	30	5.23	84	.286	.381	37-0-2	.243	2	135	-9		-0.6
1949	Bos A	0	0	—	4	0	0	0	6.2	7	3	1	1	4	1	4.05	108	.292	.414	1	1.000	1		0	73	0.1
1950	Bos A	0	0	—	1	0	0	0	1	2	2	0	0	1	1	18.00	17	.500	.600	0	—	0		-1		-0.1
Total	6	65	30	.684	144	103	67-12	8	880	914	392	42	25	314	296	3.64	103	.272	.338	372-1-5	.250	23	126	15	73	4.7

FERRY, CY Alfred Joseph B9.27.1878 Hudson NY D9.17.1938 Pittsfield MA BR/TR/6-1/170 d5.12 b-Jack Col Manhattan

YEAR	TM LG	W	L	PCT	G	GS	CG-SHO	SV-BS	IP	H	R	HR	HB	BB-IB	SO	ERA	AERA	OAV	OOB	AB-HR-SH	AVG	PB	SUP	APR	DL	PW
1904	Det A	0	1	.000	3	1	1	0	13	12	9	0	1	11	4	6.23	41	.245	.393	6	.333	1	196	-4		-0.2
1905	Cle A	0	0	—	1	1	0	0	2	3	3	1	2	0	2	13.50	19	.333	.455	1	.000	-0	135	-2		-0.1
Total	2	0	1	.000	4	2	1	0	15	15	12	1	3	11	6	7.20	36	.259	.403	7	.286	1	167	-6		-0.3

FERRY, JACK John Francis B4.7.1887 Pittsfield MA D8.29.1954 Pittsfield MA BR/TR/5-11/175 d9.4 b-Cy Col Seton Hall

YEAR	TM LG	W	L	PCT	G	GS	CG-SHO	SV-BS	IP	H	R	HR	HB	BB-IB	SO	ERA	AERA	OAV	OOB	AB-HR-SH	AVG	PB	SUP	APR	DL	PW
1910	Pit N	1	2	.333	6	3	2	0	31	26	10	0	1	8	12	2.32	133	.230	.287	9-0-2	.333	1	48	3		0.4
1911	Pit N	6	4	.600	26	8	4-1	3	85.2	83	35	3	2	27	32	3.15	109	.260	.322	29-0-2	.310	3*	148	4		0.7
1912	Pit N	2	0	1.000	11	3	1-1	1	39	33	21	1	1	23	10	3.00	109	.234	.345	13	.077	-1	142	-1		-0.1
1913	Pit N	1	0	1.000	4	0	0	0	5	4	3	0	0	2	2	5.40	56	.286	.375	0	—	0		-1		-0.2
Total	4	10	6	.625	47	14	7-2	4	160.2	146	69	4	4	60	56	3.02	110	.249	.323	51-0-4	.255	3	127	5		0.8

FERSON, ALEX Alexander "Colonel" B7.14.1866 Philadelphia PA D12.5.1957 Boston MA BR/TR/5-9/165 d5.4

YEAR	TM LG	W	L	PCT	G	GS	CG-SHO	SV-BS	IP	H	R	HR	HB	BB-IB	SO	ERA	AERA	OAV	OOB	AB-HR-SH	AVG	PB	SUP	APR	DL	PW
1889	Was N	17	17	.500	36	34	28-1	0	288.1	319	199	9	12	105	85	3.90	101	.272	.338	114	.114	-5	83	0		-0.5
1890	Buf P	1	7	.125	10	10	7	0	71	88	66	5	1	40	13	5.45	75	.291	.376	32	.219	1*	104	-11		-0.7
1892	Bal N	0	1	.000	2	1	1	0	9	17	13	1	0	6	8	11.00	31	.386	.460	4	.000	-1	55	-6		-0.5
Total	3	18	25	.419	48	45	36-1	0	368.1	424	278	15	13	151	106	4.37	91	.279	.349	150	.133	-5	88	-17		-1.7

FETTE, LOU Louis Henry William B3.15.1907 Alma MO D1.3.1981 Warrensburg MO BR/TR/6-1.5/200 d4.26 Col Missouri Valley

YEAR	TM LG	W	L	PCT	G	GS	CG-SHO	SV-BS	IP	H	R	HR	HB	BB-IB	SO	ERA	AERA	OAV	OOB	AB-HR-SH	AVG	PB	SUP	APR	DL	PW
1937	Bos N	20	10	.667	35	33	23-5	0	259	243	93	5	4	81	70	2.88	124	.251	.311	92-0-7	.239	3*	103	23		2.8
1938	Bos N	11	13	.458	33	32	17-3	1	239.2	235	95	11	4	79	43	3.15	109	.258	.320	85-0-2	.188	0	89	10		1.0
1939	Bos N★	10	10	.500	27	26	11-6	0	146	123	62	7	1	61	35	2.96	125	.229	.309	49-0-4	.061	-4	87	10		0.9
1940	Bos N	0	5	.000	7	5	0	0	32.1	38	23	0	1	18	2	5.57	67	.302	.393	8-0-1	.375	1	56	-7		-0.8
	Bro N	0	0	—	2	0	0	0	3	3	0	0	0	2	0	0.00	—	.300	.417	0	—	0		-0		0.1
	Year	0	5	.000	9	5	0	0	35.1	41	23	0	1	20	2	5.09	73	.301	.395	8-0-1	.375	1	56	-5		-0.7
1945	Bos N	0	2	.000	5	1	0	0	11	16	10	1	1	7	4	5.73	67	.356	.453	2	.000	-0	0	-3		-0.5
Total	5	41	40	.506	109	97	51-14	1	691	658	283	24	11	248	194	3.15	113	.253	.321	236-0-14	.186	-0	91	34		3.5

FETTERS, MIKE Michael Lee B12.19.1964 Van Nuys CA BR/TR/6-4/224(200-230) [CalA86 1/27] d9.1 Col Pepperdine

YEAR	TM LG	W	L	PCT	G	GS	CG-SHO	SV-BS	IP	H	R	HR	HB	BB-IB	SO	ERA	AERA	OAV	OOB	AB-HR-SH	AVG	PB	SUP	APR	DL	PW
1989	Cal A	0	0	—	1	0	0	0-0	3.1	5	4	1	0	1-0	4	8.10	47	.333	.375	0	—	0		-2		-0.1
1990	Cal A	1	1	.500	26	2	0	1-0	67.2	77	33	9	2	20-0	35	4.12	93	.287	.341	0	—	0	261	-1		0.0
1991	Cal A	2	5	.286	19	4	0	0-1	44.2	53	29	4	3	28-2	24	4.84	85	.305	.410	0	—	0	94	-5		-0.7
1992	Mil A	5	1	.833	50	0	0	2-3	62.2	38	15	3	7	24-2	43	1.87	207	.185	.290	0	—	0	14	16		1.3
1993	Mil A	3	3	.500	45	0	0	0-0	59.1	59	29	4	2	22-4	23	3.34	129	.278	.344	0	—	0	4			0.4
1994	Mil A	1	4	.200	42	0	0	17-3	46	41	16	0	1	27-5	31	2.54	200	.243	.345	0	—	0	12			1.8
1995	Mil A	0	3	.000	40	0	0	22-5	34.2	40	16	3	0	20-4	33	3.38	149	.286	.373	0	—	0	5	15		1.8
1996	Mil A	3	3	.500	61	0	0	32-6	61.1	65	28	4	1	26-4	53	3.38	154	.274	.343	0	—	0	11			1.8
1997	Mil A	1	5	.167	51	0	0	6-5	70.1	62	30	4	1	33-3	62	3.45	134	.244	.329	0	—	0	9	31		0.8
1998	Oak A	1	6	.143	48	0	0	5-3	47.1	48	26	3	0	21-2	34	3.99	116	.258	.333	0	—	0	2	20		-0.2
	Ana A	1	2	.333	12	0	0	0-1	11.1	14	8	2	0	4-0	9	5.56	85	.304	.360	0	—	0	-1			-0.2
	Year	2	8	.200	60	0	0	5-4	58.2	62	34	5	1	25-2	43	4.30	108	.267	.338	0	—	0	1			-0.5
1999	Bal A	1	0	1.000	27	0	0	0-3	31	35	23	5	2	22-2	22	5.81	81	.278	.393	0	—	0	-5	86		-0.2
2000	LA N	6	2	.750	51	0	0	5-2	50	35	18	7	1	25-2	40	3.24	137	.205	.313	0	—	0	8	21		1.3
2001	LA N	2	1	.667	34	0	0	1-2	29.2	33	23	4	1	13-0	26	6.07	68	.273	.341	0	—	0	-7	15		-0.7
	Pit N	1	1	.500	20	0	0	8-1	17.2	16	9	1	0	13-1	11	4.58	98	.235	.381	0	—	0	0			0.1
	Year	3	2	.600	54	0	0	9-3	47.1	49	32	7	4	26-1	37	5.51	77	.259	.356	0	—	0	-7			-0.5
2002	Pit N	1	0	1.000	32	0	0	0-1	30.1	25	13	2	1	18-1	29	3.26	129	.219	.328	0	—	0	3			0.1
	†Ari N	2	3	.400	33	0	0	0-1	24.2	28	18	1	2	19-5	24	5.11	88	.292	.415	0	—	0	-3			-0.5
	Year	3	3	.500	65	0	0	0-2	55	53	31	4	3	37-6	53	4.09	106	.252	.369	0	—	0	-3			-0.4
2003	Min A	0	0	—	5	0	0	1-0	6	2	0	0	0	1-0	5	0.00	—	.100	.182	0	—	0	3	170		0.1
2004	Ari N	1	0	1.000	23	0	0	1-0	18.2	32	21	3	1	14-2	14	8.68	53	.299	.404	0	—	0	-9			-0.5
Total	16	31	41	.431	620	6	0	100-37	716.2	699	360	62	31	351-39	518	3.86	116	.259	.348	0	—	0	134	38	374	6.0

FICK, JOHN John Ralph B5.18.1921 Baltimore MD D6.9.1958 Somers Point NJ BL/TL/5-10/150 d7.29

YEAR	TM LG	W	L	PCT	G	GS	CG-SHO	SV-BS	IP	H	R	HR	HB	BB-IB	SO	ERA	AERA	OAV	OOB	AB-HR-SH	AVG	PB	SUP	APR	DL	PW
1944	Phi N	0	0	—	4	0	0	0-0	5.1	3	2	0	1	3	2	3.38	107	.150	.292	0	—	0		0		0.0

FIDRYCH, MARK Mark Steven "The Bird" B8.14.1954 Worcester MA BR/TR/6-3/175* [DetA74 10/232] d4.20

YEAR	TM LG	W	L	PCT	G	GS	CG-SHO	SV-BS	IP	H	R	HR	HB	BB-IB	SO	ERA	AERA	OAV	OOB	AB-HR-SH	AVG	PB	SUP	APR	DL	PW
1976	Det A★	19	9	.679	31	29	24-4	0-0	250.1	217	76	12	3	53-3	97	2.34	159	.235	.277	0	—	0	85	36		4.5
1977	Det A*	6	4	.600	11	11	7-1	0-0	81	82	29	2	4	12-2	42	2.89	149	.269	.295	0	—	0	95	12	118	0.3
1978	Det A	2	0	1.000	3	3	2	0-0	22	17	6	1	0	5-0	10	2.45	159	.213	.259	0	—	0	146	4	135	0.4
1979	Det A	0	3	.000	4	4	0	0-0	14.2	23	17	2	2	9-2	5	10.43	42	.371	.458	0	—	0	99	-9	157	-1.3

YEAR	TM LG	W	L	PCT	G	GS	CG-SHO	SV-BS	IP	H	R	HR	HB	BB-IB	SO	ERA	AERA	OAV	OOB	AB-HR-SH	AVG	PB	SUP	APR	DL	PW
1980	Det A	2	3	.400	9	9	1	0-0	44.1	58	35	5	1	20-2	16	5.68	73	.309	.376	0	—	0*	147	-10		-0.9
Total 5		29	19	.604	58	56	34-5	0-0	412.1	397	163	23	6	99-9	170	3.10	126	.255	.300	0	—		102	33	410	4.1

FIEBER, CLARENCE Clarence Thomas "Lefty" B9.4.1913 San Francisco CA D8.20.1985 Redwood City CA BL/TL/6-4/187 d5.18 Col San Francisco

YEAR	TM LG	W	L	PCT	G	GS	CG-SHO	SV-BS	IP	H	R	HR	HB	BB-IB	SO	ERA	AERA	OAV	OOB	AB-HR-SH	AVG	PB	SUP	APR	DL	PW
1932	Chi A	1	0	1.000	3	0	0	0-0	5.1	6	1	0	0	3	1	1.69	256	.273	.360	0		0	2			0.3

FIELD, JIM James C. B4.24.1863 Philadelphia PA D5.13.1953 Atlantic City NJ 6-1/170 d6.2.1883 ▲

YEAR	TM LG	W	L	PCT	G	GS	CG-SHO	SV-BS	IP	H	R	HR	HB	BB-IB	SO	ERA	AERA	OAV	OOB	AB-HR-SH	AVG	PB	SUP	APR	DL	PW
1890	Roc AA	1	0	1.000	2	1	1	1	9.2	7	4	0	1	4	2	2.79	128	.194	.293	188-4	.202	1*	189	1		0.1

FIELD, NATE Nathan Patrick B12.11.1975 Denver CO BR/TR/6-2/185(185-205) d4.12 Col Fort Hays St.

YEAR	TM LG	W	L	PCT	G	GS	CG-SHO	SV-BS	IP	H	R	HR	HB	BB-IB	SO	ERA	AERA	OAV	OOB	AB-HR-SH	AVG	PB	SUP	APR	DL	PW
2002	KC A	0	0	—	5	0	0	0-0	5	8	5	2	0	3-1	3	9.00	55	.364	.440	0	—	0		-2		-0.1
2003	KC A	1	1	.500	19	0	0	0-0	21.2	19	10	3	1	14-1	19	4.15	116	.235	.351	0	—	0		2		0.2
2004	KC A	2	3	.400	43	0	0	3-2	44.1	40	25	5	2	19-2	30	4.26	109	.240	.321	0	—	0		1	54	0.1
2005	KC A	0	0	—	7	0	0	0-0	6.2	13	7	1	0	5-2	4	9.45	45	.433	.514	0	—	0		-4		-0.2
Total 4		3	4	.429	74	0	0	3-2	77.2	80	47	11	3	41-6	56	4.98	94	.267	.357	0	—	0		-3	54	0.0

FIENE, LOU Louis Henry "Big Finn" B12.29.1884 Ft.Dodge IA D12.22.1964 Chicago IL BR/TR/6-0/175 d5.7

YEAR	TM LG	W	L	PCT	G	GS	CG-SHO	SV-BS	IP	H	R	HR	HB	BB-IB	SO	ERA	AERA	OAV	OOB	AB-HR-SH	AVG	PB	SUP	APR	DL	PW
1906	Chi A	1	1	.500	6	2	1	0	31	35	17	0	4	9	12	2.90	87	.287	.356	10	.200	0	57	-2		-0.1
1907	Chi A	0	1	.000	6	1	1	1	26	30	17	0	2	7	15	4.15	58	.291	.348	11	.182	-0*	113	-6		-0.3
1908	Chi A	0	1	.000	1	1	1	0	9	9	7	0	0	1	3	4.00	58	.257	.278	3	.000	-0	30	-2		-0.3
1909	Chi A	2	5	.286	13	6	4	0	72	75	37	1	5	18	24	4.13	57	.284	.341	29-0-1	.069	-2*	65	-11		-1.2
Total 4		3	8	.273	26	10	7	1	138	149	78	1	11	35	54	3.85	62	.284	.342	53-0-1	.113	-2	64	-21		-1.9

FIFE, DANNY Danny Wayne B10.5.1949 Harrisburg IL BR/TR/6-3/175(175-190) d8.18 Col Michigan

YEAR	TM LG	W	L	PCT	G	GS	CG-SHO	SV-BS	IP	H	R	HR	HB	BB-IB	SO	ERA	AERA	OAV	OOB	AB-HR-SH	AVG	PB	SUP	APR	DL	PW
1973	Min A	3	2	.600	10	7	1	0-0	51.2	54	26	2	3	29-0	18	4.35	91	.270	.369	0	—	0	129	-1		-0.1
1974	Min A	0	0	—	4	0	0	0-0	4.2	10	11	0	1	4-0	3	17.36	22	.417	.517	0	—	0		-7		-0.4
Total 2		3	2	.600	14	7	1	0-0	56.1	64	37	2	4	33-0	21	5.43	73	.286	.385	0	—	0	129	-8		-0.5

FIFIELD, JACK John Proctor B10.5.1871 Enfield NH D11.27.1939 Syracuse NY BR/TR/5-11/160 d4.28

YEAR	TM LG	W	L	PCT	G	GS	CG-SHO	SV-BS	IP	H	R	HR	HB	BB-IB	SO	ERA	AERA	OAV	OOB	AB-HR-SH	AVG	PB	SUP	APR	DL	PW
1897	Phi N	5	18	.217	27	26	.21	0	210.2	263	163	8	9	80	38	5.51	76	.303	.368	77-2-2	.234	3	88	-28		-2.0
1898	Phi N	11	9	.550	21	21	18-2	0	171.1	170	91	2	18	60	31	3.31	104	.257	.336	64-0-3	.109	-4	123	3		-0.2
1899	Phi N	3	8	.273	14	11	9-1	1	92.2	110	64	0	4	36	12	4.08	90	.294	.362	35	.257	1	106	-5		-0.4
	Was N	2	4	.333	6	6	6	0	47	73	44	1	2	17	8	6.13	64	.353	.407	20	.200	-0*	123	-11		-1.1
	Year	5	12	.294	20	17	15-1	1	139.2	183	108	1	6	53	20	4.77	79	.315	.378	55	.236	1	112	-15		-1.5
Total 3		21	39	.350	68	64	54-3	1	521.2	616	362	11	33	193	89	4.59	83	.292	.360	196-2-5	.194	-0	105	-41		-3.7

FIGGEMEIER, FRANK Frank Y. B4.22.1873 St.Louis MO D4.15.1915 St.Louis MO d9.25

YEAR	TM LG	W	L	PCT	G	GS	CG-SHO	SV-BS	IP	H	R	HR	HB	BB-IB	SO	ERA	AERA	OAV	OOB	AB-HR-SH	AVG	PB	SUP	APR	DL	PW
1894									4	14	11		3	4	2	11.25	46	.343	.452	3-0-1	.333	0	97	-6		-0.4

FIGUEROA, ED Eduardo (Padilla) B10.14.1948 Ciales, PR BR/TR/6-1/190(174-194) d4.9

YEAR	TM LG	W	L	PCT	G	GS	CG-SHO	SV-BS	IP	H	R	HR	HB	BB-IB	SO	ERA	AERA	OAV	OOB	AB-HR-SH	AVG	PB	SUP	APR	DL	PW
1974	Cal A	2	8	.200	25	12	5-1	0-0	105.1	119	46	3	4	36-2	49	3.67	94	.294	.355	0	—	0	80	-1		-0.1
1975	Cal A	16	13	.552	33	32	16-2	0-0	244.2	213	96	14	5	84-6	139	2.91	123	.233	.299	0	—	0	100	17		2.0
1976	†NY A	19	10	.655	34	34	14-4	0-0	256.2	237	101	13	3	94-0	119	3.02	113	.246	.312	0	—	0	132	9		0.8
1977	†NY A	16	11	.593	32	32	12-2	0-0	239.1	228	102	19	3	75-1	104	3.57	111	.252	.308	0	—	0	103	13		1.2
1978	NY A	20	9	.690	35	35	12-2	0-0	253	233	96	22	3	77-4	96	2.99	122	.248	.305	0	—	0	111	19		2.0
1979	NY A	4	6	.400	16	16	4-1	0-0	104.2	109	49	6	0	35-1	42	4.13	100	.275	.333	0	—	0	103	-18		-1.6
1980	NY A	3	3	.500	15	9	0	1-0	58	90	47	3	1	24-2	16	6.98	57	.309	.417	0	—	0	58	-9		-1.3
	Tex A	0	7	.000	8	8	0	0-0	39.2	62	29	9	0	12-0	9	5.90	66	.365	.400	0	—	0	82	-26		-2.9
	Year	3	10	.231	23	17	0	1-0	97.2	152	76	12	1	36-2	25	6.54	60	.364	.410	0	—	0	102	-2		-0.1
1981	Oak A	0	0	—	2	1	0	0-0	8.1	8	5	1	0	6-0	1	5.40	65	.258	.378	0	—	0	105	30	88	3.0
Total 8		80	67	.544	200	179	63-12	1-0	1309.2	1299	571	90	19	443-16	571	3.51	105	.261	.322	0	—	0	105	30	88	3.0

FIGUEROA, NELSON Nelson B5.18.1974 Brooklyn NY BB/TR/6-1/155(155-180) [NYN95 30/833] d6.3 Col Brandeis

YEAR	TM LG	W	L	PCT	G	GS	CG-SHO	SV-BS	IP	H	R	HR	HB	BB-IB	SO	ERA	AERA	OAV	OOB	AB-HR-SH	AVG	PB	SUP	APR	DL	PW
2000	Ari N	0	1	.000	3	3	0	0-0	15.2	17	13	4	0	5-0	7	7.47	64	.283	.328	3-0-1	.333	0	115	-4		-0.2
2001	Phi N	4	5	.444	19	13	0	0-0	89	95	40	8	7	37-3	57	3.94	104	.275	.357	24-0-1	.250	2	109	3		0.3
2002	Mil N	1	7	.125	30	11	0	0-0	93	96	59	18	4	37-6	51	5.03	82	.270	.342	15-0-4	.133	-0	108	-11	15	-0.9
2003	Pit N	2	1	.667	12	3	0	0-0	35.1	28	13	8	2	13-2	23	3.31	131	.220	.299	7	.000	-1	101	4		0.2
2004	Pit N	0	3	.000	10	3	0	0-0	28.1	32	14	4	0	11-1	10	5.72	76	.302	.368	7	.143	-0	71	-4		-0.4
Total 5		7	17	.292	74	33	0	0-0	261.1	268	143	42	13	103-12	152	4.65	91	.270	.343	56-0-6	.179	1	105	-12	15	-1.0

FIKAC, JEREMY Jeremy Joseph B4.8.1975 Shiner TX BR/TR/6-2/185* [SDN98 19/562] d8.16 Col Southwest Texas

YEAR	TM LG	W	L	PCT	G	GS	CG-SHO	SV-BS	IP	H	R	HR	HB	BB-IB	SO	ERA	AERA	OAV	OOB	AB-HR-SH	AVG	PB	SUP	APR	DL	PW
2001	SD N	2	0	1.000	23	0	0	0-2	26.1	15	6	2	1	5-1	19	1.37	303	.165	.216	0	—	0		8		0.5
2002	SD N	4	7	.364	65	0	0	0-6	69	74	50	13	3	34-8	66	5.35	73	.267	.351	2	.000	-0		-14		-2.1
2003	Oak A	0	1	.000	14	0	0	0-0	16	14	8	4	3	11-1	9	4.50	102	.246	.394	0	—	0		1		0.0
2004	Mon N	1	2	.333	19	0	0	0-0	25	26	16	5	0	13-4	22	5.40	85	.274	.358	0	—	0		-2		-0.2
Total 4		7	10	.412	121	0	0	0-8	136.1	129	80	24	7	63-14	116	4.49	92	.248	.336	2	.000	-0		-7		-1.8

FILE, BOB Robert Michael B1.28.1977 Philadelphia PA BR/TR/6-4/215* [TorA98 19/561] d4.14 Col Philadelphia [DL 2003 Tor A 142]

YEAR	TM LG	W	L	PCT	G	GS	CG-SHO	SV-BS	IP	H	R	HR	HB	BB-IB	SO	ERA	AERA	OAV	OOB	AB-HR-SH	AVG	PB	SUP	APR	DL	PW
2001	Tor A	5	3	.625	60	0	0	0-2	74.1	57	28	6	7	29-8	38	3.27	140	.220	.314	0	—	0		11		1.1
2002	Tor A	0	1	.000	5	0	0	0-0	3.1	8	7	0	0	2-0	2	18.90	24	.471	.526	0	—	0		-5	44	-0.9
2004	Tor A	1	0	1.000	24	0	0	0-0	33.2	45	19	4	2	12-2	15	4.81	102	.331	.383	1	.000	-0		0	40	0.0
Total 3		6	4	.600	89	0	0	0-2	111.1	110	54	10	9	43-10	55	4.20	111	.267	.345	1	.000	-0		6	226	0.2

FILER, TOM Thomas Carson B12.1.1956 Philadelphia PA BR/TR/6-1/198* d6.8 Col LaSalle [DL 1986 Tor A 182]

YEAR	TM LG	W	L	PCT	G	GS	CG-SHO	SV-BS	IP	H	R	HR	HB	BB-IB	SO	ERA	AERA	OAV	OOB	AB-HR-SH	AVG	PB	SUP	APR	DL	PW
1982	Chi N	1	2	.333	8	8	0	0-0	40.2	50	25	5	0	18-2	15	5.53	68	.301	.370	12-0-1	.083	-1	88	-6		-0.4
1985	Tor A	7	0	1.000	11	9	0	0-0	48.2	38	21	6	0	18-0	24	3.88	109	.222	.295	0	—	0	155	3	15	0.3
1988	Mil A	5	8	.385	19	16	2-1	0-0	101.2	108	54	8	1	33-4	39	4.43	91	.281	.333	0	—	0*	130	3	35	0.5
1989	Mil A	7	3	.700	13	13	0	0-0	72.1	74	30	6	4	23-1	20	3.61	107	.271	.337	0	—	0	47	-5	93	-1.0
1990	Mil A	2	3	.400	7	4	0	0-0	22	26	17	2	0	9-0	7	6.14	63	.289	.354	0	—	-0	26	2		-0.1
1992	NY N	1	0	1.000	9	1	0	0-0	22	18	8	2	0	6-2	9	2.05	171	.222	.276	3	.000	-0	111	-7	325	-0.8
Total 6		22	17	.564	67	51	2-1	0-0	307.1	314	155	29	5	107-9	115	4.25	91	.269	.331	15-0-1	.067	-1	111	-7	325	-0.8

FILES, EDDIE Charles Edward B5.19.1883 Portland ME D5.10.1954 Cornish ME BR/TR d10.3 Col Bowdoin

YEAR	TM LG	W	L	PCT	G	GS	CG-SHO	SV-BS	IP	H	R	HR	HB	BB-IB	SO	ERA	AERA	OAV	OOB	AB-HR-SH	AVG	PB	SUP	APR	DL	PW
1908	Phi A	0	0	—	2	0	0	0	9	8	7	0	2	3	6	6.00	43	.286	.394	3	.000	-0		-3		-0.2

FILLEY, MARC Marcus Lucius B2.28.1912 Lansingburgh NY D1.20.1995 Yarmouth ME BR/TR/5-11/172 d4.19 Col Williams

YEAR	TM LG	W	L	PCT	G	GS	CG-SHO	SV-BS	IP	H	R	HR	HB	BB-IB	SO	ERA	AERA	OAV	OOB	AB-HR-SH	AVG	PB	SUP	APR	DL	PW
1934	Was A	0	0	—	1	0	0	0	3	1	1	0	0	1	0	27.00	16	.667	.667	0	—	0		-1		0.0

FILLINGIM, DANA Dana B11.6.1893 Columbus GA D2.3.1961 Tuskegee AL BL/TR/5-10/175 d8.2 Mil 1918

YEAR	TM LG	W	L	PCT	G	GS	CG-SHO	SV-BS	IP	H	R	HR	HB	BB-IB	SO	ERA	AERA	OAV	OOB	AB-HR-SH	AVG	PB	SUP	APR	DL	PW
1915	Phi A	0	5	.000	8	4	1	0	39.1	42	25	0	1	32	17	3.43	85	.313	.449	12-0-1	.167	-0	62	-4		-0.5
1918	Bos N	7	6	.538	14	13	10-4	0	113	99	37	0	5	28	29	2.23	120	.243	.300	42-0-1	.214	0	104	6		0.7
1919	Bos N	6	13	.316	32	18	9	2	186.1	185	80	2	2	39	50	3.38	85	.270	.312	65-0-4	.246	1	79	-5		-0.5
1920	Bos N	12	21	.364	37	31	22-2	0	272	292	123	8	3	79	66	3.11	98	.287	.340	92-0-1	.174	-2*	75	-5		-0.5
1921	Bos N	15	10	.600	44	23	11-**3**	1	239.2	249	108	10	2	56	54	3.45	106	.272	.316	85-2-1	.247	5*	107	5		0.9
1922	Bos N	5	9	.357	25	12	5-1	2	117	143	74	6	1	37	25	4.54	88	.311	.363	38-0-1	.158	-2	75	-7		-0.9
1923	Bos N	1	9	.100	35	12	1	0	100.1	141	74	6	1	36	27	5.20	77	.345	.399	31-0-1	.226	1*	69	-15		-1.2
1925	Phi N	1	0	1.000	5	1	0	0	8.2	19	12	0	0	6	3	10.38	46	.432	.500	1	.000	0	230	-5		-0.4
Total 8		47	73	.392	200	114	59-10	5	1076.1	1170	533	32	15	313	270	3.56	93	.287	.340	368-2-10	.209	4	86	-33		-2.4

FILSON, PETE William Peter B9.28.1958 Darby PA BB/TL/6-2/195(175-195) [NYA79 9/233] d5.15 Col Temple

YEAR	TM LG	W	L	PCT	G	GS	CG-SHO	SV-BS	IP	H	R	HR	HB	BB-IB	SO	ERA	AERA	OAV	OOB	AB-HR-SH	AVG	PB	SUP	APR	DL	PW
1982	Min A	0	2	.000	7	1	0	0-0	12.1	17	12	2	0	8-1	10	8.76	49	.321	.397	0	—	0	71	-5		-0.7
1983	Min A	4	1	.800	26	8	0	1-0	90	87	34	9	1	29-0	49	3.40	126	.252	.310	0	—	0	90	10	21	0.2
1984	Min A	6	5	.545	55	7	0	1-2	118.2	106	56	14	3	54-7	59	4.10	103	.238	.323	0	—	0	98	3		0.2
1985	Min A	4	5	.444	40	6	1	2-1	95.2	93	42	13	0	30-4	42	3.67	121	.251	.305	0	—	0	92	8		0.7
1986	Min A	0	0	—	4	0	0	0-0	6.1	13	4	1	1	2-0	4	5.68	76	.406	.457	0	—	0		-1		-0.2
	Chi A	0	1	.000	3	1	0	0-0	11.2	14	9	4	0	5-0	4	6.17	70	.286	.352	0	—	0	42	-2		-0.2
	Year	0	1	.000	7	1	0	0-0	18	27	13	5	1	7-0	8	6.00	72	.333	.393	0	—	0	42	-3		-0.2
1987	NY A	1	0	1.000	7	2	0	0-0	22	26	14	3	0	5-1	10	3.27	136	.299	.371	0	—	0	72	2		0.1

YEAR	TM LG	W	L	PCT	G	GS	CG-SHO	SV-BS	IP	H	R	HR	HB	BB-IB	SO	ERA	AERA	OAV	OOB	AB-HR-SH	AVG	PB	SUP	APR	DL	PW
1990	KC A	0	4	.000	8	7	0	0-0	35	42	31	6	2	13-0	9	5.91	65	.282	.345	0	—	0	71	-10	53	-1.0
Total	7	15	18	.455	148	34	1	4-3	391.2	398	198	51	8	150-13	187	4.18	102	.260	.327	0	—	0	83	5	74	-0.5

FINCH, JOEL Joel D B8.20.1956 South Bend IN BR/TR/6-2/175 [BosA74 9/212] d6.12

YEAR	TM LG	W	L	PCT	G	GS	CG-SHO	SV-BS	IP	H	R	HR	HB	BB-IB	SO	ERA	AERA	OAV	OOB	AB-HR-SH	AVG	PB	SUP	APR	DL	PW
1979	Bos A	0	3	.000	15	7	0	0-0	57.1	65	31	5	1	25-3	25	4.87	92	.289	.361	1	.000	-0	79	-1		0.0

FINCHER, BILL William Allen B5.26.1894 Atlanta GA D5.7.1946 Shreveport LA BR/TR/6-1/180 d4.23

YEAR	TM LG	W	L	PCT	G	GS	CG-SHO	SV-BS	IP	H	R	HR	HB	BB-IB	SO	ERA	AERA	OAV	OOB	AB-HR-SH	AVG	PB	SUP	APR	DL	PW
1916	StL A	0	1	.000	12	1	0	0	21	22	11	0	0	7	5	2.14	128	.282	.341	4	.250	0	55	0		0.1

FINE, TOMMY Thomas Morgan B10.10.1914 Cleburne TX D1.10.2005 Little Elm TX BB/TR/6-0/180* d4.26 Col Baylor

YEAR	TM LG	W	L	PCT	G	GS	CG-SHO	SV-BS	IP	H	R	HR	HB	BB-IB	SO	ERA	AERA	OAV	OOB	AB-HR-SH	AVG	PB	SUP	APR	DL	PW
1947	Bos A	1	2	.333	9	7	1	0	36	41	24	0	1	19	10	5.50	71	.285	.372	9-0-2	.333	1	124	-6		-0.3
1950	StL A	0	1	.000	14	0	0	0	36.2	53	38	6	0	25	6	8.10	61	.342	.433	12	.333	1*		-12		-0.4
Total	2	1	3	.250	23	7	1	0	72.2	94	62	6	1	44	16	6.81	65	.314	.404	21-0-2	.333	2	124	-18		-0.7

FINGERS, ROLLIE Roland Glen B8.25.1946 Steubenville OH BR/TR/6-4/195(180-200) d9.15 HF1992 Col Chaffey (CA) JC [DL 1983 Mil A 182]

YEAR	TM LG	W	L	PCT	G	GS	CG-SHO	SV-BS	IP	H	R	HR	HB	BB-IB	SO	ERA	AERA	OAV	OOB	AB-HR-SH	AVG	PB	SUP	APR	DL	PW
1968	Oak A	0	0	—	1	0	0		1.1	4	4	1	1	1-0	0	27.00	10	.571	.667	0	—	0		-4		-0.2
1969	Oak A	6	7	.462	60	8	1-1	12-6	119	116	60	13	4	41-5	61	3.71	93	.257	.323	25-0-3	.200	0	135	-6		-0.7
1970	Oak A	7	9	.438	45	19	1	2-1	148	137	65	13	2	48-5	79	3.65	97	.250	.310	39-1-4	.103	0	89	-1		-0.1
1971	Oak A	4	6	.400	48	8	2-1	17-3	129.1	94	46	14	8	30-3	98	2.99	111	.207	.266	33-0-5	.212	1	88	6		0.8
1972	†Oak A	11	9	.550	65	0	0	21-5	111.1	85	35	8	1	32-7	113	2.51	114	.212	.271	19-1-1	.316	3		5		1.3
1973	†Oak A★	7	8	.467	62	2	0	22-5	126.2	107	41	5	4	39-6	110	1.92	186	.226	.288	1	.000	0	25	20		3.0
1974	†Oak A★	9	5	.643	76	0	0	18-7	119	104	41	5	4	29-6	95	2.65	126	.240	.282	0	—	0		10		1.6
1975	†Oak A☆	10	6	.625	75	0	0	24-8	126.2	95	43	13	6	33-5	115	2.98	122	.213	.274	1	.000	-0*		12		1.9
1976	Oak A☆	13	11	.542	70	0	0	20-14	134.2	118	40	7	4	40-10	113	2.47	136	.243	.304	0	—	0		15		3.2
1977	SD N	8	9	.471	78	0	0	35-11	132.1	123	47	12	1	36-12	113	2.99	120	.248	.298	20-0-1	.050	-2		11		1.7
1978	SD N★	6	13	.316	67	0	0	37-10	107.1	84	33	4	1	29-12	72	2.52	133	.212	.265	12-0-2	.167	-0		11		2.4
1979	SD N	9	9	.500	54	0	0	13-10	83.2	91	47	7	1	37-8	65	4.52	78	.281	.351	12-0-1	.083	-1		-9		-2.0
1980	SD N	11	9	.550	66	0	0	23-6	103	101	36	5	1	32-13	69	2.80	122	.263	.315	18-0-1	.278	2		8		1.8
1981	†Mil A★	6	3	.667	47	0	0	28-6	78	55	9	3	1	13-5	61	1.04	334	.196	.235	0	—	0	23			4.6
1982	Mil A★	5	6	.455	50	0	0	29-6	79.2	63	23	4	3	20-5	71	2.60	148	.220	.268	0	—	0		13		2.6
1984	Mil A	1	2	.333	33	0	0	23-3	46	38	13	5	0	13-2	40	1.96	199	.213	.267	0	—	0		9	69	1.5
1985	Mil A	1	6	.143	47	0	0	17-8	55.1	59	33	9	0	19-5	24	5.04	83	.272	.329	0	—	0		-4		-0.7
Total	17	114	118	.491	944	37	4-2	341-109	1701.1	1474	615	123	39	492-109	1299	2.90	120	.235	.292	180-2-18	.172	2	95	119	251	22.7

FINK, HERMAN Herman Adam B8.22.1911 Concord NC D8.24.1980 Salisbury NC BR/TR/6-2/198 d9.16

YEAR	TM LG	W	L	PCT	G	GS	CG-SHO	SV-BS	IP	H	R	HR	HB	BB-IB	SO	ERA	AERA	OAV	OOB	AB-HR-SH	AVG	PB	SUP	APR	DL	PW
1935	Phi A	0	3	.000	5	3	0	0	15.2	18	19	0	1	10	2	9.19	49	.290	.397	5	.200	1	57	-8		-1.2
1936	Phi A	8	16	.333	34	24	9	3	188.2	222	126	18	0	78	53	5.39	95	.294	.360	64	.125	-4	65	-5		-0.9
1937	Phi A	2	1	.667	28	3	1	1	80	82	43	6	1	35	18	4.05	116	.263	.339	24	.208	-1	99	6		0.2
Total	3	10	20	.333	67	30	10	4	284.1	322	188	24	2	123	73	5.22	95	.285	.356	93	.151	-5	68	-7		-1.9

FINLAYSON, PEMBROKE Pembroke B7.31.1888 Cheraw SC D3.6.1912 Brooklyn NY BR/TR/5-6/140 d6.6

YEAR	TM LG	W	L	PCT	G	GS	CG-SHO	SV-BS	IP	H	R	HR	HB	BB-IB	SO	ERA	AERA	OAV	OOB	AB-HR-SH	AVG	PB	SUP	APR	DL	PW
1908	Bro N	0	0	—	1	0	0		0.1	0	5	0	0	4	0	135.00	2	.000	.800	0	—	0		-4		-0.2
1909	Bro N	0	0	—	1	0	0		7	7	4	0	0	4	2	5.14	50	.212	.297	3	.000	-0		-2		-0.1
Total	2	0	0	—	2	0	0		7.1	7	9	0	0	8	2	11.05	23	.206	.357	3	.000	-0		-6		-0.3

FINLEY, CHUCK Charles Edward B11.26.1962 Monroe LA BL/TL/6-6/214(212-226) [CalA85*S1/4] d5.29 Col Louisiana-Monroe

YEAR	TM LG	W	L	PCT	G	GS	CG-SHO	SV-BS	IP	H	R	HR	HB	BB-IB	SO	ERA	AERA	OAV	OOB	AB-HR-SH	AVG	PB	SUP	APR	DL	PW
1986	†Cal A	3	1	.750	25	0	0	0-0	46.1	40	17	2	1	23-1	37	3.30	125	.235	.330	0	—	0		5		0.5
1987	Cal A	2	7	.222	35	3	0	0-2	90.2	102	54	7	3	43-3	63	4.67	93	.287	.367	0	—	0	141	-4		-0.3
1988	Cal A	9	15	.375	31	31	2	0-0	194.1	191	95	15	6	82-7	111	4.17	93	.263	.339	0	—	0	91	-4		-0.5
1989	Cal A	16	9	.640	29	29	9-1	0-0	199.2	171	64	13	2	82-0	156	2.57	149	.233	.311	0	—	0	91	28	24	3.2
1990	Cal A★	18	9	.667	32	32	7-2	0-0	236	210	77	17	2	81-3	177	2.40	160	.243	.308	0	—	0	107	36		4.0
1991	Cal A	18	9	.667	34	34	4-2	0-0	227.1	205	102	23	8	101-1	171	3.80	108	.244	.330	0	—	0	106	10		0.9
1992	Cal A	7	12	.368	31	31	4	0-0	204.1	212	99	24	3	98-2	124	3.96	101	.277	.358	0	—	0	92	1	16	-0.1
1993	Cal A	16	14	.533	35	35	13-2	0-0	251.1	243	108	22	6	82-1	187	3.15	144	.253	.314	0	—	0	80	33		3.5
1994	Cal A	10	10	.500	25	25	7-2	0-0	183.1	178	95	21	4	71-0	148	4.32	114	.260	.329	0	—	0	79	11		1.0
1995	Cal A☆	15	12	.556	32	32	2-1	0-0	203	192	106	20	7	93-1	195	4.21	112	.249	.333	0	—	0	112	10		1.0
1996	†Cal A★	15	16	.484	35	35	4-1	0-0	238	241	124	27	11	94-5	215	4.16	121	.263	.336	0	—	0	69	23		2.5
1997	Ana A	13	6	.684	25	25	3-1	0-0	164	152	79	20	5	65-0	155	4.23	109	.248	.323	6	.000	-1	106	9	54	0.8
1998	Ana A	11	9	.550	34	34	1-1	0-0	223.1	210	97	20	6	109-1	212	3.39	140	.246	.334	4	.000	-0	84	31		2.4
1999	Ana A	12	11	.522	33	33	1	0-0	213.1	197	117	23	8	94-2	200	4.43	110	.246	.330	4-0-1	.000	-0	90	9		0.8
2000	Cle A☆	16	11	.593	34	34	3	0-0	218	211	108	23	2	101-3	189	4.17	120	.256	.337	7	.000	-1	111	19		1.9
2001	†Cle A	8	7	.533	22	22	1	0-0	113.2	131	78	14	2	35-0	96	5.54	83	.290	.341	4	.000	-0	114	-12	62	-1.4
2002	Cle A	4	11	.267	18	18	1	0-0	105.1	114	56	6	0	48-3	91	4.44	100	.284	.356	4	.000	-0	65	0		0.0
	†StL N	7	4	.636	14	14	1-1	0-0	85.1	69	41	7	3	30-3	81	3.80	106	.219	.288	28-0-5	.107	-1	113	1		0.0
Total	17	200	173	.536	524	467	63-15	0-2	3197.1	3069	1517	304	76	1332-36	2610	3.85	116	.255	.331	53-0-6	.057	-1	94	206	156	20.2

FINNERAN, HAPPY Joseph Ignatius "Smokey Joe" B10.29.1891 E.Orange NJ D2.3.1942 Orange NJ BR/TR/5-10.5/169 d8.20

YEAR	TM LG	W	L	PCT	G	GS	CG-SHO	SV-BS	IP	H	R	HR	HB	BB-IB	SO	ERA	AERA	OAV	OOB	AB-HR-SH	AVG	PB	SUP	APR	DL	PW
1912	Phi N	0	2	.000	14	4	0	1	46.1	50	27	2	1	10	10	2.53	144	.282	.324	10	.200	0	86	2		0.1
1913	Phi N	0	0	—	3	0	0		5	12	7	0	0	2	0	7.20	46	.462	.500	3	.667	1		-3		0.0
1914	Bro F	12	11	.522	27	23	13-2	1	175.1	153	77	6	6	60	54	3.18	90	.237	.308	55-0-4	.127	-5	92	-4		-1.1
1915	Bro F	10	12	.455	37	24	12-1	2	215.1	197	90	2	9	87	68	2.80	97	.249	.331	74	.149	-5*	91	-2		-0.7
1918	Det A	0	2	.000	5	2	0	1	13.2	22	17	0	0	8	2	9.88	47	.393	.469	1	.000	-0*	170	-11		-1.5
	NY A	3	6	.333	23	13	4	0	114.1	134	52	7	2	35	34	3.78	75	.305	.359	39-0-1	.231	1	123	-9		-0.7
	Year	3	8	.273	28	15	4	1	128	156	69	7	2	43	36	4.43	63	.315	.372	42-0-1	.214	0	129	-18		-2.2
Total	5	25	33	.431	109	66	29-3	5	570	568	270	17	18	202	168	3.30	87	.266	.335	184-0-5	.168	-7	99	-27		-3.9

FINNVOLD, GAR Anders Gar B3.11.1968 Boynton Beach FL BR/TR/6-5/195 [BosA90 6/173] d5.10 Col Florida St.

YEAR	TM LG	W	L	PCT	G	GS	CG-SHO	SV-BS	IP	H	R	HR	HB	BB-IB	SO	ERA	AERA	OAV	OOB	AB-HR-SH	AVG	PB	SUP	APR	DL	PW
1994	Bos A	0	4	.000	8	8	0	0-0	36.1	45	27	4	3	15-0	17	5.94	85	.304	.377	0	—	0	78	-4	48	-0.4

FIORE, TONY Anthony James B10.12.1971 Oak Park IL BR/TR/6-4/210* [PhiN92 28/781] d8.27 Col Triton (IL) JC

YEAR	TM LG	W	L	PCT	G	GS	CG-SHO	SV-BS	IP	H	R	HR	HB	BB-IB	SO	ERA	AERA	OAV	OOB	AB-HR-SH	AVG	PB	SUP	APR	DL	PW
2000	TB A	1	1	.500	11	0	0	0-1	15	21	16	3	2	9-2	8	8.40	58	.333	.432	0	—	0		-6		-0.7
2001	TB A	0	0	—	3	0	0	0-0	3.1	4	2	0	1	1-0	3	5.40	83	.308	.400	0	—	0		0		-0.1
	Min A	0	1	.000	4	0	0	0-0	6.1	5	4	0	0	2-0	5	5.68	82	.208	.269	0	—	0		-1		-0.1
	Year	0	1	.000	7	0	0	0-0	9.2	9	6	0	1	3-0	8	5.59	83	.243	.317	0	—	0		-1		-0.1
2002	†Min A	10	3	.769	48	2	0	0-0	91	74	32	10	5	43-4	55	3.16	141	.224	.320	3	.000	-0	135	14		1.8
2003	Min A	1	1	.500	21	0	0	0-0	36	32	25	5	3	21-1	23	5.50	82	.242	.352	1	.000	-0		-5		-0.2
Total	4	12	6	.667	87	2	0	0-1	151.2	136	79	18	11	76-7	94	4.39	103	.242	.340	4	.000	-0	135	2		0.4

FIREOVID, STEVE Stephen John B6.6.1957 Bryan OH BB/TR/6-2/195(195-210) [SDN78 7/161] d9.6 Col Miami-Ohio

YEAR	TM LG	W	L	PCT	G	GS	CG-SHO	SV-BS	IP	H	R	HR	HB	BB-IB	SO	ERA	AERA	OAV	OOB	AB-HR-SH	AVG	PB	SUP	APR	DL	PW
1981	SD N	0	1	.000	5	4	0	0-0	26.1	30	8	2	0	7-0	11	2.73	119	.294	.336	7	.143	-0	82	2		0.1
1983	SD N	0	0	—	3	0	0	0-0	5	4	1	1	0	2-0	1	1.80	195	.235	.316	0	—	0		1		0.0
1984	Phi N	0	0	—	6	0	0	0-0	5.2	4	1	1	0	0-0	3	1.59	230	.200	.200	0	—	0		1		0.1
1985	Chi A	0	0	—	4	0	0	0-0	7	7	4	1	0	2-0	2	5.14	85	.472	.500	0	—	0		-1		0.0
1986	Sea A	2	0	1.000	10	1	0	0-0	21	28	11	1	1	4-0	10	4.29	100	.333	.371	0	—	0	43	2		0.0
1992	Tex A	1	0	1.000	3	0	0	0-0	6.2	10	4	0	1	4-2	0	4.05	94	.370	.452	0	—	0		-1		-0.1
Total	6	3	1	.750	31	5	0	0-0	71.2	93	31	3	1	19-2	27	3.39	110	.325	.368	7	.143	-0	67	3		0.1

FIRTH, TED John E. B5.6.1855 Lowell MA D6.23.1902 Tewksbury MA d8.15

YEAR	TM LG	W	L	PCT	G	GS	CG-SHO	SV-BS	IP	H	R	HR	HB	BB-IB	SO	ERA	AERA	OAV	OOB	AB-HR-SH	AVG	PB	SUP	APR	DL	PW
1884	Ric AA	0	1	.000	1	1	1	0	9	14	13	0	0	5	0	8.00	41	.326	.396	3	.333	0	55	-5		-0.4

FISCHER, CARL Charles William B11.5.1905 Medina NY D12.10.1963 Medina NY BR/TL/6-0/180 d7.19

YEAR	TM LG	W	L	PCT	G	GS	CG-SHO	SV-BS	IP	H	R	HR	HB	BB-IB	SO	ERA	AERA	OAV	OOB	AB-HR-SH	AVG	PB	SUP	APR	DL	PW
1930	Was A	1	1	.500	8	1	0	1	33.1	37	22	0	2	18	21	4.86	95	.285	.380	9	.000	-1	93	-2		-0.2
1931	Was A	13	9	.591	46	23	7	3	191	207	98	12	2	80	96	4.38	98	.273	.344	66-0-5	.121	-5	103	3		-0.3
1932	Was A	3	2	.600	12	7	1-1	0	50.2	57	30	4	0	31	23	4.97	87	.282	.378	15-0-2	.200	1	169	-3		-0.3
	StL A	3	7	.300	24	11	4	0	97	122	65	12	0	45	35	5.57	87	.310	.380	34-0-3	.265	0	69	-5		-0.4
	Year	6	9	.400	36	18	5-1	0	147.2	179	95	16	0	76	58	5.36	87	.300	.379	49-0-5	.245	1	104	-6		-0.7
1933	Det A	11	15	.423	35	22	9	3	182.2	176	86	5	3	84	93	3.55	122	.251	.334	62-0-4	.145	-3	73	15		1.5
1934	Det A	6	4	.600	20	15	4-1	0	95	107	50	7	4	38	39	4.36	101	.288	.356	31-0-5	.065	-3	119	2		-0.2

YEAR	TM LG	W	L	PCT	G	GS	CG-SHO	SV-BS	IP	H	R	HR	HB	BB-IB	SO	ERA	AERA	OAV	OOB	AB-HR-SH	AVG	PB	SUP	APR	DL	PW
1935	Det A	0	1	.000	3	1	0	0	12	16	8	2	1	5	7	6.00	69	.320	.393	2	.000	-0	62	-2		-0.2
	Chi A	5	5	.500	24	11	3-1	0	88.2	102	67	7	2	39	31	6.19	75	.283	.356	21-0-2	.190	-0	80	-14		-1.4
	Year	5	6	.455	27	12	3-1	0	100.2	118	75	9	3	44	38	6.17	74	.287	.360	23-0-2	.174	-0	79	-16		-1.6
1937	Cle A	0	1	.000	2	0	0	0	0.2	2	2	0	0	1	1	27.00	17	.667	.750	0	—	0		-2		-0.3
	Was A	4	5	.444	17	11	2	2	72	74	43	6	0	31	30	4.38	101	.270	.340	22-0-2	.136	-1	106	0		-0.2
	Year	4	6	.400	19	11	2	2	72.2	76	45	6	0	32	31	4.58	97	.274	.350	22-0-2	.136	-1	106	-2		-0.5
Total	7	46	50	.479	191	105	31-3	11	823	900	471	53	11	372	376	4.63	96	.277	.354	262-0-23	.145	-12	96	-8		-2.0

FISCHER, HANK Henry William "Bulldog" B1.11.1940 Yonkers NY BR/TR/6-0/190* d4.16 Col Seton Hall

YEAR	TM LG	W	L	PCT	G	GS	CG-SHO	SV-BS	IP	H	R	HR	HB	BB-IB	SO	ERA	AERA	OAV	OOB	AB-HR-SH	AVG	PB	SUP	APR	DL	PW
1962	Mil N	2	3	.400	29	6	1	4	37.1	43	27	4	0	20-1	29	5.30	72	.291	.373	4	.000	-0		-7		-1.1
1963	Mil N	4	3	.571	31	6	1	0	74.1	74	46	8	5	28-4	72	4.96	65	.262	.333	19-0-2	.105	-0	219	-15		-1.6
1964	Mil N	11	10	.524	37	28	9-5	2	168.1	177	95	17	3	39-5	99	4.01	88	.265	.308	52-0-4	.154	1*	117	-14		-1.6
1965	Mil N	8	9	.471	31	19	2	0	122.2	126	61	18	3	39-5	79	3.89	91	.270	.329	37-0-2	.108	-1*	80	-6		-1.0
1966	Atl N	2	3	.400	14	8	0	0	48.1	55	23	3	1	14-1	22	3.91	93	.296	.343	13-0-2	.000	-1	73	-1		-0.3
	Cin N	0	6	.000	11	9	0	0	38	53	31	3	3	15-0	24	6.63	59	.331	.394	11	.091	-1	100	-11		-1.6
	Year	2	9	.182	25	17	0	0	86.1	108	54	6	4	29-1	46	5.11	73	.312	.367	24-0-2	.042	-2	88	-13		-1.9
	Bos A	2	3	.400	6	5	1	0	31	35	12	4	1	11-1	26	2.90	131	.287	.351	9	.222	-0	46	3		0.5
1967	Bos A	1	2	.333	9	2	1	1	26.2	24	15	3	1	8-0	18	2.36	148	.229	.289	7-0-1	.143	-0	137	0	73	73	0.6
Total	6	30	39	.435	168	77	14-5	7	546.2	587	310	60	17	174-17	369	4.23	84	.275	.332	152-0-11	.118	-3	104	-51	73	73	-6.5

FISCHER, JEFF Jeffrey Thomas B8.17.1963 W.Palm Beach FL BR/TR/6-3/185* [MonN85 7/166] d6.19 Col Florida

YEAR	TM LG	W	L	PCT	G	GS	CG-SHO	SV-BS	IP	H	R	HR	HB	BB-IB	SO	ERA	AERA	OAV	OOB	AB-HR-SH	AVG	PB	SUP	APR	DL	PW
1987	Mon N	0	1	.000	4	0	0	0-0	13.2	21	14	3	0	6	6	8.56	50	.362	.400	5	.200	0	149	-6		-0.4
1989	LA N	0	0	—	2	0	0	0-0	3.1	7	5	1	0	2	2	13.50	25	.438	.438	0	—	0		-4		-0.2
Total	2	0	1	.000	6	0	0	0-0	17	28	19	4	0	5-0	8	9.53	43	.378	.407	5	.200	0	149	-10		-0.6

FISCHER, RUBE Reuben Walter B9.19.1916 Carlock SD D7.16.1997 Green Bay WI BR/TR/6-4/190 d9.12

YEAR	TM LG	W	L	PCT	G	GS	CG-SHO	SV-BS	IP	H	R	HR	HB	BB-IB	SO	ERA	AERA	OAV	OOB	AB-HR-SH	AVG	PB	SUP	APR	DL	PW
1941	NY N	1	0	1.000	2	1	1	0	11	10	3	0	0	6	9	2.45	151	.238	.333	3	.333	0	161	2		0.2
1943	NY N	5	10	.333	22	17	4	1	130.2	140	69	4	2	59	47	4.61	75	.281	.360	43-1-1	.256	3	71	-14		-1.2
1944	NY N	6	14	.300	38	18	2-1	2	128.2	128	83	7	6	87	39	5.18	71	.266	.384	40-0-2	.125	-2	93	-19		-3.0
1945	NY N	3	7	.273	31	4	0	1	76.2	90	55	6	1	49	27	5.63	69	.288	.387	19-1-0	.211	2	92	-15		-1.7
1946	NY N	1	2	.333	15	1	0	0	35.2	48	32	3	0	21	14	6.31	55	.316	.399	9	.111	-1	124	-12		-1.0
Total	5	16	34	.320	108	41	7-1	4	382.2	416	242	20	9	222	136	5.10	71	.280	.377	114-2-3	.193	2	86	-58		-6.7

FISCHER, TODD Todd Richard B9.15.1960 Columbus OH BR/TR/5-10/170 d5.29 Col Edison (FL) CC

YEAR	TM LG	W	L	PCT	G	GS	CG-SHO	SV-BS	IP	H	R	HR	HB	BB-IB	SO	ERA	AERA	OAV	OOB	AB-HR-SH	AVG	PB	SUP	APR	DL	PW
1986	Cal A	0	0	—	9	0	0	0-0	17	18	8	4	0	8-2	7	4.24	98	.286	.361	0	—	0	0	0		0.0

FISCHER, BILL William Charles B10.11.1930 Wausau WI BR/TR/6-0/190* d4.21 C14

YEAR	TM LG	W	L	PCT	G	GS	CG-SHO	SV-BS	IP	H	R	HR	HB	BB-IB	SO	ERA	AERA	OAV	OOB	AB-HR-SH	AVG	PB	SUP	APR	DL	PW
1956	Chi A	0	0	—	3	0	0	0	1.2	6	4	0	0	1-0	2	21.60	19	.545	.583	0	—	0		-3		-0.1
1957	Chi A	7	8	.467	33	11	3-1	0	124	139	50	1	3	35-6	48	3.48	107	.291	.342	40-0-3	.150	-0	91	5		0.3
1958	Chi A	2	3	.400	17	3	0	0	36.1	43	28	6	0	13-1	16	6.69	54	.301	.357	7-0-1	.143	-0	82	-12		-1.4
	Det A	2	4	.333	22	0	0	2	30.2	46	34	6	0	13-2	16	7.63	53	.362	.415	1-0-1	.000	0	16	0		-2.5
	Was A	0	3	.000	3	3	0	0	21	24	9	1	1	5-1	10	3.86	99	.320	.366	5	.200	0	47	-13		0.1
	Year	4	10	.286	42	6	0	2	88	113	71	13	1	31-4	42	6.34	60	.328	.381	13-0-2	.154	-2	106	-5		-3.8
1959	Was A	9	11	.450	34	29	6-1	0	187.1	211	98	16	4	43-2	62	4.28	92	.281	.321	54-0-7	.130	-2	65	-7		-0.5
1960	Was A	3	5	.375	20	7	1	0	77	85	45	7	0	17-2	31	4.91	79	.281	.318	19-1-2	.158	1	65	-7		-0.5
	Det A	5	3	.625	20	6	1	0	55	50	23	6	0	18-3	24	3.44	115	.244	.301	11-0-2	.364	2	111	3		0.7
	Year	8	8	.500	40	13	2	0	132	135	68	13	0	35-5	55	4.30	91	.266	.311	30-1-4	.233	3	87	-4		0.2
1961	Det A	3	2	.600	26	1	0	3	46.2	54	28	10	0	17-2	18	5.01	82	.292	.351	7	.000	-0	86	-4		0.1
	KC A	1	0	1.000	15	0	0	2	21	26	9	1	0	6-0	12	3.86	108	.321	.364	2-0-1	.000	-1	86	-3		-0.4
	Year	4	2	.667	41	1	0	5	67.2	80	37	11	0	23-2	30	4.66	89	.301	.355	9-0-1	.000	-1	86	-7		-0.2
1962	KC A	4	12	.250	34	16	5	2	127.2	150	61	16	1	8-2	38	3.95	107	.293	.302	38-0-1	.105	-2	171	2		0.3
1963	KC A	9	6	.600	45	2	0	3	95.2	86	44	13	3	29-5	34	3.57	109	.242	.302	15-0-3	.067	-0	67	3		0.3
1964	Min A	0	1	.000	9	0	0	0	7.1	16	6	2	0	5-3	2	7.36	49	.471	.525	0	—	0		-3		-0.1
Total	9	45	58	.437	281	78	16-2	13	831.1	936	439	85	12	210-29	313	4.34	91	.287	.330	199-1-21	.136	-4	90	-32		-4.1

FISHEL, LEO Leo B12.13.1877 Babylon NY D5.19.1960 Hempstead NY BR/TR/6-0/175 d5.3 Col Columbia

YEAR	TM LG	W	L	PCT	G	GS	CG-SHO	SV-BS	IP	H	R	HR	HB	BB-IB	SO	ERA	AERA	OAV	OOB	AB-HR-SH	AVG	PB	SUP	APR	DL	PW
1899	NY N	0	1	.000	1	1	1	0	9	9	7	0	2	6	6	6.00	63	.257	.395	4	.250	-0	57	-2		-0.1

FISHER, BRIAN Brian Kevin B3.18.1962 Honolulu HI BR/TR/6-4/210* [AtlN80 2/29] d5.7

YEAR	TM LG	W	L	PCT	G	GS	CG-SHO	SV-BS	IP	H	R	HR	HB	BB-IB	SO	ERA	AERA	OAV	OOB	AB-HR-SH	AVG	PB	SUP	APR	DL	PW
1985	NY A	4	4	.500	55	0	0	14-4	98.1	77	32	4	0	29-3	85	2.38	170	.216	.273	0	—	0		17		1.8
1986	NY A	9	5	.643	62	0	0	6-9	96.2	105	61	14	0	37-2	67	4.93	84	.277	.341	0	—	0		-9		-1.4
1987	Pit N	11	9	.550	37	26	6-3	0-0	185.1	185	99	27	4	72-7	117	4.52	92	.262	.332	58-2-5	.190	4	99	-5		-0.2
1988	Pit N	8	10	.444	33	22	1-1	1-1	146.1	157	78	13	5	57-4	66	4.61	75	.277	.345	42-0-2	.048	-2	115	-17	15		-2.2
1989	Pit N	0	3	.000	9	3	0	1-0	17	25	17	2	0	10-3	8	7.94	43	.329	.402	5	.000	-1	78	-9	101		-1.8
1990	Hou N	0	0	—	4	0	0	0-0	5	9	5	1	0	0-0	1	7.20	52	.409	.375	0	—	0		-2		-0.2
1992	Sea A	4	3	.571	22	14	0	1-0	91.1	80	49	9	1	47-2	26	4.53	88	.234	.326	0	—	0	114	-5	116		-0.2
Total	7	36	34	.514	222	65	7-4	23-14	640	638	341	70	11	252-21	370	4.39	90	.261	.330	105-2-7	.124	2	105	-30	116		-3.8

FISHER, CHAUNCEY Chauncey Burr "Peach","Whoa Bill" B1.8.1872 Anderson IN D4.27.1939 Los Angeles CA BR/TR/5-11/175 d9.20 b-Tom

YEAR	TM LG	W	L	PCT	G	GS	CG-SHO	SV-BS	IP	H	R	HR	HB	BB-IB	SO	ERA	AERA	OAV	OOB	AB-HR-SH	AVG	PB	SUP	APR	DL	PW
1893	Cle N	0	2	.000	2	2	2	0	18	26	18	0	0	9	9	5.50	89	.329	.398	8	.250	-0	79	-1		-0.1
1894	Cle N	0	2	.000	3	2	0	0	11	22	17	0	1	5	0	11.45	48	.407	.467	4	.000	-1	52	-6		-0.2
	Cin N	2	8	.200	12	12	11	0	100	153	123	4	1	46	17	7.47	74	.347	.410	47-1-0	.213	-2	67	-22		-2.1
	Year	2	10	.167	15	14	11	0	111	175	140	4	2	51	17	7.86	70	.354	.416	51-1-0	.196	-3	65	-28		-2.2
1896	Cin N	10	7	.588	27	15	13-2	2	159.2	199	111	9	5	36	25	4.45	104	.303	.344	57-0-4	.246	0	122	2		0.2
1897	Bro N	9	7	.563	20	13	11-1	1	149	184	96	5	2	43	31	4.23	97	.301	.349	59-0-1	.203	-1	153	-2		-0.1
1901	NY N	0	0	—	1	1	0	0	4	11	9	0	0	2	1	15.75	21	.500	.542	1	.000	-0	279	-5		-0.1
	StL N	0	0	—	1	0	0	0	3	7	5	0	0	1	0	15.00	21	.438	.471	1	.000	-0	284	-8		-0.1
	Year	0	0	—	2	1	0	0	7	18	14	0	0	3	1	15.43	21	.474	.512	2	.000	-0	284	-13		-0.3
Total	5	21	26	.447	66	45	37-3	3	444.2	602	379	18	9	142	83	5.44	85	.320	.371	178-1-5	.213	-4	111	-37		-3.1

FISHER, CLARENCE Clarence Henry B8.27.1898 Letart WV D11.2.1965 Point Pleasant WV BR/TR/6-0/174 d9.14 Col Rio Grande

YEAR	TM LG	W	L	PCT	G	GS	CG-SHO	SV-BS	IP	H	R	HR	HB	BB-IB	SO	ERA	AERA	OAV	OOB	AB-HR-SH	AVG	PB	SUP	APR	DL	PW
1919	Was A	0	0	—	2	0	0	0	4	8	6	0	0	3	1	13.50	24	.421	.500	0	—	0		-4		-0.1
1920	Was A	0	1	.000	2	0	0	0	3.2	5	4	0	0	5	0	9.82	38	.714	.833	1	.000	-0		-2		-0.1
Total	2	0	1	.000	4	0	0	0	7.2	13	10	0	0	8	1	11.74	29	.500	.618	1	.000	-0		-6		-0.1

FISHER, DON Donald Raymond B2.6.1916 Cleveland OH D7.29.1973 Mayfield Heights OH BR/TR/6-0/210 d8.25

YEAR	TM LG	W	L	PCT	G	GS	CG-SHO	SV-BS	IP	H	R	HR	HB	BB-IB	SO	ERA	AERA	OAV	OOB	AB-HR-SH	AVG	PB	SUP	APR	DL	PW
1945	NY N	1	0	1.000	2	1	1-1	0	18	12	4	0	2	7	4	2.00	196	.190	.292	7	.143	-0	22	4		0.2

FISHER, EDDIE Eddie Gene B7.16.1936 Shreveport LA BR/TR/6-2.5/200* d6.22 Col Oklahoma

YEAR	TM LG	W	L	PCT	G	GS	CG-SHO	SV-BS	IP	H	R	HR	HB	BB-IB	SO	ERA	AERA	OAV	OOB	AB-HR-SH	AVG	PB	SUP	APR	DL	PW
1959	SF N	2	6	.250	17	5	0	1	40	57	37	8	1	8-0	15	7.87	48	.339	.369	8	.000	-1	75	-17		-3.1
1960	SF N	1	0	1.000	3	1	0	0	12.2	11	5	2	0	2-0	7	3.55	98	.244	.260	5	.600	1	279	2		0.2
1961	SF N	0	2	.000	15	1	0	0	33.2	36	23	7	0	9-3	16	6.35	71	.267	.313	7	.143	-0	442	-6		-0.6
1962	Chi A	9	5	.643	57	12	2-1	5	182.2	169	74	17	1	45-1	88	3.10	126	.245	.291	46-0-8	.130	-0	116	14		1.3
1963	Chi A	9	8	.529	33	15	2-1	0	120.2	114	57	14	2	28-2	67	3.95	89	.244	.286	36-0-1	.139	-0	110	-5		-0.2
1964	Chi A	6	3	.667	59	2	0	9	125	86	43	13	3	32-3	74	3.02	114	.192	.249	18-0-1	.167	-0	206	8		1.0
1965	Chi A★	15	7	.682	82	0	0	24	165.1	118	51	13	2	43-8	90	2.40	133	.205	.259	29-0-1	.138	0		15		2.1
1966	Chi A	1	3	.250	23	0	0	6	35.1	27	11	1	1	17-1	18	2.29	138	.214	.310	2	.000	-0		4		0.3
	Bal A	5	3	.625	44	0	0	13	71.2	60	26	4	2	19-1	39	2.64	126	.226	.280	13	.154	0		4		0.7
	Year	6	6	.500	67	0	0	19	107	87	37	5	3	36-2	57	2.52	130	.222	.290	15	.133	-0		-5		1.0
1967	Bal A	4	3	.571	46	0	0	4	89.2	82	40	7	4	26-3	53	3.61	87	.245	.304	5-0-2	.200	-0		1		0.4
1968	Cal A	4	2	.667	54	0	0	4	94.2	87	36	8	2	17-3	42	2.85	104	.248	.283	12	.000	-1		6		0.9
1969	Cal A	3	2	.600	52	0	0	2-0	96.2	100	46	9	1	28-3	47	3.63	96	.272	.322	13-0-2	.091	-1	101	-2		-0.2
1970	Cal A	4	4	.500	57	0	0	8-4	130.1	117	50	15	0	35-1	74	3.04	119	.239	.291	11-0-3	.091	-1	147	5		0.5
1971	Cal A	10	8	.556	57	0	0	3-2	119	92	46	11	2	50-5	82	2.72	119	.211	.293	16-0-1	.063	-0	30	-6		0.3
1972	Cal A	4	5	.444	43	0	0	4-2	81.1	73	35	6	3	31-3	30	3.76	78	.247	.314	17	.118	-1	121	-3		-0.2
	Chi A	0	1	.000	6	4	0	0	22.1	31	13	1	0	9-0	12	5.24	55	.326	.375			-0				
	Year	4	6	.400	49	4	0	4-2	103.2	104	48	7	0	40-3	42	3.91	76	.271	.335	24	.083	-1	107	-10		-0.1

YEAR	TM LG	W	L	PCT	G	GS	CG-SHO	SV-BS	IP	H	R	HR	HB	BB-IB	SO	ERA	AERA	OAV	OOB	AB-HR-SH	AVG	PB	SUP	APR	DL	PW
1973	Chi A	6	7	.462	26	16	2	0-0	110.2	135	64	12	3	38-1	57	4.88	81	.301	.358	0	—	0	107	-9		-1.0
	StL N	2	1	.667	6	0	0	0-0	7	3	1	1	1	1-0	1	1.29	286	.125	.192	1	1.000	0		2		0.5
Total	15	85	70	.548	690	63	7-2	81-8	1538.2	1398	659	149	27	438-38	812	3.41	101	.243	.297	246-0-19	.122	-5	127	8		0.4

FISHER, ED Edward Fredrick B10.31.1876 Wayne MI D7.24.1951 Spokane WA BR/TR/6-2/200 d9.5

YEAR	TM LG	W	L	PCT	G	GS	CG-SHO	SV-BS	IP	H	R	HR	HB	BB-IB	SO	ERA	AERA	OAV	OOB	AB-HR-SH	AVG	PB	SUP	APR	DL	PW
1902	Det A	0	0	—	1	0	0	0	4	4	4	0	0	0-1	0	0.00	—	.267	.313	2	.000	-0		2		0.0

FISHER, FRITZ Frederick Brown B11.28.1941 Adrian MI BL/TL/6-1/180 d4.19 Col Michigan

| 1964 | Det A | 0 | 0 | — | 1 | 0 | 0 | 0 | 0.1 | 2 | 4 | 0 | 0 | 2-0 | 1 | 108.00 | 3 | .667 | .800 | 0 | | 0 | | -4 | | -0.2 |

FISHER, HARRY Harry Devereux B1.3.1926 Newbury ON, Can. D9.20.1981 Waterloo ON, Can. BL/TR/6-0/180* d9.16.1951 ▲

| 1952 | Pit N | 1 | 2 | .333 | 8 | 3 | 0 | 0 | 18.1 | 17 | 14 | 4 | 2 | 13 | 5 | 6.87 | 58 | .266 | .405 | 15 | .333 | 1* | 74 | -5 | | -0.6 |

FISHER, J. J. B Philadelhia PA d7.17

1884	Phi U	1	7	.125	8	8	8	0	70.2	76	49	0		13	42	3.57	65	.257	.288	36	.222	-1*	69	-10		-1.0
1885	Buf N	0	1	.000	1	1	1	0	9	10	9	0		2	4	5.00	60	.256	.293	4	.000	-1	95	-2		-0.2
Total	2	1	8	.111	9	9	9	0	79.2	86	58	0		15	46	3.73	64	.257	.289	40	.200	-2	72	-12		-1.2

FISHER, JACK John Howard "Fat Jack" B3.4.1939 Frostburg MD BR/TR/6-2/215* d4.14

1959	Bal A	1	6	.143	27	7	1-1	2	88.2	76	36	7	1	38-1	52	3.05	124	.230	.307	23	.130	-1	57	6		0.4
1960	Bal A	12	11	.522	40	20	8-3	2	197.2	174	87	13	2	78-4	99	3.41	111	.241	.315	60-1-4	.183	2	110	8		1.1
1961	Bal A	10	13	.435	36	25	10-1	1	196	205	104	17	4	75-3	118	3.90	99	.270	.335	56-0-10	.089	-2	94	-5		-0.9
1962	Bal A	7	9	.438	32	25	4	1	152	173	101	23	2	56-3	81	5.09	73	.284	.345	49-0-3	.102	-1*	128	-27	30	-2.6
1963	SF N	6	10	.375	36	12	2	1	116	132	77	12	5	38-3	57	4.58	70	.284	.342	29-0-0	.103	1	106	-22		-2.8
1964	NY N	10	17	.370	40	34	8-1	0	227.2	256	124	23	10	56-0	115	4.23	85	.283	.330	76-0-2	.158	-1	105	-17		-1.8
1965	NY N	8	24	.250	43	36	10	0	253.2	252	121	22	4	68-6	116	3.94	90	.259	.309	78-0-4	.154	0	69	-9		-0.9
1966	NY N	11	14	.440	38	33	10-2	0	230	229	108	26	8	54-2	127	3.68	99	.260	.308	67-0-6	.090	-2	84	-1		-0.1
1967	NY N	9	18	.333	39	30	7-1	0	220.1	251	121	21	4	64-10	117	4.70	72	.287	.336	70-0-6	.100	-2	77	-10		-3.3
1968	Chi A	8	13	.381	35	28	2	0	180.2	176	68	14	7	48-4	80	2.99	101	.257	.310	53-0-5	.113	-1	62	2		0.0
1969	Cin N	4	4	.500	34	15	0	1-0	113	137	77	15	5	30-3	55	5.50	68	.295	.344	33-0-3	.121	-1	129	-20		-1.6
Total	11	86	139	.382	400	265	62-9	9-0	1975.2	2061	1024	193	52	605-39	1017	4.06	88	.269	.325	594-1-45	.125	-6	92	-113	30	-12.5

FISHER, MAURICE Maurice Wayne B2.16.1931 Uniondale NY BR/TR/6-5/210 d4.16

| 1955 | Cin N | 0 | 0 | — | 1 | 0 | 0 | 0 | 2.2 | 5 | 2 | 1 | 0 | 2-0 | 1 | 6.75 | 63 | .385 | .467 | 1 | .000 | -0 | | -1 | | 0.0 |

FISHER, RAY Ray Lyle "Pick" B10.4.1887 Middlebury VT D11.3.1982 Ann Arbor MI BR/TR/5-11.5/180 d7.2 Mil 1918 Col Middlebury

1910	NY A	5	3	.625	17	7	3	1	92.1	95	41	0	3	18	42	2.92	91	.274	.315	29-0-1	.103	-2	101	-3		-0.3
1911	NY A	10	11	.476	29	22	8-2	0	171.2	178	85	3	5	55	99	3.25	111	.269	.330	59-1-3	.119	-3	88	6		0.5
1912	NY A	2	8	.200	17	13	5	0	90.1	107	70	2	2	32	47	5.88	61	.312	.374	31-0-3	.065	-4	74	-17		-1.9
1913	NY A	12	16	.429	43	31	14-1	1	246.1	244	113	3	9	71	92	3.18	94	.263	.321	79-0-6	.278	3	84	-3		0.1
1914	NY A	10	12	.455	39	26	17-2	1	209	177	66	2	4	61	86	2.28	121	.241	.303	65-0-5	.138	-2	78	12		1.2
1915	NY A	18	11	.621	30	28	20-4	0	247.2	219	82	7	5	62	97	2.11	139	.243	.295	83-0-4	.108	-5	100	19		1.7
1916	NY A	11	8	.579	31	21	9-1	2	179	191	81	4	4	51	56	3.17	91	.285	.339	62-0-1	.177	1	113	-6		-0.6
1917	NY A	8	9	.471	23	18	12-3	0	144	126	49	3	2	42	64	2.19	123	.243	.304	50-1-2	.180	-0	89	7		0.9
1919	†Cin N	14	5	.737	26	20	12-5	1	174.1	141	55	4	1	38	41	2.17	128	.226	.271	59-0-2	.271	3	136	12		1.9
1920	Cin N	10	11	.476	33	21	14	0	201	189	86	5	8	50	56	2.73	111	.249	.302	70-0-3	.243	1	113	4		0.6
Total	10	100	94	.515	278	207	110-19	7	1755.2	1667	727	33	43	481	680	2.82	106	.257	.312	587-2-30	.179	-8	97	31		4.1

FISHER, TOM Thomas Chalmers "Red" B11.1.1880 Anderson IN D9.3.1972 Anderson IN BR/TR/5-10.5/185 d4.17 b-Chauncey

| 1904 | Bos N | 6 | 16 | .273 | 31 | 21 | 19-2 | 0 | 214 | 257 | 165 | 5 | 10 | 82 | 84 | 4.25 | 65 | .302 | .370 | 99-2-0 | .212 | 3* | 78 | -42 | | -3.7 |

FISHER, TOM Thomas Gene B4.4.1942 Cleveland OH BR/TR/6-0/190 d9.20 Col Ohio U.

| 1967 | Bal A | 0 | 0 | — | 2 | 0 | 0 | 0 | 3.1 | 2 | 0 | 0 | 0 | 2-0 | 1 | 0.00 | — | .182 | .308 | 0 | — | 0 | | 1 | | 0.1 |

FISHER, CHEROKEE William Charles B12.1845 Philadelphia PA D9.26.1912 New York NY BR/TR/5-9/164 d5.6 ▲

1871	Rok NA	4	16	.200	24	24	22-1	0	213	295	257	3		31	15	4.35	94	.281	.302	123-1	.228	-3*	89	-3		-0.2
1872	Bal NA	10	1	.909	19	11	9-1	1	110	93	78	0		11	20	1.80	204	.197	.216	225-1	.231	-1*	172	19		1.2
1873	Ath NA	3	4	.429	13	5	5	2	84.1	90	73	1		10	14	1.81	188	.231	.250	253-1	.261	1*	75	10		0.6
1874	Har NA	13	23	.361	39	35	31	0	322.1	416	277	1		13	25	2.32	100	.277	.284	241	.224	-4*	98	1		-0.3
1875	Phi NA	22	19	.537	41	41	36-2	0	358	345	189	6		9	18	1.99	115	.229	.233	177	.232	-1	99	13		0.9
1876	Cin N	4	20	.167	28	24	22	0	229.1	294	206	6	6	6	29	3.02	73	.285	.289	129	.248	-1*	60	-26		-2.2
1878	Pro N	0	1	.000	1	1	1	0	9	14	12	0	0	0	2	4.00	55	.304	.304	3	.000	-0	79	-3		-0.2
Total	5 NA	52	63	.452	136	116	103-4	3	1087.2	1239	874	11		74	92	2.52	115	.252	.263	1019-3	.237	-8	102	40		2.2
Total	2	4	21	.160	29	25	23	0	238.1	308	218	6	6	6	31	3.06	72	.285	.289	132	.242	-2	61	-29		-2.4

FISKE, MAX Maximilian Patrick "Ski" B10.12.1888 Chicago IL D5.25.1928 Chicago IL BR/TR/5-11/185 d4.19

| 1914 | Chi F | 12 | 12 | .500 | 38 | 22 | 7 | 0 | 198 | 161 | 84 | 7 | 7 | 59 | 87 | 3.14 | 85 | .231 | .298 | 68-0-1 | .235 | 0* | 105 | -8 | | -0.9 |

FITTERY, PAUL Paul Clarence B10.10.1887 Lebanon PA D1.28.1974 Cartersville GA BR/TL/5-8.5/156 d9.5

1914	Cin N	0	2	.000	8	4	2	0	43.2	41	20	0	1	12	21	3.09	95	.246	.300	17-0-1	.059	-1*	79	0		-0.2
1917	Phi N	1	1	.500	17	2	1	0	55.2	69	36	1	5	27	13	4.53	62	.317	.404	22-0-1	.091	-1*	188	-10		-0.5
Total	2	1	3	.250	25	6	3	0	99.1	110	56	1	6	39	34	3.90	73	.286	.360	39-0-2	.077	-2	116	-10		-0.7

FITZGERALD, BRIAN Brian Michael B12.26.1974 Woodbridge VA BL/TL/5-11/175 [SeaA96 20/597] d4.17 Col VPI

| 2002 | Sea A | 0 | 0 | — | 6 | 0 | 0 | 0-0 | 6.1 | 11 | 8 | 2 | 1 | 2-0 | 1 | 8.53 | 51 | .344 | .389 | 0 | — | 0 | | -4 | | -0.2 |

FITZGERALD, JOHN John Francis B9.15.1933 Brooklyn NY BL/TL/6-3/190 d9.28

| 1958 | SF N | 0 | 0 | — | 1 | 0 | 0 | 0 | 3 | 1 | 1 | 1 | 0 | 1-0 | 3 | 3.00 | 127 | .111 | .200 | 1 | .000 | -0 | 165 | 0 | | 0.0 |

FITZGERALD, JOHN John H. B5.30.1870 Natick MA D3.31.1921 Boston MA d7.18

| 1891 | Bos AA | 1 | 1 | .500 | 6 | 3 | 2 | 1 | 32 | 49 | 32 | 2 | 1 | 11 | 16 | 5.63 | 62 | .340 | .395 | 14 | .071 | -2 | 89 | -8 | | -0.5 |

FITZGERALD, JOHN John J. B1866 D12.20.1892 Waterbury CT d4.18

| 1890 | Roc AA | 3 | 8 | .273 | 11 | 11 | 8-1 | 0 | 78 | 77 | 51 | 0 | 6 | 45 | 35 | 4.04 | 88 | .250 | .357 | 31 | .194 | -0 | 91 | -3 | | -0.4 |

FITZGERALD, WARREN Warren Bartholomew B4.1868 PA D11.7.1930 Phoenix AZ TL/5-9/162 d6.4

1891	Lou AA	14	17	.452	32	31	28-3	0	267	265	157	5	12	89	110	3.34	110	.250	.316	108-1	.176	1*	84	8		0.6
1892	Lou N	1	3	.250	4	4	4	0	34	45	27	2	1	11	3	4.24	72	.306	.358	15	.133	-0	98	-5		-0.5
Total	2	15	20	.429	36	35	32-3	0	301	310	184	7	13	100	113	3.44	104	.257	.321	123-1	.171	0	86	3		0.1

FITZKE, PAUL Robert Paul "Bob" (b Frederick Herman Fitzke) B7.30.1900 LaCrosse WI D6.30.1950 Sacramento CA BR/TR/5-11.5/185 d9.1 Col Idaho

| 1924 | Cle A | 0 | 0 | — | 1 | 0 | 0 | 0 | 4 | 5 | 2 | 0 | 0 | 3 | 1 | 4.50 | 95 | .313 | .421 | 1 | .000 | -0 | 0 | 0 | | 0.0 |

FITZMORRIS, AL Alan James B3.21.1946 Buffalo NY BB/TR/6-2/190(185-200) d9.8

1969	KC A	1	1	.500	7	0	0	2-0	9	5	1	0	4	4-0	3	4.00	88	.237	.310	1	.000	-0		-9		-0.1
1970	KC A	8	5	.615	43	11	2	1-1	117.2	112	60	14	0	52-6	47	4.44	84	.254	.330	31	.290	4*	178	-6		-0.2
1971	KC A	7	5	.583	36	15	2-1	0-1	127.1	112	61	6	1	55-2	53	4.17	83	.245	.324	44-0-2	.250	2	135	-8		-0.5
1972	KC A	2	5	.286	38	2	0	3-1	101	99	46	10	1	28-5	51	3.74	81	.252	.303	23	.174	1*	102	-8		-0.4
1973	KC A	8	3	.727	15	13	3-1	0-0	89	88	29	5	0	25-3	26	2.83	145	.259	.309	0		0	95	13		1.6
1974	KC A	13	6	.684	34	27	9-4	1-1	190	189	73	8	0	63-10	53	2.79	137	.260	.317	0	—	0	98	19		2.0
1975	KC A	16	12	.571	35	35	11-3	0-0	242	239	104	16	5	76-6	78	3.57	108	.262	.320	0	—	0	106	10		1.1
1976	KC A	15	11	.577	35	33	8-2	0-0	220.1	227	89	6	2	56-6	80	3.06	114	.273	.316	0	—	0*	90	10		1.3
1977	Cle A	6	10	.375	29	21	1	0-0	133	164	87	12	1	53-4	54	5.41	74	.306	.367	0	—	0	108	-20		-2.1
1978	Cle A	0	1	.000	7	0	0	0-0	14.1	19	10	3	1	7-2	5	6.28	60	.333	.415	0	—	0		-3	34	-0.2
	Cal A	1	0	1.000	9	2	0	0-0	31.2	26	9	2	0	14-3	8	1.71	213	.236	.317	0	—	0		6		0.3
	Year	1	1	.500	16	2	0	0-0	46	45	19	5	1	21-5	13	3.13	118	.269	.351	0	—	0	183	3		0.1
Total	10	77	59	.566	288	159	36-11	7-4	1277	1284	573	83	11	433-47	458	3.65	101	.265	.324	99-0-2	.242	7	111	13	34	2.8

YEAR	TM LG	W	L	PCT	G	GS	CG-SHO	SV-BS	IP	H	R	HR	HB	BB-IB	SO	ERA	AERA	OAV	OOB	AB-HR-SH	AVG	PB	SUP	APR	DL	PW
FITZSIMMONS, FREDDIE					Frederick Landis "Fat Freddie"			B7.28.1901 Mishawaka IN		D11.18.1979 Yucca Valley CA			BR/TR/5-11/185		d8.12		M3/C14									
1925	NY N	6	3	.667	10	8	6-1	0	74.2	70	25	4	0	18	17	2.65	152	.248	.293	29-0-1	.310	2	120	13		1.7
1926	NY N	14	10	.583	37	26	12	0	219	224	90	7	4	58	48	2.88	130	.272	.322	86-0-1	.128	-6	117	19		1.3
1927	NY N	17	10	.630	42	31	14-1	3	244.2	260	127	15	4	67	78	3.72	104	.275	.325	87-0-8	.207	-0	128	0		0.1
1928	NY N	20	9	.690	40	32	16-1	0	261.1	264	119	13	4	65	67	3.68	106	.268	.316	94-0-5	.191	1	103	9		1.0
1929	NY N	15	11	.577	37	30	14-4	1	221.2	242	122	14	2	66	55	4.10	112	.285	.338	82-0-2	.183	-2	135	11		1.1
1930	NY N	19	7	**.731**	41	29	17-1	1	224.1	230	125	26	1	59	76	4.25	111	.266	.314	83-2-5	.265	5	148	12		1.8
1931	NY N	18	11	.621	35	33	19-4	0	253.2	242	111	16	0	62	78	3.05	121	.251	.296	92-4-3	.228	9	130	15		2.9
1932	NY N	11	11	.500	35	31	11	0	237.2	287	132	18	3	83	65	4.43	84	.299	.356	86-2-6	.221	4	139	-16		-0.6
1933	†NY N	16	11	.593	36	**35**	13-1	0	251.2	243	106	14	2	72	65	2.90	111	.251	.305	95-2-3	.200	3	110	6		1.2
1934	NY N	18	14	.563	38	37	14-3	1	263.1	266	114	12	1	51	65	3.04	127	.261	.297	95-2-3	.232	5	105	22		3.2
1935	NY N	4	8	.333	18	15	6-4	0	94	104	43	7	1	22	23	4.02	96	.281	.323	31-0-2	.258	1	81	0		0.2
1936	†NY N	10	7	.588	28	17	7-1	2	141	147	58	6	0	39	35	3.32	117	.274	.327	47-0-5	.149	-2	96	10		1.0
1937	NY N	2	2	.500	6	4	1-1	0	27.1	28	14	3	0	8	13	4.61	84	.272	.324	10-1-1	.300	2	144	-1		0.0
	Bro N	4	8	.333	13	13	4	0	90.2	91	47	2	1	32	29	4.27	95	.263	.327	30-0-1	.167	-1	72	0		0.0
	Year	6	10	.375	19	17	5-1	0	118	119	61	5	1	40	42	4.35	92	.265	.302	40-1-2	.200	1	89	-2		0.0
1938	Bro N	11	8	.579	27	26	12-3	0	202.2	205	83	8	3	43	38	3.02	129	.261	.302	70-0-4	.171	-1	98	18		1.8
1939	Bro N	7	9	.438	27	20	5	3	151.1	178	79	6	3	28	44	3.87	104	.293	.327	47-1-3	.234	3	76	0		0.6
1940	Bro N	16	2	**.889**	20	18	11-4	0	134.1	120	43	5	1	25	35	2.81	142	.233	.269	47-0-4	.106	-2	121	19		2.3
1941	†Bro N	6	1	.857	12	8	3-1	0	82.2	78	33	3	2	26	19	2.07	177	.245	.305	28-0-1	.143	-0	106	10		0.9
1942	Bro N	0	0	—	1	1	0	0	3	6	5	1	0	1	0	15.00	22	.400	.438	2	.500	1	154	-4		-0.1
1943	Bro N	3	4	.429	9	7	1	0	44.2	52	29	-6	1	21	12	5.44	62	.281	.360	14-0-1	.071	-1	97	-10		-1.4
Total	19	217	146	.598	513	425	186-30	13	3223.2	3335	1505	186	33	846	870	3.51	111	.268	.316	1155-14-58	.200	21	115	133		19.0
FLAHERTY, PATSY					Patrick Joseph		B6.29.1876 Mansfield PA		D1.23.1968 Alexandria LA		BL/TL/5-8/165		d9.8 ▲												
1899	Lou N	2	3	.400	5	4	4	0	39	41	21	0	1	9	5	2.31	167	.270	.297	24	.208	1*	75	5		0.5
1900	Pit N	0	0	—	4	1	0	0	22	30	16	0	5	9	5	6.14	59	.323	.411	9	.111	-1	152	-4		-0.2
1903	Chi A	11	25	.306	40	34	29-2	1	293.2	338	173	9	14	50	65	3.74	75	.288	.324	102-0-3	.137	-3	80	-29		-3.4
1904	Chi A	1	2	.333	5	5	4	0	43	36	19	1	1	10	14	2.09	117	.228	.278	12	.333	2	134	0		0.3
	Pit N	19	9	.679	29	28	28-5	0	242	210	81	3	11	59	54	2.05	134	.232	.287	104-2-4	.212	5*	135	16		2.8
1905	Pit N	10	10	.500	27	20	15	1	187.2	197	87	2	6	49	44	3.50	86	.272	.324	76-0-1	.197	2*	125	-8		-0.5
1907	Bos N	12	15	.444	27	25	23	0	217	197	90	4	7	59	34	2.70	95	.248	.306	115-2-0	.191	2*	95	-5		-0.2
1908	Bos N	12	18	.400	31	31	21	0	244	221	109	6	8	81	50	3.25	74	.236	.303	86-0-5	.140	-0*	94	-17		-2.0
1910	Phi N	0	0	—	1	0	0	0	0.1	1	4	0	0	1	0	0.00	—	—	.333	2	.500	0*		-1		-0.1
1911	Bos N	0	2	.000	4	2	1	0	14	21	15	0	3	8	0	7.07	54	.350	.451	94-2-1	.287	1*	98	-5		-0.5
Total	9	67	84	.444	173	150	125-7	2	1302.2	1292	615	25	56	331	271	3.10	89	.259	.312	624-6-14	.197	10	104	-48		-3.3
FLANAGAN, MIKE					Michael Kendall	B12.16.1951 Manchester NH		BL/TL/6-0/195(185-199)		[BalA73 7/159]		d9.5 C2		Col Massachusetts										
1975	Bal A	0	1	.000	2	1	0	0-0	9.2	9	4	0	0	6-1	7	2.79	127	.250	.357	0	—	0	50	0		0.1
1976	Bal A	3	5	.375	20	10	4	0-0	85	83	41	7	0	33-0	56	4.13	80	.260	.326	0	—	0	101	-7		-0.6
1977	Bal A	15	10	.600	36	33	15-2	1-0	235	235	100	17	2	70-5	149	3.64	105	.266	.318	0	—	0	106	7		0.7
1978	Bal A☆	19	15	.559	40	**40**	17-2	0-0	281.1	271	128	22	3	87-2	167	4.03	88	.257	.314	0	—	0	109	-10		-1.2
1979	†Bal A	**23**	9	.719	39	38	16-**5**	0-0	265.2	245	107	23	3	70-1	190	3.08	131	.245	.296	0	—	0*	101	9		3.0
1980	Bal A	16	13	.552	37	37	12-2	0-0	251.1	278	121	27	2	71-3	128	4.12	96	.287	.333	0	—	0	102	-4		-0.5
1981	Bal A	9	6	.600	20	20	3-2	0-0	116	108	55	11	2	37-1	72	4.19	87	.244	.305	0	—	0	105	3		0.3
1982	Bal A	15	11	.577	36	35	11-1	0-0	236	233	110	24	4	76-5	103	3.97	102	.259	.317	0	—	0	118	9	81	1.0
1983	†Bal A	12	4	.750	20	20	3-1	0-0	125.1	135	53	10	2	31-2	50	3.30	121	.278	.321	0	—	0	99	8		0.9
1984	Bal A	13	13	.500	34	34	10-2	0-0	226.2	213	103	24	1	81-5	115	3.53	111	.250	.314	0	—	0	89	-8	103	-0.7
1985	Bal A	4	5	.444	15	15	1	0-0	86	101	49	14	2	28-0	42	5.13	79	.297	.352	0	—	0	89	-4	19	-0.4
1986	Bal A	7	11	.389	29	28	2	0-1	172	179	95	15	1	66-4	96	4.24	98	.270	.334	0	—	0	103	-5	60	-0.4
1987	Bal A	3	6	.333	16	16	4	0-0	94.2	102	57	9	0	36-1	50	4.94	90	.278	.342	0	—	0	78	11		1.0
	Tor A	3	2	.600	7	7	0	0-0	49.1	46	15	3	0	15-3	43	2.37	191	.237	.292	0	—	0	95	6		0.6
	Year	6	8	.429	23	23	4	0-0	144	148	72	12	0	51-4	93	4.06	110	.264	.325	0	—	0	115	-4		-0.4
1988	Tor A	13	13	.500	34	34	2-1	0-0	211	220	106	23	6	80-1	99	4.18	95	.271	.339	0	—	0	105	-2		-0.1
1989	†Tor A	8	10	.444	30	30	1-1	0-0	171.2	186	82	10	5	47-0	47	3.93	96	.283	.331	0	—	0	147	-4		-0.6
1990	Tor A	2	2	.500	5	5	0	0-0	20.1	28	14	3	0	8-0	5	5.31	75	.329	.387	0	—	0	69	18		1.7
1991	Bal A	2	7	.222	64	0	0	3-2	98.1	84	27	6	3	25-6	55	2.38	167	.236	.289	0	—	0		-15		-0.7
1992	Bal A	0	0	—	42	0	0	0-0	34.2	50	34	5	6	26-1	17	8.05	51	.338	.438	0	—	0	104	17	263	2.9
Total	18	167	143	.539	526	404	101-19	4-3	2770	2806	1301	251	41	890-41	1491	3.90	101	.266	.323	0	—	0	104	17	263	2.9
FLANIGAN, RAY					Raymond Arthur	B1.8.1923 Morgantown WV		D3.28.1993 Baltimore MD		BR/TR/6-0/190		d9.20												
1946	Cle A	0	1	.000	3	1	0	0	9	11	12	1	0	8	2	11.00	30	.289	.413	2	.500	1	78	-8		-0.7
FLANIGAN, TOM					Thomas Anthony	B9.6.1934 Cincinnati OH		BR/TL/6-3/175*		d4.14													
1954	Chi A	0	0	—	2	0	0	0	1.2	1	0	0	0	1	0	0.00	—	.200	.286	0	—	0		1		0.0
1958	StL N	0	0	—	1	0	0	0	1	2	1	1	0	1-0	0	9.00	46	.500	.600	0	—	0	0	0		0.0
Total	2	0	0	—	3	0	0	0	2.2	3	1	1	0	2-0	0	3.38	115	.333	.417	0	—	0		1		0.0
FLATER, JACK					John William	B9.22.1883 Sandymount MD		D3.20.1970 Westminster MD		BR/TR/5-10/175		d9.18												
1908	Phi A	1	3	.250	5	3	3	0	39.1	35	15	0	2	12	8	2.06	124	.252	.320	15-0-1	.133	-0	62	1		0.2
FLAVIN, JOHN					John Thomas	B5.7.1942 Albany CA		BL/TL/6-2/208		d8.25													
1964	Chi N	0	1	.000	4	0	0	0	4.2	11	7	0	0	3-1	5	13.50	28	.500	.538	1	.000	-0	95	-5		-0.9
FLEET, FRANK					Frank H.	B1848 New York NY		D6.13.1900 New York NY		d10.18 ▲													
1871	Mut NA	0	1	.000	1	1	1	0	9	20	21	0		3	0	10.00	38	.370	.404	6	.333	0	73	-6		-0.3
1873	Res NA	0	3	.000	3	3	2	0	24	57	47	0		0	3	5.25	64	.404	.404	89	.258	0*	53	-3		-0.2
1875	StL NA	2	1	.667	3	3	3	0	27	33	17	0		3	3	3.33	60	.277	.295	16	.063	-1*	140	-3		-0.3
	Atl NA	0	1	.000	2	1	1	0	15.1	26	20	0		0	1	4.70	44	.333	.333	111	.225	-0*	118	-4		-0.2
	Year	2	2	.500	5	4	4	0	42.1	59	37	0		3	4	3.83	53	.299	.310	127	.205	-1	134	-7		-0.5
Total	3 NA	2	6	.250	9	8	7	0	75.1	136	105	0		6	4	5.02	53	.347	.357	222	.230	-1	90	-16		-1.0
FLEMING, DAVE					David Anthony	B11.7.1969 Jackson Heights NY		BL/TL/6-3/200*		[SeaA90 3/79]		d8.6 Col Georgia											
1991	Sea A	1	0	1.000	9	3	0	0-0	17.2	19	13	3	3	3-0	11	6.62	63	.284	.342	0	—	0	132	-2		-0.2
1992	Sea A	17	10	.630	33	33	7-4	0-0	228.1	225	95	13	4	60-3	112	3.39	118	.257	.306	0	—	0	106	3	48	1.7
1993	Sea A	12	5	.706	26	26	1-1	0-0	167.1	189	84	15	6	67-6	75	4.36	103	.290	.357	0	—	0	104	-19		-2.3
1994	Sea A	7	11	.389	23	23	0	0-0	117	152	93	17	1	65-4	65	6.46	76	.311	.391	0	—	0	100	-14		-1.5
1995	Sea A	1	5	.167	16	7	1	0-1	48	57	44	15	0	34-3	26	7.50	64	.294	.394	0	—	0	54	3		0.1
	KC A	0	1	.000	9	5	0	0-0	32	27	17	4	2	19-1	14	3.66	131	.229	.343	0	—	0	81	-13		-1.4
	Year	1	6	.143	25	12	1	0-1	80	84	61	19	2	53-4	40	5.96	80	.269	.375	0	—	0	101	-16	48	-1.8
Total	5	38	32	.543	116	97	9-5	0-1	610.1	669	346	67	16	248-17	303	4.67	94	.279	.349	0	—	0	101	-16	48	-1.8
FLEMING, BILL					Leslie Fletchard	B7.31.1913 Rowland CA		BR/TR/6-0/190		d8.21 Mil 1945		Col St. Marys (CA)											
1940	Bos A	1	2	.333	10	6	1	0	46.1	53	27	4	2	20	24	4.86	93	.290	.366	13-0-2	.000	-2	94	-2		-0.3
1941	Bos A	1	1	.500	16	1	0	1	41.1	32	21	4	0	24	20	3.92	106	.212	.320	9	.222	1	125	1		0.1
1942	Chi N	5	6	.455	33	14	4-2	0	134.1	117	51	9	3	63	59	3.01	106	.230	.318	39-0-1	.051	-0	79	4		0.4
1943	Chi N	0	1	.000	11	0	0	0	32.1	41	24	2	3	12	12	6.40	54	.311	.381	8	.000	-1		-10		-0.5
1944	Chi N	9	10	.474	39	18	9-1	0	158.1	163	74	6	1	62	42	3.13	113	.269	.337	53-0-4	.170	-1*	104	4		0.4
1946	Chi N	0	1	.000	14	1	0	0	29.1	37	23	2	1	12	10	6.14	54	.301	.368	3	.000	-0	26	-9		-0.5
Total	6	16	21	.432	123	40	14-3	1	442	443	220	27	10	193	167	3.79	94	.260	.339	125-0-7	.104	-3	94	-12		-1.0
FLENER, HUCK					Gregory Alan	B2.25.1969 Austin TX		BB/TL/5-11/185*		[TorA90 9/258]		d9.14 Col Cal St.-Fullerton											
1993	Tor A	0	0	—	6	0	0	0-0	6.2	7	4	0	0	4-1	2	4.05	108	.269	.367	0	—	0		1		0.0
1996	Tor A	3	2	.600	15	11	0	0-0	70.2	68	40	9	1	33-1	44	4.58	109	.251	.330	0	—	0	89	3		-0.1
1997	Tor A	0	1	.000	8	1	0	0-0	17.1	40	18	3	0	6-0	9	9.87	47	.444	.474	0	—	0	60	-9		-0.5
Total	3	3	3	.500	29	12	0	0-0	94.2	115	62	12	1	43-2	55	5.51	89	.297	.365	0	—	0	88	-6		-0.3

YEAR	TM LG	W	L	PCT	G	GS	CG-SHO	SV-BS	IP	H	R	HR	HB	BB-IB	SO	ERA	AERA	OAV	OOB	AB-HR-SH	AVG	PB	SUP	APR	DL	PW

FLETCHER, VAN Alfred Vanoide B8.6.1924 East Bend NC BR/TR/6-2/185 d4.12

YEAR	TM LG	W	L	PCT	G	GS	CG-SHO	SV-BS	IP	H	R	HR	HB	BB-IB	SO	ERA	AERA	OAV	OOB	AB-HR-SH	AVG	PB	SUP	APR	DL	PW
1955	Det A	0	0	—	9	0	0	0	12	13	10	1	0	2-1	4	3.00	128	.260	.288	0	—	0		-1		0.0

FLETCHER, PAUL Edward Paul B1.14.1967 Gallipolis OH BR/TR/6-1/185* [PhiN88 40/1029] d7.11 Col West Virginia St.

YEAR	TM LG	W	L	PCT	G	GS	CG-SHO	SV-BS	IP	H	R	HR	HB	BB-IB	SO	ERA	AERA	OAV	OOB	AB-HR-SH	AVG	PB	SUP	APR	DL	PW
1993	Phi N	0	0	—	1	0	0	0-0	0.1	0	0	0	0	0-0	0	0.00	—	.000	.000	0	—	0		0		0.0
1995	Phi N	1	0	1.000	10	0	0	0-0	13.1	15	8	2	1	9-2	10	5.40	78	.288	.397	0	—	0		-1		-0.1
1996	Oak A	0	0	—	1	0	0	0-0	1.1	6	3	0	0	1-0	0	20.25	25	.667	.700	0	—	0		-2		-0.1
Total 3		1	0	1.000	12	0	0	0-0	15	21	11	2	1	10-2	10	6.60	65	.339	.432	0	—	0		-3		-0.2

FLETCHER, SAM Samuel S. B1881 Bedford PA TR/6-2/210 d10.6

YEAR	TM LG	W	L	PCT	G	GS	CG-SHO	SV-BS	IP	H	R	HR	HB	BB-IB	SO	ERA	AERA	OAV	OOB	AB-HR-SH	AVG	PB	SUP	APR	DL	PW
1909	Bro N	0	1	.000					9	13	8	0	0	2	5	8.00	32	.351	.385	3	.000	-0	108	-4		-0.4
1912	Cin N	0	0	—	2	0	0	0	9.2	15	15	1	0	11	3	12.10	28	.366	.500	4	.500	1		-8		-0.3
Total 2		0	1	.000	3	1	1		18.2	28	23	1	0	13	8	10.13	30	.359	.451	7	.286	0	108	-12		-0.7

FLETCHER, TOM Thomas Wayne B6.28.1942 Elmira NY BB/TL/6-0/170 d9.12 s-Darrin Col Illinois

YEAR	TM LG	W	L	PCT	G	GS	CG-SHO	SV-BS	IP	H	R	HR	HB	BB-IB	SO	ERA	AERA	OAV	OOB	AB-HR-SH	AVG	PB	SUP	APR	DL	PW
1962	Det A	0	0	—	1	0	0	0	1					2-0		0.00	—	.250	.400	0	—	0		1		0.0

FLINN, JOHN John Richard B9.2.1954 Merced CA BR/TR/6-0/175* [BalA73*S2/39] d5.6 Col Los Angeles Valley (CA) JC

YEAR	TM LG	W	L	PCT	G	GS	CG-SHO	SV-BS	IP	H	R	HR	HB	BB-IB	SO	ERA	AERA	OAV	OOB	AB-HR-SH	AVG	PB	SUP	APR	DL	PW
1978	Bal A	1	1	.500	13	0	0	0-1	15.2	24	18	3	0	13-3	8	8.04	44	.348	.446	0	—	0		-10		-1.1
1979	Bal A	1	0	1.000	4	0	0	0-0	2.2	2	0	0	1	1-0	0	0.00	—	.222	.273	0	—	0		1		0.1
1980	Mil A	2	1	.667	20	1	0	2-1	37	31	20	3	0	20-2	15	3.89	101	.220	.313	0	—	0	320	-1		0.1
1982	Bal A	2	0	1.000	5	0	0	0	13.2	13	3	1	0	3-1	13	1.32	308	.260	.302	0	—	0	320	4		0.5
Total 4		5	2	.714	42	1	0	2-2	69	70	41	7	0	37-6	36	4.17	92	.260	.345	0	—	0	320	-6		-0.6

FLITCRAFT, HILLY Hildreth Milton B8.21.1923 Woodstown NJ D4.2.2003 Boulder CO BL/TL/6-2/180 d8.31 Col Rutgers

YEAR	TM LG	W	L	PCT	G	GS	CG-SHO	SV-BS	IP	H	R	HR	HB	BB-IB	SO	ERA	AERA	OAV	OOB	AB-HR-SH	AVG	PB	SUP	APR	DL	PW
1942	Phi N	0	0	—	3	0	0	0	3.1	6	4	0	0	2	1	8.10	41	.429	.500	0	—	0		-2		-0.1

FLOHR, MORT Moritz Herman "Dutch" B8.15.1911 Canisteo NY D6.2.1994 Hornell NY BL/TL/6-0/173 d6.8 Col Duke

YEAR	TM LG	W	L	PCT	G	GS	CG-SHO	SV-BS	IP	H	R	HR	HB	BB-IB	SO	ERA	AERA	OAV	OOB	AB-HR-SH	AVG	PB	SUP	APR	DL	PW
1934	Phi A	0	2	.000	14	3	0	0	30.2	34	21	3	1	33	6	5.87	75	.296	.456	12	.333	1*	73	-5		-0.1

FLORENCE, DON Donald Emery B3.16.1967 Manchester NH BR/TL/6-0/195 d8.8 Col Crowder (MO) CC

YEAR	TM LG	W	L	PCT	G	GS	CG-SHO	SV-BS	IP	H	R	HR	HB	BB-IB	SO	ERA	AERA	OAV	OOB	AB-HR-SH	AVG	PB	SUP	APR	DL	PW
1995	NY N	3	0	1.000	14	0	0	0-0	12	17	3	1	0	6-0	5	1.50	269	.340	.411	1	.000	-0		3		0.6

FLORES, JESSE Jesse (Sandoval) B11.2.1914 Guadalajara, Jalisco, Mexico D12.17.1991 Orange CA BR/TR/5-10/175* d4.16

YEAR	TM LG	W	L	PCT	G	GS	CG-SHO	SV-BS	IP	H	R	HR	HB	BB-IB	SO	ERA	AERA	OAV	OOB	AB-HR-SH	AVG	PB	SUP	APR	DL	PW
1942	Chi N	0	1	.000	4	0	0	0	5.1	5	5	1	0	2	6	3.38	95	.227	.292	0	—	0		-1		-0.2
1943	Phi A	12	14	.462	31	27	13	0	231.1	208	88	13	5	70	113	3.11	109	.240	.301	80-0-5	.175	-0	82	9		1.0
1944	Phi A	9	11	.450	27	25	11-2	0	185.2	172	75	8	4	49	65	3.39	103	.245	.298	64-0-6	.172	-0	92	5		0.4
1945	Phi A	7	10	.412	29	24	9-4	1	191.1	180	79	6	4	63	52	3.43	100	.250	.314	61-0-7	.148	-2	103	2		-0.2
1946	Phi A	9	7	.563	29	15	8-4	1	155	147	51	6	1	38	48	2.32	153	.249	.295	44-0-5	.250	3	85	19		2.2
1947	Phi A	4	13	.235	28	20	4	0	151.1	139	72	10	0	59	41	3.39	112	.244	.315	44-0-2	.227	1	59	4		0.4
1950	Cle A	3	3	.500	28	2	1-1	4	53	53	24	3	1	25	27	3.74	116	.261	.345	11	.000	-2	73	4		0.2
Total 7		44	59	.427	176	113	46-11	6	973	904	394	49	15	306	352	3.18	112	.246	.307	304-0-25	.181	-0	84	42		3.8

FLORES, RANDY Randy Alan B7.31.1975 Bellflower CA BL/TL/6-0/180* [NYA97 9/289] d4.23 Col USC

YEAR	TM LG	W	L	PCT	G	GS	CG-SHO	SV-BS	IP	H	R	HR	HB	BB-IB	SO	ERA	AERA	OAV	OOB	AB-HR-SH	AVG	PB	SUP	APR	DL	PW
2002	Tex A	0	0	—	20	0	0	1-1	12	11	7	2	0	8-2	7	4.50	106	.268	.373	0	—	0		0		0.0
	Col N	0	2	.000	8	2	0	0-0	17	29	19	5	3	8-1	7	9.53	50	.382	.460	4	.000	-0	107	-8		-0.8
2004	StL N	1	0	1.000	9	1	0	0-0	14	13	3	0	3	3-1	7	1.93	221	.265	.339	2	.000	-0	195	4		0.2
2005	†StL N	3	1	.750	50	0	0	1-2	41.2	37	22	5	3	13-0	43	3.46	121	.240	.306	1	.000	-0	141	-2	15	0.1
Total 3		4	3	.571	87	3	0	2-3	84.2	90	51	12	9	32-4	64	4.57	96	.281	.357	7	.000	-1	141	-2	15	-0.5

FLORES, RON Ronald Joel B8.9.1979 Whittier CA BL/TL/5-11/190 d6.17 Col USC

YEAR	TM LG	W	L	PCT	G	GS	CG-SHO	SV-BS	IP	H	R	HR	HB	BB-IB	SO	ERA	AERA	OAV	OOB	AB-HR-SH	AVG	PB	SUP	APR	DL	PW
2005	Oak A	0	0	—	11	0	0	0-0	8.2	8	1	1	0	0-0	6	1.04	430	.235	.235	0	—	0		3		0.2

FLORIE, BRYCE Bryce Bettencourt B5.21.1970 Charleston SC BR/TR/5-11/190* [SDN88 5/110] d7.17

YEAR	TM LG	W	L	PCT	G	GS	CG-SHO	SV-BS	IP	H	R	HR	HB	BB-IB	SO	ERA	AERA	OAV	OOB	AB-HR-SH	AVG	PB	SUP	APR	DL	PW
1994	SD N	0	0	—	9	0	0	0-0	9.1	8	1	0	0	3-0		0.96	429	.242	.297	0	—	0		3		0.2
1995	SD N	2	2	.500	47	0	0	1-3	68.2	49	30	8	4	38-3	51	3.01	135	.202	.319	2	.000	-0		7		0.3
1996	SD N	2	2	.500	39	0	0	0-1	49.1	45	24	1	0	27-3	51	4.01	100	.239	.351	3	.000	-0		0		0.0
	Mil A	0	1	1.000	15	0	0	0-2	19	20	16	3	0	13-2	12	6.63	78	.270	.371	0	—	0		-3		-0.2
1997	Mil A	4	4	.500	32	8	0	0-1	75	74	43	4	3	42-2	53	4.32	107	.262	.360	0	—	0	87	1	18	0.0
1998	Det A	8	9	.471	42	16	0	0-0	133	141	80	16	4	59-6	97	4.80	99	.275	.354	3-0-1	.333	1	72	-2	27	-0.1
1999	Det A	2	1	.667	27	3	0	0-0	51.1	61	31	6	1	20-2	40	4.56	110	.292	.355	1	.000	-0	93	1	31	0.0
	Bos A	2	0	1.000	14	2	0	0-0	30	33	19	2	1	15-3	25	4.80	104	.282	.366	0	—	0	140	0		0.0
	Year	4	1	.800	41	5	0	0-0	81.1	94	50	8	2	35-5	65	4.65	107	.288	.359	1	.000	-0	112	1		0.0
2000	Bos A	0	4	.000	29	0	0	1-1	49.1	57	30	5	1	19-6	34	4.56	110	.294	.355	0	—	0		1	91	0.2
2001	Bos A	0	1	.000	7	0	0	0-0	8.2	12	11	1	0	7-3	7	11.42	39	.316	.422	0	—	0		6	87	-0.6
Total 8		20	24	.455	261	29	0	2-8	493.2	500	285	46	20	243-30	395	4.47	104	.265	.352	9-0-1	.111	0	85	2	254	-0.6

FLOWERS, BEN Bennett B6.15.1927 Wilson NC BR/TR/6-4/195* d9.29

YEAR	TM LG	W	L	PCT	G	GS	CG-SHO	SV-BS	IP	H	R	HR	HB	BB-IB	SO	ERA	AERA	OAV	OOB	AB-HR-SH	AVG	PB	SUP	APR	DL	PW
1951	Bos A	0	0	—	1	0	0	0	2	0	0	0	0	1	2	0.00	—	.200	.273	1	.000	-0		0		0.0
1953	Bos A	1	4	.200	32	6	1-1	3	79.1	87	39	6	1	24	36	3.86	109	.280	.333	19-0-1	.158	-0	74	3		0.2
1955	Det A	0	0	—	6	0	0	0	6	5	4	1	0	2-0	2	6.00	64	.238	.292	1	.000	-0		-1		-0.1
	StL N	1	0	1.000	4	4	0	0	27.1	27	12	1	0	12-0	19	3.62	112	.255	.328	10	.100	-1	104	1		0.0
1956	StL N	1	1	.500	3	1	0	0	11.2	15	9	1	0	5-1	5	6.94	54	.341	.392	3	.000	-0	147	-4		-0.5
	Phi N	0	2	.000	32	0	0	0	41	54	29	9	1	10-1	22	5.71	65	.331	.369	2	.000	-0		-9		-0.4
	Year	1	3	.250	35	1	0	0	52.2	69	38	10	1	15-2	27	5.98	62	.333	.374	5	.000	-0	149	-13		-0.9
Total 4		3	7	.300	76	13	1-1	3	168.1	190	93	18	2	54-2	86	4.49	90	.290	.343	36-0-1	.111	-2	100	-9		-0.8

FLOWERS, WES Charles Wesley B8.13.1913 Vanndale AR D12.31.1988 Wynne AR BL/TL/6-1.5/190 d8.8

YEAR	TM LG	W	L	PCT	G	GS	CG-SHO	SV-BS	IP	H	R	HR	HB	BB-IB	SO	ERA	AERA	OAV	OOB	AB-HR-SH	AVG	PB	SUP	APR	DL	PW
1940	Bro N	1	1	.500	5	2	0	0	21	23	10	2	3	10	8	3.43	117	.299	.400	5	.200	-0	54	1		0.1
1944	Bro N	1	1	.500	9	1	0	0	17.1	26	17	3	1	13	3	7.79	46	.333	.435	5	.600	1	212	-8		-0.7
Total 2		2	2	.500	14	3	0	0	38.1	49	27	5	4	23	11	5.40	70	.316	.418	10	.400	1	105	-7		-0.6

FLOYD, GAVIN Gavin Christopher B1.27.1983 Annapolis MD BR/TR/6-4/225* [PhiN01 1/4] d9.3

YEAR	TM LG	W	L	PCT	G	GS	CG-SHO	SV-BS	IP	H	R	HR	HB	BB-IB	SO	ERA	AERA	OAV	OOB	AB-HR-SH	AVG	PB	SUP	APR	DL	PW
2004	Phi N	2	0	1.000	6	4	0	0-0	28.1	25	11	1	5	16-0	24	3.49	127	.240	.368	10	.000	-1	115	3		0.1
2005	Phi N	1	2	.333	7	4	0	0-0	26	30	31	5	3	16-2	17	10.04	43	.283	.389	9	.111	-0	107	-16		-1.5
Total 2		3	2	.600	13	8	0	0-0	54.1	55	42	6	8	32-2	41	6.63	66	.262	.378	19	.053	-2	111	-13		-1.4

FLYNN, CARNEY Cornelius Francis Xavier B1.23.1875 Cincinnati OH D2.10.1947 Cincinnati OH BL/TL/5-11/165 d7.17

YEAR	TM LG	W	L	PCT	G	GS	CG-SHO	SV-BS	IP	H	R	HR	HB	BB-IB	SO	ERA	AERA	OAV	OOB	AB-HR-SH	AVG	PB	SUP	APR	DL	PW
1894	Cin N	0	2	.000	3	2	1	0	7.2	16	15	4	1	10		17.61	31	.421	.551	3	.000	-1	115	-8		-1.0
1896	NY N	0	2	.000	3	2	1	0	10.2	18	22	0	5	8	4	11.81	36	.367	.500	4-1-0	.500	2	177	-10		-1.1
	Was N	0	1	.000	4	1	1	0	20	43	31	0	2	10	3	8.55	52	.430	.491	6	.250	-0	97	-9		-0.4
	Year	0	3	.000	7	3	2	0	30.2	61	53	0	7	18	7	9.68	45	.409	.494	12-1-0	.333	1	147	-21		-1.5
Total		0	5	.000	9	4	2	0	38.1	77	68	4	8	28	11	11.27	41	.412	.507	15-1-0	.267	1	140	-27		-2.5

FLYNN, JOCKO John A. B6.30.1864 Lawrence MA D12.31.1907 Lawrence MA BR/TR/5-6.5/143 d5.1

YEAR	TM LG	W	L	PCT	G	GS	CG-SHO	SV-BS	IP	H	R	HR	HB	BB-IB	SO	ERA	AERA	OAV	OOB	AB-HR-SH	AVG	PB	SUP	APR	DL	PW
1886	Chi N	23	6	.793	32	29	28-2	1	257	207	127	9		63	146	2.24	161	.210	.257	205-4	.200	1*	122	32		3.3

FLYTHE, STU Stuart McGuire B12.5.1911 Conway NC D10.18.1963 Durham NC BR/TR/6-2/175 d5.31 Col North Carolina St.

YEAR	TM LG	W	L	PCT	G	GS	CG-SHO	SV-BS	IP	H	R	HR	HB	BB-IB	SO	ERA	AERA	OAV	OOB	AB-HR-SH	AVG	PB	SUP	APR	DL	PW
1936	Phi A	0	0	—	17	3	0	0	39.1	49	63	4	3	61	6	13.04	39	.302	.500	15	.267	0	172	-33		-1.4

FODGE, GENE Gene Arlan "Suds" B7.9.1931 South Bend IN BR/TR/6-0/175 d4.20

YEAR	TM LG	W	L	PCT	G	GS	CG-SHO	SV-BS	IP	H	R	HR	HB	BB-IB	SO	ERA	AERA	OAV	OOB	AB-HR-SH	AVG	PB	SUP	APR	DL	PW
1958	Chi N	1	1	.500	16	4	1	0	39.2	47	22	5	0	11-3	15	4.76	82	.296	.337	7-0-1	.000	-1	132	-3		-0.2

FOGARTY, JIM James G. B2.12.1864 San Francisco CA D5.20.1891 Philadelphia PA BR/TR/5-10.5/180 d5.1 M1 b-Joe Col St. Marys (CA) ▲

YEAR	TM LG	W	L	PCT	G	GS	CG-SHO	SV-BS	IP	H	R	HR	HB	BB-IB	SO	ERA	AERA	OAV	OOB	AB-HR-SH	AVG	PB	SUP	APR	DL	PW
1884	Phi N	0	0	—	1				1	2	2	0	0			0.00	—	.333		378-1	.212	0*		0		0.0
1886	Phi N	0	1	.000	3	2	1	0	6	7	6	0	0	4		9.00	—	.250	.250	280-3	.293	0*		0		0.0
1887	Phi N	0	0	—	1	1	0	0	3	4	4	0	0	1		9.00	47	.200	.250	495-8	.261	0*		-1		-0.1
1889	Phi N	0	0	—	4	0	0	0	4	4	4	0	0			9.00	48	.333	.250	499-3	.259	1*		-1		-0.1
Total 4		0	1	.000					14	16	16	0	0	5		4.50	84	.246	.279	1652-15	.254	2		-2		-0.1

YEAR	TM LG	W	L	PCT	G	GS	CG-SHO	SV-BS	IP	H	R	HR	HB	BB-IB	SO	ERA	AERA	OAV	OOB	AB-HR-SH	AVG	PB	SUP	APR	DL	PW
1985	†StL N	9	6	.600	34	19	3-1	2-0	136	132	63	11	2	47-4	48	3.90	92	.258	.322	45-1-2	.244	4	117	-3		0.0
1986	StL N	14	10	.583	33	33	3	0-0	230	211	91	19	2	68-11	104	3.25	114	.247	.301	76-2-11	.171	3*	104	12		1.5
1987	†StL N	11	7	.611	33	30	2-1	0-0	179	189	90	15	4	45-4	89	4.32	97	.273	.318	57-2-11	.298	8*	121	-1		0.7
1988	StL N	9	4	.692	30	12	1-1	0-0	108.2	111	51	8	1	38-8	40	3.73	95	.270	.330	25-0-5	.280	2*	97	-3		-0.2
	Hou N	1	4	.200	6	6		0-0	27.2	42	22	2	2	6-1	14	6.51	51	.359	.385	7-0-1	.143	0	62	-10		-1.5
	Year	10	8	.556	36	18	1-1	0-0	136.1	153	73	10	3	44-9	54	4.29	81	.290	.342	32-0-6	.250	2	85	-12		-1.7
1989	Hou N	4	5	.444	37	15		0-0	108.1	133	68	10	1	46-6	40	5.32	64	.303	.367	24-0-6	.167	-0	107	-22		-1.8
Total	16	168	136	.553	498	422	67-19	3-2	2794.2	2777	1319	216	45	832-84	1133	3.76	98	.261	.315	893-12-115	.213	47	106	-21	94	2.9

FORSTER, SCOTT Scott Christian B10.27.1971 Philadelphia PA BR/TL/6-1/194 [MonN94 6/168] d6.18 Col James Madison

YEAR	TM LG	W	L	PCT	G	GS	CG-SHO	SV-BS	IP	H	R	HR	HB	BB-IB	SO	ERA	AERA	OAV	OOB	AB-HR-SH	AVG	PB	SUP	APR	DL	PW
2000	Mon N	0	1	.000	42	0	0	2-1	32	28	31	5	2	25-1	23	7.88	60	.230	.362	0	—	0		-11		-0.5

FORSTER, TERRY Terry Jay B1.14.1952 Sioux Falls SD BL/TL/6-3/210(185-230) [ChiA70 2/30] d4.11

YEAR	TM LG	W	L	PCT	G	GS	CG-SHO	SV-BS	IP	H	R	HR	HB	BB-IB	SO	ERA	AERA	OAV	OOB	AB-HR-SH	AVG	PB	SUP	APR	DL	PW
1971	Chi A	2	3	.400	45	3	0	1-0	49.2	46	23	5	1	23-3	48	3.99	89	.241	.323	5	.400	1	75	-1		0.0
1972	Chi A	6	5	.545	62	0	0	29-6	100	75	31	0	3	44-3	104	2.25	139	.208	.296	19-0-2	.526	4*	8			2.1
1973	Chi A	6	11	.353	51	12	4	16-3	172.2	174	69	7	0	78-6	120	3.23	122	.266	.342	1	.000	-0*	68	14		1.8
1974	Chi A	7	8	.467	59	1	0	24-10	134.1	120	57	6	8	48-3	105	3.62	104	.245	.319	0	—	0	24	4		0.7
1975	Chi A	3	3	.500	17	1	0	4-3	37	30	12	0	0	24-4	32	2.19	178	.236	.358	0	—	0	136	6	101	1.2
1976	Chi A	2	12	.143	29	16	1	1-0	111.1	126	61	7	1	41-4	70	4.37	82	.288	.350	0	—	0	82	-11		-1.2
1977	Pit N	6	4	.600	33	6	0	1-2	87.1	90	47	7	2	32-3	58	4.43	91	.269	.332	26-0-1	.346	3*	77	-3		-0.1
1978	†LA N	5	4	.556	47	0	0	22-4	65.1	56	19	2	0	23-4	46	1.93	182	.233	.300	8-0-1	.500	2	10			2.2
1979	LA N	1	2	.333	17	0	0	2-0	16.1	18	11	0	0	11-4	8	5.51	66	.295	.397	0	—	0	1		100	-0.2
1980	LA N	0	0	—	9	0	0	0-0	11.2	10	4	0	0	4-0	2	3.09	113	.222	.286	0	—	0	1		123	-0.1
1981	†LA N	0	1	.000	21	0	0	0-1	30.2	37	14	1	0	15-3	17	4.11	80	.308	.385	2	.000	-0	-2			-0.1
1982	LA N	5	6	.455	56	0	0	3-2	83	66	38	3	4	31-9	52	3.04	114	.221	.298	2	.000	-0	1			0.2
1983	Atl N	3	2	.600	56	0	0	13-3	79.1	60	19	3	2	31-9	54	2.16	179	.217	.301	8-0-1	.500	2	15			1.8
1984	Atl N	2	0	1.000	25	0	0	5-0	26.2	30	9	1	0	7-3	10	2.70	143	.297	.339	3	.667	1	3		79	0.4
1985	Atl N	2	3	.400	46	0	0	1-2	59.1	49	22	7	0	28-4	37	2.28	169	.222	.307	4-0-1	.000	-0	8		55	0.4
1986	Cal A	4	1	.800	41	0	0	5-3	47	48	23	2	3	17-1	28	3.51	118	.297	.374	0	—	0	3	55	458	0.4
Total	16	54	65	.454	614	39	5	127-39	1105.2	1034	454	51	24	457-63	791	3.23	115	.251	.327	78-0-6	.397	11	77	53	458	9.5

FORTUGNO, TIM Timothy Shawn B4.11.1962 Clinton MA BL/TL/6-1/185* d7.20 Col Vanguard

YEAR	TM LG	W	L	PCT	G	GS	CG-SHO	SV-BS	IP	H	R	HR	HB	BB-IB	SO	ERA	AERA	OAV	OOB	AB-HR-SH	AVG	PB	SUP	APR	DL	PW
1992	Cal A	1	1	.500	14	5	1-1	1-0	41.2	37	24	5	0	19-0	31	5.18	78	.236	.316	0	—	0	127	-4		-0.2
1994	Cin N	1	0	1.000	25	0	0	0-0	30	32	14	2	3	14-0	29	4.20	100	.288	.380	3	.333	0	1			-0.3
1995	Chi A	1	3	.250	37	0	0	0-1	38.2	30	24	7	0	19-2	24	5.59	80	.213	.302	0	—	0		-4		-0.3
Total	3	3	4	.429	76	5	1-1	1-1	110.1	99	62	14	3	52-2	84	5.06	84	.242	.329	3	.333	0	127	-7		-0.8

FORTUNATO, BARTOLOME Bartolome B8.24.1974 Santo Domingo, D.R. BR/TR/6-1/195 d6.29 [DL 2005 NY N 183]

YEAR	TM LG	W	L	PCT	G	GS	CG-SHO	SV-BS	IP	H	R	HR	HB	BB-IB	SO	ERA	AERA	OAV	OOB	AB-HR-SH	AVG	PB	SUP	APR	DL	PW
2004	TB A	0	0	—	3	0	0	0-0	7.1	10	3	1	0	2-0	5	3.68	127	.357	.400	0	—	0	1			0.1
	NY N	1	0	1.000	15	0	0	1-1	18.2	14	8	2	0	13-0	20	3.86	111	.203	.329	0	—	0	1			0.1
Total	1	1	0	1.000	18	0	0	1-1	26	24	11	3	0	15-0	25	3.81	116	.247	.348	0	—	0	2	183		0.1

FORTUNE, GARY Garrett Reese B10.11.1894 High Point NC D9.23.1955 Washington DC BB/TR/5-11.5/176 d10.5

YEAR	TM LG	W	L	PCT	G	GS	CG-SHO	SV-BS	IP	H	R	HR	HB	BB-IB	SO	ERA	AERA	OAV	OOB	AB-HR-SH	AVG	PB	SUP	APR	DL	PW
1916	Phi N	0	1	.000	1	1	0	0	5	2	2	0	0	4	3	3.60	74	.118	.286	2	.000	-0	28	0		-0.1
1918	Phi N	0	2	.000	5	2	1	0	31	41	30	2	1	19	10	8.13	37	.333	.427	10	.200	-0	114	-14		-0.8
1920	Bos A	0	2	.000	14	3	1	0	41.2	46	32	0	0	23	10	5.83	63	.282	.371	12	.167	-0	94	-11		-0.9
Total	3	0	5	.000	20	6	2	0	77.2	89	64	2	1	46	23	6.61	51	.294	.389	24	.167	-0	89	-25		-1.8

FOSNOW, JERRY Gerald Eugene B9.21.1940 Deshler OH BR/TL/6-4/195* d6.29

YEAR	TM LG	W	L	PCT	G	GS	CG-SHO	SV-BS	IP	H	R	HR	HB	BB-IB	SO	ERA	AERA	OAV	OOB	AB-HR-SH	AVG	PB	SUP	APR	DL	PW
1964	Min A	0	1	.000	7	0	0	0	10.2	13	13	3	0	8-0	9	10.97	33	.302	.404	0	—	0	-8			-0.1
1965	Min A	3	3	.500	29	0	0	2	46.2	33	29	7	1	25-2	35	4.44	80	.193	.299	5	.000	-1	-5			-0.5
Total	2	3	4	.429	36	0	0	2	57.1	46	42	10	1	33-2	44	5.65	65	.215	.321	5	.000	-1	-13			-0.6

FOSS, LARRY Larry Curtis B4.18.1936 Castleton KS BR/TR/6-2/195* d9.18 Col Wichita St.

YEAR	TM LG	W	L	PCT	G	GS	CG-SHO	SV-BS	IP	H	R	HR	HB	BB-IB	SO	ERA	AERA	OAV	OOB	AB-HR-SH	AVG	PB	SUP	APR	DL	PW
1961	Pit N	1	1	.500	3	3	0	0	15.1	15	11	3	2	11-0	9	5.87	68	.273	.406	6	.167	-0	96	-3		-0.2
1962	NY N	0	1	.000	5	1	0	0	11.2	17	6	2	1	7-0	3	4.63	90	.362	.446	1	.000	-0	126	0		-0.1
Total	2	1	2	.333	8	4	0	0	27	32	17	5	3	18-0	12	5.33	76	.314	.424	7	.143	-0	103	-3		-0.3

FOSSAS, TONY Emilio Antonio (Morejon) B9.23.1957 Havana, Cuba BL/TL/6-0/187(187-198) [TexA79 12/303] d5.15 Col South Florida

YEAR	TM LG	W	L	PCT	G	GS	CG-SHO	SV-BS	IP	H	R	HR	HB	BB-IB	SO	ERA	AERA	OAV	OOB	AB-HR-SH	AVG	PB	SUP	APR	DL	PW
1988	Tex A	0	0	—	5	0	0	0-0	5.2	11	3	0	0	2-0	5	4.76	86	.423	.464	0	—	0	0			0.4
1989	Mil A	2	2	.500	51	0	0	1-2	61	57	27	3	1	22-7	42	3.54	109	.256	.321	0	—	0	2			0.4
1990	Mil A	2	3	.400	32	0	0	0-2	29.1	44	23	5	0	10-2	24	6.44	60	.331	.375	0	—	0	-8			-1.3
1991	Bos A	3	2	.600	64	0	0	1-1	57	49	27	3	1	28-9	29	3.47	125	.236	.335	0	—	0	4			0.4
1992	Bos A	1	2	.333	60	0	0	2-1	29.2	31	9	1	1	14-3	19	2.43	175	.279	.365	0	—	0	6			0.4
1993	Bos A	1	1	.500	71	0	0	0-2	40	38	28	4	0	15-4	39	5.17	90	.242	.314	0	—	0	-3			-0.5
1994	Bos A	2	0	1.000	44	0	0	1-0	34	35	18	6	5	15-1	31	4.76	106	.263	.342	0	—	0	2			0.1
1995	StL N	3	0	1.000	58	0	0	0-0	36.2	28	6	1	1	10-3	40	1.47	291	.214	.273	0	—	0	12			0.9
1996	†StL N	0	4	.000	65	0	0	2-5	47	43	19	7	0	21-3	36	2.68	158	.231	.308	1	.000	-0	6			0.4
1997	StL N	2	7	.222	71	0	0	0-1	51.2	62	32	7	1	26-3	41	3.83	109	.298	.377	0	—	0	-5			-0.4
1998	Sea A	0	3	.000	23	0	0	0-1	11.1	19	11	1	0	6-0	10	8.74	54	.404	.463	0	—	0	-2			-0.3
	Chi N	0	0	—	8	0	0	0-0	4	8	4	0	0	6-0	4	9.00	49	.421	.560	0	—	0	-2			-0.2
	Tex A	1	0	1.000	10	0	0	0-0	7.1	3	0	0	0	4-0	7	0.00	—	.120	.241	0	—	0	4			0.4
1999	NY A	0	0	—	5	0	0	0-0	2	6	4	1	0	1-1	0	36.00	13	.667	.700	0	—	0	-3			-0.2
Total	12	17	24	.415	567	0	0	7-15	415.2	434	211	39	10	180-36	324	3.90	110	.269	.344	1	.000	-0	14			0.8

FOSSUM, CASEY Casey Paul B1.6.1978 Cherry Hill NJ BL/TL/6-1/160* [BosA99 1/48] d7.28 Col Texas A&M-Commerce

YEAR	TM LG	W	L	PCT	G	GS	CG-SHO	SV-BS	IP	H	R	HR	HB	BB-IB	SO	ERA	AERA	OAV	OOB	AB-HR-SH	AVG	PB	SUP	APR	DL	PW
2001	Bos A	3	2	.600	13	7	0	0-0	44.1	44	26	4	6	20-1	26	4.87	91	.259	.355	0	—	0	119	-2		-0.2
2002	Bos A	5	4	.556	43	12	0	1-0	106.2	113	56	12	4	30-0	101	3.46	129	.268	.320	0	—	0*	97	7		0.2
2003	Bos A	6	5	.545	19	14	0	1-0	79	82	55	9	4	34-0	63	5.47	85	.270	.348	0	—	0	137	-8	39	-0.9
2004	Ari N	4	15	.211	27	27	0	0-0	142	171	111	31	10	63-5	117	6.65	69	.302	.379	42-0-3	.095	-2*	65	-28	40	-3.2
2005	TB A	8	12	.400	36	25	0	0-1	162.2	170	100	21	18	60-3	128	4.92	89	.266	.343	2-0-1	.000	-0	89	-11		-1.0
Total	5	26	38	.406	138	85	0	2-1	534.2	580	348	77	42	207-9	435	5.17	87	.276	.350	44-0-4	.091	-2	93	-42	79	-5.1

FOSTER, ALAN Alan Benton B12.8.1946 Pasadena CA BR/TR/6-0/180* [LAN65 2/28] d4.25

YEAR	TM LG	W	L	PCT	G	GS	CG-SHO	SV-BS	IP	H	R	HR	HB	BB-IB	SO	ERA	AERA	OAV	OOB	AB-HR-SH	AVG	PB	SUP	APR	DL	PW
1967	LA N	0	1	.000	4	2	0		16.2	10	4	0	0	3-0	15	2.16	143	.169	.210	4	.000	-0	28	2		0.2
1968	LA N	1	1	.500	3	3	0	0	15.2	11	4	1	0	2-0	10	1.72	161	.200	.228	4	.250	0	63	2		0.1
1969	LA N	3	9	.250	24	15	2-2	0-0	102.2	119	55	11	4	29-4	59	4.38	76	.290	.341	27-0-3	.074	-1	93	-12		-1.1
1970	LA N	10	13	.435	33	33	7-1	0-0	198.2	200	104	22	2	81-2	83	4.26	90	.264	.334	64-0-8	.109	-2	112	-10		-1.1
1971	Cle A	8	12	.400	36	26	3	0	181.2	158	93	19	4	82-5	97	4.16	93	.232	.316	51-0-7	.039	-4*	69	-6		-1.1
1972	Cal A	0	1	.000	9	4	0	0-1	12.2	12	8	3	2	6-0	11	4.97	59	.245	.351	0		0	-3			-0.0
1973	StL N	13	9	.591	35	29	6-2	0-0	203.2	195	82	17	5	63-3	106	3.14	117	.254	.313	68-0-5	.191	-1	107	12		1.0
1974	StL N	7	10	.412	31	25	5-1	0-0	162.1	167	81	16	3	61-7	92	3.88	93	.268	.335	48-0-7	.167	-1*	94	-6		-0.6
1975	SD N	3	1	.750	17	4	1	0-0	44.2	41	14	1	0	21-5	20	2.42	145	.244	.326	11	.091	-1*	94	6	71	0.6
1976	SD N	3	6	.333	26	11	2	0-0	86.2	75	39	6	1	35-2	22	3.22	102	.235	.311	18-0-3	.056	-0*	73	0	71	0.2
Total	10	48	63	.432	217	148	26-6	0-1	1025.1	988	481	99	21	383-28	501	3.74	97	.254	.322	295-0-34	.119	-8	94	-15	71	-1.6

FOSTER, ED Eddy Lee "Slim" B GA D3.1.1929 Montgomery AL BR/TR/6-1/? d7.31

YEAR	TM LG	W	L	PCT	G	GS	CG-SHO	SV-BS	IP	H	R	HR	HB	BB-IB	SO	ERA	AERA	OAV	OOB	AB-HR-SH	AVG	PB	SUP	APR	DL	PW
1908	Cle A	1	0	1.000	6	1	1	2	21	16	5	1	2	12	11	2.14	111	.229	.357	6	.000	-0	143	1		0.3

FOSTER, RUBE George B1.5.1888 Lehigh OK D3.1.1976 Bokoshe OK BR/TR/5-7.5/170 d4.10

YEAR	TM LG	W	L	PCT	G	GS	CG-SHO	SV-BS	IP	H	R	HR	HB	BB-IB	SO	ERA	AERA	OAV	OOB	AB-HR-SH	AVG	PB	SUP	APR	DL	PW
1913	Bos A	3	3	.500	19	8	4-1	0	68.1	64	35	1	4	28	36	3.16	93	.252	.336	21	.095	-1*	88	-2		-0.2
1914	Bos A	14	8	.636	32	27	17-5	0	211.2	164	68	2	7	52	89	1.70	158	.218	.274	63-0-5	.175	0*	89	18		2.5
1915	†Bos A	19	8	.704	37	33	21-5	1	255.1	217	83	3	10	86	82	2.11	131	.237	.310	83-1-9	.277	7*	105	19		2.8
1916	†Bos A	14	7	.667	33	19	9-3	2	182.1	173	73	0	4	66	53	3.06	90	.263	.352	62-0-2	.177	0*	98	-5		0.5
1917	Bos A	8	7	.533	17	16	9-1	0	124.2	108	43	0	4	53	34	2.53	102	.243	.329	41-0-3	.268	2	110	2		0.7
Total	5	58	33	.637	138	103	60-15	3	842.1	726	302	6	29	305	294	2.36	116	.240	.316	270-1-19	.215	9	99	32		6.8

YEAR	TM LG	W	L	PCT	G	GS	CG-SHO	SV-BS	IP	H	R	HR	HB	BB-IB	SO	ERA	AERA	OAV	OOB	AB-HR-SH	AVG	PB	SUP	APR	DL	PW
FOSTER, KRIS	John Kristian	B8.30.1974 Riverdale NJ		BR/TR/6-1/200		[MonN92 39/1079]	d8.3	Col Edison (FL) CC						[DL 2000 LA N 181]												
2001	Bal A	0	0	—	7	0	0	0-0	10	9	4	1	0	8-0	8	2.70	160	.231	.362	0	—	0	2			0.1
FOSTER, JOHN	John Norman	B5.17.1978 Stockton CA		BL/TL/6-0/200(180-200)		[AtlN99 25/774]	d4.24	Col Lewis-Clark St.																		
2002	Atl N	1	0	1.000	5	0	0	0-0	5	6	6	3	1	6-0	6	10.80	37	.286	.464	0	—	0	-4	43		-0.6
2003	Mil N	2	0	1.000	23	0	0	0-2	21	30	11	5	1	8-2	16	4.71	92	.341	.398	0	—	0	-1			-0.1
2005	†Atl N	4	2	.667	62	0	0	1-1	34.2	27	17	3	2	19-0	32	4.15	103	.213	.324	0	—	0	0			0.1
Total	3	7	2	.778	90	0	0	1-3	60.2	63	34	11	4	33-2	54	4.90	87	.267	.365	0	—	0	-5	43		-0.6
FOSTER, KEVIN	Kevin Christopher	B1.13.1969 Evanston IL		BR/TR/6-1/170(160-175)		[MonN87 29/746]	d9.12	Col Kishwaukee (IL) CC																		
1993	Phi N	0	1	.000	2	1	0	0-0	6.2	13	11	4	0	7-0	6	14.85	27	.394	.500	2	.000	-0	23	-8		-0.8
1994	Chi N	3	4	.429	13	13	0	0-0	81	70	31	7	1	35-1	75	2.89	146	.234	.315	27-0-3	.074	-2	81	11		0.6
1995	Chi N	12	11	.522	30	28	0	0-0	167.2	149	90	32	6	65-4	146	4.51	93	.240	.315	60-1-5	.250	5*	117	-4		-0.1
1996	Chi N	7	6	.538	17	16	1	0-0	87	98	63	16	2	35-3	53	6.21	70	.288	.354	27-0-3	.296	5*	103	-16		-1.5
1997	Chi N	10	7	.588	26	25	1	0-0	146.1	141	79	27	2	66-4	118	4.61	94	.255	.333	47-0-11	.128	-1*	106	-4	15	-0.6
1998	Chi N	0	0	—	3	0	0	0-0	3.1	8	6	1	0	2-0	3	16.20	17	.500	.500	0	—	0	-4	70		-0.2
2001	Tex A	0	1	.000	9	0	0	0-0	17.2	21	14	2	3	10-0	16	6.62	72	.309	.415	0	—	0	-3			-0.2
Total	7	32	30	.516	100	83	2	0-0	509.2	500	294	88	14	220-12	417	4.86	88	.259	.336	163-1-22	.190	7	104	-28	85	-2.8
FOSTER, LARRY	Larry Lynn	B12.24.1937 Lansing MI		BL/TR/6-0/185		d9.18	Col Michigan St.																			
1963	Det A	0	0	—	1	0	0	0	2	4	3	0	0	1	1	13.50	28	.364	.417	0	—	0	-2			-0.1
FOSTER, STEVE	Stephen Eugene	B8.16.1966 Dallas TX		BR/TR/6-0/180*		[CinN88 12/306]	d8.22	Col Texas-Arlington	[DL 1994 Cin N 131]																	
1991	Cin N	0	0	—	11	0	0	0-0	14	7	5	1	0	4-0	11	1.93	197	.143	.208	0	—	0	2			0.1
1992	Cin N	1	1	.500	31	1	0	2-1	50	52	16	4	0	13-1	34	2.88	125	.275	.319	5	.200	0	25	5		0.3
1993	Cin N	2	2	.500	17	0	0	0-0	25.2	23	8	1	0	5-2	16	1.75	230	.235	.279	0-0-1	—	0	5	134		0.3
Total	3	3	3	.500	59	1	0	2-1	89.2	82	29	6	1	22-3	61	2.41	156	.244	.291	5-0-1	.200	0	25	12	265	1.1
FOUCAULT, STEVE	Steven Raymond	B10.3.1949 Duluth MN		BL/TR/6-0/205(180-205)		[TexA69 43/910]	d4.7	Col South Georgia JC																		
1973	Tex A	2	4	.333	32	0	0	8-6	55.2	54	26	6	3	31-4	28	3.88	97	.262	.364	0	—	0	0	59	0.0
1974	Tex A	8	9	.471	69	0	0	12-8	144.1	123	51	8	5	40-5	106	2.24	160	.234	.291	0	—	0	17		2.3
1975	Tex A	8	4	.667	59	0	0	10-9	107	96	57	10	4	55-15	56	4.12	92	.249	.344	0	—	0	-4		-0.6
1976	Tex A	8	8	.500	46	0	0	5-5	75.2	68	31	9	4	25-7	41	3.33	108	.249	.318	0	—	0	3		0.7
1977	Det A	7	7	.500	44	0	0	13-5	74.1	64	29	7	0	17-4	58	3.15	137	.226	.270	0	—	0	9		1.8
1978	Det A	2	4	.333	24	0	0	4-0	37.1	48	18	1	1	21-4	18	3.13	124	.324	.405	0	—	0	1		0.2
	KC A	0	0	—	3	0	0	0-0	2.1	5	1	0	0	1-1	0	3.86	99	.417	.462	0	—	0	0		0.0
	Year	2	4	.333	27	0	0	4-0	39.2	53	19	1	1	22-5	18	3.18	123	.331	.409	0	—	0	2		0.2
Total	6	35	36	.493	277	0	0	52-33	496.2	458	213	41	17	190-40	307	3.18	118	.250	.323	0	—	0	26	59		4.4
FOULKE, KEITH	Keith Charles	B10.19.1972 San Diego CA		BR/TR/6-0/200(195-210)		[SFN94 9/256]	d5.21	Col Lewis-Clark St.																		
1997	SF N	1	5	.167	11	8	0	0-1	44.2	60	41	9	4	18-1	33	8.26	50	.324	.396	13-0-2	.154	-0	70	-19		-2.0
	Chi A	3	0	1.000	16	0	0	3-2	28.2	28	11	4	0	5-1	21	3.45	128	.255	.284	0	—	0	4		0.4
1998	Chi A	3	2	.600	54	0	0	1-1	65.1	51	31	9	4	21-4	57	4.13	111	.213	.283	0	—	0	4	31	0.3
1999	Chi A	3	3	.500	67	0	0	9-4	105.1	72	28	11	3	21-4	123	2.22	222	.188	.235	2	.000	-0	32		2.0
2000	†Chi A	3	1	.750	72	0	0	34-5	88	66	31	9	2	22-2	91	2.97	171	.207	.261	0	—	0	21		2.1
2001	Chi A	4	9	.308	72	0	0	42-3	81	57	21	9	8	22-1	75	2.33	200	.199	.274	0	—	0	21		4.2
2002	Chi A	2	4	.333	65	0	0	11-3	77.2	65	26	7	2	13-2	58	2.90	156	.225	.263	1	.000	0	14		1.3
2003	†Oak A★	9	1	.900	72	0	0	43-5	86.2	57	21	10	7	20-2	88	2.08	221	.184	.249	0	—	0	24		4.8
2004	†Bos A	5	3	.625	72	0	0	32-7	83	63	22	8	6	15-5	79	2.17	225	.206	.254	0	—	0	24		3.8
2005	Bos A	5	5	.500	43	0	0	15-4	45.2	53	30	8	5	18-1	34	5.91	78	.288	.365	0	—	0	-5	58	-1.1
Total	9	38	33	.535	544	8	0	190-35	706	572	262	78	41	174-22	659	3.23	146	.219	.277	16-0-2	.125	-1	70	120	89	15.8
FOURNIER, HENRY	Julius Henry "Frenchy"	B8.8.1865 Syracuse NY	D12.8.1945 Detroit MI	TL		d8.22																				
1894	Cin N	1	3	.250	6	4	0	0	45	71	51	4	2	30	5	5.40	103	.353	.417	19	.105	-3	73	-4		-0.4
FOUTZ, DAVE	David Luther "Scissors"	B9.7.1856 Carroll Co. MD	D3.5.1897 Waverly MD	BR/TR/6-2/161		d7.29 M4	b-Frank ▲																			
1884	StL AA	15	6	.714	25	25	19-2	0	206.2	167	100	7	9	36	95	2.18	150	.212	.255	119	.227	1*	100	22		2.2
1885	†StL AA	33	14	.702	47	46	46-2	0	407.2	351	200	8	18	92	147	2.63	125	.227	.278	238	.248	5*	114	29		3.5
1886	†StL AA	41	16	.719	59	57	55-11	1	504	418	216	8	10	144	283	**2.11**	**163**	.216	.274	414-3	.280	11*	112	71		**7.6**
1887	†StL AA	25	12	.676	40	38	36-1	0	339.1	369	244	7	10	90	94	3.87	117	.258	.306	423-4	.357	15*	123	16		2.4
1888	Bro AA	12	7	.632	23	19	19	0	176	146	85	9	5	35	73	2.51	119	.218	.262	563-3	.277	6*	92	10		1.5
1889	†Bro AA	3	0	1.000	12	4	3	0	59.2	70	50	2	0	19	21	4.37	85	.283	.335	553-6	.275	3*	158	-7		-0.1
1890	†Bro N	2	1	.667	5	2	2	2	29	29	10	0	1	6	4	1.86	185	.252	.295	509-5	.303	2*	46	5		0.6
1891	Bro N	3	2	.600	6	5	5	0	52	51	24	1	1	16	14	3.29	100	.246	.304	521-2	.257	1*	98	2		-0.6
1892	Bro N	13	8	.619	27	20	17	1	203	210	119	3	4	63	56	3.41	93	.256	.313	220-1	.186	0*	122	-9		-0.6
1893	Bro N	0	0	—	2	1	0	0	18	28	17	2	0	8	3	7.50	59	.346	.404	557-7	.246	1*	-5			-0.1
1894	Bro N	0	0	—	1	0	0	0	2	4	3	0	1	1	0	13.50	37	.400	.455	297-0-8	.303	0*	-2			-0.1
Total	11	147	66	.690	251	216	202-16	4	1997.1	1843	1068	38	58	510	790	2.84	124	.235	.286	4414-31-8	.276	45	113	132		17.2
FOWLER, JESSE	Jesse Peter "Pete"	B10.30.1898 Spartanburg SC	D9.23.1973 Columbia SC	BR/TL/5-10.5/158		d7.29 b-Art																				
1924	StL N	1	1	.500	13	5	1	0	32.2	22	17	2	2	18	5	4.41	86	.226	.333	9	.222	0	82	-3		-0.2
FOWLER, ART	John Arthur	B7.3.1922 Converse SC		BR/TR/5-11/180*		d4.17 C15 b-Jesse																				
1954	Cin N	12	10	.545	40	29	8-1	0	227.2	256	112	20	4	85	93	3.83	109	.286	.348	60-0-12	.100	-1	90	7		0.4
1955	Cin N	11	10	.524	46	28	8-3	2	207.2	198	96	20	1	63-3	94	3.90	109	.250	.350	60-0-7	.200	-0	83	10		0.9
1956	Cin N	11	11	.500	45	23	8	1	177.2	191	92	15	0	35-3	86	4.05	98	.278	.311	48-0-5	.146	-0	92	-3		-0.3
1957	Cin N	3	0	1.000	33	7	1	0	87.2	111	65	11	2	24-2	45	6.47	64	.310	.355	17-0-3	.176	0	156	-20		-1.0
1959	LA N	3	4	.429	36	0	0	2	61	70	39	8	0	23-7	47	5.31	80	.294	.350	12-0-1	.083	-1	-6			-0.8
1961	LA A	5	8	.385	53	3	0	11	89	68	42	12	0	29-3	78	3.64	124	.209	.272	13-0-3	.077	-1	72	7		1.0
1962	LA A	4	3	.571	48	0	0	5	77	67	25	6	1	25-3	38	2.81	138	.234	.296	11	.273	-1	11			1.1
1963	LA A	5	3	.625	57	0	0	10	89.1	70	26	5	0	19-8	53	2.42	142	.219	.260	9-0-2	.222	0	11			1.3
1964	LA A	0	2	.000	4	0	0	1	7	8	8	4	1	5-2	5	10.29	32	.296	.424	1	.000	0	-5			-1.0
Total	9	54	51	.514	362	90	25-4	32	1024	1039	505	99	9	308-31	539	4.03	102	.265	.317	231-0-33	.152	-2	94	12		1.6
FOWLER, DICK	Richard John	B3.30.1921 Toronto ON, Can.	D5.22.1972 Oneonta NY	BR/TR/6-4.5/215(195-215)		d9.13 Mil 1943-45																				
1941	Phi A	1	2	.333	4	3	1	0	24	26	11	4	0	8-0	13	8.38	124	.289	.347	.000	-1	131	2			0.1
1942	Phi A	6	11	.353	31	17	4	1	140	159	90	13	0	45	38	4.95	76	.287	.341	50-0-1	.160	-1*	65	-17		-2.1
1945	Phi A	1	2	.333	7	3	2-1	0	37.1	41	21	1	0	18	21	4.82	71	.283	.362	18	.444	3*	33	-5		-0.1
1946	Phi A	9	16	.360	32	28	14-1	0	205.2	213	101	16	2	75	89	3.28	108	.263	.327	71-0-2	.183	-1	75	0		-0.1
1947	Phi A	12	11	.522	36	31	16-3	0	227.1	210	77	12	3	85	75	2.81	136	.249	.319	82-0-4	.171	-3	105	26		2.1
1948	Phi A	15	8	.652	29	26	16-2	0	204.2	221	93	15	4	76	75	3.78	113	.281	.348	82-1-4	.171	-2	113	12		0.9
1949	Phi A	15	11	.577	31	28	15-4	1	213.2	210	108	19	4	76	43	3.75	110	.262	.357	77-0-2	.234	3	102	5		0.9
1950	Phi A	1	5	.167	11	9	2	0	66.2	75	52	7	3	56	15	6.48	70	.300	.434	26	.192	-1	59	-14		-1.1
1951	Phi A	5	11	.313	22	22	4	0	125	141	89	11	1	72	29	5.62	76	.291	.384	42-0-1	.190	-0	96	-19		-2.1
1952	Phi A	2	2	.333	18	3	1	0	58.2	71	43	4	4	28	14	6.44	61	.302	.386	15	.000	-2	44	-13		-0.8
Total	10	66	79	.455	221	170	75-11	4	1303	1367	663	102	19	578	382	4.11	97	.273	.351	472-1-14	.186	-6	92	-23		-2.2
FOWLKES, ALAN	Alan Kim	B8.8.1958 Brawley CA		BR/TR/6-2/190*		[SFN80 10/241]	d4.7	Col Cal Poly-Pomona	[DL 1983 SF N 17]																	
1982	SF N	4	2	.667	21	15	1	0-0	85	111	55	14	2	24-3	50	5.19	69	.321	.366	26-0-2	.115	-1	108	-15		-1.1
1985	Cal A	0	0	—	2	0	0	0-0	7	8	7	4	0	4-0	5	9.00	46	.276	.364	0	—	0	-3	39		-0.2
Total	2	4	2	.667	23	15	1	0-0	92	119	62	16	3	28-3	55	5.48	66	.317	.365	26-0-2	.115	-1	108	-18	56	-1.3
FOX, CHAD	Chad Douglas	B9.3.1970 Coronado CA		BR/TR/6-3/194(175-210)		[CinN92 23/633]	d7.13	Col Tarleton St.	[DL 2000 Mil N 181]																	
1997	Atl N	0	1	.000	30	0	0	0-1	27.1	24	12	4	0	16-0	28	3.29	128	.231	.333	0	—	0	2			0.1
1998	Mil N	1	4	.200	49	0	0	0-2	57	56	27	4	1	20-0	64	3.95	110	.260	.326	3-0-1	.000	-0	3	52		0.1
1999	Mil N	0	0	—	6	0	0	0-0	6.2	11	8	1	0	6-1	8	10.80	43	.355	.444	0	—	0	-4	166		-0.2
2001	Mil N	5	2	.714	65	0	0	2-2	66.2	44	16	6	3	36-7	80	1.89	227	.181	.298	3	.000	-0	18			1.7

YEAR	TM LG	W	L	PCT	G	GS	CG-SHO	SV-BS	IP	H	R	HR	HB	BB-IB	SO	ERA	AERA	OAV	OOB	AB-HR-SH	AVG	PB	SUP	APR	DL	PW
2002	Mil N	1	0	1.000	3	0	0	0-0	4.2	6	3	0	0	5-1	3	5.79	71	.316	.458	0	—	0		-1	175	-0.2
2003	Bos A	1	2	.333	17	0	0	3-2	18	19	10	2	1	17-2	19	4.50	104	.264	.407	0	—	0		0	62	0.0
	†Fla N	2	1	.667	21	0	0	0-0	25.1	16	6	1	0	14-2	27	2.13	192	.190	.294	0	—	0		6		0.6
2004	Fla N	0	1	.000	12	0	0	0-2	10.2	9	8	1	1	8-0	17	6.75	61	.225	.367	0	—	0		-3	159	-0.1
2005	Chi N	0	0	—	11	0	0	1-0	8	8	6	2	0	8-0	11	6.75	65	.276	.421	0	—	0		-2	160	-0.1
Total	8	10	11	.476	214	0	0	6-9	224.1	193	96	21	9	128-12	261	3.57	120	.231	.336	7-0-1	.000	-1		19	955	1.8

FOX, HENRY Henry (b Henry Fuchs) B11.18.1874 Scranton PA D6.6.1927 Scranton PA d9.4

YEAR	TM LG	W	L	PCT	G	GS	CG-SHO	SV-BS	IP	H	R	HR	HB	BB-IB	SO	ERA	AERA	OAV	OOB	AB-HR-SH	AVG	PB	SUP	APR	DL	PW
1902	Phi N	0	0	—	1	1	1	0	1	2	3	0	0	1	1	18.00	16	.400	.500	0	—	0		-2		-0.3

FOX, HOWIE Howard Francis B3.1.1921 Coburg OR D10.9.1955 San Antonio TX BR/TR/6-3/210(195-210) d9.28 Col Oregon

YEAR	TM LG	W	L	PCT	G	GS	CG-SHO	SV-BS	IP	H	R	HR	HB	BB-IB	SO	ERA	AERA	OAV	OOB	AB-HR-SH	AVG	PB	SUP	APR	DL	PW
1944	Cin N	0	0	—	2	0	0	0	2.1	0	0	0	0	0	0	0.00	—	.222	.222	1	.000	-0		1		0.0
1945	Cin N	8	13	.381	45	15	7	0	164.1	169	102	6	6	77	54	4.93	76	.268	.353	46-0-5	.283	3	93	-21		-1.9
1946	Cin N	0	0	—	4	0	0	0	5	12	13	2	0	5	1	18.00	19	.462	.548	0		0		-9		-0.4
1948	Cin N	6	9	.400	34	24	5	1	171	185	100	11	1	62	63	4.53	86	.280	.343	60-0-1	.200	1*	93	-13		-0.8
1949	Cin N	6	19	.240	38	30	9	0	215	221	120	13	4	77	60	3.98	105	.265	.330	72-0-6	.236	2*	79	0		0.4
1950	Cin N	11	8	.579	34	22	10-1	1	187	196	97	14	2	85	64	4.33	98	.269	.347	63-1-3	.175	-0*	88	0		0.1
1951	Cin N	9	14	.391	40	30	9-4	2	228	239	105	16	2	69	57	3.83	107	.272	.326	70-1-8	.114	-2	74	10		0.7
1952	Phi N	2	7	.222	13	11	2	0	62	70	41	8	0	26	16	5.08	72	.287	.356	21-0-3	.048	-2	120	-10		-1.4
1954	Bal A	1	2	.333	38	0	0	2	73.2	80	33	2	2	34	27	3.67	98	.289	.366	16	.250	1		0		0.1
Total	9	43	72	.374	248	132	42-5	6	1108.1	1174	611	72	17	435	342	4.33	92	.274	.343	349-2-26	.189	2	87	-42		-3.2

FOX, JOHN John Joseph B2.7.1859 Roxbury MA D4.18.1893 Boston MA d6.2

YEAR	TM LG	W	L	PCT	G	GS	CG-SHO	SV-BS	IP	H	R	HR	HB	BB-IB	SO	ERA	AERA	OAV	OOB	AB-HR-SH	AVG	PB	SUP	APR	DL	PW
1881	Bos N	6	8	.429	17	16	12	0	124.1	144	90	0		39	30	3.33	80	.279	.329	118	.178	-4*	85	-11		-1.3
1883	Bal AA	6	13	.316	20	19	18	0	165.1	209	140	2		32	49	4.03	86	.289	.320	92	.152	-4*	82	-9		-1.1
1884	Pit AA	1	6	.143	7	7	7	0	59	76	59	2	3	16	22	5.64	59	.291	.339	25	.240	0*	60	-15		-1.3
1886	Was N	0	1	.000	1	1	1	0	8	11	13	0		11	3	9.00	36	.314	.478	3	.333	-1	57	-5		-0.4
Total	4	13	28	.317	45	43	38	0	356.2	440	302	4	3	98	104	4.16	76	.287	.331	238	.176	-7	79	-40		-4.1

FOX, TERRY Terrence Edward B7.31.1935 Chicago IL BR/TR/6-0/175* d9.4

YEAR	TM LG	W	L	PCT	G	GS	CG-SHO	SV-BS	IP	H	R	HR	HB	BB-IB	SO	ERA	AERA	OAV	OOB	AB-HR-SH	AVG	PB	SUP	APR	DL	PW
1960	Mil N	0	0	—	5	0	0	0	8.1	6	5	0	0	6-0	5	4.32	79	.200	.333	1	.000	-0		-1		-0.1
1961	Det A	5	2	.714	39	0	0	12	57.1	42	12	6	3	16-1	32	1.41	290	.200	.265	12-0-1	.167	-0		16		2.6
1962	Det A	3	1	.750	44	0	0	16	58	48	13	2	1	16-6	23	1.71	238	.227	.283	8-0-1	.250	2*		15		2.1
1963	Det A	8	6	.571	46	0	0	11	80.1	81	37	9	2	20-5	35	3.59	104	.263	.310	11-0-1	.091	-0		1		0.2
1964	Det A	4	3	.571	32	0	0	5	61	77	26	4	1	16-1	28	3.39	108	.316	.357	12	.250	1		1		0.3
1965	Det A	6	4	.600	42	0	0	10	77.2	59	26	7	3	31-2	34	2.78	125	.214	.298	15-0-4	.000	-1		6		0.9
1966	Det A	0	1	.000	4	0	0	1	10	9	8	3	0	2-0	6	6.30	55	.243	.282	3	.000	-0*		-3		-0.4
	Phi N	3	2	.600	36	0	0	4	44.1	57	22	3	2	17-8	22	4.47	80	.322	.384	3-0-1	.000	-0*		-3		-0.3
Total	7	29	19	.604	248	0	0	59	397	379	149	34	12	124-23	185	2.99	125	.254	.314	65-0-8	.123	1		32		5.2

FOXEN, BILL William Aloysius B5.31.1884 Tenafly NJ D4.17.1937 Brooklyn NY BL/TL/5-11.5/165 d5.5 Col St. Peters

YEAR	TM LG	W	L	PCT	G	GS	CG-SHO	SV-BS	IP	H	R	HR	HB	BB-IB	SO	ERA	AERA	OAV	OOB	AB-HR-SH	AVG	PB	SUP	APR	DL	PW
1908	Phi N	7	7	.500	22	16	10-2	0	147.1	126	45	2	8	53	52	1.95	124	.240	.319	53-0-1	.094	-3	113	7		0.5
1909	Phi N	3	7	.300	18	7	5-1	0	83.1	65	40	4	0	32	37	3.35	78	.219	.303	24-1-0	.208	3	65	-6		-0.1
1910	Phi N	5	5	.500	16	9	5	0	77.2	73	30	2	3	40	33	2.55	123	.268	.368	23-0-1	.174	-1	71	5		0.6
	Chi N	0	0	—	2	0	0	0	5	7	5	0	0	3	2	9.00	32	.350	.435	2	.000	-0		-3		-0.2
	Year	5	5	.500	18	9	5	0	82.2	80	35	2	3	43	35	2.94	106	.274	.373	25-0-1	.160	-1	72	1		0.4
1911	Chi N	1	1	.500	3	1	0	0	13	12	6	0	0	12	6	2.08	159	.255	.407	4	.250	1	113	1		0.3
Total	4	16	20	.444	61	33	20-3	0	326.1	283	126	4	15	140	130	2.56	104	.244	.333	106-1-2	.142	0	90	4		1.1

FOXX, JIMMIE James Emory "Beast","Double X" B10.22.1907 Sudlersville MD D7.21.1967 Miami FL BR/TR/6-0/195 d5.1.1925 C1 HF1951 ▲

YEAR	TM LG	W	L	PCT	G	GS	CG-SHO	SV-BS	IP	H	R	HR	HB	BB-IB	SO	ERA	AERA	OAV	OOB	AB-HR-SH	AVG	PB	SUP	APR	DL	PW
1939	Bos A☆	0	0	—	1	0	0	0	1	0	0	0	0	0	1	0.00	—	.000	.000	467-35-5	.360	1*		1		0.0
1945	Phi N	1	0	1.000	9	2	0	0	22.2	13	4	0	1	14	10	1.59	241	.171	.308	224-7-1	.268	2*	77	6		0.4
Total	2	1	0	1.000	10	2	0	0	23.2	13	4	0	1	14	11	1.52	254	.165	.298	691-42-6	.330	3	77	7		0.4

FOYTACK, PAUL Paul Eugene B11.16.1930 Scranton PA BR/TR/5-11/180* d4.21

YEAR	TM LG	W	L	PCT	G	GS	CG-SHO	SV-BS	IP	H	R	HR	HB	BB-IB	SO	ERA	AERA	OAV	OOB	AB-HR-SH	AVG	PB	SUP	APR	DL	PW
1953	Det A	0	0	—	6	0	0	0	9.2	15	12	1	1	9	7	11.17	36	.375	.500	1	.000	-0		-7		-0.4
1955	Det A	0	1	.000	22	1	0	0	49.2	48	29	4	0	36-3	38	5.26	73	.259	.375	11	.091	-1	139	-6		-0.4
1956	Det A	15	13	.536	43	33	16-1	1	256	211	114	24	2	142-4	184	3.59	115	.226	.327	90-0-6	.122	-6	122	16		0.9
1957	Det A	14	11	.560	38	27	8-1	1	212	175	79	19	4	104-12	118	3.14	123	.226	.318	63-0-12	.222	1	81	17		1.3
1958	Det A	15	13	.536	39	34	16-2	1	230	198	98	23	3	77-1	135	3.44	117	.233	.298	75-0-7	.240	2	97	14		1.8
1959	Det A	14	14	.500	39	37	11-2	1	240.1	239	137	34	2	64-3	110	4.64	87	.259	.307	81-0-6	.111	-4	106	-12		-1.7
1960	Det A	2	11	.154	28	13	1	2	96.2	108	70	11	0	49-3	38	6.14	64	.286	.366	25-0-2	.280	2*	96	-21	35	-2.4
1961	Det A	11	10	.524	32	20	6	0	169.2	152	81	27	2	56-0	89	3.93	104	.238	.300	54-1-6	.222	2	112	5		-0.7
1962	Det A	10	7	.588	29	21	5-1	0	143.2	145	80	18	0	86-2	63	4.39	93	.259	.306	42-0-2	.143	-3	105	-5		-0.7
1963	Det A	0	1	.000	9	0	0	0	17.2	18	18	4	0	8-0	7	8.66	43	.265	.338	4	.000	-0		-9		-0.3
	LA A	5	5	.500	25	8	0	0	70.1	68	35	9	0	29-6	37	3.71	92	.255	.326	15-0-2	.267	1*	84	-3		-0.3
	Year	5	6	.455	34	8	0	0	88	86	53	13	0	37-6	44	4.70	74	.257	.328	19-0-2	.211	1	83	-13		-0.5
1964	LA A	0	1	.000	12	0	0	0	2.1	4	4	2	0	2-1	1	15.43	21	.364	.462	0	—	0		-3		-0.6
Total	11	86	87	.497	312	193	63-7	7	1498	1381	757	176	15	662-35	827	4.14	97	.246	.324	461-1-43	.178	-3	103	-14	35	-1.9

FRAILING, KEN Kenneth Douglas B1.19.1948 Marion WI BL/TL/6-0/190* [ChiA66 5/98] d9.1 [DL 1977 Chi N 96]

YEAR	TM LG	W	L	PCT	G	GS	CG-SHO	SV-BS	IP	H	R	HR	HB	BB-IB	SO	ERA	AERA	OAV	OOB	AB-HR-SH	AVG	PB	SUP	APR	DL	PW
1972	Chi A	1	0	1.000	4	0	0	0-0	3	3	1	0	1	1-0	1	3.00	104	.250	.308	0	—	0		0		0.0
1973	Chi A	0	0	—	10	0	0	0-0	18.1	18	6	1	1	7-0	15	1.96	201	.254	.325	0	—	0		3		0.2
1974	Chi N	6	9	.400	55	16	1	1-1	125.1	150	65	11	4	43-10	71	3.88	99	.296	.351	31-0-4	.258	1*	87	-1		-1.0
1975	Chi N	2	5	.286	41	0	0	1-1	53	61	37	6	2	26-2	39	5.43	71	.293	.374	7-0-1	.143	-0		-9		-0.8
1976	Chi N	1	2	.333	6	3	0	0-0	18.2	20	7	1	0	5-0	10	2.41	161	.290	.316	3-0-1	.000	-0	45	2	20	-0.1
Total	5	10	16	.385	116	19	1	2-2	218.1	252	116	19	4	82-12	136	3.96	97	.290	.351	41-0-6	.220	1	80	-5	116	-0.5

FRANCE, OSSIE Osman Beverly "O. B." B10.4.1858 Greensburg OH D5.2.1947 Akron OH BL/TL/5-8/155 d7.14

YEAR	TM LG	W	L	PCT	G	GS	CG-SHO	SV-BS	IP	H	R	HR	HB	BB-IB	SO	ERA	AERA	OAV	OOB	AB-HR-SH	AVG	PB	SUP	APR	DL	PW
1890	Chi N	0	0	—	1	0	0	0	2	3	3	0	0	2	0	13.50	27	.333	.455	1	.000	-0		-2		-0.

FRANCIS, EARL Earl Coleman B7.14.1935 Slab Fork WV D7.3.2002 Pittsburgh PA BR/TR/6-2/215* d6.30

YEAR	TM LG	W	L	PCT	G	GS	CG-SHO	SV-BS	IP	H	R	HR	HB	BB-IB	SO	ERA	AERA	OAV	OOB	AB-HR-SH	AVG	PB	SUP	APR	DL	PW
1960	Pit N	1	0	1.000	7	0	0	0	18	14	5	0	1	4-0	8	2.00	188	.222	.275	5	.000	-1		3		0.
1961	Pit N	2	8	.200	23	15	0	0	102.2	110	60	4	4	47-7	53	4.21	95	.274	.348	28	.107	-1	88	-5		-0.
1962	Pit N	9	8	.529	36	23	5-1	0	176	153	68	8	2	83-10	121	3.07	128	.235	.322	61-1-3	.164	1	92	18		1.
1963	Pit N	4	6	.400	33	13	0	0	97.1	107	59	6	4	43-11	72	4.53	73	.284	.361	26	.308	3*	82	-13		-0.
1964	Pit N	0	1	.000	2	1	0	0	6.1	7	7	2	1	1-0	6	8.53	41	.269	.321	1	.000	-0	0	-4		-0.
1965	StL N	0	0	—	2	0	0	0	5.1	7	4	1	0	3-2	3	5.06	76	.318	.385	1	.000	2		-1		-0.
Total	6	16	23	.410	103	52	5-1	0	405.2	398	203	21	9	181-30	263	3.77	100	.258	.337	122-1-3	.172	2	87	-12		-0.

FRANCIS, JEFF Jeffrey William B1.8.1981 Vancouver BC, Can. BL/TL/6-5/200* [ColN02 1/9] d8.25 Col British Columbia

YEAR	TM LG	W	L	PCT	G	GS	CG-SHO	SV-BS	IP	H	R	HR	HB	BB-IB	SO	ERA	AERA	OAV	OOB	AB-HR-SH	AVG	PB	SUP	APR	DL	PW
2004	Col N	3	2	.600	7	7	0	0-0	36.2	42	22	8	1	13-1	32	5.15	92	.286	.346	10-0-4	.000	-1	111	-1		-0.
2005	Col N	14	12	.538	33	33	0	0-0	183.2	228	119	26	8	70-5	128	5.68	84	.311	.372	58-0-6	.103	-1	112	-15		-2.
Total	2	17	14	.548	40	40	0	0-0	220.1	270	141	34	9	83-6	160	5.60	85	.306	.368	68-0-10	.088	-2	112	-16		-2.

FRANCIS, RAY Ray James B3.8.1893 Sherman TX D7.6.1934 Atlanta GA BL/TL/6-1.5/182 d4.18

YEAR	TM LG	W	L	PCT	G	GS	CG-SHO	SV-BS	IP	H	R	HR	HB	BB-IB	SO	ERA	AERA	OAV	OOB	AB-HR-SH	AVG	PB	SUP	APR	DL	PW
1922	Was A	7	18	.280	39	26	15-2	2	225	265	136	7	6	66	64	4.28	90	.303	.356	78-0-3	.167	-2	85	-13		-1.
1923	Det A	5	8	.385	33	6	0	1	79.1	95	51	2	4	28	27	4.42	87	.308	.374	21	.143	-2*	96	-7		-1.
1925	NY A	0	0	—	6	4	0	0	4.2	5	4	3	1	8	4	7.71	55	.278	.409	0		0		-2		-0.
	Bos A	0	2	.000	6	4	0	0	28	44	29	3	1	13	4	7.71	59	.373	.439	8	.125	-0	79	-9		-0.
	Year	0	2	.000	10	4	0	0	32.2	49	33	3	2	16	5	7.71	58	.348	.435	8	.125	-0	79	-11		-0.
Total	3	12	28	.300	82	36	15-2	3	337	409	220	12	12	110	96	4.65	84	.310	.368	107-0-3	.159	-4	86	-31		-3.

FRANCISCO, FRANK Franklin B9.11.1979 Santo Domingo, D.R. BR/TR/6-2/180 d5.14 [DL 2005 Tex A 183]

YEAR	TM LG	W	L	PCT	G	GS	CG-SHO	SV-BS	IP	H	R	HR	HB	BB-IB	SO	ERA	AERA	OAV	OOB	AB-HR-SH	AVG	PB	SUP	APR	DL	PW
2004	Tex A	5	1	.833	45	0	0	0-3	51.1	36	19	4	3	28-2	60	3.33	148	.198	.313	0	—	0		9		0.

YEAR	TM LG	W	L	PCT	G	GS	CG-SHO	SV-BS	IP	H	R	HR	HB	BB-IB	SO	ERA	AERA	OAV	OOB	AB-HR-SH	AVG	PB	SUP	APR	DL	PW

FRANCO, JOHN John Anthony B9.17.1960 Brooklyn NY   BL/TL/5-10/185(170-188)   [LAN81 5/125] d4.24 Col St. Johns [DL 2002 NY N 183]

1984	Cin N	6	2	.750	54	0	0	4-5	79.1	74	28	3	2	36-4	55	2.61	145	.256	.338	3-0-1	.000	-0		9		0.9
1985	Cin N	12	3	.800	67	0	0	12-3	99	83	27	5	1	40-8	61	2.18	174	.234	.313	6-0-2	.333	0		17		3.0
1986	Cin N☆	6	6	.500	74	0	0	29-9	101	90	40	7	2	44-12	84	2.94	131	.242	.323	4	.000	-0		9		1.5
1987	Cin N★	8	5	.615	68	0	0	32-9	82	76	26	6	0	27-6	61	2.52	167	.245	.304	2	.000	0		15		2.9
1988	Cin N	6	6	.500	70	0	0	39-3	86	60	18	3	0	27-3	46	1.57	227	.198	.263	1	.000	0		18		4.0
1989	Cin N☆	4	8	.333	60	0	0	32-7	80.2	77	35	3	0	36-8	60	3.12	128	.258	.334	3	.333	-0		3		0.7
1990	NY N★	5	3	.625	55	0	0	33-6	67.2	66	22	4	0	21-2	56	2.53	149	.252	.306	5	.000	-1		9		1.9
1991	NY N	5	9	.357	52	0	0	30-5	55.1	61	27	2	1	18-4	45	2.93	125	.271	.328	1	.000	-0		2		0.4
1992	NY N	6	2	.750	31	0	0	15-2	33	24	6	1	0	11-2	20	1.64	214	.209	.273	1	.000	-0		7	73	1.7
1993	NY N	4	3	.571	35	0	0	10-7	36.1	46	24	6	1	19-3	29	5.20	77	.313	.393	1	.000	-0		-5	43	-0.9
1994	NY N	1	4	.200	47	0	0	30-6	50	47	20	2	1	19-0	42	2.70	155	.244	.313	3	.000	-0		7		1.3
1995	NY N	5	3	.625	48	0	0	29-7	51.2	48	17	4	0	17-2	41	2.44	166	.251	.311	0	—	0		9		1.8
1996	NY N	4	3	.571	51	0	0	28-8	54	54	15	2	0	21-0	48	1.83	220	.260	.328	1	.000	-0		13		2.6
1997	NY N	5	3	.625	59	0	0	36-6	60	49	18	3	1	20-2	53	2.55	157	.226	.293	0	—	0		11		2.2
1998	NY N	0	8	.000	61	0	0	38-8	64.2	66	28	4	4	29-7	59	3.62	114	.267	.347	2	.000	-0		3		0.8
1999	†NY N	0	2	.000	46	0	0	19-2	40.2	40	14	1	2	19-1	41	2.88	151	.255	.341	0	—	0		7	63	0.8
2000	†NY N	5	4	.556	62	0	0	4-0	55.2	46	24	6	2	26-6	56	3.40	129	.221	.314	1	.000	0		6		0.9
2001	NY N	6	2	.750	58	0	0	2-5	53.1	55	25	8	2	19-2	50	4.05	100	.264	.330	0	—	0		1		0.1
2003	NY N	0	3	.000	38	0	0	2-1	34.1	35	11	5	1	13-2	16	2.62	160	.265	.333	0	—	0		6	61	0.6
2004	NY N	2	7	.222	52	0	0	0-1	46	46	28	6	1	24-2	36	5.28	81	.258	.346	0	—	0		-4		-0.7
2005	Hou N	0	1	.000	31	0	0	0-1	25	23	15	4	0	9-2	16	7.20	58	.343	.429	0	—	0		-5		-0.3
Total 21		90	87	.508	1119	0	0	424-101	1245.2	1166	466	81	22	495-78	975	2.89	137	.249	.322	34-0-3	.088	-2		138	423	26.2

FRANKHOUSE, FRED Frederick Meloy B4.9.1904 Port Royal PA D8.17.1989 Mifflintown PA BR/TR/5-11/175 d9.7

1927	StL N	5	1	.833	6	6	5-1	0	50	41	18	2	1	16	20	2.70	146	.218	.283	20-0-1	.250	0*	133	7		0.8
1928	StL N	3	2	.600	21	10	1	1	84	91	47	6	5	36	29	3.96	101	.277	.358	27-0-2	.185	1*	133	-1		0.1
1929	StL N	7	2	.778	30	10	6	1	133.1	149	70	9	4	43	37	4.12	113	.289	.349	52-1-2	.288	4*	140	8		0.9
1930	StL N	2	3	.400	8	1	0	0	19.2	31	16	1	0	11	4	7.32	69	.373	.447	5	.000	-1*	17	-4		-0.7
	Bos N	7	6	.538	27	11	3-1	0	110.2	138	72	13	2	43	30	5.61	88	.313	.377	39-0-1	.359	4	82	-6		-0.2
	Year	9	9	.500	35	12	3-1	0	130.1	169	88	14	2	54	34	5.87	84	.323	.388	44-0-1	.318	3	76	-10		-0.9
1931	Bos N	8	8	.500	26	15	5	1	127.1	125	64	4	3	43	50	4.03	94	.252	.315	40-0-1	.150	-0	71	-3		-0.3
1932	Bos N	4	6	.400	37	6	3	0	108.2	113	56	7	3	45	35	3.56	106	.278	.355	30-0-2	.100	-1*	101	0		0.0
1933	Bos N	16	15	.516	43	30	14-2	2	244.2	249	97	12	3	77	83	3.16	97	.267	.324	80-0-7	.237	-4*	102	-2		0.4
1934	Bos N★	17	9	.654	37	30	13-2	1	233.2	239	102	10	4	77	78	3.20	120	.262	.322	85-0-7	.200	2	114	14		1.6
1935	Bos N	11	15	.423	40	29	10-1	0	230.2	278	147	12	6	81	64	4.76	80	.293	.352	76-0-1	.263	6	109	-29		-1.9
1936	Bro N	13	10	.565	41	31	9-1	2	234.1	236	112	18	3	89	84	3.65	113	.257	.325	91-0-1	.143	-4*	93	13		0.8
1937	Bro N	10	13	.435	33	25	9-1	0	179.1	214	104	8	4	78	64	4.27	95	.297	.369	58-0-7	.190	-0*	105	-4		-0.3
1938	Bro N	3	5	.375	30	8	2-1	0	93.2	92	48	6	4	44	32	4.04	97	.256	.344	26-0-3	.154	-1*	71	-1		-0.1
1939	Bro N	0	2	.000	23	0	0	4	38	37	16	3	1	18	12	2.61	142	.253	.339	7	.000	-1	3		0.1
Total 13		106	97	.522	402	212	81-10	12	1888	2033	969	111	43	701	622	3.92	100	.275	.341	636-1-35	.208	12	102	-5		1.2

FRANKLIN, WAYNE Gary Wayne B3.9.1974 Wilmington DE BL/TL/6-2/195* [LAN96 36/1078] d7.24 Col Maryland-Baltimore Co.

2000	Hou N	0	0	—	25	0	0	0-0	21.1	24	14	2	4	12-1	21	5.48	89	.282	.388	2	.000	-0		-1		-0.1
2001	Hou N	0	0	—	11	0	0	0-0	12	17	9	4	0	9-0	9	6.75	68	.333	.433	0	—	0		-2		-0.1
2002	Mil N	2	1	.667	4	4	0	0-0	24	16	8	1	0	17-1	17	2.63	157	.188	.324	6	.000	-0	62	4		0.5
2003	Mil N	10	13	.435	36	34	1-1	0-0	194.2	201	129	36	10	94-2	116	5.50	78	.268	.355	59-0-12	.169	-0	113	-26		-2.7
2004	SF N	2	1	.667	43	2	0	0-1	50.2	55	37	11	3	22-2	40	6.39	68	.281	.359	3	.333	1	160	-10	20	-0.5
2005	NY A	0	1	.000	13	0	0	0-3	12.2	11	12	1	1	8-0	10	6.39	68	.239	.357	0	—	0		-4		-0.3
Total 6		14	16	.467	132	40	1-1	0-4	315.1	324	209	55	18	162-6	213	5.51	79	.267	.359	70-0-12	.157	-0	109	-39	20	-3.2

FRANKLIN, JACK Jack Wilford B10.20.1919 Paris IL D11.15.1991 Panama City FL BR/TR/5-11.5/170 d6.12 Col Illinois

| 1944 | Bro N | 0 | 0 | — | 2 | 0 | 0 | 0-0 | 2 | 4 | 3 | 1 | 1 | 2 | 0 | 13.50 | 26 | .250 | .571 | 0 | — | 0 | | -2 | | -0.1 |

FRANKLIN, JAY John William B3.16.1953 Arlington VA BR/TR/6-2/185 [SDN71 1/2] d9.4

| 1971 | SD N | 0 | 1 | .000 | 3 | 1 | 0 | 0-0 | 5.2 | 5 | 5 | 3 | 0 | 4-0 | 4 | 6.35 | 52 | .250 | .375 | 1 | .000 | -0 | 53 | -2 | | -0.3 |

FRANKLIN, RYAN Ryan Ray B3.5.1973 Fort Smith AR BR/TR/6-3/165(165-180) [SeaA92 23/642] d5.15 Col Seminole St. (OK) JC

1999	Sea A	0	0	—	6	0	0	0-0	11.1	10	6	2	1	8-1	9	4.76	101	.238	.373	0	—	0		0		0.0
2001	Sea A	5	1	.833	38	0	0	0-1	78.1	76	32	13	4	24-4	60	3.56	120	.250	.311	0	—	0		7		0.5
2002	Sea A	7	5	.583	41	12	0	0-1	118.2	117	62	14	5	22-1	65	4.02	107	.255	.294	0	—	0	81	1	17	0.1
2003	Sea A	11	13	.458	32	32	2-1	0-0	212	199	93	34	9	61-3	99	3.57	121	.251	.310	4-0-1	.250	0	99	17		1.6
2004	Sea A	4	16	.200	32	32	2-1	0-0	200.1	224	116	33	10	61-1	104	4.90	91	.285	.340	3-0-1	.000	0	77	-10		-0.9
2005	Sea A	8	15	.348	32	30	2-1	0-0	190.2	212	110	28	7	62-4	93	5.10	83	.280	.339	4	.000	0	76	-18		-1.9
Total 6		35	50	.412	181	106	6-3	0-3	811.1	838	419	124	36	238-14	427	4.34	100	.267	.323	11-0-2	.091	0	84	-3	17	-0.6

FRASCATORE, JOHN John Vincent B2.4.1970 Ozone Park NY BR/TR/6-1/210(200-228) [StLN91 24/623] d7.21 Col Long Island-C.W.Post

1994	StL N	0	1	.000	7	1	0	0-0	3.1	7	6	2	0	2	2	16.20	26	.438	.500	1	.000	-0	21	-4		-0.6
1995	StL N	1	1	.500	14	4	0	0-0	32.2	39	19	3	2	16-1	21	4.41	97	.298	.380	7-0-1	.000	-1	95	-1		-0.1
1997	StL N	5	2	.714	59	0	0	0-4	80	74	25	5	6	33-5	58	2.47	169	.247	.329	3	.000	-0		15		1.1
1998	StL N	3	4	.429	69	0	0	0-2	95.2	95	48	11	3	36-3	49	4.14	102	.256	.326	6	.167	-0		1		0.0
1999	Ari N	1	4	.200	26	0	0	0-1	33	31	16	6	1	12-4	15	4.09	113	.256	.326	0	—	0		2		0.2
	Tor A	7	1	.875	33	0	0	1-1	37	42	16	5	1	9-4	22	3.41	145	.292	.333	0	—	0		6		1.1
2000	Tor A	2	4	.333	60	0	0	0-5	73	87	51	14	7	33-2	30	5.42	93	.301	.381	0	—	0		-4		-0.3
2001	Tor A	1	0	1.000	12	0	0	0-1	16.1	16	4	4	0	4-1	9	2.20	208	.246	.290	0	—	0		4		0.3
Total 7		20	17	.541	274	5	0	1-14	371	391	185	50	20	145-20	206	4.00	112	.272	.344	17-0-1	.059	-1	78	19		1.7

FRASER, CHICK Charles Carrolton B10.26.1873 Chicago IL D5.8.1940 Wendell ID BR/TR/5-10.5/188 d4.19 C1

1896	Lou N	12	27	.308	43	38	36	1	349.1	396	282	9	29	166	91	4.87	89	.283	.371	146	.151	-9*	89	-19		-2.2
1897	Lou N	15	19	.441	34	34	32	0	294.1	334	226	11	22	139	70	4.04	106	.283	.369	115-2-2	.157	-5*	92	0		-0.2
1898	Lou N	7	17	.292	26	26	20-1	0	203	230	157	4	23	100	58	5.32	67	.283	.369	78-0-3	.167	-2	93	-39		-3.6
	Cle N	2	3	.400	6	6	6	0	42	49	34	2	6	12	19	5.57	65	.290	.358	16	.250	0	101	-8		-0.7
	Year	9	20	.310	32	32	26-1	0	245	279	191	6	29	112	77	5.36	67	.284	.354	94-0-3	.181	-2	94	-42		-4.3
1899	Phi N	21	12	.636	35	33	29-4	0	270.2	278	146	1	22	85	68	3.36	110	.265	.333	117-0-1	.179	-2*	123	10		0.9
1900	Phi N	15	9	.625	29	26	22-1	0	223.1	250	117	7	11	93	93	3.14	115	.282	.358	85-0-5	.259	4	106	9		1.2
1901	Phi A	22	16	.579	40	37	35-2	0	331	344	210	6	32	132	110	3.81	99	.265	.347	139-0-5	.187	-3*	103	-5		-0.7
1902	Phi N	12	13	.480	27	26	24-3	0	224	238	115	2	15	74	97	3.42	82	.272	.339	86	.174	0*	81	-14		-1.4
1903	Phi N	12	17	.414	31	29	26-1	1	250	260	160	8	16	97	104	4.50	73	.267	.344	93-1-2	.204	4*	94	-30		-2.3
1904	Phi N	14	24	.368	42	36	32-2	1	302	287	164	2	15	162	127	3.25	82	.246	.311	110-0-5	.155	-1*	88	-18		-2.1
1905	Bos N	14	21	.400	39	37	35-2	0	334.1	320	174	8	15	149	130	3.28	94	.254	.340	156-0-3	.224	3*	83	-10		-0.5
1906	Cin N	10	20	.333	31	28	25-2	0	236	221	92	1	8	80	58	2.67	103	.259	.329	82-0-4	.171	-1	78	4		0.5
1907	Chi N	8	5	.615	22	15	9-2	1	138.1	112	51	1	3	46	41	2.28	110	.229	.299	45-0-3	.067	-3	80	3		0.5
1908	Chi N	11	9	.550	26	17	11-2	2	162.2	141	71	4	6	61	66	2.27	104	.244	.323	50-0-5	.120	-2	130	-5		-0.6
1909	Chi N	0	0	—	1	0	0	0	4	3	2	0	0	4	0	0.00	—	.222	.462	1	.000	-0	1			
Total 14		175	212	.452	434	388	342-22	6	3364	3462	2000	69	219	1338	1098	3.67	92	.266	.345	1319-3-38	.178	-15	95-121			-11.7

FRASER, WILLIE William Patrick B5.26.1964 New York NY BR/TR/6-1/206* [CalA85 1/15] d9.10 Col Concordia (NY)

1986	Cal A	0	0	—	1	1	0	0-0	4.1	6	4	4	0	1-0	2	8.31	50	.353	.368	0	—	0	154	-2		-0.1
1987	Cal A	10	10	.500	36	23	5-1	1-0	176.2	160	85	26	6	63-3	106	3.92	110	.240	.310	0	—	0	99	9		0.8
1988	Cal A	12	13	.480	34	32	1	0-0	194.2	203	129	33	9	80-7	86	5.41	72	.267	.340	0	—	0	109	-34		-3.7
1989	Cal A	4	7	.364	44	0	0	2-1	91.2	80	33	6	5	23-4	46	3.24	118	.235	.291	0	—	0		8		0.9
1990	Cal A	5	4	.556	45	0	0	2-3	76	69	29	4	0	24-3	32	3.08	125	.244	.297	0	—	0		9		0.9
1991	Tor A	0	2	.000	13	1	0	0-0	26.1	33	20	4	3	11-2	12	6.15	69	.303	.382	0	—	0	173	-6		-0.4
	StL N	3	3	.500	35	0	0	0-0	49.1	44	28	9	3	21-3	25	4.93	76	.242	.325	2	.000	-0		-6		-0.7
1994	Fla N	2	0	1.000	9	0	0	0-0	12.1	20	14	1	0	6-0	7	5.84	76	.370	.426	0	—	0		-2		-0.3

YEAR	TM LG	W	L	PCT	G	GS	CG-SHO	SV-BS	IP	H	R	HR	HB	BB-IB	SO	ERA	AERA	OAV	OOB	AB-HR-SH	AVG	PB	SUP	APR	DL	PW
1995	Mon N	2	1	.667	22	0	0	2-0	25.2	25	17	6	3	9-1	12	5.61	77	.248	.327	2	.000	-0		-3		-0.
Total	8	38	40	.487	239	57	7-1	7-4	657	640	354	89	29	238-26	328	4.47	90	.254	.323	4	.000	-0	107	-29		-3.

FRASIER, VIC   Victor Patrick (b Victor Patrick Frazier) B8.5.1904 Ruston LA D1.10.1977 Jacksonville TX   BR/TR/6-0/182   d4.18

YEAR	TM LG	W	L	PCT	G	GS	CG-SHO	SV-BS	IP	H	R	HR	HB	BB-IB	SO	ERA	AERA	OAV	OOB	AB-HR-SH	AVG	PB	SUP	APR	DL	PW
1931	Chi A	13	15	.464	46	29	13-2	4	254	258	156	11	5	127	87	4.46	95	.259	.345	86-0-3	.209	1	97	-8		-0.
1932	Chi A	3	13	.188	29	21	4	0	146	180	121	14	4	70	33	6.23	69	.297	.374	44-0-5	.091	-3	94	-30		-2.
1933	Chi A	1	1	.500	10	1	0	0	20.1	32	22	2	0	11	4	8.85	48	.368	.439	4	.000	-1	100	-10		-0.
	Det A	5	5	.500	20	14	4	0	104.1	129	85	9	1	59	26	6.64	65	.312	.399	37-0-4	.189	-0	116	-24		-1.9
	Year	6	6	.500	30	15	4	0	124.2	161	107	11	1	70	30	7.00	61	.321	.406	41-0-4	.171	-1	115	-34		-2.
1934	Det A	1	3	.250	8	2	0	0	22.2	30	19	0	1	12	11	5.96	74	.313	.394	7	.286	0	169	-5		-0.
1937	Bos N	0	0	—	3	0	0	0	8	12	7	1	0	1	2	5.63	64	.364	.382	1	.000	-0		-3		-0.
1939	Chi A	0	1	.000	10	1	0	0	23.2	45	27	0	0	11	7	10.27	46	.405	.459	7	.286	0	37	-13		-0.
Total	6	23	38	.377	126	68	21-2	4	579	686	437	37	11	291		4.46	75	.293	.373	186-0-12	.177	-3	101	-93		-7.

FRASOR, JASON   Jason Andrew B8.9.1977 Chicago IL   BR/TR/5-10/170*   [DetA99 33/987]   d4.16   Col Southern Illinois

YEAR	TM LG	W	L	PCT	G	GS	CG-SHO	SV-BS	IP	H	R	HR	HB	BB-IB	SO	ERA	AERA	OAV	OOB	AB-HR-SH	AVG	PB	SUP	APR	DL	PW
2004	Tor A	4	6	.400	63	0	0	17-2	68.1	64	31	4	3	36-3	54	4.08	120	.251	.345	0	—	0		7		1.
2005	Tor A	3	5	.375	67	0	0	1-2	74.2	67	31	8	3	28-2	62	3.25	142	.247	.323	0	—	0		10		0.
Total	2	7	11	.389	130	0	0	18-4	143	131	62	12	5	64-5	116	3.65	130	.249	.334	0	—	0		17		2.

FRAZIER, GEORGE   George Allen B10.13.1954 Oklahoma City OK   BR/TR/6-5/205*   [MilA76 9/196]   d5.25   Col Oklahoma

YEAR	TM LG	W	L	PCT	G	GS	CG-SHO	SV-BS	IP	H	R	HR	HB	BB-IB	SO	ERA	AERA	OAV	OOB	AB-HR-SH	AVG	PB	SUP	APR	DL	PW
1978	StL N	0	3	.000	14	0	0	0-0	22	22	14	2	0	6-2	8	4.09	87	.250	.292	3	.333	0		-2		-0.
1979	StL N	2	4	.333	25	0	0	0-2	32.1	35	19	3	1	12-2	14	4.45	86	.278	.343	1	.000	-0		-3		-0.
1980	StL N	1	4	.200	22	0	0	3-4	23	24	10	2	0	7-3	11	2.74	137	.273	.326	0	—	0		2		0.
1981	†NY A	0	1	.000	16	0	0	3-0	27.2	26	7	1	0	11-2	17	1.63	222	.245	.316	0	—	0		6		0.
1982	NY A	4	4	.500	63	0	0	1-1	111.2	103	51	7	5	39-5	69	3.47	116	.252	.321	0	—	0		6		0.
1983	NY A	4	4	.500	61	0	0	8-2	115.1	94	44	5	3	45-4	78	3.43	115	.227	.300	0	—	0		3		0.
1984	Cle A	3	2	.600	22	0	0	1-2	44.1	45	19	3	0	14-4	24	3.65	113	.259	.314	0	—	0		0		-0.
	†Chi N	6	3	.667	37	0	0	3-1	63.2	53	30	4	1	26-8	58	4.10	95	.221	.296	7	.286	0		0		-0.
1985	Chi N	7	8	.467	51	0	0	2-2	76	88	57	11	3	52-9	46	6.39	63	.299	.409	6	.000	-1		-17		-3.
1986	Chi N	4	2	.333	35	0	0	0-0	51.2	63	36	5	1	34-4	41	5.40	75	.310	.407	4	.000	0		-8		-1.
	Min A	1	1	.500	15	0	0	6-3	26.2	23	13	2	0	16-1	25	4.39	99	.232	.331	0	—	0		-3		-0.
1987	†Min A	5	5	.500	54	0	0	2-5	81.1	77	49	9	2	51-4	58	4.98	93	.258	.359	0	—	0		-7		-0.
Total	10	35	43	.449	415	0	0	29-22	675.2	653	349	54	16	313-48	449	4.20	97	.257	.338	21	.143	-1		-7		-3

FREDERICK, KEVIN   Kevin Albert Francis B11.4.1976 Evanston IL   BL/TR/6-1/208*   [MinA98 34/1009]   d7.15   Col Creighton

YEAR	TM LG	W	L	PCT	G	GS	CG-SHO	SV-BS	IP	H	R	HR	HB	BB-IB	SO	ERA	AERA	OAV	OOB	AB-HR-SH	AVG	PB	SUP	APR	DL	PW
2002	Min A	0	0	—	8	0	0	0-0	11.2	13	13	3	0	10-0	5	10.03	45	.283	.411	0	—	0		-7		-0.
2004	Tor A	0	2	.000	22	0	0	0-1	28.2	32	21	4	1	16-1	22	6.59	74	.283	.368	0	—	0		-5		-0.
Total	2	0	2	.000	30	0	0	0-1	40.1	45	34	7	1	26-1	27	7.59	63	.283	.381	0	—	0		-12		-0

FREDRICKSON, SCOTT   Scott Eric B8.19.1967 Manchester NH   BR/TR/6-3/215   [SDN90 14/390]   d4.29   Col Texas   [DL 1994 Col N 131]

YEAR	TM LG	W	L	PCT	G	GS	CG-SHO	SV-BS	IP	H	R	HR	HB	BB-IB	SO	ERA	AERA	OAV	OOB	AB-HR-SH	AVG	PB	SUP	APR	DL	PW
1993	Col N	1	1	.000	25	0	0	0	29	33	25	3	1	17-2	20	6.21	77	.287	.378	3	.000	-0		-5		-0

FREEMAN, BUCK   Alexander Vernon B7.5.1893 Mart TX D2.21.1953 Fort Sam Houston TX   BB/TR/5-10/167   d4.13

YEAR	TM LG	W	L	PCT	G	GS	CG-SHO	SV-BS	IP	H	R	HR	HB	BB-IB	SO	ERA	AERA	OAV	OOB	AB-HR-SH	AVG	PB	SUP	APR	DL	PW
1921	Chi N	9	10	.474	38	20	6	3	177.1	189	96	12	8	70	42	4.11	93	.281	.356	53-0-1	.208	0	102	-7		-0
1922	Chi N	0	1	.000	11	1	0	1	25.2	47	28	0	2	10	10	8.77	48	.412	.468	8	.125	-0	78	-12		-0
Total	2	9	11	.450	49	21	6	4	203	236	124	12	10	80	52	4.70	82	.300	.372	61-0-1	.197	-0	100	-19		-1

FREEMAN, HARVEY   Harvey Bayard "Buck" B12.22.1897 Mottville MI D1.10.1970 Kalamazoo MI   BR/TR/5-10/160   d7.10   Col Western Michigan

YEAR	TM LG	W	L	PCT	G	GS	CG-SHO	SV-BS	IP	H	R	HR	HB	BB-IB	SO	ERA	AERA	OAV	OOB	AB-HR-SH	AVG	PB	SUP	APR	DL	PW
1921	Phi A	1	4	.200	18	4	2	0	48	65	50	2	5	35	5	7.69	58	.346	.461	12-0-1	.083	-2	70	-16		-1

FREEMAN, HERSH   Hershell Baskin "Buster" B7.1.1928 Gadsden AL D1.17.2004 Orlando FL   BR/TR/6-3/220*   d9.10   Col Alabama

YEAR	TM LG	W	L	PCT	G	GS	CG-SHO	SV-BS	IP	H	R	HR	HB	BB-IB	SO	ERA	AERA	OAV	OOB	AB-HR-SH	AVG	PB	SUP	APR	DL	PW
1952	Bos A	1	0	1.000	4	1	1	0	13.2	13	5	1	1	5	5	3.29	120	.260	.339	4	.500	1	66	1		0
1953	Bos A	1	4	.200	18	2	0	0	39	50	31	2	0	17	15	5.54	76	.316	.383	11	.091	-1	21	-7		-0
1955	Bos A	0	0	—	2	0	0	0	1.2	1	0	0	0	1-1	1	0.00	—	.200	.333	0	—	0		-0		-0
	Cin N	7	4	.636	52	0	0	11	91.2	94	31	3	2	30-6	37	2.16	196	.276	.335	18-1-0	.167	1*	18			2
1956	Cin N	14	5	.737	64	0	0	18	108.2	112	44	2	1	34-11	50	3.40	117	.274	.329	18	.056	-1	7			1
1957	Cin N	7	2	.778	52	0	0	8	83.2	90	49	14	3	14-4	36	4.52	91	.277	.308	10	.200	0		-5		-0
1958	Cin N	0	0	—	3	0	0	0	7.2	4	3	0	0	5-0	7	3.52	118	.154	.281	1	.000	-0		1		-0
	Chi N	0	1	.000	9	0	0	0	13	23	13	3	0	3-0	7	8.31	47	.354	.382	1	.000	-0		-6		-0
	Year	0	1	.000	12	0	0	0	20.2	27	16	3	0	8-0	14	6.53	61	.297	.350	2	.000	-0		-5		-0
Total	6	30	16	.652	204	3	1	37	359	387	176	25	7	109-22	158	3.74	110	.281	.334	63-1-0	.143	-0	36	10		2

FREEMAN, JIMMY   Jimmy Lee B6.29.1951 Carlsbad NM   BL/TL/6-4/180*   [AtlN69 6/130]   d9.1

YEAR	TM LG	W	L	PCT	G	GS	CG-SHO	SV-BS	IP	H	R	HR	HB	BB-IB	SO	ERA	AERA	OAV	OOB	AB-HR-SH	AVG	PB	SUP	APR	DL	PW
1972	Atl N	2	2	.500	6	6	1	0-0	36	40	26	5	0	22-1	18	6.00	63	.278	.373	13	.077	-0*	120	-8		-0
1973	Atl N	0	2	.000	13	5	0	1-2	37.1	50	33	7	0	25-1	20	7.71	51	.327	.417	13	.154	-0*	142	-13		-0
Total	2	2	4	.333	19	11	1	1-2	73.1	90	59	12	0	47-2	38	6.87	57	.303	.396	26	.115	-1	130	-21		-1

FREEMAN, BUCK   John Frank B10.30.1871 Catasauqua PA D6.25.1949 Wilkes-Barre PA   BL/TL/5-9/169   d6.27 ▲

YEAR	TM LG	W	L	PCT	G	GS	CG-SHO	SV-BS	IP	H	R	HR	HB	BB-IB	SO	ERA	AERA	OAV	OOB	AB-HR-SH	AVG	PB	SUP	APR	DL	PW
1891	Was AA	3	2	.600	5	4	4	0	44	35	32	0	4	33	28	3.89	96	.211	.355	18	.222	0	96	-1		0
1899	Was N	0	0	—	2	0	0	0	7	15	13	3	3	3	0	7.71	51	.429	.512	588-25-5	.318	1*		-5		-0
Total	2	3	2	.600	7	4	4	0	51	50	45	3	7	36	28	4.41	85	.249	.381	606-25-5	.315	1	96	-6		-0

FREEMAN, JULIE   Julius Benjamin B11.7.1868 MO D6.10.1921 St.Louis MO   BR   d10.10

YEAR	TM LG	W	L	PCT	G	GS	CG-SHO	SV-BS	IP	H	R	HR	HB	BB-IB	SO	ERA	AERA	OAV	OOB	AB-HR-SH	AVG	PB	SUP	APR	DL	PW
1888	StL AA	0	1	.000	1	1	0	0	6.1	7	5	0	1	4	1	4.26	77	.269	.387	3	.333	0	71	-1		-0

FREEMAN, MARK   Mark Price B12.7.1930 Memphis TN   BR/TR/6-4/220*   d4.18   Col Louisiana St.

YEAR	TM LG	W	L	PCT	G	GS	CG-SHO	SV-BS	IP	H	R	HR	HB	BB-IB	SO	ERA	AERA	OAV	OOB	AB-HR-SH	AVG	PB	SUP	APR	DL	PW
1959	KC A	0	0	—	3	0	0	0	3.2	6	6	0	0	3-0	1	9.82	41	.375	.450	0	—	0		-3		-0
	NY A	0	0	—	1	0	0	0	7	6	2	0	1	2-0	4	2.57	142	.240	.310	2	.000	-0	48	1		-0
	Year	0	0	—	4	0	0	0	10.2	12	8	0	1	5-0	5	5.06	74	.293	.367	2	.000	-0	47	-2		-0
1960	Chi N	3	3	.500	30	8	1	1	76.2	70	51	10	5	33-3	50	5.63	67	.240	.325	20-0-1	.150	-0	146	-14		-1
Total	2	3	3	.500	34	9	1	1	87.1	82	59	10	6	38-3	55	5.56	68	.246	.331	22-0-1	.136	-1	135	-16		-1

FREEMAN, MARVIN   Marvin B4.10.1963 Chicago IL   BR/TR/6-7/222(200-222)   [PhiN84 2/49]   d9.16   Col Jackson St.

YEAR	TM LG	W	L	PCT	G	GS	CG-SHO	SV-BS	IP	H	R	HR	HB	BB-IB	SO	ERA	AERA	OAV	OOB	AB-HR-SH	AVG	PB	SUP	APR	DL	PW
1986	Phi N	2	0	1.000	3	3	0	0-0	16	6	4	0	0	10-0	6	2.25	173	.120	.262	6-0-1	.000	-1	160	3		-0
1988	Phi N	2	3	.400	11	11	0	0-0	51.2	55	36	2	1	43-2	37	6.10	59	.276	.406	14-0-3	.214	-0	101	-12		-0
1989	Phi N	0	0	—	1	1	0	0-0	3	2	2	0	0	5-0	0	6.00	60	.182	.438	2	.000	-0	197	-0		-0
1990	Phi N	0	0	—	16	3	0	1-0	32.1	34	21	5	3	14-2	26	5.57	69	.264	.349	7	.000	-1	86	-6		-0
	Atl N	1	0	1.000	9	0	0	0-0	15.2	7	3	0	2	3-0	12	1.72	234	.130	.203	0	—	0		4		-0
	Year	1	2	.333	25	3	0	1-0	48	41	24	5	5	17-2	38	4.31	91	.224	.307	7	.000	-1	85	-1		-0
1991	Atl N	1	0	1.000	34	0	0	1-0	48	37	19	2	2	13-1	34	3.00	129	.214	.275	7	.000	-1		4	50	-0
1992	†Atl N	7	5	.583	58	0	0	3-3	64.1	61	26	7	1	29-7	41	3.22	114	.251	.332	4	.500	1		3	15	0
1993	Atl N	2	0	1.000	21	0	0	0	23.2	24	16	1	1	10-2	25	6.08	67	.261	.340	0-0-2	—	0		-5	64	-0
1994	Col N	10	2	.833	19	18	0	0-0	112.2	113	39	10	4	23-2	67	2.80	178	.262	.306	36-1-3	.111	-0	97	23		0
1995	Col N	3	7	.300	22	18	0	0-1	94.2	122	64	15	2	41-1	61	5.89	91	.318	.384	23-1-6	.087	-1	88	-3	19	-0
1996	Col N	7	9	.438	26	23	0	0-1	129.2	151	100	21	6	57-1	71	6.04	86	.294	.370	41-0-4	.122	-2	112	-12		-1
	Chi A	0	0	—	1	1	0	0-0	2	4	3	0	0	1-0	1	13.50	35	.364	.417	0	—	0	253	-2		-0
Total	10	35	28	.556	221	78	0	5-5	593.2	616	333	63	23	249-18	383	4.64	98	.269	.345	140-2-19	.114	-5	111	-4	308	2

FREEZE, JAKE   Carl Alexander B4.25.1900 Huntington AR D4.9.1983 San Angelo TX   BR/TR/5-8/150   d7.1   Col Baylor

YEAR	TM LG	W	L	PCT	G	GS	CG-SHO	SV-BS	IP	H	R	HR	HB	BB-IB	SO	ERA	AERA	OAV	OOB	AB-HR-SH	AVG	PB	SUP	APR	DL	PW
1925	Chi A	0	0	—	2	0	0	0	3.2	5	1	0	1	3	1	2.45	169	.333	.444	1	.000	-0		-2		-0

FREISLEBEN, DAVE   David James B10.31.1951 Coraopolis PA   BR/TR/5-11/200*   [SDN71 5/98]   d4.26

YEAR	TM LG	W	L	PCT	G	GS	CG-SHO	SV-BS	IP	H	R	HR	HB	BB-IB	SO	ERA	AERA	OAV	OOB	AB-HR-SH	AVG	PB	SUP	APR	DL	PW
1974	SD N	9	14	.391	33	31	6-2	0-0	211.2	194	100	13	7	112-9	130	3.66	98	.241	.338	64-0-9	.172	2	85	-3		-0
1975	SD N	5	14	.263	36	27	4-1	0-0	181	206	102	11	5	70-7	77	4.28	82	.289	.366	48-0-6	.083	-1	76	-16		-0
1976	SD N	10	13	.435	34	24	6-3	1-0	172	163	73	10	5	66-7	81	3.51	94	.248	.320	37-0-9	.189	1	67	-3		-0
1977	SD N	7	9	.438	33	23	1	0-0	138.2	140	86	21	2	71-9	72	4.61	78	.266	.353	37-0-2	.135	0	111	-19		-0
1978	SD N	0	3	.000	12	4	0	0-0	26.2	41	22	3	0	15-3	16	6.08	55	.363	.427	6-0-1	.000	-1	87	-9		-0
	Cle A	1	4	.200	12	10	0	0-0	44.1	52	37	4	2	31-1	19	7.11	53	.299	.405	0	—	0	102	-15		-0

YEAR	TM LG	W	L	PCT	G	GS	CG-SHO	SV-BS	IP	H	R	HR	HB	BB-IB	SO	ERA	AERA	OAV	OOB	AB-HR-SH	AVG	PB	SUP	APR	DL	PW
1979	Tor A	2	3	.400	42	2	0	3-2	91	101	57	5	2	53-3	35	4.95	89	.294	.388	0	—	0	62	-6		-0.3
Total	6	34	60	.362	202	121	17-6	4-2	865.1	897	477	67	25	430-41	430	4.30	84	.269	.355	192-0-27	.141	2	84	-71		-6.6

FREITAS, TONY Antonio B5.5.1908 Mill Valley CA D3.14.1994 Orangevale CA BR/TL/5-8/161 d5.31

YEAR	TM LG	W	L	PCT	G	GS	CG-SHO	SV-BS	IP	H	R	HR	HB	BB-IB	SO	ERA	AERA	OAV	OOB	AB-HR-SH	AVG	PB	SUP	APR	DL	PW
1932	Phi A	12	5	.706	23	18	10-1	0	150.1	150	68	11	4	48	31	3.83	118	.263	.325	54-0-8	.148	-1	136	12		1.2
1933	Phi A	2	4	.333	19	9	2	1	64.1	90	56	8	2	24	15	7.27	59	.337	.396	16-0-2	.063	-1	130	-19		-1.6
1934	Cin N	6	12	.333	30	18	5	1	152.2	194	80	6	3	25	37	4.01	102	.311	.341	47-0-1	.191	0*	73	3		0.5
1935	Cin N	5	10	.333	31	18	5	2	143.2	174	95	6	2	38	51	4.57	87	.295	.340	46-0-4	.130	-0	90	-13		-1.2
1936	Cin N	0	2	.000	4	0	0	0	7	6	2	0	0	2	1	1.29	297	.240	.296	2	.000	-0		2		0.3
Total	5	25	33	.431	107	63	22-1	4	518	614	301	31	11	137	135	4.48	94	.296	.343	165-0-15	.145	-2	105	-15		-0.8

FRENCH, LARRY Lawrence Herbert B11.1.1907 Visalia CA D2.9.1987 San Diego CA BR/TL(BB 1934, 1940-42)/6-1/195 d4.18 Mil 1943-45

YEAR	TM LG	W	L	PCT	G	GS	CG-SHO	SV-BS	IP	H	R	HR	HB	BB-IB	SO	ERA	AERA	OAV	OOB	AB-HR-SH	AVG	PB	SUP	APR	DL	PW
1929	Pit N	7	5	.583	30	13	6	1	123	130	78	10	3	62	49	4.90	97	.276	.364	42-0-1	.190	-1	107	-2		-0.1
1930	Pit N	17	18	.486	42	35	21-3	1	274.2	325	163	20	6	89	90	4.36	114	.295	.351	91-0-11	.242	1	88	16		1.6
1931	Pit N	15	13	.536	39	33	20-1	1	275.2	301	127	9	1	70	73	3.26	118	.278	.322	95-0-6	.179	-1	97	16		1.4
1932	Pit N	18	16	.529	47	33	19-3	4	274.1	301	127	17	1	62	72	3.02	126	.276	.316	92-0-4	.207	1	96	19		2.1
1933	Pit N	18	13	.581	47	35	21-5	1	291.1	290	106	9	5	55	88	2.72	122	.257	.294	101-0-3	.149	-2	92	21		1.8
1934	Pit N	12	18	.400	49	34	16-3	1	263.2	299	135	8	3	59	103	3.58	115	.281	.321	84-0-10	.190	-0	96	9		0.8
1935	†Chi N	17	10	.630	42	30	16-4	2	246.1	279	94	10	2	44	90	2.96	133	.286	.318	85-0-9	.141	-4	104	28		2.5
1936	Chi N	18	9	.667	43	28	16-4	3	252.1	262	103	16	6	54	104	3.39	118	.266	.308	85-0-10	.212	-0	100	18		1.6
1937	Chi N	16	10	.615	42	28	11-4	0	208	229	106	17	1	65	100	3.98	100	.274	.327	71-0-4	.127	-4	104	-1		-0.5
1938	†Chi N	10	19	.345	43	27	10-3	0	201.1	210	95	17	1	62	83	3.80	101	.271	.326	62-0-6	.210	-2	79	1		0.5
1939	Chi N	15	8	.652	36	21	10-2	1	194	205	80	7	1	50	95	3.29	120	.269	.314	73-1-4	.192	1	104	15		1.8
1940	Chi N★	14	14	.500	40	33	18-3	2	246	240	93	12	4	64	107	3.29	114	.256	.306	85-0-5	.165	1	102	18		2.2
1941	Chi N	5	14	.263	26	18	6-1	0	138	161	88	10	2	43	60	4.63	76	.285	.338	47-0-3	.191	1	78	-19		-2.3
	†Bro N	0	0	—	6	1	0	0	15.2	16	6	1	1	4	8	3.45	106	.267	.323	4	.250	1	116	1		0.1
	Year	5	14	.263	32	19	6-1	0	153.2	177	94	11	3	47	68	4.51	78	.283	.336	51-0-3	.196	1	80	-20		-2.2
1942	Bro N	15	4	.789	32	19	8-4	0	147.2	127	39	1	5	36	62	1.83	178	.233	.287	40-0-9	.300	1	109	22		3.3
Total	14	197	171	.535	570	383	198-40	17	3152	3375	1440	164	42	819	1187	3.44	114	.272	.320	1057-1-84	.188	0	96	162		16.8

▶ **FRENCH, BILL** William B Baltimore MD d4.14 ▲

YEAR	TM LG	W	L	PCT	G	GS	CG-SHO	SV-BS	IP	H	R	HR	HB	BB-IB	SO	ERA	AERA	OAV	OOB	AB-HR-SH	AVG	PB	SUP	APR	DL	PW
1873	Mar NA	0	1	.000	1	1	1	0	9	30	27	0	0	0	0	12.00	27	.462	.462	18	.222	-0*	77	-7		-0.4

▶ **FREY, BENNY** Benjamin Rudolph B4.6.1906 Dexter MI D11.1.1937 Spring Arbor Twp. MI BR/TR/5-10/165 d9.18

YEAR	TM LG	W	L	PCT	G	GS	CG-SHO	SV-BS	IP	H	R	HR	HB	BB-IB	SO	ERA	AERA	OAV	OOB	AB-HR-SH	AVG	PB	SUP	APR	DL	PW
1929	Cin N	1	2	.333	3	2	0	0	24	29	12	2	0	8	1	4.13	111	.302	.356	8-0-1	.375	1	83	1		0.3
1930	Cin N	11	18	.379	44	28	14-2	1	245	295	145	15	3	62	43	4.70	103	.305	.349	88-0-3	.284	4	63	4		1.1
1931	Cin N	8	12	.400	34	17	7-1	2	133.2	166	76	2	2	36	19	4.92	76	.319	.365	44-0-1	.318	4	80	-14		-1.3
1932	StL N	0	2	.000	2	0	0	0	3	6	5	0	0	2	0	12.00	33	.600	.667	1	.000	-0		-3		-0.5
	Cin N	4	10	.286	28	15	5	0	131.1	159	72	10	1	30	27	4.32	89	.299	.338	44	.205	-0	93	-9		-0.3
	Year	4	12	.250	30	15	5	0	134.1	165	77	10	1	32	27	4.49	86	.305	.345	45	.200	-0	93	-9		-0.8
1933	Cin N	6	4	.600	37	9	1-1	5	132	144	67	4	0	21	12	3.82	89	.281	.309	42-0-1	.262	3*	79	-5		0.1
1934	Cin N	11	16	.407	39	30	12-2	2	245.1	288	118	10	2	42	33	3.52	116	.289	.319	82-0-2	.171	-0*	88	15		1.7
1935	Cin N	6	10	.375	38	13	3-1	2	114.1	164	100	6	4	32	24	6.85	58	.335	.381	32-0-3	.344	4	105	-35		-3.8
1936	Cin N	10	8	.556	31	12	5	0	131.1	164	73	5	0	30	20	4.25	90	.296	.332	44-0-2	.255	2*	92	-6		-0.6
Total	8	57	82	.410	256	127	49-7	7	1160	1415	668	54	12	263	179	4.50	90	.303	.341	385-0-13	.255	17	83	-48		-3.3

▶ **FREY, STEVE** Steven Francis B7.29.1963 Meadowbrook PA BR/TL/5-9/170* [NYA83 15/379] d5.10 Col Bucks Co. (PA) CC

YEAR	TM LG	W	L	PCT	G	GS	CG-SHO	SV-BS	IP	H	R	HR	HB	BB-IB	SO	ERA	AERA	OAV	OOB	AB-HR-SH	AVG	PB	SUP	APR	DL	PW
1989	Mon N	3	2	.600	20	0	0	0-0	21.1	29	15	4	1	11-1	15	5.48	65	.326	.398	0		0		-5		-1.0
1990	Mon N	8	2	.800	51	0	0	9-0	55.2	44	15	4	1	29-6	29	2.10	175	.219	.318	1	.000	-0		10	21	1.9
1991	Mon N	0	1	.000	31	0	0	1-1	39.2	43	31	3	1	23-4	21	4.99	73	.281	.374	2	.000	-0		-9		-0.5
1992	Cal A	4	2	.667	51	0	0	4-1	45.1	39	18	6	2	22-3	24	3.57	112	.238	.330	0	—	0		3	16	0.4
1993	Cal A	2	3	.400	55	0	0	13-3	48.1	41	20	1	2	26-1	22	2.98	152	.230	.337	0	—	0		7		1.0
1994	SF N	1	0	1.000	44	0	0	0-3	31	37	17	6	2	15-3	20	4.94	82	.322	.397	0	—	0		-2		-0.1
1995	SF N	0	1	.000	9	0	0	0-0	6.1	7	6	1	0	2-0	5	4.26	97	.280	.321	0	—	0		-1		-0.2
	Sea N	0	3	.000	13	0	0	0-0	11.1	16	7	0	1	6-1	7	4.76	100	.356	.434	0	—	0		0	20	0.0
	Phi N	0	0	—	9	0	0	1-0	10.2	3	1	1	0	2-1	2	0.84	500	.091	.143	1	.000	-0		4		0.2
1996	Phi N	0	1	.000	31	0	0	0-0	34.1	38	19	4	0	18-3	12	4.72	91	.295	.376	0	—	0		-1		0.0
Total	8	18	15	.545	314	0	0	28-8	304	297	149	30	11	154-23	157	3.76	107	.262	.351	4	.000	-0		6	57	1.7

▶ **FRICANO, MARION** Marion John B7.15.1923 Brant NY D5.18.1976 Tijuana, Baja California, Mexico BR/TR/6-0/170* d9.6 Col Cortland

YEAR	TM LG	W	L	PCT	G	GS	CG-SHO	SV-BS	IP	H	R	HR	HB	BB-IB	SO	ERA	AERA	OAV	OOB	AB-HR-SH	AVG	PB	SUP	APR	DL	PW
1952	Phi A	1	0	1.000	2	0	0	0	5	5	1	0	0	2	1	1.80	238	.238	.273	0-0-1	—	0		1		0.2
1953	Phi A	9	12	.429	39	23	10	0	211	206	105	21	6	90	67	3.88	110	.257	.337	69-0-3	.145	-3*	83	6		0.2
1954	Phi A	5	11	.313	37	20	4	1	151.2	163	98	17	4	64	43	5.16	76	.275	.347	41-0-6	.098	-3*	89	-21		-2.4
1955	KC A	0	0	—	10	0	0	0	20	19	9	2	0	9-0	5	3.15	133	.253	.333	3	.667	1		2		0.2
Total	4	15	23	.395	88	43	14	1	387.2	393	213	40	10	164-0	115	4.32	96	.264	.340	113-0-10	.142	-5	85	-12		-1.8

▶ **FRIDAY, SKIPPER** Grier William B10.26.1897 Gastonia NC D8.25.1962 Gastonia NC BR/TR/5-11/170 d6.17

YEAR	TM LG	W	L	PCT	G	GS	CG-SHO	SV-BS	IP	H	R	HR	HB	BB-IB	SO	ERA	AERA	OAV	OOB	AB-HR-SH	AVG	PB	SUP	APR	DL	PW
1923	Was A	0	1	.000	7	2	1	0	30	35	27	2	2	22	9	6.90	55	.313	.434	9	.222	1		99	-11		-0.4

▶ **FRIED, CY** Arthur Edwin B7.23.1897 San Antonio TX D10.10.1970 San Antonio TX BL/TL/5-11.5/150 d9.17

YEAR	TM LG	W	L	PCT	G	GS	CG-SHO	SV-BS	IP	H	R	HR	HB	BB-IB	SO	ERA	AERA	OAV	OOB	AB-HR-SH	AVG	PB	SUP	APR	DL	PW
1920	Det A	0	0	—	2	0	0	0	1.2	3	4	0	0	4	0	16.20	23	.500	.700	0	—	0		-2		-0.1

▶ **FRIEDRICHS, BOB** Robert George B8.30.1906 Cincinnati OH D4.15.1997 Jasper IN BR/TR/5-11.5/165 d5.17 Col Holy Cross

YEAR	TM LG	W	L	PCT	G	GS	CG-SHO	SV-BS	IP	H	R	HR	HB	BB-IB	SO	ERA	AERA	OAV	OOB	AB-HR-SH	AVG	PB	SUP	APR	DL	PW
1932	Was A	0	0	—	2	0	0	0	4	4	5	0	1	7	2	11.25	38	.250	.500	1	.000	-0		-3		-0.2

▶ **FRIEND, DANNY** Daniel Sebastian B4.18.1873 Cincinnati OH D6.1.1942 Chillicothe OH BL/TL/5-9/175 d9.10

YEAR	TM LG	W	L	PCT	G	GS	CG-SHO	SV-BS	IP	H	R	HR	HB	BB-IB	SO	ERA	AERA	OAV	OOB	AB-HR-SH	AVG	PB	SUP	APR	DL	PW
1895	Chi N	2	2	.500	5	5	5	0	41	50	27	5	3	14	10	5.27	97	.296	.360	17-0-1	.235	-1	92	2		0.0
1896	Chi N	18	14	.563	36	33	28-1	0	290.2	298	196	11	39	139	86	4.74	96	.263	.363	126-1-4	.238	-1*	78	0		-0.2
1897	Chi N	12	11	.522	24	24	23	0	203	244	144	5	17	86	58	4.52	99	.295	.373	88-0-1	.284	2*	94	1		0.2
1898	Chi N	0	2	.000	2	2	2	0	17	20	15	1	1	10	4	5.29	68	.290	.387	7	.286	0	79	-3		-0.1
Total	4	32	29	.525	67	64	58-1	0	551.2	612	382	22	60	249	158	4.71	96	.279	.368	238-1-6	.256	0	85	0		0.0

▶ **FRIEND, BOB** Robert Bartmess "Warrior" B11.24.1930 Lafayette IN BR/TR/6-0/190* d4.28 Col Purdue

YEAR	TM LG	W	L	PCT	G	GS	CG-SHO	SV-BS	IP	H	R	HR	HB	BB-IB	SO	ERA	AERA	OAV	OOB	AB-HR-SH	AVG	PB	SUP	APR	DL	PW
1951	Pit N	6	10	.375	34	22	3-1	0	149.2	173	94	12	0	68	41	4.27	94	.293	.366	44-0-1	.091	-2	104	-6		-0.7
1952	Pit N	7	17	.292	35	23	6-1	0	185	186	96	15	3	84	75	4.18	95	.258	.338	52-0-7	.058	-4	74	-3		-0.8
1953	Pit N	8	11	.421	32	24	8	0	170.2	193	103	18	3	57	66	4.90	91	.286	.344	52-0-3	.135	-2	99	-7		-0.9
1954	Pit N	7	12	.368	35	20	4-2	0	170.1	204	106	16	1	58	73	5.07	83	.293	.355	51-1-1	.275	5	93	-14		-1.0
1955	Pit N	14	9	.609	44	20	9-2	2	200.1	178	80	18	2	52-4	98	2.83	145	.242	.291	61-0-6	.164	-2	88	25		2.7
1956	Pit N★	17	17	.500	49	42	19-4	3	314.1	310	137	25	2	85-18	166	3.46	109	.258	.306	97-1-11	.165	-1	91	11		1.0
1957	Pit N	14	18	.438	40	38	17-3	0	277	273	121	28	1	68-8	143	3.38	112	.257	.301	87-0-6	.184	1	89	13		1.4
1958	Pit N★	22	14	.611	38	38	16-1	0	274	299	120	25	4	61-11	135	3.68	105	.281	.320	94-0-10	.106	-4	106	8		0.6
1959	Pit N	8	19	.296	35	35	7-2	0	234.2	267	129	19	7	52-9	104	4.03	96	.283	.324	73-0-12	.164	0	90	-9		-0.9
1960	†Pit N★	18	12	.600	38	37	16-4	1	275.2	266	97	18	0	45-10	183	3.00	125	.251	.280	88-0-11	.068	-5	106	25		2.0
1961	Pit N	14	19	.424	41	35	10-1	1	236	271	119	26	3	45-10	108	3.85	104	.289	.322	79-0-9	.139	-3	80	2		-0.2
1962	Pit N	18	14	.563	39	36	13-5	1	261.2	280	99	23	2	53-10	144	3.06	129	.273	.309	91-0-8	.121	-3	92	27		2.8
1963	Pit N	17	16	.515	39	38	12-4	0	268.2	236	87	13	6	44-9	144	2.34	141	.233	.267	86-0-10	.105	-3	88	27		2.9
1964	Pit N	13	18	.419	35	35	13-3	0	240.1	253	98	10	4	50-12	128	3.33	105	.271	.309	71-0-11	.070	-3	81	6		0.4
1965	Pit N	8	12	.400	34	34	8-2	0	222	221	89	17	8	40-17	74	3.24	108	.260	.304	71-0-6	.042	-5	91	9		-0.2
1966	NY A	1	4	.200	12	8	0	0	44.2	61	25	2	0	9-1	22	4.84	69	.330	.359	11-0-3	.000	-1	70	-7		-0.8
	NY N	5	8	.385	22	14	2-1	1	86	101	52	11	1	16-6	30	4.40	83	.289	.321	29-0-5	.034	-3	111	-9		-1.6
Total	16	197	230	.461	602	497	163-36	11	3611	3772	1652	286	46	894-115	1734	3.58	107	.269	.313	1137-2-120	.121	-36	92	98		7.1

▶ **FRIES, PETE** Peter Martin B10.30.1857 Scranton PA D7.29.1937 Chicago IL BL/TL/5-8/160 d8.10

YEAR	TM LG	W	L	PCT	G	GS	CG-SHO	SV-BS	IP	H	R	HR	HB	BB-IB	SO	ERA	AERA	OAV	OOB	AB-HR-SH	AVG	PB	SUP	APR	DL	PW
1883	Col AA	0	3	.000	3	3	3	0	25	34	31	1		14	7	6.48	48	.304	.381	10	.300	1	125	-10		-0.7

▶ **FRILL, JOHN** John Edmond B4.3.1879 Reading PA D9.28.1918 Westerly RI BR/TL/5-10.5/170 d4.16

YEAR	TM LG	W	L	PCT	G	GS	CG-SHO	SV-BS	IP	H	R	HR	HB	BB-IB	SO	ERA	AERA	OAV	OOB	AB-HR-SH	AVG	PB	SUP	APR	DL	PW
1910	NY A	2	2	.500	10	5	3-1	1	48.1	55	33	1	1	5	27	4.47	59	.289	.311	18-0-1	.111	-1	111	-9		-0.9
1912	StL A	0	1	.000	3	3	0	0	4.1	16	11	1	1	1	2	20.77	16	.571	.600	2	.500	0	163	-7		-1.2

YEAR	TM LG	W	L	PCT	G	GS	CG-SHO	SV-BS	IP	H	R	HR	HB	BB-IB	SO	ERA	AERA	OAV	OOB	AB-HR-SH	AVG	PB	SUP	APR	DL	PW
	Cin N	1	0	1.000	3	2	0	0	15	19	11	0	2	1	4	6.00	56	.345	.379	4	.250	0	87	-3		-0.2
Total	2	3	3	.500	16	10	3-1	1	67.2	90	55	2	4	7	33	5.85	49	.330	.356	24-0-1	.167	-1	125	-19		-2.3

FRISELLA, DANNY Daniel Vincent "Bear" B3.4.1946 San Francisco CA D1.1.1977 Phoenix AZ BL/TR/6-0/195* [NYN66 S3/49] d7.27 Col Washington St.

YEAR	TM LG	W	L	PCT	G	GS	CG-SHO	SV-BS	IP	H	R	HR	HB	BB-IB	SO	ERA	AERA	OAV	OOB	AB-HR-SH	AVG	PB	SUP	APR	DL	PW
1967	NY N	1	6	.143	14	11	0	2	74	68	32	6	0	33-1	51	3.41	100	.249	.325	23	.087	-1	54	0		-0.1
1968	NY N	2	4	.333	19	4	0	2	50.2	53	23	5	0	17-0	47	3.91	77	.270	.326	12	.083	-0	72	-4		-0.1
1969	NY N	0	0	—	3	0	0	0-0	4.2	8	4	1	0	3-0	5	7.71	47	.381	.458	1	.000	-0		-2		-0.1
1970	NY N	8	3	.727	30	1	0	1-1	65.2	49	23	4	0	34-11	54	3.02	135	.204	.302	13-0-1	.308	1	110	8		1.4
1971	NY N	8	5	.615	53	0	0	12-3	90.2	76	28	6	3	30-9	93	1.99	173	.227	.295	13-0-1	.231	1		12		2.2
1972	NY N	5	8	.385	39	0	0	9-4	67.1	63	31	8	0	20-5	46	3.34	101	.243	.296	7	.286	0		-1		-0.1
1973	Atl N	1	2	.333	42	0	0	8-8	45	40	27	5	1	23-2	27	4.20	94	.241	.332	2	.500	0		-2	56	-0.2
1974	Atl N	3	4	.429	36	1	0	6-4	41.2	37	26	4	0	28-8	27	5.18	73	.240	.357	1	.000	0	115	-6		-1.1
1975	SD N	1	6	.143	65	0	0	9-2	97.2	86	36	7	2	51-16	67	3.13	112	.242	.335	5	.200	0		6		0.5
1976	StL N	0	0	—	18	0	0	1-0	22.2	19	10	3	0	13-1	11	3.97	90	.232	.330	1	.000	-0		0		0.0
	Mil A	5	2	.714	32	0	0	9-3	49.1	30	16	4	1	34-5	43	2.74	128	.175	.314	0	—	0		5		0.9
Total	10	34	40	.459	351	17	0	57-25	609.1	529	256	53	7	286-58	471	3.32	107	.235	.320	78-0-2	.179	1	63	16	56	2.8

FRISK, EMIL John Emil B10.15.1874 Kalkaska MI D1.27.1922 Seattle WA BL/TR/6-1/190 d9.2 ▲

YEAR	TM LG	W	L	PCT	G	GS	CG-SHO	SV-BS	IP	H	R	HR	HB	BB-IB	SO	ERA	AERA	OAV	OOB	AB-HR-SH	AVG	PB	SUP	APR	DL	PW
1899	Cin N	3	6	.333	9	9	9	0	68.1	81	52	1	6	17	17	3.95	99	.295	.349	25	.280	1	100	-4		-0.3
1901	Det A	5	4	.556	11	7	6	0	74.2	94	60	1	2	26	22	4.34	89	.304	.362	48-1-0	.313	2*	130	-5		-0.1
Total	2	8	10	.444	20	16	15	0	143	175	112	2	8	43	39	4.15	93	.300	.356	73-1-0	.301	3	113	-9		-0.4

FRITZ, CHARLIE Charles Cornelius B6.18.1882 Mobile AL D7.30.1943 Mobile AL TL d10.5

YEAR	TM LG	W	L	PCT	G	GS	CG-SHO	SV-BS	IP	H	R	HR	HB	BB-IB	SO	ERA	AERA	OAV	OOB	AB-HR-SH	AVG	PB	SUP	APR	DL	PW
1907	Phi A	0	0	—	1	1	0	0	3	0	1	0	1	3	1	3.00	87	.000	.333	1	.000	-0	104	0		0.0

FROATS, BILL William John B10.20.1930 New York NY D2.9.1998 Minneapolis MN BL/TL/6-0/180 d4.22 Col Notre Dame

YEAR	TM LG	W	L	PCT	G	GS	CG-SHO	SV-BS	IP	H	R	HR	HB	BB-IB	SO	ERA	AERA	OAV	OOB	AB-HR-SH	AVG	PB	SUP	APR	DL	PW
1955	Det A	0	0	—	1	0	0	0	2	0	0	0	0	2-0	0	0.00	—	.000	.333	0		0		1		0.*

FROCK, SAM Samuel William B12.23.1882 Baltimore MD D11.3.1925 Baltimore MD BR/TR/6-0/168 d9.21

YEAR	TM LG	W	L	PCT	G	GS	CG-SHO	SV-BS	IP	H	R	HR	HB	BB-IB	SO	ERA	AERA	OAV	OOB	AB-HR-SH	AVG	PB	SUP	APR	DL	PW
1907	Bos N	1	2	.333	5	3	3-1	0	33.1	28	17	1	2	11	12	2.97	86	.243	.320	14	.071	-1	149	-2		-0.4
1909	Pit N	2	1	.667	8	4	3	1	36.1	44	19	0	3	4	11	2.48	110	.299	.331	14	.143	-1	161	-1		-0.1
1910	Pit N	0	0	—	1	0	0	0	2	2	4	0	1	2	1	4.50	69	.400	.625	0	—	0		-1		-0.1
	Bos N	12	19	.387	45	29	13-2	2	255.1	245	133	8	4	91	170	3.21	104	.262	.330	84-0-5	.190	-3	75	1		-0.1
	Year	12	19	.387	46	29	13-2	2	257.1	247	137	8	5	93	171	3.22	103	.263	.333	84-0-5	.190	-3	74	-4		-0.2
1911	Bos N	0	1	.000	4	1	1	0	16	29	18	0	1	5	8	5.63	68	.426	.473	5	.200	-0	39	-4		-0.3
Total	4	15	23	.395	63	37	20-3	3	343	348	191	9	11	113	202	3.23	99	.274	.339	117-0-5	.171	-5	87	-7		-1.0

FROHWIRTH, TODD Todd Gerard B9.28.1962 Milwaukee WI BR/TR/6-4/205(190-205) [PhiN84 13/335] d8.10 Col Northwest Missouri

YEAR	TM LG	W	L	PCT	G	GS	CG-SHO	SV-BS	IP	H	R	HR	HB	BB-IB	SO	ERA	AERA	OAV	OOB	AB-HR-SH	AVG	PB	SUP	APR	DL	PW
1987	Phi N	1	0	1.000	10	0	0	0-0	11	12	0	0	0	2-0	9	0.00	—	.293	.326	1-0-1	.000	-0		5		0.4
1988	Phi N	1	2	.333	12	0	0	0-1	12	16	11	2	0	11-6	11	8.25	44	.327	.443	0	—	0		-5		-1.*
1989	Phi N	1	0	1.000	45	0	0	0-1	62.2	56	26	4	3	18-0	39	3.59	100	.240	.302	1-0-1	.000	0		-1		0.*
1990	Phi N	0	1	.000	5	0	0	0-0	1	3	2	0	0	6-2	1	18.00	21	.500	.750	0	—	0		22		-0.*
1991	Bal A	7	3	.700	51	0	0	3-2	96.1	64	24	2	1	29-3	77	1.87	212	.190	.255	0	—	0		17		1.3
1992	Bal A	4	3	.571	65	0	0	4-3	106	97	33	4	3	41-4	58	2.46	165	.247	.323	0	—	0		6		0.1
1993	Bal A	6	7	.462	70	0	0	3-4	96.1	91	47	7	3	44-8	50	3.83	118	.256	.342	0	—	0		-17		-1.6
1994	Bos A	0	3	.000	22	0	0	1-0	26.2	40	36	3	2	17-2	13	10.80	47	.339	.431	0	—	0		-5		-0.7
1996	Cal A	0	0	—	4	0	0	0-0	5.2	10	11	1	1	4-0	1	11.12	45	.370	.455	0	—	0		23		1.*
Total	9	20	19	.513	284	0	0	11-11	417.2	389	192	23	13	172-25	259	3.60	115	.250	.328	2-0-2	.000	-0	23		1.*

FROMME, ART Arthur Henry B9.3.1883 Quincy IL D8.24.1956 Los Angeles CA BR/TR/6-0/178 d9.14

YEAR	TM LG	W	L	PCT	G	GS	CG-SHO	SV-BS	IP	H	R	HR	HB	BB-IB	SO	ERA	AERA	OAV	OOB	AB-HR-SH	AVG	PB	SUP	APR	DL	PW
1906	StL N	1	2	.333	3	3	3-1	0	25	19	6	0	1	10	11	1.44	183	.221	.309	9	.222	0	28	3		0.*
1907	StL N	5	13	.278	23	16	13-2	0	145.2	138	73	3	4	67	67	2.90	86	.256	.343	55-0-2	.182	-1	73	-7		-0.*
1908	StL N	5	13	.278	20	14	9-2	0	116	102	59	1	2	50	62	2.72	87	.218	.296	36-0-2	.139	-1	72	-6		-1.*
1909	Cin N	19	13	.594	37	34	22-4	2	279.1	195	84	2	3	101	126	1.90	137	.201	.278	94-0-6	.191	-2	97	23		3.*
1910	Cin N	3	4	.429	11	5	1	0	49.1	44	22	2	1	39	10	2.92	100	.248	.402	15-0-1	.133	-1	77	0		-0.*
1911	Cin N	10	11	.476	38	26	11-1	0	208	190	111	8	16	79	107	3.46	96	.248	.331	74-0-4	.189	-1	93	-4		-0.*
1912	Cin N	16	18	.471	43	37	23-3	0	296	285	126	7	11	88	120	2.74	123	.260	.321	103-0-5	.087	-9	88	20		1.*
1913	Cin N	1	4	.200	9	7	2	0	56	55	30	1	3	21	24	4.18	78	.274	.351	21	.143	-0	63	-4		-1.*
	NY N	11	6	.647	26	12	3	0	112.1	112	58	5	2	29	50	4.01	78	.260	.310	35-0-3	.171	-0	84	-8		-1.*
	Year	12	10	.545	35	19	5	0	168.1	167	88	6	5	50	74	4.06	78	.264	.323	56-0-3	.161	-1	76	-10		-0.*
1914	NY N	9	5	.643	38	12	3-1	2	138	142	57	7	7	44	57	3.20	83	.283	.349	31-0-3	.226	1	124	-7		-0.*
1915	NY N	0	1	.000	4	1	0	0	12.1	15	11	1	0	2	4	5.84	44	.306	.333	3	.333	1	87	-5		-0.*
Total	10	80	90	.471	252	167	90-14	4	1438	1297	637	37	50	530	638	2.90	100	.246	.320	476-0-26	.162	-8	88	5		3.*

FROST, DAVE Carl David B11.17.1952 Long Beach CA BR/TR/6-6/235(220-235) [ChiA74 18/412] d9.11 Col Stanford

YEAR	TM LG	W	L	PCT	G	GS	CG-SHO	SV-BS	IP	H	R	HR	HB	BB-IB	SO	ERA	AERA	OAV	OOB	AB-HR-SH	AVG	PB	SUP	APR	DL	PW
1977	Chi A	1	1	.500	4	3	0	0	23.2	30	9	0	1	3-0	15	3.04	134	.323	.343	0	—	0	95	3		0.*
1978	Cal A	5	4	.556	11	10	2-1	0-0	80.1	71	24	6	2	24-3	30	2.58	141	.240	.298	0	—	0	59	11		1.*
1979	†Cal A	16	10	.615	36	33	12-2	1-0	239.1	226	108	17	5	77-4	107	3.57	114	.251	.311	0	—	0	93	-13	58	-1.*
1980	Cal A	4	8	.333	15	15	2	0	78.1	97	53	8	2	21-1	28	5.29	75	.308	.352	0	—	0	68	-8		-1.*
1981	Cal A	1	8	.111	12	9	0	0-0	47.1	44	30	3	1	19-0	16	5.51	67	.250	.323	0	—	0	105	-12	44	-1.*
1982	KC A	6	6	.500	21	14	0	1-0	81.2	103	53	7	3	30-0	26	5.51	74	.313	.372	0	—	0	103	-6	102	-1.*
Total	6	33	37	.471	99	84	16-3	1-0	550.2	571	277	41	14	174-8	222	4.10	97	.271	.327	0	—	0				

FRY, JOHNSON Johnson "Jay" B11.21.1901 Huntington WV D4.7.1959 Carmi IL BR/TR/6-1/150 d8.24 Col Marshall

YEAR	TM LG	W	L	PCT	G	GS	CG-SHO	SV-BS	IP	H	R	HR	HB	BB-IB	SO	ERA	AERA	OAV	OOB	AB-HR-SH	AVG	PB	SUP	APR	DL	PW
1923	Cle A	0	0	—	1	0	0	0	3.2	6	5	0	0	4	0	12.27	32	.353	.476	1	1.000	1		-3		-0.*

FRYE, CHARLIE Charles Andrew B7.17.1914 Hickory NC D5.25.1945 Hickory NC BR/TR/6-1/175 d7.28

YEAR	TM LG	W	L	PCT	G	GS	CG-SHO	SV-BS	IP	H	R	HR	HB	BB-IB	SO	ERA	AERA	OAV	OOB	AB-HR-SH	AVG	PB	SUP	APR	DL	PW
1940	Phi N	0	6	.000	15	5	1	0	50.1	58	32	3	0	26	18	4.65	84	.291	.373	19-1-0	.263	1*	27	-5		-0.*

FRYMAN, WOODIE Woodrow Thompson B4.15.1940 Ewing KY BR/TL/6-2/205(197-225) d4.15

YEAR	TM LG	W	L	PCT	G	GS	CG-SHO	SV-BS	IP	H	R	HR	HB	BB-IB	SO	ERA	AERA	OAV	OOB	AB-HR-SH	AVG	PB	SUP	APR	DL	PW
1966	Pit N	12	9	.571	36	28	9-3	1	181.2	182	86	13	1	47-9	105	3.81	94	.261	.308	63-0-4	.159	-1	107	-5		-0.*
1967	Pit N	3	8	.273	28	18	3-1	1	113.1	121	67	12	4	44-3	74	4.05	83	.276	.344	34-0-1	.118	-1	104	-12		-1.*
1968	Phi N☆	12	14	.462	34	32	10-5	0	213.2	198	78	9	6	64-2	151	2.78	108	.246	.305	71-0-7	.085	-2	106	4		0.*
1969	Phi N	12	15	.444	36	35	10-1	0-0	228.1	243	123	15	11	89-3	150	4.41	81	.270	.343	76-1-8	.118	-2	109	-21		-2.*
1970	Phi N	8	6	.571	27	20	4-3	0	127.2	122	61	11	1	43-2	97	4.09	98	.253	.313	39-0-3	.128	-2	107	0	34	0.*
1971	Phi N	10	7	.588	37	17	3-2	2-2	149.1	133	61	7	3	46-1	104	3.38	105	.242	.301	37-0-5	.189	0	101	4		0.*
1972	Phi N	4	10	.286	23	14	3-2	1-0	119.2	131	64	15	2	39-9	69	4.36	83	.279	.335	33-1-2	.152	1	99	-9		-0.*
	†Det A	10	3	.769	16	14	6-1	0-0	113.2	93	31	6	7	31-3	72	2.06	154	.220	.284	40-0-4	.125	-2	114	13		1.*
1973	Det A	6	13	.316	34	29	1	0-0	169.2	200	106	23	3	64-5	119	5.36	76	.294	.356	0	—	0	83	-21		-2.*
1974	Det A	6	9	.400	27	22	4-1	0-0	141.2	120	73	16	4	67-2	92	4.32	89	.233	.324	0	—	0	84	-5		-0.*
1975	Mon N	9	12	.429	38	20	7-3	3-4	157	141	69	10	5	68-7	118	3.32	116	.239	.323	49-0-5	.204	1	76	7		0.*
1976	Mon N☆	13	13	.500	34	32	4-2	2-0	216.1	218	89	14	9	76-7	123	3.37	112	.263	.328	64-0-11	.109	-3	88	10		0.*
1977	Cin N	5	5	.500	17	12	0	1-0	75.1	83	45	13	2	45-2	57	5.38	73	.292	.390	22-0-3	.318	2	109	-10		0.*
1978	Chi N	2	4	.333	13	9	0	0-1	55.2	64	37	6	0	37-5	28	5.17	78	.309	.407	16-0-3	.063	-1	74	-7		-0.*
	Mon N	5	7	.417	19	17	4-3	1-0	94.2	93	39	4	3	37-1	53	3.61	99	.260	.334	34-0-2	.059	-2	108	1		0.*
	Year	7	11	.389	32	26	4-3	1-1	150.1	157	76	10	3	74-6	81	4.19	89	.278	.362	50-0-5	.060	-3	95	-7		-0.*
1979	Mon N	3	6	.333	44	0	0	10-1	58	52	25	4	1	32	44	2.79	133	.248	.328	7	.000	-1		4		0.*
1980	Mon N	7	4	.636	61	0	0	17-6	80	61	23	1	2	30-9	59	2.25	159	.209	.285	12-0-2	.167	-0		12		1.*
1981	†Mon N	5	5	.500	35	0	0	7-8	43	38	16	1	4	14-1	25	1.88	189	.247	.308	3-0-2	.667	1		5		0.*
1982	Mon N	9	4	.692	60	0	0	12-6	69.2	66	36	3	1	26-4	46	3.75	99	.259	.326	0	—	0		-2		-0.*
1983	Mon N	0	3	.000	6	0	0	1-0	3	6	7	1	0	1-0	1	21.00	17	.571	.600	0	—	0		-5	144	-0.*
Total	18	141	155	.476	625	322	68-27	58-30	2411.1	2367	1136	187	68	890-79	1587	3.77	96	.259	.327	609-2-63	.138	-12	98	-37	178	1.*

FUCHS, CHARLIE Charles Thomas B11.18.1912 Union Hill NJ D6.10.1969 Weehawken NJ BB/TR/5-8/168 d4.17

YEAR	TM LG	W	L	PCT	G	GS	CG-SHO	SV-BS	IP	H	R	HR	HB	BB-IB	SO	ERA	AERA	OAV	OOB	AB-HR-SH	AVG	PB	SUP	APR	DL	PW
1942	Det A	3	3	.500	9	4	1-1	0	36.2	43	27	5	1	19	15	6.63	60	.285	.368	13	.077	-1	76	-8		-0.*
1943	Phi N	2	7	.222	17	9	4-1	0	77.2	76	40	4	3	34	12	4.29	79	.266	.350	22-0-3	.091	-2	87	-7		
	StL A	0	0	—	13	0	0	0	35.2	42	22	4	1	11	9	4.04	82	.294	.348	7	.000	-1		-4		-0.*

YEAR	TM LG	W	L	PCT	G	GS	CG-SHO	SV-BS	IP	H	R	HR	HB	BB-IB	SO	ERA	AERA	OAV	OOB	AB-HR-SH	AVG	PB	SUP	APR	DL	PW
1944	Bro N	1	0	1.000	8	0	0	0	15.2	25	16	2	1	9	5	5.74	62	.347	.427	1	.000	0		-6		-0.3
Total	3	6	10	.375	47	13	5-2	1	165.2	186	105	15	6	73	41	4.89	72	.285	.363	43-0-3	.070	-4	84	-25		-2.8

FUENTES, BRIAN Brian Christopher B8.9.1975 Merced CA BL/TL/6-4/220* [SeaA95 25/678] d6.2 Col Merced (CA) JC

YEAR	TM LG	W	L	PCT	G	GS	CG-SHO	SV-BS	IP	H	R	HR	HB	BB-IB	SO	ERA	AERA	OAV	OOB	AB-HR-SH	AVG	PB	SUP	APR	DL	PW
2001	Sea A	1	1	.500	10	0	0	0-1	11.2	6	6	2	3	8-0	10	4.63	92	.171	.362	0	—	0		0		0.0
2002	Col N	2	0	1.000	31	0	0	0-0	26.2	25	14	4	3	13-0	34	4.73	100	.250	.347	0	—	0		1		0.0
2003	Col N	3	3	.500	75	0	0	4-2	75.1	64	24	7	6	34-2	82	2.75	178	.231	.325	1	.000	-0		16		1.3
2004	Col N	2	4	.333	47	0	0	0-1	44.2	46	30	5	4	19-6	48	5.64	84	.269	.356	0	—	0		-4		-0.5
2005	Col N☆	2	5	.286	78	0	0	31-3	74.1	59	25	6	10	34-4	91	2.91	164	.218	.326	0	—	0		14	69	2.2
Total	5	10	13	.435	241	0	0	35-7	232.2	200	99	24	26	108-12	269	3.67	130	.234	.336	1	.000	-0	27	69	3.0

FUENTES, MIGUEL Miguel (Pinet) B5.10.1946 Loiza Aldea, PR D1.29.1970 Loiza Aldea, PR BR/TR/6-0/165 d9.1

| 1969 | Sea A | 1 | 3 | .250 | 8 | 4 | 1 | 0 | 26 | 29 | 15 | 1 | 0 | 16-1 | 14 | 5.19 | 70 | .284 | .381 | 6-0-2 | .333 | 0 | 79 | -4 | | -0.5 |

FUHR, OSCAR Oscar Lawrence B8.22.1893 Defiance MO D3.27.1975 Dallas TX BL/TL/6-0.5/176 d4.19

1921	Chi N	0	0	—	1	0	0	0	4	11	9	1	0	0	2	9.00	42	.500	.500	1	.000	-0		-4		-0.2
1924	Bos A	3	6	.333	23	10	4-1	0	80.1	100	71	1	5	39	30	5.94	74	.310	.392	22-0-1	.182	-1	133	-17		-1.6
1925	Bos A	0	6	.000	39	5	0	0	91.1	138	83	7	3	30	27	6.60	69	.364	.415	20	.250	0	129	-20		-1.0
Total	3	3	12	.200	63	15	4-1	0	175.2	249	163	9	8	69	59	6.35	70	.344	.407	43-0-1	.209	-1	131	-41		-2.8

FULGHAM, JOHN John Thomas B6.9.1956 St.Louis MO BR/TR/6-2/205* [StLN76 S1/15] d6.19 Col Miami [DL 1981 StL N 180]

1979	StL N	10	6	.625	20	19	10-2	0-0	146	123	47	10	3	26-3	75	2.53	151	.227	.266	42-0-11	.143	1*	90	20		2.2
1980	StL N	4	6	.400	15	14	4-1	0-0	85.1	66	33	7	1	32-1	48	3.38	111	.219	.295	27-0-3	.000	-3*	82	5	45	0.2
Total	2	14	12	.538	35	33	14-3	0-0	231.1	189	80	17	4	58-4	123	2.84	133	.224	.276	69-0-14	.087	-2	87	25	225	2.4

FULLER, ED Edward Ashton B3.22.1868 Washington DC D3.16.1935 Hyattsville MD BR/TR/6-0/158 d7.17

| 1886 | Was N | 0 | 1 | .000 | 2 | 1 | 1 | 0 | 13 | 15 | 12 | 0 | | 5 | 3 | 6.92 | 47 | .375 | .444 | 7 | .143 | -0 | 76 | -4 | | -0.3 |

FULLERTON, CURT Curtis Hooper B9.13.1898 Ellsworth ME D1.9.1975 Winthrop MA BL/TR/6-0/162 d4.14

1921	Bos A	1	0	1.000	4	1	0	0	15.1	22	17	3	1	10	4	8.80	48	.355	.452	4	.000	-0	118	-8		-0.5
1922	Bos A	1	4	.200	31	3	0	0	64.1	70	40	4	5	35	17	5.46	75	.290	.391	8	.250	1	103	-7		-0.3
1923	Bos A	2	15	.118	37	15	6	1	143.1	167	108	9	6	71	37	5.09	81	.300	.385	37-0-1	.297	2	51	-17		-1.7
1924	Bos A	7	12	.368	33	20	9	2	152	166	93	1	6	73	33	4.32	101	.283	.368	42-0-2	.071	-3	77	-1		-0.5
1925	Bos A	0	3	.000	4	2	0	0	22.2	22	11	1	2	9	3	3.18	143	.259	.344	10-0-1	.200	-0	46	3		0.4
1933	Bos A	0	2	.000	6	2	2	0	25.1	36	24	1	1	13	10	8.53	51	.364	.442	9	.222	0	39	-10		-0.6
Total	6	10	37	.213	115	43	18	3	423	483	293	19	21	211	104	5.11	83	.296	.384	110-0-4	.182	-1	68	-40		-3.2

FULTON, BILL William David B10.22.1963 Pittsburgh PA BR/TR/6-3/195 [NYA83 S2/35] d9.12 Col Pensacola (FL) JC

| 1987 | NY A | 1 | 0 | 1.000 | 3 | 0 | 0 | 0-0 | 4.2 | 9 | 6 | 4 | 1 | 1-0 | 2 | 11.57 | 38 | .409 | .458 | 0 | | 0 | | -4 | | -0.6 |

FULTZ, AARON Richard Aaron B9.4.1973 Memphis TN BL/TL/6-0/196* [SFN92 6/159] d4.5 Col North Florida CC

2000	†SF N	5	2	.714	58	0	0	1-2	69.1	67	38	8	3	28-0	62	4.67	93	.263	.336	6-0-1	.333	1		-2		0.0
2001	SF N	3	1	.750	66	0	0	1-1	71	70	40	9	1	21-3	67	4.56	90	.258	.310	5	.400	1		-4		-0.1
2002	†SF N	2	2	.500	43	0	0	0-1	41.1	47	22	4	3	19-3	31	4.79	82	.294	.377	1	.000	-0*		-3		-0.3
2003	Tex A	1	3	.250	64	0	0	0-0	67.1	75	43	9	2	27-7	53	5.21	95	.287	.356	0	—	0		-2	18	-0.1
2004	Min A	3	3	.500	55	0	0	1-3	50	50	28	6	4	23-2	37	5.04	92	.267	.344	0	—	0		-1		-0.1
2005	Phi N	4	0	1.000	62	0	0	0-1	72.1	47	21	6	5	23-2	54	2.24	194	.186	.266	3	.333	0		16		0.9
Total	6	18	11	.621	348	0	0	3-8	371.1	356	192	41	15	141-17	304	4.34	102	.257	.328	15-0-1	.333	1	4	18	0.3

FUNK, FRANK Franklin Ray B8.30.1935 Washington DC BR/TR/6-0/180* d9.3 C11

1960	Cle A	4	2	.667	9	0	0	1	31.2	27	8	3	0	9-3	18	1.99	188	.248	.305	9	.111	-0		6		1.2
1961	Cle A	11	11	.500	56	0	0	11	92.1	79	35	9	4	31-6	64	3.31	119	.234	.303	17	.059	-1		8		1.5
1962	Cle A	2	1	.667	47	0	0	6	80.2	62	35	11	4	32-1	49	3.24	120	.212	.293	15	.067	-1		5		0.1
1963	Mil N	3	3	.500	25	0	0	1	43.2	42	14	3	1	13-3	19	2.68	120	.258	.315	4	.000	-0*		3		0.3
Total	4	20	17	.541	137	0	0	18	248.1	210	92	26	9	85-13	150	3.01	125	.233	.302	45	.067	-3	22		3.1

FUNK, TOM Thomas James B3.13.1962 Kansas City MO BL/TL/6-2/210 [HouN83 28/691] d7.24 Col Northwest Missouri

| 1986 | Hou N | 0 | 0 | — | 8 | 0 | 0 | 0-0 | 8.1 | 10 | 6 | 0 | 0 | 6 | 2 | 6.48 | 56 | .286 | .390 | 1 | .000 | -0 | | -2 | | -0.1 |

FUSSELBACK, EDDIE Edward L. B7.17.1856 Philadelphia PA D4.14.1926 Philadelphia PA BR/5-6/156 d5.3 ▲

| 1882 | StL AA | 1 | 2 | .333 | 4 | 2 | 2 | 1 | 23 | 34 | 24 | 0 | | 2 | 3 | 4.70 | 60 | .321 | .333 | 136 | .228 | 0* | 119 | -4 | | -0.5 |

FUSSELL, CHRIS Christopher Wren B5.19.1976 Oregon OH BR/TR/6-2/200* [BalA94 9/251] d9.15

1998	Bal A	0	1	.000	3	2	0	0-0	9.2	11	9	1	0	9-1	8	8.38	54	.306	.435	0	—	0	82	-4		-0.3
1999	KC A	0	5	.000	17	8	0	2-0	56	72	51	9	5	36-3	37	7.39	69	.329	.428	0	—	0	101	-14		-1.1
2000	KC A	5	3	.625	20	9	0	0-0	70	76	52	18	2	44-2	46	6.30	83	.286	.385	2	.000	-0	126	-8	60	-0.8
Total	3	5	9	.357	40	19	0	2-0	135.2	159	112	28	7	89-6	91	6.90	74	.305	.407	2	.000	-0	111	-26	60	-2.2

FUSSELL, FRED Frederick Morris "Moonlight Ace" B10.7.1895 Sheridan MO D10.23.1966 Syracuse NY BL/TL/5-10/155 d9.23

1922	Chi N	1	1	.500	3	2	1	0	19	24	11	0	0	8	4	4.74	89	.333	.400	6	.000	-1	78	-1		-0.1
1923	Chi N	3	5	.375	28	2	1	3	76.1	90	51	2	3	31	38	5.54	72	.298	.369	20	.200	-0	62	-11		-1.0
1928	Pit N	8	9	.471	28	20	9-2	1	159.2	183	79	6	1	41	43	3.61	113	.295	.340	58-0-1	.121	-3	108	7		0.2
1929	Pit N	2	2	.500	21	3	0	1	39.2	68	42	8	1	8	18	8.62	55	.389	.418	16-2-0	.250	2	171	-16		-1.2
Total	4	14	17	.452	80	27	11-2	5	294.2	365	183	16	5	88	103	4.86	85	.312	.363	100-2-1	.150	-2	110	-21		-2.1

FYHRIE, MIKE Michael Edwin B12.9.1969 Long Beach CA BR/TR/6-2/203(190-203) [KCA91 12/314] d9.14 Col UCLA

1996	NY N	0	1	.000	2	0	0	0-0	2.1	4	4	0	0	3-0	0	15.43	26	.364	.500	0	—	0		-3		-0.5
1999	Ana A	0	4	.000	16	7	0	0-0	51.2	61	32	8	0	21-1	26	5.05	97	.286	.349	0	—	0	71	-1		-0.1
2000	Ana A	0	0	—	32	0	0	0-0	52.2	54	14	4	0	15-4	43	2.39	216	.269	.315	0	—	0		16	23	0.7
2001	Chi N	0	2	.000	15	0	0	0-0	15	16	7	1	0	7-0	6	4.20	100	.281	.359	2	.000	0		0	73	0.0
	Oak A	0	0	—	3	0	0	0-0	5	2	0	0	1	1-0	5	0.00	—	.125	.176	0	—	0		2		0.1
2002	Oak A	1	4	.333	16	4	0	0-0	48.2	46	25	3	4	20-1	29	4.44	101	.246	.332	0	—	0	140	1		0.1
Total	5	2	11	.154	84	11	0	0-0	175.1	183	82	16	4	67-6	109	4.00	119	.267	.334	2	.000	-0	94	15	96	0.3

GABLER, FRANK Frank Harold "The Great Gabbo" B11.6.1911 E.Highlands CA D11.1.1967 Long Beach CA BR/TR/6-1/175 d4.19

1935	NY N	2	1	.667	26	1	0	0	60	79	43	6	0	20	24	5.70	68	.315	.365	16	.125	-1	154	-13		-0.7
1936	†NY N	9	8	.529	43	14	9	6	161.2	170	62	11	3	34	46	3.45	125	.274	.315	48-0-6	.208	2	110	16		1.7
1937		0	0	—	6	0	0	0	9	20	14	1	0	2	3	10.00	39	.455	.478	0		0		-7		-0.3
	Bos N	4	7	.364	19	9	2-1	2	76	84	45	7	0	16	19	5.09	70	.283	.319	22	.182	0	72	-12		-1.5
	Year	4	7	.364	25	9	2-1	2	85	104	59	8	0	18	22	5.61	64	.305	.340	22	.182	0	71	-18		-1.8
1938	Bos N	0	0	—	1	0	0	0	0.1	3	3	0	0	1	0	81.00	4	1.000	1.000	0	—	0		-3		-0.1
	Chi A	1	7	.125	18	7	3	0	69.1	101	74	12	1	34	17	9.09	54	.348	.418	21	.238	0	85	-28		-2.5
Total	4	16	23	.410	113	31	10-1	8	376.1	457	241	37	4	107	109	5.26	76	.303	.351	107-0-6	.196	1	95	-47		-3.4

GABLER, JOHN John Richard "Gab" B10.2.1930 Kansas City MO BB/TR/6-2/165* d9.18

1959	NY A	1	1	.500	1	1	0	0	19.1	21	6	1	1	10-0	11	2.79	130	.284	.376	6	.000	-1	24	2		0.1
1960	NY A	3	3	.500	21	4	0	1	52	46	27	2	0	8-0	19	4.15	86	.242	.348	11-0-1	.091	-0	86	-3		-0.4
1961	Was A	3	8	.273	29	9	0	4	92.2	104	61	5	1	37-3	33	4.86	83	.283	.349	25	.200	1*	47	-10		-1.0
Total	4	7	12	.368	53	14	0	5	164	171	94	8	2	79-4	63	4.39	87	.271	.352	42-0-1	.143	-0	56	-11		-1.3

GABLES, KEN Kenneth Harlin "Coral" B1.31.1919 Walnut Grove MO D1.2.1960 Walnut Grove MO BR/TR/5-11/210 d4.18

1945	Pit N	11	7	.611	29	16	6	1	138.2	139	69	5	4	68	49	4.15	95	.256	.319	39-0-3	.103	-3	117	0		-0.4
1946	Pit N	2	4	.333	32	7	0	1	100.2	113	64	3	1	52	39	5.27	67	.281	.365	24-0-2	.250	1	80	-17		-0.9
1947	Pit N	0	0	—	1	0	0	0	0.2	3	4	0	0	3	0	54.00	8	.750	.750	0		0		-2		-0.1
Total	3	13	11	.542	62	23	6	2	239.2	255	135	8	5	98	88	4.69	80	.269	.340	63-0-5	.159	-2	108	-19		-1.4

GADDY, JOHN John Wilson "Sheriff" B2.5.1914 Wadesboro NC D5.3.1966 Albemarle NC BR/TR/6-0.5/182 d9.27 Col Wake Forest

| 1938 | Bro N | 2 | 0 | 1.000 | 2 | 2 | 1 | 0 | 13 | 13 | 3 | 0 | 1 | 4 | 3 | 0.69 | 564 | .255 | .321 | 6 | .000 | -1 | 130 | 4 | | 0.5 |

YEAR	TM LG	W	L	PCT	G	GS	CG-SHO	SV-BS	IP	H	R	HR	HB	BB-IB	SO	ERA	AERA	OAV	OOB	AB-HR-SH	AVG	PB	SUP	APR	DL	PW
GAFF, BRENT	Brent Allen B10.5.1958 Fort Wayne IN BR/TR/6-2/200(185-200) [NYN77 6/146] d7.7 [DL 1985 NY N 182]																									
1982	NY N	0	3	.000	7	5	0	0-0	31.2	41	22	3	1	10-0	14	4.55	81	.323	.374	8-0-1	.000	-0	77	-4		-0.4
1983	NY N	1	0	1.000	4	0	0	0-0	10.1	18	9	0	0	1-1	4	6.10	60	.360	.365	3	.000	-0		-3		-0.3
1984	NY N	3	2	.600	47	0	0	1-0	84.1	77	39	4	1	36-11	42	3.63	98	.247	.320	6	.000	-1		0		-0.1
Total	3	4	5	.444	58	5	0	1-0	126.1	136	70	7	2	47-12	60	4.06	89	.278	.338	17-0-1	.000	-1	77	-7	182	-0.8
GAGNE, ERIC	Eric Serge B1.7.1976 Montreal QC, Can. BR/TR/6-2/235(195-235) d9.7 Col Seminole St. (OK) JC																									
1999	LA N	1	1	.500	5	5	0	0-0	30	18	8	3	0	15-0	30	2.10	207	.175	.280	10	.200	0	72	8		0.4
2000	LA N	4	6	.400	20	19	0	0-0	101.1	106	62	20	3	60-1	79	5.15	86	.270	.368	28-0-6	.143	-1	102	-7		-0.7
2001	LA N	6	7	.462	33	24	0	0-0	151.2	144	90	24	16	46-1	130	4.75	87	.251	.320	44-1-6	.136	2	119	-13		-0.9
2002	LA N★	4	1	.800	77	0	0	52-4	82.1	55	18	6	2	16-4	114	1.97	198	.189	.235	1	.000	0		19		3.3
2003	LA N★	2	3	.400	77	0	0	55-0	82.1	37	12	2	3	20-2	137	1.20	343	.133	.199	0	—	0		28		4.9
2004	†LA N★	7	3	.700	70	0	0	45-2	82.1	53	24	5	5	22-3	114	2.19	189	.181	.248	3	.000	-0		17		3.4
2005	LA N	1	0	1.000	14	0	0	8-0	13.1	10	4	2	0	3-0	22	2.70	152	.200	.245	0	—	0		2	153	0.4
Total	7	25	21	.543	296	48	0	160-6	543.1	423	218	62	29	182-11	626	3.28	127	.213	.287	86-1-12	.140	0	111	54	153	10.8
GAGUS, CHARLIE	Charles Frederick (b Charles Frederick Geggus) B3.25.1862 San Francisco CA D1.16.1917 San Francisco CA 5-7.5/150 d8.7 Col St. Marys (CA)																									
1884	Was U	10	9	.526	23	21	19	0	177.1	143	100	2		38	156	2.54	95	.206	.247	154	.247	-3*	98	-5		-0.6
GAILLARD, EDDIE	Julian Edward B8.13.1970 Camden NJ BR/TR/6-1/180(180-200) [DetA93 13/361] d8.11 Col Florida Southern																									
1997	Det A	1	0	1.000	16	0	0	1-1	20.1	16	12	2	0	10-2	12	5.31	87	.211	.295	0	—	0		-1	95	-0.1
1998	TB A				6	0	0	0-0	7.2	4	5	3	0	3-0	5	5.87	82	.148	.233	0	—	0		0		0.0
1999	TB A	1	0	1.000	8	0	0	0-0	8.2	12	9	1	1	4-0	7	2.08	239	.324	.405	0	—	0		0		-0.1
Total	3	2	0	1.000	30	0	0	1-1	36.2	32	26	6	1	17-2	24	4.66	102	.229	.313	0	—	0		-2	95	-0.1
GAINES, NEMO	Willard Roland B12.23.1897 Alexandria VA D1.26.1979 Warrenton VA BL/TL/6-0/180 d6.26 Col Navy																									
1921	Was A	0	0	—	4	0	0	0	4.2	5	0	0	0	2	1	0.00	—	.294	.368	1	.000	-0		2		0.1
GAISER, FRED	Frederick Jacob B8.31.1885 Stuttgart, Germany D10.9.1918 Trenton NJ d9.3																									
1908	StL N	0	0	—	1	0	0	0	2.1	4	2	0	0	3	2	7.71	31	.444	.583	1	.000	-0		-1		-0.1
GAJKOWSKI, STEVE	Stephen Robert B12.30.1969 Seattle WA BR/TR/6-2/200 [CleA90 18/487] d5.25 Col Bellevue (WA) CC																									
1998	Sea A	0	0	—	9	0	0	0-0	8.2	14	8	3	2	4-0	3	7.27	64	.389	.476	0	—	0		-3		-0.1
GAKELER, DAN	Daniel Michael B5.1.1964 Mt.Holly NJ BR/TR/6-6/215 [BosA84*S1/3] d6.9 Col Mercer Co. (NJ) CC [DL 1992 Det A 182]																									
1991	Det A	1	4	.200	31	7	0	2-2	73.2	73	52	5	1	39-6	43	5.74	73	.256	.345	0		0	100	-13		-0.8
GALASSO, BOB	Robert Joseph B1.13.1952 Connellsville PA BL/TR/6-1/205* d7.24																									
1977	Sea A	0	6	.000	11	7	0	0	35	57	36	8	3	8-0	21	9.00	46	.365	.402	0	—	0	62	-17		-2.4
1979	Mil A	3	1	.750	31	0	0	3-3	51.1	64	30	5	0	26-3	28	4.38	96	.299	.372	0	—	0		-2		-0.2
1981	Sea A	1	1	.500	13	1	0	1-0	31.2	32	19	2	0	13-1	14	4.83	80	.264	.331	0	—	0	23	-3		-0.2
Total	3	4	8	.333	55	8	0	4-3	118	153	85	15	3	47-4	63	5.87	70	.312	.371	0	—	0	58	-22		-2.8
GALE, RICH	Richard Blackwell B1.19.1954 Littleton NH BR/TR/6-7/225* [KCA75 5/105] d4.30 C2 Col New Hampshire																									
1978	KC A	14	8	.636	31	30	9-3	0-0	192.1	171	78	10	3	100-3	88	3.09	124	.244	.339	0	—	0	110	15		1.5
1979	KC A	9	10	.474	34	31	2-1	0-0	181.2	197	131	19	4	99-4	103	5.65	76	.278	.366	0	—	0	126	-28		-2.5
1980	†KC A	13	9	.591	32	28	6-1	1-1	190.2	169	90	16	2	78-2	97	3.92	103	.239	.315	0	—	0	86	-18		-2.0
1981	KC A	6	6	.500	19	15	2	0-0	101.2	107	63	14	2	38-0	102	4.23	85	.294	.370	48-1-1	.125	1	79	-12		-1.2
1982	SF N	7	14	.333	33	29	2	0-1	170.1	193	91	9	5	81-11	102	4.21	102	.285	.362	20-1-1	.150	1	96	-19		-1.9
1983	Cin N	4	6	.400	33	7	0	1-0	89.2	103	64	8	1	43-8	53	5.82	66	.286	.362	0	—	0	129	-5		-0.8
1984	Bos A	2	3	.400	13	4	0	0-0	43.2	57	27	6	1	18-0	19	5.56	76	.315	.380	0	—	0	106	-63		-6.2
Total	7	55	56	.495	195	144	21-5	2-2	970	997	544	82	18	457-28	518	4.54	86	.269	.349	68-2-2	.132	0	106	-63		-6.2
GALEHOUSE, DENNY	Dennis Ward B12.7.1911 Marshallville OH D10.12.1998 Doylestown OH BR/TR/6-1/195 d4.30 Def 1944																									
1934	Cle A	0	0	—	1	0	0	0	1	2	3	0	0	1	0	18.00	25	.500	.600	0	—	0		-2		-0.1
1935	Cle A	1	0	1.000	5	1	1	0	13	16	14	1	1	9	8	9.00	50	.314	.426	4	.250	-0	135	-6		-0.4
1936	Cle A	8	7	.533	36	15	5	1	148.1	161	86	5	2	68	71	4.85	104	.280	.358	47-0-1	.170	-0	95	6		0.4
1937	Cle A	9	14	.391	36	29	7	3	200.2	238	114	11	1	83	78	4.57	101	.302	.369	72-0-2	.208	-1	80	2		0.3
1938	Cle A	7	8	.467	36	12	5-1	3	114	119	62	12	1	65	66	4.34	107	.275	.371	39	.154	-1	104	4		0.3
1939	Bos A	9	10	.474	30	18	6-1	0	146.2	160	84	6	1	52	68	4.54	104	.276	.337	47-0-4	.064	-4	109	-9		-1.1
1940	Bos A	6	6	.500	25	20	5	0	120	155	77	10	0	41	53	5.18	87	.313	.366	39-0-7	.077	-4	100	-7		-0.7
1941	StL A	9	10	.474	30	24	11-2	1	190.1	183	85	10	4	68	61	3.64	118	.253	.320	68-0-5	.191	-0	86	14		1.3
1942	StL A	12	12	.500	32	28	12-3	1	192.1	193	91	6	4	79	75	3.60	103	.262	.337	72-0-4	.194	1	115	2		0.3
1943	StL A	11	11	.500	32	28	14-2	1	224	217	80	8	1	74	114	2.77	120	.255	.315	72-0-8	.125	-3	106	13		0.8
1944	†StL A	9	10	.474	24	19	6-2	0	153	162	64	6	1	44	80	3.12	115	.266	.316	48-0-4	.063	-3	82	7		0.5
1946	StL A	8	12	.400	30	24	11-2	0	180	194	84	10	0	68	90	3.65	102	.273	.322	55-0-6	.091	-3	88	3		-0.2
1947	StL A	1	3	.250	9	4	0	1	32.1	42	26	3	0	16	11	6.12	63	.311	.384	8-0-2	.000	-1	114	-8		-1.1
	Bos A	11	7	.611	21	21	11-3	0	149	150	60	7	0	34	38	3.32	117	.260	.301	52-0-9	.096	-4	117	2		0.8
	Year	12	10	.545	30	25	11-3	1	181.1	192	86	10	0	50	49	3.82	102	.269	.317	60-0-11	.083	-5	117	2		-0.2
1948	Bos A	8	8	.500	27	15	6-1	3	137.1	152	68	10	2	46	38	4.00	110	.282	.341	42-0-3	.167	-0	95	6		-0.1
1949	Bos A	0	0	—	2	0	0	0	2	4	3	1	0	3	0	13.50	32	.400	.538	0	—	0		-2		-0.1
Total	15	109	118	.480	375	258	100-17	13	2004	2148	999	104	18	735	851	3.97	105	.275	.338	665-0-55	.138	-25	95	44		0.6
GALLAGHER, DOUG	Douglas Eugene B2.21.1940 Fremont OH BR/TL/6-3.5/195 d4.9																									
1962	Det A	0	4	.000	9	2	0	1	25	31	18	2	0	15-1	14	4.68	87	.290	.371	6	.333	1	132	-3		-0.4
GALLAGHER, ED	Edward Michael "Lefty" B11.28.1910 Dorchester MA D12.22.1981 Hyannis MA BB/TL/6-2/197 d7.8 Col Boston College																									
1932	Bos A	0	3	.000	9	3	0	0	23.2	30	36	3	0	28	6	12.55	36	.323	.479	5	.000	-1	38	-20		-1.2
GALLAGHER, BILL	William John B Philadelphia PA TL d5.2 ▲																									
1883	Bal AA	0	5	.000	7	5	4	0	51.2	79	57	0		6	19	5.40	64	.331	.347	61	.164	-1*	89	-10		-0.2
1884	Phi U	1	2	.333	3	3	3	0	25	32	29	3		4	12	3.24	71	.291	.316	11	.091	-2	92	-7		-0.2
Total	2	1	7	.125	10	8	7	0	76.2	111	86	3		10	31	4.70	66	.318	.337	72	.153	-3	90	-17		-1.2
GALLIA, BERT	Melvin Allys B10.14.1891 Beeville TX D3.19.1976 Devine TX BR/TR/6-0/165 d9.4 Col St. Marys (TX)																									
1912	Was A	0	0	—	2	0	0	0	2	2	0	0	0	3	0	0.00	—	.000	.333	0	—	0		1		0.1
1913	Was A	1	5	.167	31	4	0	3	96	85	66	2	7	46	46	4.13	72	.232	.329	23	.087	-2	69	-15		-1.3
1914	Was A	0	0	—	2	0	0	0	6	3	4	0	4	4	4	4.50	63	.120	.241	2	.000	-0		-1		-0.1
1915	Was A	17	11	.607	43	29	14-3	1	259.2	220	90	2	4	64	130	2.29	130	.234	.286	85-0-3	.165	-2	97	20		1.3
1916	Was A	17	13	.567	49	31	13-1	2	283.2	278	109	3	8	99	120	2.76	101	.266	.334	93-0-4	.194	-3	111	2		0.4
1917	Was A	9	13	.409	42	23	9-1	1	207.2	191	92	4	9	93	48	2.99	88	.258	.344	62-0-1	.209	2*	100	-9		-0.6
1918	StL A	8	6	.571	19	17	10-1	0	124	126	63	1	6	61	48	3.48	79	.268	.359	46-0-1	.130	-3	115	-10		-1.1
1919	StL A	12	14	.462	34	25	14-1	1	222.1	220	109	10	4	92	83	3.60	94	.264	.343	72-1-4	.153	-2	99	-5		-0.4
1920	StL A	0	1	.000	2	1	0	0	3.2	7	8	0	0	3	2	7.36	53	.400	.478	1	.000	-0	81	-3		-0.1
	Phi N	2	6	.250	18	5	1	2	72	79	48	2	3	29	35	4.50	76	.287	.362	23-0-1	.174	-1*	60	-9		-1.0
Total	9	66	69	.489	242	135	61-7	10	1277	1210	588	21	40	494	550	3.14	94	.256	.332	412-1-15	.167	-7	100	-29		-3.0
GALLIVAN, PHIL	Philip Joseph B5.29.1907 Seattle WA D11.24.1969 St.Paul MN BR/TR/6-0/170 d4.21																									
1931	Bro N	0	1	.000	6	1	0	0	15.1	23	11	2	0	7	1	5.28	72	.354	.417	3	.000	-0	22	-3		-0.3
1932	Chi A	1	3	.250	13	3	1	0	33.1	49	32	4	1	24	12	7.56	57	.338	.435	8	.375	1	79	-11		-1.2
1934	Chi A	4	7	.364	35	7	4	1	126.2	155	97	14	1	64	55	5.61	84	.295	.373	40-0-3	.225	1	110	-14		-1.9
Total	3	5	11	.313	54	11	4	1	175.1	227	140	20	2	95	68	5.95	77	.309	.389	51-0-3	.235	1	95	-28		-2.4
GALLO, MIKE	Michael Dwain B4.2.1977 Long Beach CA BL/TL/6-0/170* [HouN99 5/173] d7.2 Col Cal St.-Long Beach																									
2003	Hou N	1	0	1.000	32	0	0	0-1	30	28	10	6	1	10-2	16	3.00	147	.267	.328	2	.000	-0		5		0.0
2004	†Hou N	2	0	1.000	69	0	0	0-1	49.1	55	27	12	6	20-7	34	4.74	92	.284	.367	1	.000	-0		-2		0.0
2005	†Hou N	0	1	.000	36	0	0	0-2	20.1	18	6	1	2	10-2	12	2.66	158	.250	.353	0	—	0		4		0.0
Total	3	3	1	.750	137	0	0	0-4	99.2	101	43	16	9	40-11	62	3.79	115	.272	.353	3	.000	-0		7		0.0

YEAR	TM LG	W	L	PCT	G	GS	CG-SHO	SV-BS	IP	H	R	HR	HB	BB-IB	SO	ERA	AERA	OAV	OOB	AB-HR-SH	AVG	PB	SUP	APR	DL	PW

GALVEZ, BALVINO Balvino (Jerez) B3.31.1964 San Pedro de Macoris, D.R. BR/TR/6-0/180 d5.7
| 1986 | LA N | 0 | 1 | .000 | 10 | 0 | 0 | 0-2 | 20.2 | 19 | 10 | 4 | 0 | 12-2 | 11 | 3.92 | 88 | .241 | .341 | 2 | .000 | -0 | | -1 | | -0.1 |

GALVIN, JIM James Francis "Pud","Gentle Jeems","The Little Steam Engine" B12.25.1856 St.Louis MO D3.7.1902 Pittsburgh PA BR/TR/5-8/190 d5.22 M1/U1 HF1965
1875	StL NA	4	2	.667	8	7	7	1	62	53	37	0		1	8	**1.16**	173	.209	.212	46	.130	-1*	105	3		0.2
1879	Buf N	37	27	.578	66	66	65-6	0	593	585	299	3		31	136	2.28	115	.243	.253	265	.249	5*	85	20		2.5
1880	Buf N	20	35	.364	58	54	46-5	0	458.2	528	281	5		32	128	2.71	91	.273	.284	241	.212	-4*	86	-14		-1.7
1881	Buf N	28	24	.538	56	53	48-5	0	474	546	255	4		46	136	2.37	117	.274	.291	236	.212	-1*	103	18		2.0
1882	Buf N	28	23	.549	52	51	48-3	0	445.1	476	255	8		40	162	3.17	93	.256	.272	206	.214	-5*	109	-8		-1.2
1883	Buf N	46	29	.613	**76**	75	72-5	0	656.1	676	367	9		50	279	2.72	117	.251	.265	322-1	.220	-4*	106	31		2.4
1884	Buf N	46	22	.676	72	72	71-**12**	0	636.1	566	254	23		63	369	1.99	158	.227	.246	274	.179	-14	103	81		6.3
1885	Buf N	13	19	.406	33	32	31-3	1	284	356	204	6		37	93	4.09	73	.292	.313	122-1	.189	-2	94	-30		-2.7
	Pit AA	3	7	.300	11	11	9	0	88.1	97	64	2	0	7	27	3.67	88	.266	.280	38	.105	-4	82	-6		-0.8
1886	Pit N	29	21	.580	50	50	49-2	0	434.2	457	229	3	7	75	72	2.67	127	.263	.296	194	.253	2	114	31		3.2
1887	Pit N	28	21	.571	49	48	47-3	0	440.2	490	259	12	11	67	76	3.29	117	.269	.299	193-2	.212	-2	98	20		1.9
1888	Pit N	23	25	.479	50	50	49-6	0	437.1	446	190	9	8	53	107	2.63	100	.255	.280	175-1	.143	-6	83	5		0.1
1889	Pit N	23	16	.590	41	40	38-4	0	341	392	230	19	10	78	77	4.17	90	.280	.322	150	.187	-1	109	-19		-1.7
1890	Pit P	12	13	.480	26	25	23-1	0	217	275	192	3	7	49	35	4.35	90	.296	.337	97	.206	-1	102	-16		-1.2
1891	Pit N	15	14	.517	33	30	23-2	0	246.2	256	143	9	13	62	46	2.88	114	.258	.310	109	.165	-4	106	14		0.9
1892	Pit N	5	6	.455	12	12	10	0	96	104	51	0	0	28	29	2.63	126	.265	.314	41	.122	-3	109	6		0.3
	StL N	5	6	.455	12	12	10	0	92	102	47	4	3	26	27	3.23	99	.270	.322	39	.051	-5	89	0		-0.5
	Year	10	12	.455	24	24	20	0	188	206	98	4	3	54	56	2.92	111	.268	.318	80	.087	-7	99	9		-0.2
Total	14	361	308	.540	697	681	639-57	1	5941.1	6352	3315	121	61	744	1799	2.87	108	.261	.284	2702-5	.202	-47	99	133		9.8

GALVIN, LOU Louis J. B4.1862 St.Paul MN D6.17.1895 d10.1
| 1884 | StP U | 0 | 2 | .000 | 3 | 3 | 3 | 0 | 25 | 21 | 18 | 0 | | 10 | 17 | 2.88 | 46 | .212 | .284 | 9 | .222 | -1 | 64 | -8 | | -0.5 |

GAMBLE, BOB Robert J. B2.6.1867 Philadelphia PA TR/5-10/155 d5.2
| 1888 | Phi AA | 0 | 1 | .000 | 1 | 1 | 1 | 0 | 9 | 10 | 10 | 0 | 0 | 3 | 2 | 8.00 | 37 | .270 | .325 | 3 | .333 | 0 | 19 | -4 | | -0.3 |

GANDARILLAS, GUS Gustavo B7.19.1971 Coral Gables FL BR/TR/6-0/190 [MinA92 3/94] d7.17 Col Miami
| 2001 | Mil N | 0 | 0 | — | 16 | 0 | 0 | 0-0 | 19.2 | 25 | 13 | 2 | 0 | 10-3 | 7 | 5.49 | 78 | .321 | .398 | 0 | | 0 | | -3 | | -0.1 |

GANNON, GUSSIE James Edward B11.26.1873 Erie PA D4.12.1966 Erie PA BL/TL/5-11/154 d6.15
| 1895 | Pit N | 0 | 0 | — | 1 | 0 | 0 | 0 | 5 | 7 | 4 | 0 | 0 | 2 | 0 | 1.80 | 250 | .333 | .391 | 2 | .000 | -0 | | 1 | | 0.0 |

GANNON, JOE Michael Joseph B2.22.1877 St.Louis MO D3.19.1931 St.Louis MO d8.28
| 1898 | StL N | 0 | 0 | — | 1 | 0 | 0 | | 9 | 13 | 13 | 0 | 1 | 5 | 2 | 11.00 | 34 | .333 | .422 | 0 | .000 | -0 | | 37 | -6 | | -0.5 |

GARAGOZZO, KEITH Keith John B10.25.1969 Camden NJ BL/TL/6-0/170 [NYA91 9/230] d4.5 Col Delaware
| 1994 | Min A | 0 | 0 | — | 7 | 0 | 0 | 0-0 | 9.1 | 9 | 10 | 3 | 0 | 13-2 | 3 | 9.64 | 51 | .273 | .468 | 0 | | 0 | | -4 | | -0.2 |

GARBER, GENE Henry Eugene B11.13.1947 Lancaster PA BR/TR/5-10/175* [PitN65 12/387] d6.17
1969	Pit N	0	0	—	2	1	0	0-0	5	6	3	3	0	1-0	3	5.40	64	.333	.368	1	.000	-0	102	-1		-0.1
1970	Pit N	0	3	.000	14	0	0	0-3	22.1	22	13	4	2	10-1	7	5.24	76	.275	.366	3	.667	1		-3		-0.2
1972	Pit N	0	0	—	4	0	0	0-0	6.1	7	5	3	0	3-0	3	7.11	47	.269	.345	1	.000	-0		-2		-0.1
1973	KC A	9	9	.500	48	8	4	11-5	152.2	164	78	14	2	49-15	60	4.24	97	.283	.338	0	—	0*	71	-1		-0.1
1974	KC A	1	2	.333	17	0	0	1-2	28	35	21	3	1	13-9	14	4.82	79	.313	.389	0	—	0		-4		-0.5
	Phi N	4	0	1.000	34	0	0	4-3	48	39	15	1	1	31-15	27	2.06	184	.236	.357	3	.000	-0		8		0.7
1975	Phi N	10	12	.455	**71**	0	0	14-6	110	104	48	13	2	27-11	69	3.60	105	.254	.302	12-0-1	.167	-0		3		0.5
1976	†Phi N	9	3	.750	59	0	0	11-3	92.2	78	33	4	3	30-8	92	2.82	127	.228	.295	7-0-3	.286	1		7		1.3
1977	†Phi N	8	6	.571	64	0	0	19-6	103.1	82	30	6	2	23-8	78	2.35	171	.220	.268	10	.000	-1		19		3.1
1978	Phi N	2	1	.667	22	0	0	3-1	38.2	26	6	1	3	11-3	24	1.40	259	.191	.267	3	.000	-0		10		0.9
	Atl N	4	4	.500	43	0	0	22-4	78.1	58	26	11	2	13-3	61	2.53	159	.204	.244	11	.091	-0*		11		1.8
	Year	6	5	.545	65	0	0	25-5	117	84	32	12	5	24-6	85	2.15	181	.200	.252	14	.071	-1		**20**		2.7
1979	Atl N	6	16	.273	68	0	0	25-8	106	121	66	10	5	24-9	56	4.33	93	.283	.326	10-0-2	.300	1		-6		-1.0
1980	Atl N	5	5	.500	68	0	0	7-2	82.1	95	42	6	0	24-5	51	3.83	96	.288	.335	2	.500	1		-3		-0.2
1981	Atl N	4	6	.400	35	0	0	2-3	58.2	49	23	2	0	20-9	34	2.61	135	.214	.277	5	.000	-1		4	97	0.8
1982	†Atl N	8	10	.444	69	0	0	30-8	119.1	100	40	4	2	32-16	68	2.34	158	.231	.285	15-0-2	.133	-0		15		3.2
1983	Atl N	4	4	.444	43	0	0	9-8	60.2	72	37	8	2	23-7	45	4.60	84	.300	.358	3	.000	-0		-6	32	-0.9
1984	Atl N	3	6	.333	62	0	0	11-5	106	103	45	7	2	24-9	55	3.06	126	.254	.294	14-0-1	.143	-0		7		0.7
1985	Atl N	6	6	.500	59	0	0	1-2	97.1	98	41	8	2	25-8	66	3.61	107	.263	.313	5-0-1	.200	1		4		0.5
1986	Atl N	5	5	.500	61	0	0	24-5	78	76	23	3	1	20-7	56	2.54	156	.260	.309	6-0-1	.167	1		12		2.3
1987	Atl N	8	10	.444	49	0	0	10-6	69.1	87	39	7	1	28-10	48	4.41	98	.311	.372	4	.000	-0		-1		-0.1
	KC A	0	0	—	13	0	0	8-0	14.1	13	5	1	1	1-0	3	2.51	183	.245	.273	4	—	0		0		0.4
1988	KC A	0	4	.000	26	0	0	6-2	32.2	29	15	4	2	13-2	20	3.58	122	.238	.321	0	—	0		1		0.2
Total	19	96	113	.459	931	9	4	218-82	1510	1464	654	123	37	445-155	940	3.34	116	.257	.312	115-0-11	.148	-0		76	77	129	13.2

GARBER, BOB Robert Mitchell B9.10.1928 Hunker PA D6.7.1999 Redwood City CA BR/TR/6-1/190 d5.13
| 1956 | Pit N | 0 | 0 | — | 2 | 0 | 0 | | 4 | 3 | 1 | 1 | 0 | 3-1 | 3 | 2.25 | 168 | .200 | .333 | 0 | — | 0 | | 1 | | 0.0 |

GARCES, RICH Richard Aron (Mendoza) "El Guapo" B5.18.1971 Maracay, Venez BR/TR/6-0/250(215-255) d9.18
1990	Min A	0	0	—	5	0	0	2-0	5.2	4	2	0	0	4-0	1	1.59	262	.200	.333	0	—	0		1		0.1
1993	Min A	0	0	—	3	0	0	0-0	4	4	2	0	0	2-0	3	0.00	—	.250	.333	0	—	0		1		0.0
1995	Chi N	0	0	—	7	0	0	0-0	11	11	6	0	0	3-0	6	3.27	127	.256	.304	1	.000	-0		0		0.0
	Fla N	0	2	.000	11	0	0	0-1	13.1	14	9	1	0	8-2	16	5.40	80	.264	.361	0	—	-0		0		-0.2
	Year	0	2	.000	18	0	0	0-1	24.1	25	15	1	0	11-2	22	4.44	96	.260	.336	1	.000	-0		-2		-0.2
1996	Bos A	3	2	.600	37	0	0	0-2	44	42	26	5	0	33-5	55	4.91	104	.251	.366	0	—	0		1	63	0.2
1997	Bos A	0	1	.000	12	0	0	0-2	13.2	14	9	2	1	9-0	12	4.61	101	.255	.364	0	—	0		1	46	0.0
1998	Bos A	1	1	.500	30	0	0	1-2	46	36	19	6	2	27-3	34	3.33	142	.213	.327	0	—	0		7	95	0.3
1999	†Bos A	5	1	.833	30	0	0	2-1	40.2	25	9	1	0	18-1	33	1.55	322	.171	.262	0	—	0		15		2.0
2000	Bos A	8	1	.889	64	0	0	1-4	74.2	64	28	4	0	23-5	69	3.25	154	.229	.286	0	—	0		15		1.5
2001	Bos A	6	1	.857	62	0	0	1-1	67	55	32	6	4	31-5	51	3.90	114	.219	.299	2	.000	0		4	16	0.4
2002	Bos A	0	1	.000	26	0	0	0-0	21.1	21	20	4	3	12-2	16	7.59	59	.273	.379	0	—	0		-7	23	-0.3
Total	10	23	10	.697	287	0	0	7-13	341.1	290	162	32	11	164-19	296	3.74	127	.227	.317	3	.000	-0		34	243	4.0

GARCIA, MIKE Edward Miguel "The Big Bear" B11.17.1923 San Gabriel CA D1.13.1986 Fairview Park OH BR/TR/6-1/200(200-218) d10.3
1948	Cle A	0	0	—	1	0	0	0	2	3	0	0	0	4-0	1	0.00	—	.333	.333	0		0		1		0.1
1949	Cle A	14	5	.737	41	20	8-5	2	175.2	154	51	6	2	60	94	**2.36**	169	.241	.308	51-1-8	.235	3	81	34		3.7
1950	Cle A	11	11	.500	33	29	11	0	184	191	88	15	0	74	76	3.86	112	.266	.334	65-0-5	.200	-1	111	11		1.1
1951	Cle A	20	13	.606	47	30	15-1	6	254	239	101	10	3	82	118	3.15	120	.246	.320	85-1-9	.212	2	97	20		2.6
1952	Cle A☆	22	11	.667	46	**36**	19-**6**	4	292.1	284	93	7	7	87	143	2.37	141	.253	.310	95-0-10	.137	-2	116	33		3.7
1953	Cle A★	18	9	.667	38	35	21-3	0	271.2	260	106	18	3	81	113	3.25	116	.250	.307	96-0-6	.250	4	107	18		2.1
1954	†Cle A★	19	8	.704	45	34	13-**5**	5	258.2	220	85	6	2	71	129	**2.64**	139	.229	**.282**	81-0-6	.136	-2	89	**31**		3.0
1955	Cle A	11	13	.458	38	31	6-2	1	210.2	230	101	17	3	56-6	120	4.02	99	.278	.326	69-0-5	.217	-1	92	2		0.4
1956	Cle A	11	12	.478	35	30	8-4	0	197.2	213	93	18	5	74-5	119	3.78	111	.272	.338	61-0-8	.115	-3	104	10		0.6
1957	Cle A	12	8	.600	38	27	9-1	0	211.1	221	98	14	6	73-6	111	3.75	99	.269	.331	75-0-3	.160	-1	117	1		0.0
1958	Cle A	1	0	1.000	6	1	1	0	8	15	10	2	1	7-0	2	9.00	41	.395	.500	1	.000	-0	123	-5		-0.6
1959	Cle A	6	6	.333	29	8	1	0	72	72	39	4	0	31-3	49	4.40	92	.265	.334	6	.071	-1	138	-4		-0.0
1960	Chi A	0	0	—	15	0	0	2	17.2	23	9	2	0	10-0	8	4.58	82	.338	.423	3	.333	3		-1		0.0
1961	Was A	0	1	.000	16	0	0	0	19	23	14	1	1	13-5	6	4.74	85	.287	.385	0		0		-3		-0.2
Total	14	142	97	.594	428	281	111-27	23	2174.2	2148	888	122	33	719-23	1117	3.27	117	.257	.318	696-2-58	.182	-0	105	148		15.7

GARCIA, FREDDY Freddy Antonio B6.10.1975 Caracas, Venez BR/TR/6-4/235(235-250) d4.7
1999	Sea A	17	8	.680	33	33	2-1	0-0	201.1	205	96	18	10	90-4	170	4.07	118	.263	.345	4-0-2	.250	0*	120	18		1.9
2000	†Sea A	9	5	.643	21	20	0	0-0	124.1	112	62	16	2	64-4	79	3.91	123	.241	.335	3-0-3	.667	1	111	11		1.1
2001	†Sea A★	18	6	.750	34	34	4-3	0-0	238.2	199	88	16	5	69-6	163	**3.05**	139	**.225**	.283	7-0-2	.143	-0	109	34		3.2

YEAR	TM LG	W	L	PCT	G	GS	CG-SHO	SV-BS	IP	H	R	HR	HB	BB-IB	SO	ERA	AERA	OAV	OOB	AB-HR-SH	AVG	PB	SUP	APR	DL	PW
2002	Sea A★	16	10	.615	34	34	1	0-0	223.2	227	110	30	6	63-3	181	4.39	98	.260	.311	6-0-1	.333	1	108	1		0.2
2003	Sea A	12	14	.462	33	33	1	0-0	201.1	196	109	31	11	71-2	144	4.51	96	.255	.323	5	.200	0	93	-5		-0.6
2004	Sea A	4	7	.364	15	15	1	0-0	107	96	39	8	2	32-1	82	3.20	140	.236	.294	4	.000	-0	49	16		1.6
	Chi A	9	4	.692	16	16	0	0-0	103	96	53	14	5	32-2	102	4.46	106	.247	.311	0	—	0	103	3		0.4
	Year	13	11	.542	31	31	1	0-0	210	192	92	22	7	64-3	184	3.81	120	.241	.302	4	.000	-0	77	20		2.0
2005	†Chi A	14	8	.636	33	33	2	0-0	228	225	102	26	7	60-2	146	3.87	117	.259	.307	7-0-2	.000	-1	115	18		1.5
Total	7	99	62	.615	219	218	11-4	0-0	1427.1	1356	659	159	44	481-24	1067	3.93	114	.249	.314	36-0-10	.194	1	105	96		9.3

GARCIA, JAIRO   Jairo (Paulino)   B3.7.1983 Don Gregoria, D.R.   BR/TR/6-0/165*   d8.9

YEAR	TM LG	W	L	PCT	G	GS	CG-SHO	SV-BS	IP	H	R	HR	HB	BB-IB	SO	ERA	AERA	OAV	OOB	AB-HR-SH	AVG	PB	SUP	APR	DL	PW
2004	Oak A	0	0	—	4	0	0	0-0	5.2	5	8	3	1	9-0	5	12.71	36	.227	.469	0	—	0		-5		-0.2
2005	Oak A	0	0	—	3	0	0	0-0	3	2	1	0	0	1-0	1	3.00	149	.182	.250	0	—	0		1		0.0
Total	2	0	0	—	7	0	0	0-0	8.2	7	9	3	1	10-0	6	9.35	49	.212	.409	0	—	0		-4		-0.2

GARCIA, MIKE   Michael R.   B5.11.1968 Riverside CA   BR/TR/6-2/220*   [DetA89 55/1362]   d9.10   Col Riverside (CA) CC

YEAR	TM LG	W	L	PCT	G	GS	CG-SHO	SV-BS	IP	H	R	HR	HB	BB-IB	SO	ERA	AERA	OAV	OOB	AB-HR-SH	AVG	PB	SUP	APR	DL	PW
1999	Pit N	1	0	1.000	7	0	0	0-0	7	2	1	1	0	3-0	9	1.29	358	.091	.200	0		0		3		0.3
2000	Pit N	0	2	.000	13	0	0	0-1	11.1	21	15	1	0	7-1	9	11.12	42	.429	.475	3	.333	0		-8		-1.1
Total	2	1	2	.333	20	0	0	0-1	18.1	23	16	2	0	10-1	18	7.36	63	.324	.393	3	.333	0		-5		-0.8

GARCIA, MIGUEL   Miguel Angel (Silfontes)   B4.3.1967 Caracas, Venez   BL/TL/5-11/170*   d4.30

YEAR	TM LG	W	L	PCT	G	GS	CG-SHO	SV-BS	IP	H	R	HR	HB	BB-IB	SO	ERA	AERA	OAV	OOB	AB-HR-SH	AVG	PB	SUP	APR	DL	PW
1987	Cal A	0	0	—	1	0	0	0-0	1.2	3	4	0	0	3-0	0	16.20	27	.375	.545	0	—	0		-3		-0.1
	Pit N	0	0	—	1	0	0	0-0	0.2	0	0	0	0	0-0	0	0.00	—	.000	.000	0	—	0		0		0.0
1988	Pit N	0	0	—	1	0	0	0-0	2	3	2	1	1	2-0	2	4.50	77	.375	.500	0	—	0		-1		0.0
1989	Pit N	0	2	.000	11	0	0	0-0	16	25	15	2	0	7-3	9	8.44	40	.357	.416	1	1.000	0		-8		-0.9
Total	3	0	2	.000	14	0	0	0-0	20.1	31	21	3	1	12-3	11	8.41	42	.352	.431	1	1.000	0		-12		-1.0

GARCIA, RALPH   Ralph   B12.14.1948 Los Angeles CA   BR/TR/6-0/195*   d9.26   Col Nevada-Las Vegas

YEAR	TM LG	W	L	PCT	G	GS	CG-SHO	SV-BS	IP	H	R	HR	HB	BB-IB	SO	ERA	AERA	OAV	OOB	AB-HR-SH	AVG	PB	SUP	APR	DL	PW
1972	SD N	0	0	—	3	0	0	0-0	5	4	1	0	0	3-2	3	1.80	184	.211	.318	0	—	0		1		0.1
1974	SD N	0	0	—	8	0	0	0-0	10.1	15	8	1	0	7-2	9	6.10	59	.357	.431	0	—	0		-3		-0.1
Total	2	0	0	—	11	0	0	0-0	15.1	19	9	1	0	10-4	12	4.70	75	.311	.397	0	—	0		-2		0.0

GARCIA, RAMON   Ramon (Garcia)   B3.5.1924 LaEsperanza, Cuba   BR/TR/5-10/170   d4.19

YEAR	TM LG	W	L	PCT	G	GS	CG-SHO	SV-BS	IP	H	R	HR	HB	BB-IB	SO	ERA	AERA	OAV	OOB	AB-HR-SH	AVG	PB	SUP	APR	DL	PW
1948	Was A	0	0	—	4	0	0	0-0	3.2	11	7	0	0	1-0	2	17.18	25	.524	.615	1	1.000	0		-5		-0.2

GARCIA, RAMON   Ramon Antonio (Fortunato)   B12.9.1969 Guanare, Venez   BR/TR/6-2/200*   d5.31   [DL 1998 Hou N 181]

YEAR	TM LG	W	L	PCT	G	GS	CG-SHO	SV-BS	IP	H	R	HR	HB	BB-IB	SO	ERA	AERA	OAV	OOB	AB-HR-SH	AVG	PB	SUP	APR	DL	PW
1991	Chi A	4	4	.500	16	15	0	0-0	78.1	79	50	13	2	31-2	40	5.40	74	.269	.340	0	—	0	130	-12		-1.0
1996	Mil A	4	4	.500	37	2	0	4-3	75.2	84	58	17	6	21-3	40	6.66	78	.287	.342	0	—	0	116	-11		-1.0
1997	†Hou N	9	8	.529	42	20	1-1	1-0	158.2	155	71	20	9	52-1	120	3.69	109	.262	.330	36-0-7	.111	0	124	6		0.6
Total	3	17	16	.515	95	37	1-1	5-3	312.2	318	179	50	17	104-6	200	4.84	88	.270	.335	36-0-7	.111	-0	120	-17	181	-1.4

GARCIA, REYNALDO   Reynaldo   B4.15.1974 Nagua, D.R.   BR/TR/6-3/170*   d7.19   [DL 2004 Bos A 183]

YEAR	TM LG	W	L	PCT	G	GS	CG-SHO	SV-BS	IP	H	R	HR	HB	BB-IB	SO	ERA	AERA	OAV	OOB	AB-HR-SH	AVG	PB	SUP	APR	DL	PW
2002	Tex A	0	0	—	3	0	0	0-0	2	7	7	3	0	1-0	2	31.50	15	.538	.571	0		0		-5		-0.2
2003	Tex A	0	0	—	17	0	0	0-0	18	19	18	6	2	14-0	15	9.00	55	.275	.407	0		0		-7		-0.3
Total	2	0	0	—	20	0	0	0-0	20	26	25	9	2	15-0	17	11.25	44	.317	.430	0		0		-12	183	-0.5

GARCIA, ROSMAN   Rosman Jose   B1.3.1979 Maracay, Venez   BR/TR/6-2/160(160-215)   d4.19

YEAR	TM LG	W	L	PCT	G	GS	CG-SHO	SV-BS	IP	H	R	HR	HB	BB-IB	SO	ERA	AERA	OAV	OOB	AB-HR-SH	AVG	PB	SUP	APR	DL	PW
2003	Tex A	1	2	.333	46	0	0	0-2	46.1	63	33	4	2	23-0	25	6.02	83	.320	.395	0		0		-5		-0.3
2004	Tex A	0	0	—	4	0	0	0-0	6.2	9	5	1	0	5-0	5	5.40	91	.310	.400	0		0		-1		0.0
Total	2	1	2	.333	50	0	0	0-2	53	72	38	5	2	28-0	30	5.94	84	.319	.395	0		0		-6		-0.3

GARDINER, ART   Arthur Cecil   B12.26.1899 Brooklyn NY   D10.21.1954 Copiague NY   BR/TR   d9.25

YEAR	TM LG	W	L	PCT	G	GS	CG-SHO	SV-BS	IP	H	R	HR	HB	BB-IB	SO	ERA	AERA	OAV	OOB	AB-HR-SH	AVG	PB	SUP	APR	DL	PW
1923	Phi N	0	0	—	1	0	0	0-0	1	1	0	0	0	0-0	0	—	—	1.000	1.000	0	—	0		0		0.0

GARDINER, MIKE   Michael James   B10.19.1965 Sarnia ON, Can.   BB/TR/6-0/200(185-200)   [SeaA87 18/449]   d9.8   Col Indiana St.

YEAR	TM LG	W	L	PCT	G	GS	CG-SHO	SV-BS	IP	H	R	HR	HB	BB-IB	SO	ERA	AERA	OAV	OOB	AB-HR-SH	AVG	PB	SUP	APR	DL	PW
1990	Sea A	0	2	.000	5	3	0	0-0	12.2	22	17	1	2	5-0	6	10.66	37	.379	.439	0	—	0	92	-9		-1.2
1991	Bos A	9	10	.474	22	22	0	0-0	130	140	79	18	4	47-2	91	4.85	89	.274	.333	0	—	0	103	-8	18	-1.0
1992	Bos A	4	10	.286	28	18	0	0-0	130.2	126	78	12	2	58-2	79	4.75	89	.253	.330	0	—	0	140	-5		-0.6
1993	Mon N	2	3	.400	24	2	0	0-1	38	40	28	3	1	19-2	21	5.21	80	.268	.349	4	.000	0	1		0.0
	Det A	0	0	—	10	0	0	0-1	11.1	12	5	0	0	7-1	4	3.97	110	.279	.380	0	—	0	168	3		0.1
1994	Det A	2	2	.500	38	1	0	5-1	58.2	53	35	10	0	23-5	31	4.14	119	.233	.302	0	—	0	105	-0.6
1995	Det A	0	0	—	9	0	0	0-1	12.1	27	20	5	0	2-1	7	14.59	33	.458	.460	0	—	-0	-12	123	-0.6
Total	6	17	27	.386	136	46	0	5-4	393.2	420	262	49	5	161-13	239	5.21	84	.272	.339	4	.000	-0	91	-36	123	-3.9

GARDNER, CHRIS   Christopher John   B3.30.1969 Long Beach CA   BR/TR/6-0/175   [HouN88 6/142]   d9.10

YEAR	TM LG	W	L	PCT	G	GS	CG-SHO	SV-BS	IP	H	R	HR	HB	BB-IB	SO	ERA	AERA	OAV	OOB	AB-HR-SH	AVG	PB	SUP	APR	DL	PW
1991	Hou N	1	2	.333	5	4	0	0-0	24.2	19	12	5	0	14-1	12	4.01	88	.218	.327	5	.000	-0	76	-1		-0.1

GARDNER, GID   Franklin Washington   B5.6.1859 Boston MA   D8.1.1914 Cambridge MA   ?/165   d8.23 ▲

YEAR	TM LG	W	L	PCT	G	GS	CG-SHO	SV-BS	IP	H	R	HR	HB	BB-IB	SO	ERA	AERA	OAV	OOB	AB-HR-SH	AVG	PB	SUP	APR	DL	PW
1879	Tro N	0	2	.000	2	2	2		14	27	21	0		0	3	5.79	43	.365	.365	6	.167	0	37	-5		-0.5
1880	Cle N	1	8	.111	9	9	9		77	80	53	2		20	21	2.57	91	.254	.299	32	.188	-0*	58	-4		-0.4
1883	Bal AA	1	0	1.000	2	0	0		7	9	7	1		1	2	5.14	68	.290	.313	161-1	.273	1*	18	-2		-0.1
1884	CP U	0	1	.000	1	1	1		6	10	8	0		1	4	6.00	40	.345	.367	149	.255	-0*	18	-2		-0.4
1885	Bal AA	0	1	.000	1	1	0		9	16	13	2	1	6	3	10.00	33	.372	.460	170	.218	0*	36	-6		-0.4
Total	5	2	12	.143	15	13	12		113	142	102	5	1	28	33	3.90	64	.289	.328	518-1	.243	0	49	-18		-1.7

GARDNER, HARRY   Harry Ray   B6.1.1887 Quincy MI   D8.2.1961 Canby OR   BR/TR/6-2/180   d4.17

YEAR	TM LG	W	L	PCT	G	GS	CG-SHO	SV-BS	IP	H	R	HR	HB	BB-IB	SO	ERA	AERA	OAV	OOB	AB-HR-SH	AVG	PB	SUP	APR	DL	PW
1911	Pit N	1	1	.500	13	3	2	0	42	39	25	2	2	20	24	4.50	76	.244	.335	14	.214	0	95	-4		-0.3
1912	Pit N	0	0	—	1	0	0	0	0.1	3	6	0	0	1	0	0.00	—	.500	.571	0	—	0	-2		-0.1
Total	2	1	1	.500	14	3	2	0	42.1	42	31	2	2	21	24	4.46	77	.253	.344	14	.214	0	95	-6		-0.4

GARDNER, JIM   James Anderson   B10.4.1874 Pittsburgh PA   D4.24.1905 Pittsburgh PA   TR   d6.20

YEAR	TM LG	W	L	PCT	G	GS	CG-SHO	SV-BS	IP	H	R	HR	HB	BB-IB	SO	ERA	AERA	OAV	OOB	AB-HR-SH	AVG	PB	SUP	APR	DL	PW
1895	Pit N	8	2	.800	11	10	8	0	85.1	99	53	1	6	27	31	2.64	171	.286	.348	34	.265	1	120	13		1.2
1897	Pit N	5	5	.500	14	11	8	0	95.1	115	72	4	9	32	35	5.19	80	.296	.363	76-1-2	.158	-1*	88	-10		-0.8
1898	Pit N	10	13	.435	25	22	19-1	0	185.1	179	96	3	8	48	41	3.21	111	.252	.306	91-0-2	.154	-2*	71	6		-0.6
1899	Pit N	1	0	1.000	6	3	0	0	32.1	52	37	1	0	13	2	7.52	51	.361	.414	13	.231	1	163	-13		-0.7
1902	Chi N	1	2	.333	3	3	2	0	25	23	12	0	0	10	6	2.88	94	.245	.317	10	.200	-0	101	0		0.0
Total	5	25	22	.532	59	49	37-1	0	423.1	468	270	9	23	130	115	3.85	100	.278	.338	224-1-4	.179	-1	93	-4		0.0

GARDNER, MARK   Mark Allan   B3.1.1962 Los Angeles CA   BR/TR/6-1/205(190-224)   [MonN85 8/192]   d5.16   C3   Col Cal St.-Fresno

YEAR	TM LG	W	L	PCT	G	GS	CG-SHO	SV-BS	IP	H	R	HR	HB	BB-IB	SO	ERA	AERA	OAV	OOB	AB-HR-SH	AVG	PB	SUP	APR	DL	PW
1989	Mon N	0	3	.000	7	4	0	0-0	26.1	26	16	2	2	11-1	21	5.13	70	.250	.333	6-0-1	.167	-0	56	-4		-0.5
1990	Mon N	7	9	.438	27	26	3-3	0-0	152.2	129	62	13	9	61-5	135	3.42	108	.230	.312	44-0-8	.114	-1	93	5	14	-0.2
1991	Mon N	9	11	.450	27	27	0	0-0	168.1	139	78	17	4	75-1	107	3.85	95	.230	.318	55-0-4	.091	-3	87	-3	36	-0.3
1992	Mon N	12	10	.545	33	30	0	0-0	179.2	179	91	15	9	60-2	132	4.36	80	.259	.324	50-0-8	.140	1	107	-16		-1.8
1993	KC A	4	6	.400	17	16	0	0-0	91.2	92	65	17	4	36-0	54	6.19	75	.271	.342	0	—	0	81	-14	51	-1.4
1994	Fla N	4	4	.500	14	6	0	0-0	92.1	97	53	14	1	30-2	57	4.87	91	.276	.331	25-0-4	.040	-2	97	-3	19	-0.4
1995	Fla N	5	5	.500	39	11	1-1	1-0	102.1	109	60	14	4	43-5	87	4.49	96	.272	.350	21-0-4	.190	-0	101	-4		-0.4
1996	SF N	12	7	.632	30	28	4-1	0-0	179.1	200	105	28	8	57-3	145	4.42	94	.283	.341	68-0-8	.162	0*	131	-8	18	-0.3
1997	SF N	12	9	.571	30	30	2-1	0-0	180.1	188	92	28	7	57-6	136	4.29	93	.272	.326	61-0-3	.115	-2*	100	-2		-0.3
1998	SF N	13	6	.684	33	33	4-2	0-0	212	203	106	29	6	57-2	151	6.47	66	.267	.341	39-1-6	.103	1	116	-33	22	-3.7
1999	SF N	5	11	.313	29	21	1	0-1	139	142	103	27	8	57-2	86	4.05	107	.270	.322	43-0-7	.116	-2	82	6		-0.5
2000	†SF N	11	7	.611	30	20	0	0-0	149	155	72	16	9	42-2	92	5.40	76	.263	.330	21-0-4	.152	2	95	-13	56	-0.3
2001	SF N	5	5	.500	23	15	0	0-0	91.2	93	57	17	3	34-3	53	5.40	89	.261	.327	506-1-61	.123	-9	103	-95	216	-10.1
Total	13	99	93	.516	345	275	15-8	1-1	1764.2	1752	960	237	65	628-37	1256	4.56	89	.261	.327	506-1-61	.123	-9	103	-95	216	-10.1

GARDNER, GLENN   Miles Glenn   B1.25.1916 Burnsville NC   D7.7.1964 Rochester NY   BR/TR/5-11/180   d7.19

YEAR	TM LG	W	L	PCT	G	GS	CG-SHO	SV-BS	IP	H	R	HR	HB	BB-IB	SO	ERA	AERA	OAV	OOB	AB-HR-SH	AVG	PB	SUP	APR	DL	PW
1945	StL N	3	1	.750	17	4	2-1	0	54.2	50	21	2	0	27	20	3.29	114	.242	.329	21-0-1	.333	2	130	4		0.4

GARDNER, ROB   Richard Frank   B12.19.1944 Binghamton NY   BR/TL/6-1/176(165-185)   d9.1

YEAR	TM LG	W	L	PCT	G	GS	CG-SHO	SV-BS	IP	H	R	HR	HB	BB-IB	SO	ERA	AERA	OAV	OOB	AB-HR-SH	AVG	PB	SUP	APR	DL	PW
1965	NY N	0	2	.000	5	4	0	0	28	23	13	4	3	7-0	19	3.21	110	.217	.265	7-0-1	.000	-1	62	0		0.4
1966	NY N	4	8	.333	41	17	3	1	133.1	147	82	15	3	64-4	74	5.12	71	.285	.366	41-0-1	.171	-0*	87	-19		-1.5
1967	Chi N	0	2	.000	18	5	0	0	31.2	33	14	2	0	6-0	16	3.98	89	.260	.289	6	.000	-0	89	-1		0.0

YEAR	TM LG	W	L	PCT	G	GS	CG-SHO	SV-BS	IP	H	R	HR	HB	BB-IB	SO	ERA	AERA	OAV	OOB	AB-HR-SH	AVG	PB	SUP	APR	DL	PW
1968	Cle A	0	0	—	5	0	0	0	2.2	5	3	0	0	2-0	6	6.75	44	.417	.467	0	—	0		-1		-0.1
1970	NY A	1	0	1.000	1	1	0	0-0	7.1	8	4	2	0	4-0	6	4.91	73	.276	.364	3	.333	1	150	-1		0.0
1971	Oak A	0	0	—	4	1	0	0-0	7.2	8	2	1	0	3-0	5	2.35	142	.267	.333	2	.500	0	135	1		0.1
	NY A	0	0	—	2	0	0	0-0	3	3	1	0	0	2-0	2	3.00	110	.273	.385	0	—	0		0		0.0
	Year	0	0	—	6	1	0	0-0	10.2	11	3	1	0	5-0	7	2.53	131	.268	.348	2	.500	0	135	1		0.1
1972	NY A	8	5	.615	20	14	1	0-1	97	91	43	9	0	28-3	58	3.06	98	.243	.295	28-0-5	.107	-1	110	-3		-0.6
1973	Oak A	0	0	—	3	0	0	0-0	7.1	10	4	2	0	4-0	2	4.91	73	.370	.452	0	—	0		-1		-0.1
	Mil A	1	1	.500	10	0	0	1-0	12.2	17	14	0	1	13-1	5	9.95	38	.327	.470	0	—	0		-8		-1.2
	Year	1	1	.500	13	0	0	1-0	20	27	18	2	1	17-1	7	8.10	46	.342	.464	0	—	0		-9		-1.3
Total	8	14	18	.438	109	42	4	2-1	331	345	180	35	4	133-8	193	4.35	78	.269	.338	87-0-7	.138	-2	94	-33		-3.7

GARDNER, LEE Terrence Lee B1.16.1975 Hartland MI BR/TR/6-0/219* d5.24 Col Central Michigan

YEAR	TM LG	W	L	PCT	G	GS	CG-SHO	SV-BS	IP	H	R	HR	HB	BB-IB	SO	ERA	AERA	OAV	OOB	AB-HR-SH	AVG	PB	SUP	APR	DL	PW
2002	TB A	1	1	.500	12	0	0	0-2	13.1	12	11	3	3	8-0	8	4.05	112	.235	.359	0	—	0		-1		-0.2
2005	TB A	0	0	—	5	0	0	0-0	7.1	12	9	2	0	2-0	4	4.91	89	.353	.378	0	—	0		-3		-0.1
Total	2	1	1	.500	17	0	0	0-2	20.2	24	20	5	3	10-0	12	4.35	103	.282	.366	0	—	0		-4		-0.3

GARDNER, WES Wesley Brian B4.29.1961 Benton AR BR/TR/6-4/197* [NYN82 22/551] d7.29 Col Central Arkansas

YEAR	TM LG	W	L	PCT	G	GS	CG-SHO	SV-BS	IP	H	R	HR	HB	BB-IB	SO	ERA	AERA	OAV	OOB	AB-HR-SH	AVG	PB	SUP	APR	DL	PW
1984	NY N	1	1	.500	21	0	0	1-2	25.1	34	19	0	0	8-2	19	6.39	56	.321	.365	1	.000	-0		-7		-0.6
1985	NY N	0	2	.000	9	0	0	0-0	12	18	14	1	0	8-2	11	5.25	67	.375	.456	0	—	0		-5		-0.8
1986	Bos A	0	0	—	1	0	0	0-0	1	1	1	0	0	0-0	1	9.00	47	.333	.250	0	—	0		0	175	-0.5
1987	Bos A	3	6	.333	49	1	0	10-2	89.2	98	55	17	2	42-7	70	5.42	84	.279	.358	0	—	0	80	-7		-0.8
1988	†Bos A	8	6	.571	36	18	1	2-0	149	119	61	17	3	64-2	106	3.50	118	.220	.302	0	—	0	98	11	15	1.0
1989	Bos A	3	7	.300	22	16	0	0-0	86	97	64	10	1	47-7	81	5.97	69	.287	.372	0	—	0	116	-17	57	-1.7
1990	Bos A	3	7	.300	34	9	0	0-2	77.1	77	43	6	2	35-0	58	4.89	84	.259	.339	0	—	0	74	-5	30	-0.6
1991	SD N	0	1	.000	14	0	0	1-0	20.1	27	16	1	0	12-1	9	7.08	54	.310	.394	2	.000	-0		-6		-0.4
	KC A	0	0	—	3	0	0	0-0	5.2	5	4	0	0	2-0	3	1.59	261	.208	.269	0	—	0		0		0.0
Total	8	18	30	.375	189	44	1	14-6	466.1	476	277	52	8	218-21	358	4.90	85	.265	.344	3	.000	-0	99	-36	277	-3.9

GARDNER, BILL William A. B9.1868 Baltimore MD d8.9

YEAR	TM LG	W	L	PCT	G	GS	CG-SHO	SV-BS	IP	H	R	HR	HB	BB-IB	SO	ERA	AERA	OAV	OOB	AB-HR-SH	AVG	PB	SUP	APR	DL	PW
1887	Bal AA	0	1	.000	3	2	1	0	13	23	20	0	1	10	3	11.08	37	.426	.523	11	.273	0*	124	-9		-0.5

GARFIELD, BILL William Milton B10.26.1867 Sheffield OH D12.16.1941 Danville IL BR/TR/5-11.5/160 d7.10 Col Oberlin

YEAR	TM LG	W	L	PCT	G	GS	CG-SHO	SV-BS	IP	H	R	HR	HB	BB-IB	SO	ERA	AERA	OAV	OOB	AB-HR-SH	AVG	PB	SUP	APR	DL	PW
1889	Pit N	0	2	.000	4	2	2	0	29	45	35	2	1	17	4	7.76	48	.344	.423	13	.000	-2	81	-14		-0.8
1890	Cle N	1	7	.125	9	8	7	0	70	91	64	3	8	35	16	4.89	73	.304	.392	26	.154	-1	42	-12		-1.1
Total	2	1	9	.100	13	10	9	0	99	136	99	5	9	52	20	5.73	64	.316	.401	39	.103	-3	50	-26		-1.9

GARIBALDI, BOB Robert Roy B3.3.1942 Stockton CA BL/TR/6-4/210* d7.15 Col Santa Clara

YEAR	TM LG	W	L	PCT	G	GS	CG-SHO	SV-BS	IP	H	R	HR	HB	BB-IB	SO	ERA	AERA	OAV	OOB	AB-HR-SH	AVG	PB	SUP	APR	DL	PW
1962	SF N	0	0	—	9	0	0	1	12.1	13	7	1	0	5-0	9	5.11	74	.265	.327	1	.000	-0		-1		-0.1
1963	SF N	0	1	.000	4	0	0	1	8	8	2	0	1	4-2	4	1.13	284	.276	.382	1	.000	-0		-2		0.2
1966	SF N	0	0	—	1	0	0	0	1	1	0	0	0	0-0	1	0.00	—	.250	.250	0	—	0		0		0.0
1969	SF N	0	1	.000	1	1	0	0-0	5	6	4	0	0	2-0	0	1.80	195	.316	.381	2	.000	-0	101	0		-0.1
Total	4	0	2	.000	15	1	0	2-0	26.1	28	13	1	1	11-2	14	3.08	116	.277	.351	4	.000	-0	101	1		0.0

GARIBAY, DANIEL Daniel (Bravo) B2.14.1973 Maneadero, Baja California, Mexico BL/TL/5-8/160 d4.9

YEAR	TM LG	W	L	PCT	G	GS	CG-SHO	SV-BS	IP	H	R	HR	HB	BB-IB	SO	ERA	AERA	OAV	OOB	AB-HR-SH	AVG	PB	SUP	APR	DL	PW
2000	Chi N	2	8	.200	30	8	0	0-2	74.2	88	54	9	1	39-1	46	6.03	76	.299	.376	15-0-4	.133	-1	65	-13		-1.4

GARLAND, JON Jon Steven B9.27.1979 Valencia CA BR/TR/6-6/205* [ChiN97 1/10] d7.4

YEAR	TM LG	W	L	PCT	G	GS	CG-SHO	SV-BS	IP	H	R	HR	HB	BB-IB	SO	ERA	AERA	OAV	OOB	AB-HR-SH	AVG	PB	SUP	APR	DL	PW
2000	Chi A	4	8	.333	15	13	0		69.2	82	55	10	1	40-0	42	6.46	78	.292	.380	0	—	0	101	-10	14	-1.4
2001	Chi A	6	7	.462	35	16	0	1-0	117	123	59	16	4	55-2	61	3.69	126	.277	.358	2	.000	-0	86	9		0.9
2002	Chi A	12	12	.500	33	33	1-1	0-0	192.2	188	109	23	9	83-1	112	4.58	98	.258	.340	2-0-1	.000	-0	86	-2		-0.3
2003	Chi A	12	13	.480	32	32	0	0-0	191.2	188	103	28	4	74-1	108	4.51	102	.260	.329	2-0-1	.000	-0	100	2		0.3
2004	Chi A	12	11	.522	34	33	1	0-0	217	223	125	34	4	76-2	113	4.89	96	.269	.332	4-0-1	.250	-0	99	-4		-0.3
2005	†Chi A★	18	10	.643	32	32	3-3	0-0	221	212	93	26	7	47-3	115	3.50	129	.255	.298	2	.500	0	94	24		2.9
Total	6	64	61	.512	181	159	5-4	1-0	1009	1016	544	137	29	375-9	551	4.42	105	.265	.332	12-0-3	.167	-0	94	19	14	2.1

GARLAND, LOU Louis Lyman B7.16.1905 Archie MO D8.30.1990 Idaho Falls ID BR/TR/6-2.5/200 d8.31

YEAR	TM LG	W	L	PCT	G	GS	CG-SHO	SV-BS	IP	H	R	HR	HB	BB-IB	SO	ERA	AERA	OAV	OOB	AB-HR-SH	AVG	PB	SUP	APR	DL	PW
1931	Chi A	0	2	.000	7	2	0	0	16.2	30	24	2	1	14	4	10.26	41	.400	.500	3	.000	-0	109	-12		-1.1

GARLAND, WAYNE Marcus Wayne B10.26.1950 Nashville TN BR/TR/6-0/195(190-205) [BalA69 S1/5] d9.13 Col Gulf Coast (FL) CC

YEAR	TM LG	W	L	PCT	G	GS	CG-SHO	SV-BS	IP	H	R	HR	HB	BB-IB	SO	ERA	AERA	OAV	OOB	AB-HR-SH	AVG	PB	SUP	APR	DL	PW
1973	Bal A	0	1	.000	4	1	0	0-0	16	14	8	1	0	7-0	10	3.94	96	.233	.313	0	—	0	47	0		0.0
1974	†Bal A	5	5	.500	20	6	0	1-0	91	68	37	5	3	26-3	40	2.97	117	.211	.272	0	—	0	97	4		0.4
1975	Bal A	2	5	.286	29	1	0	4-1	87.1	80	37	7	1	31-6	46	3.71	96	.252	.316	0	—	0	124	-1		-0.1
1976	Bal A	20	7	.741	38	25	14-4	1-1	232.1	224	81	10	6	64-9	113	2.67	123	.255	.306	0	—	0	107	15		1.8
1977	Cle A	13	19	.406	38	38	21-1	0-0	282.2	281	130	23	2	88-8	118	3.60	111	.261	.316	0	—	0	94	11		1.1
1978	Cle A	2	3	.400	6	6	0	0-0	29.2	43	27	6	1	16-1	13	7.89	48	.347	.423	0	—	0	103	-13	153	-1.7
1979	Cle A	4	10	.286	18	14	2	0-0	94.2	120	70	11	3	34-2	40	5.23	82	.318	.371	0	—	0	75	-14	60	-1.8
1980	Cle A	6	9	.400	25	20	4-1	0-0	150.1	163	85	18	6	48-2	55	4.61	90	.276	.334	0	—	0	118	-8		-0.8
1981	Cle A	3	7	.300	12	10	2-1	0-0	56	89	40	8	0	14-0	15	5.79	64	.374	.399	0	—	0	76	-13		-2.0
Total	9	55	66	.455	190	121	43-7	6-2	1040	1082	515	89	22	328-31	450	3.89	97	.272	.327	0	—	0	98	-19	213	-3.1

GARMAN, MIKE Michael Douglas B9.16.1949 Caldwell ID BR/TR/6-3/215(198-215) [BosA67 1/3] d9.22

YEAR	TM LG	W	L	PCT	G	GS	CG-SHO	SV-BS	IP	H	R	HR	HB	BB-IB	SO	ERA	AERA	OAV	OOB	AB-HR-SH	AVG	PB	SUP	APR	DL	PW
1969	Bos A	1	0	1.000	2	2	0	0-0	12.1	13	6	0	0	10-0	10	4.38	87	.277	.404	5	.400	1	116	0		0.0
1971	Bos A	1	1	.500	3	3	0	0-0	18.2	15	8	3	1	9-1	6	3.86	97	.217	.313	6	.333	0	104	0		0.0
1972	Bos A	0	1	.000	3	1	0	0-0	3.1	4	4	1	0	2-0	1	10.80	30	.286	.375	0	—	0	82	-2		-0.5
1973	Bos A	0	0	—	12	0	0	0-0	22	32	15	1	0	15-3	9	5.32	76	.352	.439	0	—	0		-3		-0.2
1974	StL N	7	2	.778	64	0	0	6-3	81.2	66	26	4	2	27-10	45	2.64	137	.227	.297	10-0-1	.100	-1		9		1.1
1975	StL N	3	8	.273	66	0	0	10-6	79	73	31	9	1	48-23	48	2.39	159	.245	.347	2	.000	-0		9		1.4
1976	Chi N	2	4	.333	47	2	0	1-1	76.1	79	48	7	3	35-8	37	4.95	78	.273	.351	7	.000	-1	23	-8		-0.7
1977	†LA N	4	4	.500	49	0	0	12-5	62.2	60	20	7	2	22-5	29	2.73	141	.254	.323	4	.000	-1		8		1.2
1978	LA N	0	1	.000	10	0	0	0-1	16.1	15	8	3	0	3-0	5	4.41	80	.259	.295	0	—	0		-1		-0.1
	Mon N	4	6	.400	47	0	0	13-6	61.1	54	32	5	0	31-8	23	4.40	81	.238	.327	5	.000	-1		-5		-1.1
	Year	4	7	.364	57	0	0	13-7	77.2	69	40	8	0	34-8	28	4.40	81	.242	.321	5	.000	-1		-7		-1.2
Total	9	22	27	.449	303	8	0	42-22	433.2	411	198	34	9	202-58	213	3.63	103	.254	.337	42-0-1	.119	-2	83	7		1.1

GARONI, WILLIE William B7.28.1877 Ft.Lee NJ D9.9.1914 Ft.Lee NJ BR/TR/6-1/165 d9.7

YEAR	TM LG	W	L	PCT	G	GS	CG-SHO	SV-BS	IP	H	R	HR	HB	BB-IB	SO	ERA	AERA	OAV	OOB	AB-HR-SH	AVG	PB	SUP	APR	DL	PW
1899	NY N	0	1	.000	3	1	1	0	10	12	7	0	0	2	2	4.50	83	.300	.333	4	.000	-1	77	-1		-0.1

GARRELTS, SCOTT Scott William B10.30.1961 Urbana IL BR/TR/6-4/195(195-210) [SFN79 1/15] d10.2 [DL 1992 SF N 177]

YEAR	TM LG	W	L	PCT	G	GS	CG-SHO	SV-BS	IP	H	R	HR	HB	BB-IB	SO	ERA	AERA	OAV	OOB	AB-HR-SH	AVG	PB	SUP	APR	DL	PW
1982	SF N	0	0	—	1	0	0	0-0	2	3	3	0	0	2-0	4	13.50	27	.333	.455	0	—	0		-2		-0.1
1983	SF N	2	2	.500	5	5	1-1	0-0	35.2	33	11	4	2	19-4	16	2.52	141	.254	.358	9-0-3	.222	0	65	4		0.5
1984	SF N	2	3	.400	21	3	0	0-1	43	45	33	6	1	34-1	32	5.65	63	.274	.398	10	.100	-0		4		-0.3
1985	SF N☆	9	6	.600	74	0	0	13-8	105.2	76	37	2	3	58-12	106	2.30	151	.198	.306	9	.222	-1	217	-11		-1.3
1986	SF N	13	9	.591	53	18	2	10-6	173.2	144	65	17	2	74-11	125	3.11	114	.231	.311	45-1-7	.178	-1	90	12		2.1
1987	†SF N	11	7	.611	64	0	0	12-10	106.1	70	41	10	0	55-4	127	3.22	120	.192	.297	10	.200	1*		8		1.5
1988	SF N	5	9	.357	65	0	0	13-6	98	80	42	3	2	46-10	86	3.58	91	.226	.317	13	.077	-1		-3		-0.5
1989	†SF N	14	5	.737	30	29	2-1	0-0	193.1	149	58	11	0	46-10	119	2.28	148	.212	.258	66-0-2	.136	1*	120	23	16	2.3
1990	SF N	12	11	.522	31	31	4-2	0-0	182	190	91	16	3	70-8	80	4.15	88	.272	.339	66	.061	-3*	94	-10		-1.6
1991	SF N	1	1	.500	9	0	0	4-0	19.2	25	14	5	0	9-0	8	6.41	56	.313	.378	4-0-1	.000	-0*	200	-6	141	-0.6
Total	10	69	53	.566	352	89	9-4	48-31	959.1	815	395	74	13	413-53	703	3.29	107	.232	.313	232-1-13	.125	-0*	107	25	334	3.9

GARRETT, CLARENCE Clarence Raymond "Laz" B3.6.1891 Reader WV D2.11.1977 Moundsville WV BR/TR/6-5.5/185 d9.13 Col West Liberty St.

YEAR	TM LG	W	L	PCT	G	GS	CG-SHO	SV-BS	IP	H	R	HR	HB	BB-IB	SO	ERA	AERA	OAV	OOB	AB-HR-SH	AVG	PB	SUP	APR	DL	PW
1915	Cle A	2	2	.500	4	4	2	0	23.1	19	13	1	1	6	5	2.31	132	.224	.283	8	.000	-0	102	0		0.1

GARRETT, GREG Gregory B3.12.1947 Atascadero CA D6.7.2003 Newhall CA BB/TL/6-0/200* d4.24 Col Washington St.

YEAR	TM LG	W	L	PCT	G	GS	CG-SHO	SV-BS	IP	H	R	HR	HB	BB-IB	SO	ERA	AERA	OAV	OOB	AB-HR-SH	AVG	PB	SUP	APR	DL	PW
1970	Cal A	5	6	.455	32	7	0	0-0	74.2	48	23	6	1	44-9	53	2.65	137	.190	.309	15-0-1	.067	-1	88	9		1.2
1971	Cin N	0	1	.000	2	1	0	0-0	8.2	7	1	0	0	10-0	2	1.04	325	.250	.447	3	.333	0	0	2		0.3
Total	2	5	7	.417	34	8	0	0-0	83.1	55	24	6	1	54-9	55	2.48	145	.196	.324	18-0-1	.111	-1	77	11		1.5

GARRISON, CLIFF Clifford William B8.13.1906 Bellemont OK D8.25.1994 Woodland CA BR/TR/6-0/180 d4.16

YEAR TM LG	W	L	PCT	G	GS	CG-SHO	SV-BS	IP	H	R	HR	HB	BB-IB	SO	ERA	AERA	OAV	OOB	AB-HR-SH	AVG	PB	SUP	APR	DL	PW
1928 Bos A	0	0	—	6	0	0	0	16	22	15	2	0	6	0	7.88	52	.361	.418	3	.000	-0		-6		-0.3

GARRY, JIM James Thomas B9.21.1869 Great Barrington MA D1.13.1917 Pittsfield MA BL/TL/5-10/165 d5.2

YEAR TM LG	W	L	PCT	G	GS	CG-SHO	SV-BS	IP	H	R	HR	HB	BB-IB	SO	ERA	AERA	OAV	OOB	AB-HR-SH	AVG	PB	SUP	APR	DL	PW
1893 Bos N	0	1	.000	1	0	0	0	1	5	8	0	0	4	2	63.00	8	.625	.750	1	.000	-0		-6		-0.7

GARVER, NED Ned Franklin B12.25.1925 Ney OH BR/TR/5-10.5/180* d4.28

YEAR TM LG	W	L	PCT	G	GS	CG-SHO	SV-BS	IP	H	R	HR	HB	BB-IB	SO	ERA	AERA	OAV	OOB	AB-HR-SH	AVG	PB	SUP	APR	DL	PW
1948 StL A	7	11	.389	38	24	7	5	198	200	92	14	1	95	75	3.41	134	.268	.352	66-1-9	.288	4*	78	20		2.2
1949 StL A	12	17	.414	41	32	16-1	3	223.2	245	126	14	3	102	70	3.98	114	.277	.354	75-0-4	.187	1*	78	9		1.2
1950 StL A	13	18	.419	37	31	22-2	0	260	264	120	18	4	108	85	3.39	146	.264	.338	91-1-7	.286	4*	75	39		4.9
1951 StL A★	20	12	.625	33	30	24-1	0	246	237	114	17	5	96	84	3.73	118	.255	.328	95-1-5	.305	7*	97	17		2.5
1952 StL A	7	10	.412	21	21	7-2	0	148.2	130	67	14	4	55	60	3.69	106	.235	.309	49-0-1	.184	0*	76	5		0.6
Det A	1	0	1.000	1	1	1	0	9	9	2	1	0	3	3	2.00	190	.265	.324	2	.000	0	92	2		0.9
Year	8	10	.444	22	22	8-2	0	157.2	139	69	15	4	58	63	3.60	109	.237	.310	51-0-1	.176	0	77	7		0.9
1953 Det A	11	11	.500	30	26	13	1	198.1	228	107	16	2	66	69	4.45	91	.290	.347	72-1-4	.153	-1	93	-7		-0.8
1954 Det A	14	11	.560	35	32	16-3	1	246.1	216	93	20	4	62	93	2.81	131	.236	.286	79-0-5	.165	-0*	106	22		2.2
1955 Det A	12	16	.429	33	32	16-1	1	230.2	251	115	21	5	67-10	83	3.98	97	.279	.330	76-1-3	.224	5	111	-3		0.1
1956 Det A	0	2	.000	6	3	1	0	17.2	15	10	2	1	13-0	6	4.08	101	.234	.367	5	.000	-0	79	0	61	-0.1
1957 KC A	6	13	.316	24	23	6-1	0	145.1	120	72	13	5	55-5	61	3.84	103	.223	.298	44-0-2	.182	0	82	1		0.1
1958 KC A	12	11	.522	31	28	10-3	1	201	192	97	24	2	66-8	72	4.03	97	.244	.303	69-0-4	.174	0	103	-2		0.2
1959 KC A	10	13	.435	32	30	9-2	1	201.1	214	94	22	3	42-0	61	3.71	108	.270	.308	71-2-4	.282	6	104	7		1.4
1960 KC A	4	9	.308	28	15	5-2	0	122.1	110	57	15	2	35-2	50	3.83	104	.240	.293	27-0-4	.074	-1	65	3		-0.5
1961 LA A	0	3	.000	12	2	0	0	29	40	18	2	0	16-0	15	5.59	84	.313	.427	6-0-1	.000	-1	29	-2		-0.5
Total 14	129	157	.451	402	330	153-18	12	2477.1	2471	1184	213	41	881-25	881	3.73	112	.260	.325	827-7-53	.218	24	89	111	61	15.2

GARVIN, JERRY Theodore Jared B10.21.1955 Oakland CA BL/TL/6-3/195* [MinA74*S1/11] d4.10 Col Merced (CA) JC

YEAR TM LG	W	L	PCT	G	GS	CG-SHO	SV-BS	IP	H	R	HR	HB	BB-IB	SO	ERA	AERA	OAV	OOB	AB-HR-SH	AVG	PB	SUP	APR	DL	PW
1977 Tor A	10	18	.357	34	34	12-1	0-0	244.2	247	127	33	4	85-5	127	4.19	101	.264	.326	0	—	0	76	2		0.8
1978 Tor A	4	12	.250	26	22	3	0-1	144.2	189	92	20	4	48-4	67	5.54	71	.319	.372	0	—	0	88	-23		-2.2
1979 Tor A	0	1	.000	8	1	0	0-1	22.2	15	9	2	2	10-0	14	2.78	158	.197	.300	0	—	0	165	3	89	2.1
1980 Tor A	4	7	.364	61	4	0	8-5	82.2	70	23	6	0	27-7	52	2.29	189	.233	.296	0	—	0	62	4		2.0
1981 Tor A	1	2	.333	35	4	0	0-1	53	46	20	3	0	23-4	25	3.40	117	.240	.318	0	—	0	106	-14		-0.1
1982 Tor A	1	1	.500	32	4	0	0-1	58.1	81	48	10	1	26-2	35	7.25	62	.335	.400	0	—	0	82	-10	89	-0.9
Total 6	20	41	.328	196	65	15-1	8-9	606	648	319	74	11	219-22	320	4.43	95	.277	.340	0	—	0			89	0.

GARVIN, NED Virgil Lee B1.1.1874 Navasota TX D6.16.1908 Fresno CA BR/TR/6-3.5/160 d7.13

YEAR TM LG	W	L	PCT	G	GS	CG-SHO	SV-BS	IP	H	R	HR	HB	BB-IB	SO	ERA	AERA	OAV	OOB	AB-HR-SH	AVG	PB	SUP	APR	DL	PW
1896 Phi N	0	1	.000	2	1	1	0	13	19	13	0	0	7	4	7.62	57	.339	.413	6	.000	-1	132	-4		-0.
1899 Chi N	9	13	.409	24	23	22-4	0	199	202	101	3	0	7 42	69	2.85	132	.263	.311	71-0-5	.155	-5	102	19		1.
1900 Chi N	10	18	.357	30	28	25-1	0	246.1	225	126	4	18	63	107	2.41	150	.243	.304	91	.154	-5	73	28		2.
1901 Mil A	8	20	.286	37	27	22-1	1	257.1	258	155	4	14	90	122	3.46	104	.258	.328	93-0-4	.108	-9	63	2		-0.
1902 Chi A	10	10	.500	23	19	16-2	0	175.1	169	68	3	8	43	55	2.21	153	.254	.307	59-0-1	.153	-2	76	19		1.
Bro N	1	1	.500	2	2	2-1	0	18	15	3	0	0	4	7	1.00	277	.227	.271	7	.143	0	98	3		-0.
1903 Bro N	15	18	.455	38	34	30-2	2	298	277	163	2	13	84	154	3.08	104	.248	.308	106-0-5	.075	-8	109	-1		0.
1904 Bro N	5	15	.250	23	22	16-2	0	181.2	141	81	6	6	78	86	1.68	163	.218	.308	63-0-3	.127	-4	66	12		1.
NY A	0	1	.000	2	2	0	0	12	14	4	0	0	2	8	2.25	121	.292	.320	4	.000	-1	53	1		0.
Total 7	58	97	.374	181	158	134-13	3	1400.2	1320	714	20	71	413	612	2.72	125	.249	.312	500-0-18	.122	-35	83	79		1.

GASPAR, HARRY Harry Lambert B4.28.1883 Kingsley IA D5.14.1940 Orange CA BR/TR/6-0/180 d4.21

YEAR TM LG	W	L	PCT	G	GS	CG-SHO	SV-BS	IP	H	R	HR	HB	BB-IB	SO	ERA	AERA	OAV	OOB	AB-HR-SH	AVG	PB	SUP	APR	DL	PW
1909 Cin N	19	11	.633	44	29	19-4	2	260	228	97	0	9	57	65	2.01	129	.242	.291	82-0-10	.122	-3	103	14		1
1910 Cin N	15	17	.469	48	31	16-4	7	275	257	103	6	15	75	74	2.59	113	.255	.317	87-0-1	.115	-3	100	14		1
1911 Cin N	11	17	.393	44	32	11-2	4	253.2	272	112	9	14	69	76	3.30	100	.283	.340	85-0-1	.153	-2	92	6		0
1912 Cin N	1	3	.250	7	6	2-1	0	36.2	38	21	0	1	16	13	4.17	81	.277	.357	12	.250	0	127	-3		-0
Total 4	46	48	.489	143	98	48-11	13	825.1	795	333	15	39	217	228	2.69	110	.261	.318	266-0-12	.135	-9	100	31		2

GASSAWAY, CHARLIE Charles Cason "Sheriff" B8.12.1918 Gassaway TN D1.15.1992 Miami FL BL/TL/6-2.5/210 d9.25

YEAR TM LG	W	L	PCT	G	GS	CG-SHO	SV-BS	IP	H	R	HR	HB	BB-IB	SO	ERA	AERA	OAV	OOB	AB-HR-SH	AVG	PB	SUP	APR	DL	PW
1944 Chi N	0	1	.000	2	2	0	0	11.2	20	11	3	0	10	7	7.71	46	.385	.484	4	.250	0	95	-5		-0.
1945 Phi A	4	7	.364	24	11	4	0	118	114	59	4	2	55	50	3.74	92	.252	.336	39	.154	-2	72	-5		-0.
1946 Cle A	1	1	.500	13	6	0	0	50.2	54	25	2	4	26	23	3.91	85	.273	.368	15	.067	-1	99	-4		-0.
Total 3	5	9	.357	39	19	4	0	180.1	188	95	9	6	91	80	4.04	84	.268	.357	58	.138	-3	83	-14		-1.

GASSNER, DAVE David K. B12.14.1978 Hortonville WI BR/TL/6-2/190 d4.16 Col Purdue

YEAR TM LG	W	L	PCT	G	GS	CG-SHO	SV-BS	IP	H	R	HR	HB	BB-IB	SO	ERA	AERA	OAV	OOB	AB-HR-SH	AVG	PB	SUP	APR	DL	PW
2005 Min A	1	0	1.000	2	2	0	0-0	7.2	9	7	1	0	1-0	2	5.87	75	.281	.294		—	0	171	-2		-0.

GASTON, MILT Nathaniel Milton B1.27.1896 Ridgefield Park NJ D4.26.1996 Barnstable MA BR/TR(BB 1933)/6-1/185 d4.20 b-Alex

YEAR TM LG	W	L	PCT	G	GS	CG-SHO	SV-BS	IP	H	R	HR	HB	BB-IB	SO	ERA	AERA	OAV	OOB	AB-HR-SH	AVG	PB	SUP	APR	DL	PW
1924 NY A	5	3	.625	29	2	0	1	86	92	48	3	6	44	24	4.50	92	.286	.382	27-0-2	.222	-1	51	-3		-0
1925 StL A	15	14	.517	42	29	16	0	238.2	284	146	8	5	101	84	4.41	106	.305	.376	80-1-6	.262	2	102	4		0
1926 StL A	10	18	.357	32	28	14-1	0	214.1	227	116	13	4	101	39	4.33	99	.283	.366	78-1-2	.167	-2	79	2		0
1927 StL A	13	17	.433	37	30	21	1	254	275	117	18	3	100	77	5.00	87	.281	.350	96-3-5	.260	5	102	-20		-1
1928 Was A	6	12	.333	28	22	8-3	0	148.2	179	103	9	0	53	45	5.51	73	.302	.360	49-0-4	.143	-3	108	-23		-2
1929 Bos A	12	19	.387	39	28	20-1	2	243.2	265	121	15	3	81	99	3.73	115	.289	.348	78-1-4	.192	0	76	14		1
1930 Bos A	13	20	.394	38	34	20-2	2	273	272	138	15	0	98	99	3.92	117	.259	.323	98-0-5	.204	-4	81	20		1
1931 Bos A	2	13	.133	23	18	4	0	119	137	76	4	0	41	33	4.46	96	.291	.348	38-0-1	.158	-2	60	-6		-0
1932 Chi A	7	17	.292	28	25	7-1	1	166.2	183	101	10	1	73	44	4.00	108	.279	.352	60	.233	2	80	3		0
1933 Chi A	8	12	.400	30	25	7-1	0	167	177	106	9	1	60	39	4.85	87	.272	.334	52-0-2	.154	0	84	-11		-1
1934 Chi A	6	19	.240	29	28	10-1	0	194	247	146	16	1	84	48	5.85	81	.313	.379	68-0-1	.147	-3	77	-23		-2
Total 11	97	164	.372	355	269	127-10	8	2105	2338	1277	114	24	816	615	4.55	97	.287	.355	724-6-32	.200	-5	85	-43		-4

GASTON, WELCOME Welcome Thornburg B12.19.1874 Senecaville OH D12.13.1944 Columbus OH TL d10.6

YEAR TM LG	W	L	PCT	G	GS	CG-SHO	SV-BS	IP	H	R	HR	HB	BB-IB	SO	ERA	AERA	OAV	OOB	AB-HR-SH	AVG	PB	SUP	APR	DL	PW
1898 Bro N	1	1	.500	2	2	2	0	16	17	9	0	0	9	0	2.81	127	.270	.361	8	.125	-0	178	1		0
1899 Bro N	0	0	—	1	0	0	0	3	3	1	0	1	4	0	3.00	130	.250	.391	1	1.000	1		1		
Total 2	1	1	.500	3	2	2	0	19	20	10	0	1	13	0	2.84	127	.267	.382	9	.222	1	178	1		0

GASTRIGHT, HANK Henry Carl (b Henry Carl Gastreich) B3.29.1865 Covington KY D10.9.1937 Cold Spring KY BR/TR/6-2/190 d4.19

YEAR TM LG	W	L	PCT	G	GS	CG-SHO	SV-BS	IP	H	R	HR	HB	BB-IB	SO	ERA	AERA	OAV	OOB	AB-HR-SH	AVG	PB	SUP	APR	DL	PW
1889 Col AA	10	16	.385	32	26	21	0	222.2	255	175	8	5	104	115	4.57	79	.279	.355	94	.181	-4	76	-24		-2
1890 Col AA	30	14	.682	48	45	41-4	0	401.1	312	204	8	18	135	199	2.94	122	.208	.281	169	.213	3	131	30		2
1891 Col AA	12	19	.387	35	33	28-1	0	283.2	280	196	7	11	136	109	3.78	91	.249	.336	117	.197	-4	105	-16		-1
1892 Was N	3	3	.500	11	8	6	0	79.2	94	54	3	4	38	32	5.08	64	.282	.361	29	.138	0*	136	-10		-C
1893 Pit N	3	1	.750	9	5	3	0	59	74	54	3	3	39	12	6.25	73	.297	.399	24	.042	-4	120	-10		-C
Bro N	12	4	.750	19	18	16	0	156	179	117	9	9	76	27	5.13	96	.279	.364	68	.191	-3*	105	-1		-C
Year	15	5	.750	28	23	19	0	215	253	171	12	12	115	39	5.44	89	.284	.374	92	.152	-6	108	-4		-C
1894 Bro N	2	6	.250	16	6	6-1	2	93	135	85	1	6	55	20	6.39	78	.335	.422	41	.171	-3	112	-13		-C
1896 Cin N	0	0	—	1	0	0	0	6	8	6	0	0	1	0	4.50	103	.320	.346	2	.000	-0		-1		-C
Total 7	72	63	.533	171	143	121-6	2	1301.1	1337	891	39	55	584	514	4.20	92	.258	.339	544	.186	-8	110	-45		-3

GATEWOOD, AUBREY Aubrey Lee B11.17.1938 Little Rock AR BR/TR/6-1/170* d9.11 Col Arkansas St.

YEAR TM LG	W	L	PCT	G	GS	CG-SHO	SV-BS	IP	H	R	HR	HB	BB-IB	SO	ERA	AERA	OAV	OOB	AB-HR-SH	AVG	PB	SUP	APR	DL	PW
1963 LA A	1	1	.500	4	3	1	0	24	12	5	0	0	16-0	13	1.50	228	.148	.283	8	.000	-1	69	5		0
1964 LA A	3	3	.500	15	7	0	0	60.1	59	18	4	1	12-1	25	2.24	147	.258	.295	20	.100	-1*	85	8		0
1965 Cal A	4	5	.444	46	3	0	0	92	91	41	6	1	37-3	37	3.42	99	.266	.336	14	.214	0	43	-1		-C
1970 Atl N	0	0	—	3	0	0	0	6	4	3	0	1	2-1	0	4.50	96	.364	.500	0	—	0		-2		-C
Total 4	8	9	.471	68	13	1	0-0	178.1	166	70	9	3	67-5	75	2.78	122	.250	.318	42	.119	-1	70	10		C

GAUDIN, CHAD Chad Edward B3.24.1983 Metairie LA BR/TR/5-10/170* [TBA01 34/1009] d8.1

YEAR TM LG	W	L	PCT	G	GS	CG-SHO	SV-BS	IP	H	R	HR	HB	BB-IB	SO	ERA	AERA	OAV	OOB	AB-HR-SH	AVG	PB	SUP	APR	DL	PW
2003 TB A	2	0	1.000	15	5	0	0-0	40	37	18	4	1	16-0	23	3.60	127	.240	.312	—		0	114	4		C
2004 TB A	1	2	.333	26	4	0	0-1	42.2	59	27	4	1	16-4	30	4.85	96	.337	.397	1-0-1	.000	-0*	105	-2		C
2005 Tor A	1	3	.250	5	3	0	0-0	13	31	19	6	1	6-0	12	13.15	35	.470	.514	—		0	88	-11		C
Total 3	4	5	.444	46	10	0	0-1	95.2	127	64	14	6	38-4	65	5.46	85	.322	.383	—	.000	0	102	-9		C

YEAR	TM LG	W	L	PCT	G	GS	CG-SHO	SV-BS	IP	H	R	HR	HB	BB-IB	SO	ERA	AERA	OAV	OOB	AB-HR-SH	AVG	PB	SUP	APR	DL	PW

GAW, CHIPPY   George Joseph B3.13.1892 W.Newton MA D5.26.1968 Boston MA BR/TR/5-11/180   d4.20   Col Tufts

| 1920 | Chi N | 1 | 1 | .500 | 6 | 1 | 0 | 0 | 13 | 16 | 9 | 1 | 1 | 3 | 4 | 4.85 | 66 | .320 | .370 | 4 | .250 | -0 | 74 | -2 | | -0.4 |

GEAR, DALE   Dale Dudley B2.2.1872 Lone Elm KS D9.23.1951 Topeka KS BR/TR/5-11/165   d8.15   Col Kansas ▲

1896	Cle N	0	2	.000	3	2	2	0	23	35	23	1	2	6	6	5.48	83	.347	.394	15	.400	2*	102	-3		-0.1
1901	Was A	4	11	.267	24	16	14-1	1	163	199	100	9	4	22	35	4.03	91	.297	.324	199-0-2	.236	0*	78	-5		-0.3
Total	2	4	13	.235	27	18	16-1	1	186	234	123	10	6	28	41	4.21	90	.304	.333	214-0-2	.248	2	81	-8		-0.4

GEARIN, DINTY   Dennis John B10.15.1897 Providence RI D3.11.1959 Providence RI BL/TL/5-4/148   d8.6

1923	†NY N	1	1	.500	6	2	1	0	24	23	11	1	0	10	9	3.38	113	.264	.340	7	.286	0	65	1		0.1
1924	NY N	1	2	.333	6	3	2	0	29	30	9	3	0	16	4	2.48	148	.275	.368	9	.333	0*	154	4		0.4
	Bos N	0	1	.000	1	0	0	0	0	3	5	0	0	2	0	∞	—	1.000	1.000	0	—	0*	178	-5		-0.4
	Year	1	3	.250	7	4	2	0	29	33	14	3	0	18	4	4.03	91	.295	.392	9	.333	0	162	-1		0.0
Total	2	2	4	.333	13	6	3	0	53	56	25	4	0	28	13	3.74	100	.281	.370	16	.313	1	127	-0		0.1

GEARY, GEOFF   Geoffrey Michael B8.26.1976 Buffalo NY BR/TR/6-0/170* [PhiN98 15/434] d8.27   Col Oklahoma

2003	Phi N	0	0	—	5	0	0	0-0	6	8	3	0	0	3-0	3	4.50	88	.333	.407	0	—	0	0	0		0.0
2004	Phi N	1	0	1.000	33	0	0	0-0	44.2	52	29	8	3	16-3	30	5.44	81	.292	.357	1	.000	-0	-5		15	-0.3
2005	Phi N	2	1	.667	40	0	0	0-1	58	54	29	5	1	21-4	42	3.72	117	.247	.310	6	.167	-0	3	15	0.1
Total	3	3	1	.750	78	0	0	0-1	108.2	114	61	13	4	40-7	75	4.47	97	.271	.335	7	.143	-0	-2	15	-0.2

GEARY, BOB   Robert Norton "Speed" B5.10.1891 Cincinnati OH D1.3.1980 Cincinnati OH BR/TR/5-11/168   d4.25   Mil 1918

1918	Phi A	2	5	.286	16	7	6-2	0	87	94	37	0	3	31	22	2.69	109	.289	.357	27-0-1	.148	-1	81	1		-0.1
1919	Phi A	0	3	.000	9	2	1	0	32.1	32	22	1	0	18	9	4.73	72	.264	.360	10	.500	2	69	-5		-0.2
1921	Cin N	1	1	.500	10	1	0	4	29	38	17	1	0	2	10	4.34	82	.333	.345	8	.250	0	138	-2		-0.2
Total	3	3	9	.250	35	10	7-2	4	148.1	164	76	2	3	51	41	3.46	92	.293	.355	45-0-1	.244	1	83	-6		-0.2

GEBHARD, BOB   Robert Henry B1.3.1943 Lamberton MN BR/TR/6-2/210* [MinA65 15/547] d8.2   C1   Col Iowa

1971	Min A	1	2	.333	17	0	0	0-0	18	17	6	0	1	11-3	13	3.00	118	.243	.354	0	—	0	1		0.3
1972	Min A	0	1	.000	13	0	0	1-0	21	36	29	3	2	13-2	13	8.57	37	.371	.447	0	—	0	-14		-0.8
1974	Mon N	0	0	—	1	0	0	0-0	2	5	1	1	0	0-0	0	4.50	86	.500	.500	0	—	0	0		0.0
Total	3	1	3	.250	31	0	0	1-0	41	58	36	4	3	24-5	26	5.93	57	.328	.413	0	—	0	-13		-0.5

GEBRIAN, PETE   Peter "Gabe" B8.10.1923 Bayonne NJ D5.6.2005 Stuart FL BR/TR/6-0/170   d5.6

| 1947 | Chi A | 2 | 3 | .400 | 27 | 4 | 0 | 5 | 66.1 | 61 | 40 | 7 | 2 | 33 | 17 | 4.48 | 82 | .247 | .340 | 13-0-1 | .000 | -2 | 48 | -7 | | -0.8 |

GEDDES, JIM   James Lee B3.23.1949 Columbus OH BR/TR/6-2/190* d4.28   Col Ohio St.

1972	Chi A	0	0	—	5	1	0	0-0	10.1	12	9	1	1	10-0	3	6.97	45	.293	.442	1-0-1	.000	-0*	170	-4		-0.3
1973	Chi A	0	0	—	6	1	0	0-0	15.2	14	6	0	3	14-0	7	2.87	138	.255	.431	0	—	0	45	2		0.1
Total	2	0	0	—	11	2	0	0-0	26	26	15	1	4	24-0	10	4.50	80	.271	.435	1-0-1	.000	-0	98	-2		-0.2

GEDNEY, COUNT   Alfred W. B5.10.1849 Brooklyn NY D3.26.1922 Hackensack NJ 5-9/140   d4.27.1872 ▲

| 1875 | Mut NA | 1 | 0 | 1.000 | 2 | 1 | 1 | 0 | 11 | 7 | 4 | 0 | 1 | 2 | 0.82 | 285 | .167 | .186 | 267 | .206 | -0* | 136 | 1 | | 0.1 |

GEE, JOHNNY   John Alexander "Whiz" B12.7.1915 Syracuse NY D1.23.1988 Cortland NY BL/TL/6-9/225   d9.17   Def 1945   Col Michigan

1939	Pit N	1	2	.333	3	1	1	0	19.2	20	17	0	0	10	16	4.12	93	.253	.337	6	.000	-1	83	-4		-0.5
1941	Pit N	0	2	.000	3	2	0	0	7.1	10	10	0	0	5	2	6.14	59	.294	.385	3	.333	0	106	-4		-0.7
1943	Pit N	4	4	.500	15	10	2	0	82	89	42	5	0	27	18	4.28	81	.280	.336	26-0-2	.115	-1	122	-4		-0.6
1944	Pit N	0	0	—	4	0	0	0	11.1	11	7	0	0	5	3	7.15	52	.377	.431	2	.500	0	-4		-0.2
	NY N	0	0	—	4	0	0	0	4.2	5	1	0	0	0	3	0.00	—	.263	.263	0	—	0	1		0.1
	Year	0	0	—	8	0	0	0	16	16	8	0	0	5	6	5.06	73	.347	.390	2	.500	0	-2		-0.1
1945	NY N	0	0	—	2	0	0	0	3	5	3	0	0	2	1	9.00	43	.385	.467	1	.000	0	-1		-0.1
1946	NY N	2	4	.333	13	6	1	0	47.1	60	27	3	2	15	22	3.99	86	.308	.363	13-0-1	.231	0	46	-4		-0.5
Total	6	7	12	.368	44	21	4	1	175.1	209	110	8	2	64	65	4.41	80	.294	.354	51-0-3	.157	-1	93	-20		-2.5

GEHRING, HENRY   Henry B1.24.1881 St.Paul MN D4.18.1912 Kansas City MO BR/TR   d7.16

1907	Was A	3	7	.300	15	9	8-2	0	87	92	44	1	1	14	31	3.31	73	.274	.305	44-1-0	.205	3*	93	-8		-0.7
1908	Was A	0	1	.000	3	1	0	0	5	9	8	0	2	2	0	14.40	16	.450	.542	5	.600	2*	90	-6		-0.7
Total	2	3	8	.273	18	10	8-2	0	92	101	52	1	3	16	31	3.91	62	.284	.320	49-1-0	.245	5	93	-14		-1.4

GEHRMAN, PAUL   Paul Arthur "Dutch" B5.3.1912 Marquam OR D10.23.1986 Bend OR BR/TR/6-0/195   d9.15

| 1937 | Cin N | 0 | 1 | .000 | 2 | 1 | 0 | 0 | 9.1 | 11 | 8 | 0 | 0 | 5 | 1 | 2.89 | 129 | .282 | .364 | 3 | .000 | -0 | 116 | -1 | | -0.1 |

GEIS, EMIL   Emil Michael B3.1861 Villmar, Germany BR/TR/5-11/170   d7.19

| 1882 | Bal AA | 4 | 9 | .308 | 13 | 13 | 10-1 | 0 | 95.2 | 84 | 73 | 2 | | 22 | 10 | 4.80 | 57 | .220 | .263 | 41 | .146 | -2 | 59 | -16 | | -1.9 |

GEISEL, DAVE   John David B1.18.1955 Windber PA BL/TL/6-3/210* [ChiN73 5/112] d6.13

1978	Chi N	1	0	1.000	18	1	0	0-0	23.1	27	12	0	0	11-4	15	4.24	95	.278	.352	3	.000	-0	89	0		-0.1
1979	Chi N	0	0	—	7	0	0	0-0	15	10	1	0	1	4-1	5	0.60	693	.189	.259	1	.000	-0	5		0.3
1981	Chi N	2	0	1.000	11	2	0	0-1	16	11	3	0	0	10-1	7	0.56	666	.204	.318	3	.000	-0	118	5		0.5
1982	Tor A	1	1	.500	16	2	0	0-0	31.2	32	15	6	2	17-2	22	3.98	113	.260	.359	0	—	0	81	2		0.1
1983	Tor A	0	3	.000	47	0	0	5-3	52.1	47	28	4	2	31-5	50	4.64	94	.240	.349	0	—	0	-1		-0.1
1984	Sea A	1	1	.500	20	3	0	3-0	43.1	47	22	2	2	9-3	28	4.15	97	.273	.314	0	—	0	97	-1		-0.1
1985	Sea A	0	0	—	12	0	0	0-0	27	35	21	3	0	15-3	17	6.33	67	.310	.391	0	—	0	-6		-0.3
Total	7	5	5	.500	131	8	0	8-4	208.2	209	102	15	7	97-19	144	4.01	105	.259	.342	7	.000	-1	94	4		0.3

GEISHERT, VERN   Vernon William B1.10.1946 Madison WI BR/TR/6-1/215 [AnaA66*2/26] d8.26   Col Wisconsin-Madison

| 1969 | Cal A | 1 | 1 | .500 | 11 | 3 | 0 | 1-0 | 31 | 32 | 18 | 4 | 1 | 7-3 | 18 | 4.65 | 75 | .267 | .308 | 9 | .000 | -1 | 143 | -4 | | -0.3 |

GEISS, EMIL   Emil August B3.20.1867 Chicago IL D10.4.1911 Chicago IL BR/TR/5-11/170   d5.18   b-Bill ▲

| 1887 | Chi N | 0 | 1 | .000 | 1 | 1 | 1 | 0 | 9 | 17 | 11 | 0 | 0 | 3 | 8 | 8.00 | 56 | .395 | .435 | 12 | .083 | -1* | 58 | -3 | | -0.2 |

GELNAR, JOHN   John Richard B6.25.1943 Granite OK BR/TR/6-1.5/190* d8.4   Col Oklahoma

1964	Pit N	0	0	—	7	0	0	1-0	9	11	5	2	0	1-0	4	5.00	70	.314	.333	0	—	0	-1		-0.1
1967	Pit N	0	1	.000	10	1	0	0	19	30	18	4	2	11-1	5	8.05	42	.375	.453	6	.167	-0	104	-9		-0.5
1969	Sea A	3	10	.231	39	10	0	3-2	108.2	103	49	7	5	26-5	69	3.31	110	.250	.299	19-0-3	.053	-2*	61	2		0.1
1970	Mil A	4	3	.571	53	0	0	4-2	92.1	98	46	7	5	23-5	48	4.19	90	.277	.326	12	.083	-1	-3		-0.3
1971	Mil A	0	0	—	2	0	0	0-0	1.1	3	2	0	0	1-0	0	13.50	26	.429	.500	0	—	0	-1		-0.1
Total	5	7	14	.333	111	11	0	7-4	230.1	245	120	20	12	62-11	126	4.18	88	.276	.328	37-0-3	.081	-2	64	-12		-0.9

GENEWICH, JOE   Joseph Edward B1.15.1897 Elmira NY D12.21.1985 Lockport NY BR/TR/6-0/174   d9.3

1922	Bos N	0	2	.000	6	2	1	0	23	29	19	2	0	11	4	7.04	57	.319	.392	6	.167	-0	102	-7		-0.5
1923	Bos N	13	14	.481	43	24	12-1	1	227.1	272	110	15	7	46	54	3.72	107	.303	.341	77-0-1	.247	-2	83	9		1.2
1924	Bos N	10	19	.345	34	27	11-2	1	200.1	258	136	4	8	65	43	5.21	73	.329	.386	60-0-5	.167	-2	72	-32		-4.0
1925	Bos N	12	10	.545	34	21	10	0	169	185	87	6	6	41	34	3.99	100	.279	.327	55-0-4	.273	1	94	2		0.3
1926	Bos N	8	16	.333	37	26	12-2	2	216	239	114	6	6	63	59	3.88	92	.288	.342	67-0-5	.164	1	88	-10		-1.1
1927	Bos N	11	8	.579	40	19	7	1	181	199	79	7	2	54	37	3.83	97	.279	.332	57-0-3	.193	-1	93	-3		-0.4
1928	Bos N	3	7	.300	13	11	4	0	80.2	88	43	14	3	18	15	4.13	95	.280	.325	26-0-4	.038	-3	77	-1		-0.4
	NY N	11	4	.733	26	18	10-2	3	158.1	136	62	10	1	54	37	3.18	123	.232	.298	64-0-2	.203	-1	112	14		1.2
	Year	14	11	.560	39	29	14-2	3	239	224	105	24	4	72	52	3.50	112	.249	.307	90-0-6	.156	-4	93	13		0.8
1929	NY N	3	7	.300	21	9	1	1	85	133	70	9	1	30	19	6.78	68	.359	.409	32	.375	3*	104	-19		-1.6
1930	NY N	2	5	.286	18	9	3	3	61	71	44	6	1	29	9	5.61	84	.297	.354	20-0-1	.150	-1*	92	-6		-0.6
Total	9	73	92	.442	272	166	71-7	12	1401.2	1610	778	77	35	402	316	4.29	91	.293	.345	464-0-25	.207	-4	89	-53		-5.9

GENTRY, GARY   Gary Edward B10.6.1946 Phoenix AZ BR/TR/6-0/183(165-183) [NYN67 S3/60] d4.10   Col Arizona St.

1969	†NY N	13	12	.520	35	35	6-3	0-0	233.2	192	94	24	5	81-5	154	3.43	107	.222	.291	74-0-7	.081	-4	90	8		0.5
1970	NY N	9	9	.500	32	29	5-2	1-1	188.1	155	88	19	9	86-7	134	3.68	110	.224	.280	59-0-5	.068	-2	100	7		0.3
1971	NY N	12	11	.522	32	31	8-3	0-0	203.1	167	84	16	6	82-8	155	3.23	106	.224	.304	68-0-6	.074	-5	92	4		-0.2
1972	NY N	7	10	.412	32	26	3	0-0	164	153	82	20	6	75-5	120	4.01	85	.250	.334	48-0-3	.104	-5	94	-11		-1.1

YEAR	TM LG	W	L	PCT	G	GS	CG-SHO	SV-BS	IP	H	R	HR	HB	BB-IB	SO	ERA	AERA	OAV	OOB	AB-HR-SH	AVG	PB	SUP	APR	DL	PW
1973	Atl N	4	6	.400	16	14	3	1-0	86.2	74	37	7	1	35-3	42	3.43	116	.231	.305	30-0-3	.233	1*	100	5	34	0.5
1974	Atl N	0	0	—	3	1	0	0-0	6.2	4	1	1	1	2-0	0	1.35	281	.167	.259	1	.000	-0	46	2	164	0.1
1975	Atl N	1	1	.500	7	2	0	0-1	20	25	14	3	0	8-1	10	4.95	76	.313	.365	5-0-1	.000	-1	46	-3		-0.3
Total	7	46	49	.484	157	138	25-8	2-2	902.2	770	400	90	28	369-29	615	3.56	103	.231	.310	285-0-25	.095	-12	94	12	198	-0.2

GENTRY, RUFE   James Ruffus B5.18.1918 Daisy Station (now Ogburn) NC D7.3.1997 Winston-Salem NC BR/TR/6-1/180 d9.10 b-Harvey

YEAR	TM LG	W	L	PCT	G	GS	CG-SHO	SV-BS	IP	H	R	HR	HB	BB-IB	SO	ERA	AERA	OAV	OOB	AB-HR-SH	AVG	PB	SUP	APR	DL	PW
1943	Det A	1	3	.250	4	4	2	0	29.1	30	12	2	2	12	8	3.68	96	.268	.349	10	.000	-1	60	0		-0.1
1944	Det A	12	14	.462	37	30	10-3	0	203.2	211	104	9	4	108	68	4.24	84	.273	.365	76-0-2	.197	1	85	-10		-1.2
1946	Det A	0	0	—	2	0	0	0	3	4	5	0	0	5	0	15.00	24	.333	.579	—		0		-3		-0.2
1947	Det A	0	0	—	1	0	0	0	0.1	1	3	0	0	2	1	81.00	5	.500	.750			0		-3		-0.1
1948	Det A	0	0	—	4	0	0	0	6.2	5	2	0	1	5	1	2.70	162	.208	.367	1	1.000	0		1		-0.1
Total	5	13	17	.433	48	34	12-3	0	243	251	126	11	7	134	78	4.37	82	.272	.368	87-0-2	.184	-1	82	-15		-1.5

GEORGE, CHRIS   Christopher Coleman B9.16.1979 Houston TX BL/TR/6-2/200* [KCA98 1/31] d7.26

YEAR	TM LG	W	L	PCT	G	GS	CG-SHO	SV-BS	IP	H	R	HR	HB	BB-IB	SO	ERA	AERA	OAV	OOB	AB-HR-SH	AVG	PB	SUP	APR	DL	PW
2001	KC A	4	8	.333	13	13	1	0-0	74	83	48	14	0	18-0	32	5.59	89	.288	.326	0	—	0	93	-4		-0.5
2002	KC A	0	4	.000	6	6	0	0-0	27.1	37	17	2	1	8-0	13	5.60	89	.325	.371	0	—	0	84	-1	32	-0.1
2003	KC A	9	6	.600	18	18	0	0-0	93.2	120	75	22	3	44-2	39	7.11	68	.309	.380	1-0-2	1.000	0	106	-21		-2.6
2004	KC A	1	2	.333	10	7	0	0-0	42.1	60	39	1	0	25-1	15	7.23	65	.331	.411	2	.000	0	83	-13		-0.7
Total	4	14	20	.412	47	44	1	0-0	237.1	300	179	39	4	95-3	99	6.48	75	.309	.369	3-0-2	.333	1	96	-39	32	-3.9

GEORGE, CHRIS   Christopher Sean B9.24.1966 Pittsburgh PA BR/TR/6-2/200 [MilA88 7/185] d10.1 Col Kent St.

YEAR	TM LG	W	L	PCT	G	GS	CG-SHO	SV-BS	IP	H	R	HR	HB	BB-IB	SO	ERA	AERA	OAV	OOB	AB-HR-SH	AVG	PB	SUP	APR	DL	PW
1991	Mil A	0	0	—	2	1	0	0-0	6	8	2	0	0	0-0	2	3.00	133	.333	.320	0		0	46	1		0.0

GEORGE, LEFTY   Thomas Edward B8.13.1886 Pittsburgh PA D5.13.1955 York PA BL/TL/6-0/155 d4.14

YEAR	TM LG	W	L	PCT	G	GS	CG-SHO	SV-BS	IP	H	R	HR	HB	BB-IB	SO	ERA	AERA	OAV	OOB	AB-HR-SH	AVG	PB	SUP	APR	DL	PW
1911	StL A	4	9	.308	27	13	6-1	0	116.1	136	81	3	9	51	23	4.18	81	.256	.332	44-0-2	.114	-3	82	-12		-1.8
1912	Cle A	0	5	.000	11	5	2	0	44.1	69	38	1	2	18	18	4.87	70	.373	.434	14-0-1	.214	1	74	-9		-0.7
1915	Cin N	2	2	.500	5	3	2-1	0	28	24	12	1	5	8	11	3.86	74	.242	.330	12	.333	2*	78	-2		0.0
1918	Bos N	1	5	.167	9	5	4	0	54.1	56	23	0	3	21	22	2.32	116	.281	.359	22	.091	-2*	90	0		0.1
Total	4	7	21	.250	52	26	14-2	0	243	285	154	5	19	98	74	3.85	82	.281	.355	92-0-3	.152	-2	82	-23		-2.3

GEORGE, BILL   William M. B1.27.1865 Bellaire OH D8.23.1916 Wheeling WV BR/TL/5-8/165 d5.11

YEAR	TM LG	W	L	PCT	G	GS	CG-SHO	SV-BS	IP	H	R	HR	HB	BB-IB	SO	ERA	AERA	OAV	OOB	AB-HR-SH	AVG	PB	SUP	APR	DL	PW
1887	NY N	3	9	.250	13	13	10	0	108	126	112	1	14	89	49	5.25	72	.292	.429	53	.170	-4	146	-23		-2.0
1888	†NY N	2	1	.667	4	3	3-1	0	33.2	18	9	0	1	11	26	1.34	205	.149	.226	39-1	.231	1*	164	5		0.5
1889	Col AA	0	0	—	2	0	0	0	8	11	13	1	0	3	3	7.88	46	.314	.368	17	.235	-0*		-5		-0.2
Total	3	5	10	.333	19	16	13-1	0	149.2	155	134	2	15	103	78	4.51	78	.264	.387	109-1	.202	-3	149	-23		-1.7

GEORGY, OSCAR   Oscar John B11.25.1916 New Orleans LA D1.15.1999 New Orleans LA BR/TR/6-3.5/180 d6.4

YEAR	TM LG	W	L	PCT	G	GS	CG-SHO	SV-BS	IP	H	R	HR	HB	BB-IB	SO	ERA	AERA	OAV	OOB	AB-HR-SH	AVG	PB	SUP	APR	DL	PW
1938	NY N	0	0	—	1	0	0	0	1	2	2	0	1	2	0	18.00	50	.400	.500	0	—	0		-1		-0.1

GERARD, DAVE   David Frederick B8.6.1936 New York NY D10.10.2001 Newtown PA BR/TR/6-2/205 d4.10

YEAR	TM LG	W	L	PCT	G	GS	CG-SHO	SV-BS	IP	H	R	HR	HB	BB-IB	SO	ERA	AERA	OAV	OOB	AB-HR-SH	AVG	PB	SUP	APR	DL	PW
1962	Chi N	2	3	.400	39	0	0	3	58.2	67	40	10	1	28-5	30	4.91	84	.289	.365	8	.375	1		-6		-0.5

GERBERMAN, GEORGE   George Alois B3.8.1942 ElCampo TX BR/TR/6-0/180 d9.23

YEAR	TM LG	W	L	PCT	G	GS	CG-SHO	SV-BS	IP	H	R	HR	HB	BB-IB	SO	ERA	AERA	OAV	OOB	AB-HR-SH	AVG	PB	SUP	APR	DL	PW
1962	Chi N	0	0	—	1	1	0	0	5.1	3	1	1	0	5-0	1	1.69	246	.158	.333	1	.000	0	21	1		0.1

GERHARDT, RUSTY   Allen Russell B8.13.1950 Baltimore MD BB/TL/5-9/175 d7.27 Col Clemson

YEAR	TM LG	W	L	PCT	G	GS	CG-SHO	SV-BS	IP	H	R	HR	HB	BB-IB	SO	ERA	AERA	OAV	OOB	AB-HR-SH	AVG	PB	SUP	APR	DL	PW
1974	SD N	2	1	.667	23	1	0	1-0	35.2	44	28	1	2	17-5	22	7.07	51	.308	.384	6	.167	-0	73	-12		-1.1

GERHEAUSER, AL   Albert "Lefty" B6.24.1917 St.Louis MO D5.28.1972 Springfield MO BL/TL/6-3/190 d4.24

YEAR	TM LG	W	L	PCT	G	GS	CG-SHO	SV-BS	IP	H	R	HR	HB	BB-IB	SO	ERA	AERA	OAV	OOB	AB-HR-SH	AVG	PB	SUP	APR	DL	PW
1943	Phi N	10	19	.345	38	31	11-2	0	215	222	108	10	2	70	92	3.60	94	.263	.321	71-0-1	.113	-3	92	-9		-1.1
1944	Phi N	8	16	.333	30	29	10-2	0	182.2	210	102	8	1	65	66	4.58	79	.285	.344	65-1-1	.231	3*	77	-17		-1.3
1945	Pit N	5	10	.333	32	14	5	1	140.1	170	72	5	1	54	55	3.91	101	.304	.366	48	.250	2*	107	1		0.3
1946	Pit N	2	2	.500	35	3	1	0	81.2	92	42	2	1	25	32	3.97	89	.286	.339	21	.333	2*	97	-4		-0.1
1948	StL A	0	3	.000	14	2	0	0	23.1	32	23	0	1	10	10	7.33	62	.317	.384	6	.333	0	50	-8		-0.5
Total	5	25	50	.333	149	79	27-4	1	643	726	347	25	6	224	255	4.13	88	.283	.342	211-1-2	.209	5	88	-37		-3.1

GERKIN, STEVE   Stephen Paul "Splinter" B11.19.1912 Grafton WV D11.9.1978 Bay Pines FL BR/TR/6-1/162 d5.13

YEAR	TM LG	W	L	PCT	G	GS	CG-SHO	SV-BS	IP	H	R	HR	HB	BB-IB	SO	ERA	AERA	OAV	OOB	AB-HR-SH	AVG	PB	SUP	APR	DL	PW
1945	Phi A	0	12	.000	21	12	3	0	102	112	49	4	3	27	25	3.62	95	.285	.336	34-0-1	.059	-4	70	-3		-0.7

GERMAN, FRANKLYN   Franklyn Miguel (Made) B1.20.1980 San Cristobal, D.R. BR/TR/6-6/245(245-270) d9.7

YEAR	TM LG	W	L	PCT	G	GS	CG-SHO	SV-BS	IP	H	R	HR	HB	BB-IB	SO	ERA	AERA	OAV	OOB	AB-HR-SH	AVG	PB	SUP	APR	DL	PW
2002	Det A	1	0	1.000	7	0	0	1-0	6.2	3	0	0	1	2-1	6	0.00	—	.150	.261	0	—	0		3		0.1
2003	Det A	2	4	.333	45	0	0	5-2	44.2	47	32	5	2	45-3	41	6.04	72	.273	.427	0	—	0		-8		-1.0
2004	Det A	1	0	1.000	16	0	0	0-1	14.2	17	15	4	0	11-1	8	7.36	61	.279	.389	1	.000	-0		-6		-0.6
2005	Det A	4	0	1.000	58	0	0	1-2	59	63	26	7	7	34-4	38	3.66	116	.284	.388	0	—	0		4		0.1
Total	4	8	4	.667	126	0	0	7-5	125	130	73	16	10	92-9	93	4.75	91	.274	.398	1	.000	-0		-7		-1.4

GERMAN, LES   Lester Stanley B6.1.1869 Baltimore MD D6.10.1934 Germantown MD BR/TR/5-8/165 d8.27

YEAR	TM LG	W	L	PCT	G	GS	CG-SHO	SV-BS	IP	H	R	HR	HB	BB-IB	SO	ERA	AERA	OAV	OOB	AB-HR-SH	AVG	PB	SUP	APR	DL	PW
1890	Bal AA	5	11	.313	17	16	15	0	132.1	147	95	2	13	54	37	4.83	84	.273	.353	51	.118	-2	75	-10		-1.4
1893	NY N	8	8	.500	20	18	14	0	152	162	109	6	9	70	35	4.14	112	.265	.349	74	.311	2*	98	6		0.7
1894	NY N	9	8	.529	24	16	11	1	143	186	139	7	12	68	21	5.54	95	.311	.392	60-0-2	.300	0	114	-6		-1.0
1895	NY N	7	11	.389	25	18	16	0	178.1	243	159	7	9	78	36	5.96	78	.320	.390	111-2-1	.261	3*	99	-23		-1.1
1896	NY N	0	0	—	1	0	0	0	2.2	9	6	0	0	1	0	13.50	31	.529	.556	1	.000	-0		-3		-0.1
	Was N	2	20	.091	28	20	14	1	166.2	240	174	6	5	74	20	6.32	70	.334	.400	70-1-0	.229	0*	84	-32		-3.2
	Year	2	20	.091	29	20	14	1	169.1	249	180	6	5	75	20	6.43	69	.339	.404	71-1-0	.225	-0	84	-41		-3.3
1897	Was N	3	5	.375	15	5	4	0	83.2	117	74	7	7	33	2	5.59	78	.328	.395	44-0-1	.341	2*	92	-10		-0.7
Total	6	34	63	.351	130	93	74	2	858.2	1104	756	30	55	378	151	5.45	84	.307	.381	411-3-4	.260	5	95	-78		-6.7

GERMANO, JUSTIN   Justin William B8.6.1982 Pasadena CA BR/TR/6-1/190 [SDN00 13/379] d5.22

YEAR	TM LG	W	L	PCT	G	GS	CG-SHO	SV-BS	IP	H	R	HR	HB	BB-IB	SO	ERA	AERA	OAV	OOB	AB-HR-SH	AVG	PB	SUP	APR	DL	PW
2004	SD N	1	2	.333	7	5	0	0	21.1	31	24	2	0	14-0	16	8.86	45	.341	.425	7-0-1	.000	-1	113	-13		-1.1

GERNER, ED   Edwin Frederick "Lefty" B7.22.1897 Philadelphia PA D5.15.1970 Philadelphia PA BL/TL/5-8.5/175 d5.14

YEAR	TM LG	W	L	PCT	G	GS	CG-SHO	SV-BS	IP	H	R	HR	HB	BB-IB	SO	ERA	AERA	OAV	OOB	AB-HR-SH	AVG	PB	SUP	APR	DL	PW
1919	Cin N	1	0	1.000	5	1	0	0	17	22	10	0	2	3	2	3.18	87	.333	.380	6	.167	0*	230	-2		-0.1

GERVAIS, LEFTY   Lucien Edward B7.6.1890 Grover WI D10.19.1950 Los Angeles CA BL/TL/5-10/165 d4.17

YEAR	TM LG	W	L	PCT	G	GS	CG-SHO	SV-BS	IP	H	R	HR	HB	BB-IB	SO	ERA	AERA	OAV	OOB	AB-HR-SH	AVG	PB	SUP	APR	DL	PW
1913	Bos N	0	1	.000	5	2	1	0	15.2	18	11	0	0	4	1	5.74	57	.383	.431	5	.000	-0*	80	-3		-0.2

GESSNER, CHARLIE   Charles R. B12.1863 Philadelphia PA D5.25.1922 Washington DC 5-8/? d7.19

YEAR	TM LG	W	L	PCT	G	GS	CG-SHO	SV-BS	IP	H	R	HR	HB	BB-IB	SO	ERA	AERA	OAV	OOB	AB-HR-SH	AVG	PB	SUP	APR	DL	PW
1886	Phi AA	0	1	.000	1	1	1	0	8	13	14	0	2	5	0	9.00	39	.351	.455	4	.250	-0	136	-5		-0.1

GETTEL, AL   Allen Jones B9.17.1917 Norfolk VA D4.8.2005 Norfolk VA BR/TR/6-3.5/200* d4.20

YEAR	TM LG	W	L	PCT	G	GS	CG-SHO	SV-BS	IP	H	R	HR	HB	BB-IB	SO	ERA	AERA	OAV	OOB	AB-HR-SH	AVG	PB	SUP	APR	DL	PW
1945	NY A	9	8	.529	27	17	9	3	154.2	141	70	11	7	53	67	3.90	89	.243	.314	57-0-2	.281	2	93	-4		-0.8
1946	NY A	6	7	.462	26	11	5-2	0	103	89	40	6	2	40	54	2.97	116	.229	.305	32-0-3	.125	-2	81	5		0.4
1947	Cle A	11	10	.524	31	21	9-2	0	149	122	54	12	3	62	64	3.20	109	.229	.313	51-0-2	.294	4*	93	7		0.5
1948	Cle A	0	1	.000	5	2	0	0	7.2	15	15	2	1	10	4	17.61	23	.385	.520	3	.000	-0	211	-11		-1.3
	Chi A	8	10	.444	22	19	7	1	148	154	76	7	4	60	49	4.01	106	.268	.342	54-0-3	.241	0*	96	3		-0.1
	Year	8	11	.421	27	21	7	1	155.2	169	91	9	5	70	53	4.68	91	.276	.355	57-0-3	.228	-0	106	-8		-0.6
1949	Chi A	2	5	.286	19	7	1-1	0	63	69	48	12	2	26	22	6.43	65	.283	.357	18	.167	-0	95	-15		-0.8
	Was A	0	2	.000	16	1	0	1	34.2	43	24	4	0	24	7	5.45	78	.314	.416	8	.000	-1	96	-20		-0.6
	Year	2	7	.222	35	8	1-1	1	97.2	112	72	16	2	50	29	6.08	69	.294	.379	26	.115	-1	158	-6		-1.4
1951	NY N	1	3	.333	30	1	0	0	57.1	52	37	12	0	25	36	4.87	80	.240	.318	12	.083	-1		-9		-0.5
1955	StL N	1	0	1.000	8	0	0	0	17	26	18	6	0	10-0	7	9.00	45	.361	.429	6	.500	1		-9		-0.5
Total	7	38	45	.458	184	79	31-5	6	734.1	711	382	72	19	310-0	310	4.28	88	.255	.334	241-0-10	.228	3	96	-35		-2.4

GETTIG, CHARLIE   Charles Henry B12.1870 Baltimore MD D4.11.1935 Baltimore MD BR/5-10/172 d8.5 ▲

YEAR	TM LG	W	L	PCT	G	GS	CG-SHO	SV-BS	IP	H	R	HR	HB	BB-IB	SO	ERA	AERA	OAV	OOB	AB-HR-SH	AVG	PB	SUP	APR	DL	PW
1896	NY N	1	0	1.000	4	1	1	0	14	20	17	0	2	8	7	9.64	44	.333	.429	9	.333	1*	253	-7		-0.6
1897	NY N	1	1	.500	3	2	2	0	19	23	23	0	2	9	7	5.21	80	.295	.382	75	.200	0*	120	-4		-0.3
1898	NY N	6	3	.667	17	8	7	0	115	141	72	1	4	43	19	3.83	91	.299	.363	196-0-1	.250	2*	186	-4		-0.5
1899	NY N	7	8	.467	18	15	12	1	128	161	102	3	8	50	25	4.43	85	.307	.376	97-0-3	.247	1*	103	-15		-0.9
Total	4	15	12	.556	42	26	22	1	276	345	214	4	16	110	51	4.50	82	.304	.374	377-0-4	.241	4	136	-30		-2.4

GETZIEN, CHARLIE Charles H. "Pretzels" B2.14.1864 , Germany D6.19.1932 Chicago IL BR/TR/5-10/172 d8.13

YEAR	TM-LG	W	L	PCT	G	GS	CG-SHO	SV-BS	IP	H	R	HR	HB	BB-IB	SO	ERA	AERA	OAV	OOB	AB-HR-SH	AVG	PB	SUP	APR	DL	PW
1884	Det N	5	12	.294	17	17	17-1	0	147.1	118	73	2		25	107	1.95	148	.204	.237	55	.109	-4	61	13		0.9
1885	Det N	12	25	.324	37	37	37-1	0	330	360	222	8		92	110	3.03	94	.264	.311	137	.212	-1*	96	-10		-1.1
1886	Det N	30	11	.732	43	43	42-1	0	386.2	388	203	6		85	172	3.03	110	.250	.288	165	.176	-3	121	11		0.5
1887	†Det N	29	13	**.690**	43	42	41-2	0	366.2	373	217	24	2	106	135	3.73	109	.254	.305	156-1	.186	-2	109	14		1.0
1888	Det N	19	25	.432	46	46	45-2	0	404	411	225	13	8	54	202	3.05	92	.251	.279	167-1	.246	9	107	-9		-0.2
1889	Ind N	18	22	.450	45	44	36	1	349	395	256	27	9	100	139	4.54	92	.277	.328	139-2	.180	2	94	-16		-1.3
1890	Bos N	23	17	.575	40	40	39-4	0	350	342	201	5	3	82	140	3.19	118	.248	.291	147-2	.231	5*	88	17		1.9
1891	Bos N	4	5	.444	11	9	7	0	89	112	62	4	0	23	29	3.84	95	.296	.337	41-1	.171	1*	82	-1		0.1
	Cle N	0	1	.000	1	1	1	0	9	12	9	1	0	4	4	8.00	43	.308	.372	4	.000	-1	52	-3		-0.3
	Year	4	6	.400	12	10	8	0	98	124	71	5	0	27	33	4.22	86	.297	.340	45-1	.156	0	79	-3		-0.2
1892	StL N	5	8	.385	13	13	12	0	108	159	87	5	6	31	32	5.67	56	.329	.377	45-1	.200	0	81	-26		-2.4
Total 9		145	139	.511	296	292	277-11	1	2539.2	2670	1555	95	28	602	1070	3.46	99	.259	.302	1056-8	.198	7	99	-10		-0.9

GEYER, RUBE Jacob Bowman B3.26.1884 Allegheny (now part of Pittsburgh) PA D10.12.1962 Ford Twp. MN BR/TR/5-10/170 d4.24

YEAR	TM-LG	W	L	PCT	G	GS	CG-SHO	SV-BS	IP	H	R	HR	HB	BB-IB	SO	ERA	AERA	OAV	OOB	AB-HR-SH	AVG	PB	SUP	APR	DL	PW
1910	StL N	0	1	.000	4	0	0	0	4	5	3	0	0	3	5	4.50	66	.294	.400	1	.000	-0		-1		-0.2
1911	StL N	9	6	.600	29	11	7-1	0	148.2	141	80	7	6	56	46	3.27	103	.259	.335	57-0-2	.228	1	103	-2		-0.2
1912	StL N	7	14	.333	41	18	5	0	181	191	110	4	4	84	61	3.28	104	.288	.371	53-0-1	.208	-0	70	-3		-0.3
1913	StL N	1	5	.167	30	4	2	1	78.2	83	57	6	2	38	21	5.26	61	.282	.368	22-0-1	.091	-2	76	-19		-1.6
Total 4		17	26	.395	104	33	14-1	1	412.1	420	250	17	12	181	133	4.67	92	.276	.358	133-0-4	.195	-1	82	-25		-2.3

GHELFI, TONY Anthony Paul B8.23.1961 LaCrosse WI BR/TR/6-3/185 [PhiN80*1/14] d9.1 [DL 1984 Phi N 107]

YEAR	TM-LG	W	L	PCT	G	GS	CG-SHO	SV-BS	IP	H	R	HR	HB	BB-IB	SO	ERA	AERA	OAV	OOB	AB-HR-SH	AVG	PB	SUP	APR	DL	PW
1983	Phi N	1	1	.500	3	3	0	0-0	14.1	15	5	2	0	6-0	14	3.14	115	.268	.339	4	.250		57	1		0.2

GIALLOMBARDO, BOB Robert Paul B5.20.1937 Brooklyn NY BL/TL/6-0/175 d6.21

YEAR	TM-LG	W	L	PCT	G	GS	CG-SHO	SV-BS	IP	H	R	HR	HB	BB-IB	SO	ERA	AERA	OAV	OOB	AB-HR-SH	AVG	PB	SUP	APR	DL	PW
1958	LA N	1	1	.500	6	5	0	0	26.1	29	14	3	0	15-0	14	3.76	109	.284	.376	6-0-3	.167	-0*	92	0		0.0

GIARD, JOE Joseph Oscar "Peco" B10.7.1898 Ware MA D7.10.1956 Worcester MA BL/TL/5-10.5/170 d4.18

YEAR	TM-LG	W	L	PCT	G	GS	CG-SHO	SV-BS	IP	H	R	HR	HB	BB-IB	SO	ERA	AERA	OAV	OOB	AB-HR-SH	AVG	PB	SUP	APR	DL	PW
1925	StL A	10	5	.667	30	21	9-4	0	160.2	179	96	13	9	87	43	5.04	93	.295	.388	53-0-3	.057	-6	98	-1		-0.6
1926	StL A	3	10	.231	22	15	2	0	90	113	81	7	1	67	18	7.00	61	.318	.428	29-0-3	.276	0	94	-24		-2.9
1927	NY A	0	0	—	16	0	0	0	27	38	25	1	0	19	10	8.00	48	.352	.449	7	.286	0		-12		-0.5
Total 3		13	15	.464	68	36	11-4	0	277.2	330	202	21	6	173	71	5.96	75	.309	.408	89-0-6	.146	-6	97	-37		-4.0

GIBBON, JOE Joseph Charles B4.10.1935 Hickory MS BR/TL/6-4/210* d4.17 Col U. of Mississippi

YEAR	TM-LG	W	L	PCT	G	GS	CG-SHO	SV-BS	IP	H	R	HR	HB	BB-IB	SO	ERA	AERA	OAV	OOB	AB-HR-SH	AVG	PB	SUP	APR	DL	PW
1960	†Pit N	4	2	.667	27	9	0	0	80.1	87	40	5	0	31-5	60	4.03	93	.277	.341	19-0-4	.211	1	115	-3		-0.1
1961	Pit N	13	10	.565	39	29	7-3	0	195.1	185	85	16	4	57-4	145	3.32	120	.251	.306	59-0-10	.136	-2*	107	13		1.2
1962	Pit N	3	4	.429	19	8	0	0	57	53	29	4	0	24-3	26	3.63	108	.250	.326	17-0-1	.176	-0	112	1		0.1
1963	Pit N	5	12	.294	37	22	5	1	147.1	147	61	7	5	54-15	110	3.30	108	.258	.326	43-0-3	.093	-2*	87	1		0.0
1964	Pit N	10	7	.588	28	24	3	0	146.2	145	66	10	6	54-10	97	3.68	95	.262	.331	47-0-5	.255	3*	118	-2		0.2
1965	Pit N	4	9	.308	31	15	1	1	105.2	85	57	7	4	34-6	63	4.51	78	.221	.288	26-0-2	.115	-0	101	-10		-1.1
1966	SF N	4	6	.400	37	10	1	1	81	86	41	4	2	16-1	48	3.67	100	.275	.310	15	.200	-0	96	-1		0.0
1967	SF N	6	2	.750	28	10	3-1	1	82	65	31	4	3	33-4	63	3.07	107	.220	.302	24-0-1	.042	-1	142	3		0.2
1968	SF N	1	2	.333	29	0	0	1	40	33	10	3	2	19-4	22	1.57	187	.234	.331	1	.000	-0		5		0.5
1969	SF N	1	3	.250	16	0	0	2-1	20	15	10	1	1	13-4	15	3.60	98	.211	.341	3	.000	-0		5		-0.1
	Pit N	5	1	.833	35	0	0	9-0	51.1	38	14	5	2	17-2	35	1.93	181	.208	.281	5-0-2	.000	-1		8		1.3
	Year	6	4	.600	51	0	0	11-1	71.1	53	24	6	3	30-6	44	2.40	146	.209	.299	5-0-2	.000	-1		8		1.2
1970	†Pit N	0	1	.000	41	0	0	5-1	41	44	25	2	2	24-8	26	4.83	82	.280	.380	3	.000	-0		-4	24	-0.2
1971	Cin N	5	6	.455	50	0	0	11-4	64.1	54	25	3	1	32-11	34	2.94	115	.239	.332	1-0-1	.000	-0		2		0.5
1972	Cin N	0	0	—	2	0	0	0-0	0.1	3	2	1	0	1-1	1	54.00	6	.750	.800	0	—	-0		-2		-0.1
	Hou N	0	0	—	9	0	0	0-0	7.1	13	9	2	1	5-2	4	9.82	34	.394	.487	0	—	0		-6		-0.3
	Year	0	0	—	11	0	0	0-0	7.2	16	11	3	1	6-3	5	11.74	29	.432	.523	0	—	0		-7		-0.4
Total 13		61	65	.484	419	127	20-4	32-6	1119.2	1053	505	74	33	414-80	743	3.52	102	.251	.321	263-0-29	.144	-3	109	5	24	2.1

GIBSON, NORWOOD Norwood Ringold "Gibby" B3.11.1877 Peoria IL D7.7.1959 Peoria IL BR/TR/5-10/165 d4.29 Col Notre Dame

YEAR	TM-LG	W	L	PCT	G	GS	CG-SHO	SV-BS	IP	H	R	HR	HB	BB-IB	SO	ERA	AERA	OAV	OOB	AB-HR-SH	AVG	PB	SUP	APR	DL	PW
1903	Bos A	13	9	.591	24	21	17-2	0	183.1	166	95	2	7	65	76	3.19	95	.241	.313	64-0-5	.266	5*	96	-4		-0.1
1904	Bos A	17	14	.548	33	32	29-1	0	273	216	111	8	4	81	112	2.21	121	.219	.281	92-0-5	.065	-6	91	8		0.0
1905	Bos A	4	7	.364	23	17	9	0	134	118	77	9	5	55	67	3.69	73	.238	.321	42-0-2	.095	-2	97	-16		-1.6
1906	Bos A	0	2	.000	5	2	1	0	18.2	25	21	2	0	7	3	5.30	52	.325	.381	5	.200	0	13	-7		-0.7
Total 4		34	32	.515	85	72	56-3	0	609	525	304	21	16	208	258	2.93	95	.233	.303	203-0-12	.138	-4	92	-19		-2.4

GIBSON, PAUL Paul Marshall B1.4.1960 Southampton NY BR/TL/6-0/185(165-195) [CinN78*3/70] d4.8

YEAR	TM-LG	W	L	PCT	G	GS	CG-SHO	SV-BS	IP	H	R	HR	HB	BB-IB	SO	ERA	AERA	OAV	OOB	AB-HR-SH	AVG	PB	SUP	APR	DL	PW
1988	Det A	4	2	.667	40	1	0	0-2	92	83	33	6	2	34-8	50	2.93	131	.240	.307	0	—	0	190	10		0.6
1989	Det A	4	8	.333	45	13	0	0-2	132	129	71	11	6	57-12	77	4.64	83	.259	.339	0	—	0	76	-9		-0.8
1990	Det A	5	4	.556	61	0	0	3-3	97.1	99	36	10	4	44-12	56	3.05	130	.269	.344	0	—	0		10		0.9
1991	Det A	5	7	.417	68	0	0	8-5	96	112	51	10	3	48-8	52	4.59	91	.297	.379	0	—	0		-3		-0.4
1992	NY N	0	1	.000	43	1	0	0-0	62	70	37	7	0	25-0	49	5.23	67	.287	.352	6-0-1	.000	-0	103	-11	33	-0.6
1993	NY N	1	1	.500	8	0	0	0-1	8.2	14	6	1	0	2-0	12	5.19	77	.350	.381	0	—	0		-1		-0.2
	NY A	2	0	1.000	20	0	0	0-0	35.1	31	15	4	0	9-0	25	3.06	137	.238	.282	0	—	0		4		-0.2
	Year	3	1	.750	28	0	0	0-1	44	45	21	5	0	11-0	37	3.67				0	—	0				
1994	NY A	1	1	.500	30	0	0	0-2	29	26	17	5	1	17-3	21	4.97	93	.236	.338	0	—	0		-1	22	-0.1
1996	NY A	0	0	—	4	0	0	0-0	4.1	6	3	1	0	0-0	3	6.23	79	.316	.316	0	—	-0		-1		0.0
Total 8		22	24	.478	319	15	0	11-15	556.2	570	269	55	13	236-43	345	4.07	97	.267	.341	6-0-1	.000	-0	83	-2	55	-0.4

GIBSON, BOB Robert (b Pack Robert Gibson) B11.9.1935 Omaha NE BR/TR/6-1.5/195* d4.15 C5 HF1981 Col Creighton

YEAR	TM-LG	W	L	PCT	G	GS	CG-SHO	SV-BS	IP	H	R	HR	HB	BB-IB	SO	ERA	AERA	OAV	OOB	AB-HR-SH	AVG	PB	SUP	APR	DL	PW
1959	StL N	3	5	.375	13	9	2-1	0	75.2	77	35	4	1	39-2	48	3.33	127	.273	.360	26-0-1	.115	-1*	61	5		0.4
1960	StL N	3	6	.333	27	12	2	0	86.2	97	61	7	1	48-6	69	5.61	73	.284	.371	28-0-1	.179	-0*	92	-14		-1.3
1961	StL N	13	12	.520	35	27	10-2	1	211.1	186	91	13	6	119-7	166	3.24	136	.239	.342	66-1-3	.197	2*	81	24		2.9
1962	StL N★	15	13	.536	32	30	15-5	1	233.2	174	84	15	10	95-9	208	2.85	**150**	.204	.291	76-2-6	.263	6*	84	34		4.7
1963	StL N	18	9	.667	36	33	14-2	0	254.2	224	110	19	13	96-1	204	3.39	105	.233	.309	87-3-5	.207	7*	116	5		1.2
1964	†StL N	19	12	.613	40	36	17-2	1	287.1	250	106	25	9	86-9	245	3.01	127	.232	.293	96-0-6	.156	1	94	27		2.9
1965	StL N★	20	12	.625	38	36	20-6	1	299	243	110	34	11	103-6	270	3.07	125	.222	.293	104-5-8	.240	8*	107	25		3.5
1966	StL N★	21	12	.636	35	35	20-5	0	280.1	210	90	20	5	78-5	225	2.44	147	.207	.265	100-1-7	.200	3*	81	35		4.4
1967	†StL N★	13	7	.650	24	24	10-2	0	175.1	151	62	10	3	40-3	147	2.98	110	.231	.278	60-0-6	.133	1*	125	8	50	1.0
1968	†StL N☆	22	9	.710	34	34	28-13	0	304.2	198	49	11	7	62-6	**268**	**1.12**	**258**	**.184**	.233	94-0-7	.170	4*	91	**60**		7.6
1969	StL N★	20	13	.606	35	35	28-4	0-0	314	251	84	12	10	95-7	269	2.18	165	.219	.283	118-1-5	.246	8*	88	50		6.3
1970	StL N★	23	7	.767	34	34	23-3	0-0	294	262	111	13	4	88-9	274	3.12	133	.237	.291	109-2-6	.303	12*	108	34		4.5
1971	StL N★	16	13	.552	31	31	20-5	0-0	245.2	215	96	14	7	76-11	185	3.04	120	.232	.294	87-2-2	.172	2	99	14	20	1.8
1972	StL N★	19	11	.633	34	34	23-4	0-0	278	226	83	14	3	88-11	208	2.46	139	.224	.286	103-5-2	.194	7	99	31		4.4
1973	StL N	12	10	.545	25	25	13-1	0	195	159	71	12	3	57-6	142	2.77	133	.224	.281	65-2-2	.185	2	96	18	43	2.2
1974	StL N	11	13	.458	33	33	9-1	0	240	236	111	24	5	104-14	129	3.83	94	.259	.335	81-0-1	.210	3	108	-4		-0.2
1975	StL N	3	10	.231	22	14	1	2-1	109	120	66	10	4	62-6	60	5.04	75	.287	.382	28-0-4	.179	0	86	-12		-1.3
Total 17		251	174	.591	528	482	255-56	6-1	3884.1	3279	1420	257	102	1336-118	3117	2.91	127	.228	.297	1328-24-72	.206	65	97	340	113	45.0

GIBSON, BOB Robert Louis B6.19.1957 Philadelphia PA BR/TR/6-0/195* d4.13 Col Bloomsburg

YEAR	TM-LG	W	L	PCT	G	GS	CG-SHO	SV-BS	IP	H	R	HR	HB	BB-IB	SO	ERA	AERA	OAV	OOB	AB-HR-SH	AVG	PB	SUP	APR	DL	PW
1983	Mil A	3	4	.429	27	7	0	2-3	80.2	71	40	6	1	46-2	46	3.90	97	.237	.334	0	—	0	96	-2		-0.2
1984	Mil A	2	5	.286	18	9	1	1-1	69	61	43	10	0	47-2	54	4.96	79	.236	.352	0	—	0	101	-8		-0.7
1985	Mil A	6	7	.462	41	1	0	11-3	92.1	86	44	10	1	49-3	53	3.90	108	.260	.353	0	—	0	43	4		0.5
1986	Mil A	1	2	.333	11	1	0	0-0	26.2	23	18	3	0	23-1	11	4.73	92	.232	.374	0	—	0	125	-2		-0.2
1987	NY N	0	0	—	1	0	0	0-0	1	1	0	0	0	1-0	2	0.00	—	.250	.250	0	—	0		0		0.0
Total 5		12	18	.400	98	18	1-1	13-6	269.2	241	145	29	2	166-8	166	4.24	95	.243	.349	0	—	0	94	-8		-0.6

GIBSON, ROBERT Robert Murray B8.20.1869 Duncansville PA D12.19.1949 Pittsburgh PA BR/TR/6-3/185 d6.4 Col Penn St.

YEAR	TM-LG	W	L	PCT	G	GS	CG-SHO	SV-BS	IP	H	R	HR	HB	BB-IB	SO	ERA	AERA	OAV	OOB	AB-HR-SH	AVG	PB	SUP	APR	DL	PW
1890	Chi N	1	0	1.000	1	1	1	0	9	6	1	0	0	2	1	0.00	—	.182	.229	4	.000	-0	17	3		0.3
	Pit N	0	3	.000	3	3	2	0	12	24	38	0	3	23	1	17.25	19	.400	.581	13	.231	-0	153	-21		-2.5
	Year	1	3	.250	4	4	3	0	21	30	39	0	3	25	3	9.86	45	.323	.479	17	.176	-0	114	-17		-2.2

YEAR	TM LG	W	L	PCT	G	GS	CG-SHO	SV-BS	IP	H	R	HR	HB	BB-IB	SO	ERA	AERA	OAV	OOB	AB-HR-SH	AVG	PB	SUP	APR	DL	PW
GIBSON, SAM Samuel Braxton B8.5.1899 King NC D1.31.1983 High Point NC BL/TR/6-2/198 d4.19 Col Catawba																										
1926	Det A	12	9	.571	35	24	16-2	0	196.1	199	94	6	6	75	61	3.48	117	.269	.341	72-0-1	.250	2*	93	12		1.3
1927	Det A	11	12	.478	33	26	11	0	184.2	201	113	9	8	86	76	3.80	111	.285	.369	66-0-3	.212	-1	126	2		0.1
1928	Det A	5	8	.385	20	18	5-1	0	119.2	155	83	4	7	52	29	5.42	76	.322	.396	42-0-1	.286	2	102	-15		-1.3
1930	NY A	0	1	.000	2	2	0	0	6	14	11	1	0	6	3	15.00	29	.424	.513	3	.333	0	260	-7		-0.8
1932	NY N	4	8	.333	41	5	1-1	3	81.2	107	51	7	2	30	39	4.85	77	.322	.382	19-0-1	.263	0	82	-10		-1.3
Total	5	32	38	.457	131	75	33-4	3	588.1	676	352	27	23	249	208	4.28	95	.295	.370	202-0-6	.248	3	112	-18		-2.0
GICK, GEORGE George Edward B10.18.1915 Dunnington IN BB/TR/6-0/190 d10.3																										
1937	Chi A	0	0	—	1	0	0	1	2	0	0	0	0	0	1	0.00	—	.000	.000	0	—	0		1		0.
1938	Chi A	0	0	—	1	0	0	0	1	0	0	0	1	0	1	0.00	—	.000	.250	0	—	0		1		0.0
Total	2	0	0	—	2	0	0	1	3	0	0	0	1	0	2	0.00	—	.000	.100	0	—	0		2		0.
GIDEON, BRETT Byron Brett B8.8.1963 Ozona TX BR/TR/6-2/195* [PitN85 6/138] d7.5 Col Mary Hardin-Baylor																										
1987	Pit N	1	5	.167	29	0	0	3-3	36.2	34	22	6	1	10-3	31	4.66	89	.243	.298	1	1.000	1		-2		-0.1
1989	Mon N	0	0	—	4	0	0	0-0	4.2	5	1	1	0	5-1	2	1.93	185	.294	.455	0	—	0		1		0.
1990	Mon N	0	0	—	1	0	0	0-0	1	2	1	0	0	4-1	0	9.00	41	.500	.750	0	—	0		-1	176	-0.
Total	3	1	5	.167	34	0	0	3-3	42.1	41	24	7	1	19-5	33	4.46	92	.255	.337	1	1.000	1		-2	176	-0.3
GIDEON, JIM James Leslie B9.26.1953 Taylor TX BR/TR/6-3/190 [TexA75 1/17] d9.14 Col Texas																										
1975	Tex A	0	0	—	2	1	0	0	5.2	7	6	1	0	5-0	2	7.94	48	.292	.414		—	0	210	-3		-0.
GIEBELL, FLOYD Floyd George B12.10.1909 Pennsboro WV D4.28.2004 Wilkesboro NC BL/TR/6-2.5/172 d4.21 Col Salem International																										
1939	Det A	1	1	.500	9	0	0	0	15.1	19	7	1	0	12	9	2.93	167	.317	.431	2-0-1	.000	-0		3		0.1
1940	Det A	2	0	1.000	2	2	2-1	0	18	14	2	2	0	4	11	1.00	476	.206	.250	6-0-1	.000	-1	139	7		0.
1941	Det A	0	0	—	17	2	0	0	34.1	45	29	3	0	26	10	6.03	75	.313	.418	6-0-1	.333	0	162	-6		0.
Total	3	3	1	.750	28	4	2-1	0	67.2	78	38	6	0	42	30	3.99	117	.287	.382	14-0-3	.143	-1	149	4		0.
GIEL, PAUL Paul Robert B2.29.1932 Winona MN D5.22.2002 Minneapolis MN BR/TR/5-11/185* d7.10 Mil 1956-57 Col Minnesota																										
1954	NY N	0	0	—	6	0	0	0	4.1	8	4	0	0	2	4	8.31	49	.421	.455	0	—	0		-2		-0.
1955	NY N	4	4	.500	34	2	0	0	82.1	70	36	8	2	50-5	47	3.39	119	.233	.345	19-0-1	.053	-2	55	6		0.
1958	SF N	4	5	.444	29	9	0	0	92	89	56	12	2	55-4	55	4.70	81	.259	.363	27-0-4	.074	-2	86	-10		-1.
1959	Pit N	0	0	—	4	0	0	0	7.2	17	12	0	0	6-1	3	14.09	27	.472	.548	0	—	0		-8		-0.
1960	Pit N	2	0	1.000	16	0	0	0	33	35	25	0	0	15-1	21	5.73	65	.276	.350	7-0-1	.000	-1		-8		-0.
1961	Min A	1	0	1.000	12	0	0	0	19.1	24	27	6	0	17-1	14	9.78	43	.289	.406	2	.500	0*		-13		-0.
	KC A	0	0	—	1	0	0	0	1.2	6	7	1	0	3-0	1	37.80	11	.600	.692	0	—	0		-6		-0.
	Year	1	0	1.000	13	0	0	0	21	30	34	7	0	20-1	15	12.00	35	.323	.439	2	.500	0		-18		-0.
Total	6	11	9	.550	102	11	0	0	240.1	249	167	30	4	148-12	145	5.39	73	.271	.372	55-0-6	.073	-4	79	-41		-2.
GIGGIE, BOB Robert Thomas B8.13.1933 Dorchester MA BR/TR/6-1/200* d4.18																										
1959	Mil N	1	0	1.000	13	0	0	1	20	24	10	2	0	10-0	15	4.05	87	.316	.395	1	.000	-0		-1		-0.
1960	Mil N	0	0	—	3	0	0	0	4.1	5	2	0	0	4-1	5	4.15	83	.278	.409	0	—	0		0		-0.
	KC A	1	0	1.000	10	0	0	0	18.2	24	12	1	0	15-2	8	5.79	69	.333	.443	2	.000	-0		0		-0.
1962	KC A	1	1	.500	4	2	0	0	14.1	17	11	5	1	3-0	4	6.28	67	.293	.339	4	.000	-0	74	-3		-0.
Total	3	3	1	.750	30	2	0	1	57.1	70	35	8	1	32-3	32	5.18	74	.313	.399	7	.000	-1	74	-7		-0.
GILBERT, BILL Alfred Gideon B3.13.1868 Havre de Grace MD D12.17.1927 Havre de Grace MD 6-0/180 d9.15																										
1892	Bal N	0	1	.000	2	1	1	0	14	14	15	1	0	17	5	5.79	59	.250	.425	6	.333	1	37	-4		
GILBERT, JOE Joe Dennis B4.20.1952 Jasper TX BR/TL/6-1/163* [MonN70 9/201] d4.30																										
1972	Mon N	0	1	.000	22	0	0	0-0	33	41	31	3	0	18-3	25	8.45	42	.306	.386	3	.000	-0		-16		-0.
1973	Mon N	1	2	.333	21	0	0	1-0	29	30	18	1	0	19-1	17	4.97	77	.270	.374	2	.000	-0		-3		-0.
Total	2	1	3	.250	43	0	0	1-0	62	71	49	4	0	37-4	42	6.82	54	.290	.380	5	.000	-0		-19		-0.
GILBRETH, BILL William Freeman B9.3.1947 Abilene TX BL/TL/6-0/180* [DetA69 3/67] d6.25 Col Abilene Christian																										
1971	Det A	2	1	.667	9	5	2	0-0	30	28	17	4	2	21-1	14	4.80	76	.264	.395	11	.182	-0	119	-4		-0.
1972	Det A	0	0	—	2	0	0	0-0	5	10	9	1	0	4-0	2	16.20	20	.476	.519	1	.000	-0		-7		-0.
1974	Cal A	0	0	—	3	0	0	0-1	1.1	2	2	0	0	1-0	0	13.50	26	.400	.429	0	—	0		-1		-0.
Total	3	2	1	.667	14	5	2	0-1	36.1	40	28	5	2	26-1	16	6.69	53	.303	.417	12	.167	-0	119	-12		-0.
GILFILLAN, JASON Jason Edward B8.31.1976 Shelby NC BR/TR/6-5/220 [KCA97 12/361] d5.16 Col Charleston (SC)/Limestone																										
2003	KC A	2	0	1.000	13	0	0	0-1	16.1	22	14	3	1	10-1	12	7.71	62	.310	.402	0	—	0		-4		-0
GILKS, BOB Robert James B7.2.1864 Cincinnati OH D8.21.1944 Brunswick GA BR/TR/5-8/178 d8.25 ▲																										
1887	Cle AA	7	5	.583	13	13	12-1	0	108	104	66	1	9	42	28	3.08	141	.245	.326	83	.313	2*	98	15		1
1888	Cle AA	2	2	.500	4	2	2	1	21	26	23	1	1	8	3	8.14	38	.292	.357	484-1	.229	0*	103	-9		-0
1890	Cle N	2	2	.500	4	3	3	0	31.2	34	17	0	4	9	5	4.26	84	.266	.333	544	.213	-0*	70	0		-0
Total	3	9	9	.500	21	18	17-1	1	160.2	164	106	2	14	59	36	3.98	101	.256	.332	1111-1	.228	2	96	6		-0
GILL, ED Edward James B8.7.1895 Somerville MA D10.10.1995 Brockton MA BL/TR/5-10/165 d7.5 Col Holy Cross																										
1919	Was A	1	1	.500	16	1	0	0	37.1	38	25	0	2	21	7	4.82	67	.260	.361	7	.000	-1	110	-6		-0
GILL, GEORGE George Lloyd B2.13.1909 Catchings MS D2.21.1999 Jackson MS BR/TR/6-1/185 d5.4 Col Mississippi College																										
1937	Det A	11	4	.733	31	10	4-1	1	127.2	146	74	11	1	42	40	4.51	104	.285	.340	50-0-1	.140	-3	130	2		-0
1938	Det A	12	9	.571	24	23	13-1	0	164	195	82	15	2	50	30	4.12	121	.296	.348	57-0-5	.105	-4	98	16		-0
1939	Det A	0	1	.000	3	1	0	0	8.2	14	8	1	0	3	1	8.31	59	.368	.415	2	.000	-0	72	-3		-0
	StL A	1	12	.077	27	11	5	0	95	139	89	10	3	34	24	7.11	68	.343	.398	26-0-1	.154	-2	86	-24		-3
	Year	1	13	.071	30	12	5	0	103.2	153	97	11	3	37	25	7.21	68	.345	.400	28-0-1	.143	-2	85	-27		-3
Total	3	24	26	.480	85	45	22-2	1	395.1	494	253	37	6	129	95	5.05	96	.306	.360	135-0-7	.126	-9	102	-9		-0
GILL, HADDIE Harold Edward B1.23.1899 Brockton MA D8.1.1932 Brockton MA BL/TL/5-11/165 d8.16 Col Holy Cross																										
1923	Cin N	0	0	—.	1	0	0	0	1	1	1	0	0	0	0		—	.333	.500		—	0		0		-0
GILLENWATER, CLARAL Claral Lewis B5.20.1900 Sims IN D2.26.1978 Bradenton FL BR/TR/6-0/187 d8.20																										
1923	Chi A	1	3	.250	5	3	1-1	0	21.1	28	15	2	1	6	2	5.48	72	.337	.389	6-0-1	.000	-1	56	-3		-0
GILLES, TOM Thomas Bradford B7.2.1962 Peoria IL BR/TR/6-1/185 [NYA84 47/834] d6.7 Col Indiana St.																										
1990	Tor A	1	0	1.000	2	0	0	0-0	1.1	2	1	0	0	0-0	1	6.75	59	.333	.333	0	—	0		0		-0
GILLESPIE, DUKE John Patrick "Silent John" B2.25.1900 Oakland CA D2.15.1954 Vallejo CA BR/TR/5-11.5/172 d4.12																										
1922	Cin N	3	3	.500	31	4	1	0	77.2	84	43	2	4	29	21	4.52	88	.294	.367	15-0-1	.133	-1	153	-2		-0
GILLESPIE, BOB Robert William "Bunch" B10.8.1919 Columbus OH D11.4.2001 Winston-Salem NC BR/TR/6-4/187* d5.11																										
1944	Det A	0	0	—	7	0	0	0	11	9	7	0	0	12	4	6.55	54	.194	.396	2	.000	-0		-3		-0
1947	Chi A	5	8	.385	25	17	1	0	118	133	71	4	1	53	36	4.73	77	.291	.364	33	.061	-3	90	-13		-1
1948	Chi A	0	4	.000	25	6	1	0	72	81	45	3	1	33	19	5.13	83	.287	.364	16-0-1	.000	-0	53	-7		-0
1950	Bos A	0	0	—	1	0	0	0	1.1	2	3	1	0	4	0	20.25	24	.333	.600	0	—	0		-2		-0
Total	4	5	13	.278	58	23	2	0	202.1	223	127	8	2	102	59	5.07	76	.286	.369	51-0-1	.039	-5	78	-25		-0
GILLIFORD, PAUL Paul Gant "Gorilla" B1.12.1945 Bryn Mawr PA BR/TL/5-11/210 d9.20																										
1967	Bal A	0	0	—	2	0	0	1-0	2	4	2	0	0	0	2	12.00	26	.429	.467	0	—	0		-3		-0
GILLIGAN, JACK John Patrick (b John Peter Gilgen) B10.18.1885 Chicago IL D11.19.1980 Modesto CA BB/TR/6-0/190 d9.16																										
1909	StL A	1	2	.333	3	3	3	0	23	28	19	1	2	9	4	5.48	44	.315	.390	9-0-1	.111	-1	58	-8		-0
1910	StL A	0	3	.000	9	5	2	0	39.1	37	21	0	1	28	10	3.66	68	.253	.377	15	.200	-0	119	-4		-0
Total	2	1	5	.167	12	8	5	0	62.1	65	40	1	3	37	14	4.33	57	.277	.382	24-0-1	.167	-1	97	-12		-0
GILLPATRICK, GEORGE George F. B2.28.1875 Holden MO D12.15.1941 Kansas City MO BR/TR/6-0/210 d5.22																										
1898	StL N	0	2	.000	7	3	1	0	35	42	38	0	2	19	12	6.94	55	.296	.387	16	.125	-2	87	-12		-0

YEAR	TM LG	W	L	PCT	G	GS	CG-SHO	SV-BS	IP	H	R	HR	HB	BB-IB	SO	ERA	AERA	OAV	OOB	AB-HR-SH	AVG	PB	SUP	APR	DL	PW
GILMORE, FRANK			Frank T. "Shadow" B4.27.1864 Webster MA D7.21.1929 Hartford CT BR/5-11.5/164 d9.11																							
1886	Was N	4	4	.500	9	9	9-1	0	75	57	35	3		22	75	2.52	128	.200	.257	29	.000	-4	80	5		0.1
1887	Was N	7	20	.259	28	27	27-1	0	234.2	247	172	7	13	92	114	3.87	104	.262	.336	93	.065	-11	59	1		-1.0
1888	Was N	1	9	.100	12	11	10	0	95.2	131	101	4	7	29	23	6.59	42	.323	.378	41	.024	-5*	115	-39		-3.6
Total	3	12	33	.267	49	47	46-2	0	405.1	435	308	14	20	143	212	4.26	84	.266	.333	163	.043	-20	73	-33		-4.5
GILMORE, LEN			Leonard Preston "Meow" B11.3.1917 Fairview Park IN BR/TR/6-3/175 d10.1 Col Indiana (PA)																							
1944	Pit N	0	1	.000	1	1	1	0	8	13	7	2	0	0	0	7.88	47	.361	.361	2	.000	-0	23	-3		-0.3
GILROY, JOHN			John M. B10.26.1869 Washington DC D8.4.1897 Norfolk VA d8.30																							
1895	Was N	1	4	.200	8	4	2	0	41.1	63	48	3	4	24	2	6.53	74	.344	.431	29	.241	-1*	82	-6		-0.7
1896	Was N	0	0	—	1	0	0	0	2	0	0	0	0	1	0	0.00	—	.000	.143	1	.000	-0		1		-0.0
Total	2	1	4	.200	9	4	2	0	43.1	63	48	3	4	25	2	6.23	77	.333	.422	30	.233	-1	82	-7		-0.7
GILSON, HAL			Harold "Lefty" B2.9.1942 Los Angeles CA BR/TL/6-5/195 d4.14 Col San Jose (CA) City																							
1968	StL N	0	2	.000	13	0	0	2	21.2	27	11	1	0	11-1	19	4.57	63	.310	.388	4-0-1	.000	-0		-3		-0.5
	Hou N	0	0	—	2	0	0	0	3.2	7	4	0	1	1-1	1	7.36	40	.412	.474	0	—	0*		-2		-0.1
	Year	0	2	.000	15	0	0	2	25.1	34	15	1	1	12-2	20	4.97	58	.327	.402	4-0-1	.000	-0		-6		-0.6
GING, BILLY			William Joseph B11.7.1872 Elmira NY D9.14.1950 Elmira NY BR/TR/5-10/170 d9.25																							
1899	Bos N	1	0	1.000	1	1	1	0	8	5	1	0	0	5	2	1.13	370	.179	.303	2-0-1	.000	-0	35	3		0.2
GINGRAS, JOE			Joseph Elzead John B1.10.1894 New York NY D9.6.1947 Jersey City NJ BR/TR/6-2/188 d6.18																							
1915	KC F	0	0	—	2	0	0	0	4	6	3	0	1	2	2	6.75	39	.353	.389	1	.000	-0		-2		-0.1
GINTER, MATT			Matthew Shane B12.24.1977 Lexington KY BR/TR/6-2/220* [ChiA99 1/22] d9.1 Col Mississippi St.																							
2000	Chi A	1	0	1.000	7	0	0	0-1	9.1	18	14	5	0	7-0	6	13.50	37	.409	.481	0	—	0		-8		-0.7
2001	Chi A	1	0	1.000	20	0	0	0-0	39.2	34	23	2	7	14-2	24	5.22	89	.238	.329	0	—	0		-1		-0.1
2002	Chi A	1	0	1.000	33	0	0	1-0	54.1	59	34	6	1	21-0	37	4.47	101	.278	.343	0	—	0		-2		-0.1
2003	Chi A	0	0	—	3	0	0	0-0	3.1	2	5	1	2	1-0	0	13.50	34	.182	.357	0	—	0		-0		-0.1
2004	NY N	1	3	.250	15	14	0	0-0	69.1	82	41	8	5	20-5	38	4.54	95	.289	.345	14-0-3	.214	1	97	-3	23	-0.1
2005	Det A	0	1	.000	14	1	0	0-0	35	49	25	6	2	9-1	15	6.17	69	.340	.385	0	—	0	67	-7		-0.3
Total	6	4	4	.500	92	15	0	1-1	211	244	142	28	17	72-8	120	5.46	81	.291	.356	14-0-3	.214	1	92	-24	23	-1.4
GIRARD, CHARLIE			Charles August B12.16.1884 Brooklyn NY D8.6.1936 Brooklyn NY BR/TR/5-10/175 d9.14																							
1910	Phi N	1	2	.333	7	1	0	1	26.2	33	26	2	2	12	11	6.41	49	.308	.388	8	.125	-0	95	-10		-1.1
GISSELL, CHRIS			Christopher Odell B1.4.1978 Tacoma WA BR/TR/6-5/210 [ChiN96 4/112] d8.22																							
2004	Col N	0	1	.000	5	1	0	0	8.2	20	14	4	0	3-0	11	14.54	33	.465	.489	1	.000	-0	58	-8		-0.8
GIUSTI, DAVE			David John B11.27.1939 Seneca Falls NY BR/TR/5-11/195* d4.13 Col Syracuse																							
1962	Hou N	2	3	.400	22	5	0	0	73.2	82	49	7	0	30-1	43	5.62	66	.280	.346	24-0-1	.292	3*	117	-14		-0.6
1964	Hou N	0	0	—	8	0	0	0	25.2	24	10	1	0	8-1	16	3.16	108	.253	.308	7	.286	1		1		0.2
1965	Hou N	8	7	.533	38	13	4-1	3	131.1	132	67	13	1	46-11	92	4.32	78	.259	.319	35-1-3	.171	2	96	-13		-1.1
1966	Hou N	15	14	.517	34	33	9-4	0	210	215	112	23	5	54-3	131	4.20	81	.260	.309	74-0-6	.230	5*	117	-19		-1.9
1967	Hou N	11	15	.423	37	33	8-1	1	221.2	231	114	20	3	58-4	157	4.18	79	.265	.311	84-3-2	.155	3*	119	-20		-2.0
1968	Hou N	11	14	.440	37	34	12-2	1	251	226	95	15	4	67-7	186	3.19	93	.239	.291	82-0-5	.183	2*	79	-4		-0.1
1969	StL N	3	7	.300	22	12	2-1	0-0	99.2	96	46	7	1	37-2	62	3.61	99	.255	.321	25-0-1	.200	1	51	-1	21	0.1
1970	†Pit N	9	3	.750	66	1	0	26-6	103	92	38	7	0	39-9	85	3.06	129	.259	.325	16-0-1	.188	2	159	11		1.9
1971	†Pit N	5	6	.455	58	0	0	30-6	86	79	31	5	1	31-8	55	2.93	116	.241	.305	17	.059	-1		5		0.8
1972	†Pit N	7	4	.636	54	0	0	22-5	74.2	59	18	3	0	20-6	54	1.93	172	.219	.271	10-0-1	.000	-1		12		2.6
1973	Pit N★	9	2	.818	67	0	0	20-6	98.2	89	31	9	0	37-13	64	2.37	149	.241	.308	13-0-2	.308	1		13		1.9
1974	†Pit N	7	5	.583	64	0	0	12-6	105.2	101	43	2	0	40-11	53	3.32	105	.258	.323	9-0-1	.111	-0	63	-3		0.4
1975	Pit N	5	4	.556	61	0	0	17-6	91.2	79	38	3	0	42-17	38	2.95	122	.237	.320	10-0-4	.300	1		5		0.8
1976	Pit N	5	4	.556	40	0	0	6-2	58.1	59	31	5	0	27-9	24	4.32	82	.267	.345	4	—	-0		-5	36	-0.8
1977	Oak A	3	3	.500	40	0	0	6-1	60.1	54	22	4	0	20-5	28	2.98	135	.245	.308	4	—	0		8		0.9
	Chi N	0	2	.000	20	0	0	1-1	25.1	30	19	2	0	14-2	15	6.04	73	.297	.379	2	—	-0		-4		-0.4
Total	15	100	93	.518	668	133	35-9	145-39	1716.2	1654	764	126	15	570-109	1103	3.60	96	.253	.313	412-4-27	.187	18	96	-24	57	2.7
GIVENS, BRIAN			Brian Allen B11.6.1965 Lompoc CA BR/TL/6-6/220* [NYN84*10/234] d6.24 Col Trinidad St. (CO) JC																							
1995	Mil A	5	7	.417	19	19	0	0-0	107.1	116	71	11	3	54-0	73	4.95	101	.275	.360	0	—	0	99	-2		-0.3
1996	Mil A	1	3	.250	4	4	0	0-0	14	32	22	3	0	7-0	10	12.86	40	.438	.481	0	—	0	94	-12	32	-1.7
Total	2	6	10	.375	23	23	0	0-0	121.1	148	93	14	3	61-0	83	5.86	86	.299	.378	0	—	0	98	-14	32	-2.0
GLADDING, FRED			Fred Earl B6.28.1936 Flat Rock MI BL/TR/6-0/225* d7.1 C3																							
1961	Det A	1	0	1.000	8	0	0	0	16.1	18	7	1	2	11-1	11	3.31	124	.286	.397	3	.000	-0		1		0.0
1962	Det A	0	0	—	6	0	0	0	5	3	0	0	0	2-0	4	0.00	—	.176	.263	0	—	-0		2		0.1
1963	Det A	1	1	.500	22	0	0	7	27.1	19	6	4	0	14-1	24	1.98	189	.198	.297	1	.000	-0		6		0.7
1964	Det A	7	4	.636	42	0	0	7	67.1	57	23	7	2	27-4	59	3.07	119	.233	.312	9	.000	-1		5		0.9
1965	Det A	6	2	.750	46	0	0	5	70	63	22	6	4	29-5	43	2.83	123	.239	.323	7-0-1	.000	-1		6		0.6
1966	Det A	5	0	1.000	51	0	0	2	74	62	33	6	1	29-6	57	3.28	106	.230	.306	2	.000	-0		0		0.0
1967	Det A	6	4	.600	42	0	0	12	77	62	20	6	4	19-0	64	1.99	164	.227	.286	18-0-1	.000	-2	27	10		1.5
1968	Hou N	0	0	—	7	0	0	2	4.1	8	7	1	0	3-1	2	14.54	20	.421	.500	0	—	0		-5	125	-0.6
1969	Hou N	4	8	.333	57	0	0	29-6	72.2	83	39	2	1	27-6	40	4.21	84	.289	.352	10	.100	-1		-5		-1.1
1970	Hou N	7	4	.636	63	0	0	18-4	71	84	39	4	3	24-8	46	4.06	96	.293	.352	6-0-1	.000	-1		-3		-0.6
1971	Hou N	4	5	.444	48	0	0	12-4	51.1	51	17	0	7	22-7	17	2.10	160	.268	.362	2	.000	-0		4		1.1
1972	Hou N	5	6	.455	48	0	0	14-2	48.2	38	16	1	2	12-5	18	2.77	121	.222	.278	5-0-1	.000	-1		3		0.6
1973	Hou N	2	0	1.000	16	0	0	1-2	16	18	8	4	0	4-1	9	4.50	81	.290	.333	0	—	0		-1		-0.1
Total	13	48	34	.585	450	0	0	109-18	601	566	237	38	27	223-45	394	3.13	113	.252	.325	63-0-4	.016	-6	27	25	125	3.1
GLADE, FRED			Frederick Monroe "Lucky" B1.25.1876 Dubuque IA D11.21.1934 Grand Island NE BR/TR/6-0/190 d5.27																							
1902	Chi N	0	1	.000	1	1	1	0	8	13	11	0	1	3	3	9.00	30	.361	.425	3	.333	1	50	-5		-0.4
1904	StL A	18	15	.545	35	34	30-6	1	289	248	101	2	13	58	156	2.27	109	.233	.281	102-0-3	.186	1	87	6		1.0
1905	StL A	6	25	.194	32	32	28-2	0	275	257	109	3	11	58	127	2.81	90	.249	.296	98	.092	-6	69	-3		-0.8
1906	StL A	15	14	.517	35	32	28-4	1	266.2	215	91	4	10	59	96	2.36	109	.224	.276	95-0-2	.137	-4	100	11		0.7
1907	StL A	13	9	.591	24	22	18-2	0	202	187	81	2	9	45	71	2.67	94	.248	.298	73-0-2	.205	2	121	-3		-0.3
1908	NY A	0	4	.000	5	5	2	0	32	30	18	0	4	14	11	4.22	59	.275	.378	10	.000	-1	66	-5		-0.7
Total	6	52	68	.433	132	126	107-14	2	1072.2	950	411	11	48	237	464	2.62	97	.240	.291	381-0-7	.150	-7	91	1		-0.5
GLAISER, JOHN			John Burke "Bert" B7.28.1894 Yoakum TX D3.7.1959 Houston TX BL/TR/5-8/165 d4.20 Col St. Edwards																							
1920	Det A	0	0	—	9	1	0	1	17	23	12	1	1	8	3	6.35	59	.354	.432	3	.000	-0	171	-4		-0.1
GLASS, TOM			Thomas Joseph B4.29.1898 Greensboro NC D12.15.1981 Greensboro NC BR/TR/6-3/170 d6.12																							
1925	Phi A	1	0	1.000	2	0	0	0	5	9	4	0	1	5	1	5.40	86	.409	.409	2-0-1	.000	-0		-1		-0.1
GLAUBER, KEITH			Keith Harris B1.18.1972 Brooklyn NY BR/TR/6-2/190* [StLN94 42/1169] d9.8 Col Montclair St.																							
1998	Cin N	0	0	—	3	0	0	0-0	7.2	6	2	0	1	1-0	4	2.35	183	.214	.226	2	.000	-0		2	154	0.0
2000	Cin N	0	0	—	4	0	0	0-0	7.1	5	3	0	1	2-0	4	3.68	129	.185	.267	1	.000	-0		1		0.0
Total	2	0	0	—	7	0	0	0-0	15	11	5	0	2	3-0	8	3.00	151	.200	.246	3	.000	-0		3	154	0.0
GLAVENICH, LUKE			Luke Frank B1.17.1893 Jackson CA D5.22.1935 Stockton CA BR/TR/5-9.5/189 d4.12 Col St. Marys (CA)																							
1913	Cle A	0	0	—	1	0	0	0	3	5	5	0	0	3	1	9.00	34	.500	.667	0		0		-2		-0.1
GLAVINE, TOM			Thomas Michael B3.25.1966 Concord MA BL/TL/6-1/190(175-190) [AtlN84 2/47] d8.17 b-Mike																							
1987	Atl N	2	4	.333	9	9	0	0-0	50.1	55	34	5	3	33-4	20	5.54	78	.279	.386	16	.125	-0	86	-6		-0.6
1988	Atl N	7	17	.292	34	34	1	0-0	195.1	201	111	12	8	63-7	84	4.56	80	.270	.329	60-0-8	.183	1*	96	-18		-1.9
1989	Atl N	14	8	.636	29	29	6-4	0-0	186	172	88	20	2	40-3	90	3.68	99	.243	.283	67-0-4	.149	0*	127	-1		0.2
1990	Atl N	10	12	.455	33	33	1	0-0	214.1	232	111	18	1	78-10	129	4.28	94	.281	.343	62-0-7	.113	0*	94	-4		-0.2
1991	†Atl N★	**20**	11	.645	34	34	**9-1**	0-0	246.2	201	83	17	2	69-6	192	2.55	152	.222	.277	74-0-15	.230	4*	106	**33**		**4.9**

YEAR	TM LG	W	L	PCT	G	GS	CG-SHO	SV-BS	IP	H	R	HR	HB	BB-IB	SO	ERA	AERA	OAV	OOB	AB-HR-SH	AVG	PB	SUP	APR	DL	PW
1992	†Atl N★	**20**	8	.714	33	33	7-**5**	0-0	225	197	81	6	2	70-7	129	2.76	133	.235	.293	77-0-9	.247	4*	114	20		3.0
1993	†Atl N☆	**22**	6	.786	36	**36**	4-2	0-0	239.1	236	91	16	2	90-7	120	3.20	127	.259	.327	81-0-11	.173	1	122	24		2.7
1994	Atl N	13	9	.591	25	25	2	0-0	165.1	173	76	10	1	70-10	140	3.97	109	.268	.338	56-0-9	.179	1*	114	8		1.2
1995	†Atl N	16	7	.696	29	29	3-1	0-0	198.2	182	76	9	5	66-0	127	3.08	140	.246	.310	63-1-8	.222	3	91	26		3.3
1996	†Atl N★	15	10	.600	36	**36**	1	0-0.	235.1	222	91	14	0	85-7	181	2.98	149	.249	.314	76-0-15	.289	6*	89	35		4.4
1997	†Atl N☆	14	7	.667	33	33	5-2	0-0	240	197	86	20	4	79-9	152	2.96	142	.226	.292	63-0-17	.222	4	104	34		3.2
1998	†Atl N★	**20**	6	.769	33	33	4-3	0-0	229.1	202	67	13	2	74-2	157	2.47	168	.238	.300	71-0-14	.239	3	114	45		5.6
1999	†Atl N	14	11	.560	35	**35**	2	0-0	234	259	115	18	4	83-14	138	4.12	109	.287	.346	65-0-7	.138	-0*	106	11		1.3
2000	†Atl N★	**21**	9	.700	35	**35**	4-2	0-0	241	222	101	24	4	65-6	152	3.40	133	.244	.296	68-0-14	.147	1*	110	30		3.5
2001	†Atl N	16	7	.696	35	**35**	1-1	0-0	219.1	213	92	24	2	97-10	116	3.57	121	.261	.338	57-0-17	.140	0	107	20		2.1
2002	†Atl N☆	18	11	.621	36	**36**	2-1	0-0	224.2	210	85	21	8	78-8	127	2.96	136	.252	.320	68-0-13	.103	-2*	100	26		3.1
2003	NY N	9	14	.391	32	32	0	0-0	183.1	205	94	24	2	66-7	82	4.52	93	.288	.348	53-0-10	.151	0*	76	-5		-0.3
2004	NY N★	11	14	.440	33	33	1-1	0-0	212.1	204	94	20	0	70-10	109	3.60	119	.252	.308	54-0-8	.204	4*	91	17		2.4
2005	NY N	13	13	.500	33	33	2-1	0-0	211.1	227	88	12	3	61-5	105	3.53	118	.279	.330	64-0-5	.203	1	92	16		2.0
Total	19	275	184	.599	603	603	55-24	0-0	3951.2	3810	1664	300	55	1337-132	2350	3.44	120	.255	.317	1195-1-191	.187	32	102	311		39.7

GLAZE, RALPH Daniel Ralph B3.13.1881 Denver CO D10.31.1968 Atascadero CA BR/TR/5-9/165 d6.1 Col Dartmouth

YEAR	TM LG	W	L	PCT	G	GS	CG-SHO	SV-BS	IP	H	R	HR	HB	BB-IB	SO	ERA	AERA	OAV	OOB	AB-HR-SH	AVG	PB	SUP	APR	DL	PW
1906	Bos A	4	6	.400	19	10	7	0	123	110	58	4	5	32	56	3.59	77	.242	.299	55-0-1	.182	0*	107	-8		-0.6
1907	Bos A	9	13	.409	32	21	11-1	0	182.1	150	75	4	4	48	53	2.32	111	.227	.283	61-1-2	.180	0	97	3		0.1
1908	Bos A	2	2	.500	10	3	2	0	34.2	43	24	1	0	5	13	3.38	73	.253	.274	13	.077	-1	111	-5		-0.7
Total	3	15	21	.417	61	34	20-1	0	340	303	157	9	9	85	137	2.89	91	.236	.288	129-1-3	.171	-1	102	-10		-1.2

GLAZNER, WHITEY Charles Franklin B9.17.1893 Sycamore AL D6.6.1989 Orlando FL BR/TR/5-9/165 d9.26

YEAR	TM LG	W	L	PCT	G	GS	CG-SHO	SV-BS	IP	H	R	HR	HB	BB-IB	SO	ERA	AERA	OAV	OOB	AB-HR-SH	AVG	PB	SUP	APR	DL	PW
1920	Pit N	0	0	—	2	0	0	0	8.2	9	3	1	0	3		3.12	103	.300	.344	3	.000	-0		0		-0.1
1921	Pit N	14	5	.737	36	25	15	1	234	214	88	5	12	58	88	2.77	139	**.250**	.306	76-0-6	.132	-3.	96	26		1.4
1922	Pit N	11	12	.478	34	26	10-1	1	.193	238	118	9	2	52	77	4.38	93	.309	.354	65-1-5	.246	3	86	-9		-0.6
1923	Pit N	2	1	.667	7	4	1-1	1	30	29	18	5	0	11	8	3.30	122	.250	.315	12-1-0	.333	2	149	0		0.2
	Phi N	7	14	.333	28	23	12-2	1	161.1	195	104	11	6	63	51	4.69	98	.304	.371	53-0-1	.170	-1	81	-2		-0.2
	Year	9	15	.375	35	27	13-3	2	191.1	224	122	16	6	74	59	4.47	101	.296	.363	65-1-1	.200	1	90	-5		0.0
1924	Phi N	7	16	.304	35	24	8-2	0	156.2	210	108	14	4	63	41	5.92	75	.339	.403	51-0-3	.157	-4	69	-18		-2.5
Total	5	41	48	.461	142	102	46-6	4	783.2	895	439	44	24	249	266	4.21	99	.295	.353	260-2-15	.181	-3	86	-3		-1.8

GLEASON, JOE Joseph Paul B7.9.1895 Phelps NY D9.8.1990 Phelps NY BR/TR/5-10.5/175 d9.11

YEAR	TM LG	W	L	PCT	G	GS	CG-SHO	SV-BS	IP	H	R	HR	HB	BB-IB	SO	ERA	AERA	OAV	OOB	AB-HR-SH	AVG	PB	SUP	APR	DL	PW
1920	Was A	0	0	—	3	0	0	0	8	14	13	2	1	6	2	13.50	28	.326	.420	2	.000	1		-8		-0.3
1922	Was A	2	2	.500	8	5	3	0	40.2	53	26	3	1	18	12	4.65	83	.319	.389	14	.143	-0	141	-4		-0.4
Total	2	2	2	.500	11	5	3	0	48.2	67	39	5	2	24	14	6.10	63	.321	.396	16	.125	0	141	-12		-0.7

GLEASON, BILL William B1868 Cleveland OH D12.2.1893 Cleveland OH d4.24

YEAR	TM LG	W	L	PCT	G	GS	CG-SHO	SV-BS	IP	H	R	HR	HB	BB-IB	SO	ERA	AERA	OAV	OOB	AB-HR-SH	AVG	PB	SUP	APR	DL	PW
1890	Cle P	0	1	.000	1	1	0	0	4	14	16	1	0	6	0	27.00	15	.538	.625	2	.000	-0	230	-9		-1.0

GLEASON, KID William J. B10.26.1866 Camden NJ D1.2.1933 Philadelphia PA BB/TR/5-7/158 d4.20 M5/C16 b-Harry ▲

YEAR	TM LG	W	L	PCT	G	GS	CG-SHO	SV-BS	IP	H	R	HR	HB	BB-IB	SO	ERA	AERA	OAV	OOB	AB-HR-SH	AVG	PB	SUP	APR	DL	PW
1888	Phi N	7	16	.304	24	23	23	0	199.2	199	112	11	12	53	89	2.84	105	.252	.309	83	.205	-0	84	0		-0.1
1889	Phi N	9	15	.375	29	21	15	1	205	242	177	8	9	97	64	5.58	78	.285	.364	99	.253	2*	92	-23		-1.9
1890	Phi N	38	17	.691	60	55	54-6	**2**	506	479	253	8	15	167	222	2.63	139	.242	.306	224	.210	-6*	94	51		4.0
1891	Phi N	24	22	.522	53	44	40-1	1	418	431	237	11	13	165	100	3.51	97	.256	.328	214	.248	6*	93	-2		0.2
1892	StL N	20	24	.455	47	45	43-2	0	400	389	244	11	10	151	133	3.33	96	.245	.314	233-3	.215	8*	112	-16		1.3
1893	StL N	21	22	.488	48	45	37-1	0	380.1	436	276	18	10	187	86	4.61	103	.279	.360	199	.256	4*	93	11		1.3
1894	StL N	2	6	.250	8	8	6	0	58	75	50	2	3	21	9	6.05	90	.310	.372	28	.250	-0*	60	-2		-0.2
	†Bal N	15	5	.750	21	20	19	0	172	224	113	3	3	44	35	4.45	123	.312	.354	86-0-4	.349	4*	109	19		1.9
	Year	17	11	.607	29	28	25	0	230	299	161	5	6	65	44	4.85	112	.311	.359	114-0-4	.325	4	95	21		1.7
1895	†Bal N	2	4	.333	9	5	3	1	52.1	77	51	4	3	21	6	6.97	83	.345	.409	42-1-0	.309	2*	185	-12		-1.0
Total	8	138	131	.513	299	266	240-10	6	2389.1	2552	1511	76	78	906	744	3.79	103	.265	.333	1587-3-10	.258	20	98	26		3.8

GLEATON, JERRY DON Jerry Don B9.14.1957 Brownwood TX BL/TL/6-3/210* [TexA79 1/17] d7.11 Col Texas

YEAR	TM LG	W	L	PCT	G	GS	CG-SHO	SV-BS	IP	H	R	HR	HB	BB-IB	SO	ERA	AERA	OAV	OOB	AB-HR-SH	AVG	PB	SUP	APR	DL	PW
1979	Tex A	0	1	.000	5	2	1		9.2	15	7	0	1	2-0	2	6.52	64	.375	.409	0	—	0	66	-2		-0.2
1980	Tex A	0	0	—	5	0	0	0-0	7	5	2	0	0	4-2	2	2.57	151	.208	.300	0	—	0		1		0.1
1981	Sea A	4	7	.364	20	13	1	0-0	85.1	88	50	10	2	38-2	31	4.75	82	.273	.350	0	—	0	125	-8		-0.9
1982	Sea A	0	0	—	3	0	0	0-0	4.2	7	7	3	1	2-0	1	13.50	32	.333	.417	0	—	0		-4		-0.2
1984	Chi A	1	2	.333	-11	1	0	2-1	18.1	20	12	2	1	6-0	4	3.44	122	.286	.333	0	—	0	0	0		-0.1
1985	Chi A	0	1	.000	31	0	0	1-1	29.2	37	19	3	0	13-3	22	5.76	75	.316	.382	0	—	0		-4		-0.2
1987	KC A	4	4	.500	48	0	0	5-2	50.2	38	28	4	0	28-3	44	4.26	108	.216	.319	0	—	0		2		0.3
1988	KC A	0	4	.000	42	0	0	3-1	38	33	17	2	3	17-1	29	3.55	113	.232	.327	0	—	0		2		-0.1
1989	KC A	0	0	—	15	0	0	0-0	14.1	20	10	0	0	6-0	9	5.65	69	.345	.394	0	—	0		-3		-0.1
1990	Det A	1	3	.250	57	0	0	13-3	82.2	62	27	5	3	25-2	56	2.94	135	.213	.279	0	—	0		10		0.7
1991	Det A	3	2	.600	47	0	0	2-1	75.1	74	37	7	0	39-8	47	4.06	103	.269	.355	0	—	0		1	38	-0.1
1992	Pit N	1	0	1.000	23	0	0	0-2	31.2	34	16	4	0	19-3	18	4.26	81	.283	.379	2-0-1	.000	0		-3		-0.1
Total	12	15	23	.395	307	16	1	26-11	447.1	433	232	40	11	199-22	265	4.25	96	.261	.340	2-0-1	.000	0	106	-9	38	-0.4

GLENDON, MARTIN Martin J. B2.8.1877 Milwaukee WI D11.6.1950 Norwood Park IL BR/TR/5-8/165 d4.18

YEAR	TM LG	W	L	PCT	G	GS	CG-SHO	SV-BS	IP	H	R	HR	HB	BB-IB	SO	ERA	AERA	OAV	OOB	AB-HR-SH	AVG	PB	SUP	APR	DL	PW
1902	Cin N	0	1	.000	1	1	0	0	5	5	5	0	0	4	0	12.00	25	.357	.500	1	.000	-0	45	-2		-0.4
1903	Cle A	1	2	.333	3	3	3	0	27.2	20	9	0	0	7	9	0.98	292	.202	.255	8-0-1	.000	-1	117	5		0.4
Total	2	1	3	.333	4	4	3	0	32.2	25	14	0	0	11	9	2.05	140	.221	.290	9-0-1	.000	-1	99	3		0.0

GLENN, BOB Burdette B6.16.1894 W.Sunbury PA D6.3.1977 Richmond CA BR/TR d7.27 Col Michigan

YEAR	TM LG	W	L	PCT	G	GS	CG-SHO	SV-BS	IP	H	R	HR	HB	BB-IB	SO	ERA	AERA	OAV	OOB	AB-HR-SH	AVG	PB	SUP	APR	DL	PW
1920	StL N	0	0	—	2	0	0	0	2	2	0	0	0	0	0	0.00	—	.222	.222	0	—	0		1		0.0

GLIATTO, SAL Salvador Michael B5.7.1902 Chicago IL D11.2.1995 Tyler TX BB/TR/5-8.5/150 d4.19

YEAR	TM LG	W	L	PCT	G	GS	CG-SHO	SV-BS	IP	H	R	HR	HB	BB-IB	SO	ERA	AERA	OAV	OOB	AB-HR-SH	AVG	PB	SUP	APR	DL	PW
1930	Cle A	0	0	—	8	0	0	2	15	21	15	1	2	9	7	6.60	73	.328	.427	2	.000	-0*		-3		-0.2

GLINATSIS, GEORGE George B6.29.1969 Youngstown OH BR/TR/6-4/195 [SeaA91 32/838] d7.18 Col Cincinnati

YEAR	TM LG	W	L	PCT	G	GS	CG-SHO	SV-BS	IP	H	R	HR	HB	BB-IB	SO	ERA	AERA	OAV	OOB	AB-HR-SH	AVG	PB	SUP	APR	DL	PW
1994	Sea A	0	1	.000	2	2	0	0-0	5.1	9	8	2	0	6-0	1	13.50	37	.429	.536	0	—	0	84	-5		-0.6

GLOVER, GARY John Gary B12.3.1976 Cleveland OH BR/TR/6-5/205(200-220) [TorA94 15/427] d9.30

YEAR	TM LG	W	L	PCT	G	GS	CG-SHO	SV-BS	IP	H	R	HR	HB	BB-IB	SO	ERA	AERA	OAV	OOB	AB-HR-SH	AVG	PB	SUP	APR	DL	PW
1999	Tor A	0	0	—	1	0	0	0-0	1	1	0	0	0	1-0	1	0.00	—	.000	.333	0	—	0		1		0.0
2001	Chi A	5	5	.500	46	11	0	0-1	100.1	98	61	16	4	32-3	63	4.93	94	.252	.314	0	—	0	90	-3		-0.3
2002	Chi A	7	8	.467	41	22	0	1-0	138.1	136	86	21	7	52-1	70	5.20	87	.253	.326	1	.000	-0	125	-10		-0.9
2003	Chi A	1	0	1.000	24	0	0	0-0	35.2	43	18	3	2	14-2	23	4.54	101	.305	.369	0	—	0		-1		-0.1
	Ana A	1	0	1.000	18	0	0	0-0	27	34	15	3	1	8-1	14	5.00	88	.315	.361	0	—	0		-1		-0.1
	Year	2	0	1.000	42	0	0	0-0	62.2	77	33	6	3	22-3	37	4.74	95	.309	.366	0	—	0		0		-0.1
2004	Mil N	2	1	.667	4	3	0	0-0	18	18	9	2	2	8-1	8	3.50	125	.265	.350	7	.000	-1	112	1		0.1
2005	Mil N	5	4	.556	15	11	0	0-0	64.2	74	41	10	2	20-0	58	5.57	77	.288	.342	20-0-3	.100	-0	114	-8		-1.0
Total	6	21	18	.538	149	47	0	1-1	385	403	230	55	18	135-8	236	5.03	90	.268	.333	28-0-3	.071	-1	112	-19		-2.2

GLYNN, ED Edward Paul B6.3.1953 Flushing NY BR/TL/6-2/180* d9.19

YEAR	TM LG	W	L	PCT	G	GS	CG-SHO	SV-BS	IP	H	R	HR	HB	BB-IB	SO	ERA	AERA	OAV	OOB	AB-HR-SH	AVG	PB	SUP	APR	DL	PW
1975	Det A	0	2	.000	3	1	0	0-0	14.2	11	8	1	0	8-0	8	4.30	94	.220	.322	0	—	0	0	0		0.0
1976	Det A	1	3	.250	5	4	1	0-0	23.2	22	18	4	0	20-1	17	6.08	61	.265	.396	0	—	0	112	-6		-0.9
1977	Det A	2	1	.667	8	3	0	0-0	27.1	36	17	3	0	12-1	13	5.27	82	.316	.372	0	—	0	153	-2		-0.2
1978	Det A	0	0	—	10	0	0	0-0	14.2	11	5	3	0	4-0	9	3.07	127	.208	.259	0	—	0		2		0.1
1979	NY N	1	4	.200	46	0	0	7-4	60	57	22	3	2	40-10	32	3.00	124	.259	.372	4	.000	0		-1		0.1
1980	NY N	3	3	.500	38	0	0	1-1	52.1	49	26	5	0	23-4	32	4.13	87	.246	.321	6-0-2	.000	-1		-3	21	-0.3
1981	Cle A	0	0	—	4	0	0	0-0	7.2	5	1	0	0	4-0	4	1.17	314	.192	.300	0	—	0		2		0.0
1982	Cle A	5	2	.714	47	0	0	4-4	49.2	43	27	6	0	30-5	54	4.17	100	.233	.336	0	—	0		-1		-0.1
1983	Cle A	0	2	.000	11	0	0	0-1	12.1	22	11	2	0	6-0	13	5.84	73	.373	.424	0	—	0		-3		-0.4
1985	Mon N	0	0	—	3	0	0	0-0	2.1	5	5	0	0	4-0	2	19.29	18	.455	.600	0	—	0		-4		-0.2
Total	10	12	17	.414	175	8	1	12-10	264.2	261	140	27	2	151-21	184	4.25	91	.261	.354	10-0-2	.000	-1	118	-10	21	-1.5

YEAR	TM LG	W	L	PCT	G	GS	CG-SHO	SV-BS	IP	H	R	HR	HB	BB-IB	SO	ERA	AERA	OAV	OOB	AB-HR-SH	AVG	PB	SUP	APR	DL	PW
GLYNN, RYAN			Ryan David B11.1.1974 Portsmouth VA BR/TR/6-3/195* [TexA95 4/94] d5.16 Col VMI																							
1999	Tex A	2	4	.333	13	10	0	0-0	54.2	71	46	10	1	35-0	39	7.24	71	.316	.408	1	.000	-0	133	-12		-1.1
2000	Tex A	5	7	.417	16	16	0	0-0	88.2	107	65	15	3	41-2	33	5.58	91	.293	.369	2	.000	-0	82	-6	30	-0.7
2001	Tex A	1	5	.167	12	9	0	0-0	46	59	38	7	0	26-1	15	7.04	68	.309	.388	0	—	0	78	-11	29	-1.2
2004	Tor A	1	0	1.000	6	2	0	0-0	20	19	9	4	3	8-1	14	4.05	121	.250	.341	0	—	0	190	2		0.1
2005	Oak A	0	4	.000	5	3	0	0-0	17	24	16	5	0	7-0	15	6.88	65	.320	.378	1	.000	-0	70	-5		-0.9
Total	5	9	20	.310	52	40	0	0-0	226.1	280	174	41	7	117-4	116	6.24	80	.300	.381	4	.000	0	99	-32	59	-3.8
GOAR, JOT			Joshua Mercer B1.31.1870 New Lisbon IN D4.4.1947 New Castle IN BR/TR/5-9/160 d4.18																							
1896	Pit N	0	1	.000	3	0	0	0	13.1	36	33	1	1	8	3	16.88	25	.486	.542	6	.167	-1		-19		-1.0
1898	Cin N	0	0	—	1	0	0	0	2	4	3	0	1	0	9.00	43	.400	.455	0	—	0		-1		0.0
Total	2	0	1	.000	4	0	0	0	15.1	40	36	1	1	9	3	15.85	26	.476	.532	6	.167	-1		-20		-1.0
GOBBLE, JIMMY			Billy James B7.19.1981 Bristol TN BL/TL/6-3/190* [KCA99 1/43] d8.3																							
2003	KC A	4	5	.444	9	9	0	0-0	52.2	56	32	8	4	15-0	31	4.61	104	.271	.328	0		0	72	0		-0.1
2004	KC A	9	8	.529	25	24	1	0-0	148	157	94	24	3	43-0	49	5.35	87	.270	.320	2	.000	-0	103	-10		-1.0
2005	KC A	1	1	.500	28	4	0	0-0	53.2	64	34	9	1	30-4	38	5.70	74	.299	.386	0	—	0	139	-8		-0.4
Total	3	14	14	.500	62	37	1	0-0	254.1	277	160	41	8	88-4	118	5.27	87	.276	.336	2	.000	-0	100	-18		-1.5
GOETZ, GEORGE			George Burt B Greencastle PA 6-2/180 d6.17																							
1889	Bal AA	1	0	1.000	1	1	0	0	9	12	6	0	0	2	4.00	99	.308	.308	4	.000	-1	157	0		0.0
GOETZ, JOHN			John Hardy B10.24.1937 Goetzville MI BR/TR/6-0/185 d4.16 Col Western Michigan																							
1960	Chi N	0	0	—	4	0	0	0	6.1	10	9	2	0	6	6	12.79	30	.370	.452	1	.000	0		-6		-0.3
GOGOLEWSKI, BILL			William Joseph B10.26.1947 Oshkosh WI BL/TR/6-4/190* [TexA65 13/468] d9.3																							
1970	Was A	2	2	.500	8	5	0	0-0	33.2	33	18	2	1	25-1	19	4.81	75	.260	.386	7-0-2	.000	0	64	-4		-0.4
1971	Was A	6	5	.545	27	17	4-1	0-0	124.1	112	39	5	2	39-6	70	2.75	123	.241	.301	32-0-4	.156	0	98	11		1.0
1972	Tex A	4	11	.267	36	21	2-1	2-0	150.2	136	74	9	6	58-9	95	4.24	72	.239	.315	40-0-2	.125	-1	83	-16		-1.8
1973	Tex A	3	6	.333	49	11	0	6-2	123.2	139	67	10	1	48-16	77	4.22	89	.286	.348	0	—	0	95	-7		-0.4
1974	Cle A	0	0	—	5	0	0	0-0	13.2	15	7	1	1	2-0	3	4.61	79	.283	.321	0	—	0		-1		0.0
1975	Chi A	0	0	—	19	0	0	2-1	55	61	35	5	1	28-3	37	5.24	74	.292	.377	0	—	0		-8	54	-0.4
Total	6	15	24	.385	144	44	6-2	10-3	501	496	240	32	12	200-35	301	4.02	86	.260	.332	79-0-8	.127	-1	82	-25	54	-2.0
GOHR, GREG			Gregory James B10.29.1967 Santa Clara CA BR/TR/6-3/205* [DetA89 1/21] d4.7 Col Santa Clara																							
1993	Det A	0	0	—	16	0	0	0-1	22.2	26	15	1	2	14-2	23	5.96	73	.289	.393	0				-3		-0.2
1994	Det A	2	2	.500	8	6	0	0-0	34	36	19	3	0	21-1	21	4.50	109	.263	.358	0	—	0	68	-3	21	0.1
1995	Det A	1	0	1.000	10	0	0	0-0	10.1	9	1	0	0	3-0	12	0.87	553	.243	.300	0	—	0		4	129	0.4
1996	Det A	4	8	.333	17	16	0	0-0	91.2	129	76	24	3	34-2	60	7.17	71	.328	.383	0	—	0	81	-19	25	-2.0
	Cal A	1	1	.500	15	0	0	1-0	24	34	20	7	0	10-0	15	7.50	67	.337	.393	0	—	0		-5		-0.4
	Year	5	9	.357	32	16	0	1-0	115.2	163	96	31	3	44-2	75	7.24	70	.330	.385	0	—	0	81	-25		-2.4
Total	4	8	11	.421	66	22	0	1-1	182.2	234	131	35	5	82-5	131	6.21	80	.309	.377	0	—	0	79	-22	175	-2.1
GOLDEN, JIM			James Edward B3.20.1936 Eldon MO BL/TR/6-0/175* d9.30																							
1960	LA N	1	0	1.000	1	1	0	0	7	6	5	1	0	4-0	4	6.43	62	.240	.333	3	.333	0	156	-2		-0.1
1961	LA N	1	1	.500	28	0	0	0	42	52	30	7	0	20-2	18	5.79	75	.306	.377	3	.000	-0		-6		-0.4
1962	Hou N	7	11	.389	37	18	5-2	0	152.2	163	84	13	0	50-4	88	4.07	92	.270	.324	54-0-3	.222	4*	108	-3		-0.4
1963	Hou N	0	1	.000	3	1	0	0	6.1	12	4	0	0	2-0	5	5.68	55	.429	.467	0	—	0	0	-2		-0.2
Total	4	9	13	.409	69	20	5-2	0	208	233	123	21	0	76-6	115	4.54	85	.282	.340	60-0-3	.217	4	103	-18		-1.1
GOLDEN, MIKE			Michael Henry B9.11.1851 Shirley MA D1.11.1929 Rockford IL BR/TR/5-8/168 d5.4 ▲																							
1875	Wes NA	1	12	.077	13	13	13	0	113	111	88	0		12	20	1.83	133	.225	.243	46	.130	-4	50	7		0.3
	Chi NA	6	7	.462	14	14	12-1	0	119	129	95	0		8	14	1.89	120	.247	.258	155	.258	1*	95	5		0.4
	Year	7	19	.269	27	27	25-1	0	232	240	183	0		20	34	1.86	126	.236	.251	201	.229	-3	73	1		0.7
1878	Mil N	3	13	.188	22	18	15	0	161	217	171	1		33	52	4.14	63	.295	.325	214	.206	-2*	79	-22		-1.8
GOLDEN, ROY			Roy Kramer B7.12.1888 Madisonville OH D10.4.1961 Norwood OH BR/TR/6-1/195 d9.7																							
1910	StL N	2	3	.400	7	6	3	0	42.2	44	28	3	2	33	31	4.43	67	.286	.418	15-0-2	.267	1	92	-7		-0.7
1911	StL N	4	9	.308	30	25	6	0	148.2	127	90	6	5	129	81	5.02	67	.240	.394	44-0-1	.114	-1	125	-21		-1.7
Total	2	6	12	.333	37	31	9	0	191.1	171	118	9	7	162	112	4.89	67	.250	.399	59-0-3	.153	-1	119	-28		-2.4
GOLDSMITH, FRED			Fredrick Ernest B5.15.1852 New Haven CT D3.28.1939 Berkley MI BR/TR/6-1/195 d10.23.1875 U2																							
1879	Tro NA	2	4	.333	7	7	7	0	63	67	38	0		1	31	1.57	159	.237	.240	38	.237	0*	69	4		0.4
1880	Chi N	21	3	.875	26	24	22-4	1	210.1	189	80	2		18	90	1.75	138	.231	.247	142	.261	2*	123	15		1.7
1881	Chi N	24	13	.649	39	39	37-5	0	330	328	166	4		44	76	2.59	106	.247	.271	158	.241	3*	131	9		1.2
1882	Chi N	28	17	.622	45	45	45-4	0	405	377	192	7		38	109	2.42	119	.236	.254	183	.230	-2	129	23		1.8
1883	Chi N	25	19	.568	46	45	40-2	0	383.1	456	256	14		39	82	3.15	105	.277	.294	235-1	.221	-1*	108	10		0.8
1884	Chi N	9	11	.450	21	21	20-1	0	188	245	140	11		29	34	4.26	74	.298	.322	81-2	.136	-2*	125	-15		-1.6
	Bal AA	3	1	.750	4	4	3	0	30	29	12	0		2	11	2.70	128	.238	.256	14	.143	-0	87	3		0.4
Total	6	112	68	.622	189	185	174-16	1	1609.2	1685	884	38	1	171	433	2.73	107	.256	.275	851-3	.224	-1	120	49		4.7
GOLDSMITH, HAL			Harold Eugene B8.18.1898 Peconic NY D10.20.1985 Riverhead NY BR/TR/6-0/174 d6.23 Col St. Lawrence																							
1926	Bos N	5	7	.417	19	15	5	0	101	135	62	2	1	28	15	4.37	81	.333	.377	38-0-1	.211	0	119	-12		-1.1
1927	Bos N	1	3	.250	22	5	1	1	71.2	83	34	4	0	26	13	3.52	106	.289	.348	21-0-1	.238	0	128	1		0.1
1928	Bos N	0	0	—	4	0	0	0	8.1	14	5	2	0	1	1	3.24	121	.359	.375	2	.000	-0	0	0		0.0
1929	StL N	0	0	—	2	0	0	0	4	3	3	1	0	1	0	6.75	69	.214	.267	1	.000	0		-1		-0.1
Total	4	6	10	.375	47	20	6	1	185	235	104	9	1	56	30	4.04	90	.315	.364	62-0-2	.210	0	120	-12		-1.1
GOLDSTEIN, IZZY			Isidore B6.6.1908 Odessa, Russia D9.24.1993 Delray Beach FL BB/TR/6-0/160 d4.24																							
1932	Det A	3	2	.600	16	6	2	0	56.1	63	42	2	3	41	14	4.47	105	.276	.393	17	.294	1	82	-2		-0.1
GOLTZ, DAVE			David Allan B6.23.1949 Pelican Rapids MN BR/TR/6-4/215(200-215) [MinA67 5/97] d7.18																							
1972	Min A	3	3	.500	15	11	2	1-0	91	75	30	5	0	26-3	38	2.67	120	.224	.278	29-0-3	.103	-1	98	6		0.3
1973	Min A	6	4	.600	32	10	1	1-1	106.1	138	68	11	2	32-1	65	5.25	76	.318	.363	0	—	0	133	-13		-1.1
1974	Min A	10	10	.500	28	24	5-1	1-0	174.1	192	81	14	7	45-1	89	3.25	115	.282	.330	0	—	0	109	5		0.6
1975	Min A	14	14	.500	32	32	15-1	0-0	243	235	112	18	6	72-2	128	3.67	104	.255	.312	0	—	0	96	5		0.6
1976	Min A	14	14	.500	36	35	13-4	0-0	249.1	239	113	14	5	91-4	133	3.36	106	.254	.320	0	—	0*	97	4		0.4
1977	Min A	20	11	.645	39	39	19-2	0-0	303	284	129	23	2	91-4	186	3.36	119	.247	.303	0	—	0*	124	20		1.8
1978	Min A	15	10	.600	29	29	13-2	0-0	220.1	209	72	12	1	67-4	116	2.49	154	.253	.307	0	—	0	91	31		3.5
1979	Min A	14	13	.519	36	35	12-1	0-0	250.2	282	124	22	1	69-3	132	4.16	106	.288	.334	0	—	0	96	7		0.7
1980	LA N	7	11	.389	35	27	2-2	1-1	171.1	198	91	12	0	59-3	91	4.31	81	.299	.353	47-0-7	.128	0	111	-17		-1.6
1981	†LA N	2	7	.222	26	8	0	1-4	77	83	35	9	4	25-3	48	4.09	81	.288	.343	17-0-2	.059	-1	118	-6		-0.7
1982	LA N	0	1	.000	2	1	0	0-0	3.2	6	4	0	0	0-0	3	4.91	71	.353	.353	1	.000	0	76	-1		-0.3
	†Cal A	8	5	.615	28	7	1	3-0	86	82	43	4	1	32-1	49	4.08	100	.252	.317	0	—	0	127	0	21	-0.1
1983	Cal A	0	6	.000	15	6	0	0-2	63.2	81	48	10	1	37-2	27	6.22	65	.315	.399	0	—	0	97	-15		-1.3
Total	12	113	109	.509	353	264	83-13	8-8	2039.2	2104	950	149	26	646-28	1105	3.69	104	.269	.325	94-0-12	.106	-1	105	26	21	2.8
GOMES, WAYNE			Wayne Maurice B1.15.1973 Hampton VA BR/TR/6-2/220* [PhiN93 1/4] d6.13 Col Old Dominion																							
1997	Phi N	5	1	.833	37	0	0	0-1	42.2	45	26	4	1	24-0	24	5.27	80	.274	.370	2	.000	0		-4		-0.6
1998	Phi N	9	6	.600	71	0	0	1-7	93.1	94	48	9	3	35-4	86	4.24	102	.258	.328	2	.000	-0		0		0.4
1999	Phi N	5	5	.500	73	0	0	19-5	74	70	38	5	2	56-2	58	4.26	110	.255	.381	1	.000	0		3		0.4
2000	Phi N	4	6	.400	65	0	0	7-4	73.2	72	41	6	3	35-3	49	4.40	104	.262	.347	0	—	0		1		0.0
2001	Phi N	4	3	.571	35	0	0	1-4	48	51	23	4	1	22-4	35	4.31	95	.276	.351	1	1.000	1		0	31	0.0
	SF N	2	0	1.000	13	0	0	0-0	15	21	14	3	0	7-2	17	8.40	49	.350	.412	0	—	0		-7	15	-0.8
	Year	6	3	.667	55	0	0	1-4	63	72	37	7	1	29-6	52	5.29	78	.294	.366	1	1.000	1		-7		-0.8
2002	Bos A	1	2	.333	20	0	0	1-0	21.1	20	11	2	3	12-2	15	4.64	96	.241	.357	0	—	0		0		0.0
Total	6	30	23	.566	321	0	0	29-21	368	373	201	33	13	191-17	284	4.60	96	.265	.356	6	.167	1		-7	66	-1.0

YEAR	TM LG	W	L	PCT	G	GS	CG-SHO	SV-BS	IP	H	R	HR	HB	BB-IB	SO	ERA	AERA	OAV	OOB	AB-HR-SH	AVG	PB	SUP	APR	DL	PW
GOMEZ, PAT	Patrick Alexander B3.17.1968 Roseville CA BL/TL/5-11/185* [ChiN86 4/90] d4.6																									
1993	SD N	1	2	.333	27	1	0	0-0	31.2	35	19	2	0	19-4	26	5.12	81	.292	.378	5	.000	-1*	87	-3	100	-0.3
1994	SF N	0	1	.000	26	0	0	0-0	33.1	23	14	2	0	20-1	14	3.78	107	.211	.328	2-0-1	.000	-0	2			0.0
1995	SF N	0	0	—	18	0	0	0-0	14	16	8	2	0	12-1	15	5.14	80	.276	.400	1	.000	-0	-1	101		-0.1
Total	3	1	3	.250	71	1	0	0-0	79	74	41	6	0	51-6	55	4.56	90	.258	.363	8-0-1	.000	-1	87	-2	201	-0.4
GOMEZ, RUBEN	Ruben (Colon) B7.13.1927 Arroyo, PR D7.26.2004 Carolina, PR BR/TR/6-0/175* d4.17																									
1953	NY N	13	11	.542	29	26	13-3	0	204	166	89	17	4	101	113	3.40	126	.218	.313	72-0-6	.208	-0*	81	20		2.2
1954	†NY N	17	9	.654	37	32	10-4	0	221.2	202	85	20	7	109	106	2.88	140	.244	.336	81-2-4	.173	0*	104	27		3.0
1955	NY N	9	10	.474	33	31	9-3	1	185.1	207	103	20	7	63-6	79	4.56	88	.285	.345	60-0-4	.300	4*	103	-9		-1.6
1956	NY N	7	17	.292	40	31	4-2	0	196.1	191	108	19	9	77-8	76	4.58	83	.259	.334	60-0-1	.183	-0*	84	-15		0.9
1957	NY N	15	13	.536	38	36	16-1	0	238.1	233	110	28	5	71-10	92	3.78	104	.254	.309	87-1-4	.184	1*	103	5		0.9
1958	SF N	10	12	.455	42	30	8-1	1	207.2	204	107	21	8	77-3	112	4.38	87	.261	.330	70-0-4	.200	1*	126	-10		-0.7
1959	Phi N	3	8	.273	20	12	2-1	0	72.1	90	55	12	0	24-2	37	6.10	67	.300	.350	17-0-3	.176	0*	82	-15		-2.0
1960	Phi N	0	3	.000	22	1	0	1	52.1	68	37	7	1	9-2	24	5.33	73	.321	.344	12-0-1	.083	-1	273	-9		-0.1
1962	Cle A	1	2	.333	15	4	0	1	45.1	50	23	5	2	25-3	21	4.37	89	.292	.383	13	.231	0*	104	-2		-0.1
	Min A	1	1	.500	6	2	1	0	19.1	17	11	3	0	11-2	8	4.66	88	.254	.354	5	.000	-0	87	-1		-0.1
	Year	2	3	.400	21	6	1	1	64.2	67	34	8	2	36-5	29	4.45	88	.282	.375	18	.167	-0	98	-3		-0.2
1967	Phi N	0	0	—	7	0	0	0	11.1	15	7	0	0	7-3	9	3.97	86	.211	.333	0	—	0		-1		0.0
Total	10	76	86	.469	289	205	63-15	5	1454	1436	734	154	43	574-39	677	4.09	97	.259	.331	477-3-27	.199	6	100	-10		0.7
GOMEZ, LEFTY	Vernon Louis "Goofy" B11.26.1908 Rodeo CA D2.17.1989 Greenbrae CA BL/TL/6-2/173 d4.29 Def 1943 HF1972																									
1930	NY A	2	5	.286	15	6	2	1	60	66	41	12	1	28	47	5.55	78	.280	.358	20-0-3	.150	-2	120	-7		-0.8
1931	NY A	21	9	.700	40	26	17-1	3	243	206	88	7	4	85	150	2.67	149	.254	.295	83-0-4	.133	-3	126	36		3.6
1932	†NY A	24	7	.774	37	31	21-1	1	265.1	266	140	23	2	105	176	4.21	97	.259	.329	104-0-5	.173	-1	145	-2		-0.5
1933	NY A★	16	10	.615	35	30	14-4	2	234.2	218	108	16	0	106	**163**	3.18	122	.240	.319	80-0-5	.112	-3	107	15		1.0
1934	NY A★	**26**	5	**.839**	38	33	**25-6**	1	281.2	223	86	12	0	96	158	**2.33**	174	**.215**	**.282**	90-0-4	.131	-3	125	**59**		5.5
1935	NY A★	12	15	.444	34	30	15-2	1	246	223	104	18	2	86	138	3.18	127	.242	.309	83-0-7	.120	-6	96	26		1.8
1936	†NY A☆	13	7	.650	31	30	10	0	188.2	184	104	6	1	122	105	4.39	106	.254	.362	69-0-8	.145	-3	117	6		0.2
1937	†NY A★	**21**	11	.656	34	34	25-6	0	278.1	233	88	10	1	93	**194**	**2.33**	191	**.223**	.287	105-0-5	.200	-1	106	**67**		6.8
1938	†NY A★	18	12	.600	32	32	20-4	0	239	239	110	7	1	99	129	3.35	135	.260	.332	86-0-9	.151	-2	107	31		3.2
1939	†NY A☆	12	8	.600	26	26	14-2	0	198	173	80	11	3	84	102	3.41	128	.235	.316	73-0-4	.151	-2	100	24		1.3
1940	NY A	3	3	.500	9	5	0	0	27.1	37	20	2	1	18	14	6.59	61	.325	.421	9	.000	-1	129	-7		-1.4
1941	NY A	15	5	**.750**	23	23	8-2	0	156.1	151	76	10	1	103	76	3.74	105	.250	.360	59-0-4	.153	-1	128	3		0.7
1942	NY A	6	4	.600	13	13	2	0	80	67	42	4	2	65	41	4.27	80	.237	.383	33-0-1	.152	-1	153	-7		-1.0
1943	Was A	0	1	.000	1	1	0	0	4.2	4	4	0	1	5	0	5.79	55	.250	.429	1	.000	-0	26	-2		-0.3
Total	14	189	102	.649	368	320	173-28	9	2503	2290	1091	138	19	1095	1468	3.34	125	.242	.321	904-0-68	.147	-30	117	242		20.1
GONZALES, JOE	Joe Madrid "Smokey" B3.19.1915 San Francisco CA D11.16.1996 Torrance CA BR/TR/5-9/175 d8.25 Col USC																									
1937	Bos A	1	2	.333	8	2	2	0	31	37	16	1	0	11	11	4.35	109	.291	.348	10-0-1	.000	-2	73	2		0.4
GONZALES, VINCE	Wenceslao (O'Reilly) B9.28.1925 Quivican, Cuba D3.11.1981 Ciudad Del Carmen, Mex BL/TL/6-1/165 d4.13																									
1955	Was A	0	0	—	1	0	0	0	2	6	6	1	0	3-0	1	27.00	14	.500	.600	0		0		-5		-0.2
GONZALEZ, DICKY	Dicky Angel B12.21.1978 Bayamon, PR BR/TR/5-11/170* [NYN96 16/468] d5.1																									
2001	NY N	3	2	.600	16	7	0	0-0	59	72	33	4	1	17-3	31	4.88	83	.306	.347	20-0-1	.100	-1	137	-5		-0.4
2004	TB A	0	0	—	4	0	0	0-0	7.1	9	5	1	0	2-0	7	6.14	76	.310	.344	0	—	0		-1		0.0
Total	2	3	2	.600	20	7	0	0-0	66.1	81	38	5	1	19-3	38	5.02	82	.307	.347	20-0-1	.100	-1	137	-6		-0.4
GONZALEZ, EDGAR	Edgardo Gerardo (Elizondo) B2.23.1983 San Nicolas de los Garza, Nuevo Leon, Mexico BR/TR/6-0/220* d6.1																									
2003	Ari N	2	1	.667	9	2	0	0-1	18.1	28	10	3	0	7-2	14	4.91	94	.368	.417	4-0-1	.250	0	132	0		-3.6
2004	Ari N	0	9	.000	10	10	0	0-0	46.1	72	49	15	5	18-4	31	9.32	49	.362	.426	13-0-1	.154	-0	59	-21		-3.3
2005	Ari N	0	0	—	1	0	0	0-0	0.1	2	4	1	0	2-0	1	108.00	4	.667	.800	0	—	0		-4		-0.2
Total	3	2	10	.167	20	12	0	0-1	65	102	63	19	5	27-6	46	8.58	53	.367	.429	17-0-2	.176	-0	71	-25		-3.7
GONZALEZ, GABE	Gabriel B5.24.1972 Long Beach CA BB/TL/6-1/160 [FlaN95 16/429] d4.1 Col Cal St.-Long Beach																									
1998	Fla N	0	0	—	3	0	0	0-0	1	1	1	1	0	1-0	0	9.00	45	.333	.600	0	—	0		-1		0.0
GONZALEZ, JEREMI	Geremis Segundo (Acosta) B1.8.1975 Maracaibo, Venez BR/TR/6-2/200(180-220) d5.27 [DL 2000 Chi N 186]																									
1997	Chi N	11	9	.550	23	23	1-1	0-0	144	126	73	16	2	69-5	93	4.25	102	.236	.323	40-0-8	.100	-1	98	1		0.4
1998	Chi N	7	7	.500	20	20	1-1	0-0	110	124	72	13	3	41-5	70	5.32	83	.281	.344	32-0-8	.188	0*	111	-12	65	-1.4
2003	TB A	6	11	.353	25	25	2-1	0-0	156.1	131	71	18	12	69-1	97	3.91	117	.228	.319	6	.000	-1	71	13		1.3
2004	TB A	0	5	.000	11	8	0	0-0	50.1	72	42	9	3	20-0	22	6.97	67	.346	.406	0	—	0	67	-12		-1.3
2005	†Bos A	2	1	.667	28	3	0	0-0	56	64	39	7	2	16-2	28	6.11	75	.288	.336	0	—	0	109	-8		-0.4
Total	5	26	33	.441	107	79	4-2	0-0	516.2	517	297	63	22	215-13	310	4.84	93	.261	.337	78-0-16	.128	-2	89	-18	251	-1.4
GONZALEZ, GERMAN	German Jose (Caraballo) B3.7.1962 Rio Caribe, Venez BR/TR/6-0/170* d8.5																									
1988	Min A	0	0	—	16	0	0	1-0	21.1	20	8	4	1	8-1	19	3.38	121	.244	.319	0	—	0		2		0.4
1989	Min A	3	2	.600	22	0	0	0-0	29	32	17	2	4	11-1	25	4.66	89	.274	.353	0	—	0		-2	38	-0.1
Total	2	3	2	.600	38	0	0	1-0	50.1	52	25	6	5	19-2	44	4.11	100	.261	.339	0	—	0		0	38	-0.2
GONZALEZ, JULIO	Julio Enrique (Herrera) B12.20.1920 Banes, Cuba D2.15.1991 Banes, Cuba BR/TR/5-11/150 d8.9																									
1949	Was A	0	0	—	13	0	0	0-0	34.1	33	20	3	1	27	5	4.72	90	.256	.389	5	.200	0		-2		-0.4
GONZALEZ, LARIEL	Lariel Alfonso B5.25.1976 San Cristobal, D.R. BR/TR/6-4/228 d9.22																									
1998	Col N	0	0	—	1	0	0	0-0	1	0	0	0	0	0-0	0	0.00	—	.000	.000	0	—	0		0		0.0
GONZALEZ, MIKE	Michael Vela B5.23.1978 Corpus Christi TX BR/TL/6-2/210* [PitN97 30/902] d8.11 Col San Jacinto (TX) JC																									
2003	Pit N	0	1	.000	16	0	0	0-0	8.1	7	7	4	0	6-0	6	7.56	57	.233	.351	0	—	0		-3		-0.2
2004	Pit N	3	1	.750	47	0	0	1-3	43.1	32	7	2	1	6-0	55	1.25	348	.204	.235	1	1.000	1		15		1.9
2005	Pit N	1	3	.250	51	0	0	3-0	50	35	15	2	1	31-2	58	2.70	157	.197	.316	0	—	0		9	54	1.1
Total	3	4	5	.444	114	0	0	4-3	101.2	74	29	8	2	43-2	119	2.48	173	.202	.287	1	1.000	1		21	54	1.9
GOOD, ANDREW	Andrew Richard B9.19.1979 San Diego CA BR/TR/6-3/170(170-210) [AriN98 8/253] d4.18																									
2003	Ari N	4	2	.667	16	10	0	0-0	66.1	74	44	15	3	16-3	42	5.29	87	.281	.325	16-0-4	.125	-1	89	-4		-0.4
2004	Ari N	1	2	.333	17	2	0	0-0	40.2	43	25	8	3	13-0	26	5.31	86	.272	.335	5	.000	-1	81	-2	87	-0.2
2005	Det A	0	0	—	2	0	0	0-0	5	4	1	1	0	1-0	7	5.40	78	.211	.250	0	—	0		-1		0.1
Total	3	5	4	.556	35	12	0	0-0	112	121	70	24	6	30-3	75	5.30	86	.275	.326	21-0-4	.095	-1	88	-7	87	-0.6
GOOD, RALPH	Ralph Nelson "Holy" B4.25.1886 Monticello ME D11.24.1965 Waterville ME BR/TR/6-0/165 d7.1 Col Colby																									
1910	Bos N	0	0	—	2	0	0	0-0	9	6	4	0	2	2	4	2.00	166	.188	.278	3	.000	-0		1		0.1
GOOD, WILBUR	Wilbur David "Lefty" B9.28.1885 Punxsutawney PA D12.30.1963 Brooksville FL BL/TL/5-11.5/180 d8.18 ▲																									
1905	NY A	0	2	.000	5	2	0	0-0	19	18	17	1	0	14	13	4.74	62	.250	.372	8	.375	1		24	-4		-0.1
GOODALL, HERB	Herbert Frank B3.10.1870 Mansfield PA D1.20.1938 Mansfield PA BR/TR/5-9/180 d4.29																									
1890	Lou AA	8	5	.615	18	13	8-1	**4**	109	94	73	2	10	51	46	3.39	114	.225	.324	45	.422	6*	104	5		1.1
GOODELL, JOHN	John Henry William "Lefty" B4.5.1907 Muskogee OK D9.21.1993 Mesquite TX BR/TL/5-10/165 d4.19																									
1928	Chi A	0	0	—	2	0	0	0-0	3	6	9	0	1	9-1	0	18.00	23	.500	.600	0	—	0		-4		-0.1
GOODEN, DOC	Dwight Eugene "Doctor K" B11.16.1964 Tampa FL BR/TR/6-3/210(190-210) [NYN82 1/5] d4.7																									
1984	NY N★	17	9	.654	31	31	7-3	0-0	218	161	72	7	2	73-2	**276**	2.60	137	**.202**	**.269**	70-0-10	.200	1	92	**24**		3.7
1985	NY N☆	**24**	4	**.857**	35	35	**16-8**	0-0	276.2	198	51	13	2	69-4	268	**1.53**	229	.201	.254	93-1-9	.226	6	123	**63**		7.8
1986	†NY N★	17	6	.739	33	33	12-2	0-0	250	197	92	17	4	80-3	200	2.84	126	.215	.278	81-0-13	.086	-3	115	20		1.8
1987	NY N	15	7	**.682**	25	25	7-3	0-0	179.2	162	68	11	2	53-2	148	3.21	120	.244	.299	64-0-5	.219	2	119	15	60	1.6
1988	†NY N★	18	9	.667	34	34	10-3	0-0	248.1	242	98	8	6	57-4	175	3.19	102	.256	.301	90-0-9	.178	2	152	3		0.5
1989	NY N	9	4	.692	19	17	0	1-0	118.1	93	42	9	2	47-2	101	2.89	114	.211	.288	40-0-3	.200	2	96	6	62	0.3
1990	NY N	19	7	.731	34	34	2-1	0-0	232.2	229	106	10	7	70-3	223	3.83	98	.258	.314	75-1-14	.187	4*	141	0		0.7

YEAR	TM LG	W	L	PCT	G	GS	CG-SHO	SV-BS	IP	H	R	HR	HB	BB-IB	SO	ERA	AERA	OAV	OOB	AB-HR-SH	AVG	PB	SUP	APR	DL	PW
1991	NY N	13	7	.650	27	27	3-1	0-0	190	185	80	12	3	56-2	150	3.60	102	.257	.311	63-1-8	.238	4	123	4	44	0.9
1992	NY N	10	13	.435	31	31	3	0-0	206	197	93	11	3	70-7	145	3.67	95	.255	.317	72-1-4	.264	6*	84	-4	21	0.3
1993	NY N	12	15	.444	29	29	7-2	0-0	208.2	188	89	16	9	61-1	149	3.45	116	.242	.302	70-2-6	.200	4*	91	14		2.2
1994	NY N	3	4	.429	7	7	0	0-0	41.1	46	32	9	1	15-1	40	6.31	66	.282	.346	12-0-4	.167	-0	112	-10	48	-1.3
1996	NY A	11	7	.611	29	29	1-1	0-0	170.2	169	101	19	9	88-4	126	5.01	99	.259	.352	0	—	0	94	-1		-0.1
1997	†NY A	9	5	.643	20	19	0	0-0	106.1	116	61	14	7	53-1	66	4.91	91	.283	.373	4	.000	0	100	-4	70	-0.5
1998	†Cle A	8	6	.571	23	23	0	0-0	134	135	59	13	9	51-0	83	3.76	127	.262	.337	2	.000	-0	48	15	53	1.4
1999	Cle A	3	4	.429	26	22	0	0-0	115	127	90	18	0	67-3	88	6.26	81	.282	.382	2-1-0	.500	2	140	-16	28	-0.6
2000	Hou N	0	0	—	1	1	0	0-0	4	6	4	1	0	3-0	1	9.00	55	.353	.450	1	.000	-0	150	-2		-0.1
	TB A	2	3	.400	8	8	0	0-0	36.2	47	32	14	3	20-0	23	6.63	74	.315	.407	0	—	0	86	-8		-0.9
	†NY A	4	2	.667	18	5	0	2-0	64.1	66	28	8	0	21-3	31	3.36	142	.266	.321	0	.000	0	110	9		0.8
	Year	6	5	.545	26	13	0	2-0	101	113	60	22	3	41-3	54	4.54	106	.285	.354	2	.000	0	96	2		-0.1
Total	16	194	112	.634	430	410	68-24	3-0	2800.2	2564	1198	210	78	954-42	2293	3.51	111	.244	.309	741-8-85	.196	29	113	128	386	18.4

GOODWIN, ART Arthur Ingram B2.27.1877 Whiteley Twnshp PA D6.19.1943 Franklin Twp. PA TR/5-8/195 d10.7

| 1905 | NY A | 0 | 0 | — | 1 | 0 | 0 | 0 | 0.1 | 2 | 4 | 0 | 2 | 0 | 2 | 0 | 81.00 | 4 | .667 | .800 | 0 | — | 0 | | -3 | | -0.1 |

GOODWIN, CLYDE Clyde Samuel B11.12.1886 Athens OH D10.12.1963 Dayton OH BR/TR/5-11/145 d9.18 Col Purdue

| 1906 | Was A | 0 | 2 | .000 | 4 | 3 | 1 | 0 | 22.1 | 20 | 16 | 0 | 1 | 13 | 9 | 4.43 | 59 | .244 | .354 | 5-0-1 | .200 | -0 | 118 | -5 | | -0.4 |

GOODWIN, JIM James Patrick B8.15.1926 St.Louis MO BL/TL/6-1/170 d4.24

| 1948 | Chi A | 0 | 0 | — | 8 | 1 | 0 | 1 | 11 | 11 | 0 | 1 | 0 | 12 | 3 | 8.71 | 49 | .237 | .431 | 2 | .500 | 0 | 85 | -5 | | -0.2 |

GOODWIN, MARV Marvin Mardo B1.16.1891 Gordonsville VA D10.21.1925 Houston TX BR/TR/5-11/168 d9.7 Mil 1918

1916	Was A	0	0	—	3	0	0	0	5.2	5	4	0	0	3	1	3.18	88	.217	.308	1	.000	-0		-1		-0.1
1917	StL N	6	4	.600	14	12	6-3	0	85.1	70	33	1	0	19	38	2.21	122	.222	.266	23-0-5	.174	-0	100	1		0.2
1919	StL N	11	9	.550	33	17	7	0	179	163	66	3	8	33	48	2.51	111	.245	.289	60-0-1	.200	1*	127	5		0.6
1920	StL N	3	8	.273	32	12	3	1	116.1	153	79	1	5	28	23	4.95	60	.314	.357	35-0-3	.200	-0	119	-26		-2.5
1921	StL N	1	2	.333	14	4	1	1	36.1	47	21	1	1	9	7	3.72	99	.315	.358	6-0-3	.000	-1	157	-1		-0.1
1922	StL N	0	0	—	2	0	0	0	4	3	1	0	0	3	0	2.25	172	.250	.400	1	—	0		1		0.1
1925	Cin N	0	2	.000	4	3	2	0	20.2	26	14	2	1	5	4	4.79	86	.317	.364	4-0-1	.250	0	62	-2		-0.1
Total	7	21	25	.457	102	48	19-3	2	447.1	467	218	8	15	100	121	3.30	90	.269	.315	129-0-13	.186	0	117	-23		-1.9

GORDINIER, RAY Raymond Cornelius "Gordy" B4.11.1892 Rochester NY D11.15.1960 Rochester NY BB/TR/5-8.5/170 d9.17

1921	Bro N	0	0	—	3	0	0	0	12	10	8	0	0	8	4	5.25	74	.227	.346	4	.250	0	134	-2		-0.1
1922	Bro N	1	0	1.000	5	0	0	0	11.1	13	11	3	0	8	5	8.74	47	.289	.396	2	.000	-0		-5		-0.3
Total	2	1	0	1.000	8	0	0	0	23.1	23	19	3	0	16	9	6.94	57	.258	.371	6	.167	-0	134	-7		-0.4

GORDON, DON Donald Thomas B10.10.1959 New York NY BR/TR/6-1/175* [DetA82 31/769] d4.10 Col South Carolina-Aiken

1986	Tor A	0	1	.000	14	0	0	1-1	21.2	28	20	1	4	8-1	13	7.06	60	.311	.366	0	—	0		-7		-0.4
1987	Tor A	0	0	—	5	0	0	0-0	11	8	5	2	0	3-0	3	4.09	111	.200	.256	0	—	0		1		0.0
	Cle A	0	3	.000	21	0	0	1-0	39.2	49	31	3	4	12-3	20	4.08	112	.295	.353	0	—	0		-2		-0.1
	Year	0	3	.000	26	0	0	1-0	50.2	57	36	5	4	15-3	23	4.09	112	.277	.335	0	—	0		-3		-0.1
1988	Cle A	3	4	.429	38	0	0	1-2	59.1	65	33	5	3	19-3	20	4.40	94	.284	.341	0	—	0		-2		-0.2
Total	3	3	8	.273	78	0	0	3-3	131.2	150	89	11	8	42-7	56	4.72	92	.286	.343	0	—	0		-10		-0.7

GORDON, TOM Thomas B11.18.1967 Sebring FL BR/TR/5-9/180(160-195) [KCA86 6/157] d9.8 [DL 2000 Bos A 181]

1988	KC A	0	2	.000	5	2	0	0-0	15.2	16	9	1	0	7-0	18	5.17	78	.267	.343	0	—	0	57	-2		-0.2
1989	KC A	17	9	.654	49	16	1-1	1-6	163	122	67	10	1	86-4	153	3.64	106	.210	.311	0	—	0	85	7		1.2
1990	KC A	12	11	.522	32	32	6-1	0-0	195.1	192	99	17	3	99-1	175	3.73	104	.257	.346	0	—	0	115	0		0.0
1991	KC A	9	14	.391	45	14	1	1-3	158	129	76	16	4	87-6	167	3.87	107	.221	.324	0	—	0*	99	5		0.7
1992	KC A	6	10	.375	40	11	0	0-2	117.2	116	67	9	4	55-4	98	4.59	89	.258	.340	0	—	0	87	-7	20	-0.9
1993	KC A	12	6	.667	48	14	2	1-5	155.2	125	65	11	7	77-5	143	3.58	129	.223	.315	0	—	0	103	17		1.9
1994	KC A	11	7	.611	24	24	0	0-0	155.1	136	79	15	3	87-3	126	4.35	116	.237	.336	0	—	0	87	13		1.3
1995	KC A	12	12	.500	31	31	2	0-0	189	204	110	12	4	89-4	119	4.43	108	.279	.355	0	—	0*	88	3	16	0.4
1996	Bos A	12	9	.571	34	34	4-1	0-0	215.2	249	143	28	4	105-5	171	5.59	91	.284	.359	0	—	0	130	-8		-0.6
1997	Bos A	6	10	.375	42	25	2-1	11-2	182.2	155	85	10	3	78-1	159	3.74	124	.226	.306	0	—	0	96	17		1.5
1998	†Bos A★	7	4	.636	73	0	0	46-1	79.1	55	24	2	0	25-1	78	2.72	174	.191	.254	0	—	0		18		3.5
1999	†Bos A	0	2	.000	21	0	0	11-2	17.2	17	11	2	1	12-2	24	5.60	89	.246	.366	0	—	0		-1	129	-0.1
2001	Chi N	1	2	.333	47	0	0	27-4	45.1	32	18	4	1	16-1	67	3.38	124	.188	.262	0	—	0	5	30		0.7
2002	Chi N	1	1	.500	19	0	0	0-0	23.2	27	12	1	1	10-1	31	3.42	118	.293	.369	0	—	0	1	93		0.1
	Hou N	0	2	.000	15	0	0	0-0	19	15	7	2	0	6-2	17	3.32	130	.217	.280	1	.000	-0	2			0.2
	Year	1	3	.250	34	0	0	0-0	42.2	42	19	3	1	16-3	48	3.38	124	.261	.331	1	.000	-0	3			0.3
2003	Chi A	7	6	.538	66	0	0	12-5	74	57	29	4	4	31-3	91	3.16	145	.213	.301	0	—	0	11			2.1
2004	†NY A★	9	4	.692	80	0	0	4-6	89.2	56	23	5	1	23-5	96	2.21	208	.180	.237	1	.000	-0	**24**			3.3
2005	†NY A	5	4	.556	79	0	0	2-7	80.2	59	25	8	0	29-4	69	2.57	170	.203	.272	0	—	0	16			1.7
Total	17	127	115	.525	750	203	18-4	116-43	1977.1	1762	949	157	35	922-52	1802	3.93	114	.238	.323	2	.000	-0	103	121	469	16.8

GORECKI, RICK Richard John B8.27.1973 Evergreen Park IL BR/TR/6-3/167* [LAN91 19/507] d9.10 [DL 1996 LA N 182, 1999 TB A 182]

1997	LA N	1	0	1.000	4	1	0	0-0	6	9	10	3	0	6-1	6	15.00	26	.346	.469	0-0-1	—	0	212	-7		-1.0
1998	TB A	1	2	.333	3	3	0	0-0	16.2	15	9	1	0	10-0	7	4.86	99	.259	.357	0	—	0	58	0	163	0.0
Total	2	2	2	.500	7	4	0	0-0	22.2	24	19	4	0	16-1	13	7.54	60	.286	.392	0-0-1	—	0	92	-7	527	-1.0

GORIN, CHARLIE Charles Perry B2.6.1928 Waco TX BL/TL/5-10/165* d5.29 Col Texas

1954	Mil N	0	1	.000	5	0	0	0	9.2	5	3	0	0	6	12	1.86	200	.152	.282	3	.000	-0		2		0.1
1955	Mil N	0	0	—	2	0	0	0	0.1	1	2	0	0	3-0	0	54.00	7	.500	.800	0	—	0		-2		-0.1
Total	2	0	1	.000	7	0	0	0	10	6	5	0	0	9-0	12	3.60	103	.171	.341	3	.000	-0		0		0.0

GORMAN, JACK John F. "Stooping Jack" B1859 St.Louis MO D9.9.1889 St.Louis MO d7.1.1883 ▲

| 1884 | Pit AA | 1 | 2 | .333 | 3 | 3 | 3 | 0 | 25 | 22 | 27 | 3 | 5 | 10 | 5 | 4.68 | 71 | .212 | .255 | 27 | .148 | -0* | 91 | -4 | | -0.4 |

GORMAN, TOM Thomas Aloysius B1.4.1925 New York NY D12.26.1992 Valley Stream NY BR/TR/6-1/190* d7.16

1952	†NY A	6	2	.750	12	6	1-1	1	60.2	63	34	8	2	22	31	4.60	72	.272	.340	23	.087	-1	127	-9		-1.2
1953	†NY A	4	5	.444	40	1	0	6	77	65	32	5	6	32	38	3.39	109	.226	.317	15-0-1	.133	-1	48	3		0.3
1954	NY A	0	0	—	23	0	0	2	36.2	30	14	1	1	14	31	2.21	156	.222	.300	4	.000	-1		7		0.1
1955	KC A	7	6	.538	57	0	0	18	109	98	48	11	4	36-5	46	3.55	118	.246	.311	24-0-1	.083	-1		7		0.8
1956	KC A	9	10	.474	52	13	1	3	171.1	168	83	23	2	68-7	56	3.83	113	.258	.329	39-0-1	.051	-4	77	9		0.5
1957	KC A	5	9	.357	38	12	3-1	3	124.2	125	59	18	1	33-7	66	3.83	103	.261	.307	33-0-1	.121	-2	83	2		0.0
1958	KC A	4	4	.500	50	0	0	8	89.2	86	41	8	3	20-0	44	3.51	111	.258	.305	17	.118	-1	46	3		0.1
1959	KC A	1	0	1.000	17	0	0	1	20.1	24	21	3	1	14-0	9	7.08	57	.293	.398	0	—	0		-8		-0.5
Total	8	36	36	.500	289	33	5-2	42	689.1	659	332	77	20	239-19	321	3.77	105	.254	.320	155-0-4	.090	-10	86	11		0.1

GORMAN, TOM Thomas David "Big Tom" B3.16.1916 New York NY D8.11.1986 Closter NJ BR/TL/6-2/200 d9.14 U26

| 1939 | NY N | 0 | 0 | — | 4 | 0 | 0 | 0 | 5 | 7 | 4 | 0 | 0 | 2 | 2 | 7.20 | 55 | .350 | .381 | 1 | .000 | -0 | | -2 | | -0.1 |

GORMAN, TOM Thomas Patrick B12.16.1957 Portland OR BL/TL/6-4/200* [MonN80 4/99] d9.2 Col Gonzaga

1981	Mon N	0	0	—	9	0	0	0-0	15	12	7	0	1	6-2	13	4.20	85	.222	.306	0	—	0		-1		-0.1
1982	Mon N	1	0	1.000	7	0	0	0-0	7	8	4	0	0	4-0	6	5.14	72	.286	.364	0	—	0		-1		-0.1
	NY N	0	1	.000	3	1	0	0-0	9.1	8	1	0	0	4-0	7	0.96	381	.235	.235	1-0-1	.000	0	24	3		0.3
	Year	1	1	.500	10	1	0	0-0	16.1	16	5	0	0	8-0	13	2.76	134	.258	.299	1-0-1	.000	0	24	2		0.2
1983	NY N	1	4	.200	25	4	0	0-0	49.1	45	29	3	0	15-4	30	4.93	75	.245	.299	4-0-1	.250	0	48	-6		-0.6
1984	NY N	6	0	1.000	36	0	0	0-2	57.2	51	20	6	4	13-3	40	2.97	120	.238	.284	3	.000	-0		5		0.4
1985	NY N	4	4	.500	34	2	0	0-3	52.2	56	32	8	0	18-2	32	5.13	68	.277	.335	5-0-1	.000	-1	126	-9		-1.3
1986	Phi N	0	1	.000	6	0	0	0-0	11.2	21	10	0	0	5-1	5	7.71	51	.382	.426	1	.000	-0		-4		-0.3
1987	SD N	0	0	—	6	0	0	0-0	11	11	5	1	0	5-0	8	4.09	97	.262	.340	0	—	0		0	37	0.0
Total	7	12	10	.545	126	7	0	0-5	213.2	212	108	24	9	66-12	144	4.34	84	.261	.315	14-0-3	.071	-1	66	-13	37	-1.6

YEAR	TM LG	W	L	PCT	G	GS	CG-SHO	SV-BS	IP	H	R	HR	HB	BB-IB	SO	ERA	AERA	OAV	OOB	AB-HR-SH	AVG	PB	SUP	APR	DL	PW

GORMLEY, JOE Joseph B12.20.1866 Summit Hill PA D7.2.1950 Summit Hill PA BL/TL d6.16

1891	Phi N	0	1	.000	1	1	1	0	8	10	8	0	0	5	2	5.63	61	.294	.385	4	.000	-1	53	-2		-0.2

GORNICKI, HANK Henry Frank B1.14.1911 Niagara Falls NY D2.16.1996 Riviera Beach FL BR/TR/6-1/145 d4.17 Mil 1944-45

1941	StL N	1	0	1.000	4	1	1-1	0	11.1	6	4	0	0	9	6	3.18	118	.158	.333	4	.250	0	135	1		0.1
	Chi N	0	0	—	1	0	0	0	2	3	1	0	0	0	2	4.50	78	.375	.375	0	—	0	0	0		0.0
	Year	1	0	1.000	5	1	1-1	0	13.1	9	5	0	1	9	8	3.38	110	.196	.339	4	.250	0	137	1		0.1
1942	Pit N	5	6	.455	25	14	7-2	2	112	89	45	2	1	40	48	2.57	132	.215	.286	35-1-2	.114	-1	113	7		0.5
1943	Pit N	9	13	.409	42	18	4-1	4	147	165	86	10	2	47	63	3.98	87	.286	.342	40-0-2	.175	-1	80	-10		-1.5
1946	Pit N	0	0	—	7	0	0	0	12.2	12	10	0	0	11	4	3.55	99	.255	.397	3	.000	-0		-2		-0.1
Total	4	15	19	.441	79	33	12-4	6	285	275	146	12	4	107	123	3.38	102	.254	.323	82-1-4	.146	-2	96	-4		-1.0

GORSICA, JOHNNY John Joseph Perry (b John Joseph Perry Gorczyca) B3.29.1915 Bayonne NJ D12.16.1998 Charlottesville VA BR/TR/6-2/180 d4.22 Mil 1945-46 Col West Virginia

1940	†Det A	7	7	.500	29	20	5-2	0	160	170	85	10	4	57	68	4.33	110	.272	.337	62-1-1	.194	0	102	9		0.9
1941	Det A	9	11	.450	33	21	8-1	2	171	193	98	14	2	55	59	4.47	102	.281	.336	57-0-3	.298	4	75	1		0.7
1942	Det A	3	2	.600	28	0	0	4	53	63	31	2	3	26	19	4.75	83	.310	.397	10-0-1	.100	-0*		-3		-0.2
1943	Det A	4	5	.444	35	4	1	5	96.1	88	43	3	2	40	45	3.36	105	.247	.327	23-0-2	.174	0*	84	1		0.3
1944	Det A	6	14	.300	34	19	8-1	4	162	192	88	5	4	32	47	4.11	87	.296	.333	52	.135	-1*	88	-9		-1.0
1946	Det A	0	0	—	14	0	0	1	23.2	28	13	5	0	11	14	4.56	80	.301	.375	3	.667	1		-2		0.0
1947	Det A	2	0	1.000	31	0	0	1	57.2	44	27	5	2	26	20	3.75	101	.208	.300	10	.200	0	0	0		0.0
Total	7	31	39	.443	204	64	22-4	17	723.2	778	385	44	17	247	272	4.18	98	.276	.338	217-1-7	.207	4	91	-3		0.8

GORZELANNY, TOM Thomas Stephen B7.12.1982 Evergreen Park IL BL/TL/6-2/205 d9.20 Col Triton (IL) JC

2005	Pit N	0	1	.000	3	1	0	0-0	6	10	8	1	0	3-0	3	12.00	35	.357	.419	1-0-1	.000	-0	88	-5		-0.6

GOSLING, MIKE Michael F. B9.23.1980 Madison WI BL/TL/6-2/210* [AriN01 2/66] d9.9 Col Stanford

2004	Ari N	1	1	.500	6	4	0	0-0	25.1	26	13	5	2	13-1	14	4.62	99	.274	.373	6-0-1	.000	-0	71	1		0.0
2005	Ari N	0	3	.000	13	5	0	0-0	32.1	40	20	2	0	19-2	14	4.45	99	.301	.388	6-0-1	.000	-1	93	-1		-0.2
Total	2	1	4	.200	19	9	0	0	57.2	66	33	7	2	32-3	28	4.53	99	.289	.382	12-0-2	.000	-1	83	0		-0.2

GOSSAGE, RICH Richard Michael "Goose" B7.5.1951 Colorado Springs CO BR/TR/6-3/217(180-226) [ChiA70 9/204] d4.16

1972	Chi A	7	1	.875	36	1	0	2-0	80	72	44	2	4	44-3	57	4.27	73	.247	.351	16-0-1	.000	-2	57	-11		-1.4
1973	Chi A	0	4	.000	20	4	1	0-0	49.2	57	44	9	3	37-2	33	7.43	53	.311	.427	0	—	0*	23	-18		-1.3
1974	Chi A	4	6	.400	39	3	0	1-1	89.1	92	45	4	2	47-7	64	4.13	91	.272	.361	0	—	0	78	-3		-0.3
1975	Chi A★	9	8	.529	62	0	0	26-5	141.2	99	32	3	5	70-15	130	1.84	211	.201	.306	0	—	0		31		5.1
1976	Chi A☆	9	17	.346	31	29	15	1-1	224	214	104	16	9	90-3	135	3.94	91	.254	.330	0	—	0	75	-8		-0.9
1977	Pit N★	11	9	.550	72	0	0	26-10	133	78	27	9	2	49-6	151	1.62	248	.170	.250	23-0-1	.217	1		34		6.4
1978	†NY A★	10	11	.476	63	0	0	27-10	134.1	87	41	9	2	59-8	122	2.01	182	.187	.277	0	—	0		22		4.3
1979	NY A	5	3	.625	36	0	0	18-3	58.1	48	18	5	0	19-4	41	2.62	157	.227	.291	0	—	0	10	79		1.9
1980	†NY A★	6	2	.750	64	0	0	33-4	99	74	29	5	1	37-3	103	2.27	174	.211	.285	0	—	0	19	24		3.0
1981	†NY A★	3	2	.600	32	0	0	20-3	46.2	22	6	2	1	14-1	48	0.77	469	.141	.215	0	—	0	14			3.0
1982	NY A☆	4	5	.444	56	0	0	30-9	93	63	23	5	0	28-5	102	2.23	181	.196	.259	0	—	0	20			3.2
1983	NY A	13	5	.722	57	0	0	22-13	87.1	82	27	5	1	25-5	90	2.27	174	.248	.298	0	—	0	16			3.1
1984	†SD N★	10	6	.625	62	0	0	25-11	102.1	75	34	6	1	36-4	84	2.90	124	.204	.275	22-0-2	.182	0	9			1.8
1985	SD N★	5	3	.625	62	0	0	26-6	79	64	21	1	1	17-1	52	1.82	195	.226	.269	11	.000	-1	14	24		2.2
1986	SD N	5	7	.417	45	0	0	21-11	64.2	69	36	8	2	20-0	63	4.45	82	.273	.326	7	.000	-1	-6			-0.1
1987	SD N	5	4	.556	40	0	0	11-6	52	47	18	4	0	19-6	44	3.12	127	.244	.307	4	.000	-0	6	19		1.1
1988	Chi N	4	4	.500	46	0	0	13-10	43.2	50	23	3	3	15-5	30	4.33	84	.291	.356	1	.000	-0	-3	15		-0.7
1989	SF N	2	1	.667	31	0	0	4-1	43.2	32	16	2	0	27-3	24	2.68	126	.212	.328	1	.000	-0	3			0.3
	NY A	1	0	1.000	11	0	0	1-0	14.1	14	6	0	1	3-1	6	3.77	103	.275	.327	0	—	0	0			0.0
1991	Tex A	4	2	.667	44	0	0	1-4	40.1	33	16	4	3	16-1	28	3.57	113	.228	.317	0	—	0	4	51		0.2
1992	Oak A	0	2	.000	30	0	0	0-1	38	32	13	5	2	19-4	26	2.84	133	.230	.327	0	—	0	1	78		0.2
1993	Oak A	4	5	.444	39	0	0	1-3	47.2	49	24	6	1	26-2	40	4.53	91	.266	.357	0	—	0	-1	26		-0.3
1994	Sea A	3	0	1.000	36	0	0	1-0	47.1	44	23	6	3	15-1	29	4.18	118	.251	.318	0	—	0	5			0.2
Total	22	124	107	.537	1002	37	16	310-112	1809.1	1497	670	119	47	732-90	1502	3.01	126	.228	.308	85-0-4	.106	-3	66	160	292	29.7

GOTT, JIM James William B8.3.1959 Hollywood CA BR/TR/6-4/220(200-230) [StLN77 4/84] d4.9

1982	Tor A	5	10	.333	30	23	1-1	0-0	136	134	76	15	3	66-0	82	4.43	102	.255	.340	0	—	0	64	0		0.0
1983	Tor A	9	14	.391	34	30	6-1	0-1	176.2	195	103	15	5	68-5	121	4.74	92	.280	.347	0	—	0	97	-7		-0.9
1984	Tor A	7	6	.538	35	12	1-1	2-3	109.2	93	54	7	3	49-3	73	4.02	103	.233	.317	0	—	0	97	-7		0.1
1985	SF N	7	10	.412	26	26	2	0-0	148.1	144	73	10	1	51-3	78	3.88	89	.254	.315	51-3-4	.196	4	97	-7		-0.2
1986	SF N	0	0	—	9	2	0	1-0	13	16	12	0	1	13-2	9	7.62	46	.314	.446	3	.000	-0	177	-6	150	-0.2
1987	SF N	1	0	1.000	30	3	0	0-1	56	53	32	4	2	32-5	63	4.50	86	.244	.345	10-1-0	.100	1	165	-5		-0.2
	Pit N	0	2	.000	25	0	0	13-3	31	28	11	0	0	8-2	27	1.45	287	.233	.281	1	.000	-0		7		0.9
	Year	1	2	.333	55	3	0	13-4	87	81	43	4	2	40-7	90	3.41	116	.240	.324	11-1-0	.091	1	160	3		0.7
1988	Pit N	6	6	.500	67	0	0	34-6	77.1	68	30	9	2	22-5	76	3.49	99	.243	.300	1	.000	-0	1			0.2
1989	Pit N	0	0	—	1	0	0	0-0	0.2	1	0	0	0	1-0	1	0.00	—	.333	.500	0	—	0		0	178	0.0
1990	LA N	3	5	.375	50	0	0	3-2	62	59	27	5	0	34-7	44	2.90	127	.257	.347	1	.000	-0	4	46		0.4
1991	LA N	4	3	.571	55	0	0	2-3	76	63	28	5	1	32-7	73	2.96	122	.223	.304	2-0-1	.500	1	6			0.6
1992	LA N	3	3	.500	68	0	0	6-5	88	72	27	4	5	41-13	75	2.45	141	.225	.314	4	.500	1	10			2.8
1993	LA N	4	8	.333	62	0	0	25-4	77.2	71	23	6	1	17-5	67	2.32	167	.248	.291	1	.000	-0	14			1.4
1994	LA N	5	3	.625	37	0	0	2-5	36.1	46	24	3	3	20-4	29	5.94	67	.322	.413	0	—	-0	-7	35		-1.4
1995	Pit N	2	4	.333	25	0	0	3-0	31.1	38	26	2	1	12-2	19	6.03	72	.288	.349	1	.000	-0	-7	91		-1.2
Total	14	56	74	.431	554	96	10-3	91-29	1120	1081	546	85	23	466-63	837	3.87	101	.254	.329	73-4-5	.178	5	96	4	500	1.7

GOULAIT, TED Theodore Lee B8.12.1889 St.Clair MI D7.15.1936 St.Clair MI BR/TR/5-9.5/172 d9.28

1912	NY N	0	0	—	1	1	1	0	4	7	5	1	0	2-0	1	6.43	53	.367	.441	2-0-1	.500	1	130	-2		-0.1

GOULD, AL Albert Frank "Pudgy" B1.20.1893 Muscatine IA D8.8.1982 San Jose CA BR/TR/5-6.5/160 d7.11

1916	Cle A	5	6	.455	30	9	6-1	1	106.2	101	37	0	3	40	41	2.53	119	.256	.329	29-0-3	.103	-2	112	6		0.4
1917	Cle A	4	4	.500	27	7	1	0	94	95	44	1	3	52	24	3.64	78	.281	.382	24-0-1	.208	1	109	-5		-0.3
Total	2	9	10	.474	57	16	7-1	1	200.2	196	81	1	6	92	65	3.05	96	.267	.354	53-0-4	.151	-1	111	1		0.1

GOWELL, LARRY Lawrence Clyde B5.2.1948 Lewiston ME BR/TR/6-2/190 [NYA67 4/61] d9.21

1972	NY A	1	0	1.000	1	1	0	0-0	7	1	1	0	0	2-0	7	1.29	233	.143	.208	1	1.000	1	0	1		0.3

GOZZO, MAURO Mauro Paul B3.7.1966 New Britain CT BR/TR/6-3/212* [NYN84 13/315] d8.8

1989	Tor A	4	1	.800	9	3	0	0-1	31.2	35	19	1	1	9-1	10	4.83	79	.289	.338	0	—	0	159	-4		-0.5
1990	Cle A	0	0	—	2	0	0	0-0	3	2	0	0	0	2-0	2	0.00	—	.182	.308	0	—	0		1		0.1
1991	Cle A	0	0	—	2	0	0	0-0	4.2	9	10	0	0	7-0	3	19.29	22	.450	.571	0	—	0	164	-7		-0.3
1992	Min A	0	0	—	2	0	0	0-0	1.2	7	5	2	0	0-0	1	27.00	15	.583	.583	0	—	0		-4		-0.2
1993	NY N	0	1	.000	10	0	0	1-0	14	11	5	1	0	5-1	6	2.57	156	.212	.281	0	—	0		2		0.1
1994	NY N	3	5	.375	23	8	0	0-1	69	86	48	5	1	28-10	33	4.83	87	.304	.363	16-0-1	.250	1	120	-8		-0.2
Total	6	7	7	.500	48	13	0	1-2	124	150	87	9	2	51-12	55	5.30	76	.301	.363	16-0-1	.250	1	136	-20		-1.5

GRABOW, JOHN John William B11.4.1978 Arcadia CA BL/TL/6-2/190(190-210) [PitN97 3/92] d9.14

2003	Pit N	0	0	—	5	0	0	0-0	5	6	3	0	0	0-0	9	3.60	120	.273	.273	0	—	0	0	0		0.0
2004	Pit N	2	5	.286	68	0	0	1-6	61.2	81	39	8	0	28-7	64	5.11	85	.323	.389	1	.000	-0		-6		-0.1
2005	Pit N	2	3	.400	63	0	0	0-1	52	46	31	6	2	25-2	42	4.85	87	.238	.332	0	—	-0		-4		-0.8
Total	4	4	8	.333	136	0	0	1-7	118.2	133	73	14	2	53-9	115	4.93	87	.285	.360	1	.000	-0		-10		-0.8

GRABOWSKI, AL Alfons Francis B9.4.1901 Syracuse NY D10.29.1966 Memphis NY BL/TL/5-11.5/175 d9.11 b-Reggie

1929	StL N	3	2	.600	6	6	4-2	0	50	44	18	0	0	8	22	2.52	185	.227	.257	16-0-1	.250	2	97	11		1.2
1930	StL N	6	4	.600	33	8	1	1	107	120	66	7	3	49	43	4.79	105	.290	.369	33	.364	3*	122	3		0.4
Total	2	9	6	.600	39	14	5-2	1	157	164	84	7	3	57	65	4.07	120	.270	.335	49-0-1	.327	4	111	14		1.6

YEAR	TM LG	W	L	PCT	G	GS	CG-SHO	SV-BS	IP	H	R	HR	HB	BB-IB	SO	ERA	AERA	OAV	OOB	AB-HR-SH	AVG	PB	SUP	APR	DL	PW
GRABOWSKI, REGGIE	Reginald John B7.16.1907 Syracuse NY D4.2.1955 Syracuse NY BR/TR/6-0.5/185 d4.15 b-Al																							
1932	Phi N	2	2	.500	14	2	0	0	34.1	38	18	2	2	22	15	3.67	120	.273	.380	6-0-1	.000	-1	95	2		0.1
1933	Phi N	1	3	.250	10	5	4-1	0	48	38	13	4	1	10	9	2.44	157	.220	.266	16	.125	-1	52	7		0.5
1934	Phi N	1	3	.250	27	5	0	0	65.1	114	72	13	3	23	13	9.23	51	.384	.433	18-0-1	.056	-2	88	-26		-1.6
Total 3		4	8	.333	51	12	4-1	0	147.2	190	103	19	6	55	37	5.73	76	.312	.375	40-0-2	.075	-3	75	-17		-1.0
GRACE, MIKE	Michael James B6.20.1970 Joliet IL BR/TR/6-4/222(210-224) [PhiN91 10/265] d9.1 Col Bradley																							
1995	Phi N	1	1	.500	2	2	0	0-0	11.1	10	4	1	0	4-0	7	3.18	133	.238	.304	2-0-2	.000	-0	43	1		0.2
1996	Phi N	7	2	.778	12	12	1-1	0-0	80	72	33	9	1	16-1	49	3.49	124	.238	.279	29-0-1	.138	-0	101	8	119	0.9
1997	Phi N	3	2	.600	6	6	1-1	0-0	39	32	16	3	1	10-1	26	3.46	122	.230	.285	12	.083	-1	95	3	85	0.3
1998	Phi N	4	7	.364	21	15	0	0-0	90.1	116	61	10	8	30-1	46	5.48	79	.312	.375	23-0-3	.087	-1	108	-12		-1.4
1999	Phi N	1	4	.200	27	5	0	0-0	55	80	48	5	6	30-0	28	7.69	61	.346	.430	7-0-3	.000	-1	63	-17		-1.3
Total 5		16	16	.500	68	40	2-2	0-0	275.2	310	162	27	16	90-3	156	4.96	88	.285	.348	73-0-9	.096	-2	94	-17	204	-1.3
GRACESQUI, FRANKLYN	Franklyn Benjamin B8.20.1979 Santo Domingo, D.R. BB/TL/6-5/210 [TorA98 21/621] d4.29																							
2004	Fla N	0	1	.000	7	0	0	1-0	4	6	5	0	2	3-0	1	11.25	37	.333	.478	0	—	0		-3		-0.6
GRAFF, JOHN	John J. B11.1866 Washington DC D4.2.1932 Washington DC d7.19																							
1893	Was N	0	1	.000	2	1	1	0	12	21	21	2	1	13	4	11.25	41	.368	.493	5	.200	-0	60	-9		-0.5
GRAHAM, SKINNY	Kyle B8.14.1899 Oak Grove AL D12.1.1973 Oak Grove AL BR/TR/6-2/172 d9.3																							
1924	Bos N	0	4	.000	5	4	0	0	33	33	14	0	0	11	15	3.82	100	.287	.349	7-0-2	.000	-1	17	1		0.0
1925	Bos N	7	12	.368	34	23	5	1	157	177	90	6	3	62	32	4.41	91	.296	.365	44-0-7	.136	-2	81	-6		-0.9
1926	Bos N	3	3	.500	15	4	1	0	36.1	54	32	3	2	19	7	7.93	45	.370	.449	12	.167	-1	153	-16		-2.3
1929	Det A	1	3	.250	13	6	2	1	51.2	70	41	2	3	33	7	5.57	77	.340	.438	19-1-0	.105	-1	183	-8		-0.7
Total 4		11	22	.333	67	37	9	2	278	334	177	11	8	125	61	5.02	79	.314	.390	82-1-9	.122	-5	100	-29		-3.9
GRAHAM, OSCAR	Oscar M. B7.20.1878 Plattsmouth NE D10.15.1931 Moline IL BL/TL/6-0.5/180 d4.16																							
1907	Was A	4	9	.308	20	14	6	0	104	116	66	3	10	29	44	3.98	61	.284	.347	48-1-1	.229	3*	128	-18		-1.8
GRAHAM, BILL	William Albert B1.21.1937 Flemingsburg KY BR/TR/6-3/217* d10.2 Col Florida																							
1966	Det A	0	0	—	1	0	0	0	2	2	0	0	0	0-0	2	0.00	—	.250	.250	0	—	0		1		0.0
1967	NY N	1	2	.333	5	3	1	0	27.1	20	10	3	0	11-0	14	2.63	129	.200	.279	8	.125	-0	43	2		0.1
Total 2		1	2	.333	6	3	1	0	29.1	22	10	3	0	11-0	16	2.45	138	.204	.277	8	.125	-0	43	3		0.1
GRAHAME, BILL	William James B7.22.1884 Owosso MI D2.15.1936 Holt MI TL/6-0/? d4.18																							
1908	StL A	6	7	.462	21	13	7	0	117.1	104	46	0	12	32	47	2.30	104	.240	.310	42-0-2	.119	-3	83	0		-0.3
1909	StL A	8	14	.364	34	21	13-3	1	187.1	171	78	3	5	60	82	3.12	77	.256	.322	63	.159	-0	86	-12		-1.4
1910	StL A	0	8	.000	9	6	1	0	43	46	31	2	4	13	12	3.56	70	.297	.366	13	.154	-0	41	-7		-1.3
Total 3		14	29	.326	64	40	21-3	1	347.2	321	155	5	21	105	141	2.90	83	.256	.323	118-0-2	.144	-3	78	-19		-3.0
GRAHE, JOE	Joseph Milton B8.14.1967 W.Palm Beach FL BR/TR/6-0/200(185-200) [CalA89 2/39] d8.4 Col Miami																							
1990	Cal A	3	4	.429	8	8	0	0-0	43.1	51	30	3	3	23-1	25	4.98	77	.293	.385	0	—	0	101	-7		-0.9
1991	Cal A	3	7	.300	18	10	1	0-0	73	84	43	2	3	33-0	40	4.81	86	.288	.365	0	—	0	64	-6		-0.7
1992	Cal A	5	6	.455	46	7	0	21-3	94.2	85	37	5	6	39-2	39	3.52	114	.246	.329	0	—	0	107	7		1.0
1993	Cal A	4	1	.800	45	0	0	11-2	56.2	54	22	5	2	25-4	31	2.86	159	.251	.331	0	—	0	9		40	1.1
1994	Cal A	2	5	.286	40	0	0	13-6	43.1	68	33	5	6	18-4	26	6.65	74	.362	.428	0	—	0		-8		-1.4
1995	Col N	4	3	.571	17	9	0	0-0	56.2	69	42	6	3	27-2	27	5.08	106	.301	.378	12-0-6	.417	1	99	-1	45	0.0
1999	Phi N	1	4	.200	13	5	0	0-0	32.2	40	16	1	3	17-0	16	3.86	121	.308	.392	7	.143	0	43	2		0.3
Total 7		22	30	.423	187	39	1	45-11	400.1	451	223	27	26	182-13	204	4.41	101	.287	.366	19-0-6	.316	1	85	-4	85	-0.6
GRAMAN, ALEX	Alex Joseph B11.17.1977 Huntingburg IN BL/TL/6-4/210* [NYA99 3/111] d4.20 Col Indiana St.																							
2004	NY A	0	0	—	3	2	0	0-0	5	14	11	1	0	2-0	4	19.80	23	.500	.516	0	—	0	182	-8		-0.4
2005	NY A	0	0	—	2	0	0	0-0	1.1	3	2	1	0	2-1	0	13.50	32	.429	.556	0	—	0		-1		-0.1
Total 2		0	0	—	5	2	0	0-0	6.1	17	13	2	0	4-1	4	18.47	25	.486	.525	0	—	0	182	-9		-0.5
GRAMLY, TOMMY	Bert Thomas B4.19.1945 Dallas TX BR/TR/6-3/175 [CleA66 S4/75] d4.18 Col TCU																							
1968	Cle A	0	1	.000	3	0	0	0	3.1	3	1	0	0	2-2	1	2.70	110	.250	.357	0	—	0*		0		0.0
GRAMPP, HANK	Henry Erchardt B9.28.1903 New York NY D3.24.1986 New York NY BR/TR/6-1/185 d6.21																							
1927	Chi N	0	0	—	2	0	0	0	3	4	3	0	0	1	3	9.00	43	.333	.385	0	—	0		-2		-0.1
1929	Chi N	0	1	.000	1	1	0	0	2	4	6	0	1	3	0	27.00	17	.500	.667	0	—	0	57	-5		-0.6
Total 2		0	1	.000	3	1	0	0	5	8	9	0	1	4	3	16.20	26	.400	.520	0	—	0	57	-7		-0.7
GRANGER, JEFF	Jeffrey Adam B12.16.1971 San Pedro CA BR/TL/6-4/200* [KCA93 1/5] d9.16 Col Texas A&M-Commerce																							
1993	KC A	0	0	—	1	0	0	0-0	1	3	3	0	0	2-0	1	27.00	17	.500	.625	0	—	0		-2		-0.1
1994	KC A	0	1	.000	2	2	0	0-0	9.1	13	8	2	0	6-0	3	6.75	74	.325	.404	0	—	0	73	-2		-0.2
1996	KC A	0	0	—	15	0	0	0-0	16.1	21	13	3	2	10-0	11	6.61	76	.313	.412	0	—	0		-3		-0.1
1997	Pit N	0	0	—	9	0	0	0-0	5	10	10	3	0	8-1	4	18.00	24	.417	.563	0	—	0		-7		-0.3
Total 4		0	1	.000	27	2	0	0-0	31.2	47	34	8	2	26-1	19	9.09	54	.343	.449	0	—	0	73	-14		-0.7
GRANGER, WAYNE	Wayne Allan B3.15.1944 Springfield MA BR/TR/6-2/165* d6.5 Col Springfield																							
1968	†StL N	4	2	.667	34	0	0	4	44	40	14	2	4	12-3	27	2.25	129	.238	.297	5	.200	0		3		0.5
1969	Cin N	9	6	.600	90	0	0	27-10	144.2	143	64	10	7	40-14	68	2.80	134	.262	.316	21-0-3	.095	-0		10		1.4
1970	†Cin N	6	5	.545	67	0	0	35-4	84.2	79	33	5	1	27-8	38	2.66	152	.252	.311	10	.100	-1		11		2.3
1971	Cin N	7	6	.538	70	0	0	11-0	100	94	39	8	1	28-7	51	3.33	101	.251	.303	7-1-1	.143	1		1		0.4
1972	Min A	4	6	.400	63	0	0	19-6	89.2	83	42	7	2	28-6	45	3.01	107	.243	.303	10	.200	0		0		-0.1
1973	StL N	2	4	.333	33	0	0	5-4	46.2	50	29	3	2	21-7	14	4.24	87	.284	.363	3	.000	-0		-5		-0.7
	NY A	0	1	.000	7	0	0	0-0	15.1	19	7	1	1	3-1	10	1.76	211	.279	.319	0	—	0		2		0.1
1974	Chi A	0	0	—	5	0	0	0-0	7.2	16	8	1	0	3-0	4	8.22	44	.432	.475	0	—	0		-4		-0.2
1975	Hou N	2	5	.286	55	0	0	5-3	74	76	39	7	4	23-7	30	3.65	93	.264	.324	9	.000	-1		-5		-0.6
1976	Mon N	1	0	1.000	27	0	0	2-2	32	32	15	3	2	16-4	16	3.66	103	.264	.355	3-0-2	.000	-0		0		0.0
Total 9		35	35	.500	451	0	0	108-29	638.2	632	290	47	22	201-57	303	3.14	113	.260	.319	68-1-6	.103	-1		13		3.1
GRANT, GEORGE	George Addison B1.6.1903 E.Tallassee AL D3.25.1986 Montgomery AL BR/TR/5-11.5/175 d9.17 Col Auburn-Montgomery																							
1923	StL A	0	0	—	4	0	0	0	8.2	15	7	0	0	3	2	5.19	80	.395	.439	2	.000	-0		-1		-0.1
1924	StL A	1	2	.333	22	2	0	0	51.1	69	43	4	1	25	11	6.31	72	.325	.399	13	.000	-2	75	-10		0.7
1925	StL A	0	2	.000	12	0	0	0	16.1	26	15	2	0	8	7	6.06	77	.400	.466	4	.250	-0		-3		-0.3
1927	Cle A	4	6	.400	25	3	2	1	74.2	85	46	1	0	40	19	4.46	94	.300	.387	21-0-2	.095	-2	146	-3		-0.5
1928	Cle A	10	8	.556	28	18	6-1	0	155.1	196	102	7	2	76	39	5.04	82	.319	.395	60-0-2	.183	-2*	91	-14		-1.4
1929	Cle A	0	2	.000	12	0	0	0	24	41	29	2	0	23	5	10.50	42	.414	.525	2	.000	-0		-14		-0.9
1931	Pit N	0	0	—	11	0	0	1	17	28	16	0	1	7	6	7.41	52	.364	.424	2	.000	-0		-6		-0.3
Total 7		15	20	.429	114	23	8-1	1	347.1	460	258	16	4	182	89	5.65	75	.331	.410	104-0-4	.135	-8	95	-51		-4.2
GRANT, JIM	James Ronald B8.4.1894 Coalville IA D11.30.1985 Des Moines IA BR/TL/5-11/180 d4.21																							
1923	Phi N	0	0	—	2	0	0	0	4	10	8	0	1	4	0	13.50	34	.588	.682	1	.000	-0		-4		-0.2
GRANT, MUDCAT	James Timothy "Jim" B8.13.1935 Lacoochee FL BR/TR/6-1/186(184-195) d4.17																							
1958	Cle A	10	11	.476	44	28	11-1	4	204	173	93	20	1	104-5	111	3.84	95	.228	.317	66-0-4	.076	-4*	106	-3		-0.8
1959	Cle A	10	7	.588	38	19	6-1	3	165.1	140	80	23	2	81-4	85	4.14	89	.232	.323	55-1-1	.200	1*	100	-6		-0.5
1960	Cle A	9	8	.529	33	19	5	0	159.2	147	88	26	2	78-4	75	4.40	85	.243	.330	57-0-1	.281	4*	133	-12		-0.8
1961	Cle A	15	9	.625	35	35	11-3	0	244.2	207	118	32	3	109-3	146	3.86	102	.227	.310	88-1-5	.170	1*	123	2		0.3
1962	Cle A	7	10	.412	26	23	6-1	0	149.2	128	75	24	0	81-4	90	4.27	91	.233	.330	53-0-1	.151	-0*	99	-5		-0.5
1963	Cle A☆	13	14	.481	38	32	10-2	1	229.1	213	107	30	4	87-3	157	3.69	98	.243	.312	69-1-7	.188	3*	100	-2		-0.1
1964	Cle A	3	4	.429	38	12	0	1	62	82	41	11	1	25-2	43	5.95	60	.324	.384	22-2-1	.273	4*	112	-14		-1.0
	Min A	11	9	.550	26	23	10-1	1	166	162	73	21	0	36-2	75	2.82	127	.248	.286	60-0-2	.167	0*	139	9		1.0
	Year	14	13	.519	39	32	11-1	1	228	244	114	32	1	61-4	118	3.67	98	.270	.314	82-2-3	.195	4*	132	-5		0.0
1965	†Min A★	21	7	.750	41	39	14-6	1	270.1	252	99	34	2	61-2	142	3.30	108	.247	.287	97-0-5	.155	2*	135	12		1.4

YEAR	TM LG	W	L	PCT	G	GS	CG-SHO	SV-BS	IP	H	R	HR	HB	BB-IB	SO	ERA	AERA	OAV	OOB	AB-HR-SH	AVG	PB	SUP	APR	DL	PW
1966	Min A	13	13	.500	35	35	10-3	0	249	248	104	23	6	49-2	110	3.25	111	.260	.298	78-0-10	.192	2	96	9		1.3
1967	Min A	5	6	.455	27	14	2	0	95.1	121	56	10	1	17-0	50	4.72	73	.315	.343	28-0-2	.179	-1	131	-12		-1.4
1968	LA N	6	4	.600	37	4	1	3	95	77	29	1	6	14-1	35	2.08	133	.226	.275	31-1-0	.129	0*	94	6		0.8
1969	Mon N	1	6	.143	11	10	1	0-0	50.2	64	33	7	1	14-1	20	4.80	77	.299	.343	16	.125	-1	91	-7		-0.9
	StL N	7	5	.583	30	3	1	7-2	63.1	62	31	9	2	22-8	35	4.12	87	.252	.319	17-0-2	.294	2*	82	-3		-0.5
	Year	8	11	.421	41	13	2	7-2	114	126	64	16	3	36-9	55	4.42	82	.274	.330	33-0-2	.212	1	90	-10		-1.4
1970	Oak A	6	2	.750	72	0	0	24-1	123.1	104	26	8	3	30-8	54	1.82	193	.235	.287	9-0-5	.222	2		26		2.8
	Pit N	2	1	.667	8	0	0	0-1	12	8	3	2	0	2-0	4	2.25	176	.190	.227	2	.000	-0		2		0.5
1971	Pit N	5	3	.625	42	0	0	7-4	75	79	32	8	1	28-8	22	3.60	94	.274	.340	8	.250	1		-1		0.0
	†Oak A	1	0	1.000	15	0	0	3-1	27.1	25	9	3	0	6-0	13	1.98	168	.243	.284	3-0-2	.333	0		3		0.2
Total	14	145	119	.549	571	293	89-18	53-9	2442	2292	1105	292	33	849-59	1267	3.63	100	.248	.311	759-6-48	.178	16	115	4		1.8

GRANT, MARK Mark Andrew B10.24.1963 Aurora IL BR/TR/6-2/205(195-215) [SFN81 1/10] d4.27 [DL 1991 Atl N 182]

YEAR	TM LG	W	L	PCT	G	GS	CG-SHO	SV-BS	IP	H	R	HR	HB	BB-IB	SO	ERA	AERA	OAV	OOB	AB-HR-SH	AVG	PB	SUP	APR	DL	PW
1984	SF N	1	4	.200	11	10	0	1-0	53.2	56	40	6	1	19-0	32	6.37	55	.272	.332	17-0-2	.000	-2	110	-16	19	-1.5
1986	SF N	0	1	.000	4	1	0	0-0	10	6	4	0	0	5-0	5	3.60	98	.176	.282	1-0-1	.000	-0	25	0		0.0
1987	SF N	1	2	.333	16	8	0	1-0	61	66	29	6	1	21-5	32	3.54	109	.282	.342	12-0-3	.083	-0	94	1		0.0
	SD N	6	7	.462	17	17	2-1	0-0	102.1	104	59	16	0	52-3	58	4.66	85	.263	.348	32-0-3	.094	-1*	87	-8		-1.0
	Year	7	9	.438	33	25	2-1	1-0	163.1	170	88	22	1	73-8	90	4.24	92	.270	.346	44-0-6	.091	-1	89	-7		-1.0
1988	SD N	2	8	.200	33	11	0	0-1	97.2	97	41	14	2	36-6	61	3.69	92	.268	.334	16-0-4	.000	-1	62	-2		-0.3
1989	SD N	8	2	.800	50	0	0	2-1	116.1	105	45	11	3	32-6	69	3.33	105	.248	.304	20-0-1	.050	-0		4		0.3
1990	SD N	1	1	.500	26	0	0	0-1	39	47	23	5	0	19-8	29	4.85	79	.305	.375	2	.500	0		-4		-0.1
	Atl N	1	2	.333	33	1	0	3-2	52.1	61	30	4	1	18-3	40	4.64	87	.293	.349	4	.250	1	90	-3		-0.2
	Year	2	3	.400	59	1	0	3-3	91.1	108	53	9	1	37-11	69	4.73	84	.298	.360	6	.333	1	91	-7		-0.3
1992	Sea A	2	4	.333	23	10	0	0-0	81	100	39	6	2	22-2	42	3.89	103	.311	.357	0	—	0	103	-1		0.0
1993	Hou N	0	0	—	6	0	0	0-0	11	11	4	0	0	5-2	6	0.82	474	.275	.348	0	—	0		3		0.2
	Col N	0	1	.000	14	0	0	1-1	14.1	23	20	4	0	6-1	8	12.56	38	.377	.426	0	—	0		-10	34	-0.7
	Year	0	1	.000	20	0	0	1-1	25.1	34	24	4	0	11-3	14	7.46	59	.337	.395	0	—	0		-8		-0.5
Total	8	22	32	.407	233	58	2-1	8-6	638.2	676	334	72	10	235-36	382	4.31	87	.277	.341	104-0-14	.067	-3	89	-34	235	-3.3

GRAPENTHIN, RICK Richard Ray B4.16.1958 Linn Grove IA BR/TR/6-2/205(190-210) d5.3 Col Indiana St.

YEAR	TM LG	W	L	PCT	G	GS	CG-SHO	SV-BS	IP	H	R	HR	HB	BB-IB	SO	ERA	AERA	OAV	OOB	AB-HR-SH	AVG	PB	SUP	APR	DL	PW
1983	Mon N	0	1	.000	4	0	0	0-0	4	4	3	0	0	1-0	3	9.00	40	.267	.313	1	.000	-0		-2		-0.4
1984	Mon N	1	2	.333	13	1	0	2-0	23	19	9	3	0	7-0	9	3.52	98	.235	.289	5	.200	0	77	0		0.1
1985	Mon N	0	0	—	5	0	0	0-0	7	13	11	0	1	8-2	4	14.14	24	.394	.512	1	1.000	0		-8		-0.4
Total	3	1	3	.250	19	1	0	2-0	34	36	24	5	1	16-2	16	6.35	55	.279	.356	7	.286	0	77	-10		-0.7

GRASMICK, LOU Louis Junior B9.11.1924 Baltimore MD BR/TR/6-0/195 d4.22

YEAR	TM LG	W	L	PCT	G	GS	CG-SHO	SV-BS	IP	H	R	HR	HB	BB-IB	SO	ERA	AERA	OAV	OOB	AB-HR-SH	AVG	PB	SUP	APR	DL	PW
1948	Phi N	0	0	—	2	0	0	0	5	3	4	1	0	8	2	7.20	55	.176	.440	1	1.000	0		-2		0.0

GRATE, DON Donald "Buckeye" B8.27.1923 Greenfield OH BR/TR/6-2.5/180 d7.6 Col Ohio St.

YEAR	TM LG	W	L	PCT	G	GS	CG-SHO	SV-BS	IP	H	R	HR	HB	BB-IB	SO	ERA	AERA	OAV	OOB	AB-HR-SH	AVG	PB	SUP	APR	DL	PW
1945	Phi N	0	1	.000	4	2	0	0	8.1	18	16	0	0	12	6	17.28	22	.439	.566	3	.000	-0*	55	-11		-1.1
1946	Phi N	1	0	1.000	3	0	0	0	8	4	1	0	0	2	2	1.13	305	.160	.222	1	.000	0		2		0.3
Total	2	1	1	.500	7	2	0	0	16.1	22	17	0	0	14	8	9.37	39	.333	.450	4	.000	-0	55	-9		-0.8

GRATER, MARK Mark Anthony B1.19.1964 Rochester PA BR/TR/5-10/205* [StLN86 23/594] d6.12 Col Florida International

YEAR	TM LG	W	L	PCT	G	GS	CG-SHO	SV-BS	IP	H	R	HR	HB	BB-IB	SO	ERA	AERA	OAV	OOB	AB-HR-SH	AVG	PB	SUP	APR	DL	PW
1991	StL N	0	0	—	3	0	0	0-0	3	5	0	0	0	2-0	0	0.00	—	.385	.467	0	—	0		1		0.1
1993	Det A	0	0	—	6	0	0	0-0	5	6	3	0	0	4-1	4	5.40	81	.286	.400	0	—	0		0		0.0
Total	2	0	0	—	9	0	0	0-0	8	11	3	0	0	6-1	4	3.38	122	.324	.425	0	—	0		1		0.1

GRATEROL, BEIKER Beiker B11.9.1974 Lara, Venez BR/TR/6-2/165 d4.9

YEAR	TM LG	W	L	PCT	G	GS	CG-SHO	SV-BS	IP	H	R	HR	HB	BB-IB	SO	ERA	AERA	OAV	OOB	AB-HR-SH	AVG	PB	SUP	APR	DL	PW
1999	Det A	0	1	.000	1	1	0	0-0	4	4	7	3	0	4-1	2	15.75	32	.250	.400	0	—	0	56	-4		-0.6

GRAVES, DANNY Daniel Peter B8.7.1973 Saigon, South Vietnam BR/TR/5-11/185(185-200) [CleA94 4/101] d7.13 Col Miami

YEAR	TM LG	W	L	PCT	G	GS	CG-SHO	SV-BS	IP	H	R	HR	HB	BB-IB	SO	ERA	AERA	OAV	OOB	AB-HR-SH	AVG	PB	SUP	APR	DL	PW
1996	Cle A	2	0	1.000	15	0	0	0-1	29.2	29	18	2	0	10-0	22	4.55	107	.246	.302	0	—	0		0		0.0
1997	Cle A	0	0	—	5	0	0	0-0	11.1	15	8	2	0	9-0	4	4.76	99	.326	.429	1	.000	-0		-1		-0.1
	Cin N	0	0	—	10	0	0	0-0	14.2	24	14	0	0	11-1	7	6.14	70	.413	.493	1	.000	-0		-4		-0.2
1998	Cin N	2	1	.667	62	0	0	8-0	81.1	76	31	6	2	28-4	44	3.32	129	.251	.314	4	.000	-0		9		0.4
1999	Cin N	8	7	.533	75	0	0	27-9	111	90	42	10	2	49-4	69	3.08	152	.227	.314	5	.000	-1		19		3.1
2000	Cin N★	10	5	.667	66	0	0	30-5	91.1	81	31	8	3	42-7	53	2.56	186	.243	.330	2-1-0	.500	2		21		4.3
2001	Cin N	6	5	.545	66	0	0	32-7	80.1	83	41	7	4	18-6	49	4.15	111	.268	.314	4-1-0	.250	1		4		0.9
2002	Cin N	7	3	.700	68	4	0	32-7	98.2	99	37	7	3	25-9	58	3.19	134	.264	.311	6-0-2	.000	-1*	43	12		1.9
2003	Cin N	4	15	.211	30	26	2-1	2-0	169	204	108	30	7	41-6	60	5.33	78	.298	.343	54-0-3	.111	-2*	88	-22		-2.3
2004	Cin N☆	1	6	.143	68	0	0	41-9	68.1	77	39	12	2	13-6	40	3.95	109	.282	.317	0	—	0		0	15	-0.1
2005	Cin N	1	1	.500	20	0	0	10-2	18.1	30	18	4	0	12-3	8	7.36	57	.357	.433	0	—	0		-7		-1.4
	NY N	0	0	—	20	0	0	0-0	20.1	29	17	5	3	8-1	12	5.75	72	.337	.412	0	—	0		-5		-0.3
	Year	1	1	.500	40	0	0	10-2	38.2	59	35	9	3	20-4	20	6.52	64	.347	.423	0	—	0		-13		-1.7
Total	10	41	43	.488	505	30	2-1	182-40	794.1	804	404	93	26	266-47	426	4.02	110	.273	.334	76-2-5	.105	-2	77	26	15	6.2

GRAY, CHARLIE Charles A. B6.1864 Indianapolis IN D6.1.1900 Indianapolis IN d4.23

YEAR	TM LG	W	L	PCT	G	GS	CG-SHO	SV-BS	IP	H	R	HR	HB	BB-IB	SO	ERA	AERA	OAV	OOB	AB-HR-SH	AVG	PB	SUP	APR	DL	PW
1890	Pit N	1	4	.200	5	4	3	0	31	48	35	0	1	24	10	7.55	44	.343	.442	15	.200	-0	43	-14		-1.6

GRAY, DAVE David Alexander B1.7.1943 Ogden UT BR/TR/6-1/195 d6.14 Col Weber St.

YEAR	TM LG	W	L	PCT	G	GS	CG-SHO	SV-BS	IP	H	R	HR	HB	BB-IB	SO	ERA	AERA	OAV	OOB	AB-HR-SH	AVG	PB	SUP	APR	DL	PW
1964	Bos A	0	0	—	9	1	0	0	13	18	20	3	0	20-0	17	9.00	43	.321	.494	1	1.000	0	138	-9		-0.4

GRAY, CHUMMY George Edward B7.17.1873 Rockland ME D8.14.1913 Rockland ME TR/5-11.5/163 d9.14

YEAR	TM LG	W	L	PCT	G	GS	CG-SHO	SV-BS	IP	H	R	HR	HB	BB-IB	SO	ERA	AERA	OAV	OOB	AB-HR-SH	AVG	PB	SUP	APR	DL	PW
1899	Pit N	3	3	.500	9	7	6	0	70.2	85	35	1	4	24	9	3.44	111	.297	.360	26	.038	-3	81	4		0.1

GRAY, JEFF Jeffrey Edward B4.10.1963 Richmond VA BR/TR/6-1/185(175-190) d6.21 Col Florida St. [DL 1992 Bos A 182]

YEAR	TM LG	W	L	PCT	G	GS	CG-SHO	SV-BS	IP	H	R	HR	HB	BB-IB	SO	ERA	AERA	OAV	OOB	AB-HR-SH	AVG	PB	SUP	APR	DL	PW
1988	Cin N	0	0	—	5	0	0	0-0	9.1	12	4	0	0	4-2	5	3.86	93	.333	.381	1-0-1	.000	-0		0		0.0
1990	†Bos A	2	4	.333	41	0	0	9-3	50.2	53	27	3	1	15-3	50	4.44	92	.268	.321	0	—	0		-1		-0.2
1991	Bos A	2	3	.400	50	0	0	1-3	61.2	39	17	7	1	10-4	41	2.34	185	.181	.219	0	—	0	13		70	1.0
Total	3	4	7	.364	96	0	0	10-6	121.2	104	48	10	2	29-9	96	3.33	125	.231	.278	1-0-1	.000	-0	12		252	0.8

GRAY, JOHNNY John Leonard B12.11.1926 W.Palm Beach FL BR/TR/6-4/226* d7.18 Col Rollins

YEAR	TM LG	W	L	PCT	G	GS	CG-SHO	SV-BS	IP	H	R	HR	HB	BB-IB	SO	ERA	AERA	OAV	OOB	AB-HR-SH	AVG	PB	SUP	APR	DL	PW
1954	Phi A	3	12	.200	18	16	5	0	105	111	83	10	0	91	51	6.51	60	.273	.406	34-0-1	.029	-4*	66	-28		-3.7
1955	KC A	0	3	.000	8	5	0	0	26.2	28	23	2	1	24-0	11	6.41	65	.277	.417	8	.125	-0	85	-7		-0.8
1957	Cle A	1	3	.250	7	3	1-1	0	20	21	17	1	0	13-1	3	5.85	64	.288	.395	4-0-1	.000	-1	72	-6		-1.0
1958	Phi N	0	0	—	15	0	0	0	17.1	12	9	3	0	14-3	10	4.15	95	.222	.377	1	.000	-0		0		0.0
Total	4	4	18	.182	48	24	6-1	0	169	172	132	16	1	142-4	75	6.18	64	.271	.404	47-0-2	.043	-5	71	-41		-5.5

GRAY, DOLLY Samuel David "Sam" B10.15.1897 Van Alstyne TX D4.16.1953 McKinney TX BR/TR/5-11/175 d4.19

YEAR	TM LG	W	L	PCT	G	GS	CG-SHO	SV-BS	IP	H	R	HR	HB	BB-IB	SO	ERA	AERA	OAV	OOB	AB-HR-SH	AVG	PB	SUP	APR	DL	PW
1924	Phi A	8	7	.533	34	19	8-2	2	151.2	169	95	5	6	89	54	3.98	108	.284	.383	57	.175	-2	98	-1		-0.4
1925	Phi A	16	8	.667	32	28	14-4	3	203.2	199	90	11	3	63	80	3.27	142	.260	.319	67-0-2	.179	-2	106	29		2.7
1926	Phi A	11	12	.478	38	18	5	0	150.2	164	79	4	4	60	82	3.64	114	.279	.340	51-0-5	.216	1	97	7		1.0
1927	Phi A	9	6	.600	37	13	3-1	3	133.1	153	79	4	4	51	49	4.59	93	.295	.362	42-0-3	.190	-1	123	-4		-0.5
1928	StL A	20	12	.625	35	31	21-2	3	262.2	256	119	11	1	86	102	3.19	132	.260	.320	101-1-4	.188	-2	100	24		2.7
1929	StL A	18	15	.545	43	37	23-4	1	305	336	142	18	1	96	109	3.72	119	.285	.349	103-0-9	.184	-2	88	24		2.0
1930	StL A	4	15	.211	27	24	7	0	167.2	215	133	17	4	52	51	6.28	78	.316	.368	54-0-1	.204	-2	73	-25		-2.3
1931	StL A	11	24	.314	43	37	13	2	258	323	187	20	4	54	88	5.09	91	.297	.332	79-1-5	.177	-1	76	-17		-2.0
1932	StL A	7	18	.368	52	18	7-3	4	206.2	250	126	9	1	53	79	4.53	107	.294	.336	62-0-1	.210	-0	77	5		0.8
1933	StL A	7	4	.636	38	6	0	4	112	131	55	7	1	45	36	4.10	114	.301	.368	32-0-1	.219	-1	94	7		0.8
Total	10	111	115	.491	379	231	101-16	22	1951.1	2196	1107	111	29	639	730	4.18	108	.286	.343	648-2-31	.191	-10	91	49		4.4

GRAY, TED Ted Glenn B12.31.1924 Detroit MI BB/TL(BR 1946)/5-11/175(160-175) d5.15

YEAR	TM LG	W	L	PCT	G	GS	CG-SHO	SV-BS	IP	H	R	HR	HB	BB-IB	SO	ERA	AERA	OAV	OOB	AB-HR-SH	AVG	PB	SUP	APR	DL	PW
1946	Det A	0	2	.000	3	2	0	1	11.2	17	12	4	0	5	5	8.49	43	.340	.400	3	.000	-0	129	-6		-0.9
1948	Det A	6	2	.750	26	11	3-1	1	85.1	73	43	2	2	72	60	4.22	104	.236	.385	29-0-2	.241	1	117	3		0.2
1949	Det A	10	10	.500	34	27	8-3	1	195	163	83	11	5	103	96	3.51	119	.227	.328	63-0-3	.127	-3*	96	15		1.2
1950	Det A★	10	7	.588	27	21	7	1	149.1	139	85	22	2	72	102	4.40	107	.248	.335	50-0-4	.140	-3	102	3		0.0
1951	Det A	7	14	.333	34	28	9-1	1	197.1	194	103	17	6	95	131	4.06	103	.256	.343	63-0-4	.143	-3*	77	1		-0.2

YEAR	TM LG	W	L	PCT	G	GS	CG-SHO	SV-BS	IP	H	R	HR	HB	BB-IB	SO	ERA	AERA	OAV	OOB	AB-HR-SH	AVG	PB	SUP	APR	DL	PW
1952	Det A	12	17	.414	35	32	13-2	0	224	212	118	21	3	101	138	4.14	92	.249	.331	76-0-8	.171	-2*	73	-9		-1.2
1953	Det A	10	15	.400	30	28	9	0	176	166	102	25	7	76	115	4.60	88	.252	.336	61-1-0	.230	2*	83	-11		-1.2
1954	Det A	3	5	.375	19	10	2	0	72	70	48	8	2	56	29	5.38	69	.268	.395	22	.045	-2	93	-13		-1.6
1955	Chi A	0	0	—	2	1	0	0	3	9	6	0	0	2-0	1	18.00	22	.500	.550	0	—	0	180	-4		-0.2
	Cle A	0	0	—	2	0	0	0	2	5	4	1	0	2-0	1	18.00	22	.455	.538	0	—	0		-3		-0.1
	NY A	0	0	—	1	1	0	0	3	3	1	0	0	0-0	1	3.00	125	.300	.273	1	.000	-0	190	0		0.0
	Bal A	1	2	.333	9	1	0	0	15.1	21	19	3	0	11-1	8	8.22	46	.344	.438	2	.000	-0	93	-9		-1.5
	Year	1	2	.333	14	3	0	0	23.1	38	30	4	0	15-1	11	9.64	40	.380	.453	3	.000	-0	154	-16		-1.8
Total	9	59	74	.444	222	162	50-7	4	1134	1072	624	114	28	595-1	687	4.37	94	.251	.346	370-0-22	.159	-10	90	-33		-5.5

GRAY, DOLLY William Denton B12.3.1878 Houghton MI D4.3.1956 Yuba City CA BL/TL/6-2/160 d4.13

1909	Was A	5	19	.208	36	26	19	0	218	210	123	9	1	77	57	3.59	68	.258	.329	89-0-1	.146	-1*	81	-29	-3.2
1910	Was A	8	19	.296	34	29	21-3	0	229	216	106	3	3	65	84	2.63	95	.249	.309	85-0-1	.247	4*	74	-6	-0.2
1911	Was A	2	13	.133	28	15	6	0	121	160	90	4	3	40	42	5.06	65	.331	.385	44	.227	1	85	-21	-2.1
Total	3	15	51	.227	98	70	46-3	0	568	586	319	8	22	182	213	3.52	75	.271	.333	218-0-2	.202	3	79	-56	-5.5

GRBA, ELI Eli B8.9.1934 Chicago IL BR/TR/6-2/207* d7.10

1959	NY A	2	5	.286	19	6	0	0	50.1	52	44	6	0	39-0	23	6.44	57	.269	.387	14-0-1	.214	1	109	-18	-2.0
1960	†NY A	6	4	.600	24	9	1	1	80.2	65	45	9	2	46-3	32	3.68	97	.226	.333	21-1-3	.238	2*	90	-4	-0.3
1961	LA A	11	13	.458	40	30	8	2	211.2	197	119	26	7	114-10	105	4.25	106	.242	.339	64-2-8	.234	4*	103	3	0.7
1962	LA A	8	9	.471	40	29	1	1	176.1	185	101	19	2	75-5	90	4.54	85	.267	.338	58-1-3	.207	3*	110	-12	-0.8
1963	LA A	1	2	.333	12	1	0	0	17.1	14	9	2	1	10-1	5	4.67	73	.222	.333	3	.000	-0	130	-2	-0.3
Total	5	28	33	.459	135	75	10	4	536.1	513	318	62	12	284-19	255	4.48	90	.250	.342	160-4-15	.219	10	106	-33	-2.7

GREASON, JOHN John A. B7.29.1851 Washington DC D7.22.1889 Washington DC TL d8.27

1873	Was NA	1	6	.143	7								3		10	5	5.86	57	.359	.378	27	.148	-2	52	-13	-1.0

GREASON, BILL William Henry "Booster" B9.3.1924 Atlanta GA BR/TR/5-10/170 d5.31 Negro Lg 1948-51

1954	StL N	0	1	.000	3	2	0	0	4	8	8	4	0	4-1	2	13.50	30	.421	.522	1	.000	-0	130	-5	-0.8

GREEN, CHRIS Christopher De Wayne B9.5.1960 Los Angeles CA BL/TL/6-2/214 [PitN79 4/94] d4.17

1984	Pit N	0	0	—	4	0	0	0-0	3	5	2	0	0	1-0	3	6.00	61	.417	.429	0	—	0		-1	0.0

GREEN, JASON David Jason B6.5.1975 Port Hope ON, Can. BR/TR/6-1/205 [HouN93 30/840] d7.23 Col Chipola (FL) JC

2000	Hou N	1	1	.500	14	0	0	0-0	17.2	15	16	3	1	20-1	19	6.62	74	.234	.424	1	.000	-0		-4	-0.4

GREEN, ED Edward M. B1850 Philadelphia PA d4.22

1890	Phi AA	7	15	.318	25	22	20-1	1	191	267	184	4	6	94	56	5.80	67	.321	.393	126	.119	-4*	70	-43	-3.9

GREEN, FRED Fred Allen B9.14.1933 Titusville NJ D12.22.1996 Titusville NJ BR/TL/6-4/190* d4.15 s-Gary

1959	Pit N	1	2	.333	17	1	0	0	37.1	37	16	2	0	15-8	20	3.13	123	.259	.327	6	.000	-1	0	2	0.1
1960	†Pit N	8	4	.667	45	0	0	3	70	61	26	4	1	33-8	49	3.21	117	.243	.328	8-2-0	.375	3		5	1.1
1961	Pit N	0	0	—	13	0	0	0	20.2	27	16	2	0	9-2	4	4.79	83	.321	.387	3	.000	-0		-3	-0.2
1962	Was A	0	1	.000	5	0	0	0	7	7	6	3	0	6-1	2	6.43	63	.280	.382	0	—	0		-2	-0.3
1964	Pit N	0	0	—	8	0	0	0	7.1	10	1	1	0	0-0	2	1.23	286	.323	.313	0	—	0		2	0.1
Total	5	9	7	.563	88	1	0	4	142.1	142	65	12	1	63-19	77	3.48	110	.264	.339	17-2-0	.176	2	0	4	0.8

GREEN, DALLAS George Dallas B8.4.1934 Newport DE BL/TR/6-5/210* d6.18 M8 Col Delaware

1960	Phi N	3	6	.333	23	10	5-1	0	108.2	100	54	10	2	44-4	51	4.06	96	.248	.321	34-0-2	.206	0*	75	-2	-0.1
1961	Phi N	2	4	.333	42	10	1-1	1	128	160	77	8	2	47-6	51	4.85	84	.315	.372	33-0-1	.152	0	102	-11	-0.5
1962	Phi N	6	6	.500	37	10	2	1	129.1	145	58	10	5	43-6	58	3.83	101	.289	.350	32-0-3	.063	-1*	84	2	0.2
1963	Phi N	7	5	.583	40	14	4	2	120	134	53	10	2	38-8	68	3.23	100	.286	.339	35	.086	-1*	103	-1	-0.2
1964	Was A	2	1	.667	25	0	0	0	42	63	31	4	2	14-0	21	5.79	60	.362	.414	3	.000	-0*		-11	-0.8
1965	Was A	0	0	—	6	2	0	0	14.1	14	6	0	0	3-0	5	3.14	111	.241	.279	4	.000	-0	139	0	0.0
1966	NY N	0	0	—	4	0	0	0	5	6	3	2	0	2-1	1	5.40	67	.333	.400	0	—	-0		0	0.0
1967	Phi N	0	0	—	8	0	0	0	15	25	16	2	1	6-2	12	9.00	38	.362	.421	1	.000	-0		-9	-0.4
Total	8	20	22	.476	185	46	12-2	4	562.1	647	298	46	14	197-27	268	4.26	88	.294	.353	142-0-6	.120	-3	93	-33	-1.8

GREEN, HARVEY Harvey George "Buck" B2.9.1915 Kenosha WI D7.24.1970 Franklin LA BB/TR/6-2.5/185 d9.12

1935	Bro N	0	0	—	2	0	0	0	1	2	1	0	1	3	0	9.00	44	.400	.667	0	—	0		0	0.0

GREEN, STEVE Steve B1.26.1978 Greenfield Park QC, Can. BR/TR/6-2/195 [AnaA97 10/297] d4.7 Col Fort Scott (KS) CC [DL 2002 Ana A 183]

2001	Ana A	0	0	—	1	1	0	0-0	6	4	2	0	0	6-0	4	3.00	155	.190	.370	0		0	40	1	0.1

GREEN, TYLER Tyler Scott B2.18.1970 Springfield OH BR/TR/6-5/185(185-210) [PhiN91 1/10) d4.9 Col Wichita St. [DL 1996 Phi N 182, 1999 Phi N 80]

1993	Phi N	0	0	—	3	2	0	0-0	7.1	16	9	1	0	5-0	7	7.36	54	.444	.512	2-0-1	.000	0	147	-4	-0.2
1995	Phi N★	8	9	.471	26	25	4-2	0-0	140.2	157	86	15	4	66-3	85	5.31	79	.290	.367	44-1-8	.182	2*	113	-15	-1.4
1997	Phi N	4	4	.500	14	14	0	0-0	76.2	72	50	8	1	45-4	58	4.93	85	.247	.347	26-0-1	.308	3	109	-8	-0.5
1998	Phi N	6	12	.333	27	27	0	0-0	159.1	142	97	23	9	85-1	113	5.03	86	.239	.340	41-0-6	.146	-0	92	-13	62	-1.4
Total	4	18	25	.419	70	68	4-2	0-0	384	387	242	47	14	201-8	263	5.16	83	.265	.356	113-1-16	.195	4	105	-40	355	-3.5

GREENE, TOMMY Ira Thomas B4.6.1967 Lumberton NC BR/TR/6-5/227* [AtlN85 1/14] d9.10

1989	Atl N	1	2	.333	4	4	1-1	0-0	26.1	22	12	5	0	6-1	17	4.10	89	.234	.275	10	.100	-1	54	-1	-0.1
1990	Atl N	1	0	1.000	5	2	0	0-0	12.1	14	11	3	1	9-0	4	8.03	50	.286	.407	1-0-1	.000	-0	123	-5	-0.4
	Phi N	2	3	.400	10	7	0	0-0	39	36	20	5	0	17-1	17	4.15	93	.247	.325	11-0-2	.182	0	57	-1	-0.1
	Year	3	3	.500	15	9	0	0-0	51.1	50	31	8	1	26-1	21	5.08	77	.256	.347	12-0-3	.167	0	72	-6	-0.5
1991	Phi N	13	7	.650	36	27	3-2	0-0	207.2	177	85	19	3	66-4	154	3.38	109	.230	.290	71-2-3	.268	7*	101	7	1.3
1992	Phi N	3	3	.500	13	12	0	0-0	64.1	75	39	5	0	34-2	39	5.32	66	.291	.371	24	.125	-1	116	-12	111	-1.1
1993	†Phi N	16	4	.800	31	30	7-2	0-0	200	175	84	12	3	62-3	167	3.42	116	.233	.291	72-2-6	.222	6*	136	14	15	1.8
1994	Phi N	2	0	1.000	7	7	0	0-0	35.2	37	20	5	0	22-0	28	4.54	94	.272	.371	13-0-1	.385	2	149	-1	99	0.2
1995	Phi N	0	5	.000	11	6	0	0-0	33.2	45	32	6	3	20-0	24	8.29	51	.319	.412	8-0-1	.000	-0	68	-14	112	-1.8
1997	Hou N	0	1		2	0	0	0-0	9	10	7	2	0	5-0	11	7.00	57	.286	.375	3-0-1	.333	1	138	-3	81	-0.2
Total	8	38	25	.603	119	97	11-5	0-0	628	591	310	62	11	241-11	461	4.14	93	.249	.317	213-4-15	.221	14	112	-16	418	-0.4

GREENE, JUNE Julius Foust B6.25.1899 Ramseur NC D3.19.1974 Glendora CA BL/TR/6-2.5/185 d4.20 ▲

1928	Phi N	0	0	—	1	0	0	0	2	5	2	0	0	0	0	9.00	47	.556	.556	6-0-1	.500	2*		-1	0.2
1929	Phi N	0	0	—	5	0	0	0	13.2	33	32	3	3	9	4	19.76	26	.465	.542	19	.211	0*		-19	-0.8
Total	2	0	0	—	6	0	0	0	15.2	38	34	3	3	9	4	18.38	28	.475	.543	25-0-1	.280	2		-20	-0.6

GREENE, NELSON Nelson George "Lefty" B9.20.1900 Philadelphia PA D4.6.1983 Lebanon PA BL/TL/6-0/185 d4.28 Col Villanova

1924	Bro N	0	1	.000	4	1	0	0	9	14	6	1	0	2	3	4.00	94	.350	.381	1	.000	-0	45	-1	-0.1
1925	Bro N	2	0	1.000	11	0	0	0	22	45	28	4	0	7	4	10.64	39	.417	.452	7	.286	0		-15	-1.2
Total	2	2	1	.667	15	1	0	0	31	59	34	5	0	9	7	8.71	47	.399	.433	8	.250	-0	45	-16	-1.3

GREENE, RICK Richard Douglas B1.2.1971 Fort Knox KY BR/TR/6-5/200 [DetA92 1/16] d6.19 Col Louisiana St.

1999	Cin N	0	0	—	1	0	0	0-0	5.2	7	4	2	0	1-0	5	4.76	99	.292	.320	2	.000	-0		0	0.0

GREENFIELD, KENT Kent B7.1.1902 Guthrie KY D3.14.1978 Guthrie KY BR/TR/6-1/180 d9.28

1924	NY N	0	1	.000	1	1	0	0	3	9	8	1	0	1	1	15.00	24	.500	.526	0	—	0	139	-5	-0.7
1925	NY N	12	8	.600	29	20	12	0	171.2	195	86	4	2	64	66	3.88	104	.288	.352	62-0-3	.081	-6	85	4	-0.2
1926	NY N	13	12	.520	39	28	8-1	1	222.2	206	111	17	5	82	74	3.96	95	.251	.322	65-0-3	.092	-5	90	-3	-0.9
1927	NY N	2	2	.500	12	1	0	0	20	29	25	3	2	13	4	9.45	41	.411	.491	2-0-1	.000	-0	110	-13	-2.1
	Bos N	11	14	.440	27	26	11-1	0	190	203	92	3	5	59	59	3.84	97	.282	.341	64-0-7	.172	-2	82	-1	-0.3
	Year	13	16	.448	39	27	11-1	0	210	242	117	6	7	72	63	4.37	86	.297	.359	66-0-8	.167	-2	83	-13	-2.4
1928	Bos N	3	11	.214	32	20	5	0	143.2	173	100	6	5	60	30	5.32	73	.307	.378	38-0-7	.053	-4	88	-22	-2.2
1929	Bos N	0	0	—	6	2	0	0	15.2	33	19	1	2	15	7	10.91	40	.465	.568	1	.000	-1	140	-10	-0.5
	Bro N	0	0	—	6	0	0	0	8.2	13	8	1	0	3	1	8.31	56	.382	.432	1	.000	-0*		-3	-0.1
	Year	0	0	—	12	2	0	0	24.1	46	27	2	2	18	8	9.99	47	.438	.528	1	.000	-1	140	-13	-0.6
Total	6	41	48	.461	152	98	36-2	1	775.1	871	449	36	21	297	242	4.54	85	.290	.358	237-0-21	.101	-18	88	-53	-7.0

YEAR	TM LG	W	L	PCT	G	GS	CG-SHO	SV-BS	IP	H	R	HR	HB	BB-IB	SO	ERA	AERA	OAV	OOB	AB-HR-SH	AVG	PB	SUP	APR	DL	PW

GREENIG, JOHN John A. B1848 Philadelphia PA D7.28.1913 Philadelphia PA d5.9

| 1888 | Was N | 0 | 1 | .000 | 1 | 1 | 1 | 0 | 9 | 17 | 13 | 2 | 0 | 4 | 2 | 11.00 | 25 | .405 | .457 | 3 | .000 | -0 | 44 | -7 | | -0.6 |

GREENWOOD, BOB Robert Chandler "Greenie" B3.13.1928 Cananea, Sonora, Mexico D9.1.1994 Hayward CA BR/TR/6-5/190* d4.21 Col St. Marys (CA)

1954	Phi N	1	2	.333	11	4	0	0	36.2	28	16	2	0	18	9	3.19	127	.209	.301	9-0-1	.000	-1*	99	3		0.2
1955	Phi N	0	0	—	1	0	0	0	2.1	7	4	1	0	0-0	0	15.43	26	.500	.500	1	.000	-0		-3		-0.1
Total	2	1	2	.333	12	4	0	0	39	35	20	3	0	18-0	9	3.92	103	.236	.317	10-0-1	.000	-1	99	0		0.1

GREER, KENNY Kenneth William B5.12.1967 Boston MA BR/TR/6-2/210* [NYA88 10/261] d9.29 Col Massachusetts

1993	NY N	1	0	1.000	1	0	0	0-0	1	0	0	0	0	0-0	2	0.00	—	.000	.000	0		0	0			0.1
1995	SF N	0	2	.000	8	0	0	0-1	12	15	12	3	1	5-2	7	5.25	79	.288	.356	1	.000	-0		-3		-0.5
Total	2	1	2	.333	9	0	0	0-1	13	15	12	3	1	5-2	9	4.85	85	.273	.339	1	.000	-0		-3		-0.4

GREGG, DAVE David Charles "Highpockets" B3.14.1891 Chehalis WA D11.12.1965 Clarkston WA BR/TR/6-1/185 d6.15 b-Vean

| 1913 | Cle A | 0 | 0 | — | 1 | 0 | 0 | 0 | 1 | 5 | 2 | 0 | 0 | 1 | 0 | 18.00 | 17 | .400 | .500 | -0 | | 0 | | -1 | | -0.1 |

GREGG, HAL Harold Dana "Skeets" B7.11.1921 Anaheim CA D5.13.1991 Bishop CA BR/TR/6-3.5/195* d8.18

1943	Bro N	0	3	.000	5	4	0	0	18.2	21	21	2	0	21	7	9.64	35	.304	.467	2-0-1	.000	0	88	-12		-1.6
1944	Bro N	9	16	.360	39	31	6	2	197.2	201	142	12	9	137	92	5.46	65	.258	.376	68-0-4	.206	-0*	117	-43		-4.9
1945	Bro N*	18	13	.581	42	34	13-2	2	254.1	221	116	5	8	120	139	3.47	108	.232	.323	91-1-8	.220	-1	106	11		1.6
1946	Bro N	6	4	.600	26	16	4-1	0	117.1	103	46	3	1	44	54	2.99	113	.236	.308	32-0-6	.125	-1	95	5		0.2
1947	†Bro N	4	5	.444	37	16	2-1	1	104.1	115	79	6	4	55	59	5.87	70	.272	.361	34	.265	2	107	-20		-1.4
1948	Pit N	2	4	.333	22	8	1	1	74.1	72	40	3	3	34	25	4.60	88	.255	.342	22-1-2	.273	-0	131	-3		-0.1
1949	Pit N	1	1	.500	8	1	0	0	18.2	20	10	1	0	8	9	3.38	125	.303	.387	5-0-2	.000	-0	126	1		0.0
1950	Pit N	0	1	.000	5	1	0	0	5.1	10	10	2	1	7	3	13.50	32	.400	.545	1	.000	-0	60	-5		-0.3
1952	NY N	0	1	.000	16	4	1	1	36.1	42	22	7	2	17	13	4.71	79	.286	.367	8	.125	-0	138	-4		-0.3
Total	9	40	48	.455	200	115	27-4	9	827	805	486	41	29	443	401	4.54	82	.253	.350	263-2-23	.205	4	110	-70		-7.3

GREGG, KEVIN Kevin Marschall B6.20.1978 Corvallis OR BR/TR/6-6/200(200-220) [OakA96 15/435] d8.9

2003	Ana A	2	0	1.000	5	3	0	0-0	24.2	18	9	3	1	8-0	14	3.28	133	.205	.278	0	—	0	49	3		0.2
2004	†Ana A	5	2	.714	55	0	0	1-1	87.2	86	43	6	3	28-3	84	4.21	106	.255	.314	0	—	0		3		0.1
2005	†LA A	1	2	.333	33	2	0	0-1	64.1	70	37	8	3	29-2	52	5.04	86	.273	.353	0	—	0	120	-4		0.2
Total	3	8	4	.667	93	5	0	1-2	176.2	174	89	17	7	65-5	150	4.38	100	.256	.324	0	—	0	76	2		0.1

GREGG, VEAN Sylveanus Augustus B4.13.1885 Chehalis WA D7.29.1964 Aberdeen WA BR/TL/6-1/185 d4.12 b-Dave Col South Dakota St.

1911	Cle A	23	7	.767	34	26	22-5	0	244.2	172	67	2	10	86	125	**1.80**	**189**	**.205**	.286	85-0-5	.165	-4	93	43		4.6
1912	Cle A	20	13	.606	37	34	26-1	2	271.1	242	99	4	10	90	184	2.59	132	.246	.316	97-0-8	.175	-3	94	27		2.8
1913	Cle A	20	13	.606	44	34	23-3	3	285.2	258	103	2	13	124	166	2.24	136	.250	.338	99-0-4	.131	-4	93	22		1.9
1914	Cle A	9	3	.750	17	12	6-1	0	96.2	88	46	0	3	48	56	3.07	94	.251	.340	34-0-1	.176	1	120	-2		-0.2
	Bos A	3	4	.429	12	9	4	0	68.1	71	39	0	0	37	24	3.95	82	.283	.375	19-0-2	.211	0	117	-9		-0.9
	Year	12	7	.632	29	21	10-1	0	165	159	85	0	3	85	80	3.44	82	.265	.358	53-0-3	.189	1	119	-11		-1.1
1915	Bos A	4	2	.667	18	9	3-1	3	75	73	37	2	5	32	43	3.36	83	.260	.348	20-0-2	.350	2	137	-5		-0.2
1916	Bos A	2	5	.286	21	7	3	0	77.2	71	30	0	3	30	41	3.01	92	.259	.339	18	.111	0	94	-1		-0.2
1918	Phi A	9	14	.391	30	25	17-3	0	199.1	180	85	4	5	67	63	3.12	94	.251	.320	71-0-1	.169	-3	75	-2		-0.6
1925	Was A	2	2	.500	26	5	1	2	74.1	87	41	3	2	38	18	4.12	103	.318	.404	14-0-4	.214	0	143	1		0.0
Total	8	92	63	.594	239	161	105-14	9	1393	1240	547	17	51	552	720	2.70	117	.248	.329	457-0-27	.171	-12	97	74		7.2

GREGORY, FRANK Frank Ernst B7.25.1888 Spring Valley Twp. WI D11.5.1955 Beloit WI BR/TR/5-11/185 d9.5

| 1912 | Cin N | 2 | 0 | 1.000 | 4 | 2 | 1 | 0 | 15.2 | 19 | 12 | 0 | 1 | 4 | 4 | 4.60 | 73 | .297 | .375 | 5 | .200 | 0 | 109 | -3 | | -0.3 |

GREGORY, LEE Grover Leroy B6.2.1938 Bakersfield CA BL/TL/6-1/180 d4.17 Col Cal St.-Fresno

| 1964 | Chi N | 0 | 0 | — | 11 | 0 | 0 | 0 | 18 | 23 | 8 | 3 | 0 | 5-2 | 8 | 3.50 | 106 | .333 | .373 | 13 | .077 | 0* | 0 | | | 0.0 |

GREGORY, HOWIE Howard Watterson B11.18.1886 Hannibal MO D5.30.1970 Tulsa OK BL/TR/6-0/175 d4.16

| 1911 | StL A | 0 | 1 | .000 | 3 | 1 | 0 | 0 | 7 | 11 | 5 | 0 | 0 | 4 | 1 | 5.14 | 66 | .393 | .469 | 2 | .000 | -0 | 21 | -1 | | -0.2 |

GREGORY, PAUL Paul Edwin "Pop" B6.9.1908 Tomnolen MS D9.16.1999 Southaven MS BR/TR/6-2/180 d4.20 Col Mississippi St.

1932	Chi A	5	3	.625	33	9	3	0	117.2	125	75	8	2	51	39	4.51	96	.273	.348	38-0-3	.079	-3	105	-3		-0.3
1933	Chi A	4	11	.267	23	17	5	0	103.2	124	75	10	1	47	18	4.95	86	.296	.368	35-0-1	.143	-1	93	-11		-1.4
Total	2	9	14	.391	56	26	8	0	221.1	249	150	18	3	98	57	4.72	91	.284	.358	73-0-4	.110	-4	97	-14		-1.7

GREIF, BILL William Briley B4.25.1950 Ft.Stockton TX BR/TR/6-5/196* [HouN68 3/43] d7.19

1971	Hou N	1	1	.500	7	3	0	0-0	16	18	10	1	2	8-0	14	5.06	67	.290	.384	3	.333	0	105	-3		-0.3
1972	SD N	5	16	.238	34	22	2-1	2-1	125.1	143	86	18	8	47-4	91	5.60	59	.287	.353	33-0-5	.030	-3	69	-32		-5.2
1973	SD N	10	17	.370	36	31	9-3	1-0	199.1	181	88	20	5	62-12	120	3.21	110	.246	.306	61-0-2	.098	-2	77	5		0.4
1974	SD N	9	19	.321	43	35	7-1	1-1	226	244	126	17	14	95-11	137	4.66	77	.279	.366	56-0-9	.071	-2*	86	-25		-2.9
1975	SD N	4	6	.400	59	1	0	9-3	72	74	44	7	5	38-17	43	3.88	90	.269	.366	1-0-1	.000	-0	201	-6		-1.1
1976	SD N	1	3	.250	5	5	0	0-0	22.1	27	20	2	2	11-0	5	8.06	41	.297	.369	8	.000	-0		-3		-0.4
	StL N	1	5	.167	47	0	0	6-0	54.2	60	28	5	2	26-5	32	4.12	87	.290	.367	4	.000	-1	131	-13		-2.1
	Year	2	8	.200	52	5	0	6-0	77	87	48	7	2	37-5	37	5.26	67	.292	.367	12	.000	-1	131	-13		-2.1
Total	6	31	67	.316	231	97	18-5	19-5	715.2	747	402	70	36	287-49	442	4.41	79	.272	.345	166-0-17	.072	-7	83	-75		-11.2

GREINKE, ZACK Donald Zackary B10.21.1983 Orlando FL BR/TR/6-2/200(175-200) [KCA02 1/6] d5.22

2004	KC A	8	11	.421	24	24	0	0-0	145	143	64	26	8	26-3	100	3.97	117	.255	.297	2	.000	-0	81	14		1.6
2005	KC A	5	17	.227	33	33	2	0-0	183	233	125	23	13	53-0	114	5.80	73	.309	.362	2-1-0	.500	1	87	-33		-3.1
Total	2	13	28	.317	57	57	2	0-0	328	376	189	49	21	79-3	214	4.99	88	.286	.335	4-1-0	.250	1	84	-19		-1.5

GREISINGER, SETH Seth Adam B7.29.1975 Kansas City KS BR/TR/6-4/200* [DetA96 1/6] d6.3 Col Virginia [DL 2001 Det A 190]

1998	Det A	6	-9	.400	21	21	0	0-0	130	142	79	17	4	48-2	66	5.12	93	.282	.346	4	.250	0	75	-5		-0.5
2002	Det A	2	2	.500	8	8	0	0-0	37.2	46	26	4	1	13-2	14	6.21	70	.303	.359	0	—	0	85	-6		-0.6
2004	Min A	2	5	.286	12	9	0	0-0	51	68	40	12	2	15-1	36	6.18	75	.319	.366	0	—	0	71	-10		-1.1
2005	Atl N	0	0	—	1	1	0	0-0	5	7	2	1	0	1-0	2	3.60	119	.350	.381	2	.000	0	43	0		0.0
Total	4	10	16	.385	42	39	0	0-0	223.2	263	147	34	7	77-5	118	5.51	84	.296	.354	6	.167	0	75	-21	190	-2.2

GREVELL, BILL William J. B3.5.1898 Williamstown NJ D6.21.1923 Philadelphia PA BR/TR/5-11/170 d5.14

| 1919 | Phi A | 0 | 0 | — | 5 | 2 | 0 | 0 | 18 | 20 | 14 | 0 | 1 | 18 | 3 | 14.25 | 24 | .306 | .500 | 5 | .000 | -1 | 183 | -12 | | -0.6 |

GRIFFETH, LEE Leon Clifford B5.20.1925 Carmel NY BB/TL/5-11.5/180 d6.25 Col Duke

| 1946 | Phi A | 0 | 0 | — | 10 | 0 | 0 | 0 | 15.1 | 13 | 7 | 1 | 2 | 6 | 4 | 2.93 | 121 | .232 | .328 | 1 | .000 | 0 | | 1 | | 0.0 |

GRIFFIN, HANK James Linton "Pepper" B7.11.1886 Whitehouse TX D2.11.1950 Terrell TX BR/TR/6-0/165 d5.5

1911	Chi N	0	0	—	1	1	0	0	1	1	2	1	0	3	1	18.00	18	.250	.571	0		0	45	-1		-0.9
	Bos N	0	6	.000	15	6	1	0	82.2	96	70	3	6	34	30	5.23	73	.305	.383	30	.233	-0	92	-14		-0.9
	Year	0	6	.000	16	7	1	0	83.2	97	72	4	6	37	31	5.38	71	.304	.387	30	.233	-0	84	-15		-1.0
1912	Bos N	0	0	—	3	0	0	0	1.2	3	5	0	1	3	0	27.00	13	.750	.875	0	—	0		-4		-0.2
Total	2	0	6	.000	19	7	1	0	85.1	100	77	4	7	40	31	5.80	66	.310	.397	30	.233	-0	84	-19		-1.2

GRIFFIN, MARTY Martin John B9.2.1901 San Francisco CA D11.19.1951 Los Angeles CA BR/TR/6-2/200 d7.25

| 1928 | Bos A | 0 | 3 | .000 | 11 | 3 | 0 | 0 | 37.2 | 42 | 21 | 0 | 0 | 17 | 9 | 5.02 | 82 | .300 | .376 | 13 | .308 | 1* | 27 | -2 | | -0.1 |

GRIFFIN, MIKE Michael Leroy B6.26.1957 Colusa CA BR/TR/6-5/197(195-210) [TexA76 3/60] d9.17

1979	NY A	0	0	—	3	0	0	1-0	4.1	5	2	0	0	2-0	5	4.15	99	.313	.389	0	—	0		0		0.0
1980	NY A	2	4	.333	13	9	0	0-0	54	64	36	6	1	23-2	25	4.83	82	.287	.353	0	—	0	123	-7		-0.7
1981	NY A	0	0	—	2	0	0	0-0	4.1	5	1	0	0	0-0	4	2.08	174	.278	.278	0	—	0		1		0.1
	Chi N	2	5	.286	16	9	0	1-0	52	64	27	4	0	20	20	4.50	83	.302	.327	13-0-2	.154	-0	66	-3		-0.4
1982	SD N	0	1	.000	2	0	0	0-0	10.1	9	4	0	0	3-0	4	3.48	98	.237	.293	1	.000	-0		-0		0.0
1987	Bal A	3	5	.375	23	6	1	1-1	74.1	78	39	9	3	33-3	42	4.36	102	.269	.347	0	—	0	51	1		-0.1
1989	Cin N	0	0	—	8	0	0	0-0	4.1	10	6	0	0	3-2	1	12.46	37	.500	.520	1	1.000	-0		-4		-0.1
Total	6	7	15	.318	67	24	1	3-1	203.2	235	115	19	4	73-7	101	4.60	88	.288	.346	15-0-2	.200	-0	82	-12		-1.0

YEAR	TM LG	W	L	PCT	G	GS	CG-SHO	SV-BS	IP	H	R	HR	HB	BB-IB	SO	ERA	AERA	OAV	OOB	AB-HR-SH	AVG	PB	SUP	APR	DL	PW

GRIFFIN, PAT Patrick Richard B5.6.1893 Niles OH D6.7.1927 Youngstown OH BR/TR/6-2/180 d7.23

| 1914 | Cin N | 0 | 0 | — | 1 | 0 | 0 | | 1 | 3 | 2 | 0 | 0 | 2 | 0 | 9.00 | 33 | .750 | .833 | 0 | — | 0 | | -1 | | 0.0 |

GRIFFIN, TOM Thomas James B2.22.1948 Los Angeles CA BR/TR/6-3/210* [HouN66*1/4] d4.10

1969	Hou N	11	10	.524	31	31	6-3	0-0	188.1	156	80	19	7	93-4	200	3.54	101	.220	.317	62-2-4	.145	2	113	3		0.5
1970	Hou N	3	13	.188	23	20	2-1	0-0	111.1	118	72	9	3	72-1	72	5.74	68	.275	.381	33-0-4	.061	-2	89	-20		-2.7
1971	Hou N	0	6	.000	10	6	0	0-1	37.2	44	22	4	2	20-1	29	4.78	70	.288	.375	9	.111	-0	44	-6		-0.9
1972	Hou N	5	4	.556	39	5	1-1	3-3	94.1	92	39	7	3	38-5	83	3.24	104	.258	.333	25-1-3	.280	3	110	0		0.4
1973	Hou N	4	6	.400	25	12	4	0-0	99.2	83	51	10	2	46-6	69	4.15	88	.229	.316	28-1-4	.107	0	91	-6	25	-0.5
1974	Hou N	14	10	.583	34	34	8-3	0-0	211	202	97	14	5	89-7	110	3.54	99	.250	.326	68-2-9	.294	8*	128	-3		0.6
1975	Hou N	3	8	.273	17	13	3-1	0-0	79.1	89	52	11	2	46-5	56	5.33	64	.288	.384	22-0-2	.136	-0	92	-19	89	-2.3
1976	Hou N	5	3	.625	20	2	0	0-0	41.2	44	29	4	1	37-2	33	6.05	53	.278	.412	5-0-1	.000	-0	96	-13		-2.2
	SD N	4	3	.571	11	11	2	0-0	70.1	56	27	0	1	42-1	36	2.94	112	.222	.333	26-0-3	.077	-2*	90	3		0.0
	Year	9	6	.600	31	13	2	0-0	112	100	56	4	2	79-3	69	4.10	80	.244	.365	31-0-4	.065	-2	91	-10		-2.2
1977	SD N	6	9	.400	38	20	0	0-0	151.1	144	88	17	5	88-8	79	4.46	80	.254	.356	45-2-3	.133	1*	112	-17		-1.4
1978	Cal A	3	4	.429	24	4	0	0-0	56	63	39	8	1	31-2	35	4.02	90	.279	.364	0	—	0	93	-8		-0.8
1979	SF N	5	6	.455	59	3	0	2-2	94.1	83	46	9	4	46-8	82	3.91	89	.237	.331	14-0-1	.071	-1	42	-5		-0.5
1980	SF N	5	1	.833	42	4	0	0-0	107.2	80	35	8	4	49-6	79	2.76	127	.212	.312	18-1-2	.111	0*	95	10		0.6
1981	SF N	8	8	.500	22	22	3-1	0-0	129.1	121	62	8	7	57-8	83	3.76	91	.249	.335	41-1-6	.195	2	98	-6		-0.4
1982	Pit N	1	3	.250	6	4	0	0-0	22.1	32	23	5	1	15-2	15	8.87	42	.330	.425	9	.222	0	106	-12		-1.6
Total	14	77	94	.450	401	191	29-10	5-6	1494.2	1407	762	133	52	769-66	1054	4.07	86	.249	.343	405-10-42	.163	12	103	-99	114	-11.2

GRIFFITH, CLARK Clark Calvin "The Old Fox" B11.20.1869 Clear Creek MO D10.27.1955 Washington DC BR/TR/5-6.5/156 d4.11 M20 HF1946

1891	StL AA	11	8	.579	27	17	12	2	186.1	195	122	8	15	58	68	3.33	126	.260	.326	77-1	.156	-3	106	15*		0.9
	Bos AA	3	1	.750	7	4	3	0	40	47	33	3	5	15	20	5.62	62	.283	.360	23-1	.174	2*	161	-3		-0.4
	Year	14	9	.609	34	21	15	2	226.1	242	155	11	20	73	88	3.74	109	.264	.332	100-2	.160	-1	115	9		0.5
1893	Chi N	1	2	.333	4	2	2	0	19.2	24	14	1	1	5	9	5.03	92	.293	.341	11	.182	-1	113	0		-0.1
1894	Chi N	21	14	.600	36	30	28	0	261.1	328	193	12	14	85	71	4.92	114	.303	.362	142	.232	-0*	107	25		2.3
1895	Chi N	26	14	.650	42	41	39	0	353	434	238	11	22	91	79	3.93	130	.298	.348	144-1-2	.319	5*	93	40		3.9
1896	Chi N	23	11	.676	36	35	35	0	317.2	370	189	3	12	70	81	3.54	128	.289	.331	135-1-2	.267	3*	86	29		2.7
1897	Chi N	21	18	.538	41	38	**38-1**	1	343.2	410	231	3	17	86	102	3.72	120	.293	.342	162-0-3	.235	3*	90	20		2.2
1898	Chi N	24	10	.706	38	38	36-4	0	325.2	305	105	1	20	64	97	**1.88**	**191**	.266	.294	122-0-2	.164	-2	106	**63**		5.9
1899	Chi N	22	14	.611	38	38	35	0	319.2	329	163	5	14	65	73	2.79	134	.266	.310	120-0-4	.258	6*	113	31		3.9
1900	Chi N	14	13	.519	30	30	27-4	0	248	245	126	6	16	51	61	3.05	118	.258	.306	95-1-1	.253	5	79	25		2.2
1901	Chi A	24	7	**.774**	35	30	26-5	1	266.2	275	114	4	4	50	67	2.67	131	.263	.299	89-2-3	.303	14	142	29		4.2
1902	Chi A	15	9	.625	28	24	20-3	0	213	247	117	11	16	47	51	4.18	81	.290	.339	92-0-3	.217	2*	105	-15		-1.3
1903	NY A	14	11	.560	25	24	22-2	0	213	201	92	5	3	33	69	2.70	116	.249	.283	69-1-2	.159	2	76	8		1.0
1904	NY A	7	5	.583	16	11	8-1	0	100.1	91	40	3	4	16	36	2.87	94	.243	.281	42-0-1	.143	-1	112	-1		-0.2
1905	NY A	9	6	.600	25	17	4-2	1	101.2	82	30	1	1	15	46	1.68	174	.223	.255	32-0-2	.219	1*	76	12		1.8
1906	NY A	2	2	.500	17	2	1	2	59.2	58	30	0	4	15	16	3.02	98	.266	.316	18-0-2	.111	-1	146	-2		-0.1
1907	NY A	0	0	—	4	0	0	0	8.1	15	16	0	0	6	3	8.64	32	.395	.477	2	.000	-0*		-6		-0.3
1909	Cin N	0	1	.000	1	1	1	0	6	11	8	0	0	2	3	6.00	43	.379	.419	2	.000	-0	27	-3		-0.4
1912	Was A	0	0	—	1	0	0	0	1	0	0	0	0	0	0	∞	—	1.000	1.000	1	.000	-0		-1		-0.1
1913	Was A	0	0	—	1	0	0	0	1	1	0	0	0	0	0	0.00	—	.250	.250	1	1.000	1		0		0.1
1914	Was A	0	0	—	1	0	0	1	1	1	0	0	0	0	1	0.00	—	.250	.250	1	1.000	1		0		0.1
Total	20	237	146	.619	453	372	337-22	8	3385.2	3670	1852	76	171	774	955	3.31	121	.274	.322	1380-8-27	.233	35	101	256		28.3

GRIFFITH, FRANK Frank Wesley B11.18.1872 Gilman IL D12.8.1908 Waterman IL BL/TL d8.13 Col Northwestern

1892	Chi N	0	1	.000	1	1	1	0	4	3	5	1	0	6	3	11.25	30	.200	.429	1	.000	-0	38	-3		-0.4
1894	Cle N	1	2	.333	7	6	3	0	42.1	64	62	5	9	37	15	9.99	55	.344	.474	24-0-1	.333	2	125	-19		-0.8
Total	2	1	3	.250	8	7	3	0	46.1	67	67	6	9	43	18	10.10	52	.333	.470	25-0-1	.320	2	114	-22		-1.2

GRIFFITHS, JEREMY Jeremy Richard B3.22.1978 Fairview OH BR/TR/6-6/240* [NYN99 3/106] d6.5 Col Toledo

2003	NY N	1	4	.200	9	6	0	0-0	41	57	34	6	2	19-2	25	7.02	60	.328	.400	9-0-1	.000	-1	90	-13		-1.4
2004	Hou N	0	0	—	1	1	0	0-0	4.1	4	5	1	0	3-0	5	10.38	42	.235	.350	1	.000	0	212	-3		-0.1
Total	2	1	4	.200	10	7	0	0-0	45.1	61	39	6	2	22-2	30	7.35	57	.319	.395	10-0-1	.000	-0	108	-16		-1.5

GRIGGS, HAL Harold Lloyd B8.24.1928 Shannon GA D5.10.2005 Tucson AZ BR/TR/6-0/170* d4.18

1956	Was A	1	6	.143	34	12	1	1	98.2	120	82	14	1	76-2	48	6.02	72	.307	.415	16-0-2	.000	-1*	72	-21		-1.4
1957	Was A	0	1	.000	2	2	0	0	13.2	11	5	1	0	7-0	12	3.29	118	.229	.327	4	.250	-0	46	1		0.1
1958	Was A	3	11	.214	32	21	3	0	137	138	91	20	2	74-1	69	5.52	69	.262	.353	41-0-2	.122	-2	85	-26		-2.6
1959	Was A	2	8	.200	37	10	2	2	97.2	103	63	8	1	52-4	43	5.25	75	.270	.356	18	.056	-2	59	-13		-1.5
Total	4	6	26	.188	105	45	6-1	3	347	372	241	43	4	209-7	172	5.50	73	.276	.372	79-0-4	.089	-5	73	-59		-5.4

GRILLI, GUIDO Guido John B1.9.1939 Memphis TN BL/TL/6-0/188 d4.12 Col Memphis

1966	Bos A	0	1	.000	6	0	0	1	4.2	5	6	1	0	9-0	4	7.71	49	.278	.519	2	.500	0		-2		-0.4
	KC A	0	1	.000	16	0	0	1	15.2	19	15	0	3	11-4	8	6.89	49	.302	.429	0	—	0		-7		-0.5
	Year	0	2	.000	22	0	0	1	20.1	24	21	1	3	20-4	12	7.08	49	.296	.452	2	.500	0		-9		-0.9

GRILLI, JASON Jason Michael B11.11.1976 Royal Oak MI BR/TR/6-4/185(185-220) [SFN97 1/4] d5.11 f-Steve Col Seton Hall

2000	Fla N	1	0	1.000	1	1	0	0-0	6.2	11	4	1	2	2-0	5	5.40	81	.379	.455	2	.500	0	105	-1		0.0
2001	Fla N	2	2	.500	6	5	0	0-0	26.2	30	18	6	2	11-0	17	6.08	69	.297	.377	7-1-2	.286	1	120	-5		-0.5
2004	Chi A	2	3	.400	8	8	1	0-0	45	52	38	11	3	20-0	26	7.40	64	.294	.373	0	—	0	121	-13		-1.1
2005	Det A	1	1	.500	3	2	0	0-0	16	14	6	1	0	6-0	5	3.38	125	.255	.323	0	—	0	100	2		0.2
Total	4	6	6	.500	18	16	1	0-0	94.1	107	66	18	7	39-0	53	6.20	72	.296	.373	9-1-2	.333	2	118	-17		-1.4

GRILLI, STEVE Stephen Joseph B5.2.1949 Brooklyn NY BR/TR/6-2/170* d9.19 s-Jason Col Gannon

1975	Det A	0	0	—	3	0	0	0-0	6.2	3	2	0	0	6-1	5	1.35	299	.136	.310	0	—	0		2		0.1
1976	Det A	3	1	.750	36	0	0	3-1	66	63	43	5	5	41-5	36	4.64	80	.258	.369	0	—	0		-8		-0.4
1977	Det A	1	2	.333	30	2	0	0-0	72.2	71	42	8	4	49-2	49	4.83	89	.265	.383	0	—	0	63	-3		-0.2
1979	Tor A	0	0	—	1	0	0	0-0	2.1	1	0	0	0	0-0	1	0.00	—	.143	.143	0	—	0		1		0.1
Total	4	4	3	.571	70	2	0	3-1	147.2	138	87	13	8	96-8	91	4.51	90	.255	.371	0	—	0	63	-8		-0.4

GRIM, BOB Robert Anton B3.8.1930 New York NY D10.23.1996 Shawnee KS BR/TR/6-1/185* d4.18

1954	NY A	20	6	.769	37	20	8-1	0	199	175	78	9	3	85	108	3.26	106	.244	.322	70-1-7	.143	-1	141	6		0.5
1955	†NY A	7	5	.583	26	11	1-1	4	92.1	81	49	9	3	42-2	63	4.19	89	.238	.321	25-0-4	.120	-1	134	-5	47	-0.7
1956	NY A	6	1	.857	26	6	1	5	74.2	64	27	3	2	31-0	48	2.77	139	.235	.317	16-0-1	.063	-0	123	9		0.8
1957	†NY A★	12	8	.600	46	2	1	**19**	72	60	22	5	0	36-5	52	2.63	137	.239	.330	9-1-3	.111	1		9		2.0
1958	NY A	1	0	1.000	11	0	0	0	16.1	12	10	1	1	10-0	11	5.51	64	.211	.338	1-0-1	.000	-0		-3		-0.2
	KC A	7	6	.538	26	14	5-1	0	113.2	118	54	7	3	41-4	54	3.56	110	.269	.334	32-0-3	.188	-0	87	2		0.1
	Year	7	7	.500	37	14	5-1	0	130	130	64	10	4	51-4	65	3.81	101	.263	.335	33-0-4	.182	-1	88	0		-0.1
1959	KC A	6	10	.375	40	9	3-1	4	125.1	124	69	10	3	57-6	65	4.09	98	.260	.341	32-1-6	.094	-1	125	-3		-0.5
1960	Cle A	0	1	.000	3	0	0	0	2.1	6	3	0	0	1-0	2	11.57	32	.500	.538	0	—	-0		-2		-0.4
	Cin N	2	2	.500	26	0	0	2	30.1	32	18	2	0	10-2	22	4.45	86	.274	.321	0	—	0		-3		-0.4
	StL N	1	0	1.000	12	0	0	0	20.2	22	7	1	0	9-1	15	3.05	134	.272	.337	1	.000	-0		1		0.1
	Year	3	2	.600	41	0	0	2	51	54	25	4	0	19-3	37	3.88	101	.273	.327	2	.000	-0		0		-0.3
1962	KC A	1	0	1.000	12	0	0	1	13	14	9	0	0	6-1	4	6.23	68	.292	.393	2	.000	-0		-2		-0.3
Total	8	61	41	.598	268	60	18-4	37	759.2	708	346	50	15	330-22	443	3.64	104	.252	.330	189-3-25	.127	-4	122	11	47	1.0

GRIMES, BURLEIGH Burleigh Arland "Ol' Stubblebeard" B8.18.1893 Emerald WI D12.6.1985 Clear Lake WI BR/TR/5-10/175 d9.10 M2/C1 HF1964

1916	Pit N	2	3	.400	6	5	4	0	45.2	40	19	1	0	10	20	2.36	114	.241	.284	17-0-1	.176	-0	78	1		0.0
1917	Pit N	3	16	.158	37	17	8-1	0	194	186	101	5	6	70	72	3.53	80	.260	.331	69-0-4	.232	2*	67	-17		-1.3
1918	Bro N	19	9	.679	**40**	30	19-7	1	270	210	94	8	4	76	113	2.13	131	.216	.276	90-0-6	.200	0*	91	16		1.9
1919	Bro N	10	11	.476	25	21	13-1	0	181.1	179	97	2	7	60	82	3.47	86	.256	.321	69-0-2	.246	1*	107	-12		-1.1
1920	†Bro N	23	11	**.676**	40	33	25-5	2	303.2	271	101	5	4	67	131	2.22	144	.238	.282	111-0-6	.306	10*	116	30		4.9
1921	Bro N	**22**	13	.629	37	35	30-2	0	302.1	313	120	6	5	76	**136**	2.83	138	.274	.322	114-1-4	.237	2	92	**33**		4.0

YEAR	TM LG	W	L	PCT	G	GS	CG-SHO	SV-BS	IP	H	R	HR	HB	BB-IB	SO	ERA	AERA	OAV	OOB	AB-HR-SH	AVG	PB	SUP	APR	DL	PW
1922	Bro N	17	14	.548	36	34	18-1	1	259	324	159	17	7	84	99	4.76	85	.308	.363	93-0-4	.237	4	104	-17		-1.1
1923	Bro N	21	18	.538	39	38	33-2	0	327	356	165	9	11	100	119	3.58	108	.280	.338	126-0-7	.238	3*	104	11		1.8
1924	Bro N	22	13	.629	38	36	30-1	1	310.2	351	161	15	6	91	135	3.82	98	.287	.339	124-0-3	.298	6*	114	-3		0.6
1925	Bro N	12	19	.387	33	31	19	0	246.2	305	164	15	7	102	73	5.04	83	.309	.377	96-1-2	.250	5*	109	-23		-1.5
1926	Bro N	12	13	.480	30	29	18-1	0	225.1	238	114	4	5	88	64	3.71	103	.276	.346	81-0-3	.222	1*	95	2		0.5
1927	NY N	19	8	.704	39	34	15-2	2	259.2	274	116	12	4	87	102	3.54	109	.276	.337	96-0-5	.188	-0	117	11		1.3
1928	Pit N	25	14	.641	48	37	28-4	3	330.2	311	146	11	9	77	97	2.99	136	.248	.297	131-0-5	.321	11	138	32		4.9
1929	Pit N	17	7	.708	33	29	18-2	2	232.2	245	108	11	4	70	62	3.13	152	.269	.324	91-0-2	.286	6	118	36		4.0
1930	Bos N	3	5	.375	11	9	1	0	49	72	53	4	3	22	15	7.35	67	.353	.424	16-0-2	.188	-0	112	-17		-2.0
	†StL N	13	6	.684	22	19	10-1	0	152.1	174	66	5	4	43	58	3.01	166	.293	.345	57-0-3	.263	2*	122	31		3.6
	Year	16	11	.593	33	28	11-1	0	201.1	246	119	9	7	65	73	4.07	123	.308	.366	73-0-5	.247	2	118	13		1.6
1931	†StL N	17	9	.654	29	28	17-3	0	212.1	240	97	11	10	59	67	3.65	108	.286	.340	76-0-9	.184	-2	112	8		0.8
1932	†Chi N	6	11	.353	30	18	5-1	0	141.1	174	89	8	1	50	36	4.78	79	.297	.354	44-0-5	.250	1	104	-17		-1.6
1933	Chi N	3	6	.333	17	7	3-1	1	69.2	71	29	2	1	29	12	3.49	94	.277	.353	20-0-2	.150	-1	109	0		-0.1
	StL N	0	1	.000	4	3	0	1	13.2	15	13	1	1	8	4	5.27	66	.263	.364	5	.200	0	144	-4		-0.4
	Year	3	7	.300	21	10	3-1	4	83.1	86	42	3	2	37	16	3.78	87	.275	.355	25-0-2	.160	-1	121	-5		-0.5
1934	StL N	2	1	.667	4	0	0	0	7.2	5	3	1	0	2	1	3.52	120	.179	.233	0-0-1	—	0		1		0.2
	NY A	1	2	.333	10	0	0	1	18	22	11	0	1	14	5	5.50	74	.319	.440	2	.000	-0		-2		-0.3
	Pit N	1	2	.333	8	4	0	0	27.1	36	24	0	1	10	9	7.24	57	.310	.370	7	.143	-0	73	-9		-0.8
Total	19	270	212	.560	616	497	314-35	18	4180	4412	2050	148	101	1295	1512	3.53	107	.273	.331	1535-2-76	.248	52	109	91		18.3

GRIMES, JOHN   John Thomas   B4.17.1869 Woodstock MD   D1.17.1964 San Francisco CA   BR/TR/5-11/160   d7.28

YEAR	TM LG	W	L	PCT	G	GS	CG-SHO	SV-BS	IP	H	R	HR	HB	BB-IB	SO	ERA	AERA	OAV	OOB	AB-HR-SH	AVG	PB	SUP	APR	DL	PW
1897	StL N	0	2	.000	3	1	1	0	19.2	24	23	0	6	8	4	5.95	74	.300	.404	7	.286	1	81	-5		-0.2

GRIMSLEY, JASON   Jason Alan   B8.7.1967 Cleveland TX   BR/TR/6-3/180(180-205)   [PhiN85 10/252]   d9.8

YEAR	TM LG	W	L	PCT	G	GS	CG-SHO	SV-BS	IP	H	R	HR	HB	BB-IB	SO	ERA	AERA	OAV	OOB	AB-HR-SH	AVG	PB	SUP	APR	DL	PW
1989	Phi N	1	3	.250	4	4	0	0-0	18.1	19	13	2	0	19-1	7	5.89	61	.268	.422	5-0-2	.000	-1	62	-4		-0.8
1990	Phi N	3	2	.600	11	11	0	0-0	57.1	47	21	1	2	43-0	41	3.30	117	.227	.364	16-0-3	.188	0*	104	4		0.5
1991	Phi N	1	7	.125	12	12	0	0-0	61	54	34	4	3	41-3	42	4.87	76	.242	.364	17	.059	-1	73	-7	77	-0.8
1993	Cle A	3	4	.429	10	6	0	0-0	42.1	52	26	3	1	20-1	27	5.31	82	.302	.378	0	—	0	53	-4		-0.5
1994	Cle A	5	2	.714	14	13	1	0-0	82.2	91	47	7	6	34-1	59	4.57	104	.283	.360	0	—	0	122	2		0.1
1995	Cle A	0	0	—	15	2	0	1-0	34	37	24	4	2	32-1	25	6.09	78	.289	.433	0	—	0	108	-5		-0.2
1996	Cal A	5	7	.417	35	20	2-1	0-0	130.1	150	110	14	13	74-5	82	6.84	74	.286	.385	0	—	0	101	-26		-1.8
1999	†NY A	7	2	.778	55	0	0	1-3	75	66	39	7	4	40-5	49	3.60	131	.231	.330	0	—	0	7	7		0.7
2000	†NY A	3	2	.600	63	4	0	1-3	96.1	100	58	10	5	42-1	53	5.04	95	.268	.345	1	.000	0	138	-3		-0.1
2001	KC A	1	5	.167	73	0	0	0-7	80.1	71	32	8	2	28-5	61	3.02	164	.241	.311	0	—	0	15	15		1.0
2002	KC A	4	7	.364	70	0	0	1-2	71.1	64	32	4	1	37-8	59	3.91	128	.236	.330	0	—	0	8	21	18	1.1
2003	KC A	2	6	.250	76	0	0	0-7	75	88	47	6	5	36-5	58	5.16	93	.299	.379	0	—	0	-3			-0.2
2004	KC A	3	3	.500	32	0	0	0-3	26.2	24	11	1	1	15-3	18	3.38	138	.238	.342	0	—	0	-1			0.8
	Bal A	2	4	.333	41	0	0	0-6	36.1	37	25	3	2	20-3	-21	4.21	111	.261	.358	0	—	0	4			0.7
	Year	5	7	.417	73	0	0	0-9	63	61	36	4	3	35-6	39	3.86	121	.251	.351	0	—	0	3			0.7
2005	Bal A	1	2	.333	22	0	0	0-3	22	24	15	5	0	11-2	10	5.73	77	.289	.355	0	—	0	-9	117		-0.7
Total	14	41	56	.423	527	72	3-1	4-34	909	924	551	79	47	490-44	612	4.76	98	.265	.360	39-0-5	.103	-0	94	-16	212	-0.7

GRIMSLEY, ROSS   Ross Albert I   B6.4.1922 Americus KS   D2.6.1994 Memphis TN   BL/TL/6-0/175   d9.3   s-Ross

YEAR	TM LG	W	L	PCT	G	GS	CG-SHO	SV-BS	IP	H	R	HR	HB	BB-IB	SO	ERA	AERA	OAV	OOB	AB-HR-SH	AVG	PB	SUP	APR	DL	PW
1951	Chi A	0	0	—	7	0	0	0	14	12	8	1	0	10	8	3.86	105	.235	.361	2-0-1	.000	-0		0		-0.1

GRIMSLEY, ROSS   Ross Albert II   B1.7.1950 Topeka KS   BL/TL/6-3/200*   [CinN69*S1/17]   d5.16   f-Ross   Col Jackson St. (TN) CC   [DL 1981 Cle A 48]

YEAR	TM LG	W	L	PCT	G	GS	CG-SHO	SV-BS	IP	H	R	HR	HB	BB-IB	SO	ERA	AERA	OAV	OOB	AB-HR-SH	AVG	PB	SUP	APR	DL	PW
1971	Cin N	10	7	.588	26	26	6-3	0-0	161.1	151	67	15	2	43-2	67	3.57	95	.250	.301	51-0-6	.118	-1	118	-3		-0.4
1972	†Cin N	14	8	.636	30	28	4-1	1-0	197.2	194	73	18	0	50-8	79	3.05	106	.260	.305	66-0-11	.121	-2	114	5		0.3
1973	†Cin N	13	10	.565	38	36	8-1	1-0	242.1	245	96	24	0	68-11	90	3.23	107	.266	.315	82-0-8	.061	-6*	102	6		-0.2
1974	†Bal A	18	13	.581	40	39	17-4	1-0	295.2	267	111	26	3	76-9	158	3.07	113	.244	.292	0	—	0	101	16		1.6
1975	Bal A	10	13	.435	35	32	8-1	0-0	197	210	95	29	4	47-1	89	4.07	87	.276	.317	0	—	0	90	-12		-1.2
1976	Bal A	8	7	.533	28	19	2	0-0	136.2	143	66	8	1	35-2	41	3.95	83	.270	.315	0	—	0	98	-4		-0.2
1977	Bal A	14	10	.583	34	34	11-2	0-0	218.1	230	105	24	1	74-2	53	3.96	97	.277	.335	0	—	0	106	13		1.5
1978	Mon N☆	20	11	.645	36	36	19-3	0-0	263	237	103	17	2	67-6	84	3.05	117	.243	.291	90-0-11	.144	-1	106	13		1.5
1979	Mon N	10	9	.526	32	27	2	0-1	151.1	199	102	18	3	41-1	42	5.35	69	.322	.363	55-0-3	.200	1	115	-27		-2.9
1980	Mon N	2	4	.333	11	7	0	0-0	41.1	61	31	5	1	12-1	11	6.31	57	.351	.385	9	.222	1	84	-12		-1.4
	Cle A	4	5	.444	14	11	2	0-0	74.2	103	63	11	1	24-1	18	6.75	61	.331	.376	0	—	0	114	-22		-2.2
1982	Bal A	1	2	.333	21	0	0	2-2	60	65	35	7	0	22-5	18	5.25	77	.283	.343	0	—	0	-7			-0.3
Total	11	124	99	.556	345	295	79-15	3-3	2039.1	2105	947	202	15	559-49	750	3.81	93	.270	.318	353-0-39	.127	-10	106	-57	48	-6.5

GRINER, DAN   Donald Dexter "Rusty"   B3.7.1888 Centerville TN   D6.3.1950 Bishopville SC   BL/TR/6-1.5/200   d8.17

YEAR	TM LG	W	L	PCT	G	GS	CG-SHO	SV-BS	IP	H	R	HR	HB	BB-IB	SO	ERA	AERA	OAV	OOB	AB-HR-SH	AVG	PB	SUP	APR	DL	PW
1912	StL N	3	4	.429	12	7	2	0	54	59	35	3	3	15	20	3.17	108	.278	.335	13	.077	-0	89	-1		-0.2
1913	StL N	10	22	.313	34	34	18-1	0	225	279	150	12	10	66	79	5.08	64	.312	.366	81-0-2	.259	5	91	-46		-5.0
1914	StL N	9	13	.409	37	17	11-2	2	179	163	66	3	3	57	74	2.51	111	.254	.318	55-0-3	.255	4	70	7		1.4
1915	StL N	5	11	.313	37	17	9-3	3	150.1	137	59	4	8	46	46	2.81	99	.259	.328	52-0-2	.269	4*	78	1		0.5
1916	StL N	0	0	—	4	0	0	1	11	15	5	0	1	3	3	4.09	65	.341	.396	4	.250	0		-1		-0.1
1918	Bro N	1	5	.167	11	6	3-1	0	54.1	47	16	0	7	15	22	2.15	129	.267	.348	14	.071	-1*	50	4		0.4
Total	6	28	55	.337	135	81	43-7	6	673.2	700	331	22	32	202	244	3.49	86	.280	.342	219-0-7	.237	12	83	-36		-3.0

GRISSOM, LEE   Lee Theo   B10.23.1907 Sherman TX   D10.4.1998 Corning CA   BB/TL(BR 1934, 37)/6-3/200   d9.2   Mil 1942-45   b-Marv

YEAR	TM LG	W	L	PCT	G	GS	CG-SHO	SV-BS	IP	H	R	HR	HB	BB-IB	SO	ERA	AERA	OAV	OOB	AB-HR-SH	AVG	PB	SUP	APR	DL	PW
1934	Cin N	0	1	.000	4	1	0	0	7	13	12	0	0	7	4	15.43	26	.382	.488	1	.000	-0	42	-8		-0.9
1935	Cin N	1	1	.500	3	3	1	0	21	31	10	0	0	4	13	3.86	103	.333	.361	7-0-1	.000	-1	114	1		0.0
1936	Cin N	1	1	.500	6	4	0	0	24.1	33	18	1	0	9	13	6.29	61	.320	.375	9	.000	-1	133	-6		-0.5
1937	Cin N★	12	17	.414	50	30	14-5	6	223.2	193	89	7	4	93	149	3.26	114	.232	.313	64-0-6	.109	-3*	74	15		1.5
1938	Cin N	2	3	.400	14	7	0	0	51	60	38	4	2	22	16	5.29	69	.300	.375	16	.188	-0	76	-11		-1.0
1939	†Cin N	9	7	.563	33	21	3	0	153.2	145	77	14	1	56	53	4.10	93	.249	.316	47-0-3	.085	-2	114	-3		-0.6
1940	NY A	0	0	—	5	0	0	0	4.2	4	0	0	0	4	2	0.00	—	.250	.333	0	—	0		2		0.1
	Bro N	2	5	.286	14	10	3-1	0	73.2	59	30	3	0	34	56	2.81	142	.215	.302	23	.217	-0	52	7		0.6
1941	Bro N	0	0	—	4	1	0	1	11.1	10	3	2	0	8	5	2.38	154	.238	.360	2-0-1	.500	0	232	2		0.1
	Phi N	2	13	.133	29	18	2	0	131.1	120	69	4	2	70	74	3.97	93	.242	.338	36-0-3	.167	-1	84	-5		-0.6
	Year	2	13	.133	33	19	2	1	142.2	130	72	6	2	78	79	3.85	96	.242	.340	38-0-4	.184	-1	92	-3		-0.5
Total	8	29	48	.377	162	95	23-6	7	701.2	668	346	35	9	305	384	3.89	97	.250	.329	205-0-14	.127	-8	88	-6		-1.3

GRISSOM, MARV   Marvin Edward   B3.31.1918 Los Molinos CA   D9.19.2005 Red Bluff CA   BR/TR/6-3/195*   d9.10   C15   b-Lee

YEAR	TM LG	W	L	PCT	G	GS	CG-SHO	SV-BS	IP	H	R	HR	HB	BB-IB	SO	ERA	AERA	OAV	OOB	AB-HR-SH	AVG	PB	SUP	APR	DL	PW
1946	NY N	0	2	.000	9	1	0	0	18.2	17	11	1	1	13	9	4.34	79	.254	.383	5	.200	-0	75	-2		-0.2
1949	Det A	4	4	.333	27	2	0	0	39.1	56	32	6	1	34	17	6.41	65	.335	.450	9	.222	1	140	-10		-1.3
1952	Chi A	12	10	.545	28	24	7-1	0	166	156	79	6	3	79	97	3.74	98	.250	.337	53-0-8	.151	-1	101	-3		-0.5
1953	Bos A	2	6	.250	13	11	1-1	0	59.1	61	34	5	1	30	31	4.70	89	.266	.354	18-0-2	.000	-3	109	-2		-0.6
	NY N	4	2	.667	21	7	3	0	84.1	83	40	6	1	31	46	3.95	109	.255	.321	27-0-1	.074	-2	140	4		0.2
1954	†NY N★	10	7	.588	56	3	1-1	19	122.1	100	37	13	2	50	64	2.35	171	.226	.312	32-0-2	.156	-1	74	23		3.7
1955	NY N	5	4	.556	55	0	0	8	89.1	76	35	6	6	41-5	49	2.92	138	.237	.332	13-0-1	.154	-1		10		1.1
1956	NY N	1	1	.500	43	0	0	7	80.2	71	15	3	1	16-3	49	1.56	242	.241	.279	11	.091	-0	70	20		1.0
1957	NY N	4	4	.500	55	0	0	14	82.2	74	36	6	2	23-6	51	2.61	151	.243	.300	12	.167	1		8		1.1
1958	SF N	7	5	.583	51	0	0	10	65.1	71	34	11	5	26-7	46	3.99	95	.287	.367	9-0-1	.000	-1		2		-0.4
1959	StL N	0	0	—	3	0	0	0	2	6	5	2	0	0	0	22.50	19	.500	.500	0	—	0		-4	36	-0.2
Total	10	47	45	.511	356	52	12-3	58	810	771	358	65	28	343-21	459	3.41	115	.254	.334	189-0-15	.122	-7	105	42	36	3.9

GROB, CONNIE   Conrad George   B11.9.1932 Cross Plains WI   D9.28.1997 Madison WI   BL/TR/6-0.5/180   d4.22

YEAR	TM LG	W	L	PCT	G	GS	CG-SHO	SV-BS	IP	H	R	HR	HB	BB-IB	SO	ERA	AERA	OAV	OOB	AB-HR-SH	AVG	PB	SUP	APR	DL	PW
1956	Was A	4	5	.444	19	1	0	1	79.1	121	79	14	1	26	27	7.83	55	.353	.396	18-0-1	.333	1	82	-30		-2.7

GRODZICKI, JOHNNY   John "Grod"   B2.26.1917 Nanticoke PA   D5.2.1998 Daytona Beach FL   BR/TR/6-1.5/200   d4.18   Mil 1942-46   C1

YEAR	TM LG	W	L	PCT	G	GS	CG-SHO	SV-BS	IP	H	R	HR	HB	BB-IB	SO	ERA	AERA	OAV	OOB	AB-HR-SH	AVG	PB	SUP	APR	DL	PW
1941	StL N	2	1	.667	5	1	0	0	13.1	6	7	0	0	11	10	1.35	279	.130	.298	2-0-1	.000	0	90	2		0.4
1946	StL N	0	0	—	3	0	0	0	4	4	5	1	0	4	2	9.00	38	.250	.400	0	—	0	-3		63	-0.1
1947	StL N	0	1	.000	16	0	0	0	23.1	21	17	5	0	19	8	5.40	77	.253	.392	1	.000	-0	-4			-0.2
Total	3	2	2	.500	24	1	0	0	40.2	31	29	6	0	34	20	4.43	89	.214	.363	3-0-1	.000	0	90	-5	63	0.1

YEAR	TM LG	W	L	PCT	G	GS	CG-SHO	SV-BS	IP	H	R	HR	HB	BB-IB	SO	ERA	AERA	OAV	OOB	AB-HR-SH	AVG	PB	SUP	APR	DL	PW

GROMEK, STEVE Stephen Joseph B1.15.1920 Hamtramck MI D3.12.2002 Clinton Twp. MI BB/TR/6-2/180(180-195) d8.18

1941	Cle A	1	1	.500	9	2	1	2	23.1	25	12	0	0	11	19	4.24	93	.266	.343	6	.167	-0	143	-1		-0.1
1942	Cle A	2	0	1.000	14	0	0	0	44.1	46	24	2	0	23	14	3.65	94	.267	.354	15	.333	3		-2		0.1
1943	Cle A	0	0	—	3	0	0	0	4	6	4	0	0	4	4	9.00	35	.353	.353	2	1.000	1		-2		0.0
1944	Cle A	10	9	.526	35	21	12-2	1	203.2	160	74	5	3	70	115	2.56	129	.219	.290	73-0-5	.260	5*	102	15		1.7
1945	Cle A*	19	9	.679	33	33	21-3	1	251	229	80	6	4	66	101	2.55	128	.243	.295	91-0-3	.231	3*	101	21		2.6
1946	Cle A	5	15	.250	29	21	5-2	4	153.2	159	79	20	3	47	75	4.33	76	.264	.321	56	.196	0*	75	-16		-2.0
1947	Cle A	3	5	.375	29	7	0	4	84.1	77	43	8	1	36	39	3.74	93	.240	.318	22	.318	2*	127	-5		-0.3
1948	†Cle A	9	3	.750	38	9	4-1	2	130	109	52	10	6	51	50	2.84	143	.226	.307	41-0-1	.146	-1	106	16		1.2
1949	Cle A	4	6	.400	27	12	3	0	92	86	41	8	2	40	22	3.33	120	.250	.332	24-0-2	.167	-0	107	6		0.5
1950	Cle A	10	7	.588	31	13	4-1	0	113.1	94	50	10	3	36	43	3.65	119	.226	.292	38-0-2	.158	-2	90	10		1.1
1951	Cle A	7	4	.636	27	8	4	1	107.1	98	41	6	4	29	41	2.77	137	.238	.295	27-0-1	.296	3	123	12		1.4
1952	Cle A	7	7	.500	29	13	3-1	1	122.2	109	55	14	2	28	65	3.67	91	.232	.278	30-0-3	.100	-0*	108	-3		-0.5
1953	Cle A	1	1	.500	5	1	0	0	11	11	4	0	1	3	8	3.27	115	.268	.333	2-0-1	.000	-0	24	1		0.1
	Det A	6	8	.429	19	17	6-1	1	125.2	138	70	17	8	36	59	4.51	90	.276	.335	41-0-5	.073	-4	94	-6		-1.1
	Year	7	9	.438	24	18	6-1	1	136.2	149	74	17	9	39	67	4.41	92	.275	.334	43-0-6	.070	-4	90	-6		-1.0
1954	Det A	18	16	.529	36	32	17-4	1	252.2	236	85	26	12	57	102	2.74	135	.246	.294	79-0-10	.190	2	84	28		**3.7**
1955	Det A	13	10	.565	28	25	8-2	0	181	183	89	26	9	37-5	73	3.98	97	.261	.305	54-0-4	.167	4	138	-2		0.1
1956	Det A	8	6	.571	40	13	4	4	141	142	74	25	9	47-7	64	4.28	96	.263	.329	27-0-3	.148	2	83*	-2		-0.1
1957	Det A	0	1	.000	15	1	0	1	23.2	32	16	3	1	13-3	11	6.08	63	.333	.414	2	.000	-0	69	-5		-0.3
Total	17	123	108	.532	447	225	92-17	23	2064.2	1940	893	186	68	630-15	904	3.41	108	.247	.308	630-0-40	.197	15	101	65		8.1

GROOM, BOB Robert B9.12.1884 Belleville IL D2.19.1948 Belleville IL BR/TR/6-2/175 d4.13

1909	Was A	7	26	.212	44	31	17-1	0	260.2	218	114	2	13	105	131	2.87	85	.229	.314	88-0-7	.091	-6*	60	-12		-2.0
1910	Was A	12	17	.414	34	30	22-3	0	257.2	244	117	8	9	77	98	2.76	90	.260	.322	92-0-3	.120	-6	81	-8		-1.6
1911	Was A	13	17	.433	37	32	20-2	2	254.2	280	148	9	8	67	135	3.82	86	.282	.332	82-0-6	.134	-6	81	-13		-1.7
1912	Was A	24	13	.649	43	40	28-2	1	316	287	133	3	5	94	179	2.62	127	.246	.305	103-0-12	.117	-7	105	25		1.8
1913	Was A	16	16	.500	37	36	17-4	0	264.1	258	118	8	5	81	156	3.23	91	.261	.320	92-0-5	.163	-1	95	-5		-0.5
1914	StL F	13	20	.394	42	34	23-1	1	280.2	281	141	8	4	75	167	3.24	94	.262	.312	94-0-1	.160	-4	77	-10		-1.5
1915	StL F	11	11	.500	37	26	11-4	2	209	200	93	6	2	73	111	3.27	88	.261	.327	66-0-3	.152	-3	86	-9		-1.2
1916	StL A	13	9	.591	41	26	8-1	4	217.1	174	82	1	3	98	92	2.57	107	.226	.315	63-0-6	.111	-2	121	4		0.3
1917	StL A	8	19	.296	38	28	11-4	3	232.2	193	80	3	5	95	82	2.94	88	.233	.315	72-0-3	.111	-4	77	0		-0.5
1918	Cle A	2	2	.500	14	5	0	0	43.1	70	42	0	1	18	18	7.06	43	.380	.438	12-0-1	.083	-1	125	-17		-1.6
Total	10	119	150	.442	367	288	157-22	13	2336.1	2205	1068	49	55	783	1159	3.10	93	.255	.320	764-0-47	.128	-35	88	-45		-8.5

GROOM, BUDDY Wedsel Gary B7.10.1965 Dallas TX BL/TL/6-2/205* [ChiA87 12/297] d6.20 Col Mary Hardin-Baylor

1992	Det A	0	5	.000	12	5	0	1-1	38.2	48	28	4	0	22-4	15	5.82	69	.320	.402	0	—	0	75	-8		-1.0
1993	Det A	0	2	.000	19	3	0	0-0	36.2	48	25	4	2	13-5	15	6.14	71	.322	.375	0	—	0	113	-6		-0.3
1994	Det A	0	1	.000	40	0	0	1-0	32	31	14	4	2	13-2	27	3.94	125	.256	.331	0	—	0	4	4		0.1
1995	Det A	1	3	.250	23	4	0	1-2	40.2	55	35	6	2	26-4	23	7.52	64	.322	.413	0	—	0	102	-11		-1.0
	Fla N	1	2	.333	14	0	0	0-0	15	26	12	2	0	6-0	12	7.20	60	.400	.451	0	—	0		-4		-0.7
1996	Oak A	5	0	1.000	72	1	0	2-2	77.1	85	37	8	3	34-3	57	3.84	129	.281	.360	0	—	0	56	9		0.5
1997	Oak A	2	2	.500	78	0	0	3-2	64.2	75	38	9	1	24-1	45	5.15	89	.292	.347	0	—	0		-3		-0.2
1998	Oak A	3	1	.750	75	0	0	0-6	57.1	62	30	4	1	20-1	36	4.24	109	.274	.332	0	—	0		3		0.1
1999	Oak A	3	2	.600	**76**	0	0	0-3	46	48	29	1	1	18-5	32	5.09	93	.274	.345	0	—	0		-2		-0.1
2000	Bal A	6	3	.667	70	0	0	4-7	59.1	63	37	5	0	21-2	44	4.85	97	.275	.329	0	—	0		-2		-0.3
2001	Bal A	1	4	.200	70	0	0	11-2	66	64	28	4	1	9-0	54	3.55	122	.252	.279	0	—	0		6		0.6
2002	Bal A	3	2	.600	60	0	0	2-2	62	44	11	4	2	12-3	48	1.60	272	.196	.243	0	—	0		20		1.5
2003	Bal A	1	3	.250	60	0	0	1-2	45.1	58	27	7	3	14-2	34	5.36	86	.309	.364	0	—	0		-3		-0.2
2004	Bal A	4	1	.800	60	0	0	0-2	52.2	67	30	6	1	16-1	32	4.78	98	.309	.356	0	—	0		-1		-0.1
2005	NY A	1	0	1.000	24	0	0	0-0	25.2	32	14	3	0	7-2	13	4.91	89	.305	.362	0	—	0		-1		-0.1
	Ari N	0	1	.000	23	0	0	1-0	15.1	19	8	2	0	5-1	7	4.70	94	.302	.348	0	—	0		0		0.0
Total	14	31	32	.492	786	15	0	27-31	734.2	825	403	73	21	260-36	494	4.64	99	.285	.345	0	—	0	85	2		-1.2

GROSS, DON Donald John B6.30.1931 Weidman MI BL/TL/5-11/186* d7.21 Col Michigan St.

1955	Cin N	4	5	.444	17	11	2-1	0	67.1	79	33	11	1	16-0	33	4.14	102	.298	.337	19-0-3	.158	-1	97	2		0.1
1956	Cin N	3	0	1.000	19	7	2	0	69.1	69	25	4	1	20-2	47	1.95	204	.257	.309	19	.105	-1	114	11		0.6
1957	Cin N	7	9	.438	43	16	5	1	148.1	152	75	21	3	33-3	73	4.31	95	.264	.304	46-0-6	.109	-2	100	-2		-0.5
1958	Pit N	5	7	.417	40	3	0	7	74.2	67	37	5	1	38-7	59	3.98	97	.241	.333	18-0-1	.056	-1	124	-1		-0.3
1959	Pit N	1	1	.500	21	0	0	2	33	28	16	3	1	10-3	15	3.55	109	.228	.289	2-0-1	.000	-0		1		0.1
1960	Pit N	0	0	—	5	0	0	0	5.1	5	2	1	0	0-0	3	3.38	111	.238	.238	0	—	0	0	0		0.0
Total	6	20	22	.476	145	37	9-1	10	398	400	188	45	7	117-15	230	3.73	108	.261	.314	104-0-11	.106	-5	106	11		0.0

GROSS, KEVIN Kevin Frank B6.8.1961 Downey CA BR/TR/6-5/215(203-227) [PhiN81*S11/1] d6.25 Col California Lutheran

1983	Phi N	4	6	.400	17	17	1-1	0-0	96	100	46	13	3	35-3	66	3.56	101	.265	.332	33-0-1	.091	-1	98	0		-0.1
1984	Phi N	8	5	.615	44	14	1	1-2	129	140	66	8	5	44-4	84	4.12	89	.277	.339	30-0-2	.067	-2	91	-5		-0.6
1985	Phi N	15	13	.536	38	31	6-2	0-1	205.2	194	86	11	7	81-6	151	3.41	109	.251	.326	65-1-8	.138	0*	80	8		1.1
1986	Phi N	12	12	.500	37	36	7-2	0-0	241.2	240	115	28	4	94-2	154	4.02	99	.259	.331	80-1-9	.188	3	103	0		0.3
1987	Phi N	9	16	.360	34	33	3-1	0-0	200.2	205	107	26	10	87-7	110	4.35	99	.267	.347	63-1-8	.190	2	75	-1		0.3
1988	Phi N★	12	14	.462	33	33	5-1	0-0	231.2	209	101	18	11	89-5	162	3.69	98	.239	.315	75-0-8	.173	1	89	0		0.1
1989	Mon N	11	12	.478	31	31	4-3	0-0	201.1	188	105	20	4	88-6	158	4.38	81	.247	.329	64-0-6	.141	1	89	-16		-1.7
1990	Mon N	9	12	.429	31	26	2-1	0-0	163.1	171	86	9	4	65-7	111	4.57	80	.272	.340	50-1-7	.200	4*	90	-15	22	-1.5
1991	LA N	10	11	.476	46	10	0	3-3	115.2	123	55	10	2	50-6	95	3.58	101	.275	.348	24-0-2	.280	2*	95	-1		0.1
1992	LA N	8	13	.381	34	30	4-3	0-0	204.2	182	82	11	3	77-10	158	3.17	110	.241	.311	63-0-3	.095	-1	89	8		0.6
1993	LA N	13	13	.500	33	32	3	0-0	202.1	224	110	15	5	74-7	150	4.14	93	.281	.344	64-1-8	.203	4	119	-8		-0.3
1994	LA N	9	7	.563	25	23	1	1-0	157.1	162	64	11	2	43-2	124	3.60	111	.263	.313	47-1-4	.149	1	80	9		1.0
1995	Tex A	9	15	.375	31	30	4	0-0	183.2	200	124	27	4	89-8	106	5.54	83	.279	.362	0	—	0	92	-15		-1.6
1996	Tex A	11	8	.579	28	19	1	0-0	129.1	151	78	19	4	50-2	78	5.22	101	.293	.355	0	—	0	101	2	36	0.2
1997	Ana A	2	1	.667	12	3	0	0-0	25.1	30	20	4	1	20-1	20	6.75	66	.313	.429	1	.000	-0	133	-6		-0.3
Total	15	142	158	.473	474	368	42-14	5-6	2487.2	2519	1245	230	79	986-76	1727	4.11	95	.264	.335	660-6-66	.161	13	93	-40	58	-3.0

GROSS, KIP Kip Lee B8.24.1964 Scottsbluff NE BR/TR/6-2/195* [NYN86 4/102] d4.21 Col Nebraska

1990	Cin N	0	0	—	5	0	0	0-0	6.1	6	3	0	0	4-0	3	4.26	93	.273	.320	0	—	0		0		0.0
1991	Cin N	6	4	.600	29	5	0	0-0	85.2	93	43	8	0	40-2	40	3.47	110	.279	.355	22-0-3	.091	-1	129	1		-0.1
1992	LA N	1	1	.500	16	1	0	0-0	23.2	32	14	1	0	10-1	14	4.18	83	.323	.385	2-0-1	1.000	1	209	-2		-0.1
1993	LA N	0	0	—	10	0	0	0-0	15	13	1	0	0	4-0	12	0.60	644	.236	.288	0	—	0		6		0.3
1999	Bos A	0	2	.000	11	1	0	0-1	12.2	15	11	3	3	8-2	9	7.82	64	.294	.413	0	—	0	168	-3	18	-0.4
2000	Hou N	0	1	.000	11	0	0	0-0	4.1	9	8	2	0	2-0	3	10.38	47	.429	.478	1	.000	-0	19	-4		-0.6
Total	6	7	8	.467	73	12	0	0-1	147.2	168	80	14	3	66-5	81	3.90	100	.289	.362	25-0-4	.160	0	130	-2	18	-0.9

GROSSMAN, HARLEY Harley Joseph B5.5.1930 Evansville IN D9.5.2003 Evansville IN BR/TR/6-0/170 d4.22 Col Ball St.

| 1952 | Was A | 0 | 0 | — | 1 | 0 | 0 | 0 | 0.1 | 2 | 2 | 1 | 0 | 0 | 1 | 54.00 | 7 | .667 | .667 | 0 | — | 0 | | -2 | | -0.1 |

GROTH, ERNIE Ernest John "Dango" B12.24.1884 Cedarburg WI D5.23.1950 Milwaukee WI BR/TR/5-11/175 d9.6

| 1904 | Chi N | 0 | 2 | .000 | 3 | 2 | 1 | 1 | 16 | 22 | 13 | 1 | 1 | 6 | 9 | 5.63 | 47 | .310 | .372 | 6 | .000 | -1 | 26 | -5 | | -0.7 |

GROTH, ERNEST Ernest William B5.3.1922 Beaver Falls PA D12.27.2004 Beaver PA BR/TR/5-9/185 d9.11

1947	Cle A	0	0	—	2	0	0	0	1.1	1	0	0	0	1	1	0.00	—	.000	.250	0	—	0		1		0.0
1948	Cle A	0	0	—	1	0	0	0	1	1	1	0	0	2	0	9.00	45	.250	.500	0	—	0*		-1		0.0
1949	Chi A	0	1	.000	3	0	0	1	5	2	3	2	1	3	1	5.40	77	.125	.300	0	—	0		-1		-0.1
Total	3	0	1	.000	6	0	0	1	7.1	4	4	2	1	6	2	4.91	82	.130	.333	0	—	0		-1		-0.1

GROTT, MATT Matthew Allen B12.5.1967 LaPorte IN BL/TL/6-1/210 d5.4 Col Phoenix (AZ) JC

| 1995 | Cin N | 0 | 0 | — | 2 | 0 | 0 | 0-0 | 1.2 | 6 | 4 | 0 | 0 | 0-0 | 2 | 21.60 | 19 | .545 | .545 | 0 | — | 0 | | -3 | | -0.1 |

YEAR	TM LG	W	L	PCT	G	GS	CG-SHO	SV-BS	IP	H	R	HR	HB	BB-IB	SO	ERA	AERA	OAV	OOB	AB-HR-SH	AVG	PB	SUP	APR	DL	PW

GROVE, ORVAL Orval Leroy B8.29.1919 Mineral KS D4.20.1992 Carmichael CA BR/TR/6-3/196 d5.28

1940	Chi A	0	0	—	3	0	0	0	6	4	2	0	0	4	1	3.00	147	.182	.308	1	.000	-0		1		0.0
1941	Chi A	0	0	—	2	0	0	0	7	9	8	2	0	5	5	10.29	40	.321	.424	2	.000	-0		-4		-0.2
1942	Chi A	4	6	.400	12	8	4	0	66.1	77	47	1	1	33	21	5.16	70	.283	.363	22-1-3	.227	1	62	-13	-17	-1.5
1943	Chi A	15	9	.625	32	25	18-3	2	216.1	192	84	9	4	72	76	2.75	122	.239	.304	66-0-7	.182	2	109	12		1.6
1944	Chi A☆	14	15	.483	34	33	11-2	0	234.2	237	112	11	8	71	105	3.72	92	.263	.322	77-0-4	.104	-3	81	-6		-0.8
1945	Chi A	14	12	.538	33	30	16-4	1	217	233	100	12	5	68	54	3.44	96	.273	.322	71-0-2	.099	-4	101	-5		-0.9
1946	Chi A	8	13	.381	33	26	10-1	0	205.1	213	96	10	3	78	60	3.02	113	.272	.340	65-0-3	.108	-2	102	5		0.3
1947	Chi A	6	8	.429	25	19	6-1	0	135.2	158	78	10	4	70	33	4.44	82	.296	.382	48-0-1	.146	-0	93	-12		-1.1
1948	Chi A	2	10	.167	32	11	1	1	87.2	110	64	6	3	42	18	6.16	69	.315	.393	21-0-1	.095	-1	64	-17		-2.1
1949	Chi A	0	0	—	1	0	0	0	0.2	4	4	1	1	1	1	54.00	8	.667	.750	0	—	0		-3		-0.2
Total	10	63	73	.463	207	152	66-11	4	1176.2	1237	595	62	29	444	374	3.78	93	.272	.340	373-1-21	.129	-9	92	-42		-4.9

GROVE, LEFTY Robert Moses B3.6.1900 Lonaconing MD D5.22.1975 Norwalk OH BL/TL/6-3/190 d4.14 HF1947

1925	Phi A	10	12	.455	45	18	5	1	197	207	120	11	5	131	**116**	4.75	98	.278	.390	65-0-2	.123	-6	91	0		-0.5
1926	Phi A	13	13	.500	45	33	20-1	6	258	227	97	6	6	101	**194**	2.51	166	.244	.322	81-0-9	.099	-5	96	44		3.7
1927	Phi A	20	13	.606	51	28	14-1	9	262.1	251	116	6	2	79	**174**	3.19	134	.252	.309	80-2-9	.125	-3	110	28		3.0
1928	Phi A	24	8	.750	39	31	24-4	4	261.2	228	93	10	1	64	**183**	2.58	156	.229	.277	88-1-5	.170	1	110	41		4.7
1929	Phi A	20	6	**.769**	42	37	19-2	4	275.1	278	104	8	3	81	**170**	2.81	151	.262	.316	102-1-8	.216	1	139	43		3.6
1930	†Phi A	28	5	**.848**	50	32	22-2	**9**	291	273	101	8	5	60	**209**	2.54	184	.247	.288	110-2-4	.200	0	125	66		6.9
1931	†Phi A	31	4	**.886**	41	30	27-4	5	288.2	249	84	10	-1	62	175	2.06	218	.229	.271	115-0-4	.200	-2	103	74		8.2
1932	Phi A	25	10	.714	44	30	27-4	7	291.2	269	101	13	1	79	188	2.84	159	.241	.292	107-4-4	.168	0	115	54		5.9
1933	Phi A★	24	8	.750	45	28	21-2	6	275.1	280	113	12	4	83	114	3.20	134	.261	.316	105-1-4	.086	-1	109	35		3.1
1934	Bos A	8	8	.500	22	12	5	0	109.1	149	84	5	1	32	43	6.50	74	.320	.365	37-1-3	.162	-0	88	-15		-1.9
1935	Bos A☆	20	12	.625	35	30	23-2	1	273	269	105	6	3	65	121	2.70	176	.257	.302	89-1-6	.079	-5	76	55		5.5
1936	Bos A★	17	12	.586	35	30	22-6	2	253.1	237	90	14	4	65	130	2.81	189	.246	.297	80-0-12	.138	-3	78	67		6.6
1937	Bos A☆	17	9	.654	32	32	21-3	0	262	269	101	9	1	83	153	3.02	157	.261	.317	91-0-6	.143	-3	92	49		3.9
1938	Bos A★	14	4	.778	24	21	12-1	1	163.2	169	65	8	1	52	99	3.08	160	.263	.319	54-0-7	.148	-1	110	33		3.0
1939	Bos A☆	15	4	**.789**	23	23	17-2	0	191	180	63	8	1	58	81	2.54	186	.249	.305	67-1-9	.134	-1*	96	45		3.7
1940	Bos A	7	6	.538	22	21	9-1	0	153.1	159	73	20	1	50	62	3.99	113	.269	.328	53-1-5	.151	-1*	96	9		0.5
1941	Bos A	7	7	.500	21	21	10	0	134	155	84	7	2	42	54	4.37	95	.287	.340	45-0-6	.111	-1	125	-6		-0.8
Total	17	300	141	.680	616	457	298-35	55	3940.2	3849	1594	162	42	1187	2266	3.06	148	.255	.311	1369-15-103	.148	-37	104	622		59.1

GROVER, CHARLIE Charles Byrd "Bugs" B6.20.1890 Gallipolis OH D5.24.1971 Emmett Twp. MI BL/TR/6-1.5/185 d9.9

| 1913 | Det A | 0 | 0 | — | 3 | 1 | 0 | 0 | 10.2 | 9 | 4 | 0 | 0 | 7 | 2 | 3.38 | 86 | .273 | .400 | 3-0-1 | .000 | -0 | 51 | 0 | | 0.0 |

GRUBBS, TOM Thomas Dillard "Judge" B2.22.1894 Mt.Sterling KY D1.28.1986 Lexington KY BR/TR/6-2/165 d10.3 Col Kentucky

| 1920 | NY N | 0 | 1 | .000 | 5 | 0 | 0 | 0 | 5 | 9 | 4 | 0 | 0 | 0 | 0 | 7.20 | 42 | .409 | .409 | 1 | .000 | -0 | 26 | -2 | | -0.3 |

GRUBER, HENRY Henry John B12.14.1863 Hamden CT D9.26.1932 New Haven CT BR/TR/5-9/155 d7.28

1887	Det N	4	3	.571	7	7	7	0	62.1	63	29	3	0	21	12	2.74	149	.262	.322	24	.167	1	118	9		0.7
1888	Det N	11	14	.440	27	25	25-3	0	240	196	121	8	4	41	71	2.29	122	.213	.249	92	.141	-1	91	9		0.7
1889	Cle N	7	16	.304	25	23	23	1	205	198	125	6	8	94	74	3.64	111	.246	.331	69	.101	-1	75	8		0.6
1890	Cle P	22	23	.489	48	44	39-1	0	383.1	464	352	15	15	204	110	4.27	93	.286	.371	163	.221	6*	99	-15		-0.7
1891	Cle N	17	22	.436	44	40	35-1	0	348.2	407	258	10	7	119	79	4.13	84	.281	.333	141-1	.163	1*	96	-16		-1.2
Total	5	61	78	.439	151	139	129-5	1	1239.1	1328	885	42	34	479	346	3.67	99	.264	.332	489-1	.170	5	94	-5		0.1

GRUNDT, KEN Kenneth Allan B8.26.1969 Melrose Park IL BL/TL/6-4/195* [SFN91 53/1354] d8.8 Col Missouri Southern

1996	Bos A	0	0	—	1	0	0	0-0	0.1	1	1	0	0	0-0	0	27.00	19	.500	.500	0	—	0		-1		0.0
1997	Bos A	0	0	—	2	0	0	0-0	3	5	3	0	0	0-0	0	9.00	52	.357	.357	0	—	0		-1		-0.1
Total	2	0	0	—	3	0	0	0-0	3.1	6	4	0	0	0-0	0	10.80	44	.375	.375	0	—	0		-2		-0.1

GRUNWALD, AL Alfred Henry "Stretch" B2.13.1930 Los Angeles CA BL/TL/6-4/200(180-210) d4.18

1955	Pit N	0	0	—	3	0	0	0	7.2	7	4	1	0	7-0	2	4.70	88	.241	.389	4	.500	1		0		0.0
1959	KC A	0	1	.000	6	1	0	1	11.1	18	14	1	0	11-1	9	7.94	50	.360	.475	4	.000	-1*	88	-6		-0.6
Total	2	0	1	.000	9	1	0	1	19	25	18	2	0	18-1	11	6.63	61	.316	.443	8	.250	0	88	-6		-0.6

GRYBOSKI, KEVIN Kevin John B11.15.1973 Wilkes-Barre PA BR/TR/6-5/220(220-255) [SeaA95 16/426] d4.13 Col Wilkes

2002	†Atl N	3	2	.667	57	0	0	0-2	51.2	50	20	6	5	37-5	33	3.48	116	.256	.388	0	—	0		4	27	0.2
2003	†Atl N	6	4	.600	64	0	0	0-4	44.1	44	22	3	2	23-6	32	3.86	109	.272	.369	1	.000	-0		1	23	0.2
2004	†Atl N	3	2	.600	69	0	0	2-2	50.2	54	22	2	0	23-4	24	2.84	152	.280	.356	0	—	0		6		0.6
2005	Atl N	0	0	—	31	0	0	0-2	21.1	24	10	0	2	12-3	8	2.95	146	.300	.396	0	—	0		2	15	0.1
	Tex A	1	1	.500	11	0	0	0-0	9.2	17	15	1	1	8-2	2	11.17	41	.378	.481	0	—	0		-8		-1.3
Total	4	12	8	.600	232	0	0	2-10	177.2	189	89	12	10	103-20	99	3.75	113	.280	.382	1	.000	-0		5	65	-0.2

GRZANICH, MIKE Michael Edward B8.24.1972 Canton IL BR/TR/6-1/180 [HouN92 19/517] d5.14 Col Parkland (IL) JC

| 1998 | Hou N | 0 | 0 | — | 2 | 0 | 0 | 0-0 | 1 | 2 | 2 | 0 | 0 | 2-0 | 1 | 18.00 | 23 | .333 | .500 | 0 | — | 0 | | -1 | | -0.1 |

GRZENDA, JOE Joseph Charles B6.8.1937 Scranton PA BR/TL/6-2/180* d4.26

1961	Det A	1	0	1.000	4	0	0	0	5.2	5	5	2	0	2-1	0	7.94	52	.375	.423	1	1.000	0		-2		-0.3
1964	KC A	0	2	.000	20	0	0	0	25	34	15	2	1	13-2	17	5.40	71	.324	.400	2	.000	-0		-4		-0.3
1966	KC A	0	0	—	21	0	0	0	22	28	8	1	0	12-3	14	3.27	104	.337	.412	1	.000	-0		1		0.1
1967	NY N	0	0	—	11	0	0	0	16.2	14	4	0	1	8-4	9	2.16	157	.237	.333	1	.000	-0		2		0.1
1969	†Min A	4	1	.800	38	0	0	3-1	48.2	52	23	4	1	17-4	24	3.88	94	.281	.343	5	.000	0		-1		0.0
1970	Was A	3	6	.333	49	3	0	6-1	84.2	86	52	8	3	34-9	38	5.00	72	.267	.341	12	.000	-1	181	-13		-1.6
1971	Was A	5	2	.714	50	0	0	5-3	70.1	54	19	2	1	17-7	56	1.92	176	.217	.266	7-0-2	.143	-0		11		1.2
1972	StL N	1	0	1.000	30	0	0	0-0	35	46	24	1	3	17-8	15	5.66	61	.326	.410	1	.000	-0		-8		-0.4
Total	8	14	13	.519	219	3	0	14-5	308	323	150	20	10	120-38	173	4.00	88	.277	.346	30-0-2	.067	-2	181	-14		-1.1

GUANTE, CECILIO Cecilio (Magallane) B2.1.1960 Villa Mella, D.R. BR/TR/6-3/205(185-205) d5.1

1982	Pit N	0	0	—	10	0	0	0-0	27	28	16	1	2	5-0	26	3.33	112	.264	.299	5	.000	-1		-1		-0.1
1983	Pit N	2	6	.250	49	0	0	9-0	100.1	90	45	5	2	46-6	82	3.32	113	.241	.325	22	.091	-1		3		0.1
1984	Pit N	2	3	.400	27	0	0	2-1	41.1	32	12	3	2	16-2	30	2.61	139	.224	.305	4-0-1	.000	-0		5	17	0.6
1985	Pit N	4	6	.400	63	0	0	5-7	109	84	34	5	5	40-9	92	2.72	133	.214	.299	17	.059	-1		12	1.0	0.3
1986	Pit N	5	2	.714	52	0	0	4-4	78	65	32	11	3	29-3	63	3.35	116	.225	.300	1	.000	-0		5	29	0.3
1987	NY A	3	2	.600	23	0	0	1-1	44	42	30	4	1	20-0	46	5.73	77	.247	.323	0	—	0		-6	84	-0.7
1988	NY A	5	6	.455	56	0	0	11-6	75	59	25	10	5	22-3	61	2.88	138	.213	.282	0	—	0		10		1.5
	Tex A	0	0	—	7	0	0	1-0	4.2	8	1	1	0	4-1	4	1.93	213	.400	.500	0	—	0		1		0.1
	Year	5	6	.455	63	0	0	12-6	79.2	67	26	11	5	26-4	65	2.82	141	.226	.298	0	—	0		11		1.6
1989	Tex A	5	6	.500	50	0	0	2-3	69	66	35	7	4	36-10	69	3.91	102	.249	.343	0	—	0		0	15	0.0
1990	Cle A	2	3	.400	26	1	0	0-3	46.2	38	26	10	3	18-4	30	5.01	79	.220	.301	0	—	0	69	-4		-0.4
Total	9	29	34	.460	363	1	0	35-25	595	512	256	61	27	236-38	503	3.48	111	.232	.310	49-0-1	.061	-3	69	25	145	2.4

GUARDADO, EDDIE Edward Adrian B10.2.1970 Stockton CA BR/TL/6-0/194(190-205) [MinA90 21/570] d6.13 Col San Joaquin Delta (CA) JC

1993	Min A	3	8	.273	19	16	0	0	94.2	123	68	13	1	36-2	46	6.18	71	.319	.376	0	—	0	86	-17		-1.7
1994	Min A	0	2	.000	4	4	0	0-0	17	26	16	3	0	4-0	8	8.47	58	.351	.375	0	—	0	65	-6		-0.6
1995	Min A	4	9	.308	51	5	0	0-1	91.1	99	54	13	0	43-2	71	5.12	94	.280	.356	0	—	0	35	-2		-0.3
1996	Min A	6	5	.545	**83**	0	0	4-3	73.2	61	45	12	3	33-4	74	5.25	98	.228	.316	0	—	0		-1		-0.1
1997	Min A	0	0	.000	69	0	0	1-0	46	45	23	7	2	17-2	54	3.91	119	.251	.322	0	—	0		3		0.3
1998	Min A	3	1	.750	79	0	0	0-4	65.2	66	34	10	0	28-6	53	4.52	106	.265	.332	0	—	0		3		0.1
1999	Min A	2	5	.286	63	0	0	2-2	48	37	24	6	2	25-4	50	4.50	115	.222	.328	0	—	0		4	38	0.6
2000	Min A	7	4	.636	70	0	0	9-2	61.2	55	27	14	1	25-3	52	3.94	134	.238	.313	0	—	0		9		0.5
2001	Min A	7	1	.875	67	0	0	12-2	66.2	47	27	5	1	23-4	67	3.51	133	.197	.268	0	—	0		8	15	1.1
2002	†Min A★	1	3	.250	68	0	0	**45**-6	67.2	53	22	9	1	18-2	70	2.93	153	.215	.269	0	—	0		12		2.1
2003	†Min A★	3	5	.375	66	0	0	41-4	65.1	65	22	9	1	14-2	60	2.89	155	.207	.249	0	—	0		12		2.3
2004	Sea A	2	2	.500	41	0	0	18-7	45.1	31	14	8	1	14-0	45	2.78	161	.194	.261	1	.000	-0		9	64	1.4

YEAR	TM LG	W	L	PCT	G	GS	CG-SHO	SV-BS	IP	H	R	HR	HB	BB-IB	SO	ERA	AERA	OAV	OOB	AB-HR-SH	AVG	PB	SUP	APR	DL	PW
2005	Sea A	2	3	.400	58	0	0	36-5	56.1	52	23	7	0	15-3	48	2.72	155	.239	.285	0	—	0	7			1.3
Total	13	40	52	.435	738	25	0	170-38	799.1	745	399	114	12	297-34	698	4.28	110	.248	.314	1	.000	-0	70	41	117	8.1

GUBICZA, MARK Mark Steven B8.14.1962 Philadelphia PA BR/TR/6-5/220(210-230) [KCA81 2/34] d4.6

YEAR	TM LG	W	L	PCT	G	GS	CG-SHO	SV-BS	IP	H	R	HR	HB	BB-IB	SO	ERA	AERA	OAV	OOB	AB-HR-SH	AVG	PB	SUP	APR	DL	PW
1984	KC A	10	14	.417	29	29	4-2	0-0	189	172	90	13	5	75-0	111	4.05	100	.243	.317	0	—	0	89	1		0.2
1985	†KC A	14	10	.583	29	28	0	0-0	177.1	160	88	14	5	77-0	99	4.06	103	.238	.319	0	—	0	100	3		0.5
1986	KC A	12	6	.667	35	24	3-2	0-0	180.2	155	77	8	5	84-2	118	3.64	117	.233	.321	0	—	0	113	14	15	1.4
1987	KC A	13	18	.419	35	35	10-2	0-0	241.2	231	114	18	6	120-3	166	3.98	115	.259	.347	0	—	0	81	19		2.3
1988	KC A★	20	8	.714	35	35	8-4	0-0	269.2	237	94	11	6	83-3	183	2.70	148	.234	.294	0	—	0	112	37		3.9
1989	KC A★	15	11	.577	36	36	8-2	0-0	255	252	100	10	5	63-8	173	3.04	130	.259	.305	0	—	0	102	22		2.2
1990	KC A	4	7	.364	16	16	2	0-0	94	101	48	5	4	38-4	71	4.50	86	.283	.355	0	—	0	97	-4	95	-0.4
1991	KC A	9	12	.429	26	26	0	0-0	133	168	90	10	6	42-1	89	5.68	73	.308	.361	0	—	0	92	-20	36	-2.6
1992	KC A	7	6	.538	18	18	2-1	0-0	111.1	110	47	8	1	36-3	81	3.72	110	.259	.316	0	—	0	91	6	86	0.6
1993	KC A	5	8	.385	49	6	0	2-1	104.1	128	61	2	2	43-8	80	4.66	99	.307	.370	0	—	0	86	-2		-0.3
1994	KC A	7	9	.438	22	22	0	0-0	130	158	74	11	0	26-5	59	4.50	112	.301	.331	0	—	0	90	6		0.7
1995	KC A	12	14	.462	33	33	3-2	0-0	213.1	222	97	21	6	62-2	81	3.75	128	.272	.326	0	—	0	77	24		2.7
1996	KC A	4	12	.250	19	19	2-1	0-0	119.1	132	70	22	7	34-0	55	5.13	98	.284	.339	0	—	0	68	0	86	0.0
1997	Ana N	0	1	.000	7	0	0	0-0	4.2	13	13	2	0	3-0	5	25.07	18	.481	.533	0	—	0	110	-10	170	-1.3
Total	14	132	136	.493	384	329	42-16	2-1	2223.1	2239	1063	155	58	786-39	1371	3.96	109	.264	.327	0	—	0	92	96	488	9.9

GUDAT, MARV Marvin John B8.27.1903 Goliad TX D3.1.1954 Los Angeles CA BL/TL/5-11/162 d5.21 Col UCLA ▲

YEAR	TM LG	W	L	PCT	G	GS	CG-SHO	SV-BS	IP	H	R	HR	HB	BB-IB	SO	ERA	AERA	OAV	OOB	AB-HR-SH	AVG	PB	SUP	APR	DL	PW
1929	Cin N	1	1	.500	7	2	2	0	26.2	29	12	0	0	4	0	3.38	135	.282	.308	10	.200	-0*	48	3		0.1
1932	†Chi N	0	0	—	1	0	0	0	1	1	0	0	0	0	2	0.00	—	.250	.250	94-1-1	.255	0*	0			0.0
Total	2	1	1	.500	8	2	2	0	27.2	30	12	0	0	4	2	3.25	139	.280	.306	104-1-1	.250	-0	48	3		0.1

GUERRIER, MATT Matthew Olson B8.2.1978 Cleveland OH BR/TR/6-3/185* [ChiA99 10/309] d6.17 Col Kent St.

YEAR	TM LG	W	L	PCT	G	GS	CG-SHO	SV-BS	IP	H	R	HR	HB	BB-IB	SO	ERA	AERA	OAV	OOB	AB-HR-SH	AVG	PB	SUP	APR	DL	PW
2004	Min A	0	1	.000	9	2	0	0-0	19	22	13	5	1	6-0	11	5.68	81	.293	.354	1	.000	-0	80	-2		-0.1
2005	Min A	0	3	.000	43	0	0	0-0	71.2	71	29	6	3	24-5	46	3.39	129	.259	.325	1	.000	-0	8			0.5
Total	2	0	4	.000	52	2	0	0-0	90.2	93	42	11	4	30-5	57	3.87	115	.266	.331	2	.000	-0	80	6		0.4

GUESE, WHITEY Theodore B1.24.1872 New Bremen OH D4.8.1951 Wapakoneta OH BR/TR/6-0.5/200 d7.13

YEAR	TM LG	W	L	PCT	G	GS	CG-SHO	SV-BS	IP	H	R	HR	HB	BB-IB	SO	ERA	AERA	OAV	OOB	AB-HR-SH	AVG	PB	SUP	APR	DL	PW
1901	Cin N	1	4	.200	6	5	4	0	44.1	62	48	5	3	14	11	6.09	53	.328	.383	15	.200	1	137	-17		-1.5

GUETTERMAN, LEE Arthur Lee B11.22.1958 Chattanooga TN BL/TL/6-8/227* [SeaA81 4/80] d9.12 Col Liberty

YEAR	TM LG	W	L	PCT	G	GS	CG-SHO	SV-BS	IP	H	R	HR	HB	BB-IB	SO	ERA	AERA	OAV	OOB	AB-HR-SH	AVG	PB	SUP	APR	DL	PW
1984	Sea A	0	0	—	3	0	0	0-0	4.1	9	2	0	0	2-0	2	4.15	97	.450	.500	0	—	0	0			0.0
1986	Sea A	0	4	.000	41	4	1	0-3	76	108	67	7	4	30-3	38	7.34	58	.347	.406	0	—	0	112	-24		-1.2
1987	Sea A	11	4	.733	25	17	2-1	0-0	113.1	117	60	13	2	35-2	42	3.81	124	.267	.320	0	—	0	106	8		1.0
1988	NY A	1	2	.333	20	2	0	0-1	40.2	49	21	2	1	14-0	15*	4.65	85	.306	.364	0	—	0	23	-2		-0.2
1989	NY A	5	5	.500	70	0	0	13-0	103	98	31	6	0	26-9	51	2.45	159	.258	.304	0	—	0	17			2.0
1990	NY A	11	7	.611	64	0	0	2-5	93	80	37	6	0	26-7	48	3.39	118	.236	.288	0	—	0	7		15	1.3
1991	NY A	3	4	.429	64	0	0	6-3	88	91	42	6	3	25-5	35	3.68	113	.268	.320	0	—	0	3			0.3
1992	NY A	1	1	.500	15	0	0	0-0	22.2	35	24	7	0	13-3	5	9.53	41	.354	.421	0	—	0	-13			-1.0
	NY N	3	4	.429	43	0	0	2-1	43.1	57	28	5	1	14-5	15	5.82	60	.324	.371	2	.000	0	-10			-1.6
1993	StL N	3	3	.500	40	0	0	1-3	46	41	18	1	2	16-5	19	2.93	137	.240	.309	2	.500	1	5			0.6
1995	Sea A	0	0	—	23	0	0	1-1	17	21	13	1	3	11-0	11	6.88	69	.300	.417	0	—	0	-3			-0.1
1996	Sea A	0	2	.000	17	0	0	0	11	11	8	0	0	10-2	6	4.09	122	.275	.420	0	—	0	0			0.0
Total	11	38	36	.514	425	23	3-1	25-17	658.1	717	351	52	16	222-41	287	4.33	96	.282	.340	4	.250	0	111	-12	15	1.1

GUIDRY, RON Ronald Ames B8.28.1950 Lafayette LA BL/TL/5-11/162(157-170) [NYA71 3/65] d7.27 Col Louisiana-Lafayette [DL 1989 NY A 78]

YEAR	TM LG	W	L	PCT	G	GS	CG-SHO	SV-BS	IP	H	R	HR	HB	BB-IB	SO	ERA	AERA	OAV	OOB	AB-HR-SH	AVG	PB	SUP	APR	DL	PW
1975	NY A	0	1	.000	10	1	0	0-0	15.2	15	6	0	1	9-0	15	3.45	108	.259	.362	0	—	0	95	1		0.0
1976	†NY A	0	0	—	7	0	0	0-0	16	20	12	1	0	4-0	12	5.63	61	.294	.333	0	—	0	-4			-0.2
1977	†NY A	16	7	.696	31	25	9-5	1-0	210.2	174	72	12	0	65-2	176	2.82	141	.224	.283	0	—	0*	107	28		2.9
1978	†NY A★	25	3	.893	35	35	16-9	0-0	273.2	187	61	13	1	72-1	248	1.74	210	.193	.249	0	—	0*	116	60		6.4
1979	NY A★	18	8	.692	33	30	15-2	2-0	236.1	203	83	20	0	71-0	201	2.78	148	.236	.292	0	—	0*	100	35		3.6
1980	†NY A	17	10	.630	37	29	5-3	1-1	219.2	215	97	19	1	80-1	166	3.56	111	.260	.322	0	—	0	118	11		1.3
1981	†NY A	11	5	.688	23	21	0	0-0	127	100	41	12	1	26-0	104	2.76	131	.214	.256	0	—	0	98	13		1.7
1982	NY A☆	14	8	.636	34	33	6-1	0-0	222	216	104	22	1	69-3	162	3.81	106	.254	.309	0	—	0	124	5		0.4
1983	NY A★	21	9	.700	31	31	21-3	0-0	250.1	232	99	26	2	60-3	156	3.42	116	.244	.288	0	—	0	105	18		2.1
1984	NY A	10	11	.476	29	28	5-1	0-0	195.2	223	102	26	2	44-3	127	4.51	85	.287	.323	0	—	0*	109	-13	18	-1.2
1985	NY A	22	6	.786	34	33	11-2	0-0	259	243	104	28	0	42-3	143	3.27	124	.248	.277	0	—	0	125	24		2.3
1986	NY A	9	12	.429	30	30	5	0-0	192.1	202	94	28	1	38-2	140	3.98	104	.265	.300	0	—	0	89	4	24	0.3
1987	NY A	5	8	.385	22	17	2	0-0	117.2	111	50	14	1	38-3	96	3.67	121	.248	.307	0	—	0	86	11		1.0
1988	NY A	2	3	.400	12	10	0	0-0	56	57	28	7	3	15-3	32	4.18	95	.259	.311	0	—	0*	94	-1	100	-0.1
Total	14	170	91	.651	368	323	95-26	4-1	2392	2198	953	226	13	633-24	1778	3.29	120	.244	.292	0	—	0	108	192	220	20.5

GUINN, SKIP Drannon Eugene B10.25.1944 St.Charles MO BR/TL/5-10/180* d5.7 Col Santa Monica (CA) City

YEAR	TM LG	W	L	PCT	G	GS	CG-SHO	SV-BS	IP	H	R	HR	HB	BB-IB	SO	ERA	AERA	OAV	OOB	AB-HR-SH	AVG	PB	SUP	APR	DL	PW
1968	Atl N	0	0	—	3	0	0	0	5	3	2	0	0	3-0	4	3.60	83	.167	.286	0*		0	0			0.0
1969	Hou N	1	2	.333	28	0	0	0-2	27	34	22	3	1	21-2	33	6.67	53	.304	.412	3	.000	-0	-9			-0.9
1971	Hou N	0	0	—	4	0	0	1-0	4.2	1	0	0	0	3-1	3	0.00	—	.067	.222	0	—	0	2			0.1
Total	3	1	2	.333	35	0	0	1-2	36.2	38	24	3	1	27-3	40	5.40	64	.262	.377	3	.000	-0	-7			-0.8

GUISE, LEFTY Witt Orison B9.18.1908 Driggs AR D8.13.1968 Little Rock AR BL/TL/6-2/172 d9.3 Col Florida

YEAR	TM LG	W	L	PCT	G	GS	CG-SHO	SV-BS	IP	H	R	HR	HB	BB-IB	SO	ERA	AERA	OAV	OOB	AB-HR-SH	AVG	PB	SUP	APR	DL	PW
1940	Cin N	0	0	—	2	0	0	0	7.2	8	2	1	0	1	5	1.17	323	.296	.424	3	.333	0	2			0.1

GULLETT, DON Donald Edward B1.6.1951 Lynn KY BR/TL/6-0/190* [CinN69 1/14] d4.10 C13 [DL 1979 NY A 180, 1980 NY A 180]

YEAR	TM LG	W	L	PCT	G	GS	CG-SHO	SV-BS	IP	H	R	HR	HB	BB-IB	SO	ERA	AERA	OAV	OOB	AB-HR-SH	AVG	PB	SUP	APR	DL	PW
1970	†Cin N	5	2	.714	44	2	0	6-0	77.2	54	23	4	0	44-6	76	2.43	166	.196	.306	19	.211	1	89	14		1.5
1971	Cin N	16	6	.727	35	31	4-3	0-3	217.2	196	73	14	2	64-6	107	2.65	128	.242	.298	75-0-5	.120	-2*	94	16		1.2
1972	†Cin N	9	10	.474	31	16	2	2-2	134.2	127	61	15	1	43-5	96	3.94	82	.250	.309	38-0-5	.211	2	128	-9		-1.2
1973	†Cin N	18	8	.692	45	30	7-4	2-0	228.1	198	95	24	3	69-8	153	3.51	98	.232	.290	64-0-7	.188	3*	128	0		0.3
1974	Cin N	17	11	.607	36	35	10-3	0-1	243	201	93	22	2	88-8	183	3.04	115	.222	.291	80-0-10	.237	4*	131	13		1.8
1975	†Cin N	15	4	.789	22	22	8-3	0-0	159.2	127	49	11	2	56-4	98	2.42	148	.218	.287	62-0-3	.226	3	126	19	62	0.7
1976	†Cin N	11	3	.786	23	20	4	1-0	126	119	48	8	0	48-3	64	3.00	117	.253	.321	44-0-6	.182	-0*	131	6		0.7
1977	†NY A	14	4	.778	22	22	7-1	0-0	158.1	137	67	14	1	69-1	116	3.58	111	.232	.312	0	—	0	131	8	24	0.8
1978	NY A	4	2	.667	8	8	2	0-0	44.2	46	19	3	1	20-1	28	3.63	101	.269	.347	0	—	0	129	1	98	0.1
Total	9	109	50	.686	266	186	44-14	11-6	1390	1205	528	115	12	501-42	921	3.11	114	.233	.301	382-0-36	.194	10	123	68	544	7.8

GULLICKSON, BILL William Lee B2.20.1959 Marshall MN BR/TR/6-3/215(198-225) [MonN77 1/2] d9.26

YEAR	TM LG	W	L	PCT	G	GS	CG-SHO	SV-BS	IP	H	R	HR	HB	BB-IB	SO	ERA	AERA	OAV	OOB	AB-HR-SH	AVG	PB	SUP	APR	DL	PW
1979	Mon N	0	0	—	1	0	0	0	1	0	0	0	0	0	0	0.00	—	.500	.500	0	—	0	0			0.0
1980	Mon N	10	5	.667	24	19	5-2	0-0	141	127	53	6	2	50-2	120	3.00	121	.238	.303	40-0-10	.175	0	111	10		1.0
1981	†Mon N	7	9	.438	22	22	3-2	0-0	157.1	142	54	3	4	34-4	115	2.80	127	.239	.283	46-0-4	.152	-0	87	13		1.3
1982	Mon N	12	14	.462	34	34	6	0-0	236.2	231	101	25	4	61-2	155	3.57	103	.254	.302	82-0-9	.122	-2	107	6		0.2
1983	Mon N	17	12	.586	34	34	10-1	0-0	242.1	230	108	19	4	59-4	120	3.75	97	.251	.297	82-1-9	.134	1	113	-2		-0.1
1984	Mon N	12	9	.571	32	32	3	0-0	226.2	230	100	27	1	37-7	100	3.61	96	.265	.294	73-0-6	.110	-2	105	-3	18	-0.8
1985	Mon N	14	12	.538	29	29	4-1	0-0	181.1	187	78	19	1	47-9	68	3.52	98	.271	.315	64-0-4	.188	2	91	-1	21	0.0
1986	Cin N	15	12	.556	37	37	6-2	0-0	244.2	245	103	24	2	60-10	121	3.38	114	.264	.306	79-0-9	.076	-4	98	12		0.7
1987	Cin N	10	11	.476	27	27	3-1	0-0	165	172	99	32	1	39-6	89	4.85	87	.267	.308	53-1-4	.208	2	101	-12		-1.2
	NY A	4	2	.667	8	8	1	0-0	48	46	29	7	1	11-1	28	4.88	91	.253	.296	0	—	0	123	-3		-0.3
1990	Hou N	10	14	.417	32	32	2-1	0-0	193.1	221	100	21	2	61-14	73	3.82	98	.287	.338	57-1-7	.158	2	88	-5		-0.6
1991	Det A	20	9	.690	35	35	4	0-0	226.1	256	109	22	4	44-13	91	3.90	107	.288	.321	0-0-1	—	0	124	6		0.5
1992	Det A	14	13	.519	34	34	4-1	0-0	221.2	228	109	35	2	50-5	64	4.34	92	.267	.305	0	—	0	116	-6		-0.6
1993	Det A	13	9	.591	28	28	2	0-0	159.1	186	106	28	3	44-3	70	5.37	81	.291	.336	0	—	0	121	-18	35	-2.1
1994	Det A	4	5	.444	21	19	1	0-0	115.1	156	79	24	4	25-2	65	5.93	83	.322	.360	0	—	0	130	-10		-0.6
Total	14	162	136	.544	398	390	54-11	0-0	2560	2659	1228	282	34	622-82	1279	3.93	98	.268	.311	576-3-63	.141	-2	108	-13	74	-2.6

GUMBERT, AD Addison Courtney B10.10.1868 Pittsburgh PA D4.23.1925 Pittsburgh PA BR/TR/5-10/200 d9.15 b-Billy

YEAR	TM LG	W	L	PCT	G	GS	CG-SHO	SV-BS	IP	H	R	HR	HB	BB-IB	SO	ERA	AERA	OAV	OOB	AB-HR-SH	AVG	PB	SUP	APR	DL	PW
1888	Chi N	3	3	.500	6	6	5	0	48.2	44	24	0	5	10	16	3.14	96	.234	.291	24	.333	2*	111	1		0.2
1889	Chi N	16	13	.552	31	28	25-2	0	246.1	258	148	16	14	76	91	3.62	115	.261	.323	153-7	.288	11*	112	17		2.4

YEAR	TM LG	W	L	PCT	G	GS	CG-SHO	SV-BS	IP	H	R	HR	HB	BB-IB	SO	ERA	AERA	OAV	OOB	AB-HR-SH	AVG	PB	SUP	APR	DL	PW
1890	Bos P	23	12	.657	39	33	27-1	0	277.1	338	189	18	11	86	81	3.96	111	.288	.342	145-3	.241	5*	115	15		1.8
1891	Chi N	17	11	.607	32	31	24-1	0	256.1	282	149	5	10	90	73	3.58	93	.269	.332	105	.305	12*	103	-4		0.8
1892	Chi N	22	19	.537	46	45	39	0	382.2	399	220	11	14	107	118	3.41	97	.258	.312	178-1	.236	4*	100	0		0.4
1893	Pit N	11	7	.611	22	20	16-2	0	162.2	207	119	5	5	78	40	5.15	88	.301	.376	95	.221	1*	121	-6		-0.4
1894	Pit N	15	14	.517	38	32	26	0	271	376	245	14	6	85	67	6.04	87	.325	.374	114-1-1	.298	6*	103	-25		-1.4
1895	Bro N	11	16	.407	33	26	20	1	234	288	183	11	12	69	45	5.08	87	.298	.352	97-2-0	.361	11*	102	-23		-1.0
1896	Bro N	0	4	.000	5	4	2	0	31	34	18	2	0	11	3	3.77	109	.276	.336	11	.182	-0	43	1		0.2
	Phi N	5	3	.625	11	10	7-1	0	77.1	99	55	0	4	23	14	4.54	95	.308	.362	34-1-1	.265	1	132	-2		-0.1
	Year	5	7	.417	16	14	9-1	0	108.1	133	73	2	4	34	17	4.32	99	.300	.355	45-1-1	.244	1	107	-1		0.1
Total	9	123	102	.547	263	235	191-7	1	1987.1	2325	1350	82	81	635	548	4.28	96	.284	.341	956-15-2	.274	53	107	-26		2.9

GUMBERT, HARRY Harry Edwards "Gunboat" B11.5.1909 Elizabeth PA D1.4.1995 Wimberley TX BR/TR/6-2/185* d9.12 Mil 1945

YEAR	TM LG	W	L	PCT	G	GS	CG-SHO	SV-BS	IP	H	R	HR	HB	BB-IB	SO	ERA	AERA	OAV	OOB	AB-HR-SH	AVG	PB	SUP	APR	DL	PW
1935	NY N	1	2	.333	6	3	1	0	23.2	35	27	1	0	10	11	6.08	63	.330	.388	8	.000	-1	73	-10		-1.1
1936	†NY N	11	3	.786	39	15	3	0	140.2	157	77	7	2	54	52	3.90	100	.281	.346	44	.250	2	121	-3		0.1
1937	†NY N	10	11	.476	34	24	10-1	1	200.1	194	92	11	4	62	65	3.68	106	.257	.317	72-1-2	.181	-1	95	6		0.8
1938	NY N	15	13	.536	38	33	14-1	0	235.2	238	114	13	7	84	84	4.01	94	.261	.328	84-0-3	.155	-3*	93	-3		-0.2
1939	NY N	18	11	.621	36	34	14-2	0	243.2	257	132	21	1	81	81	4.32	91	.271	.329	90-0-6	.200	-0*	107	-10		-0.8
1940	NY N	12	14	.462	35	30	14-2	2	237	230	110	17	3	81	77	3.76	103	.252	.316	87-1-2	.195	2	86	5		0.8
1941	NY N	1	1	.500	5	5	1	0	32.1	34	20	3	0	18	9	4.45	83	.266	.356	12-0-1	.167	-0	129	-3		-0.2
	StL N	11	5	.688	33	17	8-3	1	144.1	139	52	7	1	30	53	2.74	137	.251	.291	53-2-1	.321	6*	94	16		2.4
	Year	12	6	.667	38	22	9-3	1	176.2	173	72	10	1	48	62	3.06	123	.254	.304	65-2-2	.292	5	102	12		2.2
1942	†StL N	9	5	.643	38	19	5	5	163	156	61	3	1	59	52	3.26	105	.250	.315	54-0-1	.111	-2	115	4		0.4
1943	StL N	10	5	.667	21	19	7-2	0	133	115	46	4	0	32	40	2.84	118	.237	.284	45-0-6	.156	-2	97	9		0.9
1944	StL N	4	2	.667	10	7	3	1	61.1	60	23	1	0	19	16	2.49	141	.258	.313	21	.190	-0	102	6		0.6
	Cin N	10	8	.556	24	19	11-2	2	155.1	157	61	7	2	40	40	3.30	106	.262	.310	52-0-5	.096	-2	96	6		0.5
	Year	14	10	.583	34	26	14-2	3	216.2	217	84	8	2	59	56	3.07	114	.261	.311	73-0-5	.123	-2	98	13		1.1
1946	Cin N	6	8	.429	36	10	5	4	119	112	48	4	1	42	44	3.25	103	.248	.334	32-0-1	.250	1	67	2		0.4
1947	Cin N	10	10	.500	46	0	0	10	90.1	88	42	3	0	47	43	3.89	106	.260	.351	22-0-2	.273	1		3		0.7
1948	Cin N	10	8	.556	61	0	0	17	106.1	123	50	5	0	34	25	3.47	113	.291	.344	25-1-1	.040	-1		4		0.7
1949	Cin N	4	3	.571	29	0	0	2	40.2	58	28	5	1	8	12	5.53	76	.341	.374	2	.000	-0		-6		-0.9
	Pit N	1	4	.200	16	0	0	3	27.2	30	20	5	0	18	5	5.86	72	.270	.372	4	.250			-5		-0.8
	Year	5	7	.417	45	0	0	5	68.1	88	48	10	1	26	17	5.66	74	.313	.373	6	.167	-0		-10		-1.7
1950	Pit N	0	0	—	1	0	0	0	1.2	3	3	0	0	2	0	5.40	81	.333	.455	1	1.000			0		0.0
Total	15	143	113	.559	508	235	96-13	48	2156	2186	1012	121	23	721	709	3.68	102	.263	.323	708-5-31	.184	-2	98	20		4.3

GUMBERT, BILLY William Skeen B8.8.1865 Pittsburgh PA D4.13.1946 Pittsburgh PA BR/TR/6-1.5/200 d6.19 b-Ad

YEAR	TM LG	W	L	PCT	G	GS	CG-SHO	SV-BS	IP	H	R	HR	HB	BB-IB	SO	ERA	AERA	OAV	OOB	AB-HR-SH	AVG	PB	SUP	APR	DL	PW
1890	Pit N	4	6	.400	10	10	8	0	79.1	96	71	0	8	31	18	5.22	63	.290	.365	37-1	.243	3	134	-18		-1.4
1892	Pit N	3	2	.600	6	3	2	0	39.2	30	15	1	1	23	3	1.36	242	.201	.312	18	.111	-1*	64	7		0.7
1893	Lou N	0	0	—	1	1	0	0	0.2	2	6	0	0	5	0	27.00	16	.500	.778	1	1.000	1	175	-3		-0.1
Total	3	7	8	.467	17	14	10	0	119.2	128	92	0	9	59	21	4.06	81	.264	.355	56-1	.214	3	124	-14		-0.8

GUMPERT, DAVE David Lawrence B5.5.1958 South Haven MI BR/TR/6-1/190* d7.25 Col Aquinas

YEAR	TM LG	W	L	PCT	G	GS	CG-SHO	SV-BS	IP	H	R	HR	HB	BB-IB	SO	ERA	AERA	OAV	OOB	AB-HR-SH	AVG	PB	SUP	APR	DL	PW
1982	Det A	0	0	—	5	1	0	1-1	7	6	1	0	2	2-0	1	27.00	15	.700	.750			0	89	-5		-0.5
1983	Det A	0	2	.000	26	6	0	2-0	44.1	43	16	1	0	7-3	14	2.64	150	.257	.281	0	—	0		6		0.3
1985	Chi N	1	0	1.000	9	0	0	0-0	10.1	12	7	0	0	7-1	4	3.48	115	.279	.365	1	.000	-0		-1	26	-0.1
1986	Chi N	2	0	1.000	38	0	0	2-2	59.2	60	32	4	1	28-7	45	4.37	93	.267	.349	5	.000	-1		-2		-0.2
1987	KC A	0	0	—	8	0	0	0-0	19.1	27	16	3	0	6-0	13	6.05	76	.333	.375	0	—	0		-4		-0.2
Total	5	3	2	.600	86	1	0	5-3	135.2	149	77	9	1	50-11	76	4.31	95	.283	.342	6	.000	-1	89	-6	26	-0.7

GUMPERT, RANDY Randall Pennington B1.23.1918 Monocacy PA BR/TR/6-3/205* d6.13 Mil 1943-45 C1

YEAR	TM LG	W	L	PCT	G	GS	CG-SHO	SV-BS	IP	H	R	HR	HB	BB-IB	SO	ERA	AERA	OAV	OOB	AB-HR-SH	AVG	PB	SUP	APR	DL	PW
1936	Phi A	1	2	.333	22	3	2	0	62.1	74	42	2	0	32	9	4.76	107	.295	.375	22	.273	0	46	0		0.0
1937	Phi A	0	0	—	10	1	0	0	12	16	17	1	1	15	5	12.00	39	.333	.500	3	.333	0	111	-9		-0.4
1938	Phi A	0	2	.000	4	2	0	0	12.1	24	18	1	0	10	1	10.95	44	.393	.479	4	.250	0	91	-8		-0.9
1946	NY A	11	3	.786	33	12	4	1	132.2	113	44	8	0	32	63	2.31	150	.229	.276	47-0-1	.128	-2	151	15		1.2
1947	NY A	4	1	.800	24	6	2	0	56.1	71	36	4	0	28	25	5.43	65	.311	.387	14-0-2	.071	-1*	108	-12		-1.1
1948	NY A	1	0	1.000	15	0	0	0	25	27	10	1	0	6	12	2.88	142	.267	.315	0	—	0		3		0.1
	Chi A	2	6	.250	16	11	6-1	0	97.1	103	43	2	1	13	31	3.79	112	.275	.303	29-0-3	.138	-2	50	6		0.2
	Year	3	6	.333	31	11	6-1	0	122.1	130	53	6	3	19	43	3.60	117	.273	.305	29-0-3	.138	-2	51	9		0.3
1949	Chi A	13	16	.448	34	32	18-3	1	234	223	111	22	4	83	78	3.81	110	.253	.318	84-0-6	.190	-1	92	10		1.0
1950	Chi A	5	12	.294	40	17	6-1	0	155.1	165	87	15	4	58	48	4.75	94	.275	.343	42-0-4	.071	-4*	73	-2		-0.6
1951	Chi A☆	9	8	.529	33	16	7-1	2	141.2	156	74	20	1	34	45	4.32	93	.272	.314	45-0-4	.333	3*	128	-2		-0.1
1952	Bos A	1	0	1.000	10	1	0	0	19.2	15	11	1	1	5	6	4.12	96	.205	.266	5	.000	1	66	-1		-0.1
	Was A	4	9	.308	20	12	2	0	104	112	55	12	5	30	29	4.24	84	.273	.330	34-0-3	.206	0	110	-8		-0.9
	Year	5	9	.357	30	13	2	1	123.2	127	66	13	6	35	35	4.22	86	.262	.320	39-0-3	.179	-0	106	-8		-1.0
Total	10	51	59	.464	261	113	47-6	7	1052.2	1099	548	92	16	346	352	4.17	98	.268	.328	329-0-23	.182	-8	96	-8		-1.6

GUNDERSON, ERIC Eric Andrew B3.29.1966 Portland OR BR/TL/6-0/195(175-195) [SFN87 2/48] d4.11 Col Portland St.

YEAR	TM LG	W	L	PCT	G	GS	CG-SHO	SV-BS	IP	H	R	HR	HB	BB-IB	SO	ERA	AERA	OAV	OOB	AB-HR-SH	AVG	PB	SUP	APR	DL	PW
1990	SF N	1	2	.333	7	4	0	0-0	19.2	24	14	2	0	11-1	14	5.49	67	.293	.376	6	.000	-1	80	-5		-0.7
1991	SF N	0	0	—	2	0	0	1-0	3.1	6	4	0	0	1-0	2	5.40	67	.353	.389	0	—	0		-2		-0.1
1992	Sea A	2	1	.667	9	0	0	0-0	9.1	12	12	1	1	5-3	2	8.68	46	.324	.400	0	—	0		-6		-1.1
1994	NY N	0	0	—	14	0	0	0-0	9	5	0	0	0	4-0	4	0.00	—	.185	.290	0	—	0		4		0.2
1995	NY N	1	1	.500	30	0	0	0-3	24.1	25	10	2	1	8-3	19	3.70	109	.269	.330	0	—	0		1		0.2
	Bos A	2	1	.667	19	0	0	0-0	12.1	13	7	0	2	9-1	9	5.11	95	.295	.429	0	—	0		0		0.0
1996	Bos A	0	1	.000	28	0	0	0-0	17.1	21	17	5	2	8-2	7	8.31	61	.300	.378	0	—	0		-6		-0.3
1997	Tex A	2	1	.667	60	0	0	1-3	49.2	45	19	5	2	15-3	31	3.26	149	.241	.300	0	—	0		9	20	0.4
1998	Tex A	0	3	.000	68	1	0	0-2	67.2	88	43	13	1	19-4	41	5.19	94	.315	.358	0	—	0	38	-2		-0.1
1999	Tex A	0	0	—	11	0	0	0-0	10	20	8	1	0	2-0	6	7.20	72	.417	.431	0	—	0		-2	149	-0.1
2000	Tor A	0	1	.000	6	0	0	0-0	6.1	15	5	0	0	2-1	2	7.11	71	.455	.486	0	—	0		-2		-0.2
Total	11	8	11	.421	254	5	0	2-8	229	274	140	29	10	84-18	137	4.95	93	.299	.359	6	.000	-0	60	-11	169	-1.8

GUNKEL, RED Woodward William B4.15.1894 Sheffield IL D4.19.1954 Chicago IL BB/TR/5-8/158 d6.18 Col Illinois

YEAR	TM LG	W	L	PCT	G	GS	CG-SHO	SV-BS	IP	H	R	HR	HB	BB-IB	SO	ERA	AERA	OAV	OOB	AB-HR-SH	AVG	PB	SUP	APR	DL	PW
1916	Cle A	0	0	—	1	0	0	1	1	0	2	0	1	0	1	0.00	—	.000	.500	0	—	0		0		0.0

GURA, LARRY Lawrence Cyril B11.26.1947 Joliet IL BB/TL/6-1/185(170-185) [ChiN69 2/40] d4.30 Col Arizona St.

YEAR	TM LG	W	L	PCT	G	GS	CG-SHO	SV-BS	IP	H	R	HR	HB	BB-IB	SO	ERA	AERA	OAV	OOB	AB-HR-SH	AVG	PB	SUP	APR	DL	PW
1970	Chi N	1	3	.250	20	3	1	1-1	38	35	18	6	1	23-3	21	3.79	119	.254	.364	10-0-1	.000	-1	146	3		0.2
1971	Chi N	0	0	—	6	0	0	1-0	3	6	3	0	0	1-1	2	6.00	66	.400	.438	1	.000	-0		-1		-0.1
1972	Chi N	0	0	—	7	0	0	0-0	12.1	11	5	3	0	3-1	13	3.65	104	.250	.298	1	.000	-0		0		0.0
1973	Chi N	2	4	.333	21	7	1	0-1	64.2	79	39	10	1	11-0	43	4.87	81	.296	.325	15-0-2	.200	0*	118	-6		-0.4
1974	NY A	5	1	.833	8	8	4-2	0-0	56	54	17	2	2	12-1	17	2.41	147	.248	.287	0	—	0	124	7		0.8
1975	NY A	7	8	.467	26	20	5	0-0	151.1	173	65	13	0	41-1	65	3.51	106	.295	.342	0	—	0	81	4		0.4
1976	†KC A	4	0	1.000	20	2	1-1	0-0	62.2	47	20	4	1	20-3	22	2.30	153	.213	.274	0	—	0	88	8	22	0.6
1977	†KC A	8	5	.615	52	6	1-1	10-6	106.1	108	43	8	1	28-4	46	3.13	129	.265	.310	0	—	0	108	10		1.4
1978	†KC A	16	4	.800	35	26	8-2	0-0	221.2	183	73	13	4	60-3	81	2.72	141	.229	.283	0	—	0	104	29		2.6
1979	KC A	13	12	.520	39	33	7-1	0-1	233.2	226	117	29	4	73-4	85	4.47	96	.253	.312	0	—	0	116	-7		-0.6
1980	†KC A☆	18	10	.643	36	36	16-4	0-0	283.1	272	107	20	5	76-6	113	2.95	137	.255	.304	0	—	0	115	33		3.1
1981	†KC A	11	8	.579	23	23	12-2	0-0	172.1	139	61	14	4	35-0	61	2.72	133	.223	.265	0	—	0	91	16		1.8
1982	KC A	18	12	.600	37	37	8-3	0-0	248	251	116	24	31	64-2	98	4.03	101	.261	.309	0	—	0	111	1		0.2
1983	KC A	11	18	.379	34	31	5	0-0	200.1	220	119	23	8	76-6	57	4.90	84	.284	.347	0	—	0*	80	-16		-1.8
1984	KC A	12	9	.571	31	25	3	0-0	168.2	175	102	26	4	67-3	68	5.18	78	.269	.338	0	—	0	129	-19		-2.0
1985	KC A	0	0	—	5	3	0	1-0	4.1	7	6	1	1	4-0	1	12.46	34	.368	.478	0	—	0		-4		-0.2
	Chi N	0	3	.000	5	5	0	0-0	20.1	34	19	4	1	6-0	7	8.41	48	.370	.414	6	.000	-0	88	-8		-1.0
Total	16	126	97	.565	403	261	71-16	14-9	2047	2020	958	204	46	600-38	801	3.76	106	.260	.313	33-0-3	.091	-2	106	50	22	2.1

GUTH, CHARLIE Charles J. B1856 Chicago IL D7.5.1883 Cambridge MA d9.30

YEAR	TM LG	W	L	PCT	G	GS	CG-SHO	SV-BS	IP	H	R	HR	HB	BB-IB	SO	ERA	AERA	OAV	OOB	AB-HR-SH	AVG	PB	SUP	APR	DL	PW
1880	Chi N	1	0	1.000	1	1	1	0	9	12	8	0		1	7	5.00	48	.293	.310	4	.250	0	204	-2		-0.2

YEAR	TM LG	W	L	PCT	G	GS	CG-SHO	SV-BS	IP	H	R	HR	HB	BB-IB	SO	ERA	AERA	OAV	OOB	AB-HR-SH	AVG	PB	SUP	APR	DL	PW
GUTHRIE, JEREMY					Jeremy Shane B4.8.1979 Roseburg OR BR/TR/6-1/200* [CleA02 1/22] d8.28 Col Brigham Young/Stanford																				
2004	Cle A	0	0	—	6	0	0	0-0	11.2	9	6	1	1	6-0	7	4.63	94	.214	.327	0	—	0	0	0		0.0
2005	Cle A	0	0	—	1	0	0	0-0	6	9	4	2	0	2-0	3	6.00	68	.360	.393	0	—	0	-1			0.0
Total	2	0	0	—	7	0	0	0-0	17.2	18	10	3	1	8-0	10	5.09	84	.269	.351	0	—	0	-1			0.0
GUTHRIE, MARK					Mark Andrew B9.22.1965 Buffalo NY BR/TL/6-4/207(196-215) [MinA87 7/165] d7.25 Col Louisiana St.																				
1989	Min A	2	4	.333	13	8	0	0-0	57.1	66	32	7	1	21-1	38	4.55	91	.292	.348	0	—	0	68	-3		-0.3
1990	Min A	7	9	.438	24	21	3-1	0-0	144.2	154	65	8	1	39-3	101	3.79	110	.276	.325	0	—	0	92	7		0.7
1991	†Min A	7	5	.583	41	12	0	2-0	98	116	52	11	1	41-2	72	4.32	99	.303	.369	0	—	0*	117	-1		-0.1
1992	Min A	2	3	.400	54	0	0	5-2	75	59	27	7	0	23-7	76	2.88	142	.215	.274	0	—	0		9		0.7
1993	Min A	2	1	.667	22	0	0	0-1	21	20	11	2	0	16-2	15	4.71	94	.267	.387	0	—	0		0	128	0.0
1994	Min A	4	2	.667	50	2	0	1-2	51.1	65	43	8	2	18-2	38	6.14	80	.316	.366	0	—	0	103	-9		-0.9
1995	Min A	5	3	.625	36	0	0	0-2	42.1	47	22	5	1	16-3	48	4.46	108	.290	.358	0	—	0		2		0.3
	†LA N	0	2	.000	24	0	0	0-0	19.2	19	11	1	1	9-2	19	3.66	106	.241	.326	1	.000	-0		0		0.0
1996	LA N	2	3	.400	66	0	0	1-2	73	65	21	3	1	22-2	56	2.22	176	.240	.295	3	.000	-0		15		0.9
1997	LA N	1	4	.200	62	0	0	1-3	69.1	71	44	12	0	30-6	42	5.32	73	.271	.342	4-0-1	.250	0		-11		-0.7
1998	LA N	2	1	.667	53	0	0	0-1	54	56	26	3	2	24-1	45	3.50	115	.267	.347	1	.000	0		2		0.1
1999	Bos A	1	1	.500	46	0	0	2-0	46.1	50	32	9	2	20-3	36	5.83	86	.275	.348	0	—	0	-3		20	-0.2
	Chi N	0	2	.000	11	0	0	0-0	12.1	7	6	1	0	4-2	9	3.65	125	.171	.244	0	—	0		1		0.1
2000	Chi N	2	3	.400	19	0	0	0-0	18.2	17	11	1	1	10-4	17	4.82	99	.258	.350	2	.000	-0	-1			-0.2
	TB A	1	1	.500	34	0	0	0-3	32	33	18	4	0	18-5	26	4.50	109	.262	.354	0	—	0		1		0.1
	Tor A	0	2	.000	57	0	0	0-1	20.2	20	12	1	1	9-0	20	4.79	105	.263	.345	0	—	0		1		0.0
	Year	1	3	.250	57	0	0	0-4	52.2	53	30	7	1	27-5	46	4.61	107	.262	.351	0	—	0		2		0.1
2001	†Oak A	6	2	.750	54	0	0	1-2	52.1	49	29	7	4	20-1	52	4.47	102	.249	.326	0	—	0		0		1.4
2002	NY N	5	3	.625	68	0	0	1-1	48	35	13	3	1	19-3	44	2.44	162	.207	.289	2	.000	-0		9		1.4
2003	†Chi N	2	3	.400	65	0	0	0-1	42.2	40	14	6	3	22-4	24	2.74	158	.260	.359	1	.000	-0		8	21	0.8
Total	15	51	54	.486	765	43	3-1	14-21	978.2	989	489	101	22	381-53	778	4.05	106	.266	.335	14-0-1	.071	-1	94	27	169	2.7
GUZMAN, JOHNNY					Dionini Ramon (Estrella) B1.21.1971 Hatillo Palma, D.R. BR/TL/5-10/155* d6.8																				
1991	Oak A	1	0	1.000	5	0	0	0-0	5	11	5	0	0	2-0	3	9.00	43	.500	.542	0	—	0	-3			-0.5
1992	Oak A	0	0	—	2	0	0	0-0	3	8	4	0	1	0-0	0	12.00	31	.471	.500	0	—	0	-3			-0.1
Total	2	1	0	1.000	7	0	0	0-0	8	19	9	0	1	2-0	3	10.13	38	.487	.524	0	—	0	-6			-0.6
GUZMAN, DOMINGO					Domingo Serrano B4.5.1975 San Cristobal, D.R. BR/TR/6-0/210* d9.9																				
1999	SD N	0	1	.000	7	0	0	0-0	5	13	12	1	0	3-2	4	21.60	20	.464	.516	0	—	0	-10			-1.5
2000	SD N	0	0	—	1	0	0	0-0	1	1	1	0	2	1-0	0	9.00	49	.333	.667	0	—	0	0			0.0
Total	2	0	1	.000	8	0	0	0-0	6	14	13	1	2	4-2	4	19.50	22	.452	.541	0	—	0	-10			-1.5
GUZMAN, GERALDO					Geraldo Moreno (Suarez) B11.28.1972 Tenares, D.R. BR/TR/6-2/180* d7.6																				
2000	Ari N	5	4	.556	13	10	0	0-1	60.1	66	36	8	2	22-0	52	5.37	89	.286	.352	19-0-3	.000	-2	125	-2		-0.6
2001	Ari N	0	0	—	4	0	0	0-0	9.1	7	4	2	0	3-1	4	2.89	160	.206	.270	1	.000	-0		1	12	0.0
Total	2	5	4	.556	17	10	0	0-1	69.2	73	40	10	2	25-1	56	5.04	95	.275	.341	20-0-3	.000	-2	125	-1	12	-0.6
GUZMAN, JOSE					Jose Alberto (Mirabal) B4.9.1963 Santa Isabel, PR BR/TR/6-2/195* d9.10 [DL 1990 Tex A 122, 1995 Chi N 160, 1996 Chi N 84]																				
1985	Tex A	3	2	.600	5	5	0	0-0	32.2	27	13	3	0	14-1	24	2.76	155	.214	.293	0	—	0	85	4		0.6
1986	Tex A	9	15	.375	29	29	2	0-0	172.1	199	101	23	6	60-2	87	4.54	95	.293	.353	0	—	0	80	-5		-0.7
1987	Tex A	14	14	.500	37	30	6	0-0	208.1	196	115	30	3	82-0	143	4.67	97	.251	.322	0	—	0	94	0		0.1
1988	Tex A	11	13	.458	30	30	6-2	0-0	206.2	180	99	20	5	82-3	157	3.70	111	.231	.306	0	—	0	88	8		0.8
1991	Tex A	13	7	.650	25	25	5-1	0-0	169.2	152	67	10	4	84-1	125	3.08	132	.239	.330	0	—	0	111	17		2.0
1992	Tex A	16	11	.593	33	33	5	0-0	224	229	103	17	4	73-0	179	3.66	105	.268	.326	0	—	0	108	4		0.5
1993	Chi N	12	10	.545	30	30	2-1	0-0	191	188	98	25	3	74-6	163	4.34	93	.258	.327	63-0-9	.111	-3	120	-5		-0.8
1994	Chi N	2	2	.500	4	4	0	0-0	19.2	22	20	1	1	13-0	11	9.15	46	.289	.396	8	.000	-1	113	-10	108	-1.5
Total	8	74	74	.519	193	186	26-4	0-0	1224.1	1193	616	129	26	482-13	889	4.05	102	.256	.327	71-0-9	.099	-3	100	13	474	1.0
GUZMAN, JUAN					Juan Andres (Correa) B10.28.1966 Santo Domingo, D.R. BR/TR/5-11/195* d6.7 [DL 2001 TB A 159]																				
1991	†Tor A	10	3	.769	23	23	1	0-0	138.2	98	53	6	4	66-0	123	2.99	141	.197	.294	0	—	0	104	17		1.4
1992	†Tor A★	16	5	.762	28	28	1	0-0	180.2	135	56	6	1	72-2	165	2.64	156	.207	.286	0	—	0	99	29	25	3.2
1993	†Tor A	14	3	.824	33	33	2-1	0-0	221	211	107	17	3	110-2	194	3.99	110	.252	.338	0	—	0	129	10		0.5
1994	Tor A	12	11	.522	25	25	2	0-0	147.1	165	102	20	3	76-1	124	5.68	86	.282	.364	0	—	0	117	-14		-1.8
1995	Tor A	4	14	.222	24	24	3	0-0	135.1	151	101	13	3	73-6	94	6.32	75	.281	.369	0	—	0	68	-21	39	-2.4
1996	Tor A	11	8	.579	27	27	4-1	0-0	187.2	158	68	20	7	53-3	165	**2.93**	**171**	**.228**	**.289**	0	—	0	75	43	15	3.8
1997	Tor A	3	6	.333	13	13	0	0-0	60	48	42	14	2	31-0	52	4.95	93	.213	.312	0	—	0	79	-5	104	-0.6
1998	Tor A	6	12	.333	22	22	2	0-0	145	133	83	19	6	65-1	113	4.41	106	.239	.324	2	.000	-0	83	2		0.1
	Bal A	4	4	.500	11	11	0	0-0	66	60	34	4	2	33-1	55	4.23	108	.241	.332	0	—	0	95	2		0.1
	Year	10	16	.385	33	33	2	0-0	211	193	117	23	8	98-2	168	4.35	106	.240	.326	2	.000	-0	86	4		0.2
1999	Bal A	5	9	.357	21	21	1-1	0-0	122.2	124	63	18	3	65-3	95	4.18	112	.264	.356	6	.167	-0	89	6		0.2
	Cin N	6	3	.667	12	12	1	0-0	77.1	70	33	10	1	21-3	60	3.03	155	.238	.290	26-0-3	.115	-1	124	12		1.1
2000	TB A	0	1	.000	1	1	0	0-0	1.2	7	8	2	0	2-0	3	43.20	11	.636	.692	0	—	0	96	-7	176	-0.8
Total	10	91	79	.535	240	240	17-3	0-0	1483.1	1360	750	149	35	667-22	1243	4.10	106	.243	.325	34-0-3	.118	-1	97	74	518	5.2
GUZMAN, SANTIAGO					Santiago Donovan (b Santiago Donovan (Guzman)) B7.25.1949 San Pedro de Macoris, D.R. BR/TR/6-2/180* d9.30																				
1969	StL N	0	1	.000	3	1	0	0-0	7.1	9	4	2	0	3-1	7	4.91	73	.321	.387	3	.333	0	74	-1		-0.1
1970	StL N	1	1	.500	8	3	1	0-0	13.2	14	12	1	0	13-0	9	7.24	57	.275	.422	5	.200	-0	166	-4		-0.6
1971	StL N	0	0	—	2	1	0	0-0	10	6	1	0	0	2-0	13	0.00	—	.162	.205	1-0-1	.000	-0	146	3		0.2
1972	StL N	0	0	—	1	0	0	0-0	1	1	1	1	0	0-0	0	9.00	38	.250	.250	0	—	0	-1			0.0
Total	4	1	2	.333	12	5	1	0-0	32	30	18	4	0	18-1	29	4.50	85	.250	.348	9-0-1	.222	0	149	-3		-0.5
HAAS, BRUNO					Bruno Philip "Boon" B5.5.1891 Worcester MA D6.5.1952 Sarasota FL BB/TL/5-10/180 d6.23 Col Dean (MA) JC																				
1915	Phi A	0	1	.000	6	2	1	0	14.1	23	27	0	2	28	7	11.93	25	.404	.600	18	.056	-1*	150	-15		-0.9
HAAS, MOOSE					Bryan Edmund B4.22.1956 Baltimore MD BR/TR/6-0/170* [MilA74 2/30] d9.8																				
1976	Mil A	0	1	.000	5	2	0	0-0	16	12	8	0	0	12-0	9	3.94	89	.207	.338	0	—	0	75	-1		0.0
1977	Mil A	10	12	.455	32	32	6	0-0	197.2	195	104	21	2	84-8	113	4.33	95	.261	.334	0	—	0*	89	-4		-0.5
1978	Mil A	2	3	.400	7	6	2	1-0	30.2	33	22	6	0	8-0	32	6.16	62	.273	.315	0	—	0	181	-7	142	-1.1
1979	Mil A	11	11	.500	29	28	8-1	0-0	184.2	198	112	26	0	59-2	95	4.78	88	.275	.327	0	—	0	113	-13		-1.4
1980	Mil A	16	15	.516	33	33	14-3	0-0	252.1	246	96	25	1	56-6	146	3.10	126	.258	.297	0	—	0	81	25		2.8
1981	†Mil A	11	7	.611	24	22	5	0-1	137.1	146	69	10	1	40-4	64	4.46	78	.275	.324	0	—	0	119	-14		-1.7
1982	†Mil A	11	8	.579	32	27	3	1-0	193.1	232	101	15	3	39-4	104	4.47	86	.302	.334	0	—	0	130	-12		-1.1
1983	Mil A	13	3	.813	25	25	7-3	0-0	179	170	66	12	1	42-5	75	3.27	116	.251	.294	0	—	0*	118	14		1.1
1984	Mil A	9	11	.450	31	30	4	0-0	189.1	205	91	16	0	43-3	84	3.99	98	.279	.316	0	—	0	87	0		0.1
1985	Mil A	8	8	.500	27	26	6-1	0-0	161.2	165	85	21	1	25-3	78	3.84	109	.260	.287	0	—	0	97	4		0.2
1986	Oak A	7	2	.778	12	12	1	0-0	72.1	58	23	4	1	19-1	40	2.74	142	.218	.271	0	—	0	173	11	65	1.2
1987	Oak A	2	2	.500	9	9	0	0-0	40.2	57	29	7	0	9-0	13	5.75	72	.335	.367	0	—	0	134	-8	127	-0.6
Total	12	100	83	.546	266	252	56-8	2-1	1655	1717	806	162	10	436-36	853	4.01	98	.269	.314	0	—	0	108	-5	334	-1.0
HAAS, DAVID					Robert David B10.19.1965 Independence MO BR/TR/6-1/200* d9.8 Col Wichita St.																				
1991	Det A	1	0	1.000	11	0	0	0-1	10.2	8	8	1	1	12-3	6	6.75	42	.242	.438	0	—	0	-3			-0.2
1992	Det A	5	3	.625	12	11	1-1	0-0	61.2	68	30	8	1	16-1	29	3.94	101	.276	.323	0	—	0	110	0		0.0
1993	Det A	1	2	.333	20	0	0	0-0	28	45	20	9	0	8-5	17	6.11	71	.375	.411	0	—	0	-5	112		-0.4
Total	3	7	5	.583	43	11	1-1	0-1	100.1	121	58	18	2	36-9	52	4.84	85	.303	.361	0	—	0	110	-8	112	-0.6
HABENICHT, BOB					Robert Julius "Hobby" B2.13.1926 St.Louis MO D12.24.1980 Richmond VA BR/TR/6-2/185* d4.17 Col St. Louis																				
1951	StL N	0	0	—	3	0	0	0-0	5	5	4	0	0	9	1	7.20	55	.278	.519	1	.000	0	-2			-0.1
1953	StL A	0	0	—	1	0	0	0-0	1.2	1	1	1	1	1	1	5.40	78	.167	.375	0	—	0	0			0.0
Total	2	0	0	—	4	0	0	0-0	6.2	6	5	1	1	10	2	6.75	60	.250	.486	1	.000	0	-2			-0.1

YEAR	TM LG	W	L	PCT	G	GS	CG-SHO	SV-BS	IP	H	R	HR	HB	BB-IB	SO	ERA	AERA	OAV	OOB	AB-HR-SH	AVG	PB	SUP	APR	DL	PW

HABYAN, JOHN John Gabriel B1.29.1964 Bay Shore NY BR/TR/6-2/195(178-198) [BalA82 3/78] d9.29 [DL 1989 Bal A 67]

YEAR	TM LG	W	L	PCT	G	GS	CG-SHO	SV-BS	IP	H	R	HR	HB	BB-IB	SO	ERA	AERA	OAV	OOB	AB-HR-SH	AVG	PB	SUP	APR	DL	PW
1985	Bal A	1	0	1.000	2	0	0	0-0	2.2	3	1	0	0	0-0	2	0.00	—	.250	.250	0	—	0		1		0.2
1986	Bal A	1	3	.250	6	5	0	0-0	26.1	24	17	3	0	18-2	14	4.44	94	.250	.365	0	—	0	61	-2		-0.3
1987	Bal A	6	7	.462	27	13	0	1-0	116.1	110	67	20	2	40-1	64	4.80	93	.248	.311	0	—	0	82	-4		-0.4
1988	Bal A	1	0	1.000	7	0	0	0-0	14.2	22	10	2	0	4-0	4	4.30	92	.355	.382	0	—	0		-2		-0.1
1990	NY A	0	0	—	6	0	0	0-1	8.2	10	2	0	1	2-0	4	2.08	192	.294	.351	0	—	0		2		0.1
1991	NY A	4	2	.667	66	0	0	2-2	90	73	28	2	2	20-2	70	2.30	181	.225	.274	0	—	0		17		1.1
1992	NY A	5	6	.455	56	0	0	7-5	72.2	84	32	6	2	21-5	44	3.84	103	.295	.344	0	—	0		2		0.3
1993	NY A	2	1	.667	36	0	0	1-2	42.1	45	20	5	0	16-2	29	4.04	104	.276	.337	0	—	0		1		0.1
	KC A	0	0	—	12	0	0	0-0	14	14	7	1	0	4-2	10	4.50	103	.259	.310	0	—	0		0		0.0
	Year	2	1	.667	48	0	0	1-2	56.1	59	27	6	0	20-4	39	4.15	103	.272	.331	0	—	0		2		0.1
1994	StL N	1	0	1.000	52	0	0	1-2	47.1	50	17	2	0	20-8	46	3.23	131	.275	.347	0	—	0	6	22		0.5
1995	StL N	3	2	.600	31	0	0	0-1	40.2	32	18	0	1	15-4	35	2.88	149	.222	.298	2	.000	-0	5			0.5
	Cal A	1	2	.333	28	0	0	0-1	32.2	36	16	2	1	12-0	25	4.13	114	.279	.340	0	—	0	2			-0.3
1996	Col N	1	1	.500	19	0	0	0-0	24	34	19	4	1	14-1	25	7.13	73	.347	.430	3	.000	-0	-3			-0.3
Total 11		26	24	.520	348	18	0	12-14	532.1	537	254	47	10	186-27	372	3.85	112	.265	.327	5	.000	-0	78	25	89	1.6

HACKER, WARREN Warren Louis B11.21.1924 Marissa IL D5.22.2002 Lenzburg IL BR/TR/6-1/185* d9.24

YEAR	TM LG	W	L	PCT	G	GS	CG-SHO	SV-BS	IP	H	R	HR	HB	BB-IB	SO	ERA	AERA	OAV	OOB	AB-HR-SH	AVG	PB	SUP	APR	DL	PW
1948	Chi N	0	1	.000	3	1	0	0	3	7	7	0	0	3	0	21.00	19	.438	.526	0	—	0	68	-5		-0.9
1949	Chi N	5	8	.385	30	12	3	0	125.2	141	68	7	4	53	40	4.23	95	.283	.356	38	.184	-1*	82	-3		-0.3
1950	Chi N	0	1	.000	5	3	1	1	15.1	20	11	3	0	8	5	5.28	80	.313	.389	5	.000	-1	77	-2		-0.2
1951	Chi N	0	0	—	2	0	0	0	1.1	3	2	0	1	0	2	13.50	30	.500	.571	0	—	0		-1		-0.1
1952	Chi N	15	9	.625	33	20	12-5	1	185	144	56	14	1	31	84	2.58	149	**.212**	.247	58-0-6	.121	-2*	88	27		3.1
1953	Chi N	12	19	.387	39	32	9	2	221.2	225	123	35	4	54	106	4.38	101	.254	.299	78-0-5	.218	0*	92	2		0.2
1954	Chi N	6	13	.316	39	18	4-1	2	158.2	157	89	28	4	37	80	4.25	99	.257	.299	55-0-3	.236	1*	99	-3		-0.3
1955	Chi N	11	15	.423	35	30	13	3	213	202	112	38	2	43-7	80	4.27	96	.245	.282	72	.250	-2	79	-4		-0.4
1956	Chi N	3	13	.188	34	24	4	0	168	190	103	28	1	44-11	65	4.66	81	.285	.327	54-0-1	.148	-2	97	-18		-1.8
1957	Cin N	3	2	.600	15	6	0	0	43.1	50	26	5	1	13-3	18	5.19	79	.294	.347	8	.125	-1	111	-4		-0.5
	Phi N	4	4	.500	20	10	1	0	74	72	40	10	1	18-2	33	4.50	85	.257	.303	23-0-1	.261	1	88	-5		-0.4
	Year	7	6	.538	35	16	1	0	117.1	122	66	15	4	31-5	51	4.76	82	.271	.320	31-0-1	.226	1	97	-9		-0.9
1958	Phi N	0	1	.000	9	1	0	0	17	24	17	2	0	8-1	4	7.41	53	.329	.395	1	.000	-0	45	-7		-0.4
1961	Chi A	3	3	.500	42	0	0	8	57.1	62	26	8	1	8-1	40	3.77	104	.272	.297	9	.111	-1		1		0.0
Total 12		62	89	.411	306	157	47-6	17	1283.1	1297	680	181	21	320-25	557	4.21	96	.259	.305	401-0-16	.195	-2	90	-22		-2.0

HACKETT, JIM James Joseph "Sunny Jim" B10.1.1877 Jacksonville IL D3.28.1961 Douglas MI BR/TR/6-2/185 d9.14 ▲

YEAR	TM LG	W	L	PCT	G	GS	CG-SHO	SV-BS	IP	H	R	HR	HB	BB-IB	SO	ERA	AERA	OAV	OOB	AB-HR-SH	AVG	PB	SUP	APR	DL	PW
1902	StL N	0	3	.000	8	3	3	0	30.1	46	26	0	1	16	7	6.23	44	.348	.423	21	.286	1*	107	-10		-0.8
1903	StL N	1	3	.250	7	6	5	1	48.1	47	28	0	3	18	21	3.72	88	.249	.324	351-0-2	.228	1*	86	-1		0.0
Total 2		1	6	.143	15	9	8	1	78.2	93	54	0	4	34	28	4.69	65	.290	.365	372-0-2	.231	2	93	-11		-0.8

HACKMAN, LUTHER Luther Gean B10.10.1974 Columbus MS BR/TR/6-4/195* [ColN94 6/154] d9.1

YEAR	TM LG	W	L	PCT	G	GS	CG-SHO	SV-BS	IP	H	R	HR	HB	BB-IB	SO	ERA	AERA	OAV	OOB	AB-HR-SH	AVG	PB	SUP	APR	DL	PW
1999	Col N	1	2	.333	5	3	0	0-0	16	26	19	5	0	12-0	10	10.69	54	.371	.463	5	.200	-0	74	-6		-0.9
2000	StL N	0	0	—	1	0	0	0-0	2.2	4	3	0	1	4-1	0	10.13	46	.400	.600	—	—	0		-1		-0.1
2001	StL N	1	2	.333	35	0	0	1-2	35.2	28	18	7	2	14-0	24	4.29	101	.212	.297	1-0-2	.000	-1		0	38	-0.3
2002	StL N	5	4	.556	43	6	0	0-1	81	90	42	7	4	39-3	46	4.11	98	.287	.366	16	.063	-1	149	-2		-0.3
2003	SD N	2	2	.500	65	0	0	0-2	76.2	78	51	7	8	36-2	48	5.17	78	.261	.353	2	.000	-0	130	-12		-0.6
Total 5		9	10	.474	149	9	0	1-5	212	226	133	26	15	105-6	128	5.09	83	.274	.363	24-0-2	.083	-1	130	-21	38	-1.9

HADDIX, HARVEY Harvey "The Kitten" B9.18.1925 Medway OH D1.8.1994 Springfield OH BL/TL/5-9.5/170* d8.20 C14

YEAR	TM LG	W	L	PCT	G	GS	CG-SHO	SV-BS	IP	H	R	HR	HB	BB-IB	SO	ERA	AERA	OAV	OOB	AB-HR-SH	AVG	PB	SUP	APR	DL	PW
1952	StL N	2	2	.500	7	6	3	0	42	31	18	4	2	10	31	2.79	133	.201	.259	14	.214	0*	148	3		0.3
1953	StL N☆	20	9	.690	36	33	19-6	1	253	220	97	24	4	69	163	3.06	139	.232	.287	97-1-3	.289	10*	122	33		4.5
1954	StL N*	18	13	.581	43	35	13-3	4	259.2	247	114	26	3	77	184	3.57	115	.249	.303	93	.194	3*	120	17		2.2
1955	StL N★	12	16	.429	37	30	9-2	1	208	216	111	27	5	62-7	150	4.46	91	.268	.322	73-1-1	.164	0	89	-9		-0.9
1956	StL N	1	0	1.000	4	4	1-1	0	23.2	28	15	3	0	10-0	16	5.32	71	.298	.362	9	.222	1*	175	-1		-0.1
	Phi N	12	8	.600	31	26	11-2	2	206.2	196	98	24	4	55-9	154	3.48	107	.247	.299	93	.237	4*	121	3		0.7
	Year	13	8	.619	35	30	12-3	2	230.1	224	113	26	4	65-9	170	3.67	102	.253	.306	102	.235	5	128	-3		0.6
1957	Phi N	10	13	.435	27	25	8-1	0	170.2	176	84	18	1	39-4	136	4.06	94	.264	.303	68-0-2	.309	7*	80	-4		0.1
1958	Cin N	8	7	.533	29	26	8-1	0	184	191	79	28	4	43-7	110	3.52	118	.268	.314	61-1-6	.180	3*	102	12		1.2
1959	Pit N	12	12	.500	31	29	14-2	0	224.1	189	88	26	2	49-12	149	3.13	124	.228	**.271**	83-0-1	.145	-0	94	19		1.9
1960	†Pit N	11	10	.524	29	28	4	1	172.1	189	87	13	1	38-8	101	3.97	94	.277	.315	67	.254	4	110	-6		-0.1
1961	Pit N	10	6	.625	29	22	5-2	0	156	159	72	15	2	41-6	99	4.10	97	.266	.313	56-0-5	.143	0*	124	2		0.2
1962	Pit N	9	6	.600	28	20	4	0	141.1	146	74	17	2	42-6	101	4.20	94	.264	.318	52-1-0	.250	4	94	-3		0.1
1963	Pit N	3	4	.429	49	1	0	1	70	67	27	7	4	20-4	70	3.34	99	.256	.314	11	.182	1*	105	1		0.2
1964	Bal A	5	5	.500	49	0	0	10	89.2	68	26	4	2	23-8	90	2.31	155	.211	.265	19-0-2	.000	-2		13		1.5
1965	Bal A	3	2	.600	24	0	0	1	33.2	31	22	5	2	23-6	21	3.48	100	.248	.371	2	.000	-0		-3		-0.4
Total 14		136	113	.546	453	285	99-20	21	2235	2154	1012	240	43	601-77	1575	3.63	108	.252	.303	798-4-20	.212	35	109	74		11.4

HADDOCK, GEORGE George Silas "Gentleman George" B12.25.1866 Portsmouth NH D4.18.1926 Boston MA BR/TR/5-11/155 d9.27

YEAR	TM LG	W	L	PCT	G	GS	CG-SHO	SV-BS	IP	H	R	HR	HB	BB-IB	SO	ERA	AERA	OAV	OOB	AB-HR-SH	AVG	PB	SUP	APR	DL	PW
1888	Was N	0	2	.000	2	2	2	0	16	9	8	0	1	2	3	2.25	123	.148	.188	5	.200	0	55	0		0.1
1889	Was N	11	19	.367	33	31	30	0	276.1	299	203	10	9	123	106	4.20	94	.268	.345	112-2	.223	7*	94	-9		0.0
1890	Buf P	9	26	.257	35	34	31	0	290.2	366	307	15	14	149	123	5.76	71	.295	.377	146	.247	7*	97	-62		-4.1
1891	Bos AA	34	11	.756	51	47	37-5	1	379.2	330	172	8	14	137	169	2.49	140	.226	.299	185-3	.243	9*	128	45		5.3
1892	Bro N	29	13	.690	46	44	39-3	1	381.1	340	190	11	14	163	153	3.14	101	.229	.311	158	.177	-1*	111	2		0.2
1893	Bro N	8	9	.471	23	20	12	0	151	193	145	10	7	89	37	5.60	79	.302	.393	85-1	.282	4*	102	-24		-1.7
1894	Phi N	4	3	.571	10	7	5	0	56	63	46	0	1	34	7	5.79	89	.281	.378	29	.172	-1	116	-3		-0.3
	Was N	0	4	.000	4	4	4	0	29	50	40	2	1	17	1	8.69	61	.373	.447	16	.188	-1*	87	-9		-0.8
	Year	4	7	.364	14	11	9	0	85	113	86	2	2	51	8	6.78	77	.316	.404	45	.178	-1	106	-13		-1.1
Total 7		95	87	.522	204	189	160-8	2	1580	1650	1111	56	61	714	599	4.07	93	.259	.340	736-6	.227	25	108	-60		-1.3

HADLEY, BUMP Irving Darius B7.5.1904 Lynn MA D2.15.1963 Lynn MA BR/TR/5-11/190 d4.20 Col Brown

YEAR	TM LG	W	L	PCT	G	GS	CG-SHO	SV-BS	IP	H	R	HR	HB	BB-IB	SO	ERA	AERA	OAV	OOB	AB-HR-SH	AVG	PB	SUP	APR	DL	PW
1926	Was A	0	0	—	4	0	0	0	3	6	5	0	2	2	0	12.00	32	.429	.500	0	—	0		-3		-0.1
1927	Was A	14	6	.700	30	27	13	0	198.2	177	72	2	9	86	60	2.85	142	.244	.332	70-0-2	.271	2	107	28		2.7
1928	Was A	12	13	.480	33	31	16-3	0	231.2	236	105	4	8	100	80	3.54	113	.268	.348	81-0-3	.210	1	99	13		1.4
1929	Was A	6	16	.273	37	27	7-1	0	195.1	196	139	10	5	85	98	5.62	75	.263	.342	62-0-4	.097	-4	97	-28		-2.9
1930	Was A	15	11	.577	42	34	15-1	2	260.1	242	123	6	6	105	162	3.73	123	.247	.323	93-0-1	.226	1	99	25		2.2
1931	Was A	11	10	.524	**55**	11	2-1	8	179.2	145	81	4	1	92	124	3.06	140	**.218**	.314	54-0-5	.167	-1	82	21		2.3
1932	Chi A	1	1	.500	3	2	1	1	18.2	17	8	2	0	8	13	3.86	112	.262	.342	6	.167	-0	39	2		0.2
	StL A	13	20	.394	40	33	12-1	1	229.2	244	160	21	8	163	132	5.53	88	.274	.391	78-0-6	.282	4	94	-14		-1.4
	Year	14	21	.400	43	35	13-1	2	248.1	261	168	23	8	171	145	5.40	89	.273	.388	84-0-6	.274	4	92	-10		-1.2
1933	StL A	15	20	.429	45	36	19-2	3	**316.2**	309	152	17	3	141	149	3.92	119	.256	.335	109-0-6	.156	-1	75	25		2.0
1934	StL A	10	16	.385	39	32	7-2	1	213	212	120	14	6	127	79	4.35	115	.257	.361	64-0-6	.203	-1	67	15		1.4
1935	Was A	10	15	.400	35	32	13	0	230.1	268	143	18	4	102	77	4.92	88	.292	.366	77-0-7	.195	1	110	-17		-1.3
1936	†NY A	14	4	.778	31	17	8-1	0	173.2	194	97	12	1	89	74	4.35	107	.283	.366	68-0-4	.235	-2	129	5		0.6
1937	†NY A	11	8	.579	29	25	6	0	178.1	199	122	16	3	83	70	5.30	84	.254	.358	65	.169	1	127	-16		-1.4
1938	NY A	9	8	.529	29	17	8-1	1	167.1	165	79	13	3	66	61	3.60	126	.254	.325	54-0-3	.093	-1	113	18		1.6
1939	†NY A	12	6	.667	26	18	7-1	2	154	132	62	10	3	85	65	2.98	146	.237	.342	62-0-2	.177	-1	98	23		2.4
1940	NY A	3	5	.375	25	2	0	2	80	88	62	4	1	52	39	5.74	70	.276	.379	27-0-2	.111	-0	44	-19		-1.7
1941	NY N	1	0	1.000	3	2	0	0	13	19	10	1	0	9	4	6.23	59	.345	.438	3-0-1	.000	-0	161	-3		-0.3
	Phi A	4	6	.400	25	9	1	3	102.1	131	69	13	2	47	31	5.01	84	.310	.381	31-0-1	.129	-1	83	-11		-1.0
Total 16		161	165	.494	528	355	135-14	25	2945.2	2980	1609	167	63	1442	1318	4.24	105	.263	.350	1004-0-53	.189	-1	97	64		6.7

HAEFNER, MICKEY Milton Arnold B10.9.1912 Lenzburg IL D1.3.1995 New Athens IL BL/TL/5-8/160* d4.22

YEAR	TM LG	W	L	PCT	G	GS	CG-SHO	SV-BS	IP	H	R	HR	HB	BB-IB	SO	ERA	AERA	OAV	OOB	AB-HR-SH	AVG	PB	SUP	APR	DL	PW
1943	Was A	11	5	.688	36	13	8-1	6	165.1	126	56	4	4	60	65	2.29	140	.208	.283	45-0-7	.133	0	138	15		1.6
1944	Was A	12	15	.444	31	28	18-3	0	228	221	94	7	4	71	86	3.04	107	.251	.310	70-0-8	.157	-1	91	6		0.7
1945	Was A	16	14	.533	37	28	19-1	3	238.1	226	103	10	7	69	83	3.47	89	.247	.305	82-0-6	.244	4	102	-6		-0.3
1946	Was A	14	11	.560	33	27	17-2	1	227.2	220	86	10	5	80	85	2.85	118	.251	.317	74-0-4	.203	4	97	14		1.9

YEAR	TM LG	W	L	PCT	G	GS	CG-SHO	SV-BS	IP	H	R	HR	HB	BB-IB	SO	ERA	AERA	OAV	OOB	AB-HR-SH	AVG	PB	SUP	APR	DL	PW
1947	Was A	10	14	.417	31	28	14-4		1	193	195	86	8	4	85	77	3.64	102	.264	.343	59-0-3	.136	-1	59	3		0.1
1948	Was A	5	13	.278	28	20	4		0	147.2	151	86	7	6	61	45	4.02	108	.265	.342	43-0-1	.163	-1	58	0		0.0
1949	Was A	5	5	.500	19	12	4-1		0	91.2	85	51	7	2	53	23	4.42	96	.249	.353	25-0-3	.200	1*	86	-2		0.0
	Chi A	4	6	.400	14	12	4-1		1	80.1	84	40	9	5	41	17	4.37	95	.275	.370	23-0-6	.261	2	75	0		0.2
	Year	9	11	.450	33	24	8-2		1	172	169	91	16	7	94	40	4.40	96	.261	.361	48-0-9	.229	2	81	-2		0.2
1950	Chi A	1	6	.143	24	9	2		0	70.2	83	49	11	2	45	17	5.73	78	.299	.400	20-0-3	.200	0	80	-9		-0.8
	Bos N	0	2	.000	8	2	1		1	24	23	15	3	0	12	10	5.63	68	.247	.333	7-0-1	.286	1	92	-4		-0.2
Total	8	78	91	.462	261	179	91-13		13	1466.2	1414	666	76	39	577	508	3.50	102	.252	.326	448-0-42	.188	8	86	17		3.2

HAFFORD, LEO   Leo Edgar   B9.17.1883 Somerville MA   D10.1.1911 Willimantic CT   TR/6-0/170   d4.15   Col Tufts

YEAR	TM LG	W	L	PCT	G	GS	CG-SHO	SV-BS	IP	H	R	HR	HB	BB-IB	SO	ERA	AERA	OAV	OOB	AB-HR-SH	AVG	PB	SUP	APR	DL	PW
1906	Cin N	1	1	.500	3	1	1		0	19	13	9	0	1	11	5	0.95	291	.191	.313	9	.222	-0	212	2		0.1

HAFNER, FRANK   Francis R.   B8.14.1867 Hannibal MO   D3.2.1957 Hannibal MO   TR   d5.5

YEAR	TM LG	W	L	PCT	G	GS	CG-SHO	SV-BS	IP	H	R	HR	HB	BB-IB	SO	ERA	AERA	OAV	OOB	AB-HR-SH	AVG	PB	SUP	APR	DL	PW
1888	KC AA	0	2	.000	2	2	2		0	18	24	23	2	1	16	5	7.00	49	.308	.432	6	.000	-1	68	-6		-0.6

HAGAN, ART   Arthur Charles   B3.17.1863 Providence RI   D3.25.1936 Providence RI   TR   d6.30

YEAR	TM LG	W	L	PCT	G	GS	CG-SHO	SV-BS	IP	H	R	HR	HB	BB-IB	SO	ERA	AERA	OAV	OOB	AB-HR-SH	AVG	PB	SUP	APR	DL	PW
1883	Phi N	1	14	.067	17	16	15		0	137	207	151	2		33	39	5.45	57	.342	.376	59	.102	-5	75	-39		-3.5
	Buf N	0	2	.000	2	2	1		0	15	17	12	0		6	7	3.60	88	.270	.333	7	.000	-1	51	-1		-0.2
	Year	1	16	.059	19	18	16		0	152	224	163	2		39	46	5.27	59	.335	.371	66	.091	-7	72	-33		-3.7
1884	Buf N	1	2	.333	3	3	3		0	26	53	38	1		4	4	5.88	54	.384	.401	13	.308	0	135	-9		-0.7
Total	2	2	18	.100	22	21	19		0	178	277	201	3		43	50	5.36	58	.343	.376	79	.127	-6	81	-49		-4.4

HAGEMAN, CASEY   Kurt Moritz   B5.12.1887 Mt.Oliver PA   D4.1.1964 New Bedford PA   BL/TR/5-10.5/186   d9.18   Col Geneva

YEAR	TM LG	W	L	PCT	G	GS	CG-SHO	SV-BS	IP	H	R	HR	HB	BB-IB	SO	ERA	AERA	OAV	OOB	AB-HR-SH	AVG	PB	SUP	APR	DL	PW
1911	Bos A	0	2	.000	2	2	2		0	17	16	8	2	1	6	8	2.12	155	.262	.328	4	.000	-0	33	2		0.1
1912	Bos A	0	0	—	2	1	0		0	1.1	5	5	0	0	3	1	27.00	13	.500	.615	0	—	-0	174	-3		-0.1
1914	StL N	2	4	.333	12	7	2		0	55.1	43	24	0	5	20	21	2.44	115	.215	.302	16	.125	-1	84	1		0.1
	Chi N	1	1	.500	16	1	0		1	46.2	44	26	0	3	12	17	3.47	80	.254	.314	15	.467	3	103	-3		0.1
	Year	3	5	.375	28	8	2		1	102	87	50	0	8	32	38	2.91	96	.233	.308	31	.290	2	87	-1		0.2
Total	3	3	7	.300	32	11	4		1	120.1	108	63	2	9	40	47	3.07	93	.243	.318	35	.257	2	86	-3		0.2

HAGEN, KEVIN   Kevin Eugene   B3.8.1960 Renton WA   BR/TR/6-2/185*   [StLN80*/4/94]   d6.4   Col Bellevue (WA) CC

YEAR	TM LG	W	L	PCT	G	GS	CG-SHO	SV-BS	IP	H	R	HR	HB	BB-IB	SO	ERA	AERA	OAV	OOB	AB-HR-SH	AVG	PB	SUP	APR	DL	PW
1983	StL N	2	2	.500	9	4	0	0-0		22.1	34	15	0	0	7-0	7	4.84	76	.362	.406	5	.000	-1	73	-3		-0.6
1984	StL N	1	0	1.000	4	0	0	0-0		7.1	9	2	0	1	1-0	2	2.45	143	.300	.323	0	—	0		1		0.1
Total	2	3	2	.600	13	4	0	0-0		29.2	43	17	0	1	8-0	9	4.25	85	.347	.386	5	.000	-1	73	-2		-0.5

HAGERMAN, RIP   Zerah Zequiel   B6.20.1888 Lyndon KS   D1.30.1930 Albuquerque NM   BR/TR/6-2/200   d4.16

YEAR	TM LG	W	L	PCT	G	GS	CG-SHO	SV-BS	IP	H	R	HR	HB	BB-IB	SO	ERA	AERA	OAV	OOB	AB-HR-SH	AVG	PB	SUP	APR	DL	PW
1909	Chi N	4	4	.500	13	7	4-1		0	79	64	29	0	2	28	32	1.82	139	.225	.298	23	.130	-0	79	4		0.4
1914	Cle A	9	15	.375	37	26	12-3		0	198	189	98	3	5	118	112	3.09	93	.265	.374	61-0-2	.016	-5	80	-5		-1.3
1915	Cle A	6	14	.300	29	22	7		0	151	156	85	4	6	77	69	3.52	87	.277	.370	38-0-2	.105	-2	86	-8		-1.4
1916	Cle A	0	0	—	2	0	0		0	3.2	5	6	1	2	2	1	12.27	25	.333	.474	1	.000	-0		-3		-0.2
Total	4	19	33	.365	81	55	23-4		0	431.2	414	218	8	15	225	214	3.09	93	.263	.360	123-0-4	.065	-9	83	-12		-2.5

HAHN, NOODLES   Frank George   B4.29.1879 Nashville TN   D2.6.1960 Candler NC   BL/TL/5-9/160   d4.18

YEAR	TM LG	W	L	PCT	G	GS	CG-SHO	SV-BS	IP	H	R	HR	HB	BB-IB	SO	ERA	AERA	OAV	OOB	AB-HR-SH	AVG	PB	SUP	APR	DL	PW
1899	Cin N	23	8	.742	38	34	32-4		0	309	280	128	3	10	68	**145**	2.68	146	.242	.289	109-0-4	.147	-4	98	41		2.9
1900	Cin N	16	20	.444	39	37	29-4		0	311.1	306	145	4	7	89	**132**	3.27	112	.256	.312	115-2-3	.209	0	85	18		1.7
1901	Cin N	22	19	.537	42	42	41-2		0	**375.1**	370	159	12	9	69	**239**	2.71	118	.256	.294	141-0-4	.170	-1	95	21		2.0
1902	Cin N	23	12	.657	36	36	35-6		0	321	282	97	2	6	58	142	1.77	170	.236	.275	119-0-1	.185	0*	99	41		4.4
1903	Cin N	22	12	.647	34	34	34-5		0	296	297	125	3	8	47	127	2.52	141	.262	.297	112-0-4	.161	-2	101	32		3.1
1904	Cin N	16	18	.471	35	34	33-2		0	297.2	258	101	3	7	35	98	2.06	143	.234	.262	99-0-3	.172	-1	70	27		3.2
1905	Cin N	5	3	.625	13	8	5-1		0	77	85	44	0	2	9	17	2.81	118	.272	.297	24-0-2	.167	-1	101	2		0.0
1906	NY A	3	2	.600	6	6	3-1		0	42	38	22	0	3	6	17	3.86	77	.245	.287	12	.333	1	113	-3		-0.3
Total	8	130	94	.580	243	231	212-25		0	2029.1	1916	821	27	52	381	917	2.55	133	.249	.289	731-2-21	.176	-5	92	179		17.0

HAHN, FRED   Frederick Aloys   B2.16.1929 Nyack NY   D8.16.1984 Valhalla NY   BR/TL/6-3/174   d4.19

YEAR	TM LG	W	L	PCT	G	GS	CG-SHO	SV-BS	IP	H	R	HR	HB	BB-IB	SO	ERA	AERA	OAV	OOB	AB-HR-SH	AVG	PB	SUP	APR	DL	PW
1952	StL N	0	0	—	1	0	0		0	2	2	2	0	0	1	0	0.00	—	.250	.333	0	—	0		0		0.0

HAID, HAL   Harold Augustine   B12.21.1897 Barberton OH   D8.13.1952 Los Angeles CA   BR/TR/5-10.5/150   d9.5   Col Belmont Abbey

YEAR	TM LG	W	L	PCT	G	GS	CG-SHO	SV-BS	IP	H	R	HR	HB	BB-IB	SO	ERA	AERA	OAV	OOB	AB-HR-SH	AVG	PB	SUP	APR	DL	PW
1919	StL A	0	0	—	1	0	0		0	2	5	5	0	0	3	1	18.00	18	.556	.667	0	—	0		-3		-0.1
1928	StL N	2	2	.500	27	0	0		5	47	39	24	1	1	11	21	2.30	174	.218	.267	8	.375	1		5		0.6
1929	StL N	9	9	.500	38	14	8		4	154.2	171	90	8	5	66	41	4.07	115	.284	.360	49-0-3	.082	-4	101	6		0.2
1930	StL N	3	2	.600	20	0	0		2	33	38	17	1	3	14	13	4.09	123	.297	.379	3	.000	-0*		4		0.5
1931	Bos N	0	2	.000	27	0	0		1	56	59	36	3	3	16	20	4.50	84	.263	.321	8	.125	0		-6		-0.3
1933	Chi A	0	0	—	6	0	0		0	14.2	18	15	2	1	13	7	7.98	53	.310	.452	4	.250	0		-6		-0.3
Total	6	14	15	.483	119	14	8		12	307.1	330	187	15	14	123	103	4.16	106	.275	.349	72-0-3	.125	-3	101	0		0.6

HAINES, JESSE   Jesse Joseph "Pop"   B7.22.1893 Clayton OH   D8.5.1978 Dayton OH   BR/TR/6-0/190   d7.20   C1   HF1970

YEAR	TM LG	W	L	PCT	G	GS	CG-SHO	SV-BS	IP	H	R	HR	HB	BB-IB	SO	ERA	AERA	OAV	OOB	AB-HR-SH	AVG	PB	SUP	APR	DL	PW
1918	Cin N	0	0	—	5	0	0		0	5	5	1	0	0	1	3	1.80	148	.294	.333	1	1.000	0		1		0.1
1920	StL N	13	20	.394	**47**	34	19-4		2	301.2	303	136	9	9	80	120	2.98	100	.270	.324	108-1-4	.176	-1*	109	-5		-0.9
1921	StL N	18	12	.600	37	37	13-3		0	244.1	261	112	15	8	56	84	3.50	103	.286	.333	94-0-4	.181	-3*	141	7		0.5
1922	StL N	11	9	.550	29	26	11-2		0	183	207	103	10	4	45	62	3.84	101	.284	.329	72-0-1	.167	-2*	101	-3		-0.4
1923	StL N	20	13	.606	37	36	23-1		0	266	283	125	7	5	75	73	3.11	125	.275	.328	99-0-4	.202	-2	97	18		1.8
1924	StL N	8	19	.296	35	31	16-1		0	222.2	275	129	14	5	66	69	4.41	86	.309	.360	74-0-6	.189	-2	91	-15		-1.9
1925	StL N	13	14	.481	29	25	15		0	207	234	116	11	1	52	63	4.57	95	.290	.334	74-0-3	.176	-2	95	-2		-0.5
1926	†StL N	13	4	.765	33	20	14-3		1	183	186	76	10	2	48	46	3.25	120	.265	.314	61-0-2	.213	-1	112	14		1.0
1927	StL N	24	10	.706	38	36	25-6		1	300.2	273	114	11	5	77	89	2.72	145	.245	.297	114-0-4	.202	-1	98	39		4.1
1928	StL N	20	8	.714	33	28	20-1		0	240.1	238	98	14	6	72	77	3.18	126	.266	.324	87-0-7	.184	-1	116	23		2.2
1929	StL N	13	10	.565	28	25	12		0	179.2	230	123	21	2	73	59	5.71	82	.313	.376	69-1-3	.159	-3	108	-18		-2.2
1930	†StL N	13	8	.619	29	24	14		1	182	215	107	15	1	54	68	4.30	117	.298	.348	65-0-4	.246	-1	108	12		1.1
1931	StL N	12	3	.800	19	17	8-2		0	122.1	134	48	7	3	28	27	3.02	131	.278	.318	45-0-4	.133	-2	133	12		1.0
1932	StL N	3	5	.375	20	10	4-1		0	85.1	116	51	4	1	16	24	4.75	83	.326	.357	27-1-4	.185	0	83	-7		-0.6
1933	StL N	9	6	.600	32	10	5		1	115.1	113	46	3	1	37	37	2.50	139	.252	.311	30-0-5	.067	-2*	93	9		0.8
1934	†StL N	4	4	.500	37	6	0		1	90	86	42	6	4	19	17	3.50	121	.262	.311	19-0-1	.158	-1	126	6		0.5
1935	StL N	6	5	.545	30	11	3		2	115.1	110	49	4	1	28	24	3.59	114	.252	.299	33-0-2	.273	1	116	8		0.8
1936	StL N	7	5	.583	25	9	4		1	99.1	110	44	4	1	21	19	3.90	101	.284	.323	30-0-5	.167	-1	117	3		0.2
1937	StL N	3	3	.500	16	6	2		0	65.2	81	36	5	1	23	11	4.52	88	.303	.361	22	.182	-0	101	-3		-0.3
Total	19	210	158	.571	555	386	208-24		10	3208.2	3460	1556	165	57	871	981	3.64	108	.280	.330	1124-3-59	.186	-22	108	99		7.3

HAISLIP, JIM   James Clifton "Slim"   B8.4.1891 Farmersville TX   D1.22.1970 Dallas TX   BR/TR/6-1/186   d8.27   Col TCU

YEAR	TM LG	W	L	PCT	G	GS	CG-SHO	SV-BS	IP	H	R	HR	HB	BB-IB	SO	ERA	AERA	OAV	OOB	AB-HR-SH	AVG	PB	SUP	APR	DL	PW
1913	Phi N	0	0	—	1	0	0		0	3	4	4	0	0	3	0	6.00	56	.400	.538	1	.000	-0		-1		-0.1

HALAMA, JOHN   John Thadeuz   B2.22.1972 Brooklyn NY   BL/TL/6-5/210(200-215)   [HouN94 23/640]   d4.2   Col St. Francis (NY)

YEAR	TM LG	W	L	PCT	G	GS	CG-SHO	SV-BS	IP	H	R	HR	HB	BB-IB	SO	ERA	AERA	OAV	OOB	AB-HR-SH	AVG	PB	SUP	APR	DL	PW
1998	Hou N	1	1	.500	6	6	0	0-0		32.1	37	21	0	2	13-0	21	5.85	69	.296	.361	10-0-1	.000	-0	106	-6		-0.4
1999	Sea A	11	10	.524	38	24	1-1	0-0		179	193	88	20	7	56-3	105	4.22	113	.281	.338	5	.200	1	93	13		1.4
2000	†Sea A	14	9	.609	30	30	0	0-0		166.2	206	108	19	2	56-0	87	5.08	95	.308	.361	2-0-1	.500	0	114	-8		-0.9
2001	†Sea A	10	7	.588	31	17	0	0-0		110.1	132	69	18	6	26-0	50	4.73	90	.296	.340	1-0-1	.000	-0	139	-9		-1.1
2002	Sea A	6	5	.545	31	10	0	0-0		101	112	45	9	1	33-5	70	3.56	121	.281	.336	0	—	-0	132	8		0.8
2003	Oak A	3	5	.375	35	13	0	0-0		108.2	117	68	18	2	36-2	51	4.22	109	.268	.325	0	—	0	106	-1		0.0
2004	TB A	7	6	.538	34	14	0	0-0		118.2	134	68	17	10	27-3	59	4.70	99	.284	.334	3	—	-0	98	0		-0.1
2005	Bos A	1	1	.500	30	1	0	0-0		43.2	56	33	5	1	9-3	26	6.18	74	.299	.353	0	—	0	102	-4		-0.4
	Was N	0	3	.000	10	3	0	0-0		21.1	23	11	1	0	8-0	11	4.64	87	.277	.337	5	.200	-0	15	-1		-0.1
Total	8	53	47	.530	245	118	2-2	0-0		881.2	1010	511	107	37	264-16	480	4.60	99	.288	.342	26-0-3	.115	0	109	-12		-0.8

HALBRITER, ED   Edward L.   B2.2.1860 Auburn NY   D8.9.1936 Los Angeles CA   d5.23

YEAR	TM LG	W	L	PCT	G	GS	CG-SHO	SV-BS	IP	H	R	HR	HB	BB-IB	SO	ERA	AERA	OAV	OOB	AB-HR-SH	AVG	PB	SUP	APR	DL	PW
1882	Phi AA	0	1	.000	1	1	1		0	8	17	12	1		4	4	7.88	36	.405	.457	4	.000	-1	146	-4		-0.4

YEAR	TM LG	W	L	PCT	G	GS	CG-SHO	SV-BS	IP	H	R	HR	HB	BB-IB	SO	ERA	AERA	OAV	OOB	AB-HR-SH	AVG	PB	SUP	APR	DL	PW

HALE, DAD Ray Luther B2.18.1880 Allegan MI D2.1.1946 Allegan MI BR/TR/5-10/180 d4.21

1902	Bos N	1	3	.250	8	5	3	0	40	57	38	1	1	16	11	6.07	47	.333	.394	14	.000	-1	104	-14		-1.3
	Bal A	0	1	.000	3	2	1	0	14	21	14	0	1	6	6	4.50	84	.344	.412	6	.000	-1	124	-2		-0.2
Total	1	1	4	.200	11	7	4	0	54	78	52	1	2	22	17	5.67	54	.336	.398	20	.000	-2	110	-16		-1.5

HALICKI, ED Edward Louis B10.4.1950 Newark NJ BR/TR/6-7/220* [SFN72 24/564] d7.8 Col Monmouth

1974	SF N	1	8	.111	16	11	2	0-0	74.1	84	49	6	2	31-8	40	4.24	90	.275	.341	25-1-2	.240	1	69	-6		-0.6
1975	SF N	9	13	.409	24	23	7-2	0-0	159.2	143	76	6	3	59-7	153	3.49	109	.240	.307	53-0-5	.113	-2	82	3		0.2
1976	SF N	12	14	.462	32	31	8-4	0-0	186.1	171	86	10	2	61-7	130	3.62	101	.246	.308	53-1-7	.170	1	83	2		0.3
1977	SF N	16	12	.571	37	37	7-2	0-0	257.2	241	105	27	7	70-5	168	3.32	119	.244	.298	85-2-5	.176	3	97	20		2.2
1978	SF N	9	10	.474	29	28	9-4	1-0	199	166	74	11	7	45-9	105	2.85	122	.221	.270	66-0-8	.136	-2	102	12	28	0.8
1979	SF N	5	8	.385	33	19	3-1	0-0	125.2	134	82	12	3	47-8	81	4.58	76	.266	.330	34-0-2	.206	1	97	-21	29	-1.8
1980	SF N	0	0	—	11	2	0	0-0	25	29	15	5	0	10-1	14	5.40	65	.293	.355	6	.167	-0	102	-4		-0.2
	Cal A	3	1	.750	10	6	0	0-0	35.1	39	22	5	0	11-0	16	4.84	82	.279	.327	0	—	0	113	-4	34	-0.4
Total	7	55	66	.455	192	157	36-13	1-0	1063	1007	509	82	24	334-45	707	3.62	102	.247	.306	322-3-29	.165	3	92	2	91	0.5

HALL, DREW Andrew Clark B3.27.1963 Louisville KY BL/TL/6-4/205(205-220) [ChiN84 1/3] d9.14 Col Morehead St.

1986	Chi N	1	2	.333	5	4	1	1-0	23.2	24	12	3	0	10-0	21	4.56	89	.267	.340	7	.143	0	109	-1		-0.1
1987	Chi N	1	1	.500	21	0	0	0-1	32.2	40	31	4	0	14-0	20	6.89	63	.308	.370	4	.000	-0		-10		-0.6
1988	Chi N	1	1	.500	19	0	0	1-2	22.1	26	20	4	1	9-2	22	7.66	48	.295	.360	1	.000	0		-9		-0.8
1989	Tex A	2	1	.667	38	0	0	0-0	58.1	42	24	3	3	33-1	45	3.70	108	.207	.325	0	—	0	3			-1.7
1990	Mon N	4	7	.364	42	0	0	3-2	58.1	52	35	6	0	29-5	40	5.09	72	.242	.327	4-0-1	.000	-0		-9	45	-1.7
Total	5	9	12	.429	125	4	1	5-5	195.1	184	122	20	4	95-8	148	5.21	75	.253	.339	16-0-1	.063	-1	109	-26	45	-3.0

HALL, CHARLEY Charles Louis "Sea Lion" (b Carlos Clolo) B7.27.1885 Ventura CA D12.6.1943 Ventura CA BL/TR/6-1/187 d7.12

1906	Cin N	4	8	.333	14	9	9-1	1	95	86	56	1	8	50	49	3.32	83	.258	.368	47-0-1	.128	-1*	94	-8		-1.1
1907	Cin N	4	2	.667	11	8	5	0	68	51	22	0	4	43	25	2.51	103	.226	.359	26-0-1	.269	1*	110	2		0.3
1909	Bos A	6	4	.600	11	7	3	0	59.2	59	24	0	3	17	27	2.56	98	.271	.332	19-0-2	.158	-1	109	-1		-0.2
1910	Bos A	12	9	.571	35	16	13	2	188.2	142	68	6	9	73	95	1.91	134	.207	.282	82-0-5	.207	3*	100	10		1.6
1911	Bos A	8	7	.533	32	10	6	4	146.1	149	79	3	5	72	83	3.75	87	.279	.370	64-1-6	.141	-1*	134	-3		-0.5
1912	†Bos A	15	8	.652	34	20	9-2	2	191	178	85	3	4	70	83	3.02	113	.257	.329	75-1-3	.267	5	120	8		1.4
1913	Bos A	5	4	.556	35	4	2	2	105	97	67	1	5	46	48	3.43	86	.238	.322	42-0-1	.214	1	76	-10		-0.8
1916	StL N	0	4	.000	10	5	2	1	42.2	45	27	1	0	14	15	5.48	48	.280	.337	14	.143	-1	68	-11		-1.1
1918	Det A	0	1	.000	6	1	0	0	13.1	14	10	1	0	4	2	6.75	39	.269	.345	2	.000	-0	0	-5		-0.4
Total	9	54	47	.535	188	80	49-3	12	909.2	821	438	16	38	391	427	3.09	95	.248	.334	371-2-19	.197	7	107	-18		-0.8

HALL, BERT Herbert Ernest B10.15.1888 Portland OR D7.18.1948 Seattle WA BR/TR/5-10/178 d8.21

| 1911 | Phi N | 0 | 1 | .000 | 7 | 1 | 0 | 0 | 18 | 19 | 11 | 0 | 1 | 13 | 8 | 4.00 | 86 | .297 | .423 | 3 | .333 | 0 | 218 | -1 | | -0.1 |

HALL, HERB Herbert Silas "Iron Duke" B6.5.1893 Steeleville IL D7.1.1970 Fresno CA BB/TR/6-4/220 d4.28

| 1918 | Det A | 0 | 0 | — | 3 | 0 | 0 | 0 | 6 | 12 | 11 | 0 | 2 | 7 | 1 | 15.00 | 18 | .500 | .636 | 0 | — | -0 | | -8 | | -0.4 |

HALL, JOHN John Sylvester B1.9.1924 Muskogee OK D1.17.1995 Midwest City OK BR/TR/6-2.5/170 d4.21

| 1948 | Bro N | 0 | 0 | — | 3 | 0 | 0 | 0 | 4.1 | 4 | 3 | 1 | 0 | 2 | 2 | 6.23 | 64 | .267 | .353 | 0 | — | 0 | | -1 | | 0.0 |

HALL, JOSH Joshua Alan B12.16.1980 Lynchburg VA BR/TR/6-2/190 [CinN98 7/200] d8.2 [DL 2004 Cin N 183]

| 2003 | Cin N | 0 | 2 | .000 | 6 | 5 | 0 | 0-0 | 24.2 | 33 | 22 | 4 | 0 | 15-1 | 18 | 6.57 | 63 | .314 | .397 | 6-0-1 | .167 | -0 | 86 | -8 | | -0.6 |

HALL, MARC Marcus B8.12.1887 Joplin MO D2.24.1915 Joplin MO BR/TR/6-1.5/190 d8.20

1910	StL A	1	7	.125	8	7	5	0	46.1	50	33	0	3	31	25	4.27	58	.289	.406	15	.067	-2	77	-9		-1.5
1913	Det A	10	12	.455	30	21	8-1	0	165	154	79	1	2	79	69	3.27	89	.259	.348	45-0-7	.089	-3	98	-5		-0.9
1914	Det A	4	6	.400	25	8	1	0	90.1	88	38	1	0	27	18	2.69	104	.267	.322	23	.043	-2	88	1		-0.2
Total	3	15	25	.375	63	36	14-1	0	301.2	292	150	2	5	137	112	3.25	87	.266	.350	83-0-7	.072	-7	92	-13		-2.6

HALL, DARREN Michael Darren B7.14.1964 Marysville OH BR/TR/6-3/205* [TorA86 28/706] d4.30 Col Dallas Baptist [DL 1999 Chi A 182]

1994	Tor A	2	3	.400	30	0	0	17-3	31.2	26	12	3	1	14-1	28	3.41	143	.226	.315	0	—	0		6		1.1
1995	Tor A	0	2	.000	17	0	0	3-1	16.1	21	9	2	0	9-0	11	4.41	108	.309	.390	0	—	0	1	85		0.1
1996	LA N	0	2	.000	9	0	0	0-1	12	13	9	2	0	5-0	12	6.00	65	.271	.340	0	—	0	-3	137		-0.4
1997	LA N	3	2	.600	63	0	0	2-3	54.2	58	15	3	0	26-7	39	2.30	170	.283	.362	0	—	0	11			1.0
1998	LA N	0	3	.000	11	0	0	1-1	11.1	17	14	2	1	5-0	8	10.32	39	.347	.411	0	—	0	-8	139		-1.5
Total	5	5	12	.294	130	0	0	22-9	126	135	59	12	2	59-8	98	3.93	108	.278	.358	0	—	0	7	543		0.3

HALL, DICK Richard Wallace B9.27.1930 St.Louis MO BR/TR/6-6/200(199-220) d4.15.1952 Col Swarthmore ▲

1955	Pit N	6	6	.500	15	13	4	1	94.1	92	43	8	2	28-4	46	3.91	105	.253	.308	40-1-1	.175	1*	88	4		0.5
1956	Pit N	0	7	.000	19	9	1	1	62.1	64	36	8	0	21-3	27	4.76	73	.270	.327	29	.345	2*	62	-6	41	-0.3
1957	Pit N	0	0	—	8	0	0	0	10	17	12	4	1	5-1	7	10.80	35	.362	.434	1	.000	-0*		-7	30	-0.4
1959	Pit N	0	0	—	2	1	0	0	8.2	12	5	1	0	1-1	3	3.12	124	.333	.342	2	.000	-0	92	0		0.0
1960	KC A	8	13	.381	29	28	9-1	0	182.1	183	96	28	3	38-4	79	4.05	98	.261	.299	56-0-8	.107	-2*	97	-3		-0.6
1961	Bal A	7	5	.583	29	13	4-2	4	122.1	102	47	10	0	30-5	92	3.09	124	.227	.273	36-0-4	.139	-0*	103	11		1.0
1962	Bal A	6	6	.500	43	6	1	6	118.1	102	31	9	0	19-2	71	2.28	162	.230	.261	24-0-2	.167	1*	80	21		2.4
1963	Bal A	5	5	.500	47	3	0	12	111.2	91	39	12	4	16-6	74	2.98	116	.224	.258	28-1-2	.464	6*	102	7		1.5
1964	Bal A	9	1	.900	45	0	0	7	87.2	58	19	8	0	16-5	52	1.85	193	.188	.226	16-0-3	.125	-0		17		2.2
1965	Bal A	11	8	.579	48	0	0	12	93.2	84	34	8	0	11-7	79	3.07	113	.243	.265	12-0-0	.333	3*		6		1.4
1966	Bal A	6	2	.750	32	0	0	7	66	59	30	8	3	8-4	44	3.95	84	.233	.263	12-0-4	.167	0		-4		-0.5
1967	Phi N	10	8	.556	48	1	1	8	86	83	28	5	2	12-8	49	2.20	155	.255	.286	14-0-2	.071	-1	103	10		2.2
1968	Phi N	4	1	.800	32	0	0	0	46	53	26	6	1	5-3	31	4.89	61	.296	.316	3	.333	0		-9		-0.9
1969	†Bal A	5	2	.714	39	0	0	6-2	65.2	49	14	3	1	9-6	31	1.92	187	.213	.244	7-0-2	.286	-1		13		1.7
1970	†Bal A	10	5	.667	32	0	0	3-4	61.1	51	25	8	0	6-2	30	3.08	119	.229	.247	12-0-1	.083	-1		3		0.5
1971	†Bal A	6	6	.500	27	0	0	1-3	43.1	52	27	4	1	11-9	26	4.98	68	.302	.342	5-0-1	.400	1		-8		-1.2
Total	16	93	75	.554	495	74	20-3	68-9	1259.2	1152	512	130	18	236-70	741	3.32	111	.244	.280	300-2-32	.203	10	97	55	71	9.1

HALL, BOB Robert Lewis B12.22.1923 Swissvale PA D3.12.1983 St.Petersburg FL BR/TR/6-2/195* d4.23

1949	Bos N	6	4	.600	31	6	2	0	74.1	77	40	7	1	41	43	4.36	87	.272	.366	22	.364	3	109	-4		-0.4
1950	Bos N	0	2	.000	21	4	0	0	50.1	58	43	8	2	33	22	6.97	55	.293	.399	12	.083	-1	172	-18		-0.9
1953	Pit N	3	12	.200	37	17	6-1	1	152	172	99	17	1	72	68	5.39	83	.286	.364	38-1-1	.158	0	74	-13		-1.1
Total	3	9	18	.333	89	27	8-1	1	276.2	307	182	32	4	146	133	5.40	77	.284	.371	72-1-1	.208	2	95	-35		-2.4

HALL, TOM Tom Edward B11.23.1947 Thomasville NC BL/TL/6-0/155* [MinA66*3/53] d6.9 Col Riverside (CA) CC

1968	Min A	2	1	.667	8	4	0	0	29.2	27	15	1	1	12-2	18	2.43	127	.239	.317	9-0-1	.000	-1*	127	0		-0.1
1969	†Min A	8	7	.533	31	18	5-2	0-1	140.2	129	63	12	6	50-4	92	3.33	109	.243	.308	43-0-3	.186	1*	108	3		0.3
1970	†Min A	11	6	.647	52	11	1	4-0	155.1	94	46	11	2	66-4	184	2.55	145	.173	.262	44-0-6	.182	-0*	112	22		2.3
1971	Min A	4	7	.364	48	11	0	9-1	129.2	104	54	13	0	58-5	137	3.33	106	.216	.297	34-0-1	.265	2*	97	3		0.5
1972	†Cin N	10	1	.909	44	7	1-1	8-0	124.1	77	43	13	2	56-1	134	2.61	124	.173	.268	30-0-3	.100	-1	125	8		0.6
1973	†Cin N	8	5	.615	54	7	0	8-6	103.2	74	43	13	0	48-10	96	3.47	99	.202	.293	22	.045	-2*	117	0		0.0
1974	Cin N	3	1	.750	40	1	0	1-1	64	54	32	9	0	30-0	48	4.08	86	.232	.317	5-0-3	.000	0	225	-4		-0.3
1975	Cin N	0	0	—	2	0	0	0-0	2	2	0	0	0	2-0	3	0.00	—	.250	.400	0	—	0		1		0.0
	NY N	4	3	.571	34	4	0	1-1	60.2	58	39	10	2	31-3	48	4.75	74	.254	.348	5-0-1	.400	1*	138	-10		-1.0
	Year	4	3	.571	36	4	0	1-1	62.2	60	39	10	3	33-3	51	4.60	76	.254	.350	5-0-1	.400	1	138	-8		-1.0
1976	NY N	1	1	.500	31	0	0	0-0	4.2	5	3	0	0	5-2	2	5.79	58	.250	.400	0	—	0		-1		-0.2
	†KC A	1	1	.500	31	0	0	1-0	30.1	28	19	4	0	18-1	25	4.45	79	.246	.346	0	—	0*		-4		-0.2
1977	KC A	1	0	—	9	0	0	0-0	7.2	6	6	0	0	6-0	10	3.52	115	.154	.313	0	—	0		1		0.0
Total	10	52	33	.612	358	63	7-3	32-11	852.2	656	360	88	8	382-32	797	3.27	107	.211	.297	192-0-18	.161	-1	114	19		1.6

HALL, BILL William Bernard "Beanie" B2.22.1894 Charleston WV D8.15.1947 Newport KY BR/TR/6-2/250 d7.4

| 1913 | Bro N | 0 | 0 | — | 3 | 0 | 0 | 0 | 4.2 | 4 | 3 | 0 | 1 | 5 | 3 | 5.79 | 57 | .267 | .476 | 1 | .000 | -0 | | -1 | | -0.2 |

HALLA, JOHN John Arthur B5.13.1884 St.Louis MO D9.30.1947 ElSegundo CA BL/TL/5-11/175 d8.18

| 1905 | Cle A | 0 | 0 | — | 3 | 0 | 0 | 0 | 12.2 | 12 | 6 | 0 | 1 | 0 | 4 | 2.84 | 92 | .250 | .265 | 5 | .200 | -0 | | -1 | | 0.0 |

YEAR	TM LG	W	L	PCT	G	GS	CG-SHO	SV-BS	IP	H	R	HR	HB	BB-IB	SO	ERA	AERA	OAV	OOB	AB-HR-SH	AVG	PB	SUP	APR	DL	PW

HALLADAY, ROY Harry Leroy B5.14.1977 Denver CO BR/TR/6-6/225(205-230) [TorA95 1/17] d9.20

1998	Tor A	1	0	1.000	2	2	1	0-0	14	9	4	2	0	2-0	13	1.93	242	.176	.208	0	—	0	90	4		0.3
1999	Tor A	8	7	.533	36	18	1-1	1-0	149.1	156	76	19	4	79-1	82	3.92	126	.270	.359	2-0-1	.000	-0	83	14		1.2
2000	Tor A	4	7	.364	19	13	0	0-0	67.2	107	87	14	2	42-0	44	10.64	47	.357	.435	0	—	0	112	-41		-4.8
2001	Tor A	5	3	.625	17	16	1-1	0-0	105.1	97	41	3	1	25-0	96	3.16	145	.241	.287	1-0-1	.000	-0	82	16		1.1
2002	Tor A★	19	7	.731	34	34	2-1	0-0	239.1	223	93	10	7	62-6	168	2.93	158	.244	.297	6	.000	-1	104	39		4.0
2003	Tor A☆	22	7	.759	36	36	9-2	0-0	266	253	111	26	9	32-1	204	3.25	146	.247	.275	9	.111	-0	108	40		4.2
2004	Tor A	8	8	.500	21	21	1-1	0-0	133	140	66	13	1	39-1	95	4.20	117	.272	.323	6	.000	-1	88	10	81	1.0
2005	Tor A*	12	4	.750	19	19	5-2	0-0	141.2	118	39	11	7	18-2	108	2.41	192	.225	.260	2	.000	-0	83	34	86	3.7
Total	8	79	43	.648	184	159	20-8	1-0	1116.1	1103	517	98	31	299-11	810	3.70	128	.256	.308	26-0-2	.038	-2	96	116	167	10.7

HALLAHAN, BILL William Anthony "Wild Bill" B8.4.1902 Binghamton NY D7.8.1981 Binghamton NY BR/TL/5-10.5/170 d4.16

1925	StL N	1	0	1.000	6	0	0	0	15.1	14	6	0	0	11	8	3.52	123	.259	.385	3	.333	0		2		0.1
1926	†StL N	1	4	.200	19	3	0	0	56.2	45	27	1	1	32	28	3.65	107	.260	.379	16	.250	0	78	2		0.1
1929	StL N	4	4	.500	20	12	5	0	93.2	94	51	6	0	60	52	4.42	106	.154	.376	26-0-2	.154	-1	83	3		0.2
1930	†StL N	15	9	.625	35	32	13-2	2	237.1	233	135	15	0	126	177	4.66	108	.260	.351	81-0-11	.123	-6	100	13		0.5
1931	†StL N	19	9	.679	37	30	16-3	4	248.2	242	102	10	1	112	159	3.29	120	.259	.339	81-0-10	.099	-4	125	19		1.5
1932	StL N	12	7	.632	25	22	13-1	1	176.1	169	79	10	0	69	108	3.11	126	.253	.323	56-0-4	.214	2*	96	12		1.4
1933	StL N★	16	13	.552	36	32	16-2	0	244.1	245	114	6	0	98	93	3.50	99	.260	.330	80-0-6	.150	-0*	107	-2		-0.4
1934	†StL N	8	12	.400	32	26	10-2	0	162.2	195	93	2	0	66	70	4.26	99	.294	.358	55-0-4	.182	-1	109	-2		-0.4
1935	StL N	15	8	.652	40	23	8-2	1	181.1	196	91	6	1	57	73	3.42	120	.275	.329	56-1-4	.143	-2	123	8		0.8
1936	StL N	2	2	.500	9	6	1	0	37	58	28	-4	0	17	16	6.32	62	.360	.421	9-0-3	.556	3	151	-9		-0.6
	Cin N	5	9	.357	23	19	5-2	0	135	150	78	3	1	57	32	4.33	88	.287	.359	47-1-1	.191	1	99	-9		-0.6
	Year	7	11	.389	32	25	6-2	0	172	208	106	-1	1	74	48	4.76	81	.305	.373	56-1-4	.250	3	112	-15		-1.2
1937	Cin N	3	9	.250	21	9	2	0	63	90	52	3	2	29	18	6.14	61	.345	.414	21-0-1	.095	-1	90	-18		-2.9
1938	Phi N	1	8	.111	21	10	1	0	89	107	59	4	2	45	22	5.46	71	.295	.376	26	.192	-0	59	-14		-1.2
Total	12	102	94	.520	324	224	90-14	8	1740.1	1838	915	71	8	779	856	4.03	102	.274	.351	557-2-46	.162	-9	105	5		-1.5

HALLETT, JACK Jack Price B11.13.1914 Toledo OH D6.11.1982 Toledo OH BR/TR/6-4/215 d9.13 Mil 1943-45

1940	Chi A	1	1	.500	2	2	1	0	14	15	10	1	1	6	9	6.43	69	.273	.355	5	.400	0	139	-2		-0.2
1941	Chi A	5	5	.500	22	6	3	0	74.2	96	57	7	3	38	25	6.03	68	.306	.386	26-0-1	.154	0	116	-16		-1.7
1942	Pit N	0	1	.000	3	3	2	0	22.1	23	12	0	0	8	16	4.84	70	.274	.337	8-1-0	.375	2	91	-3		0.0
1943	Pit N	1	2	.333	9	4	2-1	0	47.2	36	11	0	1	11	11	1.70	205	.212	.264	14	.286	2	98	9		0.7
1946	Pit N	5	7	.417	35	9	3-1	0	115	107	48	0	0	39	64	3.29	107	.267	.332	26-0-2	.231	2	40	4		0.4
1948	NY N	0	0	—	2	0	0	0	4	3	3	0	0	4	1	4.50	87	.214	.389	1	.000	-0		-1		0.0
Total	6	12	16	.429	73	24	11-2	0	277.2	280	141	8	5	106	128	4.05	92	.270	.340	80-1-3	.237	4	86	-9		-0.8

HALLSTROM, CHARLIE Charles E. "Swedish Wonder" B1.22.1864 Jonkoping, Sweden D5.6.1949 Chicago IL d9.23

| 1885 | Pro N | 0 | 1 | .000 | 1 | 1 | 1 | 0 | 9 | 18 | 16 | 3 | 1 | 6 | 0 | 11.00 | 24 | .409 | .480 | 4 | .000 | -1 | 169 | -8 | | -0.6 |

HALSEY, BRAD Bradford Alexander B2.14.1981 Houston TX BL/TL/6-1/180* [NYA02 8/246] d6.19 Col Texas

2004	NY A	1	3	.250	8	7	0	0-0	32	41	26	4	2	14-0	25	6.47	71	.306	.375	2	.500	0	124	-7		-0.7
2005	Ari N	8	12	.400	28	26	0	0-0	160	191	101	20	9	39-3	82	4.61	95	.300	.347	48-0-6	.063	-2	99	-9		-1.2
Total	2	9	15	.375	36	33	0	0-0	192	232	127	24	11	53-3	107	4.92	90	.301	.352	50-0-6	.080	-2	105	-16		-1.9

HAMANN, DOC Elmer Joseph B12.21.1900 New Ulm MN D1.11.1973 Milwaukee WI BR/TR/6-1/180 d9.21

| 1922 | Cle A | 0 | 0 | — | 1 | 0 | 0 | 0 | 0 | 6 | 3 | 0 | 1 | 3 | 0 | ∞ | — | 1.000 | 1.000 | 0 | | 0 | | -6 | | -0.4 |

HAMBRIGHT, ROGER Roger Dee B3.26.1949 Sunnyside WA BR/TR/5-10/180 [NYA67 67/955] d7.19

| 1971 | NY A | 3 | 1 | .750 | 18 | 0 | 0 | 2-0 | 26.2 | 22 | 13 | 5 | 0 | 10-2 | 14 | 4.39 | 75 | .224 | .294 | 2 | .500 | 0 | | -3 | | -0.4 |

HAMILL, JOHN John Alexander Charles B12.18.1860 New York NY D12.6.1911 Bristol RI BR/TR/5-8/158 d5.1

| 1884 | Was AA | 2 | 17 | .105 | 19 | 19 | 18-1 | 0 | 156.2 | 197 | 158 | 8 | 5 | 43 | 50 | 4.48 | 68 | .287 | .333 | 71 | .099 | -3* | 95 | -28 | | -2.9 |

HAMILTON, DAVE David Edward B12.13.1947 Seattle WA BL/TL/6-0/190* [OakA66 5/82] d5.29

1972	†Oak A	6	6	.500	34	14	1	0-0	101.1	94	34	7	1	31-2	55	2.93	97	.249	.304	26-0-1	.154	2	115	1		0.3
1973	Oak A	6	4	.600	16	11	1	0-0	69.2	74	37	8	1	24-0	34	4.39	81	.274	.334	0	—	0	100	-6		-0.8
1974	Oak A	7	4	.636	29	18	1-1	0-0	117	104	45	10	5	48-3	69	3.15	106	.241	.322	0	—	0	114	4		0.3
1975	Oak A	1	2	.333	11	4	0	0-0	35.2	42	19	4	0	18-1	20	4.04	90	.290	.366	0	—	0	60	-2		-0.1
	Chi A	6	5	.545	30	1	0	6-2	69.2	63	23	4	0	29-2	51	2.84	137	.246	.322	0	—	0	68	8		1.5
	Year	7	7	.500	41	5	0	6-2	105.1	105	42	8	0	47-3	71	3.25	117	.262	.338	0	—	0	60	7		1.4
1976	Chi A	6	6	.500	45	1	0	10-3	90.1	81	38	4	4	45-6	62	3.59	99	.243	.335	0	—	0	172	0		0.0
1977	Chi A	4	5	.444	55	0	0	9-6	67.1	71	33	6	0	33-4	45	3.61	113	.270	.344	0	—	0		2		0.4
1978	StL N	0	0	—	13	0	0	0-1	14	16	13	5	0	6-0	11	8.43	55	.296	.367	1	.000	-0		-5		-0.3
	Pit N	0	2	.000	16	0	0	1-1	26.1	23	16	2	0	12-2	15	3.42	109	.221	.302	6	.000	-1		-1		-0.2
	Year	0	2	.000	29	0	0	1-2	40.1	39	29	7	0	18-2	23	4.46	82	.247	.324	7	.000	-1		-7		-0.5
1979	Oak A	3	4	.429	40	7	1	5-1	82.2	80	42	5	1	43-2	52	3.70	110	.261	.349	0	—	0	67	2		0.2
1980	Oak A	0	3	.000	21	1	0	0-0	30	44	39	4	3	28-2	23	11.40	33	.344	.466	0	—	0	94	-25		-2.1
Total	9	39	41	.488	301	57	4-1	31-14	704	692	339	61	15	317-24	434	3.85	93	.259	.338	33-0-1	.121	1	95	-22		-0.8

HAMILTON, EARL Earl Andrew B7.19.1891 Gibson City IL D11.17.1968 Anaheim CA BL/TL/5-8/160 d4.14 Mil 1918

1911	StL A	5	12	.294	32	17	10-1	0	177	191	103	4	4	69	55	3.97	85	.284	.354	56-0-1	.107	-1	99	-9		-0.8
1912	StL A	11	14	.440	41	26	17-1	2	249.2	228	117	2	9	86	139	3.24	102	.248	.319	73-0-6	.178	-0	56	4		0.3
1913	StL A	13	12	.520	31	24	19-3	1	217.1	197	95	3	9	83	101	2.57	114	.244	.321	74-0-2	.135	-2	100	5		0.3
1914	StL A	16	18	.471	44	35	20-5	2	302.1	265	111	5	10	100	111	2.50	108	.239	.307	85-0-7	.176	4	85	8		1.3
1915	StL A	9	17	.346	35	28	13-1	0	204	203	98	4	12	69	63	2.87	100	.274	.346	62-0-2	.113	-2	85	-2		-0.6
1916	StL A	0	0	—	1	0	0	0	4	4	5	0	0	4	0	9.00	31	.250	.400	0	—	0		-3		-0.2
	Det A	1	2	.333	5	5	3	0	37.1	34	14	0	4	22	7	2.65	108	.254	.375	13	.077	-1	121	1		0.0
	StL A	5	7	.417	22	12	3	0	91.1	97	44	2	2	26	25	3.05	90	.284	.339	24	.000	-1	90	-5		-0.8
	Year	6	9	.400	28	17	6	0	132.2	135	63	2	6	52	32	3.12	89	.275	.352	37	.027	-2	99	-7		-1.0
1917	StL A	0	9	.000	27	8	2	1	83	86	46	1	2	41	19	3.14	83	.274	.361	19-0-2	.368	3	38	-7		-0.5
1918	Pit N	6	0	1.000	8	6	6-1	0	54	47	7	0	0	13	20	0.83	344	.242	.290	21	.286	1	141	12		1.6
1919	Pit N	8	11	.421	28	19	9-1	0	160.1	167	73	3	5	49	39	3.31	91	.280	.340	52-0-1	.135	-2	83	-7		-1.0
1920	Pit N	10	13	.435	39	23	12	3	230.1	223	99	2	6	69	74	3.24	99	.258	.314	67-0-7	.149	-3	94	0		-0.3
1921	Pit N	13	15	.464	35	30	12-2	0	225	237	103	2	8	58	59	3.36	114	.272	.323	75-0-5	.160	-2	95	11		1.3
1922	Pit N	11	7	.611	33	14	9-1	2	160	183	84	6	1	40	34	3.99	102	.296	.339	58-0-3	.155	-2	126	2		0.0
1923	Pit N	7	9	.438	28	15	5	1	141	148	79	6	1	42	42	3.77	106	.271	.324	52-0-1	.173	-2	83	5		0.4
1924	Phi N	0	1	.000	3	0	0	0	6	9	9	0	1	2	2	10.50	42	.391	.462	2	.000	-0		-4		-0.5
Total	14	115	147	.439	410	262	140-16	13	2342.2	2319	1075	43	70	773	790	3.16	102	.265	.329	733-0-37	.153	-9	89	11		0.5

HAMILTON, JACK Jack Edwin B12.25.1938 Burlington IA BR/TR/6-0/200* d4.13

1962	Phi N	9	12	.429	41	26	4-1	2	182	185	115	18	5	107-8	101	5.09	76	.268	.366	54-0-5	.056	-4	97	-25		-2.8
1963	Phi N	2	1	.667	19	1	0	3	30	22	19	3	0	17-2	23	5.40	60	.200	.307	3	.000	-0	27	-7		-0.7
1964	Det A	0	1	.000	5	1	0	0	15	24	17	2	1	8-0	5	8.40	44	.364	.434	3	.000	-0	49	-9	33	-0.5
1965	Det A	1	1	.500	4	1	0	0	4.1	6	7	1	0	4-0	3	14.54	24	.316	.417	0	—	0	76	-5		-0.9
1966	NY N	6	13	.316	57	13	3-1	13	148.2	138	89	13	6	88-4	93	3.93	92	.248	.354	38-0-1	.132	-1	102	-11		-1.6
1967	NY N	2	0	1.000	17	1	0	1	31.1	24	15	1	2	16-5	22	3.73	91	.205	.306	5-1-0	.200	1	233	-1		0.0
	Cal A	9	6	.600	26	20	0	0	119.1	104	47	6	4	63-3	74	3.24	97	.239	.334	38-0-0	.158	-0	110	0		-0.1
1968	Cal A	3	1	.750	21	1	0	2	38	34	15	0	0	15-1	18	3.32	88	.244	.316	7	.143	-0	105	-1		-0.2
1969	Cle A	0	2	.000	20	0	0	1-2	30.2	37	17	2	0	23-4	13	4.40	86	.316	.426	2	.000	-0		-2		-0.2
	Chi A	0	3	.000	8	0	0	0-0	12.1	23	16	1	0	7-3	5	11.68	33	.411	.476	0	—	0		-10		-1.8
	Year	0	5	.000	28	0	0	1-2	43	60	33	3	0	30-7	18	6.49	59	.344	.441	2	.000	-0		-12		-2.0
Total	8	32	40	.444	218	65	8-2	20-2	611.2	597	357	48	13	348-30	357	4.53	78	.259	.356	150-1-8	.107	-6	102	-71	33	-8.8

HAMILTON, JOEY Johns Joseph B9.9.1970 Statesboro GA BR/TR/6-4/230(220-240) [SDN91 1/8] d5.24 Col Georgia Southern

| 1994 | SD N | 9 | 6 | .600 | 16 | 16 | 1-1 | 0-0 | 108.2 | 98 | 40 | 7 | 6 | 29-3 | 61 | 2.98 | 139 | .241 | .300 | 40-0-5 | .000 | -4 | 103 | 14 | | 1.4 |
| 1995 | SD N | 6 | 9 | .400 | 31 | 30 | 2-2 | 0-0 | 204.1 | 189 | 89 | 11 | 11 | 56-5 | 123 | 3.08 | 132 | .246 | .305 | 65-0-5 | .108 | -2 | 98 | 19 | | 1.0 |

YEAR	TM LG	W	L	PCT	G	GS	CG-SHO	SV-BS	IP	H	R	HR	HB	BB-IB	SO	ERA	AERA	OAV	OOB	AB-HR-SH	AVG	PB	SUP	APR	DL	PW
1996	†SD N	15	9	.625	34	33	3-1	0-0	211.2	206	100	19	9	83-3	184	4.17	97	.256	.330	68-1-11	.162	1	100	1		0.2
1997	SD N	12	7	.632	31	29	1	0-0	192.2	199	100	22	12	69-2	124	4.25	92	.271	.340	54-2-9	.130	1	121	-7	23	-0.6
1998	†SD N	13	13	.500	34	34	0	0-0	217.1	220	113	15	8	106-10	147	4.27	93	.267	.353	71-1-2	.141	0*	82	-8		-0.9
1999	Tor A	7	8	.467	22	18	0	0-0	98	118	73	13	3	39-0	56	6.52	76	.298	.364	2	.000	-0	107	-15	40	-1.9
2000	Tor A	2	1	.667	6	6	0	0-0	33	28	13	3	2	12-0	15	3.55	142	.233	.311	0	—	0	115	6	137	0.4
2001	Tor A	5	8	.385	22	22	0	0-0	122.1	170	88	17	3	38-1	82	5.89	78	.339	.384	3	.333	1	101	-18		-1.5
	Cin N	2	2	.333	4	4	0	0-0	17.1	23	12	3	1	6-0	10	6.23	74	.329	.390	5	.000	-1	70	-2		-0.4
2002	Cin N	4	10	.286	39	17	0	1-1	124.2	136	78	11	6	50-2	85	5.27	81	.279	.351	28-0-4	.250	2	96	-12	44	-1.1
2003	Cin N	0	0	—	3	0	0	0-0	10.2	21	15	3	0	5-0	7	12.66	33	.404	.456	3	.000	-0		-10		-0.2
Total	10	74	73	.503	242	209		7-4	1-1	1340.2	1408	721	130	61	493-26	894	4.44	94	.273	.341	339-4-36	.127	-2	101	-32	244	-3.9

HAMILTON, STEVE   Steve Absher   B11.30.1935 Columbia KY   D12.2.1997 Morehead KY   BL/TL/6-7/195*   d4.23 C1   Col Morehead St.

YEAR	TM LG	W	L	PCT	G	GS	CG-SHO	SV-BS	IP	H	R	HR	HB	BB-IB	SO	ERA	AERA	OAV	OOB	AB-HR-SH	AVG	PB	SUP	APR	DL	PW
1961	Cle A	0	0	—	2	0	0	0	3	3	1	0	0	3-0	4	3.00	131	.200	.385	1	1.000	0		0		0.1
1962	Was A	3	8	.273	41	10	1	2	107.1	103	51	10	3	39-5	83	3.77	107	.248	.317	26-0-3	.077	-1*	88	2		0.2
1963	Was A	0	1	.000	3	0	0	0	2	5	3	0	0	2-0	1	13.50	27	.556	.583	0	—	0		-2		-0.4
	†NY A	5	1	.833	34	0	0	5	62.1	49	19	3	1	24-2	63	2.60	135	.220	.296	14-0-5	.286	1		7		1.0
	Year	5	2	.714	37	0	0	5	64.1	54	22	3	1	26-2	64	2.94	120	.233	.309	14-0-5	.286	1		5		0.6
1964	†NY A	5	1	.778	30	3	1	3	60.1	55	24	6	0	15-0	49	3.28	110	.246	.289	20	.200	1*	164	2		0.4
1965	NY A	3	1	.750	46	1	0	5	58.1	47	12	2	0	16-5	51	1.39	245	.214	.265	6	.167	0	103	12		1.0
1966	NY A	8	3	.727	44	3	1-1	8	90	69	32	8	3	22-3	57	3.00	111	.218	.273	19-0-2	.053	-2	62	4		0.3
1967	NY A	2	4	.333	44	0	0	4	62	57	25	7	1	23-4	55	3.48	90	.250	.320	9-0-1	.111	-0		-1		-0.2
1968	NY A	2	2	.500	40	0	0	11	50.2	37	13	0	1	13-4	42	2.13	137	.211	.268	3	.000	-1		5		0.7
1969	NY A	3	4	.429	38	0	0	2-2	57	39	22	7	0	21-5	39	3.32	106	.194	.269	5	.000	-1		4		0.2
1970	NY A	4	3	.571	35	0	0	3-1	45.1	36	16	3	1	16-5	33	2.78	129	.222	.294	6	.000	-1		4		0.6
	Chi A	0	0	—	3	0*	0	0-0	3	4	2	0	0	1-0	3	6.00	56	.333	.385	0	—	0		-1		0.0
	Year	4	3	.571	38	0	0	3-1	48.1	40	18	3	1	17-5	36	2.98	121	.230	.301	6	.000	-1		4		0.6
1971	†SF N	2	2	.500	39	0	0	4-3	44.2	29	15	4	1	11-6	35	3.02	113	.186	.238	2	.000	-0		3		-0.1
1972	Chi N	0	1	.000	22	0	0	0	17	24	9	1	1	8-3	13	4.76	80	.333	.398	1	.000	-0		-1		-0.1
Total	12	40	31	.563	421	17	3-1	42-6	663	556	244	51	12	214-42	531	3.05	115	.229	.293	112-0-11	.125	-2	106	36		4.1

HAMLIN, LUKE   Lewis Dennison "Hot Potato"   B7.3.1904 Ferris Center MI   D2.18.1978 Clare MI   BL/TR/6-2/168   d9.18

YEAR	TM LG	W	L	PCT	G	GS	CG-SHO	SV-BS	IP	H	R	HR	HB	BB-IB	SO	ERA	AERA	OAV	OOB	AB-HR-SH	AVG	PB	SUP	APR	DL	PW
1933	Det A	1	0	1.000	3	3	0	0	16.2	20	11	3	0	10	10	4.86	89	.294	.385	5-0-1	.400	1	118	-1		0.0
1934	Det A	3	3	.400	20	5	1	1	75.1	87	48	11	0	44	30	5.38	82	.289	.380	26-0-3	.231	-0	174	-7		-0.4
1937	Bro N	11	13	.458	39	25	11-1	1	185.2	183	96	4	0	48	93	3.59	113	.252	.298	59-0-5	.186	-1*	85	7		0.6
1938	Bro N	12	15	.444	44	30	10-3	6	237.1	243	111	14	2	65	97	3.68	106	.263	.313	78-0-4	.141	-3	92	7		0.3
1939	Bro N	20	13	.606	40	36	19-2	1	269.2	255	115	27	0	54	88	3.64	111	.248	.285	103-1-6	.126	-5	102	15		0.9
1940	Bro N	9	8	.529	33	25	9-2	0	182.1	183	77	17	2	34	58	3.06	131	.256	.292	58-0-8	.086	-4*	79	15		0.6
1941	Bro N	8	8	.500	30	20	5-1	1	136	139	75	14	2	41	58	4.24	87	.261	.316	41-0-3	.146	1	130	-9		-1.1
1942	Pit N	4	4	.500	23	14	6-1	0	112	128	58	3	1	39	38	3.94	86	.281	.312	37-0-3	.243	1	115	-7		-0.5
1944	Phi N	6	12	.333	29	23	9-2	0	190	204	94	13	3	38	58	3.74	93	.271	.309	56-0-4	.232	3	88	-6		-0.5
Total	9	73	76	.490	261	181	70-12	9	1405	1442	685	106	10	353	563	3.77	103	.262	.308	463-1-37	.164	-8	99	14		-0.1

HAMM, PETE   Peter Whitfield   B9.20.1947 Buffalo NY   BR/TR/6-5/210*   [MinA67 S9/156]   d7.29   Col Stanford

YEAR	TM LG	W	L	PCT	G	GS	CG-SHO	SV-BS	IP	H	R	HR	HB	BB-IB	SO	ERA	AERA	OAV	OOB	AB-HR-SH	AVG	PB	SUP	APR	DL	PW
1970	Min A	0	2	.000	2	1	0	0-0	16.1	17	10	3	0	7-1	5	5.51	67	.262	.333	1	.000	-0		-3		-0.3
1971	Min A	2	4	.333	13	8	1	0-0	44	55	33	7	1	18-1	16	6.75	52	.309	.372	11-0-1	.273	1	127	-14		-1.6
Total	2	2	6	.250	23	8	1	0-0	60.1	72	43	10	1	25-2	19	6.41	56	.296	.362	12-0-1	.250	1	127	-17		-1.9

HAMMAKER, ATLEE   Charlton Atlee   B1.24.1958 Carmel CA   BB/TL/6-3/200*   [KCA79 1/21]   d8.13   Col East Tennessee   [DL 1986 SF N 182]

YEAR	TM LG	W	L	PCT	G	GS	CG-SHO	SV-BS	IP	H	R	HR	HB	BB-IB	SO	ERA	AERA	OAV	OOB	AB-HR-SH	AVG	PB	SUP	APR	DL	PW
1981	KC A	1	3	.250	10	6	0	0-0	39	44	24	2	0	12-1	11	5.54	65	.286	.335	0	—	0	95	-7		-0.7
1982	SF N	12	8	.600	29	27	4-1	0-0	175	189	86	16	2	28-8	102	4.11	87	.278	.307	59-0-1	.068	-4	96	-8		-0.8
1983	SF N★	10	9	.526	23	23	8-3	0-0	172.1	147	57	9	3	32-12	127	**2.25**	**158**	.228	**.266**	59-0-3	.102	-1	88	23	26	2.4
1984	SF N	2	0	1.000	6	6	0	0-0	33	32	10	2	0	9-1	24	2.18	162	.256	.301	11	.182	1	113	5	113	0.4
1985	SF N	5	12	.294	29	29	1-1	0-0	170.2	161	81	17	0	47-5	100	3.74	93	.247	.295	47-0-6	.085	-1	86	-5		0.5
1987	†SF N	10	10	.500	31	27	2	0-0	168.1	159	73	22	3	57-10	107	3.58	107	.248	.312	57-0-2	.123	-1	114	6	24	0.5
1988	SF N	9	9	.500	43	17	3-1	5-2	144.2	136	68	11	3	41-9	65	3.73	87	.248	.302	33-0-4	.121	-0	91	-8		0.0
1989	†SF N	6	6	.500	28	9	0	0-1	76.2	78	34	5	1	23-2	30	3.76	90	.271	.323	19-0-4	.368	2	128	-2	77	-0.1
1990	SF N	4	5	.444	25	6	0	0-0	67.1	69	33	7	0	21-4	28	4.28	86	.273	.324	17-0-1	.059	-1	119	-4	23	-0.6
	SD N	0	4	.000	9	1	0	0-0	19.1	16	11	1	0	6-1	16	4.66	82	.213	.272	2	.500	0	118	-2		-0.9
	Year	4	9	.308	34	7	0	0-0	86.2	85	44	8	0	27-5	44	4.36	85	.259	.312	19-0-1	.105	-1	119	-5		-0.9
1991	SD N	0	1	.000	1	1	0	0-0	4.2	8	7	0	0	3-0	1	5.79	66	.364	.440	1	.000	-0	24	-3	143	-0.4
1994	Chi A	0	0	—	2	0	0	0-0	1.1	1	0	0	0	0-0	1	0.00	—	.200	.200	0	—	0		1		0.0
1995	Chi A	0	0	—	13	0	0	0-0	6.1	11	9	2	1	8-1	3	12.79	35	.393	.541	0	—	0		-6		-0.3
Total	12	59	67	.468	249	152	18-6	5-3	1078.2	1051	493	94	9	287-54	615	3.66	97	.253	.304	305-0-21	.118	-7	99	-10	588	-1.9

HAMMOND, CHRIS   Christopher Andrew   B1.21.1966 Atlanta GA   BL/TL/6-1/195(190-210)   [CinN86*6/148]   d7.16   b-Steve   Col Alabama-Birmingham

YEAR	TM LG	W	L	PCT	G	GS	CG-SHO	SV-BS	IP	H	R	HR	HB	BB-IB	SO	ERA	AERA	OAV	OOB	AB-HR-SH	AVG	PB	SUP	APR	DL	PW
1990	Cin N	0	2	.000	3	3	0	0-0	11.1	13	9	2	0	12-1	4	6.35	62	.302	.455	3	.000	-0	91	-3		-0.5
1991	Cin N	7	7	.500	20	18	0	0-0	99.2	92	51	4	2	48-3	50	4.06	94	.250	.339	34-0-1	.353	5	77	-3	36	0.1
1992	Cin N	7	10	.412	28	26	0	0-0	147.1	149	75	13	3	55-6	79	4.21	86	.266	.333	44-1-3	.136	2*	90	-10		-0.1
1993	Fla N	11	12	.478	32	32	1	0-0	191	207	106	18	1	66-2	108	4.66	94	.277	.336	63-2-5	.190	4*	86	-5		-0.1
1994	Fla N	4	4	.500	13	13	1-1	0-0	73.1	79	30	5	1	23-1	40	3.07	145	.281	.336	22-0-3	.136	0	87	10	53	0.9
1995	Fla N	9	6	.600	25	24	3-2	0-0	161	157	73	17	9	47-2	126	3.80	113	.256	.315	48-1-5	.271	5	111	9	34	1.2
1996	Fla N	5	8	.385	38	9	0	0-0	81	104	65	14	4	27-3	50	6.56	63	.315	.370	15-0-2	.067	-1	105	-22	35	-3.1
1997	Bos A	3	4	.429	29	8	0	1-1	65.1	81	45	5	2	27-4	48	5.92	79	.310	.375	0	—	0	121	-8	93	-0.5
1998	Fla N	0	2	.000	3	3	0	0-0	13.2	20	11	3	1	8-0	8	6.59	62	.357	.446	5	.200	0	68	-4		-0.5
2002	†Atl N	7	2	.778	63	0	0	0-2	76	53	15	1	1	31-9	63	0.95	427	.195	.278	1	.000	0		24		2.7
2003	†NY A	3	2	.600	62	0	0	1-3	63	65	23	5	2	11-0	45	2.86	154	.270	.304	0	—	0		11		0.7
2004	Oak A	4	1	.800	41	0	0	1-2	53.2	56	21	4	3	13-1	34	2.68	172	.277	.326	0	—	0		10	45	0.8
2005	SD N	5	1	.833	55	0	0	0-3	58.2	51	25	9	3	14-0	34	3.84	101	.229	.278	3	.000	0		20		0.1
Total	13	65	61	.516	412	136	5-3	3-11	1095	1127	549	100	31	382-32	689	4.07	102	.268	.332	238-4-19	.202	15	93	10	316	0.8

HAMNER, GRANNY   Granville Wilbur   B4.26.1927 Richmond VA   D9.12.1993 Philadelphia PA   BR/TR/5-10/163(160-185)   d9.14.1944 Mil 1945   b-Garvin ▲

YEAR	TM LG	W	L	PCT	G	GS	CG-SHO	SV-BS	IP	H	R	HR	HB	BB-IB	SO	ERA	AERA	OAV	OOB	AB-HR-SH	AVG	PB	SUP	APR	DL	PW
1956	Phi N	0	1	.000	3	1	0	0	8.1	10	4	0	0	2-0	4	4.32	86	.294	.333	401-4-3	.224	1*	71	0		0.0
1957	Phi N	0	0	—	1	0	0	0	1	1	0	0	0	0-0	1	0.00	—	.250	.250	502-10-7	.227	0*		0		0.0
1962	KC A	0	1	.000	3	0	0	0	4	10	6	0	0	6-1	0	9.00	47	.476	.593	0	—	0		-3		-0.5
Total	3	0	2	.000	7	1	0	0	13.1	21	10	0	0	8-1	5	5.40	72	.356	.433	903-14-10	.226	1	71	-3		-0.5

HAMNER, RALPH   Ralph Conant "Bruz"   B9.12.1916 Gibsland LA   D5.22.2001 Little Rock AR   BR/TR/6-3/165   d4.28

YEAR	TM LG	W	L	PCT	G	GS	CG-SHO	SV-BS	IP	H	R	HR	HB	BB-IB	SO	ERA	AERA	OAV	OOB	AB-HR-SH	AVG	PB	SUP	APR	DL	PW
1946	Chi A	2	7	.222	25	7	1	1	71.1	80	47	2	5	39	29	4.42	77	.276	.371	18-0-2	.167	0	54	-10		-1.2
1947	Chi N	1	2	.333	3	3	2	0	25	24	10	0	0	16	14	2.52	157	.267	.377	8	.125	-0	52	3		0.3
1948	Chi N	5	9	.357	27	17	5	0	111.1	110	63	12	5	69	53	4.69	83	.259	.369	33-1-1	.182	1	106	-8		-0.7
1949	Chi N	0	2	.000	6	1	0	0	12.1	22	13	2	1	8	3	8.76	46	.407	.492	2-0-1	.000	-0	44	-6		-0.8
Total	4	8	20	.286	61	28	8	1	220	236	133	16	11	132	99	4.58	82	.275	.378	61-1-4	.164	0	86	-21		-2.4

HAMPTON, MIKE   Michael William   B9.9.1972 Brooksville FL   BR/TL/5-10/180(180-195)   [SeaA90 6/161]   d4.17

YEAR	TM LG	W	L	PCT	G	GS	CG-SHO	SV-BS	IP	H	R	HR	HB	BB-IB	SO	ERA	AERA	OAV	OOB	AB-HR-SH	AVG	PB	SUP	APR	DL	PW
1993	Sea A	1	3	.250	13	3	0	1-0	17	28	20	3	0	17-3	8	9.53	47	.368	.479	0	—	0	89	-10		-1.7
1994	Hou N	2	1	.667	44	0	0	0-1	41.1	46	19	4	2	16-1	24	3.70	107	.282	.354	1	.000	-0		1		0.1
1995	Hou N	9	8	.529	24	24	0	0-0	150.2	141	76	13	4	49-3	115	3.35	115	.247	.308	42-0-7	.238	1	130	5	29	0.6
1996	Hou N	10	10	.500	27	27	2-1	0-0	160.1	175	79	12	3	49-1	101	3.59	108	.280	.333	47-0-7	.213	4*	116	2		0.8
1997	†Hou N	15	10	.600	34	34	7-2	0-0	223	217	105	16	2	77-2	139	3.83	104	.257	.318	73-0-10	.137	1	123	9		0.8
1998	†Hou N	11	7	.611	32	32	1-1	0-0	211.2	227	92	18	5	81-1	137	3.36	121	.278	.344	61-0-7	.262	7	110	14	18	2.2
1999	†Hou N★	22	4	.846	34	34	3-2	0-0	239	206	86	12	5	101-2	177	2.90	153	.241	.322	74-0-5	.311	11	140	41		**5.3**
2000	†NY N	15	10	.600	33	33	3-1	0-0	217.2	194	89	10	8	99-5	151	3.14	139	.241	.328	73-0-4	.274	6*	115	29		3.7
2001	Col N★	14	13	.519	32	32	2-1	0-0	203	236	138	31	8	85-7	122	5.41	99	.296	.367	75-4-5	.291	8*	105	-4		0.0
2002	Col N	7	15	.318	30	30	0	0-0	178.2	228	135	24	7	91-4	74	6.15	87	.313	.390	64-3-1	.344	7*	87	-25		-1.9
2003	†Atl N	14	8	.636	31	31	1	0-0	190	186	91	14	1	78-4	110	3.84	109	.255	.326	60-2-9	.183	5*	115	8	20	1.5
2004	†Atl N	13	9	.591	29	29	1	0-0	172.1	198	86	12	1	65-3	87	4.28	101	.290	.351	62-2-4	.172	3*	106	3		0.2

YEAR	TM LG	W	L	PCT	G	GS	CG-SHO	SV-BS	IP	H	R	HR	HB	BB-IB	SO	ERA	AERA	OAV	OOB	AB-HR-SH	AVG	PB	SUP	APR	DL	PW
2005	Atl N	5	3	.625	12	12	1-1	0-0	69.1	74	28	5	0	18-0	27	3.50	123	.281	.326	25-1-3	.320	3	144	6	107	1.0
Total	13	138	101	.577	375	321	21-9	1-1	2074	2156	1041	177	46	826-36	1272	3.95	109	.271	.341	664-15-59	.242	54	115	75	174	13.4

HAMULACK, TIM Timothy William B11.14.1976 Ithaca NY BL/TL/6-4/220 d9.2 Col Montgomery (MD) CC

YEAR	TM LG	W	L	PCT	G	GS	CG-SHO	SV-BS	IP	H	R	HR	HB	BB-IB	SO	ERA	AERA	OAV	OOB	AB-HR-SH	AVG	PB	SUP	APR	DL	PW
2005	NY N	0	0	—	6	0	0	0-0	2.1	7	6	3	0	1-1	2	23.14	18	.583	.571	0	—	0		-5		-0.2

HANCOCK, JOSH Joshua Morgan B4.11.1978 Cleveland MS BR/TR/6-3/217(205-217) [BosA98 5/145] d9.10 Col Auburn-Montgomery

YEAR	TM LG	W	L	PCT	G	GS	CG-SHO	SV-BS	IP	H	R	HR	HB	BB-IB	SO	ERA	AERA	OAV	OOB	AB-HR-SH	AVG	PB	SUP	APR	DL	PW
2002	Bos A	0	1	.000	3	1	0	0-0	7.1	5	3	1	0	2-0	6	3.68	122	.200	.259	0	—	0	41	1		0.1
2003	Phi N	0	0	—	2	0	0	0-0	3	2	1	0	0	0-0	1	3.00	132	.182	.182	0	—	0	0	0		0.0
2004	Phi N	0	1	.000	4	2	0	0-0	9	13	9	3	0	3-0	5	9.00	49	.333	.381	2	.000	-0	104	-4		-0.4
	Cin N	5	1	.833	12	9	0	0-0	54.2	60	34	14	1	25-2	31	4.45	97	.273	.347	15-0-1	.133	0	127	-3		-0.3
	Year	5	2	.714	16	11	0	0-0	63.2	73	43	17	1	28-2	36	5.09	85	.282	.352	17-0-1	.118	0	123	-6		-0.7
2005	Cin N	1	0	1.000	11	0	0	0-0	14	11	4	1	0	1-0	5	1.93	216	.208	.222	0	—	0		3	151	-0.4
Total	6	3	.667	32	12	0	0-0	88	91	51	19	1	31-2	51	4.40	98	.261	.322	17-0-1	.118	0	117	-3	151	-0.4

HANCOCK, LEE Leland David B6.27.1967 N.Hollywood CA BL/TL/6-4/220* [SeaA88 4/97] d9.3 Col Cal Poly-San Luis Obispo

YEAR	TM LG	W	L	PCT	G	GS	CG-SHO	SV-BS	IP	H	R	HR	HB	BB-IB	SO	ERA	AERA	OAV	OOB	AB-HR-SH	AVG	PB	SUP	APR	DL	PW
1995	Pit N	0	0	—	11	0	0	0-0	14	10	3	0	0	2-0	5	1.93	226	.192	.222	0	—	0		4		0.2
1996	Pit N	0	0	—	13	0	0	0-0	18.1	21	18	5	2	10-3	13	6.38	69	.276	.375	0	—	0		-5		-0.2
Total	2	0	0	—	24	0	0	0-0	32.1	31	21	5	2	12-3	18	4.45	98	.242	.317	0	—	0		-1		0.0

HANCOCK, RYAN Ryan Lee B11.11.1971 Santa Clara CA BR/TR/6-2/220 [CalA93 2/45] d6.8 Col Brigham Young

YEAR	TM LG	W	L	PCT	G	GS	CG-SHO	SV-BS	IP	H	R	HR	HB	BB-IB	SO	ERA	AERA	OAV	OOB	AB-HR-SH	AVG	PB	SUP	APR	DL	PW
1996	Cal A	4	1	.800	11	4	0	0-0	27.2	34	23	2	2	17-1	19	7.48	68	.306	.408	1	1.000	0	115	-6		-0.9

HAND, RICH Richard Allen B7.10.1948 Bellevue WA BR/TR/6-1/195* [CleA69 S1/1] d4.9 Col Puget Sound

YEAR	TM LG	W	L	PCT	G	GS	CG-SHO	SV-BS	IP	H	R	HR	HB	BB-IB	SO	ERA	AERA	OAV	OOB	AB-HR-SH	AVG	PB	SUP	APR	DL	PW
1970	Cle A	6	13	.316	35	25	3-1	3-0	159.2	132	71	27	4	69-3	110	3.83	105	.228	.313	41-0-5	.146	-1	82	4		0.3
1971	Cle A	2	6	.250	15	12	0	0-0	60.2	74	43	6	4	38-1	26	5.79	67	.311	.413	16-0-2	.125	-0*	116	-12	32	-1.5
1972	Tex A	10	14	.417	30	28	2-1	0-0	170.2	139	66	12	3	103-8	109	3.32	92	.226	.336	52-0-3	.154	-1	95	-2		-0.2
1973	Tex A	2	3	.400	8	7	1	0-0	41.2	49	29	2	2	19-5	14	5.40	70	.290	.363	0	—	0	92	-8		-0.8
	Cal A	4	3	.571	16	6	0	0-0	54.2	58	29	5	1	21-0	19	3.62	99	.274	.336	0	—	0	91	-2	25	-0.2
	Year	6	6	.500	24	13	1	0-0	96.1	107	58	7	3	40-5	33	4.39	83	.281	.348	0	—	0	92	-11		-1.0
Total	6	24	39	.381	104	78	6-2	3-0	487.1	452	238	52	14	250-17	278	4.01	89	.249	.341	109-0-10	.147	-1	93	-20	57	-2.4

HANDIBOE, JIM James Edward "Nick" B7.17.1866 Columbus OH D11.8.1942 Columbus OH BR/TR/5-11/160 d5.28

YEAR	TM LG	W	L	PCT	G	GS	CG-SHO	SV-BS	IP	H	R	HR	HB	BB-IB	SO	ERA	AERA	OAV	OOB	AB-HR-SH	AVG	PB	SUP	APR	DL	PW
1886	Pit AA	7	7	.500	14	14	12-1	0	114	82	65	1	2	33	83	3.32	102	.195	.273	44	.114	-2	94	3		0.0

HANDRAHAN, VERN James Vernon B11.27.1938 Charlottetown PE, Can. BL/TR/6-2/185* d4.14

YEAR	TM LG	W	L	PCT	G	GS	CG-SHO	SV-BS	IP	H	R	HR	HB	BB-IB	SO	ERA	AERA	OAV	OOB	AB-HR-SH	AVG	PB	SUP	APR	DL	PW
1964	KC A	0	1	.000	18	1	0	0	35.2	33	24	9	2	25-0	18	6.06	63	.252	.377	9	.222	0	23	-7		-0.4
1966	KC A	0	1	.000	16	1	0	1	25.1	20	12	5	1	15-1	18	4.26	80	.227	.343	3	.000	-0	26	-2		-0.1
Total	2	0	2	.000	34	2	0	1	61	53	36	14	3	40-1	36	5.31	69	.242	.364	12	.167	-0	24	-9		-0.5

HANDS, BILL William Alfred B5.6.1940 Hackensack NJ BR/TR/6-2/185* d6.3

YEAR	TM LG	W	L	PCT	G	GS	CG-SHO	SV-BS	IP	H	R	HR	HB	BB-IB	SO	ERA	AERA	OAV	OOB	AB-HR-SH	AVG	PB	SUP	APR	DL	PW
1965	SF N	0	2	.000	4	2	0	0	6	13	11	0	0	6-2	5	16.50	22	.433	.528	1	.000	-0	36	-8		-1.4
1966	Chi N	8	13	.381	41	26	0	2	159	168	91	17	5	59-6	93	4.58	80	.272	.338	49-0-4	.041	-3	110	-15		-2.1
1967	Chi N	7	8	.467	49	11	3-1	6	150	134	46	9	2	48-15	84	2.46	144	.239	.301	38-0-4	.105	-1	95	17		1.7
1968	Chi N	16	10	.615	38	34	11-4	0	258.2	221	91	26	6	36-0	148	2.89	109	.231	.262	82-0-7	.061	-5	109	8		0.2
1969	Chi N	20	14	.588	41	41	18-3	0-0	300	268	102	21	6	73-8	181	2.49	161	.237	.286	98-0-11	.092	-5	80	42		4.3
1970	Chi N	18	15	.545	39	38	12-2	1-0	265	278	121	20	4	76-8	170	3.70	122	.269	.321	75-0-9	.133	1	99	22		2.8
1971	Chi N	12	18	.400	36	35	14-1	0-0	242.1	248	112	27	2	50-6	128	3.42	115	.260	.297	72-0-9	.083	-3	89	9		0.7
1972	Chi N	11	8	.579	32	28	6-3	0-0	189	168	73	12	2	47-7	96	3.00	127	.237	.285	57-0-4	.018	-4	111	15		0.9
1973	Min A	7	10	.412	39	15	3-1	2-3	142	138	69	14	2	41-2	78	3.49	114	.252	.305	0	—	0	90	5		0.5
1974	Min A	4	5	.444	35	0	0	3-4	115.1	130	57	9	4	25-0	74	4.45	84	.284	.326	0	—	0	99	-5		-0.5
	Tex A	2	0	1.000	2	2	1-1	0-0	14	11	3	0	0	3-0	4	1.93	186	.208	.250	0	—	0	123	3		0.4
	Year	6	5	.545	37	12	1-1	3-4	129.1	141	60	9	4	28-0	78	4.18	89	.276	.319	0	—	0	103	-4		-0.1
1975	Tex A	6	7	.462	18	18	4-1	0-0	109.2	118	58	12	3	28-1	67	4.02	94	.271	.318	0	—	0	123	-4	38	-0.2
Total	11	111	110	.502	374	260	72-17	14-7	1951	1895	834	167	36	492-55	1128	3.35	114	.253	.301	472-0-48	.078	-20	99	89	38	7.1

HANEY, CHRIS Christopher Deane B11.16.1968 Baltimore MD BL/TL/6-3/195(185-210) [MonN90 2/51] d6.21 f-Larry Col North Carolina-Charlotte

YEAR	TM LG	W	L	PCT	G	GS	CG-SHO	SV-BS	IP	H	R	HR	HB	BB-IB	SO	ERA	AERA	OAV	OOB	AB-HR-SH	AVG	PB	SUP	APR	DL	PW
1991	Mon N	3	7	.300	16	16	0	0-0	84.2	94	49	6	1	43-1	51	4.04	90	.280	.362	27-0-2	.074	-2	79	-7		-0.8
1992	Mon N	2	3	.400	9	6	1-1	0-0	38	40	25	6	1	10-0	27	5.45	64	.270	.327	9-0-1	.222	0*	143	-8		-1.0
	KC A	2	3	.400	7	7	1-1	0-0	42	35	18	5	0	16-2	27	3.86	106	.226	.293	0	—	0	51	2		0.1
1993	KC A	9	9	.500	23	23	1-1	0-0	124	141	87	13	3	53-2	65	6.02	77	.286	.356	0	—	0	96	-17		-2.1
1994	KC A	2	2	.500	6	6	0	0-0	28.1	36	25	2	1	11-1	18	7.31	69	.333	.387	0	—	0	113	-7		-0.7
1995	KC A	3	4	.429	16	13	1	0-0	81.1	78	35	7	2	33-0	31	3.65	131	.262	.335	0	—	0	69	10	81	0.8
1996	KC A	10	14	.417	35	35	4-1	0-0	228	267	136	29	6	51-0	115	4.70	107	.291	.330	0	—	0	82	4		0.3
1997	KC A	1	2	.333	8	5	0	0-0	24.2	29	16	1	0	5-2	16	4.38	108	.290	.333	0	—	0	71	0	131	0.0
1998	KC A	6	6	.500	33	12	0	0-1	97.1	125	78	18	5	36-0	51	7.03	69	.316	.371	0	—	0	99	-20	16	-2.0
	Chi N	0	0	—	5	0	0	0-0	5	3	4	2	0	1-0	4	7.20	61	.167	.211	0	—	0		-1		-0.1
1999	Cle A	0	2	.000	13	4	0	0-0	40.1	43	22	3	3	16-0	22	4.69	109	.270	.348	0	—	0	82	2		0.1
2000	Cle A	0	0	—	1	0	0	0-0	1	1	1	0	1	1-0	1	9.00	56	.333	.400	0	—	0	0	0		0.0
2002	Bos A	0	0	—	24	0	0	1-0	30	32	14	2	4	10-2	15	4.20	107	.274	.343	0	—	0	2			0.1
Total	11	38	52	.422	196	125	8-4	1-1	824.2	924	510	94	31	286-10	442	5.07	91	.284	.344	36-0-3	.111	-1	86	-40	228	-5.3

HANKINS, DON Donald Wayne B2.9.1902 Pendleton IN D5.16.1963 Winston-Salem NC BR/TR/6-3/183 d4.23

YEAR	TM LG	W	L	PCT	G	GS	CG-SHO	SV-BS	IP	H	R	HR	HB	BB-IB	SO	ERA	AERA	OAV	OOB	AB-HR-SH	AVG	PB	SUP	APR	DL	PW
1927	Det A	2	1	.667	20	1	0	2	42.2	67	39	1	0	13	10	6.33	67	.383	.426	7	.143	-1	119	-10		-0.8

HANKINSON, FRANK Frank Edward B4.29.1856 New York NY D4.5.1911 Palisades Park NJ BR/TR/5-11/168 d5.1 ▲

YEAR	TM LG	W	L	PCT	G	GS	CG-SHO	SV-BS	IP	H	R	HR	HB	BB-IB	SO	ERA	AERA	OAV	OOB	AB-HR-SH	AVG	PB	SUP	APR	DL	PW
1878	Chi N	0	1	.000	1	1	1	0	9	11	9	0	0	4	6.00	40	.282	.282	240-1	.267	0*	108	-2		-0.2
1879	Chi N	15	10	.600	26	25	25-2	0	230.2	248	134	0	0	27	69	2.50	103	.255	.275	171	.181	-4*	92	1		-0.1
1880	Cle N	1	1	.500	4	2	2	1	25	20	10	0	0	3	8	1.08	217	.215	.240	263-1	.209	-0*	74	3		0.2
1885	NY AA	0	0	—	1	0	0	0	2	2	1	0	1	0	1	4.50	69	.250	.333	362-2	.224	0*	0			0.0
Total	4	16	12	.571	32	28	28-2	1	266.2	281	154	1	0	31	80	2.50	102	.252	.273	1036-4	.223	-4	92	2		-0.1

HANLEY, JIM James Patrick B10.13.1885 Providence RI D5.1.1961 Elmhurst NY BR/TL/5-11/165 d7.3 Col Manhattan

YEAR	TM LG	W	L	PCT	G	GS	CG-SHO	SV-BS	IP	H	R	HR	HB	BB-IB	SO	ERA	AERA	OAV	OOB	AB-HR-SH	AVG	PB	SUP	APR	DL	PW
1913	NY A	0	0	—	1	0	0	0	4	5	3	0	0	4	2	6.75	44	.313	.450	1	.000	-0		-1		-0.1

HANNA, PRESTON Preston Lee B9.10.1954 Pensacola FL BR/TR/6-1/185(180-195) [AtlN72 1/11] d9.13

YEAR	TM LG	W	L	PCT	G	GS	CG-SHO	SV-BS	IP	H	R	HR	HB	BB-IB	SO	ERA	AERA	OAV	OOB	AB-HR-SH	AVG	PB	SUP	APR	DL	PW
1975	Atl N	0	0	—	4	0	0	0-0	5.2	7	1	0	2	5-0	2	1.59	238	.304	.467	0	—	0		1		0.1
1976	Atl N	0	0	—	5	0	0	0-0	8	11	5	0	0	4-0	3	4.50	84	.333	.405	1	.000	-0		-1		-0.1
1977	Atl N	2	6	.250	17	9	1	1-0	60	69	40	6	2	34-1	37	4.95	90	.285	.378	14-0-1	.071	-0	80	-4		-0.4
1978	Atl N	7	13	.350	29	28	0	0-0	140.1	132	89	10	3	93-5	90	5.13	79	.251	.362	49-1-2	.184	1	81	-14		-1.8
1979	Atl N	1	1	.500	6	4	0	0-0	24.1	27	11	1	0	15-1	15	2.96	136	.284	.382	6	.000	-0	61	2	94	0.2
1980	Atl N	2	0	1.000	32	2	0	0-0	79.1	63	28	3	2	44-4	35	3.18	116	.224	.331	14	.143	0	109	6		0.3
1981	Atl N	2	1	.667	20	1	0	0-0	35.1	45	27	2	0	23-2	22	6.37	55	.341	.425	4	.250	0	25	-11	21	-0.7
1982	Atl N	3	0	1.000	20	1	0	0-0	36	36	15	3	0	28-2	17	3.75	98	.277	.405	4	.400	1	96	1		0.1
	Oak A	0	4	.000	23	2	1	0-0	48.1	54	34	1	3	33-1	32	5.59	71	.287	.389	0	—	0	35	-9		-0.7
Total	8	17	25	.405	156	47	2	1-0	437.1	444	250	28	11	279-16	253	4.61	86	.269	.374	93-1-3	.161	0	80	-29	115	-3.0

HANNAHS, GERRY Gerald Ellis B3.6.1953 Binghamton NY BL/TL/6-3/208* d9.8 Col Arkansas-Monticello

YEAR	TM LG	W	L	PCT	G	GS	CG-SHO	SV-BS	IP	H	R	HR	HB	BB-IB	SO	ERA	AERA	OAV	OOB	AB-HR-SH	AVG	PB	SUP	APR	DL	PW
1976	Mon N	2	0	1.000	3	3	0	0-0	16	20	14	2	0	12-0	10	6.75	56	.323	.421	8	.375	1	164	-5		-0.5
1977	Mon N	1	5	.167	9	7	0	0-0	37	43	27	7	0	17-0	21	4.86	79	.291	.364	7-0-2	.000	-0	72	-6		-0.9
1978	LA N	0	0	—	1	0	0	0-0	2	3	2	0	0	0-0	5	9.00	39	.333	.333	0	—	0		-1		-0.1
1979	LA N	2	2	.000	16	2	0	1-0	16	10	8	2	0	13-1	6	3.38	107	.175	.324	4	.250	1	49	0		0.0
Total	4	3	7	.300	16	12	0	1-0	71	76	51	11	0	42-1	42	5.07	75	.275	.368	19-0-2	.211	1	92	-12		-1.5

HANNAN, JIM James John B1.7.1940 Jersey City NJ BR/TR/6-3/205* d4.17 Col Notre Dame

YEAR	TM LG	W	L	PCT	G	GS	CG-SHO	SV-BS	IP	H	R	HR	HB	BB-IB	SO	ERA	AERA	OAV	OOB	AB-HR-SH	AVG	PB	SUP	APR	DL	PW
1962	Was A	2	4	.333	42	1	0	4	68	56	27	6	0	49-4	39	3.31	122	.230	.355	11	.091	-1	118	6		0.5
1963	Was A	2	2	.500	13	1	0	0	27.2	23	18	2	0	17-0	14	4.88	76	.228	.336	6	.000	-0	72	-4		-0.5
1964	Was A	4	7	.364	49	7	0	3	106	108	60	19	0	45-4	67	4.16	89	.266	.338	20-0-1	.150	-1	75	-7		-0.8

YEAR	TM LG	W	L	PCT	G	GS	CG-SHO	SV-BS	IP	H	R	HR	HB	BB-IB	SO	ERA	AERA	OAV	OOB	AB-HR-SH	AVG	PB	SUP	APR	DL	PW
1965	Was A	1	1	.500	4	1	1-1	0	14.2	18	8	0	1	6-1	5	4.91	71	.340	.417	3-0-1	.000	-0	227	-2		-0.3
1966	Was A	3	9	.250	30	18	2	0	114	125	58	9	3	59-5	68	4.26	81	.288	.374	30-0-2	.067	-2	86	-9		-1.1
1967	Was A	1	1	.500	8	2	0	0	21.2	28	14	3	1	7-0	14	5.40	59	.315	.367	4	.000	-0	41	-5		-0.5
1968	Was A	10	6	.625	25	22	4-1	0	140.1	147	53	4	4	50-1	75	3.01	97	.272	.338	47-0-3	.064	-2	104	-1		-0.4
1969	Was A	7	6	.538	35	28	1-1	0-1	158.1	138	73	17	2	91-2	72	3.64	96	.238	.342	52-0-3	.115	-2	92	-2		-0.4
1970	Was A	9	11	.450	42	17	1-1	0-0	128	119	65	17	1	54-8	61	4.01	90	.250	.326	31-0-2	.129	-1	87	-6	21	-0.9
1971	Det A	1	0	1.000	7	0	0	0-0	11	7	4	1	1	7-0	6	3.27	111	.189	.333	2	.000	-0		1		0.1
	Mil A	1	1	.500	21	1	0	0-1	32.1	38	23	7	1	21-4	17	5.01	70	.295	.395	3	.000	-0	180	-6		-0.4
	Year	2	1	.667	28	1	0	0-1	43.1	45	27	8	2	28-4	23	4.57	77	.271	.381	5	.000	-1	178	-6		-0.5
Total	10	41	48	.461	276	101	9-4	7-2	822	807	403	79	14	406-29	438	3.88	90	.261	.348	209-0-12	.091	-9	91	-35	21	-4.7

HANNING, LOY   Loy Vernon   B10.18.1917 Bunker MO   D6.24.1986 Anaconda MO   BR/TR/6-2/175   d9.20

YEAR	TM LG	W	L	PCT	G	GS	CG-SHO	SV-BS	IP	H	R	HR	HB	BB-IB	SO	ERA	AERA	OAV	OOB	AB-HR-SH	AVG	PB	SUP	APR	DL	PW
1939	StL A	0	1	.000	4	1	0	0	10	6	5	1	0	4	3	3.60	135	.158	.238	1	.000	-0	91	1		0.1
1942	StL A	1	1	.500	11	0	0	0	17.1	26	15	2	1	12	9	7.79	48	.356	.453	4	.250	-0		-7		-0.7
Total	2	1	2	.333	15	1	0	0	27.1	32	20	3	1	16		6.26	66	.288	.383	5	.200	-0	91	-6		-0.6

HANSELL, GREG   Gregory Michael   B3.12.1971 Bellflower CA   BR/TR/6-5/215*   [BosA89 10/267]   d4.28

YEAR	TM LG	W	L	PCT	G	GS	CG-SHO	SV-BS	IP	H	R	HR	HB	BB-IB	SO	ERA	AERA	OAV	OOB	AB-HR-SH	AVG	PB	SUP	APR	DL	PW
1995	LA N	0	1	.000	20	0	0	0-1	19.1	29	17	5	2	6-1	13	7.45	52	.349	.402	0	—	0		-8		-0.4
1996	Min A	3	0	1.000	50	0	0	3-1	74.1	83	48	14	2	31-1	46	5.69	90	.285	.356	0	—	0		-4		-0.2
1997	Mil A	0	0	—	3	0	0	0-0	4.2	5	5	1	1	1-0	5	9.64	48	.263	.333	0	—	0		-2		-0.1
1999	Pit N	1	3	.250	33	0	0	0-3	39.1	42	20	5	3	11-3	34	3.89	118	.280	.339	2	.000	-0		3		0.2
Total	4	4	4	.500	106	0	0	3-5	137.2	159	90	25	8	49-5	98	5.56	86	.293	.358	2	.000	0		-11		-0.5

HANSEN, ANDY   Andrew Viggo "Swede"   B11.12.1924 Lake Worth FL   D2.2.2002 Lake Worth FL   BR/TR/6-3/190*   d6.30   Mil 1945-46

YEAR	TM LG	W	L	PCT	G	GS	CG-SHO	SV-BS	IP	H	R	HR	HB	BB-IB	SO	ERA	AERA	OAV	OOB	AB-HR-SH	AVG	PB	SUP	APR	DL	PW
1944	NY N	3	3	.500	23	4	0	1	52.2	63	39	4	3	32	15	6.49	56	.301	.402	12	.167	0*	86	-14		-1.4
1945	NY N	4	3	.571	23	13	4	3	92.2	98	52	7	2	28	37	4.66	84	.273	.329	25-0-4	.000	-3	103	-7		-0.7
1947	NY N	1	5	.167	27	9	1	0	82.1	78	45	8	0	38	18	4.37	93	.248	.330	21	.190	-0	77	-3		-0.2
1948	NY N	5	3	.625	36	9	3	1	100	96	40	4	0	36	27	2.97	133	.255	.320	20-0-3	.050	-0	138	10		0.7
1949	NY N	2	6	.250	33	2	0	1	66.1	58	35	7	0	28	26	4.61	86	.234	.312	12-0-1	.000	-1	133	-2		-0.3
1950	NY N	0	1	.000	31	1	0	3	57	64	37	8	1	26	19	5.53	74	.279	.355	7-0-2	.000	-1	151	-8		-0.5
1951	Phi N	3	1	.750	24	0	0	0	39	34	14	4	1	7	11	2.54	152	.228	.268	3	.333	1		5		0.6
1952	Phi N	5	6	.455	43	0	0	4	77.1	76	36	6	3	27	18	3.26	112	.259	.328	11-0-2	.182	-1		2		0.4
1953	Phi N	0	2	.000	30	1	0	3	51.1	60	30	6	1	24	17	4.03	104	.296	.373	7	.286	0	0	-1		0.0
Total	9	23	30	.434	270	39	8	16	618.2	627	328	53	11	246	188	4.22	93	.263	.335	118-0-12	.102	-3	105	-18		-1.4

HANSEN, CRAIG   Craig R.   B11.15.1983 Glen Cove NY   BR/TR/6-6/210   d9.19   Col St. John's

YEAR	TM LG	W	L	PCT	G	GS	CG-SHO	SV-BS	IP	H	R	HR	HB	BB-IB	SO	ERA	AERA	OAV	OOB	AB-HR-SH	AVG	PB	SUP	APR	DL	PW
2005	Bos A	0	0	—	4	0	0	0-1	3	6	2	1	0	1-0	3	6.00	77	.429	.438	0	—	0		0		0.0

HANSEN, SNIPE   Roy Emil Frederick   B2.21.1907 Chicago IL   D9.11.1978 Chicago IL   BB/TL(BL 1930)/6-3/195   d7.5

YEAR	TM LG	W	L	PCT	G	GS	CG-SHO	SV-BS	IP	H	R	HR	HB	BB-IB	SO	ERA	AERA	OAV	OOB	AB-HR-SH	AVG	PB	SUP	APR	DL	PW
1930	Phi N	0	7	.000	22	9	1	0	84.1	123	76	24	0	38	25	6.72	81	.364	.431	27	.111	-2	71	-12		-1.0
1932	Phi N	10	10	.500	39	23	5	2	191	215	103	13	6	51	56	3.72	118	.278	.328	63-0-4	.127	-4	104	8		0.4
1933	Phi N	6	14	.300	32	22	8	1	168.1	199	103	12	4	30	47	4.44	86	.294	.328	58-0-2	.155	-3*	91	-12		-1.7
1934	Phi N	6	12	.333	50	16	5-2	3	151	194	112	15	3	61	40	5.42	87	.307	.371	43	.233	-0	99	-13		-1.3
1935	Phi N	0	1	.000	2	1	0	0	4.1	8	7	0	0	5	0	12.46	36	.421	.542	2	.000	-0	94	-3		-0.6
	StL A	0	1	.000	10	1	0	0	26.2	44	28	2	1	9	8	8.78	55	.364	.412	7	.143	-1		-10		-0.5
Total	5	22	45	.328	155	71	19-2	6	625.2	783	429	50	16	194	176	5.01	90	.306	.358	200-0-6	.155	-10	93	-42		-4.7

HANSEN, ROY   Roy Inglof "Irig"   B3.6.1898 Beloit WI   D2.9.1977 Beloit WI   BR/TR/6-0/165   d5.28

YEAR	TM LG	W	L	PCT	G	GS	CG-SHO	SV-BS	IP	H	R	HR	HB	BB-IB	SO	ERA	AERA	OAV	OOB	AB-HR-SH	AVG	PB	SUP	APR	DL	PW
1918	Was A	1	0	1.000	5	0	0	0	9	10	4	0	1	3	2	3.00	91	.278	.350	0	—	0		0		0.0

HANSFORD, FRANK   Frank Cicero   B12.26.1874 DuQuoin IL   D12.14.1952 Fort Scott KS   TL/6-0/180   d6.9

YEAR	TM LG	W	L	PCT	G	GS	CG-SHO	SV-BS	IP	H	R	HR	HB	BB-IB	SO	ERA	AERA	OAV	OOB	AB-HR-SH	AVG	PB	SUP	APR	DL	PW
1898	Bro N	0	0	—	1	0	0	0	7	10	4	0	0	5	0	3.86	93	.333	.429	3	.000	-1		0		-0.1

HANSON, OLLIE   Earl Sylvester   B1.19.1896 Holbrook MA   D8.19.1951 Clifton NJ   BR/TR/5-11/178   d4.27

YEAR	TM LG	W	L	PCT	G	GS	CG-SHO	SV-BS	IP	H	R	HR	HB	BB-IB	SO	ERA	AERA	OAV	OOB	AB-HR-SH	AVG	PB	SUP	APR	DL	PW
1921	Chi N	0	2	.000	2	2	1	0	9	9	7	0	1	2	1	7.00	55	.265	.390	3	.000	-0	86	-3		-0.5

HANSON, ERIK   Erik Brian   B5.18.1965 Kinnelon NJ   BR/TR/6-6/210*   [SeaA86 2/36]   d9.5   Col Wake Forest

YEAR	TM LG	W	L	PCT	G	GS	CG-SHO	SV-BS	IP	H	R	HR	HB	BB-IB	SO	ERA	AERA	OAV	OOB	AB-HR-SH	AVG	PB	SUP	APR	DL	PW
1988	Sea A	2	3	.400	6	6	0	0-0	41.2	35	17	4	1	12-1	36	3.24	129	.230	.291	0	—	0	65	4		0.4
1989	Sea A	9	5	.643	17	17	1	0-0	113.1	103	44	7	5	32-1	75	3.18	127	.243	.304	0	—	0	94	11	71	1.3
1990	Sea A	18	9	.667	33	33	5	0-0	236	205	88	15	2	68-6	211	3.24	123	.232	.287	0	—	0	103	6	40	2.5
1991	Sea A	8	8	.500	27	27	2-1	0-0	174.2	182	82	16	2	56-2	143	3.81	109	.269	.323	0	—	0	83	-17	20	0.4
1992	Sea A	8	17	.320	31	30	6-1	0-0	186.2	209	110	14	7	57-1	112	4.82	83	.287	.341	0	—	0	85	22		-2.0
1993	Sea A	11	12	.478	31	30	7	0-0	215	215	91	17	5	60-6	163	3.47	129	.263	.315	0	—	0*	85	22		2.2
1994	Cin N	5	5	.500	22	21	0	0	122.2	137	60	9	3	23-3	101	4.11	102	.283	.317	39-0-2	.154	-1	107	2	3	0.1
1995	†Bos A☆	15	5	.750	29	29	1-1	0-0	186.2	187	94	17	1	59-0	139	4.24	115	.258	.311	0	—	0	108	14		1.2
1996	Tor A	13	17	.433	35	35	4-1	0-0	214.2	243	143	26	2	102-0	156	5.41	93	.289	.365	0	—	0	82	-10		-1.2
1997	Tor A	0	0	—	3	2	0	0-0	15	15	13	3	0	6-0	18	7.80	59	.254	.323	0	—	0	120	-5	160	-0.2
1998	Tor A	3	3	.000	11	8	0	0-0	49	73	34	10	1	29-1	21	6.24	75	.348	.429	0	—	0	80	-7	12	-0.3
Total	11	89	84	.514	245	238	26-5	0-0	1555.1	1604	776	139	29	504-23	1175	4.15	105	.267	.325	39-0-2	.154	-1	93	43	306	4.4

HANYZEWSKI, ED   Edward Michael   B9.18.1920 Union Mills IN   D10.8.1991 Fargo ND   BR/TR/6-1/200   d5.12   Col Notre Dame

YEAR	TM LG	W	L	PCT	G	GS	CG-SHO	SV-BS	IP	H	R	HR	HB	BB-IB	SO	ERA	AERA	OAV	OOB	AB-HR-SH	AVG	PB	SUP	APR	DL	PW
1942	Chi N	1	1	.500	6	1	0	0	19	17	9	2	0	8	4	3.79	84	.254	.333	5	.200	-0	26	-1		-0.1
1943	Chi N	8	7	.533	33	16	3	0	130	120	54	2	2	45	55	2.56	130	.243	.309	41-0-2	.049	-4	97	7		0.4
1944	Chi N	2	5	.286	14	7	3	0	58.1	61	33	6	1	20	19	4.47	79	.261	.322	17	.059	-1	71	-5		-0.5
1945	Chi N	0	0	—	2	1	0	0	4.2	7	4	1	0	1	0	5.79	63	.350	.381	1	.000	-0	116	-1		-0.1
1946	Chi N	1	0	1.000	3	0	0	0	6	8	3	0	1	5	1	4.50	74	.348	.483	1	.000	-0		-1		-0.1
Total	5	12	13	.480	58	25	6	0	218	213	103	11	4	79	81	3.30	102	.254	.321	65-0-2	.062	-5	88	-1		-0.3

HARANG, AARON   Aaron Michael   B5.9.1978 San Diego CA   BR/TR/6-7/240(240-270)   [TexA99 6/195]   d5.25   Col San Diego St.

YEAR	TM LG	W	L	PCT	G	GS	CG-SHO	SV-BS	IP	H	R	HR	HB	BB-IB	SO	ERA	AERA	OAV	OOB	AB-HR-SH	AVG	PB	SUP	APR	DL	PW
2002	Oak A	5	4	.556	16	15	0	0-0	78.1	78	44	7	3	45-2	64	4.83	93	.261	.359	3	.000	-0	93	-2		-0.2
2003	Oak A	1	3	.250	7	6	0	0-0	30.1	41	19	5	0	9-0	16	5.34	86	.331	.373	1	.000	-0	84	-2		-0.3
	Cin N	4	3	.571	9	9	0	0-0*	46	48	28	6	1	10-0	26	5.28	79	.271	.314	17	.059	-1	110	-5		-0.1
2004	Cin N	10	9	.526	28	28	1-1	0-0	161	177	90	26	5	53-5	125	4.86	88	.279	.337	57-0-4	.070	-4	106	4	24	-1.2
2005	Cin N	11	13	.458	32	32	1	0-0	211.2	217	93	22	8	51-3	163	3.83	109	.267	.315	74-0-4	.027	-7	99	10		0.2
Total	4	31	32	.492	92	90	2-1	0-0	527.1	561	274	66	17	168-10	394	4.51	95	.274	.332	152-0-8	.046	-13	100	-7		-2.3

HARDEN, RICH   James Richard   B11.30.1981 Victoria BC, Can.   BL/TR/6-1/180*   [OakA00 17/510]   d7.21   Col Central Arizona JC

YEAR	TM LG	W	L	PCT	G	GS	CG-SHO	SV-BS	IP	H	R	HR	HB	BB-IB	SO	ERA	AERA	OAV	OOB	AB-HR-SH	AVG	PB	SUP	APR	DL	PW
2003	†Oak A	5	4	.556	15	13	0	0-0	74.2	72	38	5	1	40-1	67	4.46	103	.259	.351	0	—	0	105	2		0.3
2004	Oak A	11	7	.611	31	31	0	0-0	189.2	171	90	16	3	81-6	167	3.99	114	.242	.320	5	.000	-0	101	14		1.1
2005	Oak A	10	5	.667	22	19	2-1	0-0	128	93	42	7	2	43-0	121	2.53	176	.201	.271	0	—	0	97	26	38	3.0
Total	3	26	16	.619	68	63	2-1	0-0	392.1	336	170	28	6	164-7	355	3.60	127	.232	.310	5	.000	-0	101	42	38	4.2

HARDER, MEL   Melvin Leroy "Chief"   B10.15.1909 Beemer NE   D10.20.2002 Chardon OH   BR/TR/6-1/195   d4.24   M2/C23

YEAR	TM LG	W	L	PCT	G	GS	CG-SHO	SV-BS	IP	H	R	HR	HB	BB-IB	SO	ERA	AERA	OAV	OOB	AB-HR-SH	AVG	PB	SUP	APR	DL	PW
1928	Cle A	0	2	.000	23	1	0	1	49	64	42	4	0	32	15	6.61	63	.335	.430	8	.000	-1	82	-12		-0.8
1929	Cle A	0	0	1.000	11	0	0	0	17.2	24	15	2	3	5	4	5.60	79	.333	.400	1	.000	-0		-3		-0.2
1930	Cle A	11	10	.524	36	19	7	2	175.1	205	108	9	4	68	45	4.21	115	.295	.361	63-0-2	.143	-4	106	9		0.5
1931	Cle A	13	14	.481	40	24	9	1	194	229	119	8	6	72	63	4.36	106	.289	.352	75-0-4	.253	-1	101	3		0.4
1932	Cle A	15	13	.536	39	32	17-1	0	254.2	277	123	6	3	68	90	3.75	127	.272	.319	94-0-3	.181	-0	103	27		2.7
1933	Cle A	15	17	.469	43	31	14-2	4	253	254	113	10	3	67	81	2.95	174	.259	.309	84-1-2	.190	-1*	57	35		4.4
1934	Cle A★	20	12	.625	44	29	17-6	4	255.1	246	97	6	7	81	91	2.61	174	.254	.316	87-0-9	.161	-1	92	50		5.7
1935	Cle A★	22	11	.667	42	35	17-4	2	287.1	313	120	6	0	53	95	3.29	137	.275	.307	102-2-7	.206	-1	89	39		4.1
1936	Cle A★	15	15	.500	36	30	13	1	224.2	294	155	13	6	71	84	5.17	97	.313	.365	80-0-6	.138	-4	88	-6		-1.0
1937	Cle A★	15	12	.556	38	30	13	1	233.2	269	127	9	4	86	95	4.28	108	.288	.350	86-0-7	.174	-1	105	9		0.8
1938	Cle A	17	10	.630	38	29	15-2	4	240	257	115	16	5	62	102	3.83	121	.271	.319	72-1-6	.139	-5*	99	23		2.1
1939	Cle A	15	9	.625	28	26	12-1	1	208	213	89	15	3	64	67	3.50	126	.269	.326	62-0-5	.177	-0	98	4		0.4
1940	Cle A	12	11	.522	31	25	5	0	186.1	200	96	16	5	59	76	4.06	104	.278	.337	62-0-5	.177	-1	98	4		-1.2
1941	Cle A	5	4	.556	15	10	1	1	68.2	76	43	8	2	37	21	5.24	75	.279	.370	25	.080	-1	99	-10		-1.2
1942	Cle A	13	14	.481	29	29	13-4	0	198.2	179	83	8	2	72	74	3.44	100	.240	.317	67-0-3	.119	-3	77	3		0.1

YEAR	TM LG	W	L	PCT	G	GS	CG-SHO	SV-BS	IP	H	R	HR	HB	BB-IB	SO	ERA	AERA	OAV	OOB	AB-HR-SH	AVG	PB	SUP	APR	DL	PW
1943	Cle A	8	7	.533	19	18	6-1	0	135.1	126	57	7	1	61	40	3.06	102	.254	.337	47-0-4	.213	2	110	-1	59	0.1
1944	Cle A	12	10	.545	30	27	12-2	0	196.1	211	95	5	3	69	64	3.71	89	.278	.341	74-0-2	.216	1	120	-9		-0.9
1945	Cle A	3	7	.300	11	11	2	0	76	93	37	3	0	23	16	3.67	88	.303	.352	25-0-3	.080	-2	76	-4		-0.3
1946	Cle A	5	4	.556	13	12	4-1	0	92.1	85	37	4	0	31	21	3.41	97	.249	.311	35	.086	-2	95	0		-0.3
1947	Cle A	6	4	.600	15	15	4-1	0	80	91	41	3	1	27	17	4.50	77	.289	.347	28-0-5	.179	0	141	-8		-1.0
Total	20	223	186	.545	582	433	181-25	23	3426.1	3706	1714	161	59	1118	1161	3.80	113	.276	.334	1203-4-69	.165	-27	94	172	59	17.0

HARDIN, JIM   James Warren B8.6.1943 Morris Chapel TN D3.9.1991 Key West FL BR/TR/6-0/175* d6.23 Col Memphis

YEAR	TM LG	W	L	PCT	G	GS	CG-SHO	SV-BS	IP	H	R	HR	HB	BB-IB	SO	ERA	AERA	OAV	OOB	AB-HR-SH	AVG	PB	SUP	APR	DL	PW
1967	Bal A	8	3	.727	19	14	5-2	0	111	85	30	5	3	27-0	66	2.27	139	.211	.266	37-0-1	.135	-0	122	12		1.1
1968	Bal A	18	13	.581	35	35	16-2	0	244	188	79	20	10	70-5	160	2.51	117	.212	.277	82-0-11	.085	-3	97	11		1.1
1969	Bal A	6	7	.462	30	20	3-1	1-1	137.2	128	62	18	6	43-7	64	3.60	100	.248	.311	45-2-4	.156	1	120	0		0.0
1970	Bal A	6	5	.545	36	19	3-2	1-1	145.1	150	60	13	1	26-3	78	3.53	104	.267	.299	45-0-2	.067	-2	101	4		0.0
1971	Bal A	0	0	—	6	0	0	0-0	5.2	12	5	0	0	3-1	2	4.76	72	.480	.536	0	—	-0		-2		-0.1
	NY A	0	2	.000	13	3	0	0-0	28.1	35	19	3	1	9-3	14	5.08	65	.313	.366	4	.000	-0	127	-6	27	-0.5
	Year	0	2	.000	19	3	0	0-0	34	47	24	3	1	12-4	17	5.03	66	.343	.397	4	.000	-0	127	-8		-0.6
1972	Atl N	5	2	.714	26	9	1	2-1	79.2	93	47	11	2	24-4	25	4.41	86	.287	.337	21-1-3	.095	1	140	-6		-0.5
Total	6	43	32	.573	164	100	28-7	4-3	751.2	691	302	70	23	202-23	408	3.18	105	.244	.299	234-3-21	.103	-3	111	13	27	1.1

HARDING, CHARLIE   Charles Harold "Slim" B1.3.1891 Nashville TN D10.30.1971 Bold Spring TN BR/TR/6-2.5/172 d9.18

| 1913 | Det A | 0 | 0 | — | 1 | 0 | 0 | 0 | 2 | 3 | 1 | 0 | 1 | 1 | 0 | 4.50 | 65 | .375 | .444 | 0 | | 0 | | 0 | | 0.0 |

HARDY, ALEX   David Alexander "Dooney" B1877 Toronto ON, Can. D4.22.1940 Toronto ON, Can. BR/TL/5-10.5/175 d9.4

1902	Chi N	2	2	.500	4	4	4-1	0	35	29	19	0	0	12	12	3.60	75	.227	.293	14	.214	0	151	-2		-0.2
1903	Chi N	1	1	.500	3	3	1	0	12.2	21	10	0	1	7	4	6.39	49	.375	.453	6	.167	0	129	-3		-0.4
Total	2	3	3	.500	7	7	5-1	0	47.2	50	29	0	1	19	16	4.34	65	.272	.343	20	.200	1	144	-5		-0.6

HARDY, RED   Francis Joseph B1.6.1923 Marmarth ND D8.15.2003 Phoenix AZ BR/TR/5-11/175 d6.20 Col St. Thomas (MN)

| 1951 | NY N | 0 | 0 | — | 2 | 0 | 0 | 0 | 1.1 | 4 | 1 | 0 | 1 | 1 | 1 | 6.75 | 58 | .571 | .667 | 0 | — | 0 | | 0 | | 0.0 |

HARDY, HARRY   Harry B11.5.1875 Steubenville OH D9.4.1943 Steubenville OH BL/TL/5-6/155 d9.26

1905	Was A	1	1	.500	3	2	2	0	24	20	9	0	0	6	10	1.88	141	.227	.277	9	.111	-1	67	1		0.0
1906	Was A	0	3	.000	5	3	2	0	20	35	27	0	0	12	4	9.00	29	.385	.456	6	.000	-0	64	-14		-1.7
Total	2	1	4	.200	8	5	4	0	44	55	36	0	0	18	14	5.11	52	.307	.371	15	.067	-2	65	-13		-1.7

HARDY, LARRY   Howard Lawrence B1.10.1948 Goose Creek TX BR/TR/5-10/180* [SDN70 23/536] d4.28 C7 Col Texas

1974	SD N	9	4	.692	76	1	0	2-4	101.2	129	58	9	0	44-14	57	4.69	77	.317	.380	10	.000	-1	73	-12		-1.5
1975	SD N	0	0	—	3	0	0	0-0	2.2	8	6	3	0	2-0	3	13.50	26	.500	.556	0		0		-4		-0.2
1976	Hou N	0	0	—	15	0	0	3-0	21.2	34	19	2	0	10-2	10	7.06	46	.362	.423	2	.000	-0		-10		-0.5
Total	3	9	4	.692	94	1	0	5-4	126	171	83	14	0	56-16	70	5.29	67	.331	.393	12	.000	-1	73	-26		-2.2

HARDY, JACK   John Graydon B10.8.1959 St.Petersburg FL BR/TR/6-2/175 [ChiA81 21/526] d5.23 Col St. Thomas (FL)

| 1989 | Chi A | 0 | 0 | — | 5 | 0 | 0 | 0-0 | 12.1 | 14 | 9 | 1 | 1 | 5-0 | 4 | 6.57 | 58 | .286 | .357 | 0 | | 0 | | -3 | | -0.1 |

HAREN, DANNY   Daniel John B9.17.1980 Monterey Park CA BR/TR/6-5/220* [StLN01 2/72] d6.30 Col Pepperdine

2003	StL N	3	7	.300	14	14	0	0-0	72.2	84	44	9	5	22-0	43	5.08	81	.293	.351	25-0-1	.080	-0*	93	-8		-1.1
2004	†StL N	3	3	.500	14	5	0	0-0	46	45	23	4	2	17-2	32	4.50	95	.265	.335	12-0-2	.000	1	100	0		-0.2
2005	Oak A	14	12	.538	34	34	3	0-0	217	212	101	26	6	53-5	163	3.73	120	.255	.303	5	.400	1	118	17		1.8
Total	3	20	22	.476	62	53	3	0-0	335.2	341	168	39	13	92-7	238	4.13	106	.265	.318	42-0-3	.095	-1	110	9		0.5

HARGAN, STEVE   Steven Lowell B9.8.1942 Ft.Wayne IN BR/TR/6-3/180* d8.3

1965	Cle A	4	3	.571	17	8	1	0	60.1	55	26	2	1	28-2	37	3.43	101	.246	.331	19-0-2	.053	-1	107			-0.1
1966	Cle A	13	10	.565	38	21	7-3	0	192	173	60	9	1	45-8	132	2.48	138	.241	.286	58-0-3	.121	-2	81	20		2.2
1967	Cle A☆	14	13	.519	30	29	15-6	0	223	180	79	9	3	72-7	141	2.62	125	.224	.288	67-1-7	.164	1	84	14		1.9
1968	Cle A	8	15	.348	32	27	4-2	0	158.1	139	81	11	6	81-8	78	4.15	72	.241	.336	51-0-1	.176	1	86	-19		-2.7
1969	Cle A	5	14	.263	32	23	1-1	0-0	143.2	145	95	14	3	81-9	76	5.70	67	.265	.359	44-0-1	.159	-1*	69	-25		-3.0
1970	Cle A	11	3	.786	23	19	8-1	0-0	142.2	101	47	14	3	53-0	72	2.90	138	.201	.279	45-0-8	.111	-2*	99	17	22	1.5
1971	Cle A	1	13	.071	37	16	1	1-1	113.1	138	83	18	6	56-5	52	6.19	63	.304	.387	32-0-1	.063	-3	84	-25	48	-3.3
1972	Cle A	0	3	.000	12	1	0	0-0	20	23	16	1	0	15-2	10	5.85	56	.291	.392	3	.000	-0	27	-6		-0.9
1974	Tex A	12	9	.571	37	27	8-2	0-0	186.2	202	103	15	4	48-4	98	3.95	91	.275	.320	0	—	0	96	-12		-1.2
1975	Tex A	9	10	.474	33	26	8-1	0-1	189.1	203	96	17	6	62-7	93	3.80	99	.275	.334	0	—	0	101	-2		-0.1
1976	Tex A	8	8	.500	35	8	2-1	1-2	124.1	127	63	8	3	38-3	63	3.62	99	.261	.317	0	—	0	70	-3		-0.4
1977	Tor A	1	3	.250	9	2	1	0-0	29.1	36	17	2	0	14-2	11	5.22	81	.308	.382	0	—	0	76	-2		-0.2
	Tex A	1	0	1.000	6	0	0	0-0	12.1	22	13	2	0	5-0	10	8.76	47	.393	.429	0	—	0		-6		-0.4
	Year	2	3	.400	12	5	1	0-0	41.2	58	30	4	0	19-2	21	6.26	67	.335	.397	0	—	0	77	-8		-0.6
	Atl N	0	3	.000	16	5	0	0-0	36.2	49	31	3	0	16-1	18	6.87	64	.325	.385	6	.000	-1	112	-8		-0.6
Total	12	87	107	.448	354	215	56-17	4-4	1632	1593	810	125	36	614-58	891	3.92	91	.257	.326	325-1-23	.129	-7	88	-57	70	-7.3

HARGESHEIMER, ALAN   Alan Robert B11.21.1954 Chicago IL BR/TR/6-3/195* d7.14 Col Northeastern Illinois

1980	SF N	4	6	.400	15	13	0	0-0	75	82	38	3	0	32-2	40	4.32	81	.285	.355	22-0-1	.182	1	90	-6		-0.6
1981	SF N	1	2	.333	6	3	0	0-0	18.2	20	9	1	1	9-2	6	4.34	78	.299	.385	5-0-1	.200	1	70	-1		-0.2
1983	Chi N	0	0	—	5	0	0	0-0	4	6	4	0	0	2-0	5	9.00	42	.375	.444	0	—	0		-2		-0.1
1986	KC A	0	1	.000	5	1	0	0-0	13	18	9	1	1	7-2	4	6.23	69	.340	.426	0	—	0	191	-2	14	-0.2
Total	4	5	9	.357	31	17	0	0-0	110.2	126	60	5	2	50-6	55	4.72	76	.297	.372	27-0-2	.185	1	92	-11	14	-1.1

HARIKKALA, TIM   Timothy Allan B7.15.1971 W.Palm Beach FL BR/TR/6-2/185* [SeaA92 34/950] d5.27 Col Florida Atlantic

1995	Sea A	0	0	—	1	0	0	0-0	3.1	7	6	1	0	1-0	1	16.20	29	.412	.444	0		0		-4		-0.2
1996	Sea A	0	1	.000	4	1	0	0-0	4.1	4	6	1	1	2-0	1	12.46	40	.250	.368	0		0	37	-3		-0.2
1999	Bos A	1	1	.500	7	0	0	0-0	13	15	9	0	1	6-1	7	6.23	80	.306	.393	0		0		-1		-0.2
2004	Col N	6	6	.500	55	0	0	0-7	62.2	55	34	10	1	23-5	30	4.74	100	.235	.304	3-0-1	.000	-0		0		0.0
2005	Oak A	0	0	—	8	0	0	0-0	12.2	16	9	3	0	4-0	7	6.39	70	.308	.357	0		0		-2		-0.1
Total	5	7	8	.467	72	1	0	0-7	96	97	64	15	3	36-6	46	5.91	81	.264	.333	3-0-1	.000	-0	37	-10		-1.0

HARKEY, MIKE   Michael Anthony B10.25.1966 San Diego CA BR/TR/6-5/220(220-235) [ChiN87 1/4] d9.5 Col Cal St.-Fullerton

1988	Chi N	0	3	.000	5	5	0	0-0	34.2	33	14	0	2	15-3	18	2.60	140	.248	.333	11-0-2	.091	-1	58	3		0.1
1990	Chi N	12	6	.667	27	27	2-1	0-0	173.2	153	71	14	7	59-8	94	3.26	125	.234	.303	56-0-8	.250	3	97	14	15	1.7
1991	Chi N	0	2	.000	4	4	0	0-0	18.2	21	11	3	0	6-1	15	5.30	74	.273	.321	5	.400	1	121	-2	163	-0.1
1992	Chi N	4	0	1.000	7	7	0	0-0	38	34	13	4	1	15-0	21	1.89	192	.243	.316	15	.267	1*	135	5	105	0.7
1993	Chi N	10	10	.500	28	28	1	0-0	157.1	187	100	17	3	43-4	67	5.26	77	.305	.349	54-0-5	.093	-2	103	-21	31	-2.6
1994	Col N	1	6	.143	14	13	0	0-0	91.2	125	61	10	1	35-4	39	5.79	86	.336	.393	22-0-4	.182	-1	70	-6		-0.4
1995	Oak A	4	6	.400	14	12	0	0-0	66	75	46	12	4	31-0	28	6.27	72	.292	.372	0	—	0	81	-11		-1.4
	Cal A	4	3	.571	12	8	1	0-0	61.1	80	32	12	1	16-2	28	4.55	104	.311	.351	0	—	0	84	2		0.1
	Year	8	9	.471	26	20	1	0-0	127.1	155	78	24	4	47-2	56	5.44	85	.302	.362	0	—	0	82	-10		-1.3
1997	LA N	1	0	1.000	10	0	0	0-0	14.2	12	8	3	0	5-0	6	4.30	91	.211	.274	1-0-2	.000	-0		-1		-0.1
Total	8	36	36	.500	131	104	4-1	0-0	656	720	356	75	18	225-22	316	4.49	95	.281	.341	164-0-21	.183	1	93	-17	314	-2.0

HARKINS, JOHN   John Joseph "Pa" B4.12.1859 New Brunswick NJ D11.20.1940 New Brunswick NJ BR/TR/6-1/205 d5.2 Col Rutgers

1884	Cle N	12	32	.273	46	45	42-3	0	391	399	300	7		108	192	3.68	86	.249	.297	229	.205	-4*	71	-21		-2.3
1885	Bro AA	14	20	.412	34	34	33-1	0	293	303	224	1	7	56	141	3.75	84	.250	.287	159-1	.264	5*	101	-19		-1.1
1886	Bro AA	15	16	.484	34	33	33	0	292.1	286	203	6	5	114	118	3.60	97	.244	.313	142-1	.225	3*	90	-3		0.2
1887	Bro AA	10	14	.417	24	24	22	0	199	262	184	6	5	77	36	6.02	72	.309	.369	98	.235	-0*	95	-30		-2.6
1888	Bal AA	0	1	.000	1	1	1	0	8	12	12	0	1	3	2	6.75	44	.333	.385	3	.000	-0	136	-4		-0.4
Total	5	51	83	.381	139	137	131-4	0	1183.1	1262	923	26	17	358	489	4.09	85	.259	.312	631-2	.228	4	88	-77		-6.2

HARKNESS, SPEC   Frederick Harvey B12.13.1887 Los Angeles CA D5.16.1952 Compton CA BR/TR/5-11/180 d6.13

1910	Cle A	10	7	.588	26	16	6-1	1	136.1	132	61	2	3	55	60	3.04	85	.268	.345	50-0-1	.140	-1	94	-6		-0.9
1911	Cle A	2	2	.500	12	6	3	0	53.1	62	36	1	0	21	25	4.22	81	.310	.376	19	.316	1	162	-5		-0.3
Total	2	12	9	.571	38	22	9-1	1	189.2	194	97	3	3	76	85	3.37	84	.280	.354	69-0-1	.188	-0	115	-11		-1.2

YEAR	TM LG	W	L	PCT	G	GS	CG-SHO	SV-BS	IP	H	R	HR	HB	BB-IB	SO	ERA	AERA	OAV	OOB	AB-HR-SH	AVG	PB	SUP	APR	DL	PW

HARLEY, DICK Henry Risk B8.18.1874 Springfield OH D5.16.1961 Springfield OH BR/TR d4.15

| 1905 | Bos N | 2 | 5 | .286 | 9 | 4 | 4-1 | 0 | 65.2 | 72 | 45 | 5 | 1 | 19 | 19 | 4.66 | 67 | .286 | .338 | 22-0-1 | .045 | -2 | 35 | -11 | | -1.1 |

HARMAN, BILL William Bell B1.2.1919 Bridgewater VA BR/TR/6-4/200 d6.17 Mil 1942 Col Virginia ▲

| 1941 | Phi N | 0 | 0 | — | 5 | 0 | 0 | 0 | 13 | 15 | 8 | 0 | 0 | 8 | 3 | 4.85 | 76 | .319 | .418 | 14 | .071 | -0* | | -2 | | -0.2 |

HARMON, BOB Robert Green "Hickory Bob" B10.15.1887 Liberal MO D11.27.1961 Monroe LA BB/TR/6-0/187 d6.23

1909	StL N	6	11	.353	21	17	10	0	159	155	85	6	4	65	48	3.68	69	.265	.342	51-0-4	.255	4	94	-19		-1.5
1910	StL N	13	15	.464	43	33	15	2	236	227	128	1	7	133	87	4.46	67	.258	.360	76-0-4	.184	2	129	-31		-3.1
1911	StL N	23	16	.590	51	41	28-2	4	348	290	155	10	7	181	144	3.13	108	.235	.336	111-0-9	.153	0	98	10		1.2
1912	StL N	18	18	.500	43	34	15-3	0	268	284	156	4	3	116	73	3.93	87	.281	.357	99-0-2	.232	1*	93	-11		-1.1
1913	StL N	8	21	.276	42	27	16-1	2	273.1	291	135	6	6	99	66	3.92	83	.286	.353	92-0-3	.261	5*	72	-18		-1.2
1914	Pit N	13	17	.433	37	30	19-2	3	245	226	84	4	7	55	61	2.53	105	.252	.300	86-1-5	.140	-1*	64	5		0.4
1915	Pit N	16	17	.485	37	32	25-5	1	269.2	242	106	6	3	62	86	2.50	109	.247	.294	95-0-3	.147	1*	100	4		0.7
1916	Pit N	8	11	.421	31	17	10-2	0	172.2	175	78	4	1	39	62	2.81	95	.267	.309	55	.109	-3*	103	-5		-0.6
1918	Pit N	2	7	.222	16	9	5	0	82.1	76	30	3	0	12	7	2.62	109	.254	.283	27-0-1	.148	-1*	79	3		0.2
Total	9	107	133	.446	321	240	143-15	12	2054	1966	957	44	38	762	634	3.33	90	.260	.331	692-1-31	.184	7	94	-62		-5.0

HARNISCH, PETE Peter Thomas B9.23.1966 Commack NY BB/TR/6-0/207(195-228) [BalA87 1/27] d9.13 Col Fordham [DL 2002 Col N 183]

1988	Bal A	0	2	.000	2	2	0	0-0	13	13	8	1	0	9-1	10	5.54	71	.260	.373	0	—	0	70	-2		-0.2
1989	Bal A	5	9	.357	18	17	2	0-0	103.1	97	55	10	5	64-3	70	4.62	83	.249	.358	0	—	0	82	-9		-1.1
1990	Bal A	11	11	.500	31	31	3	0-0	188.2	189	96	17	1	86-5	122	4.34	88	.261	.339	0	—	0	115	-10		-1.2
1991	Hou N★	12	9	.571	33	33	4-2	0-0	216.2	169	71	14	5	83-3	172	2.70	131	.212	.288	62-0-7	.097	1	88	21		1.7
1992	Hou N	9	10	.474	34	34	0	0-0	206.2	182	92	18	5	64-3	164	3.70	92	.233	.294	67-0-5	.164	2	120	-7		-0.5
1993	Hou N	16	9	.640	33	33	5-4	0-0	217.2	171	84	20	6	79-5	185	2.98	130	.214	.289	67-0-10	.104	-1	108	21		1.9
1994	Hou N	8	5	.615	17	17	1	0-0	95	100	59	13	3	39-1	62	3.68	110	.261	.301	33-0-3	.171	-1*	136	-14	38	-0.1
1995	NY N	2	8	.200	18	18	0	0-0	110	111	55	13	3	24-4	82	4.21	96	.260	.301	33-0-3	.091	-2	98	2	61	-0.1
1996	NY N	8	12	.400	31	31	2-1	0-0	194.2	195	103	30	7	61-5	114	4.21	96	.260	.301	55-0-10	.091	-2*	103	-3	13	-0.6
1997	NY N	0	1	.000	6	5	0	0-0	25.2	35	24	5	1	11-1	12	8.06	50	.327	.388	8-0-1	.000	-1	124	-11	122	-0.6
	Mil A	1	1	.500	4	3	0	0-0	14	13	9	1	0	12-0	10	5.14	90	.245	.385	0	—	0	46	-1		-0.1
1998	Cin N	14	7	.667	32	32	2-1	0-0	209	176	79	24	6	64-4	157	3.14	137	.228	.291	66-0-9	.106	-3	115	26		2.6
1999	Cin N	16	10	.615	33	33	2-2	0-0	198.1	190	86	25	5	57-2	120	3.68	128	.252	.306	66-1-8	.152	0	110	23		0.1
2000	Cin N	8	6	.571	22	22	3-1	0-0	131	133	76	23	1	46-1	71	4.74	101	.261	.321	43-1-6	.186	1*	85	0	54	0.1
2001	Cin N	1	3	.250	7	7	0	0-0	35.1	48	29	9	1	17-0	17	6.37	72	.318	.384	11-0-1	.273	-1*	101	-7	153	-0.2
Total	14	111	103	.519	321	318	24-11	0-0	1959	1822	926	223	49	716-38	1368	3.89	103	.245	.313	513-2-62	.129	-6	105	29	624	1.7

HARPER, JACK Charles William B4.2.1878 Galloway PA D9.30.1950 Jamestown NY BR/TR/6-0/178 d9.18

1899	Cle N	1	4	.200	5	5	5	0	37	44	33	3	3	12	14	3.89	95	.295	.360	11	.182	1	101	-5		-0.4
1900	StL N	0	1	.000	1	1	0	0	3	4	7	0	0	2	0	12.00	30	.308	.400	1	.000	-0	114	-3		-0.5
1901	StL N	23	13	.639	39	37	28-1	0	308.2	294	158	7	16	99	128	3.62	88	.249	.316	116-1-3	.172	1	89	-14		-1.3
1902	StL A	15	11	.577	29	26	20-2	0	222.1	224	131	8	8	81	74	4.13	85	.262	.332	83-0-3	.205	0	97	-7		-0.5
1903	Cin N	8	9	.471	17	15	13	0	135	143	87	2	10	70	45	4.33	82	.271	.367	56	.250	2*	127	19		1.5
1904	Cin N	23	9	.719	35	35	31-6	0	293.2	262	113	2	9	85	125	2.30	128	.234	.293	60-0-4	.167	1	105	-10		-1.1
1905	Cin N	9	13	.409	26	23	15-1	1	179.1	189	116	2	8	69	70	3.86	86	.271	.344	60-0-4	.167	1	90	-5		-0.6
1906	Cin N	1	4	.200	5	5	3	0	36.2	38	23	1	2	20	10	4.17	66	.286	.387	11-0-1	.273	1	90	-5		-0.0
	Chi N	0	0	—	1	1	0	0	1	0	0	0	0	0	0	0.00	—	.000	.000	0	—	0	304	0		0.0
	Year	1	4	.200	6	6	3	0	37.2	38	23	1	2	20	10	4.06	68	.279	.380	11-0-1	.273	1	124	-5		-0.0
Total	8	80	64	.556	158	148	115-10	1	1216.2	1198	668	25	56	438	466	3.55	92	.256	.327	451-1-14	.186	3	111	-38		-4.1

HARPER, GEORGE George B. B8.17.1866 Milwaukee WI D12.11.1931 Stockton CA BR/TR/5-10/165 d7.11

1894	Phi N	6	6	.500	12	9	7	0	86.1	128	84	3	2	49	24	5.32	97	.340	.418	40	.150	-4	127	-7		-0.9
1896	Bro N	4	8	.333	16	11	7	0	86	106	72	4	3	39	22	5.55	74	.300	.375	37	.162	0	96	-13		-1.3
Total	2	10	14	.417	28	20	14	0	172.1	234	156	7	5	88	46	5.43	85	.321	.397	77	.156	-4	110	-20		-2.2

HARPER, HARRY Harry Clayton B4.24.1895 Hackensack NJ D4.23.1963 New York NY BL/TL/6-2/165 d6.27

1913	Was A	0	0	—	4	0	0	0	12.2	10	11	1	1	5	9	3.55	83	.213	.302	4	.250	0		-2		-0.1
1914	Was A	2	1	.667	23	3	1	2	57	45	29	1	4	35	50	3.47	81	.211	.336	12	.250	0	95	-4		-0.3
1915	Was A	4	4	.500	19	10	5-2	2	86.1	66	26	1	4	40	54	1.77	168	.222	.317	25-0-2	.000	-4	81	10		0.5
1916	Was A	14	10	.583	36	34	13-2	0	249.2	209	82	4	8	101	149	2.45	114	.235	.319	87-0-1	.117	-3	117	-10		1.0
1917	Was A	11	12	.478	31	31	10-4	0	179.1	145	85	1	5	106	99	3.01	87	.230	.345	60-0-2	.134	-4*	103	17		0.8
1918	Was A	11	10	.524	35	32	14-3	1	244	182	77	1	8	104	78	2.18	125	.212	.303	82-0-3	.134	-4*	72	-14		0.9
1919	Was A	6	21	.222	35	31	8	0	208	220	119	3	8	97	87	3.72	86	.284	.370	65-0-2	.169	-2	72	-14		-1.9
1920	Bos A	5	14	.263	27	22	11-1	0	162.2	163	73	9	2	66	71	3.04	120	.275	.349	50-0-2	.120	-3	58	8		0.4
1921	†NY A	4	3	.571	8	7	4	0	52.2	52	23	2	2	26	22	3.76	113	.263	.351	16	.125	-1	76	4		-0.6
1923	Bro N	0	1	.000	1	1	0	0	3.2	6	8	2	0	3	4	14.73	26	.421	.500	1	.000	-0	127	-4		-0.0
Total	10	57	76	.429	219	171	66-12	5	1256	1100	531	26	40	582	623	2.87	105	.244	.335	402-0-12	.147	-16	88	16		-1.7

HARPER, JACK John Wesley B8.5.1893 Hendricks WV D6.18.1927 Halstead KS BR/TR/5-11/180 d4.17 Col Marshall

| 1915 | Phi A | 0 | 0 | — | 3 | 0 | 0 | 0 | 8.2 | 5 | 4 | 0 | 0 | 1 | 3 | 3.12 | 94 | .161 | .188 | 2 | .000 | -0 | | 0 | | 0.0 |

HARPER, TRAVIS Travis Boyd B5.21.1976 Harrisonburg VA BL/TR/6-4/190* [BosA97 3/101] d8.4 Col James Madison

2000	TB A	1	2	.333	6	5	1-1	0-0	32	30	17	5	1	15-0	14	4.78	102	.244	.329	0	—	0	100	1		0.1
2001	TB A	0	2	.000	2	2	0	0-0	7	15	11	5	0	3-0	2	7.71	58	.455	.500	0	—	0	21	-4		-0.7
2002	TB A	5	9	.357	37	7	0	1-1	85.2	101	54	14	9	27-3	60	5.46	83	.289	.352	0	—	0	7			0.8
2003	TB A	4	8	.333	61	0	0	1-5	93	86	45	9	6	31-8	64	3.77	121	.252	.323	0	—	0	7			0.6
2004	TB A	6	2	.750	52	0	0	0-1	78.2	69	37	8	7	23-3	59	3.89	120	.234	.303	0	—	-0		-18		-2.1
2005	TB A	4	6	.400	52	0	0	0-3	73.1	88	57	14	1	24-9	40	6.75	65	.304	.358	1	.000	-0	76	-15		-2.5
Total	6	20	29	.408	210	14	1-1	2-10	369.2	389	221	55	24	123-23	239	4.94	92	.272	.337	1		-0				

HARPER, BILL William Homer "Blue Sleeve" B6.14.1889 Bertrand MO D6.17.1951 Somerville TN BB/TR/6-1/180 d6.10

| 1911 | StL A | 0 | 0 | — | 2 | 0 | 0 | 0 | 4 | 8 | 5 | 0 | 0 | 5 | 1 | 6.75 | 50 | .300 | .400 | 3 | .000 | -0 | | -3 | | -0.2 |

HARRELL, SLIM Oscar Martin B7.31.1890 Grandview TX D4.30.1971 Hillsboro TX BR/TR/6-3/180 d6.21 Col Baylor

| 1912 | Phi A | 0 | 0 | — | 1 | 0 | 0 | 0 | 3 | 4 | 0 | 0 | 0 | 0 | 1 | 0.00 | — | .364 | .364 | 1 | .000 | -0 | | 1 | | 0.0 |

HARRELL, RAY Raymond James "Cowboy" B2.16.1912 Petrolia TX D1.28.1984 Alexandria LA BR/TR/6-1/185 d4.16

1935	StL N	1	1	.500	11	1	0	0	29.2	39	26	4	0	11	13	6.67	61	.320	.376	4-0-1	.000	-1	124	-9		-0.6
1937	StL N	3	7	.300	35	15	1-1	3	96.2	99	73	7	2	59	41	5.87	68	.263	.366	22-0-2	.045	-2	110	-19		-2.0
1938	StL N	2	3	.400	32	3	1	2	63	78	37	6	3	29	32	4.86	81	.308	.386	10	.000	-1	143	-4		-0.5
1939	Chi N	0	2	.000	4	2	0	0	17.1	29	16	2	0	6	5	8.31	47	.387	.432	5	.000	-1	33	-7		-1.4
	Phi N	3	7	.300	22	10	4	0	94.2	101	77	6	4	56	35	5.42	74	.270	.371	26	.115	-1	54	-20		-2.4
	Year	3	9	.250	26	12	4	0	112	130	93	8	4	62	40	5.87	68	.290	.381	31	.097	-2	51	-27		-2.8
1940	Pit N	0	0	—	3	0	0	0	3.1	5	5	0	2	2	3	8.10	47	.333	.412	0	—	0		-2		-0.2
1945	NY N	0	0	—	12	0	0	3	25.1	34	22	1	1	14	7	4.97	79	.343	.430	5	.200	1		-6		-0.2
Total	6	9	20	.310	119	31	6-1	3	330	385	256	26	10	177	136	5.70	70	.293	.381	72-0-3	.069	-5	91	-67		-6.3

HARRELSON, BILL William Charles B11.17.1945 Tahlequah OK BB/TR/6-5/215 d7.31 Col Bakersfield (CA) JC

| 1968 | Cal A | 1 | 6 | .143 | 16 | 5 | 1 | 0 | 33.2 | 28 | 23 | 4 | 1 | 26-0 | 22 | 5.08 | 57 | .226 | .359 | 10 | .100 | -0 | 60 | -9 | | -1.1 |

HARRIGER, DENNY Dennis Scott B7.21.1969 Kittanning PA BR/TR/5-11/185 [NYN87 18/472] d6.16

| 1998 | Det A | 0 | 3 | .000 | 4 | 2 | 0 | 0-0 | 12 | 17 | 12 | 1 | 0 | 8-2 | 3 | 6.75 | 70 | .327 | .417 | 0 | — | 0 | 98 | -4 | | -0.3 |

HARRINGTON, ANDY Andrew Francis B11.13.1888 Wakefield MA D11.12.1938 Malden MA BR/TR/6-0/193 d9.8 Col Boston College

| 1913 | Cin N | 0 | 0 | — | 1 | 0 | 0 | 0 | 4 | 6 | 5 | 0 | 0 | 1 | 1 | 9.00 | 36 | .353 | .389 | 2 | .500 | 0 | | -2 | | -0.1 |

HARRINGTON, BILL William Womble B10.3.1927 Sanford NC BR/TR/5-11/160* d4.16 Mil 1953-55

| 1953 | Phi A | 0 | 0 | — | 1 | 0 | 0 | 2 | 13.50 | 32 | .500 | .500 | 0 | — | 0 | | -2 | | -0.2 | | | | | | | | |
| 1955 | KC A | 3 | 3 | .500 | 34 | 1 | 0 | 2 | 76.2 | 69 | 41 | 6 | 2 | 41-4 | 26 | 4.11 | 102 | .246 | .339 | 17 | .118 | -1 | 21 | 0 | | -0.3 |

YEAR	TM LG	W	L	PCT	G	GS	CG-SHO	SV-BS	IP	H	R	HR	HB	BB-IB	SO	ERA	AERA	OAV	OOB	AB-HR-SH	AVG	PB	SUP	APR	DL	PW
1956	KC A	2	2	.500	23	1	0	1	37.2	40	27	3	0	26-1	14	6.45	67	.274	.384	7-0-2	.000	-1	144	-7		-0.8
Total 3		5	5	.500	58	2	0	1	116.1	114	71	9	2	67-5	40	5.03	84	.261	.357	24-0-2	.083	-1	84	-9		-1.0

HARRIS, BEN Ben Franklin B12.17.1889 Donelson TN D4.29.1927 St.Louis MO BR/TR/6-0/220 d4.19

YEAR	TM LG	W	L	PCT	G	GS	CG-SHO	SV-BS	IP	H	R	HR	HB	BB-IB	SO	ERA	AERA	OAV	OOB	AB-HR-SH	AVG	PB	SUP	APR	DL	PW
1914	KC F	7	7	.500	31	14	5	1	154	179	89	7	6	41	40	4.09	68	.303	.354	45-0-3	.200	1	102	-22		-1.7
1915	KC F	0	0	—	1	0	0	0	2	1	0	0	0	0	0	0.00	—	.143	.143	0		0		1		0.0
Total 2		7	7	.500	32	14	5	1	156	180	89	7	6	41	40	4.04	69	.301	.352	45-0-3	.200	1	102	-21		-1.7

HARRIS, LUM Chalmer Luman B1.17.1915 New Castle AL D11.11.1996 Pell City AL BR/TR/6-1/180 d4.19 Mil 1945 M8/C14

YEAR	TM LG	W	L	PCT	G	GS	CG-SHO	SV-BS	IP	H	R	HR	HB	BB-IB	SO	ERA	AERA	OAV	OOB	AB-HR-SH	AVG	PB	SUP	APR	DL	PW
1941	Phi A	4	4	.500	33	10	5	2	131.2	134	77	16	2	51	49	4.78	88	.260	.329	40-0-2	.275	2	101	-7		-0.3
1942	Phi A	11	15	.423	26	20	10-1	0	166	146	80	14	1	70	60	3.74	101	.254	.313	62-0-1	.161	-2	66	1		0.0
1943	Phi A	7	21	.250	32	27	15-1	1	216.1	241	122	17	3	63	55	4.20	81	.279	.330	70-0-4	.171	-1	71	-22		-2.7
1944	Phi A	10	9	.526	23	22	12-2	0	174.1	193	70	8	0	26	33	3.30	105	.281	.308	59-0-2	.169	-1	77	6		0.5
1946	Phi A	3	14	.176	34	12	4	0	125.1	153	70	11	0	48	33	5.24	68	.308	.369	36-1-4	.222	1	75	-20		-2.2
1947	Was A	0	0	—	3	0	0	0	6.1	7	2	0	0	7	2	2.84	131	.318	.483	1	.000	1		1		-2.2
Total 6		35	63	.357	151	91	46-4	3	820	874	429	66	6	265	232	4.16	88	.273	.329	268-1-13	.190	-0	75	-41		-4.6

HARRIS, BUBBA Charles B2.15.1926 Sulligent AL BR/TR/6-4/204* d4.29

YEAR	TM LG	W	L	PCT	G	GS	CG-SHO	SV-BS	IP	H	R	HR	HB	BB-IB	SO	ERA	AERA	OAV	OOB	AB-HR-SH	AVG	PB	SUP	APR	DL	PW
1948	Phi A	5	2	.714	45	0	0	5	93.2	89	51	2	1	35	32	4.13	104	.249	.317	24-0-2	.125	-1		0		-0.1
1949	Phi A	1	1	.500	37	0	0	3	84.1	92	57	12	1	42	18	5.44	75	.286	.370	24-0-3	.125	-2		-12		-0.7
1951	Phi A	0	0	—	3	0	0	0	4	4	4	0	1	5	2	9.00	48	.250	.455	0	—	0		-2		-0.1
	Cle A	0	0	—	2	0	0	0	4	5	2	0	0	4	1	4.50	84	.333	.474	0	—	0		0		0.0
	Year	0	0	—	5	0	0	0	8	9	6	0	1	9	3	6.75	60	.290	.463	0	—	0		-2		-0.1
Total 3		6	3	.667	87	0	0	8	186	190	114	14	3	86	53	4.84	87	.267	.349	48-0-5	.125	-3		-14		-0.9

HARRIS, GREG Greg Allen B11.2.1955 Lynwood CA BB/TR/6-0/175* d5.20 Col Long Beach (CA) City

YEAR	TM LG	W	L	PCT	G	GS	CG-SHO	SV-BS	IP	H	R	HR	HB	BB-IB	SO	ERA	AERA	OAV	OOB	AB-HR-SH	AVG	PB	SUP	APR	DL	PW
1981	NY N	3	5	.375	16	14	0	1-0	68.2	65	36	8	2	28-2	54	4.46	79	.245	.321	22	.182	0*	108	-5		-0.6
1982	Cin N	2	6	.250	34	10	1	1-0	91.1	96	56	12	2	37-1	67	4.83	76	.274	.344	18	.167	-0*	84	-12		-1.0
1983	Cin N	0	0	—	1	0	0	0-0	1	2	3	0	1	3-2	1	27.00	14	.500	.750	1	.000	-0		-2		-0.1
1984	Mon N	0	1	.000	15	0	0	2-0	17.2	10	4	0	2	7-1	15	2.04	170	.172	.284	1	.000	-0		3		0.2
†SD N		2	1	.667	19	1	0	1-0	36.2	28	14	3	2	18-0	30	2.70	133	.209	.306	8	.375	1	172	3		0.4
	Year	2	2	.500	34	1	0	3-0	54.1	38	18	3	4	25-1	45	2.48	143	.198	.299	9	.333	1	174	6		0.6
1985	Tex A	5	4	.556	58	0	0	11-4	113	74	35	7	5	43-3	111	2.47	173	.186	.273	0	—	0		21		2.0
1986	Tex A	10	8	.556	73	0	0	20-11	111.1	103	40	12	1	42-6	95	2.83	153	.251	.318	0	—	0		18		3.2
1987	Tex A	5	10	.333	42	19	0	0-4	140.2	157	92	18	4	56-3	106	4.86	93	.281	.349	0	—	0	124	-8		-0.7
1988	Phi N	4	6	.400	66	1	0	1-1	107	80	34	7	4	52-14	71	2.36	153	.209	.309	9-0-1	.333	1	98	13		1.3
1989	Phi A	2	2	.500	44	0	0	1-0	75.1	64	34	7	2	43-7	51	3.58	100	.234	.340	6-0-1	.167	1		0		0.1
	Bos A	2	2	.500	15	0	0	0-1	28	21	12	1	0	15-2	25	2.57	160	.208	.308	0	—	0		3		0.4
1990	†Bos A	13	9	.591	34	30	1	0-0	184.1	186	90	13	6	77-7	117	4.00	102	.265	.338	0	—	0	99	2		0.4
1991	Bos A	11	12	.478	53	21	0	2-3	173	157	79	13	6	69-5	127	3.85	112	.243	.318	0	—	0	79	10		1.3
1992	Bos A	4	9	.308	70	2	1	4-6	107.2	82	38	6	4	60-11	73	2.51	170	.215	.324	0	—	0	32	18		2.1
1993	Bos A	6	7	.462	**80**	0	0	8-10	112.1	95	55	7	10	60-14	103	3.77	123	.232	.341	0	—	0		9		1.1
1994	Bos A	3	4	.429	35	0	0	2-4	45.2	60	44	8	1	23-6	44	8.28	61	.321	.396	0	—	0		-15		-1.9
	NY A	0	1	.000	3	0	0	0-1	5	4	5	1	2	3-1	4	5.40	85	.222	.375	0	—	0		-1		-0.2
	Year	3	5	.375	38	0	0	2-5	50.2	64	49	9	3	26-7	48	7.99	63	.312	.394	0	—	0		-16		-2.1
1995	Mon N	2	3	.400	45	0	0	0-1	48.1	45	18	6	1	16-1	47	2.61	165	.245	.308	3	.333	1		8		0.7
Total 15		74	90	.451	703	98	4	54-46	1467	1329	689	129	54	652-86	1141	3.69	113	.243	.327	68-0-2	.221	3	98	65		8.7

HARRIS, GREG Gregory Wade B12.1.1963 Greensboro NC BR/TR/6-2/187* [SDN85 10/258] d9.19 Col Elon

YEAR	TM LG	W	L	PCT	G	GS	CG-SHO	SV-BS	IP	H	R	HR	HB	BB-IB	SO	ERA	AERA	OAV	OOB	AB-HR-SH	AVG	PB	SUP	APR	DL	PW
1988	SD N	2	0	1.000	3	1	1	0-0	18	13	3	0	0	3-0	15	1.50	227	.200	.235	7	.000	-1	235	4		0.4
1989	SD N	8	9	.471	56	8	0	6-2	135	106	43	8	2	52-9	106	2.60	135	.215	.291	19-0-4	.053	-1	95	14		1.9
1990	SD N	8	8	.500	73	0	0	9-7	117.1	92	35	6	4	49-13	97	2.30	167	.220	.303	12-0-1	.083	-0		19		2.8
1991	SD N	9	5	.643	20	20	3-2	0-0	133	116	42	16	1	27-6	95	2.23	171	.233	.273	36-0-7	.083	-2	86	20	72	1.9
1992	SD N	4	8	.333	20	20	1	0-0	118	113	62	13	2	35-2	66	4.12	87	.252	.307	31-0-5	.129	1	98	-8	81	-0.7
1993	SD N	10	9	.526	22	22	4	0-0	152	151	65	18	4	39-6	83	3.67	113	.257	.306	53-0-4	.170	1	95	10		1.4
	Col N	1	8	.111	13	13	0	0-0	73.1	88	62	15	4	30-3	40	6.50	74	.299	.370	20-0-1	.050	-2	70	-13		-1.5
	Year	11	17	.393	35	35	4	0-0	225.1	239	127	33	7	69-9	123	4.59	95	.271	.328	73-0-5	.137	-0	85	-5		-0.1
1994	Col N	3	12	.200	29	19	1	1-0	130	154	99	22	5	52-4	82	6.65	75	.300	.366	40-0-4	.175	-0	67	-19		-1.8
1995	Min A	0	5	.000	7	6	0	0-0	32.2	50	35	5	0	16-0	21	8.82	55	.355	.415	0	—	0	74	-14		-1.6
Total 8		45	64	.413	243	109	10-2	16-9	909.1	883	446	103	21	303-43	605	3.98	102	.255	.317	218-0-26	.119	-3	87	13	153	2.8

HARRIS, HERB Herbert Benjamin "Hub","Lefty" B4.24.1913 Chicago IL D1.18.1991 Crystal Lake IL BL/TL/6-1/175 d7.21 Col Northwestern

YEAR	TM LG	W	L	PCT	G	GS	CG-SHO	SV-BS	IP	H	R	HR	HB	BB-IB	SO	ERA	AERA	OAV	OOB	AB-HR-SH	AVG	PB	SUP	APR	DL	PW
1936	Phi N	0	0	—	4	0	0	0	7	14	8	0	1	5	0	10.29	44	.438	.526	1	.000	-0		-3		-0.2

HARRIS, PEP Hernando Petrocelli B9.23.1972 Lancaster SC BR/TR/6-2/230(185-253) [CleA91 7/190] d8.14 [DL 1999 Ana A 182]

YEAR	TM LG	W	L	PCT	G	GS	CG-SHO	SV-BS	IP	H	R	HR	HB	BB-IB	SO	ERA	AERA	OAV	OOB	AB-HR-SH	AVG	PB	SUP	APR	DL	PW
1996	Cal A	2	0	1.000	11	3	0	0-0	32.1	31	16	4	3	17-2	20	3.90	130	.254	.349	0	—	0	171	4		0.2
1997	Ana A	5	4	.556	61	0	0	0-3	79.2	82	33	7	2	38-6	56	3.62	128	.274	.356	0	—	0		10		1.0
1998	Ana A	3	1	.750	49	0	0	0-1	60	55	32	7	0	23-4	34	4.35	109	.239	.307	0	—	0		2	18	0.2
Total 3		10	5	.667	121	3	0	0-4	172	168	81	18	5	78-12	110	3.92	121	.258	.338	0	—	0	171	16	200	1.4

HARRIS, JEFF Jeffrey Austin B7.4.1974 Alameda CA BR/TR/6-1/190 d8.2 Col San Francisco

YEAR	TM LG	W	L	PCT	G	GS	CG-SHO	SV-BS	IP	H	R	HR	HB	BB-IB	SO	ERA	AERA	OAV	OOB	AB-HR-SH	AVG	PB	SUP	APR	DL	PW
2005	Sea A	2	5	.286	11	8	0	0-0	53.2	48	27	9	3	20-2	25	4.19	100	.238	.313	0	—	0		92	0	0.0

HARRIS, JOE Joseph White B2.1.1882 Melrose MA D4.12.1966 Melrose MA BR/TR/6-1/198 d9.22

YEAR	TM LG	W	L	PCT	G	GS	CG-SHO	SV-BS	IP	H	R	HR	HB	BB-IB	SO	ERA	AERA	OAV	OOB	AB-HR-SH	AVG	PB	SUP	APR	DL	PW
1905	Bos A	1	2	.333	3	3	3	0	23	16	6	0	0	8	14	2.35	115	.198	.270	9	.111	-1	52	2		0.1
1906	Bos A	2	21	.087	30	24	20-1	2	235	211	130	5	7	67	99	3.52	78	.243	.303	81-0-1	.160	-2	44	-22		-2.0
1907	Bos A	0	7	.000	12	5	3	0	59	57	28	0	1	13	24	3.05	84	.256	.300	21	.190	-0	58	-3		-0.3
Total 3		3	30	.091	45	32	26-1	2	317	284	164	5	8	88	137	3.35	81	.242	.300	111-0-1	.162	-3	47	-23		-2.2

HARRIS, MICKEY Maurice Charles B1.30.1917 New York NY D4.15.1971 Farmington MI BL/TL/6-0/195* d4.23 Mil 1942-45

YEAR	TM LG	W	L	PCT	G	GS	CG-SHO	SV-BS	IP	H	R	HR	HB	BB-IB	SO	ERA	AERA	OAV	OOB	AB-HR-SH	AVG	PB	SUP	APR	DL	PW
1940	Bos A	4	2	.667	9	5	3	0	68.1	82	40	8	2	26	36	5.00	90	.292	.356	22-0-1	.273	2	119	-3		0.0
1941	Bos A	8	14	.364	35	22	11-1	1	194	189	86	6	2	86	111	3.25	128	.250	.328	55-0-4	.109	2	114	18		2.0
1946	†Bos A☆	17	9	.654	34	30	15	0	222.2	236	105	18	3	76	131	3.64	101	.268	.329	78-0-5	.231	4	121	-1		0.2
1947	Bos A	5	4	.556	15	6	1	0	51.2	42	20	3	0	23	35	2.44	159	.225	.310	12-0-1	.417	3	95	6		1.4
1948	Bos A	7	10	.412	20	17	6-1	0	113.2	120	73	10	1	59	42	5.30	83	.273	.360	32-0-2	.063	-1	94	-11		-1.5
1949	Bos A	2	3	.400	7	6	2	0	37.2	53	26	3	1	20	14	5.02	87	.323	.400	12-0-2	.083	-1	113	-4		-0.5
	Was A	2	12	.143	23	19	4	0	129	151	82	8	0	55	54	5.16	82	.292	.360	39-0-2	.205	-1	69	-12		-1.0
	Year	4	15	.211	30	25	6	0	166.2	204	108	11	1	75	68	5.13	83	.299	.369	51-0-4	.176	-1	79	-16		-1.5
1950	Was A	5	9	.357	53	0	0	**15**	98	93	56	9	1	46	41	4.78	94	.247	.330	17	.235	1		-1		-0.2
1951	Was A	6	8	.429	41	0	0	4	87.1	87	45	6	1	43	47	3.81	107	.260	.347	16-0-1	.188	0		1		0.2
1952	Was A	0	0	—	1	0	0	0	1	1	1	1	0	0	0	9.00	40	.250	.250	0	—	0		1		0.2
	Cle A	3	0	1.000	29	0	0	1	46.2	42	26	6	1	21	23	4.63	72	.247	.335	5	.200	0		-6		-0.4
	Year	3	0	1.000	30	0	0	1	47.2	43	27	7	1	21	23	4.72	71	.249	.333	5	.200	-0		-7		-0.4
Total 9		59	71	.454	271	109	42-2	21	1050	1097	560	78	12	455	534	4.18	98	.267	.342	288-0-18	.188	11	104	-14		0.2

HARRIS, REGGIE Reginald Allen B8.12.1968 Waynesboro VA BR/TR/6-1/180(180-217) [BosA87 1/26] d7.4

YEAR	TM LG	W	L	PCT	G	GS	CG-SHO	SV-BS	IP	H	R	HR	HB	BB-IB	SO	ERA	AERA	OAV	OOB	AB-HR-SH	AVG	PB	SUP	APR	DL	PW
1990	Oak A	1	0	1.000	16	1	0	0-0	41.1	25	16	5	2	21-1	31	3.48	107	.176	.287	0	—	0	97	2	85	0.1
1991	Oak A	0	0	—	2	0	0	0-0	3	5	4	0	0	3-1	2	12.00	32	.455	.533	0	—	0		-3		-0.1
1996	Bos A	0	0	—	4	0	0	0-1	4.1	7	6	2	1	5-0	4	12.46	41	.389	.542	0	—	0		-3		-0.1
1997	Phi N	1	3	.250	50	0	0	0-1	54.1	55	33	1	5	43-1	45	5.30	80	.263	.395	0	—	0		-6		-0.4
1998	Hou N	0	0	—	8	0	0	0-0	6	6	4	1	2	2-0	5	6.00	68	.261	.308	0	—	0		-1		-0.1
1999	Mil N	0	0	—	6	0	0	0-0	12	8	4	1	2	10-1	8	3.00	153	.186	.321	1	.000	0		2		0.1
Total 6		2	3	.400	86	1	0	0-1	121	106	67	10	10	81-3	95	4.91	84	.238	.361	1	.000	-0	97	-9	85	-0.5

HARRIS, BOB Robert Arthur B5.1.1915 Gillette WY D8.8.1989 North Platte NE BR/TR/6-0/185 d9.19 Mil 1943-45 Col Western Nebraska CC

YEAR	TM LG	W	L	PCT	G	GS	CG-SHO	SV-BS	IP	H	R	HR	HB	BB-IB	SO	ERA	AERA	OAV	OOB	AB-HR-SH	AVG	PB	SUP	APR	DL	PW
1938	Det A	1	0	1.000	3	1	1	0	10	14	9	0	0	4	7	7.20	69	.318	.375	3	.333	0	176	-2		-0.1
1939	Det A	1	0	.500	5	1	0	0	18	18	8	4	1	9	9	4.00	122	.269	.347	5	.400	0	90	2		0.2

YEAR	TM LG	W	L	PCT	G	GS	CG-SHO	SV-BS	IP	H	R	HR	HB	BB-IB	SO	ERA	AERA	OAV	OOB	AB-HR-SH	AVG	PB	SUP	APR	DL	PW
	StL A	3	12	.200	28	16	6	0	126	162	88	5	0	71	48	5.71	85	.321	.405	37-0-2	.189	-0*	67	-10		-0.9
	Year	4	13	.235	33	17	6	0	144	180	96	9	0	79	57	5.50	89	.315	.398	42-0-2	.214	-0	68	-8		-0.7
1940	StL A	11	15	.423	35	28	8-1	1	193.2	225	120	24	3	85	49	4.93	93	.290	.362	60-0-5	.250	3	86	-7		-0.5
1941	StL A	12	14	.462	34	29	9-2	1	186.2	237	117	18	2	85	57	5.21	83	.312	.383	61-0-14	.115	-3	104	-16		-2.2
1942	StL A	1	5	.167	6	6	0	0	33.2	37	24	2	0	17	9	5.61	66	.268	.348	10-0-2	.000	-1	69	-7		-1.1
	Phi A	1	5	.167	16	8	2-1	0	78	77	31	5	0	24	26	2.88	131	.253	.308	26	.269	1	79	7		0.7
	Year	2	10	.167	22	14	2-1	0	111.2	114	55	7	0	41	35	3.71	101	.258	.321	36-0-2	.194	0	75	0		-0.4
Total	5	30	52	.366	127	89	26-4	2	646	770	397	58	5	294	205	4.96	89	.297	.370	202-0-23	.193	1	87	-33		-3.9

HARRIS, GENE Tyrone Eugene B12.5.1964 Sebring FL BR/TR/5-11/190* [MonN86 5/122] d4.5 Col Tulane

YEAR	TM LG	W	L	PCT	G	GS	CG-SHO	SV-BS	IP	H	R	HR	HB	BB-IB	SO	ERA	AERA	OAV	OOB	AB-HR-SH	AVG	PB	SUP	APR	DL	PW
1989	Mon N	1	1	.500	11	0	0	0-2	20	16	11	1	0	10-0	11	4.95	72	.242	.338	1-0-1	.000	-0		-2		-0.2
	Sea A	1	4	.200	10	6	0	1-0	33.1	47	27	3	1	15-1	14	6.48	62	.353	.414	0	—	0*	97	-9	65	-1.2
1990	Sea A	1	2	.333	25	0	0	0-1	38	31	25	9	1	30-5	43	4.74	84	.217	.352	0	—	0		-4		-0.3
1991	Sea A	0	0	—	8	0	0	1-0	13.1	15	8	1	0	10-3	6	4.05	102	.273	.385	0	—	0		-1		0.0
1992	Sea A	0	0	—	8	0	0	0-0	9	8	7	3	0	6-0	6	7.00	57	.235	.350	0	—	0		-3		-0.2
	SD N	0	2	.000	14	1	0	0-0	21.1	15	8	0	1	9-0	19	2.95	122	.195	.287	3	.333	0*	126	1		0.1
1993	SD N	6	6	.500	59	0	0	23-8	59.1	57	27	3	1	37-8	39	3.03	136	.254	.360	1	.000	-0		5		1.1
1994	SD N	1	1	.500	13	0	0	0-3	12.1	21	11	2	0	8-2	9	8.03	51	.389	.468	1	.000	-0		-5		-0.7
	Det A	0	0	—	11	0	0	1-1	11.1	13	10	1	1	4-1	10	7.15	69	.271	.340	0	—	0		-3	55	0.1
1995	Phi N	2	2	.500	21	0	0	0-1	19	19	9	2	0	8-0	9	4.26	99	.260	.333	0	—	0		0	99	0.0
	Bal A	0	0	—	3	0	0	0-1	4	4	2	0	0	1-0	4	4.50	106	.267	.313	0	—	-0		0	219	0.0
Total	7	12	18	.400	183	7	0	26-17	241	246	145	21	5	138-20	170	4.71	86	.267	.363	6-0-1	.167	-0	99	-21	219	-1.4

HARRIS, BUDDY Walter Francis B12.5.1948 Philadelphia PA BR/TR/6-7/250* [HouN68 S1/15] d9.10 Col Miami

YEAR	TM LG	W	L	PCT	G	GS	CG-SHO	SV-BS	IP	H	R	HR	HB	BB-IB	SO	ERA	AERA	OAV	OOB	AB-HR-SH	AVG	PB	SUP	APR	DL	PW
1970	Hou N	0	0	—	2	0	0	0-0	6.1	6	4	3	0	4-0		5.68	69	.240	.240	1	.000	-0		-1		-0.1
1971	Hou N	1	1	.500	20	0	0	0-0	30.2	33	22	3	0	16-1	21	6.46	52	.275	.358	2	.000	-0		-10		-0.7
Total	2	1	1	.500	22	0	0	0-0	37	39	26	6	0	16-1	23	6.32	55	.269	.340	3	.000	-0		-11		-0.8

HARRIS, BILL William Milton B6.23.1900 Wylie TX D8.21.1965 Charlotte NC BR/TR/6-1/180 d4.22

YEAR	TM LG	W	L	PCT	G	GS	CG-SHO	SV-BS	IP	H	R	HR	HB	BB-IB	SO	ERA	AERA	OAV	OOB	AB-HR-SH	AVG	PB	SUP	APR	DL	PW
1923	Cin N	3	2	.600	22	3	1	0	69.2	79	42	3	3	18	18	5.17	75	.292	.342	17-0-1	.353	1	71	-7		-0.3
1924	Cin N	0	0	—	3	0	0	0	7	10	7	0	0	2	5	9.00	42	.323	.364	1	1.000	0		-4		-0.1
1931	Pit N	2	2	.500	4	4	3-1	0	31	21	6	0	0	9	10	0.87	442	.194	.256	11	.091	-1	67	9		1.2
1932	Pit N	10	9	.526	37	17	4	2	168	178	84	6	6	38	63	3.64	105	.271	.317	55	.182	-1	88	3		0.2
1933	Pit N	4	4	.500	31	0	0	5	58.2	68	28	1	1	14	19	3.22	103	.289	.332	9	.000	-1		0		-0.2
1934	Pit N	0	0	—	11	1	0	0	19	28	15	2	1	7	8	6.63	62	.350	.409	2	.500	0	231	-5		-0.2
1938	Bos A	5	5	.500	13	11	5-1	1	80.1	83	39	5	1	21	26	4.03	122	.268	.316	28-0-2	.214	-0	115	9		0.9
Total	7	24	22	.522	121	36	13-2	8	433.2	467	221	17	12	109	149	3.92	101	.276	.324	123-0-3	.203	-1	102	5		1.5

HARRIS, BILL William Thomas B12.3.1931 Duguayville NB, Can. BL/TR/5-8/187* d9.27

YEAR	TM LG	W	L	PCT	G	GS	CG-SHO	SV-BS	IP	H	R	HR	HB	BB-IB	SO	ERA	AERA	OAV	OOB	AB-HR-SH	AVG	PB	SUP	APR	DL	PW
1957	Bro N	0	1	.000	1	1	0	0	7	9	3	1	0	1-0	3	3.86	108	.321	.345	2	.500	0	42	0		0.1
1959	LA N	0	0	—	1	0	0	0	1.2	0	0	0	0	3-1	0	0.00	—	.000	.375	0	—	0		1		0.0
Total	2	0	1	.000	2	1	0	0	8.2	9	3	1	0	4-1	3	3.12	134	.273	.351	2	.500	0	42	1		0.1

HARRISON, BOB Robert Lee B9.22.1930 St.Louis MO BL/TR/5-11/178* d9.23

YEAR	TM LG	W	L	PCT	G	GS	CG-SHO	SV-BS	IP	H	R	HR	HB	BB-IB	SO	ERA	AERA	OAV	OOB	AB-HR-SH	AVG	PB	SUP	APR	DL	PW
1955	Bal A	0	0	—	1	0	0	0	2	3	2	0	0	4-0	0	9.00	42	.500	.700	0	—	0		-1		-0.1
1956	Bal A	0	0	—	1	1	0	0	1.2	3	3	0	0	5-0	0	16.20	24	.375	.615	0	—	0	136	-2		-0.1
Total	2	0	0	—	2	1	0	0	3.2	6	5	0	0	9-0	0	12.27	31	.429	.652	0	—	0	136	-3		-0.2

HARRISON, RORIC Roric Edward B9.20.1946 Los Angeles CA BR/TR/6-3/195* d4.18 Col Santa Monica (CA) City

YEAR	TM LG	W	L	PCT	G	GS	CG-SHO	SV-BS	IP	H	R	HR	HB	BB-IB	SO	ERA	AERA	OAV	OOB	AB-HR-SH	AVG	PB	SUP	APR	DL	PW
1972	Bal A	3	4	.429	39	2	0	4-1	94	68	24	2	4	34-9	62	2.30	136	.209	.291	17-1-1	.118	1	99	10		0.9
1973	Atl N	11	8	.579	38	22	3	5-2	177.1	161	90	15	3	98-6	130	4.16	95	.242	.339	54-2-5	.056	-2*	134	-3		-0.5
1974	Atl N	6	11	.353	20	20	3	0-0	126	148	70	12	3	49-1	46	4.71	81	.294	.358	38-3-6	.184	2	90	-11	70	-1.2
1975	Atl N	3	4	.429	15	7	2	1-0	54.2	58	33	7	0	19-1	22	4.77	79	.266	.324	15	.200	1	83	-5		-0.6
	Cle A	7	7	.500	19	19	4	0-0	126	137	71	9	4	46-4	52	4.79	80	.275	.338	0	—	0	107	-11		-1.2
1978	Min A	0	1	.000	9	0	0	0-0	12	18	10	0	0	11-0	7	7.50	51	.346	.453	0	—	0		-4		-0.3
Total	5	30	35	.462	140	70	12	10-3	590	590	298	45	14	257-21	319	4.24	88	.261	.338	124-6-12	.121	2	111	-24	70	-2.9

HARRISON, TOM Thomas James B1.18.1945 Trail BC, Can. BR/TR/6-3/200 d5.7

YEAR	TM LG	W	L	PCT	G	GS	CG-SHO	SV-BS	IP	H	R	HR	HB	BB-IB	SO	ERA	AERA	OAV	OOB	AB-HR-SH	AVG	PB	SUP	APR	DL	PW
1965	KC A	0	0	—	1	0	0	0	1	2	1	0	0	1-0	0	9.00	39	.667	.750	0	—	0*		-1		0.0

HARRISS, SLIM William Jennings Bryan B12.11.1896 Brownwood TX D9.19.1963 Temple TX BR/TR/6-6/180 d4.19 Col Howard Payne

YEAR	TM LG	W	L	PCT	G	GS	CG-SHO	SV-BS	IP	H	R	HR	HB	BB-IB	SO	ERA	AERA	OAV	OOB	AB-HR-SH	AVG	PB	SUP	APR	DL	PW
1920	Phi A	9	14	.391	31	25	11-1	0	192	226	111	5	5	57	60	4.08	99	.305	.359	66-0-3	.106	-7	70	2		-0.3
1921	Phi A	11	16	.407	39	28	14	2	227.2	258	136	16	9	73	92	4.27	104	.290	.350	81-0-5	.148	-7	84	4		-0.3
1922	Phi A	9	20	.310	47	32	13	3	229.2	262	148	19	3	94	102	5.02	85	.290	.359	74-0-4	.176	-4	99	-17		-2.2
1923	Phi A	10	16	.385	46	28	9	6	209.1	221	114	9	2	95	89	4.00	103	.280	.359	61-0-5	.066	-8	85	3		-0.2
1924	Phi A	6	10	.375	36	12	4-1	2	123	138	78	9	3	62	45	4.68	92	.291	.377	42	.205	-3	62	-6		-0.8
1925	Phi A	19	12	.613	46	33	15-2	1	252.2	263	118	8	6	95	95	3.49	133	.268	.336	88-1-7	.205	-3	105	31		3.2
1926	Phi A	3	5	.375	12	10	2	0	57	66	34	0	0	22	13	4.11	102	.289	.352	17-0-1	.059	-2	81	0		-0.2
	Bos A	6	10	.375	21	18	6-1	0	113	135	66	0	2	33	34	4.46	91	.300	.362	34-0-1	.206	-0	84	-5		-0.8
	Year	9	15	.375	33	28	8-1	0	170	201	100	0	2	55	47	4.34	95	.304	.359	51-0-2	.157	-2	83	-6		-0.7
1927	Bos A	14	21	.400	44	27	11-1	1	217.2	253	127	8	9	66	77	4.18	101	.298	.355	66-0-6	.121	-5	75	-2		-1.1
1928	Bos A	8	11	.421	27	15	4-1	1	128.1	141	74	5	2	33	37	4.63	89	.287	.335	36-0-5	.139	-3	64	-6		-1.1
Total	9	95	135	.413	349	228	89-7	16	1750.1	1963	1006	75	41	630	644	4.25	100	.290	.354	565-1-37	.145	-40	84	4		-3.2

HARRIST, EARL Earl "Irish" B8.20.1919 Dubach LA D9.1.1998 Simsboro LA BR/TR/6-0/178* d8.18

YEAR	TM LG	W	L	PCT	G	GS	CG-SHO	SV-BS	IP	H	R	HR	HB	BB-IB	SO	ERA	AERA	OAV	OOB	AB-HR-SH	AVG	PB	SUP	APR	DL	PW
1945	Cin N	2	4	.333	14	5	1	0	62.1	60	30	2	1	27	15	3.61	104	.249	.327	15-0-3	.000	-2	59	0		-0.2
1947	Chi A	3	8	.273	33	4	0	5	93.2	85	48	3	3	49	55	3.56	103	.248	.347	24-0-2	.208	-0	97	-1		-0.1
1948	Chi A	1	3	.250	11	1	0	0	23	23	17	4	3	13	14	5.87	73	.267	.382	4	.000	-1	127	-4		-0.7
	Was A	3	3	.500	23	4	0	0	60.2	70	35	1	3	37	21	4.60	94	.293	.394	18	.167	-1	73	-2		-0.3
	Year	4	6	.400	34	5	0	0	83.2	93	52	5	6	50	35	4.95	87	.286	.391	22	.136	-2	84	-6		-0.4
1952	StL A	2	8	.200	36	9	1	5	116.2	119	61	7	10	47	49	4.01	98	.269	.352	31-0-4	.097	-2	67	-2		-0.4
1953	Chi A	1	0	1.000	7	0	0	0	8.1	9	7	1	0	5	1	7.56	53	.290	.389	1	.000	-0		-3		-0.1
	Det A	0	2	.000	8	1	0	0	18.2	25	19	2	0	15	7	8.68	47	.333	.444	3	.000	-0	22	-9		-0.7
	Year	1	2	.333	15	1	0	0	27	34	26	3	0	20	8	8.33	49	.321	.429	4	.000	-0	22	-12		-1.1
Total	5	12	28	.300	132	24	2	10	383.1	391	217	20	20	193	162	4.34	90	.268	.361	96-0-9	.115	-7	72	-21		-3.2

HARSHMAN, JACK John Elvin B7.12.1927 San Diego CA BL/TL/6-2/185* d9.16.1948

YEAR	TM LG	W	L	PCT	G	GS	CG-SHO	SV-BS	IP	H	R	HR	HB	BB-IB	SO	ERA	AERA	OAV	OOB	AB-HR-SH	AVG	PB	SUP	APR	DL	PW
1952	NY N	0	2	.000	7	0	0	0	6.1	12	10	2	0	6	6	14.21	26	.429	.529	2	.000	-0*	48	-7		-1.1
1954	Chi A	14	8	.636	35	21	9-4	1	177	157	61	7	5	96	134	2.95	127	.238	.339	56-2-3	.143	3*	106	17		2.4
1955	Chi A	11	7	.611	32	23	9	0	179.1	144	74	16	4	97-3	116	3.36	117	.224	.327	60-2-5	.183	4	122	11		1.1
1956	Chi A	15	11	.577	34	30	15-4	0	226.2	183	85	14	3	102-4	143	3.10	132	.221	.305	71-6-4	.169	6*	98	26		1.9
1957	Chi A	8	8	.500	30	26	6	1	151.1	142	78	16	5	82-2	83	4.10	91	.250	.344	45-2-2	.222	5	108	-8		-0.5
1958	Bal A	12	15	.444	34	29	17-3	4	236.1	204	89	20	3	75-1	161	2.89	124	.231	.292	82-6-1	.195	8*	67	17		3.1
1959	Bal A	0	6	.000	14	8	0	0	47.1	58	34	6	2	28-5	24	6.85	55	.319	.409	10-1-0	.200	1*	67	-16		-1.0
	Bos A	2	3	.400	8	2	0	0	24.2	29	19	2	0	10-0	14	6.57	62	.284	.348	7-0-1	.143	0*	54	-6		-0.9
	Cle A	5	1	.833	13	6	5-1	1	66	46	21	6	0	13-0	35	2.59	142	.179	.218	34	.206	2*	128	9		1.1
	Year	7	10	.412	35	16	5-1	1	138	133	74	14	2	51-5	73	4.76	79	.246	.311	51-1-1	.196	3	87	-14		-1.1
1960	Cle A	2	4	.333	15	8	0	0	54.1	50	32	7	0	30-2	25	3.98	94	.243	.333	17-0-2	.176	-0	106	-4	86	-0.2
Total	8	69	65	.515	217	155	61-12	7	1169.1	1025	508	96	22	539-17	741	3.50	109	.235	.320	384-19-18	.182	29	98	39	86	6.1

HARSTAD, OSCAR Oscar Theander B5.24.1892 Parkland WA D11.14.1985 Corvallis OR BR/TR/6-0/174 d4.23

YEAR	TM LG	W	L	PCT	G	GS	CG-SHO	SV-BS	IP	H	R	HR	HB	BB-IB	SO	ERA	AERA	OAV	OOB	AB-HR-SH	AVG	PB	SUP	APR	DL	PW
1915	Cle A	3	5	.375	32	1	0	1	82	81	45	1	9	35	35	3.40	90	.270	.348	16-0-1	.125	-1	102	-4		-0.

HART, BILLY Robert Lee B5.16.1866 Palmyra MO D5.14.1944 Hannibal MO 5-8/? d7.13

YEAR	TM LG	W	L	PCT	G	GS	CG-SHO	SV-BS	IP	H	R	HR	HB	BB-IB	SO	ERA	AERA	OAV	OOB	AB-HR-SH	AVG	PB	SUP	APR	DL	PW
1890	StL AA	12	8	.600	26	24	20	0	201.1	188	111	6	16	66	95	3.67	118	.240	.312	78-1	.192	- -1*	92	17		1.

YEAR	TM LG	W	L	PCT	G	GS	CG-SHO	SV-BS	IP	H	R	HR	HB	BB-IB	SO	ERA	AERA	OAV	OOB	AB-HR-SH	AVG	PB	SUP	APR	DL	PW
HART, BILL	William Franklin B7.19.1865 Louisville KY D9.19.1936 Cincinnati OH TR/5-10/163 d7.26 U2																									
1886	Phi AA	9	13	.409	22	22	22-2	0	186	183	144	7	7	66	78	3.19	110	.234	.299	73	.137	-5	79	-2		-0.6
1887	Phi AA	1	2	.333	3	3	3	0	26	28	22	1	1	17	4	4.50	95	.272	.380	13	.077	-2	99	-2		-0.3
1892	Bro N	9	12	.429	28	23	16-2	1	195	188	109	3	7	96	65	3.28	97	.243	.332	125-2	.192	3*	97	-5		-0.1
1895	Pit N	14	17	.452	36	29	24	1	261.2	293	186	4	15	135	85	4.75	95	.279	.369	106-0-3	.236	-2	88	-1		0.0
1896	StL N	12	29	.293	42	41	37	0	336	411	271	11	15	141	65	5.12	85	.299	.370	161-0-4	.186	-5*	72	-31		-3.0
1897	StL N	9	27	.250	39	38	31	0	294.2	395	292	10	16	148	67	6.26	70	.318	.398	156-2-0	.250	-1*	76	-62		-5.4
1898	Pit N	5	9	.357	16	15	13-1	1	125	141	81	4	7	44	19	4.82	74	.282	.348	69	.240	0	64	-14		-1.3
1901	Cle A	7	11	.389	20	19	16	0	157.2	180	109	3	10	57	48	3.77	94	.283	.352	64-0-1	.219	-2	83	-7		-0.7
Total	8	66	120	.355	206	190	162-5	3	1582	1819	1214	43	78	704	431	4.65	86	.282	.359	748-4-8	.207	-14	80-124			-11.4
HARTENSTEIN, CHUCK	Charles Oscar "Twiggy" B5.26.1942 Seguin TX BR/TR/5-11/165* d9.11.1965 C4 Col Texas																									
1966	Chi N	0	0	—	5	0	0	0	9.1	8	2	0	1	3-0	4	1.93	191	.222	.300	0	—	0	2			0.1
1967	Chi N	9	5	.643	45	0	0	10	73	74	27	4	1	17-7	20	3.08	115	.278	.321	16-0-1	.063	-1	4			0.7
1968	Chi N	2	4	.333	28	0	0	1	35.2	41	19	3	1	11-2	17	4.54	69	.291	.346	2	.000	-0	-5			-0.9
1969	Pit N	5	4	.556	56	0	0	10-3	95.2	84	42	9	4	27-3	44	3.95	88	.241	.300	14-0-1	.071	-1	-3			-0.3
1970	Pit N	1	1	.500	17	0	0	1-0	23.2	25	15	3	0	8-4	14	4.56	87	.278	.333	1	.000	-0	-2			-0.2
	StL N	0	0	—	6	0	0	0-1	13.1	24	13	1	0	5-0	9	8.78	47	.375	.414	2	.000	-0	-4			-0.3
	Year	1	1	.500	23	0	0	1-1	37	49	28	4	0	13-4	23	6.08	66	.318	.367	3	.000	-0	-6			-0.5
	Bos A	0	3	.000	17	0	0	1-2	19	21	17	6	1	12-5	12	8.05	49	.288	.395	2	.000	-0	-7			-1.1
1977	Tor A	0	2	.000	13	0	0	0-1	27.1	40	22	8	1	6-0	15	6.59	65	.348	.385	0	—	0	-7			-0.4
Total	6	17	19	.472	187	0	0	23-7	297	317	157	34	9	89-21	135	4.52	81	.280	.335	37-0-2	.054	-2	-24			-2.4
HARTER, FRANK	Franklin Pierce "Chief" B9.19.1886 Keyesport IL D4.14.1959 Breese IL BR/TR/5-11/165 d8.31																									
1912	Cin N	1	2	.333	6	3	1	0	29.1	25	16	1	0	11	12	3.07	110	.234	.305	11	.091	-1	44	0		-0.1
1913	Cin N	1	1	.500	17	2	0	0	46.2	47	23	3	0	19	10	3.86	84	.272	.344	14	.143	-1	116	-2		-0.2
1914	Ind F	1	2	.333	6	1	1	0	24.2	33	12	0	0	7	8	4.01	78	.330	.374	8	.000	-1	154	-1		-0.3
Total	3	3	5	.375	29	6	2	0	100.2	105	51	4	0	37	30	3.67	89	.276	.341	33	.091	-3	86	-3		-0.6
HARTGRAVES, DEAN	Dean Charles B8.12.1966 Bakersfield CA BR/TL/6-0/185* [HouN87 20/522] d5.3 Col Cal St.-Fresno																									
1995	Hou N	2	0	1.000	40	0	0	0-3	36.1	30	14	2	0	16-2	24	3.22	120	.227	.309	2-0-1	.000	-0	3			0.1
1996	Hou N	0	0	—	19	0	0	0-0	19	18	11	1	1	16-3	16	5.21	74	.257	.398	0-0-1	—	-0	-2			-0.1
	Atl N	1	0	1.000	20	0	0	0-0	18.2	16	10	3	1	7-0	14	4.34	103	.232	.308	1	.000	-0	0			0.0
	Year	1	0	1.000	39	0	0	0-0	37.2	34	21	4	2	23-3	30	4.78	87	.245	.355	1-0-1	.000	-0	-2			-0.1
1998	SF N	0	0	—	5	0	0	0-0	5.2	10	7	1	0	4-0	4	9.53	42	.385	.438	0	—	-0	-4			-0.2
Total	3	3	0	1.000	84	0	0	0-3	79.2	74	42	7	2	43-5	58	4.41	91	.249	.343	3-0-2	.000	-0	-3			-0.2
HARTLEY, MIKE	Michael Edward B8.31.1961 Hawthorne CA BR/TR/6-1/197(185-197) d9.10 Col Grossmont (CA) JC																									
1989	LA N	0	1	.000	5	0	0	0-1	6	2	1	0	0	0-0	4	1.50	229	.100	.100	1	.000	-0	1			0.2
1990	LA N	6	3	.667	32	0	0	1-1	79.1	58	32	7	2	30-2	76	2.95	125	.200	.279	13-0-3	.077	-1	82	6		0.5
1991	LA N	2	0	1.000	40	0	0	1-0	57	53	29	7	3	37-7	44	4.42	82	.245	.362	4	.000	-0	4			-0.3
	Phi N	2	1	.667	18	0	0	1-2	26.1	21	11	4	3	10-1	19	3.76	98	.219	.312.	1	.000	-0	0			0.0
	Year	4	1	.800	58	0	0	2-2	83.1	74	40	11	6	47-8	63	4.21	87	.237	.347	5	.000	-1	-4			-0.3
1992	Min A	7	6	.538	46	0	0	0-4	55	54	23	5	2	23-6	53	3.44	102	.255	.332	4	.000	-0*	0	37		0.0
1993	Min A	1	2	.333	53	0	0	1-2	81	86	38	4	7	36-3	57	4.00	110	.281	.363	0	—	0	4			0.1
1995	Bos A	0	0	—	5	0	0	0-0	7	8	7	1	2	2-0	2	9.00	54	.308	.375	0	—	0	4			0.1
	Bal A	1	0	1.000	3	0	0	0-0	7	5	1	0	0	1-0	4	1.29	372	.217	.250	0	—	0	-3			-0.1
	Year	1	0	1.000	8	0	0	0-0	14	13	8	1	2	3-0	6	5.14	94	.265	.321	0	—	0	0			0.3
Total	6	19	13	.594	202	6	1-1	4-10	318.2	287	142	28	19	139-21	259	3.70	105	.241	.328	23-0-3	.043	-2	82	7	37	0.8
HARTMAN, CHARLIE	Charles Otto B8.10.1888 Los Angeles CA D10.22.1960 Los Angeles CA TL d6.24																									
1908	Bos A	0	0	—	1	0	0	0	2	1	1	0	0	2	1	4.50	55	.143	.333	0	—	0	0			0.0
HARTMAN, BOB	Robert Louis B8.28.1937 Kenosha WI BR/TL/5-11/185* d4.26																									
1959	Mil N	0	0	—	3	0	0	0	1.2	6	5	0	0	2-0	1	27.00	13	.545	.615	0	—	0	-4			-0.2
1962	Cle A	0	1	.000	8	2	0	0	17.1	14	10	1	0	8-0	11	3.12	124	.209	.289	7	.000	-1	104	0		-0.1
Total	2	0	1	.000	0	2	0	0	19	20	15	1	0	10-0	12	5.21	74	.256	.337	7	.000	-1	104	-4		-0.3
HARTRANFT, RAY	Raymond Joseph B9.19.1890 Quakertown PA D2.10.1955 Spring City PA BL/TL/6-1/195 d6.16																									
1913	Phi N	0	0	—	1	0	0	0	4	4	3	1	0	0	2	9.00	37	.500	.571	0	—	0	-1			-0.1
HARTSOCK, JEFF	Jeffrey Roger B11.19.1966 Fairfield OH BR/TR/6-0/190 [LAN88 7/166] d9.12 Col North Carolina St.																									
1992	Chi N	0	0	—	4	0	0	0-0	9.1	15	7	2	0	4-0	6	6.75	54	.375	.422	2	.000	-0	-3			-0.2
HARTUNG, CLINT	Clinton Clarence "Floppy","The Hondo Hurricane" B8.10.1922 Hondo TX BR/TR/6-4/215(200-215) d4.15 ▲																									
1947	NY N	9	7	.563	23	20	8-1	0	138	140	76	15	2	69	54	4.57	89	.263	.350	94-4-0	.309	9*	107	-6		0.3
1948	NY N	8	8	.500	36	19	6-2	1	153.1	146	89	15	7	72	42	4.75	83	.258	.347	56	.179	2*	123	-11		-0.9
1949	NY N	9	11	.450	33	25	8	0	154.2	156	98	17	4	86	48	5.00	80	.260	.357	63-4-0	.190	4*	114	-16		-1.4
1950	NY N	3	3	.500	20	8	1	0	65.1	87	56	10	2	44	23	6.61	62	.326	.425	43-3-0	.302	4*	108	-19		-1.0
Total	4	29	29	.500	112	72	23-3	1	511.1	529	319	57	13	271	167	5.02	80	.269	.361	256-11-0	.250	19	114	-52		-3.0
HARTZELL, PAUL	Paul Franklin B11.2.1953 Bloomsburg PA BR/TR/6-5/200* [AnaA75 10/217] d4.10 Col Lehigh																									
1976	Cal A	7	4	.636	37	15	7-2	2-1	166	166	64	6	10	43-5	51	2.77	121	.266	.321	0	—	0	119	9		0.6
1977	Cal A	8	12	.400	41	23	6	4-0	189.1	200	92	14	4	38-6	79	3.57	110	.274	.309	0	—	0	97	6		0.6
1978	Cal A	6	10	.375	54	12	5	6-2	157	168	67	8	5	41-9	55	3.44	106	.278	.328	0	—	0	72	4		0.4
1979	Min A	6	10	.375	28	26	4	0-0	163	193	102	8	4	44-4	44	5.36	82	.301	.346	0	—	0	92	-15	25	-1.2
1980	Bal A	0	2	.000	6	0	0	0-0	17.2	12	14	3	0	9-2	5	6.62	60	.310	.387	0	—	0	-5			-0.5
1984	Mil A	0	1	.000	4	1	0	0-0	10.1	17	11	0	0	6-0	3	7.84	50	.370	.426	0	—	0	70	-5		-0.4
Total	6	27	39	.409	170	77	22-2	12-3	703.1	766	350	49	23	181-26	237	3.90	98	.282	.329	0	—	0	97	-6	25	-0.5
HARVEY, BRYAN	Bryan Stanley B6.2.1963 Soddy-Daisy TN BR/TR/6-2/212(190-215) d5.16 Col North Carolina-Charlotte [DL 1996 Cal A 182, 1997 Atl N 96]																									
1987	Cal A	0	0	—	3	0	0	0	5	6	0	0	0	2-0	3	0.00	—	.300	.364	0	—	0	2			0.1
1988	Cal A	7	5	.583	50	0	0	17-6	76	59	22	4	1	20-6	67	2.13	182	.214	.267	0	—	0	14			2.6
1989	Cal A	3	3	.500	51	0	0	25-7	55	36	21	6	0	41-1	78	3.44	111	.183	.321	0	—	0	3			0.6
1990	Cal A	4	4	.500	54	0	0	25-6	64.1	45	24	4	0	35-6	82	3.22	119	.201	.304	0	—	0	6			1.0
1991	Cal A☆	2	4	.333	67	0	0	**46-6**	78.2	51	20	2	1	17-3	101	1.60	257	.178	.225	0	—	0	20			3.4
1992	Cal A	0	4	.000	25	0	0	13-3	28.2	22	12	4	0	11-1	34	2.83	142	.208	.275	0	—	0	3	111		0.5
1993	Fla N★	1	5	.167	59	0	0	45-4	69	45	14	4	0	13-2	73	1.70	258	.186	.222	0	—	0	19			3.7
1994	Fla N	0	0	—	12	0	0	6-0	10.1	12	6	1	0	4-0	10	5.23	85	.279	.340	0	—	0	-1	92		-0.1
1995	Fla N	0	0	—	1	0	0	0-0	0	2	3	1	0	1-0	0	∞	—	1.000	1.000	0	—	0	-3	156		-0.2
Total	9	17	25	.405	322	0	0	177-32	387	278	122	30	2	144-19	448	2.49	162	.199	.271	0	—	0	63	637		11.6
HARVEY, ZAZA	Ervin King B1.5.1879 Saratoga CA D6.3.1954 Santa Monica CA BL/TL/6-0/190 d5.3 ▲																									
1900	Chi N	0	0	—	1	0	0	0	4	3	0	0	0	1	0	0.00	—	.214	.267	3	.000	-1*	2			0.0
1901	Chi A	3	7	.300	16	9	5	1	92	91	59	2	5	34	27	3.62	96	.255	.328	40-0-2	.250	2*	108	-2		0.1
Total	2	3	7	.300	17	9	5	1	96	94	59	2	5	35	27	3.47	101	.253	.326	43-0-2	.233	2	108	0		0.1
HARVILLE, CHAD	Chad Ashley B9.16.1976 Selmer TN BR/TR/5-9/180* [OakA97 2/63] d6.23 Col Memphis																									
1999	Oak A	0	2	.000	15	0	0	0-0	14.1	18	11	2	0	10-1	15	6.91	69	.310	.406	0	—	0	-3			-0.4
2001	Oak A	0	0	—	3	0	0	0-0	3	2	1	0	0	0-0	2	0.00	—	.182	.182	0	—	0	1	69		0.1
2003	Oak A	1	0	1.000	21	0	0	1-0	21.2	25	15	3	1	17-1	18	5.82	79	.294	.413	0	—	0	-3			-0.2
2004	Oak A	0	0	—	3	0	0	0-0	2.2	2	1	0	0	1-0	0	3.38	137	.200	.273	0	—	0	0			0.0
2005	†Hou N	3	2	.600	56	0	0	0-4	53	54	35	8	2	26-2	46	4.75	92	.260	.347	1	.000	-0	-4	25		-0.4
	Bos A	0	2	.000	37	0	0	0-1	38.1	36	21	7	4	24-1	33	4.46	94	.254	.372	1	.000	-0	-1			-0.1
	Bos A	0	1	.000	8	0	0	0-0	7	7	5	1	1	3-0	5	6.43	72	.269	.367	0	—	0	-1			-0.1
Total	5	4	7	.364	143	0	0	1-5	140	144	88	21	8	81-5	117	5.01	88	.267	.368	2	.000	-0	-11	94		-1.1

YEAR	TM LG	W	L	PCT	G	GS	CG-SHO	SV-BS	IP	H	R	HR	HB	BB-IB	SO	ERA	AERA	OAV	OOB	AB-HR-SH	AVG	PB	SUP	APR	DL	PW

HASEGAWA, SHIGETOSHI Shigetoshi B8.1.1968 Kobe, Japan BR/TR/5-11/178(160-180) d4.5

1997	Ana A	3	7	.300	50	7	0	0-1	116.2	118	60	14	3	46-6	83	3.93	117	.269	.339	0	—	0	91	7		0.6
1998	Ana A	8	3	.727	61	0	0	5-2	97.1	86	37	14	2	32-2	73	3.14	151	.241	.302	0	—	0		17		1.8
1999	Ana A	4	6	.400	64	1	0	2-3	77	80	45	14	2	34-2	44	4.91	100	.276	.352	0	—	0	0	0		0.0
2000	Ana A	10	5	.667	66	0	0	9-9	95.2	100	42	11	2	38-6	59	3.48	148	.270	.339	1	.000	-0		16		2.4
2001	Ana A	5	6	.455	46	0	0	0-6	55.2	52	28	5	2	20-5	41	4.04	115	.248	.316	0	—	0	3	9	41	0.5
2002	Sea A	8	3	.727	53	0	0	1-4	70.1	60	26	4	2	30-8	39	3.20	135	.238	.323	0	—	0	25			1.3
2003	Sea A★	2	4	.333	63	0	0	16-1	73	62	12	5	0	18-3	32	1.48	293	.235	.284	0	—	0		-6		2.8
2004	Sea A	4	6	.400	68	0	0	0-5	68	67	42	5	2	31-4	46	5.16	87	.260	.339	0	—	0		1		0.1
2005	Sea A	1	3	.250	46	0	0	0-1	66.2	66	31	4	3	16-1	30	4.18	101	.259	.307	0	—	0	80	72	41	0.1
Total	9	45	43	.511	517	8	0	33-32	720.1	691	323	76	18	265-37	447	3.70	125	.256	.324	1	.000	-0	80	72	41	8.8

HASH, HERB Herbert Howard B2.13.1911 Woolwine VA BR/TR/6-1/180 d4.19 Col Richmond

1940	Bos A	7	7	.500	34	12	3-1	3	120	123	68	11	5	84	36	4.95	91	.266	.385	40-0-3	.175	-0*	103	-4		-0.4
1941	Bos A	1	0	1.000	4	0	0	1	8.1	7	5	1	0	7	3	5.40	77	.226	.368	2	.000	-0		-1	67	-0.1
Total	2	8	7	.533	38	12	3-1	4	128.1	130	73	12	5	91	39	4.98	90	.264	.384	42-0-3	.167	-1	103	-5	67	-0.5

HASSLER, ANDY Andrew Earl B10.18.1951 Texas City TX BL/TL/6-5/220* [AnaA69 25/579] d5.30

1971	Cal A	0	3	.000	6	4	0	0-0	18.2	25	10	0	1	15-2	13	3.86	84	.333	.446	5-0-1	.000	-1	48	-2		-0.3
1973	Cal A	0	4	.000	7	4	1	0-0	31.2	33	23	0	3	19-0	19	3.69	97	.262	.369	0	—	0	81	-4		-0.5
1974	Cal A	7	11	.389	23	22	10-2	1-0	162	132	64	10	9	79-2	76	2.61	133	.225	.325	0	—	0	103	12		1.4
1975	Cal A	3	12	.200	30	18	6-1	0-0	133.1	158	94	12	6	53-0	82	5.94	60	.303	.369	0	—	0	100	-34		-3.2
1976	Cal A	0	6	.000	14	4	0	0-0	47.1	50	24	3	0	17-2	16	5.13	65	.284	.342	0	—	0	79	7		0.8
	†KC A	5	6	.455	19	14	4-1	0-1	99.2	89	37	2	0	39-0	45	2.89	121	.242	.311	0	—	0*	78	-3		-0.3
	Year	5	12	.294	33	18	4-1	0-1	147	139	68	5	0	56-2	61	3.61	96	.256	.321	0	—	0	126	-5	28	-0.4
1977	†KC A	9	6	.600	29	27	3-1	0-0	156.1	166	88	7	5	75-3	83	4.32	89	.317	.381	0	—	0	110	-5	34	-0.4
1978	KC A	1	4	.200	11	9	1	0-0	58.1	76	36	1	2	24-0	26	4.32	89	.317	.381	0	—	0	142	3		0.3
	Bos A	2	1	.667	13	2	1	1-0	30	38	13	0	0	13-2	23	3.00	137	.302	.367	0	—	0	114	-2		0.1
	Year	3	5	.375	24	11	1	1-0	88.1	114	49	1	2	37-2	49	3.87	101	.311	.376	0	—	0	114	-7		-1.2
1979	Bos A	1	2	.333	8	0	0	0-0	15.1	23	17	0	1	7-0	7	8.80	51	.365	.431	0	—	0		-7		-0.5
	NY N	4	5	.444	29	8	1	4-0	80.1	74	35	5	0	42-8	53	3.70	100	.252	.344	22	.000	-2	80	1		-0.1
1980	Pit N	0	0	—	6	0	0	0-0	11.2	9	6	2	0	4-0	4	3.86	96	.243	.310	2	.000	-0	0	0		0.0
	Cal A	5	1	.833	41	0	0	10-2	83	67	25	8	1	37-8	75	2.49	159	.214	.298	0	—	0	14			1.3
1981	†Cal A	4	3	.571	42	0	0	5-2	75.2	72	29	8	0	33-8	44	3.21	114	.262	.339	0	—	0	5			0.5
1982	†Cal A	2	1	.667	54	0	0	4-2	71.1	58	24	5	4	40-5	38	2.78	147	.232	.343	0	—	0	10			0.6
1983	Cal A	0	5	.000	42	0	0	4-3	36.1	42	22	2	0	17-8	20	5.45	74	.302	.378	0	—	0	-5			-0.7
1984	StL N	1	0	1.000	3	0	0	0-0	2.1	4	3	2	0	2-1	1	11.57	30	.364	.462	0	—	0	1			0.1
1985	StL N	0	1	.000	10	0	0	0-0	10	9	5	0	0	4-0	5	1.80	199	.225	.289	0	—	0	-2			0.0
Total	14	44	71	.383	387	112	26-5	29-10	1123.1	1125	562	67	32	520-49	630	3.83	98	.264	.346	29-0-1	.000	-3	100	-21	62	-3.2

HASTINGS, CHARLIE Charles Morton B11.11.1870 Ironton OH D8.3.1934 Parkersburg WV 5-11/179 d5.3

1893	Cle N	4	5	.444	19	9	6	1	92	128	81	5	9	33	14	4.70	104	.320	.379	39	.179	0*	100	0		0.0
1896	Pit N	5	10	.333	17	13	9	1	104	126	86	1	7	44	19	5.88	71	.296	.372	37	.216	-0	79	-18		-1.9
1897	Pit N	5	4	.556	16	10	9	0	118	138	84	3	7	47	42	4.58	91	.289	.362	43-1-1	.233	3	108	-6		-0.1
1898	Pit N	4	10	.286	19	13	12	0	137.1	142	76	2	10	52	40	3.41	104	.265	.341	43-0-1	.233	2	64	1		0.1
Total	4	18	29	.383	67	45	36	2	451.1	534	327	11	29	176	115	4.55	91	.291	.362	162-1-2	.216	5	87	-23		-1.7

HASTY, BOB Robert Keller B5.3.1896 Canton GA D5.28.1972 Dallas GA BR/TR/6-3/210 d9.11

1919	Phi A	0	2	.000	2	2	1	0	12	15	10	1	0	4	5	5.25	65	.306	.358	3-0-1	.333	0	46	-3		-0.4
1920	Phi A	1	3	.250	19	4	1	0	71.2	91	53	5	0	28	12	5.02	80	.323	.384	24	.250	0	94	-7		-0.2
1921	Phi A	5	16	.238	35	22	9	0	179.1	238	120	8	2	40	46	4.87	92	.331	.368	68-0-1	.294	2	63	-8		-0.5
1922	Phi A	9	14	.391	28	26	14-1	0	192.1	225	110	20	3	41	33	4.26	100	.298	.336	75-1-0	.200	-2	95	-1		-1.1
1923	Phi A	13	15	.464	44	36	10-1	1	243.1	274	146	11	9	72	56	4.44	93	.291	.347	88-0-6	.193	-3	82	-8		-0.5
1924	Phi A	1	3	.250	18	4	0	0	52.2	57	36	4	1	30	15	5.64	76	.282	.378	13	.077	-1	59	-7		-0.3
Total	6	29	53	.354	146	94	35-2	1	751.1	900	475	49	15	215	167	4.65	91	.305	.355	271-1-8	.221	-3	80	-34		-3.0

HATFIELD, GIL Gilbert "Colonel" B1.27.1855 Hoboken NJ D5.26.1921 Hoboken NJ TR/5-9.5/168 d9.24.1885 b-John ▲

1889	NY N	2	4	.333	6	5	5	0	52	53	43	2	1	25	28	3.98	99	.256	.339	125-1	.184	-0*	163	-2		-0.2
1890	NY P	1	1	.500	3	0	0	1	7.2	8	8	1	0	4	3	3.52	129	.258	.361	287-2	.279	0*	0			0.0
1891	Was AA	0	0	—	4	0	0	0	18	29	28	1	0	14	3	11.00	34	.349	.443	500-1	.256	1*		-12		-0.5
Total	3	3	5	.375	13	5	5	1	77.2	90	79	4	2	43	34	5.56	71	.280	.369	912-4	.253	1	163	-14		-0.7

HATHAWAY, HILLY Hillary Houston B9.12.1969 Jacksonville FL BL/TL/6-4/195* [CalA89 35/903] d9.8 Col Manatee (FL) CC

1992	Cal A	0	0	—	2	1	0	0-0	5.2	8	5	1	0	3-0	1	7.94	51	.333	.393	0	—	0	91	-2		-0.1
1993	Cal A	4	3	.571	11	11	0	0-0	57.1	71	35	6	5	26-1	11	5.02	90	.326	.405	0	—	0	98	-3	24	-0.3
Total	2	4	3	.571	13	12	0	0-0	63	79	40	7	5	29-1	12	5.29	85	.326	.404	0	—	0	97	-5	24	-0.4

HATHAWAY, RAY Ray Wilson B10.13.1916 Greenville OH BR/TR/6-0/165 d4.20

| 1945 | Bro N | 0 | 1 | .000 | 4 | 1 | 0 | 0 | 9 | 11 | 7 | 1 | 0 | 6 | 3 | 4.00 | 94 | .297 | .395 | 2 | .000 | -0 | 68 | -1 | | -0.1 |

HATTEN, JOE Joseph Hilarian B11.17.1916 Bancroft IA D12.16.1988 Redding CA BR/TL/6-0/176* d4.21

1946	Bro N	14	11	.560	42	30	13-1	2	222	207	79	10	7	110	85	2.84	119	.253	.347	79-0-4	.076	-6	107	15		0.9
1947	†Bro N	17	8	.680	42	32	11-3	0	225.1	211	95	9	5	105	76	3.63	114	.252	.339	83-0-3	.205	0	104	16		1.8
1948	†Bro N	13	10	.565	42	30	11-1	0	208.2	228	93	9	3	94	73	3.58	112	.283	.360	63-0-8	.206	1*	112	11		-0.1
1949	†Bro N	12	8	.600	37	29	11-2	2	187.1	194	102	15	2	69	58	4.18	98	.271	.337	67-0-3	.179	-1*	122	-5		-0.6
1950	Bro N	2	2	.500	23	8	2-1	0	68.2	82	45	10	0	31	29	4.59	89	.294	.365	18-0-1	.111	-1*	97	-7		-0.2
1951	Bro N	1	0	1.000	11	6	0	0	49.1	55	25	3	0	21	22	4.56	86	.281	.350	15-0-1	.133	-1	139	-2		-0.5
	Chi N	2	6	.250	23	6	1	0	75.1	82	48	8	1	37	23	5.14	80	.281	.364	17-0-1	.235	-1	58	-8		-0.8
	Year	3	6	.333	34	12	1	0	124.2	137	73	11	1	58	45	4.91	82	.281	.358	32-0-2	.188	-1*	97	-9		-1.3
1952	Chi N	4	4	.500	13	8	2	0	50.1	65	35	6	1	25	15	6.08	63	.314	.391	15-0-1	.067	-1*	75	-10		-1.8
Total	7	65	49	.570	233	149	51-8	4	1087	1124	522	70	19	492	381	3.87	101	.271	.351	357-0-22	.160	-8	107	10		0.

HATTER, CLYDE Clyde Melno B8.7.1908 Poplar Hill KY D10.16.1937 Yosemite KY BR/TL/5-11/170 d4.23 Col Eastern Kentucky

1935	Det A	0	0	—	8	2	0	0	33.1	44	33	2	1	30	14	7.56	55	.319	.444	10-0-1	.300	0	156	-14		-0.6
1937	Det A	1	0	1.000	3	0	0	0	9.1	17	12	0	1	11	5	11.57	40	.415	.547	3	.000	-0		-6		-0.5
Total	2	1	0	1.000	11	2	0	0	42.2	61	45	2	2	41	19	8.44	51	.341	.468	13-0-1	.231	0	156	-20		-1.1

HAUGHEY, CHRIS Christopher Francis "Bud" B10.3.1925 Astoria NY BR/TR/6-1/180 d10.3 Mil 1944-45

| 1943 | Bro N | 0 | 1 | .000 | 1 | 0 | 0 | 0 | 7 | 5 | 6 | 0 | 0 | 9 | 0 | 3.86 | 87 | .238 | .484 | 3 | .000 | -0 | | -2 | | -0.2 |

HAUGHT, GARY Gary Allen B9.29.1970 Tacoma WA BB/TR/6-1/190 [OakA92 22/620] d7.16 Col Louisiana-Lafayette

| 1997 | Oak A | 0 | 0 | — | 6 | 0 | 0 | 0-0 | 11.1 | 9 | 9 | 3 | 2 | 6-0 | 11 | 7.15 | 64 | .279 | .385 | 0 | — | 0 | | -3 | | -0. |

HAUGSTAD, PHIL Philip Donald B2.23.1924 Black River Falls WI D10.21.1998 Black River Falls WI BR/TR/6-2/165* d9.1

1947	Bro N	1	0	1.000	6	1	0	0	12.2	14	4	1	0	4	4	2.84	145	.298	.353	2	.000	0	43	2		0.
1948	Bro N	0	0	—	1	0	0	0	1	1	0	0	0	0	1	0.00	—	.333	.333	0	—	0	0	0		0.
1951	Bro N	0	1	.000	21	1	0	0	30.2	28	25	4	3	24	22	6.46	61	.233	.374	1	.000	-0	270	-9		-0.
1952	Cin N	0	0	—	9	0	0	0	12	8	9	1	1	13	1	6.75	56	.190	.393	1	.000	-0		-4		-0.
Total	4	1	2	.333	37	2	0	0	56.1	51	38	6	4	41	28	5.59	70	.241	.374	4	.000	-0	157	-11		-0.

HAUSMAN, TOM Thomas Matthew B3.31.1953 Mobridge SD BR/TR/6-5/200* [MilA71 10/224] d4.26

1975	Mil A	3	6	.333	29	9	1	0-0	112	110	57	7	6	47-7	46	4.10	94	.258	.338	0	—	0	76	-2		-0.
1976	Mil A	0	0	—	3	0	0	0-0	3.1	3	2	0	0	3-1	1	5.40	65	.250	.400	0	—	0		-1		-0.
1978	NY N	3	5	.500	12	10	1	0-0	51.2	58	28	6	1	9-1	16	4.70	75	.287	.318	17-0-1	.176	0	94	-6		-0.
1979	NY N	2	6	.250	19	10	1	2-1	78.2	65	25	6	4	19-1	33	2.75	135	.226	.282	26-0-1	.115	-1	69	9		0.
1980	NY N	6	5	.545	55	4	0	1-0	122	125	63	12	8	26-8	53	3.98	91	.266	.307	16-0-1	.063	-1	87	-6		-0.
1981	NY N	0	1	.000	20	0	0	0-0	33	32	8	3	0	7-1	13	2.18	162	.235	.273	0	—	0		6	58	0.

YEAR	TM LG	W	L	PCT	G	GS	CG-SHO	SV-BS	IP	H	R	HR	HB	BB-IB	SO	ERA	AERA	OAV	OOB	AB-HR-SH	AVG	PB	SUP	APR	DL	PW
1982	NY N	1	2	.333	21	0	0	0-0	36.2	44	26	4	2	6-1	16	4.42	83	.295	.323	2	.000	-0		-5	85	-0.4
	Atl N	0	0	—	3	0	0	0-0	3.2	6	2	0	4	4-2	2	4.91	75	.500	.588	0	—	0		0		0.0
	Year	1	2	.333	24	0	0	0-0	40.1	50	28	4	2	10-3	18	4.46	82	.311	.348	2	.000	-0		-6		-0.4
Total 7		15	23	.395	160	33	2	3-1	441	439	211	37	16	121-22	180	3.80	97	.262	.315	63-0-3	.111	-2	80	-5	143	-0.6

HAUSMANN, CLEM Clemens Raymond B8.17.1919 Houston TX D8.29.1972 Baytown TX BR/TR/5-9/165 d4.28

YEAR	TM LG	W	L	PCT	G	GS	CG-SHO	SV-BS	IP	H	R	HR	HB	BB-IB	SO	ERA	AERA	OAV	OOB	AB-HR-SH	AVG	PB	SUP	APR	DL	PW
1944	Bos A	4	7	.364	32	12	3	2	137	139	55	6	3	69	43	3.42	99	.266	.355	38-0-1	.079	-3	74	2		-0.1
1945	Bos A	5	7	.417	31	13	4-2	2	125	131	77	5	2	60	30	5.04	68	.270	.352	39	.103	-3	65	-21		-2.1
1949	Phi A	0	0	—	1	0	0	0	1	0	1	0	0	2	0	9.00	46	.000	.500	0	—	0		0		0.0
Total 3		9	14	.391	64	25	7-2	4	263	270	133	11	5	131	73	4.21	81	.267	.354	77-0-1	.091	-5	69	-19		-2.2

HAVENS, BRAD Bradley David B11.17.1959 Highland Park MI BL/TL/6-1/196(180-196) [CalA77 8/189] d6.5

YEAR	TM LG	W	L	PCT	G	GS	CG-SHO	SV-BS	IP	H	R	HR	HB	BB-IB	SO	ERA	AERA	OAV	OOB	AB-HR-SH	AVG	PB	SUP	APR	DL	PW
1981	Min A	3	6	.333	14	12	1-1	0-0	78	76	33	6	1	24-4	43	3.58	110	.257	.314	0	—	0	61	4		0.4
1982	Min A	10	14	.417	33	32	4-1	0-1	208.2	201	112	32	0	80-4	129	4.31	99	.250	.317	0	—	0	85	-3		-0.4
1983	Min A	5	8	.385	16	14	1	0-0	80.1	110	75	11	0	38-3	40	8.18	52	.333	.393	0	—	0	111	-31		-4.0
1985	Bal A	0	1	.000	8	1	0	0-0	14.1	20	14	4	0	10-1	19	8.79	46	.333	.429	0	—	0	45	-7		-0.4
1986	Bal A	3	3	.500	46	1	0	1-1	71	64	37	7	0	29-1	57	4.56	91	.248	.323	0	—	0		-2		-0.1
1987	LA N	0	0	—	31	1	0	1-1	35.1	30	18	2	1	23-11	23	4.33	92	.227	.346	2	.000	-0	91	-1		-0.1
1988	LA N	0	0	—	9	0	0	0-0	9.2	15	5	1	0	4-0	6	4.66	72	.357	.404	1	.000	-0		-1	26	-0.1
	Cle A	2	3	.400	28	0	0	1-1	57.1	62	22	7	0	17-3	30	3.14	132	.273	.321	0	—	0		6		0.0
1989	Cle A	0	0	—	7	0	0	0-0	13.1	18	6	3	0	7-2	6	4.05	98	.353	.417	0	—	0		6		0.5
	Det A	1	2	.333	13	1	0	0-1	22.2	28	14	3	3	14-2	15	5.56	69	.308	.409	0	—	0	0	0		-0.4
	Year	1	2	.333	20	1	0	0-1	36	46	20	6	3	21-4	21	5.00	78	.324	.412	0	—	0	0	-3		-0.4
Total 8		24	37	.393	205	61	6-2	3-5	590.2	624	336	76	5	246-31	370	4.81	86	.272	.341	3	.000	0	86	-39	26	-4.5

HAWBLITZEL, RYAN Ryan Wade B4.30.1971 West Palm Beach FL BR/TR/6-2/185 [ChiN90 2/63] d6.9

YEAR	TM LG	W	L	PCT	G	GS	CG-SHO	SV-BS	IP	H	R	HR	HB	BB-IB	SO	ERA	AERA	OAV	OOB	AB-HR-SH	AVG	PB	SUP	APR	DL	PW
1996	Col N	0	1	.000	8	0	0	0-0	15	18	12	2	0	6-0	7	6.00	87	.290	.348	1	.000	-0		-1		-0.1

HAWK, ED Edward B2.22.1888 Neosho MO D3.26.1936 Neosho MO BL/TR/5-11/175 d9.7

YEAR	TM LG	W	L	PCT	G	GS	CG-SHO	SV-BS	IP	H	R	HR	HB	BB-IB	SO	ERA	AERA	OAV	OOB	AB-HR-SH	AVG	PB	SUP	APR	DL	PW
1911	StL A	0	4	.000	5	4	4	0-0	37.2	38	18	1	4	8	14	3.35	101	.253	.309	13	.154	-1	16	1		0.0

HAWKE, BILL William Victor "Dick" B4.28.1870 Elsmere DE D12.11.1902 Wilmington DE BR/TR/5-8.5/169 d7.28

YEAR	TM LG	W	L	PCT	G	GS	CG-SHO	SV-BS	IP	H	R	HR	HB	BB-IB	SO	ERA	AERA	OAV	OOB	AB-HR-SH	AVG	PB	SUP	APR	DL	PW
1892	StL N	5	5	.500	14	11	10-1	0	97.1	108	59	2	8	45	55	3.70	86	.270	.355	45	.089	-4*	103	-6		-0.9
1893	StL N	0	1	.000	1	1	0	0	5.1	9	9	0	1	3	1	5.06	93	.360	.429	3	.333	-4	74	-2		-0.2
	Bal N	11	16	.407	29	29	22-1	0	225	248	175	8	9	108	69	4.76	100	.271	.354	93-1	.172	-4	90	-2		-0.5
	Year	11	17	.393	30	30	22-1	0	230.1	257	184	8	9	111	70	4.77	100	.274	.356	96-1	.177	-4	89	-2		-0.7
1894	†Bal N	16	9	.640	32	25	17	3	206	264	174	9	12	78	68	5.81	94	.308	.374	92-1-5	.304	2	112	-7		-0.7
Total 3		32	31	.508	76	66	49-2	3	533.2	629	417	19	29	234	193	4.98	95	.286	.363	233-2-5	.210	-7	101	-17		-2.1

HAWKINS, LA TROY La Troy B12.21.1972 Gary IN BR/TR/6-5/204(193-215) [MinA91 7/180] d4.29

YEAR	TM LG	W	L	PCT	G	GS	CG-SHO	SV-BS	IP	H	R	HR	HB	BB-IB	SO	ERA	AERA	OAV	OOB	AB-HR-SH	AVG	PB	SUP	APR	DL	PW
1995	Min A	2	3	.400	6	6	1	0-0	27	39	29	3	1	12-0	9	8.67	56	.339	.397	0	—	0	93	-12		-1.6
1996	Min A	1	1	.500	7	6	0	0-0	26.1	42	24	8	0	9-0	24	8.20	63	.372	.415	0	—	0	129	-8		-0.5
1997	Min A	6	12	.333	20	20	0	0-0	103.1	134	71	19	4	47-0	58	5.84	80	.317	.389	1	.000	-0	86	-13		-1.8
1998	Min A	7	14	.333	33	33	0	0-0	190.1	227	126	27	5	61-1	105	5.25	91	.299	.350	1	.000	-0	90	-13		-1.8
1999	Min A	10	14	.417	33	33	1	0-0	174.1	238	136	29	1	60-2	103	6.66	78	.323	.373	2	.000	-0	80	-26		-3.0
2000	Min A	2	5	.286	66	0	0	14-0	87.2	85	34	7	1	32-1	59	3.39	155	.256	.322	1	.000	-0		18		1.7
2001	Min A	1	5	.167	62	0	0	28-9	51.1	59	34	3	1	39-3	36	5.96	78	.291	.401	0	—	0		-6		-1.2
2002	†Min A	6	0	1.000	65	0	0	0-3	80.1	63	23	5	0	15-1	63	2.13	210	.217	.253	0	—	0		20		1.3
2003	†Min A	9	3	.750	74	0	0	2-6	77.1	69	20	4	1	15-1	75	1.86	242	.239	.278	0-0-1	—	0		21		3.0
2004	Chi N	5	4	.556	77	0	0	25-9	82	72	27	10	2	14-5	69	2.63	168	.233	.269	0	—	0		15		2.2
2005	Chi N	1	4	.200	21	0	0	4-4	19	18	9	4	0	7-0	13	3.32	132	.250	.316	0	—	0		1		0.3
	SF N	1	4	.200	45	0	0	2-5	37.1	40	18	3	0	17-3	30	4.10	104	.272	.345	0	—	0		1		0.1
	Year	2	8	.200	66	0	0	6-9	56.1	58	27	7	0	24-3	43	3.83	112	.265	.336	0	—	0		2		0.4
Total 11		51	69	.425	509	98	2	75-36	956.1	1086	551	122	16	328-17	644	4.77	100	.287	.343	5-0-1	.000	-1	91	-2	24	-0.6

HAWKINS, ANDY Melton Andrew B1.21.1960 Waco TX BR/TR/6-3/223(200-223) [SDN78 1/5] d7.17

YEAR	TM LG	W	L	PCT	G	GS	CG-SHO	SV-BS	IP	H	R	HR	HB	BB-IB	SO	ERA	AERA	OAV	OOB	AB-HR-SH	AVG	PB	SUP	APR	DL	PW
1982	SD N	2	5	.286	15	10	0	0-0	63.2	66	33	4	2	27-3	25	4.10	84	.274	.345	15-0-3	.000	-2	124	-5		-0.7
1983	SD N	5	7	.417	21	19	4-1	0-0	119.2	106	50	8	5	48-4	59	2.93	120	.244	.324	31-0-6	.065	-1	86	5		0.4
1984	†SD N	8	9	.471	36	22	2-1	0-0	146	143	90	13	2	72-2	77	4.68	77	.254	.339	41-0-3	.195	0	122	-20		-2.1
1985	SD N	18	8	.692	33	33	5-2	0-0	228.2	229	88	18	4	65-8	69	3.15	113	.267	.317	77-0-13	.078	-4	112	12		0.8
1986	SD N	10	8	.556	37	35	3-1	0-0	209.1	218	111	24	5	75-7	117	4.30	85	.268	.332	67-0-6	.149	-1	113	-14		-1.3
1987	SD N	3	10	.231	24	20	0	0-0	117.2	131	71	16	2	49-2	51	5.05	79	.287	.356	32-0-5	.156	-0	112	-13		-1.3
1988	SD N	14	11	.560	33	33	4-2	0-0	217.2	196	88	16	6	76-4	91	3.35	102	.244	.312	62-0-10	.113	-2	83	2		-0.1
1989	NY A	15	15	.500	34	34	5-2	0-0	208.1	238	127	23	6	76-6	74	4.80	81	.290	.354	0	—	0	98	-23		-3.0
1990	NY A	5	12	.294	28	26	2-1	0-0	157.2	156	101	20	2	82-3	74	5.37	74	.260	.349	0	—	0	86	-22		-2.2
1991	NY A	0	2	.000	4	3	0	0-0	12.2	23	15	5	0	6-0	5	9.95	42	.383	.439	0	—	0	88	-8		-0.9
	Oak A	4	4	.500	15	14	1	0-0	77	68	41	5	5	36-0	40	4.79	80	.237	.329	0	—	0	120	-7		-0.7
	Year	4	6	.400	19	17	1	0-0	89.2	91	56	10	5	42-0	45	5.52	71	.262	.348	0	—	0	115	-14		-1.6
Total 10		84	91	.480	280	249	27-10	0-0	1558.1	1574	815	152	39	612-39	706	4.22	87	.265	.335	325-0-46	.117	-8	104	-93	34	-11.1

HAWKINS, WYNN Wynn Firth "Hawk" B2.20.1936 E.Palestine OH BR/TR/6-3/190* d4.22

YEAR	TM LG	W	L	PCT	G	GS	CG-SHO	SV-BS	IP	H	R	HR	HB	BB-IB	SO	ERA	AERA	OAV	OOB	AB-HR-SH	AVG	PB	SUP	APR	DL	PW
1960	Cle A	4	4	.500	15	9	1	0	66	68	32	10	1	39-2	39	4.23	88	.269	.366	20-0-1	.100	-1	86	-2		-0.3
1961	Cle A	7	9	.438	30	21	3-1	0	133	139	72	16	2	59-1	51	4.06	97	.270	.344	37-0-3	.108	-1	95	-4		-0.4
1962	Cle A	0	0	1.000	3	0	0	0	3.2	9	5	1	0	1-0	0	7.36	53	.429	.455	0	—	0		-2		-0.4
Total 3		12	13	.480	48	30	4-1	1	202.2	216	109	27	3	99-3	90	4.17	93	.274	.354	57-0-4	.105	-2	93	-8		-1.3

HAWLEY, PINK Emerson Pink B12.5.1872 Beaver Dam WI D9.19.1938 Beaver Dam WI BL/TR/5-10/185 d8.13

YEAR	TM LG	W	L	PCT	G	GS	CG-SHO	SV-BS	IP	H	R	HR	HB	BB-IB	SO	ERA	AERA	OAV	OOB	AB-HR-SH	AVG	PB	SUP	APR	DL	PW
1892	StL N	6	14	.300	20	20	18	0	166.1	160	116	4	11	63	63	3.19	100	.243	.319	71-1	.169	-2	86	-10		-1.3
1893	StL N	5	17	.227	31	24	21	1	227	249	184	5	20	103	73	4.60	103	.270	.356	91	.286	7*	80	1		0.5
1894	StL N	19	27	.413	53	41	36	0	392.2	481	306	14	21	149	120	4.90	111	.298	.365	163-2-5	.264	2	73	20		1.8
1895	Pit N	31	22	.585	56	50	44-4	0	444.1	449	242	7	33	122	142	3.18	142	.258	.319	185-5-3	.308	14*	93	66		7.4
1896	Pit N	22	21	.512	49	43	37-2	0	378	382	197	2	28	157	137	3.57	118	.260	.343	163-1-3	.239	2*	82	29		2.9
1897	Pit N	18	18	.500	40	39	33	0	311.1	362	221	7	26	94	88	4.80	87	.288	.350	130	.231	-2	87	-19		-1.8
1898	Cin N	27	11	.711	43	37	32-3	0	331	357	163	5	22	91	69	3.37	114	.273	.331	130-1-5	.185	-4	90	18		1.1
1899	Cin N	14	17	.452	34	29	25	1	250.1	289	161	7	20	65	46	4.24	92	.289	.344	101	.218	-1	108	-9		-1.1
1900	NY N	18	18	.500	41	38	34-2	0	329.1	377	204	7	20	89	80	3.53	103	.287	.341	123-1-4	.203	-2	104	2		0.2
1901	Mil A	7	14	.333	26	23	17	0	182.1	228	133	3	9	41	50	4.59	78	.302	.346	73-0-4	.260	2*	77	-18		-1.4
Total 10		167	179	.483	393	344	297-11	3	3012.2	3334	1927	61	210	974	868	3.96	107	.277	.342	1230-11-24	.241	15	87	80		8.3

HAWLEY, SCOTT Marvin Hiram B Painesville OH D4.28.1904 Alliance OH d9.22

YEAR	TM LG	W	L	PCT	G	GS	CG-SHO	SV-BS	IP	H	R	HR	HB	BB-IB	SO	ERA	AERA	OAV	OOB	AB-HR-SH	AVG	PB	SUP	APR	DL	PW
1894	Bos N	0	1	.000	1	1	1	0	7	10	6	0	2	7	1	7.71	74	.333	.487	3	.000	-1	50	-1		-0.1

HAYDEL, HAL John Harold B7.9.1944 Houma LA BR/TR/6-0/190* d9.7

YEAR	TM LG	W	L	PCT	G	GS	CG-SHO	SV-BS	IP	H	R	HR	HB	BB-IB	SO	ERA	AERA	OAV	OOB	AB-HR-SH	AVG	PB	SUP	APR	DL	PW
1970	Min A	2	1	1.000	4	0	0	0-0	9	7	3	2	0	4-0	4	3.00	123	.226	.306	3-1-0	.667	2		1		0.4
1971	Min A	4	2	.667	31	0	0	1-2	40	33	19	3	2	20-1	29	4.27	83	.243	.346	3	.333	0		-2		-0.3
Total 2		6	2	.750	35	0	0	1-2	49	40	22	5	2	24-1	33	4.04	88	.240	.338	6-1-0	.500	2		-1		0.1

HAYDEN, LEFTY Eugene Franklin B4.14.1935 San Francisco CA BL/TL/6-2/175 d6.26

YEAR	TM LG	W	L	PCT	G	GS	CG-SHO	SV-BS	IP	H	R	HR	HB	BB-IB	SO	ERA	AERA	OAV	OOB	AB-HR-SH	AVG	PB	SUP	APR	DL	PW
1958	Cin N	0	0	—	2	0	0	0-0	3.2	5	2	0	0	1-0	3	4.91	84	.313	.353	0	—	0		0		0.0

HAYES, BEN Ben Joseph B8.4.1957 Niagara Falls NY BR/TR/6-1/180* d6.25 Col South Florida

YEAR	TM LG	W	L	PCT	G	GS	CG-SHO	SV-BS	IP	H	R	HR	HB	BB-IB	SO	ERA	AERA	OAV	OOB	AB-HR-SH	AVG	PB	SUP	APR	DL	PW
1982	Cin N	2	0	1.000	26	0	0	2-1	45.2	37	12	6	0	22-5	38	1.97	186	.219	.307	4-0-2	.000	-0		8		0.3
1983	Cin N	4	6	.400	60	0	0	7-3	69.1	82	53	8	1	37-6	44	6.49	59	.301	.381	5	.000	-1		-19		-2.9
Total 2		6	6	.500	86	0	0	9-4	115	119	65	14	1	59-11	82	4.70	80	.270	.353	9-0-2	.000	-1		-11		-2.6

HAYES, JIM James Millard "Whitey" B2.25.1912 Montevallo AL D11.27.1993 Decatur GA BL/TL/6-1/168 d7.13

YEAR	TM LG	W	L	PCT	G	GS	CG-SHO	SV-BS	IP	H	R	HR	HB	BB-IB	SO	ERA	AERA	OAV	OOB	AB-HR-SH	AVG	PB	SUP	APR	DL	PW
1935	Was A	2	4	.333	7	4	1	0	28	38	24	0	0	23	9	8.36	52	.322	.433	8-0-2	.250	-0	90	-12		-2.0

HAYNER, FRED — Fred Ames B11.3.1871 Janesville WI D1.14.1929 Lake Forest IL 6-0/160 d8.19

YEAR	TM LG	W	L	PCT	G	GS	CG-SHO	SV-BS	IP	H	R	HR	HB	BB-IB	SO	ERA	AERA	OAV	OOB	AB-HR-SH	AVG	PB	SUP	APR	DL	PW
1890	Pit N	0	0	—	1	0	0		4	7	9	2	0	5	1	13.50	24	.368	.500	2	.000	-0		-5		-0.2

HAYNES, HEATH — Heath Burnett B11.30.1968 Wheeling WV BR/TR/6-0/180 d6.1 Col Western Kentucky

YEAR	TM LG	W	L	PCT	G	GS	CG-SHO	SV-BS	IP	H	R	HR	HB	BB-IB	SO	ERA	AERA	OAV	OOB	AB-HR-SH	AVG	PB	SUP	APR	DL	PW
1994	Mon N	0	0	—	4	0	0	0-0	3.2	3	1	0	0	3-0	1	0.00	⌐	.231	.353	0	—	0		1		0.1

HAYNES, JIMMY — Jimmy Wayne B9.5.1972 LaGrange GA BR/TR/6-4/203(175-220) [BalA91 7/186] d9.13

YEAR	TM LG	W	L	PCT	G	GS	CG-SHO	SV-BS	IP	H	R	HR	HB	BB-IB	SO	ERA	AERA	OAV	OOB	AB-HR-SH	AVG	PB	SUP	APR	DL	PW
1995	Bal A	2	1	.667	4	3	0	0-0	24	11	6	2	0	12-1	22	2.25	212	.136	.247	0	—	0	97	7		0.8
1996	Bal A	6	5	.333	26	11	0	1-0	89	122	84	14	2	58-1	65	8.29	60	.333	.422	0	—	0	118	-31		-2.5
1997	Oak A	3	6	.333	13	13	0	0-0	73.1	74	38	7	2	40-1	65	4.42	104	.262	.354	2	.000	-0	88	2		0.2
1998	Oak A	11	9	.550	33	33	1-1	0-0	194.1	229	124	25	5	88-4	134	5.09	91	.298	.370	3	.000	-0	118	-10		-0.9
1999	Oak A	7	12	.368	30	25	0	0-0	142	158	112	21	2	80-3	93	6.34	75	.282	.370	4-0-1	.000	-0	89	-26		-2.9
2000	Mil N	12	13	.480	33	33	0	0-0	199.1	228	128	21	7	100-7	88	5.33	87	.295	.378	64-0-5	.125	-0	97	-15		-1.6
2001	Mil N	8	17	.320	31	29	0	0-0	172.2	182	98	20	4	78-17	112	4.85	89	.279	.356	52-0-5	.154	0*	88	-9	34	-1.1
2002	Cin N	15	10	.600	34	34	0	0-0	196.2	210	97	21	3	81-4	126	4.12	104	.278	.348	61-0-10	.164	-0*	87	5		0.5
2003	Cin N	2	12	.143	18	18	1	0-0	94.1	118	74	14	3	57-3	49	6.30	66	.311	.404	23-0-7	.261	1	94	-24	95	-2.8
2004	Cin N	0	3	.000	5	4	0	0-0	15	26	17	3	2	7-0	8	9.60	45	.382	.455	4	.000	-0	81	-9		-1.4
Total 10		63	89	.414	227	203	2-1	1-0	1200.2	1358	778	148	30	601-41	762	5.37	84	.290	.371	213-0-28	.150	-1	96	-110	129	-11.7

HAYNES, JOE — Joseph Walton B9.21.1917 Lincolnton GA D1.6.1967 Hopkins MN BR/TR/6-2.5/190* d4.24 C3

YEAR	TM LG	W	L	PCT	G	GS	CG-SHO	SV-BS	IP	H	R	HR	HB	BB-IB	SO	ERA	AERA	OAV	OOB	AB-HR-SH	AVG	PB	SUP	APR	DL	PW
1939	Was A	8	12	.400	27	20	10-1	0	173	186	118	11	0	78	64	5.36	81	.276	.352	67-0-2	.209	0	90	-20		-1.9
1940	Was A	3	6	.333	22	7	1	0	63.1	85	50	4	1	34	23	6.54	64	.327	.407	19-0-1	.105	-2	114	-16		-2.0
1941	Chi A	0	0	—	8	0	0	0	28	30	13	0	0	11	18	3.86	106	.280	.347	11	.273	0		1		0.1
1942	Chi A	8	5	.615	**40**	1	1	6	103	88	37	6	3	47	35	2.62	137	.234	.324	28-0-1	.179	2	126	1		0.3
1943	Chi A	7	2	.778	35	2	1	3	109.1	114	51	2	2	32	37	2.96	113	.263	.306	34	.265	2	67	14		1.2
1944	Chi A	5	6	.455	33	12	8	2	154.1	148	55	5	0	43	44	2.57	134	.254	.306	50-0-1	.200	1	126	-1		-0.3
1945	Chi A	5	5	.500	14	13	8-1	1	104	92	44	5	1	29	34	3.76	91	.237	.291	40	.175	-2*	126	-2		0.2
1946	Chi A	7	9	.438	32	23	9	2	177.1	203	80	14	4	60	50	3.97	107	.284	.344	57-0-3	.246	3	88	-2		0.2
1947	Chi A	14	6	.700	29	22	7-2	0	149.2	167	79	13	2	52	40	**2.42**	151	.250	.312	65-0-1	.262	2	86	22		2.6
1948	Chi A☆	9	10	.474	27	22	6	0	182	174	65	14	2	61	50	3.26	125	.250	.313	65-0-3	.160	-1	77	2		0.0
1949	Was A	2	9	.182	37	10	0	2	96.1	106	77	6	3	55	19	6.26	68	.283	.380	25	.240	1	93	-21		-2.1
1950	Was A	5	5	.583	27	10	1-1	0	101.2	124	73	14	5	46	15	4.56	90	.290	.382	35-0-1	.200	2	130	-6		-1.2
1951	Was A	1	4	.200	26	3	1	2	73	85	46	9	1	37	18	4.50	79	.275	.364	19	.105	1	86	-6		-0.2
1952	Was A	2	3	.000	22	2	0	3	66	70	35	2	1	35	18	4.77		.272	.342	19	.105					-0.4
Total 14		76	82	.481	379	147	53-5	21	1581	1672	823	95	26	620	475	4.01	96	.272	.342	521-1-14	.213	7	94	-36		-2.3

HAYWARD, RAY — Raymond Alton B4.27.1961 Enid OK BL/TL/6-1/190* [SDN83 1/10] d9.20 Col Oklahoma

YEAR	TM LG	W	L	PCT	G	GS	CG-SHO	SV-BS	IP	H	R	HR	HB	BB-IB	SO	ERA	AERA	OAV	OOB	AB-HR-SH	AVG	PB	SUP	APR	DL	PW
1986	SD N	0	2	.000	3	3	0	0-0	10	16	12	1	0	4-0	6	9.00	41	.340	.392	4	.000	-0*	106	-6		-1.0
1987	SD N	0	0	—	4	0	0	0-0	6	12	11	3	0	3-0	2	16.50	24	.444	.500	1	.000	-0		-8		-0.4
1988	Tex A	4	6	.400	12	12	1-1	0-0	62.2	63	44	6	0	35-0	37	5.46	75	.276	.367	0	—	0	87	-10	57	-1.3
Total 3		4	8	.333	19	15	1-1	0-0	78.2	91	67	10	0	42-0	45	6.75	60	.301	.382	5	.000	-1	90	-24	57	-2.7

HAYWOOD, BILL — William Kiernan B4.21.1937 Colon, Pan BR/TR/6-3/205 d7.28 Col North Carolina-Asheville

YEAR	TM LG	W	L	PCT	G	GS	CG-SHO	SV-BS	IP	H	R	HR	HB	BB-IB	SO	ERA	AERA	OAV	OOB	AB-HR-SH	AVG	PB	SUP	APR	DL	PW
1968	Was A	0	0	—	14	0	0		23	27	16	1	2	12-0	10	4.70	62	.314	.406	0	—	0		-6		-0.3

HEAD, ED — Edward Marvin B1.25.1918 Selma LA D1.31.1980 Bastrop LA BR/TR/6-1/175 d7.27 Mil 1944-45

YEAR	TM LG	W	L	PCT	G	GS	CG-SHO	SV-BS	IP	H	R	HR	HB	BB-IB	SO	ERA	AERA	OAV	OOB	AB-HR-SH	AVG	PB	SUP	APR	DL	PW
1940	Bro N	1	2	.333	13	5	2	0	39.1	40	21	0	0	18	13	4.12	97	.260	.337	11	.182	-0*	113	-1		-0.2
1942	Bro N	10	6	.625	36	15	5-1	4	136.2	118	60	11	3	47	78	3.56	92	.231	.300	39-0-4	.333	4	124	-3		0.0
1943	Bro N	9	10	.474	47	18	7-3	6	169.2	166	75	7	0	66	83	3.66	92	.250	.318	46-0-9	.152	-2	111	-4		-0.6
1944	Bro N	4	3	.571	9	8	5-1	0	63.1	54	21	2	0	19	17	2.70	132	.232	.342	19-0-4	.263	1	86	7		0.8
1946	Bro N	3	2	.600	13	7	3-1	1	56	56	24	2	0	24	17	3.21	105	.267	.342	16	.313	2	109	1		0.2
Total 5		27	23	.540	118	53	22-6	11	465	434	201	24	3	174	208	3.48	98	.245	.314	131-0-17	.244	5	111	0		0.2

HEAD, RALPH — Ralph B8.30.1893 Tallapoosa GA D10.8.1962 Muscadine AL BR/TR/5-10/175 d4.18

YEAR	TM LG	W	L	PCT	G	GS	CG-SHO	SV-BS	IP	H	R	HR	HB	BB-IB	SO	ERA	AERA	OAV	OOB	AB-HR-SH	AVG	PB	SUP	APR	DL	PW
1923	Phi N	2	9	.182	35	13	5	0	132.1	185	111	13	1	57	24	6.66	69	.341	.404	42	.071	-5	91	-23		-2.1

HEALEY, TOM — Thomas F. B1853 Cranston RI D2.6.1891 Lewiston ME TR d6.13

YEAR	TM LG	W	L	PCT	G	GS	CG-SHO	SV-BS	IP	H	R	HR	HB	BB-IB	SO	ERA	AERA	OAV	OOB	AB-HR-SH	AVG	PB	SUP	APR	DL	PW
1878	Pro N	0	3	.000	3	3	3	0	24	27	17	1		7	2	3.00	74	.278	.327	9	.222	0	40	-2		-0.2
	Ind N	6	4	.600	11	10	9	1	89	98	50	1		13	18	2.22	91	.270	.295	45	.178	-1*	92	-3		-0.3
	Year	6	7	.462	14	13	12	1	113	125	67	2		20	20	2.39	87	.272	.302	54	.185	-1	79	-4		-0.5

HEALY, JOHN — John J. "Egyptian","Long John" B10.27.1866 Cairo IL D3.16.1899 St.Louis MO BR/TR/6-2/158 d9.11

YEAR	TM LG	W	L	PCT	G	GS	CG-SHO	SV-BS	IP	H	R	HR	HB	BB-IB	SO	ERA	AERA	OAV	OOB	AB-HR-SH	AVG	PB	SUP	APR	DL	PW
1885	StL N	1	7	.125	8	8	8	0	66	54	37	0		20	32	3.00	92	.210	.267	24	.042	-3	26	-2		-0.5
1886	StL N	17	23	.425	43	41	39-3	0	353.2	315	213	5		118	213	2.88	112	.230	.291	145	.097	-12	83	12		0.0
1887	Ind N	12	29	.293	41	41	40-3	0	341	415	292	24	15	108	75	5.17	80	.294	.350	138-3	.174	-4	74	-37		-3.6
1888	Ind N	12	24	.333	37	37	36-1	0	321.1	347	199	13	15	42	124	3.89	76	.267	.320	131-1	.229	4	102	-32		-2.6
1889	Was N	1	11	.083	13	12	10	0	101	139	111	2	5	38	49	6.24	63	.317	.378	45-1	.222	1	84	-27		-0.3
	Chi N	1	4	.200	5	5	5	0	46	48	35	4	4	18	22	4.50	92	.261	.340	20	.100	-2	77	-1		-2.4
	Year	2	15	.118	18	17	15	0	147	187	146	6	9	56	71	5.69	70	.301	.367	65-1	.185	-1	82	-30		4.3
1890	Tol AA	22	21	.512	46	46	44-2	0	389	326	201	5	24	127	225	2.89	137	.221	.293	156-1	.218	7*	76	40		-0.5
1891	Bal AA	8	10	.444	23	22	19	0	170.1	179	124	6	5	57	54	3.75	99	.261	.322	64	.141	-2	102	-1		-0.7
1892	Bal N	3	6	.333	9	8	5	0	68.1	82	51	4	2	21	24	4.74	72	.286	.339	27	.222	0	90	-7		-0.3
	Lou N	1	1	.500	2	2	2	0	18.1	15	7	0	0	5	4	1.96	156	.214	.267	7	.286	1	89	-5		-0.4
	Year	4	7	.364	11	10	7	0	86.2	97	58	4	2	26	28	4.15	81	.272	.325	34	.235	1	83	-53		-0.5
Total 8		78	136	.364	227	222	208-9	1	1875	1920	1274	63	70	599	822	3.84	94	.257	.318	757-6	.174	-0	83	-53		-5.7

HEARD, CHARLIE — Charles B1.30.1872 Philadelphia PA D2.20.1945 Philadelphia PA BR/TR/6-2/190 d7.14 ▲

YEAR	TM LG	W	L	PCT	G	GS	CG-SHO	SV-BS	IP	H	R	HR	HB	BB-IB	SO	ERA	AERA	OAV	OOB	AB-HR-SH	AVG	PB	SUP	APR	DL	PW
1890	Pit N	0	6	.000	6	6	5	0	44	75	65	5	2	32	13	8.39	39	.364	.454	43	.186	-1*	67	-27		-2.5

HEARD, JAY — Jehosie B1.17.1920 Athens GA D11.18.1999 Birmingham AL BL/TL/5-7/155 d4.24 Negro Lg 1945-58

YEAR	TM LG	W	L	PCT	G	GS	CG-SHO	SV-BS	IP	H	R	HR	HB	BB-IB	SO	ERA	AERA	OAV	OOB	AB-HR-SH	AVG	PB	SUP	APR	DL	PW
1954	Bal A	0	0	—	2	0	0		3.1	6	5	1	0	3	2	13.50	27	.375	.474	0	—	0		-4		-0.2

HEARN, BUNNY — Charles Bunn B5.21.1891 Chapel Hill NC D10.10.1959 Wilson NC BL/TL/5-11/190 d9.17 Col Elon

YEAR	TM LG	W	L	PCT	G	GS	CG-SHO	SV-BS	IP	H	R	HR	HB	BB-IB	SO	ERA	AERA	OAV	OOB	AB-HR-SH	AVG	PB	SUP	APR	DL	PW
1910	StL N	1	3	.250	5	5	4	0	39	49	22	2	1	16	14	5.08	59	.322	.391	15-1-0	.133	-0	130	-7		-0.6
1911	StL N	0	0	—	2	0	0	0	2.2	7	4	1	0	0	1	13.50	25	.538	.538	1	.000	-0	96	0		0.1
1913	NY N	1	1	.500	2	2	2	0	13	13	6	0	0	7	8	2.77	113	.277	.370	5	.400	1	96	0		0.1
1915	Pit F	6	11	.353	29	17	8-1	0	175.2	187	74	6	2	37	49	3.38	80	.285	.326	53-0-2	.189	-0	68	-10		-1.0
1918	Bos N	5	6	.455	17	12	9-1	0	126.1	119	43	2	0	29	30	2.49	108	.256	.300	45-0-1	.178	-1	84	-13		0.3
1920	Bos N	0	3	.000	11	4	2	0	43	54	34	3	1	11	9	5.65	54	.329	.375	14	.143	-1	80	-29		-2.2
Total 6		13	24	.351	66	40	24-2	0	399.2	429	183	14	4	100	111	3.56	78	.287	.333	133-1-3	.180	-2	80	-29		-2.2

HEARN, BUNNY — Elmer Lafayette B1.13.1904 Brooklyn NY D3.31.1974 Venice FL BL/TL/5-8/160 d4.13

YEAR	TM LG	W	L	PCT	G	GS	CG-SHO	SV-BS	IP	H	R	HR	HB	BB-IB	SO	ERA	AERA	OAV	OOB	AB-HR-SH	AVG	PB	SUP	APR	DL	PW
1926	Bos N	4	9	.308	34	12	3	2	117.1	121	63	2	0	56	40	4.22	84	.276	.358	30-0-2	.100	-2	102	-9		-1.0
1927	Bos N	0	2	.000	8	0	0	0	12.2	16	9	0	0	9	5	4.26	87	.327	.431	5	.400	1		-2		-0.2
1928	Bos N	1	0	1.000	7	0	0	0	10	6	8	0	1	8	8	6.30	62	.167	.333	1	.000	-0	112	1		-0.2
1929	Bos N	2	0	1.000	10	1	0	0	18.1	18	10	2	0	9	12	4.42	106	.277	.365	2-0-1	.000	0	112	-13		-1.3
Total 4		7	13	.389	59	13	3	2	158.1	161	90	4	1	82	65	4.38	85	.273	.363	38-0-3	.132	-2	101	-13		-1.3

HEARN, JIM — James Tolbert B4.11.1921 Atlanta GA D6.10.1998 Boca Grande FL BR/TR/6-3/205* d4.17 Col Georgia Tech

YEAR	TM LG	W	L	PCT	G	GS	CG-SHO	SV-BS	IP	H	R	HR	HB	BB-IB	SO	ERA	AERA	OAV	OOB	AB-HR-SH	AVG	PB	SUP	APR	DL	PW
1947	StL N	12	7	.632	37	21	4-1	1	162	151	67	9	1	63	57	3.22	128	.248	.319	55-0-2	.145	-1	111	16		1.5
1948	StL N	8	6	.571	34	13	3	1	89.2	92	44	9	2	35	27	4.22	97	.271	.342	25-0-1	.200	-0*	88	0		-0.2
1949	StL N	1	3	.250	17	4	0	1	48	48	27	3	2	23	18	5.14	81	.294	.388	10	.100	-0	79	-4		-0.4
1950	StL N	0	1	.000	9	2	0	0	9	12	11	1	0	6	4	10.00	43	.333	.429	1	1.000	-0		-5		3.2
	NY N	11	3	.786	21	16	11-5	0	125	72	33	8	0	38	54	1.94	211	.169	.237	44-0-2	.136	-0	113	29		2.2
	Year	11	4	.733	22	16	11-5	0	134	84	44	9	0	44	58	2.49	165	.182	.253	45-0-2	.156	-0	113	23		0.9
1951	†NY N	17	9	.654	34	34	11	0	211.1	204	102	21	2	82	66	3.62	108	.251	.321	74-1-9	.182	4	128	-3		0.9
1952	NY N☆	14	7	.667	37	34	11-1	0	223.2	208	113	19	5	97	89	4.53	95	.266	.341	66-0-6	.136	0*	110	-4		-0.2
1953	NY N	9	12	.429	36	32	6	0	196.2	206	111	22	8													

YEAR	TM LG	W	L	PCT	G	GS	CG-SHO	SV-BS	IP	H	R	HR	HB	BB-IB	SO	ERA	AERA	OAV	OOB	AB-HR-SH	AVG	PB	SUP	APR	DL	PW
1954	NY N	8	8	.500	29	18	3-2	1	130	137	71	10	2	66	45	4.15	97	.272	.357	45-1-5	.111	-1	119	-3		-0.3
1955	NY N	14	16	.467	39	33	11-1	0	226.2	225	107	27	3	66-7	86	3.73	108	.260	.312	77-4-4	.156	1*	95	8		1.2
1956	NY N	5	11	.313	30	19	2	0	129.1	124	74	17	3	44-4	66	3.97	95	.254	.317	41	.098	-3*	76	-7		-1.1
1957	Phi N	5	1	.833	36	4	1	3	74	79	35	7	2	18-4	46	3.65	104	.274	.320	17-0-1	.000	-2	150	1		-0.1
1958	Phi N	5	3	.625	39	1	0	0	73.1	88	45	6	0	27-6	33	4.17	95	.292	.348	14	.000	-1	91	-5		-0.6
1959	Phi N	0	2	.000	6	0	0	0	11	15	7	2	0	6-1	2	5.73	72	.333	.412	2	.000	0		-2		-0.2
Total	13	109	89	.551	396	229	63-10	8	1703.2	1661	847	158	25	655-22	669	3.81	105	.255	.325	548-9-35	.141	-3	110	27		3.4

HEATH, SPENCER   Spencer Paul   B11.5.1894 Chicago IL   D1.25.1930 Chicago IL   BB/TR/6-0/170   d5.4

YEAR	TM LG	W	L	PCT	G	GS	CG-SHO	SV-BS	IP	H	R	HR	HB	BB-IB	SO	ERA	AERA	OAV	OOB	AB-HR-SH	AVG	PB	SUP	APR	DL	PW
1920	Chi A	0	0	—	4	0	0	0	7	19	12	1	0	2	0	15.43	24	.475	.500	3	.000	-1		-8		-0.4

HEATHCOCK, JEFF   Ronald Jeffrey   B11.18.1959 Covina CA   BR/TR/6-4/195*   [HouN80 S1/1]   d9.3   Col Oral Roberts

1983	Hou N	2	1	.667	6	3	0	1-0	28	19	14	1	4	4-0	12	3.21	107	.181	.216	6-0-3	.000	-1	120	0		-0.1
1985	Hou N	3	1	.750	14	7	1	1-0	56.1	50	25	9	1	13-0	25	3.36	104	.239	.286	16	.063	-1	192	1		0.1
1987	Hou N	4	2	.667	19	2	0	1-1	42.2	44	15	4	1	9-1	15	3.16	124	.277	.314	10-0-1	.000	-1	81	4		0.5
1988	Hou N	0	5	.000	17	1	0	0-0	31	33	25	2	1	16-6	12	5.81	57	.275	.360	3	.000	-1		-10		-1.0
Total	4	9	9	.500	56	13	1	3-1	158	146	79	16	4	42-7	64	3.76	95	.246	.297	35-0-4	.029	-2	142	-5		-1.0

HEATHCOTT, MIKE   Michael Joseph   B5.16.1969 Chicago IL   BR/TR/6-3/180   [ChiA91 13/358]   d8.28   Col Creighton

| 1998 | Chi A | 0 | 0 | — | 1 | 0 | 0 | 0-0 | 3 | 2 | 1 | 0 | 0 | 1-0 | 1 | 3.00 | 153 | .182 | .250 | 0 | — | 0 | | 1 | | 0.0 |

HEATON, NEAL   Neal   B3.3.1960 South Ozone Park NY   BL/TL/6-1/205*   [CleA81 2/39]   d9.3   Col Miami

1982	Cle A	0	2	.000	8	4	0	0-0	31	32	21	1	0	16-0	14	5.23	79	.260	.340	0	—	0	44	-4		-0.2
1983	Cle A	11	7	.611	39	16	4-3	7-2	149.1	157	79	11	1	44-10	75	4.16	103	.269	.319	0	—	0	101	1		0.0
1984	Cle A	12	15	.444	38	34	4-1	0-0	198.2	231	128	21	1	75-5	75	5.21	79	.293	.350	0	—	0	109	-24		-2.9
1985	Cle A	9	17	.346	36	33	5-1	0-1	207.2	244	119	19	7	80-2	82	4.90	85	.298	.362	0	—	0	85	-14		-1.6
1986	Cle A	3	6	.333	12	12	2	0-0	74.1	73	42	8	1	34-4	24	4.24	99	.254	.335	0	—	0	96	-2		-0.2
	Min A	4	9	.308	21	17	3	1-0	124.1	128	60	18	4	47-4	66	3.98	109	.273	.337	0	—	0	65	5		0.5
	Year	7	15	.318	33	29	5	1-0	198.2	201	102	26	5	81-8	90	4.08	105	.264	.336	0	—	0	77	4		0.3
1987	Mon N	13	10	.565	32	32	3-1	1-0	193.1	207	103	25	3	37-3	105	4.52	94	.273	.308	67-0-6	.209	2	102	-2		-0.1
1988	Mon N	3	10	.231	32	11	0	2-0	97.1	98	54	14	3	43-5	43	4.99	73	.271	.351	21-0-4	.143	-0	100	-10		-1.4
1989	Pit N	6	7	.462	42	18	1	0-1	147.1	127	55	12	6	55-12	67	3.05	111	.233	.309	42-0-2	.214	1*	96	6	21	0.6
1990	Pit N☆	12	9	.571	30	24	0	0-1	146	143	66	17	3	38-1	68	3.45	106	.263	.311	43-0-3	.047	-2*	106	2		0.1
1991	Pit N	3	3	.500	42	1	0	0-1	68.2	72	37	6	4	21-2	34	4.33	83	.275	.334	14	.286	2*	25	-5		-0.3
1992	KC A	3	1	.750	31	0	0	0-2	41	43	21	5	1	22-2	29	4.17	98	.274	.361	0	—	0	0	0		-0.1
	Mil A	0	0	—	1	0	0	0	1	0	0	0	0	1-0	2	0.00	—	.000	.250	0	—	0		-1		-0.1
	Year	3	1	.750	32	0	0	0-2	42	43	21	5	1	23-2	31	4.07	100	.269	.358	0	—	0	0	0		-0.1
1993	NY A	1	0	1.000	18	0	0	0-0	27	34	19	2	0	11-1	15	6.00	70	.301	.375	0	—	0		-5		-0.2
Total	12	80	96	.455	382	202	22-6	10-8	1507	1589	804	163	32	524-51	699	4.37	92	.273	.334	187-0-15	.171	2	96	-53	21	-5.8

HEAVERLO, DAVE   David Wallace   B8.25.1950 Ellensburg WA   BR/TR/6-1/210(195-220)   [SFN73*S1/23]   d4.14   Col Central Washington

1975	SF N	3	1	.750	42	0	0	1-1	64	62	18	2	1	31-4	35	2.39	159	.262	.348	4	.500	1	10		0.7
1976	SF N	4	4	.500	61	0	0	1-2	85	85	42	2	5	15-3	40	4.44	82	.289	.324	3	.333	1		-7		-0.6
1977	SF N	5	1	.833	56	0	0	1-1	98.2	92	36	10	3	21-8	58	2.55	155	.251	.294	5-0-2	.000	-0	14		0.8
1978	Oak A	3	6	.333	69	0	0	10-3	130	141	56	11	4	41-9	71	3.25	112	.281	.333	0	—	0	6		0.6
1979	Oak A	4	11	.267	62	0	0	9-8	85.2	97	42	7	4	35-12	40	4.20	97	.294	.376	1	.000	-0	0		0.0
1980	Sea A	6	3	.667	60	0	0	4-5	78.2	75	37	9	5	30-12	42	3.89	107	.253	.338	0	—	0	3		0.2
1981	Oak A	1	0	1.000	6	0	0	0-1	5.2	7	1	0	0	3-1	2	1.59	222	.292	.370	0	—	0	0		0.2
Total	7	26	26	.500	356	0	0	26-21	537.2	559	235	41	18	188-55	288	3.41	113	.273	.335	13-0-2	.231	0		27		1.9

HEBERT, WALLY   Wallace Andrew "Preacher"   B8.21.1907 Lake Charles LA   D12.8.1999 Westlake LA   BL/TL/6-1/195   d5.1

1931	StL A	6	7	.462	23	13	5	0	103	128	70	11	3	43	26	5.07	91	.306	.375	43-0-1	.209	-1	116	-5		-0.7
1932	StL A	1	12	.077	35	15	2	1	108.1	145	99	6	2	45	29	6.48	75	.322	.386	34-0-2	.353	2	74	-21		-1.9
1933	StL A	4	6	.400	30	10	3	0	88.1	114	58	4	1	35	19	5.30	88	.308	.369	23-0-4	.391	3	71	-6		-0.3
1943	Pit N	10	11	.476	34	23	12-1	0	184	197	75	3	2	45	41	2.98	117	.272	.316	59-0-5	.270	1*	101	10		1.4
Total	4	21	36	.368	125	61	22-1	1	483.2	584	302	24	8	168	115	4.63	91	.298	.355	159-0-12	.270	5	92	-22		-1.5

HEBSON, BRYAN   Bryan McCall   B3.12.1976 Columbus GA   BR/TR/6-5/210   [MonN97 1/44]   d7.6   Col Auburn

| 2003 | Mon N | 0 | 0 | — | 2 | 0 | 0 | 0-0 | 2 | 4 | 3 | 1 | 0 | 1-0 | 1 | 13.50 | 33 | .444 | .500 | 0 | — | 0 | | -2 | | -0.1 |

HECKER, GUY   Guy Jackson   B4.3.1856 Youngsville PA   D12.3.1938 Wooster OH   BR/TR/6-0/190   d5.2   M1/U1 ▲

1882	Lou AA	6	6	.500	13	11	10	0	104	75	49	0		5	33	1.30	191	.188	.199	340-3	.276	4*	100	11		1.6
1883	Lou AA	28	23	.549	53	52	51-3	0	469	526	298	4		75	164	3.34	90	.266	.292	332-1	.271	12*	101	-24		-0.8
1884	Lou AA	52	20	.722	75	73	72-6	0	670.2	526	230	4	16	56	385	1.80	172	.204	.226	316-4	.297	28*	98	103		12.9
1885	Lou AA	30	23	.566	53	53	51-2	0	480	454	252	6	18	54	209	2.18	148	.237	.265	297-2	.273	9*	102	51		6.0
1886	Lou AA	26	23	.531	49	48	45-2	0	420.2	390	273	6	10	118	133	2.87	127	.231	.285	343-4	.341	18*	131	31		4.8
1887	Lou AA	18	12	.600	34	32	32-2	1	285.1	325	214	9	10	50	58	4.16	105	.272	.307	370-4	.319	11*	119	9		1.8
1888	Lou AA	8	17	.320	26	25	25	0	223.1	251	154	5	10	43	63	3.39	91	.274	.313	211	.227	2*	94	-5		-0.2
1889	Lou AA	5	13	.278	16	16	15	0	151.1	215	145	7	5	47	33	5.59	69	.324	.373	327-1	.284	4*	98	-26		-1.9
1890	Pit N	2	9	.182	14	12	11	0	119.2	160	111	4	3	44	32	5.11	65	.311	.368	340	.226	2*	75	-27		-1.7
Total	9	175	146	.545	336	322	312-15	1	2924	2922	1726	50	72	492	1110	2.93	113	.247	.281	2876-19	.282	90	106	123		22.5

HEDGPETH, HARRY   Harry Malcolm   B9.4.1888 Fayetteville NC   D7.30.1966 Richmond VA   BL/TL/6-1.5/194   d10.3   Col North Carolina-Asheville

| 1913 | Was A | 0 | 0 | — | 1 | 0 | 0 | 0 | 0 | 0 | 0 | 0 | 0 | 0 | 0 | 0.00 | — | .250 | .250 | 0 | — | 0 | | 0 | | 0.1 |

HEDLUND, MIKE   Michael David "Red"   B8.11.1946 Dallas TX   BR/TR/6-1/190*   d5.8

1965	Cle A	0	0	—	6	0	0	0	5.1	6	4	0	0	5-1	4	5.06	69	.286	.407	1	.000	-0		-1	61	-0.1
1968	Cle A	0	0	—	3	0	0	0	1.2	6	2	0	1	2-0	0	10.80	28	.545	.643	0	—	0		-1		-0.1
1969	KC A	3	6	.333	34	16	1	2-0	123	123	53	8	1	40-2	74	3.24	114	.259	.314	33-0-1	.152	-1	87	5		0.4
1970	KC A	2	3	.400	9	0	0	0-0	15	18	13	6	0	7-0	5	7.20	52	.300	.373	4-0-1	.000	-0		-5	14	-1.1
1971	KC A	15	8	.652	32	30	7-1	0-0	205.2	168	68	15	1	72-1	76	2.71	127	.227	.295	68-0-5	.088	-4	89	17		1.6
1972	KC A	5	7	.417	29	16	1	0-0	113	119	67	10	4	41-1	52	4.78	64	.275	.341	32-0-3	.188	-0	127	-23		-2.3
Total	6	25	24	.510	113	62	9-1	2-0	465.2	440	207	39	7	167-5	211	3.56	96	.253	.318	138-0-10	.123	-5	97	-8	75	-1.6

HEFFNER, BOB   Robert Frederic   B9.13.1938 Allentown PA   BR/TR/6-4/205(198-210)   d6.19

1963	Bos A	4	9	.308	20	19	3-1	0	124.2	131	61	15	2	36-1	77	4.26	89	.267	.318	43-0-2	.116	-1*	74	-5		-0.6
1964	Bos A	7	9	.438	55	10	1-1	3	158.2	152	81	20	3	44-6	112	4.08	94	.251	.305	44-1-1	.159	0	113	-4		-0.4
1965	Bos A	0	2	.000	27	1	0	0	49	59	42	9	1	18-1	42	7.16	52	.304	.364	6-0-1	.000	-1	188	-16		-0.9
1966	Cle A	0	1	.000	5	0	0	0	13	12	6	1	0	3-0	7	3.46	99	.240	.283	1	.000	0	51	0		0.0
1968	Cal A	0	0	—	7	0	0	0	8	6	2	0	0	6-1	3	2.25	130	.240	.375	0	—	0		1		0.1
Total	5	11	21	.344	114	31	4-2	3	353.1	360	192	45	6	107-9	241	4.51	84	.264	.319	94-1-4	.128	-1	90	-24		-1.8

HEFLIN, BRONSON   Bronson Wayne   B8.29.1971 Clarksville TN   BR/TR/6-3/200   [PhiN94 37/1038]   d8.1   Col Tennessee

| 1996 | Phi N | 0 | 0 | — | 2 | 0 | 0 | 0-0 | 6.2 | 11 | 7 | 1 | 1 | 2-0 | 4 | 6.75 | 64 | .367 | .412 | 0 | — | 0 | | 1 | | -0.1 |

HEFLIN, RANDY   Randolph Rutherford   B9.11.1918 Fredericksburg VA   D8.17.1999 Fredericksburg VA   BL/TR/6-0/185   d6.9

1945	Bos A	4	10	.286	20	14	6-2	0	102	102	52	3	4	61	39	4.06	84	.272	.380	35-0-1	.086	-3	73	-7		-1.2
1946	Bos A	0	1	.000	5	1	0	0	14.2	16	5	0	1	12	6	2.45	149	.296	.433	3	.667	1	210	2		0.2
Total	2	4	11	.267	25	15	6-2	0	116.2	118	57	3	5	73	45	3.86	89	.275	.387	38-0-1	.132	-2	83	-5		-1.0

HEHL, JAKE   Herman Charles   B12.10.1899 Brooklyn NY   D7.4.1961 Brooklyn NY   BR/TR/5-11/180   d6.20

| 1918 | Bro N | 0 | 0 | — | 1 | 0 | 0 | 0 | 1 | 0 | 0 | 0 | 0 | 1 | 0 | 0.00 | — | .000 | .250 | 0 | — | 0 | | 0 | | 0.0 |

HEILMAN, AARON   Aaron Michael   B11.12.1978 Logansport IN   BR/TR/6-5/220*   [NYN01 1/18]   d6.26   Col Notre Dame

2003	NY N	2	7	.222	14	13	0	0-0	65.1	79	53	13	3	41-2	51	6.75	62	.300	.397	22	.045	-2	79	-19		-2.3
2004	NY N	1	3	.250	5	5	0	0-0	28	27	17	4	0	13-0	22	5.46	79	.257	.339	7-0-3	.000	-1	86	-3		-0.4
2005	NY N	5	3	.625	53	7	1-1	5-1	108	87	40	6	6	37-4	106	3.17	131	.223	.299	14-0-2	.000	-1	93	13		0.9
Total	3	8	13	.381	72	25	1-1	5-1	201.1	193	110	23	9	91-6	179	4.65	90	.254	.340	43-0-5	.023	-4	85	-9		-1.8

YEAR	TM LG	W	L	PCT	G	GS	CG-SHO	SV-BS	IP	H	R	HR	HB	BB-IB	SO	ERA	AERA	OAV	OOB	AB-HR-SH	AVG	PB	SUP	APR	DL	PW
HEIMACH, FRED					Frederick Amos "Lefty"		B1.27.1901 Camden NJ		D6.1.1973 Ft.Myers FL		BL/TL/6-0/175		d10.1												
1920	Phi A	0	1	.000	1	1	0	0	5	13	9	0	0	1	0	14.40	28	.542	.560	1	.000	-0	59	-5		-0.6
1921	Phi A	1	0	1.000	1	0	0	0	9	7	0	0	0	1	0	0.00	—	.226	.250	4	.250	-0	75	4		0.6
1922	Phi A	7	11	.389	37	19	7	1	171.2	220	117	18	3	63	47	5.03	85	.316	.375	60-0-3	.250	2	86	-15		-1.1
1923	Phi A	6	12	.333	40	19	10	0	208.1	238	120	14	6	69	63	4.32	95	.292	.352	118-1-5	.254	2*	75	-4		0.0
1924	Phi A	14	12	.538	40	26	10	0	198	243	122	2	4	60	60	4.73	91	.306	.357	90-0-3	.322	6*	101	-9		-0.3
1925	Phi A	0	1	.000	10	0	0	0	20.1	24	10	2	1	9	6	3.98	117	.312	.391	6	.167	-0*		2		0.1
1926	Phi A	1	0	1.000	13	1	0	0	31.2	28	14	1	0	5	8	2.84	147	.239	.270	10	.100	-1*	121	4		0.2
	Bos A	2	9	.182	20	13	6	0	102	119	72	5	0	42	17	5.65	72	.303	.370	44-0-1	.295	2	88	-16		-1.1
	Year	3	9	.250	33	14	6	0	133.2	147	86	6	0	47	25	4.98	82	.288	.348	54-0-1	.259	2	90	-13		-0.9
1928	NY A	2	3	.400	13	9	5	0	68	66	30	3	1	16	25	3.31	114	.250	.295	30-0-1	.167	-1*	143	4		0.1
1929	NY A	11	6	.647	35	10	3-3	4	134.2	141	72	4	3	29	26	4.01	96	.272	.314	49-1-0	.184	1*	107	-2		-0.1
1930	Bro N	0	2	.000	9	0	0	1	7.1	14	5	0	0	3	1	4.91	100	.424	.472	1	.250	-0*		0		0.0
1931	Bro N	9	7	.563	31	10	7-1	1	135.1	145	66	6	1	23	43	3.46	110	.274	.306	61	.197	1*	81	3		0.6
1932	Bro N	9	4	.692	36	15	7	0	167.2	203	85	7	6	28	30	3.97	96	.299	.333	55-1-3	.164	1*	103	-3		-0.1
1933	Bro N	1	0	1.000	10	3	0	7	29.2	49	33	2	2	11	7	10.01	32	.374	.431	10	.200	-0	138	-20		-1.0
Total	13	62	69	.473	296	127	56-5	7	1288.2	1510	755	64	27	360	334	4.46	90	.296	.346	542-3-16	.236	12	96	-57		-2.7
HEIMUELLER, GORMAN					Gorman John		B9.24.1955 Los Angeles CA		BL/TL/6-4/195*		d7.12		Col Cal Poly-San Luis Obispo												
1983	Oak A	3	5	.375	16	14	2-1	0-0	83.2	93	43	8	1	29-2	31	4.41	88	.286	.346	0	—	0	98	-4		-0.2
1984	Oak A	0	1	.000	6	0	0	0-0	14.2	21	14	2	0	7-1	3	6.14	62	.344	.400	0	—	0		-5		-0.3
Total	2	3	6	.333	22	14	2-1	0-0	98.1	114	57	10	1	36-3	34	4.67	83	.295	.354	0	—	0	98	-9		-0.5
HEINKEL, DON					Donald Elliott		B10.20.1959 Racine WI		BL/TR/6-0/185*		[DetA82 30/752]		d4.7		Col Wichita St.										
1988	Det A	0	0	—	21	0	0	1-0	36.1	30	17	4	1	12-1	30	3.96	97	.219	.285	0	—	-0	101	-6	134	-0.4
1989	StL N	1	1	.500	7	5	0	0-0	26.1	40	19	2	0	7-0	16	5.81	63	.348	.379	6-0-2	.000	-0	101	-6	183	-0.4
Total	2	1	1	.500	28	5	0	1-0	62.2	70	36	6	1	19-1	46	4.74	80	.278	.327	6-0-2	.000	-0	101	-6		-0.4
HEINTZELMAN, KEN					Kenneth Alphonse		B10.14.1915 Peruque MO		D8.14.2000 St.Peters MO		BR/TL/5-11.5/185*		d10.3		Mil 1943-45 s-Tom										
1937	Pit N	1	0	1.000	1	1	1	0	9	6	3	0	1	3	4	2.00	193	.207	.303	4	.000	-1	89	2		0.1
1938	Pit N	0	0	—	1	0	0	0	2	1	2	0	0	3	1	9.00	42	.167	.444	0	—	0		-1		0.0
1939	Pit N	1	1	.500	17	2	1-1	0	35.2	35	23	2	0	18	18	5.05	76	.250	.335	9	.222	0	102	-5		-0.2
1940	Pit N	8	8	.500	39	16	5-2	3	165	193	86	7	4	65	71	4.47	85	.292	.359	54-0-3	.167	-1*	104	-8		-0.7
1941	Pit N	11	11	.500	35	24	13-2	0	196	206	91	8	1	83	81	3.44	105	.272	.345	63-0-5	.127	-2	110	4		0.2
1942	Pit N	8	11	.421	27	18	5-3	0	130	143	69	9	0	63	39	4.57	74	.281	.361	35-0-2	.086	-2	91	-7		-2.0
1946	Pit N	8	12	.400	32	24	6-2	1	157.2	165	84	7	0	86	57	3.77	94	.271	.362	44-0-6	.136	-1	91	-7		-0.8
1947	Pit N	0	0	—	2	1	0	0	4	9	11	2	0	6	2	20.25	21	.409	.536	0	—	0	167	-7		-0.3
	Phi N	7	10	.412	24	19	8	1	136	144	72	12	2	46	55	4.04	99	.277	.338	43-0-6	.116	-2	92	-1		-0.5
	Year	7	10	.412	26	20	8	1	140	153	83	14	2	52	57	4.50	89	.282	.347	43-0-6	.116	-2	96	-9		-0.8
1948	Phi N	6	11	.353	27	16	5-2	2	130	117	66	10	1	45	57	4.29	92	.241	.307	37-0-6	.135	-1	77	-2		-0.4
1949	Phi N	17	10	.630	33	32	15-**5**	0	250	239	96	19	4	93	65	3.02	130	.255	.325	83-0-5	.157	-1	83	25		2.3
1950	†Phi N	3	9	.250	23	17	4-1	0	125.1	122	66	10	0	54	39	4.09	99	.250	.325	38-0-3	.053	-1	86	-1		-0.5
1951	Phi N	6	12	.333	35	12	3	2	118.1	119	61	8	4	53	55	3.16	115	.266	.319	2-0-3	.000	-0	49	3		0.2
1952	Phi N	3	1	.250	23	1	0	1	42.2	41	16	1	0	12	20	3.16	115	.266	.341	440-0-42	.000	-0	90	-16		-0.9
Total	13	77	98	.440	319	183	66-18	10	1501.2	1540	746	100	14	630	564	3.93	96	.267	.341	440-0-42	.127	-16	90	-16		-3.4
HEISE, CLARENCE					Clarence Edward "Lefty"		B8.7.1907 Topeka KS		D5.30.1999 Winter Park FL		BL/TL/5-10/172		d4.22												
1934	StL N	0	0	—	1	0	0	0	2	3	3	1	0	0	1	4.50	94	.300	.300	0	—	0		-1		0.0
HEISE, JIM					James Edward		B10.2.1932 Scottdale PA		BR/TR/6-1/185		d6.29		Col West Virginia												
1957	Was A	0	3	.000	8	2	0	0	19	25	19	2	0	16-1	8	8.05	48	.329	.441	4	.000	-0	46	-9		-1.2
HEISER, ROY					Le Roy Barton		B6.22.1942 Baltimore MD		BR/TR/6-4/190		d9.2		Col Maryland-Baltimore Co.												
1961	Was A	0	0	—	3	0	0	0	5.2	6	5	1	1	9-0	1	6.35	63	.261	.485	2	.000	-0		-2		-0.1
HEISERMAN, RICK					Richard Michael		B2.22.1973 Atlantic IA		BR/TR/6-7/225		[CleA94 3/73]		d5.23		Col Creighton										
1999	StL N	0	0	—	3	0	0	0-0	4.1	8	4	2	0	4-0	4	8.31	55	.400	.500	1	.000	-0		-2		-0.1
HEISMANN, CRESE					Christian Ernest		B4.16.1880 Cincinnati OH		D11.19.1951 Cincinnati OH		BL/TL/6-0/150		d9.25												
1901	Cin N	0	1	.000	3	2	1	0	13.2	18	9	1	3	6	6	5.93	54	.316	.409	5	.400	1	33	-3		-0.1
1902	Cin N	2	1	.667	5	3	2	0	33	33	18	1	5	10	15	2.45	122	.260	.338	14	.214	0	204	1		0.1
	Bal A	0	3	.000	3	3	2	0	16	20	17	1	2	12	2	8.44	45	.308	.430	7	.143	-1	76	-6		-0.9
Total	2	2	5	.286	11	8	5	0	62.2	71	44	3	10	28	23	4.74	69	.285	.380	26	.231	1	113	-8		-0.9
HEITMANN, HARRY					Henry Anton		B10.6.1896 Albany NY		D12.15.1958 Brooklyn NY		BR/TR/6-0/175		d7.27		Mil 1918										
1918	Bro N	0	1	.000	1	1	0	0	4	4	0	0	0	0	0	∞	—	1.000	1.000	0	—	0	190	-3		-0.3
HELD, MEL					Melvin Nicholas "Country"		B4.12.1929 Edon OH		BR/TR/6-1/178		d4.27													
1956	Bal A	0	0	—	4	0	0	0	7	7	4	0	1	3-1	4	5.14	76	.318	.385	0	—	0		-1		0.0
HELLING, RICK					Ricky Allen		B12.15.1970 Devils Lake ND		BR/TR/6-3/220(215-240)		[TexA92 1/22]		d4.10		Col Stanford										
1994	Tex A	3	2	.600	9	9	1-1	0-0	52	62	34	14	0	18-0	25	5.88	82	.295	.351	0	—	0	108	-4		-0.4
1995	Tex A	0	2	.000	3	3	0	0-0	12.1	17	11	2	2	8-0	5	6.57	74	.340	.435	0	—	0	71	-3		-0.4
1996	Tex A	1	2	.333	6	2	0	0-0	20.1	23	17	7	0	9-0	16	7.52	70	.280	.348	0	—	0	70	-4		-0.5
	Fla N	2	1	.667	5	4	0	0-0	27.2	14	6	2	0	7-0	26	1.95	211	.143	.200	9	.111	-0	60	7		0.7
1997	Tex A	2	6	.250	31	8	0	0-1	76	61	38	12	4	48-2	53	4.38	93	.232	.351	11-0-1	.091	-2	82	-2		0.1
	Tex A	3	3	.500	10	8	0	0-0	55	47	29	5	2	21-0	46	4.58	106	.235	.311	3	.000	0	112	14		1.3
1998	†Tex A	**20**	7	.741	33	33	4-2	0-0	216.1	209	109	27	1	78-6	164	4.41	111	.253	.314	5-0-1	.200	0	100	7		1.3
1999	†Tex A	13	11	.542	35	**35**	3	0-0	219.1	228	127	41	6	85-5	131	4.84	107	.272	.340	2	.000	-0	100	7		0.6
2000	Tex A	16	13	.552	35	**35**	0	0-0	217	212	122	29	5	99-2	146	5.17	92	.297	.344	4	.000	-0	109	-10		-1.1
2001	Tex A	12	11	.522	34	34	2-1	0-0	215.2	256	134	38	4	63-2	154	4.51	100	.264	.316	46-0-6	.043	-2	98	-1	22	0.4
2002	†Ari N	10	12	.455	30	30	0	0-0	175.2	180	94	31	6	48-6	120	4.51	100	.264	.347	1	.000	-0	115	-15		-1.5
2003	Bal A	7	8	.467	24	24	0	0-0	138.2	156	90	30	12	40-0	86	5.71	81	.286	.347	1	.000	-0		7		0.6
	†Fla N	1	0	1.000	11	0	0	0-0	16.1	11	1	1	0	5-0	12	0.55	745	.193	.258	2	.500	1		7		0.4
2005	Mil N	3	1	.750	15	7	0	0-0	49	39	13	2	2	18-1	42	2.39	179	.219	.296	13-0-1	.000	-1	65	11		0.6
Total	11	93	79	.541	281	232	10-4	0-1	1491.1	1515	825	241	48	547-24	1026	4.69	102	.264	.330	101-0-9	.059	-5	102	23	22	0.4
HELMBOLD, HORACE					Horace		B Philadelphia PA		d10.11																
1890	Phi AA	0	1	.000	1	1	1	0	7	17	15	0	0	6	3	14.14	27	.447	.523	3	.000	-1	70	-8		-0.7
HEMAN, RUSS					Russell Frederick		B2.10.1933 Olive CA		BR/TR/6-4/200		d4.20													
1961	Cle A	0	0	—	6	0	0	1	10	8	4	0	1	8-0	4	3.60	109	.216	.370	1	.000	-0		1		0.0
	LA A	0	0	—	6	0	0	1	10	4	3	1	1	2-0	2	1.80	251	.125	.189	1	.000	-0		2		0.1
	Year	0	0	—	12	0	0	2	20	12	7	1	2	10-0	6	2.70	156	.174	.289	2	.000	-0		3		0.1
HEMMING, GEORGE					George Earl "Old Wax Figger"		B12.15.1868 Carrollton OH		D6.3.1930 Springfield MA		BR/TR/5-11/170		d4.21										
1890	Cle P	0	1	.000	3	2	2	0	21	25	23	1	2	19	3	6.86	58	.284	.422	11	.182	-1	61	-5		-0.2
	Bro P	8	4	.667	19	11	11	3	123	117	86	3	3	59	32	3.80	117	.240	.325	57	.158	-4	88	9		0.2
	Year	8	5	.615	22	12	12	**3**	144	142	109	4	5	78	35	4.25	103	.247	.341	68	.162	-5	87	3		0.2
1891	Bro N	8	15	.348	27	22	19-1	1	199.2	231	173	11	11	84	83	4.96	67	.279	.353	82	.159	-1	109	-37		-3.3
1892	Cin N	0	1	.000	1	0	0	0	6	10	6	1	0	2	0	7.50	44	.357	.400	1	.333	0		-2		-0.3
	Lou N	2	2	.500	4	4	4	0	35	36	25	0	0	17	12	4.63	66	.255	.335	13	.077	-1	98	-5		-0.5
	Year	2	3	.400	5	4	4	0	41	46	31	2	0	19	12	5.05	61	.272	.346	16	.125	-1	97	-7		-0.6
1893	Lou N	18	17	.514	41	35	32-1	1	332	369	245	7	15	175	79	5.10	86	.273	.363	158	.203	-2*	73	26		2.1
1894	Lou N	13	19	.406	35	32	32-1	0	294.1	358	213	7	9	133	66	4.37	117	.297	.371	131-2-0	.252	2*	97	10		2.1
	†Bal N	4	0	1.000	6	6	4	0	45.1	48	22	1	2	26	4	3.57	153	.268	.367	21	.286	1	97	10		0.1
	Year	17	19	.472	41	38	36-1	0	339.2	406	235	7	11	159	70	4.27	121	.293	.370	152-2-0	.257	3	77	33		2.1
1895	Bal N	20	13	.606	34	31	26-1	0	262.1	288	155	10	8	96	43	4.05	118	.275	.339	117-1-1	.282	3*	96	22		2.1

YEAR	TM LG	W	L	PCT	G	GS	CG-SHO	SV-BS	IP	H	R	HR	HB	BB-IB	SO	ERA	AERA	OAV	OOB	AB-HR-SH	AVG	PB	SUP	APR	DL	PW
1896	Bal N	15	6	.714	25	21	20-3	0	202	233	113	9	3	54	33	4.19	102	.287	.333	97-0-2	.258	4*	149	8		0.8
1897	Lou N	3	4	.429	9	8	7	0	67	80	59	5	1	25	7	5.10	84	.294	.356	28	.179	-1*	77	-7		-0.6
Total	8	91	82	.526	204	168	156-7	6	1587.2	1795	1120	55	52	690	362	4.53	98	.279	.353	718-3-3	.223	-0	97	-7		-0.7

HENDERSON, BERNIE　Bernard "Barnyard"　B4.12.1899 Douglassville TX　D6.6.1966 Linden TX　BR/TR/5-9/175　d9.5　Col Texas A&M-Commerce

1921	Cle A	0	1	.000	2	1	0	0	3	5	5	0	0	3	1	9.00	47	.333	.333	1	.000	0*	78	-2		-0.4

HENDERSON, ED　Edward J. (b Eugene J. Ball)　B12.25.1884 Newark NJ　D1.15.1964 New York NY　BL/TL/5-9/168　d5.15

1914	Pit F	0	1	.000	6	1	1	0	16	14	8	2	0	8	4	3.94	73	.241	.333	3	.000	-0	0	-2		-0.1
	Ind F	1	0	1.000	2	1	1	0	10	8	7	0	3	4	1	4.50	69	.229	.357	4	.000	-1	110	-2		-0.2
	Year	1	1	.500	8	2	2	0	26	22	15	2	3	12	5	4.15	71	.237	.343	7	.000	-1	58	-3		-0.3

HENDERSON, HARDIE　James Harding　B10.31.1862 Philadelphia PA　D2.6.1903 Philadelphia PA　BR/TR/?/200　d5.2　U2

1883	Phi N	0	1	.000	1	1	1	0	9	26	24	0		2	2	19.00	16	.481	.500	8	.250	0*	104	-14		-0.8
	Bal AA	10	32	.238	45	42	38	0	358.1	383	315	4	87	145	4.02	87	.256	.297	191-1	.162	-6*	82	-22		-2.5
1884	Bal AA	27	23	.540	52	52	50-4	0	439.1	382	235	9	16	116	346	2.62	132	.216	.271	203	.227	2*	94	37		3.9
1885	Bal AA	25	35	.417	61	61	59	0	539.1	539	311	7	19	117	263	3.19	102	.253	.298	229-1	.223	3	91	3		0.7
1886	Bal AA	3	15	.167	19	19	19	0	171.1	188	147	0	9	66	88	4.62	74	.252	.320	68	.235	2	102	-25		-1.7
	Bro AA	10	4	.714	14	14	14	0	124	112	82	0		51	49	2.90	120	.232	.306	50	.180	-1	132	5		0.3
	Year	13	19	.406	33	33	33	0	295.1	300	229	2	9	117	137	3.90	88	.244	.314	118	.212	1	115	-20		-1.4
1887	Bro AA	5	8	.385	13	12	12	0	111.2	127	85	3	5	63	28	3.95	109	.281	.375	41	.122	-3	107	2		-0.1
1888	Pit N	1	3	.250	5	5	4	0	35.1	43	31	0	2	20	9	5.35	49	.289	.380	18	.278	-1	149	-11		-0.9
Total	6	81	121	.401	210	206	197-4	0	1788.1	1800	1230	25	51	522	930	3.50	98	.247	.302	808-2	.204	-2	96	-25		-1.1

HENDERSON, JOE　Joseph Lee　B7.4.1946 Lake Cormorant MS　BL/TR/6-2/195*　[AnaA65 5/87]　d6.7　[DL 1969 Cal A 4]

1974	Chi A	1	0	1.000	5	3	0	0-0	15	21	15	2	0	11-0	12	8.40	45	.328	.427	1	.000	-0	165	-7		-0.4
1976	Cin N	2	0	1.000	4	0	0	0-0	11	9	1	0	0	8-3	7	0.00	—	.225	.354	0	—	0		4		0.8
1977	Cin N	0	2	.000	7	0	0	0-0	9	17	13	2	0	6-0	8	12.00	33	.386	.460	1	.000	-0		-8		-1.5
Total	3	3	3	.600	16	3	0	0-0	35	47	29	4	0	25-3	27	6.69	56	.318	.416	2	.000	-0	165	-11	4	-1.1

HENDERSON, ROD　Rodney Wood　B3.11.1971 Greensburg KY　BR/TR/6-4/195*　[MonN92 2/41]　d4.19　Col Kentucky　[DL 1995 Mon N 160]

1994	Mon N	0	1	.000	3	2	0	0-0	6.2	9	9	1	0	7-0	7	9.45	45	.333	.471	1	.000	-0	129	-4		-0.5
1998	Mil N	0	0	—	2	0	0	0-0	3.2	5	4	2	1	0-0	1	9.82	44	.313	.353	0	—	0		-2		-0.1
Total	2	0	1	.000	5	2	0	0-0	10.1	14	13	3	1	7-0	8	9.58	45	.326	.431	1	.000	-0	129	-6	160	-0.6

HENDERSON, BILL　William Maxwell　B11.4.1901 Pensacola FL　D10.6.1966 Pensacola FL　BR/TR/6-0/190　d6.20

1930	NY A	0	0	—	3	0	0	0	8	7	6	1	0	4	2	4.50	96	.250	.344	2	.500	0		-1		0.0

HENDLEY, BOB　Charles Robert　B4.30.1939 Macon GA　BR/TL/6-2/195*　d6.23

1961	Mil N	5	7	.417	19	13	3	0	97	96	46	8	0	39-2	44	3.90	96	.262	.332	31-0-2	.032	-3	100	-2		-0.4
1962	Mil N	11	13	.458	35	29	7-2	1	200	188	90	17	0	59-2	112	3.60	105	.247	.299	59-1-3	.119	1*	98	5		0.7
1963	Mil N	9	9	.500	41	24	7-3	3	169.1	153	80	16	1	64-4	105	3.93	82	.244	.312	47-0-5	.106	-1*	133	-12		-1.3
1964	SF N	10	11	.476	30	29	4-1	0	163.1	161	71	18	2	59-9	104	3.64	98	.253	.322	47-0-5	.106	-1	92	0		-0.2
1965	SF N	0	0	—	8	2	0	0	15	27	22	6	1	13-2	8	12.60	29	.397	.500	3	.000	-0	158	-14		-0.7
	Chi N	4	4	.500	18	10	2	0	62	59	39	9	1	25-0	38	4.35	85	.244	.317	14-0-3	.000	-1	102	-6		-0.8
	Year	4	4	.500	26	12	2	0	77	86	61	15	2	38-2	46	5.96	62	.277	.360	17-0-3	.000	-2	111	-21		-1.5
1966	Chi N	4	5	.444	43	6	0	7	89.2	98	46	10	0	39-6	65	3.91	94	.285	.353	18	.167	-1	124	-3		-0.2
1967	Chi N	2	0	1.000	7	0	0	1	12.1	17	10	4	0	3-0	10	6.57	54	.333	.351	6	.000	-1		-4		-0.7
	NY N	3	3	.500	15	13	2	0	70.2	65	35	11	1	28-4	36	3.44	99	.241	.312	18-0-4	.111	-1	92	-2		-0.3
	Year	5	3	.625	22	13	2	1	83	82	45	15	1	31-4	46	3.90	87	.253	.318	24-0-4	.083	-1	91	-6		-1.0
Total	7	48	52	.480	216	126	25-6	12	879.1	864	439	99	6	329-29	522	3.97	90	.257	.323	243-1-22	.095	-6	104	-38		-3.9

HENDRICKS, ED　Edward "Big Ed"　B6.20.1885 Zeeland MI　D11.28.1930 Jackson MI　BL/TL/6-3/200　d9.15

1910	NY N	0	1	.000	1	1	1	0	12	12	7	0	0	4	2	3.75	79	.261	.320	4	.000	-1	25	-1		-0.2

HENDRICKSON, BEN　Benjamin John　B2.4.1981 St. Cloud MN　BR/TR/6-4/190　[MilN99 10/304]　d6.2

2004	Mil N	1	8	.111	10	9	0	0-0	46.1	58	33	6	4	20-1	29	6.22	71	.310	.385	16-0-1	.125	-1	56	-8		-1.4

HENDRICKSON, DON　Donald William　B7.14.1913 Kewanna IN　D1.19.1977 Norfolk VA　BR/TR/6-2/204　d7.4

1945	Bos N	4	8	.333	37	2	1	5	73.1	74	46	8	1	39	14	4.91	78	.261	.353	18	.167	-0	210	-8		-1.4
1946	Bos N	0	1	.000	2	0	0	0	2	4	2	0	0	2	2	4.50	76	.364	.462	1	.000	-0		-1		-0.1
Total	2	4	9	.308	39	2	1	5	75.1	78	48	8	1	41	16	4.90	78	.265	.357	19	.158	-0	210	-9		-1.5

HENDRICKSON, MARK　Mark Allan　B6.23.1974 Mount Vernon WA　BL/TL/6-9/230*　[TorA97 20/599]　d8.6　Col Washington St.

2002	Tor A	3	0	1.000	16	4	0	0-1	36.2	25	11	1	2	12-3	21	2.45	188	.202	.279	0	—	0	105	8		0.6
2003	Tor A	9	9	.500	30	30	1-1	0-0	158.1	207	111	24	0	40-3	76	5.51	86	.317	.352	4-1-0	.250	1	129	-15		-1.3
2004	Tor A	10	15	.400	32	30	2	0-0	183.1	211	113	21	7	46-5	87	4.81	97	.285	.330	5	.200	0	76	-5		-0.5
2005	TB A	11	8	.579	31	31	1	0-0	178.1	227	126	24	2	49-1	89	5.90	74	.311	.353	7	.143	-0	113	-29	16	-2.6
Total	4	33	32	.508	109	95	4-1	0-1	556.2	670	361	70	11	147-12	273	5.21	88	.298	.341	16-1-0	.188	1	106	-41	16	-3.8

HENDRIX, CLAUDE　Claude Raymond　B4.13.1889 Olathe KS　D3.22.1944 Allentown PA　BR/TR/6-0/195　d6.7　Col Wichita St.

1911	Pit N	4	6	.400	22	12	6-1	1	118.2	85	52	1	1	53	57	2.73	126	.204	.295	41-1-0	.098	-1	89	7		0.6
1912	Pit N	24	9	.727	39	32	25-4	1	288.2	256	110	6	9	105	176	2.59	126	.246	.320	121-1-2	.322	16*	121	21		4.0
1913	Pit N	14	15	.483	42	25	17-2	3	241	216	95	3	5	89	138	2.84	106	.248	.321	99-1-2	.273	10*	111	6		1.8
1914	Chi F	29	10	.744	49	37	34-6	1	362	262	91	6	5	77	189	1.69	157	.203	.251	130-2-6	.231	4*	118	42		5.4
1915	Chi F	16	15	.516	40	31	26-5	4	285	256	120	7	2	84	107	3.00	84	.241	.298	113-4-3	.265	11*	125	-15		-0.7
1916	Chi N	8	16	.333	36	24	15-3	2	218	193	81	4	6	67	117	2.68	108	.242	.306	80-1-2	.200	2*	70	6		1.1
1917	Chi N	10	12	.455	40	21	13-1	1	215	202	94	3	4	72	81	2.60	112	.257	.322	91-3-5	.264	8*	140	4		1.5
1918	†Chi N	20	7	.741	32	27	21-3	0	233	229	87	2	5	54	86	2.78	100	.259	.305	91-3-5	.264	3*	106	4		0.8
1919	Chi N	10	14	.417	35	25	15-2	0	206.1	208	79	3	4	42	69	2.62	110	.266	.311	78-1-0	.192	-0*	86	6		0.7
1920	Chi N	9	12	.429	27	23	12	0	203.2	216	101	6	3	54	72	3.58	90	.273	.322	83-0-1	.181	-2*	108	-8		-0.9
Total	10	144	116	.554	360	257	184-27	17	2371.1	2123	910	41	49	697	1092	2.65	110	.243	.303	922-14-25	.241	50	109	73		14.3

HENION, LAFAYETTE　Lafayette Marion　B6.7.1899 Eureka CA　D7.22.1955 San Luis Obispo CA　BR/TR/5-11/154　d9.10

1919	Bro N	0	0	—	1	0	0	0	2	2	2	0	0	2	2	6.00	50	.200	.333	1	.000	-0		-1		-0.1

HENKE, TOM　Thomas Anthony　B12.21.1957 Kansas City MO　BR/TR/6-5/215(215-230)　[TexA80 S4/67]　d9.10　Col East Central (MO) JC

1982	Tex A	1	0	1.000	8	0	0	0-1	15.2	14	2	0	1	8-0	9	1.15	338	.246	.348	0	—	0		5		0.3
1983	Tex A	1	0	1.000	8	0	0	1-0	16	16	6	1	0	4-0	17	3.38	120	.262	.308	0	—	0		2		0.1
1984	Tex A	1	1	.500	25	0	0	2-2	28.1	36	21	0	1	20-2	25	6.35	66	.313	.407	0	—	0		-6		-0.5
1985	†Tor A	3	3	.500	28	0	0	13-1	40	29	12	4	0	8-2	42	2.02	209	.206	.245	0	—	0		8		1.8
1986	Tor A	9	5	.643	63	0	0	27-8	91.1	63	39	6	1	32-4	118	3.35	127	.191	.261	0	—	0		9		1.5
1987	Tor A★	0	6	.000	72	0	0	34-8	94	62	27	10	0	25-3	128	2.49	182	.188	.242	0	—	0		22		2.9
1988	Tor A	4	4	.500	52	0	0	25-4	68	60	23	6	2	24-3	66	2.91	136	.237	.306	0	—	0		9		1.5
1989	Tor A	8	3	.727	64	0	0	20-4	89	66	20	5	3	25-4	116	1.92	197	.205	.264	0	—	0		20		3.1
1990	Tor A	2	4	.333	61	0	0	32-6	74.2	58	18	8	1	19-2	75	2.17	183	.213	.266	0	—	0		15		2.2
1991	†Tor A	0	2	.000	49	0	0	32-3	50.1	33	13	4	0	11-2	53	2.32	182	.184	.232	0	—	0		11	35	1.5
1992	†Tor A	3	2	.600	57	0	0	34-3	55.2	40	19	5	0	22-2	46	2.26	182	.197	.272	0	—	0		11		1.7
1993	Tex A	5	5	.500	66	0	0	40-7	74.1	55	25	7	1	27-3	79	2.91	144	.205	.278	0	—	0		12		2.3
1994	Tex A	3	6	.333	37	0	0	15-6	38	33	16	6	0	12-0	39	3.79	128	.232	.290	0	—	0		5	31	1.0
1995	StL N★	1	1	.500	52	0	0	36-2	54.1	42	11	2	0	18-0	48	1.82	235	.209	.274	1	.000	-0		15		2.3
Total	14	41	42	.494	642	0	0	311-55	789.2	607	252	64	9	255-29	861	2.67	157	.211	.275	1	.000	-0		136	66	21.7

HENLEY, WELDON　Weldon　B10.25.1880 Jasper GA　D11.16.1960 Palatka FL　BR/TR/6-0/175　d4.23　Col Georgia Tech

1903	Phi A	12	10	.545	29	21	13-1	0	186.1	186	108	3	12	67	86	3.91	78	.259	.333	68-0-1	.132	-3*	124	-18		-2.3
1904	Phi A	15	17	.469	36	34	31-5	0	295.2	245	126	4	19	76	130	2.53	106	.226	.289	108-0-3	.222	2	117	2		0.6
1905	Phi A	4	11	.267	25	19	13-1	0	183.2	155	74	4	9	61	82	2.60	102	.231	.309	65-0-2	.169	-1	97	2		0.3

YEAR	TM LG	W	L	PCT	G	GS	CG-SHO	SV-BS	IP	H	R	HR	HB	BB-IB	SO	ERA	AERA	OAV	OOB	AB-HR-SH	AVG	PB	SUP	APR	DL	PW
1907	Bro N	1	5	.167	7	7	5	0	56	54	31	2	1	21	11	3.05	77	.273	.345	20-0-2	.200	1*	83	-6		-0.5
Total	4	32	43	.427	97	81	62-7	0	721.2	640	339	12	41	231	309	2.94	93	.240	.310	261-0-8	.184	-2	112	-20		-1.9

HENN, SEAN Sean Michael B4.23.1981 Fort Worth TX BR/TL/6-5/200 d5.4 Col McLennan (TX) JC

YEAR	TM LG	W	L	PCT	G	GS	CG-SHO	SV-BS	IP	H	R	HR	HB	BB-IB	SO	ERA	AERA	OAV	OOB	AB-HR-SH	AVG	PB	SUP	APR	DL	PW
2005	NY A	0	3	.000	3	3	0	0-0	11.1	18	16	3	0	11-0	3	11.12	39	.360	.475	0	—	0	107	-9		-1.3

HENNEMAN, MIKE Michael Alan B12.11.1961 St.Charles MO BR/TR/6-4/195(195-210) [DetA84 4/104] d5.11 Col Oklahoma St.

YEAR	TM LG	W	L	PCT	G	GS	CG-SHO	SV-BS	IP	H	R	HR	HB	BB-IB	SO	ERA	AERA	OAV	OOB	AB-HR-SH	AVG	PB	SUP	APR	DL	PW
1987	†Det A	11	3	.786	55	0	0	7-4	96.2	86	36	8	3	30-5	75	2.98	143	.238	.300	1	.000	-0		15		2.0
1988	Det A	9	6	.600	65	0	0	22-7	91.1	72	23	7	2	24-10	58	1.87	205	.218	.273	0	—	0		20	15	3.9
1989	Det A☆	11	4	.733	60	0	0	8-4	90	84	46	4	5	51-15	69	3.70	104	.251	.355	0	—	0		0	21	-0.1
1990	Det A	8	6	.571	69	0	0	22-6	94.1	90	36	4	3	33-12	50	3.05	130	.253	.320	0	—	0		12	16	2.1
1991	Det A	10	2	.833	60	0	0	21-3	84.1	81	29	2	0	34-8	61	2.88	145	.258	.326	0	—	0		12		0.1
1992	Det A	2	6	.250	60	0	0	24-4	77.1	75	36	6	0	20-10	58	3.96	101	.256	.299	0	—	0		12		1.8
1993	Det A	5	3	.625	63	0	0	24-5	71.2	69	28	4	2	32-8	58	2.64	165	.251	.331	0	—	0		-3	20	-0.4
1994	Det A	1	3	.250	30	0	0	8-5	34.2	43	27	5	2	17-7	27	5.19	95	.297	.376	0	—	0		11		1.5
1995	Det A	0	1	.000	29	0	0	18-2	29.1	24	5	0	0	9-1	24	1.53	314	.222	.282	0	—	0		3		0.7
	Hou N	0	1	.000	21	0	0	8-1	21	21	7	1	2	4-1	19	3.00	129	.266	.310	0	—	0		-2		-0.4
1996	†Tex A	0	7	.000	49	0	0	31-6	42	41	28	6	0	17-5	34	5.79	91	.258	.326	0	—	-0		78	72	12.4
Total	10	57	42	.576	561	0	0	193-47	732.2	686	301	47	19	271-82	533	3.21	131	.249	.318	1	.000	-0		78	72	12.4

HENNESSEY, BRAD Brad Martin B2.7.1980 Toledo OH BR/TR/6-2/185* [SFN01 1/21] d8.7 Col Youngstown St.

YEAR	TM LG	W	L	PCT	G	GS	CG-SHO	SV-BS	IP	H	R	HR	HB	BB-IB	SO	ERA	AERA	OAV	OOB	AB-HR-SH	AVG	PB	SUP	APR	DL	PW
2004	SF N	2	2	.500	7	7	0	0-0	34.1	42	24	2	0	15-1	25	4.98	87	.294	.358	13	.231	1	189	-4		-0.3
2005	SF N	5	8	.385	21	21	0	0-0	118.1	127	63	15	4	52-3	64	4.64	92	.276	.353	39-2-2	.231	3	72	-4		-0.1
Total	2	7	10	.412	28	28	0	0-0	152.2	169	87	17	4	67-4	89	4.72	91	.280	.354	52-2-2	.231	4	102	-8		-0.4

HENNESSEY, GEORGE George "Three Star" B10.28.1907 Slatington PA D1.15.1988 Princeton NJ BR/TR/5-10/168 d9.2

YEAR	TM LG	W	L	PCT	G	GS	CG-SHO	SV-BS	IP	H	R	HR	HB	BB-IB	SO	ERA	AERA	OAV	OOB	AB-HR-SH	AVG	PB	SUP	APR	DL	PW
1937	StL A	0	1	.000	5	0	0	0	7	15	8	2	0	4	4	10.29	47	.500	.583	0-0-1	—	0		-4		-0.4
1942	Phi N	1	1	.500	5	1	0	0	17	11	5	1	0	10	2	2.65	125	.180	.296	5	.000	-1	25	2		0.1
1945	Chi N	0	0	—	2	0	0	0	3.2	7	3	0	0	1	2	7.36	50	.438	.471	0	—	-1		-1		-0.1
Total	3	1	2	.333	12	1	0	0	27.2	33	16	3	0	17	8	5.20	72	.308	.403	5-0-1	.000	-1	25	-3		-0.4

HENNIGAN, PHIL Phillip Winston B4.10.1946 Jasper TX BR/TR/5-11.5/185(180-195) [CleA66* 4/60] d9.2 Col Sam Houston St.

YEAR	TM LG	W	L	PCT	G	GS	CG-SHO	SV-BS	IP	H	R	HR	HB	BB-IB	SO	ERA	AERA	OAV	OOB	AB-HR-SH	AVG	PB	SUP	APR	DL	PW
1969	Cle A	2	1	.667	9	0	0	0-2	16.1	14	6	0	1	4-1	10	3.31	115	.241	.297	2	.000	-0		1		0.2
1970	Cle A	6	3	.667	42	1	0	3-0	71.2	69	34	7	4	44-6	43	4.02	100	.263	.376	7-0-2	.143	1	222	0		0.2
1971	Cle A	4	3	.571	57	0	0	14-2	82	80	45	13	3	51-4	69	4.94	78	.261	.365	6-0-2	.000	-0		-7		-0.9
1972	Cle A	5	3	.625	38	1	0	6-0	67.1	54	20	8	2	18-4	44	2.67	122	.226	.281	12	.083	-0	81	5	33	-1.1
1973	NY N	0	4	.000	30	0	0	3-1	43.1	50	30	6	1	16-6	22	6.23	59	.289	.353	3	.333	0		-11		-1.1
Total	5	17	14	.548	176	2	0	26-5	280.2	267	135	34	11	133-21	188	4.26	87	.257	.344	30-0-4	.100	1	155	-12	33	-0.9

HENNING, PETE Ernest Herman B12.28.1887 Crown Point IN D11.4.1939 Dyer IN BR/TR/5-11/185 d4.17

YEAR	TM LG	W	L	PCT	G	GS	CG-SHO	SV-BS	IP	H	R	HR	HB	BB-IB	SO	ERA	AERA	OAV	OOB	AB-HR-SH	AVG	PB	SUP	APR	DL	PW
1914	KC F	5	10	.333	28	14	7	2	138	153	88	5	7	58	45	4.83	58	.291	.369	44	.182	0	129	-29		-2.8
1915	KC F	9	15	.375	40	20	15-1	2	207	181	88	5	3	76	73	3.17	83	.235	.307	68-0-4	.206	-1	72	-10		-1.2
Total	2	14	25	.359	68	34	22-1	4	345	334	176	10	10	134	118	3.83	70	.258	.332	112-0-4	.196	-1	96	-39		-4.6

HENNINGER, RICK Richard Lee B1.11.1948 Hastings NE BR/TR/6-6/225 [TexA68 S1/16] d9.3 Col Missouri

YEAR	TM LG	W	L	PCT	G	GS	CG-SHO	SV-BS	IP	H	R	HR	HB	BB-IB	SO	ERA	AERA	OAV	OOB	AB-HR-SH	AVG	PB	SUP	APR	DL	PW
1973	Tex A	1	0	1.000	6	2	0	0-0	23	23	8	1	0	11-0	6	2.74	137	.261	.333	0	—	0	131	3		0.

HENNIS, RANDY Randall Philip B12.16.1965 Clearlake CA BR/TR/6-6/220 [HouN87 2/54] d9.17 Col UCLA

YEAR	TM LG	W	L	PCT	G	GS	CG-SHO	SV-BS	IP	H	R	HR	HB	BB-IB	SO	ERA	AERA	OAV	OOB	AB-HR-SH	AVG	PB	SUP	APR	DL	PW
1990	Hou N	0	0	—	3	1	0	0-0	9.2	1	0	0	0	4	4	0.00	—	.033	.147	2	.000	-0	73	4		0.2

HENRIQUEZ, OSCAR Oscar Eduardo B1.28.1974 LaGuaira, Venez BR/TR/6-6/220* d9.7

YEAR	TM LG	W	L	PCT	G	GS	CG-SHO	SV-BS	IP	H	R	HR	HB	BB-IB	SO	ERA	AERA	OAV	OOB	AB-HR-SH	AVG	PB	SUP	APR	DL	PW
1997	Hou N	1	0	1.000	4	0	0	0-0	4	2	2	0	1	3-0	3	4.50	89	.167	.375	0	—	0		0		0.
1998	Fla N	0	0	—	15	0	0	0-0	20	26	22	4	1	12-0	19	8.55	47	.306	.390	1	.000	-0		-11		-0.6
2002	Det A	1	1	.500	30	0	0	2-0	28	19	14	5	1	15-4	23	4.50	97	.196	.307	0	—	0		0	10	-0.6
Total	3	1	2	.333	49	0	0	2-0	52	47	38	9	3	30-4	45	6.06	70	.242	.348	1	.000	-0		-11	10	-0.6

HENRY, DWAYNE Dwayne Allen B2.16.1962 Elkton MD BR/TR/6-3/205(205-230) [TexA80 2/40] d9.7

YEAR	TM LG	W	L	PCT	G	GS	CG-SHO	SV-BS	IP	H	R	HR	HB	BB-IB	SO	ERA	AERA	OAV	OOB	AB-HR-SH	AVG	PB	SUP	APR	DL	PW
1984	Tex A	0	1	.000	3	0	0	0-1	4.1	5	4	0	0	7-0	7	8.31	50	.294	.500	0	—	0		-2		-0.
1985	Tex A	2	2	.500	16	0	0	3-3	21	16	7	0	0	7-0	20	2.57	166	.211	.274	0	—	0		4		0.
1986	Tex A	1	0	1.000	19	0	0	0-0	19.1	14	11	1	1	22-0	17	4.66	93	.209	.402	0	—	0		-1	38	0.
1987	Tex A	0	0	—	5	0	0	0-0	10	12	10	2	0	9-0	7	9.00	50	.293	.420	0	—	0		-4		-0.
1988	Tex A	0	1	.000	11	0	0	0-1	10.1	15	10	1	3	9-1	10	8.71	47	.326	.458	0	—	0		-5		-0.
1989	Atl N	0	2	.000	12	0	0	1-1	12.2	12	6	2	0	5-1	16	4.26	86	.250	.321	0	—	0		-6		-0.
1990	Atl N	2	2	.500	34	0	0	0-1	38.1	41	26	3	0	25-0	34	5.63	72	.273	.375	0	—	0		3		0.
1991	Hou N	3	2	.600	52	0	0	2-0	67.2	51	25	7	2	39-7	51	3.19	111	.219	.333	1	.000	-0		4		0.
1992	Cin N	3	3	.500	60	0	0	0-2	83.2	59	31	4	2	44-6	72	3.33	108	.199	.301	4	.250	-0		-3		-0.
1993	Cin N	0	1	.000	3	0	0	0-0	4.2	6	8	0	0	4-1	2	3.86	105	.273	.385	1	.000	-0		-8		-0.
	Sea A	2	1	.667	31	1	0	2-0	54	56	40	6	2	35-4	35	6.67	67	.273	.378	0	—	0	330	-11	30	-0.
1995	Det A	1	0	1.000	10	0	0	5-0	8.2	11	6	0	0	10-2	9	6.23	77	.306	.457	0	—	0		-2		-0.
Total	11	14	15	.483	256	1	0	14-10	334.2	298	184	26	9	216-22	275	4.65	85	.241	.354	6	.167	-0	330	-22	68	-1.

HENRY, EARL Earl Clifford "Hook" B6.10.1917 Roseville OH D12.10.2002 Zanesville OH BL/TL/5-11/172 d9.23

YEAR	TM LG	W	L	PCT	G	GS	CG-SHO	SV-BS	IP	H	R	HR	HB	BB-IB	SO	ERA	AERA	OAV	OOB	AB-HR-SH	AVG	PB	SUP	APR	DL	PW
1944	Cle A	1	1	.500	2	2	1	0	17.2	18	9	1	0	3	5	4.58	72	.269	.300	5	.000	-0*	101	-2		-0.
1945	Cle A	0	3	.000	15	1	0	0	21.2	20	13	0	1	20	10	5.40	60	.253	.410	4	.500	1*	105	-5		-0.
Total	2	1	4	.200	17	3	1	0	39.1	38	22	1	1	23	15	5.03	65	.260	.365	9	.222	1	103	-7		-0.

HENRY, BUTCH Floyd Bluford B10.7.1968 ElPaso TX BL/TL/6-1/205* [CinN87 15/388] d4.9 [DL 1996 Bos A 182]

YEAR	TM LG	W	L	PCT	G	GS	CG-SHO	SV-BS	IP	H	R	HR	HB	BB-IB	SO	ERA	AERA	OAV	OOB	AB-HR-SH	AVG	PB	SUP	APR	DL	PW
1992	Hou N	6	9	.400	28	28	2-1	0-0	165.2	185	81	16	1	41-7	96	4.02	84	.285	.325	54-1-5	.148	1	89	-12		-0.
1993	Col N	2	8	.200	20	15	1	0-0	84.2	117	66	14	1	24-2	39	6.59	73	.331	.370	22-0-2	.091	-1	82	-13		-1.
	Mon N	1	1	.500	10	1	0	0-0	18.1	18	10	1	0	4-0	8	3.93	106	.250	.286	2-0-1	.000	-0	129	0		0.
	Year	3	9	.250	30	16	1	0-0	103	135	76	15	1	28-2	47	6.12	76	.317	.356	24-0-3	.083	-2	85	-13		-1.
1994	Mon N	8	3	.727	24	15	0	1-0	107.1	97	30	10	2	20-1	70	2.43	174	.241	.278	31-0-5	.290	3	103	22		2.
1995	Mon N	7	9	.438	21	21	1-1	0-0	126.2	133	47	11	2	28-3	60	2.84	151	.275	.315	42-0-5	.048	-4	77	18	47	1.
1997	Bos A	7	3	.700	36	5	0	6-2	84.1	89	36	6	2	19-2	51	4.00	118	.275	.315	0-0-1	—	0	138	1	174	0.
1998	Bos A	0	0	—	2	2	0	0-0	9	8	4	1	2	1-0	6	4.00	118	.235	.316	0	—	0	209	-1	126	-0.
1999	Sea A	2	0	1.000	7	4	0	0-0	25	30	15	1	2	10-0	15	5.04	95	.303	.375	0	—	0	93	25	578	0.
Total	7	33	33	.500	148	91	4-2	7-2	621	677	289	61	9	149-15	345	3.83	109	.280	.322	151-1-19	.139	-2	93	25	578	0.

HENRY, DUTCH Frank John B5.12.1902 Cleveland OH D8.23.1968 Cleveland OH BL/TL/6-1/175 d9.16

YEAR	TM LG	W	L	PCT	G	GS	CG-SHO	SV-BS	IP	H	R	HR	HB	BB-IB	SO	ERA	AERA	OAV	OOB	AB-HR-SH	AVG	PB	SUP	APR	DL	PW
1921	StL A	0	0	—	1	0	0	0	2	2	1	0	0	1	1	4.50	100	.250	.250	1	1.000	0		0		-0.
1922	StL A	0	0	—	4	0	0	0	5	7	3	0	0	5	3	5.40	77	.280	.400	0	—	0		0		-0.
1923	Bro N	4	6	.400	17	9	5-2	0	94.1	105	55	9	2	28	28	3.91	99	.281	.334	35	.229	1	82	-1		-0.
1924	Bro N	1	2	.333	16	4	0	0	46	69	33	0	0	15	11	5.67	66	.352	.398	20	.250	1	192	-9		-0.
1927	NY N	11	6	.647	45	15	7-1	4	163.2	184	93	6	0	31	40	4.23	91	.278	.311	55-0-1	.236	1	137	-8		-0.
1928	NY N	3	6	.333	17	8	4	1	64	82	36	4	0	25	23	3.80	103	.325	.388	19	.158	0	100	-1		-0.
1929	NY N	5	6	.455	27	9	4	1	101.1	129	52	10	1	31	27	3.82	120	.316	.366	28-0-1	.250	2	133	8		-0.
	Chi A	1	0	1.000	2	1	1	0	15	20	12	1	0	7	2	6.00	71	.308	.375	7	.143	0	276	-3		-0.
1930	Chi A	2	17	.105	35	16	4	0	155	211	116	12	4	48	35	4.88	95	.331	.381	51	.235	1	62	-9		-0.
Total	8	27	43	.386	164	62	25-3	6	646.1	809	401	42	8	190	170	4.39	95	.308	.356	216-0-2	.231	6	108	-23		-1.

HENRY, JIM James Francis B6.26.1910 Danville VA D8.15.1976 Memphis TN BR/TR/6-2/175 d4.23

YEAR	TM LG	W	L	PCT	G	GS	CG-SHO	SV-BS	IP	H	R	HR	HB	BB-IB	SO	ERA	AERA	OAV	OOB	AB-HR-SH	AVG	PB	SUP	APR	DL	PW
1936	Bos A	5	1	.833	21	8	2	4	76.1	75	43	10	2	40	36	4.60	116	.255	.348	26	.115	-1*	108	6		-0.
1937	Bos A	1	0	1.000	3	2	1	0	15.1	15	9	2	1	8	8	5.28	90	.263	.382	5	.000	-0	101	0		-0.
1939	Phi N	0	1	.000	9	1	0	1	23	24	13	3	1	11	7	5.09	79	.276	.344	5	.000	-1	218	-2		-0.
Total	3	6	2	.750	33	11	3	1	114.2	114	65	15	3	59	51	4.79	104	.260	.352	36	.083	-2	117	4		-0.

YEAR	TM LG	W	L	PCT	G	GS	CG-SHO	SV-BS	IP	H	R	HR	HB	BB-IB	SO	ERA	AERA	OAV	OOB	AB-HR-SH	AVG	PB	SUP	APR	DL	PW
HENRY, JOHN	John Michael B9.2.1863 Springfield MA D6.11.1939 Hartford CT TL d8.13 ▲																									
1884	Cle N	1	4	.200	5	5	5-1	0	42	46	39	2		26	23	3.64	87	.257	.351	26	.154	-1*	27	-4		-0.4
1885	Bal AA	2	7	.222	9	9	9	0	71	71	55	0	2	13	31	4.31	76	.247	.284	34	.265	1*	60	-8		-0.4
1886	Was N	1	3	.250	4	4	4	0	27.2	35	27	1		15	19	4.23	76	.285	.362	14	.357	1	99	-5		-0.5
Total	3	4	14	.222	18	18	18-1	0	140.2	152	121	3	2	54	73	4.19	103	.245	.337	74	.243	1	59	-17		-1.5
HENRY, DOUG	Richard Douglas B12.10.1963 Sacramento CA BR/TR/6-4/205(185-205) [MilA85 8/185] d7.15 Col Arizona St.																									
1991	Mil A	2	1	.667	32	0	0	15-1	36	16	4	1	0	14-1	28	1.00	399	.133	.221	0	—	0	12			1.8
1992	Mil A	1	4	.200	68	0	0	29-4	65	64	34	6	0	24-4	52	4.02	96	.256	.319	0	—	0	-2			-0.3
1993	Mil A	4	4	.500	54	0	0	17-7	55	67	37	7	3	25-8	38	5.56	78	.300	.373	0	—	0	-7			-1.3
1994	Mil A	2	3	.400	25	0	0	0-0	31.1	32	17	7	1	23-1	20	4.60	110	.271	.394	1	.000	-0	2	24		0.2
1995	NY N	3	6	.333	51	0	0	4-3	67	48	23	7	1	25-6	62	2.96	137	.198	.274	1-0-1	1.000	0	9			1.2
1996	NY N	2	8	.200	58	0	0	9-5	75	82	48	7	1	36-6	58	4.68	87	.261	.358	4	.000	-1	-7			-1.1
1997	†SF N	4	5	.444	75	0	0	3-3	70.2	70	45	5	1	41-6	69	4.71	87	.261	.358	4	.000	-0	-6			-0.9
1998	†Hou N	8	2	.800	59	0	0	2-3	71	55	25	9	0	35-5	59	3.04	133	.216	.307	4-0-1	.000	-0	9			1.1
1999	†Hou N	2	3	.400	35	0	0	2-2	40.2	45	24	8	3	24-0	36	4.65	95	.281	.385	1	.000	-0	-2	66		-0.2
2000	Hou N	1	3	.250	45	0	0	1-1	53	39	26	10	3	28-2	46	4.42	111	.204	.314	1	.000	-0	4			0.2
	†SF N	3	1	.750	27	0	0	0-2	25.1	18	10	2	1	21-1	16	2.49	175	.214	.374	0		-0	4			0.6
	Year	4	4	.500	72	0	0	1-3	78.1	57	36	12	4	49-3	62	3.79	125	.207	.333	1	.000	0	8			0.8
2001	KC A	2	2	.500	53	0	0	0-2	75.2	75	53	13	14	45-2	57	6.07	82	.262	.365	0	—	0	-7			-0.4
Total	11	34	42	.447	582	0	0	82-33	665.2	611	346	83	17	341-42	541	4.19	103	.245	.337	17-0-2	.059	-1	9	90		0.9
HENRY, BILL	William Francis B2.15.1942 Long Beach CA BL/TL/6-3/195 d9.13 Col Seton Hall																									
1966	NY A	0	0	—	2	0	0		3	0	0	0	0	2-0	3	0.00	—	.000	.200	0		0	1			0.1
HENRY, BILL	William Rodman B10.15.1927 Alice TX BL/TL/6-2/180(175-195) d4.17 Col Houston																									
1952	Bos A	5	4	.556	13	10	5	0	76.2	75	40	7	2	36	23	3.87	102	.254	.339	31	.258	2*	120	-1		0.1
1953	Bos A	5	5	.500	21	12	4-1	1	85.2	86	39	4	4	33	56	3.26	129	.260	.334	32	.188	-0	95	7		0.7
1954	Bos A	3	7	.300	24	13	3-1	0	95.2	104	56	9	1	49	38	4.52	91	.270	.351	34	.118	-1*	96	-4		-0.6
1955	Bos A	2	4	.333	17	7	0	0	59.2	56	28	7	0	21-2	23	3.32	129	.247	.306	19	.105	-1	112	5		0.3
1958	Chi N	5	4	.556	44	0	0	6	81.1	63	27	8	1	17-6	58	2.88	136	.214	.259	17	.235	1	11			1.4
1959	Chi N	9	8	.529	65	0	0	12	134.1	111	42	19	1	26-3	115	2.68	147	.227	.264	31-0-1	.194	0	20			2.7
1960	Cin N★	1	5	.167	51	0	0	17	67.2	62	25	8	4	20-5	58	3.19	120	.247	.313	8	.000	-1	5			0.7
1961	†Cin N	2	1	.667	47	0	0	16	53.1	50	18	8	0	15-4	53	2.19	185	.244	.294	5	.000	-1*	10			1.1
1962	Cin N	4	2	.667	40	0	0	11	37.1	40	21	5	1	20-5	35	4.58	88	.280	.365	3	.333	-0	-2			-0.4
1963	Cin N	1	3	.250	42	0	0	14	52	55	30	4	1	11-2	45	4.15	81	.279	.316	6-0-1	.167	-0	-6			-0.8
1964	Cin N	2	0	1.000	37	0	0	6	52	31	9	2	3	12-4	28	0.87	418	.170	.231	6	.500	1*	14			1.6
1965	Cin N	2	0	1.000	3	0	0	0	5	3	0	0	0	1-0	5	0.00	—	.176	.222	1		0	2			0.4
	SF N	2	2	.500	35	0	0	4	42	40	18	2	1	8-3	35	3.64	99	.248	.287	5	.200	1	0			0.0
	Year	4	2	.667	38	0	0	4	47	43	18	2	1	9-3	40	3.26	111	.242	.280	5	.200	1	2			0.4
1966	SF N	1	1	.500	35	0	0	1	22	15	6	3	1	10-3	15	2.45	149	.190	.286	2	.000	0	3			0.3
1967	SF N	2	0	1.000	28	1	0	2	21.2	16	5	1	2	9-4	23	2.08	158	.198	.290	1	.000	-0	27	3		0.4
1968	SF N	0	2	.000	7	1	0	0	5	4	3	0	1	3-1	0	5.40	55	.250	.400	0	—	0	-9			-0.2
	Pit N	0	0	—	10	0	0	0	16.2	19	18	2	2	3-1	9	8.10	36	.382	.420	3	.000	0	29	-1		-0.6
	Year	0	2	.000	17	1	0	0	21.2	33	21	2	3	6-2	9	7.48	39	.359	.416	3	.000	-0	30	-12		-0.8
1969	Hou N	0	0	—	3	0	0	0-0	5	2	1	0	0	2-0	2	0.00	—	.111	.200	0	—	0	2			0.1
Total	16	46	50	.479	527	44	12-2	99	843	842	386	89	25	296-43	621	3.26	119	.244	.306	203-0-2	.177	-0	106	58		7.2
HENSHAW, ROY	Roy Knikelbine B7.29.1911 Chicago IL D6.8.1993 LaGrange IL BR/TL/5-8/155 d4.15 Col Chicago																									
1933	Chi N	2	1	.667	21	0	0	1	38.2	32	22	0	4	20	16	4.19	78	.230	.335	10	.200	-0	-4			-0.4
1935	†Chi N	13	5	.722	31	18	7-3	1	142.2	135	60	6	4	68	53	3.28	120	.249	.337	51-0-5	.255	2	118	11		1.2
1936	Chi N	6	5	.545	39	14	6-2	1	129.1	152	67	8	5	56	69	3.97	100	.296	.370	44-0-2	.136	-2	102	-1		-0.5
1937	Bro N	5	12	.294	42	16	5	2	156.1	176	110	14	4	69	98	5.07	80	.289	.352	48-0-4	.167	-2*	77	-18		-1.9
1938	StL N	5	11	.313	27	15	4	0	130	132	63	7	1	48	34	4.02	99	.266	.332	41-0-1	.220	-1	84	2		0.2
1942	Det A	2	4	.333	23	2	0	1	61.2	63	32	3	1	27	24	4.09	97	.269	.347	12	.083	-1	32	0		-0.1
1943	Det A	0	2	.000	26	3	0	2	71.1	75	35	2	3	33	33	3.79	93	.276	.360	18	.111	-1	160	-2		-0.2
1944	Det A	0	0	—	7	1	0	0	12.1	17	12	1	0	6	10	8.76	41	.315	.383	5	.000	-1	117	-6		-0.4
Total	8	33	40	.452	216	69	22-5	7	742.1	782	401	40	20	327	337	4.16	94	.271	.349	229-0-12	.179	-5	98	-18		-2.1
HENSIEK, PHIL	Philip Frank "Sid" B10.13.1901 St.Louis MO D2.21.1972 St.Louis MO BR/TR/6-0/160 d8.15																									
1935	Was A	0	3	.000	6	1	0	0	13	21	15	2	0	9	6	9.69	45	.356	.441	3	.667	1	80	-5		-1.2
HENSLEY, CHUCK	Charles Floyd B3.11.1959 Tulare CA BL/TL/6-3/190 [DetA80 10/252] d5.10 Col California-Davis																									
1986	SF N	0	0	—	11	0	0	1-1	7.1	5	2	2	0	2-0	6	2.45	144	.179	.233	0	—	0	1			0.1
HENSLEY, CLAY	Clayton Allen B8.31.1979 Tomball TX BR/TR/5-11/190 d7.20 Col Lamar																									
2005	†SD N	1	1	.500	24	1	0	0	47.2	33	12	0	0	17-2	28	1.70	228	.195	.266	6	.167	0	24	11		0.6
HENSLEY, MATT	Matthew Davis B8.18.1978 San Diego CA BR/TR/6-2/220 [AnaA00 10/290] d5.4 Col Grossmont (CA) JC [DL 2005 Ala A 183]																									
2004	Ana A	0	2	.000	16	0	0	0-0	27.2	32	15	5	2	7-1	30	4.88	92	.294	.345	1	.000	-0	-1			0.0
HENTGEN, PAT	Patrick George B11.13.1968 Detroit MI BR/TR/6-2/200* [TorA86 5/133] d9.3																									
1991	Tor A	0	0	—	3	1	0	0-0	7.1	5	2	1	2	3-0	3	2.45	172	.208	.345	0	—	0	65	1		0.1
1992	Tor A	5	2	.714	28	2	0	0-1	50.1	49	30	7	0	32-5	39	5.36	77	.254	.357	0	—	0	44	-6	47	-0.7
1993	†Tor A☆	19	9	.679	34	32	3	0-0	216.1	215	103	27	7	74-0	122	3.87	113	.258	.322	0	—	0	120	12		1.3
1994	Tor A★	13	8	.619	24	24	6-3	0-0	174.2	158	74	21	3	59-1	147	3.40	143	.240	.305	0	—	0	89	27		2.9
1995	Tor A	10	14	.417	30	30	2	0-0	200.2	236	129	24	5	90-6	135	5.11	93	.290	.363	0	—	0	91	-9		-1.0
1996	Tor A	20	10	.667	35	35	10-3	0-0	265.2	238	105	20	5	94-3	177	3.22	156	.241	.308	0	—	0	103	53		5.2
1997	Tor A★	15	10	.600	35	35	9-3	0-0	264	253	116	31	7	71-2	160	3.68	125	.254	.308	7	.000	-1	96	28		2.3
1998	Tor A	12	11	.522	29	29	0	0-0	177.2	208	109	28	5	69-1	94	5.17	90	.293	.357	5-0-1	.000	-1	109	-9		-1.0
1999	Tor A	11	12	.478	34	34	1	0-0	199	225	115	32	3	65-1	118	4.79	103	.286	.338	6	.167	-0	97	3		0.3
2000	†StL N	15	12	.556	33	33	1-1	0-0	194.1	202	107	24	3	89-4	118	4.72	98	.276	.353	60-0-8	.133	-1	119	1		-0.1
2001	Bal A	2	3	.400	9	9	1	0-0	62.1	51	25	7	0	19-3	33	3.47	124	.221	.279	0	—	0	76	7	144	-0.5
2002	Bal A	0	4	.000	4	4	0	0-0	22	31	20	6	0	10-0	11	7.77	56	.337	.398	0	—	0	48	-9	161	-1.1
2003	Bal A	7	8	.467	28	22	1	1-0	160.2	150	74	25	5	58-1	100	4.09	113	.247	.316	5	.000	-0	64	11		0.8
2004	Tor A	2	9	.182	18	16	0	0-0	80.1	90	67	16	4	42-2	33	6.95	71	.283	.361	1	.000	-0	63	-18		-2.0
Total	14	131	112	.539	344	306	34-10	1-1	2075.1	2111	1076	269	49	775-29	1290	4.32	109	.264	.331	84-0-9	.107	-3	97	93	352	7.5
HEPLER, BILL	William Lewis B9.25.1945 Covington VA BL/TL/6-0/160 d4.23																									
1966	NY N	3	3	.500	37	3	0		69	71	30	3	3	51-6	25	3.52	103	.274	.397	14-0-1	.214	0	65	1		0.1
HERBEL, RON	Ronald Samuel B1.16.1938 Denver CO D1.20.2000 Tacoma WA BR/TR/6-1/195(175-195) d9.10 Col Northern Colorado																									
1963	SF N	0	0	—	2	0	0	0	1.1	1	1	0	0	1-0	1	6.75	47	.200	.333	0		0	0			0.0
1964	SF N	9	9	.500	40	22	7-2	1	161	162	65	9	3	61-9	98	3.07	116	.259	.327	47-0-5	.000	-4*	94	7		0.4
1965	SF N	12	9	.571	47	21	1	1	170.2	172	80	16	3	47-7	106	3.85	94	.261	.311	49-0-2	.020	-4	107	-3		-0.7
1966	SF N	4	5	.444	32	18	0	1	129.2	149	70	15	2	39-9	55	4.16	88	.291	.343	38	.026	-4	119	-7		-0.9
1967	SF N	4	5	.444	42	11	1-1	0	125.2	125	54	10	2	35-10	52	3.08	107	.268	.320	28-0-3	.107	-0	66	1		0.3
1968	SF N	0	0	—	28	2	0	0	43	55	26	5	1	6-5	18	3.35	88	.309	.364	3		-0	103	-5		-0.3
1969	SF N	4	1	.800	39	4	0	1-0	87.1	92	43	7	1	23-5	34	4.02	87	.275	.320	17-0-1	.000	0	102	3		-0.3
1970	SD N	7	5	.583	64	1	0	9-6	111	114	69	14	4	39-5	53	4.95	81	.266	.330	13	.000	-1	22	1		-0.4
	NY N	2	2	.500	12	0	0	1-1	13	14	3	1	0	2-0	8	1.38	293	.275	.302	0	—	0	4			0.7
	Year	9	7	.563	76	1	0	10-7	124	128	72	15	4	41-6	61	4.57	88	.267	.327	13	.000	-1	22	-3		-0.4
1971	Atl N	0	0	—	25	0	0	1-0	51.2	61	31	6	4	23-1	22	5.23	71	.300	.381	11	.091	-1	-7			-0.4
Total	9	42	37	.532	331	79	11-3	16-7	894.1	945	442	81	20	285-55	447	3.82	94	.273	.330	206-0-11	.029	-15	105	-26		-2.8

YEAR	TM LG	W	L	PCT	G	GS	CG-SHO	SV-BS	IP	H	R	HR	HB	BB-IB	SO	ERA	AERA	OAV	OOB	AB-HR-SH	AVG	PB	SUP	APR	DL	PW

HERBERT, ERNIE Ernie Albert "Tex" B1.30.1887 Hale MO D1.13.1968 Dallas TX BR/TR/5-10/165 d7.27

1913	Cin N	0	0	—	6	0	0		17.1	12	12	0	1	1	5	2.08	156	.179	.247	4	.250	0	0	0		0.0
1914	StL F	1	0	1.000	18	1	0	1	50.1	56	33	2	4	27	24	3.58	85	.293	.392	13	.538	2*	45	-6		-0.2
1915	StL F	1	0	1.000	11	1	1	0	48	48	21	1	3	18	23	3.38	85	.253	.327	18	.278	1*	122	-2		0.0
Total	3	2	0	1.000	35	2	1		115.2	116	66	3	8	50	52	3.27	92	.259	.344	35	.371	3	70	-8		-0.2

HERBERT, FRED Frederick (b Herbert Frederick Kemman) B3.4.1887 LaGrange IL D5.29.1963 Tice FL BR/TR/6-0/185 d9.25

| 1915 | NY N | 1 | 1 | .500 | 2 | 2 | 1 | 0 | 17 | 12 | 5 | 0 | 0 | 4 | 6 | 1.06 | 242 | .197 | .246 | 6 | .167 | -0 | 87 | 2 | | 0.2 |

HERBERT, RAY Raymond Ernest B12.15.1929 Detroit MI BR/TR/5-11/185* d8.27 Mil 1951-52

1950	Det A	1	2	.333	8	3	1	1	22.1	20	11	1	0	12	5	3.63	129	.244	.340	7	.286	0	90	2		0.3
1951	Det A	4	0	1.000	5	0	0	0	12.2	8	2	0	0	9	9	1.42	294	.190	.333	4	.000	-0	4			0.8
1953	Det A	4	6	.400	43	3	0	6	87.2	109	58	6	0	46	37	5.24	78	.308	.387	19	.158	-0	102	-12		-1.2
1954	Det A	3	6	.333	42	4	0	0	84.1	114	64	6	2	50	44	5.87	63	.334	.419	17-1-0	.176	2	101	-21		-1.8
1955	KC A	1	8	.111	23	11	2	0	87.2	99	65	10	1	40-9	30	6.26	67	.292	.361	21-0-1	.190	0*	81	-18		-1.5
1958	KC A	8	8	.500	42	16	5	0	175	161	76	20	4	55-3	108	3.50	112	.248	.309	52-0-2	.192	1	79	7		0.9
1959	KC A	11	11	.500	37	26	10-2	1	183.2	196	108	24	1	62-4	99	4.85	83	.275	.330	57-1-3	.211	2	99	-14		-1.4
1960	KC A	14	15	.483	37	33	14	0	252.2	256	106	17	7	72-6	122	3.28	121	.267	.320	76-0-9	.171	1	78	18		2.3
1961	KC A	3	6	.333	13	12	1	0	83.2	103	56	10	2	30-1	34	5.38	78	.303	.360	28-0-2	.107	-1	79	-10		-1.0
	Chi A	9	6	.600	21	20	4	0	137.2	142	69	15	0	36-2	50	4.05	97	.265	.308	53-2-1	.226	4	98	-2		0.2
	Year	12	12	.500	34	32	5	0	221.1	245	125	25	2	66-3	84	4.55	88	.280	.328	81-2-3	.185	3	91	-13		-0.8
1962	Chi A★	20	9	.690	35	35	12-5	0	236.2	228	90	13	1	74-4	115	3.27	119	.255	.310	82-2-3	.195	5	115	9		2.9
1963	Chi A	13	10	.565	33	33	14-7	0	224.2	230	86	12	2	35-5	105	3.24	108	.265	.295	63-1-10	.222	6	115	9		1.7
1964	Chi A	6	7	.462	20	19	1-1	0	111.2	117	50	14	2	17-2	40	3.47	100	.275	.303	36-0-2	.139	-1	93	-1	38	-0.2
1965	Phi N	5	8	.385	25	19	4-1	1	130.2	162	60	13	1	19-2	51	3.86	90	.309	.360	41-0-4	.268	3	92	-4		-0.6
1966	Phi N	2	5	.286	23	2	0	2	50.1	55	26	7	1	14-2	15	4.29	84	.293	.341	13	.077	-1	73	-4		-0.6
Total	14	104	107	.493	407	236	68-13	15	1881.1	2000	927	167	24	571-40	864	4.01	96	.276	.328	569-7-37	.192	20	95	-27	38	1.4

HEREDIA, FELIX Felix (Perez) B6.18.1975 Santa Cruz de Barahona, D.R. BL/TL/6-0/180(165-185) d8.9

1996	Fla N	1	1	.500	21	0	0	0-0	16.2	21	8	1	0	10-1	10	4.32	95	.313	.397	—		0	0			0.0
1997	†Fla N	5	3	.625	56	0	0	0-1	56.2	53	30	3	5	30-1	54	4.29	95	.241	.342	2-0-1	.500	0		-2		-0.3
1998	Fla N	0	3	.000	41	2	0	2-1	41	38	30	1	1	32-2	38	5.49	74	.241	.368	3	.000	-0	91	-8		-0.6
	†Chi N	3	0	1.000	30	0	0	0-2	17.2	19	9	1	0	6-1	16	4.08	108	.279	.338	0		-0	88	-8		-0.6
	Year	3	3	.500	71	2	0	2-3	58.2	57	39	2	1	38-3	54	4.85	82	.252	.360	3	.000	-0		-4		-0.7
1999	Chi N	3	1	.750	69	0	0	1-6	52	56	35	7	1	25-2	52	4.85	94	.272	.347	4	.500	1		-4		-0.1
2000	Chi N	7	3	.700	74	0	0	2-3	58.2	46	31	6	2	33-4	52	4.76	96	.220	.329	2	.000	-0		-8	30	-0.9
2001	Chi N	2	2	.500	48	0	0	0-3	35	45	27	6	2	16-1	28	6.17	68	.315	.384	1		-0		9		0.8
2002	Tor A	1	2	.333	53	0	0	0-2	52.1	51	29	5	2	26-3	31	3.61	108	.256	.345	0		-0	3			0.3
2003	Cin N	5	2	.714	57	0	0	1-3	72	61	27	9	2	28-5	41	3.00	139	.228	.304	3	.333	0		4		0.3
	†NY A	0	1	.000	12	0	0	0-1	15	13	5	1	0	5-2	4	1.20	366	.228	.290	0		-0		-7	30	0.1
2004	†NY A	1	1	.500	47	0	0	0-1	38.2	44	28	5	2	20-0	25	6.28	73	.278	.365	0		-0		1	167	0.1
2005	NY N	0	0	—	3	0	0	0-0	2.2	1	0	0	1	1-0	2	0.00		.125	.300	0		0			227	-1.0
Total	10	28	19	.596	511	2	0	6-23	458.1	448	259	45	18	232-22	351	4.42	98	.255	.344	15-0-1	.267	1	85	-12	227	-1.0

HEREDIA, GIL Gilbert B10.26.1965 Nogales AZ BR/TR/6-1/190(190-221) [SFN87 9/230] d9.1 Col Arizona

1991	SF N	0	2	.000	7	4	0	0-0	33	27	14	4	0	7-2	13	3.82	94	.233	.274	7	.429	1	88	0		0.1
1992	SF N	2	3	.400	13	4	0	0-0	30	32	20	3	1	16-1	15	5.40	62	.278	.371	6-0-1	.167	0	81	-7		-1.2
	Mon N	0	0	—	7	1	0	0-0	14.2	12	3	1	0	4-0	7	1.84	189	.250	.302	3	.000	-0	26	3		0.1
	Year	2	3	.400	20	5	0	0-0	44.2	44	23	4	1	20-1	22	4.23	80	.270	.351	9-0-1	.111	-0	70	-4		-1.1
1993	Mon N	4	2	.667	20	9	1	2-1	57.1	66	28	4	2	14-2	40	3.92	106	.293	.339	13-0-4	.154	-0	110	2		0.3
1994	Mon N	6	3	.667	39	3	0	0-0	75.1	85	34	7	2	13-3	62	3.46	122	.281	.311	16	.313	1	136	6		0.1
1995	Mon N	5	6	.455	40	18	0	1-2	119	137	60	7	5	21-1	74	4.31	100	.291	.326	33-0-5	.182	-0	95	1		0.1
1996	Tex A	2	5	.286	44	0	0	1-3	73.1	91	50	12	1	14-2	43	5.89	89	.301	.332	0		-0	60	9		1.2
1998	Oak A	3	3	.500	8	6	0	0-0	42.2	43	14	4	3	3-0	27	2.74	169	.256	.282	0		-0	113	-2		-0.2
1999	Oak A	13	8	.619	33	33	1	0-0	200.1	228	119	22	8	34-4	117	4.81	99	.283	.318	6-0-1	.000	-0	105	14		1.6
2000	†Oak A	15	11	.577	32	32	2	0-0	198.2	214	106	24	4	66-5	101	4.12	118	.274	.332	2-0-1	.500	0	101	14		-1.3
2001	Oak A	7	8	.467	24	18	0	0-0	109.2	144	75	27	2	29-3	48	5.58	82	.316	.357	3	.333	2	104	10		1.0
Total	10	57	51	.528	267	128	4	4-6	954	1079	523	115	28	221-23	547	4.46	102	.285	.327	89-0-12	.213	2	104	10		1.0

HEREDIA, UBALDO Ubaldo Jose (Martinez) B5.4.1956 Ciudad Bolivar, Venez BR/TR/6-2/180 d5.12

| 1987 | Mon N | 0 | 1 | .000 | 2 | 2 | 0 | 0-0 | 10 | 10 | 6 | 2 | 1 | 3-1 | 6 | 5.40 | 79 | .263 | .333 | 2 | .000 | -0 | 106 | -1 | | -0.1 |

HEREDIA, WILSON Wilson B3.30.1972 LaRomana, D.R. BR/TR/6-0/175* d4.27 [DL 1996 Fla N 182]

1995	Tex A	0	1	.000	6	0	0	0-0	12	9	5	2	0	15-2	6	3.75	129	.225	.429	0		0	2			0.1
1997	Tex A	1	0	1.000	10	0	0	0-0	19.2	14	9	2	0	16-0	8	3.20	152	.197	.337	0	—	0	3			0.1
Total	2	1	1	.500	16	0	0	0-0	31.2	23	14	4	0	31-2	14	3.41	142	.207	.372	0		0	5		182	0.2

HERGES, MATT Matthew Tyler B4.1.1970 Champaign IL BL/TR/6-0/200* d8.3 Col Illinois St.

1999	LA N	0	2	.000	17	0	0	0-2	24.1	24	13	5	1	8-0	18	4.07	107	.255	.320	1	.000	-0	0			0.6
2000	LA N	11	3	.786	59	4	0	1-2	110.2	100	43	7	8	40-5	75	3.17	140	.249	.323	13-0-1	.077	-1	57	16		1.8
2001	LA N	9	8	.529	75	0	0	1-7	99.1	97	39	8	8	46-12	50	3.44	120	.259	.350	9-0-1	.444	1	9			1.5
2002	Mon N	2	5	.286	62	0	0	6-8	64.2	80	33	10	2	26-8	50	4.04	109	.305	.370	1	.000	-0	5			0.5
2003	SD N	2	2	.500	40	0	0	3-2	44	40	16	2	2	20-2	40	2.86	140	.244	.325	1	.000	-0	7			0.5
	†SF N	1	0	1.000	27	0	0	0-1	35	28	11	1	1	9-0	28	2.31	184	.219	.273	2	.500	0	13			0.5
	Year	3	2	.600	67	0	0	3-3	79	68	27	3	3	29-2	68	2.62	157	.233	.303	3	.333	0	-8			-1.4
2004	SF N	4	5	.444	70	0	0	23-8	65.1	90	44	4	3	21-4	39	5.23	83	.338	.388	0	—	0	-7			-0.1
2005	Ari N	0	0	—	7	0	0	0-0	8	12	12	4	1	5-0	3	13.50	33	.343	.429	0	—	0	-1			-0.1
	SF N	1	1	.500	21	0	0	0-0	21	23	11	2	0	7-1	6	4.71	90	.287	.341	0	—	0	-8			-0.1
	Year	1	1	.500	28	0	0	0-0	29	35	23	6	1	12-1	9	7.14	60	.304	.369	0	—	0	-8			2.1
Total	7	30	26	.536	378	4	0	34-30	472.1	494	222	47	24	182-32	335	3.83	112	.274	.344	27-0-2	.222	1	57	23		2.8

HERMAN, ART Arthur B5.11.1871 Louisville KY D9.20.1955 Los Angeles CA d6.29

1896	Lou N	4	6	.400	14	12	9	0	94.1	122	73	4	2	36	13	5.63	77	.310	.371	36	.139	-4	89	-8		-1.1
1897	Lou N	0	1	.000	3	2	1	0	18	23	14	1	0	5	4	4.00	107	.307	.350	6	.333	1	125	0		0.1
Total	2	4	7	.364	17	14	10	0	112.1	145	87	5	2	41	17	5.37	81	.310	.368	42	.167	-2	94	-8		-1.0

HERMANSON, DUSTIN Dustin Michael B12.21.1972 Springfield OH BR/TR/6-3/205* [SDN94 1/3] d5.8 Col Kent St.

1995	SD N	3	1	.750	26	0	0	0-0	31.2	35	26	8	1	22-1	19	6.82	60	.280	.392	0	—	0	-9			-1.1
1996	SD N	1	0	1.000	8	0	0	0-0	13.2	18	15	3	0	4-0	11	8.56	47	.340	.367	0	—	0	-5			-0.3
1997	Mon N	8	8	.500	32	28	1-1	0-0	158.1	134	68	15	1	66-2	136	3.69	113	.234	.311	48-1-5	.104	-0	89	11		2.5
1998	Mon N	14	11	.560	32	30	1	0-0	187	163	80	21	3	56-3	154	3.13	134	.234	.292	52-1-5	.115	2	91	20	15	2.8
1999	Mon N	9	14	.391	34	34	0	0-0	216.1	225	110	20	7	69-4	145	4.20	106	.271	.330	64-0-8	.047	-5	79	9		-0.3
2000	Mon N	12	14	.462	38	30	2-1	4-3	198	226	128	26	4	74-5	94	4.77	99	.290	.352	55-0-8	.145	-1	88	-7		-0.3
2001	†StL N	14	13	.519	33	33	0	0-0	192.1	195	106	34	8	73-3	123	4.45	97	.264	.335	62-0-5	.081	-3*	108	-4		-0.3
2002	Bos A	1	1	.500	12	1	0	0-1	22	35	19	3	0	7-0	10	7.77	58	.354	.393	0	—	0	249	-7	139	-0.3
2003	StL N	1	2	.333	23	0	0	1-5	29.2	35	18	4	1	14-2	12	5.46	76	.315	.394	0	—	0	-4			-0.2
	†SF N	2	1	.667	9	6	0	0-0	39	35	14	5	2	10-2	27	3.00	142	.238	.294	11-0-3	.000	-1	103	5	16	0.5
	Year	3	3	.500	32	6	0	1-5	68.2	70	32	9	3	24-4	39	4.06	103	.271	.338	11-0-3	.000	-1	104	2	17	0.3
2004	SF N	6	9	.400	47	18	0	17-3	131	132	71	15	3	46-5	102	4.53	96	.262	.323	30-0-6	.100	-1	127	-2	17	-0.2
2005	†Chi A	2	4	.333	57	0	0	34-5	57.1	46	17	4	1	18-1	33	2.04	222	.222	.284	0	—	0	14	12		2.3
Total	11	73	78	.483	351	180	4-2	56-17	1276.1	1279	672	158	31	459-31	869	4.21	104	.263	.328	322-2-40	.093	-8	96	18	187	2.0

HERNAIZ, JESUS Jesus Rafael (Rodriguez) B1.8.1945 Santurce, PR BR/TR/6-2/175 d6.14

| 1974 | Phi N | 2 | 3 | .400 | 27 | 0 | 0 | 1-3 | 41.1 | 53 | 31 | 6 | 0 | 25-1 | 16 | 5.88 | 65 | .323 | .411 | 2 | .000 | -0 | -10 | | | -1.0 |

HERNANDEZ, ADRIAN Adrian B3.25.1975 Havana, Cuba BR/TR/6-1/185* d4.21

YEAR	TM LG	W	L	PCT	G	GS	CG-SHO	SV-BS	IP	H	R	HR	HB	BB-IB	SO	ERA	AERA	OAV	OOB	AB-HR-SH	AVG	PB	SUP	APR	DL	PW
2001	NY A	0	3	.000	6	3	0	0-0	22	15	10	7	2	10-1	10	3.68	121	.190	.297	0	—	0	42	2		0.2
2002	NY A	0	1	.000	2	1	0	0-0	6	10	8	2	0	6-0	9	12.00	36	.357	.471	0	—	0	64	-5		-0.6
2004	Mil N	0	2	.000	6	1	0	0-1	16	20	18	1	0	14-0	14	8.44	52	.294	.410	4-0-1	.000	-0	126	-8		-0.8
Total 3		0	6	.000	14	5	0	0-1	44	45	36	10	2	30-1	33	6.55	67	.257	.370	4-0-1	.000	-0	63	-11		-1.2

HERNANDEZ, CARLOS Carlos E. B4.22.1980 Guacara, Venez BL/TL/5-10/145(145-200) d8.18 [DL 2003 Hou N 183]

YEAR	TM LG	W	L	PCT	G	GS	CG-SHO	SV-BS	IP	H	R	HR	HB	BB-IB	SO	ERA	AERA	OAV	OOB	AB-HR-SH	AVG	PB	SUP	APR	DL	PW
2001	Hou N	1	0	1.000	3	3	0	0-0	17.2	11	2	1	0	7-0	17	1.02	451	.177	.261	5-0-1	.200	0	74	7		0.4
2002	Hou N	7	5	.583	23	21	0	0-0	111	112	56	11	3	61-5	93	4.38	99	.261	.357	35-0-4	.171	-0*	90	0	47	0.1
2004	Hou N	1	3	.250	9	9	0	0-0	42	50	31	11	3	23-0	26	6.43	68	.303	.398	12-0-4	.083	-1	120	-9		-0.8
Total 3		9	8	.529	35	33	0	0-0	170.2	173	89	23	8	91-5	136	4.54	96	.264	.359	52-0-9	.154	-1	96	-2	230	-0.3

HERNANDEZ, LIVAN Eisler Livan B2.20.1975 Villa Clara, Cuba BR/TR/6-2/225(220-245) d9.24 b-Orlando

YEAR	TM LG	W	L	PCT	G	GS	CG-SHO	SV-BS	IP	H	R	HR	HB	BB-IB	SO	ERA	AERA	OAV	OOB	AB-HR-SH	AVG	PB	SUP	APR	DL	PW
1996	Fla N	0	0	—	1	0	0	0-0	3	3	0	0	0	2-0	2	0.00	—	.273	.385	1	1.000	0		1		0.1
1997	†Fla N	9	3	.750	17	17	0	0-0	96.1	81	39	5	3	38-1	72	3.18	128	.229	.304	29-0-3	.172	1	126	9		1.2
1998	Fla N	10	12	.455	33	33	9	0-0	234.1	265	133	37	6	104-8	72	4.72	86	.289	.363	82-0-1	.195	2*	103	-17		-1.2
1999	Fla N	5	9	.357	20	20	2	0-0	136	161	78	17	2	55-3	97	4.76	92	.294	.358	45-2-1	.289	5*	97	-6		0.1
	SF N	3	3	.500	10	10	0	0-0	63.2	66	32	6	0	21-2	47	4.38	98	.267	.322	18-0-6	.222	1*	92	0		0.2
	Year	8	12	.400	30	30	2	0-0	199.2	227	110	23	2	76-5	144	4.64	94	.286	.347	63-2-7	.270	6	95	-6		0.3
2000	†SF N	17	11	.607	33	33	5-2	0-0	240	254	114	22	4	73-3	165	3.75	116	.273	.325	89-1-9	.236	5*	110	15		2.2
2001	†SF N	13	15	.464	34	34	2	0-0	226.2	266	143	24	3	85-7	138	5.24	78	.297	.355	81-1-4	.296	8*	97	-30		-2.2
2002	†SF N	12	16	.429	33	33	5-3	0-0	216	233	113	19	4	71-5	134	4.38	90	.283	.340	64-0-10	.234	4*	101	-10		-0.6
2003	Mon N	15	10	.600	33	33	8	0-0	233.1	225	92	27	10	57-3	178	3.20	139	.253	.304	74-0-6	.189	0	110	31		3.4
2004	Mon N☆	11	15	.423	35	35	9-2	0-0	255	234	105	26	10	83-9	186	3.60	128	.248	.314	81-1-15	.247	5*	72	30		3.7
2005	Was N★	15	10	.600	35	35	2	0-0	246.1	268	116	25	13.	84-14	147	3.98	102	.284	.348	82-2-14	.244	5	96	2		1.0
Total 10		110	104	.514	284	283	42-7	0-0	1950.2	2056	965	208	55	673-55	1328	4.11	103	.274	.335	646-7-69	.237	39	99	25		7.9

HERNANDEZ, FELIX Felix Abraham (Garcia) B4.8.1986 Valencia, Venez BR/TR/6-3/170 d8.4

YEAR	TM LG	W	L	PCT	G	GS	CG-SHO	SV-BS	IP	H	R	HR	HB	BB-IB	SO	ERA	AERA	OAV	OOB	AB-HR-SH	AVG	PB	SUP	APR	DL	PW
2005	Sea A	4	4	.500	12	12	0	0-0	84.1	61	26	5	2	23-0	77	2.67	158	.203	.263	0	—	0	74	15		1.4

HERNANDEZ, FERNANDO Fernando B6.16.1971 Santiago, D.R. BR/TR/6-2/185 d4.3

YEAR	TM LG	W	L	PCT	G	GS	CG-SHO	SV-BS	IP	H	R	HR	HB	BB-IB	SO	ERA	AERA	OAV	OOB	AB-HR-SH	AVG	PB	SUP	APR	DL	PW
1997	Det A	0	0	—	2	0	0	0-0	1.1	5	6	0	1	3-1	2	40.50	11	.556	.692	0	—	0		-5		-0.2

HERNANDEZ, XAVIER Francis Xavier B8.16.1965 Port Arthur TX BL/TR/6-2/185* [TorA86 4/107] d6.4 Col Louisiana-Lafayette

YEAR	TM LG	W	L	PCT	G	GS	CG-SHO	SV-BS	IP	H	R	HR	HB	BB-IB	SO	ERA	AERA	OAV	OOB	AB-HR-SH	AVG	PB	SUP	APR	DL	PW
1989	Tor A	1	0	1.000	7	0	0	0-0	22.2	25	15	2	1	8-0	4	4.76	80	.278	.337	0	—	0		-3		-0.2
1990	Hou N	2	1	.667	34	1	0	0-1	62.1	60	34	8	4	24-5	24	4.62	81	.256	.331	3	.333	0*	48	-5		-0.3
1991	Hou N	2	7	.222	32	6	0	3-3	63	66	34	6	0	32-7	55	4.71	75	.263	.345	10-0-1	.000	-0	42	-7	23	-1.1
1992	Hou N	9	1	.900	77	0	0	7-3	111	81	31	5	3	42-7	96	2.11	161	.200	.279	9	.000	-1		15		1.4
1993	Hou N	4	5	.444	72	0	0	9-8	96.2	75	37	6	1	28-3	101	2.61	149	.212	.269	5-0-2	.000	-1		12		1.1
1994	NY A	4	4	.500	31	0	0	6-2	40	48	27	7	2	21-3	37	5.85	79	.300	.384	0	—	-1		-5	15	-0.9
1995	†Cin N	7	2	.778	59	0	0	3-1	90	95	47	8	4	31-1	84	4.60	91	.273	.338	8	.000	-1		-3		-0.4
1996	Cin N	0	0	—	3	0	0	0-0	3.1	8	6	2	0	2-0	3	13.50	32	.471	.526	0	—	-1		-4		-0.2
	Hou N	5	5	.500	58	0	0	6-4	74.2	69	39	11	2	26-5	78	4.22	92	.244	.310	2-0-1	.000	-0		-4		-0.2
	Year	5	5	.500	61	0	0	6-4	78	77	45	13	2	28-5	81	4.62	84	.258	.322	2-0-1	.000	-0		-3		-0.4
1997	Tex A	4	0	.000	44	0	0	0-1	49.1	51	27	7	2	22-4	36	4.56	107	.262	.341	0	—	0		-7		-0.6
1998	Tex A	6	6	.500	46	0	0	1-5	58	43	27	5	1	30-1	41	3.57	137	.207	.307	0	—	0		2	58	0.1
Total 10		40	35	.533	463	7	0	35-28	671	621	324	67	20	266-36	562	3.90	102	.244	.318	37-0-4	.027	-3	39	6	131	0.4

HERNANDEZ, EVELIO Gregorio Evelio (Lopez) B12.24.1931 Guanabacoa, Cuba BR/TR/6-1/195* d9.12

YEAR	TM LG	W	L	PCT	G	GS	CG-SHO	SV-BS	IP	H	R	HR	HB	BB-IB	SO	ERA	AERA	OAV	OOB	AB-HR-SH	AVG	PB	SUP	APR	DL	PW
1956	Was A	1	1	.500	4	4	1	0	22.2	24	12	2	0	8-0	9	4.76	91	.276	.333	11	.182	-0	103	0		-0.1
1957	Was A	0	0	—	14	2	0	0	36	38	18	2	0	20-1	15	4.25	92	.268	.356	6	.000	-1	115	-1		-0.2
Total 2		1	1	.500	18	6	1	0	58.2	62	30	4	0	28-1	24	4.45	91	.271	.347	17	.118	-1	110	-1		-0.3

HERNANDEZ, WILLIE Guillermo (Villanueva) B11.14.1954 Aguada, PR BL/TL/6-3/180* d4.9

YEAR	TM LG	W	L	PCT	G	GS	CG-SHO	SV-BS	IP	H	R	HR	HB	BB-IB	SO	ERA	AERA	OAV	OOB	AB-HR-SH	AVG	PB	SUP	APR	DL	PW
1977	Chi N	8	7	.533	67	1	0	4-7	110	94	42	11	1	28-9	78	3.03	146	.234	.284	16-0-3	.063	-1	20	15		2.0
1978	Chi N	8	2	.800	54	0	0	3-1	59.2	57	26	6	1	35-7	38	3.77	107	.263	.363	1	.000	-0*		2		0.4
1979	Chi N	4	4	.500	51	2	0	0-0	79	85	50	8	4	39-12	53	5.01	83	.281	.364	8-0-1	.250	-0*	128	-7		-0.6
1980	Chi N	1	9	.100	53	7	0	0-2	108.1	115	58	8	2	45-4	75	4.40	90	.281	.347	19-0-1	.211	0*	48	-4		-0.2
1981	Chi N	0	0	—	12	0	0	2-0	13.2	14	7	0	0	8-2	13	3.95	95	.280	.367	0	—	0*		0		0.0
1982	Chi N	4	6	.400	75	0	0	10-2	75	74	26	3	1	24-11	54	3.00	126	.268	.326	3-0-1	.000	0		7		1.2
1983	Chi N	1	0	1.000	11	1	0	1-0	19.2	16	8	0	0	6-1	18	3.20	119	.222	.282	2	.500	-1		1		0.1
	†Phi N	8	4	.667	63	0	0	7-3	95.2	93	39	9	1	26-7	75	3.29	109	.254	.305	13	.385	2	139	1		0.1
	Year	9	4	.692	74	1	0	8-3	115.1	109	47	9	1	32-8	93	3.28	111	.249	.301	15	.400	2	146	4		0.7
1984	†Det A★	9	3	.750	80	0	0	32-1	140.1	96	30	6	4	36-8	112	1.92	206	.194	.252	0	—	0		34		4.3
1985	Det A★	8	10	.444	74	0	0	31-9	106.2	82	38	13	1	14-2	76	2.70	152	.210	.236	1	.000	-0		16		3.1
1986	Det A☆	8	7	.533	64	0	0	24-6	88.2	87	35	13	5	21-1	77	3.55	117	.251	.301	0	—	0		8		1.6
1987	†Det A	3	4	.429	45	0	0	8-5	49	53	27	8	0	20-7	30	3.67	116	.276	.340	0	—	0		1	50	0.2
1988	Det A	6	5	.545	63	0	0	10-5	67.2	50	24	8	4	31-6	59	3.06	126	.208	.306	0	—	0		7		1.3
1989	Det A	2	2	.500	32	0	0	15-2	31.1	36	21	4	1	16-2	30	5.74	67	.293	.379	0	—	0		-6	69	-1.2
Total 13		70	63	.526	744	11	0	147-43	1044.2	952	431	97	25	349-79	788	3.38	119	.245	.308	63-0-6	.206	1	69	78	119	12.9

HERNANDEZ, JEREMY Jeremy Stuart B7.6.1966 Burbank CA BR/TR/6-6/195(195-210) [StLN87 2/46] d9.2 Col Cal St.-Northridge

YEAR	TM LG	W	L	PCT	G	GS	CG-SHO	SV-BS	IP	H	R	HR	HB	BB-IB	SO	ERA	AERA	OAV	OOB	AB-HR-SH	AVG	PB	SUP	APR	DL	PW
1991	SD N	0	0	—	9	0	0	2-0	14.1	8	1	0	0	5-0	9	0.00	—	.157	.232	2	.000	-0		5		0.3
1992	SD N	1	4	.200	26	0	0	1-1	36.2	39	17	4	1	11-5	25	4.17	86	.291	.338	2	.000	-0		-2		-0.2
1993	SD N	0	2	.000	21	0	0	0-0	34.1	41	19	2	0	7-1	26	4.72	88	.301	.333	1	.000	-0		-1		-0.1
	Cle A	6	5	.545	49	0	0	8-5	77.1	75	33	12	0	27-6	44	3.14	139	.261	.320	0	—	0		9		1.3
1994	Fla N	3	3	.500	21	0	0	9-3	23.1	16	9	0	2	14-3	13	2.70	165	.205	.337	1	.000	0		4	70	0.7
1995	Fla N	0	0	—	7	0	0	1-0	7	12	9	2	1	3-1	7	11.57	37	.400	.457	1	.000	0		-5	114	-0.3
Total 5		10	14	.417	133	0	0	20-10	193	191	88	20	4	67-16	122	3.64	114	.267	.327	5	.000	-0		10	184	1.7

HERNANDEZ, MANNY Manuel Antonio (Montas) B5.7.1961 LaRomana, D.R. BR/TR/6-0/150* d6.5

YEAR	TM LG	W	L	PCT	G	GS	CG-SHO	SV-BS	IP	H	R	HR	HB	BB-IB	SO	ERA	AERA	OAV	OOB	AB-HR-SH	AVG	PB	SUP	APR	DL	PW
1986	Hou N	2	3	.400	9	4	0	0-0	27.2	33	15	2	0	12-3	9	3.90	92	.306	.372	6-0-1	.000	-1	62	-2		-0.3
1987	Hou N	0	4	.000	6	3	0	0-0	21.2	25	15	1	1	5-1	12	5.40	73	.301	.341	5	.000	-1	84	-4		-0.7
1989	NY N	0	0	—	1	0	0	0-0	1	0	0	0	0	0-0	1	0.00	—	.000	.000	0	—	0		0		0.0
Total 3		2	7	.222	16	7	0	0-0	50.1	58	30	3	1	17-4	22	4.47	84	.299	.353	11-0-1	.000	-1	72	-6		-1.0

HERNANDEZ, ORLANDO Orlando P. "El Duque" B10.11.1965 Villa Clara, Cuba BR/TR/6-2/190(190-220) d6.3 b-Livan [DL 2003 Mon N 183]

YEAR	TM LG	W	L	PCT	G	GS	CG-SHO	SV-BS	IP	H	R	HR	HB	BB-IB	SO	ERA	AERA	OAV	OOB	AB-HR-SH	AVG	PB	SUP	APR	DL	PW
1998	†NY A	12	4	.750	21	21	3-1	0-0	141	113	53	11	6	52-1	131	3.13	140	.222	.299	7-0-1	.000	-1 0	146	20		2.1
1999	†NY A★	17	9	.654	33	33	2-1	0-0	214.1	187	108	24	8	87-2	157	4.12	115	.233	.311	3	.333	0	105	15		1.6
2000	†NY A	12	13	.480	29	29	3	0-0	195.2	186	104	34	6	51-2	141	4.51	106	.247	.298	9-0-1	.000	0	82	7	22	0.7
2001	†NY A	4	7	.364	17	16	0	0-0	94.2	90	51	19	5	42-1	77	4.85	92	.248	.333	0	—	0	70	-2	87	-0.2
2002	†NY A	8	5	.615	24	22	0	1-0	146	131	63	20	8	36-2	113	3.64	119	.236	.289	0	—	0	107	13	42	1.1
2004	†NY A	8	2	.800	15	15	0	0-0	84.2	73	31	9	5	36-0	84	3.30	139	.230	.318	0	—	0	111	13	103	1.4
2005	†Chi A	9	9	.500	24	22	0	1-0	128.1	137	77	18	12	50-1	91	5.12	88	.275	.352	3	.333	0	91	-7	50	-0.8
Total 7		70	49	.588	163	158	8-2	2-0	1004.2	917	487	132	50	354-9	794	4.11	111	.242	.312	22-0-2	.091	-1	101	59	487	5.9

HERNANDEZ, RAMON Ramon (Gonzalez) B8.31.1940 Carolina, PR BB/TL/5-9/170* d4.11

YEAR	TM LG	W	L	PCT	G	GS	CG-SHO	SV-BS	IP	H	R	HR	HB	BB-IB	SO	ERA	AERA	OAV	OOB	AB-HR-SH	AVG	PB	SUP	APR	DL	PW
1967	Atl N	0	2	.000	46	0	0	5	51.2	60	27	5	2	14-3	28	4.18	79	.296	.356	4	.000	-0		-5		-0.3
1968	Chi N	0	0	—	8	0	0	0	9	14	11	1	1	0-0	3	9.00	35	.350	.366	0	—	0		-6		-0.3
1971	Pit N	0	1	.000	10	0	0	0	12.1	5	1	0	0	2-1	7	0.73	466	.122	.163	2	.500	0		4		0.7
1972	†Pit N	5	0	1.000	53	0	0	14-1	70	50	14	3	3	22-2	47	1.67	199	.194	.264	12	.167	0		11		1.7
1973	Pit N	4	5	.444	59	0	0	11-1	89.2	71	27	5	4	25-8	64	2.41	146	.218	.282	6	.125	0		12		1.5
1974	†Pit N	5	7	.714	58	0	0	7-5	68.2	68	21	3	2	18-8	33	2.75	126	.258	.310	4	.250	1		7		0.8
1975	†Pit N	7	2	.778	46	0	0	5-3	64	62	21	0	0	28-14	43	2.95	121	.252	.325	6-0-2	.000	-0		6		1.0
1976	Pit N	2	2	.500	37	0	0	3-3	43	42	17	2	1	16-5	17	3.56	99	.262	.326	3	.000	0		6		1.0
	Chi N	0	0	—	2	0	0	0	1	2	1	0	0	0-0	0	0.00	—	.333	.333	0	—	0		1		0.0
	Year	2	2	.500	39	0	0	3-3	44.2	44	17	2	1	16-5	17	3.43	103	.265	.326	3	.000	0		2		0.0

YEAR	TM LG	W	L	PCT	G	GS	CG-SHO	SV-BS	IP	H	R	HR	HB	BB-IB	SO	ERA	AERA	OAV	OOB	AB-HR-SH	AVG	PB	SUP	APR	DL	PW
1977	Chi N	0	0	—	6	0	0	1-0	7.2	11	9	1	0	3-0	4	8.22	54	.306	.359	1	.000	-0		-3		-0.2
	Bos A	0	1	.000	12	0	0	1-0	12.2	14	10	2	1	7-1	8	5.68	79	.280	.379	0	—	0		-2		-0.2
Total	9	23	15	.605	337	0	0	46-11	430.1	399	158	23	14	135-42	255	3.03	115	.245	.307	40-0-2	.125	0		29		4.7

HERNANDEZ, ROBERTO Roberto Manuel (Rodriguez) B11.11.1964 Santurce, PR BR/TR/6-4/235(220-250) [CalA86 1/16] d9.2 Col South Carolina-Aiken

YEAR	TM LG	W	L	PCT	G	GS	CG-SHO	SV-BS	IP	H	R	HR	HB	BB-IB	SO	ERA	AERA	OAV	OOB	AB-HR-SH	AVG	PB	SUP	APR	DL	PW
1991	Chi A	1	0	1.000	9	3	0	1-0	15	18	15	1	0	7-0	6	7.80	51	.290	.362	0	—	0	153	-7		-0.4
1992	Chi A	7	3	.700	43	0	0	12-4	71	45	15	4	4	20-1	68	1.65	236	.180	.249	0	—	0		18		2.9
1993	†Chi A	3	4	.429	70	0	0	38-6	78.2	66	21	6	0	20-1	71	2.29	184	.228	.276	0	—	0		18		2.9
1994	Chi A	4	4	.500	45	0	0	14-6	47.2	44	29	5	1	19-1	50	4.91	96	.238	.311	0	—	0		-1		-0.3
1995	Chi A	3	7	.300	60	0	0	32-10	59.2	63	30	9	3	28-4	84	3.92	114	.266	.351	0	—	0		3		0.6
1996	Chi A★	6	5	.545	72	0	0	38-8	84.2	65	21	2	0	38-5	85	1.91	249	.208	.292	0	—	0		27		2.1
1997	Chi A	5	1	.833	46	0	0	27-4	48	38	15	5	1	24-4	47	2.44	181	.216	.312	0	—	0		7		1.3
	†SF N	5	2	.714	28	0	0	4-4	32.2	29	9	2	0	14-1	35	2.48	166	.238	.316	2	.500	0		6		1.0
1998	TB A	2	6	.250	67	0	0	26-9	71.1	55	33	5	5	41-4	55	4.04	119	.212	.330	0	—	0		16		2.5
1999	TB A	2	3	.400	72	0	0	43-4	73.1	68	27	1	4	33-1	69	3.07	162	.244	.329	0	—	0		12		2.2
2000	TB A	4	7	.364	68	0	0	32-8	73.1	76	33	9	3	23-1	46	4.12	120	.266	.336	0	—	0		6		1.1
2001	KC A	5	6	.455	63	0	0	28-6	67.2	69	34	7	1	26-3	46	4.33	115	.300	.345	0	—	0	32	2		0.4
2002	KC A	1	3	.250	53	0	0	26-7	52	62	29	2	3	12-2	39	4.35	97	.263	.385	0	—	0	15	-3		-0.3
2003	†Atl N	5	3	.625	66	0	0	0-4	60	61	36	10	3	43-7	45	4.35	97	.297	.379	0	—	0		-5		0.2
2004	Phi N	3	5	.375	63	0	0	0-4	56.2	66	39	9	1	29-3	44	4.76	93	.297	.379	0	—	0		13		2.6
2005	NY N	8	6	.571	67	0	0	4-6	69.2	57	20	5	2	28-4	61	2.58	161	.228	.309	0	—	0	153	123	82	23.1
Total	15	64	65	.496	892	3	0	324-90	961.1	882	406	86	31	405-42	866	3.33	136	.243	.323	2	.500	0	153	123	82	23.

HERNANDEZ, RUDY Rudolph Albert (Fuentes) B12.10.1931 Santiago, D.R. BR/TR/6-3/185* d7.3

YEAR	TM LG	W	L	PCT	G	GS	CG-SHO	SV-BS	IP	H	R	HR	HB	BB-IB	SO	ERA	AERA	OAV	OOB	AB-HR-SH	AVG	PB	SUP	APR	DL	PW
1960	Was A	4	1	.800	21	0	0	0	34.2	34	24	2	1	21-3	22	4.41	88	.262	.366	6-0-1	.167	-0*		-4		-0.5
1961	Was A	0	1	.000	7	0	0	0	9	8	5	0	0	3-0	4	3.00	134	.250	.306	0	—	0		0		0.1
Total	2	4	2	.667	28	0	0	0	43.2	42	29	2	1	24-3	26	4.12	95	.259	.354	6-0-1	.167	-0		-4		-0.4

HERNANDEZ, RUNELVYS Runelvys Antonio B4.27.1978 Santo Domingo, D.R. BR/TR/6-3/185(185-250) d7.15 [DL 2004 KC A 183]

YEAR	TM LG	W	L	PCT	G	GS	CG-SHO	SV-BS	IP	H	R	HR	HB	BB-IB	SO	ERA	AERA	OAV	OOB	AB-HR-SH	AVG	PB	SUP	APR	DL	PW
2002	KC A	4	4	.500	12	12	0	0-0	74.1	79	36	8	1	22-0	45	4.36	114	.273	.324	0	—	0	105	6		0.6
2003	KC A	7	5	.583	16	16	0	0-0	91.2	87	51	9	6	37-0	48	4.61	104	.249	.328	0	—	0	101	2	98	0.2
2005	KC A	8	14	.364	29	29	0	0-0	159.2	172	101	18	7	70-0	88	5.52	76	.277	.353	5	.000	-0	82	-22	15	-1.2
Total	3	19	23	.452	57	57	0	0-0	325.2	338	188	35	14	129-0	181	5.00	91	.268	.340	5	.000	-0	93	-14	296	-1.[ ]

HERNDON, JUNIOR Harry Francis B9.11.1978 Liberal KS BR/TR/6-1/190 [SDN97 9/290] d8.2

YEAR	TM LG	W	L	PCT	G	GS	CG-SHO	SV-BS	IP	H	R	HR	HB	BB-IB	SO	ERA	AERA	OAV	OOB	AB-HR-SH	AVG	PB	SUP	APR	DL	PW
2001	SD N	2	6	.250	12	8	0	0-0	42.2	55	34	5	3	25-5	14	6.33	66	.322	.417	12-0-1	.000	-1	75	-11		-1.

HERRELL, WALT Walter William "Reds" B2.19.1889 Rockville MD D1.23.1949 Front Royal VA d6.10

YEAR	TM LG	W	L	PCT	G	GS	CG-SHO	SV-BS	IP	H	R	HR	HB	BB-IB	SO	ERA	AERA	OAV	OOB	AB-HR-SH	AVG	PB	SUP	APR	DL	PW
1911	Was A	0	0	—	1	0	0	0	2	5	4	0	0	2	0	18.00	18	.556	.636	1	.000	-0		-3		-0.

HERRERA, ALEX Alexander Jose B11.5.1979 Maracaibo, Venez BL/TL/5-11/175* d9.13

YEAR	TM LG	W	L	PCT	G	GS	CG-SHO	SV-BS	IP	H	R	HR	HB	BB-IB	SO	ERA	AERA	OAV	OOB	AB-HR-SH	AVG	PB	SUP	APR	DL	PW
2002	Cle A	0	0	—	5	0	0	0-0	5.1	3	0	0	0	1-0	5	0.00	—	.158	.200	0	—	0		3		0.
2003	Cle A	0	0	—	10	0	0	0-0	7	7	7	3	0	8-1	6	9.00	49	.250	.417	0	—	0		-3		-0.
Total	2	0	0	—	15	0	0	0-0	12.1	10	7	3	0	9-1	11	5.11	87	.213	.339	0	—	0		0		-0.

HERRERA, BOBBY Procopio Rodriguez "Tito" (b Procopio Rodriguez (Herrera)) B7.26.1926 Nuevo Laredo, Tamaulipas, Mexico BR/TR/6-0/184 d4.19

YEAR	TM LG	W	L	PCT	G	GS	CG-SHO	SV-BS	IP	H	R	HR	HB	BB-IB	SO	ERA	AERA	OAV	OOB	AB-HR-SH	AVG	PB	SUP	APR	DL	PW
1951	StL A	0	0	—	3	0	0	0	2.1	6	7	2	1	4	1	27.00	16	.462	.611	0	—	0		-5		-0.

HERRIAGE, TROY William Troy "Dutch" B12.20.1930 Tipton OK BR/TR/6-1/170 d4.25

YEAR	TM LG	W	L	PCT	G	GS	CG-SHO	SV-BS	IP	H	R	HR	HB	BB-IB	SO	ERA	AERA	OAV	OOB	AB-HR-SH	AVG	PB	SUP	APR	DL	PW
1956	KC A	1	13	.071	31	16	1	0	103	135	83	16	6	64-6	59	6.64	65	.321	.414	25-0-2	.120	-1*	63	-24		-3

HERRIN, TOM Thomas Edward B9.12.1929 Shreveport LA D11.29.1999 Homer LA BR/TR/6-3/190 d4.13 Col Louisiana Tech

YEAR	TM LG	W	L	PCT	G	GS	CG-SHO	SV-BS	IP	H	R	HR	HB	BB-IB	SO	ERA	AERA	OAV	OOB	AB-HR-SH	AVG	PB	SUP	APR	DL	PW
1954	Bos A	1	2	.333	14	1	0	0	28.1	34	23	2	0	22	8	7.31	56	.315	.424	8	.125	-0	0	-8		-0.

HERRING, ART Arthur L "Red","Sandy" B3.10.1906 Altus OK D12.2.1995 Marion IN BR/TR/5-7/168 d9.12

YEAR	TM LG	W	L	PCT	G	GS	CG-SHO	SV-BS	IP	H	R	HR	HB	BB-IB	SO	ERA	AERA	OAV	OOB	AB-HR-SH	AVG	PB	SUP	APR	DL	PW
1929	Det A	2	1	.667	4	4	2	0	32	38	17	0	1	19	15	4.78	90	.302	.397	14	.214	1	103	0		0.
1930	Det A	3	3	.500	23	6	1	0	77.2	97	54	2	3	36	16	5.33	90	.315	.392	23-0-3	.130	-2	89	-4		-0.
1931	Det A	7	13	.350	35	16	9	1	165	186	95	8	8	67	64	4.31	106	.281	.355	55-0-3	.281	-1	93	4		-0.
1932	Det A	1	2	.333	12	0	0	2	22.1	25	18	2	1	15	12	5.24	90	.284	.394	4	.000	-0		-2		-0.
1933	Det A	1	2	.333	24	3	1	0	61	61	34	6	1	20	20	3.84	112	.264	.325	13	.077	-1	171	2		0.
1934	Bro N	2	4	.333	14	4	2	0	49.1	63	36	2	0	29	15	6.20	63	.307	.393	14	.143	1	111	-11		-1.
1939	Chi A	0	0	—	7	0	0	0	14.1	13	9	2	1	5	8	5.65	84	.250	.328	4	.000	-0		-1		-0.
1944	Bro N	3	4	.429	12	6	3-1	1	55.1	59	28	3	1	17	19	3.42	104	.277	.333	15-0-3	.250	0	122	-1		0
1945	Bro N	7	4	.636	22	15	7-2	2	124	103	60	11	3	43	34	3.48	108	.222	.292	42-0-4	.095	-2*	126	4		0
1946	Bro N	7	2	.778	35	2	0	5	86	91	39	2	1	29	34	3.35	101	.277	.338	22-0-1	.182	0	76	0		0
1947	Pit N	1	3	.250	11	0	0	2	10.2	18	11	3	0	4	6	8.44	50	.360	.407	2	.000	-0		-5		-0
Total	11	34	38	.472	199	56	25-3	13	697.2	754	401	41	20	284	243	4.32	96	.276	.349	208-0-13	.149	-4	110	-14		-2

HERRING, HERB Herbert Lee B7.22.1891 Danville AR D4.22.1964 Tucson AZ BR/TR/5-11/178 d9.4

YEAR	TM LG	W	L	PCT	G	GS	CG-SHO	SV-BS	IP	H	R	HR	HB	BB-IB	SO	ERA	AERA	OAV	OOB	AB-HR-SH	AVG	PB	SUP	APR	DL	PW
1912	Was A	0	0	—	1	0	0	0	1	1	0	0	0	1	0	0.00	—	.250	.400	0	—	0		0		0.

HERRING, BILL William Francis "Smoke" B10.31.1893 New York NY D9.10.1962 Honesdale PA BR/TR/6-3/185 d6.26

YEAR	TM LG	W	L	PCT	G	GS	CG-SHO	SV-BS	IP	H	R	HR	HB	BB-IB	SO	ERA	AERA	OAV	OOB	AB-HR-SH	AVG	PB	SUP	APR	DL	PW
1915	Bro F	0	0	—	3	0	0	0	3	5	6	1	1	2	3	15.00	18	.385	.500	0	—	0		-4		-0

HERRMANN, LEROY Leroy George B2.27.1906 Steward IL D7.3.1972 Livermore CA BR/TR/5-10/185 d7.30

YEAR	TM LG	W	L	PCT	G	GS	CG-SHO	SV-BS	IP	H	R	HR	HB	BB-IB	SO	ERA	AERA	OAV	OOB	AB-HR-SH	AVG	PB	SUP	APR	DL	PW
1932	Chi N	2	1	.667	7	0	0	0	12.2	18	9	0	0	9	5	6.39	59	.346	.443	2	.500	0		-3		-0
1933	Chi N	0	1	.000	9	1	0	1	21	26	19	3	4	8	4	5.57	59	.299	.384	6	.167	-0	102	-7		-0
1935	Cin N	3	5	.375	29	8	2	0	108	124	53	9	8	31	30	3.58	111	.297	.357	30	.267	1	117	4		0
Total	3	5	7	.417	45	9	2	1	141.2	168	81	12	12	48	39	4.13	93	.302	.370	38	.263	1	117	-6		-0

HERRMANN, MARTY Martin John "Lefty" B1.10.1893 Oldenburg IN D9.11.1956 Cincinnati OH BL/TL/5-10/150 d7.10 gs-Ed

YEAR	TM LG	W	L	PCT	G	GS	CG-SHO	SV-BS	IP	H	R	HR	HB	BB-IB	SO	ERA	AERA	OAV	OOB	AB-HR-SH	AVG	PB	SUP	APR	DL	PW
1918	Bro N	0	0	—	1	0	0	0	1	0	0	0	0	1	0	0.00	—	.000	.250	0	—	0		0		0

HERSHEY, FRANK Frank B12.13.1877 Gorham NY D12.15.1949 Canandaigua NY TR/5-10/175 d4.20

YEAR	TM LG	W	L	PCT	G	GS	CG-SHO	SV-BS	IP	H	R	HR	HB	BB-IB	SO	ERA	AERA	OAV	OOB	AB-HR-SH	AVG	PB	SUP	APR	DL	PW
1905	Bos N	0	1	.000	1	1	0	0	4	5	4	0	0	2	1	6.75	46	.313	.389	1	.000	-0	47	-2		-0

HERSHISER, OREL Orel Leonard B9.16.1958 Buffalo NY BR/TR/6-3/192* [LAN79 17/440] d9.1 C4 Col Bowling Green

YEAR	TM LG	W	L	PCT	G	GS	CG-SHO	SV-BS	IP	H	R	HR	HB	BB-IB	SO	ERA	AERA	OAV	OOB	AB-HR-SH	AVG	PB	SUP	APR	DL	PW
1983	LA N	0	0	—	8	0	0	1-0	8	7	6	1	0	6-0	5	3.38	107	.233	.361	0	—	0		-1		-0
1984	LA N	11	8	.579	45	20	8-4	2-2	189.2	160	65	9	4	50-8	150	2.66	134	.225	.278	50-0-8	.200	2	103	19		3
1985	†LA N	19	3	.864	36	34	9-5	0-0	239.2	179	72	8	6	68-5	157	2.03	173	.206	.267	76-0-10	.197	3*	114	37		5
1986	LA N	14	14	.500	35	35	8-1	0-0	231.1	213	112	13	5	86-11	153	3.85	90	.243	.312	71-0-10	.239	4*	96	-11		-0
1987	LA N★	16	16	.500	37	35	10-1	1-0	264.2	247	105	17	9	74-5	190	3.06	130	.247	.304	90-0-10	.211	4*	92	26		3
1988	†LA N★	23	8	.742	35	34	15-8	1-0	267	208	73	18	4	73-10	178	2.26	148	.213	.269	85-0-19	.129	-0*	107	35		4
1989	LA N☆	15	15	.500	35	33	8-4	0-0	256.2	226	75	9	3	77-14	178	2.31	148	.240	.298	77-0-10	.182	3	85	32		4
1990	LA N	1	1	.500	4	4	0	0-0	25.1	26	12	1	1	4-0	16	4.26	86	.260	.295	7-0-1	.000	-1	92	-1	160	-0
1991	LA N	7	2	.778	21	21	0	0-0	112	112	43	3	5	32-6	73	3.46	104	.259	.316	31-0-4	.258	3	140	5	51	1
1992	LA N	10	15	.400	33	33	1	0-0	210.2	209	101	15	4	69-13	130	3.67	94	.257	.320	68-0-6	.221	4*	81	-5		1
1993	LA N	12	14	.462	33	33	5-1	0-0	215.2	201	106	17	7	72-13	141	3.59	108	.246	.311	73-0-8	.356	10*	106	1		1
1994	LA N	6	6	.500	21	21	1	0-0	135.1	146	67	15	2	42-6	72	3.79	105	.279	.333	44-0-3	.205	2*	114	1		1
1995	†Cle A	16	6	.727	26	26	1-1	0-0	167.1	151	76	21	5	51-1	111	3.87	122	.244	.304	0	—	0	113	11		
1996	†Cle A	15	9	.625	33	33	1	0-0	206	238	115	21	12	58-4	125	4.24	115	.287	.341	0	—	0	109	5	15	-0
1997	†Cle A	14	6	.700	32	32	1	0-0	195.1	199	105	26	11	69-2	107	4.47	105	.272	.340	3-0-1	.000	-0	99	8		-0
1998	SF N	11	10	.524	34	34	0	0-0	202	200	105	22	13	85-7	126	4.41	91	.259	.341	66-0-8	.152	1	99	-8		-0
1999	†NY N	13	12	.520	32	32	0	0-0	179	175	92	14	11	77-2	89	4.58	95	.263	.342	62-0-3	.145	-1	97	-4		
2000	LA N	1	5	.167	10	6	0	0-1	24.2	42	36	5	11	14-1	13	13.14	34	.389	.493	7	.000	-1	86	-23		-1
Total	18	204	150	.576	510	466	68-25	5-3	3130.1	2939	1366	235	117	1007-108	2014	3.48	112	.248	.312	810-0-101	.201	32	104	139	241	1[ ]

YEAR	TM LG	W	L	PCT	G	GS	CG-SHO	SV-BS	IP	H	R	HR	HB	BB-IB	SO	ERA	AERA	OAV	OOB	AB-HR-SH	AVG	PB	SUP	APR	DL	PW

HESKETH, JOE Joseph Thomas B2.15.1959 Lackawanna NY BR/TL/6-2/170* [MonN80 2/50] d8.7

YEAR	TM LG	W	L	PCT	G	GS	CG-SHO	SV-BS	IP	H	R	HR	HB	BB-IB	SO	ERA	AERA	OAV	OOB	AB-HR-SH	AVG	PB	SUP	APR	DL	PW
1984	Mon N	2	2	.500	11	5	1-1	1-0	45	38	12	2	0	15-3	32	1.80	192	.233	.294	10	.100	0	97	8		0.7
1985	Mon N	10	5	.667	25	21	2-1	0-0	155.1	125	52	10	0	45-2	113	2.49	138	.222	.279	44-0-5	.091	-1*	94	15	44	1.3
1986	Mon N	6	5	.545	15	15	0	0-0	82.2	92	46	11	2	31-4	67	5.01	75	.283	.347	23-0-3	.000	-2	94	-9	94	-1.3
1987	Mon N	0	0	—	18	0	0	1-0	28.2	23	12	2	2	15-3	31	3.14	136	.211	.317	4-0-1	.000	-2		3		0.1
1988	Mon N	4	3	.571	60	0	0	9-2	72.2	63	30	1	0	35-9	64	2.85	128	.242	.328	2	.000	0		5		0.7
1989	Mon N	6	4	.600	43	0	0	3-1	48.1	54	34	5	0	26-6	44	5.77	62	.292	.376	2	.500	0		-11	21	-2.3
1990	Mon N	1	0	1.000	2	0	0	0-0	3	2	0	0	0	2-1	3	0.00	—	.200	.333	2	.500	0		1		0.3
	Atl N	0	2	.000	31	0	0	5-4	31	30	23	5	1	12-0	21	5.81	69	.248	.319	1	.000	-0		-6		-0.6
	Year	1	2	.333	33	0	0	5-4	34	32	23	5	1	14-1	24	5.29	76	.244	.320	1	.000	-0		-5		-0.3
	Bos A	0	4	.000	12	2	0	0-0	25.2	37	12	2	0	11-1	26	3.51	117	.333	.393	0	—	-0		-5		0.2
1991	Bos A	12	4	.750	39	17	0	0-0	153.1	142	59	19	0	53-3	104	3.29	132	.250	.313	0	—	0	11	1		1.8
1992	Bos A	8	9	.471	30	25	1	1-0	148.2	162	84	15	2	58-9	104	4.36	98	.276	.339	0	—	0	103	18		1.8
1993	Bos A	3	4	.429	28	5	0	1-0	53.1	62	35	4	0	29-4	34	5.06	92	.294	.376	0	—	0	93	-2		-0.2
1994	Bos A	8	5	.615	25	20	0	0-0	114	117	70	9	2	46-3	83	4.26	118	.267	.334	0	—	0	99	5	45	-0.3
Total 11		60	47	.561	339	114	4-2	21-7	961.2	947	469	85	9	378-48	726	3.78	108	.259	.328	86-0-9	.070	-2	96	25	204	0.4

HESS, OTTO Otto C. B10.10.1878 Bern, Switzerland D2.25.1926 Tucson AZ BL/TL/6-1/170 d8.3 ▲

YEAR	TM LG	W	L	PCT	G	GS	CG-SHO	SV-BS	IP	H	R	HR	HB	BB-IB	SO	ERA	AERA	OAV	OOB	AB-HR-SH	AVG	PB	SUP	APR	DL	PW
1902	Cle A	2	4	.333	7	4	4	0	43.2	67	42	0	1	23	13	5.98	58	.351	.423	14	.071	-1	104	-12		-1.3
1904	Cle A	8	7	.533	21	16	15-4	0	151.1	134	60	2	5	31	64	1.67	152	.238	.284	100-0-1	.120	-3*	102	8		0.4
1905	Cle A	10	15	.400	26	25	22-4	0	213.2	179	97	1	9	72	109	3.16	83	.229	.302	173-2-3	.254	5*	88	-11		-0.7
1906	Cle A	20	17	.541	43	36	33-7	3	333.2	274	104	4	24	85	167	1.83	143	.227	.291	154-0-1	.201	1*	109	28		3.3
1907	Cle A	6	6	.500	17	14	7	0	93.1	84	37	1	12	37	36	2.89	87	.243	.337	30-0-1	.133	0*	94	-1		-0.2
1908	Cle A	0	0	—	4	0	0	0	7	11	6	0	0	1	2	5.14	46	.407	.429	14	.000	-1*		-2		-0.2
1912	Bos N	12	17	.414	33	31	21	0	254	270	142	3	15	90	80	3.76	95	.283	.354	94-0-6	.245	3	103	-5		-0.3
1913	Bos N	7	17	.292	29	27	19-2	0	218.1	231	123	13	7	70	80	3.83	86	.279	.340	83-2-4	.313	8*	104	-10		-0.2
1914	Bos N	5	6	.455	14	11	7-1	1	89	89	39	2	5	33	24	3.03	91	.271	.347	47-1-2	.234	1*	116	-3		-0.1
1915	Bos N	0	1	.000	4	1	1	0	14	16	13	0	2	6	5	3.86	67	.286	.375	5	.400	1*	115	-4		-0.2
Total 10		70	90	.438	198	165	129-18	5	1418	1355	663	26	80	448	580	2.98	98	.257	.324	714-5-18	.216	14	103	-12		0.5

HESSELBACHER, GEORGE George Edward B1.18.1895 Philadelphia PA D2.18.1980 Rydal PA BR/TR/6-2/175 d6.29 Col Penn St.

YEAR	TM LG	W	L	PCT	G	GS	CG-SHO	SV-BS	IP	H	R	HR	HB	BB-IB	SO	ERA	AERA	OAV	OOB	AB-HR-SH	AVG	PB	SUP	APR	DL	PW
1916	Phi A	0	4	.000	6	4	2	0	26	33	33	3	0	22	6	7.27	39	.349	.461	8	.125	-0	86	-15		-1.8

HESTERFER, LARRY Lawrence B6.9.1878 Newark NJ D9.22.1943 Cedar Grove NJ BR/TL/5-8/145 d9.5

YEAR	TM LG	W	L	PCT	G	GS	CG-SHO	SV-BS	IP	H	R	HR	HB	BB-IB	SO	ERA	AERA	OAV	OOB	AB-HR-SH	AVG	PB	SUP	APR	DL	PW
1901	NY N	0	1	.000	1	1	1	0	6	15	15	0	0	3	2	7.50	44	.469	.514	2	.000	0	150	-6		-0.6

HETKI, JOHNNY John Edward B5.12.1922 Leavenworth KS BR/TR/6-1/205(190-205) d9.14

YEAR	TM LG	W	L	PCT	G	GS	CG-SHO	SV-BS	IP	H	R	HR	HB	BB-IB	SO	ERA	AERA	OAV	OOB	AB-HR-SH	AVG	PB	SUP	APR	DL	PW
1945	Cin N	1	2	.333	5	2	2	0	32.2	28	13	1	0	11	9	3.58	105	.235	.300	11	.091	-1	79	1		0.1
1946	Cin N	6	6	.500	32	11	4	1	126.1	121	44	3	1	31	41	2.99	112	.253	.300	33-0-5	.333	3	88	7		1.0
1947	Cin N	3	4	.429	37	5	2	0	96	110	72	7	1	48	33	5.81	71	.287	.368	27	.222	1	69	-19		-1.1
1948	Cin N	0	1	.000	3	0	0	0	6.2	8	7	0	0	3	3	9.45	41	.286	.355	1	.000	0		-4		-0.5
1950	Cin N	1	2	.333	22	1	0	0	53	53	33	9	3	27	21	5.09	83	.265	.361	9-0-2	.222	0	42	-5		-0.2
1952	StL N	0	1	1.000	3	1	0	0	9.1	15	7	2	0	2	4	3.86	101	.357	.386	1	.000	0	67	-1		-0.1
1953	Pit N	3	6	.333	54	2	0	9	118.1	120	60	9	1	33	37	3.95	113	.266	.318	24-0-1	.208	1	80	6		0.6
1954	Pit N	4	4	.500	58	1	0	9	83	102	53	11	0	30	27	4.99	84	.297	.349	9-0-1	.222	-0	21	-7		-1.0
Total 8		18	26	.409	214	23	8	13	525.1	557	289	42	6	185	175	4.39	91	.272	.334	115-0-9	.235	5	72	-22		-1.0

HETZEL, ERIC Eric Paul B9.25.1963 Crowley LA BR/TR/6-3/175* [BosA85 S1/1] d7.1 Col Louisiana St.

YEAR	TM LG	W	L	PCT	G	GS	CG-SHO	SV-BS	IP	H	R	HR	HB	BB-IB	SO	ERA	AERA	OAV	OOB	AB-HR-SH	AVG	PB	SUP	APR	DL	PW
1989	Bos A	2	3	.400	12	11	0	0-0	50.1	61	39	7	2	28-1	33	6.26	66	.296	.382	0	—	0	132	-11	21	-1.0
1990	Bos A	1	4	.200	9	8	0	0-0	35	39	28	3	1	21-0	20	5.91	69	.281	.377	0	—	0	72	-8		-1.0
Total 2		3	7	.300	21	19	0	0-0	85.1	100	67	10	3	49-1	53	6.12	67	.290	.380	0	—	0	107	-19	21	-2.0

HEUSSER, ED Edward Burlton "The Wild Elk of the Wasatch" B5.7.1909 Salt Lake Co. UT D3.1.1956 Aurora CO BB/TR(BR 1935-36, 38)/6-0.5/187 d4.25

YEAR	TM LG	W	L	PCT	G	GS	CG-SHO	SV-BS	IP	H	R	HR	HB	BB-IB	SO	ERA	AERA	OAV	OOB	AB-HR-SH	AVG	PB	SUP	APR	DL	PW
1935	StL N	5	5	.500	33	11	2	3	123.1	125	50	5	2	27	39	2.92	140	.263	.305	34-0-1	.118	-1	90	14		0.9
1936	StL N	7	3	.700	42	3	0	3	104.1	130	73	6	4	38	26	5.43	73	.310	.373	26-1-0	.269	3	72	-18		-1.4
1938	Phi A	0	0	—	1	0	0	0	1	2	3	1	0	1	0	27.00	14	.400	.500	0	—	0		-2		-0.1
1940	Phi A	6	13	.316	41	6	2	5	110.	144	84	11	2	42	39	4.99	89	.308	.368	30-1-1	.167	1	119	-11		-1.6
1943	Cin N	4	3	.571	26	10	2-1	0	91	97	40	4	0	23	28	3.46	96	.275	.319	27-0-1	.185	-1	120	-2		-0.3
1944	Cin N	13	11	.542	30	23	17-4	2	192.2	165	59	9	1	42	42	2.38	146	.231	.275	69-0-1	.217	1	68	25		3.1
1945	Cin N	11	16	.407	31	30	18-4	1	223	248	105	10	3	60	56	3.71	101	.280	.328	77-1-5	.247	4	73	1		0.6
1946	Cin N	7	14	.333	29	21	9-1	2	167.2	167	68	11	1	39	47	3.22	104	.260	.304	53-0-4	.208	2	83	4		0.5
1948	Phi N	3	2	.600	33	0	0	3	74	89	46	9	0	28	22	4.99	79	.299	.359	19	.158	-1		-8		-0.6
Total 9		56	67	.455	266	104	50-10	18	1087	1167	528	66	13	300	299	3.69	101	.274	.324	335-3-13	.206	8	81	3		1.1

HEVING, JOE Joseph William B9.2.1900 Covington KY D4.11.1970 Covington KY BR/TR/6-1/185 d4.29 b-Johnnie

YEAR	TM LG	W	L	PCT	G	GS	CG-SHO	SV-BS	IP	H	R	HR	HB	BB-IB	SO	ERA	AERA	OAV	OOB	AB-HR-SH	AVG	PB	SUP	APR	DL	PW
1930	NY N	7	5	.583	41	2	0	6	89.2	109	57	7	1	27	37	5.22	91	.309	.360	22-0-2	.227	-0	120	-3		-0.3
1931	NY N	1	6	.143	22	0	0	2	42.1	48	27	4	2	11	26	4.89	76	.277	.328	8-0-2	.125	-0		-6		-0.9
1933	Chi A	7	5	.583	40	6	3-1	6	118	113	50	6	2	27	47	2.67	159	.249	.295	38-0-1	.211	0	50	17		1.8
1934	Chi A	1	7	.125	33	2	0	4	88	133	85	12	3	48	40	7.26	65	.343	.419	27	.185	1	92	-25		-1.9
1937	Cle A	8	4	.667	40	0	0	4	72.2	92	53	6	2	30	35	4.83	95	.311	.378	19-0-2	.263	0		-5		-0.7
1938	Cle A	1	1	.500	3	0	0	0	6	10	8	0	0	5	0	9.00	52	.370	.469	1	.000	-0		-4		-0.6
	Bos A	8	1	.889	16	11	7-1	2	82	94	35	5	1	22	34	3.73	132	.283	.300	30-0-3	.133	-1	135	12		1.2
	Year	9	2	.818	19	11	7-1	2	88	104	43	5	1	27	34	4.09	120	.290	.341	31-0-3	.129	-2	135	9		0.6
1939	Bos A	11	3	.786	46	5	1	7	107	124	65	8	2	34	43	3.70	128	.295	.350	32-0-3	.188	-1	116	6		0.6
1940	Bos A	12	7	.632	39	7	4	3	119	129	63	6	3	42	55	4.01	112	.272	.335	40-0-2	.200	0	179	4		0.6
1941	Cle A	5	2	.714	27	3	2-1	5	70.2	63	21	2	1	31	18	2.29	172	.240	.323	15-0-1	.000	-1	73	13		1.4
1942	Cle A	5	3	.625	27	2	0	9	46.1	52	28	4	2	25	13	4.86	71	.278	.360	7-0-1	.000	-1	62	-7		-1.3
1943	Cle A	1	1	.500	30	2	1	0	72	58	23	1	2	34	34	2.75	113	.230	.326	14-0-2	.071	-0	54	4		1.3
1944	Cle A	8	3	.727	63	1	0	10	119.2	106	42	2	2	41	46	1.96	169	.239	.307	22-0-2	.182	-1	25	14		1.4
1945	Bos N	1	0	1.000	3	0	0	0	5.1	5	2	0	1	3	1	3.38	114	.294	.429	1-0-1	.000	-0		0		0.1
Total 13		76	48	.613	430	40	17-3	63	1038.2	1136	559	64	24	380	429	3.90	108	.279	.344	276-0-22	.170	-4	120	20		1.7

HEWITT, JAKE Charles Jacob B6.6.1870 Maidsville WV D5.18.1959 Morgantown WV BL/TL/5-7/150 d8.6 Col West Virginia

YEAR	TM LG	W	L	PCT	G	GS	CG-SHO	SV-BS	IP	H	R	HR	HB	BB-IB	SO	ERA	AERA	OAV	OOB	AB-HR-SH	AVG	PB	SUP	APR	DL	PW
1895	Pit N	1	0	1.000	4	2	1	2	13	13	6	1	0	2	2	4.15	108	.255	.296	6	.167	-1	103	2		0.1

HEYDEMAN, GREG Gregory George B1.2.1952 Carmel CA BR/TR/6-0/205 d9.2 Col Monterey Peninsula (CA) JC

YEAR	TM LG	W	L	PCT	G	GS	CG-SHO	SV-BS	IP	H	R	HR	HB	BB-IB	SO	ERA	AERA	OAV	OOB	AB-HR-SH	AVG	PB	SUP	APR	DL	PW
1973	LA N	0	0	—	1	0	0	0-0	2	2	1	0	0	1	1	4.50	77	.222	.364	0	—	0		0		0.0

HIBBARD, GREG James Gregory B9.13.1964 New Orleans LA BL/TL/6-0/190* [KCA86 16/417] d5.31 Col Alabama [DL 1995 Sea A 160, 1996 Sea A 183, 1997 Sea A 181]

YEAR	TM LG	W	L	PCT	G	GS	CG-SHO	SV-BS	IP	H	R	HR	HB	BB-IB	SO	ERA	AERA	OAV	OOB	AB-HR-SH	AVG	PB	SUP	APR	DL	PW
1989	Chi A	6	7	.462	23	23	2	0-0	137.1	142	58	6	2	41-0	55	3.21	120	.268	.321	0	—	0	109	8		0.8
1990	Chi A	14	9	.609	33	33	3-1	0-0	211	202	80	11	6	55-2	92	3.16	122	.255	.305	0	—	0	85	17		1.7
1991	Chi A	11	11	.500	32	29	5	0-0	194	196	107	23	2	57-1	71	4.31	93	.266	.320	0	—	0	114	-10		-1.0
1992	Chi A	10	7	.588	31	28	0	1-0	176	187	92	17	7	57-2	69	4.40	88	.277	.337	0	—	0	102	-9		-0.7
1993	Chi N	15	11	.577	31	31	1	0-0	191	209	96	19	3	47-9	82	3.96	102	.286	.327	0	—	0	102	-9		-0.7
1994	Sea A	1	5	.167	15	14	0	0-0	80.2	115	78	11	2	31-1	39	6.69	74	.328	.383	65-0-3	.092	-3*	100	-20	20	-0.3
Total 6		57	50	.533	165	158	11-1	1-0	990	1051	501	86	22	288-15	408	4.05	99	.275	.327	65-0-3	.092	-3	102	-14	593	-1.2

HIBBARD, JOHN John Denison B12.2.1864 Chicago IL D11.17.1937 Hollywood CA TL d7.31 Col Michigan

YEAR	TM LG	W	L	PCT	G	GS	CG-SHO	SV-BS	IP	H	R	HR	HB	BB-IB	SO	ERA	AERA	OAV	OOB	AB-HR-SH	AVG	PB	SUP	APR	DL	PW
1884	Chi N	1	1	.500	2	2	2-1	0	17	18	10	1	1	9	4	2.65	118	.300	.391	7	.000	-1	102	1		0.0

HICKERSON, BRYAN Bryan David B10.13.1963 Bemidji MN BL/TL/6-2/203(190-203) [MinA86 7/169] d7.25 Col Minnesota

YEAR	TM LG	W	L	PCT	G	GS	CG-SHO	SV-BS	IP	H	R	HR	HB	BB-IB	SO	ERA	AERA	OAV	OOB	AB-HR-SH	AVG	PB	SUP	APR	DL	PW
1991	SF N	2	2	.500	17	6	0	0-0	50	53	20	3	0	17-3	43	3.60	100	.275	.333	12-0-1	.000	-1	92	1		-0.1
1992	SF N	5	3	.625	61	5	0	0-5	87.1	74	31	7	1	21-2	68	3.09	108	.236	.282	4	.000	0	190	3		0.2
1993	SF N	7	5	.583	47	15	0	0-0	120.1	137	58	14	1	39-3	69	4.26	92	.291	.344	28-0-4	.143	0	119	-3		-0.2
1994	SF N	4	8	.333	28	14	0	1-0	98.1	118	60	20	1	38-6	59	5.40	75	.301	.363	27-0-2	.185	1	104	-13		-1.3
1995	Chi N	2	3	.400	38	0	0	1-2	31.2	36	28	3	0	15-4	28	6.82	61	.283	.359	2	.500	1		-10		-1.3
	Col N	1	0	1.000	18	0	0	0-1	16.2	33	24	5	1	13-1	31	11.88	45	.407	.495	1-0-1	1.000	1		-9		-0.4

YEAR	TM LG	W	L	PCT	G	GS	CG-SHO	SV-BS	IP	H	R	HR	HB	BB-IB	SO	ERA	AERA	OAV	OOB	AB-HR-SH	AVG	PB	SUP	APR	DL	PW
	Year	3	3	.500	56	0	0	1-3	48.1	69	52	8	1	28-5	40	8.57	54	.332	.414	3-0-1	.667	1		-20		-1.7
Total	5	21	21	.500	209	36	0	2-8	404.1	451	221	52	4	143-19	279	4.72	82	.286	.345	74-0-8	.149	0	112	-31		-3.3

HICKEY, JIM James Robert "Sid" B10.22.1920 N.Abington MA D9.20.1997 Manchester CT BR/TR/6-1/204 d4.25 Mil 1944-45

YEAR	TM LG	W	L	PCT	G	GS	CG-SHO	SV-BS	IP	H	R	HR	HB	BB-IB	SO	ERA	AERA	OAV	OOB	AB-HR-SH	AVG	PB	SUP	APR	DL	PW
1942	Bos N	0	1	.000	1	1	0	0	1.1	4	4	1	0	2	0	20.25	16	.500	.600	1	.000	-0	25	-3		-0.5
1944	Bos N	0	0	—	8	0	0	0	9.1	15	9	0	1	5	3	4.82	79	.366	.447	1	.000	-0		-2		-0.1
Total	2	0	1	.000	9	1	0	0	10.2	19	13	1	1	7	3	6.75	56	.388	.474	2	.000	-0	25	-5		-0.6

HICKEY, JACK John William B11.3.1881 Minneapolis MN D12.28.1941 Seattle WA BR/TL/5-10/170 d4.16

YEAR	TM LG	W	L	PCT	G	GS	CG-SHO	SV-BS	IP	H	R	HR	HB	BB-IB	SO	ERA	AERA	OAV	OOB	AB-HR-SH	AVG	PB	SUP	APR	DL	PW
1904	Cle A	0	1	.000	2	2	1	0	12.1	14	13	0	0	11	5	7.30	35	.286	.417	5	.000	-1	141	-6		-0.5

HICKEY, KEVIN Kevin John B2.25.1957 Chicago IL BL/TL/6-1/200(170-201) d4.14

YEAR	TM LG	W	L	PCT	G	GS	CG-SHO	SV-BS	IP	H	R	HR	HB	BB-IB	SO	ERA	AERA	OAV	OOB	AB-HR-SH	AVG	PB	SUP	APR	DL	PW
1981	Chi A	0	2	.000	41	0	0	3-0	44.1	38	22	3	1	18-5	17	3.65	99	.232	.308	0	—	0		-1		0.0
1982	Chi A	4	4	.500	60	0	0	6-2	78	73	32	4	2	30-6	38	3.00	136	.256	.327	0	—	0		8		1.0
1983	Chi A	1	2	.333	23	0	0	5-3	20.2	23	14	5	0	11-2	8	5.23	81	.264	.347	0	—	0	-3		33	-0.5
1989	Bal A	2	3	.400	51	0	0	2-0	49.1	38	16	3	1	23-4	28	2.92	131	.220	.315	0	—	0	6			-0.5
1990	Bal A	1	3	.250	37	0	0	1-0	26.1	26	16	3	0	13-2	17	5.13	75	.265	.348	0	—	0	-4			-0.6
1991	Bal A	1	0	1.000	19	0	0	0-1	14	15	14	3	0	6-0	10	9.00	44	.278	.339	0	—	0	-8			-0.5
Total	6	9	14	.391	231	0	0	17-6	232.2	213	114	21	4	101-19	118	3.91	100	.247	.326	0	—	0	-2	33		-0.1

HICKMAN, CHARLIE Charles Taylor "Cheerful Charlie", "Piano Legs" B3.4.1876 Taylortown (Dunkard Twp.) PA D4.19.1934 Morgantown WV BR/TR/5-9/180 d9.8 Col West Virginia ▲

YEAR	TM LG	W	L	PCT	G	GS	CG-SHO	SV-BS	IP	H	R	HR	HB	BB-IB	SO	ERA	AERA	OAV	OOB	AB-HR-SH	AVG	PB	SUP	APR	DL	PW
1897	†Bos N	0	0	—	2	0	1		7.2	10	5	0	0	5	0	5.87	76	.313	.405	3-1-0	.667	2		-1		0.1
1898	Bos N	1	2	.333	6	3	3-1	2	33	22	8	0	0	13	9	2.18	169	.188	.269	58-0-1	.259	0*	83	6		0.6
1899	Bos N	6	0	1.000	11	9	5-2	1	66.1	52	38	3	8	40	14	4.48	93	.216	.346	63-0-1	.397	6*	167	0		0.3
1901	NY N	3	5	.375	9	9	6	0	65	76	42	1	3	26	11	4.57	72	.290	.361	406-4-0	.278	2*	64	-7		-0.5
1902	Cle A	0	1	.000	1	1	1	0	8	11	8	0	1	5	1	7.88	44	.324	.425	426-8-8	.378	1*	146	-3		0.0
1907	Was A	0	0	—	1	0	0	0	5	4	4	0	0	5	2	3.60	67	.222	.391	198-1-1	.278	0*		-1		0.0
Total	6	10	8	.556	30	22	15-3	4	185	175	105	4	12	94	37	4.28	86	.249	.347	1154-14-11	.321	11	117	-6		0.2

HICKMAN, ERNIE Ernest P. B1856 E.St.Louis IL D11.19.1891 E.St.Louis IL d6.7

YEAR	TM LG	W	L	PCT	G	GS	CG-SHO	SV-BS	IP	H	R	HR	HB	BB-IB	SO	ERA	AERA	OAV	OOB	AB-HR-SH	AVG	PB	SUP	APR	DL	PW
1884	KC U	4	13	.235	17	17	15	0	137.1	172	146	6		36	68	4.52	49	.287	.328	72	.167	-7*	67	-41		-4.1

HICKMAN, JESSE Jesse Owens B2.18.1939 Lecompte LA BR/TR/6-2/186* d6.5 Col Louisiana

YEAR	TM LG	W	L	PCT	G	GS	CG-SHO	SV-BS	IP	H	R	HR	HB	BB-IB	SO	ERA	AERA	OAV	OOB	AB-HR-SH	AVG	PB	SUP	APR	DL	PW
1965	KC A	0	1	.000	12	0	0	0	15.1	9	10	3	0	8-0	16	5.87	59	.184	.293	0	—	0*	-3			-0.2
1966	KC A	0	0	—	1	0	0	0	1	0	0	0	0	1-0	0	0.00	—	.000	.333	0	—	0	0			0.0
Total	2	0	1	.000	13	0	0	0	16.1	9	10	3	0	9-0	16	5.51	63	.176	.295	0	—	0	-3			-0.2

HIGBE, KIRBY Walter Kirby B4.8.1915 Columbia SC D5.6.1985 Columbia SC BR/TR/5-11/190* d10.3 Mil 1944-45

YEAR	TM LG	W	L	PCT	G	GS	CG-SHO	SV-BS	IP	H	R	HR	HB	BB-IB	SO	ERA	AERA	OAV	OOB	AB-HR-SH	AVG	PB	SUP	APR	DL	PW
1937	Chi N	1	0	1.000	1	0	0	0	5	4	3	1	0	1	2	5.40	74	.182	.217	3	.000	-0		-1		-0.2
1938	Chi N	0	0	—	2	2	0	0	10	10	6	1	0	6	4	5.40	71	.263	.364	3	.000	-0	111	-1		-0.1
1939	Chi N	2	1	.667	9	2	0	0	22.2	12	9	0	0	22	16	3.18	124	.158	.347	7-0-1	.286	1	177	2		0.3
	Phi N	10	14	.417	34	26	14-1	2	187.1	209	113	10	10	101	79	4.85	83	.283	.378	64-0-6	.167	-2	92	-17		-2.3
	Year	12	15	.444	43	28	14-1	2	210	220	122	10	10	123	95	4.67	86	.272	.374	73-0-7	.178	-1	98	-14		-2.0
1940	Phi N☆	14	19	.424	41	36	20-1	1	283	242	126	12	3	121	137	3.72	105	.232	.313	112-0-6	.188	1	126	17		1.4
1941	†Bro N	22	9	.710	48	39	19-2	3	298	244	123	17	6	132	121	3.14	117	.220	.306	77-0-7	.104	-4	127	2		-0.3
1942	Bro N	16	11	.593	38	32	13-2	0	221.2	180	89	17	2	106	115	3.25	100	.223	.315	65-1-4	.138	-2	95	-5		-0.8
1943	Bro N	13	10	.565	35	27	8-1	0	185	189	81	4	5	95	108	3.70	91	.264	.354	77-0-6	.130	-4	121	9		-0.1
1946	Bro N★	17	8	.680	42	29	11-3	1	210.2	178	82	6	1	107	134	3.03	111	.229	.323	77-0-6	.130	-4	121	9		-0.1
1947	Bro N	2	0	1.000	4	3	0	0	15.2	18	9	0	1	12	10	5.17	80	.295	.419	5	.200	-1	90	11		1.0
	Pit N	11	17	.393	46	30	10-1	5	225	204	108	22	3	110	99	3.72	113	.240	.329	72-1-6	.139	-1	90	11		1.0
	Year	13	17	.433	50	33	10-1	5	240.2	222	117	22	4	122	109	3.81	111	.243	.335	48-1-0	.208	1	97	10		0.8
1948	Pit N	8	7	.533	56	8	3	10	158	140	75	11	3	83	86	3.36	121	.240	.337		.000	-0	126	-15		-1.5
1949	Pit N	0	2	.000	7	1	0	0	15.1	25	24	2	0	12	5	13.50	31	.379	.474	3	.000	-0	122	2		0.0
	NY N	2	0	1.000	37	2	0	2	80.1	72	42	11	1	41	38	5.08	79	.242	.335	15	.067	-0	124	-12		-1.5
	Year	2	2	.500	44	3	0	2	95.2	97	66	13	1	53	43	5.08	79	.266	.361	18	.056	-1	124	-12		-1.5
1950	NY N	0	3	.000	18	1	0	0	34.2	37	19	2	0	30	17	4.93	83	.285	.419	4	.250	-1	129	-2		-0.1
Total	12	118	101	.539	418	238	98-11	24	1952.1	1763	909	116	35	979	971	3.69	102	.241	.333	660-3-39	.153	-14	104	17		-0.5

HIGGINBOTHAM, IRV Irving Clinton B4.26.1882 Homer NE D6.12.1959 Seattle WA BR/TR/6-1/196 d8.11

YEAR	TM LG	W	L	PCT	G	GS	CG-SHO	SV-BS	IP	H	R	HR	HB	BB-IB	SO	ERA	AERA	OAV	OOB	AB-HR-SH	AVG	PB	SUP	APR	DL	PW
1906	StL N	1	4	.200	7	6	4	0	47.1	50	23	1	1	11	14	3.23	81	.266	.310	18	.222	0	46	-3		-0.3
1908	StL N	3	8	.273	19	11	7-1	0	107	113	51	0	3	33	38	3.20	74	.270	.328	38-0-1	.132	-1	81	-8		-1.0
1909	StL N	1	0	1.000	3	1	1	0	11.1	5	3	0	0	2	2	1.59	159	.143	.189	3	.000	-0	138	1		0.0
	Chi N	5	2	.714	19	6	4	1	78	64	32	0	3	20	32	2.19	116	.213	.269	26-0-1	.231	1	202	1		0.1
	Year	6	2	.750	22	7	5	1	89.1	69	35	0	3	22	34	2.12	120	.205	.260	29-0-1	.207	0	193	2		0.1
Total	3	10	14	.417	48	24	16-1	1	243.2	232	109	1	7	66	86	2.81	88	.246	.300	85-0-2	.176	-1	106	-9		-1.2

HIGGINS, DENNIS Dennis Dean B8.4.1939 Jefferson City MO BR/TR/6-4/190(180-198) d4.12

YEAR	TM LG	W	L	PCT	G	GS	CG-SHO	SV-BS	IP	H	R	HR	HB	BB-IB	SO	ERA	AERA	OAV	OOB	AB-HR-SH	AVG	PB	SUP	APR	DL	PW
1966	Chi A	1	0	1.000	42	1	0	5	93	66	29	9	5	33-4	86	2.52	126	.202	.283	17	.176	0	195	9		0.5
1967	Chi A	1	2	.333	14	0	0	0	12.1	13	9	0	3	10-0	8	5.84	53	.271	.426	1	.000	-0	-4		79	-0.8
1968	Was A	4	4	.500	59	0	0	13	99.2	81	40	9	3	46-9	66	3.25	90	.226	.313	15-0-1	.133	-0	-3			-0.5
1969	Was A	10	9	.526	55	0	0	16-10	85.1	79	42	7	3	56-7	71	3.48	101	.252	.364	11-0-1	.091	-1	-2			-0.5
1970	Cle A	4	6	.400	58	0	0	11-2	90.1	82	43	6	2	54-8	82	3.99	101	.248	.356	12-0-1	.250	1	0			0.1
1971	StL N	1	0	1.000	3	0	0	0-0	7	6	3	0	0	2-0	6	3.86	94	.240	.286	1	.000	0	0			0.0
1972	StL N	1	2	.333	15	1	0	1-0	22.2	19	14	0	0	22-0	20	3.97	86	.226	.387	1	.000	-0	103	-3		-0.4
Total	7	22	23	.489	241	2	0	46-12	410.1	346	178	33	16	223-28	339	3.42	99	.233	.335	58-0-3	.155	0	144	-3	79	-1.6

HIGGINS, EDDIE Thomas Edward "Doc", "Irish" B3.18.1888 Nevada IL D2.14.1959 Elgin IL BR/TR/6-0.5/174 d5.14

YEAR	TM LG	W	L	PCT	G	GS	CG-SHO	SV-BS	IP	H	R	HR	HB	BB-IB	SO	ERA	AERA	OAV	OOB	AB-HR-SH	AVG	PB	SUP	APR	DL	PW
1909	StL N	3	3	.500	16	5	5	0	66	68	36	4	1	17	15	4.50	68	.273	.322	21	.190	-0	55	-11		-1.0
1910	StL N	0	1	.000	2	0	0	0	10.1	15	8	0	0	7	1	4.35	68	.349	.440	5	.400	1*		-2		-0.1
Total	2	3	4	.429	18	5	5	0	76.1	83	44	4	1	24	16	4.48	58	.284	.341	26	.231	1	55	-13		-1.1

HIGH, ED Edward Thomas "Lefty" B10.26.1873 Baltimore MD D2.10.1926 Baltimore MD TL d7.4

YEAR	TM LG	W	L	PCT	G	GS	CG-SHO	SV-BS	IP	H	R	HR	HB	BB-IB	SO	ERA	AERA	OAV	OOB	AB-HR-SH	AVG	PB	SUP	APR	DL	PW
1901	Det A	0	1	.000	1	1	1	0	18	21	9	0	1	6	4	3.50	110	.288	.350	7	.000	-1	88	1		0.4

HIGUERA, TEDDY Teodoro Valenzuela (Valenzuela) B11.9.1958 Los Mochis, Sinaloa, Mexico BB/TL/5-10/178* d4.23 [DL 1992 Mil A 182]

YEAR	TM LG	W	L	PCT	G	GS	CG-SHO	SV-BS	IP	H	R	HR	HB	BB-IB	SO	ERA	AERA	OAV	OOB	AB-HR-SH	AVG	PB	SUP	APR	DL	PW
1985	Mil A	15	8	.652	32	30	7-2	0-0	212.1	186	105	22	3	63-0	127	3.90	108	.235	.290	0	—	0	96	7		0.7
1986	Mil A★	20	11	.645	34	34	15-4	0-0	248.1	226	84	26	3	74-5	207	2.79	156	.241	.296	0	—	0	83	43		5.1
1987	Mil A	18	10	.643	35	35	14-3	0-0	261.2	236	120	24	2	87-2	240	3.85	120	.241	.301	0	—	0	109	22		2.3
1988	Mil A	16	9	.640	31	31	8-1	0-0	227.1	168	66	15	6	59-4	192	2.45	163	.207	**.263**	0	—	0	96	40		4.5
1989	Mil A	9	6	.600	22	22	2-1	0-0	135.1	125	56	9	4	48-2	91	3.46	112	.248	.316	0	—	0	98	7	28	0.3
1990	Mil A	11	10	.524	27	27	4-1	0-0	170	167	80	16	3	50-2	129	3.76	103	.256	.310	0	—	0	102	3	15	0.2
1991	Mil A	3	2	.600	7	6	0	0-0	36.1	37	18	7	1	10-0	33	4.46	90	.262	.314	0	—	0	137	-1	144	-0.1
1993	Mil A	1	3	.250	8	8	0	0-0	30	43	24	4	1	16-2	27	7.20	60	.333	.408	0	—	0	117	-9	131	-1.2
1994	Mil A	1	5	.167	17	12	0	0-0	58.2	74	55	13	2	36-0	35	7.06	72	.311	.403	0	—	0	89	-14		-1.1
Total	9	94	64	.595	213	205	50-12	0-0	1380	1262	608	131	25	443-17	1081	3.61	117	.243	.303	0	—	0	99	98	500	10.6

HILCHER, WHITEY Walter Frank B2.28.1909 Chicago IL D11.21.1962 Minneapolis MN BR/TR/6-0/174 d9.17 Col Alabama

YEAR	TM LG	W	L	PCT	G	GS	CG-SHO	SV-BS	IP	H	R	HR	HB	BB-IB	SO	ERA	AERA	OAV	OOB	AB-HR-SH	AVG	PB	SUP	APR	DL	PW
1931	Cin N	0	1	.000	2	1	0	0	12	16	5	0	1	4	9	3.00	125	.320	.382	4	.000	-1	69	1		0.0
1932	Cin N	0	3	.000	11	2	0	0	18.2	24	19	3	0	10	4	7.71	50	.316	.395	3	.333	-1	76	-8		-1.1
1935	Cin N	2	0	1.000	4	2	1-1	0	19.1	19	6	0	0	5	9	2.79	142	.264	.312	6	.167	-0	75	3		0.0
1936	Cin N	1	2	.333	14	1	0	0	35	44	31	3	1	14	10	6.17	62	.299	.364	8	.000	-1	178	-11		-0.7
Total	4	3	6	.333	31	6	1-1	0	85	103	61	6	2	33	28	5.29	73	.299	.363	21	.095	-2	92	-15		-1.8

HILDEBRAND, ORAL Oral Clyde B4.7.1907 Indianapolis IN D9.8.1977 Southport IN BR/TR/6-3/175 d9.8 Col Butler

YEAR	TM LG	W	L	PCT	G	GS	CG-SHO	SV-BS	IP	H	R	HR	HB	BB-IB	SO	ERA	AERA	OAV	OOB	AB-HR-SH	AVG	PB	SUP	APR	DL	PW
1931	Cle A	2	1	.667	5	2	2	0	26.2	25	16	0	3	13	6	4.39	105	.243	.345	11	.182	-1	64	0		0.0
1932	Cle A	8	6	.571	27	15	7	0	129.1	124	69	7	0	62	49	3.69	129	.249	.333	48-0-3	.146	-3	84	12		0.0
1933	Cle A☆	16	11	.593	36	31	15-6	0	220.1	205	110	8	1	88	90	3.76	118	.245	.318	84	.196	-1	93	16		1.0
1934	Cle A	11	9	.550	33	28	10-1	1	198	225	110	8	3	99	72	4.50	101	.282	.364	76-0-4	.171	-1	124	3		0.0

YEAR	TM LG	W	L	PCT	G	GS	CG-SHO	SV-BS	IP	H	R	HR	HB	BB-IB	SO	ERA	AERA	OAV	OOB	AB-HR-SH	AVG	PB	SUP	APR	DL	PW
1935	Cle A	9	8	.529	34	20	8	5	171.1	171	85	12	3	63	49	3.94	114	.263	.331	55-0-6	.164	-2	97	11		0.8
1936	Cle A	10	11	.476	36	21	9	4	174.2	197	107	10	4	83	65	4.90	103	.283	.362	63-0-2	.190	0	116	4		0.4
1937	StL A	8	17	.320	30	27	12-1	1	201.1	228	127	18	3	87	75	5.14	94	.284	.356	70-0-9	.200	-1	90	-6		-0.7
1938	StL A	8	10	.444	23	23	10	0	163	194	104	18	3	73	66	5.69	87	.297	.370	59-0-4	.254	1*	82	-8		-0.7
1939	†NY A	10	4	.714	21	15	7-1	2	126.2	102	44	11	1	41	50	3.06	143	.219	.284	44-0-3	.182	-1	113	21		2.0
1940	NY A	1	1	.500	13	0	0	0	19.1	19	7	1	1	14	5	1.86	217	.268	.395	3	.000	-0		4		0.3
Total	10	83	78	.516	258	182	80-9	13	1430.2	1490	781	99	22	623	527	4.35	107	.267	.343	513-0-31	.187	-9	99	57		4.5

HILGENDORF, TOM Thomas Eugene B3.10.1942 Clinton IA BB/TL/6-1/190(175-190) d8.15

1969	StL N	0	0	—	6	0	0	2-1	6.1	7	1	1	0	2-0	2	1.42	252	.150	.217	1	1.000	1		2		0.2
1970	StL N	0	4	.000	32	0	0	3-0	20.2	22	11	0	0	13-5	13	3.92	106	.272	.368	1	.000	-0		0		0.0
1972	Cle A	3	1	.750	19	5	1	0-2	47	51	16	4	2	21-7	25	2.68	122	.283	.361	13	.077	-1	147	3		0.2
1973	Cle A	5	3	.625	48	1	0	6-2	94.2	87	38	9	3	36-6	58	3.14	126	.242	.316	0	—	0	45	8		0.8
1974	Cle A	4	3	.571	35	0	0	3-3	48.1	58	26	6	1	17-6	23	4.84	75	.302	.353	0	—	0		-5		-0.7
1975	Phi N	7	3	.700	53	0	0	0-2	96.2	81	32	6	1	38-3	52	2.14	176	.230	.303	12-0-2	.250	1		14		1.5
Total	6	19	14	.576	184	6	2	14-10	313.2	302	124	25	7	127-27	173	3.04	123	.255	.327	27-0-2	.185	1	114	22		2.0

HILJUS, ERIK Erik Kristian B12.25.1972 Los Angeles CA BR/TR/6-5/230* [NYN91 4/121] d9.10

1999	Det A	0	0	—	6	0	0	0-0	8.2	7	5	2	0	5-0	1	5.19	96	.241	.343	0	.	0		0		0.0
2000	Det A	0	0	—	3	0	0	0-0	3.2	5	3	1	0	1-0	2	7.36	67	.333	.375	0	—	0		-1		0.0
2001	†Oak A	5	0	1.000	16	11	0	0-0	66	70	29	7	0	21-1	67	3.41	134	.263	.316	0	—	0	161	8		0.5
2002	Oak A	3	3	.500	9	9	0	0-0	45.2	52	36	11	0	21-1	29	6.50	69	.284	.356	0	—	0	94	-10		-1.1
Total	4	8	3	.727	34	20	0	0-0	124	134	73	21	0	48-2	99	4.79	95	.272	.335	0	—	0	130	-3		-0.6

HILL, CARMEN Carmen Proctor "Specs", "Bunker" B10.1.1895 Royalton MN D1.1.1990 Indianapolis IN BR/TR/6-1/180 d8.24

1915	Pit N	2	1	.667	8	3	2-1	0	47	42	8	0	2	13	24	1.15	238	.255	.317	13	.154	0	91	8		0.6
1916	Pit N	0	0	—	2	0	0	0	6.1	11	10	0	1	5	5	8.53	31	.611	.708	0	—	0		-5		-0.2
1918	Pit N	2	3	.400	6	4	3	0	43.2	24	11	0	0	17	15	1.24	232	.160	.246	12-0-1	.167	0	79	6		0.9
1919	Pit N	0	0	—	4	0	0	0	5	12	6	0	0	1	1	9.00	33	.480	.500	0	—	0		-3		-0.2
1922	NY N	2	1	.667	8	4	0	0	28.1	33	15	0	0	5	6	4.76	84	.295	.325	11	.182	-0	112	-1		-0.1
1926	Pit N	3	3	.500	6	6	4-1	0	39.2	42	17	2	2	9	8	3.40	116	.288	.338	17	.176	-1	123	3		0.4
1927	†Pit N	22	11	.667	43	31	22-2	3	277.2	260	125	12	4	80	95	3.24	127	.249	.305	104-0-3	.212	2*	107	22		2.6
1928	Pit N	16	10	.615	36	31	16-1	2	237	229	110	16	4	81	73	3.53	115	.259	.324	86-0-4	.233	2	107	14		1.4
1929	Pit N	2	3	.400	27	3	0	3	79	94	45	4	0	35	28	3.99	120	.297	.366	28	.036	-3	85	5		0.0
	StL N	0	0	—	3	1	0	0	8.2	10	10	2	1	8	1	8.31	56	.303	.452	3	.000	-0	262	-4		-0.2
	Year	2	3	.400	30	4	0	3	87.2	104	55	6	1	43	29	4.41	108	.297	.376	31	.032	-4	128	1		-0.2
1930	StL N	0	1	.000	4	2	0	0	14.2	12	12	2	0	13	8	7.36	68	.240	.397	3	.333	0	122	-3		-0.2
Total	10	49	33	.598	147	85	47-5	8	787	769	369	38	14	267	264	3.44	116	.261	.326	277-0-8	.191	-0	109	42		5.0

HILL, RED Clifford Joseph B1.20.1893 Marshall TX D8.11.1938 El Paso TX BB/TL d4.21

1917	Phi A	0	0	—	1	0	0	0	2.2	5	4	0	0	1	0	6.75	41	.385	.429	0	—	0		-2		-0.1

HILL, DAVE David Burnham B11.11.1937 New Orleans LA BR/TL/6-2/170 d8.22 Col Northwestern

1957	KC A	0	0	—	2	0	0	3-0	2.1	6	7	3	0	3-0	1	27.00	15	.462	.563	0	—	0		-5		-0.3

HILL, GARRY Garry Alton B11.3.1946 Rutherfordton NC BR/TR/6-2/195 [AtlN67 S1/8] d6.12 Col North Carolina-Asheville

1969	Atl N	0	1	.000	1	1	0	0-0	2.1	6	4	0	1	1-0	2	15.43	23	.462	.500	0	—	0	147	-3		-0.5

HILL, HERBERT Herbert Lee B8.19.1891 Hutchins TX D9.1.1970 Farmers Branch TX BR/TR/5-11.5/175 d7.17

1915	Cle A	0	0	—	1	0	0	0	2	1	0	0	0	2	1	0.00	—	.250	.500	0	—	0		1		0.0

HILL, JEREMY Jeremy Dee B8.8.1977 Dallas TX BR/TR/5-10/200* [KCA96 5/139] d9.7

2002	KC A	0	1	.000	10	0	0	0-0	9.1	8	4	1	0	8-1	7	3.86	129	.235	.372	0	—	0		1		0.1
2003	KC A	0	0	—	1	0	0	0-0	1	1	0	0	0	0-0	0	0.00	—	.250	.250	0	—	0		1		0.0
Total	2	0	1	.000	11	0	0	0-0	10.1	9	4	1	0	8-1	7	3.48	143	.237	.362	0	—	0		2		0.1

HILL, KEN Kenneth Wade B12.14.1965 Lynn MA BR/TR/6-2/175(175-215) d9.3 Col Massachusetts Liberal Arts

1988	StL N	0	1	.000	4	1	0	0-0	14	16	9	0	0	6-0	6	5.14	68	.286	.355	3	.000	-0	50	-3	35	-0.2
1989	StL N	7	15	.318	33	33	2-1	0-0	196.2	186	92	9	5	99-6	112	3.80	97	.252	.342	59-0-8	.153	-0	92	-3		-0.3
1990	StL N	5	6	.455	17	14	1	0-0	78.2	79	49	7	1	33-1	58	5.49	70	.264	.334	19-0-5	.211	1	102	-12		-1.4
1991	StL N	11	10	.524	30	30	0	0-0	181.1	147	76	15	6	67-4	121	3.57	105	.224	.299	50-0-7	.100	-1	92	5	21	0.4
1992	Mon N	16	9	.640	33	33	3-3	0-0	218	187	76	13	3	75-4	150	2.68	130	.230	.297	62-1-10	.177	5	100	17		2.7
1993	Mon N	9	7	.563	28	28	2	0-0	183.2	163	84	7	6	74-7	90	3.23	129	.238	.315	52-0-14	.115	-1*	98	16	21	1.4
1994	Mon N★	16	5	.762	23	23	2-1	0-0	154.2	145	61	12	6	44-7	85	3.32	128	.248	.304	48-0-16	.146	-0*	124	17		2.2
1995	StL N	6	7	.462	18	18	1	0-0	110.1	125	71	11	6	45-4	50	5.06	85	.286	.351	31-0-5	.194	-0	98	-9		-0.9
	†Cle A	4	1	.800	12	11	1	0-0	74.2	77	36	5	1	32-0	48	3.98	110	.268	.343	0	—	0	98	6		0.4
1996	†Tex A	16	10	.615	35	35	7-3	0-0	250.2	250	110	19	6	95-3	170	3.63	145	.263	.332	0	—	0	102	42		3.9
1997	Tex A	5	8	.385	19	19	0	0-0	111	129	69	11	2	56-3	68	5.19	94	.298	.376	0	—	0	88	-3	23	-0.2
	Ana A	4	4	.500	12	12	1	0-0	79	65	34	8	1	39-0	38	3.65	127	.223	.315	2-0-1	.500	1	83	9		0.9
	Year	9	12	.429	31	31	1	0-0	190	194	103	19	3	95-3	106	4.55	105	.268	.352	2-0-1	.500	1	86	4		0.7
1998	Ana A	9	6	.600	19	19	0	0-0	103	123	60	6	3	47-0	57	4.98	95	.311	.384	1	.000	-0	98	-2	78	-0.1
1999	Ana A	4	11	.267	26	22	0	0-0	128.1	129	72	14	4	76-1	76	4.77	103	.270	.369	3	.000	-0	80	3	35	0.3
2000	Ana A	5	7	.417	16	16	0	0-0	78.2	102	59	16	2	53-1	50	6.52	79	.323	.415	3-0-1	.333	-0	89	-10	48	-1.2
	Chi A	0	1	.000	2	1	0	0-0	3	5	8	0	0	6-0	0	24.00	21	.455	.611	0	—	0	93	-6		-0.8
	Year	5	8	.385	18	17	0	0-0	81.2	107	67	16	2	59-1	50	7.16	72	.327	.424	3-0-1	.333	-0	89	-15		-2.0
2001	TB A	0	0	—	5	0	0	0-1	7	10	11	4	1	5-2	2	12.27	37	.333	.444	0	—	0		-6		-0.7
Total	14	117	109	.518	332	315	19-8	0-1	1973	1938	977	162	47	852-43	1181	4.06	107	.260	.337	333-1-67	.150	4	98	61	261	6.4

HILL, MILT Milton Giles B8.22.1965 Atlanta GA BR/TR/6-0/180* [CinN87 28/726] d8.1 Col Georgia College

1991	Cin N	1	1	.500	22	0	0	0-1	33.1	36	14	1	0	8-2	20	3.78	101	.295	.331	1	.000	-0		1		0.0
1992	Cin N	0	0	—	14	0	0	1-0	20	15	9	1	1	5-2	10	3.15	114	.211	.269	0	—	0		0		0.0
1993	Cin N	3	0	1.000	19	0	0	0-0	28.2	34	18	5	0	9-1	23	5.65	71	.301	.344	2	.000	-0		-4		-0.5
1994	Atl N	0	0	—	10	0	0	0-0	11.1	18	10	3	0	6-1	10	7.94	54	.367	.436	0	—	0		-4		-0.2
	Sea A	1	0	1.000	13	0	0	0-0	23.2	30	19	4	0	11-3	16	6.46	76	.306	.373	0	—	0		-4		-0.2
Total	4	5	1	.833	78	0	0	1-1	117	133	70	14	1	39-9	79	5.08	81	.294	.345	3	.000	-0		-11		-0.9

HILL, RICH Richard Joseph B3.11.1980 Boston MA BL/TL/6-5/205 d6.15 Col Michigan

2005	Chi N	0	2	.000	10	4	0	0-0	23.2	25	24	3	1	17-1	21	9.13	48	.260	.377	6	.333	0	64	-11		-0.8

HILL, SHAWN Shawn Richard B4.28.1981 Mississauga ON, Can. BR/TR/6-2/185 [MonN00 6/165] d6.29

2004	Mon N	1	2	.333	3	3	0	0-0	17	16	1	1	0	7-0	10	16.00	29	.415	.490	2-0-1	.000	-0	87	-10		-1.5

HILL, BILL William Cicero "Still Bill" B8.2.1874 Chattanooga TN D1.28.1938 Cincinnati OH BL/TL/6-1/201 d4.18 b-Hugh

1896	Lou N	9	28	.243	43	39	32	2	319.2	353	229	14	18	155	104	4.31	101	.278	.364	116-0-4	.207	-5	73	2		-0.1
1897	Lou N	7	17	.292	27	26	20-1	0	199	209	127	6	17	69	55	3.62	118	.268	.341	74-0-2	.095	-8	81	13		0.6
1898	Cin N	13	14	.481	33	32	26-2	0	262	261	146	3	17	119	75	3.98	96	.258	.346	98	.133	-7	94	-0		-0.6
1899	Cle N	3	6	.333	11	10	7	0	72.1	96	67	0	4	39	26	6.97	53	.318	.403	31	.129	-2	88	-23		-2.3
	Bal N	3	4	.429	8	7	6	0	61	64	35	1	4	3	18	3.25	122	.269	.328	24	.292	1	122	4		0.4
	Bro N	1	0	1.000	2	1	1	1	11	11	3	0	0	6	3	0.82	478	.262	.354	5	.600	2	257	3		0.5
	Year	7	10	.412	21	18	14	1	144.1	171	105	1	8	63	46	4.93	78	.294	.370	60	.233	-0	111	-13		-1.4
Total	4	36	69	.343	124	115	92-3	3	925	994	607	24	59	406	280	4.16	99	.273	.355	348-0-6	.167	-20	85	-1		-1.5

HILLEBRAND, HOMER Homer Hiller Henry B10.10.1879 Freeport IL D1.20.1974 Elsinore (now Lake Elsinore) CA BR/TL/5-8/165 d4.24 Col Princeton ▲

1905	Pit N	5	2	.714	10	6	4	1	60.2	43	20	0	2	19	37	2.82	107	.198	.269	110-0-4	.236	1*	124	3		0.4
1906	Pit N	3	2	.600	7	5	4-1	0	53	42	19	1	1	21	32	2.21	121	.220	.300	21	.238	1	125	2		0.4
1908	Pit N	0	0	—	1	0	0	0	1	1	0	0	0	0	1	0.00	—	.333	.333	0	—	0		0		0.0
Total	3	8	4	.667	18	11	8-1	1	114.2	86	39	1	3	40	70	2.51	113	.209	.284	131-0-4	.237	2	125	5		0.8

YEAR	TM LG	W	L	PCT	G	GS	CG-SHO	SV-BS	IP	H	R	HR	HB	BB-IB	SO	ERA	AERA	OAV	OOB	AB-HR-SH	AVG	PB	SUP	APR	DL	PW

HILLEGAS, SHAWN Shawn Patrick B8.21.1964 Dos Palos CA BR/TR/6-2/208(208-223) [LAN84*S1/4] d8.9 Col Middle Georgia JC

YEAR	TM LG	W	L	PCT	G	GS	CG-SHO	SV-BS	IP	H	R	HR	HB	BB-IB	SO	ERA	AERA	OAV	OOB	AB-HR-SH	AVG	PB	SUP	APR	DL	PW
1987	LA N	4	3	.571	12	10	0	0-0	58	52	27	5	0	31-0	51	3.57	112	.241	.335	14-0-1	.000	-1	100	2		0.1
1988	LA N	3	4	.429	11	10	0	0-0	56.2	54	26	5	3	17-1	30	4.13	81	.250	.311	15-0-2	.133	0	85	-4		-0.5
	Chi A	3	2	.600	6	6	0	0-0	40	30	16	4	1	18-0	26	3.15	127	.207	.295	0	—	0	87	4		0.4
1989	Chi A	7	11	.389	50	13	0	3-0	119.2	132	67	12	3	51-4	76	4.74	81	.279	.352	0	—	0	102	-11		-1.5
1990	Chi A	0	0	—	7	0	0	0-0	11.1	4	1	0	0	5-1	5	0.79	484	.111	.214	0	—	0		4		0.2
1991	Cle A	3	4	.429	51	3	0	7-2	83	67	42	7	2	46-7	66	4.34	96	.223	.324	0	—	0	73	0		0.0
1992	NY A	1	8	.111	21	9	1-1	0-0	78.1	96	52	12	0	33-1	46	5.51	72	.306	.369	0	—	0	72	-13		-1.4
	Oak A	0	0	—	5	0	0	0-0	7.2	8	5	1	0	4-1	3	2.35	161	.276	.364	0	—	0		0		0.0
	Year	1	8	.111	26	9	1-1	0-0	86	104	57	13	0	37-2	49	5.23	75	.303	.368	0	—	0	72	-12		-2.3
1993	Oak A	3	6	.333	18	11	0	0-0	60.2	78	48	8	4	33-1	29	6.97	59	.264	.344	29-0-3	.069	-1	93	-37		-5.0
Total	7	24	38	.387	181	62	1-1	10-2	515.1	521	284	54	13	238-16	332	4.61	85	.264	.344							

HILLER, FRANK Frank Walter "Dutch" B7.13.1920 Irvington NJ D1.10.1987 West Chester PA BR/TR/6-0/200* d5.25 Col Lafayette

YEAR	TM LG	W	L	PCT	G	GS	CG-SHO	SV-BS	IP	H	R	HR	HB	BB-IB	SO	ERA	AERA	OAV	OOB	AB-HR-SH	AVG	PB	SUP	APR	DL	PW
1946	NY A	0	2	.000	3	1	0	0	11.1	13	7	2	0	4	4	4.76	72	.295	.380	4-0-1	.250	0	75	-2		-0.3
1948	NY A	5	2	.714	22	5	1	0	62.1	59	29	8	1	30	25	4.04	101	.244	.330	16-0-1	.375	2	133	1		0.3
1949	NY A	0	2	.000	4	0	0	1	7.2	9	5	0	0	7	3	5.87	69	.290	.421	2	.500	0		-1		-0.2
1950	Chi N	12	5	.706	38	17	9-2	0	153	153	68	16	4	32	55	3.53	119	.258	.300	44-0-4	.114	-3	96	12		1.0
1951	Chi N	6	12	.333	24	21	6-2	1	141.1	147	83	17	9	31	50	4.84	85	.268	.317	48-0-1	.125	-2	88	-10		-1.3
1952	Cin N	5	8	.385	28	15	6-1	1	124.1	129	67	7	6	37	50	4.63	81	.271	.331	30-0-7	.167	1*	124	-11		-1.0
1953	NY N	2	1	.667	19	1	0	0	33.2	43	29	6	4	15	10	6.15	70	.303	.385	4	.500	1	104	-8		-0.5
Total	7	30	32	.484	138	60	22-5	4	533.2	553	288	56	24	158	197	4.42	92	.266	.325	148-0-14	.176	-1	103	-19		-2.0

HILLER, JOHN John Frederick B4.8.1943 Toronto ON, Can. BR/TL/6-0/195(165-195) d9.6

YEAR	TM LG	W	L	PCT	G	GS	CG-SHO	SV-BS	IP	H	R	HR	HB	BB-IB	SO	ERA	AERA	OAV	OOB	AB-HR-SH	AVG	PB	SUP	APR	DL	PW
1965	Det A	0	0	—	5	0	0	1	6	5	0	0	0	1-0	4	0.00	—	.227	.261	0	—	0		2		0.1
1966	Det A	0	0	—	1	0	0	0	2	2	2	0	0	2-0	1	9.00	39	.286	.400	0	—	0		-1		-0.1
1967	Det A	4	3	.571	23	6	2-2	3	65	57	20	4	0	9-0	49	2.63	124	.233	.259	15-0-1	.133	-0	80	5		0.6
1968	†Det A	9	6	.600	39	12	4-1	2	128	92	37	9	0	51-4	78	2.39	126	.200	.279	37	.081	-2	123	9		0.9
1969	Det A	4	4	.500	40	8	1-1	4-3	99.1	97	50	13	1	44-2	74	3.99	94	.257	.334	21-0-2	.286	2*	100	-3		-0.1
1970	Det A	6	6	.500	47	5	1-1	3-3	104	82	39	12	2	46-4	89	3.03	124	.219	.302	23-0-1	.000	-2	71	8		0.4
1972	†Det A	1	2	.333	24	3	1	3-0	44.1	39	13	4	3	13-2	26	2.03	156	.232	.299	0	.000	-0	93	5		0.4
1973	Det A	10	5	.667	65	0	0	38-4	125.1	89	21	7	0	39-7	124	1.44	285	.198	.260	0	—	0		35		6.7
1974	Det A☆	17	14	.548	59	0	0	13-9	150	127	51	10	3	62-19	134	2.64	145	.231	.309	0	—	0		14	37	3.9
1975	Det A	2	3	.400	36	0	0	14-5	70.2	52	20	6	0	36-4	87	2.17	187	.205	.300	0	—	0	118	17		1.6
1976	Det A	12	8	.600	56	1	1-1	13-13	121	93	37	7	2	67-9	117	2.38	157	.219	.323	1	.000	-0	70	8		3.2
1977	Det A	8	14	.364	45	8	3	7-9	124	120	59	15	1	61-8	115	3.56	121	.258	.342	0	—	0		15	21	2.6
1978	Det A	9	4	.692	51	0	0	15-7	92.1	64	27	6	0	35-4	74	2.34	167	.202	.277	0	—	0		-6	34	-0.0
1979	Det A	4	7	.364	43	0	0	9-7	79.1	83	47	14	0	55-7	46	5.22	83	.274	.382	0	—	0		0		-0.9
1980	Det A	1	0	1.000	11	0	0	0-0	30.2	38	15	3	0	14-1	18	4.40	94	.309	.374	0	—	0		0		-0.1
Total	15	87	76	.534	545	43	13-6	125-60	1242	1040	438	110	12	535-71	1036	2.83	134	.229	.309	101-0-4	.109	-4	87	126	92	21.0

HILLMAN, DAVE Darius Dutton B9.14.1927 Dungannon VA BR/TR/5-11/168* d4.30

YEAR	TM LG	W	L	PCT	G	GS	CG-SHO	SV-BS	IP	H	R	HR	HB	BB-IB	SO	ERA	AERA	OAV	OOB	AB-HR-SH	AVG	PB	SUP	APR	DL	PW
1955	Chi N	0	0	—	25	3	0	0	57.2	63	36	10	1	25-0	23	5.31	77	.283	.352	10-0-1	.100	0*	182	-7		-0.3
1956	Chi N	0	2	.000	2	2	0	0	12.1	11	7	0	0	5-0	6	2.19	172	.216	.286	4	.000	-2*	35	1		0.1
1957	Chi N	6	11	.353	32	14	1	1	103.1	115	52	13	0	37-2	53	4.35	89	.280	.338	24-0-2	.000	-2*	86	-4		-0.8
1958	Chi N	4	8	.333	31	16	3	1	125.2	132	57	12	0	31-4	65	3.15	124	.265	.305	41-0-2	.146	-1*	85	8		0.9
1959	Chi N	8	11	.421	39	24	4-1	0	191	178	84	17	1	43-3	88	3.53	112	.248	.290	60-0-4	.150	1*	87	8		0.9
1960	Bos A	0	3	.000	16	3	0	0	36.2	41	27	6	0	12-1	14	5.65	72	.281	.333	6-0-1	.000	-0	80	-7	58	-0.5
1961	Bos A	3	2	.600	28	1	0	0	78	70	26	8	0	23-0	39	2.77	151	.242	.296	17-0-2	.000	-2	42	12		0.4
1962	Cin N	0	0	—	2	0	0	1	3.2	8	4	0	0	1-0	0	9.82	41	.421	.450	0	—	-0		-2		-0.1
	NY N	0	0	—	13	1	0	1	15.2	21	12	5	1	8-0	8	6.32	66	.333	.405	1	.000	-0	42	-3		-0.3
	Year	0	0	—	15	1	0	1	19.1	29	16	5	1	9-0	8	6.98	59	.354	.415	1	.000	-0	42	-5		-0.3
Total	8	21	37	.362	188	64	8-1	3	624	639	305	71	3	185-10	296	3.87	103	.264	.315	163-0-12	.098	-5	86	6	58	0.3

HILLMAN, ERIC John Eric B4.27.1966 Gary IN BL/TL/6-10/225* [NYN87 16/420] d5.18 Col Eastern Illinois

YEAR	TM LG	W	L	PCT	G	GS	CG-SHO	SV-BS	IP	H	R	HR	HB	BB-IB	SO	ERA	AERA	OAV	OOB	AB-HR-SH	AVG	PB	SUP	APR	DL	PW
1992	NY N	2	2	.500	11	8	0	0-0	52.1	67	31	9	2	10-2	16	5.33	66	.318	.353	13-0-5	.077	-1	90	-9		-0.8
1993	NY N	2	9	.182	27	22	3-1	0-0	145	173	83	12	4	24-2	60	3.97	101	.299	.326	44-0-6	.159	-0	95	-3		-0.3
1994	NY N	0	3	.000	11	6	0	0-0	34.2	45	30	9	2	11-3	20	7.79	54	.321	.377	8-0-1	.000	-1	91	-12		-1.0
Total	3	4	14	.222	49	36	3-1	0-0	232	285	144	30	8	45-7	96	4.85	81	.306	.340	65-0-12	.123	-2	93	-24		-2.1

HILSEY, CHARLIE Charles T. B3.23.1864 Philadelphia PA D10.31.1918 Philadelphia PA 5-7/180 d9.27

YEAR	TM LG	W	L	PCT	G	GS	CG-SHO	SV-BS	IP	H	R	HR	HB	BB-IB	SO	ERA	AERA	OAV	OOB	AB-HR-SH	AVG	PB	SUP	APR	DL	PW
1883	Phi N	0	3	.000	3	3	3	0	26	36	26	0		9	5.54	56	.305	.328	10	.100	-1	41	-7		-0.7
1884	Phi AA	2	1	.667	3	3	3	0	27	29	19	0		10	4.67	73	.257	.288	24	.208	0*	172	-3		-0.2
Total	2	2	4	.333	6	6	6	0	53	65	45	0	0	19	5.09	64	.281	.308	34	.176	-1	105	-10		-0.9

HILTON, HOWARD Howard James B1.3.1964 Oxnard CA BR/TR/6-3/230 [StLN85 22/566] d4.9 Col Arkansas-Monticello

YEAR	TM LG	W	L	PCT	G	GS	CG-SHO	SV-BS	IP	H	R	HR	HB	BB-IB	SO	ERA	AERA	OAV	OOB	AB-HR-SH	AVG	PB	SUP	APR	DL	PW
1990	StL N	0	0	—	2	0	0	0-0	3	2	0	0	0	3-0	1	0.00	—	.182	.357	0	—	0		1		0.1

HINCHLIFFE, BRETT Brett B7.21.1974 Detroit MI BR/TR/6-5/190* [SeaA92 16/446] d4.5

YEAR	TM LG	W	L	PCT	G	GS	CG-SHO	SV-BS	IP	H	R	HR	HB	BB-IB	SO	ERA	AERA	OAV	OOB	AB-HR-SH	AVG	PB	SUP	APR	DL	PW
1999	Sea A	0	4	.000	11	4	0	0-0	30.2	41	31	10	4	21-0	14	8.80	54	.323	.434	0	—	0	63	-13		-1.4
2000	Ana A	0	0	—	2	0	0	0-0	1.2	1	1	0	0	1-0	0	5.40	96	.167	.286	0	—	0		0		0.0
2001	NY N	0	1	.000	1	1	0	0-0	2	9	8	2	1	1-0	2	36.00	11	.643	.688	1	.000	-0	183	-7		-0.9
Total	3	0	5	.000	14	5	0	0-0	34.1	51	40	12	5	23-0	16	10.22	47	.347	.451	1	.000	0	82	-20		-2.3

HINDS, SAM Samuel Russell B7.11.1953 Frederick MD BR/TR/6-6/215 d5.21 Col Broward (FL) CC

YEAR	TM LG	W	L	PCT	G	GS	CG-SHO	SV-BS	IP	H	R	HR	HB	BB-IB	SO	ERA	AERA	OAV	OOB	AB-HR-SH	AVG	PB	SUP	APR	DL	PW
1977	Mil A	3	0	.000	29	1	0	2-1	72.1	72	42	5	2	40-3	46	4.73	87	.266	.355	0	—	0	0	-5		-0.3

HINRICHS, PAUL Paul Edwin "Herky" B8.31.1925 Marengo IA BR/TR/6-0/180 d5.16 Col Concordia (TX)

YEAR	TM LG	W	L	PCT	G	GS	CG-SHO	SV-BS	IP	H	R	HR	HB	BB-IB	SO	ERA	AERA	OAV	OOB	AB-HR-SH	AVG	PB	SUP	APR	DL	PW
1951	Bos A	0	0	—	4	0	0	0	3.1	7	8	1	0	4	1	21.60	21	.412	.524	0	—	0		-5		-0.3

HINRICHS, DUTCH William Louis B4.27.1889 Orange CA D8.18.1972 Kingsburg CA BR/TR/6-3/195 d6.25 Col Occidental

YEAR	TM LG	W	L	PCT	G	GS	CG-SHO	SV-BS	IP	H	R	HR	HB	BB-IB	SO	ERA	AERA	OAV	OOB	AB-HR-SH	AVG	PB	SUP	APR	DL	PW
1910	Was A	0	1	.000	3	0	1		7	10	7	0	0	3	5	2.57	97	.357	.419	4	.000	-1		-1		-0.3

HINSLEY, JERRY Jerry Dean B4.9.1944 Hugo OK BR/TR/5-11/165* d4.18

YEAR	TM LG	W	L	PCT	G	GS	CG-SHO	SV-BS	IP	H	R	HR	HB	BB-IB	SO	ERA	AERA	OAV	OOB	AB-HR-SH	AVG	PB	SUP	APR	DL	PW
1964	NY N	0	2	.000	9	2	0	0	15.1	21	17	0	0	7-0	11	8.22	44	.313	.373	1	.000	-0	61	-8		-1.0
1967	NY N	0	0	—	2	0	0	0	5	6	2	0	0	4-0	3	3.60	94	.316	.435	0	—	0		0		0.0
Total	2	0	2	.000	11	2	0	0	20.1	27	19	0	0	11-0	14	7.08	50	.314	.388	1	.000	-0	61	-8		-1.0

HINTON, RICH Richard Michael B5.22.1947 Tucson AZ BL/TL/6-2/185(170-185) [ChiA69 S3/62] d7.17 Col Arizona

YEAR	TM LG	W	L	PCT	G	GS	CG-SHO	SV-BS	IP	H	R	HR	HB	BB-IB	SO	ERA	AERA	OAV	OOB	AB-HR-SH	AVG	PB	SUP	APR	DL	PW
1971	Chi A	3	4	.429	18	2	0	0-2	24.1	27	12	1	1	6-1	15	4.44	80	.310	.358	1-0-2	.000	-0	63	-1		-0.?
1972	NY A	1	0	1.000	7	3	0	0-0	16.2	20	11	2	0	8-2	13	4.86	62	.299	.364	3	.000	0	158	-4		-0.?
	Tex A	0	1	.000	5	0	0	0-0	11.1	7	10	1	0	10-1	4	2.38	128	.171	.327	2	.500	1		-2		-0.?
	Year	1	1	.500	12	3	0	0-0	28	27	21	3	0	18-3	17	3.86	78	.250	.349	5	.200	1	157	-6		-0.?
1975	Chi A	1	0	1.000	15	0	0	0-1	37.1	41	22	0	0	15-1	30	4.82	81	.270	.331			-0	201	-7		-1.?
1976	Cin N	1	2	.333	12	1	0	0-1	17.2	30	15	4	0	11-3	8	7.64	46	.380	.451	1	.000	-0	124	-1		-0.?
1978	Chi A	2	6	.250	29	4	2	1-2	80.2	78	38	5	2	28-2	48	4.02	95	.261	.326			-0	53	-7		-0.?
1979	Chi A	1	2	.333	16	2	0	2-0	41.2	57	30	4	2	8-1	27	6.05	70	.331	.362		—	-0	41	-2		-0.?
	Sea A	0	2	.000	14	1	0	0-1	20	23	14	4	2	5-1	7	5.40	81	.284	.337		—	0		0		-0.?
	Year	1	4	.200	30	3	0	2-1	61.2	80	44	8	4	13-2	34	5.84	74	.316	.354		—	0	49	-10		-0.?
Total	6	9	17	.346	116	13	2	3-7	249.2	283	152	23	7	91-12	152	4.87	78	.289	.350	7-0-2	.143	-0	103	-28		-0.?

HIPPAUF, HERB Herbert August B5.9.1939 New York NY D7.17.1995 Santa Clara CA BR/TL/6-0/180 d4.27 Col Pasadena (CA) City

YEAR	TM LG	W	L	PCT	G	GS	CG-SHO	SV-BS	IP	H	R	HR	HB	BB-IB	SO	ERA	AERA	OAV	OOB	AB-HR-SH	AVG	PB	SUP	APR	DL	PW
1966	Atl N	0	1	.000	3	0	0	0	2.2	6	5	0	0	1-0	1	13.50	27	.462	.500	0	—	0		-3		-0.?

HISNER, HARLEY Harley Parnell B11.6.1926 Maples IN BR/TR/6-1/185 d9.30

YEAR	TM LG	W	L	PCT	G	GS	CG-SHO	SV-BS	IP	H	R	HR	HB	BB-IB	SO	ERA	AERA	OAV	OOB	AB-HR-SH	AVG	PB	SUP	APR	DL	PW
1951	Bos A	0	1	.000	1	1	0	0	6	7	3	0	0	4	3	4.50	99	.292	.393	2	.500	0	0	0		0.?

YEAR	TM LG	W	L	PCT	G	GS	CG-SHO	SV-BS	IP	H	R	HR	HB	BB-IB	SO	ERA	AERA	OAV	OOB	AB-HR-SH	AVG	PB	SUP	APR	DL	PW

HITCHCOCK, STERLING Sterling Alex B4.29.1971 Fayetteville NC BL/TL/6-1/192(192-205) [NYA89 9/233] d9.11

YEAR	TM LG	W	L	PCT	G	GS	CG-SHO	SV-BS	IP	H	R	HR	HB	BB-IB	SO	ERA	AERA	OAV	OOB	AB-HR-SH	AVG	PB	SUP	APR	DL	PW
1992	NY A	0	2	.000	3	3	0	0-0	13	23	12	2	1	6-0	6	8.31	48	.377	.441	0	—	0	123	-6		-0.7
1993	NY A	1	2	.333	6	6	0	0-0	31	32	18	4	1	14-1	26	4.65	90	.271	.348	0	—	0	117	-2		-0.2
1994	NY A	4	1	.800	23	5	1	0-0	49.1	48	24	3	0	29-1	37	4.20	110	.265	.355	0	—	0	100	3		0.2
1995	†NY A	11	10	.524	27	27	4-1	0-0	168.1	155	91	22	5	68-1	121	4.70	98	.245	.319	0	—	0	98	0		0.2
1996	Sea A	13	9	.591	35	35	0	0-0	196.2	245	131	27	7	73-4	132	5.35	93	.309	.368	0	—	0	104	-11		-1.0
1997	SD N	10	11	.476	32	28	1	0-0	161	172	102	24	4	55-2	106	5.20	76	.276	.337	50-0-8	.100	-1	112	-24	27	-2.8
1998	†SD N	9	7	.563	39	27	2-1	1-1	176.1	169	83	29	9	48-2	158	3.93	101	.251	.308	50-0-5	.140	-1	110	1		-0.1
1999	SD N	12	14	.462	33	33	1	0-0	205.2	202	99	29	5	76-6	194	4.11	104	.254	.320	61-0-7	.082	-3	95	6		0.4
2000	SD N	1	6	.143	11	11	0	0-0	65.2	69	38	12	5	26-1	61	4.93	90	.267	.345	22-0-1	.000	-3	88	-3	127	-0.5
2001	SD N	2	1	.667	3	3	0	0-0	19	22	9	1	1	3-0	15	3.32	125	.275	.310	8	.125	-0	186	1	94	0.2
	†NY A	4	4	.500	10	9	1	0-0	51.1	67	37	5	2	18-0	28	6.49	68	.315	.367	0	—	0	120	-10		-1.3
2002	NY A	1	2	.333	20	2	0	0-0	39.1	57	29	4	1	15-3	31	5.49	79	.326	.380	0	—	0	139	-6		-0.4
2003	NY A	1	3	.250	27	1	0	0-0	49.2	57	33	6	0	18-3	36	5.44	81	.285	.341	0	—	0	105	-6		-0.4
	StL N	5	1	.833	8	6	0	0-0	38	34	17	8	1	14-1	32	3.79	109	.238	.308	12-0-2	.083	-1	99	1		0.1
2004	SD N	0	3	.000	4	4	0	0-0	21.1	22	15	5	0	8-0	14	6.33	62	.265	.330	7	.000	-1	65	-5	121	-0.7
Total	13	74	76	.493	281	200	10-2	3-1	1285.2	1374	738	181	42	471-25	997	4.80	91	.273	.337	210-0-23	.090	-9	105	-61	437	-7.4

HITT, BRUCE Bruce Smith B3.14.1897 Comanche TX D11.10.1973 Portland OR BR/TR/6-1/190 d9.23 Mil 1918

| 1917 | StL N | 0 | 0 | — | 2 | 0 | 0 | | 4 | 7 | 6 | 1 | 0 | 1-1 | 1 | 9.00 | 30 | .368 | .400 | 1 | .000 | -0 | | -3 | | -0.2 |

HITT, ROY Roy Wesley "Rhino" B6.22.1884 Carleton NE D2.8.1956 Pomona CA BL/TL/5-10/200 d4.27

| 1907 | Cin N | 6 | 10 | .375 | 21 | 18 | 14-2 | 0 | 153.1 | 143 | 76 | 2 | 12 | 56 | 63 | 3.40 | 76 | .258 | .339 | 56-0-1 | .179 | -0 | 107 | -11 | | -1.2 |

HITTLE, LLOYD Lloyd Eldon "Red" B2.21.1924 Lodi CA BR/TL/5-10.5/164* d6.12

1949	Was A	5	7	.417	36	9	3-2	0	109	123	62	2	0	57	32	4.21	101	.285	.369	28-0-2	.143	-2	61	-1		-0.3
1950	Was A	2	4	.333	11	4	1	0	43.1	60	27	1	0	17	9	4.98	90	.326	.383	13-0-1	.077	-1	55	-2		-0.3
Total	2	7	11	.389	47	13	4-2	0	152.1	183	89	3	0	74	41	4.43	98	.298	.373	41-0-3	.122	-3	59	-3		-0.6

HOBAUGH, ED Edward Russell B6.27.1934 Kittanning PA BR/TR/6-0/176* d4.19 Col Michigan St.

1961	Was A	7	9	.438	26	18	3	0	126.1	142	68	12	1	64-3	67	4.42	91	.281	.362	41-0-5	.098	-2*	92	-4		-0.7
1962	Was A	2	1	.667	26	3	0	1	69.1	66	36	9	0	25-2	37	3.76	107	.258	.320	12	.167	0	88	0		0.3
1963	Was A	0	0	—	9	1	0	0	16	20	13	3	2	6-2	11	6.19	60	.308	.368	2-1-0	.500	2	192	-4		-0.1
Total	3	9	10	.474	61	21	3	1	211.2	228	117	24	3	95-7	115	4.34	92	.276	.350	55-1-5	.127	-1	96	-8		-0.8

HOBBIE, GLEN Glen Frederick B4.24.1936 Witt IL BR/TR/6-2/195* d9.20

1957	Chi N	0	0	—	2	0	0		4.1	6	5	0	0	5-0	3	10.38	37	.333	.458	2	.000	-0		-3		-0.2
1958	Chi N	10	6	.625	36	16	2-1	2	168.1	163	80	13	7	93-8	91	3.74	105	.252	.352	48-0-1	.146	-2	106	3		0.3
1959	Chi N	16	13	.552	46	33	10-3	6	234	204	105	15	6	106-1	138	3.69	107	.236	.322	79-0-3	.114	-3	106	7		0.6
1960	Chi N	16	20	.444	46	36	16-4	1	258.2	253	130	27	9	101-7	134	3.97	95	.256	.328	86-1-1	.151	1	92	-5		-0.4
1961	Chi N	7	13	.350	36	29	7-2	2	198.2	207	113	26	6	54-7	103	4.26	98	.268	.319	66-2-3	.167	2	105	-3		0.1
1962	Chi N	5	14	.263	42	23	5	0	162	198	112	18	3	62-8	87	5.22	79	.304	.365	49-0-1	.122	-1	85	-20		-2.2
1963	Chi N	7	10	.412	36	24	4-1	0	165.1	172	80	17	6	49-2	94	3.92	90	.270	.327	50-0-3	.080	-2	94	-6		-0.9
1964	Chi N	0	3	.000	8	4	0	0	27.1	39	29	4	1	10-1	14	7.90	47	.325	.382	5	.000	0	65	-13		-1.2
	StL N	1	2	.333	13	5	1	1	44.1	41	23	4	1	15-1	18	4.26	89	.241	.305	13-1-1	.154	1	125	-1		0.0
	Year	1	5	.167	21	9	1	1	71.2	80	52	8	2	25-2	32	5.65	67	.276	.336	18-1-1	.111	1	98	-14		-1.2
Total	8	62	81	.434	284	170	45-11	6	1263	1283	677	124	39	495-35	682	4.20	93	.264	.335	398-4-13	.131	-5	98	-41		-3.9

HOBBS, JACK John Douglas B11.11.1956 Philadelphia PA BR/TL/6-3/190 [SeaA78 7/162] d8.31 Col Lynchburg

| 1981 | Min A | 0 | 0 | — | 4 | 0 | 0 | 0-0 | 5.2 | 5 | 2 | 0 | 2 | 6-1 | 1 | 3.18 | 124 | .238 | .448 | 0 | — | 0 | | 1 | | 0.0 |

HOCH, HARRY Harry Keller B1.9.1887 Woodside DE D10.26.1981 Lewes DE BR/TR/5-10.5/165 d4.16 Col Kutztown

1908	Phi N	2	1	.667	3	3	2	0	26	20	10	0	2	13	4	2.77	88	.211	.318	5-0-3	.200	1	126	-1		0.0
1914	StL A	0	2	.000	15	2	1	0	54	55	31	1	2	27	13	3.00	90	.284	.377	18	.056	-2	13	-4		-0.3
1915	StL A	0	4	.000	12	3	1	0	40	52	49	2	3	26	9	7.20	40	.311	.413	10-0-1	.200	0	17	-21		-1.8
Total	3	2	7	.222	30	8	4	0	120	127	90	3	7	66	26	4.35	62	.279	.378	33-0-4	.121	-1	54	-26		-2.1

HOCKENBERY, CHUCK Charles Marion B12.15.1950 LaCrosse WI BB/TR/6-1/195 d7.4

| 1975 | Cal A | 0 | 5 | .000 | 16 | 4 | 0 | 1-0 | 41 | 48 | 27 | 3 | 3 | 19-2 | 15 | 5.27 | 68 | .296 | .378 | 0 | — | 0 | 37 | -8 | | -0.9 |

HOCKETTE, GEORGE George Edward "Lefty" B4.7.1908 Perth MS D1.20.1974 Plantation FL BL/TL/6-0/174 d9.17

1934	Bos A	2	1	.667	3	3	3-2	0	27.1	22	5	3	0	6	14	1.65	292	.218	.262	11	.273	0	72	9		1.0
1935	Bos A	2	3	.400	23	4	0	0	61	83	43	6	1	12	11	5.16	92	.329	.362	14-0-3	.143	-1	91	-3		-0.1
Total	2	4	4	.500	26	7	3-2	0	88.1	105	48	9	1	18	25	4.08	117	.297	.333	25-0-3	.200	-0	83	6		0.9

HODGE, SHOVEL Clarence Clemet B7.6.1893 Mount Andrew AL D12.31.1967 Ft.Walton Beach FL BL/TR/6-4/190 d9.6

1920	Chi A	1	1	.500	4	2	1	0	19.2	15	14	0	0	12	5	2.29	165	.224	.342	6	.000	-1	53	0		-0.1
1921	Chi A	6	8	.429	36	10	5	2	142.2	191	118	7	5	54	25	6.56	65	.335	.397	52-0-3	.327	3	116	-37		-2.6
1922	Chi A	7	6	.538	35	8	2	1	139	154	73	3	2	65	37	4.14	98	.300	.381	58-0-3	.207	-1	91	-2		-0.2
Total	3	14	15	.483	75	20	8	3	301.1	360	205	10	7	131	67	5.17	80	.313	.387	116-0-6	.250	1	100	-39		-2.9

HODGE, ED Ed Oliver B4.19.1958 Bellflower CA BL/TL/6-2/192 [MinA79*5/114] d5.1 Col Cerritos (CA) JC

| 1984 | Min A | 4 | 3 | .571 | 25 | 15 | 0 | 0-0 | 100 | 116 | 59 | 13 | 1 | 29-1 | 59 | 4.77 | 89 | .291 | .338 | 0 | — | 0 | 107 | -6 | | -0.5 |

HODGES, KEVIN Kevin Jon B6.24.1973 Houston TX BR/TR/6-4/200 [KCA91 8/210] d4.24

| 2000 | Sea A | 0 | 0 | — | 13 | 0 | 0 | 0-0 | 17.1 | 18 | 10 | 4 | 2 | 12-0 | 7 | 5.19 | 93 | .310 | .438 | 0 | — | 0 | 0 | 0 | | 0.0 |

HODGES, TREY Trey Alan B6.29.1978 Houston TX BR/TR/6-3/187* [AtlN00 17/520] d9.10 Col Louisiana St.

2002	Atl N	2	0	1.000	7	0	0	0-0	11.2	16	7	2	1	2-0	6	5.40	75	.348	.373	3	.000	-0		-1		-0.3
2003	Atl N	3	3	.500	52	1	0	0-2	65.2	69	38	11	3	31-7	66	4.66	90	.268	.350	5-0-1	.000	-1	134	-3	17	-0.3
Total	2	5	3	.625	56	1	0	0-2	77.1	85	45	13	4	33-7	72	4.77	88	.281	.354	8-0-1	.000	-1	134	-4	17	-0.6

HODKEY, ELI Aloysius Joseph B11.3.1917 Lorain OH D8.30.2005 Lorain OH BL/TL/6-4/185 d9.12

| 1946 | Phi N | 0 | 1 | .000 | 7 | 0 | 0 | 0 | 8 | 16 | 9 | 0 | 0 | 5 | 0 | 12.46 | 28 | .391 | .500 | 2 | .000 | -0 | 50 | -4 | | -0.7 |

HODNETT, CHARLIE Charles B1861 IA D4.25.1890 St.Louis MO d5.3

1883	StL AA	2	2	.500	4	4	3	0	32	28	10	1		7	6	1.41	248	.220	.261	11	.182	-0	45	7		0.7
	StL U	12	2	.857	14	14	12-1	0	121	121	56	0		16	41	2.01	119	.243	.267	58	.207	-1*	174	5		0.1
Total	2	14	4	.778	18	18	15-1	0	153	149	66	1		23	47	1.88	138	.239	.266	69	.203	-1	144	12		0.8

HODSON, GEORGE George S. (b George S. Hodgdon) B6.1870 PA D1.9.1924 San Rafael CA TR/5-7/150 d8.9

1894	Bos N	4	4	.500	12	11	8	0	74	103	66	4	5	35	12	5.84	97	.326	.402	30	.100	-4	101	0		-0.4
1895	Phi N	1	2	.333	4	2	1	0	17	27	23	4	0	9	6	9.53	50	.355	.424	5	.000	-1	52	-8		-1.0
Total	2	5	6	.455	16	13	9	0	91	130	89	8	5	44	18	6.53	84	.332	.406	35	.086	-5	95	-8		-1.4

HOEFT, BILLY William Frederick B5.17.1932 Oshkosh WI BL/TL/6-3/205(177-205) d4.18

1952	Det A	2	7	.222	34	10	1	4	125	123	66	14	5	63	67	4.32	88	.260	.353	40-0-1	.150	-1	99	-6		-0.5
1953	Det A	9	14	.391	29	27	9	2	197.2	223	113	24	4	58	90	4.83	84	.283	.335	64-0-3	.172	0*	97	-14		-1.5
1954	Det A	7	15	.318	34	25	10-4	1	175	180	93	22	4	59	114	4.58	81	.266	.327	52	.192	4*	78	-14		-1.2
1955	Det A☆	16	7	.696	32	29	17-7	0	220	187	75	17	6	75-1	133	2.99	129	.229	.296	82-0-4	.207	3*	129	25		2.7
1956	Det A	20	14	.588	38	34	18-4	0	248	276	127	22	5	104-12	172	4.06	101	.287	.356	80-0-5	.250	6*	108	1		0.6
1957	Det A	9	11	.450	34	28	10-1	1	207	188	85	15	5	69-2	111	3.48	111	.244	.308	67-3-5	.149	2*	85	10		1.0
1958	Det A	10	9	.526	36	21	6	3	143	148	70	15	1	49-3	94	4.15	97	.268	.326	44-0-1	.273	3*	103	0		0.2
1959	Det A	1	1	.500	2	2	0	0	9	6	5	0	1	4-0	2	5.00	81	.188	.297	3-0-2	.333	0*	65	-1		-0.1
	Bos A	0	3	.000	5	3	0	0	17.2	22	12	1	1	8-1	9	5.60	72	.319	.383	3	.000	-0*	80	-5		-0.4
	Bal A	1	1	.500	16	3	0	0	41	50	29	6	0	19-3	19	5.71	66	.307	.375	12	.250	1	70	-9		-0.4
	Year	2	5	.286	23	8	0	0	67.2	78	46	7	2	31-4	30	5.59	70	.295	.368	18-0-2	.222	0	74	-12		-0.9
1960	Bal A	2	1	.667	19	0	0	0	18.2	18	10	2	0	14-1	14	4.34	88	.240	.360	1	.000	-0		-1		-0.1
1961	Bal A	7	4	.636	35	12	3-1	2	138	106	37	7	1	55-3	100	2.02	190	.216	.295	39-0-2	.179	1	90	**28**		2.4

YEAR	TM LG	W	L	PCT	G	GS	CG-SHO	SV-BS	IP	H	R	HR	HB	BB-IB	SO	ERA	AERA	OAV	OOB	AB-HR-SH	AVG	PB	SUP	APR	DL	PW
1962	Bal A	4	8	.333	57	4	0	7	113.2	103	62	7	1	43-5	73	4.59	81	.243	.311	19-0-1	.158	3	91	-10		-0.8
1963	SF N	2	0	1.000	23	0	0	0	24.1	26	12	5	0	10-2	8	4.44	72	.271	.340	1-0-1	1.000	1		-3	77	-0.2
1964	Mil N	4	0	1.000	42	0	0	4	73.1	76	35	9	1	18-6	47	3.80	93	.271	.318	9-0-3	.222	1		-2		0.0
1965	Chi N	2	2	.500	29	2	1	1	51.1	41	21	3	0	20-2	44	2.81	131	.215	.285	11		.273	1	83	4		0.3
1966	Chi N	1	2	.333	36	0	0	3	41	43	28	4	1	14-3	30	4.61	80	.264	.326	4		.250	0		-6		-0.4
	SF N	0	2	.000	4	0	0	0	3.2	4	3	0	0	3-1	3	7.36	50	.250	.368	0		—	0		-9		-0.7
	Year	1	4	.200	40	0	0	3	44.2	47	31	4	1	17-4	33	4.84	76	.263	.330	4		.250	0		-8		-0.7
Total	15	97	101	.490	505	200	75-17	33	1847.1	1820	883	173	36	685-45	1140	3.94	98	.259	.325	531-3-28	.202	24	100	-2	77	1.3

HOELSKOETTER, ART Arthur "Holley","Hoss" (aka Arthur H. Hostetter) B9.30.1882 St.Louis MO D8.3.1954 St.Louis MO BR/TR/6-2/? d9.10 ▲

YEAR	TM LG	W	L	PCT	G	GS	CG-SHO	SV-BS	IP	H	R	HR	HB	BB-IB	SO	ERA	AERA	OAV	OOB	AB-HR-SH	AVG	PB	SUP	APR	DL	PW
1905	StL N	0	1	.000	1	1	1	0	6	6	6	1	0	5	4	1.50	199	.273	.407	83-0-2	.241	0*	73	-1		-0.1
1906	StL N	1	4	.200	12	3	2	0	58.1	53	37	1	1	34	20	4.63	57	.240	.344	317-0-7	.224	1*	129	-12		-0.9
1907	StL N	0	0	—	2	0	0	0	11	9	16	0	2	10	8	5.73	44	.209	.382	397-2-8	.247	0*		-6		-0.3
Total	3	1	5	.167	15	4	3	0	75.1	68	59	2	3	49	32	4.54	58	.238	.355	797-2-17	.237	1	117	-19		-1.3

HOERNER, JOE Joseph Walter B11.12.1936 Dubuque IA D10.4.1996 Hermann MO BR/TL/6-1/200(180-200) d9.27

YEAR	TM LG	W	L	PCT	G	GS	CG-SHO	SV-BS	IP	H	R	HR	HB	BB-IB	SO	ERA	AERA	OAV	OOB	AB-HR-SH	AVG	PB	SUP	APR	DL	PW
1963	Hou N	0	0	—	1	0	0	0	3	2	0	0	0	0-0	2	0.00	—	.182	.182	1		.000	-0		1		0.1
1964	Hou N	0	0	—	7	0	0	0	11	13	11	3	0	6-1	4	4.91	70	.310	.380	1		.000	-0		-4		-0.2
1966	StL N	5	1	.833	57	0	0	13	76	57	16	5	4	21-8	63	1.54	233	.212	.274	8-1-3	.125	1		17		2.0
1967	†StL N	4	4	.500	57	0	0	15	66	52	25	5	1	20-6	50	2.59	127	.225	.283	11-0-2	.182	0		4		0.6
1968	†StL N	8	2	.800	47	0	0	17	49	34	9	2	0	12-4	42	1.47	197	.192	.241	6-0-1	.000	-1		8		1.8
1969	StL N	2	3	.400	45	0	0	15-2	53.1	44	19	6	1	9-4	35	2.87	125	.230	.263	5		.000	-1		5		0.7
1970	Phi N☆	9	5	.643	44	0	0	9-3	57.2	53	20	5	1	20-7	39	2.65	152	.247	.307	10		.200	1		8		1.8
1971	Phi N	4	5	.444	49	0	0	9-5	73	57	19	6	1	21-3	57	1.97	180	.215	.272	10		.100	-1		12		1.8
1972	Phi N	0	2	.000	15	0	0	3-4	21.2	21	6	2	1	5-5	12	2.08	174	.259	.297	1-0-1	.000	-1		3		0.4
	Atl N	1	3	.250	25	0	0	2-6	23.1	34	18	4	1	8-2	19	6.56	58	.351	.394	4		.000	-1		-9		-1.2
	Year	1	5	.167	40	0	0	5-10	45	55	24	6	2	13-7	31	4.40	84	.309	.350	5-0-1	.000	-1		-3		-0.8
1973	Atl N	2	2	.500	20	0	0	2-3	12.2	17	9	1	0	4-0	10	6.39	62	.333	.382	0		—	0		-3	46	-0.2
	KC A	2	0	1.000	22	0	0	4-2	19.1	28	11	0	0	13-5	15	5.12	80	.329	.418	0		—	0		-2		-0.1
1974	KC A	2	3	.400	30	0	0	2-3	35.1	32	15	3	4	12-5	24	3.82	100	.244	.320	0		—	0		1	32	0.1
1975	Phi N	0	0	—	25	0	0	0-0	21	25	6	3	1	8-2	20	2.57	147	.298	.358	2		.000	-0		3		-0.2
1976	Tex A	0	4	.000	41	0	0	8-3	35	41	22	3	0	19-6	15	5.14	70	.315	.395	0		—	0		-6		-0.9
1977	Cin N	0	0	—	8	0	0	0-2	5.2	5	8	1	0	3-1	5	12.71	31	.375	.469	0		—	0		-5		-0.3
Total	14	39	34	.534	493	0	0	99-33	563	519	213	50	18	181-59	412	2.99	120	.249	.309	59-1-7	.102	-1		36	78	5.9

HOERST, LEFTY Frank Joseph B8.11.1917 Philadelphia PA D2.18.2000 Maple Shade NJ BL/TL/6-3/192 d4.26 Mil 1943-45 Col LaSalle

YEAR	TM LG	W	L	PCT	G	GS	CG-SHO	SV-BS	IP	H	R	HR	HB	BB-IB	SO	ERA	AERA	OAV	OOB	AB-HR-SH	AVG	PB	SUP	APR	DL	PW
1940	Phi N	1	0	1.000	6	0	0	0	12	12	7	1	0	8	5	5.25	74	.250	.357	2		.000	-0		-1		-0.1
1941	Phi N	3	10	.231	37	11	1	0	105.2	111	70	7	1	50	33	5.20	71	.275	.357	22-0-2	.182	-1	58	-17		-1.8
1942	Phi N	4	16	.200	33	22	5	1	150.2	162	99	11	0	78	52	5.20	64	.271	.357	46-0-3	.152	-1	96	-9		-3.7
1946	Phi N	1	6	.143	18	7	2	0	68.1	77	42	4	1	36	17	4.61	74	.288	.375	17-0-2	.059	-1	96	-9		-1.1
1947	Phi N	1	1	.500	4	1	0	0	11.1	19	12	1	1	3	0	7.94	50	.358	.393	4		.500	1	66	-5		-0.7
Total	5	10	33	.233	98	41	8	1	348	381	230	24	3	175	105	5.17	68	.279	.362	91-0-7	.154	-1	70	-63		-7.4

HOFF, CHET Chester Cornelius "Red" B5.8.1891 Ossining NY D9.17.1998 Daytona Beach FL BL/TL/5-9/162 d9.6

YEAR	TM LG	W	L	PCT	G	GS	CG-SHO	SV-BS	IP	H	R	HR	HB	BB-IB	SO	ERA	AERA	OAV	OOB	AB-HR-SH	AVG	PB	SUP	APR	DL	PW
1911	NY A	0	1	.000	5	1	0	0	20.2	21	8	0	0	7	10	2.18	165	.262	.322	7		.286	0	80	3		0.2
1912	NY A	0	1	.000	5	1	0	0	15.2	20	14	0	0	6	14	6.89	52	.303	.361	5		.200	-0	82	-4		-0.3
1913	NY A	0	0	—	2	0	0	0	3	0	0	0	0	1	2	0.00	—	.000	.111	1		.000	-0		1		0.0
1915	StL A	2	2	.500	11	3	2	0	43.2	26	16	0	1	24	23	1.24	232	.169	.285	17		.176	-1	76	5		0.4
Total	4	2	4	.333	23	5	2	0	83	67	38	0	1	38	49	2.49	127	.218	.305	30		.200	-1	78	5		0.4

HOFFER, BILL William Leopold "Chick","Wizard" B11.8.1870 Cedar Rapids IA D7.21.1959 Cedar Rapids IA BR/TR/5-9/155 d4.26

YEAR	TM LG	W	L	PCT	G	GS	CG-SHO	SV-BS	IP	H	R	HR	HB	BB-IB	SO	ERA	AERA	OAV	OOB	AB-HR-SH	AVG	PB	SUP	APR	DL	PW
1895	†Bal N	31	6	.838	41	38	32-4	0	314	296	146	9	19	124	80	3.21	148	.245	.325	126-0-3	.214	-3	122	56		4.6
1896	†Bal N	25	7	.781	35	35	32-3	0	309	317	151	1	12	95	93	3.38	127	.263	.323	125-0-3	.304	11	128	35		3.9
1897	†Bal N	22	11	.667	38	33	29-1	0	303.1	350	188	2	17	104	62	4.30	97	.287	.351	139-1-2	.237	2*	110	2		0.2
1898	Bal N	0	4	.000	4	4	4	0	34.1	62	44	0	1	16	5	7.34	49	.387	.446	24		.208	0*	164	-16		-1.3
	Pit N	3	0	1.000	4	3	3	0	31	26	7	0	0	15	11	1.74	204	.226	.315	11		.091	-1	66	7		0.5
	Year	3	4	.429	8	7	7	0	65.1	88	51	0	1	31	16	4.68	76	.320	.391	35		.171	-0	122	-9		-0.8
1899	Pit N	8	10	.444	23	19	15-2	0	163.2	169	98	5	10	64	44	3.63	105	.266	.343	91		.198	-1	86	-12		-1.2
1901	Cle A	3	8	.273	16	10	10	3	99	113	78	2	1	35	19	4.55	78	.283	.343	44		.136	-1*	118	73		-1.8
Total	6	92	46	.667	161	142	125-10	3	1254.1	1333	712	22	60	453	314	3.75	112	.270	.339	560-1-8	.229	6	118	73		6.7

HOFFMAN, FRANK Frank J. "The Texas Wonder" B Houston TX TR/5-9.5/163 d8.13

YEAR	TM LG	W	L	PCT	G	GS	CG-SHO	SV-BS	IP	H	R	HR	HB	BB-IB	SO	ERA	AERA	OAV	OOB	AB-HR-SH	AVG	PB	SUP	APR	DL	PW
1888	KC AA	3	9	.250	12	12	12	0	110	3	3	6	42	38	2.77	124	.248	.326	39		.154	-1	66	2		0.1

HOFFMAN, GUY Guy Alan B7.9.1956 Ottawa IL BL/TL/5-9/185* d7.4 Col Bradley

YEAR	TM LG	W	L	PCT	G	GS	CG-SHO	SV-BS	IP	H	R	HR	HB	BB-IB	SO	ERA	AERA	OAV	OOB	AB-HR-SH	AVG	PB	SUP	APR	DL	PW
1979	Chi A	0	5	.000	11	5	0	2-1	30.1	30	18	0	1	23-5	18	5.34	80	.261	.388	0		—	0		-2		-0.4
1980	Chi A	1	0	1.000	23	1	0	1-0	37.2	38	12	1	0	17-2	24	2.63	154	.268	.344	0		—	0	88	6		0.3
1983	Chi A	1	0	1.000	11	0	0	0-0	6	14	5	1	0	2-0	2	7.50	56	.483	.500	0		—	0		-2		-0.3
1986	Chi N	6	2	.750	32	8	1	0-0	84	92	37	6	2	29-7	47	3.86	106	.288	.348	15-0-3	.067	-1*	109	3		0.1
1987	Cin N	9	10	.474	36	22	0	0-0	158.2	160	83	20	4	49-5	87	4.37	97	.265	.322	45-0-3	.111	-2	106	-2		-0.1
1988	Tex A	0	0	—	11	0	0	0-0	22.1	22	14	5	1	8-0	9	5.24	78	.247	.313	0		—	0		-2		-0.1
Total	6	17	17	.500	137	31	1	3-1	339	356	169	33	8	128-19	187	4.25	98	.274	.341	60-0-6	.100	-2	107	1		-0.4

HOFFMAN, TREVOR Trevor William B10.13.1967 Bellflower CA BR/TR/6-0/205(200-215) [CinN89 11/290] d4.6 b-Glenn Col Arizona

YEAR	TM LG	W	L	PCT	G	GS	CG-SHO	SV-BS	IP	H	R	HR	HB	BB-IB	SO	ERA	AERA	OAV	OOB	AB-HR-SH	AVG	PB	SUP	APR	DL	PW
1993	Fla N	2	2	.500	28	0	0	2-1	35.2	24	13	5	1	19-7	26	3.28	133	.192	.287	2		.000	-0		4		0.5
	SD N	2	4	.333	39	0	0	3-2	54.1	56	30	5	1	20-6	53	4.31	96	.264	.325	5		.200	-0		-1		-0.1
	Year	4	6	.400	67	0	0	5-3	90	80	43	10	1	39-13	79	3.90	108	.234	.310	7		.143	-0		3		0.4
1994	SD N	4	4	.500	47	0	0	20-3	56	39	16	4	0	20-6	68	2.57	161	.193	.263	3-0-1	.000	-0		11		2.0
1995	SD N	7	4	.636	55	0	0	31-7	53.1	48	25	10	0	14-3	52	3.88	105	.235	.284	2		.500	1		2		0.4
1996	†SD N	9	5	.643	70	0	0	42-7	88	50	23	6	2	31-5	111	2.25	179	.161	.240	8-0-1	.000	-1		19		2.5
1997	SD N	8	6	.600	70	0	0	37-7	81.1	59	25	9	0	24-4	111	2.66	148	.200	.259	3		.333	0		13		2.5
1998	†SD N★	4	2	.667	66	0	0	53-1	73	41	12	2	1	21-2	86	1.48	268	.164	.232	3		.000	-0		22		4.2
1999	SD N★	4	3	.400	64	0	0	40-3	67.1	48	23	5	0	15-2	73	2.14	200	.197	.240	4		.333	1		15		2.5
2000	SD N★	4	7	.364	70	0	0	43-7	72.1	61	29	7	0	11-4	85	2.99	149	.224	.250	0		—	0		11		2.2
2001	SD N	3	4	.429	62	0	0	43-3	60.1	48	25	10	1	21-2	69	3.43	121	.216	.285	4		.000	-0		5		1.0
2002	SD N★	2	5	.286	61	0	0	38-3	59.1	52	20	2	1	18-2	69	2.73	142	.234	.292	0		—	0		8		1.4
2003	SD N	0	0	—	9	0	0	0-0	9	7	2	1	0	3-0	11	2.00	200	.212	.278	0		—	0		2	156	0.3
2004	SD N	3	3	.500	54	0	0	41-4	54.2	42	14	5	0	8-1	53	2.30	171	.211	.242	0		—	0		12		1.8
2005	†SD N	1	6	.143	60	0	0	43-3	57.2	52	23	3	1	12-1	54	2.97	130	.234	.273	0		—	0		5	156	1.8
Total	13	49	53	.480	756	0	0	436-51	822.1	627	280	74	7	237-45	915	2.76	148	.208	.265	33-0-2	.121	-1		128	156	24.4

HOFFMAN, BILL William Joseph B3.3.1918 Philadelphia PA BL/TL/5-9/170 d8.13

YEAR	TM LG	W	L	PCT	G	GS	CG-SHO	SV-BS	IP	H	R	HR	HB	BB-IB	SO	ERA	AERA	OAV	OOB	AB-HR-SH	AVG	PB	SUP	APR	DL	PW
1939	Phi N	0	0	—	3	0	0	0	4	9	6	1	3	7	1	13.50	30	.333	.529	1		.000	-0		-6		-0.1

HOFFORD, JOHN John William B5.25.1863 Philadelphia PA D12.16.1915 Philadelphia PA d9.26

YEAR	TM LG	W	L	PCT	G	GS	CG-SHO	SV-BS	IP	H	R	HR	HB	BB-IB	SO	ERA	AERA	OAV	OOB	AB-HR-SH	AVG	PB	SUP	APR	DL	PW
1885	Pit AA	0	3	.000	3	3	3	0	25	28	16	1	0	9	21	3.60	89	.275	.333	8		.125	-1	61	-1		-0.1
1886	Pit AA	3	6	.333	9	9	9	0	81	88	66	1	2	40	25	4.33	78	.261	.343	34		.294	3	91	-9		-0.1
Total	2	3	9	.250	12	12	12	0	106	116	82	2	2	49	46	4.16	80	.264	.341	42		.262	2	84	-10		-0.1

HOGAN, GEORGE George A. B9.25.1885 Marion OH D2.22.1922 Bartlesville OK BR/TR/6-0/160 d4.18 b-Willie

YEAR	TM LG	W	L	PCT	G	GS	CG-SHO	SV-BS	IP	H	R	HR	HB	BB-IB	SO	ERA	AERA	OAV	OOB	AB-HR-SH	AVG	PB	SUP	APR	DL	PW
1914	KC F	0	1	.000	2	1	0	0	13	12	9	1	1	7	2	4.15	67	.255	.364	4		.000	-1	74	-2		-0.1

HOGAN, EDDIE Robert Edward B4.6.1862 St.Louis MO D1.22.1932 Yucaipa CA 5-7/153 d7.5

YEAR	TM LG	W	L	PCT	G	GS	CG-SHO	SV-BS	IP	H	R	HR	HB	BB-IB	SO	ERA	AERA	OAV	OOB	AB-HR-SH	AVG	PB	SUP	APR	DL	PW
1882	StL AA	0	1	.000	1	1	1	0	8	10	7	0		4	1.13	249	.286	.286	3		.333	0	73	0		0.1

HOGG, BRAD Carter Bradley B3.26.1889 Buena Vista GA D4.2.1935 Buena Vista GA BR/TR/6-0/185 d9.1 Col Mercer

YEAR	TM LG	W	L	PCT	G	GS	CG-SHO	SV-BS	IP	H	R	HR	HB	BB-IB	SO	ERA	AERA	OAV	OOB	AB-HR-SH	AVG	PB	SUP	APR	DL	PW
1911	Bos N	0	3	.000	8	3	2	1	25.2	33	20	0	1	14		6.66	57	.337	.425	9-0-1	.444	1	118	-6		-0.1
1912	Bos N	1	1	.500	10	1	0	1	31	37	32	2	2	16	12	6.97	51	.308	.399	11		.091	-1	164	-11		-0.1

YEAR	TM LG	W	L	PCT	G	GS	CG-SHO	SV-BS	IP	H	R	HR	HB	BB-IB	SO	ERA	AERA	OAV	OOB	AB-HR-SH	AVG	PB	SUP	APR	DL	PW
1915	Chi N	1	0	1.000	2	2	1-1	0	13	12	1	1	1	6	0	2.08	134	.245	.339	3-0-1	.000	-0	120	1		0.1
1918	Phi N	13	13	.500	29	25	17-3	1	228	201	83	3	6	61	81	2.53	119	.245	.302	79-0-4	.228	3*	80	10		1.8
1919	Phi N	5	12	.294	22	19	13	0	150.1	163	85	7	5	55	48	4.43	73	.292	.360	60-0-1	.283	3*	86	-17		-1.6
Total 5		20	29	.408	71	50	33-4	3	448	446	223	14	15	152	149	3.70	85	.271	.338	162-0-7	.247	5	87	-23		-1.0

HOGG, BILL William Johnston "Buffalo Bill" B9.11.1881 Port Huron MI D12.8.1909 New Orleans LA BR/TR/6-0/200 d4.25

YEAR	TM LG	W	L	PCT	G	GS	CG-SHO	SV-BS	IP	H	R	HR	HB	BB-IB	SO	ERA	AERA	OAV	OOB	AB-HR-SH	AVG	PB	SUP	APR	DL	PW
1905	NY A	9	13	.409	39	22	9-3	1	205	178	104	0	13	101	125	3.20	92	.236	.336	67-0-1	.060	-6	79	-6		-1.5
1906	NY A	14	13	.519	28	25	15-3	0	206	171	77	5	12	72	107	2.93	101	.239	.307	72-0-5	.125	-5	97	4		-0.2
1907	NY A	10	8	.556	25	21	13	0	166.2	173	84	3	6	83	64	3.08	91	.270	.359	60-1-5	.183	-0*	101	-5		-0.6
1908	NY A	4	16	.200	24	21	6	0	152.1	155	89	4	4	63	72	3.01	82	.262	.337	43-0-1	.093	-3	63	-13		-2.1
Total 4		37	50	.425	116	89	43-6	1	730	677	354	13	35	319	368	3.06	92	.248	.334	242-1-12	.116	-14	86	-20		-4.4

HOGSETT, CHIEF Elon Chester B11.2.1903 Brownell KS D7.17.2001 Hays KS BL/TL/6-0/190 d9.18

YEAR	TM LG	W	L	PCT	G	GS	CG-SHO	SV-BS	IP	H	R	HR	HB	BB-IB	SO	ERA	AERA	OAV	OOB	AB-HR-SH	AVG	PB	SUP	APR	DL	PW
1929	Det A	1	2	.333	4	4	2-1	0	28.2	34	10	0	1	9	7	2.83	152	.312	.370	10	.200	-0	84	5		0.4
1930	Det A	9	8	.529	33	17	4	1	146	174	102	9	9	63	54	5.42	88	.300	.377	58-1-0	.293	3	83	-9		-0.6
1931	Det A	3	9	.250	22	12	5	2	112.1	150	80	8	5	33	47	5.93	77	.324	.375	47	.234	-0	94	-13		-1.1
1932	Det A	11	9	.550	47	15	7	7	178	201	97	8	5	66	56	3.54	133	.286	.351	57-2-4	.246	3*	87	17		2.2
1933	Det A	6	10	.375	45	2	0	9	116	137	78	7	4	56	39	4.50	96	.296	.377	38	.211	-0	128	-6		-0.8
1934	†Det A	3	2	.600	26	0	0	3	50.1	61	34	4	1	19	23	4.29	102	.303	.367	13	.231	-0		-2		-0.2
1935	†Det A	6	6	.500	40	0	0	5	96.2	109	45	1	5	49	39	3.54	118	.288	.377	23-2-0	.261	2		7		1.1
1936	Det A	0	1	.000	3	0	0	0	4	8	7	1	0	1	1	9.00	55	.400	.429	0	—	-0		-3		-0.4
	StL A	13	15	.464	39	29	10	1	215.1	278	153	15	15	90	67	5.52	97	.310	.383	70-0-2	.143	-2*	88	-2		-0.6
	Year	13	16	.448	42	29	10	1	219.1	286	160	16	15	91	68	5.58	96	.312	.384	70-0-2	.143	-2	88	-6		-1.0
1937	StL A	6	19	.240	37	26	8-1	2	177.1	245	144	19	5	75	68	6.29	77	.328	.393	62-1-0	.210	0*	56	-29		-3.3
1938	Was A	5	6	.455	31	9	1	3	91	107	73	12	8	36	33	6.03	75	.292	.368	23	.304	3*	102	-17		-1.4
1944	Det A	0	0	—	3	0	0	0	6.1	7	6	1	2	4	5	0.00	—	.250	.382	2	.000	-0		0		0.0
Total 11		63	87	.420	330	114	37-2	33	1222	1511	829	85	60	501	441	5.02	94	.305	.376	403-6-6	.226	8	84	-54		-4.7

HOGUE, CAL Calvin Grey B10.24.1927 Dayton OH D8.5.2005 Kettering OH BR/TR/6-0/185* d7.15

YEAR	TM LG	W	L	PCT	G	GS	CG-SHO	SV-BS	IP	H	R	HR	HB	BB-IB	SO	ERA	AERA	OAV	OOB	AB-HR-SH	AVG	PB	SUP	APR	DL	PW
1952	Pit N	1	8	.111	19	12	3	0	83.2	79	56	7	4	68	34	4.84	82	.258	.399	24-0-1	.250	1	71	-10		-0.9
1953	Pit N	1	1	.500	3	2	2	0	19	19	13	4	1	16	10	5.21	86	.250	.387	5-0-1	.000	-1	100	-2		-0.2
1954	Pit N	0	1	.000	3	2	0	0	11	11	6	1	0	12	7	4.91	85	.282	.442	3-0-1	.000	-0	75	0		-0.1
Total 3		2	10	.167	25	16	5	0	113.2	109	75	12	5	96	51	4.91	83	.259	.402	32-0-3	.188	-0	75	-12		-1.2

HOGUE, BOBBY Robert Clinton B4.5.1921 Miami FL D12.22.1987 Miami FL BR/TR/5-10/195* d4.24

YEAR	TM LG	W	L	PCT	G	GS	CG-SHO	SV-BS	IP	H	R	HR	HB	BB-IB	SO	ERA	AERA	OAV	OOB	AB-HR-SH	AVG	PB	SUP	APR	DL	PW
1948	Bos N	8	2	.800	40	1	0	2	86.1	88	34	4	2	19	43	3.23	119	.265	.309	21-0-7	.095	-1	162	6		0.5
1949	Bos N	2	2	.500	33	1	0	3	72	78	30	4	2	25	23	3.13	121	.280	.343	21-0-3	.286	1		5		0.5
1950	Bos N	3	5	.375	36	1	0	7	62.2	69	35	8	4	31	15	5.03	77	.280	.370	13-0-1	.231	1	115	-6		-0.7
1951	Bos N	0	0	—	3	0	0	0	5	4	3	1	0	3	0	5.40	68	.235	.350	2	.500	0		-1		0.0
	StL A	1	1	.500	18	0	0	1	29.2	31	17	1	0	23	11	5.16	85	.279	.403	3	.500	1		-2		0.1
	†NY A	1	0	1.000	7	0	0	0	7.1	4	0	0	0	3	2	0.00	—	.174	.269	0	—	0		3		0.4
	Year	2	1	.667	25	0	0	1	37	35	17	1	0	26	13	4.14	104	.261	.381	3	.667	1		1		0.5
1952	NY A	3	5	.375	27	0	0	4	47.1	52	30	6	1	25	12	5.32	62	.294	.384	11	.273	1		-11		-1.8
	StL A	0	1	.000	8	1	0	0	16.1	10	5	1	0	13	2	2.76	142	.179	.333	2	.000	-0	22	2		0.1
	Year	3	6	.333	35	1	0	4	63.2	62	35	7	1	38	14	4.66	74	.266	.371	13	.231	0	25	-7		-1.7
Total 5		18	16	.529	172	3	0	17	326.2	336	154	25	9	142	108	3.97	96	.271	.350	73-0-11	.233	3	101	-4		-0.9

HOLBOROW, WALLY Walter Albert B11.30.1913 New York NY D7.14.1986 Ft.Lauderdale FL BR/TR/5-11/187 d9.27

YEAR	TM LG	W	L	PCT	G	GS	CG-SHO	SV-BS	IP	H	R	HR	HB	BB-IB	SO	ERA	AERA	OAV	OOB	AB-HR-SH	AVG	PB	SUP	APR	DL	PW
1944	Was A	0	0	—	1	0	0	0	3	0	0	0	0	2	1	0.00	—	.000	.182	0		0		1		0.1
1945	Was A	1	1	.500	15	1	1-1	0	31.1	20	9	0	0	16	14	2.30	135	.189	.295	2-0-2	.000	-0	110	3		0.1
1948	Phi A	1	2	.333	5	1	1	0	17.1	32	12	1	0	7	3	5.71	75	.421	.470	4-0-1	.500	1	147	-3		-0.2
Total 3		2	3	.400	21	2	2-1	0	51.2	52	21	1	0	25	18	3.31	106	.272	.356	6-0-3	.333	1	137	1		0.0

HOLCOMBE, KEN Kenneth Edward B8.23.1918 Burnsville NC BR/TR/5-11.5/169* d4.27

YEAR	TM LG	W	L	PCT	G	GS	CG-SHO	SV-BS	IP	H	R	HR	HB	BB-IB	SO	ERA	AERA	OAV	OOB	AB-HR-SH	AVG	PB	SUP	APR	DL	PW
1945	NY A	3	3	.500	23	2	0	0	55.1	43	19	2	0	27	20	1.79	194	.226	.323	15	.133	-1	74	7		0.7
1948	Cin N	0	0	—	2	0	0	0	2.1	3	2	0	0	0	2	7.71	51	.300	.300	0	—	0		-1		0.0
1950	Chi A	3	10	.231	24	15	5	1	96	122	68	10	0	45	37	4.59	98	.307	.378	32-0-2	.156	-2	87	-7		-1.0
1951	Chi A	11	12	.478	28	23	12-2	0	159.1	142	69	9	1	68	39	3.78	107	.241	.321	44-0-10	.250	1	77	9		1.3
1952	Chi A	0	5	.000	7	7	1	0	35	38	24	3	2	18	12	6.17	59	.286	.379	10-0-1	.000	-1	58	-9		-1.2
	StL A	0	2	.000	12	1	0	0	21	20	10	1	0	9	7	3.86	101	.263	.341	3	.333	1	0	0		0.1
	Year	0	7	.000	19	8	1	0	56	58	34	4	2	27	19	5.30	71	.278	.366	13-0-1	.077	-1	49	-8		-1.1
1953	Bos A	1	0	1.000	3	0	0	1	6	9	4	0	0	3	1	6.00	70	.333	.400	2-0-1	.000	-0		-1		-0.2
Total 6		18	32	.360	99	48	18-2	2	375	377	196	25	4	170	118	3.98	101	.265	.345	106-0-14	.179	-3	77	-2		-0.3

HOLDRIDGE, DAVID David Allen B2.5.1969 Wayne MI BR/TR/6-3/190 [CalA87 1/31] d8.8

YEAR	TM LG	W	L	PCT	G	GS	CG-SHO	SV-BS	IP	H	R	HR	HB	BB-IB	SO	ERA	AERA	OAV	OOB	AB-HR-SH	AVG	PB	SUP	APR	DL	PW
1998	Sea A	0	0	—	7	0	0	0	6	9	4	0	0	6	6	4.05	116	.231	.323	0		0		1		0.0

HOLDSWORTH, FRED Fredrick William B5.29.1952 Detroit MI BR/TR/6-1/190* [DetA70 21/507] d7.27

YEAR	TM LG	W	L	PCT	G	GS	CG-SHO	SV-BS	IP	H	R	HR	HB	BB-IB	SO	ERA	AERA	OAV	OOB	AB-HR-SH	AVG	PB	SUP	APR	DL	PW
1972	Det A	0	1	.000	2	2	0	0-0	7	13	10	0	0	2-0	5	12.86	25	.419	.441	3	.333	0	154	-7		-0.8
1973	Det A	0	0	—	5	2	0	0-0	14.2	13	11	3	0	6-0	9	6.75	61	.236	.311	0	—	0	87	-4		-0.2
1974	Det A	0	3	.000	8	5	0	0-0	35.2	40	20	4	1	14-3	16	4.29	89	.286	.355	0	—	0	51	-2		-0.2
1976	Bal A	4	1	.800	16	0	0	2-2	39.2	24	9	0	0	13-1	24	2.04	161	.179	.250	0	—	0		6		0.8
1977	Bal A	0	1	.000	12	0	0	0-1	14.1	17	11	0	1	16-2	4	6.28	61	.333	.479	0	—	0		-4	31	-0.3
	Mon N	3	3	.500	14	0	0	0-0	42.1	35	17	6	0	18-0	21	3.19	121	.230	.306	10	.000	-1	108	3		0.3
1978	Mon N	0	0	—	6	0	0	0-0	8.2	16	10	3	0	8-3	3	7.27	49	.381	.480	0	—	0		-5	55	-0.2
1980	Mil A	0	0	—	3	0	0	0-0	19.2	24	12	2	0	9-0	12	4.58	86	.286	.355	0	—	0		-2		-0.1
Total 7		7	10	.412	72	15	0	2-3	182	182	100	18	2	86-9	94	4.40	84	.264	.344	13	.077	-1	92	-15	86	-0.7

HOLLAND, AL Alfred Willis B8.16.1952 Roanoke VA BR/TL/5-11/207(200-213) d9.5 Col North Carolina A&T

YEAR	TM LG	W	L	PCT	G	GS	CG-SHO	SV-BS	IP	H	R	HR	HB	BB-IB	SO	ERA	AERA	OAV	OOB	AB-HR-SH	AVG	PB	SUP	APR	DL	PW
1977	Pit N	0	0	—	2	0	0	0-0	2.1	4	2	0	0	0-0	1	7.71	52	.400	.400	0	—	0		-1		0.0
1979	SF N	0	0	—	7	0	0	0-0	7	3	0	0	0	5-0	7	0.00	—	.125	.276	0	—	0		3		0.1
1980	SF N	5	3	.625	54	0	0	7-4	82.1	71	21	2	1	34-8	65	1.75	201	.233	.308	5-0-2	.200	1		15		1.9
1981	SF N	7	5	.583	47	3	0	7-1	100.2	87	31	4	2	44-11	78	2.41	141	.233	.314	16-0-5	.063	-1	78	11		1.3
1982	SF N	7	3	.700	58	7	0	5-0	129.2	115	56	12	1	40-6	97	3.33	108	.231	.288	34-0-3	.059	-3	109	3	24	0.0
1983	†Phi N	8	4	.667	68	0	0	25-7	91.2	63	26	8	0	30-12	100	2.26	160	.188	.254	7-0-1	.000	-1		14	25	2.4
1984	Phi N☆	5	10	.333	68	0	0	29-7	98.1	82	38	14	1	30-6	61	3.39	108	.225	.283	5	.000	-1		5		0.9
1985	Phi N	0	1	.000	3	0	0	1-0	4	5	2	0	0	4-2	1	4.50	83	.333	.450	0	—	0		0		0.0
	Pit N	1	3	.250	38	0	0	4-4	58.2	48	25	5	0	17-6	47	3.38	108	.227	.281	5-0-1	.400	2		3		0.3
	Year	1	4	.200	41	0	0	5-4	62.2	53	24	5	0	21-8	48	3.45	105	.235	.295	5-0-1	.400	2		3		0.3
	Cal A	0	1	.000	15	0	0	0-1	24.1	17	4	4	0	10-1	14	1.48	279	.193	.276	0	—	0		7		0.4
1986	NY A	1	0	1.000	25	1	0	0-1	40.2	44	29	5	0	9-2	37	5.09	81	.268	.301	0	—	0	263	-6	15	-0.3
1987	NY A	0	0	—	3	0	0	0-0	6.1	9	10	1	0	9-0	5	14.21	31	.321	.408	0	—	0		-7	56	-0.3
Total 10		34	30	.531	384	11	0	78-25	646	548	241	55	5	232-54	513	2.98	122	.227	.293	72-0-12	.083	-2	116	47	120	6.7

HOLLAND, MUL Howard Arthur B1.6.1903 Franklin VA D2.16.1969 Winchester VA BR/TR/6-4/185 d5.25 Col Virginia

YEAR	TM LG	W	L	PCT	G	GS	CG-SHO	SV-BS	IP	H	R	HR	HB	BB-IB	SO	ERA	AERA	OAV	OOB	AB-HR-SH	AVG	PB	SUP	APR	DL	PW
1926	Cin N	0	0	—	3	0	0	0	6.2	3	1	0	0	5	0	1.35	273	.136	.296	2	.500		2			0.2
1927	NY N	1	0	1.000	2	0	0	0	2	0	0	0	0	3	0	0.00	—	.000	.333	0	—	0		1		0.2
1929	StL N	0	1	.000	8	0	0	0	14.1	13	15	3	1	7	5	9.42	50	.232	.328	4	.250	0		-7		-0.4
Total 3		1	1	.500	13	0	0	0	23	16	16	3	1	15	5	6.26	69	.190	.320	6	.333		-4			0.0

HOLLAND, BILL William David "Dutch" B6.4.1915 Varina (now Fuquay-Varina) NC D4.5.1997 Goldsboro NC BL/TL/6-1/190 d9.17 Col East Carolina

YEAR	TM LG	W	L	PCT	G	GS	CG-SHO	SV-BS	IP	H	R	HR	HB	BB-IB	SO	ERA	AERA	OAV	OOB	AB-HR-SH	AVG	PB	SUP	APR	DL	PW
1939	Was A	0	1	.000	2	0	0	0	4	6	5	1	0	4	2	11.25	39	.400	.550					-3		-0.5

HOLLEY, ED Edward Edgar B7.23.1899 Benton KY D10.26.1986 Paducah KY BR/TR/6-1.5/195 d5.24

YEAR	TM LG	W	L	PCT	G	GS	CG-SHO	SV-BS	IP	H	R	HR	HB	BB-IB	SO	ERA	AERA	OAV	OOB	AB-HR-SH	AVG	PB	SUP	APR	DL	PW
1928	Chi N	0	0	—	13	1	0	0	31	31	15	1	2	16	10	3.77	102	.265	.363	5	.000	-0	154	0		0.0
1932	Phi N	11	14	.440	34	30	16-2	0	228	247	114	15	6	55	87	3.95	112	.273	.319	91-0-2	.132	-6	85	11		0.4
1933	Phi N	13	15	.464	30	28	12-3	0	206.2	219	93	18	3	62	56	3.53	108	.273	.335	74-0-2	.162	-2	83	7		0.5

YEAR	TM LG	W	L	PCT	G	GS	CG-SHO	SV-BS	IP	H	R	HR	HB	BB-IB	SO	ERA	AERA	OAV	OOB	AB-HR-SH	AVG	PB	SUP	APR	DL	PW
1934	Phi N	1	8	.111	15	13	2	0	72.2	85	62	10	4	31	14	7.18	66	.294	.370	24	.208	-1*	91	-15		-1.7
	Pit N	0	3	.000	5	4	0	0	9.1	20	16	1	2	6	2	15.43	27	.426	.509	2	1.000	2	126	-11		-1.7
	Year	1	11	.083	20	17	2	0	82	105	78	11	6	37	16	8.12	57	.313	.391	26	.269	1	97	-24		-3.3
Total	4	25	40	.385	97	76	30-5		547.2	602	300	45	27	170	169	4.40	95	.279	.339	196-0-4	.158	-8	89	-8		-2.4

HOLLING, CARL Carl B7.9.1896 Dana CA D7.18.1962 Santa Rosa CA BR/TR/6-1/172 d4.19

YEAR	TM LG	W	L	PCT	G	GS	CG-SHO	SV-BS	IP	H	R	HR	HB	BB-IB	SO	ERA	AERA	OAV	OOB	AB-HR-SH	AVG	PB	SUP	APR	DL	PW
1921	Det A	3	7	.300	35	11	4	4	136	162	95	4	4	58	38	4.30	99	.305	.378	48-0-2	.271	1	98	-6		-0.2
1922	Det A	1	1	.500	5	1	0	0	9.1	21	16	1	2	5	2	15.43	25	.525	.596	2	.000	-0*	88	-11		-1.7
Total	2	4	8	.333	40	12	4	4	145.1	183	111	9	6	63	40	5.02	85	.320	.394	50-0-2	.260	1	97	-17		-1.9

HOLLINGSWORTH, AL Albert Wayne "Boots" B2.25.1908 St.Louis MO D4.28.1996 Austin TX BL/TL/6-0/174 d4.16 C2

YEAR	TM LG	W	L	PCT	G	GS	CG-SHO	SV-BS	IP	H	R	HR	HB	BB-IB	SO	ERA	AERA	OAV	OOB	AB-HR-SH	AVG	PB	SUP	APR	DL	PW
1935	Cin N	6	13	.316	38	22	8	0	173.1	165	90	5	1	76	89	3.89	102	.243	.321	54-0-3	.148	-2*	76	1		-0.1
1936	Cin N	9	10	.474	29	25	9	0	184	204	97	4	5	66	76	4.16	92	.281	.345	73-1-1	.315	7*	108	-6		0.1
1937	Cin N	9	15	.375	43	24	11-1	5	202.1	224	108	8	2	73	74	3.91	95	.278	.339	76	.250	3*	110	-6		-0.3
1938	Cin N	2	2	.500	9	4	1	0	34	43	28	2	0	12	13	7.15	51	.307	.362	12	.250	1	139	-12		-1.1
	Phi N	5	16	.238	24	21	11-1	0	174.1	177	89	4	0	77	80	3.82	102	.264	.340	67-0-1	.224	-0	78	0		-0.1
	Year	7	18	.280	33	25	12-1	0	208.1	220	117	6	0	89	93	4.36	88	.272	.344	79-0-1	.228	1	87	-11		-1.2
1939	Phi N	1	9	.100	15	10	3	0	60	78	48	2	0	27	24	5.85	69	.317	.385	20	.100	-1	92	-14		-2.1
	Bro N	1	2	.333	8	5	1	0	27.1	33	17	1	1	11	11	5.27	76	.311	.381	8-0-1	.125	-1*	95	-3		-0.3
	Year	2	11	.154	23	15	4	0	87.1	111	65	3	1	38	35	5.67	71	.315	.384	28-0-1	.107	-2	93	-16		-2.4
1940	Was A	1	0	1.000	3	2	0	0	18	18	12	0	0	11	7	5.50	76	.261	.363	6	.167	0	158	-2		-0.1
1942	StL A	10	6	.625	33	18	7-1	0	161	173	70	4	2	52	60	2.96	125	.272	.329	56-0-1	.179	0*	138	10		1.0
1943	StL A	6	13	.316	35	20	9-1	3	154	169	81	7	2	51	63	4.21	79	.281	.339	50-0-2	.140	-1*	91	-14		-1.9
1944	†StL A	5	7	.417	26	10	3-2	1	92.2	108	51	3	1	37	22	4.47	81	.291	.357	28	.071	-2*	65	-7		-1.1
1945	StL A	12	9	.571	26	22	15-1	1	173.1	164	60	4	0	68	64	2.70	130	.251	.322	61-1-3	.197	1*	88	15		2.0
1946	StL A	0	0		5	0	0	0	11	23	8	1	0	4	3	6.55	57	.411	.450	2	.000	-0		-3		-0.2
	Chi A	3	2	.600	21	2	0	1	55	63	29	2	0	22	22	4.58	74	.288	.353	12-0-2	.000	-1	63	-5		-0.6
	Year	3	2	.600	26	2	0	1	66	86	37	3	0	26	25	4.91	71	.313	.372	14-0-2	.000	-1	62	-9		-0.8
Total	11	70	104	.402	315	185	78-7	15	1520.1	1642	788	47	14	587	608	3.99	93	.275	.341	525-2-14	.196	3	97	-46		-4.8

HOLLINGSWORTH, BONNIE John Burnette B12.26.1895 Jacksboro TN D1.4.1990 Knoxville TN BR/TR/5-10/170 d5.30

YEAR	TM LG	W	L	PCT	G	GS	CG-SHO	SV-BS	IP	H	R	HR	HB	BB-IB	SO	ERA	AERA	OAV	OOB	AB-HR-SH	AVG	PB	SUP	APR	DL	PW
1922	Pit N	0	0		9	0	0	0	13.2	17	14	0	1	9	7	7.90	52	.315	.413	0	—	0		-6		-0.3
1923	Was A	3	7	.300	17	8	1	0	72.2	72	43	3	3	50	26	4.09	92	.272	.393	22	.091	-1	77	-4		-0.6
1924	Bro N	1	0	1.000	3	1	1	0	8.2	8	6	0	0	10	7	6.23	60	.267	.450	3	.000	-1	91	-2		-0.2
1928	Bos N	0	2	.000	7	2	0	0	22.1	30	19	2	0	13	10	5.24	75	.341	.426	6	.167	-0	130	-5		-0.4
Total	4	4	9	.308	36	11	2	0	117.1	127	82	5	4	81	50	4.91	78	.291	.406	31	.097	-2	87	-17		-1.5

HOLLINS, JESSIE Jessie Edward B1.27.1970 Conroe TX BR/TR/6-3/190 [ChiN88 40/1027] d9.19 [DL 1993 Chi N 182, 1994 Chi N 123]

YEAR	TM LG	W	L	PCT	G	GS	CG-SHO	SV-BS	IP	H	R	HR	HB	BB-IB	SO	ERA	AERA	OAV	OOB	AB-HR-SH	AVG	PB	SUP	APR	DL	PW
1992	Chi N	0	0		4	0	0-0	0	4.2	8	7	1	0	5-0	0	13.50	27	.400	.481	0		0		-5		-0.2

HOLLISON, JOHN John Henry "Swede" B5.3.1870 Chicago IL D8.19.1969 Chicago IL BR/TL/5-8/162 d8.13

YEAR	TM LG	W	L	PCT	G	GS	CG-SHO	SV-BS	IP	H	R	HR	HB	BB-IB	SO	ERA	AERA	OAV	OOB	AB-HR-SH	AVG	PB	SUP	APR	DL	PW
1892	Chi N	0	0		1	0	0	0	4	1	1	1	0	2	1	2.25	148	.077	.077	3	.000	-0		1		0.0

HOLLOMAN, BOBO Alva Lee B3.7.1925 Thomaston GA D5.1.1987 Athens GA BR/TR/6-2/207 d4.18

YEAR	TM LG	W	L	PCT	G	GS	CG-SHO	SV-BS	IP	H	R	HR	HB	BB-IB	SO	ERA	AERA	OAV	OOB	AB-HR-SH	AVG	PB	SUP	APR	DL	PW
1953	StL A	3	7	.300	22	10	1-1	0	65.1	69	41	2	1	50	25	5.23	80	.275	.397	19-0-3	.105	-2	72	-6		-1.0

HOLLOWAY, JIM James Madison B9.22.1908 Plaquemine LA D4.15.1997 Baton Rouge LA BR/TR/6-1/165 d5.17

YEAR	TM LG	W	L	PCT	G	GS	CG-SHO	SV-BS	IP	H	R	HR	HB	BB-IB	SO	ERA	AERA	OAV	OOB	AB-HR-SH	AVG	PB	SUP	APR	DL	PW
1929	Phi N	0	0		3	0	0	0	4.2	10	7	2	0	5	1	13.50	38	.455	.556	1	1.000	0		-4		-0.1

HOLLOWAY, KEN Kenneth Eugene (b Kenneth Eugene Hollaway) B8.8.1897 Barwick GA D9.25.1968 Thomasville GA BR/TR/6-0/185 d8.27 Col Georgia

YEAR	TM LG	W	L	PCT	G	GS	CG-SHO	SV-BS	IP	H	R	HR	HB	BB-IB	SO	ERA	AERA	OAV	OOB	AB-HR-SH	AVG	PB	SUP	APR	DL	PW
1922	Det A	0	0		1	0	0	0	1	1	1	0	0	1	1	0.00	—	.250	.250	0		0		0		0.0
1923	Det A	11	10	.524	42	24	7-1	1	194	232	117	12	10	75	55	4.45	87	.302	.372	65-0-3	.123	-5	106	-14		-1.8
1924	Det A	14	6	.700	49	13	5	3	181.1	209	105	6	9	61	46	4.07	101	.299	.361	58-0-2	.190	-1	118	-1		-0.2
1925	Det A	13	4	.765	38	14	6	2	157.2	170	90	8	2	67	29	4.62	93	.282	.356	48-0-4	.229	-0	120	-4		-0.5
1926	Det A	4	6	.400	36	12	3	2	139	192	94	2	8	42	43	5.12	79	.343	.397	46-0-1	.239	0	126	-15		-0.7
1927	Det A	11	12	.478	36	23	11-1	6	183.1	210	103	10	4	61	36	4.07	103	.299	.359	62-0-6	.129	-5	94	3		-0.1
1928	Det A	4	8	.333	30	11	5	2	120.1	137	67	2	5	32	32	4.34	95	.291	.343	33-0-5	.121	-2	69	-2		-0.3
1929	Cle A	6	5	.545	25	11	6-2	0	119	143	52	2	2	37	32	3.03	147	.264	.323	41	.171	-2	74	16		1.1
1930	Cle A	1	1	.500	12	2	0	2	30	49	32	5	0	14	8	8.40	57	.374	.434	12-0-2	.000	-2	98	-10		-0.8
	NY A	0	0		16	0	0	0	34.1	52	23	3	0	8	11	5.24	82	.374	.408	13	.231	-0		-3		-0.2
	Year	1	1	.500	28	2	0	2	64.1	101	55	8	0	22	19	6.72	68	.374	.421	25-0-2	.120	-3	104	-15		-1.0
Total	9	64	52	.552	285	110	43-4	18	1160	1370	684	50	37	397	293	4.40	95	.303	.364	378-0-23	.167	-18	101	-30		-3.8

HOLLY, JEFF Jeffrey Owen B3.1.1953 San Pedro CA BL/TL/6-5/210* [ChiA71 17/390] d5.1

YEAR	TM LG	W	L	PCT	G	GS	CG-SHO	SV-BS	IP	H	R	HR	HB	BB-IB	SO	ERA	AERA	OAV	OOB	AB-HR-SH	AVG	PB	SUP	APR	DL	PW
1977	Min A	2	3	.400	18	5	0	0-0	48.1	57	37	8	1	12-0	32	6.89	58	.300	.343	0	—	0	131	-14		-1.3
1978	Min A	1	1	.500	15	1	0	0-0	35.1	28	15	1	0	18-3	12	3.57	108	.222	.313	0		0	70	1		0.1
1979	Min A	0	0		6	0	0	0-0	6.1	10	7	0	0	3-0	5	7.11	62	.385	.419	0		0		-3		-0.1
Total	3	3	4	.429	39	6	0	0-0	90	95	59	9	1	33-3	49	5.60	71	.278	.338	0		0	121	-16		-1.3

HOLMAN, BRAD Bradley Thomas B2.9.1968 Kansas City MO BR/TR/6-5/200 [KCA90 35/947] d7.4 b-Brian Col Auburn-Montgomery

YEAR	TM LG	W	L	PCT	G	GS	CG-SHO	SV-BS	IP	H	R	HR	HB	BB-IB	SO	ERA	AERA	OAV	OOB	AB-HR-SH	AVG	PB	SUP	APR	DL	PW
1993	Sea A	1	3	.250	19	0	0	3-0	36.1	27	17	1	5	16-2	17	3.72	120	.208	.318	0		0		3	19	0.3

HOLMAN, BRIAN Brian Scott B1.25.1965 Denver CO BR/TR/6-4/185* [MonN83 1/16] d6.25 b-Brad [DL 1992 Sea A 182, 1993 Sea A 182]

YEAR	TM LG	W	L	PCT	G	GS	CG-SHO	SV-BS	IP	H	R	HR	HB	BB-IB	SO	ERA	AERA	OAV	OOB	AB-HR-SH	AVG	PB	SUP	APR	DL	PW
1988	Mon N	4	8	.333	18	16	1-1	0-0	100.1	101	39	3	0	34-2	58	3.23	113	.264	.323	28-0-4	.107	-1*	69	5		0.5
1989	Mon N	1	2	.333	10	3	0	0-0	31.2	34	18	2	1	15-0	23	4.83	74	.270	.350	8	.125	-0	108	-4		-0.4
	Sea A	8	10	.444	23	22	6-2	0-0	159.2	160	68	9	6	62-6	82	3.44	117	.261	.333	0	—	0	91	11		1.2
1990	Sea A	11	11	.500	28	28	3	0-0	189.2	188	92	17	6	66-2	121	4.03	99	.260	.324	1	.000	-0	87	1		1.0
1991	Sea A	13	14	.481	30	30	5-3	0-0	195.1	199	86	16	10	77-0	108	3.69	112	.268	.343	0		0	77	10		1.4
Total	4	37	45	.451	109	99	15-6	0-0	676.2	682	303	47	23	254-10	392	3.71	107	.263	.333	37-0-4	.108	-1	82	23	364	2.2

HOLMAN, SCOTT Randy Scott B9.18.1958 Santa Paula CA BR/TR/6-1/190* d9.20 Col Ventura (CA) JC

YEAR	TM LG	W	L	PCT	G	GS	CG-SHO	SV-BS	IP	H	R	HR	HB	BB-IB	SO	ERA	AERA	OAV	OOB	AB-HR-SH	AVG	PB	SUP	APR	DL	PW
1980	NY N	0	0		4	0	0	0-0	7	6	2	0	0	1-1	3	1.29	281	.250	.269	0		0		1		0.1
1982	NY N	2	1	.667	4	4	1	0-0	26.2	23	10	2	0	7-0	11	2.36	156	.232	.280	9-0-1	.222	0	78	3		0.3
1983	NY N	1	7	.125	35	10	0	0-0	101	90	48	7	1	52-8	44	3.74	98	.242	.333	23-0-2	.217	0	70	-1		0.0
Total	3	3	8	.273	43	14	1	0-0	134.2	119	60	9	1	60-9	58	3.34	110	.240	.320	32-0-3	.219	1	72	3		0.7

HOLMAN, SHAWN Shawn Leroy B11.10.1964 Sewickley PA BR/TR/6-2/186 [PitN82 14/347] d9.5

YEAR	TM LG	W	L	PCT	G	GS	CG-SHO	SV-BS	IP	H	R	HR	HB	BB-IB	SO	ERA	AERA	OAV	OOB	AB-HR-SH	AVG	PB	SUP	APR	DL	PW
1989	Det A	0	0		5	0	0	0-0	10	8	2	0	0	11-1	9	1.80	213	.211	.380	0	—	0		2		0.2

HOLMES, DARREN Darren Lee B4.25.1966 Asheville NC BR/TR/6-0/202* [LAN84 16/415] d9.1

YEAR	TM LG	W	L	PCT	G	GS	CG-SHO	SV-BS	IP	H	R	HR	HB	BB-IB	SO	ERA	AERA	OAV	OOB	AB-HR-SH	AVG	PB	SUP	APR	DL	PW
1990	LA N	0	1	.000	14	0	0	0-0	17.1	15	10	1	0	11-3	19	5.19	71	.238	.342	0	—	0		-2		-0.2
1991	Mil A	1	4	.200	40	0	0	3-3	76.1	90	43	6	4	27-1	59	4.72	85	.295	.351	0	—	0		-6	15	-0.4
1992	Mil A	4	4	.500	41	0	0	6-2	42.1	35	12	1	2	11-4	31	2.55	152	.224	.284	0	—	0		7		1.1
1993	Col N	3	3	.500	62	0	0	25-4	66.2	56	31	6	2	20-1	60	4.05	118	.222	.285	0	—	0		-6		-0.4
1994	Col N	0	3	.000	29	0	0	3-5	28.1	35	25	5	1	24-4	33	6.35	78	.313	.435	1	.000	-0		-5	46	-0.7
1995	†Col N	6	1	.857	68	0	0	14-4	66.2	59	26	3	4	28-3	61	3.24	166	.237	.313	1-0-3	.000	-0		12		1.3
1996	Col N	5	4	.556	62	0	0	1-7	77	78	41	8	1	28-2	71	3.97	131	.259	.323	2	.000	-0		7		0.0
1997	Col N	9	2	.818	42	6	0	3-1	89.1	113	58	12	0	36-3	70	5.34	97	.314	.373	19-1-3	.158	-0	149	-2	15	-0.2
1998	NY A	0	3	.000	34	0	0	2-1	51.1	53	24	9	1	14-3	35	3.33	132	.270	.321	0		0		7	36	0.6
1999	†Ari N	4	3	.571	44	0	0	0-2	48.2	50	21	3	1	25-8	35	3.70	125	.262	.350	2	.000	-0		5	45	0.4
2000	Ari N	0	0		4	0	0	1-0	2.1	5	3	0	0	1-0	2	11.57	41	.455	.462	0	—	-0		-2		-0.2
	StL N	1	0	1.000	5	0	0	3-0	8.1	12	9	2	1	3-0	5	9.72	48	.343	.410	1	.000	-0		-2		-0.2
	Year	1	0	1.000	9	0	0	1-1	10.2	17	12	2	1	4-0	7	10.13	46	.386	.423	1		0		-4		-0.4
	Bal A	0	0		5	0	0	0-0	4.2	13	13	3	1	5-0	2	25.07	19	.481	.563	0	—	-0		-11		-0.5
	Ari N	0	0		4	0	0	0-0	4	7	3	1	1	4-0	3	6.75	71	.389	.421	0		0		-1		-0.1
2002	†Atl N	2	2	.500	55	0	0	1-1	54.2	41	12	3	2	12-4	47	1.81	223	.210	.262	0	.000	-0		14	20	1.3
2003	Atl N	1	2	.333	48	0	0	0-1	42	47	22	4	0	11-0	46	4.29	98	.280	.322	0		0		0	52	0.2
Total	13	35	33	.515	557	6	0	59-32	680	709	348	63	15	256-36	581	4.25	109	.269	.334	28-1-6	.107	-1	149	25	229	4.0

YEAR	TM LG	W	L	PCT	G	GS	CG-SHO	SV-BS	IP	H	R	HR	HB	BB-IB	SO	ERA	AERA	OAV	OOB	AB-HR-SH	AVG	PB	SUP	APR	DL	PW

HOLMES, CHICK Elwood Marter B3.22.1896 Beverly NJ D4.15.1954 Camden NJ TR d6.27

| 1918 | Phi A | 0 | 0 | — | 2 | 0 | 0 | 0 | 2 | 4 | 5 | 0 | 1 | 1 | 0 | 13.50 | 22 | .400 | .500 | 0 | — | 0 | | -3 | | -0.1 |

HOLMES, JIM James Scott B8.2.1882 Lawrenceburg KY D3.10.1960 Jacksonville FL d9.8

1906	Phi A	0	1	.000	3	1	0	0	9	10	11	0	1	8	1	4.00	68	.286	.432	5	.600	1	106	-3		-0.2
1908	Bro N	1	4	.200	13	1	1	0	40	37	19	0	3	20	10	3.37	69	.270	.375	13	.077	-1	150	-4		-0.7
Total	2	1	5	.167	16	2	1	0	49	47	30	0	4	28	11	3.49	69	.273	.387	18	.222	0	132	-7		-0.9

HOLMES, DUCKY James William B1.28.1869 Des Moines IA D8.6.1932 Truro IA BL/TR/5-6/170 d8.8 ▲

1895	Lou N	1	0	1.000	2	1	1	0	14	16	11	1	0	4	0	5.79	80	.281	.339	161-3-3	.373	1*	138	-1		0.0
1896	Lou N	0	1	.000	2	1	0	0	12	26	23	0	0	8	3	7.50	58	.433	.500	141-0-4	.270	0*	213	-7		-0.4
Total	2	1	1	.500	4	2	1	0	26	42	34	1	1	12	3	6.58	68	.359	.423	302-3-7	.325	1	174	-8		-0.4

HOLSHOUSER, HERM Herman Alexander B1.20.1907 Rockwell NC D7.26.1994 Concord NC BR/TR/6-0/170 d4.15 Col North Carolina-Asheville

| 1930 | StL A | 0 | 1 | .000 | 25 | 1 | 0 | 1 | 62.1 | 103 | 63 | 8 | 3 | 28 | 37 | 7.80 | 63 | .376 | .439 | 16 | .125 | -1 | 211 | -20 | | -0.9 |

HOLT, CHRIS Christopher Michael B9.18.1971 Dallas TX BR/TR/6-4/205* [HouN92 3/69] d9.1 Col Navarro (TX) JC [DL 1998 Hou N 181]

1996	Hou N	0	1	.000	4	0	0	0-0	4.2	5	3	0	3	3-1	0	5.79	67	.263	.364	1	.000	-0		-1		-0.2
1997	Hou N	8	12	.400	33	32	0	0-0	209.2	211	98	17	8	61-4	95	3.52	114	.263	.320	67-0-9	.090	-3	94	9		0.4
1999	†Hou N	5	13	.278	32	26	0	1-1	164	193	92	12	8	57-1	115	4.66	95	.303	.363	45-0-7	.067	-2	89	-4		-0.7
2000	Hou N	8	16	.333	34	32	3-1	0-0	207	247	131	22	8	75-2	136	5.35	92	.303	.363	60-0-5	.100	-2	101	-8		-1.0
2001	Det A	7	9	.438	30	22	0	0-0	151.1	197	102	18	8	57-5	80	5.77	77	.319	.381	4	.250	-0	105	-21		-1.8
Total	5	28	51	.354	133	112	4-1	1-1	736.2	853	426	69	32	253-13	426	4.76	93	.295	.355	177-0-21	.090	-7	97	-25	181	-3.3

HOLTGRAVE, VERN Lavern George "Woody" B10.18.1942 Aviston IL BR/TR/6-1/185 d9.26

| 1965 | Det A | 0 | 0 | — | 1 | 0 | 0 | 0 | 3 | 4 | 2 | 0 | 0 | 2 | 2 | 6.00 | 58 | .308 | .400 | 0 | — | 0 | | -1 | | 0.0 |

HOLTON, BRIAN Brian John B11.29.1959 McKeesport PA BR/TR/6-0/193* [LAN78*1/22] d9.9 Col Louisburg (NC) JC

1985	LA N	1	1	.500	4	0	0	0-0	4	9	7	0	0	1-0	1	9.00	39	.450	.476	0	—	0		-3		-0.6
1986	LA N	2	3	.400	12	3	0	0-1	24.1	28	13	1	1	6-2	24	4.44	78	.292	.337	5	.000	-1	51	-3		-0.5
1987	LA N	3	2	.600	53	1	0	2-1	83.1	87	39	11	0	32-11	58	3.89	102	.269	.332	5	.200	-1	114	2		0.1
1988	†LA N	7	3	.700	45	0	0	1-0	84.2	69	19	1	1	26-7	49	1.70	197	.228	.289	10	.000	-1		16		1.8
1989	Bal A	5	7	.417	39	12	0	0-1	116.1	140	63	11	1	39-1	51	4.02	95	.300	.352	0	—	0	111	-6		-0.6
1990	Bal A	2	3	.400	33	0	0	0-1	58	68	31	7	0	21-6	27	4.50	85	.292	.348	0	—	0		-4		-0.3
Total	6	20	19	.513	185	16	0	3-4	370.2	401	172	31	3	125-27	210	3.62	103	.278	.334	20	.050	-1	101	2		-0.1

HOLTZ, MIKE Michael James B10.10.1972 Arlington VA BL/TL/5-9/175(175-188) [CalA94 17/461] d7.11 Col Clemson

1996	Cal A	3	3	.500	30	0	0	0-0	29.1	21	11	1	3	19-2	31	2.45	206	.204	.341	0	—	0		7		1.3
1997	Ana A	3	4	.429	66	0	0	2-6	43.1	38	21	7	2	15-4	40	3.32	139	.228	.296	1	.000	-0		5		0.7
1998	Ana A	2	2	.500	53	0	0	1-1	30.1	38	16	0	1	15-1	29	4.75	100	.322	.397	0	—	0		1		0.1
1999	Ana A	2	3	.400	28	0	0	0-0	22.1	26	20	3	2	15-1	17	8.06	61	.295	.410	0	—	0		-7	16	-1.3
2000	Ana A	3	4	.429	61	0	0	0-0	41	37	26	4	2	18-2	40	5.05	102	.248	.331	0	—	0		0		0.0
2001	Ana A	1	2	.333	63	0	0	0-1	37	40	24	5	2	15-4	38	4.86	96	.274	.348	0	—	0		-2	19	-0.1
2002	Oak A	0	0	—	16	0	0	0-1	14	24	11	3	1	9-0	7	6.43	70	.358	.442	0	—	0		-3		-0.1
	SD N	2	2	.500	33	0	0	0-3	21	18	14	2	1	21-3	19	4.71	82	.237	.396	2	.000	0		-3		-0.5
Total	7	16	20	.444	350	0	0	3-12	238.1	242	143	25	14	127-17	221	4.68	101	.265	.359	3	.000	-0		-2	35	0.1

HOLTZMAN, KEN Kenneth Dale B11.3.1945 St.Louis MO BR/TL/6-2/175(175-198) [ChiN65 4/61] d9.4 Mil 1967 Col Illinois

1965	Chi N	0	0	—	3	0	0	0	4	2	4	1	0	3-0	3	2.25	164	.143	.294	0	—	0		-1		0.0
1966	Chi N	11	16	.407	34	33	9	0	220.2	194	104	27	4	68-6	171	3.79	97	.235	.295	73-0-6	.123	-3	87	-1		-0.5
1967	Chi N	9	0	1.000	12	12	3	0	92.2	76	31	11	2	44-7	62	2.53	140	.222	.314	35-0-6	.200	1	165	9		1.0
1968	Chi N	11	14	.440	34	32	6-3	1	215	201	89	17	6	76-7	151	3.35	94	.248	.316	80-0-1	.125	-2*	99	-4		-0.7
1969	Chi N	17	13	.567	39	39	12-6	0-0	261.1	248	117	18	5	93-8	176	3.58	112	.247	.313	100-1-5	.150	-1	110	12		1.1
1970	Chi N	17	11	.607	39	38	15-1	0-0	287.2	271	125	30	3	94-6	202	3.38	133	.248	.307	105-0-8	.200	1*	105	31		3.0
1971	Chi N	9	15	.375	30	29	9-3	0-1	195	213	108	18	2	64-7	143	4.48	88	.276	.331	69-1-2	.130	-1	89	-10		-1.3
1972	†Oak A☆	19	11	.633	39	37	16-4	0-1	265.1	232	83	23	4	52-6	134	2.51	114	.236	.276	90-0-11	.178	-2*	139	11		1.5
1973	†Oak A★	21	13	.618	40	40	16-4	0-0	297.1	275	109	22	4	66-5	157	2.97	120	.243	.286	0	—	0*	114	23		2.5
1974	†Oak A	19	17	.528	39	38	9-3	0-0	255.1	273	111	14	7	51-3	117	3.07	109	.272	.308	0	—	0	107	4		0.6
1975	†Oak A	18	14	.563	39	38	13-2	0-0	266.1	217	111	16	7	108-1	122	3.14	116	.222	.301	2	.000	-0	104	13		1.7
1976	Bal A	5	4	.556	13	13	6-1	0-0	97.2	100	34	4	1	35-2	25	2.86	115	.271	.333	0	—	0	96	5		0.5
	NY A	9	7	.563	21	21	10-2	0-0	149	165	74	14	0	35-0	41	4.17	82	.283	.322	0	—	0	114	-11		-1.1
	Year	14	11	.560	34	34	16-3	0-0	246.2	265	108	18	1	70-2	66	3.65	92	.278	.326	0	—	0	107	-6		-0.6
1977	NY A	2	3	.400	18	11	0	0-0	71.2	105	55	7	1	24-2	14	5.78	60	.362	.410	0	—	0	120	-17		-0.9
1978	NY A	1	0	1.000	5	3	0	0-0	17.2	21	8	2	0	9-0	3	4.08	90	.313	.395	0	—	0	115	0		0.0
	Chi N	0	3	.000	23	6	0	2-0	53	61	40	10	1	35-3	36	6.11	66	.286	.388	10-0-1	.200	0	92	-11		-0.6
1979	Chi N	6	9	.400	23	20	3-2	0-0	117.2	133	70	15	6	53-7	44	4.59	91	.287	.366	43	.233	2*	95	-6		-0.6
Total	15	174	150	.537	451	410	127-31	3-2	2867.1	2787	1273	249	49	910-70	1601	3.49	105	.255	.313	607-2-40	.163	-1	108	47	21	6.2

HOLZEMER, MARK Mark Harold B8.20.1969 Littleton CO BL/TL/6-0/165(165-185) [CalA87 4/109] d8.21 Col Seminole St. (OK) JC

1993	Cal A	0	3	.000	5	4	0	0-0	23.1	34	24	2	3	13-0	10	8.87	51	.340	.431	0	—	0	81	-10		-1.0
1995	Cal A	0	1	.000	12	0	0	0-0	8.1	11	6	1	1	7-1	5	5.40	87	.306	.432	0	—	0		-1		-0.1
1996	Cal A	1	0	1.000	25	0	0	0-0	24.2	35	28	7	3	8-1	20	8.76	58	.327	.387	0	—	0		-11	83	-0.5
1997	Sea A	0	0	—	14	0	0	1-0	9	9	6	0	0	8-0	7	6.00	76	.250	.386	0	—	0		-1		-0.1
1998	Oak A	1	0	1.000	13	0	0	0-0	9.2	13	6	1	1	3-0	3	5.59	83	.333	.386	0	—	0		-1		-0.1
2000	Phi N	0	1	.000	25	0	0	0-1	25.2	36	23	4	1	8-1	19	7.71	59	.336	.388	1	.000	-0		-9	15	-0.4
Total	6	2	5	.286	94	4	0	1-1	100.2	138	93	15	9	47-3	64	7.69	61	.325	.402	1	.000	0	81	-33	98	-2.1

HONEYCUTT, RICK Frederick Wayne B6.29.1954 Chattanooga TN BL/TL/5-11/190* [PitN76 17/405] d8.24 Col Tennessee

1977	Sea A	0	1	.000	10	3	0	0-0	29	26	16	7	3	11-2	17	4.34	76	.239	.320	0	—	0	72	-1		-0.1
1978	Sea A	5	11	.313	26	24	4-1	0-0	134.1	150	81	12	3	49-5	50	4.89	79	.285	.345	0	—	0	95	-15	37	-1.5
1979	Sea A	11	12	.478	33	28	8-1	0-0	194	201	103	22	6	67-7	83	4.04	108	.268	.331	0	—	0	89	5		0.4
1980	Sea A☆	10	17	.370	30	30	9-1	0-0	203.1	221	99	22	8	60-7	79	3.94	106	.280	.330	0	—	0	69	5		0.6
1981	Tex A	11	6	.647	20	20	8-2	0-0	127.2	120	49	12	0	17-1	40	3.31	105	.246	.272	0	—	0	110	4		0.5
1982	Tex A	5	17	.227	30	26	4-1	0-1	164	201	103	20	3	54-4	64	5.27	74	.305	.356	0	—	0	79	-25		-2.8
1983	Tex A★	14	8	.636	25	25	5-2	0-0	174.2	168	59	9	6	37-2	56	**2.42**	167	.262	.306	0	—	0	100	29		3.8
	†LA N	2	3	.400	9	7	1	0-0	39	46	26	6	2	13-4	18	5.77	63	.297	.359	12-0-2	.083	-1	115	-8		-0.9
1984	LA N	10	9	.526	29	28	6-2	0-0	183.2	180	72	11	2	51-11	75	2.84	125	.258	.308	56-0-9	.143	-0	88	13		1.4
1985	†LA N	8	12	.400	31	25	1	1-0	142	141	71	9	1	49-7	67	3.42	102	.261	.321	38-0-8	.132	0*	94	-2		-0.1
1986	LA N	11	9	.550	32	28	0	0-0	171	164	71	9	3	45-4	100	3.32	105	.249	.300	43-0-6	.070	0	104	3		0.5
1987	LA N	2	12	.143	27	20	1-1	0-0	115.2	133	74	10	2	45-4	92	4.59	87	.278	.343	30-0-3	.233	2	59	-12		-1.0
	Oak A	1	4	.200	7	4	0	0-0	23.2	25	17	3	4	9-0	10	5.32	78	.275	.343	0	—	0	88	-4		-0.7
1988	†Oak A	3	2	.600	55	0	0	7-7	79.2	74	36	6	3	25-2	47	3.50	109	.253	.312	0	—	0		11		0.9
1989	†Oak A	2	2	.500	64	0	0	12-4	76.2	56	26	5	1	26-3	52	2.35	158	.207	.277	0	—	0		11		0.9
1990	†Oak A	2	2	.500	63	0	0	7-3	63.1	46	22	2	0	22-2	38	2.70	138	.204	.272	2	.000	-0*		7		0.5
1991	Oak A	2	4	.333	43	0	0	0-4	37.2	37	16	3	2	20-3	26	3.58	108	.261	.358	0	—	0		1	69	0.2
1992	†Oak A	1	4	.200	54	0	0	3-4	39	41	19	2	2	10-3	32	3.69	102	.272	.327	0	—	0		4		0.2
1993	Oak A	1	4	.200	52	0	0	1-2	41.2	37	21	4	2	20-6	21	2.81	147	.211	.305	0	—	0		4	39	0.4
1994	Tex A	1	2	.333	42	0	0	1-1	25	37	21	4	2	9-1	18	7.20	67	.349	.410	0	—	0		-6	23	-0.6
1995	Oak A	5	1	.833	49	0	0	2-3	44.2	37	13	5	1	9-0	21	2.42	187	.231	.275	0	—	0		11		1.3
	NY A	0	0	—	3	0	0	0-0	.1	1	1	0	0	1-0	0	27.00	17	.400	.500	0	—	0		-2		-0.1
	Year	5	1	.833	52	0	0	2-3	45.2	39	16	6	1	10-0	21	2.96	153	.236	.282	0	—	0		8		1.2
1996	†StL N	2	1	.667	61	0	0	4-3	47.1	42	15	3	0	7-3	30	2.85	149	.240	.265	1	.000	1		8		0.7
Total	21	109	143	.433	797	268	47-11	38-27	2160	2183	1034	185	50	657-81	1038	3.72	104	.264	.320	182-0-28	.132	2	88	26	315	3.6

YEAR	TM LG	W	L	PCT	G	GS	CG-SHO	SV-BS	IP	H	R	HR	HB	BB-IB	SO	ERA	AERA	OAV	OOB	AB-HR-SH	AVG	PB	SUP	APR	DL	PW
HOOD, DON	Donald Harris B10.16.1949 Florence SC BL/TL/6-2/180* [BalA69 1/17] d7.16																									
1973	†Bal A	3	2	.600	8	4	1-1	1-0	32.1	31	17	1	1	6-0	18	3.90	97	.256	.295	0	—	0	71	-1		-0.2
1974	Bal A	1	1	.500	20	2	0	1-1	57.1	47	26	1	0	20-1	26	3.45	101	.223	.289	0	—	0*	63	0		0.0
1975	Cle A	6	10	.375	29	19	2	0-0	135.1	136	76	16	0	57-6	51	4.39	87	.268	.340	0	—	0*	88	-9		-1.0
1976	Cle A	3	5	.375	33	6	0	1-0	77.2	89	46	5	4	41-3	32	4.87	72	.296	.386	0	—	0*	71	-11		-1.1
1977	Cle A	2	1	.667	41	5	1	0-2	105	87	42	3	4	49-7	62	3.00	133	.224	.317	0	—	0*	72	11		0.5
1978	Cle A	5	6	.455	36	19	1	0-0	154.2	166	82	13	1	77-5	73	4.48	85	.278	.357	0	—	0	110	-10		-0.6
1979	Cle A	1	0	1.000	13	0	0	1-1	22	13	9	1	1	14-1	7	3.68	117	.169	.304	0	—	0		2		0.1
	NY A	3	1	.750	27	6	0	1-0	67.1	62	24	3	2	30-1	22	3.07	134	.252	.333	0	—	0	132	9		0.5
	Year	4	1	.800	40	6	0	2-1	89.1	75	33	4	3	44-2	29	3.22	129	.232	.326	0	—	0	131	11		0.6
1980	StL N	4	6	.400	33	8	1	0-1	82.1	90	39	2	2	34-5	35	3.39	111	.288	.359	20-0-2	.200	-0*	125	1		0.2
1982	KC A	4	0	1.000	30	3	0	1-1	66.2	71	31	7	2	22-1	31	3.51	116	.276	.333	0	—	0	113	3		0.2
1983	KC A	4	2	.400	27	0	0	0-1	47.2	48	20	5	1	14-2	17	2.27	181	.273	.328	0	—	0		7	21	0.7
Total	10	34	35	.493	297	72	6-1	6-7	848.1	840	412	57	19	364-32	374	3.79	102	.263	.339	20-0-2	.200	-0	98	2	21	-0.7
HOOD, WALLY	Wallace James Jr. B9.24.1925 Los Angeles CA D6.16.2001 Glendale CA BR/TR/6-1/190 d9.23 f-Wally Col USC																									
1949	NY A	0	0	—	2	0	0	0	2.1	0	0	0	0	1	2	0.00	—	.000	.143	0	—	0		1		0.1
HOOK, CHRIS	Christopher Wayne B8.4.1968 San Diego CA BR/TR/6-5/230* d4.30 Col Northern Kentucky																									
1995	SF N	5	1	.833	45	0	0	0-0	52.1	55	33	7	3	29-3	40	5.50	75	.274	.369	3	.000	-0		-7		-0.8
1996	SF N	0	1	.000	10	0	0	0-0	13.1	16	13	3	2	14-2	4	7.43	56	.308	.464	2	.500	0		-5		-0.3
Total	2	5	2	.714	55	0	0	0-0	65.2	71	46	10	5	43-5	44	5.89	70	.281	.390	5	.200	-0		-12		-1.1
HOOK, JAY	James Wesley B11.18.1936 Waukegan IL BL/TR/6-2/182* d9.3 Col Northwestern																									
1957	Cin N	0	1	.000	3	2	0	0	10	6	7	0	0	8-0	6	4.50	91	.176	.326	3	.000	-0	86	-1		-0.1
1958	Cin N	1	1	.000	1	1	0	0	3	3	4	2	0	2-0	5	12.00	35	.250	.357	1	.000	-0	22	-2		-0.4
1959	Cin N	5	5	.500	17	15	4	0	79	79	46	10	3	39-1	37	5.13	79	.266	.356	24-0-2	.125	-1*	100	-7		-0.9
1960	Cin N	11	18	.379	36	33	10-2	0	222	222	119	31	4	73-7	103	4.50	85	.263	.323	72-0-6	.083	-3	106	-14		-2.0
1961	Cin N	1	3	.250	22	5	0	0	62.2	83	55	14	5	22-2	36	7.76	52	.322	.382	15	.133	-1	100	-23		-1.4
1962	NY N	8	19	.296	37	34	13	0	213.2	230	137	31	8	71-4	113	4.84	86	.273	.332	69-0-6	.203	2*	88	-15		-1.5
1963	NY N	4	14	.222	41	20	3	1	152.1	168	104	21	9	53-2	89	5.48	64	.281	.346	38-0-2	.237	2	86	-29		-3.1
1964	NY N	0	1	.000	3	2	0	0	9.2	17	10	2	0	7-0	5	9.31	38	.395	.471	3	.000	-0	74	-5		-0.5
Total	8	29	62	.319	160	112	30-2	1	752.2	808	482	111	30	275-16	394	5.23	75	.276	.341	225-0-16	.151	-2	94	-96		-9.9
HOOKER, BUCK	William Edward B8.28.1880 Richmond VA D7.2.1929 Richmond VA TR/5-6/? d9.5																									
1902	Cin N	0	1	.000	1	1	1	0	8	11	5	1	0	0	0	4.50	67	.324	.324	3	.000	-0	68	-1		-0.2
1903	Cin N	0	0	—	1	0	0	0	2.1	2	0	0	2	0	0.00	—	.250	.400	1	.000	-0*		1		0.0
Total	2	0	1	.000	2	1	1	0	10.1	13	5	1	0	2	0	3.48	90	.310	.341	4	.000	-1	68	0		-0.2
HOOPER, BOB	Robert Nelson B5.30.1922 Leamington ON, Can. D3.17.1980 New Brunswick NJ BR/TR/5-11/195* d4.19 Col Montclair St.																									
1950	Phi A	15	10	.600	45	20	3	5	170.1	181	108	15	1	91	58	5.02	91	.272	.361	56-1-4	.125	-2	132	-10		-1.3
1951	Phi A	12	10	.545	38	23	9	5	189	192	98	13	3	61	64	4.38	98	.267	.327	72-1-2	.208	-1	103	0		-0.1
1952	Phi A	8	15	.348	43	14	4	4	144.1	158	100	13	4	68	40	5.18	76	.279	.361	41-2-3	.195	1	60	-21		-2.9
1953	Cle A	5	4	.556	43	0	0	7	69.1	50	37	4	2	38	16	4.02	93	.206	.318	12	.083	-1		-3		-0.5
1954	Cle A	0	0	—	17	0	0	2	34.2	39	22	3	1	16	12	4.93	74	.289	.364	5	.000	-1		-5		-0.3
1955	Cin N	0	2	.000	8	0	0	0	13	20	12	2	0	6-0	6	7.62	56	.357	.419	1	.000	-0		-4		-0.6
Total	6	40	41	.494	194	57	16	25	620.2	640	377	50	11	280-0	196	4.80	87	.268	.348	187-4-9	.166	-4	106	-43		-5.7
HOOTEN, LEON	Michael Leon B4.4.1948 Downey CA BR/TR/5-11/180 d4.13 Col Arizona																									
1974	Oak A	0	0	—	4	0	0	0-0	8.1	8	3	1	0	4-0	1	3.24	103	.207	.314	0	—	0		0		0.0
HOOTON, BURT	Burt Carlton B2.7.1950 Greenville TX BR/TR/6-1/210(190-210) [ChiN71 D1/2] d6.17 C5 Col Texas																									
1971	Chi N	2	0	1.000	3	3	2-1	0-0	21.1	8	5	2	0	10-0	22	2.11	187	.111	.220	7	.000	-1	98	4		0.3
1972	Chi N	11	14	.440	33	31	9-3	0-1	218.1	201	78	13	1	81-7	132	2.80	136	.246	.313	72-1-5	.125	-1	85	22		2.4
1973	Chi N	14	17	.452	42	34	9-2	0-1	239.2	248	107	12	4	73-7	134	3.68	107	.270	.325	70-0-5	.129	-0	95	8		0.8
1974	Chi N	7	11	.389	48	21	3-1	1-2	176.1	214	112	16	3	51-6	94	4.80	80	.299	.344	50-0-7	.060	-4	108	-18		-1.9
1975	Chi N	0	2	.000	3	3	0	0-0	11	18	12	2	0	4-5	5	8.18	47	.383	.431	3	.000	-0	76	-5		-0.8
	LA N	18	7	.720	31	30	12-4	0-0	223.2	172	76	16	0	64-2	148	2.82	122	.210	.265	70-1-13	.129	1	115	17		1.8
	Year	18	9	.667	34	33	12-4	0-0	234.2	190	88	18	0	68-2	153	3.07	112	.219	.274	73-1-13	.123	0	111	13		1.0
1976	LA N	11	15	.423	33	33	8-4	0-0	226.2	203	93	16	1	60-6	116	3.26	105	.241	.290	62-0-13	.097	-2	99	3		0.0
1977	†LA N	12	7	.632	32	31	6-2	1-0	223.1	184	74	14	3	60-5	153	2.62	147	.225	.279	67-0-14	.164	-0	107	30		2.4
1978	†LA N	19	10	.655	32	32	10-3	0-0	236	196	74	17	0	61-4	104	2.71	130	.226	.275	67-0-18	.149	1	94	25		2.1
1979	LA N	11	10	.524	29	29	12-1	0-0	212	191	85	11	2	63-4	129	2.97	122	.244	.298	75-0-8	.147	-1*	117	14		1.2
1980	LA N	14	8	.636	34	33	4-2	1-0	206.2	194	90	22	0	64-1	118	3.66	95	.249	.305	64-1-14	.063	-3	108	-3		-0.7
1981	†LA N★	11	6	.647	23	23	5-4	0-0	142.1	124	42	3	2	33-2	74	2.28	145	.237	.281	42-0-7	.190	2	104	15		2.1
1982	LA N	4	7	.364	21	21	2-2	0-0	120.2	130	57	5	2	33-2	51	4.22	86	.275	.325	35-1-6	.086	-1	98	-6		-0.8
1983	LA N	9	3	.529	33	27	2	0-0	160	156	86	21	2	59-4	87	4.22	86	.254	.319	50-0-4	.160	1	112	-9		-0.2
1984	LA N	3	6	.333	54	6	0	4-1	110	109	43	5	0	43-6	62	3.44	104	.263	.331	14-0-3	.071	0	79	4		0.2
1985	Tex A	5	8	.385	29	20	2	0-0	124	149	78	18	0	40-2	62	5.23	82	.297	.346	0	—	0	85	-12		-1.2
Total	15	151	136	.526	480	377	86-29	7-5	2652	2497	1112	193	20	799-58	1491	3.38	108	.250	.304	748-4-117	.123	-9	101	89	69	8.3
HOOVER, JOHN	John Nicklaus B11.22.1962 Fresno CA BR/TR/6-2/195 [BalA84 1/25] d5.23 Col Cal St.-Fresno																									
1990	Tex A	0	0	—	2	0	0	0	4.2	8	6	0	0	3-0	1	11.57	34	.364	.440	0	—	0		-4		-0.2
HOOVER, DICK	Richard Lloyd B12.11.1925 Columbus OH D4.12.1981 Lake Placid FL BL/TL/6-0/170 d4.16																									
1952	Bos N	0	0	—	2	0	0	0	4.2	8	4	1	0	3	0	7.71	47	.348	.423	0	—	0		-2		-0.1
HOPE, JOHN	John Alan B12.21.1970 Ft.Lauderdale FL BR/TR/6-3/195(195-206) [PitN89 2/59] d8.29																									
1993	Pit N	0	2	.000	7	7	0	0-0	38	47	19	2	2	8-3	8	4.03	102	.313	.354	13	.077	-1	116	0		-0.1
1994	Pit N	0	0	—	9	0	0	0-0	14	18	12	1	2	4-0	6	5.79	76	.310	.375	3	.333	0		-3		-0.3
1995	Pit N	0	0	—	3	0	0	0-0	2.1	8	8	0	0	4-0	2	30.86	14	.615	.714	0	—	0		-6		-0.3
1996	Pit N	1	3	.250	5	4	0	0-0	19.1	17	18	5	2	11-1	13	6.98	63	.243	.357	5-0-1	.200	-0	82	-6		-0.9
Total	4	1	5	.167	24	11	0	0-0	73.2	90	57	8	9	27-4	29	5.99	71	.309	.382	21-0-1	.143	-1	103	-15		-1.4
HOPE, SAM	Samuel Everett B12.4.1878 Brooklyn NY D6.30.1946 Greenport NY BR/TR/5-10/? d8.5																									
1907	Phi A	0	0	—	1	0	0	0	0.1	3	1	0	0	0	0	0.00	—	.750	.750	0	—	0		0		0.0
HOPKINS, PAUL	Paul Henry B9.25.1904 Chester CT D1.2.2004 Middletown CT BR/TR/6-0/175 d9.29 Col Colgate																									
1927	Was A	1	0	1.000	2	1	0	0	9	13	6	1	0	4	5	5.00	81	.361	.425	3	.667	1	185	-1		0.0
1929	Was A	0	1	.000	7	0	0	0	16.1	15	5	1	0	9	5	2.20	192	.250	.348	3	.000	-1		4		0.1
	StL A	0	0	—	2	0	0	0	2	0	0	0	0	2	1	0.00	—	.000	.286	0	—	0		1		0.1
	Year	0	1	.000	9	0	0	0	18.1	15	5	1	0	11	6	1.96	217	.231	.342	3	.000	-1		5		0.1
Total	2	1	1	.500	11	1	0	0	27.1	28	11	2	0	15	11	2.96	142	.277	.371	6	.333	1	185	4		0.1
HOPPER, LEFTY	Clarence Franklin B5.27.1875 Jersey City NJ D9.27.1959 San Diego CA TL/6-0/? d10.10																									
1898	Bro N	0	2	.000	2	2	1	0	11	14	10	0	0	5	5	4.91	73	.304	.373	4	.000		59	-3		-0.4
HOPPER, JIM	James McDaniel B9.1.1919 Charlotte NC D1.23.1982 Charlotte NC BR/TR/6-1/175 d4.21																									
1946	Pit N	0	0	—	4	0	0	0	4	6	5	1	0	3	4	11.25	31	.316	.409	0	—	0	49	-3		-0.5
HOPPER, BILL	William Booth "Bird Dog" B10.26.1890 Jackson TN D1.14.1965 Allen Park MI BR/TR/6-0/175 d9.11 Col Union (TN)																									
1913	StL N	0	3	.000	4	0	0	0	24	20	14	2	3	8	3	3.75	86	.230	.316	8	.375	1	39	-2		0.0
1914	StL N	0	0	—	3	0	0	0	5	6	3	0	0	5	1	3.60	78	.286	.423	0	—	0		0		0.0
1915	Was A	0	1	.000	13	3	2	0	31.1	39	23	0	1	16	8	4.60	65	.348	.434	5	.200	1		-6		-0.3
Total	3	0	4	.000	19	3	2	1	60.1	65	40	2	4	29	12	4.18	73	.295	.387	13	.308	1	39	-8		-0.2
HORAN, JOHN	Patrick J. B1863 , Ireland 5-10.5/160 d5.17																									
1884	CP U	3	6	.333	13	10	9	0	98	94	73	0		24	55	3.49	70	.236	.279	68	.088	-8*	91	-11		-1.4

YEAR	TM LG	W	L	PCT	G	GS	CG-SHO	SV-BS	IP	H	R	HR	HB	BB-IB	SO	ERA	AERA	OAV	OOB	AB-HR-SH	AVG	PB	SUP	APR	DL	PW

HORGAN, JOE Joseph Paul B6.7.1977 Sacramento CA BL/TL/6-1/200* [CleA96 11/333] d6.12 Col Sacramento (CA) City

YEAR	TM LG	W	L	PCT	G	GS	CG-SHO	SV-BS	IP	H	R	HR	HB	BB-IB	SO	ERA	AERA	OAV	OOB	AB-HR-SH	AVG	PB	SUP	APR	DL	PW
2004	Mon N	4	1	.800	47	0	0	2-1	40	35	18	5	3	22-3	30	3.15	146	.230	.339	4	.250	0		5		0.6
2005	Was N	0	0	—	8	0	0	0-0	6	19	15	0	1	4-0	5	21.00	19	.514	.558	0	—	0		-12		-0.6
Total	2	4	1	.800	55	0	0	2-1	46	54	33	5	4	26-3	35	5.48	83	.286	.382	4	.250	0		-7		0.0

HORLEN, JOE Joel Edward B8.14.1937 San Antonio TX BR/TR/6-0/175* d9.4 Col Oklahoma St.

YEAR	TM LG	W	L	PCT	G	GS	CG-SHO	SV-BS	IP	H	R	HR	HB	BB-IB	SO	ERA	AERA	OAV	OOB	AB-HR-SH	AVG	PB	SUP	APR	DL	PW
1961	Chi A	1	3	.250	5	4	0	0	17.2	25	15	2	0	13-0	11	6.62	59	.338	.437	7-0-1	.000	-1	107	-6		-1.1
1962	Chi A	7	6	.538	20	19	5-1	0	108.2	108	62	10	2	43-2	63	4.89	80	.262	.333	38-0-4	.053	-3	120	-11	62	-1.3
1963	Chi A	11	7	.611	33	21	3	0	124	132	50	10	2	55-8	61	3.27	107	.261	.339	40-0-2	.225	1	121	4		0.7
1964	Chi A	13	9	.591	32	28	9-2	0	210.2	142	54	11	4	55-4	138	1.88	184	.190	.248	69-0-8	.159	-1	75	37		4.0
1965	Chi A	13	13	.500	34	34	7-4	0	219	203	88	16	3	39-9	125	2.88	111	.245	.279	68-0-8	.132	0	95	4		0.5
1966	Chi A	10	13	.435	37	29	4-2	1	211	185	64	14	6	53-11	124	2.43	130	.233	.285	60-0-4	.067	-4*	83	20		2.2
1967	Chi A☆	19	7	.731	35	35	13-6	0	258	188	66	13	4	58-4	103	2.06	151	.203	.253	83-0-8	.169	1*	107	34		3.8
1968	Chi A	12	14	.462	35	35	4-1	0	223.2	197	75	16	14	70-7	102	2.37	127	.238	.307	67-0-5	.104	-1*	72	14		1.6
1969	Chi A	13	16	.448	36	35	7-2	0-1	235.2	237	105	20	5	77-10	121	3.78	102	.261	.321	77-0-7	.182	-1	80	2		0.1
1970	Chi A	6	16	.273	28	26	4	0-0	172.1	198	99	18	4	41-4	77	4.86	80	.287	.330	52-0-5	.115	-2	71	-15	35	-1.7
1971	Chi A	8	9	.471	34	18	3	2-1	137.1	150	72	12	5	30-2	82	4.26	84	.284	.325	40-0-2	.100	-2*	117	-8	27	-1.2
1972	†Oak A	3	4	.429	32	6	0	1-0	84	74	33	3	4	20-4	58	3.00	95	.236	.291	17	.176	-0	88	-2		-0.2
Total	12	116	117	.498	361	290	59-18	4-2	2002	1829	783	145	53	554-65	1065	3.11	109	.243	.299	618-0-54	.134	-12	92	73	124	7.4

HORNE, TRADER Berlyn Dale "Sonny" B4.12.1899 Bachman OH D2.3.1983 Franklin OH BB/TR/5-9/155 d4.24

YEAR	TM LG	W	L	PCT	G	GS	CG-SHO	SV-BS	IP	H	R	HR	HB	BB-IB	SO	ERA	AERA	OAV	OOB	AB-HR-SH	AVG	PB	SUP	APR	DL	PW
1929	Chi N	1	1	.500	11	1	0	0	23	24	20	3	3	6	6	5.09	91	.273	.413	5-0-1	.400		76	-3		-0.2

HORNER, JACK William Frank B9.21.1863 Baltimore MD D7.14.1910 New Orleans LA BR d5.7

YEAR	TM LG	W	L	PCT	G	GS	CG-SHO	SV-BS	IP	H	R	HR	HB	BB-IB	SO	ERA	AERA	OAV	OOB	AB-HR-SH	AVG	PB	SUP	APR	DL	PW
1894	Bal N	0	1	.000	2	1	1	1	11	15	12	0	1	7	2	9.00	61	.319	.418	6	.167	-0	91	-3		-0.3

HORSEY, HANSON Hanson B11.26.1889 Galena MD D12.1.1949 Millington MD BR/TR/5-11/165 d4.27

YEAR	TM LG	W	L	PCT	G	GS	CG-SHO	SV-BS	IP	H	R	HR	HB	BB-IB	SO	ERA	AERA	OAV	OOB	AB-HR-SH	AVG	PB	SUP	APR	DL	PW
1912	Cin N	0	0	—	1	0	0	0	4	14	10	0	0	3	0	22.50	15	.609	.654	2	.000	-0		-7		-0.3

HORSMAN, VINCE Vincent Stanley Joseph B3.9.1967 Halifax NS, Can. BR/TL/6-2/180* d9.5

YEAR	TM LG	W	L	PCT	G	GS	CG-SHO	SV-BS	IP	H	R	HR	HB	BB-IB	SO	ERA	AERA	OAV	OOB	AB-HR-SH	AVG	PB	SUP	APR	DL	PW
1991	Tor A	0	0	—	4	0	0	0-0	4	2	0	0	0	3-1	2	0.00	—	.167	.333	0	—	0		2		0.1
1992	Oak A	2	1	.667	58	0	0	1-1	43.1	39	13	3	0	21-4	18	2.49	151	.252	.339	0	—	0		7		0.4
1993	Oak A	2	0	1.000	40	0	0	0-0	25	25	15	2	3	15-1	17	5.40	77	.255	.371	0	—	0		-3		-0.2
1994	Oak A	0	1	.000	33	0	0	0-0	29.1	29	17	2	1	11-2	20	4.91	91	.266	.331	0	—	0		-1		0.0
1995	Min A	0	0	—	6	0	0	0-0	9	12	8	2	0	4-1	4	7.00	69	.333	.390	0	—	0		-2		-0.1
Total	5	4	2	.667	141	0	0	2-2	110.2	107	53	9	4	54-9	61	4.07	102	.261	.349	0	—	0		3		0.2

HORSTMANN, OSCAR Oscar Theodore B6.2.1891 Alma MO D5.11.1977 Salina KS BR/TR/5-11/165 d4.18 Mil 1918

YEAR	TM LG	W	L	PCT	G	GS	CG-SHO	SV-BS	IP	H	R	HR	HB	BB-IB	SO	ERA	AERA	OAV	OOB	AB-HR-SH	AVG	PB	SUP	APR	DL	PW
1917	StL N	9	4	.692	35	11	4-1	0	138.2	111	67	5	4	54	50	3.44	78	.225	.307	46-0-2	.196	1	132	-13		-1.2
1918	StL N	0	2	.000	9	2	0	0	23	29	18	0	0	14	6	5.48	49	.349	.443	4	.000	-0	70	-7		-0.6
1919	StL N	0	1	.000	6	2	0	1	15	14	6	0	0	12	5	3.00	93	.264	.400	2-0-1	.500	1	114	0		0.0
Total	3	9	7	.563	50	15	4-1	1	176.2	154	91	5	4	80	61	3.67	74	.245	.334	52-0-3	.192	1	121	-20		-1.8

HORTON, ELMER Elmer E. "Herky Jerky" B9.4.1869 Hamilton OH D8.12.1920 Vienna NY d9.24

YEAR	TM LG	W	L	PCT	G	GS	CG-SHO	SV-BS	IP	H	R	HR	HB	BB-IB	SO	ERA	AERA	OAV	OOB	AB-HR-SH	AVG	PB	SUP	APR	DL	PW
1896	Pit N	0	2	.000	2	2	2	0	15	22	18	0	1	9	3	9.60	44	.338	.427	7	.000	-1	68	-8		-0.8
1898	Bro N	0	1	.000	1	1	1	0	9	16	13	0	0	6	0	10.00	36	.381	.458	4	.250	-0	59	-6		-0.5
Total	2	0	3	.000	3	3	3	0	24	38	31	0	1	15	3	9.75	41	.355	.439	11	.091	-1	66	-14		-1.3

HORTON, RICKY Ricky Neal B7.30.1959 Poughkeepsie NY BL/TL/6-2/195* [StLN80 4/93] d4.7 Col Virginia

YEAR	TM LG	W	L	PCT	G	GS	CG-SHO	SV-BS	IP	H	R	HR	HB	BB-IB	SO	ERA	AERA	OAV	OOB	AB-HR-SH	AVG	PB	SUP	APR	DL	PW
1984	StL N	9	4	.692	37	18	1-1	1-1	125.2	140	53	14	1	39-2	75	3.44	102	.285	.337	31-0-6	.065	-2*	125	1		0.1
1985	†StL N	3	2	.600	49	9	1-1	1-1	89.2	84	30	5	3	34-13	59	2.91	123	.251	.324	16-0-2	.063	-0	107	8		0.5
1986	StL N	4	3	.571	42	9	1	3-0	100.1	77	25	7	1	26-7	49	2.24	165	.218	.271	18-0-2	.056	0	67	18	30	1.4
1987	†StL N	8	3	.727	67	6	0	7-1	125	127	58	15	0	42-10	55	3.82	110	.263	.321	29	.172	0*	90	5		0.6
1988	Chi A	6	10	.375	52	9	0	2-1	109.1	120	64	6	5	36-4	28	4.86	82	.291	.349	0	—	0	99	-9		-1.1
	†LA N	1	1	.500	12	0	0	0-2	9	11	7	2	0	2-0	8	5.00	67	.306	.333	0	—	0		-2		-0.5
1989	LA N	0	0	—	23	0	0	0-1	26.2	35	15	1	1	11-2	12	5.06	68	.343	.405	1	.000	-0		-4		-0.2
	Year	0	3	.000	34	8	0	0-1	72.1	85	39	3	4	21-4	26	4.85	74	.305	.357	11-0-2	.250	1	62	-8		-0.3
1990	StL N	1	1	.500	32	0	0	1-1	42	52	25	3	1	22-7	18	4.93	78	.315	.397	4-0-1	.000	-0		-5		-0.2
Total	7	32	27	.542	325	53	3-1	15-8	673.1	696	301	55	15	222-47	319	3.76	101	.273	.331	110-0-13	.109	-1	94	4	30	0.5

HOSKINS, DAVE David Taylor B8.3.1925 Greenwood MS D4.2.1970 Flint MI BL/TR/6-1/180* d4.18 Negro Lg 1942-49

YEAR	TM LG	W	L	PCT	G	GS	CG-SHO	SV-BS	IP	H	R	HR	HB	BB-IB	SO	ERA	AERA	OAV	OOB	AB-HR-SH	AVG	PB	SUP	APR	DL	PW
1953	Cle A	9	3	.750	26	7	3	1	112.2	102	57	9	4	38	55	3.99	94	.243	.312	58-1-1	.259	4*	162	4		0.1
1954	Cle A	0	1	.000	14	1	0	0	26.2	29	10	3	0	10	9	3.04	121	.284	.342	8	.000	-1*	312	2		0.0
Total	2	9	4	.692	40	8	3	1	139.1	131	67	12	4	48	64	3.81	98	.251	.318	66-1-1	.227	3	181	-2		0.1

HOST, GENE Eugene Earl "Twinkles","Slick" B1.1.1933 Leeper PA D8.20.1998 Nashville TN BB/TL/5-11/190* d9.16

YEAR	TM LG	W	L	PCT	G	GS	CG-SHO	SV-BS	IP	H	R	HR	HB	BB-IB	SO	ERA	AERA	OAV	OOB	AB-HR-SH	AVG	PB	SUP	APR	DL	PW
1956	Det A	0	0	—	1	0	0	0	4.2	9	4	2	0	2-0	5	7.71	53	.409	.458	2	.000	-0	173	-2		-0.1
1957	KC A	0	2	.000	11	2	0	0	23.2	29	19	5	0	14-0	9	7.23	55	.315	.398	5	.000	-1	90	-7		-0.6
Total	2	0	2	.000	12	2	0	0	28.1	38	23	7	0	16-0	14	7.31	55	.333	.409	7	.000	-1	119	-9		-0.7

HOUCK, BYRON Byron Simon "Duke" B8.28.1891 Prosper MN D6.17.1969 Santa Cruz CA BR/TR/6-0/175 d5.15 Col Oregon

YEAR	TM LG	W	L	PCT	G	GS	CG-SHO	SV-BS	IP	H	R	HR	HB	BB-IB	SO	ERA	AERA	OAV	OOB	AB-HR-SH	AVG	PB	SUP	APR	DL	PW
1912	Phi A	8	8	.500	30	17	10	1	180.2	148	79	1	12	74	75	2.94	105	.234	.326	62-0-4	.065	-7	144	5		-0.5
1913	Phi A	14	6	.700	41	19	4-1	6	176	147	93	3	6	122	71	4.14	67	.237	.368	60-0-5	.083	-4	127	-26		-3.1
1914	Phi A	0	0	—	3	3	0	0	11	14	9	0	0	6	4	3.27	80	.318	.400	3	.333	0	195	-3		-0.1
	Bro F	2	6	.250	17	9	3	0	92	95	48	4	2	43	45	3.13	92	.272	.355	30-1-1	.233	2	95	-5		-0.3
1918	StL A	2	4	.333	27	2	0	2	71.2	58	24	0	0	29	29	2.39	115	.225	.303	20	.150	-1	96	3		0.2
Total	4	26	24	.520	118	50	17-1	3	531.1	462	253	8	20	274	224	3.30	87	.243	.344	175-1-10	.114	-9	130	-28		-3.8

HOUGH, CHARLIE Charles Oliver B1.5.1948 Honolulu HI BR/TR/6-2/190* [LAN66 8/159] d8.12 C4

YEAR	TM LG	W	L	PCT	G	GS	CG-SHO	SV-BS	IP	H	R	HR	HB	BB-IB	SO	ERA	AERA	OAV	OOB	AB-HR-SH	AVG	PB	SUP	APR	DL	PW
1970	LA N	0	0	—	8	0	0	2-0	17	19	11	7	0	11-0	9	5.29	73	.265	.367	3	.333			-3		-0.1
1971	LA N	0	0	—	4	0	0	0-0	4.1	3	3	1	0	3-0	4	4.15	78	.200	.333	0	—	0		-1		0.0
1972	LA N	0	0	—	2	0	0	0-0	2.2	2	1	0	2	1-0	2	3.38	99	.200	.385	0	—	0		0		0.0
1973	LA N	4	2	.667	37	0	0	5-2	71.2	52	24	3	6	45-2	70	2.76	126	.207	.338	14-0-1	.214			7		0.6
1974	†LA N	9	4	.692	49	0	0	1-2	96	65	45	12	4	40-2	63	3.75	91	.196	.285	12-0-3	.000	-1		-3		-0.5
1975	LA N	3	7	.300	38	0	0	4-2	61	43	25	3	8	34-0	34	2.95	116	.195	.323	6-0-1	.333	1		-2		0.4
1976	LA N	12	8	.600	77	0	0	18-4	142.2	102	43	6	8	77-3	81	2.21	154	.200	.314	21	.286	2		17		3.1
1977	†LA N	6	12	.333	70	1	0	22-5	127.1	98	53	10	7	70-6	105	3.32	116	.213	.323	22-1-0	.182	1	46	7		1.2
1978	†LA N	5	5	.500	55	0	0	7-4	93.1	69	38	6	5	48-4	66	3.28	107	.205	.313	12	.333	1		3		0.5
1979	LA N	7	5	.583	42	14	0	0-1	151.1	152	88	16	8	66-2	76	4.76	76	.264	.346	38-0-5	.158	-0	145	-18		-1.3
1980	LA N	1	3	.250	19	1	0	1-0	32.1	37	21	4	2	20-1	25	5.57	62	.291	.392	2	.500	0	103	-7		-0.9
	Tex A	2	2	.500	16	2	2-1	0-0	61.1	54	30	2	3	37-2	47	3.96	98	.240	.353	0	—	0	127	0		0.2
1981	Tex A	4	1	.800	21	5	2	1-1	82	61	30	4	3	31-1	69	2.96	117	.207	.289	0	—	0	124	5		0.2
1982	Tex A	16	13	.552	34	34	12-2	0-0	228	217	111	21	7	72-5	128	3.95	98	.251	.313	0	—	0	101	-2		-0.2
1983	Tex A	15	13	.536	34	33	11-3	0-0	252	219	96	22	3	95-0	152	3.18	127	.238	.309	0	—	0	92	27		3.0
1984	Tex A	16	14	.533	36	36	17-1	0-0	266	260	127	26	9	94-3	164	3.76	111	.255	.322	0	—	0	94	12		1.4
1985	Tex A	14	16	.467	34	34	14-1	0-0	250.1	198	102	23	7	83-1	141	3.31	129	.215	.283	0	—	0	77	25		2.9
1986	Tex A★	17	10	.630	33	33	7-2	0-0	230.1	188	115	32	9	89-2	146	3.79	114	.221	.301	0	—	0	105	11	29	1.1
1987	Tex A	18	13	.581	40	40	13	0-0	285.1	238	159	36	19	124-1	223	3.79	114	.223	.311	0	—	0	106	13		1.4
1988	Tex A	15	16	.484	34	34	10	0-0	252	202	111	20	12	126-1	174	3.32	124	.221	.321	0	—	0	80	19		2.3
1989	Tex A	10	13	.435	30	30	5-1	0-0	182	168	97	28	6	95-2	94	4.35	92	.245	.340	0	—	0	90	-6	15	-0.7
1990	Tex A	12	12	.500	32	32	5	0-0	218.2	190	108	24	11	119-2	114	4.07	97	.235	.338	0	—	0	102	-2		-0.1
1991	Chi A	9	10	.474	31	29	4-1	0-0	199.1	167	98	21	11	94-0	107	4.02	99	.229	.320	0	—	0	96	-1	7	-0.1
1992	Chi A	7	12	.368	27	27	1	0-0	176.1	160	89	19	9	94-0	76	3.93	99	.239	.311	0	—	0	87	-2		-0.3
1993	Fla N	9	16	.360	34	34	0	0-0	204.1	202	109	20	8	71-2	126	4.27	102	.259	.325	63-0-4	.032	-5	62	1		-0.4
1994	Fla N	5	9	.357	21	21	1-1	0-0	113.2	118	74	17	10	52-1	65	5.15	86	.274	.359	33-0-4	.121	-1	77	-8	16	-1.0
Total	25	216	216	.500	858	440	107-13	61-21	3801.1	3283	1807	383	174	1665-44	2362	3.75	107	.233	.319	226-1-18	.146	-2	95	96	67	12.4

YEAR	TM LG	W	L	PCT	G	GS	CG-SHO	SV-BS	IP	H	R	HR	HB	BB-IB	SO	ERA	AERA	OAV	OOB	AB-HR-SH	AVG	PB	SUP	APR	DL	PW

HOULTON, D.J. Dennis Sean B8.12.1979 Fullerton CA BR/TR/6-4/220 d4.9 Col Pacific (CA)

YEAR	TM LG	W	L	PCT	G	GS	CG-SHO	SV-BS	IP	H	R	HR	HB	BB-IB	SO	ERA	AERA	OAV	OOB	AB-HR-SH	AVG	PB	SUP	APR	DL	PW
2005	LA N	6	9	.400	35	19	0	0-0	129	145	79	24	8	52-3	90	5.16	79	.289	.362	30-0-2	.100	-0	67	-15		-1.6

HOUSE, CRAIG Craig Michael B7.8.1977 Naha A.F.B., Okinawa BR/TR/6-2/210 [ColN99 12/370] d8.6 Col Memphis

YEAR	TM LG	W	L	PCT	G	GS	CG-SHO	SV-BS	IP	H	R	HR	HB	BB-IB	SO	ERA	AERA	OAV	OOB	AB-HR-SH	AVG	PB	SUP	APR	DL	PW
2000	Col N	1	1	.500	16	0	0	0-0	13.2	13	11	3	2	17-0	8	7.24	80	.265	.464	0	—	0		-1		-0.2

HOUSE, PAT Patrick Lory B9.1.1940 Boise ID BL/TL/6-3/185* d9.6 Col Wyoming

YEAR	TM LG	W	L	PCT	G	GS	CG-SHO	SV-BS	IP	H	R	HR	HB	BB-IB	SO	ERA	AERA	OAV	OOB	AB-HR-SH	AVG	PB	SUP	APR	DL	PW
1967	Hou N	1	0	1.000	6	0	0	1	4	3	2	0	1	0-0	2	4.50	74	.214	.267	0	—	0		0		-0.1
1968	Hou N	1	1	.500	18	0	0	0	16.1	21	15	0	2	6-3	6	7.71	38	.323	.392	0	—	0		-8	21	-0.1
Total	2	2	1	.667	24	0	0	1	20.1	24	17	0	3	6-3	8	7.08	43	.304	.371	0	—	0		-8	21	-1.1

HOUSE, TOM Thomas Ross B4.29.1947 Seattle WA BL/TL/5-11/190(175-190) [AtlN67 S3/48] d6.23 C8 Col USC

YEAR	TM LG	W	L	PCT	G	GS	CG-SHO	SV-BS	IP	H	R	HR	HB	BB-IB	SO	ERA	AERA	OAV	OOB	AB-HR-SH	AVG	PB	SUP	APR	DL	PW
1971	Atl N	1	0	1.000	11	1	0	0-0	20.2	20	8	2	1	3-0	11	3.05	122	.263	.296	5	.400	1	143	1		0.1
1972	Atl N	0	0	—	8	0	0	2-0	9.1	7	3	1	1	6-0	7	2.89	131	.226	.368	1	.000	-0		1		0.0
1973	Atl N	4	2	.667	52	0	0	4-2	67.1	58	37	13	2	31-7	42	4.68	85	.243	.326	10-0-2	.200	-0		-4		-0.4
1974	Atl N	6	2	.750	56	0	0	11-5	102.2	74	26	5	3	27-8	64	1.93	197	.203	.261	10-0-3	.400	1	20			2.2
1975	Atl N	7	7	.500	58	0	0	11-4	79.1	79	39	2	4	36-10	36	3.18	119	.262	.342	9	.111	-0		3		0.1
1976	Bos A	1	3	.250	36	0	0	4-2	43.2	39	22	4	2	19-4	27	4.33	90	.241	.324	0	—	0		-1	20	-0.1
1977	Bos A	1	0	1.000	8	0	0	0-0	7.2	15	11	0	0	6-0	6	12.91	35	.405	.488	0	—	0		-6		-0.2
	Sea A	4	5	.444	26	11	1	1-0	89.1	94	42	12	4	19-2	39	3.93	106	.268	.310	0	—	0	63	3	23	0.2
	Year	5	5	.500	34	11	1	1-0	97	109	53	12	4	25-2	45	4.64	90	.281	.329	0	—	0	63	-3		-0.5
1978	Sea A	5	4	.556	34	9	3	0-0	116	130	70	10	5	35-2	29	4.66	83	.289	.339	0	—	0	127	-11		-0.8
Total	8	29	23	.558	289	21	4	33-13	536	516	258	49	20	182-33	261	3.79	103	.256	.320	35-0-5	.257	1	94	6	43	1.1

HOUSE, FRED Willard Edwin B10.3.1890 Cabool MO D11.16.1923 Kansas City MO BR/TR/6-3/190 d4.22

YEAR	TM LG	W	L	PCT	G	GS	CG-SHO	SV-BS	IP	H	R	HR	HB	BB-IB	SO	ERA	AERA	OAV	OOB	AB-HR-SH	AVG	PB	SUP	APR	DL	PW
1913	Det A	1	2	.333	19	2	0	0	53.2	64	40	1	2	17	16	5.20	56	.328	.388	10	.000	-1	127	-12		-0.7

HOUSEMAN, FRANK Frank B , Netherlands d9.2

YEAR	TM LG	W	L	PCT	G	GS	CG-SHO	SV-BS	IP	H	R	HR	HB	BB-IB	SO	ERA	AERA	OAV	OOB	AB-HR-SH	AVG	PB	SUP	APR	DL	PW
1886	Bal AA	1	1	.500	1	1	1	0	8	6	3	0	1	1	5	3.38	101	.182	.229	4	.250	-0	35	1		0.1

HOUSER, JOE Joseph William B7.3.1891 Steubenville OH D1.3.1953 Orlando FL BL/TL/5-9.5/160 d4.24

YEAR	TM LG	W	L	PCT	G	GS	CG-SHO	SV-BS	IP	H	R	HR	HB	BB-IB	SO	ERA	AERA	OAV	OOB	AB-HR-SH	AVG	PB	SUP	APR	DL	PW
1914	Buf F	0	1	1.000	7	2	0	0	23	21	16	1	0	20	6	5.48	54	.250	.394	7	.143	-0*	127	-6		-0.3

HOUTTEMAN, ART Arthur Joseph B8.7.1927 Detroit MI D5.6.2003 Rochester Hills MI BR/TR/6-2/188* d4.29 Mil 1951

YEAR	TM LG	W	L	PCT	G	GS	CG-SHO	SV-BS	IP	H	R	HR	HB	BB-IB	SO	ERA	AERA	OAV	OOB	AB-HR-SH	AVG	PB	SUP	APR	DL	PW
1945	Det A	0	2	.000	13	0	0	0	25.1	27	17	1	1	11	9	5.33	66	.270	.348	5	.000	-1		-4		-0.4
1946	Det A	0	1	.000	1	1	0	0	8	15	8	1	0	0	2	9.00	41	.385	.385	2-0-1	.500	0	164	-4		-0.4
1947	Det A	7	2	.778	23	9	7-2	0	110.2	106	51	6	1	36	58	3.42	110	.247	.306	40	.300	2	123	3		0.4
1948	Det A	2	16	.111	43	20	4	10	164.1	186	101	11	2	52	74	4.66	94	.287	.342	56-0-1	.196	-2	69	-7		-0.8
1949	Det A	15	10	.600	34	25	13-2	0	203.2	227	101	19	5	59	85	3.71	112	.282	.335	78-0-2	.244	1*	108	7		1.1
1950	Det A★	19	12	.613	41	34	21-4	4	274.2	257	112	29	8	99	88	3.54	132	.251	.309	93-0-11	.151	-3	100	38		3.7
1952	Det A	8	20	.286	35	28	10-2	1	221	218	116	19	5	65	109	4.36	87	.253	.309	69-0-6	.101	-4*	71	-11		-1.7
1953	Det A	2	6	.250	16	9	3-1	1	68.2	87	50	11	4	29	28	5.90	69	.309	.381	19-1-2	.158	0	80	-14		-1.4
	Cle A	7	7	.500	22	13	6-1	3	109	113	56	4	5	25	40	3.80	99	.269	.333	34-0-2	.147	-1*	133	-3		-0.4
	Year	9	13	.409	38	22	9-2	4	177.2	200	106	15	9	54	68	4.61	84	.285	.344	53-1-4	.151	-1	111	-18		-1.8
1954	†Cle A	15	7	.682	32	25	11-1	0	188	198	80	14	3	59	68	3.35	110	.273	.328	65-1-8	.277	5	131	7		1.3
1955	Cle A	10	6	.625	35	12	3-1	0	124.1	126	63	15	2	44-1	53	3.98	100	.265	.328	38-0-4	.158	-1	89	0		-1.0
1956	Cle A	2	2	.500	22	4	0	1	46.2	60	39	5	4	31-2	19	6.56	64	.317	.417	12-0-1	.167	-1*	95	-12		-1.0
1957	Cle A	0	0	—	3	0	0	0	4	6	3	1	0	3-0	3	6.75	55	.353	.460	0	—	0		-1		-0.1
	Bal A	0	0	—	5	1	0	0	6.2	20	13	0	0	3-0	3	17.55	20	.513	.548	2	.500	0	149	-10		-0.5
	Year	0	0	—	8	1	0	0	10.2	26	16	1	0	6-0	6	13.50	27	.464	.516	2	.500	0	147	-12		-0.6
Total	12	87	91	.489	325	181	78-14	20	1555	1646	810	136	40	516-3	639	4.14	99	.272	.333	513-2-38	.193	-4	99	-11		-0.1

HOVLIK, ED Edward Charles B8.20.1891 Cleveland OH D3.19.1955 Painesville OH BR/TR/6-0/180 d7.14 b-Joe

YEAR	TM LG	W	L	PCT	G	GS	CG-SHO	SV-BS	IP	H	R	HR	HB	BB-IB	SO	ERA	AERA	OAV	OOB	AB-HR-SH	AVG	PB	SUP	APR	DL	PW
1918	Was A	2	1	.667	8	2	1	0	28	25	10	0	0	10	16	1.29	212	.272	.343	8	.125	-1	207	3		0.2
1919	Was A	0	0	—	3	0	0	0	5.2	12	10	0	0	9	3	12.71	25	.480	.618	2	.000	-0		-6		-0.3
Total	2	2	1	.667	11	2	1	0	33.2	37	20	0	0	19	19	3.21	88	.316	.412	10	.100	-1	207	-3		-0.1

HOVLIK, JOE Joseph B8.16.1884 , Czechoslovakia D11.3.1951 Oxford Junction IA BR/TR/5-10.5/194 d7.10 b-Ed

YEAR	TM LG	W	L	PCT	G	GS	CG-SHO	SV-BS	IP	H	R	HR	HB	BB-IB	SO	ERA	AERA	OAV	OOB	AB-HR-SH	AVG	PB	SUP	APR	DL	PW
1909	Was A	0	0	—	3	0	0	0	6	13	10	0	1	3	1	4.50	54	.419	.486	2	.000	0		-3		-0.1
1910	Was A	0	0	—	1	0	0	0	1.2	6	5	0	1	0	0	16.20	15	.500	.538	0	—	0		-3		-0.1
1911	Chi A	2	0	1.000	12	3	1-1	0	47	47	21	1	0	20	24	3.06	105	.257	.330	13	.077	-0	104	1		0.1
Total	3	2	0	1.000	16	3	1-1	0	54.2	66	36	1	2	23	25	3.62	86	.292	.363	15	.067	-0	104	-5		-0.1

HOWARD, BEN Benjamin Richard B1.15.1979 Danville IL BR/TR/6-2/190(190-220) [SDN97 2/78] d4.28

YEAR	TM LG	W	L	PCT	G	GS	CG-SHO	SV-BS	IP	H	R	HR	HB	BB-IB	SO	ERA	AERA	OAV	OOB	AB-HR-SH	AVG	PB	SUP	APR	DL	PW
2002	SD N	0	1	.000	3	2	0	0-0	10.2	13	11	4	0	14-1	10	9.28	42	.302	.466	4-0-1	.000	-0	71	-6		-0.5
2003	SD N	1	3	.250	6	6	0	0-0	34.2	31	17	10	0	15-1	24	3.63	110	.235	.313	11	.091	-1	86	1		0.0
2004	Fla N	1	1	.500	31	0	0	0-0	37.2	37	23	6	1	21-3	33	5.50	75	.261	.355	3	.000	-0		-5		-0.3
Total	3	2	5	.286	40	8	0	0-0	83	81	51	20	1	50-5	67	5.20	78	.256	.356	18-0-1	.056	-1	81	-10		-0.8

HOWARD, BRUCE Bruce Ernest B3.23.1943 Salisbury MD BB/TR/6-2/180(172-185) d9.4 s-David Col Villanova

YEAR	TM LG	W	L	PCT	G	GS	CG-SHO	SV-BS	IP	H	R	HR	HB	BB-IB	SO	ERA	AERA	OAV	OOB	AB-HR-SH	AVG	PB	SUP	APR	DL	PW
1963	Chi A	2	1	.667	7	0	0	0	17	12	7	0	0	14-0	9	2.65	132	.207	.361	4	.250	0		1		0.2
1964	Chi A	2	1	.667	3	3	1-1	0	22.1	10	2	0	1	8-1	17	0.81	429	.139	.235	8	.000	-1	69	7		0.9
1965	Chi A	9	8	.529	30	22	1-1	0	148	123	61	13	1	72-5	120	3.47	92	.224	.315	41-0-6	.146	2	106	-3		-0.2
1966	Chi A	9	5	.643	27	21	4-2	0	149	110	48	14	1	44-2	85	2.30	138	.202	.262	43-0-2	.070	-1	95	14		1.2
1967	Chi A	3	10	.231	30	17	1	0	112.2	102	55	9	3	52-1	76	3.43	90	.240	.325	28-0-3	.179	1	68	-6		-0.5
1968	Bal A	0	2	.000	10	5	0	0	31	30	16	2	2	26-2	19	3.77	78	.268	.406	7-1-2	.286	-2	71	-3		0.0
	Was A	1	4	.200	13	7	0	0	48.2	62	30	7	0	23-2	23	5.36	54	.330	.401	16	.000	-2	68	-12	22	-1.3
	Year	1	6	.143	23	12	0	0	79.2	92	46	9	2	49-4	42	4.74	62	.307	.403	23-1-2	.087	-1	70	-15	22	-1.3
Total	6	26	31	.456	120	75	7-4	1	528.2	449	219	45	8	239-13	349	3.18	99	.231	.316	147-1-13	.116	-2	87	-2	22	-0.8

HOWARD, CHRIS Christian B11.18.1965 Lynn MA BR/TL/6-0/185* d9.21 Col Miami [DL 1996 Tex A 182]

YEAR	TM LG	W	L	PCT	G	GS	CG-SHO	SV-BS	IP	H	R	HR	HB	BB-IB	SO	ERA	AERA	OAV	OOB	AB-HR-SH	AVG	PB	SUP	APR	DL	PW
1993	Chi A	1	0	1.000	3	0	0	0-0	2.1	2	0	0	0	3-1	1	0.00	—	.286	.500	0	—	0		1		0.2
1994	Bos A	1	0	1.000	37	0	0	1-1	39.2	35	17	5	0	12-4	22	3.63	139	.233	.287	0	—	0		6		0.3
1995	Tex A	0	0	—	4	0	0	0-0	4	3	0	0	1	1-0	2	0.00	—	.231	.267	0	—	0		2		0.1
Total	3	2	0	1.000	44	0	0	1-1	46	40	17	5	0	16-5	25	3.13	159	.235	.296	0	—	0		9	182	0.6

HOWARD, EARL Earl Nycum B6.25.1893 Everett PA D4.4.1937 Everett PA BR/TR/6-1/160 d4.18

YEAR	TM LG	W	L	PCT	G	GS	CG-SHO	SV-BS	IP	H	R	HR	HB	BB-IB	SO	ERA	AERA	OAV	OOB	AB-HR-SH	AVG	PB	SUP	APR	DL	PW
1918	StL N	0	0	—	1	0	0	0	2	0	0	0	0	2	2	0.00	—	.000	.286	0	—	0		1		0.1

HOWARD, FRED Fred Irving B9.2.1956 Portland ME BR/TR/6-3/190 [ChiA76*6/110] d5.26 Col Maine

YEAR	TM LG	W	L	PCT	G	GS	CG-SHO	SV-BS	IP	H	R	HR	HB	BB-IB	SO	ERA	AERA	OAV	OOB	AB-HR-SH	AVG	PB	SUP	APR	DL	PW
1979	Chi A	1	5	.167	28	6	0	0-0	68	73	34	5	1	32-2	36	3.57	119	.283	.357	0	—	0	92	4		0.3

HOWARD, LEE Lee Vincent B11.11.1923 Staten Island NY BL/TL/6-2/175 d9.22

YEAR	TM LG	W	L	PCT	G	GS	CG-SHO	SV-BS	IP	H	R	HR	HB	BB-IB	SO	ERA	AERA	OAV	OOB	AB-HR-SH	AVG	PB	SUP	APR	DL	PW
1946	Pit N	0	1	.000	3	2	1	0	13.1	14	3	0	0	9	6	2.03	174	.286	.397	5	.000	-1	24	2		0.1
1947	Pit N	0	0	—	2	0	0	0	2.2	4	1	1	0	0	2	3.38	125	.333	.333	0	—	0		0		0.0
Total	2	0	1	.000	5	2	1	0	16	18	4	1	0	9	8	2.25	162	.295	.386	5	.000	-1	24	2		0.1

HOWE, CAL Calvin Earl B11.27.1924 Rock Falls IL BL/TL/6-3/230 d9.26

YEAR	TM LG	W	L	PCT	G	GS	CG-SHO	SV-BS	IP	H	R	HR	HB	BB-IB	SO	ERA	AERA	OAV	OOB	AB-HR-SH	AVG	PB	SUP	APR	DL	PW
1952	Chi N	0	0	—	2	0	0	0	2	0	0	0	1	1	2	0.00	—	.000	.143	0	—	0		1		0.0

HOWE, LES Lester Curtis "Lucky" B8.24.1895 Brooklyn NY D7.16.1976 Woodmere NY BR/TR/5-11.5/170 d8.18

YEAR	TM LG	W	L	PCT	G	GS	CG-SHO	SV-BS	IP	H	R	HR	HB	BB-IB	SO	ERA	AERA	OAV	OOB	AB-HR-SH	AVG	PB	SUP	APR	DL	PW
1923	Bos A	1	0	1.000	12	2	1	0	30	23	10	0	1	7	7	2.40	171	.211	.265	6	.000	-1	111	6		0.2
1924	Bos A	1	0	1.000	4	0	0	0	7.1	11	4	1	1	2	3	7.36	59	.423	.483	2	.500	0		-2		-0.2
Total	2	2	0	1.000	16	2	1	0	37.1	34	16	1	2	9	10	3.38	123	.252	.308	8	.125	-1	111	4		0.1

HOWE, STEVE Steven Roy B3.10.1958 Pontiac MI BL/TL/6-1/180(180-198) [LAN79 1/16] d4.11 Col Michigan

YEAR	TM LG	W	L	PCT	G	GS	CG-SHO	SV-BS	IP	H	R	HR	HB	BB-IB	SO	ERA	AERA	OAV	OOB	AB-HR-SH	AVG	PB	SUP	APR	DL	PW
1980	LA N	7	9	.438	59	0	0	17-9	84.2	83	33	1	2	22-10	39	2.66	131	.256	.305	11	.091	-1		5		1.2
1981	†LA N	5	3	.625	41	0	0	8-2	54	51	17	2	0	18-7	32	2.50	132	.254	.309	1	.000	0		5		0.8
1982	LA N★	7	5	.583	66	0	0	13-9	99.1	87	24	8	1	17-11	49	2.08	167	.240	.272	7-0-1	.000	-1		15		2.1

YEAR	TM LG	W	L	PCT	G	GS	CG-SHO	SV-BS	IP	H	R	HR	HB	BB-IB	SO	ERA	AERA	OAV	OOB	AB-HR-SH	AVG	PB	SUP	APR	DL	PW
1983	LA N	4	7	.364	46	0	0	18-5	68.2	55	15	2	1	12-7	52	1.44	250	.217	.253	8	.125	0		16	32	3.4
1985	LA N	1	1	.500	19	0	0	3-0	22	30	17	2	1	5-2	11	4.91	71	.319	.353	0	—	0		-5		-0.5
	Min A	2	3	.400	13	0	0	0-3	19	28	16	1	0	7-2	10	6.16	72	.333	.372	0	—	0		-4		-0.8
1987	Tex A	3	3	.500	24	0	0	1-2	31.1	33	15	2	3	8-1	19	4.31	105	.280	.341	0	—	0		2		0.3
1991	NY A	3	1	.750	37	0	0	3-0	48.1	39	12	1	3	7-2	34	1.68	249	.222	.262	0	—	0		12	22	1.1
1992	NY A	3	0	1.000	20	0	0	6-1	22	9	7	1	0	3-1	12	2.45	161	.122	.154	0	—	0		3		0.6
1993	NY A	3	5	.375	51	0	0	4-3	50.2	58	31	7	3	10-4	19	4.97	84	.297	.338	0	—	0		-5	29	-0.7
1994	NY A	3	0	1.000	40	0	0	15-4	40	28	8	2	0	7-1	18	1.80	256	.194	.232	0	—	0		13	18	1.8
1995	†NY A	6	3	.667	56	0	0	2-1	49	66	29	7	4	17-3	28	4.96	93	.324	.383	0	—	0		-2		-0.3
1996	NY A	0	1	.000	25	0	0	1-1	17	19	12	1	1	6-3	5	6.35	78	.284	.351	0	—	0		-2		-0.1
Total	12	47	41	.534	497	0	0	91-40	606	586	239	32	18	139-54	328	3.03	129	.255	.300	27-0-1	.074	-1		53	101	8.9

HOWELL, HARRY   Harry Taylor B11.14.1876 NJ D5.22.1956 Spokane WA BR/TR/5-9/? d10.10 U1

YEAR	TM LG	W	L	PCT	G	GS	CG-SHO	SV-BS	IP	H	R	HR	HB	BB-IB	SO	ERA	AERA	OAV	OOB	AB-HR-SH	AVG	PB	SUP	APR	DL	PW
1898	Bro N	2	0	1.000	2	2	2	0	18	15	11	0	1	11	2	5.00	72	.224	.342	8-0-1	.250	0	188	-2		-0.1
1899	Bal N	13	8	.619	28	25	21	1	209.1	248	126	1	10	69	58	3.91	101	.294	.355	82-0-3	.146	-3	103	3		-0.1
1900	†Bro N	6	5	.545	21	10	7-2	0	110.1	131	69	4	3	36	26	3.75	102	.294	.351	42-1-0	.286	4*	88	-1		0.3
1901	Bal A	14	21	.400	37	34	32-1	0	294.2	333	188	5	7	79	93	3.67	106	.281	.330	188-2-4	.218	1*	94	6		0.6
1902	Bal A	9	15	.375	26	23	19-1	0	199	243	136	6	7	48	33	4.12	92	.301	.346	347-2-8	.268	5*	93	-8		-0.1
1903	NY A	9	6	.600	25	15	13	0	155.2	140	79	4	6	44	62	3.53	89	.240	.300	106-1-3	.217	2*	119	-5		-0.1
1904	StL A	13	21	.382	34	33	32-2	0	299.2	254	99	1	13	60	122	2.19	113	.230	.278	113-1-4	.221	5*	81	10		2.4
1905	StL A	15	22	.405	38	37	35-4	0	323	252	109	2	12	101	198	1.98	129	.217	.286	135-1-1	.193	3*	91	19		3.6
1906	StL A	15	14	.517	35	33	30-6	1	276.2	233	98	1	9	61	140	2.11	122	.231	.282	103-0-3	.126	-3	113	14		1.6
1907	StL A	16	15	.516	42	35	26-2	3	316.1	258	112	3	8	88	118	1.93	130	.225	.285	114-2-9	.237	6*	94	14		2.6
1908	StL A	18	18	.500	41	32	27-2	1	324.1	279	103	1	17	70	117	1.89	127	.240	.293	120-1-1	.183	1	94	16		2.2
1909	StL A	1	1	.500	10	3	0	0	37.1	42	21	0	3	8	16	3.13	77	.294	.344	34-0-3	.176	0*	136	-5		-0.2
1910	StL A	0	0	—	1	0	0	0	3.1	7	7	0	0	2	1	10.80	23	.467	.529	2	.000	-0		-3		-0.2
Total	13	131	146	.473	340	282	244-20	6	2567.2	2435	1158	27	97	677	986	2.74	108	.252	.307	1394-11-40	.217	21	98	58		12.5

HOWELL, J.P.   James Phillip B4.25.1983 Modesto CA BL/TL/6-0/175 d6.11 Col Texas

YEAR	TM LG	W	L	PCT	G	GS	CG-SHO	SV-BS	IP	H	R	HR	HB	BB-IB	SO	ERA	AERA	OAV	OOB	AB-HR-SH	AVG	PB	SUP	APR	DL	PW
2005	KC A	3	5	.375	15	15	0	0	72.2	73	55	9	8	39-0	54	6.19	68	.264	.363	3	.000	-0	112	-17		-1.6

HOWELL, JAY   Jay Canfield B11.26.1955 Miami FL BR/TR/6-3/205(200-220) [CinN76 31/668] d8.10 Col Colorado

YEAR	TM LG	W	L	PCT	G	GS	CG-SHO	SV-BS	IP	H	R	HR	HB	BB-IB	SO	ERA	AERA	OAV	OOB	AB-HR-SH	AVG	PB	SUP	APR	DL	PW
1980	Cin N	0	0	—	5	0	0	0-0	3.1	8	5	0	1	0	4	13.50	26	.471	.474	0	—	0		-4		-0.2
1981	Chi N	2	0	1.000	10	2	0	0-0	22.1	23	13	3	2	10-2	10	4.84	77	.277	.365	2-0-2	.000	0	166	-2		-0.1
1982	NY A	2	3	.400	6	6	0	0-0	28	42	25	1	0	13-0	21	7.71	52	.341	.399	0	—	0	147	-11		-1.5
1983	NY A	1	5	.167	19	12	2	0-0	82	89	53	7	3	35-0	61	5.38	73	.275	.346	0	—	0	98	-13	30	-0.8
1984	NY A	9	4	.692	61	1	0	7-2	103.2	86	33	5	0	34-3	109	2.69	142	.223	.284	0	—	0	189	14		1.9
1985	Oak A☆	9	8	.529	63	0	0	29-7	98	98	32	5	1	31-3	68	2.85	136	.261	.316	0	—	0	13			2.6
1986	Oak A	3	6	.333	38	0	0	16-4	53.1	53	23	4	0	23-4	42	3.38	115	.262	.339	0	—	0	3		18	0.2
1987	Oak A★	3	4	.429	36	0	0	16-8	44.1	48	30	6	1	21-1	35	5.89	71	.277	.355	0	—	0	-8	41		-1.5
1988	†LA N	5	3	.625	50	0	0	21-6	65	44	16	1	1	21-2	70	2.08	161	.188	.255	2	.000	-0	10		16	1.8
1989	LA N★	5	3	.625	56	0	0	28-4	79.2	60	15	3	0	22-6	55	1.58	217	.211	.266	3	.000	-0	17			2.8
1990	LA N	5	5	.500	45	0	0	16-8	66	59	17	5	6	20-3	59	2.18	169	.242	.315	2	.000	-0	12	24		2.3
1991	LA N	6	5	.545	44	0	0	16-2	51	39	19	3	1	11-3	40	3.18	114	.213	.259	0	—	0	3	33		0.7
1992	LA N	1	3	.250	41	0	0	4-2	46.2	41	9	2	1	18-5	36	1.54	225	.230	.303	0	—	0	10	42		1.1
1993	Atl N	3	3	.500	54	0	0	0-3	58.1	48	16	3	0	16-4	37	2.31	175	.229	.278	0	—	0	11			1.1
1994	Tex A	4	1	.800	40	0	0	2-3	43	44	29	10	1	16-2	22	5.44	89	.262	.324	0	—	0	-3			-0.3
Total	15	58	53	.523	568	21	2	155-49	844.2	782	335	57	19	291-38	666	3.34	115	.246	.310	9-0-2	.000	-1	126	52	204	10.5

HOWELL, KEN   Kenneth B11.28.1960 Detroit MI BR/TR/6-3/228(200-230) [LAN82 3/73] d6.25 Col Tuskegee [DL 1991 Phi N 182, 1992 Phi N 182]

YEAR	TM LG	W	L	PCT	G	GS	CG-SHO	SV-BS	IP	H	R	HR	HB	BB-IB	SO	ERA	AERA	OAV	OOB	AB-HR-SH	AVG	PB	SUP	APR	DL	PW
1984	LA N	5	5	.500	32	1	0	6-4	51.1	51	21	1	1	9-4	54	3.33	107	.267	.298	-1	.000	-1	0	2		0.3
1985	†LA N	4	7	.364	56	0	0	12-3	86	66	41	8	0	35-3	85	3.77	93	.208	.287	4	.000	-0	-2			-0.3
1986	LA N	6	12	.333	62	0	0	12-9	97.2	86	48	7	3	63-9	104	3.87	90	.239	.354	5	.000	-1	-5			-1.1
1987	LA N	3	4	.429	40	2	0	1-5	55	54	32	7	0	29-2	60	4.91	81	.265	.356	4	.250	-1	136	-5		-0.6
1988	LA N	0	1	.000	4	1	0	0-0	12.2	16	10	0	0	4-1	12	6.39	52	.320	.370	1-0-1	.000	-0	53	-4	72	-0.3
1989	Phi N	12	12	.500	33	32	1-1	0-0	204	155	84	11	2	86-6	164	3.44	104	.215	.297	65-0-10	.092	-2	100	5		0.3
1990	Phi N	8	7	.533	18	18	2	0-0	106.2	106	60	12	3	49-6	70	4.64	83	.260	.343	30-0-8	.067	-1	92	-9	83	-1.3
Total	7	38	48	.442	245	54	3-1	31-21	613.1	534	296	46	9	275-31	549	3.95	92	.237	.320	114-0-20	.079	-5	98	-18	519	-3.0

HOWELL, DIXIE   Millard B1.7.1920 Harold KY D3.18.1960 Hollywood FL BL/TR/6-2/210(198-210) d9.14

YEAR	TM LG	W	L	PCT	G	GS	CG-SHO	SV-BS	IP	H	R	HR	HB	BB-IB	SO	ERA	AERA	OAV	OOB	AB-HR-SH	AVG	PB	SUP	APR	DL	PW
1940	Cle A	0	0	—	3	0	0	0	5	7	1	1	0	4	1	1.80	234	.143	.333	0	—	0		1		0.1
1949	Cin N	0	1	.000	5	1	0	0	13.1	21	12	3	0	8	7	8.10	52	.362	.439	9	.111	-0*	84	-5		-0.3
1955	Chi A	8	3	.727	35	0	0	9	73.2	70	27	1	0	25-5	25	2.93	135	.250	.308	21-0-1	.381	2		8		1.6
1956	Chi A	5	6	.455	34	1	0	4	64.1	79	39	2	1	36-10	28	4.62	89	.309	.398	17-2-0	.235	2	130	-5		-0.6
1957	Chi A	6	5	.545	37	0	0	6	68.1	64	25	6	0	30-4	37	3.29	113	.255	.332	27-3-0	.185	4*		4		1.2
1958	Chi A	0	0	—	1	0	0	0	1.2	0	0	0	0	0	1	0.00	—	.000	.000	0	—	0		1		0.0
Total	6	19	15	.559	115	2	0	19	226.1	236	104	13	2	103-19	99	3.78	104	.273	.350	74-5-1	.243	8	113	4		2.0

HOWELL, ROLAND   Roland Boatner "Billiken" B1.3.1892 Napoleonville LA D3.31.1973 Baton Rouge LA BR/TR/6-4/210 d6.14 Col Louisiana St.

YEAR	TM LG	W	L	PCT	G	GS	CG-SHO	SV-BS	IP	H	R	HR	HB	BB-IB	SO	ERA	AERA	OAV	OOB	AB-HR-SH	AVG	PB	SUP	APR	DL	PW
1912	StL N	0	0	—	3	0	0	0	5	12	5	0	0	5	0	27.00	13	.556	.714	0	—	0		-4		-0.2

HOWRY, BOB   Bobby Dean B8.4.1973 Phoenix AZ BL/TR/6-5/220* [SFN94 5/144] d6.21 Col McNeese St.

YEAR	TM LG	W	L	PCT	G	GS	CG-SHO	SV-BS	IP	H	R	HR	HB	BB-IB	SO	ERA	AERA	OAV	OOB	AB-HR-SH	AVG	PB	SUP	APR	DL	PW
1998	Chi A	0	3	.000	44	0	0	9-2	54.1	37	20	7	2	19-2	51	3.15	146	.194	.270	0	—	0		9		0.7
1999	Chi A	5	3	.625	69	0	0	28-6	67.2	58	34	8	3	38-3	80	3.59	138	.229	.336	0	—	0		8		1.3
2000	†Chi A	2	4	.333	65	0	0	7-5	71	54	26	6	4	29-2	60	3.17	160	.216	.303	0	—	0		15		1.3
2001	Chi A	4	5	.444	69	0	0	5-6	78.2	85	41	11	4	30-9	64	4.69	99	.279	.348	0	—	0		1		0.1
2002	Chi A	2	2	.500	47	0	0	0-0	50.2	45	22	7	3	17-2	31	3.91	115	.245	.313	0	—	0		4		0.3
	Bos A	1	3	.250	20	0	0	0-1	18	22	15	2	2	4-2	14	5.00	90	.306	.350	0	—	0		-3		-0.5
	Year	3	5	.375	67	0	0	0-1	68.2	67	37	9	5	21-4	45	4.19	107	.262	.323	0	—	0		1		-0.2
2003	Bos A	0	0	—	4	0	0	0-1	4.1	11	6	1	0	3-1	4	12.46	37	.478	.519	0	—	0		-3	38	-0.2
2004	Cle A	4	2	.667	37	0	0	0-2	42.2	37	14	5	2	12-0	39	2.74	158	.228	.288	0	—	0		8		1.0
2005	Cle A	7	4	.636	79	0	0	3-2	73	49	23	4	0	16-1	48	2.47	166	.191	.237	1	.000	-0		14		1.9
Total	8	25	26	.490	434	0	0	52-25	460.1	398	201	51	20	168-22	391	3.58	129	.235	.308	1	.000	-0		53	38	5.9

HOY, PETER   Peter Alexander B6.29.1966 Brockville ON, Can. BL/TR/6-7/220 [BosA88 33/849] d4.11 Col LeMoyne (NY)

YEAR	TM LG	W	L	PCT	G	GS	CG-SHO	SV-BS	IP	H	R	HR	HB	BB-IB	SO	ERA	AERA	OAV	OOB	AB-HR-SH	AVG	PB	SUP	APR	DL	PW
1992	Bos A	0	0	—	5	0	0	0-1	3.2	8	3	0	0	2-1	2	7.36	58	.471	.526	0	—	0		-1		0.0

HOYLE, TEX   Roland Edison B7.17.1921 Carbondale PA D7.4.1994 Carbondale PA BR/TR/6-4/170 d4.18

YEAR	TM LG	W	L	PCT	G	GS	CG-SHO	SV-BS	IP	H	R	HR	HB	BB-IB	SO	ERA	AERA	OAV	OOB	AB-HR-SH	AVG	PB	SUP	APR	DL	PW
1952	Phi A	0	0	—	3	0	0	0	2.1	9	7	2	0	1	1	27.00	15	.563	.588	0	—	0		-5		-0.2

HOYT, LA MARR   Dewey La Marr B1.1.1955 Columbia SC BR/TR/6-1/222(190-244) [NYA73 5/109] d9.14

YEAR	TM LG	W	L	PCT	G	GS	CG-SHO	SV-BS	IP	H	R	HR	HB	BB-IB	SO	ERA	AERA	OAV	OOB	AB-HR-SH	AVG	PB	SUP	APR	DL	PW
1979	Chi A	0	0	—	2	0	0	0-0	3	2	0	0	0	0-0	0	0.00	—	.200	.200	0	—	0*		1		0.1
1980	Chi A	9	3	.750	24	13	3-1	0-0	112.1	123	66	8	2	41-3	55	4.57	89	.281	.340	0	—	0	93	-6		-0.7
1981	Chi A	9	3	.750	43	1	0	10-1	90.2	80	40	10	3	28-1	60	3.57	101	.240	.303	0	—	0	0	1		0.1
1982	Chi A	19	15	.559	39	32	14-2	0-1	239.2	248	104	17	2	48-3	124	3.53	115	.266	.301	0	—	0	119	16		2.1
1983	†Chi A	24	10	.706	36	36	11-1	0-0	260.2	236	115	27	1	31-4	148	3.66	115	.238	.260	0	—	0	115	16		2.2
1984	Chi A	13	18	.419	34	34	11-1	0-0	235.2	244	127	31	5	43-3	126	4.47	94	.266	.301	0	—	0*	85	-6		-0.7
1985	SD N★	16	8	.667	31	31	8-3	0-0	210.1	210	85	20	2	20-2	83	3.47	103	.261	.280	64-0-12	.063	-4	112	5		1.1
1986	SD N	8	11	.421	35	25	1	0-0	159	170	100	27	3	68-8	85	5.15	71	.276	.350	46-0-3	.130	-1	105	-26		-2.9
Total	8	98	68	.590	244	172	48-8	10-3	1311.1	1313	637	140	20	279-24	681	3.99	99	.260	.300	110-0-15	.091	-5	106	1		0.3

HOYT, WAITE   Waite Charles "Schoolboy" B9.9.1899 Brooklyn NY D8.25.1984 Cincinnati OH BR/TR/6-0/180 d7.24 HF1969

YEAR	TM LG	W	L	PCT	G	GS	CG-SHO	SV-BS	IP	H	R	HR	HB	BB-IB	SO	ERA	AERA	OAV	OOB	AB-HR-SH	AVG	PB	SUP	APR	DL	PW
1918	NY N	0	0	—	1	0	0	0	2	1	0	0	0	0	1	0.00	—	.000	.000	1	.000	-0		0		0.0
1919	Bos A	4	6	.400	13	11	6-1	0	105.1	99	42	1	0	22	28	3.25	93	.262	.303	38-0-2	.132	-3	83	-1		-0.3
1920	Bos A	6	6	.500	22	11	6-2	1	121.1	123	72	2	1	47	45	4.38	83	.270	.339	43-0-1	.116	-3	103	-11		-1.3
1921	†NY A	19	13	.594	43	32	21-1	3	282.1	301	121	3	5	81	102	3.09	137	.276	.329	99-0-9	.222	-2	102	35		3.3
1922	†NY A	19	12	.613	37	31	17-3	0	265	271	114	3	9	76	95	3.43	117	.269	.326	92-0-3	.217	1	94	19		2.0

YEAR	TM LG	W	L	PCT	G	GS	CG-SHO	SV-BS	IP	H	R	HR	HB	BB-IB	SO	ERA	AERA	OAV	OOB	AB-HR-SH	AVG	PB	SUP	APR	DL	PW
1923	†NY A	17	9	.654	37	28	19-1	1	238.2	227	97	9	4	66	60	3.02	131	.253	.307	84-0-6	.190	-2	91	21		1.8
1924	NY A	18	13	.581	46	32	14-2	4	247	295	117	8	3	76	71	3.79	110	.300	.352	75-0-12	.133	-5	96	11		0.7
1925	NY A	11	14	.440	46	30	17-1	6	243	283	124	14	1	78	86	4.00	107	.292	.346	79-0-8	.304	6	95	8		1.3
1926	NY A	16	12	.571	40	28	12-1	4	217.2	224	112	4	2	62	79	3.85	100	.264	.316	76-0-7	.211	-0	115	1		-0.1
1927	†NY A	22	7	.759	36	32	23-3	1	256.1	242	90	10	4	54	86	2.63	146	.251	.294	99-0-9	.222	0	145	38		3.8
1928	†NY A	23	7	.767	42	31	19-3	8	273	279	118	16	1	60	67	3.36	112	.272	.313	109-0-3	.257	2	146	15		1.6
1929	NY A	10	9	.526	30	25	12	1	201.2	219	115	9	3	69	57	4.24	91	.279	.339	76-0-8	.224	1	134	-9		-0.7
1930	NY A	2	5	.500	8	7	2	0	47.2	64	27	7	0	9	10	4.53	95	.317	.346	16-0-1	.063	-2	137	0		-0.2
	Det A	9	8	.529	26	20	8-1	4	135.2	176	89	7	2	47	25	4.78	100	.313	.368	46-0-2	.196	-2	81	-1		-0.5
	Year	11	10	.524	34	27	10-1	4	183.1	240	116	14	2	56	35	4.71	99	.314	.363	62-0-3	.161	-4	95	-1		-0.7
1931	Det A	3	8	.273	16	12	5	0	92	124	70	2	2	32	10	5.87	80	.319	.374	40-0-2	.133	-2	71	-12		-1.4
	†Phi A	10	5	.667	16	14	9-2	0	111	130	60	9	0	37	30	4.22	107	.298	.353	43-0-2	.302	3	109	4		-0.7
	Year	13	13	.500	32	26	14-2	0	203	254	130	11	2	69	40	4.97	91	.308	.363	73-0-2	.233	0	91	-7		-0.7
1932	Bro N	1	3	.250	8	4	0	1	26.2	38	27	3	0	12	7	7.76	49	.342	.407	6	.000	-1	61	-12		-1.6
	NY N	5	7	.417	18	12	3	0	97.1	103	43	6	5	25	29	3.42	109	.275	.328	31-0-2	.097	-2	83	4		-0.3
	Year	6	10	.375	26	16	3	1	124	141	70	9	5	37	36	4.35	86	.290	.347	37-0-2	.081	-3	77	-8		-1.3
1933	Pit N	5	7	.417	36	8	4-1	4	117	118	45	3	1	19	44	2.92	114	.262	.293	32	.156	-1	66	6		0.6
1934	Pit N	15	6	.714	48	17	8-3	5	190.2	184	75	7	2	43	105	2.93	141	.252	.296	56-0-2	.179	-1	95	23		2.3
1935	Pit N	7	11	.389	39	11	5	6	164	187	72	8	1	27	63	3.40	121	.285	.315	54-0-3	.259	2	75	15		1.7
1936	Pit N	7	5	.583	22	9	6	1	116.2	115	44	5	3	20	37	2.70	150	.255	.291	39-0-2	.154	-1	81	16		1.5
1937	Pit N	2	3	.333	11	0	0	2	28	31	14	3	0	6	21	4.50	86	.270	.306	12	.083	-1		-1		-0.2
	Bro N	7	7	.500	27	19	10-1	0	167	180	83	5	0	30	44	3.23	125	.270	.301	48-0-8	.083	-2	93	11		0.6
	Year	8	9	.471	38	19	10-1	0	195	211	97	8	0	36	65	3.42	117	.270	.302	60-0-8	.083	-3	94	9		-0.2
1938	Bro N	0	3	.000	6	1	0	0	16.1	24	14	1	0	5	3	4.96	79	.333	.377	3	.000	-0	43	-1		-0.2
Total 21		237	182	.566	674	425	226-26	52	3762.1	4037	1780	154	49	1003	1206	3.59	112	.276	.325	1287-0-91	.198	-17	104	179		15.7

HRABOSKY, AL
Alan Thomas "The Mad Hungarian" B7.21.1949 Oakland CA BR/TL/5-11/185* [StLN69*1/19] d6.16 Mil 1971 Col Fullerton (CA) JC

YEAR	TM LG	W	L	PCT	G	GS	CG-SHO	SV-BS	IP	H	R	HR	HB	BB-IB	SO	ERA	AERA	OAV	OOB	AB-HR-SH	AVG	PB	SUP	APR	DL	PW
1970	StL N	2	1	.667	16	1	0	0-1	19	22	10	2	0	7-1	12	4.74	88	.286	.345	3	.000	-0	65	-1		-0.2
1971	StL N	0	0	—	1	0	0	0-0	2	2	0	0	0	0-0	2	0.00	—	.250	.250	—	—	0		1		0.0
1972	StL N	1	0	1.000	5	0	0	0-0	7	2	0	0	0	3-0	9	0.00	—	.087	.185	1	.000	-0		3		0.4
1973	StL N	2	4	.333	44	0	0	5-1	56	45	15	2	2	21-6	57	2.09	176	.220	.297	4-0-1	.000	-0		10		1.1
1974	StL N	8	1	.889	65	0	0	9-4	88.1	71	34	3	1	38-7	82	2.95	122	.221	.221	13-0-1	.308	1*		6		0.8
1975	StL N	13	3	.813	65	0	0	22-6	97.1	72	27	3	1	33-8	82	1.66	228	.205	.273	15-0-3	.200	0		20		4.2
1976	StL N	8	6	.571	68	0	0	13-4	95.1	89	42	5	4	39-9	73	3.30	108	.252	.328	7-0-3	.000	0		2		-0.5
1977	StL N	6	5	.545	65	0	0	10-6	86.1	82	44	12	3	41-7	68	4.38	89	.256	.340	8	.000	-1		9		-0.4
1978	†KC A	8	7	.533	58	0	0	20-3	75	52	24	6	1	35-2	60	2.88	133	.200	.290	1	—	0		7		2.0
1979	KC A	9	4	.692	58	0	0	11-2	65	67	31	3	1	41-10	39	3.74	114	.272	.377	0	—	0		4		0.7
1980	Atl N	4	2	.667	45	0	0	3-3	59.2	50	27	8	0	31-5	31	3.62	102	.223	.313	1	.000	-0		0		-0.1
1981	Atl N	1	1	.500	24	0	0	1-0	33.2	24	5	1	0	9-1	13	1.07	330	.207	.260	1	.000	-0		9	26	0.5
1982	Atl N	2	1	.667	31	0	0	3-2	37.1	41	25	5	0	17-2	20	5.54	67	.285	.354	3	.333	-1		-5	21	-0.7
Total 13		64	35	.646	545	1	0	97-32	722	619	284	50	13	315-58	548	3.10	122	.234	.314	56-0-8	.143	0	65	53	47	8.5

HUBBELL, CARL
Carl Owen "King Carl","The Meal Ticket" B6.22.1903 Carthage MO D11.21.1988 Scottsdale AZ BR/TL(BB 1928-29, 31-32)/6-0/170 d7.26 HF1947

YEAR	TM LG	W	L	PCT	G	GS	CG-SHO	SV-BS	IP	H	R	HR	HB	BB-IB	SO	ERA	AERA	OAV	OOB	AB-HR-SH	AVG	PB	SUP	APR	DL	PW
1928	NY N	10	6	.625	20	14	8-1	1	124	117	49	7	3	21	37	2.83	138	.248	.284	47-0-1	.106	-3	101	13		1.4
1929	NY N	18	11	.621	39	35	19-1	1	268	273	128	17	6	67	106	3.69	124	.265	.313	93-0-7	.129	-6	116	28		2.2
1930	NY N	17	12	.586	37	32	17-3	2	241.2	263	120	11	11	58	117	3.87	122	.278	.327	86-0-10	.151	-5	104	25		1.9
1931	NY N	14	12	.538	36	30	21-4	3	248	211	88	14	4	67	155	2.65	139	.227	.282	83-0-6	.241	4	100	30		3.4
1932	NY N	18	11	.621	40	32	22	2	284	260	96	20	4	40	137	2.50	148	.238	.268	108-1-4	.241	4	107	40		4.7
1933	†NY N★	23	12	.657	45	33	22-10	5	308.2	256	69	6	3	47	156	1.66	193	.227	.260	109-1-5	.183	1	75	55		7.3
1934	NY N★	21	12	.636	49	35	25-5	8	313	286	100	17	2	37	118	2.30	168	.239	.263	117-0-3	.197	-1	103	55		5.9
1935	NY N☆	23	12	.657	42	35	24-1	0	302.2	314	125	27	3	49	150	3.27	118	.263	.294	109-1-2	.239	4	104	21		2.9
1936	†NY N★	26	6	.813	42	34	25-3	5	304	265	81	7	5	57	123	2.31	169	.236	.276	110-0-10	.227	1	92	60		6.2
1937	†NY N★	22	8	.733	39	32	18-4	4	261.2	261	108	18	3	55	159	3.20	122	.257	.298	97-0-3	.216	1	115	20		1.5
1938	NY N	13	10	.565	24	22	13-1	1	179	171	70	16	2	33	104	3.07	123	.249	.285	58-0-10	.155	-2	96	15		2.1
1939	NY N★	11	9	.550	29	18	10	1	154	150	60	11	2	24	62	2.75	143	.259	.280	81-0-2	.185	-0	111	5		0.0
1940	NY N	11	12	.478	31	28	11-2	0	214.1	220	102	22	2	59	86	3.65	106	.266	.309	80-0-2	.140	-2	90	3		-0.9
1941	NY N☆	11	9	.550	26	22	11-1	1	164	169	73	10	2	53	75	3.57	104	.266	.325	57-0-2	.183	-0	124	-7		-0.9
1942	NY N☆	11	8	.579	24	20	11	0	157.1	158	75	17	1	34	61	3.95	85	.259	.299	57-0-2	.183	-0	116	-7		0.0
1943	NY N	4	4	.500	12	11	3	0	66	87	36	7	0	24	31	4.91	70	.322	.378	20-0-4	.200	-0	116	-9		-1.0
Total 16		253	154	.622	535	433	260-36	33	3590.1	3461	1380	227	53	725	1677	2.98	130	.251	.291	1288-4-75	.191	-5	102	372		40.2

HUBBELL, BILL
Wilbert William B6.17.1897 San Francisco CA D8.3.1980 Lakewood CO BR/TR/6-1.5/195 d9.24 Col Idaho

YEAR	TM LG	W	L	PCT	G	GS	CG-SHO	SV-BS	IP	H	R	HR	HB	BB-IB	SO	ERA	AERA	OAV	OOB	AB-HR-SH	AVG	PB	SUP	APR	DL	PW
1919	NY N	1	1	.500	2	2	2	2	18.1	19	4	0	2	2	3	1.96	143	.260	.299	8	.125	-1	128	2		0.2
1920	NY N	0	1	.000	14	0	0	2	30	26	12	2	1	15	8	2.10	143	.239	.336	5	.200	-0		2		0.1
	Phi N	9	9	.500	24	18	9-1	2	150	176	77	3	4	42	26	3.84	89	.301	.352	53-0-2	.132	-3	83	-5		-1.0
	Year	9	10	.474	38	18	9-1	4	180	202	89	5	5	57	34	3.55	94	.291	.349	58-0-2	.138	-3	85	-5		-0.9
1921	Phi N	9	16	.360	36	30	15-1	2	220.1	269	146	18	3	38	43	4.33	98	.306	.337	75-1-1	.160	-2	83	-3		-0.4
1922	Phi N	7	15	.318	35	26	11-1	1	189	257	136	14	4	41	33	5.00	93	.317	.353	70-0-2	.171	-2	85	-6		-0.7
1923	Phi N	1	6	.143	12	5	1	0	55	102	70	13	2	17	8	8.35	55	.394	.435	17-0-2	.235	0*	79	-22		-2.3
1924	Phi N	10	9	.526	36	22	9-2	0	179	233	103	9	2	45	30	4.83	92	.324	.365	59-0-3	.220	-1	107	-3		-0.3
1925	Phi N	0	0	—	2	2	1	0	2.2	5	4	0	0	1	0	0.00	—	.385	.429	1-0-1	.000	-0		0		0.0
	Bro N	3	6	.333	33	5	3	1	86.2	120	59	8	2	24	16	5.30	79	.337	.382	20-0-1	.150	-0	77	-10		-0.8
	Year	3	6	.333	35	5	3	1	89.1	125	63	8	2	25	16	5.14	82	.339	.384	21-0-2	.143	0	76	-9		-0.8
Total 7		40	63	.388	204	108	50-5	10	931	1207	611	67	20	225	167	4.68	89	.317	.359	308-1-12	.172	-5	90	-45		-5.2

HUCKLEBERRY, EARL
Earl Eugene B5.23.1910 Konawa OK D2.25.1999 Seminole OK BR/TR/5-11/165 d9.13

YEAR	TM LG	W	L	PCT	G	GS	CG-SHO	SV-BS	IP	H	R	HR	HB	BB-IB	SO	ERA	AERA	OAV	OOB	AB-HR-SH	AVG	PB	SUP	APR	DL	PW
1935	Phi A	1	0	1.000	1	1	0	1	6.2	8	7	1	0	4	2	9.45	48	.296	.387	3	.000	-0	363	-3		-0.3

HUDEK, JOHN
John Raymond B8.8.1966 Tampa FL BB/TR/6-1/200* [ChiA88 10/249] d4.23 Col Florida Southern

YEAR	TM LG	W	L	PCT	G	GS	CG-SHO	SV-BS	IP	H	R	HR	HB	BB-IB	SO	ERA	AERA	OAV	OOB	AB-HR-SH	AVG	PB	SUP	APR	DL	PW
1994	Hou N★	0	2	.000	42	0	0	16-2	39.1	24	14	5	1	18-2	39	2.97	133	.174	.270	0	—	0		5		0.5
1995	Hou N	2	2	.500	19	0	0	7-2	20	19	12	3	0	6-0	29	5.40	72	.247	.293	1	1.000	1		-3	101	-0.8
1996	Hou N	2	0	1.000	15	0	0	2-0	16	12	5	2	0	5-2	14	2.81	138	.207	.270	0	—	0		2	105	0.3
1997	Hou N	1	3	.250	40	0	0	4-4	40.2	38	27	8	3	33-2	36	5.98	67	.252	.396	0	—	0		0		-0.8
1998	NY N	1	4	.200	28	0	0	0-0	27	23	13	2	2	19-3	28	4.00	103	.237	.367	0	—	0		0		0.0
	Cin N	4	2	.667	30	0	0	0-1	37	27	14	6	2	28-1	40	2.43	176	.206	.348	3-0-1	.000	-0		6		0.8
	Year	5	6	.455	58	0	0	0-1	64	50	27	8	4	47-4	68	3.09	136	.219	.356	3-0-1	.000	-0		6		0.8
1999	Cin N	0	1	.000	2	0	0	0-1	1	4	3	1	0	3-0	0	27.00	17	.667	.778	1	—	0		-2		-0.4
	Atl N	0	1	.000	15	0	0	0-0	16.2	21	14	1	1	11-0	18	6.48	69	.296	.393	1	.000	-0		-4	44	-0.2
	Year	0	2	.000	17	0	0	0-1	17.2	25	17	2	1	14-0	18	7.64	58	.325	.430	1	.000	-0		-7		-0.1
	Tor A	0	0	—	3	0	0	0-0	3.2	6	3	1	0	1-0	2	12.27	40	.471	.474	0	—	0		-3		-0.1
Total 6		10	15	.400	194	0	0	29-10	201.1	176	107	29	6	123-10	206	4.43	93	.236	.347	5-0-1	.200	0		-7	250	-0.4

HUDLIN, WILLIS
George Willis "Ace" B5.23.1906 Wagoner OK D8.5.2002 Little Rock AR BR/TR/6-0/190 d8.15 Mil 1944 C3

YEAR	TM LG	W	L	PCT	G	GS	CG-SHO	SV-BS	IP	H	R	HR	HB	BB-IB	SO	ERA	AERA	OAV	OOB	AB-HR-SH	AVG	PB	SUP	APR	DL	PW
1926	Cle A	1	3	.250	9	4	1	1	32.1	25	13	1	2	13	21	2.78	146	.227	.320	8-0-1	.125	0	83	4		0.5
1927	Cle A	18	12	.600	43	30	18-1	0	264.2	291	132	3	11	83	65	4.01	105	.283	.343	96-1-6	.250	2	105	9		1.2
1928	Cle A	14	14	.500	42	26	10	7	220.1	231	114	7	7	90	62	4.04	103	.279	.355	72-0-2	.194	-0	97	5		0.7
1929	Cle A	17	15	.531	40	33	22-2	1	280.1	299	122	7	1	73	60	3.34	133	.272	.318	97-0-8	.196	-3	81	34		3.5
1930	Cle A	13	16	.448	37	33	13-1	1	216.2	255	133	12	1	76	60	4.57	106	.293	.351	70-3-0	.219	-1	101	7		0.9
1931	Cle A	14	11	.517	44	34	15-1	4	254.1	313	155	14	1	88	83	4.60	100	.301	.356	100-0-2	.200	1	112	1		0.4
1932	Cle A	12	8	.600	33	21	12	2	181.2	204	108	10	1	59	65	4.71	101	.278	.332	64-0-3	.203	1	114	3		0.4
1933	Cle A	5	13	.278	34	17	6	1	147.1	161	85	7	3	61	44	3.97	112	.275	.346	41-1-5	.146	-1	72	5		0.6
1934	Cle A	15	10	.600	36	26	15-1	4	195	210	109	8	5	65	58	4.75	96	.277	.338	68-1-5	.206	3	108	1		0.6
1935	Cle A	15	11	.577	36	29	14-3	5	231.2	252	107	8	3	61	45	3.69	122	.277	.324	86-1-1	.200	6*	113	22		2.8
1936	Cle A	1	5	.167	27	7	1	0	64	112	74	1	2	31	20	9.00	56	.397	.460	18	.111	-1	80	-2		-2.0
1937	Cle A	12	11	.522	35	23	10-2	2	175.2	213	106	9	2	61	31	4.10	112	.295	.337	59-0-5	.169	-1	96	4		0.5

YEAR	TM LG	W	L	PCT	G	GS	CG-SHO	SV-BS	IP	H	R	HR	HB	BB-IB	SO	ERA	AERA	OAV	OOB	AB-HR-SH	AVG	PB	SUP	APR	DL	PW
1938	Cle A	8	8	.500	29	15	8	1	127	158	80	13	2	45	27	4.89	95	.303	.361	43-0-2	.116	-2	119	-4		-0.6
1939	Cle A	9	10	.474	27	20	7	3	143	175	85	6	1	42	28	4.91	90	.303	.352	48-1-3	.188	1	88	-7		-0.5
1940	Cle A	2	1	.667	4	4	2	0	23.2	31	13	3	0	2	8	4.94	85	.316	.330	8	.125	-0	115	-1		-0.5
	Was A	1	2	.333	8	6	1	0	37.1	50	33	9	2	5	9	6.51	64	.314	.343	10-0-2	.100	-1	133	-11		-0.8
	StL A	0	1	.000	6	1	0	0	11.1	19	16	0	0	8	4	11.12	41	.358	.443	2	.500	-0	77	-8		-0.5
	Year	3	4	.429	18	11	3	0	72.1	100	62	12	2	15	21	6.72	63	.323	.358	20-0-2	.150	-1	120	-20		-1.4
	NY N	0	1	.000	1	1	0	0	5	9	6	1	0	1	1	10.80	36	.409	.435	1	.000	-0	22	-3		-0.5
1944	StL A	0	1	.000	1	0	0	0	2	3	2	0	0	0	1	4.50	80	.300	.300	0	—	0		-1		-0.1
Total	16	158	156	.503	491	328	155-11	31	2613.1	3011	1493	118	44	846	677	4.41	102	.289	.345	894-5-48	.201	4	101	32		6.9

HUDSON, CHARLIE Charles B8.18.1949 Ada OK BL/TL/6-3/185* [NYN67 10/184] d5.21

YEAR	TM LG	W	L	PCT	G	GS	CG-SHO	SV-BS	IP	H	R	HR	HB	BB-IB	SO	ERA	AERA	OAV	OOB	AB-HR-SH	AVG	PB	SUP	APR	DL	PW
1972	StL N	1	0	1.000	12	0	0	0	12.1	10	8	0	1	7-0	4	5.11	67	.233	.353	0	—	0		-2		-0.2
1973	Tex A	4	2	.667	25	4	1-1	1-1	62.1	59	35	3	0	31-2	34	4.62	81	.254	.335	0	—	0	89	-5	47	-0.5
1975	Cal A	0	1	.000	3	1	0	0-0	5.2	7	6	0	0	4-0	0	9.53	38	.304	.407	0	—	0	98	-5		-0.5
Total	3	5	3	.625	40	5	1-1	1-1	80.1	76	49	3	1	42-2	38	5.04	73	.255	.343	0	—	0	92	-11	47	-1.2

HUDSON, CHARLES Charles Lynn B3.16.1959 Ennis TX BB/TR/6-3/185* [PhiN81 12/305] d5.31 Col Prairie View A&M

YEAR	TM LG	W	L	PCT	G	GS	CG-SHO	SV-BS	IP	H	R	HR	HB	BB-IB	SO	ERA	AERA	OAV	OOB	AB-HR-SH	AVG	PB	SUP	APR	DL	PW
1983	†Phi N	8	8	.500	26	26	3	0-0	169.1	158	73	10	0	53-6	101	3.35	108	.248	.304	54-0-5	.093	-2*	125	5		0.2
1984	Phi N	9	11	.450	30	30	1-1	0-0	173.2	181	101	12	2	52-4	94	4.04	91	.265	.316	56-0-4	.089	-2	97	-11	22	-1.5
1985	Phi N	8	13	.381	38	26	3	0-0	193	198	92	23	1	74-7	122	3.78	98	.252	.319	57-0-3	.140	-1	116	-1		-0.3
1986	Phi N	7	10	.412	33	23	0	0-0	144	165	87	20	0	58-1	82	4.94	79	.291	.355	43-0-7	.047	-3*	90	-14		-1.9
1987	NY A	11	7	.611	35	16	6-2	0-0	154.2	137	63	19	3	57-1	100	3.61	123	.239	.308	0	—	0	109	16		1.6
1988	NY A	6	6	.500	28	12	1	2-0	106.1	93	53	9	4	36-4	53	4.49	89	.235	.301	0	—	0	117	-4	34	-1.4
1989	Det N	1	5	.167	18	7	0	0-0	66.2	75	49	14	2	31-3	23	6.35	60	.288	.367	0	—	0*	98	-17	30	-1.4
Total	7	50	60	.455	208	140	14-3	2-0	1007.2	997	518	110	12	361-26	580	4.14	93	.258	.321	210-0-19	.095	-8	107	-26	86	-3.7

HUDSON, HAL Hal Campbell "Bud","Lefty" B5.4.1927 Grosse Pointe MI BL/TL/5-10/175* d4.20

YEAR	TM LG	W	L	PCT	G	GS	CG-SHO	SV-BS	IP	H	R	HR	HB	BB-IB	SO	ERA	AERA	OAV	OOB	AB-HR-SH	AVG	PB	SUP	APR	DL	PW
1952	StL A	0	0	—	3	0	0	0	5.2	9	8	0	0	6	0	12.71	31	.360	.484	1	.000	-0		-5		-0.3
	Chi A	0	0	—	2	0	0	0	4	7	2	0	0	1	4	2.25	162	.389	.421	0	—	0		-5		-0.3
	Year	0	0	—	5	0	0	0	9.2	16	10	0	0	7	4	8.38	45	.372	.460	1	.000	-0		-5		-0.3
1953	Chi A	0	0	—	1	0	0	0	0.2	0	0	0	0	0	0	0.00	—	.000	.000	0	—	0		0		0.0
Total	2	0	0	—	6	0	0	0	10.1	16	10	0	0	7	4	7.84	49	.364	.451	1	.000	-0		-5		-0.3

HUDSON, JESSE Jesse James B7.22.1948 Mansfield LA BL/TL/6-2/170 d9.19

YEAR	TM LG	W	L	PCT	G	GS	CG-SHO	SV-BS	IP	H	R	HR	HB	BB-IB	SO	ERA	AERA	OAV	OOB	AB-HR-SH	AVG	PB	SUP	APR	DL	PW
1969	NY N	0	0	—	1	0	0	0-0	2	2	1	0	0	2-0	3	4.50	81	.250	.400	0	—	0		0		0.0

HUDSON, JOE Joseph Paul B9.29.1970 Philadelphia PA BR/TR/6-1/175* [BosA92 27/758] d6.10 Col West Virginia

YEAR	TM LG	W	L	PCT	G	GS	CG-SHO	SV-BS	IP	H	R	HR	HB	BB-IB	SO	ERA	AERA	OAV	OOB	AB-HR-SH	AVG	PB	SUP	APR	DL	PW
1995	†Bos A	0	1	.000	39	0	0	1-3	46	53	21	2	2	23-1	29	4.11	118	.301	.386	0	—	0		5		0.2
1996	Bos A	3	5	.375	36	0	0	1-4	45	57	35	4	0	32-4	19	5.40	94	.318	.418	0	—	0		-3		-0.5
1997	Bos A	3	1	.750	26	0	0	0-0	35.2	39	16	1	4	14-2	14	3.53	132	.289	.373	0	—	0		4		0.4
1998	Mil N	0	0	—	1	0	0	0-0	0.1	0	2	6	0	4-1	0	162.00	3	1.000	.857	0	—	0		-5		-0.2
Total	4	6	7	.462	102	0	0	2-7	127	151	78	7	6	73-8	62	4.82	101	.307	.400	0	—	0		1		-0.1

HUDSON, LUKE Luke Stephen B5.2.1977 Fountain Valley CA BR/TR/6-3/195* [ColN98 4/120] d7.1 Col Tennessee

YEAR	TM LG	W	L	PCT	G	GS	CG-SHO	SV-BS	IP	H	R	HR	HB	BB-IB	SO	ERA	AERA	OAV	OOB	AB-HR-SH	AVG	PB	SUP	APR	DL	PW
2002	Cin N	0	0	—	3	0	0	0-0	6	5	5	1	0	6-0	7	4.50	95	.227	.393	0-0-1	—	0		-1		-0.1
2004	Cin N	4	2	.667	9	9	0	0-0	48.1	36	16	3	2	25-1	38	2.42	178	.208	.312	16	.125	-0	98	9		1.0
2005	Cin N	6	9	.400	19	16	0	0-0	84.2	83	62	14	11	50-2	53	6.38	65	.268	.384	25-0-2	.320	3*	120	-20	67	-2.6
Total	3	10	11	.476	31	25	0	0-0	139	124	83	18	13	81-3	98	4.92	86	.246	.360	41-0-3	.244	3	112	-12	67	-1.7

HUDSON, NAT Nathaniel P. B1.12.1859 Chicago IL D3.14.1928 Chicago IL BR/TR d4.18

YEAR	TM LG	W	L	PCT	G	GS	CG-SHO	SV-BS	IP	H	R	HR	HB	BB-IB	SO	ERA	AERA	OAV	OOB	AB-HR-SH	AVG	PB	SUP	APR	DL	PW
1886	†StL AA	16	10	.615	29	27	25	1	234.1	224	122	3	2	62	100	3.03	113	.243	.293	150	.233	1*	119	15		1.3
1887	StL AA	4	4	.500	9	9	7	0	67	91	57	2	4	20	15	4.97	91	.305	.357	48	.250	0*	89	-3		-0.3
1888	StL AA	25	10	.714	39	37	36-5	0	333	283	155	8	15	59	130	2.54	128	.222	.264	196-2	.255	5*	120	28		2.9
1889	StL AA	3	2	.600	5	5	4	0	60	71	47	2	4	15	13	4.20	101	.285	.336	52-1	.250	0*	82	0		0.0
Total	4	48	26	.649	86	78	72-5	1	694.1	669	381	15	25	156	258	3.08	114	.244	.291	446-3	.247	6	113	40		3.9

HUDSON, REX Rex Haughton B8.11.1953 Tulsa OK BB/TR/5-11/165 d7.27

YEAR	TM LG	W	L	PCT	G	GS	CG-SHO	SV-BS	IP	H	R	HR	HB	BB-IB	SO	ERA	AERA	OAV	OOB	AB-HR-SH	AVG	PB	SUP	APR	DL	PW
1974	LA N	0	0	—	1	0	0	0-0	2	6	3	0	0	0-0	0	22.50	15	.500	.500	0	—	0		-4		-0.2

HUDSON, SID Sidney Charles B1.3.1915 Coalfield TN BR/TR/6-4/180* d4.18 Mil 1943-45 C14

YEAR	TM LG	W	L	PCT	G	GS	CG-SHO	SV-BS	IP	H	R	HR	HB	BB-IB	SO	ERA	AERA	OAV	OOB	AB-HR-SH	AVG	PB	SUP	APR	DL	PW
1940	Was A	17	16	.515	38	31	19-3	1	252	272	149	26	3	81	96	4.57	91	.274	.330	93-0-2	.237	2	93	-11		-1.0
1941	Was A★	13	14	.481	33	33	17-3	0	249.2	242	124	12	1	97	108	3.46	117	.253	.322	86-0-6	.186	-0	95	12		1.3
1942	Was A☆	10	17	.370	35	31	19-1	2	239.1	266	140	9	5	70	72	4.36	84	.276	.328	89-0-2	.213	1*	94	-20		-1.7
1946	Was A	8	11	.421	31	16	6-1	1	142.1	160	75	9	4	37	35	3.60	93	.280	.328	43-0-1	.279	3	89	-7		-0.5
1947	Was A	6	9	.400	20	17	5-1	0	106	113	66	8	1	58	37	5.60	66	.272	.363	39	.308	3	73	-18		-2.0
1948	Was A	4	16	.200	34	29	4	1	182	217	128	11	6	107	53	5.88	74	.299	.394	59-0-3	.237	2	77	-28		-2.2
1949	Was A	8	17	.320	40	27	11-2	1	209	234	117	11	5	91	54	4.22	101	.283	.357	67-0-5	.239	2	74	-1		0.2
1950	Was A	14	14	.500	30	30	17	0	237.2	261	129	17	6	98	75	4.09	110	.284	.356	93-0-3	.215	-1*	92	9		0.9
1951	Was A	5	12	.294	23	19	8	0	138.2	168	90	8	4	52	43	5.13	80	.302	.365	44-0-1	.273	2*	71	-17		-1.5
1952	Was A	3	4	.429	7	7	6	0	62.2	59	22	4	0	29	24	2.73	130	.257	.340	24-0-1	.167	-0	77	6		0.7
	Bos A	7	9	.438	21	18	7	0	134.1	145	64	9	7	36	50	3.62	109	.276	.330	46	.174	-1	89	3		0.5
	Year	10	13	.435	28	25	13	0	197	204	86	13	7	65	74	3.34	114	.270	.333	70-0-1	.171	-1	86	10		1.2
1953	Bos A	6	9	.400	30	17	4	2	156	164	65	13	4	49	60	3.52	120	.269	.327	50-0-2	.140	-2	80	14		1.0
1954	Bos A	3	4	.429	33	5	0	5	71.1	82	45	5	2	30	24	4.42	93	.296	.363	13	.154	-1	77	-3		-0.4
Total	12	104	152	.406	380	279	123-11	13	2181	2384	1212	136	48	835	734	4.28	95	.278	.345	746-0-26	.220	9	85	-61		-4.7

HUDSON, TIM Timothy Adam B7.14.1975 Columbus GA BR/TR/6-1/165* [OakA97 6/185] d6.8 Col Auburn-Montgomery

YEAR	TM LG	W	L	PCT	G	GS	CG-SHO	SV-BS	IP	H	R	HR	HB	BB-IB	SO	ERA	AERA	OAV	OOB	AB-HR-SH	AVG	PB	SUP	APR	DL	PW
1999	Oak A	11	2	.846	21	21	1	0-0	136.1	121	56	8	4	62-2	132	3.23	146	.237	.323	4	.250	1*	125	23		2.0
2000	†Oak A★	**20**	6	.769	32	32	2-2	0-0	202.1	169	100	24	7	82-5	169	4.14	117	.227	.306	3	.000	-0*	118	18		1.9
2001	†Oak A	18	9	.667	35	**35**	3-2	0-0	235	216	100	20	6	71-5	181	3.37	135	.245	.303	8	.000	-1*	96	29		3.1
2002	†Oak A	15	9	.625	34	34	4-2	0-0	238.1	237	87	19	8	62-9	152	2.98	150	.263	.314	5	.200	1	91	39		3.8
2003	†Oak A	16	7	.696	34	34	3-2	0-0	240	197	84	15	10	61-9	162	2.70	170	.223	.280	3	.333	-1	110	48		4.5
2004	Oak A*	12	6	.667	27	27	3-2	0-0	188.2	194	82	8	12	44-3	103	3.53	131	.267	.318	3	.000	-0	87	22	45	1.9
2005	†Atl N	14	9	.609	29	29	2	0-0	192	194	79	20	9	65-5	115	3.52	122	.265	.332	65-0-4	.138	-0	101	16	32	2.0
Total	7	106	48	.688	212	212	18-12	0-0	1432.2	1328	588	114	56	447-38	1014	3.33	138	.247	.309	91-0-4	.132	0	103	195	77	19.2

HUENKE, AL Albert Alfred B6.26.1891 New Bremen OH D9.20.1974 St.Marys OH BR/TR/6-0/175 d10.6

YEAR	TM LG	W	L	PCT	G	GS	CG-SHO	SV-BS	IP	H	R	HR	HB	BB-IB	SO	ERA	AERA	OAV	OOB	AB-HR-SH	AVG	PB	SUP	APR	DL	PW
1914	NY N	0	0	—	1	0	0	0	2	2	1	0	0	2	2	4.50	59	.250	.250	1	.000	-0		0		0.0

HUFFMAN, PHIL Phillip Lee B6.20.1958 Freeport TX BR/TR/6-2/180* [SFN77 2/36] d4.10

YEAR	TM LG	W	L	PCT	G	GS	CG-SHO	SV-BS	IP	H	R	HR	HB	BB-IB	SO	ERA	AERA	OAV	OOB	AB-HR-SH	AVG	PB	SUP	APR	DL	PW
1979	Tor A	6	18	.250	31	31	2-1	0-0	173	220	130	26	4	68-0	56	5.77	76	.304	.361	0	—	0	86	-28		-3.2
1985	Bal A	0	0	—	2	1	0	0-0	4.2	7	8	1	0	5-1	2	15.43	26	.350	.480	0	—	0	201	-6		-0.3
Total	2	6	18	.250	33	32	2-1	0-0	177.2	227	138	26	4	73-1	58	6.03	73	.305	.365	0	—	0	89	-34		-3.5

HUGHES, ED Edward J. B10.5.1880 Chicago IL D10.14.1927 McHenry IL BR/TR/6-1/180 d8.29.1902 b-Tom

YEAR	TM LG	W	L	PCT	G	GS	CG-SHO	SV-BS	IP	H	R	HR	HB	BB-IB	SO	ERA	AERA	OAV	OOB	AB-HR-SH	AVG	PB	SUP	APR	DL	PW
1905	Bos A	3	2	.600	6	4	2	0	33.1	38	27	0	1	9	8	4.59	59	.288	.338	14	.214	-0	144	-9		-1.2
1906	Bos A	0	0	—	2	0	0	0	10	15	7	0	0	3	3	5.40	51	.349	.391	3	.000	-0		-2		-0.2
Total	2	3	2	.600	8	4	2	0	43.1	53	34	0	1	12	11	4.78	57	.303	.351	17	.176	-1	144	-11		-1.4

HUGHES, JAY James Jay B1.22.1874 Sacramento CA D6.2.1924 Sacramento CA BR/TR/?/185 d4.18 b-Mickey

YEAR	TM LG	W	L	PCT	G	GS	CG-SHO	SV-BS	IP	H	R	HR	HB	BB-IB	SO	ERA	AERA	OAV	OOB	AB-HR-SH	AVG	PB	SUP	APR	DL	PW
1898	Bal N	23	12	.657	38	35	31-5	0	300.2	268	152	4	18	100	81	3.20	112	.237	.309	164-2-3	.226	4*	126	14		1.9
1899	Bro N	**28**	6	**.824**	35	35	30-3	0	291.2	250	121	6	14	119	99	2.68	146	.231	.316	107-0-2	.252	5	119	40		4.6
1901	Bro N	17	12	.586	31	29	24	0	250.2	265	125	9	12	102	96	3.27	103	.269	.345	91-0-5	.176	-1	125	4		0.3
1902	Bro N	15	10	.600	30	29	26	0	245	223	114	3	9	51	92	2.87	97	.243	.289	91-1-1	.209	4*	104	-5		0.0
Total	4	83	40	.675	134	128	111-8	0	1088	1006	512	16	53	372	368	3.00	114	.245	.315	453-3-11	.219	13	120	53		6.8

YEAR	TM LG	W	L	PCT	G	GS	CG-SHO	SV-BS	IP	H	R	HR	HB	BB-IB	SO	ERA	AERA	OAV	OOB	AB-HR-SH	AVG	PB	SUP	APR	DL	PW
HUGHES, JIM	James Michael			B7.2.1951 Los Angeles CA			BR/TR/6-3/185*	[MinA69 33/760]	d9.14																	
1974	Min A	0	2	.000	2	2	1	0-0	10.1	8	8	2	0	4-0	8	5.23	72	.216	.293	0	—	0	47	-2		-0.4
1975	Min A	16	14	.533	37	34	12-2	0-0	249.2	241	119	17	13	127-3	130	3.82	100	.255	.350	0	—	0	99	1		0.2
1976	Min A	9	14	.391	37	26	3	0-0	177	190	113	17	8	73-2	87	4.98	72	.281	.354	0	—	0	116	-27		-3.2
1977	Min A	0	0	—	2	0	0	0-0	4.1	4	1	0	0	1-0	1	2.08	192	.250	.278	0	—	0	1			0.0
Total	4	25	30	.455	78	62	16-2	0-0	441.1	443	241	36	21	205-5	226	4.30	87	.265	.350	0	—	0	104	-27		-3.4
HUGHES, JIM	James Robert			B3.21.1923 Chicago IL			D8.13.2001 Palos Heights IL	BR/TR/6-1/200(185-200)	d9.13																	
1952	Bro N	2	1	.667	6	0	0	0	18.2	16	4	0	0	11	8	1.45	252	.235	.342	4-0-1	.000	-0		4		0.6
1953	†Bro N	4	3	.571	48	0	0	9	85.2	80	33	6	1	41	49	3.47	123	.245	.332	14-0-1	.286	1		9		0.9
1954	Bro N	8	4	.667	60	0	0	24	86.2	76	36	7	0	44	58	3.22	127	.239	.326	16-0-1	.188	-0		8		1.3
1955	Bro N	0	2	.000	24	0	0	6	42.2	41	22	10	0	19-1	20	4.22	96	.256	.333	10	.000	-2		0		-0.1
1956	Bro N	0	0	—	5	0	0	0	12	10	7	3	0	4-1	8	5.25	76	.233	.298	2	.000	0		-1		-0.1
	Chi N	1	3	.250	25	1	0	0	45.1	43	35	4	4	30-5	20	5.16	73	.259	.379	7	.286	1	70	-9		-0.7
	Year	1	3	.250	30	1	0	0	57.1	53	42	7	4	34-6	28	5.18	74	.254	.364	9	.222	1	69	-11		-0.8
1957	Chi A	0	0	—	4	0	0	0	5	12	6	0	0	3-0	2	10.80	35	.462	.517	0	—	0		-4		-0.2
Total	6	15	13	.536	172	1	0	39	296	278	143	30	5	152-7	165	3.83	106	.251	.341	53-0-3	.170	-1	66	7		1.6
HUGHES, MICKEY	Michael J.			B10.25.1866 New York NY			D4.10.1931 Jersey City NJ	TR/5-6/165	d4.22 b-Jay																	
1888	Bro AA	25	13	.658	40	40	40-2	0	363	281	163	5	6	98	159	2.13	140	.206	.262	139	.137	-7	105	31		2.1
1889	†Bro AA	9	8	.529	20	17	13	0	153	172	120	6	7	86	54	4.35	86	.275	.369	68	.176	-3	135	-16		-1.6
1890	Bro N	4	4	.500	9	8	6	0	66.1	77	46	1	4	30	22	5.16	67	.281	.360	26	.038	-4	89	-8		-1.1
	Phi AA	1	3	.250	6	5	4	0	41.1	64	56	0	5	21	15	5.44	71	.344	.425	16	.125	-1	73	-14		-1.1
Total	3	39	28	.582	75	70	63-2	0	623.2	594	385	12	22	235	250	3.22	102	.243	.314	249	.137	-14	109	-7		-1.7
HUGHES, DICK	Richard Henry			B2.13.1938 Stephens AR			BR/TR/6-3/195*	d9.11 Col Arkansas-Monticello																		
1966	StL N	2	1	.667	6	2	1-1	1	21	12	4	0	2	7-3	22	1.71	209	.162	.253	5-0-1	.400	1	98	5		0.8
1967	†StL N	16	6	**.727**	37	27	12-3	3	222.1	164	72	22	5	48-6	161	2.67	123	**.203**	**.251**	78-0-4	.128	-1*	101	17		1.4
1968	†StL N	2	2	.500	25	5	0	4	63.2	45	25	7	0	21-3	49	3.53	82	.202	.269	15-0-1	.000	-1	150	-3	22	-0.3
Total	3	20	9	.690	68	34	13-4	8	307	221	101	29	7	76-12	230	2.79	116	.200	.255	98-0-6	.122	-2	108	19	22	1.9
HUGHES, TOM	Thomas Edward			B9.13.1934 Ancon, Canal Zone			BL/TR/6-2/180	d9.13																		
1959	StL N	0	2	.000	2	2	0	0	4	9	9	2	0	2-0	2	15.75	27	.409	.458	1	.000	-0	32	-5		-0.9
HUGHES, TOM	Thomas James "Long Tom"			B11.29.1878 Chicago IL			D2.8.1956 Chicago IL	BR/TR/6-1/175	d9.7 b-Ed																	
1900	Chi N	1	1	.500	3	3	3	0	21	31	14	0	1	7	12	5.14	70	.341	.394	6	.000	-0	77	-2		-0.2
1901	Chi N	10	23	.303	37	35	32-1	0	308.1	309	166	4	17	115	225	3.24	100	.259	.333	118-0-4	.119	-8*	89	1		-0.4
1902	Bal A	7	5	.583	13	13	12-1	0	108.1	120	57	2	2	32	45	3.90	97	.281	.334	43-0-4	.140	-2	119	2		0.0
	Bos A	3	3	.500	9	8	4	0	49.1	51	31	0	1	24	15	3.28	109	.267	.352	30	.367	2*	136	0		0.2
	Year	10	8	.556	22	21	16-1	0	157.2	171	88	2	3	56	60	3.71	100	.277	.340	73-0-4	.233	0	125	2		0.2
1903	†Bos A	20	7	.741	33	31	25-5	0	244.2	232	95	5	9	60	112	2.57	118	.249	.301	54-0-2	.241	1*	105	-13		-1.7
1904	NY A	7	11	.389	19	18	12-1	0	136.1	141	72	3	5	48	75	3.70	73	.268	.334	50-0-2	.241	1*	73	-12		-1.0
	Was A	3	12	.200	16	14	14	0	124.1	133	67	4	6	34	48	3.47	77	.274	.330	57-1-2	.228	3*	73	-12		-1.2
	Year	10	23	.303	35	32	26-1	0	260.2	274	139	7	11	82	123	3.59	75	.271	.332	111-1-4	.234	4	91	-23		-2.7
1905	Was A	17	20	.459	39	35	26-6	0	291.1	239	113	3	10	79	149	2.35	113	.225	.285	104-1-1	.212	4	104	8		1.3
1906	Was A	7	17	.292	30	24	18-1	0	204	230	118	5	3	81	90	3.62	73	.287	.355	66-1-2	.212	3	84	-24		-2.6
1907	Was A	7	14	.333	34	23	18-2	4	211	206	104	1	12	47	102	3.11	78	.258	.309	80-1-3	.237	3*	94	-16		-1.1
1908	Was A	18	15	.545	43	31	24-3	4	276.1	224	91	8	6	77	165	2.21	103	.227	.287	87-0-8	.195	-2	81	6		1.0
1909	Was A	4	7	.364	22	13	7-2	1	120.1	113	56	1	5	33	77	2.69	90	.246	.303	36-0-3	.083	-2	98	-6		-0.7
1911	Was A	11	17	.393	34	27	17-2	0	223	251	128	7	4	77	86	3.47	96	.288	.348	81-0-1	.185	-1	90	-6		-0.9
1912	Was A	13	10	.565	31	26	11-1	0	196	201	99	8	6	78	108	2.94	113	.270	.344	67-0-3	.194	1	102	6		0.7
1913	Was A	4	12	.250	36	12	4	6	129.2	129	81	6	15	61	59	4.30	69	.265	.365	36-0-1	.111	-1	84	-19		-2.4
Total	13	132	174	.431	399	313	227-25	15	2644	2610	1292	52	102	853	1368	3.09	93	.260	.324	958-6-39	.198	12	99	-62		-6.4
HUGHES, TOM	Thomas L. "Salida Tom"			B1.28.1884 Coal Creek CO			D11.1.1961 Los Angeles CA	BR/TR/6-2/175	d9.18																	
1906	NY A	1	0	1.000	3	1	1	0	15	11	8	2	0	1	5	4.20	71	.208	.222	5	.200	0	121	-1		-0.1
1907	NY A	2	0	1.000	4	3	2	0	27	16	10	0	2	11	10	2.67	105	.174	.276	7-0-1	.143	-0	121	1		0.0
1909	NY A	7	8	.467	24	15	9-2	2	118.2	109	43	3	4	37	69	2.65	94	.249	.313	39-1-1	.128	-1	104	2		0.2
1910	NY A	7	9	.438	23	15	11	1	151.2	153	77	2	3	37	64	3.50	76	.271	.320	55-0-2	.164	-1	89	-12		-1.3
1914	Bos N	2	0	1.000	2	2	1	0	17	14	7	0	0	4	11	2.65	104	.226	.273	7	.000	-1	156	0		0.2
1915	Bos N	16	14	.533	50	25	17-4	9	280.1	208	88	4	11	58	171	2.12	122	.213	.265	90-1-5	.100	-3	72	16		1.3
1916	Bos N	16	3	**.842**	40	13	7-1	5	161	121	46	2	8	51	97	2.35	106	.215	.290	52-0-2	.192	2	123	6		1.0
1917	Bos N	5	3	.625	11	8	6-2	0	74	54	21	1	3	30	44	1.95	131	.216	.307	24-0-1	.000	-3*	118	5		0.7
1918	Bos N	0	2	.000	3	3	1	0	18.1	17	10	1	0	6	9	3.44	78	.250	.311	6-1-0	.333	1	66	-2		0.0
Total	9	56	39	.589	160	85	55-9	17	863	703	309	15	31	235	476	2.56	102	.229	.291	285-3-12	.130	-4	97	15		1.2
HUGHES, TOMMY	Thomas Owen			B10.7.1919 Wilkes-Barre PA			D11.28.1990 Wilkes-Barre PA	BR/TR/6-1/190	d4.19 Mil 1943-45																	
1941	Phi N	9	14	.391	34	24	5-2	0	170	187	106	12	4	82	59	4.45	83	.280	.362	55-0-4	.200	0*	74	-18		-2.0
1942	Phi N	12	18	.400	40	31	19	1	253	224	105	8	0	99	77	3.06	108	.238	.310	80-0-7	.100	-5*	61	4		0.1
1946	Phi N	6	9	.400	29	13	3-2	1	111	123	64	5	1	44	34	4.38	78	.281	.349	31-0-2	.097	-1	58	-12		-1.7
1947	Phi N	4	11	.267	29	15	4-1	1	127	121	52	5	0	59	44	3.47	115	.265	.350	40-0-1	.050	-4*	57	10		0.7
1948	Cin N	0	4	.000	12	4	0	0	27	43	28	3	0	24	7	9.00	43	.364	.472	7	.143	-0	28	-14		-1.8
Total	5	31	56	.356	144	87	31-5	3	688	698	355	33	5	308	221	3.92	91	.266	.344	213-0-14	.117	-10	62	-30		-4.7
HUGHES, TRAVIS	Travis Wade			B5.25.1978 Newton KS			BR/TR/6-5/240*	[TexA97 19/587]	d9.26 Col Cowley Co. (KS) CC																	
2004	Tex A	0	0	—	2	0	0	0-0	1.1	1	2	0	0	2-0	4	13.50	37	.500	.600	0	—	0		-1		-0.1
2005	Was N	1	1	.500	14	0	0	0-1	13	18	8	4	1	8-1	8	5.54	73	.333	.429	0	—	0		-2		-0.3
Total	2	1	1	.500	16	0	0	0-1	14.1	22	10	4	1	10-1	12	6.28	66	.355	.452	0	—	0		-3		-0.4
HUGHES, VERN	Vernon Alexander "Lefty"			B4.15.1893 Etna PA			D9.26.1961 Sewickley PA	BL/TL/5-10/155	d7.6																	
1914	Bal F	0	0	—	3	0	0	0	5.2	5	4	0	0	3	1	3.18	95	.250	.348	1	.000	-0		-1		-0.1
HUGHES, BILL	William Nesbert			B11.18.1896 Philadelphia PA			D2.25.1963 Birmingham AL	BR/TR/5-10.5/155	d9.15																	
1921	Pit N	0	0	—	1	0	0	0	2	3	1	0	1	1	2	4.50	85	.375	.500	0	—	0		0		0.0
HUGHES, BILL	William R.			B11.25.1866 Blandinsville IL			D8.25.1943 Santa Ana CA	BL/TL	d9.28.1884 ▲																	
1885	Phi AA	0	2	.000	2	2	2	0	16.2	18	17	0	2	10	4	4.86	71	.269	.380	16	.188	0*	137	-2		-0.2
HUGHEY, JIM	James Ulysses "Coldwater Jim"			B3.8.1869 Wakeshma MI			D3.29.1945 Coldwater MI	TR/6-0/?	d9.29																	
1891	Mil AA	1	0	1.000	2	1	1	0	15	18	6	0	3	9	9	3.00	146	.286	.318	7	.143	-1	113	3		0.1
1893	Chi N	0	1	.000	2	1	1	0	9	14	16	0	1	4	2	11.00	42	.341	.400	2	.000	0	113	-6		-0.4
1896	Pit N	6	8	.429	25	14	11	0	155	191	108	3	7	67	48	4.99	84	.278	.355	65	.215	-1	121	-12		-1.7
1897	Pit N	6	10	.375	25	17	13	1	149.1	193	115	3	7	45	38	5.06	82	.310	.364	63-0-1	.127	-5	93	-15		-1.7
1898	StL N	7	24	.226	35	33	31	0	283.2	325	169	2	11	71	74	3.93	96	.285	.333	97-1-3	.113	-5	66	-3		-0.8
1899	Cle N	4	30	.118	36	34	32	0	283	403	244	9	22	88	54	5.41	68	.334	.389	111-0-3	.162	-5	76	-59		-6.0
1900	StL N	5	7	.417	20	12	11	0	112.2	147	90	4	6	40	23	5.19	70	.314	.375	41	.171	0	97	-18		-1.6
Total	7	29	80	.266	145	113	100	1	1007.2	1271	748	21	54	317	250	4.87	80	.306	.363	386-1-7	.153	-17	85	-110		-11.4
HUGHSON, TEX	Cecil Carlton			B2.9.1916 Buda TX			D8.6.1993 San Marcos TX	BR/TR/6-3/198	d4.16 Mil 1944-45 Col Texas																	
1941	Bos A	5	3	.625	12	4	3	0	61	70	30	3	1	19	22	4.13	101	.289	.328	17-0-3	.059	-1	86	1		0.1
1942	Bos A☆	22	6	.786	38	30	22-4	4	281	258	92	10	1	75	113	2.59	144	.245	.296	102-0-7	.176	1	123	35		3.1
1943	Bos A★	12	15	.444	32	32	20-4	2	266	242	87	23	2	73	114	2.64	126	.247	.300	86-0-10	.105	-4	85	20		2.1
1944	Bos A★	18	5	**.783**	28	23	19-2	5	203.1	172	57	4	2	41	112	2.26	151	.225	**.267**	66-0-10	.152	-1	140	27		3.1
1946	†Bos A	20	11	.645	39	35	21-6	3	278	252	89	15	2	51	172	2.75	133	.238	.274	91-0-10	.132	-2	90	30		3.4
1947	Bos A	12	11	.522	29	26	13-3	0	189.1	173	86	17	2	57	119	3.33	117	.244	.314	61-0-4	.033	-6	95	8		0.1
1948	Bos A	3	1	.750	15	0	0	0	19.1	21	14	0	2	8	6	5.12	86	.276	.337	2-0-1	.000	-0		-2		-0.5

YEAR	TM LG	W	L	PCT	G	GS	CG-SHO	SV-BS	IP	H	R	HR	HB	BB-IB	SO	ERA	AERA	OAV	OOB	AB-HR-SH	AVG	PB	SUP	APR	DL	PW
1949	Bos A	4	2	.667	29	2	0	3	77.2	82	49	5	1	41	35	5.33	82	.268	.356	22-0-4	.045	-3	113	-7		-0.9
Total	8	96	54	.640	225	156	99-19	17	1375.2	1270	504	77	11	372	693	3.94	125	.245	.297	447-0-49	.119	-15	103	112		10.4

HUISMAN, JUSTIN Justin Ray B4.16.1979 Harvey IL BR/TR/6-1/195 [ColN00 15/437] d4.25 Col Mississippi

YEAR	TM LG	W	L	PCT	G	GS	CG-SHO	SV-BS	IP	H	R	HR	HB	BB-IB	SO	ERA	AERA	OAV	OOB	AB-HR-SH	AVG	PB	SUP	APR	DL	PW
2004	KC A	0	0	—	14	0	0	1-0	25	36	20	3	1	8-3	13	6.84	68	.336	.388	0	—	0		-6		-0.3

HUISMAN, RICK Richard Allen B5.17.1969 Oak Park IL BR/TR/6-3/200* [SFN90 3/94] d9.4 Col Lewis [DL 1997 KC A 66]

YEAR	TM LG	W	L	PCT	G	GS	CG-SHO	SV-BS	IP	H	R	HR	HB	BB-IB	SO	ERA	AERA	OAV	OOB	AB-HR-SH	AVG	PB	SUP	APR	DL	PW
1995	KC A	0	0	—	7	0	0	0-0	9.2	14	8	4	0	1-0	12	7.45	64	.333	.349	0	—	0		-3		-0.1
1996	KC A	2	1	.667	22	0	0	1-0	29.1	25	15	4	0	18-2	23	4.60	109	.231	.336	0	—	0		2		0.2
Total	2	2	1	.667	29	0	0	1-0	39	39	23	6	0	19-2	35	5.31	94	.260	.339	0	—	0		-1	66	0.1

HUISMANN, MARK Mark Lawrence B5.11.1958 Littleton CO BR/TR/6-3/195* d8.16 Col Colorado St.

YEAR	TM LG	W	L	PCT	G	GS	CG-SHO	SV-BS	IP	H	R	HR	HB	BB-IB	SO	ERA	AERA	OAV	OOB	AB-HR-SH	AVG	PB	SUP	APR	DL	PW
1983	KC A	2	1	.667	13	0	0	0-1	30.2	29	20	1	0	17-3	20	5.58	74	.250	.343	0	—	0		-4		-0.4
1984	†KC A	3	3	.500	38	0	0	3-1	75	84	38	7	1	21-3	54	4.20	96	.286	.330	0	—	0		-1		-0.1
1985	KC A	1	0	1.000	9	0	0	0-0	18.2	14	4	1	0	3-0	9	1.93	217	.219	.246	0	—	0		5		0.2
1986	KC A	0	1	.000	10	0	0	1-2	17.1	18	8	1	0	6-0	13	4.15	103	.269	.324	0	—	0		1		0.1
	Sea A	3	3	.500	36	1	0	4-3	80	80	39	18	1	19-0	59	3.71	115	.256	.299	0	—	0	64	4		0.3
	Year	3	4	.429	46	1	0	5-5	97.1	98	47	19	1	25-0	72	3.79	113	.259	.304	0	—	0	64	5		0.4
1987	Sea A	0	0	—	6	0	0	0-0	14.2	10	10	1	2	4-0	15	4.91	97	.196	.276	0	—	0		-1		0.0
	Cle A	2	3	.400	20	0	0	2-2	35.1	38	22	6	0	8-0	23	5.09	90	.271	.307	0	—	0		-2		-0.2
	Year	2	3	.400	26	0	0	2-2	50	48	32	7	2	12-0	38	5.04	92	.251	.298	0	—	0		-3		-0.2
1988	Det A	1	0	1.000	8	0	0	0-0	5.1	6	3	0	0	2-1	5	5.06	76	.286	.348	0	—	0		-1		-0.1
1989	Bal A	0	0	—	8	0	0	1-1	11.1	13	8	0	0	6-0	13	6.35	60	.277	.271	0	—	0		-3		-0.1
1990	Pit N	1	0	1.000	3	0	0	0-0	3	6	5	2	1	1-0	2	9.00	41	.462	.533	0	—	0		-3		-0.5
1991	Pit N	0	0	—	5	0	0	0-0	5	7	6	0	0	2-1	5	7.20	50	.304	.360	0	—	0		-3		-0.1
Total	9	13	11	.542	152	1	0	11-10	296.1	305	163	37	5	83-8	219	4.40	95	.266	.314	0	—	0	65	-8	113	-0.9

HULIHAN, HARRY Harry Joseph B4.18.1899 Rutland VT D9.11.1980 Rutland VT BR/TL/5-11/170 d8.16 Col Middlebury

YEAR	TM LG	W	L	PCT	G	GS	CG-SHO	SV-BS	IP	H	R	HR	HB	BB-IB	SO	ERA	AERA	OAV	OOB	AB-HR-SH	AVG	PB	SUP	APR	DL	PW
1922	Bos N	2	3	.400	7	6	0	0	40	40	23	0	4	26	16	3.15	127	.274	.398	13-0-1	.154	-0	115	2		0.1

HULVEY, HANK James Hensel B7.18.1897 Mount Sidney VA D4.9.1982 Mount Sidney VA BB/TR/6-0/180 d9.5 Col Shenandoah

YEAR	TM LG	W	L	PCT	G	GS	CG-SHO	SV-BS	IP	H	R	HR	HB	BB-IB	SO	ERA	AERA	OAV	OOB	AB-HR-SH	AVG	PB	SUP	APR	DL	PW
1923	Phi A	0	1	.000	1	1	0	0	7	10	6	1	0	2	2	7.71	53	.357	.400	2	.500	0	60	-2		-0.2

HUME, TOM Thomas Hubert B3.29.1953 Cincinnati OH BR/TR/6-1/185* [CinN72*S1/16] d5.25 C10 Col Manatee (FL) CC

YEAR	TM LG	W	L	PCT	G	GS	CG-SHO	SV-BS	IP	H	R	HR	HB	BB-IB	SO	ERA	AERA	OAV	OOB	AB-HR-SH	AVG	PB	SUP	APR	DL	PW
1977	Cin N	3	3	.500	14	5	0	0-0	43	54	36	5	0	17-3	22	7.12	55	.305	.364	10-1-2	.200	1	122	-15		-1.7
1978	Cin N	8	11	.421	42	23	3	1-2	174	198	89	12	4	50-9	90	4.14	86	.289	.339	45-0-8	.067	-3*	108	-11		-1.4
1979	†Cin N	10	9	.526	57	12	2	17-3	163	162	54	12	0	33-9	80	2.76	134	.262	.295	46-0-1	.174	-0	106	18		2.4
1980	Cin N	9	10	.474	78	0	0	25-10	137	121	44	6	3	38-14	68	2.56	138	.240	.296	16-0-1	.188	1	14			2.6
1981	Cin N	9	4	.692	51	0	0	13-5	67.2	63	27	7	1	31-9	27	3.46	101	.259	.343	4	.000	0	1			0.2
1982	Cin N★	2	6	.250	46	0	0	17-2	63.2	57	24	2	1	21-8	22	3.11	118	.245	.306	5	.000	-1		69		0.6
1983	Cin N	3	5	.375	48	0	0	9-3	66	64	40	8	4	41-11	34	4.77	80	.264	.369	5-0-1	.000	-1	-7	25		-1.0
1984	Cin N	4	13	.235	54	8	0	3-4	113.1	142	83	14	1	41-9	59	5.64	67	.309	.363	22	.136	-0	64	-24		-3.4
1985	Cin N	3	5	.375	50	0	0	3-2	80	65	33	7	3	35-5	50	3.26	116	.224	.313	5	.000	-1	4			0.4
1986	Phi N	4	1	.800	48	1	0	4-1	94.1	89	37	5	3	34-5	51	2.77	141	.252	.317	11-0-5	.000	-1	137	10	30	0.5
1987	Phi N	1	4	.200	38	6	0	0-1	70.2	75	48	10	4	41-5	29	5.60	77	.277	.377	15	.200	-1	112	-9		-0.5
	Cin N	1	0	1.000	11	0	0	0-0	13.1	14	6	0	1	2-0	4	4.05	104	.292	.321	0	—	0	1			0.0
	Year	2	4	.333	49	6	0	0-1	84	89	54	10	5	43-5	33	5.36	80	.279	.369	15	.200	-1	113	-9		-0.5
Total	11	57	71	.445	543	55	5	92-33	1086	1106	521	88	24	384-87	536	3.85	97	.268	.330	184-1-18	.120	-4	103	-14	124	-1.3

HUMPHREY, BILL Byron William B6.17.1911 Vienna MO D2.13.1992 Springfield MO BR/TR/6-0/180 d4.24

YEAR	TM LG	W	L	PCT	G	GS	CG-SHO	SV-BS	IP	H	R	HR	HB	BB-IB	SO	ERA	AERA	OAV	OOB	AB-HR-SH	AVG	PB	SUP	APR	DL	PW
1938	Bos A	0	0	—	2	0	0	0	3	5	2	0	1	0	0	9.00	55	.500	.545	0	—	0		-1		0.0

HUMPHREYS, BOB Robert William B8.18.1935 Covington VA BR/TR/5-11/170* d9.8 Col Hampden-Sydney

YEAR	TM LG	W	L	PCT	G	GS	CG-SHO	SV-BS	IP	H	R	HR	HB	BB-IB	SO	ERA	AERA	OAV	OOB	AB-HR-SH	AVG	PB	SUP	APR	DL	PW
1962	Det A	0	1	.000	4	0	0	0	5	8	4	3	0	2-0	3	7.20	57	.381	.435	0	—	0		-1		-0.3
1963	StL N	0	1	.000	9	0	0	0	10.2	11	8	4	1	7-1	8	5.06	70	.282	.404	0	—	0		-2	31	-0.2
1964	†StL N	2	0	1.000	28	0	0	2	42.2	32	14	3	1	15-3	36	2.53	150	.213	.287	4-0-2	.250	1	6			0.4
1965	Chi N	2	0	1.000	41	0	0	0	65.2	59	25	6	2	27-6	38	3.15	117	.244	.322	3-0-1	.000	-0	5			0.2
1966	Was A	7	3	.700	58	0	0	3	111.2	91	38	6	4	28-5	88	2.82	123	.229	.285	12-0-5	.167	1	229	9		0.9
1967	Was A	6	2	.750	48	2	0	4	105.2	93	54	13	4	41-3	54	4.17	76	.238	.310	15-0-3	.133	1	69	-11		-0.9
1968	Was A	5	7	.417	56	0	0	2	92.2	78	40	13	0	30-2	56	3.69	79	.233	.293	5-0-1	.400	1	-7			-0.8
1969	Was A	3	3	.500	47	0	0	5-0	79.2	69	37	3	1	38-2	43	3.05	115	.233	.320	13	.077	-1	1			0.1
1970	Was A	0	0	—	5	0	0	0-0	6.2	4	2	1	0	9-0	6	1.35	267	.200	.448	0	—	0	1			0.1
	Mil A	2	4	.333	23	1	0	3-2	45.2	37	18	3	2	22-3	32	3.15	120	.222	.314	9-0-1	.000	-1	71	3		0.3
	Year	2	4	.333	28	1	0	3-2	52.1	41	20	4	2	31-3	38	2.92	128	.219	.332	9-0-1	.000	-1	71	5		0.4
Total	9	27	21	.563	319	4	0	20-2	566	482	240	55	13	219-25	364	3.36	102	.234	.309	61-0-12	.131	1	110	4	31	-0.2

HUMPHRIES, BERT Albert B9.26.1880 California PA D9.21.1945 Orlando FL BR/TR/5-11.5/182 d4.16

YEAR	TM LG	W	L	PCT	G	GS	CG-SHO	SV-BS	IP	H	R	HR	HB	BB-IB	SO	ERA	AERA	OAV	OOB	AB-HR-SH	AVG	PB	SUP	APR	DL	PW
1910	Phi N	0	0	—	5	0	0	2	9.2	13	8	9	1	3	3	4.66	67	.317	.378	2	.000	0		-2		-0.1
1911	Phi N	3	1	.750	11	5	2	1	41	56	25	1	6	10	13	4.17	83	.339	.398	15	.333	3	161	-3		-0.1
	Cin N	4	3	.571	14	7	3	0	65	62	25	3	6	18	16	2.35	141	.266	.335	16-0-2	.063	-1	101	6		0.6
	Year	7	4	.636	25	12	5	1	106	118	50	4	12	28	29	3.06	110	.296	.361	31-0-2	.194	2	127	2		0.5
1912	Cin N	9	11	.450	30	15	9-1	2	158.2	162	77	6	8	36	58	3.23	104	.270	.319	51-0-2	.137	-2	74	3		0.1
1913	Chi N	16	4	.800	30	20	13-2	1	181	169	70	10	2	24	61	2.69	118	.250	.277	62-0-4	.194	1	143	10		1.1
1914	Chi N	10	11	.476	34	21	8-2	0	171	162	80	5	2	37	62	2.68	104	.250	.293	55-0-3	.236	2*	96	1		0.4
1915	Chi N	8	13	.381	31	22	10-4	3	171.2	183	69	6	5	23	45	2.31	120	.280	.309	46-0-6	.174	0	72	4		0.4
Total	6	50	43	.538	153	90	45-9	9	798	807	354	31	30	151	258	2.79	110	.267	.309	247-0-17	.186	3	101	19		2.4

HUMPHRIES, JOHNNY John William B6.23.1915 Clifton Forge VA D6.24.1965 New Orleans LA BR/TR/6-1/185 d5.8 Col North Carolina-Asheville

YEAR	TM LG	W	L	PCT	G	GS	CG-SHO	SV-BS	IP	H	R	HR	HB	BB-IB	SO	ERA	AERA	OAV	OOB	AB-HR-SH	AVG	PB	SUP	APR	DL	PW
1938	Cle A	9	8	.529	45	6	1	6	103.1	105	69	6	1	63	56	5.23	89	.264	.367	29-0-2	.103	-1	76	-7		-1.2
1939	Cle A	2	4	.333	15	1	0	2	28.1	30	30	0	1	32	12	8.26	53	.294	.467	7	.000	-1	60	-13		-2.3
1940	Cle A	0	2	.000	19	1	1	1	33.2	35	35	5	2	29	17	8.29	51	.269	.410	6-0-1	.000	-1	21	-16		-0.9
1941	Chi A	4	2	.667	14	6	4-4	1	73.1	63	18	2	1	22	25	1.84	223	.230	.290	23-0-1	.087	-1	39	18		1.3
1942	Chi A	12	12	.500	28	28	17-2	1	228.1	227	85	9	7	59	71	2.68	134	.257	.309	80-0-3	.225	-1	104	21		2.6
1943	Chi A	11	11	.500	28	27	8-2	5	188.1	198	86	7	6	54	51	3.30	101	.268	.322	69	.290	5	93	-1		0.5
1944	Chi A	8	10	.444	30	20	8	1	169	170	75	4	4	57	42	3.67	93	.267	.331	53-0-3	.189	0	80	-1		-0.3
1945	Chi A	6	14	.300	22	21	10-1	1	153	172	83	11	3	48	33	4.24	78	.282	.337	54-0-3	.148	-3	84	-16		-2.3
1946	Phi N	0	0	—	10	0	0	1	24.2	24	17	1	1	9	10	4.01	85	.258	.330	8	.250	0	75	-3		-0.2
Total	9	52	63	.452	211	111	49-9	12	1002	1024	498	50	26	373	317	3.78	97	.265	.334	329-0-13	.191	4	84	-18		-2.8

HUNT, BEN Benjamin Franklin "High Pockets" B11.10.1888 Eufaula OK D9.27.1927 Greybull WY BL/TL/6-5/190 d8.24

YEAR	TM LG	W	L	PCT	G	GS	CG-SHO	SV-BS	IP	H	R	HR	HB	BB-IB	SO	ERA	AERA	OAV	OOB	AB-HR-SH	AVG	PB	SUP	APR	DL	PW
1910	Bos A	3	4	.400	7	3	3	0	46.2	45	22	4	0	20	19	4.05	63	.264	.344	18-0-1	.056	-2	105	-3		-0.7
1913	StL N	0	1	.000	2	1	0	0	8	6	5	0	1	9	6	3.38	96	.240	.457	2	.000	-0	23	-1		-0.1
Total	2	4	.333	9	4	3	0	54.2	51	27	4	1	29	25	3.95	67	.263	.362	20-0-1	.050	-2	93	-6		-0.8

HUNT, KEN Kenneth Raymond B12.14.1938 Ogden UT BR/TR/6-4/225 d4.16 Col Brigham Young

YEAR	TM LG	W	L	PCT	G	GS	CG-SHO	SV-BS	IP	H	R	HR	HB	BB-IB	SO	ERA	AERA	OAV	OOB	AB-HR-SH	AVG	PB	SUP	APR	DL	PW
1961	†Cin N	9	10	.474	29	22	4	0	136.1	130	70	13	6	66-1	75	3.96	103	.257	.348	39-0-3	.179	0	95	1		0.0

HUNTER, GEORGE George Henry B7.8.1887 Buffalo NY D1.11.1968 Harrisburg PA BB/TL/5-8.5/165 d5.4 twb-Bill ▲

YEAR	TM LG	W	L	PCT	G	GS	CG-SHO	SV-BS	IP	H	R	HR	HB	BB-IB	SO	ERA	AERA	OAV	OOB	AB-HR-SH	AVG	PB	SUP	APR	DL	PW
1909	Bro N	4	10	.286	16	13	10	0	113.1	104	48	2	3	38	43	2.46	105	.254	.322	123-0-2	.228	2*	87	-1		0.2

HUNTER, CATFISH James Augustus "Jim" B4.8.1946 Hertford NC D9.9.1999 Hertford NC BR/TR/6-0/195(190-202) d5.13 HF1987

YEAR	TM LG	W	L	PCT	G	GS	CG-SHO	SV-BS	IP	H	R	HR	HB	BB-IB	SO	ERA	AERA	OAV	OOB	AB-HR-SH	AVG	PB	SUP	APR	DL	PW
1965	KC A	8	8	.500	32	20	3-2	0	133	124	68	21	2	46-5	82	4.26	82	.246	.309	40-0-6	.150	-1	103	-10		-1.3
1966	KC A☆	9	11	.450	30	25	4	0	176.2	158	87	17	2	64-4	103	4.02	84	.239	.306	59-0-3	.153	1	95	-11	36	-1.3
1967	KC A★	13	17	.433	35	35	13-5	0	259.2	209	91	16	2	84-6	196	2.81	113	.219	.283	92-2-2	.196	4*	91	11		1.5
1968	Oak A	13	13	.500	36	34	11-2	1	234	209	100	29	4	69-10	172	3.35	84	.238	.295	82-1-8	.232	5*	126	-14		-1.2
1969	Oak A	12	15	.444	38	35	10-3	0-0	247	210	99	34	5	85-1	150	3.35	103	.234	.302	85-1-1	.224	4*	93	4		0.8
1970	Oak A★	18	14	.563	40	40	9-1	0-0	262.1	253	124	32	9	74-3	178	3.81	93	.250	.304	90-1-6	.200	4*	106	-8		-0.7
1971	†Oak A	21	11	.656	37	37	16-4	0-0	273.2	225	103	24	7	80-7	181	2.96	112	.223	.281	103-1-4	.350	13*	111	11		2.5

YEAR	TM LG	W	L	PCT	G	GS	CG-SHO	SV-BS	IP	H	R	HR	HB	BB-IB	SO	ERA	AERA	OAV	OOB	AB-HR-SH	AVG	PB	SUP	APR	DL	PW
1972	†Oak A☆	21	7	.750	38	37	16-5	0-0	295.1	200	74	21	3	70-6	191	2.04	140	.189	.241	105-0-9	.219	3*	123	29		3.1
1973	†Oak A★	21	5	.808	36	36	11-3	0-0	256.1	222	105	39	1	69-1	124	3.34	107	.232	.282	1	1.000	1*	138	9		0.7
1974	†Oak A★	25	12	.676	41	41	23-6	0-0	318.1	268	97	25	4	46-2	143	2.49	134	.229	.258	0	—	0	121	35		3.9
1975	NY A★	23	14	.622	39	39	30-7	0-0	328	248	107	25	5	83-4	177	2.58	144	.208	.261	0	—	0	110	42		4.4
1976	†NY A★	17	15	.531	36	36	21-2	0-0	298.2	268	126	28	3	68-5	173	3.53	97	.241	.283	1	.000	-0	116	-2		-0.3
1977	†NY A	9	9	.500	22	22	8-1	0-0	143.1	137	83	29	3	47-3	52	4.71	84	.250	.310	0	—	0	127	-12	21	-1.4
1978	†NY A	12	6	.667	21	20	5-1	0-0	118	98	49	16	1	35-0	56	3.58	102	.226	.283	0	—	0	119	3	44	0.4
1979	NY A	2	9	.182	19	19	1	0-0	105	128	68	15	1	34-0	34	5.31	78	.312	.361	0	—	0	87	-14		-1.3
Total	15	224	166	.574	500	476	181-42	1-0	3449.1	2958	1380	374	49	954-57	2012	3.26	104	.231	.285	658-6-39	.226	33	112	73	101	9.8

HUNTER, JIM   James Mac Gregor   B6.22.1964 Jersey City NJ   BR/TR/6-3/205   [MonN85 S1/10]   d5.17   Col Georgia

| 1991 | Mil A | 0 | 5 | .000 | 8 | 6 | 0 | 0-0 | 31 | 45 | 26 | 3 | 4 | 17-0 | 14 | 7.26 | 55 | .349 | .437 | 0 | — | 0 | 88 | -11 | | -1.4 |

HUNTER, RICH   Richard Thomas   B9.25.1974 Pasadena CA   BR/TR/6-1/185   [PhiN93 14/384]   d4.6

| 1996 | Phi N | 3 | 7 | .300 | 14 | 14 | 0-0 | | 69.1 | 84 | 54 | 10 | 5 | 33-2 | 32 | 6.49 | 66 | .303 | .382 | 18-0-4 | .167 | 0* | 82 | -16 | | -1.8 |

HUNTER, BILL   Willard Mitchell "Hawk"   B3.8.1934 Newark NJ   BR/TL/6-2/180*   d4.16

1962	LA N	0	0	—	1	0	0	0	2	6	10	1	0	4-0	1	40.50	9	.545	.625	0	—	0		-9		-0.4
	NY N	1	6	.143	27	6	1	0	63	67	41	9	1	34-0	40	5.57	75	.270	.360	13	.231	0	66	-7		-0.7
	Year	1	6	.143	28	6	1	0	65	73	51	10	1	38-0	41	6.65	63	.287	.375	13	.231	0	67	-16		-1.1
1964	NY N	3	3	.500	41	0	0	5	49	54	25	4	2	9-1	22	4.41	81	.284	.322	1-0-2	1.000	0		-3		-0.4
Total	2	4	9	.308	69	6	1	5	114	127	76	14	3	47-1	63	5.68	69	.283	.353	14-0-2	.286	1	71	-19		-1.5

HUNTZINGER, WALT   Walter Henry "Shakes"   B2.6.1899 Pottsville PA   D8.11.1981 Upper Darby PA   BR/TR/6-0/150   d9.29   Col Penn

1923	NY N	0	1	.000	2	1	0	0	8	9	7	0	0	1	2	7.88	49	.290	.313	2	.000	-0	22	-3		-0.4
1924	NY N	1	1	.500	12	2	0	1	32.1	41	19	3	0	9	6	4.45	82	.318	.362	8	.500	1	58	-3		-0.1
1925	NY N	5	1	.833	26	1	0	0	64.1	68	30	3	0	17	19	3.50	115	.281	.328	11	.091	-1	230	4		0.2
1926	StL N	0	4	.000	9	4	2	0	34	35	19	4	0	14	9	4.24	92	.267	.338	8	.000	-1	75	-1		0.0
	Chi N	1	1	.500	11	0	0	2	28.2	26	8	0	3	8	4	0.94	408	.260	.333	7	.143	-1		-7		0.5
	Year	1	5	.167	20	4	2	2	62.2	61	27	4	3	22	13	2.73	142	.264	.336	15	.067	-2	75	6		0.3
Total	4	7	8	.467	60	8	2	3	167.1	179	83	10	3	49	40	3.60	108	.283	.337	36	.167	-1	83	4		0.0

HURD, TOM   Thomas Carr "Whitey"   B5.27.1924 Danville VA   D9.5.1982 Waterloo IA   BR/TR/5-9/155*   d7.30

1954	Bos A	2	0	1.000	16	0	0	1	29.2	21	11	2	0	12	14	3.03	135	.198	.277	3	.333	0		3		0.3
1955	Bos A	8	6	.571	43	0	0	5	80.2	72	32	7	1	38-10	48	3.01	142	.242	.326	14-0-1	.071	-1		10		1.6
1956	Bos A	3	4	.429	40	0	0	5	76	84	52	5	3	47-2	34	5.33	83	.289	.386	12-0-1	.500	2		-5		-0.4
Total	3	13	10	.565	99	0	0	11	186.1	177	95	14	4	97-12	96	3.96	111	.255	.345	29-0-2	.276	1		8		1.5

HURST, BRUCE   Bruce Vee   B3.24.1958 St.George UT   BL/TL/6-3/215(185-220)   [BosA76 1/22]   d4.12

1980	Bos A	2	2	.500	12	7	0	0-0	30.2	39	33	4	2	16-0	16	9.10	47	.307	.388	0	—	0	144	-15		-1.7
1981	Bos A	2	0	1.000	5	5	0	0-0	23	23	11	1	1	12-2	11	4.30	91	.258	.346	0	—	0	115	0		0.0
1982	Bos A	3	7	.300	28	19	0	0-0	117	161	87	16	3	40-2	53	5.77	76	.331	.383	0	—	0	95	-19		-1.4
1983	Bos A	12	12	.500	33	33	6-2	0-0	211.1	241	102	22	3	62-5	115	4.09	108	.290	.340	0	—	0	93	9		1.0
1984	Bos A	12	12	.500	33	33	9-2	0-0	218	232	106	25	4	88-3	136	3.92	107	.271	.341	0	—	0	104	7		0.8
1985	Bos A	11	13	.458	35	31	6-1	0-3	229.1	243	123	31	3	70-4	189	4.51	96	.273	.327	0	—	0	126	-4		-0.3
1986	†Bos A	13	8	.619	25	25	11-4	0-0	174.1	169	63	18	0	50-2	167	2.99	140	.256	.310	0	—	0	91	24	45	2.7
1987	Bos A☆	15	13	.536	33	33	15-3	0-0	238.2	239	124	35	1	76-5	190	4.41	104	.262	.317	0	—	0	96	5		0.6
1988	†Bos A	18	6	.750	33	32	7-1	0-0	216.2	222	98	21	2	65-1	166	3.66	113	.264	.316	0	—	0	133	10	16	1.1
1989	SD N	15	11	.577	33	33	10-2	0-0	244.2	214	84	16	0	66-7	179	2.69	131	.237	.288	70-0-8	.071	-2	94	22		2.2
1990	SD N	11	9	.550	33	33	9-4	0-0	223.2	188	85	21	1	63-5	162	3.14	122	.228	.284	67-0-7	.090	-2	89	18		1.4
1991	SD N	15	8	.652	31	31	4	0-0	221.2	201	89	17	3	59-3	141	3.29	116	.241	.292	67-0-12	.134	-1	103	13		0.7
1992	SD N	14	9	.609	32	32	6-4	0-0	217.1	223	96	22	0	51-3	131	3.85	93	.267	.308	69-0-9	.159	1*	109	-3		-0.2
1993	SD N	0	1	.000	2	2	0	0-0	4.1	9	7	0	0	3-0	3	12.46	33	.409	.480	0-0-1	—	0	120	-4	101	-0.7
	Col N	0	1	.000	3	3	0	0-0	8.2	6	5	1	0	3-0	6	5.19	92	.194	.265	0	.000	-0	107	0	42	-0.0
	Year	0	2	.000	5	5	0	0-0	13	15	12	1	0	6-0	9	7.62	60	.283	.356	1-0-1	.000	0	110	-4		-0.7
1994	Tex A	0	2	.000	8	8	0	0-0	38	53	30	8	0	16-0	24	7.11	68	.342	.394	0	—	0	152	-8		-0.8
Total	15	145	113	.562	379	359	83-23	0-3	2417.1	2463	1143	258	28	740-42	1689	3.92	104	.265	.319	274-0-37	.113	-3	106	55	204	6.2

HURST, JAMES   James Lavon   B6.1.1967 Plantation FL   BL/TL/6-0/170   [CleA89 32/827]   d4.4   Col Florida Southern

| 1994 | Tex A | 0 | 0 | — | 8 | 0 | 0 | 0-0 | 10.2 | 17 | 12 | 1 | 0 | 8-1 | 5 | 10.13 | 48 | .362 | .446 | 0 | — | 0 | | -6 | | -0.1 |

HURST, JONATHAN   Jonathan   B10.20.1966 New York NY   BR/TR/6-3/175(175-190)   [TexA87 4/103]   d6.9   Col Spartanburg Methodist (SC) JC

1992	Mon N	1	1	.500	3	3	0	0-0	16.1	18	10	1	1	7-0	5	5.51	63	.281	.361	4-0-2	.000	0	95	-3		-0.4
1994	NY N	0	1	.000	7	0	0	0-1	10	15	14	5	0	5-0	6	12.60	33	.341	.400	0	—	0		-9		-0.7
Total	2	1	2	.333	10	3	0	0-1	26.1	33	24	6	1	12-0	10	8.20	46	.306	.377	4-0-2	.000	0	95	-12		-1.1

HURST, BILL   William Hansel   B4.28.1970 Miami Beach FL   BR/TR/6-7/220   [StLN89 20/510]   d9.18   Col Central Florida CC   [DL 1997 Fla N 30]

| 1996 | Fla N | 0 | 0 | — | 2 | 0 | 0 | 0-0 | 3 | 2 | 0 | 0 | 1 | 1-0 | 1 | 0.00 | — | .333 | .400 | 0 | — | 0 | | 1 | | 0.0 |

HURTADO, EDWIN   Edwin Amilgar   B2.1.1970 Barquisimeto, Venez   BR/TR/6-3/215*   d5.22

1995	Tor A	5	2	.714	14	10	1	0-0	77.2	81	50	11	5	40-3	33	5.45	87	.275	.367	0	—	0	133	-5		-0.4
1996	Sea A	2	5	.286	16	4	0	2-1	47.2	61	42	10	0	30-3	36	7.74	64	.324	.408	0	—	0	84	-14	29	-1.6
1997	Sea A	1	2	.333	13	1	0	0-0	19	25	19	5	2	15-0	10	9.00	50	.329	.447	0	—	0	142	-9		-1.1
Total	3	8	9	.471	43	15	1	2-1	144.1	167	111	26	7	85-6	79	6.67	72	.299	.392	0	—	0	120	-28	29	-3.1

HUSTED, BILL   William J.   B10.19.1866 Gloucester NJ   D5.17.1941 Gloucester NJ   d4.29

| 1890 | Phi P | 5 | 10 | .333 | 18 | 17 | 12 | 0 | 129 | 148 | 105 | 2 | 5 | 67 | 33 | 4.88 | 88 | .276 | .361 | 56 | .107 | -6 | 97 | -6 | | -1.0 |

HUSTING, BERT   Berthold Juneau "Pete"   B3.6.1878 Fond Du Lac WI   D9.3.1948 Milwaukee WI   BR/TR/5-10.5/185   d8.16   Col Wisconsin-Madison

1900	Pit N	0	0	—	2	0	0	0	8	9	5	1	2	5	7	5.63	65	.303	.410	3	.000	-1		-1		-0.1
1901	Mil A	9	15	.375	34	26	19	1	217.1	234	151	5	13	95	67	4.27	84	.272	.353	94-1-4	.202	-1*	113	-15		-1.2
1902	Bos A	0	1	.000	1	1	1	0	8	15	15	0	0	8	4	9.00	40	.395	.500	4	.250	1	80	-6		-0.5
	Phi A	14	5	.737	32	27	17-1	0	204	240	126	7	9	91	44	3.79	97	.293	.370	82-0-4	.159	-3	142	-4		-0.5
	Year	14	6	.700	33	28	18-1	0	212	255	141	7	9	99	48	3.99	92	.298	.377	86-0-4	.163	-3	140	-9		-0.9
Total	3	23	21	.523	69	54	37-1	1	437.1	499	297	14	23	199	122	4.16	87	.285	.366	183-1-8	.180	-4	126	-26		-2.4

HUTCHINGS, JOHNNY   John Richard Joseph   B4.14.1916 Chicago IL   D4.27.1963 Indianapolis IN   BB/TR/6-2/250   d4.26

1940	†Cin N	2	1	.667	19	1	0	3	54	53	21	3	1	18	18	3.50	108	.260	.323	13	.154	0	75	3		0.1
1941	Cin N	0	0	—	8	0	0	0	11	12	6	0	0	4	5	4.09	88	.279	.340	0	—	0		-1		-0.0
	Bos N	1	6	.143	36	7	1-1	2	95.2	110	59	6	4	22	36	4.14	86	.287	.333	27-0-1	.148	0	75	-9		-0.8
	Year	1	6	.143	44	7	1-1	2	106.2	122	65	6	4	26	41	4.13	86	.286	.333	27-0-1	.148	0	75	-10		-0.9
1942	Bos N	1	0	1.000	20	3	0	6	65.2	66	33	2	2	34	27	4.39	76	.260	.352	20	.050	-2	101	-6		-0.2
1944	Bos N	1	4	.200	14	7	1	1	56.2	55	30	3	1	26	26	3.97	96	.252	.335	15	.067	-1	75	-1		-0.2
1945	Bos N	7	6	.538	57	12	3-2	3	185	173	87	21	4	75	99	3.75	102	.244	.320	54-0-1	.241	2	138	3		0.1
1946	Bos N	0	1	.000	14	2	1	0	3	5	3	0	1	3	1	9.00	38	.357	.400	1	.000	-0	25	-2		-0.1
Total	6	12	18	.400	155	34	5-3	6	471	474	239	36	12	180	212	3.96	93	.260	.330	130-0-2	.162	-1	99	-13		-1.3

HUTCHINSON, CHAD   Chad Martin   B2.21.1977 Boulder CO   BR/TR/6-5/230   [StLN98 2/48]   d4.4   Col Stanford

| 2001 | StL N | 0 | 0 | — | 3 | 0 | 0 | 0-0 | 4 | 9 | 11 | 3 | 1 | 6-0 | 2 | 24.75 | 17 | .450 | .593 | 1 | .000 | -0 | | -9 | | -0.0 |

HUTCHINSON, FRED   Frederick Charles   B8.12.1919 Seattle WA   D11.12.1964 Bradenton FL   BL/TR/6-2/200*   d5.2   Mil 1942-45   M12

1939	Det A	3	6	.333	13	12	3	0	84.2	95	56	9	0	51	22	5.21	94	.287	.382	34	.382	3	89	-2		0.0
1940	†Det A	3	7	.300	17	10	1	0	76	85	52	6	2	26	32	5.68	84	.281	.342	30	.267	0	91	-6		-0.6
1946	Det A	14	11	.560	28	26	16-3	2	207	184	78	14	0	66	138	3.09	118	.236	.295	89-0-2	.315	8*	112	14		2.1
1947	Det A	18	10	.643	33	25	18-3	2	219.2	211	84	14	2	61	113	3.03	124	.251	.304	106-2-1	.302	11*	104	18		2.3
1948	Det A	13	11	.542	33	28	15	0	221	223	119	32	4	48	92	4.32	101	.258	.297	112-1-2	.205	4*	103	2		0.3
1949	Det A	15	7	.682	33	21	9-4	1	188.2	167	70	18	1	52	71	2.96	141	.237	.290	73-0-4	.247	4*	118	25		2.6
1950	Det A	17	8	.680	39	26	10-1	5	231.2	269	119	18	5	48	71	3.96	118	.290	.329	95-0-4	.326	10*	126	15		2.2

YEAR	TM LG	W	L	PCT	G	GS	CG-SHO	SV-BS	IP	H	R	HR	HB	BB-IB	SO	ERA	AERA	OAV	OOB	AB-HR-SH	AVG	PB	SUP	APR	DL	PW
1951	Det A★	10	10	.500	31	20	9-2	2	188.1	204	84	12	2	27	53	3.68	113	.275	.302	85-0-2	.188	-2*	98	11		1.0
1952	Det A	2	1	.667	12	1	0	0	37.1	40	16	4	1	9	12	3.38	113	.276	.323	18	.056	-1*	69	2		0.1
1953	Det A	0	0	—	3	0	0	0	9.2	9	3	0	0	0	4	2.79	146	.243	.243	6-1-0	.167	0*		1		0.1
Total	10	95	71	.572	242	169	81-13	7	1464	1487	681	127	14	388	591	3.73	113	.262	.311	648-4-15	.264	39	108	80		13.7

HUTCHINSON, IRA Ira Kendall B8.31.1910 Chicago IL D8.21.1973 Chicago IL BR/TR/5-10.5/180 d9.24

YEAR	TM LG	W	L	PCT	G	GS	CG-SHO	SV-BS	IP	H	R	HR	HB	BB-IB	SO	ERA	AERA	OAV	OOB	AB-HR-SH	AVG	PB	SUP	APR	DL	PW
1933	Chi A	0	0	—	1	1	0	0	4	7	6	1	0	3	2	13.50	31	.368	.455	2	.500	0	161	-4		-0.1
1937	Bos N	4	6	.400	31	8	1	0	91.2	99	44	4	1	35	29	3.73	96	.286	.353	26-0-1	.115	-1	78	-2		-0.3
1938	Bos N	9	8	.529	36	12	4-1	4	151	150	58	3	4	61	38	2.74	125	.258	.332	52-0-2	.173	-1	80	11		1.2
1939	Bro N	5	2	.714	41	1	0	1	105.2	103	54	9	1	51	46	4.34	93	.265	.352	27-0-1	.037	-3	217	-2		-0.4
1940	StL N	4	2	.667	20	2	1	1	63.1	68	27	3	0	19	19	3.13	128	.271	.322	18-0-1	.222	0	120	5		0.5
1941	StL N	1	5	.167	29	0	0	5	46.2	32	23	2	2	19	19	3.86	98	.196	.288	8	.250	0	0	0		0.0
1944	Bos N	9	7	.563	40	8	1-1	1	119.2	136	59	8	3	53	22	4.21	91	.296	.373	29-0-2	.138	-1	104	-2		-0.3
1945	Bos N	2	3	.400	11	0	0	1	28.2	33	18	2	1	8	4	5.02	76	.277	.328	9-0-1	.000	-1		-3		-0.7
Total	8	34	33	.507	209	32	7-2	13	610.2	628	289	33	12	249	179	3.76	100	.270	.344	171-0-8	.140	-7	94	3		-0.1

HUTCHISON, BILL William Forrest "Wild Bill" B12.17.1859 New Haven CT D3.19.1926 Kansas City MO BR/TR/5-9/175 d6.10 Col Yale

YEAR	TM LG	W	L	PCT	G	GS	CG-SHO	SV-BS	IP	H	R	HR	HB	BB-IB	SO	ERA	AERA	OAV	OOB	AB-HR-SH	AVG	PB	SUP	APR	DL	PW
1884	KC U	1	1	.500	2	2	2	0	17	14	11	0		1	5	2.65	84	.209	.221	8	.250	-0	143	-1		-0.1
1889	Chi N	16	17	.485	37	36	33-3	0	318	306	206	11	8	117	136	3.54	118	.245	.314	133-1	.158	-5	90	19		1.3
1890	Chi N	**42**	25	.627	**71**	66	65-5	2	**603**	505	315	20	13	199	289	2.70	136	.220	.286	261-2	.203	-4	90	51		4.5
1891	Chi N	**44**	19	.698	**66**	58	56-4	1	**561**	508	283	26	7	178	261	2.81	119	.232	.292	243-2	.185	-1*	101	29		2.4
1892	Chi N	36	36	.500	75	70	67-5	1	**622**	571	316	11	13	190	**314**	2.76	120	.234	.293	263-1	.217	3*	79	36		4.0
1893	Chi N	16	24	.400	44	40	38-2	0	348.1	420	266	9	13	156	80	4.75	97	.289	.364	162	.253	1*	97	-4		-0.3
1894	Chi N	14	16	.467	37	34	28	0	279	374	257	9	18	140	60	6.03	93	.318	.399	136-2	.309	6*	97	-6		-0.1
1895	Chi N	13	21	.382	38	35	30-2	0	291	371	218	13	13	129	85	4.73	108	.306	.378	126	.198	-7	72	11		0.3
1897	StL N	1	4	.200	6	5	2	0	40	55	41	5	2	22	5	6.07	72	.324	.407	18	.278	1	55	-8		-0.7
Total	9	183	163	.529	376	346	321-21	4	3079.1	3124	1913	104	87	1132	1235	3.59	111	.255	.323	1350-12-2	.216	-6	90	127		11.3

HUTSON, HERB George Herbert B7.17.1949 Savannah GA BR/TR/6-2/219 d4.10 Col Georgia Southern

YEAR	TM LG	W	L	PCT	G	GS	CG-SHO	SV-BS	IP	H	R	HR	HB	BB-IB	SO	ERA	AERA	OAV	OOB	AB-HR-SH	AVG	PB	SUP	APR	DL	PW
1974	Chi N	0	2	.000	20	0	0	0-0	28.2	24	15	3	1	15-1	22	3.45	111	.233	.325	2	.000	-0	11	0	27	-0.1

HUTTON, MARK Mark Steven B2.6.1970 South Adelaide, South Australia, Australia BR/TR/6-6/240(225-240) d7.23

YEAR	TM LG	W	L	PCT	G	GS	CG-SHO	SV-BS	IP	H	R	HR	HB	BB-IB	SO	ERA	AERA	OAV	OOB	AB-HR-SH	AVG	PB	SUP	APR	DL	PW
1993	NY A	1	1	.500	7	4	0	0-0	22	24	17	2	1	17-0	12	5.73	73	.293	.412	0	—	0	137	-5		-0.4
1994	NY A	0	0	—	3	2	0	0-0	3.2	4	3	0	0	4-0	1	4.91	94	.250	.250	0	—	0		-1		0.0
1996	NY A	0	2	.000	12	2	0	0-0	30.1	32	19	3	1	18-1	25	5.04	98	.269	.364	0	—	0	37	-1	44	-0.1
	Fla N	5	1	.833	13	9	0	0-0	56.1	47	23	6	3	18-0	31	3.67	112	.222	.291	19-1-1	.316	2	95	4		0.6
1997	Fla N	3	1	.750	32	0	0	0-2	47.2	50	24	7	2	19-3	29	3.78	107	.286	.357	0	—	-0	0	0		0.1
	Col N	0	1	.000	8	1	0	0-1	12.2	22	10	3	4	7-0	10	7.11	73	.407	.500	3	.000	-0	71	-2		-0.2
	Year	3	2	.600	40	1	0	0-3	60.1	72	34	10	6	26-3	39	4.48	96	.314	.392	3	.000	-0	86	-2		-0.1
1998	Cin N	0	1	.000	10	2	0	0-0	17	24	14	2	1	17-0	3	7.41	58	.348	.483	1	1.000	0	54	-5	37	-0.2
Total	5	9	7	.563	84	18	0	0-3	189.2	203	110	23	12	96-4	111	4.75	91	.279	.368	23-1-1	.304	3	90	-10	81	-0.2

HYDE, DICK Richard Elde B8.3.1928 Hindsboro IL BR/TR/5-11/170* d4.23 Col Illinois

YEAR	TM LG	W	L	PCT	G	GS	CG-SHO	SV-BS	IP	H	R	HR	HB	BB-IB	SO	ERA	AERA	OAV	OOB	AB-HR-SH	AVG	PB	SUP	APR	DL	PW
1955	Was A	0	0	—	3	0	0	0	2	2	1	0	0	1-1	1	4.50	85	.286	.375	0	—	-0		0		0.0
1957	Was A	4	3	.571	52	0	0	1	109.1	104	54	4	7	56-7	46	4.12	95	.261	.356	18	.167	-0	92	-2		-0.1
1958	Was A	10	3	.769	53	0	0	18	103	82	26	1	2	35-7	49	1.75	218	.220	.288	18-0-3	.000	-2		21		3.4
1959	Was A	2	5	.286	37	0	0	4	54.1	56	34	5	2	27-3	29	4.97	79	.269	.354	6-0-1	.000	-1		-6		-0.8
1960	Was A	0	1	.000	9	0	0	0	8.2	11	4	2	1	5-1	4	4.15	94	.355	.459	0	—	0		0		0.0
1961	Bal A	1	2	.333	15	0	0	0	21	18	14	1	1	13-3	15	5.57	69	.228	.344	1	1.000	0		-4		-0.4
Total	6	17	14	.548	169	2	0	23	298.1	273	133	13	13	137-22	144	3.56	109	.249	.336	43-0-4	.093	-2	92	9		2.1

HYNDMAN, JIM James Harvey B7.9.1866 Hamilton ON, Can. D1.16.1934 Alamosa CO d7.23

YEAR	TM LG	W	L	PCT	G	GS	CG-SHO	SV-BS	IP	H	R	HR	HB	BB-IB	SO	ERA	AERA	OAV	OOB	AB-HR-SH	AVG	PB	SUP	APR	DL	PW
1886	Phi AA	0	1	.000	1	1	0	0	2	5	10	1	1	5	1	27.00	13	.455	.647	4	.000	-1	288	-5		-0.6

HYNES, PAT Patrick J. B3.12.1884 St.Louis MO D3.12.1907 St.Louis MO TL d9.27 ▲

YEAR	TM LG	W	L	PCT	G	GS	CG-SHO	SV-BS	IP	H	R	HR	HB	BB-IB	SO	ERA	AERA	OAV	OOB	AB-HR-SH	AVG	PB	SUP	APR	DL	PW
1903	StL N	0	1	.000	1	1	1	0	9	10	6	0	0	6	1	4.00	82	.294	.400	3	.000	-0	62	-1		-0.1
1904	StL A	1	0	1.000	5	2	1	0	26	35	21	1	0	7	6	6.23	40	.321	.362	254-0-6	.236	0*	187	-10		-0.5
Total	2	1	1	.500	6	3	2	0	35	45	27	1	0	13	7	5.66	47	.315	.372	257-0-6	.233	0	140	-11		-0.6

IBURG, HAM Herman Edward B10.29.1877 San Francisco CA D2.11.1945 San Francisco CA BR/TR/5-11/165 d4.17

YEAR	TM LG	W	L	PCT	G	GS	CG-SHO	SV-BS	IP	H	R	HR	HB	BB-IB	SO	ERA	AERA	OAV	OOB	AB-HR-SH	AVG	PB	SUP	APR	DL	PW
1902	Phi N	11	18	.379	30	29	20-1	0	236	286	141	1	11	62	106	3.89	72	.299	.349	87	.138	-5*	94	-28		-3.5

IGNASIAK, GARY Gary Raymond B9.1.1949 Anchorville MI BR/TL/5-11/185 [DetA67 36/673] d9.20 b-Mike

YEAR	TM LG	W	L	PCT	G	GS	CG-SHO	SV-BS	IP	H	R	HR	HB	BB-IB	SO	ERA	AERA	OAV	OOB	AB-HR-SH	AVG	PB	SUP	APR	DL	PW
1973	Det A	0	0	—	3	0	0	0-0	4.2	5	2	0	0	3-0	4	3.86	106	.278	.364	0	—	0		0		0.0

IGNASIAK, MIKE Michael James B3.12.1966 Mt.Clemens MI BB/TR/5-11/175(175-190) [MilA88 8/211] d8.22 b-Gary Col Michigan

YEAR	TM LG	W	L	PCT	G	GS	CG-SHO	SV-BS	IP	H	R	HR	HB	BB-IB	SO	ERA	AERA	OAV	OOB	AB-HR-SH	AVG	PB	SUP	APR	DL	PW
1991	Mil A	2	1	.667	4	1	0	0-0	12.2	7	8	2	0	8-0	10	5.68	70	.163	.294	0	—	0	92	-2	28	-0.4
1993	Mil A	1	1	.500	27	0	0	0-2	37	32	17	2	2	21-4	28	3.65	118	.241	.350	0	—	0		3		0.1
1994	Mil A	3	1	.750	23	5	0	0-1	47.2	51	25	5	1	13-2	24	4.53	112	.276	.325	0	—	0	65	3	9	0.2
1995	Mil A	4	1	.800	25	0	0	0-1	39.2	51	27	5	2	23-3	26	5.90	85	.325	.411	0	—	0		-3	35	-0.4
Total	4	10	4	.714	79	6	0	0-4	137	141	77	14	5	65-9	88	4.80	99	.272	.356	0	—	0	71	1	72	-0.5

ILSLEY, BLAISE Blaise Francis B4.9.1964 Alpena MI BL/TL/6-1/195 [HouN85 4/92] d4.4 Col Indiana St.

YEAR	TM LG	W	L	PCT	G	GS	CG-SHO	SV-BS	IP	H	R	HR	HB	BB-IB	SO	ERA	AERA	OAV	OOB	AB-HR-SH	AVG	PB	SUP	APR	DL	PW
1994	Chi N	0	0	—	10	0	0	0-0	15	25	13	2	0	9-2	9	7.80	54	.385	.459	1	.000	-0		-5	19	-0.3

IMLAY, DOC Harry Miller B1.12.1889 Allentown NJ D10.7.1948 Bordentown NJ BR/TR/5-11/168 d7.7 Col Penn

YEAR	TM LG	W	L	PCT	G	GS	CG-SHO	SV-BS	IP	H	R	HR	HB	BB-IB	SO	ERA	AERA	OAV	OOB	AB-HR-SH	AVG	PB	SUP	APR	DL	PW
1913	Phi N	0	0	—	9	0	0	0	13.2	19	13	1	0	7	7	7.24	46	.358	.433	3	.000	-0		-5		-0.3

INGERSOLL, BOB Robert Randolph B1.8.1883 Rapid City SD D1.13.1927 Minneapolis MN BR/TR/5-11.5/175 d4.23

YEAR	TM LG	W	L	PCT	G	GS	CG-SHO	SV-BS	IP	H	R	HR	HB	BB-IB	SO	ERA	AERA	OAV	OOB	AB-HR-SH	AVG	PB	SUP	APR	DL	PW
1914	Cin N	0	0	—	4	0	0	0	6	5	2	0	1	5	2	3.00	98	.250	.423	1	1.000	0		0		0.1

INKS, BERT Albert John B1.27.1871 Ligonier IN D10.3.1941 Ligonier IN BL/TL/6-3/175 d9.2

YEAR	TM LG	W	L	PCT	G	GS	CG-SHO	SV-BS	IP	H	R	HR	HB	BB-IB	SO	ERA	AERA	OAV	OOB	AB-HR-SH	AVG	PB	SUP	APR	DL	PW
1891	Bro N	3	10	.231	13	13	11-1	0	96.1	99	70	2	6	43	47	4.02	82	.256	.339	35	.286	2	74	-8		-0.7
1892	Bro N	4	2	.667	9	8	4-1	0	58	48	34	0	4	33	25	3.88	82	.216	.328	25	.400	3	155	-4		0.0
	Was N	1	2	.333	3	3	3	0	21	29	27	0	2	10	11	5.14	63	.315	.394	10	.300	1	136	-6		-0.6
	Year	5	4	.556	12	11	7-1	0	79	77	61	0	6	43	36	4.22	76	.245	.347	35	.371	4	150	-9		-0.6
1894	Bal N	9	4	.692	22	14	10	1	133	181	108	4	11	54	30	5.55	99	.321	.391	57-0-1	.316	2*	95	-1		0.0
	Lou N	2	6	.250	8	8	8	0	59.2	87	70	2	1	34	8	6.49	79	.336	.415	27	.444	3	83	-11		-0.8
	Year	11	10	.524	30	22	18	1	192.2	268	178	6	12	88	38	5.84	92	.326	.399	84-0-1	.357	5	91	-10		-0.8
1895	Lou N	7	20	.259	28	27	21	0	205.1	294	197	3	15	78	42	6.40	72	.331	.394	84-0-1	.250	-0	81	-35		-3.1
1896	Phi N	0	1	.000	3	1	0	0	10.1	21	13	1	1	5	2	7.84	55	.412	.474	5	.200	-0	66	-4		-0.4
	Cin N	1	1	.500	3	3	2	0	20	21	13	0	1	9	2	4.50	103	.269	.352	7	.000	-1	62	0		-0.1
	Year	1	2	.333	6	4	2	0	30.1	42	26	1	2	14	4	5.64	80	.326	.400	12	.083	-1	63	-3		-0.5
Total	5	27	46	.370	89	77	59-2	1	603.2	780	532	12	41	266	167	5.52	81	.307	.382	250-0-2	.300	9	89	-69		-5.7

INNIS, JEFF Jeffrey David B7.5.1962 Decatur IL BR/TR/6-0/170(168-180) [NYN83 13/318] d5.16 Col Illinois

YEAR	TM LG	W	L	PCT	G	GS	CG-SHO	SV-BS	IP	H	R	HR	HB	BB-IB	SO	ERA	AERA	OAV	OOB	AB-HR-SH	AVG	PB	SUP	APR	DL	PW
1987	NY N	0	1	.000	17	0	0	0-0	25.2	29	9	5	1	4-1	28	3.16	121	.279	.312	3	.000	-0	71	3		0.1
1988	NY N	1	1	.500	12	0	0	0-0	19	19	6	0	0	2-1	14	1.89	172	.250	.266	0	—	0		2		0.2
1989	NY N	0	1	.000	29	0	0	0-0	39.2	38	16	2	1	8-0	16	3.18	104	.255	.296	2	.000	-0		0		0.0
1990	NY N	1	3	.250	18	0	0	1-1	26.1	19	9	4	1	10-3	12	2.39	157	.209	.288	0-0-1	—	0		4		0.5
1991	NY N	0	2	.000	69	0	0	0-3	84.1	66	30	2	0	23-6	47	2.66	138	.219	.270	0	—	0		9		0.6
1992	NY N	6	9	.400	76	0	0	1-3	88	85	32	4	6	36-9	39	2.86	122	.266	.347	2	.000	-0		6		1.1
1993	NY N	2	3	.400	67	0	0	3-2	76.2	81	39	5	6	38-12	36	4.11	98	.278	.372	0-0-2	—	-1		0		0.0
Total	7	10	20	.333	288	1	0	5-9	360	337	141	22	15	121-27	192	3.05	120	.253	.319	9-0-3	.000	-1	71	24		2.5

IOTT, HOOKS Clarence Eugene B12.3.1919 Mountain Grove MO D8.17.1980 St.Petersburg FL BB/TL/6-2/200 d9.6 Mil 1943-45

YEAR	TM LG	W	L	PCT	G	GS	CG-SHO	SV-BS	IP	H	R	HR	HB	BB-IB	SO	ERA	AERA	OAV	OOB	AB-HR-SH	AVG	PB	SUP	APR	DL	PW
1941	StL A	0	0	—	2	0	0	0	2	2	2	0	1	1	1	9.00	48	.250	.333	0	—	-0		-1		0.0
1947	StL A	0	1	.000	4	0	0	0	8.1	15	16	4	0	14	6	16.20	24	.375	.537	0	.000	-0		-10		-1.0

YEAR	TM LG	W	L	PCT	G	GS	CG-SHO	SV-BS	IP	H	R	HR	HB	BB-IB	SO	ERA	AERA	OAV	OOB	AB-HR-SH	AVG	PB	SUP	APR	DL	PW
	NY N	3	8	.273	20	9	2-1	0	71.1	67	50	3	1	52	46	5.93	69	.251	.375	21-0-2	.143	1	132	-13		-1.6
Total	2	3	9	.250	26	9	2-1	0	81.2	84	68	7	1	67	53	7.05	58	.267	.397	23-0-2	.130	1	132	-24		-2.6

IRABU, HIDEKI   Hideki   B5.5.1969 Hyogo, Japan   BR/TR/6-4/240*   d7.10

YEAR	TM LG	W	L	PCT	G	GS	CG-SHO	SV-BS	IP	H	R	HR	HB	BB-IB	SO	ERA	AERA	OAV	OOB	AB-HR-SH	AVG	PB	SUP	APR	DL	PW
1997	NY A	5	4	.556	13	9	0	0-0	53.1	69	47	15	1	20-0	56	7.09	63	.311	.367	1	.000	-0	144	-16		-2.2
1998	NY A	13	9	.591	29	28	2-1	0-0	173	148	79	27	9	76-1	126	4.06	108	.233	.321	4-0-1	.250	0	105	8		0.8
1999	†NY A	11	7	.611	32	27	2-1	0-0	169.1	180	98	26	6	46-0	133	4.84	98	.267	.317	4-0-2	.000	-0	144	-1		-0.2
2000	Mon N	2	5	.286	11	11	0	0-0	54.2	77	45	9	1	14-0	42	7.24	65	.339	.377	16-0-2	.125	-0	108	-13	124	-1.1
2001	Mon N	0	2	.000	3	3	0	0-0	16.2	22	9	3	0	3-0	18	4.86	89	.314	.338	3	.000	-0	36	-1	139	-0.1
2002	Tex A	3	8	.273	38	2	0	16-4	47	51	30	11	1	16-2	30	5.74	83	.279	.337	0	—	0	68	-4	79	-0.7
Total	6	34	35	.493	126	80	4-2	16-4	514	547	308	91	18	175-3	405	5.15	89	.272	.333	28-0-5	.107	-1	120	-27	342	-3.8

IRVINE, DARYL   Daryl Keith   B11.15.1964 Harrisonburg VA   BR/TR/6-3/195*   [BosA85*S1/20]   d4.28   Col Ferrum

YEAR	TM LG	W	L	PCT	G	GS	CG-SHO	SV-BS	IP	H	R	HR	HB	BB-IB	SO	ERA	AERA	OAV	OOB	AB-HR-SH	AVG	PB	SUP	APR	DL	PW
1990	Bos A	1	1	.500	11	0	0	0-0	17.1	15	10	4	1	10-3	9	4.67	88	.246	.338	0	—	0		-1		-0.1
1991	Bos A	0	0	—	9	0	0	0-0	18	25	13	2	2	9-1	8	6.00	72	.321	.404	0	—	0		-3	67	-0.1
1992	Bos A	3	4	.429	21	0	0	0-3	28	31	20	1	2	14-2	10	6.11	70	.287	.370	0	—	0		-5		-0.9
Total	3	4	5	.444	41	0	0	0-3	63.1	71	43	3	4	33-6	27	5.68	74	.287	.372	0	—	0		-9	67	-1.1

IRWIN, BILL   William Franklin "Phil"   B9.16.1859 Neville OH   D8.7.1933 Ft.Thomas KY   BR/TR/6-0/195   d8.30

YEAR	TM LG	W	L	PCT	G	GS	CG-SHO	SV-BS	IP	H	R	HR	HB	BB-IB	SO	ERA	AERA	OAV	OOB	AB-HR-SH	AVG	PB	SUP	APR	DL	PW
1886	Cin AA	0	2	.000	2	2	2	0	17	18	19	2	0	8	6	5.82	60	.247	.321	6	.000	-0	59	-5		-0.4

ISBELL, FRANK   William Frank "Bald Eagle"   B8.21.1875 Delevan NY   D7.15.1941 Wichita KS   BL/TR/5-11/190   d5.1   ▲

YEAR	TM LG	W	L	PCT	G	GS	CG-SHO	SV-BS	IP	H	R	HR	HB	BB-IB	SO	ERA	AERA	OAV	OOB	AB-HR-SH	AVG	PB	SUP	APR	DL	PW
1898	Chi N	4	7	.364	13	9	7	0	81	86	54	0	7	42	19	3.56	101	.270	.368	159-0-6	.233	-0*	101	-1		-0.1
1901	Chi A	0	0	—	1	0	0	0	1	2	1	0	0	0	0	9.00	39	.400	.400	556-3-13	.257	0*		0		0.0
1902	Chi A	0	0	—	1	0	0	0	1	3	2	0	0	1	1	9.00	38	.500	.571	515-4-23	.252	0*	212	-1		0.0
1906	†Chi A	0	0	—	1	0	0	0	2	1	0	0	0	0	2	0.00	—	.143	.143	549-0-31	.279	0*		1		0.0
1907	Chi A	0	0	—	1	0	0	1	0.1	0	0	0	0	0	0	0.00	—	.000	.000	486-0-24	.243	0*		0		0.0
Total	5	4	7	.364	17	10	7	1	85	92	57	0	7	43	19	3.59	99	.273	.367	2265-7-97	.257	1	112	-1		-0.1

ISHII, KAZUHISA   Kazuhisa   B9.9.1973 Tokyo, Japan   BL/TL/6-0/187(187-215)   d4.6

YEAR	TM LG	W	L	PCT	G	GS	CG-SHO	SV-BS	IP	H	R	HR	HB	BB-IB	SO	ERA	AERA	OAV	OOB	AB-HR-SH	AVG	PB	SUP	APR	DL	PW
2002	LA N	14	10	.583	28	28	0	0-0	154	137	82	20	4	106-3	143	4.27	91	.240	.360	50-0-4	.100	-2	112	-8	21	-1.3
2003	LA N	9	7	.563	27	27	0	0-0	147	129	72	16	6	101-4	140	3.86	107	.238	.363	34-0-9	.029	-3	82	3	31	0.0
2004	LA N	13	8	.619	31	31	2-2	0-0	172	155	97	21	4	98-2	99	4.71	88	.246	.348	55-1-6	.127	-1	128	-12		-1.5
2005	NY N	3	9	.250	19	16	0	0-0	91	87	59	13	3	49-3	53	5.14	81	.257	.354	25-0-4	.200	-5	91	-12	28	-1.3
Total	4	39	34	.534	105	102	2-2	0-0	564	508	310	70	17	354-12	435	4.44	92	.244	.356	164-1-23	.110	-5	105	-29	80	-4.1

ISRINGHAUSEN, JASON   Jason Derik   B9.7.1972 Brighton IL   BR/TR/6-3/210(196-230)   [NYN91 44/1157]   d7.5   Col Lewis & Clark (IL) CC   [DL 1998 NY N 181]

YEAR	TM LG	W	L	PCT	G	GS	CG-SHO	SV-BS	IP	H	R	HR	HB	BB-IB	SO	ERA	AERA	OAV	OOB	AB-HR-SH	AVG	PB	SUP	APR	DL	PW
1995	NY N	9	2	.818	14	14	1	0-0	93	88	29	6	2	31-2	55	2.81	144	.254	.317	27-0-4	.148	1	96	15		1.7
1996	NY N	6	14	.300	27	27	2-1	0-0	171.2	190	103	13	8	73-5	114	4.77	84	.284	.357	51-2-2	.255	6	90	-14	19	-0.8
1997	NY N	2	2	.500	6	6	0	0-0	29.2	40	27	3	1	22-0	25	7.58	53	.336	.438	7-0-1	.143	-0	150	-12	148	-1.3
1999	NY N	1	3	.250	13	5	0	1-0	39.1	43	29	7	2	22-2	31	6.41	68	.279	.374	12-0-1	.083	-0	135	-10		-0.9
	Oak A	0	1	.000	20	0	0	8-0	25.1	21	6	2	1	12-2	20	2.13	222	.223	.318	0	—	0		8		0.7
2000	†Oak A★	6	4	.600	66	0	0	33-7	69	67	34	6	3	32-5	57	3.78	128	.252	.338	0	—	0		18		1.4
2001	†Oak A	4	3	.571	65	0	0	34-9	71.1	54	24	5	0	23-5	74	2.65	172	.203	.266	0	—	0		15		2.4
2002	†StL N	3	2	.600	60	0	0	32-5	65.1	46	22	0	1	18-1	68	2.48	163	.199	.257	0	—	0		10		1.6
2003	StL N	0	1	.000	40	0	0	22-3	42	31	14	2	0	18-1	41	2.36	175	.200	.283	-2	.500	1		7	72	0.9
2004	†StL N	4	2	.667	74	0	0	47-7	75.1	55	27	5	2	23-4	71	2.87	149	.199	.265	3	.333	0		11		2.1
2005	†StL N☆	1	2	.333	63	0	0	39-4	59	43	14	4	1	27-5	51	2.14	196	.202	.293	0	—	0		14	16	2.4
Total	10	36	36	.500	448	52	3-1	216-35	741	678	329	53	21	301-32	607	3.60	118	.243	.319	102-2-8	.206	7	100	52	436	10.2

IZQUIERDO, HANSEL   Hansel   B1.2.1977 Havana, Cuba   BR/TR/6-2/205   [FlaN95 7/177]   d4.21

YEAR	TM LG	W	L	PCT	G	GS	CG-SHO	SV-BS	IP	H	R	HR	HB	BB-IB	SO	ERA	AERA	OAV	OOB	AB-HR-SH	AVG	PB	SUP	APR	DL	PW
2002	Fla N	2	0	1.000	20	2	0	0-0	29.2	33	17	2	5	21-3	20	4.55	86	.289	.413	2	.000	-0	71	-3		-0.2

JACKSON, AL   Alvin Neill   B12.26.1935 Waco TX   BL/TL/5-10/169*   d6.1   C8   Col Wiley

YEAR	TM LG	W	L	PCT	G	GS	CG-SHO	SV-BS	IP	H	R	HR	HB	BB-IB	SO	ERA	AERA	OAV	OOB	AB-HR-SH	AVG	PB	SUP	APR	DL	PW
1959	Pit N	0	0	—	8	3	0	0	18	30	14	1	0	8-3	13	6.50	60	.405	.463	5	.200	0	239	-5		-0.3
1961	Pit N	1	0	1.000	3	2	1	0	23.2	20	10	2	0	4-1	15	3.42	117	.233	.267	8	.000	-1*	167	2		0.0
1962	NY N	8	20	.286	36	33	12-4	0	231.1	244	132	16	5	78-5	118	4.40	95	.273	.333	73-0-6	.068	-5*	83	-5		-0.7
1963	NY N	13	17	.433	37	34	11	1	227	237	128	25	12	84-2	142	3.96	88	.267	.336	79-0-3	.203	2*	82	-15		-1.6
1964	NY N	11	16	.407	40	31	11-3	0	213.1	229	115	18	4	60-3	112	4.26	84	.272	.323	72-1-2	.153	2*	72	-16		-1.6
1965	NY N	8	20	.286	37	31	7-3	0	205.1	217	111	17	8	61-4	120	4.34	81	.271	.328	60-0-8	.117	-1*	64	-17		-2.2
1966	StL N	13	15	.464	36	30	11-3	0	232.2	222	82	18	3	45-10	90	2.51	143	.250	.288	74-0-5	.176	2*	75	25		3.5
1967	StL N	9	4	.692	38	11	1-1	1	107	117	61	7	1	29-5	43	3.95	83	.279	.322	31-0-1	.258	2*	172	-12		-1.0
1968	NY N	3	7	.300	25	9	0	3	92.2	88	42	5	2	17-6	59	3.69	82	.249	.285	28-0-1	.250	1*	86	-7		-0.6
1969	NY N	0	0	—	9	0	0	0-0	11	18	13	1	1	4-0	10	10.64	34	.353	.397	1	.000	-0		-8		-0.4
	Cin N	1	0	1.000	33	0	0	3-0	27.1	27	17	3	1	13-3	16	5.27	71	.260	.376	4	.250	0		-4		-0.2
	Year	1	0	1.000	42	0	0	3-0	38.1	45	30	6	4	21-3	26	6.81	55	.290	.383	5	.200	0		-11		-0.6
Total	10	67	99	.404	302	184	54-14	10-0	1389.1	1449	725	115	39	407-42	738	3.98	91	.268	.322	435-1-26	.159	3	86	-62		-5.1

JACKSON, CHARLIE   Charles Bernard   B8.4.1876 Versailles OH   D11.23.1957 Scottsbluff NE   TR   d8.11

YEAR	TM LG	W	L	PCT	G	GS	CG-SHO	SV-BS	IP	H	R	HR	HB	BB-IB	SO	ERA	AERA	OAV	OOB	AB-HR-SH	AVG	PB	SUP	APR	DL	PW
1905	Det A	0	2	.000	2	2	1	0	11	14	12	1	0	7	3	5.73	48	.311	.404	4	.250	0	39	-4		-0.6

JACKSON, DANNY   Danny Lynn   B1.5.1962 San Antonio TX   BR/TL/6-0/205(190-220)   [KCA82*S1/1]   d9.11   Col Oklahoma

YEAR	TM LG	W	L	PCT	G	GS	CG-SHO	SV-BS	IP	H	R	HR	HB	BB-IB	SO	ERA	AERA	OAV	OOB	AB-HR-SH	AVG	PB	SUP	APR	DL	PW
1983	KC A	1	1	.500	4	3	0	0-0	19	26	12	1	0	6-0	9	5.21	79	.325	.372	0	—	0	111	-2		-0.2
1984	KC A	2	6	.250	15	11	1	0-0	76	84	41	4	5	35-0	40	4.26	95	.285	.370	0	—	0	81	-3		-0.3
1985	†KC A	14	12	.538	32	32	4-3	0-0	208	209	94	7	6	76-2	114	3.42	122	.261	.328	0	—	0	82	15		1.7
1986	KC A	11	12	.478	32	27	4-1	1-0	185.2	177	83	13	4	79-1	115	3.20	134	.256	.334	0	—	0	62	17	14	1.9
1987	KC A	9	18	.333	36	34	11-2	0-1	224	219	115	11	7	109-1	152	4.02	114	.258	.344	0	—	0	67	13		1.3
1988	Cin N☆	23	8	.742	35	35	15-6	0-0	260.2	206	86	13	2	71-6	161	2.73	134	.218	.273	90-0-8	.144	-0	114	24		5.2
1989	Cin N	6	11	.353	20	20	1	0-0	115.2	122	78	10	1	57-7	70	5.60	64	.271	.351	36-0-4	.222	1*	87	-23	56	-3.0
1990	†Cin N	6	6	.500	22	21	0	0-0	117.1	119	54	11	2	40-4	76	3.61	110	.266	.325	37-0-4	.054	-2*	87	3	54	0.0
1991	Chi N	1	5	.167	17	14	0	0-0	70.2	89	59	8	1	48-4	31	6.75	58	.309	.407	23-0-2	.087	-1	119	-21	94	-1.8
1992	Chi N	4	9	.308	19	19	0	0-0	113	117	59	5	3	48-3	51	4.22	86	.270	.343	36-0-4	.083	-1	79	-7		-1.0
	†Pit N	4	4	.500	15	15	0	0-0	88.1	94	40	1	1	29-3	46	3.36	103	.276	.330	24-0-5	.083	-2	120	-1		-0.2
	Year	8	13	.381	34	34	0	0-0	201.1	211	99	6	4	77-6	97	3.84	93	.272	.337	60-0-9	.083	-3	96	-9		-1.2
1993	†Phi N	12	11	.522	32	32	2-1	0-0	210.1	214	105	12	4	80-2	120	3.77	105	.263	.329	65-0-12	.077	1*	116	3		0.0
1994	Phi N★	14	6	.700	25	25	4-1	0-0	179.1	183	71	13	2	46-1	129	3.26	131	.266	.312	57-0-9	.158	1*	123	21		2.3
1995	StL N	2	12	.143	19	19	2-1	0-0	100.2	120	82	10	6	48-1	52	5.90	73	.303	.381	31-0-4	.161	0	83	-21	69	-2.4
1996	†StL N	1	1	.500	13	4	0	0-0	36.1	33	18	3	1	16-1	27	4.46	95	.243	.325	9-0-1	.333	1	117	0	124	0.2
1997	StL N	1	2	.333	4	4	0	0-0	18.2	26	17	3	2	8-1	13	7.71	54	.347	.414	7	.143	-0	105	-7	49	-0.9
	SD N	1	7	.125	13	9	0	0-0	49	72	47	9	3	20-2	19	7.53	52	.353	.413	13-0-1	.077	-1	91	-22		-2.9
	Year	2	9	.182	17	13	0	0-0	67.2	98	64	12	5	28-3	32	7.58	53	.351	.413	20-0-1	.100	-1	96	-29	460	-3.8
Total	15	112	131	.461	353	324	44-15	1-1	2072.2	2110	1061	133	50	816-35	1225	4.01	100	.266	.336	428-0-54	.126	-6	93	-11	460	-2.3

JACKSON, DARRELL   Darrell Preston   B4.3.1956 Los Angeles CA   BB/TL/5-10/150*   [MinA77 9/223]   d6.16   Col Arizona St.

YEAR	TM LG	W	L	PCT	G	GS	CG-SHO	SV-BS	IP	H	R	HR	HB	BB-IB	SO	ERA	AERA	OAV	OOB	AB-HR-SH	AVG	PB	SUP	APR	DL	PW
1978	Min A	4	6	.400	19	15	1-1	0-0	92.1	89	53	9	2	48-1	54	4.48	86	.256	.347	0	—	0*	90	-7		-0.7
1979	Min A	4	4	.500	24	8	1	0-1	69.1	89	36	5	1	26-0	43	4.28	103	.319	.377	0	—	0*	106	1		0.1
1980	Min A	9	9	.500	32	25	1	1-0	172	161	81	15	2	69-2	90	3.87	113	.250	.323	0	—	0*	81	10		1.0
1981	Min A	3	3	.500	14	5	0	0-0	32.2	35	16	1	1	19-2	26	4.41	90	.282	.382	0	—	0*	50	-1	96	-0.2
1982	Min A	0	5	.000	13	7	0	0-0	44.2	51	33	6	1	24-3	16	6.25	68	.297	.384	0	—	0*	37	-9	52	-0.9
Total	5	20	27	.426	102	60	3-1	1-1	411	425	219	36	7	186-8	229	4.38	96	.272	.349	0	—	0*	79	-6	148	-0.7

JACKSON, EDWIN   Edwin   B9.9.1983 Neu-Ulm, West Germany   BR/TR/6-3/190*   [LAN01 6/190]   d9.9

YEAR	TM LG	W	L	PCT	G	GS	CG-SHO	SV-BS	IP	H	R	HR	HB	BB-IB	SO	ERA	AERA	OAV	OOB	AB-HR-SH	AVG	PB	SUP	APR	DL	PW
2003	LA N	2	1	.667	4	3	0	0-0	22	17	6	2	1	11-1	19	2.45	168	.221	.322	6-0-1	.000	-0	68	4		0.5
2004	LA N	2	1	.667	8	5	0	0-0	24.2	31	20	7	0	11-1	16	7.30	57	.307	.375	4-0-2	.250	-0	156	-8	60	-0.9
2005	LA N	2	2	.500	7	6	0	0-0	28.2	31	22	2	1	17-0	13	6.28	65	.272	.366	10	.200	0*	117	-7		-0.9
Total	3	6	4	.600	19	14	0	0-0	75.1	79	48	11	2	39-2	48	5.50	75	.271	.357	20-0-3	.150	-0	121	-11	60	-1.2

YEAR	TM LG	W	L	PCT	G	GS	CG-SHO	SV-BS	IP	H	R	HR	HB	BB-IB	SO	ERA	AERA	OAV	OOB	AB-HR-SH	AVG	PB	SUP	APR	DL	PW
JACKSON, GRANT	Grant Dwight "Buck"			B9.28.1942 Fostoria OH			BB/TL/6-0/190(180-204)		d9.3	C4		Col Bowling Green														
1965	Phi N	1	1	.500	6	2	0	0	13.2	17	11	4	0	5-0	15	7.24	48	.304	.361	4	.000	-0	101	-5		-0.7
1966	Phi N	0	0	—	2	0	0	0	1.2	2	1	0	0	3-0	0	5.40	67	.333	.556	0	—	0	0	0		0.0
1967	Phi N	2	3	.400	43	4	0	1	84.1	86	40	3	2	43-7	83	3.84	89	.267	.352	15	.133	-0	103	-3		-0.3
1968	Phi N	1	6	.143	33	6	1	1	61	59	28	4	0	20-3	49	2.95	102	.248	.302	10-0-1	.300	1*	149	-2		-0.1
1969	Phi N☆	14	18	.438	38	35	13-4	1-0	253	237	114	16	5	92-3	180	3.34	107	.249	.316	86-1-6	.140	-0*	87	2		0.2
1970	Phi N	5	15	.250	32	23	1	0-0	149.2	170	94	17	1	61-3	104	5.29	76	.288	.354	44-0-1	.091	-2*	49	-21		-2.6
1971	†Bal A	4	3	.571	29	9	0	0-0	77.2	72	31	7	2	20-5	51	3.13	109	.249	.299	22-1-0	.091	-0	105	2		0.2
1972	Bal A	1	1	.500	32	0	0	8-0	41	33	14	1	0	9-0	34	2.63	118	.217	.261	4	.000	-0		2		0.1
1973	†Bal A	8	0	1.000	45	0	0	9-2	80.1	54	18	5	0	24-4	47	1.90	198	.198	.260	0	—	0		17		2.1
1974	†Bal A	6	4	.600	49	0	0	12-7	66.2	48	19	7	1	22-4	56	2.57	136	.198	.265	0	—	0		8		1.5
1975	Bal A	4	3	.571	41	0	0	7-1	48.1	42	18	3	1	21-6	39	3.35	106	.241	.322	0	—	0		2		0.3
1976	Bal A	1	1	.500	13	0	0	3-0	19.1	19	11	1	2	9-2	14	5.12	64	.268	.361	0	—	0		-4		-0.5
	†NY A	6	0	1.000	21	2	1-1	1-0	58.2	38	11	1	1	16-0	25	1.69	202	.186	.244	0	—	0	206	12		1.2
	Year	7	1	.875	34	2	1-1	4-0	78	57	22	2	3	25-2	39	2.54	133	.207	.276	0	—	0	208	9		0.7
1977	Pit N	5	3	.625	49	2	0	4-2	91	81	44	11	1	39-8	41	3.86	104	.240	.318	18	.333	2	111	1		0.3
1978	Pit N	7	5	.583	60	0	0	5-3	77.1	89	32	5	1	32-9	45	3.26	115	.298	.362	12	.250	1		4		0.8
1979	†Pit N	8	5	.615	72	0	0	14-5	82	67	32	9	2	35-5	39	2.96	132	.230	.311	9	.000	-1		8		1.3
1980	Pit N	8	4	.667	61	0	0	9-3	71	71	24	4	0	20-3	31	2.92	127	.275	.322	10	.000	-1		7		1.1
1981	Pit N	1	2	.333	35	0	0	4-2	32.1	30	10	1	0	10-3	17	2.51	146	.248	.301	2	.000	-0		4		0.4
	Mon N	1	0	1.000	10	0	0	0-0	10.2	14	9	2	0	9-2	4	7.59	47	.333	.451	0	—	0		-4		-0.4
	Year	2	2	.500	45	0	0	4-2	43	44	19	3	0	19-5	21	3.77	96	.270	.342	2	.000	-0		0		0.0
1982	KC A	3	1	.750	20	0	0	0-2	38.1	42	27	7	2	21-4	15	5.17	79	.271	.363	0	—	0		-6		-0.6
	Pit N	0	0	—	1	0	0	0-0	0.2	1	1	1	0	0-0	0	13.50	28	.333	.333	0	—	0		-1		0.0
Total	18	86	75	.534	692	83	16-5	79-27	1358.2	1272	589	109	21	511-71	889	3.46	105	.251	.318	236-2-8	.136	-2	85	23		4.3

YEAR	TM LG	W	L	PCT	G	GS	CG-SHO	SV-BS	IP	H	R	HR	HB	BB-IB	SO	ERA	AERA	OAV	OOB	AB-HR-SH	AVG	PB	SUP	APR	DL	PW
JACKSON, JOHN	John Lewis			B7.15.1909 Philadelphia PA			D10.22.1956 Somers Point NJ		BR/TR/6-2/180	d6.20		Col Penn														
1933	Phi N	2	2	.500	10	7	1	0	54	74	42	3	5	35	11	6.00	64	.329	.430	21	.143	-1	112	-11		-1.0

YEAR	TM LG	W	L	PCT	G	GS	CG-SHO	SV-BS	IP	H	R	HR	HB	BB-IB	SO	ERA	AERA	OAV	OOB	AB-HR-SH	AVG	PB	SUP	APR	DL	PW
JACKSON, LARRY	Lawrence Curtis			B6.2.1931 Nampa ID			D8.28.1990 Boise ID		BR/TR/6-2/190(175-190)	d4.17		Col Boise St.														
1955	StL N	9	14	.391	37	25	4-1	0	177.1	189	93	25	9	72-11	88	4.31	94	.277	.351	57-0-1	.053	-6	86	-5		-1.2
1956	StL N	2	2	.500	51	1	0	9	85.1	75	44	9	1	45-8	50	4.11	92	.240	.337	11	.091	-0	70	-3		-0.1
1957	StL N★	15	9	.625	41	22	6-2	1	210.1	196	84	21	4	57-8	96	3.47	114	.248	.301	72-0-3	.181	0	99	14		1.8
1958	StL N★	13	13	.500	49	23	11-1	8	198	211	93	21	10	51-11	124	3.68	112	.272	.324	60-0-2	.150	-2*	101	8		0.7
1959	StL N	14	13	.519	40	37	12-3	0	256	271	103	13	4	64-3	145	3.30	128	.270	.315	80-0-7	.112	-3*	88	25		2.1
1960	StL N★	18	13	.581	43	38	14-3	0	282	277	123	22	3	70-4	171	3.48	118	.257	.302	95-0-5	.211	2*	96	17		1.8
1961	StL N	14	11	.560	33	28	12-3	0	211	203	99	20	4	56-5	113	3.75	117	.252	.301	74-0-6	.176	0*	93	16		1.8
1962	StL N	16	11	.593	36	35	11-2	0	252.1	267	121	25	4	64-6	112	3.75	114	.269	.316	89-0-5	.169	2	104	13		1.5
1963	Chi N★	14	18	.438	37	37	13-4	0	275	256	102	11	6	54-3	153	2.55	137	.245	.284	87-0-9	.195	2	79	23		3.1
1964	Chi N	24	11	.686	40	38	19-3	0	297.2	265	114	17	1	58-8	148	3.14	118	.235	.272	114-0-5	.175	1	110	18		2.5
1965	Chi N	14	21	.400	39	39	12-4	0	257.1	268	126	28	5	57-8	131	3.85	96	.267	.309	86-1-4	.128	1*	81	-3		-0.2
1966	Chi N	0	2	.000	3	2	0	0	8	14	13	3	0	4-0	5	13.50	27	.368	.429	3	.000	-0	12	-8		-1.3
	Phi N	15	13	.536	35	33	12-5	0	247	243	93	22	3	58-5	107	2.99	120	.259	.305	89-1-5	.146	-0*	93	16		1.8
	Year	15	15	.500	38	35	12-5	0	255	257	106	25	5	62-5	112	3.32	108	.264	.310	92-1-5	.141	-1	88	6		0.5
1967	Phi N	13	15	.464	40	37	11-4	0	261.2	242	111	17	6	54-11	139	3.10	110	.241	.283	87-0-4	.161	0*	89	6		0.9
1968	Phi N	13	17	.433	34	34	12-2	0	243.2	229	86	9	4	60-15	127	2.77	108	.248	.296	85-0-2	.141	-0*	91	6		0.8
Total	14	194	183	.515	558	429	149-37	20	3262.2	3206	1405	259	68	824-106	1709	3.40	113	.256	.306	1089-2-58	.156	-5	93	143		16.0

YEAR	TM LG	W	L	PCT	G	GS	CG-SHO	SV-BS	IP	H	R	HR	HB	BB-IB	SO	ERA	AERA	OAV	OOB	AB-HR-SH	AVG	PB	SUP	APR	DL	PW
JACKSON, MIKE	Michael Ray			B12.22.1964 Houston TX			BR/TR/6-0/200(185-225)		[PhiN84*S2/44]	d8.11		Col Hill (TX) JC		[DL 2000 Phi N 177]												
1986	Phi N	0	0	—	9	0	0	0-1	13.1	12	5	2	2	4-1	3	3.38	116	.250	.333	0	—	0		1		0.0
1987	Phi N	3	10	.231	55	7	0	1-1	109.1	88	55	16	2	56-6	93	4.20	102	.219	.316	17-0-3	.118	-0	105	2	15	0.1
1988	Sea A	6	5	.545	62	0	0	4-7	99.1	74	37	10	2	43-10	76	2.63	159	.209	.291	0	—	0		14		1.6
1989	Sea A	4	6	.400	65	0	0	7-3	99.1	81	43	8	6	54-6	94	3.17	127	.223	.332	0	—	0		8		0.8
1990	Sea A	5	7	.417	63	0	0	3-9	77.1	64	42	8	2	44-12	69	4.54	88	.229	.333	0	—	0		-4		-0.5
1991	Sea A	7	7	.500	72	0	0	14-8	88.2	64	35	5	6	34-11	74	3.25	128	.201	.290	0	—	0		9		1.4
1992	SF N	6	6	.500	67	0	0	2-1	82	76	35	7	4	33-10	80	3.73	89	.252	.331	2	.000	-0		-3		-0.4
1993	SF N	6	6	.500	81	0	0	1-5	77.1	58	28	7	3	24-6	70	3.03	130	.204	.272	3	.667	2		8	16	1.3
1994	SF N	3	2	.600	36	0	0	4-2	42.1	23	8	4	2	11-0	51	1.49	273	.164	.234	1-0-1	.000	-0		12	51	1.5
1995	†Cin N	6	1	.857	40	0	0	2-2	49	38	13	5	1	19-1	41	2.39	175	.213	.291	4	.250	0		10	41	1.4
1996	Sea A	1	1	.500	73	0	0	6-2	72	61	32	11	6	24-3	70	3.63	137	.225	.301	0	—	0		11		0.5
1997	†Cle A	2	5	.286	71	0	0	15-2	75	59	33	3	4	29-5	74	3.24	145	.215	.297	0	—	0		10		1.3
1998	†Cle A	1	1	.500	69	0	0	40-5	64	43	11	4	4	13-0	55	1.55	309	.195	.252	0	—	0		23		3.0
1999	†Cle A	2	4	.429	72	0	0	39-4	68.2	60	32	11	2	26-1	55	4.06	125	.232	.304	0	—	0		8		1.5
2001	†Hou N	5	3	.625	67	0	0	4-5	69	68	36	14	2	22-3	46	4.70	98	.260	.319	1	.000	-0		1		0.0
2002	†Min A	2	3	.400	58	0	0	0-2	55	59	20	5	4	13-3	29	3.27	136	.284	.333	0	—	0		8	23	0.7
2004	Chi A	2	0	1.000	45	0	0	1-3	46.2	55	27	8	1	15-2	39	5.01	94	.294	.351	0	—	0		-1		-0.1
Total	17	62	67	.481	1005	7	0	142-59	1188.1	983	492	127	56	464-80	1006	3.42	126	.226	.306	28-0-4	.179	1	105	117	323	14.1

YEAR	TM LG	W	L	PCT	G	GS	CG-SHO	SV-BS	IP	H	R	HR	HB	BB-IB	SO	ERA	AERA	OAV	OOB	AB-HR-SH	AVG	PB	SUP	APR	DL	PW
JACKSON, MIKE	Michael Warren			B3.27.1946 Paterson NJ			BL/TL/6-3/190*		d5.10																	
1970	Phi N	1	1	.500	5	0	0	0-0	6.1	6	1	0	0	4-0	4	1.42	283	.286	.400	1	1.000	0		2		0.4
1971	StL N	0	0	—	1	0	0	0-0	0.2	1	0	0	0	1-0	0	0.00	—	.333	.500	1	.000	-0		0		0.0
1972	KC A	1	2	.333	7	3	0	0-0	19.2	24	14	0	0	14-1	15	6.41	48	.320	.422	5-0-1	.000	-1	87	-7		-1.0
1973	KC A	0	0	—	9	0	0	0-0	22.1	25	17	3	1	20-1	13	6.85	60	.301	.438	0	—	0		-6		-0.3
	Cle A	0	0	—	1	0	0	0-0	0.2	1	0	0	0	0-0	1	0.00	—	.333	.333	0	—	0		0		0.0
	Year	0	0	—	10	0	0	0-0	23	26	17	3	1	20-1	14	6.65	62	.302	.435	0	—	0		-5		-0.3
Total	4	2	3	.400	23	3	0	0-0	49.2	57	32	3	1	39-2	33	5.80	63	.308	.427	7-0-1	.143	-0	87	-11		-0.9

YEAR	TM LG	W	L	PCT	G	GS	CG-SHO	SV-BS	IP	H	R	HR	HB	BB-IB	SO	ERA	AERA	OAV	OOB	AB-HR-SH	AVG	PB	SUP	APR	DL	PW
JACKSON, ROY LEE	Roy Lee			B5.1.1954 Opelika AL			BR/TR/6-2/194(190-223)		d9.13			Col Tuskegee														
1977	NY N	0	2	.000	4	4	0	0-0	24	25	16	2	3	15-1	13	6.00	63	.263	.377	6-0-1	.000	-1	94	-5		-0.5
1978	NY N	0	0	—	4	0	0	0-0	12.2	21	13	2	2	6-0	11	9.24	38	.429	.500	3	.667	1	89	-7		-0.3
1979	NY N	1	0	1.000	8	0	0	0-0	16.1	11	4	1	1	5-0	10	2.20	169	.200	.279	1	1.000	0		3		0.2
1980	NY N	1	7	.125	24	8	1	1-0	70.2	78	37	4	0	20-4	58	4.20	86	.287	.331	16	.188	0*	102	-5		-0.5
1981	Tor A	1	2	.333	39	0	0	7-1	62	65	23	5	1	25-7	27	2.61	152	.275	.346	0	—	0		8		0.6
1982	Tor A	8	8	.500	48	2	0	6-5	97	77	37	7	2	31-4	71	3.06	147	.218	.281	0	—	0	111	14		2.3
1983	Tor A	8	3	.727	49	0	0	7-5	92	92	48	6	3	41-2	48	4.50	97	.267	.344	0	—	0		0		0.0
1984	Tor A	7	8	.467	54	0	0	10-7	86	73	40	12	1	31-4	58	3.56	116	.230	.299	0	—	0		4		0.8
1985	SD N	2	3	.400	22	0	0	2-0	40	32	13	4	1	13-1	28	2.70	132	.224	.289	5-0-1	.000	-1	62	4		0.5
1986	Min A	0	1	.000	28	0	0	1-0	58.1	57	29	7	3	16-0	32	3.86	113	.256	.308	0	—	0		2		0.1
Total	10	28	34	.452	280	18	1	34-19	559	531	260	50	17	203-23	351	3.77	108	.254	.322	31-0-2	.194	1	88	18		3.2

YEAR	TM LG	W	L	PCT	G	GS	CG-SHO	SV-BS	IP	H	R	HR	HB	BB-IB	SO	ERA	AERA	OAV	OOB	AB-HR-SH	AVG	PB	SUP	APR	DL	PW
JACOBS, TONY	Anthony Robert			B8.5.1925 Dixmoor IL			D12.21.1980 Nashville TN		BB/TR/5-9/150*	d9.19																
1948	Chi N	0	0	—	1	0	0	0	2	3	1	0	0	2	2	4.50	87	.333	.333	0	—	0		0		0.0
1955	StL N	0	0	—	1	0	0	0	2	6	4	1	0	1-0	1	18.00	23	.500	.538	1	.000	-0		-3		-0.1
Total	2	0	0	—	2	0	0	0	4	9	5	1	0	3-0	3	11.25	35	.429	.455	1	.000	-0		-3		-0.1

YEAR	TM LG	W	L	PCT	G	GS	CG-SHO	SV-BS	IP	H	R	HR	HB	BB-IB	SO	ERA	AERA	OAV	OOB	AB-HR-SH	AVG	PB	SUP	APR	DL	PW
JACOBS, ART	Arthur Edward			B8.28.1902 Luckey OH			D6.8.1967 Inglewood CA		BL/TL/5-10/170	d6.18																
1939	Cin N	0	0	—	1	0	0	0	4	9	4	0	0	1	1	9.00	43	.400	.500			-0		-1		-0.1

YEAR	TM LG	W	L	PCT	G	GS	CG-SHO	SV-BS	IP	H	R	HR	HB	BB-IB	SO	ERA	AERA	OAV	OOB	AB-HR-SH	AVG	PB	SUP	APR	DL	PW
JACOBS, BUCKY	Newton Smith			B3.21.1913 Altavista VA			D6.15.1990 Richmond VA		BR/TR/5-11/155	d6.27		Col Richmond														
1937	Was A	1	1	.500	11	1	0	0	22.1	26	12	0	0	11	8	4.84	92	.295	.374	5	.000	-1	39	0		-0.1
1939	Was A	0	0	—	2	0	0	0	3	1	0	0	0	0	1	0.00	—	.100	.100	0	—	0		2		0.1
1940	Was A	0	1	.000	9	0	0	0	15	16	11	1	2	9	6	6.00	69	.271	.386	1-0-1	.000	0		-1		-0.1
Total	3	1	2	.333	22	1	0	0	40.1	43	23	1	2	20	15	4.91	88	.274	.363	6-0-1	.000	-1	39	-1		-0.1

YEAR	TM LG	W	L	PCT	G	GS	CG-SHO	SV-BS	IP	H	R	HR	HB	BB-IB	SO	ERA	AERA	OAV	OOB	AB-HR-SH	AVG	PB	SUP	APR	DL	PW

JACOBS, ELMER William Elmer B8.10.1892 Salem MO D2.10.1958 Salem MO BR/TR/6-0/165 d4.23

1914	Phi N	1	3	.250	14	7	1	0	50.2	65	38	2	3	20	17	4.80	61	.342	.413	14	.000	-2	104	-9		-0.8
1916	Pit N	6	10	.375	34	17	8	0	153	151	70	2	4	38	46	2.94	91	.258	.308	40-0-1	.075	-2	95	-5		-0.8
1917	Pit N	6	19	.240	38	25	10-1	2	227.1	214	87	3	5	76	58	2.81	101	.262	.329	67-0-3	.179	-1	69	1		0.1
1918	Pit N	0	1	.000	8	4	0	0	23.1	31	18	0	0	14	2	5.79	50	.344	.433	7	.286	0	151	-7		-0.3
	Phi N	9	5	.643	18	14	12-4	1	123	91	39	3	4	42	33	2.41	124	.210	.285	38-0-2	.158	-1	94	8		0.8
	Year	9	6	.600	26	18	12-4	1	146.1	122	57	3	4	56	35	2.95	101	.233	.312	45-0-2	.178	-1	106	2		0.5
1919	Phi N	6	10	.375	17	15	13	0	128.2	150	66	5	6	44	37	3.85	84	.304	.304	45-0-1	.178	-1	86	-8		-1.0
	StL N	3	6	.333	17	8	4-1	1	85.1	81	30	2	5	25	31	2.53	110	.264	.329	23-0-1	.348	3	89	3		0.7
	Year	9	16	.360	34	23	17-1	1	214	231	96	7	11	69	68	3.32	92	.289	.353	68-0-2	.235	2	87	-5		-0.3
1920	StL N	4	8	.333	23	9	1	1	77.2	91	56	2	5	33	21	5.21	57	.296	.374	26-0-3	.192	-0	105	-20		-2.8
1924	Chi N	11	12	.478	38	22	13-1	1	190.1	181	93	9	2	72	50	3.74	104	.258	.329	54-0-6	.111	-4	92	4		0.1
1925	Chi N	2	3	.400	18	4	1-1	1	55.2	63	37	9	1	22	19	5.17	84	.274	.340	13	.231	-0	112	-5		-0.4
1927	Chi A	2	4	.333	25	8	2-1	0	74.1	105	49	3	4	37	22	4.60	88	.354	.432	20-0-4	.150	-1	95	-6		-0.5
Total	9	50	81	.382	250	133	65-9	7	1189.1	1223	583	40	39	423	336	3.55	91	.275	.343	347-0-21	.161	-8	91	-44		-4.9

JACOBSON, BEANY Albert Leonard (b Albin Leonard Jacobson) B6.5.1881 Port Washington WI D1.31.1933 Decatur IL BL/TL/6-0/170 d4.30

1904	Was A	5	23	.179	33	30	23-1	0	253.2	276	135	6	3	57	75	3.55	75	.278	.319	88-0-1	.091	-6	66	-24		-3.0
1905	Was A	7	8	.467	22	17	12	0	144.1	139	83	1	5	35	50	3.30	80	.255	.305	44	.159	1	96	-13		-1.3
1906	StL A	9	9	.500	24	15	12	0	155	146	68	3	4	27	53	2.50	103	.252	.290	55-0-1	.091	-4	93	0		-0.5
1907	StL A	1	6	.143	7	7	6	0	57.1	55	28	1	0	26	16	2.98	84	.255	.355	18-0-1	.222	-0	54	-4		-0.5
	Bos A	0	0	—	2	1	0	0	2	2	3	0	0	3	1	9.00	29	.250	.455	0	—	0	52	-1		-0.1
	Year	1	6	.143	9	8	6	0	59.1	57	31	1	0	29	17	3.19	79	.254	.340	18-0-1	.222	-0	54	-5		-0.6
Total	4	22	46	.324	88	70	53-1	0	612.1	618	317	11	12	148	195	3.19	82	.264	.311	205-0-3	.117	-9	78	-42		-5.4

JACOBUS, LARRY Stuart Louis B12.18.1893 Cincinnati OH D8.19.1965 N.College Hill OH BB/TR/6-2/186 d7.15

1918	Cin N	0	0	1.000	5	0	0	0	17.1	25	12	0	1	9	5	5.71	47	.368	.377	5	.000	-1		-5		-0.4

JACOME, JASON Jason James B11.24.1970 Tulsa OK BL/TL/6-1/180(155-185) [NYN91 12/329] d7.2 Col Pima (AZ) CC

1994	NY N	4	3	.571	8	8	1-1	0-0	54	54	17	3	0	17-2	30	2.67	157	.269	.324	16-0-1	.063	-1	76	10		1.1
1995	NY N	0	4	.000	5	5	0	0-0	21	33	24	3	1	15-0	11	10.29	39	.359	.450	7-0-1	.000	-1	112	-14		-2.0
	KC A	4	6	.400	15	14	1	0-0	84	101	52	15	1	21-2	39	5.36	90	.300	.340	0	—	0	98	-4		-0.3
1996	KC A	0	4	.000	49	2	0	1-3	47.2	67	27	5	2	22-5	32	4.72	107	.337	.408	0	—	0	129	2		0.2
1997	KC A	0	0	—	7	0	0	0-0	6.2	13	7	2	1	5-1	3	9.45	50	.448	.543	0	—	0		-3		-0.1
	Cle A	2	0	1.000	21	4	0	0-1	42.2	45	26	8	0	15-4	24	5.27	89	.269	.328	0	—	0	112	-2		-0.1
	Year	2	0	1.000	28	4	0	0-1	49.1	58	33	10	1	20-5	27	5.84	81	.296	.362	0	—	0	112	-5		-0.2
1998	Cle A	0	1	.000	1	0	0	0-0	5	10	8	2	0	3-0	2	14.40	33	.435	.500	0	—	0	78	-5		-0.6
Total	5	10	18	.357	106	34	2-1	1-4	261	323	161	38	5	98-14	141	5.34	87	.308	.368	23-0-2	.043	-2	97	-16		-1.8

JACQUEZ, PAT Patrick Thomas B4.23.1947 Stockton CA BR/TR/6-0/200 [ChiN67*S4/67] d4.18 s-Thomas Col Santa Clara

1971	Chi A	0	0	—	2	0	0	0-0	2	4	1	0	0	2-0	1	4.50	79	.444	.500	1	.000	-0		0		0.0

JACQUEZ, THOMAS Thomas Patrick B12.29.1975 Stockton CA BL/TL/6-2/195 [PhiN97 6/176] d9.9 f-Pat Col UCLA

2000	Phi N	0	0	—	9	0	0	0-0	7.1	9	9	2	0	3-1	6	11.05	42	.333	.382	0	—	0		-5		-0.2

JAECKEL, JAKE Paul Henry B4.1.1942 E.Los Angeles CA BR/TR/5-10/180 d9.19

1964	Chi N	1	0	1.000	4	0	0	1	8	4	0	0	0	3-0	2	0.00	—	.160	.250	1	.000	-0		3		0.5

JAEGER, CHARLIE Charles Thomas B4.17.1875 Ottawa IL D9.27.1942 Ottawa IL BR/TR d9.9

1904	Det A	3	3	.500	8	6	5	0	49	49	29	0	6	15	13	2.57	99	.261	.335	17	.059	-2	65	-3		-0.6

JAEGER, JOE Joseph Peter "Zip" B3.3.1895 St.Cloud MN D12.13.1963 Hampton IA BR/TR/6-1/190 d7.28

1920	Chi N	0	0	—	2	0	0	0	3	6	4	0	0	4	2	12.00	27	.500	.625	1	.000	-0		-3		-0.2

JAKUCKI, SIG Sigmund "Jack" B8.20.1909 Camden NJ D5.28.1979 Galveston TX BR/TR/6-2.5/198 d8.30

1936	StL A	0	3	.000	7	2	0	0	20.2	32	22	2	1	12	9	8.71	62	.348	.429	6	.000	-1	90	-7		-0.8
1944	†StL A	13	9	.591	35	24	12-4	3	198	211	89	17	3	54	67	3.55	101	.268	.318	73-1-2	.151	-2*	109	3		0.2
1945	StL A	12	10	.545	30	24	15-1	2	192.1	188	84	9	1	65	55	3.51	100	.257	.318	70-2-3	.186	0	105	1		0.1
Total	3	25	22	.532	72	50	27-5	5	411	431	195	28	5	131	131	3.79	96	.268	.325	149-3-5	.161	-2	106	-3		-0.5

JAMERSON, LEFTY Charles Dewey "Charlie" B1.26.1900 Enfield IL D8.4.1980 Mocksville NC BL/TL/6-1/195 d8.16 Col Arkansas-Monticello

1924	Bos A	0	0	—	1	0	0	0	1	1	2	0	0	3	0	18.00	24	.250	.571	0	—	0		-1		-0.1

JAMES, CHUCK Charles Hamilton B11.9.1981 Atlanta GA BL/TL/6-0/170 d9.28 Col Chattahoochee Valley (AL) CC

2005	Atl N	0	0	—	5	2	0	0-0	5.2	4	1	0	0	3-0	5	1.59	271	.200	.304	1	1.000	0		2		0.1

JAMES, DELVIN Delvin Dewayne B1.3.1978 Nacogdoches TX BR/TR/6-4/222 [TBA96 14/424] d4.16

2002	TB A	0	3	.000	8	6	0	0-0	34.1	40	25	5	1	15-1	17	6.55	69	.301	.373	0	—	0	58	-7	35	-0.5

JAMES, JEFF Jeffrey Lynn "Jesse" B9.29.1941 Indianapolis IN BR/TR/6-3/196* d4.13 Col Indiana St.

1968	Phi N	4	4	.500	29	13	1-1	0	115.2	112	61	8	4	46-2	83	4.28	70	.256	.330	33-0-1	.121	-1	102	-16		-1.2
1969	Phi N	2	2	.500	6	5	1	0	31.2	36	20	5	0	14-1	21	5.40	46	.288	.357	11	.182	-0	104	-6		-0.7
Total	2	6	6	.500	35	18	2-1	0-0	147.1	148	81	13	4	60-3	104	4.52	69	.263	.336	44-0-1	.136	-1	104	-22		-1.9

JAMES, JOHNNY John Phillip B7.23.1933 Bonners Ferry ID BL/TR/5-10/160* d9.6 Col USC

1958	NY A	0	0	—	1	0	0	0	3	2	0	0	0	4-0	1	0.00	—	.250	.500	1	.000	-0		1		0.1
1960	NY A	5	1	.833	28	0	0	2	43.1	38	22	3	3	26-2	29	4.36	82	.248	.362	3	.000	-0		-3		-0.4
1961	NY A	0	0	—	1	0	0	0	1.1	1	0	0	0	0-0	2	0.00	—	.250	.250	0	—	0		1		0.0
	LA A	0	2	.000	36	3	0	0	71.1	66	44	12	2	54-1	41	5.30	85	.246	.375	13	.000	-1*	85	-4		-0.3
	Year	0	2	.000	37	3	0	0	72.2	67	44	12	2	54-1	43	5.20	86	.246	.374	13	.000	-1	85	-4		-0.3
Total	3	5	3	.625	66	3	0	2	119	107	66	15	5	84-3	73	4.76	87	.247	.373	17	.000	-2	93	-5		-0.6

JAMES, MIKE Michael Elmo B8.15.1967 Ft.Walton Beach FL BR/TR/6-3/205(180-205) [LAN87 43/1064] d4.29 Col Lurleen Wallace St. (AL) JC [DL 1999 Ana A 155]

1995	Cal A	3	0	1.000	46	0	0	1-1	55.2	49	27	6	3	26-2	36	3.88	121	.238	.332	0	—	0	5	21		0.2
1996	Cal A	5	5	.500	69	0	0	1-5	81	62	27	7	10	42-7	65	2.67	189	.214	.329	0	—	0	21			2.2
1997	Ana A	5	5	.500	58	0	0	7-6	62.2	69	32	3	5	28-4	57	4.31	107	.283	.367	0	—	0	2	24		0.4
1998	Ana A	0	0	—	11	0	0	0-0	14	10	3	0	0	7-0	12	1.93	246	.208	.309	0	—	0	4	146		0.2
2000	†StL N	2	2	.500	51	0	0	2-3	51.1	40	22	7	3	24-2	41	3.16	147	.219	.318	1	.000	-0*	7	24		0.5
2001	StL N	1	2	.333	40	0	0	0-0	38	43	24	5	4	17-2	26	5.21	83	.293	.382	1	.000	-0	-4	56		-0.3
2002	Col N	0	0	—	13	0	0	0-0	11.1	12	9	2	1	5-0	10	5.56	85	.267	.353	0	—	0	-1			-0.1
Total	7	16	14	.533	288	0	0	11-15	314	285	144	30	27	149-17	247	3.67	129	.245	.342	2	.000	-0	34	426		3.1

JAMES, RICK Richard Lee B10.11.1947 Sheffield AL BR/TR/6-2.5/205 [ChiN65 1/6] d9.20

1967	Chi N	0	1	.000	3	1	0	0	4.2	9	8	1	0	2-0	2	13.50	26	.529	.550	1	.000	-0	74	-5		-0.9

JAMES, BOB Robert Harvey B8.15.1958 Glendale CA BR/TR/6-4/230(215-230) [MonN76 1/9] d9.7

1978	Mon N	0	1	.000	4	1	0	0-0	4	4	4	1	0	4-0	3	9.00	40	.267	.421	0	—	0	101	-2		-0.4
1979	Mon N	0	0	—	2	0	0	0-0	2	2	3	0	0	3-1	1	13.50	28	.250	.455	0	—	0		-2		-0.1
1982	Mon N	0	0	—	7	0	0	0-0	9	10	6	0	0	8-1	11	6.00	62	.294	.409	0	—	0		-2		-0.1
	Det A	0	2	.000	12	1	0	0-1	19.2	22	13	4	0	8-0	20	5.03	81	.278	.345	0	—	0	156	-2		-0.2
1983	Det A	0	0	—	4	0	0	0-0	4	5	5	2	0	3-0	4	11.25	35	.313	.421	0	—	0		-3		-0.2
	Mon N	1	0	1.000	27	0	0	7-0	50	37	17	3	3	23-2	56	2.88	126	.210	.312	7	.286	0		4		0.3
1984	Mon N	6	6	.500	62	0	0	10-9	96	92	47	9	4	45-7	91	3.66	95	.251	.333	14	.143	-0		-4		-0.6
1985	Chi A	8	7	.533	69	0	0	32-9	110	90	31	5	2	23-4	88	2.13	204	.226	.268	0	—	0		25		4.5
1986	Chi A	5	4	.556	49	0	0	14-8	58.1	61	38	5	3	22-3	32	5.25	83	.268	.340	0	—	0	-5	49		-0.2
1987	Chi A	4	6	.400	43	0	0	10-2	54	54	32	10	4	17-6	34	4.67	99	.256	.321	0	—	0	-1	36		-0.2
Total	8	24	26	.480	279	2	0	73-29	407	377	194	39	17	157-24	340	3.80	106	.246	.319	21	.190	0	123	8	85	2.1

YEAR	TM LG	W	L	PCT	G	GS	CG-SHO	SV-BS	IP	H	R	HR	HB	BB-IB	SO	ERA	AERA	OAV	OOB	AB-HR-SH	AVG	PB	SUP	APR	DL	PW

JAMES, LEFTY William A. B7.1.1889 Glen Roy OH D5.3.1933 Glen Roy OH BL/TL/5-11.5/175 d4.13

1912	Cle A	0	1	.000	3	1	0	0	6	8	9	0	2	4	2	7.50	45	.348	.483	3	.000	-0	22	-3		-0.6
1913	Cle A	2	3	.400	11	4	3	0	39	42	17	0	3	9	18	3.00	101	.275	.327	13-0-1	.231	-0	116	-3		-0.4
1914	Cle A	0	3	.000	17	6	1	0	50.2	44	23	0	2	32	16	3.20	90	.251	.373	12	.000	-1	97	-1		-0.1
Total	3	2	7	.222	31	11	4	1	95.2	94	59	0	7	45	36	3.39	88	.268	.362	28-0-1	.107	-1	96	-7		-1.1

JAMES, BILL William Henry "Big Bill" B1.20.1887 Detroit MI D5.25.1942 Venice CA BB/TR/6-4/195 d6.12

1911	Cle A	2	4	.333	8	6	4	0	51.2	58	37	1	2	32	21	4.88	70	.284	.387	17-0-1	.059	-1	99	-8		-0.9
1912	Cle A	0	0	—	3	0	0	0	13.2	15	11	0	0	9	9	4.61	74	.288	.393	3-0-1	.000	-0		-2		-0.2
1914	StL A	15	14	.517	44	35	20-3	1	284	269	121	4	6	109	109	2.85	95	.257	.330	89-0-4	.112	-3	97	-4		-0.5
1915	StL A	6	10	.375	34	22	8	1	170.1	155	89	2	7	92	58	3.59	80	.255	.359	42-0-6	.190	-1	86	-11		-0.8
	Det A	7	3	.700	11	9	3-1	0	67	57	26	0	0	33	24	2.42	125	.243	.336	21-0-1	.286	2	110	4		0.8
	Year	13	13	.500	45	31	11-1	1	237.1	212	115	3	7	125	82	3.26	89	.251	.352	63-0-7	.222	2	93	-10		0.0
1916	Det A	8	12	.400	30	20	8	1	151.2	141	76	1	11	79	61	3.68	78	.255	.360	44-0-6	.068	-3	90	-12		-2.0
1917	Det A	13	10	.565	34	23	10-2	1	198	163	71	2	12	96	62	2.09	127	.229	.330	57-0-2	.211	-1	108	11		1.6
1918	Det A	6	11	.353	19	18	8-1	0	122	127	68	3	5	68	42	3.76	71	.279	.379	46	.109	-3	97	-17		-2.4
1919	Det A	1	0	1.000	2	1	0	0	9.1	12	6	0	0	7	3	5.79	55	.324	.432	4	.250	-0	343	-2		-0.2
	Bos A	3	5	.375	13	7	4	0	72.2	74	42	2	3	39	12	4.09	74	.280	.379	21-0-3	.143	-1	100	-10		-1.0
	†Chi A	3	2	.600	5	5	3-2	0	39.1	39	12	0	2	14	11	2.52	126	.281	.355	14-0-1	.143	-1	103	4		0.3
	Year	7	7	.500	20	13	7-2	0	121.1	125	60	2	5	60	26	3.71	83	.284	.376	39-0-4	.154	-2	121	-8		-0.9
Total	8	64	71	.474	203	146	68-9	4	1179.2	1110	559	16	48	578	408	3.20	88	.258	.352	358-0-25	.142	-8	99	-47		-5.3

JAMES, BILL William Lawrence "Seattle Bill" B3.12.1892 Iowa Hill CA D3.10.1971 Oroville CA BR/TR/6-3/196 d4.17 Col St. Marys (CA)

1913	Bos N	6	10	.375	24	14	10-1	0	135.2	134	75	4	7	57	73	2.79	118	.264	.347	47-0-2	.255	1	59	2		0.4
1914	†Bos N	26	7	.788	46	37	30-4	3	332.1	261	91	7	13	118	156	1.90	145	.225	.304	129-0-5	.256	4*	118	31		3.6
1915	Bos N	5	4	.556	13	9	4	0	68.1	68	28	3	2	22	23	3.03	86	.269	.332	21-0-1	.048	-2*	128	-2		-0.4
1919	Bos N	0	0	—	1	0	0	0	5.1	6	2	0	0	2	1	3.38	85	.273	.333	2	.000	-0		0		0.0
Total	4	37	21	.638	84	60	44-5	3	541.2	469	196	14	22	199	253	2.28	126	.242	.319	199-0-8	.231	4	104	31		3.6

JAMIESON, CHARLIE Charles Devine "Cuckoo" B2.7.1893 Paterson NJ D10.27.1969 Paterson NJ BL/TL/5-8.5/165 d9.20.1915 ▲

1916	Was A	0	0	—	1	0	0	0	4	2	2	0	0	3	2	4.50	62	.143	.294	145-0-5	.248	0*		-1		0.0
1917	Was A	0	0	—	1	0	0	0	2.1	10	10	0	0	2	1	38.57	7	.625	.667	35	.171	0*		-8		-0.4
1918	Phi A	2	1	.667	5	2	1	0	23	24	17	0	2	13	2	4.30	68	.261	.364	416-0-1	.202	0*	103	-4		-0.5
1919	Cle A	0	0	—	4	1	0	0	13	12	9	0	0	8	0	5.54	60	.250	.357	17	.353	0*	141	-2		0.0
1922	Cle A	0	0	—	2	0	0	0	5.2	7	3	0	0	4	2	3.18	126	.318	.423	567-3-14	.323	1*		0		0.0
Total	5	2	2	.667	13	3	1	0	48	55	41	0	2	30	7	6.19	51	.286	.388	1180-3-20	.267	2	115	-15		-0.9

JANESKI, JERRY Gerard Joseph B4.18.1946 Pasadena CA BR/TR/6-4/205* d4.10 Col Cal St.-Los Angeles

1970	Chi A	10	17	.370	35	35	4-1	0-0	205.2	247	125	22	3	63-10	79	4.73	81	.300	.351	66-0-7	.076	-4	106	-20		-2.7
1971	Was A	1	5	.167	23	10	0	1-1	61.2	72	38	5	3	34-4	19	4.96	68	.304	.395	14-0-2	.214	1	88	-11		-1.0
1972	Tex A	0	1	.000	4	1	0	0-0	12.2	11	5	0	0	7-0	7	2.84	107	.229	.321	2	.000	-0	29	0		0.0
Total	3	11	23	.324	62	46	4-1	1-1	280	330	168	27	6	104-14	105	4.72	79	.298	.360	82-0-9	.098	-4	102	-31		-3.7

JANSEN, LARRY Lawrence Joseph B7.16.1920 Verboort OR BR/TR/6-2/190* d4.17 C14

1947	NY N	21	5	.808	42	30	20-1	1	248	241	102	23	1	57	104	3.16	129	.262	.306	86-0-9	.186	-0	126	24		2.2
1948	NY N	18	12	.600	42	36	15-4	2	277	283	125	25	3	54	126	3.61	109	.265	.303	95-0-7	.137	-2	115	12		1.1
1949	NY N	15	16	.484	37	35	17-3	0	259.2	271	130	36	2	62	113	3.85	104	.263	.306	97-0-6	.165	-1	114	5		0.6
1950	NY N★	19	13	.594	40	35	21-5	3	275	238	106	31	1	55	161	3.01	136	.232	.271	96-1-9	.167	-0	101	33		3.6
1951	†NY N☆	23	11	.676	39	34	18-3	0	278.2	254	102	26	3	56	145	3.04	129	.239	.279	96-0-12	.094	-5	101	31		3.2
1952	NY N	11	11	.500	34	27	8-1	2	167.1	183	91	16	6	47	74	4.09	91	.281	.335	45-0-6	.178	3	103	-8		-0.6
1953	NY N	11	16	.407	36	26	6	1	184.2	185	96	24	2	55	88	4.14	104	.256	.311	60-0-3	.133	-1	99	4		0.3
1954	NY N	2	2	.500	13	7	0	0	40.2	57	32	5	1	15	15	5.98	68	.337	.388	14	.286	-1	98	-9		-0.6
1956	Cin N	2	3	.400	8	7	2	1	34.2	39	20	5	1	9-1	16	5.19	77	.281	.327	11	.000	-1	133	-4		-0.6
Total	9	122	89	.578	291	237	107-17	10	1765.2	1751	804	191	20	410-1	842	3.58	112	.258	.302	600-1-52	.150	-6	109	88		9.2

JANZEN, MARTY Martin Thomas B5.31.1973 Homestead FL BR/TR/6-3/200* d5.12

1996	Tor A	4	6	.400	15	11	0	0-0	73.2	95	65	16	2	38-3	47	7.33	68	.317	.394	0	—	0	99	-18		-2.0
1997	Tor A	2	1	.667	12	0	0	0-0	25	23	11	4	0	13-0	17	3.60	128	.250	.343	0	—	0		3		0.3
Total	2	6	7	.462	27	11	0	0-0	98.2	118	76	20	2	51-3	64	6.39	77	.301	.382	0	—	0	99	-15		-1.7

JARVIS, KEVIN Kevin Thomas B8.1.1969 Lexington KY BL/TR/6-2/200* [CinN91 21/561] d4.6 Col Wake Forest

1994	Cin N	-1	1	.500	6	3	0	0-0	17.2	22	14	4	0	5-0	10	7.13	59	.301	.346	4-0-2	.250	0	145	-5		-0.5
1995	Cin N	3	4	.429	19	11	1-1	0-0	79	91	56	13	3	32-2	33	5.70	73	.292	.358	21-0-1	.143	-0	114	-14		-1.1
1996	Cin N	8	9	.471	24	20	2-1	0-0	120.1	152	93	17	2	43-5	63	5.98	72	.305	.361	36-0-8	.167	-0	107	-24		-2.9
1997	Cin N	0	1	.000	9	0	0	1-0	13.1	21	16	4	1	7-0	12	10.13	42	.344	.420	1	.000	-0		-8		-0.7
	Min A	0	0	—	6	2	0	0-0	13	23	18	4	0	9	9	12.46	37	.371	.443	0	—	0	157	-10		-0.5
	Det A	0	3	.000	17	3	0	0-0	41.2	55	28	9	0	14-0	27	5.40	86	.318	.367	0	—	0	46	-4	19	-0.3
	Year	0	3	.000	23	5	0	0-0	54.2	78	46	13	0	22-0	36	7.08	65	.332	.388	0	—	0	91	-15		-0.8
1999	Oak A	0	1	.000	4	1	0	0-0	14	28	19	6	1	6-0	11	11.57	41	.418	.467	0	—	0	59	-10	46	-0.6
2000	Col N	4	4	.429	24	19	0	0-0	115	138	83	26	4	33-3	60	5.95	97	.300	.351	34-0-3	.088	-2*	119	-2	34	-0.3
2001	SD N	12	11	.522	32	32	1-1	0-0	193.1	189	107	37	5	49-4	133	4.79	87	.254	.303	61-1-5	.180	4*	113	-11		-0.6
2002	SD N	2	4	.333	7	7	0	0-0	35	36	19	5	1	10-1	24	4.37	89	.269	.322	9-0-1	.333	2	68	-2	149	-0.2
2003	SD N	4	8	.333	16	16	0	0-0	92	113	65	15	2	32-5	49	5.87	68	.300	.358	22-0-3	.136	1*	88	-21	75	-2.1
2004	Sea A	1	0	1.000	8	0	0	0-0	13	20	12	4	0	5-0	9	8.31	54	.345	.397	0	—	0	-5		-0.3
	Col N	0	0	—	2	0	0	0-0	2	6	6	1	0	4-2	0	27.00	18	.600	.714	0	—	0	-4		-0.2
2005	StL N	0	1	.000	4	0	0	0-0	3.1	3	5	1	2	3-0	2	13.50	31	.250	.471	0	—	0	-6		-0.6
Total	11	34	47	.420	178	114	4-3	1-1	752.2	897	541	146	21	251-22	440	5.97	74	.295	.351	188-1-23	.160	4	107-123	323		-10.9

JARVIS, RAY Raymond Arnold B5.10.1946 Providence RI BR/TR/6-2/198(185-198) [BosA65 11/370] d4.15

1969	Bos A	5	6	.455	29	12	2	1-0	100.1	105	59	8	4	43-1	36	4.75	80	.274	.349	29-0-3	.069	-2	110	-9	21	-1.1
1970	Bos A	0	1	.000	15	0	0	0-1	16	17	12	1	2	14-1	8	3.94	101	.274	.418	0-0-1	—	-0		-2		-0.1
Total	2	5	7	.417	44	12	2	1-1	116.1	122	71	9	5	57-2	44	4.64	83	.274	.359	29-0-4	.069	-2	110	-11	21	-1.2

JARVIS, PAT Robert Patrick B3.18.1941 Carlyle IL BR/TR/5-10.5/180* d8.4 Col Murray St.

1966	Atl N	6	2	.750	10	9	3-1	0	62.1	46	16	1	1	12-2	41	2.31	157	.206	.250	22-0-1	.000	-2	150	10		1.0
1967	Atl N	15	10	.600	32	30	7-1	0	194	195	86	15	4	62-14	118	3.66	91	.260	.317	71-0-3	.085	-3	105	-6		-1.1
1968	Atl N	16	12	.571	34	34	14-1	0	256	202	82	15	4	50-5	157	2.60	115	.214	.252	85-0-10	.141	-0	102	12		1.3
1969	†Atl N	13	11	.542	37	33	4-1	0-0	217.1	204	113	25	1	73-7	123	4.43	82	.246	.306	71-0-5	.113	-3	110	-17		-2.0
1970	Atl N	16	16	.500	36	34	11-1	0-1	254	240	110	21	0	72-5	173	3.61	119	.247	.296	82-0-11	.183	-0	83	20		2.4
1971	Atl N	6	14	.300	35	23	3-3	1-0	162.1	162	81	16	3	51-11	68	4.10	91	.261	.320	47-0-4	.106	-2	88	-5		-0.8
1972	Atl N	11	7	.611	37	6	0	2-1	98.2	94	50	7	0	44-7	56	4.10	93	.260	.337	24-0-3	.125	-0	132	-3		-0.5
1973	Mon N	2	1	.667	28	0	0	0-1	39.1	37	21	6	1	16-4	19	3.20	119	.250	.325	3	.000	-0		1	33	0.3
Total	8	85	73	.538	249	169	42-8	3-3	1284	1180	559	106	12	380-55	755	3.58	101	.243	.298	405-0-37	.121	-10	101	12	33	0.3

JASPER, HI Henry W. B11.15.1880 St.Louis MO D5.22.1937 St.Louis MO BR/TR/5-11/180 d4.19

1914	Chi A	1	0	1.000	16	0	0	0	32.1	22	22	0	1	20	9	3.34	80	.210	.341	5	.000	-1		-4		-0.2
1915	Chi A	0	1	.000	3	2	1	0	15.2	8	8	2	0	9	15	4.60	65	.157	.283	7	.286	0	98	-2		-0.7
1916	StL N	5	6	.455	21	9	2	1	107	97	54	0	7	42	37	3.28	81	.254	.339	33-1-0	.212	1	97	-8		-0.7
1919	Cle A	4	5	.444	12	10	5	0	82.2	83	41	1	0	28	25	3.59	93	.269	.330	29-0-2	.103	-2	117	-1		-0.3
Total	4	10	12	.455	52	21	8	1	237.2	210	125	3	8	99	96	3.48	84	.248	.333	74-1-2	.162	-2	110	-15		-1.2

JASTER, LARRY Larry Edward B1.13.1944 Midland MI BL/TL/6-3.5/205(190-205) d9.17

1965	StL N	3	0	1.000	4	3	0	0	28	21	5	1	0	7-0	10	1.61	239	.206	.255	10-0-1	.200	0	144	7		0.8
1966	StL N	11	5	.688	26	21	6-5	0	151.2	124	57	17	5	45-5	92	3.26	110	.227	.290	45-1-2	.178	1	83	8		0.9
1967	†StL N	9	7	.563	34	23	2-1	3	151.1	141	57	12	2	44-6	87	3.01	109	.244	.297	50-0-1	.100	-1*	109	5		0.3
1968	†StL N	9	13	.409	31	21	3-1	0	153.2	147	70	5	3	38-5	70	3.51	82	.252	.311	43-1-6	.140	0	73	-8		-1.2
1969	Mon N	1	6	.143	31	11	1	0-0	77	95	60	10	4	28-6	39	5.49	68	.302	.359	19	.421	3	81	-17		-1.2

YEAR	TM LG	W	L	PCT	G	GS	CG-SHO	SV-BS	IP	H	R	HR	HB	BB-IB	SO	ERA	AERA	OAV	OOB	AB-HR-SH	AVG	PB	SUP	APR	DL	PV
1970	Atl N	1	1	.500	14	0	0	0-2	22.1	33	18	5	0	8-0	9	6.85	63	.359	.402	3	.000	-0		-6		-0.
1972	Atl N	1	1	.500	5	1	0	0-0	12.1	12	7	4	0	8-0	6	5.11	74	.267	.377	1	.000	-0	23	-1		-0.
Total	7	35	33	.515	138	80	15-7	3-2	597.1	579	267	69	15	178-22	313	3.65	93	.256	.312	171-2-10	.170	3	89	-12		-1.

JAVERY, AL   Alva William "Beartracks"   B6.5.1918 Worcester MA   D8.16.1977 Putnam CT   BR/TR/6-3/183   d4.23

YEAR	TM LG	W	L	PCT	G	GS	CG-SHO	SV-BS	IP	H	R	HR	HB	BB-IB	SO	ERA	AERA	OAV	OOB	AB-HR-SH	AVG	PB	SUP	APR	DL	PV
1940	Bos N	2	4	.333	29	4	1	1	83.1	99	62	2	2	36	42	5.51	68	.293	.364	23-0-1	.087	-1	76	-19		-1.5
1941	Bos N	10	11	.476	34	23	9-1	1	160.2	181	88	5	6	65	54	4.31	83	.283	.355	58-0-1	.103	-4	102	-12		-1.
1942	Bos N	12	16	.429	42	37	19-5	0	261	251	106	8	3	78	85	3.03	110	.251	.307	86-0-9	.105	-5	81	7		0.
1943	Bos N★	17	16	.515	41	35	19-5	0	303	288	130	13	4	99	134	3.21	106	.248	.309	104-0-11	.163	-3	84	7		0.
1944	Bos N☆	10	19	.345	40	33	11-3	3	254	248	119	12	2	118	137	3.54	108	.262	.345	79-0-4	.152	-3	71	7		0.
1945	Bos N	2	7	.222	17	14	2-1	0	77.1	92	59	4	0	51	18	6.28	61	.295	.394	29	.207	-0	95	-19		-1.
1946	Bos N	0	1	.000	2	1	0	0	3.1	5	5	0	0	5-1	0	13.50	25	.417	.588	1	.000	-0	125	-3		-0.
Total	7	53	74	.417	205	147	61-15	5	1142.2	1164	569	44	17	452	470	3.80	94	.264	.335	380-0-26	.137	-15	84	-32		-4.

JAY, JOEY   Joseph Richard   B8.15.1935 Middletown CT   BB/TR/6-4/228(200-228)   d7.21

YEAR	TM LG	W	L	PCT	G	GS	CG-SHO	SV-BS	IP	H	R	HR	HB	BB-IB	SO	ERA	AERA	OAV	OOB	AB-HR-SH	AVG	PB	SUP	APR	DL	PV
1953	Mil N	1	0	1.000	3	1	1-1	0	10	6	0	0	0	5	4	0.00	—	.188	.297	3	.000	-0	68	5		0.
1954	Mil N	1	0	1.000	15	1	0	0	18	21	13	2	1	16	13	6.50	57	.304	.437	0	—	0	96	-5		-0.
1955	Mil N	0	0	—	12	1	0	0	19	23	11	2	0	13-2	3	4.74	79	.324	.419	3	.667	1	190	-2		0.
1957	Mil N	0	0	—	1	0	0	1	0.2	0	0	0	0	0-0	0	0.00	—	.000	.000	0	—	0	0	0		0.
1958	Mil N	7	5	.583	18	12	6-3	0	96.2	60	25	8	1	43-3	74	2.14	164	.177	.271	32-0-1	.094	-1	70	17		1.
1959	Mil N	6	11	.353	34	19	4-1	0	136.1	130	71	11	5	64-6	88	4.09	87	.248	.334	35-0-1	.086	-1	101	-9		-1.
1960	Mil N	9	8	.529	32	11	3	1	133.1	128	60	10	6	59-5	90	3.24	106	.254	.336	45-0-3	.156	0	131	0		0.
1961	†Cin N☆	21	10	.677	34	34	14-4	0	247.1	217	102	25	5	92-1	157	3.53	115	.236	.308	89-0-2	.090	-5	95	18		1.
1962	Cin N	21	14	.600	39	37	16-4	0	273	269	121	26	4	100-5	155	3.76	107	.260	.325	90-2-7	.167	3	97	11		1.
1963	Cin N	7	18	.280	30	22	4-1	1	170	172	91	19	3	73-2	116	4.29	78	.266	.340	50-0-2	.160	0	75	-17		-2.
1964	Cin N	11	11	.500	34	23	10	2	183	167	75	17	3	36-6	134	3.39	107	.245	.284	53-0-5	.057	-3	87	6		0.
1965	Cin N	9	8	.529	37	24	4-1	1	155.2	150	83	21	4	63-0	102	4.22	89	.252	.324	49-0-4	.041	-3	113	-8		-1.
1966	Cin N	6	2	.750	12	10	1-1	0	73.2	78	33	8	3	23-1	44	3.91	100	.275	.335	26-0-2	.115	-1	108	1		0.
	Atl N	0	4	.000	9	8	0	1	29.2	39	29	4	1	20-3	19	7.89	46	.315	.405	8	.125	-0	94	-14		-1.
	Year	6	6	.500	21	18	1-1	1	103.1	117	62	12	4	43-4	63	5.05	76	.287	.358	34-0-2	.118	-1	101	-13		-1.
Total	13	99	91	.521	300	203	67-34	7	1546.1	1460	714	153	36	607-34	999	3.77	99	.251	.323	483-2-27	.114	-10	97	3		-1.2

JEAN, DOMINGO   Domingo (Luisa)   B1.9.1969 San Pedro de Macoris, D.R.   BR/TR/6-2/175   d8.8

YEAR	TM LG	W	L	PCT	G	GS	CG-SHO	SV-BS	IP	H	R	HR	HB	BB-IB	SO	ERA	AERA	OAV	OOB	AB-HR-SH	AVG	PB	SUP	APR	DL	PV
1993	NY A	1	1	.500	10	6	0	0-0	40.1	37	20	7	0	19-1	20	4.46	94	.237	.318	0	—	0	106	0		0.

JEFFCOAT, GEORGE   George Edward d   B12.24.1913 New Brookland (now West Columbia) SC   D10.13.1978 Leesville SC   BR/TR/5-11.5/175   d4.20   b-Hal   Col South Carolina-Aiken

YEAR	TM LG	W	L	PCT	G	GS	CG-SHO	SV-BS	IP	H	R	HR	HB	BB-IB	SO	ERA	AERA	OAV	OOB	AB-HR-SH	AVG	PB	SUP	APR	DL	PV
1936	Bro N	5	6	.455	40	5	3	3	95.2	84	58	7	8	63	46	4.52	92	.239	.366	23-0-1	.130	-1	78	-4		-0.
1937	Bro N	1	3	.250	21	3	1-1	0	54.1	58	33	4	1	27	29	5.13	79	.274	.358	12	.000	-2	85	-4		-0.
1939	Bro N	0	0	—	1	0	0	0	2	2	0	0	0	1	1	0.00	—	.286	.286	0	—	0		1		0.
1943	Bos N	1	2	.333	8	1	0	0	17.2	15	10	1	0	10	10	3.06	112	.217	.316	4-0-1	.500	1	124	0		0.
Total	4	7	11	.389	70	9	4-1	3	169.2	159	101	12	9	100	86	4.51	89	.248	.358	39-0-2	.128	-2	85	-7		-1.

JEFFCOAT, HAL   Harold Bentley   B9.6.1924 W.Columbia SC   BR/TR/5-10.5/185(185-198)   d4.20.1948   b-George   ▲

YEAR	TM LG	W	L	PCT	G	GS	CG-SHO	SV-BS	IP	H	R	HR	HB	BB-IB	SO	ERA	AERA	OAV	OOB	AB-HR-SH	AVG	PB	SUP	APR	DL	PV
1954	Chi N	5	6	.455	43	3	1	7	104	110	63	12	4	58	35	5.19	81	.276	.368	31-1-0	.258	2*	85	-9		-0.
1955	Chi N	8	6	.571	50	1	0	6	100.2	107	46	5	4	53-12	32	2.95	139	.276	.367	23-1-2	.174	1*	65	8		1.
1956	Chi N	8	2	.800	38	16	2	2	171	189	79	12	5	55-4	55	3.84	104	.281	.337	54-0-3	.148	-1*	112	3		0.
1957	Cin N	12	13	.480	37	31	10-1	0	207	236	117	29	7	46-7	63	4.52	91	.294	.335	69-4-8	.203	6*	111	-11		-0.
1958	Cin N	6	8	.429	49	0	0	9	75	76	34	8	2	26-8	35	3.72	111	.268	.329	9	.556	2*		3		0.
1959	Cin N	0	1	.000	17	0	0	1	21.2	21	8	3	0	10-2	12	3.32	122	.253	.333	1	1.000	1	7	2		0.
	StL N	0	1	.000	11	0	0	0	17.2	33	18	4	0	9-2	7	9.17	46	.402	.462	3	.000	-0*		-8		-0.
	Year	0	2	.000	28	0	0	1	39.1	54	26	7	0	19-4	19	5.95	70	.327	.397	4	.250	1		-6		-0.
Total	6	39	37	.513	245	51	13-1	25	697	772	365	73	22	257-35	239	4.22	97	.285	.349	190-6-13	.211	10	109	-12		0.

JEFFCOAT, MIKE   James Michael   B8.3.1959 Pine Bluff AR   BL/TL/6-2/187*   [CleA80 13/322]   d8.21   Col Louisiana Tech

YEAR	TM LG	W	L	PCT	G	GS	CG-SHO	SV-BS	IP	H	R	HR	HB	BB-IB	SO	ERA	AERA	OAV	OOB	AB-HR-SH	AVG	PB	SUP	APR	DL	PV
1983	Cle A	1	3	.250	11	2	0	0-0	32.2	32	13	1	1	13-1	9	3.31	129	.256	.331	0	—	0	21	3		0.
1984	Cle A	5	2	.714	63	1	0	1-5	75.1	82	28	7	1	24-7	41	2.99	138	.281	.330	0	—	0	285	9		2.
1985	Cle A	0	0	—	9	0	0	0-0	9.2	8	5	1	0	6-1	4	2.79	149	.235	.333	0	—	0		1		0.
	SF N	0	2	.000	19	1	0	0-0	22	27	13	4	2	6-3	10	5.32	65	.307	.361	1	.000	0	230	-4		-0.
1987	Tex A	0	1	.000	2	1	0	0-0	7	11	10	4	0	4-0	1	12.86	35	.355	.429	0	—	0	91	-6		-1.
1988	Tex A	0	2	.000	5	2	0	0-0	10	19	13	1	2	5-1	5	11.70	35	.432	.510	0	—	0	22	-7		-1.
1989	Tex A	9	6	.600	22	22	2-2	0-0	130.2	139	65	7	4	33-0	64	3.58	111	.270	.317	0	—	0	110	3		0.
1990	Tex A	5	6	.455	44	12	1	5-5	110.2	122	57	12	2	28-5	58	4.47	88	.283	.328	0	—	0	83	-4	42	-0.
1991	Tex A	5	3	.625	70	0	0	1-4	79.2	104	46	8	4	25-3	43	4.63	87	.320	.372	1	1.000	1		-5		-0.
1992	Tex A	0	1	.000	6	3	0	0-0	19.2	28	17	2	0	5-0	6	7.32	52	.350	.379	0	—	0	143	-7	99	-0.
1994	Fla N	0	0	—	4	0	0	0-0	2.2	4	3	2	0	0-0	1	10.13	44	.364	.333	0	—	0		-1	141	-1.8
Total	10	25	26	.490	255	45	3-2	7-14	500	576	270	49	16	149-21	242	4.37	92	.292	.342	2	.500	1	102	-18	141	-1.8

JEFFERSON, JESSE   Jesse Harrison   B3.3.1949 Midlothian VA   BR/TR/6-3/195(192-215)   [BalA68 4/70]   d6.23

YEAR	TM LG	W	L	PCT	G	GS	CG-SHO	SV-BS	IP	H	R	HR	HB	BB-IB	SO	ERA	AERA	OAV	OOB	AB-HR-SH	AVG	PB	SUP	APR	DL	PV
1973	Bal A	6	5	.545	18	15	3	0-0	100.2	104	53	15	0	46-1	65	4.11	92	.267	.342	0	—	0	115	-4		-0.
1974	Bal A	1	0	1.000	20	2	0	0-0	57.1	55	30	2	0	38-2	31	4.40	79	.261	.371	0	—	0	190	-5		-0.
1975	Bal A	0	2	.000	4	0	0	0-0	7.2	5	3	0	0	8-2	4	2.35	151	.217	.433	0	—	0	21	1		0.
	Chi A	5	9	.357	22	21	1	0-0	107.2	100	69	11	2	94-1	67	5.10	76	.249	.391	0	—	0	82	-15		-1.7
	Year	5	11	.313	26	21	1	0-0	115.1	105	72	11	2	102-3	71	4.92	79	.248	.394	0	—	0	83	-13		-1.8
1976	Chi A	2	5	.286	19	9	0	0-0	62.1	86	62	4	2	42-0	30	8.52	42	.339	.429	0	—	0	115	-33		-3.1
1977	Tor A	9	17	.346	33	33	8	0-0	217	224	123	23	1	83-4	114	4.31	99	.269	.332	0	—	0	78	-4		-0.
1978	Tor A	7	16	.304	31	30	9-2	0-0	211.2	214	109	28	3	86-5	97	4.38	90	.267	.337	0	—	0	75	-9		-1.
1979	Tor A	2	10	.167	34	10	2	1-2	116	150	75	19	4	45-2	43	5.51	80	.328	.387	0	—	0	56	-12		-1.0
1980	Tor A	4	13	.235	29	18	2-2	0-0	121.2	130	78	12	2	52-2	53	5.47	79	.281	.353	0	—	0	64	-13		-1.5
	Pit N	1	0	1.000	2	1	0	0-0	6.2	3	1	0	0	2-0	4	1.35	273	.143	.217	1-0-1	.000	-0	73	2		0.
1981	Cal A	2	4	.333	26	5	0	0-2	77	80	39	4	2	24-4	27	3.62	101	.269	.322	0	—	0	39	-1		0.
Total	9	39	81	.325	237	144	25-4	1-4	1085.2	1151	642	118	14	520-23	522	4.81	83	.277	.368	1-0-1	.000	-0	81	-93		-8.

JENKINS, FERGIE   Ferguson Arthur   B12.13.1942 Chatham ON, Can.   BR/TR/6-5/210(195-210)   d9.10   C2   HF1991

YEAR	TM LG	W	L	PCT	G	GS	CG-SHO	SV-BS	IP	H	R	HR	HB	BB-IB	SO	ERA	AERA	OAV	OOB	AB-HR-SH	AVG	PB	SUP	APR	DL	PV
1965	Phi N	2	1	.667	7	0	0	1.	12.1	7	3	2	0	2-0	10	2.19	158	.159	.196	1	.000	-0		2		0.
1966	Phi N	0	0	—	1	0	0	0	2.1	3	2	0	0	1-1	3	3.86	93	.273	.333	0	—	0		0		0.
	Chi N	6	8	.429	60	12	2-1	5	182	147	75	24	3	51-11	148	3.31	111	.219	.275	51-1-3	.137	1	100	8		0.
	Year	6	8	.429	61	12	2-1	5	184.1	150	77	24	3	52-12	151	3.32	111	.220	.276	51-1-3	.137	1	100	6		0.
1967	Chi N★	20	13	.606	38	38	20-3	0	289.1	230	101	30	4	83-8	236	2.80	127	.217	.276	93-0-8	.151	1*	101	22		2.
1968	Chi N	20	15	.571	40	40	20-3	0	308	255	96	26	3	65-7	260	2.63	120	.222	.265	100-1-6	.160	2	92	19		2.
1969	Chi N	21	15	.583	43	42	23-7	1-0	311.1	284	122	27	4	71-15	273	3.21	125	.242	.289	108-1-4	.139	-1	93	27		3.
1970	Chi N	22	16	.579	40	39	24-3	0-1	313	265	128	30	4	60-6	274	3.39	133	.224	.264	113-3-10	.124	-3	98	37		3.
1971	Chi N★	24	13	.649	39	39	30-3	0-0	325	304	114	29	5	37-6	263	2.77	142	.246	.269	115-6-8	.243	10	92	36		5.
1972	Chi N☆	20	12	.625	36	36	23-5	0-0	289.1	253	111	32	7	62-7	184	3.20	131	.234	.278	109-1-3	.183	1	105	20		2.
1973	Chi N	14	16	.467	38	38	7-2	0-0	271	267	133	35	4	57-10	170	3.89	102	.259	.298	84-0-7	.119	-1	88	1		0.
1974	Tex A	25	12	.676	41	41	29-6	0-0	328.1	286	117	27	8	45-3	225	2.82	127	.232	.262	2	.500	0	102	28		3.
1975	Tex A	17	18	.486	37	37	22-4	0-0	270	261	130	37	9	56-7	157	3.93	96	.251	.294	0	—	0	105	-2		-0.
1976	Bos A	12	11	.522	30	29	12-2	0-0	209	201	85	20	5	43-6	142	3.27	119	.253	.292	0	—	0	97	14		1.
1977	Bos A	10	10	.500	28	28	11-1	0-0	193	190	91	30	4	36-2	105	3.68	102	.257	.290	0	—	0	103	13		1.
1978	Tex A	18	8	.692	34	30	16-4	0-0	249	228	92	21	3	41-2	157	3.04	123	.245	.278	0	—	0	118	22		2.
1979	Tex A	16	14	.533	37	37	10-3	0-0	259	252	127	40	3	81-6	164	4.07	102	.256	.311	0	—	0	115	5		0.
1980	Tex A	12	12	.500	29	29	12	0-0	198	190	90	22	4	52-8	129	3.77	103	.250	.299	0	—	0	108	5		0.
1981	Tex A	5	8	.385	19	16	1	0-0	106	122	55	14	0	40-4	63	4.50	77	.290	.351	0	—	0	113	-11		-1.
1982	Chi N	14	15	.483	34	34	4-1	0-0	217.1	221	92	19	5	68-2	134	3.15	120	.264	.319	67-0-12	.149	-1	104	12		1.
1983	Chi N	6	9	.400	33	29	1-1	0-1	167.1	176	89	19	6	46-5	96	4.30	89	.275	.327	53-0-5	.245	3	94	-9		-0.
Total	19	284	226	.557	664	594	267-49	7-2	4500.2	4142	1853	484	84	997-116	3192	3.34	115	.243	.287	896-13-66	.165	13	101	249		30.

YEAR	TM LG	W	L	PCT	G	GS	CG-SHO	SV-BS	IP	H	R	HR	HB	BB-IB	SO	ERA	AERA	OAV	OOB	AB-HR-SH	AVG	PB	SUP	APR	DL	PW

JENKINS, JACK   Warren Washington   B12.22.1942 Covington VA   D6.18.2002 Tampa FL   BR/TR/6-2/195*   d9.13   Col Lincoln Memorial

1962	Was A	0	1	.000	3	1	1	0	13.1	12	6	4	0	7-0	10	4.05	100	.245	.339	4	.000	-0	22	0		0.0
1963	Was A	0	2	.000	4	2	0	0	12.1	16	8	2	0	12-0	5	5.84	64	.340	.475	3	.333	0	48	-2		-0.3
1969	LA N	0	0	—	1	0	0	0-0	1	0	0	0	0	0-0	1	0.00	—	.000	.000	0	—	0		0		0.0
Total	3	0	3	.000	8	3	1	0-0	26.2	28	14	6	0	19-0	16	4.73	82	.283	.398	7	.143	-0	38	-2		-0.3

JENKS, BOBBY   Robert Scott   B3.14.1981 Mission Hills CA   BR/TR/6-3/270   d7.6

| 2005 | †Chi A | 1 | 1 | .500 | 32 | 0 | 0 | 6-2 | 39.1 | 34 | 15 | 3 | 1 | 15-3 | 50 | 2.75 | 165 | .225 | .299 | 0 | — | 0 | 7 | | | 0.5 |

JENNINGS, JASON   Jason Ryan   B7.17.1978 Dallas TX   BR/TR/6-2/242*   [ColN99 1/16]   d8.23   Col Baylor

2001	Col N	4	1	.800	7	7	1-1	0-0	39.1	42	21	2	1	19-0	26	4.58	117	.276	.358	15-1-1	.267	1	124	3		0.5
2002	Col N	16	8	.667	32	32	0	0-0	185.1	201	102	26	8	70-2	127	4.52	105	.280	.349	62-0-2	.306	5	100	4		0.9
2003	Col N	12	13	.480	32	32	1	0-0	181.1	212	115	20	5	88-7	119	5.11	96	.299	.377	54-0-5	.222	2*	95	-5		-0.3
2004	Col N	11	12	.478	33	33	0	0-0	201	241	125	27	7	101-14	133	5.51	86	.299	.381	71-1-5	.239	3*	101	-14		-1.1
2005	Col N	6	9	.400	20	20	1	0-0	122	130	73	11	5	62-4	75	5.02	95	.274	.361	38-0-4	.158	-0*	81	-3	74	-0.4
Total	5	49	43	.533	124	124	3-1	0-0	729	826	436	86	26	340-27	480	5.02	96	.289	.368	240-2-17	.242	11	98	-15	74	-0.6

JENSEN, RYAN   Larry Ryan   B9.17.1975 Salt Lake City UT   BR/TR/6-0/205(205-245)   [SFN96 8/222]   d5.19   Col Southern Utah

2001	SF N	1	2	.333	10	7	0	0-0	42.1	44	21	5	4	25-0	26	4.25	96	.268	.378	12	.167	0	110	0		0.0
2002	SF N	13	8	.619	32	30	1	0-0	171.2	183	93	21	5	66-4	105	4.51	88	.278	.345	56-0-9	.107	-2	121	-1		-1.4
2003	SF N	0	0	—	6	2	0	0-0	13.1	21	16	6	1	5-0	3	10.80	39	.404	.450	5	.400	1	243	-9	29	-0.4
2005	KC A	3	2	.600	9	3	0	0-1	25.1	31	20	4	2	7-1	18	7.11	59	.298	.348	1	.000	-0	112	-8		-1.3
Total	4	17	12	.586	57	42	1	0-1	252.2	279	150	36	12	103-5	152	5.06	79	.285	.357	74-0-9	.135	-1	124	-28	29	-3.1

JENSEN, WILLIE   William Christian   B11.17.1889 Philadelphia PA   D3.27.1917 Philadelphia PA   BL/TR/5-11.5/170   d9.10

1912	Det A	1	2	.333	5	4	1	0	33	43	23	1	2	18	8	4.91	66	.339	.429	11	.000	-2	130	-6		-0.6
1914	Phi A	0	1	.000	1	1	1	0	9	7	4	1	0	2	1	2.00	131	.226	.273	2	.000	0	84	0		0.0
Total	2	1	3	.250	6	5	2	0	42	50	27	2	2	20	9	4.29	73	.316	.400	13	.000	-2	123	-6		-0.6

JERZEMBECK, MIKE   Michael Joseph   B5.18.1972 Queens NY   BR/TR/6-1/185   [NYA93 5/141]   d8.8   Col North Carolina-Asheville   [DL 1999 NY A 182]

| 1998 | NY A | 0 | 1 | .000 | 3 | 2 | 0 | 0-0 | 6.1 | 9 | 9 | 2 | 4 | 4-0 | 1 | 12.79 | 34 | .346 | .419 | 0 | — | 0 | 127 | -6 | | -0.7 |

JESTER, VIRGIL   Virgil Milton   B7.23.1927 Denver CO   BR/TR/5-11/188*   d6.18   Col Northern Colorado

1952	Bos N	3	5	.375	19	8	4-1	0	73	80	31	5	1	23	25	3.33	108	.283	.339	19-0-2	.211	1	86	2		0.2
1953	Mil N	0	0	—	2	0	0	0	2	4	5	1	0	4	0	22.50	17	.400	.571	0	—	0		-4		-0.2
Total	2	3	5	.375	21	8	4-1	0	75	84	36	6	1	27	25	3.84	94	.287	.349	19-0-2	.211	1	86	-2		0.0

JIMENEZ, GERMAN   German (Camarena)   B12.5.1962 Santiago Ixcuintla, Nayarit, Mexico   BL/TL/5-11/200   d6.28

| 1988 | Atl N | 1 | 6 | .143 | 15 | 9 | 0 | 0-0 | 55.2 | 65 | 39 | 4 | 1 | 12-0 | 26 | 5.01 | 73 | .294 | .326 | 17 | .059 | -1 | 73 | -10 | | -1.3 |

JIMENEZ, JASON   Jason Jon   B1.10.1976 Modesto CA   BR/TL/6-2/206   [TBA97 28/864]   d6.3   Col San Jose St.

2002	TB A	0	0	—	5	0	0	0-0	6.2	9	4	2	0	1-0	5	5.40	84	.333	.345	0	—	0	0			0.0
	Det A	0	0	—	1	0	0	0-0	0.2	3	4	0	0	1-0	0	27.00	16	.500	.571	0	—	0		-3		-0.1
	Year	0	0	—	6	0	0	0-0	7.1	12	8	2	0	2-0	5	7.36	61	.364	.389	0	—	0		-3		-0.1

JIMENEZ, JOSE   Jose   B7.7.1973 San Pedro de Macoris, D.R.   BR/TR/6-3/228(170-230)   d9.9

1998	StL N	3	0	1.000	4	3	0	0-0	21.1	22	8	0	0	8-0	12	2.95	142	.262	.323	6-0-2	.000	-1	146	3		0.3
1999	StL N	5	14	.263	29	28	2-2	0-1	163	173	114	16	11	71-2	113	5.85	79	.275	.356	53-0-2	.094	-3*	81	-21		-2.2
2000	Col N	5	2	.714	72	0	0	24-6	70.2	63	27	4	3	28-6	44	3.18	182	.239	.316	4-0-1	.500	0		16		2.4
2001	Col N	6	1	.857	56	0	0	17-5	55	54	27	6	0	22-4	37	4.09	130	.264	.332	1	.000	-0	6	43	1.1
2002	Col N	2	10	.167	74	0	0	41-6	73.1	76	34	7	3	11-4	47	3.56	133	.265	.297	0	—	0	7		1.6
2003	Col N	2	10	.167	63	7	0	20-3	101.2	137	62	7	6	32-5	45	5.22	94	.322	.375	17-0-2	.176	-0	63	-3		-0.4
2004	Cle A	1	7	.125	31	0	0	8-3	36.1	45	37	6	4	14-2	21	8.42	52	.296	.371	0	—	0	-18	-20	25	-3.1
Total	7	24	44	.353	329	38	2-2	110-24	521.1	572	309	46	27	186-23	319	4.92	99	.289	.344	81-0-7	.123	-3	78	-10	68	-0.3

JIMENEZ, JUAN   Juan Antonio (Martes)   B3.8.1949 LaTorre, D.R.   BR/TR/6-1/165   d9.9

| 1974 | Pit N | 0 | 0 | — | 4 | 0 | 0 | 0-0 | 4 | 6 | 4 | 0 | 0 | 2-0 | 2 | 6.75 | 52 | .353 | .421 | 0 | — | 0 | -2 | | | -0.1 |

JIMENEZ, MIGUEL   Miguel Anthony   B8.19.1969 New York NY   BR/TR/6-2/205*   [OakA91 12/333]   d9.12   Col Fordham

1993	Oak A	1	0	1.000	5	4	0	0-0	27	27	12	5	1	16-0	13	4.00	103	.262	.367	0	—	0	128	1		0.0
1994	Oak A	1	4	.200	8	7	0	0-0	34	38	33	9	1	32-2	22	7.41	61	.275	.413	0	—	0	117	-13		-1.4
Total	2	2	4	.333	13	11	0	0-0	61	65	45	14	2	48-2	35	5.90	73	.270	.394	0	—	0	122	-12		-1.4

JODIE, BRETT   Brett Paul   B3.25.1977 Columbia SC   BR/TR/6-4/208   [NYA98 6/187]   d7.20   Col South Carolina-Aiken

2001	NY A	0	1	.000	1	1	0	0-0	2	7	6	3	0	1-0	0	27.00	16	.583	.615	0	—	0	83	-5		-0.7
	SD N	0	1	.000	7	2	0	0-0	23.1	19	12	7	0	12-1	13	4.63	90	.229	.326	4	.000	-0	22	-1		-0.1
Total	1	0	2	.000	8	3	0	0-0	25.1	26	18	10	0	13-1	13	6.39	65	.274	.361	4	.000	0	44	-6		-0.8

JOHN, TOMMY   Thomas Edward   B5.22.1943 Terre Haute IN   BR/TL/6-3/185(180-203)   d9.6   [DL 1975 LA N 175]

1963	Cle A	0	2	.000	6	3	0	0	20.1	23	10	1	0	6-1	9	2.21	164	.284	.330	6	.000	-1	74	1		0.0
1964	Cle A	2	9	.182	25	14	2-1	0	94.1	97	53	10	0	35-4	65	3.91	92	.262	.324	24-0-3	.208	0	101	-7		-0.7
1965	Chi A	14	7	.667	39	27	6-1	3	183.2	162	67	12	2	58-6	126	3.09	103	.237	.298	59-1-6	.169	2	133	4		0.9
1966	Chi A	14	11	.560	34	33	10-5	0	223	195	76	13	7	57-4	138	2.62	121	.235	.289	60-2-4	.145	2	89	15		2.0
1967	Chi A	10	13	.435	31	29	9-6	0	178.1	143	62	12	5	47-7	110	2.47	126	.219	.275	51-0-5	.157	-0	76	12	27	1.9
1968	Chi A★	10	5	.667	25	25	5-1	0	177.1	135	45	10	12	49-4	117	1.98	153	.212	.280	62-1-5	.194	2	110	21	39	2.5
1969	Chi A	9	11	.450	33	33	6-2	0-0	232.1	230	91	16	9	90-10	128	3.25	118	.261	.329	79-0-1	.114	-1	80	14		1.4
1970	Chi A	12	17	.414	37	37	10-3	0-0	269.1	253	117	19	9	101-16	138	3.27	118	.251	.323	84-0-9	.202	1*	86	15		1.9
1971	Chi A	13	16	.448	38	38	10-3	0-0	229.1	244	115	17	5	58-5	131	3.61	99	.274	.318	69-0-9	.145	-1	90	-4		-0.6
1972	LA N	11	5	.688	29	29	4-1	0-0	186.2	172	68	14	3	40-1	117	2.89	118	.244	.286	63-0-7	.159	-1	108	12		1.1
1973	LA N	16	7	**.696**	36	31	4-2	0-0	218	202	88	16	4	50-2	116	3.10	112	.246	.291	74-0-7	.203	2	118	9		1.5
1974	LA N	13	3	.813	22	22	5-3	0-0	153	133	51	4	1	42-0	78	2.59	133	.235	.287	51-0-9	.118	-1	128	15	78	1.5
1976	LA N	10	10	.500	31	31	6-2	0-0	207	207	76	7	0	61-4	91	3.09	110	.261	.312	64-0-10	.109	-2	90	9		0.5
1977	†LA N	20	7	.741	31	31	11-3	0-0	220.1	225	82	12	3	50-3	123	2.78	139	.267	.310	79-1-6	.177	1	118	24		3.0
1978	†LA N☆	17	10	.630	33	30	7	1-0	213	230	95	11	5	53-7	124	3.30	107	.271	.317	66-0-12	.121	-1	124	3		0.3
1979	NY A☆	21	9	.700	37	36	17-3	0-0	276.1	268	109	9	4	65-1	111	2.96	139	.260	.305	0	—	0	105	32		3.3
1980	†NY A★	22	9	.710	36	36	16-6	0-0	265.1	270	115	13	6	56-1	78	3.43	116	.268	.309	0	—	0	119	16		1.8
1981	†NY A	9	8	.529	20	20	7	0-0	140.1	135	50	10	3	39-2	50	2.63	137	.256	.309	0	—	0	92	14	65	1.7
1982	NY A	10	10	.500	30	26	9-2	0-0	186.2	190	84	11	3	34-1	54	3.66	110	.266	.299	0	—	0	102	8		0.9
	†Cal A	4	2	.667	7	7	1	0-0	35	49	18	4	0	5-0	14	3.86	108	.336	.358	0	—	0	102	0		0.0
	Year	14	12	.538	37	33	10-2	0-0	221.2	239	102	15	3	39-1	68	3.69	109	.278	.309	0	—	0	102	8		0.9
1983	Cal A	11	13	.458	34	34	9	0-0	234.2	287	126	20	2	49-5	65	4.33	93	.304	.337	0	—	0	94	-8		-0.7
1984	Cal A	7	13	.350	32	29	4-1	0-0	181.1	223	97	15	4	56-3	47	4.52	88	.304	.356	0	—	0	96	-10		-0.9
1985	Cal A	2	4	.333	12	6	0	0-0	38.1	51	23	3	1	15-1	17	4.70	88	.329	.387	0	—	0	77	-2		-0.3
	Oak A	2	6	.250	11	11	0	0-0	48	66	37	6	1	13-0	8	6.19	63	.332	.372	0	—	0	72	-13		-1.8
	Year	4	10	.286	23	17	0	0-0	86.1	117	59	9	2	28-1	25	5.53	72	.331	.379	0	—	0	74	-15		-2.1
1986	NY A	5	3	.625	13	10	1	0-0	70.2	73	27	6	3	15-1	28	2.93	141	.275	.316	0	—	0	94	9	60	1.0
1987	NY A	13	6	.684	33	33	3-1	0-0	187.2	212	95	12	6	47-7	63	4.03	110	.288	.335	0	—	0	120	6		0.5
1988	NY A	9	8	.529	35	32	2	0-0	176.1	221	96	11	6	46-4	81	4.49	88	.308	.354	0	—	0	111	-10		-0.2
1989	NY A	2	7	.222	10	10	0	0-0	63.2	87	45	6	3	22-1	18	5.80	67	.336	.392	0	—	0	72	-13		-1.5
Total	26	288	231	.555	760	700	162-46	4-0	4710.1	4783	2017	302	98	1259-102	2245	3.34	111	.265	.315	900-5-93	.157	1	102	172	444	20.4

JOHNS, AUGIE   Augustus Francis "Lefty"   B9.10.1899 St.Louis MO   D9.12.1975 San Antonio TX   BL/TL/5-8.5/170   d4.16

1926	Det A	6	4	.600	35	14	3-1	1	112.2	117	77	6	5	69	40	5.35	76	.271	.377	28-0-3	.143	-1	110	-14		-1.3
1927	Det A	0	0	—	1	0	0	0	1	1	1	0	1	1	0	9.00	47	.333	.500	0	—	0		0		0.0
Total	2	6	4	.600	36	14	3-1	1	113.2	118	78	6	5	70	41	5.38	75	.271	.378	28-0-3	.143	-1	110	-14		-1.3

YEAR	TM LG	W	L	PCT	G	GS	CG-SHO	SV-BS	IP	H	R	HR	HB	BB-IB	SO	ERA	AERA	OAV	OOB	AB-HR-SH	AVG	PB	SUP	APR	DL	PW

JOHNS, DOUG Douglas Alan B12.19.1967 South Bend IN   BR/TL/6-2/185* [OakA90 16/451] d7.8 Col Virginia

1995	Oak A	5	3	.625	11	9	1-1		54.2	44	32	5	5	26-1	25	4.61	98	.226	.330	0	—	0	87	-1		-0.1
1996	Oak A	6	12	.333	40	23	1	1-1	158	187	112	21	6	69-5	71	5.98	83	.297	.370	0	—	0*	116	-18		-1.5
1998	Bal A	3	3	.500	31	10	0	1-0	86.2	108	46	9	4	32-2	34	4.57	100	.321	.381	2	1.000	1	114	0	15	0.2
1999	Bal A	6	4	.600	32	5	0	0-0	86.2	81	45	9	8	25-2	50	4.47	105	.248	.311	1	.000	-0	67	3		0.3
Total	4	20	22	.476	114	47	2-1	2-1	386	420	235	44	23	152-10	180	5.13	93	.282	.354	3	.667	1	106	-16	15	-1.1

JOHNS, OLLIE Oliver Tracy B8.21.1879 Trenton OH D6.17.1961 Hamilton OH   BL/TL d9.24

| 1905 | Cin N | 1 | 0 | 1.000 | 1 | 1 | 0 | | 18 | 31 | 22 | 1 | 0 | 4 | 8 | 3.50 | 94 | .369 | .398 | 5-0-1 | .200 | -0 | 175 | -4 | | -0.3 |

JOHNSON, ABE Abraham B Chicago IL d7.16

| 1893 | Chi N | 0 | 0 | — | 1 | 0 | 0 | | 1 | 2 | 4 | 0 | 1 | 2 | 0 | 36.00 | 13 | .400 | .625 | 0 | — | 0 | | -3 | | -0.4 |

JOHNSON, ADAM Adam Bryant B7.12.1979 San Jose CA   BR/TR/6-2/210* [MinA00 1/2] d7.16 Col Cal St.-Fullerton

2001	Min A	1	2	.333	7	4	0	0-0	25	32	25	6	5	13-0	17	8.28	56	.323	.424	2	.000	-0	69	-10		-1.0
2003	Min A	0	1	.000	2	0	0	0-0	1.1	8	8	1	0	1-0	0	47.25	10	.667	.692	0	—	0		-7		-1.0
Total	2	1	3	.250	9	4	0	0-0	26.1	40	33	7	5	14-0	17	10.25	45	.360	.450	2	.000	-0	69	-17		-2.0

JOHNSON, RANKIN Adam Rankin Jr. B3.1.1917 Hayden AZ   BR/TR/6-3/177 d4.17 Mil 1942-45 f-Rankin

| 1941 | Phi A | 1 | 0 | 1.000 | 7 | 0 | 0 | | 10 | 14 | 10 | 0 | 0 | 3 | 3 | 3.60 | 116 | .326 | .370 | 1 | .000 | -0 | | -2 | | -0.1 |

JOHNSON, RANKIN Adam Rankin Sr. "Tex" B2.4.1888 Burnet TX D7.2.1972 Williamsport PA   BR/TR/6-1.5/185 d4.20 s-Rankin

1914	Bos A	3	9	.250	16	13	4-2	0	99.1	92	41	2	3	34	24	3.08	87	.265	.336	30-0-2	.133	-1	52	-2		-0.5
	Chi F	9	5	.643	16	14	12-2	0	120	88	29	5	4	29	60	1.58	169	.209	.267	37	.108	-3	70	15		1.3
1915	Chi F	2	4	.333	11	6	3	1	57	58	34	2	1	23	19	4.42	57	.270	.343	22	.045	-3	153	-12		-1.6
	Bal F	7	11	.389	23	19	12-2	1	150.2	143	68	3	1	58	62	3.35	86	.255	.326	51-0-3	.157	-1	94	-6		-1.1
	Year	9	15	.375	34	25	15-2	2	207.2	201	102	5	2	81	81	3.64	76	.259	.331	73-0-3	.123	-5	107	-17		-2.7
1918	StL N	1	1	.500	6	1	0	0	23	20	10	0	0	7	4	2.74	99	.263	.325	4-0-2	.250	0	28	0		0.1
Total	3	22	30	.423	72	53	31-6	2	450	401	182	12	9	151	169	2.92	93	.248	.315	144-0-7	.125	-9	83	-5		-1.9

JOHNSON, ART Arthur Gilbert B2.15.1897 Warren PA D6.7.1982 Sarasota FL   BB/TL/6-1/167 d9.18

| 1927 | NY N | 0 | 0 | — | 1 | 0 | 0 | 0 | 3 | 1 | 1 | 0 | 0 | 1 | 0 | — | — | .125 | .222 | 0 | — | 0 | | 1 | | 0.0 |

JOHNSON, ART Arthur Henry "Lefty" B7.16.1916 Winchester MA   BL/TL/6-2/185 d9.22 Mil 1942-45 [DL 1946 Bos N 108]

1940	Bos N	0	1	.000	2	1	0	0	6	10	7	0	1	3	1	10.50	35	.345	.424	1	.000	-0	23	-4		-0.6
1941	Bos N	7	15	.318	43	18	6	1	183.1	189	92	7	5	71	70	3.53	101	.270	.342	55-0-5	.145	-2*	65	-2		-0.4
1942	Bos N	0	0	—	4	0	0	0	6.1	4	1	0	1	5	0	1.42	235	.190	.370	1	.000	-0		1		0.1
Total	3	7	16	.304	49	19	6	1	195.2	203	100	7	7	79	71	3.68	97	.271	.346	57-0-5	.140	-2	63	-5	108	-0.9

JOHNSON, BEN Benjamin Franklin B5.16.1931 Greenwood SC   BR/TR/6-2/190* d9.6

1959	Chi N	0	0	—	4	0	0		16.2	17	5	1	0	4-0	6	2.16	183	.262	.304	4-0-1	.000	-0	113	3		0.1
1960	Chi N	2	1	.667	17	0	0	1	29.1	39	21	3	1	11-0	9	4.91	77	.355	.408	2-0-1	.000	-0		-5		-0.5
Total	2	2	1	.667	21	2	0	1	46	56	26	4	1	15-0	15	3.91	98	.320	.371	6-0-2	.000	-1	113	-2		-0.4

JOHNSON, CHET Chester Lillis "Chesty Chet" B8.1.1917 Redmond WA D4.10.1983 Seattle WA   BL/TL/6-0/175 d9.12 b-Earl Col Washington

| 1946 | StL A | 0 | 0 | — | 5 | 3 | 0 | | 18 | 20 | 12 | 0 | 0 | 13 | 8 | 5.00 | 75 | .286 | .398 | 6 | .000 | -1 | 184 | -3 | | -0.2 |

JOHNSON, BART Clair Barth B1.3.1950 Torrance CA   BR/TR/6-5/195(195-215) [ChiA68 S1/2] d9.8 [DL 1975 Chi A 175]

1969	Chi A	1	3	.250	4	3	0	0-0	22.1	22	11	2	0	6-0	18	3.22	119	.259	.308	6	.167	0	84	0		0.1
1970	Chi A	4	7	.364	18	15	2-1	0-0	89.2	92	53	11	2	46-2	71	4.82	81	.268	.358	29-0-2	.276	2	98	-8		-0.7
1971	Chi A	12	10	.545	53	16	4	14-5	178	148	67	9	6	111-6	153	2.93	122	.227	.342	57-0-3	.193	0	124	13		1.8
1972	Chi A	0	3	.000	9	0	0	1-1	13.2	18	20	2	1	13-2	9	9.22	34	.327	.464	1	.000	0		-11		-2.2
1973	Chi A	3	3	.500	22	9	0	0-0	80.2	76	39	6	2	34-0	56	4.13	96	.252	.338	0	—	0	103	0		0.0
1974	Chi A	10	4	.714	18	18	8-2	0-0	121.2	105	42	6	1	32-2	76	2.74	137	.229	.280	0	—	0	89	13		1.4
1976	Chi A	9	16	.360	32	32	8-3	0-0	211.1	231	115	19	1	62-1	91	4.73	75	.282	.329	0	—	0	75	-24		-2.6
1977	Chi A	4	5	.444	29	4	0	2-1	92	114	48	5	2	38-3	46	4.01	102	.302	.365	0	—	0	105	0		0.0
Total	8	43	51	.457	185	97	22-6	17-7	809.1	806	395	60	15	348-16	520	3.94	95	.261	.336	93-0-5	.215	3	93	-17	175	-2.2

JOHNSON, CONNIE Clifford B12.27.1922 Stone Mountain GA D11.28.2004 Kansas City MO   BR/TR/6-4/200* d4.17 Negro Lg 1940-50 Mil 1943-45

1953	Chi A	4	4	.500	14	10	2-1	0	60.2	55	27	4	2	38	44	3.56	113	.238	.351	20-0-1	.050	-2*	102	3		0.1
1955	Chi A	7	4	.636	17	16	5-2	0	99	95	40	5	1	52-0	72	3.45	114	.251	.342	30-0-2	.152	-1*	110	6		0.4
1956	Chi A	9	1	.000	5	2	0	0	12.1	11	5	1	0	7-0	6	3.65	112	.234	.333	3	.000	-0	43	1		0.0
	Bal A	9	10	.474	26	25	9-2	0	183.2	165	79	12	4	62-3	130	3.43	114	.239	.301	58-0-6	.259	3	90	10		1.2
	Year	9	11	.450	31	27	9-2	0	196	176	84	13	4	69-3	136	3.44	114	.239	.303	61-0-6	.246	3	86	11		1.2
1957	Bal A	14	11	.560	35	30	14-3	0	242	212	93	17	3	66-1	177	3.20	112	.235	.287	89-0-6	.135	-4	116	11		0.5
1958	Bal A	6	9	.400	26	17	4	1	118.1	116	58	10	0	32-3	68	3.88	93	.260	.309	34-0-1	.206	1	82	-5		-0.5
Total	5	40	39	.506	123	100	34-8	1	716	654	302	52	7	257-7	497	3.42	109	.243	.309	237-0-16	.169	-3	100	26		1.7

JOHNSON, DANE Dane Edward B2.10.1963 Coral Gables FL   BR/TR/6-5/205* [TorA84 2/48] d5.30 Col St. Thomas (FL)

1994	Chi A	2	1	.667	15	0	0	0-0	12.1	16	9	2	0	11-1	7	6.57	71	.327	.443	0	—	0		-2		-0.4
1996	Tor A	0	0	—	10	0	0	0-0	9	5	3	0	0	5-0	7	3.00	167	.161	.278	0	—	0		2		0.1
1997	Oak A	4	1	.800	38	0	0	2-2	45.2	49	28	4	2	31-4	43	4.53	101	.272	.378	0	—	0		-1		-0.2
Total	3	6	2	.750	63	0	0	2-2	67	70	40	6	2	47-5	57	4.70	99	.269	.379	0	—	0		-1		-0.5

JOHNSON, DAVE David Charles B10.4.1948 Abilene TX   BR/TR/6-1/183* [BalA67 5/99] d7.2

1974	Bal A	2	2	.500	11	0	0	2-0	15.1	17	5	1	0	5-3	6	2.93	119	.274	.328	0	—	0		1		0.3
1975	Bal A	0	1	.000	6	0	0	0-2	8.2	8	4	0	0	7-1	4	4.15	85	.250	.385	0	—	0		-1		-0.1
1977	Min A	2	5	.286	30	6	0	0-1	72.2	86	42	7	5	23-1	33	4.58	87	.299	.358	0	—	0	109	-5		-0.5
1978	Min A	0	2	.000	6	1	0	0-0	12	15	11	1	0	9-0	7	7.50	51	.313	.421	0	—	0	47	-5		-0.7
Total	4	4	10	.286	53	7	0	2-3	108.2	126	62	9	5	44-5	50	4.64	83	.293	.364	0	—	0	103	-9		-1.0

JOHNSON, DAVE David Wayne B10.24.1959 Baltimore MD   BR/TR/5-11/183* d5.29 Col CC of Baltimore (MD)

1987	Pit N	0	0	—	5	0	0	0-0	6.1	13	7	1	0	2-0	4	9.95	42	.448	.484	0	—	0		-4		-0.2
1989	Bal A	4	7	.364	14	14	4	0-0	89.1	90	44	11	4	28-1	26	4.23	90	.265	.325	0	—	0	71	-4		-0.4
1990	Bal A	13	9	.591	30	29	3	0-0	180	196	83	30	3	43-2	68	4.10	93	.280	.321	0	—	0	104	-3	20	-0.5
1991	Bal A	4	8	.333	22	14	0	0-0	84	127	68	18	4	24-3	38	7.07	56	.349	.394	0	—	0	90	-29	68	-3.4
1993	Det A	1	1	.500	6	0	0	0-0	8.1	13	13	3	2	5-1	7	12.96	34	.342	.435	0	—	0	92	115		-1.2
Total	5	22	25	.468	77	57	7	0-0	368	439	215	63	13	102-7	143	5.11	76	.298	.347	0	—	0	92	-48	203	-5.9

JOHNSON, DON Donald Roy B11.12.1926 Portland OR   BR/TR/6-3/200* d4.20

1947	NY A	4	3	.571	15	8	2	0	54.1	57	26	2	1	23	16	3.64	97	.270	.345	13-0-4	.000	-2	128	-2		-0.4
1950	NY A	1	0	1.000	8	0	0	0	18	35	21	2	0	12	9	10.00	43	.398	.470	3	.000	-0		-12		-0.6
	StL A	5	6	.455	25	12	4-1	1	96	126	72	14	1	55	31	6.09	81	.325	.410	29-0-3	.069	-3	77	-10		-1.3
	Year	6	6	.500	33	12	4-1	1	114	161	93	16	1	67	40	6.71	72	.338	.422	32-0-3	.063	-4	79	-21		-1.9
1951	StL A	0	1	.000	6	3	0	0	15	27	26	4	1	18	8	12.60	35	.391	.523	3-0-1	.333	-0	108	-14		-0.8
	Was A	7	11	.389	21	20	8-1	0	143.2	138	67	9	2	58	52	3.95	104	.255	.329	47-0-6	.085	-5	93	4		-0.1
	Year	7	12	.368	27	23	8-1	0	158.2	165	93	13	3	76	60	4.76	87	.270	.354	50-0-7	.100	-5	96	-10		-0.9
1952	Was A	0	5	.000	29	6	0	2	69	80	41	4	4	33	37	4.43	80	.287	.370	13-0-2	.077	-1	74	-8		-0.7
1954	Chi A	8	7	.533	46	16	3-3	7	144	129	53	14	0	43	68	3.13	119	.243	.298	35-0-7	.029	-3	96	11		0.8
1955	Bal A	2	4	.333	31	5	0	1	68	89	46	4	0	35-2	27	5.82	65	.333	.404	10	.000	-1	70	-14		-1.2
1958	SF N	0	1	.000	17	0	0	1	23	31	19	2	4	8-1	14	6.26	61	.323	.383	2-0-1	.000	-0		-7		-0.4
Total	7	27	38	.415	198	70	17-5	12	631	712	371	55	11	285-3	262	4.78	83	.299	.363	155-0-24	.058	-16	93	-52		-4.7

JOHNSON, EARL Earl Douglas "Lefty" B4.2.1919 Redmond WA D12.3.1994 Seattle WA   BL/TL/6-3/190* d7.20 Mil 1942-45 b-Chet Col St. Marys (CA)

1940	Bos A	6	2	.750	17	10	4	0	70.1	69	33	0	4	39	26	4.09	110	.260	.359	27	.074	-3*	107	4		0.2
1941	Bos A	4	5	.444	17	12	4	0	93.2	90	57	4	3	51	46	4.52	92	.247	.344	25-0-1	.294	2	125	-4		-0.2
1946	†Bos A	5	4	.556	29	5	0	3	80	78	39	5	2	38	40	3.71	99	.250	.337	22-0-1	.227	2	61	-1		0.1
1947	Bos A	12	11	.522	45	17	6-3	8	142.1	129	63	7	2	62	65	2.97	131	.246	.328	44-0-2	.273	1*	68	10		1.9

YEAR	TM LG	W	L	PCT	G	GS	CG-SHO	SV-BS	IP	H	R	HR	HB	BB-IB	SO	ERA	AERA	OAV	OOB	AB-HR-SH	AVG	PB	SUP	APR	DL	PW
1948	Bos A	10	4	.714	35	3	1	5	91.1	98	49	7	0	42	45	4.53	97	.276	.353	31-0-1	.097	-3	137	-1		-0.3
1949	Bos A	3	6	.333	19	3	0	0	49.1	65	45	1	4	29	20	7.48	58	.327	.422	11	.000	-1	75	-16		-2.6
1950	Bos A	0	0	—	11	0	0	0	13.2	18	11	0	1	8	6	7.24	68	.333	.429	2	.000	-0		-3		-0.1
1951	Det A	0	0	—	6	0	0	1	5.2	9	5	0	0	2	2	6.35	66	.375	.423	0		0		-2		-0.1
Total 8		40	32	.556	179	50	13-3	17	546.1	556	302	24	14	272	250	4.30	96	.265	.353	171-0-7	.187	-2	95	-13		-1.0

JOHNSON, WALT   Ellis Walter B12.8.1892 Minneapolis MN D1.14.1965 Minneapolis MN BR/TR/6-0.5/180 d7.6

YEAR	TM LG	W	L	PCT	G	GS	CG-SHO	SV-BS	IP	H	R	HR	HB	BB-IB	SO	ERA	AERA	OAV	OOB	AB-HR-SH	AVG	PB	SUP	APR	DL	PW
1912	Chi A	0	0	—	3	0	0	0	11.2	11	6	0	1	7	7	3.86	83	.262	.380	3	.000	-0		-1		-0.1
1915	Chi A	0	0	—	1	0	0	0	2	3	2	0	0	0	3	9.00	33	.333	.333	0	—	0		-1		-0.1
1917	Phi A	0	2	.000	4	2	0	0	13.2	15	12	0	0	5	8	7.24	38	.294	.357	1	.000	0	78	-5		-0.7
Total 3		0	2	.000	8	2	0	0	27.1	29	20	0	1	12	18	5.93	50	.284	.365	4	.000	0	78	-7		-0.9

JOHNSON, ERNIE   Ernest Thorwald B6.16.1924 Brattleboro VT BR/TR/6-4/195* d4.28

YEAR	TM LG	W	L	PCT	G	GS	CG-SHO	SV-BS	IP	H	R	HR	HB	BB-IB	SO	ERA	AERA	OAV	OOB	AB-HR-SH	AVG	PB	SUP	APR	DL	PW
1950	Bos N	2	0	1.000	16	1	0	0	20.2	37	21	1	0	13	15	6.97	55	.394	.467	2	.500		344	-9		-0.6
1952	Bos N	6	3	.667	29	10	2-1	1	92	100	53	8	2	31	45	4.11	88	.270	.329	22-0-4	.091	-0	155	-8		-0.7
1953	Mil N	4	3	.571	36	1	0	0	81	79	34	4	3	22	36	2.67	147	.263	.320	14-0-1	.071	-1	23	9		0.6
1954	Mil N	5	2	.714	40	4	1	2	99.1	77	34	11	1	34	68	2.81	133	.219	.289	13-0-5	.231	-1	138	11		0.9
1955	Mil N	5	7	.417	40	4	0	4	92	81	38	5	2	55-8	43	3.42	110	.240	.348	20-0-1	.100	-1	95	4		0.4
1956	Mil N	4	3	.571	36	0	0	6	51	54	21	9	1	21-2	26	3.71	93	.270	.341	4	.250	0		0		0.1
1957	†Mil N	7	3	.700	30	0	0	4	65	67	29	9	1	26-5	44	3.88	90	.265	.335	17-1-1	.353	3				0.1
1958	Mil N	3	1	.750	15	0	0	1	23.1	35	21	4	1	10-3	13	8.10	43	.357	.418	2	.000	0		-12		-1.9
1959	Bal A	4	1	.800	31	1	0	1	50.1	57	32	6	3	19-2	29	4.11	92	.286	.353	6	.333	0	47	-5		-0.4
Total 9		40	23	.635	273	19	3-1	19	574.2	587	283	57	14	231-20	319	3.77	98	.266	.338	100-1-12	.180	2	142	-12		-1.5

JOHNSON, FRED   Frederick Edward "Deacon","Cactus" B3.10.1894 Tolar TX D6.14.1973 Kerrville TX BR/TR/6-0/185 d9.27

YEAR	TM LG	W	L	PCT	G	GS	CG-SHO	SV-BS	IP	H	R	HR	HB	BB-IB	SO	ERA	AERA	OAV	OOB	AB-HR-SH	AVG	PB	SUP	APR	DL	PW
1922	NY N	0	2	.000	4	2	1	0	18	20	8	3	0	1	8	4.00	100	.294	.304	4-0-1	.000	-1	31	1		0.0
1923	NY N	2	0	1.000	3	2	1	0	17	11	8	2	0	7	5	4.24	90	.177	.261	6	.000	-1	108	0		-0.1
1938	StL A	3	7	.300	17	6	3	3	69	91	50	7	1	27	24	5.61	89	.316	.377	25-0-1	.240	-0	112	-6		-0.8
1939	StL A	0	1	.000	5	2	1	0	14	23	12	0	0	9	2	6.43	76	.383	.464	4-0-1	.000	-1	100	-3		-0.2
Total 4		5	10	.333	27	12	6	3	118	145	78	12	1	44	39	5.26	88	.303	.363	39-0-3	.154	-2	96	-8		-1.1

JOHNSON, CHIEF   George Howard "Murphy","Big Murph" B3.30.1886 Winnebago NE D6.12.1922 Des Moines IA BR/TR/5-11.5/190 d4.16

YEAR	TM LG	W	L	PCT	G	GS	CG-SHO	SV-BS	IP	H	R	HR	HB	BB-IB	SO	ERA	AERA	OAV	OOB	AB-HR-SH	AVG	PB	SUP	APR	DL	PW
1913	Cin N	14	16	.467	44	31	13-3	0	269	251	137	8	7	86	107	3.01	108	.256	.320	88-1-3	.114	-3	95	1		-0.1
1914	Cin N	0	0	—	1	1	0	0	4	6	4	0	0	2	1	6.75	43	.333	.400	0	—	0	122	-2		-0.1
	KC F	9	10	.474	20	19	12-2	0	134	157	76	2	4	33	78	3.16	88	.298	.345	49-1-1	.122	-2	117	-11		-1.8
1915	KC F	17	17	.500	46	34	19-4	2	281.1	253	121	5	8	71	118	2.75	96	.242	.295	87-1-4	.126	-4	103	-8		-1.2
Total 3		40	43	.482	111	85	44-9	2	688.1	667	338	15	19	192	304	2.95	98	.259	.315	224-3-8	.121	-9	103	-20		-3.2

JOHNSON, HANK   Henry Ward B5.21.1906 Bradenton FL D8.20.1982 Bradenton FL BR/TR(BB 1933)/5-11.5/175 d4.17

YEAR	TM LG	W	L	PCT	G	GS	CG-SHO	SV-BS	IP	H	R	HR	HB	BB-IB	SO	ERA	AERA	OAV	OOB	AB-HR-SH	AVG	PB	SUP	APR	DL	PW
1925	NY A	1	3	.250	24	4	2-1	0	67	88	58	3	8	37	25	6.85	62	.319	.414	17-0-2	.059	-1	99	-19		-1.0
1926	NY A	0	0	—	1	0	0	1	1	2	2	0	2	0	0	18.00	21	.400	.571	0	—	0		-1		-0.2
1928	NY A	14	9	.609	31	22	10-1	0	199	188	107	16	12	104	110	4.30	88	.250	.351	79-1-4	.241	2	122	-10		-0.9
1929	NY A	3	3	.500	12	8	2	0	42.2	37	28	5	0	39	24	5.06	76	.237	.390	14-0-2	.071	-1*	123	-6		-0.8
1930	NY A	14	11	.560	44	15	7-1	2	175.1	177	112	12	2	104	115	4.67	92	.265	.366	64-1-5	.266	5*	130	-9		-0.5
1931	NY A	13	8	.619	40	23	8	4	196.1	176	114	13	1	102	106	4.72	84	.234	.326	77-0-1	.195	2	145	-16		-1.5
1932	NY A	2	2	.500	5	4	2	0	31.1	34	18	7	0	15	27	4.88	83	.266	.343	13	.231	0*	131	-2		-0.2
1933	Bos A	8	6	.571	25	21	7 —	1	155.1	156	84	13	3	74	65	4.06	108	.263	.348	52-0-2	.231	3*	93	5		0.7
1934	Bos A	6	8	.429	31	14	7-1	1	124.1	162	95	12	5	53	66	5.36	90	.316	.385	43-0-1	.233	1	92	-10		-0.9
1935	Bos A	2	1	.667	13	2	0	1	31	41	21	3	0	14	14	5.52	86	.331	.399	8-0-1	.000	-1	119	-2		-0.3
1936	Phi A	0	2	.000	3	3	0	0	11.2	16	16	4	1	10	6	7.71	66	.296	.415	4-0-1	.250	-0	75	-5		-0.7
1939	Cin N	0	3	.000	6	1	0	0	31.1	30	10	1	0	6	10	2.01	191	.268	.344	5	.400	1		6		0.5
Total 12		63	56	.529	249	116	45-4	11	1066.1	1107	665	89	32	567	568	4.75	88	.268	.361	376-2-19	.215	9	116	-69		-5.8

JOHNSON, JIM   James Brian B11.3.1945 Muskegon MI D12.6.1987 North Muskegon MI BL/TL/5-11/175 [SFN67 S3/56] d4.13 Col Western Michigan

YEAR	TM LG	W	L	PCT	G	GS	CG-SHO	SV-BS	IP	H	R	HR	HB	BB-IB	SO	ERA	AERA	OAV	OOB	AB-HR-SH	AVG	PB	SUP	APR	DL	PW
1970	SF N	1	0	1.000	3	0	0	0-0	6.2	8	6	0	0	5-1	2	8.10	49	.320	.419	2	.000	0		-3		-0.3

JOHNSON, JASON   Jason Michael B10.27.1973 Santa Barbara CA BR/TR/6-6/235(215-235) d8.27

YEAR	TM LG	W	L	PCT	G	GS	CG-SHO	SV-BS	IP	H	R	HR	HB	BB-IB	SO	ERA	AERA	OAV	OOB	AB-HR-SH	AVG	PB	SUP	APR	DL	PW
1997	Pit N	0	0	—	3	0	0	0-0	6	10	4	2	0	1-0	3	6.00	71	.400	.407	1	.000	-0		-1		-0.1
1998	TB A	2	5	.286	13	13	0	0-0	60	74	38	9	3	27-0	36	5.70	84	.306	.381	2	.000	-0	85	-5	86	-0.5
1999	Bal A	8	7	.533	22	21	0	0-0	115.1	120	74	16	3	55-0	71	5.46	86	.266	.347	2	.000	-0	117	-10		-1.1
2000	Bal A	1	10	.091	25	13	0	0-0	107.2	119	95	21	4	61-2	79	7.02	67	.278	.369	3-0-0	.000	-0	77	-32		-2.6
2001	Bal A	10	12	.455	32	32	2	0-0	196	194	109	28	13	77-3	114	4.09	106	.257	.334	3	.333	1	91	0		-0.1
2002	Bal A	5	14	.263	22	22	1	0-0	131.1	141	68	19	6	41-2	97	4.59	95	.276	.335	3	.000	-0	68	-2	60	-0.3
2003	Bal A	10	10	.500	32	32	0	0-0	189.2	216	100	22	10	80-8	118	4.18	110	.283	.358	5	.200	1	96	6		0.5
2004	Det A	8	15	.348	33	33	2-1	0-0	196.2	222	121	22	5	60-3	125	5.13	87	.284	.334	3-0-1	.000	-0	82	-15		-1.6
2005	Det A	8	13	.381	33	33	1	0-0	210	232	117	23	6	49-4	93	4.54	93	.285	.328	2-1-0	.500	1	104	-8		-0.6
Total 9		52	86	.377	215	199	6-1	0-0	1212.2	1329	726	162	50	451-22	736	4.88	92	.278	.344	24-1-3	.125	1	91	-67	146	-6.4

JOHNSON, JERRY   Jerry Michael B12.3.1943 Miami FL BR/TR/6-3/200* d7.17

YEAR	TM LG	W	L	PCT	G	GS	CG-SHO	SV-BS	IP	H	R	HR	HB	BB-IB	SO	ERA	AERA	OAV	OOB	AB-HR-SH	AVG	PB	SUP	APR	DL	PW
1968	Phi N	4	4	.500	16	11	2	0	80.2	82	33	5	2	29-2	40	3.24	93	.264	.328	25-0-1	.080	-0	87	-2		-0.2
1969	Phi N	6	13	.316	34	21	4-2	1-2	147.1	151	76	18	3	57-11	82	4.28	83	.268	.335	43-0-3	.209	2	78	-11		-1.2
1970	StL N	2	0	1.000	7	0	0	1-1	11.1	6	4	1	0	3-0	5	3.18	131	.146	.205	1	.000	0		1		0.3
	SF N	3	4	.429	33	1	0	3-2	65.1	67	39	5	1	38-2	44	4.27	93	.266	.364	15	.067	-1	90	-4		-0.6
	Year	5	4	.556	40	1	0	4-3	76.2	73	43	6	1	41-2	49	4.11	97	.249	.343	16	.063	-1	90	-3		-0.3
1971	†SF N	12	9	.571	67	0	0	18-5	109	93	42	9	1	48-9	85	2.97	115	.230	.310	13-0-1	.154			6		1.3
1972	SF N	8	6	.571	48	0	0	8-6	73.1	73	44	4	0	40-10	77	5.42	79	.261	.385	9-0-1	.000	-1		-7		-1.5
1973	Cle A	5	6	.455	39	1	0	5-6	59.2	70	48	7	0	39-8	45	6.18	64	.299	.396	0			90	-15		-2.8
1974	Hou N	2	1	.667	34	0	0	0-0	45	47	26	2	0	24-7	32	4.80	73	.276	.360	1	.000	-0		-6		-0.4
1975	SD N	3	1	.750	21	4	0	0-0	54	60	37	3	0	31-3	18	5.17	68	.282	.368	12	.083	-0	119	-10		-0.8
1976	SD N	1	3	.250	24	1	0	0-0	39	39	27	0	0	26-6	27	5.31	62	.260	.367	3	.000	-0	27	-10		-1.0
1977	Tor A	2	4	.333	43	0	0	5-2	86	91	50	9	0	54-4	54	4.60	92	.279	.375	0		0		-3		-0.3
Total 10		48	51	.485	365	39	6-2	41-24	770.2	779	422	63	7	389-62	489	4.31	86	.268	.355	122-0-6	.123	2	80	-61		-7.2

JOHNSON, JOHNNY   John Clifford "Swede" B9.29.1914 Belmore OH D6.26.1991 Iron Mountain MI BL/TL/6-0/182 d4.19 Col Eastern Michigan [DL 1946 Chi A 119]

YEAR	TM LG	W	L	PCT	G	GS	CG-SHO	SV-BS	IP	H	R	HR	HB	BB-IB	SO	ERA	AERA	OAV	OOB	AB-HR-SH	AVG	PB	SUP	APR	DL	PW
1944	NY A	0	2	.000	22	1	0	3	26.2	25	14	0	1	24	11	4.05	86	.243	.391	6	.500	-1	24	-2		-0.1
1945	Chi A	3	0	1.000	29	0	1	4	69.2	85	39	2	1	35	38	4.26	78	.306	.385	14-0-1	.286	2		-8		-0.2
Total 2		3	2	.600	51	1	1	7	96.1	110	53	2	2	59	49	4.20	80	.289	.387	20-0-6	.350	3	24	-10	119	-0.3

JOHNSON, YOUNGY   John Godfred B7.22.1877 San Francisco CA D8.28.1936 Berkeley CA TR d4.29

YEAR	TM LG	W	L	PCT	G	GS	CG-SHO	SV-BS	IP	H	R	HR	HB	BB-IB	SO	ERA	AERA	OAV	OOB	AB-HR-SH	AVG	PB	SUP	APR	DL	PW
1897	Phi N	1	2	.333	5	2	1	0	29	39	24	0	2	12	7	4.66	90	.320	.390	13	.077	-2	93	-3		-0.4
1899	NY N	0	0	—	1	0	0	0	2	0	0	0	0	2	1	0.00	—	.000	.250	1	.000	-0		1		0.0
Total 2		1	2	.333	6	2	1	0	31	39	24	0	2	14	8	4.35	96	.305	.382	14	.071	-2	93	-2		-0.4

JOHNSON, JOHN HENRY   John Henry B8.21.1956 Houston TX BL/TL/6-2/190(185-210) [SFN74 15/355] d4.10

YEAR	TM LG	W	L	PCT	G	GS	CG-SHO	SV-BS	IP	H	R	HR	HB	BB-IB	SO	ERA	AERA	OAV	OOB	AB-HR-SH	AVG	PB	SUP	APR	DL	PW
1978	Oak A	11	10	.524	33	30	7-2	0-0	186	164	81	18	0	82-6	91	3.39	108	.238	.317	0	—	0*	108	7		0.6
1979	Oak A	2	8	.200	14	13	1	0-0	84.2	89	45	13	1	36-0	50	4.36	93	.269	.341	0	—	0	65	-2		-0.3
	Tex A	2	6	.250	17	12	1	0-0	82.1	79	50	12	1	36-3	46	4.92	84	.255	.330	0	—	0	87	-7		-0.6
	Year	4	14	.222	31	25	2	0-0	167	168	95	25	2	72-3	96	4.63	89	.262	.335	0	—	0	76	-9		-0.9
1980	Tex A	2	2	.500	32	0	0	4-3	38.2	27	12	2	1	15-4	44	2.33	167	.199	.281	0	—	0		7		0.8
1981	Tex A	3	1	.750	24	0	0	2-1	23.2	19	7	2	1	6-1	21	2.66	131	.232	.283	0	—	0		3		0.5
1983	Bos A	3	2	.600	34	1	0	1-1	53.1	58	28	3	1	20-4	51	3.71	118	.283	.342	0	—	0	21	2		0.2
1984	Bos A	1	2	.333	30	3	0	1-0	63.2	64	26	7	0	27-1	57	3.53	119	.260	.333	0	—	0	65	6		0.3
1986	Mil A	2	1	.667	19	0	0	1-0	44	43	15	2	0	10-1	42	2.66	164	.251	.293	0	—	0		8	15	0.5
1987	Mil A	0	1	.000	10	2	0	0-0	26.1	42	30	1	0	18-1	18	9.57	48	.365	.451	0	—	0	99	-14	16	-0.6
Total 8		26	33	.441	214	61	9-2	9-5	602.2	585	294	60	5	250-21	407	3.90	103	.256	.328	0	—	0	88	10	31	1.4

YEAR	TM LG	W	L	PCT	G	GS	CG-SHO	SV-BS	IP	H	R	HR	HB	BB-IB	SO	ERA	AERA	OAV	OOB	AB-HR-SH	AVG	PB	SUP	APR	DL	PW

JOHNSON, JOHN John Louis (b John Louis Mercer) B11.18.1869 Pekin IL D1.28.1941 Kansas City MO TL/5-10/165 d9.11

| 1894 | Phi N | 1 | 1 | .500 | 4 | 3 | 2 | 0 | 32.2 | 44 | 30 | 3 | 1 | 15 | 10 | 6.06 | 85 | .319 | .390 | 16-0-1 | .188 | -1 | 166 | -3 | | -0.2 |

JOHNSON, JONATHAN Jonathan Kent B7.16.1974 LaGrange GA BR/TR/6-0/180* [TexA95 1/7] d9.27 Col Florida St.

1998	Tex A	0	0	—	1	1	0	0-0	4.1	5	4	0	0	5-0	3	8.31	59	.313	.455	0	—	0	228	-1		-0.1
1999	Tex A	0	0	—	1	0	0	0-0	3	9	5	0	1	2-0	3	15.00	34	.529	.571	0	—	0		-3		-0.1
2000	Tex A	1	1	.500	15	0	0	0-0	29	34	23	3	6	19-2	23	6.21	82	.291	.410	0	—	0		-4		-0.2
2001	Tex A	0	0	—	5	0	0	0-0	10.1	13	11	2	1	7-1	11	9.58	50	.317	.404	0	—	0		-5		-0.2
2002	SD N	1	2	.333	16	0	0	0-0	15.1	15	8	2	1	5-1	21	4.11	95	.250	.318	0	—	0		-1		-0.1
2003	Hou N	0	1	.000	4	3	0	0-0	15.1	20	11	2	0	15-3	7	5.87	75	.323	.449	4	.000	-0	64	-2		-0.2
Total	6	2	4	.333	42	4	0	0-0	77.1	96	62	9	9	53-7	68	6.63	70	.307	.413	4	.000	-0	105	-16		-0.9

JOHNSON, JOE Joseph Richard B10.30.1961 Brookline MA BR/TR/6-2/195* [AtlN82 2/37] d7.25 Col Maine

1985	Atl N	4	4	.500	15	14	1	0-0	85.2	95	44	9	3	24-5	34	4.10	94	.285	.336	23-0-3	.043	-1	98	-2		-0.3
1986	Atl N	6	7	.462	17	15	2	0-0	87	101	58	8	2	35-4	49	4.97	80	.289	.357	26-0-2	.115	-1	98	-11		-1.4
	Tor A	7	2	.778	16	15	0	0-0	88	94	39	3	3	22-1	39	3.89	109	.281	.327	0	—	0	104	5		0.4
1987	Tor A	3	5	.375	14	14	0	0-0	66.2	77	44	10	2	18-0	27	5.13	88	.289	.338	0	—	0	99	-6		-0.6
Total	3	20	18	.526	62	58	3	0-0	327.1	367	185	30	10	99-10	149	4.48	92	.286	.340	49-0-5	.082	-2	100	-14		-1.9

JOHNSON, JOSH Joshua Michael B1.31.1984 Minneapolis MN BL/TR/6-7/240 d9.10

| 2005 | Fla N | 0 | 0 | — | 4 | 1 | 0 | 0-0 | 12.1 | 11 | 5 | 0 | 1 | 10-0 | 10 | 3.65 | 109 | .256 | .407 | 4 | .250 | 0 | 116 | 1 | | 0.1 |

JOHNSON, KEN Kenneth Travis B6.16.1933 W.Palm Beach FL BR/TR/6-4/210(200-222) d9.13

1958	KC A	0	0	—	2	0	0	0	2.1	6	7	1	0	3-0	1	27.00	14	.429	.529	0	—	0		-5		-0.3
1959	KC A	1	1	.500	2	2	0	0	11	11	6	2	0	5-0	8	4.09	98	.268	.340	3	.000	-0	132	0		-0.1
1960	KC A	5	10	.333	42	6	2	3	120.1	120	68	16	7	45-6	83	4.26	93	.263	.336	30-0-3	.167	-1	85	-5		-0.6
1961	KC A	0	4	.000	6	1	0	0	9.1	11	11	2	0	7-0	4	10.61	39	.297	.409	1	.000	-0	0	-6		-1.0
†Cin N	6	2	.750	15	11	3-1	0	83	71	33	11	2	22-1	42	3.25	125	.229	.283	25-0-1	.240	1	105	8		0.8
1962	Hou N	7	16	.304	33	31	5-1	0	197	195	100	18	7	46-1	178	3.84	97	.257	.302	52-0-9	.077	-3	71	-3		-0.6
1963	Hou N	11	17	.393	37	32	6-1	1	224	204	86	12	8	50-4	148	2.65	119	.242	.290	74-0-5	.068	-4*	77	9		0.8
1964	Hou N	11	16	.407	35	35	7-1	0	218	209	100	15	7	44-6	117	3.63	94	.250	.291	76-1-4.	.079	-2	75	-5		-0.6
1965	Hou N	3	2	.600	8	8	1	0	51.2	52	25	4	4	11-1	28	4.18	80	.267	.315	18	.111	-0	111	-4		-0.3
Mil N	13	8	.619	29	26	8-1	2	179.2	165	75	15	3	37-7	123	3.21	110	.240	.280	61-0-3	.115	-2	108	5		0.2
Year	16	10	.615	37	34	9-1	2	231.1	217	100	19	7	48-8	151	3.42	102	.246	.288	79-0-3	.114	-2	108	1		-0.1
1966	Atl N	14	8	.636	32	31	11-2	0	215.2	213	89	24	0	46-6	105	3.30	110	.262	.300	70-1-10	.143	0	114	8		0.8
1967	Atl N	13	9	.591	29	29	6	0	210.1	191	78	19	7	38-8	85	2.74	121	.244	.284	71-0-6	.127	-0	121	12		1.1
1968	Atl N	5	8	.385	31	16	1	0	135	145	58	10	9	25-10	57	3.47	86	.279	.323	40-0-3	.175	-0	81	-6		-0.7
1969	Atl N	0	1	.000	9	2	0	1-1	29	32	14	4	0	9-1	20	4.97	73	.283	.328	6	.000	-0	73	-4		-0.2
NY A	1	2	.333	12	0	0	0-0	26	19	11	1	0	11-2	21	3.46	102	.202	.263	3	.000	-0		4		0.2
Chi N	2	2	.333	9	1	0	1-1	19	17	8	2	0	13-3	18	2.84	141	.230	.345	4-0-1	.000	-0	44	2		0.2
1970	Mon N	0	0	—	3	0	0	0-0	6	9	6	1	2	4-1	4	7.50	55	.321	.387	0	—	0		-2		-0.1
Total	13	91	106	.462	334	231	50-7	9-2	1737.1	1670	778	157	56	413-56	1042	3.46	101	.253	.301	534-2-45	.114	-12	92	-5		-0.5

JOHNSON, KEN Kenneth Wandersee "Hook" B1.14.1923 Topeka KS D4.6.2004 Wichita KS BL/TL/6-1/185* d9.18

1947	StL N	1	0	1.000	2	1	1	0	10	7	2	0	0	11	1		—	.063	.211	4	.500	1	64	4		0.5
1948	StL N	2	4	.333	13	4	0	0	45.1	43	27	1	1	30	20	4.76	86	.262	.379	20	.300	2*	60	-4		-0.3
1949	StL N	0	1	.000	14	2	0	0.	33.2	29	28	1	3	35	18	6.42	65	.250	.435	8	.250	0*	106	-8		-0.3
1950	StL N	0	0	—	2	0	0	0	2	1	1	0	0	3	1	0.00	—	.167	.444	0	—	0		0		0.0
†Phi N	4	1	.800	14	8	3-1	0	60.2	61	32	3	1	43	32	4.01	101	.260	.376	19	.158	-0*	126	0		0.0
Year	4	1	.800	16	8	3-1	0	62.2	62	33	3	1	46	33	3.88	105	.257	.378	19	.158	-0	126	0		0.0
1951	Phi N	5	8	.385	20	18	4-3	0	106.1	103	56	8	3	68	58	4.57	84	.259	.371	35-0-1	.143	-1*	74	-7		-0.9
1952	Det A	0	0	—	9	1	0	0	11.1	12	11	1	0	11	10	6.35	60	.273	.418	3	.333	1	183	-4		-0.2
Total	6	12	14	.462	74	34	8-4	0	269.1	251	156	14	9	195	147	4.58	87	.252	.379	89-0-1	.213	1	90	-19		-1.2

JOHNSON, LLOYD Lloyd William "Eppa" B12.24.1910 Santa Rosa CA D10.8.1980 Stockton CA BL/TL/6-4/204 d4.21

| 1934 | Pit N | 0 | 0 | — | 1 | 0 | 0 | 0 | 1 | 1 | 0 | 0 | 0 | 0 | 0 | 0.00 | — | .333 | .333 | 0 | — | 0 | | 0 | | 0.0 |

JOHNSON, MARK Mark J. B5.2.1975 Dayton OH BR/TR/6-3/226 [HouN96 1/19] d4.7 Col Hawaii-Manoa

| 2000 | Det A | 0 | 1 | .000 | 9 | 3 | 0 | 0-0 | 24 | 25 | 23 | 3 | 1 | 16-1 | 11 | 7.50 | 65 | .266 | .365 | 0 | — | 0 | 134 | -7 | 35 | -0.3 |

JOHNSON, MIKE Michael Keith B10.3.1975 Edmonton AL, Can. BL/TR/6-2/170* [TorA93 17/490] d4.6

1997	Bal A	0	1	.000	14	5	0	2-0	39.2	52	36	12	1	16-2	29	7.94	56	.317	.377	0	—	0	117	-15		-0.7
Mon N	2	5	.286	11	11	0	0-0	50	54	34	8	0	21-2	28	5.94	70	.277	.344	13-0-2	.077	-1	86	-9		-1.1
1998	Mon N	0	2	.000	2	2	0	0-0	7.1	16	12	4	1	2-0	4	14.73	29	.432	.475	3	.333	0	109	-8		-1.1
1999	Mon N	0	0	—	3	1	0	0-0	8.1	12	8	2	0	7-1	6	8.64	52	.324	.432	4	.250	0	289	-3		-0.1
2000	Mon N	5	6	.455	41	13	0	0-0	101.1	107	73	18	9	53-1	70	6.39	74	.269	.366	22-0-3	.182	-0	118	-16		-1.4
2001	Mon N	0	0	—	10	0	0	0-2	11.1	13	6	3	2	4-0	10	4.76	91	.295	.380	1	.000	-0	111	0		0.0
Total	5	7	14	.333	81	32	0	2-2	218	254	169	47	13	103-6	147	6.85	65	.290	.371	43-0-5	.163	-0	111	-51		-4.4

JOHNSON, MIKE Michael Norton B3.2.1951 Slayton MN BR/TR/6-1/185 d7.25

| 1974 | SD N | 0 | 2 | .000 | 18 | 0 | 0 | 0-0 | 21 | 29 | 13 | 1 | 1 | 15-5 | 15 | 4.64 | 77 | .326 | .421 | 0 | — | 0 | | -3 | | -0.3 |

JOHNSON, RANDY Randall David "The Big Unit" B9.10.1963 Walnut Creek CA BR/TL/6-10/225* [MonN85 2/36] d9.15 Col USC

1988	Mon N	3	0	1.000	4	4	1	0-0	26	23	8	3	0	7-0	25	2.42	150	.225	.275	9	.111	-0	152	3		0.3
1989	Mon N	0	4	.000	7	6	0	0-0	29.2	29	25	2	0	26-1	26	6.67	53	.264	.393	7-0-2	.143	-0	79	-10		-1.2
Sea A	7	9	.438	22	22	2	0-0	131	118	75	11	3	70-1	104	4.40	92	.244	.338	0	—	0	91	-6		-0.6
1990	Sea A☆	14	11	.560	33	33	5-2	0-0	219.2	174	103	26	5	120-2	194	3.65	109	.216	.319	0	—	0	95	7		0.7
1991	Sea A	13	10	.565	33	33	2-1	0-0	201.1	151	96	15	12	152-0	228	3.98	94	.213	.358	0	—	0	103	4		0.4
1992	Sea A	12	14	.462	31	31	6-2	0-0	210.1	154	104	13	18	144-1	241	3.77	106	.206	.344	0	—	0	90	2	16	0.4
1993	Sea A★	19	8	.704	35	34	10-3	1-0	255.1	185	97	22	16	99-1	308	3.24	128	.203	.290	0	—	0*	103	34		3.5
1994	Sea A★	13	6	.684	23	23	9-4	0-0	172	132	65	14	6	72-2	204	3.19	154	.216	.304	0	—	0	103	34		3.5
1995	†Sea A★	18	2	.900	30	30	6-3	0-0	214.1	159	65	12	6	65-1	294	2.48	193	.201	.266	0	—	0	108	54		4.6
1996	Sea A	5	0	1.000	14	8	0	1-1	61.1	48	27	8	2	25-0	85	3.67	136	.211	.294	0	—	0	121	9	119	0.7
1997	†Sea A★	20	4	.833	30	29	5-2	0-0	213	147	60	20	10	77-2	291	2.28	199	.194	.277	0	—	0	90	53		5.6
1998	Sea A	9	10	.474	23	23	6-2	0-0	160	146	90	19	11	60-0	213	4.33	108	.240	.319	2	.143	-0	99	28		3.5
†Hou N	10	1	.909	11	11	4	4-4	84.1	57	12	4	3	26-1	116	1.28	337	.191	.261	32-0-3	.063	-3	101	62		5.1
1999	†Ari N★	17	9	.654	35	35	12-2	0-0	271.2	207	86	30	9	70-3	364	2.48	186	.208	.266	97-0-7	.124	-3	101	62		5.1
2000	Ari N★	19	7	.731	35	35	8-3	0-0	248.2	202	89	23	6	76-1	347	2.64	182	.224	.288	83-0-5	.157	-0	79	53		5.0
2001	Ari N★	21	6	.778	35	34	3-2	0-0	249.2	181	74	19	18	71-2	372	2.49	186	.203	.274	80-0-7	.100	-3	103	56		5.4
2002	†Ari N☆	24	5	.828	35	35	8-4	0-0	260	197	78	26	13	71-1	334	2.32	193	.208	.273	89-0-6	.135	-2	114	55		5.7
2003	Ari N	6	8	.429	18	18	1-1	0-0	114	125	61	16	8	27-3	125	4.26	108	.280	.330	36-1-2	.194	1	84	4	98	0.3
2004	Ari N★	16	14	.533	35	35	4-2	0-0	245.2	177	88	18	10	44-1	290	2.60	175	.197	.241	80-0-3	.125	-1	71	47		5.3
2005	†NY A	17	8	.680	34	34	4	0-0	225.2	207	102	32	12	47-2	211	3.79	115	.243	.291	8	.000	-1	121	16		1.4
Total	18	263	136	.659	523	513	96-37	2-1	3593.2	2819	1405	333	168	1349-25	4372	3.11	144	.215	.295	528-1-35	.127	-13	98	509	233	49.9

JOHNSON, BOB Robert Dale B4.25.1943 Aurora IL BL/TR/6-4/220* d9.19 Col Bradley

1969	NY N	0	0	—	2	0	0	1-0	1.2	1	1	0	0	1-0	1	0.00	—	.167	.286	0	—	0		1		0.1
1970	KC A	8	13	.381	40	26	10-1	4-2	214	178	82	18	11	82-4	206	3.07	122	.228	.307	57-0-8	.105	-1	80	17		1.4
1971	†Pit N	9	10	.474	31	27	7-1	0-0	174.2	170	73	19	7	55-8	101	3.45	99	.259	.321	48-0-4	.063	-0	95	0		-0.2
1972	†Pit N	4	4	.500	31	11	1	3-1	115.2	98	40	14	4	46-8	79	2.96	112	.231	.309	35-0-1	.143	-0	114	7		0.4
1973	Pit N	4	2	.667	50	2	0	4-0	92	98	41	12	5	34-7	68	3.62	97	.276	.346	14-0-1	.000	-1	138	0		-0.3
1974	Cle A	3	4	.429	14	10	0	0-0	72	75	42	12	3	37-5	36	4.38	83	.273	.362	0	—	-0	126	-7		-0.6
1977	Atl N	0	1	.000	15	0	0	0-0	22.1	24	18	7	2	14-1	16	7.25	61	.270	.377	3	.333	-0		-5		-0.3
Total	7	28	34	.452	183	76	18-2	12-3	692.1	644	296	82	32	269-33	507	3.48	102	.249	.325	157-0-14	.096	-4	97	13		0.0

JOHNSON, ROY Roy "Hardrock" B10.1.1895 Madill OK D1.10.1986 Scottsdale AZ BR/TR/6-0/185 d8.7 M1/C15

| 1918 | Phi A | 1 | 5 | .167 | 10 | 8 | 3 | 0 | 50 | 47 | 32 | 0 | 2 | 34 | 12 | 3.42 | 86 | .254 | .376 | 15 | .067 | -2 | 77 | -5 | | -0.8 |

YEAR	TM	LG	W	L	PCT	G	GS	CG-SHO	SV-BS	IP	H	R	HR	HB	BB-IB	SO	ERA	AERA	OAV	OOB	AB-HR-SH	AVG	PB	SUP	APR	DL	PW

JOHNSON, JING Russell Conwell B10.9.1894 Parker Ford PA D12.6.1950 Pottstown PA BR/TR/5-9/172 d6.27 Mil 1918 Col Ursinus

YEAR	TM	LG	W	L	PCT	G	GS	CG-SHO	SV-BS	IP	H	R	HR	HB	BB-IB	SO	ERA	AERA	OAV	OOB	AB-HR-SH	AVG	PB	SUP	APR	DL	PW
1916	Phi	A	2	9	.182	12	12	8	0	84.1	90	46	3	0	39	25	3.74	76	.288	.368	27-1-1	.074	-1	88	-8		-0.9
1917	Phi	A	9	12	.429	34	23	13	0	191	184	76	3	5	56	55	2.78	99	.260	.319	59-0-3	.203	2*	101	2		0.5
1919	Phi	A	9	15	.375	34	25	12	0	202	222	106	8	3	62	67	3.61	95	.291	.346	72-1-4	.194	0*	82	-5		-0.3
1927	Phi	A	4	2	.667	17	3	2	0	51.2	42	20	2	4	16	16	3.48	122	.235	.312	12-0-3	.167	-0	130	6		0.6
1928	Phi	A	0	0		3	0	0	0	10.2	13	8	1	0	5	3	5.06	79	.310	.383	4	.500	1		-2		0.0
Total	5		24	38	.387	100	63	35	0	539.2	551	256	17	12	178	166	3.35	95	.275	.338	174-2-11	.184	2	91	-7		-0.1

JOHNSON, SI Silas Kenneth B10.5.1906 Danway IL D5.12.1994 Sheridan IL BR/TR/5-11.5/185 d5.2 Mil 1943-45

YEAR	TM	LG	W	L	PCT	G	GS	CG-SHO	SV-BS	IP	H	R	HR	HB	BB-IB	SO	ERA	AERA	OAV	OOB	AB-HR-SH	AVG	PB	SUP	APR	DL	PW
1928	Cin	N	0	0		7	0	0	0	10.1	9	5	0	0	5	1	4.35	91	.250	.341	4	.250	0		0		0.0
1929	Cin	N	0	0		1	0	0	0	2	2	1	0	0	1	0	4.50	101	.250	.333	0	—	0		0		0.0
1930	Cin	N	3	1	.750	35	3	0	0	78.1	86	54	5	4	31	47	4.94	98	.286	.360	17	.235	-0	157	-3		-0.2
1931	Cin	N	11	19	.367	42	33	14	0	262.1	273	131	5	6	74	95	3.77	99	.269	.323	87-0-3	.149	-0	77	-2		-0.7
1932	Cin	N	13	15	.464	42	27	14-2	2	245	246	109	8	2	57	94	3.27	118	.259	.302	80-0-2	.125	-3	77	-2		1.2
1933	Cin	N	7	18	.280	34	28	14-4	1	211.1	212	101	7	3	54	51	3.49	97	.263	.312	72-0-3	.042	-7	63	-2		-1.0
1934	Cin	N	7	22	.241	46	31	9	3	215.2	264	150	15	7	84	84	5.22	78	.297	.362	72	.139	-3	76	-26		-3.4
1935	Cin	N	5	11	.313	30	20	4-1	0	130	155	106	14	3	59	40	6.23	64	.293	.367	41-0-1	.024	-4	78	-32		-3.7
1936	Cin	N	0	0	—	2	0	0	0	4	7	6	1	0	0	2	13.50	28	.368	.368	0	—	0		-4		-0.2
	StL	N	5	3	.625	12	9	3-1	0	61.2	82	30	4	1	11	21	4.38	90	.314	.344	21-0-1	.190	-0	100	-1		-0.2
	Year		5	3	.625	14	9	3-1	0	65.2	89	36	5	1	11	23	4.93	80	.318	.343	21-0-1	.190	-0	101	-4		-0.4
1937	StL	N	12	12	.500	38	21	12-1	1	192.1	222	92	14	1	43	64	3.32	120	.292	.330	65-0-3	.138	-3	109	11		0.8
1938	StL	N	3	0	.000	6	3	0	0	15.2	27	17	0	0	6	4	7.47	53	.380	.429	1-0-1	.000	-3	43	-6		-1.0
1940	Phi	N	5	14	.263	37	14	5	1	138.1	145	81	13	2	42	58	4.88	80	.268	.333	43-0-2	.140	-2	62	-13		-1.9
1941	Phi	N	5	12	.294	39	21	6-1	2	163.1	207	91	8	1	54	80	4.52	82	.309	.362	47-0-2	.149	-2	71	-13		-1.5
1942	Phi	N	8	19	.296	39	26	10-1	0	195.1	198	96	6	1	72	78	3.69	90	.266	.332	58-0-5	.103	-4	66	-10		-1.8
1943	Phi	N	8	3	.727	21	14	9	2	113	110	48	4	0	25	46	3.27	103	.252	.292	33-0-3	.182	0	122	1		0.1
1946	Phi	N	0	0	—	1	0	0	0	3	7	4	1	0	0	2	3.00	114	.538	.538	1	1.000	0		-1		0.0
	Bos	N	6	5	.545	28	12	5-1	1	127	134	47	8	4	35	41	2.76	124	.272	.325	37-0-4	.135	-2	121	9		0.5
	Year		6	5	.545	29	12	5-1	1	130	141	51	9	4	35	43	2.77	124	.279	.330	38-0-4	.158	-1	121	8		0.5
1947	Bos	N	6	8	.429	36	10	3	2	112.2	124	57	7	1	34	27	4.23	92	.275	.327	30	.033	-3	97	-3		-0.5
Total	17		101	165	.380	492	272	108-13	15	2281.1	2510	1226	120	36	687	840	4.09	92	.279	.333	709-0-30	.123	-37	82	-79		-13.5

JOHNSON, SYL Sylvester W (Born Sylvester Johnson) B12.31.1900 Portland OR D2.20.1985 Portland OR BR/TR/5-11/180 d4.24 C4

YEAR	TM	LG	W	L	PCT	G	GS	CG-SHO	SV-BS	IP	H	R	HR	HB	BB-IB	SO	ERA	AERA	OAV	OOB	AB-HR-SH	AVG	PB	SUP	APR	DL	PW
1922	Det	A	7	3	.700	29	8	3	1	97	99	52	7	4	30	29	3.71	105	.273	.336	36-0-1	.222	-0	183	0		-0.1
1923	Det	A	12	7	.632	37	18	7	0	176.1	181	82	12	3	47	93	3.98	97	.274	.325	62-1-2	.161	-1	106	2		-0.1
1924	Det	A	5	4	.556	29	9	2	3	104	117	63	8	5	42	55	4.93	83	.287	.360	34-0-2	.206	-0	107	-7		-0.6
1925	Det	A	0	2	.000	6	0	0	0	13	11	7	1	0	10	5	3.46	124	.250	.389	3	.000	-1		1		0.1
1926	StL	N	3	0	.000	19	6	1	1	49	54	27	3	2	15	10	4.22	92	.297	.357	12	.000	-2	68	-2		-0.3
1927	StL	N	0	0	—	2	0	0	0	3	3	2	1	0	0	2	6.00	66	.250	.250	0	—	0		0		0.0
1928	†StL	N	8	4	.667	34	6	2	3	120	117	53	4	4	33	66	3.90	103	.259	.315	38	.158	-0	92	5		0.4
1929	StL	N	13	7	.650	42	19	12-3	3	182.1	186	88	11	7	56	80	3.60	129	.265	.325	60-1-3	.117	-2	95	20		1.4
1930	†StL	N	12	10	.545	32	24	9-2	2	187.2	215	105	13	4	38	92	4.65	108	.293	.332	70-0-1	.214	-0	113	11		0.9
1931	†StL	N	11	9	.550	32	24	12-2	2	186	186	73	9	2	29	82	3.00	131	.255	.286	60-0-1	.233	2	103	18		1.9
1932	StL	N	5	14	.263	32	22	7	2	164.2	199	103	14	4	35	70	4.92	80	.299	.338	51-0-3	.196	-1	93	-17		-1.9
1933	StL	N	3	3	.500	35	1	0	3	84	89	45	7	3	16	28	4.29	81	.271	.311	21-0-1	.238	-0	144	-6		-0.6
1934	Cin	N	0	0	—	2	0	0	0	6.2	9	6	2	0	0	4	2.70	151	.310	.310	2-1-0	.500	1		0		0.1
	Phi	N	5	9	.357	42	10	4-3	3	133.2	122	58	14	1	24	54	3.50	135	.242	.277	41-0-2	.195	-1	86	16		1.4
	Year		5	9	.357	44	10	4-3	3	140.1	131	64	16	1	24	54	3.46	136	.245	.279	43-1-2	.209	1	86	16		1.5
1935	Phi	N	10	8	.556	37	18	8-1	6	174.2	182	79	15	3	31	89	3.56	128	.265	.299	58-1-6	.241	1	88	18		1.8
1936	Phi	N	5	7	.417	39	8	-1	7	111	129	60	10	3	29	46	4.30	106	.288	.335	36	.250	-0	105	5		0.4
1937	Phi	N	4	10	.286	32	15	4	3	138	155	81	19	2	22	46	5.02	86	.288	.318	48-0-2	.146	-3	72	-7		-1.0
1938	Phi	N	7	2	.222	22	6	2	0	83	87	43	4	0	11	21	4.23	92	.267	.291	29-0-1	.034	-3	47	-2		-0.6
1939	Phi	N	8	8	.500	22	13	6	2	111	112	50	10	1	15	37	3.81	105	.264	.291	33-0-4	.152	-1	84	4		0.3
1940	Phi	N	2	2	.500	17	2	2	2	40.2	37	22	6	0	5	13	4.20	93	.236	.259	8-0-1	.000	-1	123	-2		-0.3
Total	19		112	117	.489	542	209	82-11	43	2165.2	2290	1099	172	48	488	920	4.06	104	.273	.316	702-4-30	.181	-10	98	57		3.2

JOHNSON, TOM Thomas Raymond B4.2.1951 St.Paul MN BR/TR/6-1/185* d9.10

YEAR	TM	LG	W	L	PCT	G	GS	CG-SHO	SV-BS	IP	H	R	HR	HB	BB-IB	SO	ERA	AERA	OAV	OOB	AB-HR-SH	AVG	PB	SUP	APR	DL	PW
1974	Min	A	2	0	1.000	4	0	0	1-0	7	4	1	0	0	0-0	4	0.00	—	.167	.167	0	—	0		2		0.5
1975	Min	A	1	2	.333	18	0	0	3-2	38.2	40	23	4	2	21-4	17	4.19	91	.263	.356	0	—	0		-3		-0.2
1976	Min	A	3	1	.750	18	1	0	0-0	48.1	44	14	2	0	8-1	20	2.61	137	.243	.275	0	—	0	74	6		0.5
1977	Min	A	16	7	.696	71	0	0	15-7	146.2	152	57	11	5	47-8	87	3.13	127	.272	.329	0	—	0		14		2.4
1978	Min	A	1	4	.200	18	0	0	3-1	32.2	42	22	2	2	17-4	21	5.51	70	.318	.399	0	—	0		-6	72	-0.9
Total	5		23	14	.622	129	1	0	22-10	273.1	282	117	19	9	93-17	166	3.59	114	.269	.330	0	—	0	74	13	72	2.3

JOHNSON, TYLER Tyler James B6.7.1981 Columbia MO BB/TL/6-2/180 d9.6 Col Moorpark (CA) JC

YEAR	TM	LG	W	L	PCT	G	GS	CG-SHO	SV-BS	IP	H	R	HR	HB	BB-IB	SO	ERA	AERA	OAV	OOB	AB-HR-SH	AVG	PB	SUP	APR	DL	PW
2005	StL	N	0	0	—	5	0	0	3-0	2.2	3	0	0	0	3-0	4	0.00	—	.300	.462	0	—	0		1		0.1

JOHNSON, VIC Victor Oscar B8.3.1920 Eau Claire WI D5.10.2005 Eau Claire WI BR/TL/6-0/160 d5.3

YEAR	TM	LG	W	L	PCT	G	GS	CG-SHO	SV-BS	IP	H	R	HR	HB	BB-IB	SO	ERA	AERA	OAV	OOB	AB-HR-SH	AVG	PB	SUP	APR	DL	PW
1944	Bos	A	0	3	.000	7	5	0	0	27.1	42	22	0	0	15	10	6.26	54	.362	.435	10	.000	-1	123	-9		-1.0
1945	Bos	A	6	4	.600	26	9	4-1	2	85.1	90	41	4	2	46	21	4.01	85	.276	.369	30	.167	-1	100	-5		-0.6
1946	Cle	A	0	1	1.000	9	1	0	0	13.2	20	14	1	0	8	0	9.22	36	.357	.438	2	.000	-0	52	-9		-0.6
Total	3		6	8	.429	42	15	4-1	2	126.1	152	77	5	2	69	31	5.06	67	.305	.392	42	.119	-3	105	-23		-2.2

JOHNSON, WALTER Walter Perry "Barney","The Big Train" B11.6.1887 Humboldt KS D12.10.1946 Washington DC BR/TR/6-1/200 d8.2 M7 HF1937

YEAR	TM	LG	W	L	PCT	G	GS	CG-SHO	SV-BS	IP	H	R	HR	HB	BB-IB	SO	ERA	AERA	OAV	OOB	AB-HR-SH	AVG	PB	SUP	APR	DL	PW
1907	Was	A	5	9	.357	14	12	11-2	1	110.1	100	35	2	4	20	71	1.88	129	.244	.282	36	.111	-2	58	7		0.5
1908	Was	A	14	14	.500	36	30	23-6	1	256.1	194	75	0	11	53	160	1.65	139	.211	.262	79-0-5	.165	3	79	17		2.1
1909	Was	A	13	25	.342	40	36	27-4	1	296.1	247	112	1	15	84	164	2.22	110	.221	.284	101-1-3	.129	-3	52	4		0.1
1910	Was	A	25	17	.595	45	42	38-8	1	370	262	92	1	13	76	313	1.36	183	.205	.257	137-2-1	.175	1	104	43		5.5
1911	Was	A	25	13	.658	40	37	36-6	1	322.1	292	119	8	8	70	207	1.90	173	.238	.283	128-1-6	.234	3*	106	43		5.2
1912	Was	A	33	12	.733	50	37	34-7	2	369	259	89	2	16	76	303	1.39	240	.196	.248	144-2-6	.264	9*	102	77		10.6
1913	Was	A	36	7	.837	48	36	29-11	2	346	232	56	9	9	38	243	1.14	258	.190	.220	134-2-1	.261	10*	97	70		10.9
1914	Was	A	28	18	.609	51	40	33-9	1	371.2	287	88	3	11	74	225	1.72	164	.217	.265	136-3-5	.221	8*	89	45		7.2
1915	Was	A	27	13	.675	47	39	35-7	4	336.2	258	83	4	19	56	203	1.55	192	.214	.260	147-0-5	.231	6*	94	51		7.4
1916	Was	A	25	20	.556	48	38	36-3	1	369.2	290	105	0	9	82	228	1.90	147	.220	.270	142-1-4	.225	8*	88	35		5.2
1917	Was	A	23	16	.590	47	34	30-8	3	326	248	105	3	14	68	188	2.21	119	.211	.263	130-0-2	.254	10*	102	15		3.1
1918	Was	A	23	13	.639	39	29	29-8	3	326	241	71	2	8	70	162	1.27	215	.210	.260	150-1-4	.267	6*	92	51		7.6
1919	Was	A	20	14	.588	39	29	27-7	2	290.1	235	73	0	7	51	147	1.49	216	.219	.259	125-1-4	.192	2*	90	52		6.7
1920	Was	A	8	10	.444	21	15	12-4	3	143.2	135	68	5	4	27	78	3.13	119	.245	.286	64-1-2	.266	4*	67	8		1.3
1921	Was	A	17	14	.548	35	32	25-1	1	264	265	122	7	2	92	143	3.51	117	.263	.326	111-0-2	.270	4*	103	19		2.3
1922	Was	A	15	16	.484	41	31	23-4	3	280	283	115	8	7	99	105	2.99	129	.267	.334	108-1-2	.224	-1*	77	28		2.8
1923	Was	A	17	12	.586	42	34	18-3	4	261	263	112	9	20	73	130	3.48	108	.269	.333	93-0-6	.194	-1	94	14		1.4
1924	†Was	A	23	7	.767	38	38	20-6	0	277.2	233	97	9	10	77	158	2.72	148	.224	.284	113-1-2	.283	7*	117	44		4.9
1925	†Was	A	20	7	.741	30	29	16-3	0	229	217	95	7	7	78	108	3.07	138	.250	.317	97-2-6	.433*	17*	126	30		4.6
1926	Was	A	15	16	.484	33	33	22-2	0	260.2	259	120	13	6	73	125	3.63	107	.263	.317	103-1-3	.194	1*	108	8		0.7
1927	Was	A	5	6	.455	18	15	7-1	0	107.2	113	70	7	7	26	48	5.10	80	.278	.332	46-2-1	.348	6*	96	-12		-0.4
Total	21		417	279	.599	802	666	531-110	34	5914.1	4913	1902	97	205	1363	3509	2.17	147	.227	.279	2324-24-70	.235	99	96	649		89.9

JOHNSON, BILL William Charles B10.6.1960 Wilmington DE BR/TR/6-5/205* d9.6

YEAR	TM	LG	W	L	PCT	G	GS	CG-SHO	SV-BS	IP	H	R	HR	HB	BB-IB	SO	ERA	AERA	OAV	OOB	AB-HR-SH	AVG	PB	SUP	APR	DL	PW
1983	Chi	N	1	0	1.000	10	0	0	0-0	12.1	17	6	0	0	3-1	4	4.38	87	.347	.377	0	—	0		0		0.0
1984	Chi	N	0	0		4	0	0	0-0	5.1	4	1	0	0	1-1	3	1.69	232	.235	.278	0	—	0		1		0.1
Total	2		1	0	1.000	14	0	0	0-0	17.2	21	7	0	0	4-2	7	3.57	108	.318	.352	0	—	0		1		0.1

JOHNSON, JEFF William Jeffrey B8.4.1966 Durham NC BR/TL/6-3/200* [NYA88 6/157] d6.5 Col North Carolina-Charlotte

YEAR	TM	LG	W	L	PCT	G	GS	CG-SHO	SV-BS	IP	H	R	HR	HB	BB-IB	SO	ERA	AERA	OAV	OOB	AB-HR-SH	AVG	PB	SUP	APR	DL	PW
1991	NY	A	6	11	.353	23	23	0	0-0	127	156	89	15	6	33-1	62	5.95	70	.305	.351	0	—	0	90	-24		-2.6
1992	NY	A	2	3	.400	13	8	0	0-0	52.2	71	44	4	2	23-0	14	6.66	59	.329	.395	0	—	0	104	-16		-1.4

YEAR	TM LG	W	L	PCT	G	GS	CG-SHO	SV-BS	IP	H	R	HR	HB	BB-IB	SO	ERA	AERA	OAV	OOB	AB-HR-SH	AVG	PB	SUP	APR	DL	PW
1993	NY A	0	2	.000	2	2	0	0-0	2.2	12	10	1	0	2-0	0	30.38	14	.600	.636	0	—	0	44	-8		-1.2
Total	3	8	16	.333	38	33	0	0-0	182.1	239	143	20	8	58-1	76	6.52	63	.320	.372	0	—	0	90	-48		-5.2

JOHNSTON, JOEL Joel Raymond B3.8.1967 West Chester PA BR/TR/6-4/220(220-234) [KCA88 3/75] d9.5 Col Penn St.

YEAR	TM LG	W	L	PCT	G	GS	CG-SHO	SV-BS	IP	H	R	HR	HB	BB-IB	SO	ERA	AERA	OAV	OOB	AB-HR-SH	AVG	PB	SUP	APR	DL	PW
1991	KC A	1	0	1.000	13	0	0	0-0	22.1	9	1	0	0	9-3	21	0.40	1029	.120	.214	0	—	0	9			0.5
1992	KC A	0	0	—	5	0	0	0-0	2.2	3	4	2	0	2-0	1	13.50	30	.273	.385	0	—	0	-3			-0.1
1993	Pit N	2	4	.333	33	0	0	2-1	53.1	38	20	7	0	19-5	31	3.38	121	.203	.277	6-0-1	.333	1	5			0.6
1994	Pit N	0	0	—	4	0	0	0-0	3.1	14	12	0	2	4-0	5	29.70	15	.583	.667	0	—	0	-9			-0.4
1995	Bos A	0	1	.000	4	0	0	0-0	4	2	5	1	1	3-0	4	11.25	43	.143	.333	0	—	0	-3			-0.5
Total	5	3	5	.375	59	0	0	2-1	85.2	66	42	10	3	37-8	61	4.31	96	.212	.302	6-0-1	.333	1	-1			0.1

JOHNSTON, MIKE Michael Charles B3.30.1979 Philadelphia PA BL/TL/6-2/215* [PitN98 20/598] d4.7 Col Garrett (MD) CC

YEAR	TM LG	W	L	PCT	G	GS	CG-SHO	SV-BS	IP	H	R	HR	HB	BB-IB	SO	ERA	AERA	OAV	OOB	AB-HR-SH	AVG	PB	SUP	APR	DL	PW
2004	Pit N	0	3	.000	24	0	0	0-1	22.2	29	16	2	2	15-1	18	4.37	99	.315	.422	0	—	0	-2	41		-0.2
2005	Pit N	0	0	—	1	0	0	0-0	.1	4	4	2	0	0-0	2	36.00	12	.571	.571	0	—	0	-3			-0.2
Total	2	0	3	.000	25	0	0	0-1	23.2	33	20	4	2	15-1	20	5.70	76	.333	.431	0	—	0	-5	41		-0.4

JOHNSTONE, JOHN John William B11.25.1968 Liverpool NY BR/TR/6-3/195(195-210) [NYN87 20/524] d9.3 [DL 2001 SF N 190]

YEAR	TM LG	W	L	PCT	G	GS	CG-SHO	SV-BS	IP	H	R	HR	HB	BB-IB	SO	ERA	AERA	OAV	OOB	AB-HR-SH	AVG	PB	SUP	APR	DL	PW
1993	Fla N	0	2	.000	7	0	0	0-0	10.2	16	8	1	0	7-0	5	5.91	74	.340	.426	0	—	0	-2			-0.3
1994	Fla N	1	2	.333	17	0	0	0-0	21.1	23	20	4	1	16-5	23	5.91	75	.264	.385	0-0-1	—	0	-5	147		-0.6
1995	Fla N	0	0	—	4	0	0	0-0	4.2	7	2	1	0	2-1	3	3.86	111	.333	.391	0	—	0	-2			-0.2
1996	Hou N	1	0	1.000	9	0	0	0-0	13	17	8	2	0	5-0	5	5.54	70	.321	.367	0	—	0	4			0.2
1997	SF N	0	0	—	10	0	0	0-0	16.2	12	4	0	4	6-0	14	2.16	191	.218	.324	2	.000	-0	1			0.1
	Oak A	0	0	—	5	0	0	0-0	6.1	7	3	1	0	7-0	2	2.84	162	.292	.438	0	—	0	-2			-0.1
	SF N	0	0	—	3	0	0	0-0	2	3	3	1	0	1-0	1	13.50	31	.333	.400	0	—	0	-1			-0.0
1998	SF N	6	5	.545	70	0	0	0-1	88	72	32	10	1	38-8	86	3.07	131	.224	.303	2-0-1	.000	0	10			1.0
1999	SF N	4	6	.400	62	0	0	3-4	65.2	48	24	8	1	20-5	56	2.60	164	.203	.267	2	.000	0	11			1.6
2000	SF N	3	4	.429	47	0	0	0-3	50	64	35	11	2	13-2	37	6.30	69	.322	.362	2	.000	-0	-10	45		-1.2
Total	8	15	19	.441	234	0	0	3-8	278.1	269	138	38	9	115-21	234	4.01	105	.255	.329	6-0-2	.000	-1	5	382		0.5

JOINER, ROY Roy Merrill "Pop" B10.30.1906 Red Bluff CA D12.26.1989 Red Bluff CA BL/TL/6-0/170 d4.30

YEAR	TM LG	W	L	PCT	G	GS	CG-SHO	SV-BS	IP	H	R	HR	HB	BB-IB	SO	ERA	AERA	OAV	OOB	AB-HR-SH	AVG	PB	SUP	APR	DL	PW
1934	Chi N	0	1	.000	20	1	0	0	34	61	33	3	0	8	9	8.21	47	.391	.421	10	.200	-0	100	-16		-0.8
1935	Chi N	0	0	—	2	0	0	0	3.1	6	4	0	0	2	0	5.40	73	.429	.500	1	.000	-0	-1			-0.1
1940	NY N	3	2	.600	30	2	0	1	53	66	26	8	5	17	25	3.40	114	.308	.373	11-0-1	.273	1	67	2		0.2
Total	3	3	3	.500	52	4	0	1	90.1	133	63	11	5	27	34	5.28	74	.346	.397	22-0-1	.227	0	84	-15		-0.7

JOLLY, DAVE David "Gabby" B10.14.1924 Stony Point NC D5.27.1963 Durham NC BR/TR/6-0/165* d5.9

YEAR	TM LG	W	L	PCT	G	GS	CG-SHO	SV-BS	IP	H	R	HR	HB	BB-IB	SO	ERA	AERA	OAV	OOB	AB-HR-SH	AVG	PB	SUP	APR	DL	PW
1953	Mil N	0	1	.000	24	0	0	0	38.1	34	16	4	1	27	23	3.52	111	.239	.365	2	.500	1	3			0.2
1954	Mil N	11	6	.647	47	1	0	10	111.1	87	36	6	2	64	62	2.43	154	.215	.321	31-1-2	.290	3*	24	17		3.0
1955	Mil N	2	3	.400	36	0	0	1	58.1	58	42	6	1	51-7	23	5.71	66	.258	.396	6	.167	0	-14			-1.0
1956	Mil N	2	3	.400	29	0	0	7	45.2	39	21	7	0	35-4	20	3.74	92	.228	.367	4-0-1	.000	0	-1			-0.2
1957	Mil N	1	1	.500	23	0	0	1	37.2	37	22	4	3	21-0	27	5.02	70	.264	.367	5	.600	1	-6			-0.2
Total	5	16	14	.533	159	1	0	19	291.1	255	137	27	7	198-11	155	3.77	98	.236	.354	48-1-3	.292	5	24	-1		1.8

JONES, COWBOY Albert Edward "Bronco" B8.23.1874 Golden CO D2.9.1958 Inglewood CA BL/TL/5-11/160 d6.24

YEAR	TM LG	W	L	PCT	G	GS	CG-SHO	SV-BS	IP	H	R	HR	HB	BB-IB	SO	ERA	AERA	OAV	OOB	AB-HR-SH	AVG	PB	SUP	APR	DL	PW
1898	Cle N	4	4	.500	9	9	7	0	72	76	44	0	4	29	26	3.00	121	.269	.345	28-0-1	.071	-3	100	2		-0.2
1899	StL N	6	5	.545	12	12	9	0	85.1	111	51	1	6	22	28	3.59	111	.314	.364	29-0-1	.172	0	80	3		0.5
1900	StL N	13	19	.406	39	36	29-3	0	292.2	334	185	10	19	82	68	3.54	103	.286	.343	117-0-3	.179	-3	106	-2		-0.3
1901	StL N	2	6	.250	10	9	7	0	76.1	97	51	4	3	22	25	4.48	71	.307	.358	27-0-1	.148	0	114	-12		-0.9
Total	4	25	34	.424	70	66	52-3	0	526.1	618	331	15	32	155	147	3.61	100	.292	.349	201-0-6	.159	-5	101	-9		-0.9

JONES, ALEX Alexander B12.25.1869 Pittsburgh PA D4.4.1941 Woodville PA BL/TL/5-6/135 d9.25

YEAR	TM LG	W	L	PCT	G	GS	CG-SHO	SV-BS	IP	H	R	HR	HB	BB-IB	SO	ERA	AERA	OAV	OOB	AB-HR-SH	AVG	PB	SUP	APR	DL	PW
1889	Pit N	1	0	1.000	1	1	1	0	9	7	5	0	0	1	10	3.00	125	.206	.229	5	.200	0	143	1		0.1
1892	Lou N	5	11	.313	18	16	13-1	0	146.2	130	90	3	9	56	44	3.31	93	.228	.307	55	.145	-1	84	-5		-0.5
	Was N	0	3	.000	4	4	3	0	27	33	23	0	2	14	7	4.00	81	.289	.377	11	.273	0	44	-3		-0.3
	Year	5	14	.263	22	20	16-1	0	173.2	163	113	3	11	70	51	3.42	91	.238	.319	66	.167	-1	76	-7		-0.8
1894	Phi N	1	0	1.000	1	1	1	0	9	10	4	0	0	6	2	2.00	257	.278	.278	4	.250	-0	83	3		0.2
1903	Det A	0	1	.000	2	2	0	0	8.2	19	15	0	0	6	2	12.46	23	.432	.500	4	.000	-1	184	-8		-0.8
Total	4	7	15	.318	26	24	18-1	0	200.1	199	137	3	11	77	65	3.73	86	.249	.324	79	.165	-1	86	-12		-1.3

JONES, AL Alfornia B2.10.1959 Charleston MS BR/TR/5-11/165* [ChiA81 13/318] d8.6 Col Alcorn St.

YEAR	TM LG	W	L	PCT	G	GS	CG-SHO	SV-BS	IP	H	R	HR	HB	BB-IB	SO	ERA	AERA	OAV	OOB	AB-HR-SH	AVG	PB	SUP	APR	DL	PW
1983	Chi A	0	0	—	2	0	0	0-0	2.1	3	1	0	0	2	1	3.86	110	.375	.500	0	—	0	0			0.0
1984	Chi A	1	1	.500	20	0	0	5-1	20.1	23	10	3	1	11-0	15	4.43	95	.299	.385	0	—	0	0			0.0
1985	Chi A	1	0	1.000	5	0	0	0-0	6	3	2	0	0	3-0	2	1.50	290	.167	.286	0	—	0	1	134		0.2
Total	3	2	1	.667	27	0	0	5-1	28.2	29	13	3	1	16-0	19	3.77	112	.282	.377	0	—	0	1	134		0.2

JONES, ART Arthur Lennox B2.7.1906 Kershaw SC D11.25.1980 Columbia SC BR/TR/6-0/165 d4.23 Col Furman

YEAR	TM LG	W	L	PCT	G	GS	CG-SHO	SV-BS	IP	H	R	HR	HB	BB-IB	SO	ERA	AERA	OAV	OOB	AB-HR-SH	AVG	PB	SUP	APR	DL	PW
1932	Bro N	0	0	—	1	0	0	0	1	2	2	0	0	1	0	18.00	21	.667	.750	0	—	0	-1			-0.1

JONES, BARRY Barry Louis B2.15.1963 Centerville IN BR/TR/6-4/225(210-225) [PitN84 3/69] d7.18 Col Indiana

YEAR	TM LG	W	L	PCT	G	GS	CG-SHO	SV-BS	IP	H	R	HR	HB	BB-IB	SO	ERA	AERA	OAV	OOB	AB-HR-SH	AVG	PB	SUP	APR	DL	PW
1986	Pit N	3	4	.429	26	0	0	3-4	37.1	29	16	3	0	21-2	29	2.89	134	.215	.318	5-0-1	.200	0	3			0.6
1987	Pit N	4	4	.333	32	0	0	1-3	43.1	55	34	6	0	23-6	28	5.61	74	.314	.390	3	.000	-0	-9			-1.1
1988	Pit N	1	1	.500	42	0	0	2-3	56.1	57	21	3	1	21-6	31	3.04	114	.271	.335	5	.000	-0	5			0.1
	Chi A	2	2	.500	17	0	0	1-0	26	15	7	3	0	17-1	17	2.42	165	.170	.302	0	—	0	4	112		0.8
1989	Chi A	3	2	.600	22	0	0	1-0	30.1	22	12	2	1	8-0	17	2.37	162	.208	.265	0	—	0	5			0.6
1990	Chi A	11	4	.733	65	0	0	1-7	74	62	20	2	1	33-7	45	2.31	166	.235	.317	0	—	0	13			2.6
1991	Mon N	4	9	.308	77	0	0	13-8	88.2	76	35	8	1	33-8	46	3.35	109	.246	.318	1-0-1	.000	-0	-6			0.7
1992	Phi N	5	6	.455	44	0	0	0-6	54.1	65	34	3	2	24-4	19	4.64	76	.305	.378	2	.000	-0	-9			-1.2
	NY N	2	0	1.000	17	0	0	1-0	15.1	20	16	0	0	11-3	11	9.39	37	.317	.413	0	—	0	-16			-2.4
	Year	7	6	.538	61	0	0	1-6	69.2	85	46	3	2	35-7	30	5.68	62	.308	.386	2	.000	-0	-25			-0.4
1993	Chi A	0	1	.000	6	0	0	0-0	7.1	14	8	2	0	3-0	7	8.59	49	.412	.459	0	—	0	-4	112		-0.4
Total	8	33	33	.500	348	0	0	23-31	433	415	199	32	6	194-37	250	3.66	103	.260	.338	16-0-2	.063	-1	4	112		1.5

JONES, CALVIN Calvin Douglas B9.26.1963 Compton CA BR/TR/6-3/185* [SeaA84*1/1] d6.14 Col California-Riverside

YEAR	TM LG	W	L	PCT	G	GS	CG-SHO	SV-BS	IP	H	R	HR	HB	BB-IB	SO	ERA	AERA	OAV	OOB	AB-HR-SH	AVG	PB	SUP	APR	DL	PW
1991	Sea A	2	2	.500	27	0	0	2-1	46.1	33	14	0	1	29-5	42	2.53	164	.209	.335	0	—	0	8			0.7
1992	Sea A	3	5	.375	38	1	0	0-2	61.2	50	39	8	2	47-1	49	5.69	70	.226	.361	0	—	0	91	-10		-1.2
Total	2	5	7	.417	65	1	0	2-3	108	83	53	8	3	76-6	91	4.33	94	.219	.351	0	—	0	91	-2		-0.5

JONES, DEACON Carroll Elmer B12.20.1892 Arcadia KS D12.28.1952 Pittsburg KS BR/TR/6-1/174 d9.23

YEAR	TM LG	W	L	PCT	G	GS	CG-SHO	SV-BS	IP	H	R	HR	HB	BB-IB	SO	ERA	AERA	OAV	OOB	AB-HR-SH	AVG	PB	SUP	APR	DL	PW
1916	Det A	0	0	—	1	0	0	0	7	7	3	0	0	5	2	2.57	111	.269	.387	2	.000	-0	0			0.0
1917	Det A	4	4	.500	24	6	2	0	77	69	34	0	6	26	28	2.92	91	.256	.334	15-0-2	.000	-1	131	6		-0.2
1918	Det A	3	2	.600	21	4	1	0	67	60	35	0	1	38	15	3.09	86	.244	.347	25	.200	-0*	198	-6		-0.4
Total	3	7	6	.538	46	10	3	0	151	136	72	0	7	69	45	2.98	89	.251	.343	42-0-2	.119	-1	158	-8		-0.6

JONES, BUMPUS Charles Leander B1.1.1870 Cedarville OH D6.25.1938 Xenia OH BR/TR d10.15

YEAR	TM LG	W	L	PCT	G	GS	CG-SHO	SV-BS	IP	H	R	HR	HB	BB-IB	SO	ERA	AERA	OAV	OOB	AB-HR-SH	AVG	PB	SUP	APR	DL	PW
1892	Cin N	1	0	1.000	1	1	1	0	9	0	1	0	0	4	3	0.00	—	.000	.129	2	.000	-0	19	3		0.3
1893	Cin N	1	3	.250	6	5	2	0	28.2	37	37	1	5	23	6	10.05	48	.303	.433	16	.250	1	88	-14		-1.3
	NY N	0	1	.000	1	1	0	0	4	5	5	0	1	10	1	11.25	41	.294	.571	0	—	0	30	-2		-0.3
	Year	1	4	.200	7	6	2	0	32.2	42	42	1	6	33	7	10.19	47	.302	.455	16	.250	1	78	-14		-1.6
Total	2	2	4	.333	8	7	3	0	41.2	42	43	1	6	37	10	7.99	56	.253	.407	18	.222	1	73	-13		-1.3

JONES, DALE Dale Eldon "Nubs" B12.17.1918 Marquette NE D11.8.1980 Orlando FL BR/TR/6-1/172 d9.7 Mil 1942-45 Col Wayne State (NE)

YEAR	TM LG	W	L	PCT	G	GS	CG-SHO	SV-BS	IP	H	R	HR	HB	BB-IB	SO	ERA	AERA	OAV	OOB	AB-HR-SH	AVG	PB	SUP	APR	DL	PW
1941	Phi N	0	1	.000	2	1	0	0	8.1	13	11	0	0	6	2	7.56	49	.342	.432	3	.333	0	138	-5		-0.4

JONES, JACK Daniel Albion "Jumping Jack" B10.23.1860 Litchfield CT D10.19.1936 Wallingford CT TR d7.9 Col Yale

YEAR	TM LG	W	L	PCT	G	GS	CG-SHO	SV-BS	IP	H	R	HR	HB	BB-IB	SO	ERA	AERA	OAV	OOB	AB-HR-SH	AVG	PB	SUP	APR	DL	PW
1883	Det N	6	5	.545	12	12	9-1	0	92.2	103	63	0		19	33	3.50	89	.259	.293	42	.190	-2	78	-3		-0.5
	Phi AA	5	2	.714	7	7	7	0	65	58	38	1		6	28	2.63	135	.223	.241	25	.240	-0	95	6		0.5
Total	1	11	7	.611	19	19	16-1	0	157.2	161	101	1		25	61	3.14	104	.245	.273	67	.209	-2	84	3		0.5

JONES, DICK Decatur Poindexter B5.22.1902 Meadville MS D8.2.1994 Burlingame CA BL/TR/6-0/184 d9.11

YEAR	TM LG	W	L	PCT	G	GS	CG-SHO	SV-BS	IP	H	R	HR	HB	BB-IB	SO	ERA	AERA	OAV	OOB	AB-HR-SH	AVG	PB	SUP	APR	DL	PW
1926	Was A	2	1	.667	4	3	1	0	21	20	10	0	0	11	3	4.29	90	.263	.356	10-0-1	.200	-0*	123	0		-0.1
1927	Was A	0	0	—	2	0	0	0	3.1	8	11	0	0	5	1	21.60	19	.444	.565	0	—	-0		-7		-0.3
Total 2		2	1	.667	6	3	1	0	24.1	28	21	0	0	16	4	6.66	58	.298	.400	10-0-1	.200	-0	123	-7		-0.4

JONES, DOUG Douglas Reid B6.24.1957 Lebanon IN BR/TR/6-2/195(170-225) [MilA78*3/59] d4.9 Col Butler

YEAR	TM LG	W	L	PCT	G	GS	CG-SHO	SV-BS	IP	H	R	HR	HB	BB-IB	SO	ERA	AERA	OAV	OOB	AB-HR-SH	AVG	PB	SUP	APR	DL	PW
1982	Mil A	0	0	—	4	0	0	0-0	2.2	5	3	1	0	1-0	1	10.13	38	.385	.429	0	—	0		-2		-0.1
1986	Cle A	1	0	1.000	11	0	0	1-1	18	18	5	0	1	6-1	12	2.50	167	.257	.321	0	—	0		4		0.2
1987	Cle A	6	5	.545	49	0	0	8-4	91.1	101	45	4	6	24-5	87	3.15	145	.281	.332	0	—	0		10		1.3
1988	Cle A★	3	4	.429	51	0	0	37-6	83.1	69	26	1	2	16-3	72	2.27	182	.218	.260	0	—	0		15		2.5
1989	Cle A★	7	10	.412	59	0	0	32-9	80.2	76	25	4	1	13-4	65	2.34	170	.251	.279	0	—	0		14		2.9
1990	Cle A☆	5	5	.500	66	0	0	43-8	84.1	66	26	5	2	22-4	55	2.56	154	.218	.274	0	—	0		13		2.5
1991	Cle A	4	8	.333	36	4	0	7-5	63.1	87	42	7	0	17-5	66	5.54	75	.320	.357	0	—	0	99	-9		-1.6
1992	Hou N★	11	8	.579	80	0	0	36-6	111.2	96	29	5	5	17-5	93	1.85	183	.235	.274	4	.000			18		3.9
1993	Hou N	4	10	.286	71	0	0	26-8	85.1	102	46	7	5	21-6	66	4.54	85	.298	.344	0	—	0		-5		-1.1
1994	Phi N★	2	4	.333	47	0	0	27-2	54	55	14	2	0	6-0	38	2.17	198	.255	.275	1	1.000			13		2.5
1995	Bal A	0	4	.000	52	0	0	22-3	46.2	55	30	6	2	16-2	42	5.01	95	.286	.348	0	—	0		-2		-0.4
1996	Chi A	2	2	.500	28	0	0	2-5	32.1	41	24	3	2	7-4	26	5.01	87	.306	.345	0	—	0		-2		-0.3
	Mil A	5	0	1.000	24	0	0	1-3	31.2	31	13	3	2	13-2	34	3.41	152	.254	.331	0	—	0		6		0.8
1997	Mil A	6	6	.500	75	0	0	36-2	80.1	62	20	4	3	9-1	82	2.02	230	.215	.242	0	—	0		23	17	4.5
1998	Mil A	3	4	.429	46	0	0	12-8	54	65	32	15	4	11-1	43	5.17	84	.298	.339	0	—	0		-4		-0.6
	†Cle A	1	2	.333	23	0	0	1-1	31.1	34	17	2	1	6-3	28	3.45	139	.279	.305	2	.000	0		5		0.5
1999	Oak A	5	5	.500	70	0	0	10-6	104	106	43	7	3	24-3	63	3.55	133	.267	.311	0	—	0		15		1.5
2000	†Oak A	4	2	.667	50	0	0	2-0	73.1	86	34	6	2	18-4	54	3.93	124	.292	.334	0	—	0		8	5	0.6
Total 16		69	79	.466	846	4	0	303-77	1128.1	1155	465	86	39	247-53	909	3.30	130	.264	.307	7	.143		99	120	22	19.6

JONES, EARL Earl Leslie "Lefty" B6.11.1919 Fresno CA D1.24.1989 Fresno CA BL/TL/5-10.5/190 d7.6

YEAR	TM LG	W	L	PCT	G	GS	CG-SHO	SV-BS	IP	H	R	HR	HB	BB-IB	SO	ERA	AERA	OAV	OOB	AB-HR-SH	AVG	PB	SUP	APR	DL	PW
1945	StL A	0	0	—	10	0	0	1	28.1	18	10	0	0	18	13	2.54	139	.184	.310	10-1-0	.200	1		3		0.2

JONES, ELIJAH Elijah Albert "Bumpus" B1.27.1882 Oxford MI D4.29.1943 Pontiac MI BR/TR/5-11.5/? d4.13

YEAR	TM LG	W	L	PCT	G	GS	CG-SHO	SV-BS	IP	H	R	HR	HB	BB-IB	SO	ERA	AERA	OAV	OOB	AB-HR-SH	AVG	PB	SUP	APR	DL	PW
1907	Det A	0	1	.000	4	1	1	1	16	23	15	0	1	4	9	5.06	51	.338	.384	4	.000	-1	104	-5		-0.4
1909	Det A	1	1	.500	2	2	0	1	10	10	3	0	0	2	2	2.70	93	.278	.278	4	.250		154	0		0.0
Total 2		1	2	.333	6	3	1	1	26	33	18	0	1	6	11	4.15	62	.317	.349	8	.125	-0	133	-5		-0.4

JONES, GARY Gareth Howell B6.12.1945 Huntington Park CA BL/TL/6-0/191* d9.25 b-Steve Col Whittier

YEAR	TM LG	W	L	PCT	G	GS	CG-SHO	SV-BS	IP	H	R	HR	HB	BB-IB	SO	ERA	AERA	OAV	OOB	AB-HR-SH	AVG	PB	SUP	APR	DL	PW
1970	NY A	0	0	—	2	0	0	0-0	2	3	0	0	0	1-0	2	0.00	—	.375	.444	0	—	0		1		0.0
1971	NY A	0	0	—	12	0	0	0-0	14	19	14	1	0	7-1	10	9.00	37	.317	.382	1	.000	-0		-8		-0.5
Total 2		0	0	—	14	0	0	0-0	16	22	14	1	0	8-1	12	7.88	42	.324	.390	1	.000	-0		-7		-0.5

JONES, GORDON Gordon Bassett B4.2.1930 Portland OR D4.25.1994 Lodi CA BR/TR/6-0/190* d8.6 C2

YEAR	TM LG	W	L	PCT	G	GS	CG-SHO	SV-BS	IP	H	R	HR	HB	BB-IB	SO	ERA	AERA	OAV	OOB	AB-HR-SH	AVG	PB	SUP	APR	DL	PW
1954	StL N	4	4	.500	11	10	4-2	0	81	78	25	3	1	19	48	2.00	206	.248	.292	24-0-4	.125	-1	74	17		1.5
1955	StL N	1	4	.200	15	9	0	0	57	66	38	10	1	28-5	46	5.84	70	.286	.363	14-0-3	.071	-1	88	-10		-0.9
1956	StL N	0	2	.000	5	1	0	0	11.1	14	9	2	0	5-0	6	5.56	68	.311	.380	2	.000	-0	116	-3		-0.4
1957	NY N	0	1	.000	10	0	1	0	11.2	16	9	1	1	3-1	5	6.17	64	.320	.364	2	.500	0		-3		-0.2
1958	SF N	3	1	.750	11	1	0	1	30.1	33	11	2	1	5-1	8	2.37	161	.284	.320	7	.000	-1	188	4		0.5
1959	SF N	3	2	.600	31	0	0	2	43.2	45	23	6	1	19-5	29	4.33	88	.280	.355	4-0-1	.000	-0		-2		-0.3
1960	Bal A	1	1	.500	29	0	0	2	55	59	28	9	1	13-1	30	4.42	86	.281	.324	5	.400	1		-3		-0.1
1961	Bal A	0	0	—	3	0	1	1	5	5	3	3	0	0-0	4	5.40	71	.250	.250	0	—	0		-1		0.0
1962	KC A	3	2	.600	21	0	0	6	32.2	31	23	10	0	14-1	28	6.34	67	.252	.324	5-0-1	.000	-1		-6		-1.2
1964	Hou N	0	1	.000	34	0	0	0	50	58	24	3	0	14-2	28	4.14	83	.290	.333	4	.250	0		-3		-0.2
1965	Hou N	0	0	—	1	0	0	0	1	0	0	0	0	0-0	1	0.00	—	.000	.000	0	—	0		0		0.0
Total 11		15	18	.455	171	21	4-2	12	378.2	405	193	49	6	120-16	232	4.16	94	.275	.330	67-0-9	.119	-3	90	-10		-1.3

JONES, GREG Greg Alan B11.15.1976 Clearwater FL BR/TR/6-2/190* [AnaA96 42/1253] d7.30 Col Pasco-Hernando (FL) CC [DL 2004 Ana A 64]

YEAR	TM LG	W	L	PCT	G	GS	CG-SHO	SV-BS	IP	H	R	HR	HB	BB-IB	SO	ERA	AERA	OAV	OOB	AB-HR-SH	AVG	PB	SUP	APR	DL	PW
2003	Ana A	0	0	—	18	0	0	0-0	27.2	29	15	3	2	14-0	28	4.88	90	.261	.354	0	—	0		-1		-0.1
2005	LA A	0	0	—	6	0	0	0-0	5.1	7	4	2	0	2-0	6	6.75	64	.318	.375	0	—	0		-1		-0.1
Total 2		0	0	—	24	0	0	0-0	33	36	19	5	2	16-0	34	5.18	84	.271	.358	0	—	0		-2	64	-0.2

JONES, HENRY Henry "Baldy" B Pittsburgh PA ?/150 d4.22

YEAR	TM LG	W	L	PCT	G	GS	CG-SHO	SV-BS	IP	H	R	HR	HB	BB-IB	SO	ERA	AERA	OAV	OOB	AB-HR-SH	AVG	PB	SUP	APR	DL	PW
1890	Pit N	2	1	.667	5	4	2	0	31	35	25	1	0	14	13	3.48	95	.276	.348	9	.222	-0	110	-3		-0.3

JONES, JIMMY James Condia B4.20.1964 Dallas TX BR/TR/6-2/190(175-191) [SDN82 1/3] d9.21

YEAR	TM LG	W	L	PCT	G	GS	CG-SHO	SV-BS	IP	H	R	HR	HB	BB-IB	SO	ERA	AERA	OAV	OOB	AB-HR-SH	AVG	PB	SUP	APR	DL	PW
1986	SD N	2	0	1.000	3	3	1-1	0-0	18	10	6	1	0	3-0	15	2.50	147	.164	.203	6	.167	-0	114	2		0.2
1987	SD N	9	7	.563	30	22	2-1	0-0	145.2	154	85	14	5	54-2	51	4.14	96	.270	.336	49-1-8	.163	1*	114	-7		-0.5
1988	SD N	9	14	.391	29	29	3	0-0	179	192	98	14	3	44-3	82	4.12	82	.277	.319	55-1-9	.164	2*	95	-18		-1.9
1989	NY A	2	1	.667	11	6	0	0-0	48	56	29	7	2	23-0	25	5.25	74	.293	.352	0	—	0	167	-6		-0.3
1990	NY A	1	2	.333	17	7	0	0-0	50	72	42	8	1	23-0	25	6.30	63	.344	.405	0	—	0	104	-14		-0.8
1991	Hou N	6	8	.429	26	22	1-1	0-0	135.1	143	73	9	3	51-3	88	4.39	80	.270	.336	38-0-2	.184	2	91	-13	47	-1.0
1992	Hou N	10	6	.625	25	23	0	0-0	139.1	135	64	13	5	39-3	69	4.07	83	.258	.313	36-0-9	.167	2*	111	-8	36	-0.7
1993	Mon N	4	1	.800	12	6	0	0	39.2	47	34	6	0	39-3	21	6.35	66	.285	.322	9-0-3	.111	0	173	-10	34	-1.0
Total 8		43	39	.524	153	118	7-3	0-0	755	809	431	72	19	239-12	376	4.46	82	.275	.331	193-2-31	.166	7	110	-74	117	-6.0

JONES, JIM James Tilford "Sheriff" B12.25.1876 London KY D5.6.1953 London KY BR/TR/5-10/162 d6.29 Col Centre ▲

YEAR	TM LG	W	L	PCT	G	GS	CG-SHO	SV-BS	IP	H	R	HR	HB	BB-IB	SO	ERA	AERA	OAV	OOB	AB-HR-SH	AVG	PB	SUP	APR	DL	PW
1897	Lou N	0	0	—	1	0	0	0	6.2	19	22	1	2	5	3	18.90	23	.500	.578	4	.250	1*		-11		-0.4
1901	NY N	0	1	.000	1	1	1	0	5	6	6	0	0	2	3	10.80	31	.300	.364	91	.209	0*	107	-3		-0.4
Total 2		0	1	.000	2	1	1	0	11.2	25	28	1	2	7	6	15.43	25	.431	.507	95	.211	1	107	-14		-0.8

JONES, JEFF Jeffrey Allen B7.29.1956 Detroit MI BR/TR/6-3/210* [OakA77 13/329] d4.10 C5 Col Bowling Green

YEAR	TM LG	W	L	PCT	G	GS	CG-SHO	SV-BS	IP	H	R	HR	HB	BB-IB	SO	ERA	AERA	OAV	OOB	AB-HR-SH	AVG	PB	SUP	APR	DL	PW
1980	Oak A	1	3	.250	35	0	0	5-3	44.1	32	21	2	1	26-2	34	2.84	134	.204	.316	0	—	0		3		0.3
1981	†Oak A	4	1	.800	33	0	0	3-1	61	51	27	7	3	40-7	43	3.39	104	.233	.355	0	—	0		0		0.0
1982	Oak A	3	1	.750	18	2	0	0-1	37	44	29	6	1	26-1	18	5.11	77	.306	.415	0	—	0	150	-7		-0.7
1983	Oak A	1	1	.500	13	1	0	0-1	29.2	43	19	7	2	8-1	14	5.76	67	.339	.387	0	—	0	93	-5		-0.3
1984	Oak A	0	3	.000	13	0	0	4-0	33	31	14	4	0	12-1	19	3.55	106	.258	.323	0	—	0		1	64	0.1
Total 5		9	9	.500	112	3	0	8-6	205	201	110	26	7	112-12	128	3.95	95	.262	.358	0	—	0	136	-8	64	-0.6

JONES, BROADWAY Jesse Frank B11.15.1898 Millsboro DE D9.7.1977 Lewes DE BR/TR/5-9/154 d7.4

YEAR	TM LG	W	L	PCT	G	GS	CG-SHO	SV-BS	IP	H	R	HR	HB	BB-IB	SO	ERA	AERA	OAV	OOB	AB-HR-SH	AVG	PB	SUP	APR	DL	PW
1923	Phi N	0	0	—	3	0	0	0	8	5	8	0	0	7		9.00	51	.185	.353	2	.500	0		-3		-0.1

JONES, JOHNNY John Paul "Admiral" B8.25.1892 Arcadia LA D6.5.1980 Ruston LA BR/TR/6-1/151 d4.24

YEAR	TM LG	W	L	PCT	G	GS	CG-SHO	SV-BS	IP	H	R	HR	HB	BB-IB	SO	ERA	AERA	OAV	OOB	AB-HR-SH	AVG	PB	SUP	APR	DL	PW
1919	NY N	0	0	—	2	0	0	1	6.2	9	4	0	1	3	5	5.40	52	.310	.394	3	.000	-0		-2		-0.1
1920	Bos N	1	0	1.000	3	1	0	1	9.2	16	7	1	0	5	4	6.52	47	.372	.438	4	.250		206	-2		-0.1
Total 2		1	0	1.000	5	1	0	1	16.1	25	11	1	1	8	9	6.06	49	.347	.420	7	.143	0	206	-5		-0.3

JONES, STACY Joseph Stacy B5.26.1967 Gadsden AL BR/TR/6-6/225* [BalA88 3/61] d7.30 Col Auburn-Montgomery

YEAR	TM LG	W	L	PCT	G	GS	CG-SHO	SV-BS	IP	H	R	HR	HB	BB-IB	SO	ERA	AERA	OAV	OOB	AB-HR-SH	AVG	PB	SUP	APR	DL	PW
1991	Bal A	0	0	—	4	0	0	0-0	11	11	6	1	0	5-0	10	4.09	97	.256	.327	0	—	0		184	0	0.0
1996	Chi A	0	0	—	2	0	0	0-0	2	0	0	0	0	1-0	1	0.00	—	.000	.143	0	—	0		1		0.0
Total 2		0	0	—	6	0	0	0-0	13	11	6	1	0	6-0	11	3.46	118	.224	.304	0	—	0		184	1	0.0

JONES, KEN Kenneth Frederick "Broadway" B4.13.1903 Dover NJ D5.15.1991 Hartford CT BR/TR/6-3/193 d5.19 Col Georgetown

YEAR	TM LG	W	L	PCT	G	GS	CG-SHO	SV-BS	IP	H	R	HR	HB	BB-IB	SO	ERA	AERA	OAV	OOB	AB-HR-SH	AVG	PB	SUP	APR	DL	PW
1924	Det A	0	0	—	1	0	0	0	1	0	0	0	0	0	0	0.00	—	.143	.250	0	—			1		0.0
1930	Bos N	0	1	.000	8	1	0	0	19.2	28	16	1	0	4	8	5.95	83	.359	.390	5	.200	-0	71	-3		-0.1
Total 2		0	1	.000	9	1	0	0	21.2	28	16	1	0	4	8	5.40	90	.341	.378	5	.200	-0	71	-2		-0.1

JONES, MARCUS Marcus Ray B3.29.1975 Bellflower CA BR/TR/6-5/235 [OakA97 3/95] d7.17 Col Cal St.-Long Beach

YEAR	TM LG	W	L	PCT	G	GS	CG-SHO	SV-BS	IP	H	R	HR	HB	BB-IB	SO	ERA	AERA	OAV	OOB	AB-HR-SH	AVG	PB	SUP	APR	DL	PW
2000	Oak A	0	0	—	1	1	0	0	2.1	5	4	1	0	3-0	1	15.43	31	.417	.533	2	.000	0	213	-3		-0.1

JONES, MIKE Michael B7.6.1865 Hamilton ON, Can. D3.24.1894 Hamilton ON, Can. BL/TL/5-11.5/168 d8.1

YEAR	TM LG	W	L	PCT	G	GS	CG-SHO	SV-BS	IP	H	R	HR	HB	BB-IB	SO	ERA	AERA	OAV	OOB	AB-HR-SH	AVG	PB	SUP	APR	DL	PW
1890	Lou AA	2	0	1.000	3	3	2	0	22	21	12	2	0	9	6	3.27	118	.244	.316	9	.444	2	181	2		0.3

YEAR	TM LG	W	L	PCT	G	GS	CG-SHO	SV-BS	IP	H	R	HR	HB	BB-IB	SO	ERA	AERA	OAV	OOB	AB-HR-SH	AVG	PB	SUP	APR	DL	PW
JONES, MIKE Michael Carl B7.30.1959 Penfield NY BL/TL/6-6/226(215-230) [KCA77 1/21] d9.6 [DL 1982 KC A 182]
1980	KC A	0	1	.000	3	1	0	0-0	4.2	6	7	0	0	5-1	2	11.57	35	.333	.478	0	—	0	0	-4		-0.7
1981	†KC A	6	3	.667	12	11	0	0-0	75.2	74	30	7	2	28-0	29	3.21	112	.256	.324	0	—	0	131	3		0.4
1984	†KC A	2	3	.400	23	12	0	0-0	81	86	48	10	1	36-1	43	4.89	83	.270	.343	0	—	0	99	-8		-0.4
1985	KC A	3	3	.500	33	1	0	0-0	64	62	40	6	0	39-4	32	4.78	87	.257	.353	0	—	0	65	-5		-0.4
Total	4	11	10	.524	71	25	0	0-0	225.1	228	125	23	3	108-6	106	4.43	89	.263	.343	0	—	0	105	-14	182	-1.2
JONES, ODELL Odell B1.13.1953 Tulare CA BR/TR/6-3/175(174-195) d9.11
1975	Pit N	0	0	—	2	0	0	0-0	3	1	0	0	0	0-0	2	0.00	—	.100	.100	0	—	0		1		0.1
1977	Pit N	3	7	.300	34	15	1	0-1	108	118	63	14	3	31-2	65	5.08	79	.278	.330	28	.143	-1	84	-10		-1.0
1978	Pit N	2	0	1.000	3	1	0	0-0	9	7	3	0	0	4-0	10	2.00	187	.206	.289	1	.000	-0	120	1		0.3
1979	Sea A	3	11	.214	25	19	3	0-0	118.2	151	90	16	3	58-8	72	6.07	72	.317	.390	0	—	0	93	-22		-2.3
1981	Pit N	4	5	.444	13	8	0	0-0	54.1	51	23	3	2	23-6	50	3.31	131	.250	.325	10-0-3	.200	0	76	2		0.3
1983	Tex A	3	6	.333	42	0	0	10-5	67	56	28	4	2	22-1	50	3.09	131	.223	.289	0	—	0		6	21	0.3
1984	Tex A	4	3	.333	33	0	0	2-3	59.1	62	28	7	2	23-3	28	3.64	115	.281	.351	0	—	0		3		0.3
1986	Bal A	2	2	.500	21	0	0	0-0	49.1	58	22	4	0	23-6	32	3.83	109	.305	.373	0	—	0		2		0.2
1988	Mil A	3	1	.000	28	2	0	1-0	80.2	75	47	8	1	29-6	48	4.35	92	.251	.313	0	—	0	125	-5		-0.3
Total	9	24	35	.407	201	45	4	13-9	549.1	579	304	56	11	213-32	338	4.42	92	.275	.341	39-0-3	.154	-1	90	-22	21	-1.5
JONES, OSCAR Oscar Lafayette "Flip Flap" B10.22.1879 Carter Co. MO D3.16.1953 Fort Worth TX BR/TR/5-7/163 d4.20
1903	Bro N	19	14	.576	38	36	31-4	0	324.1	320	159	4	19	77	95	2.94	109	.260	.313	125-0-3	.256	3	105	7		0.7
1904	Bro N	17	25	.405	46	41	38	0	377	387	175	7	17	92	96	2.75	100	.270	.321	137-0-4	.175	-1	86	0		-3.0
1905	Bro N	8	15	.348	29	20	14	1	174	197	121	6	9	56	66	4.66	62	.285	.347	65-0-1	.200	-0*	85	-33		-4.0
Total	3	44	54	.449	113	97	83-4	1	875.1	904	455	17	45	225	257	3.20	92	.269	.324	327-0-8	.211	2	94	-26		-3.8
JONES, PERCY Percy Lee B10.28.1899 Harwood TX D3.18.1979 Dallas TX BR/TL/5-11.5/175 d8.6
1920	Chi N	0	0	—	4	0	0	0	7	15	10	1	1	3	2	11.57	28	.455	.514	2	.000	-0		-6		-0.3
1921	Chi N	3	5	.375	32	3	1	0	98.2	116	57	2	4	39	46	4.56	84	.295	.365	27	.222	-0	72	-8		-0.6
1922	Chi N	8	9	.471	44	24	7-2	1	162	197	104	10	5	68	45	4.78	88	.314	.385	47-0-4	.085	-4	94	-11		-1.3
1925	Chi N	6	6	.500	28	13	6-1	0	124	123	74	12	5	71	60	4.65	93	.263	.366	39-0-1	.154	-3	87	-5		-0.5
1926	Chi N	12	7	.632	30	20	10-2	2	160.1	151	64	3	5	90	80	3.09	125	.256	.359	50-0-4	.260	3	87	14		1.8
1927	Chi N	7	8	.467	30	11	5-1	0	112.2	123	67	3	6	72	37	4.07	95	.285	.394	40-0-1	.350	4	84	-6		-0.3
1928	Chi N	10	6	.625	39	19	9-1	3	154	167	80	4	7	56	41	4.64	101	.298	.358	56-0-2	.196	-0	130	-3		-0.3
1929	Bos N	7	15	.318	35	22	11-1	0	188.1	219	112	15	4	84	69	4.64	95	.298	.373	61-0-4	.148	-3*	72	0		-0.2
1930	Pit N	0	1	.000	9	2	0	0	19	26	20	3	3	11	3	6.63	75	.329	.430	2	.000	-0	105	-5		-0.3
Total	9	53	57	.482	251	114	49-8	6	1026	1137	588	53	40	494	381	4.34	95	.289	.374	324-0-16	.194	-5	92	-30		-2.0
JONES, RANDY Randall Leo B1.12.1950 Fullerton CA BR/TL/6-0/180* [SDN72 5/97] d6.16 Col Chapman
1973	SD N	7	6	.538	20	19	6-1	0-0	139.2	129	58	13	1	37-9	77	3.16	111	.241	.289	48-0-4	.167	-0	95	5		0.3
1974	SD N	8	22	.267	40	34	4-1	2-0	208.1	217	118	16	5	78-12	124	4.45	81	.270	.336	65-0-3	.154	-1*	74	-21		-2.8
1975	SD N★	20	12	.625	37	36	18-6	0-0	285	242	94	17	0	56-9	103	2.24	156	.232	.269	83-0-17	.133	-1*	94	37		4.5
1976	SD N★	**22**	14	.611	40	**40**	25-5	0-0	315.1	274	109	15	4	50-9	93	2.74	120	.234	**.265**	103-0-15	.058	-6	115	21		2.2
1977	SD N	6	12	.333	27	25	1	0-0	147.1	173	85	12	0	36-10	44	4.58	78	.291	.329	43-0-4	.116	-1*	73	-17	41	-1.8
1978	SD N	13	14	.481	37	36	7-2	0-1	253	263	104	6	0	64-20	71	2.88	116	.272	.314	82-0-6	.183	-1*	95	9		1.1
1979	SD N	11	12	.478	39	39	6	0-0	263	257	120	17	3	64-10	112	3.63	97	.259	.304	86-0-7	.174	0*	93	-3		0.0
1980	SD N	5	13	.278	24	24	4-3	0-0	154.1	165	71	14	0	29-5	53	3.91	88	.276	.309	45-0-7	.067	-3*	78	-8	26	-1.0
1981	NY N	1	8	.111	13	12	0	0-0	59.1	65	48	8	1	38-1	14	4.85	73	.274	.373	17-0-1	.118	-1	73	-13	23	-1.7
1982	NY N	7	10	.412	28	20	2-1	0-0	107.2	130	68	11	4	51-3	44	4.60	80	.304	.380	27-0-2	.148	0	90	-13		-1.7
Total	10	100	123	.448	305	285	73-19	2-1	1933	1915	875	129	18	503-88	735	3.42	102	.260	.306	599-0-66	.132	-12	90	-3	90	-0.7
JONES, BOBBY Robert Joseph B2.10.1970 Fresno CA BR/TR/6-4/225(210-225) [NYN91 1/36] d8.14 Col Cal St.-Fresno
1993	NY N	2	4	.333	9	9	0	0-0	61.2	61	35	6	2	22-3	35	3.65	110	.262	.327	20-0-2	.050	-2	95	0		-0.2
1994	NY N	12	7	.632	24	24	1-1	0-0	160	157	75	10	4	56-9	80	3.15	133	.257	.322	46-0-8	.109	-2	93	13		1.3
1995	NY N	10	10	.500	30	30	3-1	0-0	195.2	209	107	20	7	53-6	127	4.19	96	.274	.325	56-0-18	.161	-1	113	-6		-0.5
1996	NY N	12	8	.600	31	31	3-1	0-0	195.2	219	102	26	3	46-6	116	4.42	91	.288	.329	60-0-9	.117	-1	113	-5		-0.5
1997	NY N★	15	9	.625	30	30	2-1	0-0	193.1	177	88	24	2	63-3	125	3.63	110	.242	.303	62-0-4	.129	-0	103	8		0.9
1998	NY N	9	9	.500	30	30	0	0-0	195.1	192	94	23	2	53-2	115	4.05	102	.262	.316	48-0-12	.188	1	99	1		0.7
1999	NY N	3	3	.500	12	9	0	0-0	59.1	69	37	3	2	11-0	31	5.61	77	.295	.328	16-1-1	.313	2	115	-8	109	-0.5
2000	†NY N	11	6	.647	27	27	1	0-0	154.2	171	90	25	5	49-3	85	5.06	86	.281	.336	44-0-5	.045	-2	121	-10	30	-3.2
2001	SD N	8	19	.296	33	33	1	0-0	195	250	137	37	4	38-6	113	5.12	81	.305	.335	57-0-2	.140	0	88	-28		-3.2
2002	SD N	7	8	.467	19	18	0	0-0	108	134	68	20	1	21-1	60	5.50	71	.300	.331	33-0-1	.152	-1	103	-18	59	-2.2
Total	10	89	83	.517	245	241	11-4	0-0	1518.2	1639	833	194	38	412-39	887	4.36	94	.276	.325	442-1-64	.133	-5	104	-53	198	-6.0
JONES, BOBBY Robert Mitchell B4.11.1972 Orange NJ BR/TL/6-0/178(170-185) [MilA91 44/1140] d5.18 Col Chipola (FL) JC [DL 2001 NY N 190]
1997	Col N	1	1	.500	4	4	0	0-0	19.1	30	18	2	0	12-0	12	8.38	62	.380	.447	5-0-1	.200	0	98	-5		-0.4
1998	Col N	7	8	.467	35	20	1	0-0	141.1	153	87	12	6	66-0	109	5.22	99	.282	.362	45-0-5	.178	-1	95	0		-0.1
1999	Col N	6	10	.375	30	20	0	0-0	112.1	132	91	24	6	77-0	74	6.33	91	.292	.399	27-0-4	.148	-1	79	-8		-1.0
2000	NY N	0	1	.000	11	1	0	0-0	21.2	18	11	2	3	14-1	20	4.15	105	.222	.354	2-0-1	.500	1	168	1		0.1
2002	NY N	0	0	—	12	0	0	0-0	17	20	11	3	1	11-2	11	5.29	75	.299	.405	0	—	0*		-3		-0.2
	SD N	0	0	—	4	2	0	0-0	9.2	10	7	1	0	7-0	7	6.52	60	.270	.378	2-0-1	.000	-0	155	-3		-0.2
	Year	0	0	—	16	2	0	0-0	26.2	30	18	4	1	18-2	18	5.74	68	.288	.395	2-0-1	.000	-0	153	-5		-0.3
2004	Bos A	3	0	1.000	3	0	0	0-0	3.1	3	2	1	0	8-1	3	5.40	90	.273	.579	0	—	0		0		0.0
Total	6	14	21	.400	99	47	1	0-0	324.2	366	227	45	16	195-4	229	5.77	91	.288	.386	81-0-12	.173	-2	94	-18	190	-1.7
JONES, SAM Samuel "Toothpick Sam" B12.14.1925 Stewartsville OH D11.5.1971 Morgantown WV BR/TR/6-4/200* d9.22 Negro Lg 1946-48
1951	Cle A	0	1	.000	2	1	0	0	8.2	4	2	0	0	5	4	2.08	182	.143	.273	2	.000	-0	23	2		0.2
1952	Cle A	2	3	.400	14	4	0	1	36	38	30	6	4	37	28	7.25	46	.270	.434	10	.100	-1	98	-15		-2.0
1955	Chi N★	14	20	.412	36	34	12-4	0	241.2	175	118	22	14	185-5	**198**	4.10	100	**.206**	.355	77-0-5	.182	-2	76	2		0.0
1956	Chi N	9	14	.391	33	28	8-2	0	188.2	155	93	21	8	115-6	**176**	3.91	96	.221	.337	57-0-10	.175	-0	93	-2		-0.4
1957	StL N	12	9	.571	28	27	10-2	0	182.2	164	77	17	6	71-1	154	3.60	110	.239	.315	63-0-4	.159	-1	103	9		0.3
1958	StL N	14	13	.519	35	35	14-2	0	250	204	95	23	6	107-5	**225**	2.88	143	.223	.307	90-0-2	.100	-6	85	**31**		2.5
1959	SF N★	**21**	15	.583	50	35	16-4	4	270.2	232	99	18	8	109-6	209	**2.83**	**153**	**.228**	.306	85-0-11	.129	-2	102	30		**3.6**
1960	SF N	18	14	.563	39	35	13-3	0	234	200	112	18	4	91-5	190	3.19	109	.230	.305	80-0-7	.200	1	104	2		0.3
1961	SF N	8	8	.500	37	17	2	1	128.1	134	72	12	8	57-7	105	4.49	85	.264	.347	36-0-5	.139	-1	107	-10		-1.3
1962	Det A	2	4	.333	30	6	1	1	81.1	77	39	13	2	35-1	73	3.65	111	.254	.330	21-1-0	.095	-1	66	3		0.1
1963	StL N	2	0	1.000	11	0	0	2	11	15	12	0	0	5-1	8	9.00	39	.319	.385	1	.000	0		-6		-1.2
1964	Bal A	0	0	—	4	0	0	0	10.1	5	3	1	0	5-0	6	2.61	137	.152	.263	0	—	0		1		0.1
Total	12	102	101	.502	322	222	76-17	9	1643.1	1403	752	151	60	822-37	1376	3.59	108	.230	.326	522-1-44	.149	-11	93	47		2.9
JONES, SAM Samuel Pond "Sad Sam" B7.26.1892 Woodsfield OH D7.6.1966 Barnesville OH BR/TR/6-0/170 d6.13
1914	Cle A	0	0	—	1	0	0	0	3.1	2	1	0	2	0	2.70	107	.200	.333	2	.500	0		0		0.0
1915	Cle A	4	9	.308	48	9	2	4	145.2	121	78	0	1	63	42	3.65	84	.252	.334	32-0-3	.156	-0	82	-8		-0.7
1916	Bos A	0	1	.000	12	0	0	1	27	25	14	0	0	10	7	3.67	76	.272	.343	6	.333	0*		-3		-0.1
1917	Bos A	0	1	.000	9	1	0	1	16.1	15	9	1	0	6	5	4.41	59	.259	.328	4-0-1	.000	-1	56	-3		-0.3
1918	†Bos A	16	5	**.762**	24	21	16-5	0	184	151	66	1	4	70	44	2.25	119	.230	.312	57-0-3	.175	2	114	7		1.0
1919	Bos A	12	20	.375	35	31	21-5	1	245	258	120	2	4	95	67	3.75	81	.278	.350	81-0-5	.136	-0	103	-19		-2.2
1920	Bos A	13	16	.448	37	33	21-3	0	274	302	143	9	4	79	86	3.94	93	.288	.340	92-0-5	.217	1*	88	-6		1.1
1921	Bos A	23	16	.590	40	38	25-5	1	298.2	318	122	6	10	78	98	3.22	131	.279	.329	100-2-2	.240	5*	79	34		4.3
1922	†NY A	13	13	.500	45	28	20	**8**	260	270	132	16	3	76	81	3.67	109	.275	.329	85-0-3	.224	8	97	6		1.4
1923	†NY A	21	8	.724	39	27	18-3	4	243	239	114	11	6	69	68	3.63	109	.257	.312	87-1-4	.276	6*	136	6		0.7
1924	NY A	9	6	.600	36	21	8-3	3	178.2	187	85	6	1	76	53	3.63	115	.276	.350	51-1-6	.176	-0	82	10		0.2
1925	NY A	15	21	.417	43	31	14-1	2	246.2	267	147	14	4	104	92	4.63	92	.281	.354	81-0-10	.152	-3*	84	-10		-1.9
1926	†NY A	9	8	.529	39	23	6-1	5	161	186	104	6	4	80	69	4.98	77	.298	.381	49-0-5	.204	1*	124	-19		-1.5
1927	StL A	8	14	.364	30	26	11	0	189.2	211	121	13	3	102	72	4.32	101	.282	.371	55	.109	-2*	88	-3		-0.6
1928	Was A	17	7	**.708**	30	27	19-4	0	224.2	209	89	5	3	78	63	2.84	141	.248	.319	79-2-5	.157	6*	111	27		3.3
1929	Was A	9	9	.500	24	24	8-1	0	153.2	156	80	5	8	44	36	3.92	108	.264	.324	51-0-3	.157	0*	99	5		0.5

YEAR	TM LG	W	L	PCT	G	GS	CG-SHO	SV-BS	IP	H	R	HR	HB	BB-IB	SO	ERA	AERA	OAV	OOB	AB-HR-SH	AVG	PB	SUP	APR	DL	PW
1930	Was A	15	7	.682	25	25	14-1	0	183.1	195	95	4	3	61	60	4.07	113	.277	.337	61-0-4	.148	-1*	126	11		0.9
1931	Was A	9	10	.474	25	24	8-1	1	148	185	88	10	4	47	58	4.32	99	.304	.358	48-0-4	.313	4*	97	-2		0.2
1932	Chi A	10	15	.400	30	28	10	0	200.1	217	123	9	3	75	64	4.22	102	.270	.335	57-0-8	.193	2*	93	0		0.3
1933	Chi A	10	12	.455	27	25	11-2	0	176.2	181	80	13	4	65	60	3.36	126	.265	.333	57-0-1	.155	-0*	79	17		1.8
1934	Chi A	8	12	.400	27	26	11-1	0	183.1	217	120	16	2	60	60	5.11	93	.289	.343	60-0-4	.200	2*	100	-7		-0.5
1935	Chi A	8	7	.533	21	19	7	0	140	162	77	8	1	51	38	4.05	114	.284	.343	48-0-3	.167	0*	109	6		0.6
Total 22		229	217	.513	647	487	250-36	31	3883	4084	2008	152	69	1396	1223	3.84	104	.274	.339	1243-6-85	.197	25	100	45		7.2

JONES, SHELDON   Sheldon Leslie "Available" B2.2.1922 Tecumseh NE D4.18.1991 Greenville NC BR/TR/6-0/180* d9.9

YEAR	TM LG	W	L	PCT	G	GS	CG-SHO	SV-BS	IP	H	R	HR	HB	BB-IB	SO	ERA	AERA	OAV	OOB	AB-HR-SH	AVG	PB	SUP	APR	DL	PW
1946	NY N	1	2	.333	6	4	1	0	28	21	10	4	1	17	24	3.21	107	.208	.328	8	.250	0	44	1		0.2
1947	NY N	2	2	.500	15	6	0	0	55.2	51	27	2	3	29	24	3.88	105	.250	.352	8-0-1	.125	-1	116	1		-0.1
1948	NY N	16	8	.667	55	21	8-1	5	201.1	204	89	16	6	90	82	3.35	117	.263	.344	64-0-9	.203	1	124	13		1.6
1949	NY N	15	12	.556	42	27	11-1	0	207.1	198	93	19	10	88	79	3.34	119	.248	.331	66-0-6	.121	-3	99	14		1.3
1950	NY N	13	16	.448	40	28	11-2	2	199	188	114	26	7	90	97	4.61	89	.249	.335	57-0-10	.105	-2	93	-11		-1.7
1951	†NY N	6	11	.353	41	12	2	4	120.1	119	77	12	4	52	58	4.26	92	.260	.340	31	.097	-1	73	-9		-1.3
1952	Bos N	1	4	.200	39	1	0	1	70	81	45	7	1	31	40	4.76	76	.286	.359	8-0-1	.125	-0	74	-11		-0.8
1953	Chi N	0	2	.000	22	2	0	0	38.1	47	24	3	2	16	9	5.40	82	.299	.382	7	.000	-1	60	-3		-0.2
Total 8		54	57	.486	260	101	33-4	12	920	909	479	89	37	413	413	3.96	100	.258	.342	257-0-27	.136	-7	98	-5		-1.0

JONES, SHERMAN   Sherman Jarvis "Roadblock" B2.10.1935 Winton NC BL/TR/6-4/205(195-210) d8.2

YEAR	TM LG	W	L	PCT	G	GS	CG-SHO	SV-BS	IP	H	R	HR	HB	BB-IB	SO	ERA	AERA	OAV	OOB	AB-HR-SH	AVG	PB	SUP	APR	DL	PW
1960	SF N	1	1	.500	16	0	0	1	32	37	17	3	1	11-1	10	3.09	112	.291	.353	7	.286	0	0			0.0
1961	†Cin N	1	1	.500	24	0	0	2	55	51	32	6	2	27-6	32	4.42	92	.256	.340	11	.182	0	76	-3		-0.1
1962	NY N	0	4	.000	8	3	0	0	23.1	31	22	3	2	8-2	11	7.71	54	.326	.373	3	.429	1	70	-8		-1.0
Total 3		2	6	.250	48	5	0	3	110.1	119	71	12	5	46-9	53	4.73	83	.283	.351	25	.280	1	77	-11		-1.1

JONES, STEVE   Steven Howell B4.22.1941 Huntington Park CA BL/TL/5-10/175* d8.15 b-Gary Col Whittier

YEAR	TM LG	W	L	PCT	G	GS	CG-SHO	SV-BS	IP	H	R	HR	HB	BB-IB	SO	ERA	AERA	OAV	OOB	AB-HR-SH	AVG	PB	SUP	APR	DL	PW
1967	Chi A	2	2	.500	11	3	0	0	25.2	21	13	1	0	12-0	11	4.21	74	.223	.311	4	.250	0	84	-3		-0.4
1968	Was A	1	2	.333	7	0	0	0	10.2	8	8	3	0	7-0	11	5.91	49	.205	.326	1	.000	-0		-4		-0.8
1969	KC A	2	3	.400	20	4	0	0-0	44.2	45	25	3	3	24-2	31	4.23	87	.260	.358	8	.125	0	126	-3		-0.3
Total 3		5	7	.417	38	7	0	0-0	81	74	46	7	3	43-2	59	4.44	77	.242	.340	13	.154	0	111	-10		-1.5

JONES, RICK   Thomas Fredrick B4.16.1955 Jacksonville FL BL/TL/6-5/190(180-200) [BosA73 5/113] d4.18

YEAR	TM LG	W	L	PCT	G	GS	CG-SHO	SV-BS	IP	H	R	HR	HB	BB-IB	SO	ERA	AERA	OAV	OOB	AB-HR-SH	AVG	PB	SUP	APR	DL	PW
1976	Bos A	5	3	.625	24	14	1	0-0	104.1	133	48	6	1	26-1	45	3.36	115	.311	.348	0	—	0	113	4		0.3
1977	Sea A	1	4	.200	10	10	0	0-0	42.1	47	25	10	0	37-2	16	5.10	81	.283	.414	0	—	0	98	-4	62	-0.4
1978	Sea A	0	2	.000	3	2	0	0-0	12.1	17	8	1	0	7-0	11	5.84	66	.315	.393	0	—	0	47	-2		-0.3
Total 3		6	9	.400	37	26	1	0-0	159	197	81	17	1	70-3	72	4.02	99	.304	.370	0	—	0	102	-2	62	-0.4

JONES, TIM   Timmothy Byron B1.24.1954 Sacramento CA BB/TR/6-5/220 [PitN72 4/95] d9.4

YEAR	TM LG	W	L	PCT	G	GS	CG-SHO	SV-BS	IP	H	R	HR	HB	BB-IB	SO	ERA	AERA	OAV	OOB	AB-HR-SH	AVG	PB	SUP	APR	DL	PW
1977	Pit N	1	0	1.000	5	1	0	0-0	10	4	3	0	1	3-0	5	0.00	—	.118	.189	2	.000	-0	111	4		0.4

JONES, TODD   Todd Barton Givin B4.24.1968 Marietta GA BL/TR/6-3/230(200-230) [HouN89 1/27] d7.7 Col Jacksonville St.

YEAR	TM LG	W	L	PCT	G	GS	CG-SHO	SV-BS	IP	H	R	HR	HB	BB-IB	SO	ERA	AERA	OAV	OOB	AB-HR-SH	AVG	PB	SUP	APR	DL	PW
1993	Hou N	1	2	.333	27	0	0	2-1	37.1	28	14	4	1	15-2	25	3.13	124	.214	.297	0	—	0		4		0.3
1994	Hou N	5	2	.714	48	0	0	5-4	72.2	52	23	3	1	26-4	63	2.72	145	.202	.277	5	.400	1		11		1.1
1995	Hou N	6	5	.545	68	0	0	15-5	99.2	89	38	8	6	52-17	96	3.07	126	.237	.336	5	.200	0		10		1.2
1996	Hou N	6	3	.667	51	0	0	17-6	57.1	61	30	5	5	32-6	44	4.40	88	.274	.375	1	.000	-0		-3	49	-0.6
1997	Det A	5	4	.556	68	0	0	31-5	70	60	29	3	1	35-2	70	3.09	150	.231	.320	0	—	0		10		1.9
1998	Det A	1	4	.200	65	0	0	28-4	63.1	58	38	7	2	36-4	57	4.97	96	.249	.347	0	—	0		-1		-0.2
1999	Det A	4	4	.500	65	0	0	30-5	66.1	64	30	7	1	35-1	64	3.80	132	.259	.352	0	—	0		9		1.5
2000	Det A★	2	4	.333	67	0	0	**42-4**	64	67	28	6	1	25-1	67	3.52	140	.276	.344	0	—	0		10		1.7
2001	Det A	4	5	.444	45	0	0	11-6	48.2	60	31	6	0	22-1	39	4.62	96	.303	.368	0	—	0		10		1.7
	Min A	1	0	1.000	24	0	0	2-2	19.1	27	8	3	0	7-0	15	3.26	143	.333	.386	0	—	0		-3		-0.5
	Year	5	5	.500	69	0	0	13-8	68	87	39	9	0	29-1	54	4.24	106	.312	.373	0	—	0		0		-0.3
2002	Col N	1	4	.200	79	0	0	1-2	82.1	84	43	10	3	28-3	73	4.70	101	.269	.332	3	.000	-0		2		0.1
2003	Col N	1	4	.200	33	1	0	0-5	39.1	61	39	8	1	18-0	28	8.24	59	.361	.421	2	.000	0	96	-13		-1.4
	†Bos A	2	1	.667	26	0	0	0-0	29.1	32	19	2	0	13-2	31	5.52	84	.269	.338	0	—	0		-2		-0.2
2004	Cin N	8	2	.800	51	0	0	1-5	57	49	25	4	1	25-2	37	3.79	114	.243	.322	0	—	0		4		0.5
	Phi N	3	3	.500	27	0	0	1-1	25.1	35	14	3	5	8-3	22	4.97	89	.330	.400	0	—	0		-1		-0.2
	Year	11	5	.688	78	0	0	2-6	82.1	84	39	7	6	33-5	59	4.15	105	.273	.348	0	—	0		3		0.3
2005	Fla N	1	5	.167	58	0	0	40-5	73	61	24	2	3	14-2	62	2.10	190	.230	.276	3	.333	0		16		2.8
Total 13		51	52	.495	812	1	0	226-60	905	888	428	81	31	391-50	793	3.91	113	.260	.338	19	.211	1	96	56	49	8.2

JONNARD, CLAUDE   Claude Alfred B11.23.1897 Nashville TN D8.27.1959 Nashville TN BR/TR/6-1/165 d10.1 twb-Bubber

YEAR	TM LG	W	L	PCT	G	GS	CG-SHO	SV-BS	IP	H	R	HR	HB	BB-IB	SO	ERA	AERA	OAV	OOB	AB-HR-SH	AVG	PB	SUP	APR	DL	PW
1921	NY N	0	0	—	1	0	0	1	4	4	2	0	0	0	7	0.00	—	.267	.267	1	.000	-0		2		0.1
1922	NY N	6	1	.857	33	0	0	**5**	96	96	45	2	3	28	44	3.84	104	.272	.331	24-0-2	.042	-3		4		0.0
1923	†NY N	4	3	.571	**45**	1	1	**5**	96	105	45	6	0	35	45	3.28	116	.279	.340	26-0-1	.038	-3	86	4		-0.1
1924	†NY N	3	5	.375	34	3	1	5	89.2	80	33	2	2	40	40	2.41	152	.229	.282	22-0-1	.045	-3	123	**11**		0.7
1926	StL N	0	2	.000	12	3	0	1	36	46	29	1	0	24	13	6.00	71	.313	.409	7-0-1	.000	-1	79	-7		-0.4
1929	Chi N	0	1	.000	12	2	0	0	27.2	41	27	4	1	11	11	7.48	62	.320	.379	10	.200	1	76	-9		-0.3
Total 6		13	12	.520	137	9	2	17	349.1	372	179	20	6	122	160	3.79	104	.272	.334	90-0-5	.056	-9	94	5		-0.0

JORDAN, CHARLIE   Charles T. "Kid" B10.4.1871 Philadelphia PA D6.1.1928 Hazleton PA d7.31

YEAR	TM LG	W	L	PCT	G	GS	CG-SHO	SV-BS	IP	H	R	HR	HB	BB-IB	SO	ERA	AERA	OAV	OOB	AB-HR-SH	AVG	PB	SUP	APR	DL	PW
1896	Phi N	0	0	—	2	0	0	0	4.2	9	4	0	0	2	3	7.71	56	.409	.458	2	.500	0		-1		0.0

JORDAN, HARRY   Harry J. B2.14.1873 Pittsburgh PA D3.1.1920 Pittsburgh PA d9.25

YEAR	TM LG	W	L	PCT	G	GS	CG-SHO	SV-BS	IP	H	R	HR	HB	BB-IB	SO	ERA	AERA	OAV	OOB	AB-HR-SH	AVG	PB	SUP	APR	DL	PW
1894	Pit N	1	0	1.000	1	1	1	0	9	10	7	0	1	2	1	4.00	131	.278	.333	3	.000	-0	135	1		0.0
1895	Pit N	0	2	.000	2	2	1	0	17	24	15	0	1	6	4	4.24	106	.329	.387	7	.286	-0	87	-1		-0.1
Total 2		1	2	.333	3	3	2	0	26	34	22	0	2	8	5	4.15	115	.312	.370	10	.200	-0	105	0		-0.1

JORDAN, MILT   Milton Mignot B5.24.1927 Mineral Springs PA D5.13.1993 Ithaca NY BR/TR/6-2.5/207 d4.16

YEAR	TM LG	W	L	PCT	G	GS	CG-SHO	SV-BS	IP	H	R	HR	HB	BB-IB	SO	ERA	AERA	OAV	OOB	AB-HR-SH	AVG	PB	SUP	APR	DL	PW
1953	Det A	0	1	.000	8	1	0	0	17	26	13	3	0	5	4	5.82	70	.366	.408	2	.500	0	153	-4		-0.1

JORDAN, NILES   Niles Chapman B12.1.1925 Lyman WA BL/TL/5-11/180(165-180) d8.26

YEAR	TM LG	W	L	PCT	G	GS	CG-SHO	SV-BS	IP	H	R	HR	HB	BB-IB	SO	ERA	AERA	OAV	OOB	AB-HR-SH	AVG	PB	SUP	APR	DL	PW
1951	Phi N	2	3	.400	5	5	2-1	0	36.2	35	15	4	0	8	11	3.19	121	.250	.291	13	.077	-1	55	2		0.2
1952	Cin N	0	1	.000	3	1	0	0	6.1	14	7	1	0	3	2	9.95	38	.452	.500	1-0-1	.000	-0	47	-4		-0.5
Total 2		2	4	.333	8	6	2-1	0	43	49	22	5	0	11	13	4.19	92	.287	.330	14-0-1	.071	-1	54	-2		-0.3

JORDAN, RIP   Raymond Willis "Lanky" B9.28.1889 Portland ME D6.5.1960 Meriden CT BL/TR/6-0/172 d6.25

YEAR	TM LG	W	L	PCT	G	GS	CG-SHO	SV-BS	IP	H	R	HR	HB	BB-IB	SO	ERA	AERA	OAV	OOB	AB-HR-SH	AVG	PB	SUP	APR	DL	PW
1912	Chi A	0	0	—	4	0	0	0	12.1	13	8	2	1	3	1	5.11	63	.289	.347	4	.000	-1		-2		-0.2
1919	Was A	0	0	—	1	1	0	0	4	6	5	1	0	2	2	11.25	29	.353	.421	1	.000	-0	171	-3		-0.2
Total 2		0	0	—	5	1	0	0	16.1	19	13	3	1	5	3	6.61	48	.306	.368	5	.000	-1	171	-5		-0.4

JORDAN, RICARDO   Ricardo B6.27.1970 Boynton Beach FL BL/TL/5-11/175(165-190) [TorA90 37/995] d6.23 Col Miami-Dade Kendall (FL) CC

YEAR	TM LG	W	L	PCT	G	GS	CG-SHO	SV-BS	IP	H	R	HR	HB	BB-IB	SO	ERA	AERA	OAV	OOB	AB-HR-SH	AVG	PB	SUP	APR	DL	PW
1995	Tor A	1	0	1.000	15	0	0	1-0	15	18	11	3	2	13-1	10	6.60	72	.305	.434	0	—	0		-3		-0.2
1996	Phi N	2	2	.500	26	0	0	0-0	25	18	6	0	2	12-0	17	1.80	240	.202	.294	1	.000	-0		7		0.9
1997	NY N	1	2	.333	22	0	0	0-0	27	31*	17	1	2	15-2	19	5.33	75	.304	.397	1	.000	-0		-4		-0.4
1998	Cin N	1	0	1.000	6	0	0	0-0	3.1	4	9	2	0	7-0	1	24.30	18	.308	.524	0	—	0		-7		-1.2
Total 4		5	4	.556	69	0	0	1-0	70.1	71	43	6	4	47-3	47	5.25	82	.270	.381	2	—	0		-7		-0.9

JORGENS, ORVILLE   Orville Edward B6.4.1908 Rockford IL D1.11.1992 Colorado Springs CO BR/TR/6-1/180 d4.19 b-Art

YEAR	TM LG	W	L	PCT	G	GS	CG-SHO	SV-BS	IP	H	R	HR	HB	BB-IB	SO	ERA	AERA	OAV	OOB	AB-HR-SH	AVG	PB	SUP	APR	DL	PW
1935	Phi N	10	15	.400	**53**	24	6	2	188.1	216	129	12	8	96	57	4.83	94	.283	.370	62-0-3	.097	-5	105	-8		-1.3
1936	Phi N	8	8	.500	39	21	4	0	167.1	196	110	16	7	69	58	4.79	95	.290	.361	60-0-2	.200	-1	105	-4		-0.4
1937	Phi N	3	4	.429	52	9	1	3	140.2	159	83	12	5	68	34	4.41	98	.298	.383	35-0-1	.143	-1	93	-3		-0.2
Total 3		21	27	.438	144	54	11	5	496.1	571	322	40	20	233	149	4.70	95	.290	.370	157-0-6	.146	-7	104	-15		-1.9

JOSEPH, KEVIN   Kevin John B8.1.1976 Camp Hill PA BR/TR/6-4/200 [SFN97 6/178] d8.1 Col Rice

YEAR	TM LG	W	L	PCT	G	GS	CG-SHO	SV-BS	IP	H	R	HR	HB	BB-IB	SO	ERA	AERA	OAV	OOB	AB-HR-SH	AVG	PB	SUP	APR	DL	PW
2002	StL N	0	1	.000	11	0	0	0-0	11	16	7	1	2	6-0	2	4.91	82	.364	.462	0	—	0		-1		-0.1

YEAR	TM LG	W	L	PCT	G	GS	CG-SHO	SV-BS	IP	H	R	HR	HB	BB-IB	SO	ERA	AERA	OAV	OOB	AB-HR-SH	AVG	PB	SUP	APR	DL	PW

JOSS, ADDIE   Adrian   B4.12.1880 Woodland WI   D4.14.1911 Toledo OH   BR/TR/6-3/185   d4.26   HF1978   Col Wisconsin-Madison

1902	Cle A	17	13	.567	32	29	28-5	0	269.1	225	120	2	13	75	106	2.77	124	.228	.291	103-0-7	.117	-5*	102	23		2.0
1903	Cle A	18	13	.581	32	31	31-3	0	283.2	232	105	3	9	37	120	2.19	130	.223	.256	114-0-1	.193	0*	105	22		2.5
1904	Cle A	14	10	.583	25	24	20-5	0	192.1	160	51	0	7	30	83	1.59	159	.227	.266	76-0-3	.132	-4*	114	20		2.3
1905	Cle A	20	12	.625	33	32	31-3	0	286	246	90	4	11	46	132	2.01	131	.234	.273	97-0-6	.134	-0*	101	18		2.3
1906	Cle A	21	9	.700	34	31	28-9	1	282	220	81	3	3	43	106	1.72	152	.218	.252	100-0-10	.210	2*	110	28		3.5
1907	Cle A	27	11	.711	42	38	34-6	2	338.2	279	100	3	7	54	127	1.83	137	.227	.263	114-0-6	.114	-5	94	27		3.0
1908	Cle A	24	11	.686	42	35	29-9	2	325	232	77	2	2	30	130	1.16	205	.197	.218	97-0-3	.155	2	87	38		5.0
1909	Cle A	14	13	.519	33	28	24-4	0	242.2	198	71	0	4	31	67	1.71	150	.226	.255	80-1-2	.100	-3	76	21		2.1
1910	Cle A	5	5	.500	13	12	9-1	0	107.1	96	35	2	2	18	49	2.26	114	.245	.282	36-0-1	.111	-1	67	5		0.7
Total	9	160	97	.623	286	260	234-45	5	2327	1888	730	19	58	364	920	1.89	142	.223	.260	817-1-39	.144	-14	96	202		23.0

JOURNELL, JIMMY   James Richard   B12.29.1977 Springfield OH   BR/TR/6-4/200*   [StLN99 4/132]   d6.29   Col Illinois

2003	StL N	0	0	—	7	0	0	0-0	9	10	7	0	0	11-0	8	6.00	69	.278	.438	0	—	0		-2	19	-0.1
2005	StL N	0	1	.000	5	0	0	0-0	4.1	6	6	1	0	5-0	5	10.38	40	.333	.478	0	—	0		-3		-0.2
Total	2	0	1	.000	12	0	0	0-0	13.1	16	13	1	0	16-0	13	7.43	56	.296	.451	0	—	0		-5	19	-0.2

JOYCE, MIKE   Michael Lewis   B2.12.1941 Detroit MI   BR/TR/6-2/195*   d7.2   Col Michigan

1962	Chi A	2	1	.667	25	1	0	2	43.1	40	17	2	0	14-2	9	3.32	118	.247	.305	7	.429	1	137	3		0.3
1963	Chi A	0	0	—	6	0	0	0	10.2	13	10	1	0	8-2	7	8.44	42	.289	.396	0-0-1	—	0		-5		-0.1
Total	2	2	1	.667	31	1	0	2	54	53	27	3	0	22-4	16	4.33	88	.256	.326	7-0-1	.429	1	137	-2		0.6

JOYCE, DICK   Richard Edward   B11.18.1943 Portland ME   BL/TL/6-5/225   d9.3   Col Holy Cross

| 1965 | KC A | 0 | 1 | .000 | 5 | 3 | 0 | 0 | 13 | 12 | 7 | 0 | 0 | 4-0 | 7 | 2.77 | 126 | .240 | .291 | 4 | .000 | -0 | 84 | 0 | | -0.1 |

JOYCE, BOB   Robert Emmett   B1.14.1915 Stockton CA   D12.10.1981 San Francisco CA   BR/TR/6-1/180   d5.4

1939	Phi A	3	5	.375	30	6	1	0	107.2	156	91	13	1	37	25	6.69	70	.337	.387	35-0-1	.086	-3	53	-22		-1.5
1946	NY N	3	4	.429	14	7	2	0	60.2	79	43	3	0	20	24	5.34	64	.315	.365	19-1-1	.158	0	139	-13		-0.7
Total	2	6	9	.400	44	13	3	0	168.1	235	134	16	1	57	49	6.20	69	.329	.380	54-1-2	.111	-3	89	-35		-2.1

JUDD, MIKE   Michael Galen   B6.30.1975 San Diego CA   BR/TR/6-1/217(200-217)   [NYA95 9/254]   d9.28   Col Grossmont (CA) JC

1997	LA N	0	0	—	1	0	0	0-0	2.2	2	1	0	0	0-0	4	0.00	—	.364	.364	1	.000	-0		1		0.0
1998	LA N	0	0	—	7	0	0	0-0	11.1	19	19	4	1	9-1	14	15.09	27	.373	.475	1	.000	-0		-14		-0.4
1999	LA N	3	1	.750	7	4	0	0-0	28	30	17	4	1	12-0	22	5.46	80	.280	.358	5-0-3	.000	-0	111	-3		-0.4
2000	LA N	0	1	.000	1	1	0	.0-0	4	4	7	2	1	3-0	5	15.75	28	.250	.400	1-0-1	1.000	0	124	-5		-0.4
2001	TB A	1	0	1.000	8	2	0	0-0	20	19	14	2	1	10-0	11	4.05	111	.250	.333	0	—	0	154	-1	15	-0.1
	Tex A	0	1	.000	4	1	0	0-0	9	15	10	2	0	5-0	5	8.00	57	.357	.426	1	.000	-0	78	-4		-0.1
	Year	1	1	.500	12	3	0	0-0	29	34	24	4	1	15-0	16	5.28	87	.288	.365	1	.000	-0	121	-5	15	-0.2
Total	5	4	3	.571	28	8	0	0-0	75	90	61	14	4	39-1	61	7.20	61	.300	.384	9-0-4	.111	-0	121	-26	15	-2.1

JUDD, RALPH   Ralph Wesley   B12.7.1901 Perrysburg OH   D5.6.1957 Lapeer MI   BL/TR/5-10/170   d10.2

1927	Was A	0	0	—	1	0	0	1	4	8	3	0	0	2	2	6.75	60	.400	.455	1	.000	-0		-1		-0.1
1929	NY N	3	0	1.000	18	0	0	0	50.2	49	19	4	0	11	21	2.66	172	.261	.302	14	.000	-2		10		0.1
1930	NY N	0	0	—	2	0	0	0	7.2	13	8	0	0	3	0	5.87	81	.394	.444	3	.000	-1		-2		-0.1
Total	3	3	0	1.000	21	0	0	1	62.1	70	30	4	0	16	23	3.32	138	.290	.335	18	.000	-3		7		0.1

JUDD, OSCAR   Thomas William Oscar "Ossie"   B2.14.1908 London ON, Can.   D12.27.1995 Ingersoll ON, Can.   BL/TL/6-0.5/180   d4.16

1941	Bos A	0	0	—	7	0	0	0	12.1	15	12	1	0	10	5	8.76	48	.300	.417	4	.500	2*		-5		0.0
1942	Bos A	8	10	.444	31	19	11	2	150.1	135	72	3	2	90	70	3.89	96	.239	.346	67-2-3	.269	6*	133	-2		0.0
1943	Bos A☆	11	6	.647	23	20	8-1	0	155.1	131	58	2	3	69	53	2.90	114	.230	.317	54-0-3	.259	4*	89	6		1.4
1944	Bos A	1	1	.500	9	6	1	0	30	30	16	1	0	15	9	3.60	94	.261	.346	11	.182	1*	188	-2		-0.2
1945	Bos A	0	1	.000	2	1	0	0	6.1	10	8	1	0	3	6	8.53	40	.333	.394	2	.500	0	50	-4		-0.2
	Phi N	5	4	.556	23	9	3-1	2	82.2	80	47	3	1	40	36	3.81	101	.254	.340	30-0-1	.267	3*	64	-1		0.1
1946	Phi N	11	12	.478	30	24	12-1	2	173.1	169	86	6	1	90	65	3.53	97	.260	.350	79-1-4	.316	8*	95	-5		0.1
1947	Phi N	4	15	.211	32	19	8-1	0	146.2	155	86	8	3	69	54	4.60	87	.279	.361	64	.188	2*	73	-10		-0.2
1948	Phi N	0	2	.000	4	1	0	0	14.1	19	14	1	0	11	7	6.91	57	.317	.423	6	.167	0	90	-5		-0.1
Total	8	40	51	.440	161	99	43-4	6	771.1	744	399	24	10	397	304	3.90	93	.256	.347	317-3-11	.262	26	98	-28		0.8

JUDEN, JEFF   Jeffrey Daniel   B1.19.1971 Salem MA   BR/TR/6-8/265(245-265)   [HouN89 1/12]   d9.15

1991	Hou N	0	2	.000	4	3	0	0-0	18	19	14	3	0	7-1	11	6.00	59	.275	.329	5	.000	-1	59	-5		-0.3
1993	Hou N	0	1	.000	2	2	0	0-0	5	4	3	1	0	4-1	7	5.40	72	.222	.348	0	—	-0		-1		-0.1
1994	Phi N	1	4	.200	6	5	0	0-0	27.2	29	25	4	1	12-0	22	6.18	69	.276	.350	9-0-2	.111	-0	72	-7		-0.5
1995	Phi N	2	4	.333	13	10	1	0-0	62.2	53	31	6	5	31-0	47	4.02	105	.235	.335	18-1-3	.056	-1	94	1		0.3
1996	SF N	4	0	1.000	36	0	0	0-0	41.2	39	23	7	1	20-2	35	4.10	101	.250	.335	3	.000	-0		6		0.5
	Mon N	1	0	1.000	22	0	0	0-0	32.2	22	12	1	4	14-0	26	2.20	197	.188	.294	0-0-1	—	-0		6		1.1
	Year	5	0	1.000	58	0	0	0-0	74.1	61	35	8	5	34-2	61	3.27	129	.223	.317	3-0-1	.000	-0	119	1		1.6
1997	Mon N	11	5	.688	22	22	3	0-0	130	125	64	17	9	57-2	107	4.22	99	.255	.341	43-0-2	.140	0	94	-3		0.6
	†Cle A	0	1	.000	8	5	0	0-0	31.1	32	21	6	1	15-0	29	5.46	86	.264	.345	41-0-3	.122	-1	100	-17		-0.7
1998	Mil N	7	11	.389	24	24	2	0-0	138.1	149	91	20	10	66-0	109	6.75	70	.217	.308	0	—	0	91	-8		-0.6
	Ana A	1	3	.250	8	6	0	0-0	40	33	32	7	2	18-0	39	6.75	70	.217	.308	0	—	0	39	-2		-0.4
1999	NY A	0	1	.000	2	1	0	0-0	5.2	5	5	1	1	3-0	9	1.59	298	.200	.310	0	—	0	99	-35		-0.0
Total	8	27	32	.458	147	76	6	0-0	533	510	325	73	34	247-6	441	4.81	89	.253	.341	119-1-11	.109	-3	99	-35		-0.8

JUDSON, HOWIE   Howard Kolls   B2.16.1926 Hebron IL   BR/TR/6-1/195*   d4.22   Col Illinois

1948	Chi A	4	5	.444	40	5	1	8	107.1	102	60	7	3	56	38	4.78	89	.255	.351	29-0-4	.103	-2*	98	-5		-0.2
1949	Chi A	1	14	.067	26	12	3	1	108	114	65	13	1	70	36	4.58	91	.274	.380	31-0-3	.065	-3	61	-6		-0.2
1950	Chi A	2	3	.400	46	3	1	0	112	105	53	10	2	63	34	3.94	114	.252	.353	20-0-4	.100	-1	94	8		-0.1
1951	Chi A	5	6	.455	27	14	3	1	121.2	124	67	9	2	55	43	3.77	107	.264	.343	33-0-5	.121	-2	108	0		-0.2
1952	Chi A	0	1	.000	21	0	0	1	34	30	17	4	0	22	15	4.24	86	.244	.359	4	.000	-0		-6		-0.1
1953	Cin N	0	1	.000	10	6	0	0	38.2	58	28	8	0	11	11	5.59	78	.341	.381	9	.111	-2	104	2		-0.1
1954	Cin N	5	7	.417	37	8	0	3	93.1	86	47	9	3	42	27	3.95	106	.251	.335	24	.083	-2	97	-9		-0.1
Total	7	17	37	.315	207	48	8	14	615	619	337	60	11	319	204	4.29	98	.265	.355	150-0-16	.093	-9	97	-9		-0.9

JULIO, JORGE   Jorge Dandys   B3.3.1979 Caracas, Venez   BR/TR/6-1/190(190-235)   d4.26

2001	Bal A	1	1	.500	18	0	0	0-1	21.1	25	13	2	1	9-0	22	3.80	114	.287	.361	0	—	0		0		0.0
2002	Bal A	5	6	.455	67	0	0	25-6	68	55	22	5	2	27-3	55	1.99	219	.213	.292	0	—	0		16		1.6
2003	Bal A	0	7	.000	64	0	0	36-8	61.2	60	36	10	2	34-4	52	4.38	105	.256	.354	0	—	0		2		0.2
2004	Bal A	2	5	.286	65	0	0	22-4	69	59	35	11	3	39-4	70	4.57	102	.228	.332	0	—	0		-11		-1.1
2005	Bal A	3	5	.375	67	0	0	0-2	71.2	76	50	14	2	24-4	58	5.90	75	.269	.327	0	—	0		7		0.7
Total	5	11	24	.314	281	0	0	83-21	291.2	275	156	42	10	133-15	257	4.20	107	.245	.329	0	—	0		7		0.7

JUNGE, ERIC   Eric Debari   B1.5.1977 Manhasset NY   BR/TR/6-5/215*   [LAN99 11/344]   d9.11   Col Bucknell   [DL 2004 Phi N 37]

2002	Phi N	2	0	1.000	4	1	0	0-0	12.2	14	3	0	0	5-0	11	1.42	270	.286	.352	3	.000	-0	96	3		0.3
2003	Phi N	0	0	—	6	0	0	0-0	7.2	5	3	1	0	1-0	5	3.52	113	.185	.214	0	—	0		1		0.1
Total	2	2	0	1.000	10	1	0	0-0	20.1	19	6	1	0	6-0	16	2.21	176	.250	.305	3	.000	-0	96	4	37	0.4

JUNGELS, KEN   Kenneth Peter "Curly"   B6.23.1916 Aurora IL   D9.9.1975 West Bend WI   BR/TR/6-1/180   d9.15

1937	Cle A	0	0	—	2	0	0	0	3	3	1	0	1	0	0	0.00	—	.273	.333	0	—	0		1		0.1
1938	Cle A	1	0	1.000	9	0	0	0	15.1	21	16	1	2	18	7	8.80	53	.339	.500	5	.000	-1		-7		-0.1
1940	Cle A	1	0	1.000	4	0	0	0	3.1	3	1	0	0	4	1	2.70	156	.273	.333	1	.000	-0		1		0.1
1941	Cle A	0	1	.000	4	0	0	0	13.2	17	12	4	1	8	6	7.24	54	.293	.388	2	.000	-0		-5		-0.1
1942	Pit N	0	0	—	6	0	0	0	13.2	12	11	0	0	4	7	6.59	51	.235	.291	2	.500	0*		-4		0.0
Total	5	2	1	1.000	25	0	0	0	49	56	41	5	3	32	21	6.80	60	.290	.399	10	.100	-1		-14		-0.2

JUREWICZ, MIKE   Michael Allen   B9.20.1945 Buffalo NY   BB/TL/6-3/205   d9.7

| 1965 | NY A | 0 | 0 | — | 2 | 0 | 0 | 0 | 2.1 | 5 | 2 | 0 | 0 | 1-0 | 2 | 7.71 | 44 | .417 | .462 | 0 | — | 0 | | -1 | | -0.0 |

YEAR	TM LG	W	L	PCT	G	GS	CG-SHO	SV-BS	IP	H	R	HR	HB	BB-IB	SO	ERA	AERA	OAV	OOB	AB-HR-SH	AVG	PB	SUP	APR	DL	PW
JURISICH, AL	Alvin Joseph			B8.25.1921 New Orleans LA			D11.3.1981 New Orleans LA		BR/TR/6-2/193					d4.26												
1944	†StL N	7	9	.438	30	14	5-2	1	130	102	53	7	5	65	53	3.39	104	.221	.323	45-0-1	.178	-1	78	4		0.3
1945	StL N	3	3	.500	27	6	1	0	71.2	61	45	7	1	41	42	5.15	73	.232	.338	23	.087	-2	143	-10		-1.0
1946	Phi N	4	3	.571	13	10	2-1	1	68.1	71	30	9	1	31	34	3.69	93	.263	.341	23-0-2	.130	-0	95	-1		-0.2
1947	Phi N	1	7	.125	34	12	5	3	118.1	110	69	15	1	52	48	4.94	81	.258	.340	31-0-4	.032	-3	81	-10		-1.0
Total	4	15	22	.405	104	42	13-3	5	388.1	344	197	38	8	189	177	4.24	87	.242	.334	122-0-7	.115	-6	92	-17		-1.9
JUSTIS, WALT	Walter Newton "Smoke"			B8.17.1883 Moores Hill IN			D10.4.1941 Greendale IN		BR/TR/5-11.5/195					d7.12												
1905	Det A	0	0	—	2	0	0	0	3.1	4	3	0	1	6	0	8.10	34	.308	.550	0	—	0		-2		-0.1
JUUL, HEROLD	Earl Herold			B5.21.1893 Chicago IL			D1.4.1942 Chicago IL		BR/TR/5-9.5/150					d4.24	b-Herb											
1914	Bro F	0	3	.000	9	3	0	0	29	26	24	0	1	16	16	6.21	46	.248	.423	9	.222	-0	80	-10		-0.9
JUUL, HERB	Herbert Victor			B2.2.1886 Chicago IL			D11.14.1928 Chicago IL		BL/TL/5-11/150					d7.11	b-Herold Col Illinois											
1911	Cin N	0	0	—	1	0	0	0	4	3	2	0	0	4	4	4.50	74	.231	.412	2	.000	-0*		0		-0.1
KAAT, JIM	James Lee			B11.7.1938 Zeeland MI			BL/TL/6-4/217(190-227)		d8.2 C2 Col Hope																	
1959	Was A	0	2	.000	3	2	0	0	5	7	9	1	2	4-0	2	12.60	31	.350	.481	1	.000	-0	56	-5		-0.9
1960	Was A	1	5	.167	13	9	0	0	50	48	39	8	0	31-2	25	5.58	70	.255	.370	14	.143	-1	88	-10		-1.1
1961	Min A	9	17	.346	36	29	8-1	0	200.2	188	105	12	11	82-1	122	3.90	109	.248	.329	63-0-3	.238	3*	75	5		1.1
1962	Min A☆	18	14	.563	39	35	16-5	1	269	243	106	23	18	75-5	173	3.14	130	.243	.305	100-1-0	.180	3*	99	27		3.8
1963	Min A	10	10	.500	31	27	7-1	1	178.1	195	96	24	9	38-1	105	4.19	87	.274	.318	61-1-1	.131	3*	99	27		3.8
1964	Min A	17	11	.607	36	34	13	1	243	231	100	23	9	60-5	171	3.22	111	.251	.301	83-3-3	.169	5*	117	10		1.8
1965	†Min A	18	11	.621	45	42	7-2	2	264.1	267	121	25	5	63-6	154	2.83	126	.258	.302	93-1-3	.247	6*	116	11		2.1
1966	Min A★	25	13	.658	41	41	19-3	0	304.2	271	114	29	5	55-4	205	2.75	131	.235	.270	118-2-1	.195	4*	103	25		3.6
1967	Min A	16	13	.552	42	38	13-2	0	263.1	269	110	21	9	42-2	211	3.04	114	.260	.294	99-1-1	.172	3*	96	9		1.4
1968	Min A	14	12	.538	30	29	9-2	0	208	192	78	16	8	40-0	130	2.94	105	.243	.278	77	.156	0*	101	4	21	0.6
1969	Min A	14	13	.519	40	32	10	1-1	242.1	252	114	23	9	75-15	139	3.49	104	.265	.322	87-2-2	.207	6*	103	1		0.7
1970	†Min A	14	10	.583	45	34	4-1	0-1	230.1	244	110	26	3	58-8	120	3.56	104	.273	.316	76-1-4	.197	3*	113	2		0.5
1971	Min A	13	14	.481	39	38	15-4	0-0	260.1	275	104	16	4	47-9	137	3.32	107	.268	.302	93-0-7	.161	0*	108	8		0.8
1972	Min A	10	2	.833	15	15	5	0-0	113.1	94	36	6	0	20-2	64	2.06	156	.227	.260	45-2-1	.289	5*	114	12	83	2.0
1973	Min A	11	12	.478	29	28	7-2	0-0	181.2	206	101	26	4	39-1	93	4.41	90	.282	.321	0	—	0*	108	1		-1.0
	Chi A	4	1	.800	7	7	3-1	0-0	42.2	44	23	4	0	4-0	16	4.22	94	.260	.277	0	—	0*	152	-1		-0.2
	Year	15	13	.536	36	35	10-3	0-0	224.1	250	124	30	4	43-1	109	4.37	91	.278	.313	0	—	0	116	-11		-1.2
1974	Chi A	21	13	.618	42	39	15-3	0-0	277.1	263	106	18	6	63-3	142	2.92	128	.250	.293	1	.000	0	92	23		2.6
1975	Chi A★	20	14	.588	43	41	12-1	0-0	303.2	321	121	20	9	77-0	142	3.11	125	.274	.321	0	—	0	99	23		2.4
1976	†Phi N	12	14	.462	38	35	7-1	0-1	227.2	241	95	21	0	32-3	83	3.48	103	.250	.298	79-1-1	.177	2*	106	3		0.4
1977	Phi N	6	11	.353	35	27	2	0-0	160.1	211	100	20	2	40-6	55	5.39	75	.320	.360	53-0-1	.189	1*	108	-21		-1.9
1978	Phi N	8	5	.615	26	24	2-1	0-0	140.1	150	67	9	1	32-6	48	4.10	88	.280	.322	48-0-1	.146	-1	112	-6		-0.7
1979	Phi N	1	0	1.000	3	1	0	0-0	8.1	9	4	1	0	5-2	2	4.32	90	.281	.378	1	.000	0	160	0		0.0
	NY A	2	3	.400	40	1	0	2-2	58.1	64	29	4	2	14-2	23	3.86	107	.287	.329	0	—	0	110	1		-0.3
1980	NY A	0	1	.000	4	0	0	0-0	5	8	5	0	0	4-2	1	7.20	55	.381	.462	0	—	0		-2		-0.3
	StL N	8	7	.533	49	14	6-1	4-1	129.2	140	61	6	0	33-11	36	3.82	98	.281	.322	35-1-4	.143	0	119	-1		-0.1
1981	StL N	6	6	.500	41	1	0	4-5	53	60	25	2	0	17-8	8	3.40	107	.299	.345	1	.375	1	98	0		0.2
1982	†StL N	5	3	.625	62	2	0	2-2	75	79	40	6	2	23-9	35	4.08	90	.270	.328	12	.000	-1	96	-4		0.0
1983	StL N	0	0	—	24	0	0	0-1	34.2	48	19	5	0	10-3	19	3.89	94	.327	.367	4-0-1	.000	-0		-2		-0.1
Total	25	283	237	.544	898	625	180-31	18-14	4530.1	4620	2038	395	122	1083-116	2461	3.45	107	.264	.309	1251-16-34	.185	41	105	93	104	16.4
KAHLER, GEORGE	George Runnells "Krum"			B9.6.1889 Athens OH			D2.7.1924 Battle Creek MI		BR/TR/6-0/183					d8.13 Col Ohio U.												
1910	Cle A	6	4	.600	12	12	8-2	0	95.1	80	35	0	4	46	38	1.60	161	.237	.335	35	.143	-2	110	6		0.4
1911	Cle A	9	8	.529	30	17	10	1	154.1	153	78	1	13	66	97	3.27	104	.270	.360	54-0-3	.167	-2	91	2		-0.1
1912	Cle A	12	19	.387	40	35	17-3	1	246.1	263	135	1	11	121	104	3.69	92	.291	.382	80-0-1	.112	-5	75	-6		-1.4
1913	Cle A	5	11	.313	24	15	5	0	117.2	118	56	1	4	32	43	3.14	97	.269	.324	33-0-3	.061	-3	86	-1		-0.7
1914	Cle A	0	1	.000	2	1	0	1	14	17	10	0	0	7	3	3.86	75	.309	.387	5	.000	-0	152	-2		-0.2
Total	5	32	43	.427	109	77	41-5	2	627.2	631	314	3	32	272	285	3.17	101	.274	.359	207-0-7	.121	-13	86	-1		-2.0
KAINER, DON	Donald Wayne			B9.3.1955 Houston TX			BR/TR/6-3/205		[TexA77 13/321] d9.6 Col Texas																	
1980	Tex A	0	0	—	4	3	0	0-0	19.2	22	7	0	3	9-1	10	1.83	213	.289	.386	0	—	0	100	4		0.3
KAISER, DON	Clyde Donald "Tiger"			B2.3.1935 Byng OK			BR/TR/6-5/195*		d7.20 Col East Central																	
1955	Chi N	0	0	—	1	0	0	0	18.1	20	11	2	1	5-0	11	5.40	76	.274	.329	2	.000	-0		-2		-0.2
1956	Chi N	4	9	.308	27	22	5-1	0	150.1	144	69	15	1	52-8	74	3.59	105	.247	.308	47	.043	-5	75	3		-0.3
1957	Chi N	2	6	.250	20	13	1	0	72	91	48	4	0	28-3	23	5.00	77	.316	.372	19	.105	-1	82	-10		-1.0
Total	6	15	.286	58	35	6-1	0	240.2	255	128	21	2	85-11	108	4.15	92	.270	.329	68	.059	-6	78	-9		-1.5
KAISER, JEFF	Jeffrey Patrick			B7.24.1960 Wyandotte MI			BR/TL/6-3/195*		[OakA82 10/262] d4.11 Col Western Michigan																	
1985	Oak A	0	0	—	15	0	0	0-1	16.2	25	32	6	1	20-2	10	14.58	37	.342	.479	0	—	0		-22		-1.0
1987	Cle A	0	0	—	2	0	0	0-0	3.1	4	6	1	1	3-0	2	16.20	28	.286	.444	0	—	0		-4	22	-0.2
1988	Cle A	0	0	—	3	0	0	0-0	2.2	2	0	0	0	1-0	0	0.00	—	.286	.333	0	—	0		1		0.1
1989	Cle A	0	1	.000	6	0	0	0-1	3.2	5	5	1	0	5-0	4	7.36	54	.313	.455	0	—	0		-2		-0.4
1990	Cle A	0	0	—	5	0	0	0-0	12.2	16	5	2	0	7-1	9	3.55	111	.308	.383	0	—	0		1	58	0.0
1991	Det A	0	1	.000	10	0	0	2-0	5	6	5	1	0	5-2	4	9.00	46	.286	.423	0	—	0		-2		-0.5
1993	Cin N	0	0	—	3	0	0	0-0	3.1	4	1	0	0	2-1	4	2.70	149	.286	.375	0	—	0		1		0.0
	NY N	0	0	—	6	0	0	0-0	4.2	6	1	0	1	1-0	5	11.57	35	.353	.429	0	—	0		-4	20	-0.2
	Year	0	0	—	9	0	0	0-0	8	10	8	1	1	3-0	9	7.88	51	.323	.405	0	—	0		-3		-0.2
Total	7	0	2	.000	50	0	0	2-2	52	68	60	12	2	46-6	38	9.17	44	.318	.433	0	—	0		-31	100	-2.2
KAISER, BOB	Robert Thomas			B4.29.1950 Cincinnati OH			BB/TL/5-10/180		[CleA68 3/46] d9.3																	
1971	Cle A	0	0	—	8	0	0	0	8	3	2	2	0	3-0	4	4.50	86	.333	.448	0	—	0		0		0.0
KAISERLING, GEORGE	George			B5.12.1893 Steubenville OH			D3.2.1918 Steubenville OH		BR/TR/6-0/175		d4.20															
1914	Ind F	17	10	.630	37	33	20-1	0	275.1	288	119	8	17	72	75	3.11	100	.274	.330	98-0-3	.112	-7	121	2		-0.7
1915	New F	15	15	.500	41	29	16-5	2	261.1	246	90	1	9	73	75	2.24	114	.257	.316	79-0-9	.152	-3	104	10		0.7
Total	2	32	25	.561	78	62	36-6	2	536.2	534	209	9	26	145	150	2.68	106	.266	.323	177-0-12	.130	-10	115	12		0.0
KALFASS, BILL	William Philip "Lefty"			B3.3.1916 New York NY			D9.8.1968 Brooklyn NY		BR/TL/6-3.5/190		d9.15 Col Columbia														
1937	Phi A	1	0	1.000	3	1	1	0	9	9	6	2	1	9	9	3.00	157	.233	.377	4	.000	-1	185	3		0.1
KALLIO, RUDY	Rudolph			B12.14.1892 Portland OR			D4.6.1979 Newport OR		BR/TR/5-10/160		d4.25															
1918	Det A	8	13	.381	30	22	10-2	0	181.1	178	91	0	1	76	70	3.62	73	.261	.336	56-0-4	.161	-1*	109	-20		-2.3
1919	Det A	0	0	—	12	1	0	1	22.1	28	15	0	1	8	3	5.64	57	.326	.389	4	.000	-1	147	-5		-0.3
1925	Bos A	1	4	.200	7	4	0	0	18.2	28	18	0	1	9	2	7.71	59	.364	.437	6	.333	0	97	-6		-0.9
Total	3	9	17	.346	49	27	10-2	1	222.1	234	124	0	3	93	75	4.17	69	.277	.351	66-0-4	.167	-1	111	-31		-3.5
KAMIENIECKI, SCOTT	Scott Andrew			B4.19.1964 Mt.Clemens MI			BR/TR/6-0/195*		[NYA86 14/366] d6.18 Col Michigan																	
1991	NY A	4	4	.500	9	9	0	0-0	55.1	54	24	8	3	22-1	34	3.90	107	.256	.333	0	—	0	80	3	65	0.4
1992	NY A	6	14	.300	28	28	4	0-0	188	193	100	13	3	74-9	88	4.36	91	.269	.340	0	—	0	103	-9	23	-0.9
1993	NY A	10	7	.588	30	20	2	1-0	154.1	163	73	17	3	59-7	72	4.08	103	.277	.343	0	—	0	98	3		0.4
1994	NY A	8	6	.571	22	16	1	0-0	117.1	115	53	13	3	59-1	71	3.76	122	.261	.350	0	—	0	134	12		1.2
1995	†NY A	7	6	.538	17	16	1	0-0	89.2	83	43	8	3	49-1	43	4.01	115	.246	.346	0	—	0	99	6	70	0.7
1996	NY A	1	2	.333	7	5	0	0-1	22.2	36	30	6	2	12-1	15	11.12	45	.364	.475	0	—	0	99	2		-1.5
1997	†Bal A	10	6	.625	30	30	0	0-0	179.1	179	83	20	4	67-2	109	4.01	110	.261	.328	2	.000	-0	99	10	84	0.8
1998	Bal A	2	6	.250	12	11	0	0-0	54.2	67	41	7	0	26-0	25	6.75	67	.313	.394	0	—	0	72	-13	117	-1.5
1999	Bal A	2	4	.333	43	3	0	2-0	56.1	52	32	4	4	29-2	39	4.95	95	.250	.348	0	—	0	86	-1	33	0.0
2000	Cle A	1	3	.250	26	2	0	0-0	33.1	42	22	6	1	20-5	29	5.67	88	.311	.404	0	—	0		-1		-0.4
	Atl N	2	1	.667	26	0	0	0-0	24.2	22	18	3	0	22-1	17	5.47	82	.239	.386	0	—	0		-3		-0.4
Total	10	53	59	.473	250	138	8	5-1	975.2	1006	519	105	32	446-34	542	4.52	97	.270	.351	2	.000	-0	101	-10	392	-1.0

KAMMEYER, BOB
Robert Lynn B12.2.1950 Kansas City KS D1.27.2003 Sacramento CA BR/TR/6-4/210* [NYA72 21/492] d7.3 Col Stanford

YEAR	TM LG	W	L	PCT	G	GS	CG-SHO	SV-BS	IP	H	R	HR	HB	BB-IB	SO	ERA	AERA	OAV	OOB	AB-HR-SH	AVG	PB	SUP	APR	DL	PW
1978	NY A	0	0	—	7	0	0	0-0	21.2	24	15	1	2	6-0	11	5.82	63	.276	.327	0	—	0		-5		-0.2
1979	NY A	0	0	—	1	0	0	0-0	0	7	8	2	1	0-0	0	∞	—	1.000	1.000	0	—	0		-8		-0.6
Total	2	0	0	—	8	0	0	0-0	21.2	31	23	3	3	6-0	11	9.14	40	.330	.377	0	—	0		-13		-0.8

KAMP, IKE
Alphonse Francis B9.5.1900 Roxbury MA D2.25.1955 Boston MA BB/TL/6-0/170 d9.16 Col Boston College

YEAR	TM LG	W	L	PCT	G	GS	CG-SHO	SV-BS	IP	H	R	HR	HB	BB-IB	SO	ERA	AERA	OAV	OOB	AB-HR-SH	AVG	PB	SUP	APR	DL	PW
1924	Bos N	0	1	.000	7	1	0	0	7	9	5	0	0	5	4	5.14	74	.360	.467	1-0-1	.000	-0	67	-1		-0.1
1925	Bos N	2	4	.333	24	4	1	0	58.1	68	38	0	0	35	20	5.09	79	.301	.395	12-0-1	.167	-0	116	-7		-0.6
Total	2	2	5	.286	25	5	1	0	65.1	77	43	0	0	40	24	5.10	78	.307	.402	13-0-2	.154	-0	106	-8		-0.7

KANE, HARRY
Harry "Klondike" (b Harry Cohen) B7.27.1883 Hamburg AR D9.15.1932 Portland OR BL/TL d8.8

YEAR	TM LG	W	L	PCT	G	GS	CG-SHO	SV-BS	IP	H	R	HR	HB	BB-IB	SO	ERA	AERA	OAV	OOB	AB-HR-SH	AVG	PB	SUP	APR	DL	PW
1902	StL A	0	1	.000	4	1	1	0	23	34	21	2	0	16	7	5.48	64	.343	.435	9	.111	-1	82	-6		-0.4
1903	Det A	0	2	.000	3	3	2	0	18	26	22	0	1	8	10	8.50	34	.338	.407	7	.143	-0	106	-10		-0.9
1905	Phi N	1	1	.500	2	2	2-1	0	17	12	6	0	0	8	12	1.59	184	.203	.299	6-0-1	.167	-0	74	2		0.2
1906	Phi N	1	3	.250	6	3	2	0	28	28	16	0	3	18	14	3.86	68	.255	.374	8-0-1	.000	-1	74	-3		-0.5
Total	4	2	7	.222	15	9	7-1	0	86	100	65	2	4	50	43	4.81	62	.290	.386	30-0-1	.100	-2	83	-17		-1.6

KANTLEHNER, ERV
Erving Leslie "Peanuts" B7.31.1892 San Jose CA D2.3.1990 Santa Barbara CA BL/TL/6-0/190 d4.17 Col Santa Clara

YEAR	TM LG	W	L	PCT	G	GS	CG-SHO	SV-BS	IP	H	R	HR	HB	BB-IB	SO	ERA	AERA	OAV	OOB	AB-HR-SH	AVG	PB	SUP	APR	DL	PW
1914	Pit N	3	2	.600	21	5	3-2	0	67	51	33	1	3	39	26	3.09	86	.218	.337	15	.067	-0	108	-5		-0.4
1915	Pit N	5	12	.294	29	18	10-1	3	163	135	60	1	4	58	64	2.26	121	.230	.304	52-0-1	.288	3	73	6		1.0
1916	Pit N	5	15	.250	34	21	7-2	2	165	151	72	1	4	57	49	3.16	85	.249	.317	46	.174	-0	64	-7		-0.8
	Phi N	0	0	—	3	0	0	0	4	7	4	0	0	3	2	9.00	29	.500	.588	0	—	-0		-2		-0.1
	Year	5	15	.250	37	21	7-2	2	169	158	76	1	4	60	51	3.30	81	.254	.324	46	.174	-0	64	-10		-0.9
Total	3	13	29	.310	87	44	20-5	5	399	344	169	3	11	157	141	2.84	95	.239	.318	113-0-1	.212	2	72	-8		-0.3

KARCHNER, MATT
Matthew Dean B6.28.1967 Berwick PA BR/TR/6-4/210* [KCA89 8/205] d7.18 Col Bloomsburg

YEAR	TM LG	W	L	PCT	G	GS	CG-SHO	SV-BS	IP	H	R	HR	HB	BB-IB	SO	ERA	AERA	OAV	OOB	AB-HR-SH	AVG	PB	SUP	APR	DL	PW
1995	Chi A	4	2	.667	31	0	0	0-0	32	33	8	2	1	12-2	24	1.69	265	.275	.336	0	—	0		10		1.6
1996	Chi A	7	4	.636	50	0	0	1-8	59.1	61	42	10	2	41-8	46	5.76	83	.266	.377	0	—	0		-7	50	-1.2
1997	Chi A	3	1	.750	52	0	0	15-1	52.2	50	18	4	0	26-4	30	2.91	152	.258	.344	0	—	0		10		1.1
1998	Chi A	2	4	.333	32	0	0	11-4	36.2	33	21	2	5	19-6	30	5.15	89	.243	.348	0	—	0		-1	31	-0.2
	†Chi A	3	1	.750	29	0	0	0-3	28	30	18	6	2	14-2	22	5.14	86	.263	.354	0	—	0		-3		-0.3
1999	Chi A	1	0	1.000	16	0	0	0-1	18	16	5	3	2	9-0	9	2.50	183	.235	.342	0	—	0		4	138	0.2
2000	Chi A	1	1	.500	13	0	0	0-0	14.2	19	11	3	0	11-0	6	6.14	75	.311	.411	0-0-1	—	0		-3		-0.3
Total	6	21	13	.618	223	0	0	27-17	241.1	242	123	30	12	132-22	166	4.21	108	.262	.357	0-0-1	—	0		10	219	0.9

KARDOW, PAUL
Paul Otto "Tex" B9.19.1915 Humble TX D4.27.1968 San Antonio TX BR/TR/6-6 /210 d7.1

YEAR	TM LG	W	L	PCT	G	GS	CG-SHO	SV-BS	IP	H	R	HR	HB	BB-IB	SO	ERA	AERA	OAV	OOB	AB-HR-SH	AVG	PB	SUP	APR	DL	PW
1936	Cle A	0	0	—	2	0	0	0	4	4	2	0	1	2	0	4.50	112	.167	.375	0	—	0		0		0.0

KARGER, ED
Edwin "Loose" B5.6.1883 San Angelo TX D9.9.1957 Delta CO BL/TL/5-11/185 d4.15

YEAR	TM LG	W	L	PCT	G	GS	CG-SHO	SV-BS	IP	H	R	HR	HB	BB-IB	SO	ERA	AERA	OAV	OOB	AB-HR-SH	AVG	PB	SUP	APR	DL	PW
1906	Pit N	2	3	.400	6	2	0	0	28	21	11	0	2	9	8	1.93	139	.204	.281	11	.091	-0	95	1		0.3
	StL N	5	16	.238	25	20	17	1	191.2	193	85	0	7	43	73	2.72	97	.271	.319	73-1-0	.233	4	73	-5		0.0
	Year	7	19	.269	31	22	17	1	219.2	214	96	0	9	52	81	2.62	100	.263	.314	84-1-0	.214	3	75	-4		0.3
1907	StL N	15	19	.441	39	32	29-6	1	314	257	102	2	10	65	137	2.04	123	.223	.270	112-2-4	.179	1	65	17		2.4
1908	StL N	4	9	.308	22	15	9-1	0	141.1	148	77	1	2	50	34	3.06	77	.260	.322	54	.241	3*	70	-12		-0.8
1909	Cin N	1	3	.250	9	5	1	0	34.1	26	22	0	2	30	8	4.46	58	.217	.382	11	.273	2	156	-6		-0.5
	Bos A	5	2	.714	12	6	3	0	68	71	29	0	3	22	17	3.18	79	.273	.337	24-0-1	.125	-0	132	-3		-0.4
1910	Bos A	11	7	.611	27	25	16-1	1	183.1	162	75	5	5	53	81	3.19	80	.230	.289	68-2-3	.294	6	142	-6		-0.1
1911	Bos A	5	8	.385	25	18	6-1	0	131	134	70	4	4	42	57	3.37	97	.272	.334	47-1-2	.234	3	109	1		0.4
Total	6	48	67	.417	165	123	81-9	3	1091.2	1012	471	12	35	314	415	2.79	94	.246	.305	400-6-10	.220	18	99	-13		1.3

KARL, ANDY
Anton Andrew B4.8.1914 Mt.Vernon NY D4.8.1989 LaJolla CA BR/TR/6-1.5/175 d4.24 Col Manhattan

YEAR	TM LG	W	L	PCT	G	GS	CG-SHO	SV-BS	IP	H	R	HR	HB	BB-IB	SO	ERA	AERA	OAV	OOB	AB-HR-SH	AVG	PB	SUP	APR	DL	PW
1943	Bos A	1	1	.500	11	0	0	1	26	31	11	0	0	13	4	3.46	96	.310	.389	7	.286	0		0		0.1
	Phi N	1	2	.333	9	2	0	0	26.2	44	22	0	0	11	4	7.09	48	.383	.437	8	.250	1*	63	-10		-0.9
1944	Phi N	3	2	.600	38	0	0	2	89	76	32	1	1	21	26	2.33	155	.237	.287	15	.200	1*		11		0.7
1945	Phi N	8	8	.500	67	2	1	15	180.2	175	80	7	3	50	51	2.99	128	.253	.306	49	.143	-2	88	15		1.3
1946	Phi N	3	7	.300	39	0	0	5	65.1	84	37	6	1	22	15	4.96	69	.321	.375	10-0-2	.100	-0		-9		-1.5
1947	Bos N	2	3	.400	27	0	0	3	35	41	18	2	0	13	5	3.86	101	.318	.380	6	.167	-0	75	7		-0.3
Total	5	18	23	.439	191	4	1	26	422.2	451	200	16	5	130	107	3.51	104	.279	.334	95-0-2	.168	-0	75	7		-0.3

KARL, SCOTT
Randall Scott B8.9.1971 Fontana CA BL/TL/6-2/195(195-209) [MilA92 6/164] d5.4 Col Hawaii-Manoa

YEAR	TM LG	W	L	PCT	G	GS	CG-SHO	SV-BS	IP	H	R	HR	HB	BB-IB	SO	ERA	AERA	OAV	OOB	AB-HR-SH	AVG	PB	SUP	APR	DL	PW
1995	Mil A	6	7	.462	25	18	1	0-0	124	141	65	10	3	50-6	59	4.14	121	.288	.356	0	—	0	93	10		0.9
1996	Mil A	13	9	.591	32	32	3-1	0-0	207.1	220	124	29	11	72-0	121	4.86	107	.271	.336	0	—	0	108	6		0.5
1997	Mil A	10	13	.435	32	32	1	0-0	193.1	212	103	23	4	67-1	119	4.47	104	.279	.339	4	.000	0	79	5		0.5
1998	Mil N	10	11	.476	33	33	0	0-0	192.1	219	104	21	4	66-4	102	4.40	99	.290	.349	56-0-9	.071	-2*	87	-7		-0.3
1999	Mil N	11	11	.500	33	33	0	0-0	197.2	246	121	21	8	69-4	74	4.78	96	.312	.370	60-2-12	.183	3	88	-7		-0.2
2000	Col N	2	3	.400	17	9	0	0-0	65.2	95	56	14	3	33-3	29	7.68	76	.343	.401	14-0-2	.286	1	102	-10	20	-0.5
	Ana A	2	2	.500	6	4	0	0-0	21.2	31	21	2	1	12-0	9	6.65	78	.337	.413	0	—	0	82	-5		-0.8
Total	6	54	56	.491	178	161	5-1	0-0	1002	1164	594	120	33	369-18	513	4.81	100	.293	.356	134-2-23	.142	1	91	-3	20	0.1

KARNS, BILL
William Arthur B12.28.1875 Richmond IA D11.15.1941 Seattle WA BL/TL d8.14

YEAR	TM LG	W	L	PCT	G	GS	CG-SHO	SV-BS	IP	H	R	HR	HB	BB-IB	SO	ERA	AERA	OAV	OOB	AB-HR-SH	AVG	PB	SUP	APR	DL	PW
1901	Bal A	1	0	1.000	3	1	1	0	17	30	18	0	0	9	5	6.35	61	.380	.443	7-0-1	.143	-1*	175	-4		-0.3

KARNUTH, JASON
Jason Andre B5.15.1976 LaGrange IL BR/TR/6-2/190* [StLN97 8/254] d4.20 Col Illinois St.

YEAR	TM LG	W	L	PCT	G	GS	CG-SHO	SV-BS	IP	H	R	HR	HB	BB-IB	SO	ERA	AERA	OAV	OOB	AB-HR-SH	AVG	PB	SUP	APR	DL	PW
2001	StL N	0	0	—	4	0	0	0-0	5	6	1	1	1	4-0	1	1.80	240	.316	.458	0	—	0		1		0.1
2005	Det A	0	0	—	3	0	0	0-0	1.2	2	1	1	0	0-0	0	5.40	78	.286	.286	0	—	0		0		0.0
Total	2	0	0	—	7	0	0	0-0	6.2	8	2	1	1	4-0	1	2.70	159	.308	.419	0	—	0		1		0.1

KARP, RYAN
Ryan Jason B4.5.1970 Los Angeles CA BL/TL/6-4/217(205-220) [NYA92 9/242] d6.23 Col Florida International

YEAR	TM LG	W	L	PCT	G	GS	CG-SHO	SV-BS	IP	H	R	HR	HB	BB-IB	SO	ERA	AERA	OAV	OOB	AB-HR-SH	AVG	PB	SUP	APR	DL	PW
1995	Phi N	0	0	—	1	0	0	0-0	2	1	1	0	0	3-0	2	4.50	94	.143	.400	0	—	0		0		0.0
1997	Phi N	1	1	.500	15	1	0	0-1	15	12	12	2	2	12-0	18	5.40	78	.218	.348	0	—	0	131	-3		-0.4
Total	2	1	1	.500	16	1	0	0-1	17	13	13	2	2	12-0	20	5.29	80	.210	.355	0	—	0	131	-3		-0.4

KARPEL, HERB
Herbert "Lefty" B12.27.1917 Brooklyn NY D1.24.1995 San Diego CA BL/TL/5-9.5/180 d4.19

YEAR	TM LG	W	L	PCT	G	GS	CG-SHO	SV-BS	IP	H	R	HR	HB	BB-IB	SO	ERA	AERA	OAV	OOB	AB-HR-SH	AVG	PB	SUP	APR	DL	PW
1946	NY A	0	0	—	2	0	0	0	2	2	2	0	0	1	2	4 10.80	32	.500	.500	0	—			-1		-0.1

KARR, BENN
Benjamin Joyce "Baldy" B11.28.1893 Mt.Pleasant MS D12.8.1968 Memphis TN BL/TR/6-0/175 d4.20

YEAR	TM LG	W	L	PCT	G	GS	CG-SHO	SV-BS	IP	H	R	HR	HB	BB-IB	SO	ERA	AERA	OAV	OOB	AB-HR-SH	AVG	PB	SUP	APR	DL	PW
1920	Bos A	3	8	.273	26	2	0	1	91.2	109	55	1	1	24	21	4.81	76	.304	.349	75-1-1	.280	6*	54	-11		-0.7
1921	Bos A	8	7	.533	26	7	5	0	117.2	123	53	8	1	38	37	3.67	115	.283	.342	62-0-4	.258	1*	96	8		1.0
1922	Bos A	5	12	.294	41	13	7	1	183.1	212	115	10	5	45	41	4.47	92	.302	.348	98-0-1	.214	-1*	107	-11		-1.0
1925	Cle A	11	12	.478	32	24	12-1	0	197.2	248	127	8	6	80	41	4.78	92	.317	.355	92-1-7	.261	4*	98	-9		-0.4
1926	Cle A	5	6	.455	30	7	4	1	113.1	137	72	9	6	41	23	5.05	83	.291	.355	45-0-1	.222	2*	119	-11		-0.7
1927	Cle A	3	3	.500	22	5	1	2	76.2	92	49	5	1	32	17	4.60	90	.315	.385	20-0-1	.200	1	87	-6		-0.3
Total	6	35	48	.422	177	58	29-1	5	780.1	921	471	43	20	260	180	4.60	90	.303	.362	392-2-15	.245	12	101	-40		-2.1

KARSAY, STEVE
Stefan Andrew B3.24.1972 Flushing NY BR/TR/6-3/205(185-215) [TorA90 1/22] d8.17 [DL 1995 Oak A 160, 2003 NY A 183]

YEAR	TM LG	W	L	PCT	G	GS	CG-SHO	SV-BS	IP	H	R	HR	HB	BB-IB	SO	ERA	AERA	OAV	OOB	AB-HR-SH	AVG	PB	SUP	APR	DL	PW
1993	Oak A	3	3	.500	8	8	0	0-0	49	49	23	4	2	16-1	33	4.04	102	.258	.319	0	—	0	92	1		0.0
1994	Oak A	1	1	.500	4	4	1	0-0	28	26	8	1	1	8-0	15	2.57	175	.252	.310	0	—	0	123	7	108	0.4
1997	Oak A	3	12	.200	24	24	0	0-0	132.2	166	92	20	9	47-3	92	5.77	80	.304	.366	0	—	0*	82	-1	54	-1.7
1998	Cle A	0	2	.000	11	1	0	0-0	24.1	31	16	2	2	6-1	13	5.92	81	.310	.355	0	—	0	153	-2	52	-0.2
1999	†Cle A	10	2	.833	50	3	0	1-2	78.2	71	29	6	2	30-3	68	2.97	171	.247	.320	0	—	0		11		2.3
2000	Cle A	5	9	.357	72	0	0	20-9	76.2	79	33	5	3	25-4	66	3.76	133	.266	.327	1	.000	-0		16		0.8
2001	Cle A	1	0	1.000	31	0	0	1-0	43.1	29	6	1	0	8-2	44	1.25	368	.188	.227	0	—	0		11		0.6
	†Atl N	3	4	.429	43	0	0	7-4	44.2	44	21	4	1	17-8	39	3.43	133	.265	.332	2	.000	-0		12		1.5
2002	†NY A	6	4	.600	78	0	0	12-4	88.1	87	33	7	2	30-14	65	3.26	133	.258	.320	1	—	0		1	155	0.0
2004	NY A	0	0	—	7	0	0	0-0	6.2	5	3	2	0	2-0	4	2.70	170	.217	.259	0	—	0		-1		-0.1
2005	NY A	0	1	.000	6	0	0	0-0	6	10	5	0	0	2-1	5	6.00	73	.385	.414	0	—	0		-5		-0.3
	Tex A	0	1	.000	14	0	0	0-0	15.2	14	14	2	2	10-2	9	7.47	61	.366	.403	0	—	0		-5		-0.3

YEAR	TM LG	W	L	PCT	G	GS	CG-SHO	SV-BS	IP	H	R	HR	HB	BB-IB	SO	ERA	AERA	OAV	OOB	AB-HR-SH	AVG	PB	SUP	APR	DL	PW
	Year	0	1	.000	20	0	0	0-0	21.2	36	19	2	0	7-1	14	7.06	64	.371	.406	0	—	0		-6		-0.4
Total	10	31	39	.443	348	40	1	41-19	594	623	283	55	22	196-37	453	3.98	116	.271	.331	4	.000	-0	91	43	712	5.4

KASHIWADA, TAKASHI Takashi B5.14.1971 Tokyo, Japan BL/TL/5-11/165 d5.1

| 1997 | NY N | 3 | 1 | .750 | 35 | 0 | 0 | 0-2 | 31.1 | 35 | 15 | 4 | 3 | 18-0 | 19 | 4.31 | 93 | .289 | .389 | 1 | .000 | -0 | | 0 | | 0.0 |

KATOLL, JACK John "Big Jack" B6.24.1872 , Germany D6.18.1955 Woodstock IL BR/TR/5-11/195 d9.9

1898	Chi N	0	1	.000	2	1	1	0	11	8	4	0	0	1	3	0.82	438	.200	.220	4	.000	-1	59	3		0.1
1899	Chi N	1	1	.500	2	2	2	0	18	17	15	0	1	4	1	6.00	62	.250	.301	7	.000	-1	125	-4		-0.4
1901	Chi A	11	10	.524	27	25	19	0	208	231	126	3	11	53	59	2.81	124	.278	.330	80-1-1	.125	-4	107	8		0.3
1902	Chi A	0	0	—	1	0	0	0	.1	1	0	0	0	0	2	0.00	—	.250	.250	1	.000	-0				0.0
	Bal A	5	10	.333	15	13	13	0	123	175	106	5	2	32	25	4.02	94	.334	.334	57	.175	-0*	76	-12		-1.0
	Year	5	10	.333	16	13	13	0	124	176	106	5	2	32	27	3.99	94	.333	.374	58	.172	-0	76	-12		-1.0
Total	4	17	22	.436	47	41	35	0	361	432	251	8	14	90	90	3.32	109	.294	.341	149-1-1	.134	-6	97	-5		-1.0

KATZ, BOB Robert Clyde B1.30.1911 Lancaster PA D12.14.1962 St.Joseph MI BR/TR/5-11.5/190 d5.12

| 1944 | Cin N | 0 | 1 | .000 | 6 | 2 | 0 | 0 | 18.1 | 17 | 9 | 0 | 0 | 7 | 4 | 3.93 | 89 | .254 | .324 | 4 | .000 | -1 | 60 | -1 | | -0.1 |

KAUFMAN, CURT Curt Gerrard B7.19.1957 Omaha NE BR/TR/6-2/175* d9.10 Col Iowa St.

1982	NY A	1	0	1.000	8.2	9	5	2	0	0-0		6-1	1	5.19	78	.265	.375	0	—	0		-1		-0.1
1983	NY A	0	0	—	4	0	0	0-0	8.2	10	3	0	0	4-0	8	3.12	127	.303	.359	0	—	0		1		0.0
1984	Cal A	2	3	.400	29	1	0	1-0	69	68	37	13	0	20-4	41	4.57	88	.254	.302	0	—	0	136	-4		-0.2
Total	3	3	3	.500	40	1	0	1-0	86.1	87	45	15	0	30-5	50	4.48	89	.260	.316	0	—	0	136	-4		-0.3

KAUFMANN, TONY Anthony Charles B12.16.1900 Chicago IL D6.4.1982 Elgin IL BR/TR/5-11/165 d9.23 C4 ▲

1921	Chi N	1	0	1.000	2	1	1	1	13	12	6	0	0	3	6	4.15	92	.240	.283	5	.400	1	280	0		0.1
1922	Chi N	7	13	.350	37	14	4-1	3	153	161	81	15	5	57	45	4.06	103	.273	.343	45-1-5	.200	1*	100	3		0.4
1923	Chi N	14	10	.583	33	24	18-2	3	206.1	209	97	14	11	67	72	3.10	129	.264	.330	74-2-2	.216	3	106	16		2.0
1924	Chi N	16	11	.593	34	26	16-3	0	208.1	218	104	21	4	66	79	4.02	97	.272	.330	76-1-0	.316	6*	95	0		0.5
1925	Chi N	13	13	.500	31	23	14-2	2	196	221	107	9	7	77	49	4.50	96	.292	.363	78-2-1	.250	2*	103	14		1.4
1926	Chi N	9	7	.563	26	22	14-1	2	169.2	169	71	6	6	44	52	3.02	127	.262	.316	60-1-2	.250	2*	103	14		1.4
1927	Chi N	3	3	.500	9	6	3	0	53.1	75	44	8	4	19	21	6.41	60	.338	.400	16-1-2	.313	3	125	-15		-1.1
	Phi N	0	3	.000	5	5	1	0	18.2	37	25	2	0	8	4	10.61	39	.425	.474	7-1-0	.143	0*	87	-13		-1.5
	StL N	0	0	—	1	0	0	0	0.1	4	3	0	0	1	0	81.00	5	1.000	1.000	0	—	0*		-3		-0.1
	Year	3	6	.333	15	11	4	0	72.1	116	72	10	4	28	25	7.84	50	.371	.429	23-2-2	.261	3	108	-29		-2.7
1928	StL N	0	0	—	4	1	0	0	4.2	8	5	1	1	4	2	9.64	41	.444	.565	0	—	0*	85	-3		-0.1
1930	StL N	0	1	.000	2	1	0	0	10.1	15	9	2	0	4	2	7.84	64	.357	.413	3	.333	0	139	-3		-0.2
1931	StL N	1	1	.500	15	1	0	1	49	65	34	3	1	17	13	6.06	65	.319	.374	18	.111	-1*	131	-10		-0.6
1935	StL N	0	0	—	3	0	0	0	3.2	4	1	0	0	1	0	2.45	167	.286	.333	0	—	0*		1		0.0
Total	11	64	62	.508	202	124	71-9	12	1086.1	1198	587	81	39	368	345	4.18	97	.284	.347	382-9-12	.236	17	102	-14		0.8

KAYE, JUSTIN Justin Malcolm B6.9.1976 Fort Lauderdale FL BR/TR/6-4/195 [SeaA95 19/510] d5.9

| 2002 | Sea A | 0 | 0 | — | 3 | 0 | 0 | 0-0 | 3 | 6 | 4 | 0 | 0 | 1-0 | 1 | 12.00 | 36 | .429 | .467 | 0 | — | 0 | | -3 | | -0.1 |

KAZMIR, SCOTT Scott Edward B1.24.1984 Houston TX BL/TL/6-0/170* [NYN02 1/15] d8.23

2004	TB A	2	3	.400	8	7	0	0-0	33.1	33	22	4	2	21-0	41	5.67	82	.256	.368	0	—	0	94	-3		-0.4
2005	TB A	10	9	.526	32	32	0	0-0	186	172	90	12	10	100-3	174	3.77	116	.248	.347	1	.000	-0	89	10		0.9
Total	2	12	12	.500	40	39	0	0-0	219.1	205	112	16	12	121-3	215	4.06	109	.249	.351	1	.000	0	91	7		0.5

KEAGLE, GREG Gregory Charles B6.28.1971 Corning NY BR/TR/6-1/185* [SDN93 6/170] d4.1 Col Florida International

1996	Det A	3	6	.333	26	6	0	0-0	87.2	104	76	13	9	68-5	70	7.39	69	.298	.418	0	—	0	79	-21	45	-1.7
1997	Det A	3	5	.375	11	10	0	0-0	45.1	58	33	9	5	18-0	33	6.55	70	.309	.382	1	.000	-0	90	-8		-1.2
1998	Det A	0	5	.000	9	7	0	0-0	38.2	46	26	5	4	20-0	25	5.59	85	.295	.389	0	—	0	84	-3		-0.4
Total	3	6	16	.273	46	23	0	0-0	171.2	208	135	27	18	106-5	128	6.76	72	.300	.402	1	.000	-0	83	-32	45	-3.3

KEALEY, STEVE Steven William B5.13.1947 Torrance CA BR/TR/6-0/185* d9.9 Col El Camino (CA) JC

1968	Cal A	0	1	.000	6	0	0	0	10	10	3	0	0	5-2	4	2.70	108	.256	.341	0	—	0		0		0.0
1969	Cal A	2	0	1.000	15	3	1	1-1	0-0	36.2	48	18	4	1	13-1	17	3.93	89	.322	.380	9	.000	-1	110	-2		-0.2
1970	Cal A	1	0	1.000	17	0	0	1-0	21.2	19	11	2	0	6-2	14	4.15	87	.260	.305	4	.250	0		-1		-0.1
1971	Chi A	2	2	.500	54	1	0	6-0	77.1	69	40	10	0	26-6	50	3.84	93	.239	.299	10-1-1	.200	1	101	-3		-0.1
1972	Chi A	3	2	.600	40	0	0	4-2	57.1	50	21	4	0	12-1	37	3.30	95	.234	.273	3	—	0		0		-0.1
1973	Chi A	0	0	—	7	0	0	0	11.1	23	22	2	0	7-1	4	15.09	26	.418	.469	0	—	0		-14	73	-0.7
Total	6	8	5	.615	139	4	1-1	11-2	214.1	219	115	22	1	69-13	126	4.28	80	.267	.322	26-1-1	.115	0	110	-20	73	-1.2

KEAS, ED Edward James B2.2.1863 Dubuque IA D1.12.1940 Dubuque IA d8.25

| 1888 | Cle AA | 3 | 3 | .500 | 6 | 6 | 6 | 0 | 51 | 53 | 28 | 1 | 1 | 12 | 18 | 2.29 | 135 | .259 | .303 | 23 | .087 | -2 | 106 | 3 | | 0.1 |

KEATING, RAY Raymond Herbert B7.21.1891 Bridgeport CT D12.28.1963 Sacramento CA BR/TR/5-11/185 d9.12 Col Niagara

1912	NY A	0	3	.000	6	5	3	0	35.2	36	27	0	1	18	21	5.80	62	.265	.355	16	.375	1	119	-6		-0.3
1913	NY A	6	12	.333	28	21	9-2	0	151.1	147	77	3	2	51	83	3.21	93	.256	.318	43-0-3	.070	-3	80	-5		-1.0
1914	NY A	8	11	.421	34	25	14	0	210	198	94	1	5	67	109	2.96	93	.253	.316	71-0-3	.169	-0*	102	-8		-0.5
1915	NY A	3	6	.333	11	10	8-1	0	79.1	66	41	3	3	45	37	3.63	81	.238	.337	26	.154	-1	109	-7		-0.7
1916	NY A	5	6	.455	14	11	6	0	91	91	42	4	4	37	35	3.07	94	.272	.349	29-0-1	.241	1	116	-3		-0.1
1918	NY A	2	2	.500	15	6	1	0	48.1	39	27	0	2	30	16	3.91	72	.238	.362	16-0-1	.188	0	84	-6		-0.5
1919	Bos N	7	11	.389	22	14	9-1	0	136	129	61	2	2	45	48	2.98	96	.261	.325	46-1-3	.152	-1*	78	-4		-0.5
Total	7	31	51	.378	130	92	50-4	0	751.2	706	369	13	17	293	349	3.29	88	.254	.329	247-1-11	.170	-2	97	-39		-3.6

KEATING, BOB Robert M. B9.22.1862 Springfield MA D1.19.1922 Springfield MA BL/TL/6-4/190 d8.27

| 1887 | Bal AA | 0 | 1 | .000 | 1 | 1 | 1 | 0 | 9 | 6 | 11 | 0 | | | 0 | 11.00 | 37 | .372 | .449 | 4 | .250 | -0 | 31 | -7 | | -0.4 |

KECK, CACTUS Frank Joseph B1.13.1899 St.Louis MO D2.6.1981 Kirkwood MO BR/TR/5-11/170 d5.26

1922	Cin N	7	6	.538	27	15	5-1	1	131	138	71	4	5	29	27	3.37	119	.276	.322	44-0-3	.159	-1	105	5		0.1
1923	Cin N	3	6	.333	35	6	1	2	87	84	49	5	3	32	16	3.72	104	.254	.325	17-0-1	.059	-1	106	0		-0.1
Total	2	10	12	.455	62	21	6-1	3	218	222	120	9	8	61	43	3.51	112	.267	.323	61-0-4	.131	-2	106	5		-0.1

KEEFE, DAVE David Edwin B1.9.1897 Williston VT D2.4.1978 Kansas City MO BL/TR/5-9/165 d4.21 Mil 1918 C10

1917	Phi A	1	0	1.000	3	0	0	0	5	4	1	0	0	4	1	1.80	153	.278	.409	1	.000	-0				-0.1
1919	Phi A	0	1	.000	1	1	1	0	9	8	4	0	0	3	5	4.00	86	.242	.306	3	.000	-0	46	0		-0.1
1920	Phi A	6	7	.462	31	13	7-1	0	130.1	129	60	2	6	30	41	2.97	136	.262	.313	40-0-1	.250	-0*	58	14		1.3
1921	Phi A	2	9	.182	44	12	4	1	173	214	126	19	5	64	-68	4.68	95	.311	.374	57	.175	-3	94	-10		-0.9
1922	Cle A	0	0	—	18	1	0	0	36.1	47	30	2	0	12	11	6.19	65	.333	.386	6	.333	1	106	-9		-0.4
Total	5	9	17	.346	97	27	12-1	1	353.2	403	224	23	11	113	126	4.15	101	.294	.352	107-0-1	.206	-3	76	-5		-0.2

KEEFE, GEORGE George W. B1.7.1867 Washington DC D8.24.1935 Washington DC BL/TL/5-9/168 d7.30

1886	Was N	0	3	.000	4	4	4	0	31.1	28	22	0		15	5	5.17	62	.233	.319	14	.000	-2	109	-5		-0.6
1887	Was N	1	1	.000	1	1	1	0	8	16	20	1	2	4	0	9.00	45	.364	.440	3	.000	-1	16	-7		-0.5
1888	Was N	6	7	.462	13	13	13-1	0	114	87	55	2	4	43	52	2.84	98	.206	.286	42	.214	-1	70	-1		0.2
1889	Was N	8	18	.308	30	27	24	0	230	266	182	6	4	143	90	5.13	77	.281	.378	98	.163	-2	84	-23		-2.2
1890	Buf P	6	16	.273	25	22	22	0	196	280	229	11	5	138	55	6.52	63	.321	.417	79	.203	1	87	-58		-4.2
1891	Was AA	0	3	.000	5	4	4	1	37	44	42	0	1	17	11	2.68	140	.286	.360	14	.143	-0	62	-3		-0.2
Total	6	20	48	.294	78	71	68-1	1	721	550	20	16	360	213	5.05	74	.282	.374	250	.172	-3	82	-97		-7.5

KEEFE, JOHN John Thomas B5.5.1867 Fitchburg MA D8.9.1937 Fitchburg MA TL d4.28 Col Holy Cross

| 1890 | Syr AA | 17 | 24 | .415 | 43 | 41 | 36-2 | 0 | 352.1 | 355 | 234 | 9 | 25 | 148 | 120 | 4.32 | 82 | .254 | .336 | 157 | .191 | -5 | 90 | -34 | | -3.4 |

KEEFE, BOBBY Robert Francis B6.16.1882 Folsom CA D12.6.1964 Sacramento CA BR/TR/5-11/155 d4.15 Col Santa Clara

| 1907 | NY A | 3 | 5 | .375 | 19 | 3 | 0 | 3 | 57.2 | 60 | 18 | 1 | 1 | 20 | 20 | 2.50 | 112 | .270 | .333 | 19 | .053 | -2 | 32 | 3 | | 0.4 |
| 1911 | Cin N | 12 | 13 | .480 | 39 | 26 | 15 | 3 | 234.1 | 196 | 88 | 2 | 8 | 76 | 105 | 2.69 | 123 | .229 | .294 | 70-0-5 | .086 | -2 | 96 | 19 | | 1.4 |

YEAR	TM LG	W	L	PCT	G	GS	CG-SHO	SV-BS	IP	H	R	HR	HB	BB-IB	SO	ERA	AERA	OAV	OOB	AB-HR-SH	AVG	PB	SUP	APR	DL	PW
1912	Cin N	1	3	.250	17	6	0	2	68.2	78	52	0	4	33	29	5.24	64	.289	.375	18-0-2	.167	-1	65	-14		-0.8
Total	3	16	21	.432	75	35	15	8	360.2	334	158	8	8	129	154	3.14	103	.248	.317	107-0-7	.093	-5	86	8		1.0

KEEFE, TIM   Timothy John "Smiling Tim","Sir Timothy"   B1.1.1857 Cambridge MA   D4.23.1933 Cambridge MA   BR/TR/5-10.5/185   d8.6   U3   HF1964

YEAR	TM LG	W	L	PCT	G	GS	CG-SHO	SV-BS	IP	H	R	HR	HB	BB-IB	SO	ERA	AERA	OAV	OOB	AB-HR-SH	AVG	PB	SUP	APR	DL	PW
1880	Tro N	6	6	.500	12	12	12	0	105	68	27	0		16	39	**0.86**	294	.178	**.212**	43	.233	-0	67	16		1.8
1881	Tro N	18	27	.400	45	45	45-4	0	403	434	241	4		83	103	3.24	91	.270	.305	152	.230	4*	87	-12		-0.7
1882	Tro N	17	26	.395	43	42	41-1	0	376	367	221	4		78	111	2.49	114	.243	.280	189-1	.228	5*	89	11		1.8
1883	NY AA	41	27	.603	**68**	**68**	**68-5**	0	**619**	488	244	6		108	**359**	2.41	138	**.203**	**.237**	259	.220	4*	83	61		6.0
1884	†NY AA	37	17	.685	58	58	56-4	0	483	380	196	5	15	71	334	2.25	138	**.204**	.239	210-3	.238	12*	112	46		5.5
1885	NY N	32	13	.711	46	46	45-7	0	400	300	154	6		102	227	**1.58**	**170**	.203	.255	166	.163	-1*	123	46		4.5
1886	NY N	**42**	20	.677	**64**	**64**	**62-2**	0	**535**	479	250	9		102	297	2.56	125	.231	.267	205-1	.171	1	119	39		3.8
1887	NY N	35	19	.648	56	56	54-2	0	476.2	428	260	11	11	108	189	3.12	121	**.230**	**.276**	191-2	.220	8	108	**53**		4.7
1888	†NY N	**35**	12	**.745**	51	51	48-**8**	0	434.1	317	140	5	12	90	**335**	**1.74**	**157**	**.196**	.243	181-2	.127	-6	109	24		1.9
1889	†NY N	28	13	.683	47	45	39-3	1	364	319	216	9	18	151	225	3.36	117	**.228**	.312	149	.154	-4	109	24		2.2
1890	NY P	17	11	.607	30	30	23-1	0	229	225	137	6	8	89	89	3.38	134	.246	.318	92-2	.109	-5	105	28		2.2
1891	NY N	2	5	.286	8	7	4	0	55	70	57	1	4	27	30	5.24	61	.299	.381	21	.095	-1	117	-13		-1.3
	Phi N	3	6	.333	11	10	9	1	78.1	82	55	2	4	30	34	3.91	87	.259	.331	29	.172	0	79	-5		-1.8
	Year	5	11	.313	19	17	13	1	133.1	152	112	3	8	57	64	4.45	75	.276	.353	50	.140	-1	94	-15		-1.8
1892	Phi N	19	16	.543	39	38	31-2	0	313.1	279	142	4	13	98	136	2.36	138	.229	.293	117-1	.085	-7	98	26		-0.1
1893	Phi N	10	7	.588	22	22	17	0	178	202	131	3	13	80	56	4.40	104	.277	.359	79	.228	0	133	-1		0.1
Total	14	342	225	.603	600	594	554-39	2	5049.2	4438	2471	75	98	1233	2564	2.63	125	.226	.275	2083-12	.187	11	104	358		35.6

KEEGAN, ED   Edward Charles   B7.8.1939 Camden NJ   BR/TR/6-3/165*   d8.24

YEAR	TM LG	W	L	PCT	G	GS	CG-SHO	SV-BS	IP	H	R	HR	HB	BB-IB	SO	ERA	AERA	OAV	OOB	AB-HR-SH	AVG	PB	SUP	APR	DL	PW
1959	Phi N	0	3	.000	3	3	0	0	9	19	18	2	1	13-0	3	18.00	23	.432	.569	3	.000	-0	44	-12		-1.8
1961	KC A	0	0	—	6	0	0	1	6	6	5	0	0	5-0	3	4.50	93	.261	.393	0	—	0		-1		0.0
1962	Phi N	0	0	—	4	0	0	0	8	6	2	1	1	5-0	5	2.25	172	.214	.353	0	—	0*		2		0.1
Total	3	0	3	.000	13	3	0	1	23	31	25	3	2	23-0	11	9.00	45	.326	.467	3	.000	-0	44	-11		-1.7

KEEGAN, BOB   Robert Charles "Smiley"   B8.4.1920 Rochester NY   D6.20.2001 Rochester NY   BR/TR/6-2.5/207*   d5.24   Col Bucknell

YEAR	TM LG	W	L	PCT	G	GS	CG-SHO	SV-BS	IP	H	R	HR	HB	BB-IB	SO	ERA	AERA	OAV	OOB	AB-HR-SH	AVG	PB	SUP	APR	DL	PW
1953	Chi A	7	5	.583	22	11	4-2	1	98.2	80	34	4	2	33	32	2.74	147	.223	.293	28-0-2	.321	2	96	14	38	1.8
1954	Chi A★	16	9	.640	31	27	14-2	2	209.2	211	84	16	1	82	61	3.09	121	.266	.334	75-0-1	.120	-2*	114	13	31	1.2
1955	Chi A	5	2	.286	18	11	1	0	58.2	83	39	6	1	28-1	29	5.83	68	.336	.400	18-0-2	.333	2	102	-11		-1.0
1956	Chi A	5	7	.417	24	16	4	0	105.1	119	56	15	2	35-2	32	3.93	104	.286	.342	32-0-4	.125	-1	100	0		-0.2
1957	Chi A	10	8	.556	30	20	6-2	2	142.2	131	62	22	2	37-2	36	3.53	106	.243	.292	39-0-10	.103	-1	106	3		0.1
1958	Chi A	0	2	.000	14	2	0	0	29.2	44	25	9	0	18-4	8	6.07	60	.358	.437	4-0-1	.000	-1	124	-10		-0.6
Total	6	40	36	.526	135	87	29-6	5	644.2	668	300	70	8	233-9	198	3.66	105	.270	.332	196-0-20	.163	-2	106	9	69	1.3

KEELEY, BURT   Burton Elwood "Speed"   B11.2.1879 Wilmington IL   D5.3.1952 Ely MN   BR/TR/5-9/170   d4.18   Col Notre Dame

YEAR	TM LG	W	L	PCT	G	GS	CG-SHO	SV-BS	IP	H	R	HR	HB	BB-IB	SO	ERA	AERA	OAV	OOB	AB-HR-SH	AVG	PB	SUP	APR	DL	PW
1908	Was A	6	11	.353	28	15	12-1	1	169	173	87	3	4	48	68	2.98	77	.259	.313	49-0-6	.102	-3*	102	-15		-1.8
1909	Was A	0	0	—	2	0	0	0	7	12	13	0	1	1	0	11.57	21	.364	.400	2	.500	0		-7		-0.3
Total	2	6	11	.353	30	15	12-1	1	176	185	100	3	5	49	68	3.32	69	.264	.317	51-0-6	.118	-3	102	-22		-2.1

KEEN, VIC   Howard Victor   B3.16.1899 Bel Air MD   D12.10.1976 Salisbury MD   BR/TR/5-9/165   d8.13   Col Maryland-Baltimore Co.

YEAR	TM LG	W	L	PCT	G	GS	CG-SHO	SV-BS	IP	H	R	HR	HB	BB-IB	SO	ERA	AERA	OAV	OOB	AB-HR-SH	AVG	PB	SUP	APR	DL	PW
1918	Phi A	0	1	.000	2	1	1	0	8	9	3	1	0	1	1	3.38	87	.300	.323	1-0-1	.000	-0	77	0		0.0
1921	Chi N	0	3	.000	5	4	1	0	25	29	17	0	1	9	9	4.68	82	.319	.386	5-0-1	.000	-0	59	-3		-0.1
1922	Chi N	1	2	.333	7	2	2	1	34.2	36	20	4	1	10	11	3.89	108	.275	.331	12-0-1	.333	1	78	0		0.1
1923	Chi N	12	8	.600	35	17	10	1	177	169	70	8	5	57	46	3.00	133	.255	.319	53-0-8	.151	-3	85	20		1.7
1924	Chi N	15	14	.517	40	28	15	3	234.2	242	112	17	4	80	75	3.80	103	.272	.335	77-0-4	.156	-4	89	5		-1.2
1925	Chi N	2	6	.250	30	8	1	1	83.1	125	61	8	0	41	19	6.26	69	.359	.427	25-0-1	.240	-0	115	-15		-1.7
1926	†StL N	10	9	.526	26	21	12-1	0	152	179	89	15	1	42	29	4.56	86	.295	.342	53-0-2	.057	-6	110	-10		-1.7
1927	StL N	2	1	.667	21	0	0	0	33.2	39	21	3	2	8	12	4.81	82	.293	.343	4	.250	0		-3		-1.7
Total	8	42	44	.488	165	81	41-1	6	748.1	828	393	56	14	248	202	4.11	97	.287	.346	230-0-18	.148	-12	94	-6		-1.7

KEENAN, KID   Harry Leon   B1875 Louisville KY   D6.11.1903 Covington KY   TR/5-2/?   d8.11

YEAR	TM LG	W	L	PCT	G	GS	CG-SHO	SV-BS	IP	H	R	HR	HB	BB-IB	SO	ERA	AERA	OAV	OOB	AB-HR-SH	AVG	PB	SUP	APR	DL	PW
1891	Cin AA	0	1	.000	1	1	1	0	8	6	9	0	0	4	5	0.00	—	.200	.314	4	.500	0	46	1		0.2

KEENAN, JIM   James William   B2.10.1858 New Haven CT   D9.21.1926 Cincinnati OH   BR/TR/5-10/186   d5.17.1875 ▲

YEAR	TM LG	W	L	PCT	G	GS	CG-SHO	SV-BS	IP	H	R	HR	HB	BB-IB	SO	ERA	AERA	OAV	OOB	AB-HR-SH	AVG	PB	SUP	APR	DL	PW
1884	Ind AA	0	0	—	1	0	0	0	3	2	1	0	0	0	0	3.00	110	.182	.182	249-3	.293	0*		0		0.0
1885	Cin AA	0	0	—	1	0	0	0	8	7	2	0	0	1	0	1.13	290	.233	.258	132-1	.265	0*		2		0.1
1886	Cin AA	0	1	.000	2	0	0	0	8	8	5	0	0	3	2	3.38	104	.258	.324	148-3	.270	0*		0		0.0
Total	3	0	1	.000	4	0	0	0	19	17	8	0	0	4	2	2.37	142	.236	.276	529-7	.280	1		2		0.1

KEENAN, JIMMIE   James William "Sparkplug"   B5.25.1898 Avon NY   D6.5.1980 Seminole FL   BL/TL/5-7/155   d9.9

YEAR	TM LG	W	L	PCT	G	GS	CG-SHO	SV-BS	IP	H	R	HR	HB	BB-IB	SO	ERA	AERA	OAV	OOB	AB-HR-SH	AVG	PB	SUP	APR	DL	PW
1920	Phi N	0	0	—	1	0	0	0	3	3	1	0	1	2	2	3.00	114	.333	.400	1	.000	-0		0		0.0
1921	Phi N	1	2	.333	15	2	0	0	32.1	48	31	3	1	15	9	6.68	63	.364	.432	9	.000	-1	29	-7		-0.7
Total	2	1	2	.333	16	2	0	0	35.1	51	32	3	1	16	9	6.37	65	.362	.430	10	.000	-2	29	-7		-0.7

KEENER, JEFF   Jeffrey Bruce   B1.14.1959 Pana IL   BL/TR/6-0/170*   [StLN81 7/163]   d6.8   Col Kentucky

YEAR	TM LG	W	L	PCT	G	GS	CG-SHO	SV-BS	IP	H	R	HR	HB	BB-IB	SO	ERA	AERA	OAV	OOB	AB-HR-SH	AVG	PB	SUP	APR	DL	PW
1982	StL N	1	1	.500	19	0	0	0-0	22.1	19	8	1	0	19-4	25	1.61	228	.235	.373	0	—	0		3		0.3
1983	StL N	0	0	—	4	0	0	0-0	4.1	6	4	0	1	1-0	4	8.31	44	.333	.381	0	—	0		-2		-0.1
Total	2	1	1	.500	23	0	0	0-0	26.2	25	12	1	1	20-4	29	2.70	136	.253	.374	0	—	0		1		0.2

KEENER, JOE   Joseph Donald   B4.21.1953 San Pedro CA   BR/TR/6-4/200   d9.18   Col Antelope Valley (CA) JC

YEAR	TM LG	W	L	PCT	G	GS	CG-SHO	SV-BS	IP	H	R	HR	HB	BB-IB	SO	ERA	AERA	OAV	OOB	AB-HR-SH	AVG	PB	SUP	APR	DL	PW
1976	Mon N	0	1	.000	2	2	0	0-0	4.1	7	7	0	1	8-0	1	10.38	36	.389	.593	1-0-1	.000	-0	94	-3		-0.6

KEENER, HARRY   Joshua Harry "Beans"   B9.1869 Easton PA   D3.5.1912 Easton PA   TR   d6.27

YEAR	TM LG	W	L	PCT	G	GS	CG-SHO	SV-BS	IP	H	R	HR	HB	BB-IB	SO	ERA	AERA	OAV	OOB	AB-HR-SH	AVG	PB	SUP	APR	DL	PW
1896	Phi N	3	11	.214	16	13	11	0	113.1	144	102	5	9	39	28	5.88	73	.307	.371	51	.314	2	94	-20		-1.6

KEETON, RICKEY   Rickey   B3.18.1957 Cincinnati OH   BR/TR/6-2/190*   [MilA78 3/60]   d5.27   Col Southern Illinois

YEAR	TM LG	W	L	PCT	G	GS	CG-SHO	SV-BS	IP	H	R	HR	HB	BB-IB	SO	ERA	AERA	OAV	OOB	AB-HR-SH	AVG	PB	SUP	APR	DL	PW
1980	Mil A	2	2	.500	7	4	0	0-0	28.1	35	15	4	0	9-0	8	4.76	82	.307	.352	0	—	0	96	-2		-0.3
1981	Mil A	1	0	1.000	17	0	0	0-0	35.1	47	21	4	0	11-4	9	5.09	68	.329	.374	0	—	0		-7		-0.2
Total	2	3	2	.600	24	4	0	0-0	63.2	82	36	8	0	20-4	17	4.95	74	.319	.364	0	—	0	96	-9		-0.5

KEFFER, FRANK   Charles Franklin   B7.1861 Bradford PA   d4.19

YEAR	TM LG	W	L	PCT	G	GS	CG-SHO	SV-BS	IP	H	R	HR	HB	BB-IB	SO	ERA	AERA	OAV	OOB	AB-HR-SH	AVG	PB	SUP	APR	DL	PW
1890	Syr AA	1	1	.500	2	1	1	0	16	15	13	0	0	9	4	5.63	63	.242	.338	7	.143	-1	76	-4		0.0

KEHN, CHET   Chester Lawrence   B10.30.1921 San Diego CA   D4.5.1984 San Diego CA   BR/TR/5-11/168   d4.30   Mil 1943-45

YEAR	TM LG	W	L	PCT	G	GS	CG-SHO	SV-BS	IP	H	R	HR	HB	BB-IB	SO	ERA	AERA	OAV	OOB	AB-HR-SH	AVG	PB	SUP	APR	DL	PW
1942	Bro N	0	0	—	3	1	0	0	7.2	8	6	2	0	4	3	7.04	46	.267	.353	2	1.000	1	283	-3		0.0

KEIFER, KATSY   Sherman Carl   B9.3.1891 California PA   D2.19.1927 Outwood KY   BB/TL   d10.8

YEAR	TM LG	W	L	PCT	G	GS	CG-SHO	SV-BS	IP	H	R	HR	HB	BB-IB	SO	ERA	AERA	OAV	OOB	AB-HR-SH	AVG	PB	SUP	APR	DL	PW
1914	Ind F	0	1	.000	1	1	1	0	9	6	2	0	0	2	2	2.00	156	.194	.242	3	.333	0	88	1		0.2

KEISLER, RANDY   Randy Dean   B2.24.1976 Richards TX   BL/TL/6-3/190*   [NYA98 2/67]   d9.10   Col Louisiana St.   [DL 2002 NY A 183]

YEAR	TM LG	W	L	PCT	G	GS	CG-SHO	SV-BS	IP	H	R	HR	HB	BB-IB	SO	ERA	AERA	OAV	OOB	AB-HR-SH	AVG	PB	SUP	APR	DL	PW
2000	NY A	1	0	1.000	4	1	0	0-0	10.2	16	14	1	0	8-0	6	11.81	40	.364	.462	0	—	0	118	-8		-0.6
2001	NY A	1	2	.333	10	10	0	0-0	50.2	52	36	12	0	34-0	36	6.40	71	.259	.364	2	.000	-0	142	-9		-0.5
2003	SD N	0	1	.000	2	2	0	0-0	6	7	9	3	1	7-0	5	12.00	33	.292	.455	2	.000	-0*	117	-6		-0.5
2005	Cin N	2	1	.667	24	4	0	0-0	56	64	45	10	1	28-2	43	6.27	67	.277	.356	15-1-0	.267	2	122	-15	25	-0.6
Total	4	4	4	.500	40	17	0	0-0	123.1	139	104	26	2	77-2	90	7.01	62	.278	.375	19-1-0	.211	2	134	-38	208	-2.2

KEKICH, MIKE   Michael Dennis   B4.2.1945 San Diego CA   BR/TL/6-1/200*   d6.9

YEAR	TM LG	W	L	PCT	G	GS	CG-SHO	SV-BS	IP	H	R	HR	HB	BB-IB	SO	ERA	AERA	OAV	OOB	AB-HR-SH	AVG	PB	SUP	APR	DL	PW
1965	LA N	0	1	.000	5	1	0	0	10.1	10	12	2	0	13-0	9	9.58	34	.263	.451	2-0-1	.000	-0	80	-8		-1.0
1968	LA N	2	10	.167	25	20	1-1	0	115	116	54	9	1	46-0	84	3.91	71	.267	.336	37-0-2	.081	-2	78	-14		-1.0
1969	NY A	4	6	.400	28	13	1	1	105	91	58	11	2	49-5	66	4.54	78	.236	.323	27-0-3	.111	-1	72	-11		-1.3
1970	NY A	6	3	.667	26	14	1	0	98.2	103	59	12	1	55-3	63	4.83	74	.267	.358	32-0-2	.094	-1	109	-13	22	-1.1
1971	NY A	10	9	.526	37	24	3	0	170.1	167	77	13	4	82-11	78	3.70	81	.263	.343	59-0-6	.136	-1	106	-12		-1.5
1972	NY A	10	13	.435	29	28	2	0	175.1	172	77	13	4	76-5	78	4.07	81	.257	.341	52-0-8	.154	-0	116	-16		-1.5
1973	NY A	1	1	.500	5	4	0	0	14.2	20	15	1	2	14-0	4	9.20	40	.351	.486	0	—	0*	144	-8		-1.4
	Cle A	1	4	.200	16	6	0	0-0	49.2	73	47	6	0	35-0	26	7.02	56	.349	.437	0	—	0*	83	-18		-1.5
	Year	2	5	.286	21	10	0	0-0	64.2	93	62	7	2	49-0	30	7.52	52	.350	.449	0	—	0	105	-26		-1.8

YEAR	TM LG	W	L	PCT	G	GS	CG-SHO	SV-BS	IP	H	R	HR	HB	BB-IB	SO	ERA	AERA	OAV	OOB	AB-HR-SH	AVG	PB	SUP	APR	DL	PW
1975	Tex A	0	0	—	23	0	0	2-2	31.1	33	16	2	0	21-2	19	3.73	101	.282	.388	0	—	0	0	0		0.0
1977	Sea A	5	4	.556	41	2	0	3-1	90	90	58	11	3	51-3	55	5.60	74	.265	.363	0	—	0	22	-12	24	-1.2
Total	9	39	51	.433	235	112	8-1	6-3	860.2	875	485	80	17	442-29	497	4.59	73	.268	.355	209-0-22	.120	-5	94-112	46		-11.8

KELB, GEORGE George Francis "Pugger","Lefty" B7.17.1870 Toledo OH D10.20.1936 Toledo OH BL/TL d4.17

| 1898 | Cle N | 0 | 1 | .000 | 3 | 1 | 1 | 0 | 16.1 | 23 | 17 | 0 | 4 | 1 | 1 | 8.27 | 82 | .329 | .373 | 5 | .200 | -0 | 20 | -3 | | -0.2 |

KELLEHER, HAL Harold Joseph B6.24.1913 Philadelphia PA D8.27.1989 Cape May Court House NJ BR/TR/6-0/165 d9.17

1935	Phi N	2	0	1.000	3	3	2-1	0	25	26	7	0	1	12	12	1.80	252	.260	.345	8	.375	1	56	6		0.6
1936	Phi N	0	5	.000	14	4	1	0	44	60	38	2	3	29	13	5.32	85	.331	.432	12	.167	-0	33	-5		-0.6
1937	Phi N	2	4	.333	27	2	1	0	58.1	72	51	3	7	31	25	6.63	65	.308	.404	17	.176	-0*	20	-15		-1.3
1938	Phi N	0	0	—	6	0	0	0	7.1	16	15	0	0	9	4	18.41	21	.432	.543	2	.500	0		-11		-0.5
Total	4	4	9	.308	50	9	4-1	0	134.2	174	111	5	11	81	49	5.95	74	.315	.413	39	.231	0	39	-25		-1.8

KELLER, KRIS Kristopher Shane B3.1.1978 Williamsport PA BR/TR/6-2/225 [DetA96 4/101] d5.24 [DL 2002 Atl N 4]

| 2002 | Det A | 0 | 0 | — | 1 | 0 | 0 | 0-0 | 1 | 2 | 3 | 1 | 0 | 3-0 | 1 | 27.00 | 16 | .400 | .625 | 0 | | 0 | | -2 | 25 | -0.1 |

KELLER, RON Ronald Lee B6.3.1943 Indianapolis IN BR/TR/6-2/200* [MinA65 8/143] d7.9 Mil 1968 Col Indiana

1966	Min A	0	0	—	2	0	0	0	5.1	7	4	1	0	1-0	1	5.06	71	.318	.348	1	.000	-0*		-1		-0.1
1968	Min A	0	1	.000	7	1	0	0	16	18	6	2	1	4-1	11	2.81	110	.305	.354	1	.000	-0*	28	0		0.0
Total	2	0	1	.000	9	1	0	0	21.1	25	10	3	1	5-1	12	3.38	95	.309	.352	2	.000	-0	28	-1		-0.1

KELLETT, AL Alfred Henry B10.30.1901 Red Bank NJ D7.14.1960 New York NY BR/TR/6-3/200 d6.29 Col Columbia

1923	Phi A	0	1	.000	5	0	0	0	10	11	9	0	0	8	1	6.30	65	.282	.404	3	.333	0		-3		-0.2
1924	Bos A	0	0	—	1	0	0	0	0	0	2	0	0	2	0	∞	—	1.000	1.000	0	—	0		-2		-0.2
Total	2	0	1	.000	6	0	0	0	10	11	11	0	0	10	1	8.10	51	.282	.429	3	.333	0		-5		-0.4

KELLEY, HARRY Harry Leroy B2.13.1906 Parkin AR D3.23.1958 Parkin AR BR/TR/5-9.5/170 d4.16

1925	Was A	1	1	.500	6	1	0	0	16	30	23	0	0	12	7	9.00	47	.405	.488	4	.000	-1	40	-10		-1.0
1926	Was A	0	0	—	7	1	0	0	10	17	10	0	1	8	6	8.10	48	.405	.510	1	.000	-0	131	-5		-0.2
1936	Phi A	15	12	.556	35	27	20-1	3	235.1	250	112	21	4	75	82	3.86	132	.275	.332	91-0-7	.198	-1*	91	34		3.1
1937	Phi A	13	21	.382	41	29	14	0	205	267	154	16	3	79	68	5.36	88	.306	.365	71-0-1	.225	1	78	-18		-2.3
1938	Phi A	0	2	.000	4	3	0	0	8	17	16	0	0	10	3	16.88	29	.436	.551	2	.000	-0	67	-10		-1.5
	Was A	9	8	.529	38	14	7-2	1	148.1	162	90	12	1	46	44	4.49	100	.276	.330	48-0-1	.250	1	103	-1		0.0
	Year	9	10	.474	42	17	7-2	1	156.1	179	106	12	1	56	47	5.12	88	.286	.346	50-0-1	.240	1	97	-13		-1.5
1939	Was A	4	3	.571	15	3	2	1	53.2	69	32	2	3	14	20	4.70	93	.314	.363	15-0-2	.267	1	88	-2		-0.2
Total	6	42	47	.472	146	78	43-3	5	676.1	812	437	51	10	244	230	4.86	98	.296	.356	232-0-11	.216	0	88	-12		-2.1

KELLEY, DICK Richard Anthony B1.8.1940 Boston MA D12.11.1991 Northridge CA BR/TL/6-0/175* d4.15 [DL 1970 SD N 23]

1964	Mil N	0	0	—	2	0	0	0	2	2	4	0	0	3-0	2	18.00	20	.250	.455	0	—	0		-3	32	-0.2
1965	Mil N	1	1	.500	21	4	0	0	45	37	15	4	0	20-2	31	3.00	117	.226	.310	8	.000	-1*	81	3		0.1
1966	Atl N	7	5	.583	20	13	2-2	0	81	75	36	6	3	21-2	50	3.22	113	.247	.301	28-0-1	.036	-3	112	2		0.0
1967	Atl N	2	9	.182	39	9	1-1	2	98	88	48	8	1	42-7	75	3.77	88	.247	.324	16-0-2	.250	1	85	-5		-0.4
1968	Atl N	2	4	.333	11	11	1-1	1	98.1	86	36	4	1	45-2	73	2.75	109	.238	.323	23-0-1	.043	-1	63	2		0.1
1969	SD N	4	8	.333	27	23	1-1	0-1	136	113	60	11	5	61-8	96	3.57	100	.230	.320	47-0-1	.106	-2	75	0		-0.1
1971	SD N	2	3	.400	48	1	0	2-3	59.2	52	26	5	4	23-5	42	3.47	96	.232	.312	3	.333	-0	213	0		0.0
Total	7	18	30	.375	188	61	5-5	5-4	520	453	225	39	14	215-26	369	3.39	100	.237	.317	125-0-5	.096	-5	87	-1	55	-0.5

KELLEY, TOM Thomas Henry B1.5.1944 Manchester CT BR/TR/6-0/191(180-191) d5.5

1964	Cle A	0	0	—	6	0	0	0	9.2	9	9	1	1	9-2	7	5.59	64	.237	.396	0	—	0		-3		-0.2
1965	Cle A	2	1	.667	4	4	1	0	30	19	8	3	0	13-0	31	2.40	145	.186	.278	9-0-1	.222	0	95	4		0.5
1966	Cle A	4	8	.333	31	7	1	0	95.1	97	55	14	0	42-1	64	4.34	79	.264	.336	28	.143	-1	92	-11		-1.5
1967	Cle A	0	0	—	1	0	0	0	1	0	0	0	0	2-0	0	0.00	—	.000	.500	0	—	0		0		0.0
1971	Atl N	9	5	.643	28	20	5	0-0	143	140	56	8	1	69-6	68	2.96	126	.262	.347	43-0-2	.047	-4	94	10		0.5
1972	Atl N	5	7	.417	27	14	2-1	0-1	116.1	122	65	12	0	65-4	59	4.56	83	.272	.363	34-0-2	.088	-2	98	-9		-1.2
1973	Atl N	0	1	.000	7	0	0	0	12.2	13	5	0	0	7-3	5	2.84	140	.289	.370	2	.000	-0		1		0.1
Total	7	20	22	.476	104	45	9-1	0-1	408	400	198	38	2	207-16	234	3.75	98	.260	.347	116-0-5	.095	-6	95	-8		-1.8

KELLNER, ALEX Alexander Raymond B8.26.1924 Tucson AZ D5.3.1996 Tucson AZ BR/TL/6-0/200(190-215) d4.29 b-Walt

1948	Phi A	0	0	—	13	1	0	0	23	21	20	0	2	16	14	7.83	55	.239	.368	5	.000	-1	211	-8		-0.5
1949	Phi A☆	20	12	.625	38	27	19	1	245	243	120	18	2	129	94	3.75	110	.261	.352	92-0-4	.217	1	120	8		1.1
1950	Phi A	8	20	.286	36	29	15	0	225.1	253	157	28	2	112	85	5.47	83	.282	.363	80	.200	-1	78	-25		-2.8
1951	Phi A	11	14	.440	33	29	11-1	2	209.2	218	118	20	4	93	94	4.46	96	.272	.350	79-0-2	.228	-1	97	-6		-0.7
1952	Phi A	12	14	.462	34	33	14-2	0	231.1	223	124	21	4	86	105	4.36	91	.252	.321	82-1-4	.207	-1	100	-8		-0.9
1953	Phi A	11	12	.478	25	25	14-2	0	201.2	210	98	8	4	51	81	3.93	109	.269	.317	69-0-5	.217	1	81	7		0.7
1954	Phi A	6	17	.261	27	27	8-1	0	173.2	204	118	16	4	88	69	5.39	72	.301	.381	55-0-5	.182	-0	70	-28		-3.2
1955	KC A	11	8	.579	30	24	6-3	0	162.2	164	81	18	5	60-2	75	4.20	99	.265	.332	56-0-2	.214	2	87	1		0.0
1956	KC A	7	4	.636	20	17	5	0	91.2	103	49	15	2	33-3	44	4.32	100	.289	.351	30-0-3	.200	-0*	76	0		0.0
1957	KC A	6	5	.545	28	21	3	0	132.2	141	65	18	2	41-3	72	4.27	93	.278	.332	47-3-1	.234	4	98	-2		0.3
1958	KC A	0	2	.000	7	6	0	0	33.2	40	24	5	0	8-2	22	5.88	66	.315	.353	11-0-2	.091	-0*	84	-7		-0.4
	Cin N	7	3	.700	18	7	4	0	82	74	24	8	3	20-1	42	2.30	180	.243	.294	28	.357	3	93	15		2.0
1959	StL N	2	1	.667	12	0	0	0	37	31	17	9	1	10-2	19	3.16	134	.220	.275	9	.222	0	95	3	76	0.2
Total	12	101	112	.474	321	250	99-9	5	1849.1	1925	1015	184	37	747-11	816	4.41	95	.270	.342	643-4-28	.215	7	90	-50	76	-3.9

KELLNER, WALT Walter Joseph B4.26.1929 Tucson AZ BR/TR/6-0/200* d9.6 b-Alex Col Arizona

1952	Phi A	0	0	—	1	0	0	0	4	4	3	0	0	3	2	6.75	59	.250	.368	1	.000	-0		-1		-0.1
1953	Phi A	0	0	—	2	0	0	0	3	1	2	0	1	4	4	6.00	71	.111	.429	0	—	0		0		0.0
Total	2	0	0	—	3	0	0	0	7	5	5	0	1	7	6	6.43	64	.200	.394	1	.000	-0		-1		-0.1

KELLOGG, AL Albert C. B9.9.1886 Providence RI D7.21.1953 Portland OR TL/6-3/208 d9.25

| 1908 | Phi A | 0 | 2 | .000 | 3 | 3 | 2 | 0 | 17 | 20 | 19 | 1 | 1 | 9 | 8 | 5.82 | 44 | .294 | .385 | 8 | .125 | -0 | 89 | -7 | | -0.7 |

KELLUM, WIN Winford Ansley B4.11.1876 Waterford ON, Can. D8.10.1951 Big Rapids MI BB/TL/5-10/190 d4.26

1901	Bos A	2	3	.400	6	6	5	0	48	61	42	3	7	7	8	6.38	55	.305	.338	18	.167	-1	124	-13		-1.0
1904	Cin N	15	10	.600	31	24	22-1	2	224.2	206	98	1	10	46	70	2.60	113	.244	.291	82-0-3	.159	-4	135	7		1.0
1905	StL N	3	3	.500	11	7	5-1	0	74	70	30	1	1	10	19	2.92	102	.255	.283	25-0-1	.200	1	132	1		0.3
Total	3	20	16	.556	48	37	32-2	2	346.2	337	170	5	14	63	97	3.19	95	.255	.297	125-0-4	.168	2	133	-5		0.3

KELLY, BRYAN Bryan Keith B2.24.1959 Silver Spring MD BR/TR/6-2/195* [DetA81 6/146] d9.2 Col Alabama

1986	Det A	1	2	.333	6	4	0	0-0	20	21	11	4	0	10-1	18	4.50	93	.269	.352	0	—	0	125	-1		-0.1
1987	Det A	0	1	.000	5	0	0	0-0	10.2	12	6	2	0	7-4	10	5.06	84	.286	.388	0	—	0		-1		-0.1
Total	2	1	3	.250	11	4	0	0-0	30.2	33	17	6	0	17-5	28	4.70	89	.275	.365	0	—	0	125	-2		-0.2

KELLY, ED Edward Leo B12.10.1888 Pawtucket RI D11.4.1928 Red Lodge MT BR/TR/5-11.5/173 d4.14

| 1914 | Bos A | 0 | 0 | — | 3 | 0 | 0 | 0 | 2.1 | 1 | 1 | 0 | 1 | 4 | 1 | 0.00 | — | .100 | .182 | 1 | .000 | -0 | | 0 | | 0.0 |

KELLY, HERB Herbert Barrett "Moke" B6.4.1892 Mobile AL D5.18.1973 Torrance CA BL/TL/5-9/160 d9.25 Col Notre Dame

1914	Pit N	0	2	.000	5	2	0	0	25.2	24	11	0	1	7	6	2.45	108	.253	.304	9	.222	0	40	0		0.0
1915	Pit N	1	1	.500	5	1	0	0	11	10	9	0	1	4	6	4.09	67	.250	.333	2	.500	1	54	-3		-0.3
Total	2	1	3	.250	10	3	0	0	36.2	34	20	0	1	11	12	2.95	91	.252	.313	11	.273	1	45	-3		-0.3

KELLY, MIKE Michael J. B11.9.1902 St.Louis MO BR/TR/6-1/178 d9.3

| 1926 | Phi N | 0 | 0 | — | 9 | 0 | 0 | 0 | 6.2 | 9 | 7 | 0 | 1 | 4 | 2 | 9.45 | 44 | .346 | .452 | 3 | .000 | -0 | | -3 | | -0.2 |

KELLY, KING Michael Joseph B12.31.1857 Troy NY D11.8.1894 Boston MA BR/TR/5-10/170 d5.1.1878 M3 HF1945 ▲

1880	Chi N	0	0	—	1	0	0	0	3	3	2	0	1	0	1	0.00	—	.250	.308	344-1	.291	0*		0		0.0
1883	Chi N	0	0	—	1	1	0	0	7	7	3	0	0	3	0	0.00	—	.333	.333	428-3	.255	0*		0		0.0
1884	Chi N	0	1	.000	3	0	0	0	5.1	12	11	2	1	2	2	8.44	58	.400	.438	452-13	.354	1*		-3		-0.4
1887	Bos N	1	0	1.000	3	0	0	0	13	17	16	1	0	14	1	3.46	118	.298	.437	484-8	.322	1*		-2		-0.1

YEAR	TM LG	W	L	PCT	G	GS	CG-SHO	SV-BS	IP	H	R	HR	HB	BB-IB	SO	ERA	AERA	OAV	OOB	AB-HR-SH	AVG	PB	SUP	APR	DL	PW
1890	Bos P	1	0	1.000	1	0	0	0	2	1	1	0	0	2	2	4.50	98	.143	.333	340-4	.326	0*	0			0.0
1891	Cin AA	0	1	.000	3	0	0	0	15.1	21	15	2	1	7	0	5.28	77	.313	.387	283-1	.297	1*	-1			0.0
1892	†Bos N	0	0	—	1	0	0	0	6	8	4	0	3	4	0	1.50	234	.308	.455	281-2	.189	0*	0			0.0
Total	7	2	2	.500	12	0	0	0	45.2	63	49	5	4	30	4	4.14	92	.312	.411	2612-32	.296	4	-6			-0.5

KELLY, REN Reynolds Joseph B11.18.1899 San Francisco CA D8.24.1963 Millbrae CA BR/TR/6-0/183   d9.18   b-George

YEAR	TM LG	W	L	PCT	G	GS	CG-SHO	SV-BS	IP	H	R	HR	HB	BB-IB	SO	ERA	AERA	OAV	OOB	AB-HR-SH	AVG	PB	SUP	APR	DL	PW
1923	Phi A	0	0	—	1	0	0	0	7	7	3	0	0	4	1	2.57	160	.259	.355	3	.000	-0	1			0.0

KELLY, BOB Robert Edward B10.4.1927 Cleveland OH BR/TR/6-0/180*   d5.4   Col Case Western Reserve

YEAR	TM LG	W	L	PCT	G	GS	CG-SHO	SV-BS	IP	H	R	HR	HB	BB-IB	SO	ERA	AERA	OAV	OOB	AB-HR-SH	AVG	PB	SUP	APR	DL	PW
1951	Chi N	7	4	.636	35	11	4	0	123.2	130	70	8	1	55	48	4.66	88	.275	.352	31-0-3	.161	-1	106	-7		-0.6
1952	Chi N	4	9	.308	31	15	3-2	0	125.1	114	62	7	3	46	50	3.59	107	.236	.306	37-0-1	.216	0	99	1		0.2
1953	Chi N	0	1	.000	14	0	0	0	17	27	19	2	1	9	6	9.53	47	.375	.451	1	.000	-0		-8		-0.4
	Cin N	1	2	.333	28	5	0	2	66.1	71	36	7	0	26	29	4.34	100	.276	.343	17-0-1	.118	-1	131	0		-0.5
	Year	1	3	.250	42	5	0	2	83.1	98	55	9	1	35	35	5.40	81	.298	.367	18-0-1	.111	-1	131	-9		-0.9
1958	Cin N	0	0	—	2	1	0	0	2	3	1	0	0	3-1	1	4.50	92	.500	.667	0		0	87	0		-0.3
	Cle A	0	2	.000	13	3	0	0	27.2	29	18	4	1	13-0	12	5.20	70	.282	.368	4	.250	-1	115	-5		-0.3
Total	4	12	18	.400	123	35	7-2	2	362	374	206	28	6	152-1	146	4.50	90	.268	.343	90-0-5	.178	-1	106	-19		-1.2

KELSO, BILL William Eugene B2.19.1940 Kansas City MO BR/TR/6-4/215*   d7.31   Col Whitworth

YEAR	TM LG	W	L	PCT	G	GS	CG-SHO	SV-BS	IP	H	R	HR	HB	BB-IB	SO	ERA	AERA	OAV	OOB	AB-HR-SH	AVG	PB	SUP	APR	DL	PW
1964	LA A	2	0	1.000	10	1	1-1	0	23.2	19	6	3	1	9-0	21	2.28	144	.218	.299	6	.000	-0	54	3		0.2
1966	Cal A	1	1	.500	5	0	0	0	11.1	11	3	1	1	6-1	11	2.38	141	.244	.346	1	.000	-0		1		0.2
1967	Cal A	5	3	.625	69	1	0	11	112	85	41	6	4	63-10	91	2.97	106	.219	.329	19-0-2	.105	-1	28	3		-0.5
1968	Cin N	4	1	.800	35	0	0	1	54.1	56	26	6	3	15-5	39	3.98	80	.277	.325	8	.000	-1		-4		0.1
Total	4	12	5	.706	119	2	1-1	12	201.1	171	76	16	9	93-16	162	3.13	102	.237	.325	34-0-2	.059	-2	41	3		0.1

KEMMERER, RUSS Russell Paul "Rusty","Dutch" B11.1.1931 Pittsburgh PA BR/TR/6-3/200*   d6.27   Col Pittsburgh

YEAR	TM LG	W	L	PCT	G	GS	CG-SHO	SV-BS	IP	H	R	HR	HB	BB-IB	SO	ERA	AERA	OAV	OOB	AB-HR-SH	AVG	PB	SUP	APR	DL	PW
1954	Bos A	5	3	.625	19	9	2-1	0	75.1	71	35	4	2	41	37	3.82	108	.257	.352	21-0-2	.143	-0	79	3		0.3
1955	Bos A	1	1	.500	7	2	0	0	17.1	18	14	3	0	15-1	13	7.27	59	.269	.402	3	.000	-0	145	-5		-0.5
1957	Bos A	0	0	—	1	0	0	0	4	5	2	0	0	2-1	1	4.50	89	.333	.389	1	.000	-0	0	0		0.0
	Was A	7	11	.389	39	26	6	0	172.1	214	110	20	2	71-4	81	4.96	79	.309	.373	45-2-7	.067	-1	122	-23		-2.3
	Year	7	11	.389	40	26	6	0	176.1	219	112	20	2	73-5	82	4.95	79	.310	.373	46-2-7	.065	-1	122	-23		-2.3
1958	Was A	6	15	.286	40	30	6	0	224.1	234	122	25	4	74-5	111	4.61	83	.270	.327	69-0-2	.159	-2	82	-19		-1.8
1959	Was A	8	17	.320	37	28	8	0	206	221	116	20	4	71-3	89	4.50	87	.276	.335	60-0-5	.133	-1	81	-12		-1.4
1960	Was A	0	2	.000	3	3	0	0	17.1	18	15	2	1	10-0	10	7.79	50	.269	.367	4-0-1	.000	0	98	-6		-0.7
	Chi A	6	3	.667	36	7	2-1	2	120.2	111	45	5	1	45-4	76	2.98	127	.248	.315	29-0-7	.000	-3	147	11		0.5
	Year	6	5	.545	39	10	2-1	2	138	129	60	7	2	55-4	86	4.38	89	.278	.323	33-0-8	.000	-3	132	4		-0.1
1961	Chi A	3	3	.500	47	2	0	0	96.2	102	53	10	0	26-1	35	4.38	101	.270	.336	15	.200	1	136	-5		-0.2
1962	Chi A	2	1	.667	20	0	0	0	28	30	14	3	0	11-1	17	3.86	101	.270	.336	2-0-1	.500	1	0			-0.1
	Hou N	5	3	.625	36	2	0	0	68	72	34	10	3	15-1	23	4.10	91	.272	.318	9	.333	1		-11		-0.5
1963	Hou N	0	0	—	17	0	0	1	36.2	48	28	1	0	8-0	12	5.65	56	.320	.350	7	.286	0		-11		-0.4
Total	9	43	59	.422	302	109	24-2	8	1066.2	1144	588	103	17	389-21	505	4.46	86	.277	.339	265-2-25	.128	-5	97	-69		-6.5

KEMNER, DUTCH Herman John B3.4.1899 Quincy IL D1.16.1988 Quincy IL BR/TR/5-10.5/175   d4.19

YEAR	TM LG	W	L	PCT	G	GS	CG-SHO	SV-BS	IP	H	R	HR	HB	BB-IB	SO	ERA	AERA	OAV	OOB	AB-HR-SH	AVG	PB	SUP	APR	DL	PW
1929	Cin N	0	0	—	9	0	0	1	15.1	19	13	0	0	8	10	7.63	60	.328	.409	4	.250	0		-5		-0.2

KENNA, ED Edward Benninghaus "The Pitching Poet" B10.17.1877 Charleston WV D3.22.1912 Grant FL TR/6-0/180   d5.5   Col West Virginia

YEAR	TM LG	W	L	PCT	G	GS	CG-SHO	SV-BS	IP	H	R	HR	HB	BB-IB	SO	ERA	AERA	OAV	OOB	AB-HR-SH	AVG	PB	SUP	APR	DL	PW
1902	Phi A	1	1	.500	2	1	1	0	17	19	15	1	1	11	5	5.29	69	.284	.392	8	.125	-0	118	-3		-0.3

KENNEDY, JOE Joseph Darley B5.24.1979 LaMesa CA BR/TL/6-4/227(225-245) [TBA98 8/252]   d6.6   Col Grossmont (CA) JC

YEAR	TM LG	W	L	PCT	G	GS	CG-SHO	SV-BS	IP	H	R	HR	HB	BB-IB	SO	ERA	AERA	OAV	OOB	AB-HR-SH	AVG	PB	SUP	APR	DL	PW
2001	TB A	7	8	.467	20	20	0	0-0	117.2	122	63	16	3	34-0	78	4.44	102	.269	.321		.250	0	83	2		0.3
2002	TB A	8	11	.421	30	30	5-1	0-0	196.2	204	114	23	16	55-0	109	4.53	100	.269	.328	7	.429	1	96	-3		0.1
2003	TB A	3	12	.200	32	22	1-1	1-1	133.2	167	101	19	11	47-1	77	6.13	75	.303	.364	0	—	0	79	-24	38	-2.1
2004	Col N	9	7	.563	27	27	1	0-0	162.1	163	68	17	8	67-12	117	3.66	130	.265	.342	48-0-4	.125	-1	92	18	38	1.6
2005	Col N	4	8	.333	16	16	0	0-0	92	128	81	12	6	44-4	52	7.04	68	.334	.406	29-0-5	.172	-0	90	-23		-2.1
	Oak A	4	5	.444	19	8	0	0-2	60.2	64	33	8	1	20-2	45	4.45	100	.267	.324	0	—	0	92	0		-0.2
Total	5	35	51	.407	144	123	7-2	1-3	763	848	460	95	45	267-19	478	4.91	94	.282	.346	88-0-9	.170	-0	89	-30	76	-3.1

KENNEDY, VERN Lloyd Vernon B3.20.1907 Kansas City MO D1.28.1993 Mendon MO BL/TR/6-0/175   d9.18

YEAR	TM LG	W	L	PCT	G	GS	CG-SHO	SV-BS	IP	H	R	HR	HB	BB-IB	SO	ERA	AERA	OAV	OOB	AB-HR-SH	AVG	PB	SUP	APR	DL	PW
1934	Chi A	0	2	.000	3	3	1	0	19.1	21	8	1	0	9	7	3.72	127	.300	.380	7	.286	0	25	3		0.3
1935	Chi A	11	11	.500	31	25	16-2	0	211.2	211	110	17	4	95	65	3.91	118	.262	.343	73-0-7	.247	1	94	14		1.4
1936	Chi A☆	21	9	.700	35	34	20-1	0	274.1	282	167	13	3	147	99	4.63	112	.268	.360	113-0-6	.283	5*	111	14		1.1
1937	Chi A	14	13	.519	32	30	15-1	0	221	238	150	16	3	124	114	5.09	90	.273	.366	87-2-3	.230	2	116	-14		-1.2
1938	Det A☆	12	9	.571	33	26	11	2	190.1	215	123	13	1	113	53	5.06	99	.287	.381	79-0-7	.291	3*	105	-3		0.6
1939	Det A	0	3	.000	4	4	1	0	21	25	15	4	1	9	4	6.43	76	.301	.376	7	.286	-0	59	-2		-0.1
	StL A	9	17	.346	33	27	12-1	0	191.2	229	130	18	1	115	55	5.73	85	.297	.389	67-0-10	.149	-2*	94	-14		-1.8
	Year	9	20	.310	37	31	13-1	0	212.2	254	145	22	2	124	64	5.80	84	.297	.388	74-0-10	.162	-2	89	-17		-2.0
1940	StL A	12	17	.414	34	32	18	0	222.1	263	149	18	3	122	70	5.59	82	.297	.385	84-2-3	.298	6*	105	-21		-2.4
1941	StL A	4	4	.333	6	6	2	0	45	44	27	5	0	27	6	4.40	98	.259	.360	15-0-1	.400	-1*	91	-1		0.1
	Was A	1	7	.125	17	7	2	0	66.1	77	49	5	2	39	22	5.70	71	.297	.393	21	.143	-1*	61	-12		-1.1
	Year	3	11	.214	23	13	4	0	111.1	121	76	10	2	66	28	5.17	80	.282	.380	36-0-1	.250	-2	75	-13		-1.1
1942	Cle A	4	8	.333	28	12	4	1	108	99	57	7	1	50	37	4.08	84	.244	.328	30-0-2	.200	1*	99	11		0.1
1943	Cle A	10	7	.588	28	17	8-1	0	146.2	130	47	4	2	59	63	2.45	127	.242	.319	52-0-8	.231	1*	99	11		1.5
1944	Cle A	2	5	.286	12	10	2	0	59	66	36	0	0	37	17	5.03	66	.289	.389	23	.087	-2*	89	-11		-1.0
	Phi N	1	5	.167	12	7	3	0	55.1	60	31	2	0	20	23	4.23	80	.269	.329	21-0-2	.286	1*	113	-4		-0.2
1945	Phi N	0	3	.000	12	3	0	0	36	43	29	2	0	14	13	5.50	70	.297	.358	11	.182	0*	133	-7		-0.7
	Cin N	5	12	.294	24	20	11-1	1	157.2	170	74	10	3	69	38	4.00	94	.280	.356	53-0-1	.226	2	66	-2		-0.7
	Year	5	15	.250	36	23	11-1	1	193.2	213	103	12	3	83	51	4.28	88	.283	.356	64-0-1	.219	2	75	-10		-0.8
Total	12	104	132	.441	344	263	126-7	5	2025.2	2173	1202	130	24	1049	691	4.67	94	.277	.363	743-4-50	.244	19	98	-57		-5.1

KENNEDY, MONTE Montia Calvin B5.11.1922 Amelia VA D3.1.1997 Midlothian VA BR/TL/6-2/185*   d4.18

YEAR	TM LG	W	L	PCT	G	GS	CG-SHO	SV-BS	IP	H	R	HR	HB	BB-IB	SO	ERA	AERA	OAV	OOB	AB-HR-SH	AVG	PB	SUP	APR	DL	PW
1946	NY N	9	10	.474	38	27	10-1	0	186.2	153	80	14	4	116	71	3.42	101	.224	.340	64-0-2	.234	2*	100	2		0.1
1947	NY N	9	12	.429	34	24	9	0	148.1	158	90	8	4	88	60	4.85	84	.272	.372	48-0-1	.167	-1	116	-13		-0.5
1948	NY N	3	9	.250	25	16	7-1	0	114.1	118	64	10	3	57	63	4.01	98	.264	.351	31-0-2	.129	-1*	69	-3		-0.1
1949	NY N	12	14	.462	38	32	14-4	1	223.1	208	105	13	3	100	95	3.43	116	.242	.323	83-1-5	.145	-1*	106	12		1.2
1950	NY N	5	4	.556	36	17	5	2	114.1	120	65	14	3	53	41	4.72	87	.269	.351	36-0-2	.056	-3	96	-7		-0.6
1951	†NY N	1	2	.333	29	5	1	0	68	68	25	0	4	31	22	2.25	174	.270	.350	15-0-3	.200	-1	112	4		0.7
1952	NY N	3	4	.429	31	6	2-1	0	83.1	73	37	6	2	31	48	3.02	122	.230	.303	22-0-1	.091	-1*		-6		0.4
1953	NY N	0	0	—	18	0	0	0	22.2	30	18	2	1	11	11	7.15	60	.337	.459	2	.000	-0*	100	0		-0.6
Total	8	42	55	.433	249	127	48-7	4	961	928	484	67	20	495	411	3.84	101	.253	.344	301-1-16	.153	-5	100	-3		0.6

KENNEDY, TED Theodore A. B2.7.1865 Henry IL D10.31.1907 St.Louis MO BL/TR/5-8/178   d6.12

YEAR	TM LG	W	L	PCT	G	GS	CG-SHO	SV-BS	IP	H	R	HR	HB	BB-IB	SO	ERA	AERA	OAV	OOB	AB-HR-SH	AVG	PB	SUP	APR	DL	PW
1885	Chi N	7	2	.778	9	9	8	0	78.2	91	54	5		28	36	3.43	88	.288	.346	36	.083	-4	146	-3		-0.2
1886	Phi AA	5	15	.250	20	19	19	0	172.2	197	143	4	8	65	68	4.53	77	.272	.339	68	.044	-9	81	-17		-2.1
	Lou AA	0	4	.000	4	4	4	0	32	53	43	1	1	16	14	5.34	68	.351	.417	13	.077	-1	82	-7		-0.3
	Year	5	19	.208	24	23	23	0	204.2	250	186	5	9	81	82	4.66	76	.286	.363	81	.049	-10	81	-29		-3.7
Total	2	12	21	.364	33	32	31	0	283.1	341	240	10	9	109	118	4.32	78	.287	.351	117	.060	-14	98	-27		-3.3

KENNEDY, BILL William Aulton "Lefty" B3.14.1921 Carnesville GA D4.9.1983 Seattle WA BL/TL/6-2/195(195-210)   d4.26

YEAR	TM LG	W	L	PCT	G	GS	CG-SHO	SV-BS	IP	H	R	HR	HB	BB-IB	SO	ERA	AERA	OAV	OOB	AB-HR-SH	AVG	PB	SUP	APR	DL	PW
1948	Cle A	1	0	1.000	6	3	0	0	11.1	16	14	0	0	13	12	11.12	37	.333	.475	3-0-1	.667	1	200	-9		-0.6
	StL A	7	8	.467	26	20	3	0	132	132	82	10	5	104	77	4.70	97	.259	.389	44-0-3	.250	1	93	-4		-0.3
	Year	8	8	.500	32	23	3	0	143.1	148	96	10	5	117	89	5.21	87	.265	.397	47-0-4	.277	2	105	-12		-0.9
1949	StL A	4	11	.267	48	16	2	1	153.2	172	97	12	3	73	69	4.69	97	.285	.365	40-0-2	.150	-2	88	-4		-0.5
1950	StL A	0	0	—	1	0	0	0	1	0	0	0	0	1	0	0.00	—	.143	.333	0		-0				0.0
1951	StL A	1	5	.167	19	5	1	0	56	76	37	4	1	37	29	5.79	76	.332	.427	16	.125	-2	85	-7		-0.7
1952	Chi A	2	2	.500	47	1	0	5	70.2	64	37	5	1	46	48	2.80	130	.213	.318	13-0-1	.231	1	0	6		0.8
1953	Bos A	0	0	—	16	0	0	0	24.1	24	13	2	1	17	14	3.70	114	.255	.375	2-0-1	.500	1		1		0.1
1956	Cin N	0	0	—	2	0	0	0	2	3	4	0-0				18.00	22	.667	.600			-0		-3		-0.2

YEAR	TM LG	W	L	PCT	G	GS	CG-SHO	SV-BS	IP	H	R	HR	HB	BB-IB	SO	ERA	AERA	OAV	OOB	AB-HR-SH	AVG	PB	SUP	APR	DL	PW
1957	Cin N	0	2	.000	8	0	0	3	12.2	16	9	1	1	5-1	8	6.39	64	.314	.379	2	.000	0		-3		-0.5
Total	8	15	28	.349	172	45	6	11	464.2	497	284	34	12	289-1	256	4.73	92	.275	.379	120-0-8	.208	-1	98	-22		-2.2

KENNEDY, BILL William Gorman B12.22.1918 Alexandria VA D8.20.1995 Alexandria VA BL/TL/6-1/175 d5.1 Mil 1943-45

YEAR	TM LG	W	L	PCT	G	GS	CG-SHO	SV-BS	IP	H	R	HR	HB	BB-IB	SO	ERA	AERA	OAV	OOB	AB-HR-SH	AVG	PB	SUP	APR	DL	PW
1942	Was A	0	1	.000	8	2	1	2	18	21	18	1	0	10	4	8.00	46	.296	.383	4	.000	-1	82	-8		-0.6
1946	Was A	1	2	.333	21	2	0	3	39	40	29	1	0	29	18	6.00	56	.270	.390	8-0-1	.125	-0	102	-11		-1.0
1947	Was A	0	0	—	2	0	0	0	6.2	10	8	1	0	5	1	8.10	46	.370	.469	2	.000	-0	-4			-0.2
Total	3	1	3	.250	31	4	1	5	63.2	71	55	3	0	44	23	6.79	51	.289	.397	14-0-1	.071	-1	93	-23		-1.8

KENNEDY, BRICKYARD William Park B10.7.1867 Bellaire OH D9.23.1915 Bellaire OH BR/TR/5-11/160 d4.26

YEAR	TM LG	W	L	PCT	G	GS	CG-SHO	SV-BS	IP	H	R	HR	HB	BB-IB	SO	ERA	AERA	OAV	OOB	AB-HR-SH	AVG	PB	SUP	APR	DL	PW
1892	Bro N	13	8	.619	26	21	18	1	191	189	115	3	4	95	108	3.86	82	.248	.334	85	.165	-1	117	-14		-1.4
1893	Bro N	25	20	.556	46	44	40-2	1	382.2	376	238	15	7	168	107	3.72	119	.249	.327	157	.248	2	90	28		2.9
1894	Bro N	24	20	.545	48	41	34	2	360.2	445	291	15	11	149	107	4.92	101	.300	.368	161-0-6	.304	4	105	-3		0.1
1895	Bro N	19	12	.613	40	34	27-2	1	288.2	341	199	14	7	95	41	5.05	87	.289	.346	131-0-1	.305	4*	112	-17		-1.0
1896	Bro N	17	20	.459	42	38	28-1	1	305.2	334	211	12	12	130	76	4.42	93	.276	.352	122-0-4	.189	-7	85	-10		-1.4
1897	Bro N	18	20	.474	44	40	36-2	1	343.1	370	206	6	8	149	81	3.91	105	.273	.348	147-1-2	.272	4*	90	7		1.0
1898	Bro N	16	22	.421	40	39	38	0	339.1	360	183	12	5	123	73	3.37	106	.273	.334	135-0-1	.252	3	84	6		1.1
1899	Bro N	22	9	.710	40	33	27-2	2	277.1	297	133	11	3	86	55	2.79	140	.273	.329	109-0-1	.248	4	101	31		3.3
1900	Bro N	20	13	.606	42	35	26-2	0	292	336	160	5	8	111	75	3.91	98	.276	.344	123-0-2	.301	7*	112	2		0.9
1901	Bro N	3	5	.375	14	8	6	0	85.1	80	40	1	1	24	28	3.06	110	.246	.300	36	.167	-1	98	3		0.1
1902	NY N	1	4	.200	6	6	4-1	0	38.2	44	25	0	0	16	9	3.96	71	.286	.353	15	.267	1	65	-5		-0.5
1903	†Pit N	9	6	.600	18	15	10-1	0	125.1	130	62	0	2	57	39	3.45	94	.277	.357	58-0-2	.362	8*	135	0		0.7
Total	12	187	159	.540	406	354	294-13	9	3030	3282	1863	94	68	1203	799	3.96	103	.273	.343	1279-1-19	.261	27	99	28		5.8

KENNEY, ART Arthur Joseph B4.29.1916 Milford MA BL/TL/6-0/175 d7.1 Col Holy Cross

YEAR	TM LG	W	L	PCT	G	GS	CG-SHO	SV-BS	IP	H	R	HR	HB	BB-IB	SO	ERA	AERA	OAV	OOB	AB-HR-SH	AVG	PB	SUP	APR	DL	PW
1938	Bos N	0	0	—	2	0	0	0	2.1	3	4	0	0	8	2	15.43	22	.300	.611	0	—	0		-3		-0.1

KENSING, LOGAN Logan French B7.3.1982 San Antonio TX BR/TR/6-1/185* d9.10

YEAR	TM LG	W	L	PCT	G	GS	CG-SHO	SV-BS	IP	H	R	HR	HB	BB-IB	SO	ERA	AERA	OAV	OOB	AB-HR-SH	AVG	PB	SUP	APR	DL	PW
2004	Fla N	0	3	.000	5	3	0	0-0	13.2	19	15	5	1	9-0	7	9.88	42	.345	.439	2-0-1	.000	-0	53	-9		-1.5
2005	Fla N	0	0	—	3	0	0	0-0	5.2	11	7	2	0	3-0	4	11.12	36	.407	.452	0	—	-0		-4	130	-0.2
Total	2	0	3	.000	8	3	0	0-0	19.1	30	22	7	1	12-0	11	10.24	40	.366	.443	2-0-1	.000	-0	53	-13	130	-1.7

KENT, ED Edward C. B1859 NY BR/TR/5-6.5/152 d8.14

YEAR	TM LG	W	L	PCT	G	GS	CG-SHO	SV-BS	IP	H	R	HR	HB	BB-IB	SO	ERA	AERA	OAV	OOB	AB-HR-SH	AVG	PB	SUP	APR	DL	PW
1884	Tol AA	0	1	.000	1	1	1	0	9	14	11	0	1	3	4	6.00	.57	.298	.353	4	.000	0	124	-3		-0.2

KENT, MAURY Maurice Allen B9.17.1885 Marshalltown IA D4.19.1966 Iowa City IA BR/TR/6-0/168 d4.15 Col Iowa

YEAR	TM LG	W	L	PCT	G	GS	CG-SHO	SV-BS	IP	H	R	HR	HB	BB-IB	SO	ERA	AERA	OAV	OOB	AB-HR-SH	AVG	PB	SUP	APR	DL	PW
1912	Bro N	5	5	.500	20	9	2-1	0	93	107	74	3	1	46	24	4.84	69	.296	.377	35	.229	1	122	-18		-1.5
1913	Bro N	0	0	—	3	0	0	0	7.1	5	2	0	0	3	1	2.45	134	.192	.276	3	.000	-0*		1		0.0
Total	2	5	5	.500	23	9	2-1	0	100.1	112	76	3	1	49	25	4.66	72	.289	.371	38	.211	1	122	-17		-1.5

KENT, STEVE Steven Patrick B10.3.1978 Frankfurt, West Germany BB/TL/5-11/170 [SeaA99 9/275] d4.4 Col Florida International

YEAR	TM LG	W	L	PCT	G	GS	CG-SHO	SV-BS	IP	H	R	HR	HB	BB-IB	SO	ERA	AERA	OAV	OOB	AB-HR-SH	AVG	PB	SUP	APR	DL	PW
2002	TB A	0	2	.000	34	0	0	1-1	57.1	67	41	6	3	38-0	41	5.65	80	.294	.399	0	—	0		-8		-0.4

KEOUGH, MATT Matthew Lon B7.3.1955 Pomona CA BR/TR/6-3/190(175-190) [OakA73 7/167] d9.3 f-Marty

YEAR	TM LG	W	L	PCT	G	GS	CG-SHO	SV-BS	IP	H	R	HR	HB	BB-IB	SO	ERA	AERA	OAV	OOB	AB-HR-SH	AVG	PB	SUP	APR	DL	PW
1977	Oak A	1	3	.250	7	6	0	0-0	42.2	39	25	4	1	22-0	23	4.85	83	.247	.341	0	—	0*	74	-3		-0.3
1978	Oak A★	8	15	.348	32	32	6	0-0	197.1	178	90	9	4	85-2	108	3.24	113	.241	.322	0	—	0*	74	7		0.9
1979	Oak A	2	17	.105	30	28	7-1	0-0	176.2	220	115	18	7	78-2	95	5.04	80	.315	.385	0	—	0	66	-21		-1.9
1980	Oak A	16	13	.552	34	32	20-2	0-1	250	218	94	24	5	94-3	121	2.92	131	.236	.308	0	—	0	94	25		2.6
1981	†Oak A	10	6	.625	19	19	10-2	0-0	140.1	125	56	11	0	45-0	60	3.40	104	.239	.298	0	—	0	121	3		0.2
1982	Oak A	11	18	.379	34	34	10-2	0-0	209.1	233	144	38	2	101-1	75	5.72	69	.284	.362	0	—	0	101	-40		-4.8
1983	Oak A	2	3	.400	14	4	0	0-0	44	50	29	7	0	31-1	28	5.52	70	.284	.388	0	—	0	105	-8		-0.8
	NY A	3	4	.429	12	12	0	0-0	55.2	59	42	12	2	20-0	26	5.17	76	.266	.331	0	—	0	125	-11		-1.2
	Year	5	7	.417	26	16	0	0-0	99.2	109	71	19	2	51-1	54	5.33	74	.274	.357	0	—	0	120	-19		-2.0
1985	StL N	0	1	.000	4	1	0	0-0	10	10	5	0	1	4-1	10	4.50	79	.278	.366	2	.000	-0	74	-1		-0.1
1986	Chi N	2	2	.500	19	2	0	0-1	29	36	17	4	1	12-2	19	4.97	82	.316	.386	5	.400	1	44	-3		-0.2
	Hou N	3	2	.600	10	5	0	0-0	35	22	14	5	1	18-2	25	3.09	137	.180	.289	11	.364	1	134	2		0.4
	Year	5	4	.556	29	7	0	0-1	64	58	31	9	2	30-4	44	3.94	97	.246	.335	16	.375	2	103	0		0.2
Total	9	58	84	.408	215	175	53-7	0-2	1190	1190	631	132	27	510-14	590	4.17	92	.262	.338	18	.333	2	92	-50		-5.2

KEPSHIRE, KURT Kurt David B7.3.1959 Bridgeport CT BL/TR/6-1/180(180-195) [CinN79 25/639] d7.4 Col New Haven

YEAR	TM LG	W	L	PCT	G	GS	CG-SHO	SV-BS	IP	H	R	HR	HB	BB-IB	SO	ERA	AERA	OAV	OOB	AB-HR-SH	AVG	PB	SUP	APR	DL	PW
1984	StL N	6	5	.545	17	16	2-2	0-0	109	100	47	7	0	44-4	71	3.30	106	.249	.321	36-0-5	.056	-2	109	1		-0.2
1985	StL N	10	9	.526	32	29	1	0-0	153.1	155	89	16	0	71-3	67	4.75	75	.264	.339	51-0-7	.118	-1	122	-19		-2.3
1986	StL N	0	1	.000	2	1	0	0-0	8	8	4	2	0	4-0	6	4.50	82	.258	.343	1-0-1	.000	-0	48	-1		-0.1
Total	3	16	15	.516	51	46	2-2	0-0	270.1	263	140	25	0	119-7	144	4.16	85	.258	.332	88-0-13	.091	-3	116	-19		-2.6

KERFELD, CHARLIE Charles Patrick B9.28.1963 Knob Noster MO BR/TR/6-6/225(225-257) [HouN82 S1/5] d7.27 Col Yavapai (AZ) JC [DL 1988 Hou N 17]

YEAR	TM LG	W	L	PCT	G	GS	CG-SHO	SV-BS	IP	H	R	HR	HB	BB-IB	SO	ERA	AERA	OAV	OOB	AB-HR-SH	AVG	PB	SUP	APR	DL	PW
1985	Hou N	4	2	.667	11	6	0	0-0	44.1	44	22	2	0	25-2	30	4.06	86	.268	.359	14-0-2	.000	-1	110	-2		-0.5
1986	†Hou N	11	2	.846	61	0	0	7-5	93.2	71	32	5	2	42-3	77	2.59	139	.213	.299	9	.111	-0		10	18	1.4
1987	Hou N	0	2	.000	21	0	0	0-0	29.2	34	22	3	1	21-2	17	6.67	59	.309	.421	3	.000	-0		-8	51	-0.5
1990	Hou N	0	0	—	5	0	0	0-0	3.1	9	6	0	0	6-1	4	16.20	23	.529	.652	0	—	0		-4		-0.8
	Atl N	3	1	.750	25	0	0	2-0	30.2	31	22	2	0	23-3	27	5.58	72	.270	.386	0	—	0		-5	15	-0.7
	Year	3	1	.750	30	0	0	2-0	34	40	28	2	0	29-4	31	6.62	61	.303	.423	0	—	0		-9		-1.5
Total	4	18	9	.667	123	6	0	9-5	201.2	189	104	12	3	117-11	155	4.20	88	.256	.354	26-0-2	.038	-2	110	-9	101	-1.1

KERIAZAKOS, GUS Constantine Nicholas B7.28.1931 W.Orange NJ D5.4.1996 Hilton Head SC BR/TR/6-3/187* d10.1

YEAR	TM LG	W	L	PCT	G	GS	CG-SHO	SV-BS	IP	H	R	HR	HB	BB-IB	SO	ERA	AERA	OAV	OOB	AB-HR-SH	AVG	PB	SUP	APR	DL	PW
1950	Chi A	0	1	.000	1	1	0	0	2.1	7	5	0	0	5	1	19.29	23	.500	.632	1	1.000	0	121	-4		-0.5
1954	Was A	2	3	.400	22	3	2	0	59.2	59	29	4	0	30	33	3.77	94	.262	.346	15-0-2	.067	-1	99	-2	30	-0.3
1955	KC A	0	1	.000	5	1	0	0	11.2	15	16	4	0	7-0	8	12.34	34	.333	.415	3	.000	-0	149	-9		-0.7
Total	3	2	5	.286	28	5	2	0	73.2	81	50	8	0	42-0	42	5.62	65	.285	.374	19-0-2	.105	-1	120	-15	30	-1.4

KERKSIECK, BILL Wayman William B12.6.1913 Ulm AR D3.11.1970 Stuttgart AR BR/TR/6-1/183 d6.21 Col Arkansas-Monticello

YEAR	TM LG	W	L	PCT	G	GS	CG-SHO	SV-BS	IP	H	R	HR	HB	BB-IB	SO	ERA	AERA	OAV	OOB	AB-HR-SH	AVG	PB	SUP	APR	DL	PW
1939	Phi N	0	2	.000	23	2	1	0	62.2	81	53	12	0	32	13	7.18	56	.328	.405	12	.083	-0*	33	-20		-1.0

KERN, JIM James Lester B3.15.1949 Gladwin MI BR/TR/6-5/205(185-205) d9.6

YEAR	TM LG	W	L	PCT	G	GS	CG-SHO	SV-BS	IP	H	R	HR	HB	BB-IB	SO	ERA	AERA	OAV	OOB	AB-HR-SH	AVG	PB	SUP	APR	DL	PW
1974	Cle A	0	1	.000	4	3	1	0-0	15.1	16	9	1	0	14-1	11	4.70	78	.262	.395	0	—	0	105	-2		-0.1
1975	Cle A	1	2	.333	13	7	0	0-0	71.2	60	31	5	5	45-3	55	3.77	101	.233	.356	0	—	0	99	2		0.1
1976	Cle A	10	7	.588	50	2	0	15-1	117.2	91	38	2	6	50-7	111	2.37	148	.222	.309	0	—	0	112	13		2.3
1977	Cle A★	8	10	.444	60	0	0	18-9	92	85	39	3	6	47-8	91	3.42	117	.260	.359	0	—	0		6		1.2
1978	Cle A★	10	10	.500	58	0	0	13-4	99.1	77	36	4	4	58-7	95	3.08	123	.224	.338	1	.000	0		6		1.2
1979	Tex A★	13	5	.722	71	0	0	29-9	143	99	35	5	2	62-6	136	1.57	264	.199	.288	0	—	0		6		1.8
1980	Tex A	3	11	.214	38	1	0	2-7	63.1	65	38	4	2	45-10	40	4.83	81	.279	.392	0	—	0	39			6.3
1981	Tex A	1	2	.333	14	0	0	6-0	30	21	14	0	1	22-3	20	2.70	129	.204	.346	0	—	0	0	-6	27	-1.2
1982	Cin N	3	5	.375	50	0	0	2-4	76	61	27	3	4	48-14	43	2.84	129	.222	.338	7	.000	0	3	33		0.4
1983	Chi A	2	1	.667	13	1	0	3-1	28	20	16	3	0	12-0	23	5.14	79	.204	.288	0	—	0	7			0.7
1984	Chi A	0	0	—	1	0	0	0-0	0.2	1	1	0	0	0-0	0	0.00	—	.333	.333	0	—	0	89	-2		-0.3
	Phi N	0	1	.000	13	0	0	0-1	13.1	20	16	3	0	10-1	9	10.13	36	.339	.435	1	.000	-0		-9	180	-0.6
1985	Mil A	1	0	1.000	6	0	0	0-0	4.2	6	0	0	0	3-0	4	0.00	—	.300	.391	0	—	0		2		0.4
1986	Cle A	1	1	.500	16	0	0	0-1	27.1	34	28	1	3	5-1	3	6.55	64	.318	.388	0	—	0		-2		-0.2
Total	13	53	57	.482	416	14	1	88-36	793.1	670	332	35	29	444-61	651	3.32	116	.235	.341	9	.000	-1	93	48	240	10.1

KERR, DICKIE Richard Henry B7.3.1893 St.Louis MO D5.4.1963 Houston TX BL/TL/5-7/155 d4.25

YEAR	TM LG	W	L	PCT	G	GS	CG-SHO	SV-BS	IP	H	R	HR	HB	BB-IB	SO	ERA	AERA	OAV	OOB	AB-HR-SH	AVG	PB	SUP	APR	DL	PW
1919	†Chi A	13	7	.650	39	17	7-0	2	212.1	208	78	2	2	64	79	2.88	110	.259	.316	68-0-9	.250	5	119	10		1.5
1920	Chi A	21	9	.700	45	27	19-3	5	253.2	266	116	7	4	72	72	3.37	112	.278	.331	90-0-4	.156	-4*	105	10		0.8
1921	Chi A	19	17	.528	44	37	25-3	1	308.2	357	182	12	11	96	80	4.72	90	.295	.352	105-0-5	.238	5*	89	-1		-1.0
1925	Chi A	0	1	.000	12	2	0	0	36.2	45	23	3	1	18	4	5.15	81	.304	.383	12-0-1	.333	1*	91	-4		-0.1
Total	4	53	34	.609	140	83	54-7	6	811.1	876	399	24	18	250	235	3.84	99	.281	.338	275-0-19	.218	7	101	1		1.2

YEAR	TM LG	W	L	PCT	G	GS	CG-SHO	SV-BS	IP	H	R	HR	HB	BB-IB	SO	ERA	AERA	OAV	OOB	AB-HR-SH	AVG	PB	SUP	APR	DL	PV
KERRIGAN, JOE	Joseph Thomas B11.30.1954 Philadelphia PA BR/TR/6-5/210(205-222) [MonN74*1/10] d7.9 M1/C16 Col Temple																									
1976	Mon N	2	6	.250	38	0	0	1-2	56.2	63	27	3	2	23-5	22	3.81	99	.289	.362	2	.000	-0	0			0.
1977	Mon N	3	5	.375	67	0	0	11-5	89.1	80	37	4	3	33-3	43	3.22	120	.241	.310	8-0-2	.000	-1	6			0.
1978	Bal A	3	1	.750	26	2	0	3-0	71.2	75	44	10	2	36-5	41	4.77	74	.273	.361	0	—	0	114 -11		-0.
1980	Bal A	0	0	—	1	0	0	0-0	2.1	3	1	0	0	0-0	1	3.86	103	.273	.273	0	—	0	0			-0.
Total	4	8	12	.400	131	2	0	15-7	220	221	109	17	7	92-13	107	3.89	96	.264	.340	10-0-2	.000	-1	114 -5		-0.
KERSHNER, JASON	Jason Ashley B12.19.1976 Scottsdale AZ BL/TL/6-2/165(165-185) [PhiN95 12/325] d7.25																									
2002	SD N	0	1	.000	15	0	0	0-0	18.2	15	14	2	2	10-0	11	5.79	67	.217	.333	0-0-1	—	0	-5		-0.
	Tor A	0	0	—	10	0	0	1-1	5.1	5	2	1	0	4-1	7	1.69	274	.227	.346	0	—	0	9		0.
2003	Tor A	3	3	.500	40	0	0	0-1	54	43	21	5	2	15-2	32	3.17	150	.217	.275	0	—	0	85 -3		-0.
2004	Tor A	0	1	.000	24	0	0	0-0	22.1	30	16	3	0	8-0	15	6.04	81	.316	.369	0	—	0	85 2		0.
Total	3	3	5	.375	89	0	0	1-2	100.1	93	53	11	4	37-3	65	4.22	109	.242	.313	0-0-1	—	0	85 2		0.
KESTER, RICK	Richard Lee B7.7.1946 Iola KS BR/TR/6-0/190* d8.18 Col UCLA																									
1968	Atl N	0	0	—	6	0	0	0-0	6.1	8	4	0	0	3-0	9	5.68	53	.308	.379	0	—	0	-2		-0.
1969	Atl N	0	0	—	1	0	0	0-0	2	5	3	1	0	0-0	2	13.50	27	.455	.455	0	—	0	-2		-0.
1970	Atl N	0	0	—	15	0	0	0-0	32.1	36	24	3	0	19-0	20	5.57	77	.283	.374	9	.000	-1	-5		-0.
Total	3	0	0	—	21	0	0	0-0	40.2	49	31	4	0	22-0	31	5.98	68	.299	.380	9	.000	-1	-9		-0.
KETCHUM, GUS	Augustus Franklin B3.21.1897 Royse City TX D9.6.1980 Oklahoma City OK BR/TR/5-9.5/170 d8.7																									
1922	Phi A	0	1	.000	6	0	0	0-0	16	19	12	2	1	8	4	5.63	76	.302	.389	4	.000	-1	-2		-0.
KEUPPER, HENRY	Henry John B6.24.1887 Staunton IL D8.14.1960 Marion IL BL/TL/6-1/185 d4.19																									
1914	StL F	8	20	.286	42	25	12-1		213	256	132	3	4	49	70	4.27	71	.291	.332	68-0-4	.250	1	86 -29		-3.
KEY, JIMMY	James Edward B4.22.1961 Huntsville AL BR/TL/6-1/190(175-190) [TorA82 3/56] d4.6 Col Clemson																									
1984	Tor A	4	5	.444	63	0	0	10-7	62	70	37	8	1	32-8	44	4.65	89	.286	.369	0	—	0*	100 29		2
1985	†Tor A★	14	6	.700	35	32	3	0-0	212.2	188	77	22	2	50-1	85	3.00	141	.237	.282	0	—	0	109 19		2
1986	Tor A	14	11	.560	36	35	4-2	0-0	232	222	98	24	3	74-1	141	3.57	119	.256	.315	0	—	0	93 48		4
1987	Tor A	17	8	.680	36	36	8-1	0-0	261	210	93	24	2	66-6	161	2.76	**164**	**.221**	**.272**	0	—	0	106 9	75	1
1988	Tor A	12	5	.706	21	21	2-2	0-0	131.1	127	55	13	5	30-2	65	3.29	120	.250	.296	0	—	0	96 0	15	0
1989	†Tor A	13	14	.481	33	33	5-1	0-0	216	226	99	18	3	27-2	118	3.88	98	.270	.292	0	—	0	113 -5	30	-0
1990	Tor A	13	7	.650	27	27	0	0-0	154.2	169	79	20	1	22-2	88	4.25	93	.281	.304	0	—	0	91 24		3
1991	†Tor A★	16	12	.571	33	33	2-2	0-0	209.1	207	84	12	3	44-3	125	3.05	138	.254	.293	0	—	0	111 15		1
1992	†Tor A	13	13	.500	33	33	4-2	0-0	216.2	205	88	24	4	59-0	117	3.53	116	.248	.298	0	—	0	127 33		3
1993	NY A★	18	6	**.750**	34	34	4-2	0-0	236.2	219	84	26	4	43-1	173	3.00	139	.246	.279	0	—	0	134 25		2
1994	NY A★ ▪	17	4	.810	25	**25**	1	0-0	168	177	68	10	3	52-0	97	3.27	141	.273	.329	0	—	0	129 -3	138	3
1995	NY A	1	2	.333	5	5	0	0-0	30.1	40	20	3	0	6-1	14	5.64	82	.323	.351	0	—	0	95 5	30	0
1996	†NY A	12	11	.522	30	30	0	0-0	169.1	171	93	21	2	58-1	116	4.68	106	.266	.326	0	—	0	98 23		7
1997	†Bal A*	16	10	.615	34	34	1-1	0-0	212.1	210	90	24	5	82-1	141	3.43	129	.261	.331	2-0-1	.000	-0	93 3	68	0
1998	Bal A	6	3	.667	25	11	0	0-1	79.1	77	39	7	3	23-0	53	4.20	108	.258	.316	0	—	0	105 221	356	23
Total	15	186	117	.614	470	389	34-13	10-8	2591.2	2518	1104	254	38	668-29	1538	3.51	124	.255	.303	2-0-1	.000		105 221	356	23
KEYSER, BRIAN	Brian Lee B10.31.1966 Castro Valley CA BR/TR/6-1/180* d6.2 Col Stanford																									
1995	Chi A	5	6	.455	23	10	0	0-1	92.1	114	53	10	2	27-1	48	4.97	90	.306	.354	0	—	0	83 -4		-0
1996	Chi A	1	2	.333	28	0	0	1-1	59.2	78	35	3	0	28-8	19	4.98	96	.328	.394	0	—	0	-1		0
Total	2	6	8	.429	51	10	0	1-2	152	192	88	13	2	55-9	67	4.97	92	.314	.370	0	—	0	83 -5		-0
KIDA, MASAO	Masao B9.12.1968 Tokyo, Japan BR/TR/6-2/209* d4.5																									
1999	Det A	1	0	1.000	49	0	0	1-0	64.2	73	48	6	4	30-3	50	6.26	80	.289	.368	0	—	0	-9	28	-0
2000	Det A	0	0	—	2	0	0	0-0	2.2	5	3	1	0	0-0	0	10.13	48	.385	.385	0	—	0	-1		-0
2003	LA N	0	1	.000	3	2	0	0-0	12	15	5	0	0	3-0	8	3.00	137	.300	.340	4	.250	0	46 1		0
2004	LA N	0	0	—	3	0	0	0-0	4.2	4	0	0	1	1-0	5	0.00	—	.235	.316	0	—	0	2		-0
	Sea A	0	0	—	7	0	0	0-0	9.2	15	9	1	1	5-0	5	8.38	53	.366	.447	0	—	0	-4		-0
2005	Sea A	0	0	—	1	0	0	0-0	2	2	1	1	0	0-0	0	4.50	94	.250	.250	0	—	0	0		-0
Total	5	1	1	.500	65	2	0	1-0	95.2	114	66	9	6	39-3	68	5.83	82	.298	.369	4	.250	0	46 -11	28	-0
KIECKER, DANA	Dana Ervin B2.25.1961 Sleepy Eye MN BR/TR/6-3/180(180-195) [BosA83 8/203] d4.12 Col St. Cloud St.																									
1990	†Bos A	8	9	.471	32	25	0	0-0	152	145	74	7	9	54-2	93	3.97	103	.253	.325	0	—	0	135 -12	55	-0
1991	Bos A	2	3	.400	18	5	0	0-0	40.1	56	34	6	2	23-4	21	7.36	59	.344	.429	0	—	0	101 -10	55	-0
Total	2	10	12	.455	50	30	0	0-0	192.1	201	108	13	11	77-6	114	4.68	89	.273	.349	0	—	0			-0
KIEFER, JOE	Joseph William "Harlem Joe","Smoke" B7.19.1899 W.Leyden NY D7.5.1975 Utica NY BR/TR/5-11/190 d10.1																									
1920	Chi A	0	1	.000	2	1	0	0	4.2	7	8	0	1	5	1	15.43	24	.333	.481	2	.000	-0	148 -5		-C
1925	Bos A	0	2	.000	2	2	0	0	15	20	12	0	1	9	4	6.00	76	.351	.448	4	.000	-1	46 -2		-C
1926	Bos A	0	2	.000	11	1	0	0	30	29	19	2	2	16	8	4.80	85	.266	.370	7	.143	-0	41 -3		-C
Total	3	0	5	.000	15	4	0	0	49.2	56	39	2	4	30	13	6.16	68	.299	.407	13	.077	-1	70 -10		-C
KIEFER, MARK	Mark Andrew B11.13.1968 Orange CA BR/TR/6-4/175* [MilA87 21/539] d9.20 b-Steve Col Fullerton (CA) JC																									
1993	Mil A	0	0	—	6	0	0	1-1	9.1	9	1	0	1	8-0	8	0.00	—	.097	.243	0	—	0	4		-C
1994	Mil A	1	0	1.000	7	0	0	0-0	10.2	15	12	4	0	8-0	8	8.44	60	.357	.442	0	—	0	-4		-C
1995	Mil A	4	1	.800	24	0	0	0-0	49.2	37	20	6	0	27-2	41	3.44	146	.203	.306	0	—	0	8		-C
1996	Mil A	0	0	—	7	0	0	0-0	10	15	9	1	0	5-1	5	8.10	64	.366	.426	0	—	0	-3		-C
Total	4	5	1	.833	44	0	0	1-1	79.2	76	41	11	1	45-3	61	4.29	116	.236	.336	0	—	0	5		-C
KIELY, JOHN	John Francis B10.4.1964 Boston MA BR/TR/6-3/210* d7.26 Col Bridgewater St. (MA)																									
1991	Det A	0	1	.000	7	0	0	0-0	6.2	13	11	0	1	9-2	1	14.85	28	.448	.575	0	—	0	-7		-C
1992	Det A	4	2	.667	39	0	0	0-1	55	44	14	2	0	28-3	18	2.13	188	.224	.317	0	—	0	11		-C
1993	Det A	0	2	.000	8	0	0	0-1	11.2	13	11	2	1	13-5	5	7.71	56	.295	.466	0	—	0	-4		-C
Total	3	4	5	.444	54	0	0	0-1	73.1	70	36	4	2	50-10	24	4.17	98	.260	.375	0	—	0	0		-C
KIELY, LEO	Leo Patrick "Kiki" B11.30.1929 Hoboken NJ D1.18.1984 Montclair NJ BL/TL/6-2/180* d6.27 Mil 1952-53																									
1951	Bos A	7	7	.500	17	16	4	0	113.1	106	48	9	2	39	46	3.34	134	.251	.317	35	.143	-1*	75 13		-C
1954	Bos A	5	8	.385	28	14	4-1	0	131	153	74	12	1	58	59	3.50	117	.295	.365	50-1-1	.180	-0	91 2		-C
1955	Bos A	3	3	.500	33	4	0	6	90	91	31	5	0	37-5	36	2.80	153	.269	.341	26-0-1	.192	-0	93 14		-C
1956	Bos A	2	2	.500	23	0	0	3	31.1	47	25	1	2	14-5	9	5.17	89	.362	.429	6	.167	0	-3		-C
1958	Bos A	5	2	.714	47	0	0	12	81	77	31	9	1	18-3	26	3.00	134	.254	.299	13-0-2	.000	-2	9		-C
1959	Bos A	3	3	.500	41	0	0	7	55.2	67	26	8	1	18-3	30	4.20	97	.299	.352	8	.000	-1	0		-C
1960	KC A	1	2	.333	20	0	0	1	20.2	21	4	1	1	5-0	6	1.74	229	.266	.318	1	.000	0	5		-C
Total	7	26	27	.491	209	39	8-1	29	523	562	239	39	9	189-16	212	3.37	125	.279	.342	139-1-4	.144	-4	86 40		-C
KIESCHNICK, BROOKS	Michael Brooks B6.6.1972 Robstown TX BL/TR/6-4/230(220-250) [ChiN93 1/10] d4.3.1996 Col Texas ▲																									
2003	Mil N	1	1	.500	42	0	0	1-0	53	66	32	6	6	13-4	39	5.26	82	.299	.354	70-7-0	.300	8*	-5		25
2004	Mil N	1	1	.500	32	0	0	0-1	43	44	19	6	0	13-3	28	3.77	117	.262	.315	63-1-0	.270	6*	3	25
Total	2	2	2	.500	74	0	0	1-1	96	110	51	11	6	26-7	67	4.59	95	.283	.337	133-8-0	.286	14	-2	25
KILE, DARRYL	Darryl Andrew B12.2.1968 Garden Grove CA D6.22.2002 Chicago IL BR/TR/6-5/185(185-212) [HouN87 30/782] d4.8 Col Chaffey (CA) JC																									
1991	Hou N	7	11	.389	37	22	0	0-1	153.2	144	81	16	4	84-4	100	3.69	96	.246	.348	38-0-4	.000	-3	105 -8		
1992	Hou N	5	10	.333	22	22	2	0-0	125.1	124	61	17	8	63-4	90	3.95	86	.261	.348	32-0-5	.156	-1	121 8		
1993	Hou N	15	8	.652	32	26	4-2	0-0	171.2	152	73	12	15	69-1	141	3.51	110	.239	.324	53-1-8	.094	0	123 -11		
1994	Hou N	9	6	.600	24	24	0	0-0	147.2	153	84	13	9	82-6	105	4.57	87	.275	.375	47-0-9	.149	0	105 -18		
1995	Hou N	4	12	.250	25	21	0	0-0	127	114	81	9	4	73-2	113	4.96	78	.240	.353	36-0-5	.111	0	105 -18		
1996	Hou N	12	11	.522	35	33	4	0-0	219	233	113	16	16	97-8	219	4.19	93	.276	.300	73-0-7	.137	1*	113 -8		
1997	†Hou N☆	19	7	.731	34	34	6-4	0-0	255.2	208	87	19	16	94-4	205	2.57	156	.225	.300	89-0-10	.124	0	110 40		
1998	Col N	13	17	.433	36	**35**	4-1	0-0	230.1	257	141	28	7	96-4	158	5.20	100	.287	.358	71-0-9	.254	2*	87 0		
1999	Col N	8	13	.381	32	32	1	0-0	190.2	225	150	31	6	109-5	116	6.61	88	.298	.387	52-0-8	.135	-2	98 -14		
2000	†StL N★	20	9	.690	34	34	5-1	0-0	232.1	215	105	30	7	58-3	192	3.91	119	.247	.301	73-0-8	.123	1	97 20		

YEAR	TM LG	W	L	PCT	G	GS	CG-SHO	SV-BS	IP	H	R	HR	HB	BB-IB	SO	ERA	AERA	OAV	OOB	AB-HR-SH	AVG	PB	SUP	APR	DL	PW
2001	†StL N	16	11	.593	34	34	2-1	0-0	227.1	228	83	22	11	65-3	179	3.09	140	.265	.322	71-1-5	.127	1	85	32		3.6
2002	Stl N	5	4	.556	14	14	0	0-0	84.2	82	36	9	8	28-1	50	3.72	108	.257	.330	22-0-3	.091	-1	98	4		0.3
Total 12		133	119	.528	359	331	28-9	0-1	2165.1	2135	1099	214	117	918-41	1668	4.12	104	.260	.341	657-2-81	.132	-1	100	37		4.2

KILGUS, PAUL Paul Nelson B2.2.1962 Bowling Green KY BL/TL/6-1/185(175-190) [TexA84 43/821] d6.7 Col Kentucky [DL 1994 StL N 131]

YEAR	TM LG	W	L	PCT	G	GS	CG-SHO	SV-BS	IP	H	R	HR	HB	BB-IB	SO	ERA	AERA	OAV	OOB	AB-HR-SH	AVG	PB	SUP	APR	DL	PW
1987	Tex A	2	7	.222	25	12	0	0-0	89.1	95	45	14	2	31-2	42	4.13	109	.271	.334	0	—	0	86	5		0.4
1988	Tex A	12	15	.444	32	32	5-0	0-0	203.1	190	105	18	10	71-2	88	4.16	99	.243	.313	0	—	0	88	-1		0.0
1989	†Chi N	6	10	.375	35	23	0	2-0	145.2	164	90	9	5	49-6	61	4.39	86	.283	.342	41-0-4	.073	-3	97	-13		-1.7
1990	Tor A	0	0	—	11	0	0	0-0	16.1	19	11	2	1	7-1	7	6.06	65	.306	.370	0	—	-3		-3		-0.2
1991	Bal A	0	2	.000	38	0	0	1-0	62	60	38	8	3	24-2	32	5.08	78	.256	.328	0	—	0		-8		-0.3
1993	StL N	1	0	1.000	22	1	0	1-0	28.2	18	2	1	1	8-1	21	0.63	642	.180	.248	5	.200	0	22	11	69	0.6
Total 6		21	34	.382	163	68	5-3	4-0	545.1	546	291	52	22	190-14	251	4.19	97	.259	.325	46-0-4	.087	-2	90	-9	200	-1.2

KILKENNY, MIKE Michael David B4.11.1945 Bradford ON, Can. BR/TL/6-3.5/175* d4.11

YEAR	TM LG	W	L	PCT	G	GS	CG-SHO	SV-BS	IP	H	R	HR	HB	BB-IB	SO	ERA	AERA	OAV	OOB	AB-HR-SH	AVG	PB	SUP	APR	DL	PW
1969	Det A	8	6	.571	39	15	6-4	2-0	128.1	99	54	13	4	63-1	97	3.37	112	.211	.309	37-0-3	.054	-3	103	5		0.3
1970	Det A	7	6	.538	36	21	3	0-1	129	141	77	10	2	70-0	105	5.16	73	.279	.368	39-0-4	.077	-3*	91	-17		-1.8
1971	Det A	4	5	.444	30	11	2	1-0	86.1	83	52	8	2	44-3	47	5.00	72	.247	.337	24-0-1	.083	-2	76	-13	23	-1.5
1972	Det A	0	0	—	1	0	0	0-0	1	1	1	1	0	0-0	0	9.00	35	.250	.250	0	—	0		-1		-1.5
	Oak A	0	0	—	1	0	0	0-0	1	0	0	0	0	0-0	0	0.00	—	.000	.000	0	—	0		-1		0.0
	Year	0	0	—	2	0	0	0-0	2	1	1	1	0	0-0	0	4.50	97	.143	.143	0	—	0		0		0.0
	SD N	0	0	—	5	0	0	0-0	4.1	7	4	1	0	3-0	5	8.31	40	.350	.435	0	—	0		-2		-0.1
	Cle A	4	1	.800	22	7	1	1-0	58	51	23	5	0	39-4	44	3.41	96	.237	.353	14-0-2	.071	-1	81	0		-0.1
1973	Cle A	0	0	—	5	0	0	0-0	2	5	5	1	1	5-0	3	22.50	18	.455	.647	0	—	0		-4		-0.2
Total 5		23	18	.561	139	54	12-4	4-1	410	387	216	39	9	224-8	301	4.43	83	.248	.344	114-0-10	.070	-8	91	-32	23	-3.4

KILLEEN, EVANS Evans Henry B2.27.1936 Brooklyn NY BR/TR/6-0/195 d9.7

YEAR	TM LG	W	L	PCT	G	GS	CG-SHO	SV-BS	IP	H	R	HR	HB	BB-IB	SO	ERA	AERA	OAV	OOB	AB-HR-SH	AVG	PB	SUP	APR	DL	PW
1959	KC A	0	0	—					5.2	4	3	0	0	4-0	1	4.76	84	.211	.348	0		0		0		0.0

KILLEEN, HENRY Henry F. B5.1872 Troy NY D10.16.1916 Waterbury CT 5-9/150 d9.11

YEAR	TM LG	W	L	PCT	G	GS	CG-SHO	SV-BS	IP	H	R	HR	HB	BB-IB	SO	ERA	AERA	OAV	OOB	AB-HR-SH	AVG	PB	SUP	APR	DL	PW
1891	Cle N	0	1	.000	1	1	1	0	8.2	11	8	1	0	8	3	6.23	56	.297	.422	3	.000	-0	34	-2		-0.2

KILLEN, FRANK Frank Bissell "Lefty" B11.30.1870 Pittsburgh PA D12.3.1939 Pittsburgh PA BL/TL/6-1/200 d8.27

YEAR	TM LG	W	L	PCT	G	GS	CG-SHO	SV-BS	IP	H	R	HR	HB	BB-IB	SO	ERA	AERA	OAV	OOB	AB-HR-SH	AVG	PB	SUP	APR	DL	PW
1891	Mil AA	7	4	.636	11	11	11-2	0	96.2	73	42	1	3	51	38	1.68	262	.202	.306	35	.229	1	126	22		2.3
1892	Was N	29	26	.527	60	52	46-2	0	459.2	448	286	15	20	182	147	3.31	98	.245	.321	186-4	.199	10*	99	-2		1.0
1893	Pit N	36	14	.720	55	48	38-2	0	415	401	235	12	15	140	99	3.64	125	.246	.312	171-4	.275	14	125	46		5.5
1894	Pit N	14	11	.560	28	28	20-1	0	204	261	148	3	5	86	62	4.50	117	.308	.375	80-0-1	.262	0	99	13		1.1
1895	Pit N	5	5	.500	13	11	6	0	95	113	77	2	1	57	25	5.49	82	.291	.383	38	.342	4*	83	-8		-0.2
1896	Pit N	30	18	.625	52	50	44-5	0	432.1	476	244	7	14	119	134	3.41	123	.277	.329	173-2-3	.231	9*	117	29		3.4
1897	Pit N	17	23	.425	42	41	38-1	0	337.1	417	246	4	8	76	99	4.46	94	.301	.341	129-1-0	.248	5	83	-16		-1.1
1898	Pit N	10	11	.476	23	23	17	0	177.2	201	106	3	11	41	48	3.75	95	.283	.332	65-0-4	.262	2*	93	-5		-0.3
	Was N	9	9	.400	17	16	15	0	128.1	149	80	4	2	29	43	3.58	102	.288	.328	55	.273	3*	110	-1		0.2
	Year	16	20	.444	40	39	32	0	306	350	186	7	13	70	91	3.68	98	.285	.330	120-0-4	.267	5	100	-5		-0.1
1899	Was N	0	2	.000	2	2	1	0	12	18	11	0	1	4	3	6.00	65	.346	.404	5	.200	-0	64	-3		-0.4
	Bos N	7	5	.583	12	12	11	0	99.1	108	65	3	3	26	23	4.26	98	.276	.326	41	.171	-2	101	-2		-0.4
	Year	7	7	.500	14	14	12	0	111.1	126	76	3	4	30	26	4.45	93	.284	.330	46	.174	-2	96	-2		-0.8
1900	Chi N	3	3	.500	6	6	6	0	54	50	31	1	2	11	4	4.67	77	.297	.336	20-0-1	.150	-1	96	-2		-0.2
Total 10		164	131	.556	321	300	253-13	0	2511.1	2730	1551	55	85	822	725	3.78	109	.272	.332	998-11-9	.241	44	104	71		10.9

KILLIAN, ED Edwin Henry "Twilight Ed" B11.12.1876 Racine WI D7.18.1928 Detroit MI BL/TL/5-11/170 d8.25

YEAR	TM LG	W	L	PCT	G	GS	CG-SHO	SV-BS	IP	H	R	HR	HB	BB-IB	SO	ERA	AERA	OAV	OOB	AB-HR-SH	AVG	PB	SUP	APR	DL	PW
1903	Cle A	3	4	.429	9	8	7-3	0	61.2	61	24	1	4	13	18	2.48	115	.257	.307	28	.179	-1*	113	3		0.3
1904	Det A	15	20	.429	40	34	32-4	0	331.2	293	108	0	17	93	124	2.44	104	.238	.301	126-0-2	.143	-3	89	8		0.2
1905	Det A	23	14	.622	39	37	33-8	0	313.1	263	108	0	13	102	110	2.27	120	.230	.300	118-0-7	.271	6	90	17		2.6
1906	Det A	10	6	.625	21	16	14	2	149.2	165	71	0	5	54	47	3.43	81	.283	.348	53-0-3	.170	-1	133	-9		-1.2
1907	†Det A	25	13	.658	42	34	29-3	0	314	286	103	2	11	91	96	1.78	147	.245	.306	122-0-3	.320	10*	104	25		4.2
1908	†Det A	12	9	.571	27	23	15	1	180.2	170	78	3	8	53	47	2.99	81	.252	.314	73	.137	-3*	118	-8		-1.1
1909	Det A	11	9	.550	25	19	14-3	1	173.1	150	45	1	6	49	54	1.71	147	.236	.297	62-0-3	.161	-1	97	15		1.7
1910	Det A	4	3	.571	11	9	5-1	0	74	75	38	2	6	27	20	3.04	87	.268	.345	27-0-1	.148	-1	150	-5		-0.6
Total 8		103	78	.569	214	180	149-22	4	1598.1	1463	585	9	70	482	516	2.38	110	.246	.310	609-0-19	.209	6	105	46		6.1

KILLILAY, JACK John William B5.24.1887 Leavenworth KS D10.21.1968 Tulsa OK BR/TR/5-11/165 d5.13

YEAR	TM LG	W	L	PCT	G	GS	CG-SHO	SV-BS	IP	H	R	HR	HB	BB-IB	SO	ERA	AERA	OAV	OOB	AB-HR-SH	AVG	PB	SUP	APR	DL	PW
1911	Bos A	4	2	.667	14	1	0		61	65	26	0	10	36	28	3.54	93	.302	.425	24	.042	-2	116	2		-0.1

KILROY, MATT Matthew Aloysius "Matches" B6.21.1866 Philadelphia PA D3.2.1940 Philadelphia PA BL/TL/5-9/175 d4.17 b-Mike

YEAR	TM LG	W	L	PCT	G	GS	CG-SHO	SV-BS	IP	H	R	HR	HB	BB-IB	SO	ERA	AERA	OAV	OOB	AB-HR-SH	AVG	PB	SUP	APR	DL	PW
1886	Bal AA	29	34	.460	68	68	66-5	0	583	476	350	10	19	182	513	3.37	102	.210	.274	218	.174	-5	76	3		0.1
1887	Bal AA	46	19	.708	69	69	66-6	0	589.1	585	326	6	20	157	217	3.07	134	.253	.306	239	.247	9*	113	72		7.2
1888	Bal AA	17	21	.447	40	40	35-2	0	321	347	224	5	23	79	135	4.04	74	.266	.319	145	.179	-0*	100	-40		-3.8
1889	Bal AA	29	25	.537	59	56	55-5	0	480.2	476	283	8	27	142	217	2.85	139	.250	.312	208-1	.274	10*	89	49		5.7
1890	Bos P	9	15	.375	30	27	18	0	217.2	268	161	14	15	87	48	4.26	103	.290	.361	93	.215	-0*	98	4		0.3
1891	Cin AA	1	4	.200	7	6	4	0	45.1	51	42	1	8	19	6	2.98	137	.274	.366	20	.150	-1*	73	2		0.1
1892	Was N	1	1	.500	4	3	2	0	26.1	20	11	0	2	15	1	2.39	136	.202	.319	10	.200	-0	45	3		0.3
1893	Lou N	3	2	.600	5	5	5-1	0	35	57	41	2	4	23	4	9.00	49	.354	.447	16	.438	3	105	-17		-1.3
1894	Lou N	0	5	.000	8	7	3	0	37	46	34	2	2	20	11	3.89	131	.301	.389	17	.118	-2	97	2		0.1
1898	Chi N	6	7	.462	13	11	10	0	100.1	119	67	2	11	30	18	4.31	83	.292	.357	96-0-2	.229	2*	108	-5		-0.3
Total 10		141	133	.515	303	292	264-19	1	2435.2	2445	1539	53	131	754	1170	3.47	109	.252	.314	1062-1-2	.222	15	95	73		8.4

KILROY, MIKE Michael Joseph B11.4.1872 Philadelphia PA D10.2.1960 Philadelphia PA BR/TR/5-11/180 d9.1 b-Matt

YEAR	TM LG	W	L	PCT	G	GS	CG-SHO	SV-BS	IP	H	R	HR	HB	BB-IB	SO	ERA	AERA	OAV	OOB	AB-HR-SH	AVG	PB	SUP	APR	DL	PW
1888	Bal AA	0	1	1.000	1	1	0	0	9	12	9	1	0	5	1	8.00	37	.308	.386	4	.000	-1	0	-4		-0.4
1891	Phi N	0	2	.000	3	1	0	0	10	15	14	1	2	4	3	9.90	34	.333	.412	5	.400	-1	175	-6		-0.8
Total 2		0	3	.000	4	2	1	0	19	27	23	2	2	9	4	9.00	36	.321	.400	9	.222	0	92	-10		-1.2

KIM, BYUNG-HYUN Byung-Hyun B1.19.1979 Kwangju, South Korea BR/TR/5-11/177* d5.29

YEAR	TM LG	W	L	PCT	G	GS	CG-SHO	SV-BS	IP	H	R	HR	HB	BB-IB	SO	ERA	AERA	OAV	OOB	AB-HR-SH	AVG	PB	SUP	APR	DL	PW
1999	Ari N	1	2	.333	25	0	0	1-3	27.1	20	15	2	9	20-2	31	4.61	100	.211	.375	1	.000	-0	0		44	0.0
2000	Ari N	6	6	.500	61	1	0	14-6	70.2	52	39	9	9	46-5	111	4.46	108	.200	.336	3	.000	-0	115	2		0.3
2001	†Ari N	5	6	.455	78	0	0	19-4	98	58	32	10	8	44-3	113	2.94	158	.173	.284	6	.167	-0		18		2.6
2002	†Ari N★	8	3	.727	72	0	0	36-6	84	64	20	5	8	26-2	92	2.04	208	.208	.281	2	.500	-0		21		4.3
2003	Ari N	1	5	.167	7	7	0	0-0	43	34	17	4	6	15-0	33	3.56	130	.214	.298	13-0-2	.154	-0	52	5	27	0.8
	†Bos A	8	5	.615	49	5	0	16-3	79.1	70	38	6	8	18-3	69	3.18	147	.230	.288	7	.286	0	182	10		1.8
2004	Bos A	2	1	.667	7	1	0	0-0	17.1	17	15	1	2	7-1	6	6.23	78	.258	.338	0	—	0	121	-3	25	-0.2
2005	Col N	5	12	.294	40	20	0	0-2	148	156	82	17	14	71-8	115	4.86	98	.275	.366	38-0-4	.079	-2	75	0		-0.2
Total 7		36	40	.474	339	38	0	86-24	567.2	471	258	56	56	247-24	570	3.76	125	.225	.321	70-0-6	.129	-2	90	53	96	9.2

KIM, SUNNY Sun-Woo B9.4.1977 Inchon, South Korea BR/TR/6-2/180* d6.15

YEAR	TM LG	W	L	PCT	G	GS	CG-SHO	SV-BS	IP	H	R	HR	HB	BB-IB	SO	ERA	AERA	OAV	OOB	AB-HR-SH	AVG	PB	SUP	APR	DL	PW
2001	Bos A	0	2	.000	20	2	0	0-0	41.2	54	27	1	4	21-5	27	5.83	76	.312	.399	0	—	0	94	-5		-0.3
2002	Bos A	1	0	1.000	15	2	0	0-0	29	34	24	5	1	7-0	18	7.45	60	.288	.328	0	—	0	145	-8		-0.5
	Mon N	1	0	1.000	4	3	0	0-0	20.1	18	2	0	1	7-2	11	0.89	495	.250	.325	6	.250	0	134	8		0.4
2003	Mon N	1	1	.000	4	3	0	0-0	14	24	13	6	4	8-0	5	8.36	53	.407	.500	3	.000	-0	113	-5		-0.4
2004	Mon N	4	6	.400	43	17	0	0-0	135.2	145	81	17	13	55-11	87	4.58	100	.275	.356	28-0-4	.214	1	100	-1		-0.4
2005	Was N	1	2	.333	12	2	0	0-0	29.1	41	20	3	2	8-2	17	6.14	66	.336	.381	4-0-2	.000	-0	195	-6		-0.6
	Col N	5	1	.833	12	8	1-1	0-0	53.1	56	26	7	1	13-0	38	4.22	113	.268	.313	15-0-4	.133	-1	98	3		0.2
	Year	6	3	.667	24	10	1-1	0-0	82.2	97	46	10	3	21-2	55	4.90	92	.293	.338	19-0-6	.105	-1	118	-2		-0.4
Total 5		13	12	.520	110	37	1-1	0-0	323.1	372	192	39	26	119-20	203	5.01	90	.291	.361	58-0-10	.172	-1	110	-14		-1.2

KIMBALL, NEWT Newell W. B3.27.1915 Logan UT D3.22.2001 Las Vegas NV BR/TR/6-2.5/190 d5.7

YEAR	TM LG	W	L	PCT	G	GS	CG-SHO	SV-BS	IP	H	R	HR	HB	BB-IB	SO	ERA	AERA	OAV	OOB	AB-HR-SH	AVG	PB	SUP	APR	DL	PW
1937	Chi N	0	0	—	2	0	0	0	5	12	9	1	0	1	1	10.80	37	.444	.464	1	.000	-0		-4		-0.2
1938	Chi N	0	0	—	1	0	0	0	1	3	1	0	0	0	1	9.00	43	.500	.500	0	—	0		-1		0.0
1940	Bro N	3	1	.750	21	0	0	0	33.2	29	15	2	0	15	21	3.21	125	.238	.321	5	.000	-1		2		0.2
1941	StL N	1	0	1.000	2	1	0	0	14	11	5	1	0	6	6	2.57	155	.208	.288	6	.333	1	109	2		0.2

YEAR	TM LG	W	L	PCT	G	GS	CG-SHO	SV-BS	IP	H	R	HR	HB	BB-IB	SO	ERA	AERA	OAV	OOB	AB-HR-SH	AVG	PB	SUP	APR	DL	PW
	Year	4	1	.800	23	1	1	1	47.2	40	20	3	0	21	27	3.02	132	.229	.311	11	.182	0	109	4		0.4
1941	Bro N	3	1	.750	15	5	1	1	52	43	22	0	0	29	17	3.63	101	.225	.327	14	.214	-0	232	1		0.1
1942	Bro N	2	0	1.000	14	1	0	0	29.1	27	13	0	1	19	8	3.68	89	.265	.385	5	.200	-0		2		-0.1
1943	Bro N	1	1	.500	5	0	0	1	11	9	2	0	0	5	2	1.64	205	.214	.298	3	.000	1		2		0.1
	Phi N	1	6	.143	34	6	2	2	89.2	85	47	4	1	42	33	4.12	82	.253	.338	16-0-2	.188	1	101	-7		-0.1
	Year	2	7	.222	39	6	2	3	100.2	94	49	4	1	47	35	3.84	88	.249	.333	19-0-2	.158	1	101	-5		-0.1
Total 6		11	9	.550	94	13	4	5	235.2	219	113	8	2	117	88	3.78	94	.249	.339	50-0-2	.180	1	107	-6		0.1

KIMBER, SAM Samuel Jackson B10.29.1852 Philadelphia PA D11.7.1925 Philadelphia PA BR/TR/5-10.5/165 d5.1

YEAR	TM LG	W	L	PCT	G	GS	CG-SHO	SV-BS	IP	H	R	HR	HB	BB-IB	SO	ERA	AERA	OAV	OOB	AB-HR-SH	AVG	PB	SUP	APR	DL	PW
1884	Bro AA	18	20	.474	41	41	41-4	0	361.1	364	240	6	15	72	122	3.81	87	.247	.289	142	.148	-5	94	-18		-2.0
1885	Pro N	0	1	.000	1	1	1	0	8	15	13	1		5	4	11.25	24	.405	.476	3	.000	-0	21	-6		-2.5
Total 2		18	21	.462	42	42	42-4	0	369.1	379	253	7	15	77	126	3.97	83	.251	.294	145	.145	-6	92	-24		-2.5

KIMBERLIN, HARRY Harry Lydle "Murphy","Mule Trader" B3.13.1909 Sullivan MO D12.31.1999 Poplar Bluff MO BR/TR/6-3/175 d7.11

YEAR	TM LG	W	L	PCT	G	GS	CG-SHO	SV-BS	IP	H	R	HR	HB	BB-IB	SO	ERA	AERA	OAV	OOB	AB-HR-SH	AVG	PB	SUP	APR	DL	PW
1936	StL A	0	0		13	0	0	0	20	24	13	3	0	16	4	5.40	100	.296	.412	1	.000	-0		0		0.0
1937	StL A	0	2	.000	3	2	1	0	15.1	16	13	2	0	9	5	2.35	206	.254	.347	5	.200	-0	63	0		0.0
1938	StL A	0	0		1	1	1	0	8	8	3	1	0	3	1	3.38	147	.286	.355	1-0-2	.000	-0	53	2		-0.3
1939	StL A	1	2	.333	17	3	0	0	41	59	35	6	2	19	11	5.49	89	.326	.396	9	.333	-0	42	-6		-0.3
Total 4		1	4	.200	34	6	2	0	84.1	107	64	12	2	47	21	4.70	106	.303	.388	16-0-2	.250	-0	50	-4		-0.2

KIME, HAL Harold Lee "Lefty" B3.15.1899 W.Salem OH D5.16.1939 Columbus OH BL/TL/5-9/160 d6.19 Col Ohio St.

YEAR	TM LG	W	L	PCT	G	GS	CG-SHO	SV-BS	IP	H	R	HR	HB	BB-IB	SO	ERA	AERA	OAV	OOB	AB-HR-SH	AVG	PB	SUP	APR	DL	PW
1920	StL N	0	0		4	0	0	0	7	9	4	0	1	2	1	2.57	116	.333	.400	1	.000	-0		0		0.0

KIMSEY, CHAD Clyde Elias B8.6.1906 Copperhill TN D12.3.1942 Pryor OK BL/TR/6-2/200 d4.21

YEAR	TM LG	W	L	PCT	G	GS	CG-SHO	SV-BS	IP	H	R	HR	HB	BB-IB	SO	ERA	AERA	OAV	OOB	AB-HR-SH	AVG	PB	SUP	APR	DL	PW
1929	StL A	3	6	.333	24	3	1	1	64.1	83	42	2	0	19	13	5.04	88	.340	.388	30-2-1	.267	3*	57	-5		-0.2
1930	StL A	6	10	.375	42	4	1	1	113.1	139	87	8	2	45	32	6.35	77	.312	.377	70-2-0	.343	7*	79	-16		-1.1
1931	StL A	4	6	.400	42	1	0	7	94.1	121	60	1	2	27	27	4.39	106	.312	.360	37-2-1	.270	5*	109	1		0.7
1932	StL A	4	2	.667	33	0	0	3	78.1	85	45	3	0	33	13	4.02	121	.281	.352	18	.333	1*		5		0.5
	Chi A	1	1	.500	7	0	0	2	11	8	4	0	1	5	6	2.45	176	.211	.318	2	.000	1		8		1.0
	Year	5	3	.625	40	0	0	5	89.1	93	49	3	1	38	19	3.83	125	.274	.348	20	.300	1		8		1.0
1933	StL A	4	1	.800	28	2	0	0	96	124	67	7	4	36	19	5.53	77	.318	.381	33	.152	-2	120	-12		0.1
1936	Det A	2	3	.400	22	0	0	3	52	58	36	2	1	29	11	4.85	102	.284	.376	16	.313	2		-1		0.1
Total 6		24	29	.453	198	10	2	17	509.1	618	341	23	10	194	121	5.07	92	.307	.371	206-6-2	.282	16	83	-26		-0.2

KINDER, ELLIS Ellis Raymond "Old Folks" B7.26.1914 Atkins AR D10.16.1968 Jackson TN BR/TR/6-0/195* d4.30

YEAR	TM LG	W	L	PCT	G	GS	CG-SHO	SV-BS	IP	H	R	HR	HB	BB-IB	SO	ERA	AERA	OAV	OOB	AB-HR-SH	AVG	PB	SUP	APR	DL	PW
1946	StL A	3	3	.500	33	7	1	1	86.2	78	35	8	0	36	59	3.32	112	.241	.318	19-0-2	.053	-1	95	5		0.1
1947	StL A	8	15	.348	34	26	10-2	1	194.1	201	105	11	0	82	110	4.49	86	.264	.336	62-0-4	.129	-4	67	-11		-1.7
1948	Bos A	10	7	.588	28	22	10-1	0	178	183	84	10	2	63	53	3.74	117	.266	.330	62-0-3	.097	-4	122	12		2.2
1949	Bos A	23	6	.793	43	30	19-6	4	252	251	103	21	2	99	138	3.36	130	.260	.330	92-0-9	.130	-4	134	27		2.2
1950	Bos A	14	12	.538	48	23	11-1	9	207	212	103	25	1	78	95	4.26	115	.263	.328	34	.118	-3	149	24		1.4
1951	Bos A	11	2	.846	63	2	1	14	127	108	42	8	0	46	84	2.55	175	.234	.290	32	.000	-4	53	13	105	1.1
1952	Bos A	5	6	.455	23	10	4	4	97.2	85	33	11	1	28	50	2.58	153	.234	.290	29-0-1	.379	3		25		5.2
1953	Bos A	10	6	.625	69	0	0	27	107	84	30	8	2	38	39	1.85	227	.215	.288	27-0-5	.185	0	172	6		1.
1954	Bos A	8	8	.500	48	2	0	15	107	106	47	7	0	36	67	3.62	114	.260	.318	12-0-1	.250	0		11		2.
1955	Bos A	5	5	.500	43	0	0	18	66.2	57	22	4	1	15-4	31	2.84	151	.229	.274	2	.000	-0		1		1.
1956	StL N	2	0	1.000	22	0	0	6	25.2	23	11	3	0	9-3	19	3.51	108	.245	.305	2	.000	-0		5		1.
	Chi A	3	1	.750	29	0	0	12	29.2	33	10	2	0	8-0	19	2.73	150	.277	.318	2	.000	-0		0		1.
1957	Chi A	0	0		1	0	0	0	0	0	0	0	0	0	0	0.00		.250	0		.000	-0		0		0.0
Total 12		102	71	.590	484	122	56-10	102	1479.2	1421	627	116	9	539-8	749	3.43	125	.252	.318	444-1-29	.142	-19	112	132	105	14.9

KING, SILVER Charles Frederick (b Charles Frederick Koenig) B1.11.1868 St.Louis MO D5.21.1938 St.Louis MO BR/TR/6-0/170 d9.28

YEAR	TM LG	W	L	PCT	G	GS	CG-SHO	SV-BS	IP	H	R	HR	HB	BB-IB	SO	ERA	AERA	OAV	OOB	AB-HR-SH	AVG	PB	SUP	APR	DL	PW
1886	KC N	1	3	.250	5	5	5	0	39	43	35	1		9	23	4.85	78	.243	.280	22	.045	-2*	58	-5		-0.
1887	†StL AA	32	12	.727	46	44	43-2	1	390	401	231	4	17	109	128	3.78	120	.260	.316	222	.207	-4*	107	36		2.
1888	†StL AA	45	20	.692	66	64	64-6	1	584.2	435	203	6	30	76	258	1.63	200	.200	.237	207-1	.208	9	89	95		10.
1889	StL AA	35	16	.686	56	53	47-2	1	458	462	257	15	21	125	188	3.14	134	.254	.309	189	.228	1	117	52		4.
1890	Chi P	30	22	.577	56	56	48-4	0	461	420	233	5	15	163	185	2.69	161	.232	.301	148	.169	-6*	84	82		6.
1891	Pit N	14	29	.326	48	44	40-3	1	384.1	382	243	7	18	144	160	3.11	105	.250	.321	163-2	.209	6	104	-2		0.
1892	NY N	22	24	.478	51	47	45-1	0	410.1	392	250	15	21	171	170	3.29	98	.242	.322	17	.176	1	124	-18		-1.
1893	NY N	3	4	.429	7	7	4	0	49	69	58	4	2	26	13	8.63	54	.322	.401	17	.176	-0	80	2		0.
	Cin N	5	6	.455	17	15	8-1	1	105	119	69	2	7	56	30	4.89	98	.277	.369	37	.162	-0	80	2		-1.
	Year	8	10	.444	24	22	12-1	1	154	188	127	6	9	82	43	6.08	78	.292	.380	54	.167	1	94	-11		-1.
1896	Was N	10	7	.588	22	16	12	1	145.1	179	106	3	4	43	35	4.09	108	.300	.351	58-0-3	.276	3	129	5		0.
1897	Was N	6	9	.400	23	19	12	1	154	196	118	7	11	45	32	4.79	91	.307	.363	57	.193	0*	121	-5		-0.
Total 10		203	152	.572	397	370	328-19	6	3180.2	3098	1803	69	146	967	1222	3.18	122	.247	.308	1305-4-3	.198	7	98	253		23.

KING, CLYDE Clyde Edward B5.23.1924 Goldsboro NC BB/TR/6-1/175* d6.21 M5/C8 Col North Carolina-Asheville

YEAR	TM LG	W	L	PCT	G	GS	CG-SHO	SV-BS	IP	H	R	HR	HB	BB-IB	SO	ERA	AERA	OAV	OOB	AB-HR-SH	AVG	PB	SUP	APR	DL	PW
1944	Bro N	2	1	.667	24	3	1	0	43.2	42	18	1	1	12	14	3.09	115	.256	.311	10-0-1	.200	-0	79	2		0.
1945	Bro N	5	5	.500	42	2	0	3	112.1	131	64	8	0	48	29	4.09	92	.295	.364	32-0-2	.125	-2*	68	-4		-0.
1947	Bro N	6	5	.545	29	9	2	0	87.2	85	34	11	0	29	31	2.77	149	.252	.311	26-0-1	.115	-0	121	12		-0.
1948	Bro N	0	1	.000	9	0	0	0	12.1	14	11	3	1	6	5	8.03	50	.286	.375	2	.000	-0		-5		-0.
1951	Bro N	14	7	.667	48	3	1	6	121.1	118	64	15	3	50	33	4.15	94	.263	.341	29-0-4	.138	-1	217	-4		-0.
1952	Bro N	2	0	1.000	23	0	0	6	42.2	56	25	5	1	12	12	5.06	72	.318	.365	5	.000	-1		-6		-0.
1953	Cin N	3	6	.333	35	4	0	2	76	78	47	15	2	32	21	5.21	84	.271	.348	10-0-1	.000	-1	118	-6		-0.
Total 7		32	25	.561	200	21	4	0	496	524	263	58	8	189	150	4.14	95	.275	.343	114-0-9	.114	-4	126	-11		-1.

KING, CURTIS Curtis Albert B10.25.1970 Norristown PA BR/TR/6-5/205* [StLN94 5/138] d8.1 Col Philadelphia

YEAR	TM LG	W	L	PCT	G	GS	CG-SHO	SV-BS	IP	H	R	HR	HB	BB-IB	SO	ERA	AERA	OAV	OOB	AB-HR-SH	AVG	PB	SUP	APR	DL	PW
1997	StL N	4	2	.667	30	0	0	0-3	29.1	38	14	0	1	11-0	13	2.76	152	.325	.379	1	.000	-0		3		0.
1998	StL N	2	0	1.000	36	0	0	2-6	51	50	20	5	3	20-4	28	3.53	119	.262	.338	5	.000	-0		5		0.
1999	StL N	0	0		2	0	0	0-0	1	3	2	0	0	0-0	0	18.00	26	.500	.500	0		-1		-1	72	0.
Total 3		6	2	.750	68	0	0	2-9	81.1	91	36	5	4	31-4	42	3.43	123	.290	.356	6	.000	-1		7	72	0.

KING, ERIC Eric Steven B4.10.1964 Oxnard CA BR/TR/6-2/215(180-218) d5.15

YEAR	TM LG	W	L	PCT	G	GS	CG-SHO	SV-BS	IP	H	R	HR	HB	BB-IB	SO	ERA	AERA	OAV	OOB	AB-HR-SH	AVG	PB	SUP	APR	DL	PW
1986	Det A	11	4	.733	33	16	3-1	3-2	138.1	108	54	11	8	63-3	79	3.51	119	.216	.312	0		0	123	13		0.
1987	†Det A	6	9	.400	55	4	0	9-6	116	111	67	15	4	60-10	89	4.89	87	.251	.343	0		0	59	-7		-0.
1988	Det A	4	1	.800	23	5	0	3-0	68.2	60	28	5	5	34-2	45	3.41	113	.233	.332	0		0	142	4		0.
1989	Chi A	9	10	.474	25	25	1-1	0-0	159.1	144	69	13	4	64-1	72	3.39	113	.244	.320	0		0	113	7	37	0.
1990	Chi A	12	4	.750	25	25	2-2	0-0	151	135	59	10	6	40-0	59	3.28	117	.237	.293	0		0	110	10	31	0.
1991	Cle A	6	11	.353	25	24	2-1	0-0	150.2	166	83	7	3	44-4	59	4.60	91	.279	.328	0		0	113	-9	79	-0.
1992	Det A	4	4	.400	17	14	0	0-0	79.1	90	47	12	1	28-1	45	5.22	77	.285	.343	0		0	109	12	192	0.
Total 7		52	45	.536	203	113	8-5	16-8	863.1	814	407	73	31	333-21	459	3.97	101	.249	.322	0		0	109	12	192	1.

KING, KEVIN Kevin Ray B2.11.1969 Atwater CA BL/TL/6-4/170(170-200) [SeaA90 7/188] d9.2 Col Oklahoma

YEAR	TM LG	W	L	PCT	G	GS	CG-SHO	SV-BS	IP	H	R	HR	HB	BB-IB	SO	ERA	AERA	OAV	OOB	AB-HR-SH	AVG	PB	SUP	APR	DL	PW
1993	Sea A	0	1	.000	13	0	0	0-1	11.2	9	8	1	4	4-1	8	6.17	72	.231	.304	0		0		-2		-0.
1994	Sea A	0	2	.000	19	0	0	0-1	15.1	21	13	0	1	17-3	6	7.04	70	.333	.481	0		0		-3		-0.
1995	Sea A	0	0		2	0	0	0-0	3.2	7	5	0	1	1-0	3	12.27	39	.412	.450	0		0		-3		-0.
Total 3		0	3	.000	34	0	0	0-2	30.2	37	26	3	3	22-4	17	7.34	65	.311	.422	0		0		-8		-0.

KING, NELLIE Nelson Joseph B3.15.1928 Shenandoah PA BR/TR/6-6/185* d4.15

YEAR	TM LG	W	L	PCT	G	GS	CG-SHO	SV-BS	IP	H	R	HR	HB	BB-IB	SO	ERA	AERA	OAV	OOB	AB-HR-SH	AVG	PB	SUP	APR	DL	PW
1954	Pit N	0	0		4	0	0	0	7	10	5	0	0	1	3	5.14	81	.400	.367	0		0		-1		0.
1955	Pit N	1	3	.250	17	4	0	0	54.1	60	24	2	2	14-3	21	2.98	138	.286	.332	12-0-2	.000	-2	76	5		0.
1956	Pit N	4	1	.800	38	0	0	5	60	54	24	8	1	19-5	25	3.15	120	.241	.302	6-0-2	.000	-1		4		0.
1957	Pit N	2	1	.667	36	0	0	6	52	69	27	7	2	16-6	23	4.50	84	.337	.387	5-0-1	.000	-1		-3		-0.
Total 4		7	5	.583	95	4	0	11	173.1	193	80	17	5	50-14	72	3.58	109	.291	.340	23-0-5	.000	-3	76	5		0.

KING, RAY Raymond Keith B1.15.1974 Chicago IL BL/TL/6-1/240(225-240) [CinN95 8/223] d5.21 Col Lambuth

YEAR	TM LG	W	L	PCT	G	GS	CG-SHO	SV-BS	IP	H	R	HR	HB	BB-IB	SO	ERA	AERA	OAV	OOB	AB-HR-SH	AVG	PB	SUP	APR	DL	PW
1999	Chi N	0	0		10	0	0	0-0	10.2	11	8	2	1	10-0	5	5.91	77	.289	.449	1	.000	-0		-2		-0
2000	Mil N	3	2	.600	36	0	0	0-1	28.2	18	7	1	0	10-0	19	1.26	368	.180	.252	0			10			0

YEAR	TM LG	W	L	PCT	G	GS	CG-SHO	SV-BS	IP	H	R	HR	HB	BB-IB	SO	ERA	AERA	OAV	OOB	AB-HR-SH	AVG	PB	SUP	APR	DL	PW
2001	Mil N	0	4	.000	82	0	0	1-3	55	49	22	5	1	25-7	49	3.60	119	.241	.325	2	.000	-0		5		0.4
2002	Mil N	3	2	.600	76	0	0	0-1	65	61	24	5	3	24-6	50	3.05	135	.255	.328	0	—	0		8	15	0.7
2003	†Atl N	3	4	.429	80	0	0	0-1	59	46	30	4	3	24-0	43	3.51	120	.213	.301	0	—	0		3		0.3
2004	†StL N	5	2	.714	86	0	0	0-1	62	43	19	1	3	24-0	43	2.61	163	.197	.285	2	.000	-0		12		1.2
2005	StL N	4	4	.500	77	0	0	0-6	40	46	17	4	1	16-0	23	3.37	124	.293	.367	0	—	0		4		0.6
Total 7		18	18	.500	447	0	0	1-13	320.1	274	127	21	12	136-16	229	3.12	137	.234	.318	5	.000	-1		40	15	4.6

KINGMAN, BRIAN Brian Paul B7.27.1954 Los Angeles CA BR/TR/6-2/200* d6.28 Col California-Santa Barbara

YEAR	TM LG	W	L	PCT	G	GS	CG-SHO	SV-BS	IP	H	R	HR	HB	BB-IB	SO	ERA	AERA	OAV	OOB	AB-HR-SH	AVG	PB	SUP	APR	DL	PW
1979	Oak A	8	7	.533	18	17	5-1	0-1	112.2	113	59	10	3	33-1	58	4.31	94	.258	.313	0	—	0	95	-2		-0.4
1980	Oak A	8	20	.286	32	30	10-1	0-1	211.1	209	105	21	4	82-5	116	3.83	99	.256	.325	0	—	0	67	-2		-0.4
1981	†Oak A	3	6	.333	18	15	3-1	0-0	100.1	112	48	10	4	32-2	52	3.95	89	.286	.345	0	—	0	92	-5		-0.5
1982	Oak A	4	12	.250	23	20	3	1-0	122.2	131	64	11	7	57-0	46	4.48	88	.279	.360	0	—	0	84	-5		-0.8
1983	SF N	0	0	—	3	0	0	0-0	4.2	10	6	0	0	1-0	1	7.71	46	.417	.440	0	—	0		-3		-0.2
Total 5		23	45	.338	94	82	21-3	1-1	551.2	575	282	52	18	205-8	273	4.13	93	.269	.336	0	—	0	82	-17		-2.3

KINNEY, DENNIS Dennis Paul B2.26.1952 Toledo OH BL/TL/6-1/190(170-190) [CleA70 10/225] d4.9

YEAR	TM LG	W	L	PCT	G	GS	CG-SHO	SV-BS	IP	H	R	HR	HB	BB-IB	SO	ERA	AERA	OAV	OOB	AB-HR-SH	AVG	PB	SUP	APR	DL	PW
1978	Cle A	0	2	.000	18	0	0	5-2	38.2	37	21	3	1	14-1	19	4.42	86	.259	.325	0		0		-3		-0.2
	SD N	0	1	.000	7	0	0	0-1	7	6	5	3	0	4-0	2	6.43	52	.222	.323	1	.000	-0		-2		-0.3
1979	SD N	0	0	—	13	0	0	0-0	18	17	8	2	1	8-3	11	3.50	101	.250	.338	1	.000	-0		0		0.0
1980	SD N	4	6	.400	50	0	0	1-2	82.2	79	45	3	1	37-15	40	4.25	81	.252	.331	12-0-1	.083	-0		-9		-1.1
1981	Det A	0	0	—	6	0	0	0-0	3.2	5	4	0	0	4-1	3	9.82	39	.313	.450	0		0		-2		-0.1
1982	Oak A	0	0	—	3	0	0	0-0	4.1	9	4	1	0	4-0	0	8.31	48	.474	.565	0		0		-2		-0.1
Total 5		4	9	.308	97	0	0	6-5	154.1	153	87	12	3	71-20	75	4.55	78	.261	.341	14-0-1	.071	-1		-18		-1.8

KINNEY, MATT Matthew John B12.16.1976 Bangor ME BR/TR/6-5/220(215-230) [BosA95 6/158] d8.18

YEAR	TM LG	W	L	PCT	G	GS	CG-SHO	SV-BS	IP	H	R	HR	HB	BB-IB	SO	ERA	AERA	OAV	OOB	AB-HR-SH	AVG	PB	SUP	APR	DL	PW
2000	Min A	2	2	.500	8	8	0	0-0	42.1	41	26	7	0	25-1	24	5.10	103	.261	.355	0	—	0	98	1		0.0
2002	Min A	2	7	.222	14	12	0	0-0	66	78	39	13	1	33-0	45	4.64	96	.295	.371	2	.000	0	64	-2	50	-0.3
2003	Mil N	10	13	.435	33	31	1	0-0	190.2	201	121	27	6	80-4	152	5.19	83	.272	.343	55-0-5	.036	-4	104	-20		-2.4
2004	Mil N	3	4	.429	32	6	0	0-0	62.1	77	41	8	2	23-1	52	5.78	76	.301	.359	9-0-1	.222	0	112	-8		-0.8
	KC A	0	1	.000	11	0	0	0-0	16.1	27	14	3	2	7-1	21	7.16	65	.365	.429	0	—	0		-4		-0.2
2005	SF N	2	0	1.000	5	1	0	0-0	12	18	8	2	1	6-0	3	6.00	71	.383	.463	0	—	0		-4		-0.2
Total 5		19	27	.413	103	58	1	0-1	389.2	442	249	60	12	174-7	297	5.29	84	.287	.359	69-0-6	.072	-4	97	-35	50	-4.0

KINNEY, WALT Walter William B9.9.1893 Denison TX D7.1.1971 Escondido CA BL/TL/6-2/186 d7.26

YEAR	TM LG	W	L	PCT	G	GS	CG-SHO	SV-BS	IP	H	R	HR	HB	BB-IB	SO	ERA	AERA	OAV	OOB	AB-HR-SH	AVG	PB	SUP	APR	DL	PW
1918	Bos A	0	0	—	5	0	0	0-0	15	5	3	0	2	4	8	1.80	149	.106	.263	5	.000	-1*		2		0.0
1919	Phi A	9	15	.375	43	21	13	2	202.2	199	110	7	8	91	97	3.64	94	.262	.347	88-1-2	.284	5*	73	-7		0.2
1920	Phi A	2	4	.333	10	8	5-1	0	61	59	38	3	1	28	19	3.10	130	.261	.345	26	.346	2*	109	-3		0.5
1923	Phi A	0	1	.000	5	1	0	0	12	11	13	0	0	9	9	7.50	50	.229	.351	6-1-0	.167	1	201	-5		-0.3
Total 4		11	20	.355	63	30	18-1	2	290.2	274	164	10	11	136	129	3.59	99	.254	.343	125-2-2	.280	7	90	-7		0.4

KINNUNEN, MIKE Michael John B4.1.1958 Seattle WA BL/TL/6-1/185(185-205) [MinA79 10/245] d6.12 Col Washington St.

YEAR	TM LG	W	L	PCT	G	GS	CG-SHO	SV-BS	IP	H	R	HR	HB	BB-IB	SO	ERA	AERA	OAV	OOB	AB-HR-SH	AVG	PB	SUP	APR	DL	PW
1980	Min A	0	0	—	21	0	0	0-0	24.2	29	18	1	1	9-1	9	5.11	86	.290	.348	0	—	0		-3		-0.1
1986	Bal A	0	0	—	9	0	0	0-0	7	8	6	1	0	5-0	1	6.43	65	.308	.419	0	—	0		-2		-0.1
1987	Bal A	0	0	—	18	0	0	0-0	20	27	14	3	0	16-1	14	4.95	90	.338	.443	0	—	0		-2		-0.1
Total 3		0	0	—	48	0	0	0-0	51.2	64	38	5	1	30-2	23	5.23	84	.311	.396	0	—	0		-7		-0.3

KINSELLA, ED Edward William "Rube" B1.15.1882 Lexington IL D1.17.1976 Bloomington IL BR/TR/6-1.5/175 d9.16 Col Illinois St.

YEAR	TM LG	W	L	PCT	G	GS	CG-SHO	SV-BS	IP	H	R	HR	HB	BB-IB	SO	ERA	AERA	OAV	OOB	AB-HR-SH	AVG	PB	SUP	APR	DL	PW
1905	Pit N	0	1	.000	3	2	2	0	17	19	6	0	1	3	11	2.65	113	.292	.333	3	.000	-0	36	1		0.0
1910	StL A	1	3	.250	10	5	2	0	50	62	30	0	2	16	10	3.78	65	.321	.379	12-0-1	.250	2	114	-7		-0.3
Total 2		1	4	.200	13	7	4	0	67	81	36	0	3	19	21	3.49	75	.314	.368	15-0-1	.200	2	90	-6		-0.3

KINZER, MATT Matthew Roy B6.17.1963 Indianapolis IN BR/TR/6-2/210* [StLN84 2/35] d5.18 Col Purdue

YEAR	TM LG	W	L	PCT	G	GS	CG-SHO	SV-BS	IP	H	R	HR	HB	BB-IB	SO	ERA	AERA	OAV	OOB	AB-HR-SH	AVG	PB	SUP	APR	DL	PW
1989	StL N	0	2	.000	8	1	0	0-0	13.1	25	19	3	0	4-2	8	12.83	29	.403	.433	1-0-1	.000	-0	97	-12		-1.6
1990	Det A	0	0	—	1	0	0	0-0	1.2	3	3	0	0	3-0	1	16.20	25	.375	.545	0	—	0		-2	30	-0.1
Total 2		0	2	.000	9	1	0	0-0	15	28	23	3	0	7-2	9	13.20	28	.400	.449	1-0-1	.000	-0	97	-14	30	-1.7

KINZY, HARRY Harry Hersel "Slim" B7.19.1910 Hallsville TX D6.22.2003 Ft.Worth TX BR/TR/6-4/185 d6.8 Col TCU

YEAR	TM LG	W	L	PCT	G	GS	CG-SHO	SV-BS	IP	H	R	HR	HB	BB-IB	SO	ERA	AERA	OAV	OOB	AB-HR-SH	AVG	PB	SUP	APR	DL	PW
1934	Chi A	0	1	.000	13	2	1	0	34.1	38	23	1	4	31	12	4.98	95	.290	.440	10	.300	1	83	-1		0.0

KIPP, FRED Fred Leo B10.1.1931 Piqua KS BL/TL/6-4/200(180-200) d9.10 Col Emporia St.

YEAR	TM LG	W	L	PCT	G	GS	CG-SHO	SV-BS	IP	H	R	HR	HB	BB-IB	SO	ERA	AERA	OAV	OOB	AB-HR-SH	AVG	PB	SUP	APR	DL	PW
1957	Bro N	0	0	—	1	0	0	0	4	6	4	2	0	0	3	9.00	46	.333	.333	1	.000	-0		-2		-0.1
1958	LA N	6	6	.500	40	9	0	0	102.1	107	60	16	1	45-7	58	5.01	82	.273	.349	36	.250	1*	80	-8		-0.7
1959	LA N	0	0	—	2	0	0	0	2.2	2	0	0	0	3-1	1	0.00	—	.222	.417	0		0		1		0.1
1960	NY A	1	0	1.000	4	0	0	0	4.1	4	3	0	0	0-0	2	6.23	57	.250	.250	0	—	0		-1		-0.2
Total 4		6	7	.462	47	9	0	0	113.1	119	67	18	1	48-8	64	5.08	80	.274	.346	37	.243	1	80	-10		-0.9

KIPPER, BOB Robert Wayne B7.8.1964 Aurora IL BR/TL/6-2/200(175-200) [CalA82 1/8] C1 d4.12

YEAR	TM LG	W	L	PCT	G	GS	CG-SHO	SV-BS	IP	H	R	HR	HB	BB-IB	SO	ERA	AERA	OAV	OOB	AB-HR-SH	AVG	PB	SUP	APR	DL	PW
1985	Cal A	0	1	.000	2	1	0	0-0	3.1	7	8	3	0	3-0	0	21.60	19	.467	.500	0		0	199	-6		-0.9
	Pit N	1	2	.333	5	4	0	0-0	24.2	21	16	4	0	7-0	13	5.11	71	.221	.272	8-0-2	.250	0	91	-4		-0.4
1986	Pit N	6	8	.429	20	19	0	0-0	114	123	60	17	2	34-3	81	4.03	97	.271	.323	33-0-3	.030	-3*	83	-3		-0.7
1987	Pit N	5	9	.357	24	20	1-1	0-0	110.2	117	74	25	2	52-4	83	5.94	70	.271	.350	33-0-3	.242	2*	97	-18	64	-1.8
1988	Pit N	2	6	.250	50	0	0	0-0	65	54	33	7	2	26-4	39	3.74	92	.234	.313	4-0-1	.000	0		-3		-0.3
1989	Pit N	3	4	.429	52	0	0	4-4	83	55	29	5	0	33-6	58	2.93	126	.188	.267	9-0-1	.111	0		5	32	0.4
1990	Pit N	5	2	.714	41	1	0	3-1	62.2	44	24	7	3	26-1	35	3.02	121	.195	.283	7-0-0	.143	-0	272	-4		0.5
1991	†Pit N	2	2	.500	52	0	0	4-2	66	64	34	7	0	22-3	38	4.65	77	.276	.335	1-0-1	.000	-0		-7		-0.6
1992	Min A	3	3	.500	25	0	0	0-2	38.2	40	23	8	3	14-3	22	4.42	92	.268	.343	0	—	0		-2		-0.3
Total 8.		27	37	.422	271	45	1-1	11-9	562	527	301	81	12	217-24	369	4.34	87	.247	.317	95-0-11	.137	-1	102	-34	124	-4.1

KIPPER, THORNTON Thornton John B9.27.1928 Bagley WI BR/TR/6-3/190* d6.7 Col Wisconsin-Madison

YEAR	TM LG	W	L	PCT	G	GS	CG-SHO	SV-BS	IP	H	R	HR	HB	BB-IB	SO	ERA	AERA	OAV	OOB	AB-HR-SH	AVG	PB	SUP	APR	DL	PW
1953	Phi N	3	3	.500	20	3	0	0	45.2	59	26	8	0	12	15	4.73	89	.319	.360	11-0-2	.091	-1	35	-2		-0.3
1954	Phi N	0	0	—	11	0	0	1	13.2	22	13	0	1	12	5	7.90	51	.379	.493	0	.000	-0		-6		-0.3
1955	Phi N	0	1	.000	24	0	0	0	39.2	47	23	4	1	22-4	15	4.99	80	.301	.389	3	.333	0		-4		-0.2
Total 3		3	4	.429	55	3	0	1	99	128	62	12	2	46-4	35	5.27	78	.321	.393	16-0-2	.125	-1	35	-12		-0.8

KIRBY, CLAY Clayton Laws B6.25.1948 Washington DC D10.11.1991 Arlington VA BR/TR/6-3/185(170-185) [StLN66 3/47] d4.11

YEAR	TM LG	W	L	PCT	G	GS	CG-SHO	SV-BS	IP	H	R	HR	HB	BB-IB	SO	ERA	AERA	OAV	OOB	AB-HR-SH	AVG	PB	SUP	APR	DL	PW
1969	SD N	7	20	.259	35	35	2	0-0	215.2	204	108	18	6	100-13	113	3.80	94	.252	.337	66-0-2	.061	-2	74	-8		-1.3
1970	SD N	10	16	.385	34	34	6-1	0-0	214.2	198	118	29	9	120-5	154	4.53	89	.248	.348	74-0-3	.149	-0	91	-11		-1.3
1971	SD N	15	13	.536	38	36	13-2	0-0	267.1	213	99	20	3	103-14	231	2.83	118	.216	.291	86-0-5	.093	-3*	87	16		1.2
1972	SD N	12	14	.462	34	34	9-2	0-0	238.2	197	87	21	2	116-11	175	3.13	106	.226	.317	74-0-6	.068	-4*	82	8		0.4
1973	SD N	8	18	.308	34	31	4-2	0-0	191.2	214	122	30	1	66-7	129	4.79	73	.282	.338	54-0-11	.093	-3	100	-30		-3.9
1974	Cin N	12	9	.571	36	35	7-1	0-0	230.2	210	97	15	2	91-3	160	3.28	107	.242	.313	74-0-11	.095	-3	114	5		0.7
1975	Cin N	10	6	.625	26	19	1	0-0	110.2	113	63	13	5	54-3	48	4.72	76	.263	.351	32-0-4	.188	1	137	-15		-1.9
1976	Mon N	1	8	.111	22	15	0	0-0	78.2	81	45	9	4	63-1	51	5.72	66	.273	.399	18-0-6	.056	1	100	-17		-1.9
Total 8		75	104	.419	261	239	42-8	0-0	1548	1430	755	156	30	713-57	1061	3.84	92	.246	.329	478-0-45	.098	-15	96	-52		-8.7

KIRBY, JOHN John F. B1.13.1865 St.Louis MO D10.6.1931 St.Louis MO TR/5-8/172 d8.1

YEAR	TM LG	W	L	PCT	G	GS	CG-SHO	SV-BS	IP	H	R	HR	HB	BB-IB	SO	ERA	AERA	OAV	OOB	AB-HR-SH	AVG	PB	SUP	APR	DL	PW
1884	KC U	0	2	.000	2	2	1	0	11	13	10	0		2	11	4.09	55	.277	.306	7	.143	-1	86	-3		-0.2
1885	StL N	5	8	.385	14	14	14	0	129.1	118	66	0		44	46	3.55	77	.241	.303	50	.060	-6	82	-6		-1.1
1886	StL N	11	26	.297	41	41	38-1	0	325	329	222	9		134	129	3.30	98	.252	.322	136	.110	-9*	81	-4		-1.3
1887	Ind N	1	6	.143	8	8	5	0	62	70	64	3	2	43	7	6.10	68	.272	.381	29	.138	-2	78	-13		-1.3
	Cle AA	0	5	.000	5	5	4	0	41	62	53	1	2	28	6	9.00	48	.339	.432	18	.167	-1	38	-16		-1.3
1888	KC AA	1	4	.200	5	5	5	0	43	48	36	0	1	9	11	4.19	82	.273	.304	16	.063	-2	24	-4		-0.5
Total 6		18	50	.265	75	75	68-1	0	611.1	640	451	13	5	258	200	4.09	80	.260	.332	256	.105	-21	74	-46		-5.7

KIRBY, LA RUE La Rue B12.30.1889 Eureka MI D6.10.1961 Lansing MI BB/TR/6-0/185 d8.7 ▲

YEAR	TM LG	W	L	PCT	G	GS	CG-SHO	SV-BS	IP	H	R	HR	HB	BB-IB	SO	ERA	AERA	OAV	OOB	AB-HR-SH	AVG	PB	SUP	APR	DL	PW
1912	NY N	1	0	1.000	3	1	1	0	11	13	7	1	1	2	2	5.73	59	.295	.392	5	.200	0	152	-2		-0.1
1915	StL F	0	0	—	1	0	0	0	7	7	5	1	0	7	7	5.14	56	.269	.321	178-0-9	.213	0*		-2		-0.1
Total 2		1	0	1.000	4	1	1	0	18	20	12	2	1	9	9	5.50	58	.286	.367	183-0-9	.213	0	152	-4		-0.2

YEAR	TM LG	W	L	PCT	G	GS	CG-SHO	SV-BS	IP	H	R	HR	HB	BB-IB	SO	ERA	AERA	OAV	OOB	AB-HR-SH	AVG	PB	SUP	APR	DL	PW

KIRCHER, MIKE Michael Andrew (b Wolfgang Andrew Kerscher) B9.30.1897 Rochester NY D6.26.1972 Rochester NY BB/TR/6-0/180 d8.8

1919	Phi A	0	0	—	2	0	0	0	8	15	8	0	0	3	2	7.88	44	.429	.474	3	.000	-0		-3		-0.2
1920	StL N	2	1	.667	9	3	1	0	36.2	50	23	0	2	5	5	5.40	55	.333	.363	11	.273	0	88	-8		-0.7
1921	StL N	0	1	1.000	3	0	0	0	3.1	4	3	0	1	1	2	8.10	45	.364	.462	0		-0		-1		-0.
Total	3	2	2	.500	14	3	1	0	48	69	34	0	3	9	9	6.00	52	.352	.389	14	.214	-0	88	-12		-1.2

KIRK, BILL William Partlemore B7.19.1935 Coatesville PA BL/TL/6-0/165 d9.23

| 1961 | KC A | 0 | 0 | — | 1 | 1 | 0 | 0 | 3 | 6 | 4 | 2 | 0 | 1-0 | 3 | 12.00 | 35 | .375 | .412 | 0 | | 0 | 106 | -2 | | -0. |

KIRKWOOD, DON Donald Paul B9.24.1949 Pontiac MI BR/TR/6-3/188(175-192) d9.13 Col Oakland

1974	Cal A	0	0	—	3	0	0	0-0	7.1	12	8	0	0	6-0	4	8.59	40	.375	.474	0		0		-4		-0.2
1975	Cal A	6	5	.545	44	2	0	7-5	84	85	38	6	0	28-2	49	3.11	115	.270	.323	0		0*	98	3		0.3
1976	Cal A	6	12	.333	28	26	4	0-0	157.2	167	91	12	1	57-9	78	4.62	72	.278	.337	0		0	94	-23		-2.3
1977	Cal A	1	0	1.000	13	0	0	1-2	17.2	20	12	3	0	9-3	10	5.09	79	.290	.372	0		0		-3		-0.1
	Chi A	1	1	.500	16	0	0	0-0	40	49	27	3	1	10-2	24	5.17	79	.310	.349	0		0		-5		-0.3
	Year	2	1	.667	29	0	0	1-2	57.2	69	39	6	1	19-5	34	5.15	78	.304	.356	0		0		-8		-0.3
1978	Tor A	1	4	.444	16	9	3	0-0	68	76	36	6	0	25-1	29	4.24	93	.289	.348	0		0*	86	-3	80	-0.3
Total	5	18	23	.439	120	37	7	8-7	374.2	409	212	30	2	135-17	194	4.37	83	.284	.342	0		0	89	-35	80	-2.9

KIRSCH, HARRY Harry Louis "Casey" B10.17.1887 Pittsburgh PA D12.25.1925 Philadelphia PA BR/TR/5-11/170 d4.16

| 1910 | Cle A | 0 | 0 | — | 2 | 0 | 0 | 0 | 3 | 5 | 2 | 0 | 1 | 5 | 6.00 | 43 | .385 | .429 | 0 | | 0 | | -1 | | -0.1 |

KISER, GARLAND Garland Routhard B7.8.1968 Charlotte NC BL/TL/6-3/190 [PhiN86 24/604] d9.9

| 1991 | Cle A | 0 | 0 | — | 7 | 0 | 0 | 0 | 4.2 | 7 | 5 | 0 | 1 | 4-0 | 3 | 9.64 | 43 | .368 | .500 | 0 | | 0 | | -3 | | -0. |

KISINGER, RUBE Charles Samuel B12.13.1876 Adrian MI D7.17.1941 Huron OH BR/TR/6-0/190 d9.10 Col Adrian

1902	Det A	2	3	.400	5	5	5	0	43.1	48	20	0	3	14	7	3.12	117	.281	.346	19	.158	-1	71	3		0.2
1903	Det A	7	9	.438	16	14	13-2	0	118.2	118	58	0	2	27	33	2.96	98	.259	.303	47	.128	-3	67	-1		-0.
Total	2	9	12	.429	21	19	18-2	0	162	166	78	0	5	41	40	3.00	103	.265	.315	66	.136	-4	68	2		-0.

KISON, BRUCE Bruce Eugene B2.18.1950 Pasco WA BR/TR/6-4/178* [PitN68 14/309] d7.4 C8

1971	†Pit N	6	5	.545	18	13	2-1	0-0	95.1	93	40	6	6	36-5	60	3.40	100	.259	.335	31-0-1	.065	-1	120	0		-0.
1972	†Pit N	9	7	.563	32	18	6-1	3-2	152	123	61	11	9	69-2	102	3.26	102	.220	.316	53-0-2	.189	2	123	2	5	0.
1973	Pit N	3	0	1.000	7	7	0	0-0	43.2	36	17	4	1	24-3	26	3.09	114	.232	.339	12	.083	-0	125	-3	16	0.
1974	†Pit N	9	8	.529	40	16	1	2-2	129	123	64	8	11	57-7	71	3.49	100	.247	.335	37-0-2	.119	-2*	107	4		-0.
1975	†Pit N	12	11	.522	33	29	6	0-0	192	160	89	10	4	92-9	89	3.23	111	.227	.317	59-0-10	.119	2	109	6		1.
1976	Pit N	14	9	.609	31	29	6-1	1-0	193	180	83	10	3	52-4	98	3.08	115	.247	.297	59-0-8	.203	4	114	-16		1.
1977	Pit N	9	10	.474	33	32	3-1	0-0	193	209	113	25	6	55-6	122	4.90	82	.278	.328	69-1-3	.261	5*	114	-16		1.
1978	Pit N	6	6	.500	28	11	0	0-1	96	81	40	3	5	39-0	62	3.19	117	.229	.311	29-1-0	.138	1	88	5	39	0.
1979	†Pit N	13	7	.650	33	25	3-1	0-1	172.1	157	70	13	4	45-5	105	3.19	123	.246	.298	55-1-7	.145	-0*	101	13		1.
1980	Cal A	3	6	.333	13	13	2-1	0-0	73.1	73	46	5	3	32-2	28	4.91	81	.264	.344	0		0	120	-9	116	0.
1981	Cal A	1	1	.500	11	4	0	0-0	44	40	18	4	0	14-1	19	3.48	106	.241	.300	0		0	129	14	122	1.
1982	†Cal A	10	5	.667	33	16	3-1	1-0	142	120	54	15	4	44-3	86	4.05	100	.226	.291	0		0	111	2	28	0.
1983	Cal A	11	5	.688	26	17	4-1	2-1	126.2	128	59	13	4	43-4	66	5.37	74	.280	.362	0		0	110	-10	65	-1.
1984	Cal A	4	5	.444	20	7	0	2-1	65.1	72	42	10	6	28-3	66	4.11	105	.274	.332	0		0	112	3	22	0.
1985	Bos A	5	3	.625	22	9	0	1-1	92	98	43	9	1	32-4	56	3.66	103	.268	.319	404-3-33	.163	8	113	14	413	2.
Total	15	115	88	.567	380	246	36-8	12-9	1809.2	1693	839	150	68	662-58	1073	3.66	103	.248	.319							

KISSINGER, BILL William Francis "Shang" B8.15.1871 Dayton KY D4.20.1929 Cincinnati OH BR/TR/5-11/185 d5.30 ▲

1895	Bal N	1	0	1.000	2	2	1	0	11.1	18	11	0	0	2	3	3.97	120	.353	.377	5	.200	-0	120	-1		-0.
	StL N	4	12	.250	24	14	9	0	140.2	222	145	8	8	51	31	6.72	72	.352	.408	97-0-1	.247	-2*	64	-28		-2.
	Year	5	12	.294	26	16	10	0	152	240	156	8	8	53	34	6.51	74	.352	.406	102-0-1	.245	-2	71	-27		-2.
1896	StL N	2	9	.182	20	12	11	1	136	209	136	5	8	55	22	6.49	67	.349	.411	73-0-2	.301	1*	69	-32		-1
1897	StL N	0	4	.000	7	4	2	0	31.1	51	50	2	8	15	5	11.49	38	.362	.451	39	.333	2*	61	-22		-1
Total	3	7	25	.219	53	32	23	1	319.1	500	342	15	24	123	61	6.99	66	.352	.413	214-0-3	.280	1	69	-83		-6

KITSON, FRANK Frank R. B9.11.1869 Hopkins MI D4.14.1930 Allegan MI BL/TR/5-11/165 d5.19

1898	Bal N	8	5	.615	17	13	13-1	0	119.1	123	71	0	8	35	32	3.24	110	.265	.327	86	.314	4*	92	2		0
1899	Bal N	22	16	.579	40	37	34-2	0	326.2	327	144	6	12	65	75	2.78	142	.260	.303	134-0-1	.201	-2*	81	42		-0
1900	†Bro N	15	13	.536	40	30	21-2	4	253.1	283	152	12	9	56	55	4.19	92	.282	.326	109-0-1	.294	5*	104	10		1
1901	Bro N	19	11	.633	38	32	26-5	0	280.2	312	135	9	10	67	127	2.98	112	.279	.326	116-1-1	.263	8*	107	2		1
1902	Bro N	19	13	.594	32	31	29-3	0	268.2	256	105	4	7	52	109	2.85	97	.251	.292	116-1-1	.276	8*	107	8		0
1903	Det A	15	16	.484	31	28	28-2	0	257.2	277	112	8	7	38	69	3.07	83	.272	.312	72-1-1	.208	1*	110	-13		-1
1904	Det A	9	13	.409	26	24	19	0	199.2	211	100	7	0	37	78	3.47	79	.266	.319	87	.184	-1	80	-17		-0
1905	Det A	12	14	.462	33	27	21-3	1	225.2	230	120	3	11	57	59	3.65	72	.262	.320	90-1-0	.244	8*	101	-18		-0
1906	Was A	6	14	.300	30	21	15-1	0	197	196	97	2	6	57	11	3.94	61	.313	.366	10	.100	-0	84	-5		-0
1907	Was A	0	3	.000	5	3	2	0	32	41	20	1	2	9	14	3.10	90	.305	.360	25-0-1	.280	1	163	-2		-0
	NY A	4	0	1.000	12	4	3	0	61	75	31	0	4	17	11	4.57	76	.305	.362	10						
	Year	4	3	.571	17	7	5	0	93	116	51	1	6	26	25	3.39	79	.308	.362	35-0-1	.229	0	130	-7		-0
Total	10	129	118	.522	304	250	211-19	7	2221.2	2331	1087	52	81	491	731	3.18	99	.270	.315	978-4-11	.240	27	100	2		0

KLAERNER, HUGO Hugo Emil "Dutch" B10.15.1908 Fredericksburg TX D2.3.1982 Fredericksburg TX BR/TR/5-11/190 d9.10

| 1934 | Chi A | 0 | 2 | .000 | 3 | 3 | 1 | 0 | 17.1 | 24 | 21 | 4 | 0 | 9 | 9 | 10.90 | 43 | .329 | .449 | 6 | .333 | 1 | 98 | -10 | | -0 |

KLAGES, FRED Frederick Albert Anthony B10.31.1943 Ambridge PA BR/TR/6-2/185* d9.11

1966	Chi A	1	0	1.000	3	3	0	0	15.2	9	4	0	0	7-0	6	1.72	184	.167	.262	6	.500	1	102	3		0
1967	Chi A	4	4	.500	11	9	0	0	44.2	43	19	6	1	16-1	17	3.83	81	.256	.323	12-0-1	.000	-1*	94	-2		-0
Total	2	5	4	.556	14	12	0	0	60.1	52	23	6	1	23-1	23	3.28	95	.234	.308	18-0-1	.167	-0	96	1		-0

KLAWITTER, AL Albert "Dutch" B4.12.1888 Wilkes-Barre PA D5.2.1950 Milwaukee WI BR/TR/5-11.5/187 d9.20

1909	NY N	1	1	.500	6	3	2	1	27	24	11	1	0	13	6	2.00	128	.247	.336	9	.333	1	173	1		-0
1910	NY N	0	0	—	1	0	0	0	1	2	1	0	0	2	0	9.00	33	.400	.571	0		0		-1		
1913	Det A	1	2	.333	8	3	1	0	32	39	25	0	0	15	10	5.91	49	.307	.380	11	.000	-2	144	-9		-0
Total	3	2	3	.400	15	6	3	1	60	65	37	1	0	30	16	4.20	66	.284	.367	*20	.150	-0	157	-9		-0

KLAWITTER, TOM Thomas Carl B6.24.1958 LaCrosse WI BR/TL/6-2/195 [LAN80 19/477] d4.14 Col Wisconsin-La Crosse

| 1985 | Min A | 0 | 0 | — | 7 | 2 | 0 | 0-0 | 9.1 | 7 | 7 | 2 | 0 | 13-0 | 5 | 6.75 | 66 | .226 | .455 | 0 | | 0 | 154 | -2 | 100 | -0 |

KLEINE, HAL Harold John B6.8.1923 St.Louis MO D12.10.1957 St.Louis MO BL/TL/6-2/193 d4.26

1944	Cle A	1	2	.333	11	6	1	0	40.2	38	29	0	0	36	13	5.75	57	.248	.392	14-0-1	.143	-1*	110	-11		-0
1945	Cle A	0	0	—	3	0	0	0	7	8	4	0	0	7	5	3.86	84	.286	.429	3	.333	1		-1		-0
Total	2	1	2	.333	14	6	1	0	47.2	46	33	0	0	43	18	5.48	60	.254	.392	17-0-1	.176	-0	110	-12		-0

KLEINHANS, TED Theodore Otto (b Traugott Otto Kleinhans) B4.8.1899 Deer Park WI D7.24.1985 Redington Beach FL BR/TL/6-0/170 d4.20

1934	Phi N	0	0	—	5	0	0	0	6	11	8	1	0	3	2	9.00	52	.379	.438	1	.000	-0		-3		-
	Cin N	2	6	.250	24	9	0	0	80	107	63	2	1	38	23	5.74	71	.321	.392	23-0-2	.130	-1*	61	-15		-
	Year	2	6	.250	29	9	0	0	86	118	71	3	1	41	25	5.97	69	.326	.396	24-0-3	.125	-1	60	-19		-
1936	NY A	1	1	.500	19	0	0	0	29.1	36	25	0	0	23	10	5.83	80	.300	.413	6	.167	-0	85	2		-
1937	Cin N	1	2	.333	7	3	1	0	27.1	29	13	1	1	12	13	2.30	162	.271	.350	8	.250	0		-1		-
1938	Cin N	0	0	—	1	0	0	0	1	2	1	0	0	0	0	9.00	41	.400	.400	0		0		-1		-
Total	4	2	9	.308	56	12	1	0	143.2	185	110	4	2	76	48	5.26	79	.311	.391	38-0-2	.158	-1	64	-23		-

KLEINKE, NUB Norbert George B5.19.1911 Fond Du Lac WI D3.16.1950 Off Marin Coast CA BR/TR/6-1/170 d4.25

1935	StL N	0	0	—	4	2	0	0	12.2	19	8	1	0	3	5	4.97	82	.358	.393	2	.000	-0	155	-1		-
1937	StL N	1	1	.500	5	2	1	0	20.2	25	14	0	1	7	9	4.79	83	.321	.376	8	.000	-1	141	-2		-
Total	2	1	1	.500	9	4	1	0	33.1	44	22	1	1	10	14	4.86	83	.336	.383	10	.000	-1	149	-3		-

YEAR	TM LG	W	L	PCT	G	GS	CG-SHO	SV-BS	IP	H	R	HR	HB	BB-IB	SO	ERA	AERA	OAV	OOB	AB-HR-SH	AVG	PB	SUP	APR	DL	PW
KLEPFER, ED	Edward Lloyd "Big Ed" B3.17.1888 Summerville PA D8.9.1950 Tulsa OK BR/TR/6-0/185 d7.4 Mil 1918 Col Penn St.																									
1911	NY A	0	0	—	2	0	0	0	4	5	3	0	0	2	4	6.75	53	.250	.318	1	.000	-0		-1		-0.1
1913	NY A	0	1	.000	8	1	0	0	24.2	38	22	3	2	12	10	7.66	39	.376	.452	6	.167	0	0	-10		-0.5
1915	Chi A	1	0	1.000	3	2	1	0	12.2	11	4	0	0	5	3	2.84	105	.234	.308	3	.000	-0	122	1		0.0
	Cle A	1	6	.143	8	7	2	0	43	47	25	0	0	11	13	2.09	146	.283	.328	12-0-1	.167	-0	79	1		0.1
	Year	2	6	.250	11	9	3	0	55.2	58	29	0	0	16	16	2.26	134	.272	.323	15-0-1	.133	-0	88	1		0.1
1916	Cle A	6	6	.500	31	13	4-1	2	143	136	52	0	4	46	62	2.52	119	.262	.327	40-0-2	.025	-4	79	8		0.2
1917	Cle A	14	4	.778	41	27	9	1	213	208	84	0	0	55	66	2.37	120	.264	.312	62-0-5	.032	-6	109	8		-0.1
1919	Cle A	0	0	—	5	0	0	1	7.1	12	14	1	0	6	7	7.36	45	.375	.474	1	.000	-0		-5		-0.3
Total	6	22	17	.564	98	50	16-1	3	447.2	457	204	3	6	137	165	2.81	104	.273	.330	125-0-8	.048	-11	95	5		-0.7
KLIEMAN, ED	Edward Frederick "Specs","Babe" B3.21.1918 Norwood OH D11.15.1979 Homosassa FL BR/TR/6-1/190* d9.24																									
1943	Cle A	0	1	.000	1	1	0	0	9	8	1	0	0	5	2	1.00	311	.286	.394	3	.000	-0	0	2		0.2
1944	Cle A	11	13	.458	47	19	5-1	5	178.1	185	73	4	7	70	44	3.38	98	.274	.348	57-0-2	.105	-3	125	1		-0.2
1945	Cle A	5	8	.385	38	12	4-1	4	126.1	123	60	3	4	49	33	3.85	84	.261	.336	40-1-2	.200	1	76	-8		-0.6
1946	Cle A	0	0	—	9	0	0	1	15	18	13	0	0	10	2	6.60	50	.290	.389	1	.000	-0		-6		-0.4
1947	Cle A	5	4	.556	58	0	0	17	92	78	32	5	2	39	21	3.03	115	.231	.315	19-0-1	.105	-1		6		0.8
1948	†Cle A	3	2	.600	44	0	0	4	79.2	62	26	3	2	46	18	2.60	156	.229	.345	14	.143	-0		14		0.9
1949	Was A	0	0	—	2	0	0	0	3	8	6	0	0	3	1	18.00	24	.500	.579	1	1.000	-0		-4		-0.2
	Chi A	2	0	1.000	18	0	0	3	33	33	15	2	0	15	9	3.00	139	.273	.353	8-0-2	.250	-0		3		0.3
	Year	2	0	1.000	20	0	0	3	36	41	21	2	0	18	10	4.25	98	.299	.381	9-0-2	.333	1		-1		0.1
1950	Phi A	0	0	—	5	0	0	0	5.2	10	6	0	2	2	2	9.53	48	.357	.438	1	.000	-0		-3		-0.2
Total	8	26	28	.481	222	32	10-2	33	542	525	232	17	17	239	130	3.49	100	.261	.345	144-1-7	.146	-3	100	5		0.6
KLIMKOWSKI, RON	Ronald Bernard B3.1.1944 Jersey City NJ BR/TR/6-2/190* d9.15 Col Morehead St.																									
1969	NY A	0	0	—	3	1	0	0-0	14	6	1	0	0	5-1	9	0.64	548	.130	.212	3	.000	-0	0	5		0.2
1970	NY A	6	7	.462	45	3	1-1	1-1	98.1	80	36	7	3	33-7	40	2.65	135	.223	.293	19-0-4	.053	-2	133	9		1.0
1971	Oak A	2	2	.500	26	0	0	2-0	45.1	37	19	3	1	23-8	25	3.38	99	.220	.316	5	.400	1	0	1		0.1
1972	NY A	0	3	.000	16	2	0	1-0	31.1	32	15	1	1	15-7	11	4.02	74	.271	.356	6	.000	-1	30	-3		-0.4
Total	4	8	12	.400	90	6	1-1	4-1	189	155	71	13	5	76-23	79	2.90	118	.224	.304	33-0-4	.091	-2	78	11		0.9
KLINE, BOB	Robert George "Junior" B12.9.1909 Enterprise OH D3.16.1987 Westerville OH BR/TR/6-3/200 d9.17																									
1930	Bos A	0	0	—	1	0	0	0	1	1	0	0	0	0.00	0	.333	.333	0		0		1		0.0	
1931	Bos A	5	5	.500	28	10	3	0	98	110	54	3	3	35	25	4.41	98	.298	.364	27-0-1	.333	2	102	-1		0.3
1932	Bos A	11	13	.458	47	19	4-1	2	172	203	117	10	1	76	31	5.28	85	.294	.365	54-0-4	.130	-3	78	-13		-1.7
1933	Bos A	7	8	.467	46	8	1	4	127	127	70	5	6	67	16	4.54	97	.265	.362	34-0-3	.176	-1	104	0		0.1
1934	Phi A	6	2	.750	20	0	1	1	39.2	50	34	6	0	13	14	6.35	69	.314	.366	9-0-1	.333	1		-10		-1.5
	Was A	1	0	1.000	6	0	0	1	4	10	8	0	1	4	1	15.75	27	.500	.600	0		0		-5		-0.9
	Year	7	2	.778	26	0	1	1	43.2	60	42	6	1	17	15	7.21	61	.335	.396	9-0-1	.333	1		-15		-2.4
Total	5	30	28	.517	148	37	8-1	7	441.2	501	283	24	11	195	87	5.05	87	.291	.367	124-0-9	.202	-1	90	-28		-3.7
KLINE, RON	Ronald Lee B3.9.1932 Callery PA D6.22.2002 Callery PA BR/TR/6-3/205(190-210) d4.21 Mil 1953-54																									
1952	Pit N	0	7	.000	27	11	0	0	78.2	74	55	3	6	66	27	5.49	73	.253	.401	19	.000	-2	67	-13		-1.3
1955	Pit N	6	13	.316	36	19	2-1	2	136.2	161	78	13	5	53-5	48	4.15	99	.298	.363	38-0-1	.132	-2*	60	-3		-0.5
1956	Pit N	14	18	.438	44	39	9-2	2	264	263	110	26	5	81-8	125	3.38	112	.263	.319	79-0-5	.127	-3	80	13		1.2
1957	Pit N	9	16	.360	40	31	11-2	0	205	214	107	27	1	61-6	88	4.04	94	.268	.319	66-0-3	.061	-6	79	-6		-1.3
1958	Pit N	13	16	.448	32	32	11-2	0	237.1	220	96	25	0	92-14	109	3.53	110	.252	.321	74-0-9	.027	-6*	74	13		0.8
1959	Pit N	11	13	.458	33	29	7	0	186	186	95	23	2	70-9	91	4.26	91	.263	.329	59-0-5	.136	-2*	99	-6		-0.9
1960	StL N	4	9	.308	34	17	1	1	117.2	133	86	21	0	43-5	54	6.04	68	.284	.341	35-0-1	.143	-2	75	-23		-2.4
1961	LA A	3	6	.333	26	12	0	1	104.2	119	62	16	1	44-5	70	4.90	92	.288	.357	31-0-3	.097	-2	83	-3		-0.4
	Det A	5	3	.625	10	8	3-1	0	56.1	53	25	3	0	17-1	27	2.72	151	.245	.297	18-0-3	.167	0	92	6		0.8
	Year	8	9	.471	36	20	3-1	1	161	172	87	19	1	61-6	97	4.14	106	.273	.336	49-0-6	.122	-2	86	2		0.4
1962	Det A	3	6	.333	36	4	0	2	77.1	88	40	9	2	28-2	47	4.31	94	.284	.347	16-0-1	.125	-1	27	-1		-0.2
1963	Was A	3	8	.273	62	1	0	17	93.2	85	36	3	3	30-7	49	2.79	133	.249	.312	11	.091	-0	72	8		1.2
1964	Was A	10	7	.588	61	0	0	14	81.1	81	29	4	2	21-9	40	2.32	159	.262	.310	6-0-2	.167	0		10		2.2
1965	Was A	7	6	.538	74	0	0	29	99.1	106	36	7	2	32-14	52	2.63	132	.275	.329	7-0-3	.000	-1		0		1.4
1966	Was A	6	4	.600	63	0	0	23	90.1	79	32	12	0	17-7	46	2.39	145	.237	.274	6		-1		-2		-0.3
1967	Min A	7	1	.875	54	0	0	5	71.2	71	33	10	1	15-7	36	3.77	92	.261	.302	5-0-1	.000	-1		8		1.3
1968	Pit N	12	5	.706	56	0	0	7	112.2	94	26	3	2	31-11	48	1.68	174	.234	.291	16-0-1	.000	-1		15		2.5
1969	Pit N	1	3	.250	20	0	0	3-2	31	37	23	3	1	5-2	15	5.81	60	.296	.326	5-0-1	.000	-1		-9		-1.3
	SF N	0	2	.000	7	0	0	0-2	11	16	6	1	0	6-3	12	4.09	86	.364	.440	0		0		-9		-0.1
	Year	1	5	.167	27	0	0	3-4	42	53	29	4	1	11-5	27	5.36	65	.314	.357	5-0-1	.000	-1		-9		-1.4
	Bos A	0	1	.000	16	0	0	1-1	17	24	11	4	1	17-3	7	4.76	80	.329	.451	0		0		-9		-1.4
1970	Atl N	0	0	—	5	0	0	2-0	6.1	9	5	1	2	2-0	3	7.11	60	.321	.367	0		0		-2		-0.1
Total	17	114	144	.442	736	203	44-8	108-5	2078	2113	991	217	33	731-118	989	3.75	101	.266	.329	491-0-39	.092	-28	81	10		2.5
KLINE, STEVE	Steven Jack B10.6.1947 Wenatchee WA BR/TR/6-3/205* [NYA66 7/130] d7.10 [DL 1975 Cle A 175]																									
1970	NY A	6	6	.500	16	15	5	0-0	100.1	99	42	8	0	24-3	49	3.41	105	.254	.296	28-0-4	.179	1	88	3		0.5
1971	NY A	12	13	.480	31	30	15-1	0-0	222.1	206	87	21	0	37-7	81	2.96	111	.244	.275	66-0-5	.136	-0	95	7		0.9
1972	NY A	16	9	.640	32	32	11-4	0-0	236.1	210	79	11	10	44-6	58	2.40	125	.237	.279	76-0-12	.092	-3	101	13		1.2
1973	NY A	4	7	.364	14	13	2-1	0-1	74	76	39	5	1	31-3	19	4.01	92	.270	.342	0	—	0	85	-3	92	-0.4
1974	NY A	2	2	.500	4	4	0	0-0	26	26	12	3	1	5-0	6	3.46	102	.263	.305	0	—	0	99	0		0.0
	Cle A	3	8	.273	16	11	1	0-0	71	70	44	9	4	31-2	17	5.07	72	.266	.350	0	—	0	64	-14	46	-1.4
	Year	5	10	.333	20	15	1	0-0	97	96	56	12	5	36-2	23	4.64	78	.265	.338	0	—	0	73	-12		-1.4
1977	Atl N	0	0	—	16	0	0	1-0	20.1	21	15	4	0	12-3	10	6.64	67	.259	.355	0	—	0		-4		-0.2
Total	6	43	45	.489	129	105	34-6	1-0	750.1	708	318	61	16	184-24	240	3.26	103	.249	.297	170-0-21	.124	-2	91	5	313	0.6
KLINE, STEVE	Steven James B8.22.1972 Sunbury PA BB/TL/6-2/215(200-240) [CleA93 8/223] d4.2 Col West Virginia																									
1997	Cle A	3	1	.750	20	1	0	0-2	26.1	42	19	6	1	13-1	17	5.81	81	.365	.434	0	—	0	59	-3		-0.5
	Mon N	1	3	.250	26	0	0	0-1	26.1	31	18	4	1	10-3	20	6.15	68	.304	.365	1	.000	0		-5		-0.7
1998	Mon N	3	6	.333	78	0	0	1-1	71.2	62	25	4	3	41-7	76	2.76	152	.228	.333	4-0-1	.000	0		11		1.3
1999	Mon N	7	4	.636	82	0	0	0-2	69.2	56	32	8	3	33-6	69	3.75	119	.218	.313	1-0-1	.000	-0		6	16	0.9
2000	Mon N	1	5	.167	83	0	0	14-4	82.1	88	36	8	3	27-2	64	3.50	135	.278	.340	2	.000	-0		11		1.0
2001	†StL N	3	3	.500	89	0	0	9-1	75	53	16	2	4	29-7	54	1.80	240	.203	.288	2	.500	0		21		2.0
2002	†StL N	2	1	.667	66	0	0	6-2	58.1	54	23	3	1	21-2	41	3.39	119	.251	.318	1	.000	-0		5	32	0.3
2003	StL N	5	5	.500	78	0	0	3-4	63.2	56	29	4	3	30-5	31	3.82	108	.237	.328	2-0-1	.500	1		2		0.4
2004	†StL N	2	2	.500	67	0	0	3-1	50.1	37	12	3	4	17-4	35	1.79	238	.209	.291	0-0-1	—	0		13	32	1.1
2005	Bal A	2	4	.333	67	0	0	0-3	61	59	34	11	0	30-5	36	4.28	104	.257	.340	0	—	0		0		0.1
Total	9	29	34	.460	656	1	0	36-21	584.2	538	244	55	23	251-42	443	3.40	128	.247	.328	13-0-4	.154	0	59	61	80	5.9
KLING, BILL	William B1.14.1867 Kansas City MO D8.26.1934 Kansas City MO BL/TR/6-0/190 d8.13 b-Johnny																									
1891	Phi N	4	2	.667	12	7	4	0	75	91	61	2	2	32	26	4.32	79	.289	.358	31	.194	1*	153	-10		-0.6
1892	Bal N	0	2	.000	2	2	0	0	11	17	16	1	2	7	7	11.45	30	.340	.441	4	.250	1	111	-7		-0.8
1895	Lou N	0	0	—	1	0	0	0	1	0	0	0	0	1	0	0.00	—	.000	.250	1	.000	0		1		0.0
Total	3	4	4	.500	15	9	4	0	87	108	77	3	4	40	33	5.17	66	.293	.369	36	.194	1	143	-16		-1.4
KLINGENBECK, SCOTT	Scott Edward B2.3.1971 Cincinnati OH BR/TR/6-2/205* [BalA92 5/128] d6.2 Col Ohio St.																									
1994	Bal A	1	0	1.000	1	1	0	0	7	6	4	2	1	4-1	5	3.86	131	.240	.355	0	—	0	200	0		0.1
1995	Bal A	2	2	.500	6	5	0	0-0	31.1	32	17	4	1	18-0	15	4.88	98	.269	.365	0	—	0	97	0		0.0
	Min A	0	2	.000	18	4	0	0-0	48.1	69	48	16	4	24-0	27	8.57	56	.338	.416	0	—	0	92	-19		-0.9
	Year	2	4	.333	24	9	0	0-0	79.2	101	65	22	4	42-0	42	7.12	67	.313	.397	0	—	0	95	-19		-0.9
1996	Min A	1	1	.500	10	3	0	0-1	28.2	42	28	5	1	10-0	15	7.85	65	.339	.390	0	—	0	169	-9		-0.5
1998	Cin N	1	3	.250	4	4	0	0-0	22.2	26	17	6	1	7-0	13	5.96	72	.286	.340	6	.000	-1	75	-5		-0.7
Total	4	5	8	.385	39	17	0	0-1	138	175	114	34	7	63-1	75	6.91	69	.311	.385	6	.000	-1	110	-33		-2.0

YEAR	TM LG	W	L	PCT	G	GS	CG-SHO	SV-BS	IP	H	R	HR	HB	BB-IB	SO	ERA	AERA	OAV	QOB	AB-HR-SH	AVG	PB	SUP	APR	DL	PW
KLINGER, BOB	Robert Harold B6.4.1908 Allenton MO D8.19.1977 Villa Ridge MO BR/TR/6-0/180 d4.19 Mil 1944-45														58	2.99	127	.253	.308	60-0-1	.167	-2	119	14		1.2
1938	Pit N	12	5	.706	28	21	10-1	1	159.1	152	63	7	6	42	58	2.99	127	.253	.308	60-0-1	.167	-2	119	14		1.2
1939	Pit N	14	17	.452	37	33	10-2	0	225	251	120	11	3	81	64	4.36	88	.284	.346	84-0-1	.202	0	112	-11		-1.2
1940	Pit N	8	13	.381	39	22	3	3	142	196	102	5	5	53	48	5.39	71	.329	.388	42-0-1	.143	0	85	-26		-3.6
1941	Pit N	9	4	.692	35	9	3	4	116.2	127	58	5	1	30	36	3.93	92	.276	.322	32-0-1	.250	2	123	-3		-0.1
1942	Pit N	8	11	.421	37	19	8-1	1	152.2	151	69	6	0	45	58	3.24	104	.252	.307	40-0-5	.200	1	107	0		0.3
1943	Pit N	11	8	.579	33	25	14-3	0	195	185	77	6	0	58	65	2.72	128	.252	.307	65-0-4	.246	3	121	15		1.7
1946	†Bos A	3	2	.600	28	1	0	9	57	49	16	1	4	25	16	2.37	155	.238	.323	16-0-3	.313	1	47	8		1.1
1947	Bos A	1	1	.500	28	0	0	5	42	42	20	5	1	24	12	3.86	101	.253	.351	9-0-2	.111	-1		0		-0.1
Total	8	66	61	.520	265	130	48-7	23	1089.2	1153	525	46	20	358	357	3.68	100	.271	.331	348-0-18	.204	3	110	-3		-0.7
KLINK, JOE	Joseph Charles B2.3.1962 Johnstown PA BL/TL/5-11/175* [NYN83 36/801] d4.9 Col St. Thomas (FL) [DL 1992 Oak A 182]																									
1987	Min A	0	1	.000	12	0	0	0-0	23	37	18	4	0	11-0	17	6.65	70	.359	.417	0	—	0		-5		-0.2
1990	†Oak A	0	0	—	40	0	0	1-0	39.2	34	9	1	0	18-0	19	2.04	183	.233	.317	0	—	0		8		0.4
1991	Oak A	10	3	.769	62	0	0	2-2	62	60	30	4	5	21-5	22	4.35	89	.259	.333	0	—	0		-3	35	-0.5
1993	Fla N	0	2	.000	59	0	0	0-0	37.2	37	22	0	0	24-4	22	5.02	87	.266	.367	2-0-1	.000	-0		-2		-0.2
1996	Sea A	0	0	—	3	0	0	0-0	2.1	3	1	1	0	1-0	2	3.86	129	.300	.364	0	—	0		0		0.0
Total	5	10	6	.625	176	0	0	3-2	164.2	171	80	10	5	75-9	94	4.26	95	.271	.352	2-0-1	.000	-0		-2	217	-0.5
KLIPPSTEIN, JOHNNY	John Calvin B10.17.1927 Washington DC D10.10.2003 Elgin IL BR/TR/6-1/185(170-190) d5.3																									
1950	Chi N	2	9	.182	33	11	3	1	104.2	112	69	9	4	64	51	5.25	80	.279	.383	33-1-0	.333	4*	80	-11		-0.6
1951	Chi N	6	6	.500	35	11	1-1	2	123.2	125	71	10	6	53	56	4.29	95	.263	.344	37-1-0	.108	-2	65	-5		-0.6
1952	Chi N	9	14	.391	41	25	7-2	3	202.2	208	110	17	6	89	110	4.44	87	.265	.344	58-1-3	.155	-1	88	-11		-1.5
1953	Chi N	10	11	.476	48	19	5	6	167.2	169	115	15	8	107	113	4.83	92	.258	.369	45-0-2	.133	-2	101	-20		-2.0
1954	Chi N	4	11	.267	36	21	4	1	148	155	104	13	4	96	69	5.29	79	.272	.373	45-0-2	.133	-2	90	10		1.0
1955	Cin N	9	10	.474	39	14	3-2	0	138	120	66	13	4	60-5	68	3.39	125	.233	.317	31-0-4	.065	-2	110	-1		-0.5
1956	Cin N	12	11	.522	37	29	11	1	211	219	103	26	10	82-13	86	4.09	97	.275	.344	71-0-8	.099	-3	86	-12		-1.8
1957	Cin N	8	11	.421	46	18	3-1	1	146	146	84	17	3	68-6	99	5.05	81	.261	.342	41-0-2	.073	-3	76	-3		-0.5
1958	Cin N	3	2	.600	12	4	0	1	33	37	20	5	1	14-1	22	4.91	84	.285	.358	8-0-1	.125	-0	4			0.2
	LA N	3	5	.375	45	0	0	9	90	81	40	12	2	44-8	73	3.80	108	.248	.338	20-0-1	.050	-2	76	1		-0.3
	Year	6	7	.462	57	4	0	10	123	118	60	17	3	58-9	95	4.10	100	.259	.343	28-0-2	.071	-2		1		-0.6
1959	†LA N	4	0	1.000	28	0	0	2	45.2	48	31	8	2	33-5	30	5.91	72	.276	.392	7	.143	-0		-7		-0.6
1960	Cle A	5	5	.500	49	0	0	14	74.1	53	30	8	1	35-3	46	2.91	129	.205	.302	7	.143	-0	66	-21		-1.0
1961	Was A	2	2	.500	42	1	0	0	71.2	83	59	13	4	43-1	41	6.78	59	.297	.395	7	.143	-0	72	-8		-0.8
1962	Cin N	7	6	.538	40	7	0	8	108.2	113	66	13	4	64-5	67	4.47	90	.278	.377	24-1-1	.125	-1	53	16		1.6
1963	Phi N	5	6	.455	49	1	0	0	112	80	28	3	3	46-9	86	1.93	168	.204	.291	26-0-2	.038	-2	53	16		1.6
1964	Phi N	2	1	.667	11	0	0	1	22.1	22	10	4	2	8-1	13	4.03	86	.250	.327	4	.000	-0		-1		-0.1
	Min A	4	0	.000	33	0	0	2	54.2	44	12	4	1	20-7	39	1.97	181	.260	.340	2	.000	0		8		0.8
1965	†Min A	9	3	.750	56	0	0	5	76.1	59	22	8	3	31-4	59	2.24	159	.217	.302	8-0-2	.000	-1		11		1.7
1966	Min A	1	1	.500	26	0	0	3	39.2	35	15	2	2	20-2	26	3.40	106	.238	.335	3	.000	-0		-1		-0.1
1967	Det A	0	0	—	5	0	0	0	6.2	6	4	1	0	1-0	4	5.40	60	.250	.269	0	—	0		-1		-0.1
Total	18	101	118	.461	711	161	37-6	66	1967.2	1915	1059	203	70	978-70	1158	4.24	94	.258	.347	502-5-35	.125	-14	92	-55		-4.7
KLOBEDANZ, FRED	Frederick Augustus "Duke" B6.13.1871 Waterbury CT D4.12.1940 Waterbury CT BL/TL/5-11/190 d8.20																									
1896	Bos N	6	4	.600	10	9	9	0	80.2	69	41	5	7	31	26	3.01	151	.229	.334	41-2-0	.317	2*	115	14		1.5
1897	†Bos N	26	7	.788	38	37	30-2	0	309.1	344	198	13	23	125	92	4.60	97	.279	.357	148-1-3	.324	9*	129	2		0.8
1898	Bos N	19	10	.655	35	33	25	0	270.2	281	168	13	12	99	51	3.89	95	.266	.336	127-3-6	.213	0*	116	-8		-0.8
1899	Bos N	1	4	.200	5	5	4	0	33.1	39	22	2	2	9	8	4.86	86	.291	.345	11-1-0	.182	1	69	-2		-0.1
1902	Bos N	1	0	1.000	1	1	1	0	8	9	1	0	1	2	4	1.13	251	.281	.343	2-0-1	.500	1	289	2		0.3
Total	5	53	25	.679	89	85	69-2	0	702	742	430	33	45	266	181	4.12	101	.269	.343	329-7-10	.277	13	120	8		1.7
KLOPP, STAN	Stanley Harold "Betz" B12.22.1910 Womelsdorf PA D3.11.1980 Robesonia PA BR/TR/6-1.5/180 d4.29																									
1944	Bos N	1	2	.333	24	0	0	2	47	47	36	1	0	33	17	4.27	89	.272	.388	7	.286	0		-6		-0.4
KNACKERT, BRENT	Brent Bradley B8.1.1969 Los Angeles CA BR/TR/6-3/185* [ChiA87 2/37] d4.10																									
1990	Sea A	1	1	.500	24	2	0	0-0	37.1	50	28	5	2	21-2	28	6.51	61	.313	.395	0	—	0		57	-9	-0.5
1996	Bos A	0	1	.000	8	0	0	0-0	10	16	12	1	0	7-1	5	9.00	57	.356	.434	0	—	0		-5		-0.3
Total	2	1	2	.333	32	2	0	0-0	47.1	66	40	6	2	28-3	33	7.04	60	.322	.403	0	—	0		57	-14	-0.8
KNAPP, CHRIS	Robert Christian B9.16.1953 Cherry Point NC BR/TR/6-5/200* [ChiA75 1/11] d9.4 Col Central Michigan																									
1975	Chi A	0	0	—	2	0	0	0-0	2	2	1	0	0	4-0	3	4.50	86	.250	.500	0	—	0		0		0.0
1976	Chi A	3	1	.750	11	6	1	0-0	52.1	54	31	5	1	32-1	41	4.82	74	.273	.375	0	—	0	131	-7		-0.5
1977	Chi A	12	7	.632	27	26	4	0-0	146.1	166	90	16	7	61-1	103	4.80	85	.283	.355	0	—	0	116	-12		-1.4
1978	Cal A	14	8	.636	30	29	6	0-0	188.1	178	94	25	4	67-6	126	4.21	86	.266	.313	0	—	0	112	-10		-1.2
1979	†Cal A	5	5	.500	20	18	3	0-0	98	109	73	8	2	35-1	36	5.51	74	.275	.334	0	—	0	95	-26		-2.6
1980	Cal A	2	11	.154	32	20	1	1-0	117.1	133	83	18	8	51-1	46	6.14	65	.289	.365	0	—	0	119	-74	52	-7.3
Total	6	36	32	.529	122	99	15	1-0	604.1	642	372	72	20	250-10	355	4.99	78	.272	.344	0	—	0	119	-74	52	-7.3
KNAUSS, FRANK	Frank H. B1868 Cleveland OH BL/TL/5-10/170 d6.25																									
1890	Col AA	17	12	.586	37	34	28-3	2	275.2	206	131	3	21	106	148	2.81	128	**.202**	.290	106-1	.226	5	111	26		2.7
1891	Cle N	0	3	.000	3	3	1	0	15	23	29	2	4	8	6	7.20	48	.338	.438	6	.167	-0	115	-8		-1.1
1892	Cin N	0	0	—	1	0	0	0	8	13	9	0	0	5	2	3.38	97	.351	.429	1	.333	0		-2		0.0
1894	Cin N	0	1	.000	2	2	1	0	11	7	9	0	3	14	2	5.73	96	.179	.429	4-0-1	.000	-1	129	0		0.0
1895	NY N	0	0	—	1	1	0	0	3.2	9	7	0	0	2	1	17.18	27	.450	.500	1	.000	-0	153	-4		-0.2
Total	5	17	16	.515	44	40	30-3	2	313.1	258	185	5	28	135	159	3.30	111	.218	.312	120-1-1	.217	4	115	12		1.4
KNEISCH, RUDY	Rudolph Frank B4.10.1899 Baltimore MD D4.6.1965 Baltimore MD BR/TL/5-10.5/175 d9.21																									
1926	Det A	0	1	.000	2	2	1	0	17	18	7	2	2	6	2	2.65	153	.273	.351	5	.000	-1	73	2		0.1
KNELL, PHIL	Philip Louis B3.12.1865 San Francisco CA D6.5.1944 Santa Monica CA BR/TL/5-7.5/154 d7.6																									
1888	Pit N	1	2	.333	3	3	3	0	26.1	20	19	1	5	18	15	3.76	70	.217	.374	11	.091	-1	77	-4		-0.5
1890	Phi P	22	11	.667	35	31	30-2	0	286.2	287	199	10	28	166	99	3.83	112	.249	.358	132-1	.220	-1*	124	14		1.1
1891	Col AA	28	27	.509	58	52	47-5	0	462	363	228	4	54	226	228	2.92	118	**.209**	.319	215	.158	-9*	84	30		2.2
1892	Was N	9	13	.409	22	21	17-1	0	170	156	114	4	11	76	74	3.65	89	.234	.323	68	.118	-5	90	-6		-1.1
	Phi N	5	5	.500	11	9	7	0	80	87	47	0	11	35	43	3.78	86	.245	.354	34	.088	-3	100	-5		-0.8
	Year	14	18	.438	33	30	24-1	0	250	243	161	4	22	111	117	3.71	88	.239	.335	102	.108	-7	93	-9		-1.9
1894	Pit N	0	0	—	1	0	0	0	7	11	9	0	1	6	0	11.57	45	.355	.474	3	.000	-1		-4		-1.0
	Lou N	7	21	.250	32	28	25	0	247	330	237	8	14	104	67	5.32	96	.317	.387	113-1-1	.274	0	73	-12		-1.0
	Year	7	21	.250	33	28	25	0	254	341	246	8	15	110	67	5.49	93	.318	.383	116-1-1	.267	-0	73	-20		-1.2
1895	Lou N	0	6	.000	10	6	3	0	56.2	75	66	3	6	21	19	6.51	71	.314	.383	26	.231	-3	105	-5		-0.6
	Cle N	7	5	.583	20	13	9	0	116.2	149	100	7	6	74	30	5.40	92	.306	.381	55-0-1	.200	-3	106	-19		-1.6
	Year	7	11	.389	30	19	12	0	173.1	224	166	10	12	74	49	5.76	85	.309	.382	81-0-1	.210	-5	106	-19		-1.9
Total	6	79	90	.467	192	163	141-8	0	1452.1	1478	1019	37	136	705	575	4.05	99	.256	.351	657-2-2	.187	-20	94	-6		-1.9
KNEPPER, CHARLIE	Charles B2.18.1871 Anderson IN D2.6.1946 Muncie IN BR/TR/6-4/190 d5.26																									
1899	Cle N	4	22	.154	27	26	26	0	219.2	307	190	11	15	77	43	5.78	64	.329	.390	89	.135	-5	74	-51		-4.9
KNEPPER, BOB	Robert Wesley B5.25.1954 Akron OH BL/TL/6-2/200(190-210) [SFN72 2/43] d9.10																									
1976	SF N	1	2	.333	4	4	0	0-0	25	26	9	0	0	7-1	11	3.24	112	.277	.327	9	.111	-0	79	2		0.2
1977	SF N	11	9	.550	27	27	6-2	0-0	166	151	73	14	4	72-2	100	3.36	117	.242	.321	55-0-5	.182	1	102	10		1.3
1978	SF N	17	11	.607	36	35	16-6	0-0	260	218	85	10	4	85-11	147	2.63	132	.229	.292	79-0-8	.063	-3	92	25		2.2
1979	SF N	9	12	.429	34	34	6-2	0-0	207.1	241	117	30	4	77-8	123	4.64	75	.289	.350	66-1-9	.182	3*	121	-27		-2.1
1980	SF N	9	16	.360	35	33	8-1	0-0	215.1	242	114	15	8	61-10	103	4.10	86	.281	.333	47-1-5	.149	1	78	21		2.0
1981	†Hou N★	9	5	.643	22	22	6-5	0-0	156.2	128	41	15	4	38-1	75	2.18	150	.226	.278	44-1-5	.058	-2	85	-24		-2.6
1982	Hou N	5	15	.250	30	29	4-1	1-0	180	193	100	14	4	60-4	108	4.45	75	.278	.335	52-0-6	.058	-2	90	1		0.5
1983	Hou N	6	13	.316	35	29	4-3	0-0	203	202	93	12	4	71-3	125	3.19	107	.261	.323	66-1-4	.182	3	90	1		0.5
1984	Hou N	15	10	.600	35	34	11-3	0-0	233.2	223	92	26	4	55-5	140	3.20	105	.251	.295	71-1-6	.171	4	126	6		1.0

YEAR	TM LG	W	L	PCT	G	GS	CG-SHO	SV-BS	IP	H	R	HR	HB	BB-IB	SO	ERA	AERA	OAV	OOB	AB-HR-SH	AVG	PB	SUP	APR	DL	PW
1985	Hou N	15	13	.536	37	37	4	0-0	241	253	119	21	3	54-5	131	3.55	98	.271	.310	78-1-8	.141	0*	103	-6		-0.7
1986	†Hou N	17	12	.586	40	38	8-5	0-0	258	232	100	19	4	62-13	143	3.14	115	.242	.289	91-0-4	.099	-3*	103	14		1.3
1987	Hou N	8	17	.320	33	31	1	0-0	177.2	226	118	26	4	54-3	76	5.27	75	.313	.362	51-0-9	.098	-1	95	-29		-3.5
1988	Hou N★	14	5	.737	27	27	3-2	0-0	175	156	70	13	2	67-2	103	3.14	106	.243	.314	48-0-14	.125	-1	123	3		0.4
1989	Hou N	4	10	.286	22	20	0	0-1	113	135	78	12	2	60-4	45	5.89	58	.303	.386	31-1-2	.226	5	100	-30		-2.7
	SF N	3	2	.600	13	6	1-1	0-0	52	55	20	4	1	15-2	19	3.46	98	.270	.318	12-0-1	.083	1	105	1		0.1
	Year	7	12	.368	35	26	1-1	0-1	165	190	98	16	3	75-6	64	5.13	66	.292	.365	43-1-3	.186	6	101	-30		-2.6
1990	SF N	3	3	.500	12	7	0	0-0	44.1	56	28	7	1	19-4	24	5.68	64	.311	.376	13	.231	1	166	-9		-1.0
Total	15	146	155	.485	445	413	78-30	1-1	2708	2737	1258	228	47	857-78	1473	3.68	95	.264	.321	840-6-90	.137	7	103	-57		-5.1

KNERR, LOU Wallace Luther B8.21.1921 Strasburg PA D3.23.1980 Denver PA BR/TR/6-1/210 d4.17 Col Muhlenberg

YEAR	TM LG	W	L	PCT	G	GS	CG-SHO	SV-BS	IP	H	R	HR	HB	BB-IB	SO	ERA	AERA	OAV	OOB	AB-HR-SH	AVG	PB	SUP	APR	DL	PW
1945	Phi A	5	11	.313	27	17	5	0	130	142	77	6	1	74	41	4.22	81	.283	.376	47-0-1	.191	-1*	72	-14		-1.8
1946	Phi A	3	16	.158	30	22	6	0	148.1	171	95	11	1	67	58	5.40	66	.288	.361	50-0-1	.180	0	75	-26		-3.0
1947	Was A	0	0	—	6	0	0	0	9	17	13	1	0	8	5	11.00	34	.405	.500	1	1.000	0		-8		-0.3
Total	3	8	27	.229	63	39	11	0	287.1	330	185	20	2	149	104	5.04	69	.290	.373	98-0-2	.194	-1	73	-48		-5.1

KNETZER, ELMER Elmer Ellsworth "Baron" B7.22.1885 Carrick PA D10.3.1975 Pittsburgh PA BR/TR/5-10/180 d9.11

YEAR	TM LG	W	L	PCT	G	GS	CG-SHO	SV-BS	IP	H	R	HR	HB	BB-IB	SO	ERA	AERA	OAV	OOB	AB-HR-SH	AVG	PB	SUP	APR	DL	PW
1909	Bro N	1	3	.250	5	4	3	0	35.2	33	22	2	0	22		3.03	86	.252	.359	12	.000	-2	61	-4		-0.6
1910	Bro N	7	5	.583	20	15	10-3	0	132.2	122	63	1	1	60	56	3.19	95	.255	.339	38-0-3	.053	-3	121	-3		-0.6
1911	Bro N	11	12	.478	35	20	11-3	0	204	202	101	1	1	93	66	3.49	96	.277	.359	62-0-5	.097	-4	85	-4		-0.8
1912	Bro N	7	9	.438	33	16	4-1	0	140.1	135	86	6	4	70	61	4.55	74	.254	.345	37-0-4	.135	-1	112	-15		-1.6
1914	Pit F	20	12	.625	37	30	20-3	1	272	257	123	9	2	88	146	2.88	100	.254	.315	91-0-9	.099	-9	113	-5		-1.4
1915	Pit F	18	14	.563	41	33	22-3	3	279	256	105	5	1	89	120	2.58	105	.251	.315	91-0-8	.132	-7	106	1		-0.6
1916	Bos N	0	2	.000	2	0	0	0	5	11	9	0	0	2	2	7.20	35	.524	.565	0	—	-7		-4		-0.7
	Cin N	5	12	.294	36	16	12	1	171.1	161	76	6	3	48	70	2.89	90	.252	.307	52-0-4	.154	-1*	92	-8		-0.8
	Year	5	14	.263	38	16	12	1	176.1	172	85	6	3	50	72	3.01	86	.261	.316	52-0-4	.154	-1*	92	-12		-1.5
1917	Cin N	0	0	—	11	0	0	1	27.1	29	18	0	2	12	7	2.96	88	.282	.368	3	.000	-0		-3		-0.2
Total	8	69	69	.500	220	134	82-13	6	1267.1	1206	603	30	14	484	535	3.15	93	.258	.330	386-0-33	.109	-26	104	-45		-7.3

KNIGHT, LON Alonzo P. B6.16.1853 Philadelphia PA D4.23.1932 Philadelphia PA BR/TR/5-11.5/165 d9.4 M2/U3 ▲

YEAR	TM LG	W	L	PCT	G	GS	CG-SHO	SV-BS	IP	H	R	HR	HB	BB-IB	SO	ERA	AERA	OAV	OOB	AB-HR-SH	AVG	PB	SUP	APR	DL	PW
1875	Ath NA	6	5	.545	13	13	12	0	107	114	73	0		12	15	2.27	105	.259	.278	47	.128	-3	86	-2		-0.3
1876	Phi N	10	22	.313	34	32	27	0	282	383	288	0		34	12	2.62	93	.297	.315	240	.250	-1*	128	-17		-1.5
1884	Phi AA	0	1	.000	2	1	1	0	14	24	19	0	1	4	2	9.00	38	.348	.392	484-1	.271	0*	125	-8		-0.4
1885	Phi AA	0	0	—	1	0	0	0	5	4	1	0	0	2	1	1.80	191	.211	.286	119	.210	-0*		1		0.1
	Pro N	0	0	—	1	0	0	0	4	4	1	1	4	1	6.75	40	.235	.381	81	.160	-0*		-1		-0.1
Total	3	16	23	.303	38	33	28	0	305	415	312	1	1	44	16	2.95	84	.297	.319	924-1	.248	-1	128	-25		-1.9

KNIGHT, BRANDON Brandon Michael B10.1.1975 Oxnard CA BL/TR/6-0/170* [TexA95 14/374] d6.5 Col Ventura (CA) JC

YEAR	TM LG	W	L	PCT	G	GS	CG-SHO	SV-BS	IP	H	R	HR	HB	BB-IB	SO	ERA	AERA	OAV	OOB	AB-HR-SH	AVG	PB	SUP	APR	DL	PW
2001	NY A	0	0	—	4	0	0	0-0	10.2	18	12	5	0	3-0	7	10.13	44	.367	.404	0	—	0		-6		-0.3
2002	NY A	0	0	—	7	0	0	0-0	8.2	11	12	2	0	5-0	7	11.42	38	.324	.390	0	—	0		-7		-0.3
Total	2	0	0	—	11	0	0	0-0	19.1	29	24	7	0	8-0	14	10.71	41	.341	.398	0*	—	0		-13		-0.6

KNIGHT, JACK Elmer Russell B1.12.1895 Pittsboro MS D7.30.1976 San Antonio TX BL/TR/6-0/175 d9.20 Col Millsaps

YEAR	TM LG	W	L	PCT	G	GS	CG-SHO	SV-BS	IP	H	R	HR	HB	BB-IB	SO	ERA	AERA	OAV	OOB	AB-HR-SH	AVG	PB	SUP	APR	DL	PW
1922	StL N	0	0	—	1	1	0	0	4	9	4	0	3	1	9.00	43	.474	.545	2	.500	0	274	-2		-0.1
1925	Phi N	7	6	.538	33	11	4	3	105.1	161	100	14	1	36	19	6.84	70	.354	.402	44	.205	-1*	135	-22		-2.4
1926	Phi N	3	12	.200	35	15	5	2	142.2	206	122	14	0	48	29	6.62	63	.347	.396	56-2-2	.214	0*	86	-35		-2.9
1927	Bos N	0	0	—	3	0	0	0	3	6	5	0	0	2	0	15.00	25	.429	.500	0	—	0		-4		-0.1
Total	4	10	18	.357	72	27	9	5	255	382	231	28	1	89	49	6.85	64	.353	.403	102-2-2	.216	-1	114	-63		-5.5

KNIGHT, GEORGE George Henry B11.24.1855 Lakeville CT D10.4.1912 Salisbury CT d9.28

YEAR	TM LG	W	L	PCT	G	GS	CG-SHO	SV-BS	IP	H	R	HR	HB	BB-IB	SO	ERA	AERA	OAV	OOB	AB-HR-SH	AVG	PB	SUP	APR	DL	PW
1875	NH NA	1	0	1.000	1	1	1	0	9	12	6	0		0	0	3.00	69	.293	.293	4	.000	-1	136	0		-0.1

KNIGHT, JOE Jonah William "Quiet Joe" B9.28.1859 Port Stanley ON, Can. D10.16.1938 Lynhurst ON, Can. BL/TL/5-11/185 d5.16 ▲

YEAR	TM LG	W	L	PCT	G	GS	CG-SHO	SV-BS	IP	H	R	HR	HB	BB-IB	SO	ERA	AERA	OAV	OOB	AB-HR-SH	AVG	PB	SUP	APR	DL	PW
1884	Phi N	2	4	.333	6			0	51	66	53	2	1	8	5.47	55	.293	.354	24	.250	1	68	-12		-1.0

KNOLLS, HUB Oscar Edward B12.18.1883 Valparaiso IN D7.1.1946 Chicago IL TR/6-2/190 d5.1

YEAR	TM LG	W	L	PCT	G	GS	CG-SHO	SV-BS	IP	H	R	HR	HB	BB-IB	SO	ERA	AERA	OAV	OOB	AB-HR-SH	AVG	PB	SUP	APR	DL	PW
1906	Bro N	0	0	—	2	0	0	0	6.2	13	5	0	0	2	3	4.05	62	.382	.417	1-0-1	1.000	1		-2		0.0

KNOTT, ERIC Eric James B9.23.1974 Harvey IL BL/TL/6-0/188* [AriN96 24/725] d9.1 Col Stetson

YEAR	TM LG	W	L	PCT	G	GS	CG-SHO	SV-BS	IP	H	R	HR	HB	BB-IB	SO	ERA	AERA	OAV	OOB	AB-HR-SH	AVG	PB	SUP	APR	DL	PW
2001	Ari N	0	1	.000	3	1	0	0-0	4.2	8	9	2	0	0-0	4 *	1.93	240	.348	.400	1	.000	-0	100	-2		-0.4
2003	Mon N	1	2	.333	13	1	0	0-0	19.1	23	12	2	0	6-0	17	5.12	87	.295	.341	5	.000	-1	21	-1		-0.2
Total	2	1	3	.250	16	2	0	0-0	24	31	21	2	2	6-0	21	4.50	99	.307	.355	6	.000	-1	63	-3		-0.6

KNOTT, JACK John Henry B3.2.1907 Dallas TX D10.13.1981 Brownwood TX BR/TR/6-2.5/200 d4.13 Mil 1942-45 Col SMU

YEAR	TM LG	W	L	PCT	G	GS	CG-SHO	SV-BS	IP	H	R	HR	HB	BB-IB	SO	ERA	AERA	OAV	OOB	AB-HR-SH	AVG	PB	SUP	APR	DL	PW
1933	StL A	1	8	.111	20	9	0	0	82.2	85	51	11	2	33	19	5.01	93	.264	.340	23-0-1	.304	1	75	-3		-0.2
1934	StL A	10	3	.769	45	10	2	-4	138	149	86	17	1	67	56	4.96	101	.278	.359	30-0-3	.133	-4	82	2		0.1
1935	StL A	11	8	.579	48	19	7-2	7	187.2	219	119	8	1	89	45	4.60	104	.287	.353	61-0-8	.115	-5	95	0		-0.4
1936	StL A	9	17	.346	47	23	9	6	192.2	272	174	15	4	93	60	7.29	74	.330	.401	57-0-8	.070	-5	89	-37		-4.5
1937	StL A	8	18	.308	38	22	9	2	191.1	220	117	25	5	91	74	4.89	99	.291	.370	57-0-4	.140	-4	76	-1		-0.1
1938	StL A	1	2	.333	7	4	0	0	30	35	19	3	0	15	4	4.80	104	.285	.362	10-0-1	.100	-1	84	0		-0.1
	Chi A	5	10	.333	20	18	9	0	131	135	70	8	0	54	35	4.05	121	.271	.342	40-0-7	.125	-2	68	12		0.9
	Year	6	12	.333	27	22	9	0	161	170	89	11	0	69	43	4.19	117	.273	.346	50-0-8	.120	-3	71	11		0.8
1939	Chi A	11	6	.647	25	23	8	0	149.2	157	71	13	1	41	56	4.15	114	.269	.318	53-0-5	.151	-3	92	12		0.8
1940	Chi A	11	9	.550	25	23	4-2	0	158	166	88	12	2	52	44	4.56	97	.265	.324	57-0-4	.088	-4	98	0		-0.4
1941	Chi A	13	11	.542	27	26	11	0	194.1	212	108	20	2	81	54	4.40	95	.279	.350	65-0-5	.077	-3	109	-4		-0.9
1942	Phi A	2	10	.167	20	14	4	0	95.1	127	84	7	1	36	31	5.57	68	.310	.367	29-0-2	.138	-1	78	-24		-2.6
1946	Phi A	0	1	.000	3	1	0	0	6.1	7	4	1	1	1	2	5.68	-62	.280	.333	0-0-1	—	0	0	-1		-0.2
Total	11	82	103	.443	325	192	62-4	19	1557	1787	991	140	20	642	484	4.97	95	.287	.355	482-0-49	.120	-29	87	-44		-8.1

KNOTTS, GARY Gary Everett B2.12.1977 Decatur AL BR/TR/6-4/235* [FlaN95 11/289] d7.28 Col NW Alabama CC [DL 2005 Det A 185]

YEAR	TM LG	W	L	PCT	G	GS	CG-SHO	SV-BS	IP	H	R	HR	HB	BB-IB	SO	ERA	AERA	OAV	OOB	AB-HR-SH	AVG	PB	SUP	APR	DL	PW
2001	Fla N	0	1	.000	2	1	0	0-0	5	6	5	1	2	2-0	9	6.00	90	.280	.357	2	.500	0	67	-1		-0.1
2002	Fla N	3	1	.750	28	1	0	0-1	30.2	21	15	6	1	16-0	21	4.40	89	.193	.299	1	.000	-0		-1		-0.2
2003	Det A	3	8	.273	20	18	0	0-0	95.1	114	70	14	4	47-0	51	6.04	73	.288	.367	1	.000	-0	80	-18		-1.7
2004	Det A	7	6	.538	36	19	0	2-0	135.1	142	83	20	4	58-3	81	5.25	80	.267	.343	3-0-1	.333	1	114	-11	16	-0.9
Total	4	13	16	.448	86	38	0	2-1	267.1	281	172	41	11	122-3	162	5.45	80	.267	.348	7-0-1	.286	1	98	-31	201	-2.9

KNOUFF, ED Edward "Fred" B6.1868 Philadelphia PA D9.14.1900 Philadelphia PA BR/TR/?/160 d7.1 ▲

YEAR	TM LG	W	L	PCT	G	GS	CG-SHO	SV-BS	IP	H	R	HR	HB	BB-IB	SO	ERA	AERA	OAV	OOB	AB-HR-SH	AVG	PB	SUP	APR	DL	PW
1885	Phi AA	7	6	.538	14	13	12	0	106	103	76	0	9	44	43	3.65	94	.228	.309	48	.188	-2	111	-1		-0.2
1886	Bal AA	0	1	.000	1	1	1	0	9	12	5	0	3	5	8	2.00	171	.067	.263	3	.000	0	17	1		0.1
1887	Bal AA	2	6	.250	9	9	6	0	63	79	79	0	13	41	27	7.57	54	.295	.413	31	.290	0	123	-23		-1.9
	StL AA	4	2	.667	6	6	6-1	0	50	40	34	0	3	36	18	4.50	101	.225	.364	56	.179	-1*	103	1		0.0
	Year	6	8	.429	15	15	12-1	0	113	119	113	0	16	77	45	6.21	69	.267	.393	87	.218	-1	114	-17		-1.9
1888	StL AA	4	5	.556	9	9	9	0	81	66	45	0	8	37	25	2.67	122	.214	.314	31	.097	-2	93	4		0.1
	Cle AA	0	1	.000	2	2	1	0	9	8	2	0	4	2	1.00	309	.229	.308	6	.167	0	66	2		0.3
	Year	5	5	.500	11	11	10	0	90	74	47	0	9	44	27	2.50	130	.216	.314	37	.108	-2	88	7		0.4
1889	Phi AA	2	0	1.000	3	3	2	0	25	37	17	2	1	9	5	3.96	96	.333	.388	12	.250	0	131	0		0.0
Total	5	20	20	.500	44	43	37-1	0	343	335	258	2	38	175	128	4.17	89	.242	.344	187	.187	-4	106	-16		-1.6

KNOWLES, DAROLD Darold Duane B12.9.1941 Brunswick MO BL/TL/6-0/190(175-190) d4.18 Mil 1968-69 C3 Col Missouri

YEAR	TM LG	W	L	PCT	G	GS	CG-SHO	SV-BS	IP	H	R	HR	HB	BB-IB	SO	ERA	AERA	OAV	OOB	AB-HR-SH	AVG	PB	SUP	APR	DL	PW
1965	Bal A	0	1	.000	5	1	0	0	14.2	14	15	2	3	10-2	12	9.20	38	.250	.391	4	.000	-0	0	-8		-0.5
1966	Phi N	6	5	.545	69	0	0	13	100.1	98	38	4	7	46-10	88	3.05	119	.260	.347	16	.250	0	6			1.0
1967	Was A	6	8	.429	70	0	0	14	113.1	91	37	5	4	52-12	85	2.70	117	.228	.319	16	.063	-1	7			1.1
1968	Was A	1	1	.500	32	0	0	4	41.1	38	11	0	1	12-2	37	2.18	134	.241	.293	4-0-1	.250	-1	12			0.4
1969	Was A★	9	2	.818	53	0	0	13-9	84.1	73	25	4	4	31-3	59	2.24	156	.236	.311	13	.077	-1	12			2.0
1970	Was A	2	14	.125	71	0	0	27-11	119.1	100	36	4	4	58-16	71	2.04	177	.231	.325	20-0-2	.050	-1	19			3.2
1971	Was A	2	3	.500	15.1	0	0	2-2	15.1	17	10	2		16	3.52	96	.266	.329	2	.000	-0	0			0.0
	†Oak A	5	2	.714	43	0	0	7-3	52.2	40	22	4	3	16-4	40	3.59	93	.221	.289	8-0-1	.125	-0	-1			0.0
	Year	7	4	.636				9-5	68	57	32			22-5	56	3.57	93	.233	.299	10-0-1	.100	-1	-1			-0.1

YEAR	TM LG	W	L	PCT	G	GS	CG-SHO	SV-BS	IP	H	R	HR	HB	BB-IB	SO	ERA	AERA	OAV	OOB	AB-HR-SH	AVG	PB	SUP	APR	DL	PW
1972	Oak A	5	1	.833	54	0	0	11-3	65.2	49	12	1	0	37-4	36	1.37	208	.212	.319	12-0-1	.250	1		11	6	1.8
1973	†Oak A	6	8	.429	52	5	1-1	9-5	99	87	44	7	3	49-3	46	3.09	115	.246	.338	0	—	0*	130	3		0.6
1974	Oak A	3	5	.500	45	1	0	3-2	53.1	61	29	6	2	35-3	18	4.22	79	.296	.397	0	—	0	211	6		-0.6
1975	Chi N	6	9	.400	58	0	0	15-7	88.1	107	61	3	3	36-9	63	5.81	67	.298	.364	15-0-2	.067	-1		-16		-3.1
1976	Chi N	5	7	.417	58	0	0	9-8	71.2	61	30	6	2	22-4	39	2.89	135	.242	.302	7-0-2	.143	1		6		1.3
1977	Tex A	5	2	.714	42	0	0	4-4	50.1	50	22	3	2	23-2	14	3.22	127	.272	.354	0	—	-0	4	10	11	1.1
1978	Mon N	3	3	.500	60	0	0	6-3	72	63	20	5	0	30-3	34	2.38	150	.250	.323	6-0-1	.167	-0		10		1.1
1979	StL N	2	5	.286	48	0	0	6-4	48.2	54	27	5	0	17-7	22	4.07	94	.277	.333	2	.000	-0		-2		-0.4
1980	StL N	1	1	.000	2	0	0	0-1	1.2	3	2	1	0	0-0	1	10.80	35	.375	.375	0		0		-1		-0.2
Total 16		66	74	.471	765	8	1-1	143-62	1092	1006	437	65	38	480-85	681	3.12	113	.250	.332	125-0-10	.120	-2	107	48	17	8.2

KNOWLSON, TOM Thomas Herbert "Doc" B4.23.1895 Pittsburgh PA D4.11.1943 Miami Shores FL BB/TR/5-11/178 d7.3

YEAR	TM LG	W	L	PCT	G	GS	CG-SHO	SV-BS	IP	H	R	HR	HB	BB-IB	SO	ERA	AERA	OAV	OOB	AB-HR-SH	AVG	PB	SUP	APR	DL	PW
1915	Phi A	4	6	.400	18	9	8	0	100.2	99	53	1	6	60	24	3.49	84	.273	.386	36	.083	-3	91	-6		-0.9

KNOWLTON, BILL William Young B8.18.1892 Philadelphia PA D2.25.1944 Philadelphia PA BR/TR d9.3

YEAR	TM LG	W	L	PCT	G	GS	CG-SHO	SV-BS	IP	H	R	HR	HB	BB-IB	SO	ERA	AERA	OAV	OOB	AB-HR-SH	AVG	PB	SUP	APR	DL	PW
1920	Phi A	0	1	.000	1	1	0	0	4	9	4	0	1	5	1	4.76	84	.346	.469	2	.000	-0	99	-2		-0.3

KNUDSEN, KURT Kurt David B2.20.1967 Arlington Heights IL BR/TR/6-3/200* [DetA88 9/239] d5.16 Col Miami

YEAR	TM LG	W	L	PCT	G	GS	CG-SHO	SV-BS	IP	H	R	HR	HB	BB-IB	SO	ERA	AERA	OAV	OOB	AB-HR-SH	AVG	PB	SUP	APR	DL	PW
1992	Det A	2	3	.400	48	1	0	5-2	70.2	70	39	9	1	41-9	51	4.58	87	.264	.362	0		0	69	-5		-0.4
1993	Det A	3	2	.600	30	0	0	2-2	37.2	41	22	9	4	16-2	29	4.78	91	.281	.361	0		0		-2	31	-0.7
1994	Det A	1	0	1.000	4	0	0	0-1	5.1	7	8	2	0	11-1	1	13.50	36	.304	.529	0		0		-5		-0.7
Total 3		6	5	.545	82	1	0	7-5	113.2	118	69	20	5	68-12	81	5.07	82	.272	.373	0		0	69	-12	31	-1.3

KNUDSON, MARK Mark Richard B10.28.1960 Denver CO BR/TR/6-5/215(200-215) [HouN82 3/69] d7.8 Col Colorado St.

YEAR	TM LG	W	L	PCT	G	GS	CG-SHO	SV-BS	IP	H	R	HR	HB	BB-IB	SO	ERA	AERA	OAV	OOB	AB-HR-SH	AVG	PB	SUP	APR	DL	PW
1985	Hou N	0	2	.000	2	2	0	0-0	11	21	11	0	0	3-0	4	9.00	39	.429	.462	2	.000	0	63	-6	21	-0.8
1986	Hou N	1	5	.167	9	7	0	0-0	42.2	48	23	5	1	15-5	20	4.22	85	.279	.340	10-0-3	.000	-1	106	-3		-0.5
	Mil A	0	1	.000	4	1	0	0-0	17.2	22	15	7	0	5-1	9	7.64	57	.286	.329	0		0	21	-5		-0.3
1987	Mil A	4	4	.500	15	8	1	0-1	62	88	46	7	0	14-1	26	5.37	86	.331	.358	0		0	104	-8		0.2
1988	Mil A	0	0	—	5	0	0	0-0	16	17	3	1	0	2-0	7	1.13	356	.279	.302	0		0	158	8		0.2
1989	Mil A	8	5	.615	40	7	1	0-2	123.2	110	50	15	3	29-2	47	3.35	115	.237	.286	0		0	96	-2		-0.3
1990	Mil A	10	9	.526	30	27	4-2	0-3	168.1	187	84	14	3	40-1	56	4.12	94	.282	.321	0		0	118	-15	36	-1.5
1991	Mil A	1	3	.250	12	7	0	0-0	35	54	33	8	1	15-0	23	7.97	50	.355	.409	0		0		-9		-0.9
1993	Col N	0	0	—	4	0	0	0-0	5.2	16	14	4	0	5-0	1	22.24	22	.471	.538	1	.000	-0		-9		-3.8
Total 8		24	29	.453	121	59	6-2	0-3	482	563	279	61	8	128-10	195	4.72	84	.290	.334	13-0-3	.000	-1	105	-35	57	-3.8

KOBEL, KEVIN Kevin Richard B10.2.1953 Buffalo NY BR/TL/6-1/183(183-195) [MilA71 11/248] d9.8

YEAR	TM LG	W	L	PCT	G	GS	CG-SHO	SV-BS	IP	H	R	HR	HB	BB-IB	SO	ERA	AERA	OAV	OOB	AB-HR-SH	AVG	PB	SUP	APR	DL	PW
1973	Mil A	0	1	.000	2	1	0	0-0	8.1	9	8	2	0	8-0	4	8.64	44	.273	.415	0		0	70	-4		-0.4
1974	Mil A	6	14	.300	34	24	3-2	0-1	169.1	166	84	16	2	54-1	74	3.99	91	.258	.314	0	—	0	80	-8		-0.6
1976	Mil A	0	1	.000	3	0	0	0-1	4	6	5	3	1	3-1	1	11.25	31	.375	.476	0		0		-3		-0.6
1978	NY N	5	6	.455	32	11	1	0-1	108.1	95	42	9	2	30-9	51	2.91	122	.239	.291	25-0-4	.160	0	88	6		0.3
1979	NY N	6	8	.429	30	27	1-1	0-0	161.2	169	74	14	3	46-4	67	3.51	106	.274	.325	46-0-9	.196	-0	78	2	24	-1.7
1980	NY N	1	4	.200	14	1	0	0-0	24.1	36	21	5	0	11-3	8	7.03	51	.353	.416	2	.000	-0	74	-9	24	-1.7
Total 6		18	34	.346	115	64	5-3	0-3	476	481	234	49	8	152-18	205	3.88	94	.266	.322	73-0-13	.178	-0	80	-16	24	-2.4

KOCH, ALAN Alan Goodman B3.25.1938 Decatur AL BR/TR/6-4/195* d7.26 Col Auburn-Montgomery

YEAR	TM LG	W	L	PCT	G	GS	CG-SHO	SV-BS	IP	H	R	HR	HB	BB-IB	SO	ERA	AERA	OAV	OOB	AB-HR-SH	AVG	PB	SUP	APR	DL	PW
1963	Det A	1	1	.500	7	1	0	0	10	21	12	3	1	9-0	5	10.80	35	.467	.564	3	.667	1*	71	-7		-1.1
1964	Det A	0	0	—	3	0	0	0	4	6	3	1	0	3-0	1	6.75	54	.375	.474	0		0		-1		-0.1
	Was A	3	10	.231	32	14	1	0	114	110	64	18	3	43-2	67	4.89	76	.253	.320	32-0-3	.250	2	87	-12		-1.1
	Year	3	10	.231	35	14	1	0	118	116	67	19	3	46-2	68	4.96	75	.258	.325	32-0-3	.250	2	88	-13		-1.2
Total 2		4	11	.267	42	15	1	0	128	137	79	22	4	55-2	73	5.41	68	.277	.349	35-0-3	.286	3	86	-20		-2.3

KOCH, BILLY William Christopher B12.14.1974 Rockville Centre NY BR/TR/6-3/215(205-220) [TorA96 1/4] d5.5 Col Clemson

YEAR	TM LG	W	L	PCT	G	GS	CG-SHO	SV-BS	IP	H	R	HR	HB	BB-IB	SO	ERA	AERA	OAV	OOB	AB-HR-SH	AVG	PB	SUP	APR	DL	PW
1999	Tor A	0	5	.000	56	0	0	31-4	63.2	55	26	6	3	30-5	57	3.39	145	.235	.328	1	.000	-0		11		1.0
2000	Tor A	9	3	.750	68	0	0	33-5	78.2	78	28	6	2	18-4	60	2.63	191	.265	.304	1	.000	-0		19		3.0
2001	Tor A	2	5	.286	69	0	0	36-8	69.1	69	39	7	6	33-7	55	4.80	95	.265	.356	0		-0		-1		-0.2
2002	†Oak A	11	4	.733	84	0	0	44-6	93.2	73	38	7	4	46-6	93	3.27	137	.214	.314	0				12	21	-1.3
2003	Chi A	5	5	.500	55	0	0	11-4	53	59	36	10	1	28-1	42	5.77	80	.281	.364	0				-7		-0.1
2004	Chi A	1	1	.500	24	0	0	8-3	23.1	24	15	3	2	16-4	25	5.40	87	.255	.368	0				2		0.1
	Fla N	1	2	.333	23	0	0	0-0	25.2	21	10	3	0	20-0	25	3.51	117	.226	.360	0	.000	-0		21		0.2
Total 6		29	25	.537	379	0	0	163-30	407.1	379	192	41	18	191-27	357	3.89	120	.247	.335	2	.000	-0		34	21	6.2

KOECHER, DICK Richard Finlay "Highpockets" B3.30.1926 Philadelphia PA BL/TL/6-5/196 d9.29 Col Temple

YEAR	TM LG	W	L	PCT	G	GS	CG-SHO	SV-BS	IP	H	R	HR	HB	BB-IB	SO	ERA	AERA	OAV	OOB	AB-HR-SH	AVG	PB	SUP	APR	DL	PW
1946	Phi N	0	1	.000	1	1	0	0	2.2	7	3	0	1	2	2	10.13	34	.467	.500	1	.000	-0	25	-2		-0.3
1947	Phi N	0	2	.000	3	2	1	0	17	20	12	1	1	10	4	4.76	84	.280	.397	4	.000	-1	22	-2		-0.2
1948	Phi N	0	1	.000	3	0	0	0	6	4	2	0	0	3	2	3.00	132	.235	.350	0				1		0.0
Total 3		0	4	.000	7	3	1	0	25.2	31	17	1	1	14	8	4.91	80	.313	.404	5	.000	-1	22	-3		-0.4

KOENIG, MARK Mark Anthony B7.19.1904 San Francisco CA D4.22.1993 Willows CA BB/TR/6-0/180 d9.8.1925 ▲

YEAR	TM LG	W	L	PCT	G	GS	CG-SHO	SV-BS	IP	H	R	HR	HB	BB-IB	SO	ERA	AERA	OAV	OOB	AB-HR-SH	AVG	PB	SUP	APR	DL	PW
1930	Det A	0	1	.000	2	1	0	0	9	11	10	0	1	8	6	10.00	48	.314	.455	267-1-13	.240	0*	89	-4		-0.4
1931	Det A	0	0	—	3	0	0	0	7	7	5	0	1	11	3	6.43	71	.280	.500	364-1-2	.253	0*		-1		0.0
Total 2		0	1	.000	5	1	0	0	16	18	15	0	1	19	9	8.44	56	.300	.475	631-2-15	.247	0	89	-5		-0.4

KOENIGSMARK, WILL Willis Thomas B2.27.1896 Waterloo IL D7.1.1972 Waterloo IL BR/TR/6-4/180 d9.10

YEAR	TM LG	W	L	PCT	G	GS	CG-SHO	SV-BS	IP	H	R	HR	HB	BB-IB	SO	ERA	AERA	OAV	OOB	AB-HR-SH	AVG	PB	SUP	APR	DL	PW
1919	StL N	0	0	—	1	0	0	0	2	2	2	0	1	5	0	∞	—	1.000	1.000	0	—	0		-2		-0.0

KOESTNER, ELMER Elmer Joseph "Bob" B11.30.1885 Piper City IL D10.27.1959 Fairbury IL BR/TR/6-1.5/175 d4.23

YEAR	TM LG	W	L	PCT	G	GS	CG-SHO	SV-BS	IP	H	R	HR	HB	BB-IB	SO	ERA	AERA	OAV	OOB	AB-HR-SH	AVG	PB	SUP	APR	DL	PW
1910	Cle A	5	10	.333	27	13	8-1	2	145	145	76	0	6	63	44	3.04	85	.282	.367	48-0-6	.313	2	106	-10		-0.0
1914	Chi N	0	0	—	4	0	0	0	6.1	6	5	0	0	4	6	2.84	98	.261	.370	1	.000	-0		-1		-0.0
	Cin N	0	0	—	5	1	0	0	18.1	18	15	0	0	9	6	4.42	66	.265	.351	5	.400	1	171	-4		-0.0
	Year	0	0	—	9	1	0	0	24.2	24	20	0	0	13	12	4.01	72	.264	.356	6	.333	1	173	-4		-0.0
Total 2		5	10	.333	36	14	8-1	2	169.2	169	96	0	6	76	56	3.18	83	.279	.365	54-0-6	.315	3	110	-15		-0.0

KOHLMAN, JOE Joseph James "Blackie" B1.28.1913 Philadelphia PA D3.16.1974 Philadelphia PA BR/TR/6-0/160 d9.26

YEAR	TM LG	W	L	PCT	G	GS	CG-SHO	SV-BS	IP	H	R	HR	HB	BB-IB	SO	ERA	AERA	OAV	OOB	AB-HR-SH	AVG	PB	SUP	APR	DL	PW
1937	Was A	1	0	1.000	2	2	1	0	13	15	7	0	3	3	3	4.15	107	.283	.321	5	.200	-0	108	0		0
1938	Was A	0	0	—	7	0	0	0	14.1	12	10	1	0	11	5	6.28	72	.240	.377	3	.000	-0		-2		-0.0
Total 2		1	0	1.000	9	2	1	0	27.1	27	17	1	3	14	8	5.27	85	.262	.350	8	.125	-1	108	-2		-0.0

KOHLMEIER, RYAN Ryan Lyle B6.25.1977 Salina KS BR/TR/6-2/197(195-223) [BalA96 14/411] d7.29 Col Butler Co. (KS) CC

YEAR	TM LG	W	L	PCT	G	GS	CG-SHO	SV-BS	IP	H	R	HR	HB	BB-IB	SO	ERA	AERA	OAV	OOB	AB-HR-SH	AVG	PB	SUP	APR	DL	PW
2000	Bal A	0	1	.000	25	0	0	13-1	26.1	30	9	1	0	15-2	17	2.39	197	.291	.378	0	—	0		6		0
2001	Bal A	1	2	.333	34	1	0	6-4	40.2	48	33	13	2	19-2	29	7.30	59	.291	.371	0	—	0	0	-12		-1
Total 2		1	3	.250	59	1	0	19-5	67	78	42	14	2	34-4	46	5.37	82	.291	.374	0	—	0	0	-12		-1

KOLB, BRANDON Brandon Charles B11.20.1973 Oakland CA BR/TR/6-1/190* [SDN95 4/89] d5.12 Col Texas Tech

YEAR	TM LG	W	L	PCT	G	GS	CG-SHO	SV-BS	IP	H	R	HR	HB	BB-IB	SO	ERA	AERA	OAV	OOB	AB-HR-SH	AVG	PB	SUP	APR	DL	PW
2000	SD N	0	1	.000	11	0	0	0-1	14	16	8	0	0	11-1	12	4.50	99	.296	.409	1	.000	-0		-10		-0
2001	Mil N	0	0	—	10	0	0	0-0	9.2	16	16	6	0	8-0	8	13.03	33	.372	.453	1	.000	-0		-10		-0
Total 2		0	1	.000	21	0	0	0-1	23.2	32	24	6	0	19-1	20	7.99	55	.330	.429	2	.000	-0		-10		-0

KOLB, DAN Daniel Lee B3.29.1975 Sterling IL BR/TR/6-4/215(185-240) [TexA95 6/150] d6.4 Col Illinois St.

YEAR	TM LG	W	L	PCT	G	GS	CG-SHO	SV-BS	IP	H	R	HR	HB	BB-IB	SO	ERA	AERA	OAV	OOB	AB-HR-SH	AVG	PB	SUP	APR	DL	PW
1999	Tex A	2	1	.667	16	0	0	0-0	31	33	18	2	1	15-0	15	4.65	111	.268	.353	0	—	0		1	1	0
2000	Tex A	0	0	—	1	0	0	0-0	0.2	5	5	2	0	2-0	0	67.50	8	.833	.778	0	—	0		-4	127	-0
2001	Tex A	0	0	—	17	0	0	0-0	15.1	15	8	2	0	10-1	15	4.70	102	.259	.362	0	—	0		1	107	-0
2002	Tex A	3	6	.333	34	0	0	1-3	32	27	17	1	1	22-2	20	4.22	114	.227	.347	0	—	0		11		1
2003	Mil N	1	2	.333	37	0	0	21-2	41.1	34	12	1	1	19-3	39	1.96	220	.231	.310	0	—	0		1		0
2004	Mil N★	4	4	.000	64	0	0	39-5	57.1	50	22	3	1	15-1	21	2.98	147	.234	.292	0	—	0		-10	-2	
2005	Atl N	3	8	.273	65	0	0	11-7	57.2	78	39	5	1	29-5	21	5.93	72	.329	.403	0	.000	-0		7	336	-0
Total 7		9	21	.300	234	0	0	72-17	235.1	242	116	16	5	112-12	149	4.21	108	.266	.348	0				7	336	

KOLB, EDDIE Edward William B7.20.1880 Cincinnati OH D10.1.1949 Calgary AL, Can. BR/TR d10.15

YEAR	TM LG	W	L	PCT	G	GS	CG-SHO	SV-BS	IP	H	R	HR	HB	BB-IB	SO	ERA	AERA	OAV	OOB	AB-HR-SH	AVG	PB	SUP	APR	DL	PW
1899	Cle N	0	1	.000	1	1	1	0	8	18	19	0	1	5	1	10.13	36	.439	.511	4	.250	-0	59	-8		-0.

YEAR	TM LG	W	L	PCT	G	GS	CG-SHO	SV-BS	IP	H	R	HR	HB	BB-IB	SO	ERA	AERA	OAV	OOB	AB-HR-SH	AVG	PB	SUP	APR	DL	PW

KOLP, RAY Raymond Carl "Jockey" B10.1.1894 New Berlin (now North Canton) OH D7.29.1967 Cincinnati OH BR/TR/5-10.5/187 d4.16

1921	StL A	8	7	.533	37	18	5-1	0	166.2	208	111	12	0	51	43	4.97	90	.314	.363	55-0-8	.127	-5*	109	-9		-1.2
1922	StL A	14	4	.778	32	18	9-1	0	169.2	199	89	10	5	36	54	3.93	106	.292	.332	57-0-11	.298	5	153	5		0.7
1923	StL A	5	12	.294	34	17	11-1	1	171.1	178	91	11	6	54	44	3.89	107	.273	.335	54-0-5	.111	-4	70	4		-0.1
1924	StL A	5	7	.417	25	12	5-1	0	96.2	131	65	4	4	25	29	5.68	79	.329	.375	30-0-2	.200	-0	76	-9		-1.0
1927	Cin N	3	3	.500	24	5	2-1	3	82.1	86	38	5	1	29	28	3.06	124	.278	.342	30-0-1	.200	-0	90	5		0.4
1928	Cin N	13	10	.565	44	23	12-1	3	209	219	87	9	4	55	61	3.19	124	.280	.330	70-1-4	.214	3	98	17		2.0
1929	Cin N	8	10	.444	30	16	4-1	0	145.1	151	75	8	1	39	27	4.03	113	.278	.328	49-0-4	.163	-2	82	8		0.8
1930	Cin N	7	12	.368	30	19	5-2	3	168.1	180	86	10	0	34	40	4.22	114	.278	.314	49-1-1	.245	1	58	13		1.4
1931	Cin N	4	9	.308	30	10	2	1	107	144	66	8	4	39	24	4.96	75	.332	.392	32-0-3	.125	-1	96	-14		-1.6
1932	Cin N	6	10	.375	32	18	7-2	1	159.2	176	80	13	3	27	42	3.89	99	.280	.313	49-0-0	.184	-1	84	1		-0.1
1933	Cin N	6	9	.400	30	14	4	3	150.1	168	73	7	1	23	28	3.53	96	.290	.318	45-0-3	.156	-1	81	-2		-0.2
1934	Cin N	0	2	.000	28	2	0	3	61.2	78	36	1	2	12	19	4.52	90	.312	.348	12	.083	-1	53	-2		-0.1
Total	12	79	95	.454	383	172	66-11	18	1688	1918	897	98	31	424	439	4.08	102	.292	.338	532-2-44	.184	-7	91	17		1.0

KOLSTAD, HAL Harold Everette B6.1.1935 Rice Lake WI BR/TR/5-9/190* d4.22 Col San Jose St.

1962	Bos A	0	0	.000	27	2	0	2	61.1	65	44	11	2	35-1	36	5.43	76	.269	.363	18-0-2	.056	-2	97	-10		-0.6
1963	Bos A	0	2	.000	7	0	0	0	11	16	16	4	2	6-0	6	13.09	29	.340	.436	1-0-1	.000	-0		-10		-1.6
Total	2	0	2	.000	34	2	0	2	72.1	81	60	15	4	41-1	42	6.59	62	.280	.375	19-0-3	.053	-2	97	-20		-2.2

KOMIYAMA, SATORU Satoru B9.15.1965 Chiba, Japan BR/TR/6-0/195 d4.4

| 2002 | NY N | 0 | 3 | .000 | 25 | 0 | 0 | 0-0 | 43.1 | 53 | 29 | 7 | 3 | 12-4 | 33 | 5.61 | 71 | .301 | .351 | 1-0-1 | .000 | 0 | | -8 | 15 | -0.5 |

KONETCHY, ED Edward Joseph "Big Ed" B9.3.1885 LaCrosse WI D5.27.1947 Ft.Worth TX BR/TR/6-2.5/195 d6.29.1907 ▲

1910	StL N	0	0	—	1	0	0	0	4	4	2	0	0	1	0	4.50	66	.267	.313	520-3-11	.302	0*		0		0.0
1913	StL N	1	0	1.000	1	0	0	0	4.2	1	0	0	0	4	3	0.00	—	.071	.278	504-8-19	.278	0*		2		0.4
1918	Bos N	0	1	.000	1	1	0	0	8	14	8	0	0	2	3	6.75	40	.378	.410	437-2-16	.236	0*	0	-2		-0.4
Total	3	1	1	.500	3	1	1	0	16.2	19	10	0	0	7	6	4.32	67	.288	.356	1461-13-46	.273	1	0	-2		0.0

KONIECZNY, DOUG Douglas James B9.27.1951 Detroit MI BR/TR/6-4/220* [HouN71*A1/4] d9.11 Col Wayne State (MI)

1973	Hou N	0	1	.000	2	0	0	0-0	13	12	8	0	0	4-0	6	5.54	66	.279	.333	4	.000	-0	85	-2		-0.2
1974	Hou N	0	3	.000	6	3	0	0-0	16	18	15	0	2	12-1	8	7.88	44	.290	.421	4	.000	-1	50	-8		-1.3
1975	Hou N	6	13	.316	32	29	4-1	0-0	171	184	93	15	1	87-1	89	4.47	76	.280	.361	50-0-5	.160	1	104	-22		-2.2
1977	Hou N	1	1	.500	4	0	0	0-0	21	26	15	1	1	8-0	7	6.00	60	.302	.361	7-0-1	.143	-0	98	-6	118	-0.5
Total	4	7	18	.280	44	38	4-1	0-0	221	240	131	16	4	111-2	110	4.93	70	.283	.364	65-0-6	.138	-0	98	-38	118	-4.2

KONIKOWSKI, ALEX Alexander James "Whitey" B6.8.1928 Throop PA D9.28.1997 Seymour CT BR/TR/6-1/187* d6.16 Mil 1952-53

1948	NY N	2	3	.400	22	1	0	1	33.1	46	34	7	0	17	9	7.56	52	.346	.420	2-0-1	.000	0	23	-14		-1.8
1951	†NY N	0	0	—	3	0	0	0	4	2	0	0	0	0	5	0.00	—	.154	.154	0		0		2		0.1
1954	NY N	0	0	—	10	0	0	0	12	10	10	1	0	12	6	7.50	54	.244	.415	1	.000	-0		-4		-0.2
Total	3	2	3	.400	35	1	0	1	49.1	58	44	8	0	29	20	6.93	57	.310	.403	3-0-1	.000	0	23	-16		-1.9

KONSTANTY, JIM Casimir James B3.2.1917 Strykersville NY D6.11.1976 Oneonta NY BR/TR/6-1.5/202* d6.18 Mil 1945 Col Syracuse

1944	Cin N	6	4	.600	20	12	5-1	0	112.2	113	46	11	3	33	19	2.80	125	.266	.320	34-0-3	.294	2	108	7		0.8
1946	Bos N	0	1	.000	10	1	0	0	15.1	17	9	2	0	7	9	5.28	65	.283	.358	2	.000	0	175	-3		-0.1
1948	Phi N	1	0	1.000	6	0	0	2	9.2	7	1	0	0	2	7	0.93	424	.233	.281	3	.000	-0		3		0.4
1949	Phi N	9	5	.643	53	0	0	7	97	98	38	9	1	29	43	3.25	121	.280	.337	17-0-1	.176	-0		8		1.2
1950	†Phi N★	16	7	.696	74	0	0	22	152	108	51	11	0	50	56	2.66	152	.205	.274	37-0-2	.108	-2		24		3.8
1951	Phi N	4	11	.267	58	1	0	9	115.2	127	58	9	0	31	27	4.05	95	.282	.328	19-0-3	.158	-0	46	-3		-0.5
1952	Phi N	5	3	.625	42	2	2-1	6	80	87	44	9	0	21	16	3.94	93	.274	.319	14-0-1	.071	0	97	-4		-0.5
1953	Phi N	14	10	.583	48	19	7-1	5	170.2	198	90	18	3	42	45	4.43	95	.290	.334	50-0-3	.220	-0	115	-1		-0.2
1954	Phi N	2	3	.400	33	1	0	3	50.1	62	27	7	0	12	11	3.75	108	.316	.352	13	.000	-2	88	0		-0.2
	NY A	1	1	.500	9	0	0	2	18.1	11	2	0	0	6	3	0.98	350	.183	.254	3	.000	-0		6		0.7
1955	NY A	7	2	.778	45	0	0	11	73.2	68	28	5	0	24-2	19	2.32	161	.247	.305	8-0-3	.125	-0		10		1.4
1956	NY A	0	0	—	8	0	0	2	11	15	6	3	0	6-0	6	4.91	79	.319	.396	2	.000	-0		1		-0.1
	StL N	1	1	.500	27	0	0	5	39.1	46	20	4	1	6-1	7	4.58	83	.301	.325	0		-0		-2		-0.2
Total	11	66	48	.579	433	36	14-2	74	945.2	957	420	88	5	269-3	268	3.46	112	.268	.319	202-0-16	.163	-5	112	44		6.6

KONUSZEWSKI, DENNIS Dennis John B2.4.1971 Bridgeport MI BR/TR/6-3/210 [PitN92 7/203] d8.4 Col Michigan

| 1995 | Pit N | 0 | 0 | — | 1 | 0 | 0 | 0 | 0.1 | 3 | 2 | 0 | 0 | 1-0 | 0 | 54.00 | 8 | 1.000 | 1.000 | 0 | | 0 | | -2 | | -0.1 |

KOO, DAE-SUNG Dae-Sung B8.2.1968 Daejeon, South Korea BL/TL/6-1/185 d4.4 Col Hanyang

| 2005 | NY N | 0 | 0 | — | 33 | 0 | 0 | 0-2 | 23 | 22 | 12 | 2 | 2 | 13-1 | 23 | 3.91 | 106 | .250 | .349 | 2 | .500 | 1 | | 0 | 43 | 0.1 |

KOOB, ERNIE Ernest Gerald B9.11.1892 Keeler MI D11.12.1941 Lemay MO BL/TL/5-10/160 d6.23 Mil 1918 Col Western Michigan

1915	StL A	4	5	.444	28	13	6	1	133.2	119	50	2	10	50	37	2.36	122	.254	.339	37-0-2	.135	-1	86	8		0.3
1916	StL A	11	8	.579	33	20	10-2	2	166.2	153	54	1	6	56	26	2.54	108	.252	.321	41-0-1	.000	-1	85	7		0.6
1917	StL A	6	14	.300	39	18	3-1	1	133.2	139	81	1	6	57	47	3.91	67	.280	.361	50-0-3	.114	-1	95	-20		-3.0
1919	StL A	2	4	.333	25	4	0	0	66	77	37	3	2	23	11	4.64	72	.296	.358	15-0-1	.000	-1	83	-7		-0.8
Total	4	23	31	.426	125	55	19-3	4	500	488	222	7	24	186	121	3.13	90	.266	.342	128-0-7	.070	-5	87	-12		-2.9

KOONCE, CAL Calvin Lee B11.18.1940 Fayetteville NC D10.28.1993 Winston-Salem NC BR/TR/6-1/185* d4.14 Col Campbell

1962	Chi N	10	10	.500	35	30	3-1	0	190.2	200	93	17	7	86-3	84	3.97	105	.271	.350	64-0-3	.094	-4	88	5		0.1
1963	Chi N	2	6	.250	21	13	0	0	72.2	75	43	9	2	32-2	44	4.58	77	.273	.353	19-0-3	.105	-0	57	-8		-0.8
1964	Chi N	3	0	1.000	6	2	0	0	31	30	8	1	0	7-1	17	2.03	183	.254	.294	10	.000	-1	95	5		0.5
1965	Chi N	7	9	.438	38	23	3-1	0	173	181	83	17	6	52-8	88	3.69	100	.271	.327	49-0-3	.102	0	94	0		0.0
1966	Chi N	5	5	.500	45	5	0	2	108.2	113	57	13	1	35-9	65	3.81	97	.268	.321	23-0-3	.130	0	153	-3		-0.2
1967	Chi N	2	2	.500	34	0	0	2	51	52	27	2	1	21-6	28	4.59	77	.268	.341	7	.000	-1		-5		-0.5
	NY N	3	3	.500	11	6	2-1	0	45	45	16	2	0	7-1	24	2.80	121	.259	.287	13-0-1	.154	-0*	73	3		0.4
	Year	5	5	.500	45	6	2-1	2	96	97	43	4	1	28-7	52	3.75	93	.264	.317	20-0-1	.100	-1	72	-2		-0.1
1968	NY N	6	4	.600	55	2	0	11	96.2	80	27	4	1	32-11	50	2.42	125	.235	.301	14	.000	-1	115	7		0.9
1969	NY N	6	3	.667	40	0	0	7-4	83	85	53	8	3	42-8	51	4.99	73	.269	.358	17	.235	0		-13		-1.4
1970	NY N	0	0	—	13	0	0	0-0	22	25	9	2	1	14-5	10	3.27	124	.301	.408	1	.000	0		2		0.2
	Bos A	3	4	.429	23	8	1	2-2	76.1	64	32	7	3	29-3	37	3.54	113	.231	.309	21-0-1	.095	-0	106	5		0.5
1971	Bos A	0	1	.000	13	1	0	1	21	22	16	3	0	11-0	9	5.57	67	.278	.367	1	.000	0	241	-5		-0.2
Total	10	47	49	.490	334	90	9-3	24-7	971	972	464	85	25	368-57	504	3.78	98	.264	.333	239-0-14	.100	-6	95	-7		-0.5

KOOSMAN, JERRY Jerome Martin B12.23.1942 Appleton MN BR/TL/6-2/208(205-225) d4.14

1967	NY N	0	2	.000	9	3	0	0	22.1	22	17	3	0	19-4	11	6.04	56	.259	.390	2	.000	0	52	-7		-0.5
1968	NY N★	19	12	.613	35	34	17-7	0	263.2	221	72	16	8	69-7	178	2.08	145	.228	.283	91-1-3	.077	-3	101	25		2.8
1969	†NY N★	17	9	.654	32	32	16-6	0-0	241	187	66	14	8	68-11	180	2.28	161	.216	.275	84-0-4	.048	-8	82	37		3.2
1970	NY N	12	7	.632	30	29	5-1	0-0	212	189	87	22	2	71-14	118	3.14	129	.237	.299	70-0-8	.086	-7	107	20		1.3
1971	NY N	6	11	.353	26	24	4	0-0	165.2	160	66	12	1	51-4	96	3.04	113	.256	.305	50-0-6	.160	0	87	6	33	0.6
1972	NY N	11	12	.478	34	24	4-1	1-0	163	155	81	14	4	52-7	147	4.14	82	.250	.310	47-0-9	.085	-3	85	-12		-1.9
1973	†NY N	14	15	.483	35	35	12-3	0-0	263	234	93	18	4	76-6	156	2.84	128	.242	.298	78-0-15	.103	-3	77	23		2.1
1974	NY N	15	11	.577	35	35	13	0-0	265	258	113	16	7	85-7	188	3.36	107	.257	.316	86-0-10	.186	2	95	8		1.0
1975	NY N	14	13	.519	36	34	11-4	2-0	239.2	234	106	19	4	98-6	173	3.42	103	.261	.335	78-0-7	.179	1	99	-1		0.3
1976	NY N	21	10	.677	34	32	17-3	0-1	247.1	205	81	19	1	66-8	200	2.69	124	.226	.278	79-0-13	.215	3	108	20		2.9
1977	NY N	8	20	.286	32	32	6-1	0-0	226.2	195	102	19	4	81-8	192	3.49	109	.232	.301	72-1-5	.111	0	75	5		0.9
1978	NY N	3	15	.167	38	32	3	2-1	235.1	221	110	17	8	84-11	160	3.75	95	.255	.323	70-0-5	.086	-3	83	-6		-0.7
1979	Min A	20	13	.606	37	36	10-2	0-0	263.2	268	108	19	7	83-4	149	3.38	130	.264	.324	0	—	0	94	29		3.4
1980	Min A	16	13	.552	38	34	8	2-0	243.1	252	119	24	4	69-5	149	4.03	108	.272	.324	0	—	0	87	11		1.2
1981	Min A	3	9	.250	19	13	2-1	5-0	94.1	98	49	8	0	34-7	55	4.20	94	.272	.331	0	—	0	61	-2		-0.3
	Chi A	1	4	.200	8	3	1	0-1	27	27	10	2	0	7-0	21	3.33	109	.260	.306	0	—	0	132	2		0.3
	Year	4	13	.235	27	16	3-1	5-1	121.1	125	59	10	0	41-7	76	4.01	97	.269	.325	0	—	0	74	-1		0.0
1982	Chi A	11	7	.611	42	19	2-1	2-0	173.1	194	81	9	6	38-3	88	3.84	106	.287	.325	0	—	0	126	6		0.6
1983	†Chi A	11	7	.611	37	24	2-1	2-0	169.2	176	96	19	6	53-2	90	4.77	88	.266	.324	0	—	0	107	-9		-0.8

YEAR	TM LG	W	L	PCT	G	GS	CG-SHO	SV-BS	IP	H	R	HR	HB	BB-IB	SO	ERA	AERA	OAV	OOB	AB-HR-SH	AVG	PB	SUP	APR	DL	PW
1984	Phi N	14	15	.483	36	34	3-1	0-0	224	232	95	8	3	60-5	137	3.25	112	.267	.315	74-0-14	.108	-3	109	10		0.9
1985	Phi N	6	4	.600	19	18	3-1	0-0	99.1	107	56	14	3	34-3	60	4.62	80	.276	.336	34-0-1	.088	-2	122	-9	81	-1.0
Total	19	222	209	.515	612	527	140-33	17-4	3839.1	3635	1608	290	71	1198-121	2556	3.36	111	.252	.310	915-2-100	.119	-22	94	158	114	15.6

KOPLITZ, HOWIE   Howard Dean   B5.4.1938 Oshkosh WI   BR/TR/5-11/195*   d9.8

YEAR	TM LG	W	L	PCT	G	GS	CG-SHO	SV-BS	IP	H	R	HR	HB	BB-IB	SO	ERA	AERA	OAV	OOB	AB-HR-SH	AVG	PB	SUP	APR	DL	PW
1961	Det A	2	0	1.000	4	1	1	0	12	16	6	0	0	8-1	9	2.25	182	.327	.414	4	.000	-1	129	1		0.1
1962	Det A	3	0	1.000	10	6	1	0	37.2	54	24	5	0	10-1	10	5.26	77	.342	.379	13	.231	1*	183	-4		-0.2
1964	Was A	0	0	—	6	1	0	0	17	20	9	3	0	13-1	9	4.76	78	.290	.402	4	.000	-0	144	-1		-0.1
1965	Was A	4	7	.364	33	11	0	1	106.2	97	51	11	3	48-4	59	4.05	86	.249	.333	30-0-1	.100	-1	108	-5		-0.6
1966	Was A	0	0	—	1	0	0	0	2	0	0	0	0	1-0	0	0.00	—	.000	.200	0	—	0	1	22	22	0.0
Total	5	9	7	.563	54	19	2	1	175.1	187	90	19	3	80-7	87	4.21	87	.280	.356	51-0-1	.118	-1	138	-8	22	-0.8

KOPLOVE, MIKE   Michael Paul   B8.30.1976 Philadelphia PA   BR/TR/6-0/160(160-180)   [AriN98 29/883]   d9.6   Col Delaware

YEAR	TM LG	W	L	PCT	G	GS	CG-SHO	SV-BS	IP	H	R	HR	HB	BB-IB	SO	ERA	AERA	OAV	OOB	AB-HR-SH	AVG	PB	SUP	APR	DL	PW
2001	Ari N	0	1	.000	9	0	0	0-0	10	8	6	7	1	9-1	14	3.60	129	.211	.388	1	.000	-0	0			0.0
2002	†Ari N	6	1	.857	55	0	0	0-0	61.2	47	24	2	0	23-4	46	3.36	134	.213	.286	1	.000	-0	7			0.8
2003	Ari N	3	0	1.000	31	0	0	0-1	37.2	31	11	3	5	10-1	27	2.15	215	.225	.297	0	—	0	9	118		0.7
2004	Ari N	4	4	.500	76	0	0	2-6	86.2	86	42	7	5	37-10	55	4.05	113	.269	.353	0	—	0	6			0.6
2005	Ari N	2	1	.667	44	0	0	0-2	49.2	48	31	6	6	20-3	28	5.07	87	.257	.343	2	.000	-0	-4			-0.2
Total	5	15	7	.682	215	0	0	2-9	245.2	220	115	19	18	99-19	170	3.77	120	.243	.328	4	.000	-0	18	118		1.9

KORINCE, GEORGE   George Eugene "Moose"   B1.10.1946 Ottawa ON, Can.   BR/TR/6-3/200*   d9.10

YEAR	TM LG	W	L	PCT	G	GS	CG-SHO	SV-BS	IP	H	R	HR	HB	BB-IB	SO	ERA	AERA	OAV	OOB	AB-HR-SH	AVG	PB	SUP	APR	DL	PW
1966	Det A	0	0	—	2	0	0	0	3	1	0	0	1	3-0	2	0.00	—	.091	.333	0	—	-0	1			0.1
1967	Det A	1	0	1.000	9	0	0	0	14	10	8	1	0	11-1	11	5.14	63	.204	.339	1	.000	-0	-3			-0.2
Total	2	1	0	1.000	11	0	0	0	17	11	8	1	1	14-1	13	4.24	78	.183	.338	1	.000	-0	-2			-0.1

KORONKA, JOHN   John Vincent   B7.3.1980 Clearwater FL   BL/TL/6-1/180   d6.1

YEAR	TM LG	W	L	PCT	G	GS	CG-SHO	SV-BS	IP	H	R	HR	HB	BB-IB	SO	ERA	AERA	OAV	OOB	AB-HR-SH	AVG	PB	SUP	APR	DL	PW
2005	Chi N	1	2	.333	4	3	0	0-0	15.2	19	13	2	0	8-0	10	7.47	59	.284	.360			-0	78	-5		-0.8

KORWAN, JIM   James "Long Jim"   B3.4.1874 Brooklyn NY   D7.24.1899 Brooklyn NY   BR/TL/6-1/181   d4.24

YEAR	TM LG	W	L	PCT	G	GS	CG-SHO	SV-BS	IP	H	R	HR	HB	BB-IB	SO	ERA	AERA	OAV	OOB	AB-HR-SH	AVG	PB	SUP	APR	DL	PW
1894	Bro N	0	0	—	1	0	0	0	5	9	14	1	0	5	2	14.40	34	.391	.500	2	.000	-0	-7			-0.2
1897	Chi N	1	2	.333	5	4	3	0	34	47	36	1	1	28	12	5.82	77	.324	.437	12	.000	-2	92	-6		-0.5
Total	2	1	2	.333	6	4	3	0	39	56	50	2	1	33	14	6.92	66	.333	.446	14	.000	-2	92	-13		-0.7

KOSKI, BILL   William John "T-Bone"   B2.6.1932 Madera CA   BR/TR/6-4/185   d4.28   Mil 1952-54

YEAR	TM LG	W	L	PCT	G	GS	CG-SHO	SV-BS	IP	H	R	HR	HB	BB-IB	SO	ERA	AERA	OAV	OOB	AB-HR-SH	AVG	PB	SUP	APR	DL	PW
1951	Pit N	0	1	.000	13	1	0	0	27	26	23	2	0	28	6	6.67	63	.257	.419	4	.000	-1	63	-7		-0.4

KOSLO, DAVE   George Bernard (b George Bernard Koslowski)   B3.31.1920 Menasha WI   D12.1.1975 Menasha WI   BL/TL/5-11/180*   d9.12   Mil 1943-45

YEAR	TM LG	W	L	PCT	G	GS	CG-SHO	SV-BS	IP	H	R	HR	HB	BB-IB	SO	ERA	AERA	OAV	OOB	AB-HR-SH	AVG	PB	SUP	APR	DL	PW
1941	NY N	1	2	.333	4	3	2	0	23.2	17	10	0	0	10	12	1.90	194	.202	.287	9	.111	-1	46	5		0.5
1942	NY N	3	6	.333	19	11	3-1	0	78	79	49	7	1	32	42	5.08	66	.261	.333	25	.120	-0	89	-13		-1.8
1946	NY N	14	19	.424	40	35	17-3	1	265.1	251	119	15	5	101	121	3.63	95	.249	.320	88-0-1	.125	-3*	86	-3		-0.4
1947	NY N	15	10	.600	39	31	10-3	0	217.1	223	118	23	3	82	86	4.39	93	.259	.326	78-0-1	.128	-1	132	-7		-0.4
1948	NY N	8	10	.444	35	18	5-3	3	149	168	69	7	1	62	58	3.87	102	.290	.359	44-0-3	.114	-1	85	4		0.1
1949	NY N	11	14	.440	38	23	15	4	212	193	72	13	0	43	64	2.50	159	.239	.278	69-2-6	.145	1*	76	34		4.0
1950	NY N	13	15	.464	40	22	7-1	3	186.2	190	89	18	5	68	56	3.91	105	.268	.337	65-1-1	.123	-1	107	5		1.0
1951	†NY N	10	9	.526	39	16	5-2	3	149.2	153	68	18	2	45	54	3.31	118	.258	.313	50	.100	-1	130	9		1.6
1952	NY N	10	7	.588	41	17	8-2	5	166.1	154	66	10	2	47	67	4.76	90	.296	.349	30-0-3	.033	-3	87	-6		-1.1
1953	NY N	6	12	.333	37	12	2	2	111.2	135	70	8	1	36	36	3.14	114	.333	.365	3	.000	-0	-5			-0.4
1954	Bal A	0	1	.000	3	1	0	0	14.1	20	7	1	0	3	3	3.12	120	.228	.324	1	.000	-0	2			-0.1
	Mil N	1	1	.500	12	0	0	0	17.1	13	6	0	0	9	7	3.68	105	.260	.321	0	—	0	-1			-0.1
1955	Mil N	0	1	.000	1	0	0	0	1	1	1	0	0	0-0	1	∞	—	1.000	1.000	0	—	0	-1			-0.1
Total	12	92	107	.462	348	189	74-15	22	1591.1	1597	740	121	20	538-0	606	3.68	105	.260	.321	516-3-18	.109	-15	101	40		3.3

KOSTAL, JOE   Joseph William "Cudgey"   B6.1.1876 Chicago IL   D10.17.1933 Guelph ON, Can.   BR/TR/5-6/130   d7.14

YEAR	TM LG	W	L	PCT	G	GS	CG-SHO	SV-BS	IP	H	R	HR	HB	BB-IB	SO	ERA	AERA	OAV	OOB	AB-HR-SH	AVG	PB	SUP	APR	DL	PW
1896	Lou N	0	0	—	2	0	0	0	2	4	4	0	0	0	0	—	—	.400	.400	0	—	0	0			0.0

KOUFAX, SANDY   Sanford (b Sanford Braun)   B12.30.1935 Brooklyn NY   BR/TL/6-2/210(198-210)   d6.24   HF1972   Col Cincinnati

YEAR	TM LG	W	L	PCT	G	GS	CG-SHO	SV-BS	IP	H	R	HR	HB	BB-IB	SO	ERA	AERA	OAV	OOB	AB-HR-SH	AVG	PB	SUP	APR	DL	PW
1955	Bro N	2	2	.500	12	5	2-2	0	41.2	33	15	2	1	28-1	30	3.02	134	.216	.341	12	.000	-2	75	5	30	0.4
1956	Bro N	2	4	.333	16	10	0	0	58.2	66	37	10	0	29-0	30	4.91	81	.286	.365	17	.118	-0	80	-7		-0.4
1957	Bro N	5	4	.556	34	13	2	0	104.1	83	49	14	2	51-1	122	3.88	107	.216	.309	26-0-1	.000	-3	91	4		-0.1
1958	LA N	11	11	.500	40	26	5	1	158.2	132	89	19	1	105-6	131	4.48	91	.220	.335	49-0-5	.122	-2	96	-7		-1.3
1959	†LA N	8	6	.571	35	23	6-1	2	153.1	136	74	23	0	92-4	173	4.05	104	.235	.338	54-0-2	.111	-1	117	4		0.9
1960	LA N	8	13	.381	37	26	7-2	1	175	133	83	20	1	100-6	197	3.91	102	.207	.314	57-0-4	.123	-2	91	2		0.9
1961	LA N★	18	13	.581	42	35	15-2	1	255.2	212	117	27	3	96-6	269	3.52	123	.222	.295	77-0-8	.065	-5	100	20		1.9
1962	LA N☆	14	7	.667	28	26	11-2	1	184.1	134	61	13	2	57-4	216	2.54	143	.197	.261	69-1-2	.087	-3	119	24		2.5
1963	†LA N☆	25	5	.833	40	40	20-11	0	311	214	68	18	5	58-7	306	1.88	161	.189	.230	110-1-7	.064	-4	123	47		4.5
1964	LA N☆	19	5	.792	29	28	15-7	1	223	154	49	13	0	53-5	223	1.74	187	.191	.240	74-0-3	.095	-2	97	41		4.1
1965	†LA N★	26	8	.765	43	41	27-8	2	335.2	216	90	26	5	71-4	382	2.04	160	.179	.227	113-0-3	.177	5	108	48		6.2
1966	†LA N★	27	9	.750	41	41	27-5	0	323	241	74	19	0	77-4	317	1.73	191	.205	.252	118	.076	-5	113	60		6.6
Total	12	165	87	.655	397	314	137-40	9	2324.1	1754	806	204	18	817-48	2396	2.76	131	.205	.275	776-2-35	.097	-25	106	241	30	22

KOUKALIK, JOE   Joseph   B3.3.1880 Chicago IL   D1.2.1947 Chicago IL   5-8/160   d9.1

YEAR	TM LG	W	L	PCT	G	GS	CG-SHO	SV-BS	IP	H	R	HR	HB	BB-IB	SO	ERA	AERA	OAV	OOB	AB-HR-SH	AVG	PB	SUP	APR	DL	PW
1904	Bro N	0	1	.000	1	1	1	0	8	10	3	0	2	4	1	1.13	244	.333	.412	3	.000	-0	0	1		0.0

KOUPAL, LOU   Louis Laddie   B12.19.1898 Tabor SD   D12.8.1961 San Gabriel CA   BR/TR/5-11/175   d4.17

YEAR	TM LG	W	L	PCT	G	GS	CG-SHO	SV-BS	IP	H	R	HR	HB	BB-IB	SO	ERA	AERA	OAV	OOB	AB-HR-SH	AVG	PB	SUP	APR	DL	PW
1925	Pit N	0	0	—	6	0	0	0	9	14	10	1	0	7	0	9.00	50	.378	.477	1	.000	-0*	-4			-0.1
1926	Pit N	0	2	.000	6	2	1	0	19.2	22	9	0	1	8	7	3.20	123	.289	.365	4	.250	-2	32	1		0.1
1928	Bro N	1	0	1.000	17	1	1	1	37.1	43	22	0	1	15	10	2.41	165	.303	.373	9	.111	-1	170	3		0.4
1929	Bro N	0	1	.000	18	3	0	4	40.1	49	36	9	0	25	17	5.36	86	.308	.402	14	.071	-2	57	-7		-0.6
	Phi N	5	5	.500	15	11	3	2	86.2	106	56	5	2	29	18	4.78	109	.305	.362	32-0-2	.125	-2	95	2		0.0
	Year	5	6	.455	33	14	3	6	127	155	92	8	2	54	35	4.96	101	.306	.375	46-0-2	.109	-4	88	-5		-0.6
1930	Phi N	0	4	.000	13	4	1	0	36.2	52	35	4	1	17	11	8.59	64	.344	.414	12	.083	-1	92	-9		-0.2
1937	StL A	4	9	.308	26	13	6	0	105.2	150	87	10	0	56	20	6.56	74	.339	.412	32-0-4	.094	-3	90	-20		-2.3
Total	6	10	21	.323	101	34	12	7	335.1	436	255	23	5	156	87	5.58	86	.322	.394	104-0-4	.106	-9	90	-34		-3.0

KOWALIK, FABIAN   Fabian Lorenz   B4.22.1908 Falls City TX   D8.14.1954 Karnes City TX   BR/TR(BB 1932, 35)/5-11/185   d9.4

YEAR	TM LG	W	L	PCT	G	GS	CG-SHO	SV-BS	IP	H	R	HR	HB	BB-IB	SO	ERA	AERA	OAV	OOB	AB-HR-SH	AVG	PB	SUP	APR	DL	PW
1932	Chi A	0	1	.000	2	1	1	0	10.1	16	11	2	1	4	2	6.97	62	.340	.404	13	.385	1*	98	-4		-0.1
1935	†Chi N	2	2	.500	20	2	1	1	55	60	31	2	0	19	20	4.42	89	.280	.339	15	.200	-0	184	-3		-0.2
1936	Chi N	0	2	.000	6	0	0	1	16	24	12	1	0	7	1	6.75	59	.358	.419	5	.000	-0*	103	-6		-0.2
	Phi N	1	5	.167	22	8	2	0	77	100	57	5	2	31	19	5.38	84	.308	.372	57-0-1	.228	-0	103	-6		-0.4
	Bos N	1	0	1.000	1	1	1	0	9	18	14	0	0	3	1	8.00	48	.419	.444	5	.400	1*	133	-4		-0.1
	Year	1	8	.111	29	9	3	1	102	142	77	6	2	40	20	5.82	75	.336	.386	67-0-1	.224	-0	107	-13		-1.6
Total	3	3	11	.214	51	12	4	2	167.1	218	119	10	3	63	42	5.43	78	.313	.373	95-0-1	.242	-0	120	-21		-3.1

KOZLOWSKI, BEN   Benjamin Anthony   B8.16.1980 St.Petersburg FL   BL/TL/6-6/220   [AtlN99 12/384]   d9.19   Col Santa Fe (FL) CC

YEAR	TM LG	W	L	PCT	G	GS	CG-SHO	SV-BS	IP	H	R	HR	HB	BB-IB	SO	ERA	AERA	OAV	OOB	AB-HR-SH	AVG	PB	SUP	APR	DL	PW
2002	Tex A	0	1	.000	3	3	0	0-0	10	11	7	3	1	11-0	6	6.30	76	.289	.460	0	—	0	194	-1		-0.1

KRAEMER, JOE   Joseph Wayne   B9.10.1964 Olympia WA   BL/TL/6-2/185*   [ChiN85 16/416]   d8.22   Col Portland St.

YEAR	TM LG	W	L	PCT	G	GS	CG-SHO	SV-BS	IP	H	R	HR	HB	BB-IB	SO	ERA	AERA	OAV	OOB	AB-HR-SH	AVG	PB	SUP	APR	DL	PW
1989	Chi N	0	1	.000	1	1	0	0-0	3.2	7	6	0	0	2-1	5	4.91	77	.368	.429	1	.000	-0	47	-2		-0.1
1990	Chi N	0	0	—	18	0	0	0-1	25	31	25	2	2	14-2	16	7.20	57	.310	.398	0	—	0	-9			-0.1
Total	2	0	1	.000	19	1	0	0-1	28.2	38	31	2	2	16-3	21	6.91	59	.319	.403	1	.000	-0	47	-11		-0.2

KRAKAUSKAS, JOE   Joseph Victor Lawrence   B3.28.1915 Montreal QC, Can.   D7.8.1960 Hamilton ON, Can.   BL/TL/6-1/203   d9.9   Mil 1943-45

YEAR	TM LG	W	L	PCT	G	GS	CG-SHO	SV-BS	IP	H	R	HR	HB	BB-IB	SO	ERA	AERA	OAV	OOB	AB-HR-SH	AVG	PB	SUP	APR	DL	PW
1937	Was A	4	1	.800	5	4	3	0	40	33	14	0	0	18	28	2.70	164	.226	.327	16	.125	-0	103	8		0.8
1938	Was A	7	5	.583	29	10	5-1	0	121.1	99	61	4	3	88	104	3.12	145	.220	.352	33-0-3	.182	1	100	15		1.6
1939	Was A	11	17	.393	39	29	12	1	217.1	230	125	13	1	114	110	4.60	95	.276	.364	77-0-3	.208	3	101	-5		-0.6
1940	Was A	1	6	.143	32	10	2	0	109	137	90	7	0	73	68	6.44	65	.309	.406	32	.250	-1	110	-28		-3.2
1941	Cle A	2	3	.333	12	5	0	0	41.2	39	25	3	0	29	25	4.10	96	.245	.362	13	.077	-1	123	-3		-0.4
1942	Cle A	0	0	—	3	0	0	0	7	7	3	0	0	6	2	3.86	89	.259	.355	2	.000	-0	0			0.0

YEAR	TM LG	W	L	PCT	G	GS	CG-SHO	SV-BS	IP	H	R	HR	HB	BB-IB	SO	ERA	AERA	OAV	OOB	AB-HR-SH	AVG	PB	SUP	APR	DL	PW
1946	Cle A	2	5	.286	29	5	0	1	47.1	60	31	2	0	25	20	5.51	60	.314	.394	10	.000	-1	83	-11		-1.7
Total	7	26	36	.419	149	63	22-1	4	583.2	605	349	30	4	355	347	4.53	93	.269	.369	183-0-6	.180	2	103	-24		-1.6

KRALICK, JACK John Francis B6.1.1935 Youngstown OH BL/TL/6-2/180(166-180) d4.15 Col Michigan St.

YEAR	TM LG	W	L	PCT	G	GS	CG-SHO	SV-BS	IP	H	R	HR	HB	BB-IB	SO	ERA	AERA	OAV	OOB	AB-HR-SH	AVG	PB	SUP	APR	DL	PW
1959	Was A	0	0	—	6	0	0	0	12.1	13	9	5	0	6-0	7	6.57	60	.289	.373	2	.000	-0		-3		-0.1
1960	Was A	8	6	.571	35	18	7-2	1	151	139	54	12	4	45-4	71	3.04	128	.245	.304	41-0-3	.122	-1	92	17		1.4
1961	Min A	13	11	.542	33	33	11-2	0	242	257	101	21	3	64-1	137	3.61	118	.274	.321	86-1-6	.151	-2	90	20		1.7
1962	Min A	12	11	.522	39	37	7-1	0	242.2	239	121	31	3	61-2	139	3.86	106	.258	.302	89-2-3	.202	3	96	4		0.7
1963	Min A	1	4	.200	5	5	1-1	0	25.2	28	16	2	1	8-0	13	3.86	94	.280	.280	6-0-1	.167	1*	39	-2		-0.3
	Cle A	13	9	.591	28	27	10-3	0	197.1	187	70	19	0	41-2	116	2.92	124	.249	.286	60-1-9	.183	1	106	17		1.9
	Year	14	13	.519	33	32	11-4	0	223	215	86	21	1	49-2	129	3.03	120	.253	.292	66-1-10	.182	2	95	15		1.6
1964	Cle A☆	12	7	.632	30	29	8-3	0	190.2	196	79	17	9	51-8	119	3.21	112	.267	.320	64-0-3	.156	-1	101	7		0.6
1965	Cle A	5	11	.313	30	16	1	0	86	106	58	9	2	21-3	34	4.92	71	.298	.338	21-0-3	.143	-1	93	-15		-2.7
1966	Cle A	3	4	.429	27	4	0	0	68.1	69	30	9	1	20-8	31	3.82	90	.268	.319	13-0-1	.077	—	70	-2		-0.2
1967	Cle A	0	2	.000	2	0	0	0	2	4	3	0	0	1-0	1	9.00	36	.444	.500	0		0		-2		-0.3
Total	9	67	65	.508	235	169	45-12	1	1637.1	1761	895	92	10	682	613	4.24	96	.276	.347	501-5-40	.144	0	107	-5		-3.8

KRALY, STEVE Steve Charles "Lefty" B4.18.1929 Whiting IN BL/TL/5-10/152 d8.9

YEAR	TM LG	W	L	PCT	G	GS	CG-SHO	SV-BS	IP	H	R	HR	HB	BB-IB	SO	ERA	AERA	OAV	OOB	AB-HR-SH	AVG	PB	SUP	APR	DL	PW
1953	NY A	0	2	.000	5	3	0	1	25	19	10	2	2	16	8	3.24	114	.209	.339	7	.000	-1	40	1		0.0

KRAMER, JACK John Henry B1.5.1918 New Orleans LA D5.18.1995 Metairie LA BR/TR/6-2/190* d4.25 Def 1942

YEAR	TM LG	W	L	PCT	G	GS	CG-SHO	SV-BS	IP	H	R	HR	HB	BB-IB	SO	ERA	AERA	OAV	OOB	AB-HR-SH	AVG	PB	SUP	APR	DL	PW
1939	StL A	9	16	.360	40	31	10-2	0	211.2	269	150	18	3	127	68	5.83	84	.318	.409	66-1-7	.136	-1	103	-19		-2.0
1940	StL A	3	7	.300	16	9	1	0	64.2	86	48	4	0	26	12	6.26	73	.327	.388	20-0-1	.050	-1	89	-10		-1.4
1941	StL A	4	3	.571	29	3	0	2	59.1	69	48	5	0	40	20	5.16	83	.289	.391	8-0-1	.000	1	101	-10		-0.9
1943	StL A	0	0	—	3	0	0	0	9	11	8	0	1	8	4	8.00	42	.297	.435	2	.500	1		-4		-0.1
1944	†StL A	17	13	.567	33	31	18-1	0	257	233	94	3	1	75	124	2.49	145	.241	.297	85-2-1	.165	1	90	27		3.4
1945	StL A*	10	15	.400	29	25	15-3	2	193	190	85	13	0	73	99	3.36	105	.254	.320	61-0-7	.148	-0	80	2		0.3
1946	StL A★	13	11	.542	31	28	13-3	0	194.2	190	84	6	0	68	69	3.19	117	.257	.319	59-0-8	.136	-1	96	10		1.0
1947	StL A☆	11	16	.407	33	28	9-1	1	199.1	206	123	16	2	89	77	4.97	78	.270	.348	62-0-5	.113	-2	101	-22		-2.8
1948	Bos A	18	5	.783	29	29	14-2	0	205	233	104	12	0	64	72	4.35	101	.284	.336	73-1-7	.151	-1	152	3		0.1
1949	Bos A	6	8	.429	21	18	7-2	1	111.2	126	70	8	1	49	24	5.16	85	.286	.358	35-0-2	.257	3	117	-9		-0.8
1950	NY N	3	6	.333	35	9	1	1	86.2	91	46	6	2	39	27	3.53	116	.268	.346	20-1-1	.100	1	98	2		0.3
1951	NY N	0	0	—	4	1	0	0	4.2	11	8	0	0	3	2	15.43	25	.524	.583	0		1	271	-5		-0.3
	NY A	1	3	.250	19	3	0	0	40.2	46	27	1	0	21	15	4.65	82	.280	.362	10	.100	-0	162	-5		-0.6
Total	12	95	103	.480	322	215	88-14	7	1637.1	1761	895	92	10	682	613	4.24	96	.276	.347	501-5-40	.144	0	107	-8		-3.8

KRAMER, RANDY Randall John B9.20.1960 Palo Alto CA BR/TR/6-2/180* [TexA82 S1/10] d9.11 Col San Jose (CA) City

YEAR	TM LG	W	L	PCT	G	GS	CG-SHO	SV-BS	IP	H	R	HR	HB	BB-IB	SO	ERA	AERA	OAV	OOB	AB-HR-SH	AVG	PB	SUP	APR	DL	PW
1988	Pit N	1	2	.333	5	1	0	0-0	10	12	6	1	1	1-0	7	5.40	64	.316	.341	2	.000	-0	180	-2		-0.4
1989	Pit N	5	9	.357	35	15	1-1	2-4	111.1	90	53	10	7	61-4	52	3.96	86	.224	.334	33-0-2	.152	-0*	99	-6		-0.8
1990	Pit N	0	1	.000	12	2	0	0-0	25.2	27	15	3	2	9-4	15	4.91	74	.273	.345	1	.000	-1	87	-3		-0.2
	Chi N	0	2	.000	10	2	0	0-0	20.1	20	10	3	1	12-2	12	3.98	103	.253	.359	1-0-1	.000	0	88	0		0.0
	Year	0	3	.000	22	4	0	0-0	46	47	25	6	3	21-6	27	4.50	85	.264	.351	6-0-1	.000	-1	88	-3		-0.2
1992	Sea A	0	1	.000	4	0	0	0-0	16.1	30	14	2	1	7-0	6	7.71	52	.400	.458	0	—	-1	125	-6		-0.3
Total	4	6	15	.286	66	24	1-1	2-4	183.2	179	98	19	12	90-10	92	4.51	79	.293	.352	41-0-3	.122	-1	105	-17		-1.7

KRAMER, TOMMY Thomas Joseph B1.9.1968 Cincinnati OH BB/TR/6-0/185(185-205) [CleA87 5/125] d9.12 Col John A. Logan (IL) CC

YEAR	TM LG	W	L	PCT	G	GS	CG-SHO	SV-BS	IP	H	R	HR	HB	BB-IB	SO	ERA	AERA	OAV	OOB	AB-HR-SH	AVG	PB	SUP	APR	DL	PW
1991	Cle A	0	0	—	4	0	0	0-0	4.2	10	9	1	0	6-0	4	17.36	24	.476	.533	—		0		-6		-0.3
1993	Cle A	7	3	.700	39	16	1	0-2	121	126	60	19	2	59-7	71	4.02	109	.269	.352	0	—	0	121	5	18	0.3
Total	2	7	3	.700	43	16	1	0-2	125.2	136	69	20	2	65-7	75	4.49	97	.278	.361	0		0	121	-1	18	0.0

KRAPP, GENE Eugene Hamlet "Rubber Arm" B5.12.1887 Rochester NY D4.13.1923 Detroit MI BR/TR/5-5/165 d4.14

YEAR	TM LG	W	L	PCT	G	GS	CG-SHO	SV-BS	IP	H	R	HR	HB	BB-IB	SO	ERA	AERA	OAV	OOB	AB-HR-SH	AVG	PB	SUP	APR	DL	PW
1911	Cle A	13	9	.591	35	26	14-1	1	222	188	115	1	13	138	132	3.41	100	.232	.353	74-0-3	.230	4*	109	0		0.6
1912	Cle A	2	5	.286	9	7	4	0	58.2	57	39	0	4	42	22	4.60	74	.273	.404	22-0-1	.318	1*	96	-7		-0.5
1914	Buf F	16	14	.533	36	29	18-1	0	252.2	198	83	4	12	115	106	2.49	114	.210	.304	77-0-2	.143	-2*	89	14		1.7
1915	Buf F	9	19	.321	38	30	14-1	0	231	188	106	4	4	123	93	3.51	80	.230	.333	70-0-2	.129	-3*	77	-15		-1.7
Total	4	40	47	.460	118	92	50-3	1	764.1	631	343	11	33	418	353	3.23	95	.227	.335	243-0-8	.181	-1	92	-8		0.1

KRAUS, JACK John William "Tex","Texas Jack" B4.26.1918 San Antonio TX D1.2.1976 San Antonio TX BR/TL/6-4/190 d4.25 Mil 1944

YEAR	TM LG	W	L	PCT	G	GS	CG-SHO	SV-BS	IP	H	R	HR	HB	BB-IB	SO	ERA	AERA	OAV	OOB	AB-HR-SH	AVG	PB	SUP	APR	DL	PW
1943	Phi N	9	15	.375	34	25	10-1	2	199.2	197	83	7	0	78	48	3.16	107	.259	.328	60-0-9	.067	-5*	67	4		0.0
1945	Phi N	4	9	.308	19	13	0	0	81.2	96	55	3	4	40	28	5.40	71	.293	.376	25-0-2	.120	-1	71	-12		-1.7
1946	NY N	2	1	.667	17	1	0	0	25	25	17	4	1	15	7	6.12	56	.260	.366	3	.000	-0	100	-6		-0.7
Total	3	15	25	.375	70	39	10-1	2	306.1	318	155	14	5	133	83	4.00	88	.268	.345	88-0-11	.080	-6	70	-14		-2.4

KRAUSE, HARRY Harry William "Hal" B7.12.1887 San Francisco CA D10.23.1940 San Francisco CA BB/TL/5-10/165 d4.20 Col St. Marys (CA)

YEAR	TM LG	W	L	PCT	G	GS	CG-SHO	SV-BS	IP	H	R	HR	HB	BB-IB	SO	ERA	AERA	OAV	OOB	AB-HR-SH	AVG	PB	SUP	APR	DL	PW
1908	Phi A	1	1	.500	4	2	2	0	21	20	11	0	3	4	10	2.57	100	.247	.307	7	.000	-1	80	-1		-0.2
1909	Phi A	18	8	.692	32	21	16-7	0	213	151	49	0	3	49	139	1.39	173	.204	.266	77-0-2	.156	-1	112	23		2.7
1910	Phi A	6	6	.500	16	11	9-2	1	112.1	99	46	4	8	42	85	2.88	82	.254	.339	38-0-4	.211	-1	103	-3		-0.4
1911	Phi A	11	8	.579	27	19	12-1	2	169	155	65	2	9	47	85	3.04	104	.251	.313	59-0-4	.254	2	107	6		0.7
1912	Phi A	0	2	.000	4	2	0	0	5.1	10	8	0	1	2	3	13.50	23	.435	.500	4	.250	0	36	-6		-1.0
	Cle A	0	1	.000	2	2	0	0	4.2	11	6	0	0	2	2	11.57	29	.500	.542	0	—	0	98	-3		-0.6
	Year	0	3	.000	6	4	0	0	10	21	14	0	1	4	5	12.60	26	.467	.520	4	.250	0	69	-9		-1.6
Total	5	36	26	.581	85	57	39-10	3	525.1	446	185	8	34	146	298	2.50	107	.238	.305	185-0-10	.195	1	105	16		1.2

KRAUSSE, LEW Lewis Bernard Jr. B4.25.1943 Media PA BR/TR/5-11/186* d6.16 f-Lew

YEAR	TM LG	W	L	PCT	G	GS	CG-SHO	SV-BS	IP	H	R	HR	HB	BB-IB	SO	ERA	AERA	OAV	OOB	AB-HR-SH	AVG	PB	SUP	APR	DL	PW
1961	KC A	2	5	.286	12	8	2-1	0	55.2	49	33	3	1	46-0	32	4.85	86	.243	.382	17-0-1	.118	-1*	90	-3		-0.5
1964	KC A	0	2	.000	5	4	0	0	14.2	22	14	1	2	9-0	9	7.36	52	.349	.434	2	.000	0*	93	-6		-0.7
1965	KC A	2	4	.333	7	5	0	0	25	29	14	1	2	8-0	22	5.04	69	.284	.336	7-0-1	.000	-1*	55	-4		-0.8
1966	KC A	14	9	.609	36	22	4-1	3	177.2	144	69	8	6	63-0	87	2.99	114	.222	.294	52-0-6	.154	0*	91	7		0.9
1967	KC A	7	17	.292	48	19	0	4	160	140	85	17	4	67-6	96	4.27	75	.236	.314	41-1-1	.146	1*	58	-19		-2.8
1968	Oak A	10	11	.476	36	25	2	4	185	147	68	4	3	62-9	105	3.11	91	.217	.283	56-0-2	.161	3	91	-4		-0.2
1969	Oak A	7	7	.500	43	16	4-2	7-1	140	134	75	23	5	48-8	85	4.44	78	.256	.322	48-4-1	.167	4	127	-16		-1.3
1970	Mil A	13	18	.419	37	35	8-1	0-0	216	235	130	33	4	67-15	130	4.75	80	.275	.328	65-0-7	.138	1*	103	-24		-3.1
1971	Mil A	8	12	.400	43	22	1	0-0	180.1	164	67	23	5	62-10	101	2.94	119	.239	.306	44-0-5	.023	-3	76	11		0.8
1972	Bos A	1	3	.250	24	7	0	1-0	60.2	74	48	9	3	28-2	35	6.38	51	.308	.387	16	.125	-0	94	-19		-1.4
1973	StL N	0	0	—	1	0	0	0-0	2	2	0	0	0	1-0	1	0.00	—	.250	.333	0	—	0	1	0		0.1
	Atl N	4	3	.571	29	4	0	0-0	66.2	65	32	3	2	28-2	27	4.18	91	.258	.345	6-1-2	.333	2	81	-2		0.0
Total	12	68	91	.428	321	167	21-5	21-1	1283.2	1205	635	137	35	493-62	721	4.00	85	.248	.320	354-6-26	.133	6	91	-78		-9.0

KRAUSSE, LEW Lewis Bernard Sr. B6.8.1912 Media PA D9.6.1988 Sarasota FL BR/TR/6-0.5/167 d6.11 s-Lew

YEAR	TM LG	W	L	PCT	G	GS	CG-SHO	SV-BS	IP	H	R	HR	HB	BB-IB	SO	ERA	AERA	OAV	OOB	AB-HR-SH	AVG	PB	SUP	APR	DL	PW
1931	Phi A	1	0	1.000	3	1	1	0	11	6	6	2	0	6	1	4.09	110	.150	.261	2	.000	0	132	0		0.1
1932	Phi A	1	1	.800	20	3	2-1	0	57	64	31	3	0	24	16	4.58	99	.281	.349	15-0-2	.133	-0	239	0		0.0
Total	2	5	1	.833	23	4	3-1	0	68	70	37	5	0	30	17	4.50	100	.261	.336	17-0-2	.118	0	212	0		0.0

RAVEC, KEN Kenneth Peter B7.29.1951 Cleveland OH BL/TL/6-2/185* [ChiA73 3/69] d9.4 Col Ashland

YEAR	TM LG	W	L	PCT	G	GS	CG-SHO	SV-BS	IP	H	R	HR	HB	BB-IB	SO	ERA	AERA	OAV	OOB	AB-HR-SH	AVG	PB	SUP	APR	DL	PW
1975	Chi A	0	1	.000	2	1	0	0-0	4.1	1	3	0	0	8-0	1	6.23	62	.071	.409	0	—	0	0	-1		-0.2
1976	Chi A	1	5	.167	9	8	1	0-0	49.2	49	28	3	1	32-0	38	4.89	73	.257	.366	0	—	0	74	-7		-0.7
1977	Chi A	11	8	.579	26	25	6-1	0-0	166.2	161	87	9	6	57-0	125	4.10	100	.250	.317	0	—	0	113	-1		-0.1
1978	Chi A	11	16	.407	30	30	7-2	0-0	203	188	104	22	10	95-1	154	4.08	93	.245	.334	0	—	0	77	-7		-0.9
1979	Chi A	15	13	.536	36	35	10-3	0-0	250	208	115	20	14	111-3	132	3.74	114	.233	.323	0	—	0	94	16		1.6
1980	Chi A	3	6	.333	20	15	0	0-0	81.2	100	71	9	8	44-3	37	6.94	58	.298	.382	0	—	0	90	-25		-2.3
1981	Chi N	1	1	.500	14	5	0	0-0	78.1	80	48	9	5	39-6	50	5.06	74	.268	.351	15-0-4	.000	-1*	59	-10		-0.9
1982	Chi N	1	1	.500	13	2	0	0-0	25	27	20	3	0	18-2	20	6.12	62	.267	.375	3	.000	0	90	-4		-0.5
Total	8	43	56	.434	160	128	24-6	1-0	858.2	814	476	78	40	404-15	557	4.47	90	.251	.339	18-0-4	.000	-1	89	-42		-4.0

KRAWCZYK, RAY Raymond Allen B10.9.1959 Pittsburgh PA BR/TR/6-1/186* [PitN81 S1/4] d6.29 Col Oral Roberts

YEAR	TM LG	W	L	PCT	G	GS	CG-SHO	SV-BS	IP	H	R	HR	HB	BB-IB	SO	ERA	AERA	OAV	OOB	AB-HR-SH	AVG	PB	SUP	APR	DL	PW
1984	Pit N	0	0	—	5	1	0	0-0	5.1	7	2	0	0	4-2	3	3.38	108	.350	.440	0	—	0		0		0.0
1985	Pit N	0	2	.000	8	0	0	0-2	8.1	20	13	1	1	6-3	9	14.04	26	.455	.529	0	—	0		-9		-1.7

YEAR	TM LG	W	L	PCT	G	GS	CG-SHO	SV-BS	IP	H	R	HR	HB	BB-IB	SO	ERA	AERA	OAV	OOB	AB-HR-SH	AVG	PB	SUP	APR	DL	PV
1986	Pit N	0	1	.000	12	0	0	0-0	12.1	17	13	3	0	10-0	7	7.30	53	.321	.422	0	—	0		-5	56	-0
1988	Cal A	0	1	.000	14	1	0	1-0	24.1	29	13	2	2	8-1	17	4.81	81	.299	.361	0	—	0	94	-2		-0.
1989	Mil A	0	0	—	1	0	0	0-0	2	4	3	0	0	1-0	6	13.50	29	.400	.455	0	—	0		-2		-0.
Total	5	0	4	.000	39	1	0	1-2	52.1	77	44	6	3	29-6	42	7.05	54	.344	.421	0	—	0	94	-18	56	-2.

KREEGER, FRANK Frank D7.14.1899 Shelby Co. IL d7.28

									7	9	8	0		5	3	0.00	—	.290	.389	3	.000	-1	38	0		-0.
1884	KC U	0	1	.000	1	1	0																			

KREMER, RAY Remy Peter "Wiz" B3.23.1893 Oakland CA D2.8.1965 Pinole CA BR/TR/6-1/190 d4.18

1924	Pit N	18	10	.643	41	30	17-4	1	259.1	262	102	7	4	51	64	3.19	120	.265	.304	86-0-5	.151	-4*	109	21		1
1925	†Pit N	17	8	.680	40	27	14	2	214.2	232	106	19	9	47	62	3.69	121	.278	.323	71-0-5	.197	1	117	18		1
1926	Pit N	20	6	.769	37	26	18-3	5	231.1	221	79	9	4	51	74	2.61	151	.252	.296	83-1-6	.253	2	106	34		3
1927	†Pit N	19	8	.704	35	28	18-3	0	226	205	73	9	0	53	63	2.47	166	.244	.289	83-2-3	.169	-1	104	39		4
1928	Pit N	15	13	.536	34	31	17-1	0	219	253	124	16	4	68	61	4.64	87	.297	.352	78-0-3	.179	0	114	-10		-1.
1929	Pit N	18	10	.643	34	27	14	0	221.2	226	114	21	1	60	66	4.26	112	.271	.320	86-1-1	.128	-2	103	16		1
1930	Pit N	20	12	.625	39	38	18-1	0	276	366	181	29	1	63	58	5.02	99	.322	.359	102-1-8	.157	-4	112	-2		-0
1931	Pit N	11	15	.423	30	30	15-1	0	230	246	116	6	5	65	58	3.33	116	.271	.323	75-0-3	.227	4	80	11		1.
1932	Pit N	4	3	.571	11	10	3-1	0	56.2	61	35	5	1	16	6	4.29	89	.270	.321	19-0-2	.105	-1	106	-4		-0
1933	Pit N	1	0	1.000	7	0	0	0	20	36	26	2	0	9	4	10.35	32	.387	.441	4	.000	-1		-15		-0
Total	10	143	85	.627	308	247	134-14	10	1954.2	2108	950	123	29	483	516	3.76	113	.278	.323	687-5-36	.178	-7	107	108		10

KREMMEL, JIM James Louis B2.28.1948 Belleville IL BL/TL/6-0/175* [TexA71*A1/9] d7.4 Col New Mexico

1973	Tex A	0	2	.000	4	2	0	0-0	9	15	10	1	2	6-1	9	9.00	42	.366	.460	0	—	0	59	-5		-0
1974	Chi N	0	2	.000	23	0	0	0-1	31	37	21	3	1	18-0	22	5.23	73	.303	.386	3	.000	-0	68	-4		-0
Total	2	0	4	.000	27	4	0	0-1	40	52	31	4	3	24-1	28	6.07	63	.319	.405	3	.000	-0	63	-9		-1

KRESS, RED Ralph B1.2.1905 Columbia CA D11.29.1962 Los Angeles CA BR/TR/5-11.5/165 d9.24.1927 C15 ▲

1935	Was A	0	0	—	3	0	0	0	5.2	8	9	0	0	5	5	12.71	34	.333	.448	252-2-2	.298	.1*		-5		-0
1946	NY N	0	0	—	1	0	0	0	3.2	5	5	1	1	1	1	12.27	28	.333	.412	1	.000	0		-3		-0
Total	2	0	0	—	4	0	0	0	9.1	13	14	1	1	6	6	12.54	32	.333	.435	253-2-2	.296	1		-8		-0

KRETLOW, LOU Louis Henry "Lena" B6.27.1921 Apache OK BR/TR/6-2/185* d9.26

1946	Det A	1	0	1.000	1	1	1	0	9	7	3	2	0	2	4	3.00	122	.206	.250	4	.500	1	141	1		C
1948	Det A	2	1	.667	5	2	1	0	23.1	21	14	1	0	11	9	4.63	94	.233	.317	8-0-1	.500	1	41	-1		0C
1949	Det A	3	2	.600	25	10	1	0	76	85	58	5	1	69	40	6.16	68	.290	.427	26-0-1	.000	-4	153	-17		-1
1950	StL A	2	0	.000	9	2	0	0	14.1	25	19	2	2	18	10	11.93	41	.403	.549	3	.000	-0*	100	-9		-1
	Chi A	0	0	—	11	1	0	0	21.1	17	13	1	0	27	14	5.48	118	.221	.423	4	.000	-1	141	0		-0
	Year	0	2	.000	20	3	0	0	35.2	42	32	3	2	45	24	7.07	66	.302	.478	7	.000	-1	116	-9		-1
1951	Chi A	6	9	.400	26	18	7-1	0	137	129	77	7	3	74	89	4.20	96	.250	.347	48-0-1	.083	-5	82	-4		-1
1952	Chi A	4	4	.500	19	11	4-2	1	79	52	31	5	1	56	63	2.96	123	.186	.323	20-0-2	.050	-1	83	5		-1
1953	Chi A	0	0	—	9	3	0	0	20.2	12	11	2	1	30	11	3.48	116	.171	.426	4	.000	-0	133	0		-C
	StL A	1	5	.167	22	11	0	0	81	93	56	5	0	52	37	5.11	82	.286	.385	25-0-2	.200	-1	83	-9		-C
	Year	1	5	.167	31	14	0	0	101.2	105	67	7	1	82	52	4.78	87	.266	.393	29-0-2	.172	-1	93	-10		-C
1954	Bal A	6	11	.353	32	20	5	0	166.2	169	83	12	4	82	82	4.37	82	.269	.349	51-0-4	.157	-0	81	-11		-C
1955	Bal A	0	4	.000	15	5	0	0	38.1	50	39	3	1	27-0	26	8.22	46	.316	.411	11-0-1	.091	-1	98	-19		-7
1956	KC A	4	9	.308	25	20	3	0	118.2	121	75	17	0	74-4	61	5.31	82	.262	.362	33-0-4	.061	-3	78	-11		-7
Total	10	27	47	.365	199	104	22-3	1	785.1	781	479	62	10	522-4	450	4.87	82	.261	.370	237-0-16	.114	-13	91	-75		-7

KREUGER, RICK Richard Allen B11.3.1948 Grand Rapids MI BR/TL/6-2/185* d9.6 Col Michigan St.

1975	Bos A	0	0	—	2	0	0	0-0	4	3	2	0	0	1-0	1	4.50	90	.200	.250	0	—	0		0		C
1976	Bos A	2	1	.667	8	4	1	0-0	31	31	14	3	0	16-0	12	4.06	96	.272	.359	0	—	0	130	0		-C
1977	Bos A	0	1	.000	1	0	0	0-0	0	2	2	0	0	1-0	0	∞	—	1.000	1.000	0	—	0		-2		-C
1978	Cle A	0	0	—	6	0	0	0-0	9.1	6	4	1	0	3-0	7	3.86	98	.194	.243	0	—	0		0		C
Total	4	2	2	.500	17	4	1	0-0	44.1	42	22	4	0	20-0	20	4.47	87	.259	.333	0	—	0	130	-2		C

KREUTZER, FRANK Franklin James B2.7.1939 Buffalo NY BR/TL/6-1/190(175-190) d9.20 Col Villanova

1962	Chi A	0	0	—	1	0	0	0	1.1	0	0	0	0	1-0	1	0.00	—	.000	.200	1		0		1		1
1963	Chi A	1	0	1.000	1	1	0	0	5	3	1	1	0	1-0	0	1.80	195	.188	.235	2	.000	-0	177	1		1
1964	Chi A	3	1	.750	17	2	0	1	40.1	37	15	1	0	18-3	32	3.35	103	.239	.316	8-0-2	.125	-0	64	1		1
	Was A	2	6	.250	13	9	0	0	45.1	48	26	6	1	23-0	27	4.76	78	.267	.351	11-0-2	.000	-1	77	-5		-1
	Year	5	7	.417	30	11	0	1	85.2	85	41	7	1	41-3	59	4.10	87	.254	.335	19-0-4	.053	-1	77	-3		-1
1965	Was A	6	6	.250	33	14	2-1	0	85.1	73	48	7	2	54-1	65	4.32	80	.232	.344	22-1-0	.045	-1	108	-8		-1
1966	Was A	0	5	.000	9	6	0	0	31.1	30	24	9	1	10-1	24	6.03	57	.236	.297	8	.250	-1	64	0		-C
1969	Was A	0	0	—	4	0	0	0	4	3	1	0	0	2-0	2	4.50	78	.333	.455	0	—	0		0		C
Total	6	8	18	.308	78	32	2-1	1-0	210.2	194	115	24	4	109-5	151	4.40	80	.241	.332	51-1-4	.078	-2	91	-19		-1

KRIEGER, KURT Kurt Ferdinand "Dutch" B9.16.1926 Traisen, Austria D8.16.1970 St.Louis MO BR/TR/6-3/212* d4.21 Col Washington-St. Louis

1949	StL N	0	0	—	1	0	0	0	1	0	0	0	0	1	0	0.00	—	.000	.250	0	—	0		0		-0
1951	StL N	0	0	—	2	0	0	0	4	6	7	1	0	5	3	15.75	25	.353	.500	0	—	0		-5		-0
Total	2	0	0	—	3	0	0	0	5	6	7	1	0	6	3	12.60	32	.300	.462	0	—	0		-5		-0

KRIST, HOWIE Howard Wilbur "Spud" B2.28.1916 W.Henrietta NY D4.23.1989 Buffalo NY BL/TR/6-1/175 d9.12 Mil 1944-45

1937	StL N	3	1	.750	9	4	1	0	27.2	34	13	0	0	10	6	4.23	94	.304	.361	9-0-1	.000	-1	135	0		C
1938	StL N	0	0	—	2	0	0	0	1.1	1	0	0	0	1	1	0.00	—	.250	.250	0	—	0		1		C
1941	StL N	10	0	1.000	37	8	2	2	114	107	57	10	1	35	36	4.03	93	.246	.304	38-0-2	.237	1	163	-2		-C
1942	StL N	13	3	.813	34	8	3	1	118.1	103	34	2	2	43	47	2.51	136	.233	.304	42-0-1	.143	-1*	144	14		C
1943	†StL N	11	5	.688	34	17	9-2	3	164.1	141	57	5	4	62	57	2.90	116	.233	.309	60-0-4	.167	-2	114	11		C
1946	StL N	0	2	.000	15	0	0	0	18.2	22	15	3	1	8	8	6.75	51	.306	.383	0	—	0		-6		C
Total	6	37	11	.771	128	37	15-2	6	444.1	408	176	20	8	158	150	3.52	106	.244	.313	149-0-8	.168	-3	134	18		C

KRIVDA, RICK Rick Michael B1.19.1970 McKeesport PA BR/TL/6-1/180* [BalA91 23/602] d7.7 Col California (PA)

1995	Bal A	2	7	.222	13	13	-1	0-0	75.1	76	40	9	4	25-1	53	4.54	105	.266	.329	0	—	0	73	2		C
1996	Bal A	3	5	.375	22	11	0	0-0	81.2	89	48	14	1	39-2	54	4.96	100	.283	.361	0	—	0	127	-10		C
1997	Bal A	4	2	.667	10	10	0	0-0	50	67	36	7	0	16-1	29	6.30	70	.328	.379	0	—	0	156	4		C
1998	Cle A	2	0	1.000	11	1	0	0-0	25	24	10	2	0	16-1	10	3.24	148	.250	.357	0	—	0	64	-20		C
	Cin N	0	2	.000	16	1	0	0-1	26.1	41	34	7	3	19-1	19	11.28	38	.366	.467	4	.000	-0	94	-24		C
Total	4	11	16	.407	72	36	1	0-1	258.1	297	168	39	8	117-6	165	5.57	85	.293	.368	4	.000	-0	94	-24		C

KROCK, GUS August H. B5.9.1866 Milwaukee WI D3.22.1905 Pasadena CA BR/TR/6-0/196 d4.24

1888	Chi N	25	14	.641	39	39	39-4	0	339.2	295	143	20	9	45	161	2.44	124	.227	.258	134-1	.164	-3	102	24		C
1889	Chi N	3	5	.500	7	7	5	0	60.2	86	43	10	2	14	16	4.90	85	.323	.382	24	.167	-1	113	-2		C
	Ind N	2	2	.500	4	4	3	0	32	48	34	2	0	14	10	7.31	57	.336	.395	14	.357	1	117	-11		C
	Was N	2	4	.333	6	6	6	0	48	65	50	1	1	22	17	5.25	75	.314	.383	23	.087	-2	128	-9		C
	Year	7	9	.438	17	17	14	0	140.2	199	131	13	3	50	43	5.57	73	.323	.377	61	.180	-2	119	-23		C
1890	Buf P	0	3	.000	4	3	3	0	25	43	37	1	0	15	5	6.12	67	.364	.436	12	.083	-1	84	-9		C
Total	6	32	26	.552	60	59	56-4	0	505.1	537	311	34	12	110	209	3.49	97	.264	.306	207-1	.164	-7	106	-7		C

KROH, RUBE Floyd Myron B8.25.1886 Friendship NY D3.17.1944 New Orleans LA BL/TL/6-2/186 d9.30

1906	Bos A	1	0	1.000	1	1	1-1	0	7	4	4	0	0	4	5	0.00	—	.074	.194	3	.000	-0	52	5		C
1907	Bos A	1	4	.200	7	4	2	0	34.1	33	13	0	2	8	8	2.62	98	.256	.309	11	.273	-0	90	1		C
1908	Chi N	0	0	—	2	1	1	0	12	9	3	0	0	4	11	1.50	157	.200	.265	4	.000	-0	108	14		C
1909	Chi N	9	4	.692	17	13	10-2	0	120.1	97	26	2	1	30	51	1.65	154	.224	.276	40-0-1	.150	-0	110	-5		C
1910	Chi N	3	1	.750	6	4	1	0	34.1	33	19	1	2	15	16	4.46	65	.254	.340	12-0-1	.250	-0	102	0		C
1912	Bos N	0	0	—	3	1	0	0	6.1	8	4	0	0	4	1	5.68	63	.364	.500	2	.500	0	94	12		C
Total	6	14	9	.609	36	25	13-3	0	216.1	182	65	3	5	65	92	2.29	115	.232	.296	72-0-2	.181	-0	94	12		C

KROLL, GARY
Gary Melvin B7.8.1941 Culver City CA BR/TR/6-6/220* d7.26

AR	TM LG	W	L	PCT	G	GS	CG-SHO	SV-BS	IP	H	R	HR	HB	BB-IB	SO	ERA	AERA	OAV	OOB	AB-HR-SH	AVG	PB	SUP	APR	DL	PW
64	Phi N	0	0	—	2	0	0	0	3	3	1	0	0	2-0	2	3.00	116	.250	.357	0		0		0		0.0
	NY N	0	1	.000	8	2	0	0	21.2	19	11	1	1	15-0	24	4.15	86	.241	.365	3	.333	0	86	-1		0.0
	Year	0	1	.000	10	2	0	0	24.2	22	12	1	1	17-0	26	4.01	89	.242	.364	3	.333	0	86	-1		0.0
65	NY N	6	6	.500	32	11	1	1	87	83	48	12	6	41-0	62	4.45	79	.249	.340	26-0-3	.115	-1	119	-8		-1.2
66	Hou N	0	0	—	10	0	0	0	23.2	26	10	2	0	11-0	22	3.80	90	.280	.356	3	.000	-0				-0.1
69	Cle A	0	0	—	19	0	0	0-0	24	16	14	3	0	22-0	28	4.13	92	.188	.352	0		-0				-0.1
tal	4	6	7	.462	71	13	1	1-0	159.1	147	84	18	7	91-0	138	4.24	84	.244	.348	32-0-3	.125	-1	114	-10		-1.4

KROON, MARC
Marc Jason B4.2.1973 Bronx NY BB/TR/6-2/195* [NYN91 2/72] d7.7

AR	TM LG	W	L	PCT	G	GS	CG-SHO	SV-BS	IP	H	R	HR	HB	BB-IB	SO	ERA	AERA	OAV	OOB	AB-HR-SH	AVG	PB	SUP	APR	DL	PW
95	SD N	0	1	.000	2	0	0	0-0	1.2	1	2	1	0	2-0	2	10.80	38	.200	.429	0		0		-1		-0.2
97	SD N	0	1	.000	12	0	0	0-0	11.1	14	9	2	1	5-0	12	6.35	62	.280	.357	0		0		-3		-0.3
98	SD N	0	0	—	2	0	0	0-0	2.1	0	0	0	0	1-0	2	0.00	—	.000	.125	0		0		1		0.1
	Cin N	0	0	—	4	0	0	0-0	5.1	7	8	0	1	8-0	4	13.50	32	.333	.533	0		0		-5	36	-0.2
	Year	0	0	—	6	0	0	0-0	7.2	7	8	0	1	9-0	6	9.39	45	.250	.447	0		0		-5	36	-0.2
04	Col N	0	0	—	6	0	0	0-0	6	7	4	1	0	10-0	3	6.00	79	.350	.548	0		0		-4		-0.1
tal	4	0	2	.000	26	0	0	0-0	26.2	29	23	3	2	26-0	23	7.43	57	.282	.432	0		0		-9	36	-0.6

KRUEGER, BILL
William Culp B4.24.1958 Waukegan IL BL/TL/6-5/210* d4.10 Col Portland

AR	TM LG	W	L	PCT	G	GS	CG-SHO	SV-BS	IP	H	R	HR	HB	BB-IB	SO	ERA	AERA	OAV	OOB	AB-HR-SH	AVG	PB	SUP	APR	DL	PW
83	Oak A	7	6	.538	17	16	2	0-0	109.2	104	54	7	2	53-1	58	3.61	108	.252	.336	0		0	114	1	59	0.0
84	Oak A	10	10	.500	26	24	1	0-0	142	156	95	9	2	85-2	61	4.75	79	.285	.378	0		0	118	-22		-2.7
85	Oak A	9	10	.474	32	23	2	0-0	151.1	165	95	13	2	69-1	56	4.52	86	.276	.351	0		0	129	-17		-1.9
86	Oak A	1	3	.333	11	3	0	1-0	34.1	40	25	4	0	13-0	10	6.03	65	.301	.358	0		0	155	-9	94	-0.7
87	Oak A	0	3	.000	9	0	0	0-0	5.2	9	7	0	0	8-3	2	9.53	44	.360	.515	0		0		-4		-0.7
88	LA N	0	0	—	2	0	0	0-0	2.1	3	2	0	0	1-0	2			.250	.308	0		0		0		0.0
	LA N	0	0	—	1	1	0	0-0	2.1	4	3	0	1	2-1	1	11.57	29	.364	.500	0		0		0		0.0
89	Mil A	3	2	.600	34	5	0	3-0	93.2	96	43	9	0	33-3	72	3.84	100	.264	.324	0		0	133	-2		-0.1
90	Mil A	6	8	.429	30	17	0	0-0	129	137	70	10	3	54-6	64	3.98	98	.276	.345	0		0	108	1		0.0
91	Sea A	11	8	.579	35	25	1	0-0	175	194	82	15	4	60-4	64	3.60	115	.289	.346	0		0	121	-3	21	-0.3
92	Min A	10	6	.625	27	27	2	2-2	161.1	166	82	18	3	46-2	86	4.30	95	.263	.316	0		0	126	-3		-0.4
	Mon N	0	2	.000	9	2	0	0-0	17.1	23	13	0	1	7-0	13	6.75	52	.315	.383	3-0-1	.000	-0	169	-6		-0.7
93	Det A	6	4	.600	32	7	0	0-3	82	90	43	6	4	30-5	60	3.40	128	.285	.351	0		0	157	5	49	0.5
94	Det A	2	0	1.000	16	2	0	0-2	19.2	26	24	3	1	17-1	17	9.61	51	.321	.431	0		0	131	-10		-0.8
	SD N	3	2	.600	8	7	1	0-0	41	42	24	1	1	7-1	30	4.83	86	.259	.292	12-0-2	.500	3	110	-3		0.0
95	SD N	0	0	—	6	0	0	0-0	7.2	13	6	1	0	4-1	6	7.04	58	.371	.436	0		0		-2		-0.1
	Sea A	2	1	.667	6	5	0	0-0	20	37	17	4	0	4-1	10	5.85	82	.407	.432	0		0	152	-4		-0.5
al	13	68	66	.507	301	164	9-2	4-5	1194.1	1305	685	104	24	493-32	639	4.35	82	.280	.349	15-0-3	.400	0	120	-70	223	-7.6

KRUGER, ABE
Abraham B2.14.1885 Morris Run PA D7.4.1962 Elmira NY BR/TR/6-2/190 d10.6

AR	TM LG	W	L	PCT	G	GS	CG-SHO	SV-BS	IP	H	R	HR	HB	BB-IB	SO	ERA	AERA	OAV	OOB	AB-HR-SH	AVG	PB	SUP	APR	DL	PW
08	Bro N	0	1	.000	2	1	0	0	6.1	5	5	0	3	3	2	4.26	55	.238	.407	2	.000	-0	60	-2		-0.2

KRUKOW, MIKE
Michael Edward B1.21.1952 Long Beach CA BR/TR/6-5/205* [ChiN73 8/184] d9.6 Col Cal Poly-San Luis Obispo

AR	TM LG	W	L	PCT	G	GS	CG-SHO	SV-BS	IP	H	R	HR	HB	BB-IB	SO	ERA	AERA	OAV	OOB	AB-HR-SH	AVG	PB	SUP	APR	DL	PW
76	Chi N	0	0	—	2	0	0	0	4.1	6	4	0	0	2-0	1	8.31	47	.333	.400	1	.000	-0		-2		-0.1
77	Chi N	8	14	.364	34	33	1-1	0-0	172	195	96	16	3	61-8	106	4.40	100	.281	.340	55-0-7	.200	-0	85	0		-0.1
78	Chi N	9	3	.750	27	20	3-1	0-0	138.1	125	62	11	5	53-4	81	3.90	104	.243	.318	45-0-3	.244	2	99	4		0.6
79	Chi N	9	9	.500	28	28	0	0-0	164.2	172	84	13	3	81-12	119	4.21	99	.275	.359	51-1-7	.314	5	84	0		0.4
80	Chi N	10	15	.400	34	34	3	0-0	205	200	117	13	8	80-5	130	4.39	90	.258	.329	65-1-7	.246	2	101	-10		-1.1
81	Chi N	9	9	.500	25	25	2-1	0-0	144.1	146	68	11	2	55-6	101	3.68	102	.264	.330	50-0-6	.180	-0	103	0		0.1
82	Phi N	13	11	.542	33	33	7-2	0-0	208	211	87	8	3	82-10	138	3.12	119	.268	.336	72-0-5	.181	-0	98	10		1.2
83	SF N	11	11	.500	31	31	2-1	0-0	184.1	189	95	17	3	76-8	136	3.95	90	.261	.332	63-1-4	.254	5	118	-9	27	-0.6
84	SF N	11	12	.478	35	33	3-1	1-0	199.1	234	117	22	5	78-5	141	4.56	78	.290	.353	72-0-2	.139	-1*	129	-24		-2.8
85	SF N★	8	11	.421	28	28	6-1	0-0	194.2	176	80	19	3	49-10	150	3.38	103	.238	.287	55-1-8	.218	5	74	4		0.9
86	SF N★	20	9	.690	34	34	10-2	0-0	245	204	90	24	4	55-4	178	3.05	116	.223	.269	82-0-12	.146	0*	128	16	15	1.8
87	†SF N	5	6	.455	30	28	3	0-0	163	182	98	24	2	46-6	104	4.80	80	.288	.334	54-0-5	.167	1	133	-19	19	-1.0
88	SF N	7	4	.636	20	20	1	0-0	124.2	111	51	13	5	31-3	75	3.54	92	.236	.289	41-1-4	.073	-0	109	-2	48	-0.2
89	SF N	4	3	.571	8	8	0	0-0	43	37	20	5	1	18-3	18	3.98	85	.236	.316	16	.063	-1	108	-2	144	-0.5
al	14	124	117	.515	369	355	41-10	1-0	2190.2	2188	1069	196	47	767-84	1478	3.90	96	.260	.323	722-5-70	.193	16	105	-34	253	-1.4

KRUMM, AL
Albert B1.13.1865 Pittsburgh PA D6.15.1937 San Diego CA TR d5.17

AR	TM LG	W	L	PCT	G	GS	CG-SHO	SV-BS	IP	H	R	HR	HB	BB-IB	SO	ERA	AERA	OAV	OOB	AB-HR-SH	AVG	PB	SUP	APR	DL	PW
49	Pit N	0	1	.000	1	1	1	0	9	8	11	0	0	10	4	10.00	37	.229	.400	4	.000	-1	125	-6		-0.4

KUBENKA, JEFF
Jeffrey Scot B8.24.1974 Weimar TX BR/TR/6-2/191* [LAN96 38/1138] d9.6 Col St. Marys (TX)

AR	TM LG	W	L	PCT	G	GS	CG-SHO	SV-BS	IP	H	R	HR	HB	BB-IB	SO	ERA	AERA	OAV	OOB	AB-HR-SH	AVG	PB	SUP	APR	DL	PW
98	LA N	1	0	1.000	6	0	0	0-1	9.1	4	1	0	0	8-0	10	0.96	418	.138	.316	0		0		3		0.3
99	LA N	0	1	.000	6	0	0	0-0	7.2	13	12	1	0	4-0	2	11.74	37	.371	.425	1	1.000	0		-7		-0.7
al	2	1	1	.500	12	0	0	0-1	17	17	13	1	0	12-0	12	5.82	72	.266	.372	1	1.000	0		-4		-0.4

KUBINSKI, TIM
Timothy Mark B1.20.1972 Pullman WA BL/TL/6-4/205* [OakA93 7/209] d7.16 Col UCLA

AR	TM LG	W	L	PCT	G	GS	CG-SHO	SV-BS	IP	H	R	HR	HB	BB-IB	SO	ERA	AERA	OAV	OOB	AB-HR-SH	AVG	PB	SUP	APR	DL	PW
97	Oak A	0	0	—	11	0	0	0-0	12.2	12	9	2	1	6-1	10	5.68	81	.255	.339	0		0		-2		-0.1
99	Oak A	0	0	—	14	0	0	0-1	12.1	14	8	3	1	5-1	7	5.84	81	.280	.351	0		0		-1		0.0
al	2	0	0	—	25	0	0	0-1	25	26	17	5	2	11-2	17	5.76	81	.268	.345	0		0		-3		-0.1

KUCAB, JOHNNY
John Albert B12.17.1919 Olyphant PA D5.26.1977 Youngstown OH BR/TR/6-2/185* d9.14

AR	TM LG	W	L	PCT	G	GS	CG-SHO	SV-BS	IP	H	R	HR	HB	BB-IB	SO	ERA	AERA	OAV	OOB	AB-HR-SH	AVG	PB	SUP	APR	DL	PW
50	Phi A	1	1	.500	4	2	2	0	26	29	10	4	0	8	8	3.46	131	.282	.333	9	.111	-0	59	4		0.2
51	Phi A	4	3	.571	30	1	0	4	74.2	76	37	9	1	23	23	4.22	101	.265	.322	16	.000	-2	21	1		-0.1
52	Phi A	0	1	.000	25	0	0	2	51.1	64	37	5	1	20	17	5.26	75	.312	.376	10	.200	-0*		-8		-0.5
al	3	5	5	.500	59	3	2	6	152	169	84	18	2	51	48	4.44	95	.284	.343	35	.086	-2	49	-3		-0.4

KUCEK, JACK
John Andrew Charles B6.8.1953 Warren OH BR/TR/6-2/200* [ChiA74 2/32] d8.8 Col Miami-Ohio

AR	TM LG	W	L	PCT	G	GS	CG-SHO	SV-BS	IP	H	R	HR	HB	BB-IB	SO	ERA	AERA	OAV	OOB	AB-HR-SH	AVG	PB	SUP	APR	DL	PW
74	Chi A	1	4	.200	9	7	0	0-0	37.2	48	25	3	1	21-0	25	5.26	71	.320	.402	0		0	71	-6		-0.7
75	Chi A	0	0	—	2	0	0	0-0	3.2	9	2	0	4	4-0	2	4.91	79	.500	.591	0		0		0		0.0
76	Chi A	0	0	—	2	0	0	0-0	4.2	9	5	2	0	4-0	2	9.64	37	.429	.500	0		0		-3		-0.2
77	Chi A	0	1	.000	8	3	0	0-0	34.2	35	20	4	2	10-0	25	3.63	112	.267	.324	0		0	183	-2	21	0.2
78	Chi A	2	3	.400	10	5	3	1-0	52	42	23	5	0	27-2	30	3.29	116	.220	.315	0		0	61	2		0.2
79	Chi A	0	0	—	1	0	0	0-0	0.2	0	4	0	0	3-0	1	0.00	—	.000	.500	0		0		-1		-0.1
	Phi N	1	0	1.000	4	0	0	0-0	4.1	6	4	0	1	1-1	2	8.31	47	.333	.368	0		0		-2		-0.4
80	Tor A	3	8	.273	23	12	0	1-0	68	83	56	9	1	41-1	35	6.75	64	.300	.391	0		0	83	-17		-2.4
al	7	7	16	.304	59	27	3	2-0	205.2	232	139	25	4	111-4	121	5.12	78	.287	.373	0		0	88	-27	21	-3.6

KUCKS, JOHNNY
John Charles B7.27.1933 Hoboken NJ BR/TR/6-3/184(170-190) d4.17

AR	TM LG	W	L	PCT	G	GS	CG-SHO	SV-BS	IP	H	R	HR	HB	BB-IB	SO	ERA	AERA	OAV	OOB	AB-HR-SH	AVG	PB	SUP	APR	DL	PW
55	†NY A	8	7	.533	29	13	3-1	0	126.2	122	54	9	8	44-6	49	3.41	110	.252	.315	40-0-2	.050	-4	111	6		0.2
56	†NY A☆	18	9	.667	34	31	12-3	0	224.1	223	113	19	10	72-0	67	3.85	100	.261	.323	77-0-6	.143	-2	127	-2		-0.3
57	†NY A	8	10	.444	37	23	4-1	2	179.1	169	82	13	8	59-2	78	3.56	101	.251	.316	55-0-11	.109	-2	123	0		-0.9
58	†NY A	8	8	.500	34	15	4-1	4	126	132	67	14	6	39-2	46	3.93	90	.269	.328	40-0-6	.125	-1	122	-7		-0.9
59	NY A	0	1	.000	9	1	0	0-0	16.2	21	16	5	0	9-0	9	8.64	42	.323	.405	2	.000	-0	97	-9		-0.5
	KC A	8	11	.421	33	23	6-1	1	151.1	163	76	10	12	42-0	51	3.87	104	.278	.336	47-0-3	.085	-3	75	2		0.0
	Year	8	12	.400	42	24	6-1	1	168	184	92	15	12	51-0	60	4.34	91	.282	.343	49-0-3	.082	-3	76	-7		-0.5
60	KC A	4	10	.286	31	17	1	0	114	140	85	22	4	43-2	38	6.00	66	.306	.361	30-0-3	.133	-3	79	-24		-2.7
al	6	54	56	.491	207	123	30-7	7	938.1	970	493	91	39	308-12	338	4.10	92	.269	.330	291-0-31	.110	-12	107	-34		-4.2

KUCZYNSKI, BERT
Bernard Carl B1.8.1920 Philadelphia PA D1.19.1997 Allentown PA BR/TR/6-0/195 d6.2 Mil 1943-45 Col Penn

AR	TM LG	W	L	PCT	G	GS	CG-SHO	SV-BS	IP	H	R	HR	HB	BB-IB	SO	ERA	AERA	OAV	OOB	AB-HR-SH	AVG	PB	SUP	APR	DL	PW
43	Phi A	0	1	.000	4	2	1	0	24.2	36	15	2	2	9	8	4.01	85	.336	.398	6	.000	-0	50	-3		-0.2

KUHAULUA, FRED
Fred Mahele B2.23.1953 Honolulu HI BL/TL/5-11/175* d8.2

AR	TM LG	W	L	PCT	G	GS	CG-SHO	SV-BS	IP	H	R	HR	HB	BB-IB	SO	ERA	AERA	OAV	OOB	AB-HR-SH	AVG	PB	SUP	APR	DL	PW
77	Cal A	0	0	—	3	1	0	0	6.1	15	11	1	0	7-0	3	15.63	25	.455	.550	0		0	69	-8		-0.4
81	SD N	1	0	1.000	5	4	0	0-0	29.1	28	10	1	0	9-1	16	2.45	132	.257	.314	9-0-1	.111	-0	89	2		0.0
al	2	1	0	1.000	8	5	0	0-0	35.2	43	21	2	0	16-1	19	4.79	70	.303	.373	9-0-1	.111	-0	85	-6		-0.4

YEAR	TM LG	W	L	PCT	G	GS	CG-SHO	SV-BS	IP	H	R	HR	HB	BB-IB	SO	ERA	AERA	OAV	OOB	AB-HR-SH	AVG	PB	SUP	APR	DL	PW
KUHN, BUB	Bernard Daniel B10.12.1899 Vicksburg MI D11.20.1956 Detroit MI BL/TR/6-1.5/182 d9.1 Col Michigan St.																									
1924	Cle A	0	1	.000	1	0	0	0	1	4	3	1	0	0	0	27.00	16	.667	.667	0	—	0		-2		-0.3
KULL, JOHN	John A. (b John A Kolonauski) B6.24.1882 Shenandoah PA D3.30.1936 Schuylkill Haven PA BL/TR/6-2/190 d10.2																									
1909	Phi A	1	0	1.000	1	0	0	0	3	3	1	0	1	5	4	3.00	80	.250	.500	1	1.000	0		0		0.0
KUME, MIKE	John Michael B5.19.1926 Premier WV BR/TR/6-1/195 d8.26																									
1955	KC A	0	2	.000	6	4	0	0	23.2	35	23	1	3	15-0	7	7.99	52	.354	.445	8	.125	-0	64	-9		-0.7
KUNKEL, BILL	William Gustave James B7.7.1936 Hoboken NJ D5.4.1985 Red Bank NJ BR/TR/6-1/187(165-187) d4.15 U17 s-Jeff																									
1961	KC A	3	4	.429	58	2	0	4	88.2	103	58	11	0	32-2	46	5.18	81	.289	.345	8-0-1	.125	-0	0	-9		-0.7
1962	KC A	0	0	—	9	0	0	0	7.2	8	7	3	0	4-0	6	3.52	120	.258	.333	0	—	0		-1		-0.1
1963	NY A	3	2	.600	22	0	0	0	46.1	42	15	3	0	13-3	31	2.72	129	.239	.289	6	.333	1		4		0.5
Total 3		6	6	.500	89	2	0	4	142.2	153	80	17	0	49-5	83	4.29	92	.272	.327	14-0-1	.214	1	0	-6		-0.3
KUNZ, EARL	Earl Dewey "Pinches" B12.25.1899 Sacramento CA D4.14.1963 Sacramento CA BR/TR/5-10/170 d4.19 Col Santa Clara																									
1923	Pit N	1	2	.333	21	2	1	1	45.2	48	33	2	0	24	12	5.52	73	.293	.383	12	.083	-1	72	-8		-0.6
KUO, HONG-CHIH	Hong-Chih B7.23.1981 Tainan City, Taiwan BL/TL/6-0/200 d9.2																									
2005	LA N	0	1	.000	9	0	0	0-1	5.1	5	4	1	0	5-1	10	6.75	61	.238	.385	0	—	0		-1		-0.2
KUROSAKI, RYAN	Ryan Yoshitomo B7.3.1952 Honolulu HI BR/TR/5-10/160 d5.20 Col Nebraska																									
1975	StL N	0	0	—	7	0	0	0	13	15	11	3	0	7-1	6	7.62	50	.283	.361	1	.000	-0		-4		-0.3
KURTZ, HAL	Harold James "Bud" B8.20.1943 Washington DC BR/TR/6-3/205 d4.18																									
1968	Cle A	1	0	1.000	28	0	0	1	38	37	24	2	5	15-6	16	5.21	57	.255	.343	4	.000	-0*		-9		-0.6
KUSEL, ED	Edward Daniel B2.15.1886 Cleveland OH D10.20.1948 Cleveland OH TR/6-0/165 d9.18																									
1909	StL A	0	3	.000	3	3	3	0	24	43	28	1	0	1	2	7.13	34	.384	.389	10	.300	1	126	-14		-1.3
KUSH, EMIL	Emil Benedict B11.4.1916 Chicago IL D11.26.1969 River Grove IL BR/TR/5-11/185 d9.21 Mil 1943-45																									
1941	Chi N	0	0	—	2	0	0	0	4	2	1	0	0	0	2	2.25	156	.143	.143	1	.000	-0		1		0.0
1942	Chi N	0	0	—	1	0	0	0	2	1	0	0	0	1	1	0.00	—	.167	.286	1	.000	-0		1		0.0
1946	Chi N	9	2	.818	40	6	1-1	2	129.2	120	47	4	3	43	50	3.05	109	.253	.319	38	.211	0	120	6		0.6
1947	Chi N	8	3	.727	47	1	1	5	91	80	38	8	3	53	44	3.36	117	.247	.358	20	.250	1	112	7		1.0
1948	Chi N	1	4	.200	34	1	0	3	72	70	39	5	2	37	31	4.38	89	.253	.345	13	.154	0	68	-3		-0.2
1949	Chi N	3	3	.500	26	0	0	2	47.2	51	21	7	2	24	22	3.78	107	.283	.374	9	.333	1		2		0.4
Total 6		21	12	.636	150	8	2-1	12	346.1	324	146	24	10	158	150	3.48	106	.254	.341	82	.220	2	106	14		1.8
KUTYNA, MARTY	Marion John B11.14.1932 Philadelphia PA BR/TR/6-0/190* d9.19																									
1959	KC A	0	0	—	4	0	0	1	7.1	7	0	0	0	1-0	1	0.00	—	.250	.276	0	—	-0		3		0.2
1960	KC A	3	2	.600	51	0	0	4	61.2	64	33	7	0	32-3	20	3.94	101	.274	.358	5-0-1	.200	-0		-1		-0.1
1961	Was A	6	8	.429	50	6	0	3	143	147	79	12	2	48-2	64	3.97	101	.271	.330	34-0-4	.206	-0	92	-2		0.0
1962	Was A	5	6	.455	54	0	0	0	78	83	42	9	0	27-2	25	4.04	100	.275	.329	8	.125	-0		-2		-0.2
Total 4		14	16	.467	159	6	0	8	290	301	154	28	2	108-7	110	3.88	103	.272	.335	47-0-5	.191	-0	92	-2		-0.1
KUTZLER, JERRY	Jerry Scott B3.25.1965 Waukegan IL BL/TR/6-1/175 [ChiA87 6/141] d4.28 Col William Penn																									
1990	Chi A	2	1	.667	7	5	0	0-0	31.1	38	23	2	0	14-1	21	6.03	64	.304	.371	0	—	0	118	-8		-0.7
KUZAVA, BOB	Robert Leroy "Sarge" B5.28.1923 Wyandotte MI BB/TL/6-2/204* d9.21																									
1946	Cle A	1	0	1.000	2	2	0	0	12	9	7	0	1	11	4	3.00	110	.191	.356	5	.200	-0	155	-1		0.0
1947	Cle A	1	1	.500	4	4	1-1	0	21.2	22	10	1	1	9	9	4.15	84	.265	.344	9	.111	-1	108	-1		-0.1
1949	Chi A	10	6	.625	29	18	9-1	0	156.2	139	76	6	1	91	83	4.02	104	.240	.344	56-0-5	.036	-6	101	4		-0.4
1950	Chi A	1	3	.250	10	7	1	0	44.1	43	28	5	0	27	21	5.68	79	.257	.361	12-0-2	.083	-0	112	-4		-0.4
	Was A	8	7	.533	22	22	8-1	0	155	156	80	8	1	75	84	3.95	114	.263	.346	50-1-3	.100	-2	86	9		0.5
	Year	9	10	.474	32	29	9-1	0	199.1	199	108	13	1	102	105	4.33	104	.261	.350	62-1-5	.097	-2	92	4		0.1
1951	Was A	3	3	.500	8	8	3	0	52.1	57	34	5	2	28	22	5.50	74	.284	.377	17	.176	0	100	-7		-0.7
	†NY A	8	4	.667	23	8	4-1	5	82.1	76	27	5	1	27	50	2.40	159	.241	.303	22	.136	0*	113	13		1.9
	Year	11	7	.611	31	16	7-1	5	134.2	133	61	10	3	55	72	3.61	109	.258	.333	39	.154	0	107	5		1.2
1952	†NY A	8	8	.500	28	12	6-1	3	133	115	53	7	1	63	67	3.45	96	.240	.329	43	.093	-1	112	1		-0.1
1953	†NY A	6	5	.545	33	6	2-2	0	92.1	92	35	9	0	34	48	3.31	111	.264	.330	21-0-1	.048	-0	80	6		0.5
1954	NY A	1	3	.250	20	3	0	1	39.2	46	30	3	0	18	22	5.45	63	.297	.366	6	.000	-0	103	-11		-1.1
	Bal A	1	3	.250	4	4	0	0	23.2	30	11	0	0	11	15	4.18	86	.323	.387	7-0-1	.000	-1	62	-1		-0.3
	Year	2	6	.250	24	7	0	1	63.1	76	41	3	0	29	37	4.97	70	.306	.374	13-0-1	.000	-0	79	-12		-1.4
1955	Bal A	0	1	.000	6	1	0	0	12.1	10	7	0	0	4-1	5	3.65	105	.222	.280	1	.000	-0	0	0		-0.1
	Phi N	1	0	1.000	17	4	0	0	32.1	47	26	5	0	12-1	13	7.24	55	.333	.386	7	.143	-0	118	-10		-0.1
1957	Pit N	0	0	—	4	0	0	0	2	3	2	0	0	3-0	1	9.00	42	.333	.500	0	—	0		-1		-0.1
	StL N	0	0	—	3	0	0	0	2.1	4	1	0	0	2-0	2	3.86	103	.364	.462	0	—	0		0		0.0
	Year	0	0	—	7	0	0	0	4.1	7	3	0	0	5-0	3	6.23	62	.350	.480	0	—	0		-1		-0.1
Total 10		49	44	.527	213	99	34-7	13	862	849	427	54	8	415-2	446	4.05	97	.260	.344	256-1-12	.086	-14	100	-3		-0.9
LABINE, CLEM	Clement Walter B8.6.1926 Lincoln RI BR/TR/6-0/180(180-195) d4.18																									
1950	Bro N	0	0	—	1	0	0	0	2	2	1	0	0	1	0	4.50	91	.286	.375	0	—	0		0		0.0
1951	Bro N	5	1	.833	14	6	5-2	0	65.1	52	17	4	0	20	39	2.20	178	.223	.285	21	.143	-1	146	13		1.0
1952	Bro N	8	4	.667	25	9	0	0	77	76	44	3	1	47	43	5.14	71	.259	.364	22-0-3	.045	-2*	125	-11		-1.7
1953	†Bro N	11	6	.647	37	7	0	7	110.1	92	39	9	0	30	44	2.77	154	.225	.278	28-0-3	.071	-1	81	18		2.5
1954	Bro N	7	6	.538	47	2	0	5	108.1	101	60	7	1	56	43	4.15	98	.247	.337	30	.033	-2	87	-3		-0.5
1955	†Bro N	13	5	.722	60	8	1	11	144.1	121	61	12	0	55-4	67	3.24	125	.229	.300	31-3-3	.097	-1	82	13		1.8
1956	†Bro N☆	10	6	.625	62	3	1	19	115.2	111	48	11	3	39-8	75	3.35	119	.253	.317	23	.087	-1	96	7		0.8
1957	Bro N★	5	7	.417	58	0	0	17	104.2	104	50	8	1	27-6	67	3.44	121	.259	.301	20	.100	-1		6		0.8
1958	LA N	6	6	.500	52	2	0	14	104	112	55	8	1	33-8	43	4.15	99	.283	.336	18-0-1	.056	-1	110	-1		-0.2
1959	†LA N	5	10	.333	56	0	0	9	84.2	91	39	11	1	25-10	37	3.93	108	.282	.332	16-0-1	.000	-2		4		0.7
1960	LA N	0	1	.000	13	0	0	0	17	26	12	1	0	8-3	15	5.82	68	.356	.420	2	.500	1		-3		-0.2
	Det A	0	3	.000	14	0	0	2	19.1	19	12	2	0	12-4	6	5.12	77	.257	.360	2	.000	-0		-2		-0.4
	†Pit N	3	0	1.000	15	0	0	3	30.1	29	5	0	1	11-3	21	1.48	253	.254	.323	4-0-2	.000	-0		8		0.9
1961	Pit N	4	1	.800	56	1	0	8	92.2	102	43	4	2	31-8	49	3.69	108	.284	.343	10	.100	-1	111	3		0.1
1962	NY N	0	0	—	3	0	0	0	4	6	6	1	0	2	1	11.25	37	.278	.316	0	—	0		-3		-0.1
Total 13		77	56	.579	513	38	7-2	96	1079.2	1043	492	81	11	396-54	551	3.63	112	.256	.322	227-3-13	.075	-11	103	49		5.4
LACEY, BOB	Robert Joseph B8.25.1953 Fredericksburg VA BR/TL/6-5/210(180-210) [OakA72*10/140] d5.13 Col Central Arizona JC																									
1977	Oak A	6	8	.429	64	0	0	7-3	121.2	100	46	13	0	43-11	69	3.03	133	.234	.301	—		0		14		1.1
1978	Oak A	8	9	.471	74	0	0	5-6	119.2	126	52	10	1	35-13	60	3.01	122	.270	.320	—		0		7		1.1
1979	Oak A	1	5	.167	42	0	0	4-5	47.2	66	34	7	1	24-8	33	5.85	69	.327	.397	—		0		-9	66	-1.2
1980	Oak A	3	2	.600	47	1	1-1	6-6	79.2	68	29	7	1	21-5	45	2.94	130	.234	.284	—		0	94	8		0.8
1981	Cle A	0	0	—	14	0	0	0-0	21.1	36	20	5	0	3-0	11	7.59	49	.371	.379	—		0		-9		-0.7
	Tex A	0	0	—	1	0	0	0-0	1	1	1	0	0	0-0	0	9.00	39	.250	.250	—		0		-1		-0.1
	Year	0	0	—	15	0	0	0-0	22.1	37	21	5	0	3-0	11	7.66	48	.364	.374	—		0		-10		-0.8
1983	Cal A	1	2	.333	8	0	0	0-2	8.2	12	5	1	0	5-0	5	5.19	78	.343	.343	—		0	75	-2		-0.3
1984	SF N	1	3	.250	34	0	0	0-1	51	55	26	5	0	13-4	26	3.88	91	.276	.318	6	.333	1	82	7	66	-0.2
Total 7		20	29	.408	284	2	1-1	22-23	450.2	464	213	49	4	139-41	251	3.67	104	.269	.322	6	.333	1	82	7	66	-0.3
LACHEMANN, MARCEL	Marcel Ernest B6.13.1941 Los Angeles CA BR/TR/6-0/185* d6.4 M3/C15 b-Rene Col USC																									
1969	Oak A	4	1	.800	28	0	0	2-1	43.1	43	24	1	2	19-2	16	3.95	87	.261	.340	2-0-1	.000	-0		-4		-0.5
1970	Oak A	3	3	.500	41	0	0	3-1	58.1	58	20	6	2	18-6	39	2.78	127	.266	.326	8	.000	-1		5		0.3
1971	Oak A	0	0	—	1	0	0	0-0	0.1	2	2	0	0	1-0	0	54.00	6	1.000	1.000	—		0		-2		-0.1
Total 3		7	4	.636	70	0	0	5-2	102	103	46	7	4	38-8	55	3.44	101	.268	.337	10-0-1	.000	-1		-1		-0.3

LACHOWICZ, AL Allen Robert B9.6.1960 Pittsburgh PA BR/TR/6-3/198 [TexA81 1/24] d9.13 Col Pittsburgh

YEAR	TM	LG	W	L	PCT	G	GS	CG-SHO	SV-BS	IP	H	R	HR	HB	BB-IB	SO	ERA	AERA	OAV	OOB	AB-HR-SH	AVG	PB	SUP	APR	DL	PW
1983	Tex	A	0	1	.000	2	1	0	0-0	8	9	2	0	0	2-0	8	2.25	180	.281	.324	0	—	0	0	2		0.2

LACKEY, JOHN John Derran B10.23.1978 Abilene TX BR/TR/6-6/200(200-235) [AnaA99 2/68] d6.24 Col Texas-Arlington

YEAR	TM	LG	W	L	PCT	G	GS	CG-SHO	SV-BS	IP	H	R	HR	HB	BB-IB	SO	ERA	AERA	OAV	OOB	AB-HR-SH	AVG	PB	SUP	APR	DL	PW
2002	†Ana	A	9	4	.692	18	18	1	0-0	108.1	113	52	10	4	33-0	69	3.66	123	.267	.323	0	—	0	120	8		0.9
2003	Ana	A	10	16	.385	33	33	2-2	0-0	204	223	117	31	10	66-4	151	4.63	94	.278	.339	3	.000	-0	90	-7		-0.8
2004	Ana	A	14	13	.519	33	32	1-1	0-0	198.1	215	108	22	8	60-4	144	4.67	96	.278	.335	2	.000	-0	88	4		-0.5
2005	†LA	A	14	5	.737	33	33	1	0-0	209	208	85	13	11	71-3	199	3.44	125	.258	.325	6	.000	-1	104	21		1.6
Total 4			47	38	.553	117	116	5-3	0-0	719.2	759	362	76	33	230-11	563	4.15	106	.270	.331	11	.000	-1	98	18		1.2

LACKEY, BILL William D. B12.8.1870 St.Albans WV D5.15.1941 Columbus OH d10.2

YEAR	TM	LG	W	L	PCT	G	GS	CG-SHO	SV-BS	IP	H	R	HR	HB	BB-IB	SO	ERA	AERA	OAV	OOB	AB-HR-SH	AVG	PB	SUP	APR	DL	PW
1890	Phi	AA	0	0	—	1	0	0		2	1	4	0	0	3	1	9.00	43	.143	.400	1	.000	-0		-2		-0.1

LaCORTE, FRANK Frank Joseph B10.13.1951 San Jose CA BR/TR/6-1/180* d9.8 Col Gavilan (CA) JC [DL 1985 Cal A 182]

YEAR	TM	LG	W	L	PCT	G	GS	CG-SHO	SV-BS	IP	H	R	HR	HB	BB-IB	SO	ERA	AERA	OAV	OOB	AB-HR-SH	AVG	PB	SUP	APR	DL	PW
1975	Atl	N	0	3	.000	3	2	0	0-0	13.2	13	10	1	0	6-0	10	5.27	72	.245	.322	5	.000	-1	70	-2		-0.5
1976	Atl	N	3	12	.200	19	17	1	0-0	105.1	97	58	6	6	53-2	79	4.70	81	.249	.344	33-0-3	.000	-2*	52	-8		-1.3
1977	Atl	N	1	8	.111	14	7	0	0-0	37	67	51	10	2	29-1	28	11.68	38	.394	.485	10-0-2	.200	-0	71	-25		-4.2
1978	Atl	N	0	1	.000	2	2	0	0-0	14.2	9	6	1	0	4-1	8	3.68	109	.180	.236	4-0-1	.000	-0	33	1		0.0
1979	Atl	N	0	0	—	6	0	0	0-0	8.1	9	7	2	0	5-1	6	7.56	53	.273	.368	1	.000	-0		-3		-0.2
	Hou	N	1	2	.333	12	3	0	0-0	27	21	16	3	0	10-1	24	5.00	70	.208	.277	3	.000	-0	67	4		-0.5
	Year		1	2	.333	18	3	0	0-0	35.1	30	23	5	0	15-2	30	5.60	65	.224	.300	4	.000	-0	65	-7		-0.7
1980	†Hou	N	8	5	.615	55	0	0	11-3	83	61	29	4	0	43-5	66	2.82	116	.210	.307	6-0-2	.167	-0		5		0.8
1981	†Hou	N	4	2	.667	37	0	0	5-3	42	41	18	1	0	21-3	40	3.64	90	.258	.339	3	.333	0		-1		-0.2
1982	Hou	N	1	5	.167	55	0	0	7-4	76.1	71	44	5	0	46-5	51	4.48	74	.247	.344	7-0-1	.000	-1		-11		-1.2
1983	Hou	N	4	4	.500	37	0	0	3-2	53.1	35	32	8	2	28-3	48	5.06	68	.190	.302	5-0-1	.200	-0		-9	38	-1.3
1984	Cal	A	1	2	.333	13	1	0	0-0	29.1	33	26	9	0	13-4	13	7.06	57	.282	.351	0	—	0	136	-10	80	-0.9
Total 10			23	44	.343	253	32	1	26-12	490	457	297	49	10	258-26	372	5.01	72	.249	.341	77-0-10	.104	-4	66	-67	300	-9.5

LaCOSS, MIKE Michael James B5.30.1956 Glendale CA BR/TR/6-4/190(186-200) [CinN74 3/71] d7.18

YEAR	TM	LG	W	L	PCT	G	GS	CG-SHO	SV-BS	IP	H	R	HR	HB	BB-IB	SO	ERA	AERA	OAV	OOB	AB-HR-SH	AVG	PB	SUP	APR	DL	PW
1978	Cin	N	4	8	.333	16	15	2-1	0-0	96	104	56	5	1	46-9	41	4.50	79	.288	.365	30-0-6	.067	-2*	88	-11		-1.5
1979	†Cin	N★	14	8	.636	35	32	6-1	0-0	205.2	202	92	13	2	79-8	73	3.50	106	.263	.331	70-0-5	.129	-1	99	4		0.2
1980	Cin	N	10	12	.455	34	29	4-2	0-1	169.1	207	101	9	1	68-8	59	4.62	76	.303	.366	55-0-6	.091	-3	104	-25		-3.1
1981	Cin	N	4	7	.364	20	13	1-1	1-0	78	102	55	7	1	30-4	22	6.12	57	.325	.380	19-0-7	.000	-2	88	-21		-2.9
1982	Hou	N	6	6	.500	41	8	0	0-0	115	107	41	3	4	54-6	51	2.90	115	.252	.342	24-0-3	.250	2	100	6		0.8
1983	Hou	N	5	7	.417	38	17	2	1-1	138	142	81	10	2	56-11	53	4.43	77	.273	.342	35-0-4	.086	-2	105	-18		-1.6
1984	Hou	N	7	5	.583	39	18	2-1	3-0	132	132	64	9	2	55-5	86	4.02	83	.261	.333	31-0-6	.129	-1	100	-8	21	-0.8
1985	KC	A	1	1	.500	21	0	0	1-0	40.2	49	25	2	0	29-6	26	5.09	82	.304	.411	0	—	0		-4		-0.2
1986	SF	N	10	13	.435	37	31	4-1	0-0	204.1	179	99	14	6	70-8	79	3.57	99	.240	.309	61-2-5	.230	6	130	-4		0.2
1987	†SF	N	13	10	.565	39	26	2-1	0-2	171	184	78	16	2	63-12	79	3.68	104	.283	.346	50-0-4	.060	-2	102	3		0.3
1988	SF	N	7	7	.500	19	19	1-1	0-0	114.1	99	55	5	1	47-3	70	3.62	90	.234	.311	33-0-4	.242	3	90	-6	53	-0.3
1989	†SF	N	10	10	.500	45	18	1	6-3	150.1	143	62	3	7	65-4	78	3.17	107	.255	.336	41-0-3	.073	-1	132	2		-0.3
1990	SF	N	6	4	.600	13	12	1	0-0	77.2	75	37	5	0	39-2	39	3.94	93	.259	.342	23-0-8	.043	-1	136	-3	98	-0.5
1991	SF	N	1	5	.167	18	5	0	0-1	47.1	61	39	4	2	24-0	31	7.23	50	.314	.392	9	.222	1	105	-19		-2.0
Total 14			98	103	.488	415	243	26-9	12-10	1739.2	1786	885	99	29	725-86	783	4.02	88	.270	.343	481-2-61	.125	-4	107	-104	172	-11.2

LACY, KERRY Kerry Ardeen B8.7.1972 Chattanooga TN BR/TR/6-2/215(195-215) [TexA91 15/404] d8.16 Col Chattanooga St. (TN) CC [DL 1998 Bos A 181]

YEAR	TM	LG	W	L	PCT	G	GS	CG-SHO	SV-BS	IP	H	R	HR	HB	BB-IB	SO	ERA	AERA	OAV	OOB	AB-HR-SH	AVG	PB	SUP	APR	DL	PW
1996	Bos	A	2	0	1.000	11	0	0	0-2	10.2	15	5	2	1	8-0	9	3.38	151	.333	.444	0	—	0		2		0.3
1997	Bos	A	1	1	.500	33	0	0	3-0	45.2	60	34	7	0	22-4	18	6.11	76	.314	.381	0	—	0		-7		-0.4
Total 2			3	1	.750	44	0	0	3-2	56.1	75	39	9	1	30-4	27	5.59	85	.318	.394	0	—	0		-5	181	-0.1

LADD, PETE Peter Linwood B7.17.1956 Portland ME BR/TR/6-3/240* [BosA77 25/620] d8.17 Col U. of Mississippi

YEAR	TM	LG	W	L	PCT	G	GS	CG-SHO	SV-BS	IP	H	R	HR	HB	BB-IB	SO	ERA	AERA	OAV	OOB	AB-HR-SH	AVG	PB	SUP	APR	DL	PW
1979	Hou	N	1	1	.500	10	0	0	0-0	12.1	8	5	1	2	8-0	6	2.92	120	.178	.327	1	.000	-0		1		0.1
1982	†Mil	A	1	3	.250	16	0	0	3-2	18	16	8	5	2	6-3	12	4.00	96	.239	.297	0	—	0		0		0.0
1983	Mil	A	3	4	.429	44	0	0	25-6	49.1	30	17	3	1	16-2	41	2.55	148	.172	.242	0	—	0		6		1.3
1984	Mil	A	4	9	.308	54	1	0	3-7	91	94	58	16	1	38-6	75	5.24	74	.266	.336	0	—	0	46	-13		-1.8
1985	Mil	A	0	0	—	29	0	0	2-1	45.2	58	26	5	2	10-0	22	4.53	93	.315	.347	0	—	0		-2		-0.1
1986	Sea	A	8	6	.571	52	0	0	6-3	70.2	69	33	10	3	18-3	53	3.82	112	.258	.306	0	—	0		4		0.7
Total 6			17	23	.425	205	1	0	39-19	287	275	147	40	9	96-14	209	4.25	92	.252	.313	1	.000	-0	46	-4		0.2

LADE, DOYLE Doyle Marion "Porky" B2.17.1921 Fairbury NE D5.18.2000 Lincoln NE BR/TR(BB 1946-47)/5-10/183* d9.18

YEAR	TM	LG	W	L	PCT	G	GS	CG-SHO	SV-BS	IP	H	R	HR	HB	BB-IB	SO	ERA	AERA	OAV	OOB	AB-HR-SH	AVG	PB	SUP	APR	DL	PW
1946	Chi	N	0	2	.000	3	2	0	0-0	15.1	15	8	0	1	3	8	4.11	81	.238	.284	5-0-1	.200	-0	52	-1		-0.2
1947	Chi	N	11	10	.524	34	25	7-1	0	187.1	202	105	15	1	79	62	3.94	100	.276	.347	60-0-3	.217	2*	89	-3		0.0
1948	Chi	N	5	6	.455	19	12	6	0	87.1	99	44	4	1	31	29	4.02	97	.283	.343	32	.156	-1	110	0		-0.1
1949	Chi	N	4	5	.444	36	13	5-1	1	129.2	141	73	13	2	58	43	5.00	81	.274	.350	32-0-4	.219	2	103	-10		-0.5
1950	Chi	N	5	6	.455	34	12	2	2	117.2	126	68	14	2	50	36	4.74	89	.275	.349	35-0-2	.286	3	121	-5		0.1
Total 5			25	29	.463	126	64	20-2	3	537.1	583	298	46	7	221	178	4.39	91	.275	.346	164-0-10	.220	1	101	-19		-0.7

LAFFERTY, FLIP Frank Bernard B5.4.1854 Scranton PA D2.8.1910 Wilmington DE TR d9.15 ▲

YEAR	TM	LG	W	L	PCT	G	GS	CG-SHO	SV-BS	IP	H	R	HR	HB	BB-IB	SO	ERA	AERA	OAV	OOB	AB-HR-SH	AVG	PB	SUP	APR	DL	PW
1876	Phi	N	0	1	.000	1	1	1	0	9	5	3	0	0	0	0	0.00	—	.152	.152	3	.000	-1	0	2		0.1

LAFITTE, ED Edward Francis "Doc" B4.7.1886 New Orleans LA D4.12.1971 Jenkintown PA BR/TR/6-2/188 d4.16 Col Georgia Tech

YEAR	TM	LG	W	L	PCT	G	GS	CG-SHO	SV-BS	IP	H	R	HR	HB	BB-IB	SO	ERA	AERA	OAV	OOB	AB-HR-SH	AVG	PB	SUP	APR	DL	PW
1909	Det	A	0	1	.000	3	1	1	1	14	22	14	2	1	2	11	3.86	65	.344	.373	4	.250	0	56	-4		-0.3
1911	Det	A	11	8	.579	29	20	15	1	172.1	205	113	2	5	52	63	3.92	88	.302	.356	70-1-2	.157	-2*	102	-13		-1.6
1912	Det	A	0	0	—	1	0	0	0	1.2	2	4	0	0	2	0	16.20	20	.333	.500	0	—	0		-2		-0.1
1914	Bro	F	18	15	.545	42	33	23	2	290.2	260	110	7	16	127	137	2.63	109	.248	.338	101-1-4	.257	3	92	9		1.4
1915	Bro	F	6	9	.400	17	15	7	1	117.2	126	66	6	1	57	34	3.90	70	.288	.371	53	.264	2	90	-15		-1.7
	Buf	F	2	2	.500	14	5	1-1	1	50.1	53	25	1	2	22	17	3.40	82	.286	.368	17	.118	-1	110	-4		-0.4
	Year		8	11	.421	31	20	8-1	2	168	179	91	7	3	79	51	3.75	73	.287	.370	70	.229	1	95	-18		-2.1
Total 5			37	35	.514	106	74	47-1	6	646.2	668	332	18	25	262	262	3.33	90	.276	.353	245-2-6	.220	1	95	-29		-2.7

LAGGER, ED Edwin Joseph B7.14.1912 Joliet IL D11.10.1981 Joliet IL BR/TR/6-3/200 d6.15 Col Northwestern

YEAR	TM	LG	W	L	PCT	G	GS	CG-SHO	SV-BS	IP	H	R	HR	HB	BB-IB	SO	ERA	AERA	OAV	OOB	AB-HR-SH	AVG	PB	SUP	APR	DL	PW
1934	Phi	A	0	0	—	1	0	0		18	27	14	1	0	14	1	11.00	40	.342	.447	6	.000	-1		-13		-0.6

LaGROW, LERRIN Lerrin Harris B7.8.1948 Phoenix AZ BR/TR/6-5/220(210-230) [DetA69 6/137] d7.28 Col Arizona St.

YEAR	TM	LG	W	L	PCT	G	GS	CG-SHO	SV-BS	IP	H	R	HR	HB	BB-IB	SO	ERA	AERA	OAV	OOB	AB-HR-SH	AVG	PB	SUP	APR	DL	PW
1970	Det	A	0	1	.000	10	0	0	0-1	12.1	16	11	2	0	6-0	7	7.30	52	.308	.373	1	.000	-0		-5		-0.4
1972	†Det	A	0	1	.000	16	0	0	2-0	27.1	22	4	0	0	6-2	9	1.32	241	.222	.264	0	—	0		6		0.3
1973	Det	A	1	5	.167	21	3	0	3-0	54	54	26	3	2	23-2	33	4.33	95	.263	.335	0	—	0	87	-9	25	0.0
1974	Det	A	8	19	.296	37	34	11	0-0	216.1	245	132	21	3	80-8	85	4.66	82	.287	.349	0	—	0	81	-21		-2.2
1975	Det	A	7	14	.333	32	26	7-2	0-0	164.1	183	105	15	2	66-5	75	4.38	92	.280	.344	0	—	0	83	-10		-1.3
1976	StL	N	1	0	1.000	8	2	1	0-0	24.1	21	4	1	0	7-2	10	1.48	242	.241	.302	5	.000	-1	25	6		0.3
1977	Chi	A	7	3	.700	66	0	0	25-3	98.2	81	32	10	1	35-3	63	2.46	166	.230	.299	0	—	0		17		2.6
1978	Chi	A	5	5	.545	52	0	0	16-6	88	85	47	9	3	38-0	41	4.40	86	.240	.340	0	—	0		-6		-0.8
1979	Chi	A	0	3	.000	11	2	0	1-3	17.2	27	21	2	1	16-1	9	9.17	46	.346	.463	0	—	0	85	-10		-1.5
	LA	N	5	1	.833	25	0	0	4-3	37	38	16	2	0	18-2	22	3.41	106	.270	.350	3	.333	0		1	26	0.2
1980	Phi	N	0	2	.000	25	0	0	3-1	39	42	22	5	0	17-2	21	4.15	92	.276	.343	4	.250	0		-1		-0.1
Total 10			34	55	.382	309	67	19-2	54-17	779	814	420	74	12	312-27	375	4.11	95	.271	.339	13	.154	-0	82	-24	51	-2.9

LAHTI, JEFF Jeffrey Allen B10.8.1956 Oregon City OR BR/TR/6-0/180* [CinN78 5/121] d6.27 Col Portland St. [DL 1987 StL N 182]

YEAR	TM	LG	W	L	PCT	G	GS	CG-SHO	SV-BS	IP	H	R	HR	HB	BB-IB	SO	ERA	AERA	OAV	OOB	AB-HR-SH	AVG	PB	SUP	APR	DL	PW
1982	†StL	N	5	4	.556	33	1	0	0-1	56.2	53	27	3	2	21-8	22	3.81	97	.245	.314	13	.077	-1	96	-1		-0.2
1983	StL	N	3	3	.500	53	0	0	0-3	74	64	31	2	3	29-12	26	3.16	116	.240	.314	10	.000	-1		3	21	0.2
1984	StL	N	4	2	.667	63	0	0	1-2	84.2	69	36	6	3	34-12	45	3.72	94	.225	.303	6-0-1	.167	-0		-1		0.0
1985	StL	N	5	2	.714	52	0	0	19-1	68.1	63	15	3	4	26-10	41	1.84	194	.217	.321	9	.000	-1	14	13		2.0
1986	StL	N	0	0	—	4	0	0	0-0	2.1	4	1	0	1	1-0	3	0.00	—	.333	.400	0	—	0		2		0.0
Total 5			17	11	.607	205	1	0	20-7	286	252	109	14	5	111-42	137	3.12	115	.240	.313	38-0-1	.053	-3	96	-1	162	2.0

LAKE, EDDIE Edward Erving "Sparky" B3.18.1916 Antioch CA D6.7.1995 Castro Valley CA BR/TR/5-7/160* d9.26.1939 ▲

YEAR	TM	LG	W	L	PCT	G	GS	CG-SHO	SV-BS	IP	H	R	HR	HB	BB-IB	SO	ERA	AERA	OAV	OOB	AB-HR-SH	AVG	PB	SUP	APR	DL	PW
1944	Bos	A	0	0	—	6	0	0		19.1	20	13	6	3	11	7	4.19	81	.278	.395	126-0-4	.206	1*		-3		-0.1

YEAR	TM LG	W	L	PCT	G	GS	CG-SHO	SV-BS	IP	H	R	HR	HB	BB-IB	SO	ERA	AERA	OAV	OOB	AB-HR-SH	AVG	PB	SUP	APR	DL	PW

LAKE, JOE   Joseph Henry B1.6.1881 Brooklyn NY D6.30.1950 Brooklyn NY BR/TR/6-0/185 d4.21

YEAR	TM LG	W	L	PCT	G	GS	CG-SHO	SV-BS	IP	H	R	HR	HB	BB-IB	SO	ERA	AERA	OAV	OOB	AB-HR-SH	AVG	PB	SUP	APR	DL	PW
1908	NY A	9	22	.290	38	27	19-2	0	269.1	252	157	6	6	77	118	3.17	78	.242	.298	112-1-1	.188	0*	79	-25		-3.0
1909	NY A	14	11	.560	31	26	17-3	1	215.1	180	81	2	5	59	117	1.88	135	.225	.283	81	.173	1	107	10		1.7
1910	StL A	11	17	.393	35	29	24-1	2	261.1	243	116	2	1	77	141	2.20	112	.248	.304	91	.231	2*	78	2		0.6
1911	StL A	10	15	.400	30	25	14-2	0	215.1	245	115	3	4	40	69	3.30	102	.282	.316	80-0-1	.262	2	83	1		0.6
1912	StL A	1	7	.125	11	6	4	0	57	70	41	0	1	16	28	4.42	75	.314	.363	20	.150	-1	74	-8		-1.0
	Det A	9	11	.450	26	14	11	1	162.2	190	94	3	3	39	86	3.10	105	.296	.340	62-1-2	.145	-3	76	-3		-0.7
	Year	10	18	.357	37	20	15	1	219.2	260	135	3	4	55	114	3.44	95	.301	.346	82-1-2	.146	-5	76	-11		-1.7
1913	Det A	8	7	.533	28	12	6	1	137	149	67	3	0	24	35	3.28	89	.279	.310	45-1-1	.267	4	104	-5		0.1
Total	6	62	90	.408	199	139	95-8	5	1318	1329	671	19	20	332	594	2.85	99	.261	.309	491-3-5	.206	4	86	-28		-1.7

LaMABE, JACK   John Alexander B10.3.1936 Farmingdale NY BR/TR/6-1/198(193-205) d4.17 Col Vermont

YEAR	TM LG	W	L	PCT	G	GS	CG-SHO	SV-BS	IP	H	R	HR	HB	BB-IB	SO	ERA	AERA	OAV	OOB	AB-HR-SH	AVG	PB	SUP	APR	DL	PW
1962	Pit N	3	1	.750	46	0	0	2	78	70	35	4	2	40-8	56	2.88	136	.238	.329	9	.000	-1		7		0.3
1963	Bos A	7	4	.636	65	2	0	6	151.1	139	63	8	4	46-11	93	3.15	120	.247	.306	32-1-1	.094	-1	82	8		0.6
1964	Bos A	9	13	.409	39	25	3	1	177.1	235	123	25	2	57-5	109	5.89	65	.318	.367	52-0-1	.115	-1	106	-35		-4.0
1965	Bos A	0	3	.000	14	0	0	0	25.1	34	24	5	3	14-2	17	8.17	46	.340	.432	4-0-1	.000	-0		-10		-1.2
	Hou N	0	2	.000	3	2	0	0	12.2	17	9	3	0	3-1	6	4.26	79	.315	.351	4	.250	-0	52	-2		-0.3
1966	Chi A	7	9	.438	34	17	3-2	0	121.1	116	55	9	1	35-1	67	3.93	81	.251	.304	35-0-4	.057	-2	116	-8		-1.2
1967	Chi A	1	0	1.000	3	0	0	0	5	7	2	0	0	1-1	3	1.80	172	.318	.348	0	—	0		0		0.1
	NY N	3	0	.000	16	2	0	1	31.2	24	15	4	0	8-1	23	3.98	85	.200	.248	5	.000	0	52	-2		-0.2
	†StL N	3	4	.429	23	1	1-1	4	47.2	43	16	2	0	10-3	30	2.83	116	.244	.282	10-0-1	.200	0	160	3		0.5
	Year	3	7	.300	39	3	1-1	5	79.1	67	31	6	0	18-4	53	3.29	101	.226	.268	15-0-1	.133	-0	88	1		0.3
1968	Chi N	2	3	.600	42	0	0	0	60.2	68	33	7	1	24-7	36	4.30	73	.289	.350	5-0-1	.200	0		-8		-0.6
Total	7	33	41	.446	285	49	7-3	15	711	753	375	67	11	238-40	434	4.24	85	.272	.330	156-1-9	.096	-6	104	-47		-6.0

LaMACCHIA, AL   Alfred Anthony B7.22.1921 St.Louis MO BR/TR/5-10.5/190 d9.27

YEAR	TM LG	W	L	PCT	G	GS	CG-SHO	SV-BS	IP	H	R	HR	HB	BB-IB	SO	ERA	AERA	OAV	OOB	AB-HR-SH	AVG	PB	SUP	APR	DL	PW
1943	StL A	0	1	.000	1	1	0	0	4	9	6	0	0	2	2	11.25	30	.450	.500	2	.000	-0	101	-4		-0.6
1945	StL A	2	0	1.000	5	0	0	0	9	6	2	0	0	3	2	2.00	176	.207	.281	1	.000	-0		2		-0.3
1946	StL A	0	0	—	8	0	0	0	15	17	10	2	0	7	3	6.00	62	.279	.353	3	.000	-0		-3		-0.2
	Was A	0	1	.000	2	0	0	0	2.2	6	5	1	0	2	0	16.88	20	.462	.533	0	—	0		-4		-0.7
	Year	0	1	.000	10	0	0	0	17.2	23	15	3	0	9	3	7.64	48	.311	.386	3	.000	-0		-7		-0.9
Total	3	2	2	.500	16	1	0	0	30.2	38	23	3	0	14	7	6.46	55	.309	.380	6	.000	-1	101	-9		-1.2

LaMANNA, FRANK   Frank "Hank" B8.22.1919 Waterton PA D9.1.1980 Syracuse NY BR/TR/6-2.5/195 d4.16 Mil 1943-45

YEAR	TM LG	W	L	PCT	G	GS	CG-SHO	SV-BS	IP	H	R	HR	HB	BB-IB	SO	ERA	AERA	OAV	OOB	AB-HR-SH	AVG	PB	SUP	APR	DL	PW
1940	Bos N	1	0	1.000	5	1	1	0	13.1	13	8	1	0	8	3	4.73	79	.271	.375	5	.200	0	117	-2		-0.1
1941	Bos N	5	4	.556	35	4	0	1	72.2	77	52	5	1	56	23	5.33	67	.285	.410	32	.281	1*	119	-15		-1.5
1942	Bos N	0	1	.000	5	0	0	0	6.2	5	4	1	0	3	2	5.40	62	.208	.296	2	.000	-0*		-1		-0.2
Total	3	6	5	.545	45	5	1	1	92.2	95	64	7	1	67	28	5.24	68	.278	.398	39	.256	1	119	-18		-1.8

LAMANSKE, FRANK   Frank James "Lefty" B9.30.1906 Oglesby IL D8.4.1971 Olney IL BL/TL/5-11/170 d4.27

YEAR	TM LG	W	L	PCT	G	GS	CG-SHO	SV-BS	IP	H	R	HR	HB	BB-IB	SO	ERA	AERA	OAV	OOB	AB-HR-SH	AVG	PB	SUP	APR	DL	PW
1935	Bro N	0	0	—	2	0	0	0	3.2	5	3	0	0	1	1	7.36	54	.313	.353	1	.000	-0		-1		-0.1

LaMASTER, WAYNE   Noble Wayne B2.13.1907 Speed IN D8.4.1989 New Albany IN BL/TL/5-8/170 d4.19

YEAR	TM LG	W	L	PCT	G	GS	CG-SHO	SV-BS	IP	H	R	HR	HB	BB-IB	SO	ERA	AERA	OAV	OOB	AB-HR-SH	AVG	PB	SUP	APR	DL	PW
1937	Phi N	15	19	.441	50	30	10-1	4	220.1	255	139	24	2	82	135	5.31	82	.290	.352	79-0-2	.190	-2*	95	-19		-3.0
1938	Phi N	4	7	.364	18	12	1-1	0	63.2	80	58	8	3	31	35	7.77	50	.301	.380	22-0-3	.409	4	120	-25		-3.1
	Bro N	0	1	.000	3	0	0*	0	11.1	17	6	0	0	3	3	4.76	82	.340	.377	6	.167	-0*		-1		-0.1
	Year	4	8	.333	21	12	1-1	0	75	97	64	8	3	34	38	7.32	53	.307	.380	28-0-3	.357	4	120	-24		-3.2
Total	2	19	27	.413	71	42	11-2	4	295.1	352	203	32	5	116	173	5.82	72	.295	.360	107-0-5	.234	1	101	-45		-6.2

LAMB, JOHN   John Andrew B7.20.1946 Sharon CT BR/TR/6-3/180(180-195) d8.12

YEAR	TM LG	W	L	PCT	G	GS	CG-SHO	SV-BS	IP	H	R	HR	HB	BB-IB	SO	ERA	AERA	OAV	OOB	AB-HR-SH	AVG	PB	SUP	APR	DL	PW
1970	Pit N	0	1	.000	23	0	0	3-2	32.1	23	10	2	2	13-1	24	2.78	142	.209	.304	3	.000	-0		5		0.2
1971	Pit N	0	0	—	2	0	0	0-0	4.1	3	0	0	0	1-0	1	0.00	—	.188	.235	1	.000	-0		2	63	0.1
1973	Pit N	0	1	.000	22	0	0	2-0	29.2	37	24	3	0	10-3	11	6.07	58	.308	.359	3	.000	-0		-9		-0.5
Total	3	0	2	.000	47	0	0	5-2	66.1	63	34	5	2	24-4	36	4.07	92	.256	.326	7	.000	-1		-2	63	-0.2

LAMB, RAY   Raymond Richard B12.28.1944 Glendale CA BR/TR/6-1/175(170-190) [LAN66 40/732] d8.1 Col USC

YEAR	TM LG	W	L	PCT	G	GS	CG-SHO	SV-BS	IP	H	R	HR	HB	BB-IB	SO	ERA	AERA	OAV	OOB	AB-HR-SH	AVG	PB	SUP	APR	DL	PW
1969	LA N	0	1	.000	10	0	0	1-0	15	12	5	2	0	7-0	11	1.80	186	.235	.328	1	.000	-0		3		0.2
1970	LA N	6	1	.857	35	0	0	0-0	57	59	27	4	4	27-9	32	3.79	102	.277	.366	4	.000	-0		-1		-0.1
1971	Cle A	6	12	.333	43	21	3-1	1-0	158.1	147	67	11	1	69-7	91	3.35	116	.247	.323	43-0-4	.093	-2	92	7		0.5
1972	Cle A	5	4	.455	34	9	0	0-0	107.2	101	42	5	1	29-5	60	3.09	105	.248	.299	21-0-1	.000	-1	88	2		0.0
1973	Cle A	3	3	.500	32	1	0	2-1	86	98	44	7	2	42-6	60	4.60	86	.291	.369	0	—	0	203	-4		-0.3
Total	5	20	23	.465	154	31	3-1	4-1	424	417	183	29	8	174-27	258	3.54	105	.260	.333	69-0-5	.058	-4	94	8		0.3

LAMBERT, CLAYTON   Clayton Patrick B3.26.1917 Summit IL D4.3.1981 Ogden UT BR/TR/6-2/185 d4.22 Col Illinois College

YEAR	TM LG	W	L	PCT	G	GS	CG-SHO	SV-BS	IP	H	R	HR	HB	BB-IB	SO	ERA	AERA	OAV	OOB	AB-HR-SH	AVG	PB	SUP	APR	DL	PW
1946	Cin N	2	2	.500	23	4	2	1	52.2	48	27	3	1	20	20	4.27	78	.251	.325	13	.154	-1	109	-4		-0.5
1947	Cin N	0	0	—	3	0	0	0	5.2	12	10	3	0	6	1	15.88	26	.444	.445	1	.000	-0		-7		-0.3
Total	2	2	2	.500	26	4	2	1	58.1	60	37	6	1	26	21	5.40	63	.275	.355	14	.143	-1	109	-11		-0.8

LAMBERT, GENE   Eugene Marion B4.26.1921 Crenshaw MS D2.10.2000 Germantown TN BR/TR/5-11/175 d9.14 Mil 1943-45

YEAR	TM LG	W	L	PCT	G	GS	CG-SHO	SV-BS	IP	H	R	HR	HB	BB-IB	SO	ERA	AERA	OAV	OOB	AB-HR-SH	AVG	PB	SUP	APR	DL	PW
1941	Phi N	0	1	.000	2	1	0	0	9	11	2	0	0	2	3	2.00	185	.297	.333	2	.000	-0	0	2		0.2
1942	Phi N	0	0	—	1	0	0	0	1	3	1	0	0	0	1	9.00	37	.500	.500	0	—	0		-1		0.0
Total	2	0	1	.000	3	1	0	0	10	14	3	0	0	2	4	2.70	136	.326	.356	2	.000	-0	0	1		0.2

LAMBETH, OTIS   Otis Samuel B5.13.1890 Berlin KS D6.5.1976 Moran KS BR/TR/6-0/175 d7.16 Mil 1918

YEAR	TM LG	W	L	PCT	G	GS	CG-SHO	SV-BS	IP	H	R	HR	HB	BB-IB	SO	ERA	AERA	OAV	OOB	AB-HR-SH	AVG	PB	SUP	APR	DL	PW
1916	Cle A	4	4	.500	15	9	3	1	74	69	33	1	3	38	28	2.92	103	.256	.354	27-0-1	.111	-1*	92	0		-0.2
1917	Cle A	7	6	.538	26	10	2	2	97.1	97	48	2	11	30	27	3.14	90	.274	.349	32-0-3	.188	-0	112	-4		-0.6
1918	Cle A	0	0	—	2	0	0	0	7	10	5	0	0	6	3	6.43	47	.370	.485	1	1.000	0		-2		-0.1
Total	3	11	10	.524	43	19	5	3	178.1	176	86	3	14	74	58	3.18	92	.270	.357	60-0-4	.167	-1	102	-6		-0.9

LAMLEIN, FRED   Frederick Arthur "Dutch" B8.14.1887 Port Huron MI D9.20.1970 Port Huron MI BR/TL/5-11/171 d9.18

YEAR	TM LG	W	L	PCT	G	GS	CG-SHO	SV-BS	IP	H	R	HR	HB	BB-IB	SO	ERA	AERA	OAV	OOB	AB-HR-SH	AVG	PB	SUP	APR	DL	PW
1912	Chi N	0	0	—	1	0	0	0	2	7	7	0	0	2	1	31.50	10	.583	.643	—	0		-6		-0.2
1915	StL N	0	0	—	4	0	0	0	19	21	4	0	2	3	11	1.42	196	.300	.347	8	.125	-0		3		0.1
Total	2	0	0	—	5	0	0	0	21	28	11	0	2	5	12	4.29	66	.341	.393	8	.125	-0		-3		-0.1

LAMP, DENNIS   Dennis Patrick B9.23.1952 Los Angeles CA BR/TR/6-3/210(180-215) [ChiN71 3/62] d8.21

YEAR	TM LG	W	L	PCT	G	GS	CG-SHO	SV-BS	IP	H	R	HR	HB	BB-IB	SO	ERA	AERA	OAV	OOB	AB-HR-SH	AVG	PB	SUP	APR	DL	PW
1977	Chi N	0	2	.000	11	3	0	0-0	30	43	21	3	2	8-4	12	6.30	70	.344	.390	8	.375	1	67	-5		-0.2
1978	Chi N	7	15	.318	37	36	6-3	0-0	223.2	221	96	16	4	56-8	73	3.30	123	.258	.306	73-0-3	.205	0	82	14		1.5
1979	Chi N	11	10	.524	38	32	6-1	0-0	200.1	223	96	14	5	46-9	86	3.50	119	.287	.329	58-0-7	.155	-0	95	10		1.0
1980	Chi N	10	14	.417	41	37	2-1	0-1	203.2	259	123	16	1	82-7	83	5.20	76	.317	.378	61-0-7	.098	-3	94	-21		-2.5
1981	Chi A	7	6	.538	27	10	3	0-0	127	103	41	4	1	43-1	71	2.41	150	.222	.289	0	—	0	74	17		1.7
1982	Chi A	11	8	.579	44	27	3-2	5-2	189.2	206	96	9	6	59-3	78	3.99	102	.279	.337	0	—	0	116	2		0.3
1983	†Chi A	7	7	.500	49	5	1	15-5	116.1	123	52	6	4	29-7	44	3.71	114	.275	.324	0	—	0	77	7		0.9
1984	Tor A	8	8	.500	56	4	0	9-5	85	97	53	9	1	38-7	45	4.55	91	.285	.358	0	—	0	153	-6		-1.1
1985	†Tor A	11	0	1.000	53	1	0	2-5	105.2	96	42	7	0	27-3	68	3.32	128	.247	.292	0	—	0	43	11		1.2
1986	Tor A	2	6	.250	40	2	0	2-1	73	93	50	7	0	23-6	30	5.05	84	.309	.357	0	—	0	114	-7		-0.9
1987	Oak A	1	3	.250	36	5	0	0-0	56.2	76	38	5	1	22-4	36	5.08	82	.326	.382	0	—	0		4		-0.4
1988	Bos A	7	6	.538	46	0	0	0-1	82.2	92	39	3	2	19-3	49	3.48	119	.284	.326	0	—	0		19	18	0.6
1989	Bos A	4	2	.667	42	0	0	2-1	112.1	96	37	4	0	27-6	61	2.32	177	.235	.280	0	—	0	44	19		1.1
1990	†Bos A	3	5	.375	47	1	0	0-2	105.2	114	61	10	3	30-8	49	4.68	87	.279	.330	0	—	0		-4		-0.4
1991	Bos A	6	3	.667	51	0	0	0-1	92	100	54	8	3	31-7	57	4.70	92	.275	.335	0	—	0		-4		-0.4
1992	Pit N	1	0	1.000	21	0	0	1-0	28	33	16	3	2	7-4	15	5.14	67	.292	.355	1	.000	-0		-4		-0.3
Total	16	96	96	.500	639	163	21-7	35-24	1830.2	1975	915	122	35	549-86	857	3.93	104	.278	.331	201-0-17	.164	-3	94	21	18	2.1

LAMPE, HENRY   Henry Joseph B9.19.1872 Boston MA D9.16.1936 Dorchester MA BR/TL/5-11.5/175 d5.14

YEAR	TM LG	W	L	PCT	G	GS	CG-SHO	SV-BS	IP	H	R	HR	HB	BB-IB	SO	ERA	AERA	OAV	OOB	AB-HR-SH	AVG	PB	SUP	APR	DL	PW
1894	Bos N	0	1	.000	2	1	0	0	5.1	17	19	5	0	7	1	11.81	48	.531	.615	2	.000	-0	337	-6		-0.7
1895	Phi N	0	2	.000	7	3	2	0	44	68	54	3	1	33	18	7.57	63	.347	.443	16	.125	-1	94	-15		-0.7
Total	2	0	3	.000	9	4	2	0	49.1	85	73	8	1	40	19	8.03	61	.373	.468	18	.111	-1	168	-21		-1.4

YEAR	TM LG	W	L	PCT	G	GS	CG-SHO	SV-BS	IP	H	R	HR	HB	BB-IB	SO	ERA	AERA	OAV	OOB	AB-HR-SH	AVG	PB	SUP	APR	DL	PW

LANAHAN, DICK Richard Anthony B9.27.1911 Washington DC D3.12.1975 Rochester MN BL/TL/6-0/186 d9.15

YEAR	TM LG	W	L	PCT	G	GS	CG-SHO	SV-BS	IP	H	R	HR	HB	BB-IB	SO	ERA	AERA	OAV	OOB	AB-HR-SH	AVG	PB	SUP	APR	DL	PW
1935	Was A	0	3	.000	3	3	0	0	20.2	27	13	2	2	17	10	5.66	76	.314	.438	6-0-1	.167	-0	40	-2		-0.3
1937	Was A	0	1	.000	6	2	0	0	11.1	16	16	2	1	13	2	12.71	35	.320	.469	1	.000	0	177	-10		-0.6
1940	Pit N	6	8	.429	40	8	4	2	108	121	63	8	1	42	45	4.25	90	.279	.345	34-0-1	.118	-0	103	-7		-1.0
1941	Pit N	0	1	.000	7	0	0	0	12	13	9	1	2	3	5	5.25	69	.283	.353	1	.000	-0		-2		-0.2
Total	4	6	13	.316	56	13	4	2	152	177	101	13	6	75	62	5.15	76	.288	.371	42-0-2	.119	-2	102	-21		-2.1

LANCASTER, LES Lester Wayne B4.21.1962 Dallas TX BR/TR/6-2/200* d4.7 Col Dallas Baptist

YEAR	TM LG	W	L	PCT	G	GS	CG-SHO	SV-BS	IP	H	R	HR	HB	BB-IB	SO	ERA	AERA	OAV	OOB	AB-HR-SH	AVG	PB	SUP	APR	DL	PW
1987	Chi N	8	3	.727	27	18	0	0-0	132.1	138	76	14	1	51-5	78	4.90	88	.268	.332	49-0-1	.082	-2	100	-7		-0.8
1988	Chi N	4	6	.400	44	3	1	5-3	85.2	89	42	4	1	34-7	36	3.78	96	.273	.337	20-0-3	.050	-1	146	-2	36	-0.4
1989	†Chi N	4	2	.667	42	0	0	8-3	72.2	60	12	2	0	15-1	56	1.36	277	.232	.263	11	.182	0		18		1.9
1990	Chi N	9	5	.643	55	6	1-1	6-4	109	121	57	11	4	40-8	65	4.62	88	.283	.342	20-0-1	.050	-1	85	-4		-0.5
1991	Chi N	9	7	.563	64	11	1	3-3	156	150	68	13	4	49-7	102	3.52	111	.256	.315	28-0-6	.179	0	113	6		0.6
1992	Det A	3	4	.429	41	1	0	0-3	86.2	101	66	11	3	51-12	35	6.33	63	.294	.386	0	—	-0	0	-22		-1.6
1993	StL N	4	1	.800	50	0	0	0-0	61.1	56	24	5	1	21-5	36	2.93	137	.242	.307	4	.000	-0		7	58	0.5
Total	7	41	28	.594	323	39	3-1	22-16	703.2	715	345	60	11	261-45	408	4.05	98	.265	.329	132-0-11	.098	-4	105	-4	94	-0.3

LANCE, GARY Gary Dean B9.21.1948 Greenville SC BB/TR/6-3/202 d9.28 Col South Carolina-Aiken

YEAR	TM LG	W	L	PCT	G	GS	CG-SHO	SV-BS	IP	H	R	HR	HB	BB-IB	SO	ERA	AERA	OAV	OOB	AB-HR-SH	AVG	PB	SUP	APR	DL	PW
1977	KC A	0	1	.000	1	0	0	0	2	2	1	0	2	2-0	1	4.50	90	.286	.444	0	—	0	0	0		0.0

LANDIS, DOC Samuel H. B8.16.1854 Philadelphia PA BR/5-11/172 d5.2

YEAR	TM LG	W	L	PCT	G	GS	CG-SHO	SV-BS	IP	H	R	HR	HB	BB-IB	SO	ERA	AERA	OAV	OOB	AB-HR-SH	AVG	PB	SUP	APR	DL	PW
1882	Phi AA	1	1	.500	2	2	2	0	17	16	12	1		1	13	3.18	88	.232	.243	12	.167	-0*	101	-1		-0.1
	Bal AA	11	28	.282	42	40	35	0	343	416	257	7		46	62	3.38	81	.281	.302	175	.166	-6*	79	-29		-3.1
	Year	12	29	.293	44	42	37	0	360	432	269	8		47	75	3.38	82	.278	.300	187	.166	-7	80	-26		-3.2

LANDIS, BILL William Henry B10.8.1942 Hanford CA BL/TL/6-2/178* d9.28 Mil 1968 Col West Hills (CA) JC

YEAR	TM LG	W	L	PCT	G	GS	CG-SHO	SV-BS	IP	H	R	HR	HB	BB-IB	SO	ERA	AERA	OAV	OOB	AB-HR-SH	AVG	PB	SUP	APR	DL	PW
1963	KC A	0	0	—	1	0	0	0	1.2	0	0	0	0	1-0	3	0.00	—	.000	.167	0	—	0		1		0.0
1967	Bos A	1	0	1.000	18	1	0	0	25.2	24	16	6	0	11-3	23	5.26	66	.253	.330	2	.000	-0*	125	-4		-0.3
1968	Bos A	3	3	.500	38	1	0	3	60	48	22	4	2	30-2	59	3.15	100	.223	.320	6	.000	-1	55	1		0.0
1969	Bos A	5	5	.500	45	5	0	1-1	82.1	82	53	7	3	49-3	50	5.25	73	.269	.370	11	.000	-0*	51	-11		-1.3
Total	4	9	8	.529	102	7	0	4-1	169.2	154	91	17	5	91-8	135	4.46	79	.248	.345	19	.000	-1	64	-13		-1.6

LANDRETH, LARRY Larry Robert B3.11.1955 Stratford ON, Can. BR/TR/6-1/175* d9.16

YEAR	TM LG	W	L	PCT	G	GS	CG-SHO	SV-BS	IP	H	R	HR	HB	BB-IB	SO	ERA	AERA	OAV	OOB	AB-HR-SH	AVG	PB	SUP	APR	DL	PW
1976	Mon N	1	2	.333	3	3	0	0-0	11	13	8	1	0	10-0	7	4.09	92	.310	.434	3	.000	-0	70	-1		-0.3
1977	Mon N	0	2	.000	4	1	0	0-0	9.1	16	11	0	0	8-1	5	9.64	40	.381	.471	2	.000	-0	69	-6		-1.0
Total	2	1	4	.200	7	4	0	0-0	20.1	29	19	1	0	18-1	12	6.64	57	.345	.452	5	.000	-1	70	-7		-1.3

LANDRUM, JOE Joseph Butler B12.13.1928 Columbia SC BR/TR/5-11/180* d7.13 s-Bill Col Clemson

YEAR	TM LG	W	L	PCT	G	GS	CG-SHO	SV-BS	IP	H	R	HR	HB	BB-IB	SO	ERA	AERA	OAV	OOB	AB-HR-SH	AVG	PB	SUP	APR	DL	PW
1950	Bro N	0	0	—	7	0	0	1	6.2	12	8	2	1	1	5	8.10	51	.414	.452	0-0-1	—	0		-4		-0.2
1952	Bro N	1	3	.250	9	5	2	0	38	46	24	3	1	10	17	5.21	70	.301	.348	8-0-3	.125	-0	113	-7		-0.7
Total	2	1	3	.250	16	5	2	1	44.2	58	32	5	2	11	22	5.64	66	.319	.364	8-0-4	.125	-0	113	-11		-0.9

LANDRUM, BILL Thomas William B8.17.1957 Columbia SC BR/TR/6-2/200(185-205) d8.31 f-Joe Col South Carolina-Aiken

YEAR	TM LG	W	L	PCT	G	GS	CG-SHO	SV-BS	IP	H	R	HR	HB	BB-IB	SO	ERA	AERA	OAV	OOB	AB-HR-SH	AVG	PB	SUP	APR	DL	PW
1986	Cin N	0	0	—	10	0	0	0-0	13.1	23	11	0	0	4-0	14	6.75	57	.390	.422	2	.000	-0		-4		-0.2
1987	Cin N	3	2	.600	44	2	0	2-1	65	68	35	3	0	34-6	42	4.71	90	.292	.379	5-0-1	.200	-0	128	-2		-0.1
1988	Chi N	1	0	1.000	7	0	0	0-0	12.1	19	8	1	0	3-0	6	5.84	62	.365	.400	2	.000	-0		-3		-0.2
1989	Pit N	2	3	.400	56	0	0	26-3	81	60	18	2	0	28-8	51	1.67	204	.205	.273	3	.000	-0		16		1.9
1990	†Pit N	7	3	.700	54	0	0	13-3	71.2	69	22	4	0	21-5	39	2.13	171	.262	.314	9	.111	-0		11		1.9
1991	†Pit N	4	4	.500	61	0	0	17-5	76.1	76	32	4	0	19-5	45	3.18	113	.252	.296	4-0-1	.000	-0		3		0.3
1992	Mon N	1	1	.500	18	0	0	0-0	20	27	16	3	2	9-2	7	7.20	48	.325	.404	0	—	-0	-8	-1	61	-0.7
1993	Cin N	0	2	.000	18	0	0	0-0	21.2	18	9	1	0	6-1	14	3.74	108	.231	.286	0-0-1	—	0	1	122	0.1
Total	8	18	15	.545	268	2	0	58-12	361.1	360	151	18	2	124-27	218	3.39	109	.265	.325	25-0-3	.080	-1	128	14	183	3.0

LANE, JERRY Gerald Hal B2.7.1926 Ashland NY D7.24.1988 Chattanooga TN BR/TR/6-0.5/205(185-205) d7.7 Col Ithaca

YEAR	TM LG	W	L	PCT	G	GS	CG-SHO	SV-BS	IP	H	R	HR	HB	BB-IB	SO	ERA	AERA	OAV	OOB	AB-HR-SH	AVG	PB	SUP	APR	DL	PW
1953	Was A	1	4	.200	20	2	0	0	56.2	64	33	3	1	16	26	4.92	79	.288	.339	9-0-1	.111	-0	46	-6		-0.4
1954	Cin N	1	0	1.000	3	0	0	0	10.2	9	2	0	0	3	2	1.69	248	.237	.293	4	.000	-0		3		0.2
1955	Cin N	0	2	.000	8	0	0	1	11	11	6	2	0	6-2	5	4.91	86	.289	.386	0	—	0		0		-0.1
Total	3	2	6	.250	31	2	0	1	78.1	84	41	5	1	25-2	33	4.48	89	.282	.340	13-0-1	.077	-0	46	-3		-0.3

LANFORD, SAM Lewis Grover B1.8.1886 Woodruff SC D9.14.1970 Woodruff SC BR/TR/5-7/155 d8.19

YEAR	TM LG	W	L	PCT	G	GS	CG-SHO	SV-BS	IP	H	R	HR	HB	BB-IB	SO	ERA	AERA	OAV	OOB	AB-HR-SH	AVG	PB	SUP	APR	DL	PW
1907	Was A	0	1	.000	2	1	0	0	7	10	10	0	3	5	2	5.14	47	.333	.474	3	.333	0	56	-4		-0.4

LANFRANCONI, WALT Walter Oswald B11.9.1916 Barre VT D8.18.1986 Barre VT BR/TR/5-7.5/155 d9.12 Mil 1942-45

YEAR	TM LG	W	L	PCT	G	GS	CG-SHO	SV-BS	IP	H	R	HR	HB	BB-IB	SO	ERA	AERA	OAV	OOB	AB-HR-SH	AVG	PB	SUP	APR	DL	PW
1941	Chi N	0	1	.000	2	1	0	0	6	7	3	0	0	2	1	3.00	117	.280	.333	1	.000	-0	0			0.0
1947	Bos N	4	4	.500	36	4	1	1	64	65	23	2	0	27	18	2.95	132	.272	.346	10-0-1	.000	-1*	57	7		0.8
Total	2	4	5	.444	38	5	1	1	70	72	26	2	0	29	19	2.96	131	.273	.345	11-0-1	.000	-1	46	7		0.8

LANG, MARTY Martin John B9.27.1905 Hooper NE D1.13.1968 Lakewood CO BR/TL/5-11/160 d7.4 Col Concordia (TX)

YEAR	TM LG	W	L	PCT	G	GS	CG-SHO	SV-BS	IP	H	R	HR	HB	BB-IB	SO	ERA	AERA	OAV	OOB	AB-HR-SH	AVG	PB	SUP	APR	DL	PW
1930	Pit N	0	0	—	2	0	0	0	1.2	9	10	0	0	2	3	54.00	9	.692	.750	0	—	0		-8		-0.3

LANG, CHIP Robert David B8.21.1952 Pittsburgh PA BR/TR/6-4/195* [MonN70 2/27] d9.8

YEAR	TM LG	W	L	PCT	G	GS	CG-SHO	SV-BS	IP	H	R	HR	HB	BB-IB	SO	ERA	AERA	OAV	OOB	AB-HR-SH	AVG	PB	SUP	APR	DL	PW
1975	Mon N	0	0	—	1	1	0	0-0	1.2	1	2	0	0	3-0	2	10.80	36	.333	.556	0	—	0	136	-1		-0.1
1976	Mon N	1	3	.250	29	2	0	0-0	62.1	56	32	3	3	34-2	30	4.19	90	.242	.346	6-0-2	.167	-0	35	-2		-0.1
Total	2	1	3	.250	30	3	0	0-0	64	58	34	3	3	37-2	32	4.36	86	.245	.353	6-0-2	.167	-0	70	-3		-0.2

LANGE, ERV Erwin Henry B8.12.1887 Forest Park IL D4.24.1971 Maywood IL BR/TR/5-10/170 d4.19

YEAR	TM LG	W	L	PCT	G	GS	CG-SHO	SV-BS	IP	H	R	HR	HB	BB-IB	SO	ERA	AERA	OAV	OOB	AB-HR-SH	AVG	PB	SUP	APR	DL	PW
1914	Chi F	12	11	.522	36	22	10-2	2	190	162	69	3	3	55	87	2.23	119	.224	.282	51-0-1	.176	2	107	7		0.9

LANGE, FRANK Frank Herman "Seagan" B10.28.1883 Columbus WI D12.26.1945 Madison WI BR/TR/5-11/180 d5.16

YEAR	TM LG	W	L	PCT	G	GS	CG-SHO	SV-BS	IP	H	R	HR	HB	BB-IB	SO	ERA	AERA	OAV	OOB	AB-HR-SH	AVG	PB	SUP	APR	DL	PW
1910	Chi A	9	4	.692	32	15	6-1	0	130.2	93	48	2	9	54	98	1.65	145	.204	.301	51	.255	3	121	7		1.0
1911	Chi A	8	8	.500	29	22	8-1	0	161.2	151	77	3	3	77	104	3.23	100	.251	.339	76-0-2	.289	8*	105	1		0.9
1912	Chi A	10	10	.500	31	20	11-2	3	165.1	165	85	4	4	68	96	3.27	98	.270	.347	65-0-3	.215	2*	112	-2		-0.1
1913	Chi A	1	3	.250	12	3	0	0	40.2	46	24	0	1	20	20	4.87	60	.299	.383	18-0-1	.167	1*	76	-6		-0.4
Total	4	28	25	.528	95	60	25-4	3	498.1	455	234	9	17	219	318	2.96	100	.250	.336	210-0-6	.248	14	110	0		1.4

LANGE, DICK Richard Otto B9.1.1948 Harbor Beach MI BR/TR/5-10/185* [AnaA70 7/158] d9.9 Col Central Michigan

YEAR	TM LG	W	L	PCT	G	GS	CG-SHO	SV-BS	IP	H	R	HR	HB	BB-IB	SO	ERA	AERA	OAV	OOB	AB-HR-SH	AVG	PB	SUP	APR	DL	PW
1972	Cal A	0	0	—	2	1	0	0-0	7.2	7	4	0	0	2-0	8	4.70	63	.233	.281	3	.000	-0	60	-1		-0.1
1973	Cal A	2	1	.667	17	4	1	0-1	52.2	61	30	9	1	21-2	27	4.44	81	.292	.356	0	—	0	119	-6		-0.3
1974	Cal A	3	8	.273	21	18	1	0-0	113.2	111	63	10	4	47-0	57	3.80	91	.248	.323	0	—	0*	97	-7		-0.7
1975	Cal A	4	6	.400	30	8	1	1-0	102	119	70	12	1	53-3	45	5.21	69	.292	.371	0	—	0	86	-20		-1.8
Total	4	9	15	.375	70	31	3	1-1	276	298	167	31	6	123-5	137	4.47	79	.272	.346	3	.000	-0	96	-34		-2.9

LANGFORD, RICK James Rick B3.20.1952 Farmville VA BR/TR/6-0/180* d6.13 C1 Col Florida St.

YEAR	TM LG	W	L	PCT	G	GS	CG-SHO	SV-BS	IP	H	R	HR	HB	BB-IB	SO	ERA	AERA	OAV	OOB	AB-HR-SH	AVG	PB	SUP	APR	DL	PW
1976	Pit N	0	1	.000	12	1	0	0-1	23	27	17	2	0	14-0	17	6.26	56	.307	.398	5	.200	0	75	-6		-0.3
1977	Oak A	8	19	.296	37	31	6-1	0-1	208.1	223	107	18	2	73-3	141	4.02	100	.273	.332	0	—	0*	76	1		0.1
1978	Oak A	7	13	.350	37	24	4-2	0-1	175.2	169	77	15	3	56-8	92	3.43	107	.253	.311	0	—	0*	61	6		0.7
1979	Oak A	12	16	.429	34	29	14-1	0-1	218.2	233	114	22	4	57-6	101	4.28	95	.273	.319	0	—	0	81	-4		-0.3
1980	Oak A	19	12	.613	35	33	28-2	0-0	290	276	119	29	1	64-6	102	3.26	117	.255	.294	0	—	0	105	18		1.9
1981	†Oak A	12	10	.545	24	24	18-2	0-0	195.1	190	81	14	3	58-2	84	2.99	118	.255	.308	0	—	0	102	8		0.7
1982	Oak A	11	16	.407	32	31	15-2	0-0	237.1	265	121	33	2	49-1	79	4.21	94	.281	.316	1	.000	-0*	98	-6		-0.6
1983	Oak A	0	4	.000	7	7	0	0-0	43	28	4	2	1	10-1	2	12.15	32	.448	.495	0	—	-0	113	-18	149	-2.7
1984	Oak A	0	0	—	3	2	0	0-0	8.2	15	8	2	0	2-0	2	8.31	46	.366	.395	0	—	-0	108	-4	152	-0.2
1985	Oak A	3	5	.375	23	3	0	0-0	59	60	24	8	0	15-2	21	3.51	111	.261	.306	0	—	0	63	5	65	0.4
1986	Oak A	1	10	.091	16	11	0	0-0	55	69	49	13	1	18-0	30	7.36	53	.300	.351	0	—	0*	51	-22	15	-3.6
Total	11	73	106	.408	260	196	85-10	0-3	1491	1570	745	160	18	416-29	671	4.01	96	.271	.319	6	.167	0	87	-24	381	-3.9

LANGSTON, MARK Mark Edward B8.20.1960 San Diego CA BR/TL/6-2/190(177-190) [SeaA81 2/35] d4.7 Col San Jose St.

YEAR	TM LG	W	L	PCT	G	GS	CG-SHO	SV-BS	IP	H	R	HR	HB	BB-IB	SO	ERA	AERA	OAV	OOB	AB-HR-SH	AVG	PB	SUP	APR	DL	PW
1984	Sea A	17	10	.630	35	33	5-2	0-1	225	188	99	16	8	118-5	204	3.40	118	.230	.330	0	—	0	86	14		1.6
1985	Sea A	7	14	.333	24	24	2-0	0-0	126.2	122	85	22	2	91-2	72	5.47	77	.255	.375	0	—	0	85	-17	45	-2.3

YEAR	TM LG	W	L	PCT	G	GS	CG-SHO	SV-BS	IP	H	R	HR	HB	BB-IB	SO	ERA	AERA	OAV	OOB	AB-HR-SH	AVG	PB	SUP	APR	DL	P
1986	Sea A	12	14	.462	37	36	9	0-0	239.1	234	142	30	4	123-1	245	4.85	88	.255	.343	0	—	0	89	-14		-1
1987	Sea A★	19	13	.594	35	35	14-3	0-0	272	242	132	30	5	114-0	262	3.84	124	.238	.317	0	—	0	88	25		2
1988	Sea A	15	11	.577	35	35	9-3	0-0	261.1	222	108	32	3	110-2	235	3.34	125	.233	.313	0	—	0	91	24		2
1989	Sea A	4	5	.444	10	10	2-1	0-0	73.1	60	30	3	4	19-0	60	3.56	113	.221	.279	0	—	0	87	5		0
	Mon N	12	9	.571	24	24	6-4	0-0	176.2	138	57	13	0	93-6	175	2.39	**149**	.218	.316	64-0-1	.172	-0	89	20		2
1990	Cal A	10	17	.370	33	33	5-1	0-0	223	215	120	13	5	104-1	195	4.40	87	.259	.343	0	—	0	93	-12		-1
1991	Cal A☆	19	8	.704	34	34	7	0-0	246.1	190	89	30	2	96-3	183	3.00	138	.215	.291	0	—	0	95	31		3
1992	Cal A★	13	14	.481	32	32	9-2	0-0	229	206	103	14	6	74-2	174	3.66	110	.242	.305	2	.000	-0*	80	8		1
1993	Cal A★	16	11	.593	35	35	7	0-0	256.1	220	100	22	1	85-2	196	3.20	142	.234	.295	0	—	0	72	37		1
1994	Cal A	7	8	.467	18	18	2-1	0-0	119.1	121	67	19	0	54-1	109	4.68	105	.268	.340	0	—	0	81	3	31	-0
1995	Cal A	15	7	.682	31	31	4-1	0-0	200.1	212	109	21	3	64-1	142	4.63	102	.272	.329	0	—	0	126	3		0
1996	Cal A	6	5	.545	18	18	2	0-0	123.1	116	68	18	2	45-0	83	4.82	105	.247	.315	0	—	0	96	6	92	0
1997	Ana A	2	4	.333	9	9	0	0-0	47.2	61	34	7	0	29-1	30	5.85	79	.316	.402	0	—	0	102	-7	128	-0
1998	†SD N	4	6	.400	22	16	0	0-1	81.1	107	55	11	1	41-1	56	5.86	68	.325	.397	24-0-4	.083	-0*	130	-17	54	-1
1999	Cle A	1	2	.333	25	5	0	0-1	61.2	69	40	9	0	29-6	43	5.25	97	.287	.362	2	.500	0	66	-2	46	0
Total	16	179	158	.531	457	428	81-18	0-3	2962.2	2723	1438	311	46	1289-34	2464	3.97	108	.246	.325	92-0-5	.152	-0	91	107	396	11

LANIER, MAX Hubert Max B8.18.1915 Denton NC BR/TL/5-10/187* d4.20 Mil 1945 s-Hal

YEAR	TM LG	W	L	PCT	G	GS	CG-SHO	SV-BS	IP	H	R	HR	HB	BB-IB	SO	ERA	AERA	OAV	OOB	AB-HR-SH	AVG	PB	SUP	APR	DL	P
1938	StL N	0	3	.000	18	3	1	0	45	57	30	1	2	28	14	4.20	94	.317	.414	10	.100	-0	93	-3		0
1939	StL N	2	1	.667	7	6	2	0	37.2	29	11	0	1	13	14	2.39	172	.220	.295	14-0-1	.286	1	110	7		0
1940	StL N	9	6	.600	35	11	4-2	3	105	113	50	1	1	38	49	3.34	119	.276	.339	30-0-1	.200	-0	91	6		0
1941	StL N	10	8	.556	35	18	8-2	3	153	126	59	4	1	59	93	2.82	133	.225	.300	52-0-2	.192	-1	115	14		1
1942	†StL N	13	8	.619	34	20	8-2	2	161	137	55	4	2	60	93	2.96	116	.234	.308	47-0-4	.255	2	98	11		1
1943	†StL N☆	15	7	.682	32	25	14-2	3	213.1	195	62	3	2	75	123	1.90	**177**	.246	.312	73-0-11	.164	-2	112	31		3
1944	†StL N∗	17	12	.586	33	30	16-5	0	224.1	192	82	5	3	71	141	2.65	133	.234	.297	77-0-6	.182	-0	105	20		3
1945	StL N	2	2	.500	4	3	3	0	26	22	10	0	0	8	16	1.73	216	.222	.280	11	.182	-0	83	4		0
1946	StL N	6	0	1.000	6	6	6-2	0	56	45	13	1	1	19	36	1.93	179	.228	.300	25	.200	-0	153	10		1
1949	StL N	5	4	.556	15	15	4-1	0	92	92	42	5	0	35	37	3.82	109	.261	.328	27-0-4	.074	-2	95	5		0
1950	StL N	11	9	.550	27	27	10-2	0	181.1	173	70	13	1	68	69	3.13	137	.249	.317	68-0-4	.162	-1	99	23		2
1951	StL N	11	9	.550	31	23	9-2	1	160	149	60	14	1	50	59	3.26	122	.248	.306	53-0-3	.151	-2	66	14		0
1952	NY N	7	12	.368	37	16	6-1	5	137	124	64	11	3	65	47	3.94	94	.244	.333	41-0-5	.268	3*	71	-1		0
1953	NY N	0	0	—	3	0	0	0	5.1	8	4	1	0	3	2	6.75	64	.381	.458	1	.000	-0		-1		-0
	StL A	0	1	.000	10	1	0	0	22.1	28	18	2	0	19	19	7.25	58	.322	.443	6	.167	-0	42	-6		-0
Total	14	108	82	.568	327	204	91-21	17	1619.1	1490	630	65	18	611	821	3.01	125	.247	.318	535-0-41	.185	-3	97	134		15

LANKFORD, FRANK Frank Greenfield B3.26.1971 Atlanta GA BR/TR/6-2/190 [NYA93 17/477] d3.31 Col Virginia

YEAR	TM LG	W	L	PCT	G	GS	CG-SHO	SV-BS	IP	H	R	HR	HB	BB-IB	SO	ERA	AERA	OAV	OOB	AB-HR-SH	AVG	PB	SUP	APR	DL	P
1998	LA N	0	2	.000	12	0	0	1-0	19.2	13	7	3	1	2-0	7	5.95	68	.287	.360	2	.000	-0		-4		0

LANNING, JOHNNY John Young "Tobacco Chewin' Johnny" B9.6.1910 Asheville NC D11.8.1989 Asheville NC BR/TR/6-1/185 d4.17 Mil 1943-45 b-Tom Col North Carolina St.

YEAR	TM LG	W	L	PCT	G	GS	CG-SHO	SV-BS	IP	H	R	HR	HB	BB-IB	SO	ERA	AERA	OAV	OOB	AB-HR-SH	AVG	PB	SUP	APR	DL	P
1936	Bos N	7	11	.389	28	20	3-1	0	153	154	75	9	0	55	33	3.65	105	.263	.326	52-1-2	.135	-2	81	2		-0
1937	Bos N	5	7	.417	32	11	4-1	2	116.2	107	59	10	1	40	37	3.93	91	.236	.300	33-0-2	.121	-1	57	-5		-0
1938	Bos N	8	7	.533	32	18	4-1	0	138	146	74	5	1	52	39	3.72	92	.267	.332	48-0-2	.188	-1	103	-8		-0
1939	Bos N	5	6	.455	37	6	3	4	129	120	53	6	2	53	45	3.42	108	.252	.329	42-0-2	.143	-1	43	6		-0
1940	Pit N	8	4	.667	38	7	2	2	115.2	119	59	8	0	39	42	4.05	94	.268	.327	35-0-3	.200	-1	150	-2		-0
1941	Pit N	11	11	.500	34	23	9	1	175.2	175	72	6	0	47	41	3.13	116	.256	.304	56-0-6	.107	-2	88	10		-0
1942	Pit N	6	8	.429	34	8	2-1	1	119.1	125	52	7	1	26	31	3.32	102	.274	.314	29-0-2	.138	-0	59	1		-0
1943	Pit N	4	1	.800	12	2	0	2	27	23	10	0	0	9	11	2.33	149	.223	.286	6	.167	-0	61	3		0
1945	Pit N	0	0	—	1	0	0	0	2	8	8	1	0	0	0	36.00	11	.571	.571	0	—	0		-6		0
1946	Pit N	4	5	.444	27	9	3	1	91	97	36	3	1	31	16	3.07	115	.269	.329	21-0-3	.143	-0	70	5		0
1947	Bos N	0	0	—	3	0	0	0	3.2	4	5	0	0	6	0	9.82	40	.400	.625	0	—	0		-3		0
Total	11	58	60	.492	278	104	30-4	13	1071	1078	503	55	6	358	295	3.58	101	.261	.321	322-1-22	.146	-7	83	3		-0

LANNING, RED Lester Alfred B5.13.1895 Harvard IL D6.13.1962 Bristol CT BL/TL/5-9/165 d6.20 Col Wesleyan ▲

YEAR	TM LG	W	L	PCT	G	GS	CG-SHO	SV-BS	IP	H	R	HR	HB	BB-IB	SO	ERA	AERA	OAV	OOB	AB-HR-SH	AVG	PB	SUP	APR	DL	P
1916	Phi A	0	3	.000	6	3	1	0	24.1	38	27	1	2	17	9	8.14	35	.362	.460	33-0-1	.182	1*	53	-13		

LANNING, TOM Thomas Newton B4.22.1907 Asheville NC D11.4.1967 Marietta GA BL/TL/6-1/165 d9.14 b-Johnny Col Wake Forest

YEAR	TM LG	W	L	PCT	G	GS	CG-SHO	SV-BS	IP	H	R	HR	HB	BB-IB	SO	ERA	AERA	OAV	OOB	AB-HR-SH	AVG	PB	SUP	APR	DL	P
1938	Phi N	0	1	.000	9	1	0	0	7	9	7	0	2	6	2	6.43	60	.300	.344	1	1.000	0	22	-2		

LANSING, GENE Eugene Hewitt "Jigger" B1.11.1898 Albany NY D1.18.1945 Rensselaer NY BR/TR/6-1/185 d4.27

YEAR	TM LG	W	L	PCT	G	GS	CG-SHO	SV-BS	IP	H	R	HR	HB	BB-IB	SO	ERA	AERA	OAV	OOB	AB-HR-SH	AVG	PB	SUP	APR	DL	P
1922	Bos N	1	1	.000	15	1	0	0	40.2	46	28	1	0	22	14	5.98	67	.301	.389	11	.000	-1	61	-7		-0

LaPALME, PAUL Paul Edmore "Lefty" B12.14.1923 Springfield MA BL/TL/5-10/184* d5.28

YEAR	TM LG	W	L	PCT	G	GS	CG-SHO	SV-BS	IP	H	R	HR	HB	BB-IB	SO	ERA	AERA	OAV	OOB	AB-HR-SH	AVG	PB	SUP	APR	DL	P
1951	Pit N	1	5	.167	22	8	1-1	0	54.1	79	48	6	1	31	24	6.29	67	.333	.413	10	.100	-0	104	-13		-1
1952	Pit N	1	2	.333	31	2	0	0	59.2	56	33	6	1	37	25	3.92	102	.253	.363	10-0-1	.100	-0	123	-1		-1
1953	Pit N	8	16	.333	35	24	7-1	2	176.1	191	107	20	0	64	86	4.59	97	.272	.333	59-0-3	.085	-5	76	-5		-0
1954	Pit N	4	10	.286	33	15	2	0	120.2	147	79	15	0	54	57	5.52	76	.302	.368	35-0-3	.143	-0	97	-15		-0
1955	StL N	4	3	.571	56	0	0	3	91.2	76	36	10	1	34-9	39	2.75	148	.228	.297	19	.211	-0		11		-0
1956	StL N	0	0	—	1	0	0	0	0.2	4	6	1	0	2-0	0	81.00	5	.667	.750	0	—	0		-5		-0
	Cin N	2	4	.333	11	2	0	0	27	26	14	7	0	4-0	4	4.67	85	.257	.283	4-0-2	.500	1	100	-1		-0
	Year	2	4	.333	12	2	0	0	27.2	30	20	7	0	6-0	4	6.51	61	.280	.316	4-0-2	.500	1	100	-6		
	Chi A	3	1	.750	29	0	0	2	45.2	31	14	2	0	27-2	23	2.36	173	.195	.310	6-0-1	.000	1		9		-0
1957	Chi A	1	4	.200	35	0	0	0	40.1	35	16	5	1	19-1	16	3.35	112	.235	.325	4-0-1	.500	1*		2		
Total	7	24	45	.348	253	51	10-2	14	616.1	645	353	71	4	272-12	277	4.42	95	.269	.343	147-0-11	.136	-4	92	-18		-2

LAPIHUSKA, ANDY Andrew "Apples" B11.1.1922 Delmont NJ D2.17.1996 Millville NJ BL/TR/5-10.5/175 d9.12 Mil 1944-45

YEAR	TM LG	W	L	PCT	G	GS	CG-SHO	SV-BS	IP	H	R	HR	HB	BB-IB	SO	ERA	AERA	OAV	OOB	AB-HR-SH	AVG	PB	SUP	APR	DL	P
1942	Phi N	0	2	.000	3	2	0	0	20.2	17	13	0	2	13	8	5.23	63	.221	.348	7	.286	-0	13	-4		-0
1943	Phi N	0	0	—	1	0	0	0	2.1	5	6	1	0	3	0	23.14	15	.417	.533	2	.000	-0		-5		-0
Total	2	0	2	.000	4	2	0	0	23	22	19	1	2	16	8	7.04	47	.247	.374	9	.222	0	13	-9		-0

LaPOINT, DAVE David Jeffrey B7.29.1959 Glens Falls NY BL/TL/6-3/215(205-231) [MilA77 10/237] d9.10

YEAR	TM LG	W	L	PCT	G	GS	CG-SHO	SV-BS	IP	H	R	HR	HB	BB-IB	SO	ERA	AERA	OAV	OOB	AB-HR-SH	AVG	PB	SUP	APR	DL	P
1980	Mil A	1	0	1.000	5	3	0	1-0	15	17	14	2	0	13-1	5	6.00	65	.293	.411	0	—	0	213	-5		-1
1981	StL N	1	0	1.000	3	2	0	0	10.2	12	5	1	1	2-0	4	4.22	86	.293	.341	5	.000	-1	172	0		-1
1982	†StL N	9	3	.750	42	21	0	0-0	152.2	170	63	8	3	52-8	81	3.42	108	.290	.348	38-0-8	.053	-3	114	5		-0
1983	StL N	12	9	.571	37	29	1	0-0	191.1	191	92	12	4	84-7	113	3.95	93	.267	.342	59-0-5	.153	-1	110	-4		-0
1984	StL N	12	10	.545	33	33	2-1	0-0	193	205	94	9	1	77-8	130	3.96	88	.278	.346	59-0-9	.068	-3	99	-10	15	-0
1985	SF N	7	17	.292	31	31	2-1	0-0	206.2	215	99	18	0	74-6	122	3.57	97	.269	.329	60-0-5	.167	2	78	-4		-0
1986	Det A	3	6	.333	16	8	0	0-1	67.2	85	49	11	0	32-3	36	5.72	73	.307	.367	0	—	0	101	-12		
	SD N	1	4	.200	24	4	0	0	61.1	67	37	8	1	24-4	41	4.26	86	.276	.342	8-0-4	.000	-1	91	-6		
1987	StL N	1	1	.500	6	2	0	0	16	26	12	4	0	5-0	8	6.75	42	.351	.392	4	.000	-0	129	-4		
	Chi A	6	3	.667	14	12	2-1	0-0	82.2	69	29	7	1	31-0	43	2.94	157	.224	.297	0	—	0	105	15		
1988	Chi A	10	11	.476	25	25	1-1	0-0	161.1	151	69	10	2	47-1	79	3.40	118	.245	.299	0	—	0	88	11		
	Pit N	4	2	.667	8	8	1	0	52	54	18	4	0	10-2	19	2.77	125	.271	.305	16-0-1	.063	-1	103	4		
1989	NY A	6	9	.400	20	20	0	0-0	113.2	146	73	12	2	45-4	51	5.62	69	.310	.370	0	—	0	100	-19	77	
1990	NY A	7	10	.412	28	27	2	0-0	157.2	180	84	11	1	57-3	67	4.11	97	.292	.347	0	—	0	88	-4		
1991	Phi N	1	0	1.000	2	2	0	0	5	10	10	1	1	6-0	3	16.20	23	.435	.548	2	.000	-0	158	-7		
Total	12	80	86	.482	294	227	11-4	1-1	1486.2	1598	748	117	17	559-47	802	4.02	94	.277	.340	251-0-32	.104	-6	100	-40	92	-5

LARA, YOVANNY Yovanny B. B9.20.1975 San Cristobal, D.R. BR/TR/6-4/180 d6.28

YEAR	TM LG	W	L	PCT	G	GS	CG-SHO	SV-BS	IP	H	R	HR	HB	BB-IB	SO	ERA	AERA	OAV	OOB	AB-HR-SH	AVG	PB	SUP	APR	DL	P
2000	Mon N	0	0	—	6	0	0	0-0	5.2	5	4	0	0	8-0	3	6.35	74	.250	.448	0	—	0		-1	78	

LARKIN, ANDY Andrew Dane B6.27.1974 Chelan WA BR/TR/6-4/180(175-190) [FlaN92 25/712] d9.29

YEAR	TM LG	W	L	PCT	G	GS	CG-SHO	SV-BS	IP	H	R	HR	HB	BB-IB	SO	ERA	AERA	OAV	OOB	AB-HR-SH	AVG	PB	SUP	APR	DL	P
1996	Fla N	0	0	—	1	1	0	0	5	3	1	0	1	4-0	2	1.80	229	.176	.364		.000	-0	87	1	67	
1998	Fla N	3	8	.273	17	14	0	0-0	74.2	101	87	12	4	55-3	43	9.64	42	.329	.435	29-0-2	.138	-1	120	-48		
2000	Cin N	0	0	—	3	0	0	0	6.2	6	4	1	0	5-0	7	5.40	88	.240	.367	1	.000	0		0		
	KC A	0	3	.000	18	0	0	1-2	19.1	29	20	5	0	11-2	17	8.84	59	.349	.421	0	—	0		-7		
Total	3	3	11	.214	39	15	0	1-2	105.2	139	112	18	5	75-5	69	8.86	49	.322	.425	32-0-2	.125	-1	111	-54	67	

YEAR	TM LG	W	L	PCT	G	GS	CG-SHO	SV-BS	IP	H	R	HR	HB	BB-IB	SO	ERA	AERA	OAV	OOB	AB-HR-SH	AVG	PB	SUP	APR	DL	PW

LARKIN, TERRY Frank S. D9.16.1894 Brooklyn NY BR/TR d5.20 ▲

876	NY N	0	1	.000	1	1	0		9	9	7	0		0	0	3.00	71	.231	.231	4	.000	-1	72	-1		-0.1
877	Har N	29	25	.537	56	56	55-4	0	501	510	285	2		53	96	2.14	114	.245	.264	228-1	.228	6*	111	14		1.6
878	Chi N	29	26	.527	56	56	56-1	0	506	511	288	6		31	163	2.24	108	.246	.257	226	.288	13*	107	10		1.9
879	Chi N	31	23	.574	58	58	57-4	0	513.1	514	277	9		30	142	2.44	105	.240	.250	228	.219	1*	96	8		0.5
880	Tro N	0	5	.000	5	5	3	0	38	83	65	1		10	5	8.76	29	.421	.449	20	.150	-0*	90	-23		-2.1
otal	5	89	80	.527	176	176	172-9	0	1567.1	1627	922	12		124	406	2.43	102	.249	.263	706-1	.241	19	103	8		1.8

LARKIN, PAT Patrick Clibborn B6.14.1960 Arcadia CA BL/TL/6-0/180 d7.16 Col Santa Clara

| 983 | SF N | 0 | 0 | — | 5 | 0 | 0 | 0-0 | 10.1 | 13 | 6 | 1 | 2 | 3-1 | 6 | 4.35 | 81 | .317 | .383 | 1 | .000 | -0 | | -1 | | -0.1 |

LARKIN, STEVE Stephen Patrick B12.9.1910 Cincinnati OH D5.2.1969 Norristown PA BR/TR/6-1/195 d5.6

| 934 | Det N | 0 | 2 | — | 1 | | 2 | | 6 | 8 | 7 | 0 | | 5 | | 1.50 | 293 | .296 | .406 | 3 | .333 | 1 | 79 | -1 | | 0.1 |

LAROCHE, DAVE David Eugene B5.14.1948 Colorado Springs CO BL/TL/6-2/200(185-200) [AnaA67*S5/86] d5.11 C5 s-Adam Col Nevada-Las Vegas

970	Cal A	4	1	.800	38	0	0	4-2	49.2	41	20	6	4	21-6	44	3.44	105	.224	.316	8	.250	1		2		0.3
971	Cal A	5	1	.833	56	0	0	9-3	72	55	21	3	1	27-10	63	2.50	130	.212	.285	11-0-1	.091	-0		7		0.7
972	Min A	5	7	.417	62	0	0	10-3	95.1	72	33	9	6	39-6	79	2.83	113	.209	.300	11-0-1	.091	0		5		0.8
973	Chi N	4	1	.800	45	0	0	4-1	54.1	55	37	7	1	29-3	34	5.80	68	.274	.362	4	.500	1		-9	12	-0.8
974	Chi N	5	6	.455	49	4	0	5-6	92	103	54	9	3	47-7	49	4.79	80	.286	.371	27	.333	3*	80	-8		-0.7
975	Cle A	5	3	.625	61	0	0	17-3	82.1	61	26	5	2	57-8	94	2.19	174	.210	.344	0	—	0		13		1.9
976	Cle A☆	1	4	.200	61	0	0	21-3	96.1	57	25	2	1	49-11	104	2.24	157	.175	.282	0	—	0		14		1.4
977	Cle A	2	2	.500	13	0	0	4-1	18.2	15	13	3	0	7-1	18	5.30	75	.234	.301	0	—	0		-3		-0.6
	Cal A★	6	5	.545	46	0	0	13-2	81.1	64	31	8	2	37-8	61	3.10	127	.218	.306	0	—	0		8		1.3
	Year	8	7	.533	59	0	0	17-3	100	79	44	11	2	44-9	79	3.51	112	.221	.305	0	—	0		5		0.7
978	Cal A	10	9	.526	59	0	0	25-6	95.2	73	35	7	2	48-11	70	2.82	129	.215	.315	0	—	0		8		1.7
979	†Cal A	7	11	.389	53	1	0	10-5	85.2	107	54	13	2	32-4	59	5.57	73	.314	.372	0	—	0	0	-12		-2.3
980	Cal A	3	5	.375	52	9	1	4-4	128	122	62	14	3	39-3	89	4.08	97	.256	.314	0	—	0*	111	-1		-0.1
981	†NY A	4	1	.800	26	1	0	0-2	47	38	16	3	1	16-1	24	2.49	145	.229	.291	0	—	0	124	5		0.5
982	NY A	4	2	.667	25	0	0	0-0	50	54	19	4	1	11-2	31	3.42	118	.273	.313	0	—	0		4		0.4
983	NY A	0	0	—	1	0	0	0-0	1	2	2	1	0	0-0	0	18.00	32	.400	.400	0	—	0		-2		-0.1
otal	14	65	58	.528	647	15	1	126-41	1049.1	919	448	94	29	459-81	819	3.53	106	.239	.322	61-0-2	.246	4	100	31	12	4.4

LAROSE, JOHN Henry John B10.25.1951 Pawtucket RI BL/TL/6-1/185 [BosA70 S1/14] d9.20

| 978 | Bos A | 0 | 0 | — | 1 | 0 | 0 | 0-0 | 2 | 3 | 5 | 1 | 0 | 3-1 | 0 | 22.50 | 18 | .375 | .545 | 0 | — | 0 | | -3 | | -0.2 |

LARSEN, DON Don James B8.7.1929 Michigan City IN BR/TR/6-4/227(215-227) d4.18

953	StL A	7	12	.368	38	22	7-2	2	192.2	201	99	11	4	64	96	4.16	101	.267	.328	81-3-0	.284	5*	95	2		0.9
954	Bal A	3	21	.125	29	28	12-1	0	201.2	213	106	18	1	89	80	4.37	82	.274	.346	88-1-2	.250	8*	64	-16		-0.9
955	†NY A	9	2	.818	19	13	5-1	2	97	81	38	8	2	51-3	44	3.06	122	.229	.328	41-2-0	.146	2*	139	8		1.0
956	†NY A	11	5	.688	38	20	6-1	1	179.2	133	72	19	7	96-0	107	3.26	119	.204	.332	79-2-1	.241	6*	131	14		1.7
957	†NY A	10	4	.714	27	20	4-1	0	139.2	113	68	12	0	87-0	81	3.74	96	.220	.332	56	.250	5*	133	-3		0.2
958	†NY A	9	6	.600	19	19	5-3	0	114.1	100	43	4	4	52-3	55	3.07	115	.233	.320	49-4-2	.306	9*	134	7		1.8
959	NY A	6	7	.462	25	18	3-1	0	124.2	122	65	14	0	76-2	69	4.33	84	.260	.361	47-0-1	.255	4*	147	-8		-0.4
960	KC A	1	10	.091	22	15	0	0	83.2	97	55	11	0	42-1	43	5.38	74	.293	.370	29	.207	0*	69	-12		-1.4
961	KC A	1	0	1.000	8	1	0	0	15	21	9	2	1	11-0	13	4.20	100	.344	.452	20-1-1	.300	1*	127	0		0.1
	Chi A	7	2	.778	25	3	0	2	74.1	64	36	5	1	29-2	53	4.12	95	.231	.306	25-1-1	.320	3	128	-1		0.2
	Year	8	2	.800	33	4	0	2	89.1	85	45	7	2	40-2	66	4.13	96	.251	.334	45-2-2	.311	4	128	-1		0.3
962	†SF N	5	4	.556	49	0	0	11	86.1	83	44	9	2	47-7	58	4.38	87	.256	.352	25-0-1	.200	1*		-4		-0.5
963	SF N	7	7	.500	46	0	0	3	62	46	23	8	0	30-9	44	3.05	105	.203	.296	11-0-1	.182	0		2		0.4
964	SF N	0	1	.000	6	0	0	0	10.1	14	5	0	0	6-1	6	4.35	82	.256	.356	1	.000	-0		-1		-0.1
	Hou N	4	8	.333	30	10	2-1	0	103.1	92	36	4	1	20-4	58	2.26	151	.233	.270	31-0-1	.097	0*	67	11		1.3
	Year	4	9	.308	36	10	2-1	0	113.2	102	41	4	1	26-5	64	2.45	140	.235	.279	32-0-1	.094	0	67	10		1.2
965	Hou N	0	0	—	1	0	0	0	5.1	8	3	0	0	3-1	1	5.06	65	.348	.423	2	.000	-0	104	-1		0.0
	Bal A	1	2	.333	27	1	0	1	54	53	22	4	1	20-2	40	2.67	130	.255	.322	11	.273	1	101	3		0.3
967	Chi N	0	0	—	3	0	0	0	4	5	4	1	0	2-0	1	9.00	39	.333	.412	0	—	0		-2		-0.1
otal	14	81	91	.471	412	171	44-11	23	1548	1442	728	130	26	725-35	849	3.78	99	.247	.331	596-14-11	.242	46	109	-1		4.5

LARSON, DAN Daniel James B7.4.1954 Los Angeles CA BR/TR/6-0/180* [StLN72 1/21] d7.18

976	Hou N	5	8	.385	13	13	5	0-0	92.1	81	40	7	1	28-1	42	3.02	107	.236	.291	31-0-2	.290	4*	111	0		0.4
977	Hou N	1	7	.125	32	10	1	1-1	97.2	108	72	13	2	45-2	44	5.81	62	.280	.355	28	.214	1*	111	-26		-1.9
978	Phi N	0	0	—	1	0	0	0-0	1	1	1	0	0	1-0	2	9.00	40	.250	.400	0	—	0		-1		0.0
979	Phi N	1	1	.500	3	3	0	0-0	19	17	9	1	1	9-0	9	4.26	91	.250	.342	5-0-1	.000	-1	114	0		-0.1
980	Phi N	0	5	.000	12	7	0	0-0	45.2	46	24	4	0	24-6	17	3.15	121	.271	.359	13	.154	0	67	1		-0.1
981	Phi N	3	0	1.000	5	4	1	0-0	28	27	13	4	0	15-1	15	4.18	88	.260	.350	9-0-1	.111	0	212	-1		0.1
982	Chi N	0	4	.000	12	6	0	0-0	39.2	51	30	4	2	18-0	22	5.67	67	.327	.397	11	.273	0	89	-9		-0.7
otal	7	10	25	.286	78	43	7	1-1	323.1	331	189	30	6	140-10	151	4.40	81	.269	.342	97-0-4	.216	4	110	-36		-2.3

LARY, AL Alfred Allen B9.26.1928 Northport AL D7.10.2001 Northport AL BR/TR/6-3/185* d9.6 b-Frank Col Alabama

954	Chi N	0	0	—	1	1	0	0	6	3	2	0	0	7	4	3.00	140	.150	.370	2	.500	0*	85	1		0.1
962	Chi N	0	1	.000	15	3	0	0	34	42	27	5	0	15-0	18	7.15	58	.311	.370	6-0-2	.167	0*	56	-9		-0.4
otal	2	0	1	.000	16	4	0	0	40	45	29	5	0	22-0	22	6.52	64	.290	.370	8-0-2	.250	1	63	-8		-0.3

LARY, FRANK Frank Strong "Mule","The Yankee Killer" B4.10.1930 Northport AL BR/TR/5-11/180* d9.14 b-Al Col Alabama

954	Det A	0	0	—	3	0	0	0	3.2	4	1	0	0	3	5	2.45	150	.286	.412	0	—	0		1		0.0
955	Det A	14	15	.483	36	31	16-2	1	235	232	100	16	9	89-3	98	3.10	124	.262	.331	82-0-5	.195	1	100	16		2.0
956	Det A	21	13	.618	41	38	20-3	1	294	289	116	20	12	116-4	165	3.15	131	.257	.331	103-1-6	.184	0	115	32		3.4
957	Det A	11	16	.407	40	35	12-2	3	237.2	250	111	23	12	72-9	107	3.98	97	.276	.336	73-0-9	.123	-3	103	-1		-0.5
958	Det A	16	15	.516	39	34	19-3	1	260.1	249	91	20	12	68-4	131	2.90	139	.251	.305	88-1-9	.170	-1	94	32		3.5
959	Det A	17	10	.630	32	32	11-3	0	223	225	109	23	11	46-4	137	3.55	114	.261	.305	80-1-8	.125	-2	98	9		0.7
960	Det A★	15	15	.500	38	36	15-2	1	274.1	262	125	25	19	62-3	149	3.51	113	.249	.301	93-2-8	.183	4*	104	12		1.5
961	Det A★	23	9	.719	36	36	22-4	0	275.1	252	117	24	6	66-2	146	3.24	127	.243	.290	108-1-3	.231	4*	119	25		3.3
962	Det A	2	6	.250	17	14	2-1	0	80	98	59	17	4	21-1	41	5.74	71	.297	.345	24	.167	1*	100	-15	32	-1.3
963	Det A	4	9	.308	16	14	6	0	107.1	90	40	15	5	26-0	46	3.27	114	.226	.280	35-0-2	.229	1	107	7		1.0
964	Det A	0	2	.000	6	4	0	0	18	24	15	3	3	10-1	6	7.00	52	.316	.416	7	.000	-0	103	-6		-0.7
	NY N	2	3	.400	13	8	3-1	1	57.1	62	33	7	4	14-2	27	4.55	79	.279	.332	17-0-1	.118	1	89	-6		-0.5
	Mil N	1	0	1.000	5	2	0	0	12.1	15	7	4	0	4-0	4	4.38	84	.306	.306	3	.000	-0	187	-1		-0.1
	Year	3	5	.500	18	10	3-1	1	69.2	77	40	11	4	14-2	31	4.52	79	.284	.328	20-0-1	.100	0	108	-7		-0.6
965	NY N	1	3	.250	14	7	0	1	57.1	48	24	2	1	16-0	23	2.98	118	.233	.288	19	.211	0	85	3		0.2
	Chi A	1	0	1.000	14	1	0	2	26.2	23	12	4	2	7-2	14	4.05	79	.230	.294	2-0-1	.500	0	110	-2		-0.1
otal	12	128	116	.525	350	292	126-21	11	2162.1	2123	960	197	97	616-35	1099	3.49	113	.257	.314	734-6-52	.177	5	105	106	32	12.4

ASHER, FRED Frederick Walter B8.19.1941 Poughkeepsie NY BR/TR/6-4/210(186-210) d4.12

963	Min A	0	0	—	11	0	0		11.1	12	10	1	0	11-1	10	4.76	76	.286	.426	1	.000	-0		-3		-0.1
967	Det A	2	1	.667	17	0	0	9	30	25	14	1	1	11-1	28	3.90	84	.221	.296	9-0-1	.111	-0		-2		-0.4
968	†Det A	5	1	.833	34	0	0	5	48.2	37	19	5	0	22-7	32	3.33	90	.215	.303	9	.111	-0		-1		-0.2
969	Det A	2	1	.667	32	0	0	0-1	44	34	16	5	2	22-1	26	3.07	123	.224	.308	4-0-1	.000	-0		4		0.2
970	Det A	1	3	.250	12	0	0	3-1	9	10	6	0	1	12-1	8	5.00	75	.278	.460	1	.000	-0		-3		-0.5
	Cle A	1	7	.125	43	1	0	5-4	57.2	57	34	6	3	30-1	44	4.06	99	.264	.354	8-0-1	.000	-1	44	-3		-0.6
	Year	2	10	.167	55	1	0	8-5	66.2	67	40	6	4	42-2	52	4.18	95	.266	.372	9-0-1	.000	-1	45	-3		-0.9
971	Cal A	0	0	—	2	0	0	0-0	1.1	4	4	0	0	2-0	0	27.00	12	.667	.667	0	—	-0		-4		-0.2
otal	6	11	13	.458	151	1	0	22-6	202	179	103	18	7	110-12	148	3.88	92	.243	.342	32-0-3	.063	-2	50	-10		-1.6

ASKEY, BILL William Alan B12.20.1957 Toledo OH BR/TR/6-5/190* [KCA78 S2/27] d4.23 Col Kent St.

| 982 | SF N | 12 | 13 | .520 | 32 | 31 | 7-1 | 0-0 | 189.1 | 186 | 74 | 14 | 2 | 43-2 | 88 | 3.14 | 114 | .261 | .302 | 62-0-4 | .129 | -2 | 106 | 10 | | 1.1 |
| 983 | SF N | 13 | 10 | .565 | 25 | 25 | 1 | 0-0 | 148.1 | 151 | 75 | 18 | 3 | 45-4 | 81 | 4.19 | 85 | .266 | .321 | 47-0-1 | .106 | 0* | 109 | -8 | | -1.2 |

YEAR	TM LG	W	L	PCT	G	GS	CG-SHO	SV-BS	IP	H	R	HR	HB	BB-IB	SO	ERA	AERA	OAV	OOB	AB-HR-SH	AVG	PB	SUP	APR	DL	PW
1984	SF N	9	14	.391	35	34	2	0-0	207.2	222	112	20	6	50-6	71	4.33	82	.273	.317	63-0-4	.063	-3	94	-18		-2.3
1985	SF N	5	11	.313	19	19	0	0-0	114	110	55	10	0	39-0	42	3.55	98	.255	.314	30-0-5	.133	0	72	-2		-2.6
	Mon N	0	5	.000	11	7	0	0-0	34.1	55	36	9	2	14-1	18	9.44	37	.362	.420	7-0-3	.143	-0	103	-22		-2.6
	Year	5	16	.238	30	26	0	0-0	148.1	165	91	19	2	53-1	60	4.91	70	.283	.342	37-0-8	.135	0	81	-24		-2.9
1986	SF N	1	1	.500	20	0	0	1-0	27.1	28	14	5	0	13-1	8	4.28	83	.275	.353	1	.000	-0		-2		-0.1
1988	Cle A	1	0	1.000	17	0	0	1-0	24.1	32	16	0	0	6-0	17	5.18	80	.320	.349		—	0		-3		-0.1
Total	6	42	53	.442	159	116	10-1		745.1	784	382	76	13	210-14	325	4.14	86	.272	.322	210-0-17	.105	-4	97	-45		-5.5

LASLEY, BILL Willard Almond B7.13.1902 Gallipolis OH D8.21.1990 Seattle WA BB/TR/6-0/175 d9.19

YEAR	TM LG	W	L	PCT	G	GS	CG-SHO	SV-BS	IP	H	R	HR	HB	BB-IB	SO	ERA	AERA	OAV	OOB	AB-HR-SH	AVG	PB	SUP	APR	DL	PW
1924	StL A	0	0	—	2	0	0		4	7	3	0	0	2		6.75	67	.412	.474	1	.000	-0		-1		-0.1

LASORDA, TOM Thomas Charles B9.22.1927 Norristown PA BL/TL/5-10/175* d8.5 M21/C4 HF1997

1954	Bro N	0	0	—	4	0	0		9	8	5	2	0	5	5	5.00	82	.242	.333	1	.000	-0		-1		-0.1
1955	Bro N	0	0	—	4	1	0		4	5	6	1	1	6-0	1	13.50	30	.313	.500	0	—	0	88	-4		-0.2
1956	KC A	0	4	.000	18	5	0	1	45.1	40	38	6	3	45-3	28	6.15	70	.240	.406	13	.077	-1*	86	-10		-0.9
Total	3	0	4	.000	26	6	0	1	58.1	53	49	9	4	56-3	37	6.48	66	.245	.404	14	.071	-2	87	-15		-1.2

LATHAM, BILL William Carol B8.29.1960 Birmingham AL BL/TL/6-2/190* d4.15 Col Auburn-Montgomery

1985	NY N	1	3	.250	7	3	0	0-0	22.2	21	10	1	0	7-1	10	3.97	88	.250	.304	3-0-1	.333	1	76	-1		0.0
1986	Min A	0	1	.000	7	2	0	0-1	16	24	14	1	1	6-0	8	7.31	59	.358	.408	0	—	0	94	-5		-0.3
Total	2	1	4	.200	14	5	0	0-1	38.2	45	24	2	1	13-1	18	5.35	72	.298	.351	3-0-1	.333	1	84	-6		-0.3

LATHROP, BILL William George B8.12.1891 Hanover WI D11.20.1958 Janesville WI BR/TR/6-2.5/184 d7.29 Col Notre Dame

1913	Chi A	0	1	.000	6	0	0		17	16	11	0	1	12	9	4.24	69	.267	.397	4	.000	-1		-2		-0.2
1914	Chi A	1	2	.333	19	1	0		47.2	41	20	0	2	19	7	2.64	102	.241	.325	12-0-1	.000	-1	54	0		-0.1
Total	2	1	3	.250	25	1	0		64.2	57	31	0	3	31	16	3.06	90	.248	.345	16-0-1	.000	-2	54	-2		-0.2

LATMAN, BARRY Arnold Barry B5.21.1936 Los Angeles CA BR/TR/6-3/210* d9.10 Col USC

1957	Chi A	1	2	.333	7	2	0	1	12.1	12	11	2	1	13-0	9	8.03	47	.267	.441	1	.000	-0	120	-6		-1.1
1958	Chi A	3	0	1.000	13	3	1-1		47.2	27	7	1	1	17-0	28	0.76	481	.162	.242	12-0-1	.083	-0	66	15		0.8
1959	Chi A	8	5	.615	37	21	5-2	0	156	138	71	15	4	72-3	97	3.75	100	.235	.321	47-0-2	.128	-1	136	1		-0.2
1960	Cle A	7	7	.500	31	20	4	0	147.1	146	78	19	6	72-2	94	4.03	93	.258	.345	41-0-7	.220	1	120	-6		-0.5
1961	Cle A☆	13	5	.722	45	18	4-2	5	176.2	163	84	23	5	54-3	108	4.02	98	.244	.303	55-0-1	.073	-3	104	1		-0.4
1962	Cle A	8	13	.381	45	21	7-1	0	179.1	179	96	23	3	72-9	117	4.17	93	.261	.334	53-1-3	.189	2	82	-7		-0.6
1963	Cle A	7	12	.368	38	21	4-2	2	149.1	146	90	23	6	52-3	133	4.94	73	.257	.323	44-1-3	.182	2	83	-21		-2.1
1964	LA N	6	10	.375	40	18	2-1	2	138	128	72	15	7	52-6	81	3.85	85	.244	.319	40-0-2	.125	-1	101	-11		-1.3
1965	Cal A	1	1	.500	18	0	0	0	31.2	30	12	3	0	16-3	18	2.84	120	.254	.343	2	.000	-0		2		0.0
1966	Hou N	2	7	.222	31	9	1-1	1	103	88	42	5	7	35-4	74	2.71	126	.233	.310	26	.154	-1	57	6	18	0.5
1967	Hou N	3	6	.333	39	1	0	1	77.2	73	42	13	6	34-2	70	4.52	73	.252	.338	11-0-1	.091	-1	53	-9		-1.1
Total	11	59	68	.465	344	134	28-10	16	1219	1130	605	142	48	489-35	829	3.91	94	.246	.323	332-2-20	.145	-1	101	-35	18	-6.0

LATTIMORE, BILL William Hershel "Slothful Bill" B5.25.1884 Roxton TX D10.30.1919 Colorado Springs CO BL/TL/5-9/165 d4.17

| 1908 | Cle A | 1 | 2 | .333 | 4 | 4 | 1 | | 24 | 24 | 16 | 0 | 0 | 7 | 5 | 4.50 | 53 | .247 | .298 | 9-0-2 | .444 | 1 | 150 | -5 | | -0.5 |

LAUER, CHUCK John Charles B4.5.1865 Pittsburgh PA D5.14.1915 Buffalo NY TR d7.17 ▲

| 1884 | Pit AA | 0 | 2 | .000 | 3 | 3 | 2 | 0 | 19 | 23 | 25 | 0 | 3 | 9 | 8 | 7.58 | 44 | .277 | .368 | 44 | .114 | -1* | 85 | -9 | | -0.8 |

LAUZERIQUE, GEORGE George Albert B7.22.1947 Havana, Cuba BR/TR/6-1/180* [OakA65 8/186] d9.17

1967	KC A	0	2	.000	3	2	0	0	16	11	4	2	1	6-0	10	2.25	142	.193	.281	3	.000	-0	27	2		0.3
1968	Oak A	0	0	—	1	0	0	0	1	0	0	0	0	1-0	1	0.00	—	.000	.333	0	—	0	0	0		0.0
1969	Oak A	3	4	.429	19	8	1	0-1	61.1	58	32	14	2	27-0	39	4.70	73	.250	.331	20	.100	-1	100	-7		-0.8
1970	Mil A	1	2	.333	11	4	1	0-1	35	41	27	7	1	14-1	24	6.94	54	.295	.357	10-1-3	.200	1	177	-11		-0.8
Total	4	4	8	.333	34	14	2	0-2	113.1	110	63	23	4	48-1	73	5.00	70	.256	.333	33-1-3	.121	-0	114	-16		-1.3

LAVELLE, GARY Gary Robert B1.3.1949 Scranton PA BB/TL/6-1/200(180-210) [SFN67 20/397] d9.10 [DL 1986 Tor A 182]

1974	SF N	0	3	.000	10	1	0	0-0	16.2	14	7	1	0	10-2	12	2.16	177	.222	.329	2-0-2	.000	-0		2		0.3
1975	SF N	6	3	.667	65	0	0	8-5	82.1	80	30	3	3	48-12	51	2.95	129	.260	.364	9	.111	-0		8		1.1
1976	SF N	10	6	.625	65	0	0	12-8	110.1	102	37	6	2	52-10	71	2.69	135	.246	.331	13-0-2	.077	-1		12		1.9
1977	SF N★	7	7	.500	73	0	0	20-8	118.1	106	35	4	0	37-18	93	2.05	192	.239	.295	14	.000	-2		23		3.3
1978	SF N	13	10	.565	67	0	0	14-10	97.2	96	41	3	2	44-11	63	3.32	105	.263	.341	15-0-1	.067	-1		1		0.2
1979	SF N	7	9	.438	70	0	0	20-9	96.2	86	31	5	2	42-15	80	2.51	139	.247	.327	4-0-2	.250	0		11		2.2
1980	SF N	6	8	.429	62	0	0	9-7	100	106	43	4	0	36-11	66	3.42	103	.275	.333	11-0-3	.000	-1		1		0.1
1981	SF N	2	6	.250	34	3	0	4-3	65.2	58	33	3	2	23-4	45	3.84	89	.244	.316	11-0-2	.273	1	96	-4		-0.3
1982	SF N	10	7	.588	68	0	0	8-5	104.2	97	35	6	1	29-12	76	2.67	134	.247	.298	13-0-2	.154	0		11		2.0
1983	SF N☆	7	4	.636	56	0	0	20-9	87	73	33	4	0	19-8	52	2.59	137	.229	.270	14	.000	-2		8	21	0.9
1984	SF N	5	4	.556	77	0	0	12-7	101	92	34	5	1	42-14	71	2.76	128	.246	.321	-5	.000	-0		9		0.5
1985	†Tor A	5	7	.417	69	0	0	8-8	72.2	54	30	5	0	36-5	50	3.10	137	.214	.310	0	—	0		-4	56	1.4
1987	Tor A	2	3	.400	23	0	0	1-0	27.2	36	20	2	0	19-4	17	5.53	82	.313	.407	0	—	0		-4		-0.1
	Oak A	0	0	—	6	0	0	0-1	4.1	4	4	0	0	3-0	6	8.31	50	.267	.368	0	—	0		-2		-0.0
	Year	2	3	.400	29	0	0	1-1	32	40	24	2	0	22-4	23	5.91	76	.308	.403	0	—	0		-6		-0.2
Total	13	80	77	.510	745	3	0	136-80	1085	1004	413	51	13	440-126	769	2.93	126	.249	.322	111-0-14	.081	-6	96	84	259	13.5

LAVENDER, JIMMY James Sanford B5.26.1884 Barnesville GA D1.12.1960 Cartersville GA BR/TR/5-11/165 d4.23

1912	Chi N	16	13	.552	42	31	15-3	3	251.2	240	116	8	10	89	109	3.04	109	.257	.328	87-0-3	.149	-3	105	5		0.3
1913	Chi N	10	14	.417	40	20	10	2	204	206	111	6	13	98	91	3.66	87	.267	.359	68-0-3	.118	-4	116	-12		-1.9
1914	Chi N	11	11	.500	37	28	11-2	0	214.1	191	106	11	11	87	87	3.07	91	.247	.331	63-0-3	.175	-2	103	-5		-0.1
1915	Chi N	10	16	.385	41	24	13-1	4	220	178	77	5	10	67	117	2.58	108	.228	.298	67-0-2	.134	-2	89	6		0.7
1916	Chi N	10	14	.417	36	25	9-4	2	188	163	76	3	9	62	91	2.82	103	.240	.312	53-0-3	.151	-1	78	2		0.1
1917	Phi N	6	8	.429	28	14	7	1	129.1	119	61	5	3	44	52	3.55	79	.250	.317	36-0-2	.139	-1	100	-8		-1.1
Total	6	63	76	.453	224	142	65-10	12	1207.1	1097	547	38	56	447	547	3.09	97	.249	.325	374-0-16	.144	-9	98	-12		-2.0

LAW, RON Ronald David B3.14.1946 Hamilton ON, Can. BR/TR/6-2/165 d6.29

| 1969 | Cle A | 3 | 4 | .429 | 35 | 0 | 0 | 1-2 | 52.1 | 68 | 34 | 2 | 2 | 34-5 | 29 | 4.99 | 76 | .325 | .419 | 7 | .143 | -0 | 140 | -7 | | -0.9 |

LAW, VERN Vernon Sanders "Deacon" B3.12.1930 Meridian ID BR/TR/6-2/195* d6.11 Mil 1952-53 C2 s-Vance

1950	Pit N	7	9	.438	27	17	5-1	0	128	137	83	11	4	49	57	4.92	89	.272	.341	41	.073	-2	104	-9		-1.2
1951	Pit N	6	9	.400	28	14	2-1	2	114	109	66	9	6	51	41	4.50	94	.253	.341	32-1-3	.344	5	85	-3		0.1
1954	Pit N	9	13	.409	39	18	7	3	161.2	201	109	20	3	56	57	5.51	76	.311	.362	52-1-6	.231	3*	70	-21		-2.1
1955	Pit N	10	10	.500	43	24	8-1	1	200.2	221	98	19	1	61-7	82	3.81	108	.280	.331	63-1-2	.254	3*	88	7		1.3
1956	Pit N	8	16	.333	39	32	6	2	195.2	218	110	24	6	49-10	60	4.32	87	.281	.326	57-1-3	.175	1	98	-13		-1.4
1957	Pit N	10	8	.556	31	25	9-3	1	172.2	172	72	18	2	32-8	55	2.87	132	.256	.290	63-0-4	.190	1*	110	14		1.5
1958	Pit N	14	12	.538	35	29	6-1	3	202.1	235	103	16	1	39-5	56	3.96	98	.297	.326	62-2-7	.194	6*	119	-4		0.1
1959	Pit N	18	9	.667	34	33	20-2	1	266	245	91	25	2	53-11	110	2.98	130	.243	.286	96-1-7	.167	1*	106	31		3.1
1960	†Pit N★	20	9	.690	35	35	18-3	0	271.2	266	104	25	4	40-8	120	3.08	122	.257	.286	90-1-7	.181	3	120	19		2.1
1961	Pit N	3	4	.429	11	10	1	0	59.1	72	33	10	1	18-3	20	4.70	85	.305	.355	19-0-2	.263	1	120	-4	87	-0.2
1962	Pit N	10	7	.588	23	20	7-2	0	139.1	156	67	21	1	27-4	78	3.94	100	.276	.310	45-0-7	.311	5	128	2		0.5
1963	Pit N	4	5	.444	18	12	1-1	0	76.2	91	45	11	0	13-0	31	4.93	67	.296	.321	23-0-1	.217	1*	118	-12		-1.3
1964	Pit N	12	13	.480	35	29	7-5	0	192	203	85	18	1	32-6	93	3.61	99	.270	.299	61-1-5	.311	8*	110	-1		0.1
1965	Pit N	17	9	.654	29	28	13-4	0	217.1	182	76	17	3	35-2	101	2.15	163	.229	.261	82-1-4	.244	4*	120	31		4.3
1966	Pit N	12	8	.600	31	28	8-4	0	177.2	203	85	19	4	24-1	88	4.05	88	.292	.318	66-0-5	.242	5*	136	-8	22	-0.8
1967	Pit N	2	6	.250	25	10	1	0	97	122	57	5	1	18-9	43	4.18	81	.308	.335	27-0-1	.111	-0*	107	-11	35	-0.5
Total	16	162	147	.524	483	364	119-28	13	2672	2833	1274	268	40	597-74	1092	3.77	101	.272	.312	883-11-63	.216	45	109	18	144	8.2

LAWRENCE, BRIAN Brian Michael B5.14.1976 Fort Collins CO BR/TR/6-0/195* [SDN98 17/502] d4.15 Col Northwestern Louisiana

2001	SD N	5	5	.500	27	15	1	0-0	114.2	107	53	10	5	34-5	86	3.45	120	.244	.304	26-0-2	.115	-0	85	8		0.8
2002	SD N	12	12	.500	35	31	2-2	0-0	210	230	97	16	11	52-6	149	3.69	105	.281	.331	63-0-3	.095	-1	100	4		0.1
2003	SD N	10	15	.400	33	33	1	0-0	210.2	206	106	27	11	57-8	116	4.19	96	.258	.314	67-1-2	.224	5	99	-5		-0.5
2004	SD N	15	14	.517	34	34	2-1	0-0	203	226	101	26	7	55-7	121	4.12	96	.287	.335	60-0-8	.097	-2*	109	-4		-0.4

YEAR	TM LG	W	L	PCT	G	GS	CG-SHO	SV-BS	IP	H	R	HR	HB	BB-IB	SO	ERA	AERA	OAV	OOB	AB-HR-SH	AVG	PB	SUP	APR	DL	PW
2005	†SD N	7	15	.318	33	33	1	0-0	195.2	211	106	18	11	57-7	109	4.83	80	.273	.329	59-0-7	.085	-3	92	-19		-2.1
Total	5	49	61	.445	162	146	7-3	0-0	934	980	463	97	45	255-33	579	4.10	96	.271	.324	277-1-22	.126	-1	98	-16		-1.6

LAWRENCE, BROOKS Brooks Ulysses "Bull" B1.30.1925 Springfield OH D4.27.2000 Springfield OH BR/TR/6-0/205* d6.24 Col Miami-Ohio

YEAR	TM LG	W	L	PCT	G	GS	CG-SHO	SV-BS	IP	H	R	HR	HB	BB-IB	SO	ERA	AERA	OAV	OOB	AB-HR-SH	AVG	PB	SUP	APR	DL	PW
1954	StL N	15	6	.714	35	18	8	1	158.2	141	71	17	8	72	72	3.74	110	.243	.333	53-0-1	.189	0	125	8		1.0
1955	StL N	3	8	.273	46	10	2-1	1	96	102	73	11	7	58-7	52	6.56	62	.278	.384	21-0-2	.095	-2	99	-25		-2.7
1956	Cin N☆	19	10	.655	49	30	11-1	0	218.2	210	109	26	2	71-4	96	3.99	100	.256	.315	70-0-6	.157	-1	131	-1		0.0
1957	Cin N	16	13	.552	49	32	12-1	4	250.1	234	111	26	4	76-5	121	3.52	117	.247	.306	82-0-6	.171	-0	90	14		1.5
1958	Cin N	8	13	.381	46	23	6-2	5	181	194	89	12	4	55-7	74	4.13	100	.275	.330	53-0-1	.113	-2	98	1		-0.1
1959	Cin N	7	12	.368	43	14	3	10	128.1	144	74	17	4	45-9	64	4.77	85	.281	.343	40-0-2	.150	-1	99	-9		-1.4
1960	Cin N	1	0	1.000	7	0	0	1	7.2	9	12	1	0	8-1	2	10.57	36	.310	.447	0	—	0		-6		-0.9
Total	7	69	62	.527	275	127	42-5	22	1040.2	1034	539	110	33	385-33	481	4.25	96	.261	.330	319-0-18	.154	-5	108	-18		-2.6

LAWRENCE, BOB Robert Andrew "Larry" B12.14.1899 Brooklyn NY D11.6.1983 Jamaica NY BR/TR/5-11/180 d7.19

YEAR	TM LG	W	L	PCT	G	GS	CG-SHO	SV-BS	IP	H	R	HR	HB	BB-IB	SO	ERA	AERA	OAV	OOB	AB-HR-SH	AVG	PB	SUP	APR	DL	PW
1924	Chi A	0	0	—	1	0	0		1	1	9.00	46	.250	.400	0		0	0		0.0					

LAWRENCE, SEAN Sean Christopher B9.2.1970 Oak Park IL BL/TL/6-4/215 [PitN92 6/175] d8.25 Col St. Francis (IL)

YEAR	TM LG	W	L	PCT	G	GS	CG-SHO	SV-BS	IP	H	R	HR	HB	BB-IB	SO	ERA	AERA	OAV	OOB	AB-HR-SH	AVG	PB	SUP	APR	DL	PW
1998	Pit N	2	1	.667	7	3	0	0-0	19.2	25	16	4	0	10-0	12	7.32	58	.313	.380	6	.000	-1	122	-6		-0.8

LAWSON, ROXIE Alfred Voyle B4.13.1906 Donnellson IA D4.9.1977 Stockport IA BR/TR/6-0/170 d8.3 Col Iowa Wesleyan

YEAR	TM LG	W	L	PCT	G	GS	CG-SHO	SV-BS	IP	H	R	HR	HB	BB-IB	SO	ERA	AERA	OAV	OOB	AB-HR-SH	AVG	PB	SUP	APR	DL	PW
1930	Cle A	1	2	.333	7	4	2	0	33.2	46	27	1	0	23	10	6.15	79	.324	.418	11-0-1	.091	-1	129	-4		-0.4
1931	Cle A	0	2	.000	17	3	0	0	55.2	72	50	5	0	36	20	7.60	61	.304	.396	14	.143	-0	85	-15		-0.7
1933	Det A	0	1	.000	4	2	0	0	16	17	16	2	0	17	6	7.31	59	.270	.425	5	.000	-1	118	-5		-0.3
1935	Det A	3	1	.750	7	4	4-2	2	40	34	11	3	0	24	16	1.57	265	.233	.341	13-0-1	.308	1	109	11		1.2
1936	Det A	8	6	.571	41	8	3	3	128	139	87	13	4	71	34	5.48	90	.281	.376	45	.222	1	140	-6		-0.5
1937	Det A	18	7	.720	37	29	15	1	217.1	236	141	17	1	115	68	5.26	89	.271	.357	81-0-5	.259	3	118	-13		-1.0
1938	Det A	8	9	.471	27	16	5	1	127	154	85	13	0	82	39	5.46	92	.299	.395	45-0-1	.044	-5	81	-6		-1.1
1939	Det A	1	1	.500	2	1	0	0	11.1	7	7	1	0	7	4	4.76	103	.167	.286	4-0-1	.000	-1	108	0		0.0
	StL A	3	7	.300	36	14	5	0	150.2	181	93	10	2	83	43	5.32	92	.307	.394	43-0-5	.186	-1*	80	-4		-0.3
	Year	4	8	.333	38	15	5	0	162	188	100	11	2	90	47	5.28	92	.297	.387	47-0-6	.170	-2	82	-4		-0.3
1940	StL A	5	5	.625	30	2	0	4	72	77	45	5	0	54	18	5.13	89	.278	.396	22	.045	-3	96	-4		-0.6
Total	9	47	39	.547	208	83	34-2	11	851.2	963	562	70	7	512	258	5.37	89	.285	.380	283-0-14	.173	-6	105	-46		-3.7

LAWSON, AL Alfred William B3.24.1869 London, England D11.29.1954 San Antonio TX BR/TR/5-11/161 d5.13

YEAR	TM LG	W	L	PCT	G	GS	CG-SHO	SV-BS	IP	H	R	HR	HB	BB-IB	SO	ERA	AERA	OAV	OOB	AB-HR-SH	AVG	PB	SUP	APR	DL	PW
1890	Bos N	0	1	.000	1	1	1	0	9	12	7	0	0	4	1	4.00	94	.308	.372	2	.000	-0	34	-1		-0.1
	Pit N	0	2	.000	2	2	1	0	10	15	20	0	0	10	2	9.00	37	.333	.455	4	.000	-1	105	-8		-1.1
	Year	0	3	.000	3	3	2	0	19	27	27	0	0	14	3	6.63	53	.321	.418	6	.000	-1	78	-9		-1.2

LAWSON, BOB Robert Baker B8.23.1875 Lynchburg VA D10.28.1952 Durham NC BR/TR/5-10/170 d5.7 Col North Carolina-Asheville

YEAR	TM LG	W	L	PCT	G	GS	CG-SHO	SV-BS	IP	H	R	HR	HB	BB-IB	SO	ERA	AERA	OAV	OOB	AB-HR-SH	AVG	PB	SUP	APR	DL	PW
1901	Bos N	2	2	.500	6	4	4	0	46	45	28	0	3	28	12	3.33	109	.254	.365	27-1-2	.148	-0*	103	0		0.0
1902	Bal A	0	2	.000	3	2	1	0	13	21	11	0	2	3	5	4.85	78	.362	.413	6	.167	-0	76	-2		-0.2
Total	2	2	4	.333	9	6	5	0	59	66	39	0	5	31	17	3.66	100	.281	.376	33-1-2	.152	-1	94	-2		-0.2

LAWSON, STEVE Steven George B12.28.1950 Oakland CA BR/TL/6-1/180 d8.3

YEAR	TM LG	W	L	PCT	G	GS	CG-SHO	SV-BS	IP	H	R	HR	HB	BB-IB	SO	ERA	AERA	OAV	OOB	AB-HR-SH	AVG	PB	SUP	APR	DL	PW
1972	Tex A	0	0	—	13	0	0	1-1	16	13	6	1	0	10-0	13	2.81	108	.213	.324	1	1.000	0		0		0.1

LAXTON, BRETT Brett William B10.5.1973 Stratford NJ BL/TR/6-2/210* [OakA96 24/705] d6.21 f-Bill Col Louisiana St.

YEAR	TM LG	W	L	PCT	G	GS	CG-SHO	SV-BS	IP	H	R	HR	HB	BB-IB	SO	ERA	AERA	OAV	OOB	AB-HR-SH	AVG	PB	SUP	APR	DL	PW
1999	Oak A	0	1	.000	3	2	0	0-0	9.2	12	12	1	2	7-1	9	7.45	64	.316	.420	0	—	0	108	-4		-0.4
2000	KC A	0	1	.000	6	1	0	0-0	16.2	23	15	0	2	10-1	14	8.10	64	.348	.449	0	—	0	0	-5		-0.2
Total	2	0	2	.000	9	3	0	0-0	26.1	35	27	1	4	17-2	23	7.86	64	.337	.438	0	—	0	68	-9		-0.6

LAXTON, BILL William Harry B1.5.1948 Camden NJ BL/TL/6-1/190* [PitN66 7/135] d9.15 s-Brett

YEAR	TM LG	W	L	PCT	G	GS	CG-SHO	SV-BS	IP	H	R	HR	HB	BB-IB	SO	ERA	AERA	OAV	OOB	AB-HR-SH	AVG	PB	SUP	APR	DL	PW
1970	Phi N	0	0	—	2	0	0	0-0	2	2	3	2	1	2-0	2	13.50	30	.250	.455	0	—	0		-2		-0.1
1971	SD N	0	2	.000	18	0	0	0-0	27.2	32	25	4	1	26-0	23	6.83	49	.305	.444	0	—	0		-11		-0.8
1974	SD N	0	1	.000	30	0	0	0-0	44.2	37	25	2	5	38-8	40	4.03	89	.226	.375	5	.200	0	49	-2		-0.1
1976	Det A	0	5	.000	26	3	0	2-1	94.2	77	49	13	6	51-1	74	4.09	91	.221	.329	0	—	0	24	-3		-0.3
1977	Sea A	3	2	.600	43	0	0	3-1	72.2	62	44	10	4	39-5	49	4.95	84	.233	.335	0	—	0		-6	24	-0.5
	Cle A	0	0	—	2	0	0	0-0	1.2	2	1	0	0	2-0	1	5.40	74	.286	.444	0	—	0		0		0.0
	Year	3	2	.600	45	0	0	3-1	74.1	64	45	10	4	41-5	50	4.96	83	.234	.339	0	—	0		-6		-0.5
Total	5	3	10	.231	121	4	0	5-2	243.1	212	144	34	15	158-14	189	4.73	80	.236	.356	5	.200	0	29	-24	24	-1.8

LAYANA, TIM Timothy Joseph B3.2.1964 Inglewood CA D6.26.1999 Bakersfield CA BR/TR/6-2/195* [NYA86 3/80] d4.9 Col Loyola Marymount

YEAR	TM LG	W	L	PCT	G	GS	CG-SHO	SV-BS	IP	H	R	HR	HB	BB-IB	SO	ERA	AERA	OAV	OOB	AB-HR-SH	AVG	PB	SUP	APR	DL	PW
1990	Cin N	5	3	.625	55	0	0	2-0	80	71	33	7	2	44-5	53	3.49	113	.244	.344	5	.000	-1		4		0.4
1991	Cin N	0	2	.000	22	0	0	0-1	20.2	23	18	1	0	11-0	14	6.97	55	.277	.362	1	.000	-0*		-7		-0.6
1993	SF N	0	0	—	1	0	0	0-0	2	7	5	1	0	1-1	1	22.50	17	.538	.571	0-0-1	—	0		-4		-0.2
Total	3	5	5	.500	78	0	0	2-1	102.2	101	56	9	2	56-6	68	4.56	86	.261	.355	6-0-1	.000	-1		-7		-0.4

LAZAR, DANNY John Daniel B11.14.1943 East Chicago IN BL/TL/6-1/190* [ChiA65 15/590] d6.21 Col Indiana St.

YEAR	TM LG	W	L	PCT	G	GS	CG-SHO	SV-BS	IP	H	R	HR	HB	BB-IB	SO	ERA	AERA	OAV	OOB	AB-HR-SH	AVG	PB	SUP	APR	DL	PW
1968	Chi A	0	1	.000	8	1	0	0	13.1	14	6	1	0	4-0	11	4.05	75	.269	.316	2	.000	0	29	-1		-0.1
1969	Chi A	0	0	—	9	3	0	0-0	20.2	21	15	5	1	11-2	9	6.53	59	.280	.371	4-0-1	.000	-0	107	-5		-0.3
Total	2	0	1	.000	17	4	0	0-0	34	35	21	6	1	15-2	20	5.56	63	.276	.349	6-0-1	.000	-0	94	-6		-0.4

LAZORKO, JACK Jack Thomas B3.30.1956 Hoboken NJ BR/TR/5-11/200(200-213) [HouN78 11/271] d6.4 Col Mississippi St.

YEAR	TM LG	W	L	PCT	G	GS	CG-SHO	SV-BS	IP	H	R	HR	HB	BB-IB	SO	ERA	AERA	OAV	OOB	AB-HR-SH	AVG	PB	SUP	APR	DL	PW
1984	Mil A	0	1	.000	15	1	0	1-0	39.2	39	19	7	3	22-2	24	4.31	90	.245	.343	0	—	0	70	-1		0.0
1985	Sea A	0	0	—	15	0	0	1-0	20.1	23	10	1	3	8-1	7	3.54	119	.291	.378	0	—	0		1		0.1
1986	Det A	0	0	—	3	0	0	0-0	6.2	8	3	0	0	4-1	3	4.05	103	.296	.387	0	—	0		0		0.0
1987	Cal A	5	6	.455	26	11	2	0-0	117.2	108	68	20	2	44-5	55	4.59	94	.248	.318	0	—	0	100	-4		-0.2
1988	Cal A	0	1	.000	10	3	0	0-0	37.2	37	15	5	1	16-0	19	3.35	116	.255	.331	0	—	0	117	3		0.1
Total	5	5	8	.385	69	15	2	2-0	222	213	115	33	7	94-9	108	4.22	99	.254	.333	0	—	0	102	-1		0.0

LEA, CHARLIE Charles William B12.25.1956 Orleans, France BR/TR/6-4/197* [MonN78 9/217] d6.12 Col Memphis [DL 1986 Mon N 182]

YEAR	TM LG	W	L	PCT	G	GS	CG-SHO	SV-BS	IP	H	R	HR	HB	BB-IB	SO	ERA	AERA	OAV	OOB	AB-HR-SH	AVG	PB	SUP	APR	DL	PW
1980	Mon N	7	5	.583	21	19	0	0-0	104	103	51	5	2	55-4	56	3.72	98	.262	.353	37	.081	-2	113	-2		-0.5
1981	Mon N	5	4	.556	16	11	2-2	0-0	64.1	63	34	4	1	26-0	31	4.62	77	.268	.341	15-0-4	.133	-0	93	-6		-0.9
1982	Mon N	12	10	.545	27	27	4-2	0-0	177.2	145	70	16	0	56-6	115	3.24	114	.222	.283	65-0-1	.123	-1	106	10		1.0
1983	Mon N	16	11	.593	33	33	8-4	0-0	222	195	87	15	1	84-4	137	3.12	116	.238	.307	70-0-12	.114	-2	106	12		1.1
1984	Mon N★	15	10	.600	30	30	8	0-0	224.1	198	82	19	3	68-3	123	2.89	120	.239	.296	72-0-12	.111	-3	99	14		1.2
1987	Mon N	0	1	.000	1	1	0	0-0	1	4	4	1	0	2-0	1	36.00	12	.571	.667	0	—	0	0	-3		-0.5
1988	Min A	7	7	.500	24	23	0	0-0	130	156	79	19	5	50-2	72	4.85	84	.301	.364	0	—	0	123	-12	21	-1.2
Total	7	62	48	.564	152	144	22-8	0-0	923.1	864	407	79	12	341-19	535	3.54	103	.250	.317	259-0-29	.112	-8	107	13	203	0.2

LEACH, TERRY Terry Hester B3.13.1954 Selma AL BR/TR/6-0/215(185-215) d8.12 Col Auburn-Montgomery

YEAR	TM LG	W	L	PCT	G	GS	CG-SHO	SV-BS	IP	H	R	HR	HB	BB-IB	SO	ERA	AERA	OAV	OOB	AB-HR-SH	AVG	PB	SUP	APR	DL	PW
1981	NY N	1	1	.500	21	1	0	0-1	35.1	26	11	2	0	12-1	16	2.55	139	.205	.273	1	.000	0	75	4		0.3
1982	NY N	2	1	.667	21	1	1-1	3-1	45.1	46	22	2	0	18-5	30	4.17	88	.271	.339	8-0-1	.125	-0	24	-1		-0.2
1985	NY N	3	4	.429	22	4	1-1	1-0	55.2	48	19	3	1	14-3	30	2.91	120	.235	.285	12-0-1	.167	1	202	4		0.6
1986	NY N	0	0	—	6	0	0	0-0	6.2	6	3	0	0	3-0	4	2.70	133	.222	.300	0	—	0		0		0.0
1987	NY N	11	1	.917	44	12	1-1	0-2	131.1	132	54	14	1	29-5	61	3.22	119	.262	.303	33-0-4	.061	-2	151	9	15	0.6
1988	†NY N	7	2	.778	52	0	0	3-1	92	95	32	5	3	24-4	51	2.54	128	.268	.318	14	.143	0		7		0.8
1989	NY N	0	0	—	10	0	0	0-0	21.1	19	11	1	1	9-2	2	4.22	78	.244	.282	4	.000	0		-2		-0.1
	KC A	5	6	.455	30	3	0	0-0	73.2	78	46	4	1	36-9	34	4.15	93	.278	.357	0	—	0	62	-6		-0.8
1990	Min A	2	5	.286	55	0	0	2-4	81.2	84	31	2	1	21-10	46	3.20	130	.268	.315	0	—	0		9		0.7
1991	†Min A	1	2	.333	50	0	0	0-2	67.1	82	28	3	1	14-5	32	3.61	119	.299	.332	0	—	0		6		0.3
1992	Chi A	6	5	.545	51	0	0	0-0	73.2	57	17	2	4	20-5	22	1.95	199	.215	.279	0	—	0		16		2.3
1993	Chi A	0	0	—	14	0	0	1-0	16	15	5	1	0	2-1	3	2.81	150	.250	.281	0	—	0		3	133	0.1
Total	11	38	27	.585	376	21	3-3	10-11	700	688	279	38	13	197-48	331	3.15	120	.259	.311	72-0-6	.097	-1	137	49	148	4.6

YEAR	TM LG	W	L	PCT	G	GS	CG-SHO	SV-BS	IP	H	R	HR	HB	BB-IB	SO	ERA	AERA	OAV	OOB	AB-HR-SH	AVG	PB	SUP	APR	DL	PW
LEAGUE, BRANDON	Brandon Paul B3.16.1983 Sacramento CA BR/TR/6-3/192* [TorA01 2/59] d9.21																									
2004	Tor A	1	0	1.000	3	0	0	0-0	4.2	3	0	0	0	1-0	2	0.00	—	.176	.222	0	—	0	2			0.5
2005	Tor A	1	0	1.000	20	0	0	0-0	35.2	42	27	8	2	20-1	17	6.56	71	.302	.395	0	—	0	-7			-0.3
Total	2	2	0	1.000	23	0	0		40.1	45	27	8	2	21-1	19	5.80	80	.288	.378	0	—	0	-5			0.2
LEAL, LUIS	Luis Enrique (Alvarado) B3.21.1957 Barquisimeto, Venez BR/TR/6-3/205(205-220) d5.25																									
1980	Tor A	3	4	.429	13	10	1		59.2	72	35	6	1	31-2	26	4.53	95	.314	.394	0	—	0	114	-2		-0.2
1981	Tor A	7	13	.350	29	19	3	1-0	129.2	127	63	8	5	44-5	71	3.68	98	.254	.317	0	—	0	69	3		0.4
1982	Tor A	12	15	.444	38	38	10	0-0	249.2	250	113	24	3	79-3	111	3.93	115	.262	.317	0	—	0	86	18		1.7
1983	Tor A	13	12	.520	35	35	7-1	0-0	217.1	216	113	23	6	65-5	116	4.31	101	.257	.314	0	—	0	107	1		0.1
1984	Tor A	13	8	.619	35	35	6-2	0-0	222.1	221	106	27	4	77-6	134	3.89	106	.258	.320	0	—	0	114	6		0.5
1985	Tor A	3	6	.333	15	14	0	0-0	67.1	82	46	13	3	24-3	33	5.75	74	.303	.361	0	—	0	86	-10		-1.2
Total	6	51	58	.468	165	151	27-3	1-0	946	968	476	101	22	320-24	491	4.14	103	.265	.325	0	—	0	97	16		1.3
LEAR, KING	Charles Bernard B1.23.1891 Greencastle PA D10.31.1976 Waynesboro PA BR/TR/6-0/175 d5.2 Col Princeton																									
1914	Cin N	1	2	.333	17	4	3-1	1	55.2	55	23	3	2	19	20	3.07	95	.271	.339	16	.188	1	79	1		0.1
1915	Cin N	6	10	.375	40	15	9	0	167.2	169	73	7	6	45	46	3.01	95	.270	.324	47-0-7	.170	-1	92	-3		-0.6
Total	2	7	12	.368	57	19	12-1	1	223.1	224	96	10	8	64	66	3.02	95	.270	.328	63-0-7	.175	-0	89	-2		-0.5
LEARY, FRANK	Francis Patrick B2.26.1881 Wayland MA D10.4.1907 Natick MA TR/5-10/190 d4.30 Col Penn																									
1907	Cin N	0	1	.000	2	1	0	0	8	7	2	0	0	6	4	1.13	231	.269	.406	2	.000	-0	302	1		0.1
LEARY, JACK	John J. B7.1857 New Haven CT TL/5-11/186 d8.21 ▲																									
1880	Bos N	0	1	.000	1	1	0	0	3	8	5	0	0	0	1	15.00	15	.727	.727	3	.000	-0	43	-3		-0.5
1881	Det N	2	0	.000	2	2	1	0	13	13	6	0	0	2	2	4.15	70	.255	.283	11	.273	1*	9	-0		0.0
1882	Pit AA	1	0	1.000	3	2	1	0	18.2	28	22	0	0	3	5	6.75	39	.326	.348	257-1	.292	1*	197	-7		-0.3
	Bal AA	2	1	.667	3	3	3	0	26	29	22	1	0	8	2	1.04	265	.264	.314	18	.222	0*	137	0		0.1
	Year	3	1	.750	6	5	4	0	44.2	57	44	1	0	11	7	3.43	79	.291	.329	275-1	.287	1	160	-7		-0.2
1884	Alt U	0	3	.000	3	3	2	0	24	31	30	0	2	7	2	5.25	51	.292	.306	33	.091	-2*	43	-7		-0.8
	CP U	0	2	.000	2	1	1	0	10	14	14	0	0	5	6	5.40	45	.311	.380	40	.175	-1*	53	-4		-0.6
	Year	0	5	.000	5	4	3	0	34	45	44	0	2	7	13	5.29	49	.298	.329	73	.137	-3	45	-11		-1.4
Total	4	3	9	.250	14	12	8	0	94.2	123	99	1	2	20	23	4.56	59	.301	.333	362-1	.254	-2	84	-21		-2.1
LEARY, TIM	Timothy James B12.23.1958 Santa Monica CA BR/TR/6-3/205(190-220) [NYN79 1/2] d4.12 Col UCLA																									
1981	NY N	0	0	—	1	1	0	0-0	2	2	0	0	0	1-0	3	0.00	—	.000	.143	1	.000	-0	50	1	107	0.0
1983	NY N	1	1	.500	2	2	1	0-0	10.2	15	10	0	0	4-0	9	3.38	109	.319	.365	3	.333	0	144	-2		-0.3
1984	NY N	3	3	.500	20	7	0	0-0	53.2	61	28	2	2	18-3	29	4.02	89	.285	.343	10-1-3	.300	2	81	-3		-0.2
1985	Mil A	1	4	.200	5	5	0	0-0	33.1	40	18	5	1	8-0	29	4.05	104	.296	.340	0	—	0	43	0		-0.0
1986	Mil A	12	12	.500	33	30	3-2	0-0	188.1	216	97	20	7	53-4	110	4.21	104	.289	.339	0	—	0	92	5		0.6
1987	LA N	3	11	.214	39	12	0	1-1	107.2	121	62	15	2	36-5	61	4.76	84	.285	.343	23-0-3	.304	2	79	-9		-0.8
1988	†LA N	17	11	.607	35	34	9-6	0-0	228.2	201	87	13	6	56-4	180	2.91	115	.234	.284	67-0-13	.269	6*	93	10		1.9
1989	LA N	6	7	.462	19	17	2	0-0	117.1	107	45	9	2	37-7	59	3.38	102	.247	.306	33-0-6	.061	-2	74	3		0.1
	Cin N	2	7	.222	14	14	0	0-0	89.2	98	39	8	3	31-8	64	3.71	97	.278	.338	26-0-3	.192	1	67	0		0.2
	Year	8	14	.364	33	31	2	0-0	207	205	84	17	5	68-15	123	3.52	100	.261	.321	59-0-9	.119	-1	71	2		0.3
1990	NY A	9	19	.321	31	31	6-1	0-0	208	202	105	18	7	78-1	138	4.11	97	.257	.328	0	—	0	70	-3		-0.2
1991	NY A	4	10	.286	28	18	1	0-0	120.2	150	89	20	4	57-1	83	6.49	64	.312	.388	0	—	0	105	-28		-2.8
1992	NY A	5	6	.455	18	15	2	0-0	97	84	62	9	4	57-2	34	5.57	71	.245	.354	0	—	0	97	-16		-1.6
	Sea A	3	4	.429	8	8	1	0-0	44	47	27	3	5	30-3	12	4.91	82	.280	.394	0	—	0	105	-5		-0.6
	Year	8	10	.444	26	23	3	0-0	141	131	89	12	9	87-5	46	5.36	74	.256	.367	0	—	0	100	-19		-2.2
1993	Sea A	11	9	.550	33	27	0	0-1	169.1	202	104	21	8	58-5	68	5.05	89	.300	.362	0	—	0	95	-7	15	-1.1
1994	Tex A	1	2	.333	5	6	3	0-0	21	26	19	4	1	11-2	9	8.14	59	.306	.380	0	—	0	102	-11		-1.1
Total	13	78	105	.426	292	224	25-9	1-2	1491.1	1570	792	147	52	535-45	888	4.36	90	.273	.338	163-1-28	.221	9	88	-65	122	-5.3
LeCLAIR, GEORGE	George Lewis "Frenchy" B10.18.1886 Milton VT D10.10.1918 Farnham QC, Can. BR/TR/5-9/170 d6.5																									
1914	Pit F	5	2	.714	22	7	5-1	0	103.1	99	52	0	1	25	49	4.01	72	.262	.309	34-0-1	.147	-2	109	-10		-0.9
1915	Pit F	1	2	.333	14	3	1	1	45.2	43	20	1	0	13	10	3.35	81	.253	.306	13	.154	-1	232	-3		-0.3
	Buf F	0	0	—	1	0	0	0	3	4	2	0	0	1	2	6.00	47	.333	.385	0	—	0		-1		-0.1
	Bal F	1	8	.111	18	9	6-1	1	84	76	43	2	0	22	30	2.46	116	.246	.296	24-0-2	.083	-2	68	-2		-0.4
	Year	2	10	.167	33	12	7-1	2	132.2	123	65	3	0	36	42	2.85	99	.251	.302	37-0-2	.108	-3	108	-4		-0.8
Total	2	7	12	.368	55	19	12-2	2	236	222	117	3	1	61	91	3.36	85	.255	.305	71-0-3	.127	-5	108	-16		-1.7
LEDBETTER, RAZOR	Ralph Overton B12.8.1894 Rutherford College NC D2.1.1969 W.Palm Beach FL BR/TR/6-3/190 d4.16																									
1915	Det A	0	0	—	1	0	0	0*	1	1	0	0	0	0	0	0.00	—	.333	.333	0	—	0		-1		0.0
LEDEZMA, WILFREDO	Wilfredo Jose B1.21.1981 Guarico, Venez BL/TL/6-3/150(150-210) d4.2																									
2003	Det A	3	7	.300	34	8	0	0-1	84	99	55	12	3	35-3	49	5.79	76	.297	.365	0	—	0	58	-12		-1.2
2004	Det A	4	3	.571	15	8	0	0-1	53.1	55	28	3	2	18-0	29	4.39	102	.272	.333	0	—	0	109	0		0.0
2005	Det A	2	4	.333	10	10	0	0-0	49.2	61	46	10	2	24-0	30	7.07	60	.303	.377	0	—	0	111	-18		-1.7
Total	3	9	14	.391	59	26	0	0-2	187	215	129	25	7	77-3	108	5.73	76	.292	.360	0	—	0	93	-30		-2.9
LEE, CLIFF	Clifton Phifer B8.30.1978 Benton AR BL/TL/6-3/190* [MonN00 4/105] d9.15 Col Arkansas-Monticello																									
2002	Cle A	0	1	.000	2	2	0	0-0	10.1	6	2	0	0	8-1	6	1.74	255	.171	.326	0	—	0	21	3		0.3
2003	Cle A	3	3	.500	9	9	0	0-0	52.1	41	28	7	2	20-1	44	3.61	123	.220	.301	0	—	0	99	3	61	0.3
2004	Cle A	14	8	.636	33	33	0	0-0	179	188	113	30	11	81-1	161	5.43	80	.268	.350	3	.333	0	117	-21		-2.2
2005	Cle A	18	5	.783	32	32	1	0-0	202	194	91	22	0	52-1	143	3.79	108	.251	.295	8	.000	-1	143	9		0.6
Total	4	35	17	.673	76	76	1	0-0	443.2	429	234	59	13	161-4	354	4.38	97	.253	.320	11	.091	-0	123	-6	61	-1.0
LEE, COREY	Corey Wayne B12.26.1974 Raleigh NC BB/TL/6-2/180 [TexA96 1/32] d8.24 Col North Carolina St.																									
1999	Tex A	0	0	—	2	1	0	0-0	3	4	3	0	0	2-0	2	9.00	48	.400	.500	0	—	0	-2			-0.3
LEE, DAVID	David Emmer B3.12.1973 Pittsburgh PA BR/TR/6-1/200* [ColN95 23/627] d5.22 Col Mercyhurst																									
1999	Col N	3	2	.600	36	0	0	0-0	49	43	21	4	2	29-1	38	3.67	158	.247	.364	5	.200	-0	9			0.8
2000	Col N	0	0	—	7	0	0	1-0	5.2	10	9	3	1	6-0	6	11.12	52	.357	.486	0	—	0	-3			-0.2
2001	SD N	1	0	1.000	41	0	0	0-0	48.2	52	20	6	6	27-1	42	3.70	112	.278	.385	1	.000	-0	4		37	0.1
2003	Cle A	1	0	1.000	8	0	0	0-0	7.2	4	4	1	0	6-1	7	4.70	94	.143	.294	0	—	0	0			0.0
2004	Cle A	0	0	—	4	0	0	0-0	4.1	8	7	0	0	4-0	4	10.38	42	.348	.444	0	—	0	-4			-0.2
Total	5	5	2	.714	96	0	0	1-0	115.1	117	61	14	11	72-3	97	4.37	113	.266	.380	6	.167	-0	6		37	0.6
LEE, DON	Donald Edward B2.26.1934 Globe AZ BR/TR/6-4/210* d4.23 Mil 1970 f-Thornton Col Arizona																									
1957	Det A	1	3	.250	11	6	0	0	38.2	48	22	6	1	18-0	19	4.66	83	.308	.379	12-0-1	.167	-0	116	-3		-0.4
1958	Det A	0	0	—	1	0	0	0	2	1	2	1	1	1-0	0	9.00	45	.143	.333	0	—	0	-1			-0.1
1960	Was A	8	7	.533	44	20	1	3	165	160	72	16	3	64-3	88	3.44	113	.258	.328	43-1-1	.116	-0	110	9		0.6
1961	Min A	3	6	.333	37	10	4	3	115	93	49	12	4	35-1	65	3.52	120	.221	.286	30-0-3	.067	-3	77	10		0.6
1962	Min A	3	3	.500	9	9	1	0	52	51	27	8	7	24-0	28	4.50	91	.256	.355	19	.211	0	102	-1		-0.1
	LA A	8	8	.500	27	22	4-2	0	153.1	153	64	12	3	39-1	74	3.11	124	.256	.304	49-0-2	.184	-0	105	12		1.1
	Year	11	11	.500	36	31	5-2	0	205.1	204	91	20	10	63-1	102	3.46	113	.256	.317	68-0-2	.191	-0	104	9		1.0
1963	LA A	8	11	.421	40	22	3-2	1	154	148	74	12	9	51-4	89	3.68	93	.251	.317	46-0-5	.156	-1	104	-5		0.5
1964	LA A	5	4	.556	33	8	0	1	89.1	99	39	6	1	25-1	73	2.72	121	.279	.326	23	.261	2	91	3		0.5
1965	Cal A	0	1	.000	10	0	0	1	14	21	14	4	1	5-2	12	6.43	53	.350	.409	3	.333	1	-5			-0.0
	Hou N	0	0	—	9	0	0	0	24	18	9	1	0	3-0	15	3.38	99	.267	.353	1	.000	-0	0			0.0
1966	Hou N	2	0	1.000	9	0	0	0	18	17	5	1	0	4-1	9	2.50	137	.250	.292	1	1.000	1	2			0.3
	Chi N	2	1	.667	16	0	0	0	19	28	19	3	0	12-1	7	7.11	52	.346	.421	0	—	0	-8		15	-1.1
	Year	4	1	.800	25	0	0	0	37	45	24	4	0	16-2	16	4.86	73	.302	.365	1	1.000	1	-7			-0.8
Total	9	40	44	.476	244	97	13-4	11	828.1	827	387	81	31	281-14	467	3.61	104	.260	.324	226-1-14	.164	-1	102	13	15	0.6

YEAR	TM LG	W	L	PCT	G	GS	CG-SHO	SV-BS	IP	H	R	HR	HB	BB-IB	SO	ERA	AERA	OAV	OOB	AB-HR-SH	AVG	PB	SUP	APR	DL	PW

LEE, MARK Mark Linden B6.14.1953 Inglewood CA BR/TR/6-4/225* [SDN76 13/293] d4.23 Col Pepperdine

1978	SD N	5	1	.833	56	0	0	2-0	85	74	34	2	2	36-13	31	3.28	102	.240	.321	5-0-1	.000	-1		1		0.1
1979	SD N	2	4	.333	46	1	0	5-3	65	88	34	3	2	25-5	25	4.29	82	.332	.392	6-0-1	.333	1	176	-5		-0.4
1980	Pit N	0	1	1.000	4	0	0	0-0	5.2	5	3	0	0	3-0	2	4.76	77	.227	.320	0	—	0		-1		0.0
1981	Pit N	0	2	.000	12	0	0	2-1	19.2	17	6	1	0	5-1	5	2.75	133	.233	.282	2	.500	0		2		0.4
Total	4	7	8	.467	118	1	0	9-4	175.1	184	77	6	4	69-19	63	3.64	95	.275	.345	13-0-2	.231	1	176	-3		0.1

LEE, MARK Mark Owen B7.20.1964 Williston ND BL/TL/6-3/198* [DetA85 15/392] d9.8 Col Florida International

1988	KC A	0	0	—	4	0	0	0-0	5	6	2	0	0	1-0	0	3.60	111	.300	.333	0	—	0		0		0.0
1990	Mil A	1	0	1.000	11	0	0	0-0	21.1	20	5	0	0	4-0	14	2.11	184	.256	.286	0	—	0		5		0.2
1991	Mil A	2	5	.286	62	0	0	1-6	67.2	72	33	10	1	31-7	43	3.86	104	.283	.362	0	—	0		0		0.1
1995	Bal A	2	0	1.000	39	0	0	1-1	33.1	31	18	5	1	18-3	27	4.86	98	.246	.340	0	—	0		0		0.0
Total	4	5	5	.500	116	0	0	2-7	127.1	129	58	16	2	54-10	84	3.82	109	.270	.343	0	—	0		5		0.3

LEE, MIKE Michael Randall B5.19.1941 Bell CA BL/TL/6-5/220* d5.6 Col East Los Angeles (CA) JC

1960	Cle A	0	0	—	7	0	0	0	9	6	2	1	1	11-0	6	2.00	187	.207	.439	0	—	0		2		0.1
1963	LA A	1	1	.500	6	4	0	0	26	30	11	3	1	14-0	11	3.81	90	.300	.391	7	.000	-1	78	0		-0.1
Total	2	1	1	.500	13	4	0	0	35	36	13	4	2	25-0	17	3.34	105	.279	.404	7	.000	-1	78	2		0.0

LEE, BOB Robert Dean "Moose","Horse" B11.26.1937 Ottumwa IA BR/TR/6-3/230(215-230) d4.15

1964	LA A	6	5	.545	64	5	0	19	137	87	31	6	1	58-8	111	1.51	217	.182	.270	22	.000	-2	70	**28**		2.7
1965	Cal A☆	9	7	.563	69	0	0	23	131.1	95	35	11	4	42-8	89	1.92	177	.205	.269	21-1-4	.143	1		20		3.2
1966	Cal A	5	4	.556	61	0	0	16	101.2	90	39	8	1	31-2	46	2.74	122	.237	.294	11-0-3	.000	-0		5		0.5
1967	LA N	0	0	—	4	0	0	0	6.2	6	4	0	1	3-0	2	5.40	57	.222	.313	0	—	-0		-4		-0.2
	Cin N	3	3	.500	27	1	0	2	50.2	51	26	0	0	25-7	33	4.44	84	.262	.338	8	.375	1	351	-3		-0.3
	Year	3	3	.500	31	1	0	2	57.1	57	34	2	1	28-7	35	4.55	81	.257	.335	8	.375	1	359	-5		-0.5
1968	Cin N	2	4	.333	44	1	0	3	64.2	73	38	4	0	37-10	34	5.15	61	.302	.387	5	.200	1	192	-12		-1.3
Total	5	25	23	.521	269	7	0	63	492	402	177	31	8	196-35	315	2.71	124	.225	.300	67-1-7	.104	-1	131	34		4.6

LEE, ROY Roy Edwin B9.28.1917 Elmira NY D11.11.1985 St.Louis MO BL/TL/5-11.5/175 d9.23 Col Bowling Green

| 1945 | NY N | 0 | 2 | .000 | 3 | 1 | 0 | 0 | 7 | 8 | 9 | 0 | 0 | 8-0 | 0 | 11.57 | 34 | .267 | .333 | 1 | .000 | -0 | 87 | -5 | | -0.9 |

LEE, SANG-HOON Sang-Hoon B3.11.1971 Seoul, South Korea BL/TL/6-1/190 d6.29

| 2000 | Bos A | 0 | 0 | — | 9 | 0 | 0 | 0-0 | 11.2 | 11 | 4 | 2 | 2 | 4-0 | 6 | 3.09 | 163 | .262 | .347 | 0 | — | 0 | | 3 | | 0.1 |

LEE, TOM Thomas Frank B6.8.1862 Philadelphia PA D3.4.1886 Milwaukee WI d6.14

1884	Chi N	1	4	.200	5	5	5	0	45.1	55	43	12		15	14	3.77	83	.272	.323	24	.125	-2*	95	-5		-0.5
	Bal U	5	8	.385	15	14	12	0	122	121	88	1		29	81	3.39	79	.242	.283	82	.280	-2*	89	-8		-0.8
Total	1	6	12	.333	20	19	17	0	167.1	176	131	13		44	95	3.50	80	.250	.295	106	.245	-3	90	-13		-1.3

LEE, THORNTON Thornton Starr "Lefty" B9.13.1906 Sonoma CA D6.9.1997 Tucson AZ BL/TL/6-3/205 d9.19 s-Don Col Cal Poly-San Luis Obispo

1933	Cle A	1	1	.500	3	2	2	0	17.1	13	9	1	0	11	7	4.15	107	.203	.320	8	.375	1	115	1		0.2
1934	Cle A	1	1	.500	24	6	0	0	85.2	105	57	8	3	44	41	5.04	90	.308	.392	21	.095	-1	124	-5		-0.3
1935	Cle A	7	10	.412	32	20	8-1	1	180.2	179	90	6	4	71	81	4.04	112	.259	.331	61-0-3	.197	-1	85	11		0.9
1936	Cle A	3	5	.375	43	8	2	3	127	138	86	2	2	67	49	4.89	103	.271	.358	41	.122	-2	107	-1		-0.2
1937	Chi A	12	10	.545	30	25	13-2	1	204.2	209	91	17	1	60	80	3.52	131	.260	.312	71-0-5	.211	1	77	26		2.4
1938	Chi A	13	12	.520	33	30	18-1	1	245.1	252	123	12	3	94	77	3.49	140	.263	.331	97-4-4	.258	6*	91	33		3.4
1939	Chi A	15	11	.577	33	29	15-2	3	235	260	121	14	3	70	81	4.21	112	.285	.338	91	.165	-3	95	14		1.1
1940	Chi A	12	13	.480	28	27	24-1	0	228	223	100	13	2	56	87	3.47	127	.254	.300	84-0-5	.274	4	98	25		2.7
1941	Chi A★	22	11	.667	35	34	**30-3**	1	300.1	258	98	18	4	92	130	**2.37**	**173**	.232	**.293**	114-0-1	.254	5	83	**56**		**6.5**
1942	Chi A	2	6	.250	11	8	6-1	0	76	82	38	4	2	31	25	3.32	109	.278	.351	30	.200	1	45	0		0.0
1943	Chi A	5	9	.357	19	19	7-1	0	127	129	66	8	4	50	35	4.18	80	.266	.340	42-0-1	.071	-4	84	-10		-1.6
1944	Chi A	3	5	.250	15	14	6	0	113.1	105	51	3	1	25	39	3.02	114	.246	.290	42-0-1	.095	-3	68	3		0.0
1945	Chi A*	15	12	.556	29	28	19-1	0	228.1	208	81	6	10	76	108	2.44	136	.245	.314	78-0-2	.179	-1	92	18		2.0
1946	Chi A	2	4	.333	7	7	2	0	43.1	39	24	1	1	23	23	3.53	97	.244	.342	15	.267	1	72	-2		-0.2
1947	Chi A	3	7	.300	21	11	2-1	1	86.2	86	50	5	2	56	57	4.47	82	.261	.372	29	.207	0	79	-8		-0.8
1948	NY N	3	7	.250	11	4	1	0	32.2	41	20	3	1	12	17	4.41	89	.304	.365	11	.091	-1	96	-2		-0.3
Total	16	117	124	.485	374	272	155-14	10	2331.1	2327	1145	121	43	838	937	3.56	119	.260	.326	835-4-22	.200	1	87	159		15.8

LEE, BILL William Crutcher "Big Bill" B10.21.1909 Plaquemine LA D6.15.1977 Plaquemine LA BR/TR/6-3/195 d4.29

1934	Chi N	13	14	.481	35	29	16-4	1	214.1	218	91	9	2	74	104	3.40	114	.263	.325	76-0-3	.132	-2*	97	12		1.2
1935	†Chi N	20	6	**.769**	39	32	18-3	1	252	241	106	11	5	84	100	2.96	133	.251	.314	102-0-3	.235	2	133	24		2.4
1936	Chi N	18	11	.621	43	33	20-4	1	258.2	238	106	14	3	93	102	3.31	121	.246	.314	87-1-9	.138	-3	94	19		1.7
1937	Chi N	14	15	.483	42	34	17-2	3	272.1	289	122	14	0	73	108	3.54	113	.273	.320	87-1-12	.172	-1	93	12		1.2
1938	†Chi N★	22	9	.710	44	37	19-9	2	291	281	96	18	2	74	121	**2.66**	**144**	.252	.299	101-0-7	.198	1	102	**39**		**4.1**
1939	Chi N	19	15	.559	37	36	20-1	0	282.1	295	125	18	1	85	105	3.44	114	.272	.325	103-1-8	.126	-4	101	15		1.4
1940	Chi N	9	17	.346	37	30	9-1	0	211.1	246	129	12	2	70	70	5.03	75	.294	.350	76-0-2	.132	-2	107	-27		-3.2
1941	Chi N	8	14	.364	34	22	12	1	167.1	179	87	6	2	43	62	3.76	93	.270	.316	59-2-9	.186	1	120	-7		-0.6
1942	Chi N	13	13	.500	32	30	18-1	0	219.2	221	99	4	2	67	75	3.85	83	.258	.312	69-0-5	.159	1	90	-11		-1.1
1943	Chi N	3	7	.300	13	12	4	0	78.1	83	37	4	0	27	18	3.56	94	.273	.332	26-0-2	.269	1	76	-2		-0.2
	Phi N	1	5	.167	13	7	2	3	60.2	70	35	4	1	21	17	4.60	73	.298	.358	17	.059	-2	65	-8		-1.0
	Year	4	12	.250	26	19	6	3	139	153	72	8	1	48	35	4.01	84	.284	.344	43-0-2	.186	-0	72	-10		-1.2
1944	Phi N	10	11	.476	31	28	11-3	1	208.1	199	88	9	3	57	50	3.15	115	.248	.300	72-0-3	.194	-0	84	9		1.0
1945	Phi N	3	6	.333	13	13	2	0	77.1	107	52	0	0	30	13	4.66	82	.318	.374	24-0-3	.167	-1	100	-8		-0.8
	Bos N	6	3	.667	16	13	6-1	0	106.1	112	43	6	0	36	12	2.79	137	.279	.338	31-0-5	.129	-1	90	10		0.8
	Year	9	9	.500	29	26	8-1	0	183.2	219	95	6	0	66	25	3.58	107	.297	.354	55-0-8	.145	-1	95	0		0.0
1946	Bos N	10	9	.526	25	21	8	0	140	148	73	7	1	45	32	4.18	82	.273	.330	47-0-3	.170	-1	90	-11		-1.4
1947	Chi N	0	2	.000	14	2	0	0	24	26	16	2	1	14	9	4.50	88	.268	.366	3	.333	0	101	-2		-0.1
Total	14	169	157	.518	462	379	182-29	13	2864	2953	1304	138	24	893	998	3.54	106	.268	.322	980-5-74	.168	-10	99	64		5.4

LEE, BILL William Francis "Spaceman" B12.28.1946 Burbank CA BL/TL/6-3/206(190-210) [BosA68 22/507] d6.25 Mil 1970 Col USC

1969	Bos A	1	3	.250	20	1	0	0-1	52	56	27	6	2	28-0	45	4.50	95	.281	.372	10	.000	-1	46	-3		-0.3
1970	Bos A	2	2	.500	11	5	0	1-0	37	48	20	3	0	14-1	19	4.62	86	.320	.378	11	.000	-1	89	-2		-0.3
1971	Bos A	9	2	.818	47	2	0	2-2	102	102	35	7	1	46-7	74	2.74	136	.256	.333	23-0-3	.217	-1	112	10		1.2
1972	Bos A☆	7	4	.636	47	0	0	5-2	84.1	75	31	5	1	32-8	43	3.20	101	.248	.320	16-1-0	.188	1		2		0.6
1973	Bos A☆	17	11	.607	38	33	18-1	1-0	284.2	275	100	20	5	76-2	120	2.75	146	.257	.307	0	—	0	87	37		3.6
1974	Bos A	17	15	.531	38	37	16-1	0-0	282.1	320	123	25	4	67-0	95	3.51	104	.290	.331	0	—	0	97	9		1.2
1975	†Bos A	17	9	.654	41	34	17-4	0-0	260	274	123	20	4	69-1	78	3.95	103	.273	.319	0	—	0	105	5		0.6
1976	Bos A	5	7	.417	24	14	1	3-0	96	124	68	13	2	28-1	29	5.63	69	.307	.354	0	—	0*	102	-16	52	-1.9
1977	Bos A	9	5	.643	27	16	4	1-0	128	155	67	14	0	29-1	31	4.43	101	.306	.341	0	—	0	101	1		0.2
1978	Bos A	10	10	.500	28	24	8	0-0	177	198	89	20	2	59-2	44	3.46	119	.285	.340	0	—	0	98	7		0.8
1979	Mon N	16	10	.615	33	33	6-3	0-0	222	230	91	20	4	46-1	59	3.04	122	.265	.302	74-0-7	.216	2	100	15		1.9
1980	Mon N	4	6	.400	24	18	2	0-0	118	156	71	13	2	22-1	34	4.96	73	.319	.349	41	.220	1*	120	-17	59	-1.2
1981	†Mon N	5	6	.455	31	7	0	6-0	88.2	90	33	6	2	14-2	34	2.94	121	.265	.297	22-1-0	.364	3	86	5		1.3
1982	Mon N	0	0	—	7	0	0	0-0	12.1	19	7	1	0	1-0	8	4.38	84	.352	.357	0	—	0		-1		0.0
Total	14	119	90	.569	416	225	72-10	19-5	1944.1	2122	885	176	27	531-27	713	3.62	108	.280	.327	197-2-10	.208	5	100	52	111	7.7

LEE, WATTY Wyatt Arnold B8.12.1879 Lynch Station VA D3.6.1936 Washington DC BL/TL/5-10.5/171 d4.30 ▲

1901	Was A	16	16	.500	36	33	25-2	0	262	328	184	14	11	45	63	4.40	83	.303	.337	129-0-1	.256	4*	95	-22		-1.6
1902	Was A	5	6	.455	13	10	10	0	98	118	66	9	8	20	24	5.05	73	.298	.344	391-4-7	.256	3*	116	-11		-0.8
1903	Was A	8	12	.400	22	20	15-2	0	166.2	169	86	5	7	40	70	3.08	102	.262	.313	231-0-4	.208	1*	87	-3		0.0
1904	Pit N	1	2	.333	5	3	1	0	22.2	34	25	0	3	9	5	8.74	31	.337	.407	12	.250	1*	92	-1		-1.3
Total	4	30	36	.455	76	66	51-4	0	549.1	649	361	24	29	114	162	4.29	81	.292	.334	763-4-12	.242	10	96	-49		-3.7

LEEVER, SAM Samuel "Deacon","The Goshen Schoolmaster" B12.23.1871 Goshen OH D5.19.1953 Goshen OH BR/TR/5-10.5/175 d5.26

| 1898 | Pit N | 1 | 0 | 1.000 | 5 | 3 | 2 | 0 | 33 | 26 | 10 | 0 | | 15 | 15 | 2.45 | 145 | .215 | .252 | 12 | .250 | 0 | 113 | 5 | | 0.3 |
| 1899 | Pit N | 21 | 23 | .477 | **51** | 39 | 35-4 | **3** | 379 | 353 | 191 | 7 | 11 | 122 | 121 | 3.18 | 120 | .247 | .311 | 146-0-6 | .226 | 3 | 97 | 25 | | 2.8 |

YEAR	TM LG	W	L	PCT	G	GS	CG-SHO	SV-BS	IP	H	R	HR	HB	BB-IB	SO	ERA	AERA	OAV	OOB	AB-HR-SH	AVG	PB	SUP	APR	DL	PW
1900	†Pit N	15	13	.536	30	29	25-3	0	232.2	236	101	2	8	48	84	2.71	134	.263	.306	88-1-0	.205	0	88	25		2.5
1901	Pit N	14	5	.737	21	20	18-2	0	176	182	82	2	7	39	82	2.86	114	.265	.311	71-0-2	.183	-0	141	9		0.8
1902	Pit N	15	7	.682	28	26	23-4	2	222	203	73	2	8	31	86	2.39	115	.243	.277	90	.178	-0*	116	11		0.8
1903	†Pit N	25	7	**.781**	36	34	30-**7**	1	284.1	255	98	2	5	60	90	**2.06**	**157**	.238	.282	115-0-4	.165	-4	115	37		3.4
1904	Pit N	18	11	.621	34	32	26-1	0	253.1	224	85	2	5	54	63	2.17	127	.237	.282	99-1-2	.263	7	116	15		2.3
1905	Pit N	20	5	**.800**	33	29	20-3	1	229.2	199	94	3	12	54	81	2.70	111	.231	.286	88-0-2	.102	-4	143	6		0.2
1906	Pit N	22	7	.759	36	31	25-6	0	260.1	232	84	3	7	48	76	2.32	115	.243	.284	95-0-1	.211	2	128	14		1.4
1907	Pit N	14	9	.609	31	24	17-5	0	216.2	182	70	3	8	46	65	1.66	147	.229	.278	73-0-4	.151	-1	109	15		1.2
1908	Pit N	15	7	.682	38	20	14-4	2	192.2	179	60	1	6	41	28	2.10	110	.249	.295	61-0-2	.148	0	106	5		0.4
1909	Pit N	8	1	.889	19	4	2	2	70	74	30	0	4	14	23	2.83	96	.276	.322	24	.167	0	96	-1		-0.1
1910	Pit N	6	5	.545	26	8	4	2	111	104	45	2	6	25	33	2.76	112	.259	.313	31-0-2	.065	-3	117	4		0.1
Total 13		194	100	.660	388	299	241-39	13	2660.2	2449	1023	29	88	587	847	2.47	123	.245	.293	993-2-25	.184	1	114	170		16.1

LEFEBVRE, BILL   Wilfred Henry "Lefty"   B11.11.1915 Natick RI   BL/TL/5-11.5/180   d6.10 Mil 1945   Col Holy Cross ▲

YEAR	TM LG	W	L	PCT	G	GS	CG-SHO	SV-BS	IP	H	R	HR	HB	BB-IB	SO	ERA	AERA	OAV	OOB	AB-HR-SH	AVG	PB	SUP	APR	DL	PW
1938	Bos A	0	0	—	1	0	0	0	4	8	6	2	1	0	0	13.50	37	.400	.429	1-1-0	1.000	1		-3		0.0
1939	Bos A	1	1	.500	5	3	0	0	26.1	35	17	2	0	14	9	5.81	81	.333	.412	10	.300	1*	118	-2		-0.1
1943	Was A	2	0	1.000	6	3	1	0	32.1	33	18	3	0	16	10	4.45	72	.268	.353	14	.286	2*	123	-4		0.0
1944	Was A	2	4	.333	24	4	2	3	69.2	86	48	3	1	21	17	4.52	72	.305	.355	62	.258	3*	109	-12		-0.5
Total 4		5	5	.500	36	10	3	3	132.1	162	89	10	2	51	36	5.03	71	.306	.369	87-1-0	.276	7	119	-21		-0.6

LEFFERTS, CRAIG   Craig Lindsay   B9.29.1957 Munich, W.Germany   BL/TL/6-1/210(180-230)   [ChiN80 9/219]   d4.7 Col Arizona

YEAR	TM LG	W	L	PCT	G	GS	CG-SHO	SV-BS	IP	H	R	HR	HB	BB-IB	SO	ERA	AERA	OAV	OOB	AB-HR-SH	AVG	PB	SUP	APR	DL	PW
1983	Chi N	3	4	.429	56	5	0	1-0	89	80	35	13	2	29-3	60	3.13	122	.243	.308	18-0-1	.111	-1	65	6		0.4
1984	†SD N	3	4	.429	62	0	0	10-2	105.2	88	29	4	1	24-1	56	2.13	169	.229	.272	17-0-1	.294	1		17		1.5
1985	SD N	7	6	.538	60	0	0	2-3	83.1	75	34	7	0	30-4	48	3.35	106	.244	.311	4	.250	0		2		0.4
1986	SD N	9	8	.529	**83**	0	0	4-3	107.2	98	41	7	1	44-11	72	3.09	118	.253	.327	8-1-1	.125	1*		7		1.3
1987	SD N	2	2	.500	33	0	0	2-2	51.1	56	29	9	2	15-5	39	4.38	91	.272	.327	3	.333	0		-3		-0.2
	†SF N	3	3	.500	44	0	0	4-5	47.1	36	18	4	0	18-6	18	3.23	119	.216	.289	4	.250	1		4		0.5
	Year	5	5	.500	77	0	0	6-7	98.2	92	47	13	2	33-11	57	3.83	102	.247	.310	7	.286	1		1		0.3
1988	SF N	3	8	.273	64	0	0	11-3	92.1	74	33	7	1	23-5	58	2.92	112	.225	.275	9	.000	-1		4		0.4
1989	†SF N	2	4	.333	70	0	0	20-4	107	93	38	11	1	22-5	71	2.69	126	.233	.272	7	.000	-1		8		0.5
1990	SD N	7	5	.583	56	0	0	23-8	78.2	68	26	10	1	22-4	60	2.52	153	.228	.283	4-0-2	.250	0		11		2.2
1991	SD N	1	6	.143	54	0	0	23-7	69	74	35	5	1	14-3	48	3.91	97	.285	.318	6	.000	-1		-1		-0.3
1992	SD N	13	9	.591	27	27	0	0-0	163.1	180	76	16	0	35-2	81	3.69	97	.285	.320	52-0-9	.077	-3	108	-3		-0.7
	Bal A	1	3	.250	5	5	-1	0-0	33	34	19	3	0	6-0	23	4.09	99	.268	.299	0	—	-0	54	-1		-0.2
1993	Tex A	3	9	.250	52	8	0	0-0	83.1	102	57	17	1	28-3	58	6.05	69	.304	.357	0	—	0	113	-16	15	-1.9
1994	Cal A	1	1	.500	30	0	0	1-0	34.2	50	20	7	0	12-3	27	4.67	105	.350	.392	0	—	.0		1		0.0
Total 12		58	72	.446	696	45	1	101-37	1145.2	1108	490	120	11	322-55	719	3.43	109	.257	.308	132-1-14	.121	-3	98	36	15	3.9

LEFTWICH, PHIL   Philip Dale   B5.19.1969 Lynchburg VA   BR/TR/6-5/205*   [CalA90 2/64]   d7.29 Col Radford   [DL 1995 Cal A 124]

YEAR	TM LG	W	L	PCT	G	GS	CG-SHO	SV-BS	IP	H	R	HR	HB	BB-IB	SO	ERA	AERA	OAV	OOB	AB-HR-SH	AVG	PB	SUP	APR	DL	PW
1993	Cal A	4	6	.400	12	12	1	0-0	80.2	81	35	5	3	27-1	31	3.79	120	.262	.326	0	—	0	101	8		0.8
1994	Cal A	5	10	.333	20	20	1	0-0	114	127	75	16	3	42-2	67	5.68	86	.283	.346	0	—	0	73	-9	21	-1.0
1996	Cal A	0	1	.000	2	2	0	0-0	7.1	12	9	1	0	3-0	4	7.36	69	.375	.429	0	—	0	92	-3		-0.3
Total 3		9	17	.346	34	34	2		202	220	119	22	6	72-3	102	4.99	96	.279	.342	0	—	0	84	-4	145	-0.5

LEHENY, REGIS   Regis Francis   B1.5.1908 Pittsburgh PA   D11.2.1976 Pittsburgh PA   BL/TL/6-0.5/180   d5.21

YEAR	TM LG	W	L	PCT	G	GS	CG-SHO	SV-BS	IP	H	R	HR	HB	BB-IB	SO	ERA	AERA	OAV	OOB	AB-HR-SH	AVG	PB	SUP	APR	DL	PW
1932	Bos A	0	0	—	2	0	0	0	2.2	5	5	0	0	3	1	16.88	27	.417	.533	1	.000	-0		-3		-0.1

LEHEW, JIM   James Anthony   B8.19.1937 Baltimore MD   BR/TR/6-0/185*   d9.13

YEAR	TM LG	W	L	PCT	G	GS	CG-SHO	SV-BS	IP	H	R	HR	HB	BB-IB	SO	ERA	AERA	OAV	OOB	AB-HR-SH	AVG	PB	SUP	APR	DL	PW
1961	Bal A	0	0	—	2	0	0	0	2	1	0	0	0	0-0	0	0.00	—	.167	.167	0	—	0		1		0.0
1962	Bal A	0	0	—	6	0	0	0	9.2	10	3	0	0	3-0	2	1.86	199	.303	.351	1	.000	-0		2		0.1
Total 2		0	0	—	8	0	0	0	11.2	11	3	0	0	3-0	2	1.54	241	.282	.326	1	.000	-0		3		0.1

LEHMAN, KEN   Kenneth Karl   B6.10.1928 Seattle WA   BL/TL/6-0/186(160-186)   d9.5

YEAR	TM LG	W	L	PCT	G	GS	CG-SHO	SV-BS	IP	H	R	HR	HB	BB-IB	SO	ERA	AERA	OAV	OOB	AB-HR-SH	AVG	PB	SUP	APR	DL	PW
1952	†Bro N	1	2	.333	4	3	0	0	15.1	19	11	1	0	6	7	5.28	69	.297	.357	4	.000	0	106	-3		-0.5
1956	Bro N	2	3	.400	25	4	0	0	49.1	65	35	11	0	23-2	29	5.66	70	.325	.389	10	.300	1	61	-9		-0.7
1957	Bro N	0	0	—	3	0	0	0	7	7	0	0	0	1-0	3	0.00	—	.259	.286	2	.500	0*		3		0.2
	Bal A	8	3	.727	30	3	1	6	68	57	21	1	0	22-2	32	2.78	129	.232	.294	20	.200	1*	50	7		1.4
1958	Bal A	2	1	.667	31	1	1	0	62	64	26	5	2	18-4	36	3.48	103	.276	.326	14	.071	-1	0	1		-0.1
1961	Phi N	1	1	.500	41	2	0	1	63.1	61	32	6	1	25-8	27	4.26	96	.260	.331	6	.000	-1*	76	-1		-0.1
Total 5		14	10	.583	134	13	2	7	265	273	125	24	3	95-16	134	3.91	97	.272	.333	56	.161	1	67	-2		-0.1

LEHR, JUSTIN   Charles Larry   B8.3.1977 Orange CA   BR/TR/6-1/200*   [OakA99 8/243]   d6.20 Col California-Santa Barbara/USC

YEAR	TM LG	W	L	PCT	G	GS	CG-SHO	SV-BS	IP	H	R	HR	HB	BB-IB	SO	ERA	AERA	OAV	OOB	AB-HR-SH	AVG	PB	SUP	APR	DL	PW
2004	Oak A	1	1	.500	32.2			0-1	32.2	35	19	3	2	14-2	16	5.23	88	.280	.357	0	—	0		-1		-0.1
2005	Mil N	1	1	.500	23	0	0	0-1	34.2	32	19	4	1	18-2	23	3.89	110	.242	.336	3	.000	-0		0		0.0
Total 2		2	2	.500	50	0	0	0-2	67.1	67	38	7	3	32-4	39	4.54	98	.261	.346	3	.000	-0		-1		-0.1

LEHR, NORM   Norman Carl Michael "King"   B5.28.1901 Rochester NY   D7.17.1968 Livonia NY   BR/TR/6-0/168   d5.20

YEAR	TM LG	W	L	PCT	G	GS	CG-SHO	SV-BS	IP	H	R	HR	HB	BB-IB	SO	ERA	AERA	OAV	OOB	AB-HR-SH	AVG	PB	SUP	APR	DL	PW
1926	Cle A	0	0	—	4	0	0	0	14.2	11	5	0	0	4	4	3.07	132	.216	.273	4	.000	-1		2		0.1

LEIBER, HANK   Henry Edward   B1.17.1911 Phoenix AZ   D11.8.1993 Tucson AZ   BR/TR/6-1.5/205   d4.16.1933   Col Arizona ▲

YEAR	TM LG	W	L	PCT	G	GS	CG-SHO	SV-BS	IP	H	R	HR	HB	BB-IB	SO	ERA	AERA	OAV	OOB	AB-HR-SH	AVG	PB	SUP	APR	DL	PW
1942	NY N	0	1	.000	1	1	1	0	9	9	9	0	1	5	5	6.00	56	.290	.405	147-4-1	.218	0*	25	-3		-0.3

LEIBRANDT, CHARLIE   Charles Louis   B10.4.1956 Chicago IL   BR/TL/6-3/200*   [CinN78 9/225]   d9.17 Col Miami-Ohio

YEAR	TM LG	W	L	PCT	G	GS	CG-SHO	SV-BS	IP	H	R	HR	HB	BB-IB	SO	ERA	AERA	OAV	OOB	AB-HR-SH	AVG	PB	SUP	APR	DL	PW
1979	†Cin N	0	0	—	3	0	0	0-0	4.1	2	2	0	0	2-0	1	0.00	—	.154	.250	0	—	0		1		0.0
1980	Cin N	10	9	.526	36	27	5-2	0-0	173.2	200	84	15	2	54-4	62	4.25	83	.292	.345	56-0-4	.196	2	106	-12		-1.0
1981	Cin N	1	1	.500	7	4	1-1	0-0	30	28	12	0	0	15-2	9	3.60	97	.262	.347	8	.000	-0	82	0		0.0
1982	Cin N	3	4	.417	36	11	0	2-0	107.2	130	68	4	2	48-9	34	5.10	72	.308	.380	25-0-4	.080	-1	98	-17		-1.9
1984	†KC A	11	7	.611	23	23	0	0-0	143.2	158	65	11	3	38-2	53	3.63	111	.277	.322	0	—	0	92	6		0.6
1985	†KC A	17	9	.654	33	33	8-3	0-0	237.2	223	86	17	2	68-3	108	2.69	155	.248	.301	0	—	0	100	36		4.0
1986	KC A	14	11	.560	35	34	8-1	0-0	231.1	238	112	18	4	63-0	108	4.09	105	.268	.317	0	—	0	94	6		0.7
1987	KC A	16	11	.593	35	35	8-3	0-0	240.1	235	104	23	1	74-2	151	3.41	135	.253	.307	0	—	0	92	30		3.3
1988	KC A	13	12	.520	35	35	7-2	0-0	243	244	98	20	4	62-3	125	3.19	126	.264	.311	0	—	0	92	21		2.2
1989	KC A	5	11	.313	33	27	3-1	0-0	161	196	98	13	2	54-4	73	5.14	75	.304	.358	0	—	0	113	-21		-1.8
1990	Atl N	9	11	.450	24	24	5-2	0-0	162.1	164	72	9	4	35-3	76	3.16	128	.261	.302	50-0-5	.180	1	93	12	55	1.5
1991	†Atl N	15	13	.536	36	36	1-1	0-0	229.2	212	105	18	4	56-3	128	3.49	111	.245	.292	70-0-12	.043	-4	93	8		0.8
1992	†Atl N	15	7	.682	32	31	5-2	0-0	193	191	78	9	3	42-4	104	3.36	109	.258	.301	58-0-8	.121	-1	103	7	36	-0.4
1993	Tex A	9	10	.474	26	26	1	0-0	150.1	169	84	15	4	45-5	89	4.55	92	.284	.336	0	—	0	119	-6	91	-0.8
Total 14		140	119	.541	394	346	52-18	2-0	2308	2390	1068	172	37	656-44	1121	3.71	108	.268	.319	267-0-33	.120	-5	99	71	91	8.8

LEICESTER, JON   Jonathan David   B2.7.1979 Mariposa CA   BR/TR/6-3/230*   [ChiN00 11/313]   d6.9 Col Memphis

YEAR	TM LG	W	L	PCT	G	GS	CG-SHO	SV-BS	IP	H	R	HR	HB	BB-IB	SO	ERA	AERA	OAV	OOB	AB-HR-SH	AVG	PB	SUP	APR	DL	PW
2004	Chi N	5	1	.833	32	0	0	0-2	41.2	40	20	7	0	15-0	35	3.89	114	.256	.318	1	.000	-0		2		0.2
2005	Chi N	0	2	.000	6	1	0	0-0	9	11	10	2	2	9-0	7	9.00	49	.324	.489	0-0-1	—	0	85	-5		-0.9
Total 2		5	3	.625	38	1	0	0-2	50.2	51	30	9	2	24-0	42	4.80	92	.268	.353	1-0-1	.000	-0	85	-3		-0.7

LEIFIELD, LEFTY   Albert Peter   B9.5.1883 Trenton IL   D10.10.1970 Alexandria VA   BL/TL/6-1/165   d9.3 C9

YEAR	TM LG	W	L	PCT	G	GS	CG-SHO	SV-BS	IP	H	R	HR	HB	BB-IB	SO	ERA	AERA	OAV	OOB	AB-HR-SH	AVG	PB	SUP	APR	DL	PW
1905	Pit N	5	2	.714	8	7	6-1	0	56	52	24	0	4	18	10	2.89	104	.248	.307	20	.350	3	106	0		0.4
1906	Pit N	18	13	.581	37	31	24-8	1	255.2	214	90	3	14	68	111	1.87	143	.231	.294	88-0-4	.125	-3	106	17		1.8
1907	Pit N	20	16	.556	40	33	24-6*	1	286	270	107	1	12	100	112	2.33	105	.256	.328	102-0-2	.147	0	112	4		0.6
1908	Pit N	15	14	.517	34	26	18-5	2	218.2	168	69	1	12	86	87	2.10	110	.212	.299	75-0-3	.227	2	96	6		1.2
1909	†Pit N	19	8	.704	32	26	13-3	0	201.2	172	76	4	6	54	43	2.37	115	.229	.286	73-0-2	.192	2	131	7		0.9
1910	Pit N	15	13	.536	40	30	13-3	2	218.1	197	84	6	10	67	64	2.64	117	.253	.308	60-0-9	.183	0	116	7		1.6
1911	Pit N	16	16	.500	42	37	26-2	1	318	301	114	7	16	92	111	2.63	131	.260	.318	102-0-3	.235	6*	90	30		3.4
1912	Pit N	1	2	.333	6	1	0	0	23.2	29	15	0	2	10	8	4.18	78	.302	.380	7	.143	-1	0	-3		-0.2
	Chi N	7	2	.778	13	9	4-1	0	70.2	68	26	0	3	21	23	2.42	137	.258	.319	26-0-3	.115	-1	104	4		0.7
	Year	8	4	.667	19	10	5-1	0	94.1	97	41	0	5	31	31	2.86	116	.269	.336	33-0-3	.121	-1	104	1		0.5
1913	Chi N	0	1	.000	6	1	0	0	21.1	28	14	0	0	5	4	5.48	58	.329	.367	7	.000	-1*	189	-4		-0.3
1918	StL A	2	6	.250	15	6	3-1	0	67	61	23	1	4	22	22	2.55	107	.252	.312	18	.053	-2	46	2		0.1

YEAR	TM LG	W	L	PCT	G	GS	CG-SHO	SV-BS	IP	H	R	HR	HB	BB-IB	SO	ERA	AERA	OAV	OOB	AB-HR-SH	AVG	PB	SUP	APR	DL	PW
1919	StL A	6	4	.600	19	9	6-2	0	92	96	40	4	4	25	18	2.93	113	.270	.325	30	.100	-2	108	3		0.1
1920	StL A	0	0	—	4	0	0	0	9	17	12	0	0	3	3	7.00	56	.405	.444	2	.000	-0		-4		-0.2
Total	12	124	97	.561	296	216	138-32	7	1838	1673	694	27	85	554	616	2.47	116	.248	.313	611-0-26	.175	6	100	76		10.1

LEIPER, DAVE   David Paul   B6.18.1962 Whittier CA   BL/TL/6-1/160(160-175)   [OakA82*S1/22]   d9.2   Col Fullerton (CA) JC

1984	Oak A	1	0	1.000	8	0	0	0-1	7	12	7	2	0	5-0	3	9.00	42	.353	.436	0	—	0		-4		-0.5
1986	Oak A	2	2	.500	33	0	0	1-2	31.2	28	17	3	2	18-4	15	4.83	81	.252	.358	0	—	0		-3		-0.3
1987	Oak A	2	1	.667	45	0	0	1-3	52.1	49	28	6	1	18-0	33	3.78	110	.246	.306	0	—	0		1		0.1
	SD N	1	0	1.000	12	0	0	1-0	16	16	-8	2	0	5-0	10	4.50	88	.267	.323	0	—	0		-1		0.0
1988	SD N	3	0	1.000	35	0	0	1-0	54	45	19	1	0	14-5	33	2.17	157	.231	.276	2	.500	0	5	34		0.4
1989	SD N	0	1	.000	22	0	0	1-0	28.2	40	19	2	2	20-4	7	5.02	70	.333	.437	1	.000	-0	5	31		-0.3
1994	Oak A	0	0	—	26	0	0	1-0	18.2	13	4	0	1	6-1	14	1.93	233	.206	.278	0	—	0	6			0.3
1995	Oak A	1	1	.500	24	0	0	0-0	22.2	23	10	3	1	13-1	10	3.57	127	.258	.359	0	—	0	2			0.2
	Mon N	0	2	.000	26	0	0	2-1	22	16	9	2	0	6-0	12	2.86	150	.200	.256	1	.000	-0	3			0.3
1996	Phi N	2	0	1.000	26	0	0	0-0	21	31	16	4	0	7-2	10	6.43	67	.348	.396	0	—	0	-5			-0.4
	Mon N	0	1	.000	7	0	0	0-0	4	9	5	0	0	2-0	3	11.25	39	.474	.524	0	—	0	-3			-0.5
	Year	2	1	.667	33	0	0	0-0	25	40	21	4	0	9-2	13	7.20	60	.370	.419	0	—	0	-7			-0.9
Total	8	12	8	.600	264	0	0	7-7	278	282	141	25	7	114-17	150	3.98	100	.266	.338	4	.250	0	-4	65		-0.7

LEIPER, JACK   John Henry Thomas   B12.23.1867 Chester PA   D8.23.1960 West Goshen PA   BL/TL/5-11/?   d9.4

1891	Col AA	2	2	.500	6	5	4	0	45	41	43	3	4	39	19	5.40	64	.234	.385	21	.143	-2	101	-11		-0.9

LEISTER, JOHN   John William   B1.3.1961 San Antonio TX   BR/TR/6-2/200(200-215)   [BosA84*S3/52]   d5.28   Col Michigan St.

1987	Bos A	0	2	.000	8	6	0	0-0	30.1	49	31	9	0	12-1	16	9.20	50	.368	.418	0	—	0	140	-14		-0.8
1990	Bos A	0	0	—	2	1	0	0-0	5.2	7	5	0	0	4-0	3	4.76	86	.304	.393	0	—	0	111	-1		-0.1
Total	2	0	2	.000	10	7	0	0-0	36	56	36	9	0	16-1	19	8.50	53	.359	.414	0	—	0	136	-15		-0.9

LEITER, AL   Alois Terry   B10.23.1965 Toms River NJ   BL/TL/6-3/215(200-220)   [NYA84 2/50]   d9.15   b-Mark

1987	NY A	2	2	.500	4	4	0	0-0	22.2	24	16	2	0	15-0	28	6.35	70	.273	.379	0	—	0	72	-4		-0.6
1988	NY A	4	4	.500	14	14	0	0-0	57.1	49	27	7	5	33-0	60	3.92	101	.231	.348	0	—	0	102	0	34	0.1
1989	NY A	1	2	.333	4	4	0	0-0	26.2	23	20	1	2	21-0	22	6.08	64	.235	.377	0	—	0	99	-6		-0.6
	Tor A	0	0	—	1	1	0	0-0	6.2	9	3	1	0	2-0	4	4.05	94	.310	.355	0	—	0	96	0	144	0.0
	Year	1	2	.333	5	5	0	0-0	33.1	32	23	2	2	23-0	26	5.67	68	.252	.373	0	—	0	98	-7		-0.6
1990	Tor A	0	0	—	4	0	0	0-0	6.1	1	0	0	0	2-0	5	0.00	—	.050	.136	0	—	0	3			0.1
1991	Tor A	0	0	—	3	0	0	0-0	1.2	3	5	0	1	5-0	1	27.00	16	.429	.667	0	—	0		-4	168	-0.2
1992	Tor A	0	0	—	1	0	0	0-0	1	1	1	0	0	2-0	0	9.00	46	.200	.429	0	—	0	0			0.0
1993	†Tor A	9	6	.600	34	12	1-1	2-1	105	93	52	8	4	56-2	66	4.11	107	.240	.339	0	—	0	91	3	16	0.4
1994	Tor A	6	7	.462	20	20	1	0-0	111.2	125	68	6	2	65-3	100	5.08	96	.285	.374	0	—	0	83	-2	15	-0.2
1995	Tor A	11	11	.500	28	28	2-1	0-0	183	162	80	15	6	108-1	153	3.64	131	.238	.345	0	—	0	71	23		2.4
1996	Fla N★	16	12	.571	33	33	2-1	0-0	215.1	153	74	11	11	119-3	200	2.93	141	**.202**	.318	70-0-7	.100	-2	101	31		3.4
1997	†Fla N	11	9	.550	27	27	0	0-0	151.1	133	78	13	12	91-4	132	4.34	93	.241	.359	48-0-2	.104	-1	95	-4	35	-0.7
1998	NY N	17	6	.739	28	28	4-2	0-0	193	151	55	8	11	71-2	174	2.47	167	.216	.298	57-0-5	.105	0	105	37	21	4.2
1999	†NY N	13	12	.520	32	32	1-1	0-0	213	209	107	19	9	93-8	162	4.23	103	.262	.342	57-0-11	.105	-2	100	1		-0.2
2000	†NY N★	16	8	.667	31	31	2-1	0-0	208	176	84	19	11	76-1	200	3.20	136	.228	.304	58-0-9	.052	-3	94	27		2.5
2001	NY N	11	11	.500	29	29	0	0-0	187.1	178	81	18	4	46-3	142	3.31	122	.252	.299	62	.065	-3	87	13	26	1.1
2002	NY N	13	13	.500	33	33	2-2	0-0	204.1	194	99	23	8	69-5	172	3.48	114	.250	.317	53-0-3	.151	2	96	6		1.0
2003	NY N	15	9	.625	30	30	1-1	0-0	180.2	176	83	15	9	94-11	139	3.99	105	.260	.355	53-0-5	.019	-5	98	5	20	0.2
2004	NY N	10	8	.556	30	30	0	0-0	173.2	138	65	16	11	97-8	117	3.21	134	.218	.332	54-0-2	.093	-2	78	23	20	2.0
2005	Fla N	3	7	.300	17	16	0	0-0	80	88	61	9	6	60-2	52	6.64	60	.292	.416	18-0-4	.000	-2	96	-23		-2.6
	†NY A	4	5	.444	16	10	0	0-0	62.1	66	42	6	4	38-0	35	5.49	80	.268	.375	0	—	0	105	-8		-1.0
Total	19	162	132	.551	419	382	16-10	2-1	2391	2152	1101	198	117	1163-53	1974	3.80	112	.242	.336	530-0-48	.085	-18	92	121	499	11.3

LEITER, MARK   Mark Edward   B4.13.1963 Joliet IL   BR/TR/6-3/210*   [BalA83*4/103]   d7.24   b-Al   Col Ramapo

1990	NY A	1	1	.500	8	3	0	0-0	26.1	33	20	5	2	9-0	21	6.84	58	.314	.376	0	—	0	129	-7		-0.4
1991	Det A	9	7	.563	38	15	1	1-1	134.2	125	66	16	6	50-4	103	4.21	99	.245	.316	0	—	0	108	1	18	0.0
1992	Det A	8	5	.615	35	14	1	0-0	112	116	57	9	4	43-5	75	4.18	96	.277	.342	0	—	0	149	-3	31	-0.3
1993	Det A	6	6	.500	27	13	1	0-1	106.2	111	61	17	3	44-5	70	4.73	92	.267	.338	0	—	0	96	-4	28	-0.4
1994	Cal A	4	7	.364	40	7	0	2-1	95.1	99	56	13	9	35-6	71	4.72	104	.265	.340	0	—	0	88	1		0.1
1995	SF N	10	12	.455	30	29	7-1	0-0	195.2	185	91	19	17	55-4	129	3.82	108	.254	.318	61-0-9	.098	-2	86	7		0.4
1996	SF N	4	10	.286	23	22	1	0-0	135.1	151	93	25	9	50-7	118	5.19	80	.283	.353	42-0-7	.143	-1	111	-18		-1.7
	Mon N	4	2	.667	12	12	1	0-0	69.2	68	35	12	7	19-1	46	4.39	99	.254	.316	25-0-2	.080	-1	116	1		0.0
	Year	8	12	.400	35	34	2	0-0	205	219	128	37	16	69-8	164	4.92	86	.273	.341	67-0-9	.119	-2	113	-18		-1.7
1997	Phi N	10	17	.370	31	31	3	0-0	182.2	216	132	25	9	64-4	148	5.67	74	.292	.352	51-0-10	.118	-1	104	-32	15	-4.0
1998	Phi N	7	5	.583	69	0	0	23-12	88.2	67	36	8	8	47-5	84	3.55	122	.216	.331	2	.000	-0	8			1.3
1999	Sea A	0	0	—	2	0	0	0-0	1.1	2	1	0	0	0-0	1	6.75	71	.333	.333	0	—	0	0		178	0.0
2001	Mil N	2	1	.667	20	3	0	0-0	36	32	16	2	2	8-2	26	3.75	114	.232	.284	7	.143	-0	143	2	113	0.2
Total	11	65	73	.471	335	149	15-1	26-15	1184.1	1205	664	155	75	424-43	892	4.57	93	.265	.334	188-0-28	.112	-6	106	-44	383	-4.8

LEITH, BILL   William "Shady Bill"   B5.31.1873 Matteawan NY   D7.16.1940 Beacon NY   TR/6-1/208   d9.25

1899	Was N	0	0	—	1	1	0	0-0	4	5	0	1	2	1	18.00	22	.400	.538	1	.000	-0		-3		-0.1

LEITNER, DOC   George Aloysius   B9.14.1865 Piermont NY   D5.18.1937 New York NY   BR/TR/5-11.5/185   d8.10   Col Fordham

1887	Ind N	2	6	.250	8	8	8	0	65	69	66	6	0	41	27	5.68	73	.259	.358	27	.148	-3	90	-12		-1.3

LEITNER, DUMMY   George Michael   B6.19.1872 Parkton MD   D2.20.1960 Baltimore MD   BL/TR/5-7/120   d6.29

1901	Phi A	0	0	—	1	0	0	0	2	1	0	0	0	1	1	0.00	—	.143	.250	1	.000	-0		1		0.0
	NY N	0	2	.000	2	2	2	0	18	27	9	0	1	4	3	4.50	73	.342	.381	7	.143	-0	32	-1		-0.2
1902	Cle A	0	0	—	1	1	0	0	8	11	4	0	0	1	0	4.50	77	.324	.343	4	.250	-0	84	0		0.0
	Chi A	0	0	—	1	0	0	0	4	9	7	0	2	2	0	13.50	25	.450	.542	3	.000	-0		-4		-0.2
	Year	0	0	—	2	1	0	0	12	20	11	0	2	3	0	7.50	46	.370	.424	7	.143	-0	84	-4		-0.2
Total	2	0	2	.000	5	3	2	0	32	48	20	0	3	8	4	5.34	63	.343	.391	15	.133	-1	49	-4		-0.4

LELIVELT, BILL   William John   B10.21.1884 Chicago IL   D2.14.1968 Chicago IL   BR/TR/5-10/168   d7.19   b-Jack

1909	Det A	0	1	.000	4	2	1	1	20	27	12	0	0	2	4	4.50	56	.325	.341	6	.333	1	84	-4		-0.1
1910	Det A	0	1	.000	1	1	1	0	9	6	4	0	0	3	2	1.00	263	.207	.281	2	.500	1	0	1		0.1
Total	2	0	2	.000	5	3	2	1	29	33	16	0	0	5	6	3.41	75	.295	.325	8	.375	2	54	-3		0.0

LEMANCZYK, DAVE   David Lawrence   B8.17.1950 Syracuse NY   BR/TR/6-4/230*   [DetA72 16/380]   d4.15   Col Hartwick

1973	Det A	0	0	—	1	0	0	0-0	2.1	4	3	0	0	0-0	2	11.57	35	.364	.364	0	—	0		-2		-0.1
1974	Det A	2	1	.667	22	3	0	0-0	78.2	79	43	12	2	44-6	52	4.00	96	.261	.357	0	—	0	84	-3		-0.1
1975	Det A	2	7	.222	26	6	4	0-1	109	120	62	8	4	46-5	67	4.46	91	.281	.352	0	—	0	33	-4	24	-0.3
1976	Det A	4	6	.400	20	10	1	0-0	81.1	86	47	7	0	34-0	51	5.09	73	.271	.341	0	—	0	83	-9		-1.0
1977	Tor A	13	16	.448	34	34	11	0-0	252	278	143	20	4	87-6	105	4.25	100	.282	.340	0	—	0	84	-4		-0.4
1978	Tor A	4	14	.222	29	20	3	0-0	136.2	170	97	16	3	65-1	62	6.26	63	.313	.388	0	—	0	74	-31	20	-3.6
1979	Tor A☆	8	10	.444	22	20	11-3	0-0	143	137	65	12	6	45-2	63	3.71	118	.258	.321	0	—	0	63	11	23	1.3
1980	Tor A	2	5	.286	10	8	0	0-0	43.1	57	29	4	0	15-0	10	5.40	80	.322	.371	0	—	0	65	-5		-0.6
	Cal A	4	4	.333	21	2	0	0-0	66.2	81	40	8	2	27-2	19	4.32	92	.301	.367	0	—	0	124	-5		-0.5
	Year	4	9	.308	31	10	0	0-0	110	138	69	12	2	42-2	29	4.75	86	.309	.368	0	—	0	79	-9		-1.1
Total	8	37	63	.370	185	103	30-3	0-1	913	1012	529	87	20	363-22	429	4.62	89	.284	.351	0	—	0	74	-52	67	-5.3

LEMASTER, DENNY   Denver Clayton   B2.25.1939 Corona CA   BR/TL/6-1/185*   d7.15

1962	Mil N	3	4	.429	17	12	4	0-0	86.2	75	36	11	3	32-1	69	3.01	126	.233	.308	33-0-2	.121	-1	116	6		0.3
1963	Mil N	11	14	.440	46	31	10-1	1	237	199	87	30	1	85-14	190	3.04	106	.227	.295	74-2-6	.189	3	78	6		0.9
1964	Mil N	17	11	.607	39	35	9-3	1	221	216	112	27	4	75-4	185	4.15	85	.252	.313	67-0-7	.134	0	115	-14		-1.6
1965	Mil N	7	13	.350	32	23	4-1	0	146.1	140	75	12	3	58-7	111	4.43	80	.251	.324	45-0-2	.089	-1	95	-12		-1.7
1966	Atl N	11	8	.579	27	27	10-3	0	171	170	78	25	1	41-5	139	3.74	97	.258	.301	59-0-4	.119	-1	124	-1		-0.3
1967	Atl N★	9	9	.500	31	31	8-2	0	215.1	184	86	20	3	72-2	148	3.34	99	.229	.293	67-0-7	.104	-2	82	2		0.0

YEAR	TM LG	W	L	PCT	G	GS	CG-SHO	SV-BS	IP	H	R	HR	HB	BB-IB	SO	ERA	AERA	OAV	OOB	AB-HR-SH	AVG	PB	SUP	APR	DL	PW
1968	Hou N	10	15	.400	33	32	7-2	0	224	231	79	11	4	72-11	146	2.81	105	.262	.319	65-0-9	.031	-3	86	3		-0.1
1969	Hou N	13	17	.433	38	37	11-1	1-0	244.2	232	97	20	1	72-8	173	3.16	112	.246	.298	88-1-6	.170	3	87	12		1.8
1970	Hou N	7	12	.368	39	21	3	3-2	162	169	88	22	2	65-9	103	4.56	85	.268	.335	45-1-3	.178	-2	86	-11		-1.0
1971	Hou N	0	2	.000	42	0	0	2-1	60	59	23	4	1	22-6	28	3.45	98	.262	.331	6-0-1	.167	-0		1		0.0
1972	Mon N	2	0	1.000	13	0	0		19.2	11	6	2	1	6-1	13	7.78	46	.329	.376	3	.333	1		-8		-0.8
Total	11	90	105	.462	357	249	66-14	8-3	1787.2	1703	778	184	24	600-73	1305	3.58	96	.249	.310	552-4-47	.130	0	96	-16		-2.5

LeMAY, DICK   Richard Paul B8.28.1938 Cincinnati OH BL/TL/6-3/190* d6.13 Col Michigan

YEAR	TM LG	W	L	PCT	G	GS	CG-SHO	SV-BS	IP	H	R	HR	HB	BB-IB	SO	ERA	AERA	OAV	OOB	AB-HR-SH	AVG	PB	SUP	APR	DL	PW
1961	SF N	3	6	.333	27	5	1	3	83.1	65	35	11	4	36-7	54	3.56	107	.217	.307	26-0-1	.077	-2	140	3		0.2
1962	SF N	0	1	.000	9	0	0	1	9.1	9	8	2	0	9-1	5	7.71	49	.265	.419	0	—	0		-4		-0.4
1963	Chi N	0	1	.000	9	1	0		15.1	26	9	1	0	4-2	10	5.28	66	.394	.429	2	.000	-0	123	-2		-0.2
Total	3	3	8	.273	45	6	1	4	108	100	52	14	4	49-10	69	4.17	91	.250	.336	28-0-1	.071	-1	136	-3		-0.4

LEMON, BOB   Robert Granville B9.22.1920 San Bernardino CA D1.11.2000 Long Beach CA BL/TR/6-0/185* d9.9.1941 Mil 1943-45 M8/C6 HF1976 ▲

YEAR	TM LG	W	L	PCT	G	GS	CG-SHO	SV-BS	IP	H	R	HR	HB	BB-IB	SO	ERA	AERA	OAV	OOB	AB-HR-SH	AVG	PB	SUP	APR	DL	PW
1946	Cle A	4	5	.444	32	5	1		94	77	40	1	0	68	39	2.49	133	.229	.359	89-1-3	.180	2*	83	4		0.7
1947	Cle A	11	5	.688	37	15	6-1	3	167.1	150	68	7	4	97	65	3.44	101	.242	.348	56-2-2	.321	9*	119	2		1.5
1948	†Cle A☆	20	14	.588	43	37	20-10	2	293.2	231	104	12	3	129	147	2.82	144	.216	.302	119-5-2	.286	14*	122	42		6.6
1949	Cle A☆	22	10	.688	37	33	22-2	1	279.2	211	101	19	6	137	138	2.99	133	.211	.309	108-7-5	.269	16*	115	34		5.6
1950	Cle A★	23	11	.676	44	37	22-3	3	288	281	144	28	2	146	170	3.84	113	.257	.345	136-6-3	.272	17*	114	15		3.4
1951	Cle A★	17	14	.548	42	34	17-1	2	263.1	244	119	18	2	124	132	3.52	108	.244	.328	102-3-1	.206	5*	92	8		1.4
1952	Cle A★	22	11	.667	42	36	28-5	4	309.2	236	104	15	6	105	131	2.50	134	.208	.279	124-2-6	.226	7*	134	30		4.4
1953	Cle A☆	21	15	.583	41	36	23-5	1	286.2	283	119	16	11	110	98	3.36	112	.262	.336	112-2-6	.232	8*	114	14		3.0
1954	†Cle A★	23	7	.767	36	33	21-2	0	258.1	228	95	12	4	92	110	2.72	135	.237	.303	98-2-8	.214	6*	134	25		3.7
1955	Cle A	18	10	.643	35	31	5	2	211.1	218	103	17	5	74-3	100	3.88	103	.266	.329	78-1-6	.244	6*	115	3		1.1
1956	Cle A	20	14	.588	39	35	21-2	2	255.1	230	103	23	6	89-2	94	3.03	139	.239	.305	93-5-7	.194	5*	95	31		4.6
1957	Cle A	6	11	.353	21	17	2	0	117.1	129	70	9	7	64-6	45	4.60	81	.287	.379	46-1-0	.065	-3*	98	-12		-1.7
1958	Cle A	0	1	.000	11	1	0	0	25.1	41	15	3	1	16-2	8	5.33	68	.376	.457	13	.231	0*	148	-4	31	-0.1
Total	13	207	128	.618	460	350	188-31	22	2850	2559	1185	180	57	1251-13	1305	3.23	119	.241	.323	1174-37-49	.233	90	114	192	31	34.2

LEMONDS, DAVE   David Lee B7.5.1948 Charlotte NC BL/TL/6-1.5/180* [ChiN68 S1/1] d6.30 Col North Carolina-Asheville [DL 1973 Chi A 55]

YEAR	TM LG	W	L	PCT	G	GS	CG-SHO	SV-BS	IP	H	R	HR	HB	BB-IB	SO	ERA	AERA	OAV	OOB	AB-HR-SH	AVG	PB	SUP	APR	DL	PW
1969	Chi N	1	1	.000			0	0-0	4.2	5	2	0	0	5-0	0	3.86	104	.313	.476	1	.000	-0	44	0		0.0
1972	Chi A	4	7	.364	31	18	0	0-0	94.2	87	39	6	1	38-3	69	2.95	106	.247	.319	25-0-2	.120	-1*	93	0		-0.1
Total	2	4	8	.333	33	19	0	0-0	99.1	92	41	6	1	43-3	69	2.99	106	.250	.327	26-0-2	.115	-1	90	0	55	-0.1

LEMONGELLO, MARK   Mark B7.21.1955 Jersey City NJ BR/TR/6-1/180* d9.14

YEAR	TM LG	W	L	PCT	G	GS	CG-SHO	SV-BS	IP	H	R	HR	HB	BB-IB	SO	ERA	AERA	OAV	OOB	AB-HR-SH	AVG	PB	SUP	APR	DL	PW
1976	Hou N	3	1	.750	4	4	1	0-0	29	26	12	2	0	7-2	9	2.79	116	.236	.282	8-0-1	.000	-1	89	1		0.1
1977	Hou N	9	14	.391	34	30	5	0-0	214.2	237	88	20	3	52-4	83	3.48	104	.281	.323	69-0-5	.087	-4*	71	6		0.2
1978	Hou N	9	14	.391	33	30	9-1	1-0	210.1	204	100	20	9	66-5	77	3.94	85	.259	.318	64-0-6	.172	1	106	-15		-1.4
1979	Tor A	1	9	.100	18	10	2	0-0	83	97	64	14	3	34-8	40	6.29	70	.299	.365	0	—	0	74	-16		-1.6
Total	4	22	38	.367	89	74	17-1	1-0	537	564	264	56	15	159-19	209	4.06	89	.273	.326	141-0-12	.121	-3	85	-24		-2.7

LENNON, ED   Edward Francis B8.17.1897 Philadelphia PA D9.13.1947 Philadelphia PA BR/TR/5-11/170 d6.30 Col Niagara

YEAR	TM LG	W	L	PCT	G	GS	CG-SHO	SV-BS	IP	H	R	HR	HB	BB-IB	SO	ERA	AERA	OAV	OOB	AB-HR-SH	AVG	PB	SUP	APR	DL	PW
1928	Phi N	0	0	—	5	0	0		12.1	14	14	0	0	10	6	8.76	49	.373	.475	4	.000	-1		-6		-0.4

LEON, DANNY   Danilo Enrique (Lineco) B4.3.1967 LaConcepcion, Venez BR/TR/6-1/170 d6.6

YEAR	TM LG	W	L	PCT	G	GS	CG-SHO	SV-BS	IP	H	R	HR	HB	BB-IB	SO	ERA	AERA	OAV	OOB	AB-HR-SH	AVG	PB	SUP	APR	DL	PW
1992	Tex A	1	1	.500	15	0	0	0-0	18.1	18	14	5	3	10-0	15	5.89	65	.254	.369	0	—	0		-5	78	-0.4

LEON, IZZY   Isidoro (Becerra) B1.4.1911 Cruces, Cuba D7.25.2002 Miami FL BR/TR/5-10/160 d6.21 Negro Lg 1944-48

YEAR	TM LG	W	L	PCT	G	GS	CG-SHO	SV-BS	IP	H	R	HR	HB	BB-IB	SO	ERA	AERA	OAV	OOB	AB-HR-SH	AVG	PB	SUP	APR	DL	PW
1945	Phi N	0	4	.000	14	4	0	0	38.2	49	25	3	0	19	11	5.35	72	.312	.386	9	.111	-0	44	-5		-0.5

LEON, MAX   Maximino (Molino) B2.4.1950 Acula, Veracruz, Mexico BR/TR/6-0/170* d7.18

YEAR	TM LG	W	L	PCT	G	GS	CG-SHO	SV-BS	IP	H	R	HR	HB	BB-IB	SO	ERA	AERA	OAV	OOB	AB-HR-SH	AVG	PB	SUP	APR	DL	PW
1973	Atl N	2	2	.500	12	1	1	0-2	27	30	18	6	3	9-1	18	5.33	74	.278	.344	7-0-1	.286	0*	156	-5		-0.5
1974	Atl N	4	7	.364	34	2	1-1	3-1	75	68	22	5	1	14-3	38	2.64	144	.242	.280	15-0-1	.133	-1	81	10		1.5
1975	Atl N	2	1	.667	50	1	0	6-3	85	90	52	5	7	33-8	53	4.13	92	.274	.349	9-0-1	.333	1	186	-5		-0.1
1976	Atl N	2	4	.333	30	0	0	3-3	36	32	15	2	2	15-3	16	2.75	138	.234	.314	2	.000	-0		3	35	0.5
1977	Atl N	4	4	.500	31	9	0	1-1	81.2	89	42	9	9	25-2	44	3.97	112	.280	.347	19-0-3	.316	1*	102	4		0.4
1978	Atl N	0	0	—	5	0	0		5.2	6	4	1	1	4-0	1	6.35	63	.273	.393	0	—	0*		-1	47	-0.1
Total	6	14	18	.438	162	13	2-1	13-10	310.1	315	153	28	23	100-17	170	3.71	107	.264	.330	52-0-6	.250	1	116	7	82	1.7

LEONARD, DENNIS   Dennis Patrick B5.8.1951 Brooklyn NY BR/TR/6-1/190* [KCA72 2/42] d9.4 Col Iona [DL 1984 KC A 182]

YEAR	TM LG	W	L	PCT	G	GS	CG-SHO	SV-BS	IP	H	R	HR	HB	BB-IB	SO	ERA	AERA	OAV	OOB	AB-HR-SH	AVG	PB	SUP	APR	DL	PW
1974	KC A	0	4	.000	5	4	0	0-0	22	28	15	0	3	12-0	8	5.32	72	.329	.430	0	—	0	40	-3		-0.5
1975	KC A	15	7	.682	32	30	8	0-1	212.1	212	98	18	9	90-4	146	3.77	102	.263	.342	0	—	0	110	4		0.4
1976	†KC A	17	10	.630	35	34	16-2	0-0	259	247	113	16	11	70-5	150	3.51	100	.255	.309	0	—	0	135	2		0.0
1977	†KC A	20	12	.625	38	37	21-5	1-0	292.2	246	117	18	8	79-0	244	3.04	132	.227	.283	0	—	0*	99	30		3.0
1978	†KC A	21	17	.553	40	40	20-4	0-0	294.2	283	125	27	9	98-7	183	3.33	115	.254	.307	0	—	0	107	16		2.0
1979	KC A	14	12	.538	32	32	12-5	0-0	236	226	117	34	2	56-3	126	4.08	105	.253	.297	0	—	0	110	7		1.0
1980	†KC A	20	11	.645	38	38	9-3	0-0	280.1	271	127	30	1	80-5	155	3.79	107	.253	.304	0	—	0	117	10		1.0
1981	†KC A	13	11	.542	26	26	9-2	0-0	201.2	202	79	15	3	41-5	107	2.99	121	.258	.296	0	—	0	84	12		1.4
1982	KC A	10	6	.625	21	21	2	0-0	130.2	145	82	20	2	46-3	58	5.10	80	.279	.337	0	—	0	132	-15	78	-1.5
1983	KC A	6	3	.667	10	10	1	0-0	63	69	29	3	0	19-1	31	3.71	111	.277	.326	0	—	0	73	3	127	0.4
1985	KC A	0	0	—	2	0	0	0-0	2	1	0	0	0	0-0	1	0.00	—	.143	.143	0	—	0		1	148	0.0
1986	KC A	8	13	.381	33	30	5-2	0-0	192.2	207	106	22	4	51-6	114	4.44	96	.275	.321	0	—	0	80	-4		-0.5
Total	12	144	106	.576	312	302	103-23	1-1	2187	2137	1008	202	52	622-39	1323	3.70	107	.257	.310	0	—	0	106	63	535	6.5

LEONARD, ELMER   Elmer Ellsworth "Tiny" B11.12.1888 Napa CA D5.27.1981 Napa CA BR/TR/6-3.5/210 d6.22 Col St. Marys (CA)

YEAR	TM LG	W	L	PCT	G	GS	CG-SHO	SV-BS	IP	H	R	HR	HB	BB-IB	SO	ERA	AERA	OAV	OOB	AB-HR-SH	AVG	PB	SUP	APR	DL	PW
1911	Phi A	2	2	.500	5	1	1	0	19	26	11	0	2	10	10	2.84	111	.329	.418	7-0-1	.286	1	274	-1		-0.1

LEONARD, DUTCH   Emil John B3.25.1909 Auburn IL D4.17.1983 Springfield IL BR/TR/6-0/175(175-198) d8.31 C3

YEAR	TM LG	W	L	PCT	G	GS	CG-SHO	SV-BS	IP	H	R	HR	HB	BB-IB	SO	ERA	AERA	OAV	OOB	AB-HR-SH	AVG	PB	SUP	APR	DL	PW
1933	Bro N	2	3	.400	10	3	2	0	40	42	17	0	0	10	6	2.93	110	.261	.304	11-0-2	.000	-1	95	-1		-0.1
1934	Bro N	14	11	.560	44	21	11-2	5	183.2	210	90	12	4	33	58	3.28	119	.286	.320	67-0-5	.179	-1	128	8		1.1
1935	Bro N	2	9	.182	43	11	4	8	137.2	152	67	11	1	29	41	3.92	101	.280	.318	39-0-1	.026	-4	83	3		-0.2
1936	Bro N	0	0	—	16	0	0	1	32	34	18	2	0	5	8	3.66	113	.262	.289	5-0-1	.400	0		1		0.1
1938	Was A	12	15	.444	33	31	15-3	0	223.1	221	109	11	7	53	68	3.43	132	.256	.305	82-0-2	.232	-1	97	24		2.8
1939	Was A	20	8	.714	34	34	21-2	0	269.1	273	124	16	5	59	88	3.54	133	.262	.305	95-0-13	.221	0	94	25		2.3
1940	Was A☆	14	19	.424	35	35	23-2	0	289	328	136	19	2	78	124	3.49	120	.286	.332	101-0-8	.158	-5	84	21		1.9
1941	Was A	18	13	.581	34	33	19-4	0	256	271	117	6	3	54	91	3.45	117	.270	.309	88-0-11	.102	-5	108	17		1.3
1942	Was A	2	2	.500	6	5	1-1	0	35	28	16	1	0	5	15	4.11	98	.214	.243	10-0-1	.100	-0	89	-1		-0.1
1943	Was A★	11	13	.458	31	30	15-2	1	219.2	218	96	9	4	46	51	3.28	98	.257	.298	67-0-11	.104	-4	102	-3		-0.5
1944	Was A☆	14	14	.500	32	31	17-3	0	229.1	222	97	8	3	37	62	3.06	106	.252	.284	79-0-5	.228	2	108	5		0.9
1945	Was A★	17	7	.708	31	29	12-4	1	216	192	72	5	2	35	96	2.13	146	.248	.279	78-0-8	.231	1	125	21		2.5
1946	Was A	10	10	.500	26	23	7-2	0	161.2	182	76	9	4	36	62	3.56	94	.281	.323	53-0-5	.170	-1	106	-7		-0.7
1947	Phi N	17	12	.586	32	29	19-3	0	235	224	86	14	2	57	103	2.68	149	.258	.306	80-0-6	.175	-1	87	33		3.9
1948	Phi N	12	17	.414	34	30	16-1	0	225.2	226	85	9	4	54	92	2.51	157	.265	.312	83-0-2	.145	-3	80	31		3.7
1949	Chi N	7	16	.304	33	28	10-1	0	180	198	94	4	7	43	84	4.15	97	.272	.319	59-0-2	.203	0	73	-2		-0.1
1950	Chi N	5	1	.833	35	1	0	6	74	70	41	7	2	27	28	3.77	110	.248	.318	16-0-1	.063	-2	147	2		0.0
1951	Chi N☆	10	6	.625	41	1	0	3	81.2	69	30	3	2	28	30	2.64	155	.234	.305	21-0-1	.000	-3	129	11		2.0
1952	Chi N	2	2	.500	45	0	0	11	66.2	56	18	3	3	24	37	2.16	178	.235	.313	10	.200	1		12		1.3
1953	Chi N	2	2	.500	45	0	0	8	62.2	72	34	9	1	24	27	4.60	97	.289	.354	10	.300	-1		9		0.1
Total	20	191	181	.513	640	375	192-30	44	3218.1	3304	1432	158	56	737	1170	3.25	119	.265	.309	1054-0-85	.168	-21	97	204		22.2

LEONARD, DUTCH   Hubert Benjamin B4.16.1892 Birmingham OH D7.11.1952 Fresno CA BL/TL/5-10.5/185 d4.12 Mil 1918 Col St. Marys (CA)

YEAR	TM LG	W	L	PCT	G	GS	CG-SHO	SV-BS	IP	H	R	HR	HB	BB-IB	SO	ERA	AERA	OAV	OOB	AB-HR-SH	AVG	PB	SUP	APR	DL	PW
1913	Bos A	14	17	.452	42	28	14-3	1	259.1	245	108	0	4	94	144	2.39	123	.255	.324	83-0-3	.181	-1	120	11		1.2
1914	Bos A	19	5	.792	36	25	17-7	3	224.2	139	34	3	8	60	176	0.96	280	.180	.246	68-0-9	.147	-1	115	43		4.8
1915	†Bos A	15	7	.682	32	21	10-2	3	183.1	130	57	3	14	67	116	2.36	118	.208	.299	53-0-3	.264	5	105	12		1.7
1916	†Bos A	18	12	.600	48	34	17-6	6	274	244	87	6	8	66	144	2.36	117	.247	.300	85-0-4	.200	2	90	13		1.4
1917	Bos A	16	17	.485	37	36	26-4	1	294.1	257	88	4	5	72	144	2.17	119	.236	.286	104-0-2	.087	-6	83	16		0.8
1918	Bos A	8	6	.571	16	16	12-3	0	125.2	119	51	0	2	53	47	2.72	99	.254	.332	43-0-2	.186	-1	133	-1		-0.2

YEAR	TM LG	W	L	PCT	G	GS	CG-SHO	SV-BS	IP	H	R	HR	HB	BB-IB	SO	ERA	AERA	OAV	OOB	AB-HR-SH	AVG	PB	SUP	APR	DL	PW
1919	Det A	14	13	.519	29	28	18-4	0	217.1	212	89	7	7	65	102	2.77	115	.254	.313	71-0-6	.155	-3	94	8		0.4
1920	Det A	10	17	.370	28	27	10-3	0	191.1	192	107	8	8	63	76	4.33	86	.271	.338	57-0-3	.211	2	64	-7		-0.7
1921	Det A	11	13	.458	36	32	16-1	1	245	273	125	15	10	63	120	3.75	114	.286	.336	82-0-5	.171	-4	101	16		0.8
1924	Det A	3	2	.600	9	7	3	1	51.1	68	32	1	4	18	26	4.56	90	.327	.383	19-0-1	.211	-0	108	-3		-0.3
1925	Det A	11	4	.733	18	18	9	0	125.2	143	73	7	1	43	65	4.51	95	.289	.347	50-0-1	.200	-1	135	-3		-0.4
Total	11	139	113	.552	331	272	152-33	13	2192	2022	851	54	68	664	1160	2.76	115	.249	.312	715-0-39	.173	-5	102	105		9.5

LEONHARD, DAVE   David Paul   B1.22.1941 Arlington VA   BR/TR/5-11/165*   d9.21   Col Johns Hopkins

YEAR	TM LG	W	L	PCT	G	GS	CG-SHO	SV-BS	IP	H	R	HR	HB	BB-IB	SO	ERA	AERA	OAV	OOB	AB-HR-SH	AVG	PB	SUP	APR	DL	PW
1967	Bal A	0	0	—	3	2	0	1	14.1	15	5	1	0	6-0	9	3.14	100	.200	.290	5	.000	-1	83	0		0.0
1968	Bal A	7	7	.500	28	18	5-2	1	126.1	95	46	10	2	57-3	61	3.13	93	.216	.307	31-0-6	.129	-1*	129	-1		-0.1
1969	†Bal A	7	4	.636	37	3	1-1	1-0	94	78	28	9	0	38-8	37	2.49	144	.228	.304	21-0-4	.095	-0*	82	12		1.3
1970	Bal A	0	0	—	23	0	0	1-0	28.1	32	18	5	0	18-3	14	5.08	72	.294	.385	1	.000	0*		-5		-0.2
1971	†Bal A	2	3	.400	12	6	1-1	1-1	54	51	18	5	1	19-0	18	2.83	120	.252	.318	18-0-1	.278	1*	79	4		0.5
1972	Bal A	0	0	—	14	0	0	0-0	20	20	10	3	0	12-0	7	4.50	69	.260	.356	1	1.000	1*		-3		0.0
Total	6	16	14	.533	117	29	7-4	5-1	337	287	125	32	4	150-14	146	3.15	104	.234	.318	77-0-11	.156	1	104	7		1.5

LEOPOLD, RUDY   Rudolph Matas   B7.27.1905 Grand Cane LA   D9.3.1965 Baton Rouge LA   BL/TL/6-0/160   d7.4

YEAR	TM LG	W	L	PCT	G	GS	CG-SHO	SV-BS	IP	H	R	HR	HB	BB-IB	SO	ERA	AERA	OAV	OOB	AB-HR-SH	AVG	PB	SUP	APR	DL	PW
1928	Chi A	0	0	—	2	0	0		2.1	3	1	0	0	1	1	3.86	105	.273	.273	1	.000	-0		-1		-0.1

LERCH, RANDY   Randy Louis   B10.9.1954 Sacramento CA   BL/TL/6-5/190(170-195)   [PhiN73 8/170]   d9.14

YEAR	TM LG	W	L	PCT	G	GS	CG-SHO	SV-BS	IP	H	R	HR	HB	BB-IB	SO	ERA	AERA	OAV	OOB	AB-HR-SH	AVG	PB	SUP	APR	DL	PW
1975	Phi N	0	0	—	3	0	0	0-0	7	6	5	1	0	6	9	6.43	59	.231	.259	0	—	0		-2		-0.1
1976	Phi N	0	0	—	1	0	0	1-0	3	3	1	0	0	0-0	3	3.00	119	.250	.250	1	1.000	1		0		0.1
1977	Phi N	10	6	.625	32	28	3	0-0	168.2	207	102	20	1	75-3	81	5.07	79	.312	.379	54-0-2	.167	-0*	110	-17		-1.4
1978	†Phi N	11	8	.579	33	28	5	0-0	184	183	89	15	1	70-3	96	3.96	91	.263	.329	60-3-2	.250	7*	133	-7		0.1
1979	Phi N	10	13	.435	37	35	6-1	0-0	214	228	98	20	3	60-4	92	3.74	104	.281	.328	72-1-3	.153	1*	98	2		0.4
1980	Phi N	4	14	.222	30	22	2	0-1	150	178	98	15	0	55-5	57	5.16	74	.302	.356	45-0-4	.267	3*	88	-22		-2.0
1981	†Mil A	7	9	.438	23	18	1	0-0	110.2	134	63	8	0	43-2	53	4.31	80	.303	.361	0	—	0	93	-14		-1.8
1982	Mil A	8	7	.533	21	20	1-1	0-0	108.2	123	68	12	3	51-1	33	4.97	77	.286	.361	0	—	0	138	-15		-1.9
	Mon N	2	0	1.000	6	4	0	0-0	23.2	26	11	0	0	8-1	4	3.42	108	.289	.343	8	.250	1	131	0		0.0
1983	Mon N	1	3	.250	19	5	0	0-0	38.2	45	33	6	1	18-2	24	6.75	54	.292	.368	9-0-1	.222	1	112	-12		-1.1
	SF N	1	0	1.000	7	0	0	0-0	10.2	9	4	1	0	8-1	6	3.38	105	.231	.354	0	—	0		1		0.1
	Year	2	3	.400	26	5	0	0-0	49.1	54	33	7	1	26-3	30	6.02	60	.280	.365	9-0-1	.222	1	113	-12		-1.0
1984	SF N	5	3	.625	37	4	0	2-1	72.1	80	36	3	1	36-3	48	4.23	84	.287	.362	15	.133	0	88	-5	56	-0.4
1986	Phi N	1	1	.500	4	0	0	0-0	8	10	8	0	1	7-1	5	7.88	50	.286	.405	3	.333	1		-3		-0.6
Total	11	60	64	.484	253	164	18-2	3-2	1099.1	1232	612	101	10	432-26	507	4.53	83	.289	.351	267-4-12	.206	14	110	-94	56	-8.6

LEREW, ANTHONY   Anthony Allen   B10.28.1982 Carlisle PA   BL/TR/6-3/220   d9.4

YEAR	TM LG	W	L	PCT	G	GS	CG-SHO	SV-BS	IP	H	R	HR	HB	BB-IB	SO	ERA	AERA	OAV	OOB	AB-HR-SH	AVG	PB	SUP	APR	DL	PW
2005	Atl N	0	0	—	7	0	0	1	8	9	5	1	0	5-2	5	5.63	76	.290	.389	0	—	0		-1		0.0

LeROY, JOHN   John Michael   B4.19.1975 Bellevue WA   D6.25.2001 Sioux City IA   BR/TR/6-3/175   [AtlN93 15/432]   d9.26

YEAR	TM LG	W	L	PCT	G	GS	CG-SHO	SV-BS	IP	H	R	HR	HB	BB-IB	SO	ERA	AERA	OAV	OOB	AB-HR-SH	AVG	PB	SUP	APR	DL	PW
1997	Atl N	1	0	1.000	1	0	0	0-0	2	1	0	0	0	3-1	3	0.00	—	.143	.400	0	—	0		1		0.2

LeROY, LOUIS   Louis Paul "Chief"   B2.18.1879 Omro WI   D10.10.1944 Shawano WI   BR/TR/5-10/180   d9.22

YEAR	TM LG	W	L	PCT	G	GS	CG-SHO	SV-BS	IP	H	R	HR	HB	BB-IB	SO	ERA	AERA	OAV	OOB	AB-HR-SH	AVG	PB	SUP	APR	DL	PW
1905	NY A	1	1	.500	3	3	2	0	24	26	14	2	1	1	8	3.75	78	.277	.292	8-0-1	.125	-0	113	-2		-0.2
1906	NY A	2	0	1.000	11	2	1	1	44.2	33	19	0	2	12	28	2.22	134	.209	.273	14-0-1	.143	-1	170	2		0.1
1910	Bos A	0	0	—	1	0	0	0	4	7	9	1	0	2	3	11.25	23	.389	.450	1	.000	-0		-4		-0.2
Total	3	3¹	1	.750	15	5	3	1	72	66	42	3	3	15	39	3.22	91	.244	.292	23-0-2	.130	-1	136	-4		-0.3

LERSCH, BARRY   Barry Lee   B9.7.1944 Denver CO   BB/TR/6-0/180*   d4.8   Col Mesa St.

YEAR	TM LG	W	L	PCT	G	GS	CG-SHO	SV-BS	IP	H	R	HR	HB	BB-IB	SO	ERA	AERA	OAV	OOB	AB-HR-SH	AVG	PB	SUP	APR	DL	PW
1969	Phi N	0	3	.000	10	0	0	2-1	17.2	20	14	6	1	10-2	13	7.13	50	.286	.383	3	.000	-0		-6		-1.1
1970	Phi N	6	3	.667	42	11	3	3-0	138	119	52	17	1	47-5	92	3.26	123	.232	.295	31-0-5	.065	-2	91	13		0.6
1971	Phi N	5	14	.263	38	30	3	0-0	214.1	203	97	28	3	50-2	113	3.78	94	.252	.297	59-0-6	.169	2*	85	-3		-0.1
1972	Phi N	4	6	.400	36	8	3-1	0-0	100.2	86	37	8	3	33-7	48	3.04	119	.231	.297	23	.000	-2*	77	6	28	0.4
1973	Phi N	3	6	.333	42	4	0	1-0	98.1	105	49	10	2	27-4	51	4.39	87	.279	.324	17	.176	0*	75	-4		-0.4
1974	StL N	0	0	—	1	0	0	0-0	1.1	3	6	1	0	5-0	0	40.50	9	.429	.667	0	—	0		-5		-0.2
Total	6	18	32	.360	169	53	9-1	6-1	570.1	536	255	70	10	172-20	317	3.82	98	.250	.306	133-0-11	.113	-3	83	1	28	-0.8

LESHNOCK, DON   Donald Lee   B11.25.1946 Youngstown OH   BR/TL/6-3/195   d6.7   Col Youngstown St.

YEAR	TM LG	W	L	PCT	G	GS	CG-SHO	SV-BS	IP	H	R	HR	HB	BB-IB	SO	ERA	AERA	OAV	OOB	AB-HR-SH	AVG	PB	SUP	APR	DL	PW
1972	Det A	0	0	—	1	0	0	0-0	2	0	0	0	0	0	2	0.00	—	.400	.400	0	—	0		0		0.0

LESKANIC, CURTIS   Curtis John   B4.2.1968 Homestead PA   BR/TR/6-0/180(180-196)   [CleA89 8/203]   d6.27   Col Louisiana St.   [DL 2002 Mil N 183]

YEAR	TM LG	W	L	PCT	G	GS	CG-SHO	SV-BS	IP	H	R	HR	HB	BB-IB	SO	ERA	AERA	OAV	OOB	AB-HR-SH	AVG	PB	SUP	APR	DL	PW
1993	Col N	1	5	.167	18	8	0	0-0	57	59	40	7	2	27-1	30	5.37	89	.266	.345	13-0-1	.154	-0	71	-4		-0.4
1994	Col N	1	1	.500	8	3	0	0-0	22.1	27	14	2	0	10-0	17	5.64	88	.314	.385	6	.167	0	110	-1		-0.1
1995	†Col N	6	3	.667	76	0	0	10-6	98	83	38	7	0	33-1	107	3.40	158	.226	.288	7-0-2	.143	-0		18		1.8
1996	Col N	7	5	.583	70	0	0	6-4	73.2	82	51	12	2	38-1	76	6.23	84	.285	.369	3-0-1	.333	-0		-5	29	-0.8
1997	Col N	4	0	1.000	30	0	0	2-2	58.1	59	36	8	0	24-0	53	5.55	93	.271	.337	1	.000	-0		-1	11	-0.1
1998	Col N	6	4	.600	66	0	0	2-3	75.2	75	37	9	1	40-2	55	4.40	118	.258	.349	2-0-1	.000	-0		6		0.7
1999	Col N	6	2	.750	63	0	0	0-3	85	87	54	7	5	49-4	77	5.08	114	.272	.374	4-1-0	.500	1		4		0.5
2000	Mil N	9	3	.750	73	0	0	12-1	77.1	58	23	7	3	51-5	75	2.56	180	.212	.337	2	.000	-0		18	18	3.0
2001	Mil N	2	6	.250	70	0	0	17-7	69.1	63	30	11	2	31-5	64	3.63	118	.241	.327	1	.000	-0		5		0.7
2003	Mil N	4	0	1.000	26	0	0	0-0	26.2	22	8	1	1	18-0	28	2.70	160	.227	.353	0	—	0		5		0.7
	KC A	1	0	1.000	27	0	0	2-1	26	16	7	1	0	11-1	22	1.73	278	.180	.267	0	—	0		8		0.4
2004	KC A	0	3	.000	19	0	0	2-3	15.2	23	16	5	0	14-0	15	8.04	58	.324	.435	0	—	0		-6		-1.1
	†Bos A	3	2	.600	32	0	0	2-1	27.2	24	11	3	1	16-3	22	3.58	136	.247	.353	0	—	0		4	23	0.7
	Year	3	5	.375	51	0	0	4-4	43.1	47	27	8	1	30-3	37	5.19	93	.280	.388	0	—	0		-2		-0.4
Total	11	50	34	.595	603	11	0	55-31	712.2	678	365	80	*17	362-23	641	4.36	116	.253	.343	39-1-5	.179	0	79	51	264	6.0

LESLEY, BRAD   Bradley Jay   B9.11.1958 Turlock CA   BR/TR/6-6/230*   [CinN78 S1/9]   d7.31   Col Merced (CA) JC

YEAR	TM LG	W	L	PCT	G	GS	CG-SHO	SV-BS	IP	H	R	HR	HB	BB-IB	SO	ERA	AERA	OAV	OOB	AB-HR-SH	AVG	PB	SUP	APR	DL	PW
1982	Cin N	0	2	.000	28	0	0	4-2	38.1	27	13	1	0	13-4	29	2.58	142	.197	.267	1	.000	-0		4		0.3
1983	Cin N	0	0	—	5	0	0	0-0	8.1	9	2	1	0	4-0	5	2.16	177	.290	.281	0-0-1	—	-0		2		0.1
1984	Cin N	0	1	.000	16	0	0	2-1	19.1	17	11	3	0	14-1	7	5.12	74	.246	.369	2	.500	-0		-2		-0.1
1985	Mil A	1	0	1.000	5	0	0	0-1	6.1	8	7	2	0	2-0	5	9.95	42	.296	.345	0	—	0		-4		-0.5
Total	4	1	3	.250	54	0	0	6-4	72.1	61	33	7	0	29-5	46	3.86	98	.231	.305	3-0-1	.333	0	0			-0.2

LEVERENZ, WALT   Walter Fred "Tiny"   B7.21.1888 Chicago IL   D3.19.1973 Atascadero CA   BL/TL/5-10/175   d4.18

YEAR	TM LG	W	L	PCT	G	GS	CG-SHO	SV-BS	IP	H	R	HR	HB	BB-IB	SO	ERA	AERA	OAV	OOB	AB-HR-SH	AVG	PB	SUP	APR	DL	PW
1913	StL A	6	17	.261	30	27	13-2	5	202.2	159	80	3	12	89	87	2.58	114	.225	.322	68-0-2	.176	-1*	72	8		0.7
1914	StL A	1	12	.077	27	16	5	0	111.1	107	67	5	4	63	41	3.80	71	.264	.368	33	.182	-0*	67	-15		-1.7
1915	StL A	1	2	.333	5	5	0	0	9	11	9	0	1	8	3	8.00	36	.333	.476	1	.000	-0	51	-4		-0.9
Total	3	8	31	.205	62	48	18-2	5	323	277	156	8	17	160	131	3.15	91	.242	.343	102-0-2	.176	-1	70	-11		-1.9

LEVERETT, DIXIE   Gorham Vance   B3.29.1894 Georgetown TX   D2.20.1957 Beaverton OR   BR/TR/5-11/190   d5.6

YEAR	TM LG	W	L	PCT	G	GS	CG-SHO	SV-BS	IP	H	R	HR	HB	BB-IB	SO	ERA	AERA	OAV	OOB	AB-HR-SH	AVG	PB	SUP	APR	DL	PW
1922	Chi A	13	10	.565	33	27	16-4	2	223.2	224	95	11	3	79	60	3.34	122	.264	.329	83-0-1	.253	3	102	17		1.9
1923	Chi A	10	13	.435	38	24	9-3	2	192.2	212	108	6	6	64	64	4.06	97	.280	.341	60-0-6	.267	4	99	-5		-0.1
1924	Chi A	2	3	.400	21	11	4	0	99	123	72	2	3	41	29	5.82	71	.314	.383	32-0-2	.188	-1	110	-17		-0.9
1926	Chi A	1	1	.500	6	3	1	0	24	31	18	1	0	7	12	6.00	64	.316	.362	7-0-1	.143	-0	160	-6		-0.4
1929	Bos N	3	7	.300	24	12	3	1	97.2	135	81	5	5	30	28	6.36	74	.339	.393	32	.188	-0	93	-20		-1.6
Total	5	29	34	.460	122	77	33-4	6	637	725	374	25	17	221	193	4.51	92	.291	.353	214-0-10	.234	5	103	-31		-1.1

LEVERETTE, HOD   Horace Wilbur "Levy"   B2.4.1889 Shreveport LA   D4.10.1958 St.Petersburg FL   BR/TR/6-0/180   d4.22

YEAR	TM LG	W	L	PCT	G	GS	CG-SHO	SV-BS	IP	H	R	HR	HB	BB-IB	SO	ERA	AERA	OAV	OOB	AB-HR-SH	AVG	PB	SUP	APR	DL	PW
1920	StL A	0	2	.000	3	2	0	0	10.1	9	6	1	0	12	0	5.23	75	.250	.438	3	.000	-1	71	-1		-0.2

LEVINE, AL   Alan Brian   B5.22.1968 Park Ridge IL   BL/TR/6-4/200(180-200)   [ChiA91 11/306]   d6.22   Col Southern Illinois

YEAR	TM LG	W	L	PCT	G	GS	CG-SHO	SV-BS	IP	H	R	HR	HB	BB-IB	SO	ERA	AERA	OAV	OOB	AB-HR-SH	AVG	PB	SUP	APR	DL	PW
1996	Chi A	0	1	.000	16	0	0	0-1	18.1	22	14	1	1	7-1	12	5.40	88	.289	.353	0	—	0		-2		-0.1
1997	Chi A	2	2	.500	25	0	0	0-1	27.1	35	22	4	2	16-1	22	6.91	64	.313	.402	0	—	0		-7		-0.9
1998	Tex A	0	1	.000	30	0	0	0-0	58	68	30	6	0	16-1	19	4.50	109	.294	.336	0	—	0		3		0.1
1999	Ana A	1	1	.500	50	1	0	0-1	85	76	40	13	3	29-2	37	3.39	144	.247	.311	0	—	0	286	12		0.5
2000	Ana A	3	4	.429	51	5	0	2-0	95.1	98	44	10	2	49-5	42	3.87	133	.266	.352	0	—	0	149	13	18	0.8
2001	Ana A	8	10	.444	64	1	0	2-4	75.2	71	26	7	2	28-4	40	2.38	196	.257	.325	0	—	0	139	17		3.3

YEAR	TM LG	W	L	PCT	G	GS	CG-SHO	SV-BS	IP	H	R	HR	HB	BB-IB	SO	ERA	AERA	OAV	OOB	AB-HR-SH	AVG	PB	SUP	APR	DL	PW
2002	Ana A	4	4	.500	52	0	0	5-2	63.2	61	35	8	2	34-3	40	4.24	106	.253	.342	0	—	0	1	1	23	0.1
2003	TB A	3	5	.375	36	0	0	0-2	49.2	45	23	7	2	18-0	25	2.90	158	.243	.317	0	—	0	7			0.9
	KC A	0	1	.000	18	0	0	1-1	21.1	22	6	2	1	11-1	5	2.53	190	.268	.362	0	—	0	5			0.3
	Year	3	6	.333	54	0	0	1-3	71	67	29	9	3	29-1	30	2.79	167	.251	.331	0	—	0	12			1.2
2004	Det A	3	4	.429	65	0	0	0-1	70.2	83	37	10	1	24-1	32	4.58	98	.295	.351	0	—	0	0			0.0
2005	SF N	0	0	—	9	0	0	0-0	10.1	16	11	2	0	4-1	4	9.58	44	.340	.392	2	.000	-0	-6	-3	23	-0.2
Total	10	24	33	.421	416	7	0	10-13	575.1	597	287	70	16	236-20	278	3.96	120	.270	.341	2	.000	-0	176	43	64	4.7

LEVRAULT, ALLEN   Allen Harry   B8.15.1977 Fall River MA   BR/TR/6-3/240(230-250)   [MilA96 13/373]   d6.13   Col CC of Rhode Island

YEAR	TM LG	W	L	PCT	G	GS	CG-SHO	SV-BS	IP	H	R	HR	HB	BB-IB	SO	ERA	AERA	OAV	OOB	AB-HR-SH	AVG	PB	SUP	APR	DL	PW
2000	Mil N	0	1	.000	5	1	0	0-0	12	10	7	0	0	7-0	9	4.50	103	.238	.340	3	.000	-0	80	0		-0.1
2001	Mil N	6	10	.375	32	20	1	0-0	130.2	146	93	27	7	59-7	80	6.06	71	.281	.359	33-0-6	.061	-2	88	-25		-2.8
2003	Fla N	1	0	1.000	19	0	0	0-0	28	38	12	3	1	15-2	21	3.86	106	.333	.409	2	.000	-0	1			0.0
Total	3	7	11	.389	56	21	1	0-0	170.2	194	112	30	8	81-9	110	5.59	77	.287	.367	38-0-6	.053	-3	89	-24		-2.9

LEVSEN, DUTCH   Emil Henry   B4.29.1898 Wyoming IA   D3.12.1972 St.Louis Park MN   BR/TR/6-0/180   d9.28   Col Iowa St.

YEAR	TM LG	W	L	PCT	G	GS	CG-SHO	SV-BS	IP	H	R	HR	HB	BB-IB	SO	ERA	AERA	OAV	OOB	AB-HR-SH	AVG	PB	SUP	APR	DL	PW
1923	Cle A			—	3	0	0		4.1	4	0	0	0	0-0	1	0.00	—	.267	.267	1	.000	-0	2			0.1
1924	Cle A	1	1	.500	4	1	1	0	16.1	22	8	0	0	4	3	4.41	97	.333	.371	5	.000	-1	237	1		0.0
1925	Cle A	1	2	.333	4	3	2	0	24.1	30	16	1	1	16	9	5.55	80	.313	.416	8-0-1	.250	0	70	-2		-0.2
1926	Cle A	16	13	.552	33	31	18-2	0	237.1	235	110	11	8	85	53	3.41	119	.261	.330	83-0-6	.205	-4	105	15		1.6
1927	Cle A	3	7	.300	25	13	2-1	0	80.1	96	54	1	2	37	15	5.49	77	.303	.379	25	.200	-1	84	-10		-1.0
1928	Cle A	0	3	.000	11	3	0	0	41.1	39	30	4	2	31	7	5.44	76	.258	.391	13	.000	-2	54	-6		-0.6
Total	6	21	26	.447	80	51	23-3	0	404	426	218	17	13	173	88	4.17	99	.276	.354	135-0-7	.178	-4	97	0		-0.1

LEWALLYN, DENNIS   Dennis Dale   B8.11.1953 Pensacola FL   BR/TR/6-4/200(175-200)   [LAN72*S1/8]   d9.21   C1   Col Chipola (FL) JC

YEAR	TM LG	W	L	PCT	G	GS	CG-SHO	SV-BS	IP	H	R	HR	HB	BB-IB	SO	ERA	AERA	OAV	OOB	AB-HR-SH	AVG	PB	SUP	APR	DL	PW
1975	LA N	0	0	—	2	0	0	0-0	3	1	0	0	0	0-0	0	0.00	—	.100	.100	0	—	0	1			0.1
1976	LA N	1	1	.500	4	2	0	0-0	16.2	12	5	1	0	6-0	4	2.16	158	.207	.281	5	.000	-1	129	2		0.2
1977	LA N	3	1	.750	5	1	0	1-1	17	22	8	1	0	4-1	8	4.24	91	.306	.342	6-0-1	.000	-1	415	0		-0.2
1978	LA N	0	0	—	1	0	0	0-0	2	2	0	0	0	0-0	0	0.00	—	.250	.250	0	—	0	1			0.0
1979	LA N	0	1	.000	7	0	0	0-0	12.1	19	9	1	0	5-3	1	5.11	71	.358	.417	2	.500	0	-2			-0.1
1980	Tex A	0	0	—	4	0	0	0-1	5.2	7	5	0	0	4-1	1	7.94	49	.304	.407	0	—	0	-2			-0.1
1981	Cle A	0	0	—	7	0	0	0-0	13.1	16	8	1	0	2-0	11	5.40	68	.296	.316	0	—	0	-2			-0.1
1982	Cle A	0	1	.000	4	0	0	0-0	10.1	13	8	3	0	1-0	3	6.97	60	.310	.311	0	—	0	-3			-0.2
Total	8	4	4	.500	34	3	0	1-2	80.1	92	42	6	1	22-5	28	4.48	83	.287	.331	13-0-1	.077	-1	224	-5		-0.4

LEWANDOWSKI, DAN   Daniel William   B1.6.1928 Buffalo NY   D7.19.1996 Hamilton ON, Can.   BR/TR/6-0/180   d9.22

YEAR	TM LG	W	L	PCT	G	GS	CG-SHO	SV-BS	IP	H	R	HR	HB	BB-IB	SO	ERA	AERA	OAV	OOB	AB-HR-SH	AVG	PB	SUP	APR	DL	PW
1951	StL N	0	0	—	2	0	0	0	1	3	1	0	0	1	1	9.00	44	.500	.571	0	—	0	-1			-0.1

LEWIS   B Brooklyn NY   d7.12

YEAR	TM LG	W	L	PCT	G	GS	CG-SHO	SV-BS	IP	H	R	HR	HB	BB-IB	SO	ERA	AERA	OAV	OOB	AB-HR-SH	AVG	PB	SUP	APR	DL	PW
1890	Buf P	0	1	.000	1	1	0	0	3	13	20	3	0	7	1	60.00	7	.591	.690	5	.200	-0	238	-16		-1.4

LEWIS, COLBY   Colby Preston   B8.2.1979 Bakersfield CA   BR/TR/6-4/215(215-230)   [TexA99 1/38]   d4.1   Col Bakersfield (CA) JC   [DL 2005 Det A 183]

YEAR	TM LG	W	L	PCT	G	GS	CG-SHO	SV-BS	IP	H	R	HR	HB	BB-IB	SO	ERA	AERA	OAV	OOB	AB-HR-SH	AVG	PB	SUP	APR	DL	PW
2002	Tex A	1	3	.250	15	4	0	0-2	34.1	42	26	4	2	26-2	28	6.29	76	.304	.422	0	—	0	82	-6		-0.5
2003	Tex A	10	9	.526	26	26	0	0-0	127	163	104	23	5	70-1	88	7.30	68	.317	.402	1	.000	-0	111	-27		-3.2
2004	Tex A	1	1	.500	3	3	0	0-0	15.1	13	7	1	1	13-0	11	4.11	120	.228	.380	0	—	0	63	2	169	0.2
Total	3	12	13	.480	44	33	0	0-2	176.2	218	137	28	8	109-3	127	6.83	72	.307	.404	1	.000	-0	104	-31	352	-3.6

LEWIS, TED   Edward Morgan "Parson"   B12.25.1872 Machynlleth, Wales   D5.23.1936 Durham NH   BR/TR/5-10.5/158   d7.6   Col Williams

YEAR	TM LG	W	L	PCT	G	GS	CG-SHO	SV-BS	IP	H	R	HR	HB	BB-IB	SO	ERA	AERA	OAV	OOB	AB-HR-SH	AVG	PB	SUP	APR	DL	PW
1896	Bos N	4	4	.200	6	5	4	0	41.2	37	32	2	0	27	12	3.24	140	.236	.348	18	.111	-2	91	3		0.1
1897	†Bos N	21	12	.636	38	34	30-2	1	290	316	177	11	10	125	65	3.85	116	.275	.351	113-0-7	.248	-2	112	17		1.1
1898	Bos N	26	8	**.765**	41	33	29-1	2	313.1	267	131	9	9	109	72	2.90	127	.229	.300	131-0-5	.282	4*	130	30		3.2
1899	Bos N	17	11	.607	29	25	23-2	0	234.2	245	119	10	8	73	60	3.49	119	.269	.328	96-0-2	.260	0	93	16		1.4
1900	Bos N	13	12	.520	30	22	19-1	0	209	215	122	11	4	86	66	4.13	100	.265	.339	73-0-2	.137	-4	81	5		0.0
1901	Bos A	16	17	.485	39	34	31-1	1	316.1	299	172	14	8	91	103	3.53	100	.247	.324	121-0-1	.174	-2	105	4		0.0
Total	6	94	64	.595	183	153	136-7	4	1405	1379	753	57	39	511	378	3.53	113	.255	.324	552-0-17	.223	-5	106	75		5.8

LEWIS, JIM   James Martin   B10.12.1955 Miami FL   BR/TR/6-3/190*   d9.12   Col South Carolina-Aiken

YEAR	TM LG	W	L	PCT	G	GS	CG-SHO	SV-BS	IP	H	R	HR	HB	BB-IB	SO	ERA	AERA	OAV	OOB	AB-HR-SH	AVG	PB	SUP	APR	DL	PW
1979	Sea A	0	0	—	2	0	0	0-0	2.1	10	7	1	0	1-0	0	15.43	28	.625	.647	0	—	0	-4			-0.2
1982	NY A	0	0	—	1	0	0	0-0	0.2	3	7	0	0	3-0	1	54.00	7	.500	.667	0	—	0	-5			-0.2
1983	Min A	0	0	—	6	0	0	0-0	18	24	13	5	1	7-0	8	6.50	66	.324	.390	0	—	0	-4			-0.2
1985	Sea A	0	1	.000	2	1	0	0-0	4.2	8	4	1	2	1-0	1	7.71	55	.421	.500	0	—	0	65	-2		-0.3
Total	4	0	1	.000	11	1	0	0-0	25.2	45	31	7	3	12-0	10	8.77	49	.391	.462	0	—	0	65	-15		-0.9

LEWIS, JIM   James Steven   B7.20.1964 Jackson MI   BR/TR/6-2/200   [SDN85*5/125]   d8.9   Col Citrus (CA) JC

YEAR	TM LG	W	L	PCT	G	GS	CG-SHO	SV-BS	IP	H	R	HR	HB	BB-IB	SO	ERA	AERA	OAV	OOB	AB-HR-SH	AVG	PB	SUP	APR	DL	PW
1991	SD N	0	0	—	12	0	0	0-0	13	14	7	2	0	11-2	10	4.15	92	.275	.403	2	.000	-0	-1			0.0

LEWIS, RICHIE   Richie Todd   B1.25.1966 Muncie IN   BR/TR/5-10/175*   [MonN87 2/44]   d7.31   Col Florida St.

YEAR	TM LG	W	L	PCT	G	GS	CG-SHO	SV-BS	IP	H	R	HR	HB	BB-IB	SO	ERA	AERA	OAV	OOB	AB-HR-SH	AVG	PB	SUP	APR	DL	PW
1992	Bal N	1	1	.500	2	2	0	0-0	6.2	13	8	1	0	7-0	4	10.80	38	.406	.500	0	—	0	79	-5		-0.8
1993	Fla N	6	3	.667	57	0	0	0-2	77.1	68	37	7	1	43-6	65	3.26	134	.239	.336	2-0-1	.500	0	6			0.7
1994	Fla N	1	4	.200	45	0	0	0-0	54	62	44	7	1	38-9	45	5.67	79	.284	.391	5	.000	-0	-9			-0.8
1995	Fla N	0	1	.000	21	1	0	0-0	36	30	15	9	1	15-5	32	3.75	115	.224	.307	1	.000	-0	63	3		0.1
1996	Det A	4	6	.400	72	0	0	2-4	90.1	78	45	9	4	65-9	78	4.18	122	.238	.361	1	.000	-0	9		20	0.8
1997	Oak A	2	0	1.000	14	0	0	0-0	18.2	24	21	7	1	15-0	12	9.64	48	.316	.430	0	—	0	-10			-0.9
	Cin N	0	0	—	4	0	0	0-0	5.2	4	5	3	0	3-0	4	6.35	67	.200	.304	1	1.000	0	-2			-0.1
1998	Bal A	0	0	—	2	0	0	0-0	4.2	8	8	2	0	5-0	4	15.43	30	.421	.520	0	—	0	204	-6		-0.3
Total	7	14	15	.483	217	4	0	2-6	293.1	287	183	45	8	191-29	244	4.88	95	.258	.366	10-0-1	.200	1	99	-14	20	-1.2

LEWIS, SCOTT   Scott Allen   B12.5.1965 Grants Pass OR   BR/TR/6-3/178(178-190)   [CalA88 11/273]   d9.25   Col Nevada-Las Vegas

YEAR	TM LG	W	L	PCT	G	GS	CG-SHO	SV-BS	IP	H	R	HR	HB	BB-IB	SO	ERA	AERA	OAV	OOB	AB-HR-SH	AVG	PB	SUP	APR	DL	PW
1990	Cal A	1	1	.500	2	1	1	0-0	16.1	10	4	2	0	2-0	5	2.20	174	.172	.200	0	—	0	107	3		0.4
1991	Cal A	3	5	.375	16	11	0	0-0	60.1	81	43	9	2	21-0	37	6.27	66	.316	.373	0	—	0	121	-13		-1.5
1992	Cal A	4	0	1.000	21	2	0	0-0	38.1	36	18	3	2	14-1	18	3.99	101	.255	.325	0	—	0	136	0		0.1
1993	Cal A	1	2	.333	15	4	0	0-0	32	37	16	3	2	12-1	10	4.22	108	.311	.364	0	—	0	117	1	19	0.1
1994	Cal A	0	1	.000	20	0	0	0-0	31	46	23	5	2	10-2	10	6.10	81	.359	.414	0	—	0	-4		53	-0.2
Total	5	9	9	.500	74	19	1	0-0	178	210	104	12	8	59-4	84	5.01	86	.299	.356	0	—	0	117	-13	72	-1.1

LEWIS, BERT   William Burton   B10.3.1895 Tonawanda NY   D3.24.1950 Tonawanda NY   BR/TR/6-2/176   d4.19

YEAR	TM LG	W	L	PCT	G	GS	CG-SHO	SV-BS	IP	H	R	HR	HB	BB-IB	SO	ERA	AERA	OAV	OOB	AB-HR-SH	AVG	PB	SUP	APR	DL	PW
1924	Phi N	0	0	—	12	0	0	0	18	23	12	1	1	7	3	6.00	74	.315	.383	5	.000	-1	-2			-0.2

LEY, TERRY   Terrence Richard   B2.21.1947 Portland OR   BL/TL/6-0/190   [NYA67*S3/60]   d8.20   Col Oregon

YEAR	TM LG	W	L	PCT	G	GS	CG-SHO	SV-BS	IP	H	R	HR	HB	BB-IB	SO	ERA	AERA	OAV	OOB	AB-HR-SH	AVG	PB	SUP	APR	DL	PW
1971	NY A	0	0	—	6	0	0	0-0	9	9	9	1	2	9-2	7	5.00	66	.257	.426	0	—	0	-3			-0.2

LIBKE, AL   Albert Walter   B9.12.1918 Tacoma WA   D3.7.2003 Wenatchee WA   BL/TR/6-4/215   d4.19   ▲

YEAR	TM LG	W	L	PCT	G	GS	CG-SHO	SV-BS	IP	H	R	HR	HB	BB-IB	SO	ERA	AERA	OAV	OOB	AB-HR-SH	AVG	PB	SUP	APR	DL	PW
1945	Cin N	0	0	—	4	0	0	0	4.1	3	0	0	0	3	2	0.00	—	.200	.333	449-4-4	.283	1*	0			0.1
1946	Cin N	0	0	—	1	1	0	0	5	4	2	0	0	3	2	3.60	93	.235	.350	431-5-4	.253	0*	77	0		0.0
Total	2	0	0	—	5	1	0	0	9.1	7	2	0	0	6	4	1.93	183	.219	.342	880-9-8	.268	2	77	0		0.1

LIDDLE, DON   Donald Eugene   B5.25.1925 Mt.Carmel IL   D6.5.2000 Mt.Carmel IL   BL/TL/5-10/165*   d4.17

YEAR	TM LG	W	L	PCT	G	GS	CG-SHO	SV-BS	IP	H	R	HR	HB	BB-IB	SO	ERA	AERA	OAV	OOB	AB-HR-SH	AVG	PB	SUP	APR	DL	PW
1953	Mil N	7	6	.538	31	15	4	0	128.2	119	54	6	2	55	63	3.08	127	.248	.328	34-0-4	.088	-2	90	12		0.9
1954	†NY N	9	4	.692	28	19	4-3	0	126.2	100	48	5	3	55	44	3.06	132	.223	.308	37-0-2	.189	2*	100	15		1.5
1955	NY N	10	4	.714	33	13	4	1	106.1	97	54	18	4	61-7	56	4.23	95	.246	.351	27-0-2	.185	1	131	-1		0.0
1956	NY N	1	2	.333	11	5	1	1	41.1	45	22	5	1	14-3	21	3.92	97	.278	.333	12-0-3	.167	0	112	-1		-0.1
	StL N	1	2	.333	14	2	0	0	24.2	36	25	6	2	18-5	14	8.39	45	.353	.446	2	.000	-0*	47	-12		-1.3
	Year	2	4	.333	25	7	1	1	66	81	47	13	3	32-8	35	5.59	68	.307	.379	14-0-3	.143	-0	93	-14		-1.4
Total	4	28	18	.609	117	54	13-3	4	427.2	397	203	42	10	203-15	198	3.75	106	.250	.337	112-0-11	.152	1	104	13		1.0

LIDGE, BRAD   Bradley Thomas   B12.23.1976 Sacramento CA   BR/TR/6-5/200*   [HouN98 1/17]   d4.26   Col Notre Dame

YEAR	TM LG	W	L	PCT	G	GS	CG-SHO	SV-BS	IP	H	R	HR	HB	BB-IB	SO	ERA	AERA	OAV	OOB	AB-HR-SH	AVG	PB	SUP	APR	DL	PW
2002	Hou N	1	0	1.000	6	1	0	0-0	8.2	12	6	0	2	9-1	12	6.23	69	.333	.489	2	1.000	1	64	-2		0.0
2003	Hou N	6	3	.667	78	0	0	1-5	85	60	36	6	8	42-7	97	3.60	123	.202	.308	4	.000	-0	8			0.4
2004	†Hou N	6	5	.545	80	0	0	29-4	94.2	57	21	6	8	30-5	157	1.90	230	.174	.254	1	.000	-0	26			4.0

YEAR	TM LG	W	L	PCT	G	GS	CG-SHO	SV-BS	IP	H	R	HR	HB	BB-IB	SO	ERA	AERA	OAV	OOB	AB-HR-SH	AVG	PB	SUP	APR	DL	PW
2005	†Hou N★	4	4	.500	70	0	0	42-4	70.2	58	21	5	3	23-1	103	2.29	183	.223	.293	0	—	0		14		2.9
Total	4	17	12	.586	234	1	0	72-13	259	187	84	19	16	104-14	369	2.71	160	.203	.293	7	.286	1	64	46		7.5

LIDLE, CORY Cory Fulton B3.22.1972 Hollywood CA BR/TR/5-11/180* d5.8 [DL 1998 Ari N 181]

YEAR	TM LG	W	L	PCT	G	GS	CG-SHO	SV-BS	IP	H	R	HR	HB	BB-IB	SO	ERA	AERA	OAV	OOB	AB-HR-SH	AVG	PB	SUP	APR	DL	PW
1997	NY N	7	2	.778	54	2	0	2-1	81.2	86	38	7	3	20-4	54	3.53	114	.274	.320	5	.000	-0	196	3		0.3
1999	TB A	1	0	1.000	5	1	0	0-0	5	8	4	0	0	2-0	4	7.20	69	.364	.417	0		-0	113	-1	166	-0.2
2000	TB A	4	6	.400	31	11	0	0-0	96.2	114	61	13	3	29-3	62	5.03	97	.294	.347	2	.000	-0	84	-2		-0.2
2001	†Oak A	13	6	.684	29	29	1	0-0	188	170	84	23	10	47-7	118	3.59	127	.242	.299	2	.000	-0	107	19		1.7
2002	†Oak A	8	10	.444	31	30	2-2	0-0	192	191	90	17	6	39-3	111	3.89	115	.258	.298	1-0-1	.000	-0	103	13	17	1.3
2003	Tor N	12	15	.444	31	31	2	0-0	192.2	216	133	24	5	60-3	112	5.75	83	.282	.337	6	.333	-0	96	-19	20	-2.1
2004	Cin N	7	10	.412	24	24	3-1	0-0	149	170	95	24	5	44-4	93	5.32	81	.288	.340	42-0-4	.143	1	85	-17		-1.4
	Phi N	5	2	.714	10	10	2-2	0-0	62.1	54	28	3	5	17-1	33	3.90	114	.236	.300	20-1-4	.150	1	119	4		0.5
	Year	12	12	.500	34	34	5-3	0-0	211.1	224	123	27	10	61-5	126	4.90	89	.273	.329	62-1-8	.145	2	95	-10		-0.9
2005	Phi N	13	11	.542	31	31	0	0-0	184.2	210	105	18	6	40-5	121	4.53	96	.289	.328	58-0-8	.138	-2	110	-6	15	-0.8
Total	8	70	62	.530	246	169	11-5	2-1	1152	1219	638	129	43	298-30	708	4.52	99	.272	.322	136-1-17	.140	0	102	-6	399	-0.9

LIEBER, DUTCH Charles Edwin B2.1.1910 Alameda CA D12.31.1961 Los Angeles CA BR/TR/6-0.5/180 d4.18

YEAR	TM LG	W	L	PCT	G	GS	CG-SHO	SV-BS	IP	H	R	HR	HB	BB-IB	SO	ERA	AERA	OAV	OOB	AB-HR-SH	AVG	PB	SUP	APR	DL	PW
1935	Phi A	1	1	.500	18	1	0	2	46.2	45	18	1	1	19	14	3.09	147	.263	.340	14	.143	-1*	134	8		0.3
1936	Phi A	0	1	.000	3	0	0	0	11.2	17	11	0	0	6	1	7.71	66	.362	.434	3	.000	-0		-3		-0.2
Total	2	1	2	.333	21	1	0	2	58.1	62	29	1	1	25	15	4.01	116	.284	.361	17	.118	-2	134	5		0.1

LIEBER, JON Jonathan Ray B4.2.1970 Council Bluffs IA BL/TR/6-2/227* [KCA92 2/44] d5.15 Col South Alabama [DL 2003 NY A 183]

YEAR	TM LG	W	L	PCT	G	GS	CG-SHO	SV-BS	IP	H	R	HR	HB	BB-IB	SO	ERA	AERA	OAV	OOB	AB-HR-SH	AVG	PB	SUP	APR	DL	PW
1994	Pit N	6	7	.462	17	17	1	0-0	108.2	116	62	12	1	25-3	71	3.73	117	.271	.311	39-0-2	.103	-2	96	2		0.0
1995	Pit N	4	7	.364	21	12	0	0-1	72.2	103	56	7	4	14-0	45	6.32	69	.346	.376	21	.048	-2	95	-15		-2.1
1996	Pit N	9	5	.643	51	15	0	1-3	142	156	70	19	3	28-2	94	3.99	110	.279	.315	36-0-3	.194	2	122	6		0.8
1997	Pit N	11	14	.440	33	32	1	0-0	188.1	193	102	23	1	51-8	160	4.49	95	.263	.309	58-0-2	.121	-0	97	-3		-0.4
1998	Pit N	8	14	.364	29	28	1	1-0	171	182	93	23	3	40-4	138	4.11	104	.269	.311	48-0-7	.167	0	85	1	24	0.2
1999	Chi N	10	11	.476	31	31	3-1	0-0	203.1	226	107	28	1	46-6	186	4.07	112	.279	.315	58-0-7	.121	-1	101	9	17	0.7
2000	Chi N	12	11	.522	35	35	6-1	0-0	251	248	130	36	10	54-3	192	4.41	104	.256	.301	82-0-10	.220	3*	96	5		0.8
2001	Chi N★	20	6	.769	34	34	5-1	0-0	232.1	226	104	25	7	41-4	148	3.80	110	.255	.290	76-0-9	.158	0*	120	12		1.3
2002	Chi N	6	8	.429	21	21	3	0-0	141	153	64	15	1	12-2	85	3.70	110	.277	.290	43-0-4	.163	-0	85	5	59	0.4
2004	†NY A	14	8	.636	27	27	0	0-0	176.2	216	95	20	2	18-2	102	4.33	106	.300	.316	3	.333	-0	124	4	32	0.3
2005	Phi N	17	13	.567	35	35	1	0-0	218.1	223	107	33	5	41-6	149	4.20	103	.263	.299	73-0-3	.096	-3*	94	5		0.2
Total	11	117	104	.529	334	287	22-3	2-4	1905.1	2042	990	241	38	370-40	1372	4.20	104	.273	.308	537-0-47	.147	-2	101	31	315	2.2

LIEBHARDT, GLENN Glenn Ignatius "Sandy" B7.31.1910 Cleveland OH D3.14.1992 Winston-Salem NC BR/TR/5-10.5/170 d4.22 f-Glenn

YEAR	TM LG	W	L	PCT	G	GS	CG-SHO	SV-BS	IP	H	R	HR	HB	BB-IB	SO	ERA	AERA	OAV	OOB	AB-HR-SH	AVG	PB	SUP	APR	DL	PW
1930	Phi A	0	1	.000	5	0	0	0	9	14	12	2	0	8	2	11.00	42	.359	.468	2	.000	-0		-6		-0.6
1936	StL A	0	0	—	24	0	0	0	55.1	98	58	4	2	27	20	8.78	61	.375	.438	11	.000	-2		-18		-1.0
1938	StL A	0	0	—	2	0	0	0	3	4	2	1	0	0	1	6.00	83	.308	.308	0	—	-0		0		0.0
Total	3	0	1	.000	31	0	0	0	67.1	116	72	7	2	35	23	8.96	59	.371	.437	13	.000	-2		-24		-1.6

LIEBHARDT, GLENN Glenn John B3.10.1883 Milton IN D7.13.1956 Cleveland OH BR/TR/5-10/175 d10.2 s-Glenn

YEAR	TM LG	W	L	PCT	G	GS	CG-SHO	SV-BS	IP	H	R	HR	HB	BB-IB	SO	ERA	AERA	OAV	OOB	AB-HR-SH	AVG	PB	SUP	APR	DL	PW
1906	Cle A	2	0	1.000	2	2	2	0	18	13	4	0	1	9	1.50	175	.206	.219	8	.000	-1	192	2		0.2
1907	Cle A	18	14	.563	38	34	27-4	1	280.1	254	100	1	10	85	110	2.05	122	.244	.307	87-0-2	.161	-1	90	13		1.4
1908	Cle A	15	16	.484	38	26	19-3	0	262	222	93	2	3	81	146	2.20	109	.235	.297	80-0-10	.175	-0	75	5		0.7
1909	Cle A	1	5	.167	12	4	1	1	52.1	54	28	0	1	16	15	2.92	87	.314	.376	15-0-1	.000	-2	76	-3		-0.6
Total	4	36	35	.507	90	66	49-7	2	612.2	543	225	3	14	183	280	2.17	113	.244	.306	190-0-13	.147	-4	86	17		1.7

LIGTENBERG, KERRY Kerry Dale B5.11.1971 Rapid City SD BR/TR/6-2/215(205-220) d8.12 Col Minnesota [DL 1999 Atl N 182]

YEAR	TM LG	W	L	PCT	G	GS	CG-SHO	SV-BS	IP	H	R	HR	HB	BB-IB	SO	ERA	AERA	OAV	OOB	AB-HR-SH	AVG	PB	SUP	APR	DL	PW
1997	†Atl N	1	0	1.000	15	0	0	1-0	15	12	5	4	0	4-2	19	3.00	140	.211	.262	0	—	0		2		0.1
1998	†Atl N	3	2	.600	75	0	0	30-4	73	51	24	6	0	24-1	79	2.71	154	.193	.260	0	—	0		12		1.5
2000	†Atl N	2	3	.400	59	0	0	12-2	52.1	43	21	7	0	24-5	51	3.61	125	.226	.312	0	—	0		6		0.7
2001	†Atl N	3	3	.500	53	0	0	1-1	59.2	50	22	4	0	30-8	56	3.02	143	.226	.316	0	—	0		9		0.7
2002	†Atl N	3	4	.429	52	0	0	0-0	66.2	52	23	6	0	33-3	51	2.97	136	.213	.306	0	—	0		9		0.8
2003	Bal A	4	2	.667	68	0	0	1-3	59.1	60	23	9	1	14-3	47	3.34	138	.263	.310	0	—	0		10		0.7
2004	Tor A	1	6	.143	57	0	0	3-2	55	73	40	6	2	25-7	49	6.38	77	.313	.385	0	—	0		-8	15	-1.0
2005	Ari N	0	0	—	7	0	0	0-0	9.2	16	15	4	0	4-0	5	13.97	31	.364	.417	1	.000	-0		-9		-0.5
Total	17	20	.459	386	0	0	48-12	390.2	357	173	46	3	158-29	357	3.82	115	.241	.315	1	.000	-0		29	197	3.0

LILLARD, GENE Robert Eugene B11.12.1913 Santa Barbara CA D4.12.1991 Goleta CA BR/TR/5-10.5/178 d5.8.1936 b-Bill ▲

YEAR	TM LG	W	L	PCT	G	GS	CG-SHO	SV-BS	IP	H	R	HR	HB	BB-IB	SO	ERA	AERA	OAV	OOB	AB-HR-SH	AVG	PB	SUP	APR	DL	PW
1939	Chi N	3	5	.375	20	7	2	0	55	68	48	2	3	36	31	6.55	60	.309	.413	10	.100	1*	92	-17		-2.0
1940	StL N	0	1	.000	2	1	0	0	4.2	8	7	1	1	4	2	13.50	30	.364	.481	0	—	0	65	-4		-0.7
Total	2	3	6	.333	22	8	2	0	59.2	76	55	3	4	40	33	7.09	56	.314	.420	10	.100	1	89	-21		-2.7

LILLIE, JIM James J. "Grasshopper" (b James J. Lilly) B7.27.1861 New Haven CT D11.9.1890 Kansas City MO BR d5.17 ▲

YEAR	TM LG	W	L	PCT	G	GS	CG-SHO	SV-BS	IP	H	R	HR	HB	BB-IB	SO	ERA	AERA	OAV	OOB	AB-HR-SH	AVG	PB	SUP	APR	DL	PW
1883	Buf N	0	1	.000	3	0	1	0	12	16	12	0		2	4	3.00	106	.302	.327	201-1	.234	0*		-1		-0.1
1884	Buf N	0	1	.000	2	1	0	0	13	22	24	0		5	4	6.23	51	.324	.370	471-3	.223	-0*	84	-6		-0.3
1886	KC N	0	0	—	1	0	0	0	6	8	5	0		1	0	4.50	84	.348	.375	416	.175	-0*		-1		0.0
Total	3	0	2	.000	6	1	1	0	31	46	41	0		8	8	4.65	71	.319	.355	1088-4	.207	-0	84	-8		-0.4

LILLIQUIST, DEREK Derek Jansen B2.20.1966 Winter Park FL BL/TL/6-0/214(195-214) [AtlN87 1/6] d4.13 Col Georgia

YEAR	TM LG	W	L	PCT	G	GS	CG-SHO	SV-BS	IP	H	R	HR	HB	BB-IB	SO	ERA	AERA	OAV	OOB	AB-HR-SH	AVG	PB	SUP	APR	DL	PW
1989	Atl N	8	10	.444	32	30	0	0-1	165.2	202	87	16	2	34-5	79	3.97	92	.301	.335	63-0-3	.190	0*	85	-7		-0.7
1990	Atl N	2	8	.200	12	11	0	0-0	61.2	75	45	10	1	19-4	34	6.28	64	.301	.348	23-2-0	.348	4*	71	-13		-1.5
	SD N	3	3	.500	16	7	1-1	0-0	60.1	61	29	6	2	23-1	29	4.33	89	.266	.337	20-0-2	.150	-0	101	-2		-0.2
	Year	5	11	.313	28	18	1-1	0-0	122	136	74	16	3	42-5	63	5.31	74	.285	.343	43-2-2	.256	4	83	-15		-1.7
1991	SD N	0	2	.000	6	2	0	0-0	14.1	25	14	3	0	4-1	7	8.79	43	.379	.414	2	.000	-0	106	-7		-0.8
1992	Cle A	5	3	.625	71	0	0	6-5	61.2	39	13	5	2	18-6	47	1.75	225	.186	.252	0	—	0		15		2.1
1993	Cle A	4	4	.500	56	2	0	10-3	64	64	20	5	1	19-5	40	2.25	195	.263	.317	0	—	0	126	14		1.9
1994	Cle A	1	3	.250	36	0	0	1-2	29.1	34	17	6	1	8-1	15	4.91	97	.304	.347	0	—	0		1		0.0
1995	Bos A	2	1	.667	28	0	0	0-3	23	27	17	7	0	9-2	14	6.26	78	.303	.356	0	—	0		-3		-0.4
1996	Cin N	0	0	—	5	0	0	0-0	3.2	5	3	1	0	0-0	1	7.36	58	.357	.357	0	—	0		-1		0.0
Total	8	25	34	.424	262	52	1-1	17-15	483.2	532	245	59	7	134-25	261	4.13	97	.283	.330	108-2-5	.213	4	83	-4		0.4

LILLY, TED Theodore Roosevelt B1.4.1976 Lamita CA BL/TL/6-0/185* [LAN96 23/688] d5.14 Col Fresno (CA) City

YEAR	TM LG	W	L	PCT	G	GS	CG-SHO	SV-BS	IP	H	R	HR	HB	BB-IB	SO	ERA	AERA	OAV	OOB	AB-HR-SH	AVG	PB	SUP	APR	DL	PW
1999	Mon N	0	1	.000	9	3	0	0-0	23.2	30	20	7	3	9-0	28	7.61	59	.309	.382	5-0-1	.200	0	62	-7		-0.3
2000	NY A	0	0	—	7	0	0	0-0	8	8	6	1	0	5-0	11	5.63	85	.235	.333	0	—	0		-1	49	-0.1
2001	NY A	5	6	.455	26	21	0	0-0	120.2	126	81	20	7	51-1	112	5.37	83	.267	.344	1-0-2	.000	-0	106	-14		-1.0
2002	NY A	3	6	.333	16	11	2	0-0	76.2	57	31	10	5	24-3	59	3.40	127	.202	.274	3	.000	-0	55	9		0.9
	†Oak A	2	1	.667	6	5	0	0-0	23.1	23	12	5	1	7-0	18	4.63	97	.253	.313	0	—	0	79	-3	49	0.0
	Year	5	7	.417	22	16	2-1	0-0	100	80	43	15	6	31-3	77	3.69	118	.214	.283	3	.000	-0	62	9		0.9
2003	†Oak A	12	10	.545	32	31	0	0-0	178.1	179	92	24	5	58-3	147	4.34	106	.255	.314	5	.000	-1	87	6		0.6
2004	Tor A★	12	10	.545	32	32	2-1	0-0	197.1	171	92	26	6	89-2	168	4.06	121	.230	.316	3-0-1	.000	-0	83	18		1.6
2005	Tor A	10	11	.476	25	25	0	0-0	126.1	135	79	23	3	58-1	96	5.56	83	.272	.348	3	.000	-0	105	-10	50	-1.5
Total	7	44	45	.494	153	128	4-2	0-0	754.1	729	413	116	30	301-10	639	4.67	99	.250	.324	20-0-4	.050	-1	89	1	148	0.3

LIMA, JOSE Jose Desiderio Rodriguez (b Jose Desiderio Rodriguez (Lima)) B9.30.1972 Santiago, D.R. BR/TR/6-2/205(170-210) d4.20

YEAR	TM LG	W	L	PCT	G	GS	CG-SHO	SV-BS	IP	H	R	HR	HB	BB-IB	SO	ERA	AERA	OAV	OOB	AB-HR-SH	AVG	PB	SUP	APR	DL	PW
1994	Det A	0	1	.000	3	1	0	0-0	6.2	11	10	2	0	3-1	7	13.50	36	.355	.412	0	—	0	112	-6		-0.6
1995	Det A	3	9	.250	15	15	0	0-0	73.2	85	52	10	4	18-4	37	6.11	79	.288	.336	0	—	0	70	-9		-1.3
1996	Det A	5	6	.455	39	4	0	3-4	72.2	87	48	13	6	22-4	59	5.70	89	.296	.352	0	—	0	46	-4		-0.4
1997	†Hou N	1	6	.143	52	1	0	2-0	75	79	45	9	5	16-2	63	5.28	76	.271	.317	3-0-2	.000	-0	92	-9		-0.3
1998	Hou N	16	8	.667	33	33	3-1	0-0	233.1	229	100	34	7	32-1	169	3.70	109	.256	.285	79-0-9	.139	-1	127	11		1.0
1999	†Hou N★	21	10	.677	35	35	3	0-0	246.1	256	108	30	2	44-2	187	3.58	124	.265	.296	75-0-13	.080	-4*	101	23		2.0
2000	Hou N	7	16	.304	33	33	0	0-0	196.1	251	152	48	2	68-3	124	6.65	74	.314	.364	60-0-8	.167	-0	98	-33		-3.2
2001	Hou N	1	2	.333	14	9	0	0-0	53	77	48	12	5	16-1	41	7.30	63	.350	.400	16-0-1	.000	-2	107	-16		-0.9
	Det A	5	10	.333	18	18	2	0-0	112.2	120	66	23	4	22-2	43	4.71	94	.274	.311	1	.000	-0	80	-4		-0.6
2002	Det A	4	6	.400	20	12	0	0-0	73.1	86	60	14	5	21-0	35	7.77	56	.314	.360	0	—	0	94	-24		-2.8
2003	KC A	8	3	.727	14	14	0	0-0	73.1	80	40	17	6	26-0	32	4.91	98	.280	.347	2-0-1	.500	0	104	5	41	0.1

YEAR	TM LG	W	L	PCT	G	GS	CG-SHO	SV-BS	IP	H	R	HR	HB	BB-IB	SO	ERA	AERA	OAV	OOB	AB-HR-SH	AVG	PB	SUP	APR	DL	PW
2004	†LA N	13	5	.722	36	24	0	0-0	170.1	178	81	33	1	34-6	93	4.07	102	.271	.307	48-0-8	.188	0*	98	2		0.2
2005	KC A	5	16	.238	32	32	1	0-0	168.2	219	140	31	9	61-1	80	6.99	60	.314	.373	3-0-1	.333	0	93	-54		-5.3
Total 12		89	98	.476	344	231	9-1	5-4	1550.1	1758	950	264	51	383-27	968	5.21	85	.286	.330	287-0-43	.132	-7	98	-122	41	-12.7

LINCOLN, EZRA Ezra Perry B11.17.1868 Raynham MA D5.7.1951 Taunton MA BL/TL/5-11/160 d5.2

YEAR	TM LG	W	L	PCT	G	GS	CG-SHO	SV-BS	IP	H	R	HR	HB	BB-IB	SO	ERA	AERA	OAV	OOB	AB-HR-SH	AVG	PB	SUP	APR	DL	PW
1890	Cle N	3	11	.214	15	15	13	0	118	157	102	1	1	53	22	4.42	81	.310	.376	51	.157	-3	73	-15		-1.6
	Syr AA	0	3	.000	3	3	2	0	20	33	27	1	1	4	6	10.35	34	.359	.392	8	.000	-1	32	-15		-1.5
Total 1		3	14	.176	18	18	15	0	138	190	129	2	2	57	28	5.28	68	.317	.378	59	.136	-4	66	-30		-3.1

LINCOLN, MIKE Michael George B4.10.1975 Carmichael CA BR/TR/6-2/210* [MinA96 13/367] d4.7 Col Tennessee [DL 2005 StL N 183]

YEAR	TM LG	W	L	PCT	G	GS	CG-SHO	SV-BS	IP	H	R	HR	HB	BB-IB	SO	ERA	AERA	OAV	OOB	AB-HR-SH	AVG	PB	SUP	APR	DL	PW
1999	Min A	0	10	.231	18	15	0	0-0	76.1	102	59	11	1	26-0		6.84	76	.321	.368		.000	-0	82	-12		-1.6
2000	Min A	0	3	.000	8	4	0	0-0	20.2	36	25	10	2	13-0	15	10.89	48	.383	.468	0	—	0	107	-11	70	-1.3
2001	Pit N	2	1	.667	31	0	0	0-2	40.1	34	16	3	4	11-0	24	2.68	167	.225	.293	4-0-1	.250	0		6	15	0.3
2002	Pit N	2	4	.333	55	0	0	0-3	72.1	80	28	7	0	27-8	50	3.11	135	.290	.349	5	.000	-1		8		0.6
2003	Pit N	3	4	.429	36	0	0	5-3	36.1	38	22	5	1	13-0	28	5.20	83	.277	.342	0		0		-3	93	-0.7
2004	StL N	3	2	.600	13	0	0	0-2	17.1	10	12	1	1	6-0	14	5.19	82	.164	.243	0		0		-2	153	-0.5
Total 6		13	24	.351	161	19	0	5-10	263.1	300	162	37	9	96-8	158	5.16	90	.289	.350	10-0-1	.100	-1	97	-14	514	-3.0

LINDAMAN, VIVE Vivan Alexander B10.28.1877 Charles City IA D2.13.1927 Charles City IA BR/TR/6-1/200 d4.14

YEAR	TM LG	W	L	PCT	G	GS	CG-SHO	SV-BS	IP	H	R	HR	HB	BB-IB	SO	ERA	AERA	OAV	OOB	AB-HR-SH	AVG	PB	SUP	APR	DL	PW
1906	Bos N	12	23	.343	39	36	32-2	0	307.1	303	132	4	11	90	115	2.43	111	.264	.324	106-0-3	.132	-2	73	3		0.1
1907	Bos N	11	15	.423	34	28	24-2	1	260	252	130	10	15	108	91	3.63	70	.265	.349	90-0-2	.122	-2	102	-28		-3.0
1908	Bos N	12	16	.429	43	30	21-2	1	270.2	246	112	7	10	70	68	2.36	102	.249	.306	85-0-4	.176	0	96	-3		-0.4
1909	Bos N	1	6	.143	15	6	6-1	0	66	76	44	1	1	28	13	4.64	61	.299	.371	22	.273	1	29	-11		-1.1
Total 4		36	60	.375	131	100	83-7	2	904	876	418	22	37	296	286	2.92	88	.263	.329	303-0-9	.152	-3	85	-39		-4.4

LINDBLAD, PAUL Paul Aaron B8.9.1941 Chanute KS D1.8.2006 Arlington TX BL/TL/6-1/195* d9.15

YEAR	TM LG	W	L	PCT	G	GS	CG-SHO	SV-BS	IP	H	R	HR	HB	BB-IB	SO	ERA	AERA	OAV	OOB	AB-HR-SH	AVG	PB	SUP	APR	DL	PW
1965	KC A	0	1	.000					7.1	12	9	3	1	6-0	12	11.05	32	.353	.371	1	.000	-0		-6		-0.7
1966	KC A	5	10	.333	38	14	0	1	121	138	63	14	3	37-10	69	4.17	82	.292	.347	34-0-1	.147	0	89	-10		-1.1
1967	KC A	5	8	.385	46	10	1-1	0	115.2	106	59	15	6	35-9	83	3.58	89	.241	.304	34-1-1	.206	2*	118	-8		-0.8
1968	Oak A	4	3	.571	47	1	0	2	56.1	51	19	6	0	14-4	42	2.40	118	.237	.281	8-0-1	.375	1	0	2		0.5
1969	Oak A	9	6	.600	60	0	0	9-2	78.1	72	37	8	2	33-8	64	4.14	83	.240	.319	12	.333	1		-5		-0.9
1970	Oak A	8	2	.800	62	0	0	3-0	63.1	52	23	7	0	28-7	42	2.70	131	.222	.305	6	.000	-1		5		0.8
1971	Oak A	1	0	1.000	8	0	0	0-2	16	18	7	1	1	2-1	4	3.94	84	.295	.328	3	.333	0		-1		0.0
	Was A	6	4	.600	43	0	0	8-5	83.2	58	25	6	2	29-6	50	2.58	131	.196	.272	19	.158	1		9		1.3
	Year	7	4	.636	51	0	0	8-7	99.2	76	32	7	3	31-7	54	2.80	120	.213	.281	22	.182	1		7		1.3
1972	Tex A	5	8	.385	66	0	0	9-5	99.2	95	31	7	0	29-6	51	2.62	116	.257	.309	15-0-2	.200	0		6		0.9
1973	†Oak A	1	5	.167	36	3	0	2-0	78	89	38	8	3	28-2	33	3.69	96	.292	.354	0	—	0	25	-2		-0.2
1974	Oak A	4	4	.500	45	2	0	6-3	100.2	85	30	4	2	30-11	46	2.06	163	.231	.288	0	—	0	92	14		1.3
1975	†Oak A	9	1	.900	68	0	0	7-1	122.1	105	44	6	0	43-10	58	2.72	134	.237	.300	1	.000	0		12		1.2
1976	Oak A	6	5	.545	65	0	0	5-5	114.2	111	50	5	3	24-5	37	3.06	110	.253	.292	0	—	0		1		0.2
1977	Tex A	4	5	.444	42	1	0	4-1	98.2	103	50	16	1	29-2	46	4.20	97	.270	.322	0	—	0	44	0		0.0
1978	Tex A	1	1	.500	18	0	0	2-2	39.2	41	16	2	2	15-7	25	3.63	103	.279	.349	0	—	0		2	19	0.1
	†NY A	0	0	—	7	1	0	0-0	18.1	21	9	4	0	8-0	9	4.42	83	.284	.354	0	—	0	98	-1		0.1
	Year	1	1	.500	25	1	0	2-2	58	62	25	6	2	23-7	34	3.88	96	.281	.351	0	—	0	97	1		0.1
Total 14		68	63	.519	655	32	1-1	64-26	1213.2	1157	510	112	26	384-88	671	3.29	104	.253	.312	133-1-5	.195	4	86	18	19	2.6

LINDE, LYMAN Lyman Gilbert B9.30.1920 Rolling Prairie WI D10.24.1995 Beaver Dam WI BR/TR/5-11/185 d9.11 Col Wisconsin-Madison

YEAR	TM LG	W	L	PCT	G	GS	CG-SHO	SV-BS	IP	H	R	HR	HB	BB-IB	SO	ERA	AERA	OAV	OOB	AB-HR-SH	AVG	PB	SUP	APR	DL	PW
1947	Cle A	0	0	—	1	0	0	0	0.2	3	2	0	1	0	0	27.00	13	.600	.667	0		0		-2		-0.1
1948	Cle A	0	0	—	3	0	0	0	10	9	6	1	0	4	0	5.40	75	.243	.317	2	.000	-0		-1		-0.1
Total 2		0	0	—	4	0	0	0	10.2	12	8	1	1	4	0	6.75	60	.286	.362	2	.000	-0		-3		-0.2

LINDELL, JOHNNY John Harlan B8.30.1916 Greeley CO D8.27.1985 Newport Beach CA BR/TR/6-4.5/217* d4.18.1941 Mil 1945 ▲

YEAR	TM LG	W	L	PCT	G	GS	CG-SHO	SV-BS	IP	H	R	HR	HB	BB-IB	SO	ERA	AERA	OAV	OOB	AB-HR-SH	AVG	PB	SUP	APR	DL	PW
1942	NY A	2	1	.667	23	2	0	1	52.2	52	25	3	1	22	28	3.76	92	.254	.329	24	.250	1*	99	-2		0.0
1953	Pit N	5	16	.238	27	23	13-1	0	175.2	173	106	17	6	116	102	4.71	95	.262	.377	91-4-0	.286	6*	76	-6		1.0
	Phi N	1	1	.500	5	3	2	0	23.1	22	16	0	0	23	16	4.24	99	.259	.417	18	.389	2*	85	-2		0.1
	Year	6	17	.261	32	26	15-1	0	199	195	122	17	6	139	118	4.66	95	.261	.382	109-4-0	.303	8	77	-9		1.1
Total 2		8	18	.308	55	28	15-1	1	251.2	247	147	20	7	161	146	4.47	95	.260	.371	133-4-0	.293	9	81	-10		1.1

LINDEMANN, ERNIE Ernest B6.10.1883 New York NY D12.27.1951 Brooklyn NY BR/TR/5-10.5/182 d6.28

YEAR	TM LG	W	L	PCT	G	GS	CG-SHO	SV-BS	IP	H	R	HR	HB	BB-IB	SO	ERA	AERA	OAV	OOB	AB-HR-SH	AVG	PB	SUP	APR	DL	PW
1907	Bos N	0	0	—	1	0	0	0	6.1	6	5	0	0	4	0	5.68	45	.286	.400	2-0-1	.500	0	167	-2		-0.1

LINDQUIST, CARL Carl Emil B5.9.1919 Morris Run PA D9.3.2001 Blossburg PA BR/TR/6-2/185 d9.27 Col Mansfield

YEAR	TM LG	W	L	PCT	G	GS	CG-SHO	SV-BS	IP	H	R	HR	HB	BB-IB	SO	ERA	AERA	OAV	OOB	AB-HR-SH	AVG	PB	SUP	APR	DL	PW
1943	Bos N	0	2	.000	2	2	0	0	13	17	10	3	0	4	6	6.23	55	.315	.362	4	.000	-1	37	-4		-0.5
1944	Bos N	0	0	—	5	0	0	0	8.2	8	5	1	0	2	4	3.12	123	.222	.263	1	.000	-0		0		0.0
Total 2		0	2	.000	7	2	0	0	21.2	25	15	4	0	6	10	4.98	72	.278	.323	5	.000	-1	37	-4		-0.5

LINDSEY, JIM James Kendrick B1.24.1898 Greensburg LA D10.25.1963 Jackson LA BR/TR/6-1/175 d5.1

YEAR	TM LG	W	L	PCT	G	GS	CG-SHO	SV-BS	IP	H	R	HR	HB	BB-IB	SO	ERA	AERA	OAV	OOB	AB-HR-SH	AVG	PB	SUP	APR	DL	PW
1922	Cle A	4	5	.444	29	5	0	1	83.2	105	60	4	3	24	24	6.02	67	.324	.376	24	.167	-1	76	-17		-1.7
1924	Cle A	0	0	—	3	0	0	0	3	8	7	0	0	3	0	21.00	20	.500	.579	3	.000	-1		-5		-0.3
1929	StL N	1	1	.500	2	2	1	0	16.1	20	11	1	1	2	8	5.51	85	.290	.319	5	.200	-1	75	-1		-0.2
1930	†StL N	7	5	.583	39	6	3	5	105.2	131	59	6	4	46	50	4.43	113	.312	.385	28-0-3	.286	1	84	7		0.7
1931	†StL N	6	4	.600	35	2	1-1	7	74.2	77	32	2	0	45	32	2.77	142	.270	.370	9-0-4	.111	-0	76	7		1.0
1932	StL N	3	3	.500	33	5	0	3	89.1	96	53	6	2	38	31	4.94	80	.279	.354	21-0-3	.143	-1	154	-8		-0.7
1933	StL N	0	0	—	1	0	0	0	2	2	1	0	0	1	2	4.50	77	.286	.375	0		0		0		0.0
1934	Cin N	0	0	—	4	0	0	0	4	4	3	0	1	2	2	4.50	91	.286	.412	0		0		0		0.0
	StL N	0	1	.000	11	0	0	1	14	21	13	2	0	3	7	6.43	66	.328	.358	1	.000	-0		-4		-0.3
	Year	0	1	.000	15	0	0	1	18	25	16	2	1	5	9	6.00	70	.321	.369	1	.000	-0		-4		-0.3
1937	Bro N	0	1	.000	20	0	0	2	38.1	43	22	4	1	12	15	3.52	115	.295	.352	6	.167	0		1		0.0
Total 9		21	20	.512	177	20	5-1	19	431	507	261	25	12	176	175	4.70	91	.300	.370	97-0-10	.186	-3	99	-20		-1.5

LINDSTROM, AXEL Axel Olaf B8.26.1895 Gustavsberg, Sweden D6.24.1940 Asheville NC BR/TR/5-10/180 d10.3

YEAR	TM LG	W	L	PCT	G	GS	CG-SHO	SV-BS	IP	H	R	HR	HB	BB-IB	SO	ERA	AERA	OAV	OOB	AB-HR-SH	AVG	PB	SUP	APR	DL	PW
1916	Phi A	0	0	—	1	0	0	0	4	2	2	0	1	0	1	4.50	63	.182	.250	2	.500	0		0		0.0

LINEBRINK, SCOTT Scott Cameron B8.4.1976 Austin TX BR/TR/6-3/185(185-210) [SFN97 2/56] d4.15 Col Southwest Texas

YEAR	TM LG	W	L	PCT	G	GS	CG-SHO	SV-BS	IP	H	R	HR	HB	BB-IB	SO	ERA	AERA	OAV	OOB	AB-HR-SH	AVG	PB	SUP	APR	DL	PW
2000	SF N	0	0	—	3	0	0	0-0	2.1	7	3	1	0	2-0	0	11.57	38	.500	.563	0		0		-2		-0.1
	Hou N	0	0	—	8	0	0	0-0	9.2	11	5	3	3	6-0	6	4.66	105	.289	.426	1	1.000	0		0		0.0
	Year	0	0	—	11	0	0	0-0	12	18	8	4	3	8-0	6	6.00	80	.346	.460	1	1.000	0		-1		-0.1
2001	Hou N	0	0	—	9	0	0	0-0	10.1	6	4	0	2	6-0	9	2.61	176	.176	.326	0	—	0		2		0.1
2002	Hou N	0	0	—	22	0	0	0-0	24.1	31	21	2	1	13-4	24	7.03	62	.298	.375	0	—	0		-7	28	-0.4
2003	Hou N	1	1	.500	9	6	0	0-0	31.2	38	15	4	3	14-1	17	4.26	104	.317	.399	8-0-1	.000	-1	138	1		-0.1
	SD N	2	1	.667	43	0	0	0-0	60.2	55	22	5	3	22-3	51	2.82	142	.244	.314	4	.500	1		8		0.4
	Year	3	2	.600	52	6	0	0-0	92.1	93	37	9	6	36-4	68	3.31	125	.270	.344	12-0-1	.167	0	147	9		0.3
2004	SD N	7	3	.700	73	0	0	0-5	84	61	22	8	2	26-2	83	2.14	184	.209	.278	2-0-1	.000	-0		18		1.9
2005	†SD N	8	1	.889	73	0	0	1-5	73.2	55	17	5	6	23-4	70	1.83	211	.209	.273	1	.000	0		18		1.9
Total 6		18	6	.750	240	6	0	1-10	296.2	264	109	27	15	112-14	260	3.00	136	.242	.318	16-0-2	.188	0	148	38	28	3.7

LINES, DICK Richard George B8.17.1938 Montreal QC, Can. BR/TL/6-1/175* d4.16

YEAR	TM LG	W	L	PCT	G	GS	CG-SHO	SV-BS	IP	H	R	HR	HB	BB-IB	SO	ERA	AERA	OAV	OOB	AB-HR-SH	AVG	PB	SUP	APR	DL	PW
1966	Was A	5	2	.714	53	0	0	2	83	63	23	4	1	24-7	49	2.28	152	.213	.273	10-0-2	.000	-1		11		1.0
1967	Was A	2	5	.286	54	0	0	4	85.2	83	43	6	4	24-6	54	3.36	94	.245	.292	9	.111	-1		-5		-0.3
Total 2		7	7	.500	107	0	0	6	168.2	146	66	10	5	48-13	103	2.83	117	.230	.283	19-0-2	.053	-1		6		0.7

LINK, FRED Edward Theodore "Laddie" B3.11.1886 Columbus OH D5.22.1939 Houston TX BL/TL/6-0/170 d4.15

YEAR	TM LG	W	L	PCT	G	GS	CG-SHO	SV-BS	IP	H	R	HR	HB	BB-IB	SO	ERA	AERA	OAV	OOB	AB-HR-SH	AVG	PB	SUP	APR	DL	PW
1910	Cle A	5	6	.455	22	13	6-1	1	127.2	121	53	0	7	50	55	3.17	82	.259	.340	42-0-3	.167	-1	90	-5		-0.6
	StL A	0	1	.000	3	3	0	0	17	24	10	0	1	13	5	4.24	58	.375	.487	6	.167	-0	181	-3		-0.2
	Year	5	7	.417	25	16	6-1	1	144.2	145	63	0	8	63	60	3.30	78	.273	.359	48-0-3	.167	-1	106	-6		-0.8

YEAR	TM LG	W	L	PCT	G	GS	CG-SHO	SV-BS	IP	H	R	HR	HB	BB-IB	SO	ERA	AERA	OAV	OOB	AB-HR-SH	AVG	PB	SUP	APR	DL	PW

LINKE, ED Edward Karl "Babe" B11.9.1911 Chicago IL D6.21.1988 Chicago IL BR/TR/5-11/180 d4.27

YEAR	TM LG	W	L	PCT	G	GS	CG-SHO	SV-BS	IP	H	R	HR	HB	BB-IB	SO	ERA	AERA	OAV	OOB	AB-HR-SH	AVG	PB	SUP	APR	DL	PW
1933	Was A	1	0	1.000	3	2	0		16	15	10	0	0	11	6	5.06	83	.250	.366	6-0-1	.167	0	102	-2		-0.1
1934	Was A	2	2	.500	7	4	2	0	34.2	38	20	1	0	9	9	4.15	104	.277	.322	11-0-1	.182	0*	71	0		0.0
1935	Was A	11	7	.611	40	22	10-1	3	178	211	111	6	1	80	51	5.01	86	.296	.367	68-1-1	.294	6	131	-14		-0.7
1936	Was A	1	5	.167	13	6	1	0	52	73	46	4	0	14	11	7.10	67	.330	.370	15-1-0	.400	5	52	-13		-0.7
1937	Was A	6	1	.857	36	7	0	3	128.2	158	89	11	4	59	61	5.60	79	.304	.379	46-0-1	.217	1*	141	-15		-0.7
1938	StL A	1	7	.125	21	2	0		39.2	60	37	6	0	33	18	7.94	63	.357	.463	10	.200	0	124	-12		-1.8
Total 6		22	22	.500	120	43	13-1	6	449	555	313	28	5	206	156	5.61	79	.305	.377	156-2-4	.263	12	113	-56		-4.0

LINT, ROYCE Royce James B1.1.1921 Birmingham AL BL/TL/6-1/165 d4.13

YEAR	TM LG	W	L	PCT	G	GS	CG-SHO	SV-BS	IP	H	R	HR	HB	BB-IB	SO	ERA	AERA	OAV	OOB	AB-HR-SH	AVG	PB	SUP	APR	DL	PW
1954	StL N	2	3	.400	30	4	1	0	70.1	75	46	9	0	30	36	4.86	85	.273	.342	10-0-1	.100	1*	152	-7		-0.2

LINTON, DOUG Douglas Warren B2.9.1965 Santa Ana CA BR/TR/6-1/190* [TorA86 43/878] d8.3 Col California-Irvine

YEAR	TM LG	W	L	PCT	G	GS	CG-SHO	SV-BS	IP	H	R	HR	HB	BB-IB	SO	ERA	AERA	OAV	OOB	AB-HR-SH	AVG	PB	SUP	APR	DL	PW
1992	Tor A	1	3	.250	8	3	0	0-0	24	31	23	5	0	17-0	16	8.63	48	.323	.417	0	—	0	96	-11		-1.5
1993	Tor A	0	1	.000	4	1	0	0-0	11	11	8	0	1	9-0	4	6.55	67	.256	.382	0	—	0	63	-2		-0.2
	Cal A	2	0	1.000	19	0	0	0-1	25.2	35	22	8	0	14-1	19	7.71	59	.324	.398	0	—	0		-8		-0.5
	Year	2	1	.667	23	1	0	0-1	36.2	46	30	8	1	23-1	23	7.36	61	.305	.393	0	—	0	62	-10		-0.7
1994	NY N	6	2	.750	32	3	0	0-0	50.1	74	27	4	0	20-3	29	4.47	93	.341	.395	7-0-2	.000	-1	131	-1		-0.3
1995	KC A	0	1	.000	7	2	0	0-0	22.1	22	21	4	2	10-1	13	7.25	66	.256	.347	0	—	0	29	-7		-0.3
1996	KC A	7	9	.438	21	18	0	0-0	104	111	65	13	8	26-1	87	5.02	100	.271	.325	0	—	0	90	-1		-0.2
1999	Bal N	1	4	.200	14	8	0	0-0	59	69	41	14	2	25-1	31	5.95	79	.296	.369	0	—	0	72	-8		-0.6
2003	Tor A	0	0	—	7	0	0	0-0	9	7	3	2	0	4-0	7	3.00	158	.226	.314	0	—	0		2		0.1
Total 7		17	20	.459	112	35	0	0-1	305.1	360	210	50	13	125-7	206	5.78	81	.294	.364	7-0-2	.000	-1	87	-36		-3.5

LINZY, FRANK Frank Alfred B9.15.1940 Ft.Gibson OK BR/TR/6-1/190* d8.14 Col Oklahoma St.

YEAR	TM LG	W	L	PCT	G	GS	CG-SHO	SV-BS	IP	H	R	HR	HB	BB-IB	SO	ERA	AERA	OAV	OOB	AB-HR-SH	AVG	PB	SUP	APR	DL	PW
1963	SF N	0	0	—	8	1	0	0	16.2	22	9	0	1	10-0	14	4.86	66	.324	.418	3	.000	-0	189	-2		-0.1
1965	SF N	9	3	.750	57	0	0	21	81.2	76	19	2	3	23-8	35	1.43	251	.250	.309	18-1-0	.222	1		**18**		4.1
1966	SF N	7	11	.389	51	0	0	16	100.1	107	40	4	2	34-9	57	2.96	124	.273	.333	20-0-3	.150	0		7		1.6
1967	SF N	7	7	.500	57	0	0	17	95.2	67	21	4	0	34-7	38	1.51	218	.203	.274	15-0-3	.000	-2		18		3.5
1968	SF N	9	8	.529	57	0	0	12	95.1	76	30	1	1	27-14	36	2.08	142	.218	.274	11-0-4	.000	-1		8		1.8
1969	SF N	14	9	.609	58	0	0	11-10	116.1	129	57	9	3	38-15	62	3.64	97	.283	.341	30-0-3	.267	3		-2		0.0
1970	SF N	1	1	.667	20	0	0	1-0	25.2	33	20	2	1	11-4	16	7.01	57	.327	.391	4	.000	-0		-8		-0.9
	StL N	3	5	.375	47	0	0	2-2	61.1	66	26	3	0	23-10	19	3.67	113	.282	.344	7	.000	-1		4		0.5
	Year	5	6	.455	67	0	0	3-2	87	99	46	5	1	34-14	35	4.66	88	.296	.358	11	.000	-1		-3		-0.4
1971	StL N	4	3	.571	50	0	0	6-2	59.1	49	18	2	0	27-11	24	2.12	171	.226	.311	4	.500	1		8	22	1.3
1972	Mil A	2	2	.500	47	0	0	12-2	77.1	70	30	4	2	27-12	24	3.03	101	.248	.313	9-0-1	.111	-0		0		0.0
1973	Mil A	2	6	.250	42	1	0	13-4	63	68	34	7	1	21-6	21	3.57	107	.282	.338	0	—	0	141	-1		-0.1
1974	Phi N	3	2	.600	22	0	0	0-1	24.2	27	11	1	0	7-1	12	3.28	116	.284	.333	0	—	0		1		0.2
Total 11		62	57	.521	516	2	0	111-21	817.1	790	315	45	14	282-97	358	2.85	123	.257	.321	121-1-14	.149	0	164	51	22	11.9

LiPETRI, ANGELO Michael Angelo B7.6.1929 Brooklyn NY BR/TR/6-1.5/180* d4.25

YEAR	TM LG	W	L	PCT	G	GS	CG-SHO	SV-BS	IP	H	R	HR	HB	BB-IB	SO	ERA	AERA	OAV	OOB	AB-HR-SH	AVG	PB	SUP	APR	DL	PW
1956	Phi N	0	0	—	6	0	0	0	11	7	5	2	1	3-0	8	3.27	114	.175	.250	1	.000	-0		-0		-0.1
1958	Phi N	0	0	—	4	0	0	0	4	6	5	1	1	0-0	1	11.25	35	.353	.389	0	—	0		-3		-0.1
Total 2		0	0	—	10	0	0	0	15	13	10	3	2	3-0	9	5.40	70	.228	.290	1	.000	-0		-3		-0.1

LIPP, TOM Thomas Charles (b Thomas Charles Lieb) B6.4.1870 Baltimore MD D5.30.1932 Baltimore MD 5-11.5/170 d9.18

YEAR	TM LG	W	L	PCT	G	GS	CG-SHO	SV-BS	IP	H	R	HR	HB	BB-IB	SO	ERA	AERA	OAV	OOB	AB-HR-SH	AVG	PB	SUP	APR	DL	PW
1897	Phi N	1	0	1.000	1	1	1	0	9	15	10	1	2	3-0	1	15.00	28	.471	.526	1	1.000	1	51	-3		-0.4

LIPSCOMB, NIG Gerard B2.24.1911 Rutherfordton NC D2.27.1978 Huntersville NC BR/TR/6-0/175 d4.23 ▲

YEAR	TM LG	W	L	PCT	G	GS	CG-SHO	SV-BS	IP	H	R	HR	HB	BB-IB	SO	ERA	AERA	OAV	OOB	AB-HR-SH	AVG	PB	SUP	APR	DL	PW
1937	StL A			—	3	0	0	0	9.2	13	9	3	0	5	1	6.52	74	.333	.409	96-0-1	.323	1*		-2		-0.1

LIRA, FELIPE Antonio Felipe B4.26.1972 Santa Teresa, Venez BR/TR/6-1/205(170-215) d4.27

YEAR	TM LG	W	L	PCT	G	GS	CG-SHO	SV-BS	IP	H	R	HR	HB	BB-IB	SO	ERA	AERA	OAV	OOB	AB-HR-SH	AVG	PB	SUP	APR	DL	PW
1995	Det A	9	13	.409	37	22	0	1-2	146.1	151	74	17	8	56-7	89	4.31	112	.271	.341	0	—	0	75	9		1.1
1996	Det A	6	14	.300	32	32	0	0-0	194.2	204	123	30	10	66-2	113	5.22	97	.269	.331	0	—	0	80	-3		-0.2
1997	Det A	5	7	.417	20	15	1-1	0-0	92	101	61	15	2	45-2	64	5.77	80	.277	.358	0	—	0	105	-10		-1.1
	Sea A	0	4	.000	8	3	0	0-0	18.2	31	21	3	4	10-0	9	9.16	50	.365	.446	0	—	0	61	-10		-1.6
	Year	5	11	.313	28	18	1-1	0-0	110.2	132	82	18	6	55-2	73	6.34	73	.294	.375	0	—	0	98	-20		-2.7
1998	Sea A	1	0	1.000	7	0	0	0-0	15.2	22	10	5	0	5-0	16	4.60	102	.319	.360	0	—	0		0		0.0
1999	Det A	0	0	—	2	0	0	0-0	3.1	7	5	2	0	2-0	3	10.80	44	.389	.450	0	—	0		-2		-0.1
2000	Mon N	5	8	.385	53	7	0	0-0	101.2	129	71	11	4	36-6	51	5.40	87	.310	.363	19-2-1	.211	2*	47	-9		-0.8
2001	Mon N	0	0	—	4	0	0	0-0	5	11	7	1	0	2-0	1	12.60	34	.440	.481	0	—	0		-4		-0.2
Total 7		26	46	.361	163	79	4-3	1-2	577.1	656	372	84	28	222-17	348	5.32	91	.286	.352	19-2-1	.211	2	80	-29		-2.9

LIRIANO, FRANCISCO Francisco Casillas B10.26.1983 San Cristobal, D.R. BL/TL/6-2/185 d9.5

YEAR	TM LG	W	L	PCT	G	GS	CG-SHO	SV-BS	IP	H	R	HR	HB	BB-IB	SO	ERA	AERA	OAV	OOB	AB-HR-SH	AVG	PB	SUP	APR	DL	PW
2005	Min A	1	2	.333	6	4	0	0	23.2	19	15	4	0	7-0	33	5.70	77	.221	.280	0	—	0	70	-3		-0.3

LIRIANO, PEDRO Pedro Antonio B10.23.1980 Fantino, D.R. BR/TR/6-2/170* d8.27

YEAR	TM LG	W	L	PCT	G	GS	CG-SHO	SV-BS	IP	H	R	HR	HB	BB-IB	SO	ERA	AERA	OAV	OOB	AB-HR-SH	AVG	PB	SUP	APR	DL	PW
2004	Mil N	0	0	—	11	0	0	0-0	15.2	15	10	3	1	3-0	10	4.02	109	.238	.284	1	.000	-0		0		0.0
2005	Phi N	0	0	—	5	0	0	0-0	7.2	10	11	3	1	6-0	6	10.57	41	.313	.436	0	—	0		-6		-0.3
Total 2		0	0	—	16	0	0	0-0	23.1	25	21	6	2	9-0	16	6.17	71	.263	.340	1-0-1	.000	-0		-6		-0.3

LISENBEE, HOD Horace Milton B9.23.1898 Clarksville TN D11.14.1987 Clarksville TN BR/TR/5-11/170 d4.23 Col Rhodes

YEAR	TM LG	W	L	PCT	G	GS	CG-SHO	SV-BS	IP	H	R	HR	HB	BB-IB	SO	ERA	AERA	OAV	OOB	AB-HR-SH	AVG	PB	SUP	APR	DL	PW
1927	Was A	18	9	.667	39	34	17-4	0	242	221	114	6	3	78	105	3.57	114	.245	.307	83-0-8	.133	-5	105	13		0.7
1928	Was A	2	6	.250	16	9	3	0	77	102	58	4	5	32	13	6.08	66	.326	.397	23-0-2	.174	-0	91	-16		-1.5
1929	Bos A	0	0	—	5	0	0	0	8.2	10	5	1	0	4	2	5.19	82	.294	.368	2	.000	-0		0		0.0
1930	Bos A	10	17	.370	37	31	15	0	237.1	254	130	20	5	86	47	4.40	105	.280	.346	75-0-8	.267	1	75	7		0.6
1931	Bos A	5	12	.294	41	17	6	0	164.2	190	108	13	3	49	42	5.19	83	.281	.332	53	.226	0	89	-16		-1.4
1932	Bos A	0	4	.000	19	6	3	0	73.1	87	55	9	1	25	13	5.65	80	.296	.353	21-0-3	.048	-2	60	-9		-0.6
1936	Phi A	1	7	.125	19	7	4	0	85.2	115	69	9	0	24	17	6.20	82	.322	.365	25-0-2	.120	-1	62	-11		-0.9
1945	Cin N	1	3	.250	31	3	0	1	80.1	97	56	9	2	16	14	5.49	68	.294	.330	19	.000	-3	158	-16		-1.1
Total 8		37	58	.389	207	107	48-4	1	969	1076	595	74	19	314	253	4.81	90	.282	.340	301-0-23	.169	-10	88	-48		-4.2

LISKA, AD Adolph James B7.10.1906 Dwight NE D11.30.1998 Portland OR BR/TR/5-11.5/160 d4.17 Col Nebraska

YEAR	TM LG	W	L	PCT	G	GS	CG-SHO	SV-BS	IP	H	R	HR	HB	BB-IB	SO	ERA	AERA	OAV	OOB	AB-HR-SH	AVG	PB	SUP	APR	DL	PW
1929	Was A	3	9	.250	24	10	4	0	94.1	87	53	1	3	42	33	4.77	89	.249	.335	29	.172	-0	72	-3		-0.2
1930	Was A	9	7	.563	32	16	7-1	1	150.2	140	69	6	5	71	40	3.29	140	.250	.340	52-0-4	.096	-4	98	19		1.7
1931	Was A	0	1	.000	2	1	0	0	4	9	3	0	0	1	2	6.75	64	.450	.476	1	.000	-0	39	-1		-0.2
1932	Phi N	2	0	1.000	8	0	0	0	26.2	22	5	0	1	10	6	1.69	261	.239	.327	7	.000	-0		7		0.5
1933	Phi N	3	1	.750	45	1	0	1	75.2	96	46	5	0	26	23	4.52	84	.310	.363	14	.071	-1*	240	-16		-0.3
Total 5		17	18	.486	111	28	11-1	3	351.1	354	176	12	9	150	104	3.87	112	.266	.344	103-0-4	.107	-7	93	16		1.5

LITTELL, MARK Mark Alan B1.17.1953 Cape Girardeau MO BL/TR/6-3/210(195-210) [KCA71 12/274] d6.14

YEAR	TM LG	W	L	PCT	G	GS	CG-SHO	SV-BS	IP	H	R	HR	HB	BB-IB	SO	ERA	AERA	OAV	OOB	AB-HR-SH	AVG	PB	SUP	APR	DL	PW
1973	KC A	1	3	.250	8	7	1	0-0	38	44	25	5	0	23-1	16	5.68	72	.288	.376	0	—	0	109	-5		-0.5
1975	KC A	1	2	.333	7	3	1	0-0	24.1	19	11	1	0	15-0	19	3.70	104	.229	.347	0	—	0	61	1		0.1
1976	†KC A	8	4	.667	60	1	0	16-5	104	68	26	1	0	60-4	92	2.08	169	.188	.301	1	.000	0	201	17		2.6
1977	†KC A	8	4	.667	48	5	0	12-3	104.2	73	49	6	1	55-6	106	3.61	112	.198	.299	1	.000	0	107	4		0.5
1978	StL N	4	8	.333	72	2	0	11-4	106.1	80	38	4	0	59-16	130	2.79	128	.213	.324	7	.000	0	38	9		1.1
1979	StL N	9	4	.692	63	0	0	13-6	82.1	60	22	2	0	39-5	67	2.19	174	.206	.324	14-0-1	.000	-1		15		2.6
1980	StL N	2	0	.000	14	0	0	2-3	10.2	14	11	0	0	7-2	7	9.28	40	.318	.412	1	.000	0		-6	115	-1.2
1981	StL N	1	3	.250	20	0	0	2-0	41	36	21	2	0	31-7	22	4.39	82	.237	.366	8	.250	0	74	-3	43	-0.3
1982	StL N	1	4	.200	16	1	0	0-0	20.2	12	14	1	0	5-3	7	5.23	77	.213	.365	2	.000	0		-6		0.0
Total 9		32	31	.508	316	19	2	56-21	532	416	217	28	5	304-46	466	3.32	113	.217	.324	34-0-1	.059	-2	101	28	158	4.6

LITTLE, JEFF Donald Jeffrey B12.25.1954 Fremont OH BR/TL/6-6/220* [SFN73 3/54] d9.6

YEAR	TM LG	W	L	PCT	G	GS	CG-SHO	SV-BS	IP	H	R	HR	HB	BB-IB	SO	ERA	AERA	OAV	OOB	AB-HR-SH	AVG	PB	SUP	APR	DL	PW
1980	StL N	1	1	.500	7	2	0	0-0	18.2	18	9	0	0	9-0	17	3.86	97	.250	.333	6	.167	-0	71	0		-0.1
1982	Min A	2	0	1.000	33	0	0	0-0	36.1	33	20	6	0	27-3	26	4.21	101	.244	.368	0	—	0		-1		0.0
Total 2		3	1	.750	40	2	0	0-2	55	51	29	6	0	36-3	43	4.09	100	.246	.357	6	.167	-0	71	-1		-0.1

YEAR	TM LG	W	L	PCT	G	GS	CG-SHO	SV-BS	IP	H	R	HR	HB	BB-IB	SO	ERA	AERA	OAV	OOB	AB-HR-SH	AVG	PB	SUP	APR	DL	PW

LITTLEFIELD, JOHN   John Andrew B1.5.1954 Covina CA BR/TR/6-2/200* [StLN76 30/655] d6.8 Col Azusa Pacific

1980	StL N	5	5	.500	52	0	0	9-5	66	71	31	2	1	20-9	22	3.14	120	.282	.330	11-0-1	.000	-1		2		0.2
1981	SD N	2	3	.400	42	0	0	2-3	64	53	28	5	1	28-5	21	3.66	89	.235	.322	1-0-1	.000	-0		-3		-0.3
Total	2	7	8	.467	94	0	0	11-8	130	124	59	7	2	48-14	43	3.39	103	.259	.326	12-0-2	.000	-1		-1		-0.1

LITTLEFIELD, DICK   Richard Bernard B3.18.1926 Detroit MI D11.20.1997 Detroit MI BL/TL/6-0/180* d7.7

1950	Bos A	2	2	.500	15	2	0	1	23.1	27	25	7	1	24	13	9.26	53	.297	.448	4	.000	-1	46	-10		-1.5
1951	Chi A	1	1	.500	4	2	0	0	9.2	9	12	1	0	17	7	8.38	48	.243	.481	1	.000	0	88	-5		-0.8
1952	Det A	0	3	.000	28	1	0	1	47.2	46	24	4	0	25	32	4.34	88	.257	.348	7	.143	-0	229	-2		-0.2
	StL A	2	3	.400	7	5	3	0	46.1	35	18	4	0	17	34	2.72	144	.205	.277	16	.063	-2	76	5		0.3
	Year	2	6	.250	35	6	3	1	94	81	42	8	0	42	66	3.54	109	.231	.314	23	.087	-2	102	4		0.1
1953	StL A	7	12	.368	36	22	2	0	152.1	153	93	17	4	84	104	5.08	83	.264	.361	42-0-5	.190	-1*	80	-12		-1.5
1954	Bal A	0	0	—	3	0	0	0	6	8	7	0	1	6	5	10.50	34	.333	.484	1	.000	-0		-4		-0.2
	Pit N	10	11	.476	23	21	7-1	0	155	140	78	10	2	85	92	3.60	116	.239	.334	49-0-4	.163	0	77	7		0.8
1955	Pit N	5	12	.294	35	17	4-1	0	130	148	91	15	2	68-8	70	5.12	80	.290	.372	34-0-1	.176	0	71	-17		-2.0
1956	Pit N	0	0	—	6	2	0	0	12.2	14	8	2	0	6-0	10	4.26	88	.286	.364	2	.000	-0	93	-1		-0.1
	StL N	0	2	.000	3	2	0	0	9.2	9	9	2	0	4-1	5	7.45	51	.237	.310	2	.000	-0	58	-4		-0.7
	NY N	4	4	.500	31	7	0	2	97	78	45	16	0	39-5	65	4.08	93	.231	.306	24-0-1	.083	-2	70	-1		-0.3
	Year	4	6	.400	40	11	0	2	119.1	101	62	20	0	49-6	80	4.37	86	.238	.313	28-0-1	.071	-2	72	-7		-1.1
1957	Chi N	2	3	.400	48	2	0	4	65.2	76	46	12	1	37-4	51	5.35	72	.295	.380	11	.182	0	23	-12		-1.0
1958	Mil N	0	1	.000	4	0	0	1	6.1	7	5	2	1	1-0	7	4.26	83	.280	.333	0	—	0		-1		-0.3
Total	9	33	54	.379	243	83	16-2	9	761.2	750	461	92	12	413-18	495	4.71	86	.260	.353	193-0-11	.145	-5	77	-57		-7.5

LITTLEJOHN, CARLISLE   Charles Carlisle B10.6.1901 Irene TX D10.27.1977 Kansas City MO BR/TR/5-10/175 d5.11 Col Austin

1927	StL N	3	1	.750	14	2	1	0	42	47	21	4	0	14	16	4.50	88	.292	.349	12	.417	2*	119	-1		0.1
1928	StL N	2	1	.667	12	2	1	0	32	36	16	2	0	14	6	3.66	109	.286	.357	11	.000	-2	116	1		-0.1
Total	2	5	2	.714	26	4	2	0	74	83	37	6	0	28	22	4.14	96	.289	.352	23	.217	-0	118	0		0.0

LIVELY, BUDDY   Everett Adrian "Red" B2.14.1925 Birmingham AL BR/TR/6-0.5/200 d4.17 f-Jack [DL 1950 Cin N 64]

1947	Cin N	4	7	.364	38	17	3-1	0	123	126	75	16	0	63	52	4.68	88	.265	.351	32-0-3	.188	2	107	-9		-0.6
1948	Cin N	0	0	—	10	0	0	0	22.2	13	7	0	1	11	12	2.38	164	.165	.275	2	.000	-0		4		0.1
1949	Cin N	4	6	.400	31	10	3-1	1	103.1	91	47	11	0	53	30	3.92	107	.245	.339	26-0-1	.154	0	67	5		0.4
Total	3	8	13	.381	79	27	6-2	1	249	230	129	27	1	127	94	4.16	99	.248	.339	60-0-4	.167	1	93	0	64	-0.1

LIVELY, JACK   Henry Everett B5.29.1885 Joppa AL D12.5.1967 Arab AL BR/TR/5-9/185 d4.16 s-Buddy

1911	Det A	7	5	.583	18	14	10	0	113.2	143	73	1	7	34	45	4.59	75	.313	.369	43	.256	3*	110	-12		-0.9

LIVENGOOD, WES   Wesley Amos B7.18.1910 Salisbury NC D9.2.1996 Winston-Salem NC BR/TR/6-2/172 d5.30

1939	Cin N	0	0	—	5	0	0	0	5.2	9	6	3	0	3	4	9.53	40	.360	.429	0	—	0		-3		-0.2

LIVINGSTONE, JAKE   Jacob M. B1.1.1880 St.Petersburg, Russia D3.22.1949 Wassaic NY d9.6

1901	NY N	0	0	—	2	0	0	0	12	26	13	0	3	7	6	9.00	37	.433	.514	6	.167	0		-6		-0.3

LLEWELLYN, CLEM   Clement Manly "Lew" B8.1.1895 Dobson NC D11.27.1969 Concord NC BL/TR/6-3.5/195 d6.18 Col North Carolina-Asheville

1922	NY A	0	0	—	1	0	0	0	1	0	0	0	0	0	0	—	.250	.250	0	—	0		0		0.0

LLOYD, GRAEME   Graeme John B4.9.1967 Victoria, Victoria, Australia BL/TL/6-7/234(215-234) d4.11 [DL 2000 Mon N 181]

1993	Mil A	3	4	.429	55	0	0	0-4	63.2	64	24	5	3	13-3	31	2.83	153	.256	.299	0	—	0	10	15		1.0
1994	Mil A	2	3	.400	43	0	0	3-3	47	49	28	4	3	15-6	31	5.17	98	.269	.332	0	—	0	0			0.0
1995	Mil A	0	5	.000	33	0	0	4-2	32	28	16	4	0	8-2	13	4.50	111	.246	.286	0	—	0	2	47		0.4
1996	Mil A	2	4	.333	52	0	0	0-3	51	49	19	3	1	17-3	24	2.82	184	.254	.316	0	—	0	12			1.2
	†NY A	0	2	.000	13	0	0	0-2	5.2	12	11	1	0	5-1	6	17.47	28	.429	.486	0	—	0	-8			-1.3
	Year	2	6	.250	65	0	0	0-5	56.2	61	30	4	1	22-4	30	4.29	121	.276	.340	0	—	0	5			-0.1
1997	†NY A	1	1	.500	46	0	0	1-0	49	55	24	6	1	20-7	26	3.31	135	.293	.355	0	—	0	4			0.2
1998	†NY A	3	0	1.000	50	0	0	0-2	37.2	26	10	3	2	6-2	20	1.67	262	.191	.234	0	—	0	11	15		0.8
1999	Tor A	5	3	.625	74	0	0	3-6	72	68	36	11	4	23-4	47	3.63	136	.250	.317	0	—	0	8			0.8
2001	Mon N	9	5	.643	84	0	0	1-2	70.1	74	38	6	6	21-2	44	4.35	99	.272	.336	2	.000	0	-1			-0.1
2002	Mon N	2	3	.400	41	0	0	5-2	30.2	41	21	5	1	8-3	17	5.87	75	.325	.368	4	.000	-0	-4			-0.8
	Fla N	2	2	.500	25	0	0	0-1	26.1	26	13	1	1	11-1	20	4.44	88	.263	.336	0	—	0	-1			-0.2
	Year	4	5	.444	66	0	0	5-3	57	67	34	6	2	19-4	37	5.21	80	.298	.353	4	.000	-0	-6			-1.0
2003	NY N	1	2	.333	36	0	0	0-0	35.1	39	16	2	0	7-2	17	3.31	127	.281	.311	0	—	0	3			0.2
	KC A	0	2	.000	16	0	0	1-0	12.1	29	18	0	1	7-0	8	10.95	44	.453	.500	0	—	0	-9			-1.2
Total	30	36	.455	568	0	0	17-28	533	560	274	51	23	161-36	304	4.04	114	.271	.327	6	.000	-0	27	258		0.9

LOAIZA, ESTEBAN   Esteban Antonio (Veyna) B12.31.1971 Tijuana, Baja California, Mexico BR/TR/6-3/210(190-215) d4.29

1995	Pit N	8	9	.471	32	31	1	0-0	172.2	205	115	21	5	55-3	85	5.16	84	.300	.352	52-0-7	.192	1*	101	-17		-1.4
1996	Pit N	2	3	.400	10	10	1-1	0-0	52.2	65	32	11	2	19-2	32	4.96	89	.308	.369	17-0-5	.118	-1*	113	-3		-0.3
1997	Pit N	11	11	.500	33	32	1	0-0	196.1	214	99	17	12	56-9	122	4.13	104	.279	.335	60-0-8	.167	-0	105	4		0.3
1998	Pit N	6	5	.545	21	14	0	0-1	91.2	96	50	13	3	30-1	53	4.52	95	.275	.332	29-0-3	.241	1	88	-1		0.0
	Tex A	3	6	.333	14	14	1	0-0	79.1	103	57	15	2	22-3	55	5.90	83	.316	.358	0	—	0	91	-8		-0.8
1999	†Tex A	9	5	.643	30	15	0	0-0	120.1	128	65	10	0	40-2	77	4.56	113	.275	.329	0	—	0	102	9	54	0.3
2000	Tex A	5	7	.417	14	14	1-1	0-0	92	95	45	8	10	26-0	62	3.62	139	.270	.337	0	—	0	76	12		-0.1
	Tor A	5	6	.455	20	17	0	1-0	107.1	133	67	21	3	31-1	75	5.37	95	.302	.349	3	.000	0	86	-1		-0.1
	Year	10	13	.435	34	31	1-1	1-0	199.1	228	112	29	13	57-1	137	4.56	111	.288	.344	3	.000	0	81	11		1.3
2001	Tor A	11	11	.500	36	30	1-1	0-0	190	239	113	27	9	40-1	110	5.02	91	.307	.347	2	.000	0	106	-8		-0.9
2002	Tor A	9	10	.474	25	25	3-1	0-0	151.1	192	102	18	4	38-3	87	5.71	81	.309	.350	6	.167	-0	120	-17	44	-1.8
2003	Chi A★	21	9	.700	34	34	1	0-0	226.1	196	75	17	10	56-2	207	2.90	158	.233	.286	5-0-1	.200	0	92	44		5.5
2004	Chi A★	9	5	.643	21	21	2-1	0-0	140.2	156	81	23	1	45-3	83	4.86	97	.283	.335	5	.000	-1	106	-3		-0.2
	†NY A	1	2	.333	10	6	0	0-0	42.1	61	43	9	2	26-2	34	8.50	54	.337	.416	0	—	0	108	-19		-1.0
	Year	10	7	.588	31	27	2-1	0-0	183	217	124	32	3	71-5	117	5.70	82	.296	.356	5	.000	-1	107	-20		-1.2
2005	Was N	12	10	.545	34	34	2-1	0-0	217	227	93	18	5	55-35	173	3.77	107	.270	.318	74-0-6	.162	-0	92	9		2.3
Total	11	112	99	.531	334	297	12-5	1-1	1880	2110	1037	228	68	539-35	1255	4.60	99	.285	.336	253-0-30	.170	-0	99	98		2.3

LOCKE, CHUCK   Charles Edward B5.5.1932 Malden MO BR/TR/5-11/185 d9.16

1955	Bal A	0	0	—	2	0	0	0	3	0	0	0	0	1-0	1	0.00	—	.000	.100	0	—	0		1		0.1

LOCKE, BOBBY   Lawrence Donald B3.3.1934 Rowes Run PA BR/TR/5-11/185* d6.18

1959	Cle A	3	2	.600	24	7	0	2	77.2	66	33	6	3	41-2	40	3.13	118	.233	.333	24-1-2	.333	3	127	4		0.6
1960	Cle A	3	5	.375	32	11	2-2	2	123	121	51	10	2	37-3	53	3.37	111	.255	.311	38-0-3	.237	3*	109	6		0.8
1961	Cle A	4	4	.500	37	4	0	2	95.1	112	50	12	2	40-4	37	4.53	87	.300	.368	19	.211	0	129	-5		-0.3
1962	StL N	0	0	—	1	0	0	0	2	1	0	0	0	2-0	1	0.00	—	.143	.333	0	—	0		1		0.1
	Phi N	1	0	1.000	5	0	0	0	15.2	16	12	4	0	10-0	9	5.74	67	.262	.366	7	.286	0		-4		-0.1
	Year	1	0	1.000	6	0	0	0	17.2	17	12	4	0	12-0	10	5.09	77	.250	.363	7	.286	0		-3		0.0
1963	Phi N	0	0	—	9	0	0	0	10.2	10	7	0	0	5-1	7	5.91	55	.244	.326	1	.000	-0		-3		-0.2
1964	Phi N	0	0	—	8	0	0	0	19.1	21	6	2	0	6-3	11	2.79	124	.276	.329	2-0-1	.000	-0		2		0.1
1965	Cin N	0	0	—	11	0	0	0	17.1	20	15	2	0	8-5	8	5.71	66	.299	.368	1	.000	-0		-5		-0.2
1967	Cal A	3	0	1.000	9	1	0	2	19.1	14	6	1	1	3-0	7	2.33	135	.203	.243	3	.667	1	305	2		0.4
1968	Cal A	2	3	.400	29	0	0	2	36.1	51	29	3	1	13-3	21	6.44	45	.331	.385	3	.000	-0		-14		-2.2
Total	9	16	15	.516	165	23	2-2	10	416.2	432	209	40	9	165-21	194	4.02	91	.269	.339	98-1-6	.255	8	128	-16		-1.0

LOCKE, RON   Ronald Thomas B4.4.1942 Wakefield RI BR/TL/5-11/168 d4.23

1964	NY N	1	2	.333	25	3	0	0	41.1	46	23	3	1	22-0	17	3.48	103	.289	.377	5-0-3	.000	-0	57	-2		-0.2

LOCKER, BOB   Robert Awtry B3.15.1938 George IA BB/TR/6-3/200(185-200) d4.14 Col Iowa St. [DL 1974 Oak A 182]

1965	Chi A	5	2	.714	51	0	0	6	91.1	71	36	6	2	30-10	69	3.15	101	.216	.281	14	.000	-2		0		0.0
1966	Chi A	9	8	.529	56	0	0	12	95	73	32	2	5	23-13	70	2.46	129	.206	.264	16	.250	1		7		1.8
1967	Chi A	7	5	.583	77	0	0	20	124.2	102	34	5	10	23-5	80	2.09	148	.222	.273	10-0-1	.000	-1		15		2.2

YEAR	TM LG	W	L	PCT	G	GS	CG-SHO	SV-BS	IP	H	R	HR	HB	BB-IB	SO	ERA	AERA	OAV	OOB	AB-HR-SH	AVG	PB	SUP	APR	DL	PW
968	Chi A	5	4	.556	70	0	0	10	90.1	78	27	4	1	27-13	62	2.29	132	.234	.290	8	.000	-1		7		1.0
969	Chi A	2	3	.400	17	0	0	4-3	22	26	18	6	0	6-1	15	6.55	59	.292	.333	1	.000	-0		-7		-1.3
	Sea A	3	3	.500	51	0	0	6-4	78.1	69	29	3	3	26-8	46	2.18	167	.234	.301	12	.083	-0		9		0.9
	Year	5	6	.455	68	0	0	10-7	100.1	95	47	9	3	32-9	61	3.14	117	.247	.308	13	.077	-1		3		-0.4
970	Mil A	0	1	.000	28	0	0	3-1	31.2	37	18	1	5	10-1	19	3.41	111	.306	.380	1	.000	-0		-1		-0.1
	Oak A	3	3	.500	38	0	0	4-3	56.1	49	21	1	1	19-3	33	2.88	123	.232	.299	6	.167	-0		4		0.5
	Year	3	4	.429	66	0	0	7-4	88	86	39	2	6	29-4	52	3.07	118	.259	.329	7	.143	-0		4		0.4
971	†Oak A	7	2	.778	47	0	0	6-5	72.1	68	28	2	1	19-9	46	2.86	116	.249	.298	6	.000	-0		3		0.4
972	†Oak A	6	1	.857	56	0	0	10-3	78	69	25	1	2	16-5	47	2.65	107	.235	.277	6	.000	0		2		0.3
973	Chi N	10	6	.625	63	0	0	18-6	106.1	96	40	6	4	42-10	76	2.54	155	.244	.321	15-0-1	.067	-1		13		2.3
975	Chi N	0	1	.000	22	0	0	6	32.2	38	21	3	2	16-2	14	4.96	78	.306	.392	0	—	0		-4		-0.2
otal	10	57	39	.594	576	0	0	95-25	879	776	329	40	36	257-80	577	2.75	122	.237	.297	95-0-2	.074	-4		48	182	7.8

LOCKWOOD, SKIP   Claude Edward   B8.17.1946 Boston MA   BR/TR/6-0/190(180-200)   d4.23.1965 ▲

YEAR	TM LG	W	L	PCT	G	GS	CG-SHO	SV-BS	IP	H	R	HR	HB	BB-IB	SO	ERA	AERA	OAV	OOB	AB-HR-SH	AVG	PB	SUP	APR	DL	PW
969	Sea A	0	1	.000	6	3	0	0-0	23	24	9	3	0	6-0	10	3.52	103	.279	.323	7	.000	-1	49	1		0.0
970	Mil A	5	12	.294	27	26	3-1	0-0	173.2	173	91	22	6	79-2	93	4.30	88	.266	.347	53-1-12	.226	2	89	-9		-0.7
971	Mil A	10	15	.400	33	32	5-1	0-0	208	191	93	13	5	91-6	115	3.33	105	.246	.326	62-1-10	.081	-1*	79	2		-0.1
972	Mil A	8	15	.348	29	27	5-3	0-0	170	148	75	11	4	71-6	106	3.60	85	.232	.311	53-0-3	.132	-1*	78	-10		-1.6
973	Mil A	5	12	.294	37	15	3	0-0	154.2	164	75	10	6	59-6	87	3.90	98	.280	.349	0	—	0	67	-1		-0.1
974	Cal A	2	5	.286	37	2	0	1-4	81.1	81	42	8	5	32-4	39	4.32	80	.264	.339	0	—	0	140	-6		-0.5
975	NY N	1	3	.250	24	0	0	2-1	48.1	28	9	3	1	25-6	61	1.49	236	.174	.287	6-0-1	.167	-0		11		1.0
976	NY N	10	7	.588	56	0	0	19-5	94.1	62	31	6	2	34-8	108	2.67	125	.186	.265	18-0-3	.333	3		8		1.9
977	NY N	4	8	.333	63	0	0	20-4	104	87	40	5	4	31-11	84	3.38	113	.227	.288	15-0-3	.200	-0		6		0.3
978	NY N	7	13	.350	57	0	0	15-8	90.2	78	36	10	0	31-5	73	3.57	99	.236	.298	11-1-2	.182	1		1		0.3
979	NY N	2	5	.286	27	0	0	9-0	42.1	33	7	3	0	14-5	42	1.49	250	.224	.292	2-0-1	.000	-0*		11	103	2.2
980	Bos A	3	1	.750	24	1	0	2-1	45.2	61	31	4	0	17-3	11	5.32	80	.321	.371	0	—	0	84	-6		-0.5
otal	12	57	97	.370	420	106	16-5	68-23	1236	1130	539	98	33	490-62	829	3.55	100	.246	.320	227-3-35	.159	3	78	8	103	2.7

LOCKWOOD, MILO   Milo Hathaway   B4.7.1858 Solon OH   D10.9.1897 Economy PA   5-10/160   d4.17 ▲

YEAR	TM LG	W	L	PCT	G	GS	CG-SHO	SV-BS	IP	H	R	HR	HB	BB-IB	SO	ERA	AERA	OAV	OOB	AB-HR-SH	AVG	PB	SUP	APR	DL	PW
884	Was U	1	9	.100	11	10	6	0	67.2	99	95	4		15	48	7.32	33	.319	.351	67	.209	-2*	76	-35		-3.6

LOE, KAMERON   Kameron David   B9.10.1981 Simi Valley CA   BR/TR/6-8/225*   [TexA02 20/592]   d9.26 Col Cal St.-Northridge

YEAR	TM LG	W	L	PCT	G	GS	CG-SHO	SV-BS	IP	H	R	HR	HB	BB-IB	SO	ERA	AERA	OAV	OOB	AB-HR-SH	AVG	PB	SUP	APR	DL	PW
004	Tex A	0		—	2	1	0	0-0	6.2	6	5	0	1	6-0	3	5.40	91	.273	.448	0	—	0	132	-1		0.0
005	Tex A	9	6	.600	48	8	0	1-3	92	89	43	7	2	31-6	45	3.42	134	.252	.315	0	—	0	108	9		1.3
otal	2	9	6	.600	50	9	0	1-3	98.2	95	48	7	3	37-6	48	3.56	130	.253	.325	0	—	0	111	8		1.3

LOES, BILLY   William   B12.13.1929 Long Island City NY   BR/TR/6-1/170(165-190)   d5.18   Mil 1951

YEAR	TM LG	W	L	PCT	G	GS	CG-SHO	SV-BS	IP	H	R	HR	HB	BB-IB	SO	ERA	AERA	OAV	OOB	AB-HR-SH	AVG	PB	SUP	APR	DL	PW
950	Bro N	0	0	—	10	0	0	0	12.2	16	11	5	0	5	2	7.82	52	.314	.375	1	.000	0		-5		-0.2
952	†Bro N	13	8	.619	39	21	8-4	1	187.1	154	62	12	3	71	115	2.69	135	.224	.299	54-0-10	.093	-3*	133	20		1.8
953	†Bro N	14	8	.636	32	25	9-1	0	162.2	165	92	21	3	53	75	4.54	94	.261	.322	56-0-2	.125	-2	132	-6		-0.8
954	Bro N	13	5	.722	28	21	6	0	147.2	154	73	14	1	60	97	4.14	99	.269	.336	51-0-4	.118	-2	127	0		-0.3
955	†Bro N	10	4	.714	22	19	6	0	128	116	59	16	2	46-1	85	3.59	113	.240	.308	44-0-3	.091	-3	104	7		0.3
956	Bro N	0	1	.000	1	1	0	0	1.1	5	6	1	0	1-0	2	40.50	10	.556	.600	0	—	0	67	-5		-0.7
	Bal A	2	7	.222	21	6	1	3	56.2	65	33	4	2	23-1	22	4.76	82	.291	.360	17-0-1	.176	-1	64	-5		-0.8
957	Bal A★	12	7	.632	31	18	8-3	4	155.1	142	59	8	4	37-4	86	3.24	111	.245	.292	50-0-7	.080	-3	138	7		0.6
958	Bal A	3	9	.250	32	10	1	5	114	106	51	10	8	44-5	44	3.63	99	.252	.328	30-0-3	.067	-2	57	0		-0.3
959	Bal A	4	7	.364	37	0	0	14	64.1	58	31	6	3	25-3	34	4.06	93	.239	.315	8	.125	-0		-1		-0.3
960	SF N	3	2	.600	37	0	0	5	45.2	40	26	9	4	17-2	28	4.93	71	.247	.330	4-0-1	.250	0		-6		-0.7
961	SF N	6	5	.545	26	18	3-1	0	114.2	114	62	13	5	39-4	55	4.24	90	.258	.324	32-0-4	.156	-0	103	-6		-0.6
otal	11	80	63	.559	316	139	42-9	32	1190.1	1135	565	118	35	421-20	645	3.89	99	.252	.319	347-0-35	.110	-17	118	0		-2.0

LOEWER, CARLTON   Carlton Ernest   B9.24.1973 Lafayette LA   BR/TR/6-6/220(200-220)   [PhiN94 1/23]   d6.14 Col Mississippi St.   [DL 2000 SD N 181]

YEAR	TM LG	W	L	PCT	G	GS	CG-SHO	SV-BS	IP	H	R	HR	HB	BB-IB	SO	ERA	AERA	OAV	OOB	AB-HR-SH	AVG	PB	SUP	APR	DL	PW
998	Phi N	7	8	.467	21	21	1	0-0	122.2	154	86	18	3	39-1	58	6.09	71	.312	.360	35-0-5	.086	-1	99	-22		-2.5
999	Phi N	2	6	.250	20	13	2-1	0-0	89.2	100	54	9	0	26-0	48	5.12	91	.287	.332	22-0-2	.227	1	85	-4	92	-0.3
001	SD N	0	2	.000	2	2	0	0-0	4.1	13	12	2	0	3-0	1	24.92	17	.520	.571	0	—	0	33	-10	60	-1.3
003	SD N	1	2	.333	5	5	0	0-0	21.2	35	17	3	1	8-1	11	6.65	60	.368	.419	5-0-1	.000	-0	89	-7		-0.8
otal	4	10	18	.357	48	41	3-1	0-0	238.1	302	169	32	4	76-2	118	6.12	72	.314	.361	62-0-8	.129	-1	89	-43	333	-4.9

LOFTUS, FRANK   Francis Patrick   B3.10.1898 Scranton PA   D10.27.1980 Belchertown MA   BR/TR/5-9/190   d9.26 Col St. Bonaventure

YEAR	TM LG	W	L	PCT	G	GS	CG-SHO	SV-BS	IP	H	R	HR	HB	BB-IB	SO	ERA	AERA	OAV	OOB	AB-HR-SH	AVG	PB	SUP	APR	DL	PW
926	Was A	0	0		1	0	0	0	1	3	2	0	0	2	0	9.00	43	.600	.714	0	—	0		-1		0.0

LOGAN, BOB   Robert Dean "Lefty"   B2.10.1910 Thompson NE   D5.20.1978 Indianapolis IN   BR/TL/5-10/170   d4.18

YEAR	TM LG	W	L	PCT	G	GS	CG-SHO	SV-BS	IP	H	R	HR	HB	BB-IB	SO	ERA	AERA	OAV	OOB	AB-HR-SH	AVG	PB	SUP	APR	DL	PW
935	Bro N	0	0	1.000	2	0	0	0	2.2	1	1	0	0	1	1	3.38	118	.182	.250	0	—	0		0		0.1
937	Det A	0	0		1	0	0	0	0.2	1	0	0	0	1	1	0.00	—	.333	.500	0	—	0		0		0.0
	Chi A	0	0		4	0	0	1	6.1	6	1	0	0	4	2	1.42	280	.261	.370	1	.000	-0		2		0.1
938	Chi N	0	2	.000	14	0	0	2	22.2	18	9	0	1	17	10	2.78	138	.222	.364	3	.000	-0		2		0.2
941	Cin N	0	1	.000	2	0	0	0	3.1	5	5	0	0	5	0	8.10	44	.333	.500	0	—	0		-2		-0.4
945	Bos N	7	11	.389	34	25	5-1	1	187	213	84	9	1	53	53	3.18	121	.283	.331	61-0-6	.213	1	95	10		1.1
otal	5	7	15	.318	57	25	5-1	4	222.2	245	100	9	2	81	67	3.15	122	.277	.339	65-0-6	.200	1	95	12		1.1

LOHRMAN, BILL   William Le Roy   B5.22.1913 Brooklyn NY   D9.13.1999 Poughkeepsie NY   BR/TR/6-1/185   d6.19

YEAR	TM LG	W	L	PCT	G	GS	CG-SHO	SV-BS	IP	H	R	HR	HB	BB-IB	SO	ERA	AERA	OAV	OOB	AB-HR-SH	AVG	PB	SUP	APR	DL	PW
934	Phi N	0	1	.000	4	0	0	1	8	5	5	0	0	1	2	4.50	105	.217	.250	2	.500	0		0		0.0
937	NY N	1	0	1.000	2	1	1	1	10	5	1	0	0	-2	3	0.90	432	.152	.200	2-0-1	.000	-0	67	3		0.4
938	NY N	9	6	.600	31	14	3	0	152	152	72	9	2	33	52	3.32	114	.253	.294	49-0-3	.082	-4	117	5		0.1
939	NY N	12	13	.480	38	24	9-1	1	185.2	200	91	15	3	45	70	4.07	96	.282	.327	60-2-0	.233	4	100	-1		0.3
940	NY N	10	15	.400	31	27	11-4	1	195	200	98	19	3	43	73	3.78	103	.264	.306	65-0-4	.123	-2	87	1		-0.1
941	NY N	9	10	.474	33	20	6-2	1	159	184	87	7	0	40	61	4.02	92	.286	.327	48-0-3	.229	4	94	-8		-0.5
942	StL N	1	1	.500	5	0	0	0	12.2	11	3	0	0	2	6	1.42	241	.244	.277	3	.667	1		2		0.5
	NY N	13	4	.765	26	19	12-2	0	158	143	52	11	2	33	41	2.56	134	.240	.282	58-0-3	.121	-3	118	14		1.2
	Year	14	5	.737	31	19	12-2	0	170.2	154	55	11	2	35	47	2.48	136	.240	.281	61-0-3	.148	-2	118	17		1.7
943	NY N	5	6	.455	17	12	3	1	80.1	110	51	7	2	25	16	5.15	67	.324	.374	27-0-2	.037	-3*	107	-15		-2.2
	Bro N	0	2	.000	6	2	2	0	27.2	29	14	2	1	10	5	3.58	94	.274	.342	7	.143	0	88	-1		-0.1
	Year	5	8	.385	23	14	5	1	108	139	65	9	3	35	21	4.75	72	.312	.366	34-0-2	.059	-3	104	-15		-2.3
944	Bro N	0	0		3	0	0	0	2.2	4	0	0	0	4	1	0.00	—	.500	.667	0	—	0		1		0.0
	Cin N	0	1	.000	2	1	0	0	1.2	5	5	0	0	2	0	27.00	13	.500	.583	0	—	0		-4		-0.7
	Year	0	1	.000	5	1	0	0	4.1	9	5	0	0	6	1	10.38	34	.500	.625	0	—	0		-3		-0.7
otal	9	60	59	.504	198	120	47-9	6	990.2	1048	479	70	13	240	333	3.69	101	.271	.315	321-2-16	.153	-3	100	-3		-1.1

LOHSE, KYLE   Kyle Matthew   B10.4.1978 Chico CA   BR/TR/6-2/190*   [ChiN96 29/862]   d6.22 Col Butte (CA) CC

YEAR	TM LG	W	L	PCT	G	GS	CG-SHO	SV-BS	IP	H	R	HR	HB	BB-IB	SO	ERA	AERA	OAV	OOB	AB-HR-SH	AVG	PB	SUP	APR	DL	PW
001	Min A	4	7	.364	19	16	0	0-0	90.1	102	60	16	8	29-0	64	5.68	82	.284	.347	5	.400	1	92	-10		-0.9
002	†Min A	13	8	.619	32	31	1-1	0-1	180.2	181	92	26	9	70-2	124	4.23	105	.259	.333	4	.250	0	109	4		0.4
003	Min A	14	11	.560	33	33	2-1	0-0	201	211	107	28	5	45-1	130	4.61	98	.268	.310	3-0-3	.333	0	100	-2		-0.2
004	†Min A	9	13	.409	35	34	1-1	0-0	194	240	128	28	7	76-5	111	5.34	87	.305	.368	3-0-1	.000	-0	97	-17		-1.7
005	Min A	9	13	.409	31	30	0	0-0	178.2	211	85	22	9	44-5	86	4.18	105	.299	.345	5	.000	-1	71	7		0.7
otal	5	49	52	.485	150	144	4-3	0-1	844.2	945	479	120	38	264-13	515	4.74	94	.283	.340	20-0-4	.200	0	95	-18		-1.7

LOISELLE, RICH   Richard Frank   B1.12.1972 Neenah WI   BR/TR/6-5/240(225-253)   [SDN91 38/991]   d9.7 Col Odessa (TX) JC

YEAR	TM LG	W	L	PCT	G	GS	CG-SHO	SV-BS	IP	H	R	HR	HB	BB-IB	SO	ERA	AERA	OAV	OOB	AB-HR-SH	AVG	PB	SUP	APR	DL	PW
996	Pit N	1	0	1.000	5	5	0	0-0	20.2	22	8	3	0	8-1	9	3.05	144	.268	.333	8	.250	1	178	3		0.2
997	Pit N	1	5	.167	72	0	0	29-5	72.2	76	29	7	1	24-3	66	3.10	138	.269	.326	1	.000	-0		9		1.2
998	Pit N	2	7	.222	54	0	0	19-8	55	56	26	2	2	36-9	48	3.44	124	.262	.352	0-0-1	—	0		4	28	0.9
999	Pit N	3	2	.600	13	0	0	0-1	15.1	16	9	2	2	9-2	14	5.28	87	.281	.397	0	—	0		-1	149	-0.1
000	Pit N	2	3	.400	40	0	0	0-6	42.1	43	27	5	3	30-5	32	5.10	91	.262	.380	0	—	0		-2	86	-0.2
001	Pit N	0	1	.000	18	0	0	1-0	18	28	24	3	4	17-4	9	11.50	39	.359	.495	0	—	0		-13	72	-0.8
otal	6	9	18	.333	202	3	0	49-20	224	241	123	22	12	124-24	178	4.38	100	.274	.370	9-0-2	.222	0	178	0	335	1.2

YEAR	TM LG	W	L	PCT	G	GS	CG-SHO	SV-BS	IP	H	R	HR	HB	BB-IB	SO	ERA	AERA	OAV	OOB	AB-HR-SH	AVG	PB	SUP	APR	DL	PW

LOLICH, MICKEY Michael Stephen B9.12.1940 Portland OR BB/TL/6-0/210(185-225) d5.12 [DL 1978 Det A 80]

YEAR	TM LG	W	L	PCT	G	GS	CG-SHO	SV-BS	IP	H	R	HR	HB	BB-IB	SO	ERA	AERA	OAV	OOB	AB-HR-SH	AVG	PB	SUP	APR	DL	PW
1963	Det A	5	9	.357	33	18	4	0	144.1	145	64	13	5	56-1	103	3.55	105	.265	.336	36-0-2	.056	-1	92	3		0.2
1964	Det A	18	9	.667	44	33	12-6	2	232	196	88	26	5	64-0	192	3.26	112	.225	.282	64-0-9	.109	1	113	12		1.3
1965	Det A	15	9	.625	43	37	7-3	3	243.2	216	103	23	12	72-2	226	3.44	101	.236	.298	86-0-3	.058	-6	114	1		-0.6
1966	Det A	14	14	.500	40	33	5-1	3	203.2	204	119	24	6	83-8	173	4.77	73	.257	.329	64-0-2	.141	1	124	-28		-3.7
1967	Det A	14	13	.519	31	30	11-6	0	204	165	71	14	7	56-2	174	3.04	107	.221	.281	61-0-7	.197	3*	98	7		1.2
1968	†Det A	17	9	.654	39	32	8-4	1	220	178	84	23	11	65-4	197	3.19	94	.219	.285	70-0-4	.114	0*	109	-4		-0.5
1969	Det A☆	19	11	.633	37	36	15-1	1-0	280.2	214	111	22	14	122-10	271	3.14	120	.211	.302	91-0-12	.088	-3*	110	18		1.6
1970	Det A	14	19	.424	40	39	13-3	0-0	272.2	272	125	27	5	109-3	230	3.80	99	.260	.330	82-0-7	.134	1*	79	0		0.2
1971	Det A★	**25**	14	.641	45	45	29-4	0-0	376	336	133	36	7	92-2	**308**	2.92	124	.237	.285	115-0-16	.130	1	117	28		2.9
1972	†Det A★	22	14	.611	41	41	23-4	0-0	327.1	282	100	29	11	74-5	250	2.50	127	.234	.283	89-0-11	.067	-0	92	25		2.7
1973	Det A	16	15	.516	42	42	17-3	0-0	308.2	315	143	35	5	79-7	214	3.82	107	.266	.314	0	—	0	87	8		0.7
1974	Det A	16	21	.432	41	41	27-3	0-0	308	310	155	38	3	78-11	202	4.15	92	.268	.314	0	—	0	83	-8		-1.0
1975	Det A	12	18	.400	32	32	19-1	0-0	240.2	260	119	19	0	64-5	139	3.78	107	.279	.322	0	—	0	72	7		0.7
1976	NY N	8	13	.381	31	30	5-2	0-0	192.2	184	83	14	0	52-1	120	3.22	104	.252	.300	54-0-11	.130	-0	85	1		0.1
1978	SD N	2	1	.667	20	2	0	0-0	34.2	30	6	1	0	11-3	13	1.56	215	.240	.307	3	.000	-0	54	8		0.7
1979	SD N	0	2	.000	27	5	0	0-0	49.1	59	33	4	0	22-3	20	4.74	74	.304	.372	6-0-1	.000	-0	140	-9		-0.5
Total	16	217	191	.532	586	496	195-41	11-0	3638.1	3366	1537	347	92	1099-67	2832	3.44	105	.246	.304	821-0-85	.110	-4	98	69	80	6.0

LOLLAR, TIM William Timothy B3.17.1956 Poplar Bluff MO BL/TL/6-3/200* [NYA78 4/104] d6.28 Col Arkansas-Monticello

YEAR	TM LG	W	L	PCT	G	GS	CG-SHO	SV-BS	IP	H	R	HR	HB	BB-IB	SO	ERA	AERA	OAV	OOB	AB-HR-SH	AVG	PB	SUP	APR	DL	PW
1980	NY A	1	0	1.000	14	1	0	2-0	32.1	33	14	3	0	20-2	13	3.34	119	.280	.379	0	—	0	45	2		0.1
1981	SD N	2	8	.200	24	11	0	1-0	76.2	87	56	4	3	51-8	38	6.10	53	.293	.399	18-1-0	.167	1	104	-26		-2.8
1982	SD N	16	9	.640	34	34	4-2	0-0	232.2	192	82	20	4	87-4	150	3.13	109	.224	.297	85-3-2	.247	9*	108	13		2.4
1983	SD N	7	12	.368	30	30	1	0-0	175.2	170	98	22	4	85-1	135	4.61	76	.258	.346	58-1-0	.241	6*	95	-22		-1.6
1984	†SD N	11	13	.458	31	31	3-2	0-0	195.2	168	89	18	1	105-2	131	3.91	92	.234	.331	68-3-1	.221	7	94	-4		0.1
1985	Chi A	3	5	.375	18	13	0	0-0	83	83	48	10	1	58-1	61	4.66	93	.266	.379	0	—	0	95	-3		-0.3
	Bos A	5	5	.500	16	10	1	1-0	67	57	37	9	1	40-0	44	4.57	94	.230	.338	1	.000	-0*	103	-2		-0.3
	Year	8	10	.444	34	23	1	1-0	150	140	85	19	2	98-1	105	4.62	93	.250	.361	1	.000	-0	99	-4		-0.6
1986	Bos A	2	0	1.000	32	1	0	0-1	43	51	35	7	3	34-3	28	6.91	61	.304	.421	1	1.000	0*	259	-12		-0.5
Total	7	47	52	.475	199	131	9-4	4-1	906	841	459	93	17	480-21	600	4.27	86	.249	.343	231-8-3	.234	23	100	-54		-2.9

LOMBARDI, VIC Victor Alvin B9.20.1922 Reedley CA D12.7.1997 Fresno CA BL/TL/5-7/158* d4.18

YEAR	TM LG	W	L	PCT	G	GS	CG-SHO	SV-BS	IP	H	R	HR	HB	BB-IB	SO	ERA	AERA	OAV	OOB	AB-HR-SH	AVG	PB	SUP	APR	DL	PW
1945	Bro N	10	11	.476	38	24	9	4	203.2	195	106	11	5	86	64	3.31	113	.252	.331	71-0-3	.183	-1*	97	6		0.4
1946	Bro N	13	10	.565	41	25	13-2	3	193	170	76	10	2	84	60	2.89	117	.235	.316	61-0-10	.230	2*	111	10		1.3
1947	†Bro N	12	11	.522	33	20	7-3	2	174.2	156	73	12	2	65	72	2.99	138	.241	.312	66-0-1	.242	2*	78	19		2.6
1948	Pit N	10	9	.526	38	17	9	4	163	156	72	9	2	67	54	3.70	110	.255	.330	48-0-1	.208	1*	90	8		1.0
1949	Pit N	5	5	.500	34	12	4	1	134	149	74	12	3	68	64	4.57	92	.286	.372	49	.347	5*	114	-5		0.3
1950	Pit N	0	5	.000	39	2	0	1	76.1	93	61	14	2	48	26	6.60	66	.310	.409	16-0-1	.250	1*	91	-17		-0.9
Total	6	50	51	.495	223	100	42-5	16	944.2	919	462	68	16	418	340	3.68	106	.257	.337	311-0-16	.238	10	96	21		4.7

LOMBARDO, LOU Louis B11.18.1928 Carlstadt NJ D6.11.2001 Rock Hill SC BL/TL/6-2/210 d9.22

YEAR	TM LG	W	L	PCT	G	GS	CG-SHO	SV-BS	IP	H	R	HR	HB	BB-IB	SO	ERA	AERA	OAV	OOB	AB-HR-SH	AVG	PB	SUP	APR	DL	PW
1948	NY N	0	0	—	2	0	0	0-0	5.1	4	4	1	0	6	0	6.75	58	.250	.423	2	.000	-0		-1		-0.1

LOMON, KEVIN Kevin Dale B11.20.1971 Fort Smith AR BR/TR/6-1/195* [AtlN91 14/361] d4.27 Col Arkansas-Fort Smith [JC]

YEAR	TM LG	W	L	PCT	G	GS	CG-SHO	SV-BS	IP	H	R	HR	HB	BB-IB	SO	ERA	AERA	OAV	OOB	AB-HR-SH	AVG	PB	SUP	APR	DL	PW
1995	NY N	0	1	.000	6	0	0	0-0	9.1	17	9	0	0	5-1	6	6.75	60	.405	.468	0-0-1	—	0		-3		-0.3
1996	Atl N	0	0	—	6	0	0	0-0	7.1	7	4	0	1	3-0	1	4.91	91	.259	.355	0	—	0	0	0		0.0
Total	2	0	1	.000	12	0	0	0-0	16.2	24	12	0	1	8-1	7	5.94	71	.348	.423	0-0-1	—	0		-3		-0.3

LONBORG, JIM James Reynold B4.16.1942 Santa Maria CA BR/TR/6-5/210(195-210) d4.23 Col Stanford

YEAR	TM LG	W	L	PCT	G	GS	CG-SHO	SV-BS	IP	H	R	HR	HB	BB-IB	SO	ERA	AERA	OAV	OOB	AB-HR-SH	AVG	PB	SUP	APR	DL	PW
1965	Bos A	9	17	.346	32	31	7-1	2	185.1	193	112	20	3	65-3	113	4.47	83	.262	.323	59-0-5	.136	0	112	-16		-2.1
1966	Bos A	10	10	.500	45	23	3-1	2	181.2	173	86	18	7	55-5	131	3.86	98	.249	.308	54-0-6	.093	-2*	117	0		-0.2
1967	†Bos A☆	22	9	.710	39	39	15-2	0	273.1	228	102	23	19	83-5	246	3.16	110	.225	.294	99-0-6	.141	-1	110	12		1.0
1968	Bos A	6	10	.375	23	17	4-1	0	113.1	89	57	11	11	59-3	73	4.29	74	.216	.327	39-1-5	.282	3	104	-12	46	-1.4
1969	Bos A	7	11	.389	29	23	4	0-1	143.2	148	78	15	7	65-3	100	4.51	85	.270	.354	41-0-5	.098	-1	86	-8		-1.1
1970	Bos A	4	1	.800	9	4	0	0-0	34	33	12	3	0	9-0	21	3.18	125	.260	.304	9-1-0	.444	2	89	4	55	0.8
1971	Bos A	10	7	.588	27	26	5-1	0-0	167.2	166	86	15	14	67-6	100	4.13	90	.259	.341	53-0-2	.170	-1	129	-8		-0.7
1972	Mil A	14	12	.538	33	30	11-2	1-0	223	197	75	17	11	76-11	143	2.83	108	.238	.309	69-0-9	.145	-1	108	7		0.7
1973	Phi N	13	16	.448	38	30	6	0-1	199.1	218	124	25	9	80-7	106	4.88	78	.279	.350	59-0-4	.136	0	99	-24		-3.2
1974	Phi N	17	13	.567	39	36	16-3	0-0	283	283	113	22	6	70-11	121	3.21	118	.261	.308	94-1-11	.096	-4	99	17		1.1
1975	Phi N	8	6	.571	27	26	6-2	0-0	159.1	161	84	12	5	45-7	72	4.12	91	.257	.310	44-0-6	.023	-3	111	-7		-0.9
1976	†Phi N	18	10	.643	33	32	8-1	0-0	222	210	85	18	5	50-4	118	3.08	116	.249	.292	67-0-6	.164	1	106	12		1.4
1977	†Phi N	11	4	.733	25	25	4-1	0-0	157.2	157	77	15	5	50-5	76	4.11	98	.261	.321	48-0-9	.104	-2	121	0	49	-0.3
1978	Phi N	8	10	.444	22	22	1	0-0	113.2	132	69	16	2	45-1	48	5.23	69	.293	.359	34-0-4	.176	1	105	-19		-2.6
1979	Phi N	0	1	.000	4	1	0	0-0	7.1	14	10	3	1	4-0	7	11.05	35	.389	.463	1	.000	-0	46	-6		-0.7
Total	15	157	137	.534	425	368	90-15	4-2	2464.1	2400	1170	233	105	823-71	1475	3.86	99	.255	.320	770-3-78	.136	-5	108	-48	150	-8.2

LONG, JOEY Joey J. B7.15.1970 Sidney OH BR/TL/6-2/220 [SDN91 5/133] d4.25 Col Kent St.

YEAR	TM LG	W	L	PCT	G	GS	CG-SHO	SV-BS	IP	H	R	HR	HB	BB-IB	SO	ERA	AERA	OAV	OOB	AB-HR-SH	AVG	PB	SUP	APR	DL	PW
1997	SD N	0	0	—	10	0	0	0-0	11	17	11	1	1	8-1	8	8.18	48	.340	.441	0	—	0		-6		-0.3

LONG, LEP Lester B7.12.1888 Summit NJ D10.21.1958 Birmingham AL BR/TR/5-10/153 d6.29 Col Lafayette

YEAR	TM LG	W	L	PCT	G	GS	CG-SHO	SV-BS	IP	H	R	HR	HB	BB-IB	SO	ERA	AERA	OAV	OOB	AB-HR-SH	AVG	PB	SUP	APR	DL	PW
1911	Phi A	0	0	—	8	1	0	0-0	15	6	6	0	0	5	4	4.50	70	.405	.476	3	.000	-0		-2		-0.1

LONG, RED Nelson B9.28.1876 Burlington ON, Can. D8.11.1929 Hamilton ON, Can. BR/TR/6-1/190 d9.11

YEAR	TM LG	W	L	PCT	G	GS	CG-SHO	SV-BS	IP	H	R	HR	HB	BB-IB	SO	ERA	AERA	OAV	OOB	AB-HR-SH	AVG	PB	SUP	APR	DL	PW
1902	Bos N	0	0	—	1	1	1	0-0	8	4	2	0	1	3	5	1.13	251	.148	.258	1	.000	-0	48	1		0.0

LONG, BOB Robert Earl B11.11.1954 Jasper TN BR/TR/6-3/178* [PitN76 24/565] d9.2 Col Shorter

YEAR	TM LG	W	L	PCT	G	GS	CG-SHO	SV-BS	IP	H	R	HR	HB	BB-IB	SO	ERA	AERA	OAV	OOB	AB-HR-SH	AVG	PB	SUP	APR	DL	PW
1981	Pit N	1	2	.333	5	3	0	0-0	19.2	23	14	2	0	10-0	8	5.95	61	.299	.375	4-0-1	.000	0	65	-4		-0.7
1985	Sea A	0	0	—	28	0	0	0-0	38.1	30	17	7	2	17-1	29	3.76	113	.210	.302	0	—	0		2		0.1
Total	2	1	2	.333	33	3	0	0-0	58	53	31	9	2	27-1	37	4.50	90	.241	.328	4-0-1	.000	-0	65	-2		-0.6

LONG, TOM Thomas Francis "Little Hawk" B4.22.1898 Memphis TN D9.16.1973 Louisville KY BL/TL/5-9/154 d4.26

YEAR	TM LG	W	L	PCT	G	GS	CG-SHO	SV-BS	IP	H	R	HR	HB	BB-IB	SO	ERA	AERA	OAV	OOB	AB-HR-SH	AVG	PB	SUP	APR	DL	PW
1924	Bro N	0	0	—	1	0	0	0-0	2	2	2	0	2	2	2	9.00	142	.333	.500	0	—	0		-1		-0.1

LONG, BILL William Douglas B2.29.1960 Cincinnati OH BR/TR/6-0/185* [SDN81 2/32] d7.21 Col Miami-Ohio

YEAR	TM LG	W	L	PCT	G	GS	CG-SHO	SV-BS	IP	H	R	HR	HB	BB-IB	SO	ERA	AERA	OAV	OOB	AB-HR-SH	AVG	PB	SUP	APR	DL	PW
1985	Chi A	0	1	.000	4	3	0	0-0	14	25	17	4	0	5-2	13	10.29	42	.391	.429	0	—	0	112	-9		-0.5
1987	Chi A	8	8	.500	29	23	5-2	1-0	169	179	85	20	3	28-1	72	4.37	106	.272	.303	0	—	0	112	6		0.5
1988	Chi A	8	11	.421	47	18	3	2-1	174	187	89	21	4	43-4	77	4.03	99	.280	.323	0	—	0	80	0		-0.1
1989	Chi A	5	5	.500	30	8	0	1-0	98.2	101	49	8	4	37-0	51	3.92	98	.265	.332	0	—	0	80	-1		-0.1
1990	Chi A	0	1	.000	4	0	0	0-0	5.2	6	5	2	0	2-0	2	6.35	61	.261	.320	0	—	0		2		-0.3
	Chi N	6	1	.857	42	0	0	5-2	55.2	66	29	8	1	21-4	32	4.69	94	.301	.365	5	.000	-0		-1	21	-0.2
1991	Mon N	0	0	—	3	0	0	0-0	1.2	4	2	0	0	4-0	1	10.80	34	.500	.667	0	—	0		-1		-0.2
Total	6	27	27	.500	159	52	8-2	9-3	518.2	568	276	63	12	140-11	247	4.37	96	.281	.328	5	.000	-0	99	-8	21	-0.8

LOONEY, BRIAN Brian James B9.26.1969 New Haven CT BL/TL/5-10/180* [MonN91 10/269] d9.26 Col Boston College

YEAR	TM LG	W	L	PCT	G	GS	CG-SHO	SV-BS	IP	H	R	HR	HB	BB-IB	SO	ERA	AERA	OAV	OOB	AB-HR-SH	AVG	PB	SUP	APR	DL	PW
1993	Mon N	0	0	—	3	1	0	0-0	6	8	2	0	0	2-0	7	3.00	139	.308	.357	1	.000	-0	108	1		0.0
1994	Mon N	0	0	—	1	0	0	0-0	2	4	5	1	1	2-0	2	22.50	19	.400	.455	0	—	0		-4		-0.2
1995	Bos A	0	1	.000	3	1	0	0-0	4.2	12	9	1	1	4-1	2	17.36	28	.545	.571	0	—	0	57	-6		-0.9
Total	3	0	1	.000	7	2	0	0-0	12.2	24	16	2	1	6-1	11	11.37	39	.414	.463	1	.000	-0	82	-9		-1.1

LOOPER, AARON Aaron Joseph B9.7.1976 Ada OK BR/TR/6-2/180 [SeaA97 30/913] d8.2 Col Indian Hills (IA) CC

YEAR	TM LG	W	L	PCT	G	GS	CG-SHO	SV-BS	IP	H	R	HR	HB	BB-IB	SO	ERA	AERA	OAV	OOB	AB-HR-SH	AVG	PB	SUP	APR	DL	PW
2003	Sea A	0	0	—	6	0	0	0-0	7	7	4	1	1	2-0	6	5.14	84	.269	.345	0	—	0		-1		0.0

LOOPER, BRADEN Braden La Vern B10.28.1974 Weatherford OK BR/TR/6-5/225(210-225) [StLN96 1/3] d3.31 Col Wichita St.

YEAR	TM LG	W	L	PCT	G	GS	CG-SHO	SV-BS	IP	H	R	HR	HB	BB-IB	SO	ERA	AERA	OAV	OOB	AB-HR-SH	AVG	PB	SUP	APR	DL	PW
1998	StL N	0	1	.000	1	0	0	0-2	3.1	1	2	2	0	5-0	4	5.40	78	.357	.375	0	—	0		-1		-0.2
1999	Fla N	3	3	.500	72	0	0	0-4	83	96	43	7	1	31-6	50	3.80	115	.293	.351	0	—	0		3		0.2
2000	Fla N	5	1	.833	73	0	0	2-3	67.1	71	41	5	3	36-6	29	4.41	99	.268	.364	2	.000	-0		-3		-0.2
2001	Fla N	3	3	.500	71	0	0	3	71	63	28	8	2	30-3	55	3.55	117	.242	.322	2	.000	-0		6		0.5
2002	Fla N	2	5	.286	78	0	0	13-3	86	73	31	6	3	28-3	55	3.14	125	.230	.295	1	.000	-0		9		0.9

YEAR TM LG	W	L	PCT	G	GS	CG-SHO	SV-BS	IP	H	R	HR	HB	BB-IB	SO	ERA	AERA	OAV	OOB	AB-HR-SH	AVG	PB	SUP	APR	DL	PW
2003 †Fla N	6	4	.600	74	0	0	28-6	80.2	82	34	4	1	29-1	56	3.68	111	.264	.326	1-0-1	1.000	0		5		0.8
2004 NY N	2	5	.286	71	0	0	29-5	83.1	86	28	5	3	16-3	60	2.70	159	.266	.305	2	.000	-0		15		1.9
2005 NY N	4	7	.364	60	0	0	28-8	59.1	65	31	7	5	22-3	27	3.94	105	.271	.345	0	—	0		0		0.0
Total 8	25	29	.463	503	0	0	103-34	534	541	240	43	18	193-25	333	3.57	118	.263	.329	8-0-1	.125	-0		34		3.9

LOOS, PETE Ivan B3.23.1878 Philadelphia PA D2.23.1956 Darby PA TR/5-9/178 d5.2 Col Ursinus

YEAR TM LG	W	L	PCT	G	GS	CG-SHO	SV-BS	IP	H	R	HR	HB	BB-IB	SO	ERA	AERA	OAV	OOB	AB-HR-SH	AVG	PB	SUP	APR	DL	PW
1901 Phi A	0	1	.000	1	1	0	0	1	2	5	0	0	4	0	27.00	14	.400	.667	0	—	0	215	-3		-0.4

LOPAT, ED Edmund Walter (b Edmund Walter Lopatynski) B6.21.1918 New York NY D6.15.1992 Darien CT BL/TL/5-10/185* d4.30 M2/C3

YEAR TM LG	W	L	PCT	G	GS	CG-SHO	SV-BS	IP	H	R	HR	HB	BB-IB	SO	ERA	AERA	OAV	OOB	AB-HR-SH	AVG	PB	SUP	APR	DL	PW
1944 Chi A	11	10	.524	27	25	13-1	0	210	217	96	12	2	59	75	3.26	105	.265	.316	81-0-1	.309	6*	98	2		1.0
1945 Chi A	10	13	.435	26	24	17-1	1	199.1	226	101	8	6	56	74	4.11	81	.285	.336	82-1-1	.293	5*	109	-16		-1.2
1946 Chi A	13	13	.500	29	29	20-2	0	231	216	80	18	1	48	89	2.73	125	.248	.288	87-0-2	.253	6*	109	21		3.2
1947 Chi A	16	13	.552	31	31	22-3	0	252.2	241	88	17	2	73	109	2.81	130	.253	.307	96-0-4	.198	0*	91	26		2.9
1948 NY A	17	11	.607	33	31	13-3	0	226.2	246	106	16	2	66	83	3.65	112	.284	.336	81-0-4	.173	-1*	110	10		1.0
1949 †NY A	15	10	.600	31	30	14-4	1	215.1	222	93	19	5	69	70	3.26	124	.269	.330	76-1-1	.263	7	98	17		2.6
1950 †NY A	18	8	.692	35	32	15-3	1	236.1	244	110	19	4	65	72	3.47	124	.266	.317	82-0-5	.232	8*	124	18		2.5
1951 †NY A★	21	9	.700	31	31	20-4	0	234.2	209	86	12	3	71	93	2.91	131	.239	.298	84-3-4	.179	1	99	26		3.3
1952 †NY A	10	5	.667	20	19	10-2	0	149.1	127	47	11	4	53	56	2.53	131	.234	.307	52-0-2	.173	1	119	15		1.6
1953 †NY A	16	4	**.800**	25	24	9-3	0	178.1	169	58	13	4	32	50	**2.42**	**152**	.250	.288	63-0-5	.190	1*	126	25		2.9
1954 NY A	12	4	.750	26	23	7	0	170	189	74	14	6	33	54	3.55	97	.288	.326	57-0-4	.018	-5	117	-2		-0.7
1955 NY A	4	8	.333	16	12	3-1	0	86.2	101	45	12	1	16-3	24	3.74	100	.294	.327	29	.138	-1	83	-2		-0.4
Bal A	3	4	.429	10	7	1	0	49	57	24	8	3	9-2	10	4.22	90	.294	.332	17-0-1	.176	0	73	-1		-0.1
Year	7	12	.368	26	19	4-1	0	135.2	158	69	20	4	25-5	34	3.91	96	.294	.329	46-0-1	.152	-1	79	-3		-0.5
Total 12	166	112	.597	340	318	164-27	3	2439.1	2464	1008	179	43	650-5	859	3.21	116	.264	.315	887-5-34	.211	29	107	139		18.6

LOPATKA, ART Arthur Joseph B5.28.1919 Chicago IL BB/TL/5-10/170 d9.12 Col Chicago

YEAR TM LG	W	L	PCT	G	GS	CG-SHO	SV-BS	IP	H	R	HR	HB	BB-IB	SO	ERA	AERA	OAV	OOB	AB-HR-SH	AVG	PB	SUP	APR	DL	PW
1945 StL N	1	0	1.000	2	1	0	0	11.2	7	4	0	1	3	5	1.54	243	.159	.229	4	.250	0	68	2		0.2
1946 Phi N	0	1	.000	4	1	0	0	5.1	13	11	1	0	4	4	16.88	20	.448	.515	0	—	0	150	-8		-1.2
Total 2	1	1	.500	8	2	1	0	17	20	15	1	1	7	9	6.35	57	.274	.346	4	.250	0	105	-6		-1.0

LOPEZ, ALBIE Albert Anthony B8.18.1971 Mesa AZ BR/TR/6-2/235(185-240) [CleA91 20/528] d7.6 Col Mesa (AZ) CC

YEAR TM LG	W	L	PCT	G	GS	CG-SHO	SV-BS	IP	H	R	HR	HB	BB-IB	SO	ERA	AERA	OAV	OOB	AB-HR-SH	AVG	PB	SUP	APR	DL	PW
1993 Cle A	3	1	.750	9	9	0	0-0	49.2	49	34	9	1	32-1	25	5.98	73	.262	.371	0	—	0	145	-8		-0.5
1994 Cle A	1	2	.333	4	4	1-1	0-0	17	20	11	3	1	6-0	18	4.24	112	.290	.355	0	—	0	92	0		0.0
1995 Cle A	0	0	—	6	2	0	0-0	23	17	8	4	1	7-1	15	3.13	151	.205	.272	0	—	0	99	4		0.2
1996 Cle A	5	4	.556	13	10	0	0-0	62	80	47	14	2	22-1	45	6.39	77	.311	.369	0	—	0	121	-10		-1.2
1997 Cle A	3	7	.300	37	6	0	0-1	76.2	101	61	11	4	40-9	63	6.93	68	.321	.402	1	.000	-0	124	-17	45	-1.8
1998 TB A	7	4	.636	54	0	0	1-4	79.2	73	31	7	3	32-4	62	2.60	185	.249	.326	1	.000	-0		16	25	2.0
1999 TB A	3	2	.600	51	0	0	1-2	64	66	40	8	1	24-2	37	4.64	107	.263	.325	0	—	0		1	39	0.1
2000 TB A	11	13	.458	45	24	4-1	2-2	185.1	199	95	24	4	70-3	96	4.13	119	.277	.341	6-0-1	.000	-1	75	15		1.5
2001 TB A	5	12	.294	20	20	1-1	0-0	124.2	152	87	16	4	51-1	67	5.34	84	.302	.368	5	.000	-1	69	-13		-1.5
†Ari N	4	7	.364	13	13	2-2	0-0	81	74	36	10	0	24-2	69	4.00	116	.247	.301	24-0-2	.042	-1	81	7		0.7
2002 Atl N	1	4	.200	30	4	0	0-0	55.2	66	29	1	0	18-3	39	4.37	93	.300	.349	9	.111	-1	57	-2	39	-0.2
2003 KC A	4	2	.667	15	0	0	0-3	22.2	40	32	7	0	17-1	15	12.71	38	.383	.468	0	—	-0		-18	30	-3.0
Total 11	47	58	.448	297	92	8-5	4-12	841.1	938	511	112	18	343-28	558	4.94	95	.284	.352	46-0-3	.043	-3	90	-25	178	-3.7

LOPEZ, AQUILINO Aquilino (Roa) B4.21.1975 Villa Altagracia, D.R. BR/TR/6-3/160* d4.2

YEAR TM LG	W	L	PCT	G	GS	CG-SHO	SV-BS	IP	H	R	HR	HB	BB-IB	SO	ERA	AERA	OAV	OOB	AB-HR-SH	AVG	PB	SUP	APR	DL	PW
2003 Tor A	1	3	.250	72	0	0	14-2	73.2	58	31	5	5	34-5	64	3.42	139	.212	.309	0	—	0		10		0.8
2004 Tor A	1	1	.500	18	0	0	0-0	21	21	15	5	2	13-3	13	6.00	82	.266	.379	0	—	0		-3		-0.2
2005 Col N	0	0	—	1	0	0	0-0	4	3	1	0	0	0-0	6	2.25	212	.200	.200	1	.000	-0		1		0.2
Phi N	0	1	.000	10	0	0	0-0	12.2	13	4	2	0	7-1	16	2.13	204	.265	.357	0	—	0		3		0.2
Year	0	1	.000	11	0	0	0-0	16.2	16	5	2	0	7-1	22	2.16	206	.250	.324	1	.000	-0		4		0.2
Total 3	2	5	.286	101	0	0	14-2	111.1	95	51	12	7	54-9	99	3.72	127	.228	.325	1	.000	-0		11		0.8

LOPEZ, AURELIO Aurelio Alejandro (Rios) B9.21.1948 Tecamachalco, Puebla, Mexico D9.22.1992 Matehuala, San Luis Potosi, Mexico BR/TR/6-0/220(200-230) d9.1

YEAR TM LG	W	L	PCT	G	GS	CG-SHO	SV-BS	IP	H	R	HR	HB	BB-IB	SO	ERA	AERA	OAV	OOB	AB-HR-SH	AVG	PB	SUP	APR	DL	PW
1974 KC A	0	0	—	8	1	0	0-0	16	21	12	0	0	10-0	5	5.63	68	.344	.425	0	—	0	92	-3		-0.2
1978 StL N	4	2	.667	25	4	0	0-0	65	52	35	4	1	32-2	46	4.29	83	.218	.308	14-0-2	.214	0	157	-5		-0.5
1979 Det A	10	5	.667	61	0	0	21-5	127	95	37	12	3	51-3	106	2.41	181	.210	.292	0	—	0		27		3.9
1980 Det A	13	6	.684	67	1	0	21-5	124	125	56	15	3	45-5	97	3.77	109	.263	.328	0	—	0	87	5		0.8
1981 Det A	5	2	.714	29	3	0	3-2	81.2	70	34	8	2	31-2	53	3.64	104	.233	.306	0	—	0	103	2		0.1
1982 Det A	3	1	.750	19	0	0	3-0	41	41	27	8	0	19-4	26	5.27	78	.268	.345	0	—	0		-5	38	-0.6
1983 Det A☆	9	8	.529	57	0	0	18-8	115.1	87	36	12	1	49-7	90	2.81	141	.210	.292	0	—	0		17		2.8
1984 †Det A	10	1	.909	71	0	0	14-2	137.2	109	51	16	2	52-6	94	2.94	135	.221	.295	0	—	0		16		1.4
1985 Det A	3	7	.300	51	0	0	5-2	86.1	82	50	15	1	41-9	53	4.80	86	.250	.330	0	—	0		-6		-0.7
1986 †Hou N	3	3	.500	45	0	0	7-1	78	64	32	6	2	25-1	44	3.46	104	.221	.280	9-0-1	.000	-1		2		0.0
1987 Hou N	2	1	.667	26	0	0	1-1	38	39	22	6	1	12-0	21	4.50	87	.273	.333	1-0-1	.000	0		-3		-0.2
Total 11	62	36	.633	459	9	0	93-26	910	785	392	102	15	367-39	635	3.56	112	.234	.309	24-0-4	.125	-1	116	47	38	6.8

LOPEZ, JAVIER Javier Alfonso B6.11.1977 San Juan, PR BL/TL/6-4/200* [AriN98 4/133] d4.1 Col Virginia

YEAR TM LG	W	L	PCT	G	GS	CG-SHO	SV-BS	IP	H	R	HR	HB	BB-IB	SO	ERA	AERA	OAV	OOB	AB-HR-SH	AVG	PB	SUP	APR	DL	PW
2003 Col N	4	1	.800	75	0	0	1-1	58.1	58	25	5	4	12-2	40	3.70	132	.258	.307	5	.200	-0		7		0.6
2004 Col N	1	2	.333	64	0	0	0-1	40.2	45	34	1	3	26-4	20	7.52	63	.287	.398	2-0-1	.000	-0		-11		-0.6
2005 Ari N	1	1	.500	29	0	0	2-1	14.1	19	15	2	1	11-3	11	9.42	47	.311	.425	0	—	0		-7		-1.0
Col N	0	0	—	3	0	0	0-1	2	7	5	0	0	0-0	1	22.50	21	.538	.538	0	—	0		-3		-0.2
Year	1	1	.500	32	0	0	2-2	16.1	26	20	2	1	11-3	12	11.02	40	.351	.442	0	—	0		-11		-1.2
Total 3	6	4	.600	171	0	0	3-4	115.1	129	79	8	8	49-9	72	6.09	79	.283	.363	7-0-1	.143	-0		-14		-1.2

LOPEZ, RAMON Jose Ramon (Hevia) B5.26.1933 Las Villas, Cuba D9.4.1982 Miami FL BR/TR/6-0/175 d8.21

YEAR TM LG	W	L	PCT	G	GS	CG-SHO	SV-BS	IP	H	R	HR	HB	BB-IB	SO	ERA	AERA	OAV	OOB	AB-HR-SH	AVG	PB	SUP	APR	DL	PW
1966 Cal A	0	1	.000	4	1	0	0	7	4	5	1	0	4-0	7	5.14	65	.154	.267	0	—	0*	105	-2		-0.2

LOPEZ, MARCELINO Marcelino Pons B9.23.1943 Havana, Cuba D11.29.2001 Hialeah FL BR/TL/6-3/210(195-222) d4.14

YEAR TM LG	W	L	PCT	G	GS	CG-SHO	SV-BS	IP	H	R	HR	HB	BB-IB	SO	ERA	AERA	OAV	OOB	AB-HR-SH	AVG	PB	SUP	APR	DL	PW
1963 Phi N	1	0	1.000	4	2	0	0	6	8	5	0	0	7-1	2	6.00	54	.333	.469	2	.000	-0*	147	-2		-0.3
1965 Cal A	14	13	.519	35	32	8-1	0	215.1	185	79	12	4	82-6	122	2.93	116	.230	.304	69-1-7	.203	3*	83	11		2.0
1966 Cal A	7	14	.333	37	32	6-2	1	199	188	95	20	2	68-2	132	3.93	85	.251	.319	58-0-3	.190	2*	85	-12		-0.9
1967 Cal A	0	2	.000	4	3	0	0	9	11	10	1	0	9-0	6	9.00	35	.324	.455	2	.500	0*	120	-6	31	-1.1
Bal A	1	0	1.000	4	4	0	0	17.2	15	5	1	0	10-0	15	2.55	124	.227	.329	5	.000	-0*	131	1	51	0.0
Year	1	2	.333	8	7	0	0	26.2	26	15	2	0	19-0	21	4.73	67	.260	.375	7	.143	0	126	-4		-1.1
1969 †Bal A	5	3	.625	27	4	0	0-3	69.1	65	34	3	2	34-4	57	4.41	81	.252	.340	14-0-2	.214	1	105	-5		-0.4
1970 †Bal A	1	1	.500	25	3	0	0-0	60.2	47	19	2	0	37-3	49	2.08	177	.217	.327	13	.077	-0	178	9		0.4
1971 Mil A	2	7	.222	31	11	0	0-1	67.2	64	48	5	0	60-1	42	4.66	75	.251	.390	17-0-1	.059	-1*	84	-12		-1.6
1972 Cle A	0	0	—	4	2	0	0-0	8.1	8	5	0	0	10-0	1	5.40	60	.276	.462	1	.000	0	41	-2		-0.1
Total 8	31	40	.437	171	93	14-3	2-4	653	591	300	44	15	317-17	426	3.62	95	.243	.331	181-1-13	.171	4	91	-18	82	-2.0

LOPEZ, RODRIGO Rodrigo (Munoz) B12.14.1975 Tlalnepantla, Estado de Mexico, Mexico BR/TR/6-1/180* d4.29

YEAR TM LG	W	L	PCT	G	GS	CG-SHO	SV-BS	IP	H	R	HR	HB	BB-IB	SO	ERA	AERA	OAV	OOB	AB-HR-SH	AVG	PB	SUP	APR	DL	PW
2000 SD N	0	3	.000	6	6	0	0-0	24.2	40	24	5	0	13-0	17	8.76	51	.377	.442	9	.111	-0	117	-11		-1.1
2002 Bal A	15	9	.625	33	28	1	0-0	196.2	172	83	23	6	62-4	136	3.57	122	.234	.296	3	.000	-0	102	18		1.9
2003 Bal A	7	10	.412	26	26	3-1	0-0	147	188	101	24	10	43-6	103	5.82	79	.313	.365	2	.000	-0	95	-19	44	-1.9
2004 Bal A	14	9	.609	33	33	1-1	0-1	170.2	164	71	21	2	54-3	121	3.59	130	.252	.310	0	—	0	98	22		2.6
2005 Bal A	15	12	.556	35	**35**	5-2	0-1	209.1	232	126	28	2	63-1	118	4.90	90	.276	.330	4	.000	-0	93	-11		-1.2
Total 5	51	43	.543	137	118	5-2	0-1	748.1	796	405	101	24	235-13	495	4.56	99	.271	.329	18	.056	-1	98	-1	44	0.3

LORENZEN, LEFTY Adolph Andreas B1.12.1893 Davenport IA D3.5.1963 Davenport IA BL/TL/5-10/164 d9.12

YEAR TM LG	W	L	PCT	G	GS	CG-SHO	SV-BS	IP	H	R	HR	HB	BB-IB	SO	ERA	AERA	OAV	OOB	AB-HR-SH	AVG	PB	SUP	APR	DL	PW
1913 Det A	0	0	—	4	0	0	0-0									16	.667	.778	2	.500	0		-3		-0.1

LORRAINE, ANDREW Andrew Jason B8.11.1972 Los Angeles CA BL/TL/6-3/195* [CalA93 4/103] d7.17 Col Stanford

YEAR TM LG	W	L	PCT	G	GS	CG-SHO	SV-BS	IP	H	R	HR	HB	BB-IB	SO	ERA	AERA	OAV	OOB	AB-HR-SH	AVG	PB	SUP	APR	DL	PW
1994 Cal A	0	2	.000	4	3	0	0-0	18.2	30	23	7	1	11-0	10	10.61	46	.366	.436	0	—	0	81	-11		-0.9
1995 Chi A	0	0	—	5	0	0	0-0	8	3	3	0	1	2-0	5	3.38	133	.111	.200	0	—	0		1		0.0
1997 Oak A	3	1	.750	12	6	0	0-0	29.2	45	22	2	1	15-0	18	6.37	72	.343	.418	0	—	0	147	-6		-0.6
1998 Sea A	0	0	—	4	0	0	0-0	3.2	3	1	0	0	4-0	2	2.45	191	.250	.438	0	—	0		1		0.0

YEAR	TM LG	W	L	PCT	G	GS	CG-SHO	SV-BS	IP	H	R	HR	HB	BB-IB	SO	ERA	AERA	OAV	OOB	AB-HR-SH	AVG	PB	SUP	APR	DL	PW
1999	Chi N	2	5	.286	11	11	2-1	0-0	61.2	71	42	9	0	22-3	40	5.55	82	.293	.350	15-0-4	.133	0*	86	-7		-0.6
2000	Chi N	1	2	.333	8	5	0	0-1	32	36	25	5	0	18-1	25	6.47	71	.286	.370	8-0-2	.125	-0	120	-7		-0.6
	Cle A	0	0	—	10	0	0	0-0	9.1	8	4	1	0	5-0	5	3.86	69	.222	.317	0	—	0		1		0.1
2002	Mil N	0	1	.000	5	1	0	0-0	12	22	18	7	0	6-0	10	11.25	37	.379	.438	1-0-1	.000	-0	225	-10		-0.7
Total	7	6	11	.353	59	26	2-1	0-1	175	218	138	31	2	83-4	113	6.53	70	.307	.377	24-0-7	.125	-0	111	-38		-3.3

LOTZ, JOE Joseph Peter "Smokey" B1.2.1891 Remsen IA D1.1.1971 Castro Valley CA BR/TR/5-8.5/175 d7.15 Col Creighton

| 1916 | StL N | 0 | 3 | .000 | 12 | 3 | 1 | 0 | 40 | 31 | 20 | 1 | 1 | 17 | 18 | 4.27 | 62 | .225 | .314 | 12 | .333 | 1 | 85 | -5 | | -0.3 |

LOUDELL, ART Arthur (b Arthur Laudel) B4.10.1882 Latham MO D2.19.1961 Kansas City MO BR/TR/5-11/173 d8.13

| 1910 | Det A | 1 | 1 | .500 | 5 | 2 | 1 | 0 | 21.1 | 23 | 13 | 0 | 0 | 14 | 12 | 3.38 | 78 | .284 | .389 | 7-0-1 | .143 | -0 | 140 | -2 | | -0.3 |

LOUGHLIN, LARRY Larry John B8.16.1941 Tacoma WA D1.26.1999 Denver CO BL/TL/6-1/190 d5.27 Col Santa Clara

| 1967 | Phi N | 0 | 0 | — | 3 | 0 | 0 | 0 | 5.1 | 9 | 9 | 1 | 0 | 4-1 | 5 | 15.19 | 22 | .375 | .464 | 1 | 1.000 | 1 | | -6 | | -0.3 |

LOUN, DON Donald Nelson B11.9.1940 Frederick MD BR/TL/6-2/185 d9.23

| 1964 | Was A | 1 | 1 | .500 | 2 | 2 | 1-1 | 0 | 13 | 13 | 4 | 0 | 0 | 3-0 | 3 | 2.08 | 178 | .250 | .291 | 4 | .000 | -0 | 12 | 3 | | 0.3 |

LOUX, SHANE Shane A. B8.13.1979 Rapid City SD BR/TR/6-2/205* [DetA97 2/53] d9.10

2002	Det A	0	3	.000	3	3	0	0-0	14	19	16	4	1	3-0	7	9.00	49	.317	.359	0	—	0	71	-8		-1.1
2003	Det A	1	1	.500	11	4	0	0-0	30.1	37	24	4	4	12-1	8	7.12	62	.303	.381	0	—	0	94	-9		-0.5
Total	2	1	4	.200	14	7	0	0-0	44.1	56	40	8	5	15-1	15	7.71	57	.308	.374	0	—	0	84	-17		-1.6

LOVE, SLIM Edward Haughton B8.1.1890 Love MS D11.30.1942 Memphis TN BL/TL/6-7/195 d9.8

1913	Was A	1	0	1.000	5	1	0	1	16.2	14	5	0	0	6	5	1.62	182	.233	.303	5	.200	0	50	2		0.1
1916	NY A	2	0	1.000	20	1	0	0	47.2	46	29	2	0	23	21	4.91	59	.274	.361	14-0-1	.000	-2	79	-9		-0.7
1917	NY A	6	5	.545	33	9	2	1	130.1	115	50	0	1	57	82	2.35	114	.251	.335	36-0-2	.167	-1	71	3		-0.5
1918	NY A	13	12	.520	38	29	13-1	1	228.2	207	92	3	10	116	95	3.07	92	.253	.353	74-0-1	.230	2	91	-5		-0.1
1919	Det A	6	4	.600	22	8	4	1	89.2	92	40	3	6	40	46	3.01	106	.275	.363	27-0-1	.222	0	86	1		-0.1
1920	Det A	0	0	—	1	0	0	0	4.1	6	4	0	0	4	2	8.31	45	.375	.500	0	—	0		-2		-0.0
Total	6	28	21	.571	119	48	19-1	4	517.1	480	220	8	17	246	251	3.04	94	.259	.351	156-0-5	.192	-0	85	-10		-1.2

LOVELACE, VANCE Vance Odell B8.9.1963 Tampa FL BL/TL/6-5/205(205-235) [ChiN81 1/16] d9.10

1988	Cal A	0	0	—	3	0	0	0-0	1.1	2	2	1	0	3-0	0	13.50	29	.400	.625	0	—	0		-1		-0.1
1989	Cal A	0	0	—	1	0	0	0	1	0	0	0	0	1-1	1	0.00	—	.000	.250	0	—	0		0		0.0
1990	Sea A	0	0	—	5	0	0	0	2.1	3	1	0	1	6-0	1	3.86	103	.300	.588	0	—	0		0		0.0
Total	3	0	0	—	9	0	0	0	4.2	5	3	1	1	10-1	2	5.79	68	.278	.552	0	—	0		-1		-0.1

LOVENGUTH, LYNN Lynn Richard B11.29.1922 Camden NY D9.29.2000 Beaverton OR BL/TR/5-10.5/170* d4.18

1955	Phi N	0	1	.000	14	1	0	0	18	17	9	1	0	10-0	14	4.50	88	.258	.358	2	.000	-0		-1		-0.1
1957	StL N	0	1	.000	2	1	0	0	9	6	3	0	0	6-0	6	2.00	198	.182	.308	2	.000	-0*	44	2		0.1
Total	2	0	2	.000	16	2	0	0	27	23	12	1	2	16-0	20	3.67	108	.232	.342	4	.000	-1	44	1		-0.0

LOVETT, JOHN John B5.6.1877 Monday OH D12.5.1937 Murray City OH d5.22

| 1903 | StL N | 0 | 0 | — | 3 | 1 | 0 | 0 | 5 | 6 | 5 | 0 | 1 | 5 | 3 | 5.40 | 60 | .300 | .462 | 3 | .333 | 0 | 21 | -1 | | 0.0 |

LOVETT, LEN Leonard Walker B7.17.1852 Lancaster Co. PA D11.18.1922 Newark DE BR/TR d8.4 ▲

| 1873 | Res NA | 0 | 1 | .000 | 1 | 1 | 1 | 0 | 9 | 22 | 16 | 0 | 1 | 7 | 1 | 7.00 | 48 | .400 | .411 | 5 | .400 | 0 | 85 | -2 | | -0.1 |

LOVETT, TOM Thomas Joseph B12.7.1863 Providence RI D3.19.1928 Providence RI BR/5-8/162 d6.4

1885	Phi AA	7	8	.467	16	16	15-1	0	138.2	130	96	3	5	38	56	3.70	93	.236	.291	58	.224	-0	113	-1		-0.1
1889	†Bro AA	17	10	.630	29	28	23-1	0	229	234	132	3	8	65	92	4.32	86	.256	.311	100-2	.190	-1	125	-6		-0.7
1890	†Bro N	30	11	**.732**	44	41	39-4	0	372	327	195	14	17	141	124	2.78	124	.229	.305	164-1	.201	-1	130	24		2.0
1891	Bro N	23	19	.548	44	43	39-3	0	365.2	361	229	14	20	129	129	3.69	90	.248	.318	153	.163	-5	108	-13		-1.7
1893	Bro N	3	5	.375	14	8	6	1	96	134	92	2	6	35	15	6.56	67	.321	.381	50	.180	-2*	101	-21		-1.4
1894	Bos N	8	6	.571	15	13	10	0	104	155	96	12	3	36	23	5.97	95	.341	.394	49-1-0	.143	-5	100	-2		-2.5
Total	6	88	59	.599	162	149	132-9	1	1305.1	1341	840	48	59	444	439	3.94	94	.257	.322	574-4-0	.185	-13	116	-19		-2.5

LOVRICH, PETE Peter B10.16.1942 Blue Island IL BR/TR/6-4/200 d4.26 Mil 1964-65 Col Arizona St.

| 1963 | KC A | 1 | 1 | .500 | 20 | 1 | 0 | 0 | 20.2 | 25 | 23 | 5 | 1 | 10-1 | 16 | 7.84 | 50 | .291 | .367 | 0-0-1 | — | 0 | 46 | -10 | | -0.9 |

LOWDERMILK, GROVER Grover Cleveland "Slim" B1.15.1885 Sandborn IN D3.31.1968 Odin IL BR/TR/6-4/190 d7.3 b-Lou

1909	StL N	0	2	.000	7	3	1	0	29	28	24	0	3	30	14	6.21	41	.292	.473	10	.100	-1	83	-11		-0.8
1911	StL N	0	1	.000	11	2	1-1	0	33.1	37	30	1	2	33	15	7.29	46	.301	.456	9	.111	-1	33	-13		-0.7
1912	Chi N	0	1	.000	2	1	1	0	13	17	18	1	0	14	8	9.69	34	.304	.443	4	.000	-1	22	-9		-0.6
1915	StL A	9	17	.346	38	29	14-1	0	222.1	183	110	0	16	133	130	3.12	92	.234	.357	72	.125	-3	79	-6		-1.0
	Det A	4	1	.800	7	5	0	0	28	17	16	0	1	24	18	4.18	73	.185	.359	8-0-1	.125	-0	120	-3		-0.5
	Year	13	18	.419	45	34	14-1	0	250.1	200	126	1	17	157	148	3.24	89	.229	.357	80-0-1	.125	-3	86	-13		-1.5
1916	Det A	0	0	—	1	0	0	0	0.1	0	0	0	0	0	0	0.00	—	.000	.750	0	—	0		0		0.0
	Cle A	1	5	.167	10	9	2	0	51.1	52	33	0	3	45	28	3.16	95	.277	.424	18-0-1	.167	-0	89	-4		-0.5
	Year	1	5	.167	11	9	2	0	51.2	52	33	0	3	48	28	3.14	96	.275	.429	18-0-1	.167	-0	89	-4		-0.5
1917	StL A	2	1	.667	3	2	2-1	0	19	16	5	0	2	8	9	1.42	183	.225	.267	7	.000	-1	97	2		0.2
1918	StL A	2	6	.250	13	11	4	0	80	74	44	1	3	38	25	3.15	87	.255	.347	28	.250	1	97	-6		-0.1
1919	StL A	0	0	—	7	0	0	0	12	6	2	0	5	4	6	0.75	442	.176	.349	1	.000	-0		3		0.1
	†Chi A	5	5	.500	20	11	0	0	96.2	95	44	0	4	43	43	2.79	114	.268	.353	34	.088	-3	128	2		-0.1
	Year	5	5	.500	27	11	5	0	108.2	101	46	0	9	47	49	2.57	125	.260	.353	35	.086	-4	127	5		0.0
1920	Chi A	0	0	—	3	0	0	0	5.1	9	4	0	0	5	0	6.75	56	.409	.519	0	—	0		-1		0.0
Total	9	23	39	.371	122	73	30-3	0	590.1	534	330	4	37	376	296	3.58	82	.253	.375	191-0-2	.131	-8	91	-46		-4.2

LOWDERMILK, LOU Louis Bailey B2.23.1887 Sandborn IN D12.27.1975 Centralia IL BR/TL/6-1/180 d4.20 b-Grover

1911	StL N	3	4	.429	16	3	3	0	65	72	39	0	5	29	20	3.46	98	.304	.391	18	.111	-1	44	-3		-0.5
1912	StL N	1	1	.500	4	1	1	0	15	14	8	0	0	9	2	3.00	114	.246	.348	4-0-1	.250	0	107	0		0.0
Total	2	4	5	.444	20	4	4	0	80	86	47	0	5	38	22	3.37	100	.293	.383	22-0-1	.136	-1	61	-3		-0.5

LOWE, DEREK Derek Christopher B6.1.1973 Dearborn MI BR/TR/6-6/200(170-210) [SeaA91 8/214] d4.26

1997	Sea A	2	4	.333	12	9	0	0-0	53	59	43	11	2	20-2	39	6.96	65	.282	.349	2	.000	-0	115	-14		-1.2
	Bos A	0	2	.000	8	0	0	0-2	16	15	6	0	2	3-1	13	3.38	138	.268	.323	1	.000	-0		2		0.2
	Year	2	6	.250	20	9	0	0-2	69	74	49	11	4	23-3	52	6.13	74	.279	.344	3	.000	-0	114	-11		-1.0
1998	†Bos A	3	9	.250	63	10	0	4-5	123	126	65	5	4	42-5	77	4.02	117	.267	.329	4	.000	-0	65	7		0.8
1999	†Bos A	6	3	.667	74	0	0	15-5	109.1	84	35	7	4	25-1	80	2.63	189	.208	.260	1	—	0		28		3.5
2000	Bos A★	4	4	.500	74	0	0	**42-5**	91.1	90	27	6	2	22-5	79	2.56	196	.257	.304	1	.000	0	104	10		1.5
2001	Bos A	5	10	.333	67	3	0	24-6	91.2	103	39	7	5	29-9	82	3.53	126	.283	.343	1	.000	0	104	10		1.5
2002	Bos A★	21	8	.724	32	32	1-1	0-0	219.2	166	65	12	12	48-0	127	2.58	173	.211	.266	3-0-1	.333	1	124	48		**6.2**
2003	†Bos A	17	7	.708	33	33	1	0-0	203.1	216	113	17	11	72-4	110	4.47	104	.272	.339	4-0-1	.000	-0	128	4		-1.1
2004	†Bos A	14	12	.538	33	33	0	0-0	182.2	224	138	15	8	71-2	105	5.42	90	.299	.365	4-0-1	.250	-0	117	-16		-1.6
2005	LA N	12	15	.444	35	35	2-2	0-0	222	223	113	28	5	55-1	146	3.61	113	.260	.307	65-0-9	.154	0	101	5		0.5
Total	9	84	74	.532	431	155	4-3	85-23	1312	1306	644	108	55	387-30	858	3.83	120	.259	.317	85-0-12	.141	0	112	99		13.9

LOWE, GEORGE George Wesley "Doc" B4.25.1895 Ridgefield Park NJ D9.2.1981 Somers Point NJ BR/TR/6-2/180 d7.28

| 1920 | Cin N | 0 | 0 | — | 1 | 0 | 0 | 0 | 2 | 1 | 0 | 0 | 0 | 1 | 0 | 0.00 | — | .167 | .286 | 0 | — | 0 | | 1 | | 0.0 |

LOWE, SEAN Jonathan Sean B3.29.1971 Dallas TX BR/TR/6-2/205* [StLN92 1/15] d8.29 Col Arizona St.

1997	StL N	0	2	.000	6	4	0	0-0	17.1	27	21	2	1	10-0	8	9.35	45	.360	.432	3	.333	0	116	-10		-1.1
1998	StL N	0	3	.000	4	1	0	0-0	5.1	11	9	1	0	5-0	2	15.19	28	.440	.533	2	.000	-0	66	-6		-1.1
1999	Chi A	4	1	.800	64	0	0	0-3	95.2	90	39	10	4	46-1	62	3.67	135	.252	.347	0	—	0		15		1.2
2000	Chi A	4	1	.800	50	5	0	0-0	70.2	78	47	10	6	39-3	53	5.48	92	.284	.383	0	—	0	111	-3	24	-0.1
2001	Chi A	9	4	.692	45	11	0	3-0	127	123	55	12	7	32-2	71	3.61	129	.256	.308	3	.333	0	83	15		1.3
2002	Pit N	4	2	.667	43	1	0	0-2	69	85	45	8	4	34-6	57	5.35	78	.307	.393	13-0-2	.077	-1	110	-9		-0.8
	Col N	1	1	.500	8	1	0	0	10.1	16	14	2	0	5-0	7	8.71	54	.348	.434	1	.000	0		-5		-0.7

YEAR TM LG	W	L	PCT	G	GS	CG-SHO	SV-BS	IP	H	R	HR	HB	BB-IB	SO	ERA	AERA	OAV	OOB	AB-HR-SH	AVG	PB	SUP	APR	DL	PW
Year	5	3	.625	51	1	0	0-2	79.1	101	58	9	7	41-6	64	5.79	74	.313	.398	14-0-2	.071	-1	108	-14		-1.5
2003 KC A	1	1	.500	28	0	0	0-1	44.2	55	32	7	2	21-5	28	6.25	77	.301	.377	0		-1		-6		-0.3
Total 7	23	15	.605	248	22	0	3-6	440	485	261	51	27	194-17	288	4.95	95	.284	.362	22-0-2	.136	-1	94	-9	24	-2.0

LOWN, TURK Omar Joseph B5.30.1924 Brooklyn NY BR/TR/6-1/185* d4.24

YEAR TM LG	W	L	PCT	G	GS	CG-SHO	SV-BS	IP	H	R	HR	HB	BB-IB	SO	ERA	AERA	OAV	OOB	AB-HR-SH	AVG	PB	SUP	APR	DL	PW
1951 Chi N	4	9	.308	31	18	3-1	0	127	125	80	14	1	90	39	5.46	75	.260	.378	39-0-2	.205	1	78	-16		-1.3
1952 Chi N	4	11	.267	33	19	5	0	156.2	154	87	13	3	93	73	4.37	88	.257	.359	50-0-5	.140	-0	86	-9		-0.7
1953 Chi N	8	7	.533	49	12	2	3	148.1	166	93	20	2	84	76	5.16	86	.282	.373	48-0-2	.125	-2	89	-9		-0.9
1954 Chi N	0	2	.000	15	0	0	0	22	23	18	1	0	15	16	6.14	68	.261	.365	0		-0*		-5		-0.4
1956 Chi N	9	8	.529	61	0	0	13	110.2	95	49	10	0	78-12	74	3.58	105	.240	.363	23-1-1	.217	2		3		0.7
1957 Chi N	5	7	.417	67	0	0	12	93	74	45	10	0	51-4	51	3.77	103	.221	.321	10	.200	0		0		0.2
1958 Chi N	0	0	—	4	0	0	0	4	2	2	0	0	3-0	3	4.50	87	.154	.313	0		0		0		0.0
Cin N	0	2	.000	11	0	0	0	11.2	12	8	2	0	12-2	9	5.40	77	.273	.421	1	.000	-0		-2		-0.3
Year	0	2	.000	15	0	0	0	15.2	14	10	2	0	15-2	13	5.17	79	.246	.397	1	.000	-0		-2		-0.3
1959 †Chi A	9	2	.818	60	0	0	15	93.1	73	32	12	2	42-4	63	2.89	130	.215	.303	12	.250	1		10		1.6
1960 Chi A	2	3	.400	45	0	0	5	67.1	60	31	6	0	34-6	39	3.88	98	.239	.326	5-0-2	.200	1		0		0.1
1961 Chi A	7	5	.583	59	0	0	11	101	87	37	13	0	35-3	50	2.76	142	.238	.300	14-0-1	.000	-2*		12		1.4
1962 Chi A	4	2	.667	42	0	0	6	56.1	58	21	3	1	25-5	40	3.04	129	.266	.346	3	.000	-0		5		0.7
Total 11	55	61	.474	504	49	10-1	73	1032	978	525	105	10	590-40	574	4.12	96	.252	.351	214-1-14	.164	1	86	-14		0.7

LOWRY, NOAH Noah Ryan B10.10.1980 Ventura CA BR/TL/6-2/190(190-210) [SFN01 1/30] d9.5 Col Pepperdine

YEAR TM LG	W	L	PCT	G	GS	CG-SHO	SV-BS	IP	H	R	HR	HB	BB-IB	SO	ERA	AERA	OAV	OOB	AB-HR-SH	AVG	PB	SUP	APR	DL	PW
2003 SF N	0	0	—	4	0	0	0-0	6.1	7	2	1	0	2-0	5	0.00	—	.048	.167	2	.500	0		3		0.2
2004 SF N	6	0	1.000	16	14	2-1	0-0	92	91	41	10	0	28-1	72	3.82	114	.259	.312	33-0-3	.182	0	122	6		0.4
2005 SF N	13	13	.500	33	33	0	0-0	204.2	193	92	21	7	76-1	172	3.78	113	.249	.320	59-0-12	.271	5*	96	11		1.8
Total 3	19	13	.594	53	47	2-1	0-0	303	285	133	31	8	106-2	249	3.71	115	.248	.315	94-0-15	.245	6	104	20		2.4

LOWRY, SAM Samuel Joseph B3.25.1920 Philadelphia PA D12.1.1992 Philadelphia PA BR/TR/5-11/170 d9.19 Mil 1944-46

YEAR TM LG	W	L	PCT	G	GS	CG-SHO	SV-BS	IP	H	R	HR	HB	BB-IB	SO	ERA	AERA	OAV	OOB	AB-HR-SH	AVG	PB	SUP	APR	DL	PW
1942 Phi A	0	0	—	1	0	0	0	3	3	2	0	1	1	1	6.00	63	.250	.308	1	.000	-0		-1		0.0
1943 Phi A	0	0	—	5	0	0	0	18	18	10	1	0	9	3	5.00	68	.269	.355	6	.167	-0		-3		-0.1
Total 2	0	0	—	6	0	0	0	21	21	12	1	1	10	4	5.14	67	.266	.348	7	.143	-0		-4		-0.1

LOYND, MIKE Michael Wallace B3.26.1964 St.Louis MO BR/TR/6-4/210* [TexA86 7/163] d7.24 Col Florida St.

YEAR TM LG	W	L	PCT	G	GS	CG-SHO	SV-BS	IP	H	R	HR	HB	BB-IB	SO	ERA	AERA	OAV	OOB	AB-HR-SH	AVG	PB	SUP	APR	DL	PW
1986 Tex A	2	2	.500	9	8	0	1-0	42	49	30	4	2	19-1	33	5.36	81	.290	.365	0	—	0	118	-5		-0.5
1987 Tex A	1	5	.167	26	8	0	1-0	69.1	82	53	14	1	38-0	48	6.10	74	.287	.370	0	—	0	93	-12		-0.9
Total 2	3	7	.300	35	16	0	2-0	111.1	131	83	18	3	57-1	81	5.82	76	.288	.368	0	—	0	105	-17		-1.4

LUBY, PAT John Perkins B6.1869 Charleston SC D4.24.1899 Charleston SC TR/6-0/185 d6.16

YEAR TM LG	W	L	PCT	G	GS	CG-SHO	SV-BS	IP	H	R	HR	HB	BB-IB	SO	ERA	AERA	OAV	OOB	AB-HR-SH	AVG	PB	SUP	APR	DL	PW
1890 Chi N	20	9	.690	34	31	26	1	267.2	226	129	6	15	95	85	3.19	115	.222	.297	116-3	.267	8*	104	19		2.3
1891 Chi N	8	11	.421	30	24	18	1	206	221	148	11	19	94	52	4.76	70	.264	.352	98-2	.245	7*	113	-26		-1.3
1892 Chi N	11	16	.407	31	27	24-1	0	252.1	248	157	10	10	103	66	3.07	108	.247	.323	92-2	.190	1*	73	1		0.2
1895 Lou N	1	5	.167	11	6	5	0	71.1	115	90	5	7	19	12	6.81	68	.357	.405	53	.283	3*	72	-21		-1.0
Total 4	40	41	.494	106	88	73-1	2	797.1	810	524	32	51	311	215	3.88	92	.254	.331	430-7	.235	18	95	-27		0.2

LUCAS, RED Charles Fred "The Nashville Narcissus" B4.28.1902 Columbia TN D7.9.1986 Nashville TN BL/TR/5-9.5/170 d4.19 ▲

YEAR TM LG	W	L	PCT	G	GS	CG-SHO	SV-BS	IP	H	R	HR	HB	BB-IB	SO	ERA	AERA	OAV	OOB	AB-HR-SH	AVG	PB	SUP	APR	DL	PW
1923 NY N	0	0	—	3	0	0	1	5.1	9	5	0	0	4	3	0.00	—	.346	.433	2	.000	-0		0		0.0
1924 Bos N	1	4	.200	27	4	1	0	83.2	112	60	5	6	18	30	5.16	74	.332	.377	33	.333	2*	67	-14		-0.5
1926 Cin N	8	5	.615	39	11	7-1	2	154	161	68	6	2	30	34	3.68	100	.277	.314	76-0-5	.303	6*	98	4		1.2
1927 Cin N	18	11	.621	37	23	19-4	2	239.2	231	96	6	0	39	51	3.38	112	.256	.287	150-0-6	.313	7*	97	17		3.1
1928 Cin N	13	9	.591	27	19	13-4	1	167.1	164	73	9	0	42	35	3.39	117	.258	.304	73-0-1	.315	6*	72	10		1.9
1929 Cin N	19	12	.613	32	32	28-2	0	270	267	119	14	1	58	72	3.60	127	.257	.297	140-0-2	.293	11*	101	31		4.3
1930 Cin N	14	16	.467	33	28	18-1	1	210.2	270	135	15	1	44	53	5.38	90	.315	.349	113-2-7	.336	15*	97	-10		0.2
1931 Cin N	14	13	.519	29	28	24-3	0	238	261	110	10	0	39	56	3.59	104	.280	.309	153-0-6	.281	11*	117	5		1.7
1932 Cin N	13	17	.433	31	31	28	0	269.1	261	110	10	1	35	63	2.94	131	.249	.274	150-0-3	.287	13*	82	26		4.4
1933 Cin N	10	16	.385	29	29	21-3	0	219.2	248	106	13	2	18	40	3.40	100	.289	.305	122-1-2	.287	12*	92	-1		1.3
1934 Pit N	10	9	.526	29	22	12-1	0	172.2	198	89	14	2	40	44	4.38	94	.283	.324	105-0-1	.219	3*	125	-2		0.0
1935 Pit N	8	6	.571	20	19	8-2	0	125.2	136	60	10	2	23	29	3.44	119	.272	.307	66-0-2	.318	8*	100	9		1.7
1936 Pit N	15	4	.789	27	22	12	0	175.2	178	70	7	3	26	53	3.18	128	.257	.287	108-0-3	.241	4*	121	19		2.2
1937 Pit N	8	10	.444	20	20	9-1	0	126.1	150	69	12	1	23	20	4.27	90	.290	.322	82	.268	5*	107	-5		-0.2
1938 Pit N	6	3	.667	13	13	4	0	84	90	33	5	1	16	19	3.54	107	.283	.319	46-0-0	.109	-2*	105	5		0.2
Total 15	157	135	.538	396	302	204-22	7	2542	2736	1203	136	22	455	602	3.72	107	.275	.308	1419-3-40	.283	98	101	94		21.5

LUCAS, GARY Gary Paul B11.8.1954 Riverside CA BL/TL/6-5/200* [SDN76 19/437] d4.16 Col Chapman

YEAR TM LG	W	L	PCT	G	GS	CG-SHO	SV-BS	IP	H	R	HR	HB	BB-IB	SO	ERA	AERA	OAV	OOB	AB-HR-SH	AVG	PB	SUP	APR	DL	PW
1980 SD N	5	8	.385	46	1	0	3-1	150	138	59	8	1	43-14	85	3.24	106	.250	.302	35-0-7	.171	-0	87	3		0.3
1981 SD N	7	7	.500	57	0	0	13-4	90	78	26	1	3	36-15	53	2.00	162	.247	.325	10-0-2	.100	-1		11		2.1
1982 SD N	1	10	.091	65	0	0	16-9	97.1	89	42	5	1	29-7	64	3.24	106	.245	.298	14-0-3	.000	-1		1		0.1
1983 SD N	5	8	.385	62	0	0	17-6	91	85	38	9	0	34-11	60	2.87	122	.245	.310	12	.000	-1		4		0.5
1984 Mon N	0	3	.000	55	0	0	8-2	53	54	20	4	0	20-5	42	2.72	127	.267	.330	4	.000	-0		4		0.3
1985 Mon N	6	2	.750	49	0	0	1-3	67.2	63	29	6	0	24-8	31	3.19	108	.251	.314	5	.000	-1		1	41	0.0
1986 †Cal A	4	1	.800	27	0	0	2-2	45.2	45	19	1	0	6-0	31	3.15	131	.253	.276	0	—	0		4	101	0.5
1987 Cal A	1	5	.167	48	0	0	3-3	74.1	66	41	7	2	35-5	43	3.63	119	.241	.329	0	—	0		3		0.3
Total 8	29	44	.397	409	18	0	63-30	669	618	274	41	7	227-65	410	3.01	118	.249	.310	80-0-12	.087	-4	87	31	142	4.1

LUCAS, RAY Ray Wesley "Luke" B10.2.1908 Springfield OH D10.9.1969 Harrison MI BR/TR/6-2/175 d9.28

YEAR TM LG	W	L	PCT	G	GS	CG-SHO	SV-BS	IP	H	R	HR	HB	BB-IB	SO	ERA	AERA	OAV	OOB	AB-HR-SH	AVG	PB	SUP	APR	DL	PW
1929 NY N	0	0	—	3	0	0	0	8	3	0	0	0	3	1	0.00	—	.111	.200	2	.500	0		4		0.2
1930 NY N	0	0	—	6	0	0	0	10.1	9	8	2	1	10	1	6.97	68	.265	.444	1	.000	-0		-2		-0.1
1931 NY N	0	0	—	1	0	0	0	2	1	1	1	0	1	0	4.50	82	.143	.250	0	—	0		0		0.0
1933 Bro N	0	0	—	2	0	0	0	5	6	4	1	0	4	0	7.20	45	.316	.458	0	—	0		-2		-0.1
1934 Bro N	1	1	.500	10	2	0	0	30.2	39	24	2	3	14	3	6.75	58	.328	.412	6-0-1	.333	1	122	-9		-0.3
Total 5	1	1	.500	22	2	0	0	56	58	37	5	5	32	5	5.79	71	.282	.391	9-0-1	.333	1	122	-9		-0.3

LUCEY, JOE Joseph Earl "Scootch" B3.27.1897 Holyoke MA D7.30.1980 Holyoke MA BR/TR/6-0/168 d7.6.1920 Col Catholic America

YEAR TM LG	W	L	PCT	G	GS	CG-SHO	SV-BS	IP	H	R	HR	HB	BB-IB	SO	ERA	AERA	OAV	OOB	AB-HR-SH	AVG	PB	SUP	APR	DL	PW
1925 Bos A	1	0	1.000	11	1	0	0	18	20	16	0	1	14	2	9.00	50	.360	.500	15	.133	-1*	102	-8		-0.6

LUCID, CON Cornelius Cecil B2.24.1874 Dublin, Ireland D6.25.1931 Houston TX 5-7/170 d5.1

YEAR TM LG	W	L	PCT	G	GS	CG-SHO	SV-BS	IP	H	R	HR	HB	BB-IB	SO	ERA	AERA	OAV	OOB	AB-HR-SH	AVG	PB	SUP	APR	DL	PW
1893 Lou N	0	1	.000	2	1	0	0	6	10	14	0	1	10	0	15.00	29	.357	.538	3	.333	0	16	-8		-0.8
1894 Bro N	5	3	.625	10	9	7	0	71.1	87	68	6	9	44	15	6.56	76	.298	.406	33	.212	-2	114	-12		-1.1
1895 Bro N	10	7	.588	21	19	12-2	0	137	164	113	4	7	72	24	5.52	80	.292	.380	53-0-2	.245	2	114	-20		-1.6
Phi N	6	3	.667	10	10	7-1	0	69.2	80	56	3	9	35	19	5.94	80	.284	.380	29-0-1	.345	4	128	-7		-0.4
Year	16	10	.615	31	29	19-3	0	206.2	244	169	7	16	107	43	5.66	80	.289	.380	82-0-3	.280	6	119	-21		-2.0
1896 Phi N	1	4	.200	5	5	4	0	42	75	43	2	2	17	3	8.36	52	.383	.437	16-0-1	.125	-2	69	-15		-1.4
1897 StL N	1	5	.167	6	6	5	0	49	66	46	0	0	26	4	3.67	120	.319	.395	17	.176	-0	49	-3		-0.2
Total 5	23	23	.500	54	50	36-3	0	375	482	340	15	28	204	65	6.02	76	.308	.397	151-0-4	.238	2	103	-65		-5.5

LUCIER, LOU Louis Joseph B3.23.1918 Northbridge MA BR/TR/5-8/160 d4.23

YEAR TM LG	W	L	PCT	G	GS	CG-SHO	SV-BS	IP	H	R	HR	HB	BB-IB	SO	ERA	AERA	OAV	OOB	AB-HR-SH	AVG	PB	SUP	APR	DL	PW
1943 Bos A	3	4	.429	16	9	3	1	74	94	35	1	2	33	23	3.89	85	.322	.394	20	.200	-0	99	-5		-0.2
1944 Bos A	0	0	—	3	0	0	0	5.1	7	3	0	1	7	2	5.06	67	.292	.452	1	.000	-0		-1		-0.1
Phi N	0	0	—	1	0	0	0	2	3	3	0	0	2	1	13.50	27	.333	.455	0	—	0		-2		-0.1
1945 Phi N	0	1	.000	13	0	0	1	20.1	14	9	1	0	5	5	2.21	173	.194	.247	4	.250	0		3		0.2
Total 3	3	5	.375	33	9	3	2	101.2	118	50	2	2	47	31	3.81	90	.297	.374	25	.200	-0	99	-5		-0.2

LUDOLPH, WILLIE William Francis "Wee Willie" B1.21.1900 San Francisco CA D4.8.1952 Oakland CA BR/TR/6-1.5/170 d5.28 Col St. Marys (CA)

YEAR TM LG	W	L	PCT	G	GS	CG-SHO	SV-BS	IP	H	R	HR	HB	BB-IB	SO	ERA	AERA	OAV	OOB	AB-HR-SH	AVG	PB	SUP	APR	DL	PW
1924 Det A	0	0	—	2	0	0	0											.348							0.0

LUDWICK, ERIC Eric David B12.14.1971 Whiteman Afb MO BR/TR/6-5/210* [NYN93 2/50] d9.1 b-Ryan Col Nevada-Las Vegas

YEAR TM LG	W	L	PCT	G	GS	CG-SHO	SV-BS	IP	H	R	HR	HB	BB-IB	SO	ERA	AERA	OAV	OOB	AB-HR-SH	AVG	PB	SUP	APR	DL	PW
1996 StL N	0	1	.000	6	1	0	0-0	10	11	11	4	1	3-0	12	9.00	47	.275	.333	2	.000	-0	64	-5		-0.5
1997 StL N	0	1	.000	5	0	0	0-0	6.2	12	7	1	0	6-0	7	9.45	44	.400	.500	0	—	-0		-4		-0.5
Oak A	1	4	.200	6	5	0	0-0	24	32	24	7	1	16-1	14	8.25	56	.330	.430	2	.000	-0	72	-10		-1.5

YEAR	TM LG	W	L	PCT	G	GS	CG-SHO	SV-BS	IP	H	R	HR	HB	BB-IB	SO	ERA	AERA	OAV	OOB	AB-HR-SH	AVG	PB	SUP	APR	DL	PW
1998	Fla N	1	4	.200	13	6	0	0-1	32.2	46	31	7	0	17-1	27	7.44	55	.333	.401	7	.000	-1	147	-13	123	-1.8
1999	Tor A	0	0	—	1	0	0	0-0	1	3	3	0	0	2-0	0	27.00	18	.500	.625	0	—	0		-2		-0.1
Total 4		2	10	.167	31	12	0	0-1	74.1	104	76	19	2	44-2	60	8.35	51	.334	.417	11	.000	-1	107	-34	123	-4.4

LUEBBER, STEVE Stephen Lee B7.9.1949 Clinton MO BR/TR/6-3/195(175-210) [MinA67 13/257] d6.27

YEAR	TM LG	W	L	PCT	G	GS	CG-SHO	SV-BS	IP	H	R	HR	HB	BB-IB	SO	ERA	AERA	OAV	OOB	AB-HR-SH	AVG	PB	SUP	APR	DL	PW
1971	Min A	2	5	.286	18	12	0	1-0	68	73	42	7	4	37-3	35	5.03	70	.278	.373	19-0-2	.053	-2*	120	-11		-1.2
1972	Min A	0	0	—	2	0	0	0-0	2.1	3	0	0	0	2-1	1	0.00	—	.333	.417	0	—	0		1		0.1
1976	Min A	4	5	.444	38	12	2-1	2-0	119.1	109	57	9	1	62-3	45	4.30	89	.248	.341	0	—	0	129	-4		-0.3
1979	Tor A	0	0	—	1	0	0	0-0	0	2	1	0	0	1-0	0	∞	—	1.000	1.000	0	—	0		-1		-0.1
1981	Bal A	0	0	—	7	0	0	0-0	16.2	26	14	3	1	4-1	12	7.56	48	.366	.403	0	—	0		-6		-0.3
Total 5		6	10	.375	66	24	2-1	3-0	206.1	213	114	19	6	106-8	93	4.62	77	.271	.360	19-0-2	.053	-2	124	-21		-1.8

LUEBBERS, LARRY Larry Christopher B10.11.1969 Cincinnati OH BR/TR/6-6/190(190-210) [CinN90 8/216] d7.3 Col Kentucky

YEAR	TM LG	W	L	PCT	G	GS	CG-SHO	SV-BS	IP	H	R	HR	HB	BB-IB	SO	ERA	AERA	OAV	OOB	AB-HR-SH	AVG	PB	SUP	APR	DL	PW
1993	Cin N	2	5	.286	14	14	0	0-0	77.1	74	49	7	1	38-3	38	4.54	89	.261	.345	24-0-1	.250	1	89	-7		-0.5
1999	StL N	3	3	.500	8	8	1	0-0	45.2	46	27	8	3	16-0	16	5.12	90	.261	.348	16-0-1	.125	-0	120	-2		-0.2
2000	Cin N	0	2	.000	14	1	0	1-0	20.1	27	15	1	0	12-2	9	6.20	77	.333	.419	0	—	0	19	-3		-0.2
Total 3		5	10	.333	36	23	1	1-0	143.1	147	91	16	4	66-5	63	4.96	87	.272	.352	40-0-2	.200	1	96	-12		-0.9

LUEBKE, DICK Richard Raymond B4.8.1935 Chicago IL D12.4.1974 San Diego CA BR/TL/6-4/200 d8.11

YEAR	TM LG	W	L	PCT	G	GS	CG-SHO	SV-BS	IP	H	R	HR	HB	BB-IB	SO	ERA	AERA	OAV	OOB	AB-HR-SH	AVG	PB	SUP	APR	DL	PW
1962	Bal A	0	1	.000	10	0	0	0	13.1	12	4	0	0	6-0	7	2.70	137	.250	.327	0	—	0		2		0.1

LUECKEN, RICK Richard Fred B11.15.1960 McAllen TX BR/TR/6-6/210* [SeaA83 27/667] d6.6 Col Texas A&M-Commerce

YEAR	TM LG	W	L	PCT	G	GS	CG-SHO	SV-BS	IP	H	R	HR	HB	BB-IB	SO	ERA	AERA	OAV	OOB	AB-HR-SH	AVG	PB	SUP	APR	DL	PW
1989	KC A	2	1	.667	19	0	0	1-0	23.2	23	9	3	0	13-4	16	3.42	113	.258	.353	0	—	0		2		0.2
1990	Atl N	1	4	.200	36	0	0	1-2	53	73	36	5	3	30-7	35	5.77	70	.336	.422	3	.333	1		-9		-0.7
	Tor A	0	0	—	1	0	0	0-0	1	2	1	1	0	1-0	0	9.00	44	.500	.600	0	—	0		-1		0.0
Total 2		3	5	.375	56	0	0	2-2	77.2	98	46	9	3	44-11	51	5.10	78	.316	.405	3	.333	1		-8		-0.5

LUFF, HENRY Henry T. B9.14.1856 Philadelphia PA D10.11.1916 Philadelphia PA 5-11/175 d4.19 ▲

YEAR	TM LG	W	L	PCT	G	GS	CG-SHO	SV-BS	IP	H	R	HR	HB	BB-IB	SO	ERA	AERA	OAV	OOB	AB-HR-SH	AVG	PB	SUP	APR	DL	PW
1875	NH NA	1	6	.143	10	7	5	0	68.2	98	91		2	3	5	3.28	63	.295	.301	166-2	.271	3*	90	-12		-0.7

LUGO, URBANO Rafael Urbano (Colina) B8.12.1962 Punto Fijo, Venez BR/TR/6-0/190(185-200) d4.28

YEAR	TM LG	W	L	PCT	G	GS	CG-SHO	SV-BS	IP	H	R	HR	HB	BB-IB	SO	ERA	AERA	OAV	OOB	AB-HR-SH	AVG	PB	SUP	APR	DL	PW
1985	Cal A	3	4	.429	20	10	1	0-0	83	86	36	10	4	29-1	42	3.69	112	.274	.341	0	—	0	95	5	15	0.4
1986	Cal A	1	1	.500	6	3	0	0-0	21.1	21	9	4	0	6-0	9	3.80	109	.266	.318	0	—	0	110	1	59	0.1
1987	Cal A	0	2	.000	7	5	0	0-0	28	42	34	8	0	18-0	24	9.32	46	.339	.420	0	—	0	101	-17		-1.0
1988	Cal A	0	0	—	1	0	0	0-0	2	2	2	1	0	1-0	1	9.00	43	.250	.333	0	—	0		-1		-0.1
1989	Mon N	0	0	—	3	0	0	0-0	4	4	3	1	0	0-0	3	6.75	53	.250	.250	0	—	0		-1		-0.1
1990	Det A	2	0	1.000	13	1	0	0-1	24.1	30	19	9	3	13-1	12	7.03	57	.313	.411	0	—	0	114	-7		-0.5
Total 6		6	7	.462	50	19	1	0-1	162.2	185	103	33	7	67-2	91	5.31	78	.290	.363	0	—	0	101	-20	74	-1.2

LUHRSEN, WILD BILL William Ferdinand B4.14.1884 Buckley IL D8.15.1973 Little Rock AR BR/TR/5-9/165 d8.23

YEAR	TM LG	W	L	PCT	G	GS	CG-SHO	SV-BS	IP	H	R	HR	HB	BB-IB	SO	ERA	AERA	OAV	OOB	AB-HR-SH	AVG	PB	SUP	APR	DL	PW
1913	Pit N	3	1	.750	5	3	2	0	29	25	10	3	2	16	11	2.48	122	.248	.361	10-0-1	.000	-1	91	2		0.2

LUKASIEWICZ, MARK Mark Francis B3.8.1973 Jersey City NJ BL/TL/6-5/240* [TorA93 1/41] d5.11 Col Oklahoma St.

YEAR	TM LG	W	L	PCT	G	GS	CG-SHO	SV-BS	IP	H	R	HR	HB	BB-IB	SO	ERA	AERA	OAV	OOB	AB-HR-SH	AVG	PB	SUP	APR	DL	PW
2001	Ana A	0	2	.000	24	0	0	0-0	22.1	21	17	6	2	9-2	25	6.04	77	.247	.330	0	—	0		-4		-0.3
2002	Ana A	2	0	1.000	17	0	0	0-0	14	17	6	0	0	9-0	15	3.86	116	.298	.388	0	—	0		1		0.1
Total 2		2	2	.500	41	0	0	0-0	36.1	38	23	6	2	18-2	40	5.20	88	.268	.354	0	—	0		-3		-0.2

LUKENS, AL Albert P. B11.1868 PA TR/5-9/168 d6.23

YEAR	TM LG	W	L	PCT	G	GS	CG-SHO	SV-BS	IP	H	R	HR	HB	BB-IB	SO	ERA	AERA	OAV	OOB	AB-HR-SH	AVG	PB	SUP	APR	DL	PW
1894	Phi N	0	1	.000	3	2	1	0	15	26	22	0	3	10	0	10.20	50	.377	.476	8	.000	-2	117	-8		-0.5

LUMENTI, RALPH Raphael Anthony B12.21.1936 Milford MA BL/TL/6-3/185* d9.7 Col Massachusetts

YEAR	TM LG	W	L	PCT	G	GS	CG-SHO	SV-BS	IP	H	R	HR	HB	BB-IB	SO	ERA	AERA	OAV	OOB	AB-HR-SH	AVG	PB	SUP	APR	DL	PW
1957	Was A	0	1	.000	3	2	0	0	9.1	9	7	1	1	5-0	8	6.75	58	.250	.357	2	.000	-0	80	-3		-0.3
1958	Was A	1	2	.333	8	4	0	0	21	21	20	2	1	36-0	20	8.57	44	.266	.500	8	.250	0	71	-10		-1.2
1959	Was A	0	0	—	2	0	0	0	3	2	0	0	0	1-0	2	0.00	—	.200	.273	0	—	0		1		0.1
Total 3		1	3	.250	13	6	0	0	33.1	32	27	3	2	42-0	30	7.29	53	.256	.450	10	.200	-0	74	-12		-1.4

LUNA, MEMO Guillermo Romero B6.25.1930 Mexico City, Distrito Federal, Mexico BL/TL/6-0/168 d4.20

YEAR	TM LG	W	L	PCT	G	GS	CG-SHO	SV-BS	IP	H	R	HR	HB	BB-IB	SO	ERA	AERA	OAV	OOB	AB-HR-SH	AVG	PB	SUP	APR	DL	PW
1954	StL N	0	1	.000	1	1	0	0	0.2	2	2	0	0	2	0	27.00	15	.667	.667	0	—	0	130	-2		-0.3

LUNDBOM, JACK John Frederick B3.10.1877 Manistee MI D10.31.1949 Manistee MI BR/TR/6-0.5/187 d5.9

YEAR	TM LG	W	L	PCT	G	GS	CG-SHO	SV-BS	IP	H	R	HR	HB	BB-IB	SO	ERA	AERA	OAV	OOB	AB-HR-SH	AVG	PB	SUP	APR	DL	PW
1902	Cle A	1	1	.500	8	3	1	0	34	48	35	1	1	16	7	6.62	52	.333	.404	15	.267	1	104	-11		-0.5

LUNDGREN, CARL Carl Leonard B2.16.1880 Marengo IL D8.21.1934 Marengo IL BR/TR/5-11/175 d6.19 Col Illinois

YEAR	TM LG	W	L	PCT	G	GS	CG-SHO	SV-BS	IP	H	R	HR	HB	BB-IB	SO	ERA	AERA	OAV	OOB	AB-HR-SH	AVG	PB	SUP	APR	DL	PW
1902	Chi N	9	9	.500	18	18	17-1	0	160	158	59	2	6	45	68	1.97	137	.258	.315	66-0-2	.106	-4*	92	12		0.7
1903	Chi N	11	9	.550	27	20	16	3	193	191	103	1	6	60	67	2.94	107	.262	.323	61-0-3	.115	-1	97	3		0.6
1904	Chi N	17	9	.654	31	27	25-2	1	242	203	97	2	4	77	106	2.60	102	.226	.290	90-0-2	.222	4	99	3		1.0
1905	Chi N	13	5	.722	23	19	16-3	0	169.1	132	58	3	4	62	69	2.23	134	.220	.293	61-0-2	.180	1*	126	14		1.6
1906	Chi N	17	6	.739	27	24	21-5	2	207.2	160	63	3	8	89	103	2.21	119	.221	.313	67-0-6	.179	2*	107	13		1.2
1907	Chi N	18	7	.720	28	25	21-7	0	207	130	42	0	2	92	84	1.17	212	.185	.282	66-0-7	.106	-3	89	29		3.5
1908	Chi N	6	9	.400	23	15	9-1	0	138.2	149	72	5	0	56	38	4.22	56	.284	.353	47-0-5	.149	-1	112	-23		-2.7
1909	Chi N	0	1	.000	2	1	0	0	4.1	6	7	0	0	4	0	4.15	61	.353	.476	2	.500	0	83	0		-0.1
Total 8		91	55	.623	179	149	125-19	6	1322	1129	496	16	35	476	535	2.42	113	.235	.308	460-0-27	.157	0	102	51		6.5

LUNDGREN, DEL Ebin Delmar B9.21.1899 Lindsborg KS D10.19.1984 Lindsborg KS BR/TR/5-8/160 d4.27

YEAR	TM LG	W	L	PCT	G	GS	CG-SHO	SV-BS	IP	H	R	HR	HB	BB-IB	SO	ERA	AERA	OAV	OOB	AB-HR-SH	AVG	PB	SUP	APR	DL	PW
1924	Pit N	0	1	.000	8	1	0	0	16.2	25	13	0	1	3	4	6.48	59	.403	.439	3	.000	-1	44	-4		-0.3
1926	Bos A	0	2	.000	18	2	0	0	31	35	28	2	3	28	11	7.55	54	.307	.455	4	.000	-0	62	-11		-0.6
1927	Bos A	5	12	.294	30	17	5-2	0	136.1	160	100	7	4	87	39	6.27	67	.302	.405	44-0-3	.159	-2	91	-25		-2.1
Total 3		5	15	.250	56	20	5-2	0	184	220	141	9	8	118	54	6.51	64	.312	.416	51-0-3	.137	-3	86	-40		-3.1

LUNDQUIST, DAVID David Bruce B6.4.1973 Beverly MA BR/TR/6-2/200* [ChiA93 5/145] d4.6 Col Nevada-Las Vegas

YEAR	TM LG	W	L	PCT	G	GS	CG-SHO	SV-BS	IP	H	R	HR	HB	BB-IB	SO	ERA	AERA	OAV	OOB	AB-HR-SH	AVG	PB	SUP	APR	DL	PW
1999	Chi A	1	1	.500	17	0	0	0-0	22	28	21	3	1	12-0	18	8.59	58	.315	.394	0	—	0		-8		-0.1
2001	SD N	0	1	.000	17	0	0	0-1	19.2	20	13	1	1	7-1	19	5.95	70	.260	.326	0	—	0		-3		-0.2
2002	SD N	0	0	—	3	0	0	0-1	2.2	8	5	0	1	5-2	0	16.88	23	.615	.737	0	—	0		-4	93	-0.2
Total 3		1	2	.333	37	0	0	0-2	44.1	56	39	4	3	24-3	37	7.92	57	.313	.397	0	—	0		-15	93	-1.0

LUQUE, DOLF Adolfo Domingo De Guzman "The Pride of Havana" B8.4.1890 Havana, Cuba D7.3.1957 Havana, Cuba BR/TR/5-7/160 d5.20 C9

YEAR	TM LG	W	L	PCT	G	GS	CG-SHO	SV-BS	IP	H	R	HR	HB	BB-IB	SO	ERA	AERA	OAV	OOB	AB-HR-SH	AVG	PB	SUP	APR	DL	PW
1914	Bos N	0	1	.000	2	1	1	0	8.2	5	5	0	0	4	1	4.15	66	.167	.265	2-0-1	.000	-0	26	-1		-0.1
1915	Bos N	0	0	—	2	1	0	0	5	6	3	0	0	4	3	3.60	72	.286	.400	2	.000	-0*	115	-1		-0.1
1918	Cin N	6	3	.667	12	10	9-1	0	83	84	44	1	1	32	26	3.80	70	.277	.348	32-0-1	.321	5*	147	-10		-0.1
1919	†Cin N	10	3	.769	30	9	6-2	3	106	89	35	2	2	36	40	2.63	105	.237	.308	32-0-2	.125	-0*	118	3		0.8
1920	Cin N	13	9	.591	37	23	10-1	1	207.2	168	65	5	4	60	72	2.51	121	.225	.286	64-0-5	.266	4	114	16		2.2
1921	Cin N	17	19	.472	41	36	25-3	3	304	318	132	13	1	64	102	3.38	106	.273	.312	111-0-5	.270	6*	91	11		2.0
1922	Cin N	13	23	.361	39	33	18	0	261	266	123	7	1	72	79	3.31	121	.268	.318	86-0-3	.209	2	71	19		2.2
1923	Cin N	27	8	.771	41	37	28-6	2	322	279	90	2	5	88	151	1.93	200	.235	.291	104-1-10	.202	2*	95	70		7.4
1924	Cin N	10	15	.400	31	28	13-2	0	219.1	229	99	5	2	53	86	3.16	119	.271	.316	73-1-3	.178	-1*	88	13		1.1
1925	Cin N	16	18	.471	36	36	22-4	0	291	263	109	7	2	78	140	2.63	156	.239	.291	102-2-4	.255	5*	76	48		5.4
1926	Cin N	13	16	.448	34	31	16-1	0	233.2	231	87	7	2	77	76	3.43	108	.260	.321	83-0-7	.346	8	87	1		1.1
1927	Cin N	13	12	.520	29	29	17-2	0	230.2	225	103	10	9	56	76	3.20	118	.260	.305	83-0-7	.217	2	86	14		1.1
1928	Cin N	11	10	.524	33	29	11-1	0	234.1	254	112	12	2	84	72	3.57	111	.284	.347	67-0-5	.119	-1	90	8		0.9
1929	Cin N	5	16	.238	32	22	8	0	176	213	103	7	2	56	43	4.50	101	.310	.364	54-1-4	.278	4	73	0		1.1
1930	Bro N	14	8	.636	35	24	16-2	2	199	221	107	18	0	58	62	4.30	114	.287	.337	75-0-4	.240	1	128	17		1.1
1931	Bro N	7	6	.538	19	15	5	0	102.2	122	59	6	1	27	25	4.56	84	.297	.342	30-0-2	.133	-0	106	-8		-0.1
1932	NY N	6	7	.462	38	5	1	5	110	128	53	4	0	32	32	4.01	93	.290	.338	25	.040	-2	50	-1		-0.1
1933	†NY N	8	2	.800	35	0	0	4	80.1	75	27	4	0	19	23	2.69	119	.251	.296	19	.263	1		6		0.1
1934	NY N	4	3	.571	26	0	0	7	42.1	54	20	3	1	12	11	3.83	101	.316	.381	7-0-1	.286	1		1		0.1
1935	NY N	1	0	1.000	2	0	0	0	3.2	1	0	0	0	3	2	0.00	—	.077	.143	1-0-1	1.000	0		2		0.1
Total 20		194	179	.520	550	367	206-26	28	3220.1	3231	1412	113	26		1130	3.24	117	.265	.318	1043-5-65	.227	37	92	208		26.

YEAR	TM LG	W	L	PCT	G	GS	CG-SHO	SV-BS	IP	H	R	HR	HB	BB-IB	SO	ERA	AERA	OAV	OOB	AB-HR-SH	AVG	PB	SUP	APR	DL	PW

LUSH, JOHNNY   John Charles   B10.8.1885 Williamsport PA   D11.18.1946 Beverly Hills CA   BL/TL/5-9.5/165   d4.22 ▲

YEAR	TM LG	W	L	PCT	G	GS	CG-SHO	SV-BS	IP	H	R	HR	HB	BB-IB	SO	ERA	AERA	OAV	OOB	AB-HR-SH	AVG	PB	SUP	APR	DL	PW
1904	Phi N	0	6	.000	7	6	3	0	42.2	52	40	0	7	27	27	3.59	75	.301	.415	369-2-6	.276	2*	81	-9		-0.9
1905	Phi N	2	0	1.000	2	2	1	0	17	12	4	0	1	8	8	1.59	184	.194	.296	16-0-1	.313	1*	235	3		0.4
1906	Phi N	18	15	.545	37	36	24-5	0	281	254	128	2	16	119	151	2.37	110	.236	.321	212	.264	7*	123	0		1.0
1907	Phi N	3	5	.375	8	8	5-2	0	57.1	48	22	0	3	21	20	2.98	81	.227	.306	40	.200	1*	74	-2		-0.2
	StL N	7	10	.412	20	19	15-3	0	144	132	63	2	8	42	71	2.50	100	.246	.311	82-0-1	.280	5*	87	-1		0.7
	Year	10	15	.400	28	27	20-5	0	201.1	180	85	2	11	63	91	2.64	94	.241	.309	122-0-1	.254	6	83	-3		0.5
1908	StL N	11	18	.379	38	32	23-3	1	250.2	221	102	6	11	57	93	2.12	111	.231	.283	89-0-4	.169	1*	80	3		0.6
1909	StL N	11	18	.379	34	28	21-2	0	221.1	215	96	1	10	69	66	3.13	81	.260	.324	92-0-1	.239	4*	116	-11		-0.8
1910	StL N	14	13	.519	36	25	13-1	1	225.1	235	116	6	7	70	54	3.20	93	.276	.336	93	.226	4*	124	-11		-0.9
Total	7	66	85	.437	182	155	105-16	2	1239.1	1169	571	17	63	413	490	2.68	97	.249	.318	993-2-13	.254	24	106	-28		-0.1

LYLE, SPARKY   Albert Walter   B7.22.1944 DuBois PA   BL/TL/6-1/192(182-198)   d7.4

YEAR	TM LG	W	L	PCT	G	GS	CG-SHO	SV-BS	IP	H	R	HR	HB	BB-IB	SO	ERA	AERA	OAV	OOB	AB-HR-SH	AVG	PB	SUP	APR	DL	PW
1967	Bos A	1	2	.333	27	0	0	5	43.1	33	13	3	2	14-1	42	2.28	153	.213	.283	8	.250	1		5		0.5
1968	Bos A	6	1	.857	49	0	0	11	65.2	67	25	6	0	14-2	52	2.74	115	.261	.298	8-0-1	.125	-0		2		0.2
1969	Bos A	8	3	.727	71	0	0	17-9	102.2	91	33	8	1	48-4	93	2.54	150	.240	.323	17	.118	-1		14		2.0
1970	Bos A	1	7	.125	63	0	0	20-10	67.1	62	37	5	1	34-5	51	3.88	103	.244	.334	13	.000	-1		-1		-0.3
1971	Bos A	6	4	.600	50	0	0	16-4	52.1	41	16	5	0	23-2	37	2.75	145	.228	.311	3-0-1	1.000	1		6		1.5
1972	NY A	9	5	.643	59	0	0	35-7	107.2	84	25	3	0	29-7	75	1.92	156	.216	.268	21-0-2	.190	1		14		3.1
1973	NY A★	5	9	.357	51	0	0	27-6	82.1	66	30	4	0	18-2	63	2.51	148	.216	.258	0	—	0		10		2.0
1974	NY A	9	3	.750	66	0	0	15-7	114	93	30	6	1	43-7	89	1.66	214	.226	.297	1	.000	-0		22		2.9
1975	NY A	5	7	.417	49	0	0	6-6	89.1	94	34	1	2	36-5	65	3.12	119	.275	.345	0	—	0		6		0.9
1976	†NY A☆	7	8	.467	64	0	0	23-8	103.2	82	33	5	0	42-7	61	2.26	151	.220	.302	0	—	0		12		2.3
1977	†NY A★	13	5	.722	72	0	0	26-8	137	131	41	7	2	33-6	68	2.17	183	.257	.302	0	—	0		26		4.3
1978	†NY A	9	3	.750	59	0	0	9-2	111.2	116	46	6	4	33-8	33	3.47	105	.278	.332	0	—	0		4		0.5
1979	Tex A	5	8	.385	67	0	0	13-7	95	93	37	9	0	28-6	48	3.13	133	.226	.283	0	—	0		11		1.6
1980	Tex A	3	2	.600	49	0	0	8-4	80.2	97	47	9	0	28-6	43	4.69	83	.306	.359	0	—	0		-7		-0.5
	Phi N	0	0	—	10	0	0	2-1	14	11	5	0	0	6-1	6	1.93	198	.220	.293	0	—	0		2		0.1
1981	†Phi N	9	6	.600	48	0	0	2-2	75	85	40	4	1	33-9	29	4.44	82	.301	.372	5-0-1	.400	1		-6		-1.0
1982	Phi N	3	3	.500	34	0	0	2-5	36.2	50	23	3	0	12-3	12	5.15	72	.327	.373	2	.500	1		-6		-0.8
	Chi A	0	0	—	11	0	0	1-0	12	11	4	0	0	7-0	6	3.00	138	.262	.360	0	—	0		2		0.1
Total	16	99	76	.566	899	0	0	238-86	1390.1	1292	519	84	14	481-81	873	2.88	126	.251	.313	78-0-5	.192	2		116		19.4

LYLE, JIM   James Charles   B7.24.1900 Lake MS   D10.10.1977 Williamsport PA   BR/TR/6-1/180   d10.2   Col Mississippi St.

YEAR	TM LG	W	L	PCT	G	GS	CG-SHO	SV-BS	IP	H	R	HR	HB	BB-IB	SO	ERA	AERA	OAV	OOB	AB-HR-SH	AVG	PB	SUP	APR	DL	PW
1925	Was A	0	0	—	1	0	0	0	3	5	2	0	0	1	3	6.00	70	.333	.375	0	—	0		0		0.0

LYNCH, ADRIAN   Adrian Ryan   B2.9.1897 Laurens IA   D3.16.1934 Davenport IA   BB/TR/6-1.5/185   d8.4   Col Notre Dame

YEAR	TM LG	W	L	PCT	G	GS	CG-SHO	SV-BS	IP	H	R	HR	HB	BB-IB	SO	ERA	AERA	OAV	OOB	AB-HR-SH	AVG	PB	SUP	APR	DL	PW
1920	StL A	2	0	1.000	3	2	1	0	22.1	23	15	1	1	17	8	5.24	75	.237	.406	9	.222	0	216	-3		-0.2

LYNCH, ED   Edward Francis   B2.25.1956 Brooklyn NY   BR/TR/6-6/210(207-230)   [TexA77 22/547]   d8.31   Col South Carolina-Aiken

YEAR	TM LG	W	L	PCT	G	GS	CG-SHO	SV-BS	IP	H	R	HR	HB	BB-IB	SO	ERA	AERA	OAV	OOB	AB-HR-SH	AVG	PB	SUP	APR	DL	PW
1980	NY N	1	1	.500	5	4	0	0-0	19.1	24	12	0	1	5-0	5	5.12	70	.304	.349	6	.333	0	74	-3		-0.2
1981	NY N	4	5	.444	17	13	0	0-0	80.1	79	32	6	1	21-2	27	2.91	121	.254	.302	21-0-2	.143	1	85	5		0.6
1982	NY N	4	8	.333	43	12	0	2-1	139.1	145	57	6	1	40-4	51	3.55	103	.273	.323	33-0-3	.000	-3	86	5		0.0
1983	NY N	10	10	.500	30	27	1	0-0	174.2	208	94	17	3	41-10	44	4.28	86	.302	.341	52-0-11	.154	-1	106	-11		-1.3
1984	NY N	9	8	.529	40	13	0	2-1	124	169	77	14	4	24-3	62	4.50	79	.324	.356	27-0-3	.222	1	88	-15		-1.9
1985	NY N	10	8	.556	31	29	6-1	0-0	191	188	76	19	1	27-1	65	3.44	102	.256	.281	52-0-9	.077	-2	103	-3		-0.1
1986	NY N	0	0	—	1	0	0	0-0	1.2	2	0	0	0	0-0	1	0.00	—	.286	.286	0	—	0		1	78	0.0
	Chi N	7	5	.583	23	13	1-1	0-0	99.2	105	48	10	1	23-6	57	3.79	107	.279	.319	30-0-1	.033	-2	98	2		-0.1
	Year	7	5	.583	24	13	1-1	0-0	101.1	107	48	10	1	23-6	58	3.73	109	.279	.319	30-0-1	.033	-2	98	3		-0.1
1987	Chi N	2	9	.182	58	8	0	4-2	110.1	130	74	17	2	48-7	80	5.38	80	.295	.366	16-0-2	.188	-0	71	-13		-1.2
Total	8	47	54	.465	248	119	8-2	8-4	940.1	1050	470	89	14	229-33	396	4.00	93	.284	.326	237-0-31	.114	-6	94	-26	78	-4.2

LYNCH, JACK   John H.   B2.5.1857 New York NY   D4.20.1923 Bronx NY   BR/TR/5-8/185   d5.2   Col Fordham

YEAR	TM LG	W	L	PCT	G	GS	CG-SHO	SV-BS	IP	H	R	HR	HB	BB-IB	SO	ERA	AERA	OAV	OOB	AB-HR-SH	AVG	PB	SUP	APR	DL	PW
1881	Buf N	10	9	.526	20	19	17	0	165.2	203	112	2		29	32	3.59	77	.297	.325	78	.167	-3*	98	-11		-1.2
1883	NY AA	13	15	.464	29	29	29-1	0	255	263	161	6		25	119	4.09	82	.250	.267	107	.187	-3	89	-19		-1.9
1884	NY AA	37	15	.712	55	53	53-5	0	496	420	225	10	10	42	292	2.67	117	.215	.236	198	.152	-7	114	28		1.5
1885	NY AA	23	21	.523	44	43	43-1	0	379	410	243	17	3	42	177	3.61	86	.263	.283	153	.196	1	100	-22		-2.1
1886	NY AA	20	30	.400	51	50	50-1	0	432.2	485	307	10	12	116	193	3.95	83	.271	.320	169	.160	-5	94	-33		-3.4
1887	NY AA	7	14	.333	21	21	21	0	187	245	158	8	4	36	45	5.10	83	.305	.338	83	.169	-4*	75	-15		-1.4
1890	Bro AA	0	1	.000	1	1	1	0	9	22	18	1	0	5	1	12.00	32	.449	.500	4	.750	2	207	-8		-0.4
Total	7	110	105	.512	221	216	214-8	0	1924.1	2048	1224	54	29	295	859	3.69	89	.260	.289	792	.173	-18	98	-80		-8.9

LYNCH, MIKE   Michael Joseph   B6.28.1880 Holyoke MA   D4.2.1927 Garrison NY   BR/TR/6-2/170   d6.21   Col Brown

YEAR	TM LG	W	L	PCT	G	GS	CG-SHO	SV-BS	IP	H	R	HR	HB	BB-IB	SO	ERA	AERA	OAV	OOB	AB-HR-SH	AVG	PB	SUP	APR	DL	PW
1904	Pit N	15	11	.577	27	24	24-1	0	222.2	200	90	1	15	91	95	2.71	101	.243	.330	87-0-1	.230	4*	114	1		0.4
1905	Pit N	17	8	.680	33	22	13	2	206.1	191	102	3	5	107	106	3.79	79	.254	.351	81-0-3	.136	-1	113	-14		-1.8
1906	Pit N	6	5	.545	18	12	7	0	119	101	48	2	8	31	48	2.42	110	.232	.295	39-0-4	.205	-0	100	2		0.1
1907	Pit N	2	2	.500	7	4	2	0	36	37	21	0	1	22	9	2.25	108	.282	.390	12-0-1	.250	1	139	-2		-0.1
	NY N	3	6	.333	12	10	7	1	72	68	34	3	0	30	34	3.38	73	.249	.323	27	.296	2	112	-7		-0.6
	Year	5	8	.385	19	14	9	1	108	105	56	3	1	52	43	3.00	82	.260	.346	39-0-1	.282	3	120	-7		-0.7
Total	4	43	32	.573	97	72	53-1	3	656	597	296	9	29	281	292	3.05	91	.248	.333	246-0-9	.203	5	112	-20		-2.0

LYNCH, TOM   Thomas S.   B1863 Peru IL   D5.13.1903 Peru IL   BL/5-11/175   d8.5

YEAR	TM LG	W	L	PCT	G	GS	CG-SHO	SV-BS	IP	H	R	HR	HB	BB-IB	SO	ERA	AERA	OAV	OOB	AB-HR-SH	AVG	PB	SUP	APR	DL	PW
1884	Chi N	0	0	—	1	1	0	0	7	7	4	1		3	2	2.57	122	.241	.313	4	.000	-1	85	0		0.0

LYNN, RED   Japhet Monroe   B12.27.1913 Kenney TX   D10.27.1977 Bellville TX   BR/TR/6-0/162   d4.25   Mil 1945

YEAR	TM LG	W	L	PCT	G	GS	CG-SHO	SV-BS	IP	H	R	HR	HB	BB-IB	SO	ERA	AERA	OAV	OOB	AB-HR-SH	AVG	PB	SUP	APR	DL	PW
1939	Det A	0	1	.000	4	0	0	0	8.1	11	8	2	1	3	3	8.64	57	.324	.395	2	.000	-0		-3		-0.3
	NY N	1	0	1.000	26	0	0	1	49.2	44	21	3	2	21	22	3.08	127	.240	.325	6	.000	-1		4		0.1
1940	NY N	4	3	.571	33	0	0	3	42.1	40	21	1	1	24	25	3.83	101	.247	.348	4	.000	-1		0		-0.1
1944	Chi N	5	4	.556	22	7	4-1	1	84.1	80	41	4	1	37	35	4.06	87	.251	.331	29	.207	0	143	-3		-0.2
Total	3	10	8	.556	85	7	4-1	5	184.2	175	91	12	5	85	85	3.95	96	.251	.336	41	.146	-1	143	-2		-0.5

LYON, BRANDON   Brandon James   B8.10.1979 Salt Lake City UT   BR/TR/6-1/175*   [TorA99 14/433]   d8.4   Col Dixie (UT) JC   [DL 2003 Pit N 7, 2004 Ari N 183]

YEAR	TM LG	W	L	PCT	G	GS	CG-SHO	SV-BS	IP	H	R	HR	HB	BB-IB	SO	ERA	AERA	OAV	OOB	AB-HR-SH	AVG	PB	SUP	APR	DL	PW
2001	Tor A	5	4	.556	11	11	0	0-0	63	63	31	6	1	15-0	35	4.29	107	.266	.305	0	—	0	73	3		0.3
2002	Tor A	1	4	.200	15	10	0	0-1	62	78	47	14	2	19-2	30	6.53	71	.308	.359	0	—	0	88	-12		-0.8
2003	Bos A	4	6	.400	49	0	0	9-3	59	73	33	6	2	19-5	50	4.12	113	.296	.346	0	—	0		2		0.4
2005	Ari N	0	2	.000	32	0	0	14-1	29.1	44	25	6	2	10-2	17	6.44	68	.341	.394	0	—	0		-7	92	-1.1
Total	4	10	16	.385	107	21	0	23-5	213.1	258	136	32	7	63-9	132	5.19	88	.298	.346	0	—	0	81	-14	314	-1.2

LYONS, AL   Albert Harold   B7.18.1918 St.Joseph MO   D12.20.1965 Inglewood CA   BR/TR/6-2/195   d4.19   Mil 1944-45

YEAR	TM LG	W	L	PCT	G	GS	CG-SHO	SV-BS	IP	H	R	HR	HB	BB-IB	SO	ERA	AERA	OAV	OOB	AB-HR-SH	AVG	PB	SUP	APR	DL	PW
1944	NY A	0	0	—	11	0	0	0	39.2	43	22	2	2	24	14	4.54	77	.291	.397	26	.346	2*		-4		0.0
1946	NY A	0	1	.000	2	1	0	0	8.1	15	5	0	1	6	4	5.40	64	.314	.429	4	.000	-1	99	-1		-0.2
1947	NY A	1	0	1.000	6	0	0	0	11	18	11	2	0	9	7	9.00	39	.367	.466	6	.667	2*		-6		-0.3
	Pit N	1	2	.333	13	0	0	0	28.1	36	24	4	1	12	16	7.31	58	.300	.368	10-1-0	.200	1*		-8		-0.6
1948	Bos N	1	0	1.000	7	0	0	0	12.2	11	11	1	0	8	5	7.82	49	.309	.397	12	.167	0*		-5		-0.3
Total	4	3	3	.500	39	1	0	0	100	125	73	9	4	59	46	6.30	59	.307	.400	58-1-0	.293	5	99	-24		-1.4

LYONS, CURT   Curt Russell   B10.17.1974 Greencastle IN   BR/TR/6-5/240   [CinN92 6/157]   d9.19

YEAR	TM LG	W	L	PCT	G	GS	CG-SHO	SV-BS	IP	H	R	HR	HB	BB-IB	SO	ERA	AERA	OAV	OOB	AB-HR-SH	AVG	PB	SUP	APR	DL	PW
1996	Cin N	2	0	1.000	3	3	0	0-0	16	17	8	1	1	7-0	14	4.50	95	.274	.357	5-0-1	.000	-1	112	0		-0.1

LYONS, GEORGE   George Tony "Smooth"   B1.25.1891 Bible Grove IL   D8.12.1981 Nevada MO   BR/TR/5-11/180   d9.6

YEAR	TM LG	W	L	PCT	G	GS	CG-SHO	SV-BS	IP	H	R	HR	HB	BB-IB	SO	ERA	AERA	OAV	OOB	AB-HR-SH	AVG	PB	SUP	APR	DL	PW
1920	StL N	2	1	.667	3	1	1	0	23.1	21	8	2	1	9	5	3.09	87	.262	.344	7	.143	-0	105	1		-0.2
1924	StL A	3	2	.600	26	6	2	3	77.2	97	52	2	5	45	25	5.21	87	.323	.420	20-0-2	.250	-0	131	-5		-0.2
Total	2	5	3	.625	29	7	3	3	101	118	60	4	6	54	30	4.72	88	.311	.405	27-0-2	.222	-0	126	-4		-0.1

LYONS, HERSH   Herschel Englebert   B7.23.1915 Fresno CA   BR/TR/5-11/195   d4.17   Col Occidental

YEAR	TM LG	W	L	PCT	G	GS	CG-SHO	SV-BS	IP	H	R	HR	HB	BB-IB	SO	ERA	AERA	OAV	OOB	AB-HR-SH	AVG	PB	SUP	APR	DL	PW
1941	StL N	0	0	—	1	0	0	0	1.1	1	0	0	0	3	1	0.00	—	.200	.500	0	—	0		0		0.1

YEAR	TM LG	W	L	PCT	G	GS	CG-SHO	SV-BS	IP	H	R	HR	HB	BB-IB	SO	ERA	AERA	OAV	OOB	AB-HR-SH	AVG	PB	SUP	APR	DL	PW

LYONS, TED Theodore Amar B12.28.1900 Lake Charles LA D7.25.1986 Sulphur LA BB/TR/5-11/200 d7.2 Mil 1943-45 M3/C6 HF1955 Col Baylor

YEAR	TM LG	W	L	PCT	G	GS	CG-SHO	SV-BS	IP	H	R	HR	HB	BB-IB	SO	ERA	AERA	OAV	OOB	AB-HR-SH	AVG	PB	SUP	APR	DL	PW
1923	Chi A	2	1	.667	9	1	0	0	22.2	30	21	2	1	15	6	6.35	62	.323	.422	5	.200	0	104	-7		-0.7
1924	Chi A	12	11	.522	41	22	12	3	216.1	279	143	10	2	72	52	4.87	85	.322	.375	77-0-4	.221	0	114	-20		-2.0
1925	Chi A	21	11	.656	43	32	19-5	3	262.2	274	111	7	2	83	45	3.26	128	.278	.335	97-0-9	.186	-3	104	28		2.8
1926	Chi A	18	16	.529	39	31	24-3	2	283.2	268	108	6	1	106	51	3.01	128	.252	.320	104-0-8	.212	-0*	86	29		3.3
1927	Chi A	22	14	.611	39	34	30-2	2	307.2	291	125	7	0	67	71	2.84	143	.251	.292	110-1-7	.255	5*	102	38		4.7
1928	Chi A	15	14	.517	39	27	21	6	240	276	133	11	2	68	60	3.98	102	.295	.344	91-0-5	.253	1*	100	-1		0.0
1929	Chi A	14	20	.412	37	31	21-1	0	259.1	276	136	11	2	76	57	4.10	105	.278	.331	91-0-4	.220	1*	88	7		1.1
1930	Chi A	22	15	.595	42	36	29-1	1	297.2	331	160	12	2	57	69	3.78	122	.285	.319	122-1-6	.311	8*	98	26		3.7
1931	Chi A	4	6	.400	22	12	7	0	101	117	50	6	0	33	16	4.01	106	.296	.350	33-0-3	.152	-1*	83	5		0.2
1932	Chi A	10	15	.400	33	26	19-1	2	230.2	243	104	10	3	71	58	3.28	132	.272	.327	73-1-6	.260	5*	74	28		3.1
1933	Chi A	10	21	.323	36	27	14-2	1	228	260	142	10	7	74	74	4.38	97	.280	.333	91-1-1	.286	6*	82	-7		-0.4
1934	Chi A	11	13	.458	30	24	21	1	205.1	249	138	15	2	66	53	4.87	97	.293	.345	97-1-4	.206	1*	95	-7		-0.4
1935	Chi A	15	6	.652	23	22	19-3	0	190.2	194	79	15	3	56	48	3.02	153	.262	.317	82-0-3	.220	-0*	84	30		3.2
1936	Chi A	10	13	.435	26	24	15-1	0	182	227	115	21	3	45	48	5.14	101	.305	.347	70-0-1	.157	-3	91	2		0.1
1937	Chi A	12	7	.632	22	22	11	0	169.1	182	86	21	1	45	45	4.15	111	.278	.326	57-0-6	.211	1*	89	11		1.2
1938	Chi A	9	11	.450	23	23	17-1	0	194.2	238	93	13	0	52	54	3.70	132	.299	.342	72-0-3	.194	-1*	86	26		2.2
1939	Chi A☆	14	6	.700	21	21	16	0	172.2	162	71	7	1	26	65	2.76	171	.247	.276	61-0-6	.295	4	90	32		3.7
1940	Chi A	12	8	.600	22	22	17-4	0	186.1	188	85	17	0	37	72	3.24	137	.252	.287	75-0-2	.240	2	112	21		2.1
1941	Chi A	12	10	.545	22	22	19-2	0	187.1	199	87	9	4	37	63	3.70	111	.269	.308	74-0-2	.270	4	114	10		1.7
1942	Chi A	14	6	.700	20	20	20-1	0	180.1	167	52	11	2	26	50	2.10	172	.245	.275	67-0-2	.239	4	109	29		3.8
1946	Chi A	1	4	.200	5	5	5	0	42.2	38	17	2	0	9	10	2.32	147	.235	.275	14-0-1	.000	-1	55	4		0.3
Total 21		260	230	.531	594	484	356-27	23	4161	4489	2056	223	31	1121	1073	3.67	118	.276	.324	1563-5-83	.233	32	95	284		33.5

LYONS, TOBY Thomas Arthur B3.27.1869 Cambridge MA D8.27.1920 Boston MA d4.18

YEAR	TM LG	W	L	PCT	G	GS	CG-SHO	SV-BS	IP	H	R	HR	HB	BB-IB	SO	ERA	AERA	OAV	OOB	AB-HR-SH	AVG	PB	SUP	APR	DL	PW
1890	Syr AA	0	2	.000	3	3	2	0	22.1	40	36	1	1	21	6	10.48	34	.377	.484	12	.333	1	254	-19		-1.1

LYSANDER, RICK Richard Eugene B2.21.1953 Huntington Park CA BR/TR/6-2/190* [OakA74 19/445] d4.12 Col Cal St.-Los Angeles

YEAR	TM LG	W	L	PCT	G	GS	CG-SHO	SV-BS	IP	H	R	HR	HB	BB-IB	SO	ERA	AERA	OAV	OOB	AB-HR-SH	AVG	PB	SUP	APR	DL	PW
1980	Oak A	0	0	—	5	0	0	0-0	13.2	24	13	3	0	4-0	5	7.90	48	.381	.418	0	—	0		-6		-0.3
1983	Min A	5	12	.294	61	4	1-1	3-5	125	132	63	8	2	43-12	58	3.38	127	.275	.332	0	—	0	80	7		0.9
1984	Min A	4	3	.571	36	0	0	5-2	56.2	62	23	2	0	27-7	22	3.49	121	.283	.357	0	—	0		5		0.6
1985	Min A	0	2	.000	35	1	0	3-2	61	72	43	3	0	22-2	26	6.05	73	.305	.362	0	—	0	41	-9		-0.8
Total 4		9	17	.346	137	5	1-1	11-9	256.1	290	142	16	2	96-21	111	4.28	104	.291	.350	0	—	0	72	-3		0.2

LYSTON, JOHN John Michael B5.28.1867 Baltimore MD D10.29.1909 Baltimore MD BR/TR/5-11/185 d8.29

YEAR	TM LG	W	L	PCT	G	GS	CG-SHO	SV-BS	IP	H	R	HR	HB	BB-IB	SO	ERA	AERA	OAV	OOB	AB-HR-SH	AVG	PB	SUP	APR	DL	PW
1891	Col AA	0	1	.000	1	1	1	0	6	10	6	0	1	6	1	10.50	33	.357	.486	2	.000	-0	36	-4		-0.4
1894	Cle N	0	0	—	1	1	0	0	3.2	5	6	1	0	4	0	9.82	56	.313	.450	2	.000	-0	103	-2		-0.2
Total 2		0	1	.000	2	2	1	0	9.2	15	14	1	1	10	1	10.24	41	.341	.473	4	.000	-0	79	-6		-0.5

MAAS, DUKE Duane Fredrick B1.31.1929 Utica MI D12.7.1976 Mt.Clemens MI BR/TR/5-10/170(165-176) d4.21

YEAR	TM LG	W	L	PCT	G	GS	CG-SHO	SV-BS	IP	H	R	HR	HB	BB-IB	SO	ERA	AERA	OAV	OOB	AB-HR-SH	AVG	PB	SUP	APR	DL	PW
1955	Det A	5	6	.455	18	16	5-2	0	86.2	91	52	7	2	50-3	42	4.88	79	.271	.366	30-0-2	.167	0	117	-10		-1.1
1956	Det A	0	7	.000	26	7	0	0	63.1	81	51	9	6	32-3	34	6.54	63	.313	.398	16	.188	0	86	-17		-1.6
1957	Det A	10	14	.417	45	26	8-2	6	219.1	210	92	23	4	65-7	116	3.28	118	.252	.307	71-1-5	.085	-4	85	12		0.9
1958	KC A	4	5	.444	10	7	3-1	1	55.1	44	25	3	1	13-0	19	3.90	100	.241	.290	17-0-1	.176	0	62	1		-0.4
	†NY A	7	3	.700	22	13	2-1	0	101.1	93	51	9	2	36-0	50	3.82	92	.242	.308	34-0-1	.088	-2	145	-4		-0.4
	Year	11	8	.579	32	20	5-2	1	156.2	142	76	12	3	49-0	69	3.85	95	.242	.302	51-0-2	.118	-1	114	-14		-2.2
1959	NY A	14	8	.636	38	21	3-1	4	138	149	82	14	2	53-1	67	4.43	82	.278	.342	40-0-5	.125	-1	114	-14		-2.2
1960	†NY A	5	1	.833	35	1	0	4	70.1	70	44	6	1	35-2	28	4.09	87	.265	.346	6	.000	0	25	-8		-0.7
1961	NY A	0	0	—	1	0	0	0	0.1	2	3	0	0	0-0	0	54.00	7	1.000	1.000	0	—	0		-2		-0.1
Total 7		45	44	.506	195	91	21-7	15	734.2	745	399	71	18	284-16	356	4.19	90	.264	.333	214-1-14	.117	-7	103	-42		-5.2

MABE, BOB Robert Lee B10.8.1929 Danville VA D1.9.2005 Danville VA BR/TR/5-11/165* d4.18

YEAR	TM LG	W	L	PCT	G	GS	CG-SHO	SV-BS	IP	H	R	HR	HB	BB-IB	SO	ERA	AERA	OAV	OOB	AB-HR-SH	AVG	PB	SUP	APR	DL	PW
1958	StL N	3	9	.250	31	13	4	0	111.2	113	66	11	4	41-6	74	4.51	91	.260	.327	24-0-3	.042	-2*	69	-6		-0.8
1959	Cin N	4	2	.667	18	1	0	3	29.2	29	28	6	0	19-2	8	5.46	74	.254	.358	7-0-1	.000	-1	199	-8		-1.6
1960	Bal A	0	0	—	2	0	0	0	0.2	4	6	0	0	1-0	0	27.00	14	.571	.625	0	—	0		-3		-0.1
Total 3		7	11	.389	51	14	4	3	142	146	100	17	4	61-8	82	4.82	85	.263	.338	31-0-4	.032	-3	78	-17		-2.4

MacARTHUR, MAC Malcolm B1.19.1862 Glasgow, Scotland D10.18.1932 Detroit MI TR/5-9.5/164 d5.2

YEAR	TM LG	W	L	PCT	G	GS	CG-SHO	SV-BS	IP	H	R	HR	HB	BB-IB	SO	ERA	AERA	OAV	OOB	AB-HR-SH	AVG	PB	SUP	APR	DL	PW
1884	Ind AA	1	5	.167	6	6	6	0	52	57	49	1	2	21	19	5.02	66	.263	.333	21	.095	-0	67	-10		-1.1

MacCORMACK, FRANK Frank Louis B9.21.1954 Jersey City NJ BR/TR/6-4/210* d6.14 Col Rutgers

YEAR	TM LG	W	L	PCT	G	GS	CG-SHO	SV-BS	IP	H	R	HR	HB	BB-IB	SO	ERA	AERA	OAV	OOB	AB-HR-SH	AVG	PB	SUP	APR	DL	PW
1976	Det A	0	5	.000	9	8	0	0-0	32.2	35	24	1	1	34-0	14	5.79	64	.294	.449	3	.000	-0	80	-7		-1.1
1977	Sea A	0	0	—	3	3	0	0-0	7	4	3	0	3	12-0	4	3.86	108	.174	.500	0	—	0	130	0	16	0.1
Total 2		0	5	.000	12	11	0	0-0	39.2	39	27	1	4	46-0	18	5.45	70	.275	.459	3	.000	-0	95	-7	16	-1.1

MacDONALD, ROB Robert Joseph B4.27.1965 East Orange NJ BL/TL/6-3/208* [TorA87 19/491] d8.14 Col Rutgers

YEAR	TM LG	W	L	PCT	G	GS	CG-SHO	SV-BS	IP	H	R	HR	HB	BB-IB	SO	ERA	AERA	OAV	OOB	AB-HR-SH	AVG	PB	SUP	APR	DL	PW
1990	Tor A	0	0	—	4	0	0	0-0	2.1	0	0	0	0	2-0	0	0.00	—	.000	.250	0	—	0		1		0.0
1991	†Tor A	3	3	.500	45	0	0	0-4	53.2	51	19	5	0	25-4	24	2.85	148	.252	.332	0	—	0	8	0		0.0
1992	Tor A	1	0	1.000	27	0	0	0-0	47.1	50	24	4	1	16-3	26	4.37	94	.270	.330	0	—	0		-1		-0.2
1993	Det A	3	3	.500	68	0	0	3-3	65.2	67	42	8	1	33-5	39	5.35	82	.268	.349	0	—	0		-7		0.0
1995	NY A	1	1	.500	33	0	0	0-1	46.1	50	25	7	1	22-0	41	4.86	95	.282	.365	0	—	0		0		0.0
1996	NY N	0	2	.000	20	0	0	0-0	19	16	10	2	0	9-0	12	4.26	94	.235	.321	0	—	0		0		0.0
Total 6		8	9	.471	197	0	0	3-8	234.1	234	120	26	3	107-12	142	4.34	99	.264	.342	0	—	0		0		0.0

MACDONALD, BILL William Paul B3.28.1929 Alameda CA D5.4.1991 Shasta Lake CA BR/TR/5-10/170* d5.6 Mil 1951-52

YEAR	TM LG	W	L	PCT	G	GS	CG-SHO	SV-BS	IP	H	R	HR	HB	BB-IB	SO	ERA	AERA	OAV	OOB	AB-HR-SH	AVG	PB	SUP	APR	DL	PW
1950	Pit N	8	10	.444	32	20	6-2	1	153	138	88	17	1	88	60	4.29	102	.243	.346	49-0-1	.122	-2	75	-1		-0.6
1953	Pit N	0	1	.000	4	1	0	0	7.1	12	10	0	1	8	4	12.27	36	.400	.538	0-0-1	—	0	20	-6		-0.3
Total 2		8	11	.421	36	21	6-2	1	160.1	150	98	17	2	96	64	4.66	94	.251	.356	49-0-2	.122	-2	72	-7		-1.0

MacDOUGAL, MIKE Robert Meiklejohn B3.5.1977 Las Vegas NV BR/TR/6-4/195* [KCA99 1/25] d9.22 Col Wake Forest

YEAR	TM LG	W	L	PCT	G	GS	CG-SHO	SV-BS	IP	H	R	HR	HB	BB-IB	SO	ERA	AERA	OAV	OOB	AB-HR-SH	AVG	PB	SUP	APR	DL	PW
2001	KC A	1	1	.500	3	3	0	0-0	15.1	18	10	2	1	4-0	7	4.70	106	.290	.343	0	—	0	81	0		0.0
2002	KC A	0	1	.000	6	0	0	0-0	9	5	5	0	0	7-1	10	5.00	100	.161	.316	0	—	0		0		0.0
2003	KC A☆	3	5	.375	68	0	0	27-8	64	64	36	4	8	32-0	57	4.08	118	.267	.369	0	—	0		3		0.0
2004	KC A	1	1	.500	30	0	0	1-2	11.1	16	8	2	1	9-0	14	5.56	84	.314	.426	0	—	0		-1	20	-0.2
2005	KC A	5	6	.455	68	0	0	21-4	70.1	69	32	6	3	24-2	72	3.33	127	.257	.323	0	—	0		5		0.1
Total 5		10	14	.417	158	3	0	49-14	170	172	91	14	13	76-3	160	3.97	115	.263	.350	0	—	0	81	7	20	0.1

MACE, JIMMY Harry L. B Washington DC D4.26.1930 Norfolk VA 5-11/185 d5.5

YEAR	TM LG	W	L	PCT	G	GS	CG-SHO	SV-BS	IP	H	R	HR	HB	BB-IB	SO	ERA	AERA	OAV	OOB	AB-HR-SH	AVG	PB	SUP	APR	DL	PW
1891	Was AA	0	1	.000	3	1	0	0	16	18	14	0	1	8	3	7.31	51	.273	.360	6	.000	-1	67	-4		-0.3

MacFAYDEN, DANNY Daniel Knowles "Deacon Danny" B6.10.1905 N.Truro MA D8.26.1972 Brunswick ME BR/TR/5-11/170 d8.25

YEAR	TM LG	W	L	PCT	G	GS	CG-SHO	SV-BS	IP	H	R	HR	HB	BB-IB	SO	ERA	AERA	OAV	OOB	AB-HR-SH	AVG	PB	SUP	APR	DL	PW
1926	Bos A	0	1	.000	3	1	1	0	13	10	7	0	0	7	1	4.85	84	.217	.321	3	.333	0	21	-1		0.0
1927	Bos A	5	8	.385	34	16	6-1	2	160.1	176	88	9	6	59	42	4.27	99	.294	.363	46-1-5	.283	4*	79	0		0.0
1928	Bos A	9	15	.375	33	28	9	0	195	215	123	12	7	78	61	4.75	87	.289	.361	63-0-1	.143	-1*	87	-15		-1.3
1929	Bos A	10	18	.357	32	27	14-4	0	221	225	108	8	5	81	61	3.62	118	.271	.340	74-0-4	.176	-3	74	15		1.3
1930	Bos A	11	14	.440	36	33	18-1	2	269.1	293	141	9	6	93	76	4.21	109	.281	.343	92-0-8	.141	-4	86	14		0.8
1931	Bos A	16	12	.571	35	32	17-2	0	230.2	263	121	9	7	79	74	4.02	107	.281	.341	81-0-6	.123	-5	96	6		0.0
1932	Bos A	1	10	.091	12	11	6	0	77.2	91	55	3	1	33	29	5.10	88	.289	.358	25-0-2	.120	-2	48	-6		-0.9
	NY A	7	5	.583	17	15	9	1	121.1	137	69	11	2	37	33	3.93	104	.281	.334	49-0-2	.102	-3	138	-1		-0.9
	Year	8	15	.348	29	26	15	1	199	228	124	14	3	70	62	4.39	97	.284	.344	74-0-4	.108	-4	98	-6		-1.8
1933	NY A	3	2	.600	25	6	2	0	90.1	120	62	8	2	28	28	5.88	66	.319	.383	34-0-1	.029	-4	131	-19		-0.9
1934	NY A	4	3	.571	22	11	4	0	96	110	57	7	2	31	41	4.50	90	.288	.345	39-0-1	.103	-2	148	-6		-0.9
1935	Cin N	1	2	.333	7	4	1	0	36	39	22	1	5	13	13	4.75	84	.281	.342	11	.091	-1	75	-3		-0.2
	Bos N	5	13	.278	28	20	7-1	0	151.2	200	96	8	3	34	46	5.10	74	.314	.354	50-0-1	.157	-1	91	-22		-2.0
	Year	6	15	.286	35	24	8-1	0	187.2	239	118	9	8	47	59	5.04	76	.308	.352	62-0-1	.145	-2	88	-23		-2.2
1936	Bos N	17	13	.567	37	31	21-2	0	266.2	268	97	5	6	66	86	2.87	134	.259	.307	83-0-8	.096	-5	75	30		2.5
1937	Bos N	14	14	.500	32	32	16-2	0	246	250	96	5	2	66	70	2.93	123	.268	.313	83-0-8	.157	-4	92	17		1.4

YEAR	TM LG	W	L	PCT	G	GS	CG-SHO	SV-BS	IP	H	R	HR	HB	BB-IB	SO	ERA	AERA	OAV	OOB	AB-HR-SH	AVG	PB	SUP	APR	DL	PW
1938	Bos N	14	9	.609	29	29	19-5	0	219.2	208	82	6	5	64	58	2.95	116	.247	.304	77-0-2	.117	-4	83	14		0.9
1939	Bos N	8	14	.364	33	28	8	2	191.2	221	100	11	4	59	46	3.90	95	.291	.345	67-0-5	.179	-1	96	-6		-0.6
1940	Pit N	5	4	.556	35	8	0	2	91.1	112	47	5	4	27	24	3.55	107	.302	.356	28-0-1	.179	-0	108	0		-0.6
1941	Was A	0	1	.000	5	0	0	0	7	12	9	1	0	5	3	10.29	39	.375	.459	0	—	0		-5		-0.5
1943	Bos N	2	1	.667	10	1	0	0	21.1	31	14	1	1	9	5	5.91	58	.344	.410	4	.250	0	75	-5		-0.6
Total 17		132	159	.454	465	333	158-18	9	2706	2981	1394	112	64	872	797	3.96	101	.281	.340	910-1-55	.142	-34	90	7		-0.4

MACHADO, JULIO Julio Segundo (Rondon) B12.1.1965 San Carlos de Zulia, Venez BR/TR/5-9/165* d9.7

YEAR	TM LG	W	L	PCT	G	GS	CG-SHO	SV-BS	IP	H	R	HR	HB	BB-IB	SO	ERA	AERA	OAV	OOB	AB-HR-SH	AVG	PB	SUP	APR	DL	PW
1989	NY N	0	1	.000	10	0	0	0-1	11	9	4	0	0	3-0	14	3.27	101	.214	.267	0	—	0		0		0.0
1990	NY N	4	1	.800	27	0	0	0-1	34.1	32	13	4	2	17-4	27	3.15	120	.248	.340	0	—	0		3		0.3
	Mil A	0	0	—	10	0	0	3-0	13	9	1	0	0	8-2	12	0.69	561	.191	.304	0	—	0		3		0.2
1991	Mil A	3	3	.500	54	0	0	3-3	88.2	65	36	12	3	55-1	98	3.45	116	.211	.334	0	—	0		5		0.4
Total 3		7	5	.583	101	0	0	6-5	147	115	54	16	5	83-7	151	3.12	124	.219	.328	0	—	0		14		0.9

MACHEMEHL, CHUCK Charles Walter B4.20.1946 Brenham TX BR/TR/6-4/215 [CleA68 12/258] d4.6 Col TCU

YEAR	TM LG	W	L	PCT	G	GS	CG-SHO	SV-BS	IP	H	R	HR	HB	BB-IB	SO	ERA	AERA	OAV	OOB	AB-HR-SH	AVG	PB	SUP	APR	DL	PW
1971	Cle A	0	2	.000	14	0	0	3-2	18.1	16	16	2	0	15-3	9	6.38	61	.246	.373	2	.500	0		-5		-0.7

MACK, DENNY Dennis Joseph (b Dennis Joseph McGee) B1851 Easton PA D4.10.1888 Wilkes-Barre PA BR/TR/5-7/164 d5.6 M1/U2 Col Villanova ▲

YEAR	TM LG	W	L	PCT	G	GS	CG-SHO	SV-BS	IP	H	R	HR	HB	BB-IB	SO	ERA	AERA	OAV	OOB	AB-HR-SH	AVG	PB	SUP	APR	DL	PW
1871	Rok NA	1	1	.000		13	0	0	3	13	20	30	0	3	1	3.46	118	.299	.329	122	.246	-0*	97	-2		-0.1

MACK, FRANK Frank George "Stubby" B2.2.1900 Oklahoma City OK D7.2.1971 Clearwater FL BR/TR/6-1.5/180 d8.16 Col St. Marys (CA)

YEAR	TM LG	W	L	PCT	G	GS	CG-SHO	SV-BS	IP	H	R	HR	HB	BB-IB	SO	ERA	AERA	OAV	OOB	AB-HR-SH	AVG	PB	SUP	APR	DL	PW
1922	Chi A	2	2	.500	8	4	1-1		34.1	36	16	2	0	16	11	3.67	111	.281	.361	12	.250	1	73	1		0.2
1923	Chi A	0	1	.000	11	0	0		23.1	23	13	0	0	11	6	4.24	93	.284	.370	6	.000	-1		-1		-0.1
1925	Chi A	0	0	—	8	0	0		13.1	24	14	1	0	13	6	9.45	44	.444	.552	3	.333	0		-7		-0.3
Total 3		2	3	.400	27	4	1-1		71	83	43	3	0	40	23	4.94	82	.316	.406	21	.190	0	73	-7		-0.2

MACK, TONY Tony Lynn B4.30.1961 Lexington KY BR/TR/5-10/177 [AnaA82 3/62] d7.27 Col Lamar

YEAR	TM LG	W	L	PCT	G	GS	CG-SHO	SV-BS	IP	H	R	HR	HB	BB-IB	SO	ERA	AERA	OAV	OOB	AB-HR-SH	AVG	PB	SUP	APR	DL	PW
1985	Cal A	0	0	—	1	0	0	0-0	2.1	8	4	0	0	0-0	1	15.43	27	.571	.571	0	—	0	66	-3		-0.4

MACK, BILL William Francis B2.12.1885 Elmira NY D9.30.1971 Elmira NY BL/TL/6-1/155 d7.14 Col Syracuse

YEAR	TM LG	W	L	PCT	G	GS	CG-SHO	SV-BS	IP	H	R	HR	HB	BB-IB	SO	ERA	AERA	OAV	OOB	AB-HR-SH	AVG	PB	SUP	APR	DL	PW
1908	Chi N	0	0	—	2	0	0	0	6	5	3	1	1	2	3.00	78	.263	.333	3	.667	1		-1		0.1

MacKENZIE, KEN Kenneth Purvis B3.10.1934 Gore Bay ON, Can. BR/TL/6-0/185* d5.2 Col Yale

YEAR	TM LG	W	L	PCT	G	GS	CG-SHO	SV-BS	IP	H	R	HR	HB	BB-IB	SO	ERA	AERA	OAV	OOB	AB-HR-SH	AVG	PB	SUP	APR	DL	PW
1960	Mil N	0	1	.000	9	0	0	0	8.1	9	7	2	0	3-2	9	6.48	53	.281	.333	1	.000	-0		-3		-0.4
1961	Mil N	0	1	.000	5	0	0	0	7	8	5	1	1	2-0	5	5.14	73	.296	.367	2	.000	-0		-1		-0.2
1962	NY N	5	4	.556	42	1	0	1	80	87	47	10	3	34-3	51	4.95	84	.280	.353	12-0-1	.083	-1	0	-4		-0.5
1963	NY N	3	1	.750	34	0	0	1	58	63	35	11	2	12-2	41	4.97	70	.267	.307	10	.000	-1		-8		-0.8
	StL N	0	0	—	8	0	0	0	9	9	6	1	0	3-1	7	4.00	89	.250	.308	0	—	0		-1		-0.1
	Year	3	1	.750	42	0	0	3	67	72	41	12	2	15-3	48	4.84	72	.265	.307	10	.000	-1		-9		-0.9
1964	SF N	0	0	—	10	0	0	1	9	9	7	1	0	3-0	3	5.00	71	.267	.308	0	—	0		-2		-0.1
1965	Hou N	0	3	.000	21	0	0	1	37	46	22	7	0	6-0	26	3.89	86	.299	.325	11	.273	1		-4		-0.2
Total 6		8	10	.444	129	1	0	5	208.1	231	129	33	6	63-8	142	4.80	78	.278	.331	36-0-1	.111	-2	0	-23		-2.3

MACKINSON, JOHN John Joseph B10.29.1923 Orange NJ D10.17.1989 Reseda CA BR/TR/5-10.5/160* d4.16

YEAR	TM LG	W	L	PCT	G	GS	CG-SHO	SV-BS	IP	H	R	HR	HB	BB-IB	SO	ERA	AERA	OAV	OOB	AB-HR-SH	AVG	PB	SUP	APR	DL	PW
1953	Phi A	0	0	—	1	0	0	0	1.1	1	0	0	0	2	0	0.00	—	.200	.429	0	—	0		1		0.0
1955	StL N	0	1	.000	8	1	0	0	20.2	24	18	3	1	10-2	8	7.84	52	.296	.372	4	.000	-0*	197	-8		-0.4
Total 2		0	1	.000	9	1	0	0	22	25	18	3	1	12-2	8	7.36	55	.291	.376	4	.000	-0	197	-7		-0.4

MacLEOD, BILLY William Daniel B5.13.1942 Gloucester MA BL/TL/6-2/190 d9.13

YEAR	TM LG	W	L	PCT	G	GS	CG-SHO	SV-BS	IP	H	R	HR	HB	BB-IB	SO	ERA	AERA	OAV	OOB	AB-HR-SH	AVG	PB	SUP	APR	DL	PW
1962	Bos A	0	1	.000					1.2	4	1	0	0	1-0	1	5.40	76	.444	.500	0	—	0		0		0.0

MACON, MAX Max Cullen B10.14.1915 Pensacola FL D8.5.1989 Jupiter FL BL/TL/6-3/175 d4.21 Mil 1945-46 ▲

YEAR	TM LG	W	L	PCT	G	GS	CG-SHO	SV-BS	IP	H	R	HR	HB	BB-IB	SO	ERA	AERA	OAV	OOB	AB-HR-SH	AVG	PB	SUP	APR	DL	PW
1938	StL N	4	11	.267	38	12	5-1	2	129.1	133	83	9	4	61	39	4.11	96	.268	.352	36-0-1	.306	2*	95	-6		-0.5
1940	Bro N	1	0	1.000	2	0	0	0	2	5	5	2	0	0	1	22.50	18	.455	.455	1	1.000	0		-4		-0.6
1942	Bro N	5	3	.625	14	8	4-1	1	84	67	22	3	2	33	27	1.93	169	.220	.300	43-0-3	.279	4*	100	12		1.6
1943	Bro N	7	5	.583	25	9	0	0	77	91	54	4	4	32	21	5.96	56	.291	.364	55	.164	-1*	185	-21		-3.0
1944	Bos N	0	0	—	1	0	0	0	3	10	7	2	0	1	1	21.00	18	.556	.579	366-3-2	.273	0*		-5		-0.2
1947	Bos N	0	0	—	1	0	0	0	2	1	0	0	0	1	0	0.00	—	.167	.286	1	1.000	-0		1		0.0
Total 6		17	19	.472	81	29	9-2	3	297.1	307	171	20	10	128	90	4.24	85	.267	.345	502-3-6	.265	5	122	-23		-2.7

MacPHERSON, HARRY Harry William B7.10.1926 N.Andover MA BR/TR/5-10/150 d8.14

YEAR	TM LG	W	L	PCT	G	GS	CG-SHO	SV-BS	IP	H	R	HR	HB	BB-IB	SO	ERA	AERA	OAV	OOB	AB-HR-SH	AVG	PB	SUP	APR	DL	PW
1944	Bos N	0	0	—	1	0	0	0	1	0	0	0	0	1	0	—	.000	.250	0		—	0		0		0.0

MacRAE, SCOTT Scott Patrick B8.13.1974 Dearborn MI BR/TR/6-3/205 [CinN95 32/895] d7.24 Col Valdosta St.

YEAR	TM LG	W	L	PCT	G	GS	CG-SHO	SV-BS	IP	H	R	HR	HB	BB-IB	SO	ERA	AERA	OAV	OOB	AB-HR-SH	AVG	PB	SUP	APR	DL	PW
2001	Cin N	0	1	.000	24	0	0	0-0	31.1	33	15	0	2	8-0	18	4.02	114	.266	.316	3	.000	-0		2		0.0

MacWHORTER, KEITH Keith B12.30.1955 Worcester MA BR/TR/6-4/190 [LAN76 15/355] d5.10 Col Bryant

YEAR	TM LG	W	L	PCT	G	GS	CG-SHO	SV-BS	IP	H	R	HR	HB	BB-IB	SO	ERA	AERA	OAV	OOB	AB-HR-SH	AVG	PB	SUP	APR	DL	PW
1980	Bos A	0	3	.000	14	2	0	0-0	42.1	46	27	3	2	18-3	21	5.53	77	.280	.357	0	—	0	42	-5		-0.3

MADDEN, LEN Leonard Joseph "Lefty" B7.2.1890 Toledo OH D9.9.1949 Toledo OH BL/TL/6-2/165 d8.31

YEAR	TM LG	W	L	PCT	G	GS	CG-SHO	SV-BS	IP	H	R	HR	HB	BB-IB	SO	ERA	AERA	OAV	OOB	AB-HR-SH	AVG	PB	SUP	APR	DL	PW
1912	Chi N	0	1	.000	6	2	0	0	19						5	2.92	114	.302	.413	4	.250	0	154	-1		-0.1

MADDEN, MIKE Michael Anthony B1.13.1958 Denver CO BL/TL/6-1/190* d4.5 Col Northern Colorado

YEAR	TM LG	W	L	PCT	G	GS	CG-SHO	SV-BS	IP	H	R	HR	HB	BB-IB	SO	ERA	AERA	OAV	OOB	AB-HR-SH	AVG	PB	SUP	APR	DL	PW
1983	Hou N	9	5	.643	28	13	0	0-0	94.2	76	37	4	1	45-3	44	3.14	109	.231	.323	22-0-6	.045	-1	85	4	21	0.4
1984	Hou N	2	3	.400	17	7	0	0-0	40.2	46	27	1	0	35-3	29	5.53	60	.297	.422	6	.333	1	72	-10		-1.0
1985	Hou N	0	0	—	13	0	0	0-0	19	29	15	1	0	11-0	16	4.26	82	.363	.435	0	—	0		-4	81	-0.2
1986	Hou N	1	2	.333	13	6	0	0-0	39.2	47	20	3	0	22-3	30	4.08	88	.297	.381	9-0-4	.000	-1	95	-2		-0.2
Total 4		12	10	.545	71	26	0	0-0	194	198	99	9	1	113-9	119	3.94	88	.274	.370	37-0-10	.081	-1	84	-12	102	-1.0

MADDEN, KID Michael Joseph B10.22.1866 Portland ME D3.16.1896 Portland ME BL/TL/5-7.5/130 d5.6

YEAR	TM LG	W	L	PCT	G	GS	CG-SHO	SV-BS	IP	H	R	HR	HB	BB-IB	SO	ERA	AERA	OAV	OOB	AB-HR-SH	AVG	PB	SUP	APR	DL	PW
1887	Bos N	21	14	.600	37	37	36-3	0	321	317	203	20	20	122	81	3.79	108	.251	.327	132-1	.242	3	106	8		0.9
1888	Bos N	7	11	.389	20	18	17-1	0	165	142	76	6	15	24	53	2.95	98	.228	.273	67	.164	-2	82	4		0.2
1889	Bos N	10	10	.500	22	19	18-1	1	178	194	131	7	16	71	64	4.40	95	.269	.348	86	.291	2*	105	-6		-0.4
1890	Bos P	3	2	.600	10	7	5-1	1	62	85	55	2	8	25	24	4.79	92	.313	.387	38	.184	-1*	109	-3		-0.3
1891	Bos AA	0	1	.000	1	1	1	0	8	10	12	2	3	6	6	6.75	52	.294	.442	3	.667	1	107	-4		-0.3
	Bal AA	13	12	.520	32	27	20-1	1	224	239	168	4	24	88	56	4.10	91	.264	.345	107-1	.271	5*	102	-7		-0.1
	Year	13	13	.500	33	28	21-1	1	232	249	180	6	27	94	62	4.19	89	.265	.349	110-1	.282	6	102	-11		-0.3
Total 5		54	50	.519	122	109	97-7	3	958	987	645	41	86	336	284	3.92	98	.259	.332	433-2	.245	6	102	-8		-0.3

MADDEN, MORRIS Morris De Wayne B8.31.1960 Laurens SC BL/TL/6-0/155* [LAN79 24/617] d6.11 Col Spartanburg Methodist (SC) JC

YEAR	TM LG	W	L	PCT	G	GS	CG-SHO	SV-BS	IP	H	R	HR	HB	BB-IB	SO	ERA	AERA	OAV	OOB	AB-HR-SH	AVG	PB	SUP	APR	DL	PW
1987	Det N	0	0	—	2	0	0	0-0	1.2	4	3	0	0	3-1	0	16.20	26	.444	.583	0	—	0		-2		-0.1
1988	Pit N	0	0	—	5	0	0	0-1	5.2	5	0	0	0	7-1	3	0.00	—	.294	.500	0			0*	2		0.1
1989	Pit N	2	2	.500	9	3	0	0-0	14	17	14	0	0	13-0	6	7.07	48	.327	.455	1-0-3	.000	-0*	139	-7		-1.3
Total 3		2	2	.500	16	3	0	0-1	21.1	26	17	0	0	23-2	9	5.91	59	.333	.480	1-0-3	.000	-0	139	-7		-1.3

MADDOX, NICK Nicholas B11.9.1886 Govans MD D11.27.1954 Pittsburgh PA BL/TR/6-0/175 d9.13

YEAR	TM LG	W	L	PCT	G	GS	CG-SHO	SV-BS	IP	H	R	HR	HB	BB-IB	SO	ERA	AERA	OAV	OOB	AB-HR-SH	AVG	PB	SUP	APR	DL	PW
1907	Pit N	5	1	.833	6	6	6-1	0	54	32	8	0	4	13	38	0.83	292	.178	.249	20	.250	2	137	9		1.5
1908	Pit N	23	8	.742	36	32	22-4	1	260.2	209	89	5	11	90	70	2.28	101	.223	.298	94-0-4	.266	8	147	9		1.1
1909	†Pit N	13	8	.619	31	27	17-4	0	203.1	173	72	2	15	39	56	2.21	123	.232	.283	67-0-4	.224	4	117	10		1.4
1910	Pit N	2	3	.400	20	7	2	0	87.1	73	40	0	5	28	29	3.40	91	.246	.321	28	.214	1*	137	-2		0.0
Total 4		43	20	.683	93	72	47-9	1	605.1	487	209	7	35	170	193	2.29	112	.225	.292	209-0-8	.244	15	133	19		4.0

MADDUX, GREG Gregory Alan B4.14.1966 San Angelo TX BR/TR/6-0/170(150-185) [ChiN84 2/31] d9.3 b-Mike

YEAR	TM LG	W	L	PCT	G	GS	CG-SHO	SV-BS	IP	H	R	HR	HB	BB-IB	SO	ERA	AERA	OAV	OOB	AB-HR-SH	AVG	PB	SUP	APR	DL	PW
1986	Chi N	2	4	.333	6	5	1	0-0	31	44	20	3	1	11-2	20	5.52	74	.336	.392	12-0-1	.333	1	114	-9		-0.7
1987	Chi N	6	14	.300	30	27	1-1	0-0	155.2	181	111	17	4	74-13	101	5.61	77	.294	.373	42-0-7	.119	-2*	84	-23		-2.4
1988	Chi N☆	18	8	.692	34	34	9-3	0-0	249	230	97	13	8	81-16	140	3.18	115	.244	.309	96-0-1	.198	2*	102	12		1.6
1989	†Chi N	19	12	.613	35	35	7-1	0-0	238.1	222	90	13	6	82-13	135	2.95	128	.249	.315	81-0-8	.210	2	104	19		2.9
1990	Chi N	15	15	.500	35	35	8-2	0-0	237	242	116	11	4	71-10	144	3.46	118	.265	.319	83-0-4	.145	-2	85	9		1.3
1991	Chi N	15	11	.577	37	37	7-2	0-0	263	232	113	18	7	66-9	198	3.35	116	.237	.288	88-1-11	.205	3*	97	14		1.9

YEAR	TM LG	W	L	PCT	G	GS	CG-SHO	SV-BS	IP	H	R	HR	HB	BB-IB	SO	ERA	AERA	OAV	OOB	AB-HR-SH	AVG	PB	SUP	APR	DL	PW
1992	Chi N★	20	11	.645	35	35	9-4	0-0	268	201	68	7	14	70-7	199	2.18	166	.210	.272	88-1-13	.170	2	94	44		6.0
1993	†Atl N	20	10	.667	36	36	8-1	0-0	267	228	85	14	6	52-7	197	2.36	172	.232	.273	91-0-10	.165	-1	90	47		5.3
1994	Atl N★	16	6	.727	25	25	10-3	0-0	202	150	44	4	6	31-3	156	1.56	277	.207	.243	63-0-9	.222	2	84	58		6.8
1995	†Atl N☆	19	2	.905	28	28	10-3	0-0	209.2	147	39	8	4	23-3	181	1.63	265	.197	.224	72-0-6	.153	-1	90	62		6.5
1996	†Atl N☆	15	11	.577	35	35	5-1	0-0	245	225	85	11	3	28-11	172	2.72	164	.241	.264	68-0-11	.147	-1	82	44		4.8
1997	†Atl N★	19	4	.826	33	33	5-2	0-0	232.2	200	58	9	6	20-6	177	2.20	191	.236	.256	67-0-6	.104	-1	102	54		5.3
1998	†Atl N	18	9	.667	34	34	9-5	0-0	251	201	75	13	7	45-10	204	2.22	187	.220	.260	75-0-6	.240	4	98	52		6.4
1999	†Atl N	19	9	.679	33	33	4	0-0	219.1	258	103	16	9	37-8	136	3.57	125	.294	.323	64-2-13	.172	3	125	19		2.8
2000	†Atl N*	19	9	.679	35	35	6-3	0-0	249.1	225	91	19	10	42-12	190	3.00	151	.238	.276	80-0-7	.188	2	89	43		5.0
2001	†Atl N	17	11	.607	34	34	3-3	0-0	233	220	86	20	7	27-10	173	3.05	141	.253	.278	64-0-13	.188	1*	82	34		4.2
2002	†Atl N	16	6	.727	34	34	0	0-0	199.1	194	67	14	4	45-7	118	2.62	155	.257	.281	59-0-9	.186	1*	94	31	12	3.6
2003	†Atl N	16	11	.593	36	36	1	0-0	218.1	225	112	24	8	33-7	124	3.96	106	.268	.299	68-0-8	.147	-0*	102	4		0.6
2004	Chi N	16	11	.593	33	33	2-1	0-0	212.2	218	103	35	9	33-4	151	4.02	110	.269	.302	69-0-9	.159	-1*	100	9		1.2
2005	Chi N	13	15	.464	35	35	3	0-0	225	239	112	29	7	36-4	136	4.24	103	.275	.308	76-1-7	.171	-0	96	4		0.6
Total	20	318	189	.627	643	639	108-35		4406.1	4082	1675	298	125	907-162	3052	3.01	138	.247	.289	1406-5-159	.176	13	95	532	12	63.7

MADDUX, MIKE Michael Ausley B8.27.1961 Dayton OH BL/TR/6-2/190* [PhiN82 5/119] d6.3 C2 b-Greg Col Texas-El Paso

YEAR	TM LG	W	L	PCT	G	GS	CG-SHO	SV-BS	IP	H	R	HR	HB	BB-IB	SO	ERA	AERA	OAV	OOB	AB-HR-SH	AVG	PB	SUP	APR	DL	PW
1986	Phi N	3	7	.300	16	16	0	0-0	78	88	56	6	3	34-4	44	5.42	72	.286	.359	22-0-4	.045	-1	96	-14		-1.7
1987	Phi N	2	0	1.000	7	2	0	0-0	17	17	5	0	0	5-0	15	2.65	162	.254	.306	3-0-1	.000	-0	95	3		0.3
1988	Phi N	4	3	.571	25	11	0	0-0	88.2	91	41	6	5	34-4	59	3.76	96	.275	.349	23-0-2	.130	-0*	107	-1	41	-0.1
1989	Phi N	1	3	.250	16	4	2-1	1-0	43.2	52	29	3	2	14-3	26	5.15	70	.304	.362	10-0-1	.000	-1	99	-8		-0.7
1990	LA N	0	1	.000	11	2	0	0-0	20.2	24	15	3	1	4-0	11	6.53	56	.293	.330	2	.000	-0	135	-6		-0.3
1991	SD N	7	2	.778	64	1	0	5-2	98.2	78	30	4	1	27-3	57	2.46	155	.221	.277	13-0-3	.077	-0	0	14		1.4
1992	SD N	2	2	.500	50	1	0	0-0	79.2	71	25	2	0	24-4	60	2.37	152	.236	.290	9-0-3	.111	-0	0	0	20	0.7
1993	NY N	3	8	.273	58	0	0	5-6	75	67	34	3	4	27-7	57	3.60	112	.243	.313	3	.000	-0		4		0.6
1994	NY N	2	1	.667	27	0	0	2-2	44	45	25	7	0	13-4	32	5.11	82	.263	.312	3	.000	-0		-3	16	-0.2
1995	Pit N	1	0	1.000	8	0	0	0-0	9	14	9	0	0	3-1	4	9.00	48	.359	.405	0	—	0		-4		-0.4
	†Bos A	4	1	.800	36	4	0	1-0	89.2	86	40	5	2	15-3	65	3.61	135	.247	.281	0	—	0	139	12		0.6
1996	Bos A	3	2	.600	23	7	0	0-0	64.1	76	37	12	5	27-2	32	4.48	114	.295	.370	0	—	0	99	4	88	0.3
1997	Sea A	1	0	1.000	6	0	0	0-0	10.2	20	12	1	1	8-2	7	10.13	45	.400	.492	0	—	0		-6	21	-0.5
1998	Mon N	3	4	.429	51	0	0	1-1	55.2	50	24	1	1	15-1	33	3.72	113	.243	.293	2	.000	-0		4	56	-0.1
1999	Mon N	0	0	—	4	0	0	0-0	5	9	5	1	1	3-0	4	9.00	50	.409	.500	0	—	0		7		0.3
	LA N	1	1	.500	49	0	0	0-0	54.2	54	21	5	4	19-2	41	3.29	132	.261	.332	0	—	0		5	31	0.3
	Year	1	1	.500	53	0	0	0-0	59.2	63	26	6	5	22-2	45	3.77	116	.275	.349	0	—	0		5		0.2
2000	Hou N	2	2	.500	21	0	0	0-0	27.1	31	20	6	2	12-0	17	6.26	78	.282	.360	2	.000	-0		-4	31	-0.4
Total	15	39	37	.513	472	48	2-1	20-15	861.2	873	428	67	32	284-40	564	4.05	102	.265	.326	92-0-14	.065	-4	105	10	273	0.2

MADIGAN, TONY William J. "Tice" B7.18.1868 Washington DC D12.4.1954 Washington DC TR/5-5.5/126 d7.10

YEAR	TM LG	W	L	PCT	G	GS	CG-SHO	SV-BS	IP	H	R	HR	HB	BB-IB	SO	ERA	AERA	OAV	OOB	AB-HR-SH	AVG	PB	SUP	APR	DL	PW
1886	Was N	1	13	.071	14	13	13	0	114.2	154	110	3		44	29	4.87	66	.310	.366	48	.083	-4	50	-25		-2.6

MADISON, DAVE David Pledger B2.1.1921 Brooksville MS D12.8.1985 Macon MS BR/TR/6-3/190* d9.26 Mil 1951 Col Louisiana St.

YEAR	TM LG	W	L	PCT	G	GS	CG-SHO	SV-BS	IP	H	R	HR	HB	BB-IB	SO	ERA	AERA	OAV	OOB	AB-HR-SH	AVG	PB	SUP	APR	DL	PW
1950	NY A	0	0	—	2	0	0	0	3	3	2	1	0	1	1	6.00	72	.273	.333	0	—	0		-1		0.0
1952	StL A	4	2	.667	31	4	0	0	78	78	46	7	4	48	35	4.38	89	.264	.374	17-0-2	.118	-1	134	-5		-0.5
	Det A	1	1	.500	10	1	0	0	15	16	14	1	1	10	7	7.80	49	.291	.409	2	.000	0	0	-6		-0.7
	Year	5	3	.625	41	5	0	0	93	94	60	8	5	58	42	4.94	79	.268	.379	19-0-2	.105	-1	107	-10		-1.2
1953	Det A	3	4	.429	32	1	0	0	62	76	55	7	3	44	27	6.82	60	.303	.413	11	.091	-1	109	-20		-2.0
Total	3	8	7	.533	74	6	0	0	158	173	117	16	8	103	70	5.70	70	.282	.392	30-0-2	.100	-2	107	-32		-3.2

MADRID, ALEX Alexander B4.18.1963 Springerville AZ BR/TR/6-3/198* [MilA83 S2/44] d7.20 Col Yavapai (AZ) JC

YEAR	TM LG	W	L	PCT	G	GS	CG-SHO	SV-BS	IP	H	R	HR	HB	BB-IB	SO	ERA	AERA	OAV	OOB	AB-HR-SH	AVG	PB	SUP	APR	DL	PW
1987	Mil A	0	0	—	3	0	0	0-0	5.1	11	9	1	0	2		15.19	30	.440	.429	0	—	0		-6		-0.3
1988	Phi N	1	1	.500	5	2	1	0-0	16.1	15	5	0	0	6-2	.2	2.76	131	.246	.304	3	.000	-0	25	2		0.2
1989	Phi N	1	2	.333	6	3	0	0-0	24.2	32	16	3	1	14-4	13	5.47	66	.314	.402	6	.000	-0	58	-5		-0.3
Total	3	2	3	.400	14	5	1		46.1	58	30	4	1	21-6	16	5.63	66	.309	.374	9	.000	-1	43	-9		-0.7

MADRITSCH, BOBBY Robert Allen B2.28.1976 Oak Lawn IL BL/TL/6-2/190* [CinN98 6/170] d7.21 Col Point Park

YEAR	TM LG	W	L	PCT	G	GS	CG-SHO	SV-BS	IP	H	R	HR	HB	BB-IB	SO	ERA	AERA	OAV	OOB	AB-HR-SH	AVG	PB	SUP	APR	DL	PW
2004	Sea A	6	3	.667	15	11	1	0-0	88	74	33	3	4	33-2	60	3.27	137	.232	.312	0	—	0	108	13		1.2
2005	Sea A	0	1	.000	1	1	0	0-0	4.1	4	3	1	0	1-0	1	6.23	68	.235	.278	0	—	0	22	-1	179	-0.2
Total	2	6	4	.600	16	12	1	0-0	92.1	78	36	4	4	34-2	61	3.41	131	.232	.310	0	—	0	101	12	179	1.0

MADSON, RYAN Ryan Michael B8.28.1980 Long Beach CA BL/TR/6-6/180* [PhiN98 9/254] d9.27

YEAR	TM LG	W	L	PCT	G	GS	CG-SHO	SV-BS	IP	H	R	HR	HB	BB-IB	SO	ERA	AERA	OAV	OOB	AB-HR-SH	AVG	PB	SUP	APR	DL	PW
2003	Phi N	0	0	—	1	0	0	0-0	2	0	0	0	0	0-0	0	0.00	—	.000	.000	0	—	0		1		0.0
2004	Phi N	9	3	.750	52	1	0	1-1	77	68	23	6	5	19-4	55	2.34	190	.238	.296	3-0-1	.000	-0	230	17	39	2.3
2005	Phi N	6	5	.545	78	0	0	0-7	87	84	44	11	6	25-6	79	4.14	105	.259	.319	6-0-1	.000	-0	2			0.1
Total	3	15	8	.652	131	1	0	1-8	166	152	67	17	11	44-10	134	3.25	135	.247	.306	9-0-2	.000	-1	230	20	39	0.0

MADURO, CALVIN Calvin Gregory B9.5.1974 Santa Cruz, Aruba BR/TR/6-0/188(175-188) d9.8

YEAR	TM LG	W	L	PCT	G	GS	CG-SHO	SV-BS	IP	H	R	HR	HB	BB-IB	SO	ERA	AERA	OAV	OOB	AB-HR-SH	AVG	PB	SUP	APR	DL	PW
1996	Phi N	0	1	.000	4	2	0	0-0	15.1	13	6	1	2	3-0	11	3.52	122	.232	.295	4	.000	-0	63	2		0.0
1997	Phi N	3	7	.300	15	13	0	0-0	71	83	59	12	3	41-5	31	7.23	58	.294	.385	20-0-1	.050	-2*	87	-22		-2.7
2000	Bal A	0	0	—	15	2	0	0-0	23.1	29	25	8	2	16-1	18	9.64	49	.315	.420	0	—	0	200	-13	138	-0.8
2001	Bal A	5	6	.455	22	12	0	0-0	93.2	83	44	10	4	36-0	51	4.23	102	.240	.319	0	—	0	98	3		0.2
2002	Bal A	2	5	.286	12	10	0	0-0	56.2	64	37	12	1	22-1	29	5.56	78	.279	.344	0	—	0	77	-8	122	-0.8
Total	5	10	19	.345	68	39	0	0-0	260	272	171	43	12	118-7	140	5.78	75	.271	.352	24-0-1	.042	-2	93	-38	260	-3.1

MAESTRI, HECTOR Hector Anibal (Garcia) B4.19.1935 Havana, Cuba BR/TR/5-10/158* d9.24

YEAR	TM LG	W	L	PCT	G	GS	CG-SHO	SV-BS	IP	H	R	HR	HB	BB-IB	SO	ERA	AERA	OAV	OOB	AB-HR-SH	AVG	PB	SUP	APR	DL	PW
1960	Was A	0	0	—	1	0	0	0	2	1	0	0	0	1-0	1	0.00	—	.167	.286	0	—	0		1		0.0
1961	Was A	0	1	.000	1	1	0	0	6	6	3	1	0	2-0	2	1.50	268	.250	.308	1	.000	-0	44	1		0.0
Total	2	0	1	.000	2	1	0	0	8	7	3	1	0	3-0	3	1.13	354	.233	.303	1	.000	-0	44	2		0.0

MAGEE, BILL William J. B7.6.1875 New Brunswick, Can BR/TR/5-10/154 d5.18

YEAR	TM LG	W	L	PCT	G	GS	CG-SHO	SV-BS	IP	H	R	HR	HB	BB-IB	SO	ERA	AERA	OAV	OOB	AB-HR-SH	AVG	PB	SUP	APR	DL	PW
1897	Lou N	4	12	.250	23	17	13-1		156.1	187	137	6	10	101	44	5.41	79	.294	.399	62-0-1	.210	-2	75	-18		-1.5
1898	Lou N	16	15	.516	38	33	29-3		295.1	294	163	8	19	129	55	4.05	88	.258	.343	111-0-1	.126	-9	83	-11		-1.8
1899	Lou N	3	7	.300	12	10	6-1		71	91	58	1	9	28	13	5.20	74	.311	.388	27-0-2	.111	-2	108	-9		-1.2
	Phi N	3	5	.375	9	9	7		70	82	50	0	7	32	4	5.66	65	.292	.378	31-0-1	.161	-2	95	-11		-1.3
	Was N	1	4	.200	8	7	4		42	54	45	3	7	28	11	8.57	46	.312	.428	15-0-1	.333	1	74	-18		-1.4
	Year	7	16	.304	29	26	17-1		183	227	153	4	23	88	28	6.15	62	.304	.394	73-0-4	.178	-2	94	-37		-3.8
1901	StL N	0	0	—	1	1	0		8	8	4	0	0	4	3	4.50	71	.258	.343	4	.500	1	111	-1		0.0
	NY N	0	4	.000	6	5	4		42.1	56	36	4	4	11	14	5.95	56	.316	.370	14	.143	-1	90	-11		-0.9
	Year	0	4	.000	7	6	4		50.1	64	40	4	4	15	17	5.72	57	.308	.366	18	.222	1	94	-11		-0.9
1902	NY N	0	0	—	2	1	0		5	5	2	0	0	1	2	3.60	78	.263	.300	1	.000	-0	121	0		0.0
	Phi N	2	4	.333	8	7	6		53.2	61	28	1	3	18	15	3.69	76	.285	.349	19	.211	-0	64	-4		-0.2
	Year	2	4	.333	10	8	6		58.2	66	30	1	3	19	17	3.68	76	.283	.345	20	.200	-1	72	-5		-0.3
Total	5	29	51	.363	107	90	69-5		743.2	838	523	23	59	352	161	4.94	75	.283	.370	284-0-6	.169	-13	84	-83		-8.2

MAGLIE, SAL Salvatore Anthony "The Barber" B4.26.1917 Niagara Falls NY D12.28.1992 Niagara Falls NY BR/TR/6-2/180* d8.9 C6 Col Niagara

YEAR	TM LG	W	L	PCT	G	GS	CG-SHO	SV-BS	IP	H	R	HR	HB	BB-IB	SO	ERA	AERA	OAV	OOB	AB-HR-SH	AVG	PB	SUP	APR	DL	PW
1945	NY N	5	4	.556	13	10	7-3	0	84.1	72	22	2	2	22	32	2.35	167	.231	.286	30-0-1	.167	-1*	84	15		1.5
1950	NY N	18	4	.818	47	16	12-5	1	206	169	71	14	10	86	96	2.71	151	.226	.314	66-0-3	.121	-1	110	32		3.6
1951	†NY N★	23	6	.793	42	37	22-3	4	298	254	110	27	6	86	146	2.93	134	.230	.289	112-1-9	.152	-3	117	35		3.6
1952	NY N☆	18	8	.692	35	31	12-5	1	216	199	80	16	6	75	112	2.92	127	.244	.312	69-0-12	.072	-3	113	20		2.4
1953	NY N	8	9	.471	27	24	9-3	0	145.1	158	79	19	4	47	80	4.15	103	.278	.334	48-0-6	.271	2	126	2		0.5
1954	†NY N	14	6	.700	34	32	9-1	2	218.1	222	83	21	3	70	117	3.26	124	.262	.319	63-0-13	.127	-2	99	23		2.3
1955	NY N	9	5	.643	23	21	6	0	129.2	142	67	18	3	48-2	71	3.75	107	.278	.340	40-0-6	.125	-1	106	2		-0.5
	Cle A	0	2	.000	10	2	0	0	25.2	26	14	0	1	7-0	11	3.86	103	.252	.306	5	.000	-0	67	0		-0.2
1956	Cle A	0	0	—	2	1	0	0	5	6	2	0	0	2-0	2	3.60	117	.300	.364	0	—	0	0	0		0.0
	†Bro N	13	5	.722	28	26	9-3	0	191	154	65	21	4	52-1	108	2.87	138	.222	.281	70-0-2	.129	-3	102	23		1.9
1957	Bro N	6	6	.500	19	17	4-1	1	101.1	94	42	12	4	26-1	50	2.93	142	.245	.298	29-0-4	.034	-3	68	14		1.0
	NY A	2	0	1.000	6	3	1-1	3	26	21	7	3	0	7-0	9	1.73	207	.227	.283	7-1-0	.143	-1	93	-2		0.5
1958	NY A	1	1	.500	7	3	0	0	23.1	27	12	3	0	9-2	7	4.63	76	.300	.364	5	.250	1	100	6		-0.2

YEAR	TM LG	W	L	PCT	G	GS	CG-SHO	SV-BS	IP	H	R	HR	HB	BB-IB	SO	ERA	AERA	OAV	OOB	AB-HR-SH	AVG	PB	SUP	APR	DL	PW
	StL N	2	6	.250	10	10	2	0	53	46	31	14	2	25-2	21	4.75	87	.232	.323	16-0-1	.125	-1	63	-3		-0.6
Total	10	119	62	.657	303	232	93-25	14	1723	1591	684	169	44	562-8	862	3.15	127	.245	.309	563-2-57	.135	-16	104	164		13.8

MAGNANTE, MIKE Michael Anthony B6.17.1965 Glendale CA BL/TL/6-1/195(180-220) [KCA88 11/283] d4.22 Col UCLA

YEAR	TM LG	W	L	PCT	G	GS	CG-SHO	SV-BS	IP	H	R	HR	HB	BB-IB	SO	ERA	AERA	OAV	OOB	AB-HR-SH	AVG	PB	SUP	APR	DL	PW
1991	KC A	0	1	.000	38	0	0	0-0	55	55	19	3	0	23-3	42	2.45	169	.262	.333	0	—	0		9		0.5
1992	KC A	4	9	.308	44	12	0	0-3	89.1	115	53	5	2	35-5	31	4.94	83	.325	.382	0	—	0	95	-8	18	-0.9
1993	KC A	1	2	.333	7	0	0	0-0	35.1	37	16	3	1	11-1	16	4.08	113	.282	.340	0	—	0	57	2		0.2
1994	KC A	2	3	.400	36	1	0	0-0	47	55	27	5	0	16-1	21	4.60	109	.289	.340	0	—	0	73	2	15	0.2
1995	KC A	1	1	.500	28	0	0	0-1	44.2	45	23	6	2	16-1	28	4.23	113	.268	.335	0	—	0	3			0.2
1996	KC A	2	2	.500	38	0	0	0-1	54	58	38	5	4	24-1	32	5.67	89	.282	.361	0	—	0	-5		25	-0.2
1997	†Hou N	3	1	.750	40	0	0	1-4	47.2	39	16	2	0	11-2	43	2.27	177	.223	.266	3	.000	-0	8			0.6
1998	Hou N	4	7	.364	48	0	0	2-2	51.2	56	28	2	4	26-4	39	4.88	83	.276	.368	2	1.000	1	-4	15		-0.5
1999	Ana A	5	2	.714	53	0	0	0-3	69.1	68	30	2	3	29-4	44	3.38	145	.262	.334	0	—	0	11			1.0
2000	†Oak A	1	1	.500	55	0	0	0-3	39.2	50	22	3	2	19-7	17	4.31	113	.309	.388	1	.000	-0	-2	30		0.2
2001	†Oak A	3	1	.750	65	0	0	0-1	55.1	50	23	7	1	13-3	23	2.77	165	.244	.287	0	—	0	9			0.5
2002	†Oak A	0	2	.000	32	0	0	0-1	28.2	38	22	2	1	11-1	11	5.97	75	.317	.373	0	—	0	-5			-0.3
Total	12	26	32	.448	484	19	0	3-19	617.2	666	317	45	20	234-33	347	4.08	111	.279	.344	6	.333	1	78	24	103	1.5

MAGNUSON, JIM James Robert B8.18.1946 Marinette WI D5.30.1991 Green Bay WI BR/TL/6-2/190* [ChiA66 3/58] d6.28 Col Wisconsin-Oshkosh

YEAR	TM LG	W	L	PCT	G	GS	CG-SHO	SV-BS	IP	H	R	HR	HB	BB-IB	SO	ERA	AERA	OAV	OOB	AB-HR-SH	AVG	PB	SUP	APR	DL	PW
1970	Chi A	1	5	.167	13	6	0	0-0	44.2	45	28	7	1	16-1	20	4.84	80	.263	.328	11-0-1	.000	-1	80	-5		-0.7
1971	Chi A	1	1	.500	15	4	0	0-0	30	30	18	0	2	16-0	11	4.50	79	.265	.366	4	.000	-0	101	-3		-0.3
1973	NY A	0	1	.000	8	0	0	0-0	27.1	38	17	2	0	9-1	9	4.28	87	.342	.382	0	—	0	-3			-0.1
Total	3	2	7	.222	36	10	0	0-0	102	113	63	9	3	41-2	40	4.59	82	.286	.354	15-0-1	.000	-2	88	-11		-1.1

MAGRANE, JOE Joseph David B7.2.1964 Des Moines IA BR/TL/6-6/230* [StLN85 1/18] d4.25 Col Arizona [DL 1991 StL N 182]

YEAR	TM LG	W	L	PCT	G	GS	CG-SHO	SV-BS	IP	H	R	HR	HB	BB-IB	SO	ERA	AERA	OAV	OOB	AB-HR-SH	AVG	PB	SUP	APR	DL	PW
1987	†StL N	9	7	.563	27	26	4-2	0-0	170.1	157	75	9	10	60-6	101	3.54	119	.245	.318	52-1-6	.135	1*	89	11	19	1.1
1988	StL N	5	9	.357	24	24	4-3	0-0	165.1	133	57	6	2	51-4	100	2.18	162	.217	.278	48-1-8	.167	1*	69	19	55	1.9
1989	StL N	18	9	.667	34	33	9-3	0-0	234.2	219	81	5	6	72-7	127	2.91	126	.251	.310	80-1-8	.138	0*	109	20	15	2.4
1990	StL N	10	17	.370	31	31	3-2	0-0	203.1	204	86	10	8	59-7	100	3.59	107	.264	.320	55-0-9	.127	-0	73	8		1.1
1992	StL N	1	2	.333	5	5	0	0-0	31.1	34	15	2	2	15-0	20	4.02	85	.279	.364	10-1-1	.200	1	127	-2	148	-0.1
1993	StL N	8	10	.444	22	20	0	0-0	116	127	68	15	5	37-3	38	4.97	81	.286	.343	35-0-4	.114	-1	83	-10		-1.5
	Cal A	3	2	.600	8	8	0	0-0	48	48	27	4	0	21-0	24	3.94	115	.265	.337	0	—	0	101	1		0.3
1994	Cal A	2	6	.250	20	11	1	0-0	74	89	63	18	6	51-0	33	7.30	67	.300	.409	0	—	0	99	-19	31	-1.6
1996	Chi A	1	5	.167	19	8	0	0-0	53.2	70	45	10	3	25-1	21	6.88	69	.318	.390	0	—	0	85	-14		-1.2
Total	8	57	67	.460	190	166	21-10	0-0	1096.2	1081	517	79	42	391-28	564	3.81	104	.327	.139	280-4-36	.139	3	89	14	450	2.4

MAGRINI, PETE Peter Alexander B6.8.1942 San Francisco CA BR/TR/6-0/195 d4.13 Col Santa Clara

YEAR	TM LG	W	L	PCT	G	GS	CG-SHO	SV-BS	IP	H	R	HR	HB	BB-IB	SO	ERA	AERA	OAV	OOB	AB-HR-SH	AVG	PB	SUP	APR	DL	PW
1966	Bos A	0	1	.000	3	1	0	0-0	7.1	8	9	0	1	8-0	3	9.82	39	.308	.459	3	.000	-0	23	-4		-0.6

MAHAFFEY, ART Arthur B6.4.1938 Cincinnati OH BR/TR/6-2/200* d7.30

YEAR	TM LG	W	L	PCT	G	GS	CG-SHO	SV-BS	IP	H	R	HR	HB	BB-IB	SO	ERA	AERA	OAV	OOB	AB-HR-SH	AVG	PB	SUP	APR	DL	PW
1960	Phi N	7	3	.700	14	12	5-1	0-0	93.1	78	29	9	1	34-1	56	2.31	168	.229	.298	30-0-5	.100	-2	81	15		1.3
1961	Phi N★	11	19	.367	36	32	12-3	0-0	219.1	205	110	27	7	70-6	158	4.10	99	.249	.311	63-0-12	.127	-2	79	0		-0.2
1962	Phi N★	19	14	.576	41	39	20-2	0-0	274	253	131	36	12	81-4	177	3.94	98	.246	.306	92-2-10	.141	1*	110	-1		-0.2
1963	Phi N	7	10	.412	26	22	6-1	0-0	149	143	73	18	5	48-1	97	3.99	81	.255	.314	50-0-3	.200	2	86	-11	45	-1.0
1964	Phi N	12	9	.571	34	29	2-2	0-0	157.1	161	84	17	6	82-5	80	4.52	77	.269	.361	50-1-5	.120	0	113	-15		-2.0
1965	Phi N	2	5	.286	22	9	1	0	71	82	53	11	7	32-2	52	6.21	56	.294	.373	21-0-1	.095	-1	118	-21		-2.0
1966	StL N	1	4	.200	12	5	0	1	35	37	27	7	1	21-4	19	6.43	56	.276	.373	7	.000	-1	74	-10		-1.5
Total	7	59	64	.480	185	148	46-9	0-0	999	959	507	125	39	368-23	639	4.17	89	.255	.324	313-3-36	.134	-2	97	-43	45	-5.6

MAHAFFEY, ROY Lee Roy "Popeye" B2.9.1903 Belton SC D7.23.1969 Anderson SC BR/TR/6-0/180 d8.31

YEAR	TM LG	W	L	PCT	G	GS	CG-SHO	SV-BS	IP	H	R	HR	HB	BB-IB	SO	ERA	AERA	OAV	OOB	AB-HR-SH	AVG	PB	SUP	APR	DL	PW
1926	Pit N	0	0	—	4	0	0	0	4.2	5	4	0	1	1	3	0.00	—	.294	.368	2	.000	-0				0.0
1927	Pit N	1	0	1.000	2	1	0	0	9.1	9	8	0	3	9	4	7.71	53	.300	.500	5	.400	0	207	-3		-0.2
1930	Phi A	9	5	.643	33	17	6	0	152.2	186	108	16	4	53	38	5.01	93	.298	.357	59-1-0	.119	-5	136	-10		-1.3
1931	†Phi A	15	4	.789	30	20	8	2	162.1	161	87	9	3	82	59	4.21	107	.258	.347	63-2-3	.190	1	107	6		0.6
1932	Phi A	13	13	.500	37	28	13	0	222.2	245	136	27	5	96	106	5.09	89	.274	.348	87-1-2	.172	-1	114	-13		-1.5
1933	Phi A	13	10	.565	33	23	9	0	179.1	198	114	5	4	74	66	5.17	83	.275	.346	65-0-2	.215	-0	130	-14		-1.6
1934	Phi A	6	7	.462	37	14	4	0	129	142	88	10	1	55	37	5.37	82	.276	.347	48	.271	2	105	-15		-1.1
1935	Phi A	8	4	.667	27	17	5	0	136	153	66	11	5	42	39	3.90	116	.283	.341	51-0-1	.176	-2	105	10		0.5
1936	StL A	2	6	.250	21	9	1	1	60	82	62	6	6	40	13	8.10	66	.315	.409	16	.063	-1	76	-19		-2.0
Total	9	67	49	.578	224	129	45	5	1056	1181	673	84	27	452	365	5.01	90	.280	.353	396-4-8	.184	-7	114	-56		-6.6

MAHAFFEY, LOU Louis Wood B1.3.1874 KY D10.26.1949 Torrance CA BR/5-9/170 d4.26

YEAR	TM LG	W	L	PCT	G	GS	CG-SHO	SV-BS	IP	H	R	HR	HB	BB-IB	SO	ERA	AERA	OAV	OOB	AB-HR-SH	AVG	PB	SUP	APR	DL	PW
1898	Lou N	0	1	.000	1	1	1	0	9	10	9	0	0	5	1	3.00	119	.278	.366	4	.000	-0	158	-1		-0.2

MAHAY, RON Ronald Matthew B6.28.1971 Crestwood IL BL/TL/6-2/190* [BosA91 18/486] d5.21.1995 Col South Suburban (IL) JC

YEAR	TM LG	W	L	PCT	G	GS	CG-SHO	SV-BS	IP	H	R	HR	HB	BB-IB	SO	ERA	AERA	OAV	OOB	AB-HR-SH	AVG	PB	SUP	APR	DL	PW
1997	Bos A	3	0	1.000	28	0	0	0-2	25	19	7	3	0	11-0	22	2.52	185	.204	.288	0	—	0	6			0.6
1998	Bos A	1	1	.500	29	0	0	1-1	26	26	16	2	2	15-1	14	3.46	137	.263	.358	0	—	0	1			0.1
1999	Oak A	2	0	1.000	6	1	0	1-0	19.1	8	4	2	0	3-0	15	1.86	254	.123	.162	0	—	0	59	7		0.6
2000	Oak A	0	1	.000	5	2	0	0-0	16	26	18	4	0	9-0	5	9.00	54	.366	.432	0	—	0*	97	-8		-0.4
	Fla N	1	0	1.000	18	0	0	0-0	25.1	31	17	6	0	16-1	27	6.04	73	.310	.402	4	.500	1	-4			-0.1
2001	Chi N	0	0	—	17	0	0	0-0	20.2	14	6	4	0	15-1	24	2.61	160	.197	.337	2	.000	-0	4			0.2
2002	Chi N	2	0	1.000	11	0	0	1-0	14.2	13	14	6	0	8-0	14	8.59	47	.228	.323	0	—	0	-7	20		-0.8
2003	Tex A	3	3	.500	35	0	0	0-3	45.1	33	19	3	0	20-7	38	3.18	156	.195	.280	0	—	0	7			0.9
2004	Tex A	3	0	1.000	60	0	0	0-2	67	60	23	5	2	29-5	54	2.55	193	.235	.318	1	.000	-0	16			0.8
2005	Tex A	0	2	.000	30	0	0	1-0	35.2	47	28	4	0	16-1	30	6.81	67	.313	.377	0	—	0	-8	16		-0.4
Total	9	15	7	.682	239	3	0	3-8	295	277	152	43	4	142-16	243	4.15	113	.245	.330	7	.286	1	86	14	36	1.5

MAHLER, MICKEY Michael James B7.30.1952 Montgomery AL BB/TL/6-3/189* [AtlN74 10/221] d9.13 b-Rick Col Trinity (TX) [DL 1983 Cal A 180]

YEAR	TM LG	W	L	PCT	G	GS	CG-SHO	SV-BS	IP	H	R	HR	HB	BB-IB	SO	ERA	AERA	OAV	OOB	AB-HR-SH	AVG	PB	SUP	APR	DL	PW
1977	Atl N	1	2	.333	14	5	1	0-0	23	31	19	4	1	9	14	6.26	71	.326	.380	6-0-1	.500	2	112	-4		-0.3
1978	Atl N	4	11	.267	34	21	1	0-1	134.2	130	82	16	7	66-6	92	4.68	86	.255	.345	41-0-5	.098	-2	97	-9		-1.3
1979	Atl N	5	11	.313	26	18	1	0-0	100	123	72	11	0	47-7	71	5.85	69	.304	.374	27-0-1	.111	-1	78	-17		-2.5
1980	Pit N	0	0	—	2	0	0	0-0	1	4	7	1	0	3-0	1	63.00	6	.571	.700	0*	—	0	-6			-0.3
1981	Cal A	0	0	—	6	0	0	0-0	6.1	1	0	0	0	3-0	5	0.00	—	.056	.150	0	—	0	3			0.1
1982	Cal A	2	0	1.000	8	3	0	0-0	8	9	1	0	0	6-1	5	1.13	364	.300	.417	0	—	0	3			0.6
1985	Mon N	1	4	.200	9	7	1-1	1-0	48.1	40	22	3	1	24-1	32	3.54	97	.229	.323	16-0-1	.188	1	95	-3		0.1
	Det A	1	2	.333	3	2	0	0-0	20.2	19	4	2	0	4-2	14	1.74	236	.241	.277	0	—	0	78	5		0.5
1986	Tex A	0	2	.000	29	5	0	3-0	63	71	31	3	0	29-2	28	4.14	104	.295	.372	0	—	0	105	2		0.1
	Tor A	0	0	—	2	0	0	0-0	1	1	0	0	1	0-0	0	0.00	—	.200	.333	0	—	0	2			0.1
	Year	0	2	.000	31	5	0	3-0	64	72	31	3	1	29-2	28	4.08	106	.293	.371	0	—	0	105	2		0.1
Total	8	14	32	.304	122	58	3-1	4-1	406	429	242	40	16	190-19	262	4.68	86	.274	.354	90-0-8	.144	-1	92	-25	180	-3.2

MAHLER, RICK Richard Keith B8.5.1953 Austin TX D3.2.2005 Jupiter FL BR/TR/6-1/202(190-205) d4.20 b-Mickey Col Trinity (TX)

YEAR	TM LG	W	L	PCT	G	GS	CG-SHO	SV-BS	IP	H	R	HR	HB	BB-IB	SO	ERA	AERA	OAV	OOB	AB-HR-SH	AVG	PB	SUP	APR	DL	PW
1979	Atl N	0	0	—	15	0	0	0-0	22	28	16	4	0	11-2	12	6.14	65	.311	.386	2	.500	0	-4			-0.2
1980	Atl N	0	0	—	2	0	0	0-0	3.2	2	1	0	0	4-0	1	2.45	150	.154	.154	0	—	0	1			0.0
1981	Atl N	8	6	.571	34	14	1	2-0	112.1	109	41	5	1	43-5	54	2.80	126	.258	.326	27-0-2	.148	-0	58	8		1.0
1982	†Atl N	9	10	.474	39	33	5-2	0-1	205.1	213	105	24	2	62-5	105	4.21	88	.272	.324	58-1-11	.190	2	110	-10		-0.6
1983	Atl N	0	0	—	10	0	0	0-2	14.1	16	8	0	0	9-1	7	5.02	77	.296	.385	2	.000	-0	-1			-0.1
1984	Atl N	13	10	.565	38	29	9-1	0-0	222	209	86	24	8	62-7	106	3.12	124	.251	.303	71-0-3	.296	5	81	18		2.5
1985	Atl N	17	15	.531	39	39	6-1	0-0	266.2	272	116	24	2	79-8	107	3.48	111	.268	.321	90-0-11	.156	-1	108	11		1.2
1986	Atl N	14	18	.438	39	39	7-1	0-0	237.2	283	139	25	3	95-10	137	4.88	81	.301	.363	83-0-9	.193	2*	91	-7		-0.9
1987	Atl N	8	13	.381	39	28	3-1	0-0	197	212	118	24	2	85-8	95	4.98	87	.283	.356	65-0-7	.169	1*	93	-11		-0.9
1988	Atl N	9	16	.360	39	34	5	0-1	249	279	125	17	8	42-6	131	3.69	99	.282	.315	72-0-11	.125	-2	100	-5		-0.6
1989	Cin N	9	13	.409	40	31	5-2	0-0	220.2	242	113	15	10	51-13	102	3.83	94	.282	.325	62-0-3	.177	2	98	-8		-0.6
1990	†Cin N	7	6	.538	35	16	2-1	4-0	134.2	134	67	16	3	39-4	68	4.28	92	.261	.314	35-0-5	.114	-1	124	-4	15	-0.4
1991	Mon N	1	0	1.000	9	0	0	0-0	37.1	37	17	2	0	15-0	17	3.62	101	.268	.338	9-0-3	.111	0	70	0		0.0
	Atl N	1	1	.500	13	2	0	0-1	28.2	33	20	7	2	15-1	10	5.65	69	.282	.364	5-0-1	.200	0	174	-5		-0.3

YEAR	TM LG	W	L	PCT	G	GS	CG-SHO	SV-BS	IP	H	R	HR	HB	BB-IB	SO	ERA	AERA	OAV	OOB	AB-HR-SH	AVG	PB	SUP	APR	DL	PW
	Year	2	4	.333	23	8	0	0-2	66	70	37	4	2	28-1	27	4.50	83	.275	.350	14-0-4	.143	-0	96	-6		-0.3
Total	13	96	111	.464	392	271	43-9	6-6	1951.1	2069	972	165	35	606-70	952	3.99	96	.275	.330	581-1-66	.179	7	97	-30	15	-1.1

MAHOLM, PAUL   Paul Gurner   B6.25.1982 Greenwood MS   BL/TL/6-2/225   d8.30   Col Mississippi St.

| 2005 | Pit N | 3 | 1 | .750 | 6 | 6 | 0 | 0-0 | 41.1 | 31 | 10 | 2 | 3 | 17-0 | 26 | 2.18 | 195 | .209 | .304 | 15-0-1 | .133 | -0 | 77 | 10 | | 0.9 |

MAHOMES, PAT   Patrick Lavon   B8.9.1970 Bryan TX   BR/TR/6-4/212(175-212)   [MinA88 6/155]   d4.12

1992	Min A	3	4	.429	14	13	0	0-0	69.2	73	41	5	0	37-0	44	5.04	81	.279	.364	0	—	0	119	-6		-0.6
1993	Min A	1	5	.167	12	5	0	0-0	37.1	47	34	8	1	16-0	23	7.71	57	.309	.372	0	—	0	29	-13		-1.7
1994	Min A	9	5	.643	21	21	0	0-0	120	121	68	22	1	62-1	53	4.72	104	.269	.357	0	—	0*	119	3	17	0.2
1995	Min A	4	10	.286	47	7	0	3-4	94.2	100	74	22	2	47-1	67	6.37	76	.271	.355	0	—	0	124	-16		-2.1
1996	Min A	1	4	.200	20	5	0	0-0	45	63	38	10	0	27-0	30	7.20	71	.330	.409	0	—	0	83	-10		-0.9
	Bos A	2	0	1.000	11	0	0	2-0	12.1	9	8	3	0	6-0	6	5.84	87	.209	.306	0	—	0	-1			-0.1
	Year	3	4	.429	31	5	0	2-0	57.1	72	46	13	0	33-0	36	6.91	74	.308	.390	0	—	0	83	-10		-1.0
1997	Bos A	1	0	1.000	10	0	0	0-0	10	15	10	2	2	10-1	5	8.10	57	.366	.500	0	—	0	-4			-0.3
1999	†NY N	8	0	1.000	39	0	0	0-1	63.2	44	26	7	2	37-5	51	3.68	118	.197	.314	16	.313	2*	5			0.8
2000	NY N	5	3	.625	53	5	0	0-1	94	96	63	15	2	66-4	76	5.46	80	.263	.376	17-0-2	.235	1	84	-12		-0.7
2001	Tex A	7	6	.538	56	4	0	0-1	107.1	115	71	17	0	55-9	61	5.70	84	.280	.359	1	1.000	0	82	-10		-0.9
2002	Chi N	1	1	.500	16	2	0	0-0	32.2	36	15	3	1	17-3	23	3.86	105	.286	.355	5	.000	-1*	80	1		0.0
2003	Pit N	0	1	.000	9	1	0	0-0	22.1	19	13	2	0	12-1	13	4.84	89	.241	.326	4	.250	0	87	-1		0.0
Total	11	42	39	.519	308	63	0	5-8	709	738	461	116	11	392-25	452	5.47	84	.272	.363	43-0-2	.256	3	104	-64	17	-6.3

MAHON, AL   Alfred Gwinn "Lefty"   B9.23.1909 Albion NE   D12.26.1977 New Haven CT   BL/TL/5-11/160   d4.22

| 1930 | Phi A | 0 | 0 | — | 3 | 0 | 0 | 0-0 | 3 | 6 | 9 | 0 | 1 | 8-0 | 0 | 22.85 | 20 | .579 | .692 | 1 | .000 | 0 | -8 | | | -0.3 |

MAHONEY, CHRIS   Christopher John   B6.11.1885 Milton MA   D7.15.1954 Visalia CA   BR/TR/5-9/160   d7.12   Col Fordham

| 1910 | Bos A | 0 | 1 | .000 | 2 | 1 | 0 | 1 | 11 | 16 | 11 | 1 | 0 | 5 | 6 | 3.27 | 78 | .327 | .389 | 7 | .143 | -0* | 131 | -3 | | -0.3 |

MAHONEY, BOB   Robert Paul   B6.20.1928 LeRoy MN   D8.27.2000 Lincoln NE   BR/TR/6-1/185*   d5.3

1951	Chi A	0	0	—	3	0	0	0	6.2	5	4	1	0	5	3	5.40	75	.208	.345		—	0	-1			0.0
	StL A	2	5	.286	30	4	0	0	81	86	47	7	0	41	30	4.44	99	.274	.358	18-0-1	.222	-0	71	-1		-0.1
	Year	2	5	.286	33	4	0	0	87.2	91	51	8	0	46	33	4.52	97	.269	.357	18-0-1	.222	-0	71	-2		-0.1
1952	StL A	0	0	—	3	0	0	0	3	8	6	0	0	4	1	18.00	22	.500	.600	0	—	0	-4			-0.2
Total	2	2	5	.286	36	4	0	0	90.2	99	57	8	0	50	34	4.96	88	.280	.369	18-0-1	.222	-0	71	-6		-0.3

MAILS, DUSTER   John Walter "Walter", "The Great"   B10.1.1894 San Quentin CA   D7.5.1974 San Francisco CA   BL/TL/6-0/195   d9.28   Mil 1917-18   Col St. Marys (CA)

1915	Bro N	0	1	.000	2	1	0	0	5	6	5	2	0	5	3	3.60	77	.333	.478	1	.000	-0	-1			-0.2
1916	Bro N	0	1	.000*	11	0	0	0	17.1	15	9	1	0	9	13	3.63	74	.242	.338	4	.250	0	-1			-0.1
1920	†Cle A	7	0	1.000	9	8	6-2	0	63.1	54	18	1	0	18	25	1.85	206	.230	.285	20-0-3	.200	0	115	13		1.3
1921	Cle A	14	8	.636	34	24	10-2	2	194.1	210	103	4	2	89	87	3.94	108	.283	.361	64-0-8	.094	-4	130	6		0.1
1922	Cle A	4	7	.364	26	13	4-1	0	104	122	69	8	4	40	54	5.28	76	.291	.359	31-0-1	.161	0	99	-14		-1.3
1925	StL N	7	7	.500	21	16	9	0	131	145	78	11	7	58	49	4.60	94	.279	.360	45-0-2	.133	-2	101	-4		-0.6
1926	StL N	0	1	.000	1	0	0	0	1	2	1	0	0	1	1	0.00	—	.400	.500	0	—	0	0			0.0
Total	7	32	25	.561	104	61	29-5	2	516	554	283	27	13	220	232	4.10	100	.277	.352	165-0-14	.133	-7	115	-2		-0.8

MAIN, WOODY   Forrest Harry   B2.12.1922 Delano CA   D6.27.1992 Whittier CA   BR/TR/6-3.5/195*   d4.21

1948	Pit N	1	1	.500	17	0	0	0	27	35	27	4	0	19	12	8.33	49	.324	.425	2	.000	-0	-12			-0.8
1950	Pit N	1	0	1.000	12	0	0	0	20.1	21	12	2	1	11	12	4.87	90	.256	.351	5	.400	0	-1			-0.1
1952	Pit N	2	12	.143	48	11	2	2	153.1	149	78	14	0	52	79	4.46	90	.253	.314	37-0-3	.054	-3	59	-4		-0.9
1953	Pit N	0	0	—	2	0	0	0	4	5	5	1	0	2	4	11.25	40	.294	.368	0	—	0	-3			-0.1
Total	4	4	13	.235	79	11	2	3	204.2	210	122	21	1	84	107	5.14	79	.264	.335	44-0-3	.091	-3	59	-20		-1.8

MAIN, ALEX   Miles Grant   B5.13.1884 Montrose MI   D12.29.1965 Royal Oak MI   BL/TR/6-5/195   d4.18

1914	Det A	6	6	.500	32	12	5-1	3	138.1	131	51	2	3	59	55	2.67	105	.259	.340	40	.100	-2	93	4		0.4
1915	KC F	13	14	.481	35	28	18-2	3	230	181	88	4	5	75	91	2.54	101	.222	.291	76-0-3	.197	-0*	82	1		0.2
1918	Phi N	2	2	.500	8	4	1-1	0	35	30	20	1	5	16	14	4.63	65	.240	.349	11-0-1	.091	-1*	82	-5		-0.6
Total	3	21	22	.488	75	44	24-4	6	403.1	342	159	7	13	150	160	2.77	98	.236	.313	127-0-4	.157	-3	85	0		0.0

MAINE, JOHN   John K.   B5.8.1981 Fredericksburg VA   BR/TR/6-4/195*   [BalA02 6/166]   d7.23   Col North Carolina-Charlotte

2004	Bal A	0	1	.000	1	1	0	0-0	3.2	7	4	1	0	3-0	1	9.82	48	.438	.526	0	—	0	60	-2		-0.3
2005	Bal A	2	3	.400	10	8	0	0-0	40	39	30	8	1	24-0	24	6.30	70	.248	.348	0	—	0	101	-8		-0.8
Total	2	2	4	.333	11	9	0	0-0	43.2	46	34	9	1	27-0	25	6.60	67	.266	.365	0	—	0	96	-10		-1.1

MAINS, JIM   James Royal   B6.12.1922 Bridgton ME   D3.17.1969 Bridgton ME   BR/TR/6-2/190   d8.22   f-Willard   Col Harvard

| 1943 | Phi A | 0 | 1 | .000 | 1 | 1 | 0 | 0 | 6 | 8 | 5 | 0 | 0 | 3 | 2 | 5.63 | 60 | .281 | .343 | 2 | .000 | 0 | 50 | -2 | | -0.2 |

MAINS, WILLARD   Willard Eben "Grasshopper"   B7.7.1868 N.Windham ME   D5.23.1923 Bridgton ME   TR/6-2/190   d8.3   s-Jim

1888	Chi N	1	1	.500	2	2	1	0	11	8	10	0	1	6	5	4.91	62	.211	.333	7	.143	-0	101	-2		-0.3
1891	Cin AA	12	12	.500	30	23	19	0	204	196	127	3	12	107	76	2.69	152	.244	.342	90-1	.244	1*	83	26		2.7
	Mil AA	0	2	.000	2	2	1	0	10	14	19	1	0	10	2	10.80	41	.318	.444	5	.600	1	64	-5		-0.7
	Year	12	14	.462	32	25	20	0	214	210	146	4	12	117	78	3.07	134	.248	.347	95-1	.263	2	82	16		2.0
1896	Bos N	3	2	.600	8	5	3	1	42.2	43	35	1	2	31	13	5.48	83	.261	.384	22	.273	-0*	119	-3		-0.1
Total	3	16	17	.485	42	32	24	1	267.2	261	191	5	15	154	96	3.53	117	.249	.353	124-1	.258	2	88	16		1.4

MAIRENA, OSWALDO   Oswaldo Antonio   B7.30.1975 Chinandega, Nicaragua   BL/TL/5-11/165*   d9.5

2000	Chi N	0	0	—	2	0	0	0-0	2	7	4	1	0	2-0	0	18.00	25	.583	.643	0	—	0	-3			-0.1
2002	Fla N	2	3	.400	31	0	0	0-0	33.2	38	21	7	0	12-0	21	5.35	74	.288	.345	0	—	0	-5	15	-0.7
Total	2	2	3	.400	33	0	0	0-0	35.2	45	25	8	0	14-0	21	6.06	65	.313	.371	0	—	0	-8	15	-0.8

MAJEWSKI, GARY   Gary Wayne   B2.26.1980 Houston TX   BR/TR/6-1/215*   [ChiA98 2/59]   d8.26

2004	Mon N	0	1	.000	16	0	0	1-1	21	28	15	2	2	5-1	12	3.86	119	.326	.372	2	.000	-0	-1			-0.1
2005	Was N	4	4	.500	79	0	0	1-4	86	80	32	2	7	37-6	50	2.93	138	.248	.334	6-0-1	.000	-1	10			0.7
Total	2	4	5	.444	95	0	0	2-5	107	108	47	4	9	42-7	62	3.11	133	.264	.342	8-0-1	.000	-1	9			0.6

MAKOSKY, FRANK   Frank   B1.20.1910 Boonton NJ   D1.10.1987 Stroudsburg PA   BR/TR/6-1/185   d4.30

| 1937 | NY A | 5 | 2 | .714 | 26 | 1 | 1 | 3 | 58 | 64 | 42 | 6 | 0 | 24 | 27 | 4.97 | 90 | .277 | .345 | 16-0-1 | .313 | 1 | 59 | -5 | | -0.4 |

MAKOWSKI, TOM   Thomas Anthony   B12.22.1950 Buffalo NY   BR/TR/5-11/185   d5.1   Col Buffalo

| 1975 | Det A | 0 | 0 | — | 3 | 0 | 0 | 0-0 | 9.1 | 10 | 11 | 2 | 0 | 9-0 | 3 | 4.82 | 84 | .278 | .404 | 0 | — | 0 | -3 | | | -0.1 |

MALARKEY, JOHN   John S. "Liz"   B5.4.1872 Springfield OH   D10.29.1949 Cincinnati OH   TR/5-11/155   d9.21

1894	Was N	2	1	.667	3	3	3	0	26	42	24	1	0	5	3	4.15	127	.359	.385	14	.071	-2*	54	3		0.0
1895	Was N	0	8	.000	22	8	5	2	100.2	135	113	3	8	60	32	5.99	80	.316	.410	37	.135	-4	85	-15		-1.3
1896	Was N	0	1	.000	1	1	0	0	7	9	7	1	0	3	0	1.29	343	.310	.375	2	.500	1	97	1		0.1
1899	Chi N	0	1	.000	1	1	1	0	9	19	13	0	1	5	7	13.00	29	.422	.490	5	.200	0	38	-7		-0.5
1902	Bos N	8	10	.444	21	19	17-1	1	170.1	158	82	0	9	58	39	2.59	109	.246	.309	62-1-1	.210	2*	106	7		0.4
1903	Bos N	11	16	.407	32	27	25-2	1	253	266	150	5	11	96	98	3.09	104	.272	.344	87-0-1	.161	1	93	-3		-0.1
Total	6	21	37	.362	80	59	51-3	3	566	629	387	10	20	227	179	3.64	96	.281	.353	207-1-2	.169	-1	90	-21		

MALARKEY, BILL   William John   B11.26.1878 Port Byron IL   D12.12.1956 Phoenix AZ   BR/TR/5-10/185   d4.16

| 1908 | NY N | 2 | 2 | .500 | 15 | 0 | 0 | 2 | 35 | 31 | 16 | 1 | 1 | 10 | 12 | 2.57 | 94 | .242 | .302 | 6 | .000 | -1 | -2 | | | -0.2 |

MALASKA, MARK   Dennis Mark   B1.17.1978 Youngstown OH   BL/TL/6-3/190(190-210)   [TBA00 8/226]   d7.17   Col Akron

2003	TB A	2	1	.667	20	0	0	0-3	16	13	6	1	0	12-3	17	2.81	163	.232	.377	0	—	0	2			0.4
2004	Bos A	1	1	.500	19	0	0	0-0	20	21	11	1	2	12-1	12	4.50	100	.266	.370	0	—	0	1			0.1
Total	2	3	2	.600	41	0	0	0-3	36	34	18	2	2	24-4	29	3.75	127	.252	.373	0	—	0	3			0.5

MALDONADO, CARLOS   Carlos Cesar (Delgado)   B10.18.1966 Chepo, Pan   BB/TR/6-2/210*   d9.16

| 1990 | KC A | 0 | 0 | — | 4 | 0 | 0 | 0-0 | 6 | 9 | 6 | 0 | 0 | 4-0 | 9 | 9.00 | 43 | .346 | .419 | 0 | — | 0 | -3 | | | -0.2 |
| 1991 | KC A | 0 | 0 | — | 5 | 0 | 0 | 0-0 | 7.2 | 11 | 9 | 0 | 0 | 9-1 | 1 | 8.22 | 50 | .333 | .476 | 0 | — | 0 | -4 | | | -0.2 |

YEAR	TM LG	W	L	PCT	G	GS	CG-SHO	SV-BS	IP	H	R	HR	HB	BB-IB	SO	ERA	AERA	OAV	OOB	AB-HR-SH	AVG	PB	SUP	APR	DL	PW
1993	Mil A	2	2	.500	29	0	0	1-0	37.1	40	20	2	0	17-5	18	4.58	94	.282	.350	0	—	0		-1		-0.1
Total		2	2	.500	38	0	0	1-0	51	60	35	2	0	30-6	28	5.65	75	.299	.381	0	—	0		-8		-0.5

MALIS, CY Cyrus Sol B2.26.1907 Philadelphia PA D1.12.1971 N.Hollywood CA BR/TR/5-11/175 d8.17

| 1934 | Phi N | 0 | 0 | — | 1 | 0 | 0 | | 3.2 | 4 | 2 | 0 | 0 | 2 | 1 | 4.91 | 96 | .267 | .353 | 0 | — | 0 | | 0 | | 0.0 |

MALLETTE, BRIAN Brian Drew B1.19.1975 Dublin GA BR/TR/6-0/185 [MilA97 27/817] d4.12 Col Kennesaw St.

| 2002 | Mil N | 0 | 0 | — | 5 | 0 | 0 | 0-0 | 5 | 7 | 6 | 3 | 1 | 3-1 | 5 | 10.80 | 38 | .350 | .458 | 0 | — | 0 | | -3 | | -0.2 |

MALLETTE, MAL Malcolm Francis B1.30.1922 Syracuse NY D11.25.2005 Durham NC BL/TL/6-2/200 d9.25 Col Syracuse

| 1950 | Bro N | 0 | 0 | — | 2 | 0 | 0 | | 1.1 | 3 | 0 | 0 | 0 | 0 | 0 | 0.00 | — | .333 | .429 | 0 | — | 0 | | 1 | 85 | 0.0 |

MALLICOAT, ROB Robbin Dale B11.16.1964 St.Helens OR BL/TL/6-3/180* [HouN84*S1/16] d9.11 Col Taft (CA) JC [DL 1993 Hou N 182]

1987	Hou N	0	0	—	4	1	0		6.2	9	6	0	0	6-0	4	6.75	58	.320	.452	0	—	0	161	-2		-0.1
1991	Hou N	0	2	.000	24	0	0	1-0	23.1	22	10	2	2	13-1	18	3.86	92	.259	.363	1	.000	-0		0		-0.1
1992	Hou N	0	0	—	23	0	0	0-0	23.2	26	19	2	5	19-2	20	7.23	47	.283	.427	1	.000	-0*		-10		-0.5
Total	3	0	2	.000	51	1	0	1-0	53.2	56	34	4	7	38-3	42	5.70	62	.277	.404	2	.000	-0	161	-12	182	-0.7

MALLOY, ALEX Archibald Alexander "Lick" B10.31.1886 Laurinburg NC D3.1.1961 Ferris TX BR/TR/6-2/180 d9.10

| 1910 | StL A | 0 | 6 | .000 | 7 | 6 | 4 | 0 | 52.2 | 47 | 26 | 0 | 2 | 17 | 27 | 2.56 | 97 | .261 | .332 | 16 | .063 | -1 | 18 | -1 | | -0.3 |

MALLOY, HERM Herman "Tug" B6.1.1885 Massillon OH D5.9.1942 Louisville OH BR/TR/6-0/? d10.6

1907	Det A	0	1	.000	1	1	1	0	8	13	10	1	0	5	6	5.63	46	.371	.450	4	.250	0	78	-3		-0.3
1908	Det A	0	2	.000	3	2	2	0	17	20	11	1	2	4	8	3.71	65	.278	.333	9	.333	1	42	-3		-0.2
Total	2	0	3	.000	4	3	3	0	25	33	21	2	2	9	14	4.32	57	.308	.373	13	.308	1	55	-6		-0.5

MALLOY, BOB Robert Paul B5.28.1918 Canonsburg PA BR/TR/5-11/185 d5.4 Mil 1944-46 Col Pittsburgh

1943	Cin N	0	0	—	6	0	0	0	10	14	8	1	0	8	4	6.30	53	.778	.846	3	.667	1		-3		-0.1
1944	Cin N	1	1	.500	9	0	0	0	23.1	22	10	0	0	11	4	3.09	113	.265	.351	7	.000	-1		1		0.0
1946	Cin N	2	5	.286	27	3	1	0	72	71	29	2	2	26	24	2.75	122	.265	.334	18	.278	1	94	4		0.4
1947	Cin N	0	0	—	1	0	0	0	1	3	2	1	0	0	1	18.00	23	.600	.600	0	—	-0		-1		-0.1
1949	StL A	1	1	.500	5	0	0	0	9.2	6	3	0	0	7	2	2.79	162	.200	.351	3	.000	-0		2		0.3
Total	5	4	7	.364	48	3	1	2	116	116	52	4	2	52	35	3.26	106	.287	.371	31	.226	1	94	3		0.5

MALLOY, BOB Robert William B11.24.1964 Arlington VA BR/TR/6-5/200* [TexA86 19/475] d5.26 Col Virginia

1987	Tex A	0	0	—	2	2	0	0-0	11	13	11	6	0	3-0	6	6.55	69	.271	.314	0	—	0	182	-3		-0.2
1990	Mon N	0	0	—	1	0	0	0-0	2	1	0	0	0	1-0	1	0.00	—	.143	.250	0	—	0		1		0.0
Total	2	0	0	—	3	2	0	0-0	13	14	11	6	0	4-0	9	5.54	79	.255	.305	0	—	0	182	-2		-0.2

MALONE, CHUCK Charles Ray B7.8.1965 Harrisburg AR BR/TR/6-7/250 [PhiN86*5/112] d9.6 Col Arkansas St.

| 1990 | Phi N | 1 | 0 | 1.000 | 7 | 0 | 0 | 0-0 | 7.1 | 3 | 4 | 1 | 0 | 11-0 | 7 | 3.68 | 105 | .130 | .412 | 0 | — | 0 | | 0 | | 0.0 |

MALONE, MARTIN Martin d6.20 ▲

| 1872 | Eck NA | 0 | 2 | .000 | 2 | 2 | 2 | 0 | 18 | 51 | 50 | 1 | | 4 | 0 | 10.50 | 32 | .443 | .462 | 16 | .375 | 1* | 90 | -14 | | -0.8 |

MALONE, PAT Perce Leigh B9.25.1902 Altoona PA D5.13.1943 Altoona PA BL/TR(BB 1935-37)/6-0/200 d4.12 Col Juniata

1928	Chi N	18	13	.581	42	25	16-2	2	250.2	218	99	15	6	99	155	2.84	136	.236	.314	95-1-3	.189	1	118	27		3.1
1929	†Chi N	22	10	.688	40	30	19-5	2	267	283	120	12	6	102	166	3.57	129	.276	.345	105-2-0	.210	2	111	33		3.5
1930	Chi N	20	9	.690	45	35	22-1	4	271.2	290	145	14	6	96	142	3.94	124	.271	.334	104-4-4	.248	5	117	26		2.6
1931	Chi N	16	9	.640	36	30	12-2	0	228.1	229	115	9	4	88	112	3.90	99	.258	.328	79-1-9	.215	2	132	-1		0.0
1932	†Chi N	15	17	.469	37	32	17-2	0	237	222	111	13	6	78	120	3.38	111	.244	.308	78-1-8	.179	0	93	8		0.8
1933	Chi N	10	14	.417	31	26	13-2	0	186.1	186	91	11	5	59	72	3.91	84	.258	.318	63-0-3	.159	-2	105	-11		-1.6
1934	Chi N	14	7	.667	34	21	8-1	0	191	200	85	14	3	55	111	3.53	110	.270	.322	64-0-8	.172	-2	100	7		0.5
1935	NY A	3	5	.375	29	2	0	3	56.1	53	45	7	1	33	25	5.43	75	.252	.357	15-0-1	.000	-3	193	-12		-1.7
1936	†NY A	12	4	.750	35	9	5	9	134.2	144	60	4	4	60	72	3.81	122	.273	.352	51-0-2	.196	-1	160	16		1.6
1937	NY A	4	4	.500	28	9	3	6	92	109	65	5	4	35	49	5.48	81	.291	.357	33-0-2	.030	-5	146	-10		-1.4
Total	10	134	92	.593	357	219	115-15	26	1915	1934	936	103	45	705	1024	3.74	111	.262	.330	688-9-40	.188	-2	115	83		7.4

MALONEY, CHARLIE Charles Michael B5.22.1886 Cambridge MA D1.17.1967 Arlington MA BR/TR/5-8/155 d8.10 Col Boston College

| 1908 | Bos N | 0 | 0 | — | 1 | 0 | 0 | | 2 | 3 | 1 | 0 | 1 | 1 | 0 | 4.50 | 54 | .429 | .500 | 0 | — | 0' | | 0 | | 0.0 |

MALONEY, JIM James William B6.2.1940 Fresno CA BL/TR/6-2/207(190-214) d7.27 Col Fresno (CA) City

1960	Cin N	2	6	.250	11	10	2-1	0	63.2	61	35	5	2	37-2	48	4.66	82	.255	.360	18-0-1	.111	-0	90	-5		-0.6
1961	†Cin N	6	7	.462	27	11	1	2	94.2	86	54	16	1	59-4	57	4.37	93	.242	.349	29-1-1	.379	4*	117	-4		-0.1
1962	Cin N	9	7	.563	22	17	3	1	115.1	90	52	11	2	66-3	105	3.51	115	.214	.320	43	.186	0*	96	6		0.7
1963	Cin N	23	7	.767	33	33	13-6	0	250.1	183	84	17	6	88-1	265	2.77	121	.202	.275	89-0-5	.169	1*	131	17		2.0
1964	Cin N	15	10	.600	31	31	11-2	0	216	175	72	16	4	83-5	214	2.71	133	.222	.296	73-1-1	.151	1	96	22		2.5
1965	Cin N★	20	9	.690	33	33	14-5	0	255.1	189	77	13	5	110-3	244	2.54	148	.206	.294	89-0-8	.225	7*	111	34		4.6
1966	Cin N	16	8	.667	32	32	10-5	0	224.2	174	75	18	10	90-4	216	2.80	139	.214	.299	81-0-3	.222	3*	92	26		3.0
1967	Cin N	15	11	.577	30	29	6-3	0	196.1	181	76	8	3	72-5	153	3.25	115	.247	.315	69-0-2	.159	-0*	85	11		1.5
1968	Cin N	16	10	.615	33	32	8-5	0	207	183	100	17	2	80-6	181	3.61	88	.239	.314	74-2-4	.243	6*	125	-12		-0.9
1969	Cin N	12	5	.706	30	27	6-3	0-0	178.2	135	64	11	1	86-4	102	2.77	136	.208	.301	55-3-6	.200	6	112	18		2.3
1970	Cin N	0	1	.000	7	3	0	1-0	16.2	26	22	3	2	15-0	7	11.34	36	.366	.478	3	.000	-0	148	-13	141	-0.8
1971	Cal A	0	3	.000	13	4	0	0	30.1	35	18	3	1	24-2	13	5.04	64	.294	.414	5	.200	-0	62	-6	33	-0.6
Total	12	134	84	.615	302	262	74-30	4-0	1849	1518	729	138	36	810-39	1605	3.19	115	.224	.308	628-7-31	.201	26	106	94	174	13.6

MALONEY, SEAN Sean Patrick B5.25.1971 South Kingstown RI BR/TR/6-7/210(210-230) [MilA93 19/543] d4.28 Col Georgetown

1997	Mil A	0	0	—	3	0	0	0-0	7	7	4	1	2	2-0	5	5.14	90	.304	.379	0	—	0		0		0.0
1998	LA N	0	1	.000	11	0	0	0-0	12.2	13	7	2	2	5-0	11	4.97	81	.265	.357	1	.000	-0		-1		-0.1
Total	2	0	1	.000	14	0	0	0-0	19.2	20	11	3	4	7-0	16	5.03	84	.278	.365	1	.000	-0		-1		-0.1

MALOY, PAUL Paul Augustus "Biff" B6.4.1892 Bascom OH D3.18.1976 Sandusky OH BR/TR/5-11/185 d7.11

| 1913 | Bos A | 0 | 0 | — | 2 | 0 | 0 | 0 | 4 | 2 | 2 | 0 | 2 | 1 | 0 | 9.00 | 33 | .286 | .500 | 0 | — | 0 | | -1 | | -0.1 |

MALTZBERGER, GORDON Gordon Ralph "Maltzy" B9.4.1912 Utopia TX D12.11.1974 Rialto CA BR/TR/6-0/170 d4.27 Mil 1945-46 C3

1943	Chi A	7	4	.636	37	0	0	14	98.2	86	29	8	2	24	48	2.46	136	.236	.287	25-0-2	.120	0		11		1.6
1944	Chi A	10	5	.667	46	0	0	12	91.1	81	31	2	1	19	49	2.96	116	.235	.277	22-0-2	.136	-1		7		1.2
1946	Chi A	2	0	1.000	19	0	0	2	39.2	30	7	3	1	6	17	1.59	215	.205	.242	6	.000	-0		9		0.5
1947	Chi A	1	4	.200	33	0	0	5	63.2	61	26	4	1	25	22	3.39	108	.257	.331	7-0-1	.143	1		3		0.4
Total	4	20	13	.606	135	0	0	33	293.1	258	93	17	5	74	136	2.70	128	.236	.288	60-0-5	.117	0		30		3.7

MAMAUX, AL Albert Leon B5.30.1894 Pittsburgh PA D12.31.1962 Santa Monica CA BR/TR/6-0.5/168 d9.23 Mil 1918 Col Duquesne

1913	Pit N	0	0	—	1	0	0	0	3	2	1	0	2	2	3.00	101	.167	.286	1	.000	-0		0		0.0
1914	Pit N	5	2	.714	13	6	4-2	0	63	41	19	1	2	24	30	1.71	155	.186	.272	20	.250	1	117	5		0.8
1915	Pit N	21	8	.724	38	30	17-8	0	251.2	182	70	3	9	96	152	2.04	134	.208	.293	92-0-5	.163	-2	116	21		2.0
1916	Pit N	21	15	.583	45	37	26-1	2	310	264	123	3	9	136	163	2.53	106	.239	.327	110-0-2	.191	1	101	3		0.5
1917	Pit N	2	11	.154	16	13	5	0	85.2	92	59	1	3	50	22	5.25	54	.278	.378	31-0-1	.226	0	98	-21		-2.9
1918	Bro N	0	1	.000	2	1	0	0	8	14	6	0	0	2	2	6.75	41	.438	.471	2	.000	-0	54	-3		-0.3
1919	Bro N	10	12	.455	30	22	16-2	0	199.1	174	89	2	4	66	80	2.66	112	.245	.312	63-0-2	.175	-0	92	16		1.2
1920	†Bro N	12	8	.600	41	17	9-2	4	190.2	172	70	2	4	63	101	2.69	119	.255	.322	60-0-2	.167	-0	88	11		0.3
1921	Bro N	3	3	.500	12	1	0	1	43	36	17	1	1	13	21	3.14	124	.240	.305	11-0-1	.182	0	63	4		0.5
1922	Bro N	1	4	.200	37	7	1	3	87.2	97	46	7	2	33	35	3.70	110	.290	.358	17-1-2	.235	3	92	3		0.5
1923	Bro N	0	0	—	13	0	0	0	13	20	13	0	0	5	5	8.31	47	.385	.448	2	.500	3	0	-6		-0.7
1924	NY A	1	1	.500	14	2	0	0	38	44	28	2	1	20	5	5.68	73	.308	.396	13	.077	-1	223	-7		-0.5
Total	12	76	67	.531	254	137	78-15	10	1293	1138	541	22	35	511	625	2.90	104	.245	.325	422-1-15	.182	2	100	12		1.4

MANDERS, HAL Harold Carl B6.14.1917 Waukee IA BR/TR/6-0/187 d8.12 Col Iowa

| 1941 | Det A | 1 | 0 | 1.000 | 8 | 0 | 0 | 0 | 15.1 | 13 | 5 | 0 | 1 | 8 | 7 | 2.35 | 194 | .236 | .344 | 4 | .000 | -1 | | 3 | | 0.1 |
| 1942 | Det A | 1 | 0 | 1.000 | 18 | 0 | 0 | 0 | 33 | 39 | 15 | 1 | 1 | 14 | 14 | 4.09 | 97 | .307 | .385 | 4 | .250 | 0 | | -1 | | 0.0 |

YEAR	TM LG	W	L	PCT	G	GS	CG-SHO	SV-BS	IP	H	R	HR	HB	BB-IB	SO	ERA	AERA	OAV	OOB	AB-HR-SH	AVG	PB	SUP	APR	DL	P
1946	Det A	0	0	—	2	0	0	0	6	8	7	1	1	2	3	10.50	35	.364	.440	2	.500	0		-4		-0
	Chi N	0	1	1.000	2	1	0	0	6	11	6	1	1	3	4	9.00	37	.423	.500	2	.000	-0	26	-3		-0
Total	3	3	1	.750	30	1	0	0	60.1	71	37	6	4	28	28	4.77	84	.309	.393	12	.167	-0	26	-5		-0

MANGUM, LEO Leo Allan "Blackie" B5.24.1896 Durham NC D7.9.1974 Lima OH BR/TR/6-1/187 d7.11

YEAR	TM LG	W	L	PCT	G	GS	CG-SHO	SV-BS	IP	H	R	HR	HB	BB-IB	SO	ERA	AERA	OAV	OOB	AB-HR-SH	AVG	PB	SUP	APR	DL	P
1924	Chi A	1	4	.200	13	7	1	0	47	69	43	3	1	25	12	7.09	58	.359	.436	14	.071	-1	117	-15		-1
1925	Chi A	1	0	1.000	7	0	0	0	15	25	15	0	0	6	6	7.80	53	.373	.425	4	.500	1		-6		-0
1928	NY N	0	0	—	1	1	0	0	3	6	5	0	0	5	1	15.00	26	.500	.647	1	1.000	0	260	-3		-0
1932	Bos N	0	0	—	7	0	0	0	10.1	17	8	1	0	0	3	5.23	72	.333	.333	2	.000	-0		-2		-0
1933	Bos N	4	3	.571	25	5	2-1	0	84	93	33	2	0	11	28	3.32	92	.280	.303	22-0-2	.091	-2	92	-1		-0
1934	Bos N	5	3	.625	29	3	1	1	94.1	127	67	9	0	23	28	5.72	67	.315	.352	32	.281	2	38	-20		-1
1935	Bos N	0	0	—	3	0	0	0	4.2	6	3	0	0	2	0	3.86	98	.300	.364	0		0		0		-0
Total	7	11	10	.524	85	16	4-1	1	258.1	343	174	15	1	72	78	5.37	68	.318	.362	75-0-2	.200	0	108	-47		-3

MANN, JIM James Joseph B11.17.1974 Brockton MA BR/TR/6-3/225* [TorA93 54/1468] d5.29 Col Massasoit (MA) CC

YEAR	TM LG	W	L	PCT	G	GS	CG-SHO	SV-BS	IP	H	R	HR	HB	BB-IB	SO	ERA	AERA	OAV	OOB	AB-HR-SH	AVG	PB	SUP	APR	DL	P
2000	NY N	0	0	—	2	0	0	0-0	2.2	6	3	1	0	1-0	1	10.13	43	.429	.467	0	—	0		-2		0
2001	Hou N	0	0	—	4	0	0	0-0	5.1	3	2	0	2	4-0	5	3.38	136	.176	.391	0	—	0		1		0
2002	Hou N	0	1	.000	17	0	0	0-0	22	19	10	3	5	7-1	19	4.09	106	.235	.333	1	.000	-0		1		0
2003	Pit N	0	0	—	2	0	0	0-0	1.2	5	4	1	0	1-0	0	10.80	40	.455	.500	0		-0		-2		-0
Total	4	0	1	.000	25	0	0	0-0	31.2	33	19	5	7	13-1	25	4.83	91	.268	.371	1	.000	-0		-2		-0

MANNING, DAVID David Anthony B8.14.1972 Buffalo NY BR/TR/6-3/210 [TexA92 3/90] d8.2 Col Palm Beach (FL) CC

YEAR	TM LG	W	L	PCT	G	GS	CG-SHO	SV-BS	IP	H	R	HR	HB	BB-IB	SO	ERA	AERA	OAV	OOB	AB-HR-SH	AVG	PB	SUP	APR	DL	P
2003	Mil N	0	2	.000	2	2	0	0-0	6.2	11	13	1	0	8-0	2	16.20	27	.393	.514	1	.000	-0	22	-9		-1

MANNING, ERNIE Ernest Devon "Ed" B10.9.1890 Florala AL D4.28.1973 Pensacola FL BL/TR/6-0/175 d5.3 Col Auburn-Montgomery

YEAR	TM LG	W	L	PCT	G	GS	CG-SHO	SV-BS	IP	H	R	HR	HB	BB-IB	SO	ERA	AERA	OAV	OOB	AB-HR-SH	AVG	PB	SUP	APR	DL	P
1914	StL A	0	0	—	4	0	0	0	10	11	6	0	0	3	3	3.60	75	.297	.350	4-0-1	.000	-0*		-1		-0

MANNING, JIM James Benjamin B7.21.1943 L'Anse MI BR/TR/6-1/185 d4.15

YEAR	TM LG	W	L	PCT	G	GS	CG-SHO	SV-BS	IP	H	R	HR	HB	BB-IB	SO	ERA	AERA	OAV	OOB	AB-HR-SH	AVG	PB	SUP	APR	DL	P
1962	Min A	0	0	—	5	1	0	0	7	14	10	0	1	1-0	3	5.14	79	.389	.410	1	.000	-0	153	-3		-0

MANNING, JACK John E. B12.20.1853 Braintree MA D8.15.1929 Boston MA BR/TR/5-8.5/158 d4.23.1873 M1 ▲

YEAR	TM LG	W	L	PCT	G	GS	CG-SHO	SV-BS	IP	H	R	HR	HB	BB-IB	SO	ERA	AERA	OAV	OOB	AB-HR-SH	AVG	PB	SUP	APR	DL	P
1874	Bal NA	4	16	.200	22	20	17	0	176.2	222	168	2		12	12	2.09	107	.266	.277	174	.351	7*	50	-1		0
1875	Bos NA	16	2	.889	27	18	8-1	6	144	152	86	1		14	34	2.38	90	.247	.263	348-1	.270	4*	173	-4		-0
1876	Bos N	18	5	.783	34	20	13	5	197.1	213	139	1		32	24	2.14	105	.252	.279	288-2	.264	3*	153	-1		C
1877	Cin N	0	4	.000	10	4	2	1	44	83	65	1		7	6	6.95	38	.379	.398	252	.317	4*	55	-21		-C
1878	Bos N	1	0	1.000	3	1	1	0	11.1	24	19	1		5	2	14.29	17	.393	.439	248	.254	0*	111	-11		-C
Total	2 NA	20	18	.526	49	38	25-1	6	320.2	374	254	2		26	46	2.22	99	.258	.271	522-1	.297	11	101	-5		C
Total	19	9	.679	47	25	16	6	252.2	320	223	3		44	32	3.53	66	.284	.311	788-2	.278	7	137	-33		C

MANNING, RUBE Walter S. B4.29.1883 Chambersburg PA D4.23.1930 Williamsport PA BR/TR/6-0/180 d9.25

YEAR	TM LG	W	L	PCT	G	GS	CG-SHO	SV-BS	IP	H	R	HR	HB	BB-IB	SO	ERA	AERA	OAV	OOB	AB-HR-SH	AVG	PB	SUP	APR	DL	P
1907	NY A	0	1	.000	1	1	0	1	9	8	3	0	1	3	3	3.00	93	.242	.324	3	.000	-0	24	0		C
1908	NY A	13	16	.448	41	26	19-2	1	245	228	114	4	18	86	113	2.94	84	.256	.334	91-0-1	.187	0*	77	-11		-C
1909	NY A	7	11	.389	26	21	11-2	1	173	167	76	2	9	48	71	3.17	80	.265	.326	60-0-3	.183	-0	102	-8		-C
1910	NY A	2	4	.333	16	9	4	0	75	80	43	4	4	25	25	3.72	71	.283	.349	26	.192	0	123	-9		-C
Total	4	22	32	.407	84	57	35-4	2	502	483	236	10	32	162	212	3.14	81	.263	.333	180-0-4	.183	-0	93	-28		C

MANON, JULIO Julio Alberto B6.10.1973 Guerra, D.R. BL/TR/6-0/200 d6.5

YEAR	TM LG	W	L	PCT	G	GS	CG-SHO	SV-BS	IP	H	R	HR	HB	BB-IB	SO	ERA	AERA	OAV	OOB	AB-HR-SH	AVG	PB	SUP	APR	DL	P
2003	Mon N	2	2	.333	24	0	0	1-0	28.1	26	13	3	1	17-1	15	4.13	107	.252	.358	1	.000	-0		2		

MANON, RAMON Ramon (Reyes) B1.20.1968 Santo Domingo, D.R. BR/TR/6-0/170 d4.19

YEAR	TM LG	W	L	PCT	G	GS	CG-SHO	SV-BS	IP	H	R	HR	HB	BB-IB	SO	ERA	AERA	OAV	OOB	AB-HR-SH	AVG	PB	SUP	APR	DL	P
1990	Tex A	0	0	—	1	0	0	0-0	2	3	3	0	0	3-1	0	13.50	29	.333	.500	0	—	0		-2		-C

MANSKE, LOU Louis Hugo B7.4.1884 Milwaukee WI D4.27.1963 Milwaukee WI BL/TL/6-0/? d8.31

YEAR	TM LG	W	L	PCT	G	GS	CG-SHO	SV-BS	IP	H	R	HR	HB	BB-IB	SO	ERA	AERA	OAV	OOB	AB-HR-SH	AVG	PB	SUP	APR	DL	P
1906	Pit N	0	0	—	2	1	0	0	8	12	6	0	0	5	6	5.63	48	.387	.472	4	.000	-1	191	-2		-I

MANTEI, MATT Matthew Bruce B7.7.1973 Tampa FL BR/TR/6-1/190(181-200) [SeaA91 25/656] d6.18 [DL 1997 Fla N 181]

YEAR	TM LG	W	L	PCT	G	GS	CG-SHO	SV-BS	IP	H	R	HR	HB	BB-IB	SO	ERA	AERA	OAV	OOB	AB-HR-SH	AVG	PB	SUP	APR	DL	P
1995	Fla N	0	1	.000	12	0	0	0-0	13.1	12	8	1	1	13-0	15	4.73	91	.245	.397	0	—	0		-1	88	
1996	Fla N	1	0	1.000	14	0	0	0-1	18.1	13	13	2	1	21-1	25	6.38	65	.197	.398	1	.000	-0		-4	103	
1998	Fla N	3	4	.429	42	0	0	9-3	54.2	38	19	1	7	23-3	61	2.96	137	.203	.308	3	.333	0		7	16	
1999	Fla N	1	2	.333	35	0	0	10-2	36.1	24	11	4	2	25-1	50	2.72	161	.186	.325	1	.000	-0		7		
	†Ari N	1	1	.000	30	0	0	22-3	29	20	10	1	3	19-0	49	2.79	165	.192	.333	0	—	0		6		
	Year	1	3	.250	65	0	0	32-5	65.1	44	21	5	5	44-1	99	2.76	163	.189	.329	1	.000	-0		13		
2000	Ari N	1	1	.500	47	0	0	17-3	45.1	31	24	4	2	35-1	53	4.57	105	.193	.343	0	—	0		1	32	
2001	Ari N	0	0	—	8	0	0	2-0	7	6	2	2	0	4-0	12	2.57	180	.222	.323	0	—	0		2	166	
2002	†Ari N	2	2	.500	31	0	0	0-1	26.2	28	15	3	1	12-0	26	4.73	95	.257	.336	0	—	0		-1	88	
2003	Ari N	5	4	.556	50	0	0	29-3	55	37	17	6	6	12-0	68	2.62	177	.191	.264	0	—	0		12	33	
2004	Ari N	0	3	.000	12	0	0	4-3	10.2	17	15	5	0	6-1	13	11.81	39	.354	.418	0	—	0		-8	148	
2005	Bos A	1	0	1.000	34	0	0	0-0	26.1	23	20	1	5	24-1	22	6.49	71	.240	.416	0	—	0		-5	93	
Total	10	14	18	.438	315	0	0	93-19	322.2	249	154	30	23	200-8	396	4.07	110	.213	.337	5	.200	0		16	948	

MANUEL, BARRY Barry Paul B8.12.1965 Mamou LA BR/TR/5-11/185* [TexA87 2/51] d9.6 Col Louisiana St. [DL 1993 Tex A 76]

YEAR	TM LG	W	L	PCT	G	GS	CG-SHO	SV-BS	IP	H	R	HR	HB	BB-IB	SO	ERA	AERA	OAV	OOB	AB-HR-SH	AVG	PB	SUP	APR	DL	P
1991	Tex A	1	0	1.000	8	0	0	0-0	16	7	2	0	0	6-0	5	1.13	360	.143	.224	0	—	0		5		
1992	Tex A	1	0	1.000	3	0	0	0-0	5.2	6	3	2	1	1-0	9	4.76	80	.261	.320	0	—	0		0		
1996	Mon N	4	1	.800	53	0	0	0-0	86	70	34	10	7	26-4	62	3.24	134	.219	.291	7-0-1	.000	-0		10		
1997	NY N	1	0	1.000	19	0	0	0-0	25.2	35	18	6	1	13-1	21	5.26	76	.324	.402	2	.000	-0		-4		
1998	Ari N	1	0	1.000	13	0	0	0-0	15.2	17	14	5	1	14-3	12	7.47	57	.266	.405	0	—	0		-5		
Total	5	7	2	.778	96	0	0	0-0	149	135	71	23	10	60-8	109	3.87	109	.240	.321	9-0-1	.000	-1		6	76	

MANUEL, MOXIE Mark Garfield B10.16.1881 Metropolis IL D4.26.1924 Memphis TN BR/TR/5-11/170 d9.25

YEAR	TM LG	W	L	PCT	G	GS	CG-SHO	SV-BS	IP	H	R	HR	HB	BB-IB	SO	ERA	AERA	OAV	OOB	AB-HR-SH	AVG	PB	SUP	APR	DL	P
1905	Was A	0	0	—	3	1	1	0	10	9	14	0	1	3	3	5.40	49	.243	.317	4	.250	0	80	-3		
1908	Chi A	3	4	.429	18	6	3	1	60.1	52	25	0	2	25	25	3.28	71	.243	.328	16-0-1	.063	-1	98	-5		
Total	2	3	4	.429	21	7	4	1	70.1	61	34	0	3	28	28	3.58	66	.243	.326	20-0-1	.100	-1	96	-8		

MANVILLE, DICK Richard Wesley B12.25.1926 Des Moines IA BR/TR/6-4/192* d4.30 Col Yale

YEAR	TM LG	W	L	PCT	G	GS	CG-SHO	SV-BS	IP	H	R	HR	HB	BB-IB	SO	ERA	AERA	OAV	OOB	AB-HR-SH	AVG	PB	SUP	APR	DL	P
1950	Bos N	0	0	—	1	0	0	0	2	0	0	0	0	3	2	0.00	—	.000	.300	0		0		1		
1952	Chi N	0	0	—	11	0	0	0	17	25	17	2	0	12	6	7.94	48	.362	.457	2	.500	0		-7		
Total	2	0	0	—	12	0	0	0	19	25	17	2	0	15	8	7.11	54	.329	.440	2	.500	0		-6		

MANZANILLO, JOSIAS Josias (Adams) B10.16.1967 San Pedro de Macoris, D.R. BR/TR/6-0/190(190-205) d10.5 b-Ravelo

YEAR	TM LG	W	L	PCT	G	GS	CG-SHO	SV-BS	IP	H	R	HR	HB	BB-IB	SO	ERA	AERA	OAV	OOB	AB-HR-SH	AVG	PB	SUP	APR	DL	P
1991	Bos A	0	0	—	1	0	0	0-0	1	2	2	0	0	3-0	1	18.00	24	.400	.625	0	—	0		-1		
1993	Mil A	1	1	.500	10	1	0	1-1	17	22	20	1	2	10-3	10	9.53	45	.314	.405	0	—	0	85	-10		
	NY N	0	0	—	6	0	0	0-0	12	8	7	1	0	9-0	11	3.00	134	.186	.321	1	.000	-0		8	16	
1994	NY N	3	2	.600	37	0	0	2-3	47.1	34	15	4	3	13-2	48	2.66	157	.200	.269	4-0-1	.000	-0		0		
1995	NY N	1	2	.333	12	0	0	0-0	16	18	15	3	0	6-2	14	7.88	51	.273	.329	0	—	-0		-7		
	NY A	0	0	—	11	0	0	0-0	17.1	19	4	1	2	9-2	11	2.08	223	.279	.380	0	—	0		5	88	
1997	Sea A	0	1	.000	16	0	0	0-1	18.1	19	13	3	0	17-1	16	5.40	84	.275	.409	1	.000	-0		-2	64	
1999	NY N	0	0	—	12	0	0	0-0	18.2	19	12	5	2	4-1	25	5.79	75	.264	.316	1	1.000	0*		-3		
2000	Pit N	2	2	.500	43	0	0	0-2	58.2	50	23	6	0	32-4	39	3.38	138	.240	.339	3-0-1	.000	-0		9		
2001	Pit N	3	2	.600	71	0	0	2-5	79.2	60	30	4	5	26-3	80	3.39	132	.211	.281	0	—	0		10		
2002	Pit N	0	0	—	13	0	0	0-1	13	20	11	2	1	5-0	4	7.62	55	.364	.426	0	—	0		-4	72	
2003	Cin N	0	2	.000	9	0	0	0-0	10.2	21	20	7	0	4-0	12	12.66	33	.389	.431	0	—	0		-12		
2004	Fla N	3	3	.500	26	0	0	1-3	32.1	38	24	4	3	15-2	27	6.12	67	.292	.376	1	.000	-0		-8		
Total	11	13	15	.464	267	1	0	6-17	342	330	198	46	18	153-20	300	4.71	93	.255	.338	12-0-2	.083	-1	85	-15	240	

MANZANILLO, RAVELO Ravelo (Adams) B10.17.1963 San Pedro de Macoris, D.R. BL/TL/5-10/190* d9.25 b-Josias

YEAR	TM LG	W	L	PCT	G	GS	CG-SHO	SV-BS	IP	H	R	HR	HB	BB-IB	SO	ERA	AERA	OAV	OOB	AB-HR-SH	AVG	PB	SUP	APR	DL	P
1988	Chi A	0	1	.000	2	0	0	0-0	9	7	6	1	1	2-0	10	5.79	69	.212	.435	0	—	0	91	-1		
1994	Pit N	4	2	.667	46	2	0	1-2	50	45	30	4	3	42-5	39	4.14	106	.245	.385	3	.667	1		-1		
1995	Pit N	0	0	—	5	0	0	0-0	3.2	3	3	0	1	2-0	1	4.91	89	.231	.375	1	.000	-0		-1		
Total	3	4	3	.571	53	2	0	1-2	63	55	39	5	5	56-5	50	4.43	97	.239	.392	4	.500	1	91	-3		

YEAR	TM LG	W	L	PCT	G	GS	CG-SHO	SV-BS	IP	H	R	HR	HB	BB-IB	SO	ERA	AERA	OAV	OOB	AB-HR-SH	AVG	PB	SUP	APR	DL	PW
MAPEL, ROLLA	Rolla Hamilton "Lefty" B3.9.1890 Lees Summit MO D4.6.1966 San Diego CA BL/TL/5-11.5/165 d8.31																								
1919	StL A	0	3	.000	4	3	2	0	20	17	12	0	3	17	2	4.50	74	.262	.435	6	.167	-0	8	-2		-0.3
MARAK, PAUL	Paul Patrick B8.2.1965 Lakenheath, England BR/TR/6-2/175 [AtIN85*11/256] d9.1 Col Trinidad St. (CO) JC																								
1990	Atl N	1	2	.333	7	7	1-1	0-0	39	39	16	2	3	19-3	15	3.69	109	.267	.361	11-0-1	.091	-0	83	2		0.2
MARANDA, GEORGES	Georges Henri B1.15.1932 Levis QC, Can. D7.14.2000 Levis QC, Can. BR/TR/6-2/195* d4.26																								
1960	SF N	1	4	.200	17	4	0	0	50.2	50	32	6	0	30-7	28	4.62	75	.254	.351	12	.167	-0	51	-8		-0.6
1962	Min A	1	3	.250	32	4	0	0	72.2	69	43	10	4	35-3	36	4.46	92	.252	.343	16	.250	1	87	-4		0.0
Total	2	2	7	.222	49	8	0	0	123.1	119	75	16	4	65-10	64	4.52	85	.253	.346	28	.214	1	70	-12		-0.6
MARBERRY, FIRPO	Fredrick B11.30.1898 Streetman TX D6.30.1976 Mexia TX BR/TR/6-1/190 d8.11 U1																								
1923	Was A	4	0	1.000	11	4	2	0	44.2	42	16	1	3	17	18	2.82	133	.258	.339	14-0-1	.143	-1	148	5		0.3
1924	†Was A	11	12	.478	50	14	6	**15**	195.1	190	88	3	7	9	70	3.09	131	.262	.335	59-0-8	.136	-4	97	18		1.7
1925	†Was A	9	5	.643	55	0	0	**15**	93.1	84	50	4	4	45	53	3.47	122	.246	.341	19-0-2	.263	1		5		1.0
1926	Was A	12	7	.632	64	5	3	**22**	138	120	55	4	3	66	43	3.00	129	.243	.336	24-0-2	.176	-1	105	13		2.0
1927	Was A	10	7	.588	56	10	2	9	155.1	177	92	4	3	68	74	4.64	88	.296	.371	41-0-1	.122	-3	113	-9		-1.4
1928	Was A	13	13	.500	48	11	7-1	3	161.1	160	79	4	3	42	76	3.85	104	.268	.319	46-0-3	.109	-4	90	4		0.1
1929	Was A	19	12	.613	49	26	16	**11**	250.1	233	100	6	6	69	121	3.06	139	.252	**.308**	81-0-5	.235	2	99	33		4.0
1930	Was A	15	5	.750	33	22	9-2	1	185	190	92	15	0	53	56	4.09	113	.270	.321	73-0-4	.329	5	132	12		1.5
1931	Was A	16	4	.800	45	25	11-1	7	219	211	92	13	3	63	88	3.45	124	.252	.307	82-1-3	.232	1	125	24		2.1
1932	Was A	8	4	.667	54	15	8-1	13	197.2	202	98	13	2	72	66	4.01	108	.268	.333	66	.167	-2	105	7		0.3
1933	Det A	16	11	.593	37	32	15-1	2	238.1	232	98	13	0	61	84	3.29	131	.254	**.302**	90-0-3	.122	-5	100	29		2.3
1934	†Det A	15	5	.750	38	19	6-1	3	155.2	174	92	12	0	48	64	4.57	96	.276	.327	55-0-1	.218	2	151	-4		-0.3
1935	Det A	0	1	.000	5	1	0	0	19	22	11	2	0	9	7	4.26	98	.289	.365	5	.200	-0	62	-1		0.0
1936	NY N	0	0	—	1	0	0	0	0.1	1	1	0	0	0	0	0.00	—	.500	.500	1	.000	-0		0		0.0
	Was A	0	2	.000	5	1	0	0	14	11	7	2	1	3	4	3.86	124	.208	.263	2-0-1	.000	-0	37	2		0.1
Total	14	148	88	.627	551	186	86-7	101	2067.1	2049	971	96	38	686	822	3.63	116	.262	.325	668-1-34	.192	-8	114	138		13.7
MARBET, WALT	Walter William B9.13.1890 Plymouth Co. IA D9.24.1956 Hohenwald TN BR/TR/6-1/175 d6.17																								
1913	StL N	1	0	1.000	3	1	0	0	3.1	9	7	0	0	4	1	16.20	20	.500	.591	0	—	0	116	-5		-0.8
MARCHILDON, PHIL	Philip Joseph "Babe" B10.25.1913 Penetanguishene ON, Can. D1.10.1997 Toronto ON, Can. BR/TR/5-11/175* d9.22 Mil 1943-45																								
1940	Phi A	0	2	.000	2	2	1	0	10	12	9	1	0	8	4	7.20	62	.286	.400	2-0-1	.000	-0	30	-3		-0.4
1941	Phi A	10	15	.400	30	27	14-1	0	204.1	188	94	15	3	118	74	3.57	117	.245	.348	66-0-8	.167	1	92	13		1.4
1942	Phi A	17	14	.548	38	31	18-1	1	244	215	126	14	4	140	110	4.20	90	.235	.339	84-0-5	.238	3	91	-8		-0.7
1945	Phi A	0	1	.000	3	2	0	0	9	5	5	0	0	11	2	4.00	86	.179	.410	2	.500	1	112	-1		0.0
1946	Phi A	13	16	.448	36	35	16-1	1	226.2	197	104	14	4	114	95	3.49	101	.237	.332	75-0-7	.067	-6	92	1		-0.6
1947	Phi A	19	9	.679	35	35	21-2	0	276.2	228	110	15	7	141	128	3.22	118	.224	.323	98-1-12	.153	-2	120	19		1.5
1948	Phi A	9	15	.375	33	30	12-1	0	226.1	214	133	19	4	131	66	4.53	95	.251	.353	72-0-3	.069	-5	92	-10		-1.5
1949	Phi A	0	3	.000	7	6	0	0	16	24	23	3	1	19	2	11.81	35	.358	.506	6	.167	-0	105	-14		-2.0
1950	Bos A	0	0	—	1	0	0	0	1.1	1	1	0	0	2	0	6.75	73	.200	.429	0	—	-0		0		0.0
Total	9	68	75	.476	185	162	82-6	2	1214.1	1084	605	81	23	684	481	3.93	100	.240	.342	405-1-36	.143	-10	97	-3		-2.3
MARCUM, JOHNNY	John Alfred "Footsie" B9.9.1909 Campbellsburg KY D9.10.1984 Louisville KY BL/TR/5-11/197 d9.7																								
1933	Phi A	3	2	.600	5	5	4-2	0	37	28	12	0	0	20	14	1.95	204	.200	.300	12	.167	0	115	9		1.1
1934	Phi A	14	11	.560	37	31	17-2	0	232	257	131	13	4	88	92	4.50	97	.280	.346	112-1-2	.268	6*	116	-3		0.2
1935	Phi A	17	12	.586	39	27	19-2	3	242.2	256	125	9	2	83	99	4.08	111	.268	.328	119-2-4	.311	9*	116	13		2.1
1936	Bos A	8	13	.381	31	23	9-1	1	174	194	100	14	0	52	57	4.81	110	.281	.332	88-2-3	.205	1*	78	12		1.2
1937	Bos A	13	11	.542	37	23	9-1	3	183.2	230	104	17	2	44	59	4.85	98	.306	.348	86-0-2	.267	5*	95	2		0.7
1938	Bos A	5	6	.455	15	11	7	0	92.1	113	49	11	0	25	25	4.09	120	.298	.342	37	.135	-1*	86	8		0.7
1939	StL A	2	5	.286	12	6	2	0	47.2	66	43	12	1	10	14	7.74	63	.332	.367	22	.455	3*	66	-13		-1.2
	Chi A	3	3	.500	19	6	2	0	90	125	66	15	0	19	32	6.00	79	.326	.357	57	.281	2*	140	-12		-0.5
	Year	5	8	.385	31	12	4	0	137.2	191	109	27	1	29	46	6.60	72	.328	.361	79	.329	6	103	-25		-1.7
Total	7	65	63	.508	195	132	69-8	7	1099.1	1269	630	91	9	344	392	4.66	101	.287	.340	533-5-11	.265	25	101	16		4.3
MARCUM, SHAUN	Shaun Michal B12.14.1981 Kansas City MO BR/TR/6-0/180 d9.6 Col Missouri St.																								
2005	Tor A	0	0	—	5	0	0	0-0	8	6	0	0	0	4-0	4	0.00	—	.214	.313	0	—	0		4		0.2
MARENTETTE, LEO	Leo John B2.18.1941 Detroit MI BR/TR/6-2/200(200-220) d9.26																								
1965	Det A	0	0	—	2	0	0	0	3	1	0	0	0	1-0	3	0.00	—	.111	.200	0	—	0		1		0.1
1969	Mon N	0	0	—	3	0	0	0-1	5.1	9	4	1	0	1-1	4	6.75	55	.391	.400	1	.000	-0		-2		-0.1
Total	2	0	0	—	5	0	0	0-1	8.1	10	4	1	0	2-1	7	4.32	84	.313	.343	1	.000	-0		-1		0.0
MARGONERI, JOE	Joseph Emanuel B1.13.1930 Somerset PA BL/TL/6-0/185* d4.25																								
1956	NY N	6	6	.500	23	13	2	0	91.2	88	45	12	0	49-3	49	3.93	96	.254	.343	29-1-3	.103	-1	91	-1		-0.3
1957	NY N	1	1	.500	13	2	1	0	34.1	44	23	1	1	21-2	18	5.24	75	.314	.402	8-0-1	.000	-1	101	-5		-0.4
Total	2	7	7	.500	36	15	3	0	126	132	68	13	1	70-5	67	4.29	89	.271	.361	37-1-4	.081	-2	92	-6		-0.7
MARICHAL, JUAN	Juan Antonio (Sanchez) "Manito" B10.20.1937 Laguna Verde, D.R. BR/TR/6-0/185* d7.19 HF1983																								
1960	SF N	6	2	.750	11	11	6-1	0	81.1	59	29	5	0	28-1	58	2.66	131	.200	.269	31-0-1	.129	0	131	8		0.7
1961	SF N	13	10	.565	29	27	9-3	0	185	183	88	24	2	48-5	124	3.89	98	.257	.305	59-0-5	.119	-2*	117	-1		-0.4
1962	†SF N★	18	11	.621	37	36	18-3	1	262.2	233	112	34	3	48-5	153	3.36	113	.234	.299	89-0-7	.236	4*	108	12		1.6
1963	SF N☆	**25**	8	.758	41	40	18-5	0	**321.1**	259	102	27	2	61-6	248	2.41	133	.216	.255	112-1-4	.179	3*	116	29		3.1
1964	SF N★	21	8	.724	33	33	22-4	0	269	241	89	18	1	52-8	206	2.48	144	.236	.272	97-0-6	.144	-1	132	30		3.1
1965	SF N★	22	13	.629	39	37	24-**10**	1	295.1	224	78	27	6	46-4	240	2.13	**169**	.205	.239	98-0-9	.173	1	92	**48**		**6.0**
1966	SF N★	25	6	**.806**	37	36	25-4	0	307.1	228	80	32	5	36-3	222	2.23	165	**.202**	**.230**	112-1-5	.250	6	111	49		5.8
1967	SF N★	14	10	.583	26	26	18-2	0	202.1	195	79	20	1	42-9	166	2.76	119	.249	.287	79-0-2	.177	3	138	9		1.3
1968	SF N★	**26**	9	.743	38	38	30-5	0	325.2	295	106	21	6	46-9	218	2.43	121	.238	.268	123-0-9	.163	1	144	18		2.5
1969	SF N☆	21	11	.656	37	36	27-**8**	0-0	299.2	244	90	15	6	54-7	205	**2.10**	**167**	.222	.261	109-0-3	.138	-1*	92	45		5.0
1970	SF N	12	10	.545	34	33	14-1	0-0	242.2	269	128	28	1	48-3	123	4.12	97	.277	.309	85-0-5	.059	-6	129	-5		-0.9
1971	†SF N★	18	11	.621	37	37	18-4	0-0	279	244	113	24	3	56-6	159	2.94	116	.233	.273	105-2-7	.133	0	131	13		1.5
1972	SF N	6	16	.273	25	24	6	0-0	165	176	82	15	3	46-7	72	3.71	94	.277	.327	51-0-1	.196	-1	84	-6		-0.6
1973	SF N	11	15	.423	34	32	9-2	0-0	207.1	231	104	22	1	37-7	87	3.82	101	.277	.307	69-0-7	.188	1	100	-1		0.3
1974	Bos A	5	1	.833	11	9	0	0-0	57.1	61	32	3	2	14-1	21	4.87	79	.270	.317	0	—	1	138	-5	58	-0.5
1975	LA N	0	1	.000	2	2	0	0-0	6	11	9	2	0	1-5	1	13.50	33	.407	.500	2	.000	-0	154	-7		-0.8
Total	16	243	142	.631	471	457	244-52	2-0	3507	3153	1329	320	40	709-82	2303	2.89	122	.237	.277	1221-4-71	.165	10	116	236	58	27.7
MARION, DAN	Donald G. "Rube" B7.31.1890 Cleveland OH D1.18.1933 Milwaukee WI BR/TR/6-1/187 d4.23																								
1914	Bro F	3	2	.600	17	9	4	0	89.1	97	52	1	6	38	41	3.93	73	.281	.362	36	.194	-2	125	-11		-0.8
1915	Bro F	12	9	.571	35	25	15-2	0	208.1	193	92	1	3	64	46	3.20	85	.248	.308	74-0-2	.176	-2	147	-9		-1.1
Total	2	15	11	.577	52	34	19-2	0	297.2	290	144	2	9	102	87	3.42	81	.258	.325	110-0-2	.182	-3	140	-20		-1.9
MARKELL, DUKE	Harry Duquesne (b Harry Duquesne Makowsky) B8.17.1923 Paris, France D6.14.1984 Ft.Lauderdale FL BR/TR/6-1.5/209 d9.6																								
1951	StL A	1	1	.500	5	2	1	0	21.1	25	16	3	0	20	10	6.33	69	.298	.433	6	.167	-0	81	-4		-0.3
MARKLE, CLIFF	Clifford Monroe B5.3.1894 Dravosburg PA D5.24.1974 Temple City CA BR/TR/5-9/163 d9.18																								
1915	NY A	1	0	1.000	7	2	2	0	23	15	3	1	0	6	12	0.39	750	.185	.241	4-0-1	.000	0	124	6		0.5
1916	NY A	4	3	.571	11	7	3-1	0	45.2	41	26	0	4	31	14	4.53	64	.256	.390	13-0-1	.000	-1	138	-7		-1.2
1921	Cin N	2	6	.250	10	6	5	0	67	75	36	0	0	20	23	3.76	95	.291	.342	24	.125	-2	69	-2		-0.4
1922	Cin N	4	5	.444	25	3	2-1	0	75.2	75	41	3	0	33	34	3.81	105	.268	.345	20	.150	-0	95	1		0.1
1924	NY A	0	3	.000	7	3	0	0	23.1	29	26	4	0	20	7	8.87	47	.333	.458	8	.000	-1	95	-12		-1.4
Total	5	12	17	.414	56	21	12-2	0	234.2	235	132	9	4	110	90	4.10	80	.271	.356	69-0-2	.087	-5	99	-14		-2.4
MARLOWE, DICK	Richard Burton B6.27.1929 Hickory NC D12.30.1968 Toledo OH BR/TR/6-2/170* d9.19 Col Davidson																								
1951	Det A	0	1	.000	2	0	0	0	1.2	5	6	0	0	2	1	32.40	13	.500	.583	0	—	0	21	-5		-0.8
1952	Det A	2	0	1.000	4	1	0	0	11	21	10	1	0	2	3	7.36	52	.420	.453	2	.000	-0	23	-4		-0.7
1953	Det A	6	7	.462	42	11	2	0	119.2	152	74	13	2	42	52	5.26	77	.319	.377	32-0-1	.219	-0	77	-14		-1.4

YEAR	TM LG	W	L	PCT	G	GS	CG-SHO	SV-BS	IP	H	R	HR	HB	BB-IB	SO	ERA	AERA	OAV	OOB	AB-HR-SH	AVG	PB	SUP	APR	DL	PW
1954	Det A	5	4	.556	38	2	0	2	84	76	45	11	0	40	39	4.18	88	.244	.326	18	.167	0	60	-5		-0.5
1955	Det A	1	0	1.000	4	1	1	1	15	12	4	1	0	4-1	9	1.80	213	.218	.271	4	.000	-0	231	3		0.2
1956	Det A	1	1	.500	7	1	0	0	11	12	8	1	0	9-0	4	5.73	72	.279	.404	1	.000	-0	43	-2		-0.3
	Chi A	0	0	—	1	0	0	0	1	2	1	1	0	1-0	0	9.00	46	.500	.600	0	—	-0		-1		0.0
	Year	1	1	.500	8	1	0	0	12	14	9	2	0	10-0	4	6.00	69	.298	.421	1	.000	-0	43	-3		-0.3
Total 6		13	15	.464	98	17	3	3	243.1	280	148	28	2	101-1	108	4.99	78	.295	.362	57-0-1	.175	-1	77	-28		-3.5

MARONE, LOU Louis Stephen B12.3.1945 San Diego CA BR/TL/5-11/185* d5.30 Col San Diego Mesa (CA) JC

YEAR	TM LG	W	L	PCT	G	GS	CG-SHO	SV-BS	IP	H	R	HR	HB	BB-IB	SO	ERA	AERA	OAV	OOB	AB-HR-SH	AVG	PB	SUP	APR	DL	PW
1969	Pit N	1	1	.500	29	0	0	0-1	35.1	24	10	2	2	13-2	25	2.55	137	.195	.281	0	—	0		4		0.2
1970	Pit N	0	0	—	1	0	0	0-0	2.1	2	1	1	0	0-0	0	3.86	103	.222	.222	0	—	0		0		0.0
Total 2		1	1	.500	30	0	0	0-1	37.2	26	11	3	2	13-2	25	2.63	134	.197	.277	0	—	0		4		0.2

MAROTH, MIKE Michael Warren B8.17.1977 Orlando FL BL/TL/6-0/180* [BosA98 3/85] d6.8 Col Central Florida

YEAR	TM LG	W	L	PCT	G	GS	CG-SHO	SV-BS	IP	H	R	HR	HB	BB-IB	SO	ERA	AERA	OAV	OOB	AB-HR-SH	AVG	PB	SUP	APR	DL	PW
2002	Det A	6	10	.375	21	21	0	0-0	128.2	136	68	7	2	36-1	58	4.48	98	.276	.326	6	.167	-0	70	0		0.0
2003	Det A	9	21	.300	33	33	1	0-0	193.1	231	131	34	8	50-2	87	5.73	77	.299	.344	2-0-1	.500	1	99	-28		-3.4
2004	Det A	11	13	.458	33	33	2-1	0-0	217	244	112	25	7	59-1	108	4.31	104	.288	.338	4-0-1	.000	-0	99	4		0.1
2005	Det A	14	14	.500	34	34	0	0-0	209	235	123	30	9	51-1	115	4.74	89	.288	.333	4-0-1	.500	1*	99	-14		-1.4
Total 4		40	58	.408	121	121	3-1	0-0	748	846	434	96	26	196-5	368	4.82	91	.289	.336	16-0-3	.250	1	94	-38		-4.4

MARQUARD, RUBE Richard William B10.9.1886 Cleveland OH D6.1.1980 Baltimore MD BB/TL/6-3/180 d9.25 HF1971

YEAR	TM LG	W	L	PCT	G	GS	CG-SHO	SV-BS	IP	H	R	HR	HB	BB-IB	SO	ERA	AERA	OAV	OOB	AB-HR-SH	AVG	PB	SUP	APR	DL	PW
1908	NY N	0	1	.000	1	1	0	1	5	6	5	0	1	2	2	3.60	67	.316	.409	1	.000	-0	29	-1		-0.3
1909	NY N	5	13	.278	29	21	8	1	173	155	81	2	9	73	109	2.60	98	.248	.335	54-0-3	.148	-1	76	-3		-0.5
1910	NY N	4	4	.500	13	8	2	0	70.2	65	35	2	4	40	52	4.46	67	.254	.363	27-0-2	.111	-2	122	-7		-0.9
1911	†NY N	24	7	.774	45	33	22-5	3	277.2	221	98	9	4	106	237	2.50	135	.219	.296	104-1-3	.163	-1	110	28		2.7
1912	†NY N	26	11	.703	43	38	22-1	1	294.2	286	112	9	3	80	175	2.57	132	.255	.306	96-0-9	.219	2	119	30		3.5
1913	†NY N	23	10	.697	42	33	20-4	3	288	248	100	10	3	49	151	2.50	125	.237	.273	105-0-2	.219	2	106	23		2.4
1914	NY N	12	22	.353	39	33	15-4	2	268	261	117	9	2	47	92	3.06	87	.262	.297	84-0-5	.179	-1	79	-14		-1.8
1915	NY N	9	8	.529	27	21	10-2	2	169	178	85	8	1	33	79	3.73	69	.272	.309	55-0-2	.109	-3	130	-21		-2.4
	Bro N	2	2	.500	6	3	0	1	24.2	29	17	0	0	5	13	6.20	45	.276	.309	8-0-1	.125	0	80	-7		-1.1
	Year	11	10	.524	33	24	10-2	3	193.2	207	102	8	1	38	92	4.04	64	.273	.308	63-0-3	.111	-3	123	-27		-3.5
1916	†Bro N	13	6	.684	36	21	15-2	5	205	169	54	2	0	38	107	1.58	150	.229	.267	63-0-2	.143	-1	102	23		2.1
1917	Bro N	19	12	.613	37	29	14-2	0	232.2	200	84	5	0	60	117	2.55	110	.232	.282	75-0-3	.200	0	83	6		0.6
1918	Bro N	9	18	.333	34	29	19-4	0	239	231	97	7	1	59	89	2.64	106	.260	.307	76-0-1	.171	-1	88	2		-0.1
1919	Bro N	3	3	.500	8	7	3	0	59	54	17	1	0	10	29	2.29	130	.244	.277	23-0-1	.261	1	88	5		0.6
1920	†Bro N	10	7	.588	28	26	10-1	0	189.2	181	83	5	1	35	89	3.23	99	.251	.287	59-0-3	.169	-1	110	1		-0.3
1921	Cin N	17	14	.548	39	36	18-2	0	265.2	291	123	8	7	50	88	3.39	106	.285	.323	63-0-3	.222	-1	71	-21		-2.3
1922	Bos N	11	15	.423	39	25	7	1	198	255	131	12	0	66	57	5.09	79	.322	.374	63-0-5	.140	-6	102	4		-0.2
1923	Bos N	11	14	.440	38	29	11-3	0	239	265	127	10	2	65	78	3.73	107	.288	.337	86-0-5	.140	-6	102	4		0.2
1924	Bos N	1	2	.333	6	6	1	0	36	33	17	3	1	13	10	3.00	127	.254	.326	11	.273	0	70	2		0.2
1925	Bos N	2	8	.200	26	8	0	0	72	105	60	5	0	27	19	5.75	70	.341	.394	22	.136	-1	108	-17		-2.1
Total 18		201	177	.532	536	407	197-30	19	3306.2	3233	1443	107	39	858	1593	3.08	103	.260	.310	1107-1-48	.179	-17	99	39		0.5

MARQUEZ, ISIDRO Isidro (Espinoza) B5.15.1965 Navojoa, Sonora, Mexico BR/TR/6-3/190 d4.26

YEAR	TM LG	W	L	PCT	G	GS	CG-SHO	SV-BS	IP	H	R	HR	HB	BB-IB	SO	ERA	AERA	OAV	OOB	AB-HR-SH	AVG	PB	SUP	APR	DL	PW
1995	Chi A	0	1	.000	7	0	0	0	6.2	9	5	3	0	2-0	5	6.75	66	.321	.367	0	—	0		-2		-0.2

MARQUIS, JIM James Milburn B11.18.1900 Yoakum TX D8.5.1992 Jackson CA BR/TR/5-11/174 d8.8

YEAR	TM LG	W	L	PCT	G	GS	CG-SHO	SV-BS	IP	H	R	HR	HB	BB-IB	SO	ERA	AERA	OAV	OOB	AB-HR-SH	AVG	PB	SUP	APR	DL	PW
1925	NY A	0	0	—	2	0	0	0	7.1	12	8	1	0	6	0	9.82	43	.414	.514	2	.000	-0		-4		-0.2

MARQUIS, JASON Jason Scott B8.21.1978 Manhasset NY BL/TR/6-1/185(185-210) [AtlN96 S1/35] d6.6

YEAR	TM LG	W	L	PCT	G	GS	CG-SHO	SV-BS	IP	H	R	HR	HB	BB-IB	SO	ERA	AERA	OAV	OOB	AB-HR-SH	AVG	PB	SUP	APR	DL	PW
2000	Atl N	1	0	1.000	15	0	0	0-1	23.1	23	16	4	1	12-1	17	5.01	90	.261	.353	2	.000	-0		-2		-0.1
2001	Atl N	5	6	.455	38	16	0	0-2	129.1	113	62	14	4	59-4	98	3.48	124	.234	.320	31-0-2	.032	-2*	67	9		0.5
2002	Atl N	8	9	.471	22	22	0	0-0	114.1	127	66	19	3	49-3	84	5.04	80	.283	.356	38-1-3	.132	-0*	102	-11	26	-1.4
2003	Atl N	0	0	—	21	2	0	1-0	40.2	43	27	3	2	18-2	19	5.53	76	.270	.346	2-0-2	.500	1	168	-6		-0.2
2004	†StL N	15	7	.682	32	32	0	0-0	201.1	215	90	26	10	70-1	138	3.71	115	.275	.339	72-0-2	.292	7*	119	13		2.0
2005	†StL N	13	14	.481	33	32	3-1	0-0	207	206	110	29	5	69-2	100	4.13	102	.262	.324	87-1-2	.310	11*	91	0		1.1
Total 6		42	36	.538	161	104	3-1	1-3	716	727	371	95	25	277-13	456	4.15	102	.265	.335	232-2-11	.237	15	99	3	26	1.9

MARRERO, CONNIE Conrado Eugenio (Ramos) B4.25.1911 Sagua La Grande, Cuba BR/TR/5-5/158(158-170) d4.21

YEAR	TM LG	W	L	PCT	G	GS	CG-SHO	SV-BS	IP	H	R	HR	HB	BB-IB	SO	ERA	AERA	OAV	OOB	AB-HR-SH	AVG	PB	SUP	APR	DL	PW
1950	Was A	6	10	.375	27	19	8-1	1	152	159	84	17	4	55	63	4.50	108	.269	.335	49-0-5	.122	-1	85	1		-0.1
1951	Was A☆	11	9	.550	25	25	16-2	0	187	198	87	8	3	71	66	3.90	105	.268	.335	61-0-3	.164	-2	100	6		0.3
1952	Was A	11	8	.579	22	22	16-2	0	184.1	175	68	9	4	53	77	2.88	123	.249	.305	63-0-5	.079	-5	85	14		1.1
1953	Was A	8	7	.533	22	20	10-2	2	145.2	130	56	14	5	48	65	3.03	129	.241	.309	48-0-1	.125	-2	100	14		1.1
1954	Was A	3	6	.333	22	8	1	0	66.1	74	37	12	0	22	26	4.75	75	.287	.340	15	.000	-1	102	-8		-1.1
Total 5		39	40	.494	118	94	51-7	3	735.2	736	332	60	16	249	297	3.67	108	.260	.323	236-0-14	.114	-11	94	27		0.9

MARROW, BUCK Charles Kennon B8.29.1909 Tarboro NC D11.21.1982 Newport News VA BR/TR/6-4/200 d7.3 Col Davidson

YEAR	TM LG	W	L	PCT	G	GS	CG-SHO	SV-BS	IP	H	R	HR	HB	BB-IB	SO	ERA	AERA	OAV	OOB	AB-HR-SH	AVG	PB	SUP	APR	DL	PW
1932	Det A	2	5	.286	18	7	2	1	63.2	70	40	6	6	29	31	4.81	98	.278	.366	19-0-1	.158	-0	67	0		0.0
1937	Bro N	1	2	.333	6	3	1	0	16.1	19	13	2	0	9	2	6.61	61	.284	.368	5	.000	-1	107	-4		-0.7
1938	Bro N	0	1	.000	15	0	0	1	19.2	23	10	1	3	11	6	4.58	85	.291	.398	1	.000	-0		-1		0.0
Total 3		3	8	.273	39	10	3	1	99.2	112	63	9	9	49	39	5.06	88	.281	.373	25-0-1	.120	-1	79	-5		-0.7

MARS, ED Edward M. B12.4.1866 Chicago IL D12.9.1941 Chicago IL 5-9/166 d8.12

YEAR	TM LG	W	L	PCT	G	GS	CG-SHO	SV-BS	IP	H	R	HR	HB	BB-IB	SO	ERA	AERA	OAV	OOB	AB-HR-SH	AVG	PB	SUP	APR	DL	PW
1890	Syr AA	9	5	.643	16	14	14	0	121.1	132	80	2	5	49	59	4.67	76	.269	.341	51	.275	4	151	-14		-0.9

MARSHALL, CUDDLES Clarence Westly B4.28.1925 Bellingham WA BR/TR/6-3/200* d4.24 Col Western Washington

YEAR	TM LG	W	L	PCT	G	GS	CG-SHO	SV-BS	IP	H	R	HR	HB	BB-IB	SO	ERA	AERA	OAV	OOB	AB-HR-SH	AVG	PB	SUP	APR	DL	PW
1946	NY A	3	4	.429	23	11	1	0	81	96	49	4	0	56	32	5.33	65	.308	.413	28-0-1	.143	-1	138	-14		-1.2
1948	NY A	0	0	—	1	0	0	0	1	0	0	0	0	3	0	0.00	—	.000	.500	0	—	0		0		0.0
1949	NY A	3	0	1.000	21	2	0	3	49.1	48	31	3	2	48	13	5.11	79	.259	.417	9-0-1	.111	-0	100	-6		-0.4
1950	StL A	1	3	.250	28	2	0	1	53.2	72	52	1	1	51	24	7.88	63	.321	.449	12	.333	-0	118	-15		-1.0
Total 4		7	7	.500	73	15	1	4	185	216	132	8	3	158	69	5.98	67	.298	.426	49-0-2	.184	-1	121	-35		-2.6

MARSHALL, MIKE Michael Grant B1.15.1943 Adrian MI BR/TR/5-10/180* d5.31

YEAR	TM LG	W	L	PCT	G	GS	CG-SHO	SV-BS	IP	H	R	HR	HB	BB-IB	SO	ERA	AERA	OAV	OOB	AB-HR-SH	AVG	PB	SUP	APR	DL	PW
1967	Det A	1	3	.250	37	0	0	10	59	51	15	6	2	20-1	41	1.98	165	.233	.303	9-0-2	.222	0		8		0.9
1969	Sea A	3	10	.231	20	14	3-1	0-0	87.2	99	54	8	2	35-2	47	5.13	71	.281	.347	27-1-1	.259	3*	87	-13		-1.3
1970	Hou N	0	1	.000	4	0	0	0-0	5.1	8	5	0	1	4-0	5	8.44	46	.400	.520	0	—	0		-3		-0.4
	Mon N	3	7	.300	24	5	0	3-0	64.2	56	34	4	0	29-4	38	3.48	119	.225	.305	11-0-2	.091	0	86	2		0.4
	Year	3	8	.273	28	5	0	3-0	70	64	39	4	1	33-4	43	3.86	107	.238	.322	16-0-2	.188	0	87	0		0.0
1971	Mon N	5	8	.385	66	0	0	23-7	111.1	100	56	9	4	50-13	85	4.28	83	.247	.333	16-0-2	.188	0		-7		-1.0
1972	Mon N	14	8	.636	65	0	0	18-7	116	82	26	3	2	47-7	95	1.78	199	.202	.286	22	.136	0		22		4.9
1973	Mon N	14	11	.560	92	0	0	31-12	179	163	62	10	4	75-12	124	2.66	142	.252	.331	33-0-4	.242	1		22		4.1
1974	†LA N★	15	12	.556	106	0	0	21-12	208.1	191	66	9	1	56-11	143	2.42	142	.247	.297	34-0-2	.235	1		24		3.7
1975	LA N☆	9	14	.391	57	0	0	13-8	109.1	99	46	8	4	39-4	64	3.29	104	.242	.311	15-0-4	.067	-1*		1	27	0.2
1976	LA N	4	3	.571	30	0	0	8-5	62.2	64	33	2	1	25-2	39	4.45	76	.270	.340	5	.000	0		-7		-0.8
	Atl N	2	1	.667	24	0	0	6-2	36.2	35	15	4	1	14-0	17	3.19	119	.259	.329	6-0-1	.167	0		3	34	-0.5
	Year	6	4	.600	54	0	0	14-7	99.1	99	48	6	2	39-2	56	3.99	89	.266	.336	11-0-1	.091	1		-4		-0.5
1977	Atl N	1	0	1.000	9	0	0	0	6	12	6	1	0	2-0	6	9.00	49	.400	.438	1	1.000	0		-2		-0.4
	Tex A	2	2	.500	12	4	0	1-3	35.2	42	19	2	1	13-1	18	4.04	101	.304	.373	0	—	0	171	0	97	0.3
1978	Min A	10	12	.455	54	0	0	21-6	99	80	34	3	1	24-6	56	2.45	156	.225	.299	0	—	0		15		2.2
1979	Min A	10	15	.400	90	1	0	32-10	142.2	132	47	8	4	48-2	81	2.65	166	.254	.319	0	—	0	62	26		5.4
1980	Min A	1	3	.250	18	0	0	1-2	32.1	42	23	2	2	12-1	13	6.12	71	.323	.381	0	—	0		-5		-0.5
1981	NY N	3	2	.600	20	0	0	3-1	32.1	26	10	2	0	8-1	15	2.61	135	.224	.272	0	—	0		0		0.0
Total 14		97	112	.464	723	24	3-1	188-74	1386.2	1281	548	79	31	514-52	880	3.14	119	.249	.319	179-1-18	.196	6	103	88	158	19.4

MARSHALL, RUBE Roy De Verne "Cy" B1.19.1890 Salineville OH D6.11.1980 Dover OH BR/TR/5-11/170 d9.28

YEAR	TM LG	W	L	PCT	G	GS	CG-SHO	SV-BS	IP	H	R	HR	HB	BB-IB	SO	ERA	AERA	OAV	OOB	AB-HR-SH	AVG	PB	SUP	APR	DL	PW
1912	Phi N	0	1	.000	2	1	0	1	3	12	11	0	0	1	2	21.00	17	.632	.650	0	—	-0	40	-6		-0.9
1913	Phi N	0	1	.000	14	1	0	1	45.1	54	29	2	1	22	18	4.57	73	.297	.376	11	.091	-1	45	-6		-1.1
1914	Phi N	6	7	.462	27	17	7	1	134.1	144	77	2	5	50	49	3.75	78	.279	.349	43-0-3	.140	-2	123	-10		-1.1

YEAR	TM LG	W	L	PCT	G	GS	CG-SHO	SV-BS	IP	H	R	HR	HB	BB-IB	SO	ERA	AERA	OAV	OOB	AB-HR-SH	AVG	PB	SUP	APR	DL	PW
1915	Buf F	2	1	.667	21	4	2	0	59.1	62	34	1	2	33	21	3.94	71	.281	.379	17-0-1	.294	1*	100	-8		-0.4
Total	4	8	10	.444	64	23	9	2	242	272	151	5	8	106	90	4.17	72	.290	.367	71-0-4	.169	-2	112	-30		-2.8

MARSONEK, SAM Samuel R. B7.10.1978 Tampa FL BR/TR/6-6/225 [TexA96 1/24] d7.11

| 2004 | NY A | 0 | 0 | — | 1 | 0 | 0 | 0-0 | 1.1 | 2 | 0 | 0 | 0 | 0-0 | 0 | 0.00 | — | .333 | .333 | 0 | — | 0 | 1 | 81 | | 0.0 |

MARTE, DAMASO Damaso (Sabinon) B2.14.1975 Santo Domingo, D.R. BL/TL/6-0/170(170-205) d6.30

1999	Sea A	0	1	.000	5	0	0	0-0	8.2	16	9	3	0	6-0	3	9.35	51	.390	.468	0	—	-0	-4			-0.4
2001	Pit N	0	1	.000	23	0	0	0-0	36.1	34	21	3	5	12-3	39	4.71	95	.250	.320	4	.000	-0	-1			-0.1
2002	Chi A	1	1	.500	68	0	0	10-2	60.1	44	19	5	4	18-2	72	2.83	159	.204	.276	1	.000	-0	12			0.7
2003	Chi A	4	2	.667	71	0	0	11-7	79.2	50	16	3	3	34-6	87	1.58	290	.185	.280	0	—	0	26			2.4
2004	Chi A	6	5	.545	74	0	0	6-6	73.2	56	28	10	3	34-4	68	3.42	137	.217	.309	0	—	0	11			1.6
2005	†Chi A	3	4	.429	66	0	0	4-4	45.1	45	21	5	3	33-4	54	3.77	120	.256	.382	0	—	0	4	17		0.5
Total	6	14	14	.500	307	0	0	31-19	304	245	114	31	16	137-19	323	3.20	143	.223	.315	5	.000	-1	48	17		4.7

MARTIN, PHONNEY Alphonse Case B8.4.1845 New York NY D5.24.1933 Hollis NY 5-7/148 d4.26 M1 ▲

1872	Tro NA	1	2	.333	8	3	0	0	37.1	70	59	0		2	2	4.82	75	.350	.356	119		.303	1*	95	-5		-0.2
	Eck NA	2	7	.222	10	9	9	0	85	143	106	1		9	3	3.92	87	.326	.339	78		.192	-1*	59	-7		-0.5
	Year	3	9	.250	18	12	9	0	122.1	213	165	1		11	5	4.19	83	.333	.345	197		.259	-0*	68	-14		-0.7
1873	Mut NA	0	1	.000	6	1	1	0	34	50	37	0		6	1	3.44	92	.292	.316	140		.221	-0*	113	-1		-0.1
Total	2 NA	3	10	.231	24	13	10	0	156.1	263	202	1		17	6	4.03	84	.325	.339	337		.243	-1	72	-13		-0.8

MARTIN, BARNEY Barnes Robertson B3.3.1923 Columbia SC D10.30.1997 Columbia SC BR/TR/5-11/170 d4.22 s-Jerry

| 1953 | Cin N | 0 | 0 | — | 1 | 0 | 0 | 0 | 2 | 3 | 2 | 0 | 0 | 1 | 1 | 9.00 | 48 | .333 | .400 | 0 | — | 0 | -1 | | | 0.0 |

MARTIN, RENIE Donald Renie B8.30.1955 Dover DE BR/TR/6-4/190* [KCA77 19/486] d5.9 Col Richmond

1979	KC A	0	3	.000	25	0	0	5-2	34.2	32	20	1	1	14-3	25	5.19	82	.248	.322	0	—	0	-2			-0.2
1980	†KC A	10	10	.500	32	20	2	2-0	137.1	133	84	18	1	70-2	68	4.39	92	.255	.342	0	—	0	116	-4		-1.2
1981	†KC A	4	5	.444	29	0	0	4-1	61.2	55	25	2	0	29-7	25	2.77	130	.244	.322	0	—	0	4			0.7
1982	SF N	7	10	.412	29	25	1	0-0	141.1	148	91	14	0	64-9	63	4.65	77	.274	.347	49-0-6	.265	3*	119	-20		-1.8
1983	SF N	2	4	.333	37	6	0	1-0	94.1	95	50	11	3	51-9	43	4.20	85	.268	.363	26-0-1	.346	4	108	-6		0.1
1984	SF N	1	1	.500	12	0	0	0-1	23.1	29	13	2	0	16-0	8	3.86	92	.305	.405	6	.500	1	-2			0.0
	Phi N	0	2	.000	9	0	0	0-1	15.2	17	12	2	0	12-4	5	4.60	80	.274	.392	2	.000	-0	-3			-0.3
	Year	1	3	.250	21	0	0	0-2	39	46	25	4	0	28-4	13	4.15	86	.293	.400	8	.375	1	-4			-0.3
Total	6	24	35	.407	173	51	3	12-5	508.1	509	295	50	5	256-34	237	4.27	88	.264	.348	83-0-7	.301	8	117	-38		-2.7

MARTIN, SPEED Elwood Good B9.15.1893 Wawawai WA D6.14.1983 Lemon Grove CA BR/TR/6-0/165 d7.5

1917	StL A	0	2	.000	9	2	0	0	15.2	20	13	0	0	6-1	3	5.74	45	.339	.391	2	.000	-0*	125	-5		-0.6
1918	Chi N	5	2	.714	9	5	4-1	1	53.2	47	19	0	1	14	16	1.84	151	.246	.301	16-0-1	.188	-0	54	4		0.6
1919	Chi N	8	8	.500	35	14	7-2	2	163.2	158	58	2	4	52	44	2.47	117	.259	.321	44-0-5	.182	-1	95	8		0.8
1920	Chi N	4	15	.211	35	13	6	2	136	165	96	2	1	50	44	4.83	66	.305	.365	44-1-1	.159	-0	102	-26		-3.3
1921	Chi N	11	15	.423	37	28	13-1	1	217.1	245	115	12	2	68	86	4.35	88	.298	.353	73-0-2	.233	1	91	-10		-0.8
1922	Chi N	1	0	1.000	1	1	0	0	6	10	5	0	0	2	2	7.50	56	.385	.429	1	1.000	-0	136	-2		-0.2
Total	6	29	42	.408	126	63	30-4	6	592.1	645	306	16	8	191	207	3.78	87	.287	.344	180-1-9	.194	-0	95	-31		-3.5

MARTIN, FRED Fred Turner B6.27.1915 Williams OK D6.11.1979 Chicago IL BR/TR/6-1/185* d4.21 C6

1946	StL N	2	1	.667	6	3	2	0	28.2	29	13	0	0	8	19	4.08	85	.254	.303	11	.273	0	149	-1		-0.1
1949	StL N	6	0	1.000	21	5	3	0	70	65	24	3	0	20	30	2.44	170	.243	.295	20-0-1	.300	1	144	12		1.0
1950	StL N	4	2	.667	30	2	0	0	63.1	87	43	4	1	30	19	5.12	84	.331	.401	15-0-1	.267	1*	31	-7		-0.4
Total	3	12	3	.800	57	10	5	0	162	181	80	7	1	58	68	3.78	108	.281	.341	46-0-2	.283	2	118	4		0.5

MARTIN, DOC Harold Winthrop B9.23.1887 Roxbury MA D4.14.1935 Milton MA BR/TR/5-11/165 d10.7 Col Tufts

1908	Phi A	0	1	.000	1	1	0	0	2	2	4	0	1	3	2	13.50	19	.286	.545	1	.000	-0	27	-2		-0.4
1911	Phi A	1	1	.500	11	3	1	0	38	40	26	1	5	17	21	4.50	70	.272	.367	14	.214	0	145	-7		-0.3
1912	Phi A	0	0	—	2	0	0	0	4.1	5	5	0	1	5	4	10.38	30	.333	.524	3	.000	-1	-3			-0.2
Total	3	1	2	.333	14	4	1	0	44.1	47	35	1	7	25	27	5.48	57	.278	.393	18	.167	-0	115	-9		-0.9

MARTIN, JOHN John Robert B4.11.1956 Wyandotte MI BB/TL/6-0/190* [DetA78 27/637] d8.27 Col Eastern Michigan

1980	StL N	2	3	.400	9	5	1	0-0	42	39	20	1	0	9-1	23	4.29	88	.247	.284	11	.273	1	76	-1		-0.1
1981	StL N	8	5	.615	17	15	4	0-0	102.2	85	43	10	2	26-0	36	3.42	106	.228	.281	33-0-7	.212	2*	118	2		0.5
1982	StL N	4	5	.444	24	7	0	0-1	66	56	33	6	0	30-3	21	4.23	87	.230	.314	11-0-2	.091	-0	103	-3		-0.5
1983	StL N	3	1	.750	24	5	0	0-0	66.1	60	31	6	2	26-4	29	3.53	104	.242	.315	18-0-2	.222	1	145	0		0.1
	Det A	0	0	—	15	0	0	1-0	13.1	15	11	2	0	4-1	11	7.43	53	.294	.339	0	—	0	-5			-0.2
Total	4	17	14	.548	91	32	5	1-1	290.1	255	138	25	4	95-9	120	3.94	93	.238	.300	73-0-11	.205	3	112	-7		-0.2

MARTIN, MORRIE Morris Webster "Lefty" B9.3.1922 Dixon MO BL/TL/6-0/180* d4.25

1949	Bro N	1	3	.250	10	4	1	0	30.2	29	25	5	2	15	15	7.04	58	.320	.403	10	.200	-0	43	-9		-1.0
1951	Phi A	11	4	.733	35	13	3-1	0	.138	139	70	13	5	63	35	3.78	113	.259	.343	50-0-4	.220	-1	136	5		0.5
1952	Phi A	0	2	.000	5	5	0	0	25.1	32	19	1	2	15	13	6.39	62	.302	.398	9	.111	-1	97	-6	30	-0.5
1953	Phi A	10	12	.455	58	11	2	7	156.1	158	85	12	8	59	64	4.43	97	.262	.336	42-0-2	.095	-4	85	-3		-0.8
1954	Phi A	2	4	.333	13	6	2	0	52.2	57	32	9	2	19	24	5.47	71	.278	.339	17-0-1	.235	0	49	-7		-0.7
	Chi A	5	4	.556	35	2	1	5	70	52	18	5	1	24	31	2.06	182	.210	.281	15-0-2	.133	-0	106	13		1.7
	Year	7	8	.467	48	8	3	5	122.2	109	50	14	3	43	55	3.52	108	.241	.308	32-0-3	.188	-0	64	6		1.0
1955	Chi A	2	3	.400	37	0	0	2	52	50	27	4	2	20-2	22	3.63	109	.259	.332	10	.300	0	0			0.1
1956	Chi A	1	0	1.000	10	0	0	0	18.1	21	10	1	0	7-0	9	4.91	84	.292	.350	5	.200	0	-1			0.0
	Bal A	1	1	.500	9	0	0	0	5	10	6	1	1	2-0	3	10.80	36	.400	.464	0	—	0	-4			-0.7
	Year	2	1	.667	19	0	0	0	23.1	31	16	2	1	9-0	12	6.17	66	.320	.380	5	.200	0	-5			-0.7
1957	StL N	0	0	—	4	1	0	0	10.2	5	3	0	1	4-0	7	2.53	157	.143	.244	0	—	0				0.1
1958	StL N	3	1	.750	17	0	0	0	24.2	19	13	3	2	12-0	16	4.74	87	.211	.317	5	.000	-0	89	2		0.1
	Cle A	2	0	1.000	9	0	0	1	18.2	20	7	0	0	8-0	5	2.41	151	.294	.364	0	—	0	2			0.2
1959	Chi N	0	0	—	3	0	0	0	2.1	5	5	2	1	1-0	1	19.29	30	.455	.538	0	—	0	-4			-0.2
Total	10	38	34	.528	250	42	8-1	15	604.2	607	320	56	27	249-2	245	4.29	95	.262	.340	165-0-9	.170	-6	96	-13	30	-1.5

MARTIN, PAT Patrick Francis B4.13.1892 Brooklyn NY D2.4.1949 Brooklyn NY BL/TL/5-11.5/170 d9.20

1919	Phi A	0	2	.000	2	1	1	0	11	11	8	0	0	8	6	4.09	84	.256	.373	3	.000	-0	23	-1		-0.3
1920	Phi A	1	4	.200	8	5	2	0	32.1	48	36	2	4	25	14	6.12	66	.364	.478	10-0-2	.400	1	71	-9		-1.1
Total	2	1	6	.143	10	7	3	0	43.1	59	44	2	4	33	20	5.61	69	.337	.453	13-0-2	.308	1	58	-10		-1.4

MARTIN, PAUL Paul Charles B3.10.1932 Brownstown PA BR/TR/6-6/235 d7.2

| 1955 | Pit N | 0 | 1 | .000 | 7 | 1 | 0 | 0 | 7 | 13 | 12 | 0 | 1 | 17-0 | 3 | 14.14 | 29 | .464 | .633 | 0 | — | 0 | 22 | -7 | | -0.9 |

MARTIN, RAY Raymond Joseph B3.13.1925 Norwood MA BR/TR/6-2/177 d8.15 Mil 1943-46

1943	Bos N	0	0	—	2	0	0	0	3.1	3	1	0	0	1	1	8.10	42	.231	.286	1	.000	-0	-1			-0.1
1947	Bos N	1	0	1.000	1	1	1	0	9	7	1	0	0	4	2	1.00	389	.212	.297	3	.000	-0	45	3		0.4
1948	Bos N	0	0	—	2	0	0	0	2.1	0	0	0	0	1	0	0.00	—	.000	.125	0	—	0	1			0.0
Total	3	1	0	1.000	5	1	1	0	14.2	10	4	0	0	6	3	2.45	154	.189	.271	4	.000	-0	45	3		0.3

MARTIN, TOM Thomas Edgar B5.21.1970 Charleston SC BL/TL/6-1/200* [BalA88 6/139] d4.2

1997	†Hou N	5	3	.625	55	0	0	2-1	56	52	13	2	1	23-2	36	2.09	192	.254	.330	3	.000	-0	13	16		1.7
1998	Cle A	1	1	.500	14	0	0	0-0	14.2	29	21	3	0	12-0	9	12.89	37	.408	.488	0	—	0	-12	38		-1.3
1999	Cle A	0	1	.000	6	0	0	0-0	9.1	13	9	2	0	3-1	8	8.68	59	.325	.364	0	—	0	-3	126		-0.3
2000	Cle A	1	0	1.000	31	0	0	0-0	33.1	32	16	3	1	15-2	21	4.05	124	.254	.336	0	—	0	3	51		0.2
2001	NY N	1	0	1.000	14	0	0	0-0	17	23	22	4	1	10-2	12	10.06	40	.319	.405	3	.000	0	-13	95		-0.7
2002	TB A	0	0	—	3	0	0	0-0	1.2	5	3	0	1	1-0	1	16.20	28	.500	.545	0	—	0	-2	160		-0.1
2003	LA N	1	2	.333	80	0	0	0-1	51	36	21	6	2	24-4	51	3.53	117	.198	.295	1	.000	0	4			0.2
2004	LA N	1	0	1.000	47	0	0	1-0	28.1	32	13	3	3	14-1	18	4.13	100	.291	.380	0	—	0	0			0.0
	†Atl N	0	1	.000	29	0	0	0-3	17	17	7	4	0	5-2	12	3.71	116	.270	.314	0	—	0	1			0.1
	Year	0	2	.000	76	0	0	1-3	45.1	49	20	7	3	19-3	30	3.97	106	.283	.357	0	—	0	2			0.1

YEAR	TM LG	W	L	PCT	G	GS	CG-SHO	SV-BS	IP	H	R	HR	HB	BB-IB	SO	ERA	AERA	OAV	OOB	AB-HR-SH	AVG	PB	SUP	APR	DL	PW
2005	Atl N	0	0	—	4	0	0	0-0	2.1	6	5	1	0	2-0	0	19.29	22	.500	.571	0	—	0		-4		-0.2
Total	9	9	9	.500	282	0	0	3-5	230.2	245	130	28	8	109-14	168	4.88	88	.275	.355	7	.000	-1		-13	486	-0.4

MARTINA, JOE Joseph John "Oyster Joe" B7.8.1889 New Orleans LA D3.22.1962 New Orleans LA BR/TR/6-0/183 d4.19

YEAR	TM LG	W	L	PCT	G	GS	CG-SHO	SV-BS	IP	H	R	HR	HB	BB-IB	SO	ERA	AERA	OAV	OOB	AB-HR-SH	AVG	PB	SUP	APR	DL	PW
1924	†Was A	6	8	.429	24	14	8	0	125.1	129	69	7	6	56	57	4.67	86	.271	.355	43-0-1	.326	3*	94	-5		

MARTINEZ, ALFREDO Alfredo B3.15.1957 Los Angeles CA BR/TR/6-3/190* [NYN77 5/120] d4.20 Col Cal St.-Los Angeles

YEAR	TM LG	W	L	PCT	G	GS	CG-SHO	SV-BS	IP	H	R	HR	HB	BB-IB	SO	ERA	AERA	OAV	OOB	AB-HR-SH	AVG	PB	SUP	APR	DL	PW
1980	Cal A	7	9	.438	30	23	4-1	0-0	149.1	150	81	14	1	59-2	57	4.52	88	.259	.326	0	—	0	96	-8		-0.9
1981	Cal A	0	0	—	2	0	0-0	0-0	6	5	2	1	0	3-0	4	3.00	122	.227	.320	0	—	0		1		0.0
Total	2	7	9	.438	32	23	4-1	0-0	155.1	155	83	15	1	62-2	61	4.46	88	.257	.326	0	—	0	96	-7		-0.9

MARTINEZ, ANASTACIO Anastacio Euclides B11.3.1978 Santa Cruz de Villomello, D.R. BR/TR/6-2/180 d5.22

YEAR	TM LG	W	L	PCT	G	GS	CG-SHO	SV-BS	IP	H	R	HR	HB	BB-IB	SO	ERA	AERA	OAV	OOB	AB-HR-SH	AVG	PB	SUP	APR	DL	PW
2004	Bos A	2	1	.667	11	0	0	0-0	10.2	13	10	2	0	10-2	8	8.44	58	.289	.385	0	—	0		-3		-0.6

MARTINEZ, TIPPY Felix Anthony B5.31.1950 LaJunta CO BL/TL/5-10/180* d8.9 Col Colorado St. [DL 1987 Bal A 59]

YEAR	TM LG	W	L	PCT	G	GS	CG-SHO	SV-BS	IP	H	R	HR	HB	BB-IB	SO	ERA	AERA	OAV	OOB	AB-HR-SH	AVG	PB	SUP	APR	DL	PW
1974	NY A	0	0	—	10	0	0	0-0	12.2	14	7	0	1	9-2	10	4.26	83	.286	.400	0	—	0		-1		-0.1
1975	NY A	1	2	.333	23	2	0	8-0	37	27	15	2	1	32-3	20	2.68	139	.208	.364	0	—	0	36	3		0.4
1976	NY A	2	0	1.000	11	0	0	2-0	28	18	6	1	0	14-0	14	1.93	177	.191	.296	0	—	0		5		0.5
	Bal A	3	1	.750	28	0	0	8-0	41.2	32	13	0	1	28-3	31	2.59	127	.222	.349	0	—	0		4		0.6
	Year	5	1	.833	39	0	0	10-0	69.2	50	19	1	1	42-3	45	2.33	144	.210	.329	0	—	0		9		1.1
1977	Bal A	5	1	.833	41	0	0	9-2	50	47	17	2	0	27-2	29	2.70	142	.266	.359	0	—	0		6		1.0
1978	Bal A	3	3	.500	42	0	0	5-3	69	77	41	4	1	40-2	57	4.83	73	.281	.373	0	—	0*		-10		-0.9
1979	†Bal A	10	3	.769	39	0	0	3-4	78	59	29	0	1	31-4	61	2.88	140	.210	.288	0	—	0*		10		1.6
1980	Bal A	4	4	.500	53	0	0	10-1	80.2	69	30	5	1	34-5	68	3.01	132	.240	.320	0	—	0		5		1.1
1981	Bal A	3	3	.500	37	0	0	11-3	59	48	21	4	0	32-6	50	2.90	126	.231	.329	0	—	0		7		1.2
1982	Bal A	8	8	.500	76	0	0	16-7	95	81	39	6	1	37-5	78	3.41	119	.240	.312	0	—	0		19	22	3.0
1983	†Bal A☆	9	3	.750	65	0	0	21-6	103.1	76	30	10	0	37-3	72	2.35	170	.211	.280	0	—	0		1		2.3
1984	Bal A	4	9	.308	56	0	0	17-6	89.2	88	42	9	0	51-13	42	4.52	89	.254	.348	0	—	0		-11		-0.9
1985	Bal A	3	3	.500	49	0	0	4-8	70	70	48	4	0	37-8	47	5.40	75	.261	.346	0	—	0		-2	138	-0.3
1986	Bal A	0	2	.000	14	0	0	1-0	16	18	10	1	1	12-1	11	5.63	74	.295	.405	0	—	0		-6		-0.3
1988	Min A	0	0	—	3	0	0	0-0	4	8	9	1	0	4-0	3	18.00	23	.471	.542	0	—	0		-3		-0.3
Total	14	55	42	.567	546	2	0	115-40	834	732	357	53	8	425-57	632	3.45	112	.242	.333	0	—	0	36	38	219	7.9

MARTINEZ, JAVIER Javier Antonio B2.5.1977 Bayamon, PR BR/TR/6-2/210 [ChiN94 3/78] d4.2 [DL 1999 Pit N 111]

YEAR	TM LG	W	L	PCT	G	GS	CG-SHO	SV-BS	IP	H	R	HR	HB	BB-IB	SO	ERA	AERA	OAV	OOB	AB-HR-SH	AVG	PB	SUP	APR	DL	PW
1998	Pit N	0	1	.000	37	0	0	0-0	41	39	32	5	4	34-11	42	4.83	89	.248	.389	1	.000	-0		-5		-0.3

MARTINEZ, DENNIS Jose Dennis (Emilia) "El Presidente" B5.14.1955 Granada, Nicaragua BR/TR/6-1/185(168-185) d9.14

YEAR	TM LG	W	L	PCT	G	GS	CG-SHO	SV-BS	IP	H	R	HR	HB	BB-IB	SO	ERA	AERA	OAV	OOB	AB-HR-SH	AVG	PB	SUP	APR	DL	PW
1976	Bal A	1	2	.333	4	2	1	0-0	27.2	23	8	1	0	8-0	18	2.60	127	.237	.295	0	—	0	40	3		0.3
1977	Bal A	14	7	.667	42	13	5	4-1	166.2	157	86	10	8	64-5	107	4.10	94	.253	.327	0	—	0	139	-7		-0.8
1978	Bal A	16	11	.593	40	38	15-2	0-0	276.1	257	121	20	3	93-4	142	3.52	100	.250	.312	0	—	0	116	0		0.2
1979	†Bal A	15	16	.484	40	39	18-3	0-0	292.1	279	129	28	1	78-1	132	3.66	110	.253	.300	0	—	0*	88	15		1.6
1980	Bal A	6	4	.600	25	12	2	1-0	99.2	103	44	12	2	44-6	42	3.97	100	.272	.349	0	—	0*	100	2	37	0.2
1981	Bal A	14	5	.737	25	24	9-2	0-0	179	173	84	10	2	62-1	88	3.32	110	.254	.316	0	—	0	108	2		1.5
1982	Bal A	16	12	.571	40	39	10-2	0-0	252	262	123	30	7	87-2	111	4.21	96	.267	.329	0	—	0	94	-28		-3.3
1983	Bal A	7	16	.304	32	25	4	0-1	153	209	108	21	2	45-0	71	5.53	72	.330	.374	0	—	0	90	-14		-1.3
1984	Bal A	6	9	.400	34	20	2	0-0	141.2	145	81	26	9	37-2	77	5.02	78	.263	.312	0	—	0	138	-21		-2.3
1985	Bal A	13	11	.542	33	31	3-1	0-0	180	203	110	29	9	63-3	68	5.15	79	.288	.349	0	—	0	-2		49	-0.1
1986	Bal A	0	0	—	4	0	0	0-0	6.2	11	5	0	0	2-0	2	6.75	62	.367	.394	0	—	0		-2		-0.6
	Mon N	3	6	.333	19	15	1-1	0-0	98	103	52	11	3	28-4	63	4.59	82	.274	.328	30	.100	-1	71	-7		-0.6
1987	Mon N	11	4	.733	22	22	2-1	0-0	144.2	133	59	9	6	40-2	84	3.30	129	.244	.301	46-0-4	.065	-2	112	15		1.3
1988	Mon N	15	13	.536	34	34	9-2	0-0	235.1	215	94	21	6	55-3	120	2.72	134	.239	.286	72-0-10	.192	-1	111	11		1.1
1989	Mon N	16	7	.696	34	33	5-2	0-0	232	227	88	21	7	49-4	142	3.18	112	.257	.300	68-0-12	.103	-2	106	19		1.1
1990	Mon N★	10	11	.476	32	32	7-2	0-0	226	191	80	16	6	49-9	156	2.95	125	.228	.274	68-0-10	.103	0*	86	30		3.6
1991	Mon N★	14	11	.560	31	31	9-5	0-0	222	187	70	9	4	62-3	123	2.39	152	.226	.282	74-0-10	.153	1	101	23		3.8
1992	Mon N★	16	11	.593	32	32	6	0-0	226.1	172	75	12	9	60-3	138	2.47	141	.211	.271	74-0-11	.189	1	103	23		2.9
1993	Mon N	15	9	.625	35	34	2	1-0	224.2	211	110	27	11	64-7	138	3.85	109	.246	.306	69-0-9	.159	-0*	96	10		1.1
1994	Cle A	11	6	.647	24	24	7-3	0-0	176.2	166	75	14	7	44-2	92	3.52	135	.247	.298	0	—	0	102	26		2.3
1995	†Cle A★	12	5	.706	28	28	3-2	0-0	187	174	71	17	12	46-2	99	3.08	153	.247	.302	0	—	0	105	34		2.9
1996	Cle A	9	6	.600	20	20	1-1	0-0	112	122	63	12	2	37-2	48	4.50	109	.278	.335	0	—	0	119	-18		-1.7
1997	Sea A	1	5	.167	9	9	0	0-0	49	65	46	8	1	29-1	17	7.71	59	.327	.424	0	—	0	128	-4		-1.1
1998	†Atl N	4	6	.400	53	5	1	2-2	91	109	53	8	3	19-5	62	4.45	94	.295	.332	11-0-1	.091	-0	105	-4		-0.4
Total	23	245	193	.559	692	562	122-36	8-4	3999.2	3897	1835	372	122	1165-71	2149	3.70	107	.256	.312	520-0-65	.142	-3	105	108	138	11.8

MARTINEZ, JOSE Jose Miguel (Martinez) B4.1.1971 Guayubin, D.R. BR/TR/6-2/180 d5.10

YEAR	TM LG	W	L	PCT	G	GS	CG-SHO	SV-BS	IP	H	R	HR	HB	BB-IB	SO	ERA	AERA	OAV	OOB	AB-HR-SH	AVG	PB	SUP	APR	DL	PW
1994	SD N	0	2	.000	4	1	0	0-0	12	18	9	2	0	5-2	7	6.75	61	.375	.434	2	.000	-0	0	-3		-0.4

MARTINEZ, LUIS Luis B1.20.1980 Santo Domingo, D.R. BL/TL/6-6/200 d9.3

YEAR	TM LG	W	L	PCT	G	GS	CG-SHO	SV-BS	IP	H	R	HR	HB	BB-IB	SO	ERA	AERA	OAV	OOB	AB-HR-SH	AVG	PB	SUP	APR	DL	PW
2003	Mil N	0	3	.000	14	0	0	0-0	16.1	25	18	3	0	15-2	10	9.92	44	.373	.488	4	.000	-0	109	-9		-1.3

MARTINEZ, PEDRO Pedro (Aquino) B11.29.1968 Villa Mella, D.R. BL/TL/6-2/185(155-185) d6.29

YEAR	TM LG	W	L	PCT	G	GS	CG-SHO	SV-BS	IP	H	R	HR	HB	BB-IB	SO	ERA	AERA	OAV	OOB	AB-HR-SH	AVG	PB	SUP	APR	DL	PW
1993	SD N	3	1	.750	32	0	0	0-1	37	23	11	4	1	13-1	32	2.43	170	.172	.250	4-0-2	.000	-0		7		0.6
1994	SD N	3	2	.600	48	0	0	3-2	68.1	52	31	4	1	49-9	52	2.90	143	.210	.341	5	.000	-1	176	7		0.5
1995	Hou N	0	0	—	25	0	0	0-0	20.2	29	18	3	2	16-1	17	7.40	52	.330	.439	0	—	0		-8		-0.7
1996	NY N	0	0	—	5	0	0	0-0	7	8	7	1	0	7-4	6	6.43	63	.296	.429	0	—	0		-3		-0.1
	Cin N	0	0	—	4	0	0	0-0	3	5	2	1	0	1-0	3	6.00	71	.357	.400	0	—	0		0		0.0
	Year	0	0	—	9	0	0	0-0	10	13	9	2	0	8-4	9	6.30	65	.317	.420	0	—	0		-3		-0.1
1997	Cin N	1	1	.500	8	0	0	0-0	6.2	9	9	1	1	7-0	4	9.45	45	.286	.432	0	—	0		-4		-0.8
Total	5	7	4	.636	122	0	0	3-3	142.2	125	78	14	5	93-15	114	3.97	103	.232	.348	9-0-2	.000	-1	176	-1		0.4

MARTINEZ, PEDRO Pedro Jaime (b Pedro Jaime (Martinez)) B10.25.1971 Manoguayabo, D.R. BR/TR/5-11/175(150-180) d9.24 b-Ramon

YEAR	TM LG	W	L	PCT	G	GS	CG-SHO	SV-BS	IP	H	R	HR	HB	BB-IB	SO	ERA	AERA	OAV	OOB	AB-HR-SH	AVG	PB	SUP	APR	DL	PW
1992	LA N	0	1	.000	2	1	0	0-0	8	6	2	0	0	1-0	8	2.25	154	.200	.226	1	.000	-0	26	1		0.1
1993	LA N	10	5	.667	65	2	0	2-1	107	76	34	5	4	57-4	119	2.61	148	.201	.309	4-0-5	.091	-0*	105	16		2.0
1994	Mon N	11	5	.688	24	23	1-1	1-0	144.2	115	58	11	11	45-3	142	3.42	124	.220	.294	44-0-5	.091	-1	99	14		1.3
1995	Mon N	14	10	.583	30	30	2-2	0-0	194.2	158	79	21	11	66-1	174	3.51	122	.227	.302	63-0-5	.111	-3	96	18		1.7
1996	Mon N★	13	10	.565	33	33	4-1	0-0	216.2	189	100	19	3	70-3	222	3.70	117	.232	.294	64-0-16	.094	-2	105	14		1.7
1997	Mon N★	17	8	.680	31	31	13-4	0-0	241.1	158	65	16	9	67-5	305	1.90	220	.184	.249	69-0-9	.116	-1	79	58		5.8
1998	†Bos A☆	19	7	.731	33	33	3-2	0-0	233.2	188	82	26	8	67-3	251	2.89	164	.217	.278	7	.000	-0	103	67	15	8.2
1999	†Bos A★	23	4	.852	31	29	5-1	0-0	213.1	160	56	9	9	37-1	313	2.07	241	.205	.248	2	.000	-0	84	78	16	8.4
2000	Bos A★	18	6	.750	29	29	7-4	0-0	217	128	44	17	14	32-0	284	1.74	288	.167	.213	0	—	0	85	77	90	8.0
2001	Bos A	7	3	.700	18	18	1	0-0	116.2	84	33	5	6	25-0	163	2.39	186	.199	.253	0	—	0	122	46		2.5
2002	Bos A☆	20	4	.833	30	30	2	0-0	199.1	144	62	13	15	40-1	239	2.26	198	.198	.254	5-0-1	.000	-0	102	49	26	4.7
2003	†Bos A	14	4	.778	29	29	3	0-0	186.2	147	52	7	9	47-0	206	2.22	210	.215	.272	3	.000	-0	92	26		3.1
2004	†Bos A★	16	9	.640	33	33	1-1	0-0	217	193	99	26	16	61-0	227	3.90	125	.238	.301	2	.000	-0	92	26		2.3
2005	NY N★	15	8	.652	31	31	4-1	0-0	217	159	69	19	4	47-3	208	2.82	147	.204	.252	69-0-6	.087	-4	97	35		3.7
Total	14	197	84	.701	419	352	46-17	3-1	2513	1905	835	194	119	662-24	2861	2.72	166	.208	.269	334-0-44	.093	-12	98	496	147	50.8

MARTINEZ, RAMON Ramon Jaime (b Ramon Jaime (Martinez)) B3.22.1968 Santo Domingo, D.R. BR/TR/6-4/173(186-186) d8.13 b-Pedro

YEAR	TM LG	W	L	PCT	G	GS	CG-SHO	SV-BS	IP	H	R	HR	HB	BB-IB	SO	ERA	AERA	OAV	OOB	AB-HR-SH	AVG	PB	SUP	APR	DL	PW
1988	LA N	1	3	.250	9	6	0	0-0	35.2	27	17	0	0	22-1	23	3.79	88	.216	.333	7-0-1	.000	-1	53	-2		-0.1
1989	LA N	6	4	.600	15	15	2-2	0-0	98.2	79	39	11	5	41-1	89	3.19	108	.219	.308	37-0-2	.162	0*	127	3		0.9
1990	LA N★	20	6	.769	33	33	12-3	0-0	234.1	191	89	22	4	67-5	223	2.92	126	.220	.278	80-0-9	.125	-2	121	20		1.9
1991	LA N	17	13	.567	33	33	6-4	0-0	220.1	190	89	18	7	69-4	150	3.27	110	.229	.293	77-1-8	.117	-1	111	9		1.1
1992	LA N	8	11	.421	25	25	1-1	0-0	150.2	141	82	11	5	69-4	101	4.00	87	.245	.331	50-0-5	.120	-2*	92	13		1.0
1993	LA N	10	12	.455	32	32	4-3	0-0	211.2	202	88	15	14	104-9	127	3.44	112	.251	.342	70-0-7	.129	-2	92	13		1.1
1994	LA N	12	7	.632	24	24	4-3	0-0	170	160	83	18	6	56-2	119	3.97	100	.249	.312	66-0-5	.273	5	123	-1		0.9
1995	†LA N	17	7	.708	30	30	4-2	0-0	206.1	176	95	19	5	81-5	138	3.66	106	.231	.308	64-0-13	.172	1	113	6		1.4
1996	†LA N	15	6	.714	28	27	2-2	0-0	168.2	153	76	12	8	86-5	133	3.42	115	.245	.341	42-0-5	.190	1	123	2	66	0.6
1997	LA N	10	5	.667	22	22	1	0	133.2	123	61	14	5	68-1	120	3.64	107	.243	.337							

YEAR	TM LG	W	L	PCT	G	GS	CG-SHO	SV-BS	IP	H	R	HR	HB	BB-IB	SO	ERA	AERA	OAV	OOB	AB-HR-SH	AVG	PB	SUP	APR	DL	PW
1998	LA N	7	3	.700	15	15	1	0-0	101.2	76	41	8	3	41-1	91	2.83	142	.206	.288	34-0-5	.176	1	90	12	105	1.2
1999	†Bos A	2	1	.667	4	4	0	0-0	20.2	14	8	2	2	8-0	15	3.05	163	.192	.286	0	—	0	122	4	150	0.6
2000	Bos A	10	8	.556	27	27	0	0-0	127.2	143	94	16	9	67-3	89	6.13	82	.283	.372	0	.200	0	109	-15	31	-1.7
2001	Pit N	0	2	.000	4	4	0	0-0	15.2	16	15	4	2	16-0	9	8.62	52	.276	.442	5	.000	-1	98	-6		-0.7
Total	14	135	88	.605	301	297	37-20	0-0	1895.2	1691	880	170	66	795-41	1427	3.67	106	.239	.319	596-1-68	.153	-1	110	43	389	4.1

MARTINEZ, ROGELIO Rogelio (Ulloa) "Limonar" B11.5.1918 Cidra, Cuba BR/TR/6-0/180 d7.13

YEAR	TM LG	W	L	PCT	G	GS	CG-SHO	SV-BS	IP	H	R	HR	HB	BB-IB	SO	ERA	AERA	OAV	OOB	AB-HR-SH	AVG	PB	SUP	APR	DL	PW
1950	Was A	0	1	.000	2	1	0	0	1.1	4	4	0	0	2	0	27.00	17	.500	.600	0	—	0	161	-3		-0.5

MARTINEZ, SILVIO Silvio Ramon (Cabrera) B8.19.1955 Santiago, D.R. BR/TR/5-10/160(154-170) d4.9

YEAR	TM LG	W	L	PCT	G	GS	CG-SHO	SV-BS	IP	H	R	HR	HB	BB-IB	SO	ERA	AERA	OAV	OOB	AB-HR-SH	AVG	PB	SUP	APR	DL	PW
1977	Chi A	0	1	.000	10	0	0	0	21	28	14	4	0	12-2	10	5.57	73	.337	.408	0		0		-3		-0.2
1978	StL N	9	8	.529	22	22	5-2	0-0	138.1	114	65	11	0	71-7	45	3.64	98	.228	.322	47-0-6	.170	0	122	-2		-0.3
1979	StL N	15	8	.652	32	29	7-2	0-1	206.2	204	92	14	0	67-2	102	3.27	117	.259	.314	62-0-10	.129	-2*	102	9		0.6
1980	StL N	5	10	.333	25	20	2	0-0	119.2	127	75	9	0	48-3	39	4.81	78	.273	.340	35-0-3	.086	-2	95	-15	33	-2.0
1981	StL N	2	5	.286	18	16	0	0-0	97	95	48	4	1	39-3	34	3.99	91	.260	.340	35-0-1	.200	1	94	-4		-0.3
Total	5	31	32	.492	107	87	14-4	1-1	582.2	568	294	41	5	237-17	230	3.88	96	.258	.328	179-0-20	.145	-3	103	-15	33	-2.2

MARTINEZ, WILLIE William Jose B1.4.1978 Barquisimeto, Venez BR/TR/6-2/185 d6.14 [DL 1999 Cle A 64]

YEAR	TM LG	W	L	PCT	G	GS	CG-SHO	SV-BS	IP	H	R	HR	HB	BB-IB	SO	ERA	AERA	OAV	OOB	AB-HR-SH	AVG	PB	SUP	APR	DL	PW
2000	Cle A	0	0	—	1	0	0	0-0	3	1	1	0	0	1-0	1	3.00	167	.111	.182	0	—	0		1		0.0

MARTINI, WEDO Guido Joe "Southern" B7.1.1913 Birmingham AL D10.28.1970 Philadelphia PA BR/TR/5-10/165 d7.28

YEAR	TM LG	W	L	PCT	G	GS	CG-SHO	SV-BS	IP	H	R	HR	HB	BB-IB	SO	ERA	AERA	OAV	OOB	AB-HR-SH	AVG	PB	SUP	APR	DL	PW
1935	Phi A	0	2	.000	3	2	0	0	6.1	8	13	0	0	11	1	17.05	27	.333	.543	2	.000	-0	29	-8		-1.3

MARTZ, RANDY Randy Carl B5.28.1956 Harrisburg PA BL/TR/6-4/210* [ChiN77 1/12] d9.6 Col South Carolina-Aiken

YEAR	TM LG	W	L	PCT	G	GS	CG-SHO	SV-BS	IP	H	R	HR	HB	BB-IB	SO	ERA	AERA	OAV	OOB	AB-HR-SH	AVG	PB	SUP	APR	DL	PW
1980	Chi N	1	2	.333	6	6	0	0-0	30.1	28	14	1	0	11-1	5	2.08	191	.241	.302	9	.111	-1	71	3		0.3
1981	Chi N	5	7	.417	33	14	1	6-1	107.2	103	49	6	1	49-1	32	3.68	102	.256	.336	28-0-2	.214	1*	69	1		0.2
1982	Chi N	11	10	.524	28	24	1	1-1	147.2	157	80	17	3	36-4	40	4.21	90	.272	.317	42-0-7	.143	1	102	-8	25	-0.9
1983	Chi A	0	0	—	1	1	0	0-0	5	4	2	0	0	4-0	1	3.60	117	.211	.348	0		0	86	0		0.0
Total	4	17	19	.472	68	45	2	7-2	290.2	292	145	24	4	100-6	78	3.78	101	.262	.323	79-0-9	.165	1	88	-4	25	-0.4

MASAOKA, ONAN Onan Kainoa Satoshi B10.27.1977 Hilo HI BR/TL/6-0/188* [LAN95 3/79] d4.5

YEAR	TM LG	W	L	PCT	G	GS	CG-SHO	SV-BS	IP	H	R	HR	HB	BB-IB	SO	ERA	AERA	OAV	OOB	AB-HR-SH	AVG	PB	SUP	APR	DL	PW
1999	LA N	2	4	.333	54	0	0	1-1	66.2	55	33	8	2	47-3	61	4.32	101	.222	.348	4-0-1	.000	-0		1		0.0
2000	LA N	1	1	.500	29	0	0	0-0	27	23	12	2	1	15-1	27	4.00	111	.230	.336	0		0		2		0.1
Total	2	3	5	.375	83	0	0	1-1	93.2	78	45	10	3	62-4	88	4.23	104	.224	.345	4-0-1	.000	-0		3		0.1

MASON, DEL Adelbert William B10.29.1883 Newfane NY D12.31.1962 Winter Park FL BR/TR/6-0/160 d4.23 Col Rollins

YEAR	TM LG	W	L	PCT	G	GS	CG-SHO	SV-BS	IP	H	R	HR	HB	BB-IB	SO	ERA	AERA	OAV	OOB	AB-HR-SH	AVG	PB	SUP	APR	DL	PW
1904	Was A	0	3	.000	5	3	2	0	33	45	30	1	2	13	16	6.00	44	.326	.392	15	.000	-2	107	-12		-1.2
1906	Cin N	0	1	.000	2	1	0	0	12	10	6	1	1	6	4	4.50	61	.250	.362	5	.000	-1	79	-1		-0.2
1907	Cin N	5	12	.294	25	17	13-1	0	146	144	68	2	6	55	45	3.14	83	.277	.353	44-0-5	.182	-0	57	-7		-0.8
Total	3	5	16	.238	32	21	16-1	0	191	199	104	4	9	74	65	3.72	70	.286	.362	64-0-5	.125	-3	65	-20		-2.2

MASON, ERNIE Ernest B New Orleans LA D7.30.1904 Covington LA 6-0/150 d7.17

YEAR	TM LG	W	L	PCT	G	GS	CG-SHO	SV-BS	IP	H	R	HR	HB	BB-IB	SO	ERA	AERA	OAV	OOB	AB-HR-SH	AVG	PB	SUP	APR	DL	PW
1894	StL N	0	3	.000	4	2	2	0	22.2	34	29	1	0	10	3	7.15	76	.343	.404	12	.250	-0	59	-6		-0.5

MASON, HANK Henry B6.19.1931 Marshall MO BR/TR/6-0/185* d9.12

YEAR	TM LG	W	L	PCT	G	GS	CG-SHO	SV-BS	IP	H	R	HR	HB	BB-IB	SO	ERA	AERA	OAV	OOB	AB-HR-SH	AVG	PB	SUP	APR	DL	PW
1958	Phi N	0	0	—	1	0	0	0	5	7	7	0	1	2-0	3	10.80	37	.368	.417	2	.000	-0		-4		-0.2
1960	Phi N	0	0	—	3	0	0	0	5.2	9	6	1	0	5-1	3	9.53	41	.375	.467	1	.000	-0		-3		-0.2
Total	2	0	0	—	4	0	0	0	10.2	16	13	1	1	7-1	6	10.13	39	.372	.444	3	.000	-0		-7		-0.4

MASON, MIKE Michael Paul B11.21.1958 Faribault MN BL/TL/6-2/205* [TexA80 S1/12] d9.13 C1 Col Oral Roberts

YEAR	TM LG	W	L	PCT	G	GS	CG-SHO	SV-BS	IP	H	R	HR	HB	BB-IB	SO	ERA	AERA	OAV	OOB	AB-HR-SH	AVG	PB	SUP	APR	DL	PW
1982	Tex A	1	2	.333	4	4	0	0-0	23	21	13	3	0	9-1	8	5.09	76	.244	.316	0	—	0	111	-3		-0.3
1983	Tex A	0	2	.000	5	4	0	0-1	10.2	10	7	0	1	6-0	9	5.91	69	.244	.354	0	—	0		-2		-0.3
1984	Tex A	9	13	.409	36	24	4	0-0	184.1	159	84	18	2	51-4	113	3.61	116	.233	.285	0	—	0	74	14		1.5
1985	Tex A	8	15	.348	38	30	1-1	0-1	179	212	113	22	3	73-4	92	4.83	88	.299	.362	0	—	0	86	-14		-1.6
1986	Tex A	7	3	.700	27	22	2-1	0-0	135	135	71	11	0	56-3	85	4.33	100	.257	.327	0	—	0	128	1	35	0.1
1987	Tex A	2	2	.500	8	6	0	0-0	29	37	20	6	4	22-2	21	5.59	81	.322	.444	0	—	0	125	-3		-0.2
	Chi N	4	1	.800	17	4	0	0-0	38	43	25	4	1	23-0	28	5.68	76	.303	.396	0	—	0	178	-5	17	-0.5
1988	Min A	0	1	.000	9	0	0	0-0	6.2	8	8	1	0	9-0	7	10.80	38	.286	.459	9-0-3	.222	0*		-5		-0.6
Total	9	29	39	.426	140	90	7-2	0-2	605.2	625	335	65	11	249-14	363	4.53	94	.268	.338	9-0-3	.222	0	101	-17	52	-1.9

MASON, ROGER Roger Le Roy B9.18.1958 Bellaire MI BR/TR/6-6/220(215-226) d9.4 Col Saginaw Valley St.

YEAR	TM LG	W	L	PCT	G	GS	CG-SHO	SV-BS	IP	H	R	HR	HB	BB-IB	SO	ERA	AERA	OAV	OOB	AB-HR-SH	AVG	PB	SUP	APR	DL	PW
1984	Det A	1	1	.500	7	4	0	1-0	22	23	11	1	0	10-0	15	4.50	88	.271	.340	0	—	0	91	-1		-0.1
1985	SF N	1	3	.250	5	5	1-1	0-0	29.2	28	13	1	0	11-1	26	2.12	163	.243	.310	11	.091	-0	66	2		0.3
1986	SF N	3	4	.429	11	11	1	0-0	60	56	35	5	3	30-3	43	4.80	74	.250	.342	21-0-1	.048	-2	99	-8	123	-1.1
1987	SF N	1	1	.500	5	5	0	0-0	26	30	15	4	0	10-0	18	4.50	86	.303	.367	8	.125	-0	132	2		-0.1
1989	Hou N	0	0	—	2	0	0	0-0	1.1	2	3	0	0	2-0	3	20.25	17	.333	.500	0	—	0		-2		-0.1
1991	†Pit N	3	2	.600	24	0	0	3-0	29.2	21	9	2	1	6-1	21	3.03	199	.200	.248	0	—	0		2		0.4
1992	†Pit N	5	7	.417	65	0	0	8-2	88	80	41	11	4	33-8	56	4.09	85	.246	.320	10	.000	-1		-5		-0.9
1993	SD N	0	7	.000	34	0	0	0-0	50	43	20	1	2	18-4	39	3.24	128	.242	.313	3	.000	-0		5		0.6
	†Phi N	5	5	.500	34	0	0	0-3	49.2	47	28	9	0	16-1	32	4.89	81	.246	.301	3	.333	-0		1		-0.1
	Year	5	12	.294	68	0	0	0-3	99.2	90	48	10	2	34-5	71	4.06	100	.244	.307	6	.167	-0		-4		-0.7
1994	Phi N	1	1	.500	6	0	0	0-0	8.2	11	6	2	0	5-1	7	5.19	82	.306	.390	0	—	0		-1		-0.2
	NY N	2	4	.333	41	0	0	1-1	51.1	44	23	6	2	20-4	26	3.51	119	.232	.310	0	—	0		4		0.3
	Year	3	5	.375	47	0	0	1-1	60	55	29	8	2	25-5	33	3.75	112	.243	.323	0	—	0		2		0.1
Total	9	22	35	.386	232	23	2-1	13-6	416.1	385	206	42	12	161-23	286	4.02	94	.248	.320	56-0-2	.071	-0	95	-10	123	-1.6

MASTERS, WALT Walter Thomas B3.28.1907 Pen Argyl PA D7.10.1992 Ottawa ON, Can. BR/TR/5-10.5/180 d7.9 Col Penn

YEAR	TM LG	W	L	PCT	G	GS	CG-SHO	SV-BS	IP	H	R	HR	HB	BB-IB	SO	ERA	AERA	OAV	OOB	AB-HR-SH	AVG	PB	SUP	APR	DL	PW
1931	Was A	0	0	—	3	0	0	0	9	7	2	0	0	4	1	2.00	215	.226	.314	2	.000	-0		2		0.1
1937	Phi N	0	0	—	1	0	0	0	1	5	4	0	0	1	0	36.00	12	.714	.750	0	—	0		-3		-0.1
1939	Phi A	0	0	—	4	0	0	0	11	15	9	0	0	8	2	6.55	72	.306	.404	2	.000	-0		-3		-0.1
Total	3	0	0	—	8	0	0	0	21	27	15	0	0	13	3	6.00	75	.310	.400	4	.000	-1		-3		-0.1

MASTERSON, PAUL Paul Nicholas "Lefty" (b Paul Nicholas Nastasowski) B10.16.1915 Chicago IL D11.27.1997 Chicago IL BL/TL/5-11/165 d9.15

YEAR	TM LG	W	L	PCT	G	GS	CG-SHO	SV-BS	IP	H	R	HR	HB	BB-IB	SO	ERA	AERA	OAV	OOB	AB-HR-SH	AVG	PB	SUP	APR	DL	PW
1940	Phi N	0	0	—	2	0	0	0	5	5	4	0	0	2	3	7.20	54	.263	.333	1	.000	-0		-2		-0.1
1941	Phi N	1	0	1.000	2	1	1	0	11.1	11	6	0	0	6	8	4.76	78	.250	.340	4-0-1	.000	-1	183	-1		-0.1
1942	Phi N	0	0	—	4	0	0	0	8.1	10	6	1	0	5	3	6.48	51	.303	.395	0	—	0		-3		-0.1
Total	3	1	0	1.000	8	1	1	0	24.2	26	16	1	0	14	14	5.84	62	.271	.358	5-0-1	.000	-1	183	-6		-0.3

MASTERSON, WALT Walter Edward B6.22.1920 Philadelphia PA BR/TR/6-2/189* d5.8 Mil 1943-45

YEAR	TM LG	W	L	PCT	G	GS	CG-SHO	SV-BS	IP	H	R	HR	HB	BB-IB	SO	ERA	AERA	OAV	OOB	AB-HR-SH	AVG	PB	SUP	APR	DL	PW
1939	Was A	2	2	.500	24	5	1	0	58.1	66	44	2	2	48	12	5.55	78	.293	.422	13	.154	-0	122	-10		-0.6
1940	Was A	3	13	.188	31	19	3	2	130.1	128	92	6	3	88	68	4.90	85	.257	.371	38-0-3	.184	-1	79	-15		-1.6
1941	Was A	4	3	.571	34	6	1	3	78.1	101	56	3	1	53	40	5.97	68	.321	.420	19-0-2	.105	-1	128	-15		-1.3
1942	Was A	5	9	.357	25	15	8-4	2	142.2	138	75	2	2	54	63	3.34	109	.251	.321	45-0-3	.156	-0*	105	0		-0.1
1945	Was A	1	2	.333	4	2	1-1	0	25	21	8	1	0	10	14	1.08	287	.228	.304	9	.111	-1	220	4		0.4
1946	Was A	5	6	.455	29	9	2	1	91.1	105	70	8	3	67	61	6.01	56	.295	.411	25-0-1	.080	-1	137	-26		-3.0
1947	Was A★	12	16	.429	35	31	14-4	1	253	215	98	11	2	97	135	3.13	119	.234	.309	83-0-3	.133	-3*	67	17		1.7
1948	Was A★	8	15	.348	33	27	9-2	2	188	171	88	12	4	122	72	3.83	112	.247	.309	57-0-9	.193	-0	72	12		1.2
1949	Was A	3	2	.600	10	7	3	0	53	42	22	4	3	21	17	3.23	132	.216	.303	18-0-1	.056	-1*	87	6		0.4
	Bos A	3	4	.429	18	5	1	4	55	58	30	2	0	35	19	4.25	102	.283	.387	17	.118	-0	148	0		-0.1
	Year	6	6	.500	28	12	4	4	108	100	52	6	3	56	36	3.75	115	.251	.347	35-0-1	.086	-2	113	6		0.3
1950	Bos A	8	6	.571	33	15	6	1	129.1	145	91	15	1	82	60	5.64	87	.287	.387	44	.136	-3	118	-11		-1.2
1951	Bos A	3	0	1.000	30	1	0	0	59.1	53	24	1	0	32	39	3.34	144	.228	.322	11-0-1	.182	-1	100	7		0.3
1952	Bos A	1	1	.500	5	1	0	0	9.1	18	12	1	0	11	3	11.57	34	.400	.518	2	.000	-1	22	-7		-0.2
	Was A	8	8	.529	24	21	11	2	160.2	153	71	11	3	72	89	3.70	96	.253	.336	50-0-8	.120	-1	99	-1		-0.2
	Year	10	9	.526	29	22	11	2	170	171	83	12	3	83	92	4.13	87	.263	.350	52-0-8	.115	-1	95	-7		-1.4
1953	Was A	10	12	.455	29	20	10-4	0	166.1	145	79	16	3	62	95	3.63	107	.232	.304	51-0-3	.137	-1	78	3		0.3
1956	Det A	0	0	—	3	0	0	0	49.2	54	28	7	1	32-1	28	4.17	99	.289	.390	4	.250	-1		-1		-0.1
Total	14	78	100	.438	399	184	70-15	20	1649.2	1613	888	101	28	886-1	815	4.15	96	.258	.353	486-0-34	.140	-14	92	-37		-5.1

YEAR	TM LG	W	L	PCT	G	GS	CG-SHO	SV-BS	IP	H	R	HR	HB	BB-IB	SO	ERA	AERA	OAV	OOB	AB-HR-SH	AVG	PB	SUP	APR	DL	PW

MATARAZZO, LEN   Leonard B9.12.1928 New Castle PA   BR/TR/6-4/195   d9.6

| 1952 | Phi A | 0 | 0 | — | 1 | 0 | 0 | 0-0 | 1 | 1 | 0 | 0 | 0 | 1 | 0 | 0.00 | — | .250 | .400 | 0 | — | 0 | 0 | | | 0.0 |

MATEO, JULIO   Julio Cesar B8.2.1977 Bani, D.R.   BR/TR/6-0/180*   d5.7

2002	Sea A	0	0	—	12	0	0	0-0	21	20	10	2	1	12-0	15	4.29	100	.247	.351	0	—	0	0			0.0
2003	Sea A	4	0	1.000	50	0	0	1-0	85.2	69	32	14	5	13-1	71	3.15	137	.220	.259	0	—	0	12	49		0.5
2004	Sea A	1	2	.333	45	0	0	1-3	57.2	56	30	11	5	16-3	43	4.68	95	.251	.310	0	—	0	0	12	49	-0.1
2005	Sea A	3	6	.333	55	1	0	0-2	88.1	79	32	12	7	17-6	52	3.06	138	.237	.287	0	—	0	0	24	49	1.4
Total	4	8	8	.500	162	1	0	2-5	252.2	224	104	39	18	58-10	181	3.56	121	.236	.289	0	—	0			

MATHEWS, GREG   Gregory Inman B5.17.1962 Harbor City CA   BR/TL/6-2/180*   StLN84 10/243]   d6.3   Col Cal St.-Fullerton   [DL 1989 StL N 182]

1986	StL N	11	8	.579	23	22	1	0-0	145.1	139	61	15	2	44-3	67	3.65	101	.259	.317	43-0-7	.047	-3	83	3		-0.1
1987	†StL N	11	11	.500	32	32	2-1	0-0	197.2	184	87	17	0	71-5	108	3.73	113	.249	.314	68-0-7	.191	1	88	11	94	1.2
1988	StL N	4	6	.400	13	13	1	0-0	68	61	34	9	2	33-5	31	4.24	83	.247	.337	23-0-1	.174	0	83	-5	94	-0.6
1990	StL N	0	5	.000	11	10	0	0-0	50.2	53	34	5	2	30-1	18	5.33	72	.277	.378	14-0-1	.214	1*	84	-8		-0.5
1992	Phi N	2	3	.400	14	7	0	0-0	52.1	54	31	7	1	24-2	27	5.16	68	.270	.350	14-0-2	.000	-1	74	-9		-0.9
Total	5	28	33	.459	93	84	4-1	0-0	514	491	247	45	7	202-16	251	4.08	95	.256	.328	162-0-18	.136	-1	85	-8	276	-0.9

MATHEWS, BOBBY   Robert T. B11.21.1851 Baltimore MD   D4.17.1898 Baltimore MD   BR/TR/5-5.5/140   d5.4   U3 ▲

1871	Kek NA	6	11	.353	19	19	19-1	0	169	261	243	5		21	17	5.17	88	.305	.322	89	.270	-3	63	-10		-0.7
1872	Bal NA	25	18	.581	49	47	39	0	406	480	356	3		52	57	3.19	115	.257	.277	222	.225	-8*	96	26		1.0
1873	Mut NA	29	23	.558	52	52	47-2	0	443	489	348	5		62	79	2.58	123	.251	.274	223	.193	-2	90	37		2.5
1874	Mut NA	42	22	.656	65	65	62-4	0	578	652	371	3		20	75	1.90	118	.261	.273	298	.242	-2	100	22		1.5
1875	Mut NA	29	38	.433	70	70	69-3	0	625.2	711	421	4		20	37	2.86	75	.301	.308	218	.183	-10	83	-46		-4.5
1876	NY N	21	34	.382	56	56	55-2	0	516	693	395	8		24	37	4.04	66	.339	.357	59	.169	-3	101	-25		-2.4
1877	Cin N	3	12	.200	15	15	13	0	129.1	208	132	0		17	9	4.04	66	.258	.282	173-1	.202	-0*	135	3		0.2
1879	Pro N	12	6	.667	27	25	15-1	1	189	194	85	4		26	90	2.29	103	.258	.282	57	.193	-2*	106	-7		-0.8
1881	Pro N	4	8	.333	14	14	10-1	0	102.1	121	81	2		21	28	3.17	84	.268	.300	57	.193	-1*	204	1		0.0
	Bos N	1	0	1.000	5	1	1	2	23	22	11	0		11	5	2.35	113	.239	.320	71	.169	-1*	113	-6		-0.8
	Year	5	8	.385	19	15	11-1	2	125.1	143	92	2		32	33	3.02	88	.263	.304	128	.180	-3	91	-2		-0.7
1882	Bos N	19	15	.559	34	32	31	0	285	278	151	5		22	153	2.87	100	.232	.246	169	.186	-7*	101	38		2.8
1883	Phi AA	30	13	.698	44	44	41-1	0	381	396	224	11		31	203	2.46	144	.251	.265	167	.185	-5	114	4		-0.3
1884	Phi AA	30	18	.625	49	49	48-3	0	430.2	401	238	10	12	49	286	2.43	142	.233	.267	179	.168	-7	104	42		3.3
1885	Phi AA	30	17	.638	48	48	46-2	0	422.1	394	229	3	20	57	286	3.96	88	.267	.320	88	.239	-0	119	-9		-0.8
1886	Phi AA	13	9	.591	24	24	22	0	197.2	226	148	3	13	53	93	6.67	64	.298	.368	25	.200	-0	121	-16		-1.3
1887	Phi AA	3	4	.429	7	7	7	0	58	75	64	4	3	25	9	6.67	64	.298	.368		.200	-0	121	-16		-1.3
Total	5 NA	131	112	.539	255	253	236-10	0	2221.2	2593	1739	20		196	329	2.69	108	.262	.276	1096	.216	-25	86	65		2.3
Total	10	.166	136	.550	323	315	289-10	3	2734.1	3008	1758	50	48	336	1199	3.00	100	.261	.285	1390-1	.192	-38	104	-13		-3.9

MATHEWS, TERRY   Terry Alan B10.5.1964 Alexandria LA   BL/TR/6-2/225(200-225)   [TexA87 5/129]   d6.21   Col Louisiana-Monroe

1991	Tex A	4	0	1.000	34	2	0	1-2	57.1	54	24	5	1	18-3	51	3.61	112	.251	.312	0	—	0	226	4		0.2
1992	Tex A	2	4	.333	40	0	0	0-4	42.1	48	29	4	1	31-3	26	5.95	64	.294	.404	0	—	0	-9	45		-1.2
1994	Fla N	2	1	.667	24	2	0	0-0	43	45	16	4	1	9-1	21	3.35	133	.268	.309	6	.500	1	133	6		0.5
1995	Fla N	4	4	.500	57	0	0	3-4	82.2	70	32	9	1	27-4	72	3.38	127	.235	.300	13	.462	3	9	15		-0.6
1996	Fla N	2	4	.333	57	0	0	4-1	55	59	33	7	1	27-5	49	4.91	84	.273	.355	4	.000	-0	-5	15		-0.6
1997	†Bal A	2	2	.500	14	0	0	0-1	18.2	20	7	3	0	7-0	13	3.38	147	.282	.346	0	—	0	4			-0.1
	†Bal A	4	4	.500	57	0	0	1-1	63.1	63	35	8	0	36-2	39	4.41	100	.267	.359	0	—	0	-4	41		-0.2
1998	Bal A	0	1	.000	17	0	0	0-1	20.1	26	15	4	0	8-3	10	6.20	73	.342	.400	0	—	0	312	40		0.5
1999	KC A	2	1	.667	24	1	0	1-2	39	44	21	4	2	17-1	19	4.38	116	.289	.360	1	.000	-0	-1			-0.1
Total	8	22	21	.512	324	5	0	10-17	421.2	429	212	50	7	180-22	300	4.25	102	.269	.343	24	.375	3	211	7	156	0.5

MATHEWS, T. J.   Timothy Jay B1.9.1970 Belleville IL   BR/TR/6-2/200(200-225)   [StLN92 36/1007]   d7.28   f-Nelson   Col Nevada-Las Vegas

1995	StL N	1	1	.500	23	0	0	2-0	29.2	21	7	1	0	11-1	28	1.52	282	.200	.276	2	.000	-0	8			0.9
1996	†StL N	2	6	.250	67	0	0	6-5	83.2	62	32	8	2	32-4	80	3.01	141	.203	.282	4	.000	-0	11			1.5
1997	StL N	4	4	.500	40	0	0	0-3	46	41	14	4	1	12-1	24	4.40	105	.293	.362	0	—	-0	-1			-0.1
1998	Oak A	6	2	.750	24	0	0	3-3	28.2	34	18	5	1	12-1	24	4.58	101	.258	.328	0	—	-0	-1			-0.1
1999	Oak A	7	4	.636	66	0	0	1-3	72.2	71	44	6	4	29-3	53	3.81	124	.215	.287	0	—	-0	6	23		1.2
2000	Oak A	9	5	.643	50	0	0	3-2	59	46	28	9	2	20-4	42	6.03	80	.303	.368	0	—	-0	-6	19		-0.7
2001	Oak A	2	3	.400	50	0	0	0-1	59.2	73	40	9	0	25-5	42	5.09	90	.295	.368	0	—	-0	2			-0.2
	Oak A	0	1	.000	20	0	0	1-0	23	28	14	2	0	11-3	19	3.07	141	.204	.204	3	.000	-0	2			0.1
	StL N	1	0	1.000	10	0	0	0-0	14.2	11	6	2	0	1-0	10	3.44	126	.271	.320	1	.000	-0	2	75		0.1
2002	Hou N	0	0	—	12	0	0	0-0	18.1	19	7	2	0	5-3	13	3.44	126	.246	.316	0	.000	-1	30	117		3.1
Total	8	32	26	.552	362	0	0	16-17	435.1	406	210	49	12	164-27	357	3.82	118	.246	.316	11	.000	-1	30	117		3.1

MATHEWSON, CHRISTY   Christopher "Matty","Big Six" B8.12.1880 Factoryville PA   D10.7.1925 Saranac Lake NY   BR/TR/6-1.5/195   d7.17   M3/C2   HF1936   b-Henry   Col Bucknell

1900	NY N	0	3	.000	6	1	1	0	33.2	37	32	1	4	20	15	5.08	71	.278	.389	11	.182	0	96	-6		-0.4
1901	NY N	20	17	.541	40	38	36-5	0	336	288	131	3	13	97	221	2.41	137	.230	.292	130-0-4	.215	-1*	81	32		3.9
1902	NY N	14	17	.452	35	33	30-8	0	284.2	246	118	2	10	77	164	2.12	132	.233	.292	130-2-2	.200	1*	73	16		2.3
1903	NY N	30	13	.698	45	42	37-3	0	366.1	321	136	4	10	100	267	2.26	148	.231	.287	124-11-16	.226	3	105	39		4.4
1904	NY N	33	12	.733	48	46	33-4	1	367.2	306	120	7	4	78	212	2.03	134	.226	.270	133-0-9	.226	6	135	27		4.1
1905	†NY N	31	9	.775	43	37	32-8	3	338.2	252	85	4	1	64	206	1.28	230	.204	.245	127-2-1	.236	10*	127	57		8.1
1906	NY N	22	12	.647	38	35	22-6	1	266.2	262	100	3	3	77	128	2.97	88	.259	.313	91-0-3	.264	7	124	-3		2.3
1907	NY N	24	12	.667	41	36	31-8	2	315	250	88	5	2	53	178	2.00	124	.212	.247	107-0-3	.187	3	89	19		2.5
1908	NY N	37	11	.771	56	44	34-11	5	390.2	281	85	5	3	42	259	1.43	169	.197	.222	129-0-7	.155	7	107	41		6.2
1909	NY N	25	6	.806	37	33	26-8	2	275.1	192	57	2	0	36	149	1.14	223	.200	.228	95-1-1	.263	7	100	42		6.6
1910	NY N	27	9	.750	38	35	27-2	0	318.1	292	100	5	3	60	184	1.89	157	.248	.286	107-1-4	.234	7	125	35		5.5
1911	†NY N	26	13	.667	45	37	29-5	3	307	303	102	5	1	38	141	1.99	169	.259	.283	112-0-3	.196	0	112	42		5.5
1912	NY N	23	12	.657	43	34	27	4	310	311	107	6	2	34	134	2.12	159	.260	.281	110-0-3	.264	5	117	43		5.1
1913	†NY N	25	11	.694	40	35	25-4	2	306	291	94	4	0	21	93	3.00	88	.263	.278	105-0-4	.219	6	124	-13		-2.7
1914	NY N	24	13	.649	41	35	29-5	2	312	314	133	16	4	23	57	3.00	88	.277	.298	51-0-5	.157	3	81	-23		-2.1
1915	NY N	8	14	.364	27	24	11-1	0	186	199	97	9	1	20	57	3.58	72	.277	.298	17-0-2	.000	-1	102	-2		-0.9
1916	NY N	3	4	.429	12	6	4-1	0	65.2	59	27	3	0	7	16	2.33	104	.243	.264	17-0-2	.000	-1	102	-2		-0.9
	Cin N	1	0	1.000	1	1	1	0	9	15	8	1	0	1	3	8.00	32	.366	.381	5	.600	1	288	-5		-0.1
	Year	4	4	.500	13	7	5-1	2	74.2	74	35	4	0	8	19	3.01	81	.261	.281	22-0-2	.136	1	131	-6		-0.2
Total	17	373	188	.665	636	552	435-79	30	4788.2	4219	1620	89	59	848	2507	2.13	136	.236	.273	1687-7-69	.215	59	108	378		56.3

MATHEWSON, HENRY   Henry B12.24.1886 Factoryville PA   D7.1.1917 Factoryville PA   BR/TR/6-3/175   d9.28   b-Christy   Col Bucknell

1906	NY N	0	1	.000	2	1	1	1	10	7	7	0	1	14	2	5.40	48	.194	.431	2-0-1	.000	-0	28	-3		-0.1
1907	NY N	0	0	—	1	0	0	1	1	1	1	0	0	0	0	0.00	—	.250	.250	0	—	.0	0			0.0
Total	2	0	1	.000	3	1	1	2	11	8	8	0	1	14	2	4.91	53	.200	.418	2-0-1	.000	-0	28	-3		-0.1

MATHIAS, CARL   Carl Lynwood "Stubby" B6.13.1936 Bechtelsville PA   BB/TL/5-11/195*   d7.31

1960	Cle A	0	1	.000	7	0	0	0	15.1	14	7	2	0	8-0	13	3.52	106	.233	.324	1	.000	-0	0			0.0
1961	Was A	0	1	.000	4	3	0	0	13.2	22	19	3	1	4-0	7	11.20	36	.361	.403	5	.200	-0	176	-11		-0.5
Total	2	0	2	.000	11	3	0	0	29	36	26	5	1	12-0	20	7.14	54	.298	.363	6	.167	-0	176	-11		-0.5

MATHIS, RON   Ronald Vance B9.25.1958 Kansas City MO   BR/TR/6-0/175*   [DetA80 30/724]   d4.13   Col Missouri

1985	Hou N	3	5	.375	23	8	0	1-0	70	83	54	7	4	27-1	34	6.04	58	.293	.352	14-0-2	.071	-1	114	-20		-2.3
1987	Hou N	1	1	.500	12	0	0	0-0	12	10	8	2	1	11-0	8	5.25	75	.233	.389	2	.000	-0	-2			-0.3
Total	2	4	6	.333	18	8	0	1-0	82	93	62	9	1	38-1	42	5.93	60	.285	.358	16-0-2	.063	-1	114	-22		-2.5

MATLACK, JON   Jonathan Trumpbour B1.19.1950 West Chester PA   BL/TL/6-3/205(190-210)   [NYN67 1/4]   d7.11   C1

1971	NY N	0	3	.000	7	6	0	0-0	37	31	18	2	0	15-0	24	4.14	83	.228	.303	11	.273	1	103	-2		-0.1
1972	NY N	15	10	.600	34	32	8-4	0-0	244	215	79	14	2	71-14	169	2.32	164	.236	.289	78-0-5	.128	1	92	26		2.9
1973	†NY N	14	16	.467	34	34	14-3	0-0	242	210	93	16	2	99-12	205	3.20	114	.236	.312	65-0-12	.138	2*	75	13		1.2
1974	NY N★	13	15	.464	34	34	14-7	0-0	265.1	221	82	8	5	76-11	195	2.41	150	.226	.283	79-0-11	.101	-4	78	36		2.1

YEAR	TM LG	W	L	PCT	G	GS	CG-SHO	SV-BS	IP	H	R	HR	HB	BB-IB	SO	ERA	AERA	OAV	OOB	AB-HR-SH	AVG	PB	SUP	APR	DL	PW
1975	NY N★	16	12	.571	33	32	8-3	0-0	228.2	224	105	15	1	58-6	154	3.38	104	.254	.299	70-0-5	.100	0	105	0		-0.1
1976	NY N☆	17	10	.630	35	35	16-6	0-0	262	236	94	18	3	57-5	153	2.95	113	.242	.284	88-0-7	.193	4	120	14		1.8
1977	NY N	7	15	.318	26	26	5-3	0-0	169	175	86	19	2	43-7	123	4.21	90	.273	.317	50-0-1	.060	-2	77	-7		-1.0
1978	Tex A	15	13	.536	35	33	18-2	1-0	270	252	93	14	4	51-4	157	2.27	165	.245	.283	0	—	0	72	38		4.0
1979	Tex A	5	4	.556	13	13	2	0-0	85	98	43	9	1	15-1	35	4.13	*100	.293	.323	0	—	0	97	1		0.1
1980	Tex A	10	10	.500	35	34	8-1	1-0	234.2	265	111	17	0	48-1	142	3.68	106	.287	.321	0	—	0	97	1	87	0.1
1981	Tex A	4	7	.364	17	16	1-1	0-0	104.1	101	59	8	1	41-1	43	4.14	84	.258	.326	0	—	0	98	5		0.3
1982	Tex A	7	7	.500	33	14	1	1-1	147.2	158	64	14	2	37-4	78	3.53	110	.275	.319	0	—	0	111	-11		-1.1
1983	Tex A	2	4	.333	25	9	2	0-0	73.1	90	43	7	3	27-1	38	4.66	87	.307	.366	0	—	0	87	-5		0.5
Total 13		125	126	.498	361	318	97-30	3-1	2363	2276	970	161	26	638-69	1516	3.18	115	.254	.303	441-0-41	.129	2	91	114	87	12.0

MATTERN, AL Alonzo Albert B6.16.1883 W.Rush NY D11.6.1958 West Rush NY BL/TL/5-10/165 d9.16

YEAR	TM LG	W	L	PCT	G	GS	CG-SHO	SV-BS	IP	H	R	HR	HB	BB-IB	SO	ERA	AERA	OAV	OOB	AB-HR-SH	AVG	PB	SUP	APR	DL	PW
1908	Bos N	1	2	.333	5	3	1-1	0	30.1	30	10	0	0	6	8	2.08	116	.265	.303	8-0-2	.125	-0	68	1		0.1
1909	Bos N	15	21	.417	47	32	24-2	3	316.1	322	142	4	3	108	98	2.85	99	.268	.330	101-0-7	.168	-1	83	-2		-0.1
1910	Bos N	16	19	.457	51	37	17-6	1	305	288	145	5	6	121	94	2.98	112	.257	.332	98-0-10	.163	-4	62	10		0.6
1911	Bos N	4	15	.211	33	21	11	0	186.1	228	129	13	1	63	51	4.97	77	.320	.376	63-0-5	.175	-2	60	-1		-1.8
1912	Bos N	0	1	.000	2	1	0	0	6.1	9	11	1	0	1	3	7.11	50	.313	.333	2	.000	-0	102	-3		-0.4
Total 5		36	58	.383	138	94	53-9	4	844.1	878	435	22	10	299	254	3.37	95	.276	.340	272-0-24	.165	-8	77	-13		-1.6

MATTES, TROY Troy Walter B8.26.1975 Champaign IL BR/TR/6-8/230 [MonN93 16/454] d6.19 Col Miami-Dade Wolfson (FL) CC [DL 2002 Mon N 183]

YEAR	TM LG	W	L	PCT	G	GS	CG-SHO	SV-BS	IP	H	R	HR	HB	BB-IB	SO	ERA	AERA	OAV	OOB	AB-HR-SH	AVG	PB	SUP	APR	DL	PW
2001	Mon N	3	3	.500	8	8	0	0-0	45	51	33	9	4	21-2	26	6.00	72	.285	.371	15-0-1	.467	3	131	-9		-0.7

MATTESON, C. V. Clifford Virgil B11.24.1861 Seville OH D12.18.1931 Seville OH d6.13

YEAR	TM LG	W	L	PCT	G	GS	CG-SHO	SV-BS	IP	H	R	HR	HB	BB-IB	SO	ERA	AERA	OAV	OOB	AB-HR-SH	AVG	PB	SUP	APR	DL	PW
1884	StL U	1	0	1.000	1	1	0	0	9	11	1	0	3		3	9.00	27	.321	.387	4	.000	-1	286	-4		-0.5

MATTESON, EDDIE Henry Edson "Matty" B9.7.1884 Guys Mills PA D9.1.1943 Westfield NY BR/TR/5-10.5/160 d5.30

YEAR	TM LG	W	L	PCT	G	GS	CG-SHO	SV-BS	IP	H	R	HR	HB	BB-IB	SO	ERA	AERA	OAV	OOB	AB-HR-SH	AVG	PB	SUP	APR	DL	PW
1914	Phi N	3	2	.600	15	3	2	0	58	58	29	1	1	23	28	3.10	95	.278	.352	22	.182	-0	105	-1		-0.2
1918	Was A	5	3	.625	14	6	2	0	67.2	57	20	2	1	15	17	1.73	158	.238	.286	19	.105	-2	69	7		0.6
Total 2		8	5	.615	29	9	4	0	125.2	115	49	3	2	38	45	2.36	120	.257	.318	41	.146	-2	81	6		0.4

MATTHEWS, JOE John Joseph "Lefty" B9.29.1898 Baltimore MD D2.8.1968 Hagerstown MD BB/TL/6-0/170 d9.18

YEAR	TM LG	W	L	PCT	G	GS	CG-SHO	SV-BS	IP	H	R	HR	HB	BB-IB	SO	ERA	AERA	OAV	OOB	AB-HR-SH	AVG	PB	SUP	APR	DL	PW
1922	Bos N	0	1	.000	3	1	0	0	10	5	6	1	1	6	0	3.60	111	.143	.286	2	.000	-0	0	0		0.0

MATTHEWS, MIKE Michael Scott B10.24.1973 Fredericksburg VA BL/TL/6-2/175(175-205) [CleA92 2/40] d5.31 Col Montgomery (MD) CC

YEAR	TM LG	W	L	PCT	G	GS	CG-SHO	SV-BS	IP	H	R	HR	HB	BB-IB	SO	ERA	AERA	OAV	OOB	AB-HR-SH	AVG	PB	SUP	APR	DL	PW
2000	StL N	0	0	—	14	0	0	0-0	9.1	15	12	2	1	10-2	8	11.57	40	.349	.481	0	—	0		-7	77	-0.3
2001	†StL N	3	4	.429	51	10	0	1-2	89	74	32	11	4	33-4	72	3.24	134	.227	.305	17-1-1	.118	0*	88	12		0.8
2002	StL N	2	1	.667	43	0	0	0-2	41.2	40	21	5	2	22-2	32	3.89	104	.260	.352	6	.167	0		0	21	0.0
	Mil N	0	0	—	4	0	0	0-0	4	3	2	0	0	7-1	2	4.50	91	.214	.476	0-0-1	—	0		0		0.0
	Year	2	1	.667	47	0	0	0-2	45.2	43	23	5	2	29-3	34	3.94	103	.256	.365	6-0-1	.167	0		0		0.0
2003	SD N	6	4	.600	77	0	0	0-3	64.2	65	34	4	4	29-5	34	4.45	90	.271	.353	2-0-1	.000	0		-3		-0.4
2004	Cin N	2	1	.667	35	0	0	0-0	30	31	22	7	2	16-1	15	6.30	68	.265	.360	0	—	0		-3		-0.4
2005	NY N	1	0	1.000	9	0	0	0-0	5	9	6	0	0	4-1	2	10.80	39	.429	.481	0	—	0		-4	62	-0.6
Total 6		14	10	.583	230	10	0	1-7	243.2	237	129	29	13	121-16	175	4.54	92	.259	.349	25-1-3	.120	0	88	-8	160	-1.1

MATTHEWS, WILLIAM William Calvin B1.12.1878 Mahanoy City PA D1.23.1946 Mt.Carbon PA TR d8.28

YEAR	TM LG	W	L	PCT	G	GS	CG-SHO	SV-BS	IP	H	R	HR	HB	BB-IB	SO	ERA	AERA	OAV	OOB	AB-HR-SH	AVG	PB	SUP	APR	DL	PW
1909	Bos A	0	0	—	5	1	0	0	16.2	16	8	1	0	10	6	3.24	77	.271	.377	8	.000	-1	113	-1		-0.2

MATTHEWSON, DALE Dale Wesley B5.15.1923 Catasauqua PA D2.20.1984 Blairsville GA BR/TR/5-11.5/145 d7.3

YEAR	TM LG	W	L	PCT	G	GS	CG-SHO	SV-BS	IP	H	R	HR	HB	BB-IB	SO	ERA	AERA	OAV	OOB	AB-HR-SH	AVG	PB	SUP	APR	DL	PW
1943	Phi N	0	3	.000	11	1	0	0	26	26	14	1	0	8	4	4.85	70	.271	.327	2-0-1	.000	-0*		-3		-0.4
1944	Phi N	0	0	—	17	0	0	0	32	27	14	1	0	16	8	3.94	92	.237	.331	3	.333	0		0		0.0
Total 2		0	3	.000	28	1	0	0	58	53	28	2	0	24	16	4.34	81	.252	.329	5-0-1	.200	0	0	-3		-0.4

MATTIMORE, MIKE Michael Joseph B8.1858 North Bend PA D4.28.1931 Butte MT BL/TL/5-8.5/160 d5.3 ▲

YEAR	TM LG	W	L	PCT	G	GS	CG-SHO	SV-BS	IP	H	R	HR	HB	BB-IB	SO	ERA	AERA	OAV	OOB	AB-HR-SH	AVG	PB	SUP	APR	DL	PW
1887	NY N	3	3	.500	7	7	6-1	0	57.1	47	39	2	4	28	12	2.35	160	.218	.319	32	.250	-0*	135	5		0.3
1888	Phi AA	15	10	.600	26	24	24-4	0	221	221	146	6	13	65	80	3.38	88	.251	.312	142	.268	7*	142	-8		-0.1
1889	Phi AA	2	1	.667	5	1	1	1	31	42	27	0	1	13	6	5.81	65	.313	.378	73-1	.233	1*	131	-5		-0.3
	KC AA	0	0	—	1	0	0	1	3	3	3	1	0	2	1	3.00	142	.250	.357	75	.160	-0*		0		0.0
	Year	2	1	.667	6	1	1	1	34	45	30	1	1	15	7	5.56	69	.308	.377	148-1	.196	1	130	-5		-0.3
1890	Bro AA	6	13	.316	19	18	19	0	178.1	201	149	3	13	76	33	4.54	86	.276	.355	129	.132	-3*	93	-15		-1.4
Total 4		26	27	.491	58	51	50-5	1	490.2	514	364	12	31	184	132	3.83	90	.261	.333	451-1	.204	5	121	-23		-1.5

MATTINGLY, EARL Laurence Earl B11.4.1904 Newport MD D9.8.1993 Brookeville MD BR/TR/5-10.5/164 d4.15

YEAR	TM LG	W	L	PCT	G	GS	CG-SHO	SV-BS	IP	H	R	HR	HB	BB-IB	SO	ERA	AERA	OAV	OOB	AB-HR-SH	AVG	PB	SUP	APR	DL	PW
1931	Bro N	0	1	.000	8	0	0	0	14.1	15	4	0	2	10	3	2.51	152	.268	.397	3	.000	-0		2		0.1

MATULA, RICK Richard Carlton B11.22.1953 Wharton TX BR/TR/6-0/190* [AtlN76 14/315] d4.8 Col Sam Houston St.

YEAR	TM LG	W	L	PCT	G	GS	CG-SHO	SV-BS	IP	H	R	HR	HB	BB-IB	SO	ERA	AERA	OAV	OOB	AB-HR-SH	AVG	PB	SUP	APR	DL	PW
1979	Atl N	8	10	.444	28	28	1	0-0	171.1	193	90	14	3	64-9	67	4.15	97	.286	.348	53-0-6	.094	-3	91	-1		-0.4
1980	Atl N	11	13	.458	33	30	3-1	0-0	176.2	195	100	17	0	60-9	62	4.58	80	.286	.339	57-0-5	.105	-3	81	-18		-2.4
1981	Atl N	0	0	—	5	0	0	0-0	7	8	5	1	0	2-0	0	6.43	55	.286	.333	1	.000	-0		-2		-0.1
Total 3		19	23	.452	66	58	4-1	0-0	355	396	195	32	3	126-18	129	4.41	87	.286	.343	111-0-11	.099	-6	86	-21		-2.9

MATUZAK, HARRY Harry George "Matty" B1.27.1910 Omer MI D11.16.1978 Fairhope AL BR/TR/5-11.5/185 d4.19

YEAR	TM LG	W	L	PCT	G	GS	CG-SHO	SV-BS	IP	H	R	HR	HB	BB-IB	SO	ERA	AERA	OAV	OOB	AB-HR-SH	AVG	PB	SUP	APR	DL	PW
1934	Phi A	0	3	.000	11	1	0	0	24	28	16	2	1	10	9	4.88	90	.292	.364	6-0-1	.167	0		-2		-0.2
1936	Phi A	0	1	.000	6	1	0	0	15	21	14	0	0	4	8	7.20	71	.318	.357	3-0-1	.000	-0	207	-4		-0.2
Total 2		0	4	.000	17	2	0	0	39	49	30	2	1	14	17	5.77	81	.302	.362	9-0-2	.111	-0	207	-6		-0.4

MAUCK, HAL Alfred Maris B3.6.1869 Princeton IN D4.27.1921 Princeton IN BR/TR/5-11/185 d4.29

YEAR	TM LG	W	L	PCT	G	GS	CG-SHO	SV-BS	IP	H	R	HR	HB	BB-IB	SO	ERA	AERA	OAV	OOB	AB-HR-SH	AVG	PB	SUP	APR	DL	PW
1893	Chi N	8	10	.444	23	18	12-1	0	143	168	112	2	9	60	23	4.41	105	.284	.359	61	.148	-5	84	0		-0.4

MAUL, AL Albert Joseph "Smiling Al" B10.9.1865 Philadelphia PA D5.3.1958 Philadelphia PA BR/TR/6-0/175 d6.20 ▲

YEAR	TM LG	W	L	PCT	G	GS	CG-SHO	SV-BS	IP	H	R	HR	HB	BB-IB	SO	ERA	AERA	OAV	OOB	AB-HR-SH	AVG	PB	SUP	APR	DL	PW
1884	Phi U	0	1	.000	1	1	1	0	8	10	7	0	1		1	4.50	51	.286	.306	4	.000	-1	55	-2		-0.3
1887	Phi N	4	2	.667	7	5	4	0	50.1	72	50	2	2	15	18	5.54	77	.326	.374	56-1	.304	3*	174	-7		-0.4
1888	Pit N	0	2	.000	3	1	1	0	17	26	20	0	0	5	12	6.35	42	.342	.383	259	.208	1*	23	-8		-0.7
1889	Pit N	1	4	.200	6	4	2	0	42	64	53	3	1	28	11	9.86	38	.340	.429	257-4	.276	2*	148	-26		-1.9
1890	Pit P	16	12	.571	30	28	26-2	0	246.2	258	189	13	12	104	81	3.79	103	.257	.335	162	.259	7*	124	0		0.7
1891	Pit N	1	2	.333	8	3	3	0	39	44	22	0	3	16	13	2.31	142	.273	.350	149	.188	1*	97	4		0.3
1893	Was N	12	9	.364	37	33	29-1	0	297	355	254	17	18	144	72	5.30	87	.288	.370	134	.254	10*	92	-22		-0.9
1894	Was N	11	15	.423	28	26	21	0	201.2	272	200	12	10	73	72	5.98	88	.319	.379	124-2-1	.242	3*	99	-9		-0.5
1895	Was N	10	5	.667	16	16	14	0	135.2	136	67	5	3	37	34	**2.45**	196	.257	.309	72-0-2	.250	1*	98	33		3.0
1896	Was N	5	2	.714	8	8	7	0	62	75	50	0	4	20	18	3.63	122	.296	.357	28	.286	2	149	2		0.3
1897	Was N	0	1	.000	1	1	0	0	2	4	2	0	4		0	9.00	48	.400	.455	1	.000	-0	66	-1		-0.1
	Bal N	0	0	—	2	0	0	0	7.2	9	6	0	4		8	7.04	59	.290	.488	3	.333	0	162	-2		-0.1
	Year	0	1	.000	3	1	0	0	9.2	13	10	0	4		9	7.45	56	.317	.481	4	.250	-0	130	-3		-0.2
1898	Bal N	20	7	.741	28	28	26-1	0	239.2	207	74	4	4	49	31	2.10	170	.231	.274	93-0-1	.204	4*	127	42		4.4
1899	Bro N	2	0	1.000	4	4	2	0	26	35	19	1	2	6	4	4.50	87	.321	.368	11	.273	0	161	-2		-0.2
1900	Phi N	2	3	.400	5	4	3	0	38	53	31	2	2	9	6	6.16	59	.329	.349	15	.200	0	72	-9		-0.9
1901	NY N	0	3	.000	9	2	2	0	19	39	27	1	2	8	5	11.37	29	.419	.476	8	.375	-0	57	-15		-1.5
Total 15		84	80	.512	187	167	143-4	0	1431.2	1659	1073	59	67	518	346	4.43	96	.284	.349	1376-7-4	.241	32	112	-22		1.3

MAUN, ERNIE Ernest Gerald B2.3.1901 Clearwater KS D1.1.1987 Corpus Christi TX BR/TR/6-0/165 d5.16

YEAR	TM LG	W	L	PCT	G	GS	CG-SHO	SV-BS	IP	H	R	HR	HB	BB-IB	SO	ERA	AERA	OAV	OOB	AB-HR-SH	AVG	PB	SUP	APR	DL	PW
1924	NY N	2	1	.667	22	0	0	0	35	46	24	2	1	10	5	5.91	62	.326	.375	3	.667	1		-8		-0.6
1926	Phi N	1	4	.200	14	5	0	0	37.2	57	36	4	1	8	9	6.45	64	.339	.406	12	.250	-0	101	-10		-1.2
Total 2		3	5	.375	36	5	0	0	72.2	103	60	6	2	18	14	6.19	63	.333	.392	15	.333	1	101	-18		-1.8

MAUNEY, DICK Richard B1.26.1920 Concord NC D2.6.1970 Albemarle NC BR/TR/5-11.5/164 d6.13

YEAR	TM LG	W	L	PCT	G	GS	CG-SHO	SV-BS	IP	H	R	HR	HB	BB-IB	SO	ERA	AERA	OAV	OOB	AB-HR-SH	AVG	PB	SUP	APR	DL	PW
1945	Phi N	6	10	.375	20	16	6-2	1	122.2	127	54	7	2	27	35	3.08	124	.268	.310	41-0-1	.146	-0*	79	9		1.2
1946	Phi N	6	4	.600	24	7	3-1	2	90	98	36	4	3	18	31	2.70	127	.279	.320	24-0-3	.167	-1*	125	5		0.6
1947	Phi N	0	0	—	9	1	0	1	16.1	15	8	1	1	7	6	3.86	104	.288	.383	2	.000	-0*	66	0		0.0
Total 3		12	14	.462	53	24	9-3	4	229	240	98	12	6	52	72	2.99	123	.274	.319	67-0-4	.149	-1	92	14		1.8

YEAR	TM LG	W	L	PCT	G	GS	CG-SHO	SV-BS	IP	H	R	HR	HB	BB-IB	SO	ERA	AERA	OAV	OOB	AB-HR-SH	AVG	PB	SUP	APR	DL	PW
MAUPIN, HARRY	Harry Carr B7.11.1872 Wellsville MO D8.25.1952 Parsons KS 5-7/150 d10.5																									
1898	StL N	0	2	.000	2	2	2	0	18	22	11	0	3	3	3	5.50	69	.297	.350	7-0-1	.429	1	94	-2		-0.1
1899	Cle N	0	3	.000	5	3	2	0	25	55	36	0	1	7	3	12.60	29	.437	.470	10	.000	-2	91	-21		-1.9
Total	2	0	5	.000	7	5	4	0	43	77	47	0	4	10	6	9.63	39	.385	.429	17-0-1	.176	-1	92	-23		-2.0
MAURER, DAVE	David Charles B2.23.1975 Minneapolis MN BR/TL/6-2/205* [SDN97 11/350] d7.22 Col Oklahoma St.																									
2000	SD N	1	0	1.000	14	0	0	0-1	14.2	15	8	2	2	5-1	13	3.68	121	.263	.344	0	—	0		1		0.0
2001	SD N	0	0	—	3	0	0	0-0	5	8	6	1	0	4-0	4	10.80	38	.348	.444	1	.000	-0		-4		-0.2
2002	Cle A	0	1	.000	2	0	0	0-0	1.1	3	2	1	0	0-0	0	13.50	33	.429	.429	0	—	0		-1		-0.2
2004	Tor A	0	0	—	3	0	0	0-0	1.1	6	8	1	0	5-0	1	54.00	9	.600	.733	0	—	0		-7		-0.7
Total	4	1	1	.500	22	0	0	0-1	22.1	32	24	5	2	14-1	18	8.87	50	.330	.425	1	.000	-0		-11		-0.7
MAURIELLO, RALPH	Ralph "Tami" B8.25.1934 Brooklyn NY BR/TR/6-3/195 d9.13																									
1958	LA N	1	1	.500	3	2	0	0	11.2	10	6	1	0	8-0	11	4.63	89	.238	.360	4	.000	-1	99	0		-0.1
MAUSER, TIM	Timothy Edward B10.4.1966 Fort Worth TX BR/TR/6-0/185(185-200) [PhiN88 3/68] d7.7 Col TCU																									
1991	Phi N	0	0	—	3	0	0	0-0	10.2	18	10	3	0	3-0	6	7.59	49	.367	.404	3	.000	-0		-5		-0.3
1993	Phi N	0	0	—	8	0	0	0-0	16.1	15	9	1	1	7-0	14	4.96	80	.238	.324	4	.000	-0		-1		0.0
	SD N	0	1	.000	28	0	0	0-0	37.2	36	19	5	0	17-5	32	3.58	115	.248	.325	2	.000	-0		1		0.1
	Year	0	1	.000	36	0	0	0-0	54	51	28	6	1	24-5	46	4.00	102	.245	.325	6	.000	-0		0		0.1
1994	SD N	2	4	.333	36	0	0	2-0	49	50	21	3	1	19-3	32	3.49	116	.269	.335	4-0-1	.250	-0		4	16	0.5
1995	SD N	0	1	.000	5	0	0	0-0	5.2	4	6	0	0	9-0	9	9.53	43	.190	.433	1	.000	-0		-3		-0.5
Total	4	2	6	.250	79	0	0	2-0	119.1	123	65	12	2	55-8	93	4.37	93	.265	.343	14-0-1	.071	-0		16	16	-0.2
MAXCY, BRIAN	David Brian B5.4.1971 Amory MS BR/TR/6-1/170* [DetA92 20/560] d5.26 Col U. of Mississippi																									
1995	Det A	4	5	.444	41	0	0	0-2	52.1	61	48	6	2	31-7	20	6.88	70	.293	.385	0	—	0		-14		-1.9
1996	Det A	0	0	—	2	0	0	0-0	3.1	8	5	2	0	2-0	1	13.50	38	.471	.526	0	—	0		-3		-0.1
Total	2	4	5	.444	43	0	0	0-2	55.2	69	53	8	2	33-7	21	7.28	66	.307	.395	0	—	0		-17		-2.0
MAXIE, LARRY	Larry Hans B10.10.1940 Upland CA BR/TR/6-4/220 d8.30 Col Chaffey (CA) JC																									
1969	Atl N	0	0	—	2	0	0	0-0	3	1	1	0	0	1-1	1	3.00	121	.111	.250	0	—	0		0		0.0
MAXWELL, BERT	James Albert B10.17.1886 Texarkana AR D12.10.1961 Brady TX BB/TR/6-0/180 d9.12																									
1906	Pit N	0	1	.000	1	1	0	0	8	8	6	0	0	2	1	5.63	48	.286	.333	3	.000	-0	136	-2		-0.3
1908	Phi A	0	0	—	4	0	0	0	13	23	21	0	2	9	7	11.08	23	.348	.442	5	.000	-1		-11		-0.6
1911	NY N	1	2	.333	4	3	3	0	31	37	15	0	2	7	8	2.90	116	.311	.359	9-0-1	.111	-0	104	1		0.1
1914	Bro F	3	4	.429	12	8	6-1	1	71.1	76	31	0	1	24	19	3.28	88	.276	.337	23-0-1	.087	-2	92	-2		-0.4
Total	4	4	7	.364	21	12	9-1	1	123.1	144	73	0	5	42	35	4.16	71	.295	.357	40-0-2	.075	-3	99	-14		-1.2
MAY, DARRELL	Darrell Kevin B6.13.1972 San Bernardino CA BL/TL/6-2/170(170-185) [AtlN92 46/1293] d9.10 Col Sacramento (CA) City																									
1995	Atl N	0	0	—	2	0	0	0-0	4	10	5	0	0	0-0	1	11.25	38	.500	.476	0	—	0		-3		-0.1
1996	Pit N	0	1	.000	5	2	0	0-0	8.2	15	10	5	1	4-0	5	9.35	47	.357	.426	3	.333	0	82	-5		-0.4
	Cal A	0	0	—	5	0	0	0-0	2.2	3	3	1	0	2-0	1	10.13	50	.333	.385	0	—	0	169	-3		-0.2
1997	Ana A	2	1	.667	29	2	0	0-1	51.2	56	31	6	0	25-2	42	5.23	88	.277	.351	2	.000	-0	81	-5	47	-0.2
2002	KC A	4	10	.286	30	21	2-1	0-1	131.1	144	83	28	1	50-3	95	5.35	93	.277	.339	4	.000	-0	97	21		1.8
2003	KC A	10	8	.556	35	35	2-1	0-1	210	197	98	31	2	53-1	115	3.77	128	.246	.292	4-0-1	.000	-0	89	-20		-2.2
2004	KC A	9	19	.321	31	31	3-1	0-0	186	234	130	38	2	55-4	120	5.61	83	.306	.350	4	.000	-0	117	-11		-1.5
2005	SD N	1	3	.250	22	8	0	0-0	59.1	73	38	10	0	20-1	32	5.61	69	.303	.354	9-0-1	.111	-0	150	-9		-0.2
	NY A	0	1	.000	2	1	0	0-0	7	14	13	4	0	3-0	3	16.71	26	.400	.447	0	—	0	94	-9	47	-0.3
Total	7	26	43	.377	161	97	7-3	0-3	660.2	746	411	123	6	212-11	414	5.16	91	.283	.334	26-0-2	.077	-1	94	-36	47	-3.1
MAY, JAKIE	Frank Spruiell B11.25.1895 Youngsville NC D6.3.1970 Wendell NC BR/TL/5-8/178 d6.26 Mil 1918																									
1917	StL N	0	0	—	15	1	0	0	29.1	29	13	0	3	11	18	3.38	80	.302	.391	4	.000	-1	56	-2		-0.1
1918	StL N	5	6	.455	29	15	6	0	152.2	149	83	2	13	69	61	3.83	71	.264	.358	45-1-4	.067	-1	113	-18		-1.1
1919	StL N	3	12	.200	28	19	8-1	0	125.2	99	64	1	14	87	58	3.22	87	.230	.377	37-0-3	.162	-1	82	-9		-0.5
1920	StL N	1	4	.200	16	5	3	0	70.2	65	38	0	7	37	33	3.06	98	.251	.360	24	.227	1	74	-4		-0.2
1921	StL N	1	3	.250	5	5	1	0	21	29	14	0	0	12	5	4.71	78	.333	.414	6	.333	1	90	-3		-0.1
1924	Cin N	3	3	.500	38	3	2	6	99	104	39	2	6	29	59	3.00	126	.276	.337	27-1-1	.111	-2	68	9		0.6
1925	Cin N	8	9	.471	36	12	7-1	2	137.1	146	74	3	7	45	74	3.87	106	.272	.337	48-0-6	.146	-1	99	12		1.1
1926	Cin N	13	9	.591	45	15	9-1	3	167.2	175	66	4	7	44	121	3.51	108	.274	.337	76-0-7	.184	-0	103	8		0.6
1927	Cin N	15	12	.556	44	28	17-2	1	235.2	242	110	6	14	70	103	4.42	89	.315	.386	27-0-3	.296	1	101	-4		-0.6
1928	Cin N	3	5	.375	21	11	1-1	1	79.1	99	44	1	1	35	39	4.61	99	.285	.352	64-0-3	.203	-1	76	1		0.1
1929	Cin N	10	14	.417	41	24	10	3	199	219	111	7	5	75	92	4.61	99	.285	.352	64-0-3	.203	-1	84	-13		-1.2
1930	Cin N	3	11	.214	26	18	5-1	0	112.1	147	83	6	6	41	44	5.77	84	.320	.383	39-0-1	.128	-1	122	2		0.1
1931	Chi N	5	5	.500	31	4	1	2	79	81	35	2	3	43	38	3.87	100	.275	.372	22-0-1	.227	1	122	2		0.0
1932	†Chi N	2	2	.500	35	0	0	1	53.2	61	34	3	2	19	19	4.36	86	.281	.345	8	.125	-0		-5		-0.3
Total	14	72	95	.431	410	160	70-7	19	1562.1	1645	808	35	88	617	765	3.88	97	.278	.355	468-2-29	.171	-4	93	-22		-2.2
MAY, RUDY	Rudolph B7.18.1944 Coffeyville KS BL/TL/6-3/205(195-207) d4.18 [DL 1984 NY A 182]																									
1965	Cal A	4	9	.308	30	19	2-1	0	124	111	59	7	4	78-1	76	3.92	87	.245	.359	30-0-2	.200	3	71	-7		-0.1
1969	Cal A	10	13	.435	43	25	4	2-0	180.1	142	81	20	3	66-5	133	3.44	102	.220	.295	49-0-1	.082	-2*	76	0		-0.1
1970	Cal A	7	13	.350	38	34	2-2	0-0	208.2	190	102	20	3	81-7	164	4.01	90	.245	.318	69-0-2	.087	-2	77	-8		-1.3
1971	Cal A	11	12	.478	32	31	7-2	0-1	208.1	160	74	12	2	87-6	156	3.02	107	.215	.296	68-0-2	.147	0	77	8	23	0.8
1972	Cal A	12	11	.522	35	30	10-3	1-0	205.1	162	79	15	0	82-6	169	2.94	100	.215	.292	62-0-2	.113	-1	81	-1		0.0
1973	Cal A	7	17	.292	34	28	10-4	0-2	185	177	101	20	3	80-9	134	4.38	82	.254	.330	0	—	0	107	-17		-1.7
1974	Cal A	0	1	.000	18	3	0	2-0	27	29	24	2	1	10-0	12	7.00	50	.274	.331	0	—	0	135	-11		-0.9
	NY A	8	4	.667	17	15	8-2	0-0	114.1	75	36	5	4	48-0	90	2.28	155	.188	.280	0	—	0	129	15	21	1.4
	Year	8	5	.615	35	18	8-2	2-0	141.1	104	60	7	5	58-0	102	3.18	111	.206	.290	0	—	0	130	3		0.5
1975	NY A	14	12	.538	32	31	13-1	0-0	212	179	87	9	2	99-2	145	3.06	121	.231	.317	0	—	0	140	-2		-0.3
1976	NY A	4	3	.571	11	11	2-1	0-0	68	49	32	5	1	28-2	38	3.57	96	.206	.291	0	—	0	123	-10		-0.9
	Bal A	11	7	.611	24	21	5-1	0-1	152.1	156	73	11	0	42-3	71	3.78	87	.267	.314	0	—	0	129	-11		-1.3
	Year	15	10	.600	35	32	7-2	0-1	220.1	205	105	16	1	70-5	109	3.72	90	.249	.307	0	—	0	105	4		0.4
1977	Bal A	18	14	.563	37	37	11-4	0-0	251.2	243	114	25	4	78-2	105	3.61	105	.255	.313	42-0-7	.143	0	125	-7	43	0.4
1978	Mon N	8	10	.444	27	23	4-1	0-0	144	141	73	15	6	42-7	87	3.88	92	.255	.313	21-0-1	.143	-0	88	14		1.2
1979	Mon N	10	3	.769	33	7	2-1	0-1	93.2	88	30	4	4	31-4	67	2.31	161	.255	.320	0	—	0	94	29	13	3.0
1980	†NY A	15	5	.750	41	17	3-1	3-2	175.1	144	56	14	0	39-2	133	2.46	161	.246	**.268**	0	—	0	95	-6		0.3
1981	†NY A	6	11	.353	27	22	4	1-0	147.2	137	71	10	2	41-0	79	4.14	87	.246	.298	0	—	0	87	11	23	1.2
1982	NY A	6	6	.500	41	6	0	3-3	106	109	43	4	1	14-5	85	2.89	140	.267	.289	0	—	0		-6	76	-0.7
1983	NY A	1	5	.167	15	0	0	0-0	18.1	24	14	1	1	12-1	16	6.87	57	.293	.398	0	—	0	96	19	381	2.0
Total	16	152	156	.494	535	360	87-24	12-12	2622	2314	1150	199	42	958-56	1760	3.46	103	.238	.308	341-0-17	.123	-3	96	19	381	2.
MAY, SCOTT	Scott Francis B11.11.1961 West Bend WI BR/TR/6-1/185* [LAN83 6/150] d9.2 Col Wisconsin-Stevens Point																									
1988	Tex A	0	0	—	3	1	0	0-0	7.1	8	7	3	0	4-1	4	8.59	48	.296	.364	0	—	0	133	-3		-0.6
1991	Chi N	0	0	—	2	0	0	0-0	2	6	4	0	0	1-0	1	18.00	22	.545	.583	0	—	0		-3		-0.6
Total	2	0	0	—	5	1	0	0-0	9.1	14	11	3	0	5-1	5	10.61	38	.368	.422	0	—	0	133	-6		-0.6
MAY, BUCKSHOT	William Herbert B12.13.1899 Bakersfield CA D3.15.1984 Bakersfield CA BR/TR/6-2/169 d5.9																									
1924	Pit N	0	0	—	1	0	0	0-0	1	2	0	0	0	0	0	0.00	—	.500	.500	0	—	0				
MAYER, ED	Edwin David B11.30.1931 San Francisco CA BL/TL/6-2/185* d9.15 Col California-Davis																									
1957	Chi N	0	0	—	3	1	0	0	7.2	8	5	2	1	2-0	3	5.87	66	.258	.324	2	.500	0	159	-1		
1958	Chi N	2	2	.500	19	0	0	1	23.2	15	12	0	3	16-1	14	3.80	103	.190	.343	5	.200	-0		0		
Total	2	2	2	.500	22	1	0	1	31.1	23	17	2	4	18-1	17	4.31	91	.209	.338	7	.286	0	159	-1		
MAYER, ERSKINE	Erskine John (b James Erskine) B1.16.1889 Atlanta GA D3.10.1957 Los Angeles CA d9.4 b-Sam Col Georgia Tech																									
1912	Phi N	0	1	.000	7	1	0	0	21.1	27	15	1	1	7	5	6.33	57	.318	.376	0	.000	0	20	-4		-0.
1913	Phi N	9	9	.500	39	19	7-2	1	170.2	172	77	6	9	46	51	3.11	107	.272	.330	50	.120	-2	86	3		-0.

YEAR	TM	LG	W	L	PCT	G	GS	CG-SHO	SV-BS	IP	H	R	HR	HB	BB-IB	SO	ERA	AERA	OAV	OOB	AB-HR-SH	AVG	PB	SUP	APR	DL	PW
1914	Phi	N	21	19	.525	48	38	24-4	2	321	308	135	8	13	91	116	2.58	114	.256	.315	108-1-3	.194	2	95	12		2.0
1915	†Phi	N	21	15	.583	43	38	20-2	2	274.2	240	94	9	14	59	114	2.36	116	.243	.239	88-1-5	.239	5	90	14		2.5
1916	Phi	N	7	7	.500	28	16	7-2	0	140	148	58	7	4	33	62	3.15	84	.281	.328	38-0-2	.132	-1	92	-5		-0.4
1917	Phi	N	11	6	.647	28	18	11-1	0	160	160	62	6	4	33	64	2.76	102	.268	.310	51-0-5	.196	-0	144	2		0.2
1918	Phi	N	7	4	.636	13	13	7	0	104	108	46	2	4	26	16	3.12	96	.276	.328	37-0-3	.216	1	139	8		0.9
	Pit	N	9	3	.750	15	14	11-1	0	123.1	122	40	1	4	27	25	2.26	127	.268	.314	42-0-1	.167	1	113	-1		-0.1
	Year		16	7	.696	28	27	18-1	0	227.1	230	86	3	8	53	41	2.65	110	.272	.320	79-0-4	.190	2	126	6		0.8
1919	Pit	N	5	3	.625	18	10	6	1	88.1	100	50	2	2	12	20	4.48	67	.267	.294	29-0-1	.207	0	156	-13		-1.2
	†Chi	A	1	3	.250	6	2	0	0	23.2	30	23	1	0	11	9	8.37	38	.316	.387	7	.000	-1	123	-12		-1.7
Total 8			91	70	.565	245	164	93-12	6	1427	1415	600	43	55	345	482	2.96	99	.264	.316	453-2-20	.185	5	106	4		2.1

MAYS, AL Albert C. B5.17.1865 Canal Dover (now Dover) OH D5.7.1905 Parkersburg WV BR d5.10

YEAR	TM	LG	W	L	PCT	G	GS	CG-SHO	SV-BS	IP	H	R	HR	HB	BB-IB	SO	ERA	AERA	OAV	OOB	AB-HR-SH	AVG	PB	SUP	APR	DL	PW
1885	Lou	AA	6	11	.353	17	17	17	0	150	129	102	3	8	43	61	2.76	117	.219	.282	61	.213	0	78	5		0.5
1886	NY	AA	11	27	.289	41	40	39-1	0	350	330	231	7	14	140	163	3.39	96	.240	.317	135-1	.119	-9	80	-10		-1.6
1887	NY	AA	17	34	.333	52	52	50	0	441.1	551	359	11	20	136	124	4.73	90	.298	.353	221-2	.204	-1*	77	-22		-1.6
1888	Bro	AA	9	5	.500	18	18	17-1	0	160.2	150	81	1	11	32	67	2.80	107	.238	.287	63	.079	-4	95	5		0.2
1889	Col	AA	10	7	.588	21	19	13-1	0	140	167	119	4	4	56	52	4.82	75	.287	.354	54	.130	-1	103	-20		-1.8
1890	Col	AA	0	1	.000	1	1	1	0	9	14	13	0	1	8	2	8.00	45	.341	.460	3	.000	-0	56	-5		-0.4
Total 6			53	89	.373	150	147	137-3	0	1251	1341	905	26	58	415	469	3.91	92	.265	.328	537-3	.160	-15	83	-47		-4.7

MAYS, CARL Carl William "Sub" B11.12.1891 Liberty KY D4.4.1971 ElCajon CA BL/TR/5-11.5/195 d4.15

YEAR	TM	LG	W	L	PCT	G	GS	CG-SHO	SV-BS	IP	H	R	HR	HB	BB-IB	SO	ERA	AERA	OAV	OOB	AB-HR-SH	AVG	PB	SUP	APR	DL	PW
1915	Bos	A	6	5	.545	38	6	3	7	131.2	119	54	0	5	21	65	2.60	107	.244	.282	38-0-2	.237	2	118	2		0.4
1916	†Bos	A	18	13	.581	44	24	14-2	3	245	208	79	3	9	74	76	2.39	116	.234	.299	77-0-3	.234	7*	97	11		2.8
1917	Bos	A	22	9	.710	35	33	27-2	0	289	230	81	1	14	74	91	1.74	148	.221	.282	107-0-2	.252	6	108	25		4.0
1918	†Bos	A	21	13	.618	35	33	30-8	0	293.1	230	94	2	11	81	114	2.21	121	.221	.284	104-0-4	.288	10*	119	16		3.7
1919	Bos	A	5	11	.313	21	16	14-2	2	146	131	57	2	5	40	53	2.47	123	.247	.306	53-0-2	.151	-2*	78	6		0.6
	NY	A	9	3	.750	13	13	12-1	0	120	96	34	3	5	37	54	1.65	193	.216	.283	45-0-1	.311	3	128	18		2.3
	Year		14	14	.500	34	29	26-3	2	266	227	91	5	10	77	107	2.10	148	.233	.295	98-0-3	.224	1	101	25		2.9
1920	NY	A	26	11	.703	45	37	26-6	2	312	310	127	13	7	84	92	3.06	125	.263	.316	109-0-8	.239	2	133	28		3.5
1921	†NY	A	27	9	.750	49	38	30-1	7	336.2	332	145	11	9	76	70	3.05	139	.257	.303	143-2-8	.343	12*	152	43		5.4
1922	†NY	A	13	14	.481	34	29	21-1	2	240	257	111	12	7	50	41	3.60	111	.285	.327	92-0-3	.250	1*	110	11		1.5
1923	NY	A	5	2	.714	23	7	2	0	81.1	119	59	8	4	32	16	6.20	64	.357	.420	27-1-1	.148	1	138	-19		-1.2
1924	Cin	N	20	9	.690	37	27	15-2	0	226	238	97	3	4	36	63	3.15	120	.270	.302	83-1-0	.289	7*	107	15		3.0
1925	Cin	N	3	5	.375	12	5	3	2	51.2	60	22	0	2	13	10	3.31	124	.294	.342	16	.250	1	66	5		0.9
1926	Cin	N	19	12	.613	39	33	24-3	1	281	286	112	3	4	53	58	3.14	118	.269	.306	98-0-7	.224	2	114	21		2.9
1927	Cin	N	3	7	.300	14	9	6	0	82	89	39	1	1	17	17	3.51	108	.276	.300	32-1-1	.406	5	52	2		1.0
1928	Cin	N	4	1	.800	14	6	4-1	1	62.2	67	33	3	0	22	10	3.88	102	.275	.335	27	.296	1	119	0		0.1
1929	NY	N	7	2	.778	37	8	1	4	123	140	67	2	4	32	32	4.32	106	.287	.333	34-0-2	.353	4	119	5		0.8
Total 15			208	126	.623	490	324	231-29	31	3021.1	2912	1211	73	89	734	862	2.92	119	.257	.307	1085-5-44	.268	64	117	189		31.7

MAYS, JOE Joseph Emerson B12.10.1975 Flint MI BB/TR/6-1/185(185-200) [SeaA94 6/161] d4.7 Col Manatee (FL) CC [DL 2004 Min A 183]

YEAR	TM	LG	W	L	PCT	G	GS	CG-SHO	SV-BS	IP	H	R	HR	HB	BB-IB	SO	ERA	AERA	OAV	OOB	AB-HR-SH	AVG	PB	SUP	APR	DL	PW
1999	Min	A	6	11	.353	49	20	2-1	0-0	171	179	92	24	2	67-2	115	4.37	119	.270	.336	3	.000	0	55	13		1.1
2000	Min	A	7	15	.318	31	28	2-1	0-0	160.1	193	105	20	2	67-1	102	5.56	95	.299	.364	5-0-1	.400	1	69	-4		-0.4
2001	Min	A★	17	13	.567	34	34	4-2	0-0	233.2	205	87	25	5	64-2	123	3.16	148	.235	.289	1-0-1	.000	-0	87	38		4.4
2002	†Min	A	4	8	.333	17	17	1-1	0-0	95.1	113	60	14	2	25-0	38	5.38	83	.292	.337	0	—	-0	93	-9	96	-1.0
2003	Min	A	8	8	.500	31	21	0	0-1	130	159	92	21	4	39-2	59	6.30	71	.302	.353	3-0-1	.333	1	115	-24		-2.4
2005	Min	A	6	10	.375	31	26	1-1	0-0	156	203	109	24	4	59-1	59	5.65	78	.318	.361	3	.333	0	91	-23		-1.9
Total 6			48	65	.425	193	146	10-6	0-1	946.1	1052	545	127	18	303-8	487	4.85	98	.282	.336	15-0-3	.267	2	83	-9	279	-0.2

MAYSEY, MATT Matthew Samuel B1.8.1967 Hamilton ON, Can. BR/TR/6-4/225* [SDN85 7/180] d7.8

YEAR	TM	LG	W	L	PCT	G	GS	CG-SHO	SV-BS	IP	H	R	HR	HB	BB-IB	SO	ERA	AERA	OAV	OOB	AB-HR-SH	AVG	PB	SUP	APR	DL	PW
1992	Mon	N	0	0	—	2	0	0	0-0	2.1	4	1	1	1	0-0	1	3.86	90	.364	.417	0	—	0	0	0		0.0
1993	Mil	A	1	2	.333	23	0	0	1-1	22	28	14	4	1	13-1	10	5.73	75	.322	.408	1	1.000	0		-3		-0.3
Total 2			1	2	.333	25	0	0	1-1	24.1	32	15	5	2	13-1	11	5.55	76	.327	.409	1	1.000	0		-3		-0.3

McADAMS, JACK George D. B12.17.1886 Benton AR D5.21.1937 San Francisco CA BR/TR/6-1.5/170 d7.22

YEAR	TM	LG	W	L	PCT	G	GS	CG-SHO	SV-BS	IP	H	R	HR	HB	BB-IB	SO	ERA	AERA	OAV	OOB	AB-HR-SH	AVG	PB	SUP	APR	DL	PW
1911	StL	N	0	0	—	6	0	0	0	9.2	7	5	0	2	5	4	3.72	91	.226	.368	1	.000	-0	0*			0.0

McAFEE, BILL William Fort B9.7.1907 Smithville GA D7.8.1958 Culpeper VA BR/TR/6-2/186 d5.12 Col Michigan

YEAR	TM	LG	W	L	PCT	G	GS	CG-SHO	SV-BS	IP	H	R	HR	HB	BB-IB	SO	ERA	AERA	OAV	OOB	AB-HR-SH	AVG	PB	SUP	APR	DL	PW
1930	Chi	N	0	0	—	3	0	0	0	3	5	3	0	0	2	0	0.00	—	.375	.500	—		-0		-2		-0.1
1931	Bos	N	0	1	.000	18	1	0	0	29.2	39	23	2	0	10	5	6.37	59	.333	.386	3	.000	-0	45	-8		-0.4
1932	Was	A	6	1	.857	8	5	2	0	41.1	47	22	3	0	22	10	3.92	110	.287	.371	18-0-2	.111	-2	130	1		0.0
1933	Was	A	3	2	.600	27	1	0	5	53	64	40	3	1	21	14	6.62	63	.296	.361	15-1-2	.267	2	102	-13		-1.1
1934	StL	A	1	0	1.000	28	0	0	0	61.2	84	48	4	3	26	11	5.84	86	.332	.401	16	.188	-0		-5		-0.3
Total 5			10	4	.714	83	7	2	5	186.2	237	137	12	4	81	40	5.35	78	.313	.382	52-1-4	.173	0	111	-27		-1.9

McALLISTER, SPORT Lewis William B7.23.1874 Austin MS D7.17.1962 Wyandotte MI BB/TR/5-11/180 d8.7 ▲

YEAR	TM	LG	W	L	PCT	G	GS	CG-SHO	SV-BS	IP	H	R	HR	HB	BB-IB	SO	ERA	AERA	OAV	OOB	AB-HR-SH	AVG	PB	SUP	APR	DL	PW
1896	Cle	N	0	0	—	1	0	0	0	4	9	3	0	0	2	0	6.75	67	.450	.500	27-0-1	.222	-0*		-1		0.0
1897	Cle	N	1	2	.333	4	3	0	0	28	29	20	3	0	9	10	4.50	100	.266	.322	137-0-4	.219	-0*	106	0		0.0
1898	Cle	N	3	4	.429	9	7	6	0	65.1	73	43	2	3	9	9	4.55	80	.281	.346	57-0-1	.228	1*	95	-5		-0.5
1899	Cle	N	0	1	.000	3	1	1	0	16	29	22	0	4	10	2	9.56	39	.387	.483	418-1-12	.237	0*	20	-10		-0.5
Total 4			4	7	.364	17	11	10	0	113.1	140	88	5	7	30	21	5.32	73	.302	.371	639-1-18	.232	1	92	-16		-0.9

McANALLY, ERNIE Ernest Lee B8.15.1946 Pittsburg TX BR/TR/6-1/190* [NYN66 20/381] d4.11 Col Paris (TX) JC

YEAR	TM	LG	W	L	PCT	G	GS	CG-SHO	SV-BS	IP	H	R	HR	HB	BB-IB	SO	ERA	AERA	OAV	OOB	AB-HR-SH	AVG	PB	SUP	APR	DL	PW
1971	Mon	N	11	12	.478	31	25	8-2	0-0	177.2	150	89	8	8	87-2	98	3.90	92	.228	.324	60-1-3	.117	-2	86	-6		-1.0
1972	Mon	N	6	15	.286	29	27	4-2	0-0	170	165	79	13	4	71-6	102	3.81	93	.259	.332	53-0-5	.113	-2	74	-5		-0.6
1973	Mon	N	7	9	.438	27	24	4	0-0	147	158	84	13	3	54-6	72	4.04	94	.274	.337	49-0-4	.184	-1	113	-6		-0.8
1974	Mon	N	6	13	.316	25	21	5-2	0-0	128.2	126	73	10	4	56-5	79	4.48	86	.256	.336	42-0-2	.119	-2	80	-8	30	-1.3
Total 4			30	49	.380	112	97	21-6	0-0	623.1	599	321	44	19	268-19	351	4.03	91	.253	.332	204-1-14	.132	-6	88	-25	30	-3.7

McANDREW, JAMIE James Brian B9.2.1967 Williamsport PA BR/TR/6-2/190* [LAN89 1/28] d7.17 f-Jim Col Florida [DL 1996 Mil A 182]

YEAR	TM	LG	W	L	PCT	G	GS	CG-SHO	SV-BS	IP	H	R	HR	HB	BB-IB	SO	ERA	AERA	OAV	OOB	AB-HR-SH	AVG	PB	SUP	APR	DL	PW
1995	Mil	A	2	3	.400	10	4	0	0-0	36.1	37	21	2	1	12-2	19	4.71	107	.266	.329	0	—	0	102	1	30	0.1
1997	Mil	A	1	1	.500	5	4	0	0-0	19.1	24	19	1	2	23-0	8	8.38	55	.304	.471	0	—	0	94	-8		-0.6
Total 2			3	4	.429	15	8	0	0-0	55.2	61	40	3	3	35-2	27	5.98	82	.280	.387	0	—	0	97	-7	212	-0.5

McANDREW, JIM James Clement B1.11.1944 Lost Nation IA BR/TR/6-2/185(175-190) [NYN65 9/245] d7.21 s-Jamie Col Iowa

YEAR	TM	LG	W	L	PCT	G	GS	CG-SHO	SV-BS	IP	H	R	HR	HB	BB-IB	SO	ERA	AERA	OAV	OOB	AB-HR-SH	AVG	PB	SUP	APR	DL	PW
1968	NY	N	4	7	.364	12	12	2-1	0	79	66	20	4	4	17-4	46	2.28	133	.230	.281	22-0-2	.045	-1	38	7		0.9
1969	NY	N	6	7	.462	21	21	4-2	0-0	135	112	57	9	2	44-6	90	3.47	106	.225	.288	37-0-5	.135	0	94	3		0.2
1970	NY	N	10	14	.417	32	27	9-3	2-0	184.1	166	77	18	2	38-6	111	3.56	114	.239	.279	54-0-8	.148	1	84	12		1.5
1971	NY	N	2	5	.286	24	10	0	0-1	90.1	78	50	10	1	32-5	42	4.38	78	.227	.292	23-0-1	.043	-1	95	-10		-0.8
1972	NY	N	11	8	.579	28	23	4	1-0	160.2	133	54	12	5	38-5	81	2.80	121	.225	.276	43-0-10	.047	-2	91	12		1.1
1973	NY	N	3	8	.273	23	12	0	1-0	80.1	109	60	9	3	31-8	38	5.38	68	.330	.386	15-2-0	.133	2*	105	-19		-2.2
1974	SD	N	4	4	.200	15	5	1	0-0	41.2	48	30	7	0	13-2	16	5.62	64	.284	.332	7-0-2	.143	0	102	-10		-1.1
Total 7			37	53	.411	161	110	20-6	4-1	771.1	712	348	73	17	213-36	424	3.65	99	.245	.297	201-0-30	.100	-3	87	-5		-0.4

McARTHUR, DIXIE Oland Alexander B2.1.1892 Vernon AL D5.31.1986 West Point MS BR/TR/6-1/185 d7.10 Col Bethel

YEAR	TM	LG	W	L	PCT	G	GS	CG-SHO	SV-BS	IP	H	R	HR	HB	BB-IB	SO	ERA	AERA	OAV	OOB	AB-HR-SH	AVG	PB	SUP	APR	DL	PW
1914	Pit	N	0	0	—	1	0	0	0	4	3	1	0	0	1	0	0.00	—	.250	.250	0	—	0		0		0.0

McCAVOY, TOM Thomas John B8.12.1936 Brooklyn NY BL/TL/6-3/200 d9.27 [DL 1960 Was A 168]

YEAR	TM	LG	W	L	PCT	G	GS	CG-SHO	SV-BS	IP	H	R	HR	HB	BB-IB	SO	ERA	AERA	OAV	OOB	AB-HR-SH	AVG	PB	SUP	APR	DL	PW
1959	Was	A	0	0	—	1	0	0	0	2.2	1	0	0	0	2-0	1	0.00	—	.125	.300	1	.000	-0		1		0.0

McBEAN, AL Alvin O'Neal B5.15.1938 Charlotte Amalie, V.I. BR/TR/6-0/180(165-180) d7.2

YEAR	TM	LG	W	L	PCT	G	GS	CG-SHO	SV-BS	IP	H	R	HR	HB	BB-IB	SO	ERA	AERA	OAV	OOB	AB-HR-SH	AVG	PB	SUP	APR	DL	PW
1961	Pit	N	3	2	.600	27	2	0	0	74.1	72	35	4	4	42-5	49	3.75	106	.263	.365	15-1-1	.267	1*	33	2		0.4
1962	Pit	N	15	10	.600	33	29	6-2	0	189.2	212	93	24	7	65-2	119	3.70	106	.285	.346	67-0-4	.209	1*	96	4		0.6
1963	Pit	N	13	3	.813	55	7	2-1	11	122.1	100	42	5	2	39-9	74	2.57	128	.222	.287	31-1-1	.194	2*	131	10		1.7
1964	Pit	N	8	7	.727	58	0	0	22	89.2	76	23	4	4	17-8	41	1.91	184	.234	.279	12-0-2	.083	-1		15		2.9
1965	Pit	N	6	6	.500	62	1	0	18	114	111	33	5	3	42-11	49	2.29	153	.260	.327	27-0-2	.222	1	199	16		2.4
1966	Pit	N	3	4	.571	47	0	0	3	86.2	95	38	9	2	24-6	54	3.22	111	.280	.330	10	.100	-1*		2		0.1
1967	Pit	N	7	4	.636	51	8	5	3	131	118	46	11	6	43-6	54	2.54	132	.248	.310	29-0-1	.207	2	98	13		1.4

YEAR	TM LG	W	L	PCT	G	GS	CG-SHO	SV-BS	IP	H	R	HR	HB	BB-IB	SO	ERA	AERA	OAV	OOB	AB-HR-SH	AVG	PB	SUP	APR	DL	PW
1968	Pit N	9	12	.429	36	28	9-2	0	198.1	204	88	10	5	63-5	100	3.58	82	.269	.327	67-1-2	.194	2*	119	-13		-0.9
1969	SD N	0	1	.000	7	1	0	0-0	7	10	4	1	0	2-0	1	5.14	70	.345	.387	2	.500	0	25	-1		-0.5
	LA N	2	6	.250	31	0	0	4-0	48.1	46	22	6	2	21-4	26	3.91	86	.258	.340	3	.000	0		-2		-0.5
	Year	2	7	.222	32	1	0	4-0	55.1	56	26	7	2	23-4	27	4.07	83	.271	.346	5	.200	0	26	-3		-0.6
1970	LA N	0	0	—	1	0	0	0-0	1	1	0	0	0	0-0	0	0.00	—	.333	.333	0	—	0		0		-0.3
	Pit N	0	0	—	7	0	0	1-0	10	13	11	2	0	7-0	3	8.10	49	.317	.417	1	.000	-0		-5		-0.3
	Year	0	0	—	8	0	0	1-0	11	14	11	2	0	7-0	3	7.36	54	.318	.412	1	.000	-0		-5		-0.3
Total	10	67	50	.573	409	76	22-5	63-0	1072.1	1058	430	63	30	365-56	575	3.13	111	.262	.325	264-3-13	.197	9	104	41		7.7

McBEE, PRYOR   Pryor Edward "Lefty"   B6.20.1901 Blanco OK   D4.19.1963 Roseville CA   BR/TL/6-1/190   d5.22

YEAR	TM LG	W	L	PCT	G	GS	CG-SHO	SV-BS	IP	H	R	HR	HB	BB-IB	SO	ERA	AERA	OAV	OOB	AB-HR-SH	AVG	PB	SUP	APR	DL	PW
1926	Chi A	0	0		1	0	0	0	1.1	1	2	0	0	3	1	6.75	57	.250	.571	0	—	0		-1		0.0

McBRIDE, DICK   James Dickson   B1845 Philadelphia PA   D10.10.1916 Philadelphia PA   TR/5-9/150   d5.20 M5

1871	Ath NA	18	5	.783	25	25	25	0	222	285	223		3	40	15	4.58	88	.280	.307	132	.235	-4	137	-15		-1.2
1872	Ath NA	30	14	.682	47	47	47-1	0	419.1	508	349		3	26	44	2.85	124	.265	.275	258	.287	5	124	34		2.6
1873	Ath NA	24	19	.558	46	46	38-3	0	382.2	453	325		3	47	25	3.34	102	.262	.281	253	.281	3*	96	15		1.2
1874	Ath NA	33	22	.600	55	55	55	0	487	514	344		6	32	37	1.64	141	.240	.251	263	.217	-7	101	34		1.9
1875	Ath NA	44	14	.759	60	60	59-6	0	538	607	297		4	24	27	2.33	103	.267	.275	270	.270	3	142	5		0.3
1876	Bos N	0	4	.000	4	4	3	1	33	53	35		1	5	2	2.73	83	.353	.374	16	.188	-1	56	-4		-0.4
Total	5 NA	149	74	.668	233	233	224-10	0	2049	2367	1538		19	169	148	2.71	111	.261	.274	1176	.260	0	117	73		4.8

McBRIDE, MACAY   Joseph Macay   B10.24.1982 Augusta GA   BL/TL/5-11/210   d7.22

2005	†Atl N	1	0	1.000	23	0	0	1-0	14	18	11	0	0	7-0	22	5.79	74	.305	.373	0	—	0		-3		-0.2

McBRIDE, KEN   Kenneth Faye   B8.12.1935 Huntsville AL   BR/TR/6-0/195*   d8.4 C1

1959	Chi A	0	1	.000	11	2	0	1	22.2	20	11	1	0	17-0	12	3.18	118	.230	.356	6	.167	-0	70	1		0.0
1960	Chi A	0	1	.000	5	0	0	1	4.2	6	2	0	1	3-0	4	3.86	98	.333	.435	0	—	0		0		0.0
1961	LA A☆	12	15	.444	38	36	11-1	1	241.2	229	114	28	7	102-4	180	3.65	124	.252	.331	83-0-6	.084	-5*	82	20		1.7
1962	LA A*	11	5	.688	24	23	6-4	0	149.1	136	66	9	9	70-3	83	3.50	110	.249	.341	55-1-0	.164	0	110	7		1.0
1963	LA A★	13	12	.520	36	36	11-2	0	251	198	101	22	14	82-1	147	3.26	105	.218	.291	87-0-5	.172	2*	116	7		1.0
1964	LA A	4	13	.235	29	21	0	1	116.1	104	77	14	16	75-0	66	5.26	62	.239	.369	28-0-2	.214	3	101	-27		-3.1
1965	Cal A	0	3	.000	8	4	0	0	22	24	17	1	2	14-0	11	6.14	55	.270	.377	5	.000	-0	77	-7	36	-0.7
Total	7	40	50	.444	151	122	28-7	3	807.2	717	388	75	49	363-8	503	3.79	101	.240	.330	264-1-13	.144	0	99	1	36	-0.3

McBRIDE, PETE   Peter William   B7.9.1875 Adams MA   D7.3.1944 N.Adams MA   BR/TR/5-10/170   d9.20   Col Manhattan

1898	Cle N	0	1	.000	1	1	1	0	7	9	6	0	1	4	6	6.43	60	.310	.412	2	1.000	2	98	-2		-0.1
1899	StL N	2	4	.333	11	6	4	0	64	65	46	4	4	40	26	4.08	98	.263	.375	27-1-0	.185	0*	93	-2		-0.1
Total	2	2	5	.286	12	7	5	0	71	74	52	4	5	44	32	4.31	92	.268	.378	29-1-0	.241	2	94	-4		-0.2

McCABE, RALPH   Ralph Herbert "Mack"   B10.21.1918 Napanee ON, Can.   D5.3.1974 Windsor ON, Can.   BR/TR/6-4/195   d9.18

1946	Cle N	0	1	.000	1	1	0	0	4	5	5	1	2	3	3	11.25	39	.313	.421	1	.000	-0	26	-3		-0.5

McCABE, DICK   Richard James   B2.21.1896 Mamaroneck NY   D4.11.1950 Buffalo NY   BR/TR/5-10.5/159   d5.30

1918	Bos A	0	1	.000	3	1	0	0	9.2	13	4	0	0	2	3	2.79	96	.351	.385	2	.000	-0	0	0		0.0
1922	Chi A	1	0	1.000	3	0	0	0	3.1	4	2	0	0	1	1	5.40	75	.308	.308	0	—	0	0	0		0.0
Total	2	1	1	.500	6	1	0	0	13	17	6	0	0	2	4	3.46	88	.340	.365	2	.000	-0	0	0		-0.1

McCABE, TIM   Timothy J.   B10.19.1894 Ironton MO   D4.12.1977 Ironton MO   BR/TR/6-0/190   d8.16

1915	StL A	3	1	.750	7	4	4-1	0	41.2	25	11	1	6	9	17	1.30	221	.177	.232	15	.067	-1	115	7		0.5
1916	StL A	2	0	1.000	13	0	0	0	25.2	29	20	0	2	7	7	3.16	87	.282	.339	4	.000	0		-4		-0.3
1917	StL A	0	0	—	1	0	0	0	2.1	4	6	1	0	4	2	23.14	11	.400	.571	0	—	0		-5		-0.2
1918	StL A	0	0	—	1	0	0	0	1.1	2	2	0	0	1	0	13.50	20	.333	.429	0	—	0		-1		-0.1
Total	4	5	1	.833	22	4	4-1	0	71	60	39	2	8	21	26	2.92	96	.231	.296	19	.053	-1	115	-3		-0.1

McCAFFREY, BILL   William T.   d6.15

1885	Cin AA	1	0	1.000	1	1	1	0	9	13	9	1	2	2	2	6.00	54	.342	.405	5	.000	-1	199	-3		-0.3

McCAHAN, BILL   William Glenn   B6.7.1921 Philadelphia PA   D7.3.1986 Fort Worth TX   BR/TR/5-11/200   d9.15   Col Duke

1946	Phi A	1	1	.500	4	2	2-1	0	18	16	2	0	0	9	6	1.00	355	.246	.338	5	.400	1	36	5		0.7
1947	Phi A	10	5	.667	29	19	10-1	0	165.1	160	73	7	0	62	47	3.32	115	.252	.318	55-0-3	.164	-1	99	7		0.6
1948	Phi A	4	7	.364	17	15	5	0	86.2	98	58	8	0	65	20	5.71	75	.284	.398	31	.258	1	91	-13		-1.3
1949	Phi A	1	1	.500	7	4	0	0	20.2	23	9	0	0	9	3	2.61	157	.291	.364	5	.200	-0	93	3		0.2
Total	4	16	14	.533	57	40	17-2	0	290.2	297	142	15	0	145	76	3.84	103	.264	.348	96-0-3	.208	1	93	2		0.2

McCALL, WINDY   John William   B7.18.1925 San Francisco CA   BL/TL/6-0/180*   d4.25   Col San Francisco

1948	Bos A	0	1	.000	1	1	0	0	1.1	6	3	1	0	1	0	20.25	22	.600	.636	0	—	0	82	-2		-0.3
1949	Bos A	0	0	—	5	0	0	0	9.1	13	12	2	0	10	9	11.57	38	.333	.469	3-0-1	.667	1		-7		-0.3
1950	Pit N	0	0	—	2	0	0	0	6.2	12	7	2	0	4	5	9.45	46	.387	.457	2	.000	0		-3		-0.1
1954	NY N	2	5	.286	33	4	0	2	61	50	26	5	3	29	38	3.25	124	.219	.314	11	.000	-1	83	5		0.4
1955	NY N	6	5	.545	42	6	4	3	95	86	45	8	4	37-6	50	3.69	109	.244	.325	17-0-3	.118	-1	100	4		0.0
1956	NY N	3	4	.429	46	4	0	7	77.1	74	36	7	1	20-5	41	3.61	105	.252	.301	15	.200	-0	76	1		0.0
1957	NY N	0	0	—	5	0	0	0	3	8	5	1	1	2-0	2	15.00	26	.533	.579	0	—	0		-3		-0.1
Total	7	11	15	.423	134	15	4	12	253.2	249	134	26	11	103-11	144	4.22	94	.257	.334	48-0-4	.146	-1	88	-5		-0.1

McCALL, LARRY   Larry Stephen   B9.8.1952 Asheville NC   BL/TR/6-2/182(182-195)   d9.10

1977	NY A	0	1	.000	2	0	0	0-0	6	12	7	1	0	1-0	7	7.50	53	.375	.394	0	—	0*		-3		-0.3
1978	NY A	1	1	.500	5	1	0	0-0	16	20	10	2	1	6-0	7	5.63	65	.323	.391	0	—	0	49	-3		-0.2
1979	Tex A	1	0	1.000	2	1	0	0-0	8.1	7	2	0	0	3-0	3	2.16	192	.226	.286	0	—	0	87	2		0.2
Total	3	2	2	.500	9	2	0	0-0	30.1	39	19	3	1	10-0	17	5.04	76	.312	.365	0	—	0	70	-4		-0.3

McCALL, DUTCH   Robert Leonard   B12.27.1920 Columbia TN   D1.8.1996 Little Rock AR   BL/TL/6-1/184   d4.27

1948	Chi N	4	13	.235	30	20	5	0	151.1	158	93	14	1	85	89	4.82	81	.268	.361	53-0-2	.170	1	97	-15		-1.3

McCAMENT, RANDY   Larry Randall   B7.29.1962 Albuquerque NM   BR/TR/6-3/195(180-195)   [SFN85 15/368]   d6.28   Col Grand Canyon

1989	SF N	1	1	.500	25	0	0	0-0	36.2	32	22	4	1	23-2	12	3.93	86	.241	.354	3	.333	0		-4		-0.2
1990	SF N	0	0	—	3	0	0	0-0	6	8	2	0	0	5-0	5	3.00	122	.333	.433	1	.000	-0		1		-0.0
Total	2	1	1	.500	28	0	0	0-0	42.2	40	24	4	1	28-2	17	3.80	90	.255	.367	4	.250	0		-3		-0.2

McCANN, GENE   Henry Eugene "Mike"   B6.13.1876 Baltimore MD   D4.26.1943 New York NY   TR/5-10/185   d4.19

1901	Bro N	2	3	.400	6	5	3	0	34	34	25	1	4	16	9	3.44	97	.260	.358	10-0-1	.000	-1	127	-3		-0.
1902	Bro N	1	2	.333	3	3	3	0	30	32	18	0	0	12	9	2.40	115	.274	.341	12	.083	-1	82	-1		-0.
Total	2	3	5	.375	9	8	6	0	64	66	43	1	4	28	18	2.95	104	.266	.350	22-0-1	.045	-2	113	-4		-0.

McCARTHY, ARCH   Archibald Joseph   B Ypsilanti MI   TR/6-0/160   d8.14

1902	Det A	2	7	.222	10	8	8	0	72	90	57	2	4	31	10	6.13	60	.306	.380	28	.071	-3	72	-15		-1.

McCARTHY, BRANDON   Brandon Patrick   B7.7.1983 Glendale CA   BR/TR/6-7/190   d5.22   Col Lamar (CO) CC

2005	Chi A	3	2	.600	12	10	0	0	67	62	30	13	2	17-0	48	4.03	112	.242	.293	2	.000	-0	102	5		0.

McCARTHY, GREG   Gregory O'Neil   B10.30.1968 Norwalk CT   BL/TL/6-2/215(195-215)   [PhiN87 36/929]   d8.28   [DL 1991 Mon N 182]

1996	Sea A	0	0	—	10	0	0	0-0	9.2	8	2	0	4	4-0	7	1.86	267	.229	.364	0	—	0		3		0.
1997	Sea A	1	1	.500	37	0	0	0-0	29.2	26	21	4	1	16-0	34	5.46	83	.230	.331	0	—	0		-4		-0.
1998	Sea A	1	2	.333	29	0	0	0-1	23.1	18	13	6	3	17-2	25	5.01	93	.214	.365	0	—	0		-1	182	0.
Total	3	2	3	.400	76	0	0	0-1	62.2	52	36	10	8	37-2	66	4.74	98	.224	.349	0	—	0		-1	182	0.

McCARTHY, TOMMY   Thomas Francis Michael   B7.24.1863 Boston MA   D8.5.1922 Boston MA   BR/TR/5-7/170   d7.10 M1 HF1957 ▲

1884	Bos U	0	7	.000	7	6	5	0	56	73	53	2		14	18	4.82	49	.296	.333	209	.215	-2*	69	-14		-1.
1886	Phi N	0			1	0	0	0	1	0	1		0			0.00	—	.000	.250	27	.185	0*		0		-0.
1888	†StL AA	0	1	.000	2	1	0	0	5.1	5	5	1	0	2	1	5.06	64	.238	.304	511-1	.274	0*	53	-1		-0.
1889	StL AA	0	0	—	1	0	0	0	5	5	4		0	1	1	7.20	59	.211	.400	604-2	.291	0*		-1		-0.

YEAR	TM LG	W	L	PCT	G	GS	CG-SHO	SV-BS	IP	H	R	HR	HB	BB-IB	SO	ERA	AERA	OAV	OOB	AB-HR-SH	AVG	PB	SUP	APR	DL	PW
1891	StL AA	0	0	—	1	0	0	0	1	2	2	0	0	0	0	9.00	47	.400	.400	570-8	.309	0*		-1		0.0
1894	Bos N	0	0	—	1	0	0	0	6	3	1	0	0	3	0	4.50	126	.143	.400	539-13-9	.349	0*		0		0.0
Total	6	0	8	.000	13	7	5	0	70.1	85	65	3	0	26	21	4.99	54	.281	.338	2460-24-9	.297	-1	65	-17		-1.5

McCARTHY, TOM Thomas Michael B6.18.1961 Lundstahl, W.Germany BR/TR/6-0/180* [BosA79 7/182] d7.5

YEAR	TM LG	W	L	PCT	G	GS	CG-SHO	SV-BS	IP	H	R	HR	HB	BB-IB	SO	ERA	AERA	OAV	OOB	AB-HR-SH	AVG	PB	SUP	APR	DL	PW
1985	Bos A	0	0	—	3	0	0	0-0	5	7	6	1	0	4-0	2	10.80	40	.350	.440	0	—	0		-3		-0.2
1988	Chi A	2	0	1.000	6	0	0	1-0	13	9	2	0	2	2-0	5	1.38	289	.191	.255	0	—	0		4		0.6
1989	Chi A	1	2	.333	31	0	0	0-0	66.2	72	32	8	2	20-0	27	3.51	109	.280	.333	0	—	0		1		0.1
Total	3	3	2	.600	40	0	0	1-0	84.2	88	40	9	4	26-0	34	3.61	108	.272	.330	0	—	0		2		0.5

McCARTHY, TOM Thomas Patrick B5.22.1884 Ft.Wayne IN D3.28.1933 Mishawaka IN TR/5-7/170 d5.10

YEAR	TM LG	W	L	PCT	G	GS	CG-SHO	SV-BS	IP	H	R	HR	HB	BB-IB	SO	ERA	AERA	OAV	OOB	AB-HR-SH	AVG	PB	SUP	APR	DL	PW
1908	Cin N	0	1	.000	1	1	0	0	3.2	6	5	0	0	3	3	9.82	23	.300	.391	2	.000	-0	214	-3		-0.5
	Pit N	0	0	—	2	1	0	0	6	3	1	0	0	6	.1	0.00	—	.176	.391	4	.000	-0*	398	1		0.0
	Bos N	7	3	.700	14	11	7-2	0	94	77	24	0	1	28	27	1.63	148	.235	.298	35-0-4	.171	0	135	8		1.0
	Year	7	4	.636	17	13	7-2	0	103.2	86	30	0	1	37	31	1.82	132	.236	.308	41-0-4	.146	-1	160	6		0.5
1909	Bos N	0	5	.000	8	7	3	0	46.1	47	28	3	2	28	11	3.50	81	.272	.379	16-0-1	.125	-0*	78	-4		-0.5
Total	2	7	9	.438	25	20	10-2	0	150	133	58	3	3	65	42	2.34	108	.248	.332	57-0-5	.140	-1	129	2		0.0

McCARTHY, BILL William Thomas B4.11.1882 Ashland MA D5.29.1939 Boston MA BR/TR/5-11/180 d4.21

YEAR	TM LG	W	L	PCT	G	GS	CG-SHO	SV-BS	IP	H	R	HR	HB	BB-IB	SO	ERA	AERA	OAV	OOB	AB-HR-SH	AVG	PB	SUP	APR	DL	PW
1906	Bos N	0	0	—	1	0	0	0	2	2	6	0	0	3	0	9.00	30	.182	.357	1	.000	-0		-3		-0.1

McCARTY, JOHN John A. B St.Louis MO TR d4.18

YEAR	TM LG	W	L	PCT	G	GS	CG-SHO	SV-BS	IP	H	R	HR	HB	BB-IB	SO	ERA	AERA	OAV	OOB	AB-HR-SH	AVG	PB	SUP	APR	DL	PW
1889	KC AA	8	6	.571	15	14	13		119.2	147	108	4	6	61	36	3.91	109	.293	.376	79	.228	-2*	120	0		-0.2

McCASKILL, KIRK Kirk Edward B4.9.1961 Kapuskasing ON, Can. BR/TR/6-1/196(190-205) [CalA82 4/88] d5.1 Col Vermont

YEAR	TM LG	W	L	PCT	G	GS	CG-SHO	SV-BS	IP	H	R	HR	HB	BB-IB	SO	ERA	AERA	OAV	OOB	AB-HR-SH	AVG	PB	SUP	APR	DL	PW
1985	Cal A	12	12	.500	30	29	6-1	0-0	189.2	189	105	23	4	64-1	102	4.70	88	.258	.319	0	—	0	107	-10		-1.1
1986	†Cal A	17	10	.630	34	33	10-2	0-0	246.1	207	98	19	5	92-1	202	3.36	123	.229	.302	0	—	0	100	23		2.3
1987	Cal A	4	6	.400	14	13	1-1	0-0	74.2	84	52	14	2	34-0	56	5.67	76	.286	.363	0	—	0*	78	-11	75	-1.2
1988	Cal A	8	6	.571	23	23	4-2	0-0	146.1	155	78	9	1	61-3	98	4.31	90	.274	.342	0	—	0	130	-7	55	-0.6
1989	Cal A	15	10	.600	32	32	6-4	0-0	212	202	73	16	5	59-1	107	2.93	131	.254	.307	0	—	0	88	23		2.7
1990	Cal A	12	11	.522	29	29	2-1	0-0	174.1	161	77	9	2	72-1	78	3.25	118	.244	.320	0	—	0	93	10		1.2
1991	Cal A	10	19	.345	30	30	1	0-0	177.2	193	93	19	3	66-1	71	4.26	97	.283	.347	0	—	0	65	-3		-0.4
1992	Chi A	12	13	.480	34	34	0	0-0	209	193	116	24	6	95-5	109	4.18	93	.242	.325	0	—	0	104	-11		-1.1
1993	†Chi A	4	8	.333	30	14	0	2-0	113.2	144	71	12	1	36-6	65	5.23	81	.313	.362	0	—	0	101	-12	15	-1.1
1994	Chi A	1	4	.200	40	0	0	3-3	52.2	51	22	6	0	22-4	37	3.42	137	.252	.322	0	—	0		8		0.7
1995	Chi A	6	4	.600	55	1	0	2-3	81	97	50	10	5	33-4	50	4.89	92	.302	.373	0	—	0	125	-5		-0.5
1996	Chi A	5	5	.500	29	4	0	0-1	51.2	72	41	6	2	31-8	28	6.97	68	.344	.432	0	—	0	151	-12		-1.8
Total	12	106	108	.495	380	242	30-11	7-7	1729	1748	876	154	34	665-35	1003	4.12	99	.264	.332	0	—	0	96	-7	145	-0.9

McCATTY, STEVE Steven Earl B3.20.1954 Detroit MI BR/TR/6-3/205(195-210) d9.17 C1 Col Macomb (MI) CC

YEAR	TM LG	W	L	PCT	G	GS	CG-SHO	SV-BS	IP	H	R	HR	HB	BB-IB	SO	ERA	AERA	OAV	OOB	AB-HR-SH	AVG	PB	SUP	APR	DL	PW
1977	Oak A	0	0	—	4	2	0	0-0	14.1	16	9	1	1	7-0	9	5.02	80	.276	.364	0	—	0	89	-1		-0.1
1978	Oak A	0	0	—	9	0	0	0-0	20	26	14	1	0	9-1	10	4.50	81	.310	.361	0	—	0		-3		-0.2
1979	Oak A	11	12	.478	31	23	8	0-0	185.2	207	106	17	10	80-8	87	4.22	96	.284	.359	0	—	0	91	-7		-0.8
1980	Oak A	14	14	.500	33	31	11-1	0-1	221.2	202	104	27	8	99-2	114	3.86	99	.240	.323	0	—	0	120	0		-0.1
1981	†Oak A	14	7	.667	22	22	16-4	0-0	185.2	140	50	12	2	61-1	91	2.33	151	.211	.277	0	—	0	110	27		3.1
1982	Oak A	6	3	.667	21	20	2	0-0	128.2	124	62	16	4	70-0	66	3.99	99	.255	.351	0	—	0	130	0	21	0.0
1983	Oak A	6	9	.400	38	24	3-2	5-1	167	156	79	16	1	82-4	65	3.99	98	.247	.331	0	—	0*	87	0		-0.1
1984	Oak A	8	14	.364	33	30	4	0-0	179.2	206	101	24	1	71-0	63	4.76	79	.289	.353	0	—	0	116	-18		-2.1
1985	Oak A	4	4	.500	30	9	1	0-0	85.2	95	56	10	4	41-4	36	5.57	70	.286	.368	0	—	0	143	-16		-1.3
Total	9	63	63	.500	221	161	45-7	5-2	1188.1	1172	581	124	31	520-20	541	3.99	96	.258	.336	0	—	0	111	-18	21	-1.6

McCAULEY, AL Allen A. B3.4.1863 Indianapolis IN D8.24.1917 Wayne Twnshp. IN BL/TL/6-0/180 d6.21 ▲

YEAR	TM LG	W	L	PCT	G	GS	CG-SHO	SV-BS	IP	H	R	HR	HB	BB-IB	SO	ERA	AERA	OAV	OOB	AB-HR-SH	AVG	PB	SUP	APR	DL	PW
1884	Ind AA	2	7	.222	10	8	7	0	87	74	2	0	5	34	5.09	65	.261	.313	53	.189	2*	90	-15		-1.1

McCLAIN, JOE Joseph Fred B5.5.1933 Johnson City TN BR/TR/6-0/183* d4.14 Col Tennessee

YEAR	TM LG	W	L	PCT	G	GS	CG-SHO	SV-BS	IP	H	R	HR	HB	BB-IB	SO	ERA	AERA	OAV	OOB	AB-HR-SH	AVG	PB	SUP	APR	DL	PW
1961	Was A	8	18	.308	33	29	7-2	1	212	221	105	22	4	48-7	76	3.86	104	.270	.309	68-0-2	.206	1	71	4		0.4
1962	Was A	0	4	.000	10	4	0	0	24	33	25	8	2	11-1	6	9.38	43	.327	.397	7	.143	-0	72	-13		-1.8
Total	2	8	22	.267	43	33	7-2	1	236	254	130	30	6	59-8	82	4.42	91	.276	.319	75-0-2	.200	1	71	-9		-1.4

McCLELLAN, PAUL Paul William B2.3.1966 San Mateo CA BR/TR/6-2/180* [SFN86*S1/6] d9.2 Col San Mateo (CA) [JC]

YEAR	TM LG	W	L	PCT	G	GS	CG-SHO	SV-BS	IP	H	R	HR	HB	BB-IB	SO	ERA	AERA	OAV	OOB	AB-HR-SH	AVG	PB	SUP	APR	DL	PW
1990	SF N	0	1	.000	4	1	0	0	7.2	14	10	4	1	6-0	2	11.74	31	.389	.488	2	.500	0	148	-7		-0.7
1991	SF N	3	6	.333	13	12	1	0-0	71	68	41	12	1	25-1	44	4.56	79	.252	.316	21-0-2	.143	-0	123	-9		-1.1
Total	2	3	7	.300	17	13	1	0-0	78.2	82	51	16	2	31-1	46	5.26	68	.268	.338	23-0-2	.174	0	125	-16		-1.8

McCLOSKEY, JIM James Ellwood "Irish" B5.26.1910 Danville PA D8.18.1971 Jersey City NJ BL/TL/5-9.5/180 d4.21 Col St. Bonaventure

YEAR	TM LG	W	L	PCT	G	GS	CG-SHO	SV-BS	IP	H	R	HR	HB	BB-IB	SO	ERA	AERA	OAV	OOB	AB-HR-SH	AVG	PB	SUP	APR	DL	PW
1936	Bos N	0	0	—	4	1	0	0	8	14	10	1	3	4	2	11.25	34	.378	.439	1	.000	-0	133	-6		-0.3

McCLOSKEY, JOHN James John B8.20.1882 Wyoming PA D6.5.1919 Wilkes-Barre PA d5.3

YEAR	TM LG	W	L	PCT	G	GS	CG-SHO	SV-BS	IP	H	R	HR	HB	BB-IB	SO	ERA	AERA	OAV	OOB	AB-HR-SH	AVG	PB	SUP	APR	DL	PW
1906	Phi N	3	2	.600	9	4	3	0	41	46	21	2	1	9	6	2.85	92	.280	.322	15	.200	0	146	-2		-0.2
1907	Phi N	0	0	—	3	0	0	0	9	15	9	0	1	6	3	7.00	35	.417	.512	4	.000	-0		-4		-0.3
Total	2	3	2	.600	12	4	3	0	50	61	30	2	2	15	9	3.60	72	.305	.359	19	.158	0	146	-6		-0.5

McCLUNG, SETH Michael Seth B2.7.1981 Lewisburg WV BR/TR/6-6/230* [TBA99 5/145] d3.31 [DL 2004 TB A 126]

YEAR	TM LG	W	L	PCT	G	GS	CG-SHO	SV-BS	IP	H	R	HR	HB	BB-IB	SO	ERA	AERA	OAV	OOB	AB-HR-SH	AVG	PB	SUP	APR	DL	PW
2003	TB A	4	1	.800	12	5	0	0-0	38.2	33	23	6	3	25-1	25	5.35	86	.241	.367	0	—	0	92	-2	129	-0.3
2005	TB A	7	11	.389	34	17	0	0-1	109.1	106	85	20	7	62-1	92	6.59	66	.249	.350	0	—	0	94	-26		-3.5
Total	2	11	12	.478	46	22	0	0-1	148	139	108	26	10	87-2	117	6.26	71	.247	.354	0	—	0	93	-28	255	-3.8

McCLURE, BOB Robert Craig B4.29.1952 Oakland CA BR/TL/5-11/170(170-188) [KCA73 S3/30] d8.13 C1 Col San Mateo (CA) [JC]

YEAR	TM LG	W	L	PCT	G	GS	CG-SHO	SV-BS	IP	H	R	HR	HB	BB-IB	SO	ERA	AERA	OAV	OOB	AB-HR-SH	AVG	PB	SUP	APR	DL	PW
1975	KC A	1	0	1.000	12	0	0	1-0	15.1	4	0	0	0	14-2	15	0.00	—	.077	.273	0	—	0		6		0.5
1976	KC A	0	0	—	8	0	0	0	4	3	4	0	0	8-0	3	9.00	39	.214	.500	0	—	0*		-2		-0.1
1977	Mil A	2	1	.667	68	0	0	6-1	71.1	64	25	2	1	34-5	23	2.52	163	.249	.333	0	—	0		11		0.7
1978	Mil A	2	6	.250	44	0	0	9-4	65	53	30	4	8	30-4	47	3.74	102	.223	.322	0	—	0		0		0.0
1979	Mil A	5	2	.714	36	0	0	1	51	53	29	6	3	24-0	37	3.88	108	.269	.352	0	—	0		0		0.2
1980	Mil A	5	8	.385	52	5	2-1	10-5	90.2	83	34	6	2	37-2	47	3.08	127	.241	.314	0	—	0	87	-9		1.4
1981	†Mil A	0	0	—	4	0	0	0-0	7.2	7	3	1	0	4-1	6	3.52	98	.233	.324	0	—	0		0	146	0.0
1982	†Mil A	12	7	.632	34	26	5	0-0	172.2	160	90	21	4	74-4	99	4.22	91	.248	.327	0	—	0	141	-8		-0.8
1983	Mil A	9	9	.500	24	23	4	0-0	142	152	75	11	5	68-1	68	4.50	84	.277	.360	0	—	0	114	-11	21	-1.2
1984	Mil A	4	8	.333	39	18	1	1-0	139.2	154	76	9	2	52-4	68	4.38	89	.282	.342	0	—	0	122	-7		-0.6
1985	Mil A	4	1	.800	38	1	0	3-1	85.2	91	43	10	3	30-2	57	4.31	97	.274	.338	0	—	0	87	1		0.2
1986	Mil A	2	1	.667	13	0	0	0-0	16.1	18	7	2	0	10-1	11	3.86	113	.286	.378	0	—	0		1		0.2
	Mon N	2	5	.286	52	0	0	0-0	62.2	53	22	2	1	23-2	42	3.02	124	.232	.303	4	.250	0		6		0.7
1987	Mon N	6	1	.857	52	0	0	5-1	52.1	47	30	8	0	20-3	33	3.44	124	.241	.309	2	.000	-0		0		0.2
1988	Mon N	1	3	.250	19	0	0	2-0	19	23	13	4	1	6-0	12	6.16	59	.307	.357	2	.000	-0		-4		-0.9
	NY N	1	0	1.000	14	0	0	1-0	11	12	5	1	1	2-0	7	4.09	80	.279	.326	0	—	0		-1		-0.1
	Year	2	3	.400	33	0	0	3-0	30	35	18	4	2	8-0	19	5.40	65	.297	.346	2	.000	-0		-5		-1.0
1989	Cal A	6	1	.857	48	0	0	3-0	52.1	39	14	2	1	15-1	36	1.55	247	.212	.270	0	—	0		12		1.5
1990	Cal A	2	0	1.000	11	0	0	0-1	7	7	6	0	0	3-0	6	6.43	60	.280	.345	0	—	0		-2	127	-0.4
1991	Cal A	0	0	—	13	0	0	0-0	9.2	13	11	3	1	5-0	5	9.31	44	.317	.396	0	—	0		-6	11	-0.3
	StL N	1	1	.500	32	0	0	0-4	23	24	8	1	0	8-2	15	3.13	120	.282	.340	1	1.000	0		2		0.2
1992	StL N	2	2	.500	71	0	0	3-0	54	52	21	6	2	25-5	24	3.17	108	.261	.345	0	—	0		1		0.1
1993	Fla N	1	1	.500	14	0	0	0-2	6.1	13	5	2	0	5-0	5	7.11	61	.419	.500	0	—	0		-2		-0.3
Total	19	68	57	.544	698	96	17	52-22	1158.2	1125	551	104	34	497-39	701	3.81	102	.257	.334	9	.222	0	121	8	305	0.8

McCLUSKEY, HARRY Harry Robert B3.29.1892 Clay Center OH D6.7.1962 Toledo OH BL/TL/5-11.5/173 d7.29

YEAR	TM LG	W	L	PCT	G	GS	CG-SHO	SV-BS	IP	H	R	HR	HB	BB-IB	SO	ERA	AERA	OAV	OOB	AB-HR-SH	AVG	PB	SUP	APR	DL	PW
1915	Cin N				5				5	4	3	0	0	2	2	5.40	53	.182	.182	2	.000	-0		-1		-0.1

YEAR	TM LG	W	L	PCT	G	GS	CG-SHO	SV-BS	IP	H	R	HR	HB	BB-IB	SO	ERA	AERA	OAV	OOB	AB-HR-SH	AVG	PB	SUP	APR	DL	P

McCOLL, ALEX   Alexander Boyd "Red"   B3.29.1894 Eagleville OH   D2.6.1991 Kingsville OH   BB/TR/6-1/178   d8.27

1933	†Was A	1	0	1.000	4	1	1	0	17	13	5	0	0	7	5	2.65	158	.210	.290	6	.333	1	61	3		0
1934	Was A	3	4	.429	42	2	1	1	112	129	56	6	1	36	29	3.86	112	.291	.345	31	.097	-2	40	5		0
Total	2	4	4	.500	46	3	2	1	129	142	61	6	1	43	34	3.70	116	.281	.338	37	.135	-1	47	8		0

McCONNAUGHEY, RALPH   Ralph James   B8.5.1889 Vandergrift PA   D6.4.1966 Detroit MI   BR/TR/5-8.5/166   d7.8

| 1914 | Ind F | 0 | 2 | .000 | 7 | 2 | 1 | 0 | 26 | 23 | 15 | 3 | 1 | 16 | 7 | 4.85 | 64 | .245 | .360 | 8 | .125 | -0 | 55 | -3 | | -0 |

McCONNELL, GEORGE   George Neely "Slats"   B9.16.1877 Shelbyville TN   D5.10.1964 Chattanooga TN   BR/TR/6-3/190   d4.13 ▲

1909	NY A	1	0	1.000	2	1	0	0	4	3	2	0	0	3	4	2.25	112	.231	.375	43-0-1	.209	0*	28	0		0
1912	NY A	8	12	.400	23	20	19	0	176.2	172	96	3	4	52	91	2.75	131	.269	.328	91-0-1	.297	3*	65	8		0
1913	NY A	4	15	.211	35	20	8	3	180	162	90	2	7	60	72	3.20	94	.247	.317	67-0-3	.179	-1*	83	-5		-0
1914	Chi N	0	1	.000	1	1	0	0	7	3	1	0	0	3	3	1.29	216	.125	.222	2	.000	-0	0	1		0
1915	Chi F	25	10	.714	44	35	23-4	1	303	262	103	8	8	89	151	2.20	114	.232	.292	125-1-3	.248	4*	124	9		1
1916	Chi N	4	12	.250	28	21	8-1	0	171.1	137	66	8	5	35	82	2.57	113	.223	.271	57-0-2	.158	-2	65	5		0
Total	6	41	51	.446	133	98	58-5	4	842	739	358	21	24	242	403	2.60	112	.240	.301	385-1-10	.229	4	86	18		3

McCONNELL, SAM   John Samuel   B12.31.1975 Middletown OH   BL/TL/6-5/230   [PitN97 11/332]   d6.25   Col Ball St.

| 2004 | Atl N | 1 | 0 | 1.000 | 10 | 0 | 0 | 0-0 | 9.1 | 11 | 4 | 0 | 1 | 4-1 | 4 | 3.86 | 112 | .289 | .372 | 1 | .000 | -0 | | 1 | | |

McCOOL, BILLY   William John   B7.14.1944 Batesville IN   BR/TL/6-2/203*   d4.24

1964	Cin N	6	5	.545	40	3	0	7	89.1	66	27	3	1	29-5	87	2.42	150	.206	.272	17-0-1	.000	-2	49	12		
1965	Cin N	9	10	.474	62	2	0	21	105.1	93	53	9	4	47-7	120	4.27	88	.237	.324	27	.037	-2	70	-5		
1966	Cin N☆	8	8	.500	57	0	0	18.	105.1	76	32	5	3	41-7	104	2.48	157	.205	.288	18	.167	-0		15		
1967	Cin N	3	7	.300	31	11	0	2	97.1	92	45	8	5	56-7	83	3.42	110	.246	.351	26-0-1	.077	-1	83	2	21	
1968	Cin N	3	4	.429	30	4	0	2	50.2	59	35	4	0	41-4	30	4.97	64	.294	.408	8-0-1	.125	-0	130	-11		
1969	SD N	3	5	.375	54	0	0	7-2	58.2	59	32	2	6	42-8	35	4.30	83	.266	.393	1	.000	-0		-5	21	
1970	StL N	0	3	.000	18	0	0	1-1	21.2	20	15	0	0	16-0	12	6.23	67	.250	.367	4-0-1	.000	-0		-4		
Total	7	32	42	.432	292	20	0	58-3	528.1	465	239	31	19	272-38	471	3.59	103	.237	.334	101-0-4	.069	-6	83	4	42	

McCORMICK, JIM   James   B11.3.1856 Glasgow, Scotland   D3.10.1918 Paterson NJ   BR/TR/5-10.5/215   d5.20 M3

1878	Ind N	5	8	.385	14	14	12-1	0	117	128	47	0		15	36	1.69	120	.269	.292	56	.143	-3*	106	5		
1879	Cle N	20	40	.333	62	60	59-3	0	546.1	582	308	3		74	197	2.42	103	.259	.282	282	.220	-1*	68	6		
1880	Cle N	45	28	.616	74	74	72-7	0	657.2	585	274	2		75	260	1.85	127	.226	.247	289	.246	1*	104	39		
1881	Cle N	26	30	.464	59	58	57-2	0	526	484	267	4		84	178	2.45	107	.235	.265	309	.256	6*	104	9		
1882	Cle N	36	30	.545	68	67	65-4	0	595.2	550	274	14		103	200	2.37	118	.238	.271	262-2	.218	-4*	92	30		
1883	Cle N	28	12	.700	43	41	36-1	1	342	316	151	1		65	145	2.86	110	.247	.285	190	.263	2*	76	13		
1884	Cle N	19	22	.463	42	41	39-3	0	359	357	206	16		75	182	2.86	117	.255	.280	157	.236	-1	102	47		
	Cin U	21	3	.875	24	24	24-7	0	210	151	57	3		14	161	1.54	166	.188	.202	110	.245	-6*	114	26		
1885	Pro N	1	3	.250	4	4	4	0	37	34	26	1		20	8	2.43	110	.234	.327	14	.214	0	68	-1		
	†Chi N	20	4	.833	24	24	24-3	0	215	187	103	8		40	88	2.43	124	.224	.260	103	.223	0*	158	14		
	Year	21	7	.750	28	28	28-3	0	252	221	129	9		60	96	2.43	122	.226	.271	117	.222	1	146	10		
1886	†Chi N	31	11	.738	42	42	38-2	0	347.2	341	165	18		100	172	2.82	128	.253	.304	174-2	.236	2	134	35		
1887	Pit N	13	23	.361	36	36	36	0	322.1	377	217	12	12	84	77	4.30	89	.285	.334	136	.243	-3	75	-15		
Total	10	265	214	.553	492	485	466-33	1	4275.2	4092	2095	82	12	749	1704	2.43	117	.242	.274	2082-4	.236	-3	98	208		2

McCORMICK, MIKE   Michael Francis   B9.29.1938 Pasadena CA   BL/TL/6-2/195(185-200)   d9.3

1956	NY N	0	1	.000	3	2	0	0	6.2	7	7	1	0	10-0	4	9.45	40	.269	.472	1	.000	-0	105	-4		
1957	NY N	3	1	.750	24	5	1	0	74.2	79	37	7	3	32-2	50	4.10	96	.280	.357	22-0-1	.273	1	99	-1		
1958	SF N	11	8	.579	42	28	8-2	1	178.1	192	103	20	3	60-6	82	4.59	83	.276	.332	54-0-3	.222	1	98	-16		
1959	SF N	12	16	.429	47	31	7-3	4	225.2	213	117	24	1	86-13	151	3.99	96	.248	.314	66-0-1	.106	-2	104	-5		
1960	SF N★	15	12	.556	40	34	15-4	3	253	228	87	15	4	65-12	154	2.70	129	.241	.290	88-0-5	.182	1	111	25		
1961	SF N★	13	16	.448	40	35	13-3	0	250	235	99	33	2	75-3	163	3.20	119	.249	.305	80-0-5	.188	1	108	18		
1962	SF N	5	5	.500	28	15	1	0	98.2	112	64	18	1	45-2	42	5.38	71	.286	.356	28-1-0	.107	0*	122	-17		
1963	Bal A	6	8	.429	25	21	4	0	136	132	70	18	0	66-4	75	4.30	81	.256	.340	46-1-3	.174	1	106	-12		
1964	Bal A	0	2	.000	4	2	0	0	17.1	21	10	1	0	8-0	13	5.19	69	.288	.381	6	.167	-0	112	-3		
1965	Was A	8	8	.500	44	21	3-1	1	158	158	64	17	0	36-4	88	3.36	103	.260	.300	41-0-4	.073	-1*	91	4		
1966	Was A	11	14	.440	41	32	8-3	0	216	193	98	23	2	51-8	101	3.46	100	.236	.281	66-2-5	.212	3	87	-2		
1967	SF N	22	10	.688	40	35	14-5	0	262.1	220	88	25	5	81-18	150	2.85	115	.226	.289	84-1-6	.119	0*	115	17		
1968	SF N	12	14	.462	38	28	9-2	1	198.1	196	92	17	2	49-13	121	3.58	82	.254	.298	58-1-5	.103	1	102	6		
1969	SF N	11	9	.550	32	28	9	0-1	196.2	175	81	20	1	77-8	76	3.34	105	.237	.308	66-1-5	.136	1	110	6		
1970	SF N	3	4	.429	23	11	1	2-1	78.1	80	58	15	3	36-7	37	6.20	64	.262	.343	25-0-2	.160	0	152	-18		
	NY A	2	0	1.000	9	4	0	0-0	20.2	26	15	2	0	13-1	12	6.10	59	.295	.386	5	.200	-0	125	-6		
1971	KC A	0	0	—	4	1	0	0-0	9.2	14	10	0	0	5-0	2	9.31	37	.350	.422	2	.000	-0	260	-6		
Total	16	134	128	.511	484	333	91-23	12-2	2380.1	2281	1100	256	24	795-101	1321	3.73	95	.251	.312	738-7-55	.156	9	107	-33		

McCORMICK, HARRY   Patrick Henry   B10.25.1855 Syracuse NY   D8.8.1889 Syracuse NY   BR/TR/5-9/155   d5.1

1879	Syr N	18	33	.353	54	54	49-5	0	457.1	517	291	3		31	96	2.99	79	.266	.277	230-1	.222	-0*	79	-30		
1881	Wor N	1	8	.111	9	9	9-1	0	78.1	89	50	1		15	7	3.56	85	.275	.307	45	.133	-2*	62	-4		
1882	Cin AA	14	11	.560	25	25	24-3	0	219.2	177	87	4		42	33	1.52	174	.206	.243	93	.129	-5*	88	25		
1883	Cin AA	8	6	.571	15	15	14-1	0	128.2	139	70	1		27	21	2.87	113	.258	.294	55	.309	4	121	7		
Total	4	41	58	.414	103	103	96-10	0	884	922	498	9		115	157	2.66	98	.252	.274	423-1	.203	-4	86	-2		

McCORRY, BILL   William Charles   B7.9.1887 Saranac Lake NY   D3.22.1973 Augusta GA   BL/TR/5-9/157   d9.17

| 1909 | StL A | 0 | 2 | .000 | 2 | 2 | 2 | 0 | 15 | 29 | 21 | 1 | 0 | 6 | 10 | 9.00 | 27 | .397 | .443 | 5 | .000 | -0 | | 15 | -12 | | |

McCRABB, LES   Lester William "Buster"   B11.4.1914 Wakefield PA   BR/TR/5-11/175*   d9.7 C5

1939	Phi A	1	2	.333	4	2	0	0	35.2	42	20	4	1	19	11	4.04	117	.290	.340	13-0-2	.000	-2	103	2		
1940	Phi A	0	0	—	4	0	0	0	11.2	19	13	2	1	2	4	6.94	64	.365	.400	4	.250	0		-4		
1941	Phi A	9	13	.409	26	23	11-1	2	157.1	188	105	16	3	49	40	5.49	76	.293	.346	56-0-1	.143	-2	77	-20		
1942	Phi A	0	0	—	1	0	0	0	4	14	14	2	1	2	0	31.50	12	.560	.607	1	.000	-0		-11		
1950	Phi A	0	0	—	2	0	0	0	1.1	7	4	0	0	0	2	27.00	17	.636	.636	0	—	0		-3		
Total	5	10	15	.400	38	27	13-1	2	210	270	156	24	6	63	57	5.96	72	.309	.359	74-0-3	.122	-4	81	-36		

McCREERY, ED   Esley Porterfield "Big Ed"   B12.24.1889 Cripple Creek CO   D10.19.1960 Sacramento CA   BR/TR/6-0/190   d8.16

| 1914 | Det A | 0 | 1 | .000 | 4 | 0 | 0 | 0 | 4 | 6 | 5 | 0 | 0 | 4 | 4 | 11.25 | 25 | .316 | .409 | 1 | .000 | -0 | 337 | -3 | | |

McCREERY, TOM   Thomas Livingston   B10.19.1874 Beaver PA   D7.3.1941 Beaver PA   BB/TR/5-11/180   d6.8   Col Georgetown ▲

1895	Lou N	3	1	.750	8	4	3-1	0	48.2	51	40	0	5	38	14	5.36	86	.266	.400	108-0-2	.324	1*	108	-3		
1896	Lou N	0	1	.000	1	1	0	0	1	4	10	1	0	5	0	36.00	12	.571	.750	441-7-9	.351	0*	49	-5		
1900	Pit N	0	0	—	1	0	0	1	3	3	4	2	0	1	0	12.00	30	.250	.308	132-1-6	.220	0*		-2		
Total	3	3	2	.600	10	5	3-1	1	52.2	58	54	3	5	44	14	6.32	72	.275	.412	681-8-17	.322	2	97	-10		

McCULLERS, LANCE   Lance Graye   B3.8.1964 Tampa FL   BB/TR/6-1/218(185-218)   [PhiN82 2/41]   d8.12

1985	SD N	0	2	.000	21	0	0	5-2	35	23	15	3	1	16-3	27	2.31	154	.195	.296	4-0-2	.000	-0		3		
1986	SD N	10	10	.500	70	7	0	5-5	136	103	46	12	4	58-9	92	2.78	132	.216	.304	22-0-3	.091	0*	73	14		
1987	SD N	8	10	.444	78	0	0	16-11	123.1	115	60	11	2	59-11	126	3.72	107	.244	.330	14-0-1	.071	-1		2		
1988	SD N	3	6	.333	60	0	0	10-5	97.2	70	29	8	0	55-12	81	2.49	137	.205	.313	8	.250	1		10		
1989	NY A	4	3	.571	52	1	0	3-3	84.2	83	46	9	3	37-4	82	4.57	85	.255	.332	0	—	0	47	-6		
1990	NY A	1	0	1.000	11	0	0	0-1	15	14	8	2	0	6-2	11	3.60	111	.241	.308	0	—	0	0	229	3	15	
	Det A	1	0	1.000	9	1	0	0-0	29.2	18	11	2	0	13-1	20	2.73	146	.170	.256	0	—	0	0	229	4	77	
	Year	2	0	1.000	20	1	0	0-1	44.2	32	19	4	0	19-3	31	3.02	132	.195	.274	0	—	0					
1992	Tex A	1	0	1.000	5	0	0	0-0	5	1	3	0	0	8-0	3	5.40	71	.067	.391	48-0-6	.104	-0	88	25	92	
Total	7	28	31	.475	306	9	0	39-27	526.1	427	219	47	10	252-42	442	3.25	115	.223	.315	48-0-6	.104	0	88	25	92	

YEAR	TM LG	W	L	PCT	G	GS	CG-SHO	SV-BS	IP	H	R	HR	HB	BB-IB	SO	ERA	AERA	OAV	OOB	AB-HR-SH	AVG	PB	SUP	APR	DL	PW
McCULLOUGH, CHARLIE	Charles F. B1866 Dublin, Ireland D4.13.1898 Brooklyn NY TR/6-1/185 d4.23																									
1890	Bro AA	4	21	.160	26	25	24	0	215.2	247	174	5	16	102	61	4.59	85	.279	.364	86	.023	-12	62	-16		-2.6
	Syr AA	1	2	.333	3	3	3	0	26	29	25	1	0	14	8	7.27	49	.274	.358	9	.111	0	108	-10		-0.8
	Year	5	23	.179	29	28	27	0	241.2	276	199	6	16	116	69	4.88	79	.278	.363	95	.032	-12	66	-34		-3.4
McCULLOUGH, PAUL	Paul Willard B7.28.1898 New Castle PA D11.7.1970 New Castle PA BR/TR/5-9.5/190 d7.2																									
1929	Was A	0	0	—	3	0	0	0	7.1	7	7	1	0	2	2	8.59	49	.250	.300	1	.000	-0		-3		-0.2
McCULLOUGH, PHIL	Pinson Lamar B7.22.1917 Stockbridge GA D1.16.2003 Decatur GA BR/TR/6-4/204 d4.22 Mil 1943-45 Col Oglethorpe																									
1942	Was A	0	0	—	1	0	0	0	3	5	4	0	0	2	2	6.00	61	.333	.412	1	.000	-0		-1		-0.1
McCURRY, JEFF	Jeffrey Dee B1.21.1970 Tokyo, Japan BR/TR/6-6/215(210-225) [PitN90 14/376] d5.6 Col San Jacinto North (TX) JC																									
1995	Pit N	1	4	.200	55	0	0	1-1	61	82	38	9	5	30-4	27	5.02	87	.337	.421	3	.000	-0		-5		-0.4
1996	Det A	0	0	—	2	0	0	0-0	3.1	9	9	3	0	2-0	0	24.30	21	.474	.524		—	0		-7		-0.3
1997	Col N	1	4	.200	33	0	0	0-2	40.2	43	22	7	0	20-0	19	4.43	117	.277	.358	1	.000	-0		3		0.3
1998	Pit N	1	3	.250	16	0	0	0-0	19.1	24	14	4	1	9-0	11	6.52	66	.324	.400	0	—	0		-4		-0.7
1999	Hou N	0	1	.000	5	0	0	0-0	4	11	8	1	0	2-0	3	15.75	28	.478	.520	0	—	0		-5		-0.9
Total 5		3	12	.200	111	0	0	1-3	128.1	169	91	24	6	63-4	60	5.89	78	.329	.407	4	.000	-0		-18		-2.0
McDANIEL, LINDY	Lyndall Dale B12.13.1935 Hollis OK BR/TR/6-3/195(182-196) d9.2 b-Von Col Oklahoma																									
1955	StL N	0	0	—	4	2	0	0	19	22	10	4	0	7-1	7	4.74	86	.293	.349	5	.200	-0	110	-1		-0.1
1956	StL N	7	6	.538	39	7	1	0	116.1	121	60	7	0	42-7	59	3.40	111	.273	.333	32	.219	2	123	1		0.3
1957	StL N	15	9	.625	30	26	10-1	0	191	196	87	13	3	53-4	75	3.49	114	.266	.316	74-1-3	.257	4*	109	8		1.4
1958	StL N	5	7	.417	26	17	2-1	0	108.2	139	76	17	2	31-2	47	5.80	71	.305	.351	30-0-2	.067	-3	118	-18		-2.0
1959	StL N	14	12	.538	62	7	1	**15**	132	144	61	11	1	41-8	86	3.82	111	.283	.335	29-0-3	.034	-2	66	6		1.1
1960	StL N★	12	4	.750	65	2	1	**26**	116.1	85	28	8	1	24-3	105	2.09	196	.207	.249	26	.231	1	86	**25**		4.7
1961	StL N	10	6	.625	55	0	0	9	94.1	117	57	11	2	31-11	65	4.87	90	.305	.359	17-0-3	.235	-0		-3		-0.5
1962	StL N	3	10	.231	55	2	0	14	107	96	53	12	1	29-8	79	4.12	104	.239	.288	21-0-1	.095	-1	164	3		0.4
1963	Chi N	.13	7	.650	57	0	0	**22**	88	82	32	9	0	27-5	75	2.86	123	.251	.304	22-1-1	.091	-0		6		1.3
1964	Chi N	1	7	.125	63	0	0	15	95	104	43	4	1	23-4	71	3.88	96	.276	.318	16-0-1	.125	-1		-1		-0.1
1965	Chi N	5	6	.455	71	0	0	2	128.2	115	45	12	0	47-20	92	2.59	142	.241	.307	8	.000	-1		14		1.3
1966	SF N	10	5	.667	64	0	0	6	121.2	103	48	5	0	35-9	93	2.66	138	.228	.282	22-0-4	.091	-1		11		1.3
1967	SF N	2	6	.250	41	3	0	3	72.2	69	34	5	2	24-10	48	3.72	88	.248	.310	11	.091	-1	53	-3		-0.5
1968	SF N	0	0	—	12	0	0	1	19.1	30	15	3	0	5-0	9	7.45	40	.357	.393	2	.000	-1		-8		-0.5
	NY A	4	1	.800	24	0	0	10	51.1	30	10	5	1	12-3	43	1.75	166	.166	.221	14	.000	-1		7		1.1
1969	NY A	5	6	.455	51	0	0	5-4	83.2	84	37	4	0	23-6	60	3.55	99	.261	.305	8-0-2	.000	-1		0		0.0
1970	NY A	9	5	.643	62	0	0	29-6	111.2	88	29	7	0	23-5	81	2.01	177	.217	.258	24-0-1	.167	-0		20		3.5
1971	NY A	5	10	.333	44	0	0	4-7	69.2	82	41	12	0	24-6	39	5.04	65	.296	.360	9-0-1	.111	-0		-12		-2.6
1972	NY A	3	1	.750	37	0	0	0-0	68	54	23	4	0	25-5	47	2.25	133	.217	.287	7-1-1	.286	1		4		0.5
1973	NY A	12	6	.667	47	3	1	10-4	160.1	148	54	11	1	49-9	93	2.86	130	.250	.304	2	.000	-0	48	18		2.3
1974	KC A	1	4	.200	38	5	2	1-2	106.2	109	50	6	0	24-5	47	3.46	111	.265	.303	0	—	0	65	3		0.2
1975	KC A	5	1	.833	40	0	0	1-2	78	91	40	3	0	24-5	40	4.15	93	.273	.323	0	—	0		-2	29	-0.2
Total 21		141	119	.542	987	74	18-2	172-25	2139.1	2099	934	172	15	623-136	1361	3.45	109	.258	.309	378-3-25	.148	-4	107	78	29	13.0
McDANIEL, VON	Max Von B4.18.1939 Hollis OK D8.20.1995 Lawton OK BR/TR/6-2.5/180* d6.13 b-Lindy																									
1957	StL N	7	5	.583	17	13	4-2	0	86.2	71	37	7	1	31-3	45	3.22	123	.225	.293	26-0-1	.000	-3	68	6		0.4
1958	StL N	0	0	—	2	1	0	0	2	5	3	0	0	5-0	0	13.50	31	.500	.667	0-0-1	—	0	174	-2		-0.1
Total 2		7	5	.583	19	14	4-2	0	88.2	76	40	7	1	36-3	45	3.45	115	.233	.309	26-0-2	.000	-3	76	4		0.3
McDERMOTT, JOE	Joseph d5.4.1871																									
1872	Eck NA	0	7	.000	7	7	7	0	63	143	144	3		14	1	8.14	42	.376	.398	32	.281	2	66	-35		-2.0
McDERMOTT, MICKEY	Maurice Joseph "Maury" B8.29.1929 Poughkeepsie NY D8.7.2003 Phoenix AZ BL/TL/6-2/170(170-190) d4.24 C1 ▲																									
1948	Bos A	0	0	—	7	0	0	0	23.1	16	18	2	1	35	17	6.17	71	.208	.460	8	.375	1		-5		-0.1
1949	Bos A	5	4	.556	12	12	6-2	0	80	63	37	5	3	35	50	4.05	108	.220	.345	33	.212	1	120	4		0.5
1950	Bos A	7	3	.700	38	15	4	5	130	119	80	8	2	124	96	5.19	94	.249	.406	44	.364	6*	135	-3		0.4
1951	Bos A	8	8	.500	34	19	9-1	3	172	141	72	9	5	92	127	3.35	133	.226	.330	66-1-1	.273	2*	95	20		2.0
1952	Bos A	10	9	.526	30	21	7-2	0	162	139	70	14	3	92	117	3.72	106	.234	.340	62-1-3	.226	3*	95	6		0.9
1953	Bos A	18	10	.643	32	30	8-4	0	206.1	169	82	9	2	109	92	3.01	140	.224	.323	93-1-0	.301	7*	92	25		4.1
1954	Was A	7	15	.318	30	26	11-1	1	196.1	172	95	8	3	110	95	3.44	103	.239	.339	95-0-2	.200	3*	93	-1		0.2
1955	Was A	10	10	.500	31	20	8-1	1	156	140	75	9	9	100-2	78	3.75	102	.243	.361	95-1-1	.263	7*	96	1		0.9
1956	†NY A	2	6	.250	23	9	1	0	87	85	46	10	4	47-2	38	4.24	91	.261	.350	52-1-1	.212	3*	92	-4		-0.1
1957	KC A	1	4	.200	29	4	0	0	69	68	47	9	0	39-5	29	5.48	72	.266	.382	49-4-0	.245	3*	141	-11		-0.7
1958	Det A	0	0	—	2	0	0	0	2	6	4	0	0	2-0	1	9.00	45	.500	.571	3	.333	0*		-2		-0.1
1961	StL N	1	0	1.000	19	0	0	4	27	29	17	3	0	15-2	15	3.67	120	.271	.358	14	.071	-1*		0		-0.1
	KC A	0	0	—	4	0	0	0	5.2	14	12	0	0	10-0	3	14.29	29	.452	.585	5	.200	1*		-7		-0.3
Total 12		69	69	.500	291	156	54-11	14	1316.2	1161	655	86	28	838-8	757	3.91	105	.240	.354	619-9-8	.252	36	102	23		8.4
McDERMOTT, MIKE	Michael H. B5.6.1864 Fall River MA D5.7.1947 Fall River MA 5-10/152 d9.2																									
1889	Lou N	1	8	.111	9	9	9	0	84.1	108	65	4	3	24	22	4.16	92	.302	.365	.33	.182	-1	68	-3		-0.3
McDERMOTT, MIKE	Michael Joseph B9.7.1862 St.Louis MO D6.30.1943 St.Louis MO TR/5-8/145 d4.20																									
1895	Lou N	4	19	.174	33	26	18	0	207.1	258	203	8	11	103	42	5.99	77	.300	.382	82	.159	-2	106	-32		-2.6
1896	Lou N	2	7	.222	12	10	4-1	0	65	87	77	4	6	44	12	7.34	59	.318	.423	27-0-1	.296	1	82	-21		-1.9
1897	Cle N	4	5	.444	9	7	4	0	62	75	44	2	3	25	12	4.50	100	.296	.367	25	.320	1	68	0		-0.2
	StL N	1	2	.333	4	4	1	0	21.1	23	23	2	0	19	3	9.28	47	.274	.408	9	.222	-0	73	-9		-0.8
	Year	5	7	.417	13	11	5	0	83.1	98	67	4	3	44	15	5.72	78	.291	.378	34	.294	1	70	-9		-0.8
Total 3		11	33	.250	58	47	27-1	0	355.2	443	347	16	20	191	69	6.17	74	.301	.389	143-0-1	.217	1	92	-62		-5.3
McDEVITT, DANNY	Daniel Eugene B11.18.1932 New York NY BL/TL/5-10/175(164-175) d6.17 Col St. Bonaventure																									
1957	Bro N	7	4	.636	22	17	5-2	0	119	105	55	6	4	72-1	90	3.25	128	.238	.351	39-0-4	.154	-0	97	9		0.8
1958	LA N	2	6	.250	13	10	2	0	48.1	71	43	6	0	17-1	26	7.45	55	.355	.438	15	.133	-0	118	-17		-2.3
1959	LA N	10	8	.556	39	22	6-2	4	145	149	83	16	14	51-5	106	3.97	106	.263	.335	46-0-2	.109	-2	92	-1		-0.3
1960	LA N	0	4	.000	24	7	0	0	53	51	26	7	6	42-3	30	4.25	93	.260	.406	10-0-2	.200	-0	89	-1		-0.3
1961	NY A	1	2	.333	8	2	0	1	13	18	11	2	1	8-0	8	7.62	49	.353	.443	1	.000	0	83	-6		-1.0
	Min A	1	0	1.000	16	1	0	0	26.2	20	11	1	4	19-0	15	2.36	179	.213	.368	3	.000	0	125	4		0.2
	Year	2	2	.500	24	3	0	1	39.2	38	22	3	5	27-0	23	4.08	100	.262	.393	4	.000	-0	94	-1		-0.8
1962	KC A	0	3	.000	33	1	0	2	51	47	37	5	1	41-2	28	5.47	73	.250	.389	9	.222	0	63	-9		-0.5
Total 6		21	27	.438	155	60	13-4	7	456	461	266	42	32	264-12	303	4.40	94	.265	.370	123-0-8	.138	-3	97	-21		-3.1
McDILL, ALLEN	Allen Gabriel B8.23.1971 Greenville MS BL/TL/6-0/155(155-170) [NYN92 20/553] d5.15 Col Arkansas Tech																									
1997	KC A	0	0	—	3	0	0	0-0	4	3	6	1	1	8-0	2	13.50	35	.214	.522	0	—	0		-4		-0.2
1998	KC A	0	0	—	7	0	0	0-0	6	9	7	3	0	2-0	3	10.50	46	.333	.379	0	—	0		-3		-0.2
2001	Det A	0	0	—	13	0	0	0-0	10	13	9	2	1	1-0	7	7.20	68	.317	.349	0	—	0		-3		-0.1
2001	Bos A	0	0	—	15	0	0	0-1	14.2	13	9	1	1	7-1	16	5.52	80	.236	.328	0	—	0		-1		-0.1
Total 4		0	0	—	38	0	0	0-1	34.2	38	31	8	3	18-1	28	7.79	60	.277	.371	0		0		-11		-0.6
McDONALD, HANK	Henry Monroe B1.16.1911 Santa Monica CA D10.17.1982 Hemet CA BR/TR/6-3/200 d4.16																									
1931	Phi A	2	4	.333	19	10	1-1	0	70.1	62	43	3	1	41	23	3.71	121	.239	.346	21	.095	-1	111	2		0.0
1933	Phi A	1	1	.500	4	1	0	0	12.1	14	12	0	0	4	2	5.11	84	.264	.316	4	.000	-0	60	-3		-0.4
	StL A	0	4	.000	25	5	0	0	58.1	83	59	6	3	34	21	8.64	54	.332	.418	14	.143	-0	66	-22		-1.4
	Year	1	5	.167	29	6	0	0	70.2	97	71	6	3	38	23	8.02	57	.320	.401	18	.111	-0	65	-24		-1.8
Total 2		3	9	.250	48	16	1-1	0	141	159	114	9	4	79	46	5.87	77	.283	.375	39	.103	-2	93	-23		-1.8
McDONALD, JIM	Jimmie Le Roy "Hot Rod" B5.17.1927 Grants Pass OR BR/TR(BB 1950-51)/5-10.5/185* d7.27																									
1950	Bos A	1	0	1.000	9	0	0	0	19	23	9	1	0	10	5	3.79	129	.329	.420	3	.333	1		2		0.2
1951	StL A	1	7	.364	16	11	5	0	84	84	48	5	2	46	28	4.07	108	.260	.356	29-0-1	.207	-0*	81	1		0.1

YEAR	TM LG	W	L	PCT	G	GS	CG-SHO	SV-BS	IP	H	R	HR	HB	BB-IB	SO	ERA	AERA	OAV	OOB	AB-HR-SH	AVG	PB	SUP	APR	DL	PW
1952	NY A	3	4	.429	26	5	1	0	69.1	71	31	1	2	40	20	3.50	95	.268	.368	19	.316	3	131	-1		0.4
1953	†NY A	9	7	.563	27	18	6-2	0	129.2	128	64	4	1	39	43	3.82	97	.260	.316	41-0-3	.098	-3*	122	-3		-0.7
1954	NY A	4	1	.800	16	10	3-1	0	71	54	28	3	1	45	20	3.17	108	.213	.332	19-0-2	.211	2	159	2	60	0.4
1955	Bal A	3	5	.375	21	8	0	0	51.2	76	48	5	0	30-1	20	7.14	53	.345	.421	11-0-1	.182	1	84	-20		-2.5
1956	Chi A	0	2	.000	8	3	0	0	18.2	29	18	2	1	7-0	10	8.68	47	.377	.425	5	.000	-0	36	-9		-0.8
1957	Chi A	0	1	.000	10	0	0	0	22.1	18	8	2	.0	10-1	12	2.01	185	.234	.315	1	.000	0	3			0.2
1958	Chi A	0	0	—	3	0	0	0	2.1	6	8	1	0	4-0	0	19.29	19	.429	.556	0	—	0		-5		-0.3
Total	9	24	27	.471	136	55	15-3	1	468	489	262	24	8	231-2	158	4.27	89	.273	.357	128-0-7	.180	4	109	-30	60	-2.8

McDONALD, JOHN John Joseph (b John Joseph McDonnell) B1.27.1883 Throop PA D4.9.1950 Roselle NJ BR/TR/6-1/170 d9.3

YEAR	TM LG	W	L	PCT	G	GS	CG-SHO	SV-BS	IP	H	R	HR	HB	BB-IB	SO	ERA	AERA	OAV	OOB	AB-HR-SH	AVG	PB	SUP	APR	DL	PW
1907	Was A	0	0	—	1	0	0	0	6	12	11	0	2	9	0	9.00	27	.414	.452	3	.333	1		-5		-0.2

McDONALD, BEN Larry Benard B11.24.1967 Baton Rouge LA BR/TR/6-7/213* [BalA89 1/1] d9.6 Col Louisiana St.

YEAR	TM LG	W	L	PCT	G	GS	CG-SHO	SV-BS	IP	H	R	HR	HB	BB-IB	SO	ERA	AERA	OAV	OOB	AB-HR-SH	AVG	PB	SUP	APR	DL	PW
1989	Bal A	1	0	1.000	6	0	0	0-0	7.1	8	7	2	0	4-0	5	8.59	44	.286	.364	0	—	0		-4		-0.4
1990	Bal A	8	5	.615	21	15	3-2	0-0	118.2	88	36	9	0	35-0	65	2.43	157	.205	.262	0	—	0	76	18	43	1.9
1991	Bal A	6	8	.429	21	21	1	0-0	126.1	126	71	16	1	43-2	85	4.84	82	.261	.321	0	—	0	107	-12	50	-1.2
1992	Bal A	13	13	.500	35	35	4-2	0-0	227	213	113	32	9	74-5	158	4.24	96	.247	.311	0	—	0	113	-4		-0.3
1993	Bal A	13	14	.481	34	34	7-1	0-0	220.1	185	92	17	5	86-4	171	3.39	133	.228	.304	0	—	0	84	25		3.0
1994	Bal A	14	7	.667	24	24	5-1	0-0	157.1	151	75	14	2	54-2	94	4.06	124	.255	.319	0	—	0	79	5	80	1.9
1995	Bal A	3	6	.333	14	13	1	0-0	80	67	40	10	3	38-3	62	4.16	115	.224	.316	0	—	0	97	31		2.6
1996	Mil A	12	10	.545	35	35	2	0-0	221.1	228	104	25	6	67-0	146	3.90	133	.264	.319	0	—	-0	84	8	74	0.7
1997	Mil A	8	7	.533	21	21	1	0-0	133	120	68	13	5	36-2	110	4.06	114	.237	.294	1	.000	-0	95	83	247	8.8
Total	9	78	70	.527	211	198	24-6	0-0	1291.1	1186	606	138	31	437-18	894	3.91	116	.243	.308	1	.000	-0	95	83	247	8.8

McDOOLAN d4.14

YEAR	TM LG	W	L	PCT	G	GS	CG-SHO	SV-BS	IP	H	R	HR	HB	BB-IB	SO	ERA	AERA	OAV	OOB	AB-HR-SH	AVG	PB	SUP	APR	DL	PW
1873	Mar NA	0	1	.000	1	1	1	0	9	18	24	0			0	3.00	108	.305	.305	4	.000	-1	33	-2		-0.2

McDOUGAL, DEWEY James H. B9.19.1871 Aledo IL D4.28.1935 Galesburg IL TR/5-10/188 d4.24

YEAR	TM LG	W	L	PCT	G	GS	CG-SHO	SV-BS	IP	H	R	HR	HB	BB-IB	SO	ERA	AERA	OAV	OOB	AB-HR-SH	AVG	PB	SUP	APR	DL	PW
1895	StL N	3	10	.231	18	14	10	0	114.2	187	146	11	10	46	23	8.32	58	.360	.423	41	.146	-2	90	-43		-3.5
1896	StL N	0	1	.000	3	1	0	0	10	13	11	2	1	4	0	8.10	54	.310	.383	3	.000	-1	65	-4		-0.3
Total	2	3	11	.214	21	15	10	0	124.2	200	157	13	11	50	23	8.30	58	.357	.420	44	.136	-3	89	-47		-3.8

McDOUGAL, SANDY John Auchanbolt B5.21.1874 Buffalo NY D10.2.1910 Buffalo NY BR/TR/5-10/155 d6.12

YEAR	TM LG	W	L	PCT	G	GS	CG-SHO	SV-BS	IP	H	R	HR	HB	BB-IB	SO	ERA	AERA	OAV	OOB	AB-HR-SH	AVG	PB	SUP	APR	DL	PW
1895	Bro N	0	0	—	1	0	0	1	3	3	4	0	0	5	2	12.00	37	.250	.471	1	.000	-0		-2		-0.1
1905	StL N	1	4	.200	5	5	5	0	44.2	50	24	0	0	12	10	3.43	87	.301	.348	15-0-1	.133	-1	58	-3		-0.2
Total	2	1	4	.200	6	5	5	1	47.2	53	28	0	0	17	12	3.97	78	.298	.359	16-0-1	.125	-1	58	-5		-0.3

McDOWELL, JACK Jack Burns B1.16.1966 Van Nuys CA BR/TR/6-5/180(179-190) [ChiA87 1/5] d9.15 Col Stanford

YEAR	TM LG	W	L	PCT	G	GS	CG-SHO	SV-BS	IP	H	R	HR	HB	BB-IB	SO	ERA	AERA	OAV	OOB	AB-HR-SH	AVG	PB	SUP	APR	DL	PW
1987	Chi A	3	0	1.000	4	4	0	0-0	28	16	6	1	2	6-0	15	1.93	240	.168	.233	0	—	0	94	8		0.9
1988	Chi A	5	10	.333	26	26	1	0-0	158.2	147	85	12	7	68-5	84	3.97	101	.245	.326	0	—	0	82	-2		0.1
1990	Chi A	14	9	.609	33	33	4	0-0	205	189	93	20	7	77-0	165	3.82	101	.244	.316	0	—	0	116	21		2.1
1991	Chi A★	17	10	.630	35	35	15-3	0-0	253.2	212	97	19	4	82-2	191	3.41	122	.228	.292	0	—	0	114	24		3.1
1992	Chi A★	20	10	.667	34	34	13-1	0-0	260.2	247	95	21	7	75-9	178	3.18	122	.251	.307	0	—	0	107	26		3.1
1993	†Chi A★	22	10	.688	34	34	10-4	0-0	256.2	261	104	20	3	69-6	158	3.37	125	.266	.314	0	—	0	89	21		1.9
1994	Chi A	10	9	.526	25	25	6-2	0-0	181	186	82	12	5	42-2	127	3.73	126	.266	.310	0	—	0	99	15		1.9
1995	†NY A	15	10	.600	30	30	8-2	0-0	217.2	211	106	25	4	78-1	157	3.93	118	.254	.320	0	—	0	102	-5	18	-0.4
1996	†Cle A	13	9	.591	30	30	5-1	0-0	192	214	119	22	4	67-2	141	5.11	96	.282	.341	0	—	0	101	-2	139	-0.2
1997	Cle A	3	3	.500	9	6	0	0-0	40.2	44	25	6	1	18-1	38	5.09	92	.282	.356	0	—	0	92	-2	99	-0.2
1998	Ana A	5	3	.625	14	14	0	0-0	76	96	45	11	1	19-1	45	5.09	93	.311	.350	0	—	0	38	-6	109	-0.9
1999	Ana A	0	4	.000	4	4	0	0-0	19	31	17	4	2	5-0	12	8.05	61	.369	.413	0	—	0	101	-9	365	10.2
Total	12	127	87	.593	277	275	62-13	0-0	1889	1854	874	173	48	606-29	1311	3.85	111	.257	.317	0	—	0	101	99	365	10.2

McDOWELL, ROGER Roger Alan B12.21.1960 Cincinnati OH BR/TR/6-1/182(175-197) [NYN82 3/59] d4.11 Col Bowling Green

YEAR	TM LG	W	L	PCT	G	GS	CG-SHO	SV-BS	IP	H	R	HR	HB	BB-IB	SO	ERA	AERA	OAV	OOB	AB-HR-SH	AVG	PB	SUP	APR	DL	PW
1985	NY N	6	5	.545	62	2	0	17-6	127.1	108	43	9	1	37-8	70	2.83	124	.230	.286	19-0-2	.158	0	88	10		1.3
1986	†NY N	14	9	.609	75	0	0	22-6	128	107	48	4	3	42-5	65	3.02	119	.228	.294	18-0-1	.278	1	9			2.0
1987	NY N	7	5	.583	56	0	0	25-7	88.2	95	41	7	2	28-4	32	4.16	92	.276	.330	13	.231	1		-1	38	1.2
1988	†NY N	5	5	.500	62	0	0	16-4	89	80	31	1	3	31-7	46	2.63	124	.238	.304	9	.333	2*	6			-0.4
1989	NY N	1	5	.167	25	0	0	4-1	35.1	34	21	1	2	16-3	15	3.31	100	.254	.340	2	.500	-0	3			2.1
	Phi N	3	3	.500	44	0	0	19-4	56.2	45	15	2	1	22-5	32	1.96	178	.233	.315	1	.000	-0	9			1.7
	Year	4	8	.333	69	0	0	23-5	92	79	36	3	3	38-8	47	3.86	100	.286	.355	3	.333	-0	0			1.1
1990	Phi N	6	8	.429	72	0	0	22-6	86.1	92	41	2	2	35-9	39	3.86	100	.286	.355	2	.000	-0	1		15	0.2
1991	Phi N	3	6	.333	38	0	0	3-3	59	61	28	1	2	32-12	28	3.20	115	.266	.360	2	.000	-0*	5			1.3
	LA N	6	3	.667	33	0	0	7-2	42.1	39	12	3	0	16-8	22	2.55	141	.257	.324	0	—	0*	7			1.1
	Year	9	9	.500	71	0	0	10-5	101.1	100	40	4	2	48-20	50	2.93	125	.262	.346	2	.000	-0	7			-1.2
1992	LA N	6	10	.375	65	0	0	14-8	83.2	103	46	3	1	42-13	50	4.09	85	.306	.381	3-0-1	.000	0*	7			-0.4
1993	LA N	5	3	.625	54	0	0	2-1	68	76	32	2	2	30-10	27	2.25	172	.288	.364	2	.500	0	7			1.1
1994	LA N	0	3	.000	32	0	0	0-1	41.1	50	25	3	1	22-6	29	5.23	76	.303	.388	1	.000	-0	-6			-0.4
1995	Tex A	7	4	.636	64	0	0	4-4	85	86	39	5	6	34-7	49	4.02	120	.277	.354	0	—	0	8		67	1.1
1996	Bal A	1	5	.500	41	0	0	4-2	59.1	69	32	7	2	23-1	20	4.25	117	.296	.363	0	—	0	4		120	8.4
Total	12	70	70	.500	723	2	0	159-55	1050	1045	454	50	28	410-98	524	3.30	115	.263	.334	72-0-5	.222	6	88	46	120	8.4

McDOWELL, SAM Samuel Edward Thomas "Sudden Sam" B9.21.1942 Pittsburgh PA BL/TL/6-5/218(190-220) d9.15

YEAR	TM LG	W	L	PCT	G	GS	CG-SHO	SV-BS	IP	H	R	HR	HB	BB-IB	SO	ERA	AERA	OAV	OOB	AB-HR-SH	AVG	PB	SUP	APR	DL	PW
1961	Cle A	0	0	—	1	1	0	0	6.1	3	0	0	0	5-0	5	0.00	—	.136	.296	2	.000	-0	45	3		0.1
1962	Cle A	3	7	.300	25	13	0	1	87.2	81	64	9	4	70-1	70	6.06	64	.243	.379	26-0-1	.154	-1	99	-21		-2.2
1963	Cle A	3	5	.375	14	12	3-1	0	65	63	37	6	4	44-0	63	4.85	75	.256	.368	19-0-4	.211	0*	100	-8		-0.8
1964	Cle A	11	6	.647	31	24	6-2	1	173.1	148	80	9	3	100-6	177	2.70	133	.229	.334	56-0-3	.143	0	97	17		1.5
1965	Cle A★	17	11	.607	42	35	14-3	4	273	178	80	9	8	132-7	325	2.18	160	.185	.286	95-0-5	.126	-3*	88	37		3.8
1966	Cle A★	9	8	.529	35	28	8-5	3	194.1	130	66	12	6	102-3	225	2.87	120	.188	.297	60-0-0	.200	1*	93	14		1.7
1967	Cle A	13	15	.464	37	37	10-1	0	236.1	201	112	21	7	123-3	236	3.85	85	.233	.331	82-1-4	.183	0	98	-13		-1.4
1968	Cle A★	15	14	.517	38	37	11-3	0	269	181	78	13	10	110-9	283	1.81	164	.189	.278	85-0-6	.153	0	83	28		3.3
1969	Cle A★	18	14	.563	39	38	18-4	1-0	285	222	111	13	7	102-9	279	2.94	129	.213	.286	92-0-11	-.174	-1	83	24		2.6
1970	Cle A★	20	12	.625	39	39	19-1	0-0	305	236	108	25	7	131-10	304	2.92	137	.213	.299	105-1-8	.124	-4*	91	33		2.9
1971	Cle A★	13	17	.433	35	31	8-2	1-1	214.2	160	89	22	3	153-13	192	3.40	114	.207	.338	73-0-6	.178	-1	70	10		1.2
1972	SF N	10	8	.556	28	25	4	0-1	164.1	155	86	12	6	86-6	122	4.33	81	.253	.348	59-0-4	.119	-1	127	-13	21	-1.2
1973	SF N	1	2	.333	18	3	0	3-0	40	45	23	4	0	29-0	35	4.50	86	.285	.392	12-0-1	.167	-0	84	-3		-0.3
	NY A	5	8	.385	16	15	2-1	0-0	95.2	73	47	4	0	64-2	75	3.95	94	.212	.332	0	—	0	62	-2		-0.2
1974	NY A	1	6	.143	13	7	0	0-0	48	42	27	6	0	41-2	33	4.69	76	.236	.379	0	—	0	64	-5	68	0.2
1975	Pit N	2	1	.667	14	1	0	0-0	34.2	30	11	0	0	20-3	29	2.86	126	.242	.346	8	.000	-1	221	4		0.2
Total	15	141	134	.513	425	346	103-23	14-2	2492.1	1948	999	164	59	1312-74	2453	3.17	113	.215	.317	774-2-56	.154	-9	91	105	89	9.9

McELROY, CHUCK Charles Dwayne B10.1.1967 Port Arthur TX BL/TL/6-0/195(160-205) [PhiN86 8/192] d9.4

YEAR	TM LG	W	L	PCT	G	GS	CG-SHO	SV-BS	IP	H	R	HR	HB	BB-IB	SO	ERA	AERA	OAV	OOB	AB-HR-SH	AVG	PB	SUP	APR	DL	PW
1989	Phi N	0	0	—	11	0	0	0-0	10.1	12	2	1	0	4-1	9	1.74	206	.286	.348	0	—	0		-1		0.1
1990	Phi N	0	1	.000	16	0	0	0-0	14	24	13	0	0	10-2	16	7.71	50	.369	.447	0	—	0	17			1.5
1991	Chi N	6	2	.750	71	0	0	3-3	101.1	73	33	7	0	57-7	92	1.95	200	.210	.317	10	.300	1		-1		0.2
1992	Chi N	4	7	.364	72	0	0	6-5	83.2	73	40	7	0	51-10	83	3.55	102	.237	.341	6	.667	3		-4		-0.4
1993	Chi N	2	2	.500	49	0	0	0-0	47.1	51	30	4	1	25-5	31	4.56	88	.280	.368	6	.000	-0	13			0.2
1994	Cin N	1	2	.333	52	0	0	5-6	57.2	52	15	0	0	15-2	38	2.34	179	.244	.294	3	.167	-0	-5	16		-1.3
1995	Cin N	3	4	.429	44	0	0	0-3	40.1	46	29	7	0	15-3	27	6.02	69	.291	.350	3	.000	-0	-8	16		-1.3
1996	Cin N	2	0	1.000	12	0	0	0-0	12.1	13	10	2	0	10-1	12	6.57	65	.265	.390	2	.000	0	-3	27	17	1.
	Cal A	5	1	.833	40	0	0	0-2	36.2	32	12	2	2	13-2	32	2.95	172	.239	.313	0	—	0	9	17		1.
1997	Ana A	0	0	—	13	0	0	0-2	15.2	17	7	2	0	3-0	18	3.45	134	.270	.303	0	—	0*	3			0.1
	Chi A	1	3	.250	48	0	0	1-3	59.1	56	29	5	3	19-1	44	3.94	112	.247	.307	0	—	0	4			0.3
	Year	1	3	.250	61	0	0	1-5	75	73	36	5	3	22-1	62	3.84	116	.252	.306	0	—	0	14			-1.
1998	Col N	6	4	.600	78	0	0	2-4	68.1	68	23	3	0	24-0	61	2.90	179	.268	.327	5-0-1	.200	-0	-1			-1.
1999	Col N	3	1	.750	40	0	0	0-0	40.2	48	29	5	0	9-2	29	6.20	93	.296	.396	1-0-1	.000	-0	2			0.
	NY N	0	0	—	15	0	0	0-0	13.1	10	5	2	0	8-1	7	3.38	129	.250	.362	0	—	0	2			0.

YEAR	TM LG	W	L	PCT	G	GS	CG-SHO	SV-BS	IP	H	R	HR	HB	BB-IB	SO	ERA	AERA	OAV	OOB	AB-HR-SH	AVG	PB	SUP	APR	DL	PW
	Year	3	1	.750	56	0	0	0-3	54	60	34	9	1	36-4	44	5.50	99	.286	.388	1-0-1	.000	-0		0		0.0
2000	Bal A	3	0	1.000	43	2	0	0-1	63.1	60	36	6	2	34-2	50	4.69	100	.247	.340	0	—	0	150	0		0.0
2001	Bal A	1	2	.333	18	5	0	0-0	45.1	49	29	8	2	28-2	22	5.36	80	.269	.371	0	—	0	103	-5		-0.2
	SD N	1	1	.500	31	0	0	0-3	29.2	38	24	6	0	18-4	25	5.16	80	.306	.392	1	.000	0		-6		-0.3
Total	13	38	30	.559	654	7	0	17-35	739.1	724	366	66	11	362-46	604	3.90	112	.258	.342	42-0-2	.214	2	117	28	60	2.9

McELROY, JIM James D. B11.5.1862 Napa Co. CA D7.24.1889 Needles CA 5-10/170 d5.26 Col St. Marys (CA)

YEAR	TM LG	W	L	PCT	G	GS	CG-SHO	SV-BS	IP	H	R	HR	HB	BB-IB	SO	ERA	AERA	OAV	OOB	AB-HR-SH	AVG	PB	SUP	APR	DL	PW
1884	Phi N	1	12	.077	13	13	13	0	111	115	112	1		54	45	4.86	61	.254	.333	48	.146	-3*	49	-22		-2.2
	Wil U	0	1	.000	1	1	0	0	5	10	6	0		0	3	10.80	25	.385	.385	2	.000	-0	16	-3		-0.3
Total	1	1	13	.071	14	14	13	0	116	125	118	1		54	48	5.12	58	.261	.336	50	.140	-4	47	-25		-2.5

McENANEY, WILL William Henry B2.14.1952 Springfield OH BL/TL/6-0/180* [CinN70 8/188] d7.3

YEAR	TM LG	W	L	PCT	G	GS	CG-SHO	SV-BS	IP	H	R	HR	HB	BB-IB	SO	ERA	AERA	OAV	OOB	AB-HR-SH	AVG	PB	SUP	APR	DL	PW
1974	Cin N	2	1	.667	24	0	0	2-1	27	24	16	4	0	9-1	13	4.33	81	.250	.311	0	—	0		-3		-0.4
1975	†Cin N	5	2	.714	70	0	0	15-4	91	92	29	6	2	23-7	48	2.47	145	.264	.310	14	.000	-2		10		0.9
1976	†Cin N	2	6	.250	55	0	0	7-2	72.1	97	44	3	1	23-8	28	4.85	72	.323	.370	6-0-1	.167	1		-11		-1.4
1977	Mon N	3	5	.375	69	0	0	3-5	86.2	92	39	6	2	22-4	38	3.95	98	.271	.314	8	.000	-1		1		0.0
1978	Pit N	0	0	—	6	0	0	0-0	8.2	15	11	3	1	2-0	6	10.38	36	.395	.429	0	—	-0		-6		-0.3
1979	StL N	0	3	.000	45	0	0	2-2	64	60	26	3	2	16-8	15	2.95	129	.251	.299	3	.000	-0		5		0.3
Total	6	12	17	.414	269	0	0	29-14	349.2	380	165	25	8	95-28	148	3.76	98	.279	.326	31-0-1	.032	-2		-4		-0.9

McEVOY, LOU Louis Anthony B5.30.1902 Williamsburg KS D12.17.1953 Webster Groves MO BR/TR/6-2.5/203 d4.28

YEAR	TM LG	W	L	PCT	G	GS	CG-SHO	SV-BS	IP	H	R	HR	HB	BB-IB	SO	ERA	AERA	OAV	OOB	AB-HR-SH	AVG	PB	SUP	APR	DL	PW
1930	NY A	1	3	.250	28	1	0	3	52.1	64	51	4	2	29	14	6.71	64	.288	.375	16	.125	-1	20	-17		-1.4
1931	NY A	0	0	—	6	0	0	1	12.1	19	11	1	1	12	3	12.41	32	.358	.485	4	.000	-1		-12		-0.6
Total	2	1	3	.250	34	1	0	4	64.2	83	68	5	3	41	17	7.59	54	.302	.398	20	.100	-2	20	-29		-2.0

McFADDEN, BARNEY Bernard Joseph B3.20.1877 Eckley PA D4.28.1924 Mauch Chunk PA BR/TR/6-1/195 d4.24 Col Villanova

YEAR	TM LG	W	L	PCT	G	GS	CG-SHO	SV-BS	IP	H	R	HR	HB	BB-IB	SO	ERA	AERA	OAV	OOB	AB-HR-SH	AVG	PB	SUP	APR	DL	PW
1901	Cin N	3	4	.429	8	5	4	0	46	54	39	2	6	40	11	6.07	53	.290	.431	20	.150	-1	111	-14		-1.7
1902	Phi N	0	1	.000	1	1	1	0	9	14	13	0	0	7	3	8.00	35	.350	.447	3	.000	-0	72	-6		-0.5
Total	2	3	5	.375	9	6	5	0	55	68	52	2	6	47	14	6.38	49	.301	.434	23	.130	-2	105	-20		-2.2

McFARLAN, DAN Anderson Daniel B11.1.1873 Gainesville TX D9.23.1924 Louisville KY ?/178 d9.2 b-Alex Col Washington and Lee

YEAR	TM LG	W	L	PCT	G	GS	CG-SHO	SV-BS	IP	H	R	HR	HB	BB-IB	SO	ERA	AERA	OAV	OOB	AB-HR-SH	AVG	PB	SUP	APR	DL	PW
1895	Lou N	0	7	.000	7	7	6	0	46	80	56	4	5	15	10	6.65	70	.376	.429	21	.238	-1	77	-13		-1.3
1899	Bro N	0	0	—	1	0	0	0	6	6	1	1	0	3	0	1.50	261	.261	.346	2	.000	-0		2		0.1
	Was N	8	18	.308	32	28	22-1	0	211.2	268	166	5	11	64	41	4.76	82	.308	.363	86-0-1	.186	-0	72	-24		-2.4
	Year	8	18	.308	33	28	22-1	0	217.2	274	167	6	11	67	41	4.67	84	.307	.363	88-0-1	.182	-1	72	-17		-2.3
Total	2	8	25	.242	40	35	28-1	0	263.2	354	223	10	16	82	51	5.02	81	.320	.375	109-0-1	.193	-1	74	-35		-3.6

McFARLAND, CHAPPIE Charles Amos B3.13.1875 White Hall IL D12.14.1924 Houston TX TR/6-1/? d9.15 b-Monte

YEAR	TM LG	W	L	PCT	G	GS	CG-SHO	SV-BS	IP	H	R	HR	HB	BB-IB	SO	ERA	AERA	OAV	OOB	AB-HR-SH	AVG	PB	SUP	APR	DL	PW
1902	StL N	0	0	—	2	1	1	0	11	11	7	1	0	3	3	5.73	48	.262	.311	4	.000	-1	99	-3		-0.2
1903	StL N	9	19	.321	28	26	25-1	0	229	253	133	2	6	48	76	3.07	106	.284	.325	74-0-3	.108	-4	73	2		0.0
1904	StL N	14	18	.438	32	31	28-1	0	269.1	266	149	7	4	56	111	3.21	84	.248	.288	99-0-2	.131	-2	123	-18		-1.9
1905	StL N	8	18	.308	31	28	22-3	1	250.1	281	145	9	6	65	85	3.81	78	.284	.332	85-0-1	.165	-1	88	-24		-2.1
1906	StL N	2	1	.667	6	4	2	1	37.1	33	18	1	0	8	16	1.93	136	.219	.258	15	.133	-1	104	0		0.0
	Pit N	1	3	.250	6	5	2-1	0	35.1	39	14	0	2	7	11	2.55	105	.298	.343	13	.385	-1	109	0		0.2
	Bro N	0	1	.000	1	1	1	0	9	10	8	1	0	5	5	8.00	32	.286	.375	3	.000	-0	29	-5		-0.4
	Year	3	5	.375	13	10	5-1	1	81.2	82	40	2	2	20	32	2.87	92	.259	.307	31	.226	0	100	-4		-0.2
Total	5	34	61	.358	106	96	81-6	2	841.1	893	474	15	18	192	307	3.35	87	.270	.313	293-0-6	.143	-6	95	-48		-4.4

McFARLAND, MONTE Lamont Amos B11.7.1872 White Hall IL D11.15.1913 Peoria IL 5-10/175 d9.14 b-Chappie

YEAR	TM LG	W	L	PCT	G	GS	CG-SHO	SV-BS	IP	H	R	HR	HB	BB-IB	SO	ERA	AERA	OAV	OOB	AB-HR-SH	AVG	PB	SUP	APR	DL	PW
1895	Chi N	2	0	1.000	2	2	2	0	14	21	11	0	0	5	5	5.14	99	.339	.388	7-0-1	.143	-1	182	0		-0.1
1896	Chi N	0	4	.000	4	3	2	0	25	32	25	0	2	21	3	7.20	63	.308	.433	12-0-1	.000	-2	37	-6		-0.8
Total	2	2	4	.333	6	5	4	0	39	53	36	0	2	26	8	6.46	73	.319	.418	19-0-2	.053	-3	99	-6		-0.9

McFETRIDGE, JACK John Reed B8.25.1869 Philadelphia PA D1.10.1917 Philadelphia PA 6-0/175 d6.7 Col Penn

YEAR	TM LG	W	L	PCT	G	GS	CG-SHO	SV-BS	IP	H	R	HR	HB	BB-IB	SO	ERA	AERA	OAV	OOB	AB-HR-SH	AVG	PB	SUP	APR	DL	PW
1890	Phi N	1	0	1.000	1	1	1	0	9	5	1	0	0	2	4	1.00	366	.156	.206	4	.750	1	69	3		0.4
1903	Phi N	1	11	.083	14	13	11	0	103	120	71	2	3	49	31	4.89	67	.299	.379	34-0-3	.176	0	92	-16		-1.5
Total	2	2	11	.154	15	14	12	0	112	125	72	2	3	51	35	4.58	72	.288	.367	38-0-3	.237	2	90	-13		-1.1

McGAFFIGAN, ANDY Andrew Joseph B10.25.1956 W.Palm Beach FL BR/TR/6-3/195* [NYA78 6/156] d9.22 Col Florida Southern

YEAR	TM LG	W	L	PCT	G	GS	CG-SHO	SV-BS	IP	H	R	HR	HB	BB-IB	SO	ERA	AERA	OAV	OOB	AB-HR-SH	AVG	PB	SUP	APR	DL	PW
1981	NY A	0	0	—	2	0	0	0-0	7	5	3	1	0	3-0	2	2.57	141	.200	.267	0	—	0		0		0.0
1982	SF N	1	0	1.000	4	0	0	0-0	8	5	1	0	1	1-0	4	0.00	—	.179	.233	1	.000	-0		3		0.3
1983	SF N	3	9	.250	43	16	0	2-0	134.1	131	67	17	1	39-5	93	4.29	83	.255	.308	30-0-2	.067	-1	75	-8		-1.0
1984	Mon N	3	4	.429	21	3	0	1-1	46	37	14	2	0	15-2	39	2.54	136	.220	.283	8-0-1	.000	-1	136	5		0.7
	Cin N	0	2	.000	9	3	0	0-1	23	23	14	2	0	8-0	18	5.48	69	.261	.323	2-0-2	.000	-0	85	-3		-0.3
	Year	3	6	.333	30	6	0	1-2	69	60	28	4	0	23-2	57	3.52	101	.234	.296	10-0-3	.000	-1	111	2		0.4
1985	Cin N	3	3	.500	15	15	2	0-0	94.1	88	40	4	2	30-4	83	3.72	102	.247	.309	29-0-1	.034	-2	87	2		-0.1
1986	Mon N	10	5	.667	48	14	1-1	2-1	142.2	114	49	9	2	55-8	104	2.65	141	.223	.298	33-0-4	.061	-2*	119	16		1.4
1987	Mon N	5	2	.714	69	0	0	12-1	120.1	105	38	5	3	42-7	100	2.39	178	.235	.303	17-0-2	.000	-1		23		1.5
1988	Mon N	6	0	1.000	63	0	0	4-5	91.1	81	31	4	2	37-7	71	2.76	132	.233	.309	5	.000	-0		9	17	0.6
1989	Mon N	3	5	.375	57	0	0	2-3	75	85	40	3	3	30-4	40	4.68	76	.293	.361	1	1.000	0		-8	15	-0.8
1990	SF N	0	0	—	4	0	0	0-0	4.2	10	9	2	0	4-0	4	17.36	21	.455	.538	0	—	0		-7		-0.4
	KC A	4	3	.571	24	11	0	1-0	78.2	75	40	6	2	28-1	49	3.09	125	.248	.313	0	—	0	116	3		0.2
1991	KC A	0	0	—	4	0	0	0-0	8	14	5	0	0	2-0	3	4.50	92	.389	.410	0	—	0		-1		0.0
Total	11	38	33	.535	363	62	3-1	24-12	833.1	773	351	55	16	294-38	610	3.38	111	.247	.312	126-0-12	.048	-7	98	34	32	2.1

McGEACHY, JACK John Charles B5.23.1864 Clinton MA D4.5.1930 Cambridge MA BR/TR/5-8/165 d6.17.1886 ▲

YEAR	TM LG	W	L	PCT	G	GS	CG-SHO	SV-BS	IP	H	R	HR	HB	BB-IB	SO	ERA	AERA	OAV	OOB	AB-HR-SH	AVG	PB	SUP	APR	DL	PW
1887	Ind N	0	1	.000	1	1	0	0	6.1	13	17	2	0	4	3	11.37	37	.351	.415	405-1	.269	0*		-7		-0.6
1888	Ind N	0	0	—	1	0	0	0	5	5	5	1	0	3	0	7.20	41	.238	.333	452	.219	0*		-2		-0.1
1889	Ind N	0	0	—	3	0	0	0	4.2	7	9	2	0	6	3	11.57	36	.333	.481	532-2	.267	0*		-4		-0.2
Total	3	0	1	.000	5	1	0	0	16	25	31	5	0	13	6	10.13	37	.316	.413	1389-3	.252			-13		-0.9

McGEE, BILL William Henry "Fiddler Bill" B11.16.1909 Batchtown IL D2.11.1987 St.Louis MO BR/TR/6-1/215 d9.29

YEAR	TM LG	W	L	PCT	G	GS	CG-SHO	SV-BS	IP	H	R	HR	HB	BB-IB	SO	ERA	AERA	OAV	OOB	AB-HR-SH	AVG	PB	SUP	APR	DL	PW
1935	StL N	1	0	1.000	1	1	1	0	9	3	1	0	1	1	2	1.00	410	.103	.133	3	.333	0	41	3		0.4
1936	StL N	1	1	.500	7	2	0	0	16	23	14	3	0	4	8	7.88	50	.359	.397	4	.250	0	118	-6		-0.6
1937	StL N	1	0	1.000	4	1	1	0	14	13	4	1	1	4	9	2.57	155	.255	.321	5	.200	-0	325	2		0.2
1938	StL N	7	12	.368	47	25	10-1	5	216	216	101	4	1	78	104	3.21	123	.257	.321	67-0-4	.209	1	83	14		1.3
1939	StL N	12	5	.706	43	17	5-4	0	156	155	68	14	0	59	56	3.81	108	.261	.328	53-0-2	.145	-2	109	8		0.6
1940	StL N	16	10	.615	38	31	11-3	0	218	222	108	13	2	96	78	3.80	105	.263	.340	73-0-10	.178	-1	108	5		0.3
1941	StL N	0	1	.000	4	3	0	0	14	17	9	1	1	13	2	5.14	73	.298	.437	4-0-1	.000	-1	105	-2		-0.2
	NY N	2	9	.182	22	14	1	0	106	117	68	9	0	54	41	4.92	75	.285	.368	31-0-1	.161	-1	98	-15		-1.6
	Year	2	10	.167	26	17	1	0	120	134	77	10	1	67	43	4.95	75	.286	.377	35-0-2	.143	-2	100	-17		-1.8
	NY N	2	6	.667	31	8	2-1	1	104	95	50	8	4	46	40	2.94	114	.244	.326	29-0-2	.103	-2	100	1		-0.2
Total	8	46	41	.529	197	102	31-9	6	853	861	423	53	6	355	340	3.74	104	.263	.336	271-0-20	.170	-6	102	10		0.2

McGEEHAN, CONNY Cornelius Bernard B8.25.1882 Drifton PA D7.4.1907 Hazleton PA TR d7.15 b-Dan Col Holy Cross

YEAR	TM LG	W	L	PCT	G	GS	CG-SHO	SV-BS	IP	H	R	HR	HB	BB-IB	SO	ERA	AERA	OAV	OOB	AB-HR-SH	AVG	PB	SUP	APR	DL	PW
1903	Phi A	1	0	1.000	3	0	0	0	10	9	5	0	1	1	4	4.50	68	.237	.275	6	.000	-1*		-1		-0.1

McGEHEE, KEVIN George Kevin B1.18.1969 Alexandria LA BR/TR/6-0/190 [SFN90 8/230] d8.23 Col Louisiana Tech

YEAR	TM LG	W	L	PCT	G	GS	CG-SHO	SV-BS	IP	H	R	HR	HB	BB-IB	SO	ERA	AERA	OAV	OOB	AB-HR-SH	AVG	PB	SUP	APR	DL	PW
1993	Bal A	0	0	—	5	0	0	0	16.2	18	11	5	2	7-2	7	5.94	76	.281	.365	0	—	0		-2		-0.1

McGEHEE, PAT Patrick Henry B7.2.1888 Meadville MS D12.30.1946 Paducah KY BL/TR/6-2.5/180 d8.23 Col Tulane

YEAR	TM LG	W	L	PCT	G	GS	CG-SHO	SV-BS	IP	H	R	HR	HB	BB-IB	SO	ERA	AERA	OAV	OOB	AB-HR-SH	AVG	PB	SUP	APR	DL	PW
1912	Det A	0	0	—	1	0	0	0	1	1	0	0	0				—	1.000	1.000	0	—	0	91	0		0.0

McGILBERRY, RANDY Randall Kent B10.29.1953 Mobile AL BB/TR/6-1/195* [KCA75 14/321] d9.6 Col Louisiana Tech

YEAR	TM LG	W	L	PCT	G	GS	CG-SHO	SV-BS	IP	H	R	HR	HB	BB-IB	SO	ERA	AERA	OAV	OOB	AB-HR-SH	AVG	PB	SUP	APR	DL	PW
1977	KC A	0	1	.000	3	0	0	0-0	7	7	4	1	0	1-0	1	5.14	78	.280	.308	0	—	0		-1		-0.1
1978	KC A	0	1	.000	18	0	0	0-1	25.2	27	16	2	0	18-1	12	4.21	91	.276	.388	0	—	0		-2		-0.1
Total	2	0	2	.000	21	0	0	0-1	32.2	34	20	3	0	19-1	13	4.41	88	.276	.373	0	—	0		-3		-0.2

YEAR	TM LG	W	L	PCT	G	GS	CG-SHO	SV-BS	IP	H	R	HR	HB	BB-IB	SO	ERA	AERA	OAV	OOB	AB-HR-SH	AVG	PB	SUP	APR	DL	PW
McGILL, BILL	William Jacob "Parson" B6.29.1880 Galva KS D8.7.1959 Alva OK BR/TR/6-2/185 d9.16 Col Friends																										
1907	StL A	1	0	1.000	2	2	1	0	18.1	22	8	0	0	2	4	3.44	73	.301	.320	9	.000	-1	121	-1		-0.2
McGILL, WILLIE	William Vaness "Kid" B11.10.1873 Atlanta GA D8.29.1944 Indianapolis IN TL/5-6.5/170 d5.8																										
1890	Cle P	11	9	.550	24	20	19	0	183.2	222	146	5	12	96	82	4.12	97	.286	.373	68	.147	2	114	1		0.4
1891	Cin AA	2	5	.286	8	8	6	0	65	69	56	1	3	37	19	4.98	82	.263	.361	20	.100	0	72	-3		-0.3
	StL AA	18	9	.667	33	29	20-1	1	233	207	140	10	12	126	146	2.70	155	.230	.332	83	.157	-0	109	29		2.5
	Year	20	14	.588	41	37	26-1	1	298	276	196	11	15	163	165	3.20	130	.238	.339	103	.146	-0	101	24		2.2
1892	Cin N	1	1	.500	3	3	1	0	17	18	14	0	0	5	7	5.29	62	.261	.311	7	.286	0	129	-3		-0.3
1893	Chi N	17	18	.486	39	34	26-1	0	302.2	311	206	6	14	181	91	4.61	101	.258	.361	124	.234	2*	103	8		0.7
1894	Chi N	7	19	.269	27	23	22	0	208	272	195	2	10	117	58	5.84	97	.312	.400	82-0-1	.244	0	81	-4		-0.4
1895	Phi N	10	8	.556	20	20	13	0	146	177	122	2	4	81	70	5.55	86	.295	.382	63-0-1	.222	-0	104	-12		-0.7
1896	Phi N	5	4	.556	12	11	7	0	79.2	87	62	0	4	53	29	5.31	81	.275	.386	29-0-2	.207	-0	141	-8		-0.7
Total	7	71	73	.493	166	148	114-2	1	1235	1363	941	26	59	696	502	4.57	100	.273	.368	476-0-4	.202	4	102	8		0.8
McGILLEN, JOHN	John Joseph B8.6.1917 Eddystone PA D8.11.1987 Upland PA BL/TL/6-1/175 d4.20																										
1944	Phi A	0	0	—	2	0	0	0	1	1	2	0	0	2	0	18.00	19	.333	.600	0	—	0		-1		-0.1
McGINLEY, JIM	James William B10.2.1878 Groveland MA D9.20.1961 Haverhill MA BR/TR/5-9.5/165 d9.22																										
1904	StL N	2	1	.667	3	3	3	0	27	28	8	0	3	6	6	2.00	135	.267	.325	11	.091	-1	94	2		0.1
1905	StL N	0	1	.000	1	1	0	0	3	5	6	1	0	2	0	15.00	20	.333	.412	1	1.000	0	145	-4		-0.5
Total	2	2	2	.500	4	4	3	0	30	33	14	1	3	8	6	3.30	83	.275	.336	12	.167	-0	108	-2		-0.4
McGINN, DAN	Daniel Michael B11.29.1943 Omaha NE BL/TL/6-0/190(185-202) d9.3 Col Notre Dame																										
1968	Cin N	0	1	.000	14	0	0	0	12	13	7	1	1	11-2	16	5.25	60	.271	.417	2	.000	-0		-2		-0.2
1969	Mon N	7	10	.412	74	1	0	6-3	132.1	123	67	8	5	65-8	112	3.94	94	.245	.337	29-1-0	.172	1	48	-4		-0.3
1970	Mon N	7	10	.412	52	19	3-2	0-0	130.2	154	88	13	7	78-4	83	5.44	76	.296	.394	35-0-3	.114	-2	82	-18		-2.1
1971	Mon N	1	4	.200	28	6	1	0-0	71	74	51	7	1	42-4	40	5.96	60	.274	.374	17	.235	0	91	-18		-1.1
1972	Chi N	0	5	.000	42	2	0	4-2	62.2	78	46	5	4	29-6	42	5.89	65	.301	.379	8	.250	1*	12	-13		-1.1
Total	5	15	30	.333	210	28	4-2	10-5	408.2	442	259	34	18	225-24	293	5.11	75	.276	.371	91-1-3	.165	-0	81	-55		-4.8
McGINNIS, JUMBO	George Washington B2.22.1854 Alton MO D5.18.1934 St.Louis MO 5-10/197 d5.2																										
1882	StL AA	25	18	.581	45	45	43-3	0	388.1	391	241	2		53	134	2.60	108	.245	.269	203	.217	1*	112	10		0.8
1883	StL AA	28	16	.636	45	45	41-6	0	382.2	325	174	3		69	128	2.33	150	.215	.249	180	.200	-6	89	49		4.2
1884	StL AA	24	16	.600	40	40	39-5	0	354.1	331	196	4	12	35	141	2.84	115	.233	.258	146	.233	3	108	19		1.9
1885	StL AA	6	6	.500	13	13	12-3	0	112	98	65	1	6	19	41	3.38	97	.225	.267	50-1	.220	0	99	0		0.0
1886	StL AA	5	5	.500	10	10	10-1	0	87.2	107	75	2	7	27	30	3.80	91	.288	.347	37	.189	-1	133	-7		-0.6
	Bal AA	11	13	.458	26	25	24	0	209.1	235	141	6	14	48	70	3.48	98	.280	.329	85-1	.188	-1	70	-5		-0.5
	Year	16	18	.471	36	35	34-1	0	297	342	216	8	21	75	100	3.58	96	.282	.335	122-1	.189	-2	88	-11		-1.1
1887	Cin AA	3	5	.375	8	8	8	0	69.1	85	66	3	8	43	18	5.45	80	.296	.402	31	.194	-0	126	-8		-0.7
Total	6	102	79	.564	187	186	177-18	0	1603.2	1572	958	21	47	294	562	2.95	112	.243	.281	732-2	.210	-5	101	58		5.1
McGINNIS, GUS	Gus B8.1870 Barnesville OH D4.20.1904 Barnesville OH TL/5-11/168 d4.27																										
1893	Chi N	2	5	.286	13	5	3	0	67.1	85	67	2	3	31	13	5.35	87	.299	.374	25	.240	2	106	-8		-0.5
	Phi N	1	3	.250	5	4	4-1	0	37.1	39	20	0	2	17	12	4.34	106	.262	.345	15	.200	-1	72	3		0.2
	Year	3	8	.273	18	9	7-1	0	104.2	124	87	2	5	48	25	4.99	93	.286	.364	40	.225	0	91	-3		-0.3
McGINNITY, JOE	Joseph Jerome "Iron Man" (b Joseph Jerome McGinty) B3.19.1871 Rock Island IL D11.14.1929 Brooklyn NY BR/TR/5-11/206 d4.18 C1 HF1946																										
1899	Bal N	28	16	.636	48	41	38-4	2	366.1	358	164	3	26	93	74	2.68	148	.256	.314	145-0-5	.193	-5*	102	48		4.5
1900	†Bro N	28	8	.778	44	37	32-1	0	343	350	179	6	40	113	93	2.94	131	.264	.340	145-0-5	.193	-4	91	17		1.4
1901	Bal A	26	20	.565	48	43	39-1	1	382	412	219	7	21	96	75	3.56	109	.272	.324	148-0-8	.209	-4	104	10		1.3
1902	Bal A	13	10	.565	25	23	19	0	198.2	219	100	3	8	46	39	3.44	110	.280	.327	87-0-4	.287	-4*	92	13		0.9
	NY N	8	8	.500	19	16	16-1	0	153	122	52	1	9	32	67	2.06	136	.219	.273	66-0-8	.121	-4*	92	13		0.9
1903	NY N	31	20	.608	55	48	44-3	2	434	391	162	4	19	109	171	2.43	138	.236	.291	165-0-13	.206	-2	96	42		4.0
1904	NY N	35	8	.814	51	44	38-9	5	408	307	103	8	13	86	144	1.61	169	.206	.256	142-0-12	.176	-1	113	50		5.4
1905	†NY N	21	15	.583	46	38	26-2	3	320.1	289	131	6	14	71	125	2.87	102	.240	.290	120-0-1	.233	6	115	6		1.3
1906	NY N	27	12	.692	45	37	32-3	2	339.2	316	127	1	7	71	105	2.25	116	.246	.289	115-0-12	.130	-3	114	10		-1.8
1907	NY N	18	18	.500	47	34	23-3	4	310.1	320	126	6	15	58	120	3.16	78	.266	.308	103-0-8	.175	-0	121	-15		-0.2
1908	NY N	11	7	.611	37	20	7-5	5	186	192	73	8	7	37	55	2.27	106	.267	.310	61-0-5	.180	-0	120	-1		-0.2
Total	10	246	142	.634	465	381	314-32	24	3441.1	3276	1436	52	179	812	1068	2.66	120	.249	.302	1297-0-81	.194	-14	105	203		18.9
McGLINCHY, KEVIN	Kevin Michael B6.28.1977 Malden MA BR/TR/6-5/220* [AtlN95 5/141] d4.5 Col Central Florida CC [DL 2001 Atl N 190, 2002 TB A 183]																										
1999	†Atl N	7	3	.700	64	0	0	0-2	70.1	66	25	6	1	30-7	67	2.82	159	.255	.330	2	.000	-0		13		1.5
2000	Atl N	0	0	—	10	0	0	0-0	8.1	11	4	1	0	6-1	9	2.16	209	.314	.415	0	—	0		1	132	0.1
Total	2	7	3	.700	74	0	0	0-2	78.2	77	29	7	1	36-8	76	2.75	163	.262	.340	2	.000	-0		14	505	1.6
McGLOTHEN, LYNN	Lynn Everett B3.27.1950 Monroe LA D8.14.1984 Dubach LA BL/TR/6-2/195(182-215) [BosA68 3/60] d6.25																										
1972	Bos A	8	7	.533	22	22	4-1	0-0	145	135	66	9	7	59-1	112	3.41	95	.247	.326	53-0-3	.189	1	106	-4		-0.1
1973	Bos A	1	2	.333	14	3	0	0-1	23	30	23	6	1	8-0	16	8.22	49	.386	.429	0	—	0	133	-10		-1.1
1974	StL N★	16	12	.571	31	31	8-3	0-0	237.1	212	80	12	4	89-14	142	2.69	134	.241	.312	83-0-3	.181	-1	92	24		2.8
1975	StL N	15	13	.536	35	34	9-2	0-0	239	231	110	21	4	97-11	146	3.92	97	.254	.326	80-0-10	.087	-5	96	3		-0.4
1976	StL N	13	15	.464	33	32	10-4	0-0	205	209	96	10	4	68-6	106	3.91	92	.268	.328	71-0-7	.211	2	92	-4		-0.2
1977	SF N	2	9	.182	21	15	2	0-0	80	94	62	9	1	52-4	42	5.62	70	.299	.397	19-0-1	.105	-1	83	-16	21	-2.1
1978	SF N	0	0	—	5	1	0	0-0	12.2	15	9	0	0	4-0	9	4.97	70	.313	.358	3	.000	-0	181	-3		-0.2
	Chi N	5	3	.625	49	1	0	0-5	80	77	33	7	0	39-5	60	3.04	133	.257	.341	13	.231	1	67	7		0.4
	Year	5	3	.625	54	2	0	0-5	92.2	92	42	7	0	43-5	69	3.30	120	.264	.344	16	.188	1	113	4		0.4
1979	Chi N	13	14	.481	42	29	6-1	2-0	212	236	103	27	3	55-8	147	4.12	101	.283	.327	71-0-4	.225	1	93	3		0.4
1980	Chi N	12	14	.462	39	27	2-2	0-0	182.1	211	105	24	4	64-7	119	4.79	83	.293	.348	51-0-8	.196	2*	90	-13		-1.6
1981	Chi N	1	4	.200	20	6	0	0-0	54.2	71	32	1	4	28-4	26	4.77	78	.317	.394	12	.083	-1	71	-5		-0.5
	Chi A	0	0	—	11	0	0	0-0	21.2	14	10	1	1	7-3	12	4.15	87	.189	.268	0	—	0		-1		-0.1
1982	NY A	0	0	—	4	0	0	0-0	5	9	6	1	0	2-0	2	10.80	37	.375	.423	0	—	0		-4	21	-0.2
Total	11	86	93	.480	318	201	41-13	2-6	1497.2	1553	735	127	25	572-63	939	3.98	95	.270	.336	456-0-36	.173	-0	93	-23	42	-3.0
McGLOTHIN, PAT	Ezra Mac B10.20.1920 Coalfield TN BL/TR/6-3.5/180* d4.25 Col Tennessee																										
1949	Bro N	1	1	.500	7	0	0	0	15.2	13	8	2	0	5	11	4.60	89	.224	.286		.000	-0		-1		-0.1
1950	Bro N	0	0	—	1	0	0	0	2	5	3	0	1	2	2	13.50	30	.455	.500	0	—	0		-2		-0.1
Total	2	1	1	.500	8	0	0	0	17.2	18	11	2	0	6	13	5.60	73	.261	.320	3	.000	-0		-3		-0.2
McGLOTHLIN, JIM	James Milton "Red" B10.6.1943 Los Angeles CA D12.23.1975 Union KY BR/TR/6-1/185* d9.20																										
1965	Cal A	0	3	.000	3	3	1	0	18	18	9	1	0	7-1	9	3.50	87	.261	.329	6	.000	-1	34	-1		-0.2
1966	Cal A	3	1	.750	19	11	0	0	67.2	79	37	9	1	19-0	41	4.52	74	.292	.338	17-0-1	.059	-0	134	-9		-0.5
1967	Cal A★	12	8	.600	32	29	9-6	0	197.1	163	74	13	4	56-2	137	2.96	106	.226	.284	57-0-7	.140	-0	105	5		0.5
1968	Cal A	10	15	.400	40	32	8	3	208.1	187	87	19	8	60-5	135	3.54	82	.244	.304	63-0-6	.111	-1	99	-13		-1.6
1969	Cal A	8	16	.333	37	35	4-1	0-0	201	188	86	19	5	58-1	96	3.18	110	.249	.306	58-0-5	.121	-1	72	5		0.6
1970	†Cin N	14	10	.583	34	34	5-3	0-0	210.2	192	91	19	9	86-8	91	3.59	113	.245	.319	66-1-4	.171	-1	95	13		1.7
1971	Cin N	8	12	.400	30	26	6	0-0	170.2	151	65	15	4	47-4	93	3.22	105	.243	.300	51-1-3	.137	0	87	4		0.5
1972	†Cin N	9	8	.529	31	21	3-1	0-1	145	165	71	15	0	49-6	69	3.91	83	.283	.341	46-1-1	.174	3	142	-12		-2.0
1973	Cin N	3	3	.500	24	9	0	0-0	63.1	91	52	13	0	23-3	18	6.68	52	.340	.390	16-0-1	.125	0	45	-24		-2.2
	Chi A	0	0	—	5	1	0	0-0	18.1	13	8	2	0	13-0	14	3.93	101	.203	.333	0	—	0		23	7	0.0
Total	9	67	77	.465	256	201	36-11	3-1	1300.1	1247	580	125	25	418-30	709	3.61	94	.255	.315	380-3-28	.126	-1	99	-32		-3.3
McGLYNN, STONEY	Ulysses Simpson Grant B5.26.1872 Lancaster PA D8.26.1941 Manitowoc WI BR/TR/5-11/185 d9.20																										
1906	StL N	2	2	.500	5	6	6	0	48	43	16	0	1	15	25	2.44	108	.249	.312	17	.059	-1	97	1		0.1
1907	StL N	14	25	.359	45	39	33-3	1	352.1	329	159	6	4	112	109	2.91	86	.251	.312	125-0-6	.200	3*	85	-12		-1.1
1908	StL N	1	6	.143	16	6	4	1	75.2	76	40	0	2	17	23	3.45	68	.256	.301	26-0-1	.077	0	75	-8		-0.8
Total	3	17	33	.340	67	51	43-3	2	476	448	215	6	7	144	157	2.95	85	.252	.310	168-0-7	.167	0	86	-19		-1.8

YEAR	TM LG	W	L	PCT	G	GS	CG-SHO	SV-BS	IP	H	R	HR	HB	BB-IB	SO	ERA	AERA	OAV	OOB	AB-HR-SH	AVG	PB	SUP	APR	DL	PW

McGOWAN, DUSTIN Dustin Michael B3.24.1982 Savannah GA BR/TR/6-3/220 d7.30

| 2005 | Tor A | 1 | 3 | .250 | 13 | 7 | 0 | 0 | 45.1 | 49 | 34 | 7 | 7 | 17-0 | 34 | 6.35 | 73 | .277 | .356 | 0 | — | 0 | 90 | -8 | | -0.6 |

McGOWAN, MICKEY Tullis Earl B11.26.1921 Dothan AL D3.8.2003 Waycross GA BL/TL/6-2/200 d4.22

| 1948 | NY N | 0 | 0 | — | 3 | 0 | 0 | 0 | 3.2 | 3 | 3 | 1 | 0 | 4 | 2 | 7.36 | 53 | .231 | .412 | 1 | .000 | -0 | | -1 | | -0.1 |

McGRANER, HOWARD Howard "Muck" B9.11.1889 Hamley Run OH D10.22.1952 Zaleski OH BL/TL/5-7/155 d9.12

| 1912 | Cin N | 1 | 0 | 1.000 | 4 | 0 | 0 | 0 | 19 | 22 | 17 | 2 | 1 | 7 | 5 | 7.11 | 47 | .293 | .361 | 8 | .250 | 1 | | -7 | | -0.2 |

McGRAW, TUG Frank Edwin B8.30.1944 Martinez CA D1.5.2004 Brentwood TN BR/TL/6-0/185(170-186) d4.18 Col Solano (CA) CC

1965	NY N	2	7	.222	37	9	2	1	97.2	88	47	8	3	48-2	57	3.32	106	.249	.341	23	.130	-1*	66	0		-0.1
1966	NY N	2	9	.182	15	12	1	0	62.1	72	38	11	0	25-2	34	5.34	68	.294	.355	17-0-2	.235	1	75	-10	24	-1.5
1967	NY N	0	3	.000	4	4	0	0	17.1	13	16	3	0	13-2	18	7.79	44	.206	.338	4-0-1	.250	0	84	-8		-1.1
1969	†NY N	9	3	.750	42	4	1	12-0	100.1	89	31	6	0	47-7	92	2.24	163	.243	.329	24	.167	0*	163	14		2.1
1970	NY N	4	6	.400	57	0	0	10-2	90.2	77	40	6	1	49-17	81	3.28	124	.231	.328	13	.308	1		7		1.0
1971	NY N	11	4	.733	51	1	0	8-2	111	73	22	4	3	41-11	109	1.70	202	.189	.271	18-1-2	.222	2	52	22		3.6
1972	NY N★	8	6	.571	54	0	0	27-5	106	71	26	3	3	40-11	92	1.70	199	.197	.279	20-0-2	.100	-0		19		3.7
1973	†NY N	5	6	.455	60	2	0	25-7	118.2	106	53	11	3	55-9	81	3.87	94	.243	.329	24-0-3	.167	1	121	-1		-0.1
1974	NY N	6	11	.353	41	4	1-1	3-6	88.2	96	43	12	0	32-6	54	4.16	87	.279	.338	14-0-1	.071	-0	85	-4	25	-0.7
1975	Phi N☆	9	6	.600	56	0	0	14-3	102.2	84	38	6	3	36-6	55	2.98	126	.226	.299	13-0-1	.154	-0	9	18		1.5
1976	†Phi N	7	6	.538	58	0	0	11-6	97.1	81	34	4	0	42-10	76	2.50	143	.226	.304	7	.143	-0	10			1.5
1977	†Phi N	7	3	.700	45	0	0	9-3	79	62	25	6	1	24-5	58	2.62	154	.221	.282	10	.400	2	12	59		1.9
1978	†Phi N	8	7	.533	55	1	0	9-2	89.2	82	39	6	0	23-7	63	3.21	112	.245	.292	4-0-2	.000	-0	0	2		0.4
1979	Phi N	4	3	.571	65	1	0	16-2	83.2	83	56	9	0	29-7	57	5.16	75	.259	.321	6-0-1	.167	-0	137	-13		-1.6
1980	†Phi N	5	4	.556	57	0	0	20-5	92.1	62	16	3	2	23-9	75	1.46	261	.194	.250	8-0-3	.250	0	23	21		3.3
1981	†Phi N	2	4	.333	34	0	0	10-1	44	35	13	2	0	14-3	26	2.66	138	.219	.278	1-0-1	.000	0	5			0.9
1982	Phi N	3	3	.500	34	0	0	5-6	39.2	50	19	3	1	12-6	25	4.31	86	.305	.356	2	.000	-0	-2	77		-0.3
1983	Phi N	2	1	.667	34	1	0	0-0	55.2	58	24	4	0	19-4	30	3.56	101	.271	.326	3-0-2	.333	0	123	1		0.1
1984	Phi N	2	0	1.000	25	0	0	0-0	38	36	17	1	0	10-4	26	3.79	97	.245	.289	3	.333	0*	0	1	55	0.0
Total	19	96	92	.511	824	39	5-1	180-50	1514.2	1318	597	108	22	582-128	1109	3.14	117	.237	.309	214-1-21	.182	5	85	86	279	14.6

McGRAW, JOHN John (b Roy Elmer Hoar) B12.8.1890 Intercourse PA D4.27.1967 Torrance CA BR/TR/5-9/160 d7.29 Col Carnegie Mellon

| 1914 | Bro F | 0 | 0 | — | 1 | 0 | 0 | 0 | 2 | 2 | 0 | 0 | 1 | 0-0 | 0 | 0.00 | — | .000 | .143 | 0 | — | 0 | 1 | | | 0.0 |

McGRAW, BOB Robert Emmett B4.10.1895 LaVeta CO D6.2.1978 Boise ID BR/TR/6-2/160 d9.25 Mil 1918-19 Col Georgetown

1917	NY A	0	1	.000	2	2	1	0	11	9	5	0	0	3	3	0.82	328	.257	.316	3	.000	-0	67	1		0.0
1918	NY A	0	1	.000	1	1	0	0	0	4	0	0	4	0	4	0	∞	—	1.000	0	—	-0	107	-4		-0.3
1919	NY A	1	0	1.000	6	0	0	0	16.1	11	6	1	1	10	3	3.31	97	.216	.355	3	.000	-0	0			0.0
	Bos A	0	2	.000	10	1	0	0	26.2	33	23	3	2	17	6	6.75	45	.347	.461	10-0-1	.100	-1	182	-11		-0.9
	Year	1	2	.333	16	1	0	0	43	44	29	4	4	27	9	5.44	57	.301	.424	13-0-1	.077	-1	178	-10		-0.9
1920	NY A	0	0	—	15	0	0	0	27	24	18	1	0	20	11	4.67	82	.240	.372	7	.000	-1	-3			-0.3
1925	Bro N	2	0	.000	2	2	2	0	19.2	14	9	0	0	13	3	3.20	130	.222	.355	6-0-1	.167	-0	61	2		0.1
1926	Bro N	9	13	.409	33	21	10	1	174.1	197	104	12	2	67	49	4.59	83	.293	.358	55-0-6	.145	-2	95	-13		-1.7
1927	Bro N	0	1	.000	1	1	0	0	4	5	5	1	0	2	2	9.00	44	.313	.389	1	.000	*	64	-2		-0.4
	StL N	4	5	.444	18	12	4-1	1	94	121	65	3	0	30	37	5.07	78	.323	.373	33-1-4	.182	1	120	-12		-0.9
	Year	4	6	.400	19	13	4-1	1	98	126	70	4	0	32	39	5.23	75	.322	.374	34-1-4	.176	1	116	-14		-1.3
1928	Phi N	7	8	.467	39	3	0	1	120	148	86	7	2	56	28	5.18	83	.317	.392	36-0-3	.111	-2	106	-14		-1.8
1929	Phi N	5	5	.500	41	4	0	4	86.1	113	68	6	2	43	22	5.73	91	.324	.401	20-0-1	.200	0	126	-7		-0.7
Total	9	26	38	.406	168	47	17-1	6	579.1	675	393	31	11	265	164	5.00	81	.303	.380	174-1-16	.138	-6	101	-63		-6.9

McGRAW, TOM Thomas Virgil B12.8.1967 Portland OR BL/TL/6-2/195 [MilA90 6/169] d5.7 Col Washington St.

| 1997 | StL N | 0 | 0 | — | 2 | 0 | 0 | 0-0 | 1.2 | 2 | 1 | 0 | 0 | 1-0 | 0 | 0.00 | — | .333 | .375 | 0 | — | 0 | 1 | | | 0.0 |

McGREGOR, SCOTT Scott Houston B1.18.1954 Inglewood CA BB/TL/6-1/190* [NYA72 1/14] d9.19

1976	Bal A	0	1	.000	3	2	0	0-0	14.2	17	7	0	0	5-0	6	3.68	90	.293	.349	0	—	0	67	-1		0.0
1977	Bal A	3	5	.375	29	5	1	4-0	114	119	57	7	8	30-2	55	4.42	87	.275	.328	0	—	0	103	-6		-0.5
1978	Bal A	15	13	.536	35	32	13-4	1-1	233	217	98	19	1	47-3	94	3.32	106	.248	.286	0	—	0	91	5		0.6
1979	†Bal A	13	6	.684	27	23	7-2	0-0	174.2	165	79	19	2	23-0	81	3.35	121	.248	.273	0	—	0	109	15		1.5
1980	Bal A	20	8	.714	36	36	12-4	0-0	252	254	101	16	2	58-3	119	3.32	120	.265	.306	0	—	0*	121	18		1.8
1981	Bal A☆	13	5	.722	24	22	8-3	0-0	160	167	63	13	0	40-5	82	3.26	112	.273	.315	0	—	0	108	8		0.9
1982	Bal A	14	12	.538	37	37	7-1	0-0	226.1	238	126	31	1	52-6	84	4.61	88	.267	.306	0	—	0	106	-15		-1.6
1983	†Bal A	18	7	.720	36	36	12-2	0-0	260	271	101	24	1	45-2	86	3.18	126	.269	.298	0	—	0	123	25		2.2
1984	Bal A	15	12	.556	30	30	10-3	0-0	196.1	216	93	18	5	54-2	67	3.94	99	.280	.329	0	—	0	98	1	33	0.2
1985	Bal A	14	14	.500	35	34	8-1	0-0	204	226	118	34	1	65-2	86	4.81	85	.283	.334	0	—	0	110	-16		-1.9
1986	Bal A	11	15	.423	34	33	4-2	0-0	203	216	110	35	3	57-0	95	4.52	92	.270	.319	0	—	0	102	-7		-0.8
1987	Bal A	2	7	.222	26	15	1-1	0-0	85.1	112	69	15	3	35-1	39	6.64	67	.326	.388	0	—	0	90	-21	31	-1.7
1988	Bal A	0	3	.000	4	4	0	0-0	17.1	27	18	3	0	7-0	10	8.83	45	.370	.415	0	—	0	70	-9		-1.2
Total	13	138	108	.561	356	309	83-23	5-1	2140.2	2245	1031	235	26	518-26	904	3.99	99	.271	.313	0	—	0	107	-3	64	-0.5

McGREW, SLIM Walter Howard B8.5.1899 Yoakum TX D8.21.1967 Houston TX BR/TR/6-7.5/235 d4.18

1922	Was A	0	0	—	1	0	0	0	1.2	4	6	0	0	2	1	10.80	36	.500	.600	1	.000	-0	-3			-0.1
1923	Was A	0	0	—	3	0	0	0	5	11	9	0	0	3	1	12.60	30	.440	.500	1	.000	-0	-5			-0.3
1924	Was A	0	1	.000	6	2	0	0	23.1	25	15	1	0	12	8	5.01	80	.281	.366	1	.000	-1	84	-2		-0.3
Total	3	0	1	.000	10	2	0	0	30	40	30	1	0	17	10	6.60	60	.328	.410	10	.000	-2	84	-10		-0.7

McGUIRE d6.16

| 1894 | Cin N | 0 | 0 | — | 1 | 0 | 0 | 0 | 6 | 15 | 9 | 0 | 0 | 5 | 1 | 10.50 | 53 | .469 | .541 | 4 | .250 | -0 | -3 | | | -0.1 |

McGUIRE, TOM Thomas Patrick "Elmer" B2.1.1892 Chicago IL D12.7.1959 Phoenix AZ BR/TR/6-0/175 d4.18 Mil 1918

1914	Chi F	5	6	.455	24	12	7	0	131.1	143	76	7	4	57	37	3.70	72	.288	.366	70-1-0	.271	4*	131	-18		-0.8
1919	Chi A	0	0	—	1	0	0	0	3	5	4	0	3	3	0	9.00	35	.500	.615	1	.000	-0	-2			-0.1
Total	2	5	6	.455	25	12	7	0	134.1	148	80	7	4	60	37	3.82	70	.292	.371	71-1-0	.268	3	131	-20		-0.9

McGUNNIGLE, BILL William Henry "Gunner" B1.1.1855 Boston MA D3.9.1899 Brockton MA BR/TR/5-9/155 d5.2 M5 ▲

1879	Buf N	9.5	5	.643	14	13	13-2	0	120	113	66	0		16	62	2.63	99	.235	.260	171	.175	-2*	99	1		-0.1
1880	Buf N	2	3	.400	5	5	4-1	0	37	43	19	0		8	3	3.41	72	.279	.315	22	.182	-1*	48	-2		-0.3
Total	2	11	8	.579	19	18	17-3	0	157	156	85	0		24	65	2.81	92	.246	.274	193	.176	-3	86	-1		-0.4

McHALE, MARTY Martin Joseph B10.30.1886 Stoneham MA D5.7.1979 Hempstead NY BR/TR/5-11.5/174 d9.28 Col Maine

1910	Bos A	0	2	.000	2	2	1	0	13.2	15	8	0	1	6	14	4.61	55	.259	.338	6	.000	-1	105	-2		-0.4
1911	Bos A	0	0	—	4	1	0	0	9.1	19	12	1	1	3	6	9.64	34	.475	.523	3	.000	-0	198	-6		-0.3
1913	NY A	2	4	.333	7	6	4-1	0	48.2	49	21	1	1	10	11	2.96	101	.268	.309	15	.000	-1	54	0		-0.1
1914	NY A	6	16	.273	31	23	12	1	191	195	82	3	4	33	75	2.97	93	.268	.303	60-0-2	.200	2*	73	-6		-0.6
1915	NY A	3	7	.300	13	11	6	0	78.1	86	45	1	0	19	25	4.25	69	.277	.318	21-0-2	.143	1	102	-11		-1.2
1916	Bos A	0	1	.000	2	1	0	0	6	7	7	0	1	4	1	3.00	92	.280	.400	2	—	0	-2			-0.3
	Cle A	0	0	—	5	0	0	0	11.1	10	7	1	0	6	2	5.56	54	.270	.372	2	.000	-0	-2			-0.2
	Year	0	1	.000	7	1	0	0	17.1	17	14	1	1	10	3	4.67	63	.274	.384	2	.000	0	-4			-0.5
Total	6	11	30	.268	64	44	23-1	1	358.1	381	182	7	8	81	131	3.57	80	.276	.320	107-0-4	.140	-0	81	-29		-3.1

McILREE, VANCE Vance Elmer B10.14.1897 Riverside IA D5.6.1959 Kansas City MO BR/TR/6-0/160 d9.13 Col Iowa

| 1921 | Was A | 0 | 0 | — | 1 | 0 | 0 | 0 | 5 | 6 | 3 | 0 | 1 | 1 | 1 | 5.40 | 46 | .200 | .200 | 0 | — | -0 | 0 | | | 0.0 |

McILWAIN, STOVER Stover William "Smokey" (b William Stover McIlwain) B9.22.1939 Savannah GA D1.15.1966 Buffalo NY BR/TR/6-4/195* d9.25 Col Rollins

1957	Chi A	0	0	—	1	0	0	0	1	1	0	0	0	1-0	0	0.00	—	.500	.600	0	—	-0	0			0.0
1958	Chi A	0	0	—	1	1	0	0	4	4	1	1	0	0-0	4	2.25	162	.250	.250	1	.000	-0	272	1		0.0
Total	2	0	0	—	2	1	0	0	5	5	1	1	0	1-0	4	1.80	203	.300	.333	1	.000	-0	272	1		0.0

YEAR	TM LG	W	L	PCT	G	GS	CG-SHO	SV-BS	IP	H	R	HR	HB	BB-IB	SO	ERA	AERA	OAV	OOB	AB-HR-SH	AVG	PB	SUP	APR	DL	PW

McINTIRE, HARRY John Reid B1.11.1879 Dayton OH D1.9.1949 Daytona Beach FL BR/TR/5-11/180 d4.14

YEAR	TM LG	W	L	PCT	G	GS	CG-SHO	SV-BS	IP	H	R	HR	HB	BB-IB	SO	ERA	AERA	OAV	OOB	AB-HR-SH	AVG	PB	SUP	APR	DL	PW
1905	Bro N	8	25	.242	40	35	29-1	1	308.2	340	188	6	20	101	135	3.70	78	.285	.351	138-1-3	.246	7*	69	-31		-2.4
1906	Bro N	13	21	.382	39	31	25-4	3	276	254	123	2	14	101	121	2.97	85	.247	.316	103-0-1	.175	1*	74	-15		-1.8
1907	Bro N	7	15	.318	28	22	19-3	0	199.2	178	82	6	7	79	49	2.39	98	.248	.329	69-0-2	.217	5*	58	-3		0.2
1908	Bro N	11	20	.355	40	35	26-4	2	288	259	106	5	20	90	108	2.69	87	.252	.324	100-0-1	.200	2	89	-7		-0.7
1909	Bro N	7	17	.292	32	26	20-2	1	228	200	114	5	21	91	84	3.63	71	.246	.337	76-0-3	.171	1	84	-24		-2.3
1910	†Chi N	13	9	.591	28	19	10-2	0	176	152	70	5	10	50	65	3.07	94	.240	.305	66-1-3	.258	3*	106	-1		0.3
1911	Chi N	11	7	.611	25	17	9-1	0	149	147	81	5	4	33	56	4.11	81	.257	.302	53-0-3	.264	4*	128	-10		-0.6
1912	Chi N	1	2	.333	4	3	2	0	23.2	22	11	0	0	6	8	3.80	87	.256	.304	10-0-1	.300	1*	51	-1		0.1
1913	Cin N	0	1	.000	1	0	0	0	1	3	3	0	0	0	0	27.00	12	.600	.600	0	—	0		-2		-0.4
Total	9	71	117	.378	237	188	140-17	7	1650	1555	778	34	96	539	626	3.22	83	.256	.326	615-2-17	.218	24	84	-94		-7.6

McINTOSH, JOE Joseph Anthony B8.4.1951 Billings MT BB/TR/6-2/185* [SDN73 13/292] d4.5 Col Washington St. [DL 1976 Hou N 179]

YEAR	TM LG	W	L	PCT	G	GS	CG-SHO	SV-BS	IP	H	R	HR	HB	BB-IB	SO	ERA	AERA	OAV	OOB	AB-HR-SH	AVG	PB	SUP	APR	DL	PW
1974	SD N	0	4	.000	10	5	0	0-0	37.1	36	19	3	1	17-2	22	3.62	99	.250	.329	10-0-1	.000	-1	49	-1		-0.3
1975	SD N	8	15	.348	37	28	4-1	0-1	183	195	88	14	2	60-9	71	3.69	95	.273	.330	48-0-5	.188	2*	87	-3		-0.2
Total	2	8	19	.296	47	33	4-1	0-1	220.1	231	107	17	3	77-11	93	3.68	96	.270	.330	58-0-6	.155	1	81	-4	179	-0.5

McINTYRE, FRANK Frank W. B7.12.1859 Walled Lake MI D7.8.1887 Detroit MI d5.16

YEAR	TM LG	W	L	PCT	G	GS	CG-SHO	SV-BS	IP	H	R	HR	HB	BB-IB	SO	ERA	AERA	OAV	OOB	AB-HR-SH	AVG	PB	SUP	APR	DL	PW
1883	Det N	1	0	1.000	1	1	1	0	11	11	10	0		1	0	0.82	379	.234	.250	4	.000	-0	190	1		0.0
	Col AA	1	1	.500	2	2	2	0	19	20	19	0		7	6	5.21	59	.253	.314	7	.000	-0	178	-5		-0.4
Total	1	2	1	.667	3	3	3	0	30	31	29	0		8	6	3.60	86	.246	.291	11	.000	-1	181	-4		-0.4

McJAMES, DOC James McCutchen (b James Mc Cutchen James) B8.27.1874 Williamsburg Co. SC D9.23.1901 Charleston SC TR d9.24 Col South Carolina-Aiken

YEAR	TM LG	W	L	PCT	G	GS	CG-SHO	SV-BS	IP	H	R	HR	HB	BB-IB	SO	ERA	AERA	OAV	OOB	AB-HR-SH	AVG	PB	SUP	APR	DL	PW
1895	Was N	1	1	.500	2	2	2	0	17	17	11	0	0	16	9	1.59	302	.258	.402	7	.143	-1	96	4		0.3
1896	Was N	12	20	.375	37	33	29	1	280.1	310	208	2	6	135	103	4.27	103	.278	.359	111-0-3	.162	-9	93	5		-0.3
1897	Was N	15	23	.395	44	39	33-3	2	323.2	361	212	7	21	137	156	3.61	120	.280	.358	124	.169	-7	72	22		1.4
1898	Bal N	27	15	.643	45	42	40-2	0	374	327	148	5	12	113	178	2.36	152	.234	.296	149-0-1	.181	-4	114	49		4.3
1899	Bro N	18	15	.545	37	34	27-1	0	275.1	295	166	4	10	122	105	3.50	112	.274	.353	112	.170	-5	96	8		0.4
1901	Bro N	5	6	.455	13	12	6	0	91	104	71	1	7	40	42	4.75	71	.285	.367	34	.029	-4	125	-15		-1.9
Total	6	78	80	.494	178	162	137-6	4	1361.1	1414	816	19	56	563	593	3.43	116	.266	.343	537-0-4	.162	-30	95	73		4.2

McKAIN, ARCHIE Archie Richard "Happy" B5.12.1911 Delphos KS D5.21.1985 Salina KS BB/TL(BL 1941, 43)/5-10/175 d4.25

YEAR	TM LG	W	L	PCT	G	GS	CG-SHO	SV-BS	IP	H	R	HR	HB	BB-IB	SO	ERA	AERA	OAV	OOB	AB-HR-SH	AVG	PB	SUP	APR	DL	PW
1937	Bos A	8	8	.500	36	18	3	4	137	152	84	7	4	64	66	4.66	102	.273	.348	49-0-1	.265	3*	97	0		0.2
1938	Bos A	5	4	.556	37	5	1	6	99.1	119	60	6	2	44	27	4.52	109	.297	.369	31-0-2	.065	-2	96	3		0.2
1939	Det A	5	6	.455	32	11	4-1	4	129.2	120	66	6	0	54	49	3.68	133	.247	.322	41-2-0	.220	4	90	15		1.5
1940	†Det A	5	0	1.000	27	0	0	3	51	48	18	2	0	25	24	2.82	168	.247	.333	7-0-1	.143	0		10		1.1
1941	Det A	2	1	.667	15	0	0	0	43	58	24	3	0	11	14	5.02	90	.330	.369	11	.000	-1		-1		-0.4
	Stl A	0	1	.000	8	0	0	1	10	16	9	2	1	4	2	8.10	53	.364	.429	2	.000	-0		-4		-0.4
	Year	2	2	.500	23	0	0	1	53	74	33	5	1	15	16	5.60	80	.336	.381	13	.000	-1		-4		-0.4
1943	Stl A	1	1	.500	10	0	0	0	16	16	9	0	0	6	6	3.94	84	.242	.306	1	.000	-0		-1		-0.2
Total	6	26	21	.553	165	34	8-1	16	486.1	529	270	26	3	208	188	4.26	112	.275	.347	142-2-4	.176	3	96	22		2.4

McKAIN, HAL Harold Le Roy B7.10.1906 Logan IA D1.24.1970 Sacramento CA BL/TR/5-11/185 d9.22

YEAR	TM LG	W	L	PCT	G	GS	CG-SHO	SV-BS	IP	H	R	HR	HB	BB-IB	SO	ERA	AERA	OAV	OOB	AB-HR-SH	AVG	PB	SUP	APR	DL	PW
1927	Cle A	0	1	.000	2	1	0	0	11	18	6	0	0	4	5	4.09	103	.391	.440	4	.000	-1	40	0		0.0
1929	Chi A	6	9	.400	34	10	4-1	0	158	158	84	10	10	85	33	3.65	117	.275	.378	44-0-1	.227	2	71	8		1.1
1930	Chi A	6	4	.600	32	5	0	5	89	108	67	0	3	42	52	5.56	83	.299	.377	31-0-2	.419	7*	138	-9		-1.8
1931	Chi A	6	9	.400	27	8	3	0	112	134	82	10	3	57	39	5.71	75	.295	.377	42-0-1	.119	-1*	74	-17		-1.8
1932	Chi A	0	0	—	8	0	0	0	11.1	17	15	1	0	5	7	11.12	39	.340	.400	1	.000	-0		-8		-0.4
Total	5	18	23	.439	103	24	7-1	6	381.1	435	254	21	16	193	136	4.93	88	.293	.380	122-0-4	.230	8	85	-26		-1.3

McKAY, REEVE Reeve Stewart "Rip" B11.16.1881 Morgan TX D1.18.1946 Dallas TX TR/6-1.5/168 d10.2

YEAR	TM LG	W	L	PCT	G	GS	CG-SHO	SV-BS	IP	H	R	HR	HB	BB-IB	SO	ERA	AERA	OAV	OOB	AB-HR-SH	AVG	PB	SUP	APR	DL	PW
1915	Stl A	0	0	—	1	0	0	0	1	0	1	0	0	0	0	9.00	32	.500	.500	0	—	0		-1		0.0

McKEE, JIM James Marion B2.1.1947 Columbus OH D9.14.2002 Pickaway Co. OH BR/TR/6-7/215* [PitN69 4/80] d9.15 Col Otterbein

YEAR	TM LG	W	L	PCT	G	GS	CG-SHO	SV-BS	IP	H	R	HR	HB	BB-IB	SO	ERA	AERA	OAV	OOB	AB-HR-SH	AVG	PB	SUP	APR	DL	PW
1972	Pit N	1	0	1.000	2	0	0	0-0	5	2	0	0	0	4	0	0.00	—	.125	.176	0	—	0		2		0.4
1973	Pit N	0	1	.000	15	1	0	0-0	27	31	21	2	1	17-0	13	5.67	62	.287	.389	4	.000	-0	326	-7		-0.4
Total	2	1	1	.500	17	1	0	0-0	32	33	21	2	1	18-0	17	4.78	73	.266	.364	4	.000	-0	326	-5		0.0

McKEE, ROGERS Rogers Hornsby B9.16.1926 Shelby NC BL/TL/6-1/160 d8.18 Mil 1945-46

YEAR	TM LG	W	L	PCT	G	GS	CG-SHO	SV-BS	IP	H	R	HR	HB	BB-IB	SO	ERA	AERA	OAV	OOB	AB-HR-SH	AVG	PB	SUP	APR	DL	PW
1943	Phi N	1	0	1.000	4	1	1	0	13.1	9	9	0	0	5	1	6.08	56	.226	.293	5	.200	0	277	-3		-0.2
1944	Phi N	0	0	—	1	0	0	0	2	2	1	1	0	1	0	4.50	80	.250	.333	0	—	0		0		0.0
Total	2	1	0	1.000	5	1	1	0	15.1	11	10	1	0	6	1	5.87	58	.230	.299	5	.200	0	277	-3		-0.2

McKEITHAN, TIM Emmett James B11.2.1906 Lawndale NC D8.30.1969 Forest City NC BR/TR/6-2/182 d7.21 Col Duke

YEAR	TM LG	W	L	PCT	G	GS	CG-SHO	SV-BS	IP	H	R	HR	HB	BB-IB	SO	ERA	AERA	OAV	OOB	AB-HR-SH	AVG	PB	SUP	APR	DL	PW
1932	Phi A	0	1	.000	4	2	0	0	12.2	18	11	0	0	5	0	7.11	64	.340	.397	3	.000	0	85	-4		-0.2
1933	Phi A	1	0	1.000	3	1	0	0	9	10	4	0	0	4	3	4.00	107	.278	.350	3	.333	0	218	1		0.1
1934	Phi A	0	0	—	3	0	0	0	4	7	7	2	0	5	0	15.75	28	.389	.522	1	.000	-0		-5		-0.2
Total	3	1	1	.500	10	3	0	0	25.2	35	22	2	0	14	3	7.36	60	.327	.405	7	.143	0	129	-8		-0.2

McKELVY, RUSS Russell Errett B9.8.1854 Swissvale PA D10.19.1915 Omaha NE BR/TR d5.1 Col Allegheny ▲

YEAR	TM LG	W	L	PCT	G	GS	CG-SHO	SV-BS	IP	H	R	HR	HB	BB-IB	SO	ERA	AERA	OAV	OOB	AB-HR-SH	AVG	PB	SUP	APR	DL	PW
1878	Ind N	0	2	.000	4	1	1	0	25	38	23	1	5		3	2.16	94	.322	.339	253-2	.225	0*	107	-3		-0.1

McKENNA, KIT James William B2.10.1873 Lynchburg VA D3.31.1941 Lynchburg VA TR/5-9/180 d7.7

YEAR	TM LG	W	L	PCT	G	GS	CG-SHO	SV-BS	IP	H	R	HR	HB	BB-IB	SO	ERA	AERA	OAV	OOB	AB-HR-SH	AVG	PB	SUP	APR	DL	PW
1898	Bro N	2	6	.250	14	9	7	0	100.2	118	75	4	17	57	27	5.63	64	.290	.399	40-0-1	.225	0	66	-18		-1.1
1899	Bal N	2	3	.400	8	4	4	1	45	66	38	1	3	19	7	4.60	86	.340	.407	17	.059	-1*	118	-5		-0.5
Total	2	4	9	.308	22	13	11	1	145.2	184	113	5	20	76	34	5.31	70	.306	.402	57-0-1	.175	-0	83	-23		-1.6

McKENRY, LIMB Frank Gordon "Big Pete" B8.13.1888 Piney Flats TN D11.1.1956 Fresno CA BR/TR/6-4/205 d8.27

YEAR	TM LG	W	L	PCT	G	GS	CG-SHO	SV-BS	IP	H	R	HR	HB	BB-IB	SO	ERA	AERA	OAV	OOB	AB-HR-SH	AVG	PB	SUP	APR	DL	PW
1915	Cin N	5	5	.500	21	11	5	0	110.1	94	43	2	3	39	37	2.94	97	.238	.311	33-0-3	.152	0	83	0		0.1
1916	Cin N	1	1	.500	6	1	0	0	14.2	14	8	0	2	8	2	4.30	66	.259	.375	5	.400	2	115	-2		-0.2
Total	2	6	6	.500	27	12	5	0	125	108	51	2	5	47	39	3.10	91	.241	.319	38-0-3	.184	2	85	-2		-0.1

McKEON, JOEL Joel Jacob B2.25.1963 Covington KY BL/TL/6-0/185* [ChiA82 S1/16] d5.6 Col Miami-Dade North (FL) CC

YEAR	TM LG	W	L	PCT	G	GS	CG-SHO	SV-BS	IP	H	R	HR	HB	BB-IB	SO	ERA	AERA	OAV	OOB	AB-HR-SH	AVG	PB	SUP	APR	DL	PW
1986	Chi A	3	1	.750	30	0	0	1-2	33	18	10	2	0	17-2	18	2.45	177	.165	.273	0	—	0		7	75	0.7
1987	Chi A	1	2	.333	13	0	0	0-0	21	27	22	8	0	15-0	14	9.43	46	.318	.416	0	—	0		-10		-1.2
Total	2	4	3	.571	43	0	0	1-2	54	45	32	10	0	32-2	32	5.17	86	.232	.336	0	—	0		-3	75	-0.5

McKEON, LARRY Lawrence G. B3.25.1866 NY D7.18.1915 Indianapolis IN 5-10/168 d5.1

YEAR	TM LG	W	L	PCT	G	GS	CG-SHO	SV-BS	IP	H	R	HR	HB	BB-IB	SO	ERA	AERA	OAV	OOB	AB-HR-SH	AVG	PB	SUP	APR	DL	PW
1884	Ind AA	18	41	.305	61	60	59-2	0	512	488	350	20	18	94	308	3.50	94	.235	.275	250	.212	-3*	74	-14		-1.2
1885	Cin AA	20	13	.606	33	33	32-2	0	290	273	143	5	13	50	117	2.86	114	.241	.281	121	.165	-5	94	14		0.8
1886	Cin AA	8	8	.500	19	19	16	0	156	174	118	6	3	54	46	5.08	69	.276	.336	75	.253	1	132	-22		-1.6
	KC N	0	2	.000	3	3	3	0	21	44	32	0	0	8	3	10.71	35	.411	.452	9	.000	-1	54	-13		-0.9
Total	3	46	64	.418	116	115	110-4	0	979	979	643	31	34	206	474	3.71	90	.248	.291	455	.202	-9	90	-35		-2.9

McKNIGHT, TONY Tony Mark B6.29.1977 Texarkana AR BL/TR/6-5/205* [HouN95 1/22] d8.10

YEAR	TM LG	W	L	PCT	G	GS	CG-SHO	SV-BS	IP	H	R	HR	HB	BB-IB	SO	ERA	AERA	OAV	OOB	AB-HR-SH	AVG	PB	SUP	APR	DL	PW
2000	Hou N	4	1	.800	6	6	1	0-0	35	35	19	4	2	9-0	23	3.86	127	.245	.297	13-0-1	.000	-2	162	3		0.2
2001	Hou N	1	0	1.000	3	3	0	0-0	18	21	8	4	2	3-0	10	4.00	115	.288	.329	7	.000	-1	141	1		0.0
	Pit N	2	6	.250	12	12	0	0-0	69.1	88	44	15	3	21-4	36	5.19	86	.307	.358	17-0-4	.000	-1	81	-6		-0.7
	Year	3	6	.333	15	15	0	0-0	87.1	109	52	19	5	24-4	46	4.95	91	.303	.352	24-0-4	.000	-2	93	-4		-0.7
Total	2	7	7	.500	21	21	1	0-0	122.1	144	71	23	7	33-4	69	4.63	100	.286	.336	37-0-5	.000	-4	114	-2		-0.5

McLAIN, DENNY Dennis Dale B3.29.1944 Chicago IL BR/TR/6-1/185* d9.21

YEAR	TM LG	W	L	PCT	G	GS	CG-SHO	SV-BS	IP	H	R	HR	HB	BB-IB	SO	ERA	AERA	OAV	OOB	AB-HR-SH	AVG	PB	SUP	APR	DL	PW
1963	Det A	2	1	.667	3	3	2	0	21	20	12	2	0	16-0	22	4.29	87	.253	.375	5-1-1	.200	1	103	-2		-0.1
1964	Det A	4	5	.444	19	16	3	0	100	84	48	16	1	37-0	70	4.05	90	.225	.296	34-0-1	.135	-1*	126	-4		-0.6
1965	Det A	16	6	.727	32	29	13-4	1	220.1	174	73	25	2	62-1	192	2.61	133	.216	.273	74-0-4	.054	-4	117	20		1.6
1966	Det A★	20	14	.588	38	38	14-4	0	264.1	205	120	42	3	104-3	192	3.92	89	.214	.292	93-0-5	.183	2	110	-9		-1.0
1967	Det A	17	16	.515	37	37	10-3	0	235	209	110	35	3	73-3	161	3.79	86	.237	.295	85-0-16	.162	-3*	96	-14		-2.3
1968	†Det A★	31	6	.838	41	41	28-6	0	336	241	86	31	6	63-2	280	1.96	154	.200	.243	111-0-16	.162	0*	146	36		4.4

YEAR	TM LG	W	L	PCT	G	GS	CG-SHO	SV-BS	IP	H	R	HR	HB	BB-IB	SO	ERA	AERA	OAV	OOB	AB-HR-SH	AVG	PB	SUP	APR	DL	PW
1969	Det A★	24	9	.727	42	41	23-9	0-0	325	288	105	25	4	67-7	181	2.80	135	.237	.278	106-0-13	.160	-1	99	37		3.3
1970	Det A	3	5	.375	14	14	1	0-0	91.1	100	51	19	3	28-0	52	4.63	81	.273	.327	31-0-3	.065	-2	111	-8		-0.8
1971	Was A	10	22	.313	33	32	9-3	0-0	216.2	233	115	31	3	72-8	103	4.28	79	.281	.337	58-0-9	.103	-1	73	-22	23	-3.0
1972	Oak A	1	2	.333	5	5	0	0-0	22.1	32	17	4	0	8-0	8	6.04	47	.323	.374	4-0-2	.000	-0	118	-9		-1.1
	Atl N	3	5	.375	15	8	2	1-0	54	60	41	12	1	18-0	21	6.50	58	.279	.335	12-0-2	.167	-0	99	-14		-1.9
Total	10	131	91	.590	280	264	105-29	2-0	1886	1646	778	242	26	548-24	1282	3.39	101	.234	.290	616-1-64	.133	-9	109	11	23	-1.5

McLAUGHLIN, BARNEY Bernard B1857 , Ireland D2.13.1921 Lowell MA BR/TR d8.2 b-Frank ▲

| 1884 | KC U | 1 | 3 | .250 | 7 | 4 | 4 | 0 | 48.2 | 62 | 44 | 2 | 1 | 15 | 14 | 5.36 | 42 | .291 | .338 | 162 | .228 | -1* | 43 | -15 | | -0.9 |

McLAUGHLIN, BYRON Byron Scott B9.29.1955 Van Nuys CA BR/TR/6-1/185(175-192) d9.18

1977	Sea A	0	0		1	0	0	0-0	1.1	5	4	1	0	0-0	1	27.00	15	.625	.625	0	—	0		-3		-0.1
1978	Sea A	4	8	.333	20	17	4	0-0	107	97	58	15	6	39-0	87	4.37	88	.238	.312	0	—	0	78	-6		-0.7
1979	Sea A	7	7	.500	47	7	1	14-3	123.2	114	58	13	2	60-8	74	4.22	104	.251	.337	0	—	0	145	5		0.5
1980	Sea A	3	6	.333	45	4	0	2-3	90.2	124	74	15	2	50-14	41	6.85	61	.331	.410	0	—	0	38	-25		-2.4
1983	Cal A	2	4	.333	16	7	0	0-2	55.2	63	32	3	2	22-3	45	5.17	78	.286	.351	0	—	0	119	-6		-0.5
Total	5	16	25	.390	129	35	5	16-8	378.1	403	226	47	12	171-25	248	5.11	81	.275	.353	0	—	0	94	-35		-3.2

McLAUGHLIN, FRANK Francis Edward B6.19.1856 Lowell MA D4.5.1917 Lowell MA BR/TR/5-9/160 d8.9.1882 b-Barney ▲

1883	Pit AA	0	0		2	0	0	0	9	14	21	0		3	1	13.00	25	.333	.378	114-1	.219	0*		-10		-0.4
1884	KC U	0	0		2	1	0	0	10	15	12	0		2	3	5.40	41	.326	.354	123-1	.228	-0*	229	-4		-0.2
Total	2	0	0		4	1	0	0	19	29	33	0		5	4	9.00	30	.330	.366	237-2	.224	-0	229	-14		-0.6

McLAUGHLIN, JIM James Thomas B11.18.1860 Cleveland OH D11.16.1895 Cleveland OH BL/TL/?/157 d5.30

| 1884 | Bal AA | 1 | 2 | .333 | 3 | 2 | 2 | 0 | 22 | 27 | 22 | 2 | 0 | 11 | 3 | 3.68 | 94 | .300 | .376 | 22 | .227 | 0* | 104 | -2 | | -0.2 |

McLAUGHLIN, JOEY Joey Richard B7.11.1956 Tulsa OK BR/TR/6-2/205(192-215) [AtlN74 2/29] d6.11

1977	Atl N	0	0		3	2	0	0-0	6	10	10	3	0	3-0	0	15.00	30	.385	.448	1	.000	-0	150	-6		-0.3
1979	Atl N	5	3	.625	37	0	0	5-0	69	54	23	3	1	34-4	40	2.48	162	.224	.319	11	.182	0	44	11		1.3
1980	Tor A	6	9	.400	55	10	0	4-3	135.2	159	79	16	4	53-11	70	4.51	96	.302	.366	0	—	0	91	-4		-0.5
1981	Tor A	1	5	.167	40	0	0	10-1	60	55	24	2	0	21-2	38	2.85	139	.249	.313	0	—	0		6		0.8
1982	Tor A	8	6	.571	44	0	0	8-6	70	54	27	7	1	30-3	49	3.21	140	.212	.296	0	—	0		9		2.0
1983	Tor A	7	4	.636	50	0	0	9-11	64.2	63	33	11	0	37-7	47	4.45	98	.259	.353	0	—	0		0		0.0
1984	Tor A	0	0		6	0	0	0-0	10.2	12	6	0	0	7-1	3	2.53	163	.286	.380	0	—	0		1		0.1
	Tex A	2	1	.667	15	0	0	0-2	32.2	33	17	4	0	13-1	21	4.41	95	.260	.326	0	—	0		0		0.0
	Year	2	1	.667	21	0	0	0-2	43.1	45	23	4	0	20-2	24	3.95	106	.266	.340	0	—	0		0		0.1
Total	7	29	28	.509	250	12	0	36-23	448.2	440	219	46	6	198-29	268	3.85	110	.262	.339	12	.167	0	104	17		3.4

McLAUGHLIN, JUD Justin Theodore B3.24.1912 Brighton MA D9.27.1964 Cambridge MA BL/TL/5-11/155 d6.23 Col Boston College

1931	Bos A	0	0	—	9	0	0	0	12	23	16	1	0	8	3	12.00	36	.397	.470	0	—	0		-9		-0.4
1932	Bos A	0	0		1	0	0	0	3	5	5	0	0	4	1	15.00	30	.385	.529	1	.000	-0		-3		-0.1
1933	Bos A	0	0		6	0	0	0	8.2	14	7	1	0	5	1	6.23	70	.359	.432	0	—	0		-2		-0.1
Total	3	0	0	—	16	0	0	0	23.2	42	28	2	0	17	4	10.27	42	.382	.465	1	.000	-0		-14		-0.6

McLAUGHLIN, BO Michael Duane B10.23.1953 Oakland CA BR/TR/6-5/210(175-210) [HouN75 1/14] d7.20 Col Lipscomb [DL 1983 Cal A 25]

1976	Hou N	4	5	.444	17	11	4-2	1-0	79	71	31	6	4	17-1	32	2.85	113	.244	.288	19-0-2	.000	-1	67	3		0.1
1977	Hou N	4	7	.364	46	6	0	5-2	84.2	81	44	6	6	34-6	59	4.25	85	.260	.341	9-0-2	.000	-1	82	-6	19	-0.8
1978	Hou N	0	1	.000	12	1	0	2-0	23.1	30	17	2	2	16-2	10	5.01	67	.313	.417	3	.000	-0	108	-6		-0.4
1979	Hou N	1	2	.333	12	0	0	0-1	16.1	22	15	2	0	4-0	12	5.51	64	.314	.347	1	.000	-0		-6		-0.9
	Atl N	1	1	.500	37	1	0	0-0	49.2	63	33	2	2	16-6	45	4.89	82	.303	.357	5-0-1	.000	-1	44	-5		-0.4
	Year	2	3	.400	49	1	0	0-1	66	85	48	4	2	20-6	57	5.05	77	.306	.354	6-0-1	.000	-1	46	-11		-1.3
1981	Oak A	0	0	—	11	0	0	1-0	11.2	17	15	1	1	9-0	3	11.57	30	.333	.443	0	—	0		-10	99	-0.5
1982	Oak A	0	4	.000	21	2	1	0-0	48.1	51	31	3	1	27-1	27	4.84	82	.267	.359	0	—	0	69	-6		-0.4
Total	6	10	20	.333	156	21	5-2	9-3	313	335	186	22	14	123-16	188	4.49	80	.275	.346	37-0-5	.000	-3	70	-36	143	-3.3

McLAUGHLIN, PAT Patrick Elmer B8.17.1910 Taylor TX D11.1.1999 Houston TX BR/TR/6-2/175 d4.25 Col St. Edwards

1937	Det A	0	2	.000	10	3	0	0	32.2	39	23	3	0	16	8	6.34	74	.291	.367	10	.100	-1*	124	-5		-0.3
1940	Phi A	0	0	—	1	0	0	0	1.2	4	3	1	0	1	0	16.20	27	.444	.500	0	—	0		-2		-0.1
1945	Det A	0	0	—	1	0	0	0	1	2	2	0	0	0	0	9.00	39	.400	.400	0	—	0		-1		-0.1
Total	3	0	2	.000	12	3	0	0	35.1	45	28	4	0	17	8	6.88	67	.304	.376	10	.100	-1	124	-8		-0.5

McLAUGHLIN, WARREN Warren A. B1.22.1876 N.Plainfield NJ D10.22.1923 Plainfield NJ TL d7.7

1900	Phi N	0	0	—	1	0	0	0	6	4	4	0	0	6	1	4.50	80	.190	.370	2	.500	1		-1		0.0
1902	Pit N	3	0	1.000	3	3	3	0	26	27	13	0	1	9	13	2.77	99	.267	.333	11	.364	0	199	-1		0.0
1903	Phi N	0	3	.000	3	2	2	0	23	38	24	0	1	11	3	7.04	46	.376	.442	10	.200	0	41	-9		-0.9
Total	3	3	3	.500	7	5	5	0	55	69	41	0	2	26	17	4.75	64	.309	.386	23	.304	2	124	-11		-0.9

McLEAN, AL Albert Eldon "Elrod" B9.20.1912 Chicago IL D9.29.1990 Asheboro NC BR/TR/6-0/175 d7.16

| 1935 | Was A | 0 | 0 | — | 4 | 0 | 0 | 0 | 8.2 | 12 | 8 | 0 | 0 | 5 | 3 | 7.27 | 59 | .324 | .405 | 2 | .000 | -0 | | -3 | | -0.2 |

McLEARY, MARTY Marty Lee B10.26.1974 Kettering OH BR/TR/6-5/230 [BosA97 10/311] d8.22 Col Mount Vernon Nazarene

| 2004 | SD N | 0 | 0 | — | 3 | 0 | 0 | 0-0 | 3.2 | 7 | 6 | 2 | 0 | 2-0 | 4 | 14.73 | 27 | .438 | .474 | 0 | — | 0 | | -5 | | -0.2 |

McLELAND, WAYNE Wayne Gaffney "Nubbin" B8.29.1924 Stockport IA D5.9.2004 Houston TX BR/TR/6-0/180* d4.20

1951	Det A	0	1	.000	6	1	0	0	11	20	10	1	4	4	0	8.18	51	.400	.455	1-0-1	.000	-0	64	-4		-0.3
1952	Det A	0	0	—	4	0	0	0	2.2	4	3	0	0	6	0	10.13	38	.444	.667	0	—	0		-2		-0.1
Total	2	0	1	.000	10	1	0	0	13.2	24	13	1	4	10	0	8.56	48	.407	.500	1-0-1	.000	-0	64	-6		-0.4

McLISH, CAL Calvin Coolidge Julius Caesar Tuskahoma "Buster" B12.1.1925 Anadarko OK BB/TR/6-1/200* d5.13 Mil 1945-46 C16

1944	Bro N	3	10	.231	23	13	3	0	84	110	81	10	1	48	24	7.82	45	.321	.406	32-0-1	.219	0*	118	-24		-4.9
1946	Bro N	0	0	—	1	0	0	0	0.1	2	2	0	0	1	0	∞	—	1.000	1.000	0	—	0		-2		-0.2
1947	Pit N	0	0	—	1	0	0	0	1	2	2	0	1	0	0	18.00	23	.400	.500	0	—	0		-1		-0.1
1948	Pit N	0	0	—	2	1	0	0	5	8	5	0	0	2	1	9.00	45	.400	.455	1	.000	-0*	174	-2		-0.1
1949	Chi N	1	1	.500	8	2	0	0	23	31	21	6	0	12	6	5.87	69	.341	.417	9-1-0	.333	2*	153	-6		-0.3
1951	Chi N	4	10	.286	30	17	5-1	0	145.2	159	76	16	3	52	46	4.45	92	.283	.347	42	.119	-1*	72	-3		-0.4
1956	Cle A	2	4	.333	37	2	0	1	61.2	67	36	5	0	32-5	27	4.96	85	.282	.364	9	.111	1*	64	-4		-0.2
1957	Cle A	9	7	.563	42	7	2	1	144.1	118	55	11	2	67-10	88	2.74	135	.220	.308	43-2-4	.186	3*	130	14		1.9
1958	Cle A	16	8	.667	39	30	13	1	225.2	214	92	25	1	70-4	97	2.99	122	.251	.307	64-0-4	.094	-1	137	13		1.3
1959	Cle A★	19	8	.704	35	32	13	1	235.1	253	110	26	5	72-6	113	3.63	101	.270	.325	74-0-9	.189	-1	118	0		0.3
1960	Cin N	4	14	.222	37	21	2-1	0	151.1	170	85	26	7	48-8	56	4.16	92	.287	.345	41-0-1	.049	-3	78	-9		-1.2
1961	Chi A	10	13	.435	31	27	4	1	162.1	178	87	21	4	47-1	80	4.38	89	.280	.328	54-0-3	.167	-1	86	-8		-1.0
1962	Phi N	11	5	.688	32	24	5-1	1	154.2	184	84	15	2	45-6	71	4.25	91	.293	.341	51-0-1	.078	-2	107	-8		-0.9
1963	Phi N	13	11	.542	32	32	10-2	0	209.2	184	85	14	4	56-3	98	3.26	99	.239	.292	69-0-4	.203	4*	110	1		0.6
1964	Phi N	0	1	.000	9	0	0	0	5.1	6	3	0	0	1-1	6	3.38	103	.261	.292	1	.000	-0	76	0	77	0.0
Total	15	92	92	.500	352	209	57-5	6	1609	1685	824	165	27	552-44	713	4.01	93	.270	.331	490-3-27	.149	4	106	-54	77	-5.2

McMACKIN, SAM Samuel B1872 Cleveland OH D2.11.1903 Columbus OH BR/TL d9.4

1902	Chi A	0	0	—	1	0	0	0	3	1	1	0	0	2	0.00	—	.100	.100	1	.000	-0		1		0.0
	Det A	0	1	.000	1	1	1	0	8.1	9	5	0	1	4	2	3.24	113	.273	.368	4	.500	1	79	0		0.1
	Year	0	1	.000	2	1	1	0	11.1	10	6	0	1	4	2	2.38	150	.233	.313	5	.400	0	80	1		0.1

McMAHAN, JACK Jack Wally B7.22.1932 Hot Springs AR BR/TL/6-0/175 d4.18 Col Arkansas-Little Rock

1956	Pit N	0	0	—	11	0	0	0	13.1	18	9	1	0	9-0	9	6.08	62	.340	.435	1	.000	-0		-3		-0.1
	KC A	0	5	.000	23	9	0	0	61.2	69	40	7	2	31-0	13	4.82	90	.290	.374	14	.000	-2	69	-4		-0.5
Total	1	0	5	.000	34	9	0	0	75	87	49	8	2	40-0	22	5.04	84	.299	.385	15	.000	-2	69	-7		-0.6

YEAR	TM LG	W	L	PCT	G	GS	CG-SHO	SV-BS	IP	H	R	HR	HB	BB-IB	SO	ERA	AERA	OAV	OOB	AB-HR-SH	AVG	PB	SUP	APR	DL	PW

McMAHON, DON Donald John B1.4.1930 Brooklyn NY D7.22.1987 Los Angeles CA BR/TR/6-2/222(213-225) d6.30 C11

YEAR	TM LG	W	L	PCT	G	GS	CG-SHO	SV-BS	IP	H	R	HR	HB	BB-IB	SO	ERA	AERA	OAV	OOB	AB-HR-SH	AVG	PB	SUP	APR	DL	PW
1957	†Mil N	2	3	.400	32	0	0	9	46.2	33	13	0	0	29-4	46	1.54	227	.196	.312	8	.250	1		9		1.5
1958	†Mil N☆	7	2	.778	38	0	0	8	58.2	50	25	4	2	29-5	37	3.68	96	.235	.328	9-0-1	.111	0		0		-0.1
1959	Mil N	5	3	.625	60	0	0	**15**	80.2	81	26	5	1	37-5	55	2.57	138	.259	.335	9	.222	1		10		1.3
1960	Mil N	3	6	.333	48	0	0	10	63.2	66	48	9	2	32-4	50	5.94	58	.263	.350	11	.000	-1		-20		-3.3
1961	Mil N	6	4	.600	53	0	0	8	92	84	35	4	2	51-6	55	2.84	132	.249	.349	16-0-1	.188	0		8		1.0
1962	Mil N	0	1	1.000	2	0	0	0	3	3	2	1	0	0-0	3	6.00	63	.250	.250	0	—	0		-1		-0.1
	Hou N	5	5	.500	51	0	0	8	76.2	53	14	4	1	33-1	69	1.53	245	.201	.288	12	.083	-1		20		2.9
	Year	5	6	.455	53	0	0	8	79.2	56	16	5	1	33-1	72	1.69	221	.203	.287	12	.083	-1		19		2.8
1963	Hou N	1	5	.167	49	2	0	5	80	83	38	10	0	26-2	51	4.05	78	.270	.323	12	.083	0	68	-7		-0.5
1964	Cle A	6	4	.600	70	0	0	16	101	67	31	7	2	52-5	92	2.41	150	.189	.293	14	.143	-0		13		1.6
1965	Cle A	3	3	.500	58	0	0	11	85	79	36	8	1	37-7	60	3.28	106	.248	.328	9-0-1	.222	-0		2		0.2
1966	Cle A	1	1	.500	12	0	0	1	12.1	8	4	1	0	6-0	5	2.92	118	.190	.286	2	.000	-0		1		0.1
	Bos A	8	7	.533	49	0	0	9	78	65	29	7	3	38-8	57	2.65	143	.232	.326	11	.091	-0		8		1.7
	Year	9	8	.529	61	0	0	10	90.1	73	33	8	3	44-8	62	2.69	140	.227	.321	13	.077	-0		9		1.8
1967	Bos A	2	3	.333	11	0	0	2	17.2	14	8	3	0	13-0	10	3.57	98	.215	.346	2	.000	-0		0		-0.1
	Chi A	5	0	1.000	52	0	0	3	91.2	54	21	5	6	27-4	74	1.67	186	.173	.251	11	.182	0		15		0.9
	Year	6	2	.750	63	0	0	5	109.1	68	29	8	6	40-4	84	1.98	160	.180	.269	13	.154	0		14		0.9
1968	Chi A	2	1	.667	25	0	0	0	46	31	10	2	3	20-6	32	1.96	155	.190	.287	3	.333	0		6		0.4
	†Det A	3	1	.750	20	0	0	1	35.2	22	8	2	0	10-1	33	2.02	149	.180	.241	4	.000	-0		4		0.5
	Year	5	2	.714	45	0	0	1	81.2	53	18	4	3	30-7	65	1.98	152	.186	.268	7	.143	-0		11		0.9
1969	Det A	3	5	.375	34	0	0	11-2	37	25	17	2	1	18-1	38	3.89	97	.192	.293	6	.000	-1		0		-0.1
	SF N	3	1	.750	13	0	0	2-3	23.2	13	9	1	0	9-0	21	3.04	116	.157	.239	3-0-1	.333	0		2		0.3
1970	SF N	9	5	.643	61	0	0	19-5	94.1	70	32	9	2	45-13	74	2.96	134	.202	.297	14-0-1	.143	0		12	23	2.2
1971	†SF N	10	6	.625	61	0	0	4-5	82	73	40	9	7	37-6	71	4.06	84	.242	.335	7-0-1	.000	-1		-4		-0.9
1972	SF N	3	3	.500	44	0	0	5-2	63	46	26	8	1	21-3	45	3.71	94	.206	.274	4-0-1	.250	0		0		0.0
1973	SF N	4	0	1.000	22	0	0	6-0	30.1	21	5	1	0	7-3	20	1.48	260	.189	.237	1	1.000	0		8		1.4
1974	SF N	0	0	—	9	0	0	0	11.2	13	5	2	0	2-0	5	3.09	124	.283	.306	0	—	0		1		0.0
Total	18	90	68	.570	874	2	0	153-17	1310.2	1054	482	104	34	579-84	1003	2.96	119	.221	.308	168-0-7	.137	-1	68	87	23	10.9

McMAHON, DOC Henry John B12.19.1886 Woburn MA D12.11.1929 Woburn MA TR d10.6 Col Holy Cross

YEAR	TM LG	W	L	PCT	G	GS	CG-SHO	SV-BS	IP	H	R	HR	HB	BB-IB	SO	ERA	AERA	OAV	OOB	AB-HR-SH	AVG	PB	SUP	APR	DL	PW
1908	Bos A	1	0	1.000	1	1	1		9	14	3	0	0		3	3.00	82	.350	.350	5	.400	1	306	0		0.0

McMAHON, SADIE John Joseph B9.19.1867 Wilmington DE D2.20.1954 Wilmington DE BR/TR/5-9.5/165 d7.5

YEAR	TM LG	W	L	PCT	G	GS	CG-SHO	SV-BS	IP	H	R	HR	HB	BB-IB	SO	ERA	AERA	OAV	OOB	AB-HR-SH	AVG	PB	SUP	APR	DL	PW
1889	Phi AA	14	12	.538	28	27	27-2	0	242	230	160	5	14	102	117	3.53	107	.243	.325	104	.154	-6*	109	6		0.1
1890	Phi AA	29	18	.617	48	46	44	1	410	414	238	5	20	133	225	3.34	116	.254	.318	175-2	.229	3*	109	18		2.3
	Bal AA	7	3	.700	12	11	11-1	0	99	84	49	1	6	33	66	3.00	135	.223	.296	39	.103	-4	86	10		0.5
	Year	**36**	21	.632	**60**	57	55-1	1	**509**	498	287	6	26	166	**291**	3.27	120	.248	.314	214-2	.206	-1	104	24		2.8
1891	Bal AA	35	24	.593	61	58	53-5	1	**503**	493	259	13	17	149	219	2.81	133	.248	.306	210-1	.205	-3	92	54		4.9
1892	Bal N	19	25	.432	48	46	44-2	1	397	430	260	9	9	145	118	3.24	106	.265	.329	177	.141	-9*	109	1		1.3
1893	Bal N	23	18	.561	43	40	35	1	346.1	378	232	6	9	156	79	4.37	109	.269	.346	148	.243	-3	101	17		1.3
1894	Bal N	25	8	.758	35	33	26	0	275.2	317	175	7	9	111	60	4.21	130	.285	.355	126-0-8	.286	0	115	36		3.1
1895	†Bal N	10	4	.714	15	15	15-4	0	122.1	110	54	1	4	32	37	2.94	162	.237	.291	51-0-1	.314	1	97	25		2.3
1896	Bal N	11	9	.550	22	22	19	0	175.2	195	109	4	3	55	33	3.48	123	.279	.334	73	.123	-7	118	10		0.3
1897	Bro N	0	6	.000	9	7	5	0	63	75	56	1	3	29	13	5.86	70	.293	.372	25	.200	-1	77	-13		-0.7
Total	9	173	127	.577	321	305	279-14	4	2634	2726	1592	52	94	945	967	3.51	118	.260	.326	1128-3-9	.204	-29	107	164		13.0

McMAKIN, JOHN John Weaver "Spartanburg John" B3.6.1878 Spartanburg SC D9.25.1956 Lyman SC BR/TL/5-11/165 d4.19 Col Clemson

YEAR	TM LG	W	L	PCT	G	GS	CG-SHO	SV-BS	IP	H	R	HR	HB	BB-IB	SO	ERA	AERA	OAV	OOB	AB-HR-SH	AVG	PB	SUP	APR	DL	PW
1902	Bro N	2	2	.500	4	4	4	0	32	34	18	0	2	11	6	3.09	89	.272	.341	11	.182	1	129	-2		-0.2

McMANUS, JOE Joab Logan B9.7.1887 Palmyra IL D12.23.1955 Beckley WV BR/TR/5-11/180 d4.12

YEAR	TM LG	W	L	PCT	G	GS	CG-SHO	SV-BS	IP	H	R	HR	HB	BB-IB	SO	ERA	AERA	OAV	OOB	AB-HR-SH	AVG	PB	SUP	APR	DL	PW
1913	Cin N	0	0	—	2	0	0	0	2	3	4	0	0	4	1	18.00	18	.375	.583	0	—			-3		-0.1

McMANUS, PAT Patrick A. B10.1859 , Ireland D5.19.1917 Mount Hope NY d5.22

YEAR	TM LG	W	L	PCT	G	GS	CG-SHO	SV-BS	IP	H	R	HR	HB	BB-IB	SO	ERA	AERA	OAV	OOB	AB-HR-SH	AVG	PB	SUP	APR	DL	PW
1879	Tro N	0	2	.000	2	2	2	0	21	24	21	1		1	6	3.00	83	.258	.266	8	.125	-1	102	-2		-0.2

McMICHAEL, GREG Gregory Winston B12.1.1966 Knoxville TN BR/TR/6-3/215* [CleA88 7/163] d4.12 Col Tennessee

YEAR	TM LG	W	L	PCT	G	GS	CG-SHO	SV-BS	IP	H	R	HR	HB	BB-IB	SO	ERA	AERA	OAV	OOB	AB-HR-SH	AVG	PB	SUP	APR	DL	PW
1993	†Atl N	2	3	.400	74	0	0	19-2	91.2	68	22	3	0	29-4	89	2.06	196	.206	.269	4	.000	-0		21		1.8
1994	Atl N	4	6	.400	51	0	0	21-10	58.2	66	29	1	0	19-6	47	3.84	113	.280	.332	1	.000	-0		2		0.4
1995	†Atl N	7	2	.778	67	0	0	2-2	80.2	64	27	8	0	32-9	74	2.79	155	.213	.289	6	.000	0		13		1.3
1996	†Atl N	5	3	.625	73	0	0	2-6	86.2	84	37	4	1	27-7	78	3.22	138	.253	.309	0	—	0		10		0.9
1997	NY N	7	10	.412	73	0	0	7-11	87.2	73	34	8	2	27-6	81	2.98	134	.233	.295	3	.667	1		10		1.9
1998	NY N	1	2	.333	22	0	0	0-0	22.2	23	12	1	1	14-2	22	3.97	104	.271	.380	0	—	0		0		0.0
	LA N	0	1	.000	12	0	0	1-2	14.1	17	8	1	1	6-3	11	4.40	92	.309	.381	0	—	0		-1		-0.1
	NY N	4	1	.800	30	0	0	1-3	31	41	19	7	2	15-5	22	4.06	101	.318	.392	1	.000	0		-2		-0.3
	Year	5	4	.556	64	0	0	2-5	68	81	39	9	4	35-10	55	4.10	100	.301	.386	1	.000	0		-3		-0.3
1999	NY N	1	1	.500	19	0	0	0-1	18.2	20	10	3	0	8-3	18	4.82	90	.270	.337	0	—	-1		-1	67	0.0
	Oak A	0	0	—	17	0	0	0-0	15	15	9	3	2	12-2	3	5.40	88	.283	.426	0	—	0		-1		0.0
2000	Atl N	0	0	—	15	0	0	0-0	16.1	12	8	3	0	4-1	14	4.41	102	.214	.262	0	—	0		1	126	0.0
Total	8	31	29	.517	453	0	0	53-37	523.1	483	215	42	9	193-48	459	3.25	130	.246	.314	15	.133	-0		52	193	5.9

McMULLEN, GEORGE George B CA d7.2

YEAR	TM LG	W	L	PCT	G	GS	CG-SHO	SV-BS	IP	H	R	HR	HB	BB-IB	SO	ERA	AERA	OAV	OOB	AB-HR-SH	AVG	PB	SUP	APR	DL	PW
1887	NY AA	2	1	.667	3	3	2	0	21	25	25	2	0	19	2	7.71	55	.269	.393	12	.083	-2	130	-7		-0.7

McMULLIN, JOHN John F. "Lefty" B1848 Philadelphia PA D4.11.1881 Philadelphia PA BR/TL/5-9/160 d5.9 ▲

YEAR	TM LG	W	L	PCT	G	GS	CG-SHO	SV-BS	IP	H	R	HR	HB	BB-IB	SO	ERA	AERA	OAV	OOB	AB-HR-SH	AVG	PB	SUP	APR	DL	PW
1871	Tro NA	12	15	.444	29	29	28	0	249	430	362	4		75	12	5.53	76	.342	.379	136	.279	1	114	-37		-2.1
1872	Mut NA	1	0	1.000	3	1	1	1	15	18	15	0		2	1	3.60	94	.247	.267	236	.254	0*	125	-1		0.0
1873	Ath NA	1	0	1.000	3	1	1	0	8	10	5	0		1	0	2.25	152	.303	.324	227	.273	0*	178	1		0.1
1875	Phi NA	0	0	—	4	0	0	0	11.1	32	23	0		1	0	7.94	29	.464	.471	222-0	.257	1*		-7		-0.1
Total	4 NA	14	15	.483	37	31	30	1	283.1	490	405	4		79	15	5.43	75	.342	.376	821-2	.264	2	118	-44		-2.3

McMURTRY, CRAIG Joe Craig B11.5.1959 Troy TX BR/TR/6-5/195* [AtlN80*1/4] d4.10 Col McLennan (TX) CC [DL 1987 Tor A 73]

YEAR	TM LG	W	L	PCT	G	GS	CG-SHO	SV-BS	IP	H	R	HR	HB	BB-IB	SO	ERA	AERA	OAV	OOB	AB-HR-SH	AVG	PB	SUP	APR	DL	PW
1983	Atl N	15	9	.625	36	35	6-3	0-0	224.2	204	86	13	1	88-1	105	3.08	125	.243	.314	70-0-12	.086	-3	109	17		1.6
1984	Atl N	9	17	.346	37	30	0	0-0	183.1	184	100	16	1	102-4	99	4.32	89	.268	.359	52-0-8	.115	-1*	72	-9		-1.1
1985	Atl N	0	3	.000	17	6	0	1-0	45	56	36	6	1	27-1	28	6.60	58	.306	.394	14-0-1	.071	-1	61	-12		-0.9
1986	Atl N	1	6	.143	37	5	0	0-1	79.2	82	46	7	2	43-5	50	4.74	83	.265	.357	16-0-1	.125	-0*	90	-6	36	-0.5
1988	Tex A	3	3	.500	32	0	0	3-4	60	37	16	5	1	24-4	35	2.25	182	.180	.266	0	—	0		12		1.3
1989	Tex A	0	0	—	19	0	0	0-1	23	29	21	3	2	13-1	14	7.43	54	.312	.400	0	—	0		-8	104	-0.4
1990	Tex A	0	3	.000	23	0	0	0-0	41.2	43	25	4	1	30-0	14	4.32	91	.281	.398	0	—	0	54	-3		-0.4
1995	Hou N	0	1	.000	11	0	0	0-1	10.1	15	11	0	1	9-1	4	7.84	49	.357	.463	1	.000	0		-5		-0.4
Total	8	28	42	.400	212	79	6-3	4-7	667.2	650	341	54	10	336-17	349	4.08	96	.259	.345	153-0-22	.098	-6	88	-14	213	-0.6

McNABB, EDGAR Edgar J. "Texas" B10.24.1865 Coshocton OH D2.28.1894 Pittsburgh PA BR/TR/5.11.5/170 d5.12

YEAR	TM LG	W	L	PCT	G	GS	CG-SHO	SV-BS	IP	H	R	HR	HB	BB-IB	SO	ERA	AERA	OAV	OOB	AB-HR-SH	AVG	PB	SUP	APR	DL	PW
1893	Bal N	8	7	.533	21	14	12	0	142	167	109	5	8	53	18	4.12	115	.284	.352	67	.194	-2	100	4		0.2

McNALLY, DAVE David Arthur B10.31.1942 Billings MT D12.1.2002 Billings MT BR/TL/5-11/190* d9.26

YEAR	TM LG	W	L	PCT	G	GS	CG-SHO	SV-BS	IP	H	R	HR	HB	BB-IB	SO	ERA	AERA	OAV	OOB	AB-HR-SH	AVG	PB	SUP	APR	DL	PW
1962	Bal A	1	0	1.000	1	1	1-1		9	2	0	0	0	3-0		0.00	—	.071	.161	3	.000	-0	72	9		0.5
1963	Bal A	7	8	.467	29	20	2	1	125.2	133	67	9	5	55-4	78	4.58	76	.276	.352	38-0-3	.053	-2	104	-14		-1.8
1964	Bal A	9	11	.450	30	23	5-3	0	159.1	157	72	15	9	51-1	88	3.67	97	.260	.325	51-0-2	.137	0	84	-2		-0.2
1965	Bal A	11	6	.647	35	29	6-2	0	198.2	163	69	15	6	73-6	116	2.85	122	.222	.297	65-0-3	.092	-3	100	16		1.0
1966	†Bal A	13	6	.684	33	34	5-1	0	213	212	91	22	4	64-1	158	3.17	105	.256	.311	77-0-4	.195	3	136	0		0.4
1967	Bal A	7	7	.500	24	24	3-1	0	119	134	65	13	2	39-1	70	4.54	69	.295	.353	38-0-7	.158	0	122	-18	22	-2.1
1968	Bal A	22	10	.688	35	35	18-5	0	273	175	67	24	10	55-1	202	1.95	150	.182	**.232**	86-3-8	.128	4	110	31		4.3
1969	†Bal A★	20	7	.741	41	40	11-4	0-0	268.2	232	103	21	21	84-6	166	3.22	112	.234	.296	94-1-8	.085	-2	126	13		0.9
1970	†Bal A☆	**24**	9	.727	40	**40**	16-1	0-0	296	277	114	29	7	78-3	185	3.22	114	.250	.301	105-1-6	.133	4*	124	17		2.1
1971	†Bal A★	21	5	**.808**	30	30	11-1	0-0	224.1	188	75	24	5	58-2	91	2.89	118	.229	.282	62-2-14	.162	3	151	16	27	2.1
1972	Bal A★	13	17	.433	36	36	12-6	0-0	241	223	90	15	2	68-15	120	2.95	106	.247	.301	79-2-2	.152	1	82	6		0.9

YEAR	TM LG	W	L	PCT	G	GS	CG-SHO	SV-BS	IP	H	R	HR	HB	BB-IB	SO	ERA	AERA	OAV	OOB	AB-HR-SH	AVG	PB	SUP	APR	DL	PW
1973	†Bal A	17	17	.500	38	38	17-4	0-0	266	247	100	16	5	81-6	87	3.21	117	.251	.310	0	—	0	90	20		2.5
1974	†Bal A	16	10	.615	39	37	13-4	0-0	259	260	112	19	8	81-6	111	3.58	97	.270	.330	0	—	0	109	0		0.1
1975	Mon N	3	6	.333	12	12	0	0-0	77.1	88	50	4	4	36-4	36	5.24	74	.280	.362	21-0-1	.190	2	89	-11		-1.0
Total	14	184	119	.607	424	396	120-33	2-0	2730	2488	1070	230	72	826-56	1512	3.24	106	.245	.305	731-9-58	.133	9	111	78	49	9.7

McNAMARA, TIM Timothy Augustine B11.20.1898 Millville MA D11.5.1994 N.Smithfield RI BR/TR/5-11/170 d6.27 Col Fordham

1922	Bos N	3	4	.429	24	5	4-2	0	70.2	55	26	2	1	26	16	2.42	165	.225	.303	17-0-1	.118	-1	110	12		0.9
1923	Bos N	3	13	.188	32	16	3	0	139.1	185	95	9	5	29	32	4.91	81	.320	.357	39	.179	1	101	-15		-1.5
1924	Bos N	8	12	.400	35	21	6-2	0	179	242	119	9	3	31	35	5.18	74	.334	.364	43-0-6	.140	-1	82	-27		-2.6
1925	Bos N	0	0	—	1	0	0	0	0.2	6	6	0	0	2	1	81.00	5	.857	.889	0	—	0		-6		-0.2
1926	NY N	0	0		6	0	0	0	6	7	6	0	0	4	4	9.00	42	.304	.407	0	—	0		-3		-0.1
Total	5	14	29	.326	98	42	13-4	0	395.2	495	252	19	9	92	88	4.78	82	.314	.355	99-0-7	.152	-1	93	-39		-3.5

McNAUGHTON, GORDON Gordon Joseph B7.31.1910 Chicago IL D8.6.1942 Chicago IL BR/TR/6-1/190 d8.13 Col Loyola-Chicago

| 1932 | Bos A | 0 | 1 | .000 | 6 | 2 | 0 | 0 | 21 | 21 | 15 | 1 | 3 | 12 | 6 | 6.43 | 70 | .259 | .434 | 8 | .250 | 0 | 133 | -3 | | -0.1 |

McNEAL, HARRY John Harley B8.13.1878 Iberia OH D1.11.1945 Cleveland OH BL/TR/6-2/175 d8.5

| 1901 | Cle A | 5 | 5 | .500 | 12 | 10 | 9 | 0 | 85.1 | 120 | 68 | 4 | 8 | 30 | 15 | 4.43 | 80 | .328 | .391 | 37-0-1 | .162 | -2 | 108 | -10 | | -1.1 |

McNICHOL, BRIAN Brian David B5.20.1974 Fairfax VA BL/TL/6-5/225 [ChiN95 2/34] d9.7 Col James Madison

| 1999 | Chi N | 0 | 2 | .000 | 4 | 2 | 0 | 0-0 | 10.2 | 15 | 8 | 4 | 1 | 7-0 | 12 | 6.75 | 68 | .333 | .426 | 2-0-1 | .000 | -0 | 40 | -2 | | -0.4 |

McNICHOL, ED Edwin Briggs B1.10.1879 Martins Ferry OH D11.1.1952 Salineville OH BR/TR/5-5/170 d7.9

| 1904 | Bos N | 2 | 12 | .143 | 17 | 15 | 12-1 | 0 | 122 | 120 | 70 | 3 | 5 | 74 | 28 | 4.28 | 64 | .262 | .371 | 43 | .093 | -4 | 65 | -16 | | -2.0 |

McPARTLIN, FRANK Frank B2.16.1872 Hoosick Falls NY D11.13.1943 New York NY TR/6-0/180 d8.22

| 1899 | NY N | 0 | 0 | — | 1 | 0 | 0 | 0 | 4 | 4 | 4 | 0 | 2 | 3 | 2 | 4.50 | 83 | .267 | .450 | 1 | .000 | -0 | | -1 | | 0.0 |

McPHERSON, JOHN John Jacob B3.9.1869 Easton PA D9.30.1941 Easton PA TR d7.12

1901	Phi A	0	1	.000	1	1	0	0	4	7	5	0	1	4	0	11.25	34	.368	.500	1	.000	-0	54	-3		-0.4
1904	Phi N	1	12	.077	15	12	11-1	0	128	130	82	1	6	46	32	3.66	73	.264	.334	47-0-1	.064	-4	49	-15		-1.7
Total	2	1	13	.071	16	13	11-1	0	132	137	87	1	7	50	32	3.89	70	.268	.341	48-0-1	.063	-4	51	-18		-2.1

McQUAID, HERB Herbert George B3.29.1899 San Francisco CA D4.4.1966 Richmond CA BR/TR/6-2/185 d6.22

1923	Cin N	1	0	1.000	12	1	0	0	34.1	31	11	0	3	10	9	2.36	164	.238	.308	7	.000	-1	106	6		0.2
1926	NY A	1	0	1.000	17	1	0	0	38.1	48	34	5	2	13	6	6.10	63	.329	.391	7-0-1	.000	-1	87	-11		-0.6
Total	2	2	0	1.000	29	2	0	0	72.2	79	45	5	5	23	15	4.33	89	.286	.352	14-0-1	.000	-2	97	-5		-0.4

McQUEEN, MIKE Michael Robert B8.30.1950 Oklahoma City OK BL/TL/5-11/190(170-190) d10.2

1969	Atl N	0	0	—	1	1	0	0-0	3	2	1	0	0	3-0	3	3.00	121	.182	.357	0	—	0	73	0		0.0
1970	Atl N	1	5	.167	22	8	1	1-0	66	67	48	10	1	31-2	35	5.59	77	.266	.345	20	.300	2	68	-10		-0.7
1971	Atl N	4	1	.800	17	3	0	1-0	56	47	24	7	2	23-4	38	3.54	105	.228	.309	19-0-2	.211	-2	182	2	50	0.1
1972	Atl N	0	5	.000	23	7	1	1-0	78.1	79	45	11	1	44-3	40	4.60	83	.260	.352	23	.087	-2	56	-6	22	-0.6
1974	Cin N	0	0	—	10	0	0	0-0	15	17	10	4	0	11-0	5	5.40	65	.288	.394	1	1.000	0	68	-3		-0.1
Total	5	5	11	.313	73	19	2	3-0	218.1	212	128	32	4	112-9	140	4.66	84	.255	.343	63-0-2	.206	1	82	-17	72	-1.3

McQUILLAN, HUGH Alvin Hugh "Handsome Hugh" B9.15.1895 New York NY D8.26.1947 New York NY BR/TR/6-0/170 d7.26

1918	Bos N	1	0	1.000	1	1	1	0	9	7	3	0	0	5	1	3.00	90	.219	.324	4	.250	0	338	0		0.0
1919	Bos N	2	3	.400	16	7	2	1	60	66	34	3	1	14	13	3.45	83	.288	.332	18-0-1	.222	0*	155	-6		-0.5
1920	Bos N	11	15	.423	38	26	17-1	5	225.2	230	110	3	2	70	53	3.55	86	.273	.330	74-1-6	.257	6	96	-13		-0.8
1921	Bos N	13	17	.433	45	31	13-2	5	250	284	137	9	2	90	94	4.00	91	.291	.352	88-1-5	.205	1	113	-14		-1.3
1922	Bos N	5	10	.333	28	17	7	0	136	154	70	3	1	56	33	4.24	94	.299	.369	42-0-5	.167	-1*	77	1		0.0
	†NY N	6	5	.545	15	13	5	1	94.1	111	48	7	0	34	24	3.82	105	.301	.360	37	.189	-1	95	2		0.1
	Year	11	15	.423	43	30	12	1	230.1	265	118	10	1	90	57	4.06	98	.300	.365	79-0-5	.177	-2	85	1		0.1
1923	†NY N	15	14	.517	38	32	15-5	0	229.2	224	96	12	5	66	75	3.41	112	.259	.315	82-0-3	.171	-2*	85	12		1.1
1924	†NY N	14	8	.636	27	23	14-1	3	184	179	68	9	3	43	49	2.69	136	.259	.304	67-0-4	.209	-1*	124	19		2.0
1925	NY N	2	3	.400	14	11	2	1	70	95	49	9	1	23	23	6.04	67	.343	.395	21-0-1	.143	-1*	99	-14		-0.9
1926	NY N	11	10	.524	33	22	12-1	0	167	171	72	7	1	42	47	3.72	101	.271	.318	53-0-1	.132	-3*	95	5		0.4
1927	NY N	5	4	.556	11	9	5	0	58	73	32	4	1	22	17	4.50	86	.309	.371	19	.211	1	147	-3		-0.4
	Bos N	3	5	.375	13	12	2	0	78	109	65	2	2	24	17	5.54	67	.332	.381	22-0-5	.227	0	113	-20		-1.7
	Year	8	9	.471	24	21	7	0	136	182	97	6	3	46	34	5.10	74	.323	.377	41-0-5	.220	1	128	-22		-2.1
Total	10	88	94	.484	279	194	95-10	16	1561.2	1703	784	67	18	489	446	3.83	95	.284	.340	527-2-31	.195	0*	104	-31		-2.0

McQUILLAN, GEORGE George Watt B5.1.1885 Brooklyn NY D3.30.1940 Columbus OH BR/TR/5-11.5/175 d5.8

1907	Phi N	4	0	1.000	6	5	5-3	0	41	21	3	0	1	11	28	0.66	368	.158	.228	11-0-1	.364	3	82	9		1.3
1908	Phi N	23	17	.575	48	42	32-7	2	359.2	263	88	2	6	91	114	1.53	159	.207	.263	119-0-6	.151	-1	99	33		3.8
1909	Phi N	13	16	.448	41	28	16-4	2	247.2	202	87	5	1	54	96	2.14	121	.226	.271	76-0-7	.118	-3	103	10		0.7
1910	Phi N	9	6	.600	24	17	13-3	1	152.1	109	42	2	3	50	71	1.60	196	.204	.276	47-0-5	.149	-1	113	23		2.2
1911	Cin N	2	6	.250	19	5	2	0	77	92	60	2	4	31	28	4.68	71	.308	.380	22-0-1	.091	-1	77	-14		-1.4
1913	Pit N	8	6	.571	25	16	7	1	141.2	144	60	1	1	35	59	3.43	88	.273	.319	39-0-3	.103	-1	108	-3		-0.4
1914	Pit N	13	17	.433	45	28	15	4	259.1	248	100	8	1	60	96	2.98	89	.261	.310	73-0-8	.068	-4	87	-6		-1.1
1915	Pit N	8	10	.444	30	20	9	1	149	160	64	1	2	39	56	2.84	96	.284	.332	44-0-3	.091	-3	79	-3		-0.6
	Phi N	4	3	.571	9	8	5	0	63.2	60	31	1	1	11	13	2.12	129	.247	.282	23-0-1	.043	-2	149	1		-0.2
	Year	12	13	.480	39	28	14	1	212.2	220	95	2	3	50	69	2.62	104	.273	.317	67-0-4	.075	-5	99	-1		-0.8
1916	Phi N	1	7	.125	21	3	1	2	62	58	33	2	3	15	22	2.76	96	.251	.305	11-0-4	.091	-1	19	-3		-0.6
1918	Cle A	0	1	.000	5	1	0	1	23	25	10	0	4	7	7	2.35	128	.284	.315	4	.000	-0	0	1		0.0
Total	10	85	89	.489	273	173	105-17	14	1576.1	1382	578	23	30	401	590	2.38	114	.241	.294	469-0-39	.117	-14	96	48		3.7

McRAE, NORM Norman B9.26.1947 Elizabeth NJ D7.25.2003 Garland TX BR/TR/6-1/195* d9.13

1969	Det A	0	0	—	3	0	0	0-0	3	2	2	0	0	1-0	3	6.00	63	.200	.250	0	—	-0		-1		0.0
1970	Det A	0	0	—	19	0	0	0-0	31.1	26	13	1	1	25-0	16	2.87	131	.226	.366	1-0-1	.000	-0		2		0.1
Total	2	0	0	—	22	0	0	0-0	34.1	28	15	1	1	26-0	19	3.15	120	.224	.357	1-0-1	.000	-0		1		0.1

McTIGUE, BILL William Patrick "Rebel" B1.3.1891 Nashville TN D5.8.1920 Nashville TN BL/TL/6-1.5/175 d5.2

1911	Bos N	0	5	.000	14	8	0	0	37	37	32	3	2	49	23	7.05	54	.280	.481	12	.083	-1	74	-10		-1.2
1912	Bos N	2	0	1.000	10	1	1	0	34.2	39	26	0	0	18	17	5.45	66	.289	.373	13	.077	-1	225	-6		-0.4
1916	Det A	0	0	—	3	0	0	0	5.1	5	6	0	0	5	1	5.06	57	.278	.435	1	.000	-0		-2		-0.1
Total	3	2	5	.286	27	9	1	0	77	81	64	3	2	72	41	5.84	58	.284	.432	26	.077	-2	93	-18		-1.7

McVEY, CAL Calvin Alexander B8.30.1850 Montrose IA D8.20.1926 San Francisco CA BR/TR/5-9/170 d5.5.1871 M3 ▲

1875	Bos NA	1	0	1.000	2	1	1	0	11	15	9	0		1	4.91	44	.294	.308	389-3	.355	2*	148	-2		-0.2
1876	Chi N	5	2	.714	11	6	5	2	59.1	57	22	0		9	1.52	161	.235	.241	308-1	.347	3*	119	6		0.7
1877	Chi N	4	8	.333	17	10	6	2	92	129	81	2		11	20	4.50	66	.301	.319	266	.368	6*	93	-15		-1.3
1879	Cin N	0	2	.000	3	1	0	0	14	34	23	1		2	7	8.36	28	.453	.468	354	.297	1*	119	-8		-0.8
Total	3	9	12	.429	31	17	12	4	165.1	220	132	3		15	36	3.76	73	.295	.309	928-1	.334	10	104	-17		-1.4

McWEENY, DOUG Douglas Lawrence "Buzz" B8.17.1896 Chicago IL D1.1.1953 Melrose Park IL BR/TR/6-2/190 d4.24

1921	Chi A	3	6	.333	27	8	3	2	97.2	127	76	7	0	45	46	6.08	70	.325	.394	31-0-1	.032	-4	86	-20		-2.0
1922	Chi A	1	0	1.000	7	0	0	0	10.2	13	8	0	0	7	5	5.91	69	.325	.426	1	.000	0	0	-2		-0.2
1924	Chi A	1	3	.250	13	9	5	0	43.1	47	25	2	2	17	18	4.57	90	.294	.369	9-0-1	.000	-0	78	-2		0.0
1926	Bro N	11	13	.458	42	24	10-1	1	216.1	213	97	6	3	84	96	3.04	126	.258	.333	64-0-4	.109	-4	77	16		1.1
1927	Bro N	4	8	.333	34	22	9	1	164.1	167	80	13	8	70	73	3.56	111	.266	.347	47-0-6	.043	-4	88	7		0.1
1928	Bro N	14	14	.500	42	32	12-4	1	244	218	108	11	5	114	79	3.17	125	.235	.322	81-0-3	.173	-1	85	22		2.4
1929	Bro N	4	10	.286	36	22	4	1	146	167	119	7	3	93	59	6.10	76	.288	.390	48-0-3	.104	-2	127	-25		-2.2
1930	Cin N	0	2	.000	8	2	0	0	25.2	28	23	0	0	10	10	7.36	66	.283	.403	7	.143	-0	72	-7		-0.4
Total	8	37	57	.394	206	116	37-5	6	948	980	536	26	21	450	386	4.17	98	.269	.353	288-0-18	.104	-16	92	-11		-1.2

YEAR	TM LG	W	L	PCT	G	GS	CG-SHO	SV-BS	IP	H	R	HR	HB	BB-IB	SO	ERA	AERA	OAV	OOB	AB-HR-SH	AVG	PB	SUP	APR	DL	PW

McWILLIAMS, LARRY Larry Dean B2.10.1954 Wichita KS BL/TL/6-5/180* [AtlN74*1/6] d7.17 Col Paris (TX) JC

1978	Atl N	9	3	.750	15	15	3-1	0-0	99.1	84	38	11	2	35-4	42	2.81	143	.224	.294	32-0-4	.063	-2	120	11		1.2
1979	Atl N	3	2	.600	13	13	1	0-0	66.1	69	41	4	4	22-2	32	5.56	72	.272	.338	24-0-2	.208	1	119	-8	84	-0.4
1980	Atl N	9	14	.391	30	30	4-1	0-0	163.2	188	97	27	7	39-2	77	4.95	74	.285	.331	51-0-4	.157	0	93	-21		-2.7
1981	Atl N	2	1	.667	6	5	2-1	0-0	37.2	31	13	2	0	8-0	23	3.11	114	.230	.269	10-0-1	.100	-0	111	2		0.2
1982	Atl N	2	3	.400	27	2	0	0-1	37.2	52	30	3	2	20-5	24	6.21	59	.327	.407	6-0-1	.167	0	96	-11		-1.2
	Pit N	6	5	.545	19	18	2-2	1-0	121.2	106	49	9	4	24-1	94	3.11	121	.232	.275	32-0-9	.188	-0*	89	7		0.7
	Year	8	8	.500	46	20	2-2	1-1	159.1	158	79	12	6	44-6	118	3.84	97	.256	.311	38-0-10	.184	-0	90	-3		-0.5
1983	Pit N	15	8	.652	35	35	8-4	0-0	238	205	99	19	3	87-7	199	3.25	135	.230	.298	79-0-10	.114	-3	99	12		0.8
1984	Pit N	12	11	.522	34	32	7-2	1-1	227.1	226	86	18	2	78-7	149	2.93	124	.263	.324	74-0-12	.122	-3*	107	16		1.3
1985	Pit N	7	9	.438	30	19	2	0-0	126.1	139	70	9	7	62-11	52	4.70	77	.283	.369	40-0-4	.125	-1*	112	-14	38	-1.6
1986	Pit N	3	11	.214	49	15	0	0-1	122.1	129	75	16	7	49-5	80	5.15	76	.268	.345	29-0-3	.138	0*	107	-15		-0.9
1987	Atl N	0	1	.000	9	2	0	0-0	20.1	25	15	2	2	7-1	13	5.75	75	.301	.366	5	.200	-0	94	-3		-0.1
1988	StL N	6	9	.400	42	17	2-1	0-0	136	130	64	10	4	45-7	70	3.90	90	.253	.317	37-0-1	.162	1*	92	-5		-0.9
1989	Phi N	2	11	.154	40	16	2-1	0-1	120.2	123	67	3	4	49-4	54	4.10	87	.265	.337	27-0-3	.111	-1*	94	-9		-0.9
	KC A	2	2	.500	8	5	1	0-0	32.2	31	15	2	3	8-1	24	4.13	94	.254	.313	0	—	0	61	0		0.0
1990	KC A	0	0	—	13	0	0	0-0	8.1	10	9	2	1	9-1	7	9.72	40	.313	.476	0	—	0		-5		-0.2
Total	13	78	90	.464	370	224	34-13	3-5	1558.1	1548	768	137	52	542-58	940	3.99	94	.259	.324	446-0-54	.135	-8	101	-43	122	-4.9

MEACHAM, RUSTY Russell Loren B1.27.1968 Stuart FL BR/TR/6-2/175(155-180) [DetA87 33/858] d6.29 Col Indian River (FL) CC

1991	Det A	2	1	.667	10	4	0	0-0	27.2	35	17	4	0	11-0	14	5.20	83	.315	.368	0	—	0	148	-3		-0.3
1992	KC A	10	4	.714	64	0	0	2-4	101.2	88	39	5	1	21-5	64	2.74	149	.233	.269	0	—	0		12		1.7
1993	KC A	2	2	.500	15	0	0	0-0	21	31	15	2	3	5-1	13	5.57	83	.326	.375	0	—	0		-3	145	-0.4
1994	KC A	3	3	.500	36	0	0	4-1	50.2	51	23	7	2	12-1	36	3.73	135	.263	.307	0	—	0		7		0.8
1995	KC A	4	3	.571	49	0	0	2-1	59.2	72	36	6	1	19-5	30	4.98	96	.304	.352	0	—	0	134	-3		-0.2
1996	Sea A	1	1	.500	15	5	0	1-0	42.1	57	30	9	4	13-1	25	5.74	87	.328	.385	0	—	0		-3		-0.2
2000	Hou N	0	0	—	5	0	0	0-0	4.2	8	6	3	0	2-0	3	11.57	42	.381	.435	0	—	0		-3		-0.1
2001	TB A	1	3	.250	24	0	0	0-0	35.1	39	24	3	2	10-0	13	5.60	80	.277	.325	0	—	0		-4		-0.4
Total	8	23	17	.575	218	9	0	9-6	343	381	188	39	13	93-13	198	4.43	103	.282	.328	0	—	0	142	2	145	1.0

MEADOR, JOHNNY John Davis B12.4.1892 Madison NC D4.11.1970 Winston-Salem NC BR/TR/5-10.5/165 d4.24

| 1920 | Pit N | 0 | 2 | .000 | 12 | 2 | 0 | 0 | 36.1 | 48 | 18 | 1 | 0 | 7 | 3 | 4.21 | 76 | .340 | .372 | 6 | .167 | -0 | 61 | -3 | | -0.1 |

MEADOWS, LEE Henry Lee "Specs" B7.12.1894 Oxford NC D1.29.1963 Daytona Beach FL BL/TR(BB 1920-21, 26, 28)/6-0/190 d4.19

1915	StL N	13	11	.542	39	26	14-1	0	244	232	112	5	5	88	104	2.99	93	.259	.329	83-0-1	.096	-4	104	-7		-1.2
1916	StL N	12	23	.343	51	36	11-1	2	289	261	117	3	14	119	120	2.58	102	.247	.332	95-0-3	.158	-1	84	-1		-0.2
1917	StL N	15	9	.625	43	37	18-4	2	265.2	253	99	5	4	90	100	3.08	93	.267	.328	89-0-7	.101	-6	109	-7		-1.5
1918	StL N	8	14	.364	30	23	12	1	165.1	176	91	1	10	56	49	3.59	75	.280	.348	55-0-2	.127	-2*	95	-17		-2.5
1919	StL N	4	10	.286	22	12	3-1	0	92	100	44	3	2	30	28	3.03	92	.292	.352	29-0-1	.103	-2	81	-5		-0.7
	Phi N	8	10	.444	18	17	15-3	1	158.1	128	55	6	7	49	88	2.33	138	.229	.300	51-0-4	.118	-3*	65	12		1.0
	Year	12	20	.375	40	29	18-4	1	250.1	228	99	9	9	79	116	2.59	118	.253	.320	80-0-5	.112	-5	71	10		0.3
1920	Phi N	16	14	.533	35	33	19-3	0	247	249	104	5	8	90	95	2.84	120	.270	.341	82-0-2	.171	-3*	89	13		0.6
1921	Phi N	11	16	.407	28	27	15-2	0	194.1	226	118	10	4	62	52	4.31	98	.288	.343	62-3-4	.210	2	81	1		0.6
1922	Phi N	12	18	.400	33	33	19-2	0	237	264	127	8	11	71	62	4.03	116	.288	.346	86-0-5	.314	3	77	18		2.6
1923	Phi N	1	3	.250	8	5	0	1	19.2	40	32	0	0	15	10	13.27	35	.430	.509	10-1-0	.400	2	129	-15		-2.3
	Pit N	16	10	.615	31	25	17-1	0	227	250	97	3	3	44	66	3.01	133	.284	.319	88-0-3	.250	3	112	22		2.6
	Year	17	13	.567	39	30	17-1	1	246.2	290	129	3	3	59	76	3.83	106	.298	.339	98-1-3	.265	5	117	2		0.3
1924	Pit N	13	12	.520	36	30	15-3	0	229.2	240	99	7	4	51	61	3.26	118	.278	.322	82-0-2	.195	-1	88	14		1.1
1925	†Pit N	19	10	.655	35	31	20-1	0	255.1	272	128	11	8	67	87	3.67	122	.273	.323	97-1-5	.175	-1	124	21		2.0
1926	Pit N	20	9	.690	36	31	15-1	0	226.2	254	125	10	4	52	54	3.97	99	.287	.329	88-0-3	.227	-1	130	-2		-0.1
1927	†Pit N	19	10	.655	40	38	25-2	0	299.1	315	131	11	4	66	84	3.40	121	.273	.317	115-0-3	.157	-5	118	23		1.4
1928	Pit N	1	1	.500	4	2	1	0	10	18	11	0	0	5	3	8.10	50	.383	.442	4	.500	1	156	-5		-0.7
1929	Pit N	0	0	—	1	0	0	0	0.2	2	1	0	0	1	0	13.50	45	.500	.600	1	.000	-0		-1		0.0
Total	15	188	180	.511	490	406	219-25	7	3160.2	3280	1491	85	90	956	1063	3.37	106	.274	.332	1117-5-43	.180	-19	101	64		3.3

MEADOWS, BRIAN Matthew Brian B11.21.1975 Montgomery AL BR/TR/6-4/200(200-230) [FlaN94 3/70] d4.4

1998	Fla N	11	13	.458	31	31	1	0-0	174.1	222	106	20	3	46-3	88	5.21	78	.315	.358	54-0-2	.130	-1	77	-21	16	-2.5
1999	Fla N	11	15	.423	31	31	0	0-0	178.1	214	117	31	5	57-5	72	5.60	78	.302	.354	50-0-7	.140	0	87	-23		-2.5
2000	SD N	7	8	.467	22	22	0	0-0	124.2	150	80	24	8	50-6	53	5.34	83	.301	.373	40-0-4	.150	-1	116	-12		-1.3
	KC A	6	2	.750	11	10	2	0-0	71.2	84	39	8	0	14-0	26	4.77	109	.293	.322	0	—	0	102	4		0.2
2001	KC A	1	6	.143	10	10	0	0-0	50.1	73	41	12	1	12-2	21	6.97	71	.351	.386	0	—	0	86	-9		-1.1
2002	Pit N	1	6	.143	11	11	0	0-0	62.2	62	29	7	1	14-8	31	3.88	108	.256	.300	18-0-3	.000	-2	54	2		0.0
2003	Pit N	2	1	.667	34	7	0	1-0	76.1	91	45	8	1	11-2	38	4.72	92	.290	.315	14-0-3	.071	-1	124	-4		-0.3
2004	Pit N	2	4	.333	68	0	0	1-1	78	76	40	7	0	19-7	46	3.58	121	.259	.300	3	.000	-0		4		0.3
2005	Pit N	3	1	.750	65	0	0	0-2	74.2	84	42	8	2	21-7	44	4.58	93	.287	.325	1	.000	-0		-3		-0.2
Total	8	44	56	.440	283	122	3	2-3	891	1056	539	125	19	244-40	419	5.04	87	.298	.343	180-0-19	.117	-4	91	-62	16	-7.7

MEADOWS, RUFUS Rufus Rivers B8.25.1907 Chase City VA D5.10.1970 Wichita KS BL/TL/5-11/175 d4.23

| 1926 | Cin N | 0 | 0 | — | 1 | 0 | 0 | 0 | 0 | 0 | 0 | 0 | 0 | 0 | 0 | 0.00 | — | .000 | .000 | 1 | .000 | -0 | | 0 | | 0.6 |

MEADS, DAVE David Donald B1.7.1964 Montclair NJ BL/TL/6-0/175* [HouN84*6/148] d4.13 Col Middlesex Co. (NJ) JC [DL 1989 Hou N 182]

1987	Hou N	5	3	.625	45	0	0	0-1	48.2	60	31	8	1	16-2	32	5.55	71	.321	.372	3	.333	1		-8		-1.2
1988	Hou N	3	1	.750	22	2	0	0-0	39.2	37	20	4	0	14-0	27	3.18	105	.240	.302	4	.250	1	27	-1		0.0
Total	2	8	4	.667	67	2	0	0-1	88.1	97	51	12	1	30-2	59	4.48	82	.284	.340	7	.286	1	27	-9	182	-1.2

MEAKIM, GEORGE George Clinton B7.11.1865 Brooklyn NY D2.17.1923 Queens NY BR/TR/5-7.5/154 d5.2

1890	†Lou AA	12	7	.632	28	21	16-3	1	192	173	100	4	5	63	123	2.91	133	.233	.298	72	.153	-2*	73	22		1.6
1891	Phi AA	1	4	.200	6	6	4	0	35	51	45	1	1	22	13	6.94	55	.329	.416	15	.200	1	109	-14		-1.3
1892	Chi N	0	1	.000	1	1	1	0	9	18	14	0	0	2	1	11.00	30	.400	.426	5	.400	-0	190	-6		-0.5
	Cin N	1	1	.500	3	3	1	0	13.2	19	18	1	2	9	4	8.56	38	.317	.423	5	.000	-1	142	-8		-0.8
	Year	1	2	.333	4	4	2	0	22.2	37	32	1	2	11	4	9.53	35	.352	.424	10	.200	-0	154	-13		-1.4
1895	Lou N	1	0	1.000	1	1	1	0	7	7	2	0	0	4	2	2.57	180	.259	.355	3	.333	0	77	2		0.2
Total	4	15	13	.536	39	32	23-3	1	256.2	268	179	6	8	100	142	4.03	95	.260	.331	100	.170	-2	90	-4		-0.9

MEARS, CHRIS Christopher Peter B1.20.1978 Ottawa ON, Can. BR/TR/6-4/190 [SeaA96 5/147] d6.29

| 2003 | Det A | 1 | 3 | .250 | 29 | 3 | 0 | 5-0 | 41.1 | 50 | 28 | 5 | 3 | 11-0 | 21 | 5.44 | 80 | .307 | .360 | 0 | — | 0 | 28 | -5 | | -0.4 |

MECHE, GIL Gilbert Allen B9.8.1978 Lafayette LA BR/TR/6-3/180(180-200) [SeaA96 1/22] d7.6 [DL 2001 Sea A 190]

1999	Sea A	8	4	.667	16	15	0	0-0	85.2	73	48	9	2	57-1	47	4.73	101	.237	.357	0	—	0	78	1		0.1
2000	Sea A	4	4	.500	15	15	1-1	0-0	85.2	75	37	7	1	40-0	60	3.78	127	.240	.324	0	—	0	87	11	76	0.5
2003	Sea A	15	13	.536	32	32	1	0-0	186.1	187	97	30	3	63-2	130	4.59	94	.263	.324	5	.200	0	101	-4		-0.4
2004	Sea A	7	7	.500	23	23	1-1	0-0	127.2	139	73	21	5	47-0	99	5.01	89	.273	.339	0	—	0	93	-7		-0.4
2005	Sea A	10	8	.556	29	26	0	0-0	143.1	153	92	18	2	72-1	83	5.09	83	.274	.356	4	.250	0	110	-18	27	-1.8
Total	5	44	36	.550	115	111	3-2	0-0	628.2	627	347	85	13	279-4	419	4.70	95	.261	.339	9	.222	0	96	-17	293	-2.1

MECIR, JIM James Jason B5.16.1970 Bayside NY BB/TR/6-1/195(195-230) [SeaA91 3/84] d9.4 Col Eckerd

1995	Sea A	0	0	—	2	0	0	0-0	4.2	5	1	0	0	3-0	3	0.00	—	.263	.333	—	—	0		2		0.1
1996	NY A	1	1	.500	26	0	0	0-0	40.1	42	24	6	0	23-4	38	5.13	97	.275	.361	—	—	0		-1		0.0
1997	NY A	0	4	.000	25	0	0	0-1	33.2	36	23	5	2	10-1	25	5.88	76	.279	.338	—	—	0		-5		-0.4
1998	TB A	7	2	.778	68	0	0	0-3	84	68	30	6	4	33-5	77	3.11	154	.225	.306	1	.000	-0		16		1.8
1999	TB A	0	1	.000	17	0	0	0-2	20.2	15	7	0	1	14-0	15	2.61	190	.200	.330	0	—	0		5	145	1.2
2000	TB A	7	2	.778	38	0	0	1-3	49.2	35	17	2	1	22-0	33	3.08	159	.201	.293	0	—	0		11	25	1.4
	†Oak A	3	1	.750	25	0	0	4-5	35.1	35	14	2	1	14-2	37	2.80	173	.255	.327	—	—	0		7		0.8
	Year	10	3	.769	63	0	0	5-8	85	70	31	4	2	36-2	70	2.96	165	.225	.308	0	—	0		18		2.3
2001	†Oak A	5	3	.625	54	0	0	3-5	63	54	25	4	1	26-7	61	3.43	133	.231	.310	—	—	0		8	34	1.1
2002	†Oak A	6	4	.600	61	0	0	1-5	67.2	68	36	6	4	29-4	53	4.26	105	.259	.337	—	—	0		1		0.

AR TM LG	W	L	PCT	G	GS	CG-SHO	SV-BS	IP	H	R	HR	HB	BB-IB	SO	ERA	AERA	OAV	OOB	AB-HR-SH	AVG	PB	SUP	APR	DL	PW
'03 †Oak A	2	3	.400	41	0	0	1-1	37	40	25	4	1	16-1	25	5.59	82	.280	.352	0	—	0		-4	44	-0.4
'04 Oak A	0	5	.000	65	0	0	2-5	47.2	45	21	5	4	19-2	49	3.59	129	.239	.322	0	—	0		5		0.5
'05 Fla N	1	4	.200	52	0	0	0-4	43.1	39	17	2	5	17-2	34	3.12	128	.248	.337	0	—	0		4	27	0.4
tal 11	29	35	.453	474	0	0	12-34	527	482	240	41	23	225-28	450	3.77	123	.244	.326	1	.000	-0		49	275	5.9

EDDERS, BRANDON   Brandon Edward B1.24.1980 Tuscaloosa AL BR/TR/6-2/195 d6.20 Col Mississippi St.

AR TM LG	W	L	PCT	G	GS	CG-SHO	SV-BS	IP	H	R	HR	HB	BB-IB	SO	ERA	AERA	OAV	OOB	AB-HR-SH	AVG	PB	SUP	APR	DL	PW
'05 Ari N	4	1	.800	27	0	0	0-0	30.1	21	6	2	1	11-0	31	1.78	247	.194	.270	1	.000	-0		9		1.3

EDICH, DOC   George Francis B12.9.1948 Aliquippa PA BR/TR/6-5/227* [NYA70 30/700] d9.5 Col Pittsburgh

AR TM LG	W	L	PCT	G	GS	CG-SHO	SV-BS	IP	H	R	HR	HB	BB-IB	SO	ERA	AERA	OAV	OOB	AB-HR-SH	AVG	PB	SUP	APR	DL	PW
'72 NY A	0	0	—	1	1	0	0-0	0	2	2	0	0	2-0	0	∞	—	1.000	1.000	0	—	0	207	-2		-0.2
'73 NY A	14	9	.609	34	32	11-3	0-0	235	217	84	20	3	74-6	145	2.95	126	.241	.299	0	—	0	105	23		2.0
'74 NY A	19	15	.559	38	38	17-4	0-0	279.2	275	122	24	8	91-8	154	3.60	98	.259	.321	0	—	0*	107	2		0.1
'75 NY A	16	16	.500	38	37	15-2	0-0	272.1	271	115	25	1	72-5	132	3.50	106	.264	.309	0	—	0	105	9		0.8
'76 Pit N	8	11	.421	29	26	3	0-0	179	193	80	17	2	48-9	86	3.52	100	.281	.326	52-0-8	.096	-2	82	0		-0.1
'77 Oak A	10	6	.625	26	25	1	0-0	147.2	155	89	19	3	49-3	74	4.69	86	.265	.322	0	—	0	118	-11		-1.1
Sea A	2	0	1.000	3	3	1	0-0	22.1	26	9	1	2	4-0	3	3.63	114	.286	.327	0	—	0	145	2		0.1
Year	12	6	.667	29	28	2	0-0	170	181	98	20	5	53-3	77	4.55	89	.268	.323	0	—	0	120	-10		-1.0
NY N	0	1	.000	1	1	0	0-0	7	6	3	0	0	1-0	3	3.86	98	.261	.280	2	.000	-0	47	0		-0.1
'78 Tex A	9	8	.529	28	22	6-2	2-0	171	166	78	10	4	52-2	71	3.74	100	.255	.311	0	—	0	102	2		0.2
'79 Tex A	10	7	.588	29	19	4-1	0-1	149	156	78	9	4	49-3	58	4.17	100	.269	.328	0	—	0	112	0		0.0
'80 Tex A	14	11	.560	34	32	6	0-0	204.1	230	104	13	3	56-1	91	3.92	99	.285	.333	0	—	0*	120	-1		-0.2
'81 Tex A	10	6	.625	20	20	4-4	0-0	143.1	136	51	8	2	33-5	65	3.08	113	.252	.296	0	—	0	119	8		0.9
'82 Tex A	7	11	.389	21	21	2	0-0	122.2	146	73	8	3	61-5	37	5.06	77	.307	.383	0	—	0	83	-16		-2.0
†Mil A	5	4	.556	10	10	1	0-0	63	57	37	4	1	32-1	36	5.00	77	.242	.332	0	—	0	107	-8		-1.0
Year	12	15	.444	31	31	3	0-0	185.2	203	110	12	4	93-6	73	5.04	77	.286	.366	0	—	0	90	-23		-3.0
tal 11	124	105	.541	312	287	71-16	2-1	1996.1	2036	925	151	35	624-48	955	3.78	99	.266	.321	54-0-8	.093	-2	106	8		-0.5

EDINA, RAFAEL   Rafael Eduardo B2.15.1975 Panama City, Pan BR/TR/6-3/195(194-240) d4.2

AR TM LG	W	L	PCT	G	GS	CG-SHO	SV-BS	IP	H	R	HR	HB	BB-IB	SO	ERA	AERA	OAV	OOB	AB-HR-SH	AVG	PB	SUP	APR	DL	PW
'98 Fla N	2	6	.250	12	12	0	0-0	67.1	76	50	8	2	53-3	49	6.01	67	.289	.407	19-0-6	.053	-2	91	-15	90	-1.7
'99 Fla N	1	1	.500	20	0	0	0-0	23.1	20	15	3	1	20-2	16	5.79	76	.227	.376	0	—	0		-3		-0.3
tal 3	3	7	.300	32	12	0	0-0	90.2	96	65	11	4	72-5	65	5.96	70	.274	.399	19-0-6	.053	-2	91	-18	90	-2.0

EDLINGER, IRV   Irving John B6.18.1927 Chicago IL D9.3.1975 Wheeling IL BL/TL/5-11/185* d4.20

AR TM LG	W	L	PCT	G	GS	CG-SHO	SV-BS	IP	H	R	HR	HB	BB-IB	SO	ERA	AERA	OAV	OOB	AB-HR-SH	AVG	PB	SUP	APR	DL	PW
'49 StL A	0	0	—	3	0	0	0	4	11	13	1	0	3	4	27.00	17	.478	.538	0	—	0		-9		-0.4
'51 StL A	0	0	—	6	0	0	0	9.2	10	10	1	0	12	5	8.38	52	.270	.449	0	—	0		-4		-0.2
tal 2	0	0	—	9	0	0	0	13.2	21	23	2	0	15	9	13.83	32	.350	.480	0	—	0		-13		-0.6

EDVIN, SCOTT   Scott Howard B9.16.1961 North Olmsted OH BR/TR/6-1/190* d5.9 Col Baldwin-Wallace

AR TM LG	W	L	PCT	G	GS	CG-SHO	SV-BS	IP	H	R	HR	HB	BB-IB	SO	ERA	AERA	OAV	OOB	AB-HR-SH	AVG	PB	SUP	APR	DL	PW
'88 Pit N	3	0	1.000	17	0	0	0-0	27.2	23	16	1	1	9-2	16	4.88	71	.230	.297	3-0-1	.000	-0		-4		-0.5
'89 Pit N	0	1	.000	6	0	0	0-0	6.1	6	5	0	0	5-2	4	5.68	60	.240	.367	0	—	0		-2		-0.3
'90 Sea A	0	1	.000	5	0	0	0-1	4.1	7	4	0	1	2-0	1	6.23	64	.368	.455	0	—	0		-1		-0.2
tal 3	3	2	.600	28	0	0	0-1	38.1	36	25	1	2	16-4	21	5.17	68	.250	.331	3-0-1	.000	-0		-7		-1.0

EEGAN, PETE   Peter James "Steady Pete" B11.13.1863 San Francisco CA D3.15.1905 San Francisco CA ?/160 d8.12

AR TM LG	W	L	PCT	G	GS	CG-SHO	SV-BS	IP	H	R	HR	HB	BB-IB	SO	ERA	AERA	OAV	OOB	AB-HR-SH	AVG	PB	SUP	APR	DL	PW
'84 Ric AA	7	12	.368	22	22	22-1	0	179	177	130	7	14	29	106	4.32	77	.246	.288	75	.160	-2*	77	-18		-1.6
'85 Pit AA	7	8	.467	18	16	14-1	0	146	146	90	1	10	38	58	3.39	95	.246	.303	67	.194	-1*	95	-3		-0.4
tal 2	14	20	.412	40	38	36-2	0	325	323	220	8	24	67	164	3.90	84	.246	.295	142	.176	-3	85	-21		-2.0

EEHAN, BILL   William Thomas B9.4.1889 Osceola Mills PA D10.8.1982 Douglas WY BR/TR/5-9/155 d9.17

AR TM LG	W	L	PCT	G	GS	CG-SHO	SV-BS	IP	H	R	HR	HB	BB-IB	SO	ERA	AERA	OAV	OOB	AB-HR-SH	AVG	PB	SUP	APR	DL	PW
'15 Phi A	0	1	.000	1	1	0	0	4	7	5	0	3	4	4	11.25	26	.389	.476	1	1.000	0	150	-3		-0.4

EEKER, ROY   Charles Roy B9.15.1900 Lead Mine MO D3.25.1929 Orlando FL BL/TL/5-9/175 d9.22

AR TM LG	W	L	PCT	G	GS	CG-SHO	SV-BS	IP	H	R	HR	HB	BB-IB	SO	ERA	AERA	OAV	OOB	AB-HR-SH	AVG	PB	SUP	APR	DL	PW
'23 Phi A	3	0	1.000	5	2	2	0	25	24	10	0	0	13	12	3.60	114	.253	.343	9	.111	-1	171	2		0.2
'24 Phi A	5	12	.294	30	14	5-1	0	146	166	86	7	5	81	37	4.68	91	.288	.381	48-0-5	.229	-0	76	-5		-0.5
'26 Cin N	0	2	.000	7	1	1	0	21	24	18	1	0	9	5	6.43	57	.324	.398	6	.000	-1	23	-7		-0.6
tal 3	8	14	.364	42	17	8-1	0	192	214	114	8	5	103	54	4.73	89	.287	.377	63-0-5	.190	-2	85	-10		-0.9

EEKIN, JOUETT   George Jouett B2.21.1867 New Albany IN D12.14.1944 New Albany IN BR/TR/6-1/180 d6.13

AR TM LG	W	L	PCT	G	GS	CG-SHO	SV-BS	IP	H	R	HR	HB	BB-IB	SO	ERA	AERA	OAV	OOB	AB-HR-SH	AVG	PB	SUP	APR	DL	PW
'91 Lou AA	9	16	.360	28	25	24-2	0	221	223	154	2	6	106	141	4.28	85	.253	.338	94-1	.223	4*	88	-13		-0.9
'92 Lou AA	7	10	.412	19	18	17	0	156.1	168	108	3	6	78	67	4.03	76	.264	.350	64	.078	-5*	101	-16		-1.8
Was N	3	10	.231	14	14	13-1	0	112	112	91	2	4	48	58	3.46	94	.250	.328	45-2	.133	-1	97	-10		-0.8
Year	10	20	.333	33	32	30-1	0	268.1	280	199	5	10	126	125	3.79	83	.258	.341	109-2	.101	-5	99	-22		-2.6
'93 Was N	10	15	.400	31	28	24-1	0	245	289	201	6	7	140	91	4.96	93	.285	.376	113-3	.257	3*	85	-10		-0.5
'94 †NY N	33	9	.786	53	49	41-1	2	418	414	240	13	11	176	137	3.70	142	.256	.333	174-5-1	.276	6	90	81		6.2
'95 NY N	16	11	.593	29	29	24-1	0	225.2	296	170	10	9	73	76	5.30	88	.342	.366	96-1-0	.292	4*	99	-9		-0.5
'96 NY N	26	14	.650	42	41	34	0	334.1	378	205	8	15	127	110	3.82	110	.283	.351	144-2-0	.299	12*	119	14		2.2
'97 NY N	20	11	.645	37	34	30-2	0	303.2	328	176	9	8	99	83	3.76	110	.273	.333	137	.299	6*	105	19		1.9
'98 NY N	16	18	.471	38	37	34-1	0	320	329	185	9	12	108	82	3.77	92	.264	.328	129	.209	1	102	-3		-0.5
'99 NY N	5	11	.313	18	18	16	0	148.1	169	103	4	8	70	30	4.37	86	.286	.369	58-1-0	.207	1	92	-11		-1.0
Bos N	7	6	.538	13	13	12	0	108	111	52	0	2	23	23	2.83	147	.266	.307	41	.171	-1	66	12		1.0
Year	12	17	.414	31	31	28	0	256.1	280	155	4	10	93	53	3.72	105	.278	.344	99-1-0	.192	-1	80	7		-0.8
'00 Pit N	0	2	.000	2	2	1	0	20	21	17	1	1	8	3	6.92	53	.351	.439	4	.000	-1	38	-7		-0.8
tal 10	152	133	.533	324	308	270-9	2	2605.1	2837	1706	67	89	1056	901	4.07	103	.273	.345	1099-15-1	.243	29	97	49		4.5

EELER, PHIL   Charles Phillip B7.3.1948 South Boston VA BR/TR/6-5/215 d5.10

AR TM LG	W	L	PCT	G	GS	CG-SHO	SV-BS	IP	H	R	HR	HB	BB-IB	SO	ERA	AERA	OAV	OOB	AB-HR-SH	AVG	PB	SUP	APR	DL	PW
'72 Det A	0	1	.000	7	0	0	0-0	8.1	10	6	0	0	7-1	5	4.32	73	.303	.405	2	.000	-0		-2		-0.2

EERS, RUSS   Russell Harlan "Babe" B11.28.1918 Tilton IL D11.16.1994 Lancaster PA BL/TL/5-10/170 d9.28 Mil 1942-45

AR TM LG	W	L	PCT	G	GS	CG-SHO	SV-BS	IP	H	R	HR	HB	BB-IB	SO	ERA	AERA	OAV	OOB	AB-HR-SH	AVG	PB	SUP	APR	DL	PW
'41 Chi N	0	1	.000	1	1	0	0	8	5	2	0	1	6	5	1.13	312	.172	.200	2	.000	-0	24	2		0.2
'46 Chi N	1	2	.333	7	2	0	0	11.1	10	6	0	0	10	4	3.18	104	.238	.385	1-0-1	1.000	-0	155	0		-0.2
'47 Chi N	2	0	1.000	35	1	0	0	64.1	61	34	5	2	38	28	4.48	88	.263	.371	14	.143	-1	179	2		-0.2
tal 3	3	3	.500	43	4	0	0	83.2	76	42	5	3	48	35	3.98	96	.251	.359	17-0-1	.176	-0	120	0		0.0

EINE, HEINIE   Henry William "The Count of Luxemburg" B5.1.1896 St.Louis MO D3.18.1968 St.Louis MO BR/TR/5-11/180 d8.16

AR TM LG	W	L	PCT	G	GS	CG-SHO	SV-BS	IP	H	R	HR	HB	BB-IB	SO	ERA	AERA	OAV	OOB	AB-HR-SH	AVG	PB	SUP	APR	DL	PW
'22 StL N	0	0	—	1	0	0	0	4	5	3	1	0	2	0	4.50	92	.313	.389	1	.000	-0	0			0.0
'29 Pit N	7	6	.538	22	13	7-1	1	108	120	62	4	7	34	19	4.50	106	.291	.355	39-0-3	.103	-2	107	4		0.1
'30 Pit N	6	8	.429	20	16	4	1	117.1	168	89	6	5	46	18	6.14	81	.346	.406	41-0-2	.122	-3	84	-13		-1.3
'31 Pit N	19	13	.594	36	35	22-3	0	284	278	121	8	7	87	58	2.98	129	.254	.313	96-0-7	.146	-2	90	25		2.4
'32 Pit N	12	9	.571	28	25	13-1	1	172.1	193	92	6	3	45	32	3.86	99	.278	.324	61-0-5	.164	-2	110	-1		-0.4
'33 Pit N	15	8	.652	32	29	12-2	0	207.1	227	99	10	2	56	50	3.65	91	.278	.321	75-0-6	.173	-1	117	-6		-0.9
'34 Pit N	7	6	.538	26	14	2	0	106.1	134	60	12	1	25	22	4.32	95	.306	.345	28-0-2	.107	-1	79	-3		-0.5
tal 7	66	50	.569	165	132	60-7	3	999.1	1125	526	47	25	287	199	3.95	101	.284	.337	341-0-25	.144	-12	98	6		-0.6

EINKE, FRANK   Frank Louis B10.18.1863 Chicago IL D11.8.1931 Chicago IL BR/5-10.5/172 d5.1 s-Bob ▲

AR TM LG	W	L	PCT	G	GS	CG-SHO	SV-BS	IP	H	R	HR	HB	BB-IB	SO	ERA	AERA	OAV	OOB	AB-HR-SH	AVG	PB	SUP	APR	DL	PW
'84 Det N	8	23	.258	35	31	31-1	0	289	341	217	10		63	124	3.18	91	.275	.310	341-6	.164	-3*	72	-13		-1.4
'85 Det N	0	1	.000	1	1	0	0	5	13	12	0		4	0	3.60	79	.433	.500	3	.000	-0	20	-3		-0.4
tal 2	8	24	.250	36	32	31-1	0	294	354	229	10		67	124	3.18	91	.279	.315	344-6	.163	-3	70	-16		-1.8

EELENDEZ, JOSE   Jose Luis (Garcia) B9.2.1965 Naguabo, PR BR/TR/6-2/175(175-190) d9.11

AR TM LG	W	L	PCT	G	GS	CG-SHO	SV-BS	IP	H	R	HR	HB	BB-IB	SO	ERA	AERA	OAV	OOB	AB-HR-SH	AVG	PB	SUP	APR	DL	PW
'90 Sea A	0	0	—	2	0	0	0-0	5.1	8	8	2	1	3-0	7	11.81	34	.333	.429	0	—	0		-5		-0.2
'91 SD N	8	5	.615	31	9	0	3-1	93.2	77	35	11	1	24-3	60	3.27	117	.221	.269	20	.100	-0	84	7		0.8
'92 SD N	6	7	.462	56	3	0	0-2	89.1	82	32	9	3	20-7	82	2.92	123	.249	.295	5-0-1	.000	-0	59	6		0.8
'93 Bos A	2	1	.667	9	0	0	0-1	16	10	4	2	0	5-3	14	2.25	206	.179	.238	0	—	0		4	147	0.7
'94 Bos A	0	1	.000	10	0	0	0-0	16.1	20	11	3	2	6-2	9	6.06	83	.323	.417	0	—	0		-1		-0.1
tal 5	16	14	.533	109	12	0	3-4	220.2	197	90	27	7	60-15	172	3.47	112	.241	.294	25-0-1	.080	-1	76	11	147	2.0

ELTER, STEVE   Stephen Blasius B1.2.1886 Cherokee IA D1.28.1962 Mishawaka IN BR/TR/6-2/180 d6.27

AR TM LG	W	L	PCT	G	GS	CG-SHO	SV-BS	IP	H	R	HR	HB	BB-IB	SO	ERA	AERA	OAV	OOB	AB-HR-SH	AVG	PB	SUP	APR	DL	PW
'09 StL N	0	1	.000	23	1	0	0	64.1	79	49	1	2	20	24	3.50	72	.322	.378	15	.133	-0	166	-12		-0.6

YEAR	TM LG	W	L	PCT	G	GS	CG-SHO	SV-BS	IP	H	R	HR	HB	BB-IB	SO	ERA	AERA	OAV	OOB	AB-HR-SH	AVG	PB	SUP	APR	DL	PW
MELTON, CLIFF					Clifford George "Mickey Mouse","Mountain Music"					B1.3.1912 Brevard NC				D7.28.1986 Baltimore MD		BL/TL/6-5.5/203		d4.25							
1937	†NY N	20	9	.690	46	27	14-2	7	248	216	90	9	6	55	142	2.61	149	.233	.280	82-0-10	.122	-5	105	33		3.4
1938	NY N	14	14	.500	36	31	10-1	0	243	266	126	19	1	61	101	3.89	97	.276	.319	80-0-13	.175	-1	110	-5		-0.5
1939	NY N	12	15	.444	41	26	9-2	5	207.1	214	94	7	4	65	95	3.56	110	.269	.327	66-0-8	.182	-1	101	8		1.0
1940	NY N	10	11	.476	37	21	4-1	2	166.2	185	103	9	3	68	91	4.91	79	.285	.355	54-0-6	.222	2	113	-18		-1.8
1941	NY N	8	11	.421	42	22	9-3	1	194.1	181	83	14	2	61	100	3.01	123	.246	.305	61-0-8	.115	-3	95	11		0.9
1942	NY N*	11	5	.688	23	17	12-2	1	143.2	122	51	9	2	33	61	2.63	128	.229	.276	47-0-2	.234	2	112	11		1.6
1943	NY N	9	13	.409	34	28	6-2	0	186.1	184	85	7	3	69	55	3.19	108	.257	.325	54-0-3	.148	0	97	1		0.3
1944	NY N	2	2	.500	13	10	1	0	64.1	78	40	5	1	19	15	4.06	90	.294	.344	25-0-1	.120	-2	133	-5		-0.4
Total	8	86	80	.518	272	179	65-13	16	1453.2	1446	672	79	22	431	660	3.42	109	.259	.314	469-0-51	.164	-9	106	36		4.5
MELTON, RUBE					Reuben Franklin					B2.27.1917 Cramerton NC				D9.11.1971 Greer SC		BR/TR/6-5/205		d4.17	Mil 1945-46 Col Campbell						
1941	Phi N	1	5	.167	25	5	2	0	83.2	81	48	7	0	47	57	4.73	78	.258	.355	19-0-2	.105	-1	55	-8		-0.7
1942	Phi N	9	20	.310	42	29	10-1	4	209.1	180	95	7	3	114	107	3.70	89	.234	.335	65-1-0	.123	-1	61	-7		-1.2
1943	Bro N	5	8	.385	30	17	4-2	0	119.1	106	62	3	5	79	63	3.92	86	.243	.365	38-0-5	.105	-2	126	-9		-1.2
1944	Bro N	9	13	.409	37	23	6-1	0	187.1	178	92	1	2	96	91	3.46	103	.254	.365	57-0-9	.123	-3	83	-1		-0.4
1946	Bro N	6	3	.667	24	12	3-2	1	99.2	72	27	3	3	52	44	1.99	170	.206	.314	28-0-3	.107	-2	101	15		1.2
1947	Bro N	0	1	.000	4	1	0	0	4.2	7	7	1	0	7	1	13.50	31	.350	.519	1	1.000	0	0	-4		-0.7
Total	6	30	50	.375	162	87	25-6	5	704	624	331	22	13	395	363	3.62	95	.241	.344	208-1-19	.120	-9	83	-14		-3.0
MENDOZA, MIKE					Michael Joseph					B11.26.1955 Inglewood CA				BR/TR/6-5/215		[HouN73 5/116]		d9.7							
1979	Hou N	0	0	—	1	0	0	0-0	1	0	0	0	0	0-0	0	0.00	—	.000	.000	0	—	0*		0		0.0
MENDOZA, RAMIRO					Ramiro					B6.15.1972 Los Santos, Pan				BR/TR/6-2/170(154-195)		d5.25									
1996	NY A	4	5	.444	12	11	0	0-0	53	80	43	9	4	10-1	34	6.79	73	.343	.379	0	—	0	75	-11		-1.4
1997	†NY A	8	6	.571	39	15	0	2-2	133.2	157	67	15	5	28-2	82	4.24	105	.292	.330	0	—	0	128	4		0.5
1998	†NY A	10	2	.833	41	14	1-1	1-3	130.1	131	50	9	9	30-6	56	3.25	135	.264	.314	0-0-1	—	0	141	17		1.5
1999	†NY A	9	9	.500	53	6	0	3-3	123.2	141	68	13	4	27-3	80	4.29	110	.284	.323	0	—	0	82	5		0.7
2000	NY A	7	4	.636	14	9	1-1	0-1	65.2	66	32	9	4	20-1	30	4.25	112	.260	.321	0	—	0	140	5	95	0.6
2001	†NY A	8	4	.667	56	2	0	6-2	100.2	89	44	9	2	23-3	70	3.75	118	.241	.287	2	.000	-0	136	9	9	0.4
2002	†NY A	8	4	.667	62	0	0	4-4	91.2	102	43	4	2	16-2	61	3.44	126	.275	.305	1	.000	-0		8		0.3
2003	Bos A	3	5	.375	37	5	0	0-1	66.2	98	51	10	5	20-4	36	6.75	69	.349	.397	0	—	0	130	-13	53	-1.3
2004	†Bos A	2	1	.667	27	0	0	0-0	30.2	25	12	3	1	7-1	13	3.52	139	.225	.277	0	—	0		5	98	0.4
2005	NY A	0	0	—	1	0	0	0-0	1	2	2	1	0	0-0	0	18.00	24	.400	.400	0	—	0		-1		-0.1
Total	10	59	40	.596	342	62	2-2	16-16	797	891	412	82	35	181-23	463	4.30	106	.283	.326	3-0-1	.000	-0	120	28	263	2.9
MENEFEE, JOCK					John					B1.15.1868 Rowlesburg WV				D3.11.1953 Belle Vernon PA		BR/TR/6-0/165		d8.17 ▲							
1892	Pit N				4			0	10	6	0	0	2	0	0	11.25	29	.455	.500	3	.000	-0*		-3		-0.1
1893	Lou N	8	7	.533	15	15	14-1	0	129.1	150	95	3	3	40	30	4.24	103	.281	.335	73	.274	4*	102	-3		0.1
1894	Lou N	8	17	.320	28	24	20-1	0	211.2	258	153	4	9	50	43	4.29	119	.297	.342	79-0-8	.165	-6*	77	19		1.3
	Pit N	5	8	.385	13	13	13	0	111.2	159	95	3	2	39	33	5.40	97	.331	.383	47-0-2	.255	0	92	-4		-0.2
	Year	13	25	.342	41	37	33-1	0	323.1	417	248	7	11	89	76	4.68	110	.309	.357	126-0-10	.198	-5	83	15		1.1
1895	Pit N	0	1	.000	2	1	0	0	1.2	2	8	0	1	7	0	16.20	28	.286	.667	—	—	0	0	-4		-0.5
1898	NY N	0	1	.000	1	1	1	0	9.1	11	8	0	2	2	3	4.82	72	.289	.357	5	.000	-1	163	-2		-0.2
1900	Chi N	9	4	.692	16	13	11	0	117	140	74	1	10	35	30	3.85	94	.296	.357	46-0-2	.109	-3*	109	-1		-0.4
1901	Chi N	8	12	.400	21	20	19	0	182.1	201	102	4	6	34	55	3.80	85	.278	.315	152-0-7	.257	4*	92	-7		-0.2
1902	Chi N	12	10	.545	22	21	20-3	0	197.1	201	81	1	6	26	60	2.42	112	.264	.293	216-0-14	.231	3*	122	8		1.1
1903	Chi N	8	10	.444	20	17	13-1	0	147	157	85	3	6	38	39	3.00	105	.275	.327	64-0-2	.203	1*	99	-1		0.1
Total	9	58	70	.453	139	125	111-6	0	1111.1	1289	707	19	45	273	293	3.81	101	.288	.335	685-0-35	.222	-2	96	2		1.0
MENENDEZ, TONY					Antonio Gustavo (Remon)					B2.20.1965 Havana, Cuba				BR/TR/6-2/190*		[ChiA84 1/20]		d6.22							
1992	Cin N	1	0	1.000	4	2	1	0-0	4.2	1	1	1	0	2-0	5	1.93	187	.067	.067	0	—	0		1		0.2
1993	Pit N	2	0	1.000	14	0	0	0-0	21	20	8	4	1	4-0	13	3.00	136	.256	.298	1	.000	-0		2		0.2
1994	SF N	0	1	.000	6	0	0	0-1	3.1	8	8	2	0	2-0	2	21.60	19	.471	.526	0	—	0		-6		-1.1
Total	3	3	1	.750	23	0	0	0-1	29	29	17	7	1	6-0	20	4.97	81	.264	.305	1	.000	-0		-3		-0.7
MENHART, PAUL					Paul Gerard					B3.25.1969 St.Louis MO				BR/TR/6-2/190*		[TorA90 8/231]		d4.27	Col Western Carolina	[DL 1994 Tor A 131]					
1995	Tor A	1	4	.200	21	9	1	0-0	78.2	72	49	9	6	47-4	50	4.92	97	.248	.360	0	—	0	85	-2		-0.1
1996	Sea A	2	2	.500	11	6	0	0-0	42	55	36	9	2	25-0	16	7.29	68	.327	.421	0	—	0	121	-11	47	-0.8
1997	SD N	2	3	.400	9	8	0	0-0	44	42	23	6	0	13-0	22	4.70	84	.256	.309	12-0-2	.000	-1	138	-3		-0.4
Total	3	5	9	.357	41	23	1	0-0	164.2	169	108	24	8	85-4	90	5.47	84	.272	.364	12-0-2	.000	-1	110	-16	178	-1.3
MEOLA, MIKE					Emile Michael					B10.19.1905 New York NY				D9.1.1976 Fair Lawn NJ		BR/TR/5-11/175		d4.24							
1933	Bos A	0	0	—	3	0	0	0	2.1	5	6	0	0	2	1	23.14	19	.417	.500	0	—	0		-4		-0.2
1936	StL A	0	1	.000	9	0	0	0	19.1	29	20	0	1	13	6	9.31	58	.358	.453	2	.500	1		-7		-0.2
	Bos A	0	2	.000	6	3	1	1	21.1	29	17	0	1	10	8	5.48	97	.326	.400	7	.143	-0	50	-1		-0.1
	Year	0	3	.000	15	3	1	1	40.2	58	37	0	2	23	14	7.30	73	.341	.426	9	.222	0	49	-8		-0.3
Total	2	0	3	.000	18	3	1	1	43	63	43	0	2	25	15	8.16	65	.346	.431	9	.222	0	50	-12		-0.5
MERCADO, HECTOR					Hector Luis					B4.29.1974 Catano, PR				BL/TL/6-3/235(205-235)		[HouN92 13/349]		d4.4	[DL 1998 NY N 181]						
2000	Cin N	0	0	—	12	0	0	0-0	14	12	7	2	0	8-0	13	4.50	106	.240	.339	1	.000	-0		1		0.0
2001	Cin N	3	2	.600	56	0	0	0-2	53	55	27	6	0	30-1	59	4.08	113	.266	.356	2	.000	-0		3		0.2
2002	Phi N	2	2	.500	31	3	0	0-0	39	32	21	3	2	25-2	40	4.62	83	.224	.349	4	.250	-0	96	-3		-0.3
2003	Phi N	0	0	—	13	0	0	1-1	18.2	18	12	4	2	12-0	15	5.79	69	.254	.360	2	.000	-0		-4	38	-0.3
Total	4	5	4	.556	112	3	0	1-3	124.2	117	67	15	4	75-3	127	4.55	94	.248	.353	9	.111	-0	96	-3	219	-0.3
MERCEDES, JOSE					Jose Miguel (Santana)					B3.5.1971 Santa Cruz de El Seibo, D.R.				BR/TR/6-1/199(180-208)		d5.31								
1994	Mil A	2	0	1.000	19	0	0	0-1	31	22	9	4	2	16-1	11	2.32	216	.216	.333	0	—	0		9	57	0.5
1995	Mil A	0	1	.000	5	0	0	0-2	7.1	12	9	1	0	6-0	6	9.82	51	.375	.476	0	—	0		-4	141	-0.4
1996	Mil A	0	2	.000	11	0	0	0-1	16.2	20	18	6	0	5-0	6	9.18	57	.294	.338	0	—	0		-7		-0.7
1997	Mil A	7	10	.412	29	23	2-1	0-0	159	146	76	24	5	53-2	80	3.79	122	.248	.314	2	.000	-0	79	14		1.2
1998	Mil N	2	2	.500	7	5	0	0-0	32	42	25	5	1	9-1	11	6.75	64	.316	.359	11	.091	-0	93	-8	146	-0.9
2000	Bal A	14	7	.667	36	20	1	0-0	145.2	150	71	15	3	64-1	70	4.02	117	.270	.345	1	.000	-0	109	11		1.2
2001	Bal A	8	17	.320	33	31	2	0-0	184	219	125	20	10	63-3	123	5.82	74	.294	.354	1	.000	-0	89	-29		-3.4
2003	Mon N	0	0	—	5	0	0	0-0	7.1	6	3	0	0	5-0	3	3.68		.231	.355	0	—	0		2		0.1
Total	8	33	39	.458	145	79	5-1	0-4	583	617	336	75	21	223-8	310	4.75	96	.274	.342	19	.053	-1	90	-12	344	-2.4
MERCER, WIN					George Barclay					B6.20.1874 Chester WV				D1.12.1903 San Francisco CA		BR/TR/5-7/140		d4.21 ▲							
1894	Was N	17	23	.425	50	39	30	3	339.1	445	285	9	14	126	72	3.85	137	.313	.375	165-2-1	.291	3*	95	41		3.8
1895	Was N	13	23	.361	44	38	32	2	313.1	432	281	17	18	96	85	4.42	109	.322	.376	201-1-5	.254	-0*	90	3		0.3
1896	Was N	25	18	.581	46	45	38-2	0	366.1	456	266	10	20	117	94	4.13	107	.302	.360	156-1-2	.244	0*	100	11		1.1
1897	Was N	21	20	.512	47	43	35-3	3	342	403	219	5	28	104	91	5.18	136	.291	.353	139-0-4	.317	8*	89	33		3.9
1898	Was N	12	18	.400	33	30	24	0	233.2	309	181	3	18	71	52	4.81	76	.316	.373	249-2-9	.321	8*	90	-30		-2.5
1899	Was N	7	14	.333	23	21	21	0	186	234	128	2	14	53	28	4.60	85	.307	.365	375-1-6	.299	5*	98	-13		-0.5
1900	NY N	13	17	.433	33	29	26-1	0	242.3	303	138	5	20	58	39	3.86	94	.305	.355	248-0-3	.294	7*	89	1		0.8
1901	Was A	9	13	.409	24	22	19-1	1	179.2	217	126	8	10	50	31	4.56	80	.295	.348	140-0-3	.300	6*	86	-16		-0.9
1902	Det A	15	18	.455	35	33	28-4	1	281.2	282	129	5	10	80	40	3.04	120	.261	.318	100-0-3	.180	-2	65	20		2.0
Total	9	132	164	.446	335	300	253-11	10	2484.2	3081	1753	64	144	755	532	3.98	107	.302	.358	1773-7-36	.285	35	90	50		8.0
MERCER, JACK					Harry Vernon					B3.10.1889 Zanesville OH				D6.25.1945 Dayton OH		d8.2								
1910	Pit N	0	0	—	3	0	0	0	0	0	0	0	2		1	0.00	—	.000	.500	0	—	0		0		0.0
MERCER, MARK					Mark Kenneth					B5.22.1954 Fort Bragg NC				BL/TL/6-5/220		[PitN73 S1/2]		d9.1	Col Hill (TX) JC						
1981	Tex A	0	1	.000	7	0	0	2-1	7.2	7	4	1	0	7-0	8	4.70	74	.241	.389	0	—			-1		-0.2

YEAR	TM LG	W	L	PCT	G	GS	CG-SHO	SV-BS	IP	H	R	HR	HB	BB-IB	SO	ERA	AERA	OAV	OOB	AB-HR-SH	AVG	PB	SUP	APR	DL	PW

MERCKER, KENT Kent Franklin B2.1.1968 Indianapolis IN BL/TL/6-2/195(175-205) [AtlN86 1/5] d9.22

1989	Atl N	0	0	—	2	1	0	0-0	4.1	8	6	0	0	6-0	4	12.46	29	.400	.538	1	.000	-0	121	-4		-0.2
1990	Atl N	4	7	.364	36	0	0	7-3	48.1	43	22	6	2	24-3	39	3.17	127	.236	.329	3	.000	-0		3	27	0.6
1991	†Atl N	5	3	.625	50	4	0	6-2	73.1	56	23	5	1	35-3	62	2.58	150	.211	.303	10	.100	-0	87	10	15	1.2
1992	†Atl N	3	2	.600	53	0	0	6-3	68.1	51	27	4	3	35-1	49	3.42	107	.207	.312	5	.000	-0		8		0.1
1993	Atl N	3	1	.750	43	6	0	0-0	66	52	24	2	2	36-3	59	2.86	141	.212	.318	13	.000	-1	74	8		0.2
1994	Atl N	9	4	.692	20	17	2-1	0-0	112.1	90	46	16	0	45-3	111	3.45	125	.220	.295	37-0-3	.054	-2	96	11		0.1
1995	†Atl N	7	8	.467	29	26	0	0-0	143	140	73	16	3	61-2	102	4.15	104	.258	.332	48-0-6	.104	-2	109	2		0.1
1996	Bal A	3	6	.333	14	12	0	0-0	58	73	56	12	3	35-1	22	7.76	64	.307	.396	0	—	0	98	-19		-2.3
	Cle A	1	0	1.000	10	0	0	0-0	11.2	10	4	1	0	3-1	7	3.09	158	.244	.283	0	—	0		3		0.2
	Year	4	6	.400	24	12	0	0-0	69.2	83	60	13	3	38-2	29	6.98	71	.297	.380	0	—	0	99	-17		-2.1
1997	Cin N	8	11	.421	28	25	0	0-0	144.2	135	65	16	2	62-6	75	3.92	109	.250	.327	45-0-4	.156	1*	67	7	15	1.0
1998	StL N	11	11	.500	30	29	0	0-0	161.2	199	99	11	3	53-4	72	5.07	83	.310	.361	54-1-5	.148	1*	121	-15	17	-1.7
1999	StL N	6	5	.545	25	18	0	0-0	103.2	125	73	16	2	51-3	64	5.12	90	.303	.380	28-0-4	.179	1*	117	-10		-0.8
	†Bos A	2	0	1.000	5	5	0	0-0	25.2	23	12	0	1	13-0	17	3.51	142	.235	.327	0	—	0	82	4	16	0.3
2000	Ana A	1	3	.250	21	7	0	0-0	48.1	57	35	12	2	29-3	30	6.52	79	.300	.396	0	—	0	104	-6	89	-0.4
2002	Col N	3	1	.750	58	0	0	0-3	44	55	33	12	2	22-2	37	6.14	77	.299	.380	1	.000	-0		-6	54	-0.5
2003	Cin N	0	2	.000	49	0	0	0-3	38.1	31	13	5	0	25-2	41	2.35	177	.225	.344	0	—	0		7	15	0.4
	†Atl N	0	0	—	18	0	0	1-1	17	15	3	1	0	7-2	7	1.06	397	.231	.301	1	.000	-0		6		0.2
	Year	0	2	.000	67	0	0	1-4	55.1	46	16	6	0	32-4	48	1.95	214	.227	.331	1	.000	-0		13		0.6
2004	Chi N	3	1	.750	71	0	0	0-3	53	39	15	4	3	27-2	51	2.55	174	.205	.309	2	.000	-0		11	19	0.7
2005	Cin N	3	1	.750	58	0	0	4-3	61.2	64	27	8	3	19-4	45	3.65	114	.270	.330	0	—	0		4		0.3
Total	16	72	66	.522	640	150	2-1	24-24	1283.1	1266	656	147	32	588-45	894	4.17	104	.259	.340	248-1-22	.113	-5	102	-6	267	0.3

MEREDITH, CLA Olise Cla B6.4.1983 Richmond VA BR/TR/6-0/180 d5.8 Col Virginia Commonwealth

| 2005 | Bos A | 0 | 0 | — | 3 | 0 | 0 | 0-0 | 2.1 | 6 | 7 | 1 | 1 | 4-0 | 0 | 27.00 | 17 | .462 | .611 | 0 | — | 0 | | -5 | | -0.2 |

MERENA, SPIKE John Joseph B11.18.1909 Paterson NJ D3.9.1977 Bridgeport CT BL/TL/6-0/185 d9.16

| 1934 | Bos A | 1 | 2 | .333 | 4 | 3 | 2-1 | 0 | 24.2 | 20 | 8 | 2 | 1 | 16 | 7 | 2.92 | 165 | .222 | .346 | 7-0-2 | .143 | -0 | 60 | 5 | | 0.5 |

MERIDITH, RON Ronald Knox B11.26.1956 San Pedro CA BL/TL/6-0/175* [HouN78 4/89] d9.16 Col Oral Roberts

1984	Chi N	0	0	—	3	0	0	0-0	5.1	6	4	0	0	2-1	4	3.38	116	.273	.320	0	—	0		-1		0.0
1985	Chi N	3	2	.600	32	0	0	1-3	46.1	53	24	3	1	24-6	23	4.47	90	.301	.382	4	.250	0		-2		-0.1
1986	Tex A	1	0	1.000	5	0	0	0-0	3	2	1	0	0	1-1	2	3.00	144	.286	.333	0	—	0		0		0.1
1987	Tex A	1	0	1.000	11	0	0	0-1	20.2	25	18	7	0	12-2	17	6.10	74	.298	.385	0	—	0		-4		-0.2
Total	4	5	2	.714	51	0	0	1-4	75.1	86	48	11	1	39-10	46	4.78	87	.298	.377	4	.250	0		-7		-0.2

MERRIMAN, BRETT Brett Alan B7.15.1966 Jacksonville IL BR/TR/6-2/180(180-216) [CleA88 9/215] d4.8 Col Grand Canyon

1993	Min A	1	1	.500	19	0	0	0-0	27	36	29	3	3	23-2	14	9.67	46	.343	.466	0	—	0		-14		-0.9
1994	Min A	0	1	.000	15	0	0	0-1	17	18	13	0	4	14-0	10	6.35	78	.269	.414	0	—	0		-3		-0.1
Total	2	1	2	.333	34	0	0	0-1	44	54	42	3	7	37-2	24	8.39	55	.314	.445	0	—	0		-17		-1.0

MERRITT, GEORGE George Washington B4.14.1880 Paterson NJ D2.21.1938 Memphis TN TR/6-0/160 d9.6 ▲

1901	Pit N	3	0	1.000	3	3	3	0	24	28	18	0	2	5	5	4.88	67	.289	.337	11	.273	1*	260	-4		-0.3
1903	Pit N	0	0	—	1	0	0	0	4	4	3	0	0	1	2	2.25	144	.267	.313	27-0-1	.148	0*		0		0.0
Total	2	3	0	1.000	4	3	3	0	28	32	21	0	2	6	7	4.50	73	.286	.333	38-0-1	.184	1	260	-4		-0.3

MERRITT, JIM James Joseph B12.9.1943 Altadena CA BL/TL/6-2/180* d8.2

1965	†Min A	5	4	.556	16	9	1	2	76.2	68	29	11	0	20-1	61	3.17	112	.239	.287	22-0-4	.136	0	121	4		0.6
1966	Min A	7	14	.333	31	18	5-1	3	144	142	57	17	0	33-3	124	3.38	107	.212	.257	39-0-2	.103	-1	64	6		0.8
1967	Min A	13	7	.650	37	28	11-4	0	227.2	196	72	21	0	30-6	161	2.53	137	.230	.260	74-0-3	.135	0	100	23		2.0
1968	Min A	12	16	.429	38	34	11-1	1	238.1	207	102	21	0	52-1	181	3.25	95	.232	.277	71-0-4	.141	0	99	-4		-0.5
1969	Cin N	17	9	.654	42	36	8-1	0-0	251	269	127	33	5	61-8	144	4.37	86	.273	.316	77-1-15	.143	0	116	-11		-1.2
1970	†Cin N★	20	12	.625	35	35	12-1	0-0	234	248	114	21	0	53-12	136	4.08	99	.270	.310	83-3-6	.169	3	108	2		0.4
1971	Cin N	1	11	.083	28	11	0	0-0	107	115	55	14	3	31-8	38	4.37	77	.279	.332	29-0-2	.138	0*	62	-12		-1.3
1972	Cin N	1	0	1.000	4	1	0	0-0	8	13	4	1	0	2-1	4	4.50	72	.361	.395	2	.000	-0	55	-1		-0.1
1973	Tex A	5	13	.278	35	19	8-1	1-0	160	191	79	18	1	34-3	65	4.05	93	.296	.327	0	—	0	91	-4		-0.4
1974	Tex A	0	0	—	26	1	0	0-0	32.2	46	17	3	0	6-2	18	4.13	87	.329	.349	0	—	0	74	-2	21	-0.1
1975	Tex A	0	0	—	5	0	0	0-0	3.2	3	1	0	1	0-0	1	0.00	—	.214	.267	0	—	0		1	31	0.0
Total	11	81	86	.485	297	192	56-9	7-0	1483	1468	657	160	25	322-45	932	3.65	98	.257	.297	397-4-33	.141	3	99	-7	52	0.2

MERRITT, LLOYD Lloyd Wesley B4.8.1933 St.Louis MO BR/TR/6-0/189 d4.22 Col Washington-St. Louis

| 1957 | StL N | 1 | 2 | .333 | 14 | 0 | 0 | 4 | 65.1 | 60 | 29 | 7 | 4 | 28-5 | 35 | 3.31 | 120 | .251 | .337 | 7 | .000 | -0 | | 4 | | 0.2 |

MERTZ, JIM James Verlin B8.10.1916 Lima OH D2.4.2003 Waycross GA BR/TR/5-10.5/170 d5.1 Mil 1944-46

| 1943 | Was A | 5 | 7 | .417 | 33 | 10 | 2 | 3 | 116.2 | 109 | 65 | 7 | 0 | 58 | 53 | 4.63 | 69 | .251 | .339 | 38-0-3 | .184 | 0 | 166 | -16 | | -1.6 |

MESA, JOSE Jose Ramon Nova (b Jose Ramon Nova (Mesa)) B5.22.1966 Pueblo Viejo, D.R. BR/TR/6-3/225(170-235) d9.10

1987	Bal A	1	3	.250	6	5	0	0-0	31.1	38	23	7	0	15-0	17	6.03	74	.297	.371	0	—	0	74	-6		-0.6
1990	Bal A	3	2	.600	7	7	0	0-0	46.2	37	20	2	1	27-2	24	3.86	99	.218	.325	0	—	0	106	1		0.0
1991	Bal A	6	11	.353	23	23	2-1	0-0	123.2	151	86	11	3	62-2	64	5.97	67	.307	.385	0	—	0*	112	-27	15	-3.1
1992	Bal A	3	8	.273	13	12	0	0-0	67.2	77	41	9	2	27-1	22	5.19	78	.287	.353	0	—	0	82	-8		-1.1
	Cle A	4	4	.500	15	15	1-1	0-0	93	92	45	5	2	43-0	40	4.16	95	.262	.344	0	—	0	117	-1		-0.1
	Year	7	12	.368	28	27	1-1	0-0	160.2	169	86	14	4	70-1	62	4.59	87	.273	.348	0	—	0	102	-7		-1.2
1993	Cle A	10	12	.455	34	33	3	0-0	208.2	232	122	21	7	62-2	118	4.92	89	.286	.339	0	—	0	102	-10		-1.0
1994	Cle A	7	5	.583	51	0	0	2-4	73	71	33	3	3	26-7	63	3.82	124	.254	.321	0	—	0		9		1.2
1995	†Cle A★	3	0	1.000	62	0	0	46-2	64	49	9	3	0	17-2	58	1.13	420	.216	.268	0	—	0		25		4.3
1996	†Cle A☆	2	7	.222	69	0	0	39-5	72.1	69	32	6	3	28-4	64	3.73	131	.257	.331	0	—	0		10		1.8
1997	†Cle A	4	4	.500	66	0	0	16-5	82.1	83	28	7	3	28-3	69	2.40	196	.259	.322	0	—	0		19		2.2
1998	Cle A	3	4	.429	44	0	0	1-2	54	61	36	7	4	20-3	35	5.17	93	.282	.351	0	—	0		-4		-0.4
	SF N	5	3	.625	32	0	0	0-1	30.2	30	14	1	0	18-2	28	3.52	114	.256	.356	0	—	0		1		0.2
1999	Sea A	3	6	.333	68	0	0	33-5	68.2	84	42	11	4	40-4	42	4.98	96	.305	.396	0	—	0		-2		-0.3
2000	†Sea A	4	6	.400	66	0	0	1-2	80.2	89	48	11	5	41-0	84	5.36	90	.280	.365	0	—	0		-3		-0.3
2001	Phi N	3	3	.500	71	0	0	42-4	69.1	65	26	4	2	20-2	59	2.34	176	.246	.301	0	—	0		11		2.1
2002	Phi N	4	6	.400	74	0	0	45-9	75.2	65	26	5	4	39-7	64	2.97	129	.231	.332	0	—	0		8		1.7
2003	Phi N	5	7	.417	61	0	0	24-6	58	71	44	7	1	31-2	45	6.52	61	.296	.379	0	—	0		-17		-3.3
2004	Pit N	5	2	.714	70	0	0	43-5	69.1	78	26	6	1	20-3	37	3.25	133	.291	.340	0	—	0		9		1.7
2005	Pit N	2	8	.200	55	0	0	27-7	56.2	61	30	7	3	26-3	37	4.76	89	.285	.361	1-0-1	.000	-0		-2		-0.4
Total	17	77	101	.433	887	95	6-2	319-55	1425.2	1503	731	133	48	590-49	970	4.29	101	.273	.345	1-0-1	.000	0	99	14	15	4.6

MESSENGER, BUD Andrew Warren B2.1.1898 Grand Blanc MI D11.4.1971 Lansing MI BR/TR/6-0/175 d7.31

| 1924 | Cle A | 2 | 0 | 1.000 | 5 | 2 | 1 | 0 | 25 | 28 | 13 | 4 | 0 | 14 | 4 | 4.32 | 99 | .283 | .372 | 8-0-2 | .125 | -0 | 237 | 1 | | 0.0 |

MESSENGER, RANDY Randall Jerome B8.13.1981 Reno NV BR/TR/6-6/245 d6.22

| 2005 | Fla N | 0 | 0 | — | 37 | 0 | 0 | 0-0 | 37 | 39 | 22 | 5 | 0 | 30-7 | 29 | 5.35 | 75 | .273 | .392 | 3 | .333 | 1 | | -5 | | -0.2 |

MESSERSMITH, ANDY John Alexander B8.6.1945 Toms River NJ BR/TR/6-1/200* [AnaA66 S1/12] d7.4 Col California-Davis

1968	Cal A	4	2	.667	28	5	2-1	4	81.1	44	21	3	1	35-4	74	2.21	132	.157	.252	20-0-4	.100	-1*	78	7		0.6
1969	Cal A	16	11	.593	40	33	10-2	2-0	250	169	81	17	5	100-7	211	2.52	139	.190	.274	77-0-6	.156	2*	101	28		3.2
1970	Cal A	11	10	.524	37	26	6-1	5-0	194.2	144	75	21	6	78-6	162	3.01	121	.205	.289	70-1-5	.157	0*	91	13		1.4
1971	Cal A☆	20	13	.606	38	38	14-4	0-0	276.2	224	112	16	7	121-6	179	2.99	109	.218	.303	93-2-6	.172	4*	103	5		1.0
1972	Cal A	8	11	.421	25	21	10-3	2-0	169.2	125	56	11	4	68-8	142	2.81	104	.207	.288	53-0-2	.189	2*	75	4	49	0.8
1973	LA N	14	10	.583	33	33	10-3	0-0	249.2	196	90	24	6	77-3	177	2.70	129	.214	.278	89-0-5	.169	2*	116	21		2.1
1974	†LA N★	20	6	.769	39	39	13-3	0-0	292.1	227	93	24	3	94-0	221	2.59	133	.212	.277	96-1-4	.240	9	118	31		3.8
1975	LA N☆	19	14	.576	42	**40**	**19-7**	0-0	**321.2**	244	92	12	6	96-2	213	2.29	149	**.213**	.275	108-0-5	.157	2*	93	**43**		4.5
1976	Atl N★	11	11	.500	29	28	12-3	1-0	207.1	166	83	14	0	74-1	135	3.04	125	.219	.287	67-0-6	.179	0	85	15		1.6
1977	Atl N	5	4	.556	16	16	1	0-0	102.1	101	54	12	4	39-5	69	4.40	101	.256	.323	34-1-2	.118	-0		2	59	0.2

YEAR	TM LG	W	L	PCT	G	GS	CG-SHO	SV-BS	IP	H	R	HR	HB	BB-IB	SO	ERA	AERA	OAV	OOB	AB-HR-SH	AVG	PB	SUP	APR	DL	PW
1978	NY A	0	3	.000	6	5	0	0-0	22.1	24	21	7	1	15-0	16	5.64	65	.267	.377	0	—	0	93	-7	119	-0.9
1979	LA N	2	4	.333	11	11	1	0-0	62.1	55	34	9	0	34-2	26	4.91	74	.244	.342	22-0-1	.091	-1	125	-7	86	-0.7
Total	12	130	99	.568	344	295	98-27	15-0	2230.1	1719	812	174	40	831-44	1625	2.86	121	.212	.287	729-5-46	.170	20	101	155	313	17.6

METCALF, TOM Thomas John B7.16.1940 Amherst WI BR/TR/6-2.5/175 d8.4 Col Northwestern

YEAR	TM LG	W	L	PCT	G	GS	CG-SHO	SV-BS	IP	H	R	HR	HB	BB-IB	SO	ERA	AERA	OAV	OOB	AB-HR-SH	AVG	PB	SUP	APR	DL	PW
1963	NY A	1	0	1.000	8	0	0	0-0	13	12	4	1	0	3-1	3	2.77	127	.250	.294	0	—	0	1			0.1

METIVIER, DEWEY George Dewey B5.6.1898 Cambridge MA D3.2.1947 Cambridge MA BL/TR/5-11/175 d9.15

1922	Cle A	2	0	1.000	2	2	2	0	18	18	9	1	1	3	1	4.50	89	.265	.306	6	.167	-0	138	0		0.0
1923	Cle A	4	2	.667	26	5	1	1	73.1	111	66	1	6	38	9	6.50	61	.368	.448	20	.150	-0	159	-21		-1.5
1924	Cle A	1	5	.167	26	6	1	3	76.1	110	50	3	0	34	14	5.31	81	.358	.422	24	.125	-2	89	-6		-0.7
Total	3	7	7	.500	54	13	4	4	167.2	239	125	5	7	75	24	5.74	72	.353	.423	50	.140	-2	122	-27		-2.2

METZGER, BUTCH Clarence Edward B5.23.1952 Lafayette IN BR/TR/6-1/185* [SFN70 2/41] d9.8

1974	SF N	1	0	1.000	10	0	0	0-0	12.2	11	5	4	0	12-7	5	3.55	107	.239	.397		—	-0		1		0.0
1975	SD N	1	0	1.000	4	0	0	0-0	4.2	6	4	1	0	4-1	6	7.71	45	.316	.417	0	—	0		-2		-0.4
1976	SD N	11	4	.733	77	0	0	16-8	123.1	119	44	5	3	52-14	89	2.92	113	.258	.335	8-0-2	.000	-0		6		0.9
1977	SD N	0	0	—	17	1	0	0-1	22.2	27	16	5	1	12-4	21	5.56	64	.307	.388	3	.000	-0	273	-5		-0.3
	StL N	4	2	.667	58	0	0	7-3	92.2	78	36	8	1	38-2	48	3.11	126	.228	.305	4-0-2	.000	-0		8		0.5
	Year	4	2	.667	75	1	0	7-4	115.1	105	52	13	2	50-6	54	3.59	107	.244	.323	7-0-2	.000	-1	255	3		0.2
1978	NY N	1	3	.250	25	0	0	0-0	37.1	48	28	4	1	22-7	21	6.51	48	.324	.406	-0	—	0		-12		-1.2
Total	5	18	9	.667	191	1	0	23-12	293.1	289	133	23	6	140-35	175	3.74	95	.262	.344	15-0-4	.000	-1	274	-4		-0.5

MEYER, BRIAN Brian Scott B1.29.1963 Camden NJ BR/TR/6-0/190* [HouN86 16/406] d9.3 Col Rollins

1988	Hou N	0	0	—	8	0	0	0-0	12.1	9	2	2	0	4-0	10	1.46	228	.225	.295	0	—	0		3		-0.2
1989	Hou N	0	1	.000	12	0	0	1-0	18	16	13	0	1	13-3	13	4.50	76	.239	.366	0-0-1	—	0		-4		0.0
1990	Hou N	0	4	.000	14	0	0	1-0	20.1	16	7	3	0	6-0	6	2.21	169	.211	.268	1	.000	-0		3		0.6
Total	3	0	5	.000	34	0	0	2-0	50.2	41	22	5	1	23-3	29	2.84	124	.224	.313	1-0-1	.000	-0		2		0.4

MEYER, DAN Daniel Livingston B7.3.1981 Woodbury NJ BR/TL/6-3/210 [AtlN02 1/34] d9.14 Col James Madison

2004	Atl N	0	0	—	2	0	0	0-0	2	2	0	0	0	1-1	1	0.00	—	.286	.375	0	—	0		1		0.0

MEYER, JACK John Robert B3.23.1932 Philadelphia PA D3.9.1967 Philadelphia PA BR/TR/6-1/175* d4.16 Col Wake Forest

1955	Phi N	6	11	.353	50	5	0	16	110.1	75	50	14	3	66-6	97	3.43	116	.190	.310	20-0-1	.100	-0	67	6		0.8
1956	Phi N	7	11	.389	41	7	2	2	96	86	49	8	4	51-11	66	4.41	84	.242	.343	20-1-2	.200	1	51	-5		-0.8
1957	Phi N	0	2	.000	19	2	0	0	37.2	44	30	6	1	28-2	34	5.73	66	.297	.408	6-0-1	.167	0	139	-10		-0.4
1958	Phi N	3	6	.333	37	5	1	2	90.1	77	38	8	1	33-3	87	3.59	110	.232	.301	18-0-1	.278	1	136	5		0.5
1959	Phi N	5	3	.625	47	1	1	1	93.2	76	43	9	1	53-2	71	3.36	122	.222	.326	14	.071	-1	0	6		0.4
1960	Phi N	3	1	.750	7	4	0	0	25	25	13	2	0	11-0	18	4.32	90	.272	.336	8-0-1	.125	-0	97	-1	93	-0.3
1961	Phi N	0	0	—	1	0	0	0	2	2	1	0	0	2-0	2	9.00	45	.286	.444	0	—	0		-1	93	-0.1
Total	7	24	34	.414	202	24	4	21	455	385	225	48	10	244-24	375	3.92	100	.230	.330	86-1-6	.163	1	84	6	93	0.4

MEYER, BOB Robert Bernard B8.4.1939 Toledo OH BR/TL/6-2/185* d4.20 Col Toledo

1964	NY A	0	3	.000	7	1	0	0	18.1	16	12	1	0	12-0	12	4.91	74	.235	.350	4	.000	-0	0	-3		-0.5
	LA A	1	1	.500	6	5	0	0	18	25	10	2	1	13-0	13	5.00	66	.333	.438	5-0-2	.000	-1	162	-3		-0.3
	KC A	1	4	.200	9	7	2	0	42	37	23	2	0	33-0	30	3.86	99	.248	.378	12-0-1	.000	-1*	77	-2		-0.3
	Year	2	8	.200	22	13	2	0	78.1	78	45	5	1	58-0	55	4.37	84	.267	.387	21-0-3	.000	-2	99	-7		-1.2
1969	Sea A	0	3	.000	6	5	1	0-0	32.2	30	14	4	2	10-0	17	3.31	110	.252	.316	11	.091	-1	73	1		0.0
1970	Mil A	0	1	.000	10	0	0	0-0	18.1	24	13	2	0	12-0	20	6.38	59	.329	.424	3-0-2	.333	0		-5	108	-0.3
Total	3	2	12	.143	38	18	3	0-0	129.1	132	72	11	3	80-0	92	4.38	84	.273	.376	35-0-5	.057	-3	92	-12	108	-1.4

MEYER, RUSS Russell Charles "Rowdy","The Mad Monk" B10.25.1923 Peru IL D11.16.1998 Oglesby IL BB/TR/6-1/185* d9.13 C1

1946	Chi N	0	0	—	4	1	0	1	17	21	7	2	0	10	10	3.18	104	.309	.397	5	.200	0	129	0	62	0.4
1947	Chi N	3	2	.600	23	2	1	0	45	43	17	4	1	14	22	3.40	116	.257	.319	12	.250	0	67	4	62	0.3
1948	Chi N	10	10	.500	29	26	8-3	0	164.2	157	75	8	1	77	89	3.66	107	.254	.338	56-0-7	.107	-3	107	6		0.3
1949	Phi N	17	8	.680	37	28	14-2	1	213	199	84	14	1	70	78	3.08	128	.250	.311	70-0-6	.143	-1	93	19		1.5
1950	†Phi N	9	11	.450	32	25	3	1	159.2	193	108	21	2	67	74	5.30	76	.304	.373	50-0-7	.140	-2	99	-23		-2.5
1951	Phi N	8	9	.471	28	24	7-2	0	168	172	69	13	2	55	65	3.48	111	.263	.322	48-0-13	.104	-2	112	8		0.4
1952	Phi N	13	14	.481	32	32	14-1	1	232.1	235	99	10	2	65	92	3.14	116	.269	.311	79-1-5	.089	-2	110	12		0.4
1953	†Bro N	15	5	.750	34	32	10-2	0	191.1	201	109	25	3	63	106	4.56	93	.269	.327	75-0-6	.147	-2	143	-8		-1.0
1954	Bro N	11	6	.647	36	28	6-2	0	180.1	193	89	17	2	49	70	3.99	102	.275	.322	47-0-14	.143	-3	122	2		-0.1
1955	†Bro N	6	2	.750	18	11	2-1	0	73	86	46	8	0	31-6	25	5.42	75	.300	.364	27-0-2	.037	-3	171	-9	30	-1.1
1956	Chi N	1	6	.143	20	9	0	0	57	71	41	11	2	26-4	28	6.32	60	.313	.384	12-0-2	.083	-1	96	-14		-1.5
	Cin N	0	0	—	1	0	0	0	1	1	0	0	0	0-0	1	0.00	—	.250	.250		—	0				
	Year	1	6	.143	21	9	0	0	58	72	41	11	2	26-4	29	6.21	61	.312	.382	12-0-2	.083	-1	96	-14		-1.5
1957	Bos A	0	0	—	2	1	0	0	5	10	5	0	0	3-0	1	5.40	74	.417	.464	1	1.000	0	90	-1		-0.3
1959	KC A	1	0	1.000	18	0	0	1	24	24	12	3	1	11-0	10	4.50	89	.261	.340	2	—	-0		0		-0.2
Total	13	94	73	.563	319	219	65-13	5	1531.1	1606	761	136	15	541-10	672	3.99	99	.271	.333	484-1-62	.114	-18	116	-4	92	-1.7

MEYERLE, LEVI Levi Samuel "Long Levi" B7.1845 Philadelphia PA D11.4.1921 Philadelphia PA BR/TR/6-1/177 d5.20 ▲

1871	Ath NA	0	0	—	1	0	0	0	1	1	1	0		2	0	9.00	45	.250	.500	130-4	.492	1*		0		0.0
1876	Phi N	0	2	.000	2	2	2	0	18	28	23	0	1	0	0	5.00	48	.337	.345	256	.340	1*	64	-4		0.0

MIADICH, BART John Barton B2.3.1976 Torrance CA BR/TR/6-4/205* d9.2

2001	Ana A	0	0	—	11	0	0	0-0	10	6	5	2	0	8-0	11	4.50	103	.182	.341	0	—	0		0		-0.0
2003	Ana A	0	0	—	1	0	0	0-0	2	5	4	0	1	1-0	3	18.00	24	.500	.583	0	—	0		-3		-0.0
Total	2	0	0	—	12	0	0	0-0	12	11	9	2	1	9-0	14	6.75	68	.256	.396	0	—	0		-3		-0.0

MICELI, DAN Daniel B9.9.1970 Newark NJ BR/TR/6-0/216(205-225) d9.9

1993	Pit N	0	0	—	9	0	0	5.1	5	3	0	0	3-0	4	5.06	81	.273	.360	0	—	0		0		-0.1
1994	Pit N	2	1	.667	28	0	0	2-1	27.1	28	19	5	2	11-2	27	5.93	74	.267	.342	3	.000	-0		-4		-0.1
1995	Pit N	4	4	.500	58	0	0	21-6	58	61	30	7	4	28-5	56	4.66	93	.270	.355	1	.000	-0		-1		-0.0
1996	Pit N	2	10	.167	44	9	0	1-0	85.2	99	65	15	3	45-5	66	5.78	76	.291	.372	13	.000	-1	87	-14		-2.0
1997	Det A	3	2	.600	71	0	0	3-5	82.2	77	49	13	1	38-4	79	5.01	92	.248	.330	0	—	0		-3		-0.6
1998	†SD N	10	5	.667	67	0	0	2-6	72.2	64	28	6	1	27-4	70	3.22	123	.238	.308	1	1.000	1		7		1.3
1999	SD N	4	5	.444	66	0	0	2-2	68.2	67	39	7	2	36-5	59	4.46	96	.266	.360	1	.000	-0		-2		-0.1
2000	Fla N	6	4	.600	45	0	0	0-3	48.2	45	23	4	1	18-2	40	4.25	103	.242	.311	0	—	0		2	49	-0.1
2001	Fla N	0	0	—	29	0	0	0-3	24.2	29	21	5	0	11-2	31	6.93	60	.287	.354	0	—	0		-8		-1.4
	Col N	2	0	1.000	22	0	0	1-0	20.1	18	8	2	0	5-0	17	2.21	241	.231	.274	0	—	0		5		0.9
	Year	2	5	.286	51	0	0	1-3	45	47	29	7	0	16-2	48	4.80	98	.263	.320	0	—	0		-2		-1.1
2002	Tex A	0	2	.000	7	0	0	0-1	8.1	13	8	1	0	3-0	5	8.64	55	.333	.381	0	—	0		-3		-0.7
2003	Col N	0	0	—	14	0	0	0-0	20.2	24	13	7	1	9-1	18	5.66	86	.286	.362	0	—	0		0		-0.1
	Cle A	1	1	.500	13	0	0	0-1	15	9	4	1	0	6-1	19	1.20	369	.164	.246	0	—	0		5		0.9
	NY A	0	0	—	7	0	0	1-0	4.2	4	3	2	0	3-0	1	5.79	76	.211	.318	0	—	0		-1		-0.0
	Year	1	1	.500	20	0	0	1-1	19.2	13	7	3	0	9-1	20	2.29	193	.176	.265	0	—	0		8		0.7
	Hou N	1	1	.500	23	0	0	0-0	30	22	7	3	1	7-1	20	2.10	210	.208	.263	0	.000	-0		6		0.9
2004	†Hou N	6	6	.500	74	0	0	2-6	77.2	74	34	10	2	27-12	83	3.59	122	.247	.311	2	.500	0		6	18	0.3
2005	Col N	1	2	.333	19	0	0	0-2	18.1	19	12	1	1	13-0	19	5.89	81	.257	.393	0	—	0		-2	59	-0.2
Total	13	42	50	.457	598	9	0	35-36	668.2	659	366	89	19	290-44	614	4.51	98	.257	.334	22	.091	-1	87	-6	126	-1.4

MICHAELS, JOHN John Joseph B7.10.1907 Bridgeport CT D11.18.1996 Sebring FL BL/TL/5-10.5/154 d4.16 gs-Jason

1932	Bos A	1	6	.143	28	8	2	0	80.1	101	59	4	3	27	16	5.13	88	.304	.362	21	.143	-1*	71	-7		-0.1

MICHAELSON, JOHN John August "Mike" B8.12.1893 Tivalkoski, Finland D4.16.1968 Woodruff WI BR/TR/5-9/165 d8.28

1921	Chi A	0	0	—	2	0	0	0	2.2	4	3	0	1	0	1	10.13	42	.400	.455	0	—	0		-2		-0.1

YEAR	TM LG	W	L	PCT	G	GS	CG-SHO	SV-BS	IP	H	R	HR	HB	BB-IB	SO	ERA	AERA	OAV	OOB	AB-HR-SH	AVG	PB	SUP	APR	DL	PW

MICHALAK, CHRIS Christian Matthew B1.4.1971 Joliet IL BL/TL/6-2/195* [OakA93 12/349] d8.22 Col Notre Dame

YEAR	TM LG	W	L	PCT	G	GS	CG-SHO	SV-BS	IP	H	R	HR	HB	BB-IB	SO	ERA	AERA	OAV	OOB	AB-HR-SH	AVG	PB	SUP	APR	DL	PW
1998	Ari N	0	0	—	5	0	0	0-0	5.1	1	1	0	0	4-0	5	11.81	36	.375	.448	0	—	0		-4		-0.2
2001	Tor A	6	7	.462	24	18	0	0-0	115	133	66	14	12	49-5	57	4.62	99	.296	.377	3-0-2	.333	1	84	-1		0.1
	Tex A	2	2	.500	11	0	0	1-1	21.2	24	8	5	1	6-0	10	3.32	144	.279	.333	0*	—	0		3		0.6
	Year	8	9	.471	35	18	0	1-1	136.2	157	74	19	13	55-5	67	4.41	105	.293	.371	3-0-2	.333	1	84	3		0.7
2002	Tex A	0	2	.000	13	0	0	0-0	14.1	20	7	1	1	10-2	5	4.40	109	.339	.437	0	—	0		1		0.1
Total 3		8	11	.421	53	18	0	1-1	156.1	186	88	21	14	69-7	77	4.66	99	.301	.380	3-0-2	.333	1	84	-1		0.6

MICKENS, GLENN Glenn Roger B7.26.1930 Wilmar CA BR/TR/6-0/175 d7.19 Col UCLA

YEAR	TM LG	W	L	PCT	G	GS	CG-SHO	SV-BS	IP	H	R	HR	HB	BB-IB	SO	ERA	AERA	OAV	OOB	AB-HR-SH	AVG	PB	SUP	APR	DL	PW
1953	Bro N	0	1	.000	4	0	0	0	6.1	11	9	2	0	4	5	11.37	37	.393	.469	2	.000	-0	178	-5		-0.7

MIDDLEBROOK, JASON Jason Douglas B6.26.1975 Jackson MI BR/TR/6-3/215* [SDN96 9/260] d9.17 Col Stanford

YEAR	TM LG	W	L	PCT	G	GS	CG-SHO	SV-BS	IP	H	R	HR	HB	BB-IB	SO	ERA	AERA	OAV	OOB	AB-HR-SH	AVG	PB	SUP	APR	DL	PW
2001	SD N	2	1	.667	4	3	0	0-0	19.1	18	11	6	1	10-1	10	5.12	81	.247	.345	7	.143	-0	126	-2		-0.2
2002	SD N	1	3	.250	12	2	0	0-0	35.1	31	20	1	0	15-2	28	5.09	76	.244	.322	6-0-1	.333	1	83	-4	30	-0.4
	NY N	1	0	1.000	3	3	0	0-0	16	13	7	1	0	7-0	14	3.94	100	.220	.303	5	.000	-0	109	0	17	-0.4
	Year	2	3	.400	15	5	0	0-0	51.1	44	27	2	1	22-2	42	4.73	83	.237	.316	11-0-1	.182	0	99	-4		-0.4
2003	NY N	0	0	—	5	0	0	0-0	7	13	8	0	0	4-0	3	10.29	41	.433	.486	0	—	0		-5		-0.2
Total 3		4	4	.500	24	8	0	0-0	77.2	75	46	8	2	36-3	55	5.33	75	.260	.341	18-0-1	.167	0	110	-11	47	-0.8

MIDDLETON, JIM James Blaine "Rifle Jim" B5.28.1889 Argos IN D1.12.1974 Argos IN BR/TR/5-11.5/165 d4.18

YEAR	TM LG	W	L	PCT	G	GS	CG-SHO	SV-BS	IP	H	R	HR	HB	BB-IB	SO	ERA	AERA	OAV	OOB	AB-HR-SH	AVG	PB	SUP	APR	DL	PW
1917	NY N	1	1	.500	13	0	0	1	36	35	18	1	1	8	9	2.75	93	.255	.301	8	.000	-1		-3		-0.3
1921	Det A	6	11	.353	38	10	2	7	121.2	149	83	5	2	44	31	5.03	85	.302	.361	34-0-4	.147	-2	117	-9		-1.3
Total 2		7	12	.368	51	10	2	8	157.2	184	101	6	3	52	40	4.51	86	.292	.348	42-0-4	.119	-3	117	-12		-1.6

MIDDLETON, JOHN John Wayne "Lefty" B4.11.1900 Mt.Calm TX D11.3.1986 Amarillo TX BL/TL/6-1/185 d9.6 Col Hardin-Simmons

YEAR	TM LG	W	L	PCT	G	GS	CG-SHO	SV-BS	IP	H	R	HR	HB	BB-IB	SO	ERA	AERA	OAV	OOB	AB-HR-SH	AVG	PB	SUP	APR	DL	PW
1922	Cle A	0	1	.000	2	1	0	0	7.1	8	7	1	0	6	2	7.36	54	.286	.412	3	.333	0	106	-3		-0.3

MIDKIFF, DICK Richard B9.28.1914 Gonzales TX D10.30.1956 Temple TX BR/TR/6-2/185 d4.24 Col Texas

YEAR	TM LG	W	L	PCT	G	GS	CG-SHO	SV-BS	IP	H	R	HR	HB	BB-IB	SO	ERA	AERA	OAV	OOB	AB-HR-SH	AVG	PB	SUP	APR	DL	PW
1938	Bos A	1	1	.500	13	2	0	0	35.1	43	30	5	0	21	10	5.09	97	.305	.395	10	.200	0	107	-4		-0.2

MIELKE, GARY Gary Roger B1.28.1963 St.James MN BR/TR/6-3/185(180-199) [TexA85 26/655] d8.19 Col Mankato St.

YEAR	TM LG	W	L	PCT	G	GS	CG-SHO	SV-BS	IP	H	R	HR	HB	BB-IB	SO	ERA	AERA	OAV	OOB	AB-HR-SH	AVG	PB	SUP	APR	DL	PW
1987	Tex A	0	0	—	3	0	0	0-0	3	3	2	2	0	1-0	3	6.00	75	.250	.308	0	—	0		0		0.0
1989	Tex A	1	0	1.000	43	0	0	1-1	49.2	52	18	4	2	25-3	26	3.26	122	.280	.369	0	—	0		5		0.2
1990	Tex A	0	3	.000	33	0	0	0-1	41	42	17	4	2	15-5	13	3.73	106	.271	.343	0	—	0		2	57	0.1
Total 3		1	3	.250	79	0	0	1-2	93.2	97	37	10	4	41-8	42	3.56	112	.275	.356	0	—	0		7	57	0.3

MIKKELSEN, PETE Peter James B10.25.1939 Staten Island NY BR/TR/6-2/220* d4.17

YEAR	TM LG	W	L	PCT	G	GS	CG-SHO	SV-BS	IP	H	R	HR	HB	BB-IB	SO	ERA	AERA	OAV	OOB	AB-HR-SH	AVG	PB	SUP	APR	DL	PW
1964	†NY A	7	4	.636	50	0	0	12	86	79	35	3	4	41-5	63	3.56	102	.247	.338	16-0-4	.063	-1		2		0.2
1965	NY A	4	9	.308	41	0	0	1	82.1	78	40	10	3	36-9	69	3.28	104	.249	.332	10-0-1	.100	-0	9	-2		-0.2
1966	Pit N	9	8	.529	71	0	0	14	126	106	45	8	5	51-9	76	3.07	116	.234	.318	20-0-2	.150	-0	8			1.3
1967	Pit N	1	2	.333	32	0	0	2	56.1	50	29	7	3	19-5	30	4.31	78	.237	.308	4-0-2	.000	-0		-5		-0.4
	Chi N	0	0	—	7	0	0	0	7	9	6	1	1	5-0	0	6.43	55	.333	.455	0	—	0		-2		-0.1
	Year	1	2	.333	39	0	0	2	63.1	59	35	8	4	24-5	30	4.55	74	.248	.326	4-0-2	.000	-0		-7		-0.5
1968	Chi N	0	0	—	3	0	0	0	4.2	7	4	3	0	1-0	5	7.71	41	.350	.381	1	1.000	-0		-2		-0.1
	StL N	0	0	—	5	0	0	0	16	10	5	0	0	7-3	8	1.13	257	.179	.270	3	.000	-0		2		0.1
	Year	0	0	—	8	0	0	0	20.2	17	9	3	0	8-3	13	2.61	113	.224	.298	4	.250	-0		0		0.0
1969	LA N	7	5	.583	48	0	0	4-0	81.1	57	34	9	4	30-8	51	2.77	121	.193	.277	6-0-1	.167	-0		3		0.5
1970	LA N	4	2	.667	33	0	0	6-3	62	48	20	5	4	20-4	47	2.76	140	.211	.286	6-0-1	.333	1	8		49	1.0
1971	LA N	8	5	.615	41	0	0	5-6	74	67	38	10	1	17-5	46	3.65	89	.242	.286	10	.200	-0		-5		-0.9
1972	LA N	5	5	.500	33	0	0	2	57.2	65	32	3	5	23-4	41	4.06	83	.283	.360	7	.000	-0		-5		-0.9
Total 9		45	40	.529	364	3	0	49-10	653.1	576	288	59	30	250-52	436	3.38	103	.237	.315	83-0-11	.133	-2	9		49	0.5

MIKLOS, HANK John Joseph B11.27.1910 Chicago IL D3.29.2000 Adrian MI BL/TL/5-11/175 d4.23

YEAR	TM LG	W	L	PCT	G	GS	CG-SHO	SV-BS	IP	H	R	HR	HB	BB-IB	SO	ERA	AERA	OAV	OOB	AB-HR-SH	AVG	PB	SUP	APR	DL	PW
1944	Chi N	0	0	—	2	0	0	0	7	9	6	1	0	3	0	7.71	46	.333	.400	2	.000	-0		-3		-0.1

MILACKI, BOB Robert B7.28.1964 Trenton NJ BR/TR/6-4/234(220-234) [BalA83 S2/29] d9.18 Col Yavapai (AZ) JC

YEAR	TM LG	W	L	PCT	G	GS	CG-SHO	SV-BS	IP	H	R	HR	HB	BB-IB	SO	ERA	AERA	OAV	OOB	AB-HR-SH	AVG	PB	SUP	APR	DL	PW
1988	Bal A	2	0	1.000	3	3	1-1	0-0	25	9	2	1	0	9-0	18	0.72	547	.110	.198	0	—	0	70	9		0.8
1989	Bal A	14	12	.538	37	36	3-2	0-0	243	233	105	21	2	88-4	113	3.74	102	.254	.318	0	—	0	94	3		0.3
1990	Bal A	5	8	.385	27	24	1-1	0-0	135.1	143	73	18	0	61-2	60	4.46	86	.273	.346	0	—	0	92	-10	32	-0.9
1991	Bal A	10	9	.526	31	26	3-1	0-0	184	175	86	17	1	53-3	108	4.01	99	.253	.305	0	—	0	93	0		0.0
1992	Bal A	6	8	.429	23	20	0	1-0	115.2	140	78	16	2	44-2	51	5.84	70	.296	.356	0	—	0	101	-21		-2.3
1993	Cle A	1	1	.500	5	2	0	0-0	16	19	8	3	0	11-0	7	3.38	130	.302	.405	0	—	0	42	1		0.1
1994	KC A	0	5	.000	10	10	0	0-0	55.2	68	43	6	1	20-3	17	6.14	82	.298	.352	0	—	0	90	-7		-0.5
1996	Sea A	1	4	.200	7	4	0	0-0	21	30	20	3	0	15-3	13	6.86	73	.330	.425	0	—	0	112	-6		-1.0
Total 8		39	47	.453	143	125	8-5	1-0	795.2	817	415	85	6	301-17	387	4.38	92	.266	.330	0	—	0	94	-31	32	-3.5

MILCHIN, MIKE Michael Wayne B2.28.1968 Knoxville TN BL/TL/6-3/190 [StLN89 2/36] d5.14 Col Clemson

YEAR	TM LG	W	L	PCT	G	GS	CG-SHO	SV-BS	IP	H	R	HR	HB	BB-IB	SO	ERA	AERA	OAV	OOB	AB-HR-SH	AVG	PB	SUP	APR	DL	PW
1996	Min A	2	1	.667	26	0	0	0-1	21.2	31	21	6	0	12-1	19	8.31	62	.341	.417	0	—	0		-7		-0.8
	Bal A	1	0	1.000	13	0	0	0-0	11	13	7	0	0	5-1	10	5.73	86	.325	.375	0	—	0		-1		0.0
	Year	3	1	.750	39	0	0	0-1	32.2	44	28	6	0	17-2	29	7.44	68	.336	.404	0	—	0		-8		-0.8

MILES, CARL Carl Thomas B3.22.1918 Trenton MO BB/TL/5-11/178 d6.8 Col Missouri

YEAR	TM LG	W	L	PCT	G	GS	CG-SHO	SV-BS	IP	H	R	HR	HB	BB-IB	SO	ERA	AERA	OAV	OOB	AB-HR-SH	AVG	PB	SUP	APR	DL	PW
1940	Phi A	0	0	—	2	0	0	0	8	9	12	2	0	8	6	13.50	33	.281	.425	4	.750	2		-7		-0.2

MILES, JIM James Charlie B8.8.1943 Grenada MS BR/TR/6-2/210* d9.7 Col Delta St.

YEAR	TM LG	W	L	PCT	G	GS	CG-SHO	SV-BS	IP	H	R	HR	HB	BB-IB	SO	ERA	AERA	OAV	OOB	AB-HR-SH	AVG	PB	SUP	APR	DL	PW
1968	Was A	0	0	—	3	0	0	0	4.1	8	6	0	0	2-0	5	12.46	23	.421	.455	0	—	0		-4		-0.2
1969	Was A	0	1	.000	10	1	0	0-0	20.1	19	15	2	4	15-1	15	6.20	37	.257	.400	3	.333	0*	76	-6		-0.2
Total 2		0	1	.000	13	1	0	0-0	24.2	27	21	2	4	17-1	20	7.30	47	.290	.410	3	.333	0	76	-10		-0.4

MILITELLO, SAM Sam Salvatore B11.26.1969 Tampa FL BR/TR/6-3/200* [NYA90 6/165] d8.9 Col Tampa

YEAR	TM LG	W	L	PCT	G	GS	CG-SHO	SV-BS	IP	H	R	HR	HB	BB-IB	SO	ERA	AERA	OAV	OOB	AB-HR-SH	AVG	PB	SUP	APR	DL	PW
1992	NY A	3	3	.500	9	9	0	0-0	60	43	24	6	2	32-1	42	3.45	115	.195	.302	0	—	0	100	4		0.3
1993	NY A	1	1	.500	3	2	0	0-0	9.1	10	8	1	2	7-1	5	6.75	62	.270	.413	0	—	0	110	-3		-0.5
Total 2		4	4	.500	12	11	0	0-0	69.1	53	32	7	4	39-2	47	3.89	102	.205	.319	0	—	0	102	1		-0.2

MILJUS, JOHNNY John Kenneth "Jovo","Big Serb" B6.30.1895 Pittsburgh PA D2.11.1976 Fort Harrison MT BR/TR/6-1/178 d10.2 Mil 1918 Col Duquesne

YEAR	TM LG	W	L	PCT	G	GS	CG-SHO	SV-BS	IP	H	R	HR	HB	BB-IB	SO	ERA	AERA	OAV	OOB	AB-HR-SH	AVG	PB	SUP	APR	DL	PW
1915	Pit F	0	0	—	1	0	0	0	1	1	0	0	0	0	0	0.00	—	.250	.250	0	—	0		0		0.0
1917	Bro N	0	1	.000	4	1	1	0	15	14	3	0	3	8	9	0.60	466	.250	.373	5	.000	-1	27	3		0.1
1920	Bro N	1	0	1.000	9	0	0	0	23.1	24	10	2	0	4	9	3.09	104	.267	.298	6	.333	1*		0		0.2
1921	Bro N	6	3	.667	28	9	3	1	93.2	115	49	1	2	27	37	4.23	92	.312	.362	30	.167	-2	106	-2		-0.3
1927	†Pit N	8	3	.727	19	6	3-2	0	75.2	62	21	0	0	17	24	1.90	216	.228	.273	28-0-1	.179	-1	79	17		2.3
1928	Pit N	5	7	.417	21	10	3	1	69.2	90	48	2	3	33	26	5.30	77	.313	.389	26	.308	1	94	-9		-1.3
	Cle A	1	4	.200	11	4	1	0	50.2	46	25	1	0	20	19	2.66	156	.243	.316	15	.200	-0	51	5		0.5
1929	Cle A	8	8	.500	34	15	4	2	128.1	174	93	10	3	64	42	5.19	86	.331	.406	43-0-2	.256	1	96	-12		-1.1
Total 7		29	26	.527	127	45	15-2	4	457.1	526	209	16	11	173	166	3.92	104	.293	.359	153-0-3	.222	0	92	2		0.4

MILLER, DYAR Dyar K B5.29.1946 Batesville IN BR/TR/6-1/200(195-215) d6.9 C2 Col Utah St.

YEAR	TM LG	W	L	PCT	G	GS	CG-SHO	SV-BS	IP	H	R	HR	HB	BB-IB	SO	ERA	AERA	OAV	OOB	AB-HR-SH	AVG	PB	SUP	APR	DL	PW
1975	Bal A	6	3	.667	30	0	0	8-4	46.1	32	14	3	0	16-4	33	2.72	130	.199	.267	0	—	0		5		1.1
1976	Bal A	2	4	.333	49	0	0	7-3	88.2	79	31	5	1	36-5	37	2.94	112	.246	.321	0	—	0		4		0.3
1977	Bal A	2	2	.500	12	0	0	1-1	22.1	25	14	6	0	10-1	9	5.64	68	.278	.350	0	—	0		-1		-0.7
	Cal A	4	4	.500	41	0	0	4-3	92.1	81	35	10	0	30-7	49	3.02	130	.242	.300	0	—	0		10		0.8
	Year	6	6	.500	53	0	0	5-4	114.2	106	49	16	0	40-8	58	3.53	111	.249	.311	0	—	0		6		0.1
1978	Cal A	6	2	.750	41	0	0	1-0	84.2	85	29	3	5	41-3	34	2.66	137	.264	.352	0	—	0		9	24	0.7
1979	Cal A	1	0	1.000	14	1	0	0-0	35.1	44	14	2	1	13-0	16	3.31	123	.319	.376	0	—	0	111	3		0.1
	Tor A	0	0	—	10	0	0	0-0	15.1	27	18	3	0	5-0	7	10.57	42	.391	.427	0	—	0		-9		-0.4
	Year	1	0	1.000	24	1	0	0-0	50.2	71	32	5	1	18-0	23	5.51	76	.343	.392	0	—	0	109	-6		-0.3
1980	NY N	1	2	.333	31	0	0	1-1	42	37	9	1	0	11-3	28	1.93	187	.242	.289	1-0-1	.000	-0		8		0.6
1981	NY N	1	0	1.000	23	0	0	1-1	38.1	42	19	5	1	15-2	22	3.29	108	.327	.387	3	.333	1		0		0.0
Total 7		23	17	.575	251	1	0	22-13	465.1	459	184	35	9	177-25	235	3.23	114	.264	.331	4-0-1	.250	0	121	26	24	2.5

YEAR	TM LG	W	L	PCT	G	GS	CG-SHO	SV-BS	IP	H	R	HR	HB	BB-IB	SO	ERA	AERA	OAV	OOB	AB-HR-SH	AVG	PB	SUP	APR	DL	PW

MILLER, ELMER Elmer Joseph "Lefty" B4.17.1903 Detroit MI D1.8.1987 Corona CA BL/TL/5-11/189 d6.21 ▲

YEAR	TM LG	W	L	PCT	G	GS	CG-SHO	SV-BS	IP	H	R	HR	HB	BB-IB	SO	ERA	AERA	OAV	OOB	AB-HR-SH	AVG	PB	SUP	APR	DL	PW
1929	Phi N	0	1	.000	8	2	0	0	11.1	12	18	1	3	21	5	11.12	47	.279	.537	38-1-0	.237	0*	118	-8		-0.5

MILLER, FRANK Frank Lee "Bullet" B5.13.1886 Allegan MI D2.19.1974 Allegan MI BR/TR/6-0/188 d7.12

YEAR	TM LG	W	L	PCT	G	GS	CG-SHO	SV-BS	IP	H	R	HR	HB	BB-IB	SO	ERA	AERA	OAV	OOB	AB-HR-SH	AVG	PB	SUP	APR	DL	PW
1913	Chi A	0	1	.000	1	1	0	0	1.2	4	5	0	0	3	2	27.00	11	.571	.700	0	—	0	0	-4		-0.6
1916	Pit N	7	10	.412	30	20	10-2	1	173	135	55	4	7	49	88	2.29	117	.226	.292	51-0-7	.137	-1	97	9		0.8
1917	Pit N	10	19	.345	38	28	14-5	1	224	216	98	1	5	60	92	3.13	91	.251	.304	76-0-5	.118	-4*	76	-7		-1.4
1918	Pit N	11	8	.579	23	23	14-2	0	170.1	152	60	1	7	37	47	2.38	121	.250	.301	57-0-7	.105	-3	109	9		0.6
1919	Pit N	13	12	.520	32	26	16-3	0	201.2	170	79	6	5	34	59	3.03	99	.234	.272	66-0-6	.106	-5	106	0		-0.5
1922	Bos N	11	13	.458	31	23	14-2	1	200	213	100	7	2	60	65	3.51	114	.279	.333	68-0-5	.118	-5	85	10		0.6
1923	Bos N	0	3	.000	8	6	0	1	39.1	54	26	2	3	11	6	4.58	87	.335	.389	7-0-1	.143	-0	93	-3		-0.3
Total 7		52	66	.441	163	127	68-14	4	1010	944	423	21	29	254	359	3.01	104	.253	.306	325-0-31	.117	-18	92	14		-0.8

MILLER, FRED Frederick Holman "Speedy" B6.28.1886 Fairfield IN D5.2.1953 Brookville IN BL/TL/6-2/190 d7.8

YEAR	TM LG	W	L	PCT	G	GS	CG-SHO	SV-BS	IP	H	R	HR	HB	BB-IB	SO	ERA	AERA	OAV	OOB	AB-HR-SH	AVG	PB	SUP	APR	DL	PW
1910	Bro N	1	1	.500	6	2	0	0	21	35	19	1	3	13	2	4.71	64	.309	.423	8	.250	0	86	-6		-0.4

MILLER, BERT Herbert Alexander B10.26.1875 Riley MI D6.14.1937 Flint MI d7.15

YEAR	TM LG	W	L	PCT	G	GS	CG-SHO	SV-BS	IP	H	R	HR	HB	BB-IB	SO	ERA	AERA	OAV	OOB	AB-HR-SH	AVG	PB	SUP	APR	DL	PW
1897	Lou N	0	1	.000	4	1	0	0	17	32	23	0	0	3	3	7.94	54	.395	.417	6	.167	-1	0	-7		-0.3

MILLER, OX John Anthony B5.4.1915 Gause TX BR/TR/6-1/190 d8.7

YEAR	TM LG	W	L	PCT	G	GS	CG-SHO	SV-BS	IP	H	R	HR	HB	BB-IB	SO	ERA	AERA	OAV	OOB	AB-HR-SH	AVG	PB	SUP	APR	DL	PW
1943	Was A	0	0	—	3	0	0	0	6	10	7	1	0	5	1	10.50	31	.370	.469	1	.000	-0		-4		-0.2
	StL A	0	0	—	2	0	0	0	6	7	8	2	2	3	3	12.00	28	.304	.429	1	.000	-0		-5		-0.2
	Year	0	0	—	5	0	0	0	12	17	15	3	2	8	4	11.25	29	.340	.450	2	.000	-0		-10		-0.4
1945	StL A	2	1	.667	4	3	3	0	28.1	23	5	2	0	5	4	1.59	222	.219	.255	11-0-1	.182	-0*	65	6		0.6
1946	StL A	1	3	.250	11	3	0	1	35.1	52	28	5	0	15	12	6.88	54	.338	.396	7-0-1	.286	1	100	-10		-1.0
1947	Chi N	1	2	.333	4	4	1	0	16	31	18	2	0	5	7	10.13	39	.397	.434	7-1-0	.429	2	101	-10		-1.2
Total 4		4	6	.400	24	10	4	1	91.2	123	66	12	2	33	27	6.38	57	.318	.374	27-1-2	.259	2	92	-23		-2.0

MILLER, JOHN John Ernest B5.30.1941 Baltimore MD BR/TR/6-2/210* d9.22

YEAR	TM LG	W	L	PCT	G	GS	CG-SHO	SV-BS	IP	H	R	HR	HB	BB-IB	SO	ERA	AERA	OAV	OOB	AB-HR-SH	AVG	PB	SUP	APR	DL	PW
1962	Bal A	1	1	.500	2	1	0	0	10	2	1	0	0	5-0	4	0.90	411	.065	.194	3	.000	-0	0	3		0.7
1963	Bal A	1	1	.500	3	2	0	0	17	12	6	0	0	14-0	16	3.18	109	.194	.342	6	.000	-1	90	1		0.0
1965	Bal A	6	4	.600	16	16	1	0	93.1	75	38	4	1	58-0	71	3.18	109	.223	.336	30-0-1	.100	-1	120	3		-0.3
1966	Bal A	4	8	.333	23	16	0	0	100.2	92	59	15	0	58-3	81	4.74	70	.241	.340	34-0-4	.118	-1	104	-16		-1.9
1967	Bal A	0	0	—	2	0	0	0	6	7	5	1	2	3-0	6	7.50	42	.304	.429	0	—	0		-3		-0.1
Total 5		12	14	.462	46	35	1	0	227	188	109	20	3	138-3	178	3.89	88	.225	.336	73-0-5	.096	-3	108	-12		-1.0

MILLER, CYCLONE Joseph H. B9.24.1859 Springfield MA D10.13.1916 New London CT TL/5-9.5/165 d7.11

YEAR	TM LG	W	L	PCT	G	GS	CG-SHO	SV-BS	IP	H	R	HR	HB	BB-IB	SO	ERA	AERA	OAV	OOB	AB-HR-SH	AVG	PB	SUP	APR	DL	PW
1884	CP U	1	0	1.000	1	1	1	0	9	4	2	0		13		1.00	243	.125	.125	4	.250	-0	176	1		0.1
	Pro N	3	2	.600	6	5	2	0	34.2	36	24	0		11	12	2.08	137	.259	.313	23	.043	-3	149	1		-0.1
	Phi N	0	1	.000	1	1	1	0	9	17	19	5		6	1	10.00	30	.386	.460	4	.000	-1	124	-7		-0.6
	Year	3	3	.500	7	6	3	0	43.2	53	43	5		17	13	3.71	78	.290	.350	27	.037	-4	144	-6		-0.6
1886	Phi AA	10	8	.556	19	19	19-1	0	169.2	158	109	6	4	59	99	2.97	118	.239	.305	66	.136	-1*	84	7		0.6
Total 2		14	11	.560	27	26	23-1	0	222.1	215	154	11	4	76	125	3.04	110	.245	.308	97	.113	-5	100	2		0.1

MILLER, JUSTIN Justin Mark B8.27.1977 Torrance CA BR/TR/6-2/209* [ColN97 5/162] d4.12 Col Los Angeles Harbor (CA) JC

YEAR	TM LG	W	L	PCT	G	GS	CG-SHO	SV-BS	IP	H	R	HR	HB	BB-IB	SO	ERA	AERA	OAV	OOB	AB-HR-SH	AVG	PB	SUP	APR	DL	PW
2002	Tor A	9	5	.643	25	18	0	0-0	102.1	103	70	12	11	66-2	68	5.54	83	.268	.385	2	.000	-0	95	-11		-1.3
2004	Tor A	3	4	.429	19	15	0	0-0	81.2	101	58	14	5	42-3	47	6.06	81	.316	.397	0	—	0	86	-10	65	-1.0
2005	Tor A	0	0	—	1	0	0	0-0	2.1	5	4	3	0	0-0	2	15.43	30	.417	.417	0	—	0		-3		-0.1
Total 3		12	9	.571	45	33	0	0	186.1	209	132	29	16	108-5	117	5.89	80	.291	.390	2	.000	-0	91	-24	65	-2.1

MILLER, WHITEY Kenneth Albert B5.2.1915 St.Louis MO D4.3.1991 St.Louis MO BR/TR/6-1/195 d9.15

YEAR	TM LG	W	L	PCT	G	GS	CG-SHO	SV-BS	IP	H	R	HR	HB	BB-IB	SO	ERA	AERA	OAV	OOB	AB-HR-SH	AVG	PB	SUP	APR	DL	PW
1944	NY N	0	1	.000	4	0	0	0	5	1	2	0	0	5	2	0.00	—	.059	.238	1	.000	-0*		1		0.2

MILLER, KURT Kurt Everett B8.24.1972 Tucson AZ BR/TR/6-5/220(205-225) [PitN90 1/5] d6.11

YEAR	TM LG	W	L	PCT	G	GS	CG-SHO	SV-BS	IP	H	R	HR	HB	BB-IB	SO	ERA	AERA	OAV	OOB	AB-HR-SH	AVG	PB	SUP	APR	DL	PW
1994	Fla N	1	3	.250	4	4	0	0-0	20	26	18	3	2	7-0	11	8.10	55	.317	.380	6-0-1	.167	-0	56	-7		-1.0
1996	Fla N	1	3	.250	26	5	0	0-2	46.1	57	41	5	2	33-8	30	6.80	61	.313	.422	8-0-1	.375	1	171	-15		-1.0
1997	Fla N	0	1	.000	7	0	0	0-0	7.1	12	8	2	1	9-0	7	9.82	41	.364	.488	0	—	0		-5	153	0.1
1998	Chi N	0	0	—	3	0	0	0-0	4	3	0	0	0	0-0	6	0.00	—	.200	.200	0	—	0		2		0.1
1999	Chi N	0	0	—	4	0	0	0-0	3	6	6	1	0	3-0	1	18.00	25	.462	.563	0	—	0		-4	45	-0.2
Total 5		2	7	.222	44	9	0	0-2	80.2	104	73	11	5	50-8	55	7.48	57	.320	.416	14-0-2	.286	1	119	-29	198	-2.6

MILLER, LARRY Larry Don B6.19.1937 Topeka KS BL/TL/6-0/195* d6.21 Col Kansas

YEAR	TM LG	W	L	PCT	G	GS	CG-SHO	SV-BS	IP	H	R	HR	HB	BB-IB	SO	ERA	AERA	OAV	OOB	AB-HR-SH	AVG	PB	SUP	APR	DL	PW
1964	LA N	4	8	.333	16	14	1	0	79.2	87	44	1	2	28-4	50	4.18	78	.275	.334	26-0-2	.269	2	107	-9		-1.1
1965	NY N	1	4	.200	28	5	0	0	57.1	66	32	6	1	25-0	36	5.02	70	.289	.357	11	.182	0	40	-8		-0.6
1966	NY N	0	2	.000	4	1	0	0	8.1	9	7	3	0	4-0	7	7.56	48	.273	.351	2	.500	0	0	-3		-0.6
Total 3		5	14	.263	48	20	1	0	145.1	162	83	10	3	57-4	93	4.71	72	.281	.344	39-0-2	.256	2	82	-20		-2.3

MILLER, RED Leo Alphonso B2.11.1897 Philadelphia PA D10.20.1973 Orlando FL BR/TR/5-11/195 d7.13

YEAR	TM LG	W	L	PCT	G	GS	CG-SHO	SV-BS	IP	H	R	HR	HB	BB-IB	SO	ERA	AERA	OAV	OOB	AB-HR-SH	AVG	PB	SUP	APR	DL	PW
1923	Phi N	0	0	—	1	0	0	0	1.2	6	6	0	0	1	0	32.40	14	.545	.583	1	.000	-0		-4		-0.2

MILLER, MATT Matt Jacob B11.23.1971 Greenwood MS BR/TR/6-3/210* d6.27 Col Delta State

YEAR	TM LG	W	L	PCT	G	GS	CG-SHO	SV-BS	IP	H	R	HR	HB	BB-IB	SO	ERA	AERA	OAV	OOB	AB-HR-SH	AVG	PB	SUP	APR	DL	PW
2003	Col N	0	0	—	4	0	0	0-0	4.1	5	1	0	0	2-0	5	2.08	236	.313	.389	0	—	0		1		0.1
2004	Cle A	4	1	.800	57	0	0	1-1	55.1	42	22	1	6	23-8	55	3.09	141	.216	.317	0	—	0		8		0.6
2005	Cle A	1	0	1.000	23	0	0	1-1	29.2	22	6	1	3	10-3	23	1.82	225	.212	.297	0	—	0		8	79	0.4
Total 3		5	1	.833	84	0	0	2-2	89.1	69	29	2	9	35-11	83	2.62	164	.220	.314	0	—	0		17	79	1.1

MILLER, MATT Matthew Lincoln B8.2.1974 Lubbock TX BL/TL/6-3/175* [DetA96 2/41] d5.8 Col Texas Tech

YEAR	TM LG	W	L	PCT	G	GS	CG-SHO	SV-BS	IP	H	R	HR	HB	BB-IB	SO	ERA	AERA	OAV	OOB	AB-HR-SH	AVG	PB	SUP	APR	DL	PW
2001	Det A	0	0	—	13	0	0	0-0	9.2	16	8	0	1	4-0	6	7.45	59	.372	.438	0	—	0		-3		-0.1
2002	Det A	0	0	—	2	0	0	0-1	0.2	4	2	1	0	1-0	1	13.50	32	.571	.625	0	—	0		-1	178	-0.1
Total 2		0	0	—	15	0	0	0-1	10.1	20	10	1	1	5-0	7	7.84	56	.400	.464	0	—	0		-4	178	-0.2

MILLER, PAUL Paul Robert B4.27.1965 Burlington WI BR/TR/6-5/215* [PitN87 53/1199] d7.30 Col Carthage

YEAR	TM LG	W	L	PCT	G	GS	CG-SHO	SV-BS	IP	H	R	HR	HB	BB-IB	SO	ERA	AERA	OAV	OOB	AB-HR-SH	AVG	PB	SUP	APR	DL	PW
1991	Pit N	0	0	—	1	1	0	0-0	5	4	3	0	0	2-0	2	5.40	67	.222	.333	3	.000	-0	75	-1		-0.1
1992	Pit N	1	0	1.000	6	0	0	0-0	11.1	11	3	0	0	1-0	5	2.38	146	.256	.267	3	.000	-0		1	48	0.1
1993	Pit N	0	0	—	3	2	0	0-0	10	15	6	2	0	2-0	9	5.40	76	.349	.378	2	.000	-0	99	-1		-0.1
Total 3		1	0	1.000	10	3	0	0-0	26.1	30	12	2	0	6-0	9	4.10	91	.288	.324	8	.000	-1	97	-1	48	-0.1

MILLER, RALPH Ralph Darwin B3.15.1873 Cincinnati OH D5.8.1973 Cincinnati OH BR/TR/5-11/170 d5.4

YEAR	TM LG	W	L	PCT	G	GS	CG-SHO	SV-BS	IP	H	R	HR	HB	BB-IB	SO	ERA	AERA	OAV	OOB	AB-HR-SH	AVG	PB	SUP	APR	DL	PW
1898	Bro N	4	14	.222	23	21	16	0	151.2	161	119	4	13	86	43	5.34	67	.270	.374	62-0-1	.194	-1*	85	-27		-2.6
1899	Bal N	1	3	.250	6	4	3	1	37	44	28	0	4	14	3	4.38	91	.295	.371	-11	.182	1	86	-2		-0.1
Total 2		5	17	.227	29	25	19	1	188.2	205	147	4	17	100	46	5.15	71	.275	.374	73-0-1	.192	-0	85	-29		-2.7

MILLER, RALPH Ralph Henry "Moose","Lefty" B1.14.1899 Vinton IA D2.18.1967 White Bear Lake MN BR/TL/6-1.5/190 d9.16 b-Bing

YEAR	TM LG	W	L	PCT	G	GS	CG-SHO	SV-BS	IP	H	R	HR	HB	BB-IB	SO	ERA	AERA	OAV	OOB	AB-HR-SH	AVG	PB	SUP	APR	DL	PW
1921	Was A	0	0	—	1	0	0	0	1	1	0	0	0	0	0	0.00	—	.000	.000	0	—	0		0		0.0

MILLER, RANDY Randall Scott B3.18.1953 Oxnard CA BR/TR/6-1/180* [BalA74 5/120] d9.7 Col California-San Diego

YEAR	TM LG	W	L	PCT	G	GS	CG-SHO	SV-BS	IP	H	R	HR	HB	BB-IB	SO	ERA	AERA	OAV	OOB	AB-HR-SH	AVG	PB	SUP	APR	DL	PW
1977	Bal A	0	0	—	1	0	0	0-0	0.2	4	3	0	0	0-0	0	40.50	9	.800	.667	0	—	0		-3		-0.1
1978	Mon N	0	1	.000	5	0	0	0-0	7	11	9	1	0	3-1	6	10.29	35	.393	.424	1	.000	-0		-5		-0.7
Total 2		0	1	.000	6	0	0	0-0	7.2	15	12	1	0	3-1	6	12.91	28	.455	.462	1	.000	-0		-8		-0.7

MILLER, BOB Robert Gerald B7.15.1935 Berwyn IL BR/TL/6-1/185* d6.25

YEAR	TM LG	W	L	PCT	G	GS	CG-SHO	SV-BS	IP	H	R	HR	HB	BB-IB	SO	ERA	AERA	OAV	OOB	AB-HR-SH	AVG	PB	SUP	APR	DL	PW
1953	Det A	1	2	.333	13	1	0	0	36.1	43	25	2	1	21	9	5.94	68	.289	.380	8	.125	-1	66	-7		-0.5
1954	Det A	1	1	.500	32	1	0	0	69.2	62	25	1	0	26	27	2.45	150	.244	.312	15	.133	-0*	72	8		0.3
1955	Det A	2	1	.667	7	3	1	0	25.1	26	12	4	0	12-1	11	2.49	154	.263	.339	9	.222	0*	123	2		0.2
1956	Det A	2	0	1.000	11	3	0	0	31.2	37	23	5	0	22-2	16	5.68	72	.308	.413	7	.143	-0	108	-6		-0.3
1962	Cin N	0	0	—	6	0	0	0	5.1	14	13	1	2	3-0	4	21.94	18	.538	.576	1	.000	-0		-10		-0.5
	NY N	2	5	.500	17	1	0	0	20.1	24	16	2	1	8-0	8	7.08	59	.312	.379	1	.000	-0		-5		-0.9
	Year	2	5	.500	23	1	0	0	25.2	38	29	3	3	11-0	12	10.17	41	.369	.433	2	.000	-0		-15		-1.4
Total 5		6	8	.429	86	8	1	2	188.2	206	114	15	4	92-3	75	4.72	83	.284	.365	41	.146	-1	104	-18		-1.7

YEAR	TM LG	W	L	PCT	G	GS	CG-SHO	SV-BS	IP	H	R	HR	HB	BB-IB	SO	ERA	AERA	OAV	OOB	AB-HR-SH	AVG	PB	SUP	APR	DL	PW

MILLER, BOB Robert John B6.16.1926 Detroit MI BR/TR/6-3/190* d9.16 Col Detroit Mercy

YEAR	TM LG	W	L	PCT	G	GS	CG-SHO	SV-BS	IP	H	R	HR	HB	BB-IB	SO	ERA	AERA	OAV	OOB	AB-HR-SH	AVG	PB	SUP	APR	DL	PW
1949	Phi N	0	0		3	0	0	0	2.2	2	0	0	0	2	0	0.00	—	.200	.333	0		0		1		0.1
1950	†Phi N	11	6	.647	35	22	7-2	0	174	190	78	9	5	57	44	3.57	113	.277	.337	61-0-2	.180	-1	98	10		0.9
1951	Phi N	2	1	.667	17	3	0	0	34.1	47	33	2	1	18	10	6.82	56	.331	.410	7	.429	1	168	-14		-1.0
1952	Phi N	0	1	.000	3	1	0	0	9	13	6	2	0	1	2	6.00	61	.351	.368	1	.000	-0	0	-2		-0.2
1953	Phi N	8	9	.471	35	20	8-3	2	157.1	169	76	14	2	42	63	4.00	105	.271	.319	55-0-1	.182	-1	89	6		0.4
1954	Phi N	7	9	.438	30	16	5	0	150	176	84	14	3	39	42	4.56	89	.300	.340	50-1-3	.160	-1	116	-8		-0.7
1955	Phi N	8	4	.667	40	0	0	1	89.2	80	26	6	1	28-6	28	2.41	165	.242	.300	18-0-1	.278	1		16		2.1
1956	Phi N	3	6	.333	49	6	3-1	5	122.1	115	55	14	3	34-11	53	3.24	115	.248	.301	22-0-2	.091	-1	79	5		0.2
1957	Phi N	2	5	.286	32	1	0	6	60.1	61	18	4	1	17-5	12	2.69	142	.265	.315	8-1-0	.250	2	116	9		1.3
1958	Phi N	1	1	.500	17	0	0	0	22.1	36	30	7	0	9-2	9	11.69	34	.360	.402	1	.000	-0		-18		-1.4
Total	10	42	42	.500	261	69	23-6	15	822	889	406	72	16	247-24	263	3.96	101	.277	.329	223-2-10	.184	1	101	5		1.7

MILLER, BOB Robert Lane (b Robert Lane Gemeinweiser) B2.18.1939 St.Louis MO D8.6.1993 Rancho Bernardo CA BR/TR/6-1/182(175-195) d6.26 C4

YEAR	TM LG	W	L	PCT	G	GS	CG-SHO	SV-BS	IP	H	R	HR	HB	BB-IB	SO	ERA	AERA	OAV	OOB	AB-HR-SH	AVG	PB	SUP	APR	DL	PW
1957	StL N	0	0	—	5	0	0	0	9	13	9	2	0	5-0	7	7.00	57	.325	.391	0		0*		-3		-0.2
1959	StL N	4	3	.571	11	10	3	0	70.2	66	31	2	1	21-2	43	3.31	128	.248	.303	24-0-1	.208	0	91	6		0.6
1960	StL N	4	3	.571	15	7	0	0	52.2	53	21	2	1	17-2	33	3.42	120	.262	.320	14-0-1	.143	-1*	102	4	49	0.5
1961	StL N	1	3	.250	34	5	0	3	74.1	82	41	6	0	46-7	39	4.24	104	.290	.388	14-0-2	.357	2*	52	1		0.3
1962	NY N	1	12	.077	33	21	1	0	143.2	146	98	20	6	62-2	91	4.89	86	.259	.335	41-0-2	.122	-1*	57	-13		-1.0
1963	LA N	10	8	.556	42	23	2	1	187	171	71	7	3	65-9	125	2.89	105	.244	.310	57-0-5	.070	-3	119	3		0.3
1964	LA N	7	7	.500	74	2	0	9	137.2	115	49	1	2	63-16	91	2.62	124	.226	.312	19-0-2	.158	1	122	9		1.3
1965	†LA N	6	7	.462	61	1	0	9	103	82	37	9	3	26-3	77	2.97	110	.225	.277	16-0-1	.000	-1	54	4		0.6
1966	†LA N	4	2	.667	46	0	0	5	84.1	70	31	9	1	29-7	58	2.77	119	.230	.297	13-0-2	.077	-1		5		0.2
1967	LA N	2	9	.182	52	4	0	0	85.2	88	46	9	3	27-9	32	4.31	72	.273	.332	8-0-1	.125	-0	21	-12		-1.5
1968	Min A	0	3	.000	45	0	0	2	72.1	65	26	1	0	24-7	41	2.74	113	.239	.311	7	.143	-0		3		0.2
1969	†Min A	5	5	.500	48	11	1	3-3	119.1	118	42	9	0	32-7	57	3.02	121	.264	.311	31-0-2	.000	-3	130	10	23	0.6
1970	Cle A	2	2	.500	15	2	0	1-0	28	35	14	1	0	15-2	15	4.18	96	.310	.388	5	.200	0	133	-1		-0.1
	Chi A	4	6	.400	15	12	0	0-0	70	88	42	11	4	33-3	36	5.01	77	.315	.391	23-0-2	.174	0*	90	-7		-0.8
	Year	6	8	.429	30	14	0	1-0	98	123	56	12	4	48-5	51	4.78	82	.314	.390	28-0-2	.179	1	96	-7		-0.9
	Chi N	0	0	—	7	1	0	2-0	9	6	5	3	0	6-1	9	5.00	90	.194	.316	0		0	100	0		0.0
1971	Chi N	0	0	—	2	0	0	0-0	7	10	4	0	1	1-0	2	5.14	77	.357	.367	1	.000	-0		-1		0.0
	SD N	7	3	.700	38	0	0	7-2	63.2	53	12	0	1	26-7	36	1.41	235	.227	.308	10-0-2	.000	-1	14			2.5
	†Pit N	1	2	.333	16	0	0	3-4	28	20	8	1	0	13-4	13	1.29	265	.200	.292	1	.000	-0		5		0.7
	Year	8	5	.615	56	0	0	10-6	98.2	83	24	1	1	40-11	51	1.64	206	.230	.308	12-0-2	.000	-1		18		3.2
1972	†Pit N	5	2	.714	36	0	0	3-1	54.1	54	19	3	1	24-7	18	2.65	125	.265	.343	4-0-1	.000	-0	4	21		-0.2
1973	SD N	0	0	—	18	0	0	0-0	30.2	29	18	4	0	12-1	15	4.11	86	.244	.311	2	.000	-0		-3		-0.2
	NY N	0	0	—	1	0	0	0-0	1	0	0	0	0	0-0	1	0.00	—	.000	.000	0		0		0		0.0
	Year	0	0	—	19	0	0	0-0	31.2	29	18	4	0	12-1	16	3.98	88	.238	.304	2	.000	-0		-3		-0.2
	Det A	4	2	.667	22	0	0	1-1	42	34	16	3	0	22-2	23	3.43	120	.230	.324	0		0		3		0.5
1974	NY N	2	2	.500	58	0	0	2-2	78	89	39	2	1	39-13	35	3.58	101	.296	.375	9	.111	-0		-1		-0.1
Total	17	69	81	.460	694	99	7	51-13	1551.1	1487	679	101	32	608-111	895	3.37	105	.255	.326	299-0-24	.110	-8	95	30	93	4.9

MILLER, BOB Robert W. B1862 D5.23.1931 Newark NJ d8.30

YEAR	TM LG	W	L	PCT	G	GS	CG-SHO	SV-BS	IP	H	R	HR	HB	BB-IB	SO	ERA	AERA	OAV	OOB	AB-HR-SH	AVG	PB	SUP	APR	DL	PW
1890	Roc AA	3	7	.300	13	12	11	1	92.1	89	58	2	3	26	20	4.29	83	.246	.302	40	.150	-1*	54	-5		-0.5
1891	Was AA	2	5	.286	7	7	3	0	42	53	51	3	6	24	13	4.29	87	.298	.399	18	.111	-2	69	-8		-1.1
Total	2	5	12	.294	20	19	14	1	134.1	142	109	5	9	50	33	4.29	84	.263	.336	58	.138	-3	60	-13		-1.6

MILLER, ROGER Roger Wesley B8.1.1954 Connellsville PA D4.26.1993 Mill Run PA BR/TR/6-3/200 d9.8

YEAR	TM LG	W	L	PCT	G	GS	CG-SHO	SV-BS	IP	H	R	HR	HB	BB-IB	SO	ERA	AERA	OAV	OOB	AB-HR-SH	AVG	PB	SUP	APR	DL	PW
1974	Mil A	0	0	—	2	0	0	0-0	2.1	3	3	1	0	0-0	2	11.57	31	.300	.364	0	—	0		-2		-0.1

MILLER, RONNIE Roland Arthur B8.28.1918 Mason City IA D1.6.1998 Ferguson MO BB/TR/5-11/167 d9.10 Mil 1942-45 Col Upper Iowa

YEAR	TM LG	W	L	PCT	G	GS	CG-SHO	SV-BS	IP	H	R	HR	HB	BB-IB	SO	ERA	AERA	OAV	OOB	AB-HR-SH	AVG	PB	SUP	APR	DL	PW
1941	Was A	0	0	—	1	0	0	0	2	1	2	1	0	1	0	4.50	90	.333	.429	0		0		0		0.0

MILLER, ROSCOE Roscoe Clyde "Roxy","Rubberlegs" B12.2.1876 Greenville IN D4.18.1913 Corydon IN BR/TR/6-2/190 d4.25

YEAR	TM LG	W	L	PCT	G	GS	CG-SHO	SV-BS	IP	H	R	HR	HB	BB-IB	SO	ERA	AERA	OAV	OOB	AB-HR-SH	AVG	PB	SUP	APR	DL	PW
1901	Det A	23	13	.639	38	36	35-3	1	332	339	168	1	13	98	79	2.95	130	.261	.320	130-0-2	.208	0	106	33		3.3
1902	Det A	6	12	.333	20	18	15-1	1	148.2	158	85	3	9	57	39	3.69	99	.273	.347	60	.183	-2	65	-1		-0.2
	NY N	1	8	.111	10	9	7	0	72.2	77	40	2	1	11	15	4.58	61	.271	.310	21-0-2	.048	-2	51	-9		-1.3
1903	NY N	2	5	.286	15	8	6	3	85	101	53	1	1	24	30	4.13	81	.302	.351	31	.161	-1	70	-7		-0.7
1904	Pit N	7	7	.500	19	17	11-2	0	134.1	133	67	4	8	39	35	3.35	82	.256	.313	46	.043	-4	103	-9		-1.3
Total	4	39	45	.464	102	88	74-6	5	772.2	808	413	10	32	229	198	3.45	100	.268	.326	288-0-4	.160	-8	89	7		-0.2

MILLER, RUSS Russell Lewis B3.25.1900 Etna OH D4.30.1962 Bucyrus OH BR/TR/5-11/165 d9.24 b-Jake Col Ohio St.

YEAR	TM LG	W	L	PCT	G	GS	CG-SHO	SV-BS	IP	H	R	HR	HB	BB-IB	SO	ERA	AERA	OAV	OOB	AB-HR-SH	AVG	PB	SUP	APR	DL	PW
1927	Phi N	1	1	.500	2	2	1	0	15.1	21	9	2	1	3	4	5.28	78	.339	.379	3-0-3	.333	0	93	-1		-0.1
1928	Phi N	0	12	.000	33	12	1	1	108	137	79	14	0	34	19	5.42	79	.315	.365	27-0-1	.148	-1*	89	-15		-1.6
Total	2	1	13	.071	35	14	2	1	123.1	158	88	16	1	37	23	5.40	79	.318	.366	30-0-4	.167	-1	90	-16		-1.7

MILLER, STU Stuart Leonard B12.26.1927 Northampton MA BR/TR/5-11.5/165* d8.12

YEAR	TM LG	W	L	PCT	G	GS	CG-SHO	SV-BS	IP	H	R	HR	HB	BB-IB	SO	ERA	AERA	OAV	OOB	AB-HR-SH	AVG	PB	SUP	APR	DL	PW
1952	StL N	6	3	.667	12	11	6-2	0	88	63	25	3	2	26	64	2.05	182	.197	.262	25-0-6	.120	-1	74	15		1.6
1953	StL N	7	8	.467	40	18	8-2	4	137.2	161	86	19	2	47	79	5.56	77	.293	.351	43-0-4	.186	1*	99	-17		-1.4
1954	StL N	2	3	.400	19	4	0	2	46.2	55	36	5	3	29	22	5.79	71	.307	.405	13	.308	1*	157	-9		-0.8
1956	StL N	0	1	.000	3	0	0	1	7.1	12	6	3	0	5-0	5	4.91	77	.387	.459	1	.000	-0*		-2		-0.2
	Phi N	5	8	.385	24	15	2	0	106.2	109	65	16	4	51-12	55	4.47	83	.263	.347	25-0-1	.160	2*	87	-11		-1.0
	Year	5	9	.357	27	15	2	1	114	121	71	19	4	56-12	60	4.50	83	.271	.356	26-0-1	.154	2	87	-14		-1.2
1957	NY N	7	9	.438	38	13	0	1	124	110	53	15	3	45-6	60	3.63	108	.242	.313	35-0-1	.057	-3	91	6		0.4
1958	SF N	6	9	.400	41	20	4-1	0	182	160	60	16	2	49-3	119	**2.47**	**154**	.233	**.286**	50-0-5	.120	-0*	105	27		2.1
1959	SF N	8	7	.533	59	9	2	8	167.2	164	66	15	5	57-13	95	2.84	134	.260	.322	45-0-4	.044	-3	117	17		1.4
1960	SF N	7	6	.538	47	3	2	2	101.2	100	49	9	3	31-5	65	3.90	89	.256	.312	25-0-3	.200	-1	93	-4		-0.3
1961	SF N★	14	5	.737	63	0	0	**17**	122	95	41	4	1	37-11	89	2.66	143	.215	.277	20-0-1	.200	1		16		3.1
1962	†SF N	5	8	.385	59	0	0	19	107	107	55	8	2	42-7	78	4.12	92	.268	.337	16-0-1	.125	-0*		-4		-0.6
1963	Bal A	5	8	.385	71	0	0	27	112.1	93	36	5	3	53-13	114	2.24	155	.232	.323	16-0-2	.313	-1		14		2.6
1964	Bal A	7	7	.500	66	0	0	23	97	77	37	7	3	34-14	87	3.06	117	.222	.295	9-0-2	.111	-0		5		1.0
1965	Bal A	14	7	.667	67	0	0	24	119.1	87	26	5	1	32-10	104	1.89	184	.207	.265	16-0-4	.063	-1		22		**4.9**
1966	Bal A	9	4	.692	51	0	0	18	92	65	24	5	4	22-6	67	2.25	148	.201	.259	19-0-2	.105	-1		12		2.1
1967	Bal A	3	10	.231	42	0	0	8	81.1	63	28	5	1	36-12	60	2.55	124	.210	.307	11	.000	-1		4		0.6
1968	Atl N	0	0	—	2	0	0	0	0.2	1	4	0	0	4-2	1	54.00	6	.500	.833	0	—	0		-4		-0.2
Total	16	105	103	.505	704	93	24-5	154	1693.1	1522	697	140	39	600-114	1164	3.24	115	.242	.311	369-0-36	.133	-2	103	87		15.3

MILLER, TRAVIS Travis Eugene B11.2.1972 Dayton OH BR/TL/6-3/209(200-215) [MinA94 1/34] d8.25 Col Kent St.

YEAR	TM LG	W	L	PCT	G	GS	CG-SHO	SV-BS	IP	H	R	HR	HB	BB-IB	SO	ERA	AERA	OAV	OOB	AB-HR-SH	AVG	PB	SUP	APR	DL	PW
1996	Min A	1	2	.333	7	7	0	0-0	26.1	45	34	9	7	9-0	15	9.23	56	.388	.432	0	—	0	103	-12		-1.0
1997	Min A	1	5	.167	13	7	0	0-0	48.1	64	49	8	1	23-2	26	7.63	61	.320	.389	0	—	0	93	-18		-1.7
1998	Min A	0	0	.000	14	0	0	0-0	23.1	25	10	0	0	11-1	23	3.86	124	.272	.346	0	—	0		3		0.2
1999	Min A	2	2	.500	52	0	0	0-2	49.2	55	19	3	0	16-3	40	2.72	191	.284	.335	0	—	0		11		0.8
2000	Min A	2	3	.400	67	0	0	1-3	67	83	35	4	1	32-2	62	3.90	135	.297	.368	0	—	0		8		0.5
2001	Min A	1	4	.200	45	0	0	0-0	48.2	54	34	5	1	20-1	30	4.81	97	.283	.347	0	—	0		-2		-0.2
2002	Min A	0	0	—	5	0	0	0-0	4	5	2	0	0	2-2	3	4.50	99	.294	.368	0	—	0		0		0.0
Total	7	7	18	.280	203	14	0	1-5	267.1	331	174	27	3	113-11	199	5.05	98	.304	.367	0	—	0	98	-10		-1.4

MILLER, TREVER Trever Douglas B5.29.1973 Louisville KY BR/TL/6-4/195(175-200) [DetA91 1/41] d9.4

YEAR	TM LG	W	L	PCT	G	GS	CG-SHO	SV-BS	IP	H	R	HR	HB	BB-IB	SO	ERA	AERA	OAV	OOB	AB-HR-SH	AVG	PB	SUP	APR	DL	PW
1996	Det A	0	4	.000	5	4	0	0-0	16.2	28	17	3	2	9-0	8	9.18	55	.384	.453	0	—	0	46	-7		-1.1
1998	†Hou N	2	0	1.000	37	0	0	1-1	53.1	57	21	4	1	20-1	30	3.04	133	.266	.332	3	.333	1	91	6	15	0.3
1999	†Hou N	3	2	.600	47	0	0	1-0	49.2	58	29	6	5	29-1	37	5.07	87	.299	.400	3-0-2	.000	-0		-3		-0.3
2000	Phi N				14	0			14	19	16	3	1	9-1	10	8.36	55	.317	.408	0	—	0		-7		-0.3
	LA N				2	0			2.1	8	6	1	0	3-0	1	23.14	19	.571	.667	0	—	0		-5		-0.2
	Year				16	0			16.1	27	22	4	1	12-1	11	10.47	44	.365	.461	0	—	0		-12		-0.5
2003	Tor A	2	2	.500	79	0	0	3-1	52.2	46	30	7	5	28-3	44	4.61	103	.231	.341	0	—	0		1		0.0
2004	TB A	1	1	.500	60	0	0	1-2	49	48	21	4	3	15-4	43	3.12	150	.257	.322	0	—	0		7		0.4

YEAR	TM LG	W	L	PCT	G	GS	CG-SHO	SV-BS	IP	H	R	HR	HB	BB-IB	SO	ERA	AERA	OAV	OOB	AB-HR-SH	AVG	PB	SUP	APR	DL	PW
2005	TB A	2	2	.500	61	0	0	0-3	44.1	45	23	4	7	29-6	35	4.06	108	.278	.399	0	—	0		1	15	0.1
Total	7	10	11	.476	305	5	0	6-7	282	309	163	30	25	142-16	208	4.66	96	.280	.372	6-0-2	.167	0	58	-7	30	-1.1

MILLER, WADE Wade T. B9.13.1976 Reading PA BR/TR/6-2/185(185-220) [HouN96 20/594] d7.7 Col Alvernia

YEAR	TM LG	W	L	PCT	G	GS	CG-SHO	SV-BS	IP	H	R	HR	HB	BB-IB	SO	ERA	AERA	OAV	OOB	AB-HR-SH	AVG	PB	SUP	APR	DL	PW
1999	Hou N	0	1	.000	5	1	0	0-0	10.1	17	11	4	0	5-0	8	9.58	46	.362	.423	1	.000	-0	145	-6		-0.5
2000	Hou N	6	6	.500	16	16	2	0-0	105	104	66	14	3	42-1	89	5.14	95	.257	.331	40-0-1	.100	-2	110	-3		-0.5
2001	†Hou N	16	8	.667	32	32	1	0-0	212	183	91	31	4	76-3	183	3.40	135	.234	.304	66-0-10	.167	-0	96	25		2.7
2002	Hou N	15	4	.789	26	26	1-1	0-0	164.2	151	63	14	6	62-9	144	3.28	132	.249	.322	62-0-6	.177	-0	117	19	46	2.1
2003	Hou N	14	13	.519	33	33	1	0-0	187.1	168	96	17	10	77-1	161	4.13	107	.242	.323	63-0-5	.159	0*	102	5		0.6
2004	Hou N	7	7	.500	15	15	0	0-0	88.2	76	35	11	0	44-0	74	3.35	131	.228	.317	27-0-8	.259	1*	97	10	100	0.1
2005	Bos A	4	4	.500	16	16	0	0-0	91	96	53	8	3	47-0	64	4.95	93	.267	.354	3	.667	1	102	-3	90	-0.2
Total	7	62	43	.590	143	139	5-1	0-0	859	795	415	99	26	353-14	723	3.98	113	.246	.324	262-0-30	.172	-0	104	47	236	5.8

MILLER, JAKE Walter B2.28.1898 Wagram OH D8.20.1975 Venice FL BL/TL/6-2/170 d9.11 b-Russ

YEAR	TM LG	W	L	PCT	G	GS	CG-SHO	SV-BS	IP	H	R	HR	HB	BB-IB	SO	ERA	AERA	OAV	OOB	AB-HR-SH	AVG	PB	SUP	APR	DL	PW
1924	Cle A	0	1	.000	2	1	0	0	12	13	6	0	0	5	4	3.00	142	.265	.333	5	.000	-1	99	1		0.0
1925	Cle A	10	13	.435	32	22	13	2	190.1	207	85	4	7	62	51	3.31	133	.279	.340	71-0-3	.183	-3	80	23		2.1
1926	Cle A	7	4	.636	18	11	5-3	1	82.2	99	34	1	2	18	24	3.27	124	.307	.348	24	.083	-2	70	8		0.7
1927	Cle A	10	8	.556	34	23	11	0	185.1	189	80	4	6	48	53	3.21	131	.271	.324	58-0-3	.138	-4	86	20		1.3
1928	Cle A	8	9	.471	25	24	8	0	158	203	89	6	5	43	37	4.44	93	.332	.381	52-0-6	.135	-4	75	-3		-0.7
1929	Cle A	14	12	.538	29	29	14-2	0	206	227	98	7	7	60	58	3.58	124	.279	.334	75-0-7	.200	-3	81	19		1.9
1930	Cle A	4	4	.500	24	9	1	0	88.1	147	89	6	4	38	31	7.13	68	.373	.433	33-0-5	.303	1	105	-23		-1.5
1931	Cle A	2	1	.667	10	5	1-1	0	41.1	45	26	2	0	19	17	4.35	106	.273	.348	13	.077	-1	143	0		-0.1
1933	Chi A	5	6	.455	26	14	4-2	0	105.2	130	73	3	6	47	30	5.62	75	.297	.373	37-0-3	.189	-1*	102	-15		-1.3
Total	9	60	58	.508	200	139	58-8	3	1069.2	1260	582	33	37	340	305	4.09	106	.298	.355	368-0-27	.171	-19	86	30		2.4

MILLER, WALT Walter W. B10.19.1883 Spiceland IN D3.1.1956 Marion IN BR/TR/5-11.5/180 d9.20

YEAR	TM LG	W	L	PCT	G	GS	CG-SHO	SV-BS	IP	H	R	HR	HB	BB-IB	SO	ERA	AERA	OAV	OOB	AB-HR-SH	AVG	PB	SUP	APR	DL	PW
1911	Bro N	0	1	.000	3	2	0	0	11	16	14	0	1	6	3	6.55	51	.356	.442	4	.000	-1	56	-6		-0.5

MILLER, BILL William Francis "Wild Bill" B4.12.1910 Hannibal MO D2.26.1982 Hannibal MO BR/TR/6-0/180 d10.2

YEAR	TM LG	W	L	PCT	G	GS	CG-SHO	SV-BS	IP	H	R	HR	HB	BB-IB	SO	ERA	AERA	OAV	OOB	AB-HR-SH	AVG	PB	SUP	APR	DL	PW
1937	StL A	0	1	.000	1	1	0	0	4	7	6	1	1	4	1	13.50	36	.389	.522	1	.000	-0	36	-3		-0.5

MILLER, BILL William Paul "Lefty","Hooks" B7.26.1927 Minersville PA D7.1.2003 Lititz PA BL/TL/6-0/175* d4.20

YEAR	TM LG	W	L	PCT	G	GS	CG-SHO	SV-BS	IP	H	R	HR	HB	BB-IB	SO	ERA	AERA	OAV	OOB	AB-HR-SH	AVG	PB	SUP	APR	DL	PW
1952	NY A	4	6	.400	21	13	5-2	0	88	78	43	5	2	49	45	3.48	96	.241	.345	28-0-2	.214	1	125	-3		-0.3
1953	NY A	2	1	.667	13	3	0	1	34	46	19	3	1	19	17	4.76	77	.324	.407	10-0-1	.200	0	112	-4		-0.3
1954	NY A	0	1	.000	2	1	0	0	5.2	9	4	0	0	1	6	6.35	54	.375	.385	1	.000	-0	51	-2		-0.3
1955	Bal A	0	1	.000	5	1	0	0	4	3	6	0	0	10-1	4	13.50	28	.200	.520	1	1.000	0	163	-4		-0.7
Total	4	6	9	.400	41	18	5-2	1	131.2	136	72	8	3	79-1	72	4.24	81	.270	.371	40-0-3	.225	1	121	-13		-1.6

MILLIGAN, JOHN John Alexander B1.22.1904 Schuylerville NY D5.15.1972 Fort Pierce FL BR/TL/5-10/172 d8.11 Col Cornell

YEAR	TM LG	W	L	PCT	G	GS	CG-SHO	SV-BS	IP	H	R	HR	HB	BB-IB	SO	ERA	AERA	OAV	OOB	AB-HR-SH	AVG	PB	SUP	APR	DL	PW
1928	Phi N	2	5	.286	13	7	3	0	68	69	39	2	1	32	22	4.37	98	.274	.358	20-0-4	.050	-2	96	-1		-0.3
1929	Phi N	0	1	.000	8	3	0	0	9.2	29	19	0	2	10	2	16.76	31	.527	.612	3	.333	0	140	-11		-0.8
1930	Phi N	1	2	.333	9	2	1	0	28.1	26	16	0	2	21	7	3.18	172	.255	.392	9	.111	-1	88	5		0.4
1931	Phi N	0	0	—	3	0	0	0	8	11	5	0	1	4	6	3.38	126	.324	.410	2	.000	-0		0		-0.1
1934	Was A	0	0	—	2	0	0	0	2.2	6	3	0	0	0	1	10.13	43	.500	.500		—	0		-2		-0.1
Total	5	3	8	.273	35	12	4	0	116.2	141	82	2	6	67	38	5.17	90	.310	.405	34-0-4	.088	-3	108	-9		-0.8

MILLIGAN, BILLY William Joseph B8.19.1878 Buffalo NY D10.14.1928 Buffalo NY BR/TL/5-7/? d4.30

YEAR	TM LG	W	L	PCT	G	GS	CG-SHO	SV-BS	IP	H	R	HR	HB	BB-IB	SO	ERA	AERA	OAV	OOB	AB-HR-SH	AVG	PB	SUP	APR	DL	PW
1901	Phi A	0	3	.000	6	3	2	0	33	43	24	1	2	14	5	4.36	86	.312	.383	15-1-1	.333	2*	137	-3		0.0
1904	NY N	0	1	.000	5	1	1	2	25	36	22	2	1	4	6	5.40	51	.310	.339	9	.111	-0	0	-8		-0.4
Total	2	0	4	.000	11	4	3	2	58	79	46	3	3	18	11	4.81	69	.311	.364	24-1-1	.250	2	118	-11		-0.4

MILLIKEN, BOB Robert Fogle "Bobo" B8.25.1926 Majorsville WV BR/TR/6-0/195* d4.22 C7

YEAR	TM LG	W	L	PCT	G	GS	CG-SHO	SV-BS	IP	H	R	HR	HB	BB-IB	SO	ERA	AERA	OAV	OOB	AB-HR-SH	AVG	PB	SUP	APR	DL	PW
1953	†Bro N	8	4	.667	37	10	3	2	117.2	94	52	13	0	42	65	3.37	127	.214	.283	34-0-4	.118	-1	107	10		0.7
1954	Bro N	5	2	.714	24	3	0	0	62.2	58	31	12	2	18	25	4.02	102	.246	.304	17	.176	-0	80	0		-0.1
Total	2	13	6	.684	61	13	3	2	180.1	152	83	25	2	60	90	3.59	117	.225	.290	51-0-2	.137	-2	101	10		0.6

MILLS, ALAN Alan Bernard B10.18.1966 Lakeland FL BR/TR/6-1/192* [CalA86 S1/8] d4.14 Col Tuskegee

YEAR	TM LG	W	L	PCT	G	GS	CG-SHO	SV-BS	IP	H	R	HR	HB	BB-IB	SO	ERA	AERA	OAV	OOB	AB-HR-SH	AVG	PB	SUP	APR	DL	PW
1990	NY A	1	5	.167	36	0	0	0-2	41.2	48	21	4	1	33-6	24	4.10	97	.298	.418	0	—	0		-1		0.0
1991	NY A	1	1	.500	6	2	0	0-0	16.1	16	9	1	0	8-0	11	4.41	95	.254	.333	0	—	0	44	-1		0.0
1992	Bal A	10	4	.714	35	3	0	2-1	103.1	78	33	5	1	54-10	60	2.61	156	.215	.315	0	—	0	105	16		2.1
1993	Bal A	5	4	.556	45	0	0	4-3	100.1	80	39	14	4	51-5	68	3.23	140	.225	.324	0	—	0		14		1.2
1994	Bal A	3	3	.500	47	0	0	2-2	45.1	43	26	7	2	24-2	44	5.16	98	.251	.348	0	—	0		0		-0.0
1995	Bal A	3	0	1.000	21	0	0	0-1	23	30	20	4	2	18-4	16	7.43	64	.309	.424	0	—	0		-7		0.3
1996	†Bal A	3	2	.600	49	0	0	3-5	54.2	40	26	10	1	35-2	50	4.28	116	.208	.330	0	—	0		5	40	0.4
1997	†Bal A	2	3	.400	39	0	0	0-0	38.2	41	23	5	1	33-1	32	4.89	90	.268	.399	0	—	-0		-2	66	-0.3
1998	Bal A	3	4	.429	72	0	0	2-3	77	55	32	8	1	50-8	57	3.74	122	.203	.326	0	—	0		8		0.4
1999	LA N	3	4	.429	68	0	0	0-5	72.1	70	33	10	4	43-4	49	3.73	117	.261	.367	2	.000	-0		5		0.4
2000	LA N	2	1	.667	18	0	0	1-0	25.2	31	12	3	1	16-0	18	4.21	106	.304	.403	3	.000	-0		1		-0.1
	Bal A	2	0	1.000	23	0	0	1-0	23.2	25	17	6	1	19-1	18	6.46	73	.263	.391	0	—	0		-4	25	-0.3
2001	Bal A	2	1	.500	15	0	0	1-0	14	20	15	6	2	11-3	9	9.64	45	.333	.452	0	—	0		-8	102	-1.0
Total	12	39	32	.549	474	5	0	15-22	636	577	306	83	21	395-40	456	4.12	109	.245	.356	5	.000	-0	74	26	233	2.5

MILLS, ART Arthur Grant B3.2.1903 Utica NY D7.23.1975 Utica NY BR/TR/5-10/155 d4.16 C5 f-Willie

YEAR	TM LG	W	L	PCT	G	GS	CG-SHO	SV-BS	IP	H	R	HR	HB	BB-IB	SO	ERA	AERA	OAV	OOB	AB-HR-SH	AVG	PB	SUP	APR	DL	PW
1927	Bos N	0	1	.000	15	1	0	0	37.2	41	19	1	3	18	7	3.82	97	.287	.378	7	.000	-1	229	-1		-0.1
1928	Bos N	0	0	—	4	0	0	0	7.2	17	11	3	2	8	0	12.91	30	.472	.587	1	.000	-0		-7		-0.3
Total	2	0	1	.000	19	1	0	0	45.1	58	30	4	5	26	7	5.36	70	.324	.424	8	.000	-1	229	-8		-0.4

MILLS, LEFTY Howard Robinson B5.12.1910 Dedham MA D9.23.1982 Riverside CA BL/TL/6-1/187 d6.10

YEAR	TM LG	W	L	PCT	G	GS	CG-SHO	SV-BS	IP	H	R	HR	HB	BB-IB	SO	ERA	AERA	OAV	OOB	AB-HR-SH	AVG	PB	SUP	APR	DL	PW
1934	StL A	0	0	—	4	0	0	0	8.2	10	4	0	0	11	2	4.15	120	.303	.477	3	.333	0		1		0.0
1937	StL A	1	1	.500	2	2	1	0	12.2	16	13	1	0	10	10	6.39	75	.286	.394	5	.000	-1	81	-3		-0.5
1938	StL A	10	12	.455	30	27	15-1	0	210.1	216	139	16	8	116	134	5.31	94	.262	.358	66-0-5	.091	-3	90	-8		-1.0
1939	StL A	4	11	.267	34	14	4	2	144.1	147	114	16	8	113	103	6.55	74	.264	.395	47-1-2	.234	1	69	-24		-2.0
1940	StL A	0	6	.000	26	5	1	0	59	64	55	7	3	52	18	7.78	59	.275	.413	13	.154	-0	31	-19		-1.6
Total	5	15	30	.333	96	48	21-1	2	435	453	325	40	19	302	267	6.06	81	.266	.382	134-1-7	.149	-3	78	-53		-5.1

MILLS, DICK Richard Alan B1.29.1945 Boston MA BR/TR/6-3/199 [BosA66 S3/54] d9.7

YEAR	TM LG	W	L	PCT	G	GS	CG-SHO	SV-BS	IP	H	R	HR	HB	BB-IB	SO	ERA	AERA	OAV	OOB	AB-HR-SH	AVG	PB	SUP	APR	DL	PW
1970	Bos A	0	0	—	2	0	0	0-0	6	4	6	0	1	3-0	3	2.45	162	.353	.476	0	—	0		-1		0.0

MILLS, WILLIE William Grant "Wee Willie" B8.15.1877 Schenevus NY D7.5.1914 Norwood NY BR/TR/5-7/150 d7.13 s-Art

YEAR	TM LG	W	L	PCT	G	GS	CG-SHO	SV-BS	IP	H	R	HR	HB	BB-IB	SO	ERA	AERA	OAV	OOB	AB-HR-SH	AVG	PB	SUP	APR	DL	PW
1901	NY N	0	2	.000	2	2	2	0	16	21	15	2	1	4	3	8.44	39	.313	.361	6	.167	0	64	-7		-0.7

MILLWOOD, KEVIN Kevin Austin B12.24.1974 Gastonia NC BR/TR/6-4/220(205-235) [AtlN93 11/320] d7.14

YEAR	TM LG	W	L	PCT	G	GS	CG-SHO	SV-BS	IP	H	R	HR	HB	BB-IB	SO	ERA	AERA	OAV	OOB	AB-HR-SH	AVG	PB	SUP	APR	DL	PW
1997	Atl N	5	3	.625	12	8	0	0-0	51.1	55	26	1	2	21-1	42	4.03	104	.281	.348	12-0-1	.000	-1	132	1		0.0
1998	Atl N	17	8	.680	31	29	3-1	0-0	174.1	175	86	18	3	56-3	163	4.08	102	.258	.316	50-0-6	.080	-1	112	3		0.2
1999	†Atl N★	18	7	.720	33	33	2	0-0	228	168	80	24	4	59-2	205	2.68	167	.202	.258	78-1-6	.154	-0	100	44		4.3
2000	†Atl N	10	13	.435	36	35	0	0-0	212.2	213	115	26	3	62-2	168	4.66	97	.258	.311	59-0-14	.119	-1	98	-1		-0.3
2001	Atl N	7	7	.500	21	21	0	0-0	121	121	66	20	1	40-6	84	4.31	100	.260	.319	43-0-1	.093	-2	121	-1	74	-0.3
2002	†Atl N	18	8	.692	35	34	1-1	0-0	217	186	83	16	8	65-7	178	3.24	125	.230	.292	70-1-11	.200	-3	102	21		2.6
2003	Phi N	14	12	.538	35	35	5-3	0-0	222	210	103	19	4	68-6	169	4.01	99	.250	.307	68-0-6	.059	-3	101	0		-0.3
2004	Phi N	9	6	.600	25	25	0	0-0	141	155	81	14	7	51-5	125	4.85	91	.278	.345	46-0-5	.174	-1	99	-6	37	-0.2
2005	Cle A	9	11	.450	30	30	1	0-0	192	182	72	20	4	52-0	146	2.86	143	.248	.300	2	.000	-0	83	26	21	2.3
Total	9	107	75	.588	258	250	12-5	0-0	1559.1	1465	712	158	36	474-32	1280	3.76	113	.248	.303	428-2-50	.124	-4	102	87	132	8.0

MILNAR, AL Albert Joseph "Happy" (b Albert Joseph Mlinar) B12.26.1913 Cleveland OH D6.30.2005 Cleveland OH BL/TL/6-2/195 d4.30 Mil 1944-45

YEAR	TM LG	W	L	PCT	G	GS	CG-SHO	SV-BS	IP	H	R	HR	HB	BB-IB	SO	ERA	AERA	OAV	OOB	AB-HR-SH	AVG	PB	SUP	APR	DL	PW
1936	Cle A	1	2	.333	4	3	1	0	22	26	20	0	0	9	8	7.36	68	.286	.404	10	.300	0	70	-5		-0.5
1938	Cle A	3	1	.750	23	5	2	1	68.1	90	48	5	0	26	29	5.00	93	.320	.378	26-1-0	.154	-0*	121	-5		-0.3
1939	Cle A	14	12	.538	37	26	12-2	3	209	212	96	11	0	99	76	3.79	116	.264	.345	79	.253	4*	109	17		2.2
1940	Cle A☆	18	10	.643	37	33	15-4	3	242.1	242	110	14	1	99	99	3.27	129	.257	.328	94-0-3	.181	-1	112	18		1.5

YEAR	TM LG	W	L	PCT	G	GS	CG-SHO	SV-BS	IP	H	R	HR	HB	BB-IB	SO	ERA	AERA	OAV	OOB	AB-HR-SH	AVG	PB	SUP	APR	DL	PW
1941	Cle A	12	19	.387	35	30	9-1	0	229.1	236	128	9	1	116	82	4.36	90	.266	.352	82-2-1	.171	2	89	-13		-1.4
1942	Cle A	6	8	.429	28	19	8-2	0	157	146	82	3	4	85	35	4.13	84	.251	.350	70-1-1	.171	2*	120	-11		-0.7
1943	Cle A	1	3	.250	16	6	0	0	39	51	38	0	1	35	12	8.08	38	.329	.455	19	.211	0*	99	-21		-2.0
	StL A	1	2	.333	4	2	1	0	14.2	23	11	0	0	9	7	5.52	60	.354	.432	6-0-1	.333	1	190	-4		-0.6
	Year	2	5	.286	19	8	1	0	53.2	74	49	0	1	44	19	7.38	43	.336	.449	25-0-1	.240	1	123	-25		-2.6
1946	StL A	1	1	.500	4	2	1-1	0	14.2	15	4	1	0	6	1	2.45	152	.278	.350	4	.750	1	57	2		0.4
	Phi N	0	0	—	1	1	0	0	0	2	4	0	0	2	0	∞	—	1.000	1.000	0	—	0	225	-4		-0.3
Total	8	57	58	.496	188	127	49-10	7	996.1	1043	551	43	7	495	350	4.22	96	.270	.354	390-4-6	.203	9	106	-26		-1.7

MILSTEAD, GEORGE George Earl "Cowboy" B6.26.1903 Cleburne TX D8.9.1977 Cleburne TX BL/TL/5-10/144 d6.27

1924	Chi N	1	1	.500	13	2	1	0	29.2	41	25	3	1	13	6	6.07	64	.328	.396	6	.167	0	76	-8		-0.4
1925	Chi N	1	1	.500	5	3	1	0	21	26	12	0	0	8	7	3.00	144	.310	.370	7	.000	-1	98	1		0.0
1926	Chi N	1	5	.167	18	4	0	2	55.1	63	30	0	1	24	14	3.58	107	.309	.384	19	.053	-2	65	0		-0.1
Total	3	3	7	.300	36	9	2	2	106	130	67	3	2	45	27	4.16	95	.315	.385	32	.063	-3	80	-7		-0.5

MILTON, ERIC Eric Robert B8.4.1975 State College PA BL/TL/6-3/220(200-220) [NYA96 1/20] d4.5 Col Maryland-Baltimore Co.

1998	Min A	8	14	.364	32	32	1	0-0	172.1	195	113	25	2	70-0	107	5.64	85	.282	.347	9	.444	1	89	-15		-1.5
1999	Min A	7	11	.389	34	34	5-2	0-0	206.1	190	111	28	3	63-0	163	4.49	115	.243	.299	2	.000	0	87	14		1.0
2000	Min A	13	10	.565	33	33	0	0-0	200	205	123	35	7	44-0	160	4.86	108	.260	.303	2	.000	-0	92	5		0.4
2001	Min A☆	15	7	.682	35	34	2-1	0-0	220.2	222	109	35	5	61-0	157	4.32	108	.257	.308	2	.000	-0	102	10		0.7
2002	†Min A	13	9	.591	29	29	2-1	0-0	171	173	96	24	3	30-0	121	4.84	92	.258	.291	5	.400	1*	86	-6	26	-0.7
2003	†Min A	1	0	1.000	3	3	0	0-0	17	15	5	2	0	1-0	7	2.65	170	.234	.242	0	—	0	109	4	168	0.2
2004	Phi N	14	6	.700	34	34	0	0-0	201	196	110	43	1	75-6	161	4.75	93	.255	.320	65-0-5	.154	-0	122	-5		-0.5
2005	Cin N	8	15	.348	34	34	0	0-0	186.1	237	141	40	7	52-2	123	6.47	65	.302	.349	56-2-5	.143	2	111	-47		-4.7
Total	8	79	72	.523	234	233	10-4	0-0	1374.2	1433	808	232	28	396-10	999	4.99	94	.265	.316	141-2-10	.170	3	98	-40	194	-5.1

MILTON, LARRY Samuel Lawrence "Tug" B5.4.1879 Owensboro KY D5.15.1942 Hannibal MO TR d5.7

| 1903 | StL N | 0 | 0 | — | 1 | 0 | 0 | 0 | 4 | 3 | 1 | 0 | 0 | 1 | 0 | 2.25 | 145 | .200 | .250 | 2 | .500 | 0 | | 1 | | 0.1 |

MIMBS, MIKE Michael Randall B2.13.1969 Macon GA BL/TL/6-2/182* [LAN90 24/645] d5.6 Col Mercer

1995	Phi N	9	7	.563	35	19	2-1	1-0	136.2	127	70	10	6	75-2	93	4.15	102	.250	.348	35-0-8	.143	-1	86	0		0.0
1996	Phi N	3	9	.250	21	17	0	0-0	99.1	116	66	13	2	41-1	56	5.53	78	.294	.361	33-0-2	.121	-1	79	-12	26	-1.4
1997	Phi N	0	3	.000	17	1	0	0-0	28.2	31	27	6	3	27-1	29	7.53	56	.272	.424	2	.000	-0	22	-11		-1.0
Total	3	12	19	.387	73	37	2-1	1-0	264.2	274	163	29	11	143-4	178	5.03	85	.270	.362	70-0-10	.129	-2	81	-23	26	-2.4

MINAHAN, COTTON Edmund Joseph B12.10.1882 Springfield OH D5.20.1958 E.Orange NJ BR/TR/6-0/190 d4.21 Col Manhattan

| 1907 | Cin N | 0 | 2 | .000 | 2 | 2 | 1 | 0 | 14 | 12 | 8 | 0 | 1 | 13 | 4 | 1.29 | 202 | .261 | .433 | 5 | .000 | -1 | 82 | 0 | | -0.1 |

MINARCIN, RUDY Rudolph Anthony "Buster" B3.25.1930 N.Vandergrift PA BR/TR/6-0/195* d4.11

1955	Cin N	5	9	.357	41	12	3-1	1	115.2	116	73	17	3	51-7	45	4.90	86	.261	.339	28	.179	-1	100	-9		-0.9
1956	Bos A	1	0	1.000	3	1	0	0	9.2	9	4	2	1	8-0	5	2.79	165	.250	.400	2	.500	1	96	2		0.2
1957	Bos A	0	0	—	26	0	0	2	44.2	44	30	5	1	30-4	20	4.43	90	.267	.375	2	.000	0		-4		-0.2
Total	3	6	9	.400	70	13	3-1	3	170	169	107	24	5	89-11	70	4.66	90	.262	.352	32	.188	0	101	-11		-0.9

MINCHEY, NATE Nathan Derek B8.31.1969 Austin TX BR/TR/6-8/225* [MonN87 2/36] d9.12

1993	Bos A	1	2	.333	5	5	1	0-0	33	35	16	5	0	8-2	18	3.55	131	.265	.307	0	—	0	103	3		0.2
1994	Bos A	2	3	.400	6	5	0	0-0	23	44	26	1	0	14-2	15	8.61	59	.427	.483	0	—	0	58	-9		-1.5
1996	Bos A	0	2	.000	2	2	0	0-0	6	16	11	1	0	5-0	4	15.00	34	.533	.583	0	—	0	91	-6	94	-0.9
1997	Col N	0	0	—	2	0	0	0-0	2	5	3	0	0	1-0	1	13.50	38	.556	.600	0	—	0		-1		-0.1
Total	4	3	7	.300	15	12	1	0-0	64	100	56	7	0	28-4	38	6.75	72	.365	.418	0	—	0	82	-13	94	-2.3

MINER, RAY Raymond Theadore "Lefty" B4.4.1897 Glens Falls NY D9.15.1963 Glenridge NY BR/TL/5-11/160 d9.15

| 1921 | Phi A | 0 | 0 | — | 1 | 0 | 0 | 0 | 1 | 2 | 4 | 0 | 0 | 3 | 0 | 36.00 | 12 | .400 | .625 | 0 | — | 0 | | -3 | | -0.1 |

MINETTO, CRAIG Craig Stephen B4.25.1954 Stockton CA BL/TL/6-0/185* d7.4 Col San Joaquin Delta (CA) JC

1978	Oak A	0	0	—	4	1	0	0-0	12	13	10	1	2	7-0	3	3.75	98	.283	.393	0	—	0	221	-2		-0.1
1979	Oak A	1	5	.167	36	13	0	0-1	118.1	131	85	16	3	58-3	64	5.55	73	.282	.360	0	—	0	91	-22		-1.1
1980	Oak A	0	2	.000	7	1	0	1-0	8	11	7	2	0	3-1	5	7.88	48	.324	.368	0	—	0	47	-3	25	-0.7
1981	Oak A	0	0	—	8	0	0	0-0	6.2	7	2	0	1	4-0	4	2.70	130	.280	.387	0	—	0		1		0.0
Total	4	1	7	.125	55	15	0	1-1	145	162	104	19	6	72-4	76	5.40	74	.284	.364	0	—	0	97	-26	25	-1.9

MINGORI, STEVE Stephen Bernard B2.29.1944 Kansas City MO BL/TL/5-10/170* d8.5 Col Pittsburg St. (KS)

1970	Cle A	1	0	1.000	21	0	0	1-0	20.1	17	8	2	1	12-5	16	2.66	151	.227	.341	1	.000	-0		2		0.1
1971	Cle A	1	2	.333	54	0	0	4-2	56.2	31	10	2	1	24-6	45	1.43	271	.166	.259	2	.500	0	14	23		1.0
1972	Cle A	0	6	.000	41	0	0	10-3	57	67	28	4	2	36-8	47	3.95	83	.293	.392	8	.125	-0*		-4		-0.6
1973	Cle A	0	0	—	5	0	0	0-1	11.2	10	8	3	0	10-1	4	6.17	64	.233	.377	0	—	0		-2		-0.1
	KC A	3	3	.500	19	1	0	1-0	56.1	59	21	6	3	23-6	46	3.04	135	.267	.344	0	—	0	0	6		0.6
	Year	3	3	.500	24	1	0	1-1	68	69	29	9	3	33-7	50	3.57	114	.261	.350	0	—	0	0	4		0.5
1974	KC A	2	3	.400	36	0	0	2-4	67.1	53	31	4	2	23-5	43	2.81	136	.212	.282	0	—	0		4		0.4
1975	KC A	0	3	.000	36	0	0	2-2	50.1	42	21	2	1	20-4	25	2.50	154	.226	.300	1	.000	-0		5	21	0.4
1976	†KC A	5	5	.500	55	0	0	10-2	85.1	73	23	3	3	25-8	38	2.32	151	.238	.301	0	—	0		12		1.9
1977	†KC A	2	4	.333	43	0	0	4-2	64	59	26	4	1	19-4	19	3.09	130	.254	.307	0	—	0		6		0.6
1978	†KC A	1	4	.200	45	0	0	7-1	69	64	25	5	3	16-4	28	2.74	140	.242	.290	0	—	0		8		0.7
1979	KC A	3	3	.500	30	1	0	1-0	46.2	69	36	10	1	17-2	18	5.79	74	.348	.401	0	—	0	85	-9	23	-1.0
Total	10	18	33	.353	385	2	0	42-17	584.2	544	237	45	18	225-53	329	3.03	126	.248	.321	12	.167	-0	47	42	67	4.0

MINNER, PAUL Paul Edison "Lefty" B7.30.1923 New Wilmington PA BL/TL/6-5/210* d9.12

1946	Bro N	0	1	.000	3	0	0	0	4	6	4	1	0	3	3	6.75	50	.333	.429	—	0		-2		-0.3
1948	Bro N	4	3	.571	24	2	0	1	62.2	61	23	5	0	26	23	2.44	164	.257	.331	21	.190	1*	155	9		1.1
1949	†Bro N	3	1	.750	27	1	0	2	47.1	49	22	7	1	18	17	3.80	108	.272	.342	14	.214	-0	172	1		0.1
1950	Chi N	8	13	.381	39	24	9-1	4	190.1	217	105	18	1	72	99	4.11	102	.287	.350	65-1-1	.215	2*	89	1		0.5
1951	Chi N	6	17	.261	33	28	14-3	1	201.2	199	97	20	0	64	68	3.79	108	.277	.331	71-1-2	.254	5*	85	6		1.4
1952	Chi N	14	9	.609	28	27	12-2	0	180.2	180	84	13	1	54	61	3.74	106	.258	.312	64-1-3	.234	6*	117	3		1.1
1953	Chi N	12	15	.444	31	27	9-2	1	201	227	109	15	3	40	64	4.21	106	.283	.320	68-1-3	.221	1	71	5		1.0
1954	Chi N	11	11	.500	32	29	12	1	218	236	107	19	1	50	79	3.96	106	.280	.317	76-2-1	.171	3*	109	6		0.9
1955	Chi N	9	9	.500	22	22	7-1	0	157.2	173	67	15	1	47-10	53	3.48	117	.283	.333	56-0-1	.232	2	102	11		1.5
1956	Chi N	2	5	.286	10	9	1	0	47	60	38	9	2	19-2	14	6.89	55	.324	.389	12	.250	2	101	-15	97	-1.7
Total	10	69	84	.451	253	169	64-9	10	1310.1	1428	656	122	10	393-12	481	3.94	105	.279	.331	447-6-11	.219	22	96	25	97	5.6

MINNICK, DON Donald Athey B4.14.1931 Lynchburg VA BR/TR/6-3/195 d9.23

| 1957 | Was A | 0 | 1 | .000 | 2 | 1 | 0 | 0 | 9.1 | 14 | 8 | 1 | 0 | 2-0 | 7 | 4.82 | 81 | .341 | .372 | 2 | .000 | -0 | 23 | -2 | | -0.2 |

MINOR, BLAS Blas B3.20.1966 Merced CA BR/TR/6-3/203* [PitN88 6/148] d7.28 Col Arizona St.

1992	Pit N	0	0	—	1	0	0	0-0	2	3	2	0	0	0-0	0	4.50	77	.333	.333	0	—	0		-1		0.0
1993	Pit N	8	6	.571	65	0	0	2-1	94.1	94	43	8	4	26-3	84	4.10	100	.263	.316	10	.200	1		1		0.2
1994	Pit N	0	1	.000	17	0	0	1-0	19	27	17	4	1	9-2	17	8.05	54	.351	.420	0-0-1	—	-0		-7		-0.4
1995	NY N	4	2	.667	35	0	0	1-0	46.2	44	21	6	1	13-1	43	3.66	110	.253	.309	2	.000	-0		-2	31	0.2
1996	NY N	0	0	—	17	0	0	0-1	25.2	23	11	4	0	6-2	20	3.51	115	.237	.279	1	.000	-0.		2		0.1
	Sea A	0	1	.000	11	0	0	0-0	25.1	27	14	6	0	11-0	14	4.97	100	.276	.349	0	—	0		1		0.0
1997	Hou N	1	0	1.000	11	0	0	1-2	12	13	7	1	1	5-0	6	4.50	89	.277	.352	0	—	0		-1		-0.1
Total	6	13	10	.565	157	0	0	5-4	225	231	115	29	7	70-8	184	4.40	95	.269	.326	13-0-1	.154	0		-3	31	0.4

MINSHALL, JIM James Edward B7.4.1947 Covington KY BR/TR/6-6/205* [PitN66 2/35] d9.14

1974	Pit N	0	1	.000	5	0	0	0-1	4.1	4	1	0	0	2-1	3	0.00	—	.083	.200	0	—	0		1		0.3
1975	Pit N	0	0	—	1	0	0	0-0	1	1	0	0	0	2-0	2	0.00	—	.000	.400	0	—	0		0		0.0
Total	2	0	1	.000	6	0	0	0-1	5.1	5	1	0	0	4-1	5	0.00	—	.067	.250	0	—	0		1		0.3

YEAR	TM LG	W	L	PCT	G	GS	CG-SHO	SV-BS	IP	H	R	HR	HB	BB-IB	SO	ERA	AERA	OAV	OOB	AB-HR-SH	AVG	PB	SUP	APR	DL	PW
MINTON, GREG	Gregory Brian B7.29.1951 Lubbock TX BB/TR/6-2/190(180-207) [KCA70*3/55] d9.7 Col San Diego Mesa (CA) JC																									
1975	SF N	1	1	.500	4	2	0	0-0	17	19	14	1	1	11-3	6	6.88	55	.288	.397	6-0-1	.000	-1	92	-5		-0.6
1976	SF N	0	3	.000	10	2	0	0-0	25.2	32	18	0	1	12-1	7	4.91	74	.317	.388	5	.200	-0*	109	-4		-0.4
1977	SF N	1	1	.500	2	2	0	0-0	14	14	8	0	0	4-0	5	4.50	88	.264	.316	3-0-1	.333	1*	90	-1		0.0
1978	SF N	0	1	.000	11	0	0	0-1	15.2	22	14	3	1	8-1	6	8.04	43	.338	.413	1	.000	-0		-7		-0.5
1979	SF N	4	3	.571	46	0	0	4-3	79.2	59	25	0	2	27-7	33	1.81	193	.215	.289	4-0-1	.000	-0		13	57	1.3
1980	SF N	4	6	.400	68	0	0	19-6	91.1	81	28	0	0	34-6	42	2.46	143	.243	.312	8-0-2	.125	-0		11		1.8
1981	SF N	4	5	.444	55	0	0	21-4	84.1	84	28	0	0	36-8	29	2.88	118	.267	.340	12-0-1	.000	-1		6		0.9
1982	SF N★	10	4	.714	78	0	0	30-7	123	108	29	5	2	42-17	58	1.83	196	.244	.310	17-0-1	.176	0		**24**		**3.9**
1983	SF N	7	11	.389	73	0	0	22-6	106.2	117	51	6	0	47-13	38	3.54	100	.283	.352	11-1-0	.545	-1		-1		0.3
1984	SF N	4	9	.308	74	1	0	19-5	124.1	130	60	6	0	57-20	48	3.76	94	.267	.341	21-0-1	.048	-1	50	-4		-0.5
1985	SF N	5	4	.556	68	0	0	4-3	96.2	98	42	6	0	54-18	37	3.54	98	.272	.364	8	.000	-1		0		0.1
1986	SF N	4	4	.500	48	0	0	5-4	68.2	63	35	4	1	34-15	34	3.93	90	.251	.339	5	.400	2		-4	23	-0.2
1987	SF N	1	0	1.000	15	0	0	1-0	23.1	30	9	2	1	10-3	9	3.47	111	.323	.394	2-0-1	.000	-0		2		0.1
	Cal A	5	4	.556	41	0	0	10-2	76	71	28	4	1	29-4	35	3.08	141	.257	.328	0	—	0		12		1.6
1988	Cal A	4	5	.444	44	0	0	7-10	79	67	37	1	3	34-10	46	2.85	136	.233	.317	0	—	0		5	37	0.7
1989	Cal A	4	3	.571	62	0	0	8-3	90	76	22	4	0	37-4	42	2.20	174	.230	.310	0	—	0		17	15	1.6
1990	Cal A	1	1	.500	11	0	0	0-0	15.1	11	4	1	1	7-1	4	2.35	164	.212	.317	0	—	0		3	133	0.3
Total	16	59	65	.476	710	7	0	150-54	1130.2	1082	452	43	16	483-131	479	3.10	118	.257	.334	103-1-9	.146	2	94	67	265	10.4
MINTZ, STEVE	Stephen Wayne B11.24.1968 Wilmington NC BL/TR/5-11/190* [LAN90 17/461] d5.18 Col Mount Olive																									
1995	SF N	1	2	.333	14	0	0	0-1	19.1	26	16	4	2	12-3	7	7.45	55	.329	.426	3	.000	-0		-6		-0.9
1999	Ana A	0	0	—	3	0	0	0-0	5	8	2	1	0	2-0	2	3.60	136	.381	.435	0	.	-0		1		0.0
Total	2	1	2	.333	17	0	0	0-1	24.1	34	18	5	2	14-3	9	6.66	64	.340	.427	3	.000	-0		-5		-0.9
MINUTELLI, GINO	Gino Michael B5.23.1964 Wilmington DE BL/TL/6-0/180* d9.18 Col Southwestern (CA) CC																									
1990	Cin N	0	0	—	2	0	0	0-0	1	0	1	0	1	2-0	0	9.00	44	.000	.500	0	—	0		-1		0.0
1991	Cin N	0	2	.000	16	3	0	0-0	25.1	30	17	5	0	18-1	21	6.04	63	.288	.387	3	.000	-0	95	-5	15	-0.4
1993	SF N	0	1	.000	9	0	0	0-1	14.1	7	9	2	0	15-0	10	3.77	104	.152	.349	4	.000	-0		-1		-0.1
Total	3	0	3	.000	27	3	0	0-1	40.2	37	27	7	1	35-1	31	5.31	73	.242	.378	7	.000	-1	95	-7	15	-0.5
MIRABELLA, PAUL	Paul Thomas B3.20.1954 Belleville NJ BL/TL/6-2/196(185-196) [TexA76*S1/21] d7.28 Col Montclair St.																									
1978	Tex A	3	2	.600	10	4	0	1-0	28	30	18	2	0	17-0	23	5.79	65	.286	.379	—		0	156	-5		-0.9
1979	NY A	0	4	.000	10	1	0	0-0	14.1	16	15	3	1	10-1	4	8.79	47	.276	.391	—		0	66	-7		-1.4
1980	Tor A	5	12	.294	33	22	3-1	0-1	130.2	151	73	11	3	66-3	53	4.34	100	.294	.375	—		0	81	-1		-0.2
1981	Tor A	0	0	—	8	1	0	0-0	14.2	20	16	2	1	7-0	9	7.36	54	.313	.384	—		0	136	-6		-0.3
1982	Tex A	1	1	.500	40	0	0	3-3	50.2	46	28	4	2	22-5	29	4.80	81	.241	.324	—		0		-5		-0.2
1983	Bal A	0	0	—	3	2	0	0-0	9.2	9	6	1	0	7-0	4	5.59	72	.243	.364	—		0	136	-1		-0.1
1984	Sea A	2	5	.286	52	1	0	3-3	68	74	39	6	1	32-6	41	4.37	92	.282	.359	—		0	22	-4		-0.3
1985	Sea A	0	0	—	10	0	0	0-0	13.2	9	4	0	2	4-1	9	1.32	321	.188	.268	—		0		4		0.2
1986	Sea A	0	0	—	8	0	0	0-0	6.1	13	7	1	0	3-0	6	8.53	50	.419	.471	—		0		-3		-0.1
1987	Mil A	2	1	.667	29	0	0	2-2	29.1	30	20	0	0	16-3	14	4.91	94	.268	.351	—		0		-2		-0.2
1988	Mil A	2	2	.500	38	0	0	4-0	60	44	12	3	0	21-5	33	1.65	243	.204	.272	—		0	16	15	1.2
1989	Mil A	0	0	—	13	0	0	0-0	15.1	18	14	1	1	7-3	6	7.63	51	.290	.356	—		0	-6	117	-0.3
1990	Mil A	4	2	.667	44	2	0	0-1	59	66	32	9	2	27-2	28	3.97	98	.281	.357	—		0	82	-1		-0.1
Total	13	19	29	.396	298	33	3-1	13-10	499.2	526	284	43	13	239-29	258	4.45	92	.272	.352	0	—	0	94	-21	132	-2.7
MIRANDA, ANGEL	Angel Luis (Andujar) B11.9.1969 Arecibo, PR BL/TL/6-1/195(160-195) d6.5																									
1993	Mil A	4	5	.444	22	17	2	0-0	120	100	53	12	2	52-4	88	3.30	131	.226	.309	0	—	0	93	12	57	0.7
1994	Mil A	2	5	.286	8	8	1	0-0	46	39	28	8	0	27-0	24	5.28	96	.234	.338	0	—	0	82	0	86	-0.1
1995	Mil A	4	5	.444	30	10	0	1-2	74	83	47	8	0	49-2	45	5.23	96	.291	.391	0	—	0	87	-2	32	-0.2
1996	Mil A	7	6	.538	46	12	0	1-1	109.1	116	68	12	2	69-4	78	4.94	105	.277	.376	0	—	0	97	2		0.1
1997	Mil A	0	0	—	10	0	0	0-0	14	17	6	1	0	9-2	8	3.86	120	.309	.433	0	—	0	1	19		0.1
Total	5	17	21	.447	116	47	3	2-3	363.1	355	202	41	7	206-12	243	4.46	108	.260	.356	0	—	0	91	13	194	0.6
MISURACA, MIKE	Michael William B8.21.1968 Long Beach CA BR/TR/6-0/190 d7.27																									
1997		0	0	—	15	0	0	0-0	15	19	16	3	0	7-1	10	11.32	41	.333	.423	0	—	0		-7		-0.3
MITCHELL, ROY	Albert Roy B4.19.1885 Belton TX D9.8.1959 Temple TX BR/TR/5-9.5/170 d9.10																									
1910	StL A	4	2	.667	6	6	6	0	52	43	24	0	2	12	23	2.60	95	.244	.300	19	.211	0	113	-1		-0.1
1911	StL A	4	8	.333	28	12	8-1	0	133.1	134	79	4	6	45	40	3.85	88	.273	.341	49-0-1	.224	1*	82	-6		-0.3
1912	StL A	3	4	.429	13	7	5	0	62	81	36	2	4	17	22	4.65	71	.323	.375	19	.316	3	95	-6		-0.3
1913	StL A	13	16	.448	33	27	21-4	1	245.1	265	111	6	5	47	59	3.01	97	.282	.320	88-0-2	.148	-1*	99	-2		-0.4
1914	StL A	4	5	.444	28	9	4	4	103.1	134	77	1	6	38	38	4.35	62	.320	.384	34	.206	1	84	-22		-1.9
1918	Chi A	0	1	.000	2	2	0	0	12	18	14	1	0	4	3	7.50	36	.346	.393	2-0-1	.000	-0	124	-7		-0.5
	Cin N	4	0	1.000	5	3	3-2	0	36.1	27	3	0	0	5	9	0.74	359	.208	.237	14	.214	0	189	8		1.1
1919	Cin N	0	1	1.000	7	1	0	0	31	32	16	0	0	9	10	2.32	119	.276	.328	10	.000	-2	0	-1		-0.2
Total	7	32	37	.464	122	67	47-7	5	675.1	734	360	14	23	177	204	3.42	86	.285	.337	235-0-4	.187	3	98	-37		-2.6
MITCHELL, CHARLIE	Charles Ross B6.24.1962 Dickson TN BR/TR/6-3/170* d8.9 b-John Col Columbia St. (TN) CC																									
1984	Bos A	0	0	—	10	0	0	0-0	16.1	14	7	1	2	6-3	7	2.76	153	.226	.314	0	—	0		2		0.1
1985	Bos A	0	0	—	2	0	0	0-1	1.2	5	3	1	0	0-0	2	16.20	27	.500	.500	0	—	0		-2		-0.1
Total	2	0	0	—	12	0	0	0-1	18	19	10	2	2	6-3	9	4.00	105	.264	.338	0	—	0		0		0.0
MITCHELL, CLARENCE	Clarence Elmer B2.22.1891 Franklin NE D11.6.1963 Grand Island NE BL/TL/5-11.5/190 d6.2 Mil 1918 C2 ▲																									
1911	Det A	1	0	1.000	5	1	0	0	14.1	20	13	1	0	7	4	8.16	42	.351	.422	4	.500	1	125	-6		-0.3
1916	Cin N	11	10	.524	29	24	17-1	0	194.2	211	87	4	10	45	52	3.14	83	.285	.334	117-0-1	.239	2*	132	-12		-0.9
1917	Cin N	9	15	.375	32	20	10-2	1	159.1	166	73	2	4	34	37	3.22	81	.268	.308	90-0-2	.278	4*	91	-8		-0.7
1918	Bro N	0	1	.000	1	1	0	0	0.1	4	4	0	0	0	0	108.00	3	1.000	1.000	24-0-1	.250	0*	136	-3		-0.5
1919	Bro N	7	5	.583	29	13	11	0	108.2	123	49	0	0	23	43	3.06	97	.297	.334	49-1-0	.367	6*	129	-1		0.6
1920	†Bro N	5	2	.714	19	7	3-1	1	78.2	85	35	1	0	23	18	3.09	104	.288	.340	107-0-1	.234	1*	102	1		0.2
1921	Bro N	11	9	.550	37	18	13-3	2	190	206	91	7	5	46	39	2.89	135	.280	.327	91	.264	3*	102	14		1.9
1922	Bro N	0	3	.000	9	5	0	0	12.2	28	24	0	1	7	1	14.21	29	.467	.529	155-3-3	.290	2*	153	-14		-2.1
1923	Phi N	9	10	.474	29	19	8-1	0	139.1	170	93	8	4	46	41	4.72	98	.299	.355	78-1-0	.269	3*	93	-3		-0.1
1924	Phi N	6	13	.316	30	26	9-1	1	165	223	113	10	6	58	36	5.62	79	.321	.379	102-0-2	.255	-1*	84	-16		-1.5
1925	Phi N	10	17	.370	32	26	12-1	1	199.1	245	130	23	5	51	46	5.28	90	.302	.347	92-0-4	.196	-2*	85	-5		-0.5
1926	Phi N	9	14	.391	28	25	12	1	178.2	232	111	7	4	55	52	4.58	90	.318	.369	78-0-1	.244	1*	94	-9		-0.6
1927	Phi N	6	3	.667	13	12	8-1	0	94.2	99	44	7	2	28	17	4.09	101	.271	.327	42-1-2	.238	2*	115	2		0.4
1928	Phi N	0	0	—	3	0	0	0	5.2	13	6	0	0	2	0	9.53	45	.542	.577	4	.250	0*		-3		-0.1
	†StL N	8	9	.471	19	18	9-1	0	150	149	59	3	4	38	31	3.30	121	.265	.315	56-0-5	.125	-3	81	15		1.3
	Year	8	9	.471	22	18	9-1	0	155.2	162	65	3	4	40	31	3.53	114	.276	.326	60-0-5	.133	-3	81	10		1.2
1929	StL N	8	11	.421	25	22	16	0	173	221	89	13	5	60	39	4.27	109	.320	.379	66-0-6	.273	4*	99	10		1.2
1930	StL N	1	0	1.000	1	1	0	0	3	5	2	0	0	1	0	6.00	84	.357	.438	2	.500	0	139	0		0.0
	NY N	10	3	.769	24	16	5	0	129	151	68	0	1	36	40	3.98	119	.298	.346	47-0-2	.255	0	138	11		1.0
	Year	11	3	.786	25	17	5	0	132	156	70	0	1	38	41	4.02	118	.300	.349	49-0-2	.265	0	139	9		1.0
1931	NY N	13	11	.542	27	25	13	0	190.1	221	100	12	3	52	39	4.07	91	.285	.332	73-1-0	.219	2	128	-8		-0.8
1932	NY N	1	3	.250	28	3	1	2	30.1	41	21	1	1	11	7	4.15	89	.325	.384	10	.200	0	174	-3		-0.4
Total	18	125	139	.473	390	278	145-12	9	2217	2613	1215	116	52	624	543	4.12	95	.297	.347	1287-7-30	.252	26	105	-38		-1.9
MITCHELL, CRAIG	Craig Seton B4.14.1954 Santa Rosa CA BR/TR/6-3/190* [OakA73 S1/1] d9.25 Col Spokane Falls (WA) CC																									
1975	Oak A	0	1	1.000	1	1	0	0-0	3.2	6	5	0	0	2-0	2	12.27	30	.375	.444	—		0	48	-3		-0.5
1976	Oak A	0	0	—	1	0	0	0-0	3.1	3	1	0	0	0-0	0	2.70	125	.231	.231	—		0		0		0.0
1977	Oak A	0	1	.000	3	1	0	0-0	5.2	9	6	1	0	2-0	1	7.94	51	.346	.393	—		0	22	-3		-0.4
Total	3	0	2	.000	5	2	0	0-0	12.2	18	12	1	0	4-0	3	7.82	48	.327	.373	—		0	36	-6		-0.9

YEAR	TM	LG	W	L	PCT	G	GS	CG-SHO	SV-BS	IP	H	R	HR	HB	BB-IB	SO	ERA	AERA	OAV	OOB	AB-HR-SH	AVG	PB	SUP	APR	DL	PW

MITCHELL, FRED Frederick Francis (b Frederick Francis Yapp) B6.5.1878 Cambridge MA D10.13.1970 Newton MA BR/TR/5-9.5/185 d4.27 M7/C3 ▲

1901	Bos	A	6	6	.500	17	13	10	0	108.2	115	67	2	11	51	34	3.81	93	.268	.360	44	.159	-1*	96	-3		-0.4
1902	Bos	A	0	1	.000	1	0	0	0	4	8	5	1	0	5	2	11.25	32	.421	.542	1	.000	-0		-3		-0.4
	Phi	A	5	8	.385	18	14	9	1	107.2	120	71	4	8	59	22	3.59	102	.282	.380	48-0-3	.188	-1*	98	-2		-0.2
	Year		5	9	.357	19	14	9	1	111.2	128	76	5	8	64	24	3.87	95	.288	.388	49-0-3	.184	-1	98	-5		-0.6
1903	Phi	N	11	16	.407	28	28	24-1	0	227	250	155	4	19	102	69	4.48	73	.284	.370	95-0-2	.200	-1*	111	-30		-3.1
1904	Phi	N	4	7	.364	13	13	11	0	108.2	133	62	3	7	25	29	3.40	79	.306	.353	82-0-3	.207	1*	117	-8		-0.5
	Bro	N	2	5	.286	8	8	8-1	0	66	73	37	0	3	23	16	3.82	72	.291	.367	24-0-1	.292	2	91	-6		-0.3
	Year		6	12	.333	21	21	19-1	0	174.2	206	99	3	10	48	45	3.56	76	.300	.355	106-0-4	.226	4	107	-16		-0.8
1905	Bro	N	3	7	.300	12	10	9	0	96.1	107	73	2	5	38	44	4.76	61	.285	.358	79-0-1	.190	0*	90	-21		-1.8
Total	5		31	50	.383	97	86	71-2	1	718.1	806	470	16	53	303	216	4.10	78	.286	.366	373-0-10	.198	1	103	-73		-6.7

MITCHELL, JOHN John Kyle B8.11.1965 Dickson TN BR/TR/6-2/195(165-195) [BosA83 7/177] d9.8 b-Charlie

1986	NY	N	0	1	.000	4	1	0-0	0	10	10	4	1	1			3.60	100	.278	.350	2	.000	-0	25	0		0.0
1987	NY	N	3	6	.333	20	19	1	0-0	111.2	124	64	6	2	36-3	57	4.11	93	.279	.333	35-0-5	.114	-1	113	-7		-0.5
1988	NY	N	0	0		1	0	0	0-0	1	2	0	0	0	1-0	1	0.00		.500	.600	1	.000	-0		0		0.0
1989	NY	N	0	1	.000	2	0	0	0-0	3	3	7	0	0	4-1	4	6.00	55	.231	.412	0	—	0		-3		-0.6
1990	Bal	A	6	6	.500	24	17	0	0-0	114.1	133	63	7	3	48-3	43	4.64	82	.300	.366	0	—	0	111	-11		-1.0
Total	5		9	14	.391	51	37	1	0-0	240	272	138	14	5	93-7	107	4.35	88	.289	.352	38-0-5	.105	-1	110	-21		-2.1

MITCHELL, LARRY Larry Paul B10.16.1971 Flint MI BR/TR/6-1/219 [PhiN92 5/137] d8.11 Col James Madison

| 1996 | Phi | N | 0 | 0 | — | 7 | 0 | 0-0 | 0 | 12 | 14 | 6 | 1 | 0 | 5-1 | 7 | 4.50 | 96 | .311 | .373 | 2 | .000 | -0 | | 0 | | 0.0 |

MITCHELL, MONROE Monroe Barr B9.11.1901 Starkville MS D9.4.1976 Valdosta GA BR/TL/6-1.5/170 d7.11 Col Mississippi St.

| 1923 | Was | A | 2 | 4 | .333 | 10 | 6 | 3-1 | 2 | 41.2 | 57 | 35 | 0 | 1 | 68 | 8 | 6.48 | 58 | .350 | .430 | 12 | .250 | 1 | 84 | -13 | | -1.5 |

MITCHELL, PAUL Paul Michael B8.19.1949 Worcester MA BR/TR/6-1/195* [BalA71 D1/7] d7.1 Col Old Dominion

1975	Bal	A	3	0	1.000	11	4	0-1	0	57	41	23	8	0	19-4	31	3.63	98	.204	.271	0	—	0	224	0		0.0
1976	Oak	A	9	7	.563	26	26	4-1	0-0	142	169	74	15	1	30-0	67	4.25	79	.294	.328	0	—	0	123	-14		-1.5
1977	Oak	A	0	3	.000	5	3	0	0-0	13.2	21	16	3	0	7-0	5	10.54	38	.339	.406	0	—	0	45	-9		-1.5
	Sea	A	3	3	.500	9	9	0	0-0	39.2	50	26	7	1	16-1	20	4.99	83	.311	.370	0	—	0	80	-4		-0.6
	Year		3	6	.333	14	12	0	0-0	53.1	71	42	10	1	23-1	25	6.41	64	.318	.380	0	—	0	71	-13		-2.1
1978	Sea	A	8	14	.364	29	29	4-2	0-0	168	173	86	21	2	79-1	75	4.18	92	.270	.350	0	—	0	80	-5		-0.7
1979	Sea	A	1	4	.200	10	6	1	0-0	36.2	46	26	4	0	15-0	18	4.42	99	.309	.370	0	—	0	69	-3		-0.3
	Mil	A	3	3	.500	18	8	0	0-0	75	81	50	11	3	10-0	32	5.76	73	.276	.301	0	—	0	121	-11		-1.1
	Year		4	7	.364	28	14	1	0-0	111.2	127	76	15	3	25-0	50	5.32	80	.287	.325	0	—	0	99	-14		-1.1
1980	Mil	A	5	5	.500	17	11	1-1	1-0	89.1	92	40	7	1	15-3	29	3.53	111	.267	.298	0	—	0	96	4		0.4
Total	6		32	39	.451	125	96	11-4	1-0	621.1	673	341	76	8	191-9	277	4.45	86	.278	.330	0	—	0	100	-42		-5.0

MITCHELL, BOBBY Robert McKasha B2.6.1856 Cincinnati OH D5.1.1933 Springfield OH BL/TL/5-5/135 d9.6

1877	Cin	N	6	5	.545	12	12	11-1	0	100	123	69	0		11	41	3.51	75	.281	.299	49	.204	-0*	86	-8		-0.6
1878	Cin	N	7	2	.778	9	9	9-1	0	80	69	32	1		18	51	2.14	100	.223	.265	49	.245	1*	116	3		0.4
1879	Cle	N	7	15	.318	23	22	20	0	194.2	236	153	1		42	90	3.28	76	.283	.317	109	.147	-4*	84	-17		-2.1
1882	StL	AA	0	1	.000	1	1	0	0	7	12	13	0		2	2	7.71	36	.353	.389	4	.000	-1	110	-4		-0.4
Total	4		20	23	.465	45	44	40-2	0	381.2	440	267	2		73	184	3.18	77	.272	.304	211	.180	-5	91	-26		-2.7

MITCHELL, WILLIE William B12.1.1889 Pleasant Grove MS D11.23.1973 Sardis MS BR/TL/6-0/176 d9.22 Mil 1918 Col Mississippi St.

1909	Cle	A	1	2	.333	3	3	3	0	23	18	6	0	4	10	8	1.57	163	.225	.340	7	.286	1	46	2		0.4
1910	Cle	A	12	8	.600	35	18	11-1	0	183.2	155	77	2	15	55	102	2.60	100	.236	.310	63-0-3	.159	-3	120	-1		-0.6
1911	Cle	A	7	14	.333	30	22	9	0	177.1	190	102	1	13	60	78	3.76	91	.284	.354	64-0-2	.109	-5*	84	-1		-1.3
1912	Cle	A	5	8	.385	29	15	8	1	163.2	149	88	0	7	56	94	2.80	121	.240	.309	53-0-1	.113	-4	105	5		-0.2
1913	Cle	A	14	8	.636	35	22	14-4	0	217	153	62	1	8	88	141	1.91	159	.202	.292	70-0-6	.143	-2	108	27		2.3
1914	Cle	A	11	17	.393	39	32	16-3	1	257	228	127	3	7	124	179	3.19	91	.238	.330	81-0-8	.086	-3	103	-7		-1.4
1915	Cle	A	11	14	.440	36	30	12-1	1	236	210	103	1	2	84	149	2.82	108	.241	.309	79-0-6	.127	-5	96	6		-0.1
1916	Cle	A	2	5	.286	12	6	1	1	43.2	55	35	1	0	19	24	5.15	58	.309	.376	11-0-1	.000	-1	101	-11		-1.7
	Det	A	7	5	.583	23	17	7-2	0	127.2	119	53	1	5	48	60	3.31	86	.253	.329	36-0-1	.250	2	121	-4		-0.3
	Year		9	10	.474	35	23	8-2	1	171.1	174	88	2	5	67	84	3.78	77	.269	.342	47-0-2	.191	1	116	-15		-2.0
1917	Det	A	12	8	.600	30	22	12-5	0	185.1	172	66	2	13	46	80	2.19	121	.250	.309	59-0-4	.119	-3*	106	9		0.5
1918	Det	A	0	1	.000	1	1	0	0	4	3	4	0	0	5	2	9.00	30	.200	.400	2	.000	-0	85	-3		-0.4
1919	Det	A	1	2	.333	3	1	0	0	12	12	8	2	1	10	4	5.27	61	.255	.397	5	.200	-0	110	-2		-0.4
Total	11		83	92	.474	276	190	93-16	• 4	1632	1464	731	14	75	605	921	2.88	103	.244	.319	530-0-32	.130	-24	102	14		-3.2

MITRE, SERGIO Sergio Armando B2.16.1981 Los Angeles CA BR/TR/6-4/210* [ChiN01 7/198] d7.22 Col San Diego (CA) City

2003	Chi	N	0	1	.000	3	2	0	0	8.2	15	8	3	1	4-1	3	8.31	52	.395	.442		.500	0	65	-3		-0.3
2004	Chi	N	2	4	.333	12	9	0	0	51.2	71	38	6	4	20-1	37	6.62	67	.327	.394	15-0-3	.067	-1*	125	-11		-1.1
2005	Chi	N	2	5	.286	21	7	1-1	0-0	60.1	62	37	11	3	23-2	37	5.37	82	.261	.330	11-0-1	.364	1	115	-6		-0.4
Total	3		4	10	.286	36	18	1-1	0-0	120.2	148	83	18	7	47-4	77	6.12	72	.300	.367	28-0-4	.214	1	115	-20		-1.8

MIZELL, VINEGAR BEND Wilmer David B8.13.1930 Leakesville MS D2.21.1999 Kerrville TX BR/TL/6-3.5/205* d4.22 Mil 1954-55

1952	StL	N	10	8	.556	30	30	7-2	0	190	171	89	12	1	103	146	3.65	102	.237	.333	68-0-4	.044	-5	103	1		-0.6
1953	StL	N	13	11	.542	33	33	10-1	0	224.1	193	93	12	4	114	173	3.49	105	.227	.321	83-1-3	.084	-4	89	20		1.5
1956	StL	N	14	14	.500	33	33	11-3	0	208.2	172	93	20	7	92-5	153	3.62	104	.222	.310	75-0-5	.107	-3	94	5		0.4
1957	StL	N	8	10	.444	33	21	7-2	0	149.1	136	69	18	1	51-4	87	3.74	106	.241	.303	40-0-1	.089	-2	89	4		0.3
1958	StL	N	10	14	.417	30	29	8-2	0	189.2	178	81	17	2	91-9	80	3.42	121	.252	.335	61-0-5	.115	-3	59	14		1.3
1959	StL N*		13	10	.565	31	30	8-1	0	201.1	196	104	21	4	89-7	108	4.20	101	.252	.333	75-0-5	.187	1	109	1		0.0
1960	StL	N	1	3	.250	9	9	0	0	55.1	64	31	7	0	28-4	42	4.55	90	.291	.369	18-0-1	.111	-1	84	-3		-0.2
	†Pit	N	13	5	.722	23	23	8-3	0	155.2	141	59	7	3	46-6	71	3.12	120	.247	.305	51-0-4	.137	-1	107	11		1.0
	Year		14	8	.636	32	32	8-3	0	211	205	90	14	3	74-10	113	3.50	110	.259	.323	69-0-5	.130	-1	101	10		0.8
1961	Pit	N	7	10	.412	25	17	2-1	0	100	120	61	16	0	31-8	37	5.04	79	.299	.348	23-0-5	.130	-1	75	-11		-1.7
1962	Pit	N	1	1	.500	4	3	0	0	16.1	15	10	1	1	10-0	6	4.96	79	.254	.366	6	.000	-0	82	-2		-0.2
	NY	N	0	2	.000	17	2	0	0	38	48	35	10	1	25-0	15	7.34	57	.324	.416	8	.250	-1	105	-12		-0.6
	Year		1	3	.250	21	5	0	0	54.1	63	45	13	2	35-0	21	6.63	62	.304	.402	14	.143	-0	90	-15		-0.8
Total	9		90	88	.506	268	230	61-15	0	1528.2	1434	725	143	28	680-43	918	3.85	104	.247	.328	513-1-33	.111	-19	91	28		1.2

MLICKI, DAVE David John B6.8.1968 Cleveland OH BR/TR/6-4/205(185-205) [CleA90 17/460] d9.12 Col Oklahoma St.

1992	Cle	A	0	2	.000	4	4	0	0-0	21.2	23	14	3	1	16-0	16	4.98	79	.280	.404	0	—	0	110	-3		-0.2
1993	Cle	A	0	0		3	3	0	0-0	13.1	11	6	2	1	6-0	7	3.38	130	.220	.328	0	—	0	98	1	121	0.1
1995	NY	N	9	7	.563	29	25	0	0-0	160.2	160	82	23	4	54-2	123	4.26	95	.256	.317	39-0-12	.051	-1	111	-3		-0.4
1996	NY	N	6	7	.462	51	2	0	1-2	90	95	46	9	6	33-8	83	3.30	122	.277	.348	10	.100	0	90	4		0.4
1997	NY	N	8	12	.400	32	32	1-1	0	193.2	194	89	21	5	76-7	157	4.00	100	.259	.329	48-0-3	.188	2*	105	3		0.4
1998	NY	N	1	4	.200	10	10	1	0	57	68	38	8	5	25-4	39	5.68	73	.297	.374	16-0-3	.188	1	120	-10		-0.7
	LA	N	7	3	.700	20	20	2-1	0	124.1	120	64	15	2	38-1	78	4.05	99	.253	.308	34-0-7	.059	-2	112	-1		-0.3
	Year		8	7	.533	30	30	3-1	0	181.1	188	102	23	7	63-5	117	4.57	89	.267	.330	50-0-10	.100	-1	115	-12		-1.0
1999	LA	N	0	1	.000	2	0	0	0	7.1	10	4	1	0	2-0	1	4.91	89	.323	.364	1-0-2	1.000	0	0	0		0.0
	Det	A	14	12	.538	31	31	2	0	191.2	209	108	24	12	70-1	119	4.60	109	.276	.344	4	.000	0	81	7		0.7
2000	Det	A	6	11	.353	24	21	0	0	119.1	143	79	14	4	44-1	57	5.58	88	.291	.349	2	.000	-0	81	-8	43	-0.9
2001	Det	A	4	8	.333	15	15	0	0	81	118	69	19	6	41-0	48	7.33	60	.348	.424	1	.000	-0	84	-25		-2.9
	†Hou	N	7	3	.700	19	14	0	0	86.2	85	53	19	2	33-1	49	5.09	90	.260	.339	26-0-4	.115	-1	113	-4		-0.6
2002	Hou	N	4	1	.286	22	16	0	0	86	101	57	13	6	35-1	57	5.34	81	.290	.356	27	.185	-0	71	-10	61	-1.5
Total	10		66	80	.452	262	193	6-2	1-2	1232.2	1337	709	171	58	472-32	834	4.72	92	.276	.344	208-0-31	.125	0	96	-49	225	-5.9

MMAHAT, KEVIN Kevin Paul B11.9.1964 Memphis TN BL/TL/6-5/220 [TexA87 31/805] d9.9 Col Tulane

| 1989 | NY | A | 0 | 2 | .000 | 4 | 2 | 0 | 0 | 7.2 | 13 | 12 | 2 | 1 | 6-0 | 3 | 12.91 | 30 | .406 | .500 | 0 | — | 0 | 81 | -8 | | -1.3 |

MODAK, MIKE Michael B5.18.1922 Campbell OH D12.12.1995 Lakeland FL BR/TR/5-10.5/195 d7.4 Mil 1946 Col Indiana

| 1945 | Cin | N | 1 | 2 | .333 | 20 | 3 | 1-1 | 1 | 42.1 | 52 | 27 | 0 | 0 | 23 | 7 | 5.74 | 65 | .308 | .391 | 10 | .100 | -1 | 68 | -8 | | -0.7 |

YEAR	TM LG	W	L	PCT	G	GS	CG-SHO	SV-BS	IP	H	R	HR	HB	BB-IB	SO	ERA	AERA	OAV	OOB	AB-HR-SH	AVG	PB	SUP	APR	DL	PW

MOEHLER, BRIAN Brian Merritt B12.31.1971 Rockingham NC BR/TR/6-3/235(195-235) [DetA93 6/165] d9.22 Col North Carolina-Greensboro

1996	Det A	0	1	.000	2	2	0	0-0	10.1	11	10	1	0	8-1	2	4.35	117	.262	.380	0	—	0	82	-1		-0.1
1997	Det A	11	12	.478	31	31	2-1	0-0	175.1	198	97	22	5	61-1	97	4.67	99	.285	.343	3	.000	-0	106	-1	15	-0.1
1998	Det A	14	13	.519	33	33	4-3	0-0	221.1	229	103	30	2	56-1	123	3.90	122	.269	.306	4	.000	-0	85	21		2.2
1999	Det A	10	16	.385	32	32	2-2	0-0	196.1	229	116	22	7	59-5	106	5.04	99	.294	.347	1	.000	0	85	0		0.1
2000	Det A	12	9	.571	29	29	2	0-0	178	222	99	20	2	40-0	103	4.50	109	.305	.342	4	.000	-0	109	7	31	0.8
2001	Det A	0	0	—	1	1	0	0-0	8	6	3	0	0	1-0	2	3.38	131	.207	.233	0	—	0	105	1	185	0.1
2002	Det A	1	1	.500	3	3	0	0-0	19.2	17	5	3	0	2-0	13	2.29	191	.233	.250	0	—	0	78	5	94	0.4
	Cin N	2	4	.333	10	9	0	0-0	43.1	61	34	8	1	11-0	18	6.02	71	.330	.369	14-0-1	.000	-1	120	-9	16	-1.1
2003	Hou N	0	0	—	3	3	0	0-0	13.2	22	12	4	0	6-0	5	7.90	56	.379	.431	4	.000	-0	120	-5	165	-0.2
2005	Fla N	6	12	.333	37	25	0	0-0	158.1	198	82	16	5	42-9	95	4.55	88	.313	.359	40-0-5	.075	-2	94	-8		-0.9
Total	9	56	68	.452	181	168	10-6	0-0	1024.1	1184	561	126	22	286-17	564	4.57	102	.291	.339	70-0-6	.043	-4	97	10	506	1.2

MOELLER, DENNIS Dennis Michael B9.15.1967 Tarzana CA BR/TL/6-2/195* [KCA86 17/443] d7.28 Col Los Angeles Valley (CA) JC

1992	KC A	0	3	.000	5	4	0	0-0	18	24	17	5	0	11-2	6	7.00	58	.333	.407	0	—	0	95	-6		-0.9
1993	Pit N	1	0	1.000	10	0	0	0-0	16.1	26	20	2	1	7-1	13	9.92	49	.356	.420	0	—	0		-11		-0.6
Total	2	1	3	.250	15	4	0	0-0	34.1	50	37	7	1	18-3	19	8.39	49	.345	.413	0	—	0	95	-17		-1.5

MOELLER, JOE Joseph Douglas B2.15.1943 Blue Island IL BR/TR/6-5/208(192-225) d4.12 Mil 1962

1962	LA N	6	5	.545	19	15	1	1	85.2	87	55	10	0	58-1	46	5.25	69	.266	.375	33-0-1	.212	1	145	-15		-1.6
1964	LA N	7	13	.350	27	24	1	0	145.1	153	89	14	4	31-4	97	4.21	77	.265	.305	45-0-4	.067	-2	78	-21		-2.9
1966	†LA N	2	4	.333	29	8	0	0	78.2	73	31	4	3	14-8	31	2.52	131	.244	.283	12-0-3	.167	1	83	5		0.5
1967	LA N	0	0	—	6	0	0	0	5	9	5	1	0	3-1	2	9.00	34	.409	.462	0			-3		-0.2
1968	LA N	1	1	.500	3	3	0	0	16	17	10	1	1	2-0	11	5.06	55	.270	.299	7	.000	-1	94	-4		-0.5
1969	LA N	1	0	1.000	23	4	0	1-0	51.1	54	23	4	0	13-0	25	3.33	101	.278	.322	10	.200	0	145	-1		0.0
1970	LA N	7	9	.438	31	19	2-1	4-0	135.1	131	63	16	1	43-3	63	3.92	98	.248	.305	39-0-3	.154	0	77	0		-0.1
1971	LA N	2	4	.333	28	1	0	1-1	66.1	72	32	5	0	12-2	32	3.80	86	.279	.307	9	.000	-0	55	-5		-0.4
Total	8	26	36	.419	166	74	4-1	7-1	583.2	596	308	55	9	176-19	307	4.01	86	.263	.316	155-0-11	.129	-2	97	-44		-5.2

MOELLER, RON Ronald Ralph "The Kid" B10.13.1938 Cincinnati OH BL/TL/6-0/180* d9.8 Mil 1962

1956	Bal A	0	1	.000	4	1	0	0	6.2	10	5	0	0	3-0	1	4.15	94	.286	.333	1	.000	-0	23	-1		-0.1
1958	Bal A	0	0	—	4	0	0	0	4.1	6	2	0	0	3-0	3	4.15	87	.333	.429	0	—	0		0		0.0
1961	LA A	4	8	.333	33	18	1-1	0	112.2	122	80	15	2	83-0	87	5.83	77	.275	.391	29-0-1	.207	2*	103	-14		-1.0
1963	LA A	0	0	—	4	0	0	0	2.2	5	2	1	0	1-0	1	6.75	51	.385	.429	0	—		-1		-0.1
	Was A	2	0	1.000	8	3	0	0	24.1	31	17	4	1	10-0	10	6.29	59	.316	.385	9	.222	0	128	-6		-0.5
	Year	2	0	1.000	11	3	0	0	27	36	19	5	1	11-0	12	6.33	58	.324	.390	9	.222	0	129	-7		-0.5
Total	4	6	9	.400	52	22	1-1	0	152.2	174	106	20	3	100-0	104	5.78	74	.287	.389	39-0-1	.205	2	105	-22		-1.6

MOFFETT, SAM Samuel R. B3.14.1857 Wheeling WV D5.5.1907 Butte MT BR/TR/6-0/175 d5.15 b-Joe ▲

1884	Cle N	3	19	.136	24	22	21	0	197.2	236	165	9		58	84	3.87	81	.284	.330	256	.184	-3*	60	-16		-1.5
1887	Ind N	1	5	.167	6	6	6	0	50	47	45	1	4	23	3	3.78	110	.242	.335	41	.122	-2*	65	-2		-0.4
1888	Ind N	2	5	.286	7	7	6-1	0	56	62	40	3	2	17	7	4.66	64	.278	.335	35	.114	-1*	151	-10		-1.1
Total	3	6	29	.171	37	35	33-1	0	303.2	345	250	13	6	98	94	4.00	82	.276	.332	332	.169	-6	76	-28		-3.0

MOFFITT, RANDY Randall James B10.13.1948 Long Beach CA BR/TR/6-3/190* [SFN70*1/18] d6.11 Col Cal St.-Long Beach

1972	SF N	1	5	.167	40	0	0	4-2	70.2	72	31	5	2	30-6	37	3.69	95	.266	.341	8-0-2	.000	-1		-1		-0.1
1973	SF N	4	4	.500	60	0	0	14-4	100.1	86	30	9	1	31-4	65	2.42	159	.225	.284	17-0-1	.059	-1		16		1.4
1974	SF N	5	7	.417	61	1	0	15-4	102	99	52	9	2	29-4	49	4.50	85	.256	.308	16-0-2	.313	2	69	-4		-0.4
1975	SF N	4	5	.444	55	0	0	11-6	74	73	35	6	3	32-6	39	3.89	98	.257	.336	14	.214	1		0		0.0
1976	SF N	6	6	.500	58	0	0	14-2	103	92	36	6	4	35-9	50	2.27	160	.238	.300	14	.143	-0		13		1.8
1977	SF N	4	9	.308	64	0	0	11-7	87.2	91	41	4	3	39-13	68	3.59	110	.267	.348	3-0-1	.000	-0		3		0.5
1978	SF N	8	4	.667	70	0	0	12-9	81.2	79	35	5	3	33-13	52	3.31	105	.258	.331	7-0-1	.143	0		1		0.1
1979	SF N	2	5	.286	28	0	0	2-1	35	53	33	5	2	14-6	16	7.71	45	.356	.416	4	.000	-0*		-17	67	-3.2
1980	SF N	1	1	.500	13	0	0	0-1	16.2	18	10	2	1	4-2	10	4.86	72	.281	.333	1	.000	-0		-2	94	-0.3
1981	SF N	0	0	—	10	0	0	0-0	11.1	15	10	2	0	2-1	11	7.94	43	.313	.333	0	—	0		-5		-0.3
1982	Hou N	2	4	.333	30	0	0	3-3	41.2	36	15	3	5	13-3	20	3.02	110	.228	.305	2-0-1	.000	-0		2		0.2
1983	Tor A	6	2	.750	45	0	0	10-3	57.1	52	27	5	1	24-6	38	3.77	116	.243	.318	0	—	0		3		0.5
Total	12	43	52	.453	534	1	0	96-42	781.1	766	355	61	24	286-73	455	3.65	102	.257	.324	86-0-8	.140	-1	69	9	161	0.2

MOFORD, HERB Herbert B8.6.1928 Brooksville KY D12.3.2005 Cincinnati, OH BR/TR/6-1/175* d4.12

1955	StL N	1	1	.500	14	1	0	1	24	29	23	5	1	15-3	8	7.88	52	.299	.395	2	.000	-0	66	-10		-0.9
1958	Det A	4	9	.308	25	11	6	1	109.2	83	45	10	9	42-6	58	3.61	112	.214	.304	37-0-3	.027	-4	73	7		0.4
1959	Bos A	0	2	.000	4	2	0	0	8.2	10	11	3	0	6-0	7	11.42	36	.286	.390	1	.000	-0	98	-6		-1.1
1962	NY N	0	1	.000	7	0	0	0	15	21	15	3	0	1-0	5	7.20	58	.318	.324	4	.250	0		-5		-0.3
Total	4	5	13	.278	50	14	6	3	157.1	143	94	21	10	64-9	78	5.03	81	.244	.327	44-0-3	.045	-4	76	-14		-1.9

MOGRIDGE, GEORGE George Anthony B2.18.1889 Rochester NY D3.4.1962 Rochester NY BL/TL/6-2/165 d8.17

1911	Chi A	0	2	.000	4	1	0	0	12.2	12	10	1	0	1	7	4.97	85	.255	.271	5	.400	0	179	-3		-0.3
1912	Chi A	3	4	.429	17	8	2	3	64.2	69	32	2	1	15	31	4.04	79	.264	.307	16	.125	-0	78	-3		-0.4
1915	NY A	2	3	.400	6	5	3-1	0	41	33	11	0	3	11	11	1.76	167	.219	.285	12	.083	-1	89	5		0.5
1916	NY A	6	12	.333	30	21	10-2	0	194.2	174	71	7	4	45	66	2.31	125	.252	.305	66-0-2	.212	1	72	9		1.0
1917	NY A	9	11	.450	29	25	15-1	0	196.1	185	82	5	9	39	46	2.98	90	.255	.301	69-0-4	.159	-1	94	-5		-0.6
1918	NY A	16	13	.552	45	19	13-1	7	239.1	232	78	6	8	43	62	2.18	130	.263	.304	79-0-6	.190	-0*	125	14		2.0
1919	NY A	10	9	.526	35	18	13-3	0	169	159	68	6	7	46	58	2.77	115	.250	.307	48-0-2	.125	-1	100	7		0.7
1920	NY A	5	9	.357	26	15	7	1	125.1	146	83	4	3	36	35	4.31	89	.287	.338	42-0-1	.167	-1	103	-10		-1.0
1921	Was A	18	14	.563	38	36	21-4	0	288	301	119	12	7	66	101	3.00	137	.269	.313	98-0-3	.153	-5	75	36		3.0
1922	Was A	18	13	.581	34	32	18-3	0	251.2	300	120	12	11	72	61	3.58	108	.304	.358	86-1-9	.244	4	97	9		1.4
1923	Was A	13	13	.500	33	30	17-3	1	211	228	90	10	3	56	62	3.11	121	.285	.334	75-0-6	.227	1	105	16		2.0
1924	†Was A	16	11	.593	30	30	13-2	0	213	217	97	7	7	61	48	3.76	107	.270	.327	74-0-4	.176	-2	86	11		1.0
1925	Was A	3	4	.429	10	8	3	0	53	58	27	2	4	18	12	4.08	104	.291	.362	19-0-1	.105	-2	97	2		0.0
	StL A	1	1	.500	2	2	1	0	15.1	17	10	2	1	5	8	5.87	80	.279	.343	4	.000	-0	99	-1		-0.1
	Year	4	5	.444	12	10	4	0	68.1	75	37	4	5	23	20	4.48	97	.288	.358	23-0-1	.087	-2	97	1		-0.1
1926	Bos N	6	10	.375	39	10	2	3	142	173	82	6	3	36	46	4.50	79	.311	.356	46-0-5	.174	-1*	120	-15		-1.6
1927	Bos N	2	4	.600	20	1	0	0	48.2	48	23	4	2	16	26	3.70	100	.257	.319	15	.200	-0	23	0		0.1
Total	15	132	133	.498	398	261	138-20	20	2265.2	2352	1003	77	76	565	678	3.23	109	.273	.323	754-1-43	.182	-8	95	72		7.7

MOHART, GEORGE George Benjamin B3.6.1892 Buffalo NY D10.2.1970 Silver Creek NY BR/TR/5-9/165 d4.15

1920	Bro N	0	1	.000	13	1	0	0	35.2	33	17	0	3	7	13	1.77	181	.250	.303	8	.125	-0	123	2		0.2
1921	Bro N	0	0	—	2	0	0	0	7	8	5	0	1	1	1	3.86	101	.296	.345	2	.500	0		-1		0.0
Total	2	0	1	.000	15	1	0	0	42.2	41	22	0	4	8	14	2.11	157	.258	.310	10	.200	0	123	1		0.2

MOHLER, MIKE Michael Ross B7.26.1968 Dayton OH BR/TL/6-2/209(195-209) [OakA89 42/1101] d4.7 Col Nicholls St.

1993	Oak A	1	6	.143	42	9	0	0-1	64.1	57	45	10	2	44-4	42	5.60	74	.241	.361	0	—	0	79	-12		-1.1
1994	Oak A	0	1	.000	1	1	0	0-0	2.1	2	2	0	0	2-0	4	7.71	58	.167	.286	0	—	0	82	-1		-0.2
1995	Oak A	1	1	.500	28	0	0	1-1	23.2	16	8	0	0	18-1	15	3.04	149	.198	.343	0	—	0		4		0.3
1996	Oak A	6	3	.667	72	0	0	7-6	81	79	36	9	1	41-6	64	3.67	136	.263	.350	0	—	0		11		1.3
1997	Oak A	1	10	.091	62	10	0	1-3	101.2	116	65	11	7	54-8	66	5.13	90	.301	.391	0	—	0*	72	-7		-0.6
1998	Oak A	3	3	.500	57	0	0	0-1	61	70	38	6	4	26-3	42	5.16	90	.289	.365	0	—	0		-3		-0.3
1999	StL N	1	1	.500	48	0	0	1-1	49.1	47	26	5	3	23-2	31	4.38	105	.254	.338	3	.000	-0		1		0.0
2000	StL N	1	1	.500	22	0	0	0-2	19	26	20	2	0	15-1	9	9.00	52	.321	.439	1	1.000	0		-9		-0.8
	Cle A	0	1	.000	2	0	0	0-1	1	1	1	1	0	0-0	2	9.00	56	.250	.250	0	—	0		0		-0.1
2001	Ari N	0	0	—	13	0	0	0-2	13.2	14	11	1	0	9-0	7	7.24	64	.286	.390	0	—	0		-3		-0.2
Total	9	14	27	.341	347	20	0	10-18	417	428	253	45	17	232-25	281	4.99	92	.272	.368	4	.250	0	72	-19		-1.7

YEAR	TM LG	W	L	PCT	G	GS	CG-SHO	SV-BS	IP	H	R	HR	HB	BB-IB	SO	ERA	AERA	OAV	OOB	AB-HR-SH	AVG	PB	SUP	APR	DL	PW

MOHORCIC, DALE Dale Robert B1.25.1956 Cleveland OH BR/TR/6-3/220* d5.31 Col Cleveland St.

1986	Tex A	2	4	.333	58	0	0	7-5	79	86	25	5	1	15-6	29	2.51	173	.279	.315	0	—	0	15			1.3
1987	Tex A	7	6	.538	74	0	0	16-7	99.1	88	34	11	2	19-6	48	2.99	151	.244	.285	0	—	0	18	15		2.8
1988	Tex A	2	6	.250	43	0	0	5-3	52	62	35	6	5	20-5	25	4.85	85	.295	.363	0	—	0	-6	23		-0.9
	NY A	2	2	.500	13	0	0	1-2	22.2	21	7	1	3	9-2	19	2.78	143	.239	.327	0	—	0	3			0.5
	Year	4	8	.333	56	0	0	6-5	74.2	83	42	7	8	29-7	44	4.22	96	.279	.352	0	—	0	-3			-0.4
1989	NY A	2	1	.667	32	0	0	2-3	57.2	65	41	8	6	18-3	24	4.99	78	.286	.352	0	—	0	-10			-0.5
1990	Mon N	1	2	.333	34	0	0	2-2	53	56	21	6	4	18-3	29	3.23	114	.286	.350	8-0-1	.125	-0	3			0.1
Total	5	16	21	.432	254	0	0	33-22	363.2	378	163	37	21	99-25	174	3.49	119	.272	.327	8-0-1	.125	-0	23	38		3.3

MOISAN, BILL William Joseph B7.30.1925 Bradford MA BL/TR/6-1/170 d9.17

| 1953 | Chi N | 0 | 0 | — | 3 | 0 | 0 | 0 | 5 | 5 | 3 | 0 | 1 | 2 | 1 | 5.40 | 82 | .278 | .381 | 0 | — | 0 | 0 | | | 0.0 |

MOLESWORTH, CARLTON Carlton B2.15.1876 Frederick MD D7.25.1961 Frederick MD BL/TL/5-7.5/162 d9.14

| 1895 | Was N | 0 | 2 | .000 | 4 | 3 | 1 | 0 | 16 | 33 | 34 | 1 | 4 | 15 | 7 | 14.63 | 33 | .418 | .531 | 7 | .143 | -1 | 124 | -15 | | -1.3 |

MOLINA, GABE Cruz Gabriel B5.3.1975 Denver CO BR/TR/5-11/202(190-220) [BalA96 21/621] d5.1 Col Arizona St.

1999	Bal A	1	2	.333	20	0	0	0-1	23	22	19	4	0	16-1	14	6.65	71	.256	.373	0	—	0	-6			-0.6
2000	Bal A	0	0	—	9	0	0	0-0	13	25	14	2	0	9-0	8	9.00	52	.397	.459	0	—	0	-7			-0.3
	Atl N	0	0	—	2	0	0	0-0	2	3	4	1	1	1-0	1	9.00	50	.375	.455	0	—	0	-2			-0.1
2002	StL N	1	0	1.000	12	0	0	0-0	11.1	6	2	1	0	6-0	4	1.59	254	.162	.279	0	—	0	3			0.3
2003	StL N	0	0	—	3	0	0	0-0	2.2	5	4	1	0	1-0	1	13.50	31	.385	.429	0	—	0	-3			-0.1
Total	4	2	2	.500	46	0	0	0-1	52	61	43	9	1	33-1	28	6.58	69	.295	.389	0	—	0	-15			-0.8

MOLONEY, RICHIE Richard Henry B6.7.1950 Brookline MA BR/TR/6-3/185 [ChiA68 14/314] d9.20

| 1970 | Chi A | 0 | 0 | — | 1 | 0 | 0 | 0 | 1 | 2 | 0 | 0 | 0 | 0-0 | 1 | 0.00 | — | .400 | .400 | 0 | — | 0 | 0 | | | 0.0 |

MOLYNEAUX, VINCE Vincent Leo B8.17.1888 Lewiston NY D5.4.1950 Stamford CT BR/TR/6-0/180 d7.5 Col Villanova

1917	StL A	0	0	—	7	0	0	0	22	18	15	0	0	20	4	4.91	53	.237	.396	4	.000	-1	-5			-0.3
1918	Bos A	1	0	1.000	6	0	0	0	10.2	3	4	0	0	8	1	3.38	80	.086	.256	2	.000	-0	0			-0.1
Total	2	1	0	1.000	13	0	0	0	32.2	21	19	0	0	28	5	4.41	60	.189	.353	6	.000	-1	-5			-0.4

MONAHAN, RINTY Edward Francis B4.28.1928 Brooklyn NY BR/TR/6-1.5/195 d8.9 Col Niagara

| 1953 | Phi A | 0 | 0 | — | 4 | 0 | 0 | 0 | 10.2 | 11 | 5 | 0 | 0 | 7 | 2 | 4.22 | 102 | .275 | .383 | 2 | .000 | -0 | 0 | 101 | | 0.0 |

MONBOUQUETTE, BILL William Charles B8.11.1936 Medford MA BR/TR/5-11/195* d7.18 C3

1958	Bos A	3	4	.429	10	8	3	0	54.1	52	25	4	0	20-4	30	3.31	121	.251	.313	17-0-2	.176	-1	98	3		0.3
1959	Bos A	7	7	.500	34	17	4	0	151.2	165	86	15	3	33-1	87	4.15	98	.285	.323	46-0-3	.065	-4*	96	-5		-0.9
1960	Bos A★	14	11	.560	35	30	12-3	0	215	217	91	18	2	68-9	134	3.64	111	.263	.319	65-0-8	.092	-3*	91	12		0.9
1961	Bos A	14	14	.500	32	32	12-1	0	236.1	233	106	24	0	100-1	161	3.39	123	.254	.326	69-0-14	.131	-1*	88	18		1.9
1962	Bos A☆	15	13	.536	35	35	11-4	0	235.1	227	100	22	3	65-1	153	3.33	124	.251	.302	73-0-8	.096	-3	91	19		1.6
1963	Bos A☆	20	10	.667	37	36	13-1	0	266.2	258	119	31	0	42-6	174	3.81	99	.250	.279	88-0-10	.114	-3	119	2		-0.2
1964	Bos A	13	14	.481	36	35	7-5	1	234	258	114	34	1	40-4	120	4.04	95	.277	.306	72-0-5	.083	-2*	95	-3		-0.6
1965	Bos A	10	18	.357	35	35	10-2	0	228.2	239	114	32	1	40-5	110	3.70	101	.269	.299	71-0-6	.059	-3*	92	-1		-0.4
1966	Det A	7	8	.467	30	14	2-1	0	102.2	120	60	14	3	22-4	61	4.73	74	.293	.330	26-0-4	.154	-0	107	-14		-1.9
1967	Det A	0	0	—	2	0	0	0	2	1	0	0	0	0-0	2	0.00	—	.143	.143	0	—	0	1			0.0
	NY A	6	5	.545	33	10	2-1	1	133.1	122	39	6	4	17-7	53	2.36	132	.246	.274	32-0-3	.156	-0	86	12		1.0
	Year	6	5	.545	35	10	2-1	1	135.1	123	39	6	4	17-7	55	2.33	134	.245	.273	32-0-3	.156	-0	86	13		1.0
1968	NY A	5	7	.417	17	11	2	0	89.1	92	47	7	3	13-2	32	4.43	66	.264	.293	26-0-2	.115	-0	98	-14		-1.7
	SF N	0	1	.000	7	0	0	0	12	11	9	4	0	2-0	5	3.75	78	.239	.265	0	—	0	-2			-0.3
Total	11	114	112	.504	343	263	78-18	3	1961.1	1995	910	211	20	462-44	1122	3.68	104	.263	.305	582-0-69	.103	-20	97	28		-0.3

MONGE, SID Isidro Pedroza B4.11.1951 Agua Prieta, Sonora, Mexico BB/TL/6-2/195(165-202) [AnaA70 24/569] d9.12

1975	Cal A	0	2	.000	4	2	0	0-0	23.2	22	12	3	1	10-0	17	4.18	86	.242	.324	0	—	0	62	-1		-0.1
1976	Cal A	6	7	.462	32	13	2	0-0	117.2	108	50	10	1	49-0	53	3.37	100	.244	.324	0	—	0	89	0		0.0
1977	Cal A	0	1	.000	4	0	0	1-0	12.1	14	6	2	0	6-0	4	2.92	135	.304	.377	0	—	0	1			0.1
	Cle A	1	2	.333	33	0	0	3-1	39	47	31	6	0	27-4	25	6.23	64	.309	.407	0	—	0	-10			-0.9
	Year	1	3	.250	37	0	0	4-1	51.1	61	37	8	0	33-4	29	5.44	73	.308	.400	0	—	0	-9			-0.8
1978	Cle A	4	3	.571	48	2	0	6-4	84.2	71	36	4	0	51-6	54	2.76	137	.225	.330	0	—	0	107	6		0.6
1979	Cle A☆	12	10	.545	76	0	0	19-7	131	96	37	9	1	64-8	108	2.40	179	.209	.300	0	—	0	28			5.2
1980	Cle A	3	5	.375	67	0	0	14-7	94.1	80	39	12	3	40-6	61	3.53	117	.227	.310	0	—	0	7			0.7
1981	Cle A	3	5	.375	31	0	0	4-2	58	58	31	9	0	21-2	41	4.34	85	.266	.326	0	—	0	-4			-0.7
1982	Phi N	7	1	.875	47	0	0	2-3	72	70	35	8	2	22-3	43	3.75	99	.256	.312	9-0-2	.111	-0	-1			-0.1
1983	Phi N	3	0	1.000	14	0	0	0-0	11.2	20	10	4	0	6-1	7	6.94	52	.377	.433	1	.000	-0	-4			-0.9
	SD N	7	3	.700	47	0	0	7-1	68.2	65	24	4	1	31-6	32	3.15	112	.257	.338	10-0-1	.100	-0	4			0.6
	Year	10	3	.769	61	0	0	7-1	80.1	85	34	8	1	37-7	39	3.70	95	.284	.354	11-0-1	.091	-1	-1			-0.3
1984	SD N	2	1	.667	13	0	0	0-1	15	17	10	3	0	17-3	7	4.80	75	.293	.447	1	.000	-0	-2			-0.5
	Det A	1	0	1.000	19	0	0	0-0	36	40	21	5	2	12-0	19	4.25	79	.282	.340	0	—	0	-2			-0.1
Total	10	49	40	.551	435	17	4	56-26	764	708	342	79	11	356-39	471	3.53	108	.248	.331	21-0-3	.095	-1	80	22		3.9

MONROE, ED Edward Oliver "Peck" B2.22.1895 Louisville KY D4.29.1969 Louisville KY BR/TR/6-5/187 d5.29 Mil 1918

1917	NY A	1	0	1.000	9	1	1	1	28.2	35	15	1	2	6	12	3.45	78	.310	.355	12	.167	-0	134	-3		-0.2
1918	NY A	0	0	—	1	0	0	0	2	1	2	0	2	2	1	4.50	63	.143	.333	0	—	0	-1			0.0
Total	2	1	0	1.000	10	1	1	1	30.2	36	17	1	2	8	13	3.52	77	.300	.354	12	.167	-0	134	-4		-0.2

MONROE, LARRY Lawrence James B6.20.1956 Detroit MI BR/TR/6-4/200 [ChiA74 1/8] d8.23

| 1976 | Chi A | 0 | 1 | .000 | 8 | 2 | 0 | 0-0 | 21.2 | 23 | 11 | 0 | 4 | 13-0 | 9 | 4.15 | 86 | .284 | .379 | 0 | — | 0 | 49 | -1 | | -0.1 |

MONROE, ZACH Zachary Charles B7.8.1931 Peoria IL BR/TR/6-0/198* d6.27 Col Bradley

1958	†NY A	4	2	.667	21	6	1	1	58	57	29	8	0	27-1	18	3.26	108	.263	.344	17	.118	-1	199	-9		-0.1
1959	NY A	0	0	—	3	0	0	0	3.1	3	2	2	0	2-0	1	5.40	67	.231	.333	0	—	0	-1			0.0
Total	2	4	2	.667	24	6	1	1	61.1	60	31	10	0	29-1	19	3.38	105	.261	.344	17	.118	-1	199	-1		-0.1

MONTAGUE, JOHN John Evans B9.12.1947 Newport News VA BR/TR/6-2/205(195-213) [BalA67*S3/50] d9.9 Col Old Dominion

1973	Mon N	0	0	—	4	0	0	0-0	7.2	8	3	0	1	2-2	7	3.52	108	.286	.344	1	.000	-0	0			0.0
1974	Mon N	3	4	.429	46	1	0	3-2	82.2	73	37	5	4	38-5	43	3.16	122	.241	.329	10	.100	-0	23	4		0.3
1975	Mon N	0	1	.000	12	0	0	2-0	17.2	23	11	4	2	6-1	9	5.60	69	.324	.383	1	.000	-0*	-3			-0.2
	Phi N	0	0	—	3	0	0	0-0	5	8	5	1	0	4-1	1	9.00	42	.400	.500	0	—	0	-3			-0.1
	Year	0	1	.000	15	0	0	2-0	22.2	31	16	5	2	10-2	10	6.35	61	.341	.410	1	.000	-0	-5			-0.3
1977	Sea A	8	12	.400	47	15	2	4-1	182.1	193	95	20	4	75-5	98	4.29	97	.272	.343	0	—	0	80	-2		-0.2
1978	Sea A	1	3	.250	19	0	0	2-1	43.2	52	31	2	0	24-4	14	6.18	62	.308	.386	0	—	0	-10	104		-1.0
1979	Sea A	6	4	.600	41	0	0	1-3	116.1	125	73	14	2	47-13	60	5.57	79	.284	.349	0	—	0	21	-12		-0.9
	†Cal A	2	0	1.000	14	0	0	6-2	17.2	16	12	3	0	9-0	6	5.09	80	.242	.333	0	—	0	-2			-0.5
	Year	8	4	.667	55	0	0	7-5	134	141	85	17	2	56-13	66	5.51	79	.279	.347	0	—	0	21	-14		-1.4
1980	Cal A	4	2	.667	37	0	0	3-1	73.2	97	47	8	1	21-1	22	5.13	77	.324	.365	0	—	0	-10			-0.8
Total	7	24	26	.480	223	17	2	21-10	546.2	595	314	57	14	226-32	260	4.76	86	.283	.351	12	.083	-0	74	-38	104	-3.4

MONTALVO, RAFAEL Rafael Edgardo (Torres) B3.31.1964 Rio Piedras, PR BR/TR/6-0/185 d4.13

| 1986 | Hou N | 0 | 0 | — | 1 | 0 | 0 | 0-0 | 1 | 1 | 1 | 0 | 0 | 2-0 | 0 | 9.00 | 40 | .250 | .500 | 0 | — | 0 | -1 | | | 0.0 |

MONTEAGUDO, AURELIO Aurelio Faustino (Cintra) B11.19.1943 Caibarien, Cuba D11.10.1990 Ramos Arizpe, Coahuila, Mexico BR/TR/5-11/185(170-185) d9.1 f-Rene

1963	KC A	0	0	—	4	0	0	0	3-0	3	2.57	152	.182	.269	0	—	0	1			0.1
1964	KC A	0	4	.000	11	6	0	0	31.1	40	32	11	1	10-0	14	8.90	43	.317	.370	7	.286	1	70	-16		-1.7
1965	KC A	0	0	—	4	0	0	0	7	5	4	1	0	4-1	5	3.86	90	.185	.290	0	—	0*	-1			0.0
1966	KC A	0	0	—	6	0	0	0	12.2	12	4	0	0	7-0	3	2.84	120	.261	.352	0	—	0	1			0.1
	Hou N	0	0	—	10	0	0	0	15.1	14	8	1	0	11-1	7	4.70	73	.241	.362	1	.000	-0	-2			-0.1
1967	Chi A	1	0	1.000	1	1	0	0	1.1	4	3	1	0	2-0	0	20.25	15	.500	.600	0	—	0	0	-2		-0.4
1970	KC A	1	1	.500	21	0	0	0-0	27.1	20	11	2	1	9-0	18	2.96	126	.200	.273	2	.000	-0	2			0.1

YEAR	TM LG	W	L	PCT	G	GS	CG-SHO	SV-BS	IP	H	R	HR	HB	BB-IB	SO	ERA	AERA	OAV	OOB	AB-HR-SH	AVG	PB	SUP	APR	DL	PW
1973	Cal A	2	1	.667	15	0	0	3-2	30	23	18	2	4	16-3	8	4.20	85	.215	.336	0	—	0		-3		-0.4
Total	7	3	7	.300	72	0	0	4-2	132	122	82	18	6	62-5	58	5.05	72	.247	.336	10	.200	1	63	-20		-2.3

MONTEAGUDO, RENE Rene (Miranda) B3.12.1916 Havana, Cuba D9.14.1973 Hialeah FL BL/TL/5-7/165 d9.6 s-Aurelio ▲

YEAR	TM LG	W	L	PCT	G	GS	CG-SHO	SV-BS	IP	H	R	HR	HB	BB-IB	SO	ERA	AERA	OAV	OOB	AB-HR-SH	AVG	PB	SUP	APR	DL	PW
1938	Was A	1	1	.500	5	3	2	0	22	26	15	3	0	15	13	5.73	79	.286	.387	6-0-1	.500	1	143	-3		-0.1
1940	Was A	2	6	.250	27	8	3	2	100.2	128	70	7	3	52	64	6.08	69	.316	.398	33	.182	0	97	-18		-1.3
1945	Phi N	0	0	—	14	0	0	0	45.2	67	42	1	2	28	16	7.49	51	.347	.435	193-0-4	.301	2*		-16		-0.6
Total	3	3	7	.300	46	11	5	2	168.1	221	127	11	5	95	93	6.42	64	.321	.407	232-0-5	.289	4	113	-37		-2.0

MONTEFUSCO, JOHN John Joseph "Count" B5.25.1950 Long Branch NJ BR/TR/6-1/180(180-192) d9.3 Col Brookdale (NJ) CC

YEAR	TM LG	W	L	PCT	G	GS	CG-SHO	SV-BS	IP	H	R	HR	HB	BB-IB	SO	ERA	AERA	OAV	OOB	AB-HR-SH	AVG	PB	SUP	APR	DL	PW
1974	SF N	3	2	.600	7	5	1	0-1	39.1	41	22	3	0	19-0	34	4.81	79	.256	.335	14-2-0	.286	3	101	-3		-0.1
1975	SF N	15	9	.625	35	34	10-4	0-0	243.2	210	85	11	8	86-12	215	2.88	132	.233	.303	80-1-9	.087	-2	93	25		2.1
1976	SF N★	16	14	.533	37	36	11-6	0-0	253.1	224	90	11	4	74-8	172	2.84	128	.238	.294	78-0-6	.103	-2*	81	24		2.4
1977	SF N	7	12	.368	26	25	4	0-0	157.1	170	82	10	3	46-6	110	3.49	113	.273	.321	49-1-4	.122	-1	81	3	40	0.2
1978	SF N	11	9	.550	36	36	3	0-0	238.2	233	110	25	4	68-6	177	3.81	91	.255	.308	70-0-9	.057	-3*	108	-8		-1.1
1979	SF N	3	8	.273	22	22	0	0-0	137	145	64	15	2	51-7	76	3.94	89	.279	.343	42-0-2	.167	2*	83	-6	48	-1.3
1980	SF N	4	8	.333	22	17	1	0-0	113.1	120	61	15	2	39-6	85	4.37	80	.265	.325	30-0-3	.033	-2	94	-10	38	-1.3
1981	Atl N	2	3	.400	26	9	0	1-0	77.1	75	32	9	0	27-2	34	3.49	101	.260	.321	15	.067	-1	109	1		0.0
1982	SD N	10	11	.476	32	32	1	0-0	184.1	177	93	17	3	41-2	83	4.00	86	.251	.290	58-0-6	.086	-2	101	-12		-1.5
1983	SD N	9	4	.692	31	10	1	4-1	95.1	94	38	6	1	32-6	52	3.30	106	.265	.326	19-0-4	.053	-1	113	3		0.2
	NY A	5	0	1.000	6	6	0	0-0	38	39	14	3	1	10-0	15	3.32	119	.271	.318	0	—	0	107	3		0.4
1984	NY A	5	3	.625	11	11	0	0-0	55.1	55	26	5	1	13-2	23	3.58	107	.253	.295	0	—	0	103	1	109	0.1
1985	NY A	0	0	—	3	1	0	0-0	7	12	8	3	0	2-0	2	10.29	39	.387	.412	0	—	0	225	-5	166	-0.2
1986	NY A	0	0	—	4	0	0	0-1	12.1	9	3	2	0	5-0	3	2.19	189	.200	.280	0	—	0		3	157	0.2
Total	13	90	83	.520	298	244	32-11	5-3	1652.1	1604	728	135	29	513-57	1081	3.54	103	.255	.311	455-4-43	.097	-10	95	19	558	1.1

MONTEJO, MANNY Manuel (Bofill) B10.16.1935 Caibarien, Cuba BR/TR/5-11/150 d7.25

YEAR	TM LG	W	L	PCT	G	GS	CG-SHO	SV-BS	IP	H	R	HR	HB	BB-IB	SO	ERA	AERA	OAV	OOB	AB-HR-SH	AVG	PB	SUP	APR	DL	PW
1961	Det A	1	1	.500	12	0	0	0	16.1	13	7	2	2	6-1	15	3.86	106	.217	.309		—	0		1		0.0

MONTELEONE, RICH Richard B3.22.1963 Tampa FL BR/TR/6-2/234(205-236) [DetA82 1/20] d4.15 C4

YEAR	TM LG	W	L	PCT	G	GS	CG-SHO	SV-BS	IP	H	R	HR	HB	BB-IB	SO	ERA	AERA	OAV	OOB	AB-HR-SH	AVG	PB	SUP	APR	DL	PW
1987	Sea A	0	0	—	3	0	0	0-0	7	10	5	2	1	4-0	2	6.43	74	.345	.441	0	—	0		-1		0.0
1988	Cal A	0	0	—	3	0	0	0-0	4.1	4	0	0	1	1-1	3	0.00	—	.222	.300	0	—	0		2		0.1
1989	Cal A	2	2	.500	24	0	0	0-2	39.2	39	15	3	0	13-1	27	3.18	121	.255	.314	0	—	0		3		0.3
1990	NY A	0	1	.000	5	0	0	0-0	7.1	8	5	0	0	2-0	6	6.14	65	.276	.323	0	—	0		-1		-0.2
1991	NY A	3	1	.750	26	0	0	0-0	47	42	27	5	0	19-3	34	3.64	115	.236	.307	0	—	0		0		0.0
1992	NY A	7	3	.700	47	0	0	0-2	92.2	82	35	7	0	27-3	62	3.30	120	.235	.289	0	—	0		8		0.7
1993	NY A	7	4	.636	42	0	0	0-1	85.2	85	52	14	0	35-10	50	4.94	85	.262	.329	0	—	0		-8		-0.9
1994	SF N	4	3	.571	39	0	0	0-1	45.1	43	18	6	0	13-2	16	3.18	128	.253	.299	3	.000	0		4	32	0.5
1995	Cal A	1	0	1.000	9	0	0	0-1	9	8	2	1	0	3-0	5	2.00	236	.267	.314	0	—	0		3		0.3
1996	Cal A	0	3	.000	12	0	0	0-0	15.1	23	11	5	1	2-0	7	5.87	86	.348	.377	0	—	0		-1	52	-0.2
Total	10	24	17	.585	210	0	0	0-7	353.1	344	170	43	4	119-20	212	3.87	106	.255	.314	3	.000	0		9	84	0.6

MONTGOMERY, JEFF Jeffrey Thomas B1.7.1962 Wellston OH BR/TR/5-11/180* [CinN83 9/212] d8.1 Col Marshall

YEAR	TM LG	W	L	PCT	G	GS	CG-SHO	SV-BS	IP	H	R	HR	HB	BB-IB	SO	ERA	AERA	OAV	OOB	AB-HR-SH	AVG	PB	SUP	APR	DL	PW
1987	Cin N	2	2	.500	14	1	0	0-0	19.1	25	15	2	0	9-1	13	6.52	65	.313	.382	2	.000	-0	43	-5		-0.8
1988	KC A	7	2	.778	45	0	0	1-2	62.2	54	25	6	2	30-1	47	3.45	116	.231	.321	0	—	0		5		0.6
1989	KC A	7	3	.700	63	0	0	18-6	92	66	16	3	2	25-4	94	1.37	283	.198	.257	0	—	0		26		3.5
1990	KC A	6	5	.545	73	0	0	24-10	94.1	81	36	6	5	34-8	94	2.39	162	.227	.302	0	—	0		12		1.9
1991	KC A	4	4	.500	67	0	0	33-6	90	83	32	6	2	28-2	77	2.90	143	.246	.305	0	—	0		13		1.8
1992	KC A★	1	6	.143	65	0	0	39-7	82.2	61	23	5	2	27-2	69	2.18	188	.205	.277	0	—	0		16		2.7
1993	KC A★	7	5	.583	69	0	0	45-6	87.1	65	22	3	4	23-4	66	2.27	204	.206	.263	0	—	0		22		4.5
1994	KC A	2	3	.400	42	0	0	27-5	44.2	48	21	5	1	15-1	50	4.03	125	.276	.335	0	—	0		5		0.9
1995	KC A	2	3	.400	54	0	0	31-7	65.2	60	27	7	2	25-4	49	3.43	140	.252	.322	0	—	0		10		1.4
1996	KC A☆	4	6	.400	48	0	0	24-10	63.1	59	31	14	3	19-3	45	4.26	118	.251	.314	0	—	0		6	15	1.0
1997	KC A	1	4	.200	55	0	0	14-3	59.1	53	24	9	0	18-5	48	3.49	136	.240	.295	-0	—	0		8		-0.2
1998	KC A	2	5	.286	56	0	0	36-5	56	58	35	8	2	22-2	54	4.98	98	.264	.335	0	—	0		-1		-1.0
1999	KC A	1	4	.200	49	0	0	12-7	51.1	72	40	7	2	21-3	27	6.84	74	.343	.404	0	—	0		-31		-1.0
Total	13	46	52	.469	700	1	0	304-74	868.2	785	347	81	26	296-40	733	3.27	135	.241	.308	2	.000	-0	43	109	46	17.4

MONTGOMERY, MONTY Monty Bryson B9.1.1946 Albemarle NC BR/TR/6-3/200* [KCA68 9/204] d9.14 Col Pfeiffer

YEAR	TM LG	W	L	PCT	G	GS	CG-SHO	SV-BS	IP	H	R	HR	HB	BB-IB	SO	ERA	AERA	OAV	OOB	AB-HR-SH	AVG	PB	SUP	APR	DL	PW
1971	KC A	3	0	1.000	3	2	0	0-0	21.1	16	5	0	0	3-0	12	2.11	163	.205	.235	7-0-1	.000	-0	130	3		0.5
1972	KC A	3	3	.500	9	8	1-1	0-0	56.1	55	21	2	0	17-2	24	3.04	100	.263	.316	17-0-3	.176	0	106	0		0.0
Total	2	6	3	.667	12	10	1-1	0-0	77.2	71	26	2	0	20-2	36	2.78	113	.247	.294	24-0-4	.125	0	110	3		0.5

MONTGOMERY, STEVE Steven Lewis B12.25.1970 Westminster CA BR/TR/6-4/210(200-212) [StLN92 3/83] d4.3 Col Pepperdine

YEAR	TM LG	W	L	PCT	G	GS	CG-SHO	SV-BS	IP	H	R	HR	HB	BB-IB	SO	ERA	AERA	OAV	OOB	AB-HR-SH	AVG	PB	SUP	APR	DL	PW
1996	Oak A	1	0	1.000	8	0	0	0-0	13.2	18	14	5	0	13-2	8	9.22	54	.310	.437	0	—	0		-6		-0.4
1997	Oak A	0	1	.000	4	0	0	0-0	6.1	10	7	2	0	8-2	1	9.95	46	.385	.514	0	—	0		-4		-0.5
1999	Phi N	1	5	.167	53	0	0	3-0	64.2	54	25	10	0	31-3	55	3.34	140	.229	.318	1	1.000	0		10	16	0.9
2000	SD N	0	2	.000	7	0	0	0-0	5.2	6	6	3	0	4-0	3	7.94	56	.273	.385	0	—	0		-2	159	-0.5
Total	4	2	8	.200	72	0	0	3-0	90.1	88	52	20	0	56-7	67	4.98	94	.257	.361	1	1.000	0		-2	175	-0.5

MONZANT, RAMON Ramon Segundo (Espina) B1.4.1933 Maracaibo, Venez D8.10.2001 Maracaibo, Venez BR/TR/6-0/165* d7.2

YEAR	TM LG	W	L	PCT	G	GS	CG-SHO	SV-BS	IP	H	R	HR	HB	BB-IB	SO	ERA	AERA	OAV	OOB	AB-HR-SH	AVG	PB	SUP	APR	DL	PW
1954	NY N	0	0	—	6	1	0	0	7.2	8	5	0	0	11	5	4.70	86	.276	.463	2	.000	-0	199	-1		-0.1
1955	NY N	4	8	.333	28	12	3	0	94.2	98	47	11	3	43-5	54	3.99	101	.278	.357	24-0-2	.125	-1*	76	1		0.0
1956	NY N	1	0	1.000	4	1	1	0	13	8	7	4	0	7-0	11	4.15	91	.170	.278	4	.000	-1*	186	-1		-0.1
1957	NY N	3	5	.600	24	2	0	0	49.2	55	27	6	2	16-1	37	3.99	99	.286	.340	10	.300	1	11	-1		-0.1
1958	SF N	8	11	.421	43	16	4-1	1	150.2	160	89	20	6	57-5	93	4.72	81	.273	.339	49-0-1	.163	-1*	119	-15		-1.8
1960	SF N	0	0	—	1	0	0	0	1	1	1	1	0	0-0	1	9.00	39	.250	.250	0	—	0		-1		0.0
Total	6	16	21	.432	106	32	8-1	1	316.2	330	176	42	11	134-11	201	4.38	89	.273	.346	89-0-3	.157	-2	100	-18		-2.1

MOODY, ERIC Eric Lane B1.6.1971 Greenville SC BR/TR/6-6/185 [TexA93 24/675] d8.3 Col Erskine [DL 1998 Tex A 10]

YEAR	TM LG	W	L	PCT	G	GS	CG-SHO	SV-BS	IP	H	R	HR	HB	BB-IB	SO	ERA	AERA	OAV	OOB	AB-HR-SH	AVG	PB	SUP	APR	DL	PW
1997	Tex A	0	1	.000	10	1	0	0-1	19	26	10	4	0	2-0	12	4.26	114	.329	.341	0	—	0	38	1		0.0

MOON, LEO Leo "Lefty" B6.22.1899 Bellemont NC D8.25.1970 New Orleans LA BR/TL/5-11/165 d7.9

YEAR	TM LG	W	L	PCT	G	GS	CG-SHO	SV-BS	IP	H	R	HR	HB	BB-IB	SO	ERA	AERA	OAV	OOB	AB-HR-SH	AVG	PB	SUP	APR	DL	PW
1932	Cle A	0	0	—	1	0	0	0	5.2	11	8	3	1	9	1	11.12	43	.379	.500	2	.500	0		-4		-0.1

MOONEY, JIM Jim Irving B9.4.1906 Mooresburg TN D4.27.1979 Johnson City TN BR/TL/5-11/168 d8.14 Col East Tennessee

YEAR	TM LG	W	L	PCT	G	GS	CG-SHO	SV-BS	IP	H	R	HR	HB	BB-IB	SO	ERA	AERA	OAV	OOB	AB-HR-SH	AVG	PB	SUP	APR	DL	PW
1931	NY N	7	1	.875	10	8	6-2	0	71.2	71	19	1	1	38	38	2.01	184	.262	.306	25-0-1	.160	-1	119	14		1.4
1932	NY N	6	10	.375	29	18	4-1	0	124.2	154	79	9	4	42	37	5.05	73	.299	.352	41	.122	-2	103	-17		-2.1
1933	StL N	2	5	.286	21	8	2	1	77.1	87	36	1	0	26	14	3.72	93	.296	.353	20-0-2	.050	-2	87	-1		-0.3
1934	†StL N	2	4	.333	32	7	1	1	82.1	114	59	3	4	49	27	5.47	77	.326	.414	19-0-1	.053	-2	99	-11		-1.0
Total	4	17	20	.459	92	41	13-3	2	356	426	193	23	5	133	116	4.25	89	.298	.360	105-0-4	.105	-7	102	-15		-2.0

MOONEYHAM, BILL William Craig B8.16.1960 Livermore CA [AnaA80 S1/10] d4.19 Col Merced (CA) JC

YEAR	TM LG	W	L	PCT	G	GS	CG-SHO	SV-BS	IP	H	R	HR	HB	BB-IB	SO	ERA	AERA	OAV	OOB	AB-HR-SH	AVG	PB	SUP	APR	DL	PW
1986	Oak A	4	5	.444	45	6	0	1-3	90.2	103	53	4	3	67-4	75	4.52	86	.270	.382	0	—	0	124	-6		-0.5

MOORE, BALOR Balor Lilbon B1.25.1951 Smithville TX BL/TL/6-2/184* [MonN69 1/22] d5.21

YEAR	TM LG	W	L	PCT	G	GS	CG-SHO	SV-BS	IP	H	R	HR	HB	BB-IB	SO	ERA	AERA	OAV	OOB	AB-HR-SH	AVG	PB	SUP	APR	DL	PW
1970	Mon N	0	2	.000	6	2	0	0-0	9.2	14	9	0	0	8-0	6	7.45	56	.368	.458	3	.333	0	43	-3		-0.6
1972	Mon N	9	9	.500	22	22	6-3	0-0	147.2	122	61	15	5	59-5	161	3.47	102	.226	.305	55-0-1	.145	-0	112	2		0.2
1973	Mon N	7	16	.304	35	32	3-1	0-0	176.1	151	98	18	3	109-2	151	4.49	85	.233	.343	53-0-2	.057	-2	79	-11		-1.6
1974	Mon N	0	2	.000	8	2	0	0-0	13.2	13	7	1	0	15-0	16	3.95	97	.245	.412	2	.000	-0	45	-1		-0.1
1977	Cal A	0	2	.000	7	3	0	0-0	22.2	28	19	7	3	10-1	14	3.97	99	.298	.376	0	—	0	137	-3		-0.3
1978	Tor A	6	9	.400	37	18	2	0-3	144.1	165	85	16	7	54-1	75	4.93	80	.294	.360	0	—	0	83	-15		-1.3
1979	Tor A	5	7	.417	34	16	5	0-1	139.1	135	85	17	8	79-4	51	4.84	91	.262	.366	0	—	0	97	-7		-0.5
1980	Tor A	1	1	.500	31	3	0	1-0	64.2	76	43	6	4	31-3	22	5.29	82	.309	.391	-0	—	0	104	-7		-0.6
Total	8	28	48	.368	180	98	16-4	1-4	718.1	704	408	80	30	365-16	496	4.52	87	.261	.352	113-0-3	.106	-3	90	-45		-4.6

YEAR	TM LG	W	L	PCT	G	GS	CG-SHO	SV-BS	IP	H	R	HR	HB	BB-IB	SO	ERA	AERA	OAV	OOB	AB-HR-SH	AVG	PB	SUP	APR	DL	PW
MOORE, BRAD	Bradley Alan B6.21.1964 Loveland CO BR/TR/6-1/185* d6.14 Col Grand Canyon																									
988	Phi N	0	0	—	5	0	0	0-0	5.2	4	0	0	0	4-1	2	0.00	—	.267	.421	0	—	0		2		0.1
990	Phi N	0	0	—	3	0	0	0-0	2.2	4	1	0	0	2-1	1	3.38	114	.400	.462	0	—	0		0		0.0
otal	2	0	0	—	8	0	0	0-0	8.1	8	1	0	0	6-2	3	1.08	342	.320	.438	0	—	0		2		0.1
MOORE, CARLOS	Carlos Whitman B8.13.1906 Clinton TN D7.2.1958 New Orleans LA BR/TR/6-1.5/180 d5.4																									
930	Was A	1	0	0	0	0	0		11.2	9	3	0	0		2	2.31	199	.225	.295	4	.000	-1		3		0.1
MOORE, DONNIE	Donnie Ray B2.13.1954 Lubbock TX D7.18.1989 Anaheim CA BL/TR/6-0/185(170-192) [ChiN73*S1/3] d9.14 Col Ranger (TX) JC																									
975	Chi N	0	0	—	4	1	0	0-0	8.2	12	4	1	0	4-0	8	4.15	93	.316	.381	3	.000	-0	113	0		0.0
977	Chi N	4	2	.667	27	1	0	0-1	48.2	51	27	1	0	18-7	34	4.07	108	.285	.345	10	.300	1	182	1		0.2
978	Chi N	9	7	.563	71	1	0	4-5	102.2	117	55	7	2	31-11	50	4.12	98	.287	.337	15-0-1	.267	1	178	-2		-0.2
979	Chi N	1	4	.200	39	1	0	1-0	73	95	46	8	2	25-7	43	5.18	80	.321	.375	13	.154	1	64	-7		-0.4
980	StL N	1	1	.500	11	0	0	0-0	21.2	25	15	1	1	5-1	10	6.23	60	.298	.341	4-0-2	.750	2		-5		-0.3
981	Mil A	0	0	—	3	0	0	0-0	4	4	3	0	0	4-0	2	6.75	57	.286	.421	0	—	0		-1		-0.1
982	†Atl N	3	1	.750	16	0	0	1-2	27.2	32	13	1	2	7-3	17	4.23	87	.294	.345	1	.000	-0		-1		-0.1
983	Atl N	2	3	.400	43	0	0	6-1	68.2	72	30	6	0	10-3	41	3.67	105	.279	.300	8-0-1	.500	1		2	21	0.2
984	Atl N	4	5	.444	47	0	0	16-3	64.1	63	27	3	1	18-6	47	2.94	131	.258	.309	3	.000	-0		5	35	0.9
985	Cal A★	8	8	.500	65	0	0	31-8	103	91	28	9	0	21-3	72	1.92	215	.237	.275	0	—	0		24		4.8
986	†Cal A	4	5	.444	49	0	0	21-8	72.2	60	28	10	0	22-4	53	2.97	139	.228	.285	0	—	0		9	36	1.4
987	Cal A	2	2	.500	14	0	0	5-2	26.2	28	12	2	0	13-2	17	2.70	160	.259	.339	0	—	0		4	101	0.6
988	Cal A	5	2	.714	27	0	0	4-3	33	48	20	4	0	8-2	22	4.91	79	.343	.373	0	—	0		-4	59	-0.8
otal	13	43	40	.518	416	4	0	89-33	654.2	698	308	53	8	186-49	416	3.67	110	.276	.325	57-0-4	.281	4	138	25	252	6.2
MOORE, EARL	Earl Alonzo "Big Ebbie","Crossfire" B7.29.1879 Pickerington OH D11.28.1961 Columbus OH BR/TR/6-0/195 d4.25																									
901	Cle A	16	14	.533	31	30	28-4	0	251.1	234	129	4	8	107	99	2.90	122	.244	.325	99-0-3	.162	-5	109	17		1.0
902	Cle A	17	18	.486	36	34	29-4	1	293	304	158	8	7	101	84	2.95	117	.268	.331	113-0-3	.212	-0	93	12		1.2
903	Cle A	20	8	.714	29	27	27-3	0	247.2	196	88	0	5	62	148	1.74	164	.217	.271	87-0-5	.092	-5	127	27		2.2
904	Cle A	12	11	.522	26	24	22-1	0	227.2	186	83	2	10	61	139	2.25	113	.224	.285	86-0-2	.140	-2	130	7		0.1
905	Cle A	15	15	.500	31	30	28-3	0	269	232	111	6	18	92	131	2.64	99	.234	.311	96-0-1	.104	-4	118	-2		-0.8
906	Cle A	1	1	.500	5	4	2	0	29.2	27	15	1	2	18	8	3.94	66	.245	.362	10	.000	-1	117	-3		-0.4
907	Cle A	1	1	.500	3	2	1	0	19.1	18	14	0	1	8	7	4.66	54	.250	.333	7	.000	-1	108	-4		-0.5
	NY A	2	6	.250	12	9	3	1	64	72	49	1	4	30	28	3.94	71	.286	.371	22	.273	1	97	-10		-1.1
	Year	3	7	.300	15	11	4	1	83.1	90	63	1	5	38	35	4.10	66	.278	.362	29	.207	-0	99	-14		-1.6
908	Phi N	2	1	.667	3	3	3-1	0	26	20	4	0	2	8	16	0.00	—	.217	.294	9-0-1	.222	0	97	5		0.8
909	Phi N	18	12	.600	38	34	24-4	0	299.2	238	93	7	9	108	173	2.10	124	.210	.283	96-0-5	.094	-4	82	17		1.0
910	Phi N	22	15	.595	46	35	18-6	0	283	228	98	5	10	121	185	2.58	121	.228	.318	87-0-8	.230	2	103	20		2.6
911	Phi N	15	19	.441	42	36	21-5	1	308.1	265	123	4	17	164	174	2.63	131	.240	.345	101-0-3	.109	-6	84	26		1.9
912	Phi N	9	14	.391	31	24	10-1	0	182.1	186	101	3	7	77	79	3.31	110	.275	.355	56-0-3	.107	-4	70	4		-0.1
913	Phi N	1	3	.250	12	5	0	1	52	50	37	2	1	40	24	5.02	66	.254	.382	16-0-1	.000	-2	113	-10		-0.9
	Chi N	1	1	.500	7	2	0	0	28.1	34	19	3	0	12	12	4.45	71	.321	.390	8	.125	-0	71	-4		-0.3
	Year	2	4	.333	19	7	0	1	80.1	84	56	6	1	52	36	4.82	68	.277	.385	24-0-1	.042	-2	102	-12		-1.2
914	Buf F	11	15	.423	36	27	14-2	2	194.2	184	109	3	10	99	96	4.30	69	.263	.362	56-0-3	.161	-2	91	-26		-3.5
otal	14	163	154	.514	388	326	230-34	6	2776	2474	1231	57	106	1108	1403	2.78	110	.241	.321	949-0-38	.141	-34	100	76		3.2
MOORE, EUEL	Euel Walton "Chief" B5.27.1908 Reagan OK D2.12.1989 Tishomingo OK BR/TR/6-2/185 d7.8																									
934	Phi N	5	7	.417	20	16	3	1	122.1	145	60	9	0	41	38	4.05	117	.288	.342	46	.109	-4	63	9		0.4
935	Phi N	1	6	.143	15	8	1	0	40.1	63	40	5	2	20	15	7.81	58	.354	.425	15-0-1	.400	1	89	-12		-1.7
	NY N	1	0	1.000	6	0	0	0	8	9	5	0	0	4	3	5.63	69	.281	.361	2	.000	-0		-1		-0.2
	Year	2	6	.250	21	8	1	0	48.1	72	45	5	2	24	18	7.45	59	.343	.415	17-0-1	.353	1	91	-14		-1.9
936	Phi N	2	3	.400	20	5	1	1	54.1	76	50	4	1	12	19	6.96	65	.311	.346	18	.222	-0	101	-12		-1.1
otal	3	9	16	.360	61	29	5	3	225	293	155	18	3	77	75	5.48	84	.306	.360	81-0-1	.185	-3	77	-16		-2.6
MOORE, GENE	Eugene Sr. "Blue Goose" B11.9.1885 Lancaster TX D8.31.1938 Dallas TX BL/TL/6-2/185 d9.28 s-Gene																									
909	Pit N	0	0	—	1	0	0	1	2	4	4	0	0	3	2	18.00	15	.364	.500	1	.000	-0		-3		-0.2
910	Pit N	2	1	.667	4	1	0	0	17.1	19	7	1	0	7	9	3.12	99	.268	.333	6	.000	-1	72	0		0.0
912	Cin N	0	1	.000	5	2	0	1	14.2	17	11	0	2	11	6	4.91	68	.304	.435	4	.000	-1	44	-3		-0.3
otal	3	2	2	.500	10	3	0	1	34	40	22	1	2	21	17	4.76	67	.290	.391	11	.000	-2	54	-6		-0.5
MOORE, FRANK	Frank J. B9.12.1877 Dover OH D5.20.1964 Portsmouth OH BR/TR/6-4/200 d6.14																									
905	Pit N	0	0	—	1	0	0	0	3	2	0	0	0	0	1	0.00	—	.200	.200	1	.000	-0		1		0.0
MOORE, JIM	James Stanford B12.14.1903 Prescott AR D5.19.1973 Seattle WA BR/TR/6-0/165 d9.21 Col Hendrix																									
928	Cle A	0	1	.000	1	1	1	0	9	5	2	0	0	5	1	2.00	207	.161	.278	3	.000	-0	20	2		0.2
929	Cle A	0	0	—	2	0	0	0	5.2	6	6	1	0	6	1	9.53	47	.273	.385	2	.000	-0		-3		-0.1
930	Chi A	2	1	.667	9	5	2	1	40	42	18	0	0	12	11	3.60	128	.268	.320	13-0-2	.231	-0	104	3		0.3
931	Chi A	0	2	.000	33	4	0	0	83.2	93	52	3	1	27	15	4.95	86	.282	.338	16	.063	-1	65	-5		-0.3
932	Chi A	0	0	—	1	0	0	0	1	1	0	0	0	1	2	0.00	—	.250	.400	1	.000	-0		0		0.0
otal	5	2	4	.333	46	10	3	1	139.1	147	78	4	1	49	29	4.52	97	.270	.332	35-0-2	.114	-2	82	-1		0.1
MOORE, WHITEY	Lloyd Albert B6.10.1912 Tuscarawas OH D12.10.1987 Uhrichsville OH BR/TR/6-1/195 d9.27 Mil 1943-45																									
936	Cin N	1	0	1.000	5	3	0	0	5	3	3	0	4	3	5.40	71	.167	.286	2-0-1	.000	-0		-1		-0.1
937	Cin N	0	3	.000	13	6	0	0	38.2	32	22	1	4	39	27	4.89	76	.239	.424	8	.000	-1	58	-4		-0.4
938	Cin N	6	4	.600	19	11	3-1	0	90.1	66	41	4	3	42	38	3.49	105	.205	.302	26-0-1	.077	-2	91	1		-0.1
939	†Cin N	13	12	.520	42	24	9-2	3	187.2	177	88	10	6	95	81	3.45	111	.254	.348	61-0-7	.098	-4	100	6		0.3
940	†Cin N	8	8	.500	25	15	5-1	1	116.2	100	48	8	7	56	60	3.63	104	.231	.329	39-0-4	.128	-1	104	4		0.2
941	Cin N	2	1	.667	23	4	1	0	61.2	62	35	2	3	45	17	4.38	82	.256	.379	18	.167	-1	165	-6		-0.4
942	Cin N	0	0	—	1	0	0	0	1	0	0	0	0	1	0	0.00	—	.000	.250	0	—	0		0		0.0
	StL N	0	1	.000	9	0	0	0	12.1	10	6	0	1	11	1	4.38	78	.217	.379	2	.000	-0		-1		-0.1
	Year	0	1	.000	10	0	0	0	13.1	10	6	0	1	12	1	4.05	84	.204	.371	2	.000	-0		-1		-0.1
otal	7	30	29	.508	133	60	18-4	4	513.1	450	243	25	24	292	228	3.75	100	.237	.346	156-0-13	.103	-10	100	-1		-0.6
MOORE, MARCUS	Marcus Braymont B11.2.1970 Oakland CA BB/TR/6-5/195* [CalA88 17/429] d7.9 Col Sacramento (CA) City																									
993	Col N	3	1	.750	27	0	0	0-2	26.1	30	25	4	1	20-0	13	6.84	70	.291	.398	1	.000	-0		-6		-0.9
994	Col N	1	1	.500	29	0	0	0-0	33.2	33	26	4	5	21-2	33	6.15	81	.252	.376	1	.000	-0		-4		-0.2
996	Cin N	3	3	.500	23	0	0	2-0	26.1	26	21	3	2	22-1	27	5.81	74	.263	.397	3	.333	1		-5		-1.0
otal	3	7	5	.583	79	0	0	2-2	86.1	89	72	11	8	63-3	73	6.25	75	.267	.389	5	.200	0		-15		-2.1
MOORE, MIKE	Michael Wayne B11.26.1959 Eakly OK BR/TR/6-4/205* [SeaA81 1/1] d4.11 Col Oral Roberts																									
982	Sea A	7	14	.333	28	27	1-1	0-0	144.1	159	91	21	2	79-0	73	5.36	80	.285	.373	0	—	0	75	-15		-1.8
983	Sea A	6	8	.429	22	21	3-2	0-0	128	130	75	10	3	60-4	108	4.71	91	.267	.348	0	—	0	83	-6		-0.5
984	Sea A	7	17	.292	34	33	6	0-0	212	236	127	16	5	85-10	158	4.97	81	.282	.350	0	—	0	87	-21		-1.9
985	Sea A	17	10	.630	35	34	14-2	0-0	247	230	100	18	4	70-2	155	3.46	122	.247	.300	0	—	0	94	23	16	2.4
986	Sea A	11	13	.458	38	37	11-1	1-0	266	279	141	28	12	94-6	146	4.30	99	.273	.339	0	—	0	103	0		0.0
987	Sea A	9	19	.321	33	33	12	0-0	231	268	145	29	0	84-3	115	4.71	101	.292	.348	1	.000	-0	78	-4		-0.4
988	Sea A	9	15	.375	37	32	9-3	1-1	228.2	196	104	24	3	63-6	182	3.78	111	.232	.286	0	—	0	80	11		1.2
989	†Oak A★	19	11	.633	35	35	6-3	0-0	241.2	193	82	14	2	83-1	172	2.61	142	.219	.286	0	—	0	97	30		3.7
990	Oak A	13	15	.464	33	33	3	0-0	199.1	204	113	14	3	84-2	73	4.65	80	.267	.339	0	—	0	97	-6		-2.5
991	Oak A	17	8	.680	33	33	3-1	0-0	210	176	75	11	5	105-1	153	2.96	130	.229	.324	0	—	0*	94	21	17	2.5
992	†Oak A	17	12	.586	36	36	2	0-0	223	229	117	30	8	103-5	117	4.12	92	.268	.349	0	—	0	120	-8		-1.0
993	Det A	13	9	.591	36	36	4-3	0-0	213.2	227	135	35	3	89-10	89	5.22	83	.271	.340	0	—	0	127	-19		-1.5
994	Det A	11	10	.524	25	25	4	0-0	154.1	152	97	27	3	89-8	62	5.42	91	.263	.361	0	—	0	96	-6		-0.5
995	Det A	5	15	.250	25	25	0	0-0	132.1	179	118	24	1	68-3	64	7.53	64	.323	.396	0	—	0	93	-38		-4.4
otal	14	161	176	.478	450	440	79-16	2-1	2831.2	2858	1516	291	55	1156-61	1667	4.39	95	.264	.335	1	.000	-0	95	-53	33	-4.8

YEAR	TM LG	W	L	PCT	G	GS	CG-SHO	SV-BS	IP	H	R	HR	HB	BB-IB	SO	ERA	AERA	OAV	OOB	AB-HR-SH	AVG	PB	SUP	APR	DL	PW

MOORE, RAY Raymond Leroy "Farmer" B6.1.1926 Meadows MD D3.2.1995 Clinton MD BR/TR/6-1/205(195-210) d8.1

YEAR	TM LG	W	L	PCT	G	GS	CG-SHO	SV-BS	IP	H	R	HR	HB	BB-IB	SO	ERA	AERA	OAV	OOB	AB-HR-SH	AVG	PB	SUP	APR	DL	PW
1952	Bro N	1	2	.333	14	2	0	0	28.1	29	17	3	2	26	11	4.76	76	.274	.425	3	.000	-0	49	-4		-0.4
1953	Bro N	0	1	.000	1	1	1	0	8	6	3	1	0	4	4	3.38	126	.214	.313	3	.000	-0	21	1		0.0
1955	Bal A	10	10	.500	46	14	3-1	6	151.2	128	75	14	4	80-1	80	3.92	97	.229	.327	44-0-2	.136	-2	100	-1		-0.4
1956	Bal A	12	7	.632	32	27	9-1	0	185	161	90	12	1	99-1	105	4.18	94	.238	.332	70-2-4	.271	6	89	-3		0.2
1957	Bal A	11	13	.458	34	32	7-1	0	227.1	196	99	17	2	112-5	117	3.72	97	.236	.326	84-3-3	.214	4	86	-2		0.1
1958	Chi A	9	7	.563	32	20	4-2	2	136.2	107	63	10	0	70-2	73	3.82	95	.220	.315	44-1-5	.205	2	99	-2		-0.1
1959	†Chi A	3	6	.333	29	8	0	0	89.2	86	46	10	1	46-3	49	4.12	91	.261	.348	23-0-1	.087	-1	59	-4		-0.5
1960	Chi A	1	1	.500	14	0	0	0	20.2	19	13	5	0	11-0	3	5.66	67	.253	.345	2	.000	-0		-4		-0.4
	Was A	3	2	.600	37	0	0	13	65.2	49	24	5	1	27-3	29	2.88	135	.213	.296	14	.071	-1		8		0.7
	Year	4	3	.571	51	0	0	13	86.1	68	37	10	1	38-3	32	3.54	109	.223	.308	16	.063	-1		4		0.3
1961	Min A	4	4	.500	46	0	0	14	56.1	49	23	8	1	38-3	45	3.67	115	.233	.351	4-0-1	.000	0		5		0.9
1962	Min A	8	3	.727	49	0	0	9	64.2	55	35	8	2	30-4	58	4.73	86	.231	.319	5-0-1	.000	-1		-3		-0.7
1963	Min A	3	3	.250	31	1	0	2	38.2	50	34	8	1	17-2	38	6.98	52	.309	.378	3	.333	-3	73	-14		-1.5
Total 11		63	59	.516	365	105	24-5	46	1072.2	935	522	101	15	560-24	612	4.06	93	.238	.332	299-6-17	.187	6	86	-23		-2.1

MOORE, BARRY Robert Barry B4.3.1943 Statesville NC BL/TL/6-1/190(175-190) d5.29 Col Pfeiffer

YEAR	TM LG	W	L	PCT	G	GS	CG-SHO	SV-BS	IP	H	R	HR	HB	BB-IB	SO	ERA	AERA	OAV	OOB	AB-HR-SH	AVG	PB	SUP	APR	DL	PW
1965	Was A	0	0	—	1	0	0	0	1	1	1	0	0	1-0	0	0.00	—	.333	.500	0		0		0		0.0
1966	Was A	3	3	.500	12	11	1	0	62.1	55	26	3	1	39-2	28	3.75	92	.240	.352	19-0-1	.105	-1	93	-1		0.0
1967	Was A	7	11	.389	27	26	3-1	0	143.2	127	67	15	3	71-6	74	3.76	84	.240	.332	46-0-4	.130	-0	86	-9	21	-1.0
1968	Was A	4	6	.400	32	18	0	3	117.2	116	55	8	2	42-2	56	3.37	87	.261	.326	31-0-3	.097	-1*	108	-8		-0.8
1969	Was A	9	8	.529	31	25	4	0-0	134	123	70	12	2	67-1	51	4.30	82	.246	.334	43-0-2	.209	1*	112	-11		-1.2
1970	Cle A	3	5	.375	13	12	0	0-0	70.1	70	34	8	1	46-3	35	4.22	95	.262	.370	21-0-1	.095	-1	87	-1		-0.2
	Chi A	0	4	.000	24	7	0	0-0	70.2	85	56	12	8	34-0	34	6.37	61	.302	.386	19-0-1	.263	1	95	-18		-0.8
	Year	3	9	.250	37	19	0	0-0	141	155	90	20	9	80-3	69	5.30	74	.283	.378	40-0-2	.175	-0	90	-17		-1.0
Total 6		26	37	.413	140	99	8-1	3-0	599.2	577	309	58	17	300-14	278	4.16	82	.256	.345	179-0-12	.151	-1	98	-48	21	-4.1

MOORE, BOBBY Robert Devell B11.8.1958 Sweetwater LA BR/TR/6-4/200 [OakA76 11/264] d9.11

YEAR	TM LG	W	L	PCT	G	GS	CG-SHO	SV-BS	IP	H	R	HR	HB	BB-IB	SO	ERA	AERA	OAV	OOB	AB-HR-SH	AVG	PB	SUP	APR	DL	PW
1985	SF N	0	0	—	11	0	0	0-0	16.2	18	6	1	0	10-2	10	3.24	107	.269	.364	2	.000	0		1		0.0

MOORE, ROY Roy Daniel B10.26.1898 Austin TX D4.5.1951 Seattle WA BB/TL/6-0/185 d4.15

YEAR	TM LG	W	L	PCT	G	GS	CG-SHO	SV-BS	IP	H	R	HR	HB	BB-IB	SO	ERA	AERA	OAV	OOB	AB-HR-SH	AVG	PB	SUP	APR	DL	PW
1920	Phi A	1	13	.071	24	14	5	0	132.2	161	89	6	3	64	45	4.68	86	.314	.393	50-1-1	.200	-1*	52	-7		-0.7
1921	Phi A	10	10	.500	29	26	12	0	191.2	206	110	4	4	122	64	4.51	99	.280	.385	74-3-0	.257	3*	82	3		0.7
1922	Phi A	0	3	.000	15	6	0	0	50.2	65	43	1	3	32	29	7.64	56	.319	.418	19-0-1	.263	1	116	-15		-0.6
	Det A	0	0	—	9	0	0	2	19.2	29	14	0	5	10	9	5.95	65	.367	.468	7	.429	1		-4		-0.1
	Year	0	3	.000	24	6	0	2	70.1	94	57	1	8	42	38	7.17	58	.332	.432	26-0-1	.308	2	119	-18		-0.7
1923	Det A	0	0	—	3	0	0	1	12	15	4	0	0	11	9	3.00	129	.288	.413	5	.000	-0*		2		-0.6
Total 4		11	26	.297	80	46	17	3	406.2	476	260	11	15	239	154	4.98	85	.300	.397	155-4-2	.239	4	78	-21		-0.8

MOORE, TOMMY Tommy Joe B7.7.1948 Lynwood CA BR/TR/5-11/175* [NYN67*S10/152] d9.15 Col Cerritos (CA) JC

YEAR	TM LG	W	L	PCT	G	GS	CG-SHO	SV-BS	IP	H	R	HR	HB	BB-IB	SO	ERA	AERA	OAV	OOB	AB-HR-SH	AVG	PB	SUP	APR	DL	PW
1972	NY N	0	0	—	3	1	0	0-0	12.1	12	4	1	0	1-0	5	2.92	116	.273	.283	3	.333	0	52	1		0.1
1973	NY N	0	1	.000	3	1	0	0-0	3.1	6	5	1	0	3-0	1	10.80	34	.400	.500	0	—	0*	121	-3		-0.6
1975	StL N	0	0	—	10	0	0	0-0	18.2	15	10	2	0	12-1	6	3.86	99	.203	.314	2	.500	0*		0		-0.8
	Tex A	0	2	.000	12	0	0	0-1	21	31	21	1	1	12-4	15	8.14	46	.352	.436	0	—	0*		-10		-0.8
1977	Sea A	2	1	.667	14	1	0	0-1	33	36	22	1	3	21-2	40	4.91	84	.281	.390	0	—	0	65	-4		-1.0
Total 4		2	4	.333	42	3	0	0-2	88.1	100	62	6	4	49-7	40	5.40	71	.287	.378	5	.400	1	77	-16		-1.1

MOORE, TREY Warren Neal B10.2.1972 Houston TX BL/TL/6-1/200* [SeaA94 2/48] d4.5 Col Texas A&M-Commerce [DL 1999 Mon N 182]

YEAR	TM LG	W	L	PCT	G	GS	CG-SHO	SV-BS	IP	H	R	HR	HB	BB-IB	SO	ERA	AERA	OAV	OOB	AB-HR-SH	AVG	PB	SUP	APR	DL	PW
1998	Mon N	2	5	.286	13	11	0	0-0	61	78	37	7	4	17-3	35	5.02	84	.306	.348	17-0-1	.235	1*	68	-5	113	-0.4
2000	Mon N	1	5	.167	8	8	0	0-0	35.1	55	31	7	4	21-1	24	6.62	71	.304	.455	8-0-2	.125	-0	78	-8		-1.1
2001	Atl N	0	0	—	2	0	0	0-0	4	7	5	0	0	2-0	1	11.25	38	.368	.429	1	1.000	1		-3		-0.1
Total 3		3	10	.231	23	19	0	0-0	100.1	140	73	12	5	40-4	60	5.83	75	.329	.391	26-0-3	.231	2	73	-16	295	-1.6

MOORE, CY William Austin B2.7.1905 Elberton GA D3.28.1972 Augusta GA BR/TR/6-1/178 d6.7

YEAR	TM LG	W	L	PCT	G	GS	CG-SHO	SV-BS	IP	H	R	HR	HB	BB-IB	SO	ERA	AERA	OAV	OOB	AB-HR-SH	AVG	PB	SUP	APR	DL	PW
1929	Bro N	3	3	.500	32	3	0	2	68	87	45	3	0	31	17	5.56	83	.320	.389	16-0-1	.188	-0	63	-5		-0.5
1930	Bro N	0	0	—	1	0	0	0	2	2	1	0	0	0	—	1.000	1.000			0	—	0		0		0.0
1931	Bro N	1	2	.333	23	1	1	0	61.2	62	31	5	4	13	35	3.79	100	.262	.311	13-0-1	.154	-1	22	0		-0.0
1932	Bro N	0	3	.000	20	2	0	0	48.2	56	32	3	1	17	21	4.81	79	.293	.354	14	.214	0*	99	-6		-0.2
1933	Phi N	8	9	.471	36	18	9-3	1	161.1	177	74	7	3	42	53	3.74	102	.279	.326	48-0-1	.063	-4	81	3		-0.2
1934	Phi N	4	9	.308	35	15	3-	0	126.2	163	98	11	2	65	55	6.47	73	.309	.387	42-0-1	.143	-3	91	-18		-1.1
Total 6		16	26	.381	147	39	13-3	3	466.1	547	281	29	10	168	181	4.86	86	.293	.355	133-0-4	.128	-8	84	-26		-2.1

MOORE, BILL William Christopher B9.3.1902 Corning NY D1.24.1984 Corning NY BR/TR/6-3/195 d4.15

YEAR	TM LG	W	L	PCT	G	GS	CG-SHO	SV-BS	IP	H	R	HR	HB	BB-IB	SO	ERA	AERA	OAV	OOB	AB-HR-SH	AVG	PB	SUP	APR	DL	PW
1925	Det A	0	0	—	1	0	0	0	1	2	2	0	0	3	0	∞	—	—	1.000	0		0		-2		-0.2

MOORE, WILCY William Wilcy "Cy" B5.20.1897 Bonita TX D3.29.1963 Hollis OK BR/TR/6-0/195 d4.14

YEAR	TM LG	W	L	PCT	G	GS	CG-SHO	SV-BS	IP	H	R	HR	HB	BB-IB	SO	ERA	AERA	OAV	OOB	AB-HR-SH	AVG	PB	SUP	APR	DL	PW
1927	†NY A	19	7	.731	50	12	6-1	13	213	185	68	3	1	59	75	**2.28**	**169**	**.234**	**.289**	75-1-7	.080	-7	119	39		4.5
1928	NY A	4	4	.500	35	2	0	2	60.1	71	44	4	0	31	18	4.18	90	.286	.366	14-0-2	.143	-1	203	-8		-0.1
1929	NY A	6	4	.600	41	0	0	8	61	64	36	4	0	19	21	4.13	93	.268	.322	15-0-1	.067	-2		-3		-0.0
1931	Bos A	11	13	.458	53	15	8-1	10	185.1	195	88	7	1	55	37	3.88	111	.269	.322	56-0-2	.161	-3	64	10		1.2
1932	Bos A	4	10	.286	37	2	0	4	84.1	98	59	5	1	42	28	5.23	86	.293	.363	22	.045	-2	28	-7		-1.1
	†NY A	2	0	1.000	10	1	0	4	25	27	8	1	0	6	8	2.52	162	.273	.314	8	.000	-1	84	5		0.2
	Year	6	10	.375	47	3	0	8	109.1	125	67	6	1	48	36	4.61	95	.282	.353	30	.033	-4	45	-2		-0.5
1933	NY A	5	6	.455	35	0	0	8	62	92	53	1	0	20	17	5.52	70	.333	.378	15-0-2	.133	-1		-16		-0.3
Total 6		51	44	.537	261	32	14-2	49	691	732	356	25	3	232	204	3.70	110	.269	.327	205-1-14	.102	-17	91	20		0.3

MOORHEAD, BOB Charles Robert B1.23.1938 Chambersburg PA D12.3.1986 Lemoyne PA BR/TR/6-1/208* d4.11

YEAR	TM LG	W	L	PCT	G	GS	CG-SHO	SV-BS	IP	H	R	HR	HB	BB-IB	SO	ERA	AERA	OAV	OOB	AB-HR-SH	AVG	PB	SUP	APR	DL	PW
1962	NY N	0	2	.000	38	7	0	0	105.1	118	69	13	4	42-4	63	4.53	92	.289	.358	22-0-1	.045	-1	126	-6		-0.7
1965	NY N	0	1	.000	9	0	0	0	14.1	16	7	0	0	5-0	5	4.40	80	.271	.328	0	—	0		-1		-0.0
Total 2		0	3	.000	47	7	0	0	119.2	134	76	13	4	47-4	68	4.51	91	.287	.354	22-0-1	.045	-1	126	-7		-0.7

MOOSE, BOB Robert Ralph B10.9.1947 Export PA D10.9.1976 Martins Ferry OH BR/TR/6-0/200(170-200) [PitN65 11/348] d9.19

YEAR	TM LG	W	L	PCT	G	GS	CG-SHO	SV-BS	IP	H	R	HR	HB	BB-IB	SO	ERA	AERA	OAV	OOB	AB-HR-SH	AVG	PB	SUP	APR	DL	PW
1967	Pit N	1	0	1.000	2	2	1	0	14.2	14	6	1	4	4-0	7	3.68	91	.259	.322	6	.333	1	196	0		0.0
1968	Pit N	8	12	.400	38	22	3-3	3	170.2	136	61	5	3	41-7	126	2.74	107	.218	.268	54-0-2	.093	-2	78	4		0.6
1969	Pit N	14	3	.824	44	19	6-1	4-1	170	149	64	9	6	62-3	165	2.91	120	.231	.302	53-0-4	.075	-1	166	10		0.8
1970	†Pit N	11	10	.524	28	27	9-2	0-0	189.2	186	88	14	3	64-5	119	3.99	99	.262	.325	66-0-4	.182	3*	92	2		0.9
1971	Pit N	11	7	.611	30	18	3-1	1-0	140	169	73	12	2	35-11	68	4.11	89	.301	.340	39-0-1	.103	-1	138	-12		0.2
1972	†Pit N	13	10	.565	31	30	6-3	0-0	226	213	84	11	4	47-9	144	2.91	114	.248	.288	71-0-6	.169	3*	121	11		1.1
1973	Pit N	12	13	.480	33	29	6-3	0-0	201.1	219	86	11	4	70-11	111	3.53	100	.280	.340	67-0-4	.134	-0*	99	2		0.2
1974	Pit N	1	5	.167	7	6	0	0-0	35.2	59	30	4	2	7-3	26	7.57	46	.386	.410	11	.182	0	84	-15	126	-0.3
1975	Pit N	2	2	.500	23	5	1	0-0	67.2	63	30	4	2	25-3	34	3.72	96	.246	.318	18-0-2	.167	0	103	0	23	-0.2
1976	Pit N	3	9	.250	53	2	0	10-3	88	100	44	4	4	32-7	38	3.68	96	.244	.356	12-1-0	.250	-2	25	-3		-0.2
Total		76	71	.517	289	160	35-13	19-4	1303.2	1308	566	75	30	387-59	827	3.50	99	.262	.317	397-1-27	.141	4	111	-1	149	0.2

MOOTY, JAKE Jake T. B4.13.1912 Millsap TX D4.20.1970 Fort Worth TX BR/TR/5-10.5/170 d9.9 Col Texas A&M-Commerce

YEAR	TM LG	W	L	PCT	G	GS	CG-SHO	SV-BS	IP	H	R	HR	HB	BB-IB	SO	ERA	AERA	OAV	OOB	AB-HR-SH	AVG	PB	SUP	APR	DL	PW
1936	Cin N	0	0	—	8	0	0	1	13.2	10	6	0	0	4	11	3.95	97	.204	.264	1	.000	-0		0		0.0
1937	Cin N	0	3	.000	14	2	0	1	39	54	39	2	0	22	11	8.31	45	.327	.406	8-0-1	.000	-1*	46	-19		-1.3
1940	Chi N	6	6	.500	20	12	6	1	114	101	45	11	0	49	42	2.92	128	.243	.325	38-0-3	.263	2*	77	10		0.8
1941	Chi N	8	9	.471	33	14	7-1	4	153.1	143	69	9	2	56	45	3.35	105	.251	.320	50-0-3	.200	1	85	2		0.2
1942	Chi N	2	5	.286	19	10	1	1	84.1	89	48	11	0	44	28	4.70	68	.265	.350	28-0-1	.214	0	137	-13		-0.3
1943	Chi N	0	0	—	2	0	0	0	1	2	0	0	1	0	0.00	—	.400	.500	0	—	0		0		0.0
1944	Det A	0	0	—	15	0	0	0	28.1	35	20	0	1	18	7	4.45	80	.310	.409	7	.143	-0		-4		0.0
Total 7		16	23	.410	111	38	14-1	8	433.2	434	227	4	4	194	145	4.03	88	.263	.341	132-0-8	.205	-2	92	-24		0.0

YEAR	TM LG	W	L	PCT	G	GS	CG-SHO	SV-BS	IP	H	R	HR	HB	BB-IB	SO	ERA	AERA	OAV	OOB	AB-HR-SH	AVG	PB	SUP	APR	DL	PW

MORAGA, DAVID David Michael B7.8.1975 Torrance CA BL/TL/6-0/185 [MonN93 30/846] d6.11 Col Sacramento (CA) City

2000	Mon N	0	0	—	3	0	0	0-0	1.2	6	7	0	0	2-0	2	37.80	12	.600	.615	0	—	0		-6		-0.3
	Col N	0	0	—	1	0	0	0-0	1	4	5	1	1	0-0	0	45.00	13	.667	.625	0	—	0		-3		-0.1
	Year	0	0	—	4	0	0	0-0	2.2	10	12	1	1	2-0	2	40.50	13	.625	.619	0	—	0		-9		-0.4

MORAN, HIKER Albert Thomas B1.1.1912 Rochester NY D1.7.1998 Saratoga Springs NY BR/TR/6-4.5/185 d9.29

1938	Bos N	0	0	—	1	0	0	0	3	1	0	0	0	1	0	0.00	—	.111	.200	1	.000	-0		1		0.0
1939	Bos N	1	1	.500	6	2	1	0	20	21	10	3	0	11	4	4.50	82	.276	.368	5-0-1	.200	1	142	-1		-0.1
Total	2	1	1	.500	7	2	1	0	23	22	10	3	0	12	4	3.91	94	.259	.351	6-0-1	.167	0	142	0		-0.1

MORAN, BILL Carl William "Bugs" B9.26.1950 Portsmouth VA BR/TR/6-4/210 d4.12 Col Louisburg (NC) JC

| 1974 | Chi A | 1 | 3 | .250 | 15 | 5 | 0 | 0-0 | 46.1 | 57 | 27 | 5 | 6 | 23-2 | 17 | 4.66 | 80 | .302 | .393 | 0 | — | 0 | 113 | -5 | | -0.4 |

MORAN, CHARLIE Charles Barthell "Uncle Charlie" B2.22.1878 Nashville TN D6.14.1949 Horse Cave KY BR/TR/5-8/180 d9.9 U22 Col Vanderbilt ▲

| 1903 | StL N | 0 | 1 | .000 | 3 | 2 | 2 | 0 | 24 | 30 | 29 | 0 | 1 | 19 | 7 | 5.25 | 62 | .297 | .413 | 14 | .429 | 1* | 124 | -7 | | -0.2 |

MORAN, HARRY Harry Edwin B4.2.1889 Slater (now Thayer) WV D11.28.1962 Beckley WV BL/TL/6-1/165 d6.23 Col Washington and Lee

1912	Det A	0	1	.000	5	2	1	0	14.2	19	14	1	2	12	3	4.91	66	.339	.471	5	.200	-0	125	-4		-0.3
1914	Buf F	10	7	.588	34	16	7-2	2	154	159	87	7	11	53	73	4.27	69	.276	.348	51-0-3	.196	-0	114	-21		-2.2
1915	New F	13	9	.591	34	23	13-2	0	205.2	193	80	2	18	66	87	2.54	101	.262	.337	61-0-9	.180	-1*	96	1		0.1
Total	3	23	17	.575	73	41	21-4	2	374.1	371	181	10	31	131	163	3.34	82	.271	.348	117-0-12	.188	-1	105	-24		-2.4

MORAN, SAM Samuel B9.16.1870 Rochester NY D8.27.1897 Rochester NY TL/?/160 d8.28

| 1895 | Pit N | 2 | 4 | .333 | 10 | 6 | 6 | 0 | 62.2 | 78 | 63 | 3 | 2 | 51 | 19 | 7.47 | 60 | .300 | .420 | 26-1-0 | .154 | -1* | 103 | -17 | | -1.2 |

MORE, FORREST Forrest Thedore B9.20.1881 Hayden IN D8.17.1968 Columbus IN BR/TR/6-0/180 d4.15

1909	StL N	1	5	.167	15	2	1	0	50	48	33	0	3	20	17	5.04	50	.258	.340	13-0-1	.154	1	111	-12		-1.3
	Bos N	1	5	.167	10	4	3	0	48.2	47	47	0	4	20	10	4.44	64	.270	.359	15	.067	-1	50	-12		-1.5
	Year	2	10	.167	25	6	4	0	98.2	95	80	0	7	40	27	4.74	56	.264	.349	28-0-1	.107	-1	70	-24		-2.8

MOREHEAD, DAVE David Michael "Moe" B9.5.1942 San Diego CA BR/TR/6-1/185(180-200) d4.13

1963	Bos A	10	13	.435	29	29	6-1	0	174.2	137	82	20	0	99-2	136	3.81	99	.211	.316	57-0-3	.105	-3	89	-1		-0.4
1964	Bos A	8	15	.348	32	30	3-1	0	166.2	156	101	4	4	112-2	139	4.97	78	.248	.358	54-0-2	.093	-2	86	-19		-2.6
1965	Bos A	10	18	.357	34	33	5-2	0	192.2	157	103	18	3	113-1	163	4.06	92	.217	.325	61-0-4	.131	-0	80	-7		-1.1
1966	Bos A	1	2	.333	12	5	0	0	28	31	17	7	0	7-0	20	5.46	70	.274	.317	6	.500	1	120	-4	16	-0.3
1967	†Bos A	5	4	.556	10	9	1-1	0	47.2	48	24	0	2	22-0	40	4.34	80	.264	.348	12-0-3	.083	-0	111	-3		-0.7
1968	Bos A	1	4	.200	11	9	3-1	0	55	52	17	3	2	20-0	28	2.45	129	.249	.320	16-0-1	.125	-0	98	4		0.3
1969	KC A	2	3	.400	21	2	0	0-0	33	28	22	7	0	28-1	32	5.73	65	.239	.384	2	.000	0	24	-6	36	-0.9
1970	KC A	3	5	.375	28	17	1	1-0	121.2	121	64	9	1	62-3	69	3.62	103	.261	.347	36-0-3	.167	-0	100	-2		-0.2
Total	8	40	64	.385	177	134	19-6	1-0	819.1	730	430	78	12	463-9	627	4.15	90	.237	.336	244-0-16	.127	-5	90	-38	52	-5.9

MOREHEAD, SETH Seth Marvin "Moe" B8.15.1934 Houston TX BL/TL/6-0.5/195* d4.27 Col Baylor

1957	Phi N	1	1	.500	34	1	1	1	58.2	57	27	1	2	20-4	36	3.68	103	.254	.315	6	.000	-1	46	1		-0.1
1958	Phi N	1	6	.143	27	11	0	0	92.1	121	67	8	1	26-3	54	5.85	68	.319	.359	22-0-3	.182	-0	87	-19		-1.3
1959	Phi N	0	2	.000	3	3	0	0	10	15	11	3	1	3-0	8	9.90	41	.333	.388	3	.000	-0	138	-6		-0.9
	Chi N	0	1	.000	11	2	0	0	18.2	25	13	1	0	8-2	9	4.82	82	.313	.375	2	.500	.1	136	-3		-0.1
	Year	0	3	.000	14	5	0	0	28.2	40	24	4	1	11-2	17	6.59	61	.320	.380	5	.200	-0	138	-8		-1.0
1960	Chi N	2	9	.182	45	7	2	4	123.1	123	61	17	2	46-6	64	3.94	96	.258	.324	29-0-1	.138	-1	80	-2		-0.2
1961	Mil N	1	0	1.000	12	0	0	0	15.1	16	11	4	1	7-0	13	6.46	58	.271	.358	0	—	0		-4		-0.3
Total	5	5	19	.208	132	24	3	5	318.1	357	190	34	7	110-15	184	4.81	80	.282	.340	62-0-4	.145	-1	95	-33		-2.9

MOREL, RAMON Ramon Rafael B8.15.1974 Villa Gonzalez, D.R. BR/TR/6-2/175(175-200) d7.6

1995	Pit N	0	1	.000	5	0	0	0-1	6.1	6	2	0	0	2-1	3	2.84	153	.300	.364	0	—	0		1		0.2
1996	Pit N	2	1	.667	29	0	0	0-0	42	57	27	4	0	19-5	22	5.36	82	.324	.391	4-0-1	.000	-0		-4		-0.3
1997	Pit N	0	0	—	5	0	0	0-0	7.2	11	4	2	0	4-1	4	4.70	91	.344	.417	0	—	0		0		0.0
	Chi N	0	0	—	3	0	0	0-0	3.2	3	2	1	0	3-0	3	4.91	88	.214	.353	0	—	0		0		0.0
	Year	0	0	—	8	0	0	0-0	11.1	14	6	3	0	7-1	7	4.76	90	.304	.396	0	—	0		0		0.0
Total	3	2	2	.500	42	0	0	0-1	59.2	77	35	7	1	28-7	32	4.98	88	.318	.390	4-0-1	.000	-0		-3		-0.1

MOREN, LEW Lewis Howard "Hicks" B8.4.1883 Pittsburgh PA D11.2.1966 Pittsburgh PA BR/TR/5-11/150 d9.21 Col Duquesne

1903	Pit N	0	1	.000	1	1	1	0	6	9	7	0	1	2	2	9.00	36	.346	.414	2	.000	-0	62	-3		-0.4
1904	Pit N	0	0	—	1	0	0	0	4	7	6	1	0	4	0	9.00	30	.412	.545	2	.000	-0		-3		-0.2
1907	Phi N	11	18	.379	37	31	21-3	1	255	202	106	3	9	101	98	2.54	95	.226	.311	74-0-3	.081	-2	89	-7		-1.1
1908	Phi N	8	9	.471	28	16	9-4	0	154	146	68	3	2	49	72	2.92	83	.258	.320	49-0-2	.245	2	67	-8		-0.8
1909	Phi N	16	15	.516	40	31	19-2	1	257.2	226	103	6	4	93	110	2.65	98	.239	.309	90-0-2	.111	-3	109	-1		-0.7
1910	Phi N	13	14	.481	34	26	12-1	1	205.1	207	104	6	9	82	74	3.55	88	.269	.347	74	.149	-1	103	-8		-1.2
Total	6	48	57	.457	141	105	62-10	3	882	797	394	17	26	331	356	2.95	90	.248	.323	291-0-7	.134	-5	96	-30		-4.4

MORENO, ANGEL Angel (Veneroso) B6.6.1955 Soledad de Doblado, Veracruz, Mexico BL/TL/5-9/165* d8.15

1981	Cal A	1	3	.250	8	4	1	0-0	31.1	27	10	2	0	14-0	12	2.87	128	.233	.313	0	—	0	37	3		0.4
1982	Cal A	3	7	.300	13	8	2	1-1	49.1	55	31	7	1	23-0	22	4.74	86	.288	.364	0	—	0	67	-5		-0.9
Total	2	4	10	.286	21	12	3	1-1	80.2	82	41	9	1	37-0	34	4.02	98	.267	.345	0	—	0	58	-2		-0.5

MORENO, JUAN Juan Carlos (Vegas) B2.28.1975 Maiquetia, Venez BL/TL/6-1/205* d5.17

2001	Tex A	3	3	.500	45	0	0	0-2	41.1	22	21	6	0	28-2	36	3.92	122	.153	.291	0	—	0		3		0.3
2002	SD N	0	0	—	4	0	0	0-0	6	6	6	1	0	10-1	3	7.50	52	.261	.471	0	—	0		-3		-0.1
Total	2	3	3	.500	49	0	0	0-2	47.1	28	27	7	0	38-3	39	4.37	107	.168	.320	0	—	0		0		0.2

MORENO, JULIO Julio (Gonzalez) B1.28.1921 Guines, Cuba D1.2.1987 Miami FL BR/TR/5-8/165(158-170) d9.8

1950	Was A	1	1	.500	4	3	1	0	21.1	22	13	1	1	12	7	4.64	97	.268	.368	8-0-1	.125	-1	114	-1		-0.1
1951	Was A	5	11	.313	31	18	5	2	132.2	132	82	18	1	80	37	4.88	84	.256	.357	40-0-3	.175	-1	95	-12		-1.4
1952	Was A	9	9	.500	26	22	7	0	147.1	154	75	10	5	52	62	3.97	90	.270	.337	49-0-1	.122	-2	96	-8		-1.1
1953	Was A	3	1	.750	12	2	1	0	35.1	41	11	2	0	13	13	2.80	139	.291	.351	9	.000	-1	125	5		0.4
Total	4	18	22	.450	73	45	14	2	336.2	349	181	31	7	157	119	4.25	91	.267	.349	106-0-5	.132	-5	98	-16		-2.2

MORENO, ORBER Orber (Aquiles) B4.27.1977 Caracas, Venez BR/TR/6-2/190* d5.25 [DL 2001 KC A 57]

1999	KC A	0	0	—	7	0	0	0-1	8	4	5	1	0	6-0	7	5.63	90	.143	.294	0	—	0		0	116	0.0
2003	NY N	0	0	—	7	0	0	0-0	8	10	7	1	0	3-0	5	7.88	53	.313	.371	1	.000	-0		-3		-0.2
2004	NY N	3	1	.750	33	0	0	1-2	34.2	29	17	0	3	11-0	29	3.38	127	.221	.297	1	.000	-0		2	92	0.2
Total	3	3	1	.750	47	0	0	1-3	50.2	43	29	2	3	20-0	41	4.44	99	.225	.308	2	.000	-0		-1	265	0.2

MORET, ROGER Rogelio (Torres) B9.16.1949 Guayama, PR BB/TL/6-4/175(160-175) d9.13

1970	Bos A	1	0	1.000	3	1	0	0-0	8.1	7	3	0	0	4-0	2	3.24	123	.226	.314	3	.000	-0	89	1		0.1
1971	Bos A	4	3	.571	13	7	4-1	0-0	71	50	24	5	2	40-4	47	2.92	128	.205	.321	23	.087	-1	103	6		0.5
1972	Bos A	0	0	—	3	0	0	0	5	5	3	0	0	6	4	3.60	90	.263	.440	1	.000	0	0	0		0.0
1973	Bos A	13	2	.867	30	15	5-2	3-1	156.1	138	60	19	3	67-2	90	3.17	127	.238	.318	0	—	0	120	15	21	1.4
1974	Bos A	9	10	.474	31	21	10-1	2-0	173.1	158	79	15	2	79-4	111	3.74	103	.243	.323	0	—	0	87	2		0.1
1975	†Bos A	14	3	.824	36	16	4-1	1-0	145	132	60	8	2	76-6	80	3.60	113	.248	.341	0	—	0*	129	9		0.9
1976	Atl N	3	5	.375	27	12	1	1-2	77.1	84	44	7	1	27-2	30	5.00	76	.280	.339	23-0-2	.130	-1	118	-8	57	-0.9
1977	Tex A	3	3	.500	18	8	0	4-0	72.1	59	41	6	0	38-2	39	3.73	109	.220	.313	0	—	0	99	0	81	-0.1
1978	Tex A	0	1	.000	7	2	0	1-0	14.2	23	8	1	1	2-0	5	4.91	76	.390	.413	0	—	0	36	-1	126	-0.1
Total	9	47	27	.635	168	82	24-5	12-3	723.1	656	322	61	11	339-20	408	3.66	108	.245	.329	50-0-2	.100	-2	107	24	285	1.9

MOREY, DAVE David Beale B2.25.1889 Malden MA D1.4.1986 Oak Bluffs MA BL/TR/6-0/185 d7.4 Col Dartmouth

| 1913 | Phi A | 0 | 0 | — | 2 | 0 | 0 | 0 | 4 | 2 | 2 | 0 | 1 | 3 | 1 | 4.50 | 61 | .222 | .417 | 1 | .000 | -0 | | -1 | | 0.0 |

MORGAN, CY Cyril Arlon B11.11.1895 Lakeville MA D9.11.1946 Lakeville MA BR/TR/6-0/170 d6.8

| 1921 | Bos N | 1 | 1 | .500 | 17 | 0 | 1 | 0 | 30.1 | 37 | 24 | 0 | 1 | 17 | 8 | 6.53 | 56 | .314 | .404 | 5 | .000 | -1 | | -9 | | -0.6 |
| 1922 | Bos N | 0 | 0 | — | 1 | 0 | 0 | 0 | 1.1 | 8 | 8 | 1 | 0 | 2 | 0 | 27.00 | 15 | .667 | .714 | 0 | — | 0 | | -5 | | -0.2 |

YEAR	TM LG	W	L	PCT	G	GS	CG-SHO	SV-BS	IP	H	R	HR	HB	BB-IB	SO	ERA	AERA	OAV	OOB	AB-HR-SH	AVG	PB	SUP	APR	DL	PW
Total	2	1	1	.500	19	0	0	1	31.2	45	32	0	1	19	8	7.39	50	.346	.433	5	.000	-1		-14		-0.8

MORGAN, DAN Daniel B5.1853 MO D1.30.1910 St.Louis MO d5.4 ▲

YEAR	TM LG	W	L	PCT	G	GS	CG-SHO	SV-BS	IP	H	R	HR	HB	BB-IB	SO	ERA	AERA	OAV	OOB	AB-HR-SH	AVG	PB	SUP	APR	DL	PW
1875	RS NA	1	3	.250	7	4	4-1	0	42	40	40	0		1	7	1.29	170	.212	.216	69	.261	1*	64	1		0.2

MORGAN, CY Harry Richard B11.10.1878 Pomeroy OH D6.28.1962 Wheeling WV BR/TR/6-0/175 d9.18

YEAR	TM LG	W	L	PCT	G	GS	CG-SHO	SV-BS	IP	H	R	HR	HB	BB-IB	SO	ERA	AERA	OAV	OOB	AB-HR-SH	AVG	PB	SUP	APR	DL	PW
1903	StL A	0	2	.000	2	1	1	0	13	12	12	0	2	6	6	4.15	70	.245	.351	4	.250	0	49	-3		-0.4
1904	StL A	0	2	.000	8	3	2	0	51	51	23	3	2	10	24	3.71	67	.262	.304	18	.056	-2	57	-5		-0.4
1905	StL A	2	5	.286	13	8	5-1	0	77.1	82	59	1	9	37	44	3.61	71	.273	.370	31	.258	2	153	-15		-1.0
1907	StL A	2	5	.286	10	6	4	0	55	77	43	3	2	17	14	6.05	42	.333	.384	20	.100	-1	103	-19		-2.2
	Bos A	6	6	.500	16	13	9-2	0	114.1	77	35	1	3	34	50	1.97	131	.193	.262	35-0-1	.057	-4	61	8		0.4
	Year	8	11	.421	26	19	13-2	0	169.1	154	78	4	5	51	64	3.30	78	.245	.307	55-0-1	.073	-5	74	-10		-1.8
1908	Bos A	14	13	.519	30	26	17-2	1	205	166	78	7	10	90	99	2.46	100	.226	.319	63-0-5	.127	-3	94	1		-0.1
1909	Bos A	2	6	.250	12	10	5	1	64.2	52	19	0	6	31	30	2.37	106	.240	.350	20-0-1	.050	-2	68	3		0.3
	Phi A	16	11	.593	28	26	21-5	0	228.2	152	56	3	16	71	81	1.65	146	.191	.271	74-0-8	.108	-3	103	20		2.1
	Year	18	17	.514	40	36	26-5	1	293.1	204	75	3	22	102	111	1.81	134	**.202**	.289	94-0-9	.096	-4	93	24		2.4
1910	Phi A	18	12	.600	36	34	23-3	1	290.2	214	92	0	18	117	134	1.55	153	.216	.310	99-0-12	.141	-4	125	24		2.1
1911	Phi A	15	7	.682	38	30	15-2	1	249.2	217	109	0	21	113	136	2.70	117	.243	.341	94-0-2	.160	-5	130	9		0.3
1912	Phi A	3	8	.273	16	14	5	0	93.2	75	56	0	5	51	47	3.75	82	.226	.338	30-0-2	.033	-3	84	-9		-1.1
1913	Cin N	0	1	.000	1	1	0	0	2.1	5	4	0	1	1	2	15.43	21	.500	.583	1	.000	-0	23	-3		-0.4
Total	10	78	78	.500	210	172	107-15	3	1445.1	1180	586	18	95	578	667	2.51	105	.229	.318	489-0-31	.125	-25	105	11		-0.4

MORGAN, MIKE Michael Thomas B10.8.1959 Tulare CA BR/TR/6-2/215(185-226) [OakA78 1/4] d6.11

YEAR	TM LG	W	L	PCT	G	GS	CG-SHO	SV-BS	IP	H	R	HR	HB	BB-IB	SO	ERA	AERA	OAV	OOB	AB-HR-SH	AVG	PB	SUP	APR	DL	PW
1978	Oak A	0	3	.000	3	3	1	0-0	12.1	19	12	1	0	8-0	0	7.30	50	.373	.458	0	—	0	49	-5		-0.9
1979	Oak A	2	10	.167	13	13	2	0-0	77.1	102	57	7	3	50-0	17	5.94	68	.332	.426	0	—	0	60	-16		-2.0
1982	NY A	7	11	.389	30	23	2	0-0	150.1	167	77	15	2	67-5	71	4.37	92	.285	.358	0	—	0	89	-4		-0.4
1983	Tor A	0	3	.000	16	4	0	0-0	45.1	48	26	6	0	21-0	22	5.16	84	.273	.348	0	—	0	73	-3	52	-0.1
1985	Sea A	1	1	.500	2	2	0	0-0	6	11	8	2	0	5-0	2	12.00	35	.393	.485	0	—	0	226	-5	173	-0.8
1986	Sea A	11	17	.393	37	33	9-1	1-0	216.1	243	122	24	4	86-3	116	4.53	94	.286	.353	0	—	0	101	-6		-0.8
1987	Sea A	12	17	.414	34	31	8-2	0-0	207	245	117	25	5	53-3	85	4.65	102	.296	.340	0	—	0	79	-11	92	-1.0
1988	Bal A	1	6	.143	22	10	2	1-0	71.1	70	45	6	1	23-1	29	5.43	73	.255	.315	0	—	0	65	14		1.8
1989	LA N	8	11	.421	40	19	0	0-1	152.2	130	51	6	2	33-8	72	2.53	135	.234	.277	36-0-3	.083	-2	65	14		1.8
1990	LA N	11	15	.423	33	33	6-4	0-0	211	216	100	19	6	60-5	106	3.75	98	.266	.278	71-0-5	.113	-2	97	-1		-0.2
1991	LA N★	14	10	.583	34	33	5-1	1-0	236.1	197	85	12	3	61-10	140	2.78	130	.226	.278	84-0-6	.092	-3	90	21		1.8
1992	Chi N	16	8	.667	34	34	6-1	0-0	240	203	80	14	3	79-10	123	2.55	142	.234	.298	74-0-11	.108	-2	101	26		2.5
1993	Chi N	10	15	.400	32	32	1-1	0-0	207.2	206	100	15	7	74-8	111	4.03	100	.262	.329	66-0-5	.061	-1	101	-22	53	-2.8
1994	Chi N	2	10	.167	15	15	1	0-0	80.2	111	65	12	4	35-2	57	6.69	63	.338	.402	24-0-1	.125	-1	76	5	30	0.6
1995	Chi N	2	1	.667	4	4	0	0-0	24.2	19	8	2	1	9-1	15	2.19	191	.216	.296	7-0-1	.143	-0	88	7	20	0.5
	StL N	5	6	.455	17	17	1	0-0	106.2	114	48	10	5	25-1	46	3.88	110	.283	.329	31-0-3	.032	-2	86	11		1.1
	Year	7	7	.500	21	21	1	0-0	131.1	133	56	12	6	34-2	61	3.56	120	.271	.323	38-0-4	.053	-2	95	-10	47	-1.3
1996	StL N	4	8	.333	18	18	0	0-0	103	118	63	14	0	40-0	55	5.24	81	.291	.294	33-0-9	.061	-3	95	-10	47	0.9
	Cin N	2	3	.400	5	5	0	0-0	27.1	28	9	2	1	7-0	19	2.30	186	.267	.316	7-0-2	.000	-0	101	5		0.9
	Year	6	11	.353	23	23	0	0-0	130.1	146	72	16	1	47-0	74	4.63	92	.289	.346	40-0-11	.050	-3	96	-4		-0.4
1997	Cin N	9	12	.429	31	30	1	0-0	162	165	91	13	8	49-6	103	4.78	90	.266	.337	44-0-9	.091	-2	82	-8	16	-1.1
1998	Min A	4	2	.667	18	17	0	0-0	98	108	41	13	7	24-1	50	3.49	137	.286	.337	2	.500	0	102	14	48	0.8
	†Chi N	0	1	.000	5	5	0	0-0	22.2	30	21	8	1	15-1	10	7.15	62	.323	.422	6-0-1	.667	-2	159	-7		-0.1
1999	Tex A	13	10	.565	34	25	1	0-0	140	184	108	25	7	48-2	61	6.24	83	.323	.380	4	.250	0	107	-18	15	-2.3
2000	Ari N	5	5	.500	60	6	0	5-1	101.2	123	55	10	1	40-5	56	4.87	98	.311	.372	16-0-1	.438	0	62	1		0.3
2001	†Ari N	1	0	1.000	31	1	0	0-1	38	45	20	2	0	17-4	24	4.26	109	.306	.373	0	—	0	159	1	99	0.0
2002	Ari N	1	1	.500	29	0	0	0-1	34	41	22	7	3	9-1	13	5.29	85	.289	.344	0		0		-3	69	-0.2
Total	22	141	186	.431	597	411	46-10	8-5	2772.1	2943	1431	270	73	938-77	1403	4.23	98	.276	.337	497-0-59	.109	-16	92	-21	729	-4.6

MORGAN, TOM Tom Stephen "Plowboy" B5.20.1930 ElMonte CA D1.13.1987 Anaheim CA BR/TR/6-2/195* d4.20 Mil 1952-53 C8

YEAR	TM LG	W	L	PCT	G	GS	CG-SHO	SV-BS	IP	H	R	HR	HB	BB-IB	SO	ERA	AERA	OAV	OOB	AB-HR-SH	AVG	PB	SUP	APR	DL	PW
1951	†NY A	9	3	.750	27	16	4-2	2	124.2	119	56	11	3	36	57	3.68	104	.253	.310	44-1-1	.273	2	101	3		0.6
1952	NY A	5	4	.556	16	12	2-1	2	93.2	86	34	8	4	35	35	3.07	123	.252	.325	33-1-0	.182	1	155	4		0.6
1954	NY A	11	5	.688	32	17	7-4	1	143	149	58	8	5	40	34	3.34	103	.274	.327	49-1-1	.143	0	133	3		0.4
1955	†NY A	7	3	.700	40	1	0	10	72	72	29	3	5	27-4	17	3.25	115	.267	.337	18-0-1	.222	-0		-4		0.9
1956	†NY A	6	7	.462	41	0	0	11	71.1	74	41	2	3	27-4	20	4.16	93	.284	.347	13-0-3	.154	-1		-4		-0.8
1957	KC A	9	7	.563	46	13	5	7	143.2	160	76	7	4	61-9	32	4.64	85	.299	.359	33-0-4	.091	-2	90	-8		-0.9
1958	Det A	2	5	.286	39	1	0	4	62.2	70	28	7	1	18-3	40	3.16	128	.286	.299	10-0-1	.200	0	111	4		0.4
1959	Det A	1	4	.200	46	1	0	9	92.2	94	48	11	6	18-3	39	3.98	102	.265	.308	23-2-0	.391	4	87	0		0.4
1960	Det A	3	2	.600	22	0	0	0	29	33	17	6	1	10-1	12	4.66	85	.295	.347	0-0-1	—	0		-2		-0.3
	Was A	1	3	.250	14	0	0	1	24	36	15	6	1	5-3	11	3.75	104	.343	.375	5	.000	4		-1		-0.2
	Year	4	5	.444	36	0	0	1	53	69	32	12	2	15-4	23	4.25	92	.318	.360	5-0-1	.000	4		-3		-0.5
1961	LA A	8	2	.800	59	0	0	10	91.2	74	31	7	5	17-3	39	2.36	191	.224	.269	12	.000	-0		18		2.2
1962	LA A	5	2	.714	48	0	0	8	58.2	53	23	6	1	19-6	29	2.91	132	.247	.304	6-0-2	.000	-0		6		0.7
1963	LA A	0	0	—	13	0	0	1	16.1	20	11	1	3	6-1	7	5.51	62	.313	.392	1	.000	-0		-4		-0.2
Total	17	67	44	.588	443	61	18-7	64	1023.1	1040	467	95	40	300-34	364	3.61	106	.270	.326	247-5-14	.186	3	112	24		3.8

MORIARITY, GENE Eugene John B7.5.1855 Holyoke MA BL/TL/5-8/130 d6.18 ▲

YEAR	TM LG	W	L	PCT	G	GS	CG-SHO	SV-BS	IP	H	R	HR	HB	BB-IB	SO	ERA	AERA	OAV	OOB	AB-HR-SH	AVG	PB	SUP	APR	DL	PW
1884	Ind AA	0	2	.000	2	2	2	0	13.2	16	13	0	1	7	4	5.27	62	.267	.353	37	.216	0*	46	-3		-0.3
1885	Det N	0	0	—	1	0	0	0	2	3	3	0	1	1	1	9.00	32	.300	.364	39	.026	-0*		-1		-0.1
Total	2	0	2	.000	3	2	2	0	15.2	19	16	0	1	8	5	5.74	56	.271	.354	76	.118	-0	46	-4		-0.4

MORLAN, JOHN John Glen B11.22.1947 Columbus OH BR/TR/6-0/185* d7.20 Col Ohio U.

YEAR	TM LG	W	L	PCT	G	GS	CG-SHO	SV-BS	IP	H	R	HR	HB	BB-IB	SO	ERA	AERA	OAV	OOB	AB-HR-SH	AVG	PB	SUP	APR	DL	PW
1973	Pit N	2	2	.500	10	7	1	0-0	41	42	18	4	0	23-3	23	3.95	89	.276	.369	11	.182	1	107	-1		0.0
1974	Pit N	0	3	.000	39	0	0	0-0	65	54	37	2	3	48-5	38	4.29	81	.227	.357	7	.000	-1		-7		-0.5
Total	2	2	5	.286	49	7	1	0-0	106	96	55	6	3	71-8	61	4.16	84	.246	.362	18	.111	0	107	-8		-0.5

MORMAN, ALVIN Alvin B1.6.1969 Rockingham NC BL/TL/6-3/210* d4.2 Col Wingate

YEAR	TM LG	W	L	PCT	G	GS	CG-SHO	SV-BS	IP	H	R	HR	HB	BB-IB	SO	ERA	AERA	OAV	OOB	AB-HR-SH	AVG	PB	SUP	APR	DL	PW
1996	Hou N	4	1	.800	53	0	0	0-2	42	43	24	8	0	24-6	31	4.93	79	.261	.353	0	—	0		-4		-0.4
1997	†Cle A	0	0	—	34	0	0	2-0	18.1	19	13	2	1	14-3	13	5.89	80	.268	.395	1	.000	-0		-2	34	-0.1
1998	Cle A	0	1	.000	31	0	0	0-1	22	25	13	1	0	11-1	16	5.32	90	.298	.375	0	—	0		-1	15	0.0
	SF N	0	1	.000	9	0	0	0-1	7	8	4	4	0	3-0	7	5.14	78	.276	.344	0	—	0		-1	25	-0.1
1999	KC A	2	4	.333	49	0	0	3-6	53.1	66	27	6	4	23-0	31	4.05	126	.307	.378	0	—	0		6	74	0.0
Total	4	6	7	.462	176	0	0	3-6	142.2	161	81	21	5	75-10	98	4.79	95	.285	.371	1	.000	-0		-2	74	0.0

MOROGIELLO, DAN Daniel Joseph B3.26.1955 Brooklyn NY BL/TL/6-1/200 [AtlN76 3/51] d5.20 Col Seton Hall

YEAR	TM LG	W	L	PCT	G	GS	CG-SHO	SV-BS	IP	H	R	HR	HB	BB-IB	SO	ERA	AERA	OAV	OOB	AB-HR-SH	AVG	PB	SUP	APR	DL	PW
1983	Bal A	0	1	.000	22	0	0	1-0	37.2	39	10	1	1	10-3	15	2.39	168	.265	.314	0		0		7		0.3

MORONEY, JIM James Francis B12.4.1883 Boston MA D2.26.1929 Philadelphia PA BL/TL/6-1/175 d4.24

YEAR	TM LG	W	L	PCT	G	GS	CG-SHO	SV-BS	IP	H	R	HR	HB	BB-IB	SO	ERA	AERA	OAV	OOB	AB-HR-SH	AVG	PB	SUP	APR	DL	PW
1906	Bos N	0	3	.000	3	3	3	0	27	28	20	1	6	12	11	5.33	50	.259	.365	10	.100	-1	72	-7		-0.7
1910	Phi N	1	2	.333	12	2	1	0	42	43	20	1	4	11	13	2.14	146	.295	.360	10	.000	-1	48	2		0.1
1912	Chi N	1	1	.500	10	3	1	1	23.2	25	13	0	4	17	5	4.56	73	.316	.460	6	.500	1	95	-2		-0.1
Total	3	2	6	.250	25	8	5	2	92.2	96	53	2	14	40	29	3.69	83	.288	.388	26	.154	-1	75	-7		-0.8

MORRELL, BILL Willard Blackmer B4.9.1893 Hyde Park MA D8.5.1975 Birmingham AL BR/TR/6-0/172 d4.20 Col Tufts

YEAR	TM LG	W	L	PCT	G	GS	CG-SHO	SV-BS	IP	H	R	HR	HB	BB-IB	SO	ERA	AERA	OAV	OOB	AB-HR-SH	AVG	PB	SUP	APR	DL	PW
1926	Was A	3	3	.500	26	6	1	0	69.2	83	48	5	2	29	16	5.30	73	.311	.383	17	.235	1	109	-12		-0.9
1930	NY N	0	0	—	2	0	0	0	8	6	1	0	0	1	3	1.13	421	.214	.241	2	.000	-0		3		0.1
1931	NY N	5	3	.625	20	7	2	0	66	83	34	4	0	27	16	4.36	85	.306	.369	18-0-2	.111	-0	116	-3		-0.4
Total	3	8	6	.571	48	9	3	0	143.2	172	83	9	2	57	35	4.64	83	.304	.367	37-0-2	.162	-0	111	-12		-1.2

MORRILL, JOHN John Francis "Honest John" B2.19.1855 Boston MA D4.2.1932 Brookline MA BR/TR/5-10.5/155 d4.24.1876 M8 ▲

YEAR	TM LG	W	L	PCT	G	GS	CG-SHO	SV-BS	IP	H	R	HR	HB	BB-IB	SO	ERA	AERA	OAV	OOB	AB-HR-SH	AVG	PB	SUP	APR	DL	PW
1880	Bos N	0	0	—	3	0	0		10.2	9	3	0		1	0	0.84	269	.273	.294	342-2	.237	0*		1		0.1
1881	Bos N	0	1	.000	3	0	0		5.2	9	8	0		1	0	6.35	42	.333	.357	311-1	.289	1*		-3		-0.4
1882	Bos N	0	0	—	1	0	0		3	2	1	0			0	2.00	—	.375	.375	349-2	.289	0*		1		0.0
1883	Bos N	1	0	1.000	2	1	1		13	12	8	0		4	5	2.77	112	.268	.317	404-6	.319	1*	86	0		0.0

YEAR	TM LG	W	L	PCT	G	GS	CG-SHO	SV-BS	IP	H	R	HR	HB	BB-IB	SO	ERA	AERA	OAV	OOB	AB-HR-SH	AVG	PB	SUP	APR	DL	PW
1884	Bos N	0	1	.000	7	1	1	2	23	34	23	0		6	13	7.43	39	.315	.351	438-3	.260	1*	37	-9		-0.4
1886	Bos N	0	0	—	1	0	0	0	4	5	1	0		0	2	0.00		.313	.313	430-7	.247	0*		1		0.1
1889	Was N	0	0	—	1	0	0	0	0.1	0	0	0	0	0-0	0	0.00	—	.000	.000	146-2	.185	0*		0		0.0
Total	7	1	2	.333	18	2	2	3	58.2	75	46	0	0	12	22	4.30	66	.301	.333	2420-23	.268	4	66	-9		-0.6

MORRIS, DANNY Danny Walker B6.11.1946 Greenville KY BR/TR/6-1/200* d9.10

YEAR	TM LG	W	L	PCT	G	GS	CG-SHO	SV-BS	IP	H	R	HR	HB	BB-IB	SO	ERA	AERA	OAV	OOB	AB-HR-SH	AVG	PB	SUP	APR	DL	PW
1968	Min A	0	1	.000	3	2	0	0	10.2	11	5	0	0	4-0	6	1.69	183	.262	.326	3	.000		-0	113	1		0.0
1969	Min A	0	1	.000	3	1	0	0-0	5.1	5	4	1	0	4-1	1	5.06	72	.238	.360	0			0	24	-1		-0.2
Total	2	0	2	.000	6	3	0	0-0	16	16	9	1	0	8-1	7	2.81	116	.254	.338	3	.000		-0	80	0		-0.2

MORRIS, ED Edward "Cannonball" B9.29.1862 Brooklyn NY D4.12.1937 Pittsburgh PA BB/TL/5-7/165 d5.1 Col St. Marys (CA)

YEAR	TM LG	W	L	PCT	G	GS	CG-SHO	SV-BS	IP	H	R	HR	HB	BB-IB	SO	ERA	AERA	OAV	OOB	AB-HR-SH	AVG	PB	SUP	APR	DL	PW
1884	Col AA	34	13	.723	52	52	47-3	0	429.2	335	159	3	13	51	302	2.18	139	.204	.234	199	.186	2*	105	46		4.5
1885	Pit AA	39	24	.619	63	63	63-7	0	581	459	245	5	14	101	298	2.35	137	.208	.247	237	.186	-5*	88	58		4.7
1886	Pit AA	41	20	.672	64	63	63-12	1	555.1	455	244	5	7	118	326	2.45	138	.214	.258	227-1	.167	-7	95	62		4.8
1887	Pit N	14	22	.389	38	38	37-1	0	317.2	375	225	4	9	71	91	4.31	89	.286	.326	126	.198	-4	78	-19		-2.0
1888	Pit N	29	23	.558	55	55	54-5	0	480	470	216	7	8	74	135	2.31	115	.245	.276	189	.101	-11	85	13		0.1
1889	Pit N	6	13	.316	21	21	18	0	170	196	107	4	6	48	40	4.13	91	.280	.332	72	.097	-5	78	-6		-1.1
1890	Pit P	8	7	.533	18	15	15-1	0	144.1	178	116	5	3	35	25	4.86	80	.290	.332	63	.143	-4	93	-11		-1.2
Total	7	171	122	.584	311	307	297-29		2678	2468	1312	42	59	498	1217	2.82	116	.235	.273	1113-1	.161	-34	90	143		9.8

MORRIS, JIM James Samuel B1.19.1964 Brownwood TX BL/TL/6-3/215* [MilA83*S1/4] d9.18 Col Ranger (TX) JC

YEAR	TM LG	W	L	PCT	G	GS	CG-SHO	SV-BS	IP	H	R	HR	HB	BB-IB	SO	ERA	AERA	OAV	OOB	AB-HR-SH	AVG	PB	SUP	APR	DL	PW
1999	TB A	0	0	—	5	0	0	0-0	4.2	3	3	1	1	2-0	5	5.79	86	.167	.286	0	—		0		0		0.0
2000	TB A	0	0	—	16	0	0	0-0	10.1	10	9	1	0	7-1	10	4.35	112	.250	.362	0	—		0		-1		-0.1
Total	2	0	0	—	21	0	0	0-0	15	13	12	2	1	9-1	13	4.80	103	.224	.338	0	—		0		-1		-0.1

MORRIS, JACK John Scott B5.16.1955 St.Paul MN BR/TR/6-3/200(190-210) [DetA76 5/98] d7.26 Col Brigham Young

YEAR	TM LG	W	L	PCT	G	GS	CG-SHO	SV-BS	IP	H	R	HR	HB	BB-IB	SO	ERA	AERA	OAV	OOB	AB-HR-SH	AVG	PB	SUP	APR	DL	PW
1977	Det A	1	1	.500	7	6	1	0-0	45.2	38	20	4	0	23-0	28	3.74	115	.235	.328	0	—		0	73	3		0.2
1978	Det A	3	5	.375	28	7	0	0-0	106	107	57	6	4	49-5	48	4.33	90	.268	.345	0	—		0	115	-5		-0.4
1979	Det A	17	7	.708	27	27	9-1	0-0	197.2	179	76	19	4	59-4	113	3.28	133	.244	.301	0	—		0*	106	24		2.7
1980	Det A	16	15	.516	36	36	11-2	0-0	250	252	125	20	4	87-5	112	4.18	99	.262	.322	0	—		0*	97	-1		0.0
1981	Det A★	14	7	.667	25	25	15-1	0-0	198	153	69	14	2	78-11	97	3.05	124	.218	.295	0	—		0	126	17		1.7
1982	Det A	17	16	.515	37	37	17-3	0-0	266.1	247	131	37	0	96-7	135	4.06	101	.247	.311	0	—		0	91	2		0.2
1983	Det A	20	13	.606	37	37	20-1	0-0	293.2	257	117	30	3	83-5	232	3.34	118	.233	.287	0	—		0*	108	22		2.2
1984	†Det A★	19	11	.633	35	35	9-1	0-0	240.1	221	108	20	2	87-7	148	3.60	110	.241	.307	0	—		0	114	10		1.2
1985	Det A★	16	11	.593	35	35	13-4	0-0	257	212	102	21	5	110-7	191	3.33	123	.225	.307	0	—		0*	103	25		2.3
1986	Det A★	21	8	.724	35	35	15-6	0-0	267	229	105	40	0	82-7	223	3.27	127	.229	.287	0	—		0*	118	28		2.8
1987	†Det A★	18	11	.621	34	34	13	0-0	266	227	111	39	1	93-7	208	3.38	126	.228	.293	1	.000		-0*	111	28		2.6
1988	Det A	15	13	.536	34	34	10-2	0-0	235	225	115	20	4	83-7	168	3.94	97	.251	.317	0	—		0	103	-3		-0.4
1989	Det A	6	14	.300	24	24	10	0-0	170.1	189	102	23	2	59-3	115	4.86	79	.283	.339	0	—		0	83	-19	60	-1.9
1990	Det A	15	18	.455	36	36	11-3	0-0	249.2	231	144	26	6	97-13	162	4.51	88	.242	.313	0	—		0	110	-18		-2.2
1991	†Min A★	18	12	.600	35	35	10-2	0-0	246.2	226	107	18	5	92-5	163	3.43	125	.245	.315	0	—		0	103	21		2.3
1992	†Tor A	21	6	.778	34	34	6-1	0-0	240.2	222	114	18	10	80-2	132	4.04	102	.246	.312	0	—		0	121	3		0.3
1993	Tor A	7	12	.368	27	27	4-1	0-0	152.2	189	116	18	3	65-2	103	6.19	71	.302	.368	0	—		0	89	-31	19	-3.2
1994	Cle A	10	6	.625	23	23	1	0-0	141.1	163	96	14	4	67-2	100	5.60	85	.292	.369	0	—		0	126	-12		-1.1
Total	18	254	186	.577	549	527	175-28	0-0	3824	3567	1815	389	58	1390-99	2478	3.90	105	.247	.313	1	.000		-0	107	94	79	9.3

MORRIS, JOHN John Wallace B8.23.1941 Lewes DE BR/TL/6-1/198* d7.19

YEAR	TM LG	W	L	PCT	G	GS	CG-SHO	SV-BS	IP	H	R	HR	HB	BB-IB	SO	ERA	AERA	OAV	OOB	AB-HR-SH	AVG	PB	SUP	APR	DL	PW
1966	Phi N	1	1	.500	13	0	0		13.2	15	8	2	1	3-1	8	5.27	68	.278	.328	0	—		0		-2		-0.3
1968	Bal A	2	0	1.000	19	0	0		31.2	19	11	4	0	17-2	22	2.56	114	.173	.303	6	.000		-1		1		0.0
1969	Sea A	0	0	—	6	0	0	0-0	12.2	16	10	2	0	8-1	6	6.39	57	.308	.400	1	1.000		1		-4		-0.1
1970	Mil A	4	3	.571	20	9	2	0-0	73.1	70	33	4	2	22-3	40	3.93	96	.253	.312	17-0-1	.176		0	89	95		-0.1
1971	Mil A	1	2	.500	43	1	0	1-0	67.2	69	34	4	1	27-9	42	3.72	94	.270	.334	5-0-1	.200		0	128	-3	36	-0.1
1972	SF N	0	0	—	7	0	0		6.1	9	6	2	0	2-0	5	4.26	82	.310	.355	0	—		0		-2		-0.1
1973	SF N	1	0	1.000	7	0	0	0-1	6.1	12	8	0	0	3-0	3	8.53	45	.429	.469	1	.000		-0		-4	59	-0.5
1974	SF N	1	1	.500	17	0	0	1-0	20.2	17	7	1	0	4-1	9	3.05	125	.215	.253	1	1.000		0		2		0.2
Total	8	11	7	.611	132	10	2	2-1	232.1	227	117	19	8	86-17	137	3.95	90	.256	.325	31-0-2	.194		1	97	-12	190	-0.4

MORRIS, BUGS Joseph Harley (aka Joseph Harley Bennett in 1918) B4.19.1892 Weir City KS D11.21.1957 Noel MO BR/TR/5-9.5/163 d7.20

YEAR	TM LG	W	L	PCT	G	GS	CG-SHO	SV-BS	IP	H	R	HR	HB	BB-IB	SO	ERA	AERA	OAV	OOB	AB-HR-SH	AVG	PB	SUP	APR	DL	PW
1918	StL A	0	2	.000	4	2	0	0	10.1	12	7	1	0	7	0	3.48	79	.308	.413	4	.250		0	96	-2		-0.3
1921	Chi A	0	3	.000	3	2	1	0	17.2	19	14	1	0	16	2	6.11	69	.297	.438	6	.333		0	10	-4		-0.5
	StL A	0	0	—	3	1	0	0	5.2	11	10	1	2	6	3	14.29	31	.407	.543	1	1.000		0	93	-6		-0.2
	Year	0	3	.000	6	3	1	0	23.1	30	24	2	2	22	5	8.10	53	.330	.470	7	.429		1	39	-9		-0.7
Total	2	0	5	.000	10	5	1	0	33.2	42	31	3	2	29	5	6.68	57	.323	.453	11	.364		1	56	-12		-1.0

MORRIS, MATT Matthew Christian B8.9.1974 Middletown NY BR/TR/6-5/210* [StLN95 1/12] d4.4 Col Seton Hall [DL 1999 StL N 182]

YEAR	TM LG	W	L	PCT	G	GS	CG-SHO	SV-BS	IP	H	R	HR	HB	BB-IB	SO	ERA	AERA	OAV	OOB	AB-HR-SH	AVG	PB	SUP	APR	DL	PW
1997	StL N	12	9	.571	33	33	3	0-0	217	208	88	12	7	69-2	149	3.19	131	.258	.319	73-0-2	.205	3*	95	24		2.3
1998	StL N	7	5	.583	17	17	2-1	0-0	113.2	101	37	8	3	42-6	79	2.53	166	.243	.316	29-0-7	.069	-0	103	21	100	2.0
2000	†StL N	3	3	.500	31	0	0	4-3	53	53	22	3	2	17-1	34	3.57	130	.261	.323	3-0-3	.333	0*		7	54	0.7
2001	†StL N★	22	8	.733	34	34	2-1	0-0	216.1	218	86	13	13	54-3	185	3.16	137	.265	.318	72-0-11	.139	-1	122	27		3.3
2002	†StL N☆	17	9	.654	32	32	1-1	0-0	210.1	210	86	16	6	64-3	171	3.42	118	.261	.317	71-0-5	.169	1	112	15	17	1.7
2003	StL N	11	8	.579	27	27	5-3	0-0	172.1	164	76	20	4	39-1	120	3.76	110	.252	.297	52-1-12	.192	3	125	7	32	0.9
2004	†StL N	15	10	.600	32	32	3-2	0-0	202	205	116	35	6	56-3	131	4.72	90	.266	.319	62-0-8	.161	1	128	-11		-1.1
2005	†StL N	14	10	.583	31	31	2	0-0	192.2	209	101	22	8	37-3	117	4.11	102	.276	.314	57-0-8	.088	-2	123	1	16	-0.1
Total	8	101	62	.620	237	206	18-8	4-3	1377.1	1368	612	129	49	378-22	986	3.61	117	.261	.315	419-1-56	.155	4	116	91	401	9.7

MORRIS, ED Walter Edward "Big Ed" B12.7.1899 Foshee AL D3.3.1932 Century FL BR/TR/6-2/185 d8.5

YEAR	TM LG	W	L	PCT	G	GS	CG-SHO	SV-BS	IP	H	R	HR	HB	BB-IB	SO	ERA	AERA	OAV	OOB	AB-HR-SH	AVG	PB	SUP	APR	DL	PW
1922	Chi N	0	0	—	5	0	0	0	12	22	17	1	0	6	5	8.25	51	.386	.444	4	.250		-0		-7		-0.3
1928	Bos A	19	15	.559	47	29	20	5	257.2	255	118	7	5	80	104	3.53	121	.264	.323	91-0-2	.154	-4	95	16		1.5
1929	Bos A	14	14	.500	33	26	17-2	1	208.1	227	118	7	2	95	73	4.45	96	.282	.360	69-1-7	.232	2	81	-2		-0.1
1930	Bos A	4	9	.308	18	9	3	0	65.1	67	42	1	0	38	28	4.13	112	.260	.355	19-0-1	.316	2	35	0		0.2
1931	Bos A	5	7	.417	37	14	3	0	130.2	131	80	4	7	74	46	4.75	91	.260	.361	38-0-2	.158	-2	83	-7		-0.7
Total	5	42	45	.483	140	78	43-2	6	674	702	375	20	12	293	256	4.19	101	.271	.348	221-1-12	.195	-1	81	0		0.6

MORRISETTE, BILL William Lee B11.21.1894 Portsmouth VA D3.25.1966 Virginia Beach VA BR/TR/6-0/176 d9.19

YEAR	TM LG	W	L	PCT	G	GS	CG-SHO	SV-BS	IP	H	R	HR	HB	BB-IB	SO	ERA	AERA	OAV	OOB	AB-HR-SH	AVG	PB	SUP	APR	DL	PW
1915	Phi A	2	0	1.000	4	1	1	0	20	15	6	0	0	5	11	1.35	217	.195	.244	7	.286		0	174	3		0.3
1916	Phi A	0	0	—	1	0	0	0	4	6	3	0	0	5	2	6.75	42	.429	.579	1	.000		0		-1		0.0
1920	Det A	1	1	.500	8	3	1	0	27	25	21	0	3	19	15	4.33	86	.245	.379	8	.000		-1	92	-3		-0.4
Total	3	3	1	.750	13	4	2	0	51	46	30	0	3	29	28	3.35	100	.238	.347	16	.125		-1	115	-1		-0.1

MORRISON, JOHNNY John Dewey "Jughandle Johnny" B10.22.1895 Pellville KY D3.20.1966 Louisville KY BR/TR/5-11/188 d9.28 b-Phil

YEAR	TM LG	W	L	PCT	G	GS	CG-SHO	SV-BS	IP	H	R	HR	HB	BB-IB	SO	ERA	AERA	OAV	OOB	AB-HR-SH	AVG	PB	SUP	APR	DL	PW
1920	Pit N	1	0	1.000	2	1	1-1	0	7	4	0	0	1	9	3	0.00	—	.167	.200	3	.000		-0	147	2		0.3
1921	Pit N	9	7	.563	21	17	11-3	0	144	131	49	3	1	33	52	2.88	133	.258	.305	42-0-4	.119		-2	76	18		1.7
1922	Pit N	17	11	.607	45	33	20-5	1	286.1	315	130	10	6	87	104	3.43	119	.286	.341	101-0-10	.198	-2	113	21		1.5
1923	Pit N	25	13	.658	42	37	27-2	2	301.2	287	136	6	5	110	114	3.49	115	.253	.321	115-0-6	.183	-3	103	18		1.6
1924	Pit N	11	16	.407	41	25	10	2	237.2	213	114	7	4	73	85	3.75	102	.245	.307	77-0-11	.169	-2	80	3		0.0
1925	†Pit N	17	14	.548	44	26	10	4	211	245	113	12	7	60	60	3.88	115	.291	.343	73-0-6	.178	-2	104	12		1.2
1926	Pit N	6	8	.429	26	13	6-2	2	122.1	119	62	2	4	44	39	3.38	116	.267	.335	39	.077	-4	67	9		0.5
1927	Pit N	3	2	.600	21	2	1	3	53.2	63	27	2	0	21	21	4.19	98	.304	.368	13-0-1	.154	-0	166	0		0.1
1929	Bro N	13	7	.650	39	10	4	8	136.2	150	87	11	3	61	57	4.48	103	.279	.355	43-0-1	.163	-2	104	0		-0.4
1930	Bro N	1	2	.333	16	0	0	1	34.2	47	29	4	0	16	11	5.45	90	.346	.414	5	.000		0		-3		-0.3
Total	10	103	80	.563	297	164	90-13	23	1535	1574	737	57	28	506	546	3.65	113	.271	.332	511-0-39	.164	-18	97	79		6.0

MORRISON, MIKE Michael B2.6.1867 Erie PA D6.16.1955 Erie PA BR/TR/5-8.5/156 d4.19

YEAR	TM LG	W	L	PCT	G	GS	CG-SHO	SV-BS	IP	H	R	HR	HB	BB-IB	SO	ERA	AERA	OAV	OOB	AB-HR-SH	AVG	PB	SUP	APR	DL	PW
1887	Cle AA	12	25	.324	40	40	35	0	316.2	385	341	13	22	205	158	4.92	88	.294	.398	141	.191	-4*	93	-30		-2.4
1888	Cle AA	1	3	.250	4	4	4	0	35	40	35	3	1	19	14	5.40	57	.278	.366	17	.235	-0	89	-8		-0.8
1890	Syr AA	6	9	.400	17	14	13-1	0	127	131	112	4	13	81	69	5.88	60	.258	.374	120-1	.242	3*	97	-35		-2.7
	Bal AA	1	3	.333	4	4	3	0	26	15	24	0	2	20	13	3.81	107	.163	.325	9	.111	-1	104	-1		-0.1

YEAR	TM LG	W	L	PCT	G	GS	CG-SHO	SV-BS	IP	H	R	HR	HB	BB-IB	SO	ERA	AERA	OAV	OOB	AB-HR-SH	AVG	PB	SUP	APR	DL	PW
Year		7	11	.389	21	18	16-1	0	153	146	132	4	15	101	82	5.53	66	.244	.366	129-1	.233	3	99	-36		-2.8
Total	3	20	39	.339	65	62	55-1	0	504.2	571	508	20	38	325	254	5.14	78	.278	.387	287-1	.213	-2	95	-74		-6.0

MORRISON, PHIL Philip Melvin B10.18.1894 Rockport IN D1.18.1955 Lexington KY BB/TR/6-2/190 d9.30 b-Johnny

YEAR	TM LG	W	L	PCT	G	GS	CG-SHO	SV-BS	IP	H	R	HR	HB	BB-IB	SO	ERA	AERA	OAV	OOB	AB-HR-SH	AVG	PB	SUP	APR	DL	PW
1921	Pit N	0	0	—	1	0	0	0	0.2	1	0	0	0	0	0	0.00	—	.333	.333	0	—	0	0			0.0

MORRISON, HANK Stephen Henry B5.22.1866 Olneyville RI D9.30.1927 Attleboro MA BR/TR/5-10/180 d5.28

1887	Ind N	3	4	.429	7	7	5	0	57	79	73	2	1	27	13	7.58	55	.307	.375	26	.115	-2	96	-21		-2.0

MORRISON, GUY Walter Guy B8.29.1895 Hinton WV D8.14.1934 Grand Rapids MI BR/TR/5-11/185 d8.31

1927	Bos N	1	2	.333	11	3	1	0	34.1	40	22	1	0	15	6	4.46	83	.296	.367	8-1-0	.125	1	138	-4		-0.2
1928	Bos N	0	0	—	1	0	0	0	3	4	4	1	0	3	0	12.00	33	.308	.438	0	—	0		-2		-0.1
Total	2	1	2	.333	12	3	1	0	37.1	44	26	2	0	18	6	5.06	74	.297	.373	8-1-0	.125	1	138	-6		-0.3

MORRISSEY, FRANK Michael Joseph "Deacon" B5.5.1876 Baltimore MD D2.22.1939 Baltimore MD TR/5-4/140 d7.13

1901	Bos A	0	0	—	1	0	0	0	4.1	5	1	0	2	2	1	2.08	170	.278	.409	3	.000	-1		1		0.0
1902	Chi N	1	3	.250	5	5	5	0	40	40	16	0	2	8	13	2.25	120	.260	.305	22	.091	-1*	65	2		0.1
Total	2	1	3	.250	6	5	5	0	44.1	45	17	0	4	10	14	2.23	125	.262	.317	25	.080	-1	65	3		0.1

MORTON, CARL Carl Wendle B1.18.1944 Kansas City MO D4.12.1983 Tulsa OK BR/TR/6-0/200(180-200) d4.11 Col Oklahoma

1969	Mon N	0	3	.000	8	5	0	0-0	29.1	29	15	2	2	18-3	16	4.60	80	.264	.368	7	.000	-0	48	-2		-0.2
1970	Mon N	18	11	.621	43	37	10-4	0-1	284.2	281	123	27	4	125-17	154	3.60	115	.262	.339	93-2-11	.161	2	100	19		2.0
1971	Mon N	10	18	.357	36	35	9	1-0	213.2	252	129	22	4	83-13	84	4.80	74	.295	.358	77-2-2	.182	2	94	-30		-3.3
1972	Mon N	7	13	.350	27	27	3-1	0-0	172	170	84	16	3	53-6	51	3.92	91	.258	.314	52-0-4	.135	1*	66	-8		-0.7
1973	Atl N	15	10	.600	38	37	10-4	0-0	256.1	254	114	18	4	70-7	112	3.41	116	.259	.309	94-3-2	.181	3*	117	13		1.6
1974	Atl N	16	12	.571	38	38	7-1	0-0	274.2	293	110	10	2	89-12	113	3.15	121	.277	.331	89-0-12	.112	-4	99	18		1.3
1975	Atl N	17	16	.515	39	39	11-2	0-0	277.2	302	122	19	3	82-3	78	3.50	108	.278	.328	94-0-5	.160	-0*	93	-8		-0.6
1976	Atl N	4	9	.308	26	24	1-1	0-0	140.1	172	79	7	4	45-4	42	4.17	91	.306	.334	45-0-5	.178	3	93	13		1.3
Total	8	87	92	.486	255	242	51-13	1-1	1648.2	1753	776	120	27	565-65	650	3.73	103	.275	.334	551-7-41	.156	3	93	13		1.3

MORTON, CHARLIE Charles Hazen B10.12.1854 Kingsville OH D12.9.1921 Massillon OH BR/TR/?/150 d5.2.1882 M3/U1 ▲

1884	Tol AA	0	1	.000	1	1	0	0	23.1	18	14	0	1	5	7	3.09	111	.209	.261	111	.162	-0*	35	1		0.0

MORTON, GUY Guy Sr. "The Alabama Blossom" B6.1.1893 Vernon AL D10.18.1934 Sheffield AL BR/TR/6-1/175 d6.20 Mil 1918 s-Guy

1914	Cle A	1	13	.071	25	13	5		128	116	62	1	3	55	80	3.02	95	.257	.341	35-0-2	.029	-4	56	-2		-0.7
1915	Cle A	16	15	.516	34	27	15-6	1	240	189	75	5	2	60	134	2.14	143	.216	.268	82-0-3	.146	-4	74	25		2.7
1916	Cle A	12	6	.667	27	18	9	0	149.2	139	63	1	3	42	88	2.89	104	.246	.302	57-0-2	.211	-1	116	2		0.1
1917	Cle A	10	10	.500	35	18	6-1	0	161	158	74	3	2	59	62	2.74	103	.266	.335	47-0-3	.085	-4	86	-1		-0.7
1918	Cle A	14	8	.636	30	28	13-1	0	214.2	189	87	3	0	77	123	2.64	114	.240	.310	56-0-1	.156	-2	101	6		0.5
1919	Cle A	9	9	.500	26	20	9-3	0	147.1	128	54	3	0	47	64	2.81	119	.233	.293	46-0-1	.161	-2	98	7		0.5
1920	Cle A	8	6	.571	29	17	6-1	1	137	140	80	2	1	57	72	4.47	85	.270	.344	46-0-1	.217	-1	93	-9		-1.0
1921	Cle A	8	3	.727	30	7	3-2	0	107.2	98	45	1	2	32	45	2.76	155	.244	.303	35-0-3	.171	-2	53	16		1.1
1922	Cle A	14	6	.609	38	23	13-3	0	202.2	218	117	7	4	85	102	4.00	100	.277	.351	68-0-6	.191	-2	112	-6		-0.6
1923	Cle A	6	6	.500	33	14	3-2	1	129.1	133	67	3	2	56	54	4.24	93	.276	.354	44-0-1	.159	-2	115	0		-0.3
1924	Cle A	0	1	.000	10	0	0	0	12.1	12	12	0	0	13	6	6.57	65	.250	.410	1	.000	-0		-3		-0.3
Total	11	98	86	.533	317	185	82-19		1629.2	1520	747	26	22	583	830	3.13	108	.251	.319	548-0-22	.157	-24	93	35		1.3

MORTON, KEVIN Kevin Joseph B8.3.1968 Norwalk CT BR/TL/6-2/185 [BosA89 1/29] d7.5 Col Seton Hall

1991	Bos A	6	5	.545	16	15	1	0-0	86.1	93	49	9	1	40-2	45	4.59	94	.284	.356	0	—	0	127	-2		-0.2

MORTON, SPARROW William P. TL d7.15

1884	Phi N	0	2	.000	2	2	2	0	17	16	14	0	0	11	5	5.29	56	.222	.325	8	.375	-1	53	-5		-0.3

MOSELEY, EARL Earl Victor "Vic" B9.7.1884 Middleburg OH D7.1.1963 Alliance OH BR/TR/5-9.5/168 d6.17

1913	Bos A	8	5	.615	24	15	7-3	0	120.2	105	56	1	0	49	62	3.13	94	.248	.326	37-0-1	.081	-2	89	-2		-0.4
1914	Ind F	19	18	.514	43	38	29-4	1	316.2	303	149	5	4	123	205	3.47	90	.258	.330	88-0-7	.110	-8	98	-8		-1.7
1915	New F	15	15	.500	38	32	22-5	1	268	222	87	2	2	99	142	1.91	134	.229	.302	88-0-7	.148	-4*	94	17		1.3
1916	Cin N	7	10	.412	31	15	7	1	150.1	145	75	5	0	69	60	3.89	67	.257	.338	46-0-2	.087	-2	123	-19		-2.5
Total	4	49	48	.505	136	100	65-12	3	855.2	775	367	13	6	340	469	3.01	94	.247	.322	280-0-17	.114	-17	99	-12		-3.3

MOSER, WALTER Walter Fredrick B2.27.1881 Concord NC D12.10.1946 Philadelphia PA BR/TR/5-9/170 d9.3

1906	Phi N	0	4	.000	6	4	4	0	42.2	49	35	0	1	15	17	3.59	73	.295	.357	14	.000	-2	14	-8		-0.9
1911	Bos A	0	1	.000	6	3	1	0	24.2	37	28	0	1	11	11	4.01	82	.366	.434	7	.000	-1	132	-6		-0.4
	StL A	0	2	.000	2	2	0	0	3.1	11	12	0	0	4	2	21.60	16	.478	.556	1	1.000	0	53	-7		-1.0
	Year	0	3	.000	8	5	1	0	28	48	40	0	1	15	13	6.11	54	.387	.457	8	.125	-1	101	-14		-1.4
Total	2	0	7	.000	14	9	5	0	70.2	97	75	0	2	30	30	4.58	63	.334	.401	22	.045	-2	70	-21		-2.3

MOSKAU, PAUL Paul Richard B12.20.1953 St.Joseph MO BR/TR/6-2/210* [CinN75 3/70] d6.21 Col Azusa Pacific

1977	Cin N	6	6	.500	20	19	2-2	0-0	108	116	51	10	1	40-3	71	4.00	98	.278	.338	38-1-1	.184	2*	106	-9		0.2
1978	Cin N	6	4	.600	26	25	2-1	1-0	145	139	65	17	3	57-4	88	3.97	89	.255	.327	49-1-2	.204	4*	138	-4		0.0
1979	Cin N	5	5	.556	21	15	1	0-0	106.1	107	53	9	0	51-3	58	3.89	95	.263	.341	37-0-6	.081	-2	104	-3		-0.4
1980	Cin N	9	7	.563	33	19	2-1	2-1	152.2	147	69	13	1	41-2	94	4.01	88	.257	.305	6-0-2	.000	-0	152	-8		-0.7
1981	Cin N	2	1	.667	27	1	0	2-1	54.2	54	31	4	1	32-5	32	4.37	86	.303	.338	11-0-1	.091	-1	118	-3		-0.5
1982	Pit N	1	3	.250	13	5	0	0-1	35	43	21	7	0	8-0	15	6.75	57	.331	.395	11-0-2	.182	0	116	-9		-1.2
1983	Chi N	3	2	.600	8	8	0	0-0	32	44	25	7	0	14-1	16	6.75	57	.331	.395	11-0-3	.153	1	117	-33	66	-3.0
Total	7	32	27	.542	148	92	7-4	5-3	633.2	650	315	67	6	243-18	374	4.22	87	.268	.333	196-2-22	.153	2	117	-33	66	-3.0

MOSS, MAL Charles Malcolm B4.18.1905 Sullivan IN D2.5.1983 Savannah GA BR/TL/6-0/175 d4.29 Col Vanderbilt

1930	Chi N	0	0	—	12	1	0	1	18.2	18	14	0	0	14	6	6.27	78	.254	.376	11	.273	0	214	-2		-0.1

MOSS, DAMIAN Damian Joseph B11.24.1976 Darlinghurst, New South Wales, Australia BR/TL/6-0/187* d4.26 [DL 1999 Atl N 57]

2001	Atl N	0	0	—	5	1	0	0-0	9	3	3	1	0	9-0	8	3.00	144	.097	.300	1	.000	0	43	1	42	0.1
2002	†Atl N	12	6	.667	33	29	0	0-0	179	140	80	20	6	89-5	111	3.42	118	.221	.321	50-0-6	.100	-1	113	10		-0.5
2003	SF N	9	7	.563	21	20	0	0-0	115	121	62	12	5	63-3	57	4.70	91	.273	.367	29-0-7	.241	0	94	-5		-1.0
	Bal A	1	5	.167	9	9	0	0-0	50.2	63	40	12	6	29-2	22	6.22	74	.307	.405	0	—	0	90	-10		-1.0
2004	TB A	0	1	.000	5	2	0	0-0	8	13	15	2	1	5-0	6	16.88	28	.351	.442	0	.150	0	99	-14	99	-1.8
Total	4	22	19	.537	74	61	0		361.2	340	200	47	18	195-10	204	4.50	93	.252	.352	80-0-13	.150	0	99	-14	99	-1.8

MOSS, RAY Raymond Earl B12.5.1901 Chattanooga TN D8.9.1998 Chattanooga TN BR/TR/6-1/185 d4.17

1926	Bro N	0	0	—	1	0	0	0	2	2	2	0	0	1	1	9.00	42	.600	.600	1	.000	-0		0		0.0
1927	Bro N	1	0	1.000	1	1	0	0	8.1	11	3	0	0	1	1	3.24	122	.333	.353	3-0-1	.333	1	86	1		0.0
1928	Bro N	0	3	.000	12	5	1-1	0	60.1	62	43	5	0	35	19	4.92	81	.279	.377	25	.320	2*	98	-7		-0.
1929	Bro N	11	6	.647	39	20	7-2	0	182	214	115	9	7	81	59	5.04	92	.296	.373	66-0-2	.076	-5*	96	-6		-1.
1930	Bro N	9	6	.600	36	11	5	0	118.1	127	78	14	3	41	30	5.10	96	.270	.352	39-0-2	.154	-2	100	-1		-0.
1931	Bro N	0	0	—	1	0	0	0	2	2	2	0	1	0	0	0.00	—	.333	.500	0	—	0		0		0.0
	Bos N	1	3	.250	12	5	0	0	45	56	32	2	0	16	14	4.60	82	.306	.362	15	.133	-1	63	-7		-0.
	Year	1	3	.250	13	5	0	0	46	57	32	2	1	16	14	4.50	84	.306	.365	15	.133	-1	63	-6		-0.
Total	6	22	18	.550	112	42	13-3	2	416	474	272	29	11	189	109	4.95	91	.289	.367	149-0-5	.148	-5	94	-20		-1.

MOSSI, DON Donald Louis "The Sphinx" B1.11.1929 St.Helena CA BL/TL/6-1/195* d4.17

1954	†Cle A	6	1	.857	40	1	0	7	93	56	22	6	1	39	55	1.94	190	.176	.267	19-0-1	.158	0	67	19		1.
1955	Cle A	4	3	.571	57	1	0	9	81.2	81	28	4	1	18-2	69	2.42	164	.253	.292	9	.111	0	156	13		1.
1956	Cle A	6	5	.545	48	3	0	11	87.2	79	38	6	1	33-5	59	3.59	117	.240	.311	20	.150	0	85	7		1.
1957	Cle A★	11	10	.524	36	22	6-1	0	159	165	82	16	2	57-5	55	4.13	90	.263	.327	26	.115	-2	64	-3		-0.
1958	Cle A	7	8	.467	43	5	1	6	101.2	106	49	6	4	30-6	125	3.36	121	.263	.284	77-1-5	.169	0*	94	19		2.
1959	Det A	17	9	.654	34	30	15-3	0	228	210	92	20	3	49-0	125	3.47	114	.258	.293	43-0-3	.116	0	86	9		0.
1960	Det A	9	8	.529	23	22	9-2	0	158.1	158	68	17	1	32-4	93	3.47	114	.258	.292	79-1-6	.165	1	121	28		2
1961	Det A	15	7	.682	35	34	12-1	1	240.2	237	97	29	0	47-3	137	2.96	139	.258	.292	55-0-1	.164	1*	103	-1		2
1962	Det A	11	13	.458	35	27	8-1	1	180.1	195	92	24	0	36-1	121	4.19	97	.270	.303	55-0-1	.164	-1	103	-1		

YEAR	TM LG	W	L	PCT	G	GS	CG-SHO	SV-BS	IP	H	R	HR	HB	BB-IB	SO	ERA	AERA	OAV	OOB	AB-HR-SH	AVG	PB	SUP	APR	DL	PW
1963	Det A	7	7	.500	24	16	3	2	122.2	110	58	20	4	17-0	68	3.74	100	.236	.268	39-0-2	.205	2	108	-1		0.2
1964	Chi A	3	1	.750	34	0	0	7	40	37	16	9	1	7-2	36	2.93	118	.240	.278	6	.167	-0		2		0.2
1965	KC A	5	8	.385	51	0	0	7	55.1	59	30	0	0	20-6	41	3.74	93	.278	.333	8	.000	-1		-3		-0.8
Total	12	101	80	.558	460	165	55-8	50	1548	1493	672	156	19	385-34	932	3.43	114	.252	.297	436-2-18	.163	4	103	83		7.8

MOSSOR, EARL Earl Dalton B7.21.1925 Forbus TN D12.29.1988 Batavia OH BL/TR/6-1/175 d4.30

| 1951 | Bro N | 0 | 0 | — | 3 | 0 | 0 | 0 | 1.2 | 2 | 6 | 1 | 0 | 7 | 1 | 32.40 | 12 | .333 | .692 | 1 | 1.000 | 0 | | -5 | | -0.2 |

MOTA, DANNY Daniel (Avila) B10.9.1975 Seybo, D.R. BR/TR/6-0/180 d9.15

| 2000 | Min A | 0 | 0 | — | 4 | 0 | 0 | 0 | 5.1 | 10 | 5 | 1 | 0 | 1-0 | 5 | 8.44 | 62 | .370 | .393 | 0 | — | 0 | | -2 | | -0.1 |

MOTA, GUILLERMO Guillermo B7.25.1973 San Pedro de Macoris, D.R. BR/TR/6-4/205(185-210) d5.2

1999	Mon N	2	4	.333	51	0	0	0-1	55.1	54	24	5	2	25-3	27	2.93	152	.257	.338	1-1-0	1.000	1		8		0.9
2000	Mon N	1	1	.500	29	0	0	0-0	30	27	21	3	2	12-0	24	6.00	79	.245	.328	1	.000	-0		-4		-0.2
2001	Mon N	1	3	.250	53	0	0	0-3	49.2	51	30	9	1	18-1	31	5.26	82	.271	.335	3	.333	0		-4		-0.3
2002	LA N	1	3	.250	43	0	0	0-1	60.2	45	30	4	2	27-6	49	4.15	94	.202	.292	4	.250	0	50	-4		-0.3
2003	LA N	6	3	.667	76	0	0	1-2	105	78	23	7	1	26-4	99	1.97	209	.206	.258	9-1-0	.222	1		27		2.2
2004	LA N	8	4	.667	52	0	0	1-0	63	51	30	4	2	27-5	52	2.14	193	.228	.314	6	.000	-1		15		2.5
	Fla N	1	4	.200	26	0	0	3-4	33.2	24	18	4	2	10-1	33	4.81	85	.200	.271	6	.333	1		-2		-0.2
	Year	9	8	.529	78	0	0	4-4	96.2	75	33	8	4	37-6	85	3.07	134	.218	.294	12	.167	0		14		2.3
2005	Fla N	2	2	.500	56	0	0	2-2	67	65	38	5	1	32-7	60	4.70	85	.254	.336	3	.000	-0	26	-6		-0.4
Total	7	22	24	.478	386	0	0	7-13	464.1	395	199	41	13	177-27	375	3.61	116	.231	.306	33-2-0	.212	3	32	76		4.4

MOULDER, GLEN Glen Hubert B9.28.1917 Cleveland OK D11.27.1994 Decatur GA BR/TR/6-0/180 d4.28

1946	Bro N	0	0	—	1	0	0	0	2	2	1	1	0	1	1	4.50	75	.286	.375		—	0		0		0.0
1947	StL A	4	2	.667	32	2	0	2	73	78	37	4	0	43	23	3.82	101	.283	.379	17-0-1	.235	0	114	0		0.0
1948	Chi A	3	6	.333	33	9	0	2	85.2	108	67	8	1	54	26	6.41	66	.316	.411	20-0-4	.300	2	78	-20		-1.8
Total	3	7	8	.467	66	11	0	4	160.2	188	105	13	1	98	50	5.21	78	.301	.396	37-0-5	.270	1	86	-20		-1.8

MOUNCE, TONY Anthony David B2.8.1975 Sacramento CA BL/TL/6-2/170 [HouN94 7/192] d6.13

| 2003 | Tex A | 1 | 5 | .167 | 11 | 11 | 0 | 0-0 | 50.2 | 65 | 42 | 9 | 5 | 25-0 | 30 | 7.11 | 70 | .317 | .403 | 2 | .000 | -0 | 62 | -11 | | -1.0 |

MOUNTAIN, FRANK Frank Henry B5.17.1860 Ft.Edward NY D11.19.1939 Schenectady NY BR/TR/5-11/185 d7.19 Col Union (NY) ▲

1880	Tro N	1	1	.500	2	2	2	0	17	23	17	0		6	2	5.29	48	.307	.358	9	.222	-0	157	-4		-0.4
1881	Det N	3	4	.429	7	7	7	0	60	80	63	2		18	13	5.25	56	.292	.336	25	.160	-0	114	-13		-1.3
1882	Wor N	0	5	.000	5	5	5	0	42	47	30	0		11	5	3.00	104	.255	.297	16	.063	-2	27	0		-0.2
	Phi AA	2	6	.250	8	8	8	0	69	72	49	1		11	15	3.91	72	.251	.279	36	.333	3*	89	-7		-0.3
	Wor N	2	11	.154	13	13	11	0	102	138	93	4		24	24	3.97	78	.299	.334	70-2	.271	2*	45	-9		-0.7
1883	Col AA	26	33	.441	59	59	57-4	0	503	546	345	8		123	159	3.60	86	.259	.300	276-3	.217	7*	88	-27		-1.8
1884	Col AA	23	17	.575	42	41	40-5	1	360.2	289	163	7	11	78	156	2.45	124	.209	.257	210-4	.238	9*	94	23		3.3
1885	Pit AA	1	4	.200	5	5	5	0	46	56	31	1	2	24	7	4.30	75	.320	.408	20	.100	-1	88	-4		-0.4
1886	Pit AA	0	2	.000	2	2	2	0	16	22	21	0	5	14	2	7.88	43	.319	.466	55	.145	0*	105	-7		-0.6
Total	7	58	83	.411	143	142	137-9	1	1215.2	1273	812	23	18	309	383	3.47	88	.254	.322	717-9	.220	17	86	-48		-2.4

MOUNTJOY, BILL William Henry "Medicine Bill" B12.11.1858 London ON, Can. D5.19.1894 London ON, Can. BL/TR/5-6/150 d9.29

1883	Cin AA	1	0	1.000	1	1	1	0	8	9	4	0		2	3	2.25	144	.265	.306	3	.000	-1	18	1		0.0
1884	Cin AA	19	12	.613	33	33	32-3	0	289	274	148	5	16	43	96	2.93	114	.238	.275	119	.151	-3*	118	7		0.3
1885	Cin AA	10	7	.588	17	17	17-1	0	153.2	149	89	5	7	52	50	3.16	103	.247	.314	60	.167	0	123	-1		0.0
	Bal AA	2	4	.333	6	6	6-1	0	53	72	47	1	4	13	15	5.43	60	.316	.363	18	.056	-0*	85	-11		-0.9
	Year	12	11	.522	23	23	23-2	0	206.2	221	136	6	11	65	65	3.75	87	.266	.327	78	.141	0	113	-10		-0.9
Total	3	31	24	.564	57	57	56-5	0	503.2	504	288	11	27	110	164	3.25	102	.250	.297	200	.145	-4	114	-2		-0.6

MOYER, ED Charles Edward B8.15.1885 Andover OH D11.18.1962 Jacksonville FL d7.20

| 1910 | Was N | 0 | 3 | .000 | 6 | 3 | 2 | 0 | 25 | 22 | 15 | 1 | 3 | 13 | 3 | 3.24 | 77 | .253 | .369 | 8 | .125 | -1 | 90 | -3 | | -0.3 |

MOYER, JAMIE Jamie B11.18.1962 Sellersville PA BL/TL/6-0/170* [ChiN84 6/135] d6.16 Col St. Josephs (PA)

1986	Chi N	7	4	.636	16	16	1-1	0-0	87.1	107	52	10	3	42-1	45	5.05	81	.311	.388	22-0-4	.091	-0	105	-8		-0.9
1987	Chi N	12	15	.444	35	33	1	0-0	201	210	127	28	5	97-9	147	5.10	85	.271	.353	61-0-7	.230	3*	79	-17		-1.6
1988	Chi N	9	15	.375	34	30	3-1	0-2	202	212	84	20	4	55-7	121	3.48	105	.272	.322	60-0-8	.083	-2	80	4		0.5
1989	Tex A	4	9	.308	15	15	1	0-0	76	84	51	10	2	33-0	44	4.86	82	.283	.354	0	—	0	80	-9	93	-1.3
1990	Tex A	2	6	.250	33	10	1	0-0	102.1	115	59	6	4	39-4	58	4.66	84	.290	.354	0	—	0	95	-8		-0.5
1991	StL N	0	5	.000	8	7	0	0-0	31.1	38	21	5	1	16-0	20	5.74	65	.319	.399	8	.000	-1	62	-6		-0.9
1993	Bal A	12	9	.571	25	25	3-1	0-0	152	154	63	11	6	38-2	90	3.43	132	.265	.316	0	—	0	106	17		2.3
1994	Bal A	5	7	.417	23	23	0	0-0	149	158	81	23	2	38-3	87	4.77	106	.271	.316	0	—	0	85	5		0.3
1995	Bal A	8	6	.571	27	18	0	0-0	115.2	117	70	18	3	30-0	65	5.21	92	.265	.314	0	—	0	103	-5		-0.5
1996	Bos A	7	1	.875	23	10	0	0-0	90	111	50	14	1	27-2	50	4.50	113	.300	.347	0	—	0	129	6		0.5
	Sea A	6	2	.750	11	11	0	0-0	70.2	66	36	9	1	19-3	29	3.31	150	.243	.292	0	—	0	122	9		0.9
	Year	13	3	.813	34	21	0	0-0	160.2	177	86	23	2	46-5	79	3.98	127	.276	.323	0	—	0	125	14		1.4
1997	†Sea A	17	5	.773	30	30	2	0-0	188.2	187	82	21	7	43-2	113	3.86	117	.256	.303	3	.333	0	149	17	28	1.9
1998	Sea A	15	9	.625	34	34	4-3	0-0	234.1	234	99	23	10	42-2	158	3.53	133	.256	.295	2	.000	-0	95	30		2.8
1999	Sea A	14	8	.636	32	32	4	0-0	228	235	108	23	4	48-1	137	3.87	124	.267	.311	2-0-1	.500	1	88	23		2.2
2000	Sea A	13	10	.565	26	26	0	0-0	154	173	103	22	3	53-2	98	5.49	88	.281	.339	2	.000	1	111	-13	47	-1.5
2001	†Sea A	20	6	.769	33	33	1	0-0	209.2	187	84	24	10	44-4	119	3.43	124	.239	.285	1-0-1	.000	0	118	22		2.4
2002	Sea A	13	8	.619	34	34	4-2	0-0	230.2	198	89	28	9	50-4	147	3.32	130	.230	.278	5	.200	0	108	27		2.4
2003	Sea A★	21	7	.750	33	33	1	0-0	215	199	83	19	8	66-3	129	3.27	133	.246	.307	5-0-1	.400	1	116	26		3.3
2004	Sea A	7	13	.350	34	33	1	0-0	202	217	127	44	11	63-3	125	5.21	86	.272	.331	2	.500	0	96	-18		-1.5
2005	Sea A	13	7	.650	32	32	1	0-0	200	225	99	23	8	52-2	102	4.28	98	.283	.331	1-0-1	.000	-0	115	-1		0.0
Total	19	205	152	.574	538	485	28-8	0-2	3139.2	3227	1568	381	107	895-54	1884	4.16	107	.266	.320	174-0-23	.155	2	103	101	168	10.8

MROZINSKI, RON Ronald Frank B9.16.1930 White Haven PA D10.19.2005 Washington NJ BR/TL/5-11/160* d6.20

1954	Phi N	1	1	.500	15	4	1	0	48	49	26	10	0	25	26	4.50	90	.261	.347	12-0-2	.083	-1	83	-5		-0.2
1955	Phi N	0	2	.000	22	1	0	1	34.1	38	26	2	4	19-2	18	6.55	61	.299	.396	4	.000	-1	67	-9		-0.6
Total	2	1	3	.250	37	5	1	1	82.1	87	52	12	4	44-2	44	5.36	75	.276	.368	16-0-2	.063	-2	80	-11		-0.8

MUDROCK, PHIL Philip Ray B6.12.1937 Louisville CO BR/TR/6-1/190 d4.19

| 1963 | Chi N | 0 | 0 | — | 1 | 0 | 0 | 0 | 1 | 2 | 1 | 0 | 0 | 0-0 | 0 | 9.00 | 39 | .400 | .400 | 0 | — | 0 | | -1 | | 0.0 |

MUELLER, GORDIE Joseph Gordon B12.10.1922 Baltimore MD BR/TR/6-4/200 d4.19 Col Loyola-Maryland

| 1950 | Bos A | 0 | 0 | — | 7 | 0 | 0 | 0 | 7 | 11 | 8 | 1 | 0 | 13 | 1 | 10.29 | 48 | .344 | .533 | 1 | .000 | -0 | | -4 | | -0.2 |

MUELLER, LES Leslie Clyde B3.4.1919 Belleville IL BR/TR/6-3/190 d8.15 Mil 1942-44

1941	Det A	0	0	—	4	0	0	0	13	9	9	1	0	10	8	4.85	94	.205	.352	3	.000	0		-1		-0.1
1945	†Det A	6	8	.429	26	18	6-2	1	134.2	117	63	8	2	58	42	3.68	96	.234	.316	44-1-1	.182	0	79	-3		-0.1
Total	2	6	8	.429	30	18	6-2	1	147.2	126	72	9	2	68	50	3.78	95	.231	.319	47-1-1	.170	0	79	-2		-0.2

MUELLER, WILLIE Willard Lawrence B8.30.1956 West Bend WI BR/TR/6-4/220* d8.12

1978	Mil A	1	0	1.000	5	0	0	0-0	12.2	16	11	1	0	6-0	6	6.39	59	.291	.361	0	—	0		-4		-0.3
1981	Mil A	0	0	—	1	0	0	0-0	2	4	1	0	1	0-0	1	4.50	77	.400	.400	0	—	0		0		0.0
Total	2	1	0	1.000	6	0	0	0-0	14.2	20	12	1	1	6-0	7	6.14	61	.308	.366	0	—	0		-4		-0.3

MUFFETT, BILLY Billy Arnold "Muff" B9.21.1930 Hammond IN BR/TR/6-1/198(186-198) d8.3 C18

1957	StL N	3	2	.600	23	0	0	5	44	35	11	6	0	13-4	21	2.25	176	.222	.279	7-0-1	.000	-1		9		1.2
1958	StL N	4	6	.400	35	6	1	5	84	107	52	11	5	42-9	41	4.93	84	.316	.397	20-0-1	.200	0	91	-7		-0.9
1959	SF N	0	0	—	5	0	0	1	6.2	11	4	2	1	3	3	5.40	71	.407	.467	0	—	0		-2		-0.1
1960	Bos A	6	4	.600	23	14	4-1	0	125	116	53	6	5	36-2	75	3.24	125	.242	.299	41-0-1	.268	2	67	9		0.5
1961	Bos A	3	11	.214	38	11	2	2	112.2	130	87	18	2	36-2	47	5.67	73	.291	.344	23-1-1	.217	2	62	-20		-2.1
1962	Bos A	0	0	—	1	1	0	0	4	8	4	0	0	2-0	1	9.00	46	.471	.500	1	.000	-0	130	-2		-0.1
Total	6	16	23	.410	125	32	7-1	15	376.1	407	213	38	12	132-18	188	4.33	94	.277	.339	92-1-4	.217	3	72	-13		-1.1

YEAR	TM	LG	W	L	PCT	G	GS	CG-SHO	SV-BS	IP	H	R	HR	HB	BB-IB	SO	ERA	AERA	OAV	OOB	AB-HR-SH	AVG	PB	SUP	APR	DL	PW

MUICH, JOE   Ignatius Andrew   B11.23.1903 St.Louis MO   D7.2.1993 St.Louis MO   BR/TR/6-2/175   d9.4

| 1924 | Bos | N | 0 | 0 | — | 3 | 0 | 0 | 0 | 9 | 19 | 12 | 1 | 0 | 5 | 1 | 11.00 | 35 | .432 | .490 | 3 | .000 | -1 | | -7 | | -0.4 |

MUIR, JOE   Joseph Allen   B11.26.1922 Oriole MD   D6.25.1980 Baltimore MD   BL/TL/6-1/172*   d4.21

1951	Pit	N	0	2	.000	9	1	0	0	16.1	11	6	2	0	7	5	2.76	153	.180	.265	1	.000	-0	21	2		0.3
1952	Pit	N	2	3	.400	12	5	1	0	35.2	42	28	3	0	18	17	6.31	63	.288	.366	9	.111	-0	94	-9		-1.1
Total	2		2	5	.286	21	6	1	0	52	53	34	5	0	25	22	5.19	78	.256	.336	10	.100	-0	80	-7		-0.8

MULCAHY, HUGH   Hugh Noyes "Losing Pitcher"   B9.9.1913 Brighton MA   D10.19.2001 Aliquippa PA   BR/TR/6-2/190   d7.24   Mil 1941-45   C1   Col Dean (MA) JC

1935	Phi	N	1	5	.167	18	5	0	0	52.2	62	35	2	5	25	11	4.78	95	.295	.383	17	.000	-2*	45	-2		-0.4
1936	Phi	N	1	1	.500	3	2	2	0	22.2	20	8	0	2	12	2	3.18	143	.238	.347	5	.250	0	84	4		0.3
1937	Phi	N	8	18	.308	56	26	9-1	3	215.2	256	147	17	9	97	54	5.13	84	.296	.372	73-0-3	.151	-3	107	-21		-2.4
1938	Phi	N	10	20	.333	46	34	15	1	267.1	294	162	14	6	120	90	4.61	84	.278	.354	94-0-7	.170	-2*	80	-23		-2.4
1939	Phi	N	9	16	.360	38	32	14-1	4	225.2	246	144	19	11	93	59	4.99	80	.282	.359	76-0-5	.158	-3	82	-26		0.6
1940	Phi	N☆	13	22	.371	36	36	21-3	0	280	283	141	12	3	91	82	3.60	108	.261	.320	94-0-6	.202	1*	78	3		-0.1
1945	Phi	N	1	3	.250	5	4	1	0	28.1	33	17	1	0	9	2	3.81	101	.295	.347	7-0-1	.000	-1	55	-1		-0.1
1946	Phi	N	2	4	.333	16	5	1	0	62.2	69	34	3	5	33	12	4.45	77	.295	.393	16-0-1	.188	1	80	-6		0.0
1947	Pit	N	0	0	—	2	1	0	0	6.2	8	7	1	0	7	2	4.05	104	.333	.484	3	.333	0	230	-1		0.0
Total	9		45	89	.336	220	145	63-5	9	1161.2	1271	695	69	39	487	314	4.49	89	.280	.355	388-0-24	.165	-9	84	-73		-7.5

MULDER, MARK   Mark Alan   B8.5.1977 South Holland IL   BL/TL/6-6/200*   [OakA98 1/2]   d4.18   Col Michigan St.

2000	Oak	A	9	10	.474	27	27	0	0-0	154	191	106	22	4	69-3	88	5.44	89	.308	.376	4	.000	-0	100	-11		-1.1
2001	†Oak	A	21	8	.724	34	34	6-4	0-0	229.1	214	92	16	5	51-4	153	3.45	132	.249	.294	5	.200	-0	107	30		3.6
2002	†Oak	A	19	7	.731	30	30	2-1	0-0	207.1	182	88	21	11	55-3	159	3.47	129	.232	.290	5	.000	-1	101	23	28	2.7
2003	Oak	A★	15	9	.625	26	26	9-2	0-0	186.2	180	66	15	2	40-2	128	3.13	146	.259	.300	4-0-1	.000	-0	94	32	40	4.0
2004	Oak	A★	17	8	.680	33	33	5-1	0-0	225.2	223	119	25	12	83-1	140	4.43	104	.264	.337	4	.000	0	121	6		0.8
2005	†StL	N	16	8	.667	32	32	3-2	0-0	205	212	90	19	9	70-1	111	3.64	115	.273	.339	62-0-1	.145	-1	116	14		1.7
Total	6		97	50	.660	182	182	25-10	0-0	1208	1202	561	118	43	368-14	779	3.87	117	.262	.321	84-0-2	.119	-2	107	94	68	11.7

MULHOLLAND, TERRY   Terence John   B3.9.1963 Uniontown PA   BR/TL/6-3/206(200-220)   [SFN84 1/24]   d6.8   Col Marietta

1986	SF	N	1	7	.125	15	10	0	0-0	54.2	51	33	3	1	35-2	27	4.94	72	.251	.363	19-0-1	.053	-1	63	-9		-1.3
1988	SF	N	2	1	.667	9	6	2-1	0-0	46	50	20	3	1	7-0	18	3.72	88	.281	.312	14	.000	-1	118	-2	63	-0.2
1989	SF	N	0	0	—	5	1	0	0-0	11	15	5	0	0	4-0	6	4.09	83	.319	.373	2-0-1	.000	-0	79	-1		0.0
	Phi	N	4	7	.364	20	17	2-1	0-0	104.1	122	61	8	4	32-3	60	5.00	72	.292	.347	34-0-2	.059	-2	81	-14		-1.5
	Year		4	7	.364	25	18	2-1	0-0	115.1	137	66	8	4	36-3	66	4.92	73	.295	.350	36-0-3	.056	-2	81	-15		-1.5
1990	Phi	N	9	10	.474	33	26	6-1	0-1	180.2	172	78	15	2	42-7	75	3.34	115	.252	.292	62-0-4	.097	-2	86	8	16	0.4
1991	Phi	N	16	13	.552	34	34	8-3	0-0	232	231	100	15	3	49-2	142	3.61	103	.260	.299	80-0-5	.087	-4*	91	3		-0.1
1992	Phi	N	13	11	.542	32	32	12-2	0-0	229	227	101	14	3	46-3	125	3.81	92	.261	.298	83-0-6	.096	-2	119	-5		-0.7
1993	†Phi	N★	12	9	.571	29	28	7-2	0-0	191	177	80	20	3	40-2	116	3.25	122	.241	.282	62-0-8	.065	-4	113	15		1.0
1994	NY	A	6	7	.462	24	19	2	0-0	120.2	150	94	24	3	37-1	72	6.49	71	.303	.353	0		0	135	-26		-2.3
1995	SF	N	5	13	.278	29	24	2	0-0	149	190	112	25	4	38-1	65	5.80	71	.313	.354	49-1-3	.102	-0*	107	-31	28	-3.2
1996	Phi	N	8	7	.533	21	21	3	0-0	133.1	157	74	17	3	21-1	52	4.66	93	.293	.320	45-1-4	.178	1	91	-4		0.3
	Sea	A	5	4	.556	12	12	0	0-0	69.1	75	38	5	2	28-3	34	4.67	106	.286	.356	0		0	113	3		-0.2
1997	Chi	N	6	12	.333	25	25	1	0-0	157	162	79	20	9	45-2	74	5.16	80	.248	.295	6-0-1	.167	0	101	-4		-0.4
	SF	N	0	1	.000	15	2	0	0-0	29.2	28	21	4	2	6-1	25	5.16	80	.248	.295	0		2	66	-1		0.2
	Year		6	13	.316	40	27	1	0-0	186.2	190	100	24	11	51-3	99	4.82	101	.267	.324	55-0-4	.164	2	94	-13		-0.2
1998	†Chi	N	6	5	.545	70	6	0	3-2	112	100	49	7	4	39-7	72	2.89	152	.235	.304	17-0-1	.294	2	94	13		1.4
1999	Chi	N	6	6	.500	26	16	0	0-0	110	137	71	16	1	32-4	44	5.15	89	.309	.355	32-0-3	.094	-2	83	-8		-0.5
	†Atl	N	4	2	.667	16	8	0	1-0	60.1	64	24	5	0	13-2	39	2.98	150	.274	.310	16-0-2	.125	-0	98	9		0.5
	Year		10	8	.556	42	24	0	1-0	170.1	201	95	21	1	45-6	83	4.39	103	.297	.340	48-0-5	.104	-2	88	1		-0.0
2000	†Atl	N	9	9	.500	54	20	1	1-2	156.2	198	96	24	4	41-7	78	5.11	88	.308	.351	36-0-9	.250	2	104	-10		-0.8
2001	Pit	N	0	0	—	22	1	0	0-0	36.1	38	15	5	1	10-1	25	3.72	120	.277	.329	3	.000	-0	124	4	67	-0.2
	LA	N	1	1	.500	19	3	0	0-0	29.1	40	20	7	1	7-0	17	5.83	71	.315	.356	6	.000	-1	67	-6	1	-0.4
	Year		1	1	.500	41	4	0	0-0	65.2	78	35	12	2	17-1	42	4.66	93	.295	.342	9	.000	-1	80	-2		-0.6
2002	LA	N	0	0	—	21	0	0	0-0	32	45	29	10	2	7-0	17	7.31	53	.331	.367	1		-0	-13	-1	31	-0.7
	Cle	A	3	2	.600	16	3	0	0-0	47	56	27	5	4	14-3	21	4.60	97	.301	.356	0	—	0	125	-1		-0.3
2003	Cle	A	3	4	.429	45	3	0	0-2	99	117	60	17	6	37-6	42	5.18	89	.295	.360	1	.000	-0	88	-7		-0.6
2004	†Min	A	5	9	.357	39	15	0	0-0	123.1	163	76	17	5	33-3	60	5.18	88	.327	.371	2	.000	0	1	1		-0.9
2005	Min	A	0	2	.000	49	0	0	0-1	59	61	30	6	2	17-4	18	4.27	103	.276	.332	0	—	0	98	-87	206	-9.?
Total	19		124	142	.466	680	332	46-10	5-8	2572.2	2826	1393	292	70	680-65	1324	4.40	94	.284	.328	619-2-53	.111	-16	98	-87	206	-9.?

MULLANE, TONY   Anthony John "Count","The Apollo of the Box"   B1.20.1859 Cork, Ireland   D4.25.1944 Chicago IL   BB/TR(BL 1882, TB 1882p, 1893p)/5-10.5/165   d8.27 ▲

1881	Det	N	4	5	.200	5	5	5	0	44	55	42	2		17	7	4.91	59	.302	.362	19	.263		100	-8		-0.?
1882	Lou	AA	30	24	.556	55	55	51-5	0	460.1	418	212	3		78	170	1.88	132	.226	.257	303	.257	11*	107	34		5.?
1883	StL	AA	35	15	.700	53	49	49-3	1	460.2	372	222	3		74	191	2.19	159	.216	.238	307	.225	1*	83	60		7.?
1884	Tol	AA	36	26	.581	67	65	64-7	0	567	481	276	5	32	89	325	3.70	95	.242	.303	324	.225	2*	103	-8		1.?
1886	Cin	AA	33	27	.550	63	56	55-1	0	529.2	501	315	11	18	166	250	3.24	134	.257	.322	199-3	.221	2*	100	51		4.?
1887	Cin	AA	31	17	.646	48	48	47-6		416.1	414	234	11	32	121	97	2.84	112	.231	.282	175-1	.251	5*	110	15		1.?
1888	Cin	AA	26	16	.619	44	42	41-4	1	380.1	341	194	9	29	75	186	2.99	131	.251	.329	196	.296	9*	87	17		1.?
1889	Cin	AA	11	9	.550	33	24	17	5	220	218	133	4	13	89	112	3.43	159	.220	.310	286	.276	7*	94	27		3.?
1890	Cin	N	12	10	.545	25	21	21	1	209	175	101	7	8	96	91	2.24	159	.220	.310	209	.148	-5*	83	7		0.?
1891	Cin	N	23	26	.469	51	47	42-1	0	426.1	390	250	15	18	187	124	3.23	104	.234	.318	209	.169	-1*	93	21		2.?
1892	Cin	N	21	13	.618	37	34	30-3	1	295	222	131	12	12	127	109	2.59	126	.201	.290	118	.169	-1*	81	4		0.?
1893	Cin	N	6	6	.500	15	13	11	1	122.1	130	84	4	9	65	24	4.41	108	.264	.360	52-1	.288	3*	81	4		0.?
	Bal	N	12	16	.429	34	26	23	1	244.2	277	177	4	7	124	71	4.45	107	.277	.360	114	.228	-3*	93	7		0.?
	Year		18	22	.450	49	39	34	2	367	407	261	8	16	189	95	4.44	107	.273	.360	166-1	.247	-0	89	20		-0.?
1894	Bal	N	6	9	.400	21	15	9	4	122.2	155	117	4	7	90	43	6.31	87	.305	.417	53	.396	5	111	-13		-0.?
	Cle	N	1	2	.333	4	4	3	0	33	46	35	3	0	10	3	7.64	72	.326	.371	13-0-1	.077	-1	120	-6		-0.?
	Year		7	11	.389	25	19	12	4	155.2	201	152	7	7	100	46	6.59	83	.310	.407	66-0-1	.333	4	113	-15		-0.?
Total	13		284	220	.563	555	504	468-30	15	4531.1	4195	2523	97	185	1408	1803	3.05	118	.235	.298	2720-8-1	.243	50	94	263		30.?

MULLEN, SCOTT   Kenneth Scott   B1.17.1975 San Benito TX   BR/TL/6-2/190*   [KCA96 7/199]   d8.31   Col Dallas Baptist

2000	KC	A	0	0	—	11	0	0	0-0	10.1	10	5	2	0	3-0	7	4.35	120	.244	.295	0	—	0		1		0.?
2001	KC	A	0	0	—	17	0	0	0-0	10	13	6	0	0	9-0	3	4.50	110	.310	.423	0	—	0	0	0	33	1
2002	KC	A	4	5	.444	44	0	0	0-2	40	40	16	5	2	13-2	21	3.15	158	.267	.329	0	—	0	7	1		1
2003	KC	A	0	0	—	2	0	0	0-0	4.1	11	8	2	0	5-0	3	16.62	29	.458	.552	0	—	0	-5			-0
	LA	N	0	0	—	1	1	0	0-0	3	2	3	0	1	5-0	1	9.00	46	.200	.471	1	.000	-0	182	-2		-0
Total	4		4	5	.444	75	1	0	0-2	67.2	76	38	9	3	35-2	35	4.66	107	.285	.369	1	.000	-0	182	1	33	-0

MULLIGAN, JOE   Joseph Ignatius "Big Joe"   B7.31.1913 Weymouth MA   D6.5.1986 W.Roxbury MA   BR/TR/6-4/210   d6.28   Col Holy Cross

| 1934 | Bos | A | 1 | 0 | 1.000 | 14 | 2 | 1 | 0 | 44.2 | 46 | 21 | 1 | 2 | 27 | 13 | 3.63 | 132 | .279 | .387 | 12-0-1 | .000 | -1 | 190 | 6 | | -0 |

MULLIGAN, DICK   Richard Charles   B3.18.1918 Swoyersville PA   D12.15.1992 Victoria TX   BL/TL/6-0/167   d9.24   Mil 1942-45

1941	Was	A	0	1	.000	1	1	1	0	9	11	5	0	4	9	5	5.00	81	.306	.342	3	.000	-0	86	-1		-0
1946	Phi	N	2	1	.500	19	5	1	1	54.2	61	32	0	4	27	16	4.77	72	.289	.380	11-0-1	.000	-1	90	-7		-0
	Bos	N	1	0	1.000	4	0	0	0	15.1	6	4	1	0	9	4	2.35	146	.122	.259	4	.000	0		2		0
	Year		3	1	.750	23	5	1	1	70	67	36	1	4	36	20	4.24	81	.258	.357	15-0-1	.000	-1*	90	-5		-0
1947	Bos	N	0	0	—	1	0	0	0	2	4	2	0	1	1	1	9.00	43	.400	.455	0	—	-1	90	-1		-0
Total	3		3	2	.600	25	6	2	1	81	82	43	1	4	39	23	4.44	79	.268	.358	18-0-1	.000	-1	90	-7		-0

MULLIN, GEORGE   George Joseph "Wabash George"   B7.4.1880 Toledo OH   D1.7.1944 Wabash IN   BR/TR/5-11/188   d5.4

1902	Det	A	13	16	.448	35	30	25	0	260	282	155	4	7	95	78	3.67	99	.277	.343	120-0-1	.325	9*	106	-3		-0
1903	Det	A	19	15	.559	41	36	31-6	2	320.2	284	128	4	6	80	170	2.25	130	.237	.303	126-1-4	.278	8*	110	21		2
1904	Det	A	17	23	.425	44	44	42-7	0	382.1	345	154	1	10	131	161	2.40	106	.242	.310	155-0-3	.290	11*	74	3		2
1905	Det	A	21	21	.500	44	41	35-1	0	347.2	303	149	4	8	138	168	2.51	109	.236	.314	135-0-3	.259	6*	79	4		1
1906	Det	A	21	18	.538	40	40	35-2	0	330	315	139	4		124	123	2.78	99	.254	.322	142-0-1	.225	3*	88	-2		0?

YEAR	TM LG	W	L	PCT	G	GS	CG-SHO	SV-BS	IP	H	R	HR	HB	BB-IB	SO	ERA	AERA	OAV	OOB	AB-HR-SH	AVG	PB	SUP	APR	DL	PW
1907	†Det A	20	20	.500	46	42	35-5	3	357.1	346	153	1	15	106	146	2.59	100	.256	.318	157	.217	3*	120	1		0.8
1908	†Det A	17	13	.567	39	30	26-1	0	290.2	301	142	1	7	71	121	3.10	78	.271	.319	125-1-3	.256	8*	139	-20		-1.1
1909	†Det A	29	8	.784	40	35	29-3	1	303.2	258	96	4	8	78	124	2.22	113	.234	.289	126-0-2	.214	5*	129	12		2.3
1910	Det A	21	12	.636	38	32	27-5	0	289	260	125	7	14	102	98	2.87	92	.254	.330	129-1-0	.256	6*	126	-8		-0.1
1911	Det A	18	10	.643	30	29	25-2	0	234.1	245	99	7	12	61	87	3.07	113	.276	.331	98-0-1	.286	8*	100	13		2.1
1912	Det A	12	17	.414	30	29	22-2	0	226	214	112	3	4	92	88	3.54	92	.255	.335	90-0-2	.278	9*	97	-4		0.6
1913	Det A	1	6	.143	7	7	4	0	52.1	53	28	1	2	18	16	2.75	106	.270	.338	20	.350	3*	40	-1		0.2
	Was A	3	5	.375	11	9	3	0	57.1	69	34	1	5	25	14	5.02	59	.294	.374	21	.190	0*	103	-10		-1.2
	Year	4	11	.267	18	16	7	0	109.2	122	62	2	7	43	30	3.94	75	.283	.358	41	.268	3	76	-11		-1.0
1914	Ind F	14	10	.583	36	20	11-1	3	203	202	100	4	10	91	74	2.70	115	.261	.346	77-0-4	.312	8*	90	2		0.8
1915	New F	2	2	.500	5	4	3	0	32.1	41	22	0	0	16	14	5.85	44	.318	.393	10-0-1	.100	-0*	96	-10		-1.1
Total	14	228	196	.538	487	428	353-35	8	3686.2	3518	1636	42	130	1238	1482	2.82	101	.255	.322	1531-3-25	.262	87	103	-2		11.9

MULLINS, GREG Gregory Eugene B12.13.1971 Palatka FL BL/TL/5-10/160 d9.18 Col North Florida

| 1998 | Mil N | 0 | 0 | | 2 | 0 | 0 | 0-0 | 1 | 1 | 1 | 0 | 0 | 1 | 0 | 0.00 | — | .250 | .400 | 0 | | 0 | | 0 | | 0.0 |

MULRENAN, DOMINIC Dominic Joseph B12.18.1893 Woburn MA D7.27.1964 Melrose MA BR/TR/5-11/170 d4.24

| 1921 | Chi A | 2 | 8 | .200 | 12 | 10 | 3 | 0 | 56 | 84 | 52 | 2 | 2 | 36 | 10 | 7.23 | 59 | .359 | .449 | 20-0-1 | .150 | -1 | 77 | -19 | | -2.7 |

MULRONEY, FRANK Francis Joseph B4.8.1903 Mallard IA D11.11.1985 Aberdeen WA BR/TR/6-0/170 d4.15 Col Iowa

| 1930 | Bos A | 0 | 1 | .000 | 2 | 0 | 0 | 0 | 3 | 3 | 2 | 0 | 0 | 2 | 2 | 3.00 | 154 | .273 | .273 | 0 | | — | 0 | | 0 | | 0.0 |

MUNCRIEF, BOB Robert Cleveland B1.28.1916 Madill OK D2.6.1996 Duncanville TX BR/TR/6-2/190* d9.30

1937	StL A	0	0	—	1	1	0	0	2	3	2	1	0	2	0	4.50	107	.300	.417	0		0	180	0		0.0
1939	StL A	0	0	—	2	0	0	0	3	7	5	1	0	3	1	15.00	32	.500	.588	0		—	0	-3		-0.1
1941	StL A	13	9	.591	36	24	12-2	1	214.1	221	95	18	5	53	67	3.65	118	.266	.314	76-0-5	.237	2	102	16		1.6
1942	StL A	6	8	.429	24	18	7-1	0	134.1	149	61	11	0	31	39	3.89	95	.280	.319	45-0-1	.111	-1	91	0		-0.1
1943	StL A	13	12	.520	35	27	12-3	1	205	211	80	13	2	48	80	2.81	118	.264	.307	66-0-8	.152	-2	100	9		0.7
1944	†StL A★	13	8	.619	33	27	12-3	1	219.1	216	83	11	3	50	88	3.08	117	.258	.302	78-0-5	.231	1	108	15		1.5
1945	StL A	13	4	.765	27	15	10	1	145.2	132	51	8	2	44	54	2.72	130	.239	.297	45-0-8	.067	-4*	132	12		0.9
1946	StL A	3	12	.200	34	14	4-1	0	115.1	149	75	6	0	31	49	4.99	75	.314	.356	32-0-2	.031	-3	79	-15		-2.2
1947	StL A	8	14	.364	31	23	7	0	176.1	210	108	14	2	51	74	4.90	79	.299	.348	57-0-4	.105	-3	83	-19		-2.4
1948	†Cle A	5	4	.556	21	9	1-1	0	72.1	76	37	8	0	31	24	3.98	102	.279	.348	18-0-2	.111	-1	89	0		-0.1
1949	Pit N	1	5	.167	14	4	1	3	35.2	44	27	8	0	13	11	6.31	67	.310	.368	7-0-3	.143	-0	73	-8		-1.2
	Chi N	5	6	.455	34	3	1	2	75	80	42	7	1	31	36	4.56	88	.276	.348	14-0-1	.286	1	102	-4		-0.4
	Year	6	11	.353	47	7	2	5	110.2	124	69	15	1	44	47	5.12	80	.287	.354	21-0-4	.238	1	86	-10		-1.6
1951	NY A	0	0	—	2	0	0	0	3	6	6	2	0	4	2	9.00	43	.417	.563	0		—	0	-2		-0.1
Total	12	80	82	.494	288	165	67-11	9	1401.1	1503	669	106	15	392	525	3.80	100	.275	.325	438-0-39	.155	-10	98	-1		-1.9

MUNGER, RED George David B10.4.1918 Houston TX D7.23.1996 Houston TX BR/TR/6-2/200* d5.1 Mil 1944-46

1943	StL N	9	5	.643	32	9	5	2	93.1	101	47	2	0	42	45	3.95	85	.281	.357	28	.214	1	146	-6		-0.7
1944	StL N★	11	3	.786	21	12	7-2	1	121	92	23	2	2	41	55	1.34	263	.212	.284	44	.114	-3	65	29		3.4
1946	†StL N	2	2	.500	10	7	2	1	48.2	47	19	0	0	12	28	3.33	104	.255	.301	16	.250	1	117	2		0.3
1947	StL N☆	16	5	.762	40	31	13-6	3	224.1	218	94	12	2	76	123	3.37	123	.255	.318	81-0-3	.185	1	120	20		1.9
1949	StL N★	15	8	.652	35	28	12-2	0	188.1	179	86	13	2	87	82	3.87	108	.255	.339	50-0-2	.160	0	101	-8		-0.8
1950	StL N	7	8	.467	32	20	5-1	0	154.2	158	73	15	3	70	61	3.90	110	.262	.342	51-0-3	.137	-2	93	7		0.5
1951	StL N	4	6	.400	23	11	3	0	94.2	106	58	13	0	44	44	5.32	74	.286	.365	29-0-1	.172	-0	81	-13		-1.1
1952	StL N	0	1	.000	1	1	0	0	4.1	7	6	2	1	1	1	12.46	30	.389	.450	2	.000	-0	24	-4		-0.6
	Pit N	0	3	.000	5	4	0	0	26.1	30	21	5	0	10	8	7.18	58	.283	.345	7-0-1	.000	-1	50	-8		-0.9
	Year	0	4	.000	6	5	0	0	30.2	37	27	7	1	11	9	7.92	50	.298	.360	9-0-1	.000	-1	45	-11		-1.4
1956	Pit N	3	4	.429	35	13	0	2	107	126	56	8	0	41-6	45	4.04	93	.299	.359	28-0-2	.107	-0	86	-4		-0.3
Total	10	77	56	.579	273	161	54-13	12	1228.2	1243	574	85	11	500-6	564	3.83	103	.264	.336	402-1-17	.174	0	104	24		3.2

MUNGO, VAN Van Lingle B6.8.1911 Pageland SC D2.12.1985 Pageland SC BR/TR/6-2/185 d9.7 C1

1931	Bro N	3	1	.750	9	4	2-1	0	31	27	9	0	1	13	12	2.32	164	.241	.325	12	.250	1	67	5		0.7
1932	Bro N	13	11	.542	39	33	11-1	2	223.1	224	120	9	6	115	107	4.43	86	.260	.351	79-0-4	.203	0	103	-13		-1.2
1933	Bro N	16	15	.516	41	28	18-3	0	248	223	89	7	0	84	110	2.72	118	.236	.298	84-0-4	.179	-0	91	15		1.8
1934	Bro N★	18	16	.529	45	38	22-3	3	315.1	300	137	15	3	104	184	3.37	116	.249	.310	121-0-1	.248	4*	100	20		2.6
1935	Bro N	16	10	.615	37	26	18-4	0	214.1	205	100	13	2	90	143	3.65	109	.252	.328	90-0-1	.289	5*	106	10		1.6
1936	Bro N☆	18	19	.486	45	37	22-2	3	311.2	275	137	8	3	118	238	3.35	123	.234	.305	123-0-4	.179	-4*	92	28		2.7
1937	Bro N★	9	11	.450	25	21	14	3	161	136	65	3	6	56	122	2.91	139	.229	.290	64	.250	2*	87	19		2.8
1938	Bro N	4	11	.267	24	18	6-2	0	133.1	133	78	11	2	72	72	3.92	100	.259	.353	47-0-4	.191	1*	94	-4		-0.2
1939	Bro N	4	5	.444	14	10	1	0	77.1	70	36	7	3	33	34	3.26	124	.239	.322	29-0-1	.345	2*	95	5		0.8
1940	Bro N	1	0	1.000	7	0	0	1	22	24	6	1	0	10	9	2.45	163	.282	.358	7	.000	-1*	4	0		0.1
1941	Bro N	0	0	—	2	0	0	0	2	1	1	0	0	2	0	4.50	81	.143	.333	0	—	-0		-0		0.0
1942	NY N	1	2	.333	9	5	2	0	36.1	38	32	4	0	21	27	5.94	57	.273	.369	14	.214	-0	115	-12		-0.9
1943	NY N	3	7	.300	45	13	2-2	2	154.1	140	68	7	6	79	83	3.91	88	.243	.341	44-0-2	.159	-1*	100	-4		-0.4
1945	NY N★	14	7	.667	26	26	7-2	0	183	161	77	4	4	71	101	3.20	122	.238	.314	73	.233	4*	106	13		1.7
Total	14	120	115	.511	364	259	123-20	16	2113	1957	955	89	33	868	1242	3.47	110	.245	.321	787-0-21	.221	13	98	86		12.1

MUNIZ, MANNY Manuel (Rodriguez) B12.31.1947 Caguas, PR BR/TR/5-11/190 d9.3

| 1971 | Phi N | 0 | 1 | .000 | 5 | 0 | 0 | 0 | 10.1 | 9 | 8 | 2 | 0 | 8-1 | 6 | 6.97 | 51 | .225 | .354 | 1 | .000 | -0- | | -3 | | -0.3 |

MUNNINGHOFF, SCOTT Scott Andrew B12.5.1958 Cincinnati OH BR/TR/6-0/180 [PhiN77 1/22] d4.13

| 1980 | Phi N | 0 | 0 | — | 4 | 0 | 0 | 0-0 | 6 | 8 | 3 | 0 | 0 | 5-0 | 2 | 4.50 | 85 | .320 | .419 | 1 | 1.000 | 1 | | 0 | | 0.1 |

MUNNS, LES Leslie Ernest "Big Ed","Nemo" B12.1.1908 Fort Bragg CA D2.28.1997 Cedar Rapids IA BR/TR/6-5/212 d4.22

1934	Bro N	3	7	.300	33	9	4	0	99.1	106	67	7	0	60	41	4.71	83	.280	.378	29	.241	2*	76	-12		-0.8
1935	Bro N	1	3	.250	21	5	0	1	58.1	74	47	5	4	33	13	5.55	72	.319	.413	16	.188	-0*	115	-12		-0.9
1936	StL N	0	3	.000	7	1	0	1	24	23	18	2	0	12	4	3.00	131	.240	.324	9	.111	-1*	129	-1		-0.2
Total	3	4	13	.235	61	15	4	2	181.2	203	132	14	4	105	58	4.76	83	.287	.382	54	.204	1	93	-25		-1.9

MUNOZ, ARNIE Arnaldo Rafel B6.21.1982 Mao, D.R. BL/TL/5-9/170 d6.19

| 2004 | Chi A | 0 | 1 | .000 | 11 | 1 | 0 | 0-0 | 14.1 | 20 | 16 | 4 | 1 | 12-1 | 11 | 10.05 | 47 | .339 | .446 | | .000 | -0 | 277 | -8 | | -0.5 |

MUNOZ, OSCAR Juan Oscar B9.25.1969 Hialeah FL BR/TR/6-3/222 [CleA90 5/136] d8.6 Col Miami

| 1995 | Min A | 2 | 1 | .667 | 10 | 3 | 0 | 0 | 35.1 | 40 | 28 | 6 | 1 | 17-0 | 25 | 5.60 | 86 | .276 | .354 | 0 | | — | 0 | 122 | -5 | | -0.4 |

MUNOZ, MIKE Michael Anthony B7.12.1965 Baldwin Park CA BL/TL/6-2/200* [LAN86 3/74] d9.6 Col Cal Poly-Pomona

1989	LA N	0	0	—	2	0	0	0	2.2	5	5	1	0	2	3	16.88	20	.417	.500	0		—	-0		-4		-0.2
1990	LA N	0	1	.000	8	0	0	0-1	5.2	6	2	1	0	3-0	2	3.18	116	.300	.391	1	.000	-0		0		0.1
1991	Det A	0	0	—	6	0	0	0-0	9.1	14	10	0	0	5-0	3	9.64	43	.350	.413	0		—	-0		-5		-0.2
1992	Det A	1	2	.333	65	0	0	2-1	48	44	16	2	4	25-6	23	3.00	133	.246	.335	0		—	-0		-5		0.5
1993	Det A	0	1	.000	8	0	0	0-0	3	4	2	1	0	6-1	1	6.00	73	.308	.526	0		—	0	6		-0.1
	Col N	2	1	.667	21	0	0	0-2	18	21	12	1	0	9-3	16	4.50	106	.309	.380	0		—	0	0		0.0
1994	Col N	4	2	.667	57	0	0	1-1	45.2	37	22	3	4	31-5	32	3.74	133	.223	.343	0		—	0	5		0.7
1995	†Col N	4	4	.333	64	0	0	2-1	43.2	54	38	5	3	23-1	37	7.42	72	.307	.398	2	.500	1	-7		-0.8
1996	Col N	2	2	.500	54	0	0	0-3	44.2	55	33	4	1	16-2	45	6.65	78	.302	.360	1	.000	-0	-5	19	-0.3
1997	Col N	3	3	.500	64	0	0	2-0	45.2	52	25	4	0	13-0	26	4.53	114	.294	.339	1	.000	-0	3		-0.3
1998	Col N	2	2	.500	40	0	0	3-1	41.1	53	32	2	1	16-2	14	5.66	91	.312	.372	0		—	-0	3		-0.3
1999	Tex A	2	1	.667	56	0	0	1-2	52.2	52	24	5	1	18-2	27	3.93	132	.263	.323	0		—	0	7		0.4
2000	Tex A	0	1	.000	9	0	0	0-0	1.1	6	6	2	0	1-0	1	13.50	38	.524	.583	0		—	-0	-3		-0.2
Total	12	18	20	.474	453	0	0	11-14	364.1	408	227	34	4	174-22	240	5.19	95	.287	.363	7-0-1	.143		-6	176		-0.5

MUNOZ, BOBBY Roberto (Sbert) B3.3.1968 Rio Piedras, PR BR/TR/6-7/259(237-259) [NYA88 15/391] d5.29 Col Palm Beach (FL) CC

| 1993 | NY A | 3 | 3 | .500 | 38 | 0 | 0 | 0-2 | 45.2 | 48 | 27 | 1 | 0 | 26-5 | 33 | 5.32 | 79 | .270 | .357 | 0 | | — | 0 | -5 | | -0.6 |
| 1994 | Phi N | 7 | 5 | .583 | 21 | 14 | 1 | 1-1 | 104.1 | 101 | 40 | 8 | 1 | 35-0 | 59 | 2.67 | 160 | .252 | .310 | 34-1-2 | .206 | 1 | 90 | 16 | | 1.9 |

YEAR	TM LG	W	L	PCT	G	GS	CG-SHO	SV-BS	IP	H	R	HR	HB	BB-IB	SO	ERA	AERA	OAV	OOB	AB-HR-SH	AVG	PB	SUP	APR	DL	PV
1995	Phi N	0	2	.000	3	3	0	0-0	15.2	15	13	3	3	9-0	6	5.74	73	.268	.386	5	.000	-1	57	-4	148	-0.
1996	Phi N	0	3	.000	6	6	0	0-0	25.1	42	28	5	1	7-1	8	7.82	55	.375	.413	7-0-1	.143	0	70	-11	159	-1.
1997	Phi N	1	5	.167	8	7	0	0-0	33.1	47	35	4	2	15-1	20	8.91	47	.338	.403	10-0-1	.300	1	75	-17		-0.
1998	Bal A	0	0	—	9	1	0	0-0	12	18	13	4	1	6-0	6	9.75	47	.383	.439	0	—	0	163	-7		-0.
2001	Mon N	0	4	.000	15	7	0	0-0	42	53	25	6	2	21-1	21	5.14	84	.321	.404	11	.000	-1	46	-3		-0.
Total 7		11	22	.333	100	38	1	1-3	278.1	324	181	30	10	119-8	153	5.17	83	.295	.364	67-1-4	.164	-2	76	-31	307	-3.

MUNRO, PETE Peter Daniel B6.14.1975 Flushing NY BR/TR/6-2/200* [BosA93 6/163] d4.6 Col Okaloosa-Walton (FL) CC

YEAR	TM LG	W	L	PCT	G	GS	CG-SHO	SV-BS	IP	H	R	HR	HB	BB-IB	SO	ERA	AERA	OAV	OOB	AB-HR-SH	AVG	PB	SUP	APR	DL	PV
1999	Tor A	0	2	.000	31	6	0	0-1	55.1	70	38	6	2	23-0	38	6.02	82	.318	.382	0		0	114	-6		-0.
2000	Tor A	1	1	.500	9	3	0	0-0	25.2	38	22	1	3	16-0	16	5.96	84	.355	.452	1	.000	-0	106	-4	29	0
2002	Hou N	5	5	.500	19	14	0	0-0	80.2	89	37	5	3	23-3	45	3.57	121	.283	.338	22-0-1	.136	-1	90	5		0
2003	Hou N	3	4	.429	40	2	0	0-1	54	63	30	7	1	26-2	27	4.67	95	.294	.382	1-0-2	.000	0	96	-1		-0.
2004	†Hou N	4	7	.364	21	19	0	0-0	99.2	120	59	12	10	26-2	65	5.15	85	.302	.357	29-0-5	.069	-1*	96	-7		-0.
Total 5		13	19	.406	120	40	0	0-2	315.1	380	186	31	23	114-7	189	4.88	93	.304	.370	53-0-6	.094	-2	94	-13	29	-0.

MUNTER, SCOTT Scott Michael B3.7.1980 Norfolk NE BR/TR/6-6/235 d5.11 Col Butler Co.(KS) CC

YEAR	TM LG	W	L	PCT	G	GS	CG-SHO	SV-BS	IP	H	R	HR	HB	BB-IB	SO	ERA	AERA	OAV	OOB	AB-HR-SH	AVG	PB	SUP	APR	DL	PV
2005	SF N	2	0	1.000	45	0	0	0-3	38.2	40	15	1	1	12-1	11	2.56	166	.280	.338	0-0-1		0	6	21		0.

MURA, STEVE Stephen Andrew B2.12.1955 New Orleans LA BR/TR/6-2/190* [SDN76 2/29] d9.5 Col Tulane

YEAR	TM LG	W	L	PCT	G	GS	CG-SHO	SV-BS	IP	H	R	HR	HB	BB-IB	SO	ERA	AERA	OAV	OOB	AB-HR-SH	AVG	PB	SUP	APR	DL	PV
1978	SD N	0	2	.000	5	2	0	0-0	7.2	15	10	1	0	5-0	5	11.74	29	.441	.500	1	.000	-0	54	-7		-1.
1979	SD N	4	4	.500	38	5	0	2-3	73	57	30	6	1	37-2	59	3.08	115	.217	.314	10-0-3	.000	-1	80	3	36	-0.
1980	SD N	8	7	.533	37	23	3-1	2-1	168.2	149	74	9	3	86-4	109	3.68	93	.246	.338	51	.137	-0*	106	-4		-2
1981	SD N	5	14	.263	23	22	2	0-0	138.2	156	72	10	0	50-2	70	4.28	76	.285	.344	44-0-2	.136	-0*	87	-17		-2
1982	StL N	12	11	.522	35	30	7-1	0-0	184.1	196	89	16	0	80-4	84	4.05	91	.278	.348	53-0-10	.057	-4	117	-6		-1
1983	Chi A	0	0	—	6	0	0	0-0	12.1	13	11	1	0	6-0	4	4.38	96	.260	.333	0	—	0		-2		-0
1985	Oak A	1	1	.500	23	1	0	1-0	48	41	25	3	0	25-4	29	4.13	94	.225	.317	0		0	70	-2		-0
Total 7		30	39	.435	167	83	12-2	5-4	632.2	627	311	46	4	289-16	360	4.00	88	.263	.340	159-0-15	.101	-5	101	-35	36	-5

MURAKAMI, MASANORI Masanori B5.6.1944 Otsuki, Japan BL/TL/6-0/180* d9.1

YEAR	TM LG	W	L	PCT	G	GS	CG-SHO	SV-BS	IP	H	R	HR	HB	BB-IB	SO	ERA	AERA	OAV	OOB	AB-HR-SH	AVG	PB	SUP	APR	DL	PV
1964	SF N	1	0	1.000	9	0	0	0	15	8	3	1	0	1-0	15	1.80	198	.163	.176	3	.000	-0		3		0.
1965	SF N	4	1	.800	45	1	0	8	74.1	57	31	9	3	22-5	85	3.75	96	.205	.271	13	.154	-0	364	1		0.
Total 2		5	1	.833	54	1	0	9	89.1	65	34	10	3	23-5	100	3.43	105	.199	.257	16	.125	-1	364	4		0.

MURCHISON, TIM Thomas Malcolm B10.8.1896 Liberty NC D10.20.1962 Liberty NC BR/TL/6-0/185 d6.21 Col Guilford

YEAR	TM LG	W	L	PCT	G	GS	CG-SHO	SV-BS	IP	H	R	HR	HB	BB-IB	SO	ERA	AERA	OAV	OOB	AB-HR-SH	AVG	PB	SUP	APR	DL	PV
1917	StL N	0	0	—	1	0	0	0	1	0	0	0	0	2	2	0.00	—	.200	.400	0		0		0		0
1920	Cle A	0	0	—	2	0	0	0	5	3	1	0	0	4	2	0.00	—	.200	.368	1	.000	-0		2		0
Total 2		0	0	—	3	0	0	0	6	3	1	0	0	6	2	0.00	—	.167	.375	1	.000	-0		2		0

MURFF, RED John Robert B4.1.1921 Burlington TX BR/TR/6-3/195* d4.21 Col Gettysburg

YEAR	TM LG	W	L	PCT	G	GS	CG-SHO	SV-BS	IP	H	R	HR	HB	BB-IB	SO	ERA	AERA	OAV	OOB	AB-HR-SH	AVG	PB	SUP	APR	DL	PV
1956	Mil N	0	0	—	14	1	0	1	24.1	25	14	3	0	7-0	18	4.44	78	.272	.320	5	.200	0	127	-3	66	-0
1957	Mil N	2	2	.500	12	1	0	2	26	31	14	3	0	11-1	13	4.85	72	.301	.368	6-0-1	.000	-1	252	-3		-0
Total 2		2	2	.500	26	2	0	3	50.1	56	28	6	0	18-1	31	4.65	75	.287	.346	11-0-1	.091	-1	190	-6	66	-0

MURPHY, CON Cornelius B. "Monk","Razzle Dazzle" B10.15.1863 Worcester MA D8.1.1914 Worcester MA TR/5-9/130 d9.11

YEAR	TM LG	W	L	PCT	G	GS	CG-SHO	SV-BS	IP	H	R	HR	HB	BB-IB	SO	ERA	AERA	OAV	OOB	AB-HR-SH	AVG	PB	SUP	APR	DL	PV
1884	Phi N	0	3	.000	3	3	3	0	26	37	34	1	6	10	6	6.58	45	.319	.352	10	.000	-1	36	-10		-0
1890	Bro P	4	10	.286	20	14	11	2	139	168	134	2	6	82	29	4.79	93	.286	.379	69	.217	-1*	85	-7		-0
Total 2		4	13	.235	23	17	14	2	165	205	168	3	6	88	39	5.07	83	.292	.375	79	.190	-3	78	-17		-0

MURPHY, DANNY Daniel Francis B8.23.1942 Beverly MA BL/TR/5-11/185* d6.18.1960 ▲

YEAR	TM LG	W	L	PCT	G	GS	CG-SHO	SV-BS	IP	H	R	HR	HB	BB-IB	SO	ERA	AERA	OAV	OOB	AB-HR-SH	AVG	PB	SUP	APR	DL	PV
1969	Chi A	2	1	.667	17	0	0	4-1	31.1	28	14	2	1	10-0	16	2.01	191	.252	.323	1	.000	0		6		
1970	Chi A	2	3	.400	51	0	0	5-3	80.2	82	55	11	4	49-8	42	5.69	68	.273	.378	6-1-0	.333	2		-14		
Total 2		4	4	.500	68	0	0	9-4	112	110	63	13	6	59-8	58	4.66	83	.268	.364	7-1-0	.286	2		-8		

MURPHY, DAN Daniel Lee B9.18.1964 Artesia CA BR/TR/6-2/195 d8.10

YEAR	TM LG	W	L	PCT	G	GS	CG-SHO	SV-BS	IP	H	R	HR	HB	BB-IB	SO	ERA	AERA	OAV	OOB	AB-HR-SH	AVG	PB	SUP	APR	DL	PV
1989	SD N	0	0	—	7	0	0	0-0	6.1	6	6	1	0	4-1	1	5.68	62	.231	.333	0	—	0		-2		

MURPHY, ED Edward J. B1.22.1877 Auburn NY D1.29.1935 Weedsport NY TR/6-1/186 d4.23

YEAR	TM LG	W	L	PCT	G	GS	CG-SHO	SV-BS	IP	H	R	HR	HB	BB-IB	SO	ERA	AERA	OAV	OOB	AB-HR-SH	AVG	PB	SUP	APR	DL	PV
1898	Phi N	1	2	.333	7	3	2	0	30	41	23	3	1	10	8	5.10	67	.323	.377	14-0-1	.357	1	96	-5		
1901	StL N	10	9	.526	23	21	16	0	165	201	105	5	1	32	42	4.20	76	.298	.331	64-1-1	.250	3	141	-21		
1902	StL N	10	6	.625	23	17	12-1	1	164	187	86	7	2	31	37	3.02	91	.286	.321	61	.262	1	123	-7		
1903	StL N	4	8	.333	15	12	9	0	106	108	62	2	6	38	16	3.31	99	.262	.333	64-0-2	.203	-1*	115	-33		
Total 4		25	25	.500	68	53	39-1	1	465	537	276	17	10	111	103	3.64	84	.288	.331	203-1-4	.246	5				

MURPHY, JOHN John Henry 5-11/165 d4.17

YEAR	TM LG	W	L	PCT	G	GS	CG-SHO	SV-BS	IP	H	R	HR	HB	BB-IB	SO	ERA	AERA	OAV	OOB	AB-HR-SH	AVG	PB	SUP	APR	DL	PV
1884	Alt U	5	6	.455	14	10	10	0	111.2	141	90	3	9	46		3.87	69	.289	.302	94	.149	-7*	59	-14		
	Wil U	0	6	.000	7	6	5	0	48	52	36	3	2	27		3.00	89	.259	.266	31	.065	-4*	32	-1		
	Year	5	12	.294	21	16	15	0	159.2	193	126	6	11	73		3.61	74	.280	.291	125	.128	-11	49	-17		

MURPHY, JOHNNY John Joseph "Grandma","Fireman","Fordham Johnny" B7.14.1908 New York NY D1.14.1970 New York NY BR/TR/6-2/190 d5.19 Def 1944-45 Col Fordham

YEAR	TM LG	W	L	PCT	G	GS	CG-SHO	SV-BS	IP	H	R	HR	HB	BB-IB	SO	ERA	AERA	OAV	OOB	AB-HR-SH	AVG	PB	SUP	APR	DL	PV
1932	NY A	0	0	—	2	0	0	0	3.1	7	6	0	0	3	2	16.20	25	.438	.526	1	1.000	1		-4		
1934	NY A	14	10	.583	40	20	10	4	207.2	193	79	11	0	76	70	3.12	130	.250	.317	71-0-5	.099	-3	94	26		
1935	NY A	10	5	.667	40	8	4	5	117	110	67	7	0	55	28	4.08	99	.243	.325	32-0-2	.156	2	123	-2		
1936	†NY A	9	3	.750	27	5	2	5	88	90	38	5	1	36	34	3.38	108	.262	.330	36	.361	4	189	13		
1937	†NY A☆	13	4	.765	39	4	0	10	110	121	59	7	1	50	36	4.24	107	.256	.336	32-0-2	.063	-3	87	5		
1938	†NY A☆	8	2	.800	32	2	1	11	91.1	90	47	5	1	41	43	4.40	99	.252	.335	11-0-1	.182	1		9		
1939	†NY A☆	3	6	.333	38	0	0	19	61.1	57	33	2	0	28	30	3.69	109	.247	.292	13-0-2	.077	1	109	4		
1940	NY A	8	4	.667	35	1	0	9	63.1	58	27	5	0	15	23	1.98	199	.237	.330	18-0-3	.056	-1		18		
1941	NY A	8	3	.727	35	0	0	15	77.1	68	20	1	0	40	29	3.41	101	.293	.364	13-0-2	.154	0		-1		
1942	†NY A	4	10	.286	31	0	0	11	58	66	27	2	2	23	24	3.40	102	.240	.317	6-0-1	.000	-0		6		
1943	†NY A	12	4	.750	37	0	0	8	68	44	22	2	0	30	19	2.51	128	.183	.273	19-0-1	.053	-2		6		
1946	NY A	4	2	.667	27	0	0	7	45	40	24	1	0	19	19	2.80	139	.206	.304	11	.273	1		7		
1947	Bos A	0	0	—	32	0	0	3	54.2	41	17	1	5	18	9											
Total 13		93	53	.637	415	40	17	107	1045	985	464	52	5	444	378	3.50	117	.249	.326	298-0-22	.154	-0	123	75		

MURPHY, JOE Joseph Akin B9.7.1866 St.Louis MO D3.28.1951 Coral Gables FL 5-11/160 d4.28 Col St.Louis

YEAR	TM LG	W	L	PCT	G	GS	CG-SHO	SV-BS	IP	H	R	HR	HB	BB-IB	SO	ERA	AERA	OAV	OOB	AB-HR-SH	AVG	PB	SUP	APR	DL	PV
1886	Cin AA	2	3	.400	5	5	5	0	46	50	34	0	1	21	11	4.89	72	.256	.332	18	.000	-3	54	-6		
	StL N	0	4	.000	4	4	3	0	33	45	41	3	0	16	11	8.18	39	.319	.389	14	.214	0	62	-15		
	StL AA	1	0	1.000	1	1	1	0	7	5	4	0	0	3	3	3.86	89	.179	.258	3	.000	-1	155	0		
1887	StL AA	1	0	1.000	1	1	1	0	9	13	8	0	0	4	5	5.00	91	.317	.378	6	.167	-1	309	-1		
Total 2		4	7	.364	11	11	10	0	95	113	87	3	1	44	30	5.97	59	.279	.351	41	.098	-4	94	-22		

MURPHY, ROB Robert Albert B5.26.1960 Miami FL BL/TL/6-2/215(200-215) [CinN81*S1/3] d9.13 Col Florida

YEAR	TM LG	W	L	PCT	G	GS	CG-SHO	SV-BS	IP	H	R	HR	HB	BB-IB	SO	ERA	AERA	OAV	OOB	AB-HR-SH	AVG	PB	SUP	APR	DL	PV
1985	Cin N	0	0	—	2	0	0	0-0	3	6	2	1	0	3-0	1	6.00	63	.200	.333	0	—	0		-1		
1986	Cin N	6	0	1.000	34	0	0	1-2	50.1	26	4	0	0	21-2	36	0.72	539	.155	.245	3	.000	-0		17		
1987	Cin N	8	5	.615	87	0	0	3-4	100.2	91	37	7	0	32-5	99	3.04	139	.239	.297	5-0-1	.200	0		13		
1988	Cin N	0	6	.000	76	0	0	3-3	84.2	69	31	3	1	38-6	74	3.08	116	.229	.317	0	—	0		5		
1989	Bos A	5	7	.417	74	0	0	9-7	105	97	38	7	1	41-8	107	2.74	150	.251	.323	0	—	0		14		
1990	†Bos A	0	6	.000	68	0	0	7-3	57	85	46	10	1	32-3	54	6.32	65	.348	.420	0	—	0		-14		
1991	Sea A	0	1	.000	57	0	0	4-0	48	47	17	4	1	19-4	34	3.00	138	.250	.322	0	—	0		-4	19	
1992	Hou N	3	1	.750	59	0	0	1-3	55.2	56	25	2	1	21-4	42	4.04	84	.260	.322	1-0-1	.000	-0		-5		
1993	StL N	5	7	.417	73	0	0	1-3	64.2	73	35	8	1	20-6	41	4.87	83	.290	.342	2-0-1	.500	1		-5		
1994	StL N	4	3	.571	50	0	0	2-1	40.1	35	18	7	0	13-2	25	3.79	112	.230	.291	0	—	0		-2		
	NY A	0	1	.000	6	0	0	0-0	1.2	5	3	2	0	0-0	0	16.20	28	.375	.375	0	—	0		-5		
1995	LA N	0	1	.000	6	0	0	0-0	5	6	7	2	0	3-0	2	12.60	31	.300	.391	1	1.000	1		-4		
	Fla N	1	1	.500	8	0	0	0-0	7.1	8	9	1	0	5-1	5	9.82	44	.286	.394	0	—	0		-9		
	Year	1	2	.333	14	0	0	0-0	12.1	14	16	3	0	8-1	7	10.95	38	.292	.393	1	1.000	1		-9		
Total 11		32	38	.457	597	0	0	30-25	623.1	598	277	54	5	247-41	520	3.64	109	.254	.324	12-0-3	.250	0		22	19	

YEAR	TM LG	W	L	PCT	G	GS	CG-SHO	SV-BS	IP	H	R	HR	HB	BB-IB	SO	ERA	AERA	OAV	OOB	AB-HR-SH	AVG	PB	SUP	APR	DL	PW

MURPHY, BOB   Robert J.   B12.26.1866 Dutchess Co. NY   6-0/173   d5.27

YEAR	TM LG	W	L	PCT	G	GS	CG-SHO	SV-BS	IP	H	R	HR	HB	BB-IB	SO	ERA	AERA	OAV	OOB	AB-HR-SH	AVG	PB	SUP	APR	DL	PW
1890	NY N	1	0	1.000	3	2	1	0	18	23	17	0	0	10	8	5.50	64	.303	.384	9	.111	-1	90	-3		-0.2
	Bro AA	3	9	.250	12	12	10	0	96	121	95	6	5	46	26	5.72	68	.299	.377	50-1	.180	0*	81	-19		-1.6
Total	1	4	9	.308	15	14	11	0	114	144	112	6	5	56	34	5.68	67	.299	.378	59-1	.169	-1	82	-22		-1.8

MURPHY, TOM   Thomas Andrew   B12.30.1945 Cleveland OH   BR/TR/6-3/185(185-205)   [AnaA67*S1/6]   d6.13   Col Ohio U.

YEAR	TM LG	W	L	PCT	G	GS	CG-SHO	SV-BS	IP	H	R	HR	HB	BB-IB	SO	ERA	AERA	OAV	OOB	AB-HR-SH	AVG	PB	SUP	APR	DL	PW
1968	Cal A	5	6	.455	15	15	3	0	99.1	67	30	5	5	28-0	56	2.17	134	.191	.258	28-0-5	.000	-3	100	7		0.4
1969	Cal A	10	16	.385	36	35	4	0-0	215.2	213	110	12	21	69-3	100	4.21	83	.260	.332	71-0-5	.141	-0	81	-15		-1.7
1970	Cal A	16	13	.552	39	38	5-2	0-0	227	223	114	32	7	81-10	99	4.24	85	.261	.329	76-1-8	.184	3	100	-14		-1.4
1971	Cal A	6	17	.261	37	36	7	0-0	243.1	228	108	24	9	82-9	89	3.77	86	.256	.323	75-0-6	.173	1	86	-12		-0.9
1972	Cal A	0	0	—	6	0	0	0	10	13	6	0	0	8-1	2	5.40	54	.342	.447	1	.000	-0		-2		-0.1
	KC A	4	4	.500	18	9	1-1	1-0	70.1	77	26	3	6	16-0	34	3.07	99	.287	.341	13-0-5	.000	-1*	142	0		-0.1
	Year	4	4	.500	24	9	1-1	1-0	80.1	90	32	3	6	24-1	36	3.36	90	.294	.356	14-0-5	.000	-1	143	-2		-0.2
1973	StL N	3	7	.300	19	13	2	0-0	88.2	89	38	5	3	22-0	42	3.76	98	.269	.317	23-0-3	.174	0	80	1		0.2
1974	Mil N	10	10	.500	70	0	0	20-7	123	97	27	6	2	51-18	47	1.90	191	.224	.306	2	.500	0		24		5.0
1975	Mil A	1	9	.100	52	0	0	20-9	72.1	85	43	5	5	27-5	32	4.60	84	.295	.362	0	—	0*		-6	20	-1.2
1976	Mil A	0	1	.000	15	0	0	1-2	18.1	25	18	2	2	9-3	7	7.36	48	.313	.396	0	—	0		-8		-0.5
	Bos A	4	5	.444	37	0	0	8-5	81	91	43	5	2	25-11	32	3.44	113	.290	.343	0	—	0		-8		-0.5
	Year	4	6	.400	52	0	0	9-7	99.1	116	61	7	4	34-14	39	4.17	92	.294	.354	0	—	0		1		0.1
1977	Bos A	0	1	.000	16	0	0	0-0	30.2	44	25	6	0	12-0	13	6.75	67	.338	.392	0	—	0		-7		-0.4
	Tor A	2	1	.667	19	1	0	2-0	52	63	22	6	1	18-3	26	3.63	117	.304	.358	0	—	0	127	4		0.2
	Year	2	2	.500	35	1	0	2-0	82.2	107	47	12	1	30-3	39	4.79	91	.318	.371	0	—	0	124	-3		-0.1
1978	Tor A	6	9	.400	50	0	0	7-4	94	87	43	11	0	37-10	36	3.96	101	.256	.322	0	—	0		1		0.2
1979	Tor A	1	2	.333	10	0	0	0-2	18.1	23	11	1	0	8-0	6	5.40	81	.311	.378	0	—	0		-1		-0.2
Total	12	68	101	.402	439	147	22-3	59-29	1444	1425	664	123	63	493-73	621	3.78	94	.263	.329	289-1-32	.145	0	89	-27	20	-0.3

MURPHY, WALTER   Walter Joseph   B9.27.1907 New York NY   D3.23.1976 Houston TX   BR/TR/6-1.5/180   d4.19

YEAR	TM LG	W	L	PCT	G	GS	CG-SHO	SV-BS	IP	H	R	HR	HB	BB-IB	SO	ERA	AERA	OAV	OOB	AB-HR-SH	AVG	PB	SUP	APR	DL	PW
1931	Bos A	0	0	—	2	0	0	0	4	2	2	0	0	1	0	9.00	48	.444	.500	0	—	0		-1		0.0

MURRAY, AMBY   Ambrose Joseph   B6.4.1913 Fall River MA   D2.6.1997 Port Salerno FL   BL/TL/5-7/150   d7.5   Col Brown

YEAR	TM LG	W	L	PCT	G	GS	CG-SHO	SV-BS	IP	H	R	HR	HB	BB-IB	SO	ERA	AERA	OAV	OOB	AB-HR-SH	AVG	PB	SUP	APR	DL	PW
1936	Bos N	0	0	—	4	1	0	0	11	15	5	1	0	3	2	4.09	94	.319	.360	4	.250	0	199	0		0.0

MURRAY, DALE   Dale Albert   B2.2.1950 Cuero TX   BR/TR/6-4/205*   [MonN70 18/418]   d7.7   Col Blinn (TX) JC

YEAR	TM LG	W	L	PCT	G	GS	CG-SHO	SV-BS	IP	H	R	HR	HB	BB-IB	SO	ERA	AERA	OAV	OOB	AB-HR-SH	AVG	PB	SUP	APR	DL	PW
1974	Mon N	1	1	.500	32	0	0	10-0	69.2	46	12	1	0	23-2	31	1.03	372	.187	.256	10	.000	-1		19		1.1
1975	Mon N	15	8	.652	63	0	0	9-10	111.1	134	59	0	3	39-10	43	3.96	98	.305	.361	14	.214	1		-3	36	-0.4
1976	Mon N	4	9	.308	81	0	0	13-8	113.1	117	47	1	0	37-12	35	3.26	115	.277	.331	8-0-3	.000	-1		6		0.9
1977	Cin N	7	4	.778	61	1	0	4-4	102	125	60	13	2	46-6	42	4.94	80	.314	.382	12-0-2	.167	-0	339	-4		-1.0
1978	Cin N	1	1	.500	15	0	0	2-0	32.2	34	20	1	0	17-4	25	4.13	86	.272	.356	3-0-2	.000	-0		-4		-0.3
	NY N	8	5	.615	53	0	0	5-2	86.1	85	39	4	2	36-19	37	3.65	97	.266	.340	7	.000	-0		-1		-0.2
	Year	9	6	.600	68	0	0	7-2	119	119	59	5	2	53-23	62	3.78	94	.268	.344	10-0-2	.000	-0		-5		-0.5
1979	NY N	4	8	.333	58	0	0	4-7	97	105	48	6	0	52-14	37	4.82	77	.287	.373	6-0-2	.000	-0		-12		-1.5
	Mon N	1	2	.333	9	0	0	1-1	13.1	14	4	1	0	3-2	4	2.70	138	.292	.327	2	.000	-0		2		0.3
	Year	5	10	.333	67	0	0	5-8	110.1	119	52	7	0	55-16	41	4.57	81	.287	.368	8-0-2	.000	-1		-10		-1.2
1980	Mon N	0	1	.000	16	0	0	0-0	29.1	39	23	3	0	12-2	16	6.14	59	.315	.372	3	.000	-0		-8		-0.5
1981	Tor A	1	0	1.000	11	0	0	0-0	15.1	12	2	0	0	5-0	12	1.17	338	.211	.274	0	—	0		5		0.3
1982	Tor A	8	7	.533	56	0	0	11-7	111	115	48	3	0	32-5	60	3.16	143	.268	.323	0	—	0		13		2.1
1983	NY A	2	4	.333	40	0	0	1-2	94.1	113	56	5	1	22-4	45	4.48	88	.297	.333	0	—	0		-7		-0.4
1984	NY A	1	2	.333	19	0	0	0-1	23.2	30	15	2	2	5-0	13	4.94	78	.306	.352	0	—	0		-3	96	-0.4
1985	NY A	0	0	—	3	0	0	0-0	2	4	3	0	0	0-0	0	13.50	30	.400	.400	0	—	0		-2		-0.1
	Tex A	0	0	—	1	0	0	0-0	1	3	2	0	0	0-0	0	18.00	24	.750	.750	0	—	0		-1		-0.1
	Year	0	0	—	4	0	0	0-0	3	7	5	0	0	0-0	0	15.00	27	.500	.500	0	—	0		-3		-0.1
Total	12	53	50	.515	518	1	0	60-42	902.1	976	448	40	14	329-80	400	3.85	101	.282	.343	65-0-9	.077	-3	339	-7	132	-0.2

MURRAY, DAN   Daniel Saffle   B11.21.1973 Los Alamitos CA   BR/TR/6-1/193*   [NYN95 10/273]   d8.9   Col San Diego St.

YEAR	TM LG	W	L	PCT	G	GS	CG-SHO	SV-BS	IP	H	R	HR	HB	BB-IB	SO	ERA	AERA	OAV	OOB	AB-HR-SH	AVG	PB	SUP	APR	DL	PW
1999	NY N	0	0	—	1	0	0	0-0	2	4	3	0	0	2-0	1	13.50	32	.444	.500	0	—	0		-2		-0.1
	KC A	0	0	—	4	0	0	0-0	8.1	9	8	4	1	4-0	1	6.48	78	.265	.359	0	—	0		-2		-0.1
2000	KC A	0	0	—	10	0	0	0-0	19.1	20	10	7	1	10-0	16	4.66	112	.278	.369	0	—	0		1		0.1
Total	2	0	0	—	15	0	0	0-0	29.2	33	21	11	2	16-0	18	5.76	89	.287	.369	0	—	0		-3		-0.1

MURRAY, GEORGE   George King "Smiler"   B9.23.1898 Charlotte NC   D10.18.1955 Memphis TN   BR/TR/6-2/200   d5.8   Col North Carolina St.

YEAR	TM LG	W	L	PCT	G	GS	CG-SHO	SV-BS	IP	H	R	HR	HB	BB-IB	SO	ERA	AERA	OAV	OOB	AB-HR-SH	AVG	PB	SUP	APR	DL	PW
1922	NY A	3	2	.600	22	2	0	0	56.2	53	27	0	1	26	14	3.97	101	.255	.340	18-1-0	.278	2	85	1		0.2
1923	Bos A	7	11	.389	39	18	5	0	177.2	190	111	9	7	87	40	4.91	84	.291	.380	55-0-6	.164	-3	69	-11		-1.3
1924	Bos A	2	9	.182	28	7	0	0	80.1	97	68	6	7	32	27	6.72	65	.307	.383	22-0-1	.182	-1	55	-19		-2.2
1926	Was A	6	3	.667	12	12	5	0	81.1	89	56	9	6	37	28	5.64	69	.287	.374	36-0-3	.139	-2	140	-15		-1.6
1927	Was A	1	1	.500	7	3	0	0	18	18	18	1	2	15	5	7.00	58	.265	.412	6-0-1	.167	-0	130	-7		-0.6
1933	Chi A	0	0	—	2	0	0	0	2.1	3	2	0	0	2	0	7.71	55	.375	.500	0	—	0		-1		0.0
Total	6	19	26	.422	110	42	10	0	416.1	450	282	17	23	199	114	5.38	76	.288	.376	137-1-11	.175	-4	90	-52		-5.5

MURRAY, HEATH   Heath Robertson   B4.19.1973 Troy OH   BL/TL/6-4/205*   [SDN94 3/66]   d5.24   Col Michigan   [DL 1998 SD N 9]

YEAR	TM LG	W	L	PCT	G	GS	CG-SHO	SV-BS	IP	H	R	HR	HB	BB-IB	SO	ERA	AERA	OAV	OOB	AB-HR-SH	AVG	PB	SUP	APR	DL	PW
1997	SD N	1	2	.333	17	3	0	0-0	33.1	50	25	3	4	21-3	16	6.75	58	.376	.472	6	.000	-1	109	-10	20	-0.9
1999	SD N	0	4	.000	22	8	0	0-0	50	60	33	7	1	26-4	25	5.76	74	.297	.377	13-0-1	.154	0	108	-8		-0.5
2001	Det A	1	7	.125	40	4	0	0-2	63.1	82	48	11	3	40-5	42	6.54	68	.322	.418	0	—	0	63	-14		-1.5
2002	Cle A	0	2	.000	9	0	0	0-0	12	12	10	3	2	7-0	11	7.50	59	.267	.389	0	—	0		-4	70	-0.5
Total	4	2	15	.118	88	15	0	0-2	158.2	204	116	24	10	94-12	94	6.41	67	.321	.415	19-0-1	.105	-1	95	-36	99	-3.4

MURRAY, JIM   James Francis "Big Jim"   B12.31.1900 Scranton PA   D7.15.1973 Queens NY   BB/TL/6-2/210   d7.3   Col Syracuse

YEAR	TM LG	W	L	PCT	G	GS	CG-SHO	SV-BS	IP	H	R	HR	HB	BB-IB	SO	ERA	AERA	OAV	OOB	AB-HR-SH	AVG	PB	SUP	APR	DL	PW
1922	Bro N	0	0	—	4	0	0	1	6	8	3	0	0	3	3	4.50	90	.320	.393	2	.500	0		0		0.0

MURRAY, JOE   Joseph Ambrose   B11.11.1920 Wilkes-Barre PA   D10.19.2001 San Clemente CA   BL/TL/6-0/165   d8.17

YEAR	TM LG	W	L	PCT	G	GS	CG-SHO	SV-BS	IP	H	R	HR	HB	BB-IB	SO	ERA	AERA	OAV	OOB	AB-HR-SH	AVG	PB	SUP	APR	DL	PW
1950	Phi A	0	3	.000	8	2	0	0	30	34	17	1	5	16	9	5.70	80	.283	.390	11	.000	-2	99	-3		-0.4

MURRAY, MATT   Matthew Michael   B9.26.1970 Boston MA   BL/TR/6-6/240   [AtlN88 2/41]   d8.12   [DL 1993 Atl N 97]

YEAR	TM LG	W	L	PCT	G	GS	CG-SHO	SV-BS	IP	H	R	HR	HB	BB-IB	SO	ERA	AERA	OAV	OOB	AB-HR-SH	AVG	PB	SUP	APR	DL	PW
1995	Atl N	0	2	.000	4	1	0	0-0	10.2	18	8	3	1	5-0	3	6.75	64	.256	.356	2	.500	0	84	-2		-0.3
	Bos A	0	1	.000	2	1	0	0-0	3.1	11	10	1	0	3-0	1	18.90	26	.524	.583	0	—	0	77	-6		-0.9
Total	1	0	3	.000	6	2	0	0-0	14	21	18	4	1	8-0	4	9.64	46	.350	.435	2	.500	0	82	-8	97	-1.2

MURRAY, PAT   Patrick Joseph   B7.18.1897 Scottsville NY   D11.5.1983 Rochester NY   BR/TL/6-0/175   d7.1   Col Notre Dame

YEAR	TM LG	W	L	PCT	G	GS	CG-SHO	SV-BS	IP	H	R	HR	HB	BB-IB	SO	ERA	AERA	OAV	OOB	AB-HR-SH	AVG	PB	SUP	APR	DL	PW
1919	Phi N	0	2	.000	8	2	1	0	34.1	50	28	0	4	12	11	6.29	51	.347	.412	12	.000	-1	37	-10		-0.7

MUSGRAVES, DENNIS   Dennis Eugene   B12.25.1943 Indianapolis IN   BR/TR/6-4/190   d7.9   Col Missouri

YEAR	TM LG	W	L	PCT	G	GS	CG-SHO	SV-BS	IP	H	R	HR	HB	BB-IB	SO	ERA	AERA	OAV	OOB	AB-HR-SH	AVG	PB	SUP	APR	DL	PW
1965	NY N	0	0	—	5	1	0	0	16	11	2	0	2	7-0	11	0.56	627	.200	.313	2	.000	-0	25	5	44	0.2

MUSSELMAN, JEFF   Jeffrey Joseph   B6.21.1963 Doylestown PA   BL/TL/6-0/180*   [TorA85 6/157]   d9.2   Col Harvard

YEAR	TM LG	W	L	PCT	G	GS	CG-SHO	SV-BS	IP	H	R	HR	HB	BB-IB	SO	ERA	AERA	OAV	OOB	AB-HR-SH	AVG	PB	SUP	APR	DL	PW
1986	Tor A	0	0	—	6	0	0	0	5.1	7	5	1	0	5-1	4	10.13	42	.333	.448	0	—	0		-4		-0.2
1987	Tor A	12	5	.706	68	1	0	3-5	89	75	43	7	3	54-12	54	4.15	109	.237	.353	0	—	0	101	4		0.8
1988	Tor A	8	5	.615	15	15	0	0-0	85	80	34	4	3	30-2	39	3.18	125	.252	.320	0	—	0	126	7	72	1.0
1989	Tor A	0	1	.000	5	3	0	0-0	11	19	15	2	0	9-0	5	10.64	36	.404	.491	0	—	0	103	-9	69	-0.7
	NY N	3	2	.600	20	0	0	0-0	26.1	27	11	1	0	14-3	11	3.08	107	.267	.357	0	—	0		0		0.2
1990	NY N	0	2	.000	28	0	0	0-1	32	40	22	3	1	15-2	14	5.63	67	.310	.364	1	.000	0		-6		-0.4
Total	5	23	15	.605	142	19	0	3-6	248.2	249	132	18	7	123-19	125	4.31	94	.266	.354	1	.000	0	118	-8	141	0.7

MUSSELMAN, RON   Ralph Ronald   B11.11.1954 Wilmington NC   BR/TR/6-2/185*   [SeaA77 5/130]   d8.18   Col Clemson

YEAR	TM LG	W	L	PCT	G	GS	CG-SHO	SV-BS	IP	H	R	HR	HB	BB-IB	SO	ERA	AERA	OAV	OOB	AB-HR-SH	AVG	PB	SUP	APR	DL	PW
1982	Sea A	1	0	1.000	12	0	0	0-0	15.2	18	7	2	1	6-1	9	3.45	124	.300	.362	0	—	0		1		0.1
1984	Tor A	0	0	—	11	0	0	1-0	21.1	18	7	2	0	10-2	9	2.11	196	.225	.304	0	—	0		4		0.4
1985	Tor A	3	0	1.000	25	4	0	0-0	52.1	59	28	2	0	24-2	29	4.47	95	.284	.352	0	—	0	123	-1		-0.1
Total	3	4	2	.667	48	4	0	1-0	89.1	95	42	6	1	40-5	47	3.73	113	.273	.343	0	—	0	123	4		0.4

YEAR	TM LG	W	L	PCT	G	GS	CG-SHO	SV-BS	IP	H	R	HR	HB	BB-IB	SO	ERA	AERA	OAV	OOB	AB-HR-SH	AVG	PB	SUP	APR	DL	PW
MUSSER, PAUL	Paul B6.24.1889 Millheim PA D7.7.1973 State College PA BR/TR/6-0/175 d6.6 Mil 1918-19 Col Susquehanna																									
1912	Was A	0	0	—	7	2	0	2	20.2	16	7	0	2	16	10	2.61	128	.225	.382	7	.000	-1	144	2		0.0
1919	Bos A	0	2	.000	5	4	1	0	19.2	26	16	0	0	8	14	4.12	73	.342	.405	8	.000	-1	123	-5		-0.6
Total	2	0	2	.000	12	6	1	2	40.1	42	23	0	2	24	24	3.35	95	.286	.393	15	.000	-2	127	-3		-0.6
MUSSILL, BARNEY	Bernard James B10.1.1919 Bower Hill PA BR/TL/6-1/200 d4.20 Col Bowling Green																									
1944	Phi N	0	1	.000	16	0	0	0	19.1	20	16	1	0	13	5	6.05	60	.267	.375	1	.000	-0		-6		-0.3
MUSSINA, MIKE	Michael Cole B12.8.1968 Williamsport PA BR/TR/6-1/180* [BalA90 1/20] d8.4 Col Stanford																									
1991	Bal A	4	5	.444	12	12	2	0-0	87.2	77	31	7	1	21-0	52	2.87	138	.239	.286	0	—	0	96	11		1.0
1992	Bal A★	18	5	**.783**	32	32	8-4	0-0	241	212	70	16	2	48-2	130	2.54	160	.239	**.278**	0	—	0	100	41		3.8
1993	Bal A☆	14	6	.700	25	25	3-2	0-0	167.2	163	84	20	3	44-2	117	4.46	101	.256	.306	0	—	0	119	4	29	0.3
1994	Bal A★	16	5	.762	24	24	3	0-0	176.1	163	63	19	1	42-1	99	3.06	165	.248	.291	0	—	0	95	37		4.0
1995	Bal A	**19**	9	.679	32	32	7-4	0-0	221.2	187	86	24	1	50-4	158	3.29	145	.226	.270	0	—	0	124	5		0.5
1996	†Bal A	19	11	.633	36	**36**	4-1	0-0	243.1	264	137	31	3	69-0	204	4.81	103	.275	.325	0	—	0	109	31		2.8
1997	†Bal A☆	15	8	.652	33	33	4-1	0-0	224.2	197	87	27	3	54-3	218	3.20	138	.234	.282	4	.250	-0	101	24	38	2.5
1998	Bal A	13	10	.565	29	29	4-2	0-0	206.1	189	85	22	4	41-3	175	3.49	130	.242	.282	2	.000	-0	129	27		2.5
1999	Bal A★	18	7	.720	31	31	4	0-0	203.1	207	88	16	1	52-0	172	3.50	134	.268	.312	11	.273	-1	66	26		2.4
2000	Bal A	11	15	.423	34	34	6-1	0-0	237.2	236	105	28	3	46-0	210	3.79	124	.255	.291	6	.000	-1	86	33		2.4
2001	†NY A	17	11	.607	34	34	4-3	0-0	228.2	202	87	20	4	42-2	214	3.15	141	.237	**.274**	7	.143	-0	125	9		1.3
2002	†NY A	18	10	.643	33	33	2-2	0-0	215.2	208	103	27	5	48-1	182	4.05	107	.253	.296	5-0-1	.600	1	93	26		2.8
2003	†NY A	17	8	.680	31	31	2-1	0-0	214.2	192	86	21	3	40-4	195	3.40	129	.238	.275	2	.000	-0	110	0	42	2.8
2004	†NY A	12	9	.571	27	27	1	0-0	164.2	178	91	22	2	40-1	132	4.59	100	.276	.318	1	.000	-0	117	1		0.1
2005	†NY A	13	8	.619	30	30	2-2	0-0	179.2	199	93	23	7	47-0	142	4.41	99	.283	.333	3	.000	-0	104	1		0.1
Total	15	224	127	.638	443	443	56-23	0-0	3013	2874	1296	323	43	684-23	2400	3.64	125	.251	.294	41-0-1	.195	1	104	311	109	32.5
MUSTAIKIS, ALEX	Alexander Dominick B3.26.1909 Chelsea MA D1.17.1970 Scranton PA BR/TR/6-3/180 d7.7																									
1940	Bos A	0	1	.000	6	1	0	0	15	15	18	1	0	15	5	9.00	50	.254	.405	6	.333	1	78	-8		-0.3
MUTIS, JEFF	Jeffrey Thomas B12.20.1966 Allentown PA BL/TL/6-2/185* [CleA88 1/27] d6.15 Col Lafayette																									
1991	Cle A	0	3	.000	3	3	0	0-0	12.1	23	16	1	0	7-1	6	11.68	36	.397	.455	0	—	0	66	-9		-1.4
1992	Cle A	0	2	.000	3	2	0	0-0	11.1	14	14	4	0	6-0	8	9.53	41	.429	.469	0	—	0	58	-7		-1.0
1993	Cle A	3	6	.333	17	13	1-1	0-0	81	93	56	14	7	33-2	29	5.78	76	.289	.365	3	.000	-0		-3		-1.1
1994	Fla N	1	0	1.000	35	0	0	0-0	38.1	51	25	6	1	15-3	30	5.40	82	.331	.390	3	.000	-0	79	-14		-0.2
Total	4	4	11	.267	58	18	1-1	0-0	143	191	111	25	8	61-6	73	6.48	67	.324	.390	3	.000	-0	79	-31		-3.7
MYERS, BRETT	Brett Allen B8.17.1980 Jacksonville FL BR/TR/6-4/215* [PhiN99 1/12] d7.24																									
2002	Phi N	4	5	.444	12	12	1	0-0	72	73	38	11	6	29-1	34	4.25	90	.277	.359	23-0-3	.130	-0	107	-4		-0.5
2003	Phi N	14	9	.609	32	32	1-1	0-0	193	205	99	20	9	76-8	143	4.43	90	.272	.344	62-0-5	.145	-0*	129	-9		-1.0
2004	Phi N	11	11	.500	32	31	1-1	0-0	176	196	113	31	6	62-4	116	5.52	80	.281	.343	51-0-8	.196	2	117	-19		-1.9
2005	Phi N	13	8	.619	34	34	2	0-0	215.1	193	94	31	11	68-2	208	3.72	117	.237	.304	65-0-11	.154	-0	119	16		1.5
Total	4	42	33	.560	110	109	5-2	0-0	656.1	667	344	93	32	235-15	501	4.47	94	.264	.333	201-0-27	.159	1	120	-16		-1.9
MYERS, ELMER	Elmer Glenn B3.2.1894 York Springs PA D7.29.1976 Collingswood NJ BR/TR/6-2/185 d10.6 Mil 1918																									
1915	Phi A	1	0	1.000	1	1	1-1	1	9	2	2	0	0	5	12	0.00	—	.074	.219	3-0-1	.000	-0	100	3		0.2
1916	Phi A	14	23	.378	44	35	31-2	1	315	280	169	7	14	168	182	3.66	78	.248	.353	126-0-4	.214	2*	85	-28		-2.5
1917	Phi A	9	16	.360	38	23	13-2	3	201.2	221	122	2	5	79	88	4.42	62	.283	.353	73-0-2	.247	-2	97	-31		-3.4
1918	Phi A	4	8	.333	18	15	5-1	1	95.1	101	66	4	4	42	17	4.63	63	.283	.365	35	.143	-2	89	-18		-2.3
1919	Cle A	8	7	.533	23	15	6-1	1	134.2	134	68	3	10	43	38	3.74	89	.264	.334	46-0-1	.239	2	87	-4		-0.7
1920	Cle A	2	4	.333	16	7	2	1	71.2	93	52	1	4	23	16	4.77	80	.316	.374	25-0-2	.240	0	96	-10		-0.7
	Bos A	9	1	.900	12	10	9-1	0	97	90	30	1	2	24	34	2.13	171	.249	.299	38	.316	3	142	16		1.4
	Year	11	5	.688	28	17	11-1	1	168.2	183	82	2	6	47	50	3.25	114	.279	.333	63-0-2	.286	3	122	7		1.1
1921	Bos A	8	12	.400	30	20	11	0	172	217	107	11	10	53	40	4.87	80	.315	.373	65-0-1	.215	-2	94	-12		-1.1
1922	Bos A	0	1	.000	3	1	0	0	5.2	10	11	1	2	3	1	17.47	24	.370	.469	1	.000	-0	41	-7		-1.4
Total	8	55	72	.433	185	127	78-8	7	1102	1148	625	30	51	440	640	4.06	80	.275	.352	412-0-11	.226	4	94	-91		-9.2
MYERS, HENRY	Henry C. B5.1858 Philadelphia PA D4.18.1895 Philadelphia PA BR/TR/5-9/159 d8.20.1881 M1 ▲																									
1882	Bal AA	0	2	.000	2	1	0	0	26	30	28	2		4	7	6.58	42	.270	.296	294	.180	-1*	84	-9		-0.6
MYERS, JIMMY	James Xavier B4.28.1969 Oklahoma City OK BR/TR/6-1/190 [SFN87 35/902] d4.6																									
1996	Bal A	0	0	—	11	0	0	0-0	14	18	13	4	0	3-1	6	7.07	70	.305	.328	0	—	0		-4		-0.1
MYERS, JOSEPH	Joseph William B3.18.1882 Wilmington DE D2.11.1956 Delaware City DE BR/TR/5-10.5/205 d10.7																									
1905	Phi N	0	1	—	1	1	1	0	5	3	3	0	1	3	2	3.60	74	.176	.333	2	.000	-0	80	-1		-0.1
MYERS, MIKE	Michael Stanley B6.26.1969 Cook Co. IL BL/TL/6-4/214(197-220) [SFN90 4/122] d4.25 Col Iowa St. [DL 1994 Fla N 60]																									
1995	Fla N	0	0	—	2	0	0	0-0	1	0	0	0	0	3-0	0	0.00	—	.167	.444	0	—	0		1		0.1
	Det A	1	0	1.000	11	0	0	0-1	6.1	10	7	1	2	4-0	4	9.95	48	.385	.485	0	—	0		-3		-0.2
1996	Det A	1	5	.167	**83**	0	0	6-2	64.2	70	41	6	4	34-8	69	5.01	102	.272	.365	0	—	0		-6		-0.8
1997	Det A	0	4	.000	**88**	0	0	2-3	53.2	58	36	12	2	25-2	50	5.70	81	.274	.351	0	—	0		8		0.3
1998	Mil N	2	2	.500	70	0	0	1-2	50	44	19	5	6	22-1	40	2.70	161	.249	.348	1	.000	-0		-2		-0.6
1999	Mil N	2	1	.667	71	0	0	0-3	41.1	46	24	7	3	13-1	35	5.23	88	.291	.356	0	—	0		16		-0.1
2000	Col N	0	1	.000	78	0	0	1-1	45.1	24	10	2	2	24-3	41	1.99	292	.160	.284	0	—	0		6		0.7
2001	Col N	4	3	.400	73	0	0	0-0	40	32	17	2	1	24-7	36	3.60	148	.225	.339	0	—	0		6		0.5
2002	†Ari N	4	3	.571	69	0	0	4-5	37	39	18	2	8	17-0	31	4.38	102	.275	.381	0	—	0		-3		-0.3
2003	Ari N	0	1	.000	64	0	0	0-3	36.1	38	23	4	5	21-1	25	5.70	81	.262	.374	0	—	0		-1		-0.5
2004	Sea A	4	1	.800	50	0	0	0-0	27.2	29	15	3	2	17-4	23	4.88	92	.279	.387	0	—	0		1		0.1
	†Bos A	1	0	1.000	25	0	0	0-1	15	16	7	2	0	6-1	9	4.20	116	.267	.333	0	—	0		1		-0.1
	Year	5	1	.833	75	0	0	0-1	42.2	45	22	5	2	23-5	32	4.64	99	.274	.368	0	—	0		6		0.0
2005	†Bos A	1	3	.250	65	0	0	0-1	37.1	30	14	3	2	13-2	21	3.13	147	.224	.300	1	.000	-0		24	60	0.2
Total	11	20	22	.476	749	0	0	14-23	456.2	437	231	49	37	223-30	380	4.30	112	.255	.351	3	.000	-0		24	60	2.5
MYERS, RANDY	Randall Kirk B9.19.1962 Vancouver WA BL/TL/6-1/215(190-230) [NYN82 S1/9] d10.6 Col Clark (WA) CC [DL 1999 SD N 181, 2000 SD N 181]																									
1985	NY N	0	0	—	1	0	0	0-0	2	0	0	0	0	1-0	2	0.00	—	.000	.143	0	—	0		0		0.1
1986	NY N	0	0	—	10	0	0	0-0	10.2	11	5	1	1	9-1	13	4.22	85	.256	.396	7	.286	0		-1		0.2
1987	NY N	3	6	.333	54	0	0	6-3	75	61	36	6	0	30-5	92	3.96	97	.225	.296	7	.286	0		-1		0.2
1988	†NY N	7	3	.700	55	0	0	26-3	68	45	15	5	2	17-2	69	1.72	190	.190	.248	4	.250	1		12		2.3
1989	NY N	7	4	.636	65	0	0	24-5	84.1	62	23	4	0	40-4	88	2.08	190	.206	.297	5	.000	-1		10		1.5
1990	†Cin N★	4	6	.400	66	0	0	31-6	86.2	59	24	6	3	38-8	98	2.08	190	.193	.287	4	.250	0	79	3		1.8
1991	Cin N	6	13	.316	58	12	1	6-4	132	116	61	8	1	80-5	108	3.55	107	.242	.347	29-0-3	.172	0	79	-4		0.3
1992	SD N	3	6	.333	66	0	0	38-8	79.2	84	38	7	1	34-3	66	4.29	84	.279	.349	7-0-1	.143	-0		-4		-0.7
1993	Chi N	4	4	.333	73	0	0	**53**-6	75.1	65	29	7	1	26-2	86	3.11	130	.230	.295	2-0-1	.500	1*		9		1.0
1994	Chi N★	1	5	.167	38	0	0	21-5	40.1	40	18	3	0	16-1	32	3.79	111	.260	.327	1	.000	-0		2		0.3
1995	Chi N★	1	2	.333	57	0	0	**38**-6	55.2	49	25	7	0	28-1	59	3.88	108	.237	.324	0	—	0		10		1.0
1996	†Bal A	4	4	.500	62	0	0	31-7	58.2	60	24	7	0	29-4	74	3.53	140	.265	.347	0	—	0		19		1.3
1997	†Bal A★	2	3	.400	61	0	0	**45**-1	59.2	47	12	2	0	22-2	56	1.51	293	.217	.289	0	—	0		22		2.5
1998	Tor A	3	4	.429	41	0	0	28-5	42.1	44	21	4	2	19-4	32	4.46	104	.265	.346	1	.000	-0		-4		-0.4
	†SD N	1	3	.250	21	0	0	0-1	14.1	15	10	2	0	7-1	9	6.28	63	.273	.355	0	—	0		4		-0.3
Total	14	44	63	.411	728	12	1	347-60	884.2	758	338	69	12	396-43	884	3.19	123	.233	.316	60-0-5	.183	2	79	78	362	15.3
MYERS, RODNEY	Rodney Luther B6.26.1969 Rockford IL BR/TR/6-1/205(200-215) [KCA90 12/342] d4.3 Col Wisconsin-Madison																									
1996	Chi N	2	1	.667	45	0	0	0-0	67.1	61	38	6	3	38-3	50	4.68	93	.243	.343	5	.000	-1		-2		-0.2
1997	Chi N	0	0	—	5	0	0	0-0	9	12	6	1	1	7-1	6	6.00	72	.333	.455	0	—	0	85	-1		-0.2
1998	Chi N	0	0	—	12	0	0	0-1	18	26	14	3	0	6-0	15	7.00	63	.342	.390	1	.000	-0		-5		-0.7
1999	Chi N	3	1	.750	46	0	0	0-0	63.2	71	34	10	1	25-2	41	4.38	104	.289	.354	7	.429	1		1	173	0.0
2000	SD N	0	0	—	3	0	0	0-0	2	2	1	0	0	0-0	3	4.50	99	.250	.250	0	—	0		0		0.0
2001	SD N	1	2	.333	37	0	0	1-1	47.1	53	31	6	4	20-0	29	5.32	78	.291	.367	2		-0		-6	29	-0.7

YEAR	TM LG	W	L	PCT	G	GS	CG-SHO	SV-BS	IP	H	R	HR	HB	BB-IB	SO	ERA	AERA	OAV	OOB	AB-HR-SH	AVG	PB	SUP	APR	DL	PW
2002	SD N	1	1	.500	14	0	0	0-0	21.1	29	20	1	3	10-0	11	5.91	66	.333	.420	1	.000	-0		-7		-0.6
2003	LA N	0	0	—	4	0	0	0-0	9	10	7	1	1	4-0	5	6.00	69	.270	.357	2	.000	-0		-2		-0.1
2004	LA N	0	0	—	1	0	0	0-0	2	1	0	0	0	0-0	1	0.00	—	.167	.167	0	—	0		1		0.0
Total 9		7	5	.583	167	1	0	1-3	239.2	265	151	28	13	110-6	161	5.07	85	.285	.365	18	.167	0	85	-21	202	-1.5

MYETTE, AARON   Aaron Kenneth B9.26.1977 New Westminster BC, Can. BR/TR/6-4/195(195-210) [ChiA97 1/43] d9.7 Col Washington

YEAR	TM LG	W	L	PCT	G	GS	CG-SHO	SV-BS	IP	H	R	HR	HB	BB-IB	SO	ERA	AERA	OAV	OOB	AB-HR-SH	AVG	PB	SUP	APR	DL	PW
1999	Chi A	0	2	.000	4	3	0	0-0	15.2	17	11	2	2	14-1	11	6.32	78	.266	.412	0	—	0	38	-2		-0.2
2000	Chi A	0	0	—	2	0	0	0-0	2.2	0	0	0	1	0-0	1	0.00	—	.000	.333	0	—	0		1	35	0.1
2001	Tex A	4	5	.444	19	15	0	0-0	80.2	94	65	12	11	37-0	67	7.14	67	.293	.381	0	—	0	109	-19		-1.7
2002	Tex A	2	5	.286	15	12	0	0-0	48.1	64	57	11	6	41-0	48	10.06	48	.325	.448	0	—	0	115	-26		-3.0
2003	Cle A	0	0	—	2	0	0	0-0	2.2	7	7	1	1	2-0	1	23.63	19	.467	.556	0	—	0		-5	20	-0.2
2004	Cin N	0	0	—	5	0	0	0-0	4.1	3	4	0	2	8-0	6	8.31	52	.188	.500	0	—	0		-2		-0.1
Total 6		6	12	.333	47	30	0	0-0	154.1	185	144	26	22	106-1	134	8.16	59	.298	.413	0	—	0	104	-53	55	-5.1

MYRICK, BOB   Robert Howard B10.1.1952 Hattiesburg MS BR/TL/6-1/200* [NYN74 20/461] d5.28 Col Mississippi St. [DL 1979 NY N 33]

YEAR	TM LG	W	L	PCT	G	GS	CG-SHO	SV-BS	IP	H	R	HR	HB	BB-IB	SO	ERA	AERA	OAV	OOB	AB-HR-SH	AVG	PB	SUP	APR	DL	PW
1976	NY N	1	1	.500	21	1	0	0-0	27.2	34	13	2	0	13-1	11	3.25	103	.306	.376	3	.000	-0	53	0		0.0
1977	NY N	2	2	.500	44	4	0	2-0	87.1	86	39	5	1	33-5	49	3.61	105	.265	.331	11	.182	-0	82	2	24	0.1
1978	NY N	0	3	.000	17	0	0	0-2	24.2	18	10	3	0	13-2	13	3.28	108	.207	.310	2	.000	-0		1		0.1
Total 3		3	6	.333	82	5	0	2-2	139.2	138	62	10	1	59-8	73	3.48	105	.264	.337	16	.125	-1	78	3	57	0.2

NABHOLZ, CHRIS   Christopher William B1.5.1967 Harrisburg PA BL/TL/6-5/212* [MonN88 2/49] d6.11 Col Towson

YEAR	TM LG	W	L	PCT	G	GS	CG-SHO	SV-BS	IP	H	R	HR	HB	BB-IB	SO	ERA	AERA	OAV	OOB	AB-HR-SH	AVG	PB	SUP	APR	DL	PW
1990	Mon N	6	2	.750	11	11	1-1	0-0	70	43	23	6	2	32-1	53	2.83	130	.176	.274	21-0-2	.000	-2	87	7		0.6
1991	Mon N	8	7	.533	24	24	1	0-0	153.2	134	66	5	2	57-4	99	3.63	100	.237	.307	52-0-3	.115	-1	103	2	48	0.1
1992	Mon N	11	12	.478	32	32	1-1	0-0	195	176	80	11	5	74-2	130	3.32	105	.244	.317	65-0-7	.123	-1	107	3		0.5
1993	Mon N	9	8	.529	26	21	1	0-0	116.2	100	57	9	8	63-4	74	4.09	102	.236	.343	39-0-3	.128	-1	104	4	31	0.3
1994	Cle A	0	1	.000	6	4	0	0-0	11	23	16	1	1	9-0	5	11.45	42	.418	.500	0	—	0	126	-8	40	-0.6
	Bos A	3	4	.429	8	8	0	0-0	42	44	32	5	2	29-1	23	6.64	76	.282	.399	0	—	0	71	-6		-0.8
	Year	3	5	.375	14	12	0	0-0	53	67	48	6	3	38-1	28	7.64	65	.318	.425	0	—	0	88	-14		-1.4
1995	Chi N	0	1	.000	34	0	0	0-0	23.1	22	15	4	0	14-3	21	5.40	77	.253	.350	1	.000	-0		-3	35	-0.1
Total 6		37	35	.514	141	100	4-2	0-0	611.2	542	289	41	20	278-15	405	3.94	97	.240	.327	178-0-15	.107	-5	101	-1	154	-0.0

NABORS, JACK   Herman John B11.19.1887 Montevallo AL D10.29.1923 Wilton AL BR/TR/6-3/185 d8.9

YEAR	TM LG	W	L	PCT	G	GS	CG-SHO	SV-BS	IP	H	R	HR	HB	BB-IB	SO	ERA	AERA	OAV	OOB	AB-HR-SH	AVG	PB	SUP	APR	DL	PW
1915	Phi A	0	5	.000	10	7	2	0	54	58	46	1	5	35	18	5.50	83	.304	.424	16-0-1	.125	-1	93	-16		-1.4
1916	Phi A	1	20	.048	40	30	11	1	212.2	206	110	2	3	95	74	3.47	82	.266	.349	69	.101	-4	68	-15		-2.0
1917	Phi A	0	0	—	2	0	0	0	3	2	1	0	0	1	2	3.00	92	.200	.273	0	—	0		0		0.0
Total 3		1	25	.038	52	37	13	1	269.2	266	157	3	8	131	94	3.87	74	.273	.364	85-0-1	.106	-6	73	-31		-3.4

NAGEOTTE, CLINT   Clinton Scott B10.25.1980 Parma OH BR/TR/6-3/200(200-225) [SeaA99 5/155] d6.1

YEAR	TM LG	W	L	PCT	G	GS	CG-SHO	SV-BS	IP	H	R	HR	HB	BB-IB	SO	ERA	AERA	OAV	OOB	AB-HR-SH	AVG	PB	SUP	APR	DL	PW
2004	Sea A	1	6	.143	12	5	0	0-0	36.2	48	31	3	4	27-1	24	7.36	61	.324	.436	2	.000	-0	96	-12	37	-1.7
2005	Sea A	0	0	—	3	0	0	0-0	4	6	3	0	1	1-0	1	6.75	62	.353	.421	0	—	0		-1		0.0
Total 2		1	6	.143	15	5	0	0-0	40.2	54	34	3	5	28-1	25	7.30	61	.327	.435	2	.000	-0	96	-13	37	-1.7

NAGLE, JUDGE   Walter Harold "Lucky" B3.10.1880 Santa Rosa CA D5.26.1971 Santa Rosa CA BR/TR/6-0/176 d4.26

YEAR	TM LG	W	L	PCT	G	GS	CG-SHO	SV-BS	IP	H	R	HR	HB	BB-IB	SO	ERA	AERA	OAV	OOB	AB-HR-SH	AVG	PB	SUP	APR	DL	PW
1911	Pit N	4	2	.667	8	3	1	1	27.1	33	16	3	1	6	11	3.62	95	.324	.367	7	.143	-0	73	-1		-0.3
	Bos A	1	1	.500	5	1	0	0	27	27	12	2	0	6	12	3.33	98	.262	.303	10-0-1	.100	-1	110	1		-0.1
Total 1		5	3	.625	13	4	1	1	54.1	60	28	5	1	12	23	3.48	97	.293	.335	17-0-1	.118	-1	82	0		-0.4

NAGY, CHARLES   Charles Harrison B5.5.1967 Bridgeport CT BL/TR/6-3/200* [CleA88 1/17] d6.29 Col Connecticut

YEAR	TM LG	W	L	PCT	G	GS	CG-SHO	SV-BS	IP	H	R	HR	HB	BB-IB	SO	ERA	AERA	OAV	OOB	AB-HR-SH	AVG	PB	SUP	APR	DL	PW
1990	Cle A	2	4	.333	9	8	0	0-0	45.2	58	31	7	1	21-1	26	5.91	67	.315	.386	0	—	0	87	-9		-1.0
1991	Cle A	10	15	.400	33	33	6-1	0-0	211.1	228	103	15	4	66-7	109	4.13	101	.275	.330	0	—	0	71	3		0.3
1992	Cle A★	17	10	.630	33	33	10-3	0-0	252	245	91	11	2	57-1	169	2.96	133	.260	.300	0	—	0	95	28		3.1
1993	Cle A	2	6	.250	9	9	1	0-0	48.2	66	38	6	2	13-1	30	6.29	70	.322	.367	0	—	0	112	-10	138	-1.3
1994	Cle A	10	8	.556	23	23	3	0-0	169.1	175	76	15	5	48-1	108	3.45	138	.265	.319	0	—	0	117	24		2.2
1995	†Cle A	16	6	.727	29	29	2-1	0-0	178	194	95	20	6	61-0	139	4.55	104	.278	.339	0	—	0	135	5		0.7
1996	†Cle A★	17	5	.773	32	32	5	0-0	222	217	89	21	3	61-2	167	3.41	144	.255	.306	0	—	0	105	39		3.5
1997	Cle A	15	11	.577	34	34	1-1	0-0	227	253	115	27	7	77-4	149	4.28	110	.282	.342	5	.200	0	106	11		1.3
1998	†Cle A	15	10	.600	33	33	2	0-0	210.1	250	139	34	9	66-12	120	5.22	92	.297	.352	5	.000	-1	109	-13		-1.2
1999	†Cle A☆	17	11	.607	33	32	1	0-0	202	238	120	26	6	59-4	126	4.95	103	.293	.344	6	.000	-1*	115	3		0.4
2000	Cle A	2	7	.222	11	11	0	0-0	57	71	53	15	2	21-2	41	8.21	61	.300	.359	0	—	0	95	-19	125	-2.2
2001	Cle A	5	6	.455	15	13	0	0-0	70.1	102	53	10	0	20-1	29	6.40	72	.342	.379	1-0-1	1.000	0	126	-13	106	-1.6
2002	Cle A	1	4	.200	19	7	0	0-0	48.2	76	51	10	2	13-1	22	8.88	50	.360	.399	0	—	0*	75	-24	45	-2.0
2003	SD N	0	2	.000	5	0	0	0-0	12.1	15	7	0	0	3-0	7	4.38	92	.313	.353	2	.000	-0		-1		-0.1
Total		129	105	.551	318	297	31-6	0-0	1954.2	2188	1061	217	51	586-37	1242	4.51	102	.284	.336	19-0-1	.105	-1	106	24	414	2.1

NAGY, MIKE   Michael Timothy B3.25.1948 Bronx NY BR/TR/6-3/200* d4.21

YEAR	TM LG	W	L	PCT	G	GS	CG-SHO	SV-BS	IP	H	R	HR	HB	BB-IB	SO	ERA	AERA	OAV	OOB	AB-HR-SH	AVG	PB	SUP	APR	DL	PW
1969	Bos A	12	2	.857	33	28	7-1	0-0	196.2	183	84	10	11	106-3	84	3.11	123	.245	.347	65-0-4	.077	-2*	128	12		0.6
1970	Bos A	6	5	.545	23	20	4	0-0	128.2	138	71	16	2	64-2	56	4.48	89	.275	.358	44-0-2	.250	-2	114	-5		-0.3
1971	Bos A	1	3	.250	12	7	0	0-1	38	46	29	4	0	20-1	9	6.63	56	.315	.395	12	.083	-1	89	-11		-1.1
1972	Bos A	0	0	—	1	0	0	0-0	2	3	2	0	1	0-0	2	9.00	36	.375	.400	0	—	0		-1		-0.1
1973	StL N	0	2	.000	9	7	0	0-0	40.2	44	21	4	1	15-2	14	4.20	87	.282	.345	11	.091	-1	86	-2		-0.2
1974	Hou N	1	1	.500	9	0	0	0-0	12.2	17	13	3	1	5-1	5	8.53	41	.309	.371	1	.000	-0		-7		-1.0
Total 6		20	13	.606	87	62	11-1	0-1	418.2	431	220	37	16	210-8	170	4.15	92	.267	.356	133-0-6	.135	-2	115	-14		-2.1

NAGY, STEVE   Stephen B5.28.1919 Franklin NJ BL/TL/5-10/170* d4.20 Col Seton Hall

YEAR	TM LG	W	L	PCT	G	GS	CG-SHO	SV-BS	IP	H	R	HR	HB	BB-IB	SO	ERA	AERA	OAV	OOB	AB-HR-SH	AVG	PB	SUP	APR	DL	PW
1947	Pit N	1	3	.250	6	1	0	0	14	18	10	1	0	9	4	5.79	73	.310	.403	4	.250	0	21	-2		-0.4
1950	Was A	2	5	.286	9	9	2	0	53.1	69	50	5	0	29	17	6.58	68	.307	.386	22-1-1	.227	2*	85	-15		-1.3
Total 2		3	8	.273	15	10	2	0	67.1	87	60	6	0	38	21	6.42	69	.307	.389	26-1-1	.231	2	79	-17		-1.7

NAHEM, SAM   Samuel Ralph "Subway Sam" B10.19.1915 New York NY D4.19.2004 Berkeley CA BR/TR/6-1.5/190 d10.2 Mil 1943-45

YEAR	TM LG	W	L	PCT	G	GS	CG-SHO	SV-BS	IP	H	R	HR	HB	BB-IB	SO	ERA	AERA	OAV	OOB	AB-HR-SH	AVG	PB	SUP	APR	DL	PW
1938	Bro N	1	0	1.000	1	1	1	0	9	6	3	0	0	4	2	3.00	130	.194	.286	5	.400	0	152	1		0.2
1941	StL N	5	2	.714	26	8	2	1	81.2	76	35	2	2	38	31	2.98	126	.243	.329	23-0-6	.174	-1	135	6		0.4
1942	Phi N	1	3	.250	35	2	0	0	74.2	72	48	2	2	40	38	4.94	67	.254	.350	20	.100	-1	102	-14		-0.8
1948	Phi N	3	3	.500	28	1	0	1	59	68	52	4	3	45	30	7.02	56	.288	.408	13	.154	-0	90	-19		-1.8
Total 4		10	8	.556	90	12	3	1	224.1	222	138	8	7	127	101	4.69	78	.257	.357	61-0-6	.164	-2	130	-26		-2.0

NAKAMURA, MICHEAL   Micheal Yoshihide B9.6.1976 Nara, Japan BR/TR/5-10/170* d6.7 Col South Alabama

YEAR	TM LG	W	L	PCT	G	GS	CG-SHO	SV-BS	IP	H	R	HR	HB	BB-IB	SO	ERA	AERA	OAV	OOB	AB-HR-SH	AVG	PB	SUP	APR	DL	PW
2003	Min A	0	0	—	12	0	0	1-0	12.2	20	11	4	1	2-0	14	7.82	58	.339	.371	0	—	0		-4		-0.2
2004	Tor A	0	3	.000	19	0	0	0-0	25.2	27	23	7	2	7-0	24	7.36	67	.262	.319	0	—	0		-7		-0.7
Total 2		0	3	.000	31	0	0	1-0	38.1	47	34	11	3	9-0	38	7.51	65	.290	.337	0	—	0		-11		-0.9

NAKTENIS, PETE   Peter Ernest B6.12.1914 Aberdeen WA BL/TL/6-1/185 d6.13 Col Duke

YEAR	TM LG	W	L	PCT	G	GS	CG-SHO	SV-BS	IP	H	R	HR	HB	BB-IB	SO	ERA	AERA	OAV	OOB	AB-HR-SH	AVG	PB	SUP	APR	DL	PW
1936	Phi A	0	1	.000	7	1	0	0	18.2	24	26	2	4	27	18	12.54	41	.324	.515	5	.200	-0	34	-14		-0.6
1939	Cin N	0	0	—	3	0	0	0	4	2	1	0	2	0	1	2.25	170	.154	.267	0	—	0		1		0.1
Total 2		0	1	.000	10	1	0	0	22.2	26	27	2	4	27	19	10.72	45	.299	.483	5	.200	-0	34	-13		-0.5

NANCE, SHANE   Joseph Shane B9.7.1977 Houston TX BL/TL/5-8/180* [LAN00 11/327] d8.24 Col Houston

YEAR	TM LG	W	L	PCT	G	GS	CG-SHO	SV-BS	IP	H	R	HR	HB	BB-IB	SO	ERA	AERA	OAV	OOB	AB-HR-SH	AVG	PB	SUP	APR	DL	PW
2002	Mil N	0	0	—	4	0	0	0-0	6.1	4	3	1	0	4-0	5	4.26	97	.174	.296	3	.333	0	0		29	0.0
2003	Mil N	0	2	.000	26	0	0	0-1	24.1	34	16	5	1	10-1	25	4.81	90	.327	.385	0	—	0		-2		-0.1
2004	Ari N	1	1	.500	19	0	0	0-1	12.1	19	11	2	3	12-4	9	5.84	78	.352	.493	0	—	0		-2	33	-0.4
Total 3		1	3	.250	49	0	0	0-2	43	57	30	8	4	26-5	39	5.02	87	.315	.408	3	.333	0		-4	62	-0.5

NAPIER, BUDDY   Skelton Le Roy B12.18.1889 Byromville GA D3.29.1968 Hutchins TX BR/TR/5-11/165 d8.14

YEAR	TM LG	W	L	PCT	G	GS	CG-SHO	SV-BS	IP	H	R	HR	HB	BB-IB	SO	ERA	AERA	OAV	OOB	AB-HR-SH	AVG	PB	SUP	APR	DL	PW
1912	StL N	2	2	.333	7	4	2	0	25.1	33	21	0	3	5	10	4.97	67	.317	.366	7	.000	-1	22	-5		-0.7
1918	Chi N	0	0	—	1	0	0	0	6.2	10	4	0	0	4	2	5.40	52	.357	.438	3	.333	0		-1		-0.1
1920	Cin N	4	2	.667	9	5	5-1	0	49	47	12	0	1	7	17	1.29	236	.254	.285	14	.214	1	119	9		1.2
1921	Cin N	0	2	.000	22	6	1	1	56.2	72	38	2	0	13	14	5.56	64	.320	.366	14	.143	1	100	-11		-0.4
Total 4		5	6	.455	39	13	6-1	1	137.2	162	75	2	4	29	43	3.92	69	.304	.343	38	.158	1	94	-8		-0.4

YEAR	TM LG	W	L	PCT	G	GS	CG-SHO	SV-BS	IP	H	R	HR	HB	BB-IB	SO	ERA	AERA	OAV	OOB	AB-HR-SH	AVG	PB	SUP	APR	DL	PW

NARANJO, CHOLLY   Lazaro Ramon Gonzalo "Gonzalo" B11.25.1934 Havana, Cuba BL/TR/5-11.5/165   d7.8

1956	Pit N	1	2	.333	17	3	0	0	34.1	37	22	7	1	17-1	26	4.46	85	.282	.364	7	.143	0	62	-4		-0.2

NARLESKI, RAY   Raymond Edmond B11.25.1928 Camden NJ BR/TR/6-1/175* d4.17 f-Bill [DL 1960 Det A 156]

1954	†Cle A	3	3	.500	42	2	1	13	89	59	25	8	2	44	52	2.22	165	.189	.293	16-0-2	.000	-2	60	15		1.2
1955	Cle A	9	1	.900	60	1	1	19	111.2	91	47	11	0	52-3	94	3.71	108	.220	.306	24-0-3	.292	1	67	6		0.7
1956	Cle A*	3	2	.600	32	0	0	4	59.1	36	11	5	1	19-0	42	1.52	277	.170	.240	8	.250	0		18		1.6
1957	Cle A	11	5	.688	46	15	7-1	6	154.1	136	65	15	4	70-6	93	3.09	120	.235	.320	43-1-4	.093	-2	112	9		0.7
1958	Cle A★	13	10	.565	44	24	7	1	183.1	179	87	21	3	91-10	102	4.07	90	.255	.341	54-0-4	.204	1	126	-6		-0.8
1959	Det A	4	12	.250	42	10	1	5	104.1	105	83	21	1	59-3	71	5.78	70	.254	.343	21-0-4	.095	-1	100	-21		-3.3
Total	6	43	33	.566	266	52	17-1	58	702	606	318	81	11	335-22	454	3.60	106	.230	.318	166-1-17	.157	-2	110	21	156	0.1

NARRON, SAM   Samuel Franklin B7.12.1981 Goldsboro NC BL/TL/6-7/210 [TexA02 15/442] d7.30 gf-Sam Col East Carolina

2004	Tex A	0	0	—	1	1	0	0-0	2.2	5	4	3	0	4-0	1	13.50	37	.385	.529	0	—	0	132	-2		-0.1

NARUM, BUSTER   Leslie Ferdinand B11.16.1940 Philadelphia PA D5.17.2004 Clearwater FL BR/TR/6-1/200* d4.14

1963	Bal A	0	0	—	7	0	0	0	9	8	3	0	0	5-2	5	3.00	116	.242	.342	1-1-0	1.000	1		1		0.2
1964	Was A	9	15	.375	38	32	7-2	0	199	195	104	31	5	73-4	121	4.30	86	.259	.325	66-1-5	.061	-5	89	-10		-1.8
1965	Was A	4	12	.250	46	24	2	0	173.2	176	98	16	7	91-11	86	4.46	78	.267	.360	46-1-6	.043	-2	93	-18		-1.7
1966	Was A	0	0	—	3	0	0	0	3.1	11	9	2	0	4-0	1	21.60	16	.579	.652	0	—	0		-7		-0.3
1967	Was A	1	0	1.000	2	2	0	0	11.2	8	4	1	0	4-0	8	3.09	103	.195	.267	5	.000	-1	96	0		0.0
Total	5	14	27	.341	96	58	9-2	0	396.2	398	218	50	12	177-17	220	4.45	80	.264	.344	118-3-11	.059	-6	91	-34		-3.6

NASH, JIM   James Edwin B2.9.1945 Hawthorne NV BR/TR/6-5/220(215-230) d7.3

1966	KC A	12	1	.923	18	17	5	1	127	95	32	6	0	47-3	98	2.06	165	.204	.276	49-0-3	.102	-2	140	20		1.8
1967	KC A	12	17	.414	37	34	8-2	0	222.1	200	103	21	4	87-5	186	3.76	85	.242	.314	70-0-3	.100	-2	93	-14		-2.0
1968	Oak A	13	13	.500	34	33	12-6	0	228.2	185	63	18	3	55-12	169	2.28	124	.219	.269	74-2-6	.068	-2	100	16		1.5
1969	Oak A	8	8	.500	26	19	3-1	0-0	115.1	112	53	17	2	30-3	75	3.67	94	.247	.296	36-0-3	.111	-1	122	-4	24	-0.6
1970	Atl N	13	9	.591	34	33	6-2	0-0	212.1	211	105	22	5	90-7	153	4.07	75	.255	.332	80-2-3	.087	-3	107	6		0.2
1971	Atl N	9	7	.563	32	19	2	2-0	133	166	81	17	0	50-3	65	4.94	75	.314	.370	47	.149	-1*	120	-16		-2.0
1972	Atl N	1	1	.500	11	4	0	1-0	31.1	35	20	2	0	25-1	10	5.46	70	.307	.420	9	.222	-0	99	-5		-0.3
	Phi N	0	8	.000	9	8	0	0	37.1	46	33	5	3	17-2	15	6.27	58	.311	.384	10	.100	-0	61	-12	36	-2.2
	Year	1	9	.100	20	12	0	1-0	68.2	81	53	7	3	42-3	25	5.90	63	.309	.400	19	.158	-0	74	-16		-2.5
Total	7	68	64	.515	201	167	36-11	4-0	1107.1	1050	490	108	17	401-36	771	3.58	96	.250	.316	375-4-18	.101	-11	108	-9	60	-3.6

NASTU, PHILIP   Philip B3.8.1955 Bridgeport CT BL/TL/6-2/180* d9.15 Col Bridgeport

1978	SF N	0	1	.000	3	1	0	0-0	8	8	5	1	0	2-0	5	5.63	62	.258	.303	1	.000	-0	0	-2		-0.2
1979	SF N	3	4	.429	25	14	1	0-0	100	105	51	14	2	41-5	47	4.32	81	.272	.344	24-0-4	.042	-1	110	-8		-0.6
1980	SF N	0	0	—	6	0	0	0-0	6	10	9	1	0	5-1	1	6.00	59	.357	.455	0	—	0		-4		-0.2
Total	3	3	5	.375	34	15	1	0-0	114	123	65	16	2	48-6	53	4.50	78	.276	.349	25-0-4	.040	-1	103	-14		-1.0

NATHAN, JOE   Joseph Michael B11.22.1974 Houston TX BR/TR/6-4/195(195-220) [SFN95 6/159] d4.21 Col Stony Brook

1999	SF N	7	4	.636	19	14	0	1-0	90.1	84	45	12	1	46-0	54	4.18	102	.243	.333	28-0-5	.179	1	112	1		0.2
2000	SF N	5	2	.714	20	15	0	0-1	93.1	89	63	12	4	63-4	61	5.21	84	.255	.371	32-2-4	.156	2	139	-11	58	-0.5
2002	SF N	0	0	—	4	0	0	0	3.2	1	0	0	0	0-0	2	0.00	—	.083	.083	0	—	-0		2		0.1
2003	†SF N	12	4	.750	78	0	0	0-3	79	51	26	7	3	33-3	83	2.96	144	.186	.277	1-0-1	.000	-0		24		3.6
2004	†Min A★	1	2	.333	73	0	0	44-3	72.1	48	14	3	2	23-3	89	1.62	286	.187	.259	1	.000	-0		13		2.6
2005	Min A★	7	4	.636	69	0	0	43-5	70	46	22	5	0	22-1	94	2.70	163	.183	.247	0	—	0	126	41	58	8.2
Total	6	32	16	.667	263	29	0	88-12	408.2	319	170	44	10	187-11	383	3.44	127	.214	.304	62-2-10	.161	3	126	41	58	8.2

NATION, JOEY   Joseph Paul B9.28.1978 Oklahoma City OK BL/TL/6-2/205 [AtlN97 2/80] d9.23

2000	Chi N	0	2	.000	2	2	0	0-0	11.2	12	9	2	1	6-0	8	6.94	66	.279	.407	4	.500	1	70	-3		-0.3

NAULTY, DAN   Daniel Donovan B1.6.1970 Los Angeles CA BR/TR/6-6/211(210-224) [MinA92 14/402] d4.2 Col Cal St.-Fullerton

1996	Min A	3	2	.600	49	0	0	4-5	57	43	26	6	0	35-3	56	3.79	135	.207	.321	0	—	0	8		56	0.7
1997	Min A	1	1	.500	29	0	0	1-2	30.2	29	20	8	0	10-0	23	5.87	80	.254	.305	0	—	0	-3		98	-0.2
1998	Min A	2	0	1.000	19	0	0	0-1	23.2	25	16	3	0	10-1	15	4.94	97	.269	.337	0	—	0	-1		78	-0.1
1999	NY A	1	0	1.000	33	0	0	0-0	49.1	40	24	8	4	22-0	25	4.38	108	.225	.322	0	—	0	3			0.2
Total	4	5	5	.500	130	0	0	5-8	160.2	137	86	24	4	77-4	119	4.54	107	.231	.321	0	—	0	7	232		0.6

NAVARRO, JAIME   Jaime (Cintron) B3.27.1967 Bayamon, PR BR/TR/6-4/210(210-250) [MilA87 3/71] d6.20 f-Julio Col Miami-Dade Wolfson (FL) CC

1989	Mil A	7	8	.467	19	17	1	0	109.2	119	47	6	1	32-3	56	3.12	124	.277	.327	0	—	0	77	7		0.9
1990	Mil A	8	7	.533	32	22	3	1-1	149.1	176	83	11	8	41-3	75	4.46	87	.293	.340	0	—	0	124	-9		-0.8
1991	Mil A	15	12	.556	34	34	10-2	0-0	234	237	117	18	6	73-3	114	3.92	102	.261	.318	0	—	0	105	-1		-0.1
1992	Mil A	17	11	.607	34	34	5-3	0-0	246	224	98	14	6	64-4	100	3.33	116	.246	.295	0	—	0	101	16		1.5
1993	Mil A	11	12	.478	35	34	5-1	0-0	214.1	254	135	21	11	73-4	114	5.33	81	.300	.356	0	—	0	78	-22		-2.1
1994	Mil A	4	9	.308	29	10	0	0	89.2	115	71	10	4	35-4	65	6.62	77	.314	.377	0	—	0	78	-14		-1.7
1995	Chi N	14	6	.700	29	29	1-1	0	200.1	194	79	19	3	56-7	128	3.28	127	.251	.303	65-0-8	.185	1	108	21		1.9
1996	Chi N	15	12	.556	35	35	4-1	0-0	236.2	244	116	25	10	72-5	158	3.92	112	.269	.327	77-0-8	.130	-2	98	10		0.6
1997	Chi A	9	14	.391	33	33	2	0	209.2	267	155	22	3	73-6	142	5.79	76	.309	.359	1-0-1	.000	-0	109	-36		-3.3
1998	Chi A	8	16	.333	37	27	1	1-0	172.2	223	135	30	7	77-1	71	6.36	72	.315	.384	3-0-1	.000	-0	94	-23		-2.5
1999	Chi A	8	13	.381	32	27	0	0-0	159.2	206	126	29	11	71-1	74	6.09	81	.313	.387	0	—	0	103	-18		-2.6
2000	Mil N	0	5	.000	5	5	0	0	18.2	34	31	6	0	18-3	7	12.54	37	.410	.505	5	.000	-1	64	-18		-2.6
	Cle A	0	1	.000	7	2	0	0	14.2	20	13	3	1	5-0	9	7.98	63	.328	.377	0	—	0	140	-4		-0.3
Total	12	116	126	.479	361	309	32-8	2-1	2055.1	2313	1206	214	67	690-44	1113	4.72	91	.285	.342	152-0-18	.145	-2	102	-107		-12.5

NAVARRO, JULIO   Julio (Ventura) "Whiplash" B1.9.1936 Vieques, PR BR/TR/5-11/190* d9.3 s-Jaime

1962	LA A	1	1	.500	9	0	0	0	15.1	20	9	2	0	4-2	11	4.70	82	.317	.353	2	.500	0		-1		-0.1
1963	LA A	4	5	.444	57	0	0	12	90.1	75	36	7	2	32-6	53	2.89	134	.228	.296	15-0-1	.200	1		5		0.7
1964	LA A	0	0	—	5	0	0	1	9.1	5	2	0	2	5-0	8	1.93	170	.167	.324	2	.000	-0		-1		0.2
	Det A	2	1	.667	26	0	0	2	41	40	19	9	2	16-1	36	3.95	93	.250	.324	5	.000	-0		1		-0.1
	Year	2	1	.667	31	0	0	3	50.1	45	21	9	4	21-1	44	3.58	100	.237	.324	7	.000	-1		1		-0.1
1965	Det A	0	2	.000	15	1	0	1	30	25	14	0	0	12-1	22	4.20	83	.238	.308	4-0-1	.000	-0	126	-3		-0.2
1966	Det A	0	0	—	1	0	0	0	0	2	3	2	1	0-0	0	∞	—	1.000	1.000	0	—	0		-3		-0.3
1970	Atl N	0	0	—	17	0	0	1	26.1	24	12	7	1	1-0	21	4.10	105	.233	.248	6	.167	-0		1		0.0
Total	6	7	9	.438	130	1	0	17-1	212.1	191	97	32	8	70-10	151	3.65	99	.241	.306	34-0-2	.147	0	126	0		0.0

NAYLOR, EARL   Earl Eugene B5.19.1919 Kansas City MO D1.16.1990 Winter Haven FL BR/TR/6-0/190 d4.15 Mil 1944-45 ▲

1942	Phi N	0	5	.000	20	4	1	0	60.1	68	43	5	0	29	19	6.12	54	.286	.363	168-0-3	.196	1*	38	-17		-1.2

NAYLOR, ROLLIE   Roleine Cecil B2.4.1892 Krum TX D6.18.1966 Fort Worth TX d9.14 Mil 1918

1917	Phi A	2	2	.500	5	5	3	0	33	30	10	1	1	11	11	1.64	168	.265	.336	11	.091	-1	94	3		0.4
1919	Phi A	5	18	.217	31	23	17	0	204.2	210	109	2	4	64	68	3.34	103	.280	.339	71-0-4	.169	-2	51	-3		-0.6
1920	Phi A	10	23	.303	42	36	20	0	251.1	306	147	7	6	86	90	3.47	116	.312	.371	86-0-2	.163	-6	69	10		0.7
1921	Phi A	3	13	.188	32	19	6	0	169.1	214	106	10	3	55	39	4.84	92	.315	.369	52-0-1	.115	-4*	93	-4		-0.7
1922	Phi A	10	15	.400	35	26	11	0	171.1	212	115	7	3	51	37	4.73	90	.309	.359	55-1-2	.200	1*	104	10		-1.3
1923	Phi A	12	7	.632	26	20	9-2	0	143	149	68	5	0	59	27	3.46	119	.273	.344	8	.375	1	43	-7		-0.7
1924	Phi A	0	5	.000	10	7	1	0	38.1	53	29	2	0	20	10	6.34	68	.333	.408							-1.0
Total	7	42	83	.336	181	136	67-2	0	1011	1174	584	34	17	346	282	3.93	102	.300	.359	328-1-9	.177	-11	80	-3		-1.0

NAYMICK, MIKE   Michael John B8.26.1917 Berlin PA D10.12.2005 Stockton CA BR/TR/6-8/225 d9.24

1939	Cle A	0	1	.000	2	1	0	0	4.2	3	1	0	0	5	3	1.93	228	.188	.381	3	.000	-0	0	1		0.2
1940	Cle A	1	2	.333	13	4	0	0	30	36	17	1	1	17	15	5.10	83	.290	.389	6	.167	-0	78	-2		-0.1
1943	Cle A	4	4	.500	29	4	0	2	62.2	32	23	3	3	47	41	2.30	135	.160	.328	16-0-2	.188	-0	61	4		0.5
1944	Cle A	0	0	—	7	0	0	0	13	16	15	1	0	10	4	9.69	34	.314	.426	1	.000	-0		-9		-0.5
	StL N	0	0	—	1	0	0	0	2	2	1	0	0	1	1	4.50	78	.333	.429	0	—	0		0		0.0
Total	4	5	7	.417	52	9	1	2	112.1	89	57	5	4	64	64	3.93	89	.224	.362	26-0-2	.154	-0	65	-6		0.0

YEAR	TM LG	W	L	PCT	G	GS	CG-SHO	SV-BS	IP	H	R	HR	HB	BB-IB	SO	ERA	AERA	OAV	OOB	AB-HR-SH	AVG	PB	SUP	APR	DL	PW

NEAGLE, DENNY Dennis Edward B9.13.1968 Gambrills MD BL/TL/6-2/225(200-225) [MinA89 3/85] d7.27 Col Minnesota [DL 2004 Col N 183]

1991	Min A	0	1	.000	7	3	0	0-0	20	28	9	3	0	7-2	14	4.05	106	.329	.380	0	—	0	100	1	15	0.0
1992	†Pit N	4	6	.400	55	6	0	2-2	86.1	81	46	9	2	43-8	77	4.48	77	.247	.335	11-0-2	.000	0	88	-10		-1.3
1993	Pit N	3	5	.375	50	7	0	1-0	81.1	82	49	10	3	37-3	73	5.31	77	.258	.340	14-0-2	.000	-2	88	-10		-1.1
1994	Pit N	9	10	.474	24	24	2	0-0	137	135	80	18	3	49-3	122	5.12	85	.259	.322	42-1-5	.190	1	82	-8		-0.9
1995	Pit N★	13	8	.619	31	31	5-1	0-0	209.2	221	91	20	3	45-3	150	3.43	127	.273	.312	74-1-5	.122	-1*	103	19		1.8
1996	Pit N	14	6	.700	27	27	1	0-0	182.2	186	67	21	3	34-2	131	3.05	144	.267	.303	55-0-16	.182	-0*	93	27		2.7
	†Atl N	2	3	.400	6	6	1	0-0	38.2	40	26	5	0	14-0	18	5.59	80	.268	.329	14	.143	-0	81	-4		-0.5
	Year	16	9	.640	33	33	2	0-0	221.1	226	93	26	3	48-2	149	3.50	126	.267	.308	69-0-16	.174	-0	91	23		2.2
1997	†Atl N☆	20	5	.800	34	34	4-4	0-0	233.1	204	87	18	6	49-5	172	2.97	141	.233	.277	72-1-9	.153	1	113	32		3.3
1998	†Atl N	16	11	.593	32	31	5-2	0-0	210.1	196	91	25	6	60-3	165	3.55	117	.250	.307	63-0-9	.175	1	113	15		1.8
1999	Cin N	9	5	.643	20	19	0	0-0	111.2	95	54	23	4	40-3	76	4.27	110	.229	.300	37-0-5	.162	-0	120	7	87	0.6
2000	Cin N	8	2	.800	18	18	0	0-0	117.2	111	48	15	3	50-3	88	3.52	136	.247	.325	37-0-7	.189	1*	116	17		1.3
	†NY A	7	7	.500	16	15	1	0-0	91.1	99	61	16	2	31-1	58	5.81	82	.278	.335	0	—	0	114	-10		-1.2
2001	Col N	9	8	.529	30	30	0	0-0	170.2	192	107	29	7	60-3	139	5.38	99	.284	.344	56-2-8	.196	2	104	0	15	-0.2
2002	Col N	8	11	.421	35	28	1	0-0	164.1	170	101	26	10	63-5	111	5.26	90	.288	.338	45-0-5	.267	2	84	-7		-0.6
2003	Col N	2	4	.333	7	7	0	0-0	35.1	47	31	12	1	12-0	21	7.90	62	.320	.375	11-0-2	.000	-1	74	-9	149	-1.4
Total	13	124	92	.574	392	286	20-7	3-2	1890.1	1887	948	250	53	594-44	1415	4.24	105	.260	.319	531-5-75	.164	3	103	60	449	4.8

NEAGLE, JACK John Henry B1.2.1858 Syracuse NY D9.20.1904 Syracuse NY BR/TR/5-6/155 d7.8 ▲

1879	Cin N	0	1	.000	2	1	1	0	13	13	12	0		5	4	3.46	67	.241	.305	12	.167	-0*	99	-2		-0.2
1883	Phi N	1	7	.125	8	7	6	0	61.1	88	77	1		21	13	6.90	45	.315	.363	73	.164	-2*	74	-25		-2.4
	Bal AA	1	4	.200	6	5	4	0	46	48	48	1		20	4	4.89	71	.251	.322	35	.286	1*	76	-7		-0.4
	Pit AA	3	12	.200	16	16	12	0	114	156	123	9		25	41	5.84	56	.306	.338	101	.188	-1*	73	-34		-3.3
	Year	4	16	.200	22	21	16	0	160	204	171	10		45	50	5.57	60	.291	.334	136	.213	-0	73	-42		-3.7
1884	Pit AA	11	26	.297	38	38	37-2	0	326	354	219	6	18	70	85	3.73	89	.255	.300	148	.149	-5*	61	-17		-2.1
Total	3	16	50	.242	70	68	60-2	0	560.1	659	479	17	18	141	152	4.59	71	.272	.317	369	.176	-8	67	-85		-8.4

NEAL, BLAINE Blaine B4.6.1978 Marlton NJ BL/TR/6-5/205(205-250) [FlaN96 4/104] d9.3

2001	Fla N	0	0	—	4	0	0	0-0	5.1	7	4	0	0	5-0	3	6.75	62	.304	.429	0	—	0		-1		-0.1
2002	Fla N	3	0	1.000	32	0	0	0-0	33	32	12	1	0	14-2	33	2.73	144	.248	.322	0	—	0		4		0.3
2003	Fla N	0	0	—	18	0	0	0-0	21	38	20	2	1	9-1	10	8.14	50	.413	.449	0	—	0		-10		-0.5
2004	SD N	1	1	.500	40	0	0	0-2	42	49	19	6	2	11-3	36	4.07	97	.295	.343	0	—	0		0		0.1
2005	Bos A	0	1	.000	8	0	0	0-0	8	15	9	2	0	3-0	5	9.00	51	.429	.462	0	—	0		-4		-0.4
	Col N	1	2	.333	11	0	0	0-0	14.2	20	10	2	0	9-2	8	6.14	78	.339	.414	1	.000	-0		-4	84	-0.3
Total	5	5	4	.556	113	0	0	0-4	124	161	74	13	3	51-8	93	5.08	81	.319	.379	1	.000	-0		-13	84	-0.9

NEALE, JOE Joseph Hunt B5.7.1866 Wadsworth OH D12.30.1913 Akron OH BR/TR/5-8/153 d6.21

1886	Lou AA	0	1	.000	1	1	1	0	7	11	12	0	1	7	0	7.71	47	.393	.528	5	.000	-0*	82	-3		-0.3
1887	Lou AA	1	4	.200	5	4	4	0	41.1	60	50	4	2	15	11	6.97	63	.326	.383	19	.053	-2	80	-11		-1.0
1890	StL AA	5	3	.625	10	9	8	0	69	53	37	4	4	15	23	3.39	127	.206	.261	30	.067	-3*	104	7		0.3
1891	StL AA	6	4	.600	15	11	9-1	3	110.1	109	73	4	7	36	24	4.24	99	.249	.317	51-1	.118	-3	114	3		0.0
Total	4	12	12	.500	31	25	21-1	3	227.2	233	172	12	14	73	58	4.59	93	.257	.322	105-1	.086	-9	103	-4		-1.0

NECCIAI, RON Ronald Andrew B6.18.1932 Gallatin PA BR/TR/6-5/185 d8.10 Mil 1953 [DL 1953 Pit N 77]

1952	Pit N	1	6	.143	12	9	0	0	54.2	63	45	5	1	32	31	7.08	56	.296	.390	17	.059	-1	62	-16		-1.9

NEGRAY, RON Ronald Alvin B2.26.1930 Akron OH BR/TR/6-1/185* d9.14

1952	Bro N	0	0	—	4	1	0	0	13	15	5	0	0	5	5	3.46	105	.294	.357	2	.000	-0	122	0		0.0
1955	Phi N	4	3	.571	19	10	2	0	71.2	71	31	13	0	21-2	30	3.52	113	.257	.308	24-0-2	.000	-3	92	4		0.0
1956	Phi N	2	3	.400	39	4	0	3	66.2	72	36	6	1	24-9	44	4.18	89	.280	.340	7-0-1	.429	1	89	-4		-0.2
1958	LA N	0	0	—	4	0	0	0	11.1	12	9	4	0	7-0	2	7.15	57	.279	.373	2	.000	-0		-3		-0.2
Total	4	6	6	.500	66	15	2	3	162.2	170	81	23	1	57-11	81	4.04	95	.271	.330	35-0-3	.086	-3	94	-3		-0.4

NEHER, JIM James Gilmore B2.5.1889 Rochester NY D11.11.1951 Buffalo NY BR/TR/5-11/185 d9.10

1912	Cle A	0	0	—	1	0	0	0	1	0	0	0	0	0	0	0.00	—	.000	.000	0		0		0		0.0

NEHF, ART Arthur Neukom B7.31.1892 Terre Haute IN D12.18.1960 Phoenix AZ BL/TL/5-9.5/176 d8.13 Col Rose-Hulman Tech

1915	Bos N	5	4	.556	12	10	6-4	0	78.1	60	29	0	3	21	39	2.53	103	.214	.276	28-0-1	.143	-1	98	1		0.0
1916	Bos N	7	5	.583	22	13	6-1	0	121	110	40	1	3	20	36	2.01	124	.244	.281	40	.125	-0*	113	5		0.4
1917	Bos N	17	8	.680	38	23	16-4	0	233.1	197	78	4	4	39	101	2.16	118	.231	.268	70-0-3	.171	5	109	7		1.4
1918	Bos N	15	15	.500	32	31	28-2	0	284.1	274	107	2	6	76	96	2.69	100	.259	.312	95-0-6	.168	1*	104	1		0.6
1919	Bos N	8	9	.471	22	19	13-1	0	168.2	151	66	6	4	40	53	3.09	92	.242	.294	63-0-1	.206	2*	97	-2		0.1
	NY N	9	2	.818	13	12	9-2	0	102	70	23	2	2	19	24	1.50	187	.196	.240	35-1-1	.229	3	130	15		2.1
	Year	17	11	.607	35	31	22-3	0	270.2	221	89	8	6	59	77	2.49	114	.221	.275	98-1-2	.214	5	109	13		2.2
1920	NY N	21	12	.636	40	33	22-4	0	280.2	273	113	8	8	59	79	3.08	97	.260	.291	97-0-4	.268	5	139	0		0.6
1921	†NY N	20	10	.667	41	34	18-2	1	260.2	266	116	18	2	55	67	3.63	101	.271	.311	89-0-8	.202	0*	121	4		0.6
1922	†NY N	19	13	.594	37	35	20-2	1	268.1	286	122	15	4	64	60	3.29	122	.276	.321	88-0-8	.255	4	107	21		2.5
1923	†NY N	13	10	.565	34	27	7-1	2	196	219	112	14	2	49	50	4.50	85	.281	.326	63-0-1	.190	1	141	-16		-1.5
1924	NY N	14	4	.778	30	20	11	2	171.2	167	75	14	2	42	72	3.62	101	.254	.301	57-5-4	.228	6*	157	3		1.0
1925	NY N	11	9	.550	29	20	8-1	1	155	193	86	7	1	50	63	3.77	107	.308	.360	51-0-1	.216	1	102	1		-0.3
1926	NY N	0	0	—	2	0	0	0	1.2	2	2	0	0	1	0	10.80	35	.286	.375	1	.000	-0		-1		-0.1
	Cin N	0	1	.000	7	1	0	0	17	25	10	1	5	5	4	3.71	100	.379	.431	5	.200	-0	68	-1		0.0
	Year	0	1	.000	9	1	0	0	18.2	27	12	1	5	6	4	4.34	85	.370	.425	6	.167	-0	68	-2		-0.1
1927	Cin N	3	5	.375	21	5	1	4	45.1	59	33	2	0	14	21	5.56	68	.319	.367	13-0-1	.077	-1	90	-9		-1.5
	Chi N	1	1	.500	8	2	2-1	1	26.1	25	5	0	0	9	12	1.37	283	.260	.324	7	.429	1	66	7		0.7
	Year	4	6	.400	29	7	3-1	5	71.2	84	38	2	0	23	33	4.02	95	.299	.352	20-0-1	.200	0	83	-1		-0.8
1928	Chi N	13	7	.650	31	21	10-2	0	176.2	190	62	3	1	52	40	2.65	145	.281	.334	58-1-5	.190	2	102	24		2.8
1929	†Chi N	8	5	.615	32	14	4	1	120.2	148	85	11	2	39	27	5.59	83	.310	.365	45-0-1	.289	0	130	-12		-0.7
Total	15	184	120	.605	451	320	181-27	13	2707.2	2715	1164	107	40	640	844	3.20	105	.265	.310	915-8-41	.210	34	119	48		9.3

NEIBAUER, GARY Gary Wayne B10.29.1944 Billings MT BR/TR/6-3/200* [AtlN66 S2/27] d4.12 Col Nebraska

1969	†Atl N	2	2	.333	29	0	0	0-0	57.2	42	28	9	1	31-2	42	3.90	93	.204	.310	10	.000	-1		-2		-0.2
1970	Atl N	0	3	.000	7	0	0	0-0	12.2	11	7	0	0	8-1	9	4.97	86	.239	.352	2	.000	-0		-1		-0.1
1971	Atl N	1	0	1.000	6	1	0	1-0	21	14	5	3	1	9-1	6	2.14	174	.187	.282	5-0-1	.000	-0		4		0.2
1972	Atl N	0	0	—	9	2	0	0-0	17.1	27	15	6	1	6-0	7	7.27	52	.360	.410	4-0-1	.000	-0		-6		-0.4
	Phi N	0	2	.000	9	2	0	0-1	18.2	17	12	1	1	14-0	7	5.30	68	.239	.372	4	.250	-0	61	-3	24	-0.3
	Year	0	2	.000	18	4	0	0-1	36	44	27	7	2	20-0	14	6.25	59	.301	.391	8-0-1	.125	-0	60	-9		-0.7
1973	Atl N	2	1	.667	16	1	0	0-2	21.1	24	19	3	2	19-1	9	7.17	55	.282	.421	4-1-1	.250	1	67	-7		-0.6
Total	5	5	8	.333	75	4	0	1-3	148.2	135	86	22	6	87-5	81	4.78	79	.242	.349	29-1-3	.069	-1	53	-15	24	-1.6

NEIDLINGER, JIM James Llewellyn B9.24.1964 Vallejo CA BB/TR/6-4/180 d8.1 Col Marin (CA) CC

1990	LA N	5	3	.625	12	12	0	0-0	74	67	30	4	1	15-1	46	3.28	112	.241	.279	25	.120	-0	121	4		0.3

NEIGER, AL Alvin Edward B3.26.1939 Wilmington DE BL/TL/6-0/195 d7.30 Col Delaware

1960	Phi N	0	0	—	6	0	0	0	12.2	16	8	2	1	4-1	3	5.68	68	.340	.393	2	.500	0		-2		-0.1

NEKOLA, BOTS Francis Joseph B12.10.1906 New York NY D3.11.1987 Rockville MD BL/TL/5-11.5/175 d7.19 Col Holy Cross

1929	NY A	0	0	—	9	1	0	0	18.2	21	10	0	0	15	2	4.34	89	.296	.419	4-0-1	.500	1	241	-1		0.1
1933	Det A	0	0	—	2	0	0	0	1.1	4	4	1	0	1	0	27.00	16	.500	.556	0	—	0		-3		-0.1
Total	2	0	0	—	11	1	0	0	20	25	14	1	0	16	2	5.85	68	.316	.432	4-0-1	.500	1	241	-4		0.0

NELSON, RED Albert Francis (b Albert W. Horazdovsky) B5.19.1886 Cleveland OH D10.26.1956 St.Petersburg FL BR/TR/5-11/190 d9.9

1910	StL A	5	1	.833	7	6	6-1	0	60	57	26	0	4	14	30	2.55	97	.261	.318	23-1-0	.261	2	117	0		0.4
1911	StL A	3	9	.250	16	13	6	0	81	103	68	1	7	44	24	5.22	65	.324	.417	27-0-1	.111	2	85	-17		-2.3
1912	StL A	0	2	.000	8	3	0	1	18	21	14	0	0	13	9	7.00	47	.318	.430		.333	1	82	-5		-0.5
	Phi N	1	0	1.000	4	2	1	0	19.1	25	14	0	0	6	2	3.72	97	.305	.367	10	.100	-1	202	0		-0.1

YEAR	TM LG	W	L	PCT	G	GS	CG-SHO	SV-BS	IP	H	R	HR	HB	BB-IB	SO	ERA	AERA	OAV	OOB	AB-HR-SH	AVG	PB	SUP	APR	DL	PW
1913	Phi N	0	0	—	2	0	0	0	8.1	9	2	0	4	4	3	2.16	154	.290	.371	3	.333	0		1		0.1
	Cin N	0	0	—	2	0	0	0	1.2	6	7	1	1	4	0	37.80	9	.667	.786	0	—	0		-5		-0.3
	Year	0	0	—	4	0	0	0	10	15	9	1	5	8	3	8.10	41	.375	.490	3	.333	0		-4		-0.2
Total 4		10	12	.455	39	24	13-1	1	188.1	221	127	4	14	85	68	4.54	68	.305	.389	66-1-1	.182	0	104	-26		-2.7

NELSON, ANDY Andrew Anthony "Peaches" B11.30.1884 St.Paul MN TL d5.26
YEAR	TM LG	W	L	PCT	G	GS	CG-SHO	SV-BS	IP	H	R	HR	HB	BB-IB	SO	ERA	AERA	OAV	OOB	AB-HR-SH	AVG	PB	SUP	APR	DL	PW
1908	Chi A	0	0	—	2	1	0	0	9	11	4	0	1	4	1	2.00	116	.282	.364	2	.000	0	148	0		0.0

NELSON, EMMETT George Emmett "Ramrod" B2.26.1905 Viborg SD D8.25.1967 Sioux Falls SD BR/TR/6-3/180 d6.24
YEAR	TM LG	W	L	PCT	G	GS	CG-SHO	SV-BS	IP	H	R	HR	HB	BB-IB	SO	ERA	AERA	OAV	OOB	AB-HR-SH	AVG	PB	SUP	APR	DL	PW
1935	Cin N	4	4	.500	19	7	3-1	1	60.1	70	31	2	2	23	14	4.33	92	.295	.363	15-0-1	.133	-1	79	-1		-0.2
1936	Cin N	1	0	1.000	6	1	0	0	17	24	8	1	1	4	3	3.18	120	.333	.377	6	.167	-0	133	1		0.0
Total 2		5	4	.556	25	8	3-1	1	77.1	94	39	3	3	27	17	4.07	97	.304	.366	21-0-1	.143	-1	86	0		-0.2

NELSON, JIM James Lorin B7.4.1947 Birmingham AL D8.22.2004 Sacramento CA BR/TR/6-0/180* [PitN65 15/588] d5.30
YEAR	TM LG	W	L	PCT	G	GS	CG-SHO	SV-BS	IP	H	R	HR	HB	BB-IB	SO	ERA	AERA	OAV	OOB	AB-HR-SH	AVG	PB	SUP	APR	DL	PW
1970	Pit N	4	2	.667	15	10	1-1	0-0	68.1	64	32	5	3	38-5	42	3.42	116	.255	.355	20-0-1	.200	0	116	3		0.2
1971	Pit N	2	2	.500	17	2	0	0-0	34.2	27	9	0	2	26-4	11	2.34	146	.225	.382	6	.500	2	26	5		0.7
Total 2		6	4	.600	32	12	1-1	0-0	103	91	41	5	5	64-9	53	3.06	123	.245	.364	26-0-1	.269	2	105	8		0.9

NELSON, JEFF Jeffrey Allan B11.17.1966 Baltimore MD BR/TR/6-8/235* [LAN84 22/569] d4.16 Col Catonsville (MD) CC
YEAR	TM LG	W	L	PCT	G	GS	CG-SHO	SV-BS	IP	H	R	HR	HB	BB-IB	SO	ERA	AERA	OAV	OOB	AB-HR-SH	AVG	PB	SUP	APR	DL	PW
1992	Sea A	1	7	.125	66	0	0	6-8	81	71	34	7	6	44-12	46	3.44	116	.245	.353	0	—	0	5			0.5
1993	Sea A	5	3	.625	71	0	0	1-10	60	57	30	6	8	34-10	61	4.35	103	.258	.371	0	—	0	1			0.2
1994	Sea A	0	0	—	28	0	0	0-0	42.1	35	18	3	6	20-4	44	2.76	178	.226	.342	0	—	0	8			0.3
1995	†Sea A	7	3	.700	62	0	0	2-2	78.2	58	21	4	6	27-5	96	2.17	219	.209	.291	0	—	0	22			2.0
1996	†NY A	4	4	.500	73	0	0	2-2	74.1	75	38	6	2	36-11	91	4.36	114	.262	.348	0	—	0	12			1.1
1997	†NY A	3	7	.300	77	0	0	2-6	78.2	53	32	7	4	37-12	81	2.86	156	.191	.294	0	—	0	3			1.7
1998	†NY A	5	3	.625	45	0	0	3-3	40.1	44	18	1	8	22-4	35	3.79	115	.278	.387	1-0-1	.000	-0	3	71		0.5
1999	†NY A	2	1	.667	39	0	0	1-1	30.1	27	14	2	3	22-2	35	4.15	114	.245	.380	0	—	0	3	86		0.4
2000	†NY A	8	4	.667	73	0	0	0-4	69.2	44	24	2	2	45-1	71	2.45	195	.183	.314	1	.000	-0	17			2.5
2001	†Sea A★	4	3	.571	69	0	0	4-1	65.1	30	21	3	6	44-1	88	2.76	155	.136	.295	0	—	0	12			1.2
2002	Sea A	3	2	.600	41	0	0	2-2	45.2	36	20	4	3	27-3	55	3.94	109	.221	.335	0	—	0	4	52		0.3
2003	Sea A	3	2	.600	46	0	0	7-4	37.2	34	16	3	2	14-1	47	3.35	129	.248	.323	0	—	0	0			0.8
	†NY A	1	0	1.000	24	0	0	1-2	17.2	17	9	1	2	10-2	21	4.58	96	.246	.358	0	—	0	4			0.6
	Year	4	2	.667	70	0	0	8-6	55.1	51	25	4	4	24-3	68	3.74	116	.248	.335	0	—	0	-1	105		-0.1
2004	Tex A	1	2	.333	29	0	0	1-0	23.2	17	16	3	4	19-0	22	5.32	93	.207	.353	0	—	0	1			0.6
2005	Sea A	1	3	.250	49	0	0	1-3	36.2	32	17	3	4	22-0	34	3.93	107	.237	.358	0	—	-0	95	314		10.1
Total 14		48	44	.522	792	0	0	33-48	782	630	328	54	64	423-58	827	3.41	133	.223	.335	2-0-1	.000	-0	95	314		10.1

NELSON, JOE Joseph George B10.25.1974 Alameda CA BR/TR/6-2/185* [AtlN96 4/122] d6.13 Col San Francisco
YEAR	TM LG	W	L	PCT	G	GS	CG-SHO	SV-BS	IP	H	R	HR	HB	BB-IB	SO	ERA	AERA	OAV	OOB	AB-HR-SH	AVG	PB	SUP	APR	DL	PW
2001	Atl N	0	0	—	2	0	0	0-0	2	7	9	1	1	2-0	0	36.00	12	.583	.625	0	—	0	-7	110		-0.5
2004	Bos A	0	0	—	3	0	0	0-0	2.2	4	5	0	2	3-0	5	16.88	29	.364	.563	0	—	0	-3			-0.2
Total 2		0	0	—	5	0	0	0-0	4.2	11	14	1	3	5-0	5	25.07	18	.478	.594	0	—	0	-10	110		-0.4

NELSON, LUKE Luther Martin B12.4.1893 Cable IL D11.14.1985 Moline IL BR/TR/6-0/180 d5.25
YEAR	TM LG	W	L	PCT	G	GS	CG-SHO	SV-BS	IP	H	R	HR	HB	BB-IB	SO	ERA	AERA	OAV	OOB	AB-HR-SH	AVG	PB	SUP	APR	DL	PW
1919	NY A	3	0	1.000	9	0	0	0	24.1	22	9	1	1	11	11	2.96	108	.244	.333	7	.143	-0	246	1		0.

NELSON, LYNN Lynn Bernard "Line Drive" B2.24.1905 Sheldon ND D2.15.1955 Kansas City MO BL/TR/5-10.5/170 d4.18
YEAR	TM LG	W	L	PCT	G	GS	CG-SHO	SV-BS	IP	H	R	HR	HB	BB-IB	SO	ERA	AERA	OAV	OOB	AB-HR-SH	AVG	PB	SUP	APR	DL	PW
1930	Chi N	3	2	.600	37	3	0	0	81.1	97	52	10	6	28	29	5.09	96	.300	.367	18	.222	0	149	-1		0.
1933	Chi N	5	5	.500	24	3	3	1	75.2	65	34	2	0	30	20	3.21	102	.232	.306	21-0-2	.238	2*	85	0		0.
1934	Chi N	0	1	.000	2	1	0	0	4	4	4	1	0	1	0	36.00	11	.667	.714	0	—	0	134	-4		-0.
1937	Phi A	4	9	.308	30	4	1	2	116	140	78	12	2	51	49	5.90	80	.300	.371	113-4-1	.354	6*	111	-10		-1.
1938	Phi A	10	11	.476	32	23	13	2	191	215	142	29	5	79	75	5.65	85	.277	.347	112	.277	4*	108	-17		-1.
1939	Phi A	10	13	.435	35	24	12-2	1	197.2	233	117	27	3	64	75	4.78	98	.292	.347	80	.188	-2*	74	1		-0.
1940	Det A	1	1	.500	6	2	0	0	14	23	19	5	0	9	7	10.93	44	.371	.451	23-1-0	.348	2*	83	-9		-0.
Total 7		33	42	.440	166	60	29-2	6	676.2	777	446	86	16	262	255	5.25	88	.287	.353	367-5-3	.281	13	97	-40		-2.

NELSON, MEL Melvin Frederick B5.30.1936 San Diego CA BR/TL/6-0/185* d9.27 Col San Bernardino Valley (CA) JC
YEAR	TM LG	W	L	PCT	G	GS	CG-SHO	SV-BS	IP	H	R	HR	HB	BB-IB	SO	ERA	AERA	OAV	OOB	AB-HR-SH	AVG	PB	SUP	APR	DL	PW
1960	StL N	0	1	.000	2	1	0	0	8	7	3	1	0	2-1	7	3.38	121	.226	.273	2	.500	0	43	1		0.
1963	LA A	2	3	.400	36	3	0	1	52.2	55	34	7	2	32-5	41	5.30	65	.263	.365	11	.091	-1*	43	-11		-1.
1965	Min A	0	4	.000	28	3	0	3	54.2	57	29	7	2	23-3	31	4.12	86	.261	.337	9-0-1	.111	-0	107	-3		-0.
1967	Min A	0	0	—	1	0	0	0	0.1	3	2	1	0	0-0	0	54.00	6	.750	.750	0	—	0	-2			-0.
1968	†StL N	2	1	.667	18	4	1	1	52.2	49	20	3	0	9-3	16	2.91	100	.254	.284	12	.167	0	120	0		0.
1969	StL N	0	1	.000	8	0	0	0-0	5	13	7	0	0	3-0	3	11.81	30	.520	.533	0	—	0	-4			-0.
Total 6		4	10	.286	93	11	1	5-0	173.2	184	95	19	4	69-12	98	4.40	76	.271	.339	34-0-1	.147	-1	86	-19		-2.

NELSON, ROGER Roger Eugene "Spider" B6.7.1944 Altadena CA BR/TR/6-3/205(190-205) d9.9 Col Mt. San Antonio (CA) JC
YEAR	TM LG	W	L	PCT	G	GS	CG-SHO	SV-BS	IP	H	R	HR	HB	BB-IB	SO	ERA	AERA	OAV	OOB	AB-HR-SH	AVG	PB	SUP	APR	DL	PW
1967	Chi A	0	1	.000	5	0	0	0	7	4	1	1	2	0-0	4	1.29	241	.182	.250	0	—	0	2			0.
1968	Bal A	4	3	.571	19	6	0	1	71	49	21	3	1	26-3	70	2.41	121	.192	.270	16-0-4	.063	-0	74	5		0.
1969	KC A	7	13	.350	29	29	8-1	0	193.1	170	78	12	6	65-4	82	3.31	112	.243	.309	58-0-5	.138	-1	82	9		0.
1970	KC A	0	2	.000	4	2	0	0-0	9	18	10	3	1	0-0	3	10.00	37	.419	.422	0	—	0	119	-6	21	-1.
1971	KC A	0	1	.000	13	1	0	0	34	35	20	1	0	5-0	29	5.29	65	.269	.294	6	.333	1	182	-6		-0.
1972	KC A	11	6	.647	34	19	10-6	2-0	173.1	120	41	13	1	31-1	120	2.08	147	.196	.234	54-0-4	.093	-2	89	20		2.
1973	†Cin N	3	2	.600	14	8	1	0	54.2	49	25	4	3	24-1	42	3.46	100	.246	.333	18-0-1	.111	-1	131	1	60	0.
1974	Cin N	4	4	.500	14	12	1	1-0	85.1	67	36	7	1	35-1	42	3.38	104	.213	.293	28-0-2	.179	-1	77	1	73	0.
1976	KC A	0	0	—	3	0	0	0-0	8.2	4	2	0	2	4-1	4	2.08	169	.138	.278	0	—	0	91	26	154	2.
Total 9		29	32	.475	135	77	20-7	4-0	636.1	516	234	44	17	190-11	371	3.06	110	.224	.286	180-0-16	.128	-3	91	26	154	2.

NELSON, GENE Wayland Eugene B12.3.1960 Tampa FL BR/TR/6-0/174* [TexA78 30/690] d5.4
YEAR	TM LG	W	L	PCT	G	GS	CG-SHO	SV-BS	IP	H	R	HR	HB	BB-IB	SO	ERA	AERA	OAV	OOB	AB-HR-SH	AVG	PB	SUP	APR	DL	PW
1981	NY A	3	1	.750	9	7	0	0-0	39.1	40	24	5	1	23-1	16	4.81	75	.261	.358	0	—	0	138	-5	24	-0.
1982	Sea A	6	9	.400	22	19	2-1	0-0	122.2	133	70	16	2	60-1	71	4.62	93	.279	.360	0	—	0	84	-4		-0.
1983	Sea A	0	3	.000	10	5	1	0-0	32	38	29	6	1	21-2	11	7.88	54	.295	.397	0	—	0	67	-1		-0.
1984	Chi A	3	5	.375	20	9	2	1-0	74.2	72	38	9	1	17-0	36	4.46	94	.254	.297	0	—	0	94	2		0.
1985	Chi A	10	10	.500	46	18	1	2-2	145.2	144	74	23	7	67-4	101	4.26	102	.258	.344	1	.000	-0*	21	7		0.
1986	Chi A	6	6	.500	54	1	0	6-5	114.2	118	52	7	3	41-5	70	3.85	113	.271	.337	0	—	0*	70	5		0.
1987	Oak A	6	5	.545	54	0	0	3-3	123.2	120	58	12	5	35-0	94	3.93	106	.249	.304	0	—	0*	96	9		0.
1988	†Oak A	9	6	.600	54	1	0	3-3	111.2	93	42	9	3	38-4	67	3.06	129	.228	.296	0	—	0*	4	15		0.
1989	†Oak A	3	5	.375	50	0	0	3-1	80	60	33	6	2	30-3	70	3.26	113	.203	.277	0	—	0	19	1		0.
1990	†Oak A	3	3	.500	51	0	0	5-3	74.2	55	14	5	3	17-1	38	1.57	239	.208	.259	0	—	0	-17	40		-1.
1991	Oak A	1	5	.167	44	0	0	0-0	48.2	60	38	12	0	23-1	23	6.84	56	.306	.381	0	—	0*	109	-14		-1.
1992	Oak A	3	1	.750	28	2	0	0-1	51.2	68	37	5	0	22-5	23	6.45	59	.335	.391	0	—	0	6			-0.
1993	Cal A	0	5	.000	46	0	0	4-2	52.2	50	25	3	2	21-4	31	3.08	148	.251	.329	0	—	0	1			0.
	Tex A	0	0	—	6	0	0	1-1	8	10	3	0	0	1-1	4	3.38	124	.303	.324	0	—	0	7			0.
	Year	0	5	.000	52	0	0	5-3	60.2	60	28	3	2	22-5	35	3.12	144	.259	.328	0	—	0	92	1	79	0.
Total 13		53	64	.453	493	68	6	28-26	1080	1061	537	117	33	418-32	655	4.13	99	.258	.328	1	.000	-0*	92	1	79	-0.

NELSON, BILL William F. B9.28.1863 Terre Haute IN D6.23.1941 Terre Haute IN TR d9.3
YEAR	TM LG	W	L	PCT	G	GS	CG-SHO	SV-BS	IP	H	R	HR	HB	BB-IB	SO	ERA	AERA	OAV	OOB	AB-HR-SH	AVG	PB	SUP	APR	DL	PW
1884	Pit AA	1	2	.333	3	3	3	0	26	26	21	1	4	8	6	4.50	73	.252	.330	12	.167	-1	97	-4		-0.

NEN, ROBB Robert Allen B11.28.1969 San Pedro CA BR/TR/6-5/210(200-222) [TexA87 32/831] d4.10 f-Dick [DL 2003 SF N 183, 2004 SF N 183]
YEAR	TM LG	W	L	PCT	G	GS	CG-SHO	SV-BS	IP	H	R	HR	HB	BB-IB	SO	ERA	AERA	OAV	OOB	AB-HR-SH	AVG	PB	SUP	APR	DL	PW
1993	Tex A	1	1	.500	9	3	0	0-0	22.2	28	17	1	0	26-0	12	6.35	68	.326	.478	0	—	0	183	-5	35	-0.
	Fla N	1	0	1.000	15	1	0	0-0	33.1	35	28	5	0	20-0	27	7.02	62	.255	.348	4	.000	-0	144	-9		-0.
1994	Fla N	5	5	.500	44	0	0	15-0	58	46	20	6	0	17-2	60	2.95	151	.222	.280	3	.000	0	10			0.
1995	Fla N	0	7	.000	62	0	0	23-6	65.2	62	26	6	4	23-3	68	3.29	131	.244	.308	0	—	0	7			0.
1996	Fla N	5	1	.833	75	0	0	35-7	83	67	21	2	1	21-6	92	1.95	211	.225	.277	2	.000	0	20			2.
1997	†Fla N	9	3	.750	73	0	0	35-7	74	72	35	7	0	40-7	81	3.89	104	.250	.338	0	—	0	1			0.
1998	SF N★	7	7	.500	78	0	0	40-5	88.2	59	21	4	1	25-5	110	1.52	265	.180	.239	3	.000	0	24			3.
1999	SF N*	4	3	.273	72	0	0	37-9	72.1	79	36	8	0	27-3	77	3.98	107	.275	.337	0	—	0	2			0.
2000	†SF N	4	3	.571	68	0	0	41-5	66	37	15	4	2	19-1	92	1.50	290	.162	.230	0	—	0	21			2.

YEAR	TM LG	W	L	PCT	G	GS	CG-SHO	SV-BS	IP	H	R	HR	HB	BB-IB	SO	ERA	AERA	OAV	OOB	AB-HR-SH	AVG	PB	SUP	APR	DL	PW
2001	SF N	4	5	.444	79	0	0	**45**-7	77.2	58	28	6	1	22-6	93	3.01	136	.203	.260	1	.000	-0		10		1.9
2002	†SF N★	6	2	.750	68	0	0	43-8	73.2	64	19	2	1	20-8	81	2.20	180	.232	.286	2	.500	0		15		3.1
Total	10	45	42	.517	643	4	0	314-54	715	607	266	51	7	260-41	793	2.98	140	.227	.295	15	.067	-1	175	96	401	19.5

NEU, MIKE Michael David B3.9.1978 Napa CA BB/TR/5-10/190(175-190) [CinN99 29/878] d4.9 Col Miami

2003	Oak A	0	0	—	32	0	0	1-0	42	43	18	2	2	26-2	20	3.64	126	.261	.368	0	—	0		5		0.3
2004	Fla N	0	0	—	1	0	0	0-0	4	5	2	1	0	2-0	2	4.50	91	.313	.389	0	—	0		0		0.0
Total	2	0	0	—	33	0	0	1-0	46	48	20	3	2	28-2	22	3.72	122	.265	.370	0	—	0		5		0.3

NEUBAUER, HAL Harold Charles B5.13.1902 Hoboken NJ D9.9.1949 Providence RI BR/TR/6-0.5/185 d6.12 Col Brown

| 1925 | Bos A | 1 | 0 | 1.000 | 7 | 0 | 0 | | 10.1 | 17 | 18 | 2 | 0 | 11 | 4 | 12.19 | 37 | .378 | .500 | 0 | | 0 | | -9 | | -0.7 |

NEUER, TEX John S. B6.8.1877 Fremont OH D1.14.1966 Northumberland PA TL d8.28

| 1907 | NY A | 4 | 2 | .667 | 7 | 6 | 6-3 | 0 | 54 | 40 | 21 | 1 | 0 | 19 | 22 | 2.17 | 129 | .208 | .280 | 21 | .095 | -2 | 133 | 3 | | 0.1 |

NEUGEBAUER, NICK Nickolas Donald B7.15.1980 Riverside CA BR/TR/6-3/235* [MilN98 2/56] d8.19 [DL 2003 Mil N 183]

2001	Mil N	1	1	.500	2	2	0	0-0	6	6	5	1	0	6-0	11	7.50	57	.250	.400	3		129	-2	44		-0.4
2002	Mil N	1	7	.125	12	12	0	0-0	55.1	56	33	10	0	44-3	47	4.72	87	.264	.389	19-0-1	.105	-1	71	-4	113		-0.7
Total	2	2	8	.200	14	14	0	0-0	61.1	62	38	11	0	50-3	58	4.99	83	.263	.390	22-0-1	.091	-1	80	-6	340		-1.1

NEUMEIER, DAN Daniel George B3.9.1948 Shawano WI BR/TR/6-5/205 [ChiA68 S3/42] d9.8 Col Wisconsin-Oshkosh

| 1972 | Chi A | 0 | 0 | — | 3 | 0 | 0 | 0 | 3 | 2 | 3 | 0 | 0 | 3-0 | 0 | 9.00 | 35 | .200 | .385 | 1 | .000 | | | -2 | | -0.1 |

NEVEL, ERNIE Ernie Wyre B8.17.1918 Charleston MO D7.10.1988 Springfield MO BR/TR/6-1/200* d9.26

1950	NY A	0	1	.000	6	1	0		6.1	10	7	0	0	6	3	9.95	43	.345	.457	1-0-1	.000	-0	63	-4		-0.5
1951	NY A	0	0	—	1	0	0		4	1	0	0	1	1	0.00	—	.083	.154	1	.000	-0		2		0.1
1953	Cin N	0	0	—	10	0	0		10.1	16	7	0	0	1	5	6.10	71	.390	.405	0	—	0		-2		-0.1
Total	3	0	1	.000	14	1	0		20.2	27	14	0	0	8	9	6.10	69	.329	.389	2-0-1	.000	-0	63	-4		-0.5

NEVERS, ERNIE Ernest Alonzo B6.11.1902 Willow River MN D5.3.1976 San Rafael CA BR/TR/6-0/205 d4.26 Col Stanford

1926	StL A	2	4	.333	11	7	4	0	74.2	82	41	4	1	24	16	4.46	96	.290	.347	27	.185	-1*	67	0		0.0
1927	StL A	3	8	.273	27	5	2	2	94.2	105	61	8	2	35	22	4.94	88	.311	.379	32-0-1	.219	-1	65	-5		-0.5
1928	StL A	1	0	1.000	6	0	0	0	9	9	4	1	0	2	1	3.00	140	.281	.324	1	.000	-0		1		0.1
Total	3	6	12	.333	44	12	6	2	178.1	196	106	13	3	61	39	4.64	93	.300	.363	60-0-1	.200	-2	66	-4		-0.4

NEWCOMBE, DON Donald "Newk" B6.14.1926 Madison NJ BL/TR/6-4/225(225-248) d5.20 Mil 1952-53 Negro Lg 1944-45

1949	†Bro N★	17	8	.680	38	31	19-**5**		244.1	223	89	17	3	73	149	3.17	129	.243	.301	96-0-1	.229	3*	119	27		2.9
1950	Bro N★	19	11	.633	40	35	20-4	3	267.1	258	120	22	2	75	130	3.70	111	.254	.306	97-1-3	.247	7	116	12		1.9
1951	Bro N★	20	9	.690	40	36	18-3	0	272	235	115	19	6	91	164	3.28	120	.230	.297	103-0-2	.223	5	138	17		2.2
1954	*Bro N	9	8	.529	29	25	6	0	144.1	158	81	24	5	49	82	4.55	90	.274	.335	47-0-3	.319	4*	116	-7		-0.4
1955	†Bro N★	20	5	**.800**	34	31	17-1	0	233.2	222	103	35	1	38-1	143	3.20	127	.249	**.279**	117-7-1	.359	20*	156	19		4.0
1956	†Bro N	27	7	.794	38	36	18-5	0	268	219	101	33	3	46-8	139	3.06	130	**.221**	**.257**	111-2-3	.234	8*	129	26		4.1
1957	Bro N	11	12	.478	28	28	12-4	0	198.2	199	86	28	1	33-4	90	3.49	119	.258	.288	74-1-1	.230	5*	106	14		2.1
1958	LA N	0	6	.000	18	8	1	0	34.1	53	37	11	0	8-1	16	7.86	52	.346	.377	12	.417	2	88	-15		-2.0
	Cin N	7	7	.500	20	18	7	1	133.1	159	61	20	1	28-4	53	3.85	108	.298	.333	60-1-0	.350	8*	107	4		1.2
	Year	7	13	.350	31	26	8	1	167.2	212	98	31	1	36-5	69	4.67	89	.309	.343	72-1-0	.361	10	101	-10		-0.8
1959	Cin N	13	8	.619	30	29	17-2	1	222	216	87	25	5	27-3	100	3.16	128	.253	.279	105-3-1	.305	15*	131	22		3.6
1960	Cin N	4	6	.400	16	15	1	0	82.2	99	48	12	3	14-0	36	4.57	84	.304	.333	36-0-2	.139	-0*	86	-7		-0.9
	Cle A	2	3	.400	20	2	0	1	54	61	28	6	0	8-0	27	4.33	86	.289	.315	20	.300	2*	83	-3		-0.1
Total	10	149	90	.623	344	294	136-24	7	2154.2	2102	956	252	30	490-**21**	1129	3.56	114	.254	.298	878-15-17	.271	79	122	109		18.6

NEWELL, TOM Thomas Dean B5.17.1963 Monrovia CA BR/TR/6-1/185 [PhiN83 24/610] d9.9 Col Lassen (CA) CC

| 1987 | Phi N | 0 | 0 | — | 4 | 0 | 0 | | 4 | 4 | 1 | 0 | 3 | 1 | 36.00 | 12 | .571 | .700 | 0 | | 0 | | -3 | | -0.2 |

NEWHAUSER, DON Donald Louis B11.7.1947 Miami FL BR/TR/6-4/200* [BosA67*2/24] d6.15 Col Broward (FL) CC

1972	Bos A	4	2	.667	31	0	0	4-1	37	30	11	2	2	25-5	27	2.43	133	.226	.354	2	.000	-0		3		0.6
1973	Bos A	0	0	—	9	0	0	1-0	12	9	2	0	1	13-2	8	0.00	—	.205	.390	0	—	0		4	49	0.2
1974	Bos A	0	1	.000	2	0	0	0-0	3.2	5	4	0	0	4-1	2	9.82	58	.357	.474	0	—	0		-2		-0.4
Total	3	4	3	.571	42	0	0	5-1	52.2	44	17	2	3	42-8	37	2.39	145	.230	.372	2	.000	-0		5	49	0.4

NEWHOUSER, HAL Harold "Prince Hal" B5.20.1921 Detroit MI D11.10.1998 Detroit MI BL/TL/6-2/192* d9.29 HF1992

1939	Det A	0	1	.000	1	1	1	0	5	3	3	0	4	4	5.40	91	.188	.350	1	.000	-0	0	0		0.0
1940	Det A	9	9	.500	28	20	7	0	133.1	149	81	12	2	76	89	4.86	98	.282	.374	40-0-4	.200	-1	88	0		0.0
1941	Det A	9	11	.450	33	27	5-1	0	173	166	109	6	1	137	106	4.79	95	.249	.378	60-0-5	.150	-2	108	-5		-0.6
1942	Det A☆	8	14	.364	38	23	11-1	5	183.2	137	73	4	2	114	103	2.45	161	**.207**	.325	52-0-3	.154	-1*	64	23		2.9
1943	Det A★	8	17	.320	37	25	10-1	1	195.2	163	88	3	0	111	144	3.04	116	.224	.327	65-0-4	.185	-1	79	6		0.9
1944	Det A★	29	9	.763	47	34	25-6	2	312.1	264	94	6	1	102	**187**	2.22	161	.230	.293	120-0-6	.242	3	117	45		6.1
1945	†Det A★	25	9	**.735**	40	36	**29**-8	2	313.1	239	73	5	0	110	**212**	**1.81**	**194**	**.211**	.284	109-0-8	.257	4	106	**58**		**7.6**
1946	Det A★	26	9	.743	37	34	29-6	1	292.2	215	77	10	0	98	275	**1.94**	**189**	.201	**.269**	103-2-8	.126	-1	104	51		6.4
1947	Det A★	17	17	.500	40	36	24-3	1	285	268	105	9	2	110	176	2.87	131	.249	.320	96-0-5	.198	2	86	28		3.7
1948	Det A★	21	12	.636	39	35	19-2	1	272.1	249	109	10	1	99	143	3.01	145	.242	.309	92-0-6	.207	1	86	38		4.5
1949	Det A★	18	11	.621	38	35	22-3	1	292	277	118	19	0	111	144	3.36	124	.251	.319	91-0-14	.198	2	106	28		2.9
1950	Det A	15	13	.536	35	30	15-1	3	213.2	232	110	23	4	81	87	4.34	108	.279	.346	74-0-5	.176	-2	85	10		0.9
1951	Det A	6	6	.500	15	14	7-1	0	96.1	98	47	9	3	19	37	3.92	106	.268	.310	29-0-4	.310	2*	102	3		0.6
1952	Det A	9	9	.500	25	19	8	0	154	148	72	13	0	47	57	3.74	102	.254	.310	46-0-1	.217	3*	99	1		0.5
1953	Det A	0	1	.000	7	4	0	1	21.2	31	22	4	2	8	6	7.06	58	.348	.414	8	.500	2	131	-8		-0.3
1954	†Cle A	7	2	.778	26	1	0	7	46.2	34	16	7	0	18	25	2.51	147	.209	.286	13-0-1	.154	-0	72	6		1.1
1955	Cle A	2	0	—	2	0	0	0	2.1	1	0	0	0	4-1	1	0.00	—	.125	.417	0	—	0		1		0.0
Total	17	207	150	.580	488	374	212-33	26	2993	2674	1197	136	19	1249-**1**	1796	3.06	130	.239	.316	999-2-72	.201	12	96	285		37.2

NEWKIRK, FLOYD Floyd Elmo "Three-Finger" B7.16.1908 Norris City IL D4.15.1976 Clayton MO BR/TR/5-11/178 d8.21 b-Joel Col Illinois College

| 1934 | NY A | 0 | 0 | — | 1 | 0 | 0 | | 1 | 0 | 0 | 0 | 1 | 0 | 0.00 | — | .333 | .500 | 0 | | 0 | | 0 | | 0.0 |

NEWKIRK, JOEL Joel Inez "Sailor" B5.1.1896 Kyana IN D1.22.1966 Eldorado IL BR/TR/6-0/180 d8.20 b-Floyd

1919	Chi N	0	0	—	2	0	0		2	3	0	1	3	1	13.50	21	.286	.545	1	.000	-0		-2		-0.1
1920	Chi N	0	1	.000	2	1	0		6.2	8	6	1	0	6	2	5.40	59	.333	.467	3	.000	-0	74	-2		-0.3
Total	2	0	1	.000	3	1	0		8.2	10	9	1	1	9	3	7.27	43	.323	.488	4	.000	-1	74	-4		-0.4

NEWLIN, MAURY Maurice Milton B6.22.1914 Bloomingdale IN D8.14.1978 Houston TX BR/TR/6-0/176 d9.20 Mil 1942-45

1940	StL A	1	0	1.000	1	1	0	0	6	4	4	1	0	2	3	6.00	76	.190	.261	2	.500	0	134	-1		-0.1
1941	StL A	0	2	.000	14	0	0	1	27.2	43	24	4	0	12	10	6.51	66	.361	.420	6	.000	-1		-7		-0.5
Total	2	1	2	.333	15	1	0	1	33.2	47	28	5	0	14	13	6.42	66	.336	.396	8	.125	-1	134	-8		-0.6

NEWMAN, AL Alan Spencer B10.2.1969 LaHabra CA BL/TL/6-6/240* [MinA88 2/50] d5.14 Col Fullerton (CA) JC

1999	TB A	2	2	.500	18	0	0	0-1	15.2	22	12	4	1	9-0	20	6.89	72	.333	.421	0	—	0		-3		-0.5
2000	Cle A	0	0	—	1	0	0	0-0	1.1	6	3	1	0	1-0	0	20.25	25	.667	.700	0	—	0		-2		-0.1
Total	2	2	2	.500	19	0	0	0-1	17	28	15	3	1	10-0	20	7.94	63	.373	.453	0	—	0		-5		-0.6

NEWMAN, FRED Frederick William B2.21.1942 Boston MA D6.24.1987 Framingham MA BR/TR/6-3/190* d9.16

1962	LA A	0	1	.000	4	1	0	0	6.1	11	7	0	0	3-1	5	9.95	39	.393	.452	1	.000	-0	69	-4		-0.5
1963	LA A	1	5	.167	12	8	0	0	44	56	27	6	1	15-2	16	5.32	64	.316	.374	16	.250	1	101	-8		-1.0
1964	LA A	13	10	.565	32	28	7-2	0	190	177	68	9	7	39-8	83	2.75	120	.246	.291	61-1-5	.180	2*	83	13		2.0
1965	Cal A	14	16	.467	36	36	10-2	0	260.2	225	94	15	1	64-10	109	2.93	116	.234	.282	74-1-7	.095	-0	82	14		2.0
1966	Cal A	4	7	.364	21	19	1	0	102.2	112	54	7	9	31-2	42	4.73	71	.289	.349	30-0-3	.200	1	101	-13	41		-1.2
1967	Cal A	1	0	1.000	3	1	0	0	6.1	8	5	1	1	2-0	0	1.42	221	.320	.393	1	.000	-0		2	41	-0.1
Total	6	33	39	.458	108	93	18-4	0	610	589	255	38	17	154-23	254	3.41	99	.256	.307	183-2-15	.153	3	87	2	41	1.2

YEAR	TM LG	W	L	PCT	G	GS	CG-SHO	SV-BS	IP	H	R	HR	HB	BB-IB	SO	ERA	AERA	OAV	OOB	AB-HR-SH	AVG	PB	SUP	APR	DL	PW
NEWMAN, RAY Raymond Francis B6.20.1945 Evansville IN BL/TL/6-5/205* d5.16 Col Muskegon (MI) CC																										
1971	Chi N	1	2	.333	30	0	0	2-0	38.1	30	15	4	0	17-0	35	3.52	112	.219	.305	6	.000	-1		2		0.1
1972	Mil A	0	0	—	4	0	0	1-0	7	4	0	0	0	2-0	1	0.00	—	.182	.250	1	1.000	0		2		0.2
1973	Mil A	2	1	.667	11	0	0	1-2	18.1	19	6	2	0	5-1	10	2.95	129	.260	.304	0	—	0		2		0.4
Total	3	3	3	.500	45	0	0	4-2	63.2	53	21	6	0	24-1	46	2.97	128	.228	.300	7	.143	-0		6		0.7
NEWSOM, BOBO Louis Norman "Buck" B8.11.1907 Hartsville SC D12.7.1962 Orlando FL BR/TR/6-2/220(195-220) d9.11																										
1929	Bro N	0	3	.000	3	2	0	0	9.1	15	12	0	0	5	6	10.61	44	.375	.444	2	.000	-0	57	-6		-0.9
1930	Bro N	0	0	—	2	0	0	0	3	2	2	0	0	2	1	0.00	—	.167	.286	0	—	0		1		0.0
1932	Chi N	0	0	—	1	0	0	0	1	1	0	0	0	0	0	0.00	—	.333	.333	0	—	0		0		0.0
1934	StL A	16	20	.444	47	32	15-2	5	262.1	259	138	15	1	149	135	4.01	124	.261	.358	93-0-3	.183	-3*	67	26		2.9
1935	StL A	0	6	.000	7	6	1	1	42.2	54	29	2	0	13	22	4.85	99	.303	.351	11-0-2	.091	-1	39	-1		-0.3
	Was A	11	12	.478	28	23	17-2	2	198.1	222	108	9	4	84	65	4.45	97	.288	.361	73-0-4	.301	3	94	2		0.1
	Year	11	18	.379	35	29	18-2	3	241	276	137	11	4	97	87	4.52	97	.291	.359	84-0-6	.274	3	82	-3		-0.2
1936	Was A	17	15	.531	43	**38**	24-4	2	285.2	294	160	13	3	146	156	4.32	117	.268	.355	108-0-4	.213	0*	110	15		1.4
1937	Was A	3	4	.429	11	10	3	0	67.2	76	49	4	3	48	39	5.85	76	.287	.402	25-1-0	.120	-1*	110	-10		-0.9
	Bos A	13	10	.565	30	27	14-1	0	207.2	193	114	14	3	119	127	4.46	106	.243	.344	75-0-4	.253	2*	82	8		0.8
	Year	16	14	.533	41	**37**	17-1	0	275.1	269	163	18	6	167	166	4.81	97	.254	.359	100-1-4	.220	1	96	-3		-0.2
1938	StL A☆	20	16	.556	44	**40**	**31**	1	**329.2**	334	205	30	3	192	226	5.08	98	.265	.364	124-0-14	.250	-0	112	1		0.1
1939	StL A	3	1	.750	6	6	3	0	45.2	50	26	5	1	22	28	4.73	103	.266	.346	18	.222	-0	112	1		0.1
	Det A☆	17	10	.630	35	31	21-3	2	246	222	100	14	2	104	164	3.37	145	.238	.316	97-0-4	.186	-4	91	42		3.7
	Year	20	11	.645	41	**37**	24-3	2	291.2	272	126	19	3	126	192	3.58	136	.243	.321	115-0-4	.191	-4	95	42		3.8
1940	†Det A★	21	5	.808	36	34	20-3	0	264	235	110	19	3	100	164	**2.83**	**168**	.238	.310	107-0-4	.215	-1	109	47		3.9
1941	Det A	12	20	.375	43	36	12-2	2	250.1	265	140	15	3	118	175	4.60	90	.264	.343	88-0-5	.102	-6	70	2		-0.5
1942	Was A	11	17	.393	30	29	15-2	0	213.2	236	135	6	3	92	**113**	4.93	74	.280	.353	75-0-4	.160	-2	81	-28		-3.5
	Bro N	2	2	.500	6	5	2-1	0	32	28	13	1	1	14	21	3.38	97	.235	.321	11-0-1	.000	-1	103	0		-0.2
1943	Bro N	9	4	.692	22	12	6-1	1	125	113	51	4	2	35	75	3.02	111	.244	.329	44-0-3	.250	1	87	-22		-2.4
	StL A	1	6	.143	10	9	0	0	52.1	69	45	7	1	35	37	7.39	45	.318	.415	15-0-1	.333	1	127	-3		-3.0
	Was A	3	3	.500	6	2	2	0	40	38	22	1	2	21	11	3.82	84	.247	.345	15	.133	-1	103	-25		-3.0
	Year	4	9	.308	16	15	2	0	92.1	107	67	8	3	56	48	5.85	56	.288	.386	30-0-1	.233	0	103	-25		-3.0
1944	Phi A★	13	15	.464	37	33	18-2	1	265	243	100	11	4	82	142	2.82	123	.244	.304	88-0-9	.114	-6	76	18		1.2
1945	Phi A	8	20	.286	36	34	16-3	0	257.1	255	111	12	3	103	127	3.29	104	.260	.332	86-0-7	.163	-4	76	3		-0.4
1946	Phi A	3	5	.375	10	9	3-1	0	58.2	61	27	2	5	30	32	3.38	105	.266	.364	19-0-4	.105	-2	101	13		1.0
	Was A	11	8	.579	24	22	14-2	1	178	163	63	5	2	60	82	2.78	120	.242	.306	62-0-7	.161	-2	103	11		0.9
	Year	14	13	.519	34	31	17-3	1	236.2	224	90	7	7	90	114	2.93	116	.248	.321	81-0-11	.148	-3	97	11		0.9
1947	Was A	4	6	.400	14	13	1	0	83.2	99	44	2	1	37	40	4.09	91	.296	.368	29-0-2	.241	1	88	-4		-0.4
	†NY A	7	5	.583	17	15	6-2	0	115.2	109	38	8	2	30	42	2.80	126	.250	.301	42-0-1	.095	-3	127	11		0.2
	Year	11	11	.500	31	28	7-2	0	199.1	208	82	10	3	67	82	3.34	108	.270	.331	71-0-3	.155	-3	108	7		0.2
1948	NY N	0	4	.000	11	4	0	0	25.2	35	16	1	0	13	9	4.21	94	.330	.403	7-0-1	.429	1	79	-2		-0.2
1952	Was A	1	1	.500	10	0	0	2	12.2	16	7	2	0	9	5	4.97	72	.302	.403	2	.000	-0		-2		-0.3
	Phi A	3	3	.500	14	5	1	1	47.2	38	19	2	2	23	22	3.59	110	.220	.318	15-0-1	.133	-1	93	3		0.3
	Year	4	4	.500	24	5	1	3	60.1	54	26	4	2	32	27	3.88	100	.239	.338	17-0-1	.118	-1	95	2		0.0
1953	Phi A	2	1	.667	17	2	1	1	38.2	44	24	3	5	24	16	4.89	88	.282	.395	6-0-1	.167	-0	124	-3		-0.1
Total	20	211	222	.487	600	483	246-31	21	3759.1	3769	1908	206	61	1732	2082	3.98	107	.261	.342	1337-1-86	.189	-26	89	108		5.3
NEWSOME, DICK Heber Hampton B12.13.1909 Ahoskie NC D12.15.1965 Ahoskie NC BR/TR/6-0/185 d4.25 Col Wake Forest																										
1941	Bos A	19	10	.655	36	29	17-2	0	213.2	235	115	13	7	79	58	4.13	101	.277	.344	78-0-6	.244	3	112	1		0.5
1942	Bos A	8	10	.444	24	23	11	0	158	174	98	11	0	67	40	5.01	74	.278	.348	55-0-6	.236	2	105	-21		-1.9
1943	Bos A	8	13	.381	25	22	8-2	0	154.1	166	83	8	5	68	40	4.49	74	.274	.352	48-0-2	.146	-1*	90	-19		-2.5
Total	3	35	33	.515	85	74	36-4	0	526	575	296	32	12	214	138	4.57	84	.276	.347	181-0-14	.215	3	104	-39		-3.9
NEWTON, DOC Eustace James B10.26.1877 Indianapolis IN D5.14.1931 Memphis TN BL/TL/6-0/185 d4.27																										
1900	Cin N	9	15	.375	36	27	22-1	0	235.2	255	146	4	12	100	89	4.12	89	.275	.354	86-0-4	.198	-1	74	-11		-1.2
1901	Cin N	4	13	.235	20	18	17	0	168.1	190	117	6	14	59	65	4.12	78	.282	.353	69-0-1	.130	-4	90	-21		-2.2
	Bro N	6	5	.545	13	12	9	0	105	110	42	1	7	30	45	2.83	119	.268	.328	41	.220	1	107	8		0.8
	Year	10	18	.357	33	30	26	0	273.1	300	159	7	21	89	110	3.62	90	.277	.343	110-0-1	.164	-4	97	-9		-1.4
1902	Bro N	15	14	.517	31	28	26-4	0	264.1	208	95	2	11	87	107	2.42	114	**.217**	.289	109-0-2	.174	-1*	97	11		1.0
1905	NY A	2	2	.500	11	7	2	0	59.2	61	23	1	2	24	15	2.11	139	.266	.341	22	.136	-0	94	-1		-0.1
1906	NY A	7	5	.583	21	15	6-2	0	125	118	53	3	7	33	52	3.17	94	.252	.311	41-0-1	.220	-0	95	-4		-0.4
1907	NY A	7	10	.412	19	15	10	0	133	132	66	0	7	31	70	3.18	88	.261	.313	37-0-5	.108	-1	95	-4		-0.4
1908	NY A	4	5	.444	23	13	6-1	1	88.1	78	52	0	7	41	49	2.95	84	.242	.341	25-0-1	.160	-0	134	-7		-0.7
1909	NY A	0	3	.000	4	4	1	0	22.1	27	17	0	3	11	11	2.82	90	.300	.394	6	.167	0	63	-3		-0.3
Total	8	54	72	.429	178	139	99-8	1	1201.2	1119	611	17	70	416	503	3.22	96	.257	.328	436-0-14	.172	-9	93	-24		-3.3
NICHOLS, KID Charles Augustus B9.14.1869 Madison WI D4.11.1953 Kansas City MO BB/TR/5-10.5/175 d4.23 M2 HF1949																										
1890	Bos N	27	19	.587	48	47	47-7	0	424	374	175	8	11	112	222	2.23	169	.229	.283	174	.247	1*	75	63		5.9
1891	Bos N	30	17	.638	52	48	45-5	3	425.1	413	219	15	17	103	240	2.39	**153**	.245	.295	183	.197	-3	96	48		4.5
1892	†Bos N	35	16	.686	53	51	49-5	0	453	404	211	15	10	121	192	2.84	124	.229	.283	197-2	.203	1*	85	34		3.3
1893	Bos N	34	14	.708	52	44	43-1	1	425	426	222	15	15	118	94	3.52	140	.253	.308	177-2	.220	-2*	93	66		5.5
1894	Bos N	32	13	.711	50	46	40-**3**	0	407	488	308	23	9	121	113	4.75	119	.294	.345	170-0-2	.294	3*	104	39		3.2
1895	Bos N	26	16	.619	48	43	43-1	3	390.2	434	222	15	5	90	102	2.83	161	.266	.316	147-1-9	.190	-3*	103	**59**		5.1
1896	Bos N	**30**	14	.682	49	43	37-3	1	372.1	387	211	14	7	101	127	2.64	169	.255	**.291**	147-3-2	.265	4	106	**70**		6.1
1897	†Bos N	**31**	11	.738	46	40	37-2	3	368	362	152	9	3	68	127	2.13	173	**.221**	**.272**	158-2-3	.241	3*	95	62		6.4
1898	Bos N	**31**	12	.721	**50**	42	40-5	4	388	316	136	7	14	85	138	2.99	139	.250	.298	136-2-1	.191	-5	86	40		3.3
1899	Bos N	21	19	.525	42	37	37-4	0	343.1	326	155	11	6	82	108	3.07	134	.246	.311	90-1-2	.200	-2	105	23		2.3
1900	Bos N	13	16	.448	29	27	25-**4**	0	231.1	215	116	11	11	72	53	3.07	134	.246	.311	163-4-4	.282	9*	81	16		2.8
1901	Bos N	19	16	.543	38	34	33-4	0	321	306	146	8	10	90	143	3.22	112	.250	.306	109	.156	-1	78	27		2.8
1904	StL N	21	13	.618	36	35	35-3	1	317	268	97	3	5	50	134	2.02	134	.222	.256	22	.227	0*	83	-16		-1.8
1905	StL N	1	5	.167	7	7	5	0	51.2	64	47	1	4	28	16	5.40	55	.296	.350	22	.227	0	88	11		1.1
	Phi N	10	6	.625	17	16	15-1	0	138.2	129	47	1	4	28	50	2.27	129	.250	.294	53	.189	0	87	-6		-0.7
	Year	11	11	.500	24	23	20-1	0	190.1	193	94	2	4	46	66	3.12	94	.264	.311	75	.200	0	87	-6		-0.7
1906	Phi N	0	1	.000	4	2	1	0	11	17	16	0	2	13	1	9.82	27	.386	.542	3	.000	-0	279	-8		-0.7
Total	15	361	208	.634	621	562	532-48	17	5067.1	4929	2480	156	129	1272	1881	2.96	139	.250	.300	2090-16-25	.226	-0	94	601		56.1
NICHOLS, CHET Chester Raymond Jr. B2.22.1931 Pawtucket RI D3.27.1995 Lincoln RI BB/TL/6-1.5/195(170-195) d4.19 Mil 1952-53 f-Chet																										
1951	Bos N	11	8	.579	33	19	12-3	2	156	142	61	4	1	69	71	**2.88**	127	.246	.327	51-0-4	.137	-2	92	13		1.1
1954	Mil N	9	11	.450	35	20	5-1	1	122.1	132	68	6	2	64	55	4.41	84	.286	.376	35-0-4	.086	-3	109	-10		-1.1
1955	Mil N	9	8	.529	34	21	6	1	144	139	79	20	0	67-6	44	4.00	94	.253	.334	52-0-1	.154	-2	123	-7		-0.7
1956	Mil N	0	1	.000	2	0	0	0	4	9	3	1	0	3-1	0	6.75	51	.563	.632	1	.000	-0		-1		-0.1
1960	Bos A	0	2	.000	6	1	0	0	12.2	12	6	0	0	4-0	11	4.26	95	.240	.296	3	.000	0	22	0		0.1
1961	Bos A	3	2	.600	26	2	0	1	51.2	40	24	3	0	26-1	33	2.09	199	.221	.317	9	.111	-0	42	12	31	1.1
1962	Bos A	1	1	.500	29	1	0	3	57	61	25	3	0	22-1	27	3.00	138	.276	.339	9-0-2	.000	-1	195	5		0.5
1963	Bos A	1	3	.250	21	7	0	0	52.2	61	30	8	0	24-0	27	4.78	95	.298	.365	13-0-1	.231	0	101	-5		-0.5
1964	Cin N	0	0	—	3	0	0	0	3	4	2	1	0	2-0	3	6.00	60	.308	.308	0	—	0		-1	31	-0.1
Total	9	34	36	.486	189	71	23-4	10	603.1	600	286	45	6	280-9	266	3.64	105	.264	.344	173-0-12	.127	-8	104	6		0.1
NICHOLS, CHET Chester Raymond Sr. "Nick" B7.3.1897 Woonsocket RI D7.11.1982 Pawtucket RI BR/TR/5-11/160 d7.30 s-Chet																										
1926	Pit N	0	0	—	3	0	0	0	7.2	13	11	0	0	5	2	8.22	48	.342	.419	3	.333	-0		-5		-0.1
1927	Pit N	0	3	.000	8	0	0	0	27.2	34	19	1	1	17	9	5.86	70	.309	.406	9	.111	-0		-8		-0.2
1928	NY N	0	0	—	3	0	0	0	2.2	11	13	0	1	3	1	23.63	17	.611	.682	0	—	0		-4		-0.1
1930	Phi N	1	2	.333	16	5	0	0	59.2	76	51	2	8	16	15	6.79	80	.306	.353	20	.300	0*	93	-7		-0.4
1931	Phi N	0	1	.000	3	0	0	0	5.2	10	6	0	0	1	0	9.53	45	.435	.458	2	.000	-0		-3		-0.1
1932	Phi N	0	2	.000	11	0	0	1	19.1	23	16	2	0	14	5	6.98	63	.299	.407	4	.000	-1		-4		-0.1
Total	6	1	8	.111	44	5	0	1	122.2	167	116	5	10	56	33	7.19	67	.325	.395	38	.211	-1	93	-31		-0.9

YEAR	TM LG	W	L	PCT	G	GS	CG-SHO	SV-BS	IP	H	R	HR	HB	BB-IB	SO	ERA	AERA	OAV	OOB	AB-HR-SH	AVG	PB	SUP	APR	DL	PW

NICHOLS, DOLAN Dolan Levon "Nick" B2.28.1930 Tishomingo MS D11.20.1989 Tupelo MS BR/TR/6-0/195 d4.15

| 1958 | Chi N | 0 | 4 | .000 | 24 | 0 | 0 | 1 | 41.1 | 46 | 27 | 1 | 1 | 16-2 | 9 | 5.01 | 78 | .295 | .362 | 5 | .000 | -1 | | -5 | | -0.5 |

NICHOLS, TRICKY Frederick C. B7.26.1850 Bridgeport CT D8.22.1897 Bridgeport CT BR/TR/5-7.5/150 d4.19

1875	NH NA	4	29	.121	34	33	30	0	288	321	245	2		9	48	2.38	87	.242	.248	119	.193	-2	56	-11		-0.7
1876	Bos N	1	0	1.000	1	1	1	0	9	7	5	0		0	0	1.00	226	.200	.200	4	.000	-1	103	1		0.0
1877	StL N	18	23	.439	42	39	35-1	0	350	376	195	2		53	80	2.60	100	.263	.289	186	.167	-6*	80	2		-0.4
1878	Pro N	4	7	.364	11	10	10	0	98	157	98	0		8	21	4.22	52	.344	.356	49	.184	-0	138	-21		-1.8
1880	Wor N	0	2	.000	2	2	2	0	17.2	29	16	0		4	4	4.08	64	.358	.388	7	.000	-1	57	-3		-0.4
1882	Bal AA	1	12	.077	16	13	12	0	118.1	155	113	2		17	21	5.02	55	.296	.319	95	.158	-2*	78	-27		-2.4
Total	5	24	44	.353	72	65	60-1	0	593	724	427	4		82	126	3.37	85	.287	.309	341	.161	-10	88	-48		-5.0

NICHOLS, ROD Rodney Lea B12.29.1964 Burlington IA BR/TR/6-2/190* [CleA85 5/115] d7.30 Col New Mexico

1988	Cle A	1	7	.125	11	10	3	0-0	69.1	73	41	9	5	23-1	31	5.06	82	.272	.332	0	—	0	64	-6	38	-0.6
1989	Cle A	4	6	.400	15	11	0	0-0	71.2	81	42	9	2	24-0	42	4.40	91	.285	.343	0	—	0	83	-5	70	-0.6
1990	Cle A	0	3	.000	4	2	0	0-0	16	24	14	5	2	6-0	3	7.88	50	.343	.410	0	—	0	58	-6		-1.0
1991	Cle A	2	11	.154	31	16	3-1	1-1	137.1	145	63	6	6	30-3	76	3.54	118	.273	.316	0	—	0	49	8		0.7
1992	Cle A	4	3	.571	30	9	0	0-0	105.1	114	58	13	2	31-1	56	4.53	87	.273	.323	0	—	0	113	-7		-0.4
1993	LA N	0	1	.000	9	0	0	0-1	6.1	9	5	1	0	2-2	5	5.68	68	.360	.407	0	—	0		-2		-0.2
1995	Atl N	0	0	—	5	0	0	0-0	6.2	14	11	3	0	5-1	1	5.40	68	.424	.500	0	—	0		-4		-0.2
Total	7	11	31	.262	100	48	6-1	1-2	412.2	460	234	42	14	121-8	214	4.43	92	.282	.335	0	—	0	72	-22	108	-2.3

NICHOLSON, FRANK Frank Collins B8.29.1889 Berlin PA D11.10.1972 Jersey Shore PA BR/TR/6-2/175 d9.6

| 1912 | Phi N | 0 | 0 | — | 2 | 0 | 0 | 0 | 4 | 8 | 3 | 1 | 0 | 2 | 1 | 6.75 | 54 | .471 | .526 | 0 | — | 0 | | -1 | | 0.0 |

NICHTING, CHRIS Christopher Thomas B5.13.1966 Cincinnati OH BR/TR/6-1/205(205-220) [LAN87 3/66] d5.15 Col Northwestern [DL 1996 Tex A 155]

1995	Tex A	0	0	—	13	0	0	0-0	24.1	36	19	1	1	13-1	6	7.03	69	.343	.413	0	—	0		-5		-0.2
2000	Cle A	0	0	—	7	0	0	0-1	9	13	7	0	2	5-1	7	7.00	72	.342	.435	0	—	0		-2		-0.1
2001	Cin N	0	3	.000	36	0	0	1-2	36.1	46	24	6	0	8-1	33	4.46	103	.307	.338	1	.000	-0		-1		-0.1
	Col N	0	0	—	7	0	0	0-0	6	9	3	2	0	0-0	7	4.50	119	.346	.346	0-0-1		0		1		0.1
	Year	0	3	.000	43	0	0	1-2	42.1	55	27	8	0	8-1	40	4.46	105	.313	.339	1-0-1	.000	-0		-1		0.0
2002	Col N	1	1	.500	29	0	0	0-0	36.1	40	18	7	1	5-0	25	4.46	106	.280	.307	3	.333	0		2		0.1
Total	4	1	4	.200	92	0	0	1-3	112	144	71	16	4	31-3	78	5.22	91	.312	.356	4-0-1	.250	0		-5	155	-0.2

NICKLE, DOUG Douglas Alan B10.2.1974 Sonoma CA BR/TR/6-4/210* [AnaA97 13/387] d9.18 Col California-Davis

2000	Phi N	0	0	—	4	0	0	0-0	2.2	5	4	1	1	2-0	1	13.50	34	.417	.533	0	—	0		-3		-0.1
2001	Phi N	0	0	—	2	0	0	0-0	2	1	0	0	0	1-0	1	0.00	—	.143	.143	0	—	0		1		0.0
2002	Phi N	0	0	—	4	0	0	0-0	4.1	6	3	2	0	4-0	2	6.23	62	.316	.435	1	.000	-0		-1		-0.1
	SD N	1	0	1.000	10	0	0	0-0	11.2	20	13	1	1	9-0	7	8.49	46	.357	.448	0	—	0		-7		-0.5
	Year	1	0	1.000	14	0	0	0-0	16	26	16	3	1	13-0	9	7.88	49	.347	.444	1	.000	-0		-8		-0.6
Total	3	1	0	1.000	20	0	0	0-0	20.2	32	20	3	2	15-0	10	7.84	51	.340	.438	1	.000	-0		-10		-0.7

NICOL, GEORGE George Edward B10.17.1870 Barry IL D8.4.1924 Milwaukee WI BR/TL/5-7/155 d9.23 ▲

1890	StL AA	2	1	.667	3	3	2	0	17	11	13	1	2	19	16	4.76	91	.180	.390	7	.286	1	161	-1		0.0
1891	Chi N	1	0	1.000	3	2	0	0	11	14	20	0	1	10	12	4.91	68	.298	.431	6	.333	1	233	-5		-0.3
1894	Pit N	3	4	.429	9	5	3	0	46.1	58	38	2	5	39	13	6.22	84	.304	.434	22-0-2	.409	2	62	-3		-0.3
	Lou N	0	1	.000	2	2	2	0	17	35	35	4	1	16	4	13.76	37	.417	.515	112-0-1	.339	1*	76	-16		-0.5
	Year	3	5	.375	11	7	5	0	63.1	93	73	6	6	55	17	8.24	63	.338	.458	134-0-3	.351	2	66	-18		-0.8
Total	3	5	7	.417	17	12	7	0	91.1	118	106	7	9	84	45	7.19	67	.308	.443	147-0-3	.347	4	108	-25		-1.1

NIED, DAVID David Glen B12.22.1968 Dallas TX BR/TR/6-2/188(175-188) [AtlN87 14/350] d9.1

1992	Atl N	3	0	1.000	6	2	0	0-0	23	10	3	0	0	5-0	19	1.17	312	.130	.183	7	.286	0	74	6		0.9
1993	Col N	5	9	.357	16	16	1	0-0	87	99	53	8	1	42-4	46	5.17	92	.296	.369	23-0-3	.174	-0	88	-2	99	-0.3
1994	Col N	9	7	.563	22	22	2-1	0-0	122	137	70	15	4	47-5	74	4.80	104	.287	.354	40-0-3	.100	-2	91	2		-0.1
1995	Col N	0	0	—	2	0	0	0-0	4.1	11	10	2	0	3-0	3	20.77	26	.458	.519	0	—	-0		-5	102	-0.3
1996	Col N	0	2	.000	6	1	0	0-0	5.1	5	8	1	0	8-0	4	13.50	39	.250	.448	1	.000	-0	52	-4		-0.3
Total	5	17	18	.486	52	41	3-1	0-0	241.2	262	144	26	5	105-9	146	5.06	95	.281	.353	71-0-6	.141	-2	90	-3	201	-0.5

NIEDENFUER, TOM Thomas Edward B8.13.1959 St.Louis Park MN BR/TR/6-5/225(217-230) d8.15 Col Washington St.

1981	†LA N	3	1	.750	17	0	0	2-1	26	25	11	1	1	6-2	12	3.81	87	.258	.305	0	—	0		-1		-0.2
1982	LA N	3	4	.429	55	0	0	9-5	69.2	71	22	3	2	25-8	60	2.71	128	.269	.333	3	.000	-0		7		0.8
1983	†LA N	8	3	.727	66	0	0	11-4	94.2	55	22	6	1	29-11	66	1.90	190	.170	.237	4	.000	-0		19		2.5
1984	LA N	2	5	.286	33	0	0	11-3	47.1	39	14	3	2	23-7	45	2.47	144	.227	.325	3-0-1	.000	-0		6	52	1.1
1985	†LA N	7	9	.438	64	0	0	19-6	106.1	86	32	6	1	24-5	102	2.71	129	.223	.268	9-0-1	.111	-0		12		2.1
1986	LA N	6	6	.500	60	0	0	11-6	80	86	35	11	1	29-15	55	3.71	93	.280	.341	4-0-1	.500	1		-1	15	-0.2
1987	LA N	1	0	1.000	15	0	0	1-1	16.1	13	5	1	1	9-1	10	2.76	145	.220	.329	0	—	0		3		0.2
	Bal A	3	5	.375	45	0	0	13-3	52.1	55	32	11	1	22-3	37	4.99	89	.266	.335	0	—	0		-3		-0.6
1988	Bal A	3	4	.429	52	0	0	18-5	59	59	23	8	2	19-3	40	3.51	112	.259	.320	0	—	0		4		0.6
1989	Sea A	0	3	.000	25	0	0	0-3	36.1	46	29	7	1	15-5	15	6.69	60	.309	.371	0	—	0		-10	48	-0.7
1990	StL N	0	6	.000	52	0	0	2-1	65	66	26	3	0	25-7	32	3.46	111	.269	.331	3	.000	-0		4		0.3
Total	10	36	46	.439	484	0	0	97-38	653	601	251	60	13	226-67	474	3.29	112	.247	.311	26-0-3	.115	-1		40	115	5.9

NIEHAUS, DICK Richard J. B10.24.1892 Covington KY D3.12.1957 Atlanta GA BL/TL/5-11/165 d9.9

1913	StL N	0	2	.000	3	3	1	0	24	20	17	1	0	13	4	4.13	78	.241	.344	7	.286	1	62	-4		-0.2
1914	StL N	1	0	1.000	8	1	1	0	17.1	18	11	1	0	8	6	3.12	90	.269	.347	4	.250	1	102	-1		0.0
1915	StL N	2	1	.667	15	2	1	0	45.1	48	35	2	1	22	21	3.97	70	.281	.366	14	.071	-1	147	-9		-0.6
1920	Cle A	1	2	.333	19	3	0	2	40	42	21	0	1	16	12	3.60	106	.269	.341	9	.444	2	70	0		0.1
Total	4	4	5	.444	45	9	3	2	126.2	128	84	4	2	59	43	3.84	85	.270	.349	34	.235	2	87	-14		-0.7

NIEKRO, JOE Joseph Franklin B11.7.1944 Martins Ferry OH BR/TR/6-1/190* [ChiN66 S3/43] d4.16 b-Phil s-Lance Col West Liberty St.

1967	Chi N	10	7	.588	36	22	7-2	0	169.2	171	68	15	2	32-7	77	3.34	106	.257	.291	46-0-9	.196	1	114	4		0.5
1968	Chi N	14	10	.583	34	29	2-1	2	177.1	204	93	18	3	59-8	65	4.31	73	.294	.349	60-0-9	.100	-2	128	-21		-3.0
1969	Chi N	0	1	.000	4	3	0	0-0	19.1	24	9	3	0	6-0	7	3.72	108	.304	.349	5-0-1	.200	-0	74	1		0.1
	SD N	8	17	.320	37	31	8-3	0-0	202	213	91	15	0	45-9	55	3.70	97	.273	.311	51-0-5	.118	0*	76	-2		-0.3
	Year	8	18	.308	41	34	8-3	0-0	221.1	237	100	18	0	51-9	62	3.70	98	.276	.314	56-0-6	.125	0	76	-1		-0.2
1970	Det A	12	13	.480	38	34	6-2	0-0	213	221	107	28	2	72-4	101	4.06	93	.266	.325	66-0-15	.197	4*	66	-1		-0.4
1971	Det A	6	7	.462	31	15	1-0	1-0	122.1	136	62	13	2	49-3	43	4.49	81	.283	.350	30-0-6	.133	-0*	111	-9		-1.0
1972	†Det A	3	2	.600	18	7	1	1-0	47	62	20	3	1	8-1	24	3.83	83	.330	.360	12-0-1	.250	1	108	-2	25	-0.1
1973	Atl N	2	4	.333	20	0	0	3-4	24	23	11	2	0	11-1	12	4.13	96	.277	.351	3	.333	0		0		0.1
1974	Atl N	3	2	.600	27	2	0	0-3	43	36	19	5	2	18-2	31	3.56	107	.237	.322	5-0-1	.000	-1	115	1		0.1
1975	Hou N	6	4	.600	40	4	1-1	4-0	88	79	32	3	2	39-4	54	3.07	111	.240	.320	14-0-2	.214	1	117	4		0.5
1976	Hou N	4	8	.333	36	13	0	0-1	118	107	60	8	1	56-1	77	3.36	96	.238	.322	27-1-4	.185	2	120	-6		-0.4
1977	Hou N	13	8	.619	44	14	9-2	5-3	180.2	155	66	14	1	64-3	101	3.04	119	.237	.304	50-0-3	.140	-1	111	14		1.5
1978	Hou N	14	14	.500	35	29	10-1	0-0	202.2	190	97	13	9	73-1	97	3.86	86	.248	.318	60-0-3	.120	-2	98	15		1.5
1979	Hou N☆	21	11	.656	38	38	11-5	0-0	263.2	221	102	17	7	107-1	119	3.00	117	.228	.308	83-0-13	.138	-1*	99	-14		-1.9
1980	†Hou N	20	12	.625	37	36	11-2	0-0	256	268	119	12	4	79-3	127	3.55	92	.270	.323	80-0-18	.275	8	132	-10		-0.4
1981	†Hou N	9	9	.500	24	24	5-2	0-0	166	150	60	8	0	47-4	77	2.82	116	.243	.294	51-0-1	.176	1	105	8		0.9
1982	Hou N	17	12	.586	35	35	16-5	0-0	270	224	79	12	5	64-1	130	2.47	135	.229	.278	89-0-7	.090	-4	90	30		2.8
1983	Hou N	15	14	.517	38	38	9-1	0-0	263.2	238	115	15	3	101-5	152	3.48	98	.241	.311	85-0-12	.094	-3	106	-1		-0.5
1984	Hou N	16	12	.571	38	38	6-1	0-0	248.1	223	104	16	4	89-4	127	3.04	110	.241	.308	83-0-11	.133	-2	127	7		0.6
1985	Hou N	9	12	.429	32	32	4-1	0-0	213	197	100	21	5	99-6	117	3.72	94	.247	.329	68-0-10	.250	4	99	-5		-0.1
	NY A	2	1	.667	3	3	0	0-0	12.1	14	8	3	0	8-0	4	5.84	69	.280	.379	0	—	0	99	1		-0.2
1986	NY A	9	10	.474	25	25	0	0-0	125.2	139	84	15	1	63-3	59	4.87	85	.275	.356	0	—	0	142	-2		-1.8
1987	NY A	3	4	.429	14	8	0	0-0	50.2	40	25	4	4	19-0	30	3.55	125	.215	.300	0	—	0	69	3	18	0.4
	†Min A	4	9	.308	19	18	1	0-0	96.1	115	76	11	6	45-0	54	6.26	74	.296	.375	0	—	0	81	-18		-2.0
	Year	7	13	.350	33	26	1	0-0	147	155	101	15	10	64-0	84	5.33	86	.270	.351	0	—	0	78	-15		-1.6

YEAR	TM LG	W	L	PCT	G	GS	CG-SHO	SV-BS	IP	H	R	HR	HB	BB-IB	SO	ERA	AERA	OAV	OOB	AB-HR-SH	AVG	PB	SUP	APR	DL	PW
1988	Min A	1	1	.500	5	2	0	0-0	11.2	16	13	2	0	9-0	7	10.03	41	.320	.424	0	—	0	123	-7		-1.
Total	22	221	204	.520	702	500	107-29	16-11	3584.1	3466	1620	276	65	1262-71	1747	3.59	98	.255	.319	973-1-147	.156	6	106	-31	43	-4.

NIEKRO, PHIL Philip Henry B4.1.1939 Blaine OH BR/TR/6-1/180(180-195) d4.15 HF1997 b-Joe

YEAR	TM LG	W	L	PCT	G	GS	CG-SHO	SV-BS	IP	H	R	HR	HB	BB-IB	SO	ERA	AERA	OAV	OOB	AB-HR-SH	AVG	PB	SUP	APR	DL	PW
1964	Mil N	0	0	—	10	0	0	0-	15	15	10	1	0	7-0	7	4.80	73	.273	.365	0		0		-3		-0.
1965	Mil N	2	3	.400	41	1	0	6	74.2	73	32	5	3	26-3	49	2.89	122	.258	.323	10	.100	-0*	223	3		0.
1966	Atl N	4	3	.571	28	0	0	2	50.1	48	32	4	2	23-5	17	4.11	88	.249	.335	8-0-3	.000	-1		-5		1.
1967	Atl N	11	9	.550	46	20	10-1	9	207	164	64	9	7	55-3	129	1.87	178	.218	.275	57-0-6	.123	-0	87	27		3.
1968	Atl N	14	12	.538	37	34	15-5	3	256.2	228	83	16	5	45-3	140	2.59	115	.239	.276	77-2-18	.104	-1	89	12		1.
1969	†Atl N★	23	13	.639	40	35	21-4	1-1	284.1	235	93	21	5	57-7	193	2.56	141	.221	.264	95-0-9	.211	3	101	32		4.
1970	Atl N	12	18	.400	34	32	10-3	0-1	229.2	222	124	40	4	68-2	168	4.27	100	.248	.304	79-1-6	.152	1	86	0		-0.
1971	Atl N	15	14	.517	42	36	18-4	2-0	268.2	248	112	27	3	70-6	173	2.98	125	.245	.294	92-0-7	.152	-2	94	16		1.
1972	Atl N	16	12	.571	38	36	17-1	0-1	282.1	254	112	22	5	53-3	164	3.06	124	.236	.274	93-1-11	.194	1	96	19		2.
1973	Atl N	13	10	.565	42	30	9-1	4-1	245	214	103	21	5	89-4	131	3.31	124	.234	.305	82-1-7	.122	-2	109	16		1.
1974	Atl N	**20**	13	.606	41	39	**18-6**	0-0	302.1	249	91	19	6	88-3	195	2.38	159	.225	.284	104-0-9	.192	-0	102	**45**		5.
1975	Atl N☆	15	15	.500	39	37	13-1	0-1	275.2	285	115	29	11	72-3	144	3.20	118	.269	.321	99-0-4	.172	0	80	18		1.
1976	Atl N	17	11	.607	38	37	10-2	0-0	270.2	249	116	18	8	101-7	173	3.29	115	.242	.313	94-1-9	.191	1	103	12		1.
1977	Atl N	16	20	.444	44	**43**	**20-2**	0-0	330.1	315	166	26	8	164-12	**262**	4.03	110	.255	.344	109-0-12	.174	-3	81	15		1.
1978	Atl N★	19	18	.514	44	**42**	**22-4**	1-0	334.1	295	129	16	13	102-5	248	2.88	140	.235	.298	120-0-4	.225	3*	81	**35**		4.
1979	Atl N	**21**	20	.512	44	**44**	**23-1**	0-0	342	311	160	41	11	113-8	208	3.39	118	.241	.306	123-0-7	.195	-2	100	18		2.
1980	Atl N	15	18	.455	40	**38**	11-3	1-0	275	256	119	30	3	85-3	176	3.63	101	.249	.306	90-0-5	.133	-2	84	3		0.
1981	Atl N	7	7	.500	22	22	3-3	0-0	139.1	120	56	6	1	56-2	62	3.10	114	.233	.309	52-0-3	.077	-4	100	6		0.
1982	†Atl N☆	17	4	**.810**	35	35	4-2	0-0	234.1	225	106	23	3	73-1	144	3.61	102	.255	.313	87-1-3	.195	0	129	2	16	-0.
1983	Atl N	11	10	.524	34	33	2	0-0	201.2	212	94	18	2	105-3	128	3.97	97	.276	.362	65-0-6	.185	0	100	-1		-0.
1984	NY A☆	16	8	.667	32	31	5-1	0-0	215.2	219	85	15	3	76-0	136	3.09	124	.267	.327	0	—	0	124	17		-0.
1985	NY A	16	12	.571	33	33	7-1	0-0	220	203	110	29	2	120-1	149	4.09	99	.245	.341	0	—	0	108	-8		-0.
1986	Cle A	11	11	.500	34	32	5	0-0	210.1	241	126	24	6	95-1	81	4.32	97	.287	.362	0	—	0	60	-4		-0.
1987	Tor A	0	2	.000	3	3	0	0-0	12	15	11	4	0	7-0	7	8.25	57	.306	.393	0	—	0	85	-14		-1
	Cle A	7	11	.389	22	22	2	0-0	123.2	142	83	18	4	53-1	57	5.89	77	.286	.356	0	—	0	82	-21		-2
	Year	7	13	.350	25	25	2	0-0	135.2	157	94	22	4	60-1	64	6.10	75	.288	.359	0	—	0	82	-21		-2
	Atl N	0	0	—	1	1	0	0-0	3	6	5	0	0	6-0	0	15.00	29	.429	.600	1	.000	-0	125	-3		-0.
Total	24	318	274	.537	864	716	245-45	29-5	5404	5044	2337	482	123	1809-86	3342	3.35	115	.247	.311	1537-7-129	.169	-5	97	258	16	29

NIELSEN, JERRY Gerald Arthur B8.5.1966 Sacramento CA BL/TL/6-3/185* [NYA88 18/469] d7.12 Col Florida St.

YEAR	TM LG	W	L	PCT	G	GS	CG-SHO	SV-BS	IP	H	R	HR	HB	BB-IB	SO	ERA	AERA	OAV	OOB	AB-HR-SH	AVG	PB	SUP	APR	DL	PW
1992	NY A	1	0	1.000	20	0	0	0-0	19.2	17	10	1	0	18-2	12	4.58	86	.243	.393	0	—	0		-1		-0
1993	Cal A	0	0	—	10	0	0	0-0	12.1	18	13	1	1	4-0	8	8.03	57	.340	.377	0	—	0		-5		-0
Total	2	1	0	1.000	30	0	0	0-0	32	35	23	2	1	22-2	20	5.91	71	.285	.387	0	—	0		-6		-0

NIELSEN, SCOTT Jeffrey Scott B12.18.1958 Salt Lake City UT BR/TR/6-1/190* [SeaA83 6/139] d7.7 Col Brigham Young

YEAR	TM LG	W	L	PCT	G	GS	CG-SHO	SV-BS	IP	H	R	HR	HB	BB-IB	SO	ERA	AERA	OAV	OOB	AB-HR-SH	AVG	PB	SUP	APR	DL	PW
1986	NY A	4	4	.500	10	9	2-2	0-0	56	66	29	12	2	12-0	20	4.02	103	.299	.340	0	—	0	129	0		0
1987	Chi A	3	5	.375	19	7	1-1	2-0	66.1	83	48	9	1	25-1	23	6.24	74	.307	.366	0	—	0	127	-11		-1
1988	NY A	1	2	.333	7	2	0	0-0	19.2	27	16	5	0	13-2	4	6.86	58	.333	.426	0	—	0	126	-6		-0
1989	NY A	1	0	1.000	2	0	0	0-0	0.2	2	1	0	0	1-0	0	13.50	29	.500	.600	0	—	0		-1		-0
Total	4	9	11	.450	38	18	3-3	2-0	142.2	178	94	26	3	51-3	47	5.49	79	.309	.367	0	—	0	127	-18		-2

NIEMANN, RANDY Randal Harold B11.15.1955 Scotia CA BL/TL/6-4/200(200-215) [NYA75 S2/30] d5.20 C5 Col Redwoods (CA) [JC] [DL 1981 Hou N 33]

YEAR	TM LG	W	L	PCT	G	GS	CG-SHO	SV-BS	IP	H	R	HR	HB	BB-IB	SO	ERA	AERA	OAV	OOB	AB-HR-SH	AVG	PB	SUP	APR	DL	PW
1979	Hou N	3	2	.600	26	7	3-2	1-0	67	68	32	1	1	22-3	24	3.76	93	.272	.324	15-0-1	.133	-0	108	-2		-0
1980	Hou N	0	1	.000	22	1	0	1-0	33	40	21	2	0	12-1	18	5.45	60	.299	.354	6	.333	1	109	-8		-0
1982	Pit N	1	1	.500	20	0	0	1-0	35.1	34	22	1	2	17-4	26	5.09	74	.254	.344	2	1.000	1		-5		-0
1983	Pit N	0	1	.000	8	1	0	0-0	13.2	20	14	2	1	7-1	8	9.22	41	.357	.431	1	.000	-0	95	-7		-0
1984	Chi A	0	0	—	5	0	0	0-0	5.1	5	1	0	0	5-1	5	1.69	248	.263	.417	0	—	0		2		0
1985	NY N	0	0	—	4	0	0	0-0	4.2	5	0	0	0	0-0	2	0.00	—	.278	.278	0	—	0		1		0
1986	NY N	2	3	.400	31	1	0	0-0	35.2	44	17	2	0	12-2	13	3.79	95	.308	.359	6	.333	1	224	-1		0
1987	Min A	1	0	1.000	6	0	0	0-0	5.1	3	5	0	0	7-0	1	8.44	55	.158	.429	0	—	0	116	-2		-0
Total	8	7	8	.467	122	10	3-2	3-0	200	219	112	8	5	82-12	102	4.64	77	.283	.352	30-0-1	.267	2	116	-22	33	-0

NIEMES, JACK Jacob Leland B10.19.1919 Cincinnati OH D3.4.1966 Hamilton OH BR/TL/6-1/180 d5.30 Mil 1944-46 Col Cincinnati

YEAR	TM LG	W	L	PCT	G	GS	CG-SHO	SV-BS	IP	H	R	HR	HB	BB-IB	SO	ERA	AERA	OAV	OOB	AB-HR-SH	AVG	PB	SUP	APR	DL	PW
1943	Cin N	0	0	—	3	0	0	0-0	3	5	3	0	0	2-1	1	6.00	55	.385	.467	0	—	0		-1		-0

NIESON, CHUCK Charles Bassett B9.24.1942 Hanford CA BR/TR/6-2/185 d9.18 Col Cal St.-Fresno

YEAR	TM LG	W	L	PCT	G	GS	CG-SHO	SV-BS	IP	H	R	HR	HB	BB-IB	SO	ERA	AERA	OAV	OOB	AB-HR-SH	AVG	PB	SUP	APR	DL	PW
1964	Min A	0	0	—	2	0	0	0	2	1	1	1	0	1-0	5	4.50	79	.143	.250	0	—	0		0		-0

NIEVES, JUAN Juan Manuel (Cruz) B1.5.1965 Las Lomas, PR BL/TL/6-3/175(175-190) d4.10 [DL 1989 Mil A 182, 1990 Mil A 58]

YEAR	TM LG	W	L	PCT	G	GS	CG-SHO	SV-BS	IP	H	R	HR	HB	BB-IB	SO	ERA	AERA	OAV	OOB	AB-HR-SH	AVG	PB	SUP	APR	DL	PW
1986	Mil A	11	12	.478	35	33	4-3	0-0	184.2	224	124	17	1	77-0	116	4.92	89	.299	.363	0	—	0	102	-15		-1
1987	Mil A	14	8	.636	34	33	3-1	0-0	195.2	199	112	24	2	100-5	163	4.88	95	.264	.348	0	—	0	114	-4		-0
1988	Mil A	7	5	.583	25	15	1-1	1-0	110.1	84	53	13	1	50-4	73	4.08	98	.208	.295	0	—	0	112	0	63	-1
Total	3	32	25	.561	94	81	8-5	1-0	490.2	507	289	54	4	227-9	352	4.71	93	.266	.343	0	—	0	109	-19	303	-1

NIGGELING, JOHNNY John Arnold B7.10.1903 Remsen IA D9.16.1963 LeMars IA BR/TR/6-0/170 d4.30

YEAR	TM LG	W	L	PCT	G	GS	CG-SHO	SV-BS	IP	H	R	HR	HB	BB-IB	SO	ERA	AERA	OAV	OOB	AB-HR-SH	AVG	PB	SUP	APR	DL	PW
1938	Bos N	1	0	1.000	2	0	0	0	5	8	5	1	0	1	9	9.00	38	.400	.455	0	—	0		-1		-0
1939	Cin N	2	1	.667	10	5	2-1	0	40.1	51	28	2	2	13	20	5.80	66	.309	.367	13-0-2	.154	-0	132	-8		-0
1940	StL A	7	11	.389	28	20	10	0	153.2	148	88	9	5	69	82	4.45	103	.250	.333	51-0-1	.176	-1	81	1		-0
1941	StL A	7	9	.438	24	20	13-1	0	168.1	168	83	17	1	63	68	3.80	113	.255	.320	60-0-4	.167	-1	83	8		-0
1942	StL A	15	11	.577	28	27	16-3	0	206.1	173	76	10	11	93	107	2.66	139	.226	.319	72-0-5	.139	-2	86	22		-0
1943	StL A	6	8	.429	20	20	7	0	150.1	122	61	7	6	57	73	3.17	105	.220	.299	49-0-5	.061	-4	92	3		-0
	Was A	4	2	.667	6	6	5-3	0	51	27	6	0	0	17	24	0.88	363	.153	.247	18	.278	1	79	14		-0
	Year	10	10	.500	26	26	12-3	0	201.1	149	67	7	6	74	97	2.59	127	.204	.282	67-0-5	.119	-3	90	16		-0
1944	Was A	10	8	.556	24	24	14-2	0	206	164	65	5	4	88	121	2.32	141	.221	.307	69-0-4	.130	-2	92	23		-0
1945	Was A	7	12	.368	26	25	8-2	0	176.2	161	80	7	3	73	90	3.16	98	.240	.318	59	.119	-4	96	-3		-0
1946	Was A	3	2	.600	8	6	3	0	38	39	22	1	1	21	10	4.03	83	.265	.361	11-0-2	.182	-2	128	-4		-0
	Bos N	2	5	.286	9	8	3	0	58	54	23	2	1	21	24	3.26	105	.243	.311	18-0-2	.111	-1	59	2		-0
Total	9	64	69	.481	184	161	81-12	0	1250.2	1111	534	60	34	516	620	3.22	113	.236	.316	420-0-25	.140	-14	89	57		-0

NIPPER, AL Albert Samuel B4.2.1959 San Diego CA BR/TR/6-0/194* [BosA80 8/206] d9.6 C4 Col Truman St.

YEAR	TM LG	W	L	PCT	G	GS	CG-SHO	SV-BS	IP	H	R	HR	HB	BB-IB	SO	ERA	AERA	OAV	OOB	AB-HR-SH	AVG	PB	SUP	APR	DL	PW
1983	Bos A	1	1	.500	3	2	1	0-0	16	17	4	0	1	7-0	5	2.25	195	.293	.373	0	—	0	41	4		-0
1984	Bos A	11	6	.647	29	24	6	0-0	182.2	183	86	18	7	52-1	84	3.89	108	.257	.313	0	—	0	86	3	7	-0
1985	Bos A	9	12	.429	25	25	5	0-0	162	157	83	14	9	82-3	85	4.06	106	.256	.350	0	—	0	105	-22	37	-0
1986	†Bos A	10	12	.455	26	26	3	0-0	159	186	108	24	4	47-2	79	5.38	78	.290	.340	0	—	0	111	-17	24	-0
1987	Bos A	11	12	.478	30	30	6	0-0	174	196	115	30	7	62-1	89	5.43	84	.284*	.345	0	—	0	102	2	41	-0
1988	Chi N	4	4	.333	22	12	0	1-0	80	72	37	9	3	34-2	27	3.04	120	.238	.321	23-0-2	.087	-1	92	-7		-0
1990	Cle A	2	3	.400	9	5	0	0-0	24	35	19	2	2	9-2	12	6.75	58	.354	.448	0	—	0	92	-7		-0
Total	7	46	50	.479	144	124	21	1-0	797.2	846	452	97	33	303-9	381	4.52	94	.271	.339	23-0-2	.087	-1	102	-29	115	-0

NIPPERT, DUSTIN Dustin David B5.6.1981 Wheeling WV BR/TR/6-7/215 d9.8 Col West Virginia

YEAR	TM LG	W	L	PCT	G	GS	CG-SHO	SV-BS	IP	H	R	HR	HB	BB-IB	SO	ERA	AERA	OAV	OOB	AB-HR-SH	AVG	PB	SUP	APR	DL	PW
2005	Ari N	1	0	1.000	3	3	0	0-0	14.2	10	9	1	1	13-0	11	5.52	80	.185	.353	4	.250	0	106	-1		

NIPPERT, MERLIN Merlin Lee B9.1.1938 Mangum OK BR/TR/6-1/175 d9.12 Col Oklahoma St.

YEAR	TM LG	W	L	PCT	G	GS	CG-SHO	SV-BS	IP	H	R	HR	HB	BB-IB	SO	ERA	AERA	OAV	OOB	AB-HR-SH	AVG	PB	SUP	APR	DL	PW
1962	Bos A	0	0	—	4	0	0	0	6	4	3	1	0	4-1	3	4.50	92	.200	.320	0	—	0		0		-0

NISCHWITZ, RON Ronald Lee B7.1.1937 Dayton OH BB/TL/6-3/205* d9.4 Col Ohio St.

YEAR	TM LG	W	L	PCT	G	GS	CG-SHO	SV-BS	IP	H	R	HR	HB	BB-IB	SO	ERA	AERA	OAV	OOB	AB-HR-SH	AVG	PB	SUP	APR	DL	PW
1961	Det A	0	1	.000	6	1	0	0	11.1	13	12	2	0	8-1	8	5.56	74	.295	.382	2	.000	-0	108	-3		-0
1962	Det A	4	5	.444	48	1	0	4	64.2	73	30	5	1	26-1	28	3.90	104	.285	.351	12	.417	2		2		-0
1963	Cle A	0	2	.000	14	0	0	1	16.2	17	13	3	0	8-2	10	6.48	56	.262	.342	1	.000	-0		1		-0
1965	Det A	1	0	1.000	20	0	0	1	22.2	21	10	2	0	6-1	12	2.78	125	.259	.307	3	.000	-0	108	-5		-0
Total	4	5	8	.385	88	1	0	6	115.1	124	65	12	1	48-5	58	4.21	92	.278	.345	18	.278	1	108	-5		-0

NITCHOLAS, OTHO Otho James B9.13.1908 McKinney TX D9.11.1986 McKinney TX BR/TR/6-0/190 d4.18

YEAR	TM LG	W	L	PCT	G	GS	CG-SHO	SV-BS	IP	H	R	HR	HB	BB-IB	SO	ERA	AERA	OAV	OOB	AB-HR-SH	AVG	PB	SUP	APR	DL	PW
1945	Bro N	1	0	1.000	7	0	0	0	18.2	19	14	4	0	7-4	4	5.30	71	.257	.267	4	.250	0		-3		

NITKOWSKI, C. J. Christopher John B3.9.1973 Suffern NY BL/TL/6-3/205(190-210) [CinN94 1/9] d6.3 Col St. Johns

YEAR TM LG	W	L	PCT	G	GS	CG-SHO	SV-BS	IP	H	R	HR	HB	BB-IB	SO	ERA	AERA	OAV	OOB	AB-HR-SH	AVG	PB	SUP	APR	DL	PW
'95 Cin N	1	3	.250	9	7	0	0-1	32.1	41	25	4	2	15-1	18	6.12	68	.306	.382	10	.200	0	71	-8		-0.8
'96 Det A	1	4	.200	11	11	0	0-0	39.1	53	32	7	3	20-2	13	7.09	68	.335	.413	0	—	0	70	-9		-0.9
'96 Hou N	2	3	.400	11	8	0	0-0	45.2	62	44	7	7	38-1	36	8.08	63	.332	.457	0	—	0	141	-15	18	-1.2
'98 Det A	3	3	.500	43	0	0	3-2	59.2	49	27	4	6	23-2	44	3.77	108	.228	.317	4-0-1	.000	-0	2			0.2
'99 Det A	4	5	.444	68	7	0	0-0	81.2	63	44	11	3	45-3	66	4.30	116	.213	.319	1	.000	-0*	104	5		0.5
'00 Det A	4	9	.308	67	11	0	0-2	109.2	124	79	13	4	49-3	81	5.25	93	.286	.358	0	—	0	96	-8		-0.7
'01 Det A	0	3	.000	56	0	0	0-6	45.1	51	30	7	5	31-7	38	5.56	80	.283	.401	0	—	0		-5		-0.3
NY N	1	0	1.000	5	0	0	0-0	5.2	3	0	0	0	3-1	4	0.00	—	.167	.286	0	—	0		-5		-0.3
'02 Tex A	0	1	.000	12	0	0	0-0	13.2	11	4	0	0	13-0	14	2.63	182	.224	.387	0	—	0		3		0.4
'03 Tex A	0	0	—	6	0	0	0-0	9.2	17	8	0	0	8-1	5	7.45	67	.415	.490	0	—	0		3		0.2
'04 Atl N	1	0	1.000	22	0	0	0-0	20	22	11	3	2	10-0	16	4.50	96	.275	.362	0	—	0		-2		-0.1
NY A	1	1	.500	19	0	0	0-0	13	18	11	1	4	6-0	10	7.62	60	.327	.431	0	—	0		-4		-0.5
'05 Was N	0	0	—	7	0	0	0-0	3.1	5	3	0	0	2-0	2	8.10	50	.357	.438	0	—	0		-1		-0.1
Total 10	18	32	.360	336	44	0	3-11	479	519	318	57	36	263-21	347	5.37	87	.279	.375	15-0-1	.133	-1	99	-39	18	-3.3

NIXON, WILLARD Willard Lee B6.17.1928 Taylorsville GA D12.10.2000 Rome GA BL/TR/6-2/195* d7.7 Col Auburn-Montgomery

YEAR TM LG	W	L	PCT	G	GS	CG-SHO	SV-BS	IP	H	R	HR	HB	BB-IB	SO	ERA	AERA	OAV	OOB	AB-HR-SH	AVG	PB	SUP	APR	DL	PW
'50 Bos A	8	6	.571	22	15	2	2	101.1	126	75	7	2	58	57	6.04	81	.310	.398	36-0-3	.139	-1	103	-12		-1.6
'51 Bos A	7	4	.636	33	14	2-1	0	125	136	79	12	7	56	70	4.90	91	.285	.368	45-1-1	.289	3*	129	-7		-0.3
'52 Bos A	5	4	.556	23	13	5	0	103.2	115	64	12	4	61	50	4.86	81	.290	.390	53	.208	1*	128	-10		-0.7
'53 Bos A	8	8	.333	23	15	5-1	0	116.2	114	57	6	1	59	57	3.93	107	.254	.343	42-0-1	.190	0	99	4		0.4
'54 Bos A	11	12	.478	31	30	8-2	0	199.2	182	102	16	9	87	102	4.06	101	.248	.333	68-1-2	.265	5	88	2		0.8
'55 Bos A	12	10	.545	31	31	7-3	0	208	207	102	10	3	85-2	95	4.07	105	.259	.330	69-0-4	.261	5	84	7		1.3
'56 Bos A	9	8	.529	23	22	9-1	0	145.1	142	79	9	8	57-2	74	4.21	110	.255	.331	54-0-2	.204	-1	106	6		0.6
'57 Bos A	12	13	.480	29	29	11-1	0	191	207	86	10	7	56-3	96	3.68	108	.280	.335	75	.293	5*	114	7		1.3
'58 Bos A	1	7	.125	10	8	2	0	43.1	48	30	7	0	11-0	15	6.02	67	.281	.324	17	.294	1	73	-8	77	-1.2
Total 9	69	72	.489	225	177	51-9	3	1234	1277	674	89	41	530-7	616	4.39	97	.270	.348	459-2-13	.242	17	101	-11	77	0.6

NOLAN, THE ONLY Edward Sylvester B11.7.1857 Paterson NJ D5.18.1913 Paterson NJ BL/TR/5-8/171 d5.1

YEAR TM LG	W	L	PCT	G	GS	CG-SHO	SV-BS	IP	H	R	HR	HB	BB-IB	SO	ERA	AERA	OAV	OOB	AB-HR-SH	AVG	PB	SUP	APR	DL	PW
'78 Ind N	13	22	.371	38	38	37-1	0	347	357	208	1		56	125	2.57	79	.253	.281	152	.243	6	99	-21		-1.0
'81 Cle N	8	14	.364	22	21	20	0	180	183	111	3		38	54	3.05	86	.251	.288	168	.244	1*	79	-9		-0.9
'83 Pit AA	0	7	.000	7	7	6	0	55	81	44	0		10	23	4.25	76	.321	.347	26	.308	1	73	-7		-0.5
'84 Wil U	1	4	.200	5	5	5	0	40	44	28	1		7	52	2.93	91	.262	.291	33	.273	-0*	32	0		0.0
'85 Phi N	1	5	.167	7	7	6	0	54	55	43	1		24	20	4.17	67	.256	.294	26	.077	-2	49	-7		-0.7
Total 5	23	52	.307	79	78	74-1	0	676	720	434	6		135	274	2.98	80	.259	.294	405	.240	6	82	-44		-3.1

NOLAN, GARY Gary Lynn B5.27.1948 Herlong CA BR/TR/6-2.5/197* [CinN66 1/13] d4.15

YEAR TM LG	W	L	PCT	G	GS	CG-SHO	SV-BS	IP	H	R	HR	HB	BB-IB	SO	ERA	AERA	OAV	OOB	AB-HR-SH	AVG	PB	SUP	APR	DL	PW
'67 Cin N	14	8	.636	33	32	8-5	0	226.2	193	73	18	5	62-7	206	2.58	145	.228	.282	67-0-8	.104	-1	69	27		2.4
'68 Cin N	9	4	.692	23	22	4	0	150	105	48	10	3	49-1	111	2.40	132	.196	.266	46-1-7	.130	2	122	11		1.1
'69 Cin N	8	8	.500	16	15	2-1	0-0	108.2	100	45	11	0	40-3	83	3.56	106	.247	.312	35-0-8	.229	3*	107	4		0.8
'70 †Cin N	18	7	.720	37	37	4-2	0-0	250.2	226	102	25	1	96-9	181	3.27	124	.240	.304	82-0-9	.159	1	100	23		2.1
'71 †Cin N	12	15	.444	35	35	9	0-0	244.2	208	91	12	2	59-11	146	3.16	107	.227	.275	75-0-6	.147	-1	92	7		0.7
'72 †Cin N*	15	5	.750	25	25	6-2	0-0	176	147	48	13	1	30-5	90	1.99	163	.227	.259	60-0-4	.117	-1	130	24		2.6
'73 Cin N	0	1	.000	2	2	0	0-0	10.1	6	4	1	0	7-1	3	3.48	99	.167	.295	2	.000	-1	13	0	166	0.0
'75 †Cin N	15	9	.625	32	32	5-1	0-0	210.2	202	75	18	3	29-5	74	3.16	113	.251	.275	68-0-6	.176	2	124	12		1.4
'76 †Cin N	15	9	.625	34	34	7-1	0-0	239.1	232	96	28	1	27-3	113	3.46	101	.254	.275	79-0-6	.101	-3	119	4		-0.2
'77 Cin N	4	1	.800	8	8	0	0-0	39.1	53	22	5	0	12-1	28	4.81	82	.321	.367	15-0-2	.067	-2	141	-3		-0.5
Cal A	0	3	.000	5	5	0	0-0	18.1	31	19	5	0	2-0	4	8.84	44	.365	.371	0	—	0*	87	-10	43	-1.2
Total 10	110	70	.611	250	247	45-14	0-0	1674.2	1505	623	146	14	413-46	1039	3.08	116	.239	.285	529-1-56	.138	0	106	99	209	9.2

NOLD, DICK Richard Louis B5.4.1943 San Francisco CA BR/TR/6-2/190 d8.19 Col San Francisco (CA) City

YEAR TM LG	W	L	PCT	G	GS	CG-SHO	SV-BS	IP	H	R	HR	HB	BB-IB	SO	ERA	AERA	OAV	OOB	AB-HR-SH	AVG	PB	SUP	APR	DL	PW
'67 Was A	0	2	.000	7	3	0	0	20.1	19	13	1	0	13-0	10	4.87	65	.241	.348	3	.000	-0	92	-4		-0.4

NOLES, DICKIE Dickie Ray B11.19.1956 Charlotte NC BR/TR/6-2/190(178-190) [PhiN75 4/84] d7.5

YEAR TM LG	W	L	PCT	G	GS	CG-SHO	SV-BS	IP	H	R	HR	HB	BB-IB	SO	ERA	AERA	OAV	OOB	AB-HR-SH	AVG	PB	SUP	APR	DL	PW
'79 Phi N	3	4	.429	14	14	0	0	90	80	40	6	2	38-2	42	3.80	102	.246	.325	30-0-1	.100	-1	87	1		0.0
'80 †Phi N	1	4	.200	48	3	0	6-1	81	80	40	5	1	42-11	57	3.89	98	.254	.342	13-0-2	.308	-1	148	-2		-0.1
'81 †Phi N	2	2	.500	13	8	0	0-0	58.1	57	30	2	3	23-2	34	4.17	88	.260	.336	19-0-2	.105	-1	112	-3		-0.4
'82 Chi N	10	13	.435	31	30	2-2	0-0	171	180	99	11	5	61-2	85	4.42	86	.274	.336	56-0-4	.107	-2	96	-14	21	-1.9
'83 Chi N	5	10	.333	24	18	1-1	0-0	116.1	133	69	9	1	37-3	59	4.72	81	.287	.339	38-0-3	.237	-1	89	-12	53	-1.3
'84 Chi N	2	2	.500	21	1	0	0-3	50.2	60	29	4	1	16-1	14	5.15	76	.305	.356	10	.000	-1	0	-5		-0.5
Tex A	2	3	.400	18	6	0	0-0	57.2	60	38	6	5	30-0	39	5.15	81	.262	.360	0	—	0	130	-6		-0.5
'85 Tex A	4	8	.333	28	13	0	1-0	110.1	129	67	11	6	33-1	59	5.06	84	.289	.346	0	—	-1	82	-9	20	-0.5
'86 Cle N	3	2	.600	32	0	0	0-0	54.2	56	33	9	1	30-4	32	5.10	82	.269	.367	0	—	0		-5	61	-0.4
'87 Chi N	4	2	.667	41	1	0	2-2	64.1	59	31	1	5	27-1	33	3.50	124	.239	.325	11	.000	0	0	4	50	0.3
Det A	0	0	—	4	0	0	2-1	2	2	1	0	0	1-0	1	4.50	95	.250	.333	0	—	0		0		0.3
'88 Bal A	2	0	2.000	2	2	0	0-0	3.1	11	10	2	1	0-0	1	24.30	16	.500	.522	0	—	0	116	-8		-1.1
'90 Phi N	0	1	.000	1	0	0	0-0	0.1	2	1	0	0	0-0	0	27.00	14	.667	.667	0	—	0		-1	82	-0.2
Total 11	36	53	.404	277	96	3-3	11-7	860	909	490	66	35	338-27	455	4.56	87	.272	.343	177-0-12	.136	-4	93	-60	287	-7.0

NOLTE, ERIC Eric Carl B4.28.1964 Canoga Park CA BL/TL/6-3/200* [SDN85 6/154] d8.1 Col UCLA

YEAR TM LG	W	L	PCT	G	GS	CG-SHO	SV-BS	IP	H	R	HR	HB	BB-IB	SO	ERA	AERA	OAV	OOB	AB-HR-SH	AVG	PB	SUP	APR	DL	PW
'87 SD N	2	6	.250	12	12	1	0-0	67.1	57	28	6	2	36-2	44	3.21	124	.226	.326	21-0-3	.095	-1	78	5		0.5
'88 SD N	0	0	—	2	0	0	0-0	3	3	2	1	0	2-0	1	6.00	57	.273	.385	0	—	0		-1		0.0
'89 SD N	0	0	—	3	1	0	0-0	9	15	12	1	0	7-1	8	11.00	32	.375	.458	2	.000	-0		-2		0.0
'91 SD N	3	2	.600	6	6	0	0-0	22	37	27	6	0	10-0	15	11.05	34	.378	.423	9-0-2	.111	-0	126	-16	35	-2.6
Tex A	0	0	—	3	0	0	0-0	2.2	3	1	0	0	3-0	1	3.38	120	.273	.429	0	—	0		0		0.0
Total 5	5	8	.385	26	19	1	0-0	104	115	70	14	2	58-3	69	5.63	69	.279	.367	32-0-5	.094	-1	103	-19	35	-2.5

NOMO, HIDEO Hideo B8.31.1968 Osaka, Japan BR/TR/6-2/220(200-235) d5.2

YEAR TM LG	W	L	PCT	G	GS	CG-SHO	SV-BS	IP	H	R	HR	HB	BB-IB	SO	ERA	AERA	OAV	OOB	AB-HR-SH	AVG	PB	SUP	APR	DL	PW
'95 †LA N★	13	6	.684	28	28	4-3	0-0	191.1	124	63	14	5	78-2	236	2.54	152	.182	.269	66-0-5	.091	-4	104	30		2.2
'96 †LA N	16	11	.593	33	33	3-2	0-0	228.1	180	93	23	2	85-6	234	3.19	123	.218	.290	75-0-10	.133	-0	97	20		2.1
'97 LA N	14	12	.538	33	33	1	0-0	207.1	193	104	23	9	92-2	233	4.25	92	.243	.328	69-0-5	.159	2	119	-7		-0.7
'98 LA N	2	7	.222	12	12	2	0-0	67.2	57	39	8	3	38-0	73	5.05	80	.228	.334	20-1-2	.050	-1	51	-7		-0.9
NY N	4	5	.444	17	16	1	0-0	89.2	73	49	11	1	56-2	94	4.82	86	.224	.337	30-0-2*	.267	2	110	-6		-0.4
Year	6	12	.333	29	28	3	0-0	157.1	130	88	19	4	94-2	167	4.92	83	.226	.336	50-1-4	.180	1	85	-13		-1.3
'99 Mil N	12	8	.600	28	28	0	0-0	176.1	176	97	27	3	78-2	161	4.54	101	.256	.333	56-0-7	.214	2*	110	2		0.3
'00 Det A	8	12	.400	32	31	1	0-0	190	191	102	31	3	89-1	181	4.74	104	.263	.344	6	.000	-1	88	7	18	0.5
'01 Bos A	13	10	.565	33	33	2-2	0-0	198	171	105	26	9	96-2	220	4.50	99	.231	.320	5	.200	0	108	1		0.1
'02 LA N	16	6	.727	34	34	0	0-0	220.1	189	92	26	2	101-5	193	3.39	115	.236	.321	63-1-6	.063	-1	115	12		0.8
'03 LA N	16	13	.552	33	33	2-2	0-0	218.1	175	82	24	1	98-6	177	3.09	133	.233	.309	65-1-6	.138	-0	75	26		3.2
'04 LA N	4	11	.267	18	18	0	0-0	84	105	77	19	4	42-1	54	8.25	50	.312	.391	26-1-1	.115	-0	94	-38	81	-5.1
'05 TB A	4		.385	19	19	0	0-0	100.2	127	92	21	2	51-2	59	7.24	60	.314	.386	4	.000	-0	108	-29		-3.0
Total 11	123	109	.530	320	318	16-9	0-0	1972	1758	984	248	38	904-31	1915	4.21	99	.239	.324	485-4-44	.134	-1	101	11	99	-0.9

NOMURA, TAKAHITO Takahito B1.10.1969 Kouchi Prefecture, Japan BL/TL/5-7/175 d4.3

YEAR TM LG	W	L	PCT	G	GS	CG-SHO	SV-BS	IP	H	R	HR	HB	BB-IB	SO	ERA	AERA	OAV	OOB	AB-HR-SH	AVG	PB	SUP	APR	DL	PW
'02 Mil N	0	0	—	21	0	0	0-1	13.2	11	14	2	2	18-4	9	8.56	48	.224	.437	0	—	0		-7		-0.3

NOPS, JERRY Jeremiah H. B6.23.1875 Toledo OH D3.26.1937 Camden NJ BL/TL/5-8.5/168 d9.7

YEAR TM LG	W	L	PCT	G	GS	CG-SHO	SV-BS	IP	H	R	HR	HB	BB-IB	SO	ERA	AERA	OAV	OOB	AB-HR-SH	AVG	PB	SUP	APR	DL	PW
'96 Phi N	1	0	1.000	1	1	1	0	7	11	5	0	0	1		5.14	84	.355	.375	4	.000	-1	165	0		-0.1
Bal N	2	1	.667	3	3	3	0	22	29	15	0	0	3		6.14	70	.315	.330	9	.111	-1	105	-2		-0.3
Year	3	1	.750	4	4	4	0	29	40	20	0	0	3		5.90	73	.325	.341	13	.077	-2	120	-3		-0.4
'97 †Bal N	20	6	.769	30	25	23-1	0	220.2	235	107	5	9	52	69	2.81	148	.270	.318	92-0-2	.196	-3	97	31		2.5
'98 Bal N	16	9	.640	33	29	23-2	0	235	241	130	6	16	78	91	3.56	100	.263	.332	91-0-1	.220	2	99	2		0.1
'99 Bal N	17	11	.607	33	33	26-2	0	259	296	156	11	11	71	60	4.03	98	.287	.339	105	.276	1*	93	2		0.1
'00 Bro N	4	4	.500	9	8	6-1	0	68	79	44	0	3	16	22	3.84	100	.289	.338	25	.160	-1	104	-2		-0.3
'01 Bal A	12	10	.545	27	23	17-1	1	176.2	192	123	5	13	59	43	4.08	95	.274	.341	59-0-4	.220	-0	96	-3		-0.6
Total 6	72	41	.637	136	122	99-7	1	988.1	1083	581	17	51	281	294	3.70	106	.277	.333	385-0-7	.221	-2	97	28		1.4

YEAR	TM LG	W	L	PCT	G	GS	CG-SHO	SV-BS	IP	H	R	HR	HB	BB-IB	SO	ERA	AERA	OAV	OOB	AB-HR-SH	AVG	PB	SUP	APR	DL	P
NORIEGA, JOHN	John Alan B12.20.1943 Ogden UT BR/TR/6-4/180* [CinN66*S4/62] d5.1 Col Utah																									-0
1969	Cin N	0	0	—	5	0	0	0-0	7.2	12	6	1	0	3-0	4	5.87	64	.400	.429	0	—	0		-2		-0
1970	Cin N	0	0	—	8	0	0	0-0	18	25	17	0	2	10-1	6	8.00	51	.333	.420	4	.250	0		-7		-0
Total	2	0	0	—	13	0	0	0-0	25.2	37	23	1	2	13-1	10	7.36	54	.352	.423	4	.250	0		-9		-0
NORMAN, FRED	Fredie Hubert B8.20.1942 San Antonio TX BB/TL/5-8/160(158-170) d9.21																									C
1962	KC A	0	0	—	2	0	0	0	4	4	1	0	0	1-0	2	2.25	188	.250	.294	1	.000	-0	80	1		C
1963	KC A	0	1	.000	2	2	0	0	6.1	9	9	1	0	7-0	6	11.37	34	.346	.471	1	.000	-0	80	-5		
1964	Chi N	0	4	.000	8	5	0	0	31.2	34	25	9	1	21-5	20	6.54	57	.279	.389	11	.091	-1	62	-9		-1
1966	Chi N	0	0	—	2	0	0	0	4	5	2	0	0	2-1	6	4.50	82	.313	.389	0	—	0		0		C
1967	Chi N	0	0	—	1	0	0	0	1	0	0	0	0	0-0	3	0.00	—	.000	.000	0	—	0		0		C
1970	LA N	2	0	1.000	30	0	0	1-1	62	65	40	8	2	33-1	47	5.23	74	.273	.364	7-0-2	.143	0		-10		-0
	StL N	0	0	—	1	0	0	0-0	1	1	0	0	0	0-0	0	0.00	—	.333	.250	0	—	0		0		-0
	Year	2	0	1.000	31	0	0	1-1	63	66	40	8	2	33-1	47	5.14	75	.274	.362	7-0-2	.143	0		-9		-0
1971	StL N	0	0	—	4	0	0	0-0	3.2	7	5	1	0	7-0	4	12.27	30	.438	.583	0	—	0		-3		
	SD N	3	12	.200	20	18	5	0-1	127.1	114	48	7	2	56-7	77	3.32	100	.240	.321	38-0-3	.237	2*	50	3		C
	Year	3	12	.200	24	18	5	0-1	131	121	53	8	2	63-7	81	3.57	93	.246	.332	38-0-3	.237	2*	50	-1		C
1972	SD N	9	11	.450	42	28	10-6	2-0	211.2	195	88	18	2	88-12	167	3.44	83	.244	.332	64-0-5	.125	1*	103	-2		C
1973	SD N	1	7	.125	12	11	1	0-0	74	72	35	9	1	29-2	49	4.26	83	.262	.332	22-0-1	.136	0	57	-4		C
†	Cin N	12	6	.667	24	24	7-3	0-0	166.1	136	67	18	1	72-9	112	3.30	104	.224	.304	58-0-6	.052	-4	132	3		C
	Year	13	13	.500	36	35	8-3	0-0	240.1	208	102	27	2	101-11	161	3.60	97	.236	.313	80-0-7	.075	-4	108	0		C
1974	Cin N	13	12	.520	35	26	8-2	0-1	186.1	170	84	15	0	84-5	119	3.73	96	.235	.316	60-0-9	.117	-2	131	-4		C
1975	†Cin N	12	4	.750	34	26	2	0	188	163	85	20	0	84-5	119	3.09	113	.231	.305	50-0-7	.140	-1	119	7		C
1976	†Cin N	12	7	.632	33	24	8-3	0-0	180.1	153	71	10	3	70-5	126	3.38	117	.241	.322	73-0-6	.110	-2	100	10		C
1977	Cin N	14	13	.519	35	34	8-1	0-1	221.1	200	97	28	3	99-8	160	3.70	96	.255	.325	50-0-8	.140	-1	102	-5		C
1978	Cin N	11	9	.550	36	31	0	1-0	177.1	173	86	19	3	82-6	111	3.64	102	.258	.309	59-0-6	.153	-1	106	3		C
1979	†Cin N	11	13	.458	34	31	5	0-0	195.1	193	86	14	0	57-4	95	3.84	95	.262	.315	68-0-9	.154	-0	89	-5		C
1980	Mon N	4	4	.500	48	8	2	4-0	98	96	50	8	2	40-4	58	4.13	88	.259	.333	20-0-2	.050	-2	89	-5		C
Total	16	104	103	.502	403	268	56-15	8-4	1939.2	1790	864	188	23	815-79	1303	3.64	98	.246	.321	574-0-62	.125	-11	105	-10		
NORRIS, MIKE	Michael Kelvin B3.19.1955 San Francisco CA BR/TR/6-2/175(160-190) d4.10 [OakA73*1/24] [DL 1985 Oak A 182]																									
1975	Oak A	1	0	1.000	4	3	1-1	0-0	16.2	6	2	0	0	8-0	5	0.00	—	.107	.215	0	—	0	137	6	144	
1976	Oak A	4	5	.444	24	19	1-1	0-0	96	91	53	10	2	56-2	44	4.78	70	.250	.350	0	—	0	117	-14		
1977	Oak A	2	7	.222	16	12	1-1	0-0	77.1	77	45	14	4	31-1	35	4.77	85	.260	.336	1	.000	-0*	78	-5		-0
1978	Oak A	0	5	.000	14	5	1	0-0	49	46	35	2	3	35-1	36	5.51	66	.249	.373	0	—	0*	64	-10		-0
1979	Oak A	5	8	.385	29	18	3	0-0	146.1	146	87	11	9	94-9	96	4.80	85	.265	.376	0	—	0	83	-12	26	-0
1980	Oak A	22	9	.710	33	33	24-1	0-0	284.1	215	88	18	6	83-2	180	2.53	151	.209	.270	0	—	0	110	44		
1981	†Oak A★	12	9	.571	23	23	12-2	0-0	172.2	145	77	17	10	63-0	78	3.75	94	.228	.305	0	—	0	105	-3		
1982	Oak A	7	11	.389	28	28	7-1	0-0	166.1	154	103	25	4	84-1	83	4.76	83	.242	.335	0	—	0*	91	-18	21	-0
1983	Oak A	4	5	.444	16	16	2	0-0	88.2	68	42	11	3	36-0	63	3.76	104	.213	.297	0	—	0	98	1	91	
1990	Oak A	1	0	1.000	14	0	0	0-0	27	24	10	0	2	9-0	16	3.00	125	.242	.315	0	—	0		2		
Total	10	58	59	.496	201	157	52-7	0-0	1124.1	972	542	108	45	499-16	636	3.89	98	.233	.319	1	.000	-0	99	-9	464	
NORTH, LOU	Louis Alexander B6.15.1891 Elgin IL D5.15.1974 Shelton CT BR/TR/5-11/175 d8.22 Mil 1918																									
1913	Det A	0	1	.000	1	1	0	0	6	10	11	1	0	9	3	15.00	19	.370	.528	2	.000	-0	178	-1		
1917	StL N	0	0	—	5	0	0	0	11.1	14	5	1	0	4	4	3.97	68	.350	.409	3	.000	-0		-1		
1920	StL N	3	2	.600	24	6	3	1	88	90	43	3	2	32	37	3.26	91	.278	.346	31-0-1	.226	0*	145	-4		
1921	StL N	4	4	.500	40	0	0	7	86.1	81	39	5	1	32	28	3.54	103	.256	.327	19	.158	-1		2		
1922	StL N	10	3	.769	53	10	4	4	149.2	164	90	4	6	64	84	4.45	87	.283	.361	47-1-2	.234	2	131	-10		
1923	StL N	3	4	.429	34	3	0	1	71.2	90	50	8	3	31	24	5.15	76	.308	.380	22	.182	-1	211	-9		
1924	StL N	0	0	—	6	1	0	0	14.2	15	12	1	0	6	9	6.75	56	.273	.375	4	.250	-0	135	-4		
	Bos N	1	2	.333	9	4	1	0	35.1	45	25	1	0	19	11	5.35	71	.321	.403	9	.111	-1	89	-6		
	Year	1	2	.333	15	5	1	0	50	60	37	2	0	25	19	5.76	66	.308	.395	13	.154	-1	98	-11		
Total	7	21	16	.568	172	25	8	13	463	509	274	24	12	200	199	4.43	82	.287	.363	137-1-3	.197	-1	139	-40		
NORTHROP, JAKE	George Howard "Jerky" B3.5.1888 Monroeton PA D11.16.1945 Monroeton PA BL/TR/5-11/170 d7.29 Col Bucknell																									
1918	Bos N	5	1	.833	7	4	4-1	0	40	26	9	0	0	3	4	1.35	199	.183	.200	13-0-2	.154	-1	106	6		
1919	Bos N	1	5	.167	11	3	2	0	37.1	43	22	2	1	10	9	4.58	62	.301	.351	8-0-1	.500	3	74	-7		
Total	2	6	6	.500	18	7	6-1	0	77.1	69	31	2	1	13	13	2.91	95	.242	.278	21-0-3	.286	2	92	-1		
NORTON, EFFIE	Elisha Strong "Leiter" B8.17.1873 Conneaut OH D3.5.1950 Aspinwall PA BR/TR/5-10.5/170 d8.8 Col Ohio St.																									
1896	Was N	3	1	.750	8	5	2	0	44	49	25	2	6	14	13	3.07	144	.280	.354	19	.211	-0	87	6		
1897	Was N	2	1	.667	4	2	1	0	17	31	18	0	0	11	3	6.88	63	.387	.462	18	.278	1*	90	-4		
Total	2	5	2	.714	12	7	3	0	61	80	43	2	6	25	16	4.13	106	.314	.388	37	.243	0	88	2		
NORTON, PHIL	Phillip Douglas B2.1.1976 Texarkana TX BR/TL/6-1/190(190-215) [ChiN96 10/292] d8.3 Col Texarkana (TX) JC																									
2000	Chi N	0	1	.000	2	2	0	0-0	8.2	14	10	5	0	7-0	6	9.35	49	.350	.447	3-0-1	.667	1	100	-5		
2003	Chi N	0	0	—	4	0	0	0-0	3.1	3	2	0	0	3-0	5	5.40	80	.182	.357	0	—	0		3		
	Cin N	0	0	—	17	0	0	0-0	14.2	7	4	0	0	6-0	7	2.45	170	.149	.245	1	.000	-0		3		
	Year	0	0	—	21	0	0	0-0	18	9	6	0	0	9-0	7	3.00	140	.155	.269	1	.000	-0		-6		
2004	Cin N	2	5	.286	69	0	0	0-2	65.2	71	41	5	2	38-7	48	5.07	85	.284	.380	0	—	0		-6		
Total	3	2	6	.250	92	2	0	0-2	92.1	94	57	10	2	54-7	61	5.07	85	.270	.369	4-0-1	.500	1	100	-8		
NORTON, TOM	Thomas John B4.26.1950 Elyria OH BR/TR/6-1/200 d4.18 Col St. Clair Co. (MI) CC																									
1972	Min A	0	1	.000	21	0	0	0-0	32.1	31	14	1	1	14-0	22	2.78	115	.252	.333	0	—	0		1	63	
NOSEK, RANDY	Randall William B1.8.1967 Omaha NE BR/TR/6-4/216* [DetA85 1/26] d5.27																									
1989	Det A	0	2	.000	2	2	0	0-0	5.1	7	7	0	0	10-0	4	13.50	28	.333	.548	0	—	0	47	-5		
1990	Det A	1	1	.500	3	2	0	0-0	7	7	7	1	0	9-1	3	7.71	52	.280	.457	0	—	0	103	-3		
Total	2	1	3	.250	5	4	0	0-0	12.1	14	15	3	0	19-1	7	10.22	38	.304	.500	0	—	0	75	-8		
NOTTEBART, DON	Donald Edward B1.23.1936 West Newton MA BR/TR/6-1/190(190-208) d7.1																									
1960	Mil N	1	0	1.000	5	1	0	1	15.1	14	10	0	0	15-2	8	4.11	83	.233	.387	5	.000	-1	180	-2		
1961	Mil N	6	7	.462	38	11	2	3	126.1	117	61	11	2	48-2	66	4.06	92	.251	.321	38-0-1	.184	0	103	-4		
1962	Mil N	2	2	.500	39	0	0	2	64	64	30	4	4	20-3	36	3.23	117	.258	.321	6	.333	1		2		
1963	Hou N	11	8	.579	31	27	9-2	0	193	170	80	10	1	39-1	118	3.17	99	.234	.272	66-0-3	.167	0	101	-1		
1964	Hou N	6	11	.353	28	24	2	0	157	165	76	12	1	37-1	90	3.90	88	.275	.314	47-0-5	.064	-2	99	-7		
1965	Hou N	4	15	.211	29	25	3	0	158	166	99	14	5	55-11	77	4.67	72	.273	.337	48-0-4	.104	-1	104	-27		
1966	Cin N	5	4	.556	59	1	0	11	111.1	97	45	11	2	43-5	69	3.07	127	.235	.309	24-0-1	.167	-0	45	8		
1967	Cin N	0	3	.000	47	0	0	4	79.1	75	25	4	2	19-4	48	1.93	194	.253	.299	3-0-2	.000	0		12		
1969	NY A	0	0	—	4	0	0	0-0	6	6	3	1	1	0-0	5	4.50	78	.261	.292	0	—	0		0		
	Chi N	1	1	.500	7	0	0	0	18	28	14	2	0	7-0	8	7.00	57	.350	.398	1	.000	0		-5		
Total	9	36	51	.414	296	89	16-2	21-0	928.1	902	443	69	18	283-29	525	3.65	96	.256	.312	238-0-16	.134	-3	95	-24		
NOURSE, CHET	Chester Linwood B8.7.1887 Ipswich MA D4.20.1958 Clearwater FL BR/TR/6-3/185 d7.27 Col Brown																									
1909	Bos A	0	0	—	3	0	0	0	5	5	5	0	0	5	3	7.20	35	.263	.417	2	.000	-0		-2		
NOVOA, RAFAEL	Rafael Angel B10.26.1967 New York NY BL/TL/6-0/180* [SFN89 9/232] d7.31 Col Villanova																									
1990	SF N	0	1	.000	7	2	0	1-0	18.2	21	14	3	0	13-1	14	6.75	54	.284	.386	5	.200	0	111	-6		
1993	Mil A	0	3	.000	15	7	2	0-0	56	58	32	7	4	22-2	17	4.50	96	.267	.343	0	—	0	67	-2	15	
Total	2	0	4	.000	22	9	2	1-0	74.2	79	46	10	4	35-3	31	5.06	82	.271	.354	5	.200	0	76	-8	15	
NOVOA, ROBERTO	Roberto B8.15.1979 Las Matas de Farfan, D.R. BR/TR/6-5/200* d7.29																									
2004	Det A	1	1	.500	16	0	0	0-1	21	25	15	4	0	6-0	15	5.57	80	.309	.355	0	—	0		-3		
2005	Chi N	4	5	.444	49	0	0	0-5	44.2	47	22	4	2	25-6	47	4.43	99	.264	.355	1	.000	-0		0		
Total	2	5	6	.455	65	0	0	0-6	65.2	72	37	8	2	31-6	62	4.80	92	.278	.355	1	.000	-0		-3		

YEAR	TM LG	W	L	PCT	G	GS	CG-SHO	SV-BS	IP	H	R	HR	HB	BB-IB	SO	ERA	AERA	OAV	OOB	AB-HR-SH	AVG	PB	SUP	APR	DL	PW
NOYES, WIN	Winfield Charles B6.16.1889 Pleasanton NE D4.8.1969 Cashmere WA BR/TR/6-0/180 d5.19 Mil 1918 Col Nebraska Wesleyan																									
1913	Bos N	0	0	—	11	0	0	0	20.2	22	18	1	4	6	5	4.79	69	.289	.372	4	.250	0		-4		-0.2
1917	Phi A	10	10	.500	27	22	11-1	1	171	156	74	5	4	77	64	2.95	93	.258	.345	52-0-2	.115	-2	95	-2		-0.5
1919	Phi A	1	5	.167	10	6	3	0	49	66	34	1	1	15	20	5.69	60	.332	.381	16	.125	-1	88	-10		-1.1
	Chi A	0	0	—	1	1	0	0	6	10	5	0	0	0	4	7.50	42	.385	.385	2	.500	0	123	-2		-0.1
	Year	1	5	.167	11	7	3	0	55	76	39	1	1	15	24	5.89	58	.338	.382	18	.167	-1	92	-12		-1.2
Total	3	11	15	.423	49	29	14-1	1	246.2	254	131	7	9	98	93	3.76	78	.280	.356	74-0-2	.135	-3	93	-18		-1.9
NUNEZ, EDWIN	Edwin (Martinez) B5.27.1963 Humacao, PR BR/TR/6-5/237(220-240) d4.7																									
1982	Sea A	1	2	.333	8	5	0	0-0	35.1	36	18	7	0	16-0	27	4.58	93	.269	.347	0	—	0	106	0	22	0.0
1983	Sea A	0	4	.000	14	5	0	0-0	37	40	21	3	3	22-1	35	4.38	98	.278	.385	0	—	0	51	-1		-0.1
1984	Sea A	2	2	.500	37	0	0	7-2	67.2	55	26	8	3	21-2	57	3.19	126	.218	.283	0	—	0	7			0.5
1985	Sea A	7	3	.700	70	0	0	16-5	90.1	79	36	13	0	34-5	58	3.09	137	.234	.302	0	—	0	10			1.4
1986	Sea A	1	2	.333	14	1	0	0-2	21.2	25	15	5	0	5-1	17	5.82	73	.284	.323	0	—	0	64	-3	37	-0.4
1987	Sea A	3	4	.429	48	0	0	12-5	47.1	45	20	7	1	18-3	34	3.80	125	.262	.328	0	—	0	6		15	1.0
1988	Sea A	1	4	.200	14	3	0	0-0	29.1	45	33	4	2	14-3	19	7.98	52	.366	.427	0	—	0	65	-13		-1.9
	NY N	1	0	1.000	10	0	0	0-0	14	21	7	1	0	3-0	8	4.50	73	.339	.369	0	—	0	-2			-0.1
1989	Det A	3	4	.429	27	0	0	1-2	54	49	33	6	0	36-13	41	4.17	92	.254	.366	0	—	0	-4			-0.5
1990	Det A	3	1	.750	42	0	0	6-1	80.1	65	26	4	2	37-6	66	2.24	178	.218	.308	0	—	0	13		38	0.7
1991	Mil A	2	1	.667	23	0	0	8-1	25.1	28	20	6	0	13-2	24	6.04	66	.277	.353	0	—	0	-7		86	-1.0
1992	Mil A	1	1	.500	10	0	0	0-0	13.2	12	5	1	0	6-0	10	2.63	147	.231	.310	0	—	0	2			0.2
	Tex A	0	2	.000	39	0	0	3-1	45.2	51	29	5	2	16-0	39	5.52	69	.279	.337	0	—	0	-8			-0.4
	Year	1	3	.250	49	0	0	3-1	59.1	63	34	6	2	22-0	49	4.85	79	.268	.331	0	—	0	-6			-0.2
1993	Oak A	3	6	.333	56	0	0	1-3	75.2	89	36	2	6	29-2	58	3.81	109	.298	.369	0	—	0	2			0.2
1994	Oak A	0	0	—	15	0	0	0-0	15	26	20	2	0	10-0	15	12.00	37	.382	.456	0	—	0	-12			-0.5
Total	13	28	36	.438	427	14	0	54-22	652.1	666	345	74	19	280-38	508	4.19	98	.266	.341	0	—	0	77	-10	198	-0.9
NUNEZ, FRANKLIN	Franklin B1.18.1977 Nagua, D.R. BR/TR/6-0/175* d8.14																									
2004	TB A	0	3	.000	8	0	0	0-1	10.2	11	8	1	3	7-0	14	5.91	79	.268	.396	0	—	0	-2			-0.3
2005	TB A	1	0	1.000	5	0	0	0-0	5	5	6	0	0	4-0	2	10.80	40	.278	.409	0	—	0	-3	55		-0.6
Total	2	1	3	.250	13	0	0	0-1	15.2	16	14	1	3	11-0	16	7.47	61	.271	.400	0	—	0	-5	55		-0.9
NUNEZ, JOSE	Jose (Jimenez) B1.13.1964 Jarabacoa, D.R. BR/TR/6-3/175(175-190) d4.9																									
1987	Tor A	5	2	.714	37	9	0	0-0	97	91	57	12	0	58-8	99	5.01	91	.256	.356	0	—	0*	130	-4		-0.3
1988	Tor A	0	1	.000	13	2	0	0-1	29.1	28	11	3	1	17-3	18	3.07	129	.259	.365	0	—	0	81	3	15	0.1
1989	Tor A	0	0	—	6	1	0	0-0	10.2	8	3	0	0	2-0	14	2.53	150	.200	.238	0	—	0	119	2		0.1
1990	Chi N	4	7	.364	21	10	0	0-0	60.2	61	47	5	0	34-4	40	6.53	63	.270	.361	11-0-3	.000	-1	113	-14		-2.4
Total	4	9	10	.474	77	22	0	0-1	197.2	188	118	20	1	111-15	171	5.05	85	.258	.353	11-0-3	.000	-1	117	-13	15	-2.5
NUNEZ, JOSE	Jose Antonio B3.14.1979 Monte Cristi, D.R. BL/TL/6-2/173* d4.3																									
2001	LA N	0	1	.000	6	0	0	0-1	7.1	14	15	4	0	5-0	11	13.50	31	.389	.463	0	—	0	-10			-1.1
	SD N	4	1	.800	56	0	0	0-1	51.2	48	20	3	4	20-3	49	3.31	125	.245	.324	3	.000	-0	6			0.4
	Year	4	2	.667	62	0	0	0-2	59	62	35	7	4	25-3	60	4.58	91	.267	.346	3	.000	-0	-4			-0.7
2002	SD N	0	0	—	1	0	0	0-0	1	0	0	0	0	1-0	0	0.00	—	.000	.250	0	—	0	0	181		0.0
Total	2	4	2	.667	63	0	0	0-2	60	62	35	7	4	26-3	60	4.50	92	.264	.345	3	.000	-0	-4	181		-0.7
NUNEZ, LEO	Leonel (Morales) B8.14.1983 Jamao Norte, D.R. BR/TR/6-1/160 d5.9																									
2005	KC A	3	2	.600	41	0	0	0	53.2	73	45	9	3	18-2	32	7.55	56	.329	.384	0	—	0	-19			-1.5
NUNEZ, VLADIMIR	Vladimir (Zarabaza) B3.15.1975 Havana, Cuba BR/TR/6-4/235(224-240) d9.11																									
1998	Ari N	0	0	—	4	0	0	0-0	5.1	7	6	0	0	2-0	2	10.13	42	.318	.360	0	—	0	-3			-0.2
1999	Ari N	3	2	.600	27	0	0	1-1	34	29	15	2	1	20-5	28	2.91	159	.242	.347	3	.000	-0	5			0.6
	Fla N	4	8	.333	17	12	0	0-1	74.2	66	48	9	3	34-1	58	4.58	96	.243	.330	25-0-2	.160	-0	80	-5		-0.7
	Year	7	10	.412	44	12	0	1-2	108.2	95	63	11	4	54-6	86	4.06	110	.242	.336	28-0-2	.143	-1	79	0		-0.1
2000	Fla N	0	6	.000	17	12	0	0-0	68.1	88	63	12	2	34-2	45	7.90	55	.319	.391	17-1-4	.118	-0	89	-27		-1.9
2001	Fla N	4	5	.444	52	3	0	0-1	92	79	33	9	5	30-5	64	2.74	152	.234	.302	9-0-2	.111	-0	81	14	15	1.2
2002	Fla N	6	5	.545	77	0	0	20-8	97.2	80	38	8	0	37-1	73	3.41	115	.224	.294	5	.200	0	7			0.9
2003	Fla N	0	3	.000	14	0	0	0-3	10.2	21	21	7	0	7-0	10	16.03	26	.396	.452	0	—	0	-15			-2.7
2004	Col N	3	3	.500	22	0	0	0-3	25.2	26	22	6	1	14-0	22	7.01	68	.280	.363	0	—	0	-6			-1.2
Total	7	20	32	.385	230	27	0	21-17	408.1	396	246	53	12	178-14	302	4.83	88	.259	.335	59-1-8	.136	-0	87	-30	15	-4.0
NUNN, HOWIE	Howard Ralph B10.18.1935 Westfield NC BR/TR/6-0/173* d4.11																									
1959	StL N	2	2	.500	16	0	0	0	21.1	23	18	3	0	15-5	20	7.59	56	.291	.404	1-0-1	.000	-0	-7			-1.1
1961	Cin N	2	1	.667	24	0	0	0	37.2	35	17	0	1	24-4	26	3.58	113	.252	.357	8	.250	0	2	44		0.1
1962	Cin N	0	0	—	6	0	0	0	9.2	15	6	0	0	3-1	4	5.59	72	.375	.400	1	.000	-0	-1			-0.1
Total	3	4	3	.571	46	0	0	0	68.2	73	41	3	1	42-10	50	5.11	80	.283	.378	10-0-1	.200	-0	-6	44		-1.1
NUXHALL, JOE	Joseph Henry B7.30.1928 Hamilton OH BL/TL/6-3/219(219-234) d6.10																									
1944	Cin N	0	0	—	1	0	0	0	0.2	2	5	0	0	5	0	67.50	5	.500	.778	0	—	0	-5			-0.2
1952	Cin N	1	4	.200	37	5	2	1	92.1	83	33	4	3	42	52	3.22	117	.246	.334	23	.087	-1	71	7		0.3
1953	Cin N	9	11	.450	30	17	5-1	2	141.2	136	77	13	8	69	52	4.32	101	.252	.345	49-3-2	.327	4*	83	0		0.7
1954	Cin N	12	5	.706	35	14	5-1	0	166.2	188	77	11	6	59	85	3.89	108	.292	.353	52-3-4	.173	4*	125	7		1.0
1955	Cin N★	17	12	.586	50	33	14-5	3	257	240	108	25	5	78-6	98	3.47	122	.249	.307	86-3-4	.198	4*	116	23		2.8
1956	Cin N☆	13	11	.542	44	32	10-2	3	200.2	196	96	18	4	87-6	120	3.72	107	.257	.336	59-2-4	.186	3*	92	4		0.7
1957	Cin N	10	10	.500	39	28	6-2	1	174.1	192	104	24	7	53-3	99	4.75	87	.275	.331	59-0-5	.237	3*	111	-13		-1.2
1958	Cin N	12	11	.522	36	26	5	0	175.2	169	78	15	1	63-5	111	3.79	109	.257	.322	62-0-2	.210	0	95	7		0.9
1959	Cin N	9	9	.500	28	21	6-1	1	131.2	155	76	10	1	35-1	75	4.24	96	.292	.335	44-0-2	.250	3	119	-5		-0.4
1960	Cin N	1	8	.111	38	6	0	0	112	130	58	8	4	27-6	72	4.42	86	.297	.340	26	.077	-1*	50	-6		-0.5
1961	KC A	5	8	.385	37	13	1	1	128	135	81	12	3	65-2	81	5.34	78	.268	.352	65-2-5	.292	7*	85	-13		-0.5
1962	LA A	0	0	—	5	0	0	0	5.1	7	6	0	1	5-0	2	10.13	38	.304	.448	0	—	0	-3			-0.2
	Cin N	5	0	1.000	1	1	1	1	66	59	20	4	1	25-1	57	2.45	164	.240	.311	26-1-3	.269	1	160	11		1.1
1963	Cin N	15	8	.652	35	29	14-2	2	217.1	194	73	14	6	39-2	169	2.61	128	.237	.275	76-0-4	.158	0	110	17		1.7
1964	Cin N	9	8	.529	32	22	7-4	2	154.2	146	73	19	6	51-3	111	4.07	89	.250	.316	54-1-1	.130	-1*	99	-5		-0.7
1965	Cin N	11	4	.733	32	16	5-1	2	148.2	142	57	18	3	31-2	117	3.45	109	.252	.294	45-0-6	.178	1	112	8		0.7
1966	Cin N	6	8	.429	35	16	2-1	0	130	136	71	14	9	42-7	71	4.50	87	.270	.336	40-0-1	.100	-2	96	-8	15	-1.1
Total	16	135	117	.536	526	287	83-20	19	2302.2	2310	1093	209	70	776-44	1372	3.90	102	.262	.325	766-15-43	.198	28	104	26	15	5.1
NYE, RICH	Richard Raymond B8.4.1944 Oakland CA BL/TL/6-4/185* [ChiN66 14/265] d9.16 Col California-Davis																									
1966	Chi N	0	2	.000	3	2	1	0	17	16	4	1	0	7-2	9	2.12	174	.254	.329	4	.250	0	0	3		0.0
1967	Chi N	13	10	.565	35	30	7	0	205	179	82	15	2	52-4	119	3.20	111	.234	.282	75-0-3	.213	3	92	7		1.1
1968	Chi N	7	12	.368	27	20	6-1	1	132.2	145	65	16	1	34-4	74	3.80	83	.276	.319	44-0-1	.182	-0	85	-10		-1.5
1969	Chi N	3	5	.375	34	5	1	3-1	68.2	72	43	13	1	21-4	39	5.11	79	.271	.324	16	.063	-1*	75	-7		-1.0
1970	StL N	0	0	—	6	0	0	0-0	8	13	5	2	0	6-1	5	4.50	92	.371	.452	2	.500	1	-1			0.0
	Mon N	3	2	.600	8	6	2	0-0	46.1	47	23	3	0	20-3	21	4.08	102	.260	.330	17-0-1	.176	0*	112	1		0.0
	Year	3	2	.600	14	6	2	0-0	54.1	60	28	5	0	26-4	26	4.14	100	.278	.351	19-0-1	.211	1	112	0		0.0
Total	5	26	31	.456	113	63	16-1	4-1	477.2	472	222	50	4	140-18	267	3.71	96	.257	.309	158-0-5	.190	2	86	-7		-1.0

YEAR	TM LG	W	L	PCT	G	GS	CG-SHO	SV-BS	IP	H	R	HR	HB	BB-IB	SO	ERA	AERA	OAV	OOB	AB-HR-SH	AVG	PB	SUP	APR	DL	PW

NYE, RYAN   Ryan Craig B6.24.1973 Biloxi MS   BR/TR/6-2/195* [PhiN94 2/57] d6.7 Col Texas Tech

1997	Phi N	0	2	.000	4	2	0	0-0	12	20	11	2	2	9-0	7	8.25	51	.392	.484	2-0-1	.000	-0	44	-5	25	-0.7
1998	Phi N	0	0	—	1	0	0	0-0	1	3	3	1	0	0-0	3	27.00	16	.500	.500	0	—		44	-2		-0.8
Total	2	0	2	.000	5	2	0	0-0	13	23	14	3	2	9-0	10	9.69	44	.404	.486	2-0-1	.000	-0	44	-7	25	-0.8

NYMAN, JERRY   Gerald Smith B11.23.1942 Logan UT   BL/TL/5-10/170* d8.24 Col Brigham Young

1968	Chi A	2	1	.667	8	7	1-1	0-0	40.1	38	13	1	0	16-1	27	2.01	151	.247	.314	13-0-1	.154	-0	74	3		0.2
1969	Chi A	4	4	.500	20	10	2-1	0-0	64.2	58	40	7	0	39-1	40	5.29	73	.244	.346	20-0-1	.050	-1*	110	-9		-1.2
1970	SD N	0	2	.000	2	2	0	0-0	5.1	8	9	1	0	2-0	2	15.19	26	.364	.400	0	—	0*	101	-6		-0.9
Total	3	6	7	.462	30	19	3-2	0-0	110.1	104	62	9	0	57-2	69	4.57	78	.251	.338	33-0-2	.091	-1	98	-12		-1.9

OANA, PRINCE   Henry Kawaihoa B1.22.1908 Waipahu HI D6.19.1976 Austin TX   BR/TR/6-2/193 d4.22.1934 ▲

1943	Det A	3	2	.600	10	0	0	0	34	34	21	4	2	19	15	4.50	78	.262	.364	26-1-0	.385	4*		-4		-0.1
1945	Det A	0	0	—	3	1	0	1	11.1	3	2	0	0	7	3	1.59	221	.086	.238	5	.200	-0*	48	2		0.1
Total	2	3	2	.600	13	1	0	1	45.1	37	23	4	2	26	18	3.77	93	.224	.337	31-1-0	.355	4	48	-2		0.1

OBERBECK, HENRY   Henry A. B5.17.1858 MO D8.26.1921 St.Louis MO d5.7.1883 ▲

1884	Bal U	0	0	—	2	1	0	0	6	9	3	0		2	1	3.00	89	.321	.367	125	.184	-1*	80	0		0.0
	KC U	0	5	.000	6	4	3	0	29.2	47	35	0		3	6	5.76	39	.338	.352	90	.189	-1*	19	-12		-1.5
	Year	0	5	.000	8	5	3	0	35.2	56	38	0		5	7	5.30	44	.335	.355	215	.186	-2	33	-12		-1.5

OBERLANDER, DOC   Hartman Louis B5.12.1864 Waukegan IL D11.14.1922 Pryor MT   TL/5-10.5/165 d5.16 Col Syracuse

| 1888 | Cle AA | 1 | 2 | .333 | 3 | 3 | 3 | 0 | 25.2 | 27 | 33 | 2 | 1 | 18 | 23 | 5.26 | 59 | .260 | .374 | 14 | .214 | 0 | 200 | -8 | | -0.7 |

OBERLIN, FRANK   Frank Rufus "Flossie" B3.29.1876 Elsie MI D1.6.1952 Ashley IN   BR/TR/6-1/165 d9.20

1906	Bos A	1	3	.250	4	4	4	0	34	38	20	0	2	13	13	3.18	87	.286	.358	13	.154	-0	79	-3		-0.3
1907	Bos A	1	5	.167	12	4	2	0	46	48	31	2	2	24	18	4.30	60	.271	.365	13	.154	-0	20	-8		-1.1
	Was A	2	6	.250	11	8	3	0	48.2	57	38	0	2	12	18	4.62	52	.294	.341	18	.056	-2*	87	-13		-2.2
	Year	3	11	.214	23	12	5	0	94.2	105	69	2	4	36	36	4.47	56	.283	.353	31	.097	-2	63	-22		-3.3
1909	Was A	1	4	.200	9	4	1	0	41	41	22	0	1	16	13	3.73	65	.266	.358	14	.143	-1*	65	-5		-0.5
1910	Was A	0	6	.000	8	6	6	0	57.1	52	32	0	2	23	18	2.98	84	.259	.341	19	.053	-2	45	-5		-0.4
Total	4	5	24	.172	44	26	16	0	227	236	143	2	14	88	80	3.77	67	.275	.352	77	.104	-4	62	-34		-4.9

OBERMUELLER, WES   Wesley Mitchell B12.22.1976 Cedar Rapids IA   BR/TR/6-2/195(195-210) [KCA99 2/58] d9.20 Col Iowa

2002	KC A	0	2	.000	2	2	0	0-0	7.2	14	10	3	0	2-0	5	11.74	43	.378	.410	0	—		47	-5		-0.8
2003	Mil N	2	5	.286	12	11	0	0-0	65.2	81	40	10	6	25-2	34	5.07	85	.301	.371	23-0-2	.130	-1	81	-6		-0.6
2004	Mil N	6	8	.429	25	20	1-1	0-0	118	138	80	15	3	42-0	59	5.80	76	.291	.349	39-0-2	.385	5*	97	-16		-1.1
2005	Mil N	1	4	.200	23	8	0	0-0	65	74	41	7	5	36-2	33	5.65	81	.289	.382	15-0-1	.200	1*	95	-7		-0.2
Total	4	9	19	.321	62	41	1-1	0-0	256.1	307	171	35	14	105-4	131	5.65	77	.296	.365	77-0-5	.273	6	90	-34		-2.7

O'BRIEN, DAN   Daniel Jogues B4.22.1954 St.Petersburg FL   BR/TR/6-4/215* [StLN76*S3/61] d9.4 Col Florida St.

1978	StL N	2	2	.000	7	2	0	0	18	22	12	1	2	8-2	12	4.50	79	.301	.381	3-0-1	.000	-0	88	-3		-0.1
1979	StL N	1	1	.500	6	0	0	0	11	21	10	0	0	3-0	5	8.18	47	.420	.436	2	.000	-0		-8		-0.6
Total	2	1	3	.250	13	2	0	0	29	43	22	1	2	11-2	17	5.90	62	.350	.403	5-0-1	.000	-1	88	-8		-1.2

O'BRIEN, EDDIE   Edward Joseph B12.11.1930 S.Amboy NJ   BR/TR/5-9/165* d4.25.1953 Mil 1954-55 C1 twb-Johnny Col Seattle ▲

1956	Pit N	0	0	—	1	0	0	0	2	1	1	0	0	0-0	0	0.00	—	.167	.286	53-0-3	.264	0*		1		0.5
1957	Pit N	1	0	1.000	3	1	1	0	12.1	11	3	2	0	3-0	10	2.19	173	.229	.275	4	.000	-1	70	2		0.2
1958	Pit N	0	0	—	1	0	0	0	2	4	3	1	0	1-0	1	13.50	29	.444	.500	0	—		70	-2		-0.1
Total	3	1	0	1.000	5	1	1	0	16.1	16	6	3	1	4-0	11	3.31	115	.254	.309	57-0-3	.246	-0	70	1		0.6

O'BRIEN, DARBY   John F. B4.15.1867 Troy NY D3.11.1892 W.Troy NY   BR/TR/5-10/165 d6.23

1888	Cle AA	11	19	.367	30	30	30-1	0	259	245	162	5	12	99	135	3.30	94	.241	.315	109	.183	-3*	88	-5		-0.5
1889	Cle N	22	17	.564	41	41	39-1	0	346.2	345	216	9	24	167	122	4.15	97	.251	.343	140	.250	4	95	3		0.7
1890	Cle P	8	16	.333	25	25	22	0	206.1	229	171	9	19	93	54	3.40	117	.269	.354	96	.156	-6*	91	8		0.1
1891	Bos AA	18	13	.581	40	30	22	2	268.2	300	197	13	20	127	87	3.65	95	.273	.359	128	.234	1*	153	-11		-1.1
Total	4	59	65	.476	136	126	113-2	2	1080.2	1119	746	36	75	486	398	3.68	100	.258	.343	473	.211	-4	106	-5		-1.2

O'BRIEN, JOHNNY   John Thomas B12.11.1930 S.Amboy NJ   BR/TR/5-9/170* d4.19.1953 Mil 1954-55 twb-Eddie Col Seattle ▲

1956	Pit N	1	0	1.000	8	0	0	0	19	8	6	2	2	9-0	9	2.84	133	.133	.260	104-0-4	.173	-0*		2		0.0
1957	Pit N	0	3	.000	16	1	0	0	40	46	32	7	1	24-2	19	6.07	62	.293	.384	35-0-1	.314	2*	70	-11		-0.5
1958	StL N	0	0	—	1	0	0	0	2	7	5	0	0	2-0	2	22.50	18	.538	.600	2	.000	0*		-4		-0.2
Total	3	1	3	.250	25	1	0	0	61	61	43	9	3	35-2	30	5.61	68	.265	.363	141-0-5	.206	2	70	-13		-0.7

O'BRIEN, BOB   Robert Allen B4.23.1949 Pittsburgh PA   BL/TL/5-10/170 [LAN69*4/74] d4.11 Col Arizona

| 1971 | LA N | 2 | 2 | .500 | 14 | 4 | 1-1 | 0-0 | 42 | 42 | 18 | 4 | 1 | 13-1 | 15 | 3.00 | 108 | .262 | .320 | 9-0-2 | .111 | -0 | 75 | 0 | | -0.1 |

O'BRIEN, BUCK   Thomas Joseph B5.9.1882 Brockton MA D7.25.1959 Boston MA   BR/TR/5-10/188 d9.9

1911	Bos A	5	1	.833	6	5	5-2	0	47.2	30	9	0	1	21	31	0.38	868	.180	.275	16	.125	-1	66	14		2.2
1912	†Bos A	20	13	.606	37	34	25-2	0	275.2	237	107	3	10	90	115	2.58	132	.237	.306	94-0-4	.138	-5	91	24		2.1
1913	Bos A	4	9	.308	15	12	6	0	90.1	103	42	0	4	35	54	3.69	80	.307	.373	30-0-1	.167	0	99	-4		-0.6
	Chi A	0	2	.000	6	3	0	0	18.1	21	14	0	0	13	4	3.93	74	.323	.436	3	.000	-0	76	-3		-0.4
	Year	4	11	.267	21	15	6	0	108.2	124	56	0	4	48	58	3.73	79	.310	.384	33-0-1	.152	-0	94	-8		-1.0
Total	3	29	25	.537	64	54	36-4	0	432	391	172	3	11	159	204	2.63	125	.250	.323	143-0-5	.140	-6	89	31		2.6

O'BRIEN, BILLY   William Smith B3.14.1860 Albany NY D5.26.1911 Kansas City MO   BR/TR/6-0/185 d9.27 ▲

| 1884 | StP U | 0 | 1 | 1.000 | 1 | 1 | 1 | 0 | 10 | 8 | 5 | 0 | | 3 | 4 | 1.80 | 74 | .205 | .262 | 30 | .233 | -0* | | -1 | | -0.2 |

OCKEY, WALTER   Walter Andrew "Footie" (b Walter Andrew Okpych) B1.4.1920 New York NY D12.4.1971 Staten Island NY   BR/TR/6-0/175 d5.3

| 1944 | NY N | 0 | 0 | — | 2 | 0 | 0 | 0 | 2.2 | 1 | 1 | 0 | 2 | 1 | 3.38 | 109 | .200 | .333 | — | | 0 | | 0 | | -0.1 |

O'CONNOR, ANDY   Andrew James B9.14.1884 Roxbury MA D9.26.1980 Norwood MA   BR/TR/6-0/160 d10.6

| 1908 | NY A | 0 | 1 | .000 | 1 | 1 | 1 | 0 | 8 | 15 | 11 | 0 | 3 | 7 | 5 | 10.13 | 24 | .429 | .556 | 3 | .000 | -0 | 83 | -6 | | -0.7 |

O'CONNOR, BRIAN   Brian Michael B1.4.1977 Cincinnati OH   BL/TL/6-2/190 [PitN95 11/293] d5.13

| 2000 | Pit N | 0 | 0 | — | 6 | 1 | 0 | 0 | 12.1 | 12 | 11 | 2 | 1 | 11-0 | 7 | 5.11 | 91 | .250 | .393 | .500 | 0 | 218 | -2 | | -0.4 |

O'CONNOR, FRANK   Frank Henry B9.15.1870 Keeseville NY D12.26.1913 Brattleboro VT   BL/TL/6-0/185 d8.3 Col Dartmouth

| 1893 | Phi N | 0 | 0 | — | 3 | 1 | 0 | 1 | 4 | 2 | 5 | 0 | 0 | 9 | 0 | 11.25 | 41 | .143 | .478 | 2-1 | 1.000 | 2 | 335 | -2 | | -0.4 |

O'CONNOR, JACK   Jack William B6.2.1958 Twentynine Palms CA   BL/TL/6-3/215(200-215) [MonN76 9/201] d4.9

1981	Min A	3	2	.600	28	0	0	0-3	35.1	46	27	3	2	30-6	16	5.86	67	.336	.462	0	—	0		-7		-0.7
1982	Min A	8	9	.471	23	19	6-1	0-0	126	122	63	13	2	57-4	56	4.29	100	.255	.336	0	—	0	89	1		-0.1
1983	Min A	2	3	.400	27	8	0	0-0	83	107	59	13	0	36-1	56	5.86	73	.315	.376	0	—	0	114	-14		-1.5
1984	Min A	0	0	—	2	0	0	0	4.2	1	1	1	0	4-0	0	1.93	220	.067	.263	0	—	0	51	-4		-0.1
1985	Mon N	0	2	.000	20	1	0	0-1	23.2	21	14	1	0	13-7	16	4.94	70	.239	.330	0	—	0	51	-4		-0.4
1987	Bal A	1	1	.500	29	1	0	2-1	46	46	23	5	0	23-4	33	4.30	103	.263	.343	0	—	0	96	-22	45	-0.9
Total	6	14	17	.452	129	28	6-1	2-5	318.2	343	187	36	4	163-22	177	4.89	86	.278	.361	0	—	0			45	-2.8

O'DAY, HANK   Henry Francis B7.8.1862 Chicago IL D7.2.1935 Chicago IL   TR/6-0/180 d5.2 M2/U30 Col St.Marys (CA)

1884	Tol AA	9	28	.243	41	40	35-2	1	326.2	335	241	6	18	66	163	3.75	91	.252	.297	242	.211	-1*	73	-12		-1.4
1885	Pit AA	5	7	.417	12	12	10	0	103	110	77	4	7	16	36	3.67	88	.258	.296	49	.245	-1*	115	-8		-0.7
1886	Was N	2	2	.500	6	6	6	0	49	41	17	1	7	17	47	1.65	195	.219	.284	19	.053	-2	44	8		0.9
1887	Was N	8	20	.286	30	30	29	0	254.2	255	197	15	9	109	86	4.17	96	.254	.332	116	.198	-3*	87	-7		-0.8
1888	Was N	16	29	.356	46	46	46-2	0	403	359	208	19	16	112	186	3.10	89	.232	.293	166	.139	-6*	66	-12		-1.3
1889	Was N	0	1	.167	13	13	11	0	108	117	88	7	6	57	23	4.33	91	.266	.360	44	.182	-1	51	-7		-0.6
	†NY N	9	1	.900	10	10	8	0	78	83	51	2	7	35	51	4.27	92	.264	.351	31	.097	-1	135	0		0.2
	Year	11	11	.500	23	23	19	0	186	200	139	9	13	92	51	4.31	92	.266	.356	75	.147	-2	87	-10		-0.4
1890	NY P	22	13	.629	43	35	32-1	3	329	355	249	11	18	161	94	4.21	108	.264	.350	150-1	.227	-3	110	11		1.4
Total	7	73	110	.399	201	192	177-5	4	1651.1	1655	1128	61	81	578	663	3.74	96	.251	.319	817-1	.190	-16	86	-27		-2.3

YEAR	TM LG	W	L	PCT	G	GS	CG-SHO	SV-BS	IP	H	R	HR	HB	BB-IB	SO	ERA	AERA	OAV	OOB	AB-HR-SH	AVG	PB	SUP	APR	DL	PW

O'DELL, BILLY William Oliver B2.10.1932 Whitmire SC BB/TL/5-11/170* d6.20 Mil 1955-56 Col Clemson

YEAR	TM LG	W	L	PCT	G	GS	CG-SHO	SV-BS	IP	H	R	HR	HB	BB-IB	SO	ERA	AERA	OAV	OOB	AB-HR-SH	AVG	PB	SUP	APR	DL	PW
1954	Bal A	1	1	.500	7	2	1	0	16.1	15				5	6	2.76	130	.242	.299	3	.000	-0	25	1		0.1
1956	Bal A	0	0	—	4	1	0	0	8	6	1	0	0	6-1	6	1.13	349	.222	.353	1	.000	-0	91	3		0.1
1957	Bal A	4	10	.286	35	15	2-1	4	140.1	107	48	12	5	39-2	97	2.69	133	.212	.275	34-0-5	.147	-1*	58	14		1.2
1958	Bal A★	14	11	.560	41	25	12-3	8	221.1	201	83	13	4	51-6	137	2.97	121	.241	.284	72-1-4	.111	-1*	108	15		1.7
1959	Bal A★	10	12	.455	38	24	6-2	1	199.1	163	74	18	1	67-7	88	2.93	129	.220	.284	60-1-2	.083	-3*	77	19		1.7
1960	SF N	8	13	.381	43	24	6-1	2	202.2	198	80	16	2	72-8	145	3.20	109	.252	.314	56-0-3	.107	1*	99	9		0.9
1961	SF N	7	5	.583	46	14	4-1	2	130.1	132	63	10	1	33-6	110	3.59	106	.260	.305	39-0-4	.103	-1*	116	7		-0.2
1962	†SF N	19	14	.576	43	39	20-2	0	280.2	282	126	18	7	66-1	195	3.53	108	.258	.303	90-0-10	.133	-1*	126	1		0.6
1963	SF N	14	10	.583	36	33	10-3	1	222.1	218	90	14	7	70-12	116	3.16	101	.253	.313	78-0-5	.205	4*	131	2		0.3
1964	SF N	8	7	.533	36	8	1	2	85.	82	55	10	4	35-6	54	5.40	66	.252	.329	22	.000	-2*	74	-16		-2.9
1965	Mil N	10	6	.625	62	1	0	18	111.1	87	35	10	2	30-8	78	2.18	161	.215	.269	23-0-2	.174	1	50	14		2.7
1966	Atl N	2	3	.400	24	0	0	6	41.1	44	14	3	2	18-1	20	2.40	152	.272	.352	8	.250	0*		5		0.8
	Pit N	3	2	.600	37	2	0	6	71.1	74	24	3	4	23-1	47	2.78	129	.275	.339	16	.063	-1	86	7		0.4
	Year	5	5	.500	61	2	0	10	112.2	118	38	6	6	41-2	67	2.64	136	.274	.344	24	.125	-1	86	11		1.2
1967	Pit N	5	6	.455	27	11	1	0	86.2	88	38	6	6	41-2	34	5.82	58	.265	.347	26-0-1	.115	-0*	138	-21		-2.5
Total 13		105	100	.512	479	199	63-13	48	1817	1697	758	137	42	556-66	1133	3.29	109	.246	.304	528-2-36	.125	-7	104	60		4.9

ODENWALD, TED Theodore Joseph "Lefty" B1.4.1902 Hudson WI D10.23.1965 Shakopee MN BR/TL/5-10/147 d4.13

YEAR	TM LG	W	L	PCT	G	GS	CG-SHO	SV-BS	IP	H	R	HR	HB	BB-IB	SO	ERA	AERA	OAV	OOB	AB-HR-SH	AVG	PB	SUP	APR	DL	PW
1921	Cle A	1	0	1.000	10	0	0	0	17.1	16	5	0	1	6	4	1.56	274	.262	.338	3	.000	-1		5		0.2
1922	Cle A	0	0	—	1	0	0	0	1.1	6	6	0	0	2	2	40.50	10	.600	.667	0	—	0		-5		-0.2
Total 2		1	0	1.000	11	0	0	0	18.2	22	11	0	1	8	6	4.34	98	.310	.387	3	.000	-1		0		0.0

ODOM, DAVE David Everett "Blimp","Porky" B6.5.1918 Dinuba CA D11.19.1987 Myrtle Beach SC BR/TR/6-1/220 d5.31

YEAR	TM LG	W	L	PCT	G	GS	CG-SHO	SV-BS	IP	H	R	HR	HB	BB-IB	SO	ERA	AERA	OAV	OOB	AB-HR-SH	AVG	PB	SUP	APR	DL	PW
1943	Bos N	0	3	.000	22	3	1	2	54.2	54	32	3	4	30	17	5.27	65	.269	.374	12	.000	-2	58	-8		-0.8

ODOM, BLUE MOON Johnny Lee B5.29.1945 Macon GA BR/TR/6-0/185* d9.5

YEAR	TM LG	W	L	PCT	G	GS	CG-SHO	SV-BS	IP	H	R	HR	HB	BB-IB	SO	ERA	AERA	OAV	OOB	AB-HR-SH	AVG	PB	SUP	APR	DL	PW
1964	KC A	1	2	.333	5	5	1-1	0	17	29	21	5	0	11-0	10	10.06	38	.363	.440	5	.000	-0	135	-11		-1.6
1965	KC A	0	0	—	1	0	0	0	1	2	1	0	0	2-0	0	9.00	39	.400	.571	0	—	0		-1		-0.1
1966	KC A	5	5	.500	14	14	4-2	0	90.1	70	31	1	2	53-2	47	2.49	136	.215	.326	31-0-1	.097	-1*	87	8		0.9
1967	KC A	3	8	.273	29	17	0	0	103.2	94	67	9	3	68-7	67	5.04	63	.243	.359	28	.286	2*	109	-22		-2.0
1968	Oak A★	16	10	.615	32	31	9-4	0	231.1	179	74	9	7	98-9	143	2.45	115	.216	.302	78-1-4	.218	6*	121	9		1.9
1969	Oak A★	15	6	.714	32	32	10-3	0-0	231.1	179	87	15	6	112-5	150	2.92	118	.215	.310	79-5-8	.266	11*	133	12		2.3
1970	Oak A	9	8	.529	29	29	4-1	0-0	156.1	128	77	14	8	100-1	88	3.80	93	.227	.348	54-3-3	.241	6*	98	-6	45	0.1
1971	Oak A	10	12	.455	25	25	3-1	0-0	140.2	147	78	13	0	71-7	69	4.29	78	.271	.352	50-1-1	.160	6*	93	-17	33	-2.3
1972	†Oak A	15	6	.714	31	30	4-2	0-0	194.1	164	62	10	3	87-2	86	2.50	114	.234	.319	66-2-5	.121	0*	125	9		0.9
1973	†Oak A	5	12	.294	30	24	3	0-0	150.1	153	86	14	2	67-3	83	4.49	79	.263	.339	1.	.000	-0*	101	-16		-1.7
1974	†Oak A	1	5	.167	34	5	1	1-2	87.1	85	39	4	3	52-3	52	3.81	88	.267	.373	0	—	0*	47	-3		-0.2
1975	Oak A	2	0	2.000	7	2	0	0	11	19	15	1	0	11-1	10	12.27	30	.422	.534	0	—	0*	145	-10		-1.5
	Cle A	1	0	1.000	3	1	1-1	0-1	10.1	4	3	1	0	8-0	10	2.61	146	.118	.286	0	—	0	92	2		0.1
	Year	1	2	.333	10	3	1-1	0-1	21.1	23	18	2	1	19-1	14	7.59	49	.291	.430	0	—	0	126	-8		-1.4
	Atl N	1	7	.125	15	10	0	0-0	56	78	46	5	0	28-0	18	7.07	54	.342	.411	13-0-1	.077	-1	81	-17		-2.2
1976	Chi A	2	2	.500	8	4	0	0	28	31	21	2	1	20-0	18	5.79	62	.282	.394	0	—	-1	129	-7	21	-1.0
Total 16		84	85	.497	295	229	40-15	1-3	1509	1362	708	103	36	788-40	857	3.70	89	.244	.339	405-12-21	.195	26	109	-71	99	-6.3

O'DONNELL, GEORGE George Dana B5.27.1929 Winchester IL BR/TR/6-3/175 d4.18

YEAR	TM LG	W	L	PCT	G	GS	CG-SHO	SV-BS	IP	H	R	HR	HB	BB-IB	SO	ERA	AERA	OAV	OOB	AB-HR-SH	AVG	PB	SUP	APR	DL	PW
1954	Pit N	3	9	.250	21	10	3	1	87.1	105	50	4	2	21	8	4.53	92	.315	.348	23-1-0	.087	-1	45	-3		-0.4

O'DONOGHUE, JOHN John Eugene B10.7.1939 Kansas City MO BR/TL/6-3/210(197-210) d9.29 s-John Col Missouri

YEAR	TM LG	W	L	PCT	G	GS	CG-SHO	SV-BS	IP	H	R	HR	HB	BB-IB	SO	ERA	AERA	OAV	OOB	AB-HR-SH	AVG	PB	SUP	APR	DL	PW
1963	KC A	0	1	.000	1	1	0	0	6	6	2	0	0	2-0	1	1.50	260	.286	.348	2	.000	-0	23	1		0.1
1964	KC A	10	14	.417	39	32	2-1	0	173.2	202	104	24	3	65-4	79	4.92	78	.286	.347	55-1-7	.236	-0	90	-20		-2.4
1965	KC A☆	9	18	.333	34	30	4-1	0	177.2	183	92	15	1	66-8	83	3.95	88	.267	.331	55-1-6	.218	3*	76	-11		-1.3
1966	Cle A	6	8	.429	32	13	2	0	108	109	50	13	2	23-2	49	3.83	90	.264	.303	33	.152	-0	108	-4		-0.5
1967	Cle A	8	9	.471	33	17	5-2	2	130.2	120	52	10	2	33-3	81	3.24	101	.247	.296	40-1-1	.100	-0	89	1		0.4
1968	Bal A	0	0	—	16	0	0	2	22	34	15	2	0	7-3	11	6.14	48	.374	.414	2	.000	-0		-7		-0.4
1969	Sea A	2	2	.500	55	0	0	6-2	70	58	28	5	3	37-4	48	2.96	123	.230	.331	13-0-3	.077	-1		4		0.3
1970	Mil A	2	0	1.000	25	0	0	0-3	23.1	29	15	4	0	9-1	15	5.01	75	.299	.358	2	.000	-0		-3		-0.3
	Mon N	2	3	.400	9	3	0	0-1	22.1	20	14	2	2	11-1	6	5.24	79	.263	.359	4	.000	0	86	-2		-0.5
1971	Mon N	0	0	—	13	0	0	0-0	17.1	19	10	3	0	7-1	7	4.67	76	.271	.333	0	—	0		-2		-0.1
Total 9		39	55	.415	257	96	13-4	10-6	751	780	382	78	13	260-27	377	4.07	87	.269	.330	206-3-17	.170	2	88	-43		-4.7

O'DONOGHUE, JOHN John Preston B5.26.1969 Wilmington DE BL/TL/6-6/198 d6.27 f-John Col Louisiana St.

YEAR	TM LG	W	L	PCT	G	GS	CG-SHO	SV-BS	IP	H	R	HR	HB	BB-IB	SO	ERA	AERA	OAV	OOB	AB-HR-SH	AVG	PB	SUP	APR	DL	PW
1993	Bal A	0	1	.000	11	0	0	0	19.2	22	12	1	1	16	16	4.58	99	.278	.367	0	—	0	102	-1		-0.1

O'DOUL, LEFTY Francis Joseph B3.4.1897 San Francisco CA D12.7.1969 San Francisco CA BL/TL/6-0/180 d4.29 ▲

YEAR	TM LG	W	L	PCT	G	GS	CG-SHO	SV-BS	IP	H	R	HR	HB	BB-IB	SO	ERA	AERA	OAV	OOB	AB-HR-SH	AVG	PB	SUP	APR	DL	PW
1919	NY A	0	0	—	3	0	1	0	5	7	6	0	0	4	2	3.60	98	.304	.407	16	.250	0*		-2		-0.1
1920	NY A	0	0	—	2	0	0	0	3.2	4	2	0	1	2	2	4.91	78	.286	.412	12	.167	-0*		0		0.0
1922	NY A	0	0	—	6	0	0	0	16	24	13	0	0	12	5	3.38	119	.353	.450	9	.333	1*		-1		0.0
1923	Bos A	1	1	.500	23	1	0	0	53	69	50	2	4	31	10	5.43	76	.337	.433	35-0-2	.143	-1*	121	-11		-0.7
Total 4		1	1	.500	34	1	0	0	77.2	104	71	2	5	49	19	4.87	83	.335	.434	72-0-2	.194	-1	121	-14		-0.8

OELKERS, BRYAN Bryan Alois B3.11.1961 Zaragoza, Spain BL/TL/6-3/192* [MinA82 1/4] d4.9 Col Wichita St.

YEAR	TM LG	W	L	PCT	G	GS	CG-SHO	SV-BS	IP	H	R	HR	HB	BB-IB	SO	ERA	AERA	OAV	OOB	AB-HR-SH	AVG	PB	SUP	APR	DL	PW
1983	Min A	0	5	.000	10	8	0	0-0	34.1	56	34	7	0	17-0	13	8.65	50	.376	.437	0	—	0	87	-15		-1.8
1986	Cle A	3	3	.500	35	4	0	1-1	69	70	38	13	6	40-2	33	4.70	89	.262	.368	0	—	0	103	-3		-0.3
Total 2		3	8	.273	45	12	0	1-1	103.1	126	72	20	6	57-2	46	6.01	70	.303	.392	0	—	0	93	-18		-2.1

OESCHGER, JOE Joseph Carl B5.24.1892 Chicago IL D7.28.1986 Rohnert Park CA BR/TR/6-0/190 d4.21 Col St. Marys (CA)

YEAR	TM LG	W	L	PCT	G	GS	CG-SHO	SV-BS	IP	H	R	HR	HB	BB-IB	SO	ERA	AERA	OAV	OOB	AB-HR-SH	AVG	PB	SUP	APR	DL	PW
1914	Phi N	4	8	.333	32	12	5	1	124	129	74	6	10	54	47	3.77	78	.279	.366	40-0-1	.075	-4	102	-10		-1.4
1915	Phi N	1	0	1.000	6	1	1	0	23.2	21	13	1	0	9	9	3.42	80	.247	.319	7	.000	-1	81	-2		-0.2
1916	Phi N	1	0	1.000	14	0	0	0	30.1	18	8	2	1	14	17	2.37	112	.184	.292	5-0-1	.000	-1		2		0.1
1917	Phi N	15	14	.517	42	30	18-5	1	262	241	108	7	6	72	123	2.75	102	.249	.305	88-0-2	.114	-4*	95	1		-0.6
1918	Phi N	6	18	.250	30	23	13-2	3	184	159	87	3	7	83	60	3.03	99	.238	.328	60-0-1	.083	-4	78	-4		-1.0
1919	Phi N	0	1	.000	5	4	2	0	38	52	29	1	2	16	5	5.92	54	.340	.409	15	.000	-2	179	-10		-0.7
	NY N	0	0	—	5	1	0	0	8	12	4	0	0	2	3	4.50	62	.400	.438	1	.000	-0	57	-1		-0.2
	Bos N	4	4	.667	7	7	4-1	0	56.2	63	19	0	1	21	16	2.54	112	.300	.366	22	.091	-1	88	2		0.0
	Year	4	4	.500	17	12	6-1	0	102.2	127	52	1	3	39	24	3.94	76	.323	.389	38	.053	-4	118	-9		-0.9
1920	Bos N	15	13	.536	38	30	20-5	0	299	294	124	10	8	99	80	3.46	88	.265	.329	101-0-5	.178	-3	86	-7		-1.0
1921	Bos N	20	14	.588	46	36	19-3	0	299	303	148	11	15	97	68	3.52	104	.274	.341	110-0-2	.255	2	93	8		1.1
1922	Bos N	6	21	.222	46	23	10-1	1	195.2	234	137	8	9	81	51	5.06	79	.303	.375	63-0-1	.190	-0	73	-23		-2.6
1923	Bos N	5	15	.250	44	19	6-1	2	166.1	227	117	4	5	54	33	5.68	70	.330	.383	52-0-2	.231	-0	78	-27		-2.8
1924	NY N	2	0	1.000	10	2	0	0	29	35	17	1	0	14	6	3.10	118	.287	.360	7	.429	-1	208	-1		0.0
	Phi N	2	7	.222	19	8	0	0	65.1	88	44	6	3	16	8	4.41	101	.333	.378	20	.250	-1	62	-2		-0.3
	Year	4	7	.364	29	10	0	0	94.1	123	61	7	3	30	14	4.01	105	.319	.372	27	.296	-1	89	-3		-0.3
1925	Bro N	1	2	.333	21	3	1	0	37	60	38	2	1	19	6	6.08	69	.382	.452	8-0-1	.125	-0	101	-11		-0.5
Total 12		82	116	.414	365	199	99-18	8	1818	1936	947	61	67	651	535	3.81	88	.281	.349	599-0-16	.165	-18	88	-85		-10.4

OGDEN, JACK John Mahlon B11.5.1897 Ogden PA D11.9.1977 Philadelphia PA BR/TR/6-0/190 d6.22 b-Curly Col Swarthmore

YEAR	TM LG	W	L	PCT	G	GS	CG-SHO	SV-BS	IP	H	R	HR	HB	BB-IB	SO	ERA	AERA	OAV	OOB	AB-HR-SH	AVG	PB	SUP	APR	DL	PW
1918	NY N	0	0	—	5	0	0	0	8.2	8	4	0	2	3	1	3.12	84	.296	.406	1	—	0		-1		-0.1
1928	StL A	15	16	.484	38	31	18-1	2	242.2	257	121	23	1	80	67	4.15	101	.274	.331	85-0-2	.200	-1	93	5		0.3
1929	StL A	4	8	.333	34	14	7	0	131.1	154	83	8	0	44	32	4.93	90	.301	.357	45-0-2	.244	0	95	-7		-0.5
1931	Cin N	4	8	.333	22	9	3-1	1	89	79	42	3	0	32	24	2.93	127	.242	.310	27-0-1	.148	-1	61	5		0.4
1932	Cin N	2	2	.500	24	3	1	0	57	72	40	5	0	22	20	5.21	74	.310	.370	12	.167	0*	58	-9		-0.5
Total 5		25	34	.424	123	57	29-2	3	528.2	570	290	39	3	181	144	4.24	97	.280	.340	170-0-5	.200	-1	88	-7		-0.4

OGDEN, CURLY Warren Harvey B1.24.1901 Ogden PA D8.6.1964 Upland PA BR/TR/6-1.5/180 d7.18 b-Jack Col Swarthmore

YEAR	TM LG	W	L	PCT	G	GS	CG-SHO	SV-BS	IP	H	R	HR	HB	BB-IB	SO	ERA	AERA	OAV	OOB	AB-HR-SH	AVG	PB	SUP	APR	DL	PW
1922	Phi A	1	4	.200	15	6	1	0	72.1	59	29	4	5	26	21	3.11	124	.238	.338	29	.241	-0*	50	5		0.5
1923	Phi A	1	2	.333	18	2	1	0	46.1	63	39	2	4	26	14	5.63	73	.330	.434	17	.294	1*	50	-9		-0.4

YEAR	TM LG	W	L	PCT	G	GS	CG-SHO	SV-BS	IP	H	R	HR	HB	BB-IB	SO	ERA	AERA	OAV	OOB	AB-HR-SH	AVG	PB	SUP	APR	DL	PW
1924	Phi A	0	3	.000	5	1	0	0	12.2	14	9	1	1	7	4	4.97	86	.275	.373	3	.000	-1	118	-1		-0.3
	†Was A	9	5	.643	16	16	9-3	0	108	83	36	3	2	51	23	2.58	156	.221	.317	47-0-1	.277	2*	114	19		2.4
	Year	9	8	.529	21	17	9-3	0	120.2	97	45	4	3	58	27	2.83	143	.227	.324	50-0-1	.260	1	114	17		2.1
1925	Was A	3	1	.750	17	4	2-1	0	42	45	24	1	2	18	6	4.50	94	.288	.369	12	.250	-0	124	-1		-0.1
1926	Was A	4	4	.500	22	9	4	0	96.1	114	55	2	5	45	21	4.30	90	.305	.387	27-0-1	.185	-1	123	-5		-0.5
Total 5		18	19	.486	93	38	19-4	0	377.2	378	192	13	18	186	88	3.79	108	.271	.364	135-0-2	.244	1	103	12		1.6

OGEA, CHAD Chad Wayne B11.9.1970 Lake Charles LA BR/TR/6-2/200(200-220) [CleA91 3/86] d5.3 Col Louisiana St.

YEAR	TM LG	W	L	PCT	G	GS	CG-SHO	SV-BS	IP	H	R	HR	HB	BB-IB	SO	ERA	AERA	OAV	OOB	AB-HR-SH	AVG	PB	SUP	APR	DL	PW
1994	Cle A	0	1	.000	4	1	0	0-0	16.1	21	11	2	1	10-2	11	6.06	78	.304	.400	0	—	0	19	-2		-0.1
1995	†Cle A	8	3	.727	20	14	1	0-0	106.1	95	38	11	1	29-0	57	3.05	155	.233	.283	0	—	0	114	20		1.8
1996	†Cle A	10	6	.625	29	21	1-1	0-0	146.2	151	82	22	5	42-3	101	4.79	102	.266	.321	0	—	0	106	3	30	0.2
1997	†Cle A	8	9	.471	21	21	1	0-0	126.1	139	79	13	5	47-4	80	4.99	94	.283	.346	2-0-2	.000	-0	106	-5	69	-0.6
1998	†Cle A	4	4	.556	19	9	0	0-1	69	74	44	9	7	25-1	43	5.61	83	.273	.346	0	—	0	104	-5	108	-0.6
1999	Phi N	6	12	.333	36	28	0	0-0	168	192	110	36	4	61-1	77	5.63	83	.288	.349	44-0-7	.091	-2	93	-16		-1.7
Total 6		37	35	.514	129	94	3-1	0-1	632.2	672	364	93	23	214-11	369	4.88	97	.272	.333	46-0-9	.087	-2	102	-5	207	-1.0

OGRODOWSKI, JOE Joseph Anthony B11.20.1906 Hoytville PA D6.24.1959 Elmira NY BR/TR/5-11/165 d4.27

YEAR	TM LG	W	L	PCT	G	GS	CG-SHO	SV-BS	IP	H	R	HR	HB	BB-IB	SO	ERA	AERA	OAV	OOB	AB-HR-SH	AVG	PB	SUP	APR	DL	PW
1925	Bos N	0	0	—	1	0	0	0	1	6	8	0	0	3	0	54.00	7	.600	.692	0	—	0		-6		-0.3

OHKA, TOMO Tomokazu B3.18.1976 Kyoto, Japan BR/TR/6-1/180(179-200) d7.19

YEAR	TM LG	W	L	PCT	G	GS	CG-SHO	SV-BS	IP	H	R	HR	HB	BB-IB	SO	ERA	AERA	OAV	OOB	AB-HR-SH	AVG	PB	SUP	APR	DL	PW
1999	Bos A	1	2	.333	8	2	0	0-0	13	21	12	2	0	6-0	8	6.23	80	.362	.415	0	—	0	112	-3		-0.5
2000	Bos A	3	6	.333	13	12	0	0-0	69.1	70	25	7	2	26-0	40	3.12	161	.263	.331	0	—	0	50	15		1.7
2001	Bos A	2	5	.286	12	11	0	0-0	52.1	69	40	7	2	19-0	37	6.19	72	.317	.375	3	.000	-0	93	-10		-1.2
	Mon N	1	4	.200	10	10	0	0-0	54.2	65	30	8	1	10-0	31	4.77	90	.302	.335	15-0-3	.200	-0	83	-2		-0.2
2002	Mon N	13	8	.619	32	31	2	0-0	192.2	194	83	19	7	45-7	118	3.18	138	.264	.310	55-0-8	.127	-1	97	21		2.1
2003	Mon N	10	12	.455	34	34	2	0-0	199	233	106	24	9	45-11	118	4.16	107	.292	.335	55-0-8	.182	0*	95	4		0.5
2004	Mon N	3	7	.300	15	15	0	0-0	84.2	98	40	11	1	20-1	38	3.40	135	.288	.328	25	.080	1*	135	9	95	0.8
2005	Was N	4	3	.571	10	9	0	0-0	54	44	23	6	1	27-1	17	3.33	121	.224	.320	16-0-1	.250	1*	135	9		0.8
	Mil N	7	6	.538	22	20	1-1	0-0	126.1	145	65	16	2	28-4	81	4.35	99	.285	.323	38-0-2	.053	-3	120	3		-0.3
	Year	11	9	.550	32	29	1-1	0-0	180.1	189	88	22	3	55-5	98	4.04	104	.268	.322	54-0-3	.111	-2	125	3		0.2
Total 7		44	53	.454	156	144	5-1	0-0	846	939	424	100	25	226-24	488	3.95	113	.281	.330	207-0-22	.135	-4	92	38	95	3.4

OHL, JOE Joseph Earl (b Joseph Earl Von Ohl) B1.10.1888 Jobstown NJ D12.18.1951 Camden NJ BL/TL/6-1/175 d7.29

YEAR	TM LG	W	L	PCT	G	GS	CG-SHO	SV-BS	IP	H	R	HR	HB	BB-IB	SO	ERA	AERA	OAV	OOB	AB-HR-SH	AVG	PB	SUP	APR	DL	PW
1909	Was A	0	0	—	4	0	0	0	8.2	7	4	1	0	6	2	2.08	117	.194	.237	2	.000	-0		0		0.0

OHMAN, WILL William McDaniel B8.13.1977 Frankfurt, West Germany BL/TL/6-2/195* [ChiN98 8/226] d9.19 Col Pepperdine [DL 2002 Chi N 183, 2003 Chi N 183]

YEAR	TM LG	W	L	PCT	G	GS	CG-SHO	SV-BS	IP	H	R	HR	HB	BB-IB	SO	ERA	AERA	OAV	OOB	AB-HR-SH	AVG	PB	SUP	APR	DL	PW
2000	Chi N	1	0	1.000	6	0	0	0-0	3.1	4	3	0	0	4-1	2	8.10	57	.308	.471	0	—	0		-1		-0.2
2001	Chi N	0	1	.000	11	0	0	0-0	11.2	14	10	2	0	6-0	12	7.71	54	.292	.370	0	.000	-0		-4		-0.4
2005	Chi N	2	2	.500	69	0	0	0-3	43.1	32	14	6	3	24-3	45	2.91	151	.201	.317	0	—	0		7		0.6
Total 3		3	3	.500	86	0	0	0-3	58.1	50	27	8	3	34-4	59	4.17	105	.227	.339	0	.000	0		2	366	0.0

OHME, KEVIN Kevin Arthur B4.13.1971 Palm Beach FL BL/TL/6-1/180 [MinA93 9/261] d4.14 Col North Florida

YEAR	TM LG	W	L	PCT	G	GS	CG-SHO	SV-BS	IP	H	R	HR	HB	BB-IB	SO	ERA	AERA	OAV	OOB	AB-HR-SH	AVG	PB	SUP	APR	DL	PW
2003	StL N	0	0	—	4	0	0	0-0	4.1	3	0	0	0	1-1	2	0.00	—	.200	.235	1	1.000	0		2		0.2

OJALA, KIRT Kirt Stanley B12.24.1968 Kalamazoo MI BL/TL/6-2/210(200-215) [NYA90 4/111] d8.18 Col Michigan

YEAR	TM LG	W	L	PCT	G	GS	CG-SHO	SV-BS	IP	H	R	HR	HB	BB-IB	SO	ERA	AERA	OAV	OOB	AB-HR-SH	AVG	PB	SUP	APR	DL	PW
1997	Fla N	1	2	.333	7	5	0	0-0	28.2	28	10	4	0	18-0	19	3.14	129	.252	.354	7-0-1	.000	-1	100	3		0.3
1998	Fla N	2	7	.222	41	13	1	0-0	125	128	71	14	4	59-4	75	4.25	96	.267	.351	26-0-2	.154	1	77	-6		-0.2
1999	Fla N	0	1	.000	8	1	0	0-0	10.2	21	17	1	0	6-0	5	14.34	31	.438	.482	0	—	0	42	-12		-0.9
Total 3		3	10	.231	56	19	1	0-0	164.1	177	98	19	4	83-4	99	4.71	87	.277	.362	33-0-3	.121	0	81	-15		-0.8

OJEDA, BOB Robert Michael B12.17.1957 Los Angeles CA BL/TL/6-1/190* d7.13 Col Sequoias (CA) [JC]

YEAR	TM LG	W	L	PCT	G	GS	CG-SHO	SV-BS	IP	H	R	HR	HB	BB-IB	SO	ERA	AERA	OAV	OOB	AB-HR-SH	AVG	PB	SUP	APR	DL	PW
1980	Bos A	1	1	.500	7	1	0	0-0	26	39	20	2	0	14-1	12	6.92	62	.361	.434	0	—	0	105	-6		-0.4
1981	Bos A	6	2	.750	10	10	2	0-0	66.1	50	25	6	2	25-2	28	3.12	126	.212	.292	0	—	0	119	6		0.7
1982	Bos A	4	6	.400	22	14	0	0-0	78.1	95	53	13	1	29-0	52	5.63	77	.296	.355	0	—	0	97	-10	21	-1.2
1983	Bos A	12	7	.632	29	28	5	0-0	173.2	173	85	15	3	73-2	94	4.04	109	.265	.336	0	—	0	100	6	16	0.7
1984	Bos A	12	12	.500	33	32	8-5	0-0	216.2	211	106	17	2	96-2	137	3.99	105	.259	.336	0	—	0	80	6		0.3
1985	Bos A	9	11	.450	39	22	5	1-0	157.2	166	74	11	2	48-9	102	4.00	108	.273	.327	0	—	0	120	25		2.3
1986	†NY N	18	5	.783	32	30	7-2	0-0	217.1	185	72	15	2	52-3	148	2.57	140	.230	.278	71-0-8	.113	-2	120	25		2.3
1987	NY N	3	5	.375	10	7	0	0-0	46.1	45	24	9	1	10-1	21	3.88	99	.253	.291	14	.071	-0	118	-1	113	-0.2
1988	NY N	10	13	.435	29	29	5-5	0-0	190.1	158	74	6	4	33-2	133	2.88	113	.225	.261	61-0-4	.164	1*	81	7		1.0
1989	NY N	13	11	.542	31	31	5-2	0-0	192	179	83	16	2	78-5	95	3.47	95	.245	.317	66-0-6	.106	-2*	112	-4		-0.6
1990	NY N	7	6	.538	38	12	0	0-2	118	123	53	10	2	40-4	62	3.66	103	.272	.332	30-0-1	.133	-0	108	2		0.3
1991	LA N	12	9	.571	31	31	2-1	0-0	189.1	181	78	15	3	70-9	120	3.18	113	.257	.323	56-1-6	.161	-1	95	8		1.1
1992	LA N	6	9	.400	29	29	2-1	0-0	166.1	169	80	7	1	81-8	94	3.63	96	.268	.349	49-0-5	.102	-1	97	-4		-0.4
1993	Cle A	2	1	.667	9	7	0	0-0	43	48	22	5	0	21-0	27	4.40	100	.289	.363	0	—	0	105	0	124	-0.3
1994	NY A	0	0	—	2	2	0	0-0	3	11	8	1	0	6-0	3	24.00	19	.611	.680	0	—	0	120	-6		-0.3
Total 15		115	98	.540	351	291	41-16	1-2	1884.1	1833	856	145	24	676-48	1128	3.65	104	.257	.321	347-1-30	.127	-4	101	36	274	4.7

OKRIE, FRANK Frank Anthony "Lefty" B10.28.1896 Detroit MI D10.16.1959 Detroit MI BL/TL/5-11/175 d4.20 s-Len

YEAR	TM LG	W	L	PCT	G	GS	CG-SHO	SV-BS	IP	H	R	HR	HB	BB-IB	SO	ERA	AERA	OAV	OOB	AB-HR-SH	AVG	PB	SUP	APR	DL	PW
1920	Det A	1	2	.333	21	1	1	0-0	41	44	29	2	5	18	9	5.27	71	.295	.390	5-0-1	.200	-0	107	-6		-0.1

OLDHAM, RED John Cyrus B7.15.1893 Zion MD D1.28.1961 Costa Mesa CA BB/TL(BL 1922, 25-26)/6-0/176 d8.19

YEAR	TM LG	W	L	PCT	G	GS	CG-SHO	SV-BS	IP	H	R	HR	HB	BB-IB	SO	ERA	AERA	OAV	OOB	AB-HR-SH	AVG	PB	SUP	APR	DL	PW
1914	Det A	2	4	.333	9	7	3	0	45.1	42	22	1	3	8	23	3.38	83	.243	.288	15-0-1	.267	1	78	-2		-0.2
1915	Det A	3	0	1.000	17	2	1	4	57.2	52	22	1	4	17	17	2.81	108	.243	.311	14	.143	-0	84	2		0.1
1920	Det A	8	13	.381	39	22	10-1	1	215.1	248	132	5	6	91	62	3.85	97	.302	.376	69-0-4	.174	-1	93	-6		-0.5
1921	Det A	11	14	.440	40	28	12-1	1	229.1	258	129	11	6	81	67	4.24	101	.288	.351	85-2-2	.224	2*	117	3		0.6
1922	Det A	10	13	.435	43	28	9	3	212	256	130	14	11	59	72	4.67	83	.305	.358	73-0-1	.260	4	123	-19		-1.3
1925	†Pit N	3	2	.600	11	4	3	1	53	66	27	2	2	18	10	3.91	114	.313	.372	18	.333	2	80	4		-0.5
1926	Pit N	2	2	.500	17	2	0	2	41.2	56	27	1	1	18	16	5.62	70	.359	.429	9-0-1	.222	0	85	-6		-0.5
Total 7		39	48	.448	176	93	38-2	12	854.1	978	489	35	33	292	267	4.15	93	.305	.368	283-2-9	.226	9	108	-24		-1.3

OLIN, STEVE Steven Robert B10.4.1965 Portland OR D3.22.1993 Little Lake Nellie FL BR/TR/6-3/185* [CleA87 16/411] d7.29 Col Portland St.

YEAR	TM LG	W	L	PCT	G	GS	CG-SHO	SV-BS	IP	H	R	HR	HB	BB-IB	SO	ERA	AERA	OAV	OOB	AB-HR-SH	AVG	PB	SUP	APR	DL	PW
1989	Cle A	1	4	.200	25	0	0	1-0	36	35	16	1	0	14-2	24	3.75	106	.255	.325	0	—	0		1		0.2
1990	Cle A	4	4	.500	50	1	0	1-2	92.1	96	41	3	6	26-2	64	3.41	116	.270	.329	0	—	0	92	4		0.4
1991	Cle A	3	6	.333	48	0	0	17-5	56.1	61	26	2	1	23-7	38	3.36	124	.274	.344	0	—	0		4		0.8
1992	Cle A	8	5	.615	72	0	0	29-7	88.1	80	25	8	4	27-6	47	2.34	168	.248	.313	0	—	0		16		3.2
Total 4		16	19	.457	195	1	0	48-14	273	272	108	14	11	90-17	173	3.10	129	.262	.327	0	—	0	92	25		4.6

OLIVARES, OMAR Omar (Palqu) B7.6.1967 Mayaguez, PR BR/TR/6-1/193(185-210) d8.18 f-Ed Col Miami-Dade Wolfson (FL) CC

YEAR	TM LG	W	L	PCT	G	GS	CG-SHO	SV-BS	IP	H	R	HR	HB	BB-IB	SO	ERA	AERA	OAV	OOB	AB-HR-SH	AVG	PB	SUP	APR	DL	PW
1990	StL N	1	1	.500	9	6	0	0-0	49.1	46	17	2	2	17-0	20	2.92	132	.249	.320	17-1-0	.176	1	82	5		0.4
1991	StL N	11	7	.611	28	24	0	1-0	167.1	148	72	13	5	61-1	91	3.71	101	.243	.316	53-0-4	.226	3	101	3		0.7
1992	StL N	9	9	.500	32	30	1	0-0	197	189	84	20	4	63-5	124	3.84	89	.257	.316	68-1-3	.235	4*	101	-6	17	0.0
1993	StL N	5	3	.625	58	9	0	1-4	118.2	134	60	10	9	54-7	63	4.17	97	.288	.370	26-0-3	.269	2*	112	-1	16	-1.0
1994	StL N	3	4	.429	14	12	1	0-0	73.2	84	53	10	4	37-0	26	5.74	74	.294	.379	28-1-2	.214	2*	120	-14		-1.0
1995	Col N	1	1	.250	11	6	0	0-0	31.2	44	28	4	2	21-0	15	7.39	73	.349	.447	11-0-1	.143	0*	79	-5		-0.6
	Phi N	0	1	1.000	11	0	0	0-0	10	11	6	1	1	2-0	7	5.40	78	.282	.326	2-1-0	.500	1		-1		0.0
	Year	1	4	.200	16	6	0	0-0	41.2	55	34	5	3	23-0	22	6.91	74	.333	.420	9-1-1	.222	1	83	-6	44	-0.6
1996	Det A	7	11	.389	25	25	4	0-0	160	169	90	16	9	75-4	81	4.89	104	.275	.359	0	—	0	88	6	44	0.0
1997	Det A	5	6	.455	19	19	3-2	0-0	115	110	64	9	9	53-1	74	4.70	98	.253	.344	3	.667	1*	107	-3		0.0
	Sea A	1	4	.200	13	12	0	0-0	62.1	81	45	10	4	28-3	29	5.49	83	.315	.387	2	.500	0	100	-7		-0.4
	Year	6	10	.375	32	31	3-2	0-0	177.1	191	109	18	13	81-4	103	4.97	92	.276	.360	5	.600	1	104	-9		-0.4
1998	Ana A	8	9	.500	37	26	1	0-0	183	189	92	19	5	91-1	112	4.03	118	.270	.357	2	.000	0*	91	13		1.3
1999	Ana A	8	9	.471	20	20	3	0-0	131	135	62	11	6	49-0	49	4.05	121	.273	.342	6-0-1	.333	1	73	13		0.2
	Oak A	7	2	.778	12	12	1	0-0	74.2	82	43	8	3	32-0	36	4.34	109	.283	.358	0	—	0	123	2		1.8
	Year	15	11	.577	32	32	4	0-0	205.2	217	105	19	9	81-0	85	4.16	116	.276	.348	6-0-1	.333	1	92	15	55	1.8
2000	Oak A	4	8	.333	21	16	1	0-0	108	134	64	7	6	46-0	57	6.75	72	.309	.396	0	1.000	0	99	-21	55	0.2

YEAR	TM LG	W	L	PCT	G	GS	CG-SHO	SV-BS	IP	H	R	HR	HB	BB-IB	SO	ERA	AERA	OAV	OOB	AB-HR-SH	AVG	PB	SUP	APR	DL	PW
2001	Pit N	6	9	.400	45	12	1	1-1	110	123	87	17	10	42-8	69	6.55	68	.283	.356	27-1-0	.222	2*	108	-25		-2.7
Total	12	77	86	.472	349	229	16-2	4-5	1591.2	1678	889	159	80	685-30	853	4.67	94	.275	.353	242-5-14	.240	18	98	-41	132	-1.5

OLIVER, DARREN   Darren Christopher   B10.6.1970 Rio Linda CA   BR/TL/6-2/210(170-220)   [TexA88 3/63]   d9.1 f-Bob

YEAR	TM LG	W	L	PCT	G	GS	CG-SHO	SV-BS	IP	H	R	HR	HB	BB-IB	SO	ERA	AERA	OAV	OOB	AB-HR-SH	AVG	PB	SUP	APR	DL	PW
1993	Tex A	0	0	—	2	0	0	0-0	3.1	1	1	0	1	1-1	4	2.70	155	.154	.214	0	—	0		1		0.0
1994	Tex A	4	0	1.000	43	0	0	2-1	50	40	24	4	6	35-4	50	3.42	142	.223	.368	0	—	0		7		0.6
1995	Tex A	4	2	.667	17	7	0	0-0	49	47	25	3	1	32-1	39	4.22	115	.257	.369	0	—	0	88	3	97	0.4
1996	†Tex A	14	6	.700	30	30	1-1	0-0	173.2	190	97	20	10	76-3	112	4.66	113	.279	.356	0	—	0	104	11		1.0
1997	Tex A	13	12	.520	32	32	3-1	0-0	201.1	213	111	29	11	82-3	104	4.20	116	.271	.346	2	.500	1	105	11		1.1
1998	Tex A	6	7	.462	19	19	2	0-0	103.1	140	84	16	10	43-1	50	6.53	75	.325	.394	6	.167	0	116	-19	15	-1.9
	StL N	4	4	.500	10	10	0	0-0	57	64	31	7	0	23-1	29	4.26	99	.283	.347	23	.087	-1*	90	-1		-0.2
1999	StL N	9	9	.500	30	30	2-1	0-0	196.1	197	96	16	11	74-4	119	4.26	108	.265	.339	73-0-8	.274	5*	96	10		1.4
2000	Tex A	2	9	.182	21	21	0	0-0	108	151	95	16	4	42-3	49	7.42	69	.339	.397	2	.000	0	111	-25	63	-2.0
2001	Tex A	11	11	.500	28	28	1	0-0	154	189	100	19	3	65-0	104	6.02	79	.305	.374	6-0-2	.333	1	115	-20	29	-2.2
2002	Bos A	4	5	.444	14	9	1-1	0-0	58	70	30	7	6	27-0	32	4.66	96	.317	.401	1	.000	-0	85	0		0.1
2003	Col N	13	11	.542	33	32	1	0-0	180.1	201	108	21	8	61-3	88	5.04	97	.284	.345	67-1-2	.254	4*	109	-2		0.1
2004	Fla N	2	3	.400	18	8	0	0-0	58.2	75	44	13	1	17-1	33	6.44	64	.319	.363	19-0-2	.158	-0	127	-16		-1.1
	Hou N	1	0	1.000	9	2	0	0-0	14	12	6	1	0	4-0	15	3.86	113	.240	.296	3-0-1	.000	-0*	138	1	31	0.0
	Year	3	3	.500	27	10	0	0-0	72.2	87	50	14	1	21-1	46	5.94	70	.305	.352	22-0-3	.136	-1	129	-13		-1.1
Total	12	87	79	.524	306	228	11-4	2-1	1407	1591	861	172	74	582-25	834	5.07	95	.288	.361	202-1-15	.228	9	106	-39	235	-2.8

OLIVERAS, FRANCISCO   Francisco Javier (Noa)   B1.31.1963 Santurce, PR   BR/TR/5-10/170*   d5.3

YEAR	TM LG	W	L	PCT	G	GS	CG-SHO	SV-BS	IP	H	R	HR	HB	BB-IB	SO	ERA	AERA	OAV	OOB	AB-HR-SH	AVG	PB	SUP	APR	DL	PW
1989	Min A	3	4	.429	12	8	1	0-0	55.2	64	28	8	1	15-0	24	4.53	92	.288	.335	0	—	0	115	-1		-0.2
1990	SF N	2	2	.500	33	2	0	2-0	55.1	47	22	5	2	21-6	41	2.77	132	.230	.304	5	.000	-1	111	4	24	0.2
1991	SF N	6	6	.500	55	1	0	3-1	79.1	69	36	12	1	22-4	48	3.86	93	.242	.296	10	.200	0	75	-2		-0.3
1992	SF N	0	3	.000	16	7	0	0-0	44.2	41	19	11	1	10-2	17	3.63	92	.250	.294	7	.143	0	58	-1	17	-0.1
Total	4	11	15	.423	116	18	1	5-1	235	221	105	36	5	68-12	130	3.71	99	.253	.307	22	.136	-0	94	0	41	-0.4

OLIVO, DIOMEDES   Diomedes Antonio (Maldonado)   B1.22.1919 Guayubin, D.R.   D2.15.1977 Santo Domingo, D.R.   BL/TL/6-1/195*   d9.5   b-Chi-Chi s-Gilberto

YEAR	TM LG	W	L	PCT	G	GS	CG-SHO	SV-BS	IP	H	R	HR	HB	BB-IB	SO	ERA	AERA	OAV	OOB	AB-HR-SH	AVG	PB	SUP	APR	DL	PW
1960	Pit N	0	0	—	4	0	0	0	9.2	8	3	1	0	5-1	10	2.79	134	.216	.310	1	.000	-0		1		0.0
1962	Pit N	5	1	.833	62	1	0	7	84.1	88	30	5	0	25-7	66	2.77	142	.277	.325	16-0-2	.188	1	89	11		1.0
1963	StL N	0	5	.000	19	0	0	0	13.1	16	9	1	1	9-1	9	5.40	66	.296	.400	0	—	0	89	-2		-0.5
Total	3	5	6	.455	85	1	0	7	107.1	112	42	7	1	39-9	85	3.10	125	.274	.334	17-0-2	.176	0	89	10		0.5

OLIVO, CHI-CHI   Federico Emilio (Maldonado)   B3.18.1928 Guayubin, D.R.   D2.3.1977 Guayubin, D.R.   BR/TR/6-2/215*   d6.5   b-Diomedes

YEAR	TM LG	W	L	PCT	G	GS	CG-SHO	SV-BS	IP	H	R	HR	HB	BB-IB	SO	ERA	AERA	OAV	OOB	AB-HR-SH	AVG	PB	SUP	APR	DL	PW
1961	Mil N	0	0	—	3	0	0	0	2	3	4	1	0	5-1	1	18.00	21	.500	.727	0	—	0		-3		-0.2
1964	Mil N	2	1	.667	38	0	0	5	60	55	25	7	0	21-5	45	3.75	94	.247	.309	4	.250	-0		0		0.0
1965	Mil N	0	1	.000	8	0	0	0	13	12	2	1	0	5-2	11	1.38	254	.267	.327	0	—	0		3		0.2
1966	Atl N	5	4	.556	47	0	0	7	66	59	34	4	1	19-5	41	4.23	86	.240	.293	9	.111	-0		-4		-0.7
Total	4	7	6	.538	96	0	0	12	141	129	65	13	1	50-13	98	3.96	90	.248	.311	13	.154	-0		-4		-0.7

OLLOM, JIM   James Donald   B7.8.1945 Snohomish WA   BR/TL/6-4/210*   d9.3

YEAR	TM LG	W	L	PCT	G	GS	CG-SHO	SV-BS	IP	H	R	HR	HB	BB-IB	SO	ERA	AERA	OAV	OOB	AB-HR-SH	AVG	PB	SUP	APR	DL	PW
1966	Min A	0	0	—	3	1	0	0	10	6	4	1	1	1-0	11	3.60	100	.167	.211	2	.000	-0	123	0		0.0
1967	Min A	0	1	.000	21	2	0	0	35	33	24	4	4	11-1	17	5.40	64	.258	.331	5	.200	0	76	-7		-0.4
Total	2	0	1	.000	24	3	0	0	45	39	28	5	5	12-1	28	5.00	70	.238	.306	7	.143	-0	92	-7		-0.4

OLMSTEAD, FRED   Frederic William   B7.3.1881 Grand Rapids MI   D10.22.1936 Muskogee OK   BR/TR/5-11/170   d7.2

YEAR	TM LG	W	L	PCT	G	GS	CG-SHO	SV-BS	IP	H	R	HR	HB	BB-IB	SO	ERA	AERA	OAV	OOB	AB-HR-SH	AVG	PB	SUP	APR	DL	PW
1908	Chi A	0	0	—	1	0	0	0	2	6	3	0	0	1	1	13.50	17	.600	.636	1	.000	1		-2		-0.1
1909	Chi A	3	2	.600	8	6	5	0	54.2	52	17	1	1	12	21	1.81	129	.277	.323	21	.095	-1	105	3		0.1
1910	Chi A	10	12	.455	32	20	14-4	0	184.1	174	64	4	4	50	68	1.95	123	.260	.316	65-0-2	.154	-2	64	8		0.8
1911	Chi A	6	6	.500	25	11	7-1	2	117.2	146	78	3	6	30	45	4.21	77	.309	.358	37-0-1	.189	-0	124	-15		-1.4
Total	4	19	20	.487	66	37	26-5	2	358.2	378	162	5	11	93	135	2.74	97	.283	.334	124-0-3	.153	-3	90	-6		-0.6

OLMSTED, AL   Alan Ray   B3.18.1957 St.Louis MO   BR/TL/6-2/195   [StLN75 13/304]   d9.12

YEAR	TM LG	W	L	PCT	G	GS	CG-SHO	SV-BS	IP	H	R	HR	HB	BB-IB	SO	ERA	AERA	OAV	OOB	AB-HR-SH	AVG	PB	SUP	APR	DL	PW
1980	StL N	1	1	.500	5	5	0	0-0	34.2	32	14	2	1	14-1	14	2.86	131	.244	.322	11-0-2	.182	-0	100	3		0.2

OLMSTED, HANK   Henry Theodore   B1.12.1879 Sac Bay MI   D1.6.1969 Bradenton FL   BR/TR/5-8.5/147   d7.15   Col Notre Dame

YEAR	TM LG	W	L	PCT	G	GS	CG-SHO	SV-BS	IP	H	R	HR	HB	BB-IB	SO	ERA	AERA	OAV	OOB	AB-HR-SH	AVG	PB	SUP	APR	DL	PW
1905	Bos A	1	2	.333	3	3	3	0	25	18	10	0	0	12	6	3.24	83	.205	.300	8	.125	-0	26	-1		-0.1

OLSEN, OLE   Arthur Ole   B9.12.1894 S.Norwalk CT   D9.12.1980 Norwalk CT   BR/TR/5-10/163   d4.12   Col Cornell

YEAR	TM LG	W	L	PCT	G	GS	CG-SHO	SV-BS	IP	H	R	HR	HB	BB-IB	SO	ERA	AERA	OAV	OOB	AB-HR-SH	AVG	PB	SUP	APR	DL	PW
1922	Det A	7	6	.538	37	15	5	0	137	147	84	8	14	40	52	4.53	86	.281	.348	39-0-3	.179	-1*	112	-11		-1.0
1923	Det A	1	1	.500	17	2	1	0	41.1	42	30	1	5	17	12	6.31	61	.290	.383	8-0-1	.125	-1	193	-10		-0.6
Total	2	8	7	.533	54	17	6	3	178.1	189	114	9	19	57	64	4.95	78	.283	.356	47-0-4	.170	-2	122	-21		-1.6

OLSEN, KEVIN   Kevin Gary   B7.26.1976 Covina CA   BR/TR/6-2/200*   [FlaN98 26/790]   d9.7   Col Oklahoma

YEAR	TM LG	W	L	PCT	G	GS	CG-SHO	SV-BS	IP	H	R	HR	HB	BB-IB	SO	ERA	AERA	OAV	OOB	AB-HR-SH	AVG	PB	SUP	APR	DL	PW
2001	Fla N	0	0	—	4	0	0	0-0	15	11	2	0	0	2-1	13	1.20	347	.204	.232	3-0-1	.000	-0	22	5		0.2
2002	Fla N	0	5	.000	17	8	0	0-0	55.2	57	31	5	4	31-1	38	4.53	87	.270	.363	12	.083	-1	97	-4		-0.4
2003	Fla N	0	0	—	7	0	0	0-0	12	25	18	2	0	4-1	12	12.75	32	.431	.468	0	—	0	-12	-12	72	-0.6
Total	3	0	5	.000	28	10	0	0-0	82.2	93	51	7	4	37-3	63	5.12	78	.288	.361	15-0-1	.067	-1	81	-11	72	-0.8

OLSEN, SCOTT   Scott Matthew   B1.12.1984 Kalamazoo MI   BL/TL/6-4/200   d6.25

YEAR	TM LG	W	L	PCT	G	GS	CG-SHO	SV-BS	IP	H	R	HR	HB	BB-IB	SO	ERA	AERA	OAV	OOB	AB-HR-SH	AVG	PB	SUP	APR	DL	PW
2005	Fla N	1	1	.500	5	4	0	0-0	20.1	21	13	5	0	10-0	21	3.98	100	.259	.341	3-0-1	.000	-0	87	-2		-0.2

OLSEN, VERN   Vern Jarl   B3.16.1918 Hillsboro OR   D7.13.1989 Maywood IL   BR/TL/6-0.5/175   d9.8   Mil 1949-45

YEAR	TM LG	W	L	PCT	G	GS	CG-SHO	SV-BS	IP	H	R	HR	HB	BB-IB	SO	ERA	AERA	OAV	OOB	AB-HR-SH	AVG	PB	SUP	APR	DL	PW
1939	Chi N	1	0	1.000	4	0	0	0	7.2	2	0	0	0	7	3	0.00	—	.087	.300	1	.000	0		3		0.5
1940	Chi N	13	9	.591	34	20	9-4	0	172.2	172	64	5	2	62	71	2.97	126	.260	.325	57-0-3	.263	3*	95	16		2.5
1941	Chi N	10	8	.556	37	23	10-2	1	185.2	202	84	7	1	59	73	3.15	111	.276	.331	63-1-2	.238	3	108	5		0.9
1942	Chi N	6	9	.400	32	17	4-1	1	140.1	161	75	6	1	55	46	4.49	71	.283	.347	48-0-1	.188	1	103	-17		-1.5
1946	Chi N	0	0	—	5	0	0	0	9.2	10	3	0	0	9	8	2.79	119	.294	.442	0	—	0		1		0.0
Total	5	30	26	.536	112	60	23-7	2	516	547	226	18	4	192	201	3.40	103	.271	.335	169-1-6	.231	8	102	8		2.4

OLSON, GREGG   Greggory William   B10.11.1966 Scribner NE   BR/TR/6-4/206*   [BalA88 1/4]   d9.2   Col Auburn-Montgomery

YEAR	TM LG	W	L	PCT	G	GS	CG-SHO	SV-BS	IP	H	R	HR	HB	BB-IB	SO	ERA	AERA	OAV	OOB	AB-HR-SH	AVG	PB	SUP	APR	DL	PW
1988	Bal A	1	1	.500	10	0	0	0-1	11	10	4	1	0	10-1	9	3.27	120	.244	.392	0	—	0		1		0.2
1989	Bal A	5	2	.714	64	0	0	27-6	85	57	17	1	1	46-10	90	1.69	226	.188	.295	0	—	0		20		2.8
1990	Bal A☆	6	5	.545	64	0	0	37-5	74.1	57	20	3	3	31-3	74	2.42	158	.213	.299	0	—	0		13		2.6
1991	Bal A	4	6	.400	72	0	0	31-8	73.2	74	28	1	1	29-5	72	3.18	125	.261	.331	0	—	0		7		1.3
1992	Bal A	1	5	.167	60	0	0	36-8	61.1	46	14	3	0	24-0	58	2.05	198	.211	.287	0	—	0		14		2.7
1993	Bal A	0	2	.000	50	0	0	29-6	45	37	9	1	0	18-3	44	1.60	283	.223	.296	0	.000	0		14		2.1
1994	Atl N	0	2	.000	16	0	0	1-0	14.2	19	15	1	0	13-3	10	9.20	47	.317	.440	1	.000	-0	14	-7	42	-0.9
1995	Cle A	0	0	—	3	0	0	0-0	2.2	5	4	1	0	2-0	0	13.50	35	.417	.500	0	—	0	-2		57	-0.1
	KC A	3	3	.500	20	0	0	3-2	30.1	23	11	3	0	17-2	21	3.26	147	.215	.317	0	—	0		5		1.0
	Year	3	3	.500	23	0	0	3-2	33	28	15	4	0	19-2	21	4.09	117	.235	.336	0	—	0		3		0.9
1996	Det A	3	0	1.000	43	0	0	8-2	43	43	25	0	4	28-4	29	5.02	101	.259	.369	0	—	0		1		0.0
	Hou N	1	0	1.000	9	0	0	0-0	9.1	12	5	1	0	7-2	8	4.82	80	.308	.404	0	—	0		-1		-0.1
1997	Min A	0	0	—	11	0	0	0-0	8.1	19	17	0	0	11-1	6	18.36	25	.432	.545	0	—	0		-12		-0.5
	KC A	4	3	.571	34	0	0	1-3	41.2	39	18	3	1	17-3	28	3.02	157	.260	.337	0	—	0		6		1.0
	Year	4	3	.571	45	0	0	1-3	50	58	35	3	1	28-4	34	5.58	85	.299	.388	0	—	0		-5		0.5
1998	Ari N	3	4	.429	64	0	0	30-4	68.2	56	25	4	1	25-1	55	3.01	142	.223	.295	2-1-0	.500	1		10		1.7
1999	†Ari N	9	4	.692	61	0	0	14-9	60.2	54	29	9	2	25-2	45	3.71	124	.238	.316	0	—	0		6	15	1.1
2000	LA N	0	1	.000	13	0	0	0-1	17.2	21	11	4	1	7-0	15	5.09	87	.296	.363	0	—	0		-1	108	-0.1
2001	LA N	0	1	.000	28	0	0	0-1	24.2	26	24	4	0	20-1	24	8.03	51	.268	.383	0	—	0		-11		-0.6
Total	14	40	39	.506	622	0	0	217-56	672	598	275	46	12	330-41	588	3.46	123	.239	.328	4-1-0	.250	1		63	222	14.2

OLSON, TED   Theodore Otto   B8.27.1912 Quincy MA   D12.9.1980 Weymouth MA   BR/TR/6-2.5/185   d6.21   Col Dartmouth

YEAR	TM LG	W	L	PCT	G	GS	CG-SHO	SV-BS	IP	H	R	HR	HB	BB-IB	SO	ERA	AERA	OAV	OOB	AB-HR-SH	AVG	PB	SUP	APR	DL	PW
1936	Bos A	1	1	.500	5	3	1	0	18.1	24	16	3	0	8	5	7.36	72	.324	.390	7	.143	-0	66	-3		-0.3
1937	Bos A	0	0	—	11	0	0	0	32.1	42	28	4	0	15	11	7.24	66	.318	.388	10	.300	1		-8		-0.3
1938	Bos A	0	0	—	2	0	0	0	7	9	5	0	0	2	2	6.43	77	.310	.355	1	.000	-0		-1		-0.1
Total	3	1	1	.500	18	3	1	0	57.2	75	49	7	0	25	18	7.18	69	.319	.385	-18	.222	1	66	-12		-0.7

YEAR	TM LG	W	L	PCT	G	GS	CG-SHO	SV-BS	IP	H	R	HR	HB	BB-IB	SO	ERA	AERA	OAV	OOB	AB-HR-SH	AVG	PB	SUP	APR	DL	PW
OLWINE, ED	Edward R. B5.28.1958 Greenville OH BL/TL/6-2/165* d6.2 Col Morehead St.																									
1986	Atl N	0	0	—	37	0	0	1-0	47.2	35	20	5	1	17-7	37	3.40	117	.207	.282	3	.333	1		3		0.2
1987	Atl N	0	1	.000	27	0	0	1-1	23.1	25	16	4	1	8-1	12	5.01	86	.269	.330	0-0-1	—	0		-2		-0.3
1988	Atl N	0	0	—	16	0	0	1-0	18.2	22	15	4	1	4-1	5	6.75	54	.286	.329		—	0		-6	86	-0.3
Total	3	0	1	.000	80	0	0	3-1	89.2	82	51	13	3	29-9	54	4.52	88	.242	.306	3-0-1	.333	1		-5	86	-0.
O'NEAL, SKINNY	Oran Herbert B5.2.1899 Gatewood MO D6.2.1981 Springfield MO BR/TR/5-11/160 d4.18 Col East Central																									
1925	Phi N	0	0	—	11	1	0	0	20.1	35	23	2	0	12	9	9.30	51	.407	.480	6	.167	-0	106	-8		-0.4
1927	Phi N	0	0	—	2	0	0	0	5	9	5	0	0	2	2	9.00	46	.409	.458	1.	.000	-0		-2		-0.1
Total	2	0	0	—	13	1	0	0	25.1	44	28	2	0	14	8	9.24	50	.407	.475	7	.143	-0	106	-10		-0.5
O'NEAL, RANDY	Randall Jeffrey B8.30.1960 Ashland KY BR/TR/6-2/195* [DetA81 S1/15] d9.12 Col Florida																									
1984	Det A	2	1	.667	4	3	0	0-0	18.2	16	7	0	0	6-0	12	3.38	117	.222	.282	0	—	0	107	2		0.2
1985	Det A	5	5	.500	28	12	1	1-0	94.1	82	42	8	2	36-3	52	3.24	127	.240	.310	0	—	0	92	7		0.8
1986	Det A	3	7	.300	37	11	1	2-1	122.2	121	69	13	3	44-9	68	4.33	96	.260	.324	0	—	0	103	-4		-0.6
1987	Atl N	4	2	.667	16	10	0	0-0	61	79	41	12	2	24-3	33	5.61	77	.316	.378	19-0-1	.105	-1*	125	-7		0.1
	StL N	0	0	—	1	1	0	0-0	5	2	1	0	0	2-0	4	1.80	234	.111	.200	1	1.000	0	21	1		0.1
	Year	4	2	.667	17	11	0	0-0	66	81	42	12	2	26-3	37	5.32	81	.302	.366	20-0-1	.150	-0	116	-6		-0.5
1988	StL N	2	3	.400	19	10	8	0-0	53	57	29	7	2	10-1	20	4.58	77	.274	.314	19-0-1	.000	-2	120	-6	62	-0.6
1989	Phi N	0	1	.000	20	1	0	0-1	39	46	28	5	0	9-2	29	6.23	58	.301	.333	5	.000	-1	395	-10		-0.6
1990	SF N	1	0	1.000	26	0	0	0-0	47	58	23	3	0	18-4	30	3.83	96	.314	.371	6-0-1	.167	-0		-2	23	-0.1
Total	7	17	19	.472	142	46	2	3-2	440.2	461	240	48	9	149-22	248	4.35	92	.272	.331	50-0-3	.080	-3	114	-19	85	-1.
O'NEIL, ED	Edward J. B3.11.1859 Fall River MA D9.30.1892 Fall River MA TR/5-11/180 d6.20																									
1890	Tol AA	0	2	.000	2	2	2	0	16	27	18	0	0	13	2	7.88	50	.365	.460	9	.000	-2	145	-6		-0.8
	Phi AA	0	6	.000	6	6	6	0	52	84	77	0	7	32	17	9.69	40	.353	.444	31	.161	-1*	58	-32		-2.7
	Year	0	8	.000	8	8	8	0	68	111	95	0	7	45	19	9.26	42	.356	.448	40	.125	-2	80	-40		-3.5
O'NEILL, J.	J. B Brooklyn NY d8.20																									
1875	Atl NA	0	4	.000	5	4	3	0	34	39	45	3	0	0	0	5.03	41	.343	.343	26	.077	-2*	68	-9		-0.9
O'NEILL, TIP	James Edward B5.25.1858 Springfield ON, Can. D12.31.1915 Montreal QC, Can. BR/TR/6-1.5/167 d5.5 ▲																									
1883	NY N	5	12	.294	19	19	15	0	148	182	129	5		64	55	4.07	76	.289	.354	76	.197	-1*	83	-14		-1.
1884	StL AA	11	4	.733	17	14	14	0	141	125	95	3	4	51	36	2.68	122	.219	.288	297-3	.276	5*	112	4		0.
Total	2	16	16	.500	36	33	29	0	289	307	224	8	4	115	91	3.39	94	.256	.323	373-3	.260	3	95	-10		-0.
O'NEILL, HARRY	Joseph Henry B11.20.1892 Lindsay ON, Can. D9.5.1969 Ridgetown ON, Can. BR/TR/6-0/180 d9.15																									
1922	Phi A	0	0	—	1	0	0	0	3	2	1	0	1	1	0	3.00	142	.200	.333	1	.000	-0		0		0.0
1923	Phi A	0	0	—	3	0	0	0	2	1	0	0	0	3	2	0.00	—	.167	.444	0		-0		1		0.0
Total	2	0	0	—	4	0	0	0	5	3	1	0	1	4	2	1.80	233	.188	.381	1	.000	-0		1		0.0
O'NEILL, MIKE	Michael Joyce (aka Michael Joyce in 1901) B9.7.1877 Maam, Ireland D8.12.1959 Scranton PA BL/TL/5-11/185 d9.20 b-Jim b-Jack b-Steve Col Villanova																									
1901	StL N	2	2	.500	5	4	4-1	0	41	29	12	2	5	10	16	1.32	242	.197	.272	15	.400	3*	139	7		1.4
1902	StL N	16	15	.516	36	32	29-2	2	288.1	297	136	3	12	66	105	2.90	94	.266	.314	135-2-1	.319	9*	92	-5		0.9
1903	StL N	4	13	.235	19	17	12	0	145	184	124	2	6	43	39	3.79	86	.304	.356	110	.227	2*	66	-17		-1.
1904	StL N	10	14	.417	25	24	23-1	0	220	229	86	1	3	50	68	2.09	129	.262	.304	91-0-5	.231	5*	94	11		2.
Total	4	32	44	.421	85	77	68-4	2	694.1	739	358	8	26	169	228	2.73	105	.269	.318	351-2-6	.271	19	89	-4		2.
O'NEILL, EMMETT	Robert Emmett "Pinky" B1.13.1918 San Mateo CA D10.11.1993 Sparks NV BR/TR/6-2.5/180 d8.3 Col St. Marys (CA)																									
1943	Bos A	1	4	.200	11	5	1	0	57.2	56	31	3	1	46	20	4.53	73	.256	.387	16	.188	1	51	-7		-0.
1944	Bos A	6	11	.353	28	22	8-1	0	151.2	154	88	6	2	89	68	4.63	73	.265	.365	55	.182	-0	109	-20		-2.
1945	Bos A	8	11	.421	24	22	10-1	0	141.2	134	87	5	5	117	55	5.15	66	.258	.399	50-1-1	.180	2	107	-24		-2.
1946	Chi N	0	0	—	1	0	0	0	1	0	0	0	0	3	1	0.00	—	.000	.500	0		0		0		0.
	Chi A	0	0	—	2	0	0	0	3.2	4	2	0	0	5	0	0.00	—	.333	.529	1	.000	-0		1		0.
Total	4	15	26	.366	66	49	19-2	0	355.2	348	208	14	8	260	144	4.76	71	.261	.385	122-1-1	.180	2	103	-50		-5.
ONTIVEROS, STEVE	Steven B3.5.1961 Tularosa NM BR/TR/6-0/190* [OakA82 2/54] d6.14 Col Michigan [DL 1991 Phi N 182, 1997 Ana A 181]																									
1985	Oak A	1	3	.250	39	0	0	8-1	74.2	45	17	4	2	19-2	36	1.93	201	.174	.234	0	—	0		18		1.
1986	Oak A	2	2	.500	46	0	0	10-3	72.2	72	40	10	1	25-3	54	4.71	83	.265	.322	0	—	0*		-6	52	-0.
1987	Oak A	10	8	.556	35	22	2-1	1-3	150.1	141	78	19	4	50-3	97	4.00	104	.242	.305	0	—	0*	119	1	18	0.
1988	Oak A	3	4	.429	10	10	0	0-0	54.2	57	32	4	0	21-1	30	4.61	83	.265	.331	0	—	0*	161	-6	112	-0.
1989	Phi N	2	1	.667	6	5	0	0-0	30.2	34	15	2	0	15-1	12	3.82	94	.288	.368	12	.083	-0	113	-1	150	-0.
1990	Phi N	0	0	—	5	0	0	0-0	10	9	3	1	0	3-0	6	2.70	143	.225	.279	0	—	0		1	152	0.
1993	Sea A	0	2	.000	14	0	0	0-0	18	18	3	0	0	6-2	13	1.00	447	.277	.338	0	—	0		6		0.
1994	Oak A	6	4	.600	27	13	2	0-0	115.1	93	39	7	6	26-1	56	2.65	169	.217	**.271**	0	—	0	85	24		1.
1995	Oak A★	9	6	.600	22	22	2-1	0-0	129.2	144	75	12	4	38-0	77	4.37	104	.283	.335	0	—	0	103	-1	39	-0.
2000	Bos A	1	1	.500	3	1	0	0-0	5.1	9	6	1	0	4-0	1	10.13	50	.375	.464	0	—	0	37	-3		-0.
Total	10	34	31	.523	207	73	6-2	19-7	661.2	622	308	60	17	207-13	382	3.67	114	.248	.307	12	.083	-0	112	33	886	1.
OQUIST, MIKE	Michael Lee B5.30.1968 LaJunta CO BR/TR/6-2/170(170-190) [BalA89 13/323] d8.14 Col Arkansas-Monticello																									
1993	Bal A	0	0	—	5	0	0	0-0	11.2	12	5	0	0	4-1	8	3.86	117	.261	.320	0	—	0		1		0.
1994	Bal A	3	3	.500	15	9	0	0-0	58.1	75	41	7	6	30-4	39	6.17	82	.319	.404	0	—	0	91	-7		-0.
1995	Bal A	2	1	.667	27	0	0	0-1	54	51	27	6	2	41-3	27	4.17	115	.246	.370	0	—	0		3		-0.
1996	SD N	0	0	—	8	0	0	0-0	7.2	6	2	0	0	4-2	4	2.35	171	.231	.333	0	—	0*	106	-4	37	-0.
1997	Oak A	4	6	.400	19	17	1	0-0	107.2	111	62	15	6	43-3	72	5.02	92	.266	.340	4-0-1	.250	0*	100	-26		-2.
1998	Oak A	7	11	.389	31	29	0	0-0	175	210	125	27	5	57-1	112	6.22	74	.298	.352	1-0-1	.000	-0	102	-7		-0.
1999	Oak A	9	10	.474	28	24	0	0-0	140.2	158	86	18	2	64-5	89	5.37	88	.283	.358	2	.000	-0	102	-7	37	-0.
Total	7	25	31	.446	133	79	1	0-2	555	623	348	73	21	243-19	351	5.46	86	.284	.358	7-0-2	.143	-0	101	-38	37	-3.
O'RILEY, DON	Donald Lee B3.12.1945 Topeka KS D5.2.1997 Kansas City MO BR/TR/6-3/200(180-205) d6.20																									
1969	KC A	1	1	.500	18	0	0	1-0	23.1	32	23	0	0	15-2	10	6.94	53	.311	.395	3	.000	-0*		-9		-0.
1970	KC A	0	0	—	9	2	0	0-0	23.1	26	15	5	1	9-0	13	5.40	69	.277	.343	3-0-2	.000	-0	155	-4		-0.
Total	2	1	1	.500	27	2	0	1-0	46.2	58	38	5	1	24-2	23	6.17	60	.294	.371	6-0-2	.000	-1	155	-13		-0.
OROPESA, EDDIE	Edilberto B11.23.1971 Colon, Cuba BL/TL/6-3/215* [LAN94 14/384] d4.2																									
2001	Phi N	1	0	1.000	30	0	0	0-1	19	16	10	1	0	17-6	15	4.74	87	.232	.384	0	—	0		-1	22	-0.
2002	Ari N	2	0	1.000	32	0	0	0-0	25.1	39	30	6	2	15-0	18	10.30	44	.348	.431	0	—	0		-15		-1.
2003	Ari N	3	3	.500	47	0	0	0-0	38.2	38	27	3	2	27-2	39	5.82	79	.257	.379	0	—	0		-5		-0.
2004	SD N	2	1	.667	16	0	0	0-0	9	6	12	1	0	13-3	6	11.00	36	.188	.422	0	—	0		-8		-1.
Total	4	8	4	.667	125	0	0	0-2	92	99	79	11	4	72-11	78	7.34	60	.267	.400	0	—	0		-29	22	-3.
OROSCO, JESSE	Jesse Russell B4.21.1957 Santa Barbara CA BR/TL/6-2/185(174-205) [MinA78*2/41] d4.5 Col Santa Barbara (CA) City																									
1979	NY N	1	2	.333	18	2	0	0-0	35	33	20	4	2	22-0	22	4.89	76	.260	.377	6-0-1	.000	-1	95	-4		-0.
1981	NY N	0	1	.000	8	0	0	1-0	17.1	13	4	2	0	6-2	18	1.56	227	.213	.284	2	.000	-0		4		0.
1982	NY N	4	10	.286	54	2	0	4-1	109.1	92	37	7	2	40-2	89	2.72	135	.230	.300	14	.143	-0	108	12		1.
1983	NY N★	13	7	.650	62	0	0	17-5	110	76	27	3	1	38-7	84	1.47	249	.197	.269	12-0-2	.333	1		24		5.
1984	NY N☆	10	6	.625	60	0	0	31-8	87	58	29	7	2	34-6	85	2.59	138	.185	.267	4-0-1	.250	1		10		2.
1985	NY N	8	6	.571	54	0	0	17-8	79	66	26	6	0	34-7	68	2.73	128	.224	.303	7-0-2	.429	1		7		1.
1986	†NY N	8	6	.571	58	0	0	21-8	81	64	23	6	1	35-3	62	2.33	154	.217	.304	3	.000	1		12		2.
1987	NY N	3	9	.250	58	0	0	16-6	77	78	41	5	2	31-9	78	4.44	86	.266	.336	8-0-1	.000	-1		-5		-0.
1988	†LA N	3	2	.600	55	0	0	9-6	53	41	18	4	2	30-3	43	2.72	123	.215	.323	2	.000	-0		4		0.
1989	Cle A	3	4	.429	69	0	0	3-4	78	54	20	7	2	26-4	79	2.08	192	.198	.276		—	0		16		1.
1990	Cle A	5	6	.455	55	0	0	2-1	64.2	58	35	9	0	38-3	55	3.90	101	.239	.338		—	0		-2		-0.
1991	Cle A	2	0	1.000	47	0	0	0-0	45.2	52	29	4	1	15-8	36	3.74	111	.286	.338		—	0		3		0.
1992	Mil A	3	1	.750	59	0	0	1-1	39	33	15	5	1	13-1	40	3.23	120	.232	.297	1	.000	-0		9		0.
1993	Mil A	3	5	.375	57	0	0	8-0	56.2	47	25	3	1	17-3	65	3.18	136	.224	.289		—	0		6		0.
1994	Mil A	3	1	.750	40	0	0	0-4	39	28	24	4	2	26-2	36	5.08	100	.222	.345		—	0		-1		-0.

OROSCO (continued)

YEAR	TM LG	W	L	PCT	G	GS	CG-SHO	SV-BS	IP	H	R	HR	HB	BB-IB	SO	ERA	AERA	OAV	OOB	AB-HR-SH	AVG	PB	SUP	APR	DL	PW
1995	Bal A	2	4	.333	65	0	0	3-3	49.2	28	19	4	1	27-7	58	3.26	147	.169	.283	0	—	0	8			1.0
1996	†Bal A	3	1	.750	66	0	0	0-3	55.2	42	22	5	2	28-4	52	3.40	146	.207	.308	0	—	0	10			0.6
1997	†Bal A	6	3	.667	71	0	0	0-4	50.1	29	13	6	0	30-0	46	2.32	190	.169	.289	0	—	0	13			2.0
1998	Bal A	4	1	.800	69	0	0	7-2	56.2	46	20	6	1	28-1	50	3.18	143	.221	.314	0	—	0	9			0.9
1999	Bal A	0	2	.000	65	0	0	1-3	32	28	21	5	2	20-3	35	5.34	88	.239	.352	0	—	0	-3			-0.1
2000	StL N	0	0	—	6	0	0	0-0	2.1	3	3	1	2	3-2	4	3.86	120	.273	.500	0	—	0	-1	161		0.0
2001	LA N	0	1	.000	35	0	0	0-2	16	17	7	3	0	7-1	21	3.94	105	.279	.348	0	—	0	1	19		0.0
2002	LA N	1	2	.333	56	0	0	1-0	27	24	10	4	0	12-1	22	3.00	130	.229	.305	0	—	0	3	15		0.3
2003	SD N	1	1	.500	42	0	0	2-1	25	33	22	4	2	10-0	22	7.56	53	.317	.381	0	—	0	-10			-0.8
	NY A	0	0	—	15	0	0	0-1	4.1	4	6	0	1	6-3	4	10.38	42	.250	.435	0	—	0	-3			-0.1
	Min A	1	1	.500	8	0	0	0-0	4.2	4	3	0	1	5-0	3	5.79	78	.235	.417	0	—	0	-1			-0.1
	Year	1	1	.500	23	0	0	0-1	9	8	9	0	1	11-3	7	8.00	56	.242	.426	0	—	0	-4			-0.1
Total 24		87	80	.521	1252	4	0	144-76	1295.1	1055	512	113	34	581-86	1179	3.16	126	.223	.309	59-0-7	.169	2	97	115	195	18.9

O'ROURKE d7.9

YEAR	TM LG	W	L	PCT	G	GS	CG-SHO	SV-BS	IP	H	R	HR	HB	BB-IB	SO	ERA	AERA	OAV	OOB	AB-HR-SH	AVG	PB	SUP	APR	DL	PW
1872	Eck NA	0	1	.000	1	1	1		9	16	15	0			2	8.00	42	.327	.353	4	.000	-1	34	-4		-0.3

O'ROURKE, JIM James Henry "Orator Jim" B9.1.1850 Bridgeport CT D1.8.1919 Bridgeport CT BR/TR/5-8/185 d4.26.1872 M5/U1 HF1945 b-John s-Queenie ▲

YEAR	TM LG	W	L	PCT	G	GS	CG-SHO	SV-BS	IP	H	R	HR	HB	BB-IB	SO	ERA	AERA	OAV	OOB	AB-HR-SH	AVG	PB	SUP	APR	DL	PW
1883	Buf N	0	0	—	2	0	0	1	7	10	9	0		1	1	6.43	49	.357	.379	436-1	.328	1*	-2			-0.1
1884	Buf N	0	1	.000	4	0	0	1	12.2	7	5	0		1	3	2.84	111	.175	.195	467-5	.347	2*	1			0.1
Total 2		0	1	.000	6	0	0	2	19.2	17	14	0		2	4	4.12	77	.250	.271	903-6	.338	2	-1			0.0

O'ROURKE, MIKE Michael J. D3.3.1934 Richmond VA d9.1

YEAR	TM LG	W	L	PCT	G	GS	CG-SHO	SV-BS	IP	H	R	HR	HB	BB-IB	SO	ERA	AERA	OAV	OOB	AB-HR-SH	AVG	PB	SUP	APR	DL	PW
1890	Bal AA	1	2	.333	5	5	5		41	45	19	0	3	10	8	3.95	103	.271	.324	26	.115	-1*	60	2		0.1

ORR, DAVE David L. B9.29.1859 New York NY D6.2.1915 Richmond Hill NY BR/TR/5-11/250 d5.17.1883 M1 ▲

YEAR	TM LG	W	L	PCT	G	GS	CG-SHO	SV-BS	IP	H	R	HR	HB	BB-IB	SO	ERA	AERA	OAV	OOB	AB-HR-SH	AVG	PB	SUP	APR	DL	PW
1885	NY AA	0	0	—	3	0	0		10	11	13	2	0	5	1	7.20	43	.250	.327	444-6	.342	2*	-5			-0.2

ORRELL, JOE Forrest Gordon B3.6.1917 National City CA D1.12.1993 Chula Vista CA BR/TR/6-4/210 d8.12

YEAR	TM LG	W	L	PCT	G	GS	CG-SHO	SV-BS	IP	H	R	HR	HB	BB-IB	SO	ERA	AERA	OAV	OOB	AB-HR-SH	AVG	PB	SUP	APR	DL	PW
1943	Det A	0	0	—	10	0	0	1	19.1	18	9	0	2	11	2	3.72	95	.257	.373	4	.250	0	0			0.0
1944	Det A	2	1	.667	10	2	0		22.1	26	13	0	1	11	10	2.42	147	.286	.369	4	.250	0	105	0		0.1
1945	Det A	2	3	.400	12	5	1	0	48	46	18	1	2	24	14	3.00	117	.260	.355	15	.133	-1	53	3		0.2
Total 3		4	4	.500	32	7	1	1	89.2	90	40	1	5	46	26	3.01	117	.266	.362	23	.174	-1	68	3		0.3

ORTEGA, PHIL Filomeno Coronado "Kemo" B10.7.1939 Gilbert AZ BR/TR/6-2/175(175-195) d9.10

YEAR	TM LG	W	L	PCT	G	GS	CG-SHO	SV-BS	IP	H	R	HR	HB	BB-IB	SO	ERA	AERA	OAV	OOB	AB-HR-SH	AVG	PB	SUP	APR	DL	PW
1960	LA N	0	0	—	3	1	0		6.1	12	12	1	0	5-0	4	17.05	23	.400	.486	1	.000	-0	178	-8		-0.4
1961	LA N	0	2	.000	4	2	1	0	13	10	9	6	0	2-0	15	5.54	78	.208	.240	4	.250	-1	41	-2		-0.2
1962	LA N	0	2	.000	24	3	0	1	53.2	60	43	8	3	39-2	30	6.88	53	.276	.392	7	.000	-1	40	-19		-1.0
1963	LA N	0	0	—	1	0	0		2	1	2	1	0	0-0	1	18.00	17	.400	.400	0	—	0	-2			-0.1
1964	LA N	7	9	.438	34	25	4-3	1	157.1	149	74	22	6	56-2	107	4.00	81	.249	.317	53-0-7	.136	-0*	104	-11		-1.2
1965	Was A	12	15	.444	35	29	4-2		179.2	176	107	33	6	97-7	88	5.11	68	.262	.356	53-0-3	.208	4	97	-28		-3.4
1966	Was A	12	12	.500	33	31	5-1		197.1	158	91	29	5	53-5	121	3.92	88	.218	.274	54-0-8	.056	-2	96	-7		-1.2
1967	Was A	10	10	.500	34	34	5-2	0	219.2	189	77	16	6	57-3	122	3.03	104	.231	.286	54-0-8	.061	-3	97	7		-1.2
1968	Was A	5	12	.294	31	16	1-1		115.2	115	70	12	5	62-8	57	4.98	59	.263	.356	24-0-5	.167	1	104	-26		-3.5
1969	Cal A	0	0	—	8	0	0	0-0	8	13	13	3	0	7-1	4	10.13	35	.333	.435	0	—	0	-7	59		-0.4
Total 10		46	62	.426	204	141	20-9	2-0	951.2	884	498	131	30	378-28	549	4.43	75	.246	.321	253-0-30	.115	-1	97-103	-59	59	-11.1

ORTH, AL Albert Lewis "Smiling Al","The Curveless Wonder" B9.5.1872 Tipton IN D10.8.1948 Lynchburg VA BL/TR/6-0/200 d8.15 U6 Col DePauw ▲

YEAR	TM LG	W	L	PCT	G	GS	CG-SHO	SV-BS	IP	H	R	HR	HB	BB-IB	SO	ERA	AERA	OAV	OOB	AB-HR-SH	AVG	PB	SUP	APR	DL	PW
1895	Phi N	8	1	.889	11	10	9	1	88	103	50	0	2	22	25	3.89	123	.288	.332	45-1-2	.356	4	159	9		1.0
1896	Phi N	15	10	.600	25	23	19	0	196	244	128	10	3	46	23	4.41	98	.302	.342	82-1-0	.256	3	103	-1		0.2
1897	Phi N	14	19	.424	36	34	29-2		282.1	349	194	12	6	82	64	4.62	91	.301	.350	152-1-2	.329	7*	104	-14		-0.4
1898	Phi N	15	13	.536	32	28	25-1		250	290	131	2	8	53	52	3.02	114	.288	.329	123-1-7	.293	8*	122	9		1.7
1899	Phi N	14	3	.824	21	15	13-3		144.2	149	67	0	3	19	35	2.49	148	.266	.294	62-1-1	.210	1*	105	17		1.6
1900	Phi N	14	14	.500	33	30	24-2	1	262	302	145	4	13	60	68	3.78	96	.288	.335	129-1-0	.310	7*	105	-2		0.5
1901	Phi N	20	12	.625	35	32	30-6		281.2	250	101	3	8	32	92	2.27	150	.237	.264	128-1-0	.281	5*	95	33		4.4
1902	Was A	19	18	.514	38	37	36-1	0	324	367	181	18	7	40	76	3.97	93	.286	.312	175-2-3	.217	1*	101	-5		-0.1
1903	Was A	10	22	.313	36	30	30-2	2	279.2	326	174	8	7	62	88	4.34	72	.290	.331	162-0-1	.302	9*	75	-34		-2.4
1904	Was A	3	4	.429	10	7	7		73.2	88	49	2	3	15	23	4.76	56	.297	.338	102	.216	0*	134	-15		-1.3
	NY A	11	6	.647	20	18	11-2		137.2	122	47	0	3	19	47	2.68	101	.238	.270	64-0-1	.297	3*	98	3		0.8
	Year	14	10	.583	30	25	18-2		211.1	210	96	2	6	34	70	3.41	79	.280	.295	166-0-1	.247	3	108	-10		-0.5
1905	NY A	18	16	.529	40	37	26-6		305.1	273	122	8	7	61	121	2.86	103	.241	.284	131-1-3	.183	-1*	99	7		0.6
1906	NY A	27	17	.614	45	39	36-3		338.2	317	115	2	1	66	133	2.34	127	.251	.289	135-1-3	.274	6*	90	21		3.4
1907	NY A	14	21	.400	36	32	21-2		248.2	244	134	2	6	53	78	2.61	107	.259	.303	105-1-2	.324	7*	98	-4		0.5
1908	NY A	2	13	.133	21	17	8-1		139.1	134	62	4	4	30	22	3.42	72	.255	.300	69-0-2	.290	5*	93	-9		-0.5
1909	Cin N	0	0	—	1	1	0								1	12.00	21	.429	.467	34-0-1	.265	0*	251	-2		-0.1
Total 15		204	189	.519	440	394	324-31	6	3354.2	3564	1704	75	83	661	948	3.37	101	.272	.311	1698-12-28	.273	63	101	13		9.7

ORTIZ, RAMON Diogenes Ramon (Ortiz) B3.23.1973 Cotui, D.R. BR/TR/6-0/170* d8.19

YEAR	TM LG	W	L	PCT	G	GS	CG-SHO	SV-BS	IP	H	R	HR	HB	BB-IB	SO	ERA	AERA	OAV	OOB	AB-HR-SH	AVG	PB	SUP	APR	DL	PW
1999	Ana A	2	3	.400	9	9	0	0-0	48.1	50	35	7	2	25-0	44	6.52	75	.265	.353	0	—	0	80	-7		-0.6
2000	Ana A	8	6	.571	18	18	2	0-0	111.1	96	69	18	2	55-0	73	5.09	101	.236	.327	0	—	0	102	0	7	0.0
2001	Ana A	13	11	.542	32	32	2	0-0	208.2	223	114	25	12	76-6	135	4.36	107	.274	.343	7	.000	-1	91	5		0.3
2002	†Ana A	15	9	.625	32	32	4-1	0-0	217.1	188	97	40	5	68-0	162	3.77	119	.230	.292	7	.000	-1	127	18		1.6
2003	Ana A	16	13	.552	32	32	1	0-0	180	209	121	28	12	63-0	94	5.20	84	.287	.350	5-0-1	.000	-0	112	-21		-2.9
2004	†Ana A	5	7	.417	34	14	0	0-0	128	139	64	18	4	38-4	82	4.43	101	.280	.335	3	.000	-0	119	2		0.1
2005	Cin N	9	11	.450	30	30	1	0-0	171.1	206	110	34	7	51-1	96	5.36	78	.302	.353	54-0-6	.074	-3	117	-23	22	-2.5
Total 7		68	60	.531	187	167	10-1	0-0	1065	1111	610	170	44	376-11	686	4.72	96	.269	.334	76-0-7	.053	-5	109	-26	29	-4.0

ORTIZ, BABY Oliverio (Nunez) B12.5.1919 Camaguey, Cuba D3.27.1984 Central Senado, Cuba BR/TR/6-0/190 d9.23 b-Roberto

YEAR	TM LG	W	L	PCT	G	GS	CG-SHO	SV-BS	IP	H	R	HR	HB	BB-IB	SO	ERA	AERA	OAV	OOB	AB-HR-SH	AVG	PB	SUP	APR	DL	PW
1944	Was A	0	2	.000	2	2	1	0-0	13	13	11	0	0	6	4	6.23	52	.255	.333	6	.167	-0	103	-4		-0.6

ORTIZ, RUSS Russell Reid B6.5.1974 Van Nuys CA BR/TR/6-1/210(190-210) [SFN95 4/103] d4.2 Col Oklahoma

YEAR	TM LG	W	L	PCT	G	GS	CG-SHO	SV-BS	IP	H	R	HR	HB	BB-IB	SO	ERA	AERA	OAV	OOB	AB-HR-SH	AVG	PB	SUP	APR	DL	PW
1998	SF N	4	4	.500	22	13	0	0-0	88.1	90	51	11	4	49-5	75	4.99	81	.269	.360	25-1-5	.280	3	144	-9		-0.4
1999	SF N	18	9	.667	33	33	0	0-0	207.2	189	109	24	6	125-5	164	3.81	112	.244	.351	71-1-7	.197	3	115	5		0.9
2000	†SF N	14	12	.538	33	32	0	0-0	195.2	192	117	28	7	112-1	167	5.01	87	.261	.361	61-0-6	.197	4	116	-14		-1.1
2001	SF N	17	9	.654	33	33	1-1	0-0	218.2	187	90	13	0	94-5	169	3.29	124	.232	.309	67-0-8	.194	4	124	20		2.7
2002	†SF N	14	10	.583	33	33	2	0-0	214.1	191	89	15	4	94-5	137	3.61	109	.241	.293	69-2-7	.246	8	121	11		2.1
2003	†Atl N★	21	7	.750	34	34	1-1	0-0	212.1	177	101	24	4	102-7	149	3.81	110	.223	.312	70-2-6	.257	8*	127	9		1.8
2004	†Atl N	15	9	.625	34	34	2-1	0-0	204.2	197	98	23	3	112-7	143	4.13	104	.258	.352	59-0-10	.102	-2	102	7		0.6
2005	Ari N	5	11	.313	22	22	0	0-0	115	147	92	18	4	65-3	46	6.89	64	.313	.396	34-0-6	.206	1*	99	-29	58	-3.3
Total 7		108	71	.603	244	234	9-3	0-0	1456.2	1370	747	149	32	747-32	1050	4.23	99	.251	.341	456-6-55	.206	30	117	0	58	3.3

ORVELLA, CHAD Chad Robert B10.1.1980 Renton WA BR/TR/5-11/190 d5.31 Col North Carolina St.

YEAR	TM LG	W	L	PCT	G	GS	CG-SHO	SV-BS	IP	H	R	HR	HB	BB-IB	SO	ERA	AERA	OAV	OOB	AB-HR-SH	AVG	PB	SUP	APR	DL	PW
2005	TB A	3	3	.500	37	0	0	1-1	50	47	26	4	3			3.60	121	.246	.324	0	—	0	2			0.2

ORWOLL, OSSIE Oswald Christian B11.17.1900 Portland OR D5.8.1967 Decorah IA BL/TL/6-0/174 d4.13 Col Luther ▲

YEAR	TM LG	W	L	PCT	G	GS	CG-SHO	SV-BS	IP	H	R	HR	HB	BB-IB	SO	ERA	AERA	OAV	OOB	AB-HR-SH	AVG	PB	SUP	APR	DL	PW
1928	Phi A	6	5	.545	27	8	3	2	106	110	59	7	2	50	53	4.58	87	.274	.358	170-0-5	.306	7*	84	-4		0.0
1929	Phi A	0	2	.000	12	0	0	1	30	32	23	6	0	6	12	4.80	88	.278	.314	51	.255	1*	-4			-0.2
Total 2		6	7	.462	39	8	3	3	136	142	82	13	2	56	65	4.63	88	.275	.348	221-0-5	.294	7	84	-8		-0.2

OSBORN, OZZIE Danny Leon B6.19.1946 Springfield MO BR/TR/6-2/195 d4.26 Col Mesa St.

YEAR	TM LG	W	L	PCT	G	GS	CG-SHO	SV-BS	IP	H	R	HR	HB	BB-IB	SO	ERA	AERA	OAV	OOB	AB-HR-SH	AVG	PB	SUP	APR	DL	PW
1975	Chi A	3	0	1.000	24	0	0	0-0	58	57	29	2	2	37-1	38	4.50	86	.265	.375	0	—	0	-2			-0.2

OSBORN, BOB John Bode B4.17.1903 San Diego TX D4.19.1960 Paris AR BR/TR/6-1/175 d9.16

YEAR	TM LG	W	L	PCT	G	GS	CG-SHO	SV-BS	IP	H	R	HR	HB	BB-IB	SO	ERA	AERA	OAV	OOB	AB-HR-SH	AVG	PB	SUP	APR	DL	PW
1925	Chi N	0	0	—	1	0	0		1	0	0	0	0	0	0	0.00	—	.600	.600	0	—	0	0			0.0
1926	Chi N	6	5	.545	31	15	6	1	136.1	157	64	3	0	58	43	3.63	106	.301	.371	41-0-4	.146	-3	91	4		0.1
1927	Chi N	5	5	.500	24	12	3	1	107.2	125	54	2	1	48	45	4.18	92	.294	.367	39-0-1	.205	-0	112	-2		-0.1
1929	Chi N	0	0	—	3	1	0		8	9	8	0	0	2	2	3.00	154	.242	.286	4	.250	0	113	2		0.1
1930	Chi N	10	6	.625	35	13	3	1	126.2	147	74	9	1	53	42	4.97	98	.300	.369	42-0-3	.095	-5	136	2		-0.1

YEAR	TM LG	W	L	PCT	G	GS	CG-SHO	SV-BS	IP	H	R	HR	HB	BB-IB	SO	ERA	AERA	OAV	OOB	AB-HR-SH	AVG	PB	SUP	APR	DL	PW
1931	Pit N	6	1	.857	27	2	0	0	64.2	85	43	3	1	20	9	5.01	77	.316	.366	18	.167	-0	189	-8		-0.8
Total	6	27	17	.614	121	43	11	2	446.1	528	240	17	3	181	140	4.32	97	.302	.368	144-0-8	.153	-8	117	-2		-0.9

OSBORNE, DONOVAN Donovan Alan B6.21.1969 Roseville CA   BB/TL/6-2/195(195-210) [StLN90 1/13] d4.9 Col Nevada-Las Vegas [DL 1994 StL N 131]

YEAR	TM LG	W	L	PCT	G	GS	CG-SHO	SV-BS	IP	H	R	HR	HB	BB-IB	SO	ERA	AERA	OAV	OOB	AB-HR-SH	AVG	PB	SUP	APR	DL	PW
1992	StL N	11	9	.550	34	29	0	0-0	179	193	91	14	2	38-2	104	3.77	91	.275	.312	58-0-2	.121	-1	93	-12		-1.5
1993	StL N	10	7	.588	26	26	1	0-0	155.2	153	73	18	7	47-4	83	3.76	107	.257	.318	49-0-7	.204	2*	102	5		0.7
1995	StL N	4	6	.400	19	19	0	0-0	113.1	112	58	17	2	34-2	82	3.81	112	.260	.316	31-0-3	.161	0	66	4	60	0.5
1996	†StL N	13	9	.591	30	30	2-1	0-0	198.2	191	87	22	1	57-5	134	3.53	120	.254	.306	59-1-10	.220	4	85	15	16	1.8
1997	StL N	3	7	.300	14	14	0	0-0	80.1	84	46	10	1	23-2	51	4.93	85	.274	.323	24-0-1	.208	1	82	-5	87	-0.5
1998	StL N	5	4	.556	14	14	1-1	0-0	83.2	84	42	11	1	22-2	60	4.09	103	.256	.301	25-0-4	.040	-1	116	1	108	-0.1
1999	StL N	1	3	.250	6	6	0	0-0	29.1	34	18	4	2	10-0	21	5.52	83	.298	.362	10-0-1	.100	-0	113	-2	150	-0.2
2002	Chi N	0	1	.000	11	0	0	0-0	16	19	11	1	0	10-2	13	6.19	66	.297	.387	3	.000	-0		-3	116	-0.2
2004	NY A	2	0	1.000	9	2	0	0-0	17.2	25	16	3	2	5-0	10	7.13	64	.347	.405	0	—	0	142	-5		-0.5
Total	9	49	46	.516	163	140	4-2	0-0	873.2	895	442	100	18	246-19	558	4.03	100	.266	.317	259-1-28	.162	5	92	-2	668	0.0

OSBORNE, TINY Earnest Preston B4.9.1893 Porterdale GA D1.5.1969 Atlanta GA   BL/TR/6-4.5/215 d4.15 s-Bobo

YEAR	TM LG	W	L	PCT	G	GS	CG-SHO	SV-BS	IP	H	R	HR	HB	BB-IB	SO	ERA	AERA	OAV	OOB	AB-HR-SH	AVG	PB	SUP	APR	DL	PW
1922	Chi N	9	5	.643	41	14	7-1	3	184	183	113	7	12	95	81	4.50	93	.271	.370	67-0-2	.134	-4	112	-7		-1.0
1923	Chi N	8	15	.348	37	25	8-1	1	179.2	174	117	14	2	89	69	4.56	88	.255	.342	60	.200	-1	85	-14		-1.7
1924	Chi N	0	0		2	0	0	1	3	3	3	1	0	2	2	3.00	130	.300	.417	0		0		0		0.0
	Bro N	6	5	.545	21	13	6	0	104.1	123	67	1	4	54	52	5.09	74	.298	.384	36-0-1	.250	1	104	-14		-1.2
	Year	6	5	.545	23	13	6	1	107.1	126	68	1	4	56	54	5.03	75	.298	.385	36-0-1	.250	1	104	-15		-1.2
1925	Bro N	8	15	.348	41	22	10	1	175	210	111	9	4	75	59	4.94	85	.304	.375	57-0-1	.246	1	91	-13		-1.4
Total	4	31	40	.437	142	74	31-2	6	646	693	409	31	22	315	263	4.72	86	.280	.367	220-0-4	.200	-3	95	-48		-5.3

OSBORNE, FRED Frederick W. B Alberta, Can   BL/TL d7.14 ▲

YEAR	TM LG	W	L	PCT	G	GS	CG-SHO	SV-BS	IP	H	R	HR	HB	BB-IB	SO	ERA	AERA	OAV	OOB	AB-HR-SH	AVG	PB	SUP	APR	DL	PW
1890	Pit N	0	5	.000	8	5	5	0	58	82	87	6	7	45	14	8.38	39	.323	.438	168-1	.238	1*	100	-36		-2.1

OSBORNE, WAYNE Wayne Harold "Ossie","Fish Hook" B10.11.1912 Watsonville CA D3.13.1987 Vancouver WA   BL/TR/6-2.5/172 d4.18

YEAR	TM LG	W	L	PCT	G	GS	CG-SHO	SV-BS	IP	H	R	HR	HB	BB-IB	SO	ERA	AERA	OAV	OOB	AB-HR-SH	AVG	PB	SUP	APR	DL	PW
1935	Pit N	0	0	—	2	0	0	0	1.1	1	1	0	0	0	1	6.75	61	.250	.250		—	0*		0		0.0
1936	Bos N	1	1	.500	5	3	0	0	20	31	13	1	0	9	8	5.85	66	.352	.412	8	.250	0	133	-4		-0.3
Total	2	1	1	.500	7	3	0	0	21.1	32	14	1	0	9	9	5.91	65	.348	.406	8	.250	0	133	-4		-0.3

OSBURN, PAT Larry Patrick B5.4.1949 Murray KY   BL/TL/6-4/195* [CinN70 S1/9] d4.13 Col Florida St.

YEAR	TM LG	W	L	PCT	G	GS	CG-SHO	SV-BS	IP	H	R	HR	HB	BB-IB	SO	ERA	AERA	OAV	OOB	AB-HR-SH	AVG	PB	SUP	APR	DL	PW
1974	Cin N	0	0	—	6	0	0	0-0	9	11	9	2	2	4-0	4	8.00	44	.297	.357	2	.000	-0		-5		-0.2
1975	Mil A	0	1	.000	6	1	0	0-0	11.2	19	9	2	2	9-0	1	5.40	71	.404	.492	0	—	0	46	-2		-0.2
Total	2	0	1	.000	12	1	0	0-0	20.2	30	18	4	2	13-0	5	6.53	57	.357	.437	2	.000	-0	46	-7		-0.4

OSGOOD, CHARLIE Charles Benjamin B11.23.1926 Somerville MA   BR/TR/5-10/180 d6.18

YEAR	TM LG	W	L	PCT	G	GS	CG-SHO	SV-BS	IP	H	R	HR	HB	BB-IB	SO	ERA	AERA	OAV	OOB	AB-HR-SH	AVG	PB	SUP	APR	DL	PW
1944	Bro N	0	0	—	1	0	0	0	3	2	1	0	1	2	0	3.00	118	.222	.462	0	—	0		0		0.0

OSINSKI, DAN Daniel B11.17.1933 Chicago IL   BR/TR/6-2/195* d4.11

YEAR	TM LG	W	L	PCT	G	GS	CG-SHO	SV-BS	IP	H	R	HR	HB	BB-IB	SO	ERA	AERA	OAV	OOB	AB-HR-SH	AVG	PB	SUP	APR	DL	PW
1962	KC A	0	0	—	4	0	0	0	4.2	8	9	1	0	8-0	4	17.36	24	.381	.533	0	—	0		-6		-0.3
	LA A	6	4	.600	33	0	0	4	54.1	45	22	3	0	30-3	44	2.82	137	.223	.323	11-0-1	.000	-1		6		1.0
	Year	6	4	.600	37	0	0	4	59	53	31	4	0	38-3	48	3.97	98	.238	.347	11-0-1	.000	-1		-2		0.7
1963	LA A	8	8	.500	47	16	4-1	2	159.1	145	66	15	2	80-6	100	3.28	105	.242	.331	45-0-2	.111	-2	102	3		-0.2
1964	LA A	3	3	.500	47	4	1-1	2	93	87	47	8	2	39-7	88	3.48	94	.244	.321	18-0-2	.056	-1	108	-4		-0.3
1965	Mil N	0	3	.000	61	0	0	6	83	81	28	4	1	40-9	54	2.82	125	.261	.347	6	.167	-0		7		0.3
1966	Bos A	4	3	.571	44	1	0	2	67.1	68	33	8	1	28-6	44	3.61	105	.274	.349	6	.333	0	46	1		0.1
1967	†Bos A	3	1	.750	34	0	0	2	63.2	61	19	5	0	14-2	38	2.54	137	.243	.283	9	.333	1		7		0.6
1969	Chi A	5	5	.500	51	0	0	2-2	60.2	56	28	3	0	23-5	27	3.56	108	.251	.320	3	.000	-0		1		-0.4
1970	Hou N	0	1	.000	3	0	0	0-1	3.2	5	4	0	0	2-1	1	9.82	40	.357	.412	0	—	0		-2		-0.1
Total	8	29	28	.509	324	21	5-2	18-3	589.2	556	256	47	6	264-39	400	3.34	107	.250	.330	98-0-5	.122	-3	96	13		1.2

OSORIA, FRANQUELIS Franquelis Antonio B9.12.1981 Santiago, D.R.   BR/TR/6-0/165 d6.7

YEAR	TM LG	W	L	PCT	G	GS	CG-SHO	SV-BS	IP	H	R	HR	HB	BB-IB	SO	ERA	AERA	OAV	OOB	AB-HR-SH	AVG	PB	SUP	APR	DL	PW
2005	LA N	0	2	.000	24	0	0	0-2	29.2	28	14	3	3	8-0	15	3.94	104	.259	.328	3	.000	-0		1		0.0

OSTEEN, CLAUDE Claude Wilson B8.9.1939 Caney Spring TN   BL/TL/5-11/173* d7.6 Mil 1970 C15

YEAR	TM LG	W	L	PCT	G	GS	CG-SHO	SV-BS	IP	H	R	HR	HB	BB-IB	SO	ERA	AERA	OAV	OOB	AB-HR-SH	AVG	PB	SUP	APR	DL	PW
1957	Cin N	0	0	—	3	0	0	0	4	4	1	0	0	3-0	3	2.25	183	.250	.368	1	.000	-0		0		0.0
1959	Cin N	0	0	—	2	0	0	0	7.2	11	10	2	0	9-1	3	7.04	58	.333	.465	2	.000	-0		-4		-0.2
1960	Cin N	0	1	.000	20	3	0	0	48.1	53	29	4	1	30-4	15	5.03	76	.293	.393	12	.083	-1*	108	-6		-0.4
1961	Cin N	0	0	—	1	0	0	0	0.1	1	0	0	0	0-0	0	0.00	—	.000	.000	0	—	0*		0		0.0
	Was A	1	1	.500	3	3	0	0	18.1	14	11	3	1	9-0	14	4.91	82	.219	.320	1	.143	-0	103	-2		-0.1
1962	Was A	8	13	.381	28	22	7-2	1	150.1	140	62	12	4	47-6	59	3.65	111	.246	.308	48-0-1	.208	1*	69	9		1.3
1963	Was A	9	14	.391	40	29	8-2	0	212.1	222	101	23	4	60-4	109	3.35	111	.270	.318	70-1-5	.171	1*	78	4		0.4
1964	Was A	15	13	.536	37	36	13	0	257	256	107	20	3	64-8	133	3.33	111	.259	.304	90-1-7	.156	1*	99	12		1.1
1965	LA N	15	15	.500	40	40	9-1	0	287	253	95	19	3	78-10	162	2.79	117	.236	.290	99-0-6	.121	-1*	92	19		2.2
1966	†LA N	17	14	.548	39	38	8-3	0	240.1	238	92	6	3	65-13	137	2.85	116	.261	.309	76-1-2	.171	6	96	11		2.1
1967	LA N☆	17	17	.500	39	39	14-5	0	288.1	298	116	19	2	52-10	152	3.22	96	.270	.301	101-2-5	.178	6*	105	-4		0.9
1968	LA N	12	18	.400	39	36	5-3	0	254	267	109	14	5	54-10	119	3.08	94	.275	.314	84-0-9	.179	2*	84	-13		-1.2
1969	LA N	20	15	.571	41	41	16-7	0-0	321	293	103	17	6	74-8	183	2.66	126	.245	.291	111-1-8	.216	6*	105	28		3.9
1970	LA N★	16	14	.533	37	37	11-4	0-0	258.2	280	121	24	4	52-3	114	3.83	101	.276	.312	93-1-1	.204	5*	120	1		0.1
1971	LA N	14	11	.560	38	38	11-4	0-0	259	262	108	25	3	63-2	109	3.51	93	.266	.312	86-0-8	.186	2*	131	-5		0.1
1972	LA N	20	11	.645	33	33	14-4	0-0	252	232	82	16	4	69-4	100	2.64	127	.245	.299	88-1-6	.273	10*	95	24		2.1
1973	LA N★	16	11	.593	33	33	12-3	0-0	236.2	227	97	20	2	61-2	86	3.31	105	.258	.306	78-0-8	.154	-1	102	6		0.7
1974	Hou N	9	9	.500	23	21	7-2	0-0	138.1	158	67	8	2	47-1	45	3.71	94	.292	.348	46-0-2	.283	3	104	-5		-0.2
	StL N	0	2	.000	8	2	0	0-0	22.2	26	14	1	0	11-5	6	4.37	83	.286	.363	7	.000	-1	121	-3		-0.2
	Year	9	11	.450	31	23	7-2	0-0	161	184	81	9	2	58-6	51	3.80	92	.291	.350	53-0-2	.245	3	105	-7		-0.8
1975	Chi A	7	16	.304	37	37	5	0-0	204.1	237	110	16	2	92-2	63	4.36	89	.294	.365	0	—	0	81	-11		-0.7
Total	18	196	195	.501	541	488	140-40	1-0	3460.2	3471	1435	249	45	940-93	1612	3.30	104	.263	.313	1099-8-69	.188	38	98	62		13.7

OSTEEN, DARRELL Milton Darrell B2.14.1943 Oklahoma City OK   BR/TR/6-1/170* d9.2 Mil 1970

YEAR	TM LG	W	L	PCT	G	GS	CG-SHO	SV-BS	IP	H	R	HR	HB	BB-IB	SO	ERA	AERA	OAV	OOB	AB-HR-SH	AVG	PB	SUP	APR	DL	PW
1965	Cin N	0	0	—	3	0	0	0	4	4	0	0	0	4-0	1	0.00	—	.200	.429	0	—	0		1		0.1
1966	Cin N	0	0	—	13	0	0	1	15	26	21	3	0	9-2	17	12.00	33	.371	.443	2	.500	0*		-12		-1.0
1967	Cin N	0	2	.000	10	0	0	2	14.1	10	10	1	3	13-1	13	6.28	60	.196	.388	1-0-1	.000	-0*		-3		-0.5
1970	Oak A	1	0	1.000	3	1	0	0-0	5.2	9	4	0	0	3-0	3	6.35	56	.346	.414	2	.000	-0	126	-2		-0.2
Total	4	1	2	.200	29	1	0	3-0	39	49	35	4	3	29-3	34	8.05	47	.299	.418	5-0-1	.200	0	126	-16		-0.5

OSTENDORF, FRED Frederick K. B8.5.1892 Baltimore MD D3.2.1965 Kecoughtan (now part of Hampton) VA   BL/TL/6-0.5/169 d7.16

YEAR	TM LG	W	L	PCT	G	GS	CG-SHO	SV-BS	IP	H	R	HR	HB	BB-IB	SO	ERA	AERA	OAV	OOB	AB-HR-SH	AVG	PB	SUP	APR	DL	PW
1914	Ind F	0	0	—	1	0	0	0	2	5	5	0	1	2	0	22.50	14	.500	.615		.000	-0		-3		-0.2

OSTER, BILL William Charles B1.2.1933 New York NY   BL/TL/6-3/198 d8.23 Col NYU

YEAR	TM LG	W	L	PCT	G	GS	CG-SHO	SV-BS	IP	H	R	HR	HB	BB-IB	SO	ERA	AERA	OAV	OOB	AB-HR-SH	AVG	PB	SUP	APR	DL	PW
1954	Phi A	0	1	.000	8	1	0	0	15.2	19	15	2	0	12	5	6.32	62	.311	.425	3	.333	0	45	-5		-0.3

OSTERMUELLER, FRITZ Frederick Raymond B9.15.1907 Quincy IL D12.17.1957 Quincy IL   BL/TL/5-11/175 d4.21 Mil 1945

YEAR	TM LG	W	L	PCT	G	GS	CG-SHO	SV-BS	IP	H	R	HR	HB	BB-IB	SO	ERA	AERA	OAV	OOB	AB-HR-SH	AVG	PB	SUP	APR	DL	PW
1934	Bos A	10	13	.435	33	23	10	3	198.2	200	93	7	1	99	75	3.49	138	.262	.348	78	.167	-2	72	27		2.1
1935	Bos A	7	8	.467	22	19	10	1	137.2	135	67	0	3	78	41	3.92	121	.257	.356	49-0-2	.286	1	80	13		1.2
1936	Bos A	10	16	.385	43	23	7-1	2	180.2	210	115	8	3	84	90	4.88	109	.288	.364	64-0-4	.234	0	91	7		0.9
1937	Bos A	3	7	.300	25	7	2	1	86.2	101	64	7	1	44	29	4.98	95	.286	.367	33-0-3	.333	3	108	-6		-0.4
1938	Bos A	13	5	.722	31	18	10-1	2	176.2	199	98	15	3	58	46	4.58	108	.275	.331	74-0-3	.216	2*	127	9		0.9
1939	Bos A	11	7	.611	34	20	8	4	159.1	173	86	6	2	58	66	4.24	112	.277	.341	56-0-5	.161	-2	122	9		0.9
1940	Bos A	5	9	.357	31	16	5	0	143.2	166	86	7	0	70	80	4.95	91	.284	.361	46	.315	4*	100	-7		-0.3
1941	StL A	0	3	.000	15	2	0	0	46	45	24	6	3	23	16	4.50	96	.257	.343	14-0-2	.214	0*	121	-1		-0.1
1942	StL A	3	1	.750	10	4	2	1	43.2	46	22	4	0	17	21	3.71	100	.266	.332	16	.188	-0	144	0		-0.0
1943	StL A	0	2	.000	11	3	0	0	28.2	36	16	1	0	13	4	5.02	66	.321	.392	7	.286	-0	59	-4		-0.5
	Bro N	1	1	.500	7	5	2	0	27.1	21	11	0	0	12	15	3.29	102	.212	.297	11-0-1	.000	-1*	51	0		0.1
1944	Bro N	2	1	.667	10	4	3	0	41.2	46	17	0	0	12	17	3.24	110	.267	.315	13-0-1	.154	-0*	94	2		0.0
	Pit N	11	7	.611	28	24	14-1	1	204.2	201	79	7	1	65	80	2.73	136	.260	.318	80-0-1	.250	2*	102	21		1.9
	Year	13	8	.619	38	28	17-1	2	246.1	247	96	7	1	77	97	2.81	131	.261	.318	93-0-2	.237	2*	101	23		2.1

YEAR	TM LG	W	L	PCT	G	GS	CG-SHO	SV-BS	IP	H	R	HR	HB	BB-IB	SO	ERA	AERA	OAV	OOB	AB-HR-SH	AVG	PB	SUP	APR	DL	PW
1945	Pit N	5	4	.556	14	11	4-1	0	80.2	74	45	6	2	37	29	4.57	86	.236	.321	28-0-1	.321	2	111	-4		-0.2
1946	Pit N	13	10	.565	27	25	16-2	0	193.1	193	70	5	3	56	57	2.84	124	.263	.318	64-0-5	.328	6*	94	15		2.5
1947	Pit N	12	10	.545	26	24	12-3	0	183	181	94	18	1	68	66	3.84	110	.254	.320	64-0-6	.188	-0	124	6		0.5
1948	Pit N	8	11	.421	23	22	10-2	0	134.1	143	73	13	1	41	43	4.42	92	.262	.315	44-0-3	.182	-0	80	-5		-0.7
Total	15	114	115	.498	390	246	113-11	15	2066.2	2170	1062	105	21	835	774	3.99	109	.268	.337	749-0-37	.234	16	100	82		9.7

OSTING, JIMMY James Michael B4.7.1977 Louisville KY BR/TL/6-5/190* [AtlN95 4/113] d5.2

2001	SD N	0	0	—	3	0	0	0-0	2	1	0	0	0	2-1	3	0.00	—	.143	.333	0	—	0		1		0.0
2002	Mil N	0	2	.000	3	3	0	0-0	12	18	11	3	0	10-0	7	7.50	55	.340	.444	3-0-1	.000	-0	15	-5	33	-0.6
Total	2	0	2	.000	6	3	0	0-0	14	19	11	3	0	12-1	10	6.43	64	.317	.431	3-0-1	.000	-0	15	-5	33	-0.6

OSTROWSKI, JOE Joseph Paul "Professor","Specs" B11.15.1916 W.Wyoming PA D1.3.2003 Wilkes-Barre PA BL/TL/6-0/180* d7.18 Col Scranton

1948	StL A	4	6	.400	26	9	3	3	78.1	108	54	6	0	17	20	5.97	76	.333	.367	18-0-3	.222	1	70	-10		-1.0
1949	StL A	8	8	.500	40	13	4	2	141	185	94	16	0	27	34	4.79	95	.307	.337	37	.189	2	103	-6		-0.4
1950	StL A	2	4	.333	9	7	2	0	57.1	57	22	2	0	7	15	2.51	197	.251	.274	18	.222	1	68	13		1.4
	NY A	1	1	.500	21	4	1	3	43.2	50	26	11	0	15	15	5.15	83	.294	.351	9-0-1	.111	-0	147	-4		-0.2
	Year	3	5	.375	30	11	3	3	101	107	48	13	0	22	30	3.65	128	.270	.308	27-0-1	.185	1	95	11		1.2
1951	†NY A	6	4	.600	34	3	2	5	95.1	103	44	4	1	18	30	3.49	110	.279	.314	28	.107	-2	209	3		0.1
1952	NY A	2	2	.500	20	1	0	2	40	56	31	5	1	14	17	5.62	59	.327	.382	8-0-2	.000	-1	105	-12		-1.4
Total	5	23	25	.479	150	37	12	15	455.2	559	271	44	2	98	131	4.54	95	.300	.336	118-0-6	.161	-0	104	-16		-1.5

OSUNA, AL Alfonso B8.10.1965 Inglewood CA BR/TL/6-3/200* [HouN87 16/418] d9.2 Col Stanford

1990	Hou N	2	0	1.000	12	0	0	0-1	11.1	10	6	1	0	6-1	6	4.76	78	.270	.396	0	—	0		-1		-0.2
1991	Hou N	7	6	.538	71	0	0	12-9	81.2	59	39	5	3	46-5	68	3.42	103	.201	.311	2-0-1	.000	-0		-1		-0.2
1992	Hou N	6	3	.667	66	0	0	0-2	61.2	52	29	8	1	38-5	37	4.23	80	.236	.343	0	—	0		-5		-0.6
1993	Hou N	1	1	.500	44	0	0	2-0	25.1	17	10	3	1	13-2	21	3.20	121	.200	.301	0	—	0		2		0.2
1994	LA N	2	0	1.000	15	0	0	0-1	8.2	5	6	0	1	4-0	7	6.23	64	.333	.395	0	—	0		-2		-0.4
1996	SD N	0	0	—	10	0	0	0-1	4	5	1	0	1	2-1	4	2.25	179	.313	.400	1	.000	-0		1		0.0
Total	6	18	10	.643	218	0	0	14-14	192.2	156	91	17	9	109-14	143	3.83	93	.226	.332	3-0-1	.000	-0		-6		-1.2

OSUNA, ANTONIO Antonio Pedro B4.12.1973 Guasave, Sinaloa, Mexico BR/TR/5-11/206(160-225) d4.25

1995	†LA N	2	4	.333	39	0	0	0-2	44.2	39	22	5	1	20-2	46	4.43	87	.241	.326	2	.000	-0		-1	28	-0.2
1996	†LA N	9	6	.600	73	0	0	4-5	84	65	33	6	2	32-12	85	3.00	131	.220	.296	1	.000	0		9		1.5
1997	LA N	3	4	.429	48	0	0	0-0	61.2	46	15	6	1	19-2	68	2.19	178	.209	.274	2	.500	0		13		1.5
1998	LA N	7	1	.875	54	0	0	6-5	64.2	50	26	8	2	32-0	72	3.06	132	.214	.311	2	.000	-0		7	19	0.8
1999	LA N	0	0	—	5	0	0	0-0	4.2	4	5	0	1	3-0	5	7.71	56	.222	.364	0	—	0		-2	166	-0.1
2000	LA N	3	6	.333	46	0	0	0-3	67.1	57	30	7	2	35-2	70	3.74	119	.229	.325	2	.000	-0		6	32	0.6
2001	Chi A	0	0	—	4	0	0	0-1	4.1	8	10	3	1	2-1	6	20.77	22	.421	.478	0	—	0		-7	179	-0.3
2002	Chi A	8	2	.800	59	0	0	11-3	67.2	64	32	1	4	28-4	66	3.86	117	.250	.330	0	—	0		5		0.8
2003	NY A	2	5	.286	48	0	0	0-1	50.2	58	25	9	1	20-3	47	3.73	118	.282	.348	0	—	0		4	49	0.5
2004	SD N	2	1	.667	31	0	0	0-2	36.2	32	11	3	1	11-0	36	2.45	161	.232	.291	0	—	0		7	101	0.5
2005	Was N	0	0	—	4	0	0	0-0	2.1	9	11	2	0	7-1	0	42.43	10	.600	.696	0	—	0		-10	175	-0.5
Total	11	36	29	.554	411	0	0	21-22	488.2	432	217	44	17	209-27	501	3.68	112	.238	.320	9	.111	-0		31	749	5.1

OSWALT, ROY Roy Edward B8.29.1977 Kosciusko MS BR/TR/6-0/170(170-185) [HouN96 23/684] d5.6 Col Holmes (MS) CC

2001	Hou N	14	3	.824	28	20	3-1	0-0	141.2	126	48	13	6	24-2	144	2.73	168	.235	.273	47-0-3	.191	0	126	27		3.1
2002	Hou N	19	9	.679	35	34	0	0-0	233	215	86	17	5	62-34	208	3.01	144	.247	.299	77-0-7	.130	-1	102	32		3.5
2003	Hou N	10	5	.667	21	21	0	0-0	127.1	116	48	15	5	29-0	108	2.97	149	.246	.296	39-0-7	.179	-0	107	19	73	2.1
2004	Hou N	20	10	.667	36	35	2-2	0-0	237	233	100	17	11	62-5	206	3.49	125	.260	.315	71-0-13	.141	-1	109	22		2.5
2005	†Hou N★	20	12	.625	35	35	4-1	0-0	241.2	243	85	18	8	48-3	184	2.94	143	.262	.302	73-0-7	.178	0	86	34		4.4
Total	5	83	39	.680	155	145	9-4	0-0	980.2	933	367	80	35	225-14	850	3.07	142	.252	.299	307-0-37	.160	-1	104	134	73	15.6

OTEY, BILL William Tilford "Steamboat Bill" B12.16.1886 Dayton OH D4.23.1931 Dayton OH BL/TL/6-2/181 d9.27

1907	Pit N	0	1	.000	3	2	1	0	16.1	23	11	1	1	4	5	4.41	55	.319	.364	4	.250	0	88	-3		-0.2
1910	Was A	0	1	.000	9	1	1	0	34.2	40	17	1	1	6	12	3.38	74	.301	.336	13	.385	2	27	-3		0.0
1911	Was A	1	3	.250	12	2	0	0	49.2	68	44	2	3	15	16	6.34	52	.333	.387	17-0-1	.059	-2	66	-15		-1.1
Total	3	1	5	.167	24	5	2	0	100.2	131	72	4	5	25	33	5.01	57	.320	.367	34-0-1	.206	0	64	-21		-1.3

OTIS, HARRY Harry George "Cannonball" B10.5.1886 W.New York NJ D1.29.1976 Teaneck NJ BR/TL/6-0/180 d9.5

| 1909 | Cle A | 2 | 2 | .500 | 5 | 3 | 0 | 0 | 26.1 | 26 | 11 | 0 | 3 | 18 | 6 | 1.37 | 187 | .283 | .416 | 9-0-1 | .111 | -0 | 83 | 2 | | 0.2 |

O'TOOLE, DENNIS Dennis Joseph B3.13.1949 Chicago IL BR/TR/6-3/195* [ChiA67 6/113] d9.8 b-Jim

1969	Chi A	0	0	—	2	0	0	0-0	4	5	3	0	0	2-0	4	6.75	57	.333	.389	0	—	0		-1		-0.1
1970	Chi A	0	0	—	3	0	0	0-0	3.1	5	1	0	0	2-0	3	2.70	144	.357	.412	0	—	0		0		0.0
1971	Chi A	0	0	—	1	0	0	0-0	2	0	0	0	0	1-0	2	0.00	—	.000	.143	0	—	0		1		0.0
1972	Chi A	0	0	—	3	0	0	0-0	5	10	3	0	0	2-0	5	5.40	68	.417	.462	0	—	0		-1		-0.1
1973	Chi A	0	0	—	6	0	0	0-0	16	23	11	3	0	3-0	8	5.63	70	.329	.356	0	—	0		-3		-0.1
Total	5	0	0	—	15	0	0	0-0	30.1	43	18	3	0	10-0	22	5.04	75	.333	.376	0	—	0		-4		-0.3

O'TOOLE, JIM James Jerome B1.10.1937 Chicago IL BB/TL/6-0/198(190-205) d9.26 b-Dennis Col Wisconsin-Madison

1958	Cin N	0	1	.000	1	1	0	0	7	4	2	0	0	4	4	1.29	372	.154	.290	2	.000	-0	22	2		0.2
1959	Cin N	5	8	.385	28	19	3-1	0	129.1	144	78	14	4	73-2	68	5.15	79	.287	.380	37-0-3	.135	-0*	127	-13		-1.1
1960	Cin N	12	12	.500	34	31	7-2	1	196.1	198	94	14	4	66-4	124	3.80	100	.263	.323	66-0-7	.106	-3	86	0		-0.5
1961	†Cin N	19	9	.679	39	35	11-3	2	252.2	229	101	16	3	93-7	178	3.10	131	.240	.309	93-0-4	.172	-1	109	26		2.6
1962	Cin N	16	13	.552	36	34	11-3	0	251.2	222	115	20	4	87-4	170	3.50	115	.238	.305	91-0-3	.110	-5	116	12		0.7
1963	Cin N★	17	14	.548	33	32	12-5	0	234.1	208	85	13	3	74-4	146	2.88	116	.239	.285	74-0-6	.149	-1	104	12		1.3
1964	Cin N	17	7	.708	30	30	9-3	0	220	194	71	9	3	51-7	145	2.66	136	.235	.277	70-0-7	.100	-1	91	24		2.4
1965	Cin N	3	10	.231	29	22	2	1	127.2	154	98	14	3	47-4	71	5.92	63	.294	.352	45-0-3	.089	-2	126	-31		-3.1
1966	Cin N	5	7	.417	25	24	2	0	142	139	65	16	3	49-6	96	3.55	110	.254	.317	47-0-1	.128	-2	98	3		0.0
1967	Chi A	4	3	.571	15	10	1-1	0	54.1	53	21	4	1	18-2	37	2.82	110	.251	.313	13-0-1	.077	-1	70	2	63	0.1
Total	10	98	84	.538	270	238	58-18	4	1615.1	1545	730	119	26	546-40	1039	3.57	106	.251	.313	538-0-35	.125	-15	104	37	63	2.6

O'TOOLE, MARTY Martin James B11.27.1888 Wm.Penn PA D2.18.1949 Aberdeen WA BR/TR/5-11/175 d9.21

1908	Cin N	0	1	.000	3	2	1	0	15	15	8	0	0	7	5	2.40	96	.273	.355	5	.200	-0	214	-1		-0.1
1911	Pit N	3	2	.600	5	5	3	0	38	28	17	1	0	20	34	2.37	145	.215	.320	14	.357	2	105	3		0.5
1912	Pit N	15	17	.469	37	36	17-6	0	275.1	237	110	4	2	159	150	2.71	120	.241	.348	99-0-2	.222	2	96	16		1.9
1913	Pit N	6	8	.429	26	16	7	1	144.2	148	69	3	3	55	58	3.30	92	.271	.341	53-0-1	.132	-2	136	-5		-0.7
1914	Pit N	1	8	.111	19	9	1	1	92.1	92	56	2	0	47	36	4.68	57	.270	.358	30	.167	0	60	-20		-1.8
	NY N	1	1	.500	10	5	2	0	34	34	17	0	0	12	13	4.24	63	.262	.324	10-0-1	.300	1	92	-5		-0.2
	Year	2	9	.182	29	14	3	1	126.1	126	73	2	0	59	49	4.56	58	.268	.349	40-0-1	.200	1	71	-20		-2.0
Total	5	27	36	.429	100	73	31-6	2	599.1	554	277	10	5	300	296	3.21	95	.254	.345	211-0-4	.204	2	104	-12		-0.4

OTSUKA, AKINORI Akinori B1.13.1972 Chiba, Japan BR/TR/6-0/200* d4.6

2004	SD N	7	2	.778	73	0	0	2-5	77.1	56	16	6	2	26-6	87	1.75	226	.199	.266	1	.000	-0		21		2.3
2005	†SD N	2	8	.200	66	0	0	1-6	62.2	55	28	3	2	34-8	60	3.59	108	.234	.336	1	.000	-0		2		0.2
Total	2	9	10	.474	139	0	0	3-11	140	111	44	9	4	60-14	147	2.57	152	.215	.299	2	.000	-0		23		2.5

OTTEN, JIM James Edward B7.1.1951 Lewistown MT BR/TR/6-2/195* [ChiA73 2/45] d7.31 Col Arizona St.

1974	Chi A	1	0	1.000	5	1	0	0-0	16.1	22	11	0	1	7-2	11	5.51	68	.324	.432	0	—	0		47	-3		-0.2
1975	Chi A	0	0	—	2	0	0	0-0	5.1	4	5	1	0	7-0	3	6.75	58	.235	.440	0	—	0		-2		-0.1
1976	Chi A	0	0	—	2	0	0	0-0	6	9	6	0	0	2-0	3	4.50	79	.333	.379	0	—	0		-2		-0.1
1980	StL N	0	5	.000	31	4	0	0-0	55.1	71	38	7	0	26-7	38	5.53	68	.323	.393	5	.200	-0		65	-10		-0.9
1981	StL N	0	1	.000	24	0	0	0-0	35.2	44	23	3	0	25-7	20	5.30	68	.321	.405	2-0-1	.000	-0		-6	22	-0.4
Total	5	1	6	.143	64	5	0	0-0	118.2	150	83	7	1	67-14	75	5.46	68	.320	.404	7-0-1	.143	-0		62	-23	22	-1.7

OTTO, DAVE David Alan B11.12.1964 Chicago IL BL/TL/6-7/210* [OakA85 2/39] d9.8 Col Missouri

| 1987 | Oak A | 0 | 0 | — | 3 | 0 | 0 | 0-0 | 7 | 6 | 7 | 1 | 0 | 4-0 | 3 | 9.00 | 46 | .304 | .333 | 0 | — | 0 | | -3 | | -0.2 |
| 1988 | Oak A | 0 | 0 | — | 3 | 0 | 0 | 0-0 | 10 | 9 | 2 | 0 | 0 | 7-0 | 7 | 1.80 | 211 | .243 | .349 | 0 | — | 0 | | 108 | 2 | | 0.1 |

YEAR	TM LG	W	L	PCT	G	GS	CG-SHO	SV-BS	IP	H	R	HR	HB	BB-IB	SO	ERA	AERA	OAV	OOB	AB-HR-SH	AVG	PB	SUP	APR	DL	PW
1989	Oak A	0	0	—	1	1	0	0-0	6.2	6	2	0	0	2-0	4	2.70	137	.261	.320	0	—	0	98	1		0.0
1990	Oak A	0	0	—	2	0	0	0-0	2.1	3	3	0	0	3-0	2	7.71	48	.300	.462	0	—	0		-1	158	-0.1
1991	Cle A	2	8	.200	18	14	1	0-0	100	108	52	7	4	27-6	47	4.23	99	.283	.333	0	—	0	77	0		0.0
1992	Cle A	5	9	.357	18	16	0	0-0	80.1	110	64	12	1	33-0	32	7.06	56	.333	.395	0	—	0	71	-25	16	-3.6
1993	Pit N	3	4	.429	28	8	0	0-0	68	85	40	9	3	28-1	30	5.03	81	.317	.387	18-0-1	.222	1	91	-7		-0.5
1994	Chi N	0	1	.000	36	0	0	0-1	45	49	20	4	1	22-4	19	3.80	111	.283	.367	2	.000	-0		2		0.1
Total 8		10	22	.313	109	41	1	0-1	318.1	377	189	33	9	122-11	144	5.06	81	.303	.367	20-0-1	.200	1	78	-31	174	-4.2

OVERALL, ORVAL Orval B2.2.1881 Farmersville CA D7.14.1947 Fresno CA BB/TR/6-2/214 d4.16 Col California-Davis

YEAR	TM LG	W	L	PCT	G	GS	CG-SHO	SV-BS	IP	H	R	HR	HB	BB-IB	SO	ERA	AERA	OAV	OOB	AB-HR-SH	AVG	PB	SUP	APR	DL	PW
1905	Cin N	18	23	.439	42	39	32-2	0	318	290	146	4	14	147	173	2.86	116	.252	.343	117-0-5	.145	-2	85	16		1.7
1906	Cin N	4	5	.444	13	10	6	0	82.1	77	52	1	4	46	33	4.26	65	.253	.359	31	.194	0	130	-12		1.2
	†Chi N	12	3	.800	18	14	13-2	1	144	116	43	1	4	51	94	1.88	141	.217	.290	53-0-3	.170	-1	118	12		1.2
	Year	16	8	.667	31	24	19-2	1	226.1	193	95	2	8	97	127	2.74	98	.230	.316	84-0-3	.179	-1	123	-3		-0.1
1907	†Chi N	23	7	.767	36	30	26-**8**	3	268.1	201	62	3	11	69	141	1.68	149	.208	.268	94-0-8	.213	3	112	28		**3.9**
1908	†Chi N	15	11	.577	37	27	16-4	4	225	165	74	3	2	78	167	1.92	123	.208	.280	70-0-8	.129	-0*	101	7		0.8
1909	Chi N	20	11	.645	38	32	23-**9**	3	285	204	66	1	8	80	**205**	1.42	179	**.198**	.262	96-2-4	.229	8	100	35		5.2
1910	†Chi N	12	6	.667	23	21	11-4	1	144.2	106	44	2	1	54	92	2.68	108	.212	.291	41-0-6	.122	-1*	103	8		1.0
1913	Chi N	4	5	.444	11	9	6-1	0	68	73	33	1	1	26	30	3.31	96	.284	.352	24-0-1	.250	2	83	-1		0.1
Total 7		108	71	.603	218	182	133-30	12	1535.1	1232	520	16	45	551	935	2.23	123	.223	.298	526-2-35	.179	9	101	93		12.6

OVERMIRE, STUBBY Frank W. B5.16.1919 Moline MI D3.3.1977 Lakeland FL BR/TL/5-7/170* d4.25 C4 Col Western Michigan

YEAR	TM LG	W	L	PCT	G	GS	CG-SHO	SV-BS	IP	H	R	HR	HB	BB-IB	SO	ERA	AERA	OAV	OOB	AB-HR-SH	AVG	PB	SUP	APR	DL	PW
1943	Det A	7	6	.538	29	18	8-3	1	147	135	56	5	1	38	53	3.18	111	.243	.293	42-0-5	.167	0	89	7		0.6
1944	Det A	11	11	.500	32	28	11-3	1	199.2	214	84	2	2	41	57	3.07	116	.271	.309	63-0-5	.175	1	101	10		1.3
1945	†Det A	9	9	.500	31	22	9	4	162.1	189	81	6	3	42	36	3.88	91	.294	.341	53-0-6	.189	0	102	-5		-0.5
1946	Det A	5	7	.417	24	13	3	1	97.1	106	54	6	0	29	34	4.62	99	.274	.325	33-0-4	.152	-1	128	-9		-1.1
1947	Det A	11	5	.688	28	17	7-3	0	140.2	142	62	9	1	44	33	3.77	100	.259	.315	47-0-2	.149	-1	108	3		0.2
1948	Det A	3	4	.429	37	4	0	3	66.1	89	48	5	2	31	14	5.97	73	.326	.395	14	.071	-1	150	-11		-1.1
1949	Det A	1	3	.250	14	1	0	0	17.1	29	21	2	1	9	3	9.87	42	.377	.448	3	.333	-1	22	-11		-1.9
1950	StL A	9	12	.429	31	19	8-2	0	161	200	89	11	1	45	39	4.19	118	.298	.343	48-0-2	.167	1	69	12		1.3
1951	StL A	1	6	.143	8	7	3	0	53.1	61	26	5	0	21	13	3.54	124	.281	.345	14-0-3	.071	-1	40	4		0.3
	NY A	1	1	.500	15	4	1	0	44.2	50	27	2	2	18	14	4.63	87	.287	.361	7	.143	-0	133	-5		-0.2
	Year	2	7	.222	23	11	4	0	98	111	53	7	2	39	27	4.04	102	.284	.352	21-0-3	.095	-0	72	0		0.1
1952	StL A	0	3	.000	17	4	0	0	44	44	21	3	0	7	10	3.73	105	.270	.300	11	.182	-0	50	0		0.0
Total 10		58	67	.464	266	137	50-11	10	1130.2	1169	569	56	11	325	301	3.96	98	.280	.330	335-0-27	.161	-1	94	-5		-1.1

OVERY, MIKE Harry Michael B1.27.1951 Clinton IL BR/TR/6-2/190 [AnaA73*S2/28] d8.14 Col Olivet Nazarene

YEAR	TM LG	W	L	PCT	G	GS	CG-SHO	SV-BS	IP	H	R	HR	HB	BB-IB	SO	ERA	AERA	OAV	OOB	AB-HR-SH	AVG	PB	SUP	APR	DL	PW
1976	Cal A	0	2	.000	5	0	0	0-2	7.1	6	5	1	1	3-1	8	6.14	55	.214	.313	0	—	0		-2		-0.4

OVITZ, ERNIE Ernest Gayhart B10.7.1885 Mineral Point WI D9.11.1980 Green Bay WI BR/TR/5-8.5/156 d6.22 Col Illinois

YEAR	TM LG	W	L	PCT	G	GS	CG-SHO	SV-BS	IP	H	R	HR	HB	BB-IB	SO	ERA	AERA	OAV	OOB	AB-HR-SH	AVG	PB	SUP	APR	DL	PW
1911	Chi N	0	0	—	1	0	0	0	2	3	2	0	0	3	3	4.50	74	.375	.545	0	—	0		-1		0.0

OWCHINKO, BOB Robert Dennis B1.1.1955 Detroit MI BL/TL/6-2/195* [SDN76 1/5] d9.25 Col Eastern Michigan

YEAR	TM LG	W	L	PCT	G	GS	CG-SHO	SV-BS	IP	H	R	HR	HB	BB-IB	SO	ERA	AERA	OAV	OOB	AB-HR-SH	AVG	PB	SUP	APR	DL	PW
1976	SD N	0	2	.000	2	2	0	0-0	4.1	11	8	0	0	3-1	4	16.62	20	.478	.538	1-0-1	.000	-0	120	-6		-1.0
1977	SD N	9	12	.429	30	28	3-2	0-0	170	191	93	20	0	67-5	101	4.45	80	.287	.351	49-0-11	.082	-2	113	-16		-2.0
1978	SD N	10	13	.435	36	33	4-1	0-1	202.1	198	87	14	1	78-12	94	3.56	94	.263	.336	63-0-6	.175	1	79	-3		-0.2
1979	SD N	6	12	.333	42	20	2	0-1	149.1	144	73	16	2	55-6	66	3.74	95	.259	.327	33-0-7	.121	0	90	-5		-0.6
1980	Cle A	2	9	.182	29	14	1-1	0-0	114.1	138	71	13	2	47-2	66	5.27	78	.301	.365	0	—	0	63	-13		-1.1
1981	†Oak A	4	3	.571	29	0	0	2-4	39.1	34	15	2	1	19-2	26	3.20	110	.245	.335	0	—	0		2		0.3
1982	Oak A	2	4	.333	54	0	0	3-3	102	111	60	11	0	52-5	67	5.21	76	.275	.356	0	—	0		-12		-0.8
1983	Pit N	0	0	—	1	0	0	0-1	2	2	1	1	0	0-0	0	∞		1.000	1.000	0	—	0		-1		-0.1
1984	Cin N	3	5	.375	49	4	0	2-1	94	91	47	10	0	39-2	60	4.12	92	.253	.325	12-0-1	.167	1	99	-3	16	-0.2
1986	Mon N	1	0	1.000	3	3	0	0-0	15	17	6	1	0	3-0	6	3.60	104	.288	.323	5	.200	0	119	1		0.1
Total 10		37	60	.381	275	104	10-4	7-11	890.2	937	461	88	6	363-35	490	4.28	85	.274	.343	163-0-26	.135	-0	89	-56	16	-5.6

OWEN, FRANK Frank Malcolm "Yip" B12.23.1879 Ypsilanti MI D11.24.1942 Dearborn MI BB/TR/5-11/160 d4.26

YEAR	TM LG	W	L	PCT	G	GS	CG-SHO	SV-BS	IP	H	R	HR	HB	BB-IB	SO	ERA	AERA	OAV	OOB	AB-HR-SH	AVG	PB	SUP	APR	DL	PW
1901	Det A	1	3	.250	8	5	3	0	56	70	43	1	4	30	17	4.34	89	.302	.391	20-0-2	.050	-2*	74	-3		-0.3
1903	Chi A	8	12	.400	26	20	15-1	1	167.1	167	85	1	7	44	66	3.50	80	.259	.314	57-0-2	.123	-1	94	-9		-1.0
1904	Chi A	21	15	.583	37	36	34-4	1	315	243	95	2	11	61	103	1.94	126	.214	.261	107-2-3	.215	5	114	18		3.2
1905	Chi A	21	13	.618	42	38	32-3	0	334	276	110	4	9	56	125	2.10	117	.227	.266	124-0-8	.145	4	109	15		1.3
1906	†Chi A	22	13	.629	42	36	27-7	0	293	289	114	4	4	54	66	2.33	104	.261	.288	103-0-5	.136	-2	116	5		0.6
1907	Chi A	2	3	.400	11	4	2	0	47	43	22	1	0	13	15	2.49	96	.246	.298	16	.250	0	92	-2		-0.2
1908	Chi A	6	7	.462	25	14	5-1	0	140	142	79	2	3	37	48	3.41	68	.260	.310	50-0-1	.180	1	93	-21		-1.7
1909	Chi A	1	1	.500	3	2	1	0	16	19	8	0	1	3	3	4.50	52	.279	.319	6	.167	-0	120	-3		-0.4
Total 8		82	67	.550	194	155	119-16	2	1368.1	1249	556	17	39	298	443	2.55	100	.244	.290	483-2-21	.159	-0	106	0		1.5

OWENS, JIM James Philip "Bear" B1.16.1934 Gifford PA BR/TR/5-11/190(180-200) d4.19 Mil 1957-58 C6

YEAR	TM LG	W	L	PCT	G	GS	CG-SHO	SV-BS	IP	H	R	HR	HB	BB-IB	SO	ERA	AERA	OAV	OOB	AB-HR-SH	AVG	PB	SUP	APR	DL	PW
1955	Phi N	0	2	.000	4	2	0	0	8.2	13	8	2	0	7-0	6	8.31	48	.382	.488	1-0-1	.000	-0	79	-4		-0.7
1956	Phi N	0	4	.000	10	5	0	0	29.2	35	26	3	2	22-1	22	7.28	51	.313	.431	6-0-1	.167	0	90	-11		-1.3
1958	Phi N	1	0	1.000	1	1	0	0	7	4	4	1	0	5-0	3	2.57	154	.154	.290	2	.000	0	136	0		0.0
1959	Phi N	12	12	.500	31	30	11-1	1	221.1	203	97	14	4	73-11	135	3.21	128	.244	.306	75-0-3	.120	-1	73	18		1.7
1960	Phi N	4	14	.222	31	22	6	0	150	182	95	21	1	64-7	83	5.04	77	.299	.365	44-0-3	.068	-3	78	-19		-2.4
1961	Phi N	5	10	.333	20	17	3	0	106.2	119	62	8	0	32-2	38	4.47	91	.287	.335	27-0-5	.074	-1*	65	-6		-0.9
1962	Phi N	2	4	.333	23	12	1	0	69.2	90	53	12	0	33-1	21	6.33	61	.318	.388	14-0-3	.143	0	113	-19		-1.4
1963	Cin N	0	2	.000	19	3	0	4	42.1	42	28	6	0	24-2	29	5.31	63	.259	.353	8	.125	0	137	-9		-0.6
1964	Hou N	8	7	.533	48	11	0	6	118	115	48	7	0	32-6	88	3.28	104	.262	.309	29-0-1	.103	-1	89	3		0.2
1965	Hou N	6	5	.545	50	0	0	8	71.1	64	28	4	0	29-8	53	3.28	102	.238	.310	8-0-1	.125	-0		1		0.2
1966	Hou N	4	7	.364	40	0	0	2	50	53	29	5	1	17-7	32	4.68	73	.273	.332	4	.000	0		-7		-1.4
1967	Hou N	0	1	.000	10	0	0	1	10.2	12	5	1	0	2-1	6	4.22	78	.308	.341	0	—	0		-1		-0.1
Total 12		42	68	.382	286	103	21-1	21	885.1	932	483	84	8	340-46	516	4.31	88	.273	.338	218-0-18	.101	-7	84	-54		-6.7

OWNBEY, RICK Richard Wayne B10.20.1957 Corona CA BR/TR/6-3/185(170-185) [NYN80 13/313] d8.17 Col Santa Ana (CA) JC [DL 1985 StL N 42]

YEAR	TM LG	W	L	PCT	G	GS	CG-SHO	SV-BS	IP	H	R	HR	HB	BB-IB	SO	ERA	AERA	OAV	OOB	AB-HR-SH	AVG	PB	SUP	APR	DL	PW
1982	NY N	1	2	.333	8	8	2	0-0	50.1	44	23	3	0	43-1	28	3.75	98	.242	.382	15-0-1	.200	1*	108	0		0.0
1983	NY N	1	3	.250	10	4	0	0-0	34.2	31	19	4	1	21-0	19	4.67	79	.240	.351	9-0-1	.111	-0*	66	-3		-0.4
1984	StL N	0	3	.000	4	0	0	0-0	19	23	13	1	0	8-0	11	4.74	74	.303	.360	4-0-2	.000	-0*	50	-4		-0.5
1986	StL N	1	3	.250	17	3	0	0-0	42.2	47	20	4	2	19-0	25	3.80	97	.294	.372	7-0-3	.000	-1	72	-1		-0.2
Total 4		3	11	.214	39	19	2	0-0	146.2	145	75	12	3	91-1	83	4.11	89	.265	.369	35-0-7	.114	-1	82	-8	42	-1.1

OXSPRING, CHRIS Chris Andrew B5.13.1977 Ipswich, Queensland, Australia BL/TR/6-0/185 d9.2

YEAR	TM LG	W	L	PCT	G	GS	CG-SHO	SV-BS	IP	H	R	HR	HB	BB-IB	SO	ERA	AERA	OAV	OOB	AB-HR-SH	AVG	PB	SUP	APR	DL	PW
2005	SD N	0	0	—	5	0	0	0-0	12	9	8	2	0	6-0	11	3.75	103	.225	.313	2	.000	-0		-1		-0.1

OZMER, DOC Horace Robert B5.25.1901 Atlanta GA D12.28.1970 Atlanta GA BR/TR/5-10.5/185 d5.11 Col Milligan

YEAR	TM LG	W	L	PCT	G	GS	CG-SHO	SV-BS	IP	H	R	HR	HB	BB-IB	SO	ERA	AERA	OAV	OOB	AB-HR-SH	AVG	PB	SUP	APR	DL	PW
1923	Phi A	0	0	—	1	0	0	0	2	1	1	0	0	1	1	4.50	91	.167	.286	0	—	0		0		0.0

PABOR, CHARLIE Charles Henry B9.24.1846 New York NY D4.23.1913 New Haven CT BL/TL/5-8/155 d5.4 M2 ▲

YEAR	TM LG	W	L	PCT	G	GS	CG-SHO	SV-BS	IP	H	R	HR	HB	BB-IB	SO	ERA	AERA	OAV	OOB	AB-HR-SH	AVG	PB	SUP	APR	DL	PW
1871	Cle NA	0	2	.000	7	1	1	0	29.1	50	53	4		6	0	6.75	61	.325	.350	142	.296	0*	77	-7		-0.2
1872	Cle NA	1	1	.500	2	2	2	0	18	20	15	0		3	0	4.00	89	.247	.274	92	.207	-0*	145	-1		-0.1
1875	Atl NA	0	1	.000	1	1	1	0	4	11	14	0		1	0	9.00	23	.407	.429	153	.235	0*	102	-3		-0.4
Total 3 NA		1	4	.200	10	4	3	0	51.1	81	80	4		10	0	5.96	63	.309	.335	387	.251	-0	106	-11		-0.7

PACELLA, JOHN John Lewis B9.15.1956 Brooklyn NY BR/TR/6-3/195(180-195) [NYN74 4/89] d9.15

YEAR	TM LG	W	L	PCT	G	GS	CG-SHO	SV-BS	IP	H	R	HR	HB	BB-IB	SO	ERA	AERA	OAV	OOB	AB-HR-SH	AVG	PB	SUP	APR	DL	PW
1977	NY N	0	0	—	3	0	0	0-0	4	4	2	0	0	2-0	1	0.00	—	.133	.235	0	—	0		1		0.0
1979	NY N	0	2	.000	4	3	0	0-0	16	16	8	0	0	4-0	12	4.41	84	.246	.290	4	.000	-0	56	-1		-0.1
1980	NY N	3	4	.429	32	15	0	0-0	84	89	51	5	2	59-2	68	5.14	70	.280	.396	20-0-2	.100	-1	119	-13		-1.1
1982	NY A	0	1	.000	3	1	0	0-0	10	13	8	1	1	9-1	2	7.20	56	.342	.451	0	—	0	23	-3		-0.3
	Min A	1	2	.333	21	1	0	2-1	51.2	61	48	14	1	37-0	20	7.32	58	.299	.402	0	—	0	43	-18	24	-1.1
	Year	1	3	.250	24	2	0	2-1	61.2	74	56	14	1	46-1	22	7.30	58	.306	.410	0	—	0	32	-20		-1.4
1984	Bal A	0	1	.000	6	1	0	0-0	14.2	15	13	2	0	7-0	8	6.75	58	.268	.369	0	—	0	115	-5		-0.3

YEAR	TM LG	W	L	PCT	G	GS	CG-SHO	SV-BS	IP	H	R	HR	HB	BB-IB	SO	ERA	AERA	OAV	OOB	AB-HR-SH	AVG	PB	SUP	APR	DL	PW
1986	Det A	0	0		5	0	0	1-0	11	10	5	0	0	13-1	5	4.09	102	.294	.469	0		0	0			0.1
Total	6	4	10	.286	74	21	0	3-1	191.2	206	135	21	3	133-5	116	5.73	68	.282	.391	24-0-2	.083	-1	96	-39	24	-2.8

PACHECO, ALEX Alexander Melchor (Lara) B7.19.1973 Caracas, Venez BR/TR/6-3/200 d4.17

| 1996 | Mon N | 0 | 0 | — | 5 | 0 | 0 | 0-0 | 5.2 | 8 | 7 | 2 | 0 | 1-0 | 7 | 11.12 | 39 | .320 | .346 | 0 | | 0 | | -4 | | -0.2 |

PACILLO, PAT Patrick Michael B7.23.1963 Jersey City NJ BR/TR/6-2/205* [CinN84 1/5] d5.23 Col Seton Hall

1987	Cin N	3	3	.500	12	7	0	0-0	39.2	41	30	7	1	19-0	23	6.13	69	.270	.351	11-0-1	.091	-0*	110	-8		-1.1
1988	Cin N	1	0	1.000	6	0	0	0-0	10.2	14	7	2	0	4-0	11	5.06	71	.318	.375	1	.000	-0		-2	21	-0.2
Total	2	4	3	.571	18	7	0	0-0	50.1	55	37	9	1	23-0	34	5.90	69	.281	.356	12-0-1	.083	-0	110	-10	21	-1.3

PACKARD, GENE Eugene Milo B7.13.1887 Colorado Springs CO D5.18.1959 Riverside CA BL/TL/5-10/155 d9.27

1912	Cin N	1	0	1.000	1	1	1	0-0	9	7	3	0	0	4		3.00	112	.206	.289	4	.250	1	218	1		0.1
1913	Cin N	7	11	.389	39	21	9-2	0	190.2	208	97	2	8	64	73	2.97	109	.286	.350	61-0-4	.180	-0*	114	1		0.1
1914	KC F	20	14	.588	42	34	24-4	5	302	282	127	5	3	88	154	2.89	96	.246	.301	116-1-5	.241	2*	122	-3		0.3
1915	KC F	20	12	.625	42	31	21-5	2	281.2	250	111	3	9	74	108	2.68	98	.242	.298	95-1-8	.232	2*	99	-3		0.3
1916	Chi N	10	6	.625	37	16	5-2	5	155.1	154	60	4	3	38	36	2.78	105	.256	.306	54-0-2	.130	-1*	108	3		0.5
1917	Chi N	0	0		2	0	0		1.2	3	2	1	0	0	1	10.80	27	.375	.375	0	—	0		-1		-0.1
	StL N	9	6	.600	34	11	6	2	153.1	138	48	4	3	25	44	2.47	109	.246	.281	52	.288	3*	89	5		0.9
	Year	9	6	.600	36	11	6	2	155	141	50	5	3	25	45	2.55	105	.247	.283	52	.288	3	89	5		0.8
1918	StL N	12	12	.500	30	23	10-1	2	182.1	184	84	6	5	33	46	3.50	77	.266	.304	69-0-4	.174	-1*	119	-12		-1.7
1919	StL N	6	8	.429	21	16	10-1	1	134.1	167	70	3	4	30	24	4.15	78	.321	.363	51	.137	-2*	123	-11		-1.3
Total	8	85	69	.552	248	153	86-15	17	1410.1	1393	602	28	35	356	488	3.01	95	.262	.312	502-2-23	.205	4	113	-20		-1.0

PACTWA, JOE Joseph Martin B6.2.1948 Hammond IN BL/TL/5-11/185 [NYA66 18/350] d9.15

| 1975 | Cal A | 1 | 0 | 1.000 | 4 | 3 | 0 | 0-0 | 16.1 | 23 | 7 | 0 | 0 | 10-0 | 3 | 3.86 | 93 | .343 | .423 | 0 | | 0 | 90 | 0 | | 0.0 |

PADILLA, JUAN Juan Miguel B2.17.1977 Rio Piedras, PR BR/TR/6-0/200* [MinA98 24/709] d7.16 Col Jacksonville

2004	NY A	0	0	—	6	0	0	0-0	11.1	16	5	1	0	4-0	5	3.97	116	.348	.400	0		0	1	0		0.1
	Cin N	1	0	1.000	12	0	0	0-0	14.1	23	17	6	1	8-0	12	10.67	40	.359	.438	0	—	0		-10		-0.6
2005	NY N	3	1	.750	24	0	0	1-1	36.1	24	7	0	2	13-2	17	1.49	280	.180	.264	2	.500	0		11		1.2
Total	2	4	1	.800	42	0	0	1-1	62	63	29	7	3	25-2	34	4.06	105	.259	.336	2	.500	0		0		0.7

PADILLA, VICENTE Vicente De La Cruz B9.27.1977 Chinandega, Nicaragua BR/TR/6-2/200(200-220) d6.29

1999	Ari N	0	1	.000	5	0	0	0-1	2.2	7	5	1	0	3-0	0	16.88	27	.467	.556	0		0		-3		-0.6
2000	Ari N	2	1	.667	27	0	0	0-1	35	32	10	0	0	10-2	30	2.31	207	.242	.294	1	1.000	0		9		0.7
	Phi N	2	6	.250	28	0	0	2-4	30.1	40	23	3	1	18-5	21	5.34	86	.328	.413	0	—	0		-4		-0.8
	Year	4	7	.364	55	0	0	2-5	65.1	72	33	3	1	28-7	51	3.72	126	.283	.353	1	1.000	0		5		-0.1
2001	Phi N	3	1	.750	23	0	0	0-3	34	36	18	1	0	12-0	29	4.24	97	.273	.333	3-0-1	.333	1		-11	26	-0.1
2002	Phi N★	14	11	.560	32	32	1-1	0-0	206	198	83	16	15	53-5	128	3.28	117	.254	.312	58-0-7	.052	-4	112	13		1.0
2003	Phi N	14	12	.538	32	32	1-1	0-0	208.2	196	94	22	16	62-4	133	3.62	110	.251	.317	67-0-3	.060	-3	118	7		0.5
2004	Phi N	7	7	.500	20	20	0	0-0	115.1	119	63	16	10	36-6	82	4.53	98	.267	.333	35-0-3	.114	-1	94	-1	72	-0.4
2005	Phi N	9	12	.429	27	27	0	0-0	147	146	79	22	8	74-9	103	4.71	92	.260	.352	41-0-5	.146	1	109	-4	16	-0.4
Total	7.	51	51	.500	194	111	2-2	2-9	779	774	375	81	50	268-31	526	3.95	105	.261	.330	205-0-19	.093	-5	109	16	114	0.1

PAGAN, DAVE David Percy B9.15.1949 Nipawin SK, Can. BR/TR/6-2/175* d7.1

1973	NY A	0	0	—	4	1	0	0-0	12.2	16	4	1	0	1-0	9	2.84	131	.320	.333	0	—	0	265	-1		0.1
1974	NY A	1	3	.250	16	6	1	0-0	49.1	49	29	1	0	28-0	39	5.11	69	.265	.362	0	—	0	112	-7		-0.6
1975	NY A	0	0	—	13	0	0	1-0	31	30	16	2	2	13-5	18	4.06	91	.256	.336	0	—	0		-1		-0.1
1976	NY A	1	1	.500	7	2	1	0-0	23.2	18	7	0	0	4-0	13	2.28	150	.222	.253	0	—	0	77	3		0.2
	Bal A	1	4	.200	20	5	0	1-1	46.2	54	33	2	1	23-1	34	5.98	55	.298	.370	0	—	0	107	-14		-1.5
	Year	2	5	.286	27	7	1	1-1	70.1	72	40	2	1	27-1	47	4.73	70	.275	.336	0	—	0	98	-11		-1.3
1977	Sea A	1	1	.500	24	4	1-1	2-1	66	86	52	3	2	26-2	30	6.14	68	.323	.383	0	—	0	108	-15		-0.8
	Pit N	0	0	—	1	0	0	0-0	3	1	0	0	0	0		4	0.00	—	.100	.100	0	—	0		1	0.1
Total	5	4	9	.308	85	18	3-1	4-2	232.1	254	141	9	5	95-8	147	4.96	74	.285	.353	0	—	0	112	-31		-2.6

PAGE, JOE Joseph Francis "Fireman" B10.28.1917 Cherry Valley PA D4.21.1980 Latrobe PA BL/TL/6-2/205* d4.19

1944	NY A☆	5	7	.417	19	16	4	0-0	102.2	100	65	3	3	52	63	4.56	76	.258	.351	32-0-2	.156	-0	97	-14		-1.5
1945	NY A	6	3	.667	20	9	4	0	102	95	43	1	0	46	50	2.82	123	.246	.350	36	.250	1	139	5		0.4
1946	NY A	9	8	.529	31	17	6-1	3	136	126	66	7	4	72	77	3.57	97	.252	.351	43-1-6	.163	-0*	142	-4		-0.5
1947	†NY A★	14	8	.636	56	2	0	**17**	141.1	105	41	5	1	72	116	2.48	142	.208	.308	46-1-2	.217	1	163	**18**		3.3
1948	NY A☆	7	8	.467	**55**	1	0	16	107.2	116	59	6	1	66	77	4.26	90	.275	.374	24-0-1	.292	3	243	-3		-0.2
1949	†NY A	13	8	.619	**60**	0	0	**27**	135.1	103	44	8	5	75	99	2.59	156	.215	.328	40	.175	1		**23**		4.0
1950	NY A	3	7	.300	37	0	0	13	55.1	66	34	8	0	31	33	5.04	85	.295	.380	8	.250	1		-5		-0.9
1954	Pit N	0	0	—	7	0	0	1	9.2	16	17	4	1	11	4	11.17	37	.364	.462	0	—	0		-9		-0.4
Total	8	57	49	.538	285	45	14-1	76	790	727	369	42	15	421	519	3.53	106	.247	.344	229-2-11	.205	5	124	11		4.2

PAGE, PHIL Philippe Rausac B8.23.1905 Springfield MA D7.27.1958 Springfield MA BR/TL/6-2/175 d9.18 C6 Col Penn St.

1928	Det A	2	0	1.000	3	2	2	0	22	21	9	1	0	10	3	2.45	167	.256	.337	9	.222	-0	124	3		0.3
1929	Det A	2	0	.000	10	4	1	0	25.1	29	24	1	1	19	6	8.17	53	.296	.415	8	.125	-1	147	-9		-0.7
1930	Det A	0	1	.000	12	0	0	0	12	23	16	1	0	9	2	9.75	49	.434	.516	0	—	0		-7		-0.4
1934	Bro N	1	0	1.000	6	0	0	0	10	13	7	1	0	6	4	5.40	72	.342	.432	1	.000	-0		-2		-0.1
Total	4	3	3	.500	31	6	3	0	69.1	86	56	4	1	44	15	6.23	68	.317	.415	18	.167	-1	140	-15		-0.9

PAGE, SAM Samuel Walter B2.11.1916 Woodruff SC D5.29.2002 Greenville SC BL/TR/6-0/172 d9.11

| 1939 | Phi A | 0 | 3 | .000 | 4 | 3 | 1 | 0 | 22 | 34 | 27 | 1 | 0 | 15 | 11 | 6.95 | 68 | .343 | .430 | 7-0-1 | .429 | 1 | 106 | -8 | | -0.7 |

PAGE, VANCE Vance Linwood B9.15.1905 Elm City NC D7.14.1951 Wilson NC BR/TR/6-0/180 d8.6

1938	†Chi N	5	4	.556	13	9	3	1	68	90	33	4	0	13	18	3.84	100	.323	.353	26-0-1	.154	-1	93	0		0.0
1939	Chi N	7	7	.500	27	17	8-1	5	139.1	169	77	8	1	37	43	3.88	102	.298	.342	47-0-2	.255	3	102	-2		0.1
1940	Chi N	3	1	.250	30	1	0	2	59	65	38	1	0	26	22	4.42	85	.271	.342	13	.308	2*	278	-6		-0.2
1941	Chi N	2	2	.500	25	3	1	1	48.1	48	24	2	2	30	17	4.28	82	.254	.362	7-0-1	.286	1	64	-3		-0.1
Total	4	15	16	.484	95	30	12-1	5	314.2	372	172	15	3	106	100	4.03	95	.292	.348	93-0-4	.237	5	103	-11		-0.2

PAIGE, PAT George Lynn "Piggy" B5.5.1882 Paw Paw MI D6.8.1939 Berlin WI BL/TR/5-10/175 d5.20

| 1911 | Cle A | 1 | 0 | 1.000 | 2 | 1 | 1 | 0 | 16 | 21 | 12 | 0 | 0 | 7 | 6 | 4.50 | 76 | .339 | .406 | 7 | .143 | -0 | 169 | -2 | | -0.1 |

PAIGE, SATCHEL Leroy Robert B7.7.1906 Mobile AL D6.8.1982 Kansas City MO BR/TR/6-3.5/180* d7.9 C2 HF1971 Negro Lg 1926-67

1948	†Cle A	6	1	.857	21	7	3-2	1	72.2	61	21	2	1	22	43	2.48	164	.228	.290	23-0-2	.087	-2	121	14		1.0
1949	Cle A	4	7	.364	31	5	1	5	83	70	29	4	1	33	54	3.04	131	.230	.308	16	.063	-1	63	10		1.2
1951	StL A	3	4	.429	23	3	0	5	62	67	39	6	1	29	48	4.79	92	.276	.355	16-0-1	.125	-2	61	-3		-0.6
1952	StL A☆	12	10	.545	46	6	3-2	10	138	116	51	2	3	57	91	3.07	128	.226	.307	39-0-4	.128	-2	56	13		2.1
1953	StL A★	3	9	.250	57	4	0	11	117.1	114	51	12	1	39	51	3.53	119	.257	.319	29-0-1	.069	-3	95	9		0.6
1965	KC A	0	0	—	1	1	0	0	3	1	0	0	0	0	0.00	—	.100	.100	1	.000	0	50	1		0.0
Total	6	28	31	.475	179	26	7-4	32	476	429	191	29	7	180-0	288	3.29	124	.241	.313	124-0-8	.097	-10	80	44		4.3

PAINE, PHIL Phillips Steere "Flip" B6.8.1930 Chepachet RI D2.19.1978 Lebanon PA BR/TR/6-2/181* d7.14 Mil 1952-53

1951	Bos N	2	0	1.000	21	0	0	1	35.1	36	15	2	4	20	17	3.06	120	.271	.382	4	.000	-1		2		0.0
1954	Mil N	1	0	1.000	11	0	0	1	14	14	9	1	1	12	11	3.86	97	.292	.443	0	—	0		-1		-0.1
1955	Mil N	2	0	1.000	15	0	0	0	25.1	20	8	2	1	14-3	26	2.49	151	.225	.324	3	.333	0		4		0.3
1956	Mil N	0	0	—	1	0	0	0	2	2	0	0	0	1	0	0.00	∞	1.000	1.000	0	—	0		-2		0.0
1957	Mil N	0	0	—	1	0	0	0	1	0	0	0	0	3-0	2	0.00	—	.143	.400	0	—	0		4		0.1
1958	StL N	5	1	.833	46	0	0	1	73.1	70	33	7	5	31-4	45	3.56	116	.256	.342	7-0-1	.286	-0		4		0.4
Total	6	10	2	.909	95	0	0	3	151	142	65	12	10	80-7	101	3.46	116	.255	.350	14-0-1	.214	-0		6		0.5

PAINTER, LANCE Lance Telford B7.21.1967 Bedford, England BL/TL/6-1/197* [SDN90 25/681] d5.19 Col Wisconsin-Madison

| 1993 | Col N | 2 | 2 | .500 | 10 | 6 | 1 | 0-0 | 39 | 52 | 26 | 5 | 0 | 9-0 | 16 | 6.00 | 80 | .333 | .370 | 10-0-3 | .300 | 1 | 116 | -3 | | -0.2 |
| 1994 | Col N | 4 | 6 | .400 | 15 | 14 | 0 | 0-0 | 73.2 | 91 | 51 | 9 | 1 | 26-2 | 41 | 6.11 | 82 | .302 | .354 | 21-0-3 | .143 | -1 | 114 | -7 | | -0.8 |

YEAR	TM LG	W	L	PCT	G	GS	CG-SHO	SV-BS	IP	H	R	HR	HB	BB-IB	SO	ERA	AERA	OAV	OOB	AB-HR-SH	AVG	PB	SUP	APR	DL	PW
1995	†Col N	3	0	1.000	33	1	0	1-0	45.1	55	23	9	2	10-0	36	4.37	123	.296	.338	9-0-1	.111	-0	202	4	11	0.3
1996	Col N	4	2	.667	34	1	0	0-1	50.2	56	37	12	3	25-3	48	5.86	89	.280	.364	15	.133	-1*	17	-3	55	-0.4
1997	StL N	1	1	.500	14	0	0	0-0	17	13	9	1	0	8-2	11	4.76	88	.213	.304	1	.000	-0		-1	141	0.0
1998	StL N	4	0	1.000	65	0	0	1-1	47.1	42	24	5	4	28-3	39	3.99	105	.249	.365	1-0-1	1.000	0		1		0.2
1999	StL N	4	5	.444	56	4	0	1-2	63.1	63	37	6	2	25-1	56	4.83	95	.265	.336	7	.000	-1	65	-1	15	-0.2
2000	Tor A	2	0	1.000	42	2	0	0-1	66.2	69	37	9	2	22-1	53	4.72	107	.271	.332	0	—	0	130	3	19	0.2
2001	Tor A	0	1	.000	10	0	0	0-0	18.1	27	17	4	1	11-0	14	7.85	58	.342	.429	0	—	0	-6	31	-0.3
	Mil N	1	0	1.000	13	0	0	0-0	10.2	11	5	3	0	7-2	6	4.22	102	.268	.375	0	—	0	0	46		0.0
2003	StL N	0	1	.000	22	0	0	0-1	18	17	12	3	0	7-1	5	5.50	75	.246	.316	1	.000	-0	-3	111		-0.1
Total	10	25	18	.581	314	28	1	3-6	450	496	278	66	15	178-15	331	5.24	92	.283	.351	65-0-8	.154	-1	111	-16	429	-1.3

PALACIOS, VICENTE Vicente (Diaz) B7.19.1963 Manlio Fabio Altimirano, Veracruz, Mexico BR/TR/6-3/195(175-208) d9.4

YEAR	TM LG	W	L	PCT	G	GS	CG-SHO	SV-BS	IP	H	R	HR	HB	BB-IB	SO	ERA	AERA	OAV	OOB	AB-HR-SH	AVG	PB	SUP	APR	DL	PW
1987	Pit N	2	1	.667	6	4	0	0-0	29.1	27	14	1	0	9-1	13	4.30	97	.250	.314	9	.111	-0	119	0		-0.1
1988	Pit N	1	2	.333	7	3	0	0-0	24.1	28	18	3	0	15-1	15	6.66	52	.291	.387	8	.000	-0	197	-8		-0.9
1990	Pit N	0	0	—	7	0	0	3-0	15	4	0	0	0	2-0	9	0.00	—	.083	.120	4	.000	-0		6		0.3
1991	Pit N	6	3	.667	36	7	1-1	3-2	81.2	69	34	12	1	38-2	64	3.75	96	.230	.315	14-0-5	.071	-1	114	1	29	0.0
1992	Pit N	3	2	.600	20	8	0	0-0	53	56	25	1	0	27-1	33	4.25	82	.280	.364	14-0-2	.071	-1	111	-4	108	-0.4
1994	StL N	3	8	.273	31	17	1-1	1-0	117.2	104	60	16	3	43-2	95	4.44	96	.245	.314	33-0-3	.000	-4	67	-2		-0.5
1995	StL N	2	3	.400	20	5	0	0-0	40.1	48	29	7	2	19-1	34	5.80	74	.300	.379	6-0-1	.167	-1	93	-6	102	-0.7
2000	SD N	0	1	.000	7	0	0	0-0	10.2	12	10	4	0	5-1	6	6.75	66	.308	.378	0	—	0	-3		-0.2
Total	8	17	20	.459	134	44	2-2	7-2	372	348	190	44	7	158-9	270	4.43	89	.253	.330	88-0-11	.045	-6	98	-16	239	-2.5

PALAGYI, MIKE Michael Raymond B7.4.1917 Conneaut OH BR/TR/6-2/185 d8.18

YEAR	TM LG	W	L	PCT	G	GS	CG-SHO	SV-BS	IP	H	R	HR	HB	BB-IB	SO	ERA	AERA	OAV	OOB	AB-HR-SH	AVG	PB	SUP	APR	DL	PW
1939	Was A	0	0	—	1	0	0	0-0	2	0	3	0	0	3	0	∞	—	—	1.000	0		0	-3		-0.2

PALICA, ERV Ervin Martin (b Ervin Martin Pavliecivich) B2.9.1928 Lomita CA D5.29.1982 Huntington Beach CA BR/TR/6-1.5/180* d4.21.1945 Mil 1952-53

YEAR	TM LG	W	L	PCT	G	GS	CG-SHO	SV-BS	IP	H	R	HR	HB	BB-IB	SO	ERA	AERA	OAV	OOB	AB-HR-SH	AVG	PB	SUP	APR	DL	PW
1947	Bro N	0	1	.000	7	0	0	0-0	3	2	1	0	1	2	1	3.00	138	.182	.357			0	0		0.1
1948	Bro N	6	6	.500	41	10	3	3	125.1	111	63	13	3	58	74	4.45	90	.239	.327	39-0-1	.128	0*	109	-3		-0.3
1949	†Bro N	8	9	.471	49	1	0	6	97	93	43	6	1	49	44	3.62	113	.261	.352	19-0-4	.158	0	86	5		0.9
1950	Bro N	13	8	.619	43	19	10-2	1	201.1	176	89	13	2	98	131	3.58	115	.237	.327	68-1-3	.221	2*	117	11		1.1
1951	Bro N	2	6	.250	19	8	0	0	53	55	28	10	0	20	15	4.75	83	.259	.323	13-0-1	.154	0*	98	-4		-0.5
1953	Bro N	0	0	—	4	0	0	0	6	10	8	1	0	8	3	12.00	36	.370	.514	1	1.000	0	-5			-0.2
1954	Bro N	3	3	.500	25	3	0	0	67.2	77	45	9	1	31	25	5.32	77	.285	.357	16	.250	1*	102	-10		-0.7
1955	Bal A	5	11	.313	33	25	5-1	2	169.2	165	91	10	2	83-4	68	4.14	92	.260	.342	55-0-2	.236	2	86	-7		-0.3
1956	Bal A	4	11	.267	29	14	2	0	116.1	117	64	10	1	50-3	62	4.49	87	.264	.336	32	.156	-2*	66	-8		-1.0
Total	9	41	55	.427	246	80	20-3	12	839.1	806	432	72	11	399-7	423	4.22	94	.255	.338	243-1-11	.198	5	94	-21		-0.9

PALL, DONN Donn Steven B1.11.1962 Chicago IL BR/TR/6-1/183* [ChiA85 23/579] d8.1 Col Illinois

YEAR	TM LG	W	L	PCT	G	GS	CG-SHO	SV-BS	IP	H	R	HR	HB	BB-IB	SO	ERA	AERA	OAV	OOB	AB-HR-SH	AVG	PB	SUP	APR	DL	PW
1988	Chi A	0	2	.000	17	0	0	0-0	28.2	39	11	1	0	8-1	15	3.45	116	.328	.367	0	—	0	2			0.2
1989	Chi A	4	5	.444	53	0	0	6-4	87	90	35	9	8	19-3	58	3.31	116	.270	.323	0	—	0	6	14		0.5
1990	Chi A	3	5	.375	56	0	0	2-1	76	63	33	7	4	24-8	39	3.32	116	.232	.301	0	—	0	3			0.3
1991	Chi A	7	2	.778	51	0	0	0-1	71	59	22	7	3	20-3	40	2.41	166	.231	.295	0	—	0	12			1.4
1992	Chi A	5	2	.714	39	0	0	1-1	73	79	43	9	2	27-8	27	4.93	79	.272	.335	0	—	0	-8			-0.8
1993	Chi A	2	3	.400	39	0	0	1-1	58.2	62	25	5	2	11-3	29	3.22	131	.268	.306	0	—	0	6			0.5
	Phi N	1	0	1.000	8	0	0	0-0	17.2	15	7	1	0	3-0	11	2.55	156	.231	.265	0	—	0	2			0.1
1994	NY A	1	2	.333	26	0	0	0-0	35	43	18	3	1	9-0	21	3.60	128	.291	.338	0	—	0	3			0.2
	Chi A	0	0	—	2	0	0	0-0	4	8	2	1	0	1-0	2	4.50	94	.444	.474	0	—	0	0			0.0
1996	Fla N	1	1	.500	12	0	0	0-0	18.2	16	15	3	0	9-1	9	5.79	71	.232	.316	2	.000	-0	-4			-0.4
1997	Fla N	0	0	—	2	0	0	0-1	2.1	3	1	1	0	1-0	1	3.86	105	.300	.364	1	.000	-0	0			0.0
1998	Fla N	0	1	.000	23	0	0	0-0	33.1	42	19	5	1	7-2	26	5.13	79	.326	.362	2	.000	-0	-3			-0.2
Total	10	24	23	.511	328	0	0	10-9	505.1	519	231	52	21	139-29	278	3.63	110	.268	.322	5	.000	-0	19	14		1.8

PALM, MIKE Richard Paul B2.13.1925 Boston MA BR/TR/6-3.5/190 d7.11

YEAR	TM LG	W	L	PCT	G	GS	CG-SHO	SV-BS	IP	H	R	HR	HB	BB-IB	SO	ERA	AERA	OAV	OOB	AB-HR-SH	AVG	PB	SUP	APR	DL	PW
1948	Bos A	0	0	—	3	0	0	0-0	3	6	2	0	0	5	1	6.00	73	.400	.550	3	.000	-0	0			-0.7

PALMER, BILLY Billy B St.Louis MO d5.28

YEAR	TM LG	W	L	PCT	G	GS	CG-SHO	SV-BS	IP	H	R	HR	HB	BB-IB	SO	ERA	AERA	OAV	OOB	AB-HR-SH	AVG	PB	SUP	APR	DL	PW
1885	StL N	0	4	.000	4	4	4	0	34	46	33	2		20	9	3.44	80	.311	.393	11	.091	-0	67	-6		-0.6

PALMER, DAVID David William B10.19.1957 Glens Falls NY BR/TR/6-1/205* [MonN76 21/489] d9.9 (DL 1981 Mon N 123, 1983 Mon N 169)

YEAR	TM LG	W	L	PCT	G	GS	CG-SHO	SV-BS	IP	H	R	HR	HB	BB-IB	SO	ERA	AERA	OAV	OOB	AB-HR-SH	AVG	PB	SUP	APR	DL	PW
1978	Mon N	0	1	.000	5	1	0	0-0	9.2	9	4	1	0	2-0	7	2.79	128	.243	.282	1	.000	-0	76	1		0.1
1979	Mon N	10	2	.833	36	11	2-1	2-1	122.2	110	41	10	2	30-7	72	2.64	141	.237	.285	31-0-4	.032	-3	123	15		1.1
1980	Mon N	8	6	.571	24	19	3-1	0-0	129.2	124	53	11	2	30-1	73	2.98	122	.255	.299	45-0-2	.200	1*	109	7	37	0.9
1982	Mon N	6	4	.600	13	13	1	0-0	73.2	60	34	3	2	36-2	46	3.18	116	.224	.315	24-0-3	.042	-2	112	2	44	0.1
1984	Mon N	7	3	.700	20	19	1-1	0-0	105.1	101	45	5	0	44-4	66	3.84	90	.256	.330	33-1-6	.152	1	98	-2	27	-0.1
1985	Mon N	7	10	.412	24	23	0	0-0	135.2	128	60	3	3	67-5	106	3.71	93	.250	.340	36-0-5	.111	-1	86	-3	23	-0.4
1986	Atl N	11	10	.524	35	35	2	0-0	209.2	181	98	17	5	102-8	170	3.65	109	.234	.325	66-1-10	.182	2	84	6		0.9
1987	Atl N	8	11	.421	28	28	0	0-0	152.1	169	94	17	7	64-4	111	4.90	88	.281	.354	48-1-8	.125	-0	104	-9	36	-1.0
1988	Phi N	7	9	.438	22	22	1-1	0-0	129	129	67	8	0	48-5	85	4.47	81	.261	.324	39-2-9	.256	5	84	-10	15	-0.7
1989	Det A	3	3	.000	5	5	0	0-0	17.1	25	19	1	0	11-0	12	7.79	49	.342	.424	0	—	0	137	-9		-1.2
Total	10	64	59	.520	212	176	10-4	2-1	1085	1036	515	78	21	434-36	748	3.78	100	.252	.325	323-5-47	.149	2	98	-2	474	-0.3

PALMER, JIM James Alvin B10.15.1945 New York NY BR/TR/6-3/196* d4.17 HF1990 (DL 1968 Bal A 38)

YEAR	TM LG	W	L	PCT	G	GS	CG-SHO	SV-BS	IP	H	R	HR	HB	BB-IB	SO	ERA	AERA	OAV	OOB	AB-HR-SH	AVG	PB	SUP	APR	DL	PW
1965	Bal A	5	4	.556	27	6	0	1	92	75	49	6	2	56-1	75	3.72	93	.229	.342	26-1-0	.192	1*	72	-4		-0.3
1966	†Bal A	15	10	.600	30	30	6	0	208.1	176	83	21	0	91-1	147	3.46	96	.231	.311	73-1-2	.096	-2*	132	0		-0.3
1967	Bal A	3	1	.750	9	9	2-1	0	49	34	18	6	0	20-0	23	2.94	107	.199	.281	13-0-3	.077	0	154	1		0.1
1969	Bal A	16	4	**.800**	26	23	11-6	0-0	181	131	48	11	1	64-1	123	2.34	154	.200	.272	64-0-2	.203	2*	134	27	41	3.1
1970	†Bal A★	20	10	.667	39	39	17-**5**	0-0	**305**	263	98	21	4	100-4	199	2.71	136	.231	.293	113-1-7	.150	-1*	108	**35**		3.1
1971	†Bal A★	20	9	.690	37	37	20-3	0-0	282	231	94	19	4	106-6	184	2.68	127	.221	.294	102-0-11	.196	2*	121	23		2.6
1972	†Bal A★	21	10	.677	36	36	18-3	0-0	274.1	219	73	21	1	70-1	184	2.07	151	.217	.268	98-0-6	.224	4	117	30		4.1
1973	Bal A	22	9	.710	38	37	19-6	1-0	296.1	225	86	16	3	113-5	158	**2.40**	157	.211	.288	0	—	0	111	47		4.8
1974	Bal A	7	12	.368	26	26	5-2	0-0	178.2	176	78	12	3	69-4	84	3.27	106	.257	.340	0	—	0	86	2	54	0.3
1975	Bal A☆	**23**	11	.676	39	38	25-**10**	1-0	323	253	87	20	4	80-4	193	**2.09**	**170**	.216	.266	0	—	0	101	**53**		**5.7**
1976	Bal A	**22**	13	.629	40	**40**	23-6	0-0	**315**	255	101	20	8	84-5	159	2.51	131	.224	.278	0	—	0	90	27		3.1
1977	Bal A★	**20**	11	.645	39	**39**	22-3	0-0	**319**	263	106	24	3	99-1	193	2.91	132	.229	.290	0	—	0	99	38		3.4
1978	Bal A★	21	12	.636	38	38	19-6	0-0	**296**	246	94	19	1	97-1	138	2.46	143	.227	.290	0	—	0	94	36		4.0
1979	†Bal A	10	6	.625	23	22	7	0-0	155.2	144	66	12	0	43-0	67	3.30	123	.246	.295	0	—	0	126	12	26	1.1
1980	Bal A	16	10	.615	34	33	4	0-0	224	238	108	26	3	74-0	109	3.98	100	.275	.332	0	—	0*	114	-1		0.0
1981	Bal A	7	8	.467	22	22	5	0-0	127.1	117	60	14	2	46-1	35	3.75	97	.247	.313	0	—	0	102	-1		-0.1
1982	Bal A	15	5	**.750**	36	32	8-2	1-0	227	195	85	22	4	63-1	103	3.13	130	.231	**.286**	0	—	0	105	23		1.9
1983	†Bal A	5	4	.556	14	11	0	0-0	76.2	86	42	11	0	19-0	34	4.23	95	.281	.320	0	—	0	101	-3	98	-0.3
1984	Bal A	0	3	.000	5	4	0	0-0	17.2	19	12	9	0	17-1	4	9.17	43	.319	.443	0	—	0	77	-10		-1.3
Total	19	268	152	.638	558	521	211-53	4-0	3948	3349	1395	303	38	1311-37	2212	2.86	126	.230	.294	489-3-31	.174	6	108	335	257	35.0

PALMER, LOWELL Lowell Raymond B8.18.1947 Sacramento CA BR/TR/6-1/190* [PhiN66*S1/6] d6.21 Col American River (CA) CC

YEAR	TM LG	W	L	PCT	G	GS	CG-SHO	SV-BS	IP	H	R	HR	HB	BB-IB	SO	ERA	AERA	OAV	OOB	AB-HR-SH	AVG	PB	SUP	APR	DL	PW
1969	Phi N	2	8	.200	26	9	1-1	0-0	90	91	54	12	6	47-7	68	5.20	69	.264	.356	22-1-2	.136	1	86	-15		-1.4
1970	Phi N	1	2	.333	38	5	0	0-0	102	98	66	15	5	55-4	85	5.47	74	.255	.353	27-0-1	.114	1	125	-16		-0.7
1971	Phi N	0	0	—	3	1	0	0-0	15	13	11	3	4	13-0	6	6.00	59	.236	.411	5	.200	-0	125	-4	68	-0.2
1972	StL N	0	3	.000	16	2	0	0-0	34.2	30	16	2	1	26-1	25	3.89	88	.244	.375	0	.000	-1*	26	-1		-0.2
	Cle A	0	0	—	1	0	0	0-0	2	2	1	0	0	2-0	1	4.50	72	.222	.364	0		0	0			0.0
1974	SD N	2	5	.286	22	8	1	0-0	73	68	48	9	7	59-6	52	5.67	63	.256	.398	23	.087	-1*	97	-15		-1.5
Total	5	5	18	.217	106	25	2-1	0-0	316.2	302	196	41	23	202-18	239	5.29	70	.255	.370	82-1-3	.122	-0	94	-51	68	-4.0

PALMERO, EMILIO Emilio Antonio "Pal" B6.13.1895 Guanabacoa, Cuba D7.15.1970 Toledo OH BL/TL(BB 1915-16)/5-11/157 d9.21

YEAR	TM LG	W	L	PCT	G	GS	CG-SHO	SV-BS	IP	H	R	HR	HB	BB-IB	SO	ERA	AERA	OAV	OOB	AB-HR-SH	AVG	PB	SUP	APR	DL	PW
1915	NY N	0	2	.000	3	2	1	0	11.2	10	4	0	3	9	8	3.09	83	.233	.400		.250	0	44	0		0.0
1916	NY N	0	3	.000	4	2	0	0	15.2	17	14	2	1	8	9	8.04	30	.288	.382	3	.000	-0*	107	-9		-1.4
1921	StL A	4	7	.364	24	9	4	0	90	109	63	1	6	49	26	5.00	90	.319	.413	37	.216	1*	85	-6		-0.5
1926	Was A	2	2	.500	7	3	0	0	17	22	15	1	1	6	6	4.76	81	.344	.475	3	.333	-0	58	-4		-0.7

YEAR	TM LG	W	L	PCT	G	GS	CG-SHO	SV-BS	IP	H	R	HR	HB	BB-IB	SO	ERA	AERA	OAV	OOB	AB-HR-SH	AVG	PB	SUP	APR	DL	PW
1928	Bos N	0	1	.000	3	1	0	0	6.2	14	8	0	0	2	0	5.40	72	.452	.485	1-0-1	.000	-0	65	-2		-0.3
Total 5		6	15	.286	41	17	5	0	141	172	104	4	11	83	48	5.17	77	.319	.420	48-0-1	.208	1	76	-21		-2.9

PALMQUIST, ED Edwin Lee B6.10.1933 Los Angeles CA BR/TR/6-3/195* d6.10

YEAR	TM LG	W	L	PCT	G	GS	CG-SHO	SV-BS	IP	H	R	HR	HB	BB-IB	SO	ERA	AERA	OAV	OOB	AB-HR-SH	AVG	PB	SUP	APR	DL	PW
1960	LA N	0	1	.000	22	0	0	0	39	34	16	6	1	16-5	23	2.54	156	.243	.317	7	.000	-1		4		0.1
1961	LA N	0	1	.000	5	0	0	1	8.2	10	8	0	2	7-0	5	6.23	70	.333	.463	0	—	0		-2		-0.3
	Min A	1	1	.500	9	2	0	0	21	33	23	7	3	13-3	11	9.43	45	.359	.450	3-0-2	.000	-0	94	-11		-0.9
Total 2		1	3	.250	36	2	0	1	68.2	77	47	13	6	36-8	41	5.11	80	.294	.383	10-0-2	.000	-1	94	-9		-1.1

PANIAGUA, JOSE Jose Luis (Sanchez) B8.20.1973 San Jose de Ocoa, D.R. BR/TR/6-2/185* d4.4

YEAR	TM LG	W	L	PCT	G	GS	CG-SHO	SV-BS	IP	H	R	HR	HB	BB-IB	SO	ERA	AERA	OAV	OOB	AB-HR-SH	AVG	PB	SUP	APR	DL	PW
1996	Mon N	2	4	.333	13	11	0	0-0	51	55	24	7	3	23-0	27	3.53	123	.282	.365	11-0-1	.000	-1	81	4	21	0.3
1997	Mon N	1	2	.333	9	3	0	0-0	18	29	24	2	4	16-1	8	12.00	35	.372	.495	5	.000	-1	147	-15		-2.0
1998	Sea A	2	0	1.000	18	0	0	1-1	22	15	5	3	3	5-0	16	2.05	229	.200	.277	0	—	0		7		0.6
1999	Sea A	6	11	.353	59	0	0	3-9	77.2	75	37	5	7	52-4	74	4.06	118	.264	.387	0	—	0		7		1.3
2000	†Sea A	3	0	1.000	69	0	0	5-3	80.1	68	31	6	7	38-3	71	3.47	139	.234	.331	1	.000	-0		13		0.6
2001	†Sea A	4	3	.571	60	0	0	3-1	66	59	35	7	4	38-2	46	4.36	98	.233	.341	1	.000	-0		-1		-0.2
2002	Det A	0	1	.000	41	0	0	1-1	41.2	50	30	10	3	15-1	34	5.83	75	.294	.356	0	—	0		-7		-0.3
2003	Chi A	0	0	—	1	0	0	0-0	0.1	3	4	0	0	1-0	0	108.00	4	.750	.800	0	—	0		-4		-0.2
Total 8		18	21	.462	270	14	0	13-15	357	354	190	40	31	188-11	276	4.49	101	.262	.362	18-0-1	.000	-1	92	4	21	0.1

PANTHER, JIM James Edward B3.1.1945 Burlington IA BR/TR/6-1/190* [OakA67*S5/92] d4.5 Col Southern Illinois

YEAR	TM LG	W	L	PCT	G	GS	CG-SHO	SV-BS	IP	H	R	HR	HB	BB-IB	SO	ERA	AERA	OAV	OOB	AB-HR-SH	AVG	PB	SUP	APR	DL	PW
1971	Oak A	0	1	.000	4	0	0	0-0	5.2	10	9	1	0	5-2	4	11.12	30	.385	.484	1	.000	-0		-6		-0.9
1972	Tex A	5	9	.357	58	4	0	0-1	93.2	101	55	8	5	46-8	44	4.13	74	.277	.365	8-0-3	.125	0	36	-14		-2.0
1973	Atl N	2	3	.400	23	0	0	0-2	30.2	45	26	3	0	9-1	8	7.63	52	.363	.391	0	—	0		-10		-1.6
Total 3		7	13	.350	85	4	0	0-3	130	156	90	12	5	60-11	56	5.26	62	.303	.377	9-0-3	.111	-0	36	-30		-4.5

PAPA, JOHN John Paul B12.5.1940 Bridgeport CT BR/TR/5-11/190* d4.11 Col Bridgeport

YEAR	TM LG	W	L	PCT	G	GS	CG-SHO	SV-BS	IP	H	R	HR	HB	BB-IB	SO	ERA	AERA	OAV	OOB	AB-HR-SH	AVG	PB	SUP	APR	DL	PW
1961	Bal A	0	0	—	2	0	0	0	1	2	2	1	0	3-0	3	18.00	21	.400	.625	0	—	0		-2		-0.1
1962	Bal A	0	0	—	1	0	0	0	1	3	3	0	1	1-0	0	27.00	14	.600	.571	0	—	0		-3		-0.1
Total 2		0	0	—	3	0	0	0	2	5	5	1	0	4-0	3	22.50	17	.500	.600	0	—	0		-5		-0.2

PAPAI, AL Alfred Thomas B5.7.1917 Divernon IL D9.7.1995 Springfield IL BR/TR/6-3/185* d4.24

YEAR	TM LG	W	L	PCT	G	GS	CG-SHO	SV-BS	IP	H	R	HR	HB	BB-IB	SO	ERA	AERA	OAV	OOB	AB-HR-SH	AVG	PB	SUP	APR	DL	PW
1948	StL N	0	1	.000	10	0	0	0	16	14	10	3	0	7	8	5.06	81	.241	.323	2	.000	-0*		-2		-0.1
1949	StL N	4	11	.267	42	15	6	1	142.1	175	103	6	1	81	31	5.06	90	.298	.384	38-0-1	.079	-2	84	-11		-1.1
1950	Bos A	4	2	.667	16	3	2	0	50.2	61	41	5	0	28	19	6.75	73	.293	.377	17-0-1	.176	-0	68	-10		-1.0
	StL N	1	0	1.000	7	0	0	0	19	21	12	0	0	14	7	5.21	82	.300	.417	3	.000	-0		-2		-0.1
1955	Chi A	0	0	—	7	0	0	0	11.2	10	5	1	0	8-2	5	3.86	102	.244	.360	2	.000	-0		0		0.0
Total 4		9	14	.391	88	18	8	4	239.2	281	171	17	1	138-2	70	5.37	84	.291	.380	62-0-2	.097	-3	82	-25		-2.3

PAPE, LARRY Laurence Albert B7.21.1883 Norwood OH D7.21.1918 Swissvale PA BR/TR/5-11/175 d7.6

YEAR	TM LG	W	L	PCT	G	GS	CG-SHO	SV-BS	IP	H	R	HR	HB	BB-IB	SO	ERA	AERA	OAV	OOB	AB-HR-SH	AVG	PB	SUP	APR	DL	PW
1909	Bos A	2	0	1.000	11	3	2-1	2	57.1	46	17	0	5	12	18	2.04	123	.221	.280	21	.143	-1	103	3		0.0
1911	Bos A	10	8	.556	27	19	10-1	0	176.1	167	68	3	4	63	49	2.45	134	.264	.335	64-0-3	.203	-1	74	19		1.8
1912	Bos A	1	1	.500	13	2	1	1	48.2	74	36	0	2	16	17	4.99	68	.366	.418	17	.235	-1	98	-9		-0.3
Total 3		13	9	.591	51	24	13-2	3	282.1	287	121	3	11	91	84	2.81	112	.275	.340	102-0-3	.196	-1	80	13		1.5

PAPELBON, JONATHAN Jonathan Robert B11.23.1980 Baton Rouge LA BR/TR/6-4/230 d7.31 Col Mississippi St.

YEAR	TM LG	W	L	PCT	G	GS	CG-SHO	SV-BS	IP	H	R	HR	HB	BB-IB	SO	ERA	AERA	OAV	OOB	AB-HR-SH	AVG	PB	SUP	APR	DL	PW
2005	†Bos A	3	1	.750	17	3	0	0-1	34	33	11	4	3	17-2	34	2.65	174	.260	.361	0	—	0	130	7		0.7

PAPISH, FRANK Frank Richard "Pap" B10.21.1917 Pueblo CO D8.30.1965 Pueblo CO BR/TL/6-2/192* d5.8

YEAR	TM LG	W	L	PCT	G	GS	CG-SHO	SV-BS	IP	H	R	HR	HB	BB-IB	SO	ERA	AERA	OAV	OOB	AB-HR-SH	AVG	PB	SUP	APR	DL	PW
1945	Chi A	4	4	.500	19	5	3	1	84.1	75	36	3	0	40	45	3.74	89	.241	.328	26-0-3	.231	1	123	-2		0.0
1946	Chi A	7	5	.583	31	15	6-2	0	138	122	52	7	1	63	66	2.74	125	.243	.328	43-0-3	.186	-0	107	11		0.9
1947	Chi A	12	12	.500	38	26	6-1	3	199	185	82	6	2	98	79	3.26	112	.245	.333	58-0-6	.086	-5	78	10		0.6
1948	Chi A	2	8	.200	32	14	0	4	95.1	97	65	7	3	75	41	5.00	85	.265	.394	27-0-1	.185	-1	109	-11		-1.1
1949	Cle A	1	0	1.000	25	3	1	1	62	54	24	2	0	39	23	3.19	125	.240	.352	8-0-3	.125	-1	120	6		0.3
1950	Pit N	0	0	—	4	1	0	0	2.1	8	7	1	0	4	1	27.00	16	.533	.632	0	—	0	121	-5		-0.2
Total 6		26	29	.473	149	64	18-3	9	581	541	266	26	6	319	255	3.58	103	.249	.346	162-0-16	.154	-5	99	9		0.5

PAPPALAU, JOHN John Joseph B4.3.1875 Albany NY D5.12.1944 Albany NY BR/TR/6-0/175 d6.9 Col Holy Cross

YEAR	TM LG	W	L	PCT	G	GS	CG-SHO	SV-BS	IP	H	R	HR	HB	BB-IB	SO	ERA	AERA	OAV	OOB	AB-HR-SH	AVG	PB	SUP	APR	DL	PW
1897	Cle N	0	1	.000	2	1	1	0	12	22	16	0	2	6	3	10.50	43	.393	.469	5	.000	-0	95	-7		-0.4

PAPPAS, MILT Milton Stephen "Gimpy" (b Miltiades Stergios Papastegios) B5.11.1939 Detroit MI BR/TR/6-3/190(190-214) d8.10

YEAR	TM LG	W	L	PCT	G	GS	CG-SHO	SV-BS	IP	H	R	HR	HB	BB-IB	SO	ERA	AERA	OAV	OOB	AB-HR-SH	AVG	PB	SUP	APR	DL	PW
1957	Bal A	0	0	—	4	0	0	0	9	6	1	0	0	3-0	3	1.00	359	.200	.273	1	.000	-0		3	17	0.1
1958	Bal A	10	10	.500	31	21	3	0	135.1	135	67	8	2	48-1	72	4.06	89	.262	.326	42-1-3	.143	-0*	90	-7		-0.9
1959	Bal A	15	9	.625	33	27	15-4	3	209.1	175	82	8	4	75-2	120	3.27	116	.226	.297	79-0-1	.139	-3	98	14		1.1
1960	Bal A	15	11	.577	30	27	11-3	0	205.2	184	81	15	6	83-4	126	3.37	113	.243	.320	70-1-5	.043	-5	92	13		1.0
1961	Bal A	13	9	.591	26	23	11-4	1	177.2	134	67	16	7	78-5	89	3.04	127	.208	.300	66-3-3	.136	1	92	17		2.1
1962	Bal A★	12	10	.545	35	32	9-1	0	205.1	200	105	30	2	75-3	130	4.03	92	.257	.322	66-4-3	.087	-0	97	-8		-0.7
1963	Bal A	16	9	.640	34	32	11-4	0	216.2	186	80	21	5	69-6	120	3.03	115	.233	.296	71-2-7	.127	-0*	111	12		1.4
1964	Bal A	16	7	.696	37	36	13-7	0	251.2	225	89	21	7	48-10	157	2.97	120	.239	.280	93-0-2	.129	-2	120	18		1.4
1965	Bal A★	13	9	.591	34	34	9-3	0	221.1	192	81	22	3	52-3	127	2.60	133	.233	.279	71-0-7	.071	-3	89	19		1.3
1966	Cin N	12	11	.522	33	32	6-2	0	209.2	224	106	23	3	39-4	133	4.29	91	.275	.308	75-1-3	.107	-2*	101	-8		-1.0
1967	Cin N	16	13	.552	34	32	5-3	0	217.2	218	88	19	5	38-5	129	3.35	112	.265	.293	72-1-2	.097	-2	95	10		1.1
1968	Cin N	2	5	.286	15	11	0	0	62.2	70	41	9	2	10-3	43	5.60	56	.275	.306	16-0-4	.063	-1*	105	-15		-1.7
	Atl N	10	8	.556	22	19	3-1	0	121.1	111	36	8	3	22-6	75	2.37	126	.246	.283	37-1-2	.162	2	76	9		1.6
	Year	12	13	.480	37	30	3-1	0	184	181	77	17	5	32-9	118	3.47	88	.256	.291	53-1-6	.132	1	87	-7		-0.1
1969	†Atl N	6	10	.375	26	24	1	0-0	144	149	66	14	4	44-9	72	3.63	100	.267	.323	45-2-1	.156	3	89	-1		0.2
1970	Atl N	2	2	.500	11	3	1	0	35.2	44	25	6	2	7-1	25	6.06	71	.293	.331	10	.000	-1	84	-6		-0.7
	Chi N	10	8	.556	21	20	6-2	0	144.2	135	53	14	0	36-9	80	2.68	168	.248	.292	50-2-1	.240	4	94	25		3.4
	Year	12	10	.545	32	23	7-2	0	180.1	179	78	20	2	43-10	105	3.34	134	.258	.300	60-2-1	.200	3	93	19		2.7
1971	Chi N	17	14	.548	35	34	14-5	0-0	261.1	279	109	25	5	62-6	99	3.51	112	.274	.317	90-0-2	.154	-1	91	13		1.3
1972	Chi N	17	7	.708	29	28	10-3	0-0	195	187	72	18	8	29-3	80	2.77	138	.251	.286	68-1-4	.191	1	112	19		2.6
1973	Chi N	7	12	.368	30	29	1-1	0-0	162	192	83	20	4	40-9	48	4.28	92	.299	.342	48-1-2	.063	-2	79	-4		-0.7
Total 17		209	164	.560	520	465	129-43	4-0	3186	3046	1331	298	72	858-89	1728	3.40	110	.252	.304	1073-20-52	.123	-14	96	123	17	12.9

PARK, CHAN HO Chan Ho B6.30.1973 Kongju, South Korea BR/TR/6-2/204(185-210) d4.8

YEAR	TM LG	W	L	PCT	G	GS	CG-SHO	SV-BS	IP	H	R	HR	HB	BB-IB	SO	ERA	AERA	OAV	OOB	AB-HR-SH	AVG	PB	SUP	APR	DL	PW
1994	LA N	0	0	—	2	0	0	0-0	4	5	5	1	1	5-0	6	11.25	35	.294	.478	0	—	0		-3		-0.2
1995	LA N	0	0	—	2	1	0	0-0	4	2	2	1	0	2-0	7	4.50	86	.143	.250	1	.000	-0	93	0		0.0
1996	LA N	5	5	.500	48	10	0	0-0	108.2	82	48	7	4	71-3	119	3.64	107	.209	.335	19-0-3	.053	-1	90	5		0.4
1997	LA N	14	8	.636	32	29	2	0-0	192	149	80	24	8	70-1	166	3.38	116	.213	.290	51-0-11	.176	3	111	12		1.5
1998	LA N	15	9	.625	34	34	2	0-0	220.2	199	101	16	11	97-1	191	3.71	109	.244	.328	72-0-6	.194	2	115	8		1.1
1999	LA N	13	11	.542	33	33	0	0-0	194.1	208	120	31	14	100-4	174	5.23	83	.276	.369	59-0-6	.153	0	112	-18		-1.7
2000	LA N	18	10	.643	34	34	3-1	0-0	226	173	92	21	12	124-4	217	3.27	136	.214	.325	70-2-6	.214	5	97	30		4.1
2001	LA N★	15	11	.577	36	35	2-1	0-0	234	183	98	23	20	91-1	218	3.50	118	.216	.305	69-0-7	.145	1	96	18		2.0
2002	Tex A	9	8	.529	25	25	0	0-0	145.2	154	95	20	17	78-2	121	5.75	83	.273	.376	4	.000	-0	124	-13	56	-1.3
2003	Tex A	1	3	.250	7	7	0	0-0	29.2	34	26	5	6	25-0	16	7.58	66	.306	.448	0	—	0	85	-8	153	-0.8
2004	Tex A	4	7	.364	16	16	0	0-0	95.2	105	63	22	13	33-0	63	5.46	90	.281	.356	0	—	0	87	-5	98	-0.5
2005	Tex A	8	5	.615	20	20	0	0-0	109.2	130	70	8	6	54-1	80	5.66	81	.299	.382	5	.400	1	131	-10		-0.8
	SD N	4	3	.571	10	9	0	0-0	45.2	50	33	3	4	26-0	33	5.91	65	.278	.379	4	.214	-0	150	-12		-1.4
Total 12		106	80	.570	299	253	9-2	0-0	1610	1474	833	182	116	776-17	1411	4.33	99	.245	.340	364-2-43	.173	11	109	4	307	2.4

PARK, JIM James B11.10.1892 Richmond KY D12.17.1970 Lexington KY BR/TR/6-2/175 d9.7 Col Kentucky

YEAR	TM LG	W	L	PCT	G	GS	CG-SHO	SV-BS	IP	H	R	HR	HB	BB-IB	SO	ERA	AERA	OAV	OOB	AB-HR-SH	AVG	PB	SUP	APR	DL	PW
1915	StL A	2	0	1.000	3	3	1	0	22.2	18	8	1	0	9	5	1.19	240	.214	.290	10	.400	1	204	3		0.4
1916	StL A	1	4	.200	26	6	1	0	79	69	28	2	1	25	26	2.62	105	.244	.307	20	.100	-2	55	2		-0.1
1917	StL A	1	1	.500	13	0	0	0	20.1	27	20	1	0	12	9	6.64	39	.333	.419	2	.000	-0		-9		-0.9
Total 3		4	5	.444	42	9	2	0	122	114	56	4	1	46	40	3.02	91	.254	.325	32	.188	-0	109	-4		-0.6

PARKER, CHRISTIAN Christian Michael B7.3.1975 Albuquerque NM BR/TR/6-1/200 [MonN96 4/100] d4.6 Col Notre Dame [DL 2002 NY A 183]

YEAR	TM LG	W	L	PCT	G	GS	CG-SHO	SV-BS	IP	H	R	HR	HB	BB-IB	SO	ERA	AERA	OAV	OOB	AB-HR-SH	AVG	PB	SUP	APR	DL	PW
2001	NY A	0	1	.000	1	1	0	0-0	3	8	7	2	0	1-0	1	21.00	21	.471	.500	0	—	0	83	-5	184	-0.7

YEAR	TM LG	W	L	PCT	G	GS	CG-SHO	SV-BS	IP	H	R	HR	HB	BB-IB	SO	ERA	AERA	OAV	OOB	AB-HR-SH	AVG	PB	SUP	APR	DL	PW

PARKER, DOC   Harley Park   B6.14.1872 Theresa NY   D3.3.1941 Chicago IL   BR/TR/6-2/200   d7.11   b-Jay

1893	Chi N	0	0	—	1	0	0	1	2	5	3	0	0	1	0	13.50	34	.455	.500	1	.000	-0		-2		-0.1
1895	Chi N	4	2	.667	7	6	5-1	0	51.1	65	30	1	3	9	9	3.68	138	.304	.341	22	.318	1	98	8		0.7
1896	Chi N	1	5	.167	9	7	7	0	73	100	71	3	3	27	15	6.16	74	.323	.382	36	.278	0*	74	-13		-0.8
1901	Cin N	0	1	.000	1	1	0	0	8	26	21	1	0	2	0	15.75	20	.531	.549	3	.000	-0	66	-12		-0.9
Total	4	5	8	.385	18	14	13-1	1	134.1	196	125	5	6	39	24	5.90	79	.336	.383	62	.274	0	85	-19		-1.1

PARKER, HARRY   Harry William   B9.14.1947 Highland IL   BR/TR/6-3/190*   [StLN65 4/73]   d8.8

1970	StL N	1	1	.500	7	4	0	0-0	22.1	24	13	0	0	15-0	9	3.22	129	.276	.382	8	.250	0	97	0		0.1
1971	StL N	0	0	—	4	0	0	0-0	5	6	4	2	0	2-0	2	7.20	50	.286	.348	0	—	0		-2		-0.1
1973	†NY N	8	4	.667	38	9	0	5-1	96.2	79	40	7	3	36-3	63	3.35	109	.217	.291	23-0-5	.174	-0	105	3		0.3
1974	NY N	4	12	.250	40	16	1	4-3	131	145	64	10	3	46-5	58	3.92	92	.281	.342	36-0-3	.000	-4	56	-4		-0.9
1975	NY N	2	3	.400	18	1	0	2-0	34.2	37	17	2	0	19-5	22	4.41	80	.272	.361	2-0-1	.000	1	100	-3	25	-0.3
	StL N	0	1	.000	14	0	0	1-0	18.2	21	13	3	0	10-2	13	6.27	61	.288	.365	1-0-1	.000	0		-4		-0.2
	Year	2	4	.333	32	1	0	3-0	53.1	58	30	5	0	29-7	35	5.06	71	.278	.363	3-0-2	.000	1	97	-6		-0.5
1976	Cle A	0	0	—	3	0	0	0-0	7	3	0	0	0	0-0	5	0.00	—	.136	.136	0	—	0		3		0.2
Total	6	15	21	.417	124	30	1	12-4	315.1	315	151	24	6	128-15	172	3.85	95	.258	.330	70-0-10	.086	-3	79	-7	25	-0.9

PARKER, CLAY   James Clayton   B12.19.1962 Columbia LA   BR/TR/6-1/185*   [SeaA85 15/373]   d9.14   Col Louisiana St.

1987	Sea A	0	0	—	3	1	0	0-0	7.2	15	10	2	1	4-0	8	10.57	45	.405	.465	0	—	0	96	-5		-0.2
1989	NY A	4	5	.444	22	17	2	0-0	120	123	53	12	2	31-3	53	3.68	106	.264	.311	0	—	0	93	4	21	0.3
1990	NY A	1	1	.500	5	2	0	0-0	22	19	11	5	0	7-1	20	4.50	89	.229	.286	0	—	0	125	-1		0.1
	Det A	2	2	.500	24	1	0	0-0	51	45	18	4	1	25-5	20	3.18	125	.242	.332	0	—	0	69	5		0.4
	Year	3	3	.500	29	3	0	0-0	73	64	29	11	1	32-6	40	3.58	111	.238	.318	0	—	0	107	5		0.5
1992	Sea A	0	2	.000	8	6	0	0-0	33.1	47	28	6	2	11-0	20	7.56	53	.338	.390	0	—	0	118	-12	118	-0.6
Total	4	7	10	.412	62	27	2	0-0	234	249	120	31	6	78-9	121	4.42	90	.273	.332	0	—	0	100	-9	139	-0.2

PARKER, JAY   Jay   B7.8.1874 Theresa NY   D6.8.1935 Hartford MI   BL/TR/5-11/185   d9.27   b-Harley

| 1899 | Pit N | 0 | 0 | — | 1 | 1 | 0 | 0 | 2 | 8 | 2 | 0 | 1 | 2 | 2 | ∞ | — | 1.000 | 1.000 | 0 | — | 0 | 132 | -2 | | -0.1 |

PARKER, ROY   Roy William   B2.29.1896 Union MO   D5.17.1954 Tulsa OK   BR/TR/6-3/200   d9.10

| 1919 | StL N | 0 | 0 | — | 2 | 0 | 0 | 0 | 2 | 6 | 7 | 0 | 1 | 6 | 0 | 31.50 | 9 | .333 | .400 | 0 | — | 0 | | -6 | | -0.3 |

PARKS, SLICKER   Vernon Henry   B11.10.1895 Dallas (now Fowler) MI   D2.21.1978 Royal Oak MI   BR/TR/5-10/158   d7.11   Col Michigan

| 1921 | Det A | 3 | 2 | .600 | 10 | 1 | 0 | 0-0 | 25.1 | 33 | 17 | 2 | 1 | 16 | 10 | 5.68 | 75 | .306 | .400 | 9-0-1 | .111 | -1 | 98 | -3 | | -0.5 |

PARKS, BILL   William Robert   B6.4.1849 Easton PA   D10.10.1911 Easton PA   BR/TR/5-8/150   d4.26   M1 ▲

1875	Was NA	4	8	.333	14	11	9	0	106.2	144	120	3		5	3	3.29	72	.280	.287	111	.180	-3*	66	-9		-1.0
	Phi NA	0	0	—	2	0	0	0	5.1	13	11	0		1	0	8.44	27	.419	.438	6	.167	-0		-3		-0.2
	Year	4	8	.333	16	11	9	0	112	157	131	3		6	3	3.54	67	.288	.295	117	.179	-3	66	-17		-1.2

PARMELEE, ROY   Le Roy Earl "Tarzan"   B4.25.1907 Lambertville MI   D8.31.1981 Monroe MI   BR/TR/6-1/190   d9.28   Col Eastern Michigan

1929	NY N	1	0	1.000	2	1	0	0	7	13	7	1	1	3	1	9.00	51	.481	.548	2	.500	0	171	-3		-0.3
1930	NY N	1	0	1.000	11	1	0	0	21	18	26	3	0	26	19	9.43	50	.228	.419	4	.250	1	147	-12		-0.5
1931	NY N	2	2	.500	13	5	4	0	58.2	47	25	1	3	33	30	3.68	100	.223	.336	20-0-1	.200	-0	74	2		0.1
1932	NY N	0	3	.000	8	3	0	0	25.1	25	18	0	2	14	23	3.91	95	.250	.353	5	.400	1	60	-3		-0.2
1933	NY N	13	8	.619	32	32	14-3	0	218.1	191	94	9	14	77	132	3.17	101	.232	.309	81-1-1	.235	4*	122	1		0.5
1934	NY N	10	6	.625	22	21	7-2	0	152.2	134	59	6	6	60	83	3.42	113	.238	.335	55-2-2	.200	2	96	13		1.4
1935	NY N	14	10	.583	34	31	13	0	226	214	117	20	9	97	79	4.22	91	.249	.332	86	.209	3	115	-8		-0.4
1936	StL N	11	11	.500	37	28	9	2	221	226	125	13	10	107	79	4.56	86	.270	.360	76-0-2	.197	-0	101	-14		-1.3
1937	Chi N	7	8	.467	33	18	8	0	145.2	165	93	13	7	79	55	5.13	78	.286	.379	52-2-1	.173	0*	153	-18		-1.6
1939	Phi A	1	6	.143	14	5	0	1	44.2	42	41	2	3	35	13	6.45	73	.235	.369	15	.133	-1*	82	-10		-1.3
Total	10	59	55	.518	206	145	55-5	3	1120.1	1075	605	68	55	531	514	4.27	89	.253	.343	396-5-7	.207	9	112	-52		-3.6

PARNELL, MEL   Melvin Lloyd "Dusty"   B6.13.1922 New Orleans LA   BL/TL/6-0/180*   d4.20   [DL 1957 Bos A 86]

1947	Bos A	2	3	.400	15	5	1	0	50.2	60	41	1	1	27	23	6.39	61	.296	.381	18	.056	-2	105	-14		-1.4
1948	Bos A	15	8	.652	35	27	16-1	0	212	205	87	7	4	90	77	3.14	140	.252	.330	80-0-2	.162	-4	106	26		2.2
1949	Bos A★	25	7	.781	39	33	27-4	2	295.1	258	102	8	5	134	122	2.77	157	.237	.324	114-0-10	.254	2	123	49		5.2
1950	Bos A	18	10	.643	40	31	21-2	3	249	244	116	17	7	106	93	3.61	136	.259	.338	98-0-3	.194	-1	119	30		3.1
1951	Bos A★	18	11	.621	36	29	11-3	2	221	229	99	11	6	77	77	3.26	137	.272	.333	81-0-4	.309	4*	99	24		3.3
1952	Bos A	12	12	.500	33	29	15-3	2	214	207	94	13	5	89	107	3.62	109	.255	.332	84-1-0	.095	-3*	95	9		0.6
1953	Bos A	21	8	.724	38	34	12-5	0	241	217	89	15	4	116	136	3.06	137	.239	.328	94-0-6	.223	1	93	28		3.2
1954	Bos A	3	7	.300	19	15	4-1	0	92.1	104	45	7	1	35	38	3.70	111	.287	.349	34-0-1	.088	-2	93	3	47	0.2
1955	Bos A	2	3	.400	13	9	0	1	46	62	44	12	1	25-1	18	7.83	55	.318	.395	19	.316	1*	140	-16		-1.7
1956	Bos A	7	6	.538	21	20	6-1	0	131.1	129	71	9	0	59-2	41	3.77	123	.256	.333	46-0-4	.152	-2	95	8	30	0.5
Total	10	123	75	.621	289	232	113-20	10	1752.2	1715	797	104	28	758-3	732	3.50	125	.257	.335	668-1-30	.198	-7	106	147	163	15.5

PARNHAM, RUBE   James Arthur   B2.1.1894 Heidelberg PA   D11.25.1963 McKeesport PA   BR/TR/6-3/185   d9.20

1916	Phi A	2	1	.667	4	3	2	0	24.2	27	14	0	0	13	8	4.01	71	.300	.388	11	.273	1	150	-3		-0.2
1917	Phi A	0	1	.000	2	2	0	0	11	12	6	1	0	9	4	4.09	67	.316	.447	3	.000	-0	105	-1		-0.2
Total	2	2	2	.500	6	5	2	0	35.2	39	20	1	0	22	12	4.04	70	.305	.407	14	.214	0	132	-4		-0.4

PARONTO, CHAD   Chad Michael   B7.28.1975 Woodsville NH   BR/TR/6-5/255*   [BalA96 8/231]   d4.18   Col Massachusetts

2001	Bal A	1	3	.250	24	0	0	0-1	27	33	24	5	1	11-0	16	5.00	86	.289	.354	0	—	0		-6		-0.7
2002	Cle A	0	0	—	29	0	0	0-0	35.2	34	19	2	0	11-1	23	4.04	110	.248	.305	0	—	0	1	63	0.4
2003	Cle A	0	2	.000	6	0	0	0-0	6.2	7	8	1	0	3-0	6	9.45	47	.292	.357	0	—	0		-4		-0.7
Total	3	1	7	.125	59	0	0	0-1	69.1	74	51	9	3	25-1	45	4.93	89	.269	.330	0	—	0		-9	63	-1.4

PARQUE, JIM   Jim Vo   B2.8.1975 Norwalk CA   BL/TL/5-11/165*   [ChiA97 1/46]   d5.26   Col UCLA

1998	Chi A	7	5	.583	21	21	0	0-0	113	135	72	14	6	49-0	77	5.10	90	.299	.375	1-0-2	.000	0	107	-7		-0.6
1999	Chi A	9	15	.375	31	30	1	0-0	173.2	210	111	23	10	79-2	111	5.13	96	.299	.374	5-0-1	.400	1	89	-4		-0.5
2000	†Chi A	13	6	.684	33	32	0	0-0	187	208	105	21	11	71-1	111	4.28	118	.283	.352	4	.000	-0	126	13		1.1
2001	Chi A	0	3	.000	5	5	1	0-0	28	36	26	7	2	10-1	15	8.04	58	.308	.369	0	—	0	107	-9	164	-0.8
2002	Chi A	1	4	.200	9	8	0	0-0	25.1	34	29	11	1	16-0	13	9.95	45	.318	.405	0	—	0	67	-14		-2.1
2003	TB A	1	1	.500	5	5	0	0-0	17.1	27	23	2	1	16-0	8	11.94	38	.351	.468	0	—	0	124	-13	30	-1.2
Total	6	31	34	.477	103	97	2	0-0	544.1	650	366	78	31	241-4	335	5.42	90	.297	.372	10-0-3	.200	0	107	-34	194	-4.1

PARRA, JOSE   Jose Miguel   B11.28.1972 Jacagua, D.R.   BR/TR/5-11/165(160-175)   d5.7

1995	LA N	0	0	—	3	0	0	0-2	10.1	17	5	2	0	6-1	7	4.35	89	.256	.362	0-0-2	—	0		-2		-0.1
	Min A	1	5	.167	12	12	0	0-0	61.2	83	59	11	2	22-0	29	7.59	63	.313	.366	0	—	0	87	-20		-1.5
1996	Min A	5	5	.500	27	5	0	0-1	70	88	48	15	3	27-0	50	6.04	85	.308	.370	0	—	0	79	-6		-0.7
2000	Pit N	0	1	.000	6	0	0	0-0	11.2	17	9	3	1	7-0	9	6.94	67	.354	.446	0	—	1	59	-3		-0.1
2002	Ari N	0	1	.000	16	0	0	0-0	14	13	5	0	1	11-2	8	3.21	140	.255	.397	0	—	0	1	78	0.1
2004	NY N	1	0	1.000	13	0	0	0-0	14	14	9	2	0	6-1	14	3.21	134	.255	.328	0	—	0	1	78	0.1
Total	5	7	12	.368	82	19	0	0-1	181.2	225	135	33	8	79-4	117	6.09	79	.302	.372	0-0-2	—	1	83	-28	78	-2.2

PARRETT, JEFF   Jeffrey Dale   B8.26.1961 Indianapolis IN   BR/TR/6-3/193(185-205)   [MilA83 9/236]   d4.11   Col Kentucky

1986	Mon N	0	1	.000	12	0	0	0-0	20.1	19	11	3	0	13-0	21	4.87	77	.247	.352	2	.500	0		-2		-0.1
1987	Mon N	7	6	.538	45	0	0	6-5	62	53	33	8	0	30-4	56	4.21	101	.229	.317	5	.000	-1		0		0.0
1988	Mon N	12	4	.750	61	0	0	6-4	91.2	66	29	8	1	45-9	62	2.65	157	.214	.311	0	—	0	11	29	1.9
1989	Phi N	12	6	.667	72	0	0	6-6	105.2	90	43	6	0	44-13	69	2.98	120	.232	.307	5	.000	-1	6	23	0.9
1990	Phi N	4	9	.308	47	5	0	1-3	81.2	92	51	10	1	36-8	69	5.18	74	.293	.366	10-0-2	.000	-1	94	-11		-1.8
	Atl N	1	1	.500	20	0	0	1-3	27	27	11	1	1	19-2	17	3.00	134	.281	.392	1	1.000	0		3		0.2
	Year	5	10	.333	67	5	0	2-6	108.2	119	62	11	2	55-10	86	4.64	84	.290	.373	11-0-2	.091	-1	93	-8		-1.6
1991	Atl N	1	2	.333	18	0	0	1-0	21.1	31	18	2	0	12-2	14	6.33	61	.326	.402	0	—	0		-6		-0.7
1992	†Oak A	9	1	.900	66	0	0	0-1	98.1	81	35	7	2	42-3	78	3.02	125	.226	.308	0	—	0	10		0.9
1993	Col N	3	3	.500	40	0	0	1-3	73.2	78	47	6	2	45-9	66	5.38	89	.274	.371	11	.091	-1	119	-3	67	-0.3

YEAR	TM LG	W	L	PCT	G	GS	CG-SHO	SV-BS	IP	H	R	HR	HB	BB-IB	SO	ERA	AERA	OAV	OOB	AB-HR-SH	AVG	PB	SUP	APR	DL	PW
1995	StL N	4	7	.364	59	0	0	0-2	76.2	71	33	8	1	28-5	71	3.64	118	.243	.310	2	.500	0		6		0.8
1996	StL N	2	2	.500	33	0	0	0-2	42.1	40	20	2	1	20-2	42	4.25	100	.245	.330	2	.000	0		1		0.1
	Phi N	1	1	.500	18	0	0	0-0	24	24	5	0	0	11-2	22	1.88	230	.270	.347	0	—	0		7		0.5
	Year	3	3	.500	51	0	0	0-2	66.1	64	25	2	1	31-4	64	3.39	126	.254	.336	2	.000	0		8		0.6
total	10	56	43	.566	491	11	0	22-29	724.2	672	336	61	9	345-59	616	3.80	105	.249	.333	38-0-2	.105	-1	119	22	119	2.4

ARRIS, STEVE Steven Michael B12.17.1967 Joliet IL BR/TR/6-0/195* [PhiN89 5/118] d6.21 Col St. Francis (IL)

YEAR	TM LG	W	L	PCT	G	GS	CG-SHO	SV-BS	IP	H	R	HR	HB	BB-IB	SO	ERA	AERA	OAV	OOB	AB-HR-SH	AVG	PB	SUP	APR	DL	PW
1995	Pit N	6	6	.500	15	15	1-1	0-0	82	89	49	12	7	33-1	61	5.38	81	.283	.361	28-0-1	.250	1	84	-7		-0.7
1996	Pit N	0	3	.000	8	4	0	0-0	26.1	35	22	4	1	11-0	27	7.18	61	.321	.385	6-0-2	.167	0	103	-7	124	-0.7
1998	Cin N	6	5	.545	18	16	1-1	0-0	99	89	44	9	4	32-3	77	3.73	115	.236	.302	29-0-3	.138	-1	99	6		0.6
1999	Cin N	11	4	.733	22	21	2-1	0-0	128.2	124	59	16	6	52-4	86	3.50	134	.260	.338	38-0-5	.158	-1	91	15	37	1.4
2000	Cin N	12	17	.414	33	33	0	0-0	192.2	227	109	30	4	71-5	117	4.81	99	.294	.355	55-0-4	.127	-1*	83	1		-0.1
2001	Tor A	4	6	.400	19	19	1	0-0	105.2	126	60	17	8	41-4	49	4.60	100	.299	.362	1-0-1	.000	-0	89	-1	76	-0.1
2002	Tor A	5	5	.500	14	14	0	0-0	75.1	96	50	13	3	35-5	48	5.97	77	.314	.387	4	.000	-0	108	-9	76	-1.1
2003	TB A	0	3	.000	10	7	0	0-0	43.2	60	32	12	0	13-0	14	6.18	74	.328	.369	1	.000	-0	77	-7	27	-0.5
total	8	44	49	.473	139	129	5-3	0-0	753.1	846	425	114	27	288-22	479	4.75	96	.286	.353	162-0-16	.154	-2	90	-9	340	-1.2

ARRISH, JOHN John Henry B11.26.1977 Lancaster PA BL/TL/5-11/180(170-200) [BalA96 25/741] d7.24 [DL 2002 Bal A 183]

YEAR	TM LG	W	L	PCT	G	GS	CG-SHO	SV-BS	IP	H	R	HR	HB	BB-IB	SO	ERA	AERA	OAV	OOB	AB-HR-SH	AVG	PB	SUP	APR	DL	PW
2000	Bal A	2	4	.333	8	8	0	0-0	36.1	40	32	6	1	35-0	28	7.18	65	.288	.425	0	—	0	102	-11		-1.4
2001	Bal A	1	2	.333	16	1	0	0-0	22	22	17	5	3	17-1	20	6.14	70	.256	.396	0	—	0	107	-5		-0.6
2003	Bal A	1	0	1.000	14	0	0	0-2	23.2	17	7	2	1	8-2	15	1.90	242	.205	.280	0	—	0		6		0.3
2004	Bal A	6	3	.667	56	1	0	1-0	78	68	39	4	3	55-6	71	3.46	135	.238	.360	1	.000	-0	60	8		0.8
2005	Bal A	1	0	1.000	14	0	0	0-0	17.1	19	6	1	0	17-1	25	3.12	142	.279	.424	0	—	0		3	27	0.2
total	5	10	10	.500	108	10	0	1-2	177.1	166	101	18	8	132-10	159	4.31	107	.251	.376	1	.000	-0	99	1	210	-0.7

ARROTT, MIKE Michael Everett Arch B12.6.1954 Oxnard CA BR/TR/6-4/210* [BalA73 1/15] d9.5

YEAR	TM LG	W	L	PCT	G	GS	CG-SHO	SV-BS	IP	H	R	HR	HB	BB-IB	SO	ERA	AERA	OAV	OOB	AB-HR-SH	AVG	PB	SUP	APR	DL	PW
1977	Bal A	-	-	-	3	0	0	0-0	4.1	4	1	0	0	2-0	2	2.08	185	.250	.333	0	—	0		1		0.0
1978	Sea A	1	5	.167	27	10	0	1-1	82.1	108	59	8	3	32-5	41	5.14	75	.316	.373	0	—	0	110	-14	59	-1.0
1979	Sea A	14	12	.538	38	30	13-2	0-0	229.1	231	104	17	6	86-16	127	3.77	116	.267	.336	0	—	0	100	16		1.8
1980	Sea A	1	16	.059	27	16	1	3-1	94	136	83	16	1	42-9	53	7.28	57	.348	.411	0	—	0	64	-31	21	-4.6
1981	Sea A	3	6	.333	24	12	0	1-0	85	102	51	3	1	28-1	43	5.08	76	.299	.350	0	—	0	98	-10		-1.0
total	5	19	39	.328	119	68	14-2	5-2	495	581	298	44	11	190-31	266	4.87	85	.297	.360	0	—	0	93	-38	80	-4.8

ARROTT, TOM Thomas William "Tacky Tom" B4.10.1868 Portland OR D1.1.1932 Dundee OR BR/TR/5-10.5/170 d6.18 b-Jiggs ▲

YEAR	TM LG	W	L	PCT	G	GS	CG-SHO	SV-BS	IP	H	R	HR	HB	BB-IB	SO	ERA	AERA	OAV	OOB	AB-HR-SH	AVG	PB	SUP	APR	DL	PW
1893	Chi N	0	3	.000	4	3	2	0	27	35	30	1	0	17	7	6.67	69	.304	.394	27	.259	-0*	141	-6		-0.5
	Cin N	10	7	.588	22	17	11-1	0	154	174	95	1	9	70	33	4.09	117	.276	.357	68-1	.191	-3*	85	12		0.8
	Year	10	10	.500	26	20	13-1	0	181	209	125	2	9	87	40	4.48	106	.281	.363	95-1	.211	-3	93	11		0.3
1894	Cin N	17	19	.472	41	36	31-1	1	308.2	402	268	19	11	126	61	5.60	99	.311	.377	229-4-1	.323	8*	83	0		0.7
1895	Cin N	11	18	.379	41	31	23	3	263.1	382	228	8	5	76	57	5.47	91	.334	.378	201-3-6	.343	10*	90	-16		-0.5
1896	StL N	1	1	.500	7	2	2	0	42	62	39	4	3	18	8	6.21	70	.339	.407	474-7-14	.291	1*	82	-8		-0.3
total	4	39	48	.448	115	89	69-2	4	795	1055	660	33	28	307	166	5.33	96	.314	.376	999-15-21	.301	17	88	-18		-0.3

ARSON, JIGGS William Edwin B12.28.1885 Parker SD D5.19.1967 Los Angeles CA BR/TR/6-2/180 d5.16 Col Bucknell

YEAR	TM LG	W	L	PCT	G	GS	CG-SHO	SV-BS	IP	H	R	HR	HB	BB-IB	SO	ERA	AERA	OAV	OOB	AB-HR-SH	AVG	PB	SUP	APR	DL	PW
1910	Bos N	0	2	.000	10	4	0	0	35.1	35	23	2	2	26	7	3.82	87	.278	.409	12	.083	-1	162	-2		-0.3
1911	Bos N	0	1	.000	7	0	0	0	25	36	30	2	4	15	7	6.48	59	.375	.478	10	.200	-0		-9		-0.5
total	2	0	3	.000	17	4	0	0	60.1	71	53	4	6	41	14	4.92	72	.320	.439	22	.136	-2	162	-11		-0.8

ARSONS, CHARLIE Charles James B7.18.1863 Cherry Flats PA D3.24.1936 Mansfield PA BL/TL/5-10/160 d5.29

YEAR	TM LG	W	L	PCT	G	GS	CG-SHO	SV-BS	IP	H	R	HR	HB	BB-IB	SO	ERA	AERA	OAV	OOB	AB-HR-SH	AVG	PB	SUP	APR	DL	PW
1886	Bos N	0	2	.000	2	2	2	0	16	20	13	0		4	5	3.94	82	.308	.348	8	.375	1	48	-1		-0.1
1887	NY AA	1	1	.500	4	4	4	0	34	51	36	0	1	6	5	4.50	94	.319	.347	15	.200	-1*	116	-4		-0.2
1890	Cle N	0	1	.000	2	1	0	0	9	12	11	0	4	6	2	6.00	60	.308	.449	4	.750	1	194	-3		-0.2
total	3	1	4	.200	8	7	6	0	59	83	60	0	5	16	12	4.58	84	.314	.365	27	.333	2	109	-8		-0.5

ARSONS, TOM Thomas Anthony B9.13.1939 Lakeville CT BR/TR/6-7/210* d9.5

YEAR	TM LG	W	L	PCT	G	GS	CG-SHO	SV-BS	IP	H	R	HR	HB	BB-IB	SO	ERA	AERA	OAV	OOB	AB-HR-SH	AVG	PB	SUP	APR	DL	PW
1963	Pit N	0	1	.000	1	1	0	0	4.1	7	6	1	0	2-0	2	8.31	40	.368	.429	2	.000	-0	0	-3		-0.5
1964	NY N	1	2	.333	4	2	1	0	19.1	20	9	1	0	6-0	10	4.19	85	.274	.321	7	.000	-1	74	-1		-0.2
1965	NY N	1	10	.091	35	11	1-1	1	90.2	108	53	17	0	17-2	58	4.67	76	.290	.321	18-0-1	.056	-0	61	-11		-1.3
total	3	2	13	.133	40	14	2-1	1	114.1	135	68	19	0	25-2	70	4.72	75	.291	.325	27-0-1	.037	-2	58	-15		-2.0

ARSONS, BILL William Raymond B8.17.1948 Riverside CA BR/TR/6-6/195* d4.13 Col Utah

YEAR	TM LG	W	L	PCT	G	GS	CG-SHO	SV-BS	IP	H	R	HR	HB	BB-IB	SO	ERA	AERA	OAV	OOB	AB-HR-SH	AVG	PB	SUP	APR	DL	PW
1971	Mil A	13	17	.433	36	35	12-4	0-0	244.2	219	95	19	4	93-10	139	3.20	109	.241	.312	72-1-8	.167	3	85	10		1.6
1972	Mil A	13	13	.500	33	30	10-2	0-0	214	194	102	27	3	68-8	111	3.91	78	.240	.299	67-0-6	.164	0	99	-20		-2.4
1973	Mil A	3	6	.333	20	17	0	0-0	59.2	59	50	6	0	67-1	30	6.79	56	.257	.423	0	—	0	95	-19		-2.5
1974	Oak A	0	0	—	4	0	0	0-0	2	1	1	0	0	3-0	2	0.00	—	.143	.400	0	—	0		1		0.0
total	4	29	36	.446	93	82	22-6	0-0	520.1	473	247	52	7	231-19	282	3.89	86	.242	.322	139-1-14	.165	3	94	-28		-3.3

ARTENHEIMER, STAN Stanwood Wendell "Party" B10.21.1922 Chicopee Falls MA D1.28.1989 Wilson NC BR/TL/5-11/175 d5.27 f-Steve Col Wooster

YEAR	TM LG	W	L	PCT	G	GS	CG-SHO	SV-BS	IP	H	R	HR	HB	BB-IB	SO	ERA	AERA	OAV	OOB	AB-HR-SH	AVG	PB	SUP	APR	DL	PW
1944	Bos N	0	0	—	1	1	0	0	1	3	2	0	0	2	0	18.00	19	.500	.625	1	.000	-0	49	-2		-0.1
1945	StL N	0	0	—	8	2	0	0	13.1	12	9	2	0	16	6	6.08	62	.250	.438	3	.000	-0	170	-3		-0.2
total	2	0	0	—	9	3	0	0	14.1	15	11	2	0	18	6	6.91	54	.278	.458	4	.000	-1	129	-5		-0.3

ASCHALL, BILL William Herbert B4.22.1954 Norfolk VA BR/TR/6-0/175* [KCA76*S3/53] d9.20 Col North Carolina-Asheville

YEAR	TM LG	W	L	PCT	G	GS	CG-SHO	SV-BS	IP	H	R	HR	HB	BB-IB	SO	ERA	AERA	OAV	OOB	AB-HR-SH	AVG	PB	SUP	APR	DL	PW
1978	KC A	0	1	.000	2	0	0	1-0	8	6	3	0	1	0-0	5	3.38	113	.207	.226	0	—	0		1		0.1
1979	KC A	0	1	.000	7	0	0	0-1	13.2	18	11	2	2	5-3	3	6.59	65	.300	.368	0	—	0		-3		-0.2
1981	KC A	0	0	—	2	0	0	0-0	2	2	1	0	0	0-0	1	4.50	80	.286	.286	0	—	0		-2		0.0
total	3	0	2	.000	11	0	0	1-1	23.2	26	15	2	3	5-3	9	5.32	76	.271	.321	0	—	0		-2		-0.1

ASCUAL, CAMILO Camilo Alberto (Lus) B1.20.1934 Havana, Cuba BR/TR/5-11/185(150-185) d4.15 C3 b-Carlos

YEAR	TM LG	W	L	PCT	G	GS	CG-SHO	SV-BS	IP	H	R	HR	HB	BB-IB	SO	ERA	AERA	OAV	OOB	AB-HR-SH	AVG	PB	SUP	APR	DL	PW
1954	Was A	4	7	.364	48	4	1	3	119.1	126	65	7	6	61	60	4.22	84	.276	.368	30-0-1	.133	-0	81	-9		-0.8
1955	Was A	2	12	.143	43	16	1	3	129	158	94	5	6	70-6	82	6.14	62	.311	.395	32-0-2	.219	0	93	-32		-3.0
1956	Was A	8	18	.250	39	27	6	0	188.2	194	131	33	6	89-4	162	5.87	74	.261	.342	58-0-6	.138	-2*	81	-27		-3.1
1957	Was A	8	17	.320	29	26	8-2	0	175.2	168	85	11	3	76-5	113	4.10	95	.258	.333	50-0-5	.140	-2*	80	-3		-0.5
1958	Was A	8	12	.400	31	27	6-2	0	177.1	166	66	14	3	60-2	146	3.15	121	.248	.351	57-0-4	.158	-1	75	13		1.4
1959	Was A*	17	10	.630	32	30	17-6	0	238.2	202	80	10	3	69-7	185	2.64	148	.226	.282	86-0-5	.302	6	105	34		4.7
1960	Was A*	12	8	.600	26	22	8-3	2	151.2	139	65	12	4	53-2	143	3.03	128	.240	.305	51-1-4	.176	3*	120	12		1.9
1961	Min A★	15	16	.484	35	33	15-8	0	252.1	205	114	26	3	100-1	221	3.46	123	.217	.293	85-0-5	.165	-0	102	19		2.2
1962	Min A★	20	11	.645	34	33	18-5	0	257.2	236	100	25	2	59-5	206	3.32	123	.241	.285	97-2-0	.268	8	107	24		3.7
1963	Min A	21	9	.700	31	31	18-3	0	248.1	205	76	21	3	81-4	202	2.46	148	.224	.288	92-0-5	.250	6*	129	33		4.7
1964	Min A★	15	12	.556	36	36	14-1	0	267.1	245	121	30	3	98-6	213	3.30	108	.241	.308	94-0-4	.181	4	112	5		0.9
1965	†Min A	9	3	.750	27	27	5-1	0	156	126	67	12	6	63-0	96	3.35	106	.217	.298	60-2-2	.200	3	122	4		0.7
1966	Min A	8	6	.571	21	19	2	0	103	113	63	9	2	30-0	56	4.89	73	.278	.323	37-0-1	.216	1	103	-13	37	-1.5
1967	Was A	12	10	.545	28	27	5-1	0	164.2	147	73	16	3	43-3	106	3.28	96	.237	.288	51-0-6	.176	1	108	-4		-0.4
1968	Was A	13	12	.520	31	31	8-4	0	201	181	72	16	4	59-4	111	2.69	109	.239	.297	65-0-4	.185	1	98	4		0.6
1969	Was A	2	5	.286	14	13	0	0-0	55.1	49	42	12	5	38-1	34	6.83	51	.239	.371	17	.235	0*	117	-18		-0.2
	Cin N	0	0	—	5	1	0	0-0	7.1	14	7	2	0	4-0	3	8.59	44	.424	.486	0	—	0	448	-3	21	-0.2
1970	LA N	0	0	—	10	0	0	0-0	14	12	4	2	1	5-1	8	2.57	150	.231	.310	0	—	0		2	21	0.1
1971	Cle A	2	2	.500	9	1	0	0-0	23.1	17	9	0	1	11-0	20	3.09	126	.205	.302	5-0-1	.600	1	23	2		0.5
total	18	174	170	.506	529	404	132-36	10-0	2930.2	2703	1334	256	61	1069-51	2167	3.63	103	.244	.312	967-5-55	.205	29	103	43	113	9.9

ASCUAL, CARLOS Carlos Alberto (Lus) "Little Potato" B3.13.1931 Havana, Cuba BR/TR/5-6/165 d9.24 b-Camilo

YEAR	TM LG	W	L	PCT	G	GS	CG-SHO	SV-BS	IP	H	R	HR	HB	BB-IB	SO	ERA	AERA	OAV	OOB	AB-HR-SH	AVG	PB	SUP	APR	DL	PW
1950	Was A	1	1	.500	2	2	2	0	17	18	8		3	3		2.12	212	.194	.296	4-0-1	.250	0	60	4		0.5

ASHNICK, LARRY Larry John B4.25.1956 Lincoln Park MI BR/TR/6-3/200* d4.10 Col Michigan St.

YEAR	TM LG	W	L	PCT	G	GS	CG-SHO	SV-BS	IP	H	R	HR	HB	BB-IB	SO	ERA	AERA	OAV	OOB	AB-HR-SH	AVG	PB	SUP	APR	DL	PW
1982	Det A	4	4	.500	28	13	1	0-0	94.1	110	46	17	1	25-2	19	4.01	102	.297	.342	0	—	0	91	1		0.1
1983	Det A	1	3	.250	12	6	0	0-1	37.2	48	27	5	3	18-1	17	5.26	75	.308	.383	0	—	0	80	-7		-0.6
1984	Min A	2	1	.667	13	1	0	0-0	38.1	38	19	3	2	11-1	10	3.52	120	.260	.321	0	—	0	64	2		0.1
total	3	7	6	.467	53	20	1	0-1	170.1	196	92	25	6	54-4	46	4.17	98	.292	.347	0	—	0	85	-4		-0.4

YEAR	TM LG	W	L	PCT	G	GS	CG-SHO	SV-BS	IP	H	R	HR	HB	BB-IB	SO	ERA	AERA	OAV	OOB	AB-HR-SH	AVG	PB	SUP	APR	DL	PW
PASSEAU, CLAUDE	Claude William		B4.9.1909 Waynesboro MS			D8.30.2003 Lucedale MS		BR/TR/6-3/198		d9.29	Col Millsaps															
1935	Pit N	0	1	.000	1	1	0	0	3	7	4	0	0	2	1	12.00	34	.500	.563	1	.000	-0	124	-2		-0.
1936	Phi N	11	15	.423	49	21	8-2	3	217.1	247	118	7	4	55	85	3.48	130	.280	.325	78-2-2	.282	3*	93	18		2.
1937	Phi N	14	18	.438	50	34	18-1	2	292.1	348	158	16	5	79	135	4.34	100	.286	.343	107-1-1	.196	-0	93	0		0.
1938	Phi N	11	18	.379	44	33	15	1	239	281	147	8	8	93	100	4.52	86	.287	.354	80-0-4	.162	-2*	85	-20		-0.
1939	Phi N	2	4	.333	8	8	4-1	0	53.1	54	26	1	1	25	29	4.22	95	.263	.346	20	.200	-0	95	0		-0.
	Chi N	13	9	.591	34	27	13-1	3	221	215	86	8	4	48	108	3.05	129	.254	.297	77-1-2	.156	-1*	109	22		1.
	Year	15	13	.536	42	35	17-2	3	274.1	269	112	9	5	73	137	3.28	120	.256	.307	97-1-2	.165	-2	106	22		1.
1940	Chi N	20	13	.606	46	31	20-4	5	280.2	259	97	8	4	59	124	2.50	150	.237	.278	98-1-3	.204	6	116	37		5.
1941	Chi N★	14	14	.500	34	34	20-3	0	231	262	99	10	1	52	80	3.35	105	.281	.320	86-3-4	.221	5	115	6		1.
1942	Chi N★	19	14	.576	35	34	24-3	0	278.1	284	116	13	4	74	89	2.68	119	.260	.309	105-2-5	.181	1	110	9		1.
1943	Chi N☆	15	12	.556	35	31	18-1	1	257	245	96	10	4	66	93	2.91	115	.249	.299	96-0-6	.198	1	110	13		2.
1944	Chi N	15	9	.625	34	27	18-2	3	227	234	80	8	1	50	89	2.89	122	.266	.306	80-0-7	.162	-1	85	20		2.
1945	†Chi N✳	17	9	.654	34	27	19-**5**	1	227	205	70	4	2	59	98	2.46	149	.238	.289	91-2-3	.187	2	119	**33**		3.
1946	Chi N★	9	8	.529	21	21	10-2	0	129.1	118	53	5	1	42	47	3.13	106	.237	.298	49-3-3	.204	3	108	2		0.
1947	Chi N	2	6	.250	19	6	1-1	2	63.1	97	54	7	1	24	26	6.25	63	.353	.407	14-0-1	.000	-2	52	-18		1.
Total	13	162	150	.519	444	331	188-26	21	2719.2	2856	1204	105	39	728	1104	3.32	113	.267	.316	982-15-41	.192	13	102	120		14.
PASTORE, FRANK	Frank Enrico		B8.21.1957 Alhambra CA					BR/TR/6-3/205*		[CinN75 2/46]		d4.4														
1979	†Cin N	6	7	.462	30	9	2-1	4-2	95.1	102	47	8	1	23-5	63	4.25	87	.271	.313	25-0-2	.160	-0	106	-4		-0.
1980	Cin N	13	7	.650	27	27	9-2	0-0	184.2	161	72	13	0	42-3	110	3.27	108	.233	.275	64-0-6	.156	-1	112	5	26	0.
1981	Cin N	4	9	.308	22	22	2-1	0-0	132	125	73	11	3	35-1	81	4.02	87	.247	.297	44-0-6	.114	-2	106	-11		-1.
1982	Cin N	8	13	.381	31	29	3-2	0-0	188.1	210	86	13	4	57-8	93	3.97	93	.286	.338	58-1-5	.172	1	94	-3	25	-1.
1983	Cin N	9	12	.429	36	29	4-1	0-0	184.1	207	104	20	1	64-3	93	4.88	78	.290	.346	59-1-3	.186	2	103	-18		-1.
1984	Cin N	3	8	.273	24	16	1	0-0	98.1	110	74	10	3	40-3	53	6.50	58	.285	.353	28-0-2	.071	-2	98	-26	22	-2.
1985	Cin N	2	1	.667	17	6	1	0-0	54	60	23	1	1	16-1	23	3.83	99	.287	.336	14-0-2	.143	-0	97	1	79	-0.
1986	Min A	3	1	.750	33	1	0	2-3	49.1	54	28	4	0	24-6	18	4.01	108	.283	.356	0	—	0	105	0	21	0.
Total	8	48	58	.453	229	139	22-7	6-5	986.1	1029	507	80	13	301-30	541	4.29	86	.270	.323	292-2-26	.151	-2	102	-56	173	-6.
PASTORIUS, JIM	James W. "Sunny Jim"		B7.12.1881 Pittsburgh PA			D5.10.1941 Pittsburgh PA		BL/TL/5-9/165		d4.15																
1906	Bro N	10	14	.417	29	24	16-3	0	211.2	225	111	4	3	69	58	3.61	70	.274	.333	71-0-5	.141	-0	103	-26		-2.
1907	Bro N	16	12	.571	28	26	20-4	0	222	218	74	2	6	77	70	2.35	100	.264	.331	73-0-4	.205	3*	92	3		0.
1908	Bro N	4	20	.167	28	25	16-2	0	213.2	171	88	5	7	74	54	2.44	96	.216	.288	62-0-3	.129	-0	58	-6		0.
1909	Bro N	1	9	.100	12	9	5-1	0	79.2	91	65	4	1	58	23	5.76	45	.313	.429	25	.080	-1	57	-27		-3.
Total	4	31	55	.360	97	84	57-10	0	727	705	338	15	17	278	205	3.12	78	.258	.330	231-0-12	.152	1	81	-56		-5.
PATE, JOE	Joseph William		B6.6.1892 Alice TX			D12.26.1948 Fort Worth TX		BL/TL/5-10/184		d4.15	Col Tulane														
1926	Phi A	9	0	1.000	47	2	0	6	113	109	38	3	2	51	24	2.71	154	.262	.345	27-0-2	.148	-0	81	**20**		1.
1927	Phi A	0	3	.000	32	0	0	6	53.2	67	36	3	1	21	14	5.20	82	.318	.382	10	.300	1		-5		-0.
Total	2	9	3	.750	79	2	0	12	166.2	176	74	6	3	72	38	3.51	120	.281	.358	37-0-2	.189	1	81	15		1.
PATRICK, BRONSWELL	Bronswell Dante		B9.16.1970 Greenville NC			BR/TR/6-1/220(205-237)		[OakA88 23/593]		d5.18															
1998	Mil N	4	1	.800	32	3	0	0	78.2	83	43	9	0	29-1	49	4.69	92	.279	.339	15-1-1	.200	2	92	-2		0
1999	SF N	1	0	1.000	6	0	0	1-0	5.1	9	7	1	0	3-0	6	10.13	42	.375	.429	1	.000	-0		-4		-0.
Total	2	5	1	.833	38	3	0	1-0	84	92	50	10	0	32-1	55	5.04	86	.286	.346	16-1-1	.188	1	92	-6		0
PATTEN, CASE	Case Lyman "Casey"		B5.7.1874 Westport NY			D5.31.1935 Rochester NY		BB/TL/6-0/175		d5.4															
1901	Was A	18	10	.643	32	30	26-4	0	254.1	285	163	8	17	74	109	3.93	93	.280	.339	96-1-6	.135	-5	115	-9		-1
1902	Was A	18	17	.514	36	34	33-1	0	299.2	331	186	11	11	89	92	4.05	91	.281	.337	125-0-3	.096	-10*	94	-13		-2
1903	Was A	11	22	.333	36	34	32	1	300	313	163	11	4	80	133	3.60	87	.268	.317	106-0-5	.132	-6	68	-16		-2
1904	Was A	14	23	.378	45	39	37-2	3	357.2	367	162	3	20	79	150	3.07	87	.266	.315	126-0-4	.127	-5	77	-15		-2
1905	Was A	14	21	.400	42	36	29-2	0	309.2	300	145	3	10	86	113	3.14	84	.256	.312	103-0-4	.155	-2	94	-14		-1
1906	Was A	19	16	.543	38	32	28-7	0	282.2	253	106	2	6	79	96	2.17	122	.242	.299	94-1-1	.117	-4	72	11		0
1907	Was A	12	16	.429	36	29	20-1	0	237.1	272	135	3	6	63	58	3.56	68	.290	.339	87-0-3	.126	-3	96	-30		-3.
1908	Was A	0	2	.000	4	3	1	0	18	25	14	0	0	6	6	3.50	65	.333	.383	5	.200	-0	179	-4		-0.
	Bos A	0	1	.000	1	1	0	0	3	8	5	0	0	1	0	15.00	16	.533	.563	1	.000	-0	139	-3		-0
	Year	0	3	.000	5	4	1	0	21	33	19	0	0	7	6	5.14	45	.367	.412	6	.167	-0	170	-7		-0
Total	8	106	128	.453	270	238	206-17	4	2062.1	2154	1079	40	74	557	757	3.36	88	.270	.323	743-2-26	.127	-35	90	-93		-13
PATTERSON, DANNY	Danny Shane		B2.17.1971 San Gabriel CA			BR/TR/6-0/225(185-225)		[TexA89 47/1199]		d7.26	Col Cerritos (CA) JC														
1996	†Tex A	0	0	—	7	0	0	0-0	8.2	10	4	0	0	3-1	5	0.00	—	.286	.342	0		0		3		0.
1997	Tex A	10	6	.625	54	0	0	1-7	71	70	29	3	0	23-4	69	3.42	142	.263	.318	0	—	0	11	28	2.
1998	Tex A	2	5	.286	56	0	0	2-0	60.2	64	31	11	2	19-2	34	4.45	110	.274	.332	0		0	4	17	0.
1999	†Tex A	2	0	1.000	53	0	0	0-1	60.1	77	38	5	1	19-3	43	5.67	91	.304	.353	1	.000	-0		-2		-0
2000	Det A	5	1	.833	58	0	0	0-2	56.2	69	26	4	2	14-2	29	3.97	124	.309	.353	0	—	0	6	15	0
2001	Det A	5	4	.556	60	0	0	1-4	64.2	64	24	4	4	12-5	21	3.06	144	.274	.316	0		0	10	1	0
2002	Det A	0	2	.000	6	0	0	0-1	3	5	5	0	1	2-0	1	15.00	29	.357	.471	0		0	-3	170	-0.
2003	Det A	0	0	—	19	0	0	3-0	17.2	15	8	1	1	4-0	19	4.08	107	.227	.282	0	—	0	1	109	0
2004	Det A	0	4	.000	37	0	0	2-2	41.2	44	24	7	5	16-2	29	4.75	94	.282	.367	0	—	0	-2	24	-0.
Total	9	24	22	.522	350	0	0	9-17	384.1	418	189	35	16	112-19	250	4.14	116	.282	.337	1	.000	-0		28	363	3
PATTERSON, DARYL	Daryl Alan		B11.21.1943 Coalinga CA			BL/TR/6-4/195*		d4.10	Mil 1969		Col Sequoias (CA) [JC]														
1968	†Det A	2	3	.400	38	1	0	7	68	53	19	3	4	27-1	49	2.12	142	.213	.299	13	.000	-1	116	6		0
1969	Det A	0	2	.000	18	0	0	0-2	22.1	15	8	2	0	19-3	12	2.82	133	.205	.358	1	.000	-0		2		0
1970	Det A	7	1	.875	43	0	0	2-2	78	81	47	9	5	39-1	55	4.85	78	.269	.361	11	.000	-1		-9		-1.
1971	Det A	0	1	.000	12	0	0	0-0	9.1	14	7	1	1	6-1	9	4.82	75	.359	.457	0	—	0		-2		-0
	Oak A	0	0	—	4	0	0	0-0	5.2	5	5	3	1	4-0	2	7.94	42	.238	.385	1	.000	-0		-3		-0
	Year	0	1	.000	16	0	0	0-0	15	19	12	4	2	10-1	11	7.00	59	.317	.431	1	.000	-0		-5		-0
	StL N	0	1	.000	13	2	0	1-0	26.2	20	14	3	0	15-1	11	4.39	83	.211	.313	5	.000	-0	98	-2		-0
1974	Pit N	2	1	.667	14	0	0	1-1	21	35	19	3	0	9-1	8	7.29	48	.376	.427	4	.000	-1		-9		-1.
Total	5	11	9	.550	142	3	0	11-5	231	223	119	24	11	119-8	142	4.09	85	.256	.350	35	.000	-3	101	-17		-5
PATTERSON, DAVE	David Glenn		B7.25.1956 Springfield MO			BR/TR/6-0/170		[LAN76*2/44]		d6.9	Col Cerritos (CA) JC														
1979	LA N	4	1	.800	36	0	0	6-1	53	62	35	6	0	22-6	34	5.26	69	.292	.356	7-0-2	.143	-0*		-10		-1
PATTERSON, GIL	Gilbert Thomas		B9.5.1955 Philadelphia PA			BR/TR/6-1/185		[NYA75 S1/7]		d4.19	C4 Col Miami-Dade Kendall (FL) CC														
1977	NY A	1	2	.333	10	6	0	1-0	33.1	38	20	3	3	20-1	29	5.40	73	.290	.396	0	—	0	110	-4		0
PATTERSON, JEFF	Jeffrey Simmons		B10.1.1968 Anaheim CA			BR/TR/6-2/200		[PhiN88 58/1353]		d4.30	Col Cypress (CA) JC														
1995	NY A	0	0	—	2	0	0	0-0	3	1	1	1	0	3-0	3	2.70	171	.231	.375	0	—	0		1		0
PATTERSON, JOHN	John Hollis		B1.30.1978 Orange TX			BR/TR/6-6/200*		d7.20																		
2002	Ari N	2	0	1.000	7	5	0	0-0	30.2	27	11	7	1	7-0	31	3.23	139	.235	.285	10-0-1	.100	-0	173	4		0
2003	Ari N	1	4	.200	16	8	0	1-0	55	61	39	7	2	30-5	43	6.05	76	.281	.371	13	.077	-1	97	-7		-0
2004	Mon N	4	7	.364	19	19	0	0-0	98.1	100	58	18	8	46-4	99	5.03	91	.260	.349	33-0-5	.121	-1	83	-3	78	-3.
2005	Was N	9	7	.563	31	31	2-1	0-0	198.1	172	71	19	5	65-11	185	3.13	129	.233	.298	59-0-8	.102	-2	87	23	15	1
Total	4	16	18	.471	73	63	2-1	1-0	382.1	360	179	51	16	148-20	358	4.05	106	.247	.322	115-0-14	.104	-4	94	17	93	0
PATTERSON, KEN	Kenneth Brian		B7.8.1964 Costa Mesa CA			BL/TL/6-4/210(210-230)		[NYA85 3/77]		d7.8	Col Baylor														
1988	Chi A	0	2	.000	11	0	0	1-0	20.2	25	11	2	0	7-0	6	4.79	84	.294	.348	0	—	0	91	-1		-0
1989	Chi A	6	1	.857	50	1	0	0-1	65.2	64	37	11	2	28-3	43	4.52	85	.257	.332	0	—	0	165	-5		-0
1990	Chi A	2	1	.667	43	0	0	2-0	66.1	58	27	6	3	34-1	40	3.39	113	.242	.335	0	—	0		8		0
1991	Chi A	3	0	1.000	43	0	0	1-1	63.2	48	22	5	1	35-1	32	2.83	141	.214	.321	0	—	0		16		0
1992	Chi A	2	3	.400	32	1	0	0-0	41.2	41	25	7	1	27-6	23	3.89	93	.268	.373	1-0-1	.000	-0	249	-3	42	-0
1993	Cal A	1	1	.500	46	0	0	1-1	59	54	30	7	0	35-5	36	4.58	99	.249	.352	0	—	0		1		-0
1994	Cal A	0	0	—	2	0	0	0-0	0.2	0	0	0	0	0-0	1	0.00	—	.000	.000	0	—	0		0	110	0
Total	7	14	8	.636	224	4	0	5-5	317.2	290	152	38	6	166-16	183	3.88	103	.248	.340	1-0-1	.000	-0	143	3	152	-0

YEAR	TM LG	W	L	PCT	G	GS	CG-SHO	SV-BS	IP	H	R	HR	HB	BB-IB	SO	ERA	AERA	OAV	OOB	AB-HR-SH	AVG	PB	SUP	APR	DL	PW

PATTERSON, REGGIE Reginald Allen B11.7.1958 Birmingham AL BR/TR/6-4/180* d8.13

1981	Chi A	0	1	.000	6	1	0	0-0	7.1	14	11	1	0	6-0	2	13.50	27	.412	.500	0	—	0	149	-7		-0.9
1983	Chi N	1	2	.333	5	2	0	0-0	18.2	17	12	3	2	6-0	10	4.82	79	.246	.321	6-0-2	.000	-1	151	-2		-0.4
1984	Chi N	0	1	.000	3	1	0	0-0	6	10	7	1	0	2-0	5	10.50	37	.357	.400	2		-0	23	-4		-0.5
1985	Chi N	3	0	1.000	8	5	1	0-0	39	36	13	2	0	10-1	17	3.00	133	.250	.297	10-0-2	.100	-0	110	4		0.3
Total	4	4	4	.500	22	9	1	0-0	71	77	43	7	2	24-1	34	5.20	75	.280	.340	18-0-4	.056	-1	113	-9		-1.5

PATTERSON, BOB Robert Chandler B5.16.1959 Jacksonville FL BR/TL/6-2/192* [SDN82 21/524] d9.2 Col East Carolina

1985	SD N	0	0	—	3	0	0	0-0	4	13	11	2	0	3-0	1	24.75	14	.565	.615	0		0		-9		-0.4
1986	Pit N	2	3	.400	11	5	0	0-0	36.1	49	20	0	0	5-2	20	4.95	79	.322	.342	8-0-2	.125	-0	78	-3		-0.4
1987	Pit N	1	4	.200	15	7	0	0-0	43	49	34	5	1	22-4	27	6.70	62	.290	.369	12-0-1	.083	-1	90	-11		-1.2
1989	Pit N	4	3	.571	12	3	0	1-0	26.2	23	13	3	0	8-2	20	4.05	84	.232	.287	3-0-2	.000	0	104	-2		-0.4
1990	†Pit N	8	5	.615	55	5	0	5-3	94.2	88	33	9	3	21-7	70	2.95	124	.249	.294	19-0-1	.053	-1	104	9		1.1
1991	†Pit N	4	3	.571	54	1	0	2-1	65.2	67	32	7	0	15-1	57	4.11	88	.267	.306	6	.250	0	100	-3		-0.3
1992	†Pit N	6	3	.667	60	0	0	9-4	64.2	59	22	7	0	23-6	43	2.92	119	.246	.309	6	.333	1	4			0.8
1993	Tex A	2	4	.333	52	0	0	1-1	52.2	59	28	8	1	11-0	46	4.78	88	.282	.318	0	—	0		-2		-0.2
1994	Cal A	2	3	.400	47	0	0	1-0	42	35	21	6	2	15-2	30	4.07	121	.229	.306	0	—	0		3		0.3
1995	Cal A	5	2	.714	62	0	0	0-1	53.1	48	18	6	1	13-3	41	3.04	155	.246	.295	0	—	0	11			1.1
1996	Chi N	3	3	.500	79	0	0	8-2	54.2	46	19	6	1	22-7	53	3.13	140	.229	.303	3	.333	0		8		1.0
1997	Chi N	1	6	.143	76	0	0	0-3	59.1	47	23	9	0	10-1	58	3.34	130	.222	.252	1	.000	-0		7		0.7
1998	Chi N	1	1	.500	33	0	0	1-1	20.1	36	20	2	0	12-3	17	7.52	59	.391	.453	0-0-1	—	0		-8	17	-0.7
Total	13	39	40	.494	559	21	0	28-16	617.1	619	294	70	9	180-38	483	4.08	99	.263	.315	56-0-7	.125	-1	89	4	17	1.4

PATTERSON, ROY Roy Lewis "Boy Wonder" B12.17.1876 Stoddard WI D4.14.1953 St.Croix Falls WI BR/TR/6-0/185 d4.24

1901	Chi A	20	15	.571	41	35	30-4	0	312.1	345	164	11	11	62	127	3.37	103	.277	.317	117-1-6	.222	1	109	10		1.0
1902	Chi A	19	14	.576	34	30	26-2	0	268	262	111	5	3	67	61	3.06	111	.256	.304	105-0-5	.190	-2	99	13		1.2
1903	Chi A	15	15	.500	34	30	26-2	1	293	275	119	5	11	69	89	2.70	104	.248	.298	105-0-3	.105	-6	96	8		0.2
1904	Chi A	9	9	.500	22	17	14-4	0	165	148	52	1	7	24	64	2.29	107	.241	.277	30-0-1	.267	-4	96	5		0.1
1905	Chi A	4	6	.400	13	9	7	0	88.2	73	34	0	4	16	29	1.83	135	.226	.263	30-0-1	.267	2	83	4		0.7
1906	Chi A	10	7	.588	21	18	12-3	1	142	119	46	1	4	17	45	2.09	121	.231	.261	49-0-4	.061	-5	88	8		0.5
1907	Chi A	4	6	.400	19	13	4-1	0	96	105	42	0	2	18	27	2.63	91	.280	.316	31	.097	-3	121	-4		-0.7
Total	7	81	72	.529	184	152	119-16	2	1365	1327	568	23	38	273	442	2.75	107	.255	.297	495-1-22	.156	-16	101	44		3.0

PATTIN, MARTY Martin William B4.6.1943 Charleston IL BR/TR/5-11/180* [AnaA65 7/127] d5.14 C1 Col Eastern Illinois

1968	Cal A	4	4	.500	52	4	0	3	84	67	27	7	2	37-4	66	2.79	105	.221	.307	12-0-1	.083	-1	127	2		0.1
1969	Sea A	7	12	.368	34	27	2-1	0-0	158.2	166	104	29	2	71-5	126	5.62	65	.268	.345	58-0-2	.155	-1*	110	-31		-3.5
1970	Mil A	14	12	.538	37	29	11	0-0	233.1	204	91	20	6	71-9	161	3.39	111	.235	.296	70-0-7	.129	-2*	84	13		1.2
1971	Mil A☆	14	14	.500	36	36	9-5	0-0	264.2	225	100	29	4	73-11	169	3.13	112	.235	.289	83-0-11	.084	-3	85	13		1.0
1972	Bos A	17	13	.567	38	35	13-4	0-1	253	232	102	19	9	65-3	168	3.24	100	.243	.295	86-2-7	.140	0	106	1		0.2
1973	Bos A	15	15	.500	34	30	11-2	1-0	219.1	238	112	31	8	69-7	119	4.31	93	.277	.335	0	—	0	123	-5		-0.6
1974	KC A	3	7	.300	25	11	2	0-1	117.1	121	55	10	2	28-3	50	3.99	96	.264	.306	0	—	0	84	0		-0.1
1975	KC A	10	10	.500	44	15	5-1	5-1	177	173	77	13	3	45-6	89	3.25	119	.253	.300	0	—	0*	117	10		1.1
1976	†KC A	8	14	.364	44	15	4-1	5-3	141	114	51	9	3	38-9	65	2.49	141	.216	.271	0	—	0	105	14		2.2
1977	†KC A	10	3	.769	31	10	4	0-0	128.1	115	56	16	2	37-2	55	3.58	113	.242	.297	0	—	0	100	7		0.6
1978	†KC A	3	3	.500	32	5	2	4-1	78.2	72	41	8	2	25-7	30	3.32	115	.248	.307	0	—	0	61	1		0.0
1979	KC A	5	2	.714	31	7	1	3-0	94.1	109	50	11	1	21-2	41	4.58	93	.293	.329	0	—	0	103	-1	20	-0.1
1980	†KC A	4	0	1.000	37	0	0	4-0	89	97	39	7	1	23-7	40	3.64	111	.277	.321	0	—	0		5		0.2
Total	13	114	109	.511	475	224	64-14	25-7	2038.2	1933	905	209	45	603-75	1179	3.62	102	.250	.306	309-2-28	.123	-7	101	29	20	2.3

PATTISON, JIMMY James Wells B12.18.1908 Bronx NY D2.22.1991 Melbourne FL BL/TL/6-0/185 d4.18

| 1929 | Bro N | 0 | 1 | .000 | 6 | 0 | 0 | 0 | 11.2 | 14 | 6 | 0 | 0 | 4 | 5 | 4.63 | 100 | .231 | .302 | 2 | .500 | 0 | | | | 0.1 |

PATTON, HARRY Harry Claude B6.29.1884 Gillespie IL D6.9.1930 St.Louis MO d8.22

| 1910 | StL N | 0 | 0 | — | 1 | 0 | 0 | 0 | 4 | 4 | 2 | 0 | 0 | 2 | 2 | 2.25 | 132 | .267 | .353 | 0 | — | 0 | | 0 | | 0.0 |

PAUL, MIKE Michael George B4.18.1945 Detroit MI BL/TL/6-0/183* d5.27 C6 Col Arizona

1968	Cle A	5	8	.385	36	7	0	3	91.2	72	42	11	5	35-5	87	3.93	76	.213	.295	24-0-1	.167	0	117	-8		-1.2
1969	Cle A	5	10	.333	47	12	0	2-0	117.1	104	48	12	2	54-11	98	3.61	105	.241	.325	27-0-1	.000	-3	45	5		0.3
1970	Cle A	2	8	.200	30	15	1	0-2	88	91	51	13	0	45-0	70	4.81	83	.271	.351	26-0-1	.154	-1	67	-8		-0.9
1971	Cle A	2	7	.222	17	12	1	0-0	62	78	42	8	5	14-3	33	5.95	65	.318	.365	19-0-1	.053	-1	64	-12		-1.7
1972	Tex A	8	9	.471	49	20	2-1	1-2	161.2	149	50	4	2	52-12	108	2.17	141	.246	.306	48-0-3	.167	1	73	14		1.6
1973	Tex A	5	4	.556	36	10	1	2-2	87.1	104	55	9	5	36-2	49	4.95	76	.295	.364	0	—	0*	83	-12		-1.1
	Chi N	0	1	.000	11	1	0	0-0	18.1	17	7	2	0	9-2	6	3.44	115	.258	.342	4	.000	-0	45	1		0.0
1974	Chi N	0	0	1.000	2	0	0	0-0	1.1	4	4	1	0	1-1	1	27.00	14	.500	.556	0	—	0		-3		-0.5
Total	7	27	48	.360	228	77	5-1	8-6	627.2	619	299	60	19	246-36	452	3.91	90	.260	.331	148-0-7	.115	-4	71	-23		-3.5

PAULSEN, GIL Guilford Paul Hans B11.14.1902 Graettinger IA D4.2.1994 Harlan IA BR/TR/6-2.5/190 d10.3 Col Cornell

| 1925 | StL N | 0 | 0 | — | 1 | 0 | 0 | 0 | 2 | 1 | 0 | 0 | 0 | 1 | 0 | 0.00 | — | .125 | .125 | 0 | — | 0 | | 1 | | 0.1 |

PAVANO, CARL Carl Anthony B1.8.1976 New Britain CT BR/TR/6-5/230(225-240) [BosA94 13/355] d5.23

1998	Mon N	6	9	.400	24	23	0	0-0	134.2	130	70	18	8	43-1	83	4.21	100	.251	.315	38-0-6	.158	-0	82	0		-0.1
1999	Mon N	6	8	.429	19	18	1-1	0-0	104	117	66	8	4	35-1	70	5.63	79	.285	.345	33-0-5	.061	-2	82	-10	61	-1.2
2000	Mon N	8	4	.667	15	15	0	0-0	97	89	40	8	8	34-1	64	3.06	154	.248	.324	35-0-3	.143	-1	101	16	98	1.7
2001	Mon N	1	6	.143	8	8	0	0-0	42.2	59	33	7	2	16-1	36	6.33	68	.331	.391	13-0-1	.077	-1	35	-10	136	-1.4
2002	Mon N	3	8	.273	15	14	0	0-0	74.1	98	55	14	7	31-5	51	6.30	70	.318	.391	24-0-3	.208	0	93	-14		-1.7
	Fla N	3	2	.600	22	8	0	0-0	61.2	76	33	5	3	14-3	41	3.79	104	.306	.348	16-0-2	.188	1	150	-1		-0.1
	Year	6	10	.375	37	22	0	0-0	136	174	88	19	10	45-8	92	5.16	81	.313	.372	40-0-5	.200	1	114	-16		-1.8
2003	†Fla N	12	13	.480	33	32	1	0-0	201	204	99	19	7	49-10	133	4.30	95	.265	.311	61-0-5	.098	-1	92	-3		-0.5
2004	Fla N★	18	8	.692	31	31	2-2	0-0	222.1	212	80	16	11	49-13	139	3.00	137	.253	.302	68-2-9	.191	4	111	28		3.5
2005	NY A	4	6	.400	17	17	1-1	0-0	100	129	66	17	8	18-1	56	4.77	92	.315	.354	7	.000	-1	111	-8	97	-0.8
Total	8	61	64	.488	184	166	6-4	0-0	1037.2	1114	542	112	58	289-36	673	4.27	100	.276	.331	295-2-34	.139	-1	96	-2	392	-0.6

PAVLAS, DAVE David Lee B8.12.1962 Frankfurt, W.Germany BR/TR/6-7/180(180-205) d8.21 Col Rice

1990	Chi N	2	0	1.000	13	0	0	0-0	21.1	23	7	2	0	6-2	12	2.11	194	.271	.312	1	.000	0		4		0.3
1991	Chi N	0	0	—	1	0	0	0-0	3	3	2	1	0	0-0	0	18.00	22	.750	.750	0	—	0		-1		-0.1
1995	NY A	0	0	—	4	0	0	0-0	5.2	8	2	0	0	0-0	3	3.18	146	.333	.333	0	—	0		1		0.0
1996	NY A	0	0	—	16	0	0	1-0	23	23	7	0	1	7-2	18	2.35	211	.264	.326	0	—	0		6		0.3
Total	4	2	0	1.000	34	0	0	1-0	51	57	18	3	1	13-4	33	2.65	172	.285	.329	1	.000	0		10		0.5

PAVLIK, ROGER Roger Allen B10.4.1967 Houston TX BB/TR/6-2/220* [TexA86 2/32] d5.2

1992	Tex A	4	4	.500	13	12	1	0-0	62	66	32	3	3	34-0	45	4.21	91	.280	.375	0	—	0	111	-2		-0.3
1993	Tex A	12	6	.667	26	26	2	0-0	166.1	151	67	18	5	80-3	131	3.41	123	.245	.334	0	—	0	112	16		1.6
1994	Tex A	2	5	.286	11	11	0	0-0	50.1	61	45	8	4	30-1	31	7.69	63	.300	.394	0	—	0	85	-14	83	-1.5
1995	Tex A	10	10	.500	31	31	2-1	0-0	191.2	174	96	19	4	90-5	149	4.37	111	.243	.329	0	—	0	84	12		1.2
1996	†Tex A★	15	8	.652	34	34	7	0-0	201	216	120	28	5	81-5	127	5.19	101	.276	.346	0	—	0	108	3		0.1
1997	Tex A	3	5	.375	11	11	0	0-0	57.2	59	29	7	1	31-1	35	4.37	111	.267	.358	0	—	0	74	4	118	0.4
1998	Tex A	1	1	.500	5	0	0	1-0	14	16	8	2	1	6-0	8	3.86	127	.286	.349	0	—	0		1	157	0.1
Total	7	47	39	.547	131	125	12-1	1-0	743	743	397	85	23	351-16	526	4.58	103	.262	.346	0	—	0	98	20	358	1.6

PAWLOWSKI, JOHN John B9.6.1963 Johnson City NY BR/TR/6-2/175* [ChiA85 6/137] d9.19 Col Clemson

1987	Chi A	0	0	—	2	0	0	0-0	3.2	1	1	0	0	3-0	2	4.91	94	.438	.500	0	—	0		0		0.0
1988	Chi A	1	0	1.000	6	0	0	0-0	14	20	14	2	0	3-0	10	8.36	48	.328	.354	0	—	0		-6		-0.4
Total	2	1	0	1.000	8	0	0	0-0	17.2	27	16	2	0	6-0	12	7.64	54	.351	.388	0	—	0		-6		-0.4

PAXTON, MIKE Michael De Wayne B9.3.1953 Memphis TN BR/TR/5-11/190* [BosA75 23/538] d5.25 Col Memphis

| 1977 | Bos A | 10 | 5 | .667 | 29 | 12 | 2-1 | 0-1 | 108 | 134 | 53 | 7 | 3 | 25-2 | 58 | 3.83 | 117 | .311 | .350 | 0 | — | 0 | 127 | 6 | | 0.7 |
| 1978 | Cle A | 12 | 11 | .522 | 33 | 27 | 5-2 | 1-2 | 191 | 179 | 89 | 13 | 8 | 63-5 | 96 | 3.86 | 98 | .247 | .313 | 0 | — | 0 | 105 | -1 | | -0.1 |

YEAR	TM LG	W	L	PCT	G	GS	CG-SHO	SV-BS	IP	H	R	HR	HB	BB-IB	SO	ERA	AERA	OAV	OOB	AB-HR-SH	AVG	PB	SUP	APR	DL	PW
1979	Cle A	8	8	.500	33	24	3	0-0	159.2	210	118	14	2	52-1	70	5.92	73	.315	.363	0	—	0	122	-29		-2.5
1980	Cle A	0	0	—	4	0	0	0-1	7.2	13	11	4	0	6-1	6	12.91	32	.394	.475	0	—	0		-7		-0.3
Total	4	30	24	.556	99	63	10-3	1-4	466.1	536	271	38	13	146-9	230	4.71	88	.289	.342	0	—	0	116	-31		-2.2

PAYNE, GEORGE   George Washington   B5.23.1890 Mt.Vernon KY   D1.24.1959 Bellflower CA   BR/TR/5-11/172   d5.8

YEAR	TM LG	W	L	PCT	G	GS	CG-SHO	SV-BS	IP	H	R	HR	HB	BB-IB	SO	ERA	AERA	OAV	OOB	AB-HR-SH	AVG	PB	SUP	APR	DL	PW
1920	Chi A	1	1	.500	12	0	0	0	29.2	39	24	2	0	9	7	5.46	69	.312	.358	8	.125	-0		-7		-0.5

PAYNE, HARLEY   Harley Fenwick "Lady"   B1.9.1868 Windsor OH   D12.29.1935 Orwell OH   BB/TL/6-0/160   d4.18

YEAR	TM LG	W	L	PCT	G	GS	CG-SHO	SV-BS	IP	H	R	HR	HB	BB-IB	SO	ERA	AERA	OAV	OOB	AB-HR-SH	AVG	PB	SUP	APR	DL	PW
1896	Bro N	14	16	.467	34	28	24-2	0	241.2	284	129	4	8	58	52	3.39	122	.290	.335	98-0-4	.214	0*	72	21		2.2
1897	Bro N	14	17	.452	40	38	30-1	0	280	350	215	8	17	71	86	4.63	88	.303	.353	110-0-3	.236	-0*	90	-24		-2.0
1898	Bro N	1	0	1.000	1	1	1	0	9	11	8	0	0	3	2	4.00	90	.297	.350	4	.750	1	178	-1		0.0
1899	Pit N	1	3	.250	5	5	2	0	26.1	33	19	2	2	4	8	3.76	101	.306	.342	10	.100	-1	79	-1		-0.1
Total	4	30	36	.455	80	72	57-3	0	557	678	371	14	27	136	148	4.04	101	.298	.345	222-0-7	.230	0	83	-5		0.1

PAYNE, MIKE   Michael Earl   B11.15.1961 Woonsocket RI   D8.4.2002 Dunnellon FL   BR/TR/5-11/167   [AtlN79 6/134]   d8.22

YEAR	TM LG	W	L	PCT	G	GS	CG-SHO	SV-BS	IP	H	R	HR	HB	BB-IB	SO	ERA	AERA	OAV	OOB	AB-HR-SH	AVG	PB	SUP	APR	DL	PW
1984	Atl N	0	1	.000	3	1	0	0	5.2	7	4	1	0	3-1	3	6.35	61	.333	.417	1	.000	-0	46	-1		-0.2

PAZIK, MIKE   Michael Joseph   B1.26.1950 Lynn MA   BL/TL/6-2/200*   [NYA71 D1/13]   d5.11   C4   Col Holy Cross

YEAR	TM LG	W	L	PCT	G	GS	CG-SHO	SV-BS	IP	H	R	HR	HB	BB-IB	SO	ERA	AERA	OAV	OOB	AB-HR-SH	AVG	PB	SUP	APR	DL	PW
1975	Min A	0	4	.000	5	3	0	0-0	19.2	28	20	5	0	10-0	8	8.24	47	.329	.400	0	—	0	54	-9		-1.5
1976	Min A	0	0	—	5	0	0	0-0	9	13	9	0	1	4-0	6	7.00	51	.342	.419	0	—	0		-4		-0.2
1977	Min A	1	0	1.000	3	3	0	0-0	18	18	5	1	0	6-0	6	2.50	160	.265	.320	0	—	0	128	3	161	0.2
Total	3	1	4	.200	13	6	0	0-0	46.2	59	34	6	1	20-0	20	5.79	66	.309	.376	0	—	0	92	-10	161	-1.5

PEARCE, FRANK   Franklin Johnson   B3.30.1860 Jefferson Co. KY   D11.13.1926 Louisville KY   d10.4

YEAR	TM LG	W	L	PCT	G	GS	CG-SHO	SV-BS	IP	H	R	HR	HB	BB-IB	SO	ERA	AERA	OAV	OOB	AB-HR-SH	AVG	PB	SUP	APR	DL	PW
1876	Lou N	0	0	—	1	0	0	0	4	5	4	0	1	0	1	4.50	60	.263	.300	2	.000	-0		0		-0.1

PEARCE, FRANK   Franklin Thomas   B8.31.1905 Middletown KY   D9.3.1950 Van Buren NY   BR/TR/6-0/170   d4.20

YEAR	TM LG	W	L	PCT	G	GS	CG-SHO	SV-BS	IP	H	R	HR	HB	BB-IB	SO	ERA	AERA	OAV	OOB	AB-HR-SH	AVG	PB	SUP	APR	DL	PW
1933	Phi N	5	4	.556	20	7	3-1	0	82	78	41	6	0	29	18	3.62	105	.251	.315	26-0-4	.192	-1	106	1		0.0
1934	Phi N	0	2	.000	7	1	0	0	20	25	16	4	0	5	4	7.20	66	.301	.341	3	.667	1	73	-4		-0.3
1935	Phi N	0	0	—	5	0	0	0	13	22	15	0	0	6	7	8.31	55	.361	.418	4	.500	1		-5		-0.2
Total	3	5	6	.455	32	8	3-1	0	115	125	72	9	0	40	29	4.77	85	.275	.333	33-0-4	.273	1	98	-8		-0.5

PEARCE, JIM   James Madison   B6.9.1925 Zebulon NC   D7.17.2005 Raleigh NC   BR/TR/6-6/180*   d9.8

YEAR	TM LG	W	L	PCT	G	GS	CG-SHO	SV-BS	IP	H	R	HR	HB	BB-IB	SO	ERA	AERA	OAV	OOB	AB-HR-SH	AVG	PB	SUP	APR	DL	PW
1949	Was A	0	1	.000	2	1	0	0	7.1	10	9	1	0	5	1	8.44	50	.375	.483	2	.000	-0	21	-4		-0.6
1950	Was A	2	1	.667	20	3	1	0	56.2	58	40	2	1	37	18	6.04	74	.270	.379	13	.154	-1	141	-8		-0.5
1953	Was A	0	1	.000	4	1	0	0	9.1	15	10	3	0	6	1	7.71	51	.405	.488	1	.000	-0	91	-5		-0.4
1954	Cin N	1	0	1.000	2	1	1	0	11	7	1	0	1	5	3	.00	—	.194	.310	3-0-1	.000	-0	64	5		0.4
1955	Cin N	0	1	.000	2	1	0	0	3.1	8	5	0	0	0-0	0	10.80	39	.471	.444	0	—	0	105	-2		-0.4
Total	5	3	4	.429	30	7	2	0	85.2	97	66	6	2	53-0	22	5.78	76	.295	.395	19-0-1	.105	-2	100	-14		-1.5

PEARCE, JOSH   Joshua Ray   B8.20.1977 Yakima WA   BR/TR/6-3/215*   [StLN99 2/82]   d4.20   Col Arizona

YEAR	TM LG	W	L	PCT	G	GS	CG-SHO	SV-BS	IP	H	R	HR	HB	BB-IB	SO	ERA	AERA	OAV	OOB	AB-HR-SH	AVG	PB	SUP	APR	DL	PW
2002	StL N	0	0	—	3	3	0	0-0	13	20	13	1	1	8-0	1	7.62	53	.377	.460	4-0-2	.250	0	115	-6	31	-0.3
2003	StL N	0	0	—	7	0	0	0	9	11	3	0	1	6-0	4	3.00	137	.306	.359	0	—	0		1		0.1
2004	StL N	0	0	—	3	0	0	0	2.1	3	1	0	0	2-0	0	3.86	111	.375	.375	0	—	0		0		0.0
Total	3	0	0	—	13	3	0	0-0	24.1	34	17	1	2	10-0	5	5.55	74	.351	.418	4-0-2	.250	0	115	-5	31	-0.2

PEARS, FRANK   Frank H.   B8.30.1866 Louisville KY   D11.29.1923 St.Louis MO   TR/5-9/145   d10.6   U2

YEAR	TM LG	W	L	PCT	G	GS	CG-SHO	SV-BS	IP	H	R	HR	HB	BB-IB	SO	ERA	AERA	OAV	OOB	AB-HR-SH	AVG	PB	SUP	APR	DL	PW
1889	KC AA	0	2	.000	3	2	2	0	22	21	16	2	1	9	5	4.91	87	.244	.323	11	.091	-1	51	0		-0.1
1893	StL N	0	0	—	1	0	0	0	4	9	7	0	1	2	0	13.50	35	.429	.500	2	.000	-0		-3		-0.2
Total	2	0	2	.000	4	2	2	0	26	30	23	2	2	11	5	6.23	70	.280	.358	13	.077	-2	51	-3		-0.3

PEARSON, ALEX   Alexander Franklin   B3.9.1877 Greensboro PA   D10.30.1966 Rochester PA   BR/TR/5-10.5/160   d8.1

YEAR	TM LG	W	L	PCT	G	GS	CG-SHO	SV-BS	IP	H	R	HR	HB	BB-IB	SO	ERA	AERA	OAV	OOB	AB-HR-SH	AVG	PB	SUP	APR	DL	PW
1902	StL N	2	6	.250	11	10	8	0	82	90	47	0	3	22	24	3.95	69	.279	.330	34	.265	0	79	-9		-0.8
1903	Cle A	1	2	.333	4	3	2	0	30.1	34	15	1	1	3	12	3.56	80	.281	.304	12	.083	-1	109	-1		-0.2
Total	2	3	8	.273	15	13	10	0	112.1	124	62	1	4	25	36	3.85	72	.279	.323	46	.217	-0	86	-10		-1.0

PEARSON, IKE   Issac Overton   B3.1.1917 Grenada MS   D3.17.1985 Sarasota FL   BR/TR/6-1/180   d6.6   Mil 1943-45   Col U. of Mississippi

YEAR	TM LG	W	L	PCT	G	GS	CG-SHO	SV-BS	IP	H	R	HR	HB	BB-IB	SO	ERA	AERA	OAV	OOB	AB-HR-SH	AVG	PB	SUP	APR	DL	PW
1939	Phi N	2	13	.133	26	13	4	0	125	144	84	15	5	56	29	5.76	70	.296	.374	37-0-4	.054	-3*	55	-21		-2.5
1940	Phi N	3	14	.176	29	20	5-1	1	145.1	160	91	13	3	57	43	5.45	72	.275	.343	44-0-4	.205	-1	75	-21		-2.0
1941	Phi N	4	14	.222	46	10	0	6	136	139	75	8	8	70	38	3.57	104	.266	.361	40	.125	-2	41	-3		-0.7
1942	Phi N	1	6	.143	35	7	0	0	85.1	87	48	4	4	50	21	4.54	73	.271	.376	23	.043	-2	65	-11		-1.1
1946	Phi N	1	0	1.000	5	2	1-1	0	14.1	16	8	1	1	8	6	3.77	91	.271	.368	5-1-0	.200	1	237	-1		0.0
1948	Chi A	2	3	.400	23	2	0	1	53	62	32	8	2	27	12	4.92	87	.292	.378	10-0-2	.200	-0	106	-4		-0.3
Total	6	13	50	.206	164	54	10-2	8	559	608	338	49	23	268	149	4.83	79	.279	.363	159-1-10	.126	-6	69	-61		-6.6

PEARSON, JASON   Jason John   B12.29.1975 Freeport IL   BL/TL/6-0/195*   d6.4   Col Illinois St.

YEAR	TM LG	W	L	PCT	G	GS	CG-SHO	SV-BS	IP	H	R	HR	HB	BB-IB	SO	ERA	AERA	OAV	OOB	AB-HR-SH	AVG	PB	SUP	APR	DL	PW
2002	SD N	0	0	—	2	0	0	0-0	1.2	1	0	0	0	0	3	0.00	—	.167	.167	0	—	0		1		0.0
2003	StL N	0	0	—	2	0	0	0	1	4	7	1	0	3-0	1	63.00	7	.571	.700	0	—	0		-7		-0.3
Total	2	0	0	—	4	0	0	0-0	2.2	5	7	1	0	3-0	4	23.63	17	.385	.500	0	—	0		-6		-0.3

PEARSON, MONTE   Montgomery Marcellus "Hoot"   B9.2.1909 Oakland CA   D1.27.1978 Fresno CA   BR/TR/6-0/175   d4.22   Col California-Davis   [DL 1942 Cin N 140]

YEAR	TM LG	W	L	PCT	G	GS	CG-SHO	SV-BS	IP	H	R	HR	HB	BB-IB	SO	ERA	AERA	OAV	OOB	AB-HR-SH	AVG	PB	SUP	APR	DL	PW
1932	Cle A	0	0	—	8	0	0	0	8	10	9	1	0	11	5	10.13	47	.323	.500	0	—	0		-4		-0.1
1933	Cle A	10	5	.667	19	16	10	0	135.1	111	45	5	0	55	54	**2.33**	191	.221	.297	50-0-2	.260	1	98	30		3.1
1934	Cle A	18	13	.581	39	33	19	2	254.2	257	144	16	1	130	140	4.52	101	.260	.346	92-1-6	.272	6	106	3		0.9
1935	Cle A	8	13	.381	30	24	10-1	0	181.2	199	117	9	0	103	90	4.90	92	.279	.371	62-0-1	.177	-0	91	-9		-0.8
1936	†NY A☆	19	7	**.731**	33	31	15-1	1	223	191	99	13	3	135	118	3.71	125	**.233**	.343	91-1-6	.253	6	152	27		3.3
1937	†NY A	9	3	.750	22	20	7-1	1	144.2	145	60	6	1	64	71	3.17	140	.261	.339	51-0-4	.216	1	121	21		1.6
1938	†NY A	16	7	.696	28	27	17-1	0	202	198	107	12	0	113	98	3.97	114	.258	.354	76-0-3	.171	1	133	13		1.3
1939	†NY A	12	5	.706	22	20	8	0	146.1	151	77	9	1	70	76	4.49	97	.272	.354	53-0-5	.321	6	158	0		0.6
1940	NY A☆	7	5	.583	16	16	7-1	0	109.2	108	48	8	0	44	43	3.69	109	.262	.333	33-0-7	.121	-1	108	6		0.6
1941	Cin N	1	3	.250	7	4	1	0	24.1	22	15	3	0	15	8	5.18	69	.242	.349	5-0-1	.000	-1*	71	-4		-0.6
Total	10	100	61	.621	224	191	94-5	4	1429.2	1392	721	82	6	740	703	4.00	112	.256	.346	513-2-35	.228	19	121	83	140	9.9

PEARSON, TERRY   Terry Bobby Gene   B11.10.1971 Tuscaloosa AL   BR/TR/6-0/200   d4.4   Col West Alabama

YEAR	TM LG	W	L	PCT	G	GS	CG-SHO	SV-BS	IP	H	R	HR	HB	BB-IB	SO	ERA	AERA	OAV	OOB	AB-HR-SH	AVG	PB	SUP	APR	DL	PW
2002	Det A	0	0	—	4	0	0	0	6	8	7	2	0	2-1	5	10.50	42	.320	.370	0	—	0		-4		-0.2

PEASLEY, MARV   Marvin Warren   B7.16.1889 Jonesport ME   D12.27.1948 San Francisco CA   BL/TL/6-1/175   d9.27

YEAR	TM LG	W	L	PCT	G	GS	CG-SHO	SV-BS	IP	H	R	HR	HB	BB-IB	SO	ERA	AERA	OAV	OOB	AB-HR-SH	AVG	PB	SUP	APR	DL	PW
1910	Det A	0	1	.000	2	1	0	0	10	13	14	0	1	11	4	8.10	32	.295	.446	3	.000	0	127	-6		-0.5

PEAVY, JAKE   Jacob Edward   B5.3.1981 Mobile AL   BR/TR/6-1/180*   [SDN99 15/472]   d6.22

YEAR	TM LG	W	L	PCT	G	GS	CG-SHO	SV-BS	IP	H	R	HR	HB	BB-IB	SO	ERA	AERA	OAV	OOB	AB-HR-SH	AVG	PB	SUP	APR	DL	PW
2002	SD N	6	7	.462	17	17	0	0-0	97.2	106	54	11	3	33-4	90	4.52	86	.274	.334	33-0-2	.212	2	102	-7		-0.6
2003	SD N	12	11	.522	32	32	0	0-0	194.2	173	94	33	6	82-3	156	4.11	97	.238	.318	55-0-8	.073	-2	96	-2		-0.4
2004	SD N	15	6	.714	27	27	0	0-0	166.1	146	49	13	11	53-4	173	**2.27**	174	.236	.305	59-0-5	.169	1	124	32	43	4.1
2005	†SD N★	13	7	.650	30	30	3-3	0-0	203	162	70	18	7	50-3	**216**	2.88	134	.217	.271	53-0-5	.189	2	97	25		2.5
Total	4	46	31	.597	106	106	3-3	0-0	661.2	587	267	75	27	218-14	635	3.33	118	.237	.303	200-0-20	.155	4	105	48	43	5.6

PECHINEY, GEORGE   George Adolphe "Pisch"   B9.20.1861 Cincinnati OH   D7.14.1943 Cincinnati OH   BR/TR/5-9/184   d8.4

YEAR	TM LG	W	L	PCT	G	GS	CG-SHO	SV-BS	IP	H	R	HR	HB	BB-IB	SO	ERA	AERA	OAV	OOB	AB-HR-SH	AVG	PB	SUP	APR	DL	PW
1885	Cin AA	7	4	.636	11	11	11-1	0	98	95	45	1	0	49	2.02	164	.247	.311	40	.150	-2	91	10		0.8
1886	Cin AA	15	21	.417	40	40	35-2	0	330.1	355	230	4	14	133	110	4.14	85	.266	.339	144-1	.208	-1*	104	-24		-2.3
1887	Cle AA	1	9	.100	10	10	10	0	86	118	124	8	3	44	24	7.12	61	.303	.378	36	.250	-0	88	-27		-2.1
Total	3	23	34	.404	61	61	56-3	0	514.1	568	399	13	23	207	134	4.23	85	.269	.341	220-1	.205	-3	99	-41		-3.6

PEEK, STEVE   Stephen George   B7.30.1914 Springfield MA   D9.20.1991 Syracuse NY   BB/TR/6-2/195   d4.16   Mil 1942-45   Col St. Lawrence

YEAR	TM LG	W	L	PCT	G	GS	CG-SHO	SV-BS	IP	H	R	HR	HB	BB-IB	SO	ERA	AERA	OAV	OOB	AB-HR-SH	AVG	PB	SUP	APR	DL	PW
1941	NY A	4	2	.667	17	8	2	0	80	85	43	6	0	39	18	5.06	78	.276	.357	28-0-1	.036	-3	121	-9		-0.8

PEERY, RED   George Allan   B8.15.1906 Payson UT   D5.6.1985 Salt Lake City UT   BL/TL/5-11/160   d9.22

YEAR	TM LG	W	L	PCT	G	GS	CG-SHO	SV-BS	IP	H	R	HR	HB	BB-IB	SO	ERA	AERA	OAV	OOB	AB-HR-SH	AVG	PB	SUP	APR	DL	PW
1927	Pit N	0	0	—	1	0	0	0	1	0	1	0	0	0	0	0.00	—	.000	.333	0	—	0		0		0.0
1929	Bos N	0	1	.000	9	1	0	0	44	53	28	1	0	9	3	5.11	91	.305	.339	14	.214	1*	56	-2		0.0
Total	2	0	1	.000	10	1	0	0	45	53	29	1	0	10	3	5.00	91	.301	.339	14	.214	0	56	-2		0.0

YEAR	TM LG	W	L	PCT	G	GS	CG-SHO	SV-BS	IP	H	R	HR	HB	BB-IB	SO	ERA	AERA	OAV	OOB	AB-HR-SH	AVG	PB	SUP	APR	DL	PW
PEITZ, HEINIE					Henry Clement		B11.28.1870 St.Louis MO			D10.23.1943 Cincinnati OH				BR/TR/5-11/165			d10.15.1892		C3	b-Joe ▲					
1894	StL N	0	0	—	1	0	0	0	3	7	7	0	1	2	0	9.00	60	.438	.526	338-3-7	.263	0*		-2		-0.1
1897	Cin N	0	1	.000	2	1	1	0	8	9	8	0	2	4	0	7.88	58	.281	.395	266-1-7	.293	0*	125	-2		-0.2
1899	Cin N	0	0	—	1	0	0	0	5	6	3	0	0	1	3	5.40	73	.300	.333	293-1-10	.270	0*		0		0.0
Total	3	0	1	.000	4	1	1	0	16	22	18	0	3	7	3	7.31	62	.324	.410	897-5-24	.274	1	125	-4		-0.3
PELTY, BARNEY					Barney		B9.10.1880 Farmington MO			D5.24.1939 Farmington MO				BR/TR/5-9/175			d8.20								
1903	StL A	3	3	.500	7	6	5	1	48.2	49	25	1	2	15	20	2.40	121	.261	.322	20	.150	-0	90	0		0.0
1904	StL A	15	18	.455	39	35	31-2	0	301	270	121	7	20	77	126	2.84	87	.241	.301	118-0-2	.127	-6*	89	-9		-1.8
1905	StL A	14	14	.500	31	28	27-1	0	258.2	222	106	3	12	68	114	2.75	93	.233	.293	98-0-4	.153	-3	119	-3		-0.6
1906	StL A	16	11	.593	34	30	25-4	2	260.2	189	77	1	18	59	92	1.59	163	**.206**	.267	91-0-3	.165	-3	110	27		2.9
1907	StL A	12	21	.364	36	31	29-5	1	273	234	101	1	18	64	85	2.57	98	.234	.292	95-0-3	.168	-2	79	1		0.0
1908	StL A	7	4	.636	20	13	7-1	0	122	104	44	0	10	32	36	1.99	120	.241	.309	42-0-4	.119	-3*	138	4		0.1
1909	StL A	11	11	.500	27	23	17-5	0	199.1	158	63	2	5	53	88	2.30	105	.222	.281	91-0-4	.165	0*	100	4		0.8
1910	StL A	5	11	.313	27	19	13-3	0	165.1	157	81	3	8	70	48	3.48	71	.263	.348	56-0-4	.089	-4*	67	-13		-1.4
1911	StL A	7	15	.318	28	22	18-1	0	197	197	87	4	4	69	59	2.97	114	.265	.331	65-0-2	.138	-3*	55	11		0.8
1912	StL A	1	5	.167	6	6	2	0	38.2	43	27	0	1	3	10	5.59	59	.297	.374	12	.000	-2	70	-8		-1.1
	Was A	1	4	.200	11	4	1	0	43.2	40	18	0	4	10	15	3.30	101	.250	.310	9	.222	0	55	2		0.2
	Year	2	9	.182	17	10	3	0	82.1	83	45	0	7	25	25	4.37	76	.272	.341	21	.095	-2	64	-6		-0.9
Total	10	92	117	.440	266	217	175-22	4	1908	1663	750	22	104	532	693	2.63	100	.239	.302	697-0-26	.143	-25	90	16		-0.1
PEMBER, DAVE					David Joseph		B5.24.1978 Cincinnati OH		BR/TR/6-5/225		[MilN99 8/244]			d9.3	Col Western Carolina										
2002	Mil N	0	1	.000	4	1	0	0	8.2	7	6	1	0	5	5	5.19	79	.219	.333	1	.000	0	22	-1		-0.2
PENA, ALEJANDRO					Alejandro (Vasquez)		B6.25.1959 Cambiaso, D.R.		BR/TR/6-1/205(190-228)		d8.13		[DL 1993 Pit N 182]												
1981	†LA N	1	1	.500	14	0	0	2-2	25.1	18	8	2	0	11-1	14	2.84	116	.194	.279	6	.000	-1		2		0.1
1982	LA N	0	2	.000	29	0	0	0-0	35.2	37	24	2	1	21-7	20	4.79	72	.272	.373	0		0		-7		-0.3
1983	†LA N	12	9	.571	34	26	4-3	1-1	177	152	67	7	1	51-7	120	2.75	131	.229	.283	60-1-1	.100	-2	89	16		1.7
1984	LA N	12	6	.667	28	28	8-4	0-0	199.1	186	67	7	3	46-7	135	**2.48**	143	.246	.291	66-0-4	.121	-1	94	23		1.8
1985	LA N	0	1	.000	2	1	0	0-0	4.1	7	5	1	0	3-1	2	8.31	42	.350	.435	1	.000	-0	126	-2	150	-0.5
1986	LA N	1	2	.333	24	10	0	1-0	70	74	40	6	1	30-5	46	4.89	71	.263	.343	17-0-3	.176	0	124	-11	49	-0.2
1987	LA N	2	7	.222	37	7	0	11-0	87.1	82	41	9	2	37-5	76	3.50	114	.251	.325	13-0-1	.077	-1	58	3	21	0.2
1988	†LA N	6	7	.462	60	0	0	12-2	94.1	75	29	4	1	27-6	83	1.91	175	.218	.275	6	.000	-1		13		2.0
1989	LA N	4	3	.571	53	0	0	5-4	76	62	20	6	2	18-4	75	2.13	161	.220	.271	1	1.000	0		11	15	1.1
1990	NY N	3	3	.500	52	0	0	5-0	76	71	31	4	1	22-5	76	3.20	118	.245	.295	6	.167	0		4		0.4
1991	NY N	6	1	.857	44	0	0	4-5	63	63	20	5	0	19-4	49	2.71	135	.267	.317	0		0		7		0.9
	†Atl N	2	0	1.000	15	0	0	11-0	19.1	11	3	1	0	3-0	13	1.40	278	.167	.203	1	.000	-0		5		1.1
	Year	8	1	.889	59	0	0	15-5	82.1	74	23	6	0	22-4	62	2.40	155	.245	.293	1	.000	-0		12		2.0
1992	Atl N	1	6	.143	41	0	0	15-3	42	40	19	7	0	13-5	34	4.07	90	.255	.310	2	.000	-0		-1	33	-0.3
1994	Pit N	3	2	.600	22	0	0	7-1	28.2	22	16	4	1	10-2	27	5.02	87	.206	.280	1	.000	-0		-1	28	-0.3
1995	Bos A	1	1	.500	17	0	0	0-0	24.1	33	23	5	0	12-2	25	7.40	66	.314	.385	0	—	0		-7		-0.5
	Fla N	2	0	1.000	13	0	0	0-1	18	11	3	2	0	3-1	21	1.50	286	.169	.206	1	.000	-0		6		0.5
	†Atl N	0	0	—	14	0	0	0-0	13	11	6	1	0	4-0	18	4.15	104	.224	.283	0		0		0		0.0
	Year	3	1	.750	44	0	0	0-1	55	55	32	8	0	19-3	64	4.42	110	.252	.318	1	.000	-0		-1		0.0
1996	Fla N	0	1	.000	4	0	0	0-0	4	4	5	2	0	1-0	5	4.50	92	.235	.278	0	—	0		-1	169	-0.3
Total	15	56	52	.519	503	72	12-7	74-19	1057.2	959	427	75	13	331-62	839	3.11	118	.240	.299	181-1-9	.110	-5	92	60	647	7.0
PENA, HIPOLITO					Hipolito (Concepcion)		B1.30.1964 Fantino, D.R.		BL/TL/6-3/165*		d9.1														
1986	Pit N	0	3	.000	10	1	0	1-0	8.1	7	10	3	1	3-1	6	8.64	45	.206	.289	0	—	0	0	-5		-0.9
1987	Pit N	0	0	—	16	1	0	1-0	25.2	16	14	2	0	26-3	16	4.56	91	.184	.372	6	.167	-0	22	-1		-0.1
1988	NY A	1	1	.500	16	0	0	0-0	14.1	10	8	1	0	9-1	10	3.14	126	.192	.306	0		0		0		0.0
Total	3	1	7	.125	42	2	0	2-0	48.1	33	32	6	1	38-5	32	4.84	84	.191	.338	6	.167	-0	11	-6		-1.0
PENA, JIM					James Patrick		B9.17.1964 Los Angeles CA		BL/TL/6-0/175		d7.7	Col Cal St.-Dominguez Hills												
1992	SF N	1	1	.500	25	2	0	0-0	44	49	19	4	1	20-5	32	3.48	96	.282	.357	5-0-3	.200	0	204	-1		0.0
PENA, JESUS					Jesus		B3.8.1975 Santo Domingo, D.R.		BL/TL/6-0/170*		d8.7														
1999	Chi A	0	0	—	26	0	0	0-1	20.1	21	15	3	1	23-5	20	5.31	93	.259	.429	0	—	0		-2		-0.1
2000	Chi A	2	1	.667	20	0	0	1-0	23.1	25	18	6	1	16-0	19	5.40	94	.278	.385	0	—	0		-2		-0.2
	Bos A	0	0	—	2	0	0	0-0	3	3	1	1	0	3-0	1	3.00	167	.273	.429	0	—	0		1		0.0
	Year	2	1	.667	22	0	0	1-0	26.1	28	19	7	1	19-0	20	5.13	99	.277	.390	0	—	0		-1		-0.2
Total	2	2	1	.667	48	0	0	1-1	46.2	49	34	10	2	42-5	40	5.21	96	.269	.408	0	—	0		-3		-0.3
PENA, JOSE					Jose (Gutierrez)		B12.3.1942 Ciudad Juarez, Chihuahua, Mexico		BR/TR/6-2/190*		d6.1														
1969	Cin N	1	1	.500	6	0	0	0-0	5	10	10	0	0	5-1	3	18.00	21	.400	.500	0	—	0		-7		-1.3
1970	LA N	4	3	.571	29	0	0	4-2	57	51	32	8	3	29-5	31	4.42	87	.241	.336	8	.125	0		-4		-0.5
1971	LA N	2	0	1.000	21	0	0	0-0	43	32	18	7	1	18-1	44	3.56	91	.211	.295	3	.667	1		-1		0.0
1972	LA N	0	0	—	5	0	0	0-0	7.1	13	8	1	0	6-1	4	8.59	39	.371	.452	0	—	0		-4		-0.2
Total	4	7	4	.636	61	0	0	5-2	112.1	106	68	16	4	58-8	82	4.97	72	.250	.341	11	.273	1		-16		-2.0
PENA, JUAN					Juan Francisco		B6.27.1977 Santo Domingo, D.R.		BR/TR/6-5/215		[BosA95 27/746]		d5.8	Col Miami-Dade Wolfson (FL) CC			[DL 2000 Bos A 181, 2001 Bos A 57]								
1999	Bos A	2	0	1.000	2	2	0	0-0	13	9	1	0	0	3-0	15	0.69	720	.196	.245	0	—	0	103	6	63	1.0
PENA, ORLANDO					Orlando Gregorio (Quevara)		B11.17.1933 Victoria de las Tunas, Cuba		BR/TR/5-11/154(150-165)		d8.24														
1958	Cin N	1	0	1.000	9	0	0	0-0	15	10	1	0	0	4-1	11	0.60	691	.185	.241	0		0		6		0.6
1959	Cin N	5	9	.357	46	8	1	5	136	150	80	26	0	39-5	76	4.76	85	.280	.325	34-0-5	.088	-0	85	-10		-1.1
1960	Cin N	0	1	.000	4	0	0	0	9.1	8	3	0	0	3-2	9	2.89	132	.222	.282	1	.000	-0		1		0.1
1962	KC A	6	4	.600	13	12	6-1	0	89.2	71	31	9	1	27-2	56	3.01	140	.213	.272	31	.161	-0	109	12		1.2
1963	KC A	12	20	.375	35	33	9-3	0	217	218	93	24	5	53-2	128	3.69	106	.260	.306	62-1-10	.145	0	70	7		0.9
1964	KC A	12	14	.462	40	32	5	0	219.1	231	116	40	8	73-2	184	4.43	86	.268	.329	75-1-3	.160	0*	90	-17		-2.0
1965	KC A	0	6	.000	12	5	0	0	35.1	42	30	4	1	13-0	24	6.88	51	.302	.368	9	.111	-0	65	-13		-2.0
	Det A	4	6	.400	30	0	0	4	57.1	54	18	5	1	20-5	55	2.51	138	.252	.318	8-0-1	.250	1		6		1.1
	Year	4	12	.250	42	5	0	4	92.2	96	48	9	2	33-5	79	4.18	83	.252	.338	17-0-1	.176	1	66	-6		-0.9
1966	Det A	4	2	.667	54	0	0	7	108	105	47	16	5	35-6	79	3.08	113	.252	.315	18-0-2	.111	-1		2		0.2
1967	Det A	0	1	.000	2	0	0	0	2	5	3	0	1	0-0	2	13.50	24	.500	.500	0	—	0		-2		-0.4
	Cle A	0	3	.000	48	1	0	8	88.1	67	34	8	1	22-5	72	3.36	97	.208	.259	8-0-1	.000	-1	27	1		-0.1
	Year	0	4	.000	50	1	0	8	90.1	72	37	8	2	22-5	74	3.59	91	.217	.267	8-0-1	.000	-1	27	-1		-0.5
1970	Pit N	2	1	.667	23	0	0	2-1	37.2	38	21	6	1	7-2	25	4.78	83	.268	.305	6-0-1	.000	-1		-3		-0.3
1971	Bal A	1	0	1.000	5	0	0	0-0	14.2	16	7	0	0	5-1	9	3.07	111	.281	.339	3	.000	-0		0		0.0
1973	Bal A	1	1	.500	11	2	0	1-1	44.2	36	20	10	2	8-1	23	4.03	94	.218	.260	0	—	0	59	0		0.0
	StL N	4	4	.500	42	0	0	6-1	62	60	17	3	0	14-4	38	2.18	169	.254	.290	7-0-1	.143	-0		10		1.5
1974	StL N	5	2	.714	42	0	0	1-2	45	45	15	0	1	20-3	23	2.60	139	.269	.342	2	.500	0		5		0.8
	Cal A	0	0	—	4	0	0	3-0	8	6	0	0	0	1-0	5	0.00	—	.214	.241	0	—	0		3		0.3
1975	Cal A	0	2	.000	7	0	0	0-0	12.2	13	7	3	0	5-1	6	2.13	168	.283	.382	0	—	0		3		0.3
Total	14	56	77	.421	427	93	21-4	40-5	1202	1175	549	151	28	352-42	818	3.71	102	.255	.309	264-2-24	.136	-3	85	10		1.1
PENA, RAMON					Ramon Arturo (Padilla)		B5.5.1962 Santiago, D.R.		BR/TR/5-10/155		d4.27	b-Tony													
1989	Det A	0	0	—	8	0	0	0-0	18	26	13	0	2	8-3	12	6.00	64	.338	.409	0	—	0		-4	21	-0.2
PENCE, RUSTY					Russell William		B3.11.1900 Marine IL		D8.11.1971 Hot Springs AR		BR/TR/6-0/185		d5.13												
1921	Chi A	0	0	—	4	0	0	0	5.1	6	5	0	1	7	2	8.44	50	.286	.483	1	.000	-0		-2		-0.1
PENN, HAYDEN					Hayden Andrew		B10.13.1984 LaJolla CA		BR/TR/6-3/195		d5.28														
2005	Bal A	3	2	.600	8	8	0	0-0	38.1	46	30	6	0	21-3	18	6.34	70	.295	.379	1-0-1	.000	0	98	-8		-0.8

YEAR	TM LG	W	L	PCT	G	GS	CG-SHO	SV-BS	IP	H	R	HR	HB	BB-IB	SO	ERA	AERA	OAV	OOB	AB-HR-SH	AVG	PB	SUP	APR	DL	PW

PENNER, KEN Kenneth William B4.24.1896 Boonville IN D5.28.1959 Sacramento CA BL/TR/5-11.5/170 d9.11

YEAR	TM LG	W	L	PCT	G	GS	CG-SHO	SV-BS	IP	H	R	HR	HB	BB-IB	SO	ERA	AERA	OAV	OOB	AB-HR-SH	AVG	PB	SUP	APR	DL	PW
1916	Cle A	1	1	.500	4	2	0	0	12.2	14	6	0	0	4	5	4.26	71	.304	.360	2	.000	-0	88	-1		-0.1
1929	Chi N	0	1	.000	5	0	0	0	12.2	14	11	1	0	6	3	12.00	42	.280	.357	4	.250	0		0		0.0
Total	2	1	2	.333	9	2	0	0	25.1	28	17	1	0	10	8	3.55	108	.292	.358	6	.167	-0	88	-1		-0.1

PENNINGTON, BRAD Brad Lee B4.14.1969 Salem IN BL/TL/6-5/205* [BalA89 12/297] d4.17 Col Vincennes (IN) JC

YEAR	TM LG	W	L	PCT	G	GS	CG-SHO	SV-BS	IP	H	R	HR	HB	BB-IB	SO	ERA	AERA	OAV	OOB	AB-HR-SH	AVG	PB	SUP	APR	DL	PW
1993	Bal A	3	2	.600	34	0	0	4-3	33	34	25	7	2	25-0	39	6.55	69	.266	.391	0	—	0		-7		-1.0
1994	Bal A	0	1	.000	8	0	0	0-1	6	9	8	2	0	8-0	7	12.00	42	.346	.500	0	—	0		-4		-0.6
1995	Bal A	0	1	.000	8	0	0	0-1	6.2	3	7	1	0	11-1	10	8.10	59	.136	.404	0	—	0		-3		-0.3
	Cin N	0	0	—	6	0	0	0-0	9.2	9	8	0	1	11-0	7	5.59	75	.273	.447	2	.000	-0		-2		-0.1
1996	Bos A	0	2	.000	14	0	0	0-0	13	6	5	1	0	15-1	13	2.77	184	.140	.356	0	—	0		3		0.4
	Cal A	0	0	—	8	0	0	0-0	7.1	5	10	1	0	16-0	7	12.27	41	.185	.488	0	—	0		-5	25	-0.2
	Year	0	2	.000	22	0	0	0-0	20.1	11	15	2	0	31-1	20	6.20	82	.157	.412	0	—	0		-2		0.2
1998	TB A	0	0	—	1	0	0	0-0	0	1	1	0	0	3-0	0	∞		1.000	1.000	0	—	0		-1		-0.1
Total	5	3	6	.333	79	0	0	4-5	75.2	67	64	12	3	89-2	83	7.02	67	.239	.423	2	.000	-0		-19	25	-1.9

PENNINGTON, KEWPIE George Louis B9.24.1896 New York NY D5.3.1953 Newark NJ BR/TR/5-8.5/168 d4.14

YEAR	TM LG	W	L	PCT	G	GS	CG-SHO	SV-BS	IP	H	R	HR	HB	BB-IB	SO	ERA	AERA	OAV	OOB	AB-HR-SH	AVG	PB	SUP	APR	DL	PW
1917	StL A	0	0	—	1	0	0	0	1	1	0	0	0	0	0	0.00	—	.250	.250	0		0		0		0.0

PENNOCK, HERB Herbert Jefferis "The Knight of Kennett Square" B2.10.1894 Kennett Square PA D1.30.1948 New York NY BB/TL/6-0/160 d5.14 Mil 1918 C4 HF1948

YEAR	TM LG	W	L	PCT	G	GS	CG-SHO	SV-BS	IP	H	R	HR	HB	BB-IB	SO	ERA	AERA	OAV	OOB	AB-HR-SH	AVG	PB	SUP	APR	DL	PW
1912	Phi A	1	2	.333	17	2	1	2	50	48	31	1	3	30	38	4.50	68	.262	.375	15-0-1	.133	-1	120	-8		-0.5
1913	Phi A	2	1	.667	14	3	1	0	33.1	30	24	4	0	22	17	5.13	54	.242	.356	9	.111	0	223	-10		-0.8
1914	†Phi A	11	4	.733	28	14	8-3	3	151.2	136	56	1	2	65	90	2.79	94	.248	.330	56-0-1	.214	2	140	-3		-0.1
1915	Phi A	3	6	.333	11	8	3-1	1	44	46	34	2	2	29	24	5.32	55	.266	.377	18	.278	1	81	-11		-1.9
	Bos A	0	0	—	5	1	0	0	14	23	16	0	0	10	7	9.64	29	.390	.478	6	.167	0	262	-10		-0.5
	Year	3	6	.333	16	9	3-1	1	58	69	50	2	2	39	31	6.36	45	.297	.403	24	.250	1	101	-21		-2.4
1916	Bos A	0	2	.000	9	2	0	1	26.2	23	11	0	1	8	12	3.04	91	.245	.311	8	.125	-0*	27	-1		-0.1
1917	Bos A	5	5	.500	24	5	4-1	1	100.2	90	49	2	3	23	35	3.31	78	.243	.292	24-0-1	.167	2	117	-9		-0.7
1919	Bos A	16	8	.667	32	26	16-5	0	219	223	78	2	3	48	70	2.71	111	.274	.316	75-0-6	.173	1	120	9		1.0
1920	Bos A	16	13	.552	37	31	19-4	2	242.1	244	108	9	4	61	68	3.68	99	.264	.312	77-0-7	.260	4*	97	3		0.6
1921	Bos A	13	14	.481	32	31	15-1	0	222.2	268	121	7	2	59	91	4.04	105	.307	.352	85-1-4	.212	2	79	2		0.5
1922	Bos A	10	17	.370	32	26	15-1	1	202	230	108	7	1	74	59	4.32	95	.297	.359	65-0-2	.138	-3	72	-3		-0.5
1923	†NY A	19	6	.760	35	27	21-1	1	238.1	235	86	11	2	68	93	3.13	126	.261	.314	83-0-8	.193	0	121	25		2.4
1924	NY A	21	9	.700	40	34	25-4	3	286.1	302	104	13	1	64	101	2.83	147	.273	.314	101-2-10	.158	-2	107	43		3.8
1925	NY A	16	17	.485	47	31	21-2	2	277	267	117	11	2	71	88	2.96	144	.254	.303	99-0-9	.202	-3	84	36		3.3
1926	†NY A	23	11	.676	40	33	19-1	2	266.1	294	133	11	4	43	78	3.62	107	.282	.313	85-0-16	.212	3	119	6		1.0
1927	†NY A	19	8	.704	34	26	18-1	0	209.2	225	89	5	2	48	51	3.00	128	.283	.325	69-0-13	.217	-0	134	19		2.1
1928	NY A	17	6	.739	28	24	18-5	3	211	215	71	2	0	40	53	2.56	147	.267	.302	74-0-7	.203	-1	114	31		3.1
1929	NY A	9	11	.450	27	23	8-1	0	157.1	205	101	11	3	28	49	4.92	78	.318	.349	51-0-6	.176	-1	108	-19		-2.1
1930	NY A	11	7	.611	25	19	11-1	0	156.1	194	95	8	0	20	46	4.32	100	.301	.322	60-0-1	.183	-2	137	-2		-0.5
1931	NY A	11	6	.647	25	25	12-1	0	189.1	247	96	7	1	30	65	4.28	93	.315	.342	66-1-7	.152	1	147	-3		-0.2
1932	†NY A	9	5	.643	22	21	9-1	0	146.2	191	94	8	0	38	54	4.60	89	.310	.350	53-0-5	.151	-0	143	-13		-1.0
1933	NY A	7	4	.636	23	5	2-1	4	65	96	46	4	0	21	22	5.54	70	.342	.387	21-0-6	.238	-0	180	-13		-1.9
1934	Bos A	2	0	1.000	30	2	1	1	62	68	31	2	0	16	16	3.05	158	.276	.321	14-0-1	.214	-0	163	9		0.3
Total	22	241	162	.598	617	419	247-35	33	3571.2	3900	1699	128	36	916	1227	3.60	106	.282	.328	1214-4-111	.191	3	113	78		7.3

PENNY, BRAD Bradley Wayne B5.24.1978 Broken Arrow OK BR/TR/6-4/200(200-250) [AriN96 5/155] d4.7

YEAR	TM LG	W	L	PCT	G	GS	CG-SHO	SV-BS	IP	H	R	HR	HB	BB-IB	SO	ERA	AERA	OAV	OOB	AB-HR-SH	AVG	PB	SUP	APR	DL	PW
2000	Fla N	8	7	.533	23	22	0	0-0	119.2	120	70	13	5	60-4	80	4.81	91	.263	.354	45-0-1	.111	-2*	116	-6	43	-0.8
2001	Fla N	10	10	.500	31	31	1-1	0-0	205	183	92	15	7	54-3	154	3.69	113	.240	.296	62-0-3	.161	1	86	11		0.9
2002	Fla N	8	7	.533	24	24	1-1	0-0	129.1	148	76	18	1	50-7	93	4.66	84	.288	.350	48-0-1	.167	0	109	-13	44	-1.3
2003	†Fla N	14	10	.583	32	32	0	0-0	196.1	195	96	21	3	56-6	138	4.13	99	.264	.316	68-2-5	.132	1*	116	-1		-0.1
2004	Fla N	8	8	.500	21	21	0	0-0	131.1	124	50	10	3	39-6	105	3.15	130	.249	.306	47-0-1	.064	0	80	14		1.2
	LA N	1	2	.333	3	3	0	0-0	11.2	6	5	2	0	6-0	6	3.09	134	.154	.267	4	.000	-0	30	1	44	0.1
	Year	9	10	.474	24	24	0	0-0	143	130	55	12	3	45-6	111	3.15	131	.243	.303	51-0-1	.059	-4	74	17		1.3
2005	LA N	7	9	.438	29	29	1	0-0	175.1	185	78	17	3	41-2	122	3.90	105	.270	.313	50-0-9	.160	1	101	6	21	0.6
Total	6	56	53	.514	163	162	3-2	0-0	968.2	961	467	96	22	306-28	698	4.00	103	.260	.319	324-2-20	.133	-4	100	12	152	0.6

PENSON, PAUL Paul Eugene B7.12.1931 Kansas City KS BR/TR/6-1/185 d4.21

YEAR	TM LG	W	L	PCT	G	GS	CG-SHO	SV-BS	IP	H	R	HR	HB	BB-IB	SO	ERA	AERA	OAV	OOB	AB-HR-SH	AVG	PB	SUP	APR	DL	PW
1954	Phi N	1	1	.500	5	3	0	0	14	14	11	1	0	14	3	4.50	90	.237	.368	7	.000	-1	132	-2		-0.3

PENTZ, GENE Eugene David B6.21.1953 Johnstown PA BR/TR/6-1/200(192-215) [DetA71 7/157] d7.29

YEAR	TM LG	W	L	PCT	G	GS	CG-SHO	SV-BS	IP	H	R	HR	HB	BB-IB	SO	ERA	AERA	OAV	OOB	AB-HR-SH	AVG	PB	SUP	APR	DL	PW
1975	Det A	0	4	.000	13	0	0	0-1	25.1	27	14	0	0	20-4	21	3.20	126	.293	.412	0	—	0		1		0.1
1976	Hou N	3	3	.500	40	0	0	5-2	63.2	62	26	5	1	31-2	36	2.97	109	.259	.343	5	.200	0		1	43	0.2
1977	Hou N	5	2	.714	41	4	0	2-2	87	76	41	8	1	44-5	51	3.83	94	.236	.324	13	.000	-2	117	-2		-0.3
1978	Hou N	0	0	—	10	0	0	0-0	15	12	13	1	1	13-3	8	6.00	56	.214	.366	1	.000	-0		-6	115	-0.3
Total	4	8	9	.471	104	4	0	7-5	191	177	94	14	3	108-14	116	3.63	97	.250	.346	19	.053	-1	117	-6	158	-0.3

PEOPLES, JIMMY James Elsworth B10.8.1863 Big Beaver MI D8.29.1920 Detroit MI TR/5-8/200 d5.29.1884 U1 ▲

YEAR	TM LG	W	L	PCT	G	GS	CG-SHO	SV-BS	IP	H	R	HR	HB	BB-IB	SO	ERA	AERA	OAV	OOB	AB-HR-SH	AVG	PB	SUP	APR	DL	PW
1885	Cin AA	0	2	.000	2	2	1	0	15	30	28	0	3	2	4	12.00	27	.390	.427	22	.182	-0*	118	-13		-1.1

PEPPER, LAURIN Hugh McLaurin B1.18.1931 Vaughan MS BR/TR/5-11/190* d7.4 Col Southern Mississippi

YEAR	TM LG	W	L	PCT	G	GS	CG-SHO	SV-BS	IP	H	R	HR	HB	BB-IB	SO	ERA	AERA	OAV	OOB	AB-HR-SH	AVG	PB	SUP	APR	DL	PW
1954	Pit N	1	5	.167	14	8	0	0	50.2	63	53	4	0	43	17	7.99	52	.315	.429	17	.235	0	75	-21		-2.0
1955	Pit N	0	1	.000	14	1	0	0	20	30	24	5	2	25-0	7	10.35	40	.370	.523	2	.000	-0	43	-13		-0.6
1956	Pit N	1	1	.500	11	7	0	0	30	30	17	1	0	25-1	12	5.00	126	.256	.385	6	.000	-0	67	0		-0.1
1957	Pit N	0	1	.000	5	1	0	0	9	11	8	1	0	5-2	4	8.00	47	.297	.381	0	—	0*	70	-4		-0.4
Total	4	2	8	.200	44	17	0	0	109.2	134	102	11	2	98-3	40	7.06	57	.308	.433	25	.160	-0	69	-38		-3.1

PEPPER, BOB Robert Ernest B5.3.1895 Rosston PA D4.8.1968 Ford Cliff PA BR/TR/6-2/178 d7.23

YEAR	TM LG	W	L	PCT	G	GS	CG-SHO	SV-BS	IP	H	R	HR	HB	BB-IB	SO	ERA	AERA	OAV	OOB	AB-HR-SH	AVG	PB	SUP	APR	DL	PW
1915	Phi A	0	0	—	1	0	0	0	5	6	5	0	1	4	0	1.80	163	.333	.478	2	.000	-0		-1		-0.1

PEPPERS, HARRISON William Harrison (b William Harrison Pepper) B9.1866 KY D11.5.1903 Webb City MO BL d6.30

YEAR	TM LG	W	L	PCT	G	GS	CG-SHO	SV-BS	IP	H	R	HR	HB	BB-IB	SO	ERA	AERA	OAV	OOB	AB-HR-SH	AVG	PB	SUP	APR	DL	PW
1894	Lou N	0	1	.000	2	1	0	0	8	10	7	0	0	4	0	6.75	76	.303	.378	4	.000	-1	83	-1		-0.1

PERALTA, JOEL Joel (Gutierrez) B3.23.1976 Bonao, D.R. BR/TR/5-11/170 d5.25

YEAR	TM LG	W	L	PCT	G	GS	CG-SHO	SV-BS	IP	H	R	HR	HB	BB-IB	SO	ERA	AERA	OAV	OOB	AB-HR-SH	AVG	PB	SUP	APR	DL	PW
2005	LA A	1	0	1.000	28	0	0	0-0	34.2	28	15	6	0	14-2	30	3.89	111	.219	.294	0		0		2		0.1

PERAZA, LUIS Luis (Rios) B6.17.1942 Rio Piedras, PR BR/TR/5-11/185 d4.9

YEAR	TM LG	W	L	PCT	G	GS	CG-SHO	SV-BS	IP	H	R	HR	HB	BB-IB	SO	ERA	AERA	OAV	OOB	AB-HR-SH	AVG	PB	SUP	APR	DL	PW
1969	Phi N	0	0	—	8	0	0	0	9	12	6	1	0	2-0	7	6.00	59	.364	.378	1	.000	-0		-2		-0.1

PERAZA, OSWALDO Oswald Jose B10.19.1962 Puerto Cabello, Venez BR/TR/6-4/172 d4.4 [DL 1989 Bal A 182]

YEAR	TM LG	W	L	PCT	G	GS	CG-SHO	SV-BS	IP	H	R	HR	HB	BB-IB	SO	ERA	AERA	OAV	OOB	AB-HR-SH	AVG	PB	SUP	APR	DL	PW
1988	Bal A	5	7	.417	19	15	1	0-0	86	98	62	10	2	37-2	61	5.55	71	.282	.352	0	—	0	96	-17		-2.1

PERCIVAL, TROY Troy Eugene B8.9.1969 Fontana CA BR/TR/6-3/230(200-236) [CalA90 6/179] d4.26 Col California-Riverside

YEAR	TM LG	W	L	PCT	G	GS	CG-SHO	SV-BS	IP	H	R	HR	HB	BB-IB	SO	ERA	AERA	OAV	OOB	AB-HR-SH	AVG	PB	SUP	APR	DL	PW
1995	Cal A	3	2	.600	62	0	0	3-3	74	37	19	6	1	26-2	94	1.95	242	.147	.229	0	—	0		22		1.4
1996	Cal A★	0	2	.000	62	0	0	36-3	74	38	20	8	2	31-4	100	2.31	219	.149	.246	1	.000	-0		23		1.4
1997	Ana A	5	5	.500	55	0	0	27-4	52	40	20	6	4	22-2	72	3.46	133	.205	.296	0	—	0		7	39	1.4
1998	Ana A★	2	7	.222	67	0	0	42-6	66.2	45	31	5	3	37-4	87	3.65	130	.186	.299	0	—	0		7		1.3
1999	Ana A☆	4	6	.400	60	0	0	31-8	57	38	24	9	3	22-0	58	3.79	129	.186	.274	0	—	0		8		1.4
2000	Ana A	5	5	.500	54	0	0	32-10	50	42	27	7	2	30-4	49	4.50	115	.228	.339	0	—	0		3	20	0.6
2001	Ana A★	4	2	.667	57	0	0	39-3	57.2	39	19	3	2	18-1	71	2.65	175	.187	.258	0	—	0		12		2.3
2002	†Ana A	4	1	.800	58	0	0	40-4	56.1	38	12	6	1	25-1	68	1.92	234	.188	.276	0	—	0		16	30	3.2
2003	Ana A	0	5	.000	52	0	0	33-4	49.1	33	22	7	3	23-1	48	3.47	126	.184	.286	0	—	0		5	15	0.8
2004	Ana A	2	3	.400	52	0	0	33-5	49.2	43	19	7	3	19-3	33	2.90	154	.230	.308	0	—	0		8	25	1.5
2005	Det A	1	3	.250	26	0	0	8-3	25	19	16	7	2	11-3	20	5.76	73	.207	.302	0	—	0		-4	113	-0.7
Total	11	30	41	.423	605	0	0	324-53	611.2	412	229	70	25	264-25	700	3.10	152	.187	.280	1	.000	-0		107	242	15.6

YEAR	TM LG	W	L	PCT	G	GS	CG-SHO	SV-BS	IP	H	R	HR	HB	BB-IB	SO	ERA	AERA	OAV	OOB	AB-HR-SH	AVG	PB	SUP	APR	DL	PW

PERDUE, HUB Herbert Rodney "The Gallatin Squash" B6.7.1882 Bethpage TN D10.31.1968 Gallatin TX BR/TR/5-10.5/192 d4.19

YEAR	TM LG	W	L	PCT	G	GS	CG-SHO	SV-BS	IP	H	R	HR	HB	BB-IB	SO	ERA	AERA	OAV	OOB	AB-HR-SH	AVG	PB	SUP	APR	DL	PW
1911	Bos N	6	10	.375	24	19	9	1	137.1	180	100	10	4	41	40	4.98	77	.321	.372	48-0-4	.208	-1	117	-16		-1.7
1912	Bos N	13	16	.448	37	30	20-1	3	249	295	135	11	2	54	101	3.80	94	.303	.341	87-0-6	.138	-5	83	-4		-1.1
1913	Bos N	16	13	.552	38	32	16-3	1	212.1	201	107	7	4	39	91	3.26	101	.249	.287	67-0-4	.104	-5	95	1		-0.7
1914	Bos N	2	5	.286	9	9	2	0	51	60	35	5	3	11	13	5.82	47	.311	.357	14-0-1	.071	-0	92	-15		-1.8
	StL N	8	8	.500	22	19	12	1	153.1	160	60	3	5	35	43	2.82	99	.290	.338	48-0-5	.167	-1	92	3		-0.1
	Year	10	13	.435	31	28	14	1	204.1	220	95	8	8	46	56	3.57	78	.296	.343	62-0-6	.145	-1	92	-9		-1.9
1915	StL N	6	12	.333	31	13	5-1	1	115.1	141	66	7	2	19	29	4.21	66	.311	.341	36-0-1	.111	-1	96	-16		-2.5
Total	5	51	64	.443	161	122	64-5	7	918.1	1037	503	43	20	199	317	3.85	85	.293	.334	300-0-21	.140	-13	95	-47		-7.9

PEREZ, CARLOS Carlos Gross (b Carlos Gross (Perez)) B4.14.1971 Nigua, D.R. BL/TL/6-3/210(195-210) d4.27 b-Pascual b-Melido [DL 1996 Mon N 182, 2001 LA N 34]

YEAR	TM LG	W	L	PCT	G	GS	CG-SHO	SV-BS	IP	H	R	HR	HB	BB-IB	SO	ERA	AERA	OAV	OOB	AB-HR-SH	AVG	PB	SUP	APR	DL	PW
1995	Mon N★	10	8	.556	28	23	2-1	0-0	141.1	142	61	18	5	28-2	106	3.69	116	.257	.299	45-1-4	.133	1	90	10		1.3
1997	Mon N	12	13	.480	33	32	8-5	0-0	206.2	206	109	21	4	48-1	110	3.88	108	.260	.303	64-1-5	.172	2	99	3		0.6
1998	Mon N	7	10	.412	23	23	3	0-0	163.1	177	79	12	3	33-3	82	3.75	112	.277	.314	47-1-11	.191	2	70	7		0.9
	LA N	4	4	.500	11	11	4-2	0-0	77.2	67	30	9	0	30-1	46	3.24	124	.234	.307	24-0-3	.083	-0	75	8		0.7
	Year	11	14	.440	34	34	7-2	0-0	241	244	109	21	3	63-4	128	3.59	116	.263	.312	71-1-14	.155	1	72	13		1.6
1999	LA N	2	10	.167	17	16	0	0-0	89.2	116	77	23	6	39-1	40	7.43	59	.317	.389	27-1-3	.296	4	82	-30	27	-2.8
2000	LA N	5	8	.385	30	22	0	0-1	144	192	95	25	8	33-1	64	5.56	80	.324	.367	43-0-7	.047	-3*	100	-17		-1.5
Total	5	40	53	.430	142	127	17-8	0-1	822.2	900	451	108	26	211-9	448	4.44	98	.279	.327	250-4-33	.152	6	88	-19	243	-0.8

PEREZ, GEORGE George Thomas B12.29.1937 San Fernando CA BR/TR/6-2.5/200 d4.17

YEAR	TM LG	W	L	PCT	G	GS	CG-SHO	SV-BS	IP	H	R	HR	HB	BB-IB	SO	ERA	AERA	OAV	OOB	AB-HR-SH	AVG	PB	SUP	APR	DL	PW
1958	Pit N	0	1	.000	4	0	0	1	8.1	9	5	1	0	4-0	2	5.40	72	.300	.371	2	.000	-0		-1		-0.2

PEREZ, MELIDO Melido Turpen Gross (b Melido Turpen Gross (Perez)) B2.15.1966 San Cristobal, D.R. BR/TR/6-4/180(180-210) d9.4 b-Pascual b-Carlos [DL 1996 NY A 182]

YEAR	TM LG	W	L	PCT	G	GS	CG-SHO	SV-BS	IP	H	R	HR	HB	BB-IB	SO	ERA	AERA	OAV	OOB	AB-HR-SH	AVG	PB	SUP	APR	DL	PW
1987	KC A	1	1	.500	3	3	0	0-0	10.1	18	12	2	0	5-0	5	7.84	59	.375	.434	0	—	0	126	-4		-0.7
1988	Chi A	12	10	.545	32	32	3-1	0-0	197	186	105	26	2	72-0	138	3.79	106	.248	.313	0	—	0	99	0		-0.1
1989	Chi A	11	14	.440	31	31	2	0-0	183.1	187	106	23	3	90-3	141	5.01	77	.264	.348	0	—	0	96	-20		-2.5
1990	Chi A	13	14	.481	35	35	3-3	0-0	197	177	111	14	2	86-1	161	4.61	83	.241	.320	0	—	0	102	-18		-2.2
1991	Chi A	8	7	.533	49	8	0	1-4	135.2	111	49	15	1	52-0	128	3.12	128	.224	.299	0	—	0	86	15		1.5
1992	NY A	13	16	.448	33	33	10-1	0-0	247.2	212	94	16	5	93-3	218	2.87	138	.235	.308	0	—	0	89	26		2.9
1993	NY A	6	14	.300	25	25	0	0-0	163	173	92	13	22	64-5	148	5.19	81	.267	.333	0	—	0	74	-19	13	-2.0
1994	NY A	9	4	.692	22	22	1	0-0	151.1	134	74	16	3	58-5	109	4.10	112	.238	.311	0	—	0	100	9		0.6
1995	NY A	5	5	.500	13	12	1	0-0	69.1	70	46	10	1	31-2	44	5.58	83	.261	.337	0	—	0	129	-8	69	-1.0
Total	9	78	85	.479	243	201	20-5	1-4	1354.2	1268	700	144	18	551-21	1092	4.17	98	.248	.321	0	—	0	96	-19	264	-3.5

PEREZ, MIKE Michael Irvin (Ortega) B10.19.1964 Yauco, PR BR/TR/6-0/187(187-200) [StLN86 12/312] d9.5 Col Troy St.

YEAR	TM LG	W	L	PCT	G	GS	CG-SHO	SV-BS	IP	H	R	HR	HB	BB-IB	SO	ERA	AERA	OAV	OOB	AB-HR-SH	AVG	PB	SUP	APR	DL	PW
1990	StL N	1	0	1.000	13	0	0	1-1	13.2	12	6	0	0	3-0	5	3.95	97	.240	.273	1	.000	-0		0		0.0
1991	StL N	0	2	.000	14	0	0	1-1	17	19	11	1	1	7-2	7	5.82	64	.288	.365	0	—	-0		-3		-0.4
1992	StL N	9	3	.750	77	0	0	0-3	93	70	23	4	1	32-9	46	1.84	186	.210	.278	4-0-2	.000	-0		16		2.0
1993	StL N	7	2	.778	65	0	0	7-3	72.2	65	24	4	1	20-1	58	2.48	163	.243	.294	1	.000	0		12	40	1.6
1994	StL N	2	3	.400	36	0	0	12-2	31	52	32	5	3	10-1	20	8.71	49	.391	.430	0	—	-0		-15	44	-2.9
1995	Chi N	2	6	.250	68	0	0	2-1	71.1	72	30	8	4	27-8	49	3.66	114	.268	.340	4-0-1	.000	-0		5		0.5
1996	Chi N	1	0	1.000	24	0	0	0-0	27	29	14	2	3	13-1	22	4.67	94	.264	.357	1	.000	-0		0		0.0
1997	KC A	2	0	1.000	16	0	0	0-0	20.1	15	8	2	1	8-0	17	3.54	134	.214	.304	0	—	-0		3		0.3
Total	8	24	16	.600	313	0	0	22-10	346	334	148	26	14	120-22	224	3.56	111	.257	.323	11-0-3	.000	-0		18	84	1.1

PEREZ, ODALIS Odalis Amadol B6.11.1977 Las Matas de Farfan, D.R. BL/TL/6-0/220(150-220) d9.1 [DL 2000 Atl N 181]

YEAR	TM LG	W	L	PCT	G	GS	CG-SHO	SV-BS	IP	H	R	HR	HB	BB-IB	SO	ERA	AERA	OAV	OOB	AB-HR-SH	AVG	PB	SUP	APR	DL	PW
1998	†Atl N	0	1	.000	10	0	0	0-1	10.2	10	5	1	0	4-0	5	4.22	99	.244	.311	0	—	0		0		0.0
1999	Atl N	4	6	.400	18	17	0	0-0	93	100	65	12	1	53-2	82	6.00	75	.275	.366	30-0-4	.133	-1	110	-14	73	-1.3
2001	Atl N	7	8	.467	24	16	0	0-0	95.1	108	55	7	1	39-0	71	4.91	88	.290	.357	26-0-2	.192	1	94	-5	41	-0.6
2002	LA N★	15	10	.600	32	32	4-2	0-0	222.1	182	76	21	4	38-5	155	3.00	130	.226	.262	64-1-10	.156	2	108	25		3.2
2003	LA N	12	12	.500	30	30	0	0-0	185.1	191	98	28	3	46-4	141	4.52	91	.267	.313	52-0-10	.096	-2	91	-7		-0.9
2004	†LA N	7	6	.538	31	31	0	0-0	196.1	188	76	26	3	44-4	128	3.25	127	.250	.294	62-0-6	.113	-1	93	20	20	1.1
2005	LA N	7	8	.467	19	19	0	0-0	108.2	109	59	13	0	28-2	74	4.56	90	.262	.308	33-0-8	.121	-1	93	-5	88	-0.8
Total	7	52	51	.505	164	145	4-2	0-1	911.2	880	434	108	24	252-17	656	4.07	101	.256	.308	267-1-40	.131	-3	98	14	403	0.7

PEREZ, OLIVER Oliver (Martinez) B8.15.1981 Culiacan, Sinaloa, Mexico BL/TL/6-3/160(160-200) d6.16

YEAR	TM LG	W	L	PCT	G	GS	CG-SHO	SV-BS	IP	H	R	HR	HB	BB-IB	SO	ERA	AERA	OAV	OOB	AB-HR-SH	AVG	PB	SUP	APR	DL	PW
2002	SD N	4	5	.444	16	15	0	0-0	90	71	37	13	5	48-1	94	3.50	111	.218	.325	30-0-3	.133	-1	89	5	26	0.3
2003	SD N	4	7	.364	19	19	0	0-0	103.2	103	65	20	3	65-2	117	5.38	74	.258	.365	33-0-3	.212	1	93	-16		-1.4
	Pit N	0	3	.000	5	5	0	0-0	23	26	15	2	1	12-1	24	5.87	74	.283	.371	6	.000	-1	70	-3		-0.4
	Year	4	10	.286	24	24	0	0-0	126.2	129	80	22	4	77-3	141	5.47	74	.263	.366	39-0-3	.179	0	88	-19		-1.8
2004	Pit N	12	10	.545	30	30	2-1	0-0	196	145	72	22	9	81-2	239	2.98	145	.207	.295	58-0-10	.190	1*	83	29		3.2
2005	Pit N	7	5	.583	20	20	0	0-0	103	102	68	23	6	70-1	97	5.85	72	.264	.382	33-0-7	.182	0	134	-16	68	-1.6
Total	4	27	30	.474	90	89	2-1	0-0	515.2	447	256	80	24	276-7	571	4.26	98	.235	.337	160-0-23	.175	1	97	-1	94	0.1

PEREZ, PASCUAL Pascual Gross (b Pascual Gross (Perez)) B5.17.1957 San Cristobal, D.R. BR/TR/6-2/163(162-183) d5.7 b-Melido b-Carlos

YEAR	TM LG	W	L	PCT	G	GS	CG-SHO	SV-BS	IP	H	R	HR	HB	BB-IB	SO	ERA	AERA	OAV	OOB	AB-HR-SH	AVG	PB	SUP	APR	DL	PW
1980	Pit N	0	1	.000	2	2	0	0-0	12	15	6	0	2	2-0	7	3.75	98	.341	.380	4	.250	0	85	0		0.0
1981	Pit N	2	7	.222	17	13	2	0-0	86.1	92	50	5	3	34-9	46	3.96	92	.273	.345	22-0-2	.136	-0*	82	-6		-0.6
1982	†Atl N	4	4	.500	16	11	0	0-0	79.1	85	35	4	0	17-3	29	3.06	120	.276	.311	18-0-5	.167	1	96	3		0.5
1983	Atl N★	15	8	.652	33	33	7-1	0-0	215.1	213	88	20	4	51-5	144	3.43	113	.260	.306	75-0-7	.160	-1	103	10		1.0
1984	Atl N	14	8	.636	30	30	4-1	0-0	211.2	208	96	26	4	51-5	145	3.74	103	.260	.305	66-0-6	.076	-2*	99	4	28	0.4
1985	Atl N	1	13	.071	22	22	0	0-0	95.1	115	72	10	1	57-10	57	6.14	63	.297	.386	25-0-4	.120	-0	88	-22	62	-2.9
1987	Mon N	7	0	1.000	10	10	2	0-0	70.1	52	21	5	1	16-1	58	2.30	185	.206	.256	24-0-1	.042	-2*	119	14		1.2
1988	Mon N	12	8	.600	27	27	4-2	0-0	188	133	59	15	2	44-6	131	2.44	149	.196	.252	54-0-6	.037	-3*	89	24	44	2.3
1989	Mon N	9	13	.409	33	28	2	0-1	198.1	178	85	15	4	45-13	152	3.31	108	.237	.282	54-0-9	.204	2*	93	4		0.6
1990	NY A	1	2	.333	3	3	0	0-0	14	8	3	0	0	3-0	12	1.29	311	.163	.212	0	—	0	38	4	161	0.3
1991	NY A	2	4	.333	14	14	0	0-0	73.2	68	26	7	0	24-1	41	3.18	131	.250	.311	0	—	0	83	9	112	0.7
Total	11	67	68	.496	207	193	21-4	0-1	1254.1	1167	541	107	25	344-53	822	3.44	111	.249	.302	342-0-40	.120	-5	94	44	407	4.0

PEREZ, YORKIS Yorkis Miguel Vargas (b Yorkis Miguel Vargas (Perez)) B9.30.1967 Bajos de Haina, D.R. BL/TL/6-0/180(160-213) d9.30

YEAR	TM LG	W	L	PCT	G	GS	CG-SHO	SV-BS	IP	H	R	HR	HB	BB-IB	SO	ERA	AERA	OAV	OOB	AB-HR-SH	AVG	PB	SUP	APR	DL	PW
1991	Chi N	1	0	1.000	3	0	0	0-1	4.1	5	1	0	0	2-0	3	2.08	188	.167	.250	—		0		1		0.2
1994	Fla N	3	0	1.000	44	0	0	0-2	40.2	33	18	4	1	14-3	41	3.54	126	.220	.291	2	.000	-0		4	20	0.2
1995	Fla N	2	6	.250	69	0	0	1-3	46.2	35	29	6	2	28-4	47	5.21	82	.203	.320	2	.000	-0		-4		-0.7
1996	Fla N	3	4	.429	64	0	0	0-2	47.2	51	28	2	1	31-4	47	5.29	78	.274	.377	1	.000	-0		-5		-0.6
1997	NY N	0	1	.000	9	0	0	0-1	8.2	15	8	2	0	4-0	7	8.31	48	.375	.422	1	.000	-0		-4	63	-0.4
1998	Phi N	2	0	1.000	57	0	0	0-2	52	40	23	3	0	25-0	42	3.81	113	.209	.297	2	.000	-0		3	23	0.2
1999	Phi N	3	1	.750	35	0	0	0-1	32	29	15	4	0	15-1	26	3.94	119	.244	.326	2	.000	-0		3	94	0.2
2000	Hou N	2	1	.667	33	0	0	0-2	22.2	25	18	4	0	14-2	21	5.16	95	.266	.355	1	.000	-0		-2		-0.3
2002	Bal A	0	0	—	23	0	0	1-0	27.1	21	12	4	0	14-1	25	3.29	132	.198	.292	0	—	0		3	14	0.1
Total	9	14	15	.483	337	0	0	2-12	282	251	152	29	4	147-15	259	4.44	99	.235	.326	11	.000	-1		-1	214	-1.2

PERISHO, MATT Matthew Alan B6.8.1975 Burlington IA BL/TL/6-0/205(175-205) [AnaA93 3/75] d5.27

YEAR	TM LG	W	L	PCT	G	GS	CG-SHO	SV-BS	IP	H	R	HR	HB	BB-IB	SO	ERA	AERA	OAV	OOB	AB-HR-SH	AVG	PB	SUP	APR	DL	PW
1997	Ana A	0	2	.000	11	8	0	0-0	45	59	34	6	3	28-0	35	6.00	77	.324	.419	1	.000	-0	95	-7		-0.3
1998	Tex A	2	0	.000	2	2	0	0-0	5	15	17	2	2	8-0	2	27.00	18	.500	.625	0	—	0	133	-12		-1.5
1999	Tex A	0	0	—	4	1	0	0-0	10.1	8	3	0	0	2-1	17	2.61	198	.211	.250	—		0	0	3		0.1
2000	Tex A	2	7	.222	34	13	0	0-1	105	136	99	20	6	67-3	74	7.37	69	.316	.411	4	.000	-0	84	-27		-1.9
2001	Det A	2	3	.400	30	4	0	0-2	39.1	54	29	4	4	14-1	19	5.72	77	.327	.391	0	—	0	73	-6	20	-0.7
2002	Det A	0	0	—	5	0	0	0-0	10.1	16	11	2	0	6-0	3	8.71	50	.372	.440	0	—	-0		-5		-0.2
2004	Fla N	5	3	.625	66	0	0	0-2	47	45	23	6	2	26-2	42	4.40	93	.247	.346	0	—	-0		-1		-0.2
2005	Fla N	2	0	1.000	24	0	0	0-0	14	12	4	1	1	11-0	10	1.93	207	.245	.387	0	—	0		3		0.4
	Bos A	0	0	—	1	0	0	0-0	0	4	4	0	0	0-0	0	∞	—	1.000	1.000	0	—	0		-1		-0.1
Total	8	11	17	.393	177	28	0	0-5	276	346	221	42	18	162-7	202	6.39	73	.309	.401	5	.000	-1	89	-53	20	-4.4

PERKINS, CECIL Cecil Boyce B12.1.1940 Baltimore MD BR/TR/6-0/175 d7.5 Col Shepherd

YEAR	TM LG	W	L	PCT	G	GS	CG-SHO	SV-BS	IP	H	R	HR	HB	BB-IB	SO	ERA	AERA	OAV	OOB	AB-HR-SH	AVG	PB	SUP	APR	DL	PW
1967	NY A	0	1	.000	2	1	0	0	5	6	5	1	0	2-0	1	9.00	35	.316	.381	1	.000	-0	111	-3		-0.5

YEAR	TM LG	W	L	PCT	G	GS	CG-SHO	SV-BS	IP	H	R	HR	HB	BB-IB	SO	ERA	AERA	OAV	OOB	AB-HR-SH	AVG	PB	SUP	APR	DL	PW
PERKINS, CHARLIE Charles Sullivan "Lefty" B9.9.1905 Ensley AL D5.25.1988 Salem OR BR/TL/6-1/175 d5.1 Col Williams																										
1930	Phi A	0	0	—	8	1	0	0	23.2	25	20	0	0	15	15	6.46	72	.313	.421	8	.125	-1	129	-5		-0.3
1934	Bro N	0	3	.000	11	2	0	0	24.1	37	25	3	2	14	5	8.51	46	.336	.421	7	.286	0	88	-12		-1.2
Total	2	0	3	.000	19	3	0	0	48	62	45	3	2	29	20	7.50	57	.326	.421	15	.200	-1	101	-17		-1.5
PERKINS, DAN Daniel Lee B3.15.1975 Miami FL BR/TR/6-2/193 [MinA93 2/63] d4.7																										
1999	Min A	1	7	.125	29	12	0	0-0	86.2	117	69	14	5	43-0	44	6.54	79	.326	.401	2	.500	0	75	-13		-1.0
PERKOVICH, JOHN John Joseph "Perky" B3.10.1924 Chicago IL D9.16.2000 Little Rock AR BR/TR/5-11/170 d5.6																										
1950	Chi A	0	0	—	1	0	0	0	5	3	4	3	0	1	3	7.20	62	.318	.348	1	.000	-0		-1		-0.1
PERKOWSKI, HARRY Harry Walter B9.6.1922 Dante VA BL/TL/6-2.5/196* d9.13																										
1947	Cin N	0	0	—	3	1	0	0	7.1	12	3	1	0	3	2	3.68	111	.375	.429	1	.000	0	150	1		0.0
1949	Cin N	1	1	.500	5	3	2	0	23.2	21	14	2	0	14	3	4.56	92	.236	.340	9	.333	1	91	-1		-0.1
1950	Cin N	0	0	—	22	0	0	0	34.1	36	21	6	1	23	19	5.24	81	.286	.340	20	.318	2*		-3		0.1
1951	Cin N	3	6	.333	35	7	1	1	102	96	42	2	1	46	56	2.82	144	.251	.333	25-0-3	.040	-3*	53	12		0.7
1952	Cin N	12	10	.545	33	24	11-1	0	194	197	91	9	3	89	86	3.80	99	.265	.347	75-0-1	.160	-0	119	-2		-0.1
1953	Cin N	12	11	.522	33	25	7-2	2	193	204	107	26	1	62	70	4.52	96	.271	.327	69	.203	1	94	-3		-0.1
1954	Cin N	2	8	.200	28	12	3-1	0	95.2	100	71	16	1	62	32	6.11	69	.276	.379	25-1-2	.160	1	83	-19		-1.7
1955	Chi N	3	4	.429	25	4	0	2	47.2	53	32	3	0	25-4	28	5.29	77	.283	.366	13	.154	-0*	71	-7		-0.9
Total	8	33	40	.452	184	76	24-4	5	697.2	719	381	65	7	324-4	296	4.37	94	.269	.349	239-1-6	.180	1	95	-22		-2.1
PERLMAN, JON Jonathan Samuel B12.13.1956 Dallas TX BL/TR/6-3/185* [ChiN79 1/12] d9.6 Col Baylor																										
1985	Chi N	1	0	1.000	6	0	0	0-0	8.2	10	11	3	0	8-2	4	11.42	35	.313	.439	1	.000	-0		-6		-0.6
1987	SF N	0	0	—	10	0	0	0-0	11.1	11	7	1	1	4-0	3	3.97	97	.256	.320	0	—	0		-1		-0.1
1988	Cle A	0	2	.000	10	0	0	0-1	19.2	25	12	0	0	11-3	10	5.49	75	.309	.391	0	—	-0		-2	86	-0.2
Total	3	1	2	.333	26	0	0	0-1	39.2	46	30	4	1	23-5	17	6.35	64	.295	.383	1	.000	-0		-9	86	-0.9
PERME, LEN Leonard John B11.25.1917 Cleveland OH BL/TL/6-0/170 d9.8 Mil 1943-45																										
1942	Chi A	0	1	.000	4	1	1	0	13	5	2	0	1	4	4	1.38	260	.119	.213	3	.333	0	0	3		0.3
1946	Chi A	0	0	—	4	0	0	0	4.1	6	4	0	0	7	2	8.31	41	.316	.500	0	—	0		-2		-0.1
Total	2	0	1	.000	8	1	1	0	17.1	11	6	0	1	11	6	3.12	114	.180	.315	3	.333	0	0	1		0.2
PERNOLL, HUB Henry Hubbard B3.14.1888 Grants Pass OR D2.18.1944 Grants Pass OR BR/TL/5-8/175 d4.25																										
1910	Det A	4	3	.571	11	5	4	0	54.2	54	20	1	5	14	25	2.96	89	.270	.333	16-0-1	.063	-2	122	0		-0.1
1912	Det A	0	0	—	3	0	0	0	9	9	6	0	0	4	3	6.00	54	.265	.342	3	.000	-0		-2		-0.1
Total	2	4	3	.571	14	5	4	0	63.2	63	26	1	5	18	28	3.39	80	.269	.335	19-0-1	.053	-2	122	-2		-0.2
PERRANOSKI, RON Ronald Peter (b Ronald Peter Perzanowski) B4.1.1936 Paterson NJ BL/TL/6-0/192(180-192) d4.14 C17 Col Michigan St.																										
1961	LA N	7	5	.583	53	1	0	6	91.2	82	31	5	4	41-7	56	2.65	164	.244	.330	12	.083	-0	245	16		2.1
1962	LA N	6	6	.500	70	0	0	20	107.1	103	40	1	0	36-9	68	2.85	127	.255	.314	14-0-1	.071	-1		10		1.3
1963	†LA N	16	3	.842	69	0	0	21	129	112	30	7	4	43-14	75	1.67	180	.231	.298	24-0-2	.125	0		20		3.9
1964	LA N	5	7	.417	72	0	0	14	125.1	128	62	5	1	46-19	79	3.09	105	.263	.325	19-0-3	.105	-0		-3		-0.3
1965	†LA N	6	6	.500	59	0	0	17	104.2	85	28	2	3	40-7	53	2.24	146	.226	.303	19	.158	1		14		2.1
1966	†LA N	6	7	.462	55	0	0	7	82	82	32	4	1	31-11	50	3.18	104	.269	.337	8-0-1	.250	1		2		0.6
1967	LA N	6	7	.462	70	0	0	16	110	97	36	4	3	45-13	75	2.45	126	.240	.318	10	.100	-0		8		1.2
1968	Min A	8	7	.533	66	0	0	6	87	86	36	5	0	38-12	65	3.10	99	.252	.325	7	.000	-1		0		-0.1
1969	†Min A	9	10	.474	75	0	0	31-11	119.2	85	32	4	1	52-16	62	2.11	173	.205	.292	24-0-4	.083	-1		20		4.3
1970	†Min A	7	8	.467	67	0	0	34-11	111	108	38	7	1	42-7	55	2.43	152	.259	.325	24-0-1	.042	-2		14		2.4
1971	Min A	1	4	.200	36	0	0	5-6	42.2	60	39	2	3	28-4	21	6.75	52	.337	.431	3-0-1	.000	-0		-16		-2.3
	Det A	0	1	.000	11	0	0	2-1	18	16	9	2	1	3-1	8	2.50	145	.254	.290	2	.000	-0		1		0.0
	Year	1	5	.167	47	0	0	7-7	60.2	76	48	4	4	31-5	29	5.49	65	.315	.396	5-0-1	.000	-1		-16		-2.3
1972	Det A	0	1	.000	17	0	0	0-0	18.2	23	16	2	1	8-1	10	7.71	41	.307	.381	1	.000	-0		-8		-0.5
	LA N	2	0	1.000	9	0	0	0-0	16.2	19	8	0	0	8-0	5	2.70	124	.292	.365	0	—	0		0		0.0
1973	Cal A	0	2	.000	8	0	0	0-0	11	11	5	0	1	7-0	5	4.09	88	.282	.404	0	—	0		0	74	0.0
Total	13	79	74	.516	737	1	0	179-29	1174.2	1097	442	50	24	468-121	687	2.79	123	.250	.323	167-0-13	.096	-4	245	78	74	14.7
PERRIN, BILL William Joseph "Lefty" B6.23.1910 New Orleans LA D6.30.1974 New Orleans LA BR/TL/5-11/172 d9.30																										
1934	Cle A	0	1	.000	1	1	0	0	5	13	9	0	1	2	3	14.40	32	.520	.571	2	.000	-0	96	-5		-0.6
PERRITT, POL William Dayton B8.30.1892 Arcadia LA D10.15.1947 Shreveport LA BR/TR/6-2/168 d9.7																										
1912	StL N	1	1	.500	6	3	1	2	31	25	16	0	0	10	13	3.19	107	.243	.310	9	.222	-0	71	1		0.0
1913	StL N	6	14	.300	36	21	8	0	175	205	123	9	8	64	64	5.25	62	.300	.367	59-0-1	.203	-1	82	-40		-4.0
1914	StL N	16	13	.552	41	32	18-3	2	286	248	106	7	15	93	115	2.36	118	.245	.318	92-0-7	.141	-2	100	14		1.0
1915	NY N	12	18	.400	35	29	16-4	0	220	226	95	6	12	56	91	2.66	96	.266	.323	68-0-2	.162	-1	86	-7		-1.3
1916	NY N	18	11	.621	40	29	17-5	2	251	243	82	11	7	56	115	2.62	93	.257	.304	83-0-5	.084	-4	133	-2		-0.8
1917	†NY N	17	7	.708	35	26	14-5	1	215	186	61	3	7	45	72	1.88	135	.237	.284	70-0-5	.157	-2	131	15		1.5
1918	NY N	18	13	.581	35	31	19-6	0	233	212	82	5	1	38	60	2.74	96	.246	.278	80-0-5	.175	-1*	92	0		-0.3
1919	NY N	1	1	.500	11	3	0	1	19	27	18	0	2	12	2	7.11	39	.386	.488	4	.000	-1	113	-9		-0.1
1920	NY N	0	0	—	8	0	0	2	15	9	3	0	0	4	3	1.80	167	.167	.224	4	.000	-1		2		0.1
1921	NY N	2	0	1.000	5	1	0	0	11.2	17	5	0	0	2	5	3.86	95	.321	.345	3	.000	-0	112	-2		-0.3
	Det A	0	0	—	1	0	0	0	2	5	1	0	1	1	3	4.85	88	.383	.473	5	.400	-0	137	-1		0.0
	Year	2	0	1.000	6	1	0	0	13.2	22	6	0	1	3	8	3.95	93	.333	.361	8	.250	-0	117	-3		-0.3
Total	10	92	78	.541	256	177	93-23	8	1469.2	1416	604	41	53	390	543	2.89	94	.259	.315	477-0-22	.151	-13	103	-29		-5.2
PERRY, GAYLORD Gaylord Jackson B9.15.1938 Williamston NC BR/TR/6-4/215(205-220) d4.14 HF1991 b-Jim																										
1962	SF N	3	1	.750	13	7	1	0	43	54	29	3	0	14-2	20	5.23	73	.310	.354	13-0-2	.231	0	158	-8		-0.6
1963	SF N	1	6	.143	31	4	0	2	76	84	41	10	2	29-7	52	4.03	79	.279	.345	18	.222	1*	121	-8		-0.7
1964	SF N	12	11	.522	44	19	5-2	5	206.1	179	65	16	5	43-6	155	2.75	130	.232	.275	56-0-7	.054	-3*	82	21		2.0
1965	SF N	8	12	.400	47	26	6	1	195.2	194	105	21	6	70-16	170	4.19	86	.256	.322	64-0-5	.156	-0*	96	-13		-1.1
1966	SF N★	21	8	.724	36	35	13-3	0	255.2	242	92	15	5	40-3	201	2.99	123	.247	.279	86-0-6	.186	-0	105	22	15	2.6
1967	SF N	15	17	.469	39	37	18-3	1	293	231	98	20	4	84-17	230	2.61	126	.214	.273	91-0-15	.143	-1*	90	23		2.6
1968	SF N	16	15	.516	39	38	19-3	1	290.2	240	93	10	4	59-12	173	2.45	120	.222	.264	97-0-8	.113	-3	92	17		1.8
1969	SF N	19	14	.576	40	39	26-3	0-1	325.1	290	115	23	11	91-14	233	2.49	141	.237	.295	117-1-7	.120	-2	102	35		3.5
1970	SF N★	23	13	.639	41	41	23-5	0-0	328.2	292	138	27	8	84-8	214	3.20	124	.237	.289	120-1-10	.117	-4	111	26		2.5
1971	†SF N	16	12	.571	37	37	14-2	0-0	280	255	116	20	5	67-4	158	2.76	123	.242	.287	98-1-10	.102	-3*	110	15		1.1
1972	Cle A★	24	16	.600	41	40	29-5	1-0	342.2	253	79	17	12	82-16	234	1.92	170	.205	.261	110-1-14	.155	-0	79	49		6.8
1973	Cle A	19	19	.500	41	41	29-7	0-0	344	315	143	34	5	115-9	238	3.38	117	.246	.310	0	—	0	90	21		2.3
1974	Cle A★	21	13	.618	37	37	28-4	0-0	322.1	230	98	25	6	99-7	216	2.51	145	.204	.270	0	—	0	101	42		4.5
1975	Cle A	6	9	.400	15	15	10-1	0-0	121.2	120	57	16	1	34-5	85	3.55	107	.256	.308	0	—	0	68	3		0.4
	Tex A	12	8	.600	22	22	15-4	0-0	184	157	70	12	3	36-1	148	3.03	124	.227	.267	0	—	0	107	16		1.6
	Year	18	17	.514	37	37	25-5	0-0	305.2	277	127	28	4	70-6	233	3.24	117	.239	.284	0	—	0	91	18		2.0
1976	Tex A	15	14	.517	32	32	21-2	0-0	250.1	232	93	14	0	52-3	143	3.24	111	.247	.285	0	—	0	94	14		1.4
1977	Tex A	15	12	.556	34	34	13-4	0-0	238	239	108	21	5	56-4	177	3.37	121	.262	.307	0	—	0	86	15		1.1
1978	SD N	21	6	.778	37	37	5-2	0-0	260.2	241	96	9	2	66-8	154	2.73	123	.248	.295	87-0-13	.092	-3	119	17		1.3
1979	SD N★	12	11	.522	32	32	10	0-0	232.2	225	90	12	4	67-10	140	3.06	116	.257	.312	71-1-11	.085	-2	82	13		1.1
1980	Tex A	6	9	.400	24	24	6-2	0-0	155	159	74	12	7	46-3	107	3.43	114	.268	.327	0	—	0	100	6		0.5
	NY A	4	4	.500	10	8	0	0-0	50.2	65	33	2	1	18-0	28	4.44	89	.320	.372	0	—	0	90	-5		-0.7
	Year	10	13	.435	34	32	6-2	0-0	205.2	224	107	14	8	64-3	135	3.68	106	.281	.338	0	—	0	97	1		-0.2
1981	Atl N	8	9	.471	23	23	3	0-0	150.2	182	70	9	4	24-1	60	3.94	89	.304	.342	48-1-5	.250	3*	108	-5		-0.3
1982	Sea A	10	12	.455	32	32	6	0-0	216.2	245	117	27	4	54-4	116	4.40	97	.287	.331	0	—	0	85	-2		-0.2
1983	Sea A	3	10	.231	16	16	2	0-0	102	116	60	18	3	23-3	42	4.94	87	.286	.327	0	—	0	60	-6		-0.7
	KC A	4	4	.500	14	14	1-1	0-0	84.1	98	48	6	1	26-1	40	4.27	96	.292	.342	0	—	0	81	-3		-0.2
	Year	7	14	.333	30	30	3-1	0-0	186.1	214	108	24	4	49-4	82	4.64	91	.289	.334	0	—	0	69	-9		-0.9
Total	22	314	265	.542	777	690	303-53	11-1	5350	4938	2128	399	108	1379-164	3534	3.11	117	.245	.296	1076-6-113	.131	-16	96	305	15	32.9

PERRY, SCOTT
Herbert Scott B4.17.1891 Denison TX D10.27.1959 Kansas City MO BR/TR/6-0/175 d5.13

YEAR	TM LG	W	L	PCT	G	GS	CG-SHO	SV-BS	IP	H	R	HR	HB	BB-IB	SO	ERA	AERA	OAV	OOB	AB-HR-SH	AVG	PB	SUP	APR	DL	PW
1915	StL A	0	0						2	5	3	0	1	1	0	13.50	21	.455	.538	0	—	0	153	-2		-0.1
1916	Chi N	2	1	.667	4	3	2-1	0	28.1	30	9	0	0	3	10	2.54	115	.291	.311	11	.273	1	68	2		0.3
1917	Cin N	0			4	1		0	13.1	17	15	0	1	8	4	6.75	39	.321	.419	5	.000	-1	288	-7		-0.4
1918	Phi A	20	19	.513	44	36	30-3	2	332.1	295	97	1	2	111	81	1.98	148	.247	.312	112-0-6	.134	-6	73	32		3.5
1919	Phi A	4	17	.190	25	21	12	1	183.2	193	92	4	2	72	38	3.58	96	.282	.352	59-0-5	.136	-3	78	-3		-0.2
1920	Phi A	11	25	.306	42	34	20-1	1	263.2	310	151	14	7	65	79	3.62	111	.300	.345	83-1-5	.157	-4	67	10		0.8
1921	Phi A	3	6	.333	12	8	5	1	70	77	36	4	1	24	19	4.11	108	.288	.349	26	.038	-4	75	4		0.1
Total 7		40	68	.370	132	104	69-5	5	893.1	927	403	23	14	284	231	3.07	113	.277	.336	296-1-16	.135	-17	75	36		4.0

PERRY, JIM
James Evan B10.30.1935 Williamston NC BB/TR/6-4/200(185-205) d4.23 b-Gaylord Col Campbell

YEAR	TM LG	W	L	PCT	G	GS	CG-SHO	SV-BS	IP	H	R	HR	HB	BB-IB	SO	ERA	AERA	OAV	OOB	AB-HR-SH	AVG	PB	SUP	APR	DL	PW
1959	Cle A	12	10	.545	44	13	8-2	4	153	122	54	10	2	55-7	79	2.65	139	.225	.295	50-0-1	.300	3	109	17		2.7
1960	Cle A	18	10	.643	41	36	10-4	1	261.1	257	118	35	4	91-3	120	3.62	103	.260	.321	91-0-5	.242	-1	97	4		0.7
1961	Cle A☆	10	17	.370	35	35	6-1	0	223.2	238	132	28	6	87-5	90	4.71	84	.273	.341	73-0-5	.164	-1	87	-19		-2.1
1962	Cle A	12	12	.500	35	27	7-3	0	193.2	213	94	21	2	59-1	74	4.14	94	.285	.337	60-0-7	.183	0	100	-3		-0.3
1963	Cle A	0	0	—	5	0	0	0	10.1	12	6	0	0	2-0	7	5.23	69	.293	.326	2	.000	-0		-1		-0.1
	Min A	9	9	.500	35	25	5-1	1	168.1	167	77	17	2	57-4	65	3.74	97	.256	.315	51-0-1	.216	3	101	-1		0.2
	Year	9	9	.500	40	25	5-1	1	178.2	179	83	17	2	59-4	72	3.83	95	.258	.316	53-0-1	.208	3	101	-2		0.1
1964	Min A	6	3	.667	42	1	0	2	65.1	61	26	7	1	23-4	55	3.44	104	.245	.309	13	.154	-0	174	2		0.3
1965	†Min A	12	7	.632	36	19	4-2	0	167.2	142	57	18	3	47-2	88	2.63	135	.232	.286	53-0-4	.170	1	96	17		1.9
1966	Min A	11	7	.611	33	25	8-1	0	184.1	149	61	17	5	53-4	122	2.54	142	.227	.281	59-1-2	.220	4	106	20		2.4
1967	Min A	8	7	.533	37	11	3-2	0	130.2	123	51	8	3	50-5	94	3.03	114	.255	.325	42-1-0	.190	1*	98	6		0.7
1968	Min A	8	6	.571	32	18	3-2	1	139	113	37	8	4	26-2	69	2.27	136	.219	.262	42-2-4	.143	2	96	14		1.8
1969	†Min A	20	6	.769	46	36	12-3	0-0	261.2	244	87	18	9	66-10	153	2.82	129	.244	.298	93-0-3	.172	1*	128	27		2.6
1970	†Min A★	24	12	.667	40	40	13-4	0-0	278.2	258	112	20	7	57-10	168	3.04	129	.243	.286	97-1-10	.247	5*	107	20		3.1
1971	Min A☆	17	17	.500	40	39	8	1-0	270	263	135	39	5	102-10	126	4.23	84	.259	.326	92-0-4	.185	1	110	-17		-2.0
1972	Min A	13	16	.448	35	35	5-2	0-0	217.2	191	93	14	8	60-5	85	3.35	96	.236	.292	71-0-5	.155	-1	88	-1		-0.3
1973	Det A	14	13	.519	35	34	7-1	0-0	203	225	96	22	4	55-5	66	4.03	102	.282	.329	0	—	0	88	2		0.2
1974	Cle A	17	12	.586	36	36	8-3	0-0	252	242	94	11	5	64-10	71	2.96	123	.254	.303	0	—	0	95	19		2.1
1975	Cle A	1	6	.143	8	6	0	0-0	37.2	46	34	8	0	18-5	11	6.69	57	.309	.383	0	—	0	69	-13		-1.9
	Oak A	3	4	.429	15	11	2-1	0-1	67.2	61	43	7	7	26-1	33	4.66	78	.237	.319	0	—	0	90	-9		-0.9
	Year	4	10	.286	23	17	2-1	0-1	105.1	107	77	15	7	44-6	44	5.38	69	.264	.342	0	—	0	82	-22		-2.8
Total 17		215	174	.553	630	447	109-32	10-1	3285.2	3127	1407	308	80	998-93	1576	3.45	106	.252	.309	889-5-51	.199	24	100	84		11.1

PERRY, PAT
William Patrick B2.4.1959 Taylorville IL BL/TL/6-1/170(170-190) [HouN78*2/38] d9.12 Col Lincoln Land (IL) CC

YEAR	TM LG	W	L	PCT	G	GS	CG-SHO	SV-BS	IP	H	R	HR	HB	BB-IB	SO	ERA	AERA	OAV	OOB	AB-HR-SH	AVG	PB	SUP	APR	DL	PW
1985	StL N	1	0	1.000	6	0	0	0-0	12.1	3	0	0	0	3-1	6	0.00	—	.077	.143	2	.500	0		5		0.4
1986	StL N	2	3	.400	46	0	0	2-0	68.2	59	31	5	0	34-9	29	3.80	97	.234	.323	8	.000	-1		0		-0.1
1987	StL N	4	2	.667	45	0	0	1-1	65.2	54	34	7	2	21-3	33	4.39	96	.222	.288	7	.143	-0		-1		-0.1
	Cin N	1	0	1.000	12	0	0	1-1	15.1	6	0	0	1	4-1	6	0.00	—	.122	.204	0	—	0		7		0.5
	Year	5	2	.714	57	0	0	2-2	81	60	34	7	3	25-4	39	3.56	118	.205	.274	7	.143	-0		7		0.4
1988	Cin N	2	2	.500	12	0	0	0-0	20.2	21	17	4	0	9-4	11	5.66	63	.262	.326	2	.000	-0		-6		-1.1
	Chi N	2	2	.500	35	0	0	1-3	38	40	15	5	1	7-0	24	3.32	110	.270	.304	1-1-0	1.000	1	1		21	0.3
	Year	4	4	.500	47	0	0	1-3	58.2	61	32	9	1	16-4	35	4.14	87	.268	.312	3-1-0	.333	1		-4		-0.8
1989		0	1	.000	19	0	0	0-0	35.2	23	8	2	0	16-3	20	1.77	214	.187	.279	6	.167	-0		7	93	0.4
1990	LA N	0	0	—	7	0	0	0-0	6.2	9	7	0	1	5-1	2	8.10	45	.310	.417	1	.000	-0		-3	125	-0.2
Total 6		12	10	.545	182	0	0	6-5	263	215	112	23	5	99-22	131	3.46	111	.224	.296	27-1-0	.148	0		10	239	0.1

PERRYMAN, PARSON
Emmett Key B10.24.1888 Everett Springs GA D9.12.1966 Starke FL BR/TR/6-4.5/193 d4.14 Col Emory

YEAR	TM LG	W	L	PCT	G	GS	CG-SHO	SV-BS	IP	H	R	HR	HB	BB-IB	SO	ERA	AERA	OAV	OOB	AB-HR-SH	AVG	PB	SUP	APR	DL	PW
1915	StL A	2	4	.333	24	3	0	0	50.1	52	27	2	1	16	19	3.93	73	.281	.342	6	.000	-1	102	-5		-0.6

PERSON, ROBERT
Robert Alan B10.6.1969 Lowell MA BR/TR/6-0/195(180-195) [CleA89 25/645] d9.18 Col Seminole St. (OK) JC

YEAR	TM LG	W	L	PCT	G	GS	CG-SHO	SV-BS	IP	H	R	HR	HB	BB-IB	SO	ERA	AERA	OAV	OOB	AB-HR-SH	AVG	PB	SUP	APR	DL	PW
1995	NY N	1	0	1.000	3	1	0	0-0	12	5	1	0	2	2-0	6	0.75	538	.119	.159	3	.667	1	112	5		0.4
1996	NY N	4	5	.444	27	13	0	0-0	89.2	86	50	16	2	35-3	76	4.52	89	.247	.316	21-0-5	.143	-0*	102	-4		-0.5
1997	Tor A	5	10	.333	23	22	0	0-0	128.1	125	86	19	5	60-2	99	5.61	82	.255	.338	4	.000	-0	72	-14	39	-1.4
1998	Tor A	3	1	.750	27	0	0	6-2	38.1	45	31	9	2	22-1	31	7.04	66	.294	.379	0	—	0		-9		-1.1
1999	Tor A	0	2	.000	11	0	0	2-0	11	9	12	1	4	15-1	12	9.82	50	.231	.467	0	—	0		-5	7	-1.0
	Phi N	10	5	.667	31	22	0	0-0	137	130	72	23	2	70-1	127	4.27	109	.252	.341	41-0-4	.073	-2	119	5		0.2
2000	Phi N	9	7	.563	28	28	1-1	0-0	173.1	144	73	13	6	95-1	164	3.63	126	.229	.332	53-0-8	.132	-0	91	20	32	1.5
2001	Phi N	15	7	.682	33	33	3-1	0-0	208.1	179	103	34	8	80-3	183	4.19	98	.234	.311	67-2-5	.119	1	102	-1		-0.1
2002	Phi N	4	5	.444	16	16	0	0-0	87.2	79	58	13	5	51-0	61	5.44	70	.241	.350	24-2-3	.083	1*	124	-17	102	-1.5
2003	Bos A	0	0	—	7	0	0	1-0	11.2	11	10	1	0	8-0	10	7.71	60	.250	.364	1	.000	-0		-3	157	-0.2
Total 9		51	42	.548	206	135	4	9-2	897.1	813	496	129	35	438-12	773	4.64	94	.242	.332	214-4-25	.117	-0	99	-23	337	-3.7

PERTICA, BILL
William Andrew B8.17.1898 Santa Barbara CA D12.28.1967 Los Angeles CA BR/TR/5-9/165 d8.7

YEAR	TM LG	W	L	PCT	G	GS	CG-SHO	SV-BS	IP	H	R	HR	HB	BB-IB	SO	ERA	AERA	OAV	OOB	AB-HR-SH	AVG	PB	SUP	APR	DL	PW
1918	Bos A	0	0	—	1	0	0	0	3	3	1	0	0	1	1	3.00	89	.273	.273	1	.000	-0		0		0.0
1921	StL N	14	10	.583	38	31	15-2	1	208.1	212	104	9	10	70	67	3.37	109	.267	.334	70-0-5	.143	-3	110	4		-0.1
1922	StL N	8	8	.500	34	15	2	0	117.1	153	94	5	3	65	30	5.91	65	.333	.419	33	.182	-0*	121	-28		-3.1
1923	StL N	0	0	—	1	1	0	0	2.1	2	2	0	1	2	0	3.86	101	.250	.500	1	.000	-0	42	0		0.1
Total 4		22	18	.550	74	47	17-2	1	331	370	201	14	14	138	98	4.27	87	.291	.367	105-0-5	.152	-4	112	-24		-3.2

PERZANOWSKI, STAN
Stanley B8.25.1950 East Chicago IN BB/TR/6-2/170* [ChiA68 16/362] d6.20

YEAR	TM LG	W	L	PCT	G	GS	CG-SHO	SV-BS	IP	H	R	HR	HB	BB-IB	SO	ERA	AERA	OAV	OOB	AB-HR-SH	AVG	PB	SUP	APR	DL	PW
1971	Chi A	0	1	.000	5	0	0	1-0	6	14	10	1	0	3-0	5	12.00	30	.412	.447	2	.000	-0		-6		-1.0
1974	Chi A	0	0	—	2	1	0	0-0	2.1	8	7	1	0	2-0	2	19.29	19	.533	.588	0	—	0	94	-4		-0.2
1975	Tex A	3	3	.500	12	8	1	0-0	66	59	25	1	5	25-2	26	3.00	126	.246	.327	0	—	0	70	6		0.6
1976	Tex A	0	0	—	5	0	0	0-0	11.2	20	15	3	2	4-0	6	10.03	36	.385	.448	0	—	0		-8		-0.4
1978	Min A	2	7	.222	13	7	1	1-0	56.2	59	37	1	4	26-0	31	5.24	73	.276	.362	2	.000	-0	114	-9		-1.2
Total 5		5	11	.313	37	16	2	2-0	142.2	160	94	7	11	60-2	70	5.11	74	.288	.366	4	.000	-0	91	-21		-2.2

PETEREK, JEFF
Jeffrey Allen B9.22.1963 Michigan City IN BR/TR/6-2/195 d8.14 Col Mary Hardin-Baylor

YEAR	TM LG	W	L	PCT	G	GS	CG-SHO	SV-BS	IP	H	R	HR	HB	BB-IB	SO	ERA	AERA	OAV	OOB	AB-HR-SH	AVG	PB	SUP	APR	DL	PW
1989	Mil A	0	2	.000	7	4	0	0-0	31.1	31	14	3	0	14-1	16	4.02	96	.252	.328	0	—	0	59	0		0.0

PETERS, CHRIS
Christopher Michael B1.28.1972 Fort Thomas KY BL/TL/6-1/175(162-175) [PitN93 37/1046] d7.19 Col Indiana

YEAR	TM LG	W	L	PCT	G	GS	CG-SHO	SV-BS	IP	H	R	HR	HB	BB-IB	SO	ERA	AERA	OAV	OOB	AB-HR-SH	AVG	PB	SUP	APR	DL	PW
1996	Pit N	2	4	.333	16	10	0	0-0	64	72	43	9	1	25-0	28	5.63	78	.287	.350	19-0-1	.211	0	70	-8		-0.6
1997	Pit N	2	2	.500	31	1	0	0-1	37.1	38	23	6	3	21-4	17	4.58	93	.277	.383	4	.250	0	86	-2		-0.2
1998	Pit N	8	10	.444	39	21	1	1-0	148	142	63	13	8	55-4	103	3.47	123	.252	.319	39-0-4	.231	1	106	14		1.6
1999	Pit N	5	4	.556	19	11	0	0-0	71	98	59	17	4	27-0	46	6.59	70	.322	.381	22-0-1	.273	2	116	-16	89	-1.4
2000	Pit N	0	1	.000	18	0	0	1-0	28.1	23	9	2	1	14-2	16	2.86	162	.221	.319	6	.167	-0		6	55	0.3
2001	Mon N	2	4	.333	13	6	0	0-1	31	47	26	7	2	15-1	14	7.55	57	.367	.435	11	.091	-1	93	-10		-1.7
Total 6		19	25	.432	136	49	1	2-2	379.2	420	223	54	14	157-11	224	4.81	91	.282	.353	101-0-6	.218	2	99	-16	144	-2.0

PETERS, GARY
Gary Charles B4.21.1937 Grove City PA BL/TL/6-2/200* d9.10 Col Grove City

YEAR	TM LG	W	L	PCT	G	GS	CG-SHO	SV-BS	IP	H	R	HR	HB	BB-IB	SO	ERA	AERA	OAV	OOB	AB-HR-SH	AVG	PB	SUP	APR	DL	PW
1959	Chi A	0	0	—	2	0	0	0	1	2	0	0	0	2-0	1	0.00	—	.400	.571	0	—	0		0		0.0
1960	Chi A	0	0	—	2	0	0	0	3.1	4	1	0	0	1-0	4	2.70	140	.286	.333	0	—	0		0		0.0
1961	Chi A	0	0	—	2	0	0	0	10.1	10	2	0	0	2-0	6	1.74	225	.270	.308	3	.333	-0		3		0.2
1962	Chi A	0	1	.000	5	0	0	0	6.1	8	5	0	1	1-0	4	5.68	69	.308	.345	0	—	0		-2		-0.2
1963	Chi A	19	8	.704	41	30	13-4	1	243	192	69	9	8	68-2	189	2.33	150	.216	.277	81-3-2	.259	9*	96	34		4.8
1964	Chi A☆	20	8	.714	37	36	11-3	0	273.2	217	89	20	7	104-9	205	2.50	138	.219	.296	120-4-3	.208	8*	109	29		3.9
1965	Chi A	10	12	.455	33	30	6-2	0	176.1	181	76	19	4	63-8	95	3.62	88	.265	.329	72-1-0	.181	2*	98	-7		-0.6
1966	Chi A	12	10	.545	30	27	11-4	0	204.2	156	54	11	3	45-6	129	1.98	160	.212	.260	81-1-3	.235	6*	102	29		4.0
1967	Chi A★	16	11	.593	38	36	11-3	0	260	187	81	15	11	91-8	215	2.28	136	.199	.276	99-2-4	.212	7*	109	24		3.6
1968	Chi A	4	13	.235	31	25	6-1	0	162.2	146	79	7	7	60-6	110	3.76	80	.242	.315	72-2-0	.208	7*	93	-13		-0.6
1969	Chi A	10	15	.400	36	32	7-3	0	218.2	238	118	21	5	78-1	140	4.53	85	.280	.344	71-2-6	.169	2*	106	-15		-1.4
1970	Bos A	16	11	.593	34	34	10-4	0-0	221.2	221	114	20	7	83-2	155	4.06	98	.257	.325	82-1-2	.244	6*	122	-1		0.5
1971	Bos A	14	11	.560	34	32	9-1	1-0	214	241	111	25	6	70-3	100	4.37	85	.288	.346	96-3-5	.271	8*	112	-14		-0.8
1972	Bos A	3	3	.500	33	4	0	1-1	85.1	91	48	10	3	38-8	67	4.32	75	.279	.356	30	.200	1	130	-10		-0.7
Total 14		124	103	.546	359	286	79-23	5-1	2081	1894	847	157	62	706-53	1420	3.25	106	.243	.309	807-19-25	.222	57	107	57		12.7

YEAR	TM LG	W	L	PCT	G	GS	CG-SHO	SV-BS	IP	H	R	HR	HB	BB-IB	SO	ERA	AERA	OAV	OOB	AB-HR-SH	AVG	PB	SUP	APR	DL	PW

PETERS, RUBE Oscar Casper B3.15.1885 Grantfork IL D2.7.1965 Pequannock NJ BR/TR/6-1/195 d4.13

1912	Chi A	5	6	.455	28	11	4	0	108.2	134	73	2	6	33	39	4.14	77	.309	.366	31-0-2	.194	-1	86	-14		-1.1
1914	Bro F	2	2	.500	11	3	1	0	37.2	52	27	1	0	16	13	3.82	75	.335	.398	11-0-1	.091	-1	151	-6		-0.7
Total	2	7	8	.467	39	14	5	0	146.1	186	100	3	6	49	52	4.06	77	.316	.374	42-0-3	.167	-1	100	-20		-1.8

PETERS, RAY Raymond James B8.27.1946 Buffalo NY BR/TR/6-5.5/220 [MilA69*S1/22] d6.4 Col Harvard

| 1970 | Mil A | 0 | 2 | .000 | 2 | 2 | 0 | 0-0 | 2 | 7 | 7 | 0 | 0 | 5-0 | 1 | 31.50 | 12 | .583 | .667 | 0 | — | 0 | 83 | -6 | | -0.9 |

PETERS, STEVE Steven Bradley B11.14.1962 Oklahoma City OK BL/TL/5-10/170* [StLN85 5/124] d8.11 Col Oklahoma

1987	StL N	0	0	—	12	0	0	1-0	15	17	3	1	0	6-1	11	1.80	234	.298	.365	2	.000	-0	4			0.2
1988	StL N	3	3	.500	44	0	0	0-1	45	57	34	8	0	22-7	30	6.40	55	.313	.382	3	.000	-0	-13			-1.7
Total	2	3	3	.500	56	0	0	1-1	60	74	37	9	0	28-8	41	5.25	70	.310	.378	5	.000	-1	-9			-1.5

PETERSON, ADAM Adam Charles B12.11.1965 Long Beach CA BR/TR/6-3/190* [ChiA84 5/132] d9.19

1987	Chi A	0	0	—	1	1	0	0-0	4	8	6	1	0	3-0	1	13.50	34	.444	.500	0	—	0	197	-4		-0.2
1988	Chi A	0	1	.000	2	2	0	0-0	6	6	9	0	0	6-1	5	13.50	30	.240	.387	0	—	0	91	-6		-0.7
1989	Chi A	0	1	.000	3	2	0	0-0	5.1	13	9	1	0	2-0	3	15.19	25	.464	.500	0	—	0	165	-6		-0.9
1990	Chi A	2	5	.286	20	11	2	0-0	85	90	46	12	2	26-0	29	4.55	85	.278	.332	0	—	0	108	-6		-0.6
1991	SD N	3	4	.429	13	11	0	0-0	54.2	50	33	10	0	28-2	37	4.45	86	.242	.329	13-0-1	.000	-1	90	-5		-0.7
Total	5	5	11	.313	39	27	2	0-0	155	167	103	24	2	65-3	75	5.46	71	.277	.347	13-0-1	.000	-1	108	-27		-3.1

PETERSON, ADAM Adam L. B5.18.1979 Savannah GA BR/TR/6-3/220 [TorA02 4/116] d6.24 Col Wichita St.

| 2004 | Tor A | 0 | 0 | — | 2 | 0 | 0 | 0-0 | 3 | 7 | 6 | 2 | 0 | 2-0 | 2 | 16.88 | 29 | .467 | .556 | 0 | — | 0 | | -3 | | -0.2 |

PETERSON, FRITZ Fritz Fred (b Fred Ingels Peterson) B2.8.1942 Chicago IL BB/TL/6-0/200(185-207) d4.15 Col Northern Illinois

1966	NY A	12	11	.522	34	32	11-2	0	215	196	89	15	3	40-6	96	3.31	101	.241	.277	67-0-8	.224	4	110	1		0.6
1967	NY A	8	14	.364	36	30	6-1	0	181.1	179	88	11	3	43-9	102	3.47	90	.256	.301	48-0-3	.146	1	78	-10		-1.0
1968	NY A	12	11	.522	36	27	6-2	0	212.1	187	72	13	4	29-9	115	2.63	111	.241	.270	63-0-5	.079	-2	100	7		0.8
1969	NY A	17	16	.515	37	37	16-4	0	272	228	95	15	3	43-11	150	2.55	138	.229	.261	80-0-7	.112	-0	74	27		3.4
1970	NY A★	20	11	.645	39	37	8-2	0-0	260.1	247	102	24	3	40-6	127	2.90	123	.248	**.279**	90-2-7	.222	5	111	18		2.8
1971	NY A	15	13	.536	37	35	16-4	1-0	274	269	106	25	4	42-7	139	3.05	108	.258	.287	85-0-14	.082	-3	101	8		0.6
1972	NY A	17	15	.531	35	35	12-3	0-0	250.1	270	98	17	5	44-5	100	3.24	92	.276	.309	82-0-15	.232	3	121	-5		-0.2
1973	NY A	8	15	.348	31	31	6	0-0	184.1	207	93	18	7	49-10	59	3.95	94	.286	.336	0	—	0	73	-5		-0.6
1974	NY A	0	0	—	3	1	0	0-0	7.2	13	4	1	0	2-1	5	4.70	76	.361	.395	0	—	0	149	-1		0.0
	Cle A	9	14	.391	29	29	3	0-0	152.2	187	89	16	4	37-7	52	4.36	83	.305	.346	0	—	0	97	-14		-1.9
	Year	9	14	.391	32	30	3	0-0	160.1	200	93	17	4	39-8	57	4.38	83	.308	.349	0	—	0	99	-17		-1.9
1975	Cle A	14	8	.636	25	25	6-2	0-0	146.1	154	73	15	6	40-4	47	3.94	97	.275	.330	0	—	0	123	-2	28	-0.2
1976	Cle A	0	3	.000	9	9	0	0-0	47	59	31	3	0	10-0	19	5.55	63	.309	.342	0	—	0	128	-10		-0.6
	Tex A	1	0	1.000	4	2	0	0-1	15	21	7	0	0	7-0	4	3.60	100	.344	.412	0	—	0	122	0	68	0.0
	Year	1	3	.250	13	11	0	0-1	62	80	38	3	0	17-0	23	5.08	70	.317	.359	0	—	0	127	-10		-0.6
Total	11	133	131	.504	355	330	90-20	1-1	2218.1	2217	947	173	42	426-75	1015	3.30	102	.261	.298	515-2-59	.159	8	100	14	96	3.7

PETERSON, JIM James Niels B8.18.1908 Philadelphia PA D4.8.1975 Palm Beach FL BR/TR/6-0.5/200 d7.9 Col Penn

1931	Phi A	0	1	.000	6	1	1	0	13	18	10	0	4	7	6.23	72	.321	.367	2	.500	1	94	-2		-0.1
1933	Phi A	2	5	.286	32	5	0	0	90.2	114	64	6	0	36	18	4.96	86	.305	.366	27	.148	-1	115	-9		-0.5
1937	Bro N	0	0	—	3	0	0	0	5.2	8	5	3	0	2	4	7.94	51	.333	.385	0	—	0		-2		-0.1
Total	3	2	6	.250	41	6	1	0	109.1	140	79	9	0	42	22	5.27	82	.308	.367	29	.172	0	112	-13		-0.7

PETERSON, KENT Kent Franklin "Pete" B12.21.1925 Goshen UT D4.27.1995 Highland UT BR/TL/5-10/175* d7.15 Mil 1945-46

1944	Cin N	0	0	—	1	0	0	0	0	0	0	0	0	0	0	0.00		.000	.000	0	—	0	0	0		0.0
1947	Cin N	6	13	.316	37	17	3-1	2	152.1	156	74	8	3	62	78	4.25	96	.265	.338	44-0-4	.068	-3	62	1		-0.4
1948	Cin N	2	15	.118	43	17	2	1	137	146	82	10	6	59	64	4.60	85	.271	.350	36-0-2	.139	-2	67	-12		-1.5
1949	Cin N	4	5	.444	30	7	2	0	66.1	66	54	8	4	46	28	6.24	67	.261	.383	18-0-2	.056	-2	78	-15		-2.0
1950	Cin N	0	3	.000	9	2	0	0	20	25	20	4	0	17	6	7.20	59	.305	.424	3-0-1	.333	0	42	-7		-0.9
1951	Cin N	1	1	.500	9	0	0	1	9.2	13	8	0	1	8	5	6.52	63	.317	.440	1	.000	0		-2		-0.5
1952	Phi N	0	0	—	3	0	0	2	7	2	0	0	0	2	7	0.00		.091	.167	1	.000	-0		3		0.2
1953	Phi N	0	1	.000	15	0	0	0	27	26	20	3	1	21	20	6.67	63	.252	.384	7	.000	-1		-6		-0.4
Total	8	13	38	.255	147	43	7-1	5	420.1	434	258	33	15	215	208	4.95	82	.266	.357	110-0-9	.091	-8	65	-38		-5.5

PETERSON, KYLE Kyle Johnathan B4.9.1976 Elkhorn NE BL/TR/6-3/215* [MilA97 1/13] d7.19 Col Stanford [DL 2000 Mil N 181]

1999	Mil N	4	7	.364	17	12	0	0-1	77	87	46	3	4	25-2	34	4.56	101	.285	.344	22-0-2	.136	-0	90	-1		-0.3
2001	Mil N	1	2	.333	3	2	0	0-0	14.2	19	10	3	0	4-2	12	5.52	78	.302	.343	5	.200	0	86	-2		-0.3
Total	2	5	9	.357	20	14	0	0-1	91.2	106	56	6	4	29-4	46	4.71	97	.288	.344	27-0-2	.148	0	89	-3	181	-0.6

PETERSON, SID Sidney Herbert B1.31.1918 Havelock ND D8.29.2001 Wichita Falls TX BR/TR/6-3/220 d5.4

| 1943 | StL A | 2 | 0 | 1.000 | 3 | 0 | 0 | 0 | 10 | 15 | 3 | 0 | 1 | 3 | 0 | 2.70 | 123 | .341 | .396 | 2 | .000 | -0 | | 1 | | 0.1 |

PETKOVSEK, MARK Mark Joseph B11.18.1965 Beaumont TX BR/TR/6-0/185(185-198) [TexA87 1/29] d6.8 Col Texas

1991	Tex A	0	1	.000	4	1	0	0-0	9.1	21	16	4	0	4-0	6	14.46	28	.438	.472	0	—	0	158	-11		-0.9
1993	Pit N	3	0	1.000	26	0	0	0-0	32.1	43	25	7	0	9-2	14	6.96	59	.328	.369	0	—	0		-10		-0.7
1995	StL N	6	6	.500	26	21	1-1	0-0	137.1	136	71	11	6	35-3	71	4.00	107	.262	.313	37-0-3	.081	-1	88	4		0.1
1996	†StL N	11	2	.846	48	6	0	0-3	88.2	83	37	9	5	35-2	45	3.55	119	.251	.331	16	.188	2	74	7	18	1.0
1997	StL N	4	7	.364	55	2	0	2-0	96	109	61	14	6	31-4	51	5.06	83	.292	.354	11-0-1	.091	-0	99	-9		-0.9
1998	StL N	7	4	.636	48	10	0	0-5	105.2	131	63	9	8	36-3	55	4.77	88	.312	.375	22-0-2	.318	2	109	-7		-0.5
1999	Ana A	10	4	.714	64	0	0	1-3	83	85	37	6	2	21-2	43	3.47	141	.269	.314	0	—	0		12		1.4
2000	Ana A	4	2	.667	64	1	0	2-2	81	86	40	8	3	23-6	31	4.33	119	.277	.332	0	—	0	36	8	25	0.5
2001	Tex A	1	2	.333	55	0	0	0-4	76.2	103	61	14	5	28-4	42	6.69	71	.323	.379	1	.000	-0		-16		-0.8
Total	9	46	28	.622	390	41	1-1	5-17	710	797	411	82	35	222-26	358	4.74	94	.288	.346	87-0-6	.161	1	89	-22	43	-0.4

PETRY, DAN Daniel Joseph B11.13.1958 Palo Alto CA BR/TR/6-4/200(180-215) [DetA76 4/74] d7.8

1979	Det A	6	5	.545	15	15	2	0-0	98	90	46	11	4	33-5	43	3.95	110	.254	.321	0	—	0	86	5		0.4
1980	Det A	10	9	.526	27	25	4-3	0-0	164.2	156	82	9	1	83-14	88	3.94	105	.253	.340	0	—	0	105	2		0.3
1981	Det A	10	9	.526	23	22	7-2	0-0	141	115	53	10	1	57-4	79	3.00	126	.224	.301	0	—	0	78	10		1.5
1982	Det A	15	9	.625	35	35	8-1	0-0	246	220	98	15	4	100-5	132	3.22	127	.241	.317	0	—	0	112	24		2.4
1983	Det A	19	11	.633	38	**38**	9-2	0-0	266.1	256	126	37	6	99-7	122	3.92	101	.256	.325	0	—	0	121	2		0.3
1984	†Det A	18	8	.692	35	35	7-2	0-0	233.1	231	94	21	3	66-4	144	3.24	122	.259	.312	0	—	0	120	19		2.2
1985	Det A★	15	13	.536	34	34	8	0-0	238.2	190	94	24	3	81-9	109	3.36	122	.217	.285	0	—	0	89	21		2.3
1986	Det A	5	10	.333	20	20	2	0-0	116	122	78	14	0	53-3	56	4.66	89	.268	.348	0	—	0	90	-12	74	-1.2
1987	†Det A	9	7	.563	30	21	0	0-0	134.2	148	101	22	10	76-5	93	5.61	76	.279	.375	0	—	0	149	-24	65	-2.3
1988	Cal A	3	9	.250	22	22	4-1	0-0	139.2	139	70	18	6	59-5	64	4.38	89	.263	.341	0	—	0	94	-6		-0.3
1989	Cal A	3	2	.600	19	4	0	0-0	51	53	32	8	1	23-0	21	5.47	70	.275	.347	0	—	0	89	-9		-0.8
1990	Det A	10	9	.526	32	23	1	0-0	149.2	148	78	14	1	77-7	73	4.45	89	.263	.349	0	—	0	96	-7		-0.7
1991	Det A	2	3	.400	17	6	0	0-0	54.2	66	35	9	0	19-3	18	4.94	85	.300	.356	0	—	0	109	-6		-0.4
	Atl N	0	0	—	10	0	0	0-0	24.1	29	17	2	1	14-1	9	5.55	70	.296	.389	5	.200			-4		-0.2
	Bos A	0	0	—	13	0	0	0-0	22.1	17	13	1	1	12-2	12	4.43	98	.250	.347	0	—	0		-2		-0.1
Total	13	125	104	.546	370	300	52-11	1-0	2080.1	1984	1025	218	47	852-74	1063	3.95	103	.253	.328	5	.200	0	105	13	139	3.4

PETTIBONE, JAY Harry Jonathan B6.21.1957 Mt.Clemens MI BR/TR/6-4/182 [TexA79 30/743] d9.11 Col Chapman

| 1983 | Min A | 0 | 4 | .000 | 4 | 4 | 1 | 0-0 | 27 | 28 | 16 | 8 | 2 | 8-0 | 10 | 5.33 | 80 | .280 | .345 | 0 | — | 0 | 48 | -2 | | -0.3 |

PETTIT, PAUL George William Paul "Lefty" B11.29.1931 Los Angeles CA BL/TL/6-2/195* d5.4

1951	Pit N	0	0	—	2	0	0	0	2.2	2	1	1	0	1	0	3.38	125	.200	.273	1	.000	-0		0		0.0
1953	Pit N	1	2	.333	10	5	0	0	28	33	27	1	0	20	14	7.71	58	.297	.405	8-0-1	.250	1*	112	-10		-0.8
Total	2	1	2	.333	12	5	0	0	30.2	35	28	2	0	21	14	7.34	61	.289	.394	9-0-1	.222	1	112	-10		-0.8

YEAR	TM LG	W	L	PCT	G	GS	CG-SHO	SV-BS	IP	H	R	HR	HB	BB-IB	SO	ERA	AERA	OAV	OOB	AB-HR-SH	AVG	PB	SUP	APR	DL	PW

PETTIT, LEON Leon Arthur "Lefty" B6.23.1902 Waynesburg PA D11.21.1974 Columbia TN BL/TL/5-10.5/165 d4.18

YEAR	TM LG	W	L	PCT	G	GS	CG-SHO	SV-BS	IP	H	R	HR	HB	BB-IB	SO	ERA	AERA	OAV	OOB	AB-HR-SH	AVG	PB	SUP	APR	DL	PW
1935	Was A	8	5	.615	41	7	1	3	109	129	65	6	4	58	45	4.95	87	.301	.390	25-0-1	.080	0	126	-7		-0.7
1937	Phi N	0	1	.000	3	1	0	0	4	6	5	1	0	4	0	11.25	39	.353	.476	0	—	0	80	-3		-0.5
Total 2		8	6	.571	44	8	1	3	113	135	70	7	4	62	45	5.18	84	.303	.393	25-0-1	.080	0	120	-10		-1.2

PETTITTE, ANDY Andrew Eugene B6.15.1972 Baton Rouge LA BL/TL/6-5/235* d4.29 Col San Jacinto North (TX) JC

YEAR	TM LG	W	L	PCT	G	GS	CG-SHO	SV-BS	IP	H	R	HR	HB	BB-IB	SO	ERA	AERA	OAV	OOB	AB-HR-SH	AVG	PB	SUP	APR	DL	PW
1995	†NY A	12	9	.571	31	26	3	0-0	175	183	86	15	1	63-3	114	4.17	111	.272	.333	0	—	0	91	9		0.9
1996	†NY A☆	21	8	.724	35	34	2	0-0	221	229	105	23	3	72-2	162	3.87	128	.271	.330	0	—	0	102	25		2.8
1997	†NY A	18	7	.720	35	35	4-1	0-0	240.1	233	86	7	3	65-0	166	2.88	154	.256	.307	0	—	0	128	42		4.1
1998	†NY A	16	11	.593	33	32	5	0-0	216.1	226	110	20	6	87-1	146	4.24	103	.274	.344	4-0-2	.000	-0	102	3		0.3
1999	†NY A	14	11	.560	31	31	0	0-0	191.2	216	105	20	3	89-3	121	4.70	101	.288	.364	5	.200	-0	109	3	12	0.5
2000	†NY A	19	9	.679	32	32	3-1	0-0	204.2	219	111	17	4	80-4	125	4.35	110	.271	.338	5	.000	-0	130	8	17	1.0
2001	†NY A★	15	10	.600	31	31	2	0-0	200.2	224	103	14	1	41-3	164	3.99	111	.281	.319	4-0-1	.000	-0	109	8	15	0.9
2002	†NY A	13	5	.722	22	22	3-1	0-0	134.2	144	58	6	4	32-2	97	3.27	132	.272	.317	3	.333	1	117	15	59	2.0
2003	†NY A	21	8	.724	33	33	1	0-0	208.1	227	109	21	1	50-3	180	4.02	109	.272	.312	7	.143	-0	138	6		0.7
2004	Hou N	6	4	.600	15	15	0	0-0	83	71	37	8	0	31-2	79	3.90	112	.226	.296	23-0-3	.174	1	75	5	102	0.7
2005	†Hou N	17	9	.654	33	33	0	0-0	222.1	188	66	17	3	41-0	171	2.39	176	.230	.268	62-0-15	.081	-4	99	44		4.7
Total 11		172	91	.654	331	324	23-3	0-0	2098	2160	976	168	34	651-23	1525	3.78	120	.267	.322	113-0-21	.106	-3	111	168	205	18.6

PETTY, CHARLIE Charles E. B6.28.1866 Nashville TN TR/?/175 d7.30

YEAR	TM LG	W	L	PCT	G	GS	CG-SHO	SV-BS	IP	H	R	HR	HB	BB-IB	SO	ERA	AERA	OAV	OOB	AB-HR-SH	AVG	PB	SUP	APR	DL	PW
1889	Cin AA	2	3	.400	5	5	5	0	44	44	29	3	6	20	10	5.52	71	.253	.350	20	.300	1	98	-3		-0.2
1893	NY N	5	2	.714	9	6	4	0	54	66	36	0	1	28	12	3.33	140	.292	.373	22-1	.318	3	168	6		0.8
1894	Was N	3	8	.273	16	12	8	0	103	156	114	4	9	32	14	5.59	95	.344	.399	41-0-5	.195	-2	85	-6		-0.6
	Cle N	0	2	.000	4	3	2	0	27	42	37	4	3	14	4	8.67	63	.363	.431	12	.083	-2	103	-9		-0.6
	Year	3	10	.231	20	15	10	0	130	198	151	8	12	46	18	6.23	85	.346	.406	53-0-5	.170	-4	89	-21		-1.2
Total 3		10	15	.400	34	26	19	0	228	308	216	11	19	94	40	5.41	91	.317	.388	95-1-5	.232	-0	107	-12		-0.6

PETTY, JESSE Jesse Lee "The Silver Fox" B11.23.1894 Orr OK D10.23.1971 St.Paul MN BR/TL/6-0/195 d4.14

YEAR	TM LG	W	L	PCT	G	GS	CG-SHO	SV-BS	IP	H	R	HR	HB	BB-IB	SO	ERA	AERA	OAV	OOB	AB-HR-SH	AVG	PB	SUP	APR	DL	PW
1921	Cle N	0	0	—	4	0	0	0	9	10	2	0	0	0	0	2.00	213	.345	.345	2	.000	-0		2		0.1
1925	Bro N	9	9	.500	28	21	7	0	153	188	97	15	2	47	39	4.88	86	.304	.355	50-0-3	.140	-3	95	-11		-1.4
1926	Bro N	17	17	.500	38	33	23-1	1	275.2	246	118	9	3	79	101	2.84	135	.240	.296	97-0-3	.175	-3	71	25		2.4
1927	Bro N	13	18	.419	42	33	19-2	1	271.2	263	108	13	4	53	101	2.98	133	.254	.293	91-0-1	.099	-7	53	29		2.2
1928	Bro N	15	15	.500	40	31	15-2	1	234	264	119	18	5	56	74	4.04	98	.289	.334	81-0-4	.111	-5	93	4		-0.3
1929	Pit N	11	10	.524	36	25	12+1	0	184.1	197	100	12	0	42	58	3.71	129	.277	.317	67-0-1	.104	-5	95	17		1.0
1930	Pit N	1	6	.143	10	7	0	1	41.1	67	43	8	2	13	16	8.27	60	.362	.410	12-0-1	.083	-1	88	-14		-2.0
	Chi N	1	3	.250	9	3	0	0	39.1	51	18	2	0	6	18	2.97	164	.317	.341	13-0-1	.231	0	30	7		0.6
	Year	2	9	.182	19	10	0	1	80.2	118	61	10	2	19	34	5.69	87	.341	.379	25-0-2	.160	-1	71	-8		-1.4
Total 7		67	78	.462	207	153	76-6	4	1208.1	1286	605	77	16	296	407	3.68	113	.275	.320	413-0-14	.128	-25	80	59		2.6

PETTYJOHN, ADAM Adam Christopher B6.11.1977 Phoenix AZ BR/TL/6-3/190 [DetA98 2/73] d7.16 Col Cal St.-Fresno [DL 2002 Det A 183]

YEAR	TM LG	W	L	PCT	G	GS	CG-SHO	SV-BS	IP	H	R	HR	HB	BB-IB	SO	ERA	AERA	OAV	OOB	AB-HR-SH	AVG	PB	SUP	APR	DL	PW
2001	Det A	1	6	.143	16	9	0	0-0	65	81	48	10	4	21-2	40	5.82	76	.309	.366	2	.000	-0	67	-11		-1.0

PEZZULLO, PRETZEL John B12.10.1910 Bridgeport CT D5.16.1990 Dallas TX BL/TL/5-11.5/180 d4.18

YEAR	TM LG	W	L	PCT	G	GS	CG-SHO	SV-BS	IP	H	R	HR	HB	BB-IB	SO	ERA	AERA	OAV	OOB	AB-HR-SH	AVG	PB	SUP	APR	DL	PW
1935	Phi N	3	5	.375	41	7	2	1	84.1	115	75	5	7	45	24	6.40	71	.321	.407	24	.250	0	78	-16		-1.4
1936	Phi N	0	0	—	1	0	0	0	2	1	1	0	0	6	0	4.50	101	.167	.583	0	—	0		0		0.0
Total 2		3	5	.375	42	7	2	1	86.1	116	75	5	7	51	24	6.36	71	.319	.412	24	.250	0	78	-16		-1.4

PFANN, BILL William F. B6.1863 Hamilton ON, Can. D6.3.1904 Hamilton ON, Can. TR/6-0/205 d6.16

YEAR	TM LG	W	L	PCT	G	GS	CG-SHO	SV-BS	IP	H	R	HR	HB	BB-IB	SO	ERA	AERA	OAV	OOB	AB-HR-SH	AVG	PB	SUP	APR	DL	PW
1894	Cin N	0	1	.000	1	1	0	0	3	10	10	1	0	4	0	27.00	21	.526	.609	1	.000	-0	115	-6		-0.7

PFEFFER, JEFF Edward Joseph B3.4.1888 Seymour IL D8.15.1972 Chicago IL BR/TR/6-3/210 d4.16 Mil 1918 b-Big Jeff

YEAR	TM LG	W	L	PCT	G	GS	CG-SHO	SV-BS	IP	H	R	HR	HB	BB-IB	SO	ERA	AERA	OAV	OOB	AB-HR-SH	AVG	PB	SUP	APR	DL	PW
1911	StL A	0	0	—	2	0	0	0	10	11	11	0	0	4	4	7.20	47	.297	.366	4	.000	-1		-4		-0.3
1913	Bro N	0	1	.000	5	2	1	0	24.1	28	16	0	4	13	13	3.33	99	.311	.421	7-0-1	.000	-1	103	-2		-0.2
1914	Bro N	23	12	.657	43	34	27-3	4	315	264	99	9	7	91	135	1.97	145	.232	.293	116-0-1	.198	-1*	104	30		3.2
1915	Bro N	19	14	.576	40	34	26-6	3	291.2	243	93	8	17	76	84	2.10	132	.231	.293	106-0-1	.255	5	114	22		2.9
1916	†Bro N	25	11	.694	41	36	30-6	1	328.2	291	91	5	17	63	128	1.92	140	.230	.278	122-0-3	.279	7*	110	30		4.1
1917	Bro N	11	15	.423	30	30	24-3	0	266	225	84	4	16	66	115	2.23	125	.234	.294	100-0-5	.130	-4*	92	16		1.0
1918	Bro N	1	0	1.000	1	1	1-1	0	9	9	2	0	0	3	1	0.00	—	.071	.161		.250	0	54	3		0.4
1919	Bro N	17	13	.567	30	30	26-4	0	267	270	95	7	12	49	92	2.66	112	.267	.308	97-0-3	.206	1	101	12		1.5
1920	†Bro N	16	9	.640	30	28	20-2	0	215	225	81	5	9	45	80	3.01	106	.273	.314	74-0-6	.243	1	110	8		0.8
1921	Pit N	1	5	.167	6	5	2	0	31.2	36	19	0	1	9	8	4.55	86	.310	.365	11	.000	-2	51	-2		-0.5
	StL N	9	3	.750	18	13	7-1	0	98.1	115	51	3	5	28	22	4.29	86	.305	.361	29-0-4	.138	-1	128	-4		-0.6
	Year	10	8	.556	24	18	9-1	0	130.1	151	70	6	6	37	30	4.35	86	.306	.362	40-0-4	.100	-2	106	-7		-1.1
1922	StL N	19	12	.613	44	32	19-1	2	261.1	286	126	12	11	58	83	3.58	108	.279	.324	98-0-2	.245	4*	111	9		1.4
1923	StL N	8	9	.471	26	18	7-1	0	152.1	171	80	8	9	46	32	4.02	97	.287	.341	55-0-1	.127	-4	98	-1		-0.5
1924	StL N	4	5	.444	16	12	3	0	78	102	52	3	1	30	20	5.31	71	.318	.378	26-0-1	.115	-2	82	-12		-1.5
	Pit N	5	3	.625	15	4	1	0	58.2	68	23	3	0	17	19	3.07	125	.293	.341	25-0-1	.240	-0	116	5		0.5
	Year	9	8	.529	31	16	4	0	136.2	170	75	6	1	47	39	4.35	88	.307	.363	51-0-2	.176	-3	90	-8		-1.0
Total 13		158	112	.585	347	279	194-28	10	2407.1	2320	921	67	105	592	836	2.77	114	.258	.311	874-0-29	.206	2	104	110		12.2

PFEFFER, BIG JEFF Francis Xavier B3.31.1882 Champaign IL D12.19.1954 Kankakee IL BR/TR/6-1/185 d4.15 b-Jeff Col Illinois

YEAR	TM LG	W	L	PCT	G	GS	CG-SHO	SV-BS	IP	H	R	HR	HB	BB-IB	SO	ERA	AERA	OAV	OOB	AB-HR-SH	AVG	PB	SUP	APR	DL	PW
1905	Chi N	4	4	.500	11	9	9	0	101	84	36	2	4	36	56	2.50	120	.240	.318	40-0-1	.200	1	77	6		0.5
1906	Bos N	13	22	.371	36	36	33-4	0	302.1	270	138	6	16	114	158	2.95	91	.246	.325	158-1-2	.196	3*	78	-9		-0.4
1907	Bos N	6	8	.429	19	16	12-1	0	144	129	62	3	7	61	65	3.00	85	.253	.341	60-0-1	.250	3*	99	-7		-0.3
1908	Bos N	0	0	—	4	0	0	0	10	18	16	1	0	8	3	12.60	19	.383	.473	2	.000	-0		-10		-0.6
1910	Chi N	1	0	1.000	13	1	1	0	41.1	43	31	1	6	16	11	3.27	88	.281	.353	17-0-1	.176	1*	77	-7		-0.3
1911	Bos N	7	5	.583	26	6	4-1	2	97	116	74	3	0	57	24	4.73	81	.301	.391	46-1-0	.196	1*	95	-11		-1.1
Total 6		31	39	.443	113	70	59-6	2	695.2	660	357	14	28	292	317	3.30	87	.260	.342	323-2-5	.204	8	83	-38		-2.2

PFEFFER, FRED Nathaniel Frederick "Fritz","Dandelion" B3.17.1860 Louisville KY D4.10.1932 Chicago IL BR/TR/5-10.5/184 d5.1.1882 M1 ▲

YEAR	TM LG	W	L	PCT	G	GS	CG-SHO	SV-BS	IP	H	R	HR	HB	BB-IB	SO	ERA	AERA	OAV	OOB	AB-HR-SH	AVG	PB	SUP	APR	DL	PW
1884	Chi N	0	0	—	1	0	1	0	3	2	0	1	0	1	0	9.00	35	.333	.400	467-25	.289	0*		-1		0.0
1885	†Chi N	2	1	.667	5	2	2	2	31.2	26	15	1	4	8	13	2.56	118	.222	.272	469-5	.241	1*	94	2		0.2
1892	Lou N	0	0	—	1	0	0	0	5	4	3	0	0	5	0	1.80	170	.211	.375	470-2	.257	0*		0		0.0
1894	Lou N	0	0	—	1	0	0	0	7	8	6	0	1	6	0	2.57	198	.286	.429	414-5-15	.309	0*		1		0.0
Total 4		2	1	.667	8	2	2	2	44.2	41	26	2	1	20	13	2.62	129	.237	.320	1820-37-15	.273	2	94	2		0.2

PFIESTER, JACK John Albert "Jack the Giant Killer" (b John Albert Hagenbush) B5.24.1878 Cincinnati OH D9.3.1953 Loveland OH BR/TL/5-11/180 d9.8

YEAR	TM LG	W	L	PCT	G	GS	CG-SHO	SV-BS	IP	H	R	HR	HB	BB-IB	SO	ERA	AERA	OAV	OOB	AB-HR-SH	AVG	PB	SUP	APR	DL	PW
1903	Pit N	0	3	.000	3	3	1	0	19	26	21	0	2	10	15	6.16	53	.321	.409	6	.000	-1	69	-7		-0.9
1904*	Pit N	1	1	.500	3	2	1	0	20	28	18	0	0	9	6	7.20	38	.318	.381	7	.286	1	125	-8		-0.6
1906	†Chi N	20	8	.714	31	29	20-4	0	250.2	173	63	3	13	63	153	1.51	175	.194	.258	84-0-2	.048	-7	129	30		2.6
1907	†Chi N	14	9	.609	30	22	13-3	0	195	143	61	1	5	48	90	1.15	216	.207	.263	64-0-8	.094	-3	126	21		2.1
1908	†Chi N	12	10	.545	33	29	18-3	0	252	204	82	1	11	70	117	2.00	118	.223	.287	79-0-4	.101	-4	113	7		0.1
1909	†Chi N	17	6	.739	29	25	13-5	0	196.2	179	67	1	5	49	73	2.43	150	.240	.291	65-0-3	.169	0	131	6		0.8
1910	†Chi N	6	3	.667	14	13	5-2	0	100.1	82	28	0	1	26	34	1.79	161	.225	.279	33-0-1	.091	-2	83	12		0.7
1911	Chi N	1	4	.200	6	5	3	0	33.2	34	25	0	2	18	15	4.01	83	.262	.360	11-0-1	.182	0	77	-5		-0.6
Total 8		71	44	.617	149	128	75-17	0	1067.1	869	365	6	39	293	503	2.02	128	.223	.284	349-0-19	.103	-15	117	56		4.2

PFISTER, DAN Daniel Albin B12.20.1936 Plainfield NJ BR/TR/6-0/187* d9.9

YEAR	TM LG	W	L	PCT	G	GS	CG-SHO	SV-BS	IP	H	R	HR	HB	BB-IB	SO	ERA	AERA	OAV	OOB	AB-HR-SH	AVG	PB	SUP	APR	DL	PW
1961	KC A	0	0	—	2	0	0	0	2.1	4	2	0		4-0	3	15.43	27	.417	.563	0	—	0		-3		-0.1
1962	KC A	4	14	.222	41	26	2	1	196.1	175	112	27	9	106-2	123	4.54	93	.238	.340	65-0-2	.185	-1*	85	-8		-0.8
1963	KC A	1	0	1.000	8	2	0	0	9.1	8	2	1	1	3-0	9	1.93	202	.229	.308	2	.000	-0*	159	2		0.2
1964	KC A	1	5	.167	14	5	0	1	41.1	50	32	10	6	29-4	21	6.53	58	.311	.431	6	.000	-0*	93	-11		-1.6
Total 4		6	19	.240	65	26	2	2	249.1	238	150	41	16	142-6	156	4.87	85	.252	.358	74-0-2	.162	-2	89	-20	123	-2.3

PFUND, LEE Le Roy Herbert B10.10.1919 Oak Park IL BR/TR/6-1/185 d4.21

YEAR	TM LG	W	L	PCT	G	GS	CG-SHO	SV-BS	IP	H	R	HR	HB	BB-IB	SO	ERA	AERA	OAV	OOB	AB-HR-SH	AVG	PB	SUP	APR	DL	PW
1945	Bro N	3	2	.600	15	10	2	0	62.1	69	51	4	5	35	27	5.20	72	.274	.373	22-0-1	.182	0	203	-12	62	-0.8

YEAR	TM LG	W	L	PCT	G	GS	CG-SHO	SV-BS	IP	H	R	HR	HB	BB-IB	SO	ERA	AERA	OAV	OOB	AB-HR-SH	AVG	PB	SUP	APR	DL	PW
PHEBUS, BILL	Raymond William							B8.2.1909	Cherryvale KS		D10.11.1989	Bartow FL		BR/TR/5-9/170	d9.6										
1936	Was A	0	0	—	2	1	0	0	7.1	4	6	1	1	4	1	2.45	195	.114	.225	1	.000	0	129	0		0.0
1937	Was A	3	2	.600	6	5	4-1	1	40.2	33	13	2	2	24	12	2.21	200	.232	.351	8-0-1	.000	1	67	10		1.2
1938	Was A	0	0	—	5	0	0	1	6.1	9	9	1	0	7	2	11.37	40	.346	.485	1	.000	-0		-5		-0.2
Total	3	3	2	.600	13	6	4-1	2	54.1	46	28	4	3	35	18	3.31	135	.227	.349	10-0-1	.000	1	78	5		1.0
PHELPS, RAY	Raymond Clifford							B12.11.1903	Dunlap TN		D7.7.1971	Fort Pierce FL		BR/TR/6-2/200	d4.23										
1930	Bro N	14	7	.667	36	24	11-2	0	179.2	198	98	21	3	52	64	4.11	120	.280	.332	68-1-1	.147	-2	113	16		1.4
1931	Bro N	7	9	.438	28	26	3-1	0	149.1	184	88	3	4	44	50	5.00	76	.306	.357	51	.157	-1	108	-16		-1.6
1932	Bro N	4	5	.444	20	9	4-1	0	79.1	101	58	5	3	27	21	5.90	65	.323	.382	23-0-2	.087	-1	122	-18		-1.8
1935	Chi A	4	8	.333	27	17	4	1	125	126	77	10	3	55	38	4.82	96	.262	.341	41-0-1	.122	-4	90	-3		-0.5
1936	Chi A	4	6	.400	15	4	2	0	68.2	91	54	9	2	42	17	6.03	86	.331	.423	26	.231	1	68	-7		-0.7
Total	5	33	35	.485	126	80	24-4	1	602	700	375	48	15	220	190	4.93	90	.294	.358	209-1-4	.148	-8	103	-28		-3.2
PHELPS, TOMMY	Thomas Allen							B3.4.1974	Seoul, South Korea		BL/TL/6-3/190(190-215)		[MonN92 8/211]	d3.31										
2003	Fla N	3	2	.600	27	7	0	0-0	63	70	32	3	2	23-1	43	4.00	103	.282	.345	11-0-1	.091	0	121	0	30	0.0
2004	Fla N	1	1	.500	19	4	0	0-0	34	34	20	6	0	12-0	28	4.76	86	.268	.326	6	.000	-1	118	-3		-0.2
2005	Mil N	0	2	.000	29	0	0	1-1	23.1	25	12	2	2	12-4	14	4.63	92	.272	.368	0	—	0		0		0.0
Total	4	5	.444	75	11	0	1-1	120.1	129	64	11	4	47-5	85	4.34	95	.276	.345	17-0-1	.059	-1	119	-3	30	-0.1	
PHELPS, TRAVIS	Travis Howard							B7.25.1977	Neosho MO		BR/TR/6-2/170(165-195)		[TBA96 89/1721]	d4.19		Col Crowder (MO) CC									
2001	TB A	2	2	.500	49	0	0	5-1	62	53	30	6	3	24-1	54	3.48	129	.226	.301	0	—	0		6		0.4
2002	TB A	1	2	.333	26	0	0	0-0	37.2	30	20	7	5	27-0	36	4.78	95	.222	.367	0	—	0		0		0.0
2004	Mil N	0	1	.000	4	0	0	0-0	6	8	7	2	0	3-0	3	10.50	42	.286	.355	1	.000	-0		-4		-0.5
Total	3	3	5	.375	79	0	0	5-1	105.2	91	57	15	8	54-1	93	4.34	104	.229	.328	1	.000	-0		2		-0.1
PHILLIPPE, DEACON	Charles Louis							B5.23.1872	Rural Retreat VA		D3.30.1952	Avalon PA		BR/TR/6-0.5/180	d4.21										
1899	Lou N	21	17	.553	42	38	33-2	1	321	331	178	10	7	64	68	3.17	122	.266	.306	128-0-5	.203	-1*	97	22		2.0
1900	†Pit N	20	13	.606	38	33	29-1	0	279	274	127	7	7	42	75	2.84	128	.257	.289	105-0-4	.181	-2*	83	26		2.2
1901	Pit N	22	12	.647	37	32	30-1	2	296	274	115	7	10	38	103	2.22	147	.244	.275	113-1-2	.230	5*	120	33		4.1
1902	Pit N	20	9	.690	31	30	29-5	0	272	265	90	1	4	26	122	2.05	134	.255	.276	113-1-3	.221	3*	135	19		2.1
1903	†Pit N	25	9	.735	36	33	31-4	2	289.1	269	116	4	4	29	123	2.43	133	.241	.263	124	.210	2*	125	27		2.9
1904	Pit N	10	10	.500	21	19	17-3	1	166.2	183	82	7	1	26	82	3.24	85	.272	.302	65-0-1	.123	-4	77	-9		-1.4
1905	Pit N	20	13	.606	38	33	25-5	0	279	235	95	0	10	48	133	2.19	137	.233	.274	97-0-2	.093	-4	93	22		2.0
1906	Pit N	15	10	.600	33	24	19-3	0	218.2	216	78	3	2	26	90	2.47	108	.252	.276	82	.244	3	89	7		1.1
1907	Pit N	14	11	.560	35	26	17-1	2	214	214	83	2	5	36	61	2.61	93	.264	.300	60-0-5	.185	1	124	-2		-0.2
1908	Pit N	0	0	—	5	0	0	0	12	20	15	0	0	3	1	11.25	20	.357	.390	4	.250	0		-10		-0.5
1909	†Pit N	8	3	.727	22	13	7-1	0	131.2	121	41	2	4	14	38	2.32	117	.253	.280	42-0-1	.071	-3	101	8		0.2
1910	Pit N	14	2	.875	31	8	5-1	4	121.2	111	46	4	3	9	30	2.29	135	.239	.258	41-1-1	.220	1	153	9		1.1
1911	Pit N	0	0	—	3	0	0	0	6	5	5	0	0	2	3	7.50	46	.238	.304	1	1.000	1		-2		0.0
Total	13	189	109	.634	372	289	242-27	12	2607	2518	1071	41	59	363	929	2.59	120	.253	.283	980-3-24	.189	2	107	150		15.6
PHILLIPS, BUZ	Albert Abernathy							B5.25.1904	Newton NC		D11.6.1964	Baltimore MD		BR/TR/5-11.5/185	d8.5		Col Lenoir-Rhyne								
1930	Phi N	0	0	—	14	1	0	0	43.2	68	44	8	1	18	9	8.04	68	.354	.412	13-1-0	.462	2	80	-11		-0.3
PHILLIPS, RED	Clarence Lemuel							B11.3.1908	Pauls Valley OK		D2.1.1988	Wichita KS		BR/TR/6-3.5/195	d7.24		Col East Central								
1934	Det A	2	0	1.000	7	1	1	1	23.1	31	17	1	0	16	3	6.17	71	.316	.412	12	.250	1	317	-4		-0.3
1936	Det A	2	4	.333	22	6	3	0	87.1	124	67	12	0	22	15	6.49	76	.332	.370	33	.303	2	86	-13		-0.5
Total	2	4	4	.500	29	7	4	1	110.2	155	84	13	0	38	18	6.42	75	.329	.379	45	.289	3	117	-17		-0.8
PHILLIPS, JASON	Jason Charles							B3.22.1974	Williamsport PA		BR/TR/6-6/225*		[PitN92 14/399]	d4.5											
1999	Pit N	0	0	—	6	0	0	0-0	7	11	9	2	0	6-1	7	11.57	40	.393	.486	0	—	0		-5		-0.2
2002	Cle A	1	3	.250	8	6	0	0-0	41.2	41	24	7	4	20-0	23	4.97	89	.259	.353	0	—	0	112	-2	33	-0.2
2003	Cle A	0	1	.000	3	0	0	0-0	5	9	5	1	0	2-0	2	9.00	49	.409	.440	0	—	0		-2		-0.4
Total	3	1	4	.200	17	6	0	0-0	53.2	61	38	10	4	28-1	32	6.20	72	.293	.381	0	—	0	112	-9	33	-0.8
PHILLIPS, JACK	John Stephen							B5.24.1919	St.Louis MO		D6.16.1958	St.Louis MO		BR/TR/6-1/185	d7.13										
1945	NY N	0	0	—	1	0	0	0	4.1	5	5	1	1	4	0	10.38	38	.294	.455	2	.500	0*		-3		-0.1
PHILLIPS, ED	Norman Edwin							B9.20.1944	Ardmore OK		BR/TR/6-1/190		[BosA66 16/304]	d4.9		Col Colby									
1970	Bos A	0	2	.000	18	0	0	4	23.2	29	14	4	2	10-1	23	5.32	75	.312	.387	0	.000	-0		-2		-0.3
PHILLIPS, TOM	Thomas Gerald							B4.5.1889	Philipsburg PA		D4.12.1929	Philipsburg PA		BR/TR/6-2/190	d9.13										
1915	StL A	1	3	.250	5	4	1	0	27.1	28	13	0	2	12	5	2.96	97	.283	.372	9-0-1	.111	-1	57	0		-0.2
1919	Cle A	3	2	.600	22	3	1	0	55	55	27	2	3	34	18	2.95	114	.272	.385	11	.364	1	86	1		0.1
1921	Was A	1	0	1.000	1	1	1	0	9	9	2	0	0	3	2	2.00	206	.290	.353	3	.000	-0	61	2		0.2
1922	Was A	3	7	.300	17	7	2-1	0	70	72	43	2	4	22	19	4.89	79	.273	.338	20-0-1	.150	-1	78	-7		-0.9
Total	4	8	12	.400	45	15	5-1	0	161.1	164	85	4	9	71	44	3.74	95	.275	.361	43-0-2	.186	-1	73	-4		-0.8
PHILLIPS, BILL	William Corcoran "Whoa Bill","Silver Bill"							B11.9.1868	Allenport PA		D10.25.1941	Charleroi PA		BR/TR/5-11/180	d8.11	M2								
1890	Pit N	1	9	.100	10	10	9	0	82	123	97	8	1	29	25	7.57	44	.336	.386	46	.239	1*	69	-38		-3.1
1895	Cin N	6	7	.462	18	9	6	2	109	126	90	6	7	44	15	6.03	82	.285	.359	48	.313	2*	120	-9		-0.6
1899	Cin N	17	9	.654	33	27	18-1	1	227.2	234	121	3	14	71	43	3.32	118	.265	.330	92-0-4	.130	-5*	115	13		0.7
1900	Cin N	9	11	.450	29	24	16-3	0	207.1	229	140	5	13	67	50	4.30	85	.280	.344	79-0-1	.165	-4	115	-16		-1.3
1901	Cin N	14	18	.438	37	36	29-1	0	281.1	364	196	7	12	67	109	4.64	69	.311	.354	109-0-1	.202	2*	93	-45		-3.8
1902	Cin N	16	16	.500	33	33	30	0	269	267	121	3	9	55	85	2.51	119	.259	.302	114-0-2	.342	10*	116	12		2.6
1903	Cin N	7	6	.538	16	13	11-1	0	118.1	134	74	0	7	30	46	3.35	106	.279	.330	57	.175	-1*	118	1		0.0
Total	7	70	76	.479	176	152	119-6	3	1294.2	1477	839	32	63	363	373	4.09	87	.284	.339	545-0-8	.224	4	103	-82		-5.5
PHILLIPS, TAYLOR	William Taylor "Tay"							B6.18.1933	Atlanta GA		BL/TL/5-11/185*		d6.8												
1956	Mil N	5	3	.625	23	6	3	2	87.2	69	25	6	7	33-8	36	2.26	153	.223	.310	21-0-1	.000	-2	81	13		1.1
1957	Mil N	3	2	.600	27	6	0	2	73	82	46	3	1	40-3	36	5.55	63	.300	.388	20	.100	-1	130	-16		-1.2
1958	Chi N	7	10	.412	39	27	5-1	1	170.1	178	102	22	6	79-5	102	4.76	82	.266	.348	54-0-5	.056	-4	106	-16		-1.8
1959	Chi N	0	2	.000	7	2	0	0	16.2	22	14	3	2	11-2	5	7.56	52	.319	.422	4	.000	-0	57	-6		-0.7
	Phi N	1	4	.200	32	3	1	1	63	72	35	4	4	31-1	35	5.00	82	.303	.389	11	.091	-1	80	-4		-0.4
	Year	1	6	.143	39	5	1	1	79.2	94	49	7	6	42-3	40	5.54	74	.306	.397	15	.067	-1	70	-10		-1.1
1960	Phi N	0	1	.000	10	1	0	0	14	21	13	2	1	4-0	6	8.36	46	.356	.388	1	.000	-0	182	-6		-0.4
1963	Chi A	0	0	—	9	0	0	0	14	16	16	2	1	13-5	13	10.29	34	.302	.441	2	.000	-0		-10		-0.5
Total	6	16	22	.421	147	45	9-1	6	438.2	460	251	42	22	211-24	233	4.82	78	.275	.362	113-0-6	.053	-9	104	-45		-3.9
PHOEBUS, TOM	Thomas Harold							B4.7.1942	Baltimore MD		BR/TR/5-8/185*		d9.15												
1966	Bal A	2	1	.667	3	3	2-2	0	22	16	3	0	0	6-0	17	1.23	271	.213	.272	6-0-1	.167	0	62	5		0.9
1967	Bal A	14	9	.609	33	33	7-4	0	208	177	84	16	0	114-1	179	3.33	95	.227	.325	76-1-3	.145	1	142	-4		-0.5
1968	Bal A	15	15	.500	36	36	9-3	0	240.2	186	81	10	4	105-5	193	2.62	112	.212	.299	82-1-7	.183	3	98	8		1.4
1969	Bal A	14	7	.667	35	33	6-2	0	202	180	89	23	4	87-5	117	3.52	102	.241	.321	75-0-5	.200	2	119	1		0.2
1970	†Bal A	5	5	.500	27	21	3	0-1	135	106	58	11	6	62-2	72	3.07	120	.219	.312	43-0-3	.163	-0	119	6		0.4
1971	SD N	3	11	.214	29	21	2	0-0	133.1	144	67	14	3	64-6	80	4.45	75	.280	.361	36-0-2	.167	1	89	-13		-1.1
1972	SD N	0	1	.000	1	1	0	0	5.2	3	5	2	0	6-0	8	7.94	42	.150	.346	2	.000	-0	27	-3		-0.4
	Chi N	3	3	.500	37	1	0	6-3	83.1	76	40	9	2	45-4	59	3.78	101	.247	.343	15-0-1	.133	-1*	46	0		-0.4
	Year	3	4	.429	38	2	0	6-3	89	79	45	11	2	51-4	67	4.04	93	.241	.343	17-0-1	.118	-1	35	-2		-0.4
Total	7	56	52	.519	201	149	29-11	6-4	1030	888	427	85	19	489-23	725	3.33	100	.233	.322	335-2-22	.170	5	112	0		0.9
PHOENIX, STEVE	Steven Robert							B1.31.1968	Phoenix AZ		BR/TR/6-2/175*		d7.30			Col Grand Canyon								
1994	Oak A	0	0	—	2	0	0	0-0	4.1	4	3	0	0	2-0	3	6.23	72	.235	.316	0	—	0		-1		0.0
1995	Oak A	0	0	—	1	0	0	0-0	1.2	3	6	1	0	3-0	3	32.40	14	.429	.600	0	—	0		-5		-0.2
Total	2	0	0	—	3	0	0	0-0	6	7	9	1	0	5-0	6	13.50	33	.292	.414	0	—	0		-6		-0.2

YEAR	TM LG	W	L	PCT	G	GS	CG-SHO	SV-BS	IP	H	R	HR	HB	BB-IB	SO	ERA	AERA	OAV	OOB	AB-HR-SH	AVG	PB	SUP	APR	DL	PW

PHYLE, BILL William Joseph B6.25.1875 Duluth MN D8.6.1953 Los Angeles CA TR d9.17 ▲

YEAR	TM LG	W	L	PCT	G	GS	CG-SHO	SV-BS	IP	H	R	HR	HB	BB-IB	SO	ERA	AERA	OAV	OOB	AB-HR-SH	AVG	PB	SUP	APR	DL	PW
1898	Chi N	2	1	.667	3	3	3-2	0	23	24	15	0	2	6	4	0.78	458	.267	.327	9	.111	-0*	119	4		0.4
1899	Chi N	1	8	.111	10	9	9	1	83.2	92	58	2	4	29	10	4.20	89	.279	.344	34	.176	-2	77	-4		-0.5
1901	NY N	7	10	.412	24	19	16	1	168.2	208	121	2	6	54	62	4.27	77	.301	.356	66	.182	-1*	126	-21		-1.8
Total	3	10	19	.345	37	31	28-2	2	275.1	324	194	4	12	89	76	3.96	88	.291	.350	109	.174	-4	110	-21		-1.9

PIATT, DOUG Douglas William B9.26.1965 Beaver PA BL/TR/6-1/185 d6.11 Col Western Kentucky

YEAR	TM LG	W	L	PCT	G	GS	CG-SHO	SV-BS	IP	H	R	HR	HB	BB-IB	SO	ERA	AERA	OAV	OOB	AB-HR-SH	AVG	PB	SUP	APR	DL	PW
1991	Mon N	0	0	—	21	0	0	0-0	34.2	29	11	3	0	17-0	29	2.60	140	.230	.322	1	.000	-0		4		0.2

PIATT, WILEY Wiley Harold "Iron Man" B7.13.1874 Blue Creek OH D9.20.1946 Cincinnati OH BL/TL/5-10/175 d4.22 Col Ohio U.

YEAR	TM LG	W	L	PCT	G	GS	CG-SHO	SV-BS	IP	H	R	HR	HB	BB-IB	SO	ERA	AERA	OAV	OOB	AB-HR-SH	AVG	PB	SUP	APR	DL	PW
1898	Phi N	24	14	.632	39	37	33-6	0	306	285	156	2	19	97	121	3.18	108	.245	.314	122-0-1	.262	4*	100	10		1.3
1899	Phi N	23	15	.605	39	38	31-2	0	305	323	173	6	23	86	89	3.45	107	.271	.332	122-0-3	.270	4*	115	7		0.8
1900	Phi N	9	10	.474	22	20	16-1	0	160.2	194	120	5	16	71	47	4.65	78	.298	.380	68-0-1	.250	2	111	-21		-2.0
1901	Phi A	5	12	.294	18	16	15	1	140	176	112	3	3	60	45	4.63	82	.303	.372	58-0-1	.224	0	115	-16		-1.7
	Chi A	4	2	.667	7	6	4-1	0	51.2	42	29	2	4	14	19	2.79	125	.220	.287	17	.118	-1	110	3		0.1
	Year	9	14	.391	25	22	19-1	1	191.2	218	141	5	7	74	64	4.13	89	.283	.351	75-0-1	.200	-1	114	-13		-1.6
1902	Chi A	12	12	.500	32	30	22-2	0	246	263	129	3	9	66	96	3.51	96	.274	.327	85-0-4	.200	2	115	-5		-0.4
1903	Bos N	9	14	.391	25	23	18	0	181	198	107	5	4	61	100	3.18	101	.280	.340	71-0-2	.225	2*	107	-3		-0.2
Total	6	86	79	.521	182	170	139-12	1	1390.1	1481	828	26	78	455	517	3.60	98	.272	.337	543-0-12	.239	13	110	-25		-2.1

PICHARDO, HIPOLITO Hipolito Antonio (Balbina) B8.22.1969 Jicome Esperanza, D.R. BR/TR/6-1/185(160-195) d4.21 [DL 1999 KC A 182]

YEAR	TM LG	W	L	PCT	G	GS	CG-SHO	SV-BS	IP	H	R	HR	HB	BB-IB	SO	ERA	AERA	OAV	OOB	AB-HR-SH	AVG	PB	SUP	APR	DL	PW
1992	KC A	9	6	.600	31	24	1-1	0-0	143.2	148	71	9	3	49-1	59	3.95	104	.267	.327	0	—	0	116	1		0.1
1993	KC A	7	8	.467	30	25	0	0-0	165	183	85	10	6	53-2	70	4.04	114	.282	.338	0	—	0	85	7	18	0.7
1994	KC A	5	3	.625	45	0	0	3-2	67.2	82	42	4	7	24-5	36	4.92	102	.308	.378	0	—	0	0	0		0.1
1995	KC A	8	4	.667	44	0	0	1-1	64	66	34	4	4	30-7	43	4.36	110	.265	.352	2	.000	-0	3	17		0.5
1996	KC A	3	5	.375	57	0	0	3-2	68	74	41	5	2	26-5	43	5.43	93	.284	.351	0	—	0	-2			-0.1
1997	KC A	3	5	.375	47	0	0	11-2	49	51	24	7	1	24-8	34	4.22	112	.271	.357	0	—	0	3	52		0.7
1998	KC A	7	8	.467	27	18	0	1-0	112.1	126	73	11	4	43-2	55	5.13	95	.280	.346	2	.000	-0	91	-5	55	-0.5
2000	Bos N	6	3	.667	38	1	0	1-1	65	63	29	1	3	26-2	37	3.46	145	.260	.337	1	.000	-0	75	10		1.2
2001	Bos N	2	1	.667	30	0	0	0-3	34.2	42	23	3	5	10-3	17	4.93	90	.300	.363	0	—	0	-3	58		-0.2
2002	Hou N	0	1	.000	1	0	0	0-0	0.1	3	3	0	0	2-1	0	81.00	5	.750	.833	0	—	0	-3	28		-0.4
Total	10	50	44	.532	350	68	3-1	20-11	769.2	838	425	54	35	287-36	394	4.44	105	.279	.346	5	.000	-1	94	11	410	2.1

PICHE, RON Ronald Jacques B5.22.1935 Verdun QC, Can. BR/TR/5-11/165* d5.30 C1

YEAR	TM LG	W	L	PCT	G	GS	CG-SHO	SV-BS	IP	H	R	HR	HB	BB-IB	SO	ERA	AERA	OAV	OOB	AB-HR-SH	AVG	PB	SUP	APR	DL	PW
1960	Mil N	3	5	.375	37	0	0	9	48	48	26	3	3	23-4	38	3.56	96	.258	.346	7	.000	0	-3			-0.6
1961	Mil N	2	2	.500	12	1	1	0	23.1	20	12	1	0	16-2	16	3.47	108	.238	.353	5-0-1	.000	-1	71	0		-0.1
1962	Mil N	3	2	.600	14	8	2	0	52	54	32	6	3	29-3	28	4.85	78	.273	.369	18	.056	-1*	118	-6		-0.6
1963	Mil N	1	1	.500	37	1	0	0	53	53	32	4	0	25-6	40	3.40	95	.256	.333	7	.000	-1	80	-5		-0.3
1965	Cal A	0	3	.000	14	1	0	0	19.2	20	15	5	0	12-2	14	6.86	50	.267	.364	1	.000	-0	77	-7		-1.0
1966	StL N	1	3	.250	20	0	0	2	25.1	21	13	4	1	18-4	21	4.26	84	.214	.339	4-0-1	.000	-0	-2			-0.3
Total	6	10	16	.385	134	11	3	12	221.1	216	130	23	7	123-21	157	4.19	84	.255	.350	42-0-2	.024	-3	113	-23		-2.9

PICKETT, RICKY Cecil Lee B1.19.1970 Fort Worth TX BL/TL/6-1/220 [CinN92 28/773] d4.28 Col NE Oklahoma A&M JC

YEAR	TM LG	W	L	PCT	G	GS	CG-SHO	SV-BS	IP	H	R	HR	HB	BB-IB	SO	ERA	AERA	OAV	OOB	AB-HR-SH	AVG	PB	SUP	APR	DL	PW
1998	Ari N	0	0	—	2	0	0	0-0	0.2	3	6	0	0	4-0	2	81.00	5	.600	.778	0	—	0	-5			-0.2

PICKETT, CHARLIE Charles Albert B3.1.1883 Delaware OH D5.20.1969 Springfield OH BR/TR/6-1/175 d6.21

YEAR	TM LG	W	L	PCT	G	GS	CG-SHO	SV-BS	IP	H	R	HR	HB	BB-IB	SO	ERA	AERA	OAV	OOB	AB-HR-SH	AVG	PB	SUP	APR	DL	PW
1910	StL N	0	0	—	2	0	0	0	6	7	2	0	0	2	2	1.50	199	.280	.333	0	—	0	1			0.1

PICKFORD, KEVIN Kevin Patrick B3.12.1975 Fresno CA BL/TL/6-4/200 [PitN93 2/54] d5.16

YEAR	TM LG	W	L	PCT	G	GS	CG-SHO	SV-BS	IP	H	R	HR	HB	BB-IB	SO	ERA	AERA	OAV	OOB	AB-HR-SH	AVG	PB	SUP	APR	DL	PW
2002	SD N	0	2	.000	16	4	0	0-0	30	37	23	3	3	20-1	18	6.00	65	.314	.423	5	.000	-1	89	-8		-0.5

PICKREL, CLARENCE Clarence Douglas B3.28.1911 Gretna VA D11.4.1983 Rocky Mount VA BR/TR/6-1/180 d4.22

YEAR	TM LG	W	L	PCT	G	GS	CG-SHO	SV-BS	IP	H	R	HR	HB	BB-IB	SO	ERA	AERA	OAV	OOB	AB-HR-SH	AVG	PB	SUP	APR	DL	PW
1933	Phi N	1	0	1.000	9	0	0	0	13.2	20	7	0	1	3	6	3.95	97	.357	.400	1	.000	-0	0			-0.1
1934	Bos N	0	0	—	10	1	0	0	16	24	9	0	0	7	9	5.06	76	.333	.392	2	.000	-0	203	-2		-0.1
Total	2	1	0	1.000	19	1	0	0	29.2	44	16	0	1	10	15	4.55	85	.344	.396	3	.000	-0	203	-2		-0.1

PICO, JEFF Jeffrey Mark B2.12.1966 Antioch CA BR/TR/6-1/170(170-190) [ChiN84 13/317] d5.31

YEAR	TM LG	W	L	PCT	G	GS	CG-SHO	SV-BS	IP	H	R	HR	HB	BB-IB	SO	ERA	AERA	OAV	OOB	AB-HR-SH	AVG	PB	SUP	APR	DL	PW
1988	Chi N	6	7	.462	29	13	3-2	1-1	112.1	108	57	6	0	37-6	57	4.15	88	.252	.309	34-0-2	.147	-0	103	-6		-0.7
1989	Chi N	3	1	.750	53	0	0	2-1	90.2	99	43	8	0	31-10	38	3.77	100	.278	.334	10-0-3	.100	-1	117	0		0.0
1990	Chi N	4	4	.500	31	8	0	2-1	92	120	53	7	1	37-10	37	4.79	85	.321	.382	22-0-1	.273	2	144	-6		-0.2
Total	3	13	12	.520	113	26	3-2	5-3	295.1	327	153	21	1	105-26	132	4.24	90	.282	.340	66-0-6	.182	1	119	-12		-0.9

PICONE, MARIO Mario Peter "Babe" B7.5.1926 Brooklyn NY BR/TR/5-11/180* d9.27

YEAR	TM LG	W	L	PCT	G	GS	CG-SHO	SV-BS	IP	H	R	HR	HB	BB-IB	SO	ERA	AERA	OAV	OOB	AB-HR-SH	AVG	PB	SUP	APR	DL	PW
1947	NY N	0	0	—	2	1	0	0	7	10	6	1	2	2	1	7.71	53	.345	.387	2	.500	1	152	-2		0.0
1952	NY N	0	1	.000	2	1	0	0	9	11	8	2	0	5	3	7.00	53	.306	.390	2-0-1	.000	-0	72	-3		-0.3
1954	NY N	0	0	—	5	0	0	0	13.2	13	8	1	0	11	6	5.27	77	.283	.421	1	.000	0	-1			-0.1
	Cin N	0	1	.000	4	1	0	0	10.1	9	7	3	0	7	1	6.10	69	.243	.364	1	.000	0	43	-2		-0.1
	Year	0	1	.000	9	1	0	0	24	22	15	4	0	18	7	5.63	73	.265	.396	2	.000	0	43	-3		-0.2
Total	3	0	2	.000	13	3	0	0	40	43	29	7	0	25	11	6.30	64	.291	.393	6-0-1	.167	0	89	-8		-0.5

PIECHOTA, AL Aloysius Edward "Pie" B1.19.1914 Chicago IL D6.13.1996 Chicago IL BR/TR/6-0/195 d5.7

YEAR	TM LG	W	L	PCT	G	GS	CG-SHO	SV-BS	IP	H	R	HR	HB	BB-IB	SO	ERA	AERA	OAV	OOB	AB-HR-SH	AVG	PB	SUP	APR	DL	PW
1940	Bos N	2	5	.286	21	8	2	0	61	68	45	6	0	41	18	5.75	65	.278	.381	20-0-1	.200	1	93	-15		-1.4
1941	Bos N	0	0	—	1	0	0	0	1	0	0	0	0	1	0	0.00	—	.000	.250	0	—	0	0			0.0
Total	2	2	5	.286	22	8	2	0	62	68	45	6	0	42	18	5.66	66	.274	.379	20-0-1	.200	1	93	-15		-1.4

PIEH, CY Edwin John B9.29.1886 Waunakee WI D9.12.1945 Jacksonville FL BR/TR/6-2/190 d9.6

YEAR	TM LG	W	L	PCT	G	GS	CG-SHO	SV-BS	IP	H	R	HR	HB	BB-IB	SO	ERA	AERA	OAV	OOB	AB-HR-SH	AVG	PB	SUP	APR	DL	PW
1913	NY A	1	0	1.000	4	0	0	0	10.1	10	8	0	0	7	6	4.35	69	.256	.370	4	.250	1	-2			-0.1
1914	NY A	3	4	.429	18	4	1	0	62.1	68	41	6	0	29	24	5.05	55	.289	.367	17-0-1	.118	-0*	86	-15		-1.6
1915	NY A	4	5	.444	21	8	3-2	0	94	78	40	2	5	39	46	2.87	102	.234	.324	30	.067	-3	75	0		-0.4
Total	3	8	9	.471	43	12	4-2	0	166.2	156	89	8	5	75	76	3.78	76	.257	.344	51-0-1	.098	-3	78	-17		-2.1

PIERCE, ED Edward John B10.6.1968 Arcadia CA BL/TL/6-1/185 [KCA89 7/179] d9.6 Col California-Santa Barbara

YEAR	TM LG	W	L	PCT	G	GS	CG-SHO	SV-BS	IP	H	R	HR	HB	BB-IB	SO	ERA	AERA	OAV	OOB	AB-HR-SH	AVG	PB	SUP	APR	DL	PW
1992	KC A	0	0	—	2	1	0	0-0	5.1	9	2	1	0	4-0	3	3.38	121	.429	.500	0	—	0	67	0		0.0

PIERCE, GEORGE George Thomas "Filbert" B1.10.1888 Shabbona Grove IL D10.11.1935 Joliet IL BL/TL/5-10.5/175 d4.16

YEAR	TM LG	W	L	PCT	G	GS	CG-SHO	SV-BS	IP	H	R	HR	HB	BB-IB	SO	ERA	AERA	OAV	OOB	AB-HR-SH	AVG	PB	SUP	APR	DL	PW
1912	Chi N	0	0	—	3	2	0	0	14.2	15	13	0	0	12	9	5.52	60	.185	.290	6	.167	0	77	-4		-0.2
1913	Chi N	13	5	.722	25	21	14-3	0	164	137	60	4	3	59	73	2.30	138	.234	.308	55-0-3	.073	-3	129	14		1.1
1914	Chi N	9	12	.429	30	17	4	1	141	122	82	3	2	65	78	3.51	79	.239	.327	45-0-2	.089	-3	109	-11		-1.8
1915	Chi N	13	9	.591	36	20	8-2	0	176	158	83	1	4	77	96	3.32	84	.244	.328	56-0-3	.196	1	92	-11		-1.2
1916	Chi N	0	0	—	4	1	0	0	4.1	6	5	0	0	1	0	2.08	140	.300	.333	0	—	0	103	-1		-0.1
1917	StL N	1	1	.500	5	0	0	0	10.1	7	7	0	1	3	4	3.48	77	.184	.262	4	.000	-1	-2			-0.4
Total	6	36	27	.571	103	61	26-5	1	510.1	445	250	8	10	217	260	3.10	94	.236	.318	166-0-8	.120	-6	110	-15		-2.6

PIERCE, JEFF Jeffrey Charles B6.7.1969 Poughkeepsie NY BR/TR/6-1/190 d4.26 Col North Carolina St.

YEAR	TM LG	W	L	PCT	G	GS	CG-SHO	SV-BS	IP	H	R	HR	HB	BB-IB	SO	ERA	AERA	OAV	OOB	AB-HR-SH	AVG	PB	SUP	APR	DL	PW
1995	Bos A	0	3	.000	12	0	0	0-1	15	12	12	0	0	14-4	12	6.60	74	.286	.423	0	—	0	-3			-0.5

PIERCE, RAY Raymond Lester "Lefty" B6.6.1897 Emporia KS D5.4.1963 Denver CO BL/TL/5-7/156 d5.12 Col Kansas

YEAR	TM LG	W	L	PCT	G	GS	CG-SHO	SV-BS	IP	H	R	HR	HB	BB-IB	SO	ERA	AERA	OAV	OOB	AB-HR-SH	AVG	PB	SUP	APR	DL	PW
1924	Chi N	0	0	—	6	0	0	0	7.1	7	6	2	0	4	2	7.36	53	.269	.367	0	—	0	-2			-0.1
1925	Phi N	5	4	.556	23	8	4	0	90	134	67	7	1	24	18	5.50	87	.356	.397	28-0-4	.179	-0	115	-6		-0.5
1926	Phi N	2	7	.222	37	7	1	0	84.2	128	71	3	1	35	18	5.63	74	.348	.406	24-0-2	.125	-2*	80	-16		-1.7
Total	3	7	11	.389	66	15	5	0	182	269	144	12	2	63	38	5.64	79	.349	.400	52-0-6	.154	-2	101	-24		-2.3

PIERCE, TONY Tony Michael B1.29.1946 Brunswick GA BR/TL/6-1/190* d4.14

YEAR	TM LG	W	L	PCT	G	GS	CG-SHO	SV-BS	IP	H	R	HR	HB	BB-IB	SO	ERA	AERA	OAV	OOB	AB-HR-SH	AVG	PB	SUP	APR	DL	PW
1967	KC A	3	4	.429	49	6	0	7	97.2	79	42	6	5	30-6	61	3.04	105	.221	.290	20-0-1	.000	-2	77	-1		-0.3
1968	Oak A	1	2	.333	17	3	0	1	32.2	39	16	3	1	10-2	16	3.86	73	.295	.347	6-0-1	.000	-1	113	-4		-0.4
Total	2	4	6	.400	66	9	0	8	130.1	118	58	9	6	40-8	77	3.25	95	.241	.305	26-0-2	.000	-3	88	-5		-0.7

YEAR	TM LG	W	L	PCT	G	GS	CG-SHO	SV-BS	IP	H	R	HR	HB	BB-IB	SO	ERA	AERA	OAV	OOB	AB-HR-SH	AVG	PB	SUP	APR	DL	PW

PIERCE, BILLY Walter William B4.2.1927 Detroit MI BL/TL/5-10/160(155-175) d6.1

YEAR	TM LG	W	L	PCT	G	GS	CG-SHO	SV-BS	IP	H	R	HR	HB	BB-IB	SO	ERA	AERA	OAV	OOB	AB-HR-SH	AVG	PB	SUP	APR	DL	PW
1945	Det A	0	0	—	5	0	0	0	10	6	2	1	1	10	10	1.80	195	.182	.386	2	.000	-0		2		0.1
1948	Det A	3	0	1.000	22	5	0	0	55.1	47	40	5	1	51	36	6.34	69	.234	.391	17	.294	2	145	-10		-0.3
1949	Chi A	7	15	.318	32	26	8	0	171.2	145	89	11	0	112	95	3.88	108	.228	.344	51-0-6	.176	-1*	88	3		0.4
1950	Chi A	12	16	.429	33	29	15-1	1	219.1	189	112	11	2	137	118	3.98	113	.228	.339	77-0-4	.260	4*	82	11		1.5
1951	Chi A	15	14	.517	37	28	18-1	2	240.1	237	93	14	1	73	113	3.03	133	.258	.313	79-0-5	.203	-0*	94	28		3.1
1952	Chi A	15	12	.556	33	32	14-4	1	255.1	214	76	12	3	79	144	2.57	142	.227	.289	91-0-5	.187	0*	102	33		3.5
1953	Chi A★	18	12	.600	40	33	19-7	3	271.1	216	94	20	3	102	186	2.72	148	.218	.292	87-0-10	.218	-4*	82	38		3.5
1954	Chi A	9	10	.474	36	26	12-4	3	188.2	179	86	15	3	86	148	3.48	107	.249	.330	57-0-6	.193	0*	96	3		0.2
1955	Chi A★	15	10	.600	33	26	16-6	1	205.2	162	50	16	3	64-5	157	1.97	200	.213	.277	70-0-8	.171	-1*	81	45		5.3
1956	Chi A★	20	9	.690	35	33	21-1	1	276.1	261	108	24	3	100-7	192	3.32	123	.249	.316	102-0-7	.157	-4*	124	26		1.9
1957	Chi A★	20	12	.625	37	34	16-4	2	257	228	98	18	1	71-9	171	3.26	115	.234	.287	99-0-3	.172	-2*	96	15		1.6
1958	Chi A☆	17	11	.607	35	32	19-3	2	245	204	83	33	1	66-2	144	2.68	136	.227	.279	83-0-6	.205	2	95	26		3.0
1959	†Chi A☆	14	15	.483	34	33	12-2	0	224	217	98	26	3	62-4	114	3.62	104	.253	.305	68-0-6	.191	3	79	5		0.9
1960	Chi A	14	7	.667	32	30	8-1	0	196.1	201	81	24	0	46-1	108	3.62	104	.266	.307	67-0-3	.179	1	115	7		0.7
1961	Chi A☆	10	9	.526	39	28	5-1	3	180	190	85	17	1	54-3	106	3.80	103	.275	.326	56-0-6	.143	-2	104	2		0.0
1962	†SF N	16	6	.727	30	23	7-2	1	162.1	147	67	19	3	35-2	76	3.49	109	.239	.283	56-0-7	.214	2	131	7		1.0
1963	SF N	3	11	.214	38	13	3-1	8	99	106	49	12	1	20-1	52	4.27	75	.272	.308	31-0-1	.129	-0	116	-9		-1.4
1964	SF N	3	0	1.000	34	1	0	4	49	40	14	6	0	11-0	31	2.20	162	.222	.260	9	.333	1	123	7		0.6
Total	18	211	169	.555	585	432	193-38	32	3306.2	2989	1325	284	30	1178-35	1999	3.27	119	.240	.307	1102-0-83	.184	-0	98	239		25.6

PIERCY, BILL William Benton "Wild Bill" B5.2.1896 ElMonte CA D8.28.1951 Long Beach CA BR/TR/6-1/185 d10.3

YEAR	TM LG	W	L	PCT	G	GS	CG-SHO	SV-BS	IP	H	R	HR	HB	BB-IB	SO	ERA	AERA	OAV	OOB	AB-HR-SH	AVG	PB	SUP	APR	DL	PW
1917	NY A	0	1	.000	1	1	1	0	9	9	3	0	0	2	4	3.00	90	.257	.297	2	.214	0	27			0.0
1921	†NY A	5	4	.556	14	10	5-1	0	81.2	82	40	4	7	28	35	2.98	142	.263	.337	28	.214	0	97	9		0.9
1922	Bos A	3	9	.250	29	12	7-1	0	121.1	140	77	2	6	62	24	4.67	88	.304	.394	34-0-4	.147	-1	59	-9		-0.8
1923	Bos A	8	17	.320	30	24	11	0	187.1	193	105	5	14	73	51	3.41	121	.277	.357	53-0-8	.132	-3	74	8		0.8
1924	Bos A	5	7	.417	23	18	3	0	121	156	87	4	10	66	20	5.95	73	.335	.429	39-0-5	.154	-2	108	-17		-1.5
1926	Chi N	6	5	.545	19	5	1	0	90.1	96	52	1	6	37	31	4.48	86	.280	.360	35	.257	1	126	-5		-0.5
Total	6	27	43	.386	116	70	28-2	0	610.2	676	364	16	43	268	165	4.26	97	.292	.376	191-0-17	.173	-5	88	-14		-1.1

PIERETTI, MARINO Marino Paul "Chick" B9.23.1920 Lucca, Italy D1.30.1981 San Francisco CA BR/TR/5-7/158* d4.19

YEAR	TM LG	W	L	PCT	G	GS	CG-SHO	SV-BS	IP	H	R	HR	HB	BB-IB	SO	ERA	AERA	OAV	OOB	AB-HR-SH	AVG	PB	SUP	APR	DL	PW
1945	Was A	14	13	.519	44	27	14-3	2	233.1	235	114	3	1	91	93	6.32	94	.257	.325	81-0-4	.222	2	102	-10		-0.9
1946	Was A	2	5	.500	30	2	1	0	62	70	48	9	2	40	20	5.95	56	.292	.397	14-0-1	.214	0	102	-18		-1.0
1947	Was A	2	4	.333	23	10	2-1	0	83.1	97	50	3	2	47	32	4.21	88	.287	.377	26-0-2	.231	-0	126	-7		-0.5
1948	Was A	0	2	.000	8	1	0	0	11.2	18	14	1	0	7	6	10.80	40	.375	.455	2	.000	-0*	83	-7		-1.1
	Chi A	8	10	.444	21	18	4	1	120	117	70	6	0	52	28	4.95	86	.262	.339	39-0-1	.179	-1*	80	-8		-1.0
	Year	8	12	.400	29	19	4	1	131.2	135	84	7	0	59	34	5.47	78	.273	.351	41-0-1	.171	-1*	80	-15		-2.1
1949	Chi A	4	6	.400	39	9	0	4	116	131	77	10	0	54	25	5.51	76	.289	.364	38-0-1	.237	-1*	93	-16		-1.2
1950	Cle A	0	1	.000	29	1	0	0	47.1	45	24	2	0	30	11	4.18	104	.253	.361	7	.286	0*	146	-1		0.1
Total	6	30	38	.441	194	68	21-4	8	673.2	713	397	34	5	321	188	4.53	81	.272	.353	207-0-9	.217	2	98	-65		-5.6

PIEROTTI, AL Albert Felix B10.24.1895 Boston MA D2.12.1964 Everett MA BR/TR/5-10.5/195 d8.9 Col Washington and Lee

YEAR	TM LG	W	L	PCT	G	GS	CG-SHO	SV-BS	IP	H	R	HR	HB	BB-IB	SO	ERA	AERA	OAV	OOB	AB-HR-SH	AVG	PB	SUP	APR	DL	PW
1920	Bos N	1	1	.500	6	2	1	0	25	23	9	2	0	9	11	2.88	106	.250	.317	8-0-1	.250	0	90	1		0.1
1921	Bos N	0	1	.000	2	0	1	0	1.2	3	4	0	0	3	2	21.60	17	.375	.545	1	.000	-0		-3		-0.6
Total	2	1	2	.333	8	2	2	0	26.2	26	13	2	0	12	13	4.05	76	.260	.339	9-0-1	.222	-0	90	-2		-0.5

PIERRO, BILL William Leonard "Wild Bill" B4.15.1926 Brooklyn NY BR/TR/6-1/155 d7.17 [DL 1951 Pit N 94]

YEAR	TM LG	W	L	PCT	G	GS	CG-SHO	SV-BS	IP	H	R	HR	HB	BB-IB	SO	ERA	AERA	OAV	OOB	AB-HR-SH	AVG	PB	SUP	APR	DL	PW
1950	Pit N	0	2	.000	12	3	0	0	29	33	34	2	2	28	13	10.55	42	.289	.438	9	.222	-0*	74	-17		-1.0

PIERSOLL, CHRIS Christopher Earl B9.25.1977 Van Nuys CA BR/TR/6-4/195 [ChiN97 19/574] d8.31 Col Fullerton (CA) JC

YEAR	TM LG	W	L	PCT	G	GS	CG-SHO	SV-BS	IP	H	R	HR	HB	BB-IB	SO	ERA	AERA	OAV	OOB	AB-HR-SH	AVG	PB	SUP	APR	DL	PW
2001	Cin N	0	0	—	11	0	0	0-0	11.1	12	4	1	1	6-0	7	2.38	193	.267	.365	0	—	0		2		0.1

PIERSON, WILLIAM William Morris B6.14.1899 Atlantic City NJ D2.20.1959 Atlantic City NJ BL/TL/6-2/180 d7.4

YEAR	TM LG	W	L	PCT	G	GS	CG-SHO	SV-BS	IP	H	R	HR	HB	BB-IB	SO	ERA	AERA	OAV	OOB	AB-HR-SH	AVG	PB	SUP	APR	DL	PW
1918	Phi A	0	1	.000	8	1	0	0	21.2	20	10	2	0	20	6	3.32	88	.286	.457	4	.250	-0	26	-1		-0.1
1919	Phi A	0	0	—	2	1	0	0	7.2	9	3	0	0	8	4	3.52	97	.333	.486	3	.333	0	160	0		0.0
1924	Phi A	0	0	—	1	0	0	0	2.2	3	1	0	0	3	0	3.38	127	.300	.462	0	—	0		0		0.0
Total	3	0	1	.000	11	2	0	0	32	32	14	2	0	31	10	3.38	94	.299	.464	7	.286	0	97	-1		-0.1

PIKTUZIS, GEORGE George Richard B1.3.1932 Chicago IL D11.28.1993 Long Beach CA BR/TL/6-2/200 d4.25

YEAR	TM LG	W	L	PCT	G	GS	CG-SHO	SV-BS	IP	H	R	HR	HB	BB-IB	SO	ERA	AERA	OAV	OOB	AB-HR-SH	AVG	PB	SUP	APR	DL	PW
1956	Chi N	0	0	—	2	0	0	0	5	6	4	1	0	2-0	3	7.20	52	.333	.400	0	—	0		-2		-0.1

PILLETTE, DUANE Duane Xavier "Dee" B7.24.1922 Detroit MI BR/TR/6-3/205* d7.19 f-Herman Col Santa Clara

YEAR	TM LG	W	L	PCT	G	GS	CG-SHO	SV-BS	IP	H	R	HR	HB	BB-IB	SO	ERA	AERA	OAV	OOB	AB-HR-SH	AVG	PB	SUP	APR	DL	PW
1949	NY A	2	4	.333	12	3	2	0	37.1	43	20	6	0	19	9	4.34	93	.299	.380	11-0-2	.000	-1	89	-1		-0.2
1950	NY A	0	0	—	4	0	0	0	7	9	3	0	0	3	4	1.29	334	.321	.387	0	—	0		2		0.1
	StL A	3	5	.375	24	7	1	2	73.2	104	62	6	2	44	18	7.09	70	.337	.423	22-0-1	.136	-1	81	-14		-1.4
	Year	3	5	.375	28	7	1	2	80.2	113	65	6	2	47	22	6.58	74	.335	.420	22-0-1	.136	-1	82	-13		-1.3
1951	StL A	6	14	.300	35	24	6-1	0	191	205	113	14	5	115	65	4.99	88	.276	.376	59-0-6	.136	-3*	60	-10		-1.3
1952	StL A	10	13	.435	30	30	9-1	0	205.1	222	94	14	7	55	62	3.59	109	.274	.325	66-0-6	.182	0*	99	7		0.6
1953	StL A	7	13	.350	31	25	5-1	0	166.2	181	90	16	2	62	58	4.48	94	.277	.341	53-1-2	.132	-1	73	-3		-0.5
1954	Bal A	10	14	.417	25	24	11-1	0	179	158	79	9	1	67	66	3.12	115	.234	.303	53-0-6	.132	-1	81	5		0.8
1955	Bal A	0	3	.000	7	5	0	0	20.2	31	16	0	0	14-1	13	6.53	58	.344	.433	6	.167	0	65	-6	51	-0.7
1956	Phi N	0	0	—	20	0	0	0	23.1	32	21	2	0	12-4	10	6.56	57	.330	.396	1	.000	-0		-8		-0.4
Total	8	38	66	.365	188	119	34-4	2	904	985	498	67	17	391-5	305	4.40	93	.277	.351	271-1-23	.140	-7	78	-28	51	-3.0

PILLETTE, HERMAN Herman Polycarp "Old Folks" B12.26.1895 St.Paul OR D4.30.1960 Sacramento CA BR/TR/6-2/190 d7.30 s-Duane

YEAR	TM LG	W	L	PCT	G	GS	CG-SHO	SV-BS	IP	H	R	HR	HB	BB-IB	SO	ERA	AERA	OAV	OOB	AB-HR-SH	AVG	PB	SUP	APR	DL	PW
1917	Cin N	0	0	—	1	0	0	0	4	4	2	0	0	0	0	18.00	15	.571	.571	0	—	0		-1		-0.1
1922	Det A	19	12	.613	40	37	18-4	1	274.2	270	110	6	15	95	71	2.85	136	.258	.328	99-0-3	.172	-3	120	30		2.9
1923	Det A	14	19	.424	47	36	14	1	250.1	280	138	7	6	83	64	3.85	100	.288	.347	85-0-2	.247	4	106	-4		0.0
1924	Det A	1	1	.500	19	3	1	1	37.2	46	30	1	3	14	13	4.78	86	.297	.366	11	.364	1	150	-5		-0.2
Total	4	34	32	.515	107	76	33-4	3	563.2	600	280	14	24	192	148	3.45	113	.275	.340	195-0-5	.215	2	115	20		2.6

PILLION, SQUIZ Cecil Randolph B4.13.1894 Hartford CT D9.30.1962 Pittsburgh PA BL/TL/6-0/178 d8.20

YEAR	TM LG	W	L	PCT	G	GS	CG-SHO	SV-BS	IP	H	R	HR	HB	BB-IB	SO	ERA	AERA	OAV	OOB	AB-HR-SH	AVG	PB	SUP	APR	DL	PW
1915	Phi A	0	0	—	2	0	0	0	5.1	10	5	0	1	2	0	6.75	43	.400	.464	1	.000	-0		-2		-0.1

PINA, HORACIO Horacio (Garcia) B3.12.1945 Matamoros, Coahuila, Mexico BR/TR/6-2/177* d8.14

YEAR	TM LG	W	L	PCT	G	GS	CG-SHO	SV-BS	IP	H	R	HR	HB	BB-IB	SO	ERA	AERA	OAV	OOB	AB-HR-SH	AVG	PB	SUP	APR	DL	PW
1968	Cle A	1	1	.500	12	3	0	2	31.1	24	7	0	1	15-1	24	1.72	172	.218	.315	6-0-2	.000	-1	108	4		0.3
1969	Cle A	4	2	.667	31	4	0	1-2	46.2	44	29	6	5	27-2	32	5.21	73	.256	.371	6	.500	1	99	-6		-0.7
1970	Was A	5	3	.625	61	0	0	6-4	71	66	25	4	3	35-9	41	2.79	129	.250	.341	1	.000	-0		7		0.8
1971	Was A	1	1	.500	56	0	0	2-2	57.2	47	26	2	4	31-7	38	3.59	94	.227	.335	1	.000	-0		-1		0.0
1972	Tex A	2	7	.222	60	0	0	15-3	76	61	33	3	8	43-7	60	3.20	95	.228	.351	5-0-2	.200	-0		-2		-0.1
1973	†Oak A	6	3	.667	47	0	0	8-2	88	58	31	6	8	34-5	41	2.76	129	.193	.290	0	—	0		9		1.1
1974	Chi N	3	4	.429	34	0	0	4-3	47.1	49	22	4	2	28-4	32	3.99	96	.268	.367	5	.200	-0		4		0.1
	Cal A	1	2	.333	11	0	0	0-1	11.2	9	3	1	0	3-2	6	2.31	150	.209	.261			-0		-1		0.0
1978	Phi N	0	0	—	2	0	0	0-0	2.1	6	4	0	0	0-0	4	0.00	—	.000	.000	1	.000	-0		4		0.0
Total	8	23	23	.500	314	7	0	38-17	432	358	176	28	31	216-37	278	3.25	107	.231	.334	27-0-4	.185	0	102	14		1.9

PINEDA, LUIS Luis A. B10.17.1974 San Cristobal, D.R. BR/TR/6-1/160* d8.4

YEAR	TM LG	W	L	PCT	G	GS	CG-SHO	SV-BS	IP	H	R	HR	HB	BB-IB	SO	ERA	AERA	OAV	OOB	AB-HR-SH	AVG	PB	SUP	APR	DL	PW
2001	Det A	0	1	.000	16	0	0	0-0	18.1	16	10	2	0	14-2	13	4.91	90	.239	.366	0	—	0		-1		0.0
2002	Cin N	1	3	.250	26	2	0	0-0	32.1	25	16	4	2	24-1	31	4.18	102	.221	.362	3	.000	-0	184	1	91	0.0
Total	2	1	4	.200	42	2	0	0-0	50.2	41	26	6	2	38-3	44	4.44	97	.228	.363	3	.000	-0	184	0	91	0.0

PINEIRO, JOEL Joel Alberto B9.25.1978 Rio Piedras, PR BR/TR/6-1/180(180-200) [SeaA97 12/373] d8.8 Col Edison (FL) CC

YEAR	TM LG	W	L	PCT	G	GS	CG-SHO	SV-BS	IP	H	R	HR	HB	BB-IB	SO	ERA	AERA	OAV	OOB	AB-HR-SH	AVG	PB	SUP	APR	DL	PW
2000	Sea A	1	0	1.000	8	1	0	0-0	19.1	25	13	3	0	13	10	5.59	86	.316	.404	0	—	0	234	-2		-0.1
2001	Sea A	6	4	.750	17	11	0	0-0	75.1	50	24	2	3	21-0	56	2.03	210	.191	.257	0	—	0	79	17		1.6
2002	Sea A	14	7	.667	37	28	2-1	0-0	194.1	189	75	24	7	54-0	136	3.24	133	.256	.310	7	.143	-0	112	24		2.4
2003	Sea A	16	11	.593	32	32	3-2	0-0	211.2	192	94	19	6	76-3	151	3.78	114	.241	.309	4-0-1	.000	-0	113	14		1.5
2004	Sea A	6	11	.353	21	21	1	0-0	140.2	144	77	21	4	43-1	111	4.67	96	.265	.321	5	.200	-0	89	-3	70	-0.3

YEAR	TM LG	W	L	PCT	G	GS	CG-SHO	SV-BS	IP	H	R	HR	HB	BB-IB	SO	ERA	AERA	OAV	OOB	AB-HR-SH	AVG	PB	SUP	APR	DL	PW
2005	Sea A	7	11	.389	30	30	2	0-0	189	224	118	23	6	56-4	107	5.62	75	.299	.350	4-0-1	.000	-0	109	-28	12	-2.2
Total 6		50	42	.543	145	123	8-3	0-0	830.1	824	401	92	26	263-9	571	4.11	105	.260	.319	20-0-2	.100	-0	105	22	82	2.9

PINKHAM, ED Edward B1849 Brooklyn NY BL/TL/5-7/142 d5.8 ▲

YEAR	TM LG	W	L	PCT	G	GS	CG-SHO	SV-BS	IP	H	R	HR	HB	BB-IB	SO	ERA	AERA	OAV	OOB	AB-HR-SH	AVG	PB	SUP	APR	DL	PW
1871	Chi NA	1	0	1.000	3	0	0	1	10.1	10	8	0		3	0	3.48	132	.208	.255	95-1	.263	1*		2		0.1

PINNANCE, ED Elijah Edward "Peanuts" B10.22.1879 Walpole Island ON, Can. D12.12.1944 Walpole Island ON, Can. BL/TR/6-1/180 d9.14 Col Michigan St.

YEAR	TM LG	W	L	PCT	G	GS	CG-SHO	SV-BS	IP	H	R	HR	HB	BB-IB	SO	ERA	AERA	OAV	OOB	AB-HR-SH	AVG	PB	SUP	APR	DL	PW
1903	Phi A	2	1	0	2	1	0	1	7	5	2	2	0	2		2.57	119	.200	.259	3	.000	-0	117	1		0.0

PINTO, LERTON William Lerton B4.8.1899 Chillicothe OH D5.13.1983 Oxnard CA BL/TL/6-0/190 d5.23

YEAR	TM LG	W	L	PCT	G	GS	CG-SHO	SV-BS	IP	H	R	HR	HB	BB-IB	SO	ERA	AERA	OAV	OOB	AB-HR-SH	AVG	PB	SUP	APR	DL	PW
1922	Phi N	0	1	.000	9	0	0	0	24.2	31	20	1	0	14	5	5.11	91	.320	.405	9	.111	-1		-2		-0.2
1924	Phi N	0	0		3	0	0	0	4	7	4	1	0	0	1	9.00	50	.467	.467	1	.000	-0		-2		-0.1
Total 2		0	1	.000	12	0	0	0	28.2	38	24	2	0	14	5	5.65	65	.339	.413	10	.100	-1		-4		-0.3

PIPGRAS, ED Edward John B6.15.1904 Schleswig IA D4.13.1964 Currie MN BR/TR/6-2.5/175 d8.25 b-George

YEAR	TM LG	W	L	PCT	G	GS	CG-SHO	SV-BS	IP	H	R	HR	HB	BB-IB	SO	ERA	AERA	OAV	OOB	AB-HR-SH	AVG	PB	SUP	APR	DL	PW
1932	Bro N	0	1	.000	5	1	0	0	10	16	11	2	0	6	5	5.40	71	.348	.423	2	.000	-0	154	-4		-0.3

PIPGRAS, GEORGE George William B12.20.1899 Ida Grove IA D10.19.1986 Gainesville FL BR/TR/6-1.5/185 d6.9 U9 b-Ed

YEAR	TM LG	W	L	PCT	G	GS	CG-SHO	SV-BS	IP	H	R	HR	HB	BB-IB	SO	ERA	AERA	OAV	OOB	AB-HR-SH	AVG	PB	SUP	APR	DL	PW
1923	NY A	1	3	.250	8	2	2	0	33.1	34	22	2	1	25	12	5.94	66	.276	.403	9	.000	-1	84	-6		-0.7
1924	NY A	0	1	.000	9	1	0	1	15.1	20	18	0	4	18	4	9.98	42	.351	.532	3	.333	0	101	-9		-0.6
1927	†NY A	10	3	.769	29	21	9-1	0	166.1	148	81	2	1	77	81	4.11	94	.247	.334	67-1-2	.239	2	156	0		0.1
1928	NY A	24	13	.649	46	38	22-4	3	300.2	314	132	4	3	103	139	3.38	111	.272	.333	115-0-6	.157	-4	127	15		1.1
1929	NY A	18	12	.600	39	33	13-3	0	225.1	229	132	16	5	95	125	4.23	91	.264	.340	84-0-4	.143	-0	129	-12		-1.8
1930	NY A	15	15	.500	44	30	15-3	4	221	230	133	9	8	70	111	4.11	105	.263	.324	80-1-6	.150	-2	143	0		-0.3
1931	NY A	7	6	.538	36	14	6-1	3	137.2	134	73	8	2	58	59	3.79	105	.251	.327	41-0-1	.024	-6	99	0		-0.6
1932	†NY A	16	9	.640	32	27	14-2	0	219	235	120	15	6	87	111	4.19	97	.269	.340	82-0-5	.220	1	130	-4		-0.4
1933	NY A	2	2	.500	4	4	3	0	33	32	13	1	0	12	14	3.27	119	.252	.371	11	.091	-1	99	3		0.3
	Bos A	9	8	.529	22	17	9-2	1	128.1	140	65	5	2	45	56	4.07	108	.276	.337	46-0-2	.196	-1	102	6		0.5
	Year	11	10	.524	26	21	12-2	1	161.1	172	78	6	2	57	70	3.90	110	.271	.333	57-0-2	.175	-1	101	9		0.8
1934	Bos A	0	0		2	1	0	0	3.1	4	3	1	0	3	0	8.10	59	.308	.438	1	.000	0	109	-1		-0.0
1935	Bos A	0	1	.000	5	1	0	0	5	9	9	3	1	5	2	14.40	33	.391	.517	0-0-1	—	0	37	-5		-0.8
Total 11		102	73	.583	276	189	93-16	12	1488.1	1529	801	66	33	598	714	4.09	98	.266	.339	539-2-27	.163	-15	127	-13		-3.2

PIPPEN, COTTON Henry Harold B4.2.1911 Cisco TX D2.15.1981 Williams CA BR/TR/6-2/180 d8.28 Col Texas A&M-Commerce

YEAR	TM LG	W	L	PCT	G	GS	CG-SHO	SV-BS	IP	H	R	HR	HB	BB-IB	SO	ERA	AERA	OAV	OOB	AB-HR-SH	AVG	PB	SUP	APR	DL	PW
1936	StL N	0	2	.000	6	3	0	0	21	37	18	5	2	8	8	7.71	51	.402	.461	6	.167	0	72	-6		-0.6
1939	Phi A	4	11	.267	25	17	5	1	118.2	169	97	13	1	40	33	5.99	79	.329	.378	35-0-3	.086	-2	77	-18		-2.0
	Det A	0	1	.000	3	2	0	0	14	18	13	1	0	6	5	7.07	69	.310	.375	0	.400	0	108	-3		-0.2
	Year	4	12	.250	28	19	5	1	132.2	187	110	14	1	46	38	6.11	77	.327	.378	40-0-3	.125	-2	80	-23		-2.2
1940	Det A	1	2	.333	4	3	0	0	21.1	29	16	3	1	10	9	6.75	70	.326	.400	8	.000	-1	49	-3		-0.5
Total 3		5	16	.238	38	25	5	1	175	253	144	22	4	64	55	6.38	73	.336	.391	54-0-3	.111	-3	76	-32		-3.3

PIRTLE, GERRY Gerald Eugene B12.3.1947 Tulsa OK BR/TR/6-1/185 [NYA67 S7/128] d7.2 Col Bacone

YEAR	TM LG	W	L	PCT	G	GS	CG-SHO	SV-BS	IP	H	R	HR	HB	BB-IB	SO	ERA	AERA	OAV	OOB	AB-HR-SH	AVG	PB	SUP	APR	DL	PW
1978	Mon N	0	2	.000	19	0	0	0-1	25.2	33	24	5	2	23-6	14	5.96	60	.314	.446	0	—	0		-9		-0.7

PISCIOTTA, MARC Marc George B8.7.1970 Edison NJ BR/TR/6-5/225(225-240) [PitN91 19/513] d6.30 Col Georgia Tech

YEAR	TM LG	W	L	PCT	G	GS	CG-SHO	SV-BS	IP	H	R	HR	HB	BB-IB	SO	ERA	AERA	OAV	OOB	AB-HR-SH	AVG	PB	SUP	APR	DL	PW
1997	Chi N	3	1	.750	24	0	0	0-1	28.1	20	10	1	1	16-0	21	3.18	136	.200	.314	1	.000	-0		4		0.5
1998	Chi N		2	.333	43	0	0	0-0	44	44	21	4	2	32-3	31	4.09	108	.259	.380	3	.333	0		2		0.1
1999	KC A	0	2	.000	8	0	0	0-0	8.1	9	8	1	0	10-0	3	8.64	59	.281	.452	0	—	0		-3		-0.5
Total 3		5	4	.444	75	0	0	0-1	80.2	73	39	6	3	58-3	55	4.24	105	.242	.367	4	.250	0		3		0.1

PITLOCK, SKIP Lee Patrick Thomas B11.6.1947 Hillside IL BL/TL/6-2/180* [SFN69 11/256] d6.12 Col Southern Illinois

YEAR	TM LG	W	L	PCT	G	GS	CG-SHO	SV-BS	IP	H	R	HR	HB	BB-IB	SO	ERA	AERA	OAV	OOB	AB-HR-SH	AVG	PB	SUP	APR	DL	PW
1970	SF N	5	5	.500	18	15	1	0	87	92	48	13	4	48-2	56	4.66	85	.274	.369	25-1-3	.080	-0	105	-5		-0.5
1974	Chi A	3	3	.500	40	5	0	1-1	105.2	103	58	7	7	55-4	68	4.43	85	.257	.353	0	—	0	113	-7		-0.5
1975	Chi A	0	0	—	1	0	0	0	0	0	0	0	0	0	0		—	1.000	1.000	0	—	0	0	0		0.0
Total 3		8	8	.500	59	20	1	1-1	192.2	196	106	20	11	103-6	124	4.53	85	.266	.361	25-1-3	.080	-0	108	-12		-1.0

PITTINGER, TOGIE Charles Reno B1.12.1872 Greencastle PA D1.14.1909 Greencastle PA BL/TR/6-2/175 d4.26

YEAR	TM LG	W	L	PCT	G	GS	CG-SHO	SV-BS	IP	H	R	HR	HB	BB-IB	SO	ERA	AERA	OAV	OOB	AB-HR-SH	AVG	PB	SUP	APR	DL	PW
1900	Bos N	2	9	.182	18	13	8	0	114	135	97	7	8	54	27	5.13	80	.293	.377	46	.130	-4	88	-12		-1.4
1901	Bos N	13	16	.448	34	33	27-1	0	281.1	288	135	7	8	76	129	3.01	120	.263	.316	100-0-2	.110	-8	65	15		0.7
1902	Bos N	27	16	.628	46	40	36-7	0	389.1	360	139	4	16	128	174	2.52	112	.245	.313	147-0-4	.136	-8	100	18		0.9
1903	Bos N	18	22	.450	44	39	35-3	1	351.2	396	205	12	17	143	140	3.48	92	.294	.329	128-1-3	.109	-9	76	-10		-1.9
1904	Bos N	15	21	.417	38	37	35-5	0	335.1	298	149	1	14	144	146	2.66	104	.242	.329	121-0-3	.107	-9	74	2		-0.5
1905	Phi N	23	14	.622	46	37	29-4	2	337.1	311	155	3	16	104	136	3.09	94	.247	.313	122-0-12	.156	-3	126	-5		-1.0
1906	Phi N	8	10	.444	20	16	9-2	0	129.2	128	62	2	12	50	43	3.40	77	.252	.334	44-0-1	.091	-1	92	-8		-1.3
1907	Phi N	9	5	.643	16	12	8-1	0	102	101	43	3	5	35	37	3.00	81	.261	.330	36	.139	-1	105	-6		-0.9
Total 8		115	113	.504	262	227	187-23	3	2040.2	2017	985	39	96	734	832	3.10	98	.260	.332	744-1-25	.124	-43	89	-6		-5.4

PITTSLEY, JIM James Michael B4.3.1974 DuBois PA BR/TR/6-7/215(215-230) [KCA92 1/17] d5.23 [DL 1996 KC A 96]

YEAR	TM LG	W	L	PCT	G	GS	CG-SHO	SV-BS	IP	H	R	HR	HB	BB-IB	SO	ERA	AERA	OAV	OOB	AB-HR-SH	AVG	PB	SUP	APR	DL	PW
1995	KC A	0	0	—	1	1	0	0-0	3.1	7	5	3	0	1-0	0	13.50	36	.438	.471	0	—	0	116	-9	46	-0.1
1997	KC A	5	8	.385	21	21	0	0-0	112	120	72	15	6	54-1	52	5.46	87	.277	.361	2	.500	1	92	-8		-0.8
1998	KC A	1	1	.500	39	2	0	0-0	68.1	88	56	13	2	37-1	44	6.59	74	.322	.361	2-0-1	.000	-0	38	-13		-0.6
1999	KC A	1	2	.333	5	5	0	0-0	23.1	33	22	2	1	15-0	7	6.94	73	.337	.426	0	—	0	95	-6		-0.6
	Mil N	0	1	.000	15	0	0	0-1	18.2	20	12	3	1	10-0	13	4.82	95	.274	.365	1	.000	0		-1		0.0
Total 4		7	12	.368	81	29	0	0-1	225.2	268	167	36	10	117-2	116	6.02	80	.300	.382	5-0-1	.200	1	90	-31	142	-2.1

PITULA, STAN Stanley B3.23.1931 Hackensack NJ D8.15.1965 Hackensack NJ BR/TR/5-10/170 d4.24

YEAR	TM LG	W	L	PCT	G	GS	CG-SHO	SV-BS	IP	H	R	HR	HB	BB-IB	SO	ERA	AERA	OAV	OOB	AB-HR-SH	AVG	PB	SUP	APR	DL	PW
1957	Cle A	2	2	.500	23	5	1	0	59.2	67	37	8	2	32-4	17	4.98	75	.296	.384	15	.200	0*	130	-8	36	-0.5

PIZARRO, JUAN Juan Ramon (Cordova) B2.7.1937 Santurce, PR BL/TL/5-11/190(170-197) d5.4

YEAR	TM LG	W	L	PCT	G	GS	CG-SHO	SV-BS	IP	H	R	HR	HB	BB-IB	SO	ERA	AERA	OAV	OOB	AB-HR-SH	AVG	PB	SUP	APR	DL	PW
1957	†Mil N	5	6	.455	24	10	3	0	99.1	99	58	16	1	51-2	68	4.62	76	.261	.348	36-1-0	.250	3*	101	-14		-1.1
1958	†Mil N	6	4	.600	16	10	7-1	1	96.2	75	36	12	4	47-0	84	2.70	130	.212	.311	32	.250	3	107	8		1.1
1959	Mil N	6	2	.750	29	14	6-2	0	133.2	117	61	13	8	70-3	126	3.77	94	.237	.340	41-0-2	.122	-0	133	-2		-0.1
1960	Mil N	6	7	.462	21	17	3	0	114.2	105	63	13	4	72-1	126	4.55	75	.244	.354	40-0-1	.275	3*	123	-14		-1.2
1961	Chi A	14	7	.667	39	25	12-1	2	194.2	164	73	17	4	89-1	188	3.05	128	.226	.312	69-0-1	.246	5*	110	19		2.5
1962	Chi A	12	14	.462	36	32	9-1	1	203.1	182	97	16	1	97-3	173	3.81	103	.236	.320	69-0-3	.159	-0	94	1		0.0
1963	Chi A★	16	8	.667	32	28	10-3	1	214.2	177	69	14	3	63-1	163	2.39	147	.224	.282	73-2-3	.178	3	110	25		3.0
1964	Chi A☆	19	9	.679	33	33	11-4	0	239	193	78	24	3	55-5	162	2.56	135	.219	.267	90-3-2	.211	5	105	24		3.3
1965	Chi A	6	3	.667	18	18	2-1	0	97	96	42	9	1	37-3	65	3.43	93	.254	.321	34-1-1	.235	3*	119	-3	31	0.1
1966	Chi A	8	6	.571	34	9	1	3	88.2	91	49	9	1	39-7	42	3.76	84	.269	.346	26-0-3	.154	0	120	-9		-1.3
1967	Pit N	8	10	.444	50	9	1-1	9	107	99	55	10	2	52-15	96	3.95	85	.245	.332	27	.259	2	67	-8		-1.2
1968	Pit N	1	1	.500	12	0	0	0	11	14	7	2	1	10-2	6	3.27	89	.311	.439	2	.000	-0*		-1		-0.3
	Bos A	6	8	.429	19	12	6	2	107.2	97	46	9	4	44-4	84	3.59	88	.242	.315	31-0-4	.161	1*	97	-4		-0.3
1969	Bos A	0	1	.000	9	1	0	0	9	14	7	2	0	6-0	6	6.00	64	.359	.444	3	.333	0		-2		-0.3
	Cle A	3	3	.500	48	4	1	4-3	82.2	67	34	6	2	49-7	44	3.16	120	.229	.335	15-0-1	.200	0	122	5		0.5
	Oak A	1	1	.500	3	0	0	1-0	7.2	3	2	1	0	3-0	1	2.35	147	.125	.214	2	.500	0		1		0.3
	Year	4	5	.444	57	4	1	7-3	99.1	84	43	9	2	58-7	52	3.35	113	.236	.339	20-0-1	.250	1	123	4		0.5
1970	Chi N	0	0	—	12	0	0	1-0	15.2	16	9	2	1	9-0	8	4.60	98	.262	.366	3	.000	-0		0		0.0
1971	Chi N	7	6	.538	16	14	6-3	0	101.1	78	43	10	2	40-3	67	3.46	114	.209	.288	34-1-2	.176	1	80	5		0.7
1972	Chi N	5	4	.444	16	7	1	1	59.1	66	28	7	1	32-5	24	3.94	97	.293	.384	21	.143	-0	63	0		0.0
1973	Chi N	0	1	.000	2	0	0	0-1	4	4	5	1	0	1-0	3	11.25	35	.353	.400	1	.000	-0		-3	21	-0.5
	Hou N	2	2	.500	15	1	0	0-0	23.1	28	17	1	1	11-3	10	6.56	56	.301	.381	3-0-1	.000	-0	73	-7		-1.0
	Year	2	3	.400	17	1	0	0-1	27.1	34	22	2	1	12-3	13	7.24	51	.309	.384	4-0-1	.000	-0	72	-9		-1.5
1974	†Pit N	1	1	.500	7	2	0	0	24	20	11	2	0	11-2	17	1.88	186	.220	.298	6	.333	-0	163	2		0.2
Total 18		131	105	.555	488	245	79-17	28-4	2034.1	1807	890	201	41	888-67	1522	3.43	104	.237	.319	658-8-24	.202	29	105	23	52	4.4

PLADSON, GORDIE Gordon Cecil B7.31.1956 New Westminster BC, Can. BR/TR/6-4/210* d9.7

YEAR	TM LG	W	L	PCT	G	GS	CG-SHO	SV-BS	IP	H	R	HR	HB	BB-IB	SO	ERA	AERA	OAV	OOB	AB-HR-SH	AVG	PB	SUP	APR	DL	PW
1979	Hou N	0	4		6	0	0	0-0	9	12	9	2	0	2-0	2	4.50	78	.450	.500	0	—	0				0.0
1980	Hou N	0	4	.000	12	6	0	0-0	41.1	38	23	3	0	16-0	13	4.35	75	.244	.312	10	.000	-1	86	-5		-0.6

YEAR	TM LG	W	L	PCT	G	GS	CG-SHO	SV-BS	IP	H	R	HR	HB	BB-IB	SO	ERA	AERA	OAV	OOB	AB-HR-SH	AVG	PB	SUP	APR	DL	PW
1981	Hou N	0	0	—	2	0	0	0-0	4	9	4	0	0	3-0	3	9.00	36	.429	.500	0	—	0		-2		-0.1
1982	Hou N	0	0	—	2	0	0	0-0	1.1	10	8	0	0	2-0	0	54.00	6	.769	.750	0	—	0		-8		-0.4
Total	4	0	4	.000	20	6	0	0-0	50.2	66	37	4	0	23-0	18	6.04	55	.314	.379	10	.000	-1	86	-15		-1.1

PLANETA, EMIL Emil Joseph B1.31.1909 Higganum CT D2.2.1963 Rocky Hill CT BR/TR/6-0/190 d9.20

1931	NY N	0	0	—	2	0	0	0-0	5.1	7	7	0	0	4	0	10.13	36	.292	.393	1	.000	-0		-4		-0.2

PLANK, ED Edward Arthur B4.9.1952 Chicago IL BR/TR/6-1/195* [SFN73 10/222] d9.6 Col Nevada-Reno

1978	SF N	0	0	—	5	0	0	0-0	6.2	9	6	0	0	2-1	1	4.05	86	.273	.320	0	—	0		0		0.0
1979	SF N	0	0	—	4	0	0	0-0	3.2	9	5	0	0	2-1	1	7.36	47	.450	.500	0	—	0		-2		-0.1
Total	2	0	0	—	9	0	0	0-0	10.1	15	8	1	0	4-2	2	5.23	67	.357	.404	0	—	0		-2		-0.1

PLANK, EDDIE Edward Stewart "Gettysburg Eddie" B8.31.1875 Gettysburg PA D2.24.1926 Gettysburg PA BL/TL/5-11.5/175 d5.13 HF1946 Col Gettysburg

1901	Phi A	17	13	.567	33	32	28-1	0	260.2	254	133	3	7	68	90	3.31	114	.252	.304	99-0-2	.182	-3	96	14		0.9
1902	Phi A	20	15	.571	36	32	31-1	0	300	319	140	5	18	61	107	3.30	111	.273	.319	120-0-4	.292	6	107	18		2.3
1903	Phi A	23	16	.590	43	40	33-3	0	336	317	128	5	23	65	176	2.38	128	.249	.297	134-1-2	.187	-1*	100	20		2.0
1904	Phi A	26	17	.605	44	43	37-7	0	357.1	311	111	2	19	86	201	2.17	124	.235	.292	129-0-6	.240	3*	93	23		3.2
1905	†Phi A	24	12	.667	41	41	35-4	0	346.2	287	113	3	24	75	210	2.26	118	.227	.283	126-0-2	.230	3	108	20		2.2
1906	Phi A	19	6	.760	26	25	21-5	0	211.2	173	70	1	15	51	108	2.25	121	.226	.288	73-0-5	.233	2	126	13		1.6
1907	Phi A	24	16	.600	43	40	33-8	0	343.2	282	115	5	17	85	183	2.20	118	.226	.285	123-1-8	.211	2	84	17		2.2
1908	Phi A	14	16	.467	34	28	21-4	1	244.2	202	71	1	9	46	135	2.17	118	.224	.269	89-0-1	.180	-1*	80	14		1.4
1909	Phi A	19	10	.655	34	33	24-3	0	265.1	215	74	1	8	62	132	1.76	136	.224	.277	96-1-2	.219	4*	111	19		2.6
1910	Phi A	16	10	.615	38	32	22-1	2	250.1	218	89	3	8	85	123	2.01	118	.237	.286	86-0-2	.128	-3	138	10		0.6
1911	†Phi A	23	8	.742	40	30	24-6	4	256.2	237	85	2	14	77	149	2.10	150	.255	.322	94-0-6	.191	-1	121	29		3.2
1912	Phi A	26	6	.813	37	30	23-5	2	259.2	234	90	1	6	83	110	2.22	139	.245	.306	90-0-11	.267	4	132	25		3.2
1913	†Phi A	18	10	.643	41	30	18-7	4	242.2	211	87	3	5	57	151	2.60	106	.243	.293	76-0-6	.105	-0	145	4		0.4
1914	†Phi A	15	7	.682	34	22	12-4	3	185.1	178	68	2	6	42	110	2.87	91	.266	.315	60-0-7	.150	0	142	-4		-0.6
1915	StL F	21	11	.656	42	31	23-6	3	268.1	212	75	1	3	54	147	2.08	138	.218	.262	93-0-4	.258	3	101	23		3.0
1916	StL A	16	15	.516	37	26	17-3	3	235.2	203	78	2	4	67	88	2.33	118	.237	.297	81-0-4	.185	-1	121	12		1.4
1917	StL A	5	6	.455	20	14	8-1	1	131	105	39	2	2	38	26	1.79	145	.225	.287	38-0-4	.105	-1	83	11		0.7
Total	17	326	194	.627	623	529	410-69	23	4495.2	3958	1566	42	190	1072	2246	2.35	122	.239	.293	1607-3-76	.206	17	109	268		30.3

PLANTENBERG, ERIK Erik John B10.30.1968 Renton WA BB/TL/6-1/180* [BosA90 16/443] d7.31 Col San Diego St.

1993	Sea A	0	0	—	20	0	0	1-0	9.2	11	7	0	1	12-1	3	6.52	69	.282	.462	0	—	0		-2		-0.1
1994	Sea A	0	0	—	6	0	0	0-0	7	4	0	0	1	7-0	1	0.00	—	.174	.387	0	—	0		4		0.2
1997	Phi N	0	0	—	35	0	0	0-0	25.2	25	14	1	1	12-0	12	4.91	86	.255	.339	0	—	0		-1		-0.1
Total	3	0	0	—	61	0	0	1-0	42.1	40	21	1	3	31-1	16	4.46	98	.250	.379	0	—	0		1		0.0

PLEIS, BILL William B8.5.1937 St.Louis MO BL/TL/5-10/175* d4.16

1961	Min A	4	2	.667	37	0	-0	2	56.1	59	35	4	4	34-5	32	4.95	86	.266	.370	9	.111	-1		-4		-0.5
1962	Min A	2	5	.286	21	4	0	3	45	46	27	7	1	14-2	31	4.40	93	.264	.319	14	.286	1	66	-2		-0.3
1963	Min A	6	2	.750	36	4	1	0	68	67	37	10	0	16-2	37	4.37	83	.258	.297	16-0-1	.125	0	165	-5		-0.6
1964	Min A	4	1	.800	47	0	0	4	50.2	43	23	6	1	31-3	42	3.91	92	.232	.342	4-0-1	.250	0		-1		0.0
1965	†Min A	4	4	.500	41	2	0	4	51.1	49	20	3	0	27-5	33	2.98	119	.250	.336	7-0-1	.000	-1	25	3		0.4
1966	Min A	1	2	.333	8	0	0	0	9.1	5	6	1	0	5-6	9	1.93	186	.152	.243	0	—	0		0		0.0
Total	6	21	16	.568	190	10	1	13	280.2	269	148	31	6	126-17	184	4.07	93	.251	.330	50-0-3	.160	0	96	-9		-1.0

PLESAC, DAN Daniel Thomas B2.4.1962 Gary IN BL/TL/6-5/215* [MilA83 1/26] d4.11 Col North Carolina St.

1986	Mil A	10	7	.588	51	0	0	14-4	91	81	34	6	0	29-1	75	2.97	147	.240	.296	0	—	0		14		2.7
1987	Mil A★	5	6	.455	57	0	0	23-13	79.1	63	30	8	3	23-1	89	2.61	177	.213	.275	0	—	0		15		2.7
1988	Mil A★	1	2	.333	50	0	0	30-5	52.1	46	14	2	0	12-2	52	2.41	166	.234	.278	0	—	0		10		1.6
1989	Mil A★	3	4	.429	52	0	0	33-7	61.1	47	16	6	0	17-1	52	2.35	164	.213	.264	0	—	0		11		2.3
1990	Mil A	3	7	.300	66	0	0	24-10	69	67	36	5	3	31-6	65	4.43	88	.257	.340	0	—	0		-3		-0.4
1991	Mil A	2	7	.222	45	10	0	8-4	92.1	92	49	12	3	39-1	61	4.29	93	.263	.336	0	—	0	121	-3		-0.4
1992	Mil A	5	4	.556	44	4	0	1-2	79	64	28	5	3	35-5	54	2.96	131	.229	.317	0	—	0	124	8		0.9
1993	Chi N	2	1	.667	57	0	0	0-2	62.2	74	37	10	0	21-6	47	4.74	85	.298	.349	1	.000	-0		-5		-0.3
1994	Chi N	2	3	.400	54	0	0	1-2	54.2	61	30	9	1	13-0	53	4.61	92	.279	.321	4	.000	-0		-2		-0.3
1995	Pit N	4	4	.500	58	0	0	3-2	60.1	53	26	3	1	27-7	57	3.58	122	.237	.318	4	.250	0		5		0.7
1996	Pit N	6	5	.545	73	0	0	11-6	70.1	67	35	4	0	24-6	76	4.09	107	.247	.305	5	.000	-1		2		0.3
1997	Tor A	2	4	.333	73	0	0	1-4	50.1	47	22	8	0	19-4	61	3.58	128	.244	.310	0	—	0		6		0.6
1998	Tor A	4	3	.571	78	0	0	4-1	50	41	23	4	1	16-1	55	3.78	123	.224	.286	0	—	0		5		0.6
1999	Tor A	0	3	.000	30	0	0	0-2	22.2	28	21	4	0	9-1	26	8.34	59	.308	.366	0	—	0		-8		-0.8
	†Ari N	2	1	.667	34	0	0	1-0	21.2	22	9	3	0	8-1	27	3.32	139	.259	.323	1	.000	-0		3		0.4
2000	Ari N	5	1	.833	62	0	0	0-4	40	34	21	4	0	26-2	45	3.15	152	.228	.341	0	—	0		6		1.0
2001	Tor A	4	5	.444	62	0	0	1-1	45.1	34	18	4	0	24-5	68	3.57	128	.207	.311	0	—	0		5		0.6
2002	Tor A	1	2	.333	19	0	0	0-1	13.1	15	5	1	0	6-0	14	3.38	137	.216	.293	0	—	0		-2		-0.2
	Phi N	2	1	.667	41	0	0	1-2	23	16	12	5	0	12-3	27	4.70	82	.190	.292	0	—	0		4		0.4
2003	Phi N	2	1	.667	58	0	0	2-2	33.1	29	12	3	1	11-1	37	2.70	147	.228	.295	0	—	0		4		0.4
Total	18	65	71	.478	1064	14	0	158-74	1072	977	478	105	17	402-54	1041	3.64	117	.242	.311	15	.067	-1	114	72		12.5

PLITT, NORMAN Norman William B2.21.1893 York PA D2.1.1954 New York NY BR/TR/5-11/180 d4.26

1918	Bro N	0	0	—	1	0	0	0	2	3	1	0	0	1	0	4.50	62	.429	.500	1	1.000	-0		0		0.0
1927	Bro N	2	6	.250	19	8	1	0	62.1	73	40	3	1	36	9	4.91	81	.303	.396	18-0-2	.222	-0	75	-6		0.1
	NY N	1	0	1.000	3	0	0	0	7.1	9	3	0	1	1	0	3.68	105	.310	.355	1	.000	-0		0		0.1
	Year	3	6	.333	22	8	1	0	69.2	82	43	3	2	37	9	4.78	83	.304	.392	19-0-2	.211	-0	75	-6		-0.6
Total	2	3	6	.333	23	8	1	0	71.2	85	44	3	2	38	9	4.77	82	.307	.394	20-0-2	.250	-0	76	-6		-0.6

PLODINEC, TIM Timothy Alfred B1.27.1947 Aliquippa PA BR/TR/6-4/190 [StLN68 33/738] d6.2 Col Arizona

1972	StL N	0	0	—	2	0	0	0-0	0.1	3	1	0	0	0-0	0	27.00	13	.750	.750	0	—	0		-1		0.0

PLUNK, ERIC Eric Vaughn B9.3.1963 Wilmington CA BR/TR/6-5/217(210-224) [NYA81 4/103] d5.12

1986	Oak A	4	7	.364	26	15	0	0-0	120.1	91	75	14	5	102-2	98	5.31	73	.214	.370	0	—	0	95	-19		-1.6
1987	Oak A	4	6	.400	32	11	0	2-3	95	91	53	8	2	62-3	90	4.74	88	.253	.361	0	—	0	94	-5		-0.5
1988	†Oak A	7	2	.778	49	0	0	5-4	78	62	27	6	1	39-4	79	3.00	127	.217	.311	0	—	0		8	15	0.9
1989	Oak A	1	1	.500	23	0	0	1-2	28.2	17	7	1	1	12-0	24	2.20	168	.172	.268	0	—	0		5		0.4
	NY A	7	5	.583	27	7	0	0-0	75.2	65	36	9	0	52-2	61	3.69	106	.237	.355	0	—	0	116	1		0.1
	Year	8	6	.571	50	7	0	1-2	104.1	82	43	10	1	64-2	85	3.28	117	.220	.333	0	—	0	118	6		0.5
1990	NY A	6	3	.667	47	0	0	0-1	72.2	58	27	6	2	43-4	67	2.72	147	.225	.340	0	—	0		9		-0.6
1991	NY A	2	5	.286	43	8	0	0-0	111.2	128	69	18	0	62-1	103	4.76	86	.286	.371	0	—	0	69	-9		-0.8
1992	Cle A	9	6	.600	58	0	0	4-4	71.2	61	31	5	0	38-2	50	3.64	108	.229	.324	0	—	0		10		1.5
1993	Cle A	4	5	.444	70	0	0	15-3	71	61	29	5	0	30-4	77	2.79	157	.226	.301	0	—	0		17		1.9
1994	Cle A	7	2	.778	41	0	0	3-4	71	61	25	3	2	37-5	73	2.54	188	.231	.329	0	—	0		15		1.9
1995	†Cle A	6	2	.750	56	0	0	2-3	64	48	19	5	4	27-2	71	2.67	177	.211	.303	0	—	0		23		1.3
1996	†Cle A	3	2	.600	56	0	0	2-1	77.2	65	21	6	3	34-2	85	2.43	201	.203	.293	0	—	0		0		0.0
1997	†Cle A	4	5	.444	55	0	0	0-2	65.2	62	37	12	1	36-7	66	4.66	101	.245	.339	0	.000	-0*		2		0.0
1998	Cle A	3	1	.750	30	0	0	0-3	41	44	23	6	2	15-1	38	4.83	99	.282	.349	0	.000	-0		2		-0.3
	Mil N	1	2	.333	26	0	0	1-2	31.2	33	14	3	3	15-1	36	3.69	117	.270	.359	0	—	0		-3		-0.3
1999	Mil N	4	4	.500	68	0	0	0-3	75.1	71	44	15	5	43-5	81	5.02	92	.251	.357	0	.000	-0		0	15	-0.4
Total	14	72	58	.554	714	41	0	35-35	1151	1009	512	122	32	647-45	1081	3.82	112	.236	.339	0	.000	0	88	57	15	4.4

PLYMPTON, JEFF Jeffrey Hunter B11.24.1965 Framingham MA BR/TR/6-2/205 [BosA87 10/266] d6.15 Col Maine

1991	Bos A	0	0	—	4	0	0	0-0	5.1	5	0	0	0	4-0	1	0.00	—	.263	.375	0	—	0		2		0.1

POAT, RAY Raymond Willis B12.19.1917 Chicago IL D4.29.1990 Oak Lawn IL BR/TR/6-2/200 d4.15 Def 1945 Col Illinois

1942	Cle A	1	3	.250	4	4	1-1	0	18.1	24	11	1	9	9	5.40	64	.296	.374	5	.000	-0	93	-3		-0.6
1943	Cle A	2	5	.286	17	4	1	0	45	44	22	0	4	20	31	4.40	71	.259	.337	13	.154	-1	108	-5		-0.8
1944	Cle A	4	8	.333	36	6	1	1	80.2	82	50	9	0	44	40	5.13	64	.265	.343	17-0-2	.000	-2	105	-15		-2.3

YEAR	TM LG	W	L	PCT	G	GS	CG-SHO	SV-BS	IP	H	R	HR	HB	BB-IB	SO	ERA	AERA	OAV	OOB	AB-HR-SH	AVG	PB	SUP	APR	DL	PW
1947	NY N	4	3	.571	7	7	5	0	60	53	18	8	0	13	25	2.55	160	.238	.280	21-1-1	.190	2	99	11		1.4
1948	NY N	11	10	.524	39	24	7-3	0	157.2	162	95	21	8	67	57	4.34	91	.262	.337	56-0-1	.125	-1	146	-10		-1.3
1949	NY N	0	0	—	2	0	0	0	2.1	8	6	0	0	1	0	19.29	21	.615	.643	0	—	0		-4		-0.2
	Pit N	0	1	.000	11	2	0	0	36	52	29	6	0	15	17	6.25	67	.335	.394	10	.100	-1	52	-8		-0.5
	Year	0	1	.000	13	2	0	0	38.1	60	35	6	0	16	17	7.04	59	.357	.413	10	.100	-1	53	-11		-0.7
Total	6	22	30	.423	116	47	15-4	0	400	425	231	48	4	162	178	4.55	82	.271	.340	122-1-4	.115	-3	124	-34		-4.3

PODBIELAN, BUD Clarence Anthony B3.6.1924 Curlew WA D10.26.1982 Syracuse NY BR/TR/6-1.5/170* d4.25

1949	Bro N	0	1	.000	7	1	0	0	12.1	9	9	1	1	9	5	3.65	112	.205	.352	3	.000	-0	107	-1		-0.1
1950	Bro N	5	4	.556	20	10	2	1	72.2	93	47	10	2	29	28	5.33	77	.307	.371	28-0-2	.107	-1	131	-10		-1.2
1951	Bro N	2	2	.500	27	5	1	0	79.2	67	32	9	2	36	26	3.50	112	.233	.322	23	.304	-1	103	5		0.4
1952	Bro N	0	0	—	3	0	0	0	2	4	5	1	0	3	1	18.00	20	.444	.583	0	—	0*		-4		-0.2
	Cin N	4	5	.444	24	7	4-1	1	86.2	78	30	8	1	26	22	2.80	135	.245	.304	25	.160	-0	64	9		0.9
	Year	4	5	.444	27	7	4-1	1	88.2	82	35	9	1	29	23	3.15	120	.251	.314	25	.160	-0	64	7		0.7
1953	Cin N	6	16	.273	36	24	8-1	1	186.1	214	112	21	8	67	74	4.73	92	.290	.356	56-0-3	.125	-3	85	-9		-1.2
1954	Cin N	7	10	.412	27	24	4	0	131	157	92	20	2	58	42	5.36	78	.300	.370	42-0-3	.143	-1	105	-19		-2.2
1955	Cin N	1	2	.333	17	2	0	0	42	36	16	4	1	11-0	26	3.21	132	.234	.284	5-0-1	.400	-1	42	5	34	0.4
1957	Cin N	0	1	.000	5	3	1	0	16	18	11	4	0	4-0	13	6.19	66	.290	.333	5	.000	-1	114	-3		-0.3
1959	Cle A	0	1	.000	6	0	0	0	12.1	17	8	1	0	2-0	5	5.84	63	.354	.380	1	.000	-0		-3		-0.2
Total	9	25	42	.373	172	76	20-2	3	641	693	362	79	17	245-0	242	4.49	92	.279	.347	188-0-9	.154	-4	98	-30	34	-3.7

PODGAJNY, JOHNNY John Sigmund "Specs" B6.10.1920 Chester PA D3.2.1971 Chester PA BR/TR/6-2/173 d9.15

1940	Phi N	1	3	.250	4	4	3	0	35	33	14	0	1	.1	12	2.83	138	.250	.261	12	.167	-0	45	3		0.4
1941	Phi N	9	12	.429	34	24	8	0	181.1	191	96	8	4	70	53	4.62	80	.270	.339	62-0-3	.129	-3*	88	-13		-1.6
1942	Phi N	6	14	.300	43	23	6	0	186.2	191	95	9	11	63	40	3.91	85	.268	.337	60-0-2	.183	-0*	84	-13		-1.4
1943	Phi N	4	4	.500	13	5	3	0	64	77	32	4	0	16	13	4.22	80	.310	.352	20-0-1	.250	1	116	-5		-0.4
	Pit N	0	4	.000	15	5	0	0	34.1	37	28	1	0	13	7	4.72	74	.266	.329	7	.143	-0*	73	-7		-0.7
	Year	4	8	.333	28	10	3	0	98.1	114	60	5	0	29	20	4.39	78	.295	.344	27-0-1	.222	1	95	-12		-1.1
1946	Cle A	0	0	—	6	0	0	0	9	13	8	0	2	4	5.00	66	.302	.333	0	—	0		-3		-0.1
Total	5	20	37	.351	115	61	20	0	510.1	542	273	22	16	165	129	4.20	84	.273	.334	161-0-6	.168	-3	85	-38		-3.8

PODRES, JOHNNY John Joseph B9.30.1932 Witherbee NY BL/TL/5-11/192(170-192) d4.17 Mil 1956 C13

1953	†Bro N	9	4	.692	33	18	3-1	0	115	126	62	12	1	64	82	4.23	101	.282	.373	36-0-1	.306	2*	120	-1		0.1
1954	Bro N	11	7	.611	29	21	6-2	0	151.2	147	77	13	1	53	79	4.27	96	.255	.317	60-0-3	.283	5*	116	-2	30	0.2
1955	†Bro N	9	10	.474	27	24	5-2	0	159.1	160	80	15	4	57-2	114	3.95	103	.259	.325	60-0-4	.183	-0*	126	2		0.1
1957	Bro N	12	9	.571	31	27	10-**6**	0	196	168	64	15	1	44-1	109	**2.66**	**156**	.230	**.273**	72-0-3	.208	1*	95	31		3.4
1958	LA N☆	13	15	.464	39	31	10-2	1	210.1	208	96	27	4	78-8	143	3.72	110	.261	.326	71-0-4	.127	-3*	95	9		0.7
1959	†LA N	14	9	.609	34	29	6-2	0	195	192	.93	23	3	74-7	145	4.11	103	.261	.330	65-0-3	.246	3	98	5		1.0
1960	LA N★	14	12	.538	34	33	8-1	0	227.2	217	88	25	1	71-9	159	3.08	129	.250	.307	66-0-10	.136	-1	85	21		2.1
1961	LA N	18	5	**.783**	32	29	6-1	0	182.2	192	81	27	4	51-2	124	3.74	116	.271	.322	69-0-4	.232	1	111	13		1.5
1962	LA N★	15	13	.536	40	40	8	0	255	270	121	20	3	71-14	178	3.81	95	.272	.321	88-1-5	.159	1	110	-3		-0.4
1963	†LA N	14	12	.538	37	34	10-5	1	198.1	196	91	16	3	64-13	134	3.54	85	.257	.315	64-1-3	.141	1	115	-12		-1.4
1964	LA N	0	2	.000	2	2	0	0	2.2	5	5	1	0	3-1	0	16.88	19	.417	.533	0	—	0	54	-4	96	-0.7
1965	LA N	7	6	.538	27	22	2-1	0	134	126	57	17	2	39-4	63	3.43	95	.247	.301	45-0-1	.178	1	83	-2		-0.3
1966	LA N	0	0	—	1	0	0	0	1.2	2	0	0	0	1-1	1	0.00	—	.400	.429	0	—	0		1		0.0
1967	Det A	4	5	.444	36	13	2-1	4	107.2	106	48	12	1	34-3	53	3.43	102	.259	.313	30	.233	2	94	0		0.2
1968	Det A	3	1	.750	21	8	0	1	63.1	58	29	12	1	11-2	34	3.84	85	.244	.280	20	.100	-1	117	-4	22	0.4
1969	SD N	5	6	.455	17	9	1	0-1	64.2	66	34	7	1	28-3	17	4.31	83	.264	.337	16-0-2	.063	-1	88	-5		-0.3
Total	15	148	116	.561	440	340	77-24	11-1	2265	2239	1026	242	28	743-70	1435	3.68	105	.259	.318	762-2-43	.190	11	103	49	148	5.2

POETZ, JOE Joseph Frank "Bull Montana" B6.22.1900 St.Louis MO D2.7.1942 St.Louis MO BR/TR/5-10.5/175 d9.14

| 1926 | NY N | 0 | 1 | .000 | 2 | 1 | 0 | 0 | 3 | 8 | 13 | 0 | 0 | 5 | 1 | 3.38 | 111 | .192 | .400 | 1 | .000 | 0 | 44 | 1 | | 0.1 |

POFFENBERGER, BOOTS Cletus Elwood B7.1.1915 Williamsport MD D9.1.1999 Williamsport MD BR/TR/5-10/178 d6.11

1937	Det A	10	5	.667	29	16	5	3	137.1	147	83	8	4	79	35	4.65	100	.277	.375	51-0-2	.216	-0	144	-1		-0.1
1938	Det A	6	7	.462	25	15	8-1	1	125	147	74	8	2	66	28	4.82	104	.297	.382	44-0-1	.182	-1	80	2		0.0
1939	Bro N	0	0	—	3	1	0	0	5	7	3	1	0	4	2	5.40	75	.318	.423	1	.000	-0	130	-1		0.0
Total	3	16	12	.571	57	32	13-1	4	267.1	301	160	17	6	149	65	4.75	101	.287	.379	96-0-3	.198	-2	113	0		-0.1

POHOLSKY, TOM Thomas George B8.26.1929 Detroit MI D1.6.2001 Kirkwood MO BR/TR/6-3/205(190-205) d4.20 Mil 1952-53

1950	StL N	0	0	—	5	1	0	0	14.2	16	6	2	0	3	2	3.68	117	.281	.317	2	.000	-0	41	1		0.0
1951	StL N	7	13	.350	38	26	10-1	1	195	204	106	15	0	68	70	4.43	89	.271	.331	67-0-6	.209	0	125	-10		-0.8
1954	StL N	5	7	.417	25	13	4	0	106	101	43	11	4	20	55	3.06	135	.254	.293	27-0-6	.148	-1	120	11		1.1
1955	StL N	9	11	.450	30	24	8-2	0	151	143	71	26	2	35-4	66	3.81	106	.244	.289	44-0-5	.182	-0	91	3		0.3
1956	StL N	9	14	.391	33	29	7-2	0	203	210	100	27	5	44-7	95	3.59	105	.268	.309	69-0-3	.159	-1	88	1		0.0
1957	Chi N	1	7	.125	28	11	1	0	84	117	55	9	2	22-4	28	4.93	79	.330	.366	19-0-1	.105	-1	103	-11		-1.0
Total	6	31	52	.373	159	104	30-5	1	753.2	791	381	90	13	192-15	316	3.93	101	.270	.316	228-0-21	.171	-3	103	-5		-0.4

POINDEXTER, JENNINGS Chester Jennings "Jinx" B9.30.1910 Pauls Valley OK D3.3.1983 Norman OK BL/TL/5-10/165 d9.15

1936	Bos A	0	2	.000	3	3	0	0	10.2	13	11	0	0	16	2	6.75	79	.302	.492	4	.000	-1	44	-2		-0.4
1939	Phi N	0	0	—	11	1	0	0	30.1	29	19	0	0	15	12	4.15	96	.250	.336	10	.200	-0	153	-2		-0.1
Total	2	0	2	.000	14	4	0	0	41	42	30	0	0	31	14	4.83	90	.264	.384	14	.143	-1	76	-4		-0.5

POLCHOW, LOU Louis William B3.14.1881 Mankato MN D8.15.1912 Good Thunder MN 5-9/? d9.14

| 1902 | Cle A | 0 | 1 | .000 | 1 | 1 | 1 | 0 | 8 | 9 | 5 | 0 | 0 | 4 | 2 | 5.63 | 61 | .281 | .361 | 4 | .000 | -1 | 63 | -1 | | -0.2 |

POLE, DICK Richard Henry B10.13.1950 Trout Creek MI BR/TR/6-3/200(195-210) d8.3 C17

1973	Bos A	3	2	.600	12	7	0	0-0	54.2	70	35	4	0	18-0	24	5.60	72	.318	.370	0	—	0	155	-8		-0.7
1974	Bos A	1	1	.500	15	2	0	1-0	45	55	28	6	1	13-0	32	4.20	92	.304	.352	0	—	0	160	-4		-0.2
1975	†Bos A	4	6	.400	18	11	2-1	0-0	89.2	102	46	11	2	32-4	42	4.42	92	.290	.349	0	—	0	79	-2	62	-0.2
1976	Bos A	6	5	.545	31	15	1	0-0	120.2	131	62	8	2	48-3	49	4.33	90	.279	.346	1	.000	-0	83	-3		-0.4
1977	Sea A	7	12	.368	25	24	3	0-0	122.1	127	76	16	6	57-2	51	5.15	81	.270	.353	0	—	0	80	-13	26	-1.8
1978	Sea A	4	11	.267	18	12	2	0-1	98.2	122	76	16	3	41-3	41	6.48	59	.306	.371	0	—	0	103	-29		-3.8
Total	6	25	37	.403	122	77	8-1	1-1	531	607	329	61	14	209-12	239	5.00	79	.290	.356	1	.000	-0	94	-59	88	-7.1

POLITTE, CLIFF Clifford Anthony B2.27.1974 Kirkwood MO BR/TR/5-11/185(185-200) [StLN95 54/1439] d4.2 Col Jefferson (MO) CC

1998	StL N	2	3	.400	8	8	0	0-0	37	45	32	6	1	18-0	22	6.32	67	.302	.379	14-0-1	.071	-1	117	-10		-1.2
1999	Phi N	1	0	1.000	13	0	0	0-0	17.2	19	14	2	0	15-0	15	7.13	65	.275	.405	0		-2		-4		-0.2
2000	Phi N	4	3	.571	12	8	0	0-0	59	55	24	8	0	27-1	50	3.66	125	.248	.328	15-0-2	.133	-0	83	7		0.8
2001	Phi N	2	3	.400	23	0	0	0-0	26	24	8	2	1	8-3	23	2.42	170	.250	.306	2	.000	0		5	96	0.9
2002	Phi N	2	0	1.000	13	0	0	0-1	16.1	19	10	0	1	9-1	15	3.86	90	.288	.382	1	.000	0		-1		-0.2
	Tor A	1	3	.250	55	0	0	1-2	57.1	38	23	5	1	19-1	57	3.61	128	.186	.258	0	—	-1		7		0.4
2003	Tor A	1	5	.167	54	0	0	12-6	49.1	52	32	11	1	17-4	40	5.66	84	.268	.326	0	—	0		-4	26	-0.6
2004	Chi A	3	0	1.000	54	0	0	1-0	51.1	52	26	6	2	21-3	48	4.38	107	.261	.348	0	—	0		2		0.1
2005	†Chi A	7	1	.875	68	0	0	1-1	67.1	42	15	7	3	21-4	57	2.00	226	.181	.254	1	1.000	0		19		2.0
Total	8	20	21	.488	300	16	0	15-10	381.1	346	184	47	10	156-19	327	4.06	111	.242	.318	33-0-3	.121	-0	97	21	122	2.0

POLIVKA, KEN Kenneth Lyle "Soup" B1.21.1921 Chicago IL D7.23.1988 Aurora IL BL/TL/5-10.5/175 d4.18

| 1947 | Cin N | 0 | 0 | — | 2 | 0 | 0 | 0 | 3 | 3 | 1 | 0 | 0 | 3 | 1 | 3.00 | 137 | .250 | .400 | 0 | | 0 | | -0 | | 0.0 |

POLLET, HOWIE Howard Joseph B6.26.1921 New Orleans LA D8.8.1974 Houston TX BL/TL/6-1.5/175* d8.20 Mil 1944-45 C7

1941	StL N	5	2	.714	9	8	6-2	0	70	55	18	1	1	27	37	1.93	195	.212	.289	28-0-1	.179	-0	107	14		1.4
1942	†StL N	7	5	.583	24	13	5-2	0	109.1	102	43	7	2	39	42	2.88	194	.249	.309	31-0-2	.226	3	123	6		0.9
1943	StL N*	8	4	.667	16	14	12-5	0	118.1	83	26	2	2	32	61	1.75	192	.200	.261	43-0-1	.163	-1	92	3		2.1
1946	†StL N☆	**21**	10	.677	40	32	22-4	5	**266**	228	84	12	5	86	107	2.10	165	.234	.300	87-0-7	.161	-0	99	**35**		4.3
1947	StL N	9	11	.450	34	24	9	2	176.1	195	96	11	3	87	73	4.34	95	.286	.369	65	.231	-2	103	-3		-0.1
1948	StL N	13	8	.619	36	26	11	0	186.1	216	102	10	2	67	80	4.54	90	.289	.349	68-0-5	.118	-3*	123	-9		-1.1

YEAR	TM LG	W	L	PCT	G	GS	CG-SHO	SV-BS	IP	H	R	HR	HB	BB-IB	SO	ERA	AERA	OAV	OOB	AB-HR-SH	AVG	PB	SUP	APR	DL	PW
1949	StL N★	20	9	.690	39	28	17-**5**	1	230.2	228	80	9	2	59	108	2.77	150	.256	.304	82-0-3	.195	1	100	**35**		**4.2**
1950	StL N	14	13	.519	37	30	14-2	2	232.1	228	103	19	1	68	117	3.29	130	.256	.310	84-0-2	.143	-2*	96	22		2.1
1951	StL N	0	3	.000	6	2	0	1	12.1	10	10	1	0	8	10	4.38	91	.208	.321	1	.000	1	111	-2		-0.3
	Pit N	6	10	.375	21	21	4-1	0	128.2	149	81	24	1	51	47	5.04	84	.294	.360	36-0-4	.139	0	86	-10		-1.1
	Year	6	13	.316	27	23	4-1	0	141	159	91	25	1	59	57	4.98	84	.287	.357	37-0-4	.135	1	88	-11		-1.4
1952	Pit N	7	16	.304	31	30	9-1	0	214	217	111	22	3	71	90	4.12	97	.266	.322	68-0-2	.191	2	70	-3		0.0
1953	Pit N	1	1	.500	5	2	0	0	12.2	27	15	2	0	6	8	10.66	42	.482	.532	3-0-1	.333	-2	200	-8		-0.9
	Chi N	5	6	.455	25	17	2	1	111.1	120	62	6	1	44	45	4.12	108	.271	.338	31-0-3	.129	-1	78	3		0.1
	Year	6	7	.462	30	19	2	1	124	147	77	8	1	50	53	4.79	93	.295	.360	34-0-4	.147	-1	91	-7		-0.8
1954	Chi N	8	10	.444	20	20	4-2	0	128.1	131	60	4	0	54	58	3.58	117	.263	.332	47-0-3	.277	2	94	7		1.2
1955	Chi N	4	3	.571	24	7	1-1	5	61	62	41	11	0	27-3	27	5.61	73	.265	.337	15-0-1	.400	3	112	-10		-0.8
1956	Chi A	3	1	.750	11	4	0	0	26.1	27	15	2	0	11-0	14	4.10	100	.252	.322	8-0-1	.375	1*	174	-1		0.0
	Pit N	0	4	.000	19	0	0	3	23.1	18	10	3	0	8-1	10	3.09	122	.212	.277	1-0-1	.000	0		1		0.3
Total	14	131	116	.530	403	278	116-25	20	2107.1	2096	957	146	23	745-4	934	3.51	113	.260	.324	698-0-37	.185	7	99	99		12.3

POLLEY, DALE Ezra Dale B8.9.1965 Georgetown KY BR/TL/6-0/185 d6.23 Col Kentucky St.

YEAR	TM LG	W	L	PCT	G	GS	CG-SHO	SV-BS	IP	H	R	HR	HB	BB-IB	SO	ERA	AERA	OAV	OOB	AB-HR-SH	AVG	PB	SUP	APR	DL	PW
1996	NY A	1	3	.250	32	0	0	0	21.2	23	20	5	3	11-1	14	7.89	63	.264	.363	0	—	0		-7		-1.1

POLLI, LOU Louis Americo "Crip" B7.9.1901 Baveno, Italy D12.19.2000 Berlin VT BR/TR/5-10.5/165 d4.18

1932	StL A	0	0	—	5	0	0	0	6.2	13	8	0	0	3	5	5.40	90	.406	.457	2	.500	0		-2		-0.1
1944	NY N	0	2	.000	19	0	0	3	35.2	42	25	3	0	20	6	4.54	81	.294	.380	6	.000	-1		-5		-0.4
Total	2	0	2	.000	24	0	0	3	42.1	55	33	3	0	23	11	4.68	82	.314	.394	8	.125	-1		-7		-0.5

POLONI, JOHN John Paul B2.28.1954 Dearborn MI BL/TL/6-5/210 [TexA75 6/137] d9.16 Col Arizona St.

| 1977 | Tex A | 1 | 0 | 1.000 | 2 | 1 | 0 | 0-0 | 13 | 9 | 7 | 1 | 0 | 1-0 | 5 | 6.43 | 63 | .286 | .310 | 0 | — | 0 | 176 | -2 | | -0.2 |

POMORSKI, JOHN John Leon B12.30.1905 Brooklyn NY D12.6.1977 Brampton ON, Can. BR/TR/6-0/178 d4.17

| 1934 | Chi A | 0 | 0 | — | 3 | 0 | 0 | 0 | 1.2 | 1 | 2 | 0 | 0 | 2 | 0 | 5.40 | 88 | .143 | .333 | 0 | — | 0 | | 0 | | 0.0 |

POND, ARLIE Erasmus Arlington B1.19.1873 Saugus MA D9.19.1930 Cebu, Philippines BR/TR/5-10/160 d7.4 Mil 1898 Col Vermont

1895	Bal N	0	1	.000	6	1	1	2	13.2	10	13	0	1	12	13	5.93	80	.200	.365	6	.333	1*	45	-2		-0.1
1896	Bal N	16	8	.667	28	26	21-2	0	214.1	232	133	4	6	57	80	3.49	123	.274	.324	81-0-5	.235	0	112	13		1.0
1897	Bal N	18	9	.667	32	28	23	0	248	267	131	4	15	72	59	3.52	118	.273	.332	90-0-3	.244	2*	122	21		1.9
1898	Bal N	1	1	.500	3	2	1-1	0	20	8	4	0	2	9	4	0.45	795	.123	.250	7	.286	1	178	6		0.6
Total	4	35	19	.648	69	57	46-3	2	496	517	281	8	24	150	156	3.45	122	.266	.327	184-0-8	.245	3	117	38		3.4

PONDER, ELMER Charles Elmer B6.26.1893 Reed OK D4.20.1974 Albuquerque NM BR/TR/6-0/178 d9.18 Mil 1918-19 Col Oklahoma

1917	Pit N	1	1	.500	3	2	1-1	0	21.1	12	5	0	1	6	11	1.69	168	.167	.241	7	.000	-1	13	3		0.1
1919	Pit N	0	5	.000	9	5	0	0	47.1	55	26	0	3	6	6	3.99	76	.297	.330	15	.133	-1	37	-6		-0.7
1920	Pit N	11	15	.423	33	23	13-2	0	196	182	76	3	2	40	62	2.62	123	.246	.286	59-0-3	.119	-4	71	10		0.1
1921	Pit N	2	0	1.000	8	1	1	0	24.2	29	8	1	0	3	3	2.19	175	.305	.327	10	.000	-2	150	4		-1.1
	Chi N	3	6	.333	16	11	5	0	89.1	117	58	7	3	17	31	4.74	81	.321	.350	33-0-2	.121	-2	92	-10		-1.1
	Year	5	6	.455	24	12	6	0	114	146	66	8	3	20	34	4.18	91	.317	.350	43-0-2	.093	-4	97	-6		-1.0
Total	4	17	27	.386	69	42	20-3	0	378.2	395	173	11	9	72	113	3.21	105	.271	.309	124-0-5	.105	-10	73	1		-0.7

PONSON, SIDNEY Sidney Alton B11.2.1976 Noord, Aruba BR/TR/6-2/225(200-265) d4.19

1998	Bal A	8	9	.471	31	20	0	1-1	135	157	82	19	3	42-2	85	5.27	86	.293	.345	4	.500	1	100	-11		-1.2
1999	Bal A	12	12	.500	32	32	6	0-0	210	227	118	35	1	80-2	112	4.71	100	.282	.345	3-0-1	.000	-0	104	0		-0.1
2000	Bal A	9	13	.409	32	32	6-1	0-0	222	223	125	30	1	83-0	152	4.82	97	.258	.323	1-0-2	.000	-0	97	-2		-0.2
2001	Bal A	5	10	.333	23	23	3-1	0-0	138.1	161	83	21	6	37-0	84	4.94	87	.289	.339	3	.000	-1	90	-10	23	-0.3
2002	Bal A	7	9	.438	28	28	3	0-0	176	172	84	26	2	63-1	120	4.09	106	.258	.323	4	.333	-1	106	6	25	1.7
2003	Bal A	14	6	.700	21	21	4	0-0	148	147	65	10	4	43-2	100	3.77	122	.258	.313	22-0-3	.091	-1	75	5		1.7
	†SF N	3	6	.333	10	10	0	0-0	68	64	29	6	1	18-3	34	3.71	115	.255	.305	5	.000	-1	98	-14		-1.4
2004	Bal A	11	15	.423	33	33	5-2	0-0	215.2	265	136	23	8	69-3	115	5.30	88	.305	.361	5	.000	-1	107	-24	24	-1.2
2005	Bal A	7	11	.389	23	23	1	0-0	130.1	177	97	16	3	48-1	68	6.21	71	.331	.384	4	.250	-0	101	-36	72	-3.7
Total	8	76	91	.455	233	222	28-4	1-1	1443.1	1593	819	186	29	483-14	870	4.81	95	.282	.340	50-0-6	.120	-1	101	-36	72	

POOLE, ED Edward I. B9.7.1874 Canton OH D3.11.1919 Malvern OH BR/TR/5-10/175 d10.6

1900	Pit N	1	0	1.000	1	0	0	0	7	4	1	0	0	4	3	1.29	283	.167	.167	4-1-0	.500	1*		2		0.4
1901	Pit N	5	4	.556	12	10	8-1	0	80	78	45	3	6	30	26	3.60	91	.254	.332	78-1-0	.205	1*	126	-2		-0.1
1902	Pit N	0	0	—	1	0	0	0	8	7	4	0	0	3	2	1.13	244	.233	.303	4	.250	0		0		0.0
	Cin N	12	4	.750	16	16	16-2	0	138	129	47	2	8	54	55	2.15	139	.248	.328	61	.115	-4*	108	13		1.0
	Year	12	4	.750	17	16	16-2	0	146	136	51	2	8	57	57	2.10	142	.247	.326	65	.123	-4	108	12		1.0
1903	Cin N	7	13	.350	25	21	18-1	0	184	188	105	4	12	77	73	3.28	109	.270	.352	70-0-3	.243	-3	87	-7		0.8
1904	Bro N	8	14	.364	25	23	19-1	1	178	178	86	4	8	74	67	3.39	81	.268	.349	62-0-3	.183	-6	103	11		0.8
Total	5	33	35	.485	80	70	61-5	1	595	584	288	13	34	238	226	3.04	103	.260	.340	279-2-6	.183					

POOLE, JIM James Richard B4.28.1966 Rochester NY BL/TL/6-2/203(190-203) [LAN88 9/218] d6.15 Col Georgia Tech

1990	LA N	0	0	—	16	0	0	0-0	10.2	7	5	1	0	8-4	6	4.22	87	.184	.326	0	—	0		0		0.0
1991	Tex A	0	0	—	5	0	0	1-0	6	10	4	0	0	3-0	4	4.50	90	.370	.419	0	—	0		-1		0.0
	Bal A	3	2	.600	24	0	0	0-0	36	19	10	3	0	9-2	34	2.00	198	.157	.212	0	—	0		7		1.1
	Year	3	2	.600	29	0	0	1-0	42	29	14	3	0	12-2	38	2.36	169	.196	.252	0	—	0		7		1.0
1992	Bal A	0	0	—	6	0	0	0-1	3.1	3	3	0	0	1-0	3	0.00		.231	.286	0	—	0		10	78	0.1
1993	Bal A	2	1	.667	55	0	0	2-1	50.1	30	18	2	0	21-5	29	2.15	211	.175	.263	0	—	0		10		0.8
1994	Bal A	1	0	1.000	38	0	0	0-0	20.1	32	15	4	0	11-2	18	6.64	76	.372	.430	0	—	0		-3		-0.7
1995	†Cle A	3	3	.500	42	0	0	0-0	50.1	40	22	7	2	17-0	41	3.75	126	.217	.288	0	—	0		6		0.1
1996	Cle A	4	1	1.000	32	0	0	0-1	26.2	29	15	3	0	14-4	19	3.04	161	.274	.355	0	—	-0		4		0.6
	SF N	1	2	.667	35	0	0	0-3	23.2	15	7	2	1	13-3	24	2.66	156	.188	.309	2	.000	-0		0		0.7
1997	SF N	3	1	.750	63	0	0	0-0	49.1	73	44	6	4	25-4	26	7.11	58	.353	.429	0-0-1	—	0		-17		-1.2
1998	SF N	1	3	.250	26	0	0	0-2	32.1	38	20	5	0	9-5	16	5.29	76	.302	.346	4-0-2	.250	0		-5		-0.7
	†Cle A	0	0	—	12	0	0	0-1	7	9	4	0	1	3-1	11	5.14	93	.300	.382	0	—	0		1		0.3
1999	Phi N	1	1	.500	51	0	0	1-1	35.1	48	20	3	4	15-1	22	4.33	108	.327	.400	0	—	0		-1		-0.1
	Cle A	1	0	1.000	3	0	0	0-0	1	2	2	0	0	3-1	5	18.00	28	.667	.714	0	—	0		-2		-0.1
2000	Det A	1	0	1.000	5	0	0	0-1	8.2	13	8	4	1	1-0	5	7.27	68	.361	.375	0	—	0		-5		-0.2
	Mon N	0	0	—	5	0	0	0-0	2	8	6	1	0	1-0	3	27.00	17	.571	.647	0	—	0		-3	78	-0.3
Total	11	22	12	.647	431	0	0	4-13	363	376	203	41	12	156-33	256	4.31	102	.277	.346	8-0-3	.125	0		-3	78	

POORMAN, TOM Thomas Iverson B10.14.1857 Lock Haven PA D2.18.1905 Lock Haven PA BL/TR/5-7/135 d5.5 ▲

1880	Buf N	1	8	.111	11	9	9	1	85	117	90	3		19	13	4.13	59	.307	.340	70	.157	-3*	51	-18		-1.4
	Chi N	2	1	1.000	2	1	1	0	15	12	5	0		8	0	2.40	101	.203	.299	25	.200	0*	102	1		-1.2
	Year	3	9	.273	13	10	9	1	100	129	95	3		27	13	3.87	63	.293	.334	95	.168	-3	56	-17		-1.7
1884	Tol AA	0	1	.000	1	1	1	0	9	13	11	1	0	1	0	3.00	114	.310	.341	382	.233	0*	18	-1		-0.4
1887	Phi AA	0	0	—	1	0	0	0	0.2	5	4	1	0	1	1	40.50	11	.714	.750	585-4	.265	0		-3		-0.1
Total	3	3	9	.250	15	11	10	1	109.2	147	110	5	0	30	14	4.02	63	.301	.341	1062-4	.245	-2	52	-21		-1.9

POPP, BILL William Peter B6.7.1877 St.Louis MO D9.5.1909 St.Louis MO TR/5-10.5/170 d4.19

| 1902 | StL N | 2 | 6 | .250 | 9 | 7 | 5 | 0 | 60.1 | 87 | 60 | 2 | 5 | 26 | 20 | 4.92 | 56 | .337 | .408 | 21-0-2 | .048 | -3 | 120 | -19 | | -2.1 |

PORRAY, ED Edmund Joseph B12.5.1888 , At Sea On Atlantic Ocean D7.13.1954 Lackawaxen PA BR/TR/5-11/170 d4.17

| 1914 | Buf F | 0 | 1 | .000 | 3 | 3 | 0 | 0 | 10.1 | 18 | 9 | 2 | 0 | 7 | 4 | 4.35 | 68 | .391 | .472 | 4 | .000 | -1 | 147 | -3 | | -0.3 |

PORTER, CHUCK Charles William B1.12.1956 Baltimore MD BR/TR/6-3/188* [AnaA76 7/150] d9.14 Col Clemson

1981	Mil A	0	0	—	3	0	0	0-0	4.1	7	2	0	0	1-0	1	4.15	84	.316	.350	0	—	0		0		0.0
1982	Mil A	0	0	—	3	0	0	0-0	3.2	5	2	1	0	1-0	3	4.91	78	.256	.308	0	—	0		0		0.0
1983	Mil A	7	9	.438	25	21	6-1	0-0	134	162	72	9	2	38-2	76	4.50	84	.298	.342	0	—	0	118	-11		-1.0
1984	Mil A	6	4	.600	17	12	1	0-0	81.1	92	37	8	0	12-2	48	3.87	101	.284	.309	0	—	0	110	1	90	0.7
1985	Mil A	0	0	—	6	1	0	0-0	13.2	15	8	1	0	2-0	8	1.98	213	.273	.298	0	—	0	117	-9	90	0.0
Total	5	13	13	.500	54	34	7-1	0-0	237	278	121	18	2	54-4	136	4.14	93	.291	.328	0	—	0				

YEAR	TM LG	W	L	PCT	G	GS	CG-SHO	SV-BS	IP	H	R	HR	HB	BB-IB	SO	ERA	AERA	OAV	OOB	AB-HR-SH	AVG	PB	SUP	APR	DL	PW

PORTER, NED Ned Swindell B5.6.1905 Apalachicola FL D6.30.1968 Gainesville FL BR/TR/6-0/173 d8.7 Col Florida

1926	NY N	0	0	—	2	0	0	0	2	2	1	1	0	0	1	4.50	83	.250	.250	0	—	0	0			0.0
1927	NY N	0	0	—	1	0	0	0	2	3	1	0	0	1	0	0.00	—	.333	.400	0	—	0	0			0.0
Total	2	0	0	—	3	0	0	0	4	5	2	1	0	1	1	2.25	169	.294	.333	0	—	0	0			0.0

PORTER, ODIE Odie Oscar B5.24.1877 Borden IN D5.2.1903 Borden IN TL d6.16 Col Indiana

| 1902 | Phi A | 0 | 1 | .000 | 1 | 1 | 1 | 0 | 8 | 12 | 10 | 0 | 0 | 5 | 2 | 3.38 | 109 | .343 | .425 | 3 | .000 | -0 | 98 | -2 | | -0.2 |

PORTER, HENRY Walter Henry B6.1858 Vergennes VT D12.30.1906 Brockton MA BR/TR/?/142 d9.27

1884	Mil U	3	3	.500	6	6	6-1	0	51	32	25	1		9	71	3.00	44	.168	.205	40	.275	1*	144	-19		-1.4
1885	Bro AA	33	21	.611	54	54	53-2	0	481.2	427	261	11	16	107	197	2.78	118	.223	.270	195	.205	-2	102	25		2.2
1886	Bro AA	27	19	.587	48	48	48-1	0	424	439	277	8	5	120	163	3.42	102	.252	.303	184	.179	-9	113	5		-0.5
1887	Bro AA	15	24	.385	40	40	38-1	0	339.2	416	264	7	7	96	74	4.21	102	.297	.345	146-1	.199	-3	92	-2		-0.5
1888	KC AA	18	37	.327	55	54	53-4	0	474	527	336	16	23	120	145	4.16	83	.277	.321	195	.144	-13	65	-29		-3.6
1889	KC AA	0	3	.000	4	4	3	0	23	52	46	0	1	14	9	12.52	34	.433	.496	10	.100	-1	84	-16		-1.4
Total	6	96	107	.473	207	206	201-9	0	1793.1	1893	1209	43	52	466	659	3.70	95	.259	.308	770-1	.184	-27	93	-36		-5.2

PORTERFIELD, BOB Erwin Coolidge B8.10.1923 Newport VA D4.28.1980 Sealy TX BR/TR/6-0/190* d8.8

1948	NY A	5	3	.625	16	12	2-1	0	78	85	42	5	0	34	30	4.50	91	.273	.345	24-0-7	.250	-3	138	-3		-0.3
1949	NY A	2	5	.286	12	8	3	0	57.2	53	26	3	1	29	25	4.06	100	.251	.344	19	.053	-2	97	1		0.0
1950	NY A	1	1	.500	10	2	0	1	19.2	28	19	2	0	8	9	8.69	49	.341	.400	3	.333	1*	84	-9	42	-0.8
1951	NY A	0	0	—	2	0	0	0	3	5	6	0	0	3	2	15.00	26	.385	.500	0	—	0	-4			-0.2
	Was A	9	8	.529	19	19	10-3	0	133.1	109	51	6	0	54	53	3.24	126	.224	.302	46	.130	-3	78	14		1.3
	Year	9	8	.529	21	19	10-3	0	136.1	114	57	6	0	57	55	3.50	117	.228	.308	46	.130	-3	78	10		1.1
1952	Was A	13	14	.481	31	29	15-3	0	231.1	222	80	7	8	85	80	2.72	131	.254	.323	79-0-3	.190	-0	68	22		2.4
1953	Was A	22	10	.688	34	32	24-9	0	255	243	99	19	1	73	77	3.35	116	.257	.310	98-3-4	.255	8*	119	19		3.3
1954	Was A★	13	15	.464	32	31	21-2	0	244	249	104	14	3	77	82	3.32	107	.266	.322	88-1-5	.102	-3	98	7		0.5
1955	Was A	10	17	.370	30	27	8-2	0	178	197	103	14	2	54-5	74	4.45	86	.282	.333	63-0-5	.190	1	100	-14		-1.8
1956	Bos A	3	12	.200	25	18	4-1	0	126	127	82	21	4	64-4	53	5.14	90	.260	.347	43-1-1	.326	3	83	-6		-0.4
1957	Bos A	4	4	.500	28	9	3-1	1	102.1	107	54	8	1	30-2	28	4.05	99	.272	.324	29	.172	-0	92	-2		-0.1
1958	Bos A	0	0	—	2	0	0	0	4	3	2	1	0	0-0	1	4.50	89	.214	.214	0	—	0	0			0.0
	Pit N	4	6	.400	37	6	2-1	5	87.2	78	33	7	1	19-3	39	3.29	118	.241	.281	20-1-0	.050	-1	93	7		0.8
1959	Pit N	0	0	—	6	0	0	0	5.1	6	2	1	0	2-1	1	1.69	229	.286	.348	0	—	0	1			0.0
	Chi N	0	0	—	4	0	0	0	6.1	14	9	1	0	3-0	1	11.37	35	.424	.472	1	.000	-0	-5			-0.3
	Pit N	1	2	.333	30	0	0	1	36	45	20	2	0	17-5	18	4.75	81	.321	.395	3	.000	-0	-3			-0.2
	Year	1	2	.333	40	0	0	1	47.2	65	31	4	0	22-6	19	5.29	73	.335	.403	4	.000	-0	-7			-0.5
Total	12	87	97	.473	318	193	92-23	8	1567.2	1571	732	113	14	552-20	572	3.79	102	.263	.326	516-6-25	.184	4	96	25	42	4.2

PORTO, AL Alfred "Lefty" B6.27.1926 Heilwood PA BL/TL/5-11/176 d4.22

| 1948 | Phi N | 0 | 0 | — | 3 | 0 | 0 | 0 | 2 | 2 | 0 | 0 | 1 | 0 | 1.000 | — | .143 | .200 | 0 | — | 0 | 2 | | | 0.1 |

PORTOCARRERO, ARNIE Arnold Mario B7.5.1931 New York NY D6.21.1986 Kansas City KS BR/TR/6-3/196(196-210) d4.18

1954	Phi A	9	18	.333	34	33	16-1	0	248	233	124	25	5	114	132	4.06	96	.249	.329	75-1-7	.107	-2	73	-4		-0.8
1955	KC A	5	9	.357	24	20	4-1	0	111.1	109	66	12	4	67-4	34	4.77	88	.259	.364	37-1-2	.108	-1	95	-7	31	-1.0
1956	KC A	0	1	.000	3	1	0	0	8	9	9	2	0	7-0	2	10.13	43	.300	.432	1	.000	-0	82	-4		-0.5
1957	KC A	4	9	.308	33	17	1	0	114.2	103	55	10	3	34-2	42	3.92	101	.240	.298	28-0-3	.107	-1	78	1		-0.1
1958	Bal A	15	11	.577	32	27	10-3	2	204.2	173	81	17	3	57-3	90	3.25	110	.229	.284	67-1-3	.164	0	93	9		0.9
1959	Bal A	2	7	.222	27	14	1	0	90	107	73	10	2	32-0	23	6.80	56	.294	.352	21-0-3	.000	-3	82	-29		-2.7
1960	Bal A	3	2	.600	13	5	1	0	40.2	44	23	6	0	9-0	15	4.43	86	.275	.312	11	.000	-1	116	-3		-0.2
Total	7	38	57	.400	166	117	33-5	2	817.1	778	431	82	17	320-9	338	4.32	89	.252	.322	240-3-18	.108	-9	85	-37	31	-4.7

PORTUGAL, MARK Mark Steven B10.30.1962 Los Angeles CA BR/TR/6-0/190(170-215) d8.14

1985	Min A	1	3	.250	6	4	0	0-0	24.1	24	16	3	0	14-0	12	5.55	80	.270	.362	0	—	0	103	-3		-0.3
1986	Min A	6	10	.375	27	15	3	1-1	112.2	112	56	10	4	50-1	67	4.31	101	.265	.342	0	—	0	110	9		0.2
1987	Min A	1	3	.250	13	7	0	0-1	44	58	40	13	1	24-1	28	7.77	60	.326	.407	0	—	0	90	-14		-1.1
1988	Min A	3	3	.500	26	0	0	3-1	57.2	60	30	11	3	17-1	31	4.53	90	.274	.325	0	—	0	111	9	21	-0.3
1989	Hou N	7	1	.875	20	15	2-1	0-0	108	91	34	7	2	37-0	86	2.75	124	.232	.301	34-1-3	.206	3	111	9		1.0
1990	Hou N	11	10	.524	32	32	1	0-0	196.2	187	90	21	4	67-4	136	3.62	103	.256	.313	66-0-5	.136	-1	83	2		0.1
1991	Hou N	10	12	.455	32	27	1	0-0	168.1	163	91	19	2	59-5	120	4.49	79	.256	.318	46-0-6	.196	-3	99	-3		-0.2
1992	Hou N	6	3	.667	18	16	1-1	0-0	101.1	76	32	7	1	41-3	62	2.66	127	.213	.295	28-0-6	.107	-1	88	9		0.7
1993	Hou N	18	4	.818	33	33	1-1	0-0	208	194	75	10	4	77-3	131	2.77	140	.248	.318	65-1-10	.231	4	115	25		2.9
1994	SF N	10	8	.556	21	21	1	0-0	137.1	135	68	17	6	45-2	87	3.93	103	.260	.324	48-0-4	.354	7	110	1	22	0.8
1995	SF N	5	5	.500	17	17	1	0-0	104	106	56	10	2	34-2	63	4.15	99	.262	.323	29-0-7	.103	-0	112	-2		-0.2
	Cin N	6	5	.545	14	14	0	0-0	77.2	79	35	7	2	22-0	33	3.82	109	.262	.316	29-0-1	.172	1	134	3		0.5
	Year	11	10	.524	31	31	1	0-0	181.2	185	91	17	4	56-2	96	4.01	103	.262	.320	58-0-8	.138	1	122	2		0.3
1996	Cin N	8	9	.471	27	26	1-1	0-0	156	146	77	20	2	42-2	93	3.98	108	.248	.297	48-0-7	.167	-0*	93	5	19	0.4
1997	Phi N	0	2	.000	3	3	0	0-0	13.2	17	8	0	0	5-0	2	4.61	91	.321	.373	4	.000	-0	51	-1	167	-0.1
1998	Phi N	10	5	.667	26	26	3	0-0	166.1	186	88	26	4	32-2	104	4.44	97	.283	.319	50-0-4	.260	4	92	-7	41	0.3
1999	Bos A	7	12	.368	31	27	1	0-0	150.1	179	100	28	4	41-1	79	5.51	90	.292	.337	3-0-1	.000	-0	92	-7		-0.7
Total	15	109	95	.534	346	283	16-4	5-4	1826.1	1813	896	209	36	607-27	1134	4.03	100	.261	.321	450-2-54	.198	19	104	7	392	2.3

PORZIO, MIKE Lawrence Michael B8.20.1972 Waterbury CT BL/TL/6-3/190(190-208) d7.9 Col Villanova

1999	Col N	0	0	—	16	0	0	0-0	14.2	21	14	5	0	10-0	10	8.59	67	.328	.419	0	—	0	-3			-0.1
2002	Chi A	2	2	.500	32	0	0	0-0	43	40	25	10	3	23-2	33	4.81	94	.248	.347	0	—	0	-1			-0.1
2003	Chi A	1	1	.500	3	3	0	0-0	14	18	10	2	2	1-0	9	6.43	71	.321	.350	0	—	0	80	-2		-0.3
Total	3	3	3	.500	51	3	0	0-0	71.2	79	49	17	5	34-2	52	5.90	81	.281	.364	0	—	0	80	-6		-0.5

POSEDEL, BILL William John "Sailor Bill","Barnacle Bill" B8.2.1906 San Francisco CA D11.28.1989 Livermore CA BR/TR/5-11/175 d4.23 Mil 1942-45 C18

1938	Bro N	8	9	.471	33	17	6-1	1	140	178	96	14	2	46	49	5.66	69	.311	.365	44-0-4	.227	1	121	-23		-2.5
1939	Bos N	15	13	.536	33	29	18-5	0	220.2	221	103	8	0	78	73	3.92	94	.268	.331	73-0-5	.110	-4	94	-1		-0.6
1940	Bos N	12	17	.414	35	32	18	1	233	263	118	16	1	81	86	4.13	90	.288	.346	82-0-2	.171	1	89	-10		-1.0
1941	Bos N	4	4	.500	18	9	3	0	57.1	61	36	6	1	30	30	4.87	73	.279	.368	25-0-1	.320	2	116	-8		-0.8
1946	Bos N	2	0	1.000	19	0	0	4	28.1	34	24	4	0	13	10	6.99	49	.304	.376	3	.000	-0	-10			-1.1
Total	5	41	43	.488	138	87	45-6	6	679.1	757	377	48	4	248	227	4.56	82	.286	.349	227-0-12	.176	0	100	-52		-6.0

POSER, BOB John Falk B3.16.1910 Columbus WI D5.21.2002 Columbus WI BL/TR/6-0/173 d4.17 Col Wisconsin-Madison

1932	Chi A	0	0	—	1	0	0	0	1	3	0	0	0	2		27.00	16	.600	.714	3	.000	-0*	-2			-0.1
1935	StL A	1	1	.500	4	1	0	0	13.2	26	15	0	0	4	1	9.22	52	.400	.435	4-0-1	.250	0	54	-6		-0.7
Total	2	1	1	.500	5	1	0	0	14.1	29	17	0	0	6	1	10.05	47	.414	.461	7-0-1	.143	0	54	-8		-0.8

POSSEHL, LOU Louis Thomas B4.12.1926 Chicago IL D10.7.1997 Sarasota FL BR/TR/6-2/180* d8.25 gf-George Rooks Col Illinois

1946	Phi N	1	2	.333	4	4	0	0	12.3	19	9	0	1	10	4	5.93	58	.339	.404	3-0-1	.000	-0	62	-3		-0.6
1947	Phi N	0	0	—	2	0	0	0	4.1	5	2	0	1	0	1	4.15	96	.385	.429	0	—	0	0			0.1
1948	Phi N	1	1	.500	2	1	0	0	14.2	17	8	3	0	4	7	4.91	80	.304	.350	4	.250	0*	135	-1		-0.1
1951	Phi N	0	1	.000	2	1	0	0	6	9	5	0	0	3	6	6.00	64	.333	.400	1	.000	-0	92	-2		-0.3
1952	Phi N	0	1	.000	5	1	0	0	12.2	12	9	3	0	7	4	4.97	73	.235	.328	2	.000	-0	73	-2		-0.2
Total	5	2	5	.286	15	8	1	0	51.1	62	33	6	2	24	22	5.26	71	.305	.384	10-0-1	.100	-0	85	-8		-1.1

POTE, LOU Louis William B8.21.1971 Evergreen Park IL BR/TR/6-3/190(190-208) [SFN90 29/787] d8.11 Col Kishwaukee (IL) CC

1999	Ana A	1	1	.500	20	0	0	3-0	29.1	23	9	1	0	12-1	20	2.15	228	.219	.299	—	—		0	8		0.6
2000	Ana A	1	1	.500	32	1	0	1-0	50.1	52	23	4	0	17-1	44	3.40	152	.267	.324	—	—		36	8		0.4
2001	Ana A	2	0	1.000	44	1	0	2-1	86.2	88	41	11	3	35-2	66	4.15	112	.258	.325	—	—		60	6		0.3
2002	Ana A	0	2	.000	31	0	0	0-1	50.1	33	20	7	3	26-2	32	3.22	139	.194	.304	—	—		0	7		0.4
2004	Cle A	0	0	—	2	0	0	0-0	3	3	3	0	0	1-0	5	9.00	48	.250	.308	—	—		0	-2		-0.1
Total	5	4	4	.500	129	2	0	6-2	219.2	199	96	23	6	88-9	167	3.56	133	.242	.316	—	—		49	27		1.6

YEAR	TM LG	W	L	PCT	G	GS	CG-SHO	SV-BS	IP	H	R	HR	HB	BB-IB	SO	ERA	AERA	OAV	OOB	AB-HR-SH	AVG	PB	SUP	APR	DL	PW

POTT, NELLIE Nelson Adolph "Lefty" B7.16.1899 Cincinnati OH D12.3.1963 Cincinnati OH BL/TL/6-0/185 d4.19

| 1922 | Cle A | 0 | 0 | — | 2 | 0 | 0 | 0 | 7 | 7 | 11 | 0 | 2 | 7 | 2 | 31.50 | .13 | .583 | .643 | 0 | — | 0 | | -6 | | -0.3 |

POTTER, DYKES Maryland Dykes B11.18.1910 Ashland KY D2.27.2002 Greenup KY BR/TR/6-0/185 d4.26 b-Squire

| 1938 | Bro N | 0 | 0 | — | 2 | 0 | 0 | 0 | 2 | 4 | 1 | 1 | 0 | 0 | 1 | 4.50 | 87 | .400 | .400 | 0 | — | 0 | | 0 | | 0.0 |

POTTER, NELS Nelson Thomas "Nellie" B8.23.1911 Mt.Morris IL D9.30.1990 Mt.Morris IL BL/TR/5-11/180 d4.25 Col Manchester

1936	StL N	0	0	—	1	0	0	0	1	0	0	0	0	0	0	0.00	—	.000	.000	0	—	0		0		0.0
1938	Phi A	2	12	.143	35	9	4	5	111.1	139	95	15	2	49	43	6.47	75	.306	.376	39-0-1	.256	1*	75	-20		-2.1
1939	Phi A	8	12	.400	41	25	9	2	196.1	258	163	26	5	88	60	6.60	71	.321	.391	67-0-4	.179	-1	106	-37		-3.2
1940	Phi A	9	14	.391	31	25	13	0	200.2	213	115	18	1	71	73	4.44	100	.269	.330	71-0-6	.254	2	82	1		-1.3
1941	Phi A	1	1	.500	10	3	1	2	23.1	35	26	3	0	16	7	9.26	45	.337	.425	6-0-1	.167	-0				-1.1
	Bos A	2	0	1.000	10	0	0	0	20	21	10	0	0	16	6	4.50	93	.284	.411	3	.000	-0	0			0.0
	Year	3	-1	.750	20	3	1	2	43.1	56	36	3	0	32	13	7.06	59	.315	.419	9-0-1	.111	-1	152	-12		-1.1
1943	StL A	10	5	.667	33	13	8	1	168.1	146	56	11	3	54	80	2.78	120	.235	.299	55-0-4	.145	-1	88	12		1.0
1944	†StL A	19	7	.731	32	29	16-3	0	232	211	79	6	1	70	91	2.83	127	.244	.301	82-0-5	.159	-2	137	22		2.3
1945	StL A	15	11	.577	32	32	21-3	0	255.1	212	75	10	1	68	129	2.47	143	.226	.279	92-0-5	.304	4	88	30		3.6
1946	StL A	8	9	.471	23	19	10	0	145	152	72	9	3	59	72	3.72	100	.268	.340	52	.231	2	80	-1		0.1
1947	StL A	4	10	.286	32	10	3	2	122.2	130	61	13	2	44	65	4.04	96	.277	.342	35	.257	3	71	-1		-0.1
1948	StL A	1	1	.500	2	2	0	0	10.1	11	7	1	2	4	4	5.23	87	.262	.354	4	.500	1	79	-1		0.2
	Phi A	2	2	.500	8	0	0	1	18	17	8	1	0	5	13	4.00	107	.250	.301	4	.250	-0		1		0.2
	Year	3	3	.500	10	2	0	1	28.1	28	15	2	2	9	17	4.45	99	.255	.322	8	.375	1	82	0		0.1
	†Bos N	5	2	.714	18	7	3	2	85	77	27	4	0	8	47	2.33	165	.245	.264	29-0-2	.379	3	145	14		1.5
1949	Bos N	6	11	.353	41	3	1	7	96.2	99	49	6	1	30	57	4.19	90	.265	.321	23	.130	-0	93	-3		-0.5
Total	12	92	97	.487	349	177	89-6	22	1686	1721	843	123	21	582	747	3.99	99	.265	.328	562-0-28	.228	11	99	5		2.2

POTTER, SQUIRE Robert B3.18.1902 Flatwoods KY D1.27.1983 Ashland KY BR/TR/6-1/185 d8.7 b-Dykes

| 1923 | Was A | 0 | 0 | — | 1 | 0 | 0 | 0 | 3 | 11 | 9 | 0 | 0 | 4 | 1 | 21.00 | 18 | .688 | .750 | 0 | — | 0 | | -6 | | -0.3 |

POTTS, MIKE Michael Larry B9.5.1970 Langdale AL BL/TL/5-9/179 [AtlN90 18/480] d4.6 Col Gordon (GA) JC

| 1996 | Mil A | 1 | 2 | .333 | 24 | 0 | 0 | 1-0 | 45.1 | 58 | 39 | 7 | 0 | 30-2 | 21 | 7.15 | 73 | .319 | .407 | 0 | | 0 | | -9 | | -0.6 |

POUNDS, BILL Jeared Wells B3.11.1878 Paterson NJ D7.7.1936 Paterson NJ BR/TR/5-10.5/178 d5.2

1903	Cle A	0	0	—	1	0	0	0	5	8	7	0	0	2	2	10.80	26	.364	.364	2	.500	1		-4		-0.1
	Bro N	0	0	—	1	0	0	0	6	8	5	1	0	2	2	6.00	53	.348	.400	3	.667	1		-2		0.0
Total	1				2	0	0	0	11	16	12	1	0	2	4	8.18	37	.356	.383	5	.600	1		-6		-0.1

POWELL, ABNER Charles Abner "Ab" B12.15.1860 Shenandoah PA D8.7.1953 New Orleans LA BL/TR/5-7/160 d8.4 ▲

1884	Was U	6	12	.333	18	17	14-1	0	134	135	107	3		19	78	3.43	70	.245	.270	191	.283	0*	64	-19		-1.8
1886	Bal AA	2	5	.286	7	7	7	0	60	66	51	2	1	26	15	5.10	67	.264	.336	39	.179	-1*	77	-10		-0.9
	Cin AA	0	1	.000	4	1	1	0	15.1	16	13	0	0	9	4	5.00	75	.271	.368	74	.230	-0*	67	-2		-0.1
	Year	2	6	.250	11	8	8	0	75.1	82	64	2	1	35	19	5.02	69	.265	.342	113	.212	-1	75	-12		-1.0
Total	2	8	18	.308	29	25	22-1	0	209.1	217	171	5	1	54	97	4.00	69	.252	.297	304	.257	-1	67	-31		-2.8

POWELL, DENNIS Dennis Clay B8.13.1963 Moultrie GA BR/TL/6-3/200(200-227) d7.7

1985	LA N	1	1	.500	16	2	0	1-0	29.1	31	17	1	1	13-3	19	5.22	67	.263	.341	3-0-2	.000	-0	88	-5		-0.4
1986	LA N	2	7	.222	27	6	0	0-0	65.1	65	32	5	1	25-7	31	4.27	81	.272	.341	14	.214	1	64	-5	37	-0.3
1987	Sea A	1	3	.250	16	3	0	0-1	34.1	32	13	3	0	15-0	17	3.15	151	.250	.324	0	—	0	116	6		0.6
1988	Sea A	1	3	.250	12	2	0	0-0	18.2	29	20	2	2	11-2	15	8.68	48	.363	.442	0	—	0	153	-9		-1.6
1989	Sea A	2	2	.500	43	1	0	2-0	45	49	25	6	0	21-0	27	5.00	81	.285	.364	0	—	0	67	-3		-0.2
1990	Sea A	0	0	—	2	0	0	0-0	3	5	3	0	1	0-2	0	9.00	44	.357	.471	0	—	0		-1		-0.1
	Mil A	0	4	.000	9	7	0	0-0	39.1	59	37	0	1	19-0	23	6.86	57	.341	.405	0	—	0	90	-14		-1.2
	Year	0	4	.000	11	7	0	0-0	42.1	64	40	0	2	20-2	23	7.02	55	.342	.410	0	—	0	90	-16		-1.3
1992	Sea A	3	3	.500	49	2	0	0-0	57	49	30	5	3	29-2	35	4.58	88	.238	.340	0	—	0		-3		-0.3
1993	Sea A	0	0	—	33	2	0	0-0	47.2	42	22	7	1	24-2	32	4.15	108	.255	.349	0	—	0	62	2		0.1
Total	8	11	22	.333	207	19	0	3-1	339.2	360	201	35	12	159-16	199	4.95	81	.279	.360	17-0-2	.176	1	89	-32	37	-3.6

POWELL, GROVER Grover David B10.10.1940 Sayre PA D5.21.1985 Raleigh NC BL/TL/5-10/175 d7.13 Col Penn

| 1963 | NY N | 1 | 1 | .500 | 20 | 4 | 1-1 | 0 | 49.2 | 37 | 23 | 2 | 1 | 32-0 | 39 | 2.72 | 128 | .202 | .323 | 10 | .200 | 1 | 68 | 2 | | 0.2 |

POWELL, JAY James Willard B1.9.1972 Meridian MS BR/TR/6-4/225* [BalA93 1/19] d9.10 Col Mississippi St.

1995	Fla N	0	0	—	9	0	0	0-0	8.1	7	2	0	2	6-1	4	1.08	398	.241	.405	0	—	0		3		0.1
1996	Fla N	4	3	.571	67	0	0	2-3	71.1	71	41	5	4	36-1	52	4.54	91	.255	.348	5-0-1	.000	1		-4	20	-0.5
1997	†Fla N	7	2	.778	74	0	0	2-2	79.2	71	35	3	4	30-3	65	3.28	124	.242	.317	4	.500	1		6		0.7
1998	Fla N	4	4	.500	33	0	0	3-3	36.1	36	19	5	2	22-6	24	4.21	96	.263	.370	1	.000	-0		-1		-0.1
	†Hou N	3	3	.500	29	0	0	4-1	34	22	9	1	3	15-3	38	2.38	170	.182	.277	1	.000	-0		7		1.2
	Year	7	7	.500	62	0	0	7-4	70.1	58	28	6	5	37-9	62	3.33	122	.225	.328	1		-0		6		1.1
1999	†Hou N	5	4	.556	67	0	0	4-3	75	82	38	3	3	40-4	77	4.32	102	.282	.372	0	—	0		1		0.1
2000	Hou N	1	1	.500	29	0	0	0-0	27	29	18	1	0	19-1	16	5.67	87	.271	.381	1	.000	-0*		-2	107	-0.1
2001	Col N	3	1	.750	39	0	0	7-1	38.2	34	18	5	0	19-0	28	3.72	124	.275	.355	1	.000	-0		3		0.9
	Tex A	2	2	.500	35	0	0	0-5	36.1	41	18	4	1	12-3	26	2.79	191	.245	.314	0	—	0		7		0.9
	Year	5	3	.625	74	0	0	7-6	75	75	36	9	2	31-3	54	3.24	154	.260	.335	1	.000	0		10		1.1
2002	Tex A	4	2	.600	51	0	0	0-4	49.2	50	28	5	1	24-4	35	3.44	139	.253	.336	0	—	0		4	71	0.3
2003	Tex A	3	0	1.000	51	0	0	0-0	58.2	75	58	7	2	34-3	40	7.82	64	.318	.399	0	—	0		-18	20	-0.9
2004	Tex A	1	1	.500	23	0	0	0-0	24	24	11	3	0	11-1	17	3.38	146	.267	.343	0	—	0		3	121	0.1
2005	Atl N	0	0	—	5	0	0	0-0	3.1	1	0	0	0	4-0	4	0.00	—	.091	.333	0	—	0		2	65	0.1
Total	11	36	23	.610	512	0	0	22-22	542.1	543	295	42	21	272-30	423	4.17	108	.261	.350	12-0-1	.167	-0		11	404	2.2

POWELL, JEREMY Jeremy Robert B6.18.1976 Bellflower CA BR/TR/6-5/230* [MonN94 4/112] d7.23

1998	Mon N	1	5	.167	7	6	0	0-0	25	27	25	5	4	11-0	14	7.92	53	.290	.382	6	.000	-1	95	-10		-1.9
1999	Mon N	4	8	.333	17	17	0	0-0	97	113	60	14	8	44-2	44	4.73	94	.302	.385	30-0-1	.133	0	86	-4		-0.4
2000	Mon N	0	3	.000	11	4	0	0-0	26	35	27	6	0	9-0	19	7.96	59	.321	.370	5	.600	1	97	-10		-0.8
Total	3	5	16	.238	35	27	0	0-0	148	175	112	25	12	64-2	77	5.84	76	.304	.381	41-0-1	.171	1	89	-24		-3.1

POWELL, JACK John Joseph "Red" B7.9.1874 Bloomington IL D10.17.1944 Chicago IL BR/TR/5-11/195 d6.23

1897	Cle N	15	10	.600	27	26	24-3	0	225	245	117	2	9	62	61	3.16	142	.275	.328	97-0-4	.206	-4*	111	29		2.2
1898	Cle N	23	15	.605	42	41	36-6	0	342	328	154	8	16	112	93	3.00	121	.251	.317	136-0-2	.132	-7	100	27		1.8
1899	StL N	23	19	.548	48	43	40-2	0	373	433	197	15	15	85	87	3.52	113	.290	.334	134-1-4	.201	-1*	87	24		2.0
1900	StL N	17	16	.515	38	37	28-3	0	287.2	325	194	9	3	77	77	4.44	82	.284	.331	109-1-4	.284	10	107	7		-1.1
1901	StL N	19	19	.500	45	37	33-2	3	338.1	351	168	14	12	50	133	3.54	90	.266	.299	119-2-9	.176	1	108	-11		-1.2
1902	StL A	22	17	.564	42	39	36-3	2	328.1	320	144	12	9	93	137	3.21	124	.266	.312	127-1-3	.205	-4	99	16		1.7
1903	StL A	15	19	.441	38	34	33-4	2	306.1	294	131	11	5	58	169	2.91	100	.252	.290	120-0-3	.208	2*	84	3		0.5
1904	NY A	23	19	.548	47	45	38-3	0	390.1	340	154	15	10	92	202	2.44	111	.235	.286	146-0-4	.178	-3	90	7		0.1
1905	NY A	8	13	.381	37	23	13-1	1	203	214	107	4	6	57	84	3.50	84	.272	.326	65-1-0	.185	-0	95	-10		-1.4
	StL A	2	1	.667	3	3	3	0	28	22	6	0	1	5	12	1.61	158	.218	.262	10	.100	-0	83	3		0.1
	Year	10	14	.417	40	26	16-1	1	231	236	113	4	7	62	96	3.27	88	.266	.319	75-1-0	.173	-1	74	21		2.6
1906	StL A	13	14	.481	28	26	25-3	0	244	196	77	2	8	55	132	1.77	146	.223	.275	91-1-2	.231	-3	92	-4		-1.0
1907	StL A	13	16	.448	32	31	27-4	1	255.2	229	104	4	5	62	96	2.68	94	.242	.292	92-0-1	.132	-3	92	13		1.4
1908	StL A	16	13	.552	33	32	23-5	1	256	208	73	1	6	47	85	2.11	113	.231	.274	89-0-4	.236	3	77	5		0.4
1909	StL A	12	16	.429	34	27	18-4	3	239	221	83	1	4	42	82	2.11	115	.250	.287	78-0-4	.179	0	77	5		0.3
1910	StL A	7	11	.389	21	18	8-3	0	129.1	121	45	0	1	28	52	2.30	108	.250	.292	40-0-3	.163	-1	63	5		-0.8
1911	StL A	8	19	.296	31	27	18-1	1	207.2	224	120	7	7	44	52	3.29	102	.262	.304	73-0-4	.164	-3*	94	-2		0.2
1912	StL A	9	17	.346	32	27	19	0	235.1	248	117	3	5	52	67	3.10	107	.276	.318	82-1-1	.183	-1	83	4		0.2
Total	16	245	254	.491	578	516	422-46	15	4389	4319	1991	102	120	1021	1621	2.97	106	.258	.305	1610-8-50	.192	-1	94	109		

POWELL, JACK Reginald Bertrand B8.17.1891 Holcomb MO D3.12.1930 Memphis TN TR/6-2/? d6.14

| 1913 | StL A | 0 | 0 | — | 2 | 0 | 0 | 0 | 2 | 1 | 0 | 0 | 0 | 2 | 0 | 0.00 | — | .143 | .333 | 0 | — | 0 | | 0 | | 0.0 |

YEAR	TM LG	W	L	PCT	G	GS	CG-SHO	SV-BS	IP	H	R	HR	HB	BB-IB	SO	ERA	AERA	OAV	OOB	AB-HR-SH	AVG	PB	SUP	APR	DL	PW
POWELL, ROSS	Ross John B1.24.1968 Grand Rapids MI BL/TL/6-0/180* [CinN89 3/80] d9.5 Col Michigan																								
1993	Cin N	0	3	.000	9	1	0	0-0	16.1	13	8	1	0	6-0	17	4.41	91	.224	.297	1	.000	-0	45	0		-0.1
1994	Hou N	0	0	—	12	0	0	0-0	7.1	6	1	0	1	5-0	5	1.23	322	.240	.387	0	—	-0	2			0.1
1995	Hou N	0	0	—	15	0	0	0-0	9	16	12	1	0	11-4	8	11.00	35	.381	.500	0	—	0		-8		-0.4
	Pit N	0	2	.000	12	3	0	0-0	20.2	20	14	5	2	10-0	12	5.23	83	.253	.352	3-0-1	.000	-0	131	-2		-0.2
	Year	0	2	.000	27	3	0	0-0	29.2	36	26	6	2	21-4	20	6.98	60	.298	.407	3-0-1	.000	-0	136	-9		-0.6
Total	3	0	5	.000	48	4	0	0-0	53.1	55	35	7	3	32-4	42	5.40	76	.270	.375	4-0-1	.000	-0	115	-8		-0.6
POWELL, BRIAN	William Brian B10.10.1973 Bainbridge GA BR/TR/6-2/205* [DetA95 2/41] d6.27 Col Georgia																								
1998	Det A	3	8	.273	18	16	0	0-0	83.2	101	67	17	2	36-2	46	6.35	75	.294	.364	1	.000	-0	79	-16		-1.7
2000	Hou N	2	1	.667	9	5	0	0-0	31.1	34	21	8	1	13-0	14	5.74	85	.279	.348	9	.222	1	142	-2		-0.2
2001	Hou N	0	1	.000	1	1	0	0-0	3	5	6	1	0	3-0	3	18.00	26	.357	.471	1	.000	-0	101	-4		-0.6
2002	Det A	1	5	.167	13	9	0	0-0	57.2	64	34	11	1	21-0	30	4.84	90	.278	.339	0	—	0	64	-3		-0.3
2003	SF N	0	1	.000	1	1	0	0-0	4.2	8	7	3	0	1-0	5	13.50	32	.381	.409	2	.000	0	66	-5		-0.6
2004	Phi N	1	2	.333	17	2	0	0-0	39.1	39	23	5	1	16-4	24	5.03	88	.275	.341	8-0-1	.125	-0	115	-2	45	-0.2
Total	6	7	18	.280	59	34	0	0-0	219.2	251	158	45	5	90-6	120	5.94	78	.288	.354	21-0-1	.143	-0	88	-32	45	-3.6
POWELL, BILL	William Burris "Big Bill" B5.8.1885 Taylor Co. WV D9.28.1967 E.Liverpool OH BR/TR/6-2.5/182 d4.16																								
1909	Pit N	0	1	.000	3	1	0	0	7.1	7	6	0	1	6	2	3.68	74	.292	.452	3	.333	0	77	-1		-0.2
1910	Pit N	4	6	.400	12	9	4-2	0	75	65	32	0	5	34	23	2.40	129	.242	.338	23-0-1	.261	1	61	4		0.6
1912	Chi N	0	0	—	1	0	0	0	2	2	2	0	1	1	0	9.00	37	.250	.333	0	—	0		-1		0.0
1913	Chi N	0	1	.000	1	1	0	0	0.1	2	2	0	0	2	0	54.00	6	1.000	1.000	0	—	0	116	-2		-0.3
Total	4	4	8	.333	17	11	4-2	0	84.2	76	42	0	6	43	25	2.87	107	.251	.355	26-0-1	.269	1	68	0		0.1
POWER, TED	Ted Henry B1.31.1955 Guthrie OK BR/TR/6-4/225* [LAN76 5/115] d9.9 Col Kansas St. [DL 1994 Sea A 131]																								
1981	LA N	1	3	.250	5	2	0	0-0	14.1	16	16	4	0	7-2	1	3.14	105	.286	.364	3	.000	-0	13	0		-0.1
1982	LA N	1	1	.500	12	4	0	0-0	33.2	38	27	4	0	23-1	15	6.68	52	.288	.391	6-0-1	.000	-1	127	-12		-0.7
1983	Cin N	5	6	.455	49	6	1	2-0	111	120	62	10	1	49-3	57	4.54	84	.286	.357	16-0-3	.000	-1	77	-8		-1.1
1984	Cin N	9	7	.563	**78**	0	0	11-4	108.2	93	37	4	0	46-8	81	2.82	135	.237	.311	5-0-1	.000	-0		11		1.8
1985	Cin N	8	6	.571	64	0	0	27-9	80	65	27	2	1	45-8	42	2.70	140	.227	.330	0	—	0		9		1.9
1986	Cin N	10	6	.625	56	10	0	1-1	129	115	59	13	1	52-10	95	3.70	104	.245	.318	24-0-3	.125	0	137	2		0.3
1987	Cin N	10	13	.435	34	34	2-1	0-0	204	213	115	28	3	71-7	133	4.50	94	.267	.327	59-1-9	.119	0*	96	-7		-0.9
1988	KC A	5	6	.455	22	12	2-2	0-0	80.1	98	54	7	3	30-3	44	5.94	88	.305	.366	0	—	0	121	-15	16	-1.8
	Det A	1	1	.500	4	2	0	0-0	18.2	23	13	1	0	8-4	13	5.79	66	.305	.373	0	—	0	59	-4		-0.4
	Year	6	7	.462	26	14	2-2	0-0	99	121	67	8	3	38-7	57	5.91	67	.306	.367	0	—	0	113	-19		-2.2
1989	StL N	7	5	.500	23	15	0	0-0	97	96	47	7	1	21-3	43	3.71	99	.255	.294	33-0-3	.091	-2	100	-2	33	-0.5
1990	†Pit N	1	3	.250	40	0	0	7-0	51.2	50	23	5	0	17-6	42	3.66	100	.255	.312	8	.125	0		0	54	0.2
1991	Cin N	5	3	.625	68	0	0	3-1	87	87	37	6	2	31-5	51	3.62	105	.265	.329	3	.000	-0		3		0.2
1992	Cle A	3	3	.500	64	0	0	6-5	99.1	83	37	3	4	35-9	51	2.54	155	.248	.316	0	—	0	15	15	15	1.0
1993	Cle A	0	2	.000	20	0	0	0-1	20	30	17	2	0	8-3	11	7.20	61	.333	.384	0	—	0		-6	55	-0.5
	Sea A	2	2	.500	25	0	0	13-2	25.1	27	11	1	0	9-1	16	3.91	114	.287	.346	0	—	0		2		0.4
	Year	2	4	.333	45	0	0	13-3	45.1	57	28	3	0	17-4	27	5.36	83	.310	.365	0	—	0		-3		-0.1
Total	13	68	69	.496	564	85	5-3	70-23	1160	1159	568	97	17	452-73	701	4.00	98	.264	.331	157-1-20	.089	-4	104	-12	304	-0.4
POWERS, JIM	James T. B1868 New York NY 5-10/150 d4.18																								
1890	Bro AA	1	2	.333	4	2	2	0	30	38	29	1	1	16	3	5.70	68	.299	.382	13	.154	-0	43	-6		-0.5
POWERS, IKE	John Lloyd B3.13.1906 Hancock MD D12.22.1968 Hancock MD BR/TR/6-0.5/188 d7.26																								
1927	Phi A	1	1	.500	11	1	0	0	26	26	16	1	0	7	3	4.50	95	.271	.320	5	.400	1	98	-1		0.0
1928	Phi A	1	0	1.000	9	0	0	2	12	8	6	1	1	10	4	4.50	89	.222	.404	0	—	0		0		0.0
Total	2	2	1	.667	20	1	0	2	38	34	22	2	1	17	7	4.50	93	.258	.347	5	.400	1	98	-1		0.0
PRALL, WILLIE	Wilfred Anthony B4.20.1950 Hackensack NJ BL/TL/6-3/200 [SFN71 3/64] d9.3																								
1975	Chi N	0	2	.000	9	1	0	0	14.2	11	9	1	0	8-0	7	8.59	45	.339	.408	4-0-2	.000	-0	98	-7		-0.8
PRATT, AL	Albert George "Uncle Al" B11.19.1848 Allegheny (now part of Pittsburgh) PA D11.21.1937 Pittsburgh PA TR/5-7/140 d5.4 M2/U2																								
1871	Cle NA	10	17	.370	28	28	22	0	224.2	296	288	9		47	**34**	3.77	110	.277	.307	130	.262	2*	83	7		0.8
1872	Cle NA	2	9	.182	15	12	8	0	105.2	150	133	3		14	7	5.79	61	.286	.305	65	.277	0*	72	-26		-1.6
Total	2 NA	12	26	.316	43	40	30	0	330.1	446	421	12		61	41	4.41	89	.280	.306	195	.267	3	80	-19		-0.8
PRATT, ANDY	Andrew Elias B8.27.1979 Mesa AZ BL/TL/5-11/160(160-185) [TexA98 9/263] d9.28																								
2002	Atl N	0	0	—	1	0	0	0-0	1.1	1	1	0	0	4-0	1	6.75	60	.200	.556	0	—	0		0		0.0
2004	Chi N	0	1	.000	4	0	0	0-0	1.2	0	4	0	1	7-1	1	21.60	21	.000	.615	0	—	0		-3		-0.5
Total	2	0	1	.000	5	0	0	0-0	3	1	5	0	1	11-1	2	15.00	28	.100	.591	0	—	0		-3		-0.5
PREGENZER, JOHN	John Arthur B8.2.1935 Burlington WI BR/TR/6-5/220* d4.20 Col Illinois Wesleyan																								
1963	SF N	0	0	—	6	0	0	1	9.1	8	5	0	1	8-2	5	4.82	66	.242	.405	0	—	0		-1		-0.1
1964	SF N	2	0	1.000	13	0	0	0	18.1	21	15	1	1	11-3	8	4.91	73	.296	.398	0	—	0		-4		-0.5
Total	2	2	0	1.000	19	0	0	1	27.2	29	20	1	2	19-5	13	4.88	70	.279	.400	0	—	0		-5		-0.6
PRENDERGAST, JIM	James Bartholomew B8.23.1917 Brooklyn NY D8.23.1994 Amherst NY BL/TL/6-1/208 d4.25																								
1948	Bos N	1	1	.500	10	2	0	0	16.2	30	20	1	0	5	3	10.26	37	.380	.417	5	.000	-1	116	-12		-1.4
PRENDERGAST, MIKE	Michael Thomas B12.15.1888 Arlington IL D11.18.1967 Omaha NE BR/TR/5-9.5/165 d4.26																								
1914	Chi F	5	9	.357	30	19	7-1	0	136	131	65	5	3	40	71	2.38	111	.255	.313	37-0-4	.108	-3	73	3		-0.1
1915	Chi F	14	12	.538	42	30	16-3	0	253.2	220	93	6	4	67	95	2.48	101	.240	.295	80-0-4	.075	-9	88	0		-1.0
1916	Chi N	6	11	.353	35	10	4-2	2	152	127	53	5	1	23	56	2.31	126	.228	.260	46-0-1	.152	-2	62	8		0.7
1917	Chi N	3	6	.333	35	8	1	1	99.1	112	42	6	0	21	43	3.35	86	.302	.339	28	.250	1	114	-2		0.0
1918	Phi N	13	14	.481	33	30	20	1	252.1	257	102	6	3	46	41	2.89	104	.273	.308	85-0-2	.082	-8	80	3		-0.6
1919	Phi N	0	1	.000	5	0	0	0	15	20	15	0	1	10	5	8.40	38	.351	.456	3	.333	0	25	-7		-0.4
Total	6	41	53	.436	180	98	48-6	4	908.1	867	358	28	10	207	311	2.74	102	.258	.304	279-0-11	.115	-19	81	5		-1.4
PRENTISS, GEORGE	George Pepper (aka George Pepper Wilson in 1901) B6.10.1876 Wilmington DE D9.8.1902 Wilmington DE BB/TR/5-11/175 d9.23																								
1901	Bos A	1	0	1.000	2	1	1	0	10	7	4	0	0	4	0	1.80	196	.194	.310	3	.333	1	134	2		0.2
1902	Bos A	2	2	.500	7	4	3	0	41	55	31	0	0	10	9	5.27	68	.322	.359	16	.313	1	136	-6		-0.5
	Bal A	0	1	.000	2	2	0	0	6.2	14	10	1	0	5	1	10.80	35	.424	.500	4	.000	-0	124	-4		-0.6
	Year	2	3	.400	9	6	3	0	47.2	69	41	1	0	15	10	6.04	60	.338	.384	20	.250	-0	133	-11		-1.1
Total	3	3	3	.500	11	7	4	0	57.2	76	45	1	0	21	10	5.31	68	.317	.372	23	.261	1	133	-8		-0.9
PRESKO, JOE	Joseph Edward "Baby Joe" B10.7.1928 Kansas City MO BR/TR/6-0/170* d5.3																								
1951	StL N	7	4	.636	15	12	5	2	88.2	88	36	9	2	20	38	3.45	115	.251	.296	37	.162	-1	113	6		0.5
1952	StL N	7	10	.412	28	18	5-1	0	146.2	140	74	16	1	57	63	4.05	92	.247	.317	43-0-3	.093	-2	99	-5		-0.8
1953	StL N	6	13	.316	34	25	4	1	161.2	165	95	19	5	65	56	5.01	85	.261	.335	59-0-4	.220	1*	106	-12		-1.1
1954	StL N	4	9	.308	37	6	1-1	0	71.2	97	56	14	5	41	36	6.91	60	.327	.416	16	.250	0*	101	-19		-3.0
1957	Det A	1	1	.500	7	0	0	0	11	10	3	0	1	4-1	3	1.64	236	.278	.357	1	.000	-0		2		0.4
1958	Det A	0	0	—	7	0	0	2	10.2	13	4	0	0	1-0	6	3.38	120	.317	.326	0	—	0		1		0.1
Total	6	25	37	.403	128	61	15-2	5	490.1	511	268	58	14	188-1	202	4.61	87	.267	.336	156-0-7	.173	-1	105	-27		-3.9
PRESSNELL, TOT	Forest Charles B8.8.1906 Findlay OH D1.6.2001 Findlay OH BR/TR/5-10/175 d4.21																								
1938	Bro N	11	14	.440	43	19	6-1	6	192	209	86	11	8	56	57	3.56	110	.276	.332	63-0-1	.143	-1	91	8		0.9
1939	Bro N	9	7	.563	31	18	10-2	1	156.2	171	76	9	1	33	43	4.02	100	.273	.311	51-0-3	.196	-1	111	1		0.9
1940	Bro N	6	5	.545	24	8	1-1	2	68.1	58	31	4	2	17	21	3.69	108	.221	.274	17-0-4	.000	-2	71	2		0.1
1941	Chi N	5	3	.625	29	1	0	1	70	69	26	2	4	23	27	3.09	114	.253	.320	15-0-1	.200	0	73	**5**		0.5
1942	Chi N	1	1	.500	27	0	0	4	39.1	40	28	5	5	5	9	5.49	58	.260	.305	3	.667	1		-10		-0.6
Total	5	32	30	.516	154	42	17-4	12	526.1	547	247	26	30	134	157	3.80	101	.264	.315	149-0-9	.161	-3	100	6		0.9

YEAR	TM LG	W	L	PCT	G	GS	CG-SHO	SV-BS	IP	H	R	HR	HB	BB-IB	SO	ERA	AERA	OAV	OOB	AB-HR-SH	AVG	PB	SUP	APR	DL	PW

PRICE, JOE   Joseph Walter B11.29.1956 Inglewood CA   BR/TL/6-4/220*   [CinN77 4/102]   d6.14   Col Oklahoma

YEAR	TM LG	W	L	PCT	G	GS	CG-SHO	SV-BS	IP	H	R	HR	HB	BB-IB	SO	ERA	AERA	OAV	OOB	AB-HR-SH	AVG	PB	SUP	APR	DL	PW
1980	Cin N	7	3	.700	24	13	2	0-0	111.1	95	45	10	1	37-0	44	3.56	99	.236	.302	39-0-3	.128	-2	107	1		-0.2
1981	Cin N	6	1	.857	41	0	0	4-2	53.2	42	19	3	0	18-2	41	2.52	139	.222	.286	3	.000	-0		5		0.7
1982	Cin N	3	4	.429	59	1	0	3-5	72.2	73	26	7	4	32-8	71	2.85	129	.263	.346	3-0-2	.333	0	96	6		0.6
1983	Cin N	10	6	.625	21	21	5	0-0	144	118	46	12	0	46-2	83	2.88	133	.225	.285	41-0-3	.098	-1	66	17	25	1.7
1984	Cin N	7	13	.350	30	30	3-1	0-0	171.2	176	91	19	2	61-5	129	4.19	90	.261	.322	48-0-9	.146	-1	92	-8		-1.1
1985	Cin N	2	2	.500	26	8	0	1-0	64.2	59	35	10	0	23-7	52	3.90	97	.242	.301	14-0-1	.000	-1	105	-2	31	-0.3
1986	Cin N	1	2	.333	25	2	0	0-1	41.2	49	30	5	0	22-2	30	5.40	71	.293	.366	7	.143	0	127	-8	46	-0.5
1987	†SF N	2	2	.500	20	0	0	1-0	35	19	10	5	1	13-2	42	2.57	150	.154	.241	6	.167	-0		6		0.6
1988	SF N	1	6	.143	38	3	0	4-1	61.2	59	33	5	1	27-6	49	3.94	83	.249	.328	8-0-2	.000	0	127	-6	41	-0.8
1989	SF N	1	1	.500	7	1	0	0-1	14	16	9	3	0	4-2	10	5.79	58	.314	.357	2	.000	0	157	-3		-0.4
	Bos A	2	5	.286	31	5	0	0-1	70.1	71	35	8	0	30-3	52	4.35	95	.262	.332	0	—	0	79	0		-0.1
1990	Bal A	3	4	.429	50	0	0	0-2	65.1	62	29	8	0	24-2	54	3.58	107	.253	.319	0	—	0		1	18	0.1
Total	11	45	49	.479	372	84	10-1	13-13	906	839	408	95	9	337-41	657	3.65	102	.246	.313	171-0-20	.111	-5	92	9	161	0.3

PRICE, BILL   William B Philadelphia PA   d4.27

YEAR	TM LG	W	L	PCT	G	GS	CG-SHO	SV-BS	IP	H	R	HR	HB	BB-IB	SO	ERA	AERA	OAV	OOB	AB-HR-SH	AVG	PB	SUP	APR	DL	PW
1890	Phi AA	1	0	1.000	1	1	1	0	9	6	3	0	1	7	1	2.00	194	.182	.341	4	.250	-0	87	2		0.2

PRIDDY, BOB   Robert Simpson B12.10.1939 Pittsburgh PA   BR/TR/6-1/200*   d9.20

YEAR	TM LG	W	L	PCT	G	GS	CG-SHO	SV-BS	IP	H	R	HR	HB	BB-IB	SO	ERA	AERA	OAV	OOB	AB-HR-SH	AVG	PB	SUP	APR	DL	PW
1962	Pit N	1	0	1.000	2	0	0	0	3	4	1	0	0	1-0	1	3.00	131	.308	.357	0	—	0		0		0.1
1964	Pit N	1	2	.333	19	0	0	1	34.1	35	16	2	1	15-1	23	3.93	89	.282	.354	3	.000	0		-1		-0.2
1965	SF N	1	0	1.000	8	0	0	0	10.1	6	2	1	0	2-0	7	1.74	207	.176	.216	1	.000	-0*		2		0.2
1966	SF N	6	3	.667	38	3	0	1	91	88	45	8	3	28-3	51	3.96	93	.259	.317	17	.176	0*	40	-2		-0.1
1967	Was A	3	7	.300	46	8	1	4	110	98	48	12	0	33-5	57	3.44	92	.240	.295	22-0-2	.182	1*	62	-3		-0.1
1968	Chi A	3	11	.214	35	18	2	0	114	106	50	14	4	41-1	66	3.63	83	.244	.314	24-1-3	.042	-1*	96	-6		-0.9
1969	Chi A	0	0	—	4	0	0	0-0	8	10	5	2	0	2-0	5	4.50	86	.303	.343	0	—	0		-1		0.0
	Cal A	0	1	.000	15	0	0	0-0	26.1	24	14	4	0	7-1	15	4.78	73	.242	.292	2-0-1	.000	0		-3		-0.1
	Year	0	1	.000	19	0	0	0-0	34.1	34	19	6	0	9-1	20	4.72	76	.258	.305	2-0-1	.000	0		-4		-0.1
	Atl N	0	0	—	1	0	0	0-0	2	1	0	0	0	1-0	1	0.00	—	.143	.250	0	—	0		1		0.0
1970	Atl N	5	5	.500	41	0	0	8-2	73	75	46	9	3	24-2	32	5.42	79	.269	.331	15-0-2	.200	0		-7		-1.0
1971	Atl N	4	9	.308	40	0	0	4-3	64	71	36	8	1	44-5	36	4.22	88	.289	.396	11	.182	0	72	-4		-0.8
Total	9	24	38	.387	249	29	3	18-5	536	518	263	60	12	198-18	294	4.00	88	.257	.324	95-1-8	.137	1	72	-24		-3.1

PRIEST, EDDIE   Eddie Lee B4.8.1974 Boaz AL   BR/TL/6-1/200   [CinN94 9/240]   d5.27   Col Southern Union St. (AL) CC

YEAR	TM LG	W	L	PCT	G	GS	CG-SHO	SV-BS	IP	H	R	HR	HB	BB-IB	SO	ERA	AERA	OAV	OOB	AB-HR-SH	AVG	PB	SUP	APR	DL	PW
1998	Cin N	0	1	.000	8	2	0	0	12	8	12	8	2	6	12	10.50	41	.444	.448	2	.000	-0	107	-4		-0.6

PRIETO, ARIEL   Ariel B10.22.1969 Havana, Cuba   BR/TR/6-3/230(225-247)   [OakA95 1/5]   d7.2   [DL 1999 Oak A 182]

YEAR	TM LG	W	L	PCT	G	GS	CG-SHO	SV-BS	IP	H	R	HR	HB	BB-IB	SO	ERA	AERA	OAV	OOB	AB-HR-SH	AVG	PB	SUP	APR	DL	PW
1995	Oak A	2	6	.250	14	9	1	0-0	58	57	35	4	5	32-1	37	4.97	91	.264	.369	0	—	0	78	-3	15	-0.4
1996	Oak A	6	7	.462	21	21	0	0-0	125.2	130	66	9	2	54-2	75	4.15	120	.273	.352	0	—	0	89	10	70	0.8
1997	Oak A	6	8	.429	22	22	0	0-0	125	155	84	16	5	70-3	90	5.04	91	.306	.393	0	—	0	101	-10	72	-0.5
1998	Oak A	0	1	.000	2	2	0	0-0	8.1	17	11	2	1	5-1	8	11.88	39	.415	.489	0	—	0	90	-6		-0.5
2000	Oak A	1	2	.333	8	6	0	0-0	31.2	42	21	3	1	13-0	19	5.12	95	.321	.384	2	.000	-0	122	-1		-0.1
2001	TB A	0	0	—	3	0	0	0-0	3.2	6	1	0	1	2-0	2	2.45	184	.375	.474	0	—	0		1	150	0.0
Total	6	15	24	.385	70	60	3	0-0	352.1	407	218	34	20	176-7	231	4.85	98	.294	.378	2	.000	-0	95	-9	489	-1.7

PRIM, RAY   Raymond Lee "Pop" B12.30.1906 Salitpa AL   D4.29.1995 Monte Rio CA   BR/TL/6-0/178   d9.24   Col Auburn-Montgomery

YEAR	TM LG	W	L	PCT	G	GS	CG-SHO	SV-BS	IP	H	R	HR	HB	BB-IB	SO	ERA	AERA	OAV	OOB	AB-HR-SH	AVG	PB	SUP	APR	DL	PW
1933	Was A	0	1	.000	7	2	1	0	14.1	13	6	0	0	2	6	3.14	133	.232	.259	5-0-1	.000	-1*	0	2		0.1
1934	Was A	0	2	.000	8	1	0	0	14.2	19	11	1	0	8	3	6.75	64	.339	.422	3	.000	0	60	-4		-0.4
1935	Phi N	3	4	.429	29	6	1	0	73.1	110	54	4	0	15	27	5.77	79	.340	.369	24	.083	-2	69	-8		-0.9
1943	Chi N	4	3	.571	29	5	0	1	60	67	24	2	0	14	27	2.55	131	.282	.321	12-0-2	.167	-0	122	4		0.5
1945	†Chi N	13	8	.619	34	19	9-2	2	165.1	142	58	9	1	23	88	2.40	153	.228	.256	51-0-5	.255	3	99	21		2.1
1946	Chi N	2	3	.400	14	2	0	1	23.1	28	17	5	0	10	10	5.79	57	.289	.355	5	.200	0	90	-6	60	-1.2
Total	6	22	21	.512	116	34	10-2	4	351	379	170	21	1	72	161	3.56	107	.272	.308	100-0-8	.180	-0	90	9	60	0.2

PRINCE, DON   Donald Mark B4.5.1938 Clarkton NC   BR/TR/6-4/215   d9.21   Col Campbell

YEAR	TM LG	W	L	PCT	G	GS	CG-SHO	SV-BS	IP	H	R	HR	HB	BB-IB	SO	ERA	AERA	OAV	OOB	AB-HR-SH	AVG	PB	SUP	APR	DL	PW
1962	Chi N	0	0	—	1	0	0	0	1	0	0	0	1	1-0	0	0.00	—	.000	.500	0	—	0		0		0.0

PRINZ, BRET   Bret Randolph B6.15.1977 Chicago Heights IL   BR/TR/6-3/185(185-215)   [AriN98 18/553]   d4.22   Col Phoenix (AZ) JC

YEAR	TM LG	W	L	PCT	G	GS	CG-SHO	SV-BS	IP	H	R	HR	HB	BB-IB	SO	ERA	AERA	OAV	OOB	AB-HR-SH	AVG	PB	SUP	APR	DL	PW
2001	Ari N	4	1	.800	46	0	0	9-3	41	33	13	4	1	19-1	27	2.63	176	.220	.310	0	—	0		9		1.1
2002	Ari N	0	2	.000	20	0	0	0-2	13.1	23	14	1	1	10-1	10	9.45	47	.404	.493	0	—	0		-6		-0.7
2003	Ari N	0	0	—	1	0	0	0-0	1	1	0	0	0	1-1	1	0.00	—	.250	.400	0	—	0		0	114	-0.0
	NY A	0	0	—	2	0	0	0-0	2	6	4	1	0	3-1	1	18.00	24	.500	.600	0	—	0		-3		-0.2
2004	NY A	1	0	1.000	26	0	0	0-0	28.1	28	17	5	1	14-0	22	5.08	90	.259	.347	0	—	0		-1		-0.1
2005	LA A	0	1	.000	3	0	0	0-0	3	4	1	0	1	1-0	1	3.00	144	.308	.357	0	—	0		0	143	-0.0
Total	5	5	4	.556	98	0	0	9-5	88.2	95	49	12	4	48-4	63	4.77	96	.276	.367	0	—	0		-1	257	0.1

PRIOR, MARK   Mark William B9.7.1980 San Diego CA   BR/TR/6-5/225*   [ChiN01 1/2]   d5.22   Col USC

YEAR	TM LG	W	L	PCT	G	GS	CG-SHO	SV-BS	IP	H	R	HR	HB	BB-IB	SO	ERA	AERA	OAV	OOB	AB-HR-SH	AVG	PB	SUP	APR	DL	PW
2002	Chi N	6	6	.500	19	19	1	0-0	116.2	98	45	14	7	38-0	147	3.32	122	.226	.296	35-0-2	.171	1	98	11	15	1.6
2003	†Chi N☆	18	6	.750	30	30	3-1	0-0	211.1	183	67	15	9	50-4	245	2.43	179	.231	.283	72-1-7	.250	5*	101	43	23	5.1
2004	Chi N	6	4	.600	21	21	0	0-0	118.2	112	53	14	3	48-2	139	4.02	110	.251	.325	36-0-6	.139	-1	105	7	61	0.5
2005	Chi N	11	7	.611	27	27	1	0-0	166.2	143	73	25	4	59-2	188	3.67	119	.227	.296	48-0-6	.229	2	97	12	38	1.6
Total	4	41	23	.641	97	97	5-1	0-0	613.1	536	238	68	23	195-8	719	3.24	133	.233	.297	191-1-21	.209	8	100	73	137	8.8

PROCTOR, JIM   James Arthur B9.9.1935 Brandywine MD   BR/TR/6-0/165   d9.14

YEAR	TM LG	W	L	PCT	G	GS	CG-SHO	SV-BS	IP	H	R	HR	HB	BB-IB	SO	ERA	AERA	OAV	OOB	AB-HR-SH	AVG	PB	SUP	APR	DL	PW
1959	Det A	0	1	.000	2	0	0	0	2.2	8	5	0	0	3-0	0	16.88	24	.533	.611	0	—	0	109	-3		-0.1

PROCTOR, RED   Noah Richard B10.27.1900 Williamsburg VA   D12.17.1954 Richmond VA   BR/TR/6-1/165   d8.6

YEAR	TM LG	W	L	PCT	G	GS	CG-SHO	SV-BS	IP	H	R	HR	HB	BB-IB	SO	ERA	AERA	OAV	OOB	AB-HR-SH	AVG	PB	SUP	APR	DL	PW
1923	Chi A	0	0	—	2	0	0	0	4	11	8	0	0	2	0	13.50	29	.550	.591	0		0		-5		-0.1

PROCTOR, SCOTT   Scott Christopher B1.2.1977 Stuart FL   BR/TR/6-1/200*   [LAN98 5/156]   d4.20   Col Florida St.

YEAR	TM LG	W	L	PCT	G	GS	CG-SHO	SV-BS	IP	H	R	HR	HB	BB-IB	SO	ERA	AERA	OAV	OOB	AB-HR-SH	AVG	PB	SUP	APR	DL	PW
2004	NY A	2	1	.667	26	0	0	0-0	25	29	18	5	0	14-0	21	5.40	85	.284	.364	0	—	0		-3		-0.2
2005	†NY A	1	0	1.000	29	0	0	0-0	44.2	46	32	10	2	17-4	36	6.04	72	.257	.327	0	—	0	193	-8		-0.2
Total	2	3	1	.750	55	0	0	0-0	69.2	75	50	15	2	31-4	57	5.81	77	.267	.341	0	—	0	193	-11		-0.5

PROESER, GEORGE   George "Yatz" B5.30.1864 Cincinnati OH   D10.13.1941 New Burlington OH   BL/TL/5-10/190   d9.15 ▲

YEAR	TM LG	W	L	PCT	G	GS	CG-SHO	SV-BS	IP	H	R	HR	HB	BB-IB	SO	ERA	AERA	OAV	OOB	AB-HR-SH	AVG	PB	SUP	APR	DL	PW
1888	Cle AA	3	4	.429	7	7	7-1	0	59	53	47	3	7	30	20	3.81	81	.231	.338	23	.304	2	83	-3		-0.1

PROKOPEC, LUKE   Kenneth Luke B2.23.1978 Blackwood, South Australia, Australia   BL/TR/5-11/166*   d9.4   [DL 2003 Cin N 183]

YEAR	TM LG	W	L	PCT	G	GS	CG-SHO	SV-BS	IP	H	R	HR	HB	BB-IB	SO	ERA	AERA	OAV	OOB	AB-HR-SH	AVG	PB	SUP	APR	DL	PW
2000	LA N	1	1	.500	5	3	0	0-0	21	19	10	2	2	9-0	12	3.00	148	.253	.345	5-0-1	.000	-1*	110	2		0.2
2001	LA N	8	7	.533	29	22	0	0-0	138.1	146	80	27	4	40-1	91	4.88	84	.268	.321	36-0-7	.194	1*	123	-12	16	-1.2
2002	Tor A	2	9	.182	22	12	0	0-0	71.2	90	57	19	7	25-2	41	6.78	68	.302	.364	0	—	0	65	-16	81	-2.0
Total	3	11	17	.393	56	37	0	0-0	231	255	147	48	13	74-3	144	5.30	81	.278	.337	41-0-8	.171	0	102	-26	280	-3.0

PROLY, MIKE   Michael James B12.15.1950 Jamaica NY   BR/TR/6-0/185*   [StLN72 9/213]   d4.10   Col St. Johns

YEAR	TM LG	W	L	PCT	G	GS	CG-SHO	SV-BS	IP	H	R	HR	HB	BB-IB	SO	ERA	AERA	OAV	OOB	AB-HR-SH	AVG	PB	SUP	APR	DL	PW
1976	StL N	1	0	1.000	14	0	0	0-1	17	21	9	0	0	6-1	4	3.71	97	.328	.370	0-0-1	—	0		-1		0.0
1978	Chi A	5	2	.714	14	6	2	1-0	65.2	63	24	4	0	12-0	19	2.74	139	.250	.282	0	—	0	122	7	33	0.7
1979	Chi A	3	8	.273	38	6	0	9-2	88.1	89	43	6	4	40-7	32	3.87	110	.260	.337	0	—	0	89	4	44	0.4
1980	Chi A	5	10	.333	62	3	0	8-6	146.2	136	67	7	6	58-9	56	3.07	132	.253	.323	0	—	0	88	12		1.1
1981	Phi N	2	1	.667	35	2	0	2-0	63	66	29	6	1	19-5	19	3.86	95	.282	.335	7	.000	-1	85	-1		-0.1
1982	Chi N	5	3	.625	44	1	0	1-5	82	77	22	5	2	22-5	24	2.30	164	.257	.310	14-0-5	.286	1	93	14		1.3
1983	Chi N	5	5	.167	60	0	0	1-2	83	79	35	5	1	38-13	31	3.58	107	.259	.339	11-0-2	.091	-0		3	19	0.2
Total	7	22	29	.431	267	18	2	22-16	545.2	531	229	33	8	195-40	185	3.23	121	.261	.324	32-0-8	.156	-0	100	38	96	4.0

PROUGH, BILL   Herschel Clinton "Clint" B11.28.1887 Markle IN   D12.29.1936 Richmond IN   BR/TR/6-3/185   d4.27

YEAR	TM LG	W	L	PCT	G	GS	CG-SHO	SV-BS	IP	H	R	HR	HB	BB-IB	SO	ERA	AERA	OAV	OOB	AB-HR-SH	AVG	PB	SUP	APR	DL	PW
1912	Cin N	0	0	—	1	0	0	0	3	7	5	0	0	2	0	6.00	56	.538	.571	1	.000	0		-2		-0.0

PRUDHOMME, AUGIE   John Olgus B11.20.1902 Frierson LA   D10.4.1992 Shreveport LA   BR/TR/6-2/186   d4.19

YEAR	TM LG	W	L	PCT	G	GS	CG-SHO	SV-BS	IP	H	R	HR	HB	BB-IB	SO	ERA	AERA	OAV	OOB	AB-HR-SH	AVG	PB	SUP	APR	DL	PW
1929	Det A	1	6	.143	34	6	2	1	94	119	78	7	2	53	26	6.22	69	.322	.410	21	.238	1	157	-20		-1.1

YEAR	TM LG	W	L	PCT	G	GS	CG-SHO	SV-BS	IP	H	R	HR	HB	BB-IB	SO	ERA	AERA	OAV	OOB	AB-HR-SH	AVG	PB	SUP	APR	DL	PW
PRUETT, HUB								Hubert Shelby "Shucks"	B9.1.1900 Malden MO		D1.28.1982 Ladue MO			BL/TL/5-10.5/165		d4.26	Col Missouri								
1922	StL A	7	7	.500	39	8	4	7	119.2	99	48	2	5	59	70	2.33	178	.235	.336	34-0-3	.147	-1	82	19		2.3
1923	StL A	4	7	.364	32	8	3	2	104.1	109	57	3	3	64	59	4.31	97	.279	.385	23-0-4	.130	-1	79	0		0.0
1924	StL A	3	4	.429	33	1	0	0	65	64	42	1	4	42	27	4.57	99	.270	.389	15-0-1	.200	-1	37	-2		-0.2
1927	Phi N	7	17	.292	31	28	12-1	1	186	238	147	6	12	89	90	6.05	68	.314	.395	60-0-5	.217	1	86	-41		-4.1
1928	Phi N	2	4	.333	13	9	4	0	71.1	78	49	2	3	49	35	4.54	94	.291	.406	24-0-2	.208	-0	86	-5		-0.4
1930	NY N	4	5	.556	45	8	1	3	135.2	152	83	11	4	63	49	4.78	99	.287	.367	37-0-2	.135	-1	94	0		-0.1
1932	Bos N	1	5	.167	18	7	4	0	63	76	42	4	6	30	27	5.14	73	.308	.396	19	.105	-1	48	-10		-0.8
Total	7	29	48	.377	211	69	28-1	13	745	816	468	28	37	396	357	4.63	92	.286	.380	212-0-17	.170	-3	80	-39		-3.3
PRUIETT, TEX								Charles Le Roy	B4.10.1883 Osgood IN		D3.6.1953 Ventura CA			BL/TR/5-8/176		d4.26									
1907	Bos A	3	11	.214	35	17	6-2	1	173.2	166	77	1	8	59	54	3.11	83	.254	.323	51-0-1	.157	-1	59	-7		-0.6
1908	Bos A	1	7	.125	13	6	1-1	2	58.2	55	26	1	2	21	28	1.99	123	.275	.350	16	.063	-2	32	1		-0.1
Total	2	4	18	.182	48	23	7-3	5	232.1	221	103	2	10	80	82	2.83	90	.259	.329	67-0-1	.134	-2	52	-6		-0.7
PUCKETT, TROY								Troy Levi	B12.10.1889 Winchester IN		D4.13.1971 Winchester IN			BL/TR/6-2/186		d10.4	Col Wabash								
1911	Phi N	0	0	—	1	0	0	0	2	4	3	0	1	2	1	13.50	26	.444	.583	0	—	0		-2		-0.1
PUENTE, MIGUEL								Miguel Antonio (Aguilar)	B5.8.1948 San Luis Potosi, San Luis Potosi, Mexico		BR/TR/6-0/160			d5.3												
1970	SF N	1	3	.250	6	4	1	0-0	18.2	25	18	5	0	11-1	14	8.20	49	.325	.409	7-0-1	.000	-1	130	-8		-1.5
PUFFER, BRANDON								Brandon Duane	B10.5.1975 Downey CA		BR/TR/6-3/190*			[MinA94 27/743]		d4.17									
2002	Hou N	3	3	.500	55	0	0	0-0	69	67	37	3	5	38-8	48	4.43	98	.258	.361	6-0-1	.000	-0		-1		-0.1
2003	Hou N	0	0	—	13	0	0	0-1	21	24	13	2	1	16-3	10	5.14	86	.300	.423	0		0		-2		-0.1
2004	SD N	0	1	.000	14	0	0	0-0	18	24	13	3	1	11-1	12	5.50	72	.320	.414	3	.000	-0		-4		-0.2
2005	SF N	0	0	—	3	0	0	0-0	7	9	8	2	0	2-0	1	10.29	41	.310	.355	0		0		-4		-0.2
Total	4	3	4	.429	85	0	0	0-1	115	124	71	10	7	67-12	71	5.09	84	.279	.381	9-0-1	.000	-1		-11		-0.6
PUGH, TIM								Timothy Dean	B1.26.1967 S.Lake Tahoe CA		BR/TR/6-6/230*			[CinN89 6/160]		d9.1	Col Oklahoma St.								
1992	Cin N	4	2	.667	7	7	0	0-0	45.1	47	15	2	1	13-3	18	2.58	140	.276	.330	13-0-1	.077	-0	75	5		0.5
1993	Cin N	10	15	.400	31	27	3-1	0-0	164.1	200	102	19	7	59-1	94	5.26	77	.303	.363	54-0-7	.222	2	99	-21		-2.6
1994	Cin N	3	3	.500	10	9	1	0-0	47.2	60	37	5	3	26-0	24	6.04	69	.314	.396	14-0-1	.357	2	111	-10		-0.9
1995	Cin N	6	5	.545	28	12	0	0-0	98.1	100	46	13	1	32-2	38	3.84	109	.266	.324	28-0-4	.143	0*	115	3		0.3
1996	Cin N	1	0	1.000	9	0	0	0-0	15.1	20	18	3	1	11-2	9	10.57	41	.317	.421	0-0-1	—	0	111	-6		-0.5
	KC A	0	1	.000	19	1	0	0-0	36.1	42	24	9	2	12-1	27	5.45	92	.282	.341	0	—	0	111	-2		-0.1
	Cin N	0	1	.000	1	0	0	0-0	0.1	4	2	0	0	0-0	0	54.00	8	.800	.800	0	—	0		-2		-0.3
1997	Det A	1	1	.500	2	2	0	0-0	9	6	5	0	0	5-0	4	5.00	92	.188	.297	0	—	0	129	0		0.0
Total	6	25	28	.472	107	58	4-1	0-0	416.2	479	249	51	15	158-9	214	4.97	83	.291	.355	109-0-14	.202	4	102	-37		-3.6
PULEO, CHARLIE								Charles Michael	B2.7.1955 Glen Ridge NJ		BR/TR/6-3/200*			d9.16		Col Seton Hall								
1981	NY N	0	0	—	4	1	0	0-0	13.1	8	1	0	0	8-2	8	0.00	—	.182	.308	2	.000	-0	50	5		0.2
1982	NY N	9	9	.500	36	24	1-1	1-0	171	179	99	13	2	90-7	98	4.47	82	.275	.362	48-0-6	.125	-1	101	-15		-1.5
1983	Cin N	6	12	.333	27	24	0	0-0	143.2	145	86	18	5	91-9	71	4.89	78	.269	.375	50-0-2	.100	-2	91	-16	28	-2.0
1984	Cin N	1	2	.333	5	4	0	0-0	22	27	15	2	0	15-2	16	5.73	66	.297	.393	5-0-2	.200	0	93	-4		-0.5
1986	Atl N	1	2	.333	5	3	1	0-0	24.1	13	10	4	1	12-1	18	2.96	134	.160	.274	6-0-1	.333	0	90	2		0.3
1987	Atl N	6	8	.429	35	16	1	0-0	123.1	122	63	11	3	40-0	99	4.23	102	.262	.319	28-1-6	.179	1*	78	2		0.2
1988	Atl N	5	5	.500	53	3	0	1-1	106.1	101	46	9	3	47-7	70	3.47	106	.251	.330	13-0-4	.231	0	73	2		0.2
1989	Atl N	1	1	.500	15	1	0	0-0	29	26	15	2	0	16-1	17	4.66	79	.245	.333	1-0-1	.000	-0	24	-2	13	-0.2
Total	8	29	39	.426	180	76	3-1	2-1	633	621	335	59	14	319-29	387	4.25	90	.261	.348	153-1-22	.144	-1	90	-26	41	-3.3
PULIDO, ALFONSO								Alfonso (Manzo)	B1.23.1957 Tierra Blanca, Veracruz, Mexico		BL/TL/5-11/170*			d9.5										
1983	Pit N	0	0	—	1	0	0	0-0	2	4	3	2	0	1-0	1	9.00	42	.400	.455	0-0-1	—	0	142	-1		-0.1
1984	Pit N	0	0	—	1	0	0	0-0	2	3	2	0	0	1-0	2	9.00	40	.333	.400	0-0-1	—	0		-1		-0.1
1986	NY A	1	1	.500	10	3	0	1-0	30.2	38	17	8	0	9-0	13	4.70	88	.306	.351	0	—	0	124	-2		-0.1
Total	3	1	1	.500	12	4	0	1-0	34.2	45	22	10	0	11-0	16	5.19	79	.315	.361	0-0-1	—	0	127	-4		-0.3
PULIDO, CARLOS								Juan Carlos (Valera)	B8.5.1971 Caracas, Venez		BL/TL/6-0/195(180-205)			d4.9										
1994	Min A	3	7	.300	19	14	0	0-0	84.1	87	57	17	1	40-1	32	5.98	83	.273	.352	0	—	0	95	-8		-0.8
2003	Min A	1	0	.000	7	1	0	0-0	15.2	15	9	0	0	3-0	9	4.02	112	.254	.281	0	—	0	123	0		0.0
2004	Min A	0	0	—	6	0	0	0-0	11.1	16	13	2	1	4-1	9	8.74	53	.333	.382	0	—	0		-6		-0.3
Total	3	3	8	.273	32	15	0	0-0	111.1	118	79	19	2	47-2	47	5.98	81	.277	.346	0	—	0	98	-14		-1.1
PULSIPHER, BILL								William Thomas	B10.9.1973 Fort Benning GA		BL/TL/6-3/225(200-228)			[NYN91 2/66]		d6.17	[DL 1997 NY N 32]								
1995	NY N	5	7	.417	17	17	2	0-0	126.2	122	58	11	4	45-0	81	3.98	101	.255	.324	38-0-4	.105	0	88	3		0.3
1998	NY N	0	0	—	15	1	0	0-1	14.1	23	11	2	0	5-1	13	6.91	60	.371	.418	1	.000	-0*	156	-4		-0.2
	Mil N	3	4	.429	11	10	0	0-0	58	63	30	6	1	26-3	38	4.66	93	.289	.361	19-0-1	.158	-0	85	-1		-0.2
	Year	3	4	.429	26	11	0	0-1	72.1	86	41	8	1	31-4	51	5.10	84	.307	.373	20-0-1	.150	-1	91	-5		-0.4
1999	Mil N	5	6	.455	19	16	0	0-0	87.1	100	65	19	2	36-2	42	5.98	77	.286	.352	21-0-8	.143	-1	110	-14	77	-1.5
2000	NY N	0	2	.000	2	2	0	0-0	6.2	12	9	1	4	6-0	7	12.15	36	.387	.500	2	.000	-0	42	-6		-0.9
2001	Bos A	0	0	—	23	0	0	0-0	22	25	15	3	2	14-0	16	5.32	83	.294	.402	0	—	0		-2		-0.1
	Chi A	0	0	—	14	0	0	0-0	8	11	8	2	1	7-0	4	7.88	59	.314	.432	0	—	0		-3		-0.1
	Year	0	0	—	37	0	0	0-0	30	36	23	5	3	21-0	20	6.00	75	.300	.411	0	—	0		-5		-0.2
2005	StL N	0	0	—	5	0	0	0-0	4	5	3	0	0	2-1	1	6.75	62	.357	.412	0	—	0		-1	24	0.0
Total	6	13	19	.406	106	46	2	0-1	327	361	199	44	11	141-7	202	5.15	83	.284	.357	81-0-13	.123	-1	95	-28	133	-2.7
PUMPELLY, SPENCER								Spencer Armstrong	B4.11.1893 Owego NY		D12.5.1973 Sayre PA			TR/5-11/175		d7.11	Col Yale								
1925	Was A	0	0	—	1	0	0	0-0	1	1	1	1	0	1-0	0	9.00	47	.333	.500	0	—	0		0		0.0
PURCELL, BLONDIE								William Aloysius	B Paterson NJ		BR/TR/5-9.5/159			d5.1		M1 ▲								
1879	Syr N	4	15	.211	22	17	15	0	179.2	245	165	1		19	28	3.76	63	.303	.319	277	.260	3*	64	-33		-2.5
	Cin N	0	2	.000	2	2	2	0	18	27	15	0		2	3	4.00	58	.355	.372	50	.220	-0*	69	-2		-0.2
	Year	4	17	.190	24	19	17	0	197.2	272	180	1		21	31	3.78	63	.308	.324	327	.254	3	65	-39		-2.7
1880	Cin N	3	17	.150	25	21	21	0	196	235	149	1		32	47	3.21	77	.271	.297	325-1	.292	4*	56	-11		-0.5
1881	Buf N	4	1	.800	9	5	5	0	61.2	62	37	2		9	15	2.77	100	.248	.274	113	.292	2*	117	0		0.2
1882	Buf N	2	1	.667	6	3	2	0	31	44	30	1		4	9	4.94	59	.338	.358	380-2	.276	1*	138	-7		-0.5
1883	Phi N	2	6	.250	11	9	7	0	80	110	71	0		12	30	4.39	70	.306	.329	425-1	.268	2*	75	-13		-0.8
1884	Phi N	0	0	—	1	0	0	0	4	3	1	0		0	1	2.25	133	.188	.188	428-1	.252	0*		1		0.0
1885	Phi AA	0	1	.000	1	0	0	0	6	11	9	0		2	3	6.00	57	.423	.464	304	.296	0*		-2		-0.2
1886	Bal AA	0	0	—	1	0	0	0	3	4	1	1		0	0	9.00	38	.200	.200	85	.224	0*		0		0.0
1887	Bal AA	0	0	—	1	0	0	0	4	8	8	0		4	2	15.75	26	.381	.500	567-4	.250	0*		-4		-0.2
Total	9	15	43	.259	79	57	52	0	581.1	746	486	5		84	138	3.73	70	.292	.314	2954-9	.267	12	72	-71		-4.7
PURDIN, JOHN								John Nolan	B7.16.1942 Lynx OH		BR/TR/6-2/185(160-185)			d9.16										
1964	LA N	2	0	1.000	3	2	1-1	0	16	6	1	0	1	6-0	16	0.56	576	.115	.207	5	.200	0	176	5		0.7
1965	LA N	2	1	.667	11	2	0	0	22.2	26	19	8	0	13-3	16	6.75	48	.283	.368	3	.000	-0	120	-9		-1.2
1968	LA N	2	3	.400	35	1	0	2	55.2	42	22	2	0	21-7	38	3.07	90	.206	.276	6	.500	1*	251	-2		-0.1
1969	LA N	0	0	—	9	0	0	0-0	16.1	19	11	7	0	12-1	6	6.06	55	.292	.403	2	.000	-0		-5	23	-0.3
Total	4	6	4	.600	58	5	1-1	2-0	110.2	93	53	18	1	52-11	68	3.90	77	.225	.309	16	.250	1	173	-11	23	-0.9
PURKEY, BOB								Robert Thomas	B7.14.1929 Pittsburgh PA		BR/TR/6-2/195(175-201)			d4.14										
1954	Pit N	3	8	.273	36	11	0	1	131.1	145	78	3	7	47-3	38	5.07	83	.293	.375	26-0-3	.077	-1	75	-10		-0.5
1955	Pit N	2	7	.222	14	10	2	1	67.2	77	47	5	2	25-1	24	5.32	77	.287	.353	19-1-3	.316	2	58	-9		-0.9
1956	Pit N	0	0	—	2	0	0	0	4	2	1	1	0	0-0	1	2.25	168	.143	.143	0	—	0		1		0.0
1957	Pit N	11	14	.440	48	21	6-1	2	179.2	194	84	10	7	38-9	51	3.86	98	.278	.317	45-0-2	.111	-0	69	1		0.0
1958	Cin N☆	17	11	.607	37	34	17-3	0	250	259	106	25	4	49-3	70	3.60	115	.268	.304	81-1-6	.111	-2	87	15		1.5
1959	Cin N	13	18	.419	38	33	9-1	1	218	241	118	25	6	43-2	78	4.25	95	.279	.316	66-1-4	.167	3	90	-5		-0.4
1960	Cin N	17	11	.607	41	33	11-1	0	252.2	259	114	22	9	59-5	97	3.60	106	.265	.311	83-0-6	.133	-2	113	6		0.5

YEAR	TM LG	W	L	PCT	G	GS	CG-SHO	SV-BS	IP	H	R	HR	HB	BB-IB	SO	ERA	AERA	OAV	OOB	AB-HR-SH	AVG	PB	SUP	APR	DL	PW
1961	†Cin N★	16	12	.571	36	34	13-1	1	246.1	245	118	27	6	51-4	116	3.73	109	.255	.296	80-1-7	.100	-3	96	8		0.8
1962	Cin N★	23	5	**.821**	37	37	18-2	0	288.1	260	109	28	14	64-3	141	2.81	143	.240	.289	107-2-7	.103	-2	114	**35**		3.0
1963	Cin N	6	10	.375	21	21	4-1	0	137	143	60	12	2	33-6	55	3.55	94	.272	.317	41-0-3	.098	-1	87	-3		-0.3
1964	Cin N	11	9	.550	34	25	9-2	1	195.2	181	77	16	7	49-4	78	3.04	119	.246	.289	58-0-8	.052	-4	116	11		0.8
1965	StL N	10	9	.526	32	17	3-1	2	124.1	148	83	20	7	33-4	39	5.79	66	.294	.344	35-0-7	.029	-3	123	-23		-3.4
1966	Pit N	0	1	.000	10	0	0	1	19.2	16	3	0	0	4-0	5	1.37	260	.235	.278	4	.000	-0*		5		0.3
Total	13	129	115	.529	386	276	92-13	9	1414.2	2170	998	195	71	510-41	793	3.79	103	.266	.313	645-6-56	.110	-13	97	32		1.5

PURNER, OSCAR Oscar E. B12.9.1873 Washington DC D12.4.1915 Douglas AZ d9.2

YEAR	TM LG	W	L	PCT	G	GS	CG-SHO	SV-BS	IP	H	R	HR	HB	BB-IB	SO	ERA	AERA	OAV	OOB	AB-HR-SH	AVG	PB	SUP	APR	DL	PW
1895	Was N	0	0		1	0	0	0	2	4	2	1	0	3	0	9.00	53	.400	.538	1	.000	-0		-1		0.0

PUTTMANN, AMBROSE Ambrose Nicholas "Putty","Brose" B9.9.1880 Cincinnati OH D6.21.1936 Jamaica NY TL/6-4/185 d9.4

YEAR	TM LG	W	L	PCT	G	GS	CG-SHO	SV-BS	IP	H	R	HR	HB	BB-IB	SO	ERA	AERA	OAV	OOB	AB-HR-SH	AVG	PB	SUP	APR	DL	PW
1903	NY A	2	0	1.000	3	2	1	0	19	16	9	0	1	4	8	0.95	330	.229	.280	7	.143	-0	206	2		0.3
1904	NY A	2	0	1.000	9	3	2-1	0	49.1	40	21	0	1	17	26	2.74	99	.222	.289	18	.278	2	105	0		0.2
1905	NY A	2	7	.222	17	9	5-1	0	86.1	79	50	2	5	37	39	4.27	69	.245	.332	32	.313	3*	96	-9		-0.7
1906	StL N	2	2	.500	4	4	0	0	18.2	23	13	2	2	9	12	5.30	60	.303	.391	6	.333	0	139	-5		-0.9
Total	4	8	9	.471	33	18	8-2	0	173.1	158	93	4	8	67	85	3.58	80	.244	.322	63	.286	4	119	-12		-1.1

PUTZ, J.J. Joseph Jason B2.2.1977 Trenton MI BR/TR/6-5/220* [SeaA99 6/185] d8.11 Col Michigan

YEAR	TM LG	W	L	PCT	G	GS	CG-SHO	SV-BS	IP	H	R	HR	HB	BB-IB	SO	ERA	AERA	OAV	OOB	AB-HR-SH	AVG	PB	SUP	APR	DL	PW
2003	Sea A	0	0		3	0	0	0-0	3.2	4	2	1	0	3-0	3	4.91	88	.267	.389	0	—	0		0		0.0
2004	Sea A	0	3	.000	54	0	0	9-4	63	66	35	10	5	24-4	47	4.71	95	.274	.349	0	—	0		-2		-0.1
2005	Sea A	6	5	.545	64	0	0	1-3	60	58	27	8	2	23-2	45	3.60	117	.254	.324	0	—	0		3		0.6
Total	3	6	8	.429	121	0	0	10-7	126.2	128	64	18	7	50-6	95	4.19	104	.264	.339	0	—	0		1		0.5

PYECHA, JOHN John Nicholas B11.25.1931 Aliquippa PA BR/TR/6-5/200 d4.24 Col Appalachian St.

YEAR	TM LG	W	L	PCT	G	GS	CG-SHO	SV-BS	IP	H	R	HR	HB	BB-IB	SO	ERA	AERA	OAV	OOB	AB-HR-SH	AVG	PB	SUP	APR	DL	PW
1954	Chi N	0	1	.000	1	0	0	0	2.2	4	3	1	0	2	1	10.13	41	.333	.429	1	.000	-0		-2		-0.3

PYLE, EWALD Ewald "Lefty" B8.27.1910 St.Louis MO D1.10.2004 DuQuoin IL BL/TL/6-0.5/175 d4.23

YEAR	TM LG	W	L	PCT	G	GS	CG-SHO	SV-BS	IP	H	R	HR	HB	BB-IB	SO	ERA	AERA	OAV	OOB	AB-HR-SH	AVG	PB	SUP	APR	DL	PW
1939	StL A	0	2	.000	6	1	0	0	8.1	17	15	3	0	11	5	12.96	38	.405	.528	2	.000	-0	145	-8		-1.3
1942	StL A	0	0		2	0	0	0	5.1	6	4	0	0	4	1	6.75	55	.286	.400	3	.000	-0		-1		-0.1
1943	Was A	4	8	.333	18	11	2-1	1	72.2	70	38	0	1	45	25	4.09	78	.254	.360	20-0-1	.100	-1	60	-6		-1.2
1944	NY N	7	10	.412	31	21	3	0	164	152	89	12	6	68	79	4.34	85	.241	.321	51-0-1	.157	-0	95	-10		-1.0
1945	NY N	0	0		6	1	0	0	6.1	16	12	0	0	4	2	17.05	23	.457	.513	2	.000	-0	108	-8		-0.4
	Bos N	0	1	.000	4	2	0	0	13.2	16	15	1	0	18	10	7.24	53	.302	.479	6	.333	1	155	-6		-0.3
	Year	0	1	.000	10	3	0	0	20	32	27	1	0	22	12	10.35	37	.364	.491	8	.250	0	139	-15		-0.7
Total	5	11	21	.344	67	36	5-1	1	270.1	277	173	16	7	150	122	5.03	71	.262	.357	84-0-2	.143	-2	91	-39		-4.3

PYLE, HARLAN Harlan Albert "Firpo" B11.29.1905 Burchard NE D1.13.1993 Beatrice NE BR/TR/6-2/180 d9.21

YEAR	TM LG	W	L	PCT	G	GS	CG-SHO	SV-BS	IP	H	R	HR	HB	BB-IB	SO	ERA	AERA	OAV	OOB	AB-HR-SH	AVG	PB	SUP	APR	DL	PW
1928	Cin N	0	0		2	1	0	0	1.1	3	3	0	0	1	0	20.25	20	.143	.455	1	.000	-0	128	-2		-0.1

PYLE, SHADOW Harry Thomas B11.29.1861 Reading PA D12.26.1908 Reading PA TL/5-8/136 d10.15

YEAR	TM LG	W	L	PCT	G	GS	CG-SHO	SV-BS	IP	H	R	HR	HB	BB-IB	SO	ERA	AERA	OAV	OOB	AB-HR-SH	AVG	PB	SUP	APR	DL	PW
1884	Phi N	0	1	.000	1	1	1	0	9	9	8	0		6	4	4.00	75	.257	.366	4	.000	-1	0	-1		-0.2
1887	Chi N	1	3	.250	4	4	3	0	26.2	32	27	1	2	21	5	4.73	95	.291	.414	16-1	.188	-0	90	-2		-0.2
Total	2	1	4	.200	5	5	4	0	35.2	41	35	1	2	27	9	4.54	90	.283	.402	20-1	.150	-1	76	-3		-0.4

QUALLS, CHAD Chad Michael B8.17.1978 Lomita CA BR/TR/6-5/220* [HouN00 2/67] d7.22 Col Nevada-Reno

YEAR	TM LG	W	L	PCT	G	GS	CG-SHO	SV-BS	IP	H	R	HR	HB	BB-IB	SO	ERA	AERA	OAV	OOB	AB-HR-SH	AVG	PB	SUP	APR	DL	PW
2004	†Hou N	4	0	1.000	25	0	0	1-1	33	34	13	3	4	8-1	24	3.55	123	.266	.326	1	.000	-0		3		0.4
2005	†Hou N	6	4	.600	77	0	0	0-0	79.2	73	33	7	6	23-2	60	3.28	128	.249	.314	1	.000	-0		7		0.9
Total	2	10	4	.714	102	0	0	1-1	112.2	107	46	10	10	31-3	84	3.36	127	.254	.318	2	.000	-0		10		1.3

QUALTERS, TOM Thomas Francis "Money Bags" B4.1.1935 McKeesport PA BR/TR/6-0.5/190* d9.13

YEAR	TM LG	W	L	PCT	G	GS	CG-SHO	SV-BS	IP	H	R	HR	HB	BB-IB	SO	ERA	AERA	OAV	OOB	AB-HR-SH	AVG	PB	SUP	APR	DL	PW
1953	Phi N	0	0	—	1	0	0	0	0.1	4	6	1	1	1	0	162.00	3	.800	.857	0	—	0		-6		-0.2
1957	Phi N	0	0	—	6	0	0	0	7.1	12	6	0	0	4-1	6	7.36	52	.400	.471	0	—	0		-3		-0.
1958	Phi N	0	0	—	1	0	0	0	2	2	1	0	0	1-0	0	4.50	88	.222	.300	0	—	0		0		-0.
	Chi A	0	0	—	26	0	0	0	43	45	22	1	0	20-4	14	4.19	87	.281	.359	2	.000	-0		-3		-0.
Total	3	0	0	—	34	0	0	0	52.2	63	35	2	1	26-5	20	5.64	65	.309	.388	2	.000	-0		-12		-0.

QUANTRILL, PAUL Paul John B11.3.1968 London ON, Can. BL/TR/6-1/185(175-200) [BosA89 6/163] d7.20 Col Wisconsin-Madison

YEAR	TM LG	W	L	PCT	G	GS	CG-SHO	SV-BS	IP	H	R	HR	HB	BB-IB	SO	ERA	AERA	OAV	OOB	AB-HR-SH	AVG	PB	SUP	APR	DL	PW
1992	Bos A	2	3	.400	27	0	0	1-4	49.1	55	18	1	1	15-5	24	2.19	194	.288	.340	0	—	0		9		0.8
1993	Bos A	6	12	.333	49	14	1-1	1-1	138	151	73	13	2	44-14	66	3.91	118	.279	.334	0	—	0	68	8		0.8
1994	Bos A	1	1	.500	17	0	0	0-2	23	25	10	4	2	5-1	15	3.52	143	.278	.323	0	—	0	4	4		-0.
	Phi N	2	2	.500	18	1	0	1-1	30	39	21	3	3	10-3	13	6.00	71	.331	.394	3	.000	-0	64	-5		-0.
1995	Phi N	11	12	.478	33	29	0	0-0	179.1	212	102	20	6	44-3	103	4.67	90	.295	.338	57-0-7	.105	-2	89	-9		-1.
1996	Tor A	5	14	.263	38	20	0	0-2	134.1	172	90	27	2	51-3	86	5.43	92	.316	.373	0	—	0	82	-7		-0.
1997	Tor A	6	7	.462	77	0	0	5-5	88	103	25	5	1	17-3	56	1.94	236	.297	.329	1	.000	-0		24		3.
1998	Tor A	3	4	.429	82	0	0	7-7	80	88	26	5	5	22-6	59	2.59	180	.285	.334	0	—	0		18		1.
1999	Tor A	3	2	.600	41	0	0	0-4	48.2	53	19	5	4	17-1	28	3.33	148	.282	.351	0	—	0	9	9	71	0.
2000	Tor A	2	5	.286	68	0	0	1-2	83.2	100	45	7	2	25-1	47	4.52	111	.298	.347	0	—	0	5	5		0.
2001	Tor A★	11	2	.846	**80**	0	0	2-7	83	86	29	6	6	12-7	53	3.04	151	.274	.311	0	—	0	15	15		2.
2002	LA N	5	4	.556	**86**	0	0	1-2	76.2	80	27	1	3	25-7	53	2.70	144	.267	.328	3	.333	-0	20	10		1.
2003	LA N	2	5	.286	**89**	0	0	1-4	77.1	61	18	2	3	15-2	44	1.75	236	.227	.275	1	.000	-0		20		1.
2004	†NY A	7	3	.700	**86**	0	0	1-4	95.1	124	54	5	4	20-9	37	4.72	97	.316	.352	1	.000	-0		-1		-0.
2005	NY A	1	0	1.000	22	0	0	0-1	32	48	24	2	4	7-2	11	6.75	67	.361	.383	0	—	0		-7		-0.
	SD N	1	1	.500	22	0	0	0-0	31.2	37	13	2	1	2-1	24	3.41	113	.294	.303	1	.000	-0	2	2		-0.
	Fla N	0	1	.000	6	0	0	0-0	5.1	8	7	1	0	5-0	1	8.44	47	.348	.464	0	—	0		-4		-0.
	Year	1	2	.333	28	0	0	0-0	37	45	20	3	1	7-1	25	4.14	94	.302	.331	1	.000	-0	2	-2		-0.
Total	14	68	78	.466	841	64	1-1	21-46	1255.2	1442	601	112	45	336-68	725	3.83	118	.292	.339	67-0-7	.104	-2	83	91	71	9.

QUARLES, BILL William H. B1869 Petersburg VA D3.25.1897 Petersburg VA 6-3/? d5.21

YEAR	TM LG	W	L	PCT	G	GS	CG-SHO	SV-BS	IP	H	R	HR	HB	BB-IB	SO	ERA	AERA	OAV	OOB	AB-HR-SH	AVG	PB	SUP	APR	DL	PW
1891	Was AA	1	1	.500	3	2	2	0	22	32	27	1	2	12	10	8.18	46	.330	.414	11	.000	-2	100	-9		-0.
1893	Bos N	2	1	.667	3	3	3	0	27	31	20	2	2	5	6	4.67	106	.279	.322	9	.222	0	127	1		0.
Total	2	3	2	.600	6	5	5	0	49	63	47	3	4	17	16	6.24	70	.303	.367	20	.100	-2	119	-8		-0.

QUEEN, MEL Melvin Douglas B3.26.1942 Johnson City NY BL/TR/6-1/197* d4.13.1964 M1/C5 s-Mel ▲

YEAR	TM LG	W	L	PCT	G	GS	CG-SHO	SV-BS	IP	H	R	HR	HB	BB-IB	SO	ERA	AERA	OAV	OOB	AB-HR-SH	AVG	PB	SUP	APR	DL	PW
1966	Cin N	0	0	—	7	0	0	0	7	11	5	0	0	6-0	5	6.43	61	.367	.459	55-0-1	.127	0*	-2	28		-0.
1967	Cin N	14	8	.636	31	24	6-2	0	195.2	155	69	17	6	52-5	154	2.76	136	.215	.271	81-0-3	.210	3*	80	19		2.
1968	Cin N	0	1	.000	5	4	0	0	18.1	25	15	7	0	6-4	20	5.89	54	.333	.383	8	.125	0*	158	-6	84	-0.
1969	Cin N	1	0	1.000	2	2	0	0-0	12	7	3	2	1	3-0	7	2.25	167	.163	.234	6	.167	-0	212	2		0.
1970	Cal A	3	6	.333	34	3	0	9-3	60	58	28	5	5	28-6	44	4.20	86	.261	.354	16	.250	1*	49	-2	21	-0.
1971	Cal A	2	2	.500	44	0	0	4-3	65.2	49	17	3	8	29-6	35	1.78	182	.212	.319	8-0-1	.000	-1*	10			0.
1972	Cal A	0	0	—	17	0	0	0-0	31	31	17	2	3	19-1	19	4.35	67	.265	.376	2	.000	-0	-5			-0.
Total	7	20	17	.541	140	33	6-2	14-6	389.2	336	154	36	23	143-22	306	3.14	113	.230	.310	176-0-5	.170	3	97	16	133	2.

QUEEN, MEL Melvin Joseph B3.4.1918 Maxwell PA D4.4.1982 Fort Smith AR BR/TR/6-0.5/204* d4.18 .Mil 1945 f-Mel

YEAR	TM LG	W	L	PCT	G	GS	CG-SHO	SV-BS	IP	H	R	HR	HB	BB-IB	SO	ERA	AERA	OAV	OOB	AB-HR-SH	AVG	PB	SUP	APR	DL	PW
1942	NY A	1	0	1.000	4	0	0	0	5.2	6	2	0	2	3	0	0.00	—	.300	.440	0	—	0		2		0.
1944	NY A	6	3	.667	10	10	4-1	0	81.2	68	32	7	1	34	30	3.31	105	.227	.308	31-0-3	.194	-0	125	3		0.
1946	NY A	1	1	.500	14	3	1	0	30.1	40	28	2	0	21	26	6.53	53	.315	.412	7	.143	-0	116	-12		-0.
1947	NY A	0	0	—	5	0	0	0	6.2	9	7	2	1	4	2	9.45	37	.321	.424	0	.000	-0	-4			-0.
	Pit N	3	7	.300	14	12	2	0	74	70	39	8	1	51	34	4.01	105	.244	.360	26-0-1	.077	-2	106	1		-2.
1948	Pit N	4	4	.500	25	8	0	1	66.1	82	51	8	3	40	34	6.65	61	.308	.405	17-0-2	.059	-2	76	-17		-2.
1950	Pit N	5	14	.263	33	21	4-1	0	120.1	135	95	18	2	73	76	5.98	73	.284	.381	35-0-2	.057	-3	90	-22		-3.
1951	Pit N	7	9	.438	39	21	4-1	0	168.1	149	90	21	1	99	123	4.44	95	.233	.337	47-0-6	.106	-3	100	-2		-1.
1952	Pit N	0	2	.000	2	2	0	0	3.1	8	12	2	0	4	3	29.70	13	.381	.480	0		0	89	-9		-1.
Total	8	27	40	.403	146	77	15-3	1	556.2	567	354	68	11	329	328	5.09	80	.262	.362	164-0-14	.104	-10	100	-60		-13.

QUEVEDO, RUBEN Ruben Eduardo B1.5.1979 Valencia, Venez BR/TR/6-1/230(190-245) d4.14

YEAR	TM LG	W	L	PCT	G	GS	CG-SHO	SV-BS	IP	H	R	HR	HB	BB-IB	SO	ERA	AERA	OAV	OOB	AB-HR-SH	AVG	PB	SUP	APR	DL	PW
2000	Chi N	3	10	.231	21	15	1	0-0	88	96	81	21	3	54-4	65	7.47	61	.271	.370	30-0-1	.133	-1	78	-30		-3
2001	Mil N	4	5	.444	10	10	0	0-0	56.2	59	30	9	0	30-4	60	4.61	93	.257	.344	16-0-4	.250	0	84	-1		-0

YEAR	TM LG	W	L	PCT	G	GS	CG-SHO	SV-BS	IP	H	R	HR	HB	BB-IB	SO	ERA	AERA	OAV	OOB	AB-HR-SH	AVG	PB	SUP	APR	DL	PW
2002	Mil N	6	11	.353	26	25	1-1	0-0	139	159	100	28	4	68-3	93	5.76	71	.288	.368	42-0-3	.095	-2	106	-27		-3.1
2003	Mil N	1	4	.200	9	8	0	0-0	42.2	53	32	12	0	23-1	19	6.75	64	.314	.390	10-0-1	.300	1	84	-10	84	-1.0
Total	4	14	30	.318	66	58	2-1	0-0	326.1	364	243	70	7	175-12	237	6.15	70	.281	.367	98-0-9	.153	-2	91	-68	84	-7.8

QUICK, EDDIE Edward B12.1881 Baltimore MD D6.19.1913 Rocky Ford CO TR/5-11/? d9.28

| 1903 | NY A | 0 | 0 | — | 1 | 1 | 0 | 0 | 2 | 5 | 5 | 0 | 0 | 1 | 0 | 9.00 | 35 | .455 | .500 | 1 | | .000 | -0 | 160 | -2 | | -0.1 |

QUINN, TAD Clarence Carr B9.21.1882 Torrington CT D8.6.1946 Waterbury CT TR/6-1/210 d9.27

1902	Phi A	0	1	.000	1	1	1	0	8	12	9	1	0	1	3	4.50	82	.343	.361	3		.000	-0	78	-2		-0.2
1903	Phi A	0	0	—	2	0	0	0	9	11	6	0	1	5	1	5.00	61	.297	.395	3		.667	1		-2		0.1
Total	2	0	1	.000	3	1	1	0	17	23	15	1	1	6	4	4.76	70	.319	.380	6		.333	1	78	-4		-0.1

QUINN, FRANK Frank William B11.27.1927 Springfield MA D1.11.1993 Boynton Beach FL BR/TR/6-2/180* d5.29 Col Yale

1949	Bos A	0	0	—	8	0	0	0	22	18	7	2	1	9	4	2.86	152	.222	.308	6		.167	-0		4		0.1
1950	Bos A	0	0	—	1	0	0	0	2	2	2	0	1	1	0	9.00	54	.250	.333	0		—	.0		-1		0.0
Total	2	0	0	—	9	0	0	0	24	20	9	2	1	10	4	3.38	131	.225	.310	6		.167	-0		3		0.1

QUINN, JACK John Picus (b John Quinn Picus) B7.5.1883 Janesville PA D4.17.1946 Pottsville PA BR/TR/6-0/196 d4.15

1909	NY A	9	5	.643	23	11	8	1	118.2	110	45	1	4	24	36	1.97	128	.252	.297	45-0-1	.156	0	119	5		0.8
1910	NY A	18	12	.600	35	31	20	0	235.2	214	88	2	6	58	82	2.37	112	.247	.299	82-0-4	.232	4	102	6		1.6
1911	NY A	8	10	.444	40	16	7	2	174.2	203	111	4	4	41	71	3.76	96	.297	.341	61-1-2	.164	-1	74	-7		-0.6
1912	NY A	5	7	.417	18	11	7	0	102.2	139	89	4	4	23	47	5.79	62	.325	.365	39-0-1	.205	-1	84	-22		-2.1
1913	Bos N	4	3	.571	8	7	6-1	0	56.1	55	22	1	1	7	33	2.40	137	.261	.288	20	.200	1*	72	5		0.9
1914	Bal F	26	14	.650	46	42	27-4	1	342.2	335	129	8	8	65	164	2.60	117	.266	.307	121-2-8	.273	6*	89	15		2.5
1915	Bal F	9	22	.290	44	31	21	1	273.2	289	137	9	8	63	118	3.45	83	.278	.325	110-0-3	.264	3*	83	-18		-1.4
1918	Chi A	5	1	.833	6	5	5	0	51	38	13	0	0	7	22	2.29	119	.216	.246	18	.222	1	143	4		0.7
1919	NY A	15	14	.517	38	31	18-4	0	266	242	96	8	6	65	97	2.61	123	.244	.295	91-0-4	.209	1	99	18		2.0
1920	NY A	18	10	.643	41	32	17-2	3	253.1	271	110	8	2	48	101	3.20	119	.273	.308	88-2-3	.091	-5	105	18		1.4
1921	†NY A	8	7	.533	33	13	6	0	119	158	61	2	5	32	44	3.78	112	.327	.375	41-1-2	.220	1	97	6		0.8
1922	Bos A	13	16	.448	40	32	16-4	0	256	263	119	9	3	59	67	3.48	118	.267	.311	91-1-3	.099	-5	99	16		1.4
1923	Bos A	13	17	.433	28	28	16-1	7	243	302	125	6	6	53	71	3.89	106	.316	.356	80-0-6	.225	0	75	9		1.0
1924	Bos A	12	13	.480	44	25	13-2	7	228.2	241	109	10	12	52	64	3.27	134	.273	.322	78-0-4	.179	-4	82	23		2.2
1925	Bos A	7	8	.467	19	15	8	0	105	140	68	3	3	26	24	4.37	104	.315	.357	32-0-2	.094	-2	89	1		0.0
	Phi A	6	3	.667	18	13	4	0	99.2	119	56	3	3	16	19	3.88	120	.296	.328	31-0-1	.097	-3	90	6		0.3
	Year	13	11	.542	37	28	12	0	204.2	259	124	6	6	42	43	4.13	111	.306	.343	63-0-3	.095	-5	89	8		0.3
1926	Phi A	10	11	.476	31	21	8-3	1	163.2	191	74	4	1	36	58	3.41	122	.296	.334	46-0-6	.174	-0	98	15		1.8
1927	Phi A	15	10	.600	34	26	11-3	1	201.1	211	82	8	4	37	43	3.26	131	.278	.315	66-0-7	.091	-7	82	24		1.9
1928	Phi A	18	7	.720	31	28	18-4	1	211.1	239	92	7	3	34	43	2.90	139	.286	.320	79-0-6	.165	-3	142	22		2.1
1929	†Phi A	11	9	.550	35	18	7	2	161	182	87	8	1	39	41	3.97	107	.290	.332	60-0-4	.133	-4	104	3		-0.1
1930	†Phi A	9	7	.563	35	6	0	6	89.2	109	51	6	1	22	28	4.42	106	.302	.344	34-1-0	.265	1	61	2		0.5
1931	Bro N	5	4	.556	39	1	0	15	64.1	65	28	1	1	24	25	2.66	143	.266	.335	15-0-1	.200	0	90	6		1.1
1932	Bro N	3	7	.300	42	0	0	8	87.1	102	36	1	4	24	28	3.30	116	.296	.343	20-0-3	.200	0		5		0.7
1933	Cin N	0	1	.000	14	0	0	1	15.2	20	9	0	0	5	3	4.02	84	.323	.373	1	.000	-0		-1		-0.1
Total	23	247	218	.531	756	443	243-28	57	3920.1	4238	1837	102	91	860	1329	3.29	113	.280	.323	1349-8-71	.184	-16	95	161		19.4

QUINN, WIMPY Wellington Hunt B5.14.1918 Birmingham AL D9.1.1954 Santa Monica CA BR/TR/6-2/187 d6.8 Col Oregon

| 1941 | Chi N | 0 | 0 | — | 3 | 0 | 0 | 0 | 5 | 3 | 4 | 0 | 0 | 4 | 0 | 7.20 | 49 | .158 | .273 | 2 | .500 | 0 | | -2 | | -0.1 |

QUINTANA, LUIS Luis Joaquin (Santos) B12.25.1951 Vega Baja, PR BL/TL/6-2/175* d7.9 [DL 1976 Atl N 56]

1974	Cal A	2	1	.667	18	0	0	0-2	12.2	17	6	0	0	14-1	11	4.26	81	.327	.463	0	—	0		-1		-0.2
1975	Cal A	0	2	.000	4	0	0	0-0	7	13	6	2	0	6-1	5	6.43	56	.394	.487	0	—	0		-2		-0.5
Total	2	2	3	.400	22	0	0	0-2	19.2	30	12	2	0	20-2	16	5.03	70	.353	.472	0	—	0		-3	56	-0.7

QUIRICO, RAFAEL Rafael Octavio (Dottin) B9.7.1969 Santo Domingo, D.R. BL/TL/6-3/212 d6.25

| 1996 | Phi N | 0 | 1 | .000 | 1 | 1 | 0 | 0-0 | 1.2 | 4 | 7 | 1 | 0 | 5-0 | 1 | 37.80 | 11 | .444 | .643 | 0 | — | 0 | 21 | -6 | | -0.8 |

QUIRK, ART Arthur Lincoln B4.11.1938 Providence RI BR/TL/5-11/170* d4.17 Col Dartmouth

1962	Bal A	2	2	.500	7	5	0	0	27.1	36	20	3	0	18-0	18	5.93	62	.308	.400	7-0-1	.143	0	92	-7		-0.8
1963	Was A	1	0	1.000	7	3	0	0	21	23	13	3	0	8-1	12	4.29	87	.280	.341	4	.250	0	152	-2		-0.1
Total	2	3	2	.600	14	8	0	0	48.1	59	33	6	0	26-1	30	5.21	71	.296	.376	11-0-1	.182	0	114	-9		-0.9

QUISENBERRY, DAN Daniel Raymond B2.7.1953 Santa Monica CA D9.30.1998 Leawood KS BR/TR/6-2/180* d7.8 Col La Verne

1979	KC A	3	2	.600	32	0	0	5-5	40	42	16	5	0	7-5	13	3.15	135	.278	.306	0	—	0		5		0.7
1980	†KC A	12	7	.632	75	0	0	33-3	128.1	129	47	5	1	27-15	37	3.09	131	.265	.302	0	—	0		15		3.0
1981	†KC A	1	4	.200	40	0	0	18-4	62.1	59	16	1	1	15-8	20	1.73	208	.258	.301	0	—	0		12		1.9
1982	KC A★	9	7	.563	72	0	0	35-9	136.2	126	43	12	0	12-2	46	2.57	159	.252	.266	0	—	0		23		4.2
1983	KC A★	5	3	.625	69	0	0	45-8	139	118	35	4	0	11-2	48	1.94	212	.229	.243	0	—	0		33		4.0
1984	†KC A☆	6	3	.667	72	0	0	44-9	129.1	121	39	10	0	12-4	41	2.64	153	.247	.264	0	—	0		21		2.9
1985	†KC A	8	9	.471	84	0	0	37-12	129	142	41	8	1	16-5	54	2.37	176	.280	.301	0	—	0		25		4.4
1986	KC A	3	7	.300	62	0	0	12-4	81.1	92	30	2	3	24-12	36	2.77	154	.291	.342	0	—	0		12		1.8
1987	KC A	4	1	.800	47	0	0	8-3	49	58	15	3	1	10-3	17	2.76	167	.287	.322	0	—	0		11		1.4
1988	KC A	0	1	.000	20	0	0	1-0	25.1	32	11	0	0	5-2	9	3.55	113	.305	.336	0	—	0		1		0.1
	StL N	2	0	1.000	33	0	0	0-1	38	54	26	4	0	6-1	19	6.16	57	.344	.364	1	.000	0		-10		-0.5
1989	StL N	3	1	.750	63	0	0	6-1	78.1	78	25	2	0	14-9	37	2.64	139	.261	.293	4	.250	0		9		0.7
1990	SF N	0	1	.000	5	0	0	0-0	6.2	13	12	1	0	3-2	2	13.50	27	.419	.432	1	.000	-0		-8		-1.0
Total	12	56	46	.549	674	0	0	244-60	1043.1	1064	356	59	7	162-70	379	2.76	147	.267	.294	6	.167	0		149		23.6

RABE, CHARLIE Charles Henry B5.6.1932 Boyce TX BL/TL/6-1/180* d9.21

1957	Cin N	0	1	.000	2	1	0	0	9	5	2	2	0	0-0	6	2.16	190	.167	.167	0	.000	-0	21	2		0.2
1958	Cin N	0	3	.000	9	1	0	0	18.2	25	10	3	0	9-0	10	4.34	96	.321	.391	4	.000	-1	43	0		-0.1
Total	2	0	4	.000	11	2	0	0	27	30	12	5	0	9-0	16	3.67	113	.308	.333	6	.000	-1	32	2		0.1

RACHUNOK, STEVE Stephen Stepanovich "The Mad Russian" B12.5.1916 Rittman OH D5.11.2002 Corona CA BR/TR/4.5/205 d9.17

| 1940 | Bro N | 0 | 1 | .000 | 2 | 1 | 1 | 0 | 10 | 9 | 5 | 0 | 0 | 5 | 10 | 4.50 | 89 | .243 | .333 | | .000 | 0 | 87 | 0 | | 0.0 |

RACZKA, MIKE Michael B11.16.1962 New Britain CT BL/TL/6-0/200 [BalA84 5/131] d8.15 Col New Haven

| 1992 | Oak A | 0 | 0 | — | 8 | 0 | 0 | 0-0 | 6.1 | 7 | 7 | 0 | 0 | 5-0 | 2 | 8.53 | 44 | .308 | .394 | 0 | — | 0 | | -4 | | -0.2 |

RADATZ, DICK Richard Raymond "The Monster" B4.2.1937 Detroit MI D3.16.2005 Easton MA BR/TR/6-5/235* d4.10 Col Michigan St.

1962	Bos A	9	6	.600	62	0	0	24	124.2	95	32	9	4	40-2	144	2.24	184	.211	.278	31-0-2	.097	-2		26		3.9
1963	Bos A★	15	6	.714	66	0	0	25	132.1	94	31	9	5	51-13	162	1.97	192	.201	.285	29-0-2	.069	-2		26		5.0
1964	Bos A★	16	9	.640	79	0	0	29	157	103	44	13	7	58-9	181	2.29	168	.186	.269	37-0-2	.162	-0		26		4.9
1965	Bos A	9	11	.450	63	0	0	22	124.1	104	57	11	5	53-11	121	3.91	95	.227	.312	27-1-2	.185	1		0		0.1
1966	Bos A	0	2	.000	16	0	0	4	19	24	10	3	0	11-2	19	4.74	80	.304	.389	2	.000	-0		-1		-0.2
	Cle A	0	3	.000	39	0	0	10	56.2	49	33	6	3	34-6	49	4.61	75	.233	.344	9	.111	-0		-8		-0.8
	Year	0	5	.000	55	0	0	14	75.2	73	43	9	3	45-8	68	4.64	76	.253	.356	11	.091	-1		-8		-1.0
1967	Cle A	0	0	—	3	0	0	0	3	5	2	1	0	2-0	1	6.00	54	.357	.438	0	—	-0		-1		-0.1
	Chi N	1	0	1.000	20	0	0	5	23.1	12	21	4	5	24-2	18	6.56	54	.154	.380	4	.250	-0		-8		-0.4
1969	Det N	2	2	.500	11	0	0	0-1	18.2	14	8	0	1	5-0	18	3.38	112	.212	.268	2	.000	-0		1		0.1
	Mon N	0	4	.000	22	0	0	3-1	34.2	32	22	6	1	18-1	32	5.71	65	.244	.340	4	.250	-0		-6		-0.0
Total	7	52	43	.547	381	0	0	122-2	693.2	532	260	65	30	296-46	745	3.13	122	.212	.300	145-1-8	.131	-3		55		11.4

RADBOURN, CHARLEY Charles Gardner "Old Hoss" B12.11.1854 Rochester NY D2.5.1897 Bloomington IL BR/TR(BB 1886p)/5-9/168 d5.5.1880 HF1939

1881	Pro N	25	11	.694	41	36	34-3	0	325.1	309	162	1		64	117	2.43	109	.235	.270	270	.219	-1*	122	14		1.4
1882	Pro N	33	19	.635	54	51	50-6	0	466	422	213	6		51	201	2.11	134	.226	.247	326-1	.239	-1*	109	35		3.2
1883	Pro N	48	25	.658	76	68	66-4	0	632.1	563	275	7		56	315	2.05	150	.227	.244	381-3	.283	14*	118	74		8.3
1884	†Pro N	59	12	.831	75	73	73-11	1	678.2	528	216	18		98	441	1.38	206	.205	.234	361-1	.230	5*	112	116		10.7
1885	Pro N	28	21	.571	49	49	49-2	0	445.2	423	209	4		83	154	2.20	122	.241	.275	249	.233	11*	97	22		3.4

YEAR	TM LG	W	L	PCT	G	GS	CG-SHO	SV-BS	IP	H	R	HR	HB	BB-IB	SO	ERA	AERA	OAV	OOB	AB-HR-SH	AVG	PB	SUP	APR	DL	PW
1886	Bos N	27	31	.466	58	58	57-3	0	509.1	521	300	18		111	218	3.00	107	.254	.292	253-2	.237	7*	101	12		2.0
1887	Bos N	24	23	.511	50	50	48-1	0	425	505	305	20	14	133	87	4.55	90	.286	.340	175-1	.229	2*	103	-19		-1.5
1888	Bos N	7	16	.304	24	24	24-1	0	207	187	110	8	8	45	64	2.87	100	.234	.282	79	.215	1	74	1		0.1
1889	Bos N	20	11	.645	33	31	28-1	0	277	282	151	14	8	72	99	3.67	113	.256	.306	122-1	.189	-1*	114	19		1.6
1890	Bos P	27	12	.692	41	38	36-1	0	343	352	183	8	11	100	80	3.31	133	.254	.309	154	.253	0*	99	46		3.9
1891	Cin N	11	13	.458	26	24	23-2	0	218	236	149	13	13	62	54	4.25	79	.266	.323	96	.177	-1*	84	-15		-1.5
Total	11	309	194	.614	527	502	488-35	2	4527.1	4328	2273	117	54	875	1830	2.68	120	.241	.278	2466-9	.236	38	106	305		31.5

RADBOURN, GEORGE George B. "Dordy" B4.8.1856 Bloomington IL D1.1.1904 Bloomington IL ?/160 d5.30

YEAR	TM LG	W	L	PCT	G	GS	CG-SHO	SV-BS	IP	H	R	HR	HB	BB-IB	SO	ERA	AERA	OAV	OOB	AB-HR-SH	AVG	PB	SUP	APR	DL	PW
1883	Det N	1	2	.333	3	3	2	0	22	38	28	1		7	2	6.55	47	.345	.385	12	.167	-1	92	-8		-0.8

RADEBAUGH, ROY Roy B2.22.1884 Champaign IL D1.17.1945 Cedar Rapids IA BR/TR/5-7/160 d9.22

YEAR	TM LG	W	L	PCT	G	GS	CG-SHO	SV-BS	IP	H	R	HR	HB	BB-IB	SO	ERA	AERA	OAV	OOB	AB-HR-SH	AVG	PB	SUP	APR	DL	PW
1911	StL N	0	0	—	2	1	0	0	10	6	3	0	0	4		2.70	125	.176	.263	3	.000	-0	67	1		0.0

RADER, DREW Drew Leon "Lefty" B5.14.1901 Elmira NY D6.5.1975 Catskill NY BR/TL/6-2/187 d7.18 Col Syracuse

YEAR	TM LG	W	L	PCT	G	GS	CG-SHO	SV-BS	IP	H	R	HR	HB	BB-IB	SO	ERA	AERA	OAV	OOB	AB-HR-SH	AVG	PB	SUP	APR	DL	PW
1921	Pit N	0	0	—	1	0	0	0	2	2	0	0	0	0	0	—	—	.286	.286	1	.000	-0		1		0.0

RADFORD, PAUL Paul Revere "Shorty" B10.14.1861 Roxbury MA D2.21.1945 Boston MA BR/TR/5-6/148 d5.1.1883 ▲

YEAR	TM LG	W	L	PCT	G	GS	CG-SHO	SV-BS	IP	H	R	HR	HB	BB-IB	SO	ERA	AERA	OAV	OOB	AB-HR-SH	AVG	PB	SUP	APR	DL	PW
1884	†Pro N	0	2	.000	2	2	1	0	13	27	19	0		3	2	7.62	37	.403	.429	355-1	.197	0*	74	-6		-0.7
1885	Pro N	0	2	.000	3	2	2	0	18.1	34	27	1		8	3	7.85	34	.378	.429	371	.243	1*	74	-10		-0.8
1887	NY AA	0	0	—	2	0	0	0	5	15	16	1	0	3	4	18.00	24	.789	.818	486-4	.265	1*		-8		-0.3
1890	Cle P	0	0	—	1	0	0	0	5	7	5	1	0	1	3	3.60	110	.318	.348	466-2	.292	0*		0		0.0
1891	Bos AA	0	0	—	1	0	0	0	1	0	0	0	0	1		0.00	—	.000	.000	456	.259	0*		0		0.0
1893	Was N	0	0	—	1	0	0	0	1	2	2	2	0	2	1	18.00	26	.400	.571	464-2	.228	0*		-1		0.0
Total	6	0	4	.000	10	4	3	0	43.1	85	69	5	0	17	13	8.52	37	.413	.457	2598-9	.250	2	69	-25		-1.8

RADINSKY, SCOTT Scott David B3.3.1968 Glendale CA BL/TL/6-3/204(190-221) [ChiA86 3/75] d4.9 [DL 1994 Chi A 131]

YEAR	TM LG	W	L	PCT	G	GS	CG-SHO	SV-BS	IP	H	R	HR	HB	BB-IB	SO	ERA	AERA	OAV	OOB	AB-HR-SH	AVG	PB	SUP	APR	DL	PW
1990	Chi A	6	1	.857	62	0	0	4-1	52.1	47	29	1	2	36-1	46	4.82	80	.241	.362	0	—	0		-5		-0.7
1991	Chi A	5	5	.500	67	0	0	8-7	71.1	53	18	4	1	23-2	44	2.02	198	.206	.270	0	—	0		16		2.4
1992	Chi A	3	7	.300	68	0	0	15-8	59.1	54	21	3	2	34-5	48	2.73	142	.243	.347	0	—	0		7		1.5
1993	†Chi A	8	2	.800	73	0	0	4-1	54.2	61	33	3	1	19-3	44	4.28	99	.268	.327	0	—	0		-2		-0.4
1995	Chi A	2	1	.667	46	0	0	1-2	38	46	23	7	0	17-4	14	5.45	82	.309	.371	0	—	0		-3	29	-0.3
1996	†LA N	5	1	.833	58	0	0	1-3	52.1	52	19	2	0	17-5	48	2.41	163	.264	.318	1	.000	-0		8	11	0.9
1997	LA N	5	1	.833	75	0	0	3-2	62.1	54	22	4	1	21-5	44	2.89	135	.236	.298	4	.000	0		10		1.9
1998	LA N	6	6	.500	62	0	0	13-11	61.2	63	21	5	4	20-1	45	2.63	153	.272	.337	0	—	0		-1	69	-0.1
1999	StL N	2	1	.667	43	0	0	3-0	27.2	27	16	2	1	18-3	17	4.88	94	.270	.371	0	—	0		0	174	-0.2
2000	StL N	0	0	—	1	0	0	0-0	0	0	0	0	0	1-0	0	—	—	—	1.000	0	—	0		-5		-0.2
2001	Cle A	0	0	—	2	0	0	0-0	2	4	6	2	0	3-0	3	27.00	17	.400	.538	0	—	0		-5		5.8
Total	11	42	25	.627	557	0	0	52-35	481.2	461	208	33	12	209-29	358	3.44	118	.253	.330	5	.000	-1	33	414		5.8

RADKE, BRAD Brad William B10.27.1972 Eau Claire WI BR/TR/6-2/188* [MinA91 8/206] d4.29

YEAR	TM LG	W	L	PCT	G	GS	CG-SHO	SV-BS	IP	H	R	HR	HB	BB-IB	SO	ERA	AERA	OAV	OOB	AB-HR-SH	AVG	PB	SUP	APR	DL	PW
1995	Min A	11	14	.440	29	28	2-1	0-0	181	195	112	32	4	47-0	75	5.32	91	.275	.319	0	—	0	93	-8		-0.9
1996	Min A	11	16	.407	35	35	3	0-0	232	231	125	40	4	57-2	148	4.46	115	.256	.302	0	—	0	88	16		1.4
1997	Min A	20	10	.667	35	**35**	4-1	0-0	239.2	238	114	28	3	48-1	174	3.87	121	.257	.293	3-0-1	.000	-0	109	19		2.
1998	Min A★	12	14	.462	32	32	5-1	0-0	213.2	238	109	23	9	43-1	146	4.30	112	.283	.324	2	.000	-0	86	12		1.
1999	Min A	12	14	.462	33	33	4	0-0	218.2	239	97	28	1	44-0	121	3.75	138	.280	.314	2	.000	-1	70	33		3.5
2000	Min A	12	16	.429	34	34	4-1	0-0	226.2	261	119	27	5	51-1	141	4.45	118	.286	.326	2	.000	-0	67	20		2.
2001	Min A	15	11	.577	33	33	6-2	0-0	226.2	235	105	24	10	26-0	137	3.94	118	.271	.298	4	.500	1	102	17	17	2.
2002	†Min A	9	5	.643	21	21	2-1	0-0	118.1	124	64	12	7	20-0	62	4.72	95	.272	.309	0	—	0	107	-2	80	-0.
2003	†Min A	14	10	.583	33	33	3-1	0-0	212.1	242	111	32	5	28-2	120	4.49	100	.288	.314	5	.200	1	103	1		2.
2004	†Min A	11	8	.579	34	34	1-1	0-0	219.2	229	92	23	6	26-1	143	3.48	133	.267	.291	2-0-1	.000	-0	92	28		2.
2005	Min A	9	12	.429	31	31	3-1	0-0	200.2	214	98	33	7	23-1	117	4.04	109	.272	.295	5-0-2	.000	-1	105	8		2.
Total	11	136	130	.511	350	349	37-10	0-0	2288.2	2446	1146	302	61	413-9	1384	4.22	114	.273	.308	28-0-4	.107	-0	91	144	97	13.

RADLOSKY, ROB Robert Vincent B1.7.1974 W.Palm Beach FL BR/TR/6-2/204 [MinA93 22/625] d5.25 Col Central Florida CC

YEAR	TM LG	W	L	PCT	G	GS	CG-SHO	SV-BS	IP	H	R	HR	HB	BB-IB	SO	ERA	AERA	OAV	OOB	AB-HR-SH	AVG	PB	SUP	APR	DL	PW
1999	Min A	0	1	.000	1	1	0	0	8.2	15	12	7	1	4-0	3	12.46	42	.375	.444	0	—	0		-6		-0.

RAETHER, HAL Harold Herman "Bud" B10.10.1932 Lake Mills WI BR/TR/6-1/185* d7.4 Col Wisconsin-Madison

YEAR	TM LG	W	L	PCT	G	GS	CG-SHO	SV-BS	IP	H	R	HR	HB	BB-IB	SO	ERA	AERA	OAV	OOB	AB-HR-SH	AVG	PB	SUP	APR	DL	PW
1954	Phi A	0	0	—	1	0	0	0	2	1	1	0	0	4	0	4.50	87	.200	.556	0	—	0		0		0.
1957	KC A	0	0	—	1	0	0	0	2	2	2	1	0	0-0	0	9.00	44	.250	.250	0	—	0		-1		-0.
Total	2	0	0	—	2	0	0	0	4	3	3	1	0	4-0	0	6.75	58	.231	.412	0	—	0		-1		-0.

RAFFENSBERGER, KEN Kenneth David B8.8.1917 York PA D11.10.2002 York PA BR/TL/6-2/185(185-205) d4.25 Mil 1945

YEAR	TM LG	W	L	PCT	G	GS	CG-SHO	SV-BS	IP	H	R	HR	HB	BB-IB	SO	ERA	AERA	OAV	OOB	AB-HR-SH	AVG	PB	SUP	APR	DL	PW
1939	StL N	0	0	—	1	0	0	0	1	2	0	0	0	0	0	0.00	—	.200	.400	0	—	0		0		0.
1940	Chi N	7	9	.438	43	10	3	3	114.2	120	54	10	2	29	55	3.38	111	.271	.319	30-0-2	.167	-1	70	3		0.
1941	Chi N	0	1	.000	10	1	0	0	18	17	9	0	0	7	5	4.50	78	.262	.333	5-0-1	.000	-0	0	1		-0.
1943	Phi N	0	1	.000	1	1	1	0	8	7	3	0	0	2	3	1.13	300	.241	.290	3	.000	-0	0	0		1.
1944	Phi N★	13	20	.394	37	31	18-3	0	258.2	257	101	9	2	45	136	3.06	118	.252	.285	80-0-13	.138	-3*	72	17		1.
1945	Phi N	0	3	.000	5	4	1	0	24.1	28	19	3	0	14	6	4.44	86	.283	.372	8	.000	-1	88	-3		-0.
1946	Phi N	8	15	.348	39	23	14-2	6	196	203	89	10	1	39	73	3.63	95	.265	.302	60-0-9	.167	-1	72	-3		-1.
1947	Phi N	2	6	.250	10	7	3-1	0	41	50	30	4	1	8	16	5.49	73	.307	.343	15	.267	0	86	0		-1.
	Cin N	6	5	.545	19	15	7	1	106.2	132	54	11	0	29	38	4.13	99	.305	.348	37-0-2	.162	-1	86	-7		-0.
	Year	8	11	.421	29	22	10-1	1.	147.2	182	84	15	1	37	54	4.51	90	.305	.347	52-0-2	.192	-0	82	-7		-0.
1948	Cin N	11	12	.478	40	24	7-4	0	180.1	187	88	15	1	37	57	3.84	102	.259	.296	62-0-3	.113	-1	90	21		2
1949	Cin N	18	17	.514	41	**38**	20-5	0	284	289	129	23	2	80	103	4.36	123	.264	.315	90-1-12	.178	-0	95	0		1
1950	Cin N	14	19	.424	38	35	18-4	0	239	271	127	34	2	40	87	4.26	100	.279	.308	82-1-3	.134	-2	95	0		1
1951	Cin N	16	17	.485	42	33	14-5	5	248.2	232	108	29	6	38	81	3.44	119	.246	.279	82-0-6	.122	-3	89	18		1
1952	Cin N	17	13	.567	38	33	18-**6**	1	247	247	85	18	2	45	93	2.81	134	.261	.295	75-1-11	.107	-2	85	26		2
1953	Cin N	7	14	.333	26	26	9-1	0	174	200	87	23	0	33	47	3.93	111	.289	.322	57-1-8	.140	-1	84	7		2
1954	Cin N	0	2	.000	6	1	0	0	10.1	15	10	2	0	3	5	7.84	53	.333	.367	2	.500	0	276	-4		6
Total	15	119	154	.436	396	282	133-31	16	2151.2	2257	993	191	19	449	806	3.60	110	.267	.306	688-4-70	.141	-17	84	76		6

RAFFO, AL Albert Martin B11.27.1941 San Francisco CA BR/TR/6-5/210 d4.29

YEAR	TM LG	W	L	PCT	G	GS	CG-SHO	SV-BS	IP	H	R	HR	HB	BB-IB	SO	ERA	AERA	OAV	OOB	AB-HR-SH	AVG	PB	SUP	APR	DL	PW
1969	Phi N	3		.250	45	0	0	1-0	72.1	81	35	6	4	25-3	38	4.11	87	.286	.349	6-0-2	.167	0		-3		-0

RAGAN, PAT Don Carlos Patrick B11.15.1888 Blanchard IA D9.4.1956 Los Angeles CA BR/TR/5-10.5/185 d4.21 C1 Col Cornell

YEAR	TM LG	W	L	PCT	G	GS	CG-SHO	SV-BS	IP	H	R	HR	HB	BB-IB	SO	ERA	AERA	OAV	OOB	AB-HR-SH	AVG	PB	SUP	APR	DL	PW
1909	Cin N	0	1	.000	2	0	0	0	8	7	4	0	0	4	2	3.38	77	.259	.355	2	.500	-0		-1		0.
	Chi N	0	0	—	2	0	0	0	3.2	4	2	0	0	1	2	2.45	104	.286	.333	2	.000	-0		0		-0.
	Year	0	1	.000	4	0	0	0	11.2	11	6	0	0	5	4	3.09	84	.268	.348	4	.250	0		-1		-0.
1911	Bro N	4	3	.571	22	7	5-1	1	93.2	81	32	2	0	31	39	2.11	158	.252	.321	29	.138	-1	74	11		-1
1912	Bro N	7	18	.280	36	26	12-1	1	208	211	101	7	4	65	101	3.63	92	.270	.329	67-0-4	.060	-7	87	-2		-1
1913	Bro N	15	18	.455	44	32	14	0	264.2	284	145	16	4	64	109	3.77	87	.281	.327	91-0-3	.165	-2	119	-15		-1
1914	Bro N	10	15	.400	38	25	14-1	3	208.1	214	104	5	3	85	106	2.98	96	.270	.343	75-0-1	.133	-3	103	-4		-0
1915	Bro N	1	0	1.000	5	0	0	0	19.2	11	6	0	0	8	7	0.92	304	.164	.253	6	.167	-0		3		0.
	Bos N	16	12	.571	33	26	13-3	0	227	208	71	2	7	59	81	2.46	105	.255	.311	80-0-1	.150	-0	105	9		1
	Year	17	12	.586	38	26	13-3	0	246.2	219	77	2	7	67	88	2.34	112	.248	.306	86-0-1	.151	-1	104	12		1
1916	Bos N	9	9	.500	28	23	14-3	0	182	143	53	3	0	47	94	2.08	120	.218	.270	60-0-2	.217	3*	93	9		1
1917	Bos N	6	9	.400	30	13	5-1	1	147.2	138	59	6	1	35	61	2.93	87	.250	.295	48-1-3	.125	-1	100	-6		-0
1918	Bos N	8	17	.320	30	25	15-2	0	206.1	212	95	4	4	54	68	3.23	83	.270	.320	71-0-4	.183	-2	121	-12		-1
1919	Bos N	2	0	.000	4	3	0	0	12.2	16	13	0	0	3	7	7.11	40	.281	.317	4	.250	0		56	-6	-0
	NY N	1	0	1.000	7	1	1	0	22.2	19	7	0	0	6	14	1.59	177	.247	.363	7	.429	1	199	2		0
	Year	1	2	.333	11	4	1	0	35.1	35	20	0	0	9	21	3.57	79	.261	.344	11	.364	1		92	-4	-0
	Chi A	0	0	—	1	0	0	0	1	1	0	0	0	1	0	0.00	—	.250	.250	0	—	0		0		0.
1923	Phi N	0	0	—	3	0	0	0	3	6	2	1	0	4	2	6.00	77	.400	.400	0	.500	0		0		0.
Total	11	77	104	.425	283	181	93-12	6	1608.1	1555	694	38	25	470	680	2.99	97	.260	.317	544-1-18	.154	-13	103	-12		-3

YEAR	TM LG	W	L	PCT	G	GS	CG-SHO	SV-BS	IP	H	R	HR	HB	BB-IB	SO	ERA	AERA	OAV	OOB	AB-HR-SH	AVG	PB	SUP	APR	DL	PW
RAGGIO, BRADY							Brady John	B9.17.1972 Los Angeles CA	BR/TR/6-4/210*				[StLN92 20/559]		d4.15	Col Chabot (CA) JC									
1997	StL N	1	2	.333	15	4	0	0-0	31.1	44	24	1	1	16-0	21	6.89	61	.336	.407	3-0-1	.000	-0	171	-8		-0.7
1998	StL N	1	1	.500	4	1	0	0-0	7	22	12	1	1	3-0	3	15.43	27	.579	.605	1	.000	-0	153	-8		-1.4
2003	Ari N	0	0	—	10	0	0	1-0	8.1	9	6	1	0	6-1	8	6.48	71	.290	.405	0	—	0		-1		-0.1
Total	3	2	3	.400	29	5	0	1-0	46.2	75	42	3	2	25-1	32	8.10	53	.375	.443	4-0-1	.000	-0	165	-17		-2.2
RAGLAND, FRANK							Frank Roland	B5.26.1904 Water Valley MS	D7.28.1959 Paris MS	BR/TR/6-1/186						d4.17									
1932	Was A	1	0	1.000	12	1	0	0	37.2	54	33	5	3	21	11	7.41	58	.346	.433	11	.273	1	99	-13		-0.5
1933	Phi N	0	4	.000	11	5	0	0	38.1	51	32	1	1	10	4	6.81	56	.317	.360	10	.200	-0	57	-10		-0.9
Total	2	1	4	.200	23	6	0	0	76	105	65	6	4	31	15	7.11	58	.331	.398	21	.238	1	62	-23		-1.4
RAICH, ERIC							Eric James	B11.1.1951 Detroit MI	BR/TR/6-4/230*	[CleA72*1/1]						d5.24	Col USC								
1975	Cle A	7	8	.467	18	17	2	0-0	92.2	118	61	12	1	31-6	34	5.54	69	.320	.368	0	—	0	94	-16		-2.2
1976	Cle A	0	0	—	1	0	0	0-0	2.2	7	5	1	0	0-0	1	16.88	21	.467	.467	0	—	0		-4		-0.2
Total	2	7	8	.467	19	17	2	0-0	95.1	125	66	13	1	31-6	35	5.85	65	.326	.371	0	—	0	94	-20		-2.4
RAIN, STEVE							Steven Nicholas	B6.2.1975 Los Angeles CA	BR/TR/6-6/250*	[ChiN93 11/306]						d7.17									
1999	Chi N	0	1	.000	16	0	0	0-0	14.2	20	17	1	1	7-0	12	9.20	50	.418	.474	0	—	0		-8		-0.4
2000	Chi N	3	4	.429	37	0	0	0-3	49.2	46	25	10	1	27-0	54	4.35	105	.250	.347	2	.000	0	2	2		0.2
Total	2	3	5	.375	53	0	0	0-3	64.1	74	42	11	2	34-0	66	5.46	84	.295	.381	2	.000	0		-6		-0.2
RAINEY, CHUCK							Charles David	B7.14.1954 San Diego CA	BR/TR/5-11/195*	[BosA74*1/19]						d4.8	Col San Diego Mesa (CA) JC							
1979	Bos A	8	5	.615	20	16	4-1	1-0	103.2	97	47	7	3	41-1	41	3.82	117	.250	.325	0	—	0	97	8	22	0.9
1980	Bos A	8	3	.727	16	13	2-1	0-0	87	92	49	7	2	41-3	43	4.86	88	.273	.353	0	—	0	113	-4	94	-0.5
1981	Bos A	0	1	.000	11	2	0	0-0	40	39	21	2	0	13-1	20	2.70	145	.252	.306	0	—	0	103	2		0.1
1982	Bos A	7	5	.583	27	25	3-3	0-0	129	146	75	14	2	63-2	57	5.02	87	.294	.373	0	—	0	103	-7		-0.6
1983	Chi N	14	13	.519	34	34	1-1	0-0	191	219	109	17	3	74-3	84	4.48	85	.295	.358	56-0-10	.161	1	104	-15		-1.7
1984	Chi N	5	7	.417	17	16	0	0-0	88.1	102	55	4	2	38-1	45	4.28	91	.290	.361	31-0-1	.097	-1	105	-7		-1.0
	Oak A	1	1	.500	16	0	0	1-1	30.2	43	27	2	0	17-4	10	6.75	56	.333	.403	0	—	0		-11		-0.7
Total	6	43	35	.551	141	106	10-6	2-1	669.2	738	383	53	12	287-15	300	4.50	91	.284	.355	87-0-11	.138	-1	104	-34	116	-3.5
RAJSICH, DAVE							David Christopher	B9.28.1951 Youngstown OH	BL/TL/6-5/175*	d7.2	b-Gary	Col Arizona												
1978	NY A	0	0	—	4	2	0	0-0	13.1	16	6	0	0	6-0	9	4.05	90	.320	.379	0	—	0	123	6		0.0
1979	Tex A	1	3	.250	27	3	0	0-0	53.2	56	25	7	0	18-0	32	3.52	118	.267	.325	0	—	0	66	3		0.3
1980	Tex A	2	1	.667	24	1	0	2-0	48.1	56	34	7	3	22-0	35	5.96	65	.295	.370	0	—	0	23	-10		-0.7
Total	3	3	4	.429	55	6	0	2-0	115.1	128	65	14	3	46-0	76	4.60	87	.284	.350	0	—	0	75	-7		-0.4
RAKERS, AARON							Aaron James	B1.22.1977 Highland IL	BR/TR/6-3/205(205-220)	[BalA99 23/697]						d9.8	Col Southern Illinois-Edwardsville							
2004	Bal A	0	0	—	3	0	0	0-0	4.1	5	2	0	0	1-0	5	4.15	112	.278	.316	0	—	0	0	0		0.0
2005	Bal A	1	0	1.000	10	0	0	0-0	13.2	11	5	3	0	3-0	9	3.29	135	.220	.255	0	—	0	2			0.1
Total	2	1	0	1.000	13	0	0	0-0	18	16	7	3	0	4-0	14	3.50	128	.235	.270	0	—	0	2			0.1
RAKERS, JASON							Jason Paul	B6.29.1973 Pittsburgh PA	BR/TR/6-2/200*	[CleA95 25/698]						d5.6	Col New Mexico St.							
1998	Cle A	0	0	—	1	0	0	0-0	1	0	0	0	0	3-0	0	9.00	53	.000	.500	0	—	0	0	0		0.0
1999	Cle A	0	0	—	1	0	0	0-0	2	2	1	1	0	1-0	0	4.50	113	.250	.333	0	—	0	0	0	34	0.0
2000	KC A	2	0	1.000	11	0	0	0-0	21.2	33	22	5	0	7-0	16	9.14	57	.351	.392	0	—	0		-8		-0.6
Total	3	2	0	1.000	13	0	0	0-0	24.2	35	24	6	0	11-0	16	8.76	59	.337	.393	0	—	0		-8	34	-0.6
RAKOW, ED							Edward Charles "Rock"	B5.30.1935 Pittsburgh PA	D8.26.2000 West Palm Beach FL	BB/TR/5-11/178*						d4.22									
1960	LA N	0	1	.000	9	2	0	0	22	30	19	5	0	11-3	9	7.36	54	.323	.390	6	.333	0	67	-7		-0.3
1961	KC A	2	8	.200	45	11	1	1	124.2	131	80	14	8	49-1	81	4.76	88	.269	.341	29-0-3	.103	-2	98	-9		-0.8
1962	KC A	14	17	.452	42	35	11-2	1	235.1	232	126	31	4	98-5	159	4.25	99	.260	.334	82-0-5	.098	-5	92	-2		-0.7
1963	KC A	9	10	.474	34	26	7-1	0	174.1	173	85	18	5	61-4	104	3.92	99	.261	.326	57-0-2	.105	-2	91	-1		-0.2
1964	Det A	8	9	.471	42	13	1	3	152.1	155	70	14	6	59-1	96	3.72	98	.266	.337	39-0-4	.000	-4	95	-2		-0.5
1965	Det A	0	0	—	6	0	0	0	13.1	14	11	2	0	11-0	10	6.08	57	.280	.403	3	.000	-0		-4		-0.3
1967	Atl N	3	2	.600	17	3	0	0	39.1	36	23	4	1	15-3	25	5.26	63	.240	.311	10	.000	-1	132	-7		-1.0
Total	7	36	47	.434	195	90	20-3	5	761.1	771	414	88	24	304-17	484	4.33	92	.264	.336	226-0-14	.084	-13	94	-32		-3.8
RALEIGH, JOHN							John Austin	B4.21.1890 Elkhorn WI	D8.24.1955 Escondido CA	BR/TL/5-9/165						d8.4									
1909	StL N	1	10	.091	15	10	3	0	80.2	85	42	0	3	21	26	3.79	67	.285	.339	23-0-1	.087	-2	39	-10		-1.4
1910	StL N	0	0	—	3	1	0	0	5	8	5	0	0	0	2	9.00	33	.364	.364	1	.000	-0	125	-3		-0.2
Total	2	1	10	.091	18	11	3	0	85.2	93	47	0	3	21	28	4.10	62	.291	.340	24-0-1	.083	-2	47	-13		-1.6
RAMBERT, PEP							Elmer Donald	B8.1.1916 Cleveland OH	D11.16.1974 W.Palm Beach FL	BR/TR/6-0/175						d9.23									
1939	Pit N	0	0	—	2	0	0	0	3.2	7	4	0	1	4	4	9.82	39	.389	.421	0	—	0		-2		-0.1
1940	Pit N	0	1	.000	3	1	0	0	8.1	12	8	0	3	1	0	7.56	50	.333	.442	2	.000	0	68	-3		-0.3
Total	2	0	1	.000	5	1	0	0	12	19	12	0	3	5	4	8.25	46	.352	.435	2	.000	0	68	-5		-0.4
RAMBO, PETE							Warren Dawson	B11.1.1906 Thorofare NJ	D6.19.1991 Camden NJ	BR/TR/5-9/150						d9.16									
1926	Phi N	0	0	—	1	0	0	0	3.2	6	8	0	0	4	1	14.73	28	.353	.476	1	1.000	0		-4		-0.2
RAMIREZ, ALLAN							Daniel Allan	B5.1.1957 Victoria TX	BR/TR/5-10/190	[BalA79 5/123]						d6.8	Col Rice							
1983	Bal A	4	4	.500	11	10	1	0-0	57	46	22	6	0	30-1	20	3.47	115	.229	.328	0	—	0	113	5		0.6
RAMIREZ, ELIZARDO							Elizardo (De Palma)	B1.28.1983 Villa Mella, D.R.	BL/TR/6-0/180*	d5.25														
2004	Phi N	0	0	—	7	0	0	0-0	15	17	8	3	1	5-1	9	4.80	92	.283	.343	0	—	0	0			0.0
2005	Cin N	0	3	.000	6	4	0	0-0	22.1	33	22	5	2	10-2	9	8.46	49	.344	.417	8	.000	-1	117	-10		-1.2
Total	2	0	3	.000	13	4	0	0-0	37.1	50	30	8	3	15-3	18	6.99	61	.321	.389	8	.000	-1	117	-10		-1.2
RAMIREZ, ERASMO							Erasmo	B4.29.1976 Santa Ana CA	BL/TL/6-0/180*	[SFN98 11/338]						d4.30	Col Cal St.-Fullerton/Cal St.-Northridge							
2003	Tex A	3	1	.750	34	0	0	0-1	49	46	21	4	4	9-0	28	3.86	129	.251	.298	0	—	0	6			0.4
2004	Tex A	5	3	.625	34	0	0	0-2	35.2	34	19	5	3	7-1	21	4.29	115	.252	.301	0	—	0	2		15	0.4
2005	Tex A	0	0	—	16	0	0	0-1	23	24	10	3	2	3-0	6	3.91	117	.273	.312	0	—	0	2		88	0.1
Total	3	8	4	.667	84	0	0	0-4	107.2	104	50	12	9	19-1	55	4.01	121	.256	.302	0	—	0	10		103	0.9
RAMIREZ, HECTOR							Hector Bienvenido	B12.15.1971 Santa Cruz de El Seibo, D.R.	BR/TR/6-3/218*	d8.28														
1999	Mil N	1	2	.333	15	0	0	0-3	21	19	8	1	0	11-2	9	3.43	134	.247	.341	3	.000	-0	3			0.3
2000	Mil N	0	1	.000	6	0	0	0-0	9	11	10	1	0	5-0	4	10.00	46	.289	.372	1	1.000	0	-5			-0.4
Total	2	1	3	.250	21	0	0	0-3	30	30	18	2	0	16-2	13	5.40	85	.261	.351	4	.250	0	-2			-0.1
RAMIREZ, HORACIO							Horacio	B11.24.1979 Carson CA	BL/TL/6-1/170(170-220)	[AtlN97 5/172]				d4.2	[DL 2002 Atl N 76]								
2003	Atl N	12	4	.750	29	29	1	0-0	182.1	181	91	21	6	72-10	100	4.00	105	.263	.337	61-0-6	.098	-3	142	4		0.1
2004	Atl N	2	4	.333	10	9	1	0-0	60.1	51	24	7	0	35-5	31	2.39	184	.226	.315	21-0-1	.095	-1*	69	10	122	0.9
2005	Atl N	11	9	.550	33	32	1-1	0-0	202.1	214	108	31	2	67-4	80	4.63	93	.282	.339	73-0-3	.219	2*	105	-6		-0.2
Total	3	25	17	.595	72	70	3-1	0-0	445	446	223	59	8	169-19	211	4.07	105	.266	.335	155-0-10	.155	-2	115	8	198	0.8
RAMIREZ, ROBERTO							Roberto Sanchez	B8.17.1972 Vega de Alatorre, Veracruz, Mexico	BL/TL/6-0/171*	d6.12														
1998	SD N	1	0	1.000	21	0	0	1-0	14.2	12	13	4	0	12-1	17	6.14	65	.211	.348	0	—	0	-5			-0.3
1999	Col N	1	5	.167	32	4	0	1-0	40.1	68	42	8	0	22-2	32	8.26	70	.368	.435	7-0-1	.143	-0	115	-10		-1.2
Total	2	2	5	.286	53	4	0	2-0	55	80	55	12	0	34-3	49	7.69	69	.331	.413	7-0-1	.143	-0	115	-15		-1.5
RAMOS, EDGAR							Edgar Jose (Malave)	B3.6.1975 Cumana, Venez	BR/TR/6-4/210	d5.21														
1997	Phi N	0	2	.000	4	2	0	0-0	14	15	9	1	0	6-0	4	5.14	82	.288	.373	3-0-1	.000	0	33	-2	45	-0.2
RAMOS, MARIO							Mario Martin	B10.19.1977 Aurora IL	BL/TL/6-1/180	[OakA99 6/183]						d6.19	Col Rice							
2003	Tex A	1	1	.500	3	3	0	0-0	13	11	9	3	2	13-0	8	6.23	80	.224	.406	1	.000	-0	105	-1		-0.2
RAMOS, PEDRO							Pedro (Guerra) "Pete"	B4.28.1935 Pinar Del Rio, Cuba	BB/TR/6-0/185(175-189)	d4.11														
1955	Was A	5	11	.313	45	9	3-1	5	130	121	62	13	11	39-3	34	3.88	99	.253	.319	38	.079	-3*	90	0		-0.3
1956	Was A	12	10	.545	37	18	4	0	152	178	95	23	8	76-0	54	5.27	82	.299	.377	44-0-4	.205	0*	106	-13		-1.6

YEAR	TM LG	W	L	PCT	G	GS	CG-SHO	SV-BS	IP	H	R	HR	HB	BB-IB	SO	ERA	AERA	OAV	OOB	AB-HR-SH	AVG	PB	SUP	APR	DL	PW
1957	Was A	12	16	.429	43	30	7-1	0	231	251	131	43	7	69-4	91	4.79	81	.271	.325	76-1-3	.171	-1*	93	-21		-2.4
1958	Was A	14	18	.438	43	37	10-4	3	259.1	277	133	38	5	77-9	132	4.23	90	.273	.325	88-0-7	.239	1*	98	-13		-1.4
1959	Was A☆	13	19	.406	37	35	11	0	233.2	233	127	30	9	52-4	95	4.16	94	.257	.301	75-1-6	.147	-0*	90	-7		-0.9
1960	Was A	11	18	.379	43	36	14-1	2	274	254	126	24	7	99-8	160	3.45	113	.245	.313	86-2-7	.116	-2*	94	12		0.8
1961	Min A	11	20	.355	42	34	9-3	2	264.1	265	134	39	4	79-6	174	3.95	107	.258	.312	93-3-2	.172	1*	90	8		0.8
1962	Cle A	10	12	.455	37	27	7-2	1	201.1	189	104	28	5	85-5	96	3.71	104	.246	.323	68-3-2	.147	2*	86	-1		0.1
1963	Cle A	9	8	.529	36	22	5	0	184.2	156	74	29	4	41-6	169	3.12	116	.226	.272	55-3-4	.109	1*	107	10		0.8
1964	Cle A	7	10	.412	36	19	3-1	0	133	144	84	18	4	26-6	98	5.14	70	.273	.310	39-2-1	.179	2*	105	-23		-2.5
	NY A	1	0	1.000	13	0	0	8	21.2	13	3	1	0	0-0	21	1.25	291	.183	.176	5-0-1	.000	-1		6		0.6
	Year	8	10	.444	49	19	3-1	8	154.2	157	87	19	4	26-6	119	4.60	78	.263	.294	44-2-2	.159	1	105	-15		-1.9
1965	NY A	5	5	.500	65	0	0	19	92.1	80	34	7	1	27-9	68	2.92	116	.237	.294	12-0-2	.083	-1		5		0.6
1966	NY A	3	9	.250	52	1	0	13	89.2	98	43	10	1	18-4	58	3.61	92	.283	.317	13	.154	-0	53	-4		-0.2
1967	Phi N	0	0	—	6	0	0	0	8	14	8	1	2	8-1	1	9.00	38	.412	.545	1	.000	-0		-4		-0.2
1969	Pit N	0	1	.000	5	0	0	0-0	6	8	4	2	0	0-0	4	6.00	58	.320	.320	1	.000	-0		-2		-0.2
	Cin N	4	3	.571	38	0	0	2-2	66.1	73	41	8	5	24-11	40	5.16	73	.284	.357	8-0-2	.000	-1		-9		-1.0
	Year	4	4	.500	43	0	0	2-2	72.1	81	45	10	5	24-11	44	5.23	72	.287	.354	9-0-2	.000	-1		-10		-1.2
1970	Was A	0	0	—	4	0	0	0-0	8.1	10	7	2	0	4-0	10	7.56	48	.294	.368	1	.000	0*		-3		-0.1
Total	15	117	160	.422	582	268	73-13	55-2	2355.2	2364	1210	316	68	724-76	1305	4.08	95	.261	.318	703-15-41	.155	-0	96	-59		-7.3

RAMSAY, ROBERT   Robert Arthur B12.3.1973 Vancouver WA BL/TL/6-5/220(215-230) [BosA96 7/211] d8.27 Col Washington St. [DL 2002 SD N 183]

YEAR	TM LG	W	L	PCT	G	GS	CG-SHO	SV-BS	IP	H	R	HR	HB	BB-IB	SO	ERA	AERA	OAV	OOB	AB-HR-SH	AVG	PB	SUP	APR	DL	PW
1999	Sea A	0	2	.000	-6	-3	0	0-0	18.1	23	13	3	0	9-1	11	6.38	75	.324	.395	0	—	0	84	-3		-0.3
2000	†Sea A	1	1	.500	37	1	0	0-0	50.1	43	22	3	1	40-3	32	3.40	142	.234	.368	0	—	0	58	7	14	0.4
Total	2	1	3	.250	43	4	0	0-0	68.2	66	35	6	1	49-4	43	4.19	115	.259	.375	0	—	0	78	4	197	0.1

RAMSDELL, WILLIE   James Willard "The Knuck" B4.4.1916 Williamsburg KS D10.8.1969 Wichita KS BR/TR/5-10/180* d9.24

YEAR	TM LG	W	L	PCT	G	GS	CG-SHO	SV-BS	IP	H	R	HR	HB	BB-IB	SO	ERA	AERA	OAV	OOB	AB-HR-SH	AVG	PB	SUP	APR	DL	PW
1947	Bro N	1	1	.500	2	0	0	0	2.2	4	6	0	1	3	3	6.75	61	.333	.500	1	1.000	0		-2		-0.4
1948	Bro N	4	4	.500	27	1	0	4	50.1	48	35	6	3	41	34	5.19	77	.251	.391	11	.091	-1	22	-7		-1.2
1950	Bro N	1	2	.333	5	0	0	1	6.1	7	3	0	1	2	2	2.84	144	.292	.391	3	.000	-0		1		0.1
	Cin N	7	12	.368	27	22	8-1	0	157.1	151	77	17	2	75	83	3.72	114	.255	.341	50-0-6	.200	1	90	7		0.8
	Year	8	14	.364	32	22	8-1	1	163.2	158	80	17	3	77	85	3.68	115	.257	.342	53-0-6	.189	0	90	8		0.9
1951	Cin N	9	17	.346	31	31	10-1	0	196	204	103	18	9	70	88	4.04	101	.266	.333	58-0-5	.155	-1	73	1		-0.1
1952	Chi N	2	3	.400	19	4	0	0	67	41	22	5	5	24	30	2.42	159	.173	.263	18	.056	-1	69	10		0.6
Total	5	24	39	.381	111	58	18-2	5	479.2	455	246	46	20	215	240	3.83	107	.250	.335	141-0-11	.156	-2	79	10		-0.2

RAMSEY, TOAD   Thomas H. B8.8.1864 Indianapolis IN D3.27.1906 Indianapolis IN BR/TL d9.5

YEAR	TM LG	W	L	PCT	G	GS	CG-SHO	SV-BS	IP	H	R	HR	HB	BB-IB	SO	ERA	AERA	OAV	OOB	AB-HR-SH	AVG	PB	SUP	APR	DL	PW
1885	Lou AA	3	6	.333	9	9	9	0	79	44	38	1	1	28	83	1.94	167	.150	.227	31	.129	-2	87	10		0.8
1886	Lou AA	38	27	.585	67	67	66-3	0	588.2	447	297	3	12	207	499	2.45	149	.198	.269	241	.241	-3	87	77		6.7
1887	Lou AA	37	27	.578	65	64	61	0	561	544	358	9	16	167	355	3.43	128	.242	.299	225	.191	-10	96	58		3.7
1888	Lou AA	8	30	.211	40	40	37-1	0	342.1	362	278	10	11	86	228	5.59	69	.262	.310	142	.120	-7*	74	-19		-2.5
1889	Lou AA	1	16	.059	18	18	15	0	140	175	152	7	2	71	60	5.59	73	.297	.374	57	.263	0	62	-29		-2.6
	StL AA	3	1	.750	5	3	3	0	41	44	29	0	1	10	33	3.95	107	.265	.311	17	.294	0	108	1		0.1
	Year	4	17	.190	23	21	18	0	181	219	181	7	3	81	93	5.22	75	.290	.361	74	.270	1	68	-27		-2.5
1890	StL AA	23	17	.575	44	40	34-1	0	348.2	325	221	10	8	102	257	3.69	117	.239	.296	145	.228	-1	94	20		1.4
Total	6	113	124	.477	248	241	225-5	0	2100.2	1941	1373	40	51	671	1515	3.29	117	.234	.295	858	.204	-22	87	118		7.8

RANDALL, SCOTT   Scott Philip B10.29.1975 Fullerton CA BR/TR/6-3/200 [ColN95 11/291] d8.26 Col California-Santa Barbara/Santa Barbara (CA) City

YEAR	TM LG	W	L	PCT	G	GS	CG-SHO	SV-BS	IP	H	R	HR	HB	BB-IB	SO	ERA	AERA	OAV	OOB	AB-HR-SH	AVG	PB	SUP	APR	DL	PW
2003	Cin N	2	5	.286	15	2	0	0-1	27.2	34	20	1	2	11-3	25	6.51	64	.304	.376	4	.250	0	11	-7		-1.2

RANDOLPH, STEPHEN   Stephen Le Charles B5.1.1974 Okinawa, Japan BL/TL/6-3/180(180-200) [NYA95 18/506] d3.31 Col Texas

YEAR	TM LG	W	L	PCT	G	GS	CG-SHO	SV-BS	IP	H	R	HR	HB	BB-IB	SO	ERA	AERA	OAV	OOB	AB-HR-SH	AVG	PB	SUP	APR	DL	PW
2003	Ari N	8	1	.889	50	0	0	0-0	60	50	28	7	2	43-3	50	4.05	114	.226	.357	3-0-1	.000	-0		4	26	0.5
2004	Ari N	2	5	.286	45	6	0	0-0	81.2	73	56	11	1	76-2	62	5.51	83	.235	.384	12	.417	2*	85	-8		-0.4
Total	2	10	6	.625	95	6	0	0-0	141.2	123	84	18	3	119-5	112	4.89	94	.232	.373	15-0-1	.333	2	85	-4	26	0.

RANEY, RIBS   Frank Robert Donald (b Frank Robert Donald Raniszewski) B2.16.1923 Detroit MI D7.7.2003 Warren MI BR/TR/6-4/190* d9.18 Col Western Michigan

YEAR	TM LG	W	L	PCT	G	GS	CG-SHO	SV-BS	IP	H	R	HR	HB	BB-IB	SO	ERA	AERA	OAV	OOB	AB-HR-SH	AVG	PB	SUP	APR	DL	PW
1949	StL A	1	2	.333	3	3	1	0	16.1	23	15	2	0	12	5	7.71	59	.333	.432	0	.000	-1	92	-5		-0.4
1950	StL A	0	1	.000	1	0	0	0	2	2	2	0	0	2		4.50	110	.250	.400	1	.000	-0		0		-0.1
Total	2	1	3	.250	4	3	1	0	18.1	25	17	2	0	14	7	7.36	62	.325	.429	7	.000	-1	92	-5		-0.5

RAPP, PAT   Patrick Leland B7.13.1967 Jennings LA BR/TR/6-3/215(195-230) [SFN89 15/388] d7.10 Col Southern Mississippi

YEAR	TM LG	W	L	PCT	G	GS	CG-SHO	SV-BS	IP	H	R	HR	HB	BB-IB	SO	ERA	AERA	OAV	OOB	AB-HR-SH	AVG	PB	SUP	APR	DL	PW
1992	SF N	0	2	.000	3	2	0	0-0	16	8	8	0	1	6-1	3	7.20	46	.235	.366	2-0-1	.000	-0	41	-4		-0.1
1993	Fla N	4	6	.400	16	16	1	0-0	94	101	49	7	2	39-1	57	4.02	109	.281	.351	31-0-2	.194	0	80	2		0.2
1994	Fla N	7	8	.467	24	23	2-1	0-0	133.1	132	67	13	7	69-3	75	3.85	116	.266	.361	41-0-4	.122	-2*	88	7		0.1
1995	Fla N	14	7	.667	28	28	3-2	0-0	167.1	158	72	10	7	76-2	102	3.44	125	.253	.340	56-0-9	.107	-2	109	15		1.4
1996	Fla N	8	16	.333	30	29	0	0-0	162.1	184	95	12	3	91-6	86	5.10	81	.301	.390	58	.121	-2	102	-15		-2.2
1997	Fla N	4	6	.400	19	19	1-1	0-0	108.2	121	59	11	3	51-3	64	4.47	91	.286	.365	35-1-4	.143	-1	111	-5		-0.0
	SF N	1	2	.333	8	6	0	0-0	33	37	24	4	2	21-1	28	6.00	69	.294	.395	12	.000	-1	112	-7	17	-0.2
	Year	5	8	.385	27	25	1-1	0-0	141.2	158	83	16	5	72-4	92	4.83	84	.288	.372	47-1-4	.106	-1	111	-12		-1.1
1998	KC A	12	13	.480	32	32	1-1	0-0	188.1	200	117	24	10	107-7	132	5.30	92	.285	.381	2-0-1	.000	-0	85	-7		0.5
1999	†Bos A	6	7	.462	37	26	0	0-0	146.1	147	78	13	7	69-1	90	4.12	121	.263	.351	3	.000	1	105	13		0.9
2000	Bal A	9	12	.429	31	30	0	0-0	174	203	125	18	5	83-5	106	5.90	80	.289	.365	3	.000	0	125	-26		-2.0
2001	Ana A	5	12	.294	31	28	1	0-0	170	169	96	20	2	71-2	82	4.76	98	.261	.332	5	.000	-1	86	-1		-0.8
Total	10	70	91	.435	259	239	9-5	0-0	1387.1	1468	790	133	49	683-32	825	4.68	96	.276	.361	247-1-21	.117	-8	99	-28	17	-4.

RASCHI, VIC   Victor John Angelo B3.28.1919 W.Springfield MA D10.14.1988 Groveland NY BR/TR/6-1/205(185-210) d9.23 Col William and Mary

YEAR	TM LG	W	L	PCT	G	GS	CG-SHO	SV-BS	IP	H	R	HR	HB	BB-IB	SO	ERA	AERA	OAV	OOB	AB-HR-SH	AVG	PB	SUP	APR	DL	PW
1946	NY A	2	0	1.000	2	2	2	0	16	14	7	0	0	5	11	3.94	88	.230	.288	4-0-3	.250	0	137	0		0.
1947	†NY A	7	2	.778	15	14	6-1	0	104.2	89	47	11	4	38	51	3.87	91	.226	.296	40-0-1	.250	2	139	-3		-0.
1948	NY A★	19	8	.704	36	31	18-6	1	222.2	208	103	15	3	74	124	3.84	106	.247	.310	81-0-4	.235	2	134	8		1.
1949	†NY A★	21	10	.677	38	37	21-3	0	274.2	247	120	16	6	138	124	3.34	121	.241	.334	83-0-11	.157	1	123	20		1.
1950	†NY A★	21	8	.724	33	32	17-2	1	256.2	232	120	19	3	116	155	4.00	107	.243	.327	86-1-10	.198	1	116	11		1.
1951	†NY A★	21	10	.677	35	34	15-4	0	258.1	233	110	20	5	103	164	3.27	117	.242	.319	85-0-13	.176	-2	123	16		1.
1952	†NY A★	16	6	.727	31	31	13-4	0	223	174	78	12	6	91	127	2.78	119	.216	.300	69-0-10	.188	3	113	16		1.
1953	†NY A	13	6	.684	28	26	7-4	1	181	150	74	11	1	55	76	3.33	111	.224	.283	63-0-5	.143	-2	135	9		0.
1954	StL N	8	9	.471	30	29	6-2	0	179	182	94	24	0	71	71	4.73	87	.268	.335	64-0-3	.141	0	105	-9		-0.
1955	StL N	0	1	.000	1	1	0	0	1.2	5	4	0	0	1-1	1	21.60	19	.556	.545	0	.182	-0	88	-3		-0.
	KC A	4	6	.400	20	18	1	0	101.1	132	66	10	1	35-4	10	5.42	77	.312	.364	33-0-3	.182	-0	80	-13		-1.
Total	132	66	.667	269	255	106-26	3	1819	1666	828	138	26	727-5	944	3.72	105	.244	.319	608-1-63	.184	3	119	52		5.

RASMUSSEN, DENNIS   Dennis Lee B4.18.1959 Los Angeles CA BL/TL/6-7/230(223-240) [CalA80 1/17] d9.16 gf-Bill Brubaker Col Creighton

YEAR	TM LG	W	L	PCT	G	GS	CG-SHO	SV-BS	IP	H	R	HR	HB	BB-IB	SO	ERA	AERA	OAV	OOB	AB-HR-SH	AVG	PB	SUP	APR	DL	PW
1983	SD N	0	0	—	4	1	0	0-0	13.2	10	5	1	0	8-0	13	1.98	178	.200	.310	0	.000	-0*	101	2		0.
1984	NY A	9	6	.600	24	24	1	0-0	147.2	127	79	16	4	60-0	110	4.57	84	.234	.312	0	—	0	129	-11		-1
1985	NY A	3	5	.375	22	16	2	0-0	101.2	97	56	10	1	42-1	63	3.98	102	.255	.327	0	—	0	104	-2		-0
1986	NY A	18	6	.750	31	31	3-1	0-0	202	160	91	28	2	74-0	131	3.88	107	.217	.289	0	—	0	128	9		0
1987	NY A	9	7	.563	26	25	2	0-0	146	145	78	31	4	55-1	89	4.75	93	.260	.328	0	—	0	120	-3		-0.
	Cin N	4	1	.800	7	7	0	0-0	45.1	39	22	5	1	12-0	39	3.97	106	.229	.283	15	.067	-1	119	1		0.1
1988	Cin N	2	6	.250	11	11	1-1	0-0	56.1	68	36	8	2	22-4	27	5.75	62	.300	.364	22	.227	1	90	-12		-1.1
	SD N	14	4	.778	20	20	6	0-0	148.1	131	48	9	2	36-0	85	2.55	133	.238	.286	48-0-6	.188	2	129	14		2.1
	Year	16	10	.615	31	31	7-1	0-0	204.2	199	84	17	4	58-4	112	3.43	101	.256	.309	70-0-6	.200	3	115	2		2.0
1989	SD N	10	10	.500	33	33	1	0-0	183.2	190	100	18	3	72-6	87	4.26	82	.277	.335	65-0-3	.169	1	99	-16		-1
1990	SD N	11	15	.423	32	32	3-1	0-0	187.2	217	110	28	3	62-4	86	4.51	85	.292	.348	62-0-6	.290	5*	110	-16		-1
1991	SD N	6	13	.316	24	24	1-1	0-0	146.2	155	74	12	2	49-3	75	3.74	102	.271	.328	44-0-3	.136	1*	83	-1	47	-0.3
1992	Chi N	0	0	—	3	1	0	0-0	5	7	6	2	1	2-1	0	10.80	34	.350	.417	0-0-1	—	0	100	-4	19	-0.0
	KC A	4	1	.800	5	5	1	0-0	37.2	25	7	0	0	6-0	12	1.43	285	.197	.233	0	—	0	63	11		0.4
1993	KC A	1	2	.333	9	4	0	0-0	29	40	25	4	1	14-1	12	7.45	62	.328	.399	0	—	0	125	-8	60	-0.6
1995	KC A	0	1	.000	5	1	0	0-0	10	13	10	3	0	8-2	6	9.00	53	.302	.412	0	—	0	97	-4		-0.2
Total	12	91	77	.542	256	235	21-5	0-0	1460.2	1424	747	175	26	522-23	835	4.15	94	.257	.321	259-0-19	.193	8	111	-40	126	-2.

YEAR	TM LG	W	L	PCT	G	GS	CG-SHO	SV-BS	IP	H	R	HR	HB	BB-IB	SO	ERA	AERA	OAV	OOB	AB-HR-SH	AVG	PB	SUP	APR	DL	PW
RASMUSSEN, ERIC			Eric Ralph (Born Harold Ralph Rasmussen)						B3.22.1952 Racine WI BR/TR/6-3/205* [StLN73 32/676] d7.21 Col New Orleans																
1975	StL N	5	5	.500	14	13	2-1	0-0	81	86	44	8	0	20-2	59	3.78	101	.264	.306	26-0-1	.154	-0	89	-1		-0.2
1976	StL N	6	12	.333	43	17	2-1	0-2	150.1	139	67	10	2	54-6	76	3.53	101	.247	.313	38-0-4	.105	-1	91	1		0.2
1977	StL N	11	17	.393	34	34	11-3	0-0	233	223	103	24	5	63-7	120	3.48	112	.254	.305	72-0-6	.139	0	82	10		1.1
1978	StL N	2	5	.286	10	10	2-1	0-0	60.1	61	32	4	0	20-2	32	4.18	85	.270	.324	18-0-2	.111	-1	58	-4		-0.5
	SD N	12	10	.545	27	24	3-2	0-0	146.1	154	72	16	1	43-6	59	4.06	83	.277	.327	46-0-8	.152	-1	102	-11		-1.5
	Year	14	15	.483	37	34	5-3	0-0	206.2	215	104	20	1	63-8	91	4.09	83	.275	.326	64-0-10	.141	-2	88	-17		-2.0
1979	SD N	6	9	.400	45	20	5-3	3-2	156.2	142	59	9	0	42-6	54	3.27	108	.244	.292	36-0-6	.056	-2*	93	7		0.5
1980	SD N	4	11	.267	40	14	0	1-3	111.1	130	60	9	3	33-6	50	4.37	78	.295	.347	21-0-6	.095	-1	78	-13		-1.7
1982	StL N	1	2	.333	8	3	0-	0-0	18.1	21	13	2	0	8-4	15	4.42	83	.288	.354	3-0-1	.000	-0	48	-3		-0.4
1983	StL N	0	0	—	6	0	0	1-0	7.2	16	11	1	0	4-2	6	11.74	31	.444	.500	0	—	0		-7		-0.3
	KC A	3	6	.333	11	9	2-1	0-0	52.2	61	28	4	0	22-0	18	4.78	86	.289	.355	0	—	0	76	-2		-0.4
Total	8	50	77	.394	238	144	27-12	5-7	1017.2	1033	489	87	11	309-41	489	3.85	95	.266	.319	260-0-34	.119	-6	85	-23		-3.2
RASMUSSEN, HANS			Henry Florian B4.18.1895 Chicago IL D1.1.1949 Chicago IL BR/TR/6-6/220 d8.11																							
1915	Chi F	0	0	—	2	0	0	0	2	3	3	0	2	2	13.50	19	.600	.714	1	.000	-0		-2		-0.1
RASNER, DARRELL			Darrell Wayne B1.13.1981 Carson City NV BR/TR/6-3/210 d9.6 Col Nevada-Reno																							
2005	Was N	0	1	.000	5	1	0	0-0	4	3	3.68	110	.192	.300	0	—	0	46	0		0.0				
RATH, GARY			Alfred Gary B1.10.1973 Gulfport MS BL/TL/6-2/186* [LAN94 2/47] d6.2 Col Mississippi St.																							
1998	LA N	0	0	—	3	0	0	0-0	3.1	3	4	1	0	2-0	1	10.80	37	.250	.357	0	—	0		-2		-0.1
1999	Min A	0	1	.000	5	1	0	0-0	4.2	6	6	1	0	5-0	1	11.57	45	.300	.440	0	—	0	90	-3		-0.5
Total	2	0	1	.000	8	1	0	0-0	8	9	10	2	0	7-0	2	11.25	42	.281	.410	0	—	0	90	-5		-0.6
RATH, FRED			Frederick Helsher Jr. B1.5.1973 Dallas TX BR/TR/6-3/220 d7.29 f-Fred Col South Florida																							
1998	Col N	0	0	—	2	0	0	0-0	5.1	6	1	1	0	2-0	2	1.69	307	.300	.348	2	.000	-0		2		0.1
RATH, FRED			Frederick Helsher Sr. B9.1.1943 Little Rock AR BR/TR/6-3/190* [ChiA65 4/80] d9.10 s-Fred Col Baylor																							
1968	Chi A	0	0	—	5	0	0	0	11.1	8	5	1	0	3-1	3	1.59	190	.182	.250	0	—	0		1		0.0
1969	Chi A	0	2	.000	3	2	0	0-0	11.2	11	10	4	0	8-1	4	7.71	50	.256	.373	3	.000	-0	34	-4		-0.7
Total	2	0	2	.000	8	2	0	0-0	23	19	15	4	1	11-2	7	4.70	73	.218	.313	3	.000	-0	34	-3		-0.7
RATLIFF, JON			Jon Charles B12.22.1971 Syracuse NY BR/TR/6-4/195 [ChiN93 1/24] d9.15 Col LeMoyne (NY)																							
2000	Oak A	0	0	—	1	0	0	0-0	0	0	0	0	0	0-0	0	0.00	—	.000	.000	0	—	0		1		0.0
RATZER, STEVE			Steven Wayne B9.9.1953 Paterson NJ BR/TR/6-1/192* d10.5 Col St. Johns																							
1980	Mon N	0	0	—	1	0	0	0-0	4	9	5	0	0	2-0	0	11.25	32	.450	.500	1	.000	-0	197	-3		-0.1
1981	Mon N	1	1	.500	12	0	0	0-0	17.1	23	14	2	0	7-1	4	6.23	57	.311	.370	2	.000	-0		-5		-0.6
Total	2	1	1	.500	13	1	0	0-0	21.1	32	19	2	0	9-1	4	7.17	50	.340	.398	3	.000	-0	197	-8		-0.7
RAU, DOUG			Douglas James B12.15.1948 Columbus TX BL/TL/6-2/175* [LAN70 S1/7] d9.2 Col Texas A&M-Commerce [DL 1980 LA N 180]																							
1972	LA N	2	2	.500	7	3	2	0-0	32.2	18	11	1	1	11-2	19	2.20	152	.159	.236	7-0-1	.143	1	61	4		0.6
1973	LA N	4	2	.667	31	3	0	3-1	63.2	64	28	5	1	28-2	51	3.96	88	.259	.336	11-0-2	.091	-1	34	-2		-0.3
1974	†LA N	13	11	.542	36	35	3-1	0-0	198.1	191	90	20	4	70-1	126	3.72	92	.251	.316	64-0-8	.141	-1	124	-5		-0.6
1975	LA N	15	9	.625	38	38	8-2	0-0	257.2	227	96	18	8	61-1	151	3.11	110	.236	.282	87-0-10	.195	2	116	11		1.2
1976	LA N	16	12	.571	34	32	8-3	0-0	231	231	71	18	7	69-1	98	2.57	132	.258	.317	60-0-8	.150	1	84	23		2.9
1977	†LA N	14	8	.636	32	32	4-2	0-0	212.1	232	87	15	6	49-2	126	3.43	112	.282	.325	71-0-3	.141	-1	99	11		1.0
1978	†LA N	15	9	.625	30	30	7-2	0-0	199	219	82	17	4	68-5	95	3.26	108	.284	.342	63-0-13	.143	-1	122	6		0.5
1979	LA N	1	5	.167	11	11	1-1	0-0	56	73	37	3	4	22-0	28	5.30	68	.320	.384	14-0-1	.143	1	89	-10	119	-0.9
1981	Cal A	1	2	.333	3	3	0	0-0	10.1	14	10	2	0	4-0	3	8.71	42	.341	.400	0	—	0	90	-5	74	-0.9
Total	9	81	60	.574	222	187	33-11	3-1	1261	1259	512	99	28	382-14	697	3.35	105	.262	.318	377-0-46	.154	2	106	33	373	3.5
RAUCH, JON			Jon Erich B9.27.1978 Louisville KY BR/TR/6-11/230(230-260) [ChiA99 3/99] d4.2 Col Morehead St.																							
2002	Chi A	2	1	.667	8	6	0	0-0	28.2	28	26	7	2	14-2	19	6.59	68	.248	.338	0	—	0	151	-8		-0.7
2004	Chi A	1	1	.500	2	2	0	0-0	8.2	16	6	0	0	4-0	4	6.23	75	.432	.476	0	—	0	79	-1		-0.2
	Mon N	3	0	1.000	4	3	0	0-0	23.1	14	4	1	0	7-2	18	1.54	298	.175	.241	6-1-0	.167	1	141	8	31	1.0
2005	Was N	2	4	.333	15	1	0	0-0	30	24	12	3	1	11-2	23	3.60	112	.218	.293	7-0-1	.143	-0	253	2	103	0.3
Total	3	8	6	.571	34	11	0	0-0	90.2	82	48	11	3	36-6	64	4.27	103	.241	.317	13-1-1	.154	1	148	1	134	0.4
RAUCH, BOB			Robert John B6.16.1949 Brookings SD BR/TR/6-4/200 d6.29 Col San Bernardino Valley (CA) JC																							
1972	NY N	0	1	.000	19	0	0	1-0	27	27	16	3	0	21-2	23	5.00	68	.273	.393	3	.000	-0		-5		-0.3
RAUTZHAN, LANCE			Clarence George B8.20.1952 Pottsville PA BR/TL/6-1/200* [LAN70 3/57] d7.23																							
1977	†LA N	4	1	.800	25	0	0	2-4	20.2	25	10	0	1	7-1	13	4.35	89	.313	.364	1	.000	-0		-1		-0.1
1978	†LA N	2	1	.667	43	0	0	4-2	61.1	61	22	1	1	19-3	25	2.93	120	.263	.318	4-0-2	.000	-0		4		0.3
1979	LA N	0	2	.000	12	0	0	1-2	9.2	9	9	0	1	11-2	5	7.45	49	.273	.447	0	—	0		-4		-0.8
	Mil A	0	0	—	3	0	0	0-0	3	3	3	0	0	10-0	2	9.00	47	.300	.650	0	—	0		-4		-0.3
Total	3	6	4	.600	83	0	0	7-8	94.2	98	44	1	2	47-6	45	3.90	93	.276	.359	5-0-2	.000	-1		-2		-0.7
RAWLEY, SHANE			Shane William B7.27.1955 Racine WI BR/TL/6-0/180(155-185) [MonN74 S2/29] d4.6 Col Indian Hills (IA) CC																							
1978	Sea A	4	9	.308	52	2	0	4-1	111.1	114	57	7	5	51-3	66	4.12	93	.275	.356	0	—	0*	70	-3		-0.3
1979	Sea A	5	9	.357	48	3	0	11-5	84.1	88	40	2	1	40-5	48	3.84	114	.278	.357	0	—	0*	124	5	52	0.9
1980	Sea A	7	7	.500	59	0	0	13-9	113.2	103	44	3	3	63-16	68	3.33	125	.257	.360	0	—	0		12		1.7
1981	Sea A	4	6	.400	46	0	0	8-7	68.1	64	31	1	1	38-6	35	3.95	98	.257	.354	0	—	0		0	16	0.1
1982	NY A	11	10	.524	47	17	3	3-1	164	165	79	10	2	54-5	111	4.06	99	.267	.324	0	—	0	97	1		0.2
1983	NY A	14	14	.500	34	33	13-2	1-0	238.1	246	111	19	3	79-1	124	3.78	105	.269	.327	0	—	0	96	5		0.5
1984	NY A	2	3	.400	11	10	0	0-0	42	46	33	0	0	27-0	24	6.21	62	.272	.372	0	—	0	78	-12	15	-1.2
	Phi N	10	6	.625	18	18	3	0-0	120.1	117	55	13	1	27-2	58	3.81	96	.257	.298	43	.116	-2*	102	0		-0.2
1985	Phi N	13	8	.619	36	31	6-2	0-0	198.2	188	82	16	2	48-6	106	3.31	112	.249	.321	58-0-7	.138	0	109	9		1.0
1986	Phi N☆	11	7	.611	23	23	7-1	0-0	157.2	166	67	13	1	50-4	73	3.54	110	.270	.325	52-0-10	.173	0	129	8	68	0.9
1987	Phi N	17	11	.607	36	**36**	4-1	0-0	229.2	250	118	23	5	86-8	123	4.39	98	.279	.343	79-0-12	.152	-1*	104	0		0.9
1988	Phi N	8	16	.333	32	**32**	4-1	0-0	198	220	111	27	4	78-7	87	4.18	86	.286	.351	57-0-11	.105	-1	95	-16	23	-1.9
1989	Min A	5	12	.294	27	25	1	0-0	145	167	89	19	0	60-1	68	5.21	80	.293	.359	0	—	0	85	-15		-1.6
Total	12	111	118	.485	469	230	41-7	40-23	1871.1	1934	917	153	28	734-64	991	4.02	98	.271	.338	289-0-40	.138	-3	100	-6	174	0.1
RAY, CARL			Carl Grady B1.31.1889 Danbury NC D4.2.1970 Lexington NC BL/TL/5-11/170 d9.25																							
1915	Phi A	0	1	.000	7	1	0	0	7.1	7	7	0	4	6	4.91	60	.333	.488	2	.000	-0	25	-2		-0.3
1916	Phi A	0	1	.000	9	1	0	0	9.1	9	8	0	1	14	5	4.82	59	.257	.480	3	.000	0	53	-3		-0.3
Total	2	0	2	.000	16	2	0	0	16.2	16	15	0	5	20	11	4.86	59	.294	.484	5	.000	-0	39	-5		-0.6
RAY, CHRIS			Christopher Thomas B1.12.1982 Tampa FL BR/TR/6-3/200 d6.14 Col William and Mary																							
2005	Bal A	1	3	.250	41	0	0	0-4	40.2	34	15	5	1	18-3	43	2.66	167	.222	.306	0	—	0		7		0.6
RAY, JIM			James Francis "Sting" B12.1.1944 Rock Hill SC BR/TR/6-1/195* d9.16																							
1965	Hou N	0	2	.000	3	2	0	0	7.2	11	9	1	0	6-0	7	10.57	32	.355	.447	2	.000	-0	117	-6		-1.0
1966	Hou N	0	0	—	1	0	0	0	0	1	0	0	0	1-0	0	∞	—	—	1.000	0	—	0		-1		-0.1
1968	Hou N	2	3	.400	41	2	1	1	81	65	26	5	1	25-8	71	2.67	111	.220	.278	15-0-1	.067	-1*	103	3		0.0
1969	Hou N	8	2	.800	40	13	0	0-0	115	105	55	11	2	48-4	115	3.91	91	.245	.322	26-0-3	.115	-1	92	-3		-0.4
1970	Hou N	6	3	.667	52	0	0	5-1	105	97	39	13	0	42-2	67	3.26	120	.251	.333	27	.185	-0	69	9		0.3
1971	Hou N	10	4	.714	47	1	0	3-1	97.2	72	27	2	1	31-5	46	2.12	159	.211	.277	18	.167	0	79	13		1.9
1972	Hou N	10	9	.526	54	0	0	8-9	90.1	77	50	10	3	44-6	50	4.28	78	.227	.319	16-0-1	.063	-1		-11		-2.5
1973	Hou N	6	4	.600	42	0	0	6-3	69	65	37	5	3	38-8	25	4.43	82	.253	.355	13-0-2	.231	-0		-6		-0.9
1974	Det A	1	3	.250	28	0	0	2-1	52.1	49	26	4	1	29-4	26	4.47	86	.254	.350	0	—	0		-2		-0.2
Total	12	43	30	.589	308	20	1	25-15	618	541	269	71	47	271-37	407	3.61	97	.238	.320	117-0-7	.137	-3	92	-4		-2.4
RAY, KEN			Kenneth Alan B11.27.1974 Atlanta GA BR/TR/6-2/200 [KCA93 18/497] d7.10																							
1999	KC A	1	0	1.000	10	0	0	0-0	11.1	23	12	2	1	6-0	0	8.74	58	.460	.526	0	—	0		-4		-0.3

YEAR	TM LG	W	L	PCT	G	GS	CG-SHO	SV-BS	IP	H	R	HR	HB	BB-IB	SO	ERA	AERA	OAV	OOB	AB-HR-SH	AVG	PB	SUP	APR	DL	PW

RAY, FARMER Robert Henry B9.17.1886 Ft.Lyon CO D3.11.1963 Electra TX BL/TR/5-11/160 d6.13
| 1910 | StL A | 4 | 10 | .286 | 21 | 16 | 11 | 0 | 140.2 | 146 | 77 | 3 | 7 | 49 | 35 | 3.58 | 69 | .285 | .356 | 40-0-3 | .175 | 0 | 73 | -14 | | -1.5 |

RAYDON, CURT Curtis Lowell B11.18.1933 Bloomington IL BR/TR/6-4/190 d4.15
| 1958 | Pit N | 8 | 4 | .667 | 31 | 20 | 2-1 | 1 | 134.1 | 118 | 64 | 18 | 5 | 61-4 | 85 | 3.62 | 107 | .236 | .323 | 38-0-4 | .026 | -2 | 120 | 2 | | -0.2 |

RAYMOND, BUGS Arthur Lawrence B2.24.1882 Chicago IL D9.7.1912 Chicago IL BR/TR/5-10/180 d9.23
1904	Det A	0	1	.000	5	2	1	0	14.2	14	9	0	2	6	7	3.07	83	.250	.344	5	.000	-1	14	-2		-0.1
1907	StL N	2	4	.333	8	6	6-1	0	64.2	56	34	3	1	21	34	1.67	150	.230	.294	22	.091	-0	81	1		0.0
1908	StL N	15	25	.375	48	37	23-5	2	324.1	236	116	2	14	95	145	2.03	116	.207	.277	90-0-3	.189	1	61	11		1.8
1909	NY N	18	12	.600	39	30	18-2	0	270	239	98	7	6	87	121	2.47	104	.245	.311	89-0-5	.146	-0	90	7		0.9
1910	NY N	4	11	.267	19	11	6	0	99.1	106	63	2	8	40	55	3.81	78	.280	.362	32-0-1	.156	-1	78	-12		-1.5
1911	NY N	6	4	.600	17	9	4-1	0	81.2	73	40	1	2	33	39	3.31	102	.248	.328	25-0-3	.200	-0	104	0		0.0
Total 6		45	57	.441	136	95	58-9	2	854.2	724	360	15	33	282	401	2.49	105	.235	.306	263-0-12	.160	-0	78	5		1.1

RAYMOND, HARRY Harry H. "Jack" B2.20.1862 Utica NY D3.21.1925 San Diego CA 5-9/179 d9.9.1888 ▲
| 1889 | Lou AA | 1 | 0 | 1.000 | 1 | 1 | 1 | 0 | 9 | 8 | 2 | 0 | 1 | | 1 | 1.00 | 385 | .229 | .413 | 515 | .239 | 0* | 97 | 3 | | 0.2 |

RAYMOND, CLAUDE Joseph Claude Marc "Frenchy" B5.7.1937 St.Jean QC, Can. BR/TR/5-10/175* d4.15
1959	Chi A	0	0	—	3	0	0	0	4	5	4	2	0	2-0	1	9.00	42	.333	.389	0	—	0		-2		-0.1
1961	Mil N	1	0	1.000	13	0	0	2	20.1	22	9	2	1	9-1	13	3.98	94	.275	.356	3	.000	-0		0		0.0
1962	Mil N	5	5	.500	26	0	0	10	42.2	37	15	5	2	15-2	40	2.74	138	.236	.309	8-0-1	.000	-1		5		0.9
1963	Mil N	4	6	.400	45	0	0	5	53.1	57	36	12	4	27-4	44	5.40	60	.268	.361	4	.500	2		-13		-2.3
1964	Hou N	5	5	.500	38	0	0	5	79.2	64	28	3	3	22-1	56	2.82	121	.229	.289	14-0-2	.071	-0*		6		0.7
1965	Hou N	7	4	.636	33	7	2	5	96.1	87	35	6	5	16-2	79	2.90	116	.244	.285	26	.115	-1*	97	5		0.6
1966	Hou N☆	7	5	.583	62	0	0	16	92	85	39	10	4	25-6	73	3.13	109	.242	.298	9-0-1	.111	-0		4		0.2
1967	Hou N	0	4	.000	21	0	0	5	31	31	12	5	2	7-4	17	2.62	127	.256	.305	5	.200	-0		3		0.1
	Atl N	4	1	.800	28	0	0	5	34.1	33	11	2	0	11-5	14	2.62	127	.260	.314	2	.000	-0		4		0.6
	Year	4	5	.444	49	0	0	10	65.1	64	23	7	2	18-9	31	2.89	115	.258	.310	7	.143	-0		7		0.6
1968	Atl N	3	5	.375	36	0	0	10	60.1	56	21	4	1	18-9	37	2.83	106	.256	.313	7	.143	-0		1		0.3
1969	Atl N	2	2	.500	33	0	0	1-1	48	56	34	4	2	13-2	15	5.25	69	.298	.346	7-0-1	.286	-0		-10		-0.8
	Mon N	1	2	.333	15	0	0	1-1	22	21	12	2	2	8-3	11	4.09	90	.256	.333	4	.000	-0		-1		-0.2
	Year	3	4	.429	48	0	0	2-2	70	77	46	6	4	21-5	26	4.89	75	.285	.346	11-0-1	.182	-0		-11		-1.0
1970	Mon N	6	7	.462	59	0	0	23-6	83.1	76	48	13	2	27-7	68	4.43	94	.240	.300	11-0-2	.000	-1		-3		-0.8
1971	Mon N	1	7	.125	37	0	0	0-1	53.2	81	34	5	0	25-8	29	4.70	76	.373	.433	1-0-1	.000	-0		-8		-1.1
Total 12		46	53	.465	449	7	2	83-9	721	711	338	75	28	225-54	497	3.66	96	.261	.321	101-0-8	.109	-2	97	-14		-2.0

RAZIANO, BARRY Barry John B2.5.1947 New Orleans LA BB/TR/5-10/175* [NYN65 27/815] d8.18
1973	KC A	0	0	—	2	0	0	0-0	5	6	3	1	1	1-1	9	5.40	76	.316	.381	0	—	0		-1		0.0
1974	Cal A	1	2	.333	13	0	0	1-2	16.2	15	14	1	0	8-1	9	6.48	54	.246	.333	0	—	0		-6		-1.0
Total 2		1	2	.333	15	0	0	1-2	21.2	21	17	2	1	9-2	18	6.23	58	.262	.344	0	—	0		-7		-1.0

REAGAN, RIP Arthur (b Arthur Edgar Ragan) B6.5.1878 Lincoln IL D6.8.1953 Kansas City MO BR/TR/5-11/170 d9.19
| 1903 | Cin N | 0 | 2 | .000 | 3 | 2 | 0 | 0 | 18 | 40 | 30 | 0 | 1 | 7 | 7 | 6.00 | 59 | .455 | .500 | 8 | .250 | 0 | 161 | -8 | | -0.7 |

REAMES, BRITT William Britt B8.19.1973 Seneca SC BR/TR/5-11/175* [StLN95 17/463] d8.20 Col The Citadel
2000	†StL N	2	1	.667	8	7	0	0-0	40.2	30	17	4	1	23-1	31	2.88	162	.207	.318	12-0-1	.167	-0*	76	7		0.4
2001	Mon N	4	8	.333	41	13	0	0-1	95	101	68	16	5	48-3	86	5.59	77	.273	.362	17-1-3	.118	2	74	-15		-1.4
2002	Mon N	1	4	.200	42	6	0	0-1	68	70	42	8	3	38-6	76	5.03	87	.266	.364	9-0-2	.111	-0	77	-4		-0.3
2003	Mon N	0	0	—	2	0	0	0-0	1.1	4	4	0	0	2-0	1	27.00	16	.500	.600	0	—	-0		-3		-0.2
2005	Oak A	0	0	—	2	0	0	0-0	5.2	10	6	2	1	2-0	4	9.53	47	.400	.448	0	—	-0		-3		-0.1
Total 5		7	13	.350	95	26	0	0-2	210.2	215	137	30	10	113-10	198	5.13	86	.265	.360	39-1-6	.128	1	76	-18		-1.6

REARDON, JEFF Jeffrey James B10.1.1955 Dalton MA BR/TR/6-1/195(190-205) d8.25 Col Massachusetts
1979	NY N	1	2	.333	18	0	0	2-0	20.2	12	7	2	0	9-3	10	1.74	213	.174	.266	0		0		3		0.5
1980	NY N	8	7	.533	61	0	0	6-4	110.1	96	36	10	4	47-15	101	2.61	138	.231	.306	8	.000	-1		12		1.5
1981	NY N	1	0	1.000	18	0	0	2-0	28.2	27	11	2	1	9-0	21	1.30	275	.148	.204	4-0-2	.000	-0		11		0.7
	†Mon N	2	0	1.000	25	0	0	6-1	41.2	21	6	3	1	12-4	28	2.18	163	.190	.257	5-0-2	.000	-1		12		0.7
	Year	3	0	1.000	43	0	0	8-1	70.1	48	17	5	2	21-4	49	2.06	179	.221	.287	10-0-1	.100	-0		20		1.4
1982	Mon N	7	4	.636	75	0	0	26-8	109	87	28	6	2	36-4	86	2.06	179	.221	.287	8	.125	-0		6		1.1
1983	Mon N	7	9	.438	66	0	0	21-8	92	87	34	7	1	44-9	78	3.03	120	.250	.334	9	.000	-1		6		1.1
1984	Mon N	7	7	.500	68	0	0	23-3	87	70	31	5	3	37-7	79	3.18	108	.209	.269	7-0-2	.286	-0		4		0.9
1985	Mon N★	2	8	.200	63	0	0	41-9	87.2	68	31	7	1	26-4	67	3.18	108	.209	.269	8-0-1	.125	-0		-1		-0.3
1986	Mon N☆	7	9	.438	62	0	0	35-13	89	83	42	12	1	26-2	67	3.94	95	.251	.306	8-0-1	.125	-1		-1		-0.3
1987	†Min A	8	8	.500	63	0	0	31-10	80.1	70	41	14	3	28-4	83	4.48	104	.232	.301	0		0		13		2.3
1988	Min A☆	4	4	.333	63	0	0	42-8	73	68	21	6	2	15-2	56	2.47	166	.245	.288	0	—	0		2		0.2
1989	Min A	5	4	.556	65	0	0	31-11	73	68	33	9	3	12-3	46	4.07	102	.246	.280	0	—	0		6	44	1.1
1990	†Bos A	5	3	.625	47	0	0	21-7	51.1	39	19	5	1	19-4	33	3.16	130	.206	.282	0	—	0		6		1.0
1991	Bos A★	1	4	.200	57	0	0	40-9	59.1	54	21	9	1	16-3	44	3.03	143	.236	.286	0	—	0		1		0.2
1992	Bos A	2	2	.500	46	0	0	27-8	42.1	53	20	6	1	7-0	32	4.25	100	.308	.335	0	—	0		-4		-0.5
	†Atl N	3	0	1.000	14	0	0	3-2	15.2	14	2	0	1	2-1	7	1.15	319	.241	.279	0	—	0		-2		-0.4
1993	Cin N	4	6	.400	58	0	0	8-4	61.2	66	34	4	5	10-0	35	4.09	99	.270	.308	2-0-1	.000	-3		-4		-0.1
1994	NY A	1	0	1.000	11	0	0	2-1	9.2	17	9	3	0	3-0	4	8.38	55	.386	.426	0	—	-0		94	44	13.9
Total 16		73	77	.487	880	0	0	367-106	1132.1	1000	426	109	27	358-65	877	3.16	122	.236	.297	57-0-7	.088	-3	94	44		

REARDON, JEREMIAH Jeremiah J. B9.1868 D4.22.1907 St.Louis MO d7.17
1886	StL N	0	1	.000	1	1	1	0	8	10	1	0	0		5	0	6.75	48	.323	.417	4	.250	0	57	-2		-0.2
	Cin AA	0	1	.000	1	1	0	0	2	5	4	0	4		4	0	18.00	30	.500	.643	3	.000	-1	67	-3		-0.4
Total 1		0	2	.000	2	2	1	0	10	15	12	1	0		9	0	9.00	36	.366	.480	7	.143	-1	65	-5		-0.6

REBERGER, FRANK Frank Beall "Crane" B6.7.1944 Caldwell ID BL/TR/6-5/200* d6.6 C3 Col Idaho
1968	Chi N	0	1	.000	3	0	0	6	9	4	1	0	2-0	3	4.50	70	.346	.393	0		0	220	-1		-0.
1969	SD N	1	2	.333	67	0	0	6-2	87.2	83	38	6	2	41-8	65	3.59	100	.258	.342	5	.200	0	0	0		0.
1970	SF N	7	8	.467	45	18	3	2-1	152	178	108	13	7	98-6	117	5.57	71	.293	.395	47-0-3	.234	1*	129	-28		-2.
1971	SF N	3	0	1.000	13	0	0	0-0	43.2	37	20	5	2	19-0	21	3.92	87	.228	.315	13	.231	0*	152	-1	27	-0.
1972	SF N	3	4	.429	20	11	2	0	99.1	97	49	10	5	37-2	52	3.99	88	.257	.329	35	.229	2*	117	-5		-0.
Total 5		14	15	.483	148	37	5	8-3	388.2	404	219	35	16	197-16	258	4.52	82	.270	.359	100-0-3	.230	4	132	-35	27	-2.

RECCIUS, JOHN John B10.29.1859 Louisville KY D9.1.1930 Louisville KY 5-6.5/? d5.2 b-Phil ▲
1882	Lou AA	4	6	.400	13	10	9-1	0	95	106	70	3	0	22	31	3.03	82	.264	.303	266-1	.237	3*	133	-6		-0.
1883	Lou AA	0	0	—	1	0	0	0	4	10	3	0	0	0	0	2.25	133	.455	.455	63	.143	-0*		0		-0.
Total 2		4	6	.400	14	10	9-1	0	99	116	73	3	0	22	31	3.00	83	.274	.310	329-1	.219	3	133	-6		-0.

RECCIUS, PHIL Phillip B6.7.1862 Louisville KY D2.15.1903 Louisville KY 5-9/163 d9.25.1882 b-John ▲
1884	Lou AA	6	7	.462	18	11	11	1	129.1	118	80	2	4	19	46	2.71	114	.228	.261	263-3	.240	2*	64	2		0.
1885	Lou AA	0	4	.000	5	4	1	0	40	46	35	0	1	11	10	3.82	84	.253	.299	402-1	.241	1*	88	-3		-0.
1886	Lou AA	0	1	.000	1	1	0	0	3	7	6	0	4	0	0	9.00	40	.467	.556	13	.308	0*	82	-2		-0.
1887	Cle AA	0	0	—	1	1	0	0	7	8	7	0	0	5	0	7.71	56	.320	.433	229	.205	-0*		-2		-0.
Total 4		6	12	.333	27	17	15	1	179.1	179	128	2	5	38	56	3.26	97	.242	.284	907-4	.233	4	73	-5		-0.

REDDING, PHIL Philip Hayden B1.28.1889 Crystal Springs MS D3.31.1928 Greenwood MS BL/TR/5-11.5/190 d9.14
1912	StL N	2	1	.667	3	3	2	0	25.1	31	17	2	0	11	9	4.97	69	.313	.382	8-0-1	.000	-1	100	-3		-0.
1913	StL N	0	0	—	1	0	0	0	2.2	2	2	0	0	1	1	6.75	48	.286	.375	1	.000	-0		-1		-0.
Total 2		2	1	.667	4	3	2	0	28	33	19	2	0	12	10	5.14	66	.311	.381	9-0-1	.000	-1	100	-4		-0.

REDDING, TIM Timothy James B2.12.1978 Rochester NY BR/TR/6-0/180(180-200) [HouN97 20/610] d6.24 Col Monroe (NY) CC
| 2001 | Hou N | 3 | 1 | .750 | 13 | 9 | 0 | 0-0 | 55.2 | 62 | 38 | 11 | 3 | 24-0 | 55 | 5.50 | 84 | .286 | .360 | 14-0-2 | .214 | 0 | 116 | -6 | | -0. |
| 2002 | Hou N | 3 | 6 | .333 | 18 | 14 | 0 | 0-0 | 73.1 | 78 | 49 | 10 | 0 | 35-3 | 63 | 5.40 | 80 | .276 | .352 | 20-0-1 | .100 | -1 | 111 | -9 | | -1 |

YEAR	TM LG	W	L	PCT	G	GS	CG-SHO	SV-BS	IP	H	R	HR	HB	BB-IB	SO	ERA	AERA	OAV	OOB	AB-HR-SH	AVG	PB	SUP	APR	DL	PW
2003	Hou N	10	14	.417	33	32	0	0-0	176	179	85	16	7	65-4	116	3.68	120	.261	.329	50-0-8	.200	2	80	11		1.5
2004	Hou N	5	7	.417	27	17	0	0-0	100.2	125	73	15	5	43-3	56	5.72	76	.309	.380	29-0-1	.138	-1	106	-17		-1.8
2005	SD N	0	5	.000	9	6	0	0-0	29.2	40	35	7	2	13-1	17	9.10	42	.328	.393	8-0-1	.000	-1	64	-20	44	-2.7
	NY A	0	1	.000	1	1	0	0-0	1	4	6	0	0	4-0	2	54.00	8	.571	.727	0	—	0	21	-5		-0.7
Total 5		21	34	.382	101	79	0	0-0	436.1	488	286	59	17	184-11	309	5.16	85	.284	.356	121-0-13	.157	-1	93	-46	44	-5.1

REDFERN, PETE Peter Irvine B8.25.1954 Glendale CA BR/TR/6-2/195* [MinA76*S1/1] d5.15 Col USC

YEAR	TM LG	W	L	PCT	G	GS	CG-SHO	SV-BS	IP	H	R	HR	HB	BB-IB	SO	ERA	AERA	OAV	OOB	AB-HR-SH	AVG	PB	SUP	APR	DL	PW
1976	Min A	8	8	.500	23	23	1-1	0-0	118	105	61	6	3	63-1	74	3.51	102	.241	.339	0	—	0	141	-2		-0.3
1977	Min A	6	9	.400	30	28	1	0-0	137.1	164	89	13	4	66-2	73	5.18	77	.304	.382	0	—	0	122	-19	21	-1.8
1978	Min A	0	2	.000	3	2	0	0-0	9.2	10	12	2	0	6-0	4	6.52	59	.294	.381	0	—	0	94	-5		-0.8
1979	Min A	7	3	.700	40	6	0	1-2	108.1	106	45	8	1	35-0	85	3.49	126	.258	.315	0	—	0*	141	11		0.9
1980	Min A	7	7	.500	23	16	2	2-1	104.2	117	58	11	0	33-3	73	4.56	96	.283	.333	0	—	0	82	-1	42	-0.2
1981	Min A	9	8	.529	24	23	3	0-1	141.2	140	70	12	2	52-1	77	4.07	97	.261	.326	0	—	0	86	-1		-0.2
1982	Min A	5	11	.313	27	13	0	0-1	94.1	122	74	16	1	51-3	59	6.58	65	.322	.401	0	—	0	80	-23	23	-3.3
Total 7		42	48	.467	170	111	9-1	3-5	714	764	409	68	11	306-10	426	4.54	90	.278	.350	0	—	0	106	-40	86	-5.7

REDMAN, MARK Mark Allen B1.5.1974 San Diego CA BL/TL/6-5/220(220-245) [MinA95 1/13] d7.24 Col Oklahoma

YEAR	TM LG	W	L	PCT	G	GS	CG-SHO	SV-BS	IP	H	R	HR	HB	BB-IB	SO	ERA	AERA	OAV	OOB	AB-HR-SH	AVG	PB	SUP	APR	DL	PW
1999	Min A	1	0	1.000	5	1	0	0-0	12.2	17	13	3	1	7-0	11	8.53	61	.298	.385	0	—	0	180	-5	16	-0.3
2000	Min A	12	9	.571	32	24	0	0-0	151.1	168	81	22	3	45-0	117	4.76	111	.281	.333	4-0-1	.000	-0	84	10		1.1
2001	Min A	2	4	.333	9	9	0	0-0	49	57	26	6	0	19-0	29	4.22	111	.286	.349	0	—	-0	79	2		0.2
	Det A	0	2	.000	2	2	0	0-0	9	11	6	1	1	4-0	4	6.00	74	.306	.390	0	—	-0	42	-1	68	-0.2
	Year	2	6	.250	11	11	0	0-0	58	68	32	7	1	23-0	33	4.50	103	.289	.355	0	—	-0	73	1	25	0.0
2002	Det A	8	15	.348	30	30	3	0-0	203	211	107	15	6	51-2	109	4.21	101	.268	.314	5	.200	0	67	3		0.3
2003	†Fla N	14	9	.609	29	29	3	0-0	190.2	172	82	16	5	61-3	151	3.59	114	.239	.301	61-0-6	.016	-6	112	11	30	0.5
2004	Oak A	11	12	.478	32	32	0	0-0	191	218	110	28	6	68-6	102	4.71	98	.292	.353	5	.000	0	91	-2		-0.3
2005	Pit N	5	15	.250	30	30	2-1	0-0	178.1	188	100	18	2	56-3	101	4.90	87	.278	.332	53-0-4	.113	-2	73	-11		-1.1
Total 7		53	66	.445	169	157	10-1	0-0	985	1042	525	109	24	311-14	624	4.47	101	.273	.329	128-0-9	.063	-8	85	7	139	0.2

REED, HOWIE Howard Dean "Diz" B12.21.1936 Dallas TX D12.7.1984 Corpus Christi TX BR/TR/6-1/210(195-211) d9.13 Col Texas

YEAR	TM LG	W	L	PCT	G	GS	CG-SHO	SV-BS	IP	H	R	HR	HB	BB-IB	SO	ERA	AERA	OAV	OOB	AB-HR-SH	AVG	PB	SUP	APR	DL	PW
1958	KC A	1	0	1.000	3	1	1	0	10.1	5	1	0	0	4-0	5	0.87	449	.132	.214	2-0-1	.000	0	46	3		0.3
1959	KC A	0	3	.000	6	3	0	0	20.2	26	19	3	0	10-0	11	7.40	54	.313	.379	3	.000	-0	66	-7		-0.9
1960	KC A	0	0	—	1	0	0	0	1.2	2	1	1	0	0-0	1	0.00	—	.286	.286	0	—	0	6	0		0.0
1964	LA N	3	4	.429	26	7	0	1	90	79	34	4	0	36-9	52	3.20	101	.236	.309	20	.100	-0	81	2		0.2
1965	†LA N	7	5	.583	38	5	0	1	78	73	31	6	3	27-6	47	3.12	105	.243	.311	12	.000	-0	86	1		0.2
1966	LA N	0	0	—	1	0	0	1	1.2	1	0	0	0	0-0	0	0.00	—	.167	.167	1	.000	-0	0	1		0.0
	Cal A	0	1	.000	19	1	0	1	43	39	14	5	0	15-2	17	2.93	115	.247	.307	6	.000	-1	26	3		0.1
1967	Hou N	1	1	.500	4	2	0	0	18.1	19	8	0	0	2-0	9	3.44	96	.268	.288	4	.000	0	80	0		-0.1
1969	Mon N	6	7	.462	31	15	2-1	1-0	106	119	59	7	2	50-7	59	4.84	76	.290	.365	32-1-3	.125	1	93	-10		-1.0
1970	Mon N	6	5	.545	57	1	0	5-1	89	81	34	7	2	40-5	42	3.13	133	.252	.336	10-0-1	.000	-0	151	10		1.2
1971	Mon N	2	3	.400	43	0	0	0-0	56.2	66	28	8	0	24-7	25	4.29	83	.296	.360	1	.000	-0		-4		-0.3
Total 10		26	29	.473	229	35	3-1	15-1	515.1	510	229	41	7	208-36	268	3.72	96	.261	.332	91-1-5	.066	-1	85	-1		-0.3

REED, JERRY Jerry Maxwell B10.8.1955 Bryson City NC BR/TR/6-1/190* [PhiN77 22/559] d9.11 Col Western Carolina

YEAR	TM LG	W	L	PCT	G	GS	CG-SHO	SV-BS	IP	H	R	HR	HB	BB-IB	SO	ERA	AERA	OAV	OOB	AB-HR-SH	AVG	PB	SUP	APR	DL	PW
1981	Phi N	0	1	.000	4	0	0	0-0	4.2	7	4	0	0	6-0	5	7.71	47	.333	.481	0	—	0		-2		-0.4
1982	Phi N	1	0	1.000	7	0	0	0-0	8.2	11	6	0	1	3-0	5	5.19	71	.324	.395	0	—	0		-2		-0.1
	Cle A	1	1	.500	6	1	0	0-0	15.2	15	6	1	0	3-0	10	3.45	120	.250	.286	0	—	0	22	-2		0.2
1983	Cle A	0	0	—	7	0	0	0-0	21.1	26	19	4	0	9-1	11	7.17	60	.310	.372	0	—	0		-7		-0.3
1985	Cle A	3	5	.375	33	5	0	8-2	72.1	67	41	12	3	19-2	37	4.11	101	.245	.298	0	—	0	79	-2		-0.2
1986	Sea A	4	0	1.000	11	4	0	0-0	34.2	38	13	3	0	13-0	16	3.12	137	.273	.336	0	—	0	186	5	63	0.5
1987	Sea A	1	2	.333	39	1	0	7-1	81.2	79	32	7	3	24-3	51	3.42	139	.255	.314	0	—	0	58	12	26	0.6
1988	Sea A	1	1	.500	46	0	0	1-2	86.1	82	42	8	2	33-7	48	3.96	106	.256	.325	0	—	0*		2		0.1
1989	Sea A	7	7	.500	52	1	0	0-4	101.2	89	44	10	1	43-10	50	3.19	127	.235	.313	0	—	0		2		1.0
1990	Sea A	0	1	.000	4	0	0	0-0	7.1	8	4	1	0	3-0	2	4.91	81	.286	.355	0	—	0	8	-1		1.0
	Bos A	2	1	.667	29	0	0	2-1	45	55	27	1	0	16-2	17	4.80	85	.302	.353	0	—	0		-1		-0.1
	Year	2	2	.500	33	0	0	2-1	52.1	63	31	2	0	19-2	19	4.82	85	.300	.353	0	—	0		-4		-0.2
Total 9		20	19	.513	238	12	0	18-10	479.1	477	238	47	10	172-25	248	3.94	107	.261	.325	0	—	0	102	12	89	1.0

REED, RICK Richard Allen B8.16.1964 Huntington WV BR/TR/6-0/205(190-210) [PitN86 26/644] d8.8 Col Marshall

YEAR	TM LG	W	L	PCT	G	GS	CG-SHO	SV-BS	IP	H	R	HR	HB	BB-IB	SO	ERA	AERA	OAV	OOB	AB-HR-SH	AVG	PB	SUP	APR	DL	PW
1988	Pit N	1	0	1.000	1	1	0	0-0	12	10	4	1	0	2-0	6	3.00	115	.233	.267	4	.000	0	142	1		0.0
1989	Pit N	1	4	.200	15	7	0	0-0	54.2	62	35	5	2	11-3	34	5.60	61	.290	.326	13	.077	-0	63	-12		-1.1
1990	Pit N	2	3	.400	13	8	1-1	1-0	53.2	62	32	6	1	12-6	27	4.36	84	.279	.318	16	.250	1	114	-6		-0.4
1991	Pit N	0	0	—	1	1	0	0-0	4.1	6	6	1	0	1-0	2	10.38	35	.400	.429	2	.500	1	150	-3		-0.1
1992	KC A	3	7	.300	19	18	1-1	0-0	100.1	105	47	10	5	20-3	49	3.68	111	.271	.312	2	.000	0	81	3		0.3
1993	KC A	0	0	—	1	0	0	0-0	3.2	6	4	0	1	1-0	3	9.82	47	.375	.444	0	—	0		1		-0.1
	Tex A	1	0	1.000	2	0	0	0-0	4	6	1	1	1	1-0	2	2.25	187	.375	.444	0	—	0		1		0.2
	Year	1	0	1.000	3	0	0	0-0	7.2	12	5	1	2	2-0	5	5.87	75	.375	.444	0	—	0		1		0.1
1994	Tex A	1	1	.500	4	3	0	0-0	16.2	17	13	3	1	7-0	12	5.94	81	.254	.333	0	—	0		-1		-0.2
1995	Cin N	0	0	—	4	3	0	0-0	17	18	12	5	0	3-0	10	5.82	72	.273	.304	0	—	-0	139	-2		-0.2
1997	NY N	13	9	.591	33	31	2	0-0	208.1	186	76	19	5	31-4	113	2.89	138	.239	.272	3-0-2	.000	-0	159	-3		-0.2
1998	NY N☆	16	11	.593	31	31	2-1	0-0	212.1	208	84	30	6	29-2	153	3.48	119	.261	.290	57-1-6	.175	4	100	26		2.9
1999	†NY N	11	5	.688	26	26	1-1	0-0	149.1	163	77	23	4	47-2	104	4.58	95	.281	.334	45-0-8	.244	-1	91	17		2.0
2000	†NY N	11	5	.688	30	30	0	0-0	184	192	90	28	5	34-3	121	4.11	106	.266	.302	49-0-14	.204	2*	123	-3	47	0.5
2001	NY N★	8	6	.571	20	20	3-1	0-0	134.2	119	53	16	1	17-3	99	3.48	116	.236	.262	40-0-4	.125	1	120	7	16	0.5
	Min A	4	6	.400	12	12	0	0-0	67.2	92	45	12	4	14-0	43	5.19	90	.325	.363	0	—	0	94	11		1.1
2002	†Min A	15	7	.682	33	32	2-1	0-0	188	192	89	32	6	26-0	121	3.78	118	.259	.288	4-0-1	.250	0	83	-5		-0.6
2003	†Min A	6	12	.333	27	21	0	0-1	135	155	80	21	5	29-2	71	5.07	89	.285	.325	0	—	0	70	-8	37	1.3
Total 15		93	76	.550	273	245	14-7	1-1	1545.2	1601	748	213	44	285-28	970	4.03	104	.267	.303	297-2-47	.172	8	102	34	100	4.6

REED, BOB Robert Edward B1.12.1945 Boston MA BR/TR/5-10/170* [DetA66 S2/22] d9.5 Col Michigan

YEAR	TM LG	W	L	PCT	G	GS	CG-SHO	SV-BS	IP	H	R	HR	HB	BB-IB	SO	ERA	AERA	OAV	OOB	AB-HR-SH	AVG	PB	SUP	APR	DL	PW
1969	Det A	0	0	—	8	1	0	0-0	14.2	9	7	1	0	8-0	9	1.84	205	.184	.298	2	.500	0	71	3		0.2
1970	Det A	2	4	.333	16	4	0	2-0	46.1	54	25	5	0	14-0	26	4.86	78	.292	.342	12	.083	-0*	77	-4		-0.6
Total 2		2	4	.333	24	5	0	2-0	61	63	28	5	0	22-0	35	4.13	91	.269	.332	14	.143	-0	76	-1		-0.4

REED, RON Ronald Lee B11.2.1942 LaPorte IN BR/TR/6-6/215* d9.26 Col Notre Dame

YEAR	TM LG	W	L	PCT	G	GS	CG-SHO	SV-BS	IP	H	R	HR	HB	BB-IB	SO	ERA	AERA	OAV	OOB	AB-HR-SH	AVG	PB	SUP	APR	DL	PW
1966	Atl N	1	1	.500	2	2	0	0	8.1	7	2	1	0	4-0	6	2.16	168	.226	.314	2	.000	-0	73	1		0.3
1967	Atl N	1	1	.500	3	3	0	0	21.1	21	8	1	2	3-0	11	2.95	112	.262	.299	8	.000	-1	88	1		0.0
1968	Atl N★	11	10	.524	35	28	6-1	0	201.2	189	87	10	4	49-11	111	3.35	89	.246	.294	62-0-9	.161	1	87	-8		-0.8
1969	†Atl N	18	10	.643	36	33	7-1	0-0	241.1	227	103	24	6	56-5	160	3.47	104	.246	.292	80-0-13	.125	-2*	114	4		0.2
1970	Atl N	7	10	.412	21	18	6	0-0	134.2	140	69	16	2	39-5	68	4.41	97	.266	.319	44-0-5	.091	-2*	91	0	58	-0.3
1971	Atl N	13	14	.481	32	32	8-1	0-0	222.1	221	105	26	2	54-10	129	3.72	100	.261	.304	74-0-6	.149	-3	78	0		-0.3
1972	Atl N	11	15	.423	31	30	11-1	0-0	213	222	109	18	2	60-7	111	3.93	97	.270	.321	73-0-5	.178	-1	89	-5		-0.6
1973	Atl N	4	11	.267	20	19	2	1-0	116.1	133	71	7	3	31-6	64	4.41	90	.287	.334	45-0-1	.200	-0*	89	-8	63	-0.9
1974	Atl N	10	11	.476	28	28	6-2	0-0	186	171	76	16	2	41-6	78	3.39	112	.243	.285	57-0-7	.105	-3	75	9	40	0.5
1975	Atl N	4	5	.444	10	10	1	0-0	74.2	93	39	1	0	16-2	40	4.22	90	.304	.335	26	.231	1	93	-2		-0.1
	StL N	9	8	.529	24	24	7-2	0-0	175.2	181	79	4	4	37-5	99	3.23	118	.263	.304	56-0-5	.161	-0	97	9		0.8
	Year	13	13	.500	34	34	8-2	0-0	250.1	274	118	5	4	53-7	139	3.52	108	.276	.313	82-0-5	.183	1	96	6		0.7
1976	†Phi N	8	7	.533	59	4	1	14-9	128	88	39	8	2	32-7	96	2.46	145	.193	.247	24-0-2	.167	0	117	15		2.1
1977	†Phi N	7	5	.583	60	3	0	15-3	124.1	101	41	9	1	37-7	84	2.75	146	.223	.283	18-0-1	.111	0	125	18		2.0
1978	†Phi N	3	4	.429	66	0	0	17-2	108.2	87	32	7	1	23-5	85	2.24	161	.223	.273	6	.000	0		15		1.4
1979	†Phi N	1	4	.619	61	0	0	5-5	102	110	52	9	2	32-5	58	4.15	93	.278	.332	10-0-2	.300	-1		-4		-0.6
1980	†Phi N	7	5	.583	55	0	0	9-4	91.1	88	45	4	1	30-10	54	4.04	95	.253	.311	10	.300	1		-2		-0.1
1981	†Phi N	5	3	.625	39	0	0	8-0	61.1	54	26	6	1	17-8	40	3.08	119	.237	.290	6	.500	1		2		0.5
1982	†Phi N	5	5	.500	57	2	0	14-2	98	85	30	4	3	24-5	57	2.66	139	.248	.286	12-0-1	.333	2	143	12		1.8
1983	†Phi N	9	1	.900	61	0	0	8-4	95.2	89	42	5	1	34-14	73	3.48	104	.248	.312	6-0-1	.167	-0		2		0.1
1984	Chi A	0	6	.000	51	0	0	12-5	73	67	29	7	1	14-2	57	3.08	136	.248	.286	1	.000	-0		8	15	0.9
Total 19		146	140	.510	751	236	55-8	103-36	2477.2	2374	1084	182	50	633-124	1481	3.46	108	.252	.301	620-0-58	.158	-6	91	67	176	7.0

REED, STEVE Steven Vincent B3.11.1965 Los Angeles CA BR/TR/6-2/212(200-212) d8.30 Col Lewis-Clark St.

YEAR TM LG	W	L	PCT	G	GS	CG-SHO	SV-BS	IP	H	R	HR	HB	BB-IB	SO	ERA	AERA	OAV	OOB	AB-HR-SH	AVG	PB	SUP	APR	DL	PW
1992 SF N	1	0	1.000	18	0	0	0-0	15.2	13	5	1	2		11	2.30	145	.220	.270	0	—	0		2		0.1
1993 Col N	9	5	.643	64	0	0	3-3	84.1	80	47	13	3	30-5	51	4.48	107	.259	.328	9-0-2	.000	-1		5		0.3
1994 Col N	3	2	.600	61	0	0	3-7	64	79	33	9	6	26-3	51	3.94	127	.306	.374	2	.000	0		23		1.9
1995 †Col N	5	2	.714	71	0	0	3-3	84	61	24	8	1	21-3	79	2.14	251	.203	.256	3	.333	0		8		0.6
1996 Col N	4	3	.571	70	0	0	0-6	75	66	38	11	6	19-0	51	3.96	132	.239	.298	3	.333	0		7		1.2
1997 Col N	4	6	.400	63	0	0	6-7	62.1	49	28	10	5	27-1	43	4.04	128	.219	.315	1	.000	-0		16		0.8
1998 SF N	2	1	.667	50	0	0	1-4	54.2	30	10	4	4	19-5	50	1.48	272	.160	.251	3	.333	0		-5		-0.6
†Cle A	2	2	.500	20	0	0	0-1	25.2	26	19	4	1	8-0	23	6.66	72	.260	.321	0	—	0		5		0.3
1999 †Cle A	3	2	.600	63	0	0	0-3	61.2	69	33	10	3	20-5	44	4.23	120	.285	.341	0	—	0		3		0.2
2000 Cle A	2	0	1.000	57	0	0	0-1	56	58	30	7	1	21-4	39	4.34	115	.269	.335	0	—	0		3		0.2
2001 Cle A	1	1	.500	31	0	0	0-1	27.1	22	11	3	2	10-2	21	3.62	127	.212	.293	0	—	0*		3		0.3
†Atl N	2	2	.500	39	0	0	1-0	31	30	14	3	1	13-3	25	3.48	124	.259	.336	0	—	0		3		0.3
2002 SD N	2	4	.333	40	0	0	1-2	41	33	9	2	6	10-2	36	1.98	197	.228	.304	1	.000	-0*		10		1.4
NY N	0	1	1.000	24	0	0	1-1	26	23	6	0	2	4-1	14	2.08	190	.240	.284	1	.000	-0		6		0.3
Year	2	5	.286	64	0	0	1-3	67	56	15	2	8	14-3	50	2.01	194	.232	.297	2	.000	-0		15		1.7
2003 Col N	5	3	.625	67	0	0	0-2	63.1	59	24	9	8	26-3	39	3.27	150	.254	.348	0	—	0		10		1.2
2004 Col N	3	8	.273	65	0	0	0-4	66	72	29	7	7	17-7	38	3.68	129	.281	.342	2	.500	0		7		1.0
2005 Bal A	1	2	.333	30	0	0	0-0	32.2	41	24	5	4	11-2	15	6.61	67	.308	.376	0	—	0		-7		-0.5
Total 14	49	44	.527	833	0	0	18-45	870.2	811	384	107	61	285-46	630	3.63	132	.249	.319	25-0-2	.160	-1		98		9.0

REEDER, BILL William Edgar B2.20.1922 Dike TX D3.12.2001 Sulphur Springs TX BR/TR/6-5/205 d4.23

YEAR TM LG	W	L	PCT	G	GS	CG-SHO	SV-BS	IP	H	R	HR	HB	BB-IB	SO	ERA	AERA	OAV	OOB	AB-HR-SH	AVG	PB	SUP	APR	DL	PW
1949 StL N	1	1	.500	21	1	0	0	33.2	33	22	2	1	30	21	5.08	82	.270	.418	3	.000	-0	85	-3		-0.2

REES, STAN Stanley Milton "Nellie" B2.25.1899 Cynthiana KY D8.30.1937 Lexington KY BL/TL/6-3/190 d6.12

YEAR TM LG	W	L	PCT	G	GS	CG-SHO	SV-BS	IP	H	R	HR	HB	BB-IB	SO	ERA	AERA	OAV	OOB	AB-HR-SH	AVG	PB	SUP	APR	DL	PW
1918 Was A	1	0	1.000	2	0	0	0	2	3	0	0	0	4	1	0.00	—	.500	.700	0	—	0		1		0.1

REGAN, MIKE Michael John B11.19.1888 Phoenix NY D5.22.1961 Albany NY BR/TR/5-10/160 d5.13

YEAR TM LG	W	L	PCT	G	GS	CG-SHO	SV-BS	IP	H	R	HR	HB	BB-IB	SO	ERA	AERA	OAV	OOB	AB-HR-SH	AVG	PB	SUP	APR	DL	PW
1917 Cin N	11	10	.524	32	26	16-1	0	216	228	106	4	4	41	50	2.71	97	.273	.310	75	.200	1*	107	-6		-0.3
1918 Cin N	5	5	.500	22	6	4-3	2	80	77	38	0	0	29	15	3.26	82	.262	.328	27	.296	2*	104	-6		0.0
1919 Cin N	0	0	—	2	0	0	0	2.1	1	0	0	0	1	1	0.00	—	.143	.143	1	.000	-0		0		0.0
Total 3	16	15	.516	55	32	20-4	2	298.1	306	145	4	4	70	66	2.84	93	.269	.314	103	.223	3	107	-12		-0.8

REGAN, PHIL Philip Raymond "The Vulture" B4.6.1937 Otsego MI BR/TR/6-3/200* d7.19 M1/C7

YEAR TM LG	W	L	PCT	G	GS	CG-SHO	SV-BS	IP	H	R	HR	HB	BB-IB	SO	ERA	AERA	OAV	OOB	AB-HR-SH	AVG	PB	SUP	APR	DL	PW
1960 Det A	0	4	.000	17	7	0	1	68	70	39	11	2	25-1	38	4.50	88	.267	.333	17-0-1	.059	-1	89	-4		-0.4
1961 Det A	10	7	.588	32	16	6	2	120	134	70	19	1	41-1	46	5.25	78	.281	.337	40-0-3	.075	-2*	101	-10		-1.6
1962 Det A	11	9	.550	35	23	6	0	171.1	169	89	23	1	64-0	87	4.04	101	.254	.318	63-0-4	.206	1	115	0		0.0
1963 Det A	15	9	.625	38	27	5-1	0	189	179	95	33	7	59-5	115	3.86	97	.245	.305	63-1-3	.143	-1	123	-4		-0.7
1964 Det A	5	10	.333	32	21	2	1	146.2	162	87	21	5	49-4	91	5.03	73	.282	.341	41-0-4	.317	5*	117	-21		-1.5
1965 Det A	1	5	.167	16	7	1	0	51.2	57	31	6	0	20-1	37	5.05	69	.282	.341	12-0-2	.083	-0	87	-8		-1.0
1966 †LA N☆	14	1	.933	65	0	0	21	116.2	85	24	6	2	24-9	88	1.62	203	.207	.248	21-0-2	.143	0		24		4.1
1967 LA N	6	9	.400	55	3	0	6	96.1	108	38	2	2	32-17	53	2.99	104	.284	.339	10	.100	0		28		0.1
1968 LA N	2	0	1.000	5	0	0	0	7.2	10	3	1	0	1-0	7	3.52	79	.313	.333	1	.000	0		0		-0.1
Chi N	10	5	.667	68	0	0	25	127	109	36	9	2	24-6	60	2.20	144	.232	.271	20-0-3	.150	0		12		2.2
Year	12	5	.706	73	0	0	25	134.2	119	39	10	2	25-6	67	2.27	138	.237	.274	21-0-3	.143	0		12		2.1
1969 Chi N	12	6	.667	71	0	0	17-3	112	120	49	6	2	35-13	56	3.70	109	.282	.335	15	.067	-0		5		0.9
1970 Chi N	5	9	.357	54	0	0	12-9	75.2	81	43	8	1	32-7	31	4.76	95	.287	.356	9	.000	-1	68	-1		-0.2
1971 Chi N	5	5	.500	48	1	0	6-4	73.1	84	37	4	2	33-13	28	3.93	100	.301	.374	8-0-3	.000	0		1		0.1
1972 Chi N	0	1	.000	5	0	0	0-0	4	6	1	0	0	2-0	2	2.25	169	.400	.471	0	—	-1		-1		0.0
Chi N	1	0	1.000	10	0	0	0-1	13.1	18	7	1	1	6-2	4	4.05	77	.346	.417	1	1.000	0		-1		0.0
Total 13	96	81	.542	551	105	20-1	92-17	1372.2	1392	649	150	26	447-79	743	3.84	97	.265	.322	321-1-25	.153	1	112	-7		-1.8

REGILIO, NICK Nicholas D. B9.4.1978 Miami FL BR/TR/6-2/205* [TexA99 2/72] d7.9 Col Jacksonville

YEAR TM LG	W	L	PCT	G	GS	CG-SHO	SV-BS	IP	H	R	HR	HB	BB-IB	SO	ERA	AERA	OAV	OOB	AB-HR-SH	AVG	PB	SUP	APR	DL	PW
2004 Tex A	0	4	.000	6	4	0	0-0	19.1	20	16	3	2	15-1	12	6.05	81	.278	.411	0	—	0	19	-3	116	0.0
2005 Tex A	1	2	.333	18	0	0	0-2	17.2	22	10	2	1	7-1	14	4.58	100	.297	.361	0	—	0		0	116	-0.5
Total 2	1	6	.143	24	4	0	0-2	37	42	26	5	3	22-2	26	5.35	89	.288	.387	0	—	0	19	-3	116	-0.5

REICHERT, DAN Daniel Robert B7.12.1976 Monterey CA BR/TR/6-3/175* [KCA97 1/7] d7.16 Col Pacific (CA)

YEAR TM LG	W	L	PCT	G	GS	CG-SHO	SV-BS	IP	H	R	HR	HB	BB-IB	SO	ERA	AERA	OAV	OOB	AB-HR-SH	AVG	PB	SUP	APR	DL	PW
1999 KC A	2	2	.500	8	8	0	0-0	36.2	48	38	2	2	32-1	20	9.08	56	.327	.451	3-0-1	.333	0	144	-15	41	-1.2
2000 KC A	8	10	.444	44	18	1-1	2-4	153.1	157	92	15	7	91-1	94	4.70	111	.271	.372	1	.000	-0	91	5		0.5
2001 KC A	8	8	.500	27	19	0	0-0	123	131	83	14	8	67-2	77	5.63	88	.278	.374	5	.000	-1	94	-8		-0.9
2002 KC A	3	5	.375	30	6	0	0-0	66	77	48	10	4	25-2	36	5.32	94	.306	.373	0	—	0	68	-5		-0.4
2003 Tor A	0	0	—	15	0	0	0-1	16.1	28	12	2	2	8-3	13	6.06	78	.389	.463	0	—	0		-2		-0.1
Total 5	21	25	.457	124	51	1-1	2-6	395.1	441	273	43	23	223-9	240	5.55	91	.290	.385	9-0-1	.111	-0	98	-25	41	-2.1

REID, EARL Earl Percy B6.8.1913 Bangor AL D5.11.1984 Cullman AL BL/TR/6-3/190 d5.8

YEAR TM LG	W	L	PCT	G	GS	CG-SHO	SV-BS	IP	H	R	HR	HB	BB-IB	SO	ERA	AERA	OAV	OOB	AB-HR-SH	AVG	PB	SUP	APR	DL	PW
1946 Bos N	1	0	1.000	3	0	0	0-0	3	4	3	0	0	3	2	3.00	114	.308	.438	0	—	0		-1		-0.1

REIDY, BILL William Joseph B10.9.1873 Cleveland OH D10.14.1915 Cleveland OH BR/TR/5-10/175 d7.21

YEAR TM LG	W	L	PCT	G	GS	CG-SHO	SV-BS	IP	H	R	HR	HB	BB-IB	SO	ERA	AERA	OAV	OOB	AB-HR-SH	AVG	PB	SUP	APR	DL	PW
1896 NY N	0	1	.000	2	1	1	0	13	24	11	0	3	2	2	7.62	55	.393	.439	5	.000	-1	34	-3		-0.3
1899 Bro N	1	0	1.000	2	1	1	0	7	9	2	0	0	2	2	2.57	152	.310	.355	3	.000	-1	129	1		0.2
1901 Mil A	16	20	.444	37	33	28-2	0	301.1	364	183	14	9	62	50	4.21	85	.295	.333	112-0-7	.143	-6	94	-11		-1.8
1902 StL A	3	5	.375	12	9	7	0	95	111	52	0	7	13	16	4.45	79	.292	.327	41	.195	-0*	82	-6		-0.5
1903 StL A	1	4	.200	5	5	5-1	0	43	53	31	1	3	7	8	3.98	73	.301	.339	15	.067	-2	59	-7		-0.7
Bro N	6	7	.462	15	13	11	0	104	130	54	0	6	14	21	3.46	92	.315	.346	37-0-1	.243	1	107	-2		-0.2
1904 Bro N	0	4	.000	6	4	2	1	38.1	49	33	0	2	6	11	4.46	82	.293	.326	32	.156	-0*	63	-9		-0.9
Total 6	27	41	.397	79	66	55-3	2	601.2	740	366	15	30	106	109	4.17	82	.301	.337	245-0-8	.159	-9	90	-37		-4.3

REINHART, ART Arthur Conrad B5.29.1899 Ackley IA D11.11.1946 Houston TX BL/TL/6-1/170 d4.26 Col Iowa

YEAR TM LG	W	L	PCT	G	GS	CG-SHO	SV-BS	IP	H	R	HR	HB	BB-IB	SO	ERA	AERA	OAV	OOB	AB-HR-SH	AVG	PB	SUP	APR	DL	PW
1919 StL N	0	0	—	1	0	0	0	0	0	0	0	0	0	0	—	—	1.000		0	—	0				
1925 StL N	11	5	.688	20	16	15-1	0	144.2	149	61	7	4	47	26	3.05	142	.278	.341	67-0-2	.328	5*	115	19		
1926 †StL N	10	5	.667	27	11	9	0	143	159	75	5	3	47	26	4.22	93	.295	.355	63-0-3	.317	4*	151	-3		
1927 StL N	5	2	.714	21	9	4-2	1	81.2	82	47	5	0	36	15	4.19	94	.267	.344	32-0-1	.313	2*	108	-2		
1928 StL N	4	6	.400	23	9	5	0	75.1	80	39	3	0	27	12	2.87	140	.272	.333	24	.167	-0*	73	5		
Total 5	30	18	.625	92	45	31-4	3	444.2	470	222	20	8	157	79	3.60	113	.280	.345	186-0-6	.301	10	114	19		

REIS, JACK Harrie Crane B6.14.1890 Cincinnati OH D7.20.1939 Cincinnati OH BR/TR/5-10.5/160 d9.9 Col Cincinnati

YEAR TM LG	W	L	PCT	G	GS	CG-SHO	SV-BS	IP	H	R	HR	HB	BB-IB	SO	ERA	AERA	OAV	OOB	AB-HR-SH	AVG	PB	SUP	APR	DL	PW
1911 StL N	0	0	—	3	0	0	0	9.1	5	3	0	0	8	4	0.96	350	.156	.325	2	.000	-0		2		

REIS, LAURIE Lawrence P. B11.20.1858 IL D1.24.1921 Chicago IL BB/TR/?/160 d10.1

YEAR TM LG	W	L	PCT	G	GS	CG-SHO	SV-BS	IP	H	R	HR	HB	BB-IB	SO	ERA	AERA	OAV	OOB	AB-HR-SH	AVG	PB	SUP	APR	DL	PW
1877 Chi N	3	1	.750	4	4	4-1	0	36	29	8	1	0	6	11	0.75	396	.213	.246	16	.125	-2	111	8		
1878 Chi N	1	3	.250	4	4	0	0	36	55	34	0	0	10	8	3.25	75	.335	.351	20	.150	-1*	148	-4		
Total 2	4	4	.500	8	8	8-1	0	72	84	42	1	1	16	19	2.00	135	.280	.303	36	.139	-2	129	4		

REIS, BOBBY Robert Joseph Thomas B1.2.1909 Woodside NY D5.1.1973 St.Paul MN BR/TR/6-1/175 d9.19.1931 ▲

YEAR TM LG	W	L	PCT	G	GS	CG-SHO	SV-BS	IP	H	R	HR	HB	BB-IB	SO	ERA	AERA	OAV	OOB	AB-HR-SH	AVG	PB	SUP	APR	DL	PW
1935 Bro N	3	2	.600	14	2	1	0	41.1	46	26	0	1	24	7	2.83	140	.277	.372	85	.247	1*	128	1		
1936 Bos N	6	5	.545	35	5	2	0	138.2	152	77	7	5	74	25	4.48	86	.283	.375	60	.217	1*	75	-9		
1937 Bos N	0	0	—	4	0	0	0	5	3	1	0	0	0	5	1.80	199	.158	.333	86	.244	1*		1		
1938 Bos N	1	6	.143	16	2	1	0	57.2	61	35	6	6	41	20	4.99	69	.271	.397	49-0-2	.184	-0*	62	-10		
Total 4	10	13	.435	69	9	5	2	242.2	262	139	12	12	144	52	4.27	88	.277	.379	280-0-2	.229	3	85	-17		

REIS, TOMMY Thomas Edward B8.6.1914 Newport KY BR/TR/6-2/180 d4.27

YEAR TM LG	W	L	PCT	G	GS	CG-SHO	SV-BS	IP	H	R	HR	HB	BB-IB	SO	ERA	AERA	OAV	OOB	AB-HR-SH	AVG	PB	SUP	APR	DL	PW
1938 Phi N	0	1	.000	8	0	0	0	8	11	8	1	0	8	2	19.29	20	.364	.533	2	.000	-0		-8		
Bos N	0	0	—	4	0	0	0	6.1	8	5	1	0	1	4	7.11	48	.296	.321	0	—	-0		-2		
Year	0	1	.000	12	0	0	0	14.1	19	13	2	0	9	6	12.27	30	.327	.431	2	.000	-0		-10		

REISIGL, BUGS Jacob B12.12.1887 Brooklyn NY D2.24.1957 Amsterdam NY BR/TR/5-10.5/175 d9.20

YEAR TM LG	W	L	PCT	G	GS	CG-SHO	SV-BS	IP	H	R	HR	HB	BB-IB	SO	ERA	AERA	OAV	OOB	AB-HR-SH	AVG	PB	SUP	APR	DL	PW
1911 Cle A	0	1	.000	2	1	1	0	13	19	11	0	3	9	6	6.23	55	.271	.314	5	.000	-1	85	-3		

YEAR	TM LG	W	L	PCT	G	GS	CG-SHO	SV-BS	IP	H	R	HR	HB	BB-IB	SO	ERA	AERA	OAV	OOB	AB-HR-SH	AVG	PB	SUP	APR	DL	PW

REISLING, DOC Frank Carl B7.25.1874 Martins Ferry OH D3.4.1955 Tulsa OK BR/TR/5-10/180 d9.10 Col Ohio U.

YEAR	TM LG	W	L	PCT	G	GS	CG-SHO	SV-BS	IP	H	R	HR	HB	BB-IB	SO	ERA	AERA	OAV	OOB	AB-HR-SH	AVG	PB	SUP	APR	DL	PW
1904	Bro N	3	4	.429	7	7	6-1	0	51	45	16	0	9	10	19	2.12	130	.238	.308	13	.154	0	43	4		0.6
1905	Bro N	0	1	.000	2	0	0	0	3	3	1	0	0	4	2	3.00	96	.273	.467	1	.000	0		0		0.1
1909	Was A	2	4	.333	10	6	6-1	0	66.2	70	29	0	0	17	22	2.43	100	.270	.315	24-0-2	.167	0*	145	-1		-0.1
1910	Was A	10	10	.500	30	20	13-2	1	191	185	77	3	5	44	57	2.54	98	.264	.312	60-0-5	.200	2*	96	0		0.2
Total	4	15	19	.441	49	33	25-4	1	311.2	303	123	3	14	75	100	2.45	103	.261	.314	98-0-7	.184	2	92	3		0.8

REITH, BRIAN Brian Eric B2.28.1978 Fort Wayne IN BR/TR/6-5/220(190-220) [NYA96 6/179] d5.16

YEAR	TM LG	W	L	PCT	G	GS	CG-SHO	SV-BS	IP	H	R	HR	HB	BB-IB	SO	ERA	AERA	OAV	OOB	AB-HR-SH	AVG	PB	SUP	APR	DL	PW
2001	Cin N	0	7	.000	9	8	0	0-0	40.1	56	37	13	2	16-0	22	7.81	59	.333	.394	12	.250	0	50	-13		-1.8
2003	Cin N	2	3	.400	42	1	0	1-0	61.1	61	32	8	1	36-6	39	4.11	101	.263	.358	7	.000	-1	90	0		-0.2
2004	Cin N	2	2	.500	22	0	0	0-1	26	30	21	5	3	19-1	24	7.27	59	.288	.413	0	—	0		-8		-1.0
Total	3	4	12	.250	73	9	0	1-1	127.2	147	90	26	6	71-7	85	5.92	73	.292	.381	19	.158	-0	57	-21		-3.0

REITSMA, CHRIS Christopher Michael B12.31.1977 Minneapolis MN BR/TR/6-5/214(214-235) [BosA96 1/34] d4.4

YEAR	TM LG	W	L	PCT	G	GS	CG-SHO	SV-BS	IP	H	R	HR	HB	BB-IB	SO	ERA	AERA	OAV	OOB	AB-HR-SH	AVG	PB	SUP	APR	DL	PW
2001	Cin N	7	15	.318	36	29	0	0-0	182	209	121	23	5	49-6	96	5.29	87	.288	.334	48-0-7	.104	-1*	94	-14		-1.5
2002	Cin N	6	12	.333	32	21	1-1	0-0	138.1	144	73	17	5	45-5	84	3.64	117	.267	.327	30-0-7	.100	-1	79	5		0.4
2003	Cin N	9	5	.643	57	3	0	12-6	84	92	41	14	0	19-6	53	4.29	97	.281	.320	8	.125	-0	113	0		-0.1
2004	†Atl N	6	4	.600	84	0	0	2-7	79.2	89	38	9	3	20-3	60	4.07	106	.284	.327	0	—	-0		3		0.3
2005	†Atl N	3	6	.333	76	0	0	15-9	73.1	79	32	3	0	14-3	42	3.93	109	.272	.304	1	.000	-0		4		0.6
Total	5	31	42	.425	285	53	1-1	29-22	557.1	613	305	66	13	147-23	335	4.38	100	.279	.325	87-0-14	.103	-3	91	-2		-0.3

REKAR, BRYAN Bryan Robert B6.3.1972 Oak Lawn IL BR/TR/6-3/210(208-220) [ColN93 2/70] d7.19 Col Bradley

YEAR	TM LG	W	L	PCT	G	GS	CG-SHO	SV-BS	IP	H	R	HR	HB	BB-IB	SO	ERA	AERA	OAV	OOB	AB-HR-SH	AVG	PB	SUP	APR	DL	PW
1995	Col N	4	6	.400	15	14	1	0-0	85	95	51	11	3	24-2	60	4.98	108	.282	.332	26-0-4	.038	-2	75	3		0.1
1996	Col N	2	4	.333	14	11	0	0-1	58.1	87	61	11	5	26-1	25	8.95	58	.345	.413	15-0-1	.267	1	112	-19		-1.6
1997	Col N	1	0	1.000	2	2	0	0-0	9.1	11	7	3	0	6-0	6	5.79	89	.282	.378	4	.250	0	143	-1		-0.1
1998	TB A	2	8	.200	16	15	1	0-0	86.2	95	56	16	2	21-0	55	4.98	96	.282	.321	0	—	0	83	-4	97	-0.4
1999	TB A	6	6	.500	27	12	0	0-0	94.2	121	68	14	5	41-2	55	5.80	86	.313	.385	5	.200	0	127	-8		-0.8
2000	TB A	7	10	.412	30	27	2	0-0	173.1	200	92	22	4	39-0	95	4.41	111	.291	.328	3	.333	1	87	10	26	0.4
2001	TB A	3	13	.188	25	25	0	0-0	140.2	167	104	21	6	45-2	87	5.89	77	.294	.348	2	.000	-0	74	-21	37	-2.0
2002	KC A	0	2	.000	2	2	0	0-0	7	12	12	1	0	6-0	2	15.43	32	.387	.474	0	—	0	65	-7		-1.0
Total	8	25	49	.338	131	108	4	0-1	655	788	451	99	25	208-7	383	5.62	88	.299	.351	55-0-5	.145	-1	89	-47	160	-5.0

REMLINGER, MIKE Michael John B3.23.1966 Middletown NY BL/TL/6-1/215(195-215) [SFN87 1/16] d6.15 Col Dartmouth

YEAR	TM LG	W	L	PCT	G	GS	CG-SHO	SV-BS	IP	H	R	HR	HB	BB-IB	SO	ERA	AERA	OAV	OOB	AB-HR-SH	AVG	PB	SUP	APR	DL	PW
1991	SF N	2	1	.667	8	6	1-1	0-0	35	36	17	5	0	20-1	19	4.37	82	.271	.364	7-0-4	.000	-0	183	-2		-0.2
1994	NY N	1	5	.167	10	9	0	0-0	54.2	55	30	9	1	35-4	33	4.61	91	.261	.364	16-0-3	.000	-1	70	-2		-0.4
1995	NY N	0	1	.000	5	0	0	0-1	5.2	7	5	1	0	2-0	6	6.35	64	.292	.346	1	.000	-0		-2		-0.3
	Cin N	0	0	—	2	0	0	0	1	2	1	0	0	3-0	1	9.00	46	.500	.714	0	—	0		-1		0.0
	Year	0	1	.000	7	0	0	0-1	6.2	9	6	1	0	5-0	7	6.75	60	.321	.424	1	.000	-0		-3		-0.3
1996	Cin N	1	0	1.000	19	4	0	0-0	27.1	24	17	4	3	19-2	19	5.60	77	.242	.377	7	.143	0	111	-3		-0.1
1997	Cin N	8	8	.500	69	12	2	0-0	124	100	61	11	7	60-6	145	4.14	103	.223	.322	21-0-3	.095	0*	106	2		0.3
1998	Cin N	8	15	.348	35	28	1-1	0-0	164.1	164	96	23	5	87-1	144	4.82	89	.266	.358	47-0-7	.106	-2	88	-10		-1.5
1999	†Atl N	10	1	.909	73	0	0	1-2	83.2	66	24	9	1	35-5	81	2.37	189	.215	.297	2-0-2	.000	-0		20	13	2.3
2000	†Atl N	5	3	.625	71	0	0	12-4	72.2	55	29	6	3	37-1	72	3.47	130	.207	.308	3	.000	-0		10	19	1.2
2001	†Atl N	3	3	.500	74	0	0	1-4	75	67	25	9	2	23-4	93	2.76	156	.234	.296	2	.000	-0*		13		0.9
2002	†Atl N★	3	1	.700	73	0	0	0-5	68	48	17	3	1	28-3	69	1.99	204	.198	.284	2	.000	-0		16	16	2.1
2003	†Chi N	6	5	.545	73	0	0	0-1	69	54	30	11	2	39-4	83	3.65	119	.211	.318	1	.000	-0		6		0.8
2004	Chi N	1	2	.333	48	0	0	2-4	36.2	33	16	3	1	16-3	35	3.44	129	.246	.323	1	.000	-0		3	65	0.3
2005	Chi N	3	0	.000	35	0	0	0	33	31	19	5	2	12-2	30	4.91	89	.250	.326	0	—	0		-2	15	-0.1
	Bos A	0	0	—	8	0	0	0-0	6.2	15	14	2	0	5-0	5	14.85	31	.417	.488	0	—	0		-2		-0.4
Total	13	51	51	.500	603	59	4-2	18-22	856.2	757	401	101	28	421-36	835	3.90	110	.238	.330	110-0-19	.073	-4	98	40	128	4.9

REMMERSWAAL, WIN Wilhelmus Abraham B3.8.1954 The Hague, Netherlands BR/TR/6-2/160* d8.3

YEAR	TM LG	W	L	PCT	G	GS	CG-SHO	SV-BS	IP	H	R	HR	HB	BB-IB	SO	ERA	AERA	OAV	OOB	AB-HR-SH	AVG	PB	SUP	APR	DL	PW
1979	Bos A	1	0	1.000	8	0	0	0-0	20.1	26	16	1	1	12-1	16	7.08	63	.317	.402	0		0		-5		-0.3
1980	Bos A	2	1	.667	14	0	0	0-0	35.1	39	18	4	0	9-1	20	4.58	93	.295	.338	0		0		0		-0.1
Total	2	3	1	.750	22	0	0	0-0	55.2	65	34	5	1	21-2	36	5.50	79	.304	.364	0		0		-5		-0.4

REMNEAS, ALEX Alexander Norman B2.21.1886 Minneapolis MN D8.27.1975 Phoenix AZ BR/TR/6-1/180 d4.15

YEAR	TM LG	W	L	PCT	G	GS	CG-SHO	SV-BS	IP	H	R	HR	HB	BB-IB	SO	ERA	AERA	OAV	OOB	AB-HR-SH	AVG	PB	SUP	APR	DL	PW
1912	Det A	0	0	—	1	0	0	0	1.2	5	5	0	0	0	0	27.00	12	.455	.455	0		-0		-4		-0.1
1915	StL A	0	0	—	2	0	0	0	6	3	4	0	1	3	5	1.50	191	.136	.269	1	.000	-0		0		0.0
Total	2	0	0	—	3	0	0	0	7.2	8	9	0	1	3	5	7.04	42	.242	.324	1	.000	0		-4		-0.1

RENFER, ERWIN Erwin Arthur B12.11.1891 Elgin IL D10.26.1957 Sycamore IL BR/TR/6-0/180 d9.18 Col VPI

YEAR	TM LG	W	L	PCT	G	GS	CG-SHO	SV-BS	IP	H	R	HR	HB	BB-IB	SO	ERA	AERA	OAV	OOB	AB-HR-SH	AVG	PB	SUP	APR	DL	PW
1913	Det A	0	1	.000	1	1	0	0	6	5	5	0	1	3	1	6.00	49	.227	.346	2	.000	-0	25	-2		-0.3

RENFROE, LADDIE Cohen Williams B5.9.1962 Natchez MS BB/TR/5-11/200 [ChiN84 25/622] d7.3 Col U. of Mississippi

YEAR	TM LG	W	L	PCT	G	GS	CG-SHO	SV-BS	IP	H	R	HR	HB	BB-IB	SO	ERA	AERA	OAV	OOB	AB-HR-SH	AVG	PB	SUP	APR	DL	PW
1991	Chi N	0	1	.000	4	0	0	0-1	4.2	11	7	1	0	2-1	3	13.50	29	.440	.481	1	.000	-0		-4		-0.8

RENFROE, MARSHALL Marshall Daniel B5.25.1936 Century FL D12.10.1970 Pensacola FL BL/TL/6-0/180 d9.27

YEAR	TM LG	W	L	PCT	G	GS	CG-SHO	SV-BS	IP	H	R	HR	HB	BB-IB	SO	ERA	AERA	OAV	OOB	AB-HR-SH	AVG	PB	SUP	APR	DL	PW
1959	SF N	0	0	—	1	1	0	0	2	3	6	1	0	3-0	3	27.00	14	.333	.500	1	.000	-0	188	-5		-0.2

RENIFF, HAL Harold Eugene "Porky" B7.2.1938 Warren OH D9.7.2004 Ontario CA BR/TR/6-0/215* d6.8

YEAR	TM LG	W	L	PCT	G	GS	CG-SHO	SV-BS	IP	H	R	HR	HB	BB-IB	SO	ERA	AERA	OAV	OOB	AB-HR-SH	AVG	PB	SUP	APR	DL	PW
1961	NY A	2	0	1.000	25	0	0	2	45.1	31	14	1	0	31-3	21	2.58	144	.197	.330	5	.000	-1		6		0.2
1962	NY A	0	0	—	2	0	0	0	3.2	6	3	0	1	5-1	1	7.36	51	.400	.545	0	—	0		-1		-0.1
1963	†NY A	4	3	.571	48	0	0	18	89.1	63	31	3	2	42-5	56	2.62	134	.202	.300	15-0-1	.000	-1		8		1.0
1964	†NY A	6	4	.600	41	0	0	9	69.1	47	26	3	0	30-4	38	3.12	116	.199	.287	10	.100	-1*		4		0.6
1965	NY A	3	4	.429	51	0	0	3	85.1	74	40	4	5	48-7	74	3.80	90	.232	.340	2-0-1	.000	-0		-3		-0.3
1966	NY A	3	7	.300	56	0	0	9	95.1	80	37	2	5	49-8	79	3.21	104	.229	.330	14-0-2	.286	1		2		0.3
1967	NY A	0	2	.000	24	0	0	1	40	40	22	0	3	14-2	24	4.27	73	.256	.328	2-0-1	.000	-0		-5		-0.3
	NY N	3	3	.500	29	0	0	4	43	42	20	1	1	23-4	21	3.35	101	.266	.361	4	.000	-0		-1		-0.2
Total	7	21	23	.477	276	0	0	45	471.1	383	193	14	17	242-34	314	3.27	106	.225	.326	52-0-5	.096	-2		10		1.2

RENINGER, JIM James David B3.7.1915 Aurora IL D8.23.1993 N.Fort Myers FL BR/TR/6-3/210 d9.17

YEAR	TM LG	W	L	PCT	G	GS	CG-SHO	SV-BS	IP	H	R	HR	HB	BB-IB	SO	ERA	AERA	OAV	OOB	AB-HR-SH	AVG	PB	SUP	APR	DL	PW
1938	Phi A	0	2	.000	4	4	1	0	22.2	28	18	3	0	14	9	7.15	68	.295	.385	7	.000	-0	73	-4		-0.3
1939	Phi A	0	2	.000	4	2	0	0	16.1	24	15	3	0	12	3	7.71	61	.369	.468	6	.167	-0	28	-5		-0.5
Total	2	0	4	.000	8	6	1	0	39	52	33	6	0	26	12	7.38	65	.325	.419	13	.077	-1	58	-9		-0.8

RENKO, STEVE Steven B12.10.1944 Kansas City KS BR/TR/6-5/230(220-240) [NYN65 16/620] d6.27 Col Kansas

YEAR	TM LG	W	L	PCT	G	GS	CG-SHO	SV-BS	IP	H	R	HR	HB	BB-IB	SO	ERA	AERA	OAV	OOB	AB-HR-SH	AVG	PB	SUP	APR	DL	PW
1969	Mon N	6	7	.462	18	15	4	0-0	103.1	94	54	14	2	50-6	68	4.01	92	.243	.330	36-1-2	.167	1	117	-4		-0.4
1970	Mon N	13	11	.542	41	33	7-1	1-0	222.2	203	121	27	6	104-7	142	4.32	96	.241	.327	80-1-3	.200	2	115	-5		-0.2
1971	Mon N	15	14	.517	40	37	9-3	0-1	275.2	256	128	24	3	135-11	129	3.75	95	.247	.333	100-2-4	.210	4*	95	-6		-0.2
1972	Mon N	1	10	.091	30	12	0	0-0	97	96	60	11	0	67-10	66	5.20	69	.262	.375	24	.292	1*	64	-17		-1.6
1973	Mon N	15	11	.577	36	34	9	1-0	249.2	201	94	26	1	108-12	164	2.81	136	.218	.299	84-0-6	.273	7*	94	26		3.5
1974	Mon N	12	16	.429	37	35	8-1	0-0	227.2	222	115	17	0	81-8	138	4.03	95	.257	.318	81-1-2	.210	4	95	-8		0.1
1975	Mon N	6	12	.333	31	25	3-1	1-0	170.1	175	89	20	1	76-7	99	4.07	95	.265	.340	54-1-5	.278	5*	95	-5		0.0
1976	Mon N	0	1	.000	5	1	0	0-1	13	15	8	2	0	4	4	5.54	68	.288	.327	3	.333	0		-2		-0.1
	Chi N	8	11	.421	28	27	4-1	0-0	163.1	164	79	12	0	43-8	112	3.86	101	.258	.304	53-0-4	.094	-3*	73	0		-0.4
	Year	8	12	.400	33	28	4-1	0-1	176.1	179	87	14	0	46-8	116	3.98	97	.260	.306	56-0-4	.107	-3	71	-1		-0.5
1977	Chi N	3	3	.500	13	8	0	1-0	51.1	51	32	10	1	21-6	34	4.56	97	.258	.330	12	.167	0	91	-2	54	-0.2
	Oak A	5	0	1.000	8	8	0	0-0	53.1	55	23	3	1	17-0	36	3.54	115	.274	.330	0	—	0	107	4		0.3
1978	Oak A	6	12	.333	27	25	3-1	0-0	151	152	77	10	2	67-4	89	4.29	85	.265	.342	0	—	0	72	-7		-0.8
1979	Bos A	11	9	.550	27	27	4-1	0-0	171	174	86	22	2	53-1	99	4.11	108	.260	.315	0	—	0	109	7		0.6
1980	Bos A	9	9	.500	32	23	1	0-0	165.1	180	86	17	1	56-4	90	4.19	102	.281	.337	0	—	0	92	0		0.4
1981	Cal A	8	4	.667	22	15	0	1-0	102	93	40	7	1	42-1	50	3.44	107	.250	.323	0	—	0	108	4		0.4
1982	Cal A	11	6	.647	31	23	4	0-1	156	163	78	17	1	51-0	81	4.44	92	.269	.325	0	—	0	107	-4		-0.5
1983	KC A	6	11	.353	25	17	1	1-0	121.1	144	63	9	0	36-1	54	4.30	96	.293	.338	0	—	0	107	-2		-0.2
Total	15	134	146	.479	451	365	57-9	6-3	2494	2438	1233	248	22	1010-86	1455	3.99	98	.256	.327	531-6-24	.215	20	96	-16	54	0.3

YEAR	TM LG	W	L	PCT	G	GS	CG-SHO	SV-BS	IP	H	R	HR	HB	BB-IB	SO	ERA	AERA	OAV	OOB	AB-HR-SH	AVG	PB	SUP	APR	DL	PW
REPLOGLE, ANDY Andrew David B10.7.1953 South Bend IN BR/TR/6-5/205* [StLN75 9/208] d4.11 Col Kansas St.																								
1978	Mil A	9	5	.643	32	18	3-2	0-1	149.1	177	75	14	1	47-3	41	3.92	97	.301	.350	0	—	0	113	-3		-0.4
1979	Mil A	0	0	—	3	0	0	0-0	8	13	5	0	0	2-0	2	5.63	75	.382	.417	0	—	0		-1		0.0
Total	2	9	5	.643	35	18	3-2	0-1	157.1	190	80	14	1	49-3	43	4.00	95	.305	.353	0	—	0	113	-4		-0.4
RESCIGNO, XAVIER Xavier Frederick "Mr. X" B10.13.1913 New York NY BR/TR/5-10.5/175 d4.22 Col Manhattan																								
1943	Pit N	6	9	.400	37	14	5-1	2	132.2	125	52	6	2	45	41	2.98	117	.252	.317	35	.143	0	94	8		0.8
1944	Pit N	10	8	.556	48	6	2	5	124	146	69	9	1	34	45	4.35	85	.291	.337	22-0-1	.091	-1	90	-7		-1.0
1945	Pit N	3	5	.375	44	1	0	9	78.2	95	57	6	1	34	29	5.72	69	.303	.372	15-0-1	.133	-0	0	-14		-1.6
Total	3	19	22	.463	129	21	7-1	16	335.1	366	178	21	4	113	115	4.13	89	.279	.338	72-0-2	.125	-1	85	-13		-1.8
RESOP, CHRIS Christopher Paul B11.4.1982 Naples FL BR/TR/6-3/220 d6.28																								
2005	Fla N	2	0	1.000	15	0	0	0-0	17	22	16	1	1	9-0	15	8.47	47	.324	.400	1	.000	-0				-0.9
RETTGER, GEORGE George Edward B7.29.1868 Cleveland OH D6.5.1921 Lakewood OH BR/TR/5-11/175 d8.13																								
1891	StL AA	7	3	.700	14	12	10-1	1	92.2	85	63	4	8	51	49	3.40	123	.235	.343	42-1	.071	-3*	104	6		0.3
1892	Cle N	1	3	.250	6	5	3	0	38	32	27	2	1	31	12	4.26	80	.219	.360	15	.133	-0	93	-3		-0.3
	Cin N	1	0	1.000	1	1	1	0	9	8	5	0	1	10	1	4.00	82	.229	.413	8	.125	-0*	310	-0		-0.3
	Year	2	3	.400	7	6	4	0	47	40	32	2	2	41	13	4.21	80	.221	.371	23	.130	-0	128	-3		-0.3
Total	2	9	6	.600	21	18	14-1	1	139.2	125	95	6	10	92	62	3.67	106	.231	.352	65-1	.092	-3	111	3		0.0
RETTIG, OTTO Adolph John B1.29.1894 New York NY D6.16.1977 Stuart FL BR/TR/5-11/165 d7.19 Col Seton Hall																								
1922	Phi A	1	2	.333	4	4	1	0	18.1	18	14	1	2	9	3	4.91	87	.265	.383	6	.000	-1	40	-1		-0.2
REULBACH, ED Edward Marvin "Big Ed" B12.1.1882 Detroit MI D7.17.1961 Glens Falls NY BR/TR/6-1/190 d5.16 Col Vermont																								
1905	Chi N	18	14	.563	34	29	28-5	1	291.2	208	71	4	18	73	152	1.42	210	**.201**	.266	110-0-2	.127	-6*	81	48		4.6
1906	†Chi N	19	4	**.826**	33	24	20-6	3	218	129	51	2	13	92	94	1.65	160	**.175**	.278	83-0-6	.157	-2*	123	26		2.8
1907	†Chi N	17	4	.810	27	22	16-4	0	192	147	48	1	9	64	96	1.69	148	.217	.294	63-0-6	.175	0	99	19		2.2
1908	†Chi N	24	7	.774	46	35	25-7	1	297.2	227	81	4	12	106	133	2.03	116	.214	.292	99-0-9	.232	7	143	14		2.2
1909	†Chi N	19	10	.655	35	32	23-6	0	262.2	194	69	1	11	82	105	1.78	143	.212	.285	86-0-7	.140	-1	90	24		2.9
1910	†Chi N	12	8	.600	24	23	14-1	0	173.1	161	76	1	9	49	55	3.12	92	.250	.312	56-0-6	.107	-3	126	-3		-0.8
1911	Chi N	16	9	.640	33	29	15-2	0	221.2	191	97	3	4	103	79	3.78	88	.259	.332	55-0-1	.109	-3	131	-7		1.0
1912	Chi N	10	6	.625	39	19	8	4	169	161	86	1	1	21	75	4.42	72	.281	.375	12	.250	0	126	-6		-0.6
1913	Chi N	1	3	.250	10	3	1	0	38.2	41	27	1	1	21	10	2.05	161	.202	.274	29-0-3	.103	0	65	14		1.6
	Bro N	7	6	.538	15	12	8-2	0	110	77	34	3	4	34	46	2.66	123	.203	.303	41-0-3	.146	0	77	10		1.6
	Year	8	9	.471	25	15	9-2	0	148.2	118	61	4	5	55	56	2.66	123	.223	.303	70-0-6	.122	-0	89	6		0.7
1914	Bro N	11	18	.379	44	29	14-3	3	256	228	108	5	10	83	119	2.64	108	.242	.310	74-0-3	.122	-0	89	6		0.7
1915	New F	21	10	.677	33	30	23-4	1	270	233	88	3	6	69	117	2.23	115	.236	.287	92-0-8	.196	-2	117	12		1.2
1916	Bos N	7	6	.538	21	11	6	0	109.1	99	38	1	4	41	44	2.47	101	.251	.328	33-0-2	.091	-1	101	1		0.6
1917	Bos N	0	1	.000	5	2	1	0	22.1	21	13	0	1	15	9	2.82	90	.256	.378	3	.000	1	89	-2		0.6
Total	13	182	106	.632	399	300	201-40	13	2632.1	2117	887	33	107	892	1137	2.28	122	.224	.299	862-1-58	.147	-11	107	154		17.
REUSCHEL, PAUL Paul Richard B1.12.1947 Quincy IL BR/TR/6-4/210(210-225) [ChiN68 S4/61] d7.25 b-Rick Col Western Illinois																								
1975	Chi N	1	3	.250	28	0	0	5-2	36	44	15	1	1	13-2	25	3.50	111	.312	.372	4	.000	-0	2			0.2
1976	Chi N	4	2	.667	50	2	0	3-0	87	94	46	12	1	33-4	55	4.55	85	.278	.341	13	.154	-0	113	-4		-0.3
1977	Chi N	5	6	.455	69	0	0	4-5	107	105	58	9	0	40-8	62	4.37	101	.262	.326	11-0-1	.000	-1		1		0.
1978	Chi N	2	0	1.000	16	0	0	0-0	28	29	16	4	1	13-3	13	5.14	79	.269	.352	4	.000	-0		-2	28	-0.
1979	Cle A	2	4	.333	18	6	1	0-0	89.2	95	33	5	2	22-1	24	3.11	122	.271	.316	0	—	0	51	7		0.
	Cle A	2	1	.667	17	1	0	1-0	45.1	73	43	7	0	11-0	22	7.94	54	.365	.398	0	—	0	148	-18	75	-1.
Total	5	16	16	.500	198	9	1	13-7	393	440	211	38	5	132-18	188	4.51	90	.286	.342	32-0-1	.063	-2	73	-14	103	-0.
REUSCHEL, RICK Rickey Eugene B5.16.1949 Quincy IL BR/TR/6-3/235(210-250) [ChiN70 3/67] d6.19 b-Paul Col Western Illinois [DL 1982 NY A 182, 1983 NY A 66]																								
1972	Chi N	10	8	.556	21	18	5-4	0-0	129	127	46	3	2	29-6	87	2.93	130	.259	.302	44-0-6	.136	-1	107	12		1.
1973	Chi N	14	15	.483	36	36	7-3	0-0	237	244	95	15	5	62-6	168	3.00	131	.263	.312	73-0-9	.123	-3	73	21		2.
1974	Chi N	13	12	.520	41	38	8-2	0-0	240.2	262	130	18	6	83-12	160	4.30	89	.276	.335	86-0-9	.221	2	101	-9		-0.
1975	Chi N	11	17	.393	38	37	6	1-0	234	244	116	17	7	67-8	155	3.73	104	.268	.322	77-1-6	.208	2	88	1		1.
1976	Chi N	14	12	.538	38	37	9-2	0-0	260	260	117	17	8	64-5	146	3.46	112	.265	.311	83-0-7	.229	4	96	9		1.
1977	Chi N★	20	10	.667	39	37	8-4	1-0	252	233	84	13	5	74-11	166	2.79	158	.247	.304	87-1-6	.207	1*	71	42		5.
1978	Chi N	14	15	.483	35	35	9-1	0-0	242.2	235	98	16	5	54-8	115	3.41	119	.254	.297	73-0-10	.137	-1	83	17		1.
1979	Chi N	18	12	.600	36	36	5-1	0-0	239	251	104	16	10	75-8	125	3.62	115	.274	.333	79-0-5	.165	1*	105	15		2.
1980	Chi N	11	13	.458	38	**38**	6	0-0	257	281	111	13	4	76-10	140	3.40	117	.286	.336	82-0-10	.159	-1*	78	1		1.
1981	Chi N	4	7	.364	13	13	1	0-0	85.2	87	40	4	4	23-4	53	3.47	108	.267	.323	25-0-4	.080	-1*	78	1		1.
	†NY A	4	4	.500	12	11	3	0-0	70.2	75	24	4	1	10-0	22	2.67	135	.280	.306	0	—	0	104	7		1.
1983	Chi N	1	1	.500	4	4	0	0-0	20.2	18	9	1	0	10-2	9	3.92	97	.234	.318	7	.143	0	75	0		0.
1984	Chi N	5	5	.500	19	14	1	0-0	92.1	123	57	7	3	23-0	43	5.17	76	.339	.374	29-0-4	.241	2*	108	-11	28	0.
1985	Pit N	14	8	.636	31	26	9-1	1-0	194	153	58	7	8	52-10	138	2.27	160	.215	.271	59-1-6	.169	2	90	27		3.
1986	Pit N	9	16	.360	35	34	4-2	0-0	215.2	232	106	20	8	57-2	125	3.96	98	.274	.322	70-0-8	.157	0*	96	-2		0.
1987	Pit N★	8	6	.571	25	25	9-3	0-0	177	163	63	6	1	35-1	80	2.75	152	.246	.287	60-1-6	.150	0	92	26		2.
	†SF N	5	3	.625	9	8	3-1	0-0	50	44	28	1	2	7-2	27	4.32	89	.230	.264	19-0-1	.105	-0	138	-3		-0.
	Year	13	9	.591	34	33	12-4	0-0	227	207	91	13	8	42-3	107	3.09	132	.242	.282	79-1-7	.139	1	106	24		1.
1988	SF N	19	11	.633	36	**36**	7-2	0-0	245	242	88	11	6	42-8	92	3.12	105	.260	.293	73-0-19	.110	-1	121	8		1.
1989	†SF N★	17	8	.680	32	32	2	0-0	208.1	195	75	18	2	54-4	111	2.94	115	.247	.294	61-0-16	.164	1	110	11	110	1.
1990	SF N	3	6	.333	15	13	0	1-0	87	102	40	8	1	31-9	49	3.93	93	.297	.353	26-0-3	.154	0	103	-2	56	-0.
1991	SF N	0	2	.000	4	1	0	0-1	10.2	17	14	0	0	7-1	4	4.22	85	.370	.453	2	.000	-0	50	-1		-0.
Total	19	214	191	.528	557	529	102-26	5-1	3548.1	3588	1494	221	88	935-117	2015	3.37	115	.264	.313	1115-4-135	.168	7	94	184	459	23
REUSS, JERRY Jerry B6.19.1949 St.Louis MO BL/TL/6-5/217(195-227) [StLN67 2/30] d9.27																								
1969	StL N	1	0	1.000	1	1	0	0-0	7	2	0	2	3	2	3	0.00	—	.091	.259	3	.333	0	49	3		0
1970	StL N	7	8	.467	20	20	5-2	0-0	127.1	132	62	9	4	49-2	74	4.10	101	.271	.337	40-0-5	.050	-3	82	2		0
1971	StL N	14	14	.500	36	35	7-2	0-0	211	228	125	15	7	109-11	131	4.78	76	.279	.366	65-0-11	.123	0	119	-26		-2
1972	Hou N	9	13	.409	33	30	4-1	1-0	192	177	101	14	10	83-3	174	4.17	81	.246	.329	66-0-1	.106	-1	122	-19		-2
1973	Hou N	16	13	.552	41	**40**	12-3	0-0	279.1	271	123	17	3	117-6	177	3.74	98	.256	.330	95-0-9	.137	-1*	105	-1		-0
1974	†Pit N	16	11	.593	35	35	14-1	0-0	260	259	115	20	1	101-16	105	3.50	100	.261	.323	86-0-4	.151	0	108	0		-0
1975	†Pit N★	18	11	.621	32	32	15-6	0-0	237.1	224	73	10	0	78-8	131	2.54	141	.253	.313	71-0-10	.197	2	92	30		1
1976	Pit N	14	9	.609	31	29	11-3	2-0	209.1	209	98	16	2	51-10	108	3.53	100	.256	.301	66-0-3	.242	6	116	-2		0
1977	Pit N	10	13	.435	33	33	8-2	0-0	208	225	109	11	4	71-2	116	4.11	98	.280	.339	70-0-4	.171	1*	100	-3		-0
1978	Pit N	3	2	.600	23	12	3-1	0-0	82.2	97	48	5	3	23-1	42	4.90	76	.297	.346	27	.185	0	84	-5		-0
1979	LA N	7	14	.333	39	21	4	3-3	160	178	88	4	3	60-7	83	3.54	102	.282	.347	42-0-3	.167	1	112	24		0
1980	LA N	18	6	.750	37	29	10-**6**	3-2	229.1	193	74	12	0	40-9	111	2.51	138	.227	.260	51-0-7	.196	0	127	17		3
1981	†LA N	10	4	.714	22	22	8-2	0-0	152.2	138	44	6	4	27-3	51	2.30	144	.243	.282	51-0-7	.196	3	113	11		1
1982	LA N	18	11	.621	39	37	8	0-0	254.2	232	98	11	2	50-10	138	3.11	112	.246	.277	77-0-16	.221	3	92	14		2
1983	†LA N	12	11	.522	32	31	7	0-0	223.1	233	94	12	2	50-5	143	2.94	123	.271	.311	71-0-10	.282	3	92	14		2
1984	LA N	5	7	.417	30	15	2	1-1	99	102	51	4	0	31-7	44	3.82	93	.266	.310	24-0-2	.167	1	93	-4	34	0
1985	†LA N	14	10	.583	34	33	5-3	0-0	212.2	210	78	13	9	58-7	84	2.92	120	.260	.310	74-0-6	.135	-1	102	16	48	1
1986	LA N	2	6	.250	19	13	0	1-0	74	96	57	13	2	17-4	29	5.84	59	.313	.353	20	.250	2	113	-23		-1
1987	LA N	0	0	—	1	0	0	0-0	2	2	1	1	0	0	4.50	89	.333	.286	0	—	0	67	-1		0
	Cin N	0	5	.000	7	7	0	0-0	34.2	52	31	2	1	12-2	10	7.79	54	.351	.404	8-0-2	.125	0	67	-12		-1
	Year	0	5	.000	8	7	0	0-0	36.2	54	32	2	1	12-2	12	7.61	55	.351	.399	8-0-2	.125	0	68	-12		-1
	Cal A	2	5	.444	17	16	1-1	0-0	82.1	112	60	16	2	17-1	37	5.25	83	.327	.361	0	—	0	115	-11	15	-1
1988	Chi A	13	9	.591	32	29	1-1	0-0	183	183	79	15	3	43-1	73	3.44	116	.263	.307	0	—	0	114	-14		1
1989	Chi A	8	5	.615	23	19	1-1	0-1	106.2	135	65	12	3	21-1	27	5.06	76	.308	.340	0	—	0	77	-6	15	-0
	Mil A	1	4	.200	7	7	0	0-0	33.2	36	23	7	1	13-1	13	3.48	116	.273	.342	0	—	0	104	-20		-0
	Year	9	9	.500	30	26	1-1	0-1	140.1	171	88	19	4	34-2	40	5.13	75	.300	.340	0	—	0	74	0		-0
1990	Pit N	0	0	—	4	1	0	0-0	7.2	10	4	2	0	3-1	1	3.52	104	.267	.333	0-0-2	—	0	106	-6	112	-0
Total	22	220	191	.535	628	547	127-39	11-7	3669.2	3734	1700	245	59	1127-118	1907	3.64	100	.265	.320	1024-1-99	.167	14	106	-6	112	

YEAR	TM LG	W	L	PCT	G	GS	CG-SHO	SV-BS	IP	H	R	HR	HB	BB-IB	SO	ERA	AERA	OAV	OOB	AB-HR-SH	AVG	PB	SUP	APR	DL	PW

REVENIG, TODD Todd Michael B6.28.1969 Brainerd MN BR/TR/6-1/185 [OakA90 37/999] d8.24 Col Mankato St. [DL 1993 Oak A 182]

YEAR	TM LG	W	L	PCT	G	GS	CG-SHO	SV-BS	IP	H	R	HR	HB	BB-IB	SO	ERA	AERA	OAV	OOB	AB-HR-SH	AVG	PB	SUP	APR	DL	PW
1992	Oak A	0	0	—	2	0	0	0-0	2.0	0	0	0	0	0-0	1	0.00	—	.286	.286	0	—	0		1		0.0

REYES, ANTHONY Anthony Loza B10.16.1981 Downey CA BR/TR/6-2/215 d8.9 Col Southern California

YEAR	TM LG	W	L	PCT	G	GS	CG-SHO	SV-BS	IP	H	R	HR	HB	BB-IB	SO	ERA	AERA	OAV	OOB	AB-HR-SH	AVG	PB	SUP	APR	DL	PW
2005	StL N	1	1	.500	4	1	0	0-0	13.1	6	4	2	0	4-1	12	2.70	155	.133	.200	4	.000	-0	111	2		0.3

REYES, CARLOS Carlos Alberto B4.4.1969 Miami FL BB/TR/6-1/190* d4.7 Col Florida Southern

YEAR	TM LG	W	L	PCT	G	GS	CG-SHO	SV-BS	IP	H	R	HR	HB	BB-IB	SO	ERA	AERA	OAV	OOB	AB-HR-SH	AVG	PB	SUP	APR	DL	PW
1994	Oak A	0	3	.000	27	9	0	1-0	78	71	38	10	2	44-1	57	4.15	108	.242	.342	0	—	0	75	4	17	0.1
1995	Oak A	4	6	.400	40	0	0	0-1	69	71	43	10	5	28-4	48	5.09	89	.264	.344	0	—	0	82	-5		-0.6
1996	Oak A	7	10	.412	46	10	0	0-0	122.1	134	71	19	2	61-8	78	4.78	104	.281	.359	0	—	0	62	2		0.1
1997	Oak A	3	4	.429	37	6	0	0-1	77.1	101	52	13	2	25-2	43	5.82	79	.316	.367	0	—	0	67	-10	22	-0.7
1998	SD N	2	2	.500	22	0	0	1-1	27.2	23	11	4	2	6-0	24	3.58	111	.235	.290	0-0-1	—	0		2		0.2
	Bos A	1	1	.500	24	0	0	0-0	38.1	35	15	2	1	14-2	23	3.52	134	.246	.316	0	—	0		6		0.3
1999	SD N	2	4	.333	65	0	0	1-1	77.1	76	38	11	0	24-4	57	3.72	115	.254	.307	1	.000	-0		4		0.3
2000	Phi N	0	2	.000	10	0	0	0-0	10.1	10	6	2	0	5-0	8	5.23	88	.270	.357	0	—	0		-1	9	-0.1
	SD N	1	1	.500	12	0	0	1-2	18	15	12	5	1	8-0	13	6.00	74	.221	.312	1	.000	-0		-3		-0.3
	Year	1	3	.250	22	0	0	1-2	28.1	25	18	7	1	13-0	21	5.72	79	.238	.328	1	.000	-0		-3		-0.4
2003	TB A	0	3	.000	10	3	0	0-0	39.2	40	23	10	2	5-0	13	5.22	88	.265	.294	1	.000	-0	60	-2		-0.1
Total	8	20	36	.357	293	29	0	4-6	558	576	309	86	17	220-21	360	4.66	98	.267	.337	3-0-1	.000	-0	69	-3	48	-0.8

REYES, DENNYS Dennys (Valarde) B4.19.1977 Higuera de Zaragoza, Sinaloa, Mexico BL/TL/6-3/246* d7.13

YEAR	TM LG	W	L	PCT	G	GS	CG-SHO	SV-BS	IP	H	R	HR	HB	BB-IB	SO	ERA	AERA	OAV	OOB	AB-HR-SH	AVG	PB	SUP	APR	DL	PW
1997	LA N	2	3	.400	14	5	0	0-0	47	51	21	4	1	18-3	36	3.83	102	.280	.347	9-0-1	.000	-1	118	1		0.1
1998	LA N	0	4	.000	11	3	0	0-0	28.2	27	17	1	0	20-4	33	4.71	86	.255	.370	5-0-1	.000	-1	114	-2		-0.3
	Cin N	3	1	.750	8	7	0	0-0	38.2	35	19	2	1	27-1	44	4.42	97	.255	.380	12	.083	-0	126	0		0.0
	Year	3	5	.375	19	10	0	0-0	67.1	62	36	3	1	47-5	77	4.54	92	.255	.375	17-0-1	.059	-1	123	-3		-0.3
1999	Cin N	2	2	.500	65	1	0	2-1	61.2	53	30	5	3	39-1	72	3.79	124	.232	.348	4	.000	-0	20	5		0.3
2000	Cin N	2	1	.667	62	0	0	0-0	43.2	43	31	5	-1	29-0	36	4.53	105	.262	.371	2	.000	0		-2		-0.1
2001	Cin N	2	6	.250	35	6	0	0-0	53	51	35	5	1	35-1	52	4.92	93	.248	.357	0	—	0		-2		-0.1
2002	Col N	0	1	.000	43	0	0	0-0	40.1	43	19	1	0	24-3	30	4.24	112	.279	.372	11	.182	-0*	54	-3	33	-0.4
	Tex A	4	3	.571	15	5	0	0-0	42.1	55	33	9	0	21-1	29	6.38	75	.316	.390	0	—	0		3		0.1
2003	Pit N	0	0	—	12	0	0	0-0	10.1	10	13	1	0	9-1	11	10.45	41	.263	.388	0	—	0	116	-7		-1.0
	Ari N	0	0	—	3	0	0	0-0	2.1	5	3	1	0	1-0	5	11.57	40	.417	.462	0	—	0		-7		-0.3
	Year	0	0	—	15	0	0	0-0	12.2	15	16	2	0	10-1	16	10.66	41	.300	.403	0	—	0		-9		-0.4
2004	KC A	4	8	.333	40	12	0	0-1	108	114	64	12	4	50-3	91	4.75	98	.273	.353	6	.000	-1	71	-1		-0.2
2005	SD N	3	2	.600	36	1	0	0-1	43.2	57	30	3	1	32-2	35	5.15	75	.315	.421	5	.200	0	48	-8		-0.8
Total	9	22	31	.415	344	40	0	2-4	519.2	544	315	49	12	305-20	474	4.80	93	.272	.369	54-0-2	.074	-3	89	-23	33	-2.7

REYES, AL Rafael Alberto B4.10.1971 San Cristobal, D.R. BR/TR/6-1/209(193-210) d4.27

YEAR	TM LG	W	L	PCT	G	GS	CG-SHO	SV-BS	IP	H	R	HR	HB	BB-IB	SO	ERA	AERA	OAV	OOB	AB-HR-SH	AVG	PB	SUP	APR	DL	PW
1995	Mil A	1	1	.500	27	0	0	1-0	33.1	19	9	3	3	18-2	29	2.43	206	.167	.292	0	—	0		9	75	0.5
1996	Mil A	1	0	1.000	5	0	0	1-0	5.2	8	5	1	0	2-0	2	7.94	65	.320	.370	0	—	0		-1		-0.2
1997	Mil A	1	2	.333	19	0	0	1-0	29.2	32	19	4	3	9-0	28	5.46	85	.274	.341	0	—	0		-2		-0.2
1998	Mil N	5	1	.833	50	0	0	0-1	57	55	26	9	2	31-1	58	3.95	110	.253	.351	5	.200	0		3	45	0.3
1999	Mil N	2	0	1.000	26	0	0	0-1	36	27	17	5	3	25-1	39	4.25	108	.206	.344	2	.000	-0		2		0.1
	Bal A	2	3	.400	27	0	0	0-3	29.2	23	16	4	3	16-2	28	4.85	97	.225	.341	0	—	0		0		0.0
2000	Bal A	1	0	1.000	13	0	0	0-1	13	13	10	2	0	11-1	10	6.92	68	.271	.393	0	—	0		-3		-0.2
	LA N	0	0	—	6	0	0	0-0	6.2	2	0	0	0	1-0	8	0.00	—	.087	.125	0	—	0		-3		0.1
2001	LA N	2	1	.667	19	0	0	1-1	25.2	28	13	3	1	13-1	23	3.86	107	.269	.350	3-0-1	.333	0		3		0.2
2002	Pit N	0	0	—	15	0	0	0-1	17	9	5	1	2	7-0	21	2.65	158	.161	.273	0	—	0		3		0.1
2003	NY A	0	0	—	13	0	0	0-1	17	13	7	1	0	9-1	9	3.18	138	.203	.301	0	—	0		3		0.2
2004	†StL N	0	0	—	12	2	0	0-0	12	3	1	0	0	2-0	11	0.75	568	.081	.128	1	1.000	0	152	5		0.3
2005	StL N	4	2	.667	65	0	0	3-0	62.2	38	15	5	5	20-2	67	2.15	195	.177	.261	1-0-1	.000	0		15		1.5
Total	11	19	10	.655	297	2	0	6-9	345.1	270	143	38	22	164-11	333	3.60	124	.215	.314	12-0-2	.000	1	152	36	120	2.7

REYNOLDS, ALLIE Allie Pierce "Superchief" B2.10.1917 Bethany OK D12.26.1994 Oklahoma City OK BR/TR/6-0/195* d9.17 Col Oklahoma St.

YEAR	TM LG	W	L	PCT	G	GS	CG-SHO	SV-BS	IP	H	R	HR	HB	BB-IB	SO	ERA	AERA	OAV	OOB	AB-HR-SH	AVG	PB	SUP	APR	DL	PW
1942	Cle A	0	0	—	2	0	0	0	5	5	1	0	0	4	2	0.00	—	.250	.375	2	.000	-0		2		0.0
1943	Cle A	11	12	.478	34	21	11-3	3	198.2	140	72	3	7	109	151	2.99	104	.202	.316	67-0-5	.149	-1*	112	5		0.5
1944	Cle A	11	8	.579	28	21	5-1	1	158	141	63	7	4	91	84	3.30	100	.240	.346	57-0-3	.123	-3*	102	2		-0.1
1945	Cle A*	18	12	.600	44	30	16-2	4	247.1	227	102	7	5	130	112	3.20	101	.247	.343	85-0-7	.094	-7	108	1		-0.7
1946	Cle A	11	15	.423	31	28	9-3	0	183.1	180	93	10	1	108	107	3.88	85	.259	.359	63-0-6	.222	1*	96	-14		-1.7
1947	†NY A	19	8	.704	34	30	17-4	2	241.2	207	94	23	4	123	129	3.20	110	.227	.322	89-0-7	.146	-2*	153	9		0.7
1948	NY A	16	7	.696	39	31	11-1	3	236.1	240	108	17	4	111	101	3.77	108	.268	.351	83-1-5	.193	0*	129	10		0.7
1949	†NY A☆	17	6	.739	35	31	4-2	1	213.2	200	102	15	4	123	105	4.00	101	.250	.353	78-0-2	.218	6*	126	4		0.8
1950	†NY A★	16	12	.571	35	29	14-2	2	240.2	215	108	12	8	138	160	3.74	115	.242	.349	81-0-9	.185	1*	122	16		1.7
1951	†NY A	17	8	.680	40	26	16-7	7	221	171	84	12	5	100	126	3.05	125	.213	.304	76-0-5	.184	0*	140	21		2.2
1952	†NY A☆	20	8	.714	35	29	24-6	6	244.1	194	70	10	7	97	160	2.06	161	.218	.300	85-0-4	.153	-1*	118	35		4.1
1953	†NY A★	13	7	.650	41	15	5-1	13	145	140	64	9	5	61	86	3.41	100	.253	.333	41	.122	1*	106	4		0.5
1954	NY A*	13	4	.765	36	18	5-4	7	157.1	133	65	13	4	66	100	3.32	104	.233	.314	50-0-5	.160	-0	185	2		0.2
Total	13	182	107	.630	434	309	137-36	49	2492.1	2193	1026	133	57	1261	1423	3.30	110	.238	.333	857-1-58	.163	-5	125	97		8.9

REYNOLDS, ARCHIE Archie Edward B1.3.1946 Glendale CA BR/TR/6-2/205* [ChiN66 38/703] d8.15 Col Paris (TX) JC

YEAR	TM LG	W	L	PCT	G	GS	CG-SHO	SV-BS	IP	H	R	HR	HB	BB-IB	SO	ERA	AERA	OAV	OOB	AB-HR-SH	AVG	PB	SUP	APR	DL	PW
1968	Chi N	0	1	.000	7	1	0	0	13.1	14	10	1	1	7-0	6	6.75	47	.259	.355	2	.500	1	110	-5		-0.3
1969	Chi N	0	1	.000	2	2	0	0-0	7.1	11	5	1	0	7-1	4	2.45	164	.379	.500	1	.000	1	99	0		0.1
1970	Chi N	0	2	.000	7	1	0	0-0	15	17	11	2	1	9-0	9	6.60	68	.298	.403	2	.000	0	20	-3		-0.3
1971	Cal A	0	3	.000	15	1	0	0-0	27.1	32	15	2	0	18-5	15	4.61	70	.305	.407	2	.000	-0	0	-4		-0.4
1972	Mil A	0	1	.000	5	2	0	0-0	18.2	26	18	2	0	8-1	13	7.23	42	.338	.391	4	.500	1	101	-9		-0.4
Total	5	0	8	.000	36	7	0	0-0	81.2	100	59	8	2	49-7	47	5.73	61	.311	.403	11	.273	2	77	-21		-1.3

REYNOLDS, CHARLIE Charles E. B7.31.1857 Allegany NY D5.1.1913 Buffalo NY d5.18

YEAR	TM LG	W	L	PCT	G	GS	CG-SHO	SV-BS	IP	H	R	HR	HB	BB-IB	SO	ERA	AERA	OAV	OOB	AB-HR-SH	AVG	PB	SUP	APR	DL	PW
1882	Phi AA	1	1	.500	2	2	1	0	12	18	11	0		3	4	5.25	53	.327	.362	8	.125	-1	110	-3		-0.4

REYNOLDS, KEN Kenneth Lee B1.4.1947 Trevose PA BL/TL/6-0/180* [PhiN66 4/69] d9.5 Col New Mexico Highlands

YEAR	TM LG	W	L	PCT	G	GS	CG-SHO	SV-BS	IP	H	R	HR	HB	BB-IB	SO	ERA	AERA	OAV	OOB	AB-HR-SH	AVG	PB	SUP	APR	DL	PW
1970	Phi N	0	0	—	4	0	0	0	2.1	3	0	0	0	4-0	1	0.00	—	.333	.538	0	—	0		1		0.1
1971	Phi N	5	9	.357	35	25	2-1	0-0	162.1	163	89	11	6	82-1	81	4.49	79	.269	.358	50-0-1	.200	2*	97	-15		-1.1
1972	Phi N	2	15	.118	33	23	2	0-0	154.1	149	76	17	1	60-6	87	4.26	85	.258	.327	40-0-1	.200	1*	75	-8		-0.7
1973	Mil A	0	1	.000	5	0	0	0-0	7.1	5	7	1	1	10-2	3	7.36	52	.200	.444	0	—	0	23	-3		-0.3
1975	StL N	0	1	.000	10	0	0	0-0	17	12	4	0	0	11-2	7	1.59	239	.214	.343	2	.000	-0		4		0.2
1976	SD N	0	3	.000	19	2	0	1-0	32.1	38	27	0	0	29-4	18	6.40	51	.309	.435	5	.000	-1	134	-12		-1.2
Total	6	7	29	.194	103	51	4-1	1-0	375.2	370	203	29	8	196-13	197	4.46	80	.265	.356	97-0-2	.186	2	86	-33		-3.0

REYNOLDS, SHANE Richard Shane B3.26.1968 Bastrop LA BR/TR/6-3/210* [HouN89 3/72] d7.20 Col Texas

YEAR	TM LG	W	L	PCT	G	GS	CG-SHO	SV-BS	IP	H	R	HR	HB	BB-IB	SO	ERA	AERA	OAV	OOB	AB-HR-SH	AVG	PB	SUP	APR	DL	PW
1992	Hou N	1	3	.250	8	5	0	0-0	25.1	42	22	2	0	6-1	10	7.11	48	.385	.414	4-0-2	.500	1	133	-11		-1.4
1993	Hou N	0	0	—	5	1	0	0-0	11	11	4	0	0	6-1	10	0.82	474	.256	.347	2	.500	0	93	3		0.2
1994	Hou N	8	5	.615	33	14	1-1	0-0	124	128	46	10	6	21-3	110	3.05	130	.263	.302	33-0-7	.091	-2	107	14		1.1
1995	Hou N	10	11	.476	30	30	3-2	0-0	189.1	196	87	15	2	37-6	175	3.47	111	.263	.300	63-0-10	.127	-2*	118	7		0.7
1996	Hou N	16	10	.615	35	35	4-1	0-0	239	227	103	20	8	44-3	204	3.65	106	.249	.288	76-2-14	.184	4	98	9		1.3
1997	†Hou N	9	10	.474	30	30	0	0-0	181	189	92	19	3	47-5	152	4.23	95	.267	.313	53-0-7	.113	-0	112	-4	34	-0.3
1998	†Hou N	19	8	.704	35	35	3-1	0-0	233.1	257	99	25	2	53-2	209	3.51	115	.280	.318	82-0-7	.159	1	135	15		1.8
1999	†Hou N	16	14	.533	35	35	4-2	0-0	231.2	250	108	24	1	37-0	197	3.85	115	.275	.303	66-1-17	.167	1	94	15		2.0
2000	Hou N☆	7	8	.467	22	22	0	0-0	131	150	86	20	6	45-2	93	5.22	94	.287	.345	40-1-4	.225	2	101	-6	63	0.4
2001	Hou N	14	11	.560	28	28	3	0-0	182.2	208	95	24	4	36-2	102	4.34	106	.290	.327	52-1-10	.077	-2	98	5	35	0.4
2002	Hou N	3	6	.333	13	13	0	0-0	74	80	43	13	1	26-2	47	4.86	89	.274	.334	21-0-9	.048	-2	98	5		-0.6
2003	Atl N	11	9	.550	30	29	0	0-0	167.1	191	104	20	8	59-6	94	5.43	77	.293	.358	54-0-10	.093	-3	143	-19	108	-2.3
2004	Ari N	0	1	.000	2	2	0	0-0	6	6	6	0	0	2-0	1	4.50	101	.500	.571	0	—	0	102	-2	182	-0.3
Total	13	114	96	.543	305	278	20-7	0-0	1791.2	1935	895	191	41	419-33	1403	4.09	102	.275	.318	546-5-97	.141	-0	111	22	422	2.3

REYNOLDS, BOB Robert Allen B1.21.1947 Seattle WA BR/TR/6-0/205(192-205) [SFN66 1/17] d9.19

YEAR	TM	LG	W	L	PCT	G	GS	CG-SHO	SV-BS	IP	H	R	HR	HB	BB-IB	SO	ERA	AERA	OAV	OOB	AB-HR-SH	AVG	PB	SUP	APR	DL	PW
1969	Mon	N	0	0	—	1	1	0	0-0	1.1	3	6	0	0	3-0	2	20.25	18	.429	.545	0	—	0	240	-3		-0.2
1971	StL	N	0	0	—	4	0	0	0-0	7	15	8	2	1	6-1	4	10.29	35	.441	.537	1	.000	-0		-5		-0.3
	Mil	A	0	1	.000	3	0	0	0-0	6	4	2	0	0	3-0	4	3.00	116	.222	.318	1	.000	-0		0		-0.3
1972	Bal	A	0	0	—	3	0	0	0-0	9.2	8	2	0	0	7-2	5	1.86	167	.258	.395	2	.000	-0		1		0.0
1973	†Bal	A	7	5	.583	42	1	0	9-3	111	88	27	3	0	31-6	77	1.95	194	.219	.272	0	—	0	142	23	9	2.7
1974	†Bal	A	7	5	.583	54	0	0	7-3	69.1	75	23	4	1	14-3	43	2.73	128	.278	.314	0	—	0		6		1.2
1975	Bal	A	0	1	.000	7	0	0	0-2	6	11	6	1	0	1-0	1	9.00	39	.423	.429	0	—	0		-4		-0.5
	Det	A	0	2	.000	21	0	0	3-1	34.2	40	20	8	1	14-1	26	4.67	86	.288	.355	0	—	0		-2		-0.1
	Cle	A	0	2	.000	5	0	0	2-0	9.2	11	7	0	0	3-1	5	4.66	82	.289	.341	0	—	0		-7		-0.3
	Year		0	5	.000	33	0	0	5-3	50.1	62	33	9	1	18-2	32	5.19	76	.305	.362	0	—	0	192	15	9	-0.9
Total	6		14	16	.467	140	2	0	21-9	254.2	255	101	18	3	82-14	167	3.15	117	.264	.320	4	.000	-0	192	15	9	2.6

REYNOLDS, ROSS Ross Ernest "Doc" B8.20.1887 Barksdale TX D6.23.1970 Ada OK BR/TR/6-2/185 d5.2

YEAR	TM	LG	W	L	PCT	G	GS	CG-SHO	SV-BS	IP	H	R	HR	HB	BB-IB	SO	ERA	AERA	OAV	OOB	AB-HR-SH	AVG	PB	SUP	APR	DL	PW
1914	Det	A	5	3	.625	26	7	3-1	0	78	62	26	0	6	39	31	2.08	135	.230	.340	21-0-1	.048	-2	67	6		0.3
1915	Det	A	0	1	.000	4	2	0	0	11.1	17	9	0	1	5	2	6.35	48	.378	.451	3	.000	-0	60	-3		-0.3
Total	2		5	4	.556	30	9	3-1	0	89.1	79	35	0	7	44	33	2.62	108	.251	.355	24-0-1	.042	-2	66	3		0.0

REYNOSO, ARMANDO Armando Martin (Gutierrez) B5.1.1966 San Luis Potosi, San Luis Potosi, Mexico BR/TR/6-0/204(186-210) d8.11

YEAR	TM	LG	W	L	PCT	G	GS	CG-SHO	SV-BS	IP	H	R	HR	HB	BB-IB	SO	ERA	AERA	OAV	OOB	AB-HR-SH	AVG	PB	SUP	APR	DL	PW
1991	Atl	N	2	1	.667	6	5	0	0-0	23.1	26	18	4	3	10-1	10	6.17	63	.299	.390	7	.000	-0	139	-6		-0.6
1992	Atl	N	1	0	1.000	3	1	0	1-0	7.2	11	4	2	1	2-1	2	4.70	78	.393	.452	2-0-1	.000	-0	198	-1		-0.1
1993	Col	N	12	11	.522	30	30	4	0-0	189	206	101	22	9	63-7	117	4.00	120	.277	.337	63-2-6	.127	-1*	92	11		1.3
1994	Col	N	3	4	.429	9	9	1	0-0	52.1	54	30	5	6	22-1	25	4.82	104	.278	.366	17-0-3	.176	-0	116	1	83	0.2
1995	†Col	N	7	7	.500	20	18	0	0-0	93	116	61	12	5	36-3	40	5.32	101	.316	.383	30-0-2	.133	-2	82	0	54	0.5
1996	Col	N	8	9	.471	30	30	0	0-0	168.2	195	97	27	9	49-0	88	4.96	105	.291	.347	52-0-7	.173	-1	95	5		0.5
1997	NY	N	6	3	.667	16	16	1-1	0-0	91.1	95	47	7	6	29-4	47	3.82	108	.256	.351	30-0-1	.167	-0	95	2	115	0.4
1998	NY	N	7	3	.700	11	11	0	0-0	68.1	64	31	4	5	32-3	40	3.82	106	.276	.347	16-0-0	.163	-0	119	4		0.4
1999	Ari	N	10	6	.625	31	27	0	0-0	167	178	90	20	6	67-7	79	5.27	93	.291	.273	48-0-8	.104	-2	93	-6		-0.8
2000	Ari	N	11	12	.478	31	30	2	0-0	170.2	179	102	22	8	52-5	89	5.98	78	.312	.366	10-0-3	.100	-0	89	-6	144	-0.8
2001	Ari	N	1	6	.143	9	9	0	0-0	53	68	32	13	4	13-2	15	5.43	75	.312	.366	0	—	0		-1	158	-0.1
2002	Ari	N	0	0	—	2	0	0	0-0	1.2	3	2	0	0	1-0	2	10.80	42	.375	.444	0	—	0		-1	158	-0.1
Total	12		68	62	.523	198	186	8-1	1-0	1079.2	1185	615	138	60	376-34	554	4.74	100	.283	.349	337-3-38	.148	-4	101	-1	642	0.6

RHEM, FLINT Charles Flint "Shad" B1.24.1901 Rhems SC D7.30.1969 Columbia SC BR/TR/6-2/180 d9.6 Col Clemson

YEAR	TM	LG	W	L	PCT	G	GS	CG-SHO	SV-BS	IP	H	R	HR	HB	BB-IB	SO	ERA	AERA	OAV	OOB	AB-HR-SH	AVG	PB	SUP	APR	DL	PW
1924	StL	N	2	2	.500	6	3	3	1	32.1	31	18	1	0	17	20	4.45	85	.254	.345	12	.167	-0	135	-2		-0.3
1925	StL	N	8	13	.381	30	24	8-1	1	170	204	114	16	4	58	66	4.92	88	.299	.357		.237	1	109	-13		-1.2
1926	†StL	N	**20**	7	.741	34	34	20-1	0	258	241	121	12	1	75	72	3.21	122	.250	.305	59-0-3	.068	-5	97	-9		-1.8
1927	StL	N	10	12	.455	27	26	9-2	0	169.1	189	102	9	4	54	51	4.14	97	.296	.365	67-1-1	.164	-1	124	-2		-0.2
1928	†StL	N	11	8	.579	28	22	9	3	169.2	199	91	13	9	71	47	4.45	113	.306	.352	52-0-4	.231	-1	144	5		0.1
1930	StL	N	12	8	.600	26	19	9	0	139.2	173	90	11	3	37	47	4.45	113	.306	.352	52-0-4	.188	0	116	6		0.1
1931	†StL	N	11	10	.524	33	26	10-2	1	207.1	214	100	17	3	60	72	3.56	111	.268	.321	69-0-5	.130	-4	116	6		0.1
1932	StL	N	4	2	.667	6	6	5-1	0	50	48	19	3	0	10	18	3.06	129	.257	.294	16-0-3	.188	0	128	5		0.7
	Phi	N	11	7	.611	26	20	10	1	168.2	177	79	13	0	49	35	3.74	118	.269	.319	62-0-4	.113	-5	117	12		0.7
	Year		15	9	.625	32	26	15-1	1	218.2	225	98	16	0	59	53	3.58	120	.266	.314	78-0-7	.128	-5	120	18		1.
1933	Phi	N	5	14	.263	28	19	3	2	125	182	109	10	2	33	27	6.62	58	.340	.381	46-0-1	.087	-4	100	-34		-5.
1934	StL	N	1	0	1.000	5	0	1	0	15.2	26	12	0	0	7	6	4.60	92	.394	.452	2	.000	-0	163	-2		-0.2
	Bos	N	8	8	.500	25	20	5-1	0	152.2	164	71	5	0	38	56	3.60	106	.273	.317	54-0-1	.058	-5	78	4		-0.
	Year		9	8	.529	30	21	5-1	1	168.1	190	83	5	0	45	62	3.69	105	.285	.331	54-0-1	.056	-5	82	3		-0.
1935	Bos	N	0	5	.000	10	6	0	0	40.1	61	37	4	0	11	10	5.36	71	.341	.379	10-0-1	.000	-1	67	-12		-1.
1936	StL	N	1	1	.667	10	4	0	0	26.2	49	26	2	0	9	7	6.75	58	.405	.446	8	.125	-0	172	-10		-1.
Total	12		105	97	.520	294	230	91-8	10	1725.1	1958	989	113	20	529	534	4.20	98	.287	.340	610-3-33	.144	-28	117	-37		-8.

RHINES, BILLY William Pearl "Bunker" B3.14.1869 Ridgway PA D1.30.1922 Ridgway PA BR/TR/5-11/168 d4.22 Col Bucknell

YEAR	TM	LG	W	L	PCT	G	GS	CG-SHO	SV-BS	IP	H	R	HR	HB	BB-IB	SO	ERA	AERA	OAV	OOB	AB-HR-SH	AVG	PB	SUP	APR	DL	PW
1890	Cin	N	28	17	.622	46	45	45-6	0	401.1	337	163	6	15	113	182	**1.95**	**183**	**.221**	**.281**	154	.188	-5	71	**68**		6.
1891	Cin	N	17	24	.415	48	43	40-1	1	372.2	364	224	4	22	124	138	2.87	124	.246	.314	148	.122	-9	84	12		0.
1892	Cin	N	3	4	.300	11	9	6	0	74.2	102	71	0	4	36	10	5.42	60	.313	.388	27-1	.185	1*	84	-19		-1.
1893	Lou	N	1	4	.200	5	5	3	0	31	49	37	3	3	19	6	8.71	50	.348	.436	11	.091	-2	86	-15		-1.
1895	Cin	N	19	10	.655	38	33	25	0	267.2	322	195	4	21	76	72	4.81	103	.293	.351	113-0-2	.221	-3	116	6		0.
1896	Cin	N	8	6	.571	19	17	11-3	0	143	128	52	1	9	48	32	**2.45**	**188**	**.238**	**.311**	52-0-1	.192	-3	71	33		2.
1897	Cin	N	21	15	.583	41	32	26-1	0	288.2	311	175	4	17	86	65	4.08	111	.273	.333	107-0-2	.159	-6	71	14		0.
1898	Pit	N	12	16	.429	31	29	27-2	0	258	289	143	0	13	61	48	3.52	101	.281	.329	100-0-1	.150	-4	80	-5		-0.
1899	Pit	N	4	4	.500	9	7	4	0	54	59	42	3	4	13	6	6.00	64	.277	.330	22-0-1	.435	4*	113	-10		-0.
Total	9		113	103	.523	248	222	187-13	1	1891	1961	1102	25	108	576	553	3.48	114	.262	.324	735-1-7	.177	-27	85	89		5.

RHOADS, BOB Robert Barton "Dusty" (b Barton Emory Rhoads) B10.4.1879 Wooster OH D2.12.1967 San Bernardino CA BR/TR/6-1/215 d4.19

YEAR	TM	LG	W	L	PCT	G	GS	CG-SHO	SV-BS	IP	H	R	HR	HB	BB-IB	SO	ERA	AERA	OAV	OOB	AB-HR-SH	AVG	PB	SUP	APR	DL	PW
1902	Chi	N	4	8	.333	16	12	12-1	0	118	131	66	0	6	42	43	3.20	84	.281	.348	45	.222	0	61	-6		-0.
1903	StL	N	5	8	.385	17	13	12-1	0	129	154	88	3	3	47	52	4.60	71	.303	.366	50-1-2	.140	-2*	87	-14		-1.
	Cle	A	2	3	.400	5	5	5	0	41	55	34	2	2	3	21	5.27	54	.320	.339	17	.118	-1	90	-10		-1.
1904	Cle	A	10	9	.526	22	19	18	0	175.1	175	72	1	5	48	72	2.87	88	.261	.315	92	.196	0*	104	-4		-0.
1905	Cle	A	16	9	.640	28	26	24-4	0	235	219	96	4	10	55	61	2.83	93	.249	.300	95-1-3	.221	4*	111	-4		0.
1906	Cle	A	22	10	.688	38	34	31-7	0	315	259	95	5	5	92	89	1.80	145	.227	.288	118-0-6	.161	-3	114	**28**		2.
1907	Cle	A	15	14	.517	35	31	23-5	1	275	258	105	0	14	84	76	2.29	109	.250	.316	92-0-6	.185	-1	90	7		0.
1908	Cle	A	18	12	.600	37	30	20-1	0	270	229	82	2	7	73	62	1.77	135	.234	.298	90-0-5	.222	4	104	16		2.
1909	Cle	A	5	9	.357	20	15	9-2	0	133.1	124	63	0	8	50	46	2.90	88	.281	.361	43-0-4	.163	-0	118	-5		1.
Total	8		97	82	.542	218	185	154-21	2	1691.2	1604	701	19	58	494	522	2.61	100	.256	.316	642-2-26	.188	-0	100	8		1.

RHODEN, RICK Richard Alan B5.16.1953 Boynton Beach FL BR/TR/6-3/195(190-203) [LAN71 1/20] d7.5

YEAR	TM	LG	W	L	PCT	G	GS	CG-SHO	SV-BS	IP	H	R	HR	HB	BB-IB	SO	ERA	AERA	OAV	OOB	AB-HR-SH	AVG	PB	SUP	APR	DL	PW
1974	LA	N	1	0	1.000	4	0	0	0-0	9	5	2	1	0	4-1	7	2.00	172	.161	.257	2	.500	0		2		0.
1975	LA	N	3	3	.500	26	11	1	0-1	99.1	94	40	8	1	32-1	40	3.08	111	.253	.310	28-0-1	.071	-2	100	3		0.
1976	LA N★		12	3	.800	27	26	10-3	0-0	181	165	66	17	1	53-2	77	2.98	114	.242	.296	65-1-7	.308	7	120	9		1.
1977	†LA	N	16	10	.615	31	31	4-1	0-0	216.1	223	98	20	2	63-1	122	3.74	103	.270	.321	78-3-6	.231	5*	106	3		0.
1978	†LA	N	10	8	.556	30	23	6-3	0-0	164.2	160	77	13	3	51-0	79	3.66	96	.255	.311	52-0-6	.135	-0	128	-3		-0.
1979	Pit	N	0	1	.000	1	1	0	0-0	5	5	4	0	2	2-0	2	7.20	54	.263	.333	1	1.000	0	23	-2	142	-0.
1980	Pit	N	7	5	.583	20	19	2	0-0	126.2	133	58	9	3	40-4	70	3.84	96	.273	.330	40-1-4	.375	6	102	-1		0.
1981	Pit	N	9	4	.692	21	21	4-2	0-0	136.1	147	66	6	2	53-2	76	3.89	94	.283	.348	48-0-3	.265	8*	107	-8		0.
1982	Pit	N	11	14	.440	35	35	6-1	0-0	230.1	239	115	14	2	70-8	128	4.14	91	.267	.320	83-3-2	.151	-2	91	17		3.
1983	Pit	N	13	13	.500	36	35	7-2	1-0	244.1	256	95	13	2	68-15	153	3.09	121	.276	.325	86-0-2	.333	9*	91	24		3.
1984	Pit	N	14	9	.609	33	33	6-3	0-0	238.1	216	81	13	1	62-0	136	2.72	134	.243	.292	84-0-5	.189	2*	88	-20		2.
1985	Pit	N	10	15	.400	35	35	2	0-0	213.1	254	119	16	6	69-3	128	4.47	81	.296	.352	74-0-2	.278	9*	102	31		2.
1986	Pit N☆		15	12	.556	34	34	12-1	0-0	253.2	211	82	15	4	76-8	159	2.84	137	.228	.286	90-1-7	.278	9*	83	12		2.
1987	NY	A	16	10	.615	30	29	4	0-0	181.2	184	84	22	3	61-5	107	3.86	115	.268	.327	0	—	-0*	100	-9	22	-1.
1988	NY	A	12	12	.500	30	30	5-1	0-0	197	206	107	20	8	56-4	99	4.29	92	.269	.322	1	.000	1	86	-9	79	-0.
1989	Hou	N	2	6	.250	20	17	0	0-0	96.2	108	49	7	3	41-8	41	3.59	104	.264	.319	29-0-2	.207	1	86	-9	79	-0.
Total	16		151	125	.547	413	380	69-17	1-0	2593.2	2606	1143	198	39	801-62	1419	3.59	104	.264	.319	761-9-47	.238	44	99	46	243	1.

RHODES, ARTHUR Arthur Lee B10.24.1969 Waco TX BL/TL/6-2/205(190-210) [BalA88 2/34] d8.21

YEAR	TM	LG	W	L	PCT	G	GS	CG-SHO	SV-BS	IP	H	R	HR	HB	BB-IB	SO	ERA	AERA	OAV	OOB	AB-HR-SH	AVG	PB	SUP	APR	DL	PW
1991	Bal	A	0	3	.000	8	8	0	0-0	36	47	35	4	0	23-0	23	8.00	50	.320	.405		—	0	89	-17		-1.
1992	Bal	A	7	5	.583	15	15	2-1	0-0	94.1	87	39	6	1	38-2	77	3.63	112	.249	.324		—	0	102	5		0.
1993	Bal	A	5	6	.455	17	17	0	0-0	85.2	91	62	16	1	49-1	49	6.51	69	.274	.366		—	0	102	-14	18	-1.
1994	Bal	A	3	5	.375	10	10	3-2	0-0	52.2	51	34	8	2	30-1	47	5.81	87	.254	.352		—	0	104	-11	38	-0.
1995	Bal	A	2	5	.286	19	9	0	0-0	75.1	68	53	13	0	48-1	77	6.21	77	.239	.349		—	0	122	4	71	0.
1996	†Bal	A	9	1	.900	28	2	0	1-0	53	48	28	6	0	23-3	62	4.08	121	.241	.318		—	0		16		0.
1997	†Bal	A	10	3	.769	53	0	0	1-1	95.1	75	32	9	4	26-5	102	3.02	146	.218	.278	2	.000	-0*		16	43	0.
1998	Bal	A	4	4	.500	45	0	0	4-4	77	65	30	8	1	34-2	83	3.51	130	.233	.313		.500			10		-0.
1999	Bal	A	3	4	.429	43	0	0	3-2	53	48	28	6	0	45-6	59	5.43	87	.221	.364		—			-6		-0.

YEAR	TM LG	W	L	PCT	G	GS	CG-SHO	SV-BS	IP	H	R	HR	HB	BB-IB	SO	ERA	AERA	OAV	OOB	AB-HR-SH	AVG	PB	SUP	APR	DL	PW
2000	†Sea A	5	8	.385	72	0	0	0-7	69.1	51	34	6	0	29-3	77	4.28	112	.205	.286	0	—	0		5		0.8
2001	†Sea A	8	0	1.000	71	0	0	3-4	68	46	14	5	1	12-0	83	1.72	247	.189	.230	1	.000	-0*		20		2.3
2002	Sea A	10	4	.714	66	0	0	2-5	69.2	45	18	4	1	13-1	81	2.33	185	.187	.227	0	—	0		17		3.0
2003	Sea A	3	3	.500	67	0	0	3-3	54	53	25	4	1	18-2	48	4.17	104	.256	.319	0	—	0		2		0.2
2004	Oak A	3	3	.500	37	0	0	9-5	38.2	46	23	9	0	21-4	34	5.12	90	.293	.374	0	—	0		-2	51	-0.3
2005	Cle A	3	1	.750	47	0	0	0-3	43.1	33	13	2	1	12-2	43	2.08	197	.206	.263	0	—	0		9	21	0.8
Total	15	75	55	.577	598	61	5-3	26-35	965.1	849	477	109	12	421-33	945	4.26	106	.237	.317	4	.250	0	99	32	320	5.8

RHODES, CHARLIE Charles Anderson "Dusty" B4.7.1885 Caney KS D10.26.1918 Caney KS BR/TR/5-7/180 d7.26

YEAR	TM LG	W	L	PCT	G	GS	CG-SHO	SV-BS	IP	H	R	HR	HB	BB-IB	SO	ERA	AERA	OAV	OOB	AB-HR-SH	AVG	PB	SUP	APR	DL	PW
1906	StL N	3	4	.429	9	6	3	0	45	37	21	0	6	20	32	3.40	77	.223	.328	16	.188	-0	97	-3		-0.5
1908	Cin N	0	0	—	1	0	0	0	4	1	2	0	1	2	4	0.00	—	.077	.250	1	.000	-0		0		0.0
	StL N	1	2	.333	4	4	3	0	33	23	14	2	1	12	15	3.00	79	.200	.281	12	.250	1	104	-1		0.0
	Year	1	2	.333	5	4	3	0	37	24	16	2	2	14	19	2.68	88	.188	.278	13	.231	1	105	-2		0.0
1909	StL N	3	5	.375	12	10	4	0	61	55	36	0	2	33	25	3.98	63	.256	.360	19	.211	1	113	-10		-0.9
Total	3	7	11	.389	26	20	10	0	143	116	73	2	10	67	76	3.46	73	.228	.328	48	.208	2	107	-14		-1.4

RHODES, GORDON John Gordon "Dusty" B8.11.1907 Winnemucca NV D3.22.1960 Long Beach CA BR/TR/6-0/187 d4.29

YEAR	TM LG	W	L	PCT	G	GS	CG-SHO	SV-BS	IP	H	R	HR	HB	BB-IB	SO	ERA	AERA	OAV	OOB	AB-HR-SH	AVG	PB	SUP	APR	DL	PW
1929	NY A	0	4	.000	10	4	0	0	42.2	57	32	3	2	16	13	4.85	80	.333	.397	10-0-3	.300	1	82	-7		-0.5
1930	NY A	0	0	—	3	0	0	0	2	3	3	0	0	4	1	9.00	48	.500	.700	0	—	0		-1		-0.1
1931	NY A	6	3	.667	18	11	4	0	87	82	49	3	0	52	36	3.41	116	.235	.334	28-0-4	.214	1	147	1		0.1
1932	NY A	1	2	.333	10	2	1	0	24	25	22	0	0	21	15	7.88	52	.275	.411	7	.286	0	230	-10		-0.9
	Bos A	1	8	.111	12	11	4	0	79.1	79	46	5	0	31	22	5.11	88	.261	.329	27	.074	-2	45	-2		-0.4
	Year	2	10	.167	22	13	5	0	103.1	104	68	5	0	52	37	5.75	76	.264	.350	34	.118	-2	72	-11		-1.3
1933	Bos A	12	15	.444	34	29	14	0	232	242	126	13	1	93	85	4.03	109	.265	.334	86-1-4	.267	4*	114	7		1.2
1934	Bos A	12	12	.500	44	31	10	2	219	247	133	10	4	98	79	4.56	105	.285	.360	75-1-1	.133	-3	103	5		0.2
1935	Bos A	2	10	.167	34	19	1	2	146.1	195	103	14	1	60	44	5.41	88	.324	.387	48-0-1	.146	-4*	83	-10		-1.1
1936	Phi A	9	20	.310	35	28	13-1	5	216.1	266	162	26	2	102	61	5.74	89	.304	.378	75-0-2	.213	-2	68	-17		-2.0
Total	8	43	74	.368	200	135	47-1	5	1048.2	1196	676	74	10	477	356	4.85	95	.286	.361	356-2-15	.194	-5	95	-34		-3.5

RHODES, BILL William Clarence B Pottstown PA d6.14

YEAR	TM LG	W	L	PCT	G	GS	CG-SHO	SV-BS	IP	H	R	HR	HB	BB-IB	SO	ERA	AERA	OAV	OOB	AB-HR-SH	AVG	PB	SUP	APR	DL	PW
1893	Lou N	5	12	.294	20	19	17	0	151.2	244	173	10	10	66	22	7.60	58	.352	.416	70	.129	-4	127	-59		-4.7

RIBANT, DENNIS Dennis Joseph B9.20.1941 Detroit MI BR/TR/5-11/175* d8.9

YEAR	TM LG	W	L	PCT	G	GS	CG-SHO	SV-BS	IP	H	R	HR	HB	BB-IB	SO	ERA	AERA	OAV	OOB	AB-HR-SH	AVG	PB	SUP	APR	DL	PW
1964	NY N	1	5	.167	14	7	1-1	1	57.2	65	35	8	0	9-1	35	5.15	69	.281	.308	20	.100	-0*	105	-9		-0.9
1965	NY N	1	3	.250	19	1	0	3	35.1	29	16	5	0	6-0	13	3.82	92	.228	.261	6	.000	-1	25	-1		-0.2
1966	NY N	11	9	.550	39	26	10-1	3	188.1	184	78	20	1	40-5	84	3.20	114	.254	.291	61-0-4	.197	0*	99	9		1.0
1967	Pit N	9	8	.529	38	22	2-1	0	172	186	78	16	3	40-5	75	4.08	82	.280	.323	60-0-2	.267	5*	108	-9		-0.2
1968	Det N	2	2	.500	14	0	0	1	24.1	20	7	1	3	10-2	7	2.22	136	.217	.301	5	.200	0*		2		0.4
	Chi A	0	2	.000	17	0	0	1	31.1	42	24	3	2	17-4	20	6.03	50	.318	.399	7	.000	-1		-10		-0.8
	Year	2	4	.333	31	0	0	2	55.2	62	31	4	5	27-6	27	4.37	69	.277	.359	12	.083	-0		-8		-0.4
1969	StL N	0	0	—	1	0	0	0	1.1	1	2	1	0	1-0	0	13.50	27	.571	.556	0	—	0*		-1		-0.1
	Cin N	0	0	—	7	0	0	0-1	8.1	6	5	1	0	3-0	7	1.08	348	.188	.257	0	—	0		-1		0.0
	Year	0	0	—	9	0	0	0-1	9.2	7	7	2	0	4-0	7	2.79	134	.256	.318	0	—	0		-1		-0.1
Total	6	24	29	.453	149	56	13-2	9-1	518.2	536	245	55	7	126-17	241	3.87	90	.267	.310	159-0-6	.195	4	103	-18		-0.8

RICCELLI, FRANK Frank Joseph B2.24.1953 Syracuse NY BL/TL/6-3/205(190-205) [SFN71 1/18] d9.11

YEAR	TM LG	W	L	PCT	G	GS	CG-SHO	SV-BS	IP	H	R	HR	HB	BB-IB	SO	ERA	AERA	OAV	OOB	AB-HR-SH	AVG	PB	SUP	APR	DL	PW
1976	SF N	1	1	.500	4	3	0	0-0	16	16	10	1	0	5-0	11	5.63	65	.258	.309	6	.167	-0	97	-3		-0.3
1978	Hou N	0	0	—	2	0	0	0-0	3	1	0	0	0	5-0	1	0.00	—	.100	.100	0	—	0		1		0.1
1979	Hou N	2	2	.500	11	2	0	0-0	22	22	11	0	0	18-0	20	4.09	86	.262	.392	6	.333	1	139	-1	70	-0.1
Total	3	3	3	.500	17	5	0	0-0	41	39	21	1	0	23-0	32	4.39	81	.250	.344	12	.250	1	114	-3	70	-0.3

RICCI, CHUCK Charles Mark B11.20.1968 Abington PA BR/TR/6-2/180 [BalA87 4/91] d9.8

YEAR	TM LG	W	L	PCT	G	GS	CG-SHO	SV-BS	IP	H	R	HR	HB	BB-IB	SO	ERA	AERA	OAV	OOB	AB-HR-SH	AVG	PB	SUP	APR	DL	PW
1995	Phi N	1	0	1.000	7	0	0	0-0	10	9	2	0	1	3-0	9	1.80	234	.273	.333	0	—	0		3		0.2

RICE, SAM Edgar Charles B2.20.1890 Morocco IN D10.13.1974 Rossmoor MD BL/TR/5-9/150 d8.7 Mil 1918 HF1963 ▲

YEAR	TM LG	W	L	PCT	G	GS	CG-SHO	SV-BS	IP	H	R	HR	HB	BB-IB	SO	ERA	AERA	OAV	OOB	AB-HR-SH	AVG	PB	SUP	APR	DL	PW
1915	Was A	0	1	.000	4	2	1	0	18	13	8	0	0	9	9	2.00	148	.213	.314	8	.375	1	147	1		0.1
1916	Was A	0	0	.000	5	1	0	0	21.1	18	10	0	0	10	3	2.95	95	.237	.326	197-1-1	.299	2*	54	-1		0.1
Total	2	0	1	.500	9	3	1	0	39.1	31	18	0	0	19	12	2.52	114	.226	.321	205-1-1	.302	2	121	0		0.2

RICE, PAT Patrick Edward B11.2.1963 Rapid City SD BR/TR/6-2/200 d5.18 Col Arkansas-Monticello

YEAR	TM LG	W	L	PCT	G	GS	CG-SHO	SV-BS	IP	H	R	HR	HB	BB-IB	SO	ERA	AERA	OAV	OOB	AB-HR-SH	AVG	PB	SUP	APR	DL	PW
1991	Sea A	1	1	.500	21	1	0	1-0	21	18	10	3	1	10-1	21	3.00	138	.234	.319	0	—	0		77	2	0.1

RICH, WOODY Woodrow Earl B3.9.1916 Morganton NC D4.18.1983 Morganton NC BL/TR/6-2/185 d4.22 Mil 1945

YEAR	TM LG	W	L	PCT	G	GS	CG-SHO	SV-BS	IP	H	R	HR	HB	BB-IB	SO	ERA	AERA	OAV	OOB	AB-HR-SH	AVG	PB	SUP	APR	DL	PW
1939	Bos A	4	3	.571	21	12	3	1	77	78	46	2	5	35	24	4.91	96	.264	.352	27-0-1	.259	0	138	0		0.1
1940	Bos A	1	0	1.000	3	1	1	0	11.2	9	3	2	0	1	8	0.77	583	.214	.233	4	.000	-1	78	4		0.2
1941	Bos A	0	0	—	2	1	0	0	3.2	8	7	1	0	2	1	17.18	24	.421	.476	0	—	0	166	-5		-0.2
1944	Bos N	1	1	.500	7	2	1	0	25	32	17	1	0	12	9	5.76	66	.327	.416	8-0-1	.125	-1	110	-4		-0.4
Total	4	6	4	.600	33	16	5	1	117.1	127	73	8	5	50	42	5.06	89	.280	.361	39-0-2	.205	-1	135	-5		-0.3

RICHARD, J.R. James Rodney B3.7.1950 Vienna LA BR/TR/6-8/222(222-237) [HouN69 1/2] d9.5 [DL 1981 Hou N 146, 1982 Hou N 150, 1983 Hou N 182]

YEAR	TM LG	W	L	PCT	G	GS	CG-SHO	SV-BS	IP	H	R	HR	HB	BB-IB	SO	ERA	AERA	OAV	OOB	AB-HR-SH	AVG	PB	SUP	APR	DL	PW
1971	Hou N	2	1	.667	4	4	1	0-0	21	17	9	1	0	16-0	29	3.43	98	.215	.344	7-0-2	.000	0	92	0		-0.1
1972	Hou N	1	0	1.000	4	1	0	0-0	6	10	9	2	0	8-0	8	13.50	25	.385	.556	0	—	0	184	-7		-0.9
1973	Hou N	6	2	.750	16	10	2-1	0-0	72	54	37	2	1	38-0	75	4.00	91	.210	.313	28-0-1	.179	-0	153	-4		-0.5
1974	Hou N	2	3	.400	15	9	0	0-0	64.2	58	31	3	1	36-0	42	4.18	84	.243	.343	21-1-1	.143	0	108	-4		-0.3
1975	Hou N	12	10	.545	33	31	7-1	0-0	203	178	107	8	4	138-0	176	4.39	77	.238	.358	74-1-5	.203	4	141	-24		-2.0
1976	Hou N	20	15	.571	39	39	14-3	0-0	291	221	105	14	4	151-4	214	2.75	117	.212	.312	100-2-1	.140	0	104	15		1.8
1977	Hou N	18	12	.600	36	36	13-3	0-0	267	212	94	18	0	104-1	214	2.97	122	.218	.292	87-0-11	.230	6	105	23		3.3
1978	Hou N	18	11	.621	36	36	16-3	0-0	275.1	192	104	12	2	141-4	303	3.11	105	.196	.298	101-1-5	.178	1*	124	7		1.0
1979	Hou N	18	13	.581	38	38	19-4	0-0	292.1	220	98	13	3	98-5	313	2.71	130	.209	.276	95-2-11	.126	-0	85	29		2.8
1980	Hou N★	10	4	.714	17	17	4-4	0-0	113.2	65	31	2	0	40-1	119	1.90	173	.166	.242	39-1-4	.154	1	93	18	82	2.3
Total	10	107	71	.601	238	221	76-19	0-0	1606	1227	625	73	17	770-15	1493	3.15	109	.212	.305	552-10-41	.168	11	111	53.	560	7.4

RICHARDS, DUANE Duane Lee B12.16.1936 Spartanburg IN BR/TR/6-3/200 d9.25

YEAR	TM LG	W	L	PCT	G	GS	CG-SHO	SV-BS	IP	H	R	HR	HB	BB-IB	SO	ERA	AERA	OAV	OOB	AB-HR-SH	AVG	PB	SUP	APR	DL	PW
1960	Cin N	0	0	—	2	0	0	0	3	5	4	0	0	2-0	2	9.00	42	.385	.438	0	—	0		-2		-0.1

RICHARDS, RUSTY Russell Earl B1.27.1965 Houston TX BL/TR/6-4/200* d9.20 Col Texas

YEAR	TM LG	W	L	PCT	G	GS	CG-SHO	SV-BS	IP	H	R	HR	HB	BB-IB	SO	ERA	AERA	OAV	OOB	AB-HR-SH	AVG	PB	SUP	APR	DL	PW
1989	Atl N	0	0	—	2	2	0	0-0	9.1	10	5	2	1	6-0	4	4.82	76	.278	.395	3-0-1	.000	-0	133	-1		-0.1
1990	Atl N	0	0	—	1	0	0	0-0	1	2	3	1	0	1-0	0	27.00	15	.400	.500	0	—	0		-2		-0.1
Total	2	0	0	—	3	2	0	0-0	10.1	12	8	3	1	7-0	4	6.97	53	.293	.408	3-0-1	.000	-0	133	-3		-0.2

RICHARDSON, HARDY Abram Harding "Old True Blue" B4.21.1855 Clarksboro NJ D1.14.1931 Utica NY BR/TR/5-9.5/170 d5.1.1879 ▲

YEAR	TM LG	W	L	PCT	G	GS	CG-SHO	SV-BS	IP	H	R	HR	HB	BB-IB	SO	ERA	AERA	OAV	OOB	AB-HR-SH	AVG	PB	SUP	APR	DL	PW
1885	Buf N	0	0	—	1	0	0	0	4	5	2	0		3		2.25	133	.294	.400	426-9	.319	0*		0		0.0
1886	Det N	3	0	1.000	4	0	0	0	12	11	8	1	0	10	5	4.50	74	.208	.333	538-11	.351	2*		-1		-0.1
Total	2	3	0	1.000	16				16	10	1			13	6	3.94	82	.229	.349	964-17	.337	3		-1		-0.1

RICHARDSON, DANNY Daniel B1.25.1863 Elmira NY D9.12.1926 New York NY BR/TR/5-8/165 d5.22.1884 M1 ▲

YEAR	TM LG	W	L	PCT	G	GS	CG-SHO	SV-BS	IP	H	R	HR	HB	BB-IB	SO	ERA	AERA	OAV	OOB	AB-HR-SH	AVG	PB	SUP	APR	DL	PW
1885	NY N	7	1	.875	9	8	7-1	0	75	58	30	0		18	21	2.40	111	.252	.263	198	.263	2*	175	5		0.5
1886	NY N	0	2	.000	5	1	1	0	25	33	24	1		11	17	5.76	56	.320	.386	237-1	.232	1*	19	-7		-0.3
1887	NY N	0	0	—	1	0	0	0	0	0	0	0	1	0	—	—	1.000		450-3	.278	0*		0		0.0
Total	3	7	3	.700	15	9	8-1	0	100	91	54	1	0	30	38	3.24	86	.236	.291	885-4	.262	3	154	-2		0.2

RICHARDSON, GORDIE Gordon Clark B7.19.1938 Colquitt GA BR/TL/6-0/185* d7.26

YEAR	TM LG	W	L	PCT	G	GS	CG-SHO	SV-BS	IP	H	R	HR	HB	BB-IB	SO	ERA	AERA	OAV	OOB	AB-HR-SH	AVG	PB	SUP	APR	DL	PW
1964	†StL N	4	2	.667	19	6	1	1	47	40	18	2	1	15-0	28	2.30	166	.231	.296	13	.077	-0	104	5		0.7
1965	NY N	2	2	.500	35	0	0	2	52.1	41	27	5	2	16-2	43	3.78	93	.224	.289	7-0-1	.000	-1	48	-3		-0.3
1966	NY N	0	2	.000	15	1	0	0	18.2	24	19	7	0	6-1	15	9.16	40	.312	.353	0	—	-0	48	-10		-0.7
Total	3	6	6	.500	69	7	1	3	118	105	64	14	3	37-3	86	4.04	90	.242	.303	21-0-1	.048	-1	99	-6		-0.7

RICHARDSON, JEFF Jeffrey Scott B8.29.1963 Wichita KS BR/TR/6-3/185 d9.19 Col Connors St. (OK) JC [DL 1991 Cal A 182]

YEAR	TM LG	W	L	PCT	G	GS	CG-SHO	SV-BS	IP	H	R	HR	HB	BB-IB	SO	ERA	AERA	OAV	OOB	AB-HR-SH	AVG	PB	SUP	APR	DL	PW
1990	Cal A	0	0	—	1	0	0	0-0	0.1	1	0	0	0	0	0	0.00	—	.500	.500	0	—	0		0		0.0

YEAR	TM LG	W	L	PCT	G	GS	CG-SHO	SV-BS	IP	H	R	HR	HB	BB-IB	SO	ERA	AERA	OAV	OOB	AB-HR-SH	AVG	PB	SUP	APR	DL	PV

RICHARDSON, JACK   John William   B10.3.1891 Central City IL   D1.18.1970 Marion IL   BB/TR/6-3/197   d9.17

YEAR	TM LG	W	L	PCT	G	GS	CG-SHO	SV-BS	IP	H	R	HR	HB	BB-IB	SO	ERA	AERA	OAV	OOB	AB-HR-SH	AVG	PB	SUP	APR	DL	PV
1915	Phi A	0	1	.000	3	3	2	0	24	21	13	0	1	14	11	2.63	111	.253	.367	8	.000	-1	116	0		-0.2
1916	Phi A	0	0	—	1	0	0	0	0.2	2	3	0	0	1	1	40.50	7	.667	.750	0	—	0		-2		-0.1
Total	2	0	1	.000	4	3	2	0	24.2	23	16	0	1	15	12	3.65	.80	.267	.382	8	.000	-1	116	-2		-0.3

RICHERT, PETE   Peter Gerard   B10.29.1939 Floral Park NY   BL/TL/6-0/184(170-196)   d4.12 Mil 1968

YEAR	TM LG	W	L	PCT	G	GS	CG-SHO	SV-BS	IP	H	R	HR	HB	BB-IB	SO	ERA	AERA	OAV	OOB	AB-HR-SH	AVG	PB	SUP	APR	DL	PV
1962	LA N	5	4	.556	19	12	1	0	81.1	77	35	6	1	45-1	75	3.87	94	.249	.346	25-0-1	.080	-1	137	0	33	-0.2
1963	LA N	5	3	.625	20	12	1	0	78	80	40	7	1	28-3	54	4.50	67	.262	.326	22-0-2	.182	1	138	-11		-1.0
1964	Was A	2	3	.400	8	6	1-1	0	34.2	38	17	2	2	18-2	25	4.15	78	.271	.360	11	.091	-0	113	-3		-0.4
1965	Was A★	15	12	.556	34	29	6	0	194	146	64	18	2	84-7	161	2.60	134	.210	.296	64-0-3	.156	-0*	78	19		2.0
1966	Was A★	14	14	.500	36	34	7	0	245.2	196	106	36	1	69-6	195	3.37	103	.215	.270	86-1-5	.163	2*	94	1		0.2
1967	Was A	2	6	.250	11	10	1-1	0	54.1	49	29	5	1	15-0	41	4.64	68	.237	.288	17-0-1	.059	-1*	44	-8		-1.2
	Bal A	7	10	.412	26	19	5-1	2	132.1	107	53	11	1	41-1	90	2.99	105	.220	.279	37-0-5	.108	-1*	71	0		-1.2
	Year	9	16	.360	37	29	6-2	2	186.2	156	82	16	2	56-1	131	3.47	91	.225	.282	54-0-6	.093	-2	62	-6		-1.2
1968	Bal A	6	3	.667	36	0	0	0	62.1	51	25	7	3	12-1	47	3.47	84	.225	.273	10-0-1	.200	-0		-3		-0.1
1969	†Bal A	7	4	.636	44	0	0	12-3	57.1	42	17	7	0	14-2	54	2.20	163	.202	.249	8-0-2	.125	-0		8		-1.8
1970	†Bal A	7	2	.778	50	0	0	13-4	54.2	36	14	5	1	24-3	66	1.98	186	.194	.284	4	.000	-0		10		2.2
1971	†Bal A	3	5	.375	35	0	0	4-1	36.1	26	15	3	1	22-6	35	3.47	98	.205	.325	2-0-1	.000	-0		0		0.1
1972	LA N	2	3	.400	37	0	0	6-3	52	42	17	3	1	18-5	38	2.25	149	.219	.286	6-0-1	.500	1		6		0.4
1973	LA N	3	3	.500	39	0	0	7-6	51	44	18	5	1	19-5	31	3.18	110	.234	.306	5-0-1	.200	0		3		0.1
1974	StL N	0	0	—	13	0	0	1-0	11.1	10	7	1	0	11-1	0	2.38	152	.244	.389	0	—	0		0		0.1
	Phi N	2	1	.667	21	0	0	0-0	20.1	15	6	0	0	4-3	9	2.21	172	.205	.244	0	—	0		3		0.1
	Year	2	1	.667	34	0	0	1-0	31.2	25	13	1	0	15-4	9	2.27	164	.219	.303	0	—	0		3		0.2
Total	13	80	73	.523	429	122	22-3	51-17	1165.2	959	463	116	16	424-46	925	3.19	106	.223	.294	297-1-23	.145	-1	92	25	33	5.

RICHIE, LEW   Elwood Lewis   B8.23.1883 Ambler PA   D8.15.1936 South Mountain PA   BR/TR/5-8/165   d5.8

YEAR	TM LG	W	L	PCT	G	GS	CG-SHO	SV-BS	IP	H	R	HR	HB	BB-IB	SO	ERA	AERA	OAV	OOB	AB-HR-SH	AVG	PB	SUP	APR	DL	PV
1906	Phi N	9	11	.450	33	22	14-3	0	205.2	170	86	3	6	79	65	2.41	109	.230	.309	60-0-1	.050	-3	82	2		-0.1
1907	Phi N	6	6	.500	25	12	9-2	0	117	88	37	0	5	38	40	1.77	137	.215	.290	43-0-2	.163	0	64	6		0.9
1908	Phi N	7	10	.412	25	15	13-2	1	157.2	125	50	1	6	49	58	1.83	133	.233	.304	52	.212	2	62	8		1.1
1909	Phi N	1	1	.500	11	1	0	1	45	40	14	0	2	18	11	2.00	130	.263	.349	16	.250	1	188	3		-0.2
	Bos N	7	7	.500	22	13	9-2	2	131.2	118	58	2	1	44	42	2.32	121	.247	.312	44-0-1	.114	-2	82	3		-0.1
	Year	8	8	.500	33	14	9-2	3	176.2	158	72	2	3	62	53	2.24	123	.251	.321	60-0-1	.150	-1	90	7		0.1
1910	Bos N	0	3	.000	4	2	0	0	16.1	20	11	0	0	9	7	2.76	121	.317	.403	4	.000	-1	34	0		0.1
	†Chi N	11	4	.733	30	11	8-3	4	130	117	45	1	3	51	53	2.70	107	.257	.336	40-0-2	.225	3	131	5		0.3
	Year	11	7	.611	34	13	8-3	4	146.1	137	56	1	3	60	60	2.71	108	.264	.344	44-0-2	.205	2	115	4		0.3
1911	Chi N	15	11	.577	36	29	18-4	1	253	213	88	6	2	103	78	2.31	143	.235	.315	91-0-2	.154	-3	100	28		3.0
1912	Chi N	16	8	.667	39	27	15-4	0	238	222	102	5	6	74	69	2.95	113	.261	.324	76-0-6	.132	-3	100	9		0.1
1913	Chi N	2	4	.333	16	5	1	0	65	77	53	3	1	30	15	5.82	55	.304	.380	17-0-1	.118	-1	109	-18		-1.1
Total	8	74	65	.532	241	137	87-20	9	1359.1	1190	544	21	32	495	438	2.54	115	.246	.320	443-0-15	.147	-7	92	46		3.3

RICHMOND, BERYL   Beryl Justice   B8.24.1907 Glen Easton WV   D4.24.1980 Cameron WV   BB/TL(BR 1933)/6-1/185   d4.21

YEAR	TM LG	W	L	PCT	G	GS	CG-SHO	SV-BS	IP	H	R	HR	HB	BB-IB	SO	ERA	AERA	OAV	OOB	AB-HR-SH	AVG	PB	SUP	APR	DL	PV
1933	Chi N	0	0	—	4	0	0	0	4.2	10	1	0	0	2	2	1.93	170	.455	.500	1	.000	-0*		1		0.1
1934	Cin N	1	2	.333	6	2	1	0	19.1	23	11	0	0	10	9	3.72	110	.303	.384	5	.000	-1	85	0		0.1
Total	2	1	2	.333	10	2	1	0	24	33	12	0	0	12	11	3.38	116	.337	.409	6	.000	-1	85	1		0.1

RICHMOND, LEE   J Lee   B5.5.1857 Sheffield OH   D10.1.1929 Toledo OH   TL/5-10/155   d9.27 Col Brown ▲

YEAR	TM LG	W	L	PCT	G	GS	CG-SHO	SV-BS	IP	H	R	HR	HB	BB-IB	SO	ERA	AERA	OAV	OOB	AB-HR-SH	AVG	PB	SUP	APR	DL	PV
1879	Bos N	1	0	1.000	1	1	1	0	9	4	6	0		1	11	2.00	124	.114	.139	6	.333	0	224	0		0.1
1880	Wor N	32	32	.500	74	66	57-5	3	590.2	541	278	7		74	243	2.15	121	.232	.255	309	.227	-4*	97	25		-1.1
1881	Wor N	25	26	.490	53	52	50-3	0	462.1	547	302	7		68	156	3.39	89	.284	.309	252	.250	-1*	98	-19		-1.0
1882	Wor N	14	33	.298	48	46	44	0	411	525	343	11		88	123	3.74	83	.294	.327	228-2	.281	7*	90	-23		-1.0
1883	Pro N	3	7	.300	12	12	8	0	92	122	67	2		27	13	3.33	93	.314	.358	194-1	.284	3*	88	-3		-0.0
1886	Cin AA	0	2	.000	3	2	1	0	18	24	22	0	2	11	6	8.00	44	.308	.407	29	.276	0*	126	-8		-0.1
Total	6	75	100	.429	191	179	161-8	3	1583	1763	1018	27	2	269	552	3.06	95	.269	.298	1018-3	.257	7	96	-28		-4

RICHMOND, RAY   Raymond Sinclair   B6.15.1896 Fillmore IL   D10.21.1969 DeSoto MO   BR/TR/6-0/175   d9.25 Col Eastern Illinois

YEAR	TM LG	W	L	PCT	G	GS	CG-SHO	SV-BS	IP	H	R	HR	HB	BB-IB	SO	ERA	AERA	OAV	OOB	AB-HR-SH	AVG	PB	SUP	APR	DL	PV
1920	StL A	2	0	1.000	2	2	1	0	17	18	12	0	0	9	4	6.35	62	.273	.360	6-0-1	.167	-0	233	-3		-0.0
1921	StL A	0	1	.000	6	2	0	0	14.1	21	19	1	3	13	6	11.30	40	.362	.500	4	.000	-1	93	-9		-0.1
Total	2	2	1	.667	8	4	1	0	31.1	39	31	1	3	22	10	8.62	48	.315	.430	10-0-1	.100	-1	161	-12		-0.1

RICHTER, REGGIE   Emil Henry   B9.14.1888 Dusseldorf, Germany   D8.2.1934 Winfield IL   BR/TR/6-2/180   d5.30

YEAR	TM LG	W	L	PCT	G	GS	CG-SHO	SV-BS	IP	H	R	HR	HB	BB-IB	SO	ERA	AERA	OAV	OOB	AB-HR-SH	AVG	PB	SUP	APR	DL	PV
1911	Chi N	1	3	.250	12	5	3-1	0	54.2	62	30	1	3	20	34	3.13	106	.307	.378	10	.100	-1	118	-1		-0.0

RICKETTS, DICK   Richard James   B12.4.1933 Pottstown PA   D3.6.1988 Rochester NY   BL/TR/6-7/225   d6.14 b-Dave Col Duquesne

YEAR	TM LG	W	L	PCT	G	GS	CG-SHO	SV-BS	IP	H	R	HR	HB	BB-IB	SO	ERA	AERA	OAV	OOB	AB-HR-SH	AVG	PB	SUP	APR	DL	PV
1959	StL N	1	6	.143	12	9	0	0	55.2	68	42	7	0	30-4	25	5.82	73	.301	.381	18-0-2	.056	-2	70	-10		-1

RIDDLE, ELMER   Elmer Ray   B7.31.1914 Columbus GA   D5.14.1984 Columbus GA   BR/TR/5-11.5/170   d10.1 b-Johnny

YEAR	TM LG	W	L	PCT	G	GS	CG-SHO	SV-BS	IP	H	R	HR	HB	BB-IB	SO	ERA	AERA	OAV	OOB	AB-HR-SH	AVG	PB	SUP	APR	DL	PV
1939	Cin N	0	0	—	1	0	0	0	2	1	0	0	0	0	0	0.00	—	.143	.143	0	—	0		1		0
1940	†Cin N	1	2	.333	15	1	1	2	33.2	30	12	0	0	17	9	1.87	202	.250	.343	7	.143	0	23	5		3
1941	Cin N	19	4	.826	33	22	15-4	1	216.2	180	68	8	5	59	80	2.24	160	.234	.282	71-0-9	.225	3	115	30		3
1942	Cin N	7	11	.389	24	19	7-1	0	158.1	157	74	7	4	79	79	3.69	89	.260	.349	58	.259	3	89	-5		-0
1943	Cin N	21	11	.656	36	33	19-5	3	260.1	235	87	6	2	107	69	2.63	126	.245	.322	93-0-6	.194	1	112	19		2
1944	Cin N	2	2	.500	4	4	2	0	26.2	25	12	0	0	12	6	4.05	86	.250	.330	8-0-1	.125	-0	84	-1		-0
1945	Cin N	1	4	.200	12	3	0	0	29.2	39	27	4	0	27	5	8.19	46	.333	.458	11	.273	-1	90	-13		-0
1947	Cin N	1	0	1.000	16	3	0	0	30.1	42	30	5	1	31	8	8.31	49	.333	.468	5-0-1	.000	-0	143	-13		-0
1948	Pit N☆	12	10	.545	28	27	12-3	1	191	184	83	20	3	81	63	3.49	117	.250	.327	64-1-6	.188	-1*	86	12		-1
1949	Pit N	1	8	.111	16	12	1	1	74.1	81	45	9	4	45	24	5.33	79	.281	.386	22-0-1	.136	-1	82	-7		-1
Total	10	65	52	.556	190	124	57-13	8	1023	974	438	59	19	458	342	3.40	107	.252	.335	339-1-24	.204	7	99	28		3

RIDDLEBERGER, DENNY   Dennis Michael   B11.22.1945 Clifton Forge VA   BR/TL/6-3/195*   d9.15 Col Old Dominion

YEAR	TM LG	W	L	PCT	G	GS	CG-SHO	SV-BS	IP	H	R	HR	HB	BB-IB	SO	ERA	AERA	OAV	OOB	AB-HR-SH	AVG	PB	SUP	APR	DL	PV
1970	Was A	0	0	—	8	0	0	0-0	9.1	7	2	1	0	2-0	5	0.96	374	.219	.257	0	—	0		2		0
1971	Was A	3	1	.750	57	0	0	1-0	69.2	67	27	9	1	32-7	56	3.23	105	.260	.341	4	.000	0		2		0
1972	Cle A	1	3	.250	38	0	0	0-1	54	45	23	5	2	22-3	34	2.50	130	.237	.319	4	.000	-0		2		0
Total	3	4	4	.500	103	0	0	1-1	133	119	52	15	3	56-10	95	2.77	121	.248	.327	8	.000	-0		6		0

RIDDLEMOSER, DORSEY   Dorsey Lee   B3.25.1875 Frederick MD   D5.11.1954 Frederick MD   BR/TR   d8.22

YEAR	TM LG	W	L	PCT	G	GS	CG-SHO	SV-BS	IP	H	R	HR	HB	BB-IB	SO	ERA	AERA	OAV	OOB	AB-HR-SH	AVG	PB	SUP	APR	DL	PV
1899	Was N	0	0	—	1	0	0	0	2	7	4	0	2	0	0	18.00	22	.538	.600	1	.000	-0		-3		-0

RIDGWAY, JACK   Jacob A.   B7.23.1889 Philadelphia PA   D2.23.1928 Philadelphia PA   BL/TR/5-11/174   d5.20

YEAR	TM LG	W	L	PCT	G	GS	CG-SHO	SV-BS	IP	H	R	HR	HB	BB-IB	SO	ERA	AERA	OAV	OOB	AB-HR-SH	AVG	PB	SUP	APR	DL	PV
1914	Bal F	0	1	.000	4	1	0	0	9	20	11	1	1	3	2	11.00	28	.444	.490	1	.000	-0	136	-6		-0

RIDZIK, STEVE   Stephen George   B4.29.1929 Yonkers NY   BR/TR/5-11/170(170-195)   d9.4

YEAR	TM LG	W	L	PCT	G	GS	CG-SHO	SV-BS	IP	H	R	HR	HB	BB-IB	SO	ERA	AERA	OAV	OOB	AB-HR-SH	AVG	PB	SUP	APR	DL	PV
1950	Phi N	0	0	—	1	0	0	0	3	3	2	1	0	1	2	6.00	67	.300	.364	0	—	0		-1		0
1952	Phi N	4	2	.667	24	9	2	0	92.2	74	37	11	1	37	43	3.01	121	.218	.297	22-0-2	.136	0	100	6		0
1953	Phi N	9	6	.600	42	12	1	0	124	119	61	15	5	48	53	3.77	112	.256	.332	36-1-2	.194	2	74	6		0
1954	Phi N	4	5	.444	35	6	0	0	80.2	72	42	7	0	44	45	4.13	98	.233	.326	22-0-1	.227	1	63	-1		0
1955	Phi N	0	1	.000	3	1	0	0	11	7	9	1	3	8-0	6	2.45	162	.179	.360	4	.000	-1	45	-1		0
	Cin N	0	3	.000	13	2	0	0	30	35	16	4	1	14-1	6	4.50	94	.299	.376	6	.167	-0	53	0		0
	Year	0	4	.000	16	3	0	0	41	42	25	5	4	22-1	12	3.95	105	.269	.372	10	.100	-1	50	-1		0
1956	NY N	6	2	.750	41	6	1-1	0	92.1	80	42	7	6	65-5	53	3.80	99	.240	.286	28	.250	1*	98	-1		0
1957	NY N	2	2	.500	15	0	0	0	26.2	19	14	3	2	19-1	13	4.73	83	.213	.360	5	.200	0		-2		0
1958	Cle A	0	2	.000	6	0	0	0	8.2	9	7	1	0	5-2	6	2.08	176	.257	.341	1	.000	-0		-1		0
1963	Was A	5	6	.455	20	10	1	0	89.2	82	53	16	5	35-0	47	4.82	77	.240	.316	29	.172	0	93	-10		0
1964	Was A	5	5	.500	49	3	0	2	112	96	46	10	7	31-6	60	2.89	128	.236	.298	27-0-2	.222	1	64	8		0
1965	Was A	6	4	.600	63	0	0	8	109.2	108	61	18	7	43-4	72	4.02	86	.257	.333	18-0-2	.167	0		-9		0
1966	Phi N	0	0	—	5	0	0	0	2.1	5	2	0	0	1-0	0	7.71	47	.455	.462	0	—	0	83	-5		0
Total	12	39	38	.506	314	48	4-1	11	782.2	709	392	94	36	351-19	406	3.79	101	.243	.330	198-1-9	.192	4	83	-5		0

YEAR	TM LG	W	L	PCT	G	GS	CG-SHO	SV-BS	IP	H	R	HR	HB	BB-IB	SO	ERA	AERA	OAV	OOB	AB-HR-SH	AVG	PB	SUP	APR	DL	PW

RIEDLING, JOHN John Richard B8.29.1975 Ft.Lauderdale FL BR/TR/5-11/190* [CinN94 22/604] d8.30

2000	Cin N	3	1	.750	13	0	0	1-1	15.1	11	7	1	1	8-0	18	2.35	203	.208	.323	2	.000	-0		3		0.5
2001	Cin N	1	1	.500	29	0	0	1-2	33.2	22	9	1	2	14-0	23	2.41	191	.186	.284	1	.000	-0		8	115	0.5
2002	Cin N	2	4	.333	14	0	0	0-0	46.2	39	16	2	3	26-6	30	2.70	158	.234	.345	1	.000	-0		8	46	0.9
2003	Cin N	2	3	.400	55	8	0	1-3	101	107	61	7	3	47-0	65	4.90	85	.270	.347	18-0-1	.222	0	127	-9	15	-0.4
2004	Cin N	5	3	.625	70	0	0	0-7	77.2	90	54	10	4	40-5	46	5.10	84	.286	.370	3	.000	-0		-10		-0.9
2005	Fla N	4	1	.800	29	0	0	0-0	27.2	34	23	3	1	13-2	16	7.16	56	.298	.372	2	.000	-0		-10	47	-1.6
Total	6	17	13	.567	229	8	0	3-13	302	303	170	24	14	148-13	198	4.41	97	.260	.348	27-0-1	.148	-1	127	-10	223	-1.0

RIEGER, ELMER Elmer Jay B2.25.1889 Perris CA D10.21.1959 Los Angeles CA BB/TR/6-0/175 d4.20

| 1910 | StL N | 0 | 2 | .000 | 13 | 1 | 0 | | 21.1 | 26 | 16 | 1 | 1 | 7 | 9 | 5.48 | 54 | .325 | .386 | 3 | .000 | 0 | 125 | -6 | | -0.5 |

RIGBY, BRAD Bradley Kenneth B5.14.1973 Milwaukee WI BR/TR/6-6/203(195-215) [OakA94 2/36] d6.28 Col Georgia Tech [DL 1998 Oak A 10]

1997	Oak A	1	7	.125	14	14	0	0-0	77.2	92	44	14	2	22-2	34	4.87	95	.302	.344	3	.000	-0	81	-2	15	-0.2
1999	Oak A	3	4	.429	29	0	0	0-1	62.1	69	31	5	5	26-7	26	4.33	109	.284	.361	0	—	0		4		0.3
	KC A	1	2	.333	20	0	0	0-1	21.1	33	20	6	2	5-0	10	7.17	71	.351	.388	0	—	0		-5		-0.6
	Year	4	6	.400	49	0	0	0-2	83.2	102	51	11	7	31-7	36	5.06	95	.303	.368	0	—	0		-2		-0.3
2000	KC A	0	0	—	4	0	0	1-0	8.1	19	16	6	1	5-0	3	16.20	32	.422	.490	0	—	0		-10		-0.4
	Mon N	0	0	—	6	0	0	1-0	5.1	8	5	0	1	3-0	2	5.06	93	.348	.444	1	.000	-0		-1		-0.1
Total	3	5	13	.278	73	14	0	2-2	175	221	116	31	11	61-9	75	5.50	86	.311	.369	4	.000	-0	81	-14	25	-1.0

RIGDON, PAUL Paul David B11.2.1975 Jacksonville FL BR/TR/6-5/210(210-242) [CleA96 6/183] d5.21 Col Florida [DL 2002 Mil N 183]

2000	Cle A	1	1	.500	5	4	0	0-0	17.2	21	15	4	0	9-1	15	7.64	66	.300	.380	0	—	0	140	-5	15	-0.4
	Mil N	4	4	.500	12	12	0	0-0	69.2	68	37	14	1	26-4	48	4.52	102	.255	.318	16-1-7	.188	1	106	1		0.3
2001	Mil N	3	5	.375	15	15	0	0-0	79.1	86	52	13	3	46-6	49	5.79	74	.287	.385	20-0-5	.200	0	96	-12	115	-1.0
Total	2	8	10	.444	32	31	0	0-0	166.2	175	104	31	4	81-11	112	5.45	83	.275	.357	36-1-12	.194	2	106	-16	313	-1.1

RIGGAN, JERROD Jerrod Ashley B5.16.1974 Brewster WA BR/TR/6-3/197* [CalA96 8/235] d8.29 Col San Diego St.

2000	NY N	0	0	—	1	0	0	0-0	2	3	2	0	0	0-0	1	0.00	—	.300	.300	0	—	-0		0		0.0
2001	NY N	3	3	.500	35	0	0	0-1	47.2	42	19	5	0	24-7	41	3.40	119	.243	.330	2	.000	-0		4		0.4
2002	Cle A	2	1	.667	29	0	0	0-0	33	53	28	3	0	18-4	22	7.64	58	.373	.433	0	—	-0		-11		-0.8
2003	Cle A	0	0	—	2	0	0	0-0	4	7	4	0	0	1-0	2	9.00	49	.412	.421	0	—	-0		-2		-0.1
Total	4	5	4	.556	67	0	0	0-1	86.2	105	53	8	0	43-11	66	5.19	81	.307	.377	2	.000	-0		-9		-0.5

RIGHETTI, DAVE David Allan B11.28.1958 San Jose CA BL/TL/6-3/198(175-220) [TexA77*1/9] d9.16 C6 Col San Jose (CA) City

1979	NY A	0	1	.000	3	3	0	0-0	17.1	10	7	2	0	10-0	13	3.63	113	.182	.303	0	—	0	73	1		0.1
1981	†NY A	8	4	.667	15	15	2	0-0	105.1	75	25	1	0	38-0	89	2.05	176	.196	.268	0	—	0	96	19		2.2
1982	NY A	11	10	.524	33	27	4	1-0	183	155	88	11	6	108-4	163	3.79	107	.229	.338	0	—	0	94	4		0.3
1983	NY A	14	8	.636	31	31	7-2	0-0	217	194	96	12	2	67-2	169	3.44	115	.237	.296	0	—	0	119	11		1.0
1984	NY A	5	6	.455	64	0	0	31-9	96.1	79	29	5	0	37-7	90	2.34	164	.223	.293	0	—	0	16	15		2.7
1985	NY A	12	7	.632	74	0	0	29-10	107	96	36	5	0	45-3	92	2.78	146	.241	.316	0	—	0	16			3.2
1986	NY A★	8	8	.500	74	0	0	46-10	106.2	88	31	4	2	35-7	83	2.45	169	.226	.291	0	—	0	16			3.2
1987	NY A★	8	6	.571	60	0	0	31-13	95	95	45	9	2	44-4	77	3.51	127	.262	.341	0	—	0	21			4.2
1988	NY A	5	4	.556	60	0	0	25-9	87	86	39	5	1	37-2	70	3.52	113	.257	.332	0	—	0	7			1.4
1989	NY A	2	6	.250	55	0	0	25-9	69	73	32	3	1	26-6	51	3.00	130	.277	.341	0	—	0	5			0.7
1990	NY A	1	1	.500	53	0	0	36-3	53	48	24	8	2	26-2	43	3.57	112	.234	.325	0	—	0	4			0.7
1991	SF N	2	7	.222	61	0	0	24-5	71.2	64	29	4	3	28-6	51	3.39	106	.240	.317	3-0-1	.000	-0	2			0.2
1992	SF N	2	7	.222	54	4	0	3-2	78.1	79	47	4	0	36-5	47	5.06	66	.269	.344	7-0-4	.143	-0	75	-15		-1.8
1993	SF N	1	1	.500	51	0	0	1-2	47.1	58	31	11	1	17-0	31	5.70	69	.305	.365	1	.000	-0		-9		-0.4
1994	Oak A	0	0	—	7	0	0	0-1	7	13	13	3	1	9-0	4	16.71	27	.419	.548	0	—	0		-10		-0.4
	Tor A	0	1	.000	13	0	0	0-1	13.1	9	10	2	0	4-0	10	6.75	72	.188	.322	0	—	0		-2		-0.1
	Year	0	1	.000	20	0	0	0-2	20.1	22	23	5	1	13-0	14	10.18	47	.278	.416	0	—	0		-11		-0.5
1995	Chi A	3	2	.600	10	9	0	0-0	49.1	65	24	6	0	18-0	29	4.20	107	.325	.377	0	—	0	113	2		0.2
Total	16	82	79	.509	718	89	13-2	252-74	1403.2	1287	602	95	21	591-48	1112	3.46	114	.244	.321	11-0-5	.182	-0	103	74	15	14.5

RIGHTNOWAR, RON Ronald Gene B9.5.1964 Toledo OH BR/TR/6-3/190 d5.20 Col Eastern Michigan

| 1995 | Mil A | 2 | 1 | .667 | 34 | 0 | 0 | 1-3 | 36.2 | 35 | 23 | 3 | 5 | 18-3 | 22 | 5.40 | 93 | .271 | .374 | 0 | — | 0 | | -1 | | -0.1 |

RIGNEY, JOHNNY John Dungan B10.28.1914 Oak Park IL D10.21.1984 Lombard IL BR/TR/6-2/190 d4.21 Mil 1942-45 Col St. Thomas (MN)

1937	Chi A	2	5	.286	22	4	0	1	90.2	107	65	10	3	46	38	4.96	93	.290	.373	30-0-2	.167	-0	80	-7		-0.5
1938	Chi A	9	9	.500	38	12	7-1	1	167	164	74	16	2	72	84	3.56	138	.256	.333	55-0-3	.145	-3	66	26		2.1
1939	Chi A	15	8	.652	35	29	11-2	0	218.2	208	103	10	2	84	119	3.70	128	.247	.316	80-0-5	.200	-1	98	23		1.9
1940	Chi A	14	18	.438	39	33	19-2	3	280.2	240	117	22	2	90	141	3.11	142	.230	.292	93-0-12	.215	1*	82	39		4.1
1941	Chi A	13	13	.500	30	29	18-3	0	237	224	116	21	2	92	119	3.84	107	.249	.320	84-0-2	.202	2	92	8		0.9
1942	Chi A	3	3	.500	7	7	6	0	59	40	23	2	1	16	34	3.20	112	.185	.245	19-0-2	.053	-1	92	3		0.2
1946	Chi A	5	5	.500	15	11	3-2	0	82.2	76	37	6	2	35	51	4.03	85	.240	.319	26-0-4	.154	-1	78	-2		-0.3
1947	Chi A	2	3	.400	11	7	2	0	50.2	42	15	3	0	15	21	1.95	187	.228	.286	14-0-1	.000	-2	62	9		0.7
Total	8	63	64	.496	197	132	66-10	5	1186.1	1101	550	90	14	450	605	3.59	121	.244	.314	401-0-31	.177	-6	85	99		9.1

RIJO, JOSE Jose Antonio (Abreu) B5.13.1965 San Cristobal, D.R. BR/TR/6-2/200(160-215) d4.5 [DL 1997 Cin N 181]

1984	NY A	2	8	.200	24	5	0	2-1	62.1	74	40	5	1	33-1	47	4.76	80	.298	.382	0	—	0	61	-8		-1.2
1985	Oak A	6	4	.600	12	9	0	0-1	63.2	57	26	6	1	28-2	65	3.53	110	.239	.322	0	—	0	86	3		0.5
1986	Oak A	9	11	.450	39	26	4	1-2	193.2	172	116	24	4	108-7	176	4.65	84	.237	.336	0	—	0	111	-20		-1.9
1987	Oak A	2	7	.222	21	14	1	0-0	82.1	106	67	10	2	41-1	67	5.90	70	.305	.378	0	—	0	86	-20		-1.8
1988	Cin N	13	8	.619	49	19	0	0-2	162	120	47	7	3	63-7	160	2.39	149	.209	.288	37-1-4	.054	-2	94	21	21	2.5
1989	Cin N	7	6	.538	19	19	1-1	0-0	111	101	39	6	2	48-3	86	2.84	127	.249	.328	38-0-1	.211	1	87	9	46	1.2
1990	†Cin N	14	8	.636	29	29	7-1	0-0	197	151	65	10	2	78-1	152	2.70	147	.212	.291	62-0-11	.161	-0	100	26	22	2.9
1991	Cin N	15	6	.714	30	30	3-1	0-0	204.1	165	69	8	3	55-4	172	2.51	152	.219	.272	67-0-9	.209	1*	121	26	34	2.8
1992	Cin N	15	10	.600	33	33	2	0-0	211	185	67	15	3	44-1	171	2.56	141	.238	.281	72-0-6	.194	1	100	23	15	3.0
1993	Cin N	14	9	.609	36	36	2-1	0-0	257.1	218	76	19	2	62-2	227	2.48	162	.230	.278	82-1-12	.268	7	88	45		4.8
1994	Cin N★	9	6	.600	26	26	2-1	0-0	172.1	177	73	16	4	52-1	171	3.08	136	.265	.321	49-0-10	.204	2	103	18		1.7
1995	Cin N	5	4	.556	14	14	0	0-0	69	76	33	6	0	22-1	62	4.17	100	.285	.326	22-0-2	.136	-0	105	1	90	0.0
2001	Cin N	0	0	—	13	0	0	0-0	17	19	6	2	0	9-2	12	2.12	217	.271	.354	0	—	0		4		0.2
2002	Cin N	5	4	.556	31	9	0	0-0	77	89	48	13	1	21-0	38	5.14	83	.283	.327	16-0-3	.125	-1	115	-7	41	-0.8
Total	14	116	91	.560	376	269	22-4	3-6	1880	1710	772	147	28	663-34	1606	3.24	121	.243	.308	445-2-58	.191	9	99	121	450	13.9

RILEY, GEORGE George Michael B10.6.1956 Philadelphia PA BL/TL/6-4/200* [ChiN74 4/79] d9.15

1979	Chi N	0	1	.000	4	1	0	0-0	13	16	9	1	2	6-1	5	5.54	75	.320	.414	2-0-1	.000	-0	21	-2		-0.7
1980	Chi N	0	4	.000	22	0	0	0-0	36	41	29	2	2	20-5	18	5.75	69	.293	.389	1-0-1	.000	-0		-8		-0.7
1984	SF N	1	0	1.000	5	4	0	0-0	29.1	39	14	1	2	7-0	12	3.99	89	.315	.358	10-0-1	.100	-0	94	-1		-0.1
1986	Mon N	0	0	—	10	0	0	0-0	8.2	7	4	0	1	8-3	5	4.15	90	.212	.372	0	—	0		0		0.0
Total	4	1	5	.167	41	5	0	0-0	87	103	56	4	7	41-9	40	4.97	77	.297	.380	13-0-3	.077	-0	74	-11		-0.9

RILEY, MATT Matthew Paul B8.2.1979 Antioch CA BL/TL/6-1/205(201-220) [BalA97 3/105] d9.9 Col Sacramento (CA) City [DL 2001 Bal A 190]

1999	Bal A	0	3	.000	3	3	0	0-0	11	17	9	4	0	13-0	6	7.36	64	.378	.508	0	—	0	152	-3		-0.4
2003	Bal A	1	0	1.000	2	2	0	0-0	10	7	2	1	0	5-0	8	1.80	256	.194	.293	0	—	0	70	3		0.3
2004	Bal A	3	4	.429	14	13	0	0-0	64	60	43	11	1	44-0	60	5.63	83	.244	.361	2	.000	-0	100	-7	15	-0.7
2005	Tex A	1	0	1.000	7	0	0	0-0	12.2	16	14	2	1	10-0	4	9.95	46	.320	.435	0	—	0		-7		-0.5
Total	4	5	.556	26	18	0	0-0	97.2	100	68	18	2	72-0	78	5.99	78	.265	.384	2	.000	-0	105	-14	205	-1.0

RINCON, ANDY Andrew John B3.5.1959 Monterey Park CA BR/TR/6-3/195* [StLN77 5/110] d9.15

1980	StL N	3	1	.750	4	4	1	0-0	31	23	9	1	0	7-1	22	2.61	144	.215	.263	12-0-1	.250	0	83	4		0.6
1981	StL N	3	1	.750	5	5	1-1	0-0	35.2	27	8	0	2	5-0	13	1.77	205	.214	.256	13-0-2	.231	1	162	7	31	0.9
1982	StL N	2	3	.400	11	11	1	0-0	40	35	22	1	0	25-0	11	4.72	78	.241	.351	10-0-1	.100	-0	92	-4		-0.5
Total	3	8	5	.615	20	20	3-1	0-0	106.2	85	39	2	2	37-2	46	3.12	118	.225	.297	35-0-4	.200	1	113	7	31	1.0

YEAR	TM LG	W	L	PCT	G	GS	CG-SHO	SV-BS	IP	H	R	HR	HB	BB-IB	SO	ERA	AERA	OAV	OOB	AB-HR-SH	AVG	PB	SUP	APR	DL	PW
RINCON, JUAN	Juan Manuel B1.23.1979 Maracaibo, Venez BR/TR/5-11/190(187-215) d6.7																									
2001	Min A	0	0	—	4	0	0	0-0	5.2	7	5	1	0	5-0	4	6.35	74	.318	.444	1	1.000	0		-1		0.0
2002	Min A	0	2	.000	10	3	0	0-1	28.2	44	23	5	0	9-0	21	6.28	71	.352	.393	0	—	0	69	-6		-0.4
2003	†Min A	5	6	.455	58	0	0	0-1	85.2	74	38	5	4	38-7	63	3.68	122	.231	.315	0	—	0	7			0.9
2004	†Min A	11	6	.647	77	0	0	2-4	82	52	27	5	2	32-1	106	2.63	176	.181	.265	1	.000	-0	18			3.2
2005	Min A	6	6	.500	75	0	0	0-5	77	63	26	2	3	30-3	84	2.45	179	.224	.305	0	—	0	15			2.1
Total	5	22	20	.524	224	3	0	2-11	279	240	119	18	9	114-11	278	3.35	134	.232	.311	2	.500	0	69	33		5.8
RINCON, RICARDO	Ricardo (Espinoza) B4.13.1970 Cuitlahuac, Veracruz, Mexico BL/TL/5-10/187* d4.3																									
1997	Pit N	4	8	.333	62	0	0	4-2	60	51	26	5	2	24-6	71	3.45	124	.230	.309	1-0-1	.000	-0		5	15	1.0
1998	Pit N	2	2	.000	60	0	0	14-3	65	50	31	6	0	29-2	64	2.91	147	.208	.292	2	.000	-0		7	14	0.4
1999	†Cle A	2	3	.400	59	0	0	0-2	44.2	41	22	6	1	24-5	30	4.43	115	.248	.346	0	—	0	4	33		0.4
2000	Cle A	2	0	1.000	35	0	0	0-0	20	17	7	1	1	13-1	20	2.70	186	.224	.344	0	—	0	5	97		0.6
2001	†Cle A	2	1	.667	67	0	0	2-2	54	44	18	3	0	21-5	50	2.83	162	.223	.294	0	—	0	11			0.6
2002	Cle A	1	4	.200	46	0	0	0-3	35.2	36	21	3	1	8-1	30	4.79	93	.263	.304	1	.000	-0	-2			-0.2
	†Oak A	0	0	—	25	0	0	1-1	20.1	11	7	1	0	3-0	19	3.10	145	.164	.194	0	—	0	3			0.7
	Year	1	4	.200	71	0	0	1-4	56	47	28	4	1	11-1	49	4.18	107	.230	.268	1	.000	-0	2			1.6
2003	†Oak A	8	4	.667	64	0	0	0-3	55.1	45	21	4	3	32-4	40	3.25	141	.230	.343	0	—	0	4			0.1
2004	Oak A	1	1	.500	67	0	0	0-4	44	45	22	3	1	22-4	40	3.68	126	.256	.340	0	—	0	1			0.2
2005	Oak A	1	1	.500	67	0	0	0-5	37.1	34	19	7	1	20-4	27	4.34	103	.246	.344	0	—	0	1			0.0
Total	9	21	24	.467	552	0	0	21-22	436.1	374	194	39	10	196-32	391	3.53	129	.232	.316	4-0-1	.000	0	47	159		4.5
RINEER, JEFF	Jeffrey Alan B7.3.1955 Lancaster PA BL/TL/6-4/210 [BalA75 S3/43] d9.30 Col Franklin & Marshall																									
1979	Bal A	0	0	—	1	0	0	0-0	1	1	0	0	0	0-0	0	0.00	—	.000	.000	0	—	0		0		0.0
RING, JIMMY	James Joseph B2.15.1895 Brooklyn NY D7.6.1965 Queens NY BR/TR/6-1/170 d4.13																									
1917	Cin N	3	7	.300	24	7	3	2	88	90	47	2	1	35	33	4.40	60	.272	.343	26	.077	-2	173	-13		-1.6
1918	Cin N	9	5	.643	21	18	13-4	0	142.1	130	57	5	3	48	26	2.85	94	.247	.314	50-0-4	.120	-3	161	-2		-0.7
1919	†Cin N	10	9	.526	32	18	12-2	5	183	150	53	2	3	51	61	2.26	123	.232	.291	62-0-2	.097	-5	86	13		1.0
1920	Cin N	17	16	.515	42	33	18-1	1	266.2	268	134	4	5	92	73	3.54	86	.264	.329	96-0-2	.198	-0	113	-16		-1.9
1921	Phi N	10	19	.345	34	30	21	1	246	258	161	8	5	88	88	4.24	100	.274	.340	83-0-5	.145	-4	86	-1		-0.4
1922	Phi N	12	18	.400	40	33	17	1	249.1	292	160	19	3	103	116	4.58	102	.297	.365	88-1-4	.148	-5	90	4		0.2
1923	Phi N	18	16	.529	39	36	23	0	304.1	336	151	13	1	115	112	3.87	112	.283	.347	113-1-9	.106	-9*	86	25		1.8
1924	Phi N	10	12	.455	32	31	16-1	0	215.1	236	123	9	4	108	72	3.97	112	.286	.371	74-0-5	.230	-1	95	5		0.6
1925	Phi N	14	16	.467	38	37	21-1	0	270	325	166	14	1	119	93	4.37	109	.297	.367	101-2-5	.109	-7	86	9		0.3
1926	NY N	11	10	.524	39	23	5	2	183.1	207	114	12	1	74	76	4.57	82	.290	.357	56-0-3	.143	-3	105	-18		-2.2
1927	StL N	0	4	.000	13	3	1	0	33	39	28	3	1	17	13	6.55	60	.300	.385	8	.375	1	93	-9		-0.8
1928	Phi N	4	17	.190	35	25	4	1	176	220	135	14	2	103	70	6.44	66	.320	.410	60-0-1	.183	-2	79	-36		-3.7
Total	12	118	149	.442	389	294	154-9	11	2357.1	2551	1329	105	30	953	833	4.13	95	.281	.351	817-4-40	.147	-40	97	-39		-7.4
RING, ROYCE	Roger Royce B12.21.1980 LaMesa CA BL/TL/6-0/220 d4.29 Col San Diego St.																									
2005	NY N	2	2	.000	15	0	0	0-0	10.2	10	6	0	0	10-1	8	5.06	82	.250	.400	0	—	0		-1		-0.1
RIOS, DANNY	Daniel B11.11.1972 Madrid, Spain BR/TR/6-2/192* d5.30 Col Miami																									
1997	NY A	0	0	—	2	0	0	0-0	2.1	9	5	3	1	2-0	1	19.29	23	.563	.632	0	—	0		-4		-0.2
1998	KC A	0	1	.000	5	0	0	0-0	7.1	9	9	1	1	6-0	6	6.14	79	.300	.421	0	—	0		-3		-0.3
Total	2	0	1	.000	7	0	0	0-0	9.2	18	14	4	2	8-0	7	9.31	51	.391	.491	0	—	0		-7		-0.5
RIPLEY, ALLEN	Allen Stevens B10.18.1952 Norwood MA BR/TR/6-3/190(180-200) d4.10 f-Walt																									
1978	Bos A	2	5	.286	15	11	1	0-0	73	92	49	10	3	22-2	26	5.55	74	.311	.362	0	—	0	83	-10		-0.9
1979	Bos A	3	1	.750	16	3	0	1-1	64.2	77	42	9	3	25-5	34	5.15	86	.295	.362	0	—	0	109	-5		-0.5
1980	SF N	9	10	.474	23	20	2	0-1	112.2	119	59	10	4	36-6	65	4.15	85	.274	.331	40-0-3	.150	-0	94	-8		-1.3
1981	SF N	4	4	.500	19	14	1	0-0	90.2	103	45	5	3	27-2	47	4.07	84	.289	.342	30-0-2	.133	-1	108	-6		-0.6
1982	Chi N	5	7	.417	28	19	0	0-0	122.2	130	61	12	2	38-6	57	4.26	89	.285	.338	38-0-2	.132	-2	77	-4	20	-0.3
Total	5	23	27	.460	101	67	4	1-2	463.2	521	256	46	15	148-21	229	4.52	84	.289	.345	108-0-7	.139	-3	89	-33	20	-3.7
RIPLEY, WALT	Walter Franklin B11.26.1916 Worcester MA D10.7.1990 Attleboro MA BR/TR/6-0/168 d8.17 s-Allen																									
1935	Bos A	0	0	—	2	0	0	0	4	7	4	0	0	3	0	9.00	53	.412	.500	0	—	0		-1		-0.1
RIPPELMEYER, RAY	Raymond Roy B7.9.1933 Valmeyer IL BR/TR/6-3/200 d4.14 C9 Col Southern Illinois																									
1962	Was A	1	2	.333	18	1	0	0	39.1	47	24	7	0	17-2	17	5.49	74	.294	.358	6-1-0	.500	2	0	-5		0.0
RIPPLE, CHARLIE	Charles Dawson B12.1.1921 Bolton NC D5.6.1979 Wilmington NC BL/TL/6-2/210 d9.25 Col Wake Forest																									
1944	Phi N	0	0	—	1	1	0	0	2.1	6	4	0	0	4	2	15.43	23	.500	.625	1	1.000	0	139	-3		-0.1
1945	Phi N	0	1	.000	4	0	0	0	7.2	7	6	0	0	10	5	7.04	54	.241	.436	1	.000	-0		-2		-0.3
1946	Phi N	1	0	1.000	6	0	0	0	3.1	5	4	0	0	6	3	10.80	32	.385	.579	0	—	0		-2		-0.5
Total	3	1	1	.500	11	1	0	0	13.1	18	14	0	0	20	10	9.45	39	.333	.514	2	.500	0	139	-7		-0.9
RISKE, DAVID	David Richard B10.23.1976 Renton WA BR/TR/6-2/175(175-195) [CleA96 56/1560] d8.14 Col Green River (WA) CC [DL 2000 Cle A 17]																									
1999	Cle A	1	1	.500	12	0	0	0-1	14	20	15	2	0	6-0	16	8.36	61	.333	.388	0	—	0	-5	16		-0.6
2001	†Cle A	2	0	1.000	26	0	0	1-0	27.1	20	7	3	2	18-3	29	1.98	232	.206	.339	0	—	0	8			0.6
2002	Cle A	2	2	.500	51	0	0	1-0	51.1	49	32	8	4	35-4	65	5.26	84	.257	.378	0	—	0	-5	28		-0.3
2003	Cle A	2	2	.500	68	0	0	8-5	74.2	52	21	9	3	20-3	82	2.29	193	.196	.260	0	—	0	18			1.2
2004	Cle A	7	3	.700	72	0	0	5-7	77.1	69	32	11	4	41-4	78	3.72	117	.240	.336	0	—	0	7			0.8
2005	Cle A	3	4	.429	58	0	0	1-0	72.2	55	28	11	4	15-0	48	3.10	132	.208	.260	0	—	0	31	61		0.7
Total	6	17	12	.586	287	0	0	16-13	317.1	265	135	44	15	135-14	318	3.55	123	.227	.313	0	—	0	31	61		2.4
RISLEY, BILL	William Charles B5.29.1967 Chicago IL BR/TR/6-2/215(210-230) [CinN87 14/362] d7.8 Col Truman (IL) JC [DL 1999 Tor A 182]																									
1992	Mon N	0	0	1.000	5	1	0	0-0	5	4	1	0	0	1-0	5	1.80	194	.235	.278	2	.000	-0	104	1		0.2
1993	Mon N	0	0	—	2	0	0	0-0	3	2	3	1	1	2-0	2	6.00	70	.200	.385	0	—	0	10			0.0
1994	Sea A	9	6	.600	37	0	0	0-2	52.1	31	20	7	0	19-4	61	3.44	143	.170	.246	0	—	0	12	15		1.8
1995	†Sea A	2	1	.667	45	0	0	1-6	60.1	55	21	7	1	18-1	65	3.13	152	.244	.300	0	—	0	5	67		0.5
1996	Tor A	0	1	.000	25	0	0	0-2	41.2	33	20	7	0	25-0	29	3.89	129	.221	.330	0	—	0	-2	164		-0.3
1997	Tor A	0	1	.000	3	0	0	0-1	4.1	3	4	2	0	2-0	2	8.31	55	.188	.278	0	—	0	-5			-0.5
1998	Tor A	3	4	.429	44	0	0	0-0	54.2	52	37	7	4	34-4	42	5.27	88	.259	.372	0	—	0	104	20	428	1.9
Total	7	15	13	.536	157	1	0	1-11	221.1	180	106	31	6	101-9	203	3.98	120	.225	.313	2	.000	-0	104	20	428	1.9
RITCHIE, JAY	Jay Seay B11.20.1936 Salisbury NC BR/TR/6-4/190(175-190) d8.4																									
1964	Bos A	1	1	.500	21	0	0	0	46	43	21	4	0	14-2	35	2.74	141	.249	.303	9	.111	-1	3			0.1
1965	Bos A	1	2	.333	44	0	0	2	71	83	30	3	1	26-5	55	3.17	118	.302	.361	5	.200	0	4			0.2
1966	Atl N	0	1	.000	22	0	0	4	35.1	32	17	3	0	12-4	33	4.08	89	.241	.303	4-0-1	.500	1	-1			0.4
1967	Atl N	4	6	.400	52	0	0	9	82.1	75	32	6	4	29-11	57	3.17	105	.245	.317	10	.300	1	2			0.4
1968	Cin N	2	3	.400	28	2	0	0	56.2	68	32	7	1	13-2	32	4.61	69	.293	.332	7	.000	-1	55	-8		-0.2
Total	5	8	13	.381	167	2	0	15	291.1	301	132	23	6	94-24	212	3.49	101	.269	.327	35-0-1	.200	0	55	0		0.9
RITCHIE, TODD	Todd Everett B11.7.1971 Portsmouth VA BR/TR/6-3/222(190-222) [MinA90 1/12] d4.3																									
1997	Min A	2	3	.400	42	0	0	0-2	74.2	87	41	11	2	28-0	44	4.58	102	.290	.353	2	.000	-0	1			0.0
1998	Min A	0	0	—	15	0	0	0-0	24	30	17	1	0	9-0	21	5.63	85	.288	.345	0	—	0	-3			-0.2
1999	Pit N	15	9	.625	28	26	2	0-0	172.2	169	79	17	4	54-3	107	3.49	132	.259	.318	53-0-8	.151	-1*	113	20	15	2.3
2000	Pit N	9	8	.529	31	31	1-1	0-0	187	208	111	26	3	51-1	124	4.81	96	.282	.329	60-0-2	.217	2	103	-3	17	0.0
2001	Pit N	11	15	.423	33	33	4-2	0-0	207.1	211	118	23	7	52-7	144	4.47	100	.259	.308	59-0-8	.153	0*	66	-3		-3.0
2002	Chi A	5	15	.250	26	23	0	0-0	133.2	176	104	18	5	52-2	77	6.06	74	.318	.378	4	.250	0*	95	-25	37	-3.6
2003	Mil N	1	2	.333	5	5	0	0-0	28.1	36	17	4	0	10-0	15	5.08	85	.319	.388	9-0-2	.222	0	78	-2	157	-0.2
2004	TB A	0	2	.000	4	2	0	0-0	8	12	9	4	1	6-0	4	9.00	52	.343	.452	0	—	0	50	-4	226	-0.7
Total	8	43	54	.443	184	120	7-3	0-2	835.2	929	496	104	26	262-13	516	4.71	97	.281	.336	187-0-20	.176	2	91	-19	226	-2.1

RITCHIE, WALLY Wallace Reid B7.12.1965 Glendale CA BL/TL/6-2/180* [PhiN85 4/96] d5.1 Col Brigham Young

YEAR	TM	LG	W	L	PCT	G	GS	CG-SHO	SV-BS	IP	H	R	HR	HB	BB-IB	SO	ERA	AERA	OAV	OOB	AB-HR-SH	AVG	PB	SUP	APR	DL	PW
1987	Phi	N	3	2	.600	49	0	0	3-0	62.1	60	27	8	1	29-11	45	3.75	114	.254	.336	4	.250	0		4		0.4
1988	Phi	N	0	0	—	19	0	0	0-0	26	19	14	1	0	17-2	21	3.12	116	.207	.327	0	—	0		0		0.0
1991	Phi	N	1	2	.333	39	0	0	0-3	50.1	44	17	4	2	17-5	26	2.50	148	.234	.299	3	.000	0		0		0.3
1992	Phi	N	2	1	.667	40	0	0	1-1	39	44	17	3	0	17-3	19	3.00	117	.288	.359	1	.000	0		6	22	0.3
Total	4		6	5	.545	147	0	0	4-4	177.2	167	75	16	4	80-21	98	3.14	123	.250	.329	8	.125	0		11	22	0.8

RITTER, REGGIE Reggie Blake B1.23.1960 Malvern AR BL/TR/6-2/195* d5.17 Col Henderson St.

YEAR	TM	LG	W	L	PCT	G	GS	CG-SHO	SV-BS	IP	H	R	HR	HB	BB-IB	SO	ERA	AERA	OAV	OOB	AB-HR-SH	AVG	PB	SUP	APR	DL	PW
1986	Cle	A	0	0	—	5	0	0	0-0	10	14	10	1	1	4-0	6	6.30	66	.341	.396	0	—	0		-3		-0.1
1987	Cle	A	1	1	.500	14	0	0	0-1	26.2	33	21	5	0	16-1	11	6.08	75	.300	.386	0	—	0		-5	34	-0.3
Total	2		1	1	.500	19	0	0	0-1	36.2	47	31	6	1	20-1	17	6.14	73	.311	.389	0	—	0		-5	34	-0.4

RITTER, HANK William Herbert B10.12.1893 McCoysville PA D9.3.1964 Akron OH BR/TR/6-0/180 d8.3 Col Albright

YEAR	TM	LG	W	L	PCT	G	GS	CG-SHO	SV-BS	IP	H	R	HR	HB	BB	SO	ERA	AERA	OAV	OOB	AB-HR-SH	AVG	PB	SUP	APR	DL	PW
1912	Phi	N	0	0	—	3	0	0	0	6	5	5	0	0	5	1	4.50	81	.192	.323	1	.000	0		-1		-0.1
1914	NY	N	1	0	1.000	1	0	0	0	8	4	1	0	0	4	1	1.13	236	.160	.276	3	.000	-0		-1		0.1
1915	NY	N	2	1	.667	22	1	0	2	58.1	66	38	4	5	15	35	4.63	55	.291	.348	16	.125	-1*	87	-14		-0.9
1916	NY	N	1	0	1.000	3	0	0	0	5	3	0	0	1	0	3	0.00	—	.200	.250	0	—	0*		1		0.3
Total	4		4	1	.800	29	1	0	2	77.1	78	44*	4	6	24	43	3.96	67	.266	.334	20	.100	-1	87	-12		-0.6

RITTWAGE, JIM James Michael B10.23.1944 Cleveland OH BR/TR/6-3/190 d9.7

YEAR	TM	LG	W	L	PCT	G	GS	CG-SHO	SV-BS	IP	H	R	HR	HB	BB-IB	SO	ERA	AERA	OAV	OOB	AB-HR-SH	AVG	PB	SUP	APR	DL	PW
1970	Cle	A	1	1	.500	8	3	1	0-0	26	18	12	0	0	21-0	16	4.15	96	.194	.342	8	.375	1	104	0		0.1

RITZ, KEVIN Kevin D B6.8.1965 Eatontown NJ BR/TR/6-4/220(195-226) [DetA85 S4/85] d7.15 Col William Penn [DL 1993 Col N 182, 1999 Col N 182]

YEAR	TM	LG	W	L	PCT	G	GS	CG-SHO	SV-BS	IP	H	R	HR	HB	BB-IB	SO	ERA	AERA	OAV	OOB	AB-HR-SH	AVG	PB	SUP	APR	DL	PW
1989	Det	A	4	6	.400	12	12	1	0-0	74	75	41	2	1	44-5	56	4.38	88	.265	.360	0	—	0	91	-5		-0.6
1990	Det	A	0	4	.000	4	4	0	0-0	7.1	14	12	0	0	14-2	3	11.05	36	.400	.571	0	—	0	69	-7		-1.1
1991	Det	A	0	3	.000	11	5	0	0-1	15.1	17	22	1	2	22-1	9	11.74	36	.288	.482	0	—	0	118	-13		-2.0
1992	Det	A	2	5	.286	23	11	0	0-0	80.1	88	52	4	3	44-4	57	5.60	71	.278	.368	0	—	0	102	-13		-1.0
1994	Col	N	5	6	.455	15	15	0	0-0	73.2	88	49	6	4	35-4	53	5.62	89	.303	.384	20-0-5	.000	-2	87	-4	62	-1.0
1995	†Col	N	11	11	.500	31	28	0	2-0	173.1	171	91	6	16	65-3	120	4.21	128	.259	.329	48-0-11	.188	-1	77	17		2.1
1996	Col	N	17	11	.607	35	35	2	0-0	213	236	135	24	12	105-3	105	5.28	99	.282	.368	65-1-11	.231	-1	109	-3		0.3
1997	Col	N	6	8	.429	18	18	1	0-0	107.1	142	72	16	1	46-3	56	5.87	88	.330	.392	35-0-2	.057	-2	98	-5	80	-0.8
1998	Col	N	0	2	.000	2	2	0	0-0	9	17	11	1	1	2-0	3	11.00	47	.395	.435	3	.333	0	62	-4	170	-0.7
Total	9		45	56	.446	151	130	4	2-1	753.1	848	485	69	30	377-25	462	5.35	92	.287	.371	171-1-29	.158	-3	94	-35	676	-4.5

RIVERA, BEN Bienvenido Santana B1.11.1968 San Pedro de Macoris, D.R. BR/TR/6-6/210(210-250) d4.9

YEAR	TM	LG	W	L	PCT	G	GS	CG-SHO	SV-BS	IP	H	R	HR	HB	BB-IB	SO	ERA	AERA	OAV	OOB	AB-HR-SH	AVG	PB	SUP	APR	DL	PW
1992	Atl	N	0	1	.000	8	0	0	0-0	15.1	21	8	1	2	13-2	11	4.70	78	.339	.462	1	.000	-0		-1		-0.1
	Phi	N	7	3	.700	20	14	4-1	0-0	102	78	32	8	2	32-2	66	2.82	124	.211	.277	32-0-2	.094	-1	151	9	21	0.7
	Year		7	4	.636	28	14	4-1	0-0	117.1	99	40	9	4	45-4	77	3.07	115	.230	.307	33-0-2	.091	-1	150	8		0.7
1993	†Phi	N	13	9	.591	30	28	1-1	0-0	163	175	99	16	6	85-4	123	5.02	79	.273	.361	51-0-13	.098	-2	146	-17		-2.3
1994	Phi	N	3	4	.429	9	7	0	0-0	38	44	29	7	1	22-0	19	6.87	62	.274	.371	9-0-3	.000	-1	91	-9	78	-1.4
Total	3		23	17	.575	67	49	5-2	0-0	318.1	314	168	32	11	152-8	219	4.52	85	.258	.343	93-0-18	.086	-3	140	-18	99	-3.0

RIVERA, LUIS Luis (Gutierrez) B6.21.1978 Chihuahua, Chihuahua, Mexico BR/TR/6-3/163 d4.4 [DL 2001 Bal A 190, 2002 Bal A 183]

YEAR	TM	LG	W	L	PCT	G	GS	CG-SHO	SV-BS	IP	H	R	HR	HB	BB-IB	SO	ERA	AERA	OAV	OOB	AB-HR-SH	AVG	PB	SUP	APR	DL	PW
2000	Atl	N	1	0	1.000	5	0	0	0-0	6.2	4	1	0	0	5-1	5	1.35	334	.190	.346	0	—	0		2		0.3
	Bal	A	0	0	—	1	0	0	0-0	0.2	1	0	0	0	1-0	0	0.00	—	.333	.500	0	—	0		0		0.0
Total	1		1	0	1.000	6	0	0	0-0	7.1	5	1	0	0	6-1	5	1.23	369	.208	.367	0	—	0		2	373	0.3

RIVERA, MARIANO Mariano B11.29.1969 Panama City, Pan BR/TR/6-2/170(168-185) d5.23

YEAR	TM	LG	W	L	PCT	G	GS	CG-SHO	SV-BS	IP	H	R	HR	HB	BB-IB	SO	ERA	AERA	OAV	OOB	AB-HR-SH	AVG	PB	SUP	APR	DL	PW
1995	†NY	A	5	3	.625	19	10	0	0-1	67	71	43	11	2	30-0	51	5.51	84	.266	.342	0	—	0	105	-6		-0.6
1996	†NY	A	8	3	.727	61	10	0	5-3	107.2	73	25	1	2	34-3	130	2.09	237	.189	.258	0	—	0		**35**		3.3
1997	†NY	A★	6	4	.600	66	0	0	43-9	71.2	65	17	5	0	20-6	68	1.88	236	.237	.285	0	—	0		21		4.1
1998	†NY	A	3	0	1.000	54	0	0	36-5	61.1	48	13	3	1	17-1	36	1.91	230	.215	.270	0	—	0		23		4.5
1999	†NY	A★	4	3	.571	66	0	0	**45-4**	69	43	15	2	3	18-3	52	1.83	259	.176	.239	0	—	0		18	18	2.6
2000	†NY	A★	7	4	.636	66	0	0	36-5	75.2	58	26	4	0	25-3	58	2.85	167	.208	.271	0	—	0		23		4.5
2001	†NY	A★	4	6	.400	71	0	0	**50-7**	80.2	61	24	5	1	12-2	83	2.34	190	.209	.242	0	—	0		19		3.8
2002	†NY	A	1	4	.200	45	0	0	28-4	46	35	16	3	2	11-2	41	2.74	158	.203	.259	0	—	0		8	67	1.6
2003	†NY	A	5	2	.714	64	0	0	40-6	70.2	61	15	3	4	10-1	63	1.66	265	.235	.272	0	—	0		22	30	4.3
2004	†NY	A★	4	2	.667	74	0	0	**53-4**	78.2	65	17	3	5	20-3	66	1.94	236	.225	.287	0	—	0		24		4.9
2005	†NY	A★	7	4	.636	71	0	0	43-4	78.1	50	18	2	4	18-0	80	1.38	317	.177	.235	0	—	0		**24**		**4.9**
Total	11		54	35	.607	657	10	0	379-52	806.2	630	229	42	24	215-24	728	2.33	196	.212	.269	0	—	0	105	205	115	36.6

RIVERA, ROBERTO Roberto (Diaz) B1.1.1969 Bayamon, PR BL/TL/6-0/175(175-200) d9.3

YEAR	TM	LG	W	L	PCT	G	GS	CG-SHO	SV-BS	IP	H	R	HR	HB	BB-IB	SO	ERA	AERA	OAV	OOB	AB-HR-SH	AVG	PB	SUP	APR	DL	PW
1995	Chi	N	0	0	—	7	0	0	0-0	5	8	3	1	0	2-0	2	5.40	77	.381	.435	0	—	0		-1		0.0
1999	SD	N	1	2	.333	12	0	0	0-0	7	6	4	1	0	3-0	3	3.86	111	.240	.310	0	—	0		-1		0.0
Total	2		1	2	.333	19	0	0	0-0	12	14	7	2	0	5-0	5	4.50	94	.304	.365	0	—	0		-1		0.0

RIVIERE, TINK Arthur Bernard B8.2.1899 Liberty TX D9.27.1965 Liberty TX BR/TR/5-10/167 d4.15

YEAR	TM	LG	W	L	PCT	G	GS	CG-SHO	SV-BS	IP	H	R	HR	HB	BB	SO	ERA	AERA	OAV	OOB	AB-HR-SH	AVG	PB	SUP	APR	DL	PW
1921	StL	N	1	0	1.000	18	2	0	0	38.1	45	30	2	2	20	15	6.10	60	.280	.366	8	.375	2	79	-10		-0.4
1925	Chi	A	0	0	—	3	0	0	0	4.2	6	7	0	1	7	1	13.50	31	.429	.636	1	.000	-0		-5		-0.2
Total	2		1	0	1.000	21	2	0	0	43	51	37	2	3	27	16	6.91	54	.291	.395	9	.333	2	79	-15		-0.6

RIXEY, EPPA Eppa "Jeptha" B5.3.1891 Culpeper VA D2.28.1963 Cincinnati OH BR/TL/6-5/210 d6.21 Mil 1918-19 HF1963 Col Virginia

YEAR	TM	LG	W	L	PCT	G	GS	CG-SHO	SV-BS	IP	H	R	HR	HB	BB	SO	ERA	AERA	OAV	OOB	AB-HR-SH	AVG	PB	SUP	APR	DL	PW
1912	Phi	N	10	10	.500	23	20	10-3		162	147	57	2	2	54	59	2.50	145	.256	.322	53-0-2	.170	-2	64	21		2.2
1913	Phi	N	9	5	.643	35	19	9-1	2	155.2	148	67	4	6	56	75	3.12	107	.258	.331	47-0-3	.191	-0	106	4		0.3
1914	Phi	N	2	11	.154	24	15	2	0	103	124	73	0	3	45	41	4.37	67	.313	.387	26	.038	-1	105	-15		-1.9
1915	†Phi	N	11	12	.478	29	22	10-2	1	176.2	163	67	2	2	64	88	2.39	115	.250	.319	55-0-5	.164	-0	95	6		0.8
1916	Phi	N	22	10	.688	38	33	20-3	0	287	239	91	2	7	74	134	1.85	143	.229	.284	97-0-4	.155	-2	124	21		2.5
1917	Phi	N	16	21	.432	39	36	23-4	1	281.1	249	102	1	5	67	121	2.27	124	.241	.290	94-0-6	.191	-1	75	13		1.8
1919	Phi	N	6	12	.333	23	18	11-1	0	154	160	88	4	3	50	63	3.97	81	.278	.339	47-0-3	.149	-2	84	-14		-1.6
1920	Phi	N	11	22	.333	41	34	25	2	284.1	288	137	5	4	69	109	3.48	98	.274	.321	101-1-3	.248	1*	68	0		0.3
1921	Cin	N	19	18	.514	40	37	21-2	1	301	324	128	1	5	66	76	2.78	129	.282	.324	101-0-9	.129	-5	91	23		2.2
1922	Cin	N	**25**	13	.658	40	**38**	26-2	0	**313.1**	337	146	13	4	45	80	3.53	113	.275	.303	109-0-11	.193	-1	102	19		1.9
1923	Cin	N	20	15	.571	42	37	23-3	1	309	334	124	3	4	65	97	2.80	138	.280	.320	107-0-9	.159	-5	97	37		3.3
1924	Cin	N	15	14	.517	35	29	15-**4**	1	238.1	219	86	3	2	47	57	2.76	137	.246	.285	84-1-6	.214	1	99	29		3.4
1925	Cin	N	21	11	.656	39	36	22-2	1	287.1	302	109	8	7	47	69	2.88	143	.273	.307	103-0-5	.214	-1	102	43		4.1
1926	Cin	N	14	8	.636	37	29	14-3	0	233	271	104	12	2	58	61	3.40	109	.265	.313	84-0-6	.226	0	128	9		0.7
1927	Cin	N	12	10	.545	34	29	11-1	1	219.2	240	106	3	3	43	42	3.48	109	.287	.325	81-0-3	.247	4	115	6		0.9
1928	Cin	N	19	18	.514	43	**37**	17-3	2	291.1	317	127	4	4	67	58	3.43	115	.288	.330	104-1-3	.173	-1	82	17		1.8
1929	Cin	N	10	13	.435	35	24	11	1	201	235	102	6	3	60	37	4.16	110	.296	.348	65-0-5	.231	-0	76	11		1.0
1930	Cin	N	9	13	.409	32	21	5	0	164	207	103	11	7	47	37	5.10	96	.317	.370	65-0-5	.200	-1	88	-4		-0.5
1931	Cin	N	4	7	.364	22	17	4	0	126.2	143	71	4	0	30	22	3.91	96	.291	.332	40-0-1	.150	-1	90	-5		-0.3
1932	Cin	N	5	5	.500	25	11	6-2	0	111.2	108	50	3	4	16	14	2.66	145	.254	.288	34	.265	1	71	11		1.1
1933	Cin	N	6	3	.667	16	12	5-1	0	94.1	118	48	1	0	12	10	3.15	108	.298	.319	35	.257	2	116	0		0.2
Total	21		266	251	.515	692	554	290-37	14	4494.2	4633	1986	92	76	1082	1350	3.15	116	.272	.318	1522-3-87	.191	-15	94	232		24.2

RIZZO, TODD Todd Michael B5.24.1971 Media PA BR/TL/6-3/220* d4.2 Col Delaware Co. (PA) CC

YEAR	TM	LG	W	L	PCT	G	GS	CG-SHO	SV-BS	IP	H	R	HR	HB	BB-IB	SO	ERA	AERA	OAV	OOB	AB-HR-SH	AVG	PB	SUP	APR	DL	PW
1998	Chi	A	0	0	—	9	0	0	0-0	6.2	12	12	0	0	6-0	3	13.50	34	.387	.474	0	—	0		-7		-0.3
1999	Chi	A	0	2	.000	3	0	0	0-0	1.1	4	2	0	0	3-1	2	6.75	73	.500	.636	0	—	0		-1		-0.1
Total	2		0	2	.000	12	0	0	0-0	8	16	14	0	0	9-1	5	12.38	37	.410	.510	0	—	0		-8		-0.4

ROA, JOE Joseph Rodger B10.11.1971 Southfield MI BR/TR/6-1/195* [AtlN89 18/454] d9.20

YEAR	TM	LG	W	L	PCT	G	GS	CG-SHO	SV-BS	IP	H	R	HR	HB	BB-IB	SO	ERA	AERA	OAV	OOB	AB-HR-SH	AVG	PB	SUP	APR	DL	PW
1995	Cle	A	0	1	.000	1	1	0	0-0	6	9	4	1	0	2-0	0	6.00	79	.360	.407	0	—	0	59	-1		-0.1
1996	Cle	A	0	0	—	1	0	0	0-0	1.2	2	2	0	0	3-0	0	10.80	45	.500	.636	0	—	0		-1		0.0
1997	SF	N	2	5	.286	28	3	0	0-0	65.2	76	40	8	2	20-5	34	5.21	79	.333	.380	5	.133	0	127	-7		-0.6
2002	Phi	N	4	4	.500	14	11	0	0-0	71.1	78	33	11	1	13-2	35	4.04	95	.279	.310	25-0-3	.240	2	107	-1		0.0
2003	Phi	N	0	2	.000	6	3	0	0-0	19.1	28	13	3	1	4-0	16	6.05	66	.341	.379	4	.250	0	55	-4		-0.3
	Col	N	0	0	—	3	0	0	0-0	6.2	7	3	2	0	1-0	4	4.05	121	.269	.269	0	—	0		1		0.0

YEAR	TM LG	W	L	PCT	G	GS	CG-SHO	SV-BS	IP	H	R	HR	HB	BB-IB	SO	ERA	AERA	OAV	OOB	AB-HR-SH	AVG	PB	SUP	APR	DL	PW
	SD N	1	1	.500	18	1	0	0-0	25.1	34	20	5	1	6-0	18	6.75	59	.315	.353	3	.333	0	94	-8		-0.5
	Year	1	3	.250	28	4	0	0-0	51.1	69	36	10	2	10-0	38	6.14	67	.319	.354	7	.286	0	63	-11		-0.8
2004	Min A	2	3	.400	48	0	0	0-1	70	84	38	9	5	24-0	47	4.50	103	.297	.360	0	—	0		1		0.1
Total	6	9	16	.360	120	19	0	0-1	266	330	153	39	10	72-7	154	4.94	85	.308	.355	47-0-3	.213	2	93	-20		-1.4

ROACH, JASON   Jason Glenn   B4.20.1976 Kinston NC   BR/TR/6-4/190   [NYN97 20/600]   d6.14   Col North Carolina-Wilmington

YEAR	TM LG	W	L	PCT	G	GS	CG-SHO	SV-BS	IP	H	R	HR	HB	BB-IB	SO	ERA	AERA	OAV	OOB	AB-HR-SH	AVG	PB	SUP	APR	DL	PW
2003	NY N	0	2	.000	2	2	0	0-0	9	14	12	3	1	4-0	2	12.00	35	.350	.422	2	1.000	1	67	-8		-1.0

ROACH, JOHN   John F.   B11.19.1867 North Bend PA   D4.2.1934 Peoria IL   BR/TL/5-9/175   d5.14   b-Mike

YEAR	TM LG	W	L	PCT	G	GS	CG-SHO	SV-BS	IP	H	R	HR	HB	BB-IB	SO	ERA	AERA	OAV	OOB	AB-HR-SH	AVG	PB	SUP	APR	DL	PW
1887	NY N	0	1	.000	1	1	0		8	18	17	0	1	4	3	11.25	33	.419	.479	4	.250	-0	34	-7		-0.6

ROACH, SKEL   Rudolph Charles (b Rudolph Charles Weichbrodt)   B10.20.1871 Danzig, Germany   D3.9.1958 Oak Park IL   BR/TR/6-2/?   d8.9

YEAR	TM LG	W	L	PCT	G	GS	CG-SHO	SV-BS	IP	H	R	HR	HB	BB-IB	SO	ERA	AERA	OAV	OOB	AB-HR-SH	AVG	PB	SUP	APR	DL	PW
1899	Chi N	1	0	1.000	1	1	1	0-0	9	13	5	0	1	0	0	3.00	125	.333	.350	4	.000	-1	115	1		0.0

ROBBINS, BRUCE   Bruce Duane   B9.10.1959 Portland IN   BL/TL/6-1/190*   [DetA77 14/343]   d7.28

YEAR	TM LG	W	L	PCT	G	GS	CG-SHO	SV-BS	IP	H	R	HR	HB	BB-IB	SO	ERA	AERA	OAV	OOB	AB-HR-SH	AVG	PB	SUP	APR	DL	PW
1979	Det A	3	3	.500	10	8	0	0-0	46	45	21	3	0	21-0	22	3.91	111	.265	.342	0	—	0	120	3		0.3
1980	Det A	4	2	.667	15	6	0	0-0	51.2	60	40	12	0	28-0	23	6.62	62	.287	.368	0	—	0	130	-13		-1.3
Total	2	7	5	.583	25	14	0	0-0	97.2	105	61	15	0	49-0	45	5.34	79	.277	.356	0	—	0	125	-10		-1.0

ROBBINS, JAKE   Philip Jacob   B5.23.1976 Charlotte NC   BR/TR/6-5/190   [NYA94 11/311]   d9.20

YEAR	TM LG	W	L	PCT	G	GS	CG-SHO	SV-BS	IP	H	R	HR	HB	BB-IB	SO	ERA	AERA	OAV	OOB	AB-HR-SH	AVG	PB	SUP	APR	DL	PW
2004	Cle A	0	0	—	2	0	0	0-0	1.2	3	1	0	0	1-0	0	5.40	80	.375	.375		—	0	0	0		0.0

ROBERGE, BERT   Bertrand Roland   B10.3.1954 Lewiston ME   BR/TR/6-4/190*   [HouN76 17/385]   d5.28   Col Maine

YEAR	TM LG	W	L	PCT	G	GS	CG-SHO	SV-BS	IP	H	R	HR	HB	BB-IB	SO	ERA	AERA	OAV	OOB	AB-HR-SH	AVG	PB	SUP	APR	DL	PW
1979	Hou N	3	0	1.000	26	0	0	4-1	32	20	6	0	0	17-0	13	1.69	208	.196	.308	2	.000	-0		7	21	0.8
1980	Hou N	2	0	1.000	14	0	0	0-0	24.1	24	16	2	2	10-1	9	5.92	55	.261	.343	3-0-1	.000	-0		-7		-0.5
1982	Hou N	1	2	.333	22	0	0	3-2	25.2	29	12	0	0	6-3	18	4.21	79	.284	.324	1	.000	-0		-2		-0.3
1984	Chi A	3	3	.500	21	0	0	0-2	40.2	36	18	2	3	15-1	25	3.76	111	.240	.320	0	—	0		2	32	0.3
1985	Mon N	3	3	.500	42	0	0	2-5	68	58	28	5	2	22-5	34	3.44	105	.232	.299	1	.000	-0		0	39	-0.4
1986	Mon N	0	4	.000	21	0	0	1-0	28.2	33	20	2	1	10-3	20	6.28	60	.295	.352	2	.000	-0		-7		-1.0
Total	6	12	12	.500	146	0	0	10-10	219.1	200	100	11	8	80-13	119	3.98	90	.248	.320	9-0-1	.000	-1		-7	92	-0.7

ROBERSON, SID   Sidney Dean   B9.7.1971 Jacksonville FL   BL/TL/5-9/170   [MilA92 29/808]   d5.20   Col North Florida

YEAR	TM LG	W	L	PCT	G	GS	CG-SHO	SV-BS	IP	H	R	HR	HB	BB-IB	SO	ERA	AERA	OAV	OOB	AB-HR-SH	AVG	PB	SUP	APR	DL	PW
1995	Mil A	6	4	.600	26	13	0	0-0	84.1	102	55	16	8	37-3	40	5.76	87	.307	.388	0	—	0	99	-5		-0.6

ROBERTS, DALE   Dale "Mountain Man"   B4.12.1942 Owenton KY   BR/TL/6-4/180   d9.9

YEAR	TM LG	W	L	PCT	G	GS	CG-SHO	SV-BS	IP	H	R	HR	HB	BB-IB	SO	ERA	AERA	OAV	OOB	AB-HR-SH	AVG	PB	SUP	APR	DL	PW
1967	NY A	0	0	—	2	0	0	0-0	2	3	3	2	0	2-1	0	9.00	35	.429	.636	0	—	0		-1		-0.1

ROBERTS, DAVE   David Arthur   B9.11.1944 Gallipolis OH   BL/TL/6-2/197(185-197)   d7.6   [DL 1983 Phi N 39]

YEAR	TM LG	W	L	PCT	G	GS	CG-SHO	SV-BS	IP	H	R	HR	HB	BB-IB	SO	ERA	AERA	OAV	OOB	AB-HR-SH	AVG	PB	SUP	APR	DL	PW
1969	SD N	0	3	.000	22	5	0	1-0	48.2	65	30	6	3	19-0	19	4.81	74	.322	.387	15	.267	1*	69	-7		-0.3
1970	SD N	8	14	.364	43	21	3-2	1-2	181.2	182	80	16	1	43-10	102	3.81	105	.261	.304	59-2-4	.153	-4	73	7		0.9
1971	SD N	14	17	.452	37	34	14-2	0-0	269.2	238	79	9	5	61-9	135	2.10	158	.240	.285	86-0-8	.221	2*	62	36		4.7
1972	Hou N	12	7	.632	35	28	7-3	2-0	192	227	100	24	2	57-3	111	4.50	75	.296	.345	67-2-6	.239	6	144	-22		-1.6
1973	Hou N	17	11	.607	39	36	12-6	0-1	249.1	264	92	15	2	62-8	119	2.85	128	.271	.314	85-0-12	.129	-3*	102	20		1.8
1974	Hou N	10	12	.455	34	30	8-2	1-0	204	216	83	6	3	65-2	72	3.40	103	.276	.332	73-1-2	.219	5*	100	4		1.1
1975	Hou N	8	14	.364	32	27	7	1-1	198.1	182	98	16	2	73-4	101	4.27	80	.244	.310	63-0-10	.143	-0	90	-19		-1.8
1976	Det A	16	17	.485	36	36	18-4	0-0	252	254	122	16	4	63-4	79	4.00	93	.264	.309	0	—	0	82	4		-0.4
1977	Det A	4	10	.286	22	22	5	0-0	129.1	143	88	20	2	41-2	46	5.15	84	.274	.328	0	—	0	91	-13		-1.3
	Chi N	1	1	.500	17	6	1	1-0	53	55	22	1	1	12-8	23	3.23	137	.275	.315	17	.059	-2	74	6		0.2
1978	Chi N	6	8	.429	35	20	2-1	1-0	142.1	159	87	17	3	56-15	54	5.25	77	.288	.353	52-2-3	.327	6*	109	-15	14	-0.7
1979	SF N	0	2	.000	26	1	0	3-5	42	42	15	6	1	18-3	23	2.57	136	.262	.339	5	.000	-1	177	4		0.2
	†Pit N	5	2	.714	21	3	0	1-0	38.2	47	18	1	1	12-4	15	3.26	120	.318	.366	5	.000	-1	136	2		0.3
	Year	5	4	.556	47	4	0	4-5	80.2	89	33	4	2	30-7	38	2.90	127	.289	.352	10	.000	-1	150	5		0.5
1980	Pit N	0	1	.000	2	0	0	0-0	2.1	2	1	0	0	1-0	1	3.86	96	.250	.333	0	—	0	0	0		0.0
	Sea A	2	3	.400	37	4	0	3-1	80.1	86	46	7	1	27-7	47	4.37	95	.270	.324	0	—	0	70	-3		-0.2
1981	NY N	0	3	.000	7	1	0	0-0	15.1	26	18	5	0	5-0	10	9.39	38	.366	.408	4	.250	0	50	-9		-1.6
Total	13	103	125	.452	445	277	77-20	15-10	2099	2188	979	155	31	615-80	957	3.78	97	.270	.321	531-7-45	.194	15	93	-13	53	1.3

ROBERTS, GRANT   Grant William   B9.13.1977 ElCajon CA   BR/TR/6-3/205*   [NYN95 11/301]   d7.27

YEAR	TM LG	W	L	PCT	G	GS	CG-SHO	SV-BS	IP	H	R	HR	HB	BB-IB	SO	ERA	AERA	OAV	OOB	AB-HR-SH	AVG	PB	SUP	APR	DL	PW
2000	NY N	0	0	—	4	1	0	0-0	7	11	10	0	0	4-1	6	11.57	38	.344	.395	0-0-1	.000	0	189	-6		-0.3
2001	NY N	1	0	1.000	16	0	0	0-1	26	24	11	2	0	8-1	29	3.81	106	.240	.294	3	.000	-0		1		0.0
2002	NY N	3	1	.750	34	0	0	0-0	45	43	12	3	1	16-7	31	2.20	180	.253	.317	1	1.000	0	9	80		0.8
2003	NY N	0	3	.000	18	0	0	1-0	19	19	9	0	1	3-1	10	3.79	111	.257	.295	0	—	0	1	130		0.1
2004	NY N	0	0	—	4	0	0	0-0	4.2	9	9	2	0	6-1	1	17.36	25	.429	.536	0	—	0	-6	132		-0.3
Total	5	4	4	.500	76	1	0	1-1	101.2	106	51	7	2	37-11	77	4.25	96	.267	.328	4-0-1	.250	0	189	-1	342	0.1

ROBERTS, JIM   James Newson "Big Jim"   B10.13.1895 Artesia MS   D6.24.1984 Columbus MS   BR/TR/6-3/205   d7.27   Col Mississippi St.

YEAR	TM LG	W	L	PCT	G	GS	CG-SHO	SV-BS	IP	H	R	HR	HB	BB-IB	SO	ERA	AERA	OAV	OOB	AB-HR-SH	AVG	PB	SUP	APR	DL	PW
1924	Bro N	0	3	.000	11	5	0	0	25.1	41	28	1	2	8	10	7.46	50	.360	.411	7	.143	-0	72	-12		-1.2
1925	Bro N	0	0	—	1	0	0	0	1	1	1	0	0	0	0	0.00		.500	.500	0	—	0	0	0		0.0
Total	2	0	3	.000	12	5	0	0	26.1	42	29	1	2	8	10	7.18	52	.362	.413	7	.143	-0	72	-12		-1.2

ROBERTS, RAY   Raymond   B8.25.1895 Cruger MS   D1.30.1962 Cruger MS   BL/TR/5-11/180   d9.12   Col Mississippi St.

YEAR	TM LG	W	L	PCT	G	GS	CG-SHO	SV-BS	IP	H	R	HR	HB	BB-IB	SO	ERA	AERA	OAV	OOB	AB-HR-SH	AVG	PB	SUP	APR	DL	PW
1919	Phi A	1	2	.333	21	14	0	0	3	21	14	0	3	3	2	2.71	44	.368	.400	4	.250	0	114	-6		-0.7

ROBERTS, ROBIN   Robin Evan   B9.30.1926 Springfield IL   BB/TR/6-0/190*   d6.18   HF1976   Col Michigan St.

YEAR	TM LG	W	L	PCT	G	GS	CG-SHO	SV-BS	IP	H	R	HR	HB	BB-IB	SO	ERA	AERA	OAV	OOB	AB-HR-SH	AVG	PB	SUP	APR	DL	PW
1948	Phi N	7	9	.438	20	20	9	0	146.2	148	63	10	4	61	84	3.19	124	.278	.356	44-1-3	.250	4*	70	12		1.6
1949	Phi N	15	15	.500	43	31	11-3	4	226.2	229	101	15	5	75	95	3.69	107	.273	.357	67-0-5	.075	-3	99	7		0.4
1950	†Phi N	20	11	.645	40	39	21-5	1	304.1	282	112	29	2	77	146	3.02	134	.248	.297	102-0-7	.118	-4	99	**38**		3.2
1951	Phi N★	21	15	.583	44	39	22-6	2	315	284	115	20	3	64	127	3.03	127	.237	**.278**	87-0-14	.172	5	99	30		3.8
1952	Phi N☆	28	7	.800	39	37	30-3	2	330	292	104	22	5	45	148	2.59	141	.234	.263	112-0-13	.125	2	122	**43**		4.6
1953	Phi N★	23	16	.590	44	41	33-5	2	346.2	324	119	30	2	61	198	2.75	153	.242	.276	123-1-9	.179	-4	96	59		6.4
1954	Phi N★	23	15	.605	45	38	29-4	2	336.2	289	116	35	5	56	185	2.97	136	.231	**.266**	122-0-4	.123	-3	107	44		4.3
1955	Phi N★	23	14	.622	41	38	26-1	3	305	292	137	41	2	53-3	160	3.28	121	.246	.279	107-2-5	.252	14*	104	18		3.4
1956	Phi N☆	19	18	.514	43	37	22-1	2	297.1	328	155	46	2	40-3	157	4.45	84	.282	.305	100-1-3	.200	4	103	-18		-1.7
1957	Phi N	10	22	.313	39	32	14-2	0	249.2	246	122	40	1	43-16	128	4.07	93	.252	.283	80-0-4	.162	0	79	-6		-0.6
1958	Phi N	17	14	.548	35	34	21-1	0	269.2	270	112	30	2	51-5	130	3.24	122	.259	.282	99-0-3	.202	4*	95	21		2.4
1959	Phi N	15	17	.469	35	35	19-2	0	257.1	267	137	34	5	35-4	137	4.27	96	.263	.290	89-0-2	.191	3	77	-4		-0.1
1960	Phi N	12	16	.429	35	33	13-2	1	237.1	256	113	31	2	34-7	122	4.02	97	.275	.300	33-0-1	.091	-2	89	-23	30	-0.3
1961	Phi N	1	10	.091	26	18	2	0	117	154	85	19	2	23-6	54	5.85	70	.326	.354	33-0-1	.152	-1	81	-1		-0.3
1962	Bal A	10	9	.526	27	25	6	0	191.1	176	63	17	4	41-7	102	2.78	133	.244	.288	52-0-7	.192	2	84	23		2.4
1963	Bal A	14	13	.519	35	35	9-2	0	251.1	230	100	35	3	40-8	124	3.33	104	.240	.272	70-0-8	.203	2	104	6		0.8
1964	Bal A	13	7	.650	31	31	8-4	0	204	203	69	18	3	52-6	109	2.91	123	.261	.308	68-0-4	.132	0	97	17		1.3
1965	Bal A	5	7	.417	20	15	5-1	0	114.2	110	51	17	1	20-3	63	3.38	103	.252	.282	35-0-3	.171	1	94	1		0.2
	Hou N	5	2	.714	10	10	3-2	0	76	76	22	1	0	10-1	34	1.89	177	.216	.243	21-0-3	.238	3	104	11		1.4
1966	Hou N	3	5	.375	13	12	1-1	1	63.2	79	31	7	1	10-0	26	3.82	90	.307	.331	16-0-3	.063	-0	88	-3		-0.4
	Chi N	2	3	.400	11	9	1	0	48.1	62	35	8	0	11-0	28	6.14	60	.313	.349	10-0-3	.200	1	88	-12		-1.0
	Year	5	8	.385	24	21	2-1	1	112	141	66	15	1	21-0	54	4.82	73	.310	.339	26-0-6	.115	-0	88	-17		-1.4
Total	19	286	245	.539	676	609	305-45	25	4688.2	4582	1962	505	54	902-69	2357	3.41	113	.255	.292	1525-5-108	.167	34	95	263	30	30.3

ROBERTS, WILLIS   Willis Augusto (De Leon)   B6.19.1975 San Cristobal, D.R.   BR/TR/6-3/175(175-240)   d7.2

YEAR	TM LG	W	L	PCT	G	GS	CG-SHO	SV-BS	IP	H	R	HR	HB	BB-IB	SO	ERA	AERA	OAV	OOB	AB-HR-SH	AVG	PB	SUP	APR	DL	PW
1999	Det A	0	1	.000	1	0	0	0-0	1.1	3	4	0	1	0-0	0	13.50	37	.500	.500	0	—	0		-2		-0.1
2001	Bal A	9	10	.474	46	18	1	6-4	132	142	75	15	11	55-1	95	4.91	88	.274	.343	4-0-1	.250	0	97	-7		0.9
2002	Bal A	5	4	.556	66	0	0	1-2	75	79	34	5	4	32-3	51	3.36	129	.270	.345	0	—	0		7		0.7
2003	Bal A	3	1	.750	26	0	0	0-0	39.1	41	26	7	7	16-2	26	5.72	80	.273	.370	0	—	0	-4	92		-0.4
2004	Pit N	0	0	—	9	0	0	0-0	12	12	7	0	2	9-0	7	5.25	83	.279	.411	1	.000	-0		-1		-0.1
Total	5	17	15	.531	148	18	1	7-6	259.2	277	146	27	25	112-6	179	4.64	94	.274	.358	5-0-1	.200	0	97	-7	92	-0.7

YEAR	TM LG	W	L	PCT	G	GS	CG-SHO	SV-BS	IP	H	R	HR	HB	BB-IB	SO	ERA	AERA	OAV	OOB	AB-HR-SH	AVG	PB	SUP	APR	DL	PW

ROBERTSON, CHARLIE Charles Culbertson B1.31.1896 Dexter TX D8.23.1984 Fort Worth TX BL/TR/6-0/175 Col Austin

1919	Chi A	0	1	.000	1	1	0	0	2	5	2	0	0	1	1	9.00	35	.556	.556	0	—	0	25	-1		-0.2
1922	Chi A	14	15	.483	37	34	21-3	0	272	294	124	9	4	89	83	3.64	112	.286	.345	87-0-8	.184	-2	95	13		0.8
1923	Chi A	13	18	.419	38	34	18-1	0	255	262	126	8	5	104	91	3.81	104	.272	.346	85-0-8	.247	0	88	5		0.4
1924	Chi A	4	10	.286	17	14	5	0	97.1	108	65	2	0	54	29	4.99	83	.293	.383	33-0-3	.182	-1	70	-10		-1.4
1925	Chi A	8	12	.400	24	23	6-2	0	137	181	96	8	2	47	27	5.26	79	.327	.381	45-0-2	.222	0	91	-19		-2.3
1926	StL A	1	2	.333	8	7	1	0	28	38	27	2	2	21	11	8.36	51	.333	.445	10	.300	1	109	-10		-0.8
1927	Bos N	7	17	.292	28	21	6	0	154.1	188	90	2	4	46	49	4.72	79	.308	.360	50-0-3	.240	1	70	-16		-2.1
1928	Bos N	2	5	.286	13	7	3	1	59.1	73	40	5	0	16	17	5.31	74	.308	.352	17-0-2	.000	-1	114	-9		-1.0
Total	8	49	80	.380	166	141	60-6	1	1005	1149	570	38	17	377	310	4.44	90	.296	.361	327-0-26	.208	-2	88	-47		-6.6

ROBERTSON, JERIOME Jeriome Paul B3.30.1977 San Jose CA BL/TL/6-1/190* d9.2

2002	Hou N	0	2	.000	11	1	0	0-0	9.2	13	8	4	0	5-3	6	6.52	66	.394	.439	0	—	0	43	-2		-0.4
2003	Hou N	15	9	.625	32	31	0	0-0	160.2	180	98	23	6	64-8	99	5.10	87	.287	.356	52-0-5	.154	-0*	116	-11		-1.4
2004	Cle A	1	1	.500	8	0	0	0-1	14	22	22	5	2	9-2	6	12.21	36	.349	.440	0	—	0		-14		-1.5
Total	3	16	12	.571	51	32	0	0-1	184.1	215	128	32	8	78-13	111	5.71	77	.297	.368	52-0-5	.154	-0	114	-27		-3.3

ROBERTSON, JERRY Jerry Lee B10.13.1943 Winchester KS D3.24.1996 Burlington KS BB/TR/6-2/200* [StLN65 14/532] d4.8 Col Washburn Topeka

1969	Mon N	5	16	.238	38	27	3	1-0	179.2	186	97	17	4	81-11	133	3.96	93	.272	.348	56-0-2	.089	-3	67	-3		-0.8
1970	Det A	0	0	—	11	0	0	0-0	14.2	19	8	1	0	5-1	11	3.68	102	.306	.353	0	—	0	0	0		0.0
Total	2	5	16	.238	49	27	3	1-0	194.1	205	95	18	4	86-12	144	3.94	94	.274	.348	56-0-2	.089	-3	67	-3		-0.8

ROBERTSON, NATE Nathan Daniel B9.3.1977 Wichita KS BR/TL/6-2/215* [FlaN99 5/146] d9.7 Col Wichita St.

2002	Fla N	0	1	.000	6	1	0	0-0	8.1	15	11	3	2	4-1	3	11.88	33	.375	.457	2	.000	-0	24	-7		-0.8
2003	Det A	1	2	.333	8	8	0	0-0	44.2	55	27	6	0	23-2	33	5.44	81	.306	.384	0	—	0	94	-4		-0.2
2004	Det A	12	10	.545	34	32	1	0-0	196.2	210	116	30	4	66-1	155	4.90	91	.274	.333	3	.000	-0	124	-10		-1.0
2005	Det A	7	16	.304	32	32	2	0-0	196.2	202	113	28	7	65-2	122	4.48	94	.266	.325	3-0-1	.000	-0	84	-9		-0.9
Total	4	20	29	.408	80	73	3	0-0	446.1	482	267	67	13	158-6	313	4.90	89	.276	.338	8-0-1	.000	-1	103	-30		-2.9

ROBERTSON, DICK Preston B1891 Washington DC D10.2.1944 New Orleans LA BR/TR/5-9/160 d9.16

1913	Cin N	0	1	.000	1	0	0	0	10	13	9	0	0	9	1	7.20	45	.342	.468	3	.000	-0	0	-4		-0.4
1918	Bro N	3	6	.333	13	9	7-1	0	87	87	34	0	0	28	18	2.59	108	.272	.330	30	.300	2*	60	1		0.3
1919	Was A	0	1	.000	7	4	0	0	27.2	25	11	1	0	9	7	2.28	141	.253	.315	7	.000	-1	61	2		0.0
Total	3	3	8	.273	22	14	8-1	0	124.2	125	54	1	0	46	26	2.89	101	.274	.340	40	.225	-0	56	-1		-0.1

ROBERTSON, RICH Richard Paul B10.14.1944 Albany CA BR/TR/6-2/210(195-215) [SFN65 5/92] d9.10 Col Santa Clara

1966	SF N	0	0	—	1	0	0	0	2.1	3	3	0	0	2-0	2	7.71	48	.300	.417	0	—	0		-1		-0.1
1967	SF N	0	0	—	1	0	0	0	2	3	1	0	0	0-0	1	4.50	73	.333	.333	0	—	0		0		0.0
1968	SF N	2	0	1.000	3	1	0	0	9	9	6	0	0	3-0	8	6.00	49	.265	.324	2-0-1	.500	0	324	-3		-0.5
1969	SF N	1	3	.250	17	7	1-1	0	44.1	53	32	4	1	21-1	20	5.48	64	.298	.368	10-0-1	.000	-1	130	-10		-0.9
1970	SF N	8	9	.471	41	26	6	1-1	183.2	199	113	22	1	96-3	131	4.85	82	.277	.359	59-2-7	.102	-0	109	-19		-1.6
1971	SF N	2	2	.500	23	6	1	1-0	61	66	40	5	2	31-3	32	4.57	75	.267	.351	15	.067	-1	113	-9		-0.8
Total	6	13	14	.481	86	40	8-1	2-1	302.1	333	195	31	4	153-7	184	4.94	76	.278	.358	86-2-9	.093	-2	118	-42		-3.9

ROBERTSON, RICH Richard Wayne B9.15.1968 Nacogdoches TX BL/TL/6-4/175* [PitN90 9/241] d4.30 Col Texas A&M-Commerce

1993	Pit N	0	1	.000	9	0	0	0-0	9	15	6	0	0	4-0	5	6.00	68	.385	.442	0	—	0		-2		-0.2
1994	Pit N	0	0	—	8	0	0	0-0	15.2	20	12	2	0	10-4	8	6.89	63	.313	.400	4	.250	0		-4		-0.2
1995	Min A	2	0	1.000	25	4	1	0-1	51.2	48	28	4	0	31-4	38	3.83	126	.253	.354	0	—	0	97	4		0.1
1996	Min A	7	17	.292	36	31	5-3	0-1	186.1	197	113	22	9	116-2	114	5.12	100	.273	.378	0	—	0	79	0		0.1
1997	Min A	8	12	.400	31	26	0	0-0	147	169	105	19	6	70-3	69	5.69	82	.292	.370	5	.200	0	79	-19		-2.2
1998	Ana A	0	0	—	5	0	0	0-0	5.2	11	11	3	0	2-0	3	15.88	30	.393	.419	0	—	0		-7		-0.3
Total	6	17	30	.362	114	61	6-3	0-2	415.1	460	275	50	15	233-13	237	5.40	90	.284	.375	9	.222	0	81	-28		-2.7

ROBINSON, DEWEY Dewey Everett B4.28.1955 Evanston IL BR/TR/6-0/180(180-195) [ChiA77 19/467] d4.6 C2 Col Southern Illinois

1979	Chi A	0	1	.000	11	0	0	0-0	14.1	11	12	1	0	9-2	5	6.28	68	.212	.328	0	—	0		-3		-0.2
1980	Chi A	1	1	.500	15	0	0	0-1	35	26	13	2	0	16-0	28	3.09	132	.215	.302	0	—	0		4		0.2
1981	Chi A	1	0	1.000	4	0	0	0-0	4	5	2	1	0	3-1	2	4.50	80	.357	.471	0	—	0		0		-0.1
Total	3	2	2	.500	30	0	0	0-1	53.1	42	27	4	0	28-3	35	4.05	101	.225	.323	0	—	0		1		-0.1

ROBINSON, DON Don Allen B6.8.1957 Ashland KY BR/TR/6-4/231(225-240) [PitN75 3/68] d4.10

1978	Pit N	14	6	.700	35	32	9-1	1-0	228.1	203	98	20	3	57-4	135	3.47	112	.236	.283	85-0-4	.235	2	111	8		0.9
1979	†Pit N	8	8	.500	29	25	4	0-0	160.2	171	74	12	4	52-5	96	3.87	101	.277	.335	49-0-4	.204	-1	114	3		0.2
1980	Pit N	7	10	.412	29	24	3-2	1-0	160.1	157	74	14	5	45-5	103	3.99	93	.257	.312	57-1-0	.333	6*	90	3	22	0.3
1981	Pit N	0	3	.000	16	2	0	2-1	38.1	47	27	4	0	23-4	17	5.87	62	.313	.400	12	.250	1*	122	-8	59	-0.6
1982	Pit N	15	13	.536	38	30	6	0-0	227	213	123	26	3	103-11	165	4.28	88	.250	.331	85-2-2	.282	8*	114	-14		-0.8
1983	Pit N	2	2	.500	9	6	0	0-1	36.1	43	21	5	0	21-3	28	4.46	84	.297	.386	13-1-0	.154	1*	110	-3	102	-0.3
1984	Pit N	5	6	.455	51	1	0	10-4	122	99	45	6	0	49-4	110	3.02	120	.226	.298	31-1-0	.290	4*	49	9		1.3
1985	Pit N	5	11	.313	44	6	0	3-5	95.1	95	49	6	2	42-11	65	3.87	94	.255	.334	21-1-0	.238	2	73	-4		-0.4
1986	Pit N	3	4	.429	50	0	0	14-11	69.1	61	27	5	2	27-3	53	3.38	115	.237	.310	6	.667	2	5	47		0.8
1987	Pit N	6	6	.500	42	0	0	12-7	65.1	66	29	6	0	22-3	53	3.86	108	.267	.326	7	.143	0*	5	3		0.6
	†SF N	5	1	.833	25	0	0	7-0	42.2	39	13	1	0	18-3	26	2.74	140	.239	.311	11-1-0	.273	2	6			1.2
	Year	11	7	.611	67	0	0	19-7	108	105	42	7	0	40-6	79	3.42	118	.256	.320	18-1-0	.222	2	9			1.8
1988	SF N	10	5	.667	51	19	3-2	6-3	176.2	152	63	11	3	49-12	122	2.45	133	.231	.284	52-1-2	.173	3*	103	13		1.4
1989	†SF N	12	11	.522	34	32	5-1	0-0	197	184	80	22	2	37-6	96	3.43	99	.248	.283	81-3-0	.185	4*	113	1		0.3
1990	SF N	10	7	.588	26	25	4	0-0	157.2	173	84	18	1	41-8	78	4.57	80	.280	.324	63-2-3	.143	1*	103	-15	44	-1.5
1991	SF N	5	9	.357	34	16	0	1-0	121.1	123	64	12	1	50-7	78	4.38	82	.265	.334	40	.150	0*	98	-11	16	-1.2
1992	Cal A	1	0	1.000	3	3	0	0-0	16.1	19	4	1	0	3-0	9	2.20	182	.292	.324	0	—	0	76	3	22	0.2
	Phi N	1	4	.200	8	4	0	0-0	43.2	49	32	6	1	4-0	17	6.18	57	.290	.300	18	.389	3*	116	-13	15	-1.0
Total	15	109	106	.507	524	229	34-6	57-22	1958.1	1894	907	175	27	643-89	1251	3.79	97	.255	.314	631-13-15	.231	40	105	-20	327	1.4

ROBINSON, HUMBERTO Humberto Valentino B6.25.1930 Colon, Pan BR/TR/6-1/155* d4.20

1955	Mil N	3	1	.750	13	2	1	2	38	31	13	1	4	25-2	19	3.08	122	.235	.368	13	.077	-1	119	4		0.3
1956	Mil N	0	0	—	1	0	0	0	2	1	0	0	0	2-0	0	0.00	—	.167	.375	0	—	0		1		0.1
1958	Mil N	2	4	.333	19	0	0	1	41.2	30	15	4	2	13-2	26	3.02	116	.203	.276	6	.167	1		3		0.5
1959	Cle A	1	0	1.000	5	0	0	0	8.2	9	4	0	0	4-1	6	4.15	89	.281	.361	0	—	0		0		0.0
	Phi N	2	4	.333	31	4	1	1	73	79	36	6	0	24-6	32	3.33	123	.251	.308	13-0-1	.231	1	60	4		0.4
1960	Phi N	0	4	.000	33	1	0	0	49.2	48	24	6	0	22-5	31	3.44	113	.255	.333	6	.167	-0	23	1		0.1
Total	5	8	13	.381	102	7	2	4	213	189	92	17	6	90-16	114	3.25	119	.241	.322	38-0-1	.158	0	73	13		1.4

ROBINSON, JEFF Jeffrey Daniel B12.13.1960 Santa Ana CA BR/TR/6-4/200* [SFN83 2/44] d4.7 Col Cal St.-Fullerton

1984	SF N	7	15	.318	34	33	1-1	0-0	171.2	195	99	12	7	52-4	102	4.56	78	.288	.341	61-0-1	.115	-2	87	-20		-2.5
1985	SF N	0	0	—	8	0	0	0-0	12.1	16	11	2	0	10-1	8	5.11	68	.333	.441	0	—	0		-4		-0.2
1986	SF N	6	3	.667	64	1	0	8-1	104.1	92	46	8	1	32-7	90	3.36	105	.234	.291	15-0-1	.067	-1*	177	1		0.0
1987	SF N	6	8	.429	63	0	0	10-6	96.2	69	34	10	1	48-10	82	2.79	138	.207	.306	18	.111	-1	12	6		1.7
	Pit N	2	1	.667	18	0	0	4-1	26.2	20	9	1	0	6-1	19	3.04	137	.215	.263	4-1-1	.250	1	4			0.6
	Year	8	9	.471	81	0	0	14-7	123.1	89	43	11	1	54-11	101	2.85	138	.209	.297	22-1-1	.136	0	16			2.3
1988	Pit N	11	5	.688	75	0	0	9-4	124.2	113	44	6	3	39-5	87	3.03	114	.244	.303	16-0-5	.188	0	7			1.0
1989	Pit N	7	13	.350	50	19	0	4-4	141.1	161	92	14	1	59-11	95	4.58	74	.283	.347	35-1-5	.229	2	119	-24		-3.0
1990	NY A	3	6	.333	54	0	0	0-2	88.2	82	35	8	1	34-3	43	3.45	116	.248	.319	0	—	0	74	6		0.7
1991	Cal A	0	3	.000	39	0	0	3-2	57	56	34	9	2	29-4	57	5.37	77	.259	.349	0	—	0		-6		-0.4
1992	Chi N	3	4	.571	19	5	0	1-3	78	79	29	5	2	20-4	46	3.00	121	.264	.354	12-0-2	.000	0	70	5		0.4
Total	9	46	57	.447	454	62	2-1	39-23	901.1	880	433	75	18	349-53	629	3.79	96	.258	.327	161-2-15	.137	0	94	-19		-1.7

ROBINSON, JEFF Jeffrey Mark B12.14.1961 Ventura CA BR/TR/6-6/240(210-240) [DetA83 3/69] d4.12 Col Azusa Pacific

1987	†Det A	9	6	.600	29	21	2-1	0-0	127.1	132	86	16	7	54-3	98	5.37	79	.262	.340	0	—	0	122	-17		-1.7
1988	Det A	13	6	.684	24	23	6-2	0-0	172	121	61	19	3	72-5	114	2.98	129	.197	.282	0	—	0	105	18	40	1.9
1989	Det A	4	5	.444	16	16	1-1	0-0	78	76	44	17	1	46-1	40	4.73	81	.259	.358	0	—	0	139	-8	61	-0.9

YEAR	TM LG	W	L	PCT	G	GS	CG-SHO	SV-BS	IP	H	R	HR	HB	BB-IB	SO	ERA	AERA	OAV	OOB	AB-HR-SH	AVG	PB	SUP	APR	DL	PW
1990	Det A	10	9	.526	27	27	1-1	0-0	145	141	101	23	6	88-9	76	5.96	67	.255	.361	0	—	0	123	-30		-3.4
1991	Bal A	4	9	.308	21	19	0	0-0	104.1	119	62	12	6	51-2	65	5.18	77	.289	.375	0	—	0	82	-13		-1.5
1992	Tex A	4	4	.500	16	4	0	0-2	45.2	50	30	6	0	21-1	18	5.72	67	.281	.351	0	—	0	119	-9		-1.3
	Pit N	3	1	.750	8	7	0	0-0	36.1	33	18	2	1	15-0	14	4.46	78	.244	.322	11-0-2	.091	-1	164	-3		-1.0
Total	6	47	40	.540	141	117	10-5	0-2	708.2	672	405	88	24	347-21	425	4.79	82	.250	.339	11-0-2	.091	-1	117	-62	101	-7.3

ROBINSON, JACK John Edward B2.20.1921 Orange NJ D3.2.2000 Ormond Beach FL BR/TR/6-0/175 d5.4

YEAR	TM LG	W	L	PCT	G	GS	CG-SHO	SV-BS	IP	H	R	HR	HB	BB-IB	SO	ERA	AERA	OAV	OOB	AB-HR-SH	AVG	PB	SUP	APR	DL	PW
1949	Bos A	0	0	—	3	0	0	0	4	4	1	0	1	1	1	2.25	194	.267	.353	0	—	0	1			0.1

ROBINSON, HANK John Henry "Rube" (b John Henry Roberson) B8.16.1889 Floyd AR D7.3.1965 N.Little Rock AR BR/TL/5-11.5/160 d9.2

YEAR	TM LG	W	L	PCT	G	GS	CG-SHO	SV-BS	IP	H	R	HR	HB	BB-IB	SO	ERA	AERA	OAV	OOB	AB-HR-SH	AVG	PB	SUP	APR	DL	PW
1911	Pit N	0	1	.000	5	0	0	0	13	13	7	0	1	5	8	2.77	124	.283	.365	3	.000	-0	0			0.0
1912	Pit N	12	7	.632	33	16	11	2	175	146	54	3	10	30	79	2.26	144	.237	.284	59	.254	3	91	21		2.4
1913	Pit N	14	9	.609	43	22	8-1	0	196.1	184	72	1	7	41	50	2.38	127	.255	.301	61-0-3	.180	-1	96	13		1.2
1914	StL N	7	8	.467	26	16	6-1	0	126	128	61	1	4	32	30	3.00	93	.274	.325	35-0-3	.171	-0	98	-3		-0.3
1915	StL N	7	8	.467	32	15	6-1	0	143	128	54	1	7	35	57	2.45	114	.245	.301	47	.106	-2	123	4		0.3
1918	NY N	2	4	.333	11	3	1	0	48	47	21	0	3	16	14	3.00	94	.269	.340	13	.000	-2	71	-1		-0.4
Total	6	42	37	.532	150	72	32-3	2	701.1	646	269	6	32	159	238	2.53	118	.253	.305	218-0-6	.170	-3	99	34		3.2

ROBINSON, KEN Kenneth Neal B11.3.1969 Barberton OH D2.28.1999 Tucson AZ BR/TR/5-7/170* [TorA91 10/276] d7.20 Col Florida St. [DL 1998 Ari N 181]

YEAR	TM LG	W	L	PCT	G	GS	CG-SHO	SV-BS	IP	H	R	HR	HB	BB-IB	SO	ERA	AERA	OAV	OOB	AB-HR-SH	AVG	PB	SUP	APR	DL	PW
1995	Tor A	1	2	.333	21	0	0	0-0	39	25	19	7	2	22-1	31	3.69	129	.179	.295	0	—	0	3			0.2
1996	KC A	1	0	1.000	5	0	0	0-0	6	9	4	0	0	3-1	5	6.00	84	.346	.400	0	—	0	-1			-0.1
1997	Tor A	0	0	—	3	0	0	0-1	3.1	1	1	1	0	1-0	4	2.70	170	.100	.182	0	—	0	1			0.1
Total	3	2	2	.500	29	0	0	0-1	48.1	35	26	8	2	26-2	40	3.91	122	.199	.304	0	—	0	3		181	0.2

ROBINSON, RON Ronald Dean B3.24.1962 Exeter CA BR/TR/6-4/235(200-235) [CinN80 1/19] d8.14

YEAR	TM LG	W	L	PCT	G	GS	CG-SHO	SV-BS	IP	H	R	HR	HB	BB-IB	SO	ERA	AERA	OAV	OOB	AB-HR-SH	AVG	PB	SUP	APR	DL	PW
1984	Cin N	1	2	.333	12	5	1	0-0	39.2	35	18	3	0	13-3	24	2.72	139	.232	.291	8-0-1	.000	-1	107	2		0.1
1985	Cin N	7	7	.500	33	12	0	1-0	108.1	107	53	11	1	32-3	76	3.99	95	.259	.311	22-0-5	.091	-1	74	-2		-0.4
1986	Cin N	10	3	.769	70	0	0	14-6	116.2	110	44	10	2	43-8	117	3.24	119	.253	.321	14	.071	-1	9			1.1
1987	Cin N	7	5	.583	48	18	0	4-2	154	148	71	14	4	43-8	99	3.68	115	.256	.305	36-0-5	.194	0	131	8		0.5
1988	Cin N	3	7	.300	17	16	0	0-0	78.2	88	47	5	2	26-4	38	4.12	87	.285	.339	25-0-1	.200	1	81	-8	67	-0.9
1989	Cin N	5	3	.625	15	15	0	0-0	83.1	80	36	8	2	28-2	36	3.35	108	.252	.316	28-0-2	.214	1	126	2	105	0.3
1990	Cin N	2	5	.500	6	5	0	0-0	31.1	36	18	2	0	14-0	14	4.88	81	.295	.368	11-0-1	.091	-1	137	-3		0.0
	Mil A	12	5	.706	22	22	7-2	0-0	148.1	158	60	5	6	37-1	57	2.91	133	.275	.322	0	—	0	131	14		1.5
1991	Mil A	0	1	.000	1	1	0	0-0	4.1	6	3	0	1	3-1	1	6.23	64	.353	.476	0	—	0	69	-1	178	-0.2
1992	Mil A	1	4	.200	8	8	0	0-0	35.1	51	26	3	2	14-0	12	5.86	66	.331	.392	0	—	0	97	-8	114	-1.0
Total	9	48	39	.552	232	102	8-2	19-8	800	819	376	61	17	253-30	473	3.63	107	.267	.323	144-0-15	.153	-2	111	13	464	0.6

ROBINSON, YANK William H. B9.19.1859 Philadelphia PA D8.25.1894 St.Louis MO BR/TR/5-6.5/170 d8.24 ▲

YEAR	TM LG	W	L	PCT	G	GS	CG-SHO	SV-BS	IP	H	R	HR	HB	BB-IB	SO	ERA	AERA	OAV	OOB	AB-HR-SH	AVG	PB	SUP	APR	DL	PW
1882	Det N	0	0	—	1	0	0	0	2	0	0	0		1	0	0.00	—	.000	.125	39	.179	-0*	1			0.0
1884	Bal U	3	3	.500	11	3	3	0	75	96	61	1		18	61	3.48	77	.292	.329	415-3	.267	-0*	101	-7		-0.6
1886	†StL AA	0	1	.000	1	1	1	0	9	10	11	0	0	7	1	3.00	115	.286	.405	481-3	.274	0*	121	-1		-0.1
1887	†StL AA	0	0	—	1	0	0	1	3	3	2	0	1	3	0	3.00	151	.333	.538	430-1	.305	0*	0			-0.1
Total	4	3	4	.429	14	4	4	1	89	109	74	1	1	29	62	3.34	85	.287	.339	1365-7	.279	0	104	-7		-0.7

ROBITAILLE, CHICK Joseph Anthony B3.2.1879 Whitehall NY D7.30.1947 Waterford NY BR/TR/5-8/150 d9.2

YEAR	TM LG	W	L	PCT	G	GS	CG-SHO	SV-BS	IP	H	R	HR	HB	BB-IB	SO	ERA	AERA	OAV	OOB	AB-HR-SH	AVG	PB	SUP	APR	DL	PW
1904	Pit N	4	3	.571	9	8	8	0	66	52	22	1	1	13	34	1.91	144	.208	.250	21	.095	-2	47	5		0.2
1905	Pit N	8	5	.615	17	12	10	0	120.1	126	54	1	3	28	32	2.92	103	.276	.322	45-0-1	.133	-2	80	0		-0.3
Total	2	12	8	.600	26	20	18	0	186.1	178	76	2	4	41	66	2.56	114	.252	.297	66-0-1	.121	-4	67	5		-0.1

ROCHE, ARMANDO Armando (Baez) B12.7.1926 Havana, Cuba D6.26.1997 Chicago IL BR/TR/6-0/190 d5.10

YEAR	TM LG	W	L	PCT	G	GS	CG-SHO	SV-BS	IP	H	R	HR	HB	BB-IB	SO	ERA	AERA	OAV	OOB	AB-HR-SH	AVG	PB	SUP	APR	DL	PW
1945	Was A	0	0	—	2	0	0	0	6	10	4	0	0	2	0	6.00	52	.400	.444	1	.000	-0	-2			-0.1

ROCHFORD, MIKE Michael Joseph B3.14.1963 Methuen MA BL/TL/6-4/205* [BosA82*1/17] d9.3 Col Santa Fe (FL) CC

YEAR	TM LG	W	L	PCT	G	GS	CG-SHO	SV-BS	IP	H	R	HR	HB	BB-IB	SO	ERA	AERA	OAV	OOB	AB-HR-SH	AVG	PB	SUP	APR	DL	PW
1988	Bos A	0	0	—	2	0	0	0-0	2.1	4	0	0	0	1-0	1	0.00	—	.364	.417	0	—	0	1			0.0
1989	Bos A	0	0	—	4	0	0	0-0	4	4	7	1	0	4-1	1	6.75	61	.267	.400	0	—	0	-3			-0.1
1990	Bos A	0	1	.000	2	1	0	0-0	4	10	10	1	0	4-0	0	18.00	23	.526	.583	0	—	0	156	-6		-1.1
Total	3	0	1	.000	8	1	0	0-0	10.1	18	17	2	0	9-1	2	9.58	43	.400	.482	0	—	0	156	-8		-1.1

ROCKER, JOHN John Loy B10.17.1974 Statesboro GA BR/TL/6-4/225(210-225) [AtlN93 18/516] d5.5

YEAR	TM LG	W	L	PCT	G	GS	CG-SHO	SV-BS	IP	H	R	HR	HB	BB-IB	SO	ERA	AERA	OAV	OOB	AB-HR-SH	AVG	PB	SUP	APR	DL	PW
1998	†Atl N	1	3	.250	47	0	0	2-2	38	22	10	4	3	22-4	42	2.13	195	.172	.307	0	—	0	9			0.5
1999	†Atl N	4	5	.444	74	0	0	38-7	72.1	47	24	5	1	37-4	104	2.49	180	.180	.284	0	—	0	15			3.4
2000	†Atl N	1	1	.333	59	0	0	24-3	53	42	25	5	2	48-4	77	2.89	156	.210	.368	0	—	0	7			0.9
2001	Atl N	2	2	.500	30	0	0	19-4	32	25	13	2	2	16-1	36	3.09	139	.216	.319	0	—	0	-4			-0.1
	†Cle A	3	7	.300	38	0	0	4-3	34.2	33	21	5	3	25-3	43	5.45	84	.250	.379	0	—	0	-3			-0.4
2002	Tex A	2	3	.400	30	0	0	1-3	24.1	29	19	5	0	13-1	30	6.66	72	.299	.372	0	—	0	-5	88	-0.8
2003	TB A	0	0	—	2	0	0	0-0	1	2	1	0	1	3-0	0	9.00	51	.500	.750	0	—	0	0	88	0.0
Total	6	13	22	.371	280	0	0	88-22	255.1	200	115	23	12	164-17	332	3.42	130	.213	.336	0	—	0	27	88	4.2

RODAS, RICH Richard Martin B11.7.1959 Roseville CA BL/TL/6-1/180* d9.6 Col Sacramento (CA) City

YEAR	TM LG	W	L	PCT	G	GS	CG-SHO	SV-BS	IP	H	R	HR	HB	BB-IB	SO	ERA	AERA	OAV	OOB	AB-HR-SH	AVG	PB	SUP	APR	DL	PW
1983	LA N	0	0	—	7	0	0	0-0	4.2	4	1	0	0	3-1	5	1.93	187	.222	.333	0	—	0	1			0.1
1984	LA N	0	0	—	3	0	0	0-0	5	5	3	2	0	1-0	1	5.40	66	.250	.286	1	.000	-0	-1		103	0.1
Total	2	0	0	—	10	0	0	0-0	9.2	9	4	2	0	4-1	6	3.72	96	.237	.310	1	.000	0	0		103	0.1

RODNEY, FERNANDO Fernando B3.18.1977 Samana, D.R. BR/TR/5-11/170(170-210) d5.4 [DL 2004 Det A 183]

YEAR	TM LG	W	L	PCT	G	GS	CG-SHO	SV-BS	IP	H	R	HR	HB	BB-IB	SO	ERA	AERA	OAV	OOB	AB-HR-SH	AVG	PB	SUP	APR	DL	PW
2002	Det A	1	3	.250	20	0	0	0-4	18	25	15	2	0	10-2	10	6.00	73	.329	.402	0	—	0	-4			-0.1
2003	Det A	1	3	.250	27	0	0	3-3	29.2	35	20	2	1	17-1	33	6.07	72	.294	.379	0	—	0	-5			-0.1
2005	Det A	2	3	.400	39	0	0	9-6	44	39	14	5	2	17-3	42	2.86	148	.238	.317	0	—	0	7	67	1.1
Total	3	4	9	.308	86	0	0	12-13	91.2	99	49	9	3	44-6	85	4.52	95	.276	.356	0	—	0	-2	250	-0.1

RODRIGUEZ, EDDY Eddy B8.8.1981 San Pedro de Macoris, D.R. BR/TR/6-1/195 d5.31

YEAR	TM LG	W	L	PCT	G	GS	CG-SHO	SV-BS	IP	H	R	HR	HB	BB-IB	SO	ERA	AERA	OAV	OOB	AB-HR-SH	AVG	PB	SUP	APR	DL	PW
2004	Bal A	1	0	1.000	29	0	0	0-0	43.1	36	23	5	5	30-5	37	4.78	98	.231	.370	0	.000	-0	0			0.1

RODRIGUEZ, EDUARDO Eduardo (Reyes) B3.6.1952 Barceloneta, PR BR/TR/6-0/185* d6.20

YEAR	TM LG	W	L	PCT	G	GS	CG-SHO	SV-BS	IP	H	R	HR	HB	BB-IB	SO	ERA	AERA	OAV	OOB	AB-HR-SH	AVG	PB	SUP	APR	DL	PW
1973	Mil A	9	7	.563	30	6	2	5-5	76.1	71	33	6	2	47-7	49	3.30	115	.247	.354	1	1.000	1	156	4		0.1
1974	Mil A	7	4	.636	43	6	0	4-4	111.2	97	49	7	5	51-5	58	3.63	100	.241	.330	0	—	0	73	0		0.1
1975	Mil A	7	0	1.000	43	1	0	7-0	87.2	77	37	9	5	44-9	65	3.49	111	.235	.332	0	—	0	160	4		0.4
1976	Mil A	5	13	.278	45	12	3	8-3	136	124	68	10	3	65-6	77	3.64	97	.249	.334	0	—	0	67	-5		-0.5
1977	Mil A	5	6	.455	42	5	1-1	4-2	142.2	126	70	15	3	56-6	104	4.35	94	.238	.310	0	—	0	79	-1		-0.2
1978	Mil A	5	5	.500	32	8	0	2-2	105.1	107	49	9	2	26-3	51	3.93	97	.262	.306	0	—	0	121	-1		-0.1
1979	KC A	4	1	.800	29	1	1	2-0	74.1	79	42	9	3	34-4	26	4.84	88	.276	.355	0	—	0	297	-3	22	-0.2
Total	7	42	36	.538	264	39	7-1	32-16	734	681	348	65	23	323-40	430	3.89	99	.248	.329	1	1.000	1	101	-2	22	0.0

RODRIGUEZ, FELIX Felix Antonio B9.9.1972 Monte Cristi, D.R. BR/TR/6-1/190(180-200) d5.13

YEAR	TM LG	W	L	PCT	G	GS	CG-SHO	SV-BS	IP	H	R	HR	HB	BB-IB	SO	ERA	AERA	OAV	OOB	AB-HR-SH	AVG	PB	SUP	APR	DL	PW
1995	LA N	1	1	.500	11	0	0	0-1	10.2	11	3	2	0	5-0	5	2.53	153	.275	.356	0	—	0	2			0.0
1997	Cin N	0	0	—	26	0	0	0-0	46	48	23	6	2	28-2	34	4.30	99	.271	.387	3-0-1	.000	-0	151	0		-0.1
1998	Ari N	0	2	.000	43	0	0	5-3	44	44	31	5	1	29-1	36	6.14	70	.259	.365	0	—	0	-8	39	-0.5
1999	SF N	2	3	.400	47	0	0	0-1	66.1	67	32	6	2	29-2	55	3.80	112	.262	.338	6-1-1	.333	2	3		0.0
2000	†SF N	4	2	.667	76	0	0	3-5	81.2	65	29	4	3	42-2	95	2.64	164	.220	.320	4	.000	-0	15		0.5
2001	SF N	9	1	.900	80	0	0	0-3	80.1	53	16	5	4	27-2	91	1.68	243	.188	.259	0	—	0	23		2.9
2002	†SF N	8	6	.571	71	0	0	0-6	69	53	33	5	4	29-1	58	4.17	95	.212	.301	1	1.000	1	-1		0.0
2003	†SF N	8	2	.800	68	0	0	2-1	61	59	21	9	4	29-2	46	3.10	137	.259	.351	1	1.000	1	9	15	1.0
2004	SF N	3	5	.375	50	0	0	0-3	44.2	43	17	7	1	19-2	34	3.43	127	.250	.337	1	1.000	-0	3		0.0
	Phi N	2	3	.400	23	0	0	1-0	21	18	7	1	1	10-2	28	3.00	148	.231	.326	0	—	0	6		0.0
	Year	5	8	.385	76	0	0	1-3	65.2	61	25	8	5	29-4	62	3.29	133	.244	.333	1	1.000	-0	9		1.0
2005	NY A	0	0	—	34	0	0	0-0	32.1	33	18	2	2	20-0	18	5.01	87	.264	.374	0	—	0	-2	73	-0.1
Total	10	37	25	.597	532	1	0	11-23	557	494	231	45	28	267-16	497	3.51	121	.238	.331	16-1-2	.250	2	151	49	127	6.3

YEAR	TM LG	W	L	PCT	G	GS	CG-SHO	SV-BS	IP	H	R	HR	HB	BB-IB	SO	ERA	AERA	OAV	OOB	AB-HR-SH	AVG	PB	SUP	APR	DL	PW
RODRIGUEZ, FREDDY				Fernando Pedro (Borrego)		B4.29.1924 Havana, Cuba	BR/TR/6-0/185*	d4.18																		
1958	Chi N	0	0	—	7	0	0	2	7.1	8	6	2	1	5-0	5	7.36	53	.267	.389	1	.000	-0		-2		-0.2
1959	Phi N	0	0	—	1	0	0	0	2	4	3	1	1	0-0	1	13.50	30	.400	.455	0	—	0		-2		-0.1
Total	2	0	0	—	8	0	0	2	9.1	12	9	3	2	5-0	6	8.68	46	.300	.404	1	.000	-0		-4		-0.3
RODRIGUEZ, FRANK				Francisco	B12.11.1972 Brooklyn NY	BR/TR/6-0/200(195-210)	[BosA90 2/41]	d4.26																		
1995	Bos A	0	2	.000	9	2	0	0-0	15.1	21	19	3	0	10-1	14	10.57	46	.323	.413	0	—	0	201	-9		-0.9
	Min A	5	6	.455	16	16	0	0-0	90.1	93	64	8	5	47-0	45	5.38	90	.269	.361	0	—	0	98	-8		-0.7
	Year	5	8	.385	25	18	0	0-0	105.2	114	83	11	5	57-1	59	6.13	79	.277	.369	0	—	0	109	-18		-1.6
1996	Min A	13	14	.481	38	33	3	2-0	206.2	218	129	27	5	78-1	110	5.05	102	.272	.337	0	—	0	98	-1		-0.1
1997	Min A	3	6	.333	43	15	0	0-2	142.1	147	82	12	4	60-9	65	4.62	101	.271	.346	1	.000	-0	104	-1		0.0
1998	Min A	4	6	.400	20	11	0	0-0	70	88	58	6	3	30-0	62	6.56	73	.303	.369	0	—	0	93	-15		-1.7
1999	Sea A	2	4	.333	28	5	0	3-1	73.1	94	47	11	4	30-2	47	5.65	85	.314	.383	3	.333	0*	93	-6		-0.4
2000	Sea A	2	1	.667	23	0	0	0-0	47.1	60	33	8	0	22-2	19	6.27	77	.317	.383	1	.000	-0		-7	61	-0.3
2001	Cin N	0	0	—	7	0	0	0-0	8.2	16	12	1	0	5-2	9	11.42	40	.400	.457	1	.000	-0		-6		-0.3
Total	7	29	39	.426	184	82	3	5-3	654	737	444	76	21	282-17	371	5.53	88	.286	.358	6	.167	-0	101	-53	61	-4.4
RODRIGUEZ, FRANCISCO				Francisco Jose	B1.7.1982 Caracas, Venez	BR/TR/6-0/165(165-180)	d9.18																		
2002	†Ana A				5	0	0		5.2	3	0	0	1	2-1	13	0.00	—	.167	.286	0	—	0		3		0.1
2003	Ana A	8	3	.727	59	0	0	2-4	86	50	30	12	2	35-5	95	3.03	144	.172	.262	0	—	0		14		1.6
2004	†Ana A★	4	1	.800	69	0	0	12-7	84	51	21	2	1	33-1	123	1.82	245	.171	.255	0	—	0		24		1.9
2005	†LA A	2	5	.286	66	0	0	45-5	67.1	45	20	7	0	32-3	91	2.67	161	.184	.277	0	—	0		13	17	2.6
Total	4	14	9	.609	199	0	0	59-16	243	149	71	21	4	102-10	322	2.44	180	.175	.265	0	—	0		54	17	6.2
RODRIGUEZ, JOSE				Jose Ilich (Jose)	B12.18.1974 Cayey, PR	BL/TL/6-1/205*	[StLN97 24/734]	d5.18	Col Florida International																
2000	StL N	0	0	—	6	0	0	0-0	4	2	2	0	1	3-0	2	0.00	—	.143	.316	1	.000	-0		1		0.0
2002	StL N	0	0	—	2	0	0	0-0	0.1	4	2	0	0	2-0	0	54.00	7	.800	.857	0	—	0		-2		-0.1
	Min A	0	1	.000	4	0	0	0-0	3.2	8	6	0	0	4-1	1	14.73	30	.421	.522	0	—	0		-4	78	-0.7
Total	2	0	1	.000	12	0	0	0-0	8	14	10	0	1	9-1	3	9.00	50	.368	.490	1	.000	-0		-5	78	-0.8
RODRIGUEZ, NERIO				Nerio	B3.4.1971 San Pedro de Macoris, D.R.	BR/TR/6-0/185(165-205)	d8.16																		
1996	Bal A	0	1	.000	8	1	0	0-0	16.2	18	11	2	1	7-0	12	4.32	115	.265	.338	0	—	0	19	0		0.0
1997	Bal A	2	1	.667	6	2	0	0-1	22	21	15	2	1	8-0	11	4.91	90	.250	.309	0	—	0	52	-2		-0.2
1998	Bal A	1	3	.250	6	4	0	0-0	19	25	17	0	0	9-0	8	8.05	57	.321	.382	0	—	0	87	-7	35	-1.2
	Tor A	1	0	1.000	7	0	0	0-0	8.1	10	9	1	1	8-0	3	9.72	48	.286	.432	0	—	0		-4		-0.4
	Year	2	3	.400	13	4	0	0-0	27.1	35	26	1	1	17-0	11	8.56	54	.310	.398	0	—	0	86	-11		-1.6
1999	Tor A	0	1	.000	2	0	0	0-0	2	3	2	2	0	2-0	2	13.50	36	.250	.400	0	—	0		-2		-0.3
2002	Cle A	0	0	—	1	0	0	0-0	0.1	0	0	0	0	0-0	0	0.00	—	.000	.000	0	—	0		0		0.0
	StL N	0	0	—	2	0	0	0-0	4.1	4	3	1	0	1-0	2	4.15	97	.222	.263	1	.000	-0		0		0.0
Total	5	4	6	.400	32	7	0	0-1	72.2	80	58	8	3	35-0	38	6.32	73	.274	.350	1	.000	-0	66	-15	35	-2.1
RODRIGUEZ, RICK				Ricardo	B9.21.1960 Oakland CA	BR/TR/6-3/190*	[OakA81 2/41]	d9.17	Col California-Riverside																
1986	Oak A	1	2	.333	3	3	0	0-0	16.1	17	12	4	0	7-0	2	6.61	59	.262	.333	0	—	0	70	-5		-0.7
1987	Oak A	1	0	1.000	15	0	0	0-0	24.1	32	8	1	1	15-1	9	2.96	141	.337	.432	0	—	0	4		0.2
1988	Cle A	1	2	.333	10	5	0	0-0	33	43	28	4	1	17-1	9	7.09	58	.323	.401	0	—	0	97	-10		-0.8
1990	SF N	0	0	—	3	0	0	0-0	3.1	5	3	0	0	2-0	2	8.10	45	.357	.438	0	—	0		-2		-0.1
Total	4	3	4	.429	31	8	0	0-0	77	97	51	9	2	41-2	22	5.73	71	.316	.399	0	—	0	86	-13		-1.4
RODRIGUEZ, RICARDO				Ricardo Antonio	B5.21.1978 Guayubin, D.R.	BL/TR/6-3/195*	d8.21	[DL 2003 Tex A 73]																	
2002	Cle A	2	2	.500	7	7	0	0-0	41.1	40	27	5	8	18-3	24	5.66	78	.255	.361	0	—	0	105	-5		-0.4
2003	Cle A	3	9	.250	15	15	0	0-0	81.2	89	57	16	3	28-1	41	5.73	77	.275	.336	3	.000	-0	72	-11	33	-1.3
2004	Tex A	3	1	.750	5	4	1-1	0-0	26.2	28	10	1	0	12-0	15	2.03	243	.262	.336	2	.000	-0	108	7	73	0.9
2005	Tex A	2	3	.400	12	10	0	0-0	57	67	39	11	1	17-0	24	5.53	83	.289	.339	3	.333	-0	113	-6	55	-0.4
Total	4	10	15	.400	39	36	1-1	0-0	206.2	224	133	33	12	75-4	104	5.18	88	.273	.342	8	.125	-0	94	-15	234	-1.2
RODRIGUEZ, RICH				Richard Anthony	B3.1.1963 Downey CA	BL/TL/6-0/200(194-205)	[NYN84 9/211]	d6.30	Col Tennessee																
1990	SD N	1	1	.500	32	0	0	1-0	47.2	52	17	2	1	16-4	22	2.83	136	.287	.347	3	.000	-0		5		0.3
1991	SD N	3	1	.750	64	1	0	0-2	80	66	31	8	0	44-8	40	3.26	117	.234	.335	5	.000	-1*	24	5		0.2
1992	SD N	6	3	.667	61	1	0	0-1	91	77	28	4	0	29-4	64	2.37	151	.229	.289	6-0-2	.000	-0	0	11		1.1
1993	SD N	2	3	.400	34	0	0	2-3	30	34	15	2	1	9-3	22	3.30	125	.281	.336	0	—	-0		2		0.3
	Fla N	0	1	.000	36	0	0	1-1	46	39	23	8	1	24-5	21	4.11	106	.229	.328	2	.000	0		1		0.1
	Year	2	4	.333	70	0	0	3-4	76	73	38	10	2	33-8	43	3.79	113	.251	.331	2	.000	-0		3		0.4
1994	StL N	3	5	.375	56	0	0	0-3	60.1	62	30	6	1	26-4	43	4.03	105	.270	.345	1	.000	-0		1		0.0
1995	StL N	0	0	—	1	0	0	0-0	1.2	0	0	0	0	0-0	0	0.00	—	.000	.000	0	—	0		1		0.0
1997	†SF N	4	3	.571	71	0	0	1-4	65.1	65	24	7	1	21-4	32	3.17	130	.264	.325	3	.333	1		8	158	0.9
1998	SF N	4	0	1.000	68	0	0	2-4	65.2	69	28	7	0	20-5	44	3.70	109	.272	.322	6-0-1	.167	-0		3		0.2
1999	SF N	3	0	1.000	62	0	0	0-2	56.2	60	33	8	1	28-5	44	5.24	82	.274	.356	1-0-1	1.000	1		-5		-0.1
2000	NY N	0	1	.000	32	0	0	0-0	37	59	40	7	3	15-0	18	7.78	56	.364	.416	1	.000	-0		-17		-0.8
2001	Cle A	2	2	.500	53	0	0	0-2	39	41	24	2	2	17-3	31	4.15	110	.270	.349	0	—	0		0		0.0
2002	Tex A	3	2	.600	36	0	0	1-2	16.2	14	10	1	1	11-1	12	5.40	89	.237	.366	0	—	0		-1	98	-0.1
2003	Ana A	0	0	—	3	0	0	0-0	3.2	4	1	0	0	2-1	2	2.45	178	.308	.333	0	—	0		1		0.0
Total	13	31	22	.585	609	2	0	8-24	640.2	642	304	62	12	261-46	396	3.81	107	.264	.337	28-0-4	.107	-0	11	15	256	2.1
RODRIGUEZ, ROSARIO				Rosario Isabel (Echavarria)	B7.8.1969 Los Mochis, Sinaloa, Mexico	BR/TL/6-0/185*	d9.1																		
1989	Cin N	1	1	.500	7	0	0	0-1	4.1	3	2	0	0	3-1	5	4.15	87	.188	.316	0	—	0		0		0.0
1990	Cin N	0	0	—	9	0	0	0-0	10.1	15	7	3	1	2-0	8	6.10	65	.357	.391	0	—	0		-2		-0.1
1991	†Pit N	1	1	.500	18	0	0	6-0	15.1	14	7	1	1	8-0	10	4.11	88	.246	.348	1	.000	-0		0		-0.1
Total	3	2	2	.500	34	0	0	6-1	30	32	16	4	2	13-1	18	4.80	77	.278	.359	1	.000	-0		-2		-0.2
RODRIGUEZ, WANDY				Wandy E.	B1.18.1979 Santiago Rodriguez, D.R.	BB/TL/5-11/160	d5.23																		
2005	†Hou N	10	10	.500	25	22	0	0-0	128.2	135	82	21	3	47-3	80	5.53	76	.274	.352	40-0-1	.150	-0	110	-18		-2.3
RODRIGUEZ, WILFREDO				Wilfredo Jose	B3.20.1979 Ciudad Bolivar, Venez	BL/TL/6-3/180	d9.21																		
2001	Hou N	0	0	—	2	0	0	0-0	3	6	5	2	0	1-0	3	15.00	31	.429	.438	0	—	0		-3		-0.1
RODRIGUEZ, ROBERTO				Roberto (Munoz)	B11.29.1941 Caracas, Venez	BR/TR/6-3/185*	d5.13																		
1967	KC A	1	1	.500	15	5	0	2	40.1	42	17	4	1	14-1	29	3.57	89	.268	.331	9	.000	-1	93	-1		-0.2
1970	Oak A	0	0	—	6	0	0	0-0	12.1	10	5	2	0	3-0	8	2.92	121	.227	.271	1	.000	-0		1		0.0
	SD N	0	0	—	10	0	0	3-1	16.1	26	16	1	0	5-0	8	6.61	61	.366	.408	3	.000	-0		-6		-0.3
	Chi N	3	2	.600	26	0	0	2-1	43.1	50	33	6	0	15-2	46	5.82	78	.289	.340	8-1-0	.125	1		-6		-0.6
	Year	3	2	.600	36	0	0	5-2	59.2	76	49	7	0	20-2	54	6.03	72	.311	.360	11-1-0	.091	0		-12		-0.9
Total	2	4	3	.571	57	5	0	7-2	112.1	128	71	13	1	37-3	91	4.81	80	.288	.341	21-1-0	.048	-1	93	-12		-1.1
ROE, PREACHER				Elwin Charles	B2.26.1915 Ash Flat AR	BR/TL/6-2/170*	d8.22	Col Harding																	
1938	StL N	0	0	—	1	0	0	0	2.2	6	4	0	0	2	1	13.50	29	.429	.500	1	.000	-0		-2		-0.1
1944	Pit N	13	11	.542	39	25	7-1	1	185.1	182	82	7	2	59	88	3.11	120	.253	.311	53-0-6	.132	-2	92	11		1.0
1945	Pit N★	14	13	.519	33	31	15-3	1	235	228	77	11	1	46	148	2.87	137	.259	.296	75-0-8	.107	-3	87	32		3.2
1946	Pit N	3	8	.273	21	10	1	2	70	83	50	5	2	25	28	5.14	69	.294	.356	15	.067	-1	83	-13		-2.0
1947	Pit N	4	15	.211	38	22	4-1	2	144	156	93	19	0	63	59	5.25	80	.276	.348	40-0-4	.125	-2	66	-15		-1.9
1948	Bro N	12	8	.600	34	22	8-2	2	177.2	156	60	14	2	33	86	2.63	152	.233	.271	51-0-9	.098	-2	104	27		2.6
1949	†Bro N★	15	6	.714	30	27	13-3	1	212.2	201	69	25	2	52	109	2.79	147	.252	.293	70-0-7	.114	-2	105	32		2.6
1950	Bro N☆	19	11	.633	36	32	16-2	1	250.2	245	96	34	4	66	113	3.30	124	.257	.308	91-0-8	.154	-2	102	35		2.3
1951	Bro N☆	22	3	.880	34	33	19-2	0	257.2	247	91	30	6	64	113	3.04	129	.258	.306	89-0-9	.112	-5	112	28		1.9
1952	†Bro N★	11	2	.846	27	25	8-2	0	158.2	163	59	16	3	39	83	3.12	117	.270	.317	57-0-5	.070	-3	131	10		0.4
1953	†Bro N	11	3	.786	25	24	9-1	0	157	171	78	27	1	40	85	4.36	98	.278	.323	57-1-5	.053	-4	134	1		-0.3
1954	Bro N	3	4	.429	15	8	1-0	0	63	69	40	11	0	23	31	5.00	82	.279	.339	21-0-2	.143	-0	103	-7		-0.7
Total	12	127	84	.602	333	261	101-17	10	1914.1	1907	799	199	17	504	956	3.43	116	.261	.310	620-1-63	.110	-27	103	129		9.0

YEAR	TM LG	W	L	PCT	G	GS	CG-SHO	SV-BS	IP	H	R	HR	HB	BB-IB	SO	ERA	AERA	OAV	OOB	AB-HR-SH	AVG	PB	SUP	APR	DL	PW
ROE, CLAY	James Clay "Shad" B1.7.1904 Greenbrier TN D4.4.1956 Cleveland MS BL/TL/6-1/180 d10.3																									
1923	Was A	0	1	.000	1	1	0	0	1.2	0	4	0	0	6	2	0.00	—	.000	.500	0	—	0	176	-1		-0.2
ROEBUCK, ED	Edward Jack B7.3.1931 East Millsboro PA BR/TR/6-2/185(180-197) d4.18																									
1955	†Bro N	5	6	.455	47	0	0	12	84	96	51	14	3	24-5	33	4.71	86	.288	.341	18	.111	-1		-6		-1.0
1956	†Bro N	5	4	.556	43	0	0	1	89.1	83	49	15	2	29-2	60	3.93	101	.251	.314	18-0-1	.333	2		-2		0.0
1957	Bro N	8	2	.800	44	1	0	8	96.1	70	37	9	2	46-6	73	2.71	154	.205	.303	21-2-0	.238	2	0	13		1.9
1958	LA N	0	1	.000	32	0	0	5	44	45	22	9	2	15-3	26	3.48	118	.271	.315	4	.500	1		2		0.2
1960	LA N	8	3	.727	58	0	0	8	116.2	109	42	13	0	38-11	77	2.78	143	.256	.315	24-0-4	.167	-0		14		1.6
1961	LA N	2	0	1.000	5	0	0	0	9	12	5	1	0	2-0	9	5.00	87	.324	.359	2	.000	-0		0	144	-0.1
1962	LA N	10	2	.833	64	0	0	9	119.1	102	60	11	6	54-6	72	3.09	117	.232	.321	28	.214	1		2		0.3
1963	LA N	2	4	.333	29	0	0	0	40.1	54	25	4	2	21-5	26	4.24	71	.321	.399	4	.250	-0		-7		-1.0
	Was A	2	1	.667	26	0	0	4	57.1	63	27	5	2	29-2	25	3.30	113	.284	.359	11-0-1	.182	-0		1		0.1
1964	Was A	0	0	—	2	0	0	0	1	0	1	0	0	2-0	0	9.00	41	.000	.333	0	—	0		-1		0.0
	Phi N	5	3	.625	60	0	0	12	77.1	55	21	7	4	25-6	42	2.21	157	.196	.270	6-0-1	.000	-1		11		1.5
1965	Phi N	5	3	.625	44	0	0	3	50.1	55	27	2	5	15-5	29	3.40	102	.288	.349	1-0-1	.000	-0		-2		-0.4
1966	Phi N	2	0	1.000	6	0	0	0	6	9	7	0	0	2-0	5	6.00	60	.333	.367	0	—	0		-3		-0.6
Total	11	52	31	.627	460	1	0	62	791	753	374	90	28	302-51	477	3.35	114	.254	.326	137-2-8	.204	3	0	22	144	2.5
ROESLER, MIKE	Michael Joseph B9.12.1963 Fort Wayne IN BR/TR/6-5/195* [CinN85 17/422] d8.9 Col Ball St.																									
1989	Cin N	0	1	.000	17	0	0	0-0	25	22	11	4	0	9-1	14	3.96	97	.239	.307	0		0		0		-0.1
1990	Pit N	1	0	1.000	5	0	0	0-0	6	5	2	1	0	2-0	4	3.00	122	.217	.280	1	.000	-0		1		0.1
Total	2	1	1	.500	22	0	0	0-0	31	27	13	5	0	11-1	18	3.77	96	.235	.302	1	.000	-0		1		0.0
ROETTGER, OSCAR	Oscar Frederick Louis "Okkie" B2.19.1900 St.Louis MO D7.4.1986 St.Louis MO BR/TR/6-0/170 d7.7 b-Wally ▲																									
1923	NY A	0	0	—	5	0	0	1	11.2	16	15	3	1	12	7	8.49	46	.340	.483	2	.000			-7		-0.4
1924	NY A	0	0	—	1	0	0	0	0	1	0	0	0	2	0	—	—	1.000	1.000	0	—	0		0		0.0
Total	2	0	0	—	6	0	0	1	11.2	17	15	3	1	14	7	8.49	46	.354	.508	2	.000	-0		-7		-0.4
ROGALSKI, JOE	Joseph Anthony B7.16.1915 Ashland WI D11.20.1951 Ashland WI BR/TR/6-2/187 d9.14																									
1938	Det A	0	0	—	2	0	0	0	7	12	4	0	0	7	2	2.57	194	.400	.400	2	.000	-0		1		0.0
ROGERS, KEVIN	Charles Kevin B8.20.1968 Cleveland MS BB/TL/6-2/190* [SFN88 9/230] d9.4 Col Mississippi Delta JC [DL 1995 SF N 160]																									
1992	SF N	0	2	.000	6	6	0	0-0	34	37	17	4	1	13-1	26	4.24	79	.280	.349	9-0-3	.222	0	86	-3		-0.2
1993	SF N	2	2	.500	64	0	0	0-2	80.2	71	28	3	4	28-5	62	2.68	147	.236	.308	3	.000	-0		11		0.5
1994	SF N	0	0	—	9	0	0	0-1	10.1	10	4	1	0	6-0	7	3.48	117	.250	.348	0	—	0		1	102	0.0
Total	3	2	4	.333	79	6	0	0-3	125	118	49	8	5	47-6	95	3.17	119	.249	.323	12-0-3	.167	-0	86	9	262	0.3
ROGERS, JIMMY	James Randall B1.3.1967 Tulsa OK BR/TR/6-2/200 d7.30 Col Seminole St. (OK) JC																									
1995	Tor A	2	4	.333	19	0	0	0	23.2	21	15	4	0	18-4	13	5.70	83	.239	.364			0		-2		-0.3
ROGERS, KENNY	Kenneth Scott B11.10.1964 Savannah GA BL/TL/6-1/205(200-217) [TexA82 39/816] d4.6																									
1989	Tex A	3	4	.429	73	0	0	2-3	73.2	60	28	2	4	42-9	63	2.93	136	.232	.344	0		0		8		0.9
1990	Tex A	10	6	.625	69	3	0	15-8	97.2	93	40	6	1	42-5	74	3.13	126	.249	.323	0		0	62	8		1.5
1991	Tex A	10	10	.500	63	9	0	5-1	109.2	121	80	14	6	61-7	73	5.42	75	.281	.375	0		0	120	-20		-3.3
1992	Tex A	3	6	.333	81	0	0	6-4	78.2	80	32	7	0	26-8	70	3.09	124	.261	.318	0		0		6		0.8
1993	Tex A	16	10	.615	35	33	5	0-0	208.1	210	108	18	4	71-2	140	4.10	102	.263	.325	0		0	124	0		0.8
1994	Tex A	11	8	.579	24	24	6-2	0-0	167.1	169	93	24	3	52-1	120	4.46	108	.260	.315	0		0	107	7		0.8
1995	Tex A★	17	7	.708	31	31	3-1	0-0	208	192	87	26	2	76-1	140	3.38	143	.243	.309	0		0	99	32		3.4
1996	†NY A	12	8	.600	30	30	2-1	0-0	179	179	97	16	8	83-2	92	4.68	106	.261	.346	0		0	106	6		0.7
1997	NY A	6	7	.462	31	22	1	0-0	145	161	100	18	7	62-1	78	5.65	79	.280	.354	3	.000	-0	130	-20		-1.3
1998	Oak A	16	8	.667	34	34	7-1	0-0	238.2	215	96	19	7	67-0	138	3.17	146	.242	.299	4	.000	0	112	38		3.8
1999	Oak A	5	3	.625	19	19	3	0-0	119.1	135	66	8	9	41-0	68	4.30	110	.288	.353	3	.000	0	112	5		0.3
	†NY N	5	1	.833	12	12	2-1	0-0	76	71	35	8	4	28-1	58	4.03	110	.253	.328	25-0-3	.120	-0	129	3		0.3
2000	Tex A	13	13	.500	34	34	2	0-0	227.1	257	126	20	11	78-2	127	4.55	112	.285	.348	4-0-1	.500	1	90	14		1.6
2001	Tex A	5	7	.417	20	20	0	0-0	120.2	150	88	18	8	49-2	74	6.19	77	.307	.376	2	.000	-0	106	-18	76	-1.3
2002	Tex A	13	8	.619	33	33	2-1	0-0	210.2	212	101	21	6	70-1	107	3.84	125	.261	.324	3	.667	1*	87	18		2.0
2003	†Min A	13	8	.619	33	31	0	0-0	195	227	108	22	11	50-5	116	4.57	98	.292	.342	4	.000	-0	107	-3		-0.1
2004	Tex A☆	18	9	.667	35	35	2-1	0-0	211.2	248	117	24	9	66-0	126	4.76	104	.292	.348	5	.000	1	109	6		0.8
2005	Tex A★	14	8	.636	30	30	1-1	0-0	195.1	205	86	15	8	53-1	87	3.46	133	.271	.323	3	.333	1	107	21		2.5
Total	17	190	131	.592	687	400	36-9	28-16	2862	2985	1488	286	108	1017-48	1715	4.21	109	.269	.334	56-0-4	.143	0	107	111	76	13.9
ROGERS, LEE	Lee Otis "Buck" B10.8.1913 Tuscaloosa AL D11.23.1995 Little Rock AR BR/TL/5-11/170 d4.27 Col Alabama																									
1938	Bos A	1	1	.500	14	1	0	0	27.2	32	24	4	0	18	7	6.51	76	.302	.403	6	.000	-0	80	-5		-0.3
	Bro N	0	2	.000	12	2	0	0	23.2	23	16	0	1	10	11	5.70	68	.256	.337	1	.000	0*	54	-4		-0.2
Total	1	1	3	.250	26	4	0	0	51.1	55	40	4	1	28	18	6.14	73	.281	.373	7	.000	-0	68	-9		-0.5
ROGERS, BUCK	Orlin Woodrow "Lefty" B11.5.1912 Spring Garden VA D2.20.1999 Winston-Salem NC BR/TL/5-8.5/164 d9.15 Col Virginia																									
1935	Was A	0	1	.000	2	1	0	0	10	16	15	0	0	6	7	7.20	60	.340	.415	3	.000	-1	80	-6		-0.5
ROGERS, STEVE	Stephen Douglas B10.26.1949 Jefferson City MO BR/TR/6-1/182(175-190) [MonN71 D1/4] d7.18 Col Tulsa																									
1973	Mon N	10	5	.667	17	17	7-3	0-0	134	93	28	5	1	49-3	64	1.54	247	.199	.274	41-0-5	.098	-1	68	32		3.8
1974	Mon N☆	15	22	.405	38	38	11-1	0-0	253.2	255	139	19	5	80-7	154	4.47	86	.265	.322	79-0-7	.139	-1	75	-14		-1.9
1975	Mon N	11	12	.478	35	35	12-3	0-0	251.2	248	104	13	4	88-8	137	3.29	118	.260	.324	77-0-6	.169	1	87	15		1.4
1976	Mon N	7	17	.292	33	32	8-4	1-0	230	212	93	10	4	69-7	150	3.21	117	.250	.307	74-0-6	.149	-2*	67	14	33	1.4
1977	Mon N	17	16	.515	40	40	17-4	0-0	301.2	272	122	16	5	81-3	206	3.10	124	.242	.294	96-0-12	.104	-5	90	23		2.0
1978	Mon N★	13	10	.565	30	29	11-1	1-0	219	186	64	12	2	64-2	126	2.47	145	.235	.293	71-0-8	.113	-2	77	28		2.8
1979	Mon N	13	12	.520	37	37	13-5	0-0	248.2	232	97	14	4	78-9	143	3.00	124	.251	.311	77-0-2	.156	1*	98	19		2.0
1980	Mon N	16	11	.593	37	37	14-4	0-0	281	247	101	16	3	85-7	147	2.98	122	.238	.296	81-0-15	.160	1*	106	22		2.1
1981	†Mon N	12	8	.600	22	22	7-3	0-0	160.2	149	64	7	2	41-4	87	3.42	104	.248	.296	55-0-4	.145	-1*	100	4		0.3
1982	Mon N★	19	8	.704	35	35	14-4	0-0	277	245	84	12	6	65-7	179	2.40	154	.237	.285	85-0-12	.129	1*	102	39		3.8
1983	Mon N☆	17	12	.586	36	36	13-5	0-0	273	258	108	14	5	78-12	146	3.23	112	.252	.306	82-0-20	.146	-1	96	12		1.0
1984	Mon N	6	15	.286	31	28	1	0-0	169.1	171	93	12	2	78-5	64	4.31	80	.267	.346	49-0-4	.143	0	80	-18	17	-2.0
1985	Mon N	2	4	.333	8	7	1	0-0	38	51	25	1	0	20-1	18	5.68	61	.329	.401	14	.143	0	88	-9		-1.2
Total	13	158	152	.510	399	393	129-37	2-0	2837.2	2619	1122	151	43	876-75	1621	3.17	117	.248	.306	881-0-101	.138	-9	88	167	50	15.5
ROGERS, TOM	Thomas Andrew "Shotgun" B2.12.1892 Sparta TN D3.7.1936 Nashville TN BR/TR/6-0.5/180 d4.14																									
1917	StL A	3	6	.333	24	8	3	0	108.2	112	58	2	3	44	27	3.89	67	.277	.352	29-0-2	.172	-1	76	-13		-1.2
1918	StL A	8	10	.444	29	16	11	2	154	148	66	3	3	49	29	3.27	84	.267	.330	53-0-3	.245	2	95	-6		-0.5
1919	StL A	0	1	.000	2	0	0	0	1	7	6	0	0	0	1	27.00	12	.700	.700	0	—	0		-3		-0.6
	Phi A	4	12	.250	23	18	7-1	0	140	152	82	9	1	60	37	4.31	80	.292	.369	49-1-1	.224	-0	83	-13		-1.0
	Year	4	13	.235	25	18	7-1	0	141	159	88	9	1	60	38	4.47	77	.300	.374	49-1-1	.224	-0	83	-15		-1.6
1921	†NY A	0	1	.000	5	0	0	1	11	12	9	1	1	9	0	7.36	58	.300	.440	3	.333	0*		-3		-0.2
Total	4	15	30	.333	83	42	21-1	3	414.2	431	221	15	10	162	94	3.95	75	.282	.354	134-1-6	.224	-0	86	-37		-3.5
ROGGE, CLINT	Francis Clinton B7.19.1889 Memphis MI D1.6.1969 Mt.Clemens MI BL/TR/5-10/185 d4.11 Col Adrian																									
1915	Pit F	17	11	.607	37	31	17-5	0	254.1	240	96	6	9	93	93	2.55	106	.257	.330	81-0-8	.173	-1	94	1		0.1
1921	Cin N	1	2	.333	6	2	0	0	35.1	43	19	2	0	9	12	4.08	88	.307	.349	10	.100	0	103	-2		-0.1
Total	2	18	13	.581	43	33	17-5	0	289.2	283	115	8	9	102	105	2.73	103	.264	.332	91-0-8	.165	0	94	-1		0.0
ROGGENBURK, GARRY	Garry Earl B4.16.1940 Cleveland OH BL/TL/6-6/195* d4.20 Col Dayton [DL 1964 Min A 161]																									
1963	Min A	2	4	.333	36	2	0	4	50	47	26	3	5	22-3	24	2.16	169	.253	.344	7	.143	0	98	3		0.4
1965	Min A	1	0	1.000	12	0	0	2	21	21	10	1	0	12-2	6	3.43	104	.266	.359	3-0-2	.000	0		0		0.0
1966	Min A	1	2	.333	12	0	0	0	12.1	14	8	4	0	10-0	3	5.84	62	.292	.414	0	—	-0		-2		-0.5
	Bos A	0	0	—	1	0	0	0	0.1	1	0	0	0	1-0	0	0.00	—	.500	.667	0		0		0		0.0
	Year	1	2	.333	13	0	0	0	12.2	15	8	4	0	11-0	3	5.68	63	.300	.426	0		-0		-2		-0.5
1968	Bos A	0	0	—	4	0	0	0	8.1	9	2	0	0	3-0	4	2.16	146	.257	.316	0		0		1	65	0.0

YEAR	TM LG	W	L	PCT	G	GS	CG-SHO	SV-BS	IP	H	R	HR	HB	BB-IB	SO	ERA	AERA	OAV	OOB	AB-HR-SH	AVG	PB	SUP	APR	DL	PW
1969	Bos A	0	1	.000	7	0	0	0-0	9.2	13	9	1	1	5-0	8	8.38	46	.342	.432	2	.000	-0		-4		-0.4
	Sea A	2	2	.500	7	4	1	0-1	24.1	27	12	6	1	11-0	11	4.44	82	.276	.351	8-0-1	.125	-0	85	-1		-0.3
	Year	2	3	.400	14	4	1	0-1	34	40	21	7	2	16-0	19	5.56	66	.294	.374	10-0-1	.100	-1	84	-6		-0.7
Total 5		6	9	.400	79	6	1	7-1	126	132	67	15	7	64-5	56	4.06	99	.272	.362	20-0-3	.100	-1	90	-3	226	-0.8

ROGOVIN, SAUL Saul Walter B10.10.1923 Brooklyn NY D1.23.1995 New York NY BR/TR/6-2/205* d4.28

YEAR	TM LG	W	L	PCT	G	GS	CG-SHO	SV-BS	IP	H	R	HR	HB	BB-IB	SO	ERA	AERA	OAV	OOB	AB-HR-SH	AVG	PB	SUP	APR	DL	PW
1949	Det A	0	1	.000	5	0	0	0	5.2	13	9	1	0	7	2	14.29	29	.464	.571	0	—	0		-6		-0.8
1950	Det A	2	1	.667	11	5	1	0	40	39	21	5	2	26	11	4.50	104	.258	.374	16-1-0	.188	0	119	1		0.1
1951	Det A	1	1	.500	5	4	0	0	24	23	15	4	0	7	5	5.25	80	.247	.300	7	.286	1	144	-3		-0.1
	Chi A	11	7	.611	22	22	17-3	0	192.2	166	64	11	1	67	77	2.48	163	.234	.301	74	.203	-0*	90	33		2.9
	Year	12	8	.600	27	26	17-3	0	216.2	189	79	15	1	74	82	**2.78**	**146**	.235	.301	81	.210	1	99	30		2.8
1952	Chi A	14	9	.609	33	30	12-3	1	231.2	224	104	14	3	79	-121	3.85	95	.255	.318	84-1-4	.202	3	106	-2		0.0
1953	Chi A	7	12	.368	22	19	4-1	1	131	151	82	17	2	48	62	5.22	77	.289	.351	37-0-2	.135	-0	94	-16	36	-2.1
1955	Bal A	1	8	.111	14	12	1	0	71	79	42	5	2	27-1	35	4.56	84	.288	.355	22	.091	-1*	52	-6		-0.9
	Phi N	5	3	.625	12	11	5-2	0	73	60	25	3	0	17-2	27	3.08	129	.230	.274	24-1-2	.250	2*	94	9		1.1
1956	Phi N	7	6	.538	22	18	3	0	106.2	122	65	22	0	27-3	48	4.98	75	.282	.324	36-0-3	.111	-2	128	-14		-1.8
1957	Phi N	0	0	—	4	0	0	0	8	11	8	1	0	3-1	0	9.00	42	.333	.378	0	—	-0		-4		-0.2
Total 8		48	48	.500	150	121	43-9	2	883.2	888	435	83	10	308-7	388	4.06	96	.262	.325	300-3-11	.180	2	100	-8	36	-1.8

ROHR, LES Leslie Norvin B3.5.1946 Lowestoft, England BL/TL/6-5/205* [NYN65 1/2] d9.19

YEAR	TM LG	W	L	PCT	G	GS	CG-SHO	SV-BS	IP	H	R	HR	HB	BB-IB	SO	ERA	AERA	OAV	OOB	AB-HR-SH	AVG	PB	SUP	APR	DL	PW
1967	NY N	2	1	.667	3	3	0	0	17	13	7	1	0	9-0	15	2.12	160	.224	.319	6	.000	-1	112	1		0.1
1968	NY N	0	2	.000	2	1	0	0	6	9	4	0	0	7-3	5	4.50	67	.333	.471	0	—	0	57	-1		-0.2
1969	NY N	0	0	—	1	0	0	0-0	1.1	5	4	0	0	1-0	0	20.25	18	.625	.667	0	—	0		-3		-0.1
Total 3		2	3	.400	6	4	0	0-0	24.1	27	15	1	0	17-3	20	3.70	90	.290	.393	6	.000	-0	99	-3		-0.2

ROHR, BILLY William Joseph B7.1.1945 San Diego CA BL/TL/6-3/170* d4.14

YEAR	TM LG	W	L	PCT	G	GS	CG-SHO	SV-BS	IP	H	R	HR	HB	BB-IB	SO	ERA	AERA	OAV	OOB	AB-HR-SH	AVG	PB	SUP	APR	DL	PW
1967	Bos A	2	3	.400	10	8	2-1	0	42.1	43	27	4	2	22-2	16	5.10	68	.256	.349	10-0-3	.000	-1	103	-7		-0.9
1968	Cle A	1	0	1.000	17	0	0	1	18.1	18	16	5	0	10-2	5	6.87	43	.265	.354	1	.000	-0		-8		-0.5
Total 2		3	3	.500	27	8	2-1	1	60.2	61	43	9	2	32-4	21	5.64	59	.258	.351	11-0-3	.000	-1	103	-15		-1.4

ROJAS, MEL Melquiades (Medrano) B12.10.1966 Haina, D.R. BR/TR/5-11/185(175-212) d8.1

YEAR	TM LG	W	L	PCT	G	GS	CG-SHO	SV-BS	IP	H	R	HR	HB	BB-IB	SO	ERA	AERA	OAV	OOB	AB-HR-SH	AVG	PB	SUP	APR	DL	PW
1990	Mon N	3	1	.750	23	0	0	1-1	40	34	17	5	2	24-4	26	3.60	102	.234	.351	3-0-3	.000	-0		1		0.0
1991	Mon N	3	3	.500	37	0	0	6-3	48	42	21	4	1	13-1	37	3.75	97	.228	.280	4-0-1	.000	-0		-1		-0.1
1992	Mon N	7	1	.875	68	0	0	10-1	100.2	71	17	2	2	34-8	70	1.43	244	.199	.271	15	.067	-1		**23**		2.2
1993	Mon N	5	8	.385	66	0	0	10-9	88.1	80	39	6	4	30-3	48	2.95	141	.242	.308	12	.083	-1		10	15	1.4
1994	Mon N	3	2	.600	58	0	0	16-2	84	71	35	11	4	21-0	84	3.32	127	.227	.283	10	.200	0		8		0.7
1995	Mon N	1	4	.200	59	0	0	30-9	67.2	69	32	2	7	29-4	61	4.12	104	.262	.350	6-0-2	.000	-1		2		0.2
1996	Mon N	7	4	.636	74	0	0	36-4	81	56	30	5	2	28-3	92	3.22	134	.193	.265	8	.375	1		11		2.3
1997	Chi N	0	4	.000	54	0	0	13-6	59	54	30	11	5	30-1	61	4.42	98	.244	.346	1	.000	-0		0		-0.1
	NY N	0	2	.000	23	0	0	2-1	26.1	24	17	4	2	6-1	32	5.13	78	.235	.288	0	—	0		-4		-0.3
	Year	0	6	.000	77	0	0	15-7	85.1	78	47	15	7	36-2	93	4.64	91	.241	.329	1	.000	-0		-3		-0.4
1998	NY N	5	2	.714	50	0	0	2-4	58	68	39	9	3	30-5	41	6.05	68	.305	.391	0	—	0		-12		-1.3
1999	LA N	0	0	—	5	0	0	0-0	5	5	7	3	0	3-1	3	12.60	35	.250	.348	0	—	0		-4		-0.2
	Det A	0	0	—	5	0	0	0-0	6.1	12	16	3	3	4-0	6	22.74	22	.387	.487	0	—	0		-12		-0.5
	Mon N	0	0	—	3	0	0	0-0	2.2	5	5	0	2	2-0	1	16.88	26	.417	.529	0	—	0		-3		-0.2
Total 10		34	31	.523	525	0	0	126-40	667	591	305	65	37	254-31	562		106	.237	.315	59-0-6	.119	-2		20	15	4.1

ROJAS, MINNIE Minervino Alejandro (Landin) B11.26.1933 Remidios, Cuba D3.23.2002 Los Angeles CA BR/TR/6-1/182(170-185) d5.30

YEAR	TM LG	W	L	PCT	G	GS	CG-SHO	SV-BS	IP	H	R	HR	HB	BB-IB	SO	ERA	AERA	OAV	OOB	AB-HR-SH	AVG	PB	SUP	APR	DL	PW
1966	Cal A	7	4	.636	47	2	0	10	84.1	83	28	9	1	15-2	37	2.88	117	.262	.296	14-0-1	.071	-0	92	6		0.8
1967	Cal A	12	9	.571	72	0	0	**27**	121.2	106	45	7	3	38-17	83	2.52	125	.232	.292	17-0-3	.059	-1		6		1.2
1968	Cal A	4	3	.571	38	0	0	6	55	55	29	11	0	15-4	33	4.25	69	.252	.299	10	.100	-0		-8	56	-1.4
Total 3		23	16	.590	157	2	0	43	261	244	102	27	4	68-23	153	3.00	105	.246	.295	41-0-4	.073	-2	92	4	56	0.6

ROLAND, JIM James Ivan B12.14.1942 Franklin NC BR/TL/6-3/190(185-200) d9.20

YEAR	TM LG	W	L	PCT	G	GS	CG-SHO	SV-BS	IP	H	R	HR	HB	BB-IB	SO	ERA	AERA	OAV	OOB	AB-HR-SH	AVG	PB	SUP	APR	DL	PW
1962	Min A	0	0	—	1	0	0	0	2	1	0	0	0	0-0	1	0.00	—	.143	.143	0	—	0		1		0.0
1963	Min A	4	1	.800	10	7	2-1	0	49	32	17	4	0	27-1	34	2.57	142	.185	.292	15-0-3	.000	-2	129	5	68	0.4
1964	Min A	2	6	.250	30	13	1	3	94.1	76	48	12	4	55-2	63	4.10	87	.218	.329	27	.148	-1	88	-5		-0.6
1966	Min A	0	0	—	1	0	0	0	2	0	0	0	0	0-0	1	0.00	—	.000	.000	0	—	0		1		0.0
1967	Min A	0	1	.000	25	0	0	2	35.2	33	12	3	0	17-5	16	3.03	114	.244	.325	3	.000	-0		2		0.1
1968	Min A	4	1	.800	28	4	1	0	61.2	55	33	3	2	24-2	36	3.50	88	.238	.314	8-0-2	.000	-1*	113	-5		-0.4
1969	Oak A	5	1	.833	39	3	2	1-0	86.1	59	24	6	6	46-6	48	2.19	197	.197	.314	21	.095	-1	154	12		0.8
1970	Oak A	3	3	.500	28	2	0	2-0	43.1	28	14	2	0	23-1	26	2.70	131	.181	.285	6	.000	-0	114	4	27	0.6
1971	Oak A	1	3	.250	31	0	0	1-0	45.1	34	18	4	5	19-3	30	3.18	105	.214	.310	3-0-1	.000	-0		1		0.0
1972	Oak A	0	0	—	2	0	0	0-0	2.1	5	2	0	0	0-0	0	3.86	74	.455	.455	0	—	-0		-1		0.0
	NY A	0	1	.000	16	0	0	0-0	25	27	14	3	1	16-1	13	5.04	59	.287	.396	1	.000	-0		-5		-0.3
	Tex A	0	0	—	5	0	0	0-0	3.1	7	3	1	1	2-1	4	8.10	38	.412	.500	0	—	0		-2		-0.1
	Year	0	1	.000	23	0	0	0-0	30.2	39	19	4	2	18-2	17	5.28	57	.320	.415	1	.000	-0		-7		-0.4
Total 10		19	17	.528	216	29	6-1	9-0	450.1	357	185	34	19	229-22	272	3.22	106	.218	.319	84-0-6	.071	-5	112	8	95	0.5

ROMAN, JOSE Jose Rafael (Sarita) B5.21.1963 Santo Domingo, D.R. BR/TR/6-0/175* d9.5

YEAR	TM LG	W	L	PCT	G	GS	CG-SHO	SV-BS	IP	H	R	HR	HB	BB-IB	SO	ERA	AERA	OAV	OOB	AB-HR-SH	AVG	PB	SUP	APR	DL	PW
1984	Cle A	0	2	.000	3	2	0	0-0	6	9	12	1	0	11-0	3	18.00	23	.391	.541	0	—	0	77	-8		-1.3
1985	Cle A	0	4	.000	5	3	0	0-0	16.1	13	17	3	0	14-0	12	6.61	63	.200	.342	0	—	0	29	-6		-1.1
1986	Cle A	1	2	.333	6	5	0	0-0	22	23	20	3	1	17-0	9	6.55	64	.280	.394	0	—	0	91	-7		-0.8
Total 3		1	8	.111	14	10	0	0-0	44.1	45	49	7	1	42-0	24	8.12	51	.265	.400	0	—	0	70	-21		-3.2

ROMANICK, RON Ronald James B11.6.1960 Burley ID BR/TR/6-4/195* [AnaA81*S1/4] d4.5 Col Arizona St.

YEAR	TM LG	W	L	PCT	G	GS	CG-SHO	SV-BS	IP	H	R	HR	HB	BB-IB	SO	ERA	AERA	OAV	OOB	AB-HR-SH	AVG	PB	SUP	APR	DL	PW
1984	Cal A	12	12	.500	33	33	8-2	0-0	229.2	240	107	23	4	61-3	87	3.76	106	.270	.316	0	—	0	90	5		0.3
1985	Cal A	14	9	.609	31	31	6-1	0-0	195	210	101	29	4	62-1	64	4.11	100	.280	.334	0	—	0	106	-1		-0.2
1986	Cal A	5	8	.385	18	18	1-1	0-0	106.1	124	68	13	0	44-0	38	5.50	75	.297	.360	0	—	0	106	-15		-1.6
Total 3		31	29	.517	82	82	15-4	0-0	531	574	276	65	8	167-4	189	4.24	96	.279	.332	0	—	0	100	-11		-1.5

ROMANO, JIM James King B4.6.1927 Brooklyn NY D9.12.1990 New York NY BR/TR/6-4/190 d9.21

YEAR	TM LG	W	L	PCT	G	GS	CG-SHO	SV-BS	IP	H	R	HR	HB	BB-IB	SO	ERA	AERA	OAV	OOB	AB-HR-SH	AVG	PB	SUP	APR	DL	PW
1950	Bro N	0	0	—	3	0	0	0	3	6	2	0	0	5-0	1	5.68	72	.296	.345	1	.000	-0	216	-2		-0.1

ROMANO, MIKE Michael Desport B3.3.1972 New Orleans LA BR/TR/6-2/195 [TorA93 3/85] d9.5 Col Tulane

YEAR	TM LG	W	L	PCT	G	GS	CG-SHO	SV-BS	IP	H	R	HR	HB	BB-IB	SO	ERA	AERA	OAV	OOB	AB-HR-SH	AVG	PB	SUP	APR	DL	PW
1999	Tor A	0	0	—	3	0	0	0-0	5.1	8	8	1	0	5-0	3	11.81	42	.364	.464	0	—	0		-4		-0.2

ROMBERGER, DUTCH Allen Isaiah B5.26.1927 Klingerstown PA D5.26.1983 Weikert PA BR/TR/6-0/185 d5.31

YEAR	TM LG	W	L	PCT	G	GS	CG-SHO	SV-BS	IP	H	R	HR	HB	BB-IB	SO	ERA	AERA	OAV	OOB	AB-HR-SH	AVG	PB	SUP	APR	DL	PW
1954	Phi A	1	1	.500	10	0	0	0	15.2	28	20	3	0	12	6	11.49	34	.406	.488	2	.000	0		-12		-1.3

ROMERO, J.C. Juan Carlos B6.4.1976 Rio Piedras, PR BB/TL/5-11/195(193-205) [MinA97 21/633] d9.15 Col Mobile

YEAR	TM LG	W	L	PCT	G	GS	CG-SHO	SV-BS	IP	H	R	HR	HB	BB-IB	SO	ERA	AERA	OAV	OOB	AB-HR-SH	AVG	PB	SUP	APR	DL	PW
1999	Min A	0	0	—	5	0	0	0-0	9.2	13	4	0	0	0-0	4	3.72	139	.333	.333	0	—	0		2		0.1
2000	Min A	2	7	.222	12	11	0	0-0	57.2	72	51	8	1	30-0	50	7.02	75	.312	.390	0	—	0	84	-12	36	-1.4
2001	Min A	1	4	.200	14	11	0	0-0	65	71	48	10	1	24-1	39	6.23	75	.277	.339	2	.500	1	97	-11		-0.6
2002	†Min A	9	2	.818	81	0	0	1-4	81	62	17	3	4	36-4	76	1.89	236	.213	.308	0	—	0		**24**		2.9
2003	†Min A	2	0	1.000	73	0	0	0-4	63	66	37	7	6	42-7	50	5.00	90	.272	.392	1	.000	-0		-4		-0.1
2004	†Min A	7	4	.636	74	0	0	1-7	74.1	61	32	4	5	38-6	69	3.51	132	.224	.329	0	—	0		9		1.2
2005	Min A	4	3	.571	68	0	0	0-1	57	50	26	6	6	39-8	48	3.47	126	.235	.367	0	—	0	96	5		0.6
Total 7		25	20	.556	327	22	0	2-16	407.2	395	215	38	23	209-26	336	4.35	107	.256	.352	3	.333	1	96	13	36	2.7

ROMERO, RAMON Ramon (De Los Santos) B1.8.1959 San Pedro de Macoris, D.R. BL/TL/6-4/170* d9.18

YEAR	TM LG	W	L	PCT	G	GS	CG-SHO	SV-BS	IP	H	R	HR	HB	BB-IB	SO	ERA	AERA	OAV	OOB	AB-HR-SH	AVG	PB	SUP	APR	DL	PW
1984	Cle A	0	0	—	1	0	0	0-0	3	0	0	0	0	3	3	0.00	—	.000	.111	0	—	0		1		0.1
1985	Cle A	2	3	.400	19	10	0	0-0	64.1	69	48	13	5	38-0	38	6.58	63	.276	.381	0	—	0	85	-15		-1.1
Total 2		2	3	.400	20	10	0	0-0	67.1	69	48	13	6	38-0	41	6.28	66	.267	.373	0	—	0	85	-14		-1.0

ROMMEL, EDDIE Edwin Americus B9.13.1897 Baltimore MD D8.26.1970 Baltimore MD BR/TR/6-2/197 d4.19 C2/U22

YEAR	TM LG	W	L	PCT	G	GS	CG-SHO	SV-BS	IP	H	R	HR	HB	BB-IB	SO	ERA	AERA	OAV	OOB	AB-HR-SH	AVG	PB	SUP	APR	DL	PW
1920	Phi A	7	7	.500	33	12	8-2	1	173.2	165	68	5	4	43	43	2.85	141	.259	.309	51-0-8	.216	-0*	74	24		2.0
1921	Phi A	16	23	.410	46	32	20	3	285.1	312	155	21	1	87	71	3.94	113	.289	.337	94-0-10	.191	-2	77	16		1.8

YEAR	TM LG	W	L	PCT	G	GS	CG-SHO	SV-BS	IP	H	R	HR	HB	BB-IB	SO	ERA	AERA	OAV	OOB	AB-HR-SH	AVG	PB	SUP	APR	DL	PW
1922	Phi A	**27**	13	.675	51	33	22-3	2	294	294	128	21	5	63	54	3.28	130	.267	.309	94-0-6	.181	-3	91	30		3.6
1923	Phi A	18	19	.486	56	31	19-3	5	297.2	306	141	14	3	108	76	3.27	126	.271	.336	101-0-4	.238	1	75	24		3.2
1924	Phi A	18	15	.545	43	34	21-3	1	278	302	139	8	3	94	72	3.95	108	.284	.344	95-0-6	.158	-6*	95	13		1.0
1925	Phi A	21	10	.677	52	28	14-1	3	261	285	127	10	7	95	67	3.69	126	.281	.346	81-1-11	.185	-1	99	27		2.9
1926	Phi A	11	11	.500	37	26	12-3	0	219	225	91	10	2	54	52	3.08	135	.268	.354	61-0-10	.098	-4	82	27		2.2
1927	Phi A	11	3	.786	30	17	8-2	1	146.2	166	83	6	3	48	33	4.36	98	.286	.343	51-0-4	.157	-2	125	-1		-0.2
1928	Phi A	13	5	.722	43	11	6	4	173.2	177	70	11	2	26	37	3.06	131	.266	.295	47-0-4	.255	3	100	19		2.2
1929	†Phi A	12	2	.857	32	6	4	4	113.2	135	52	10	1	34	25	2.85	148	.294	.344	39-0-4	.205	-0	156	14		1.5
1930	Phi A	9	4	.692	35	9	5	3	130.1	142	66	11	1	27	35	4.28	109	.277	.315	38-0-3	.263	3	102	8		1.0
1931	†Phi A	7	5	.583	25	10	8-1	0	118	136	50	5	1	27	18	2.97	151	.291	.331	54	.259	2*	113	18		1.8
1932	Phi A	1	2	.333	17	0	0	2	65.1	84	43	6	0	18	16	5.51	82	.315	.358	20	.300		-2	-7		0.0
Total	13	171	119	.590	500	249	147-18	29	2556.1	2729	1213	138	33	724	599	3.54	122	.277	.329	826-1-70	.199	-7	92	212		23.0

ROMO, ENRIQUE Enrique (Navarro) B7.15.1947 Santa Rosalia, Baja California, Mexico BR/TR/5-11/185* d4.7 b-Vicente

YEAR	TM LG	W	L	PCT	G	GS	CG-SHO	SV-BS	IP	H	R	HR	HB	BB-IB	SO	ERA	AERA	OAV	OOB	AB-HR-SH	AVG	PB	SUP	APR	DL	PW
1977	Sea A	8	10	.444	58	3	0	16-7	114.1	93	40	8	5	39-7	105	2.83	146	.227	.300	0	—	0	94	16	21	2.9
1978	Sea A	11	7	.611	56	0	0	10-12	107.1	88	46	12	5	39-6	62	3.69	104	.227	.302	0	—	0		3		0.5
1979	†Pit N	10	3	.667	84	0	0	5-8	129.1	122	50	11	3	43-9	106	2.99	131	.253	.317	12-0-4	.167	-0		12		1.5
1980	Pit N	5	5	.500	74	0	0	11-7	123.2	117	53	10	1	28-4	82	3.27	113	.252	.293	11-1-2	.455	3*		4		0.8
1981	Pit N	1	3	.250	33	0	0	9-1	41.2	47	27	5	0	18-7	23	4.54	80	.288	.353	4-0-2	.000	-0		-5	21	-0.8
1982	Pit N	9	3	.750	45	0	0	1-0	86.2	81	43	11	1	36-6	58	4.36	86	.245	.321	10-0-1	.300	1*		-4		-0.4
Total	6	44	33	.571	350	3	0	52-35	603	548	259	57	15	203-39	436	3.45	112	.245	.310	37-1-9	.270	4	94	26	42	4.5

ROMO, VICENTE Vicente (Navarro) "Huevo" B4.12.1943 Santa Rosalia, Baja California, Mexico BR/TR/6-1/195(180-195) d4.11 b-Enrique

YEAR	TM LG	W	L	PCT	G	GS	CG-SHO	SV-BS	IP	H	R	HR	HB	BB-IB	SO	ERA	AERA	OAV	OOB	AB-HR-SH	AVG	PB	SUP	APR	DL	PW
1968	LA N	0	0		1	0	0	1	1	1	1	0	0	0-0	1	0.00	—	.250	.200	0	—	0		0		0.0
	Cle A	5	3	.625	40	1	0	12	83.1	43	15	5	2	32-6	54	1.62	183	.154	.241	14-0-4	.143	0	88	14		1.9
1969	Cle A	1	1	.500	3	0	0	0-0	8	7	3	0	0	3-1	7	2.25	169	.233	.294	2	.500	0		1		0.3
	Bos A	7	9	.438	52	11	4-1	11-2	127.1	116	51	14	1	50-6	89	3.18	120	.247	.319	31-0-3	.129	-1	90	9		1.2
	Year	8	10	.444	55	11	4-1	11-2	135.1	123	54	14	1	53-7	96	3.13	122	.246	.318	33-0-3	.152	-0	91	10		1.5
1970	Bos A	7	3	.700	48	10	0	6-1	108	115	51	14	0	43-6	71	4.08	98	.273	.338	27-1-2	.148	0	121	1		0.2
1971	Chi A	1	7	.125	45	2	0	5-0	72	52	27	5	0	37-6	48	3.38	106	.202	.300	11-0-1	.364	1	63	4		0.7
1972	Chi A	3	0	1.000	28	0	0	1-3	51.2	47	19	5	1	18-2	46	3.31	94	.246	.311	9	.000	-1	50	-2	21	-0.1
1973	SD N	2	3	.400	49	0	0	7-3	87.2	85	43	11	0	46-8	51	3.70	95	.260	.347	16-0-2	.125	-0	50	-2		-0.2
1974	SD N	5	5	.500	54	1	0	9-5	71	78	47	6	2	37-13	26	4.56	79	.290	.374	6-0-1	.000	-1	49	-11		-1.7
1982	LA N	1	2	.333	15	6	0	1-0	35.2	25	12	1	2	14-0	24	3.03	115	.195	.285	5-0-4	.200	0	102	3	35	0.2
Total	8	32	33	.492	335	32	4-1	52-14	645.2	569	269	61	8	280-48	416	3.36	106	.239	.318	121-1-17	.149	-1	103	19	56	2.5

ROMONOSKY, JOHN John B7.7.1929 Harrisburg IL BR/TR/6-2/195* d9.6

YEAR	TM LG	W	L	PCT	G	GS	CG-SHO	SV-BS	IP	H	R	HR	HB	BB-IB	SO	ERA	AERA	OAV	OOB	AB-HR-SH	AVG	PB	SUP	APR	DL	PW
1953	StL N	0	0	—	2	2	0	0	7.2	9	6	1	1	4	3	4.70	91	.281	.378		.000	-0	105	-1		-0.1
1958	Was A	2	4	.333	18	5	1	0	55.1	52	42	6	1	28-4	38	6.51	59	.243	.328	13-1-1	.308	2*	90	-16		-1.3
1959	Was A	1	0	1.000	12	2	0	0	38.1	36	15	4	3	19-0	22	3.29	119	.254	.352	11	.182	0*	158	3		0.2
Total	3	3	4	.429	32	9	1	0	101.1	97	63	11	4	51-4	63	5.15	75	.250	.341	26-1-1	.231	2	110	-14		-1.2

RONDON, GILBERTO Gilberto B11.18.1953 Bronx NY BR/TR/6-2/200* [BalA73*S3/59] d4.10 f-Diomedes Olivo

YEAR	TM LG	W	L	PCT	G	GS	CG-SHO	SV-BS	IP	H	R	HR	HB	BB-IB	SO	ERA	AERA	OAV	OOB	AB-HR-SH	AVG	PB	SUP	APR	DL	PW
1976	Hou N	2	2	.500	19	7	0	0-0	53.2	70	37	6	0	39-0	21	5.70	57	.315	.416	14-0-2	.286	1	160	-15	27	-1.0
1979	Chi A	0	0	—	4	0	0	0-0	9.2	11	5	2	0	6-0	3	3.72	114	.282	.370	0	—	0		0		0.0
Total	2	2	2	.500	23	7	0	0-0	63.1	81	42	8	0	45-0	24	5.40	63	.310	.409	14-0-2	.286	1	160	-15	27	-1.0

RONEY, MATT Matthew Stephen B1.10.1980 Tulsa OK BR/TR/6-3/230 [ColN98 1/28] d4.2

YEAR	TM LG	W	L	PCT	G	GS	CG-SHO	SV-BS	IP	H	R	HR	HB	BB-IB	SO	ERA	AERA	OAV	OOB	AB-HR-SH	AVG	PB	SUP	APR	DL	PW
2003	Det A	1	9	.100	45	11	0	0-2	100.2	102	67	17	4	48-4	47	5.45	80	.262	.346		.500	0	76	-13		-1.1

ROOKER, JIM James Phillip B9.23.1942 Lakeview OR BR/TL/6-0/195(190-201) d6.30

YEAR	TM LG	W	L	PCT	G	GS	CG-SHO	SV-BS	IP	H	R	HR	HB	BB-IB	SO	ERA	AERA	OAV	OOB	AB-HR-SH	AVG	PB	SUP	APR	DL	PW
1968	Det A	0	0	—	2	0	0	0	4.2	4	2	0	0	1-0	4	3.86	78	.235	.278	2	.000	-0		0		0.0
1969	KC A	4	16	.200	28	22	8-1	0-0	158.1	136	80	13	1	73-3	108	3.75	99	.229	.312	57-4-0	.281	8*	86	-3		0.5
1970	KC A	10	15	.400	38	29	6-3	1-0	203.2	190	99	11	1	102-4	117	3.54	106	.252	.339	70-1-2	.200	3*	86	1		0.5
1971	KC A	2	7	.222	20	7	1-1	0-1	54	59	35	2	1	24-1	31	5.33	65	.284	.354	10-0-1	.000	-1*	60	-11		-1.8
1972	KC A	5	6	.455	18	10	4-2	0-0	72	78	37	3	1	24-0	44	4.38	70	.280	.337	20	.100	-1	93	-10		-1.6
1973	Pit N	10	6	.625	41	18	6-3	5-0	170.1	143	59	12	2	52-10	122	2.85	124	.229	.288	49-0-5	.245	3*	129	15		1.7
1974	†Pit N	15	11	.577	33	33	15-1	0-0	262.2	228	93	11	4	83-6	139	2.78	125	.238	.299	95-0-5	.305	10	104	21		3.3
1975	†Pit N	13	11	.542	28	28	7-1	0-0	196.2	177	80	16	3	76-13	102	2.97	121	.238	.309	63-0-9	.095	-3	106	12		1.1
1976	Pit N	15	8	.652	30	29	10-1	1-0	198.2	201	83	12	2	72-5	92	3.35	105	.263	.325	74-1-5	.216	3*	128	5		0.8
1977	Pit N	14	9	.609	30	30	7-2	0-0	204.1	196	87	24	0	64-4	89	3.08	131	.253	.308	70-0-1	.186	0	107	17		1.8
1978	Pit N	9	11	.450	28	28	1	0-0	163.1	160	94	13	3	81-4	76	4.24	88	.259	.346	56-0-1	.161	-0*	102	-11		-1.2
1979	†Pit N	4	7	.364	19	17	1	0-0	103.2	106	58	11	0	39-5	44	4.60	85	.266	.329	33-0-2	.121	-1	93	-7	64	-0.8
1980	Pit N	2	2	.500	4	4	0	0-0	18	16	7	0	0	12-0	1	3.50	106	.262	.319	7-1-1	.143	1	79	1	156	0.2
Total	13	103	109	.486	319	255	66-15	7-1	1810.1	1694	814	128	18	703-55	976	3.46	105	.249	.319	606-7-32	.201	22	103	30	220	4.5

ROOT, CHARLIE Charles Henry "Chinski" B3.17.1899 Middletown OH D11.5.1970 Hollister CA BR/TR/5-10.5/190 d4.18 C6

YEAR	TM LG	W	L	PCT	G	GS	CG-SHO	SV-BS	IP	H	R	HR	HB	BB-IB	SO	ERA	AERA	OAV	OOB	AB-HR-SH	AVG	PB	SUP	APR	DL	PW
1923	StL A	0	4	.000	27	9	0	2	60	68	45	4	6	18	27	5.70	73	.302	.369	13	.077	-1	50	-9		-0.7
1926	Chi N	18	17	.514	42	32	21-2	2	271.1	267	104	10	6	62	127	2.82	136	.264	.310	91-1-4	.143	-4	93	30		3.1
1927	Chi N	**26**	15	.634	48	36	21-4	2	309	296	148	16	9	117	145	3.76	103	.254	.326	122-0-5	.221	3	127	5		0.7
1928	Chi N	14	18	.438	40	30	13-1	2	237	214	109	15	7	73	122	3.57	108	.242	.305	73-0-8	.178	-0	67	8		0.9
1929	†Chi N	19	6	**.760**	43	31	19-4	5	272	286	120	12	3	83	124	3.47	133	.275	.330	96-1-5	.156	0	118	**37**		2.7
1930	Chi N	16	14	.533	37	30	15-4	3	220.1	247	122	17	7	63	124	4.33	113	.281	.334	80-1-2	.262	5	102	14		1.9
1931	Chi N	17	14	.548	39	31	19-3	2	251	240	109	7	7	71	131	3.48	111	.252	.309	76-1-2	.171	-1	103	6		0.3
1932	†Chi N	15	10	.600	39	24	11	3	216.1	211	99	10	5	55	96	3.58	105	.253	.303	85-0-4	.094	-4	102	18		1.2
1933	Chi N	15	10	.600	35	30	20-2	0	242.1	232	85	14	10	61	86	2.60	126	.252	.306	69-1-12	.203	2	131	18		1.9
1934	Chi N	4	7	.364	34	9	2	0	117.2	141	62	8	5	53	46	4.28	90	.298	.298	40-2-1	.175	2	94	-5		-0.3
1935	†Chi N	15	8	.652	38	18	11-1	1	201.1	193	85	15	3	47	94	3.08	127	.252	.298	15	.333	1	149	0		0.1
1936	Chi N	3	6	.333	33	4	0	1	73.2	81	34	3	2	20	32	4.15	96	.280	.331	67-1-2	.179	0	133	13		1.4
1937	Chi N	13	5	.722	43	15	5	5	178.2	173	71	18	4	32	74	3.38	118	.253	.299	67-1-2	.179	0	133	13		1.4
1938	†Chi N	8	7	.533	44	11	5	4	160.2	163	62	10	2	30	70	2.86	134	.258	.294	48-0-1	.167	-0	72	15		1.4
1939	Chi N	8	5	.500	35	16	8	4	167.1	189	83	11	2	34	65	4.03	98	.286	.323	57-2-3	.175	2	98	0		0.0
1940	Chi N	2	4	.333	36	8	1	1	112	118	60	9	1	33	50	3.86	97	.265	.317	31	.129	-1	125	-4		-0.3
1941	Chi N	8	7	.533	19	15	6	0	106.2	133	68	8	0	37	46	5.40	65	.306	.360	33-1-4	.152	-2	113	-20		-2.3
Total	17	201	160	.557	632	342	177-21	40	3197.1	3252	1467	187	79	889	1459	3.59	110	.264	.318	1086-11-54	.180	8	105	138		13.5

ROPER, JOHN John Christopher B11.21.1971 Southern Pines NC BR/TR/6-0/175* [CinN90 12/324] d5.16

YEAR	TM LG	W	L	PCT	G	GS	CG-SHO	SV-BS	IP	H	R	HR	HB	BB-IB	SO	ERA	AERA	OAV	OOB	AB-HR-SH	AVG	PB	SUP	APR	DL	PW
1993	Cin N	2	5	.286	16	15	0	0-0	80	92	51	10	4	36-3	54	5.62	72	.295	.372	28-0-1	.179	-0	121	-13	30	-1.0
1994	Cin N	6	2	.750	16	15	0	0-0	92	90	49	16	4	30-0	51	4.50	93	.255	.318	33-0-2	.182	0	141	-2		-0.1
1995	Cin N	0	0	—	2	2	0	0-0	7	13	9	3	0	4-0	6	10.29	41	.406	.472	1-0-1	.000	-0	162	-5	42	-0.1
	SF N	0	0	—	1	0	0	0-0	1	2	2	0	1	2-0	0	27.00	15	.500	.571	0	—	0		-2		-0.1
	Year	0	0	—	3	2	0	0-0	8	15	11	3	1	6-0	6	12.38	34	.417	.488	1-0-1	.000	0	162	-7		-0.3
Total	3	8	7	.533	32	30	0	0-0	180	197	112	29	8	72-3	111	5.35	77	.281	.352	62-0-4	.177	0	133	-22	72	-1.4

ROQUE, RAFAEL Rafael Antonio B1.1.1972 Cotui, D.R. BL/TL/6-4/186* d8.1

YEAR	TM LG	W	L	PCT	G	GS	CG-SHO	SV-BS	IP	H	R	HR	HB	BB-IB	SO	ERA	AERA	OAV	OOB	AB-HR-SH	AVG	PB	SUP	APR	DL	PW
1998	Mil N	4	2	.667	9	9	0	0-0	48	42	28	9	1	24-0	34	4.88	89	.237	.332	13-0-4	.077	-1	122	-3		-0.3
1999	Mil N	1	6	.143	43	9	0	1-1	84.1	96	52	16	4	42-1	66	5.34	86	.286	.369	17-0-1	.059	-0	82	-6		-0.5
2000	Mil N	0	0	—	4	0	0	0-0	5.1	7	6	1	0	7-1	4	10.13	46	.333	.483	0	—	0		-3		-0.1
Total	3	5	8	.385	56	18	0	1-1	137.2	145	86	26	5	73-2	104	5.36	84	.272	.362	30-0-5	.067	-2	101	-12		-0.9

ROSADO, JOSE Jose Antonio B11.9.1974 Newark NJ BL/TL/6-0/185* [KCA94 12/331] d6.12 Col Galveston (TX) CC [DL 2001 KC A 190]

YEAR	TM LG	W	L	PCT	G	GS	CG-SHO	SV-BS	IP	H	R	HR	HB	BB-IB	SO	ERA	AERA	OAV	OOB	AB-HR-SH	AVG	PB	SUP	APR	DL	PW
1996	KC A	8	6	.571	16	16	2-1	0-0	106.2	101	39	7	4	26-1	64	3.21	157	.249	.298	0	—	0	82	22		2.6
1997	KC A★	9	12	.429	33	33	2	0-0	203.1	208	117	26	4	73-3	129	4.69	101	.264	.326	2	.000	-0*	80	0		0.0
1998	KC A	8	11	.421	38	25	2-1	1-0	174.2	180	106	25	5	57-2	135	4.69	104	.260	.320	2	.500	0	89	25		2.4
1999	KC A★	10	14	.417	33	33	5	0-0	208	197	103	24	5	72-1	141	3.85	132	.248	.314	0	—	0	86	-1	153	-0.2
2000	KC A	2	2	.500	5	5	0	0-0	27.2	29	18	4	4	9-0	15	5.86	89	.271	.347	0	—	0	85	-1	190	-0.2
Total	5	37	45	.451	125	112	11-2	1-0	720.1	715	383	86	22	237-7	484	4.27	115	.257	.318		.111	0	85	46	343	4.9

YEAR	TM	LG	W	L	PCT	G	GS	CG-SHO	SV-BS	IP	H	R	HR	HB	BB-IB	SO	ERA	AERA	OAV	OOB	AB-HR-SH	AVG	PB	SUP	APR	DL	PW
ROSARIO, RODRIGO				Rodrigo B12.14.1977 LaRomana, D.R. BR/TR/6-2/160 d6.21																							
2003	Hou	N	1	0	1.000	2	2	0	0-0	8	5	2	0	1	3-1	6	1.13	393	.172	.273	0	—	0	170	2	93	0.3
ROSE, BRIAN				Brian Leonard B2.13.1976 New Bedford MA BR/TR/6-3/215* [BosA94 3/75] d7.25																							
1997	Bos	A	0	0	—	1	1	0	0-0	3	5	4	0	0	2-0	3	12.00	39	.357	.438	0	—	0	99	-2		-0.1
1998	Bos	A	1	4	.200	8	8	0	0-0	37.2	43	32	9	2	14-0	18	6.93	68	.285	.351	0	—	0	118	-9	138	-1.0
1999	Bos	A	7	6	.538	22	18	0	0-0	98	112	59	19	2	29-2	51	4.87	102	.280	.332	2-0-1	.000	-0	83	-2		0.2
2000	Bos	A	3	5	.375	15	12	0	0-0	53	58	37	11	3	21-3	24	6.11	82	.274	.345	3	.000	-0	87	-5		-0.7
	Col	N	4	5	.444	12	12	0	0-0	63.2	72	41	10	3	30-6	40	5.51	105	.281	.361	21-0-3	.048	-2	79	2		0.0
2001	NY	N	0	1	.000	3	0	0	0-0	8.2	10	4	3	0	2-1	4	4.15	97	.286	.324	1	.000	-0	0	0		0.0
	TB	A	0	2	.000	7	3	0	0-0	20.1	31	20	4	0	12-0	11	8.85	51	.356	.426	0	—	0	82	-9		-0.7
Total	5		15	23	.395	68	54	0	0-0	284.1	331	197	56	10	110-12	151	5.86	87	.287	.352	27-0-4	.037	-2	88	-21	138	-2.3
ROSE, CHUCK				Charles Alfred B9.1.1885 Macon MO D8.4.1961 Salina KS BL/TL/5-8.5/158 d9.13																							
1909	StL	A	1	2	.333	3	3	3	0	25	32	17	1	3	7	6	5.40	45	.330	.393	7-0-1	.000	-1	68	-7		-0.9
ROSE, DON				Donald Gary B3.19.1947 Covina CA BR/TR/6-3/195* d9.15 Col Stanford																							
1971	NY	N	0	0	—	1	0	0	0-0	2	2	0	0	0	0-0	1	0.00	—	.286	.286	0	—	0	0	1		0.0
1972	Cal	A	1	4	.200	16	4	0	0-0	42.2	49	25	9	0	19-5	39	4.22	70	.283	.352	10-1-1	.200	1	151	-7		-0.7
1974	SF	N	0	0	—	2	0	0	0-1	1	4	1	0	0	1-0	0	9.00	42	.667	.714	0	—	0	0	0		0.0
Total	3		1	4	.200	19	4	0	0-1	45.2	55	26	9	0	20-5	40	4.14	72	.296	.362	10-1-1	.200	1	151	-6		-0.7
ROSEBRAUGH, ZEKE				Eli Ethelbert B9.8.1876 Charleston IL D7.16.1930 Fresno CA TL d9.21																							
1898	Pit	N	0	2	.000	4	2	2	0	21.2	23	14	0	3	9	6	3.32	107	.271	.361	8	.375	1	50	-1		0.0
1899	Pit	N	0	1	.000	2	0	0	0	6	14	8	0	1	3	2	9.00	42	.452	.514	2	.000	-0	47	-3		-0.4
Total	2		0	3	.000	6	4	2	0	27.2	37	22	0	4	12	8	4.55	79	.319	.402	10	.300	1	49	-4		-0.4
ROSEMAN, CHIEF				James John B1856 New York NY D7.4.1938 Brooklyn NY BR/TR/5-7/167 d5.1.1882 M1 ▲																							
1885	NY	AA	0	1	.000	1	1	1	0	1	3	5	0	0	0	0	27.00	12	.333	.455	410-4	.278	0*	246	-3		-0.4
1886	NY	AA	0	0	—	1	0	0	0	7	6	6	0	0	0	0	5.14	63	.240	.240	559-5	.227	0*	-1			0.0
1887	NY	AA	0	0	—	2	0	0	0	8	11	14	0	2	5	1	7.88	54	.407	.529	241-1	.228	-0*	-4			-0.2
Total	3		0	1	.000	4	1	1	0	16	20	25	0	2	7	1	7.88	47	.328	.414	1210-10	.245	0	246	-8		-0.6
ROSENBERG, STEVE				Steven Allen B10.31.1964 Brooklyn NY BL/TL/6-0/185* [NYA86 4/106] d6.4 Col Florida [DL 1992 NY N 182]																							
1988	Chi	A	0	1	.000	33	0	0	1-0	46	53	22	5	0	19-0	28	4.30	93	.298	.360	0	—	0				
1989	Chi	A	4	13	.235	38	21	0	0-0	142	148	92	14	1	58-1	77	4.94	78	.273	.339	0	—	0	80	-20		-2.1
1990	Chi	A	1	0	1.000	6	0	0	0-0	10	10	6	2	0	5-0	4	5.40	71	.256	.341	0	—	0	-2			-0.1
1991	SD	N	1	1	.500	10	0	0	0-1	11.2	11	9	3	0	5-1	6	6.94	55	.250	.327	1	.000	-0	-3			-0.6
Total	4		6	15	.286	87	21	0	1-1	209.2	222	129	24	1	87-2	115	4.94	78	.276	.343	1	.000	-0	80	-25	182	-2.8
ROSENTHAL, WAYNE				Wayne Scott B2.19.1965 Brooklyn NY BR/TR/6-5/220(220-240) [TexA86 24/601] d6.26 C2 Col St. Johns																							
1991	Tex	A	1	4	.200	36	0	0	1-1	70.1	72	43	9	1	36-1	61	5.25	77	.257	.341	0	—	0	-8			-0.6
1992	Tex	A	0	0	—	6	0	0	0-0	4.2	7	4	1	0	2-0	1	7.71	50	.333	.391	0	—	0	-2			-0.1
Total	2		1	4	.200	42	0	0	1-1	75	79	47	10	1	38-1	62	5.40	75	.262	.344	0	—	0	-10			-0.7
ROSER, STEVE				Emerson Corey B1.25.1918 Rome NY D2.8.2002 Utica NY BR/TR/6-4/220 d5.5 Col Clarkson																							
1944	NY	A	4	3	.571	16	6	1	1	84	80	39	3	0	34	34	3.86	90	.256	.329	30-0-2	.100	-2	96	-2		-0.4
1945	NY	A	0	0	—	11	0	0	1	27	27	15	1	0	8	11	3.67	94	.262	.315	8	.125	-0	-2			-0.1
1946	NY	A	1	1	.500	4	1	0	0	3.1	7	6	0	0	4	1	16.20	21	.438	.550	0	—	0	124	-4		-0.8
	Bos	N	1	1	.500	14	1	0	1	35	33	15	1	0	18	18	3.60	95	.250	.340	5	.000	-1	75	0		-0.1
Total	3		6	5	.545	45	8	1	2	149.1	147	75	5	0	64	64	4.04	86	.261	.336	43-0-2	.093	-3	97	-8		-1.4
ROSS, BUSTER				Chester Franklin B3.11.1903 Kuttawa KY D4.24.1982 Mayfield KY BL/TL/6-1/195 d6.15																							
1924	Bos	A	4	3	.571	30	2	1-1	1	93.1	109	49	3	0	30	16	3.47	126	.307	.361	25	.200	-0	145	7		0.4
1925	Bos	A	3	8	.273	33	8	0	0	94.1	119	86	9	5	40	15	6.20	73	.313	.386	24-0-2	.125	-1	90	-18		-1.9
1926	Bos	A	0	1	.000	1	0	0	0	2.2	5	7	0	0	4	0	16.88	24	.385	.529	1	.000	-0	-4			-0.6
Total	3		7	12	.368	64	10	1-1	1	190.1	233	142	12	5	74	31	5.01	89	.311	.377	50-0-2	.160	-2	102	-15		-2.1
ROSS, CLIFF				Clifford David B8.3.1928 Philadelphia PA D4.12.1999 Philadelphia PA BL/TL/6-4/195 d9.11																							
1954	Cin	N	0	0	—	4	0	0	1	2.2	0	0	0	0	1	0	0.00	—	.000	.000	0	—	0	1			0.1
ROSS, ERNIE				Ernest Bertram "Curly" B3.31.1880 Toronto ON, Can. D3.28.1950 Toronto ON, Can. BL/TL/5-8/150 d9.17																							
1902	Bal	A	1	1	.500	2	2	2	0	17	20	18	0	1	12	2	7.41	51	.294	.407	8	.000	-1	76	-6		-0.6
ROSS, BOB				Floyd Robert B11.2.1928 Fullerton CA BR/TL/6-0/165* d6.16 Mil 1952-53 Col San Jose St.																							
1950	Was	A	0	1	.000	6	2	0	0	12.2	15	12	1	0	15	2	8.53	53	.300	.462	3	.000	-0	70	-5		-0.4
1951	Was	A	0	1	.000	11	1	0	0	31.2	36	25	3	0	21	23	6.54	63	.295	.399	9	.111	-0	43	-8		-0.5
1956	Phi	N	0	0	—	3	0	0	0	3.1	4	3	1	0	2-0	4	8.10	46	.333	.400	0	—	0	-1			-0.1
Total	3		0	2	.000	20	3	0	0	47.2	55	40	5	0	38-0	29	7.17	58	.299	.417	12	.083	-1	64	-14		-1.0
ROSS, GARY				Gary Douglas B9.16.1947 McKeesport PA BR/TR/6-1/190(175-195) [ChiN67*S1/7] d6.28 Col Grand View																							
1968	Chi	N	1	1	.500	13	5	1	0	41	44	22	1	0	25-3	31	4.17	76	.288	.383	11	.091	-1	82	-5		-0.3
1969	Chi	N	0	0	—	2	1	0	0-0	2	3	3	0	0	2-0	2	13.50	30	.143	.333	0	—	0	110	-2		-0.1
	SD	N	3	12	.200	46	7	0	3-4	109.2	104	58	5	5	56-8	58	4.19	86	.252	.345	23-0-5		-2	39	-8		-1.2
	Year		3	12	.200	48	8	0	3-4	111.2	105	61	5	5	58-8	60	4.35	82	.250	.345	23-0-5	.000	-2	49	-9		-1.3
1970	SD	N	2	3	.400	33	2	0	1-1	62.1	72	37	8	3	36-10	39	5.20	77	.305	.402	8-0-2	.500	2	201	-7		-0.3
1971	SD	N	1	3	.250	13	0	0	0-0	24.1	27	10	0	1	11-2	13	2.96	112	.300	.375	1-0-1	.000	-0	1			0.1
1972	SD	N	4	3	.571	60	0	0	3-3	91.2	87	35	2	4	49-12	46	2.45	135	.261	.359	13-0-1	.154	-0	6			0.5
1973	SD	N	4	4	.500	58	0	0	0-1	76.1	93	51	8	4	33-8	44	5.42	65	.304	.376	4-0-1	.000	-0	-16			-1.6
1974	SD	N	0	0	—	9	0	0	0-0	18	23	10	1	0	6-4	11	4.50	80	.315	.363	1	.000	-0	-2			-0.1
1975	Cal	A	0	1	.000	7	0	0	0-0	5	6	3	1	0	1-0	4	5.40	66	.273	.304	0	—	0	0	-1		-0.2
1976	Cal	A	8	16	.333	34	31	7-2	0-0	225	224	89	12	6	58-5	100	3.00	112	.258	.306	0	—	0	83	6		1.1
1977	Cal	A	2	4	.333	14	12	0	0-0	58.1	83	41	10	2	11-1	30	5.55	71	.337	.369	0	—	0	86	-11	83	-0.9
Total	10		25	47	.347	283	59	8-2	7-9	713.2	764	359	48	24	288-53	378	3.92	89	.278	.349	61-0-10	.115	-2	82	-37	83	-3.0
ROSS, GEORGE				George Sidney B6.27.1892 San Rafael CA D4.22.1935 Amityville NY BL/TL/5-10.5/175 d6.27																							
1918	NY	N	0	0	—	1	0	0	1	2.1	2	2	0	0	3	1	0.00	—	.222	.417	1	.000	-0	1			0.1
ROSS, BUCK				Lee Ravon B2.3.1915 Norwood NC D11.23.1978 Charlotte NC BR/TR/6-2/170 d5.7																							
1936	Phi	A	9	14	.391	30	27	12-1	0	200.2	253	146	17	0	83	47	5.83	88	.304	.367	71-0-4	.169	-1	91	-15		-1.5
1937	Phi	A	5	10	.333	28	22	7-1	0	147.1	183	102	12	2	63	37	4.89	96	.306	.373	49	.102	-3	92	-6		-0.8
1938	Phi	A	9	16	.360	29	28	10	0	184.1	218	132	23	0	80	54	5.32	91	.289	.357	63-1-5	.190	-0	79	-11		-1.2
1939	Phi	A	6	14	.300	29	28	6-1	0	174	216	143	17	0	95	43	6.00	78	.302	.384	58-0-7	.207	-1	91	-27		-2.6
1940	Phi	A	5	10	.333	24	19	10	1	156.1	160	91	15	0	60	43	4.38	102	.256	.322	53-1-2	.132	-2	89	1		-0.2
1941	Phi	A	0	1	.000	1	1	0	0	4	10	9	2	0	2	0	18.00	23	.435	.480	1	.000	-0	83	-6		-0.8
	Chi	A	3	8	.273	20	11	7	0	108.1	99	51	6	1	43	30	3.16	130	.239	.312	32-0-4	.219	1	67	9		0.8
	Year		3	9	.250	21	12	7	0	112.1	109	60	8	1	45	30	3.69	111	.249	.321	33-0-4	.212	1	69	3		0.6
1942	Chi	A	5	7	.417	22	14	4-2	1	113.1	118	63	6	0	39	37	5.00	72	.264	.323	38-0-2	.158	-0	95	-13		-1.4
1943	Chi	A	11	7	.611	21	21	7-1	0	149.1	140	61	6	2	56	41	3.19	105	.253	.323	46-1-4	.087	-1	101	3		0.2
1944	Chi	A	2	7	.222	20	9	2	0	90.1	97	56	7	2	35	20	5.18	66	.280	.350	26-0-6	.077	-2	106	-15		-1.7
1945	Chi	A	1	1	.500	13	2	0	0	37.1	51	28	3	0	17	8	5.79	57	.327	.393	11	.182	-0	51	-10		-0.6
Total	10		56	95	.371	237	182	65-6	2	1365.1	1545	882	114	7	573	360	4.89	88	.283	.351	448-3-30	.154	-8	90	-90		-9.8
ROSS, MARK				Mark Joseph B8.8.1957 Galveston TX BR/TR/6-0/195* [HouN79 7/164] d9.12 Col Texas A&M-Commerce																							
1982	Hou	N	0	0	—	4	0	0	0-0	6	3	1	0	0	0-0	4	1.50	222	.143	.143	0	—	0	1			0.1
1984	Hou	N	1	0	1.000	2	0	0	0-0	2.1	1	0	0	0	0-0	1	0.00	—	.125	.125	0	—	0	1			0.2
1985	Hou	N	0	2	.000	8	0	0	1-1	13	12	7	2	0	2-0	3	4.85	72	.240	.269	0	—	0	-2			-0.3
1987	Pit	N	0	0	—	1	0	0	0-0	1	1	1	0	0	0-0	0	9.00	46	.250	.250	0	—	-0	-0			0.0

YEAR	TM LG	W	L	PCT	G	GS	CG-SHO	SV-BS	IP	H	R	HR	HB	BB-IB	SO	ERA	AERA	OAV	OOB	AB-HR-SH	AVG	PB	SUP	APR	DL	PW
1988	Tor A	0	0	—	3	0	0	0-0	7.1	5	6	0	0	4-1	4	4.91	81	.185	.281	0	—	0		-1		-0.1
1990	Pit N	1	0	1.000	9	0	0	0-0	12.2	11	5	2	0	4-2	5	3.55	103	.244	.306	1	.000	-0		0		0.0
Total	6	2	2	.500	27	0	0	1-1	42.1	33	20	5	0	10-3	17	3.83	94	.213	.259	2	.000	-0		-1		-0.1

ROSSELLI, JOEY   Joseph Donald   B5.28.1972 Burbank CA   BR/TL/6-1/170   [SFN90 2/70]   d4.30

YEAR	TM LG	W	L	PCT	G	GS	CG-SHO	SV-BS	IP	H	R	HR	HB	BB-IB	SO	ERA	AERA	OAV	OOB	AB-HR-SH	AVG	PB	SUP	APR	DL	PW
1995	SF N	2	1	.667	9	5	0	0-0	30	39	29	5	0	20-2	7	8.70	47	.342	.428	10-0-1	.200	0	136	-14	49	-1.2

ROSSO, FRANK   Francis James   B3.1.1921 Agawam MA   D1.26.1980 Springfield MA   BR/TR/5-11/180   d9.15

YEAR	TM LG	W	L	PCT	G	GS	CG-SHO	SV-BS	IP	H	R	HR	HB	BB-IB	SO	ERA	AERA	OAV	OOB	AB-HR-SH	AVG	PB	SUP	APR	DL	PW
1944	NY N	0	0	—	0	0	0	0	5	5	5	0	0	3	1	9.00	41	.550	.609	0		0*		-2		-0.1

ROTBLATT, MARV   Marvin "Rotty"   B10.18.1927 Chicago IL   BB/TL/5-7/160*   d7.4   Col Illinois

YEAR	TM LG	W	L	PCT	G	GS	CG-SHO	SV-BS	IP	H	R	HR	HB	BB-IB	SO	ERA	AERA	OAV	OOB	AB-HR-SH	AVG	PB	SUP	APR	DL	PW
1948	Chi A	0	1	.000	7	2	0	0	18.1	19	16	0	1	23	4	7.85	54	.271	.457	4	.000	-0	74	-7		-0.4
1950	Chi A	0	0	—	2	0	0	0	8.2	11	7	2	0	5	6	6.23	72	.344	.432	2	.000	-0		-2		-0.1
1951	Chi A	4	2	.667	26	2	0	2	47.2	44	21	4	1	23	20	3.40	119	.244	.333	9-0-2	.000	-2	242	3		0.3
Total	3	4	3	.571	35	4	0	2	74.2	74	44	6	2	51	30	4.82	86	.262	.379	15-0-2	.000	-2	156	-6		-0.2

ROTHSCHILD, LARRY   Lawrence Lee   B3.12.1954 Chicago IL   BL/TR/6-2/180*   d9.11   M4/C11   Col Florida St.

YEAR	TM LG	W	L	PCT	G	GS	CG-SHO	SV-BS	IP	H	R	HR	HB	BB-IB	SO	ERA	AERA	OAV	OOB	AB-HR-SH	AVG	PB	SUP	APR	DL	PW
1981	Det A	0	0	—	5	0	0	1-0	5.2	4	1	0	0	6-1	1	1.59	238	.200	.370	0	—	0		1		0.1
1982	Det A	0	0	—	2	0	0	0	2.2	4	4	1	0	2-0	0	13.50	30	.333	.429	0	—	0		-3		-0.1
Total	2	0	0	—	7	0	0	1-0	8.1	8	5	1	0	8-1	1	5.40	72	.250	.390	0	—	0		-2		0.0

ROUNSAVILLE, GENE   Virle Gene   B9.27.1944 Konawa OK   BR/TR/6-3/205   d4.7   Col Diablo Valley (CA) JC

YEAR	TM LG	W	L	PCT	G	GS	CG-SHO	SV-BS	IP	H	R	HR	HB	BB-IB	SO	ERA	AERA	OAV	OOB	AB-HR-SH	AVG	PB	SUP	APR	DL	PW
1970	Chi A	0	1	.000	8	0	0	0-0	6.1	6	7	0	1	2-0	3	9.95	39	.357	.400	0	—	0		-4		-0.6

ROWAN, JACK   John Albert   B6.16.1887 New Castle PA   D9.29.1966 Dayton OH   BR/TR/6-1/210   d9.6

YEAR	TM LG	W	L	PCT	G	GS	CG-SHO	SV-BS	IP	H	R	HR	HB	BB-IB	SO	ERA	AERA	OAV	OOB	AB-HR-SH	AVG	PB	SUP	APR	DL	PW
1906	Det A	0	1	.000	1	1	1	0	9	15	13	0	0	6	4	11.00	25	.375	.457	4	.250	0	130	-7		-0.6
1908	Cin N	3	3	.500	8	7	4-1	0	49.1	46	17	0	0	16	24	1.82	126	.253	.313	14	.071	-0	105	2		0.2
1909	Cin N	11	12	.478	38	23	14	0	225.2	185	86	0	3	104	81	2.79	93	.233	.324	65-0-2	.092	-1	106	2		-0.2
1910	Cin N	14	13	.519	42	30	18-4	1	261	242	122	4	9	105	108	2.93	99	.254	.334	83-0-3	.229	3	100	-1		0.1
1911	Phi N	2	4	.333	12	6	2	0	45.2	59	35	3	1	20	17	4.73	73	.316	.385	13-0-1	.077	-1	80	-8		-0.9
	Chi N	0	0	—	1	0	0	0	2	1	4	0	1	2	0	4.50	74	.143	.400	1	.000	0		-1		-0.1
	Year	2	4	.333	13	6	2	0	47.2	60	39	3	2	22	17	4.72	73	.309	.385	14-0-1	.071	-1	80	-9		-1.0
1913	Cin N	0	4	.000	5	5	5	0	39	37	14	0	1	9	21	3.00	108	.264	.313	11	.182	-1	32	2		0.3
1914	Cin N	1	3	.250	12	2	0	2	39	38	22	1	0	10	16	3.46	85	.262	.310	8	.000	-1	73	-2		-0.4
Total	7	31	40	.437	119	74	44-5	3	670.2	623	313	8	15	272	267	3.07	92	.255	.333	199-0-6	.151	1	95	-13		-1.6

ROWE, DAVE   David Elwood   B10.9.1854 Harrisburg PA   D12.9.1930 Glendale CA   BR/TR/5-9/180   d5.30   M2   b-Jack ▲

YEAR	TM LG	W	L	PCT	G	GS	CG-SHO	SV-BS	IP	H	R	HR	HB	BB-IB	SO	ERA	AERA	OAV	OOB	AB-HR-SH	AVG	PB	SUP	APR	DL	PW
1877	Chi N	0	1	.000	1	1	0	0	1	3	2	0		2	0	18.00	17	.600	.714	7	.286	0*	16	-1		-0.2
1882	Cle N	0	1	.000	1	1	1	0	9	29	35	3		7	0	12.00	23	.492	.545	97-1	.258	0*	76	-13		-0.8
1883	Bal AA	0	0	—	1	0	0	0	4	12	11	1		2	1	20.25	17	.500	.538	256	.313	0*		-5		-0.2
1884	StL U	1	0	1.000	1	1	1	0	9	10	3	0		0	2	3.00	119	.263	.263	485-4	.293	0*	107	1		0.1
Total	4	1	2	.333	4	3	2	0	23	54	51	4		11	3	9.78	28	.429	.474	845-5	.295	0	66	-18		-1.1

ROWE, DON   Donald Howard   B4.3.1936 Brawley CA   D10.15.2005 Newport Beach CA   BL/TL/6-0/180   d4.9   C8   Col Compton (CA) CC

YEAR	TM LG	W	L	PCT	G	GS	CG-SHO	SV-BS	IP	H	R	HR	HB	BB-IB	SO	ERA	AERA	OAV	OOB	AB-HR-SH	AVG	PB	SUP	APR	DL	PW
1963	NY N	0	0	—	26	1	0	0	54.2	59	27	6	1	21-0	27	4.28	81	.280	.346	13	.231	0	148	-3		0.2

ROWE, KEN   Kenneth Darrell   B12.31.1933 Ferndale MI   BR/TR/6-2/185*   d4.14   C2

YEAR	TM LG	W	L	PCT	G	GS	CG-SHO	SV-BS	IP	H	R	HR	HB	BB-IB	SO	ERA	AERA	OAV	OOB	AB-HR-SH	AVG	PB	SUP	APR	DL	PW
1963	LA N	1	1	.500	14	0	0	1	27.2	28	16	2	1	11-3	12	2.93	103	.264	.336		.000	-1		-2		-0.2
1964	Bal A	1	0	1.000	6	0	0	0	4.1	10	10	1	0	1-0	4	8.31	43	.455	.478	0	—	0		-5		-0.9
1965	Bal A	0	0	—	6	0	0	0	13.1	17	5	0	0	2-1	3	3.38	103	.321	.333	1	1.000	0		1		0.0
Total	3	2	1	.667	26	0	0	1	45.1	55	31	3	1	14-4	19	3.57	90	.304	.352	6	.167	-0		-6		-1.1

ROWE, SCHOOLBOY   Lynwood Thomas   B1.11.1910 Waco TX   D1.8.1961 ElDorado AR   BR/TR/6-4.5/210   d4.15   Mil 1944-45   C2

YEAR	TM LG	W	L	PCT	G	GS	CG-SHO	SV-BS	IP	H	R	HR	HB	BB-IB	SO	ERA	AERA	OAV	OOB	AB-HR-SH	AVG	PB	SUP	APR	DL	PW
1933	Det A	7	4	.636	19	15	8-1	0	123.1	129	60	7	1	31	75	3.58	121	.269	.315	50-0-2	.220	-0*	100	9		0.8
1934	†Det A	24	8	.750	45	30	20-3	1	266	259	110	12	1	81	149	3.45	127	.256	.312	109-2-4	.303	12*	115	31		4.5
1935	†Det A☆	19	13	.594	42	34	21-6	0	275.2	272	121	11	2	68	140	3.69	113	.255	.301	109-3-3	.312	14*	141	20		3.2
1936	Det A★	19	10	.655	41	35	19-4	3	245.1	266	134	6	2	64	115	4.51	110	.275	.321	90-1-2	.256	7*	95	16		2.3
1937	Det A	1	4	.200	10	2	1	0	31.1	49	32	7	1	9	6	8.62	54	.350	.393	10-0-1	.200	-0	84	-13		-1.5
1938	Det A	0	2	.000	4	3	0	0	21	20	11	1	0	11	4	3.00	167	.256	.348	6-0-1	.167	-0	53	3		0.3
1939	Det A	10	12	.455	28	24	8-1	0	164	192	113	17	2	61	51	4.99	98	.291	.353	61-1-3	.246	2*	110	-5		-0.3
1940	†Det A	16	3	.842	27	23	11-1	0	169	170	68	15	1	43	61	3.46	137	.259	.305	67-1-1	.269	5*	137	26		3.1
1941	Det A	8	6	.571	27	14	4	1	139	155	70	6	0	33	54	4.14	110	.278	.318	55-1-1	.273	5*	95	7		1.2
1942	Det A	1	0	1.000	2	1	0	0	10.1	9	2	0	0	2	7	0.00	—	.220		4-0-1	.000	-1	87	3		0.3
	Bro N	1	0	1.000	9	2	0	0	30.1	36	19	2	1	12	6	5.34	61	.288	.355	19	.211	0*	180	-6		-0.3
1943	Phi N	14	8	.636	27	25	11-3	1	199	196	73	7	3	29	52	2.94	115	.249	.289	120-4-1	.300	16*	112	10		3.3
1946	Phi N	11	4	.733	17	16	9-2	0	136	112	39	3	6	21	51	2.12	162	.224	.263	61-1-1	.180	2*	80	19		2.3
1947	Phi N★	14	10	.583	31	28	15-1	1	195.2	232	106	23	3	45	74	4.32	93	.292	.333	79-2-2	.278	10*	105	-6		0.3
1948	Phi N	10	10	.500	30	20	8	2	148	167	74	5	2	31	46	4.07	97	.281	.319	52-1-2	.192	2*	93	0		0.2
1949	Phi N	3	7	.300	23	6	2	0	65.1	68	43	2	2	17	22	4.82	82	.300	.354	17-1-0	.235	2	67	-8		-0.9
Total	15	158	101	.610	382	278	137-22	12	2219.1	2332	1075	132	27	558	913	3.87	110	.269	.315	909-18-25	.263	76	109	106		18.8

ROWLAND, MIKE   Michael Evan   B1.31.1953 Chicago IL   BR/TR/6-3/205*   [SFN75 22/509]   d7.25   Col Millikin

YEAR	TM LG	W	L	PCT	G	GS	CG-SHO	SV-BS	IP	H	R	HR	HB	BB-IB	SO	ERA	AERA	OAV	OOB	AB-HR-SH	AVG	PB	SUP	APR	DL	PW
1980	SF N	1	1	.500	19	0	0	0-0	27	20	8	2	1	8-2	8	2.33	150	.206	.271	0		0		4		0.2
1981	SF N	0	0	—	9	1	0	0-0	15.2	13	7	1	1	6-2	8	3.45	99	.232	.313	1	1.000	0	313	0		0.0
Total	2	1	2	.333	28	1	0	0-0	42.2	33	15	3	2	14-4	16	2.74	127	.216	.287	1	1.000	0	313	4		0.2

ROY, CHARLIE   Charles Robert   B6.22.1884 Beaulieu MN   D2.10.1950 Blackfoot ID   BR/TR/5-10/190   d6.27   b-Luther

YEAR	TM LG	W	L	PCT	G	GS	CG-SHO	SV-BS	IP	H	R	HR	HB	BB-IB	SO	ERA	AERA	OAV	OOB	AB-HR-SH	AVG	PB	SUP	APR	DL	PW
1906	Phi N	0	1	.000	7	1	0	0	18.1	24	12	0	1	5	6	4.91	53	.316	.366	7-0-1	.000	-1*	84	-4		-0.3

ROY, EMIL   Emil Arthur   B5.26.1907 Brighton MA   D1.5.1997 Crystal River FL   BR/TR/5-11/180   d9.30   Col Boston College

YEAR	TM LG	W	L	PCT	G	GS	CG-SHO	SV-BS	IP	H	R	HR	HB	BB-IB	SO	ERA	AERA	OAV	OOB	AB-HR-SH	AVG	PB	SUP	APR	DL	PW
1933	Phi A	0	0	—	2	1	0	0	2.1	4	7	0	0	4	3	27.00	16	.364	.533	0	—	0	20	-5		-0.7

ROY, JEAN-PIERRE   Jean-Pierre   B6.26.1920 Montreal QC, Can.   BB/TR/5-10/160   d5.5

YEAR	TM LG	W	L	PCT	G	GS	CG-SHO	SV-BS	IP	H	R	HR	HB	BB-IB	SO	ERA	AERA	OAV	OOB	AB-HR-SH	AVG	PB	SUP	APR	DL	PW
1946	Bro N	0	0	—	3	1	0	0	6.1	5	7	2	0	5	6	9.95	34	.200	.333	2	.000	-0	177	-4		-0.2

ROY, LUTHER   Luther Franklin   B7.29.1902 Ooltewah TN   D7.24.1963 Grand Rapids MI   BR/TR/5-10.5/161   d6.12   b-Charlie

YEAR	TM LG	W	L	PCT	G	GS	CG-SHO	SV-BS	IP	H	R	HR	HB	BB-IB	SO	ERA	AERA	OAV	OOB	AB-HR-SH	AVG	PB	SUP	APR	DL	PW
1924	Cle A	0	5	.000	16	5	2	0	48.2	62	48	3	0	31	14	7.77	55	.318	.412	15-0-1	.267	-0	63	-17		-1.4
1925	Cle A	0	0	—	6	1	0	0	10	14	7	1	0	11	1	3.60	123	.368	.510	2	.000	-0	76	0		-0.1
1927	Chi N	3	1	.750	11	0	0	0	19.2	14	9	0	1	11	5	2.29	169	.209	.329	3	.333	0		2		0.4
1929	Phi N	3	6	.333	21	11	1	0	88.2	137	91	11	3	37	16	8.42	62	.350	.411	32	.281	2	108	-28		-2.0
	Bro N	0	0	—	2	0	0	0	3.2	4	2	0	0	2	0	4.91	94	.286	.375	1	.000	-0		0		0.0
	Year	3	6	.333	23	11	1	0	92.1	141	93	11	3	39	16	8.29	62	.348	.409	33	.273	2	109	-28		-2.0
Total	4	6	12	.333	56	17	3	0	170.2	231	157	15	4	92	36	7.17	64	.328	.408	53-0-1	.264	2	98	-43		-3.1

ROY, NORMIE   Norman Brooks "Jumbo"   B11.15.1928 Newton MA   BR/TR/6-0/200   d4.23

YEAR	TM LG	W	L	PCT	G	GS	CG-SHO	SV-BS	IP	H	R	HR	HB	BB-IB	SO	ERA	AERA	OAV	OOB	AB-HR-SH	AVG	PB	SUP	APR	DL	PW
1950	Bos N	4	3	.571	19	6	2	1	59.2	72	38	6	2	39	25	5.13	75	.305	.408	18-0-1	.167	0	126	-9		-0.9

ROZEK, DICK   Richard Louis   B3.27.1927 Cedar Rapids IA   D9.27.2001 LaQuinta CA   BL/TL/6-0.5/190*   d4.29

YEAR	TM LG	W	L	PCT	G	GS	CG-SHO	SV-BS	IP	H	R	HR	HB	BB-IB	SO	ERA	AERA	OAV	OOB	AB-HR-SH	AVG	PB	SUP	APR	DL	PW
1950	Cle A	0	0	—	12	2	0	0	25.1	28	15	3	0	19	14	4.97	87	.283	.398	5-0-1	.000	-1	177	-1		-0.2
1951	Cle A	0	0	—	7	1	0	0	15.1	18	12	1	1	11	5	2.93	129	.286	.400	3	.333	0	164	-1		-0.1
1952	Cle A	1	0	1.000	10	1	0	0	12.2	11	8	0	0	13	5	4.97	67	.224	.387	2	.000	-0	209	-2		-0.2
1953	Phi A	0	0	—	2	0	0	0	10.2	8	6	3	0	9	2	5.06	85	.222	.378	2	.000	-0		-1		0.0
1954	Phi A	0	0	—	2	0	0	0	1.1	0	1	0	1	3	0	6.75	58	.000	.500	0	—	0		0		0.0
Total	5	1	0	1.000	33	4	0	0	65.1	65	42	7	2	55	26	4.55	88	.260	.396	12-0-1	.083	-1	178	-5		-0.5

ROZEMA, DAVE   David Scott   B8.5.1956 Grand Rapids MI   BR/TR/6-4/200*   [DetA75*S4/71]   d4.11   Col Grand Rapids (MI) CC

YEAR	TM LG	W	L	PCT	G	GS	CG-SHO	SV-BS	IP	H	R	HR	HB	BB-IB	SO	ERA	AERA	OAV	OOB	AB-HR-SH	AVG	PB	SUP	APR	DL	PW
1977	Det A	15	7	.682	28	28	16-1	0-0	218.1	222	87	25	7	34-4	92	3.09	140	.265	.298	0	—	0	110	27		2.5
1978	Det A	9	12	.429	28	28	11-2	0-0	209.1	205	83	17	2	41-1	57	3.14	124	.260	.297	0	—	0	86	16		1.5
1979	Det A	4	4	.500	16	16	4-1	0-0	97.1	101	42	12	6	30-2	33	3.51	124	.270	.329	0	—	0	108	4	72	0.3

YEAR	TM LG	W	L	PCT	G	GS	CG-SHO	SV-BS	IP	H	R	HR	HB	BB-IB	SO	ERA	AERA	OAV	OOB	AB-HR-SH	AVG	PB	SUP	APR	DL	PW
1980	Det A	6	9	.400	42	13	2-1	4-1	144.2	152	68	11	5	49-14	49	3.92	105	.277	.339	0	—	0	117	4		0.4
1981	Det A	5	5	.500	28	9	2-2	3-2	104	99	42	12	3	25-8	46	3.63	104	.256	.305	0	—	0	58	3		0.2
1982	Det A	3	0	1.000	8	2	0	1-0	27.2	17	5	2	1	7-1	15	1.63	252	.179	.243	0	—	0	67	8	142	0.9
1983	Det A	8	3	.727	29	16	1	2-0	105	100	50	10	1	29-6	63	3.43	115	.248	.297	0	—	0	139	4		0.4
1984	Det A	7	6	.538	29	16	0	0-0	101	110	49	13	2	18-3	48	3.74	106	.274	.307	0	—	0	96	2		0.2
1985	Tex A	3	7	.300	34	4	0	7-4	88	100	45	10	2	22-3	42	4.19	102	.287	.332	0	—	0	64	1	33	0.1
1986	Tex A	0	0	—	6	0	0	0-0	10.2	19	9	1	0	3-0	3	5.91	73	.404	.423	0	—	0		-2		-0.1
Total 10		60	53	.531	248	132	36-7	17-7	1106	1125	490	113	29	258-42	448	3.47	118	.266	.310	0		0	102	67	247	6.4

RUBIO, JORGE Jorge Jesus (Chavez) B4.23.1945 Mexicali, Baja California, Mexico BR/TR/6-3/200* d4.21

YEAR	TM LG	W	L	PCT	G	GS	CG-SHO	SV-BS	IP	H	R	HR	HB	BB-IB	SO	ERA	AERA	OAV	OOB	AB-HR-SH	AVG	PB	SUP	APR	DL	PW
1966	Cal A	2	1	.667	7	4	1-1	0	27.1	22	10	2	1	16-1	27	2.96	113	.220	.333	8-0-1	.000	-1	52	1		0.0
1967	Cal A	0	2	.000	3	3	0	0	15	18	7	2	4	9-0	4	3.60	87	.316	.443	3	.333	1	18	-1		0.0
Total 2		2	3	.400	10	7	1-1	0	42.1	40	17	4	5	25-1	31	3.19	103	.255	.374	11-0-1	.091	-0	38	0		0.0

RUCKER, DAVE David Michael B9.1.1957 San Bernardino CA BL/TL/6-1/190* [DetA78 16/402] d4.12 Col La Verne

YEAR	TM LG	W	L	PCT	G	GS	CG-SHO	SV-BS	IP	H	R	HR	HB	BB-IB	SO	ERA	AERA	OAV	OOB	AB-HR-SH	AVG	PB	SUP	APR	DL	PW
1981	Det A	0	0	—	2	0	0	0	4	3	4	0	1	1-0	2	6.75	56	.188	.278	0	—	0		-2		-0.1
1982	Det A	5	6	.455	27	4	1	0-2	64	62	26	4	2	23-3	31	3.38	121	.251	.320	0	—	0	78	5		0.9
1983	Det A	1	2	.333	4	3	0	0	9	18	17	2	1	8-0	6	17.00	23	.419	.519	0	—	0	146	-13		-1.9
	StL N	5	3	.625	34	0	0	0-0	37	36	14	1	1	18-0	22	2.43	150	.263	.353	4	.000	-0		4		0.8
1984	StL N	2	3	.400	50	0	0	0-1	73	62	23	0	1	34-2	38	2.10	167	.237	.324	7	.143	-0		10		0.6
1985	Phi N	3	2	.600	39	3	0	1-1	79.1	83	42	6	2	40-6	41	4.31	86	.279	.361	12-0-1	.333	2*	119	-5		-0.1
1986	Phi N	2	0	.000	19	0	0	0-0	25	34	19	4	0	14-3	14	5.76	68	.340	.410	1	.000	-0		-5		-0.4
1988	Pit N	0	2	.000	31	0	0	0	28.1	39	19	2	0	9-1	16	4.76	72	.328	.369	2	.000	-0		-5		-0.4
Total 7		16	20	.444	206	10	1	1-4	319.2	337	164	19	8	147-15	170	3.94	95	.276	.354	26-0-1	.192	-1	115	-11		-0.6

RUCKER, NAP George B9.30.1884 Crabapple GA D12.19.1970 Alpharetta GA BR/TL/5-11/190 d4.15

YEAR	TM LG	W	L	PCT	G	GS	CG-SHO	SV-BS	IP	H	R	HR	HB	BB-IB	SO	ERA	AERA	OAV	OOB	AB-HR-SH	AVG	PB	SUP	APR	DL	PW
1907	Bro N	15	13	.536	37	30	26-4	0	275.1	242	94	3	8	80	131	2.06	114	.242	.303	97-0-3	.155	-1	104	8		0.7
1908	Bro N	17	19	.472	42	37	30-6	1	333.1	265	107	1	19	125	199	2.08	113	.231	.317	117-0-1	.179	-1	75	9		1.2
1909	Bro N	13	19	.406	38	33	28-6	1	309.1	245	95	6	14	101	201	2.24	116	.228	.303	101-0-7	.119	-5	70	14		0.8
1910	Bro N	17	18	.486	41	**39**	**27-6**	5	**320.1**	293	112	5	9	84	147	2.58	117	.251	.306	110-0-4	.209	-1	77	18		1.7
1911	Bro N	22	18	.550	48	33	23-5	4	315.2	255	102	12	8	110	190	2.71	123	.226	.300	104-1-7	.202	2	61	30		3.9
1912	Bro N	18	21	.462	45	34	23-**6**	4	297.2	272	101	6	3	72	151	2.21	152	.250	.298	102-0-4	.245	2	91	37		5.1
1913	Bro N	14	15	.483	41	33	16-4	3	260	236	99	3	7	67	111	2.87	115	.249	.304	87-0-2	.241	2	72	14		1.6
1914	Bro N	7	6	.538	16	16	5	0	103.2	113	57	2	4	27	35	3.39	84	.275	.323	34-0-3	.265	2	102	-6		-0.5
1915	Bro N	9	4	.692	19	15	7-1	1	122.2	134	42	3	2	28	38	2.42	115	.279	.322	42	.214	1	95	6		0.9
1916	†Bro N	2	1	.667	9	4	1	0	37.1	34	14	0	1	14	14	1.69	159	.241	.282	11	.091	-1	118	3		0.1
Total 10		134	134	.500	336	274	186-38	14	2375.1	2089	823	41	73	701	1217	2.42	119	.243	.306	805-1-31	.195	-1	81	133		15.5

RUDOLPH, ERNIE Ernest William B2.13.1909 Black River Falls WI D1.13.2003 Black River Falls WI BL/TR/5-8/165 d6.16

YEAR	TM LG	W	L	PCT	G	GS	CG-SHO	SV-BS	IP	H	R	HR	HB	BB-IB	SO	ERA	AERA	OAV	OOB	AB-HR-SH	AVG	PB	SUP	APR	DL	PW
1945	Bro N	0	1	1.000	7	0	0	0	8.2	12	10	1	0	7	3	5.19	72	.333	.442	0	—	1		-3		-0.2

RUDOLPH, DON Frederick Donald B8.16.1931 Baltimore MD D9.12.1968 Granada Hills CA BL/TL/5-11/195* d9.21

YEAR	TM LG	W	L	PCT	G	GS	CG-SHO	SV-BS	IP	H	R	HR	HB	BB-IB	SO	ERA	AERA	OAV	OOB	AB-HR-SH	AVG	PB	SUP	APR	DL	PW
1957	Chi A	1	0	1.000	5	0	0	0	12	6	3	2	0	2-0	2	2.25	166	.146	.186	2	.500	1		2		0.2
1958	Chi A	1	0	1.000	7	0	0	1	7	4	2	0	0	5-1	2	2.57	141	.190	.346	0	—	0		1		0.2
1959	Chi A	0	0	—	4	0	0	1	3	4	0	0	0	2-1	0	0.00	—	.333	.429	0	—	0		1		0.1
	Cin N	0	0	—	5	0	0	0	7.1	13	4	1	0	3-1	0	4.91	83	.394	.444	1	.000	0		0		0.0
1962	Cle N	0	0	—	1	0	0	0	0.1	1	0	0	0	0-0	0	0.00	—	1.000	1.000	0	—	0		0		0.0
	Was A	8	10	.444	37	23	6-2	0	176.1	187	84	13	3	42-2	68	3.62	111	.274	.316	57-0-1	.175	1	92	5		0.6
	Year	8	10	.444	38	23	6-2	0	176.2	188	84	13	3	42-2	68	3.62	112	.275	.317	57-0-1	.175	1	92	6		0.6
1963	Was A	7	19	.269	37	26	4	1	174	189	98	28	6	36-3	70	4.55	82	.275	.314	45-1-5	.178	2	77	-15		-1.9
1964	Was A	1	3	.250	28	8	0	0	70.1	81	36	10	0	12-5	32	4.09	90	.290	.317	15	.067	-1	54	-3		-0.2
Total 6		18	32	.360	124	57	10-2	3	450.1	485	227	54	9	102-13	182	4.00	96	.276	.317	120-1-6	.167	3	81	-9		-1.0

RUDOLPH, DICK Richard "Baldy" B8.25.1887 New York NY D10.20.1949 Bronx NY BR/TR(BB 1919-27)/5-9.5/160 d9.30 M1/C7 Col Fordham

YEAR	TM LG	W	L	PCT	G	GS	CG-SHO	SV-BS	IP	H	R	HR	HB	BB-IB	SO	ERA	AERA	OAV	OOB	AB-HR-SH	AVG	PB	SUP	APR	DL	PW
1910	NY N	0	1	.000	3	1	1	2	12	21	11	0	0	9	9	7.50	40	.350	.371	4	.250	0	50	-5		-0.6
1911	NY N	0	0	—	1	0	0	0	2	2	2	0	0	0	0	9.00	37	.250	.250	1	1.000	0		1		0.0
1913	Bos N	14	13	.519	33	22	17-2	0	249.1	258	101	4	2	59	109	2.92	112	.276	.320	88-0-4	.239	4*	92	14		2.2
1914	†Bos N	26	10	.722	42	36	31-6	0	336.1	288	105	9	4	61	138	2.35	117	.238	.276	120-0-5	.125	-1*	112	18		1.9
1915	Bos N	22	19	.537	44	**43**	30-3	1	341.1	304	125	4	6	64	147	2.37	109	.242	.282	116-1-4	.198	6*	109	7		1.6
1916	Bos N	19	12	.613	41	38	27-5	3	312	266	93	7	3	38	133	2.16	115	.235	**.261**	101-0-4	.158	1	93	14		1.9
1917	Bos N	13	14	.481	31	30	22-5	0	242.2	252	104	1	4	54	96	3.41	75	.272	.314	87-0-7	.230	3*	123	-20		-1.8
1918	Bos N	9	10	.474	21	20	15-3	0	154	144	63	2	0	30	48	2.57	104	.255	.292	54-0-3	.185	-1	66	0		-0.1
1919	Bos N	13	18	.419	37	32	24-2	2	273.2	282	95	2	3	54	76	2.17	132	.271	.314	88-1-1	.193	3	80	16		2.3
1920	Bos N	4	8	.333	18	11	3	0	89	104	57	4	4	24	24	4.04	75	.294	.346	27-0-2	.185	-0	96	-13		-1.7
1922	Bos N	0	2	.000	3	3	1	0	16	22	10	2	1	5	3	5.06	79	.328	.375	5	.400	1	88	-1		-0.1
1923	Bos N	1	2	.333	4	4	1-1	0	19.1	27	12	0	1	10	3	3.72	107	.333	.413	7	.000	-1	88	0		-0.1
1927	Bos N	0	0	—	1	0	0	0	1.1	1	0	0	0	1	0	0.00	—	.200	.333			0		1		0.0
Total 13		121	109	.526	279	240	172-27	8	2049	1971	778	35	27	402	786	2.66	104	.258	.298	698-2-30	.188	14	97	30		5.5

RUEBEL, MATT Matthew Alexander B10.16.1969 Cincinnati OH BL/TL/6-2/180* [PitN91 3/97] d5.21 Col Oklahoma

YEAR	TM LG	W	L	PCT	G	GS	CG-SHO	SV-BS	IP	H	R	HR	HB	BB-IB	SO	ERA	AERA	OAV	OOB	AB-HR-SH	AVG	PB	SUP	APR	DL	PW
1996	Pit N	1	1	.500	26	7	0	1-0	58.2	64	38	7	6	25-0	22	4.60	95	.277	.358	13-0-2	.231	1	120	-3		-0.1
1997	Pit N	3	2	.600	44	0	0	0-1	62.2	77	50	8	5	27-3	50	6.32	68	.301	.372	7-0-1	.000	-1		-14	16	-1.1
1998	TB A	0	2	.000	7	1	0	0-0	8.2	11	7	3	0	4-0	6	6.23	77	.314	.385	0	—	0	39	-2		-0.3
Total 3		4	5	.444	77	8	0	1-1	130	152	95	18	11	56-3	78	5.54	79	.291	.367	20-0-3	.150	-0	112	-19	16	-1.5

RUETER, KIRK Kirk Wesley B12.1.1970 Hoyleton IL BL/TL/6-3/207(190-212) [MonN91 18/477] d7.7 Col Murray St.

YEAR	TM LG	W	L	PCT	G	GS	CG-SHO	SV-BS	IP	H	R	HR	HB	BB-IB	SO	ERA	AERA	OAV	OOB	AB-HR-SH	AVG	PB	SUP	APR	DL	PW
1993	Mon N	8	0	1.000	14	14	1	0-0	85.2	85	33	5	0	18-1	31	2.73	153	.264	.303	26-0-8	.077	-1	111	12		1.1
1994	Mon N	7	3	.700	20	20	0	0-0	92.1	106	60	11	2	23-1	50	5.17	82	.294	.335	34-0-2	.118	-1	134	-10		-1.0
1995	Mon N	5	3	.625	9	9	1-1	0-0	47.1	38	17	3	1	9-0	28	3.23	133	.224	.267	16-0-2	.000	-2	96	6		0.8
1996	Mon N	5	6	.455	16	16	0	0-0	78.2	91	44	12	2	22-0	30	4.58	95	.294	.344	25-0-2	.120	-1	130	-2	16	-0.2
	SF N	1	2	.333	4	3	0	0-0	23.1	18	6	0	0	5-0	16	1.93	215	.207	.250	7	.143	0	51	6		0.7
	Year	6	8	.429	20	19	0	0-0	102	109	50	12	2	27-0	46	3.97	108	.275	.324	32-0-2	.125	-1	118	4		0.5
1997	†SF N	13	6	.684	32	32	0	0-0	190.2	194	83	17	1	51-8	115	3.45	120	.264	.311	65-0-7	.138	-1	117	14		1.4
1998	SF N	16	9	.640	33	33	1	0-0	187.2	193	100	27	1	57-3	102	4.36	92	.265	.321	67-0-9	.209	-1	139	-8		-0.8
1999	SF N	15	10	.600	33	33	1	0-0	184.2	219	118	28	2	55-2	94	5.41	79	.297	.346	58-0-8	.155	1	123	-23		-2.4
2000	†SF N	11	9	.550	32	31	0	0-0	184	205	92	23	2	62-5	71	3.96	110	.290	.345	60-0-10	.200	-2*	116	7		1.1
2001	SF N	14	12	.538	34	34	0	0-0	195.1	213	105	25	4	66-4	83	4.42	93	.283	.341	58-0-10	.172	2*	117	-8		-0.5
2002	†SF N	14	8	.636	33	33	0	0-0	203.2	204	83	22	1	54-7	76	3.23	122	.262	.308	62-0-13	.177	0*	116	15		1.6
2003	†SF N	10	5	.667	27	27	0	0-0	147	170	77	14	1	47-2	41	4.53	94	.297	.350	53-0-6	.132	-1	124	-3	45	-0.3
2004	SF N	9	12	.429	33	33	0	0-0	190.1	225	108	21	4	66-5	56	4.73	92	.296	.351	61-0-3	.131	-1*	94	-8		-0.6
2005	SF N	2	7	.222	20	18	0	0-0	107.1	131	78	12	1	47-3	25	5.95	72	.305	.368	30-0-6	.167	0*	102	-21	7	-1.3
Total 13		130	92	.586	340	336	4-1	0-0	1918	2092	1004	220	25	582-41	818	4.27	98	.281	.333	622-0-86	.153	-1	117	-23	68	-0.4

RUETHER, DUTCH Walter Henry B9.13.1893 Alameda CA D5.16.1970 Phoenix AZ BL/TL/6-1.5/180 d4.13 Mil 1918 ▲

YEAR	TM LG	W	L	PCT	G	GS	CG-SHO	SV-BS	IP	H	R	HR	HB	BB-IB	SO	ERA	AERA	OAV	OOB	AB-HR-SH	AVG	PB	SUP	APR	DL	PW
1917	Chi N	2	0	1.000	10	4	1	0	36.1	37	12	0	3	12	23	2.48	117	.285	.359	44-0-1	.273	2*	162	2		0.4
	Cin N	1	2	.333	7	4	1-1	0	35.2	43	17	0	2	14	12	3.53	74	.323	.396	24	.208	1*	101	-3		-0.1
	Year	3	2	.600	17	8	2-1	0	72	80	29	0	5	26	35	3.00	92	.304	.378	68-0-1	.250	3*	133	-1		0.3
1918	Cin N	0	1	.000	2	2	1	0	10	10	9	0	1	3	10	2.70	99	.244	.311	3	.000	-0	28	-2		-0.2
1919	†Cin N	19	6	**.760**	33	29	20-3	1	242.2	195	69	1	7	83	78	1.82	153	.223	.295	90-2-3	.261	6*	117	24		3.1
1920	Cin N	16	12	.571	37	33	23-5	3	265.2	235	87	2	9	96	99	2.47	123	.247	.321	104-0-3	.192	-1*	93	19		2.0
1921	Bro N	10	13	.435	36	27	12-1	2	211.1	247	116	7	7	67	78	4.26	91	.299	.356	97-2-2	.351	11*	89	-6		0.5
1922	Bro N	21	12	.636	35	35	26-2	0	267.1	290	123	11	6	92	92	3.53	115	.282	.345	125-2-5	.208	6*	96	18		2.5
1923	Bro N	15	14	.517	34	34	20	0	275	308	157	11	6	86	87	4.22	92	.287	.343	117-0-2	.274	4*	116	-8		-0.2
1924	Bro N	8	13	.381	30	21	13-2	3	168	190	92	4	5	45	63	3.91	96	.282	.332	62-0-1	.242	2*	86	-4		-0.2
1925	†Was A	18	7	.720	30	29	16-1	0	223.1	241	105	9	2	105	68	3.87	109	.281	.365	108-1-3	.333	6*	120	14		2.2
1926	Was A	12	6	.667	23	23	9	0	169.1	214	100	4	6	66	48	4.84	80	.311	.375	92-1-3	.250	4*	134	-16		-1.1

YEAR TM LG	W	L	PCT	G	GS	CG-SHO	SV-BS	IP	H	R	HR	HB	BB-IB	SO	ERA	AERA	OAV	OOB	AB-HR-SH	AVG	PB	SUP	APR	DL	PW
†NY A	2	3	.400	5	5	1	0	36	32	14	0	1	18	8	3.50	110	.248	.345	21	.095	-2*	79	3		0.1
Year	14	9	.609	28	28	10	0	205.1	246	116	5	5	84	56	4.60	84	.301	.370	113-1-3	.221	3	125	-14		-1.0
1927 NY A	13	6	.684	27	26	12-3	0	184	202	88	8	7	52	45	3.38	114	.287	.343	80-1-0	.262	5*	132	9		1.2
Total 11	137	95	.591	309	272	155-18	8	2124.2	2244	989	54	66	739	708	3.50	104	.277	.342	969-7-22	.258	45	109	50		10.2

RUFFCORN, SCOTT Scott Patrick B12.29.1969 Austin TX BR/TR/6-4/210* [ChiA91 1/25] d6.19 Col Baylor

YEAR TM LG	W	L	PCT	G	GS	CG-SHO	SV-BS	IP	H	R	HR	HB	BB-IB	SO	ERA	AERA	OAV	OOB	AB-HR-SH	AVG	PB	SUP	APR	DL	PW
1993 Chi A	0	2	.000	3	2	0	0-0	10	9	11	2	0	10-0	2	8.10	52	.265	.422	0	—	0	66	-5		-0.8
1994 Chi A	0	2	.000	2	2	0	0-0	6.1	15	11	1	0	5-0	3	12.79	37	.455	.513	0	—	0	49	-6		-0.9
1995 Chi A	0	0	—	4	0	0	0-0	8	10	7	0	2	13-0	5	7.88	57	.333	.556	0	—	0		-3		-0.1
1996 Chi A	0	1	.000	3	1	0	0-0	6.1	10	8	1	0	6-0	3	11.37	42	.370	.485	0	—	0	39	-5		-0.5
1997 Phi N	0	3	.000	18	4	0	0-0	39.2	42	40	4	7	36-1	33	7.71	55	.275	.423	6-0-1	.000	-0	82	-17	42	-1.1
Total 5	0	8	.000	30	9	0	0-0	70.1	86	77	8	9	70-1	46	8.57	51	.310	.455	6-0-1	.000	-0	66	-36	42	-3.4

RUFFIN, BRUCE Bruce Wayne B10.4.1963 Lubbock TX BB/TL/6-2/209* [PhiN85 2/34] d6.28 Col Texas

YEAR TM LG	W	L	PCT	G	GS	CG-SHO	SV-BS	IP	H	R	HR	HB	BB-IB	SO	ERA	AERA	OAV	OOB	AB-HR-SH	AVG	PB	SUP	APR	DL	PW
1986 Phi N	9	4	.692	21	21	6	0-0	146.1	138	53	6	1	44-6	70	2.46	159	.251	.306	55-0-1	.073	-3	110	19		1.3
1987 Phi N	11	14	.440	35	35	3-1	0-0	204.2	236	118	17	2	73-4	93	4.35	99	.298	.355	73-0-6	.055	-5	82	-5		-1.0
1988 Phi N	6	10	.375	55	15	3	3-2	144.1	151	86	7	3	80-6	82	4.43	82	.275	.368	33	.121	-0	72	-16		-1.7
1989 Phi N	6	10	.375	24	23	1	0-0	125.2	152	69	10	0	62-6	70	4.44	81	.301	.377	34-0-1	.176	2	103	-11		-1.0
1990 Phi N	6	13	.316	32	25	2-1	0-0	149	178	99	14	1	62-7	79	5.38	72	.297	.361	44-0-6	.068	-2	99	-25		-3.0
1991 Phi N	4	7	.364	31	15	1-1	0-0	119	125	52	6	1	38-3	85	3.78	98	.272	.327	24-0-6	.000	-1	83	0		-0.1
1992 Mil N	1	6	.143	25	6	1	0-2	58	66	43	7	0	41-3	45	6.67	58	.293	.398	4	.250	-0	67	-17		-1.8
1993 Col N	6	5	.545	59	12	0	2-1	139.2	145	71	10	1	69-9	126	3.87	124	.269	.350	25-0-3	.080	-1	110	11		0.7
1994 Col N	4	5	.444	56	0	0	16-5	55.2	55	28	5	2	30-2	65	4.04	123	.253	.343	4	.250		0	5		0.9
1995 †Col N	0	1	.000	37	0	0	11-1	34	26	8	1	0	19-1	23	2.12	254	.222	.331	2	.000	-0	10		76	0.8
1996 Col N	7	5	.583	71	0	0	24-5	69.2	55	35	5	3	29-3	74	4.00	130	.212	.288	1	.000		0	7		1.1
1997 Col N	0	2	.000	23	0	0	7-2	22	18	15	3	0	18-0	31	5.32	97	.220	.360	0	—	0	-1		123	-0.1
Total 12	60	82	.423	469	152	17-3	63-18	1268	1345	677	92	10	565-50	843	4.19	99	.275	.348	295-0-23	.081	-10	89	-23	199	-3.6

RUFFIN, JOHNNY Johnny Renando B7.29.1971 Butler AL BR/TR/6-3/172* [ChiA88 4/93] d8.8

YEAR TM LG	W	L	PCT	G	GS	CG-SHO	SV-BS	IP	H	R	HR	HB	BB-IB	SO	ERA	AERA	OAV	OOB	AB-HR-SH	AVG	PB	SUP	APR	DL	PW
1993 Cin N	2	1	.667	21	0	0	2-1	37.2	36	16	4	1	11-1	30	3.58	112	.247	.304	3	.333	0	2			0.2
1994 Cin N	7	2	.778	51	0	0	1-2	70	57	26	7	0	27-3	44	3.09	135	.223	.295	8	.000	-1	9			0.9
1995 Cin N	0	0	—	10	0	0	0-0	13.1	4	3	0	0	11-0	11	1.35	309	.093	.278	2	.000	0	4		31	0.2
1996 Cin N	1	3	.250	49	0	0	0-1	62.1	71	42	10	2	37-5	69	5.49	78	.292	.386	4	.500	1	-8			-0.4
2000 Ari N	0	0	—	5	0	0	0-0	9	14	9	4	0	3-1	5	9.00	53	.350	.395	0	—	0	-4		49	-0.2
2001 Fla N	0	0	—	3	0	0	0-0	3.2	5	4	0	1	4-1	4	4.91	85	.313	.476	0	—	0	-1			-0.1
Total 6	10	6	.625	139	0	0	3-4	196	187	100	25	4	93-11	163	4.13	102	.251	.336	17	.176	-0	2		80	0.6

RUFFING, RED Charles Herbert B5.3.1905 Granville IL D2.17.1986 Mayfield Hts. OH BR/TR/6-1.5/205 d5.31 Mil 1943-44 C1 HF1967 ▲

YEAR TM LG	W	L	PCT	G	GS	CG-SHO	SV-BS	IP	H	R	HR	HB	BB-IB	SO	ERA	AERA	OAV	OOB	AB-HR-SH	AVG	PB	SUP	APR	DL	PW
1924 Bos A	0	0	—	8	2	0	0	23	29	17	0	3	9	10	6.65	66	.333	.414	7	.143	-0	135	-4		-0.2
1925 Bos A	9	18	.333	37	27	13-3	1	217.1	253	135	10	2	75	64	5.01	91	.299	.357	79-0-2	.215	-0	88	-4		-0.5
1926 Bos A	6	15	.286	37	22	6	2	166	169	96	4	5	68	58	4.39	93	.274	.351	51-1-2	.196	0	69	-6		-0.8
1927 Bos A	5	13	.278	26	18	10	2	158.1	160	94	7	4	87	77	4.66	91	.277	.375	55-0-6	.255	1*	72	-6		-0.4
1928 Bos A	10	25	.286	42	34	25-1	2	289.1	303	147	8	10	96	118	3.89	106	.275	.339	121-2-7	.314	11*	71	6		1.8
1929 Bos A	9	22	.290	35	32	18-1	1	244.1	280	162	17	2	118	109	4.86	88	.297	.376	114-2-3	.307	5*	76	-18		-1.1
1930 Bos A	0	3	.000	4	3	1	0	24	32	19	1	1	6	14	6.38	72	.323	.368	11	.273	-1	56	-5		-0.4
NY A	15	5	.750	34	25	12-2	1	197.2	200	106	10	2	62	117	4.14	104	.260	.317	99-4-0	.374	17*	130	6		1.9
Year	15	8	.652	38	28	13-2	1	221.2	232	125	11	3	68	131	4.38	99	.268	.323	110-4-0	.364	18	122	1		1.5
1931 NY A	16	14	.533	37	30	19-1	2	237	240	130	11	6	87	132	4.41	90	.268	.323	109-3-6	.330	11*	143	-11		-0.1
1932 †NY A	18	7	.720	35	29	22-3	2	259	219	102	16	3	115	**190**	3.09	132	**.226**	.311	124-3-2	.306	14*	129	32		4.0
1933 NY A	9	14	.391	35	28	18	3	235	230	118	7	4	93	122	3.91	99	.258	.330	115-2-2	.252	8*	111	0		0.7
1934 NY A★	19	11	.633	36	31	19-5	0	256.1	232	134	18	1	104	149	3.93	103	.236	.310	113-2-0	.248	7*	122	2		0.7
1935 NY A	16	11	.593	30	29	19-2	0	222	201	88	17	1	76	81	3.12	130	.239	.303	109-2-1	.339	14*	103	27		4.2
1936 †NY A	20	12	.625	33	33	25-3	0	271	274	133	22	3	90	102	3.85	121	.263	.323	127-5-2	.291	16*	119	25		3.9
1937 †NY A	20	7	.741	31	31	22-4	0	256.1	242	101	17	1	68	131	2.98	149	.247	.296	129-1-2	.202	8*	137	43		4.0
1938 †NY A☆	**21**	7	**.750**	31	31	22-3	0	247.1	246	104	16	0	82	127	3.31	137	.258	.317	107-3-1	.224	10*	127	**37**		**4.5**
1939 †NY A★	21	7	.750	28	28	22-**5**	0	233.1	211	88	15	2	75	95	2.93	149	.240	.301	114-1-3	.307	9*	152	38		4.8
1940 NY A★	15	12	.556	30	30	20-3	0	226	218	98	24	3	76	97	3.38	119	.252	.314	89-1-1	.124	-3*	99	17		1.3
1941 †NY A☆	15	6	.714	23	23	13-2	0	185.2	177	87	13	1	54	60	3.54	111	.252	.306	89-2-1	.303	12*	136	7		1.7
1942 †NY A☆	14	7	.667	24	24	16-4	0	193.2	183	72	10	3	41	80	3.21	107	.250	.292	80-1-2	.250	7*	142	9		1.5
1945 NY A	7	3	.700	11	11	8-1	0	87.1	85	32	2	1	20	24	2.89	120	.251	.294	46-1-0	.217	1*	132	6		0.6
1946 NY A	5	1	.833	8	8	4-2	0	61	37	13	2	0	23	19	1.77	195	.171	.251	25	.120	-1	102	12	73	1.0
1947 Chi A	3	5	.375	9	9	1	0	53	63	39	7	0	16	11	6.11	60	.290	.339	24	.208	-0*	118	-13	65	-1.7
Total 22	273	225	.548	624	538	335-45	16	4344	4284	2115	254	58	1541	1987	3.80	109	.258	.323	1937-36-43	.269	143	112	200	138	31.4

RUHLE, VERN Vernon Gerald B1.25.1951 Coleman MI BR/TR/6-1/187(175-195) [DetA72 17/404] d9.9 C8 Col Olivet

YEAR TM LG	W	L	PCT	G	GS	CG-SHO	SV-BS	IP	H	R	HR	HB	BB-IB	SO	ERA	AERA	OAV	OOB	AB-HR-SH	AVG	PB	SUP	APR	DL	PW
1974 Det A	2	0	1.000	5	3	1	0-0	33	35	13	1	1	6	10	2.73	144	.273	.307	0	—	0	107	3		0.1
1975 Det A	11	12	.478	32	31	8-3	0-0	190	199	104	17	7	65-6	67	4.03	100	.266	.328	0	—	0	89	-1		-0.3
1976 Det A	9	12	.429	32	32	5-1	0-0	199.2	227	99	19	4	59-4	88	3.92	95	.288	.339	0	—	0	99	-4		-0.4
1977 Det A	3	5	.375	14	10	0	0-0	66.1	83	44	9	3	15-0	27	5.70	76	.305	.346	0	—	0	65	-8	26	-0.9
1978 Hou N	3	3	.500	13	10	2-2	0-0	68	57	17	0	1	20-1	27	2.12	157	.224	.282	18-0-1	.056	-1	94	10		0.7
1979 Hou N	2	6	.250	13	10	2-2	0-1	66.1	64	33	9	2	8-0	33	4.07	86	.249	.277	19-0-2	.053	-1	86	-4	110	-0.6
1980 Hou N	12	4	.750	28	22	6-2	0-0	159.1	148	51	7	3	29-1	55	2.37	138	.251	.287	49-0-4	.245	4	98	16		2.0
1981 †Hou N	4	6	.400	20	15	1	1-1	102	97	36	6	4	20-1	39	2.91	113	.250	.288	24-0-4	.250	3	97	5	21	0.8
1982 Hou N	9	13	.409	31	21	3-2	1-1	149	169	81	12	4	24-4	56	3.93	85	.289	.319	41-0-5	.098	-0	80	-14		-2.1
1983 Hou N	8	5	.615	41	9	0	3-0	114.2	107	49	13	3	36-7	43	3.69	93	.249	.308	19-0-4	.105	-0	106	-1		-0.1
1984 Hou N	1	9	.100	40	6	0	2-0	90.1	112	58	5	3	29-7	60	4.58	73	.309	.363	12	.083	-0	106	-15		-1.6
1985 Cle A	2	10	.167	42	16	1	3-1	125	139	65	16	2	30-6	54	4.32	96	.283	.324	0	—	0	71	-1	33	-0.2
1986 †Cal A	3	3	.250	16	3	0	1-0	47.2	46	25	5	1	7-0	23	4.15	100	.247	.276	0	—	0	80	0		0.0
Total 13	67	88	.432	327	188	29-12	11-4	1411.1	1483	675	119	35	348-37	582	3.73	98	.270	.316	182-0-20	.148	6	90	-14	190	-2.6

RUNYAN, SEAN Sean David B6.21.1974 Fort Smith AR BL/TL/6-3/200* [HouN92 5/125] d3.31

YEAR TM LG	W	L	PCT	G	GS	CG-SHO	SV-BS	IP	H	R	HR	HB	BB-IB	SO	ERA	AERA	OAV	OOB	AB-HR-SH	AVG	PB	SUP	APR	DL	PW
1998 Det A	1	4	.200	**88**	0	0	1-2	50.1	47	23	7	2	28-3	39	3.58	133	.255	.348	0	—	0		6		0.5
1999 Det A	0	1	.000	12	0	0	0-0	10.2	9	4	2	1	3-1	6	3.38	148	.237	.295	0	—	0		2	150	0.2
2000 Det A	0	0	—	3	0	0	0-0	3	2	2	0	0	2-0	1	6.00	82	.222	.333	0	—	0		0	61	0.0
Total 3	1	5	.167	103	0	0	1-2	64	58	29	9	3	33-4	46	3.66	131	.251	.339	0	—	0		8	211	0.7

RUPE, JOSH Joshua Matthew B8.18.1982 Portsmouth VA BR/TR/6-2/200 d9.16 Col Louisburg (NC) JC

YEAR TM LG	W	L	PCT	G	GS	CG-SHO	SV-BS	IP	H	R	HR	HB	BB-IB	SO	ERA	AERA	OAV	OOB	AB-HR-SH	AVG	PB	SUP	APR	DL	PW
2005 Tex A	1	0	1.000	4	1	0	0-0	9.2	7	4	0	2	4-0	6	2.79	164	.219	.342	0	—	0	102	1		0.1

RUPE, RYAN Ryan Kittman B3.31.1975 Houston TX BR/TR/6-5/230* [TBA98 6/192] d5.5 Col Texas A&M-Commerce

YEAR TM LG	W	L	PCT	G	GS	CG-SHO	SV-BS	IP	H	R	HR	HB	BB-IB	SO	ERA	AERA	OAV	OOB	AB-HR-SH	AVG	PB	SUP	APR	DL	PW
1999 TB A	8	9	.471	24	24	0	0-0	142.1	136	81	17	12	57-2	97	4.55	109	.253	.334	4	.000	-0	85	7		0.6
2000 TB A	5	6	.455	18	18	0	0-0	91	121	75	19	9	31-3	61	6.92	71	.321	.381	1	.000	-0	101	-20	20	-1.9
2001 TB A	5	12	.294	28	26	0	0-1	143.1	161	111	30	11	48-0	123	6.59	68	.283	.348	3	.333	1	89	-30		-2.9
2002 TB A	5	10	.333	15	15	2	0-0	90	83	60	11	10	25-0	67	5.60	81	.243	.311	1	.000	-0	75	-10	97	-1.5
2003 Bos A	1	1	.500	4	1	0	0-1	10	13	9	4	0	1-0	7	6.30	74	.302	.318	0	—	0	79	-2		-0.4
Total 5	24	38	.387	89	84	2	0-2	476.2	514	336	81	42	162-5	355	5.85	81	.275	.343	9	.111	-0	88	-55	117	-6.1

RUSCH, GLENDON Glendon James B11.7.1974 Seattle WA BL/TL/6-1/200(195-220) [KCA93 17/469] d4.6

YEAR TM LG	W	L	PCT	G	GS	CG-SHO	SV-BS	IP	H	R	HR	HB	BB-IB	SO	ERA	AERA	OAV	OOB	AB-HR-SH	AVG	PB	SUP	APR	DL	PW
1997 KC A	6	9	.400	30	27	1	0-0	170.1	206	111	28	7	32-0	116	5.50	86	.301	.353	3	.000	-0	90	-13	15	-1.1
1998 KC A	6	15	.286	29	24	1-1	0-0	154.2	191	104	22	4	50-0	94	5.88	83	.304	.358	3	.000	-0	74	-14	26	-1.6
1999 KC A	0	1	.000	3	0	0	0-0	4	7	7	1	1	3-0	4	15.75	32	.368	.478	0	—	0		-7		-0.7
NY N	0	0	—	1	0	0	0-0	1	1	0	0	0	0-0	0	0.00	—	.333	.333	0	—	0		1		0.0
2000 †NY N	11	11	.500	31	30	2	0-0	190.2	196	91	18	6	44-2	157	4.01	109	.267	.331	50-0-4	.060	-3	90	17		0.7
2001 NY N	8	12	.400	33	33	1	0-0	179	216	101	23	7	43-2	156	4.63	87	.300	.344	54-0-6	.056	-4	73	-13		-1.7
2002 Mil N	10	16	.385	34	34	4-1	0-0	210.2	227	118	30	5	76-1	140	4.70	88	.279	.343	66-1-14	.288	5*	94	-13		-1.0
2003 Mil N	1	12	.077	32	19	1	1-0	123.1	171	93	11	4	45-3	93	6.42	67	.331	.387	34-0-6	.206	1*	68	-28	24	-2.4

YEAR	TM LG	W	L	PCT	G	GS	CG-SHO	SV-BS	IP	H	R	HR	HB	BB-IB	SO	ERA	AERA	OAV	OOB	AB-HR-SH	AVG	PB	SUP	APR	DL	PW
2004	Chi N	6	2	.750	32	16	0	2-0	129.2	127	54	10	4	33-1	90	3.47	128	.255	.305	39-2-7	.154	1*	107	13		0.9
2005	Chi N	9	8	.529	46	19	1-1	0-1	145.1	175	79	14	1	53-8	111	4.52	97	.302	.357	41	.146	-0	77	-3		-0.3
Total	9	57	86	.399	271	202	11-3	4-1	1308.2	1517	758	157	39	399-17	961	4.88	90	.292	.345	290-3-35	.152	0	82	-65	65	-7.3

RUSH, ANDY   Jesse Howard   B12.26.1889 Longton KS   D3.16.1969 Fresno CA   BR/TR/6-3/180   d4.16

1925	Bro N	0	1	.000	4	2	0	0	9.2	16	14	3	0	5	4	9.31	45	.364	.429	3	.000	-0	91	-6		-0.6

RUSH, BOB   Robert Ransom   B12.21.1925 Battle Creek MI   BR/TR/6-4/205*   d4.22

1948	Chi N	5	11	.313	36	16	4	0	133.1	153	70	8	1	37	72	3.92	100	.287	.335	39-0-2	.128	-2*	54	-1		-0.2
1949	Chi N	10	18	.357	35	27	9-1	4	201	197	104	9	0	79	80	4.07	99	.255	.324	63-0-5	.032	-7	66	-1		-0.8
1950	Chi N☆	13	20	.394	39	34	19-1	1	254.2	261	124	11	6	93	93	3.71	113	.265	.332	90-1-1	.167	-1*	66	14		1.7
1951	Chi N	11	12	.478	37	29	12-2	2	211.1	212	108	16	3	68	129	3.83	107	.254	.312	68-0-4	.191	-0	100	3		0.3
1952	Chi N★	17	13	.567	34	32	17-4	0	250.1	205	99	14	6	81	157	2.70	143	.216	.282	96-0-2	.292	7	102	26		4.0
1953	Chi N	9	14	.391	29	28	8-1	0	166.2	177	97	17	5	66	84	4.54	98	.270	.341	54-0-3	.111	-2	71	-2		-0.4
1954	Chi N	13	15	.464	33	32	11	0	236.1	213	102	12	5	103	124	3.77	111	.243	.323	83-2-1	.277	7	84	15		2.5
1955	Chi N	13	11	.542	33	33	14-3	0	234	204	95	19	2	73-4	130	3.50	117	.234	.293	82-1-3	.110	-3	95	18		1.4
1956	Chi N	13	10	.565	32	32	13-1	0	239.2	210	101	30	2	59-8	104	3.19	118	.233	.280	82-0-4	.098	-3	93	14		0.9
1957	Chi N	6	16	.273	31	29	5	0	205.1	211	111	16	2	66-6	103	4.38	88	.265	.318	69-0-3	.203	2	93	-11		-1.0
1958	†Mil N	10	6	.625	28	20	5-2	0	147.1	142	59	13	1	31-7	84	3.42	103	.253	.291	45-0-3	.200	2	122	3		0.4
1959	Mil N	5	6	.455	31	9	1-1	0	101.1	102	39	5	1	23-2	64	2.40	148	.257	.298	32-0-1	.188	0	95	10		1.0
1960	Mil N	2	0	1.000	10	0	0	1	15	24	9	2	0	5-2	7	4.20	82	.369	.403	3	.333	1		-2		-0.2
	Chi A	0	0	—	9	0	0	0	14.1	16	10	4	0	5-2	12	5.65	67	.302	.362	1	1.000	0		-3		-0.1
Total	13	127	152	.455	417	321	118-16	8	2410.2	2327	1128	176	34	789-31	1244	3.65	109	.251	.311	807-4-32	.173	0	87	83		9.5

RUSIE, AMOS   Amos Wilson "The Hoosier Thunderbolt"   B5.30.1871 Mooresville IN   D12.6.1942 Seattle WA   BR/TR/6-1/200   d5.9   HF1977

1889	Ind N	12	10	.545	33	22	19-1	1	225	246	181	12	9	116	109	5.32	78	.270	.358	103	.175	-3	110	-25		-2.2
1890	NY N	29	34	.460	67	62	56-4	1	548.2	436	300	3	26	289	341	2.56	137	.211	.311	284	.278	10*	79	50		5.9
1891	NY N	33	20	.623	61	57	52-6	1	500.1	391	244	6	18	262	337	2.55	125	.207	.310	220	.245	4*	110	40		3.9
1892	NY N	32	31	.508	65	62	59-2	0	541	410	290	7	12	270	304	2.84	113	.202	.299	256-1	.215	-0	99	23		2.5
1893	NY N	33	21	.611	56	52	50-4	1	482	451	246	15	16	218	208	3.23	144	.240	.324	212-3	.269	3	103	74		6.8
1894	†NY N	36	13	.735	54	50	45-3	1	444	426	228	10	5	200	195	2.78	189	.250	.330	186-3-2	.280	2*	86	118		10.2
1895	NY N	23	23	.500	49	47	42-4	0	393.1	384	248	9	7	159	201	3.73	125	.252	.325	179-1-0	.246	-5*	100	37		2.8
1897	NY N	28	10	.737	38	37	35-2	0	322.1	314	143	6	10	87	135	2.54	163	.253	.308	144	.278	3*	126	58		5.9
1898	NY N	20	11	.645	37	36	33-4	1	300	288	149	6	9	103	114	3.03	115	.251	.317	138	.210	-1*	101	18		1.4
1901	Cin N	0	1	.000	3	2	2	0	22	43	21	1	0	3	6	8.59	37	.406	.422	8	.125	-0	44	-12		-0.5
Total	10	246	174	.586	463	427	393-30	5	3778.2	3389	2068	75	112	1707	1950	3.07	130	.234	.319	1730-8-2	.248	13	99	381		36.7

RUSKIN, SCOTT   Scott Drew   B6.8.1963 Jacksonville FL   BR/TL/6-2/185*   [PitN86 S3/64]   d4.9   Col Florida

1990	Pit N	2	2	.500	44	0	0	2-3	47.2	50*	21	2	2	28-3	34	3.02	121	.269	.367	6	.333	2		2		0.5
	Mon N	1	0	1.000	23	0	0	0-3	27.2	25	7	2	0	10-3	23	2.28	161	.243	.310	2	.000	-0		5		0.2
	Year	3	2	.600	67	0	0	2-6	75.1	75	28	4	2	38-6	57	2.75	133	.260	.347	8	.250	1		7		0.5
1991	Mon N	4	4	.500	64	0	0	6-5	63.2	57	31	4	3	30-2	46	4.24	86	.241	.333	2	.000	0		-3		-0.4
1992	Cin N	4	3	.571	57	0	0	0-3	53.2	56	31	6	1	20-4	43	5.03	72	.275	.339	3-0-0	.000	-0		-8		-0.9
1993	Cin N	0	0	—	4	0	0	0-0	1	3	2	1	0	2-0	0	18.00	22	.500	.625	0	—	0		-1		-0.1
Total	4	11	9	.550	192	0	0	8-14	193.2	191	92	15	6	90-12	146	3.95	92	.260	.343	13-0-2	.154	1		-5		-0.9

RUSSELL, ALLAN   Allan E. "Rubberarm"   B7.31.1893 Baltimore MD   D10.20.1972 Baltimore MD   BB/TR/5-11/165   d9.13   b-Lefty

1915	NY A	1	2	.333	5	3	1	0	27	21	10	1	1	21	21	2.67	110	.228	.377	8-0-1	.250	0	50	1		0.1
1916	NY A	6	10	.375	34	19	8-1	6	171.1	138	83	8	1	72	75	3.20	90	.232	.324	45-0-6	.044	-3*	84	-8		-1.1
1917	NY A	7	8	.467	25	10	6	2	104.1	89	42	2	7	39	55	2.24	120	.236	.319	31-0-1	.323	3*	72	2		0.7
1918	NY A	7	11	.389	27	18	7-2	4	141	139	68	6	5	73	54	3.26	87	.267	.363	42-0-4	.167	-1*	90	-9		-1.3
1919	NY A	5	5	.500	23	5	4-1	1	90.2	89	48	5	2	32	50	3.47	92	.251	.317	30-0-1	.233	0	85	-5		-0.4
	Bos A	10	4	.714	21	11	9-1	4	121.1	105	38	1	1	39	63	2.52	120	.246	.310	41-0-2	.122	-1	132	9		0.8
	Year	15	9	.625	44	20	13-2	5	212	194	86	6	3	71	113	2.93	106	.248	.313	71-0-3	.169	-1	110	4		0.4
1920	Bos A	5	6	.455	16	10	7	1	107.2	100	44	3	3	38	53	3.01	121	.251	.321	41-0-2	.122	-2*	98	7		0.5
1921	Bos A	6	11	.353	39	14	7	3	173	204	92	9	9	77	60	4.11	103	.303	.382	57	.123	-5*	75	2		-0.3
1922	Bos A	6	7	.462	34	11	1	2	125.2	152	81	6	5	57	34	5.01	82	.314	.392	38	.079	-3	51	-12		-1.3
1923	Was A	10	7	.588	52	5	4	9	181.1	177	81	9	2	77	67	3.03	124	.257	.348	50-0-7	.200	2*	83	13		1.2
1924	†Was A	5	1	.833	37	0	0	8	82.1	83	49	1	4	45	17	4.37	92	.282	.379	18-0-1	.278	2		-4		-0.2
1925	Was A	2	4	.333	32	2	1	2	68.2	85	57	6	1	37	25	5.77	73	.315	.399	14-0-1	.143	-1	50	-14		-1.1
Total	9	70	76	.479	345	112	54-5	42	1394.1	1382	693	58	44	610	603	3.52	99	.269	.351	415-0-26	.157	-10	80	-18		-2.4

RUSSELL, LEFTY   Clarence Dickson   B7.8.1890 Baltimore MD   D1.22.1962 Baltimore MD   BL/TL/6-1/165   d10.1   b-Allan

1910	Phi A	1	0	1.000	1	1	1-1	0	9	8	0	0	2	2	4	0.00	—	.258	.303	3	.000	-0	85	3		0.3
1911	Phi A	0	3	.000	7	2	0	0	31.2	45	32	1	5	18	5	7.67	41	.357	.456	13	.385	1	126	-16		-1.1
1912	Phi A	0	2	.000	5	2	1	0	17.1	18	18	1	3	14	9	7.27	42	.265	.412	4	.000	-0	72	-8		-0.8
Total	3	1	5	.167	13	5	2-1	0	58	71	50	2	8	34	21	6.36	47	.316	.423	20	.250	0	96	-21		-1.6

RUSSELL, REB   Ewell Albert   B4.12.1889 Jackson MS   D9.30.1973 Indianapolis IN   BL/TL/5-11/185   d4.18 ▲

1913	Chi A	22	16	.579	52	36	26-8	4	316.2	250	89	2	7	79	122	1.90	154	.220	.275	106-1-4	.189	3*	69	38		4.7
1914	Chi A	7	12	.368	38	23	8-1	1	167.1	168	80	3	3	33	79	2.90	92	.268	.308	64	.266	4*	91	-5		-0.2
1915	Chi A	11	10	.524	41	25	10-3	2	229.1	215	90	0	6	47	90	2.59	115	.249	.292	86-0-2	.244	4*	101	9		1.1
1916	Chi A	18	11	.621	56	25	16-5	3	264.1	207	88	1	1	42	112	2.42	114	.220	.254	91-0-2	.143	-4	103	13		1.0
1917	†Chi A	15	5	.750	35	24	11-5	3	189.1	170	61	1	1	32	54	1.95	136	.245	.279	68-0-4	.279	5*	121	13		2.0
1918	Chi A	7	5	.583	19	15	10-2	0	124.2	117	45	0	0	33	38	2.60	105	.252	.302	50-0-4	.140	-1*	105	3		0.0
1919	Chi A	0	0	—	1	0	0	0	1	1	0	0	1	0	1	—	—	1.000	1.000	—	—	0		0		0.0
Total	7	80	59	.576	242	148	81-24	13	1291.2	1128	453	7	18	267	495	2.33	120	.239	.282	465-1-16	.209	10	95	71		8.6

RUSSELL, JACK   Jack Erwin   B10.24.1905 Paris TX   D11.3.1990 Clearwater FL   BR/TR/6-1.5/178   d5.5

1926	Bos A	0	5	.000	36	5	1	0	98	94	44	7	1	24	17	3.58	114	.268	.316	21-0-1	.190	-0	87	8		0.6
1927	Bos A	4	9	.308	34	15	4-1	0	147	172	80	5	1	40	25	4.10	103	.298	.348	48-0-1	.125	-3*	94	2		-0.1
1928	Bos A	11	14	.440	32	26	10-2	0	201.1	233	102	6	4	41	27	3.84	107	.294	.332	62-0-7	.210	-0*	78	5		0.6
1929	Bos A	6	18	.250	35	32	13	0	227.1	263	132	12	3	40	37	3.92	109	.294	.322	70-0-5	.129	-4*	76	3		0.1
1930	Bos A	9	20	.310	35	30	15	0	229.2	302	162	11	3	53	35	5.45	85	.321	.359	79-1-2	.177	-3*	72	-23		-2.4
1931	Bos A	10	18	.357	36	31	13	0	232	298	145	7	2	65	45	5.16	83	.310	.355	82-0-4	.195	-0*	78	-19		-1.7
1932	Bos A	1	7	.125	19	6	1	0	39.2	61	35	2	0	15	7	6.81	66	.343	.394	11-0-1	.091	-1*	57	-10		-1.6
	Cle A	5	7	.417	18	11	6	1	113	146	67	5	1	27	27	4.70	101	.310	.349	40-0-1	.300	2	87	2		0.4
	Year	6	14	.300	37	17	7	1	152.2	207	102	7	1	42	34	5.25	89	.321	.361	51-0-2	.255	1	76	-7		-1.2
1933	†Was A	12	6	.667	50	3	2	13	124	119	45	3	1	32	28	2.69	156	.255	.305	34-0-2	.147	-1	122	20		3.1
1934	Was A☆	5	10	.333	54	9	3	7	157.2	179	86	6	2	56	38	4.17	104	.287	.348	44-0-2	.159	3	99	1		0.5
1935	Was A	4	9	.308	43	7	2	3	126	170	88	10	2	37	30	5.71	76	.324	.371	35	.000	-2	121	-19		-1.6
1936	Was A	3	2	.600	18	5	1	3	49.2	66	46	3	0	25	6	6.34	75	.317	.391	15-0-1	.000	-2	181	-11		-1.2
	Bos A	0	3	.000	23	2	0	0	40	57	27	2	0	16	9	5.62	94	.345	.403	7	.286	0	8	-1		0.1
	Year	3	5	.375	41	7	1	3	89.2	123	73	5	0	41	15	6.02	83	.330	.396	22-0-1	.091	-2*	125	-12		-1.1
1937	Det A	2	5	.286	25	0	0	4	40.1	63	35	4	1	20	10	7.59	60	.362	.431	7-0-1	.000	-0		-11		-1.8
1938	†Chi N	6	1	.857	42	0	0	3	102.1	100	43	1	1	30	29	3.34	115	.258	.313	32-0-1	.219	1		6		0.7
1939	Chi N	4	3	.571	39	0	0	3	68.2	78	32	3	0	24	32	3.67	107	.282	.339	17	.000	-2*		2		0.1
1940	StL N	4	3	.429	26	0	0	1	54	53	22	1	0	26	16	2.50	160	.252	.335	13	.000	-2		7		0.7
Total	15	85	141	.376	557	182	71-3	38	2050.2	2454	1187	82	24	617	457	4.46	97	.299	.346	617-1-29	.167	-11	85	-38		-3.5

RUSSELL, JEFF   Jeffrey Lee   B9.2.1961 Cincinnati OH   BR/TR/6-3/210(195-210)   [CinN79 5/126]   d8.13

1983	Cin N	4	5	.444	10	10	2	0-0	68.1	58	30	7	0	22-3	40	3.03	126	.233	.290	21-1-2	.143	1	86	4		0.6
1984	Cin N	6	18	.250	33	30	4-2	0-0	181.2	186	97	15	4	65-8	101	4.26	89	.263	.327	57-0-5	.140	-0*	72	-10		-1.2
1985	Tex A	3	6	.333	13	13	0	0-0	62	85	55	10	2	27-1	44	7.55	58	.324	.388	0	—	0	95	-21		-2.4
1986	Tex A	5	2	.714	37	0	0	2-0	82	74	40	11	2	31-2	54	3.40	127	.244	.315	0	—	0		6		0.5
1987	Tex A	5	4	.556	52	2	0	3-1	97.1	109	56	9	2	52-5	56	4.44	102	.285	.369	0	—	0	61	0	39	0.1

YEAR	TM LG	W	L	PCT	G	GS	CG-SHO	SV-BS	IP	H	R	HR	HB	BB-IB	SO	ERA	AERA	OAV	OOB	AB-HR-SH	AVG	PB	SUP	APR	DL	PW
1988	Tex A★	10	9	.526	34	24	5	0-0	188.2	183	86	15	7	66-3	88	3.82	107	.257	.324	1	.000	-0*	95	8		0.8
1989	Tex A★	6	4	.600	71	0	0	38-6	72.2	45	21	4	3	24-5	77	1.98	201	.182	.260	0	—	0		15		3.1
1990	Tex A	1	5	.167	27	0	0	10-2	25.1	23	15	1	0	16-5	16	4.26	92	.253	.361	0	—	0		-2	104	-0.3
1991	Tex A	6	4	.600	68	0	0	30-10	79.1	71	36	11	1	26-1	52	3.29	123	.235	.294	0	—	0		5		1.0
1992	Tex A	2	3	.400	51	0	0	28-9	56.2	51	14	3	2	22-3	43	1.91	201	.238	.313	0	—	0		12		2.1
	†Oak A	2	0	1.000	8	0	0	2-0	9.2	4	0	0	0	3-0	5	0.00	—	.125	.200	0	—	0		4		0.9
	Year	4	3	.571	59	0	0	30-9	66.1	55	14	3	2	25-3	48	1.63	235	.224	.298	0	—	0		17		3.0
1993	Bos A	1	4	.200	51	0	0	33-4	46.2	39	16	1	1	14-1	45	2.70	172	.231	.287	0	—	0		9	30	1.9
1994	Bos A	0	5	.000	29	0	0	12-3	28	30	17	3	1	13-2	18	5.14	98	.270	.346	0	—	0		0		0.0
	Cle A	1	1	.500	13	0	0	5-3	12.2	13	8	2	0	3-0	10	4.97	96	.265	.308	0	—	0		0		-0.1
	Year	1	6	.143	42	0	0	17-6	40.2	43	25	5	1	16-2	28	5.09	97	.269	.335	0	—	0		0		-0.1
1995	Tex A	1	0	1.000	37	0	0	20-4	32.2	36	12	3	0	9-1	21	3.03	160	.277	.324	0	—	0		6	31	0.8
1996	†Tex A	3	3	.500	55	0	0	3-3	56	58	22	5	4	22-3	23	3.38	156	.269	.341	0	—	0		11		1.1
Total	14	56	73	.434	589	79	11-2	186-45	1099.2	1065	525	100	28	415-43	693	3.75	112	.255	.323	79-1-7	.139	1	81	47	204	8.9

RUSSELL, JOHN John Albert B10.20.1894 San Mateo CA D11.19.1930 Ely NV BL/TL/6-2/195 d7.4 Mil 1918

YEAR	TM LG	W	L	PCT	G	GS	CG-SHO	SV-BS	IP	H	R	HR	HB	BB-IB	SO	ERA	AERA	OAV	OOB	AB-HR-SH	AVG	PB	SUP	APR	DL	PW
1917	Bro N	0	1	.000	5	1	1	0	16	12	8	1	0	6	1	4.50	62	.222	.300	4	.250	0	27	-2		-0.1
1918	Bro N			—	1	0	0	0	1	2	2	0	0	1	0	18.00	15	.500	.600	0	—	0		-1		-0.1
1921	Chi A	2	5	.286	11	9	4	0	66.1	82	42	3	1	35	15	5.29	80	.314	.397	25-0-1	.400	3	112	-7		-0.3
1922	Chi A	0	1	.000	4	1	0	1	6.2	7	5	0	0	4	3	6.75	60	.280	.379	1	.000	-0	125	-2		-0.1
Total	4	2	7	.222	21	11	5	1	90	103	57	4	1	46	19	5.40	73	.299	.384	30-0-1	.367	3	110	-12		-0.8

RUSSO, MARIUS Marius Ugo "Lefty" B7.19.1914 Brooklyn NY D3.26.2005 Fort Myers FL BR/TL/6-1/190 d6.6 Mil 1944-45 Col Long Island-Brooklyn

YEAR	TM LG	W	L	PCT	G	GS	CG-SHO	SV-BS	IP	H	R	HR	HB	BB-IB	SO	ERA	AERA	OAV	OOB	AB-HR-SH	AVG	PB	SUP	APR	DL	PW
1939	NY A	8	3	.727	21	11	9-2	2	116	86	37	6	1	41	55	2.41	181	.210	.283	40-0-8	.244	1	131	26		2.4
1940	NY A	14	8	.636	30	24	15	0	189.1	181	79	17	1	55	87	3.28	123	.249	.303	64-0-6	.188	2	133	17		2.1
1941	†NY A☆	14	10	.583	28	27	17-3	1	209.2	195	85	8	1	87	105	3.09	127	.247	.322	78-0-5	.231	3	108	20		2.4
1942	NY A	4	1	.800	9	5	2	0	45.1	41	15	2	1	14	15	2.78	124	.244	.306	17-0-1	.235	1	154	4		0.5
1943	†NY A	5	10	.333	24	14	5-1	1	101.2	89	53	7	2	45	42	3.72	87	.235	.319	31-0-2	.194	1	92	-7		-0.9
1946	NY A	0	2	.000	8	3	0	1	18.2	26	9	1	0	11	7	4.34	80	.333	.416	4	.000	-1*	41	-1		-0.2
Total	6	45	34	.570	120	84	48-6	5	680.2	618	278	41	6	253	311	3.13	122	.242	.312	235-0-16	.213	8	116	59		6.3

RUSTECK, RICH Richard Frank B7.12.1941 Chicago IL BR/TL/6-1/175 d6.10 Col Notre Dame

YEAR	TM LG	W	L	PCT	G	GS	CG-SHO	SV-BS	IP	H	R	HR	HB	BB-IB	SO	ERA	AERA	OAV	OOB	AB-HR-SH	AVG	PB	SUP	APR	DL	PW
1966	NY N	1	2	.333	8	3	1-1	0	24	24	10	1	0	8-0	9	3.00	121	.276	.337	5	.000	-1	113	1	33	0.1

RUTH, BABE George Herman "The Bambino","The Sultan of Swat" B2.6.1895 Baltimore MD D8.16.1948 New York NY BL/TL/6-2/215 d7.11 C1 HF1936 ▲

YEAR	TM LG	W	L	PCT	G	GS	CG-SHO	SV-BS	IP	H	R	HR	HB	BB-IB	SO	ERA	AERA	OAV	OOB	AB-HR-SH	AVG	PB	SUP	APR	DL	PW
1914	Bos A	2	1	.667	4	3	1	0	23	21	12	1	0	7	3	3.91	69	.236	.292	10	.200	0*	153	-3		-0.3
1915	†Bos A	18	8	.692	32	28	16-1	0	217.2	166	80	3	6	85	112	2.44	114	.212	.294	92-4-2	.315	16*	137	8		2.8
1916	†Bos A	23	12	.657	44	41	23-9	1	323.2	230	83	0	8	118	170	1.75	158	.201	.280	136-3-4	.272	14*	108	35		5.7
1917	Bos A	24	13	.649	41	38	35-6	2	326.1	244	93	2	11	108	128	2.01	128	.211	.284	123-2-7	.325	17*	103	22		4.9
1918	†Bos A	13	7	.650	20	19	18-1	0	166.1	125	51	2	2	49	40	2.22	121	.214	.277	317-11-3	.300	12*	112	10		2.9
1919	Bos A	9	5	.643	17	15	12	1	133.1	148	59	2	2	58	30	2.97	102	.290	.365	432-29-3	.322	14*	99	-1		1.4
1920	NY A	1	0	1.000	1	1	0	0	4	3	4	0	0	2	0	4.50	85	.200	.294	458-54-5	.376	1*	291	-1		-0.1
1921	†NY A	2	0	1.000	2	1	0	0	9	14	10	1	0	9	2	9.00	47	.350	.469	540-59-4	.378	2*	256	-4		-0.6
1930	NY A	1	0	1.000	1	1	1	0	9	11	3	0	0	2	3	3.00	143	.306	.342	518-49-21	.359	1*	180	2		0.3
1933	NY A★	1	0	1.000	1	1	1	1	9	12	5	0	0	3	0	5.00	78	.308	.357	459-34-0	.301	1*	131	-1		0.0
Total	10	94	46	.671	163	148	107-17	4	1221.1	974	400	10	29	441	488	2.28	122	.221	.297	3085-245-49	.338	78	117	67		17.0

RUTHERFORD, JOHNNY John William "Doc" B5.5.1925 Belleville ON, Can. BL/TR/5-10.5/170 d4.30 Col Detroit Mercy

YEAR	TM LG	W	L	PCT	G	GS	CG-SHO	SV-BS	IP	H	R	HR	HB	BB-IB	SO	ERA	AERA	OAV	OOB	AB-HR-SH	AVG	PB	SUP	APR	DL	PW
1952	†Bro N	7	7	.500	22	19	4	2	97.1	97	51	9	2	29	29	4.25	86	.262	.319	31-0-1	.290	2	98	-7		-0.7

RUTHVEN, DICK Richard David B3.27.1951 Sacramento CA BR/TR/6-3/190(187-200) [PhiN73*S1/1] d4.17 Col Cal St.-Fresno

YEAR	TM LG	W	L	PCT	G	GS	CG-SHO	SV-BS	IP	H	R	HR	HB	BB-IB	SO	ERA	AERA	OAV	OOB	AB-HR-SH	AVG	PB	SUP	APR	DL	PW
1973	Phi N	6	9	.400	25	23	3-1	1-0	128.1	125	69	10	3	75-9	98	4.21	91	.257	.358	38-0-6	.132	-1*	88	-6	29	-0.8
1974	Phi N	9	13	.409	35	35	6	0-0	212.2	182	106	11	3	116-7	153	4.02	95	.231	.329	68-0-5	.191	-1	83	-5		-0.7
1975	Phi N	2	2	.500	11	7	0	0-0	40.2	37	22	2	1	22-0	26	4.20	90	.243	.341	13-0-2	.154	-0*	100	-2		-0.4
1976	Atl N☆	14	17	.452	36	36	8-4	0-0	240.1	255	112	14	8	90-8	142	4.19	90	.275	.343	76-0-9	.171	-0*	85	-4		-0.4
1977	Atl N	7	13	.350	25	23	6-2	0-0	151	158	86	14	1	62-6	84	4.23	105	.267	.336	45-1-5	.267	3	76	1	63	0.4
1978	Atl N	2	6	.250	13	13	2-1	0-0	81	78	43	8	0	28-2	45	4.11	98	.257	.317	24-0-3	.083	-2	70	-1		-0.9
	†Phi N	13	5	.722	20	20	9-2	0-0	150.2	136	52	13	1	28-1	75	2.99	121	.248	.283	53-0-3	.283	4*	103	12		1.8
	Year	15	11	.577	33	33	11-3	0-0	231.2	214	95	21	1	56-3	120	3.38	110	.251	.295	77-0-6	.221	3	90	9		1.5
1979	Phi N	7	5	.583	20	20	3-2	0-0	122.1	121	59	10	2	37-6	58	4.27	91	.256	.311	41-0-2	.146	-0*	117	-4	68	-0.4
1980	†Phi N	17	10	.630	33	33	6-1	0-0	223.1	241	99	9	3	74-9	86	3.55	108	.283	.340	68-0-12	.235	3	109	6		1.0
1981	†Phi N★	12	7	.632	23	22	5	0-0	146.2	162	94	10	3	54-4	80	5.15	71	.281	.342	50-0-5	.140	3	120	-24		-2.9
1982	Phi N	11	11	.500	33	31	8-2	0-0	204.1	189	99	18	6	59-10	115	3.79	98	.246	.301	64-0-12	.109	-2	94	-3		-0.7
1983	Phi N	1	3	.250	7	7	0	0-0	33.2	46	23	5	0	10-0	26	5.61	64	.333	.368	9-0-3	.111	-0	116	-7		-0.7
	Chi N	12	9	.571	25	25	5-2	0-0	149.1	156	78	17	3	28-3	73	4.10	93	.269	.304	53-0-4	.226	2	117	-6		-0.4
	Year	13	12	.520	32	32	5-2	0-0	183	202	101	22	3	38-3	99	4.38	86	.281	.317	62-0-7	.210	2	116	-14		-1.1
1984	Chi N	6	10	.375	23	22	0	0-0	126.2	154	75	14	4	41-4	55	5.04	78	.302	.357	44-0-5	.159	0*	88	-13	-56	-1.5
1985	Chi N	4	7	.364	20	15	0	0-0	87.1	103	49	6	0	37-3	26	4.53	88	.299	.362	24-0-6	.208	-0	75	-5	51	-0.7
1986	Chi N	0	0	—	6	0	0	0-0	10.2	12	9	4	0	6-0	3	5.06	81	.293	.383	1	.000	-0		-2		-0.1
Total	14	123	127	.492	355	332	61-17	1-0	2109	2155	1075	165	38	767-72	1145	4.14	93	.267	.331	671-1-82	.183	5	95	-63	267	-6.6

RYAN, JACK Jack "Gulfport" B9.19.1884 Lawrenceville IL D10.16.1949 Handsboro MS BR/TR/5-10/165 d7.2

YEAR	TM LG	W	L	PCT	G	GS	CG-SHO	SV-BS	IP	H	R	HR	HB	BB-IB	SO	ERA	AERA	OAV	OOB	AB-HR-SH	AVG	PB	SUP	APR	DL	PW
1908	Cle A	1	1	.500	8	1	1	1	35.2	27	12	3	1	2	7	2.27	105	.220	.238	11	.091	0	143	1		0.1
1909	Bos A	3	3	.500	13	8	2	0	59.1	64	34	0	4	20	24	3.34	75	.288	.358	19-0-2	.211	0*	92	-7		-0.7
1911	Bro N	0	1	.000	3	1	0	0	6	9	7	1	1	4	1	3.00	111	.375	.483	1	.000	-0	68	-2		-0.2
Total	3	4	5	.444	24	10	3	1	101	100	53	4	6	26	32	2.94	85	.271	.329	31-0-2	.161	0	95	-8		-0.8

RYAN, JIMMY James Edward "Pony" B2.11.1863 Clinton MA D10.26.1923 Chicago IL BR/TL/5-9/162 d10.8.1885 Col Boston College ▲

YEAR	TM LG	W	L	PCT	G	GS	CG-SHO	SV-BS	IP	H	R	HR	HB	BB-IB	SO	ERA	AERA	OAV	OOB	AB-HR-SH	AVG	PB	SUP	APR	DL	PW
1886	†Chi N	0	0	—	5	0	0	1	23.1	19	13	3	3	13	15	4.63	78	.257	.368	327-4	.306	1*		0		0.1
1887	Chi N	2	1	.667	8	3	2	0	45	53	36	3	6	17	14	4.20	107	.305	.386	508-11	.285	2*	115	1		0.2
1888	Chi N	4	0	1.000	8	2	1	0	38.1	47	29	2	0	12	11	3.05	99	.297	.347	549-16	.332	4*	101	-2		0.0
1891	Chi N	0	0	—	2	0	0	1	5.2	11	7	0	0	2	2	1.59	210	.393	.433	505-9	.277	1*		-1		0.1
1893	Chi N	0	0	—	1	0	0	0	4.2	3	0	0	0	0	1	0.00	—	.176	.176	341-3	.299	0*		2		0.1
Total	5	6	1	.857	24	5	3	2	117	133	85	8	6	44	43	3.62	105	.295	.365	2230-43	.300	9	114	0		0.4

RYAN, JASON Jason Paul B1.21.1976 Long Branch NJ BB/TR/6-3/185* [ChiN94 9/246] d8.24

YEAR	TM LG	W	L	PCT	G	GS	CG-SHO	SV-BS	IP	H	R	HR	HB	BB-IB	SO	ERA	AERA	OAV	OOB	AB-HR-SH	AVG	PB	SUP	APR	DL	PW
1999	Min A	1	4	.200	8	8	1	0-0	40.2	46	23	9	3	17-0	15	4.87	106	.286	.363		—	0	59	1		0.1
2000	Min A	0	1	.000	16	1	0	0-0	26	37	24	8	1	10-0	19	7.62	69	.330	.384	0	—	0	53	-7		-0.3
Total	2	1	5	.167	24	9	1	0-0	66.2	83	47	17	4	27-0	34	5.94	88	.304	.371	0	—	0	58	-6		-0.2

RYAN, JOHN John A. B Birmingham MI BL/TR d4.19

YEAR	TM LG	W	L	PCT	G	GS	CG-SHO	SV-BS	IP	H	R	HR	HB	BB-IB	SO	ERA	AERA	OAV	OOB	AB-HR-SH	AVG	PB	SUP	APR	DL	PW
1884	Bal U	3	2	.600	6	6	5	0	51	61	42	1		16	33	3.35	80	.277	.326	25	.080	-3*	130	-5		-0.7

RYAN, JOHNNY John Joseph B10.1853 Philadelphia PA D3.22.1902 Philadelphia PA 5-7.5/150 d8.19.1873 ▲

YEAR	TM LG	W	L	PCT	G	GS	CG-SHO	SV-BS	IP	H	R	HR	HB	BB-IB	SO	ERA	AERA	OAV	OOB	AB-HR-SH	AVG	PB	SUP	APR	DL	PW
1874	Bal NA	0	0	—	1	0	0	0	3.1	13	8	0	0	0	0	16.20	14	.565	.565	181	.193	-0*		-3		-0.1
1875	NH NA	1	5	.167	10	6	4	0	59.1	70	55	1		9	1	3.19	65	.255	.279	146	.158	-1*	45	-6		-0.1
1876	Lou N	0	0	—	1	0	0	0	8	22	20	0	1	0	0	5.63	48	.449	.449	241-1	.253	-0*		-3		-0.1
Total	2 NA	1	5	.167	11	6	4	0	62.2	83	63	1	1	9	1	3.88	54	.279	.301	327	.177	-1	45	-9		-0.6

RYAN, KEN Kenneth Frederick B10.24.1968 Pawtucket RI BR/TR/6-3/230(200-230) d8.31

YEAR	TM LG	W	L	PCT	G	GS	CG-SHO	SV-BS	IP	H	R	HR	HB	BB-IB	SO	ERA	AERA	OAV	OOB	AB-HR-SH	AVG	PB	SUP	APR	DL	PW
1992	Bos A	0	0	—	7	0	0	1-0	7	4	5	2	0	5	5	6.43	66	.174	.310	0	—	0		-1		-0.1
1993	Bos A	7	2	.778	47	0	0	1-3	50	43	23	2	3	29-5	49	3.60	129	.235	.342	0	—	0		5		0.9
1994	Bos A	2	3	.400	42	0	0	13-3	48	46	14	1	1	17-3	32	2.44	207	.256	.323	0	—	0		13		1.1
1995	Bos A	0	4	.000	28	0	0	7-3	32.2	34	20	4	1	24-6	34	4.96	98	.268	.388	0	—	0		0		-0.1
1996	Phi N	3	5	.375	62	0	0	8-5	89	71	32	4	1	45-8	70	2.43	178	.223	.321	7-0-1	.143	-0		16		1.5
1997	Phi N	1	0	1.000	22	0	0	0-0	20.2	31	23	5	2	13-1	16	9.58	44	.344	.430	0	—	0		-12	123	-0.6
1998	Phi N			—	17	1	0	0-0	22.2	21	12	1	1	20-1	16	4.37	99	.253	.396	1	.000	-0	192	0	122	-0.1

YEAR	TM LG	W	L	PCT	G	GS	CG-SHO	SV-BS	IP	H	R	HR	HB	BB-IB	SO	ERA	AERA	OAV	OOB	AB-HR-SH	AVG	PB	SUP	APR	DL	PW
1999	Phi N	1	2	.333	15	0	0	0-0	15.2	16	11	2	0	11-2	9	6.32	74	.267	.380	0	—	0		-2		-0.4
Total	8	14	16	.467	240	1	0	30-14	285.2	266	140	21	9	164-26	225	3.91	117	.250	.352	8-0-1	.125		192	19	245	3.0

RYAN, NOLAN Lynn Nolan B1.31.1947 Refugio TX BR/TR/6-2/195(155-212) [NYN65 10/295] d9.11 HF1999

YEAR	TM LG	W	L	PCT	G	GS	CG-SHO	SV-BS	IP	H	R	HR	HB	BB-IB	SO	ERA	AERA	OAV	OOB	AB-HR-SH	AVG	PB	SUP	APR	DL	PW
1966	NY N	0	1	.000	2	1	0	0	3	5	5	1	0	3-1	6	15.00	24	.357	.471	0	—	0	48	-3		-0.6
1968	NY N	6	9	.400	21	18	3	0	134	93	50	12	4	75-4	133	3.09	98	.200	.314	44-0-1	.114	-1	80	-3	33	-0.3
1969	†NY N	6	3	.667	25	10	2	1-0	89.1	60	38	3	1	53-3	92	3.53	104	.189	.306	29-0-3	.103	-1	111	2	27	-0.1
1970	NY N	7	11	.389	27	19	5-2	1-1	131.2	86	59	10	4	97-2	125	3.42	119	.188	.333	45-0-2	.178	-1	78	8		0.9
1971	NY N	10	14	.417	30	26	3	0-0	152	125	78	8	15	116-4	137	3.97	87	.219	.365	47-0-3	.128	-0	86	-10		-1.6
1972	Cal A☆	19	16	.543	39	39	20-9	0-0	284	166	80	14	10	157-4	**329**	2.28	129	**.171**	.291	96-0-1	.135	0	84	22		2.9
1973	Cal A★	21	16	.568	41	39	26-4	1-0	326	238	113	18	7	162-2	**383**	2.87	125	.203	.302	0	—	0	88	30		3.2
1974	Cal A	22	16	.579	42	41	26-3	0-1	332.2	221	127	18	9	202-3	367	2.89	120	.190	.313	0	—	0	104	21		2.4
1975	Cal A☆	14	12	.538	28	28	10-5	0-0	198	152	90	13	7	132-0	186	3.45	104	.213	.339	0	—	0	93	2		0.1
1976	Cal A	17	18	.486	39	39	21-7	0-0	284.1	193	117	13	5	183-2	327	3.36	100	.195	.322	0	—	0	72	2		-0.2
1977	Cal A*	19	16	.543	37	37	**22-4**	0-0	299	198	110	12	6	204-7	341	2.77	142	.193	.329	0	—	0	91	38		4.3
1978	Cal A	10	13	.435	31	31	14-3	0-0	234.2	183	106	12	3	148-7	260	3.72	98	.220	.335	0	—	0	100	-1	38	-0.1
1979	†Cal A★	16	14	.533	34	34	17-5	0-0	222.2	169	104	15	6	114-3	223	3.60	113	.212	.311	0	—	0	109	10		1.2
1980	†Hou N	11	10	.524	35	35	4-2	0-0	233.2	205	100	10	3	98-1	200	3.35	98	.236	.314	70-1-5	.086	-1	109	-2		-0.4
1981	†Hou N★	11	5	.688	21	21	5-3	0-0	149	99	34	2	1	68-1	140	**1.69**	**194**	**.188**	.280	51-0-4	.216	3	97	**27**		**3.4**
1982	Hou N	16	12	.571	35	35	10-3	0-0	250.1	196	100	20	8	109-3	245	3.16	105	.213	.301	83-0-6	.120	-1	102	5		0.3
1983	Hou N	14	9	.609	29	29	5-2	0-0	196.1	134	74	9	4	101-3	183	2.98	115	.195	.300	69-0-4	.072	-1	96	11	46	0.8
1984	Hou N	12	11	.522	30	30	5-2	0-0	183.2	143	78	12	4	69-2	197	3.04	110	.211	.286	61-0-5	.098	-2	106	4	30	0.2
1985	Hou N★	10	12	.455	35	35	4	0-0	232	205	108	12	9	95-8	209	3.80	92	.239	.318	63-0-14	.111	-1	98	-6		-0.8
1986	†Hou N	12	8	.600	30	30	1	0-0	178	119	72	14	4	82-5	194	3.34	108	.188	.283	59-0-3	.102	-2	93	6	38	0.3
1987	Hou N	8	16	.333	34	34	0	0-0	211.2	154	75	14	4	87-2	**270**	2.76	142	.199	.284	65-1-7	.062	-3	77	**27**		2.5
1988	Hou N	12	11	.522	33	33	4-1	0-0	220	186	98	18	7	87-6	228	3.52	95	.227	.304	70-0-7	.057	-3	103	-5		-1.0
1989	Tex A★	16	10	.615	32	32	6-2	0-0	239.1	162	96	17	9	98-3	**301**	3.20	125	**.187**	.275	0	—	0	99	21		2.1
1990	Tex A	13	9	.591	30	30	5-2	0-0	204	137	86	18	7	74-2	**232**	3.44	114	**.188**	**.267**	0	—	0	99	12	19	1.1
1991	Tex A	12	6	.667	27	27	2-2	0-0	173	102	58	12	5	72-0	203	2.91	139	**.172**	**.263**	0	—	0	106	24	36	2.3
1992	Tex A	5	9	.357	27	27	2	0-0	157.1	138	75	9	12	69-0	157	3.72	103	.238	.327	0	—	0	91	1	23	0.1
1993	Tex A	5	5	.500	13	13	0	0-0	66.1	54	47	5	1	40-0	46	4.88	86	.220	.329	0	—	0	88	-9	115	-1.2
Total	27	324	292	.526	807	773	222-61	3-2	5386	3923	2178	321	158	2795-78	5714	3.19	112	.204	.307	852-2-65	.110	-17	95	236	405	22.2

RYAN, B.J. Robert Victor B12.28.1975 Bossier City LA BR/TR/6-6/230(230-260) [CinN98 17/500] d7.28 Col Louisiana-Lafayette

YEAR	TM LG	W	L	PCT	G	GS	CG-SHO	SV-BS	IP	H	R	HR	HB	BB-IB	SO	ERA	AERA	OAV	OOB	AB-HR-SH	AVG	PB	SUP	APR	DL	PW
1999	Cin N	0	0	—	7	0	0	0-0	2	4	1	0	1	1-0	1	4.50	104	.500	.556	0		0	0			0.0
	Bal A	1	0	1.000	13	0	0	0-0	18.1	9	6	0	0	12-1	28	2.95	160	.150	.288	0	—	0	4			0.2
2000	Bal A	2	3	.400	42	0	0	0-3	42.2	36	29	7	0	31-1	41	5.91	80	.225	.349	0	—	0	-6			-0.5
2001	Bal A	2	4	.333	61	0	0	2-2	53	47	31	6	2	30-4	54	4.25	102	.233	.335	1	.000	-0	-1			-0.2
2002	Bal A	2	1	.667	67	0	0	1-1	57.2	51	31	7	4	33-4	56	4.68	93	.241	.353	1	.000	-0	-2			-0.1
2003	Bal A	4	1	.800	76	0	0	0-2	50.1	42	19	1	3	27-0	63	3.40	135	.227	.330	0	—	0	7			0.6
2004	Bal A	4	6	.400	76	0	0	3-4	87	64	24	4	1	35-9	122	2.28	205	.200	.279	0	—	0	23			2.4
2005	Bal A★	1	4	.200	69	0	0	36-5	70.1	54	20	4	2	26-2	100	2.43	182	.208	.284	0	—	0	16			2.4
Total	7	16	19	.457	405	0	0	42-17	381.1	307	161	29	12	195-21	465	3.54	128	.218	.317	2	.000	-0	41			4.8

RYAN, ROSY Wilfred Patrick Dolan B3.15.1898 Worcester MA D12.10.1980 Scottsdale AZ BL/TR/6-0/185 d9.7 Col Holy Cross

YEAR	TM LG	W	L	PCT	G	GS	CG-SHO	SV-BS	IP	H	R	HR	HB	BB-IB	SO	ERA	AERA	OAV	OOB	AB-HR-SH	AVG	PB	SUP	APR	DL	PW
1919	NY N	1	2	.333	4	3	1	0	20.1	20	9	0	1	9	7	3.10	91	.260	.345	6	.000	-1	66	-1		-0.2
1920	NY N	0	1	.000	3	1	1	0	15.1	14	6	1	0	4	5	1.76	170	.259	.310	5	.000	1	52	1		0.0
1921	NY N	7	10	.412	36	16	5	3	147.1	140	72	6	1	32	58	3.73	98	.255	.297	45-0-3	.200	-1	112	-1		-0.1
1922	†NY N	17	12	.586	46	22	12-1	3	191.2	194	87	5	2	74	75	3.01	133	.269	.338	62-0-3	.194	1	94	18		2.5
1923	†NY N	16	5	.762	**45**	15	7	-4	172.2	169	77	8	2	46	58	3.49	109	.257	.308	53-0-7	.208	0	176	6		0.7
1924	†NY N	8	6	.571	37	9	2	5	124.2	137	64	1	2	37	36	4.26	86	.285	.339	36-0-1	.139	-1	111	-7		-1.0
1925	Bos N	.2	8	.200	37	7	1	2*	122.2	152	103	7	0	52	48	6.31	64	.303	.368	39-1-0	.282	3*	150	-33		-2.1
1926	Bos N	0	2	.000	7	2	0	0	19	29	19	1	0	7	1	7.58	47	.392	.444	5	.200	-0	47	-9		-0.8
1928	NY A	0	0	—	3	0	0	0	6	17	11	1	0	1	5	16.50	23	.486	.500	4	.000	-1		-8		-0.4
1933	Bro N	1	1	.500	30	0	0	2	61.1	69	38	3	3	16	22	4.55	71	.276	.327	13	.154	0		-5		-0.5
Total	10	52	47	.525	248	75	29-1	19	881	941	486	33	11	278	315	4.14	91	.277	.333	268-1-14	.190	1	121	-44		-1.9

RYBA, MIKE Dominic Joseph B6.9.1903 DeLancey PA D12.13.1971 Brookline Station MO BR/TR/5-11.5/195 d9.22 C4 Col St. Francis (PA)

YEAR	TM LG	W	L	PCT	G	GS	CG-SHO	SV-BS	IP	H	R	HR	HB	BB-IB	SO	ERA	AERA	OAV	OOB	AB-HR-SH	AVG	PB	SUP	APR	DL	PW
1935	StL N	1	1	.500	2	1	1	0	16	15	6	0	0	1	6	3.38	121	.242	.254	5-0-1	.400	1	62	2		0.3
1936	StL N	5	1	.833	14	0	0	0	45	55	33	3	2	16	25	5.40	73	.294	.356	18-0-1	.167	-0*		-8		-1.0
1937	StL N	9	6	.600	38	8	5	0	135	152	76	8	2	40	57	4.13	96	.284	.336	48-0-1	.313	4*	119	-3		0.1
1938	StL N	1	1	.500	3	0	0	0	5	11	4	1	0	1	0	5.40	73	.344	.375	0	—	0		-1		-0.1
1941	Bos A	7	3	.700	40	3	0	6	121	143	72	14	0	42	54	4.46	93	.297	.353	37-0-4	.216	1	166	-5		-0.2
1942	Bos A	3	3	.500	18	0	0	3	44.1	49	25	1	1	13	16	3.86	97	.278	.332	17	.294	1*		-2		-0.2
1943	Bos A	7	5	.583	40	8	4-1	2	143.2	142	57	4	0	57	50	3.26	102	.262	.333	43-0-4	.186	0	130	1		0.1
1944	Bos A	12	7	.632	42	7	2	2	138	119	57	7	0	39	50	3.33	102	.233	.287	41-0-5	.146	-0	116	2		0.3
1945	Bos A	7	6	.538	34	9	4-1	2	123	122	45	5	2	33	44	2.49	137	.259	.310	36-0-4	.250	2	106	10		1.2
1946	†Bos A	0	1	.000	9	0	0	1	12.2	12	7	1	0	5	5	3.55	103	.261	.333	2	1.000	1		0		0.0
Total	10	52	34	.605	240	36	16-2	16	783.2	817	381	47	7	247	307	3.66	100	.269	.326	247-0-20	.235	9	118	-4		0.5

RYERSON, GARY Gary Lawrence B6.17.1948 Los Angeles CA BR/TL/6-1/160(160-175) [SFN66 13/257] d6.28

YEAR	TM LG	W	L	PCT	G	GS	CG-SHO	SV-BS	IP	H	R	HR	HB	BB-IB	SO	ERA	AERA	OAV	OOB	AB-HR-SH	AVG	PB	SUP	APR	DL	PW
1972	Mil A	3	8	.273	20	14	4-1	0-0	102	119	48	9	0	21-5	45	3.62	85	.290	.323	24-0-2	.042	-1	68	-7		-1.0
1973	Mil A	0	1	.000	9	4	0	0-0	23	32	23	0	0	7-1	10	7.83	49	.327	.364	0	—	0	106	-10		-0.5
Total	2	3	9	.250	29	18	4-1	0-0	125	151	71	9	0	28-6	55	4.39	73	.297	.331	24-0-2	.042	-1	79	-17		-1.5

SAARLOOS, KIRK Kirk Craig B5.23.1979 Long Beach CA BR/TR/6-0/185* [HouN01 3/86] d6.18 Col Cal St.-Fullerton

YEAR	TM LG	W	L	PCT	G	GS	CG-SHO	SV-BS	IP	H	R	HR	HB	BB-IB	SO	ERA	AERA	OAV	OOB	AB-HR-SH	AVG	PB	SUP	APR	DL	PW
2002	Hou N	6	7	.462	17	17	1-1	0-0	85.1	100	59	12	6	27-5	54	6.01	72	.301	.362	30-0-5	.067	-2	111	-14		-2.0
2003	Hou N	2	1	-.667	36	4	0	0-0	49.1	55	31	4	3	17-3	44	4.93	90	.281	.346	5-0-3	.000	-0	165	-3		-0.2
2004	Oak A	2	1	.667	6	5	0	0-0	24.1	27	13	4	2	12-0	10	4.44	104	.284	.373	0	—	0	109	1	58	0.1
2005	Oak A	10	9	.526	29	27	2-1	0-0	159.2	170	75	11	11	54-8	52	4.17	107	.278	.346	1	.000	-0	91	8		1.0
Total	4	20	18	.526	88	53	3-2	0-0	318.2	352	178	31	22	110-16	160	4.80	92	.285	.353	36-0-8	.056	-2	105	-8	58	-1.1

SABATHIA, C.C. Carsten Charles B7.21.1980 Vallejo CA BL/TL/6-7/260(260-290) [CleA98 1/20] d4.8

YEAR	TM LG	W	L	PCT	G	GS	CG-SHO	SV-BS	IP	H	R	HR	HB	BB-IB	SO	ERA	AERA	OAV	OOB	AB-HR-SH	AVG	PB	SUP	APR	DL	PW
2001	†Cle A	17	5	.773	33	33	0	0-0	180.1	149	93	19	7	95-1	171	4.39	105	.228	.330	4-0-1	.000	-0	107	5		0.5
2002	Cle A	13	11	.542	33	33	2	0-0	210	198	109	17	1	88-2	149	4.37	102	.252	.324	5	.200	0	100	2		0.1
2003	Cle A☆	13	9	.591	30	30	2-1	0-0	197.2	190	85	19	6	66-3	141	3.60	123	.255	.319	6	.500	1*	80	21		2.1
2004	Cle A★	11	10	.524	30	30	1-1	0-0	188	176	90	20	7	72-3	139	4.12	106	.252	.325	4	.250	0	106	7		0.6
2005	Cle A	15	10	.600	31	31	1	0-0	196.2	185	92	19	7	62-1	161	4.03	102	.248	.311	6-1-0	.333	2	115	4	14	0.6
Total	5	69	45	.605	157	157	6-2	0-0	972.2	898	469	94	28	383-10	761	4.10	107	.247	.322	25-1-1	.280	3	102	39	14	3.9

SABEL, ERIK Erik Douglas B10.14.1974 Lafayette IN BR/TR/6-3/193* [AriN96 42/1262] d7.9 Col Tennessee Tech

YEAR	TM LG	W	L	PCT	G	GS	CG-SHO	SV-BS	IP	H	R	HR	HB	BB-IB	SO	ERA	AERA	OAV	OOB	AB-HR-SH	AVG	PB	SUP	APR	DL	PW
1999	Ari N	0	0	—	7	0	0	0-0	9.2	12	7	1	2	6-2	6	6.52	71	.300	.417	2	.000	-0	-2			-0.1
2001	Ari N	3	2	.600	42	0	0	0-0	51.1	57	26	8	3	12-3	25	4.38	106	.282	.332	0	—	0	2			0.1
2002	Det A	0	0	—	1	0	0	0-0	0	2	2	1	0	0-0	0	∞	—	1.000	1.000	0	—	0	-2			-0.2
Total	3	3	2	.600	50	0	0	0-0	61	71	35	10	5	18-5	31	5.02	92	.291	.352	2	.000	-0	-2			-0.2

SABERHAGEN, BRET Bret William B4.11.1964 Chicago Heights IL BR/TR/6-1/195(160-200) [KCA82 19/480] d4.4 [DL 1996 Col N 182, 2000 Bos A 181]

YEAR	TM LG	W	L	PCT	G	GS	CG-SHO	SV-BS	IP	H	R	HR	HB	BB-IB	SO	ERA	AERA	OAV	OOB	AB-HR-SH	AVG	PB	SUP	APR	DL	PW
1984	†KC A	10	11	.476	38	18	2-1	0-0	157.2	138	71	13	2	36-4	73	3.48	116	.237	.281	0		0*	77	8		1.0
1985	†KC A	20	6	.769	32	32	10-1	0-0	235.1	211	79	19	1	38-1	158	2.87	146	.241	**.271**	0		0	98	37		3.9
1986	KC A	7	12	.368	30	25	4-2	0-0	156	165	77	15	2	29-1	112	4.15	103	.268	.302	0		0	71	-3	22	0.4
1987	KC A★	18	10	.643	33	33	15-4	0-0	257	246	99	27	6	53-2	163	3.36	137	.252	.293	0		0	105	38		3.8
1988	KC A	14*	16	.467	35	35	9-0	0-0	260.2	271	122	18	4	59-5	171	3.80	106	.269	.309	0		0	86	7		0.7
1989	KC A	**23**	6	.793	36	35	12-4	0-0	262.1	209	74	13	2	43-6	193	**2.16**	**179**	.217	**.251**	0		0*	107	**48**		**5.3**
1990	KC A★	5	9	.357	20	20	5	0-0	135	146	52	9	1	28-1	87	3.27	118	.279	.314	0		0	108	11	56	1.2
1991	KC A	13	8	.619	28	28	7-2	0-0	196.1	165	76	12	9	45-5	136	3.07	135	.228	.280	0		0	102	23	30	2.4
1992	NY N	3	5	.375	17	15	1-1	0-1	97.2	84	39	6	4	27-1	81	3.50	100	.233	.292	28-0-3	.107	-1	81	1	99	0.2

YEAR	TM LG	W	L	PCT	G	GS	CG-SHO	SV-BS	IP	H	R	HR	HB	BB-IB	SO	ERA	AERA	OAV	OOB	AB-HR-SH	AVG	PB	SUP	APR	DL	PW
1993	NY N	7	7	.500	19	19	4-1	0-0	139.1	131	55	11	3	17-4	93	3.29	122	.250	.275	45-0-8	.111	-0	99	13	62	1.3
1994	NY N☆	14	4	.778	24	24	4	0-0	177.1	169	58	13	4	13-0	143	2.74	152	.254	.271	58-0-8	.172	1	112	30		3.1
1995	NY N	5	5	.500	16	16	3	0-0	110	105	45	13	5	20-2	71	3.35	120	.251	.291	35-0-5	.114	-1	109	9		0.7
	†Col N	2	1	.667	9	9	0	0-0	43	60	33	8	5	13-1	29	6.28	86	.323	.382	14	.071	-1	105	-3		-0.3
	Year	7	6	.538	25	25	3	0-0	153	165	78	21	10	33-3	100	4.18	106	.273	.320	49-0-5	.102	-2	110	4		0.4
1997	Bos A	0	1	.000	6	6	0	0-0	26	30	20	5	2	10-0	14	6.58	71	.288	.353	1	.000	-0	115	-5	143	-0.3
1998	†Bos A	15	8	.652	31	31	0	0-0	175	181	82	22	6	29-1	100	3.96	119	.264	.299	5	.000	-1	100	16		1.7
1999	†Bos A	10	6	.625	22	22	0	0-0	119	122	43	11	2	11-0	81	2.95	169	.265	.284	4	.000	-0	99	27	63	3.2
2001	Bos A	1	2	.333	3	3	0	0-0	15	19	11	3	1	0-0	10	6.00	74	.302	.313	0		-0	104	-3	178	-0.4
Total	16	167	117	.588	399	371	76-16	1-1	2562.2	2452	1036	218	59	471-34	1715	3.34	126	.252	.289	190-0-24	.121	-2	99	260	1016	27.9

SACKINSKY, BRIAN Brian Walter B6.22.1971 Pittsburgh PA BR/TR/6-4/220 [BalA92 2/42] d4.20 Col Stanford

YEAR	TM LG	W	L	PCT	G	GS	CG-SHO	SV-BS	IP	H	R	HR	HB	BB-IB	SO	ERA	AERA	OAV	OOB	AB-HR-SH	AVG	PB	SUP	APR	DL	PW
1996	Bal A	0	0	—	3	0	0	0-0	4.2	6	2	1	0	3-0	2	3.86	128	.316	.409	0	—	0		1		0.0

SADECKI, RAY Raymond Michael B12.26.1940 Kansas City KS BL/TL/5-11/180* d5.19

YEAR	TM LG	W	L	PCT	G	GS	CG-SHO	SV-BS	IP	H	R	HR	HB	BB-IB	SO	ERA	AERA	OAV	OOB	AB-HR-SH	AVG	PB	SUP	APR	DL	PW
1960	StL N	9	9	.500	26	26	7-1	0	157.1	148	76	15	1	86-1	95	3.78	109	.249	.342	57-0-2	.211	-0*	94	4		0.3
1961	StL N	14	10	.583	31	31	13	0	222.2	196	100	28	3	102-2	114	3.72	118	.238	.321	87-0-2	.253	2*	95	19		1.8
1962	StL N	6	8	.429	22	17	4-1	1	102.1	121	74	13	3	43-3	50	5.54	77	.296	.362	37-1-2	.081	-2*	100	-14		-1.9
1963	StL N	10	10	.500	36	28	4-1	1	193.1	198	100	13	4	78-3	136	4.10	87	.266	.338	64-0-7	.141	-1*	121	-10		-1.3
1964	†StL N	20	11	.645	37	32	9-2	1	220	232	104	16	1	60-4	119	3.68	103	.273	.319	75-0-9	.160	2*	105	4		0.6
1965	StL N	6	15	.286	36	28	4	1	172.2	192	107	26	0	64-4	122	5.21	74	.284	.344	55-0-3	.200	2	87	-23		-2.5
1966	StL N	2	1	.667	5	3	1	0	24.1	16	9	2	0	9-0	21	2.22	162	.188	.266	7-1-1	.429	2*	82	3		0.6
	SF N	3	7	.300	26	19	3-1	0	105	125	82	20	4	39-2	62	5.40	86	.293	.344	34-2-2	.324	5	110	-23		-1.5
	Year	5	8	.385	31	22	4-1	0	129.1	141	91	22	4	48-2	83	4.80	76	.276	.339	41-3-3	.341	7	106	-24		-0.9
1967	SF N	12	6	.667	35	24	10-2	0	188	165	65	8	4	58-4	145	2.78	118	.238	.298	73-0-1	.247	4*	100	12		1.6
1968	SF N	12	18	.400	38	36	13-6	0	253.2	225	94	14	3	70-17	206	2.91	101	.237	.290	85-0-4	.094	-1*	92	3		0.1
1969	SF N	5	8	.385	29	17	4-3	0-0	138.1	137	73	18	2	53-4	104	4.23	83	.259	.325	40-1-4	.125	2*	116	-9		-0.5
1970	NY N	8	4	.667	28	19	4	0-1	138.2	134	67	20	0	52-9	89	3.89	104	.255	.320	39-0-8	.205	1	117	3		0.2
1971	NY N	7	7	.500	34	20	5-2	0-0	163.1	139	56	10	4	44-5	120	2.92	118	.229	.283	50-0-5	.200	1	84	11		-0.9
1972	NY N	2	1	.667	34	2	0	0-1	75.2	73	33	3	2	31-6	38	3.09	110	.257	.331	13-0-1	.154	-0	91	1		0.0
1973	†NY N	5	4	.556	31	11	1	1-0	116.2	109	47	11	1	41-3	87	3.39	107	.248	.312	31-0-2	.226	1	103	4		0.3
1974	NY N	8	8	.500	34	10	3-1	0-1	103	107	49	7	2	35-6	46	3.41	106	.274	.332	27	.259	1	68	1		0.2
1975	StL N	1	0	1.000	8	0	0	0	11	13	7	0	0	7-2	8	3.27	116	.289	.370	0	—	0		0		0.0
	Atl N	2	3	.400	25	5	0	1-1	66.1	73	39	3	4	21-5	24	4.21	90	.286	.341	15-0-1	.200	0	93	-4		-0.3
	Year	3	3	.500	33	5	0	1-1	77.1	86	46	3	4	28-7	32	4.07	93	.287	.346	15-0-1	.200	0	93	-4		-0.3
	KC A	1	0	1.000	5	0	0	0-2	3	5	2	0	0	3-0	0	3.00	129	.333	.444	0	—	0		0		0.0
1976	KC A	0	0	—	3	0	0	0	4.2	7	0	0	0	3-0	1	0.00	—	.368	.455	0	—	0		2		0.1
	Mil A	2	0	1.000	36	0	0	1-0	37.1	38	20	2	3	20-2	27	4.34	81	.262	.363	0	—	0		-3		-0.2
	Year	2	0	1.000	39	0	0	1-1	42	45	20	2	3	23-2	28	3.86	91	.274	.374	0	—	0		-1		-0.1
1977	NY N	0	1	.000	4	0	0	0-1	3	3	2	1	0	3-0	0	6.00	63	.300	.462	0	—	0		-1		-0.1
Total	18	135	131	.508	563	328	85-20	7-8	2500.1	2456	1206	240	41	922-82	1614	3.78	97	.258	.324	789-5-54	.191	19	101	-20		-1.6

SADLER, CARL William Carl B10.11.1976 Gainesville FL BL/TL/6-2/180* [MonN96 34/1000] d7.31

YEAR	TM LG	W	L	PCT	G	GS	CG-SHO	SV-BS	IP	H	R	HR	HB	BB-IB	SO	ERA	AERA	OAV	OOB	AB-HR-SH	AVG	PB	SUP	APR	DL	PW
2002	Cle A	1	2	.333	24	0	0	0-1	20.1	15	10	2	0	11-0	23	4.43	100	.211	.317	0	—	0		0		0.0
2003	Cle A	0	0	—	18	0	0	0-0	9.2	11	2	0	2	5-0	10	1.86	238	.306	.409	0	—	0		3		0.1
Total	2	1	2	.333	42	0	0	0-1	30	26	12	2	2	16-0	33	3.60	123	.243	.349	0	—	0		3		0.1

SADOWSKI, JIM James Michael B8.7.1951 Pittsburgh PA BR/TR/6-3/195 d4.27

YEAR	TM LG	W	L	PCT	G	GS	CG-SHO	SV-BS	IP	H	R	HR	HB	BB-IB	SO	ERA	AERA	OAV	OOB	AB-HR-SH	AVG	PB	SUP	APR	DL	PW
1974	Pit N	0	0	—	9	0	0	0-0	9	7	6	1	0	9-0	1	6.00	58	.233	.400	1	.000	0		-2		-0.2

SADOWSKI, BOB Robert B2.19.1938 Pittsburgh PA BR/TR/6-2/195* d6.19 b-Ed b-Ted

YEAR	TM LG	W	L	PCT	G	GS	CG-SHO	SV-BS	IP	H	R	HR	HB	BB-IB	SO	ERA	AERA	OAV	OOB	AB-HR-SH	AVG	PB	SUP	APR	DL	PW
1963	Mil N	5	7	.417	19	18	5-1	0	116.2	99	36	8	5	30-6	72	2.62	123	.231	.288	35-0-3	.057	-2	95	9		0.7
1964	Mil N	9	10	.474	51	18	5	5	166.2	159	85	18	7	56-5	96	4.10	86	.251	.317	52-0-6	.154	-2	143	-10		-1.1
1965	Mil N	5	9	.357	34	13	3	3	123	117	62	11	3	35-5	78	4.32	82	.250	.303	35-0-2	.086	-1	78	-9		-1.2
1966	Bos A	1	1	.500	11	5	0	0	33.1	41	26	4	1	9-1	11	5.40	70	.311	.354	7-0-1	.000	-1	102	-7		-0.5
Total	4	20	27	.426	115	54	13-1	8	439.2	416	209	41	16	130-17	257	3.87	90	.250	.309	129-0-12	.101	-4	107	-17		-2.1

SADOWSKI, TED Theodore B4.1.1936 Pittsburgh PA D7.18.1993 Shaler Twp. PA BR/TR/6-1.5/190* d9.2 b-Ed b-Bob

YEAR	TM LG	W	L	PCT	G	GS	CG-SHO	SV-BS	IP	H	R	HR	HB	BB-IB	SO	ERA	AERA	OAV	OOB	AB-HR-SH	AVG	PB	SUP	APR	DL	PW
1960	Was A	1	0	1.000	9	1	0	1	17.1	17	10	4	1	9-1	12	5.19	75	.258	.351	3	.000	-0	91	-2		-0.1
1961	Min A	0	2	.000	15	1	0	0	33	49	29	6	1	11-2	12	6.82	62	.348	.396	6	.000	-1	42	-9		-0.5
1962	Min A	1	1	.500	19	0	0	0	34	37	19	6	1	11-0	15	5.03	81	.301	.363	4	.500	1		-2		-0.1
Total	3	2	3	.400	43	2	0	1	84.1	103	58	16	3	31-3	39	5.76	71	.312	.374	13	.154	-0	65	-13		-0.7

SAENZ, CHRIS Christopher Andrew B8.14.1981 Tucson AZ BR/TR/6-3/200 [MilN01 28/838] d4,24 Col Pima (AZ) CC

YEAR	TM LG	W	L	PCT	G	GS	CG-SHO	SV-BS	IP	H	R	HR	HB	BB-IB	SO	ERA	AERA	OAV	OOB	AB-HR-SH	AVG	PB	SUP	APR	DL	PW
2004	Mil N	1	0	1.000	1	1	0	0-0	6	2	0	0	1	3-0	7	0.00	—	.100	.250	2	.000	-0	63	3		0.5

SAGER, A. J. Anthony Joseph B3.3.1965 Columbus OH BR/TR/6-4/220* [SDN88 10/240] d4.4 Col Toledo

YEAR	TM LG	W	L	PCT	G	GS	CG-SHO	SV-BS	IP	H	R	HR	HB	BB-IB	SO	ERA	AERA	OAV	OOB	AB-HR-SH	AVG	PB	SUP	APR	DL	PW
1994	SD N	1	4	.200	22	3	0	0-0	46.2	62	34	4	2	16-5	26	5.98	69	.325	.379	10-0-1	.100	0	59	-9		-0.8
1995	Col N	0	0	—	10	0	0	0-1	14.2	19	16	1	0	7-1	10	7.36	73	.311	.382	3	.000	-0		-4		-0.2
1996	Det A	4	5	.444	22	9	0	0-0	79	91	46	10	2	29-2	52	5.01	102	.294	.355	0	—	0	97	2		0.1
1997	Det A	3	4	.429	38	1	0	3-1	84	81	43	10	1	24-6	53	4.18	111	.258	.307	0	—	0	0	4		0.3
1998	Det A	4	2	.667	31	3	0	2-1	59.1	79	47	7	1	23-4	23	6.52	73	.325	.383	1	.000	-0	124	-12		-1.0
Total	5	12	15	.444	123	16	0	5-3	283.2	332	186	32	6	99-18	164	5.36	88	.297	.353	14-0-1	.071	-0	91	-19		-1.6

SAIN, JOHNNY John Franklin B9.25.1917 Havana AR BR/TR/6-2/200(185-200) d4.24 Mil 1943-45 C17

YEAR	TM LG	W	L	PCT	G	GS	CG-SHO	SV-BS	IP	H	R	HR	HB	BB-IB	SO	ERA	AERA	OAV	OOB	AB-HR-SH	AVG	PB	SUP	APR	DL	PW
1942	Bos N	4	7	.364	40	3	0	6	97	79	54	8	5	63	68	3.90	86	.228	.354	27-0-2	.074	-2	50	-8		-1.2
1946	Bos N	20	14	.588	37	34	24-3	2	265	225	80	8	2	87	129	2.21	155	.230	.294	94-0-10	.298	5*	98	34		**5.4**
1947	Bos N	21	12	.636	38	35	22-3	1	266	265	117	19	4	79	132	3.52	111	.255	.310	107-0-8	.346	12*	126	12		2.7
1948	†Bos N★	24	15	.615	42	39	28-4	1	314.2	297	105	19	5	83	137	2.60	147	.245	.296	115-0-16	.217	3*	110	43		**5.3**
1949	Bos N	10	17	.370	37	36	16-1	0	243	285	150	15	4	75	73	4.81	78	.291	.344	97-0-3	.206	1*	99	-30		-2.8
1950	Bos N	20	13	.606	37	37	25-3	0	278.1	294	139	34	2	70	96	3.94	98	.269	.314	102-1-7	.206	4	112	-2		0.0
1951	Bos N	5	13	.278	26	22	6-1	1	160.1	195	88	16	3	45	63	4.21	87	.299	.347	52-1-4	.212	3	82	-11		-0.9
	†NY A	2	1	.667	7	4	1	1	37	41	17	5	0	8	21	4.14	93	.281	.318	14	.286	1	110	0		0.1
1952	†NY A	11	6	.647	35	16	8	7	148.1	149	70	15	2	38	57	3.46	96	.261	.310	71-1-1	.268	7*	144	-4		0.1
1953	†NY A☆	14	7	.667	40	19	10-1	9	189	189	68	14	3	45	84	3.00	123	.262	.308	68-0-4	.250	5*	136	17		2.4
1954	NY A	6	6	.500	45	0	0	**22**	77	66	27	11	0	15	33	3.16	109	.226	.269	17-0-1	.353	3	4			1.1
1955	NY A	0	0	—	3	0	0	1	5.1	6	4	4	0	1-0	5	6.75	55	.300	.333	2	.000	-0		-2		-0.1
	KC A	2	5	.286	25	0	0	1	44.2	54	28	10	0	10-4	12	5.44	77	.297	.332	8	.000	-1		-5		-0.9
	Year	2	5	.286	28	0	0	1	50	60	32	14	0	11-4	17	5.58	74	.297	.332	10	.000	-1		-6		-1.0
Total	11	139	116	.545	412	245	140-16	51	2125.2	2145	947	180	30	619-4	910	3.49	106	.261	.315	774-3-56	.245	40	111	48		11.2

ST.CLAIRE, RANDY Randy Anthony B8.23.1960 Glens Falls NY BR/TR/6-2/190(180-195) d9.11 C3 f-Ebba

YEAR	TM LG	W	L	PCT	G	GS	CG-SHO	SV-BS	IP	H	R	HR	HB	BB-IB	SO	ERA	AERA	OAV	OOB	AB-HR-SH	AVG	PB	SUP	APR	DL	PW
1984	Mon N	0	0	—	4	0	0	0-0	8	11	4	0	1	2-1	4	4.50	77	.344	.378	0	—	0		-1		0.0
1985	Mon N	5	0	.625	42	0	0	0-1	68.2	69	32	3	1	26-7	25	3.93	88	.265	.333	5-0-1	.200	1		-3		-0.3
1986	Mon N	2	0	1.000	11	0	0	1-0	19	13	5	2	0	6-1	21	2.37	158	.186	.250	1-0-1	.000	-0		3		0.4
1987	Mon N	3	3	.500	44	0	0	7-2	67	64	31	9	1	20-4	43	4.03	106	.249	.303	6-0-2	.333	1		3		0.3
1988	Mon N	0	0	—	6	0	0	0-0	7.1	11	5	1	0	5-1	6	6.14	59	.344	.421	0	—	0		-2		-0.1
	Cin N	1	0	1.000	10	0	0	0-0	13.2	13	8	4	0	5-2	8	2.63	136	.241	.300	1	.000	-0		-0		0.0
	Year	1	0	1.000	16	0	0	0-0	21	24	13	5	0	10-3	14	3.86	93	.279	.347	1	.000	-0		-2		-0.1
1989	Min A	1	0	1.000	8	0	0	1-0	22.1	19	13	4	2	10-2	14	5.24	79	.226	.320	0	—	0		-2		-0.1
1991	†Atl N	0	0	—	19	0	0	0-0	28.2	31	17	4	0	9-3	30	4.08	95	.282	.333	2	.500	1		-0		-0.0
1992	Atl N	0	0	—	10	0	0	0-0	15.1	17	11	1	0	8-3	7	5.87	62	.283	.368	0	—	0		-4		-0.2
1994	Tor A	0	0	—	2	0	0	0-0	2	4	4	0	0	2-1	2	9.00	54	.444	.545	0	—	0		-2		-0.1
Total	9	12	6	.667	162	0	0	9-3	252	252	130	28	5	93-25	160	4.14	92	.260	.325	15-0-4	.267	1		-10		-0.7

ST.VRAIN, JIM James Marcellin B6.6.1883 Ralls Co. MO D6.12.1937 Butte MT BR/TL/5-9/175 d4.20

YEAR	TM LG	W	L	PCT	G	GS	CG-SHO	SV-BS	IP	H	R	HR	HB	BB-IB	SO	ERA	AERA	OAV	OOB	AB-HR-SH	AVG	PB	SUP	APR	DL	PW
1902	Chi N	4	6	.400	12	11	10-1	0	95	88	36	0	5	25	51	2.08	130	.246	.304	31	.097	-2	82	6		0.5

YEAR	TM LG	W	L	PCT	G	GS	CG-SHO	SV-BS	IP	H	R	HR	HB	BB-IB	SO	ERA	AERA	OAV	OOB	AB-HR-SH	AVG	PB	SUP	APR	DL	PW

SAIPE, MIKE Michael Eric B9.10.1973 San Diego CA BR/TR/6-1/190 [ColN94 12/322] d6.25 Col San Diego

| 1998 | Col N | 0 | 1 | .000 | 2 | 0 | 0 | 0-0 | 10 | 22 | 12 | 4 | 0 | 2-0 | 2 | 10.80 | 48 | .431 | .453 | 1 | .000 | 0 | 98 | -5 | | -0.4 |

SALE, FREDDY Frederick Link B5.2.1902 Chester SC D5.27.1956 Hermosa Beach CA BR/TR/5-9/160 d6.30 Col Georgia

| 1924 | Pit N | 0 | 0 | — | 1 | 0 | 0 | 0 | 1 | 2 | 0 | 0 | 0 | 0 | 0 | 0.00 | — | .500 | .500 | 0 | — | 0 | 0 | 0 | | 0.0 |

SALISBURY, HARRY Henry H. B5.15.1855 Providence RI D3.29.1933 Chicago IL BL/5-8.5/162 d8.28 Col Brown

1879	Tro N	4	6	.400	10	10	9	0	89	103	72	0		11	31	2.22	112	.265	.285	36	.056	-4	76	-1		-0.3
1882	Pit AA	20	18	.526	38	38	38-1	0	335	315	188	1		37	135	2.63	99	.232	.253	145	.152	-6*	107	-1		-0.7
Total	2	24	24	.500	48	48	47-1	0	424	418	260	1		48	166	2.55	102	.239	.260	181	.133	-10	100	-1		-1.0

SALISBURY, BILL William Ansel "Solly" B11.12.1876 Algona IA D1.17.1952 Rowena OR BR/TR/6-0/180 d4.19

| 1902 | Phi N | 0 | 0 | — | 2 | 1 | 0 | 0 | 6 | 15 | 10 | 1 | 1 | 2 | 0 | 13.50 | 21 | .469 | .514 | 1 | .000 | -0 | 145 | -6 | | -0.3 |

SALKELD, ROGER Roger William B3.6.1971 Burbank CA BR/TR/6-5/215* [SeaA89 1/3] d9.8 gf-Bill

1993	Sea A	0	0	—	3	2	0	0-0	14.1	13	4	0	1	4-0	13	2.51	178	.232	.295	0	—	0	52	3		0.2
1994	Sea A	2	5	.286	13	13	0	0-0	59	76	47	7	1	45-1	46	7.17	69	.314	.419	0	—	0	106	-12		-1.2
1996	Cin N	8	5	.615	29	19	1-1	0-0	116	114	69	18	6	54-2	82	5.20	80	.261	.349	32-0-4	.031	-3	117	-9		-1.2
Total	3	10	10	.500	45	34	1-1	0-0	189.1	203	120	25	8	103-3	141	5.61	80	.277	.369	32-0-4	.031	-3	110	-18		-2.2

SALLEE, SLIM Harry Franklin "Scatter" B2.3.1885 Higginsport OH D3.23.1950 Higginsport OH BL/TL/6-3/180 d4.16

1908	StL N	3	8	.273	25	12	7-1	0	128.2	144	65	1	3	36	39	3.15	75	.274	.324	41-0-1	.049	-3	55	-10		-1.1
1909	StL N	10	11	.476	32	27	12-1	0	219	223	107	3	5	59	55	2.42	104	.264	.315	71-0-6	.113	-2	129	-7		-0.8
1910	StL N	7	8	.467	18	13	9-1	2	115	112	44	4	1	24	46	2.97	100	.251	.290	37-0-2	.108	-2	90	2		0.0
1911	StL N	15	9	.625	36	30	18-1	3	245	234	102	6	5	64	74	2.76	123	.257	.309	89-0-4	.169	-2	96	15		1.0
1912	StL N	16	17	.485	48	32	20-3	6	294	289	122	6	6	72	108	2.60	132	.266	.315	103-0-2	.136	-4	84	26		2.3
1913	StL N	19	15	.559	50	29	18-3	5	276	257	98	11	9	60	106	2.71	119	.255	.301	95-2-6	.211	-2	86	16		2.2
1914	StL N	18	17	.514	46	29	18-3	6	282.1	252	92	9	9	72	105	2.10	133	.246	.302	91-0-6	.231	2	87	22		3.1
1915	StL N	13	17	.433	46	33	17-2	3	275.1	245	121	6	3	57	91	2.84	98	.238	.280	92-0-4	.120	-3	86	-3		-0.8
1916	StL N	5	5	.500	16	7	4-2	1	70	75	28	2	2	23	28	3.47	76	.290	.352	18-0-2	.167	-0	56	-3		-0.6
	NY N	9	4	.692	15	11	7-2	0	111.2	96	24	2	0	10	35	1.37	178	.234	.252	35-0-1	.257	2	117	13		1.8
	Year	14	9	.609	31	18	11-4	1	181.2	171	52	4	2	33	63	2.18	115	.256	.293	53-0-3	.226	2	92	9		1.2
1917	†NY N	18	7	.720	34	24	18-1	4	215.2	199	70	4	1	34	54	2.17	118	.249	.280	77-0-6	.221	1	149	8		0.9
1918	NY N	8	8	.500	18	16	12-1	2	132	122	44	3	0	12	33	2.25	117	.241	**.259**	41-0-4	.122	-2	92	5		0.3
1919	†Cin N	21	7	.750	29	28	22-4	0	227.2	221	63	4	1	20	24	2.06	135	.258	.276	74-0-8	.189	2	116	20		2.5
1920	Cin N	5	6	.455	21	12	6	2	116	129	57	4	2	16	13	3.34	91	.293	.320	35-0-1	.171	-1	121	-6		-0.7
	NY N	1	0	1.000	5	2	1	0	17	16	7	0	0	2	0	1.59	189	.239	.239	3-0-1	.333	1	171	1		0.1
	Year	6	6	.500	26	14	7	2	133	145	64	4	2	16	15	3.11	97	.285	.310	38-0-2	.184	-0	128	-5		-0.6
1921	NY N	6	4	.600	37	0	0	2	96.1	115	48	7	0	14	23	3.64	101	.307	.332	22-0-4	.364	2		-1		0.0
Total	14	174	143	.549	476	305	189-25	36	2821.2	2729	1092	68	43	573	836	2.56	114	.258	.299	924-2-58	.171	-8	99	99		10.2

SALMON, ROGER Roger Elliott B5.11.1891 Newark NJ D6.17.1974 Belfast ME BL/TL/6-2/170 d5.3 Col Princeton

| 1912 | Phi A | 1 | 0 | 1.000 | 2 | 0 | 0 | 0 | 5 | 7 | 7 | 0 | 0 | 4 | 2 | 9.00 | 34 | .318 | .423 | 1-0-1 | .000 | -0 | 96 | -4 | | -0.6 |

SALVE, GUS Augustus William B12.29.1885 Boston MA D3.29.1971 Providence RI BL/TL/6-0/190 d9.14

| 1908 | Phi N | 0 | 1 | .000 | 2 | 1 | 1 | 0 | 15.1 | 17 | 7 | 1 | 9 | 6 | 4.11 | 62 | .266 | .365 | 5 | .000 | -1 | 27 | -2 | | -0.2 |

SALVESON, JACK John Theodore B1.5.1914 Fullerton CA D12.28.1974 Norwalk CA BR/TR/6-0.5/180 d6.3

1933	NY N	0	2	.000	8	2	2	0	30.2	30	17	4	0	14	8	3.82	84	.252	.331	9	.111	-1	26	-3		-0.2
1934	NY N	3	1	.750	12	4	0	0	38.1	43	16	2	0	13	18	3.52	110	.281	.337	10	.300	0*	134	2		0.3
1935	Pit N	0	1	.000	5	0	0	0	7	11	12	1	1	5	2	9.00	46	.306	.405	2	.000	-0		-5		-0.6
	Chi A	1	2	.333	20	2	2	1	66.2	79	39	6	0	23	22	4.86	95	.298	.298	20-1-0	.300	2	150	-1		0.1
1943	Cle A	5	3	.625	23	11	4-3	3	86	87	36	5	1	26	24	3.35	93	.266	.322	26-1-2	.231	2	94	-2		0.0
1945	Cle A	0	0	—	19	0	0	0	44	52	23	3	1	6	11	3.68	88	.294	.321	10-1-0	.400	3		-3		0.2
Total	5	9	9	.500	87	19	8-3	4	272.2	302	143	21	3	87	85	3.99	91	.280	.336	77-3-2	.260	7	99	-12		-0.2

SALVO, MANNY Manuel "Gyp" B6.30.1912 Sacramento CA D2.7.1997 Vallejo CA BR/TR/6-4/210 d4.22

1939	NY N	4	10	.286	32	18	4	1	136	150	84	11	5	75	69	4.63	85	.285	.380	41-1-0	.098	-2	101	-13		-1.3
1940	Bos N	10	9	.526	21	20	14-**5**	0	160.2	151	63	9	2	43	60	3.08	121	.248	.300	58	.103	-3	95	11		0.9
1941	Bos N	7	16	.304	35	27	11-2	0	195	192	103	9	4	93	67	4.06	88	.255	.346	62	.113	-0	89	-10		-1.2
1942	Bos N	7	8	.467	25	14	6-1	0	130.2	129	52	7	4	41	25	3.03	110	.260	.322	41-0-2	.122	-1	70	4		0.3
1943	Bos N	0	1	.000	1	1	0	0	5	5	4	0	0	6	1	7.20	47	.250	.423	2	1.000	2	75	-2		-0.2
	Phi N	0	0	—	1	0	0	0	0.1	2	1	0	0	1	0	27.00	12	.667	.750	0	—	0		-1		0.0
	Bos N	5	6	.455	20	13	5-1	0	93.2	94	45	6	1	25	25	3.27	105	.261	.311	28-0-2	.214	0	69	0		0.0
	Year	5	7	.417	22	14	5-1	0	99	101	50	6	1	32	26	3.55	96	.264	.322	30-0-2	.267	2	69	-3		-0.2
Total	5	33	50	.398	134	92	40-9	1	721.1	723	352	42	16	284	247	3.69	98	.264	.332	230-1-4	.129	-4	87	-10		-1.5

SAMBITO, JOE Joseph Charles B6.28.1952 Brooklyn NY BL/TL/6-1/190* [HouN73 17/404] d7.20 Col Adelphi [DL 1983 Hou N 182]

1976	Hou N	3	2	.600	21	4	1	1-0	53.1	45	21	4	0	14-1	26	3.54	91	.237	.286	9	.222	1	109	-1		0.1
1977	Hou N	5	5	.500	54	1	0	7-4	89	77	34	6	0	24-2	67	2.33	155	.235	.286	13	.154	-0	0	10		1.2
1978	Hou N	4	9	.308	62	0	0	11-4	88	85	32	5	0	32-7	96	3.07	109	.260	.322	6-0-1	.167	0		3		0.6
1979	Hou N★	8	7	.533	63	0	0	22-6	91.1	80	20	8	4	23-4	83	1.77	198	.235	.290	7	.286	2		19		**4.3**
1980	†Hou N	8	4	.667	64	0	0	17-5	90.1	65	26	3	2	22-3	75	2.19	150	.200	.254	9	.000	-1		12		1.9
1981	†Hou N	5	5	.500	49	0	0	10-3	63.2	43	17	4	2	22-5	41	1.84	178	.192	.269	5	.000	-1		10		1.8
1982	Hou N	0	0	—	9	0	0	4-1	12.2	7	2	0	0	2-2	7	0.71	468	.159	.196	1	.000	-0*		4	137	0.2
1984	Hou N	0	0	—	32	0	0	0-0	47.2	39	16	5	0	16-2	26	3.02	111	.228	.289	2	.000	-0		3	53	0.1
1985	NY N	0	0	—	8	0	0	0-0	10.2	21	18	1	0	8-0	3	12.66	28	.420	.492	0	—	0		-12		-0.6
1986	†Bos A	2	0	1.000	53	0	0	12-0	44.2	54	26	4	0	16-3	30	4.84	87	.298	.362	0	—	0		-3		-0.2
1987	Bos A	2	6	.250	47	0	0	0-0	37.2	46	29	8	0	16-3	35	6.93	66	.301	.367	0	—	0		-9		-1.5
Total	11	37	38	.493	461	5	1-1	84-27	629	562	241	48	10	195-32	489	3.03	116	.241	.300	52-0-1	.135	2	81	36	372	7.9

SAMPEN, BILL William Albert B1.18.1963 Lincoln IL BR/TR/6-2/195(180-200) [PitN85 12/294] d4.10 Col MacMurray

1990	Mon N	12	7	.632	59	4	0	2-1	90.1	94	34	7	2	33-6	69	2.99	123	.268	.332	8-0-2	.000	-1	233	6		1.2
1991	Mon N	9	5	.643	43	8	0	0-0	92.1	96	49	13	3	46-7	52	4.00	91	.273	.358	13-0-2	.231	0	99	-5		-0.7
1992	Mon N	1	4	.200	44	1	0	0-1	63.1	62	22	4	1	29-6	23	3.13	111	.268	.351	6-0-1	.000	-1	0	4		0.2
	KC A	0	2	.000	21	0	0	0-0	19.2	21	10	0	3	3-1	14	3.66	112	.292	.338	0	—	-1	45	0		0.2
1993	KC A	2	2	.500	18	0	0	0-4	18.1	25	12	1	4	9-0	9	5.89	78	.338	.437	0	—	0		-2		-0.4
1994	Cal A	1	1	.500	10	0	0	0-0	15.1	14	11	1	2	13-0	9	6.46	76	.241	.405	0	—	0		-2		-0.2
Total	5	25	21	.543	182	14	0	2-6	299.1	312	138	26	16	133-20	176	3.73	101	.274	.355	27-0-5	.111	-1	124	1		0.1

SAMPSON, BENJ Benjamin Damon B4.27.1975 Des Moines IA BR/TL/6-2/210* [MinA93 6/177] d9.9

1998	Min A	1	0	1.000	5	2	0	0-0	17.1	10	3	0	1	6-0	16	1.56	308	.172	.254	0	—	0	78	6		0.3
1999	Min A	3	2	.600	30	4	0	0-0	71	107	65	17	0	34-3	56	8.11	64	.351	.410	3	.000	-0	126	-20		-1.2
Total	2	4	2	.667	35	6	0	0-0	88.1	117	68	17	1	40-3	72	6.83	75	.322	.384	3	.000	-0	110	-14		-0.9

SAMUELS, JOE Joseph Jonas "Skabotch" B3.21.1905 Scranton PA D10.28.1996 Bath NY BR/TR/6-1.5/196 d4.23

| 1930 | Det A | 0 | 0 | — | 6 | 0 | 0 | 0 | 10 | 11 | 11 | 0 | 6 | 4 | 1 | 16.50 | 29 | .417 | .533 | 1 | .000 | -0 | | -7 | | -0.3 |

SAMUELS, ROGER Roger Howard B1.5.1961 San Jose CA BL/TL/6-5/210* [HouN83 10/244] d7.20 Col Santa Clara

1988	SF N	2	1	.333	15	0	0	0-0	23.1	17	10	4	1	7-0	20	3.47	94	.202	.272	3	—	-0		-1		-0.1
1989	Pit N	0	0	—	5	0	0	0-0	3.2	9	4	1	0	4-0	2	9.82	35	.474	.565	0	—	-0		-2		-0.1
Total	2	2	1	.333	20	0	0	0-0	27	26	14	5	1	11-0	22	4.33	76	.252	.330	3	.000	-0		-2		-0.2

SANCHEZ, ALEX Alex Anthony B4.8.1966 Concord CA BR/TR/6-2/185 [TorA87 1/17] d5.23 Col UCLA

| 1989 | Tor A | 0 | 1 | .000 | 4 | 3 | 0 | 0-0 | 11.2 | 16 | 13 | 1 | 0 | 14-0 | 4 | 10.03 | 38 | .356 | .492 | 0 | — | 0 | 135 | -8 | | -0.5 |

YEAR	TM LG	W	L	PCT	G	GS	CG-SHO	SV-BS	IP	H	R	HR	HB	BB-IB	SO	ERA	AERA	OAV	OOB	AB-HR-SH	AVG	PB	SUP	APR	DL	PW

SANCHEZ, DUANER Duaner B10.14.1979 Cotui, D.R. BR/TR/6-0/160(160-189) d6.14

2002	Ari N	0	0	—	6	0	0	0-1	3.2	3	2	1	0	5-0	4	4.91	91	.214	.421	0	—	0	0	0		0.0
	Pit N	0	0	—	3	0	0	0-0	2.1	3	4	1	0	2-0	2	15.43	27	.300	.417	0	—	0	-3			-0.1
	Year	0	0	—	9	0	0	0-1	6	6	6	2	0	7-0	6	9.00	49	.250	.419	0	—	0	-3			-0.1
2003	Pit N	1	0	1.000	6	0	0	0-0	6	15	11	2	2	1-0	3	16.50	26	.500	.529	0	—	0	-8			-1.0
2004	†LA N	3	1	.750	67	0	0	0-1	80	81	34	9	6	27-2	44	3.37	123	.266	.335	4-0-1	.250	0	6			0.3
2005	LA N	4	7	.364	79	0	0	8-4	82	75	36	8	3	36-6	71	3.73	110	.248	.332	4	.000	-0	4			0.1
Total	4	8	8	.500	161	0	0	8-6	174	177	87	21	11	71-8	124	4.19	99	.268	.346	8-0-1	.125	0	-1			-0.3

SANCHEZ, FELIX Felix Antonio B8.3.1981 Puerto Plata, D.R. BR/TL/6-3/180 [BosA00 11/332] d9.3

2003	Chi N	0	0	—	3	0	0	0-0	1.2	2	2	1	0	3-0	2	10.80	40	.333	.556	0	—	0	-1			-0.1

SANCHEZ, ISRAEL Israel (Matos) B8.20.1963 Falcon Lasvias, Cuba BL/TL/5-9/170* [KCA82 9/220] d7.7 [DL 1989 KC A 182]

1988	KC A	3	2	.600	19	1	0	1-0	35.2	36	20	0	0	18-2	14	4.54	88	.265	.348	0	—	0	182	-2		-0.3
1990	KC A	0	0	—	11	0	0	0-0	9.2	16	9	1	1	3-0	5	8.38	46	.381	.426	0	—	0	-4			-0.2
Total	2	3	2	.600	30	1	0	1-0	45.1	52	29	1	1	21-2	19	5.36	74	.292	.366	0	—	0	182	-6	182	-0.5

SANCHEZ, JESUS Jesus Paulino B10.11.1974 Nizao Bani, D.R. BL/TL/5-10/155(153-170) d3.31

1998	Fla N	7	9	.438	35	29	0	0-1	173	178	98	18	4	91-2	137	4.47	91	.272	.363	52-0-4	.135	-1*	105	-10		-0.7
1999	Fla N	5	7	.417	59	10	0	0-2	76.1	84	53	16	4	60-11	62	6.01	73	.291	.411	12-0-2	.083	-0*	103	-13		-1.8
2000	Fla N	9	12	.429	32	32	2-2	0-0	182	197	118	32	4	76-4	123	5.34	82	.280	.348	56-0-3	.232	2*	107	-20		-1.8
2001	Fla N	2	4	.333	16	9	0	0-0	62.2	61	33	7	2	31-2	46	4.74	88	.256	.346	17-0-2	.235	1*	108	-3		-0.6
2002	Chi N	0	0	—	8	0	0	0-0	8.1	15	12	4	1	10-1	6	12.96	31	.395	.510	1	.000	-0	-8			-0.4
2003	Col N	0	0	—	9	0	0	0-0	8	11	8	1	0	4-2	2	9.00	54	.324	.395	0	—	0	-3			-0.2
2004	Cin N	0	2	.000	3	3	0	0-0	14.1	18	12	4	0	9-0	8	7.53	57	.305	.397	4-0-1	.000	-0	43	-5		-0.6
Total	7	23	34	.404	162	83	2-2	0-3	524.2	564	334	82	15	281-22	384	5.32	80	.280	.368	142-0-12	.176	1	103	-62		-5.7

SANCHEZ, LUIS Luis Mercedes (b Luis Mercedes Escoba (Sanchez)) B8.24.1953 Cariaco, Venez D2.4.2005 LaGuaira, Venez BR/TR/6-2/210(170-215) d4.10

1981	Cal A	0	2	.000	17	0	0	2-2	33.2	39	16	4	1	11-0	13	2.94	125	.287	.342	0	—	0	1			0.1
1982	†Cal A	7	4	.636	46	0	0	5-3	92.2	89	36	3	7	34-4	58	3.21	128	.259	.337	0	—	0	9			1.1
1983	Cal A	10	8	.556	56	1	0	7-9	98.1	92	42	6	3	40-14	49	3.66	111	.254	.332	0	—	0	67	5		1.0
1984	Cal A	9	7	.563	49	0	0	11-10	83.2	84	34	10	3	33-9	62	3.33	120	.268	.340	0	—	0	6			1.1
1985	Cal A	2	0	1.000	26	0	0	2-0	61.1	67	41	9	1	27-3	34	5.72	72	.283	.354	0	—	0	-10	50		-0.5
Total	5	28	21	.571	194	1	0	27-24	369.2	371	169	32	15	145-30	216	3.75	107	.267	.340	0	—	0	67	11	50	2.9

SANCHEZ, RAUL Raul Guadalupe (Rodriguez) B12.12.1930 Marianao, Cuba BR/TR/6-0/150* d4.17

1952	Was A	1	1	.500	3	2	1-1	0	12.2	13	5	0	0	7	4	3.55	100	.260	.351	5	.000	-1	61	0		0.0
1957	Cin N	3	2	.600	38	0	0	5	62.1	61	37	7	4	25-3	37	4.76	86	.262	.341	7-0-1	.286	1	-5			-0.3
1960	Cin N	1	0	1.000	8	0	0	0	14.2	12	9	1	3	11-1	5	4.91	78	.226	.388	2	.500	0	-2			-0.1
Total	3	5	3	.625	49	2	1-1	5	89.2	86	51	8	7	43-4	48	4.62	86	.256	.351	14-0-1	.214	0	61	-7		-0.4

SANDERS, BEN Alexander Bennett B2.16.1865 Catharpin VA D8.29.1930 Memphis TN BR/TR/6-0/210 d6.6 Col Roanoke ▲

1888	Phi N	19	10	.655	31	29	28-8		275.1	240	100	3	3	33	121	1.90	157	.228	.253	236-1	.246	5*	94	30		3.7
1889	Phi N	19	18	.514	44	39	34-1	1	349.2	406	217	9	4	96	123	3.55	122	.282	.328	169	.278	6	83	24		2.4
1890	Phi P	19	18	.514	43	40	37-2	1	346.2	412	237	13	10	69	107	3.76	114	.283	.320	189	.312	9*	92	20		2.3
1891	Phi AA	11	5	.688	19	18	15	0	145	157	85	3	8	37	40	3.79	100	.267	.319	156-1	.250	2*	123	1		0.7
1892	Lou N	12	19	.387	31	31	30-3	0	268.1	281	150	6	2	62	77	3.22	95	.259	.300	198-3	.273	10*	84	-3		0.7
Total	5	80	70	.533	168	157	144-14	2	1385	1496	789	34	27	297	468	3.51	116	.266	.266	948-5	.271	33	93	72		9.4

SANDERS, DAVE David Andrew B8.29.1979 Oklahoma City OK BL/TL/6-0/200* [ChiA99 6/189] d4.23 Col Barton Co. (KS) CC

2003	Chi A	0	0	—	20	0	0	0-0	22	25	16	5	1	11-0	14	6.14	75	.281	.363	0	—	0	-4			-0.2
2005	Chi A	0	0	—	2	0	0	0-0	2	3	3	1	0	1-0	1	13.50	34	.375	.400	0	—	0	-2			-0.1
Total	2	0	0	—	22	0	0	0-0	24	28	19	6	1	12-0	15	6.75	68	.289	.366	0	—	0	-6			-0.3

SANDERS, DEE Dee Wilman B4.8.1921 Quitman TX BR/TR/6-3/195 d8.12 Col Oklahoma

1945	StL A	0	0	—	2	0	0		1.1	7	7	0	0	1	1	40.50	9	.700	.727	0	—	0	-5			-0.3

SANDERS, KEN Kenneth George "Daffy" B7.8.1941 St.Louis MO BR/TR/5-11/185(170-185) d8.6

1964	KC A	0	2	.000	21	0	0	1	27	23	12	2	1	17-4	18	3.67	104	.232	.345	0	—	0	0			0.1
1966	Bos A	3	6	.333	24	0	0	2	47.1	36	22	2	2	28-9	33	3.80	100	.214	.332	6-0-3	.000	-0	0			0.1
	KC A	3	4	.429	38	1	0	1	65.1	59	28	8	1	48-7	41	3.72	91	.250	.374	8-0-1	.250	1	130	-1		-0.1
	Year	6	10	.375	62	1	0	3	112.2	95	50	10	3	76-16	74	3.75	95	.235	.357	14-0-4	.143	0	123	0		0.0
1968	Oak A	0	1	.000	7	0	0		10.2	8	5	1	0	8-2	6	3.38	84	.229	.372	0	—	0	-1			-0.1
1970	Mil A	5	2	.714	50	0	0	13-6	92.1	64	19	6	4	25-6	64	1.75	215	.201	.266	13-0-2	.231	1	21			2.3
1971	Mil A	7	12	.368	83	0	0	31-4	136.1	111	35	9	4	34-10	80	1.91	182	.227	.282	14-0-1	.000	1	23			4.5
1972	Mil A	2	9	.182	62	0	0	17-4	92.1	88	38	10	2	31-13	51	3.12	98	.245	.308	7-0-1	.143	1	-2			-0.2
1973	Min A	2	4	.333	27	0	0	8-3	44.1	53	31	4	2	21-1	19	6.09	65	.299	.374	0	—	0	-9			-1.4
	Cle A	5	1	.833	15	0	0	5-1	27.1	18	6	2	0	9-2	14	1.65	240	.188	.257	0	—	0	7			1.4
	Year	7	5	.583	42	0	0	13-4	71.2	71	37	6	2	30-3	33	4.40	90	.260	.334	0	—	0	-3			0.0
1974	Cle A	0	1	.000	9	0	0	1-0	11	21	12	5	0	5-2	4	9.82	37	.404	.456	0	—	0	-7			-0.7
	Cal A	0	0	—	9	0	0	1-1	9.2	10	5	0	0	3-0	4	2.79	124	.278	.317	0	—	0	0			0.0
	Year	0	1	.000	18	0	0	2-1	20.2	31	17	5	0	8-2	8	6.53	55	.352	.398	0	—	0	-7			-0.7
1975	NY N	1	1	.500	29	0	0	5-1	43	31	11	2	0	14-7	8	2.30	153	.205	.271	2	.000	-0*	7	22		0.4
1976	NY N	1	2	.333	31	0	0	1-0	47	39	16	4	1	12-4	16	2.87	117	.231	.281	2	.000	-0	3			0.2
	KC A	0	0	—	3	0	0	0-0	3	3	0	0	0	3-0	2	0.00	—	.273	.429	0	—	0	1			0.1
Total	10	29	45	.392	408	1	0	86-20	656.2	564	240	50	17	258-67	360	2.97	119	.235	.312	52-0-8	.115	-0	126	42	22	6.6

SANDERS, ROY Roy Garvin "Butch","Pepe" B8.1.1892 Stafford KS D1.17.1950 Kansas City MO BR/TR/6-0.5/195 d4.16 Col William Jewell

1917	Cin N	0	1	.000	2	2	1		14	12	7	0	1	16	3	4.50	58	.273	.475	6	.000	-1*	101	-2		-0.2
1918	Pit N	7	9	.438	28	14	6-1	1	156	135	59	1	2	52	55	2.60	111	.239	.305	53-0-2	.151	-1	81	5		0.5
Total	2	7	10	.412	30	16	7-1	1	170	147	66	1	3	68	58	2.75	104	.241	.321	59-0-2	.136	-2	83	3		0.3

SANDERS, ROY Roy Lee "Simon" B6.10.1894 MO D7.8.1963 Louisville KY BR/TR/6-0/185 d8.6

1918	NY A	0	2	.000	6	2	0		25.2	28	15	0	2	16	8	4.21	67	.301	.414	7	.000	-1	27	-4		-0.5
1920	StL A	1	1	.500	8	1	0	0	17.1	20	10	1	1	17	2	5.19	75	.313	.463	4	.000	-1	243	-1		-0.2
Total	2	1	3	.250	14	3	0	0	43	48	25	1	3	33	10	4.60	71	.306	.435	11	.000	-2	110	-5		-0.7

SANDERS, SCOTT Scott Gerald B3.25.1969 Hannibal MO BR/TR/6-4/220* [SDN90 1/32] d8.6 Col Nicholls St.

1993	SD N	3	3	.500	9	9	0	0-0	52.1	54	32	4	1	23-1	37	4.13	100	.265	.339	16-0-4	.063	-1	77	-2		-0.4
1994	SD N	4	8	.333	23	20	0	1-0	111	103	63	10	5	48-4	109	4.78	86	.245	.326	32-0-6	.125	0	101	-7	16	-0.3
1995	SD N	5	5	.500	17	15	1	0-0	90	79	46	14	2	31-4	88	4.30	95	.228	.294	27-0-3	.296	2	108	-1	69	0.1
1996	†SD N	9	5	.643	46	16	0	0-0	144	117	58	10	2	48-5	157	3.38	119	.221	.284	36-0-4	.194	2	126	12		1.1
1997	Sea A	3	6	.333	33	6	0	2-2	65.1	73	48	16	3	38-5	62	6.47	70	.280	.371	0	—	0	84	-13		-1.3
	Det A	3	8	.273	14	14	1-1	0	74.1	79	44	14	1	24-1	58	5.33	87	.276	.329	0	—	0	67	-4		-0.5
	Year	6	14	.300	47	20	1-1	2-2	139.2	152	92	30	4	62-6	120	5.86	78	.278	.350	0	—	0	72	-17		-2.1
1998	Det A	0	2	.000	3	2	0	0-0	9.2	24	19	1	0	6-2	6	17.69	27	.471	.526	0	—	0	-39	-13		-1.7
	SD N	3	1	.750	27	0	0	0-0	30.2	33	20	5	0	5-1	26	4.11	97	.270	.299	0	—	0	-3			-0.3
1999	Chi N	4	7	.364	67	6	0	2-3	104.1	112	69	19	0	53-8	89	5.52	80	.277	.358	18-0-2	.278	1	70	-10		-0.8
Total	7	34	45	.430	235	88	2-1	5-5	681.2	674	399	93	14	276-31	632	4.86	88	.257	.327	129-0-20	.194	4	93	-41	85	-4.7

SANDERS, WAR Warren Williams B8.2.1877 Maynardville TN D8.3.1962 Chattanooga TN BR/TL/5-10/160 d4.18 Col Tennessee

1903	StL N	1	6	.143	9	6	3	0	40	48	37	0	2	21	9	6.07	54	.286	.372	15	.067	-2	69	-11		-1.6
1904	StL N	1	2	.333	4	3	1	0	19	25	15	1	1	1	11	4.74	57	.298	.314	6	.000	-1	60	-4		-0.7
Total	2	2	8	.200	12	9	4	0	59	73	52	1	3	22	20	5.64	55	.290	.354	21	.048	-2	66	-15		-2.3

SANDERSON, SCOTT Scott Douglas B7.22.1956 Dearborn MI BR/TR/6-5/200* [MonN77 3/54] d8.6 Col Vanderbilt

1978	Mon N	4	2	.667	10	9	1-1	0-0	61	52	20	3	1	21-0	50	2.51	142	.232	.298	19-0-2	.105	-1	87	7		0.5
1979	Mon N	9	8	.529	34	24	5-3	1-0	168	148	69	16	3	54-4	138	3.43	108	.236	.297	50-0-7	.160	-0	95	7		0.6

YEAR	TM LG	W	L	PCT	G	GS	CG-SHO	SV-BS	IP	H	R	HR	HB	BB-IB	SO	ERA	AERA	OAV	OOB	AB-HR-SH	AVG	PB	SUP	APR	DL	PW
1980	Mon N	16	11	.593	33	33	7-3	0-0	211.1	206	76	18	3	56-3	125	3.11	117	.257	.307	64-0-8	.078	-3	93	15		1.4
1981	†Mon N	9	7	.563	22	22	4-1	0-0	137.1	122	50	10	1	31-2	77	2.95	121	.236	.278	35-0-5	.114	2	121	9		1.1
1982	Mon N	12	12	.500	32	32	7	0-0	224	212	98	24	3	58-5	158	3.46	107	.251	.299	57-1-16	.140	1	106	6		0.5
1983	Mon N	6	7	.462	18	16	0	1-0	81.1	98	50	12	0	20-0	55	4.65	78	.303	.343	28-0-1	.143	0	93	-11	58	-1.7
1984	†Chi N	8	5	.615	24	24	3	0-0	140.2	140	54	5	2	24-3	76	3.14	125	.264	.294	42-0-4	.119	0	105	11	34	0.9
1985	Chi N	5	6	.455	19	19	2	0-0	121	100	49	13	0	27-4	80	3.12	128	.228	.268	31-0-6	.065	-2	96	9	54	0.7
1986	Chi N	9	11	.450	37	28	1-1	1-0	169.2	165	85	21	2	37-2	124	4.19	97	.255	.320	51-0-6	.059	-3*	84	-2		-0.6
1987	Chi N	8	9	.471	32	22	0	2-2	144.2	156	72	23	3	50-5	106	4.29	101	.274	.333	40-1-4	.075	-1	89	2	33	-0.1
1988	Chi N	1	2	.333	11	0	0	0-2	15.1	13	9	1	0	3-1	6	5.28	69	.232	.258	0	—	0		-2	140	-0.4
1989	†Chi N	11	9	.550	37	23	2	0-0	146.1	155	69	16	2	31-6	86	3.94	96	.273	.312	43-0-6	.047	-2	95	-1		-0.5
1990	†Oak A	17	11	.607	34	34	2-1	0-0	206.1	205	99	27	4	66-2	128	3.88	96	.255	.312	0	—	-2	108	-4		0.8
1991	NY A☆	16	10	.615	34	34	2-2	0-0	208	200	95	22	3	29-0	130	3.81	109	.252	.279	0	—	0	101	9		0.8
1992	NY A	12	11	.522	33	33	2-1	0-0	193.1	220	116	28	4	64-5	104	4.93	80	.286	.340	0	—	0	118	-21		-2.3
1993	Cal A	7	11	.389	21	21	4-1	0-0	135.1	153	77	15	5	27-5	66	4.46	102	.289	.325	0	—	0	86	0		0.0
	SF N	4	2	.667	11	8	0	0-0	48.2	48	20	12	1	7-2	36	3.51	112	.255	.283	14-0-1	.000	-1	112	3		0.2
1994	Chi A	8	4	.667	18	14	1	0-0	92	110	57	20	2	12-1	36	5.09	92	.296	.321	0	—	0	136	-4		-0.2
1995	Cal A	1	3	.250	7	7	0	0-0	39.1	48	23	6	2	4-1	23	4.12	114	.298	.320	0	—	0	102	1	123	0.1
1996	Cal A	0	2	.000	5	4	0	0-0	18	39	21	5	2	4-0	7	7.50	67	.433	.464	0	—	0	105	-7	28	-0.6
Total	19	163	143	.533	472	407	43-14	5-4	2561.2	2590	1209	297	43	625-51	1611	3.84	103	.263	.307	474-2-66	.097	-12	101	27	470	-0.2

SANFORD, FRED John Frederick B8.9.1919 Garfield UT BB/TR(BR 1948)/6-1/200* d5.5 Mil 1944-45

YEAR	TM LG	W	L	PCT	G	GS	CG-SHO	SV-BS	IP	H	R	HR	HB	BB-IB	SO	ERA	AERA	OAV	OOB	AB-HR-SH	AVG	PB	SUP	APR	DL	PW
1943	StL A	0	0	—	3	0	0	0	9.1	7	2	0	0	4	2	1.93	172	.219	.306	0-0-1		0		2		0.1
1946	StL A	2	1	.667	3	3	2-2	0	22	19	7	0	0	9	8	2.05	182	.235	.311	7	.286	1	46	3		0.6
1947	StL A	7	16	.304	34	23	9	4	186.2	186	89	17	0	76	62	3.71	104	.261	.332	54-0-7	.204	-0	66	3		0.2
1948	StL A	12	21	.364	42	33	9-1	2	227	250	123	19	2	91	79	4.64	98	.279	.347	73-1-2	.151	-2*	73	1		0.0
1949	NY A	7	3	.700	29	11	3	0	95.1	100	53	9	0	57	51	3.87	105	.270	.367	34-0-2	.118	-2	115	-1		-0.4
1950	NY A	5	4	.556	26	12	2	0	112.2	103	60	9	1	79	54	4.55	94	.252	.354	35-0-1	.229	1	103	-2		0.0
1951	NY A	0	3	.000	11	2	0	0	26.2	15	11	2	0	25	10	3.71	103	.169	.351	5	.000	-1	58	1		0.1
	Was A	2	3	.400	7	7	0	0	37	51	25	5	0	27	12	6.57	62	.329	.429	14-0-1	.071	-1	115	-9		-1.1
	StL A	2	4	.333	9	7	1	0	27.1	37	33	6	0	23	7	10.21	43	.308	.420	7	.286	1	136	-16		-2.6
	Year	4	10	.286	27	16	1	0	91	103	71	13	0	75	29	6.82	60	.283	.405	26-0-1	.115	-1	120	-24		-3.6
Total	7	37	55	.402	164	101	26-3	6	744	768	405	67	3	391	285	4.45	94	.268	.357	229-1-14	.170	-4	87	-18		-3.1

SANFORD, JACK John Stanley B5.18.1929 Wellesley Hills MA D3.7.2000 Beckley WV BR/TR/6-0/190(175-196) d9.16 C2

YEAR	TM LG	W	L	PCT	G	GS	CG-SHO	SV-BS	IP	H	R	HR	HB	BB-IB	SO	ERA	AERA	OAV	OOB	AB-HR-SH	AVG	PB	SUP	APR	DL	PW
1956	Phi N	1	0	1.000	3	1	0	0	13	7	2	0	1	13-0	6	1.38	269	.184	.404	3	.333	0	95	4		0.3
1957	Phi N★	19	8	.704	33	33	15-3	0	236.2	194	94	22	3	94-2	188	3.08	124	.221	.297	89-0-4	.169	-1	112	18		1.8
1958	Phi N	10	13	.435	38	27	7-2	0	186.1	197	103	15	3	81-6	106	4.44	89	.274	.347	59-0-3	.169	1	94	-9		-1.0
1959	SF N	15	12	.556	36	31	10	1	222.1	198	90	22	7	70-4	132	3.16	121	.235	.298	72-0-5	.111	-1	111	17		1.8
1960	SF N	12	14	.462	37	34	11-6	0	219	199	111	11	2	99-6	125	3.82	91	.243	.325	74-0-5	.176	1	126	-9		-1.0
1961	SF N	13	9	.591	38	33	6	0	217.1	203	114	22	5	87-7	112	4.22	90	.249	.322	74-3-5	.216	-1	112	-10		-0.4
1962	†SF N	24	7	.774	39	38	13-2	0	265.1	233	110	23	3	92-4	147	3.43	111	.234	.300	98-0-4	.153	0	130	13		1.4
1963	SF N	16	13	.552	42	42	11	0	284.1	273	123	21	5	76-8	158	3.51	91	.251	.303	94-0-7	.138	3*	128	-7		-0.3
1964	SF N	5	7	.417	18	17	3-1	1	106.1	91	44	7	4	37-3	64	3.30	108	.228	.298	30-0-3	.133	1*	88	3	84	-0.4
1965	SF N	4	5	.444	23	16	0	2	91	92	50	11	7	30-7	43	3.96	91	.256	.324	25-0-1	.120	-0	100	-5		-0.6
	Cal A	1	2	.333	9	5	0	1	29.1	35	16	2	0	10-1	13	4.60	74	.324	.381	7-0-1	.143	-0	114	-4		-0.4
1966	Cal A	13	7	.650	50	6	0	5	108	108	51	11	4	27-6	56	3.83	88	.271	.316	22-0-1	.136	1	96	-6		-0.9
1967	Cal A	3	2	.600	12	9	0	1	48.1	53	26	6	0	7-1	21	4.47	70	.288	.311	15-0-2	.200	1	142	-7		-0.5
	KC A	1	2	.333	10	1	0	0	22	24	18	1	2	14-4	13	6.55	49	.296	.408	3	.000	-0	82	-8		-1.0
	Year	4	4	.500	22	10	0	1	70.1	77	44	7	2	21-5	34	5.12	62	.291	.344	18-0-2	.167	1	135	-15		-1.5
Total	12	137	101	.576	388	292	79-14	11	2049.1	1907	952	174	46	737-59	1182	3.69	98	.247	.314	665-3-41	.158	12	115	-10	84	-0.4

SANFORD, MO Meredith Leroy B12.24.1966 Americus GA BR/TR/6-6/220(220-233) d8.9 Col Alabama

YEAR	TM LG	W	L	PCT	G	GS	CG-SHO	SV-BS	IP	H	R	HR	HB	BB-IB	SO	ERA	AERA	OAV	OOB	AB-HR-SH	AVG	PB	SUP	APR	DL	PW
1991	Cin N	1	2	.333	5	5	0	0-0	28	19	14	3	1	15-1	31	3.86	99	.186	.297	0	.000	-1	90	0		-0.1
1993	Col N	1	2	.333	11	6	0	0-0	35.2	37	25	9	0	27-0	36	5.30	90	.278	.395	8-0-1	.000	-1	82	-2		-0.3
1995	Min A	0	0	—	11	0	0	0-0	18.2	16	11	7	2	16-0	17	5.30	91	.225	.382	0	—	0		-1		-0.1
Total	3	2	4	.333	27	11	0	0-0	82.1	72	50	14	3	58-1	84	4.81	93	.235	.360	16-0-3	.000	-2	83	-3		-0.5

SANTANA, ERVIN Ervin Ramon B1.10.1983 LaRomana, D.R. BR/TR/6-2/160 d5.17

YEAR	TM LG	W	L	PCT	G	GS	CG-SHO	SV-BS	IP	H	R	HR	HB	BB-IB	SO	ERA	AERA	OAV	OOB	AB-HR-SH	AVG	PB	SUP	APR	DL	PW
2005	†LA A	12	8	.600	23	23	1-1	0-0	133.2	139	73	17	8	47-2	99	4.65	93	.266	.333	0		0	92	-5		-0.6

SANTANA, JOHAN Johan Alexander B3.13.1979 Tovar, Venez BL/TL/6-0/195* d4.3

YEAR	TM LG	W	L	PCT	G	GS	CG-SHO	SV-BS	IP	H	R	HR	HB	BB-IB	SO	ERA	AERA	OAV	OOB	AB-HR-SH	AVG	PB	SUP	APR	DL	PW
2000	Min A	2	3	.400	30	5	0	0-0	86	102	64	11	2	54-0	64	6.49	81	.302	.398	1	.000	-0	78	-10		-0.4
2001	Min A	1	0	1.000	15	4	0	0-0	43.2	50	25	6	3	16-0	28	4.74	99	.292	.358	0	—	0	149	-1	76	0.0
2002	†Min A	8	6	.571	27	14	0	1-0	108.1	84	41	7	1	49-0	137	2.99	149	.218	.298	4	.250	0	106	17		2.0
2003	†Min A	12	3	.800	45	18	0	0-0	158.1	127	56	17	3	47-1	169	3.07	147	.216	.276	3	.333	0	105	26		2.1
2004	†Min A	20	6	.769	34	34	1-1	0-0	228	156	70	24	9	54-0	265	2.61	178	.192	.249	8	.375	1	103	52		5.6
2005	Min A★	16	7	.696	33	33	3-2	0-0	231.2	180	77	22	1	45-2	238	2.87	153	.210	.250	6	.167	-0	95	40		3.7
Total	6	59	25	.702	184	108	4-3	1-0	856	699	333	87	19	265-2	901	3.31	138	.221	.284	22	.273	1	101	124	76	13.0

SANTANA, JULIO Julio Franklin B1.20.1973 San Pedro de Macoris, D.R. BR/TR/6-0/185(175-215) d4.6 [DL 1999 Bos A 74]

YEAR	TM LG	W	L	PCT	G	GS	CG-SHO	SV-BS	IP	H	R	HR	HB	BB-IB	SO	ERA	AERA	OAV	OOB	AB-HR-SH	AVG	PB	SUP	APR	DL	PW
1997	Tex A	4	6	.400	30	14	0	0-1	104	141	86	16	4	49-2	64	6.75	72	.323	.392	2	.500	0	101	-21	26	-1.6
1998	Tex A	0	0	—	3	0	0	0-0	5.1	7	5	0	0	4-1	1	8.44	58	.304	.407	0	—	0		-2		-0.1
	TB A	5	6	.455	32	19	1	0-0	140.1	144	72	18	5	58-2	60	4.23	113	.270	.344	4	.000	-0	92	8		0.4
	Year	5	6	.455	35	19	1	0-0	145.2	151	77	18	5	62-3	61	4.39	109	.272	.347	4	.000	-0	92	7		0.3
1999	TB A	1	4	.200	22	5	0	0-0	55.1	66	49	10	7	32-0	34	7.32	68	.300	.404	1	1.000	-1	56	-13	21	-1.0
2000	Mon N	4	5	.167	36	4	0	0-2	66.2	69	45	11	2	33-2	58	5.67	83	.271	.356	7	.000	-1	97	-6		-0.5
2002	Det A	3	5	.375	38	0	0	0-1	57	49	19	8	2	28-2	38	2.84	154	.238	.335	0	—	0		10	50	1.2
2005	Mil N	3	5	.375	41	0	0	1-3	42	34	21	6	0	19-4	49	4.50	95	.221	.301	1	.000	-0		0	43	-0.1
Total	6	17	31	.354	202	42	1	1-7	470.2	510	297	69	20	223-13	304	5.26	90	.279	.361	15	.133	-1	93	-24	214	-1.7

SANTANA, MARINO Marino (Castro) B5.10.1972 San Jose de los Llanos, D.R. BR/TR/6-1/175* d9.4

YEAR	TM LG	W	L	PCT	G	GS	CG-SHO	SV-BS	IP	H	R	HR	HB	BB-IB	SO	ERA	AERA	OAV	OOB	AB-HR-SH	AVG	PB	SUP	APR	DL	PW
1998	Det A	0	0	—	7	0	0	0-0	7.1	9	3	1	1	8-2	10	3.68	129	.310	.474	0	—	0		1		0.0
1999	Bos A	0	0	—	3	0	0	0-0	4	8	7	3	0	3-0	4	15.75	32	.444	.500	0	—	0		-4	69	-0.2
Total	2	0	0	—	10	0	0	0-0	11.1	17	10	4	1	11-2	14	7.94	61	.362	.483	0	—	0		-3	69	-0.2

SANTIAGO, JOSE Jose Guillermo (Guzman) "Pants" B9.4.1928 Coamo, PR BR/TR/5-10/175* d4.17 Negro Lg 1947-48

YEAR	TM LG	W	L	PCT	G	GS	CG-SHO	SV-BS	IP	H	R	HR	HB	BB-IB	SO	ERA	AERA	OAV	OOB	AB-HR-SH	AVG	PB	SUP	APR	DL	PW
1954	Cle A	0	0	—	1	0	0	0	1.2	0	1	0	0	2	1	0.00	—	.000	.286	0	—	0		0		0.0
1955	Cle A	2	0	1.000	17	0	0	0	32.2	31	11	1	5	14-1	19	2.48	161	.256	.350	4-0-2	.500	1		5		0.4
1956	KC A	1	2	.333	9	5	0	0	21.2	36	26	8	5	17-0	9	8.31	52	.387	.500	5-0-1	.400	0	169	-11		-1.2
Total	3	3	2	.600	27	5	0	0	56	67	38	9	10	33-1	29	4.66	88	.306	.414	9-0-3	.444	2	169	-6		-0.8

SANTIAGO, JOSE Jose Rafael (Alfonso) B8.15.1940 Juana Diaz, PR BR/TR/6-2/185* d9.9

YEAR	TM LG	W	L	PCT	G	GS	CG-SHO	SV-BS	IP	H	R	HR	HB	BB-IB	SO	ERA	AERA	OAV	OOB	AB-HR-SH	AVG	PB	SUP	APR	DL	PW
1963	KC A	1	0	1.000	4	0	0	0	7	8	7	4	0	2-0	6	9.00	43	.276	.323	0	—	0		-3		-0.4
1964	KC A	0	6	.000	34	8	0	0	83.2	84	53	9	4	35-1	64	4.73	81	.258	.336	18-0-2	.000	-2	102	-10		-0.9
1965	KC A	0	0	—	4	0	0	0	5	8	5	1	0	4-2	9	9.00	39	.364	.462	0	—	0		-3		-0.1
1966	Bos A	12	13	.480	35	28	7-1	0	172	155	87	17	2	58-0	119	3.66	104	.238	.300	56-0-4	.196	0*	94	0		0.3
1967	†Bos A	12	4	.750	50	11	2	5	145.1	138	61	17	2	47-3	109	3.59	97	.251	.312	42-1-1	.190	2	157	0		0.3
1968	Bos A★	9	4	.692	18	18	7-2	0	124	96	34	7	3	42-0	86	2.25	140	.215	.286	43-0-3	.163	1*	100	12	70	1.5
1969	Bos A	0	0	—	10	0	0	0	7.2	11	5	2	0	4-0	4	3.52	109	.344	.395	0	—	0		0	134	0.0
1970	Bos A	0	2	.000	8	0	0	1-0	11.1	18	13	0	0	8-1	7	10.32	39	.353	.441	3	.667	1*		-7	22	-1.1
Total	8	34	29	.540	163	65	16-3	8-0	556	518	265	57	11	200-7	404	3.74	96	.246	.313	162-1-10	.173	2	107	-11	226	-0.7

SANTIAGO, JOSE Jose Rafael (Fuentes) B11.5.1974 Fajardo, PR BR/TR/6-3/215* [KCA94 70/1627] d6.7

YEAR	TM LG	W	L	PCT	G	GS	CG-SHO	SV-BS	IP	H	R	HR	HB	BB-IB	SO	ERA	AERA	OAV	OOB	AB-HR-SH	AVG	PB	SUP	APR	DL	PW
1997	KC A	0	0	—	4	0	0	0	4.2	7	2	1	0	2-1	1	1.93	246	.333	.417	0	—	0		1	21	0.0
1998	KC A	0	0	—	2	0	0	0-0	2	4	2	0	0	0-0	2	9.00	54	.444	.444	0	—	0		-1		0.0
1999	KC A	3	4	.429	34	0	0	2-1	47.1	46	23	7	2	14-2	15	3.42	149	.251	.307	0	—	0		7	85	0.9
2000	KC A	8	6	.571	45	0	0	2-6	69	70	33	7	8	26-3	44	3.91	133	.260	.329	0	—	0		9		1.6

YEAR	TM LG	W	L	PCT	G	GS	CG-SHO	SV-BS	IP	H	R	HR	HB	BB-IB	SO	ERA	AERA	OAV	OOB	AB-HR-SH	AVG	PB	SUP	APR	DL	PW
2001	KC A	2	2	.500	20	0	0	0-1	29.1	40	22	2	1	9-1	15	6.75	74	.333	.376	0	—	0	-4			-0.5
	Phi N	2	4	.333	53	0	0	0-1	62.1	66	25	3	2	13-1	28	3.61	114	.272	.312	3	.000	0	5			0.3
2002	Phi N	1	3	.250	42	0	0	0-1	47	56	35	7	3	15-1	30	6.70	57	.290	.347	2	.000	0	-15			-1.1
2003	Cle A	1	3	.250	25	0	0	0-2	31.2	37	11	2	0	14-3	15	2.84	134	.298	.370	0	—	0	6			0.6
2005	NY N	0	0	—	4	0	0	0-0	5.2	10	2	0	1	2-0	3	3.18	131	.417	.481	0	—	0	1			0.0
Total	8	17	22	.436	229	0	0	4-12	299	336	155	28	13	95-12	153	4.36	105	.283	.340	5	.000	0	9	106		1.8

SANTORINI, AL Alan Joel B5.19.1948 Irvington NJ BR/TR/6-0/190* [AtlN66 1/11] d9.10

YEAR	TM LG	W	L	PCT	G	GS	CG-SHO	SV-BS	IP	H	R	HR	HB	BB-IB	SO	ERA	AERA	OAV	OOB	AB-HR-SH	AVG	PB	SUP	APR	DL	PW
1968	Atl N	0	1	.000	1	1	0	0	3	4	4	1	0	0-0	0	0.00	—	.286	.286	0	—	0	58	-1		-0.2
1969	SD N	8	14	.364	32	30	2-1	0-0	184.2	194	95	11	7	73-10	111	3.95	91	.270	.341	63-1-3	.111	-1	71	-10		-2.0
1970	SD N	1	8	.111	21	12	0	1-0	75.2	91	56	11	3	43-6	41	6.07	66	.294	.382	18	.000	-2	78	-17		-2.0
1971	SD N	0	2	.000	18	3	0	0-1	38.1	43	19	4	0	11-1	21	3.76	89	.285	.329	5	.400	1	62	-2		-0.1
	StL N	0	2	.000	19	5	0	2-0	49.2	51	21	2	1	19-2	21	3.81	96	.270	.340	10	.300	1	98	0		0.0
	Year	0	4	.000	37	8	0	2-1	88	94	40	6	1	30-3	42	3.78	92	.276	.335	15	.333	1	86	-2		-0.1
1972	StL N	8	11	.421	30	19	3-3	0-1	133.2	136	63	6	1	46-7	72	4.11	83	.263	.323	40-0-3	.075	-2	92	-8		-1.3
1973	StL N	0	0	—	6	0	0	0-0	8.1	14	5	1	1	2-0	2	5.40	68	.400	.436	1	.000	-0	-1			-0.1
Total	6	17	38	.309	127	70	5-4	3-2	493.1	533	263	36	13	194-26	268	4.29	84	.276	.344	137-1-6	.109	-4	79	-39		-4.9

SANTOS, VICTOR Victor Irving B10.2.1976 San Pedro de Macoris, D.R. BR/TR/6-3/175(175-190) d4.9 Col St. Peters

YEAR	TM LG	W	L	PCT	G	GS	CG-SHO	SV-BS	IP	H	R	HR	HB	BB-IB	SO	ERA	AERA	OAV	OOB	AB-HR-SH	AVG	PB	SUP	APR	DL	PW
2001	Det A	2	2	.500	33	7	0	0-0	76.1	62	33	9	3	49-4	52	3.30	134	.222	.341	0	—	0	144	9		0.4
2002	Col N	0	4	.000	24	2	0	0-0	26	41	30	3	0	22-3	25	10.38	46	.360	.460	2	.500	0	137	-13		-1.7
2003	Tex A	0	2	.000	8	4	0	0-0	25.2	29	21	5	1	16-1	15	7.01	71	.296	.397	2-0-1	.000	0	74	-5		-0.4
2004	Mil N	11	12	.478	31	28	0	0-0	154	169	95	18	7	57-5	115	4.97	88	.278	.344	39-0-6	.051	-2	81	-10		-1.7
2005	Mil N	4	13	.235	29	24	1	0-0	141.2	153	87	20	5	60-8	89	4.57	94	.269	.343	40-0-3	.075	-3	75	-8		-1.7
Total	5	17	33	.340	125	65	1	0-0	423.2	454	266	55	16	204-21	296	4.99	88	.272	.355	83-0-10	.072	-5	87	-27		-4.6

SARMIENTO, MANNY Manuel Eduardo (Aponte) B2.2.1956 Cagua, Venez BR/TR/6-0/170(136-170) d7.30 [DL 1984 Pit N 182]

YEAR	TM LG	W	L	PCT	G	GS	CG-SHO	SV-BS	IP	H	R	HR	HB	BB-IB	SO	ERA	AERA	OAV	OOB	AB-HR-SH	AVG	PB	SUP	APR	DL	PW
1976	†Cin N	5	1	.833	22	0	0	0-0	43.2	36	14	1	1	12-3	20	2.06	170	.222	.278	1	.000	-1	6			0.6
1977	Cin N	0	0	—	24	0	0	1-0	40.1	28	13	6	0	11-2	23	2.45	160	.196	.247	1-0-1	.000	-0	6			0.6
1978	Cin N	9	7	.563	63	4	0	5-3	127.1	109	65	16	1	54-10	72	4.38	81	.234	.310	16-0-1	.000	-1*	70	-10		-1.4
1979	Cin N	0	4	.000	23	1	0	0-2	38.2	47	21	2	1	7-2	23	4.66	80	.311	.337	6-0-1	.000	-1	215	-3		-0.4
1980	Sea A	0	1	.000	9	0	0	1-1	14.2	14	7	2	0	6-1	15	3.68	113	.255	.317	0	—	0				0.0
1982	Pit N	9	4	.692	35	17	4	1-0	164.2	153	69	7	0	46-4	81	3.39	111	.246	.295	40-0-7	.191	1	133	6		0.4
1983	Pit N	3	5	.375	52	0	0	4-1	84.1	74	35	8	0	36-8	49	2.99	125	.243	.318	10-0-2	.000	-1	5			0.4
Total	7	26	22	.542	228	22	4	12-7	513.2	461	224	42	3	172-30	283	3.49	106	.242	.301	87-0-12	.103	-3	126	11	182	-0.2

SASAKI, KAZUHIRO Kazuhiro B2.22.1968 Tokyo, Japan BR/TR/6-4/209(209-220) d4.5

YEAR	TM LG	W	L	PCT	G	GS	CG-SHO	SV-BS	IP	H	R	HR	HB	BB-IB	SO	ERA	AERA	OAV	OOB	AB-HR-SH	AVG	PB	SUP	APR	DL	PW
2000	†Sea A	2	5	.286	63	0	0	37-3	62.2	42	25	10	2	31-5	78	3.16	152	.184	.285	0	—	0	11			2.0
2001	†Sea A★	0	4	.000	69	0	0	45-7	66.2	48	24	6	4	11-2	62	3.24	131	.195	.241	0	—	0	9			1.4
2002	Sea A★	4	5	.444	61	0	0	37-8	60.2	44	24	6	2	20-4	73	2.52	171	.201	.268	0	—	0	10			1.9
2003	Sea A	1	2	.333	35	0	0	10-4	33.1	31	17	2	1	15-2	29	4.05	107	.238	.318	0	—	0	1	77		0.0
Total	4	7	16	.304	228	0	0	129-22	223.1	165	90	24	9	77-13	242	3.14	141	.200	.273	0	—	0	31	77		5.3

SAUCIER, KEVIN Kevin Andrew B8.9.1956 Pensacola FL BR/TL/6-1/196* [PhiN74 2/27] d10.1

YEAR	TM LG	W	L	PCT	G	GS	CG-SHO	SV-BS	IP	H	R	HR	HB	BB-IB	SO	ERA	AERA	OAV	OOB	AB-HR-SH	AVG	PB	SUP	APR	DL	PW
1978	Phi N	0	1	.000	1	0	0	0-0	2	4	4	1	0	1-0	2	18.00	20	.400	.500	10	.100	-1	-3			-0.5
1979	Phi N	1	4	.200	29	2	0	1-1	62.1	68	31	4	3	33-3	21	4.19	93	.291	.381	10	.100	-1	34	-2		-0.2
1980	†Phi N	7	3	.700	40	0	0	0-2	50	50	21	2	4	20-8	25	3.42	112	.281	.359	8	.000	-1	2	18		0.3
1981	Det A	4	2	.667	38	0	0	13-2	49	26	11	1	5	21-3	23	1.65	229	.160	.277	0	—	0	11			2.0
1982	Det A	3	1	.750	31	1	0	5-2	40.1	35	15	0	2	29-4	23	3.12	131	.254	.391	0	—	0	111	5		0.2
Total	5	15	11	.577	139	3	0	19-7	203.2	183	82	7	15	104-18	94	3.31	117	.253	.356	18	.056	-2	62	13	18	2.2

SAUERBECK, SCOTT Scott William B11.9.1971 Cincinnati OH BR/TL/6-3/197* [NYN94 23/624] d4.5 Col Miami-Ohio

YEAR	TM LG	W	L	PCT	G	GS	CG-SHO	SV-BS	IP	H	R	HR	HB	BB-IB	SO	ERA	AERA	OAV	OOB	AB-HR-SH	AVG	PB	SUP	APR	DL	PW
1999	Pit N	4	1	.800	65	0	0	2-3	67.2	53	19	6	4	38-5	55	2.00	230	.220	.336	1-0-1	.000	-0	19			1.3
2000	Pit N	5	4	.556	75	0	0	1-3	75.2	76	36	4	0	61-8	83	4.04	115	.270	.399	1	.000	-0	6	17		0.6
2001	Pit N	2	2	.500	70	0	0	2-2	62.2	61	41	4	2	40-6	79	5.60	80	.257	.369	2	.000	-0	-7			-0.5
2002	Pit N	4	5	.444	78	0	0	0-0	62.2	50	18	4	1	27-4	70	2.30	183	.220	.306	2	.000	-0*	13			1.7
2003	Pit N	3	4	.429	53	0	0	0-4	40	30	20	5	1	25-2	32	4.05	107	.207	.327	1	.000	-0	1			0.2
	†Bos A	0	1	.000	26	0	0	0-1	16.2	17	14	1	4	18-3	18	6.48	72	.266	.448	0	—	0	-4			-0.2
2005	Cle A	1	0	1.000	58	0	0	0-2	35.2	35	18	4	4	16-2	35	4.04	102	.259	.353	0	—	0	0			0.0
Total	6	20	16	.556	425	0	0	5-15	361	322	166	28	17	225-30	372	3.74	119	.242	.358	7-0-1	.000	-1	28	17		3.1

SAUNDERS, TONY Anthony Scott B4.29.1974 Baltimore MD BL/TL/6-2/205* d4.5 [DL 2000 TB A 181]

YEAR	TM LG	W	L	PCT	G	GS	CG-SHO	SV-BS	IP	H	R	HR	HB	BB-IB	SO	ERA	AERA	OAV	OOB	AB-HR-SH	AVG	PB	SUP	APR	DL	PW
1997	†Fla N	4	6	.400	22	21	0	0-0	111.1	99	62	12	2	64-1	102	4.61	88	.244	.347	37-1-1	.081	-1	116	-7	52	-0.7
1998	TB A	6	15	.286	31	31	2	0-0	192.1	191	95	15	7	111-1	172	4.12	116	.265	.364	2	1.000	1	65	14		1.4
1999	TB A	3	3	.500	9	9	0	0-0	42	53	39	6	4	29-0	30	6.43	77	.315	.424	0	—	0	102	-9	130	-1.0
Total	3	13	24	.351	62	61	2	0-0	345.2	343	196	33	13	204-2	304	4.56	100	.265	.367	39-1-1	.128	0	87	-2	363	-0.3

SAUNDERS, DENNIS Dennis James B1.4.1949 Alhambra CA BB/TR/6-3/195 [DetA67 6/115] d5.21

YEAR	TM LG	W	L	PCT	G	GS	CG-SHO	SV-BS	IP	H	R	HR	HB	BB-IB	SO	ERA	AERA	OAV	OOB	AB-HR-SH	AVG	PB	SUP	APR	DL	PW
1970	Det A	1	1	.500	8	0	0	1-2	14	16	5	1	0	5-1	8	3.21	117	.286	.355	.5	.000	-1	1			0.1

SAUNDERS, JOE Joseph Francis B6.16.1981 Falls Church VA BL/TL/6-3/210 d8.16 Col Virginia Tech

YEAR	TM LG	W	L	PCT	G	GS	CG-SHO	SV-BS	IP	H	R	HR	HB	BB-IB	SO	ERA	AERA	OAV	OOB	AB-HR-SH	AVG	PB	SUP	APR	DL	PW
2005	LA A	0	0	—	2	2	0	0-0	9.1	10	8	3	0	4-0	4	7.71	56	.270	.341	0	—	0	131	-3		0.2

SAUVEUR, RICH Richard Daniel B11.23.1963 Arlington VA BL/TL/6-4/170(163-195) [PitN83 S5/81] d7.1 Col Manatee (FL) CC

YEAR	TM LG	W	L	PCT	G	GS	CG-SHO	SV-BS	IP	H	R	HR	HB	BB-IB	SO	ERA	AERA	OAV	OOB	AB-HR-SH	AVG	PB	SUP	APR	DL	PW
1986	Pit N	0	0	—	3	3	0	0-0	12	17	8	3	2	6-0	6	6.00	65	.354	.446	3-0-1	.333	0	115	-2		-0.1
1988	Mon N	0	0	—	4	0	0	0-0	3	3	2	1	0	2-0	3	6.00	61	.250	.357	0	—	0	-1			0.0
1991	NY N	0	0	—	6	0	0	0-2	3.1	7	4	1	0	2-0	4	10.80	34	.467	.529	0	—	0	-2			-0.1
1992	KC A	0	1	.000	8	0	0	0-0	14.1	15	7	1	2	8-1	7	4.40	93	.273	.385	0	—	0	75	-2		-0.1
1996	Chi A	0	0	—	3	0	0	0-0	3	3	5	1	1	5-0	1	15.00	32	.333	.600	0	—	0	-3			-0.1
2000	Oak A	0	0	—	10	0	0	0-0	10.1	13	5	3	0	1-0	7	4.35	111	.310	.326	0	—	0	1			-0.3
Total	6	0	1	.000	34	3	0	0-2	46	58	31	10	5	24-1	28	6.07	69	.320	.414	3-0-1	.333	0	115	-7		-0.8

SAVAGE, JACK John Joseph B4.22.1964 Louisville KY BR/TR/6-3/185* [LAN85 8/194] d9.14 Col Kentucky

YEAR	TM LG	W	L	PCT	G	GS	CG-SHO	SV-BS	IP	H	R	HR	HB	BB-IB	SO	ERA	AERA	OAV	OOB	AB-HR-SH	AVG	PB	SUP	APR	DL	PW
1987	LA N	0	0	—	3	0	0	0-0	3.1	4	1	0	0	0-0	2	2.70	148	.286	.286	0	—	0	1			0.0
1990	Min A	0	2	.000	17	0	0	1-2	26	37	26	3	0	11-1	12	8.31	59	.339	.397	0	—	0	-11			-0.8
Total	2	0	2	.000	20	0	0	1-2	29.1	41	27	3	0	11-1	12	7.67	54	.333	.385	0	—	0	-10			-0.8

SAVAGE, BOB John Robert B12.1.1921 Manchester NH BR/TR/6-2/180 d6.24 Mil 1943-45 Col Staunton Mil. Academy (JC)

YEAR	TM LG	W	L	PCT	G	GS	CG-SHO	SV-BS	IP	H	R	HR	HB	BB-IB	SO	ERA	AERA	OAV	OOB	AB-HR-SH	AVG	PB	SUP	APR	DL	PW
1942	Phi A	0	1	.000	8	3	0	0	30.2	24	16	0	0	31	10	3.23	117	.220	.393	9	.111	0	113	1		0.0
1946	Phi A	3	15	.167	40	19	7-1	2	164	164	80	5	2	93	78	4.06	87	.259	.355	41-0-1	.122	1	78	-7		-0.7
1947	Phi A	8	10	.444	44	8	2-1	2	146	135	71	8	0	55	56	3.76	101	.245	.314	40-0-2	.050	-4	90	0		-0.5
1948	Phi A	5	1	.833	33	1	1	5	75.1	98	55	9	0	33	26	6.21	69	.318	.384	13-0-2	.077	-1	21	-15		-1.3
1949	StL A	0	0	—	4	0	0	0	7	12	5	1	0	3	1	6.43	70	.400	.455	1	.000	0	-1			-0.1
Total	5	16	27	.372	129	31	10-2	9	423	433	227	23	2	215	171	4.32	88	.265	.352	104-0-5	.087	-3	80	-22		-2.6

SAVIDGE, DON Donald Snyder B8.28.1908 Berwick PA D3.22.1983 Santa Barbara CA BR/TR/6-1/180 d8.6 f-Ralph Col Albright

YEAR	TM LG	W	L	PCT	G	GS	CG-SHO	SV-BS	IP	H	R	HR	HB	BB-IB	SO	ERA	AERA	OAV	OOB	AB-HR-SH	AVG	PB	SUP	APR	DL	PW
1929	Was A	0	0	—	6	0	0		12	7	11	0	2	7	1	0	2	9.00	47	.414	.452	0	—	0	-3		-0.1

SAVIDGE, RALPH Ralph Austin "The Human Whipcord" B2.3.1879 Jerseytown PA D7.22.1959 Berwick PA BR/TR/6-2/210 d9.22 s-Don

YEAR	TM LG	W	L	PCT	G	GS	CG-SHO	SV-BS	IP	H	R	HR	HB	BB-IB	SO	ERA	AERA	OAV	OOB	AB-HR-SH	AVG	PB	SUP	APR	DL	PW
1908	Cin N	0	1	.000	4	1	1	0	21	18	9	0	0	8	7	2.57	90	.247	.321	7	.000	-1	0	-1		-0.2
1909	Cin N	0	0	—	1	0	0	1	4	10	12	1	1	3	2	22.50	12	.588	.667	1	.000	-0	-8			-0.4
Total	2	0	1	.000	5	1	1	1	25	28	21	1	1	11	9	5.76	41	.311	.392	8	.000	-1	-9			-0.6

SAVRANSKY, MOE Morris B1.13.1929 Cleveland OH BL/TL/5-11/175 d4.23 Col Ohio St.

YEAR	TM LG	W	L	PCT	G	GS	CG-SHO	SV-BS	IP	H	R	HR	HB	BB-IB	SO	ERA	AERA	OAV	OOB	AB-HR-SH	AVG	PB	SUP	APR	DL	PW
1954	Cin N	0	2	.000	16	0	0	0	24	23	13	6	2	8	7	4.88	86	.247	.320	2	.500	1	-1			0.0

SAWYER, RICK Richard Clyde B4.7.1948 Bakersfield CA BR/TR/6-2/200* [CleA68*S3/45] d4.28 Col Bakersfield (CA) JC

YEAR	TM LG	W	L	PCT	G	GS	CG-SHO	SV-BS	IP	H	R	HR	HB	BB-IB	SO	ERA	AERA	OAV	OOB	AB-HR-SH	AVG	PB	SUP	APR	DL	PW
1974	NY A	0	0	—	1	0	0	0-0	1.2	2	3	0	0	1-0	1	16.20	22	.500	.600	0	—	0	-2			-0.1
1975	NY A	0	0	—	4	0	0	0-0	6	7	4	0	0	3-0	3	3.00	124	.304	.360	0	—	0	1			0.0

YEAR	TM LG	W	L	PCT	G	GS	CG-SHO	SV-BS	IP	H	R	HR	HB	BB-IB	SO	ERA	AERA	OAV	OOB	AB-HR-SH	AVG	PB	SUP	APR	DL	PW
1976	SD N	5	3	.625	13	11	4-2	0-0	81.2	84	24	2	1	38-8	33	2.53	130	.272	.351	24-0-5	.208	1	109	8		0.9
1977	SD N	7	6	.538	56	9	0	0-0	111	136	77	15	7	55-11	45	5.84	61	.316	.399	20-0-2	.150	1	138	-28		-2.7
Total	4	12	9	.571	74	20	4-2	0-0	200.1	229	108	17	8	96-19	82	4.49	77	.299	.380	44-0-7	.182	2	121	-22		-1.9

SAWYER, WILL   Willard Newton   B7.29.1864 Brimfield OH   D1.5.1936 Kent OH   BL/TL   d7.21   Col Case Western Reserve

YEAR	TM LG	W	L	PCT	G	GS	CG-SHO	SV-BS	IP	H	R	HR	HB	BB-IB	SO	ERA	AERA	OAV	OOB	AB-HR-SH	AVG	PB	SUP	APR	DL	PW
1883	Cle N	4	10	.286	17	15	15	0	141	119	79	1		47	76	2.36	133	**.217**	.279	47	.021	-7	52	11		0.2

SAYLES, BILL   William Nisbeth   B7.27.1917 Portland OR   D11.20.1996 Lincoln City OR   BR/TR/6-2/175   d7.17   Mil 1944-45   Col Oregon

YEAR	TM LG	W	L	PCT	G	GS	CG-SHO	SV-BS	IP	H	R	HR	HB	BB-IB	SO	ERA	AERA	OAV	OOB	AB-HR-SH	AVG	PB	SUP	APR	DL	PW
1939	Bos N	0	0	—	5	0	0	0	14	14	13	1	0	13	9	7.07	67	.264	.409	7	.143	-0		-4		-0.2
1943	NY N	1	3	.250	18	3	1	0	53	60	29	1	0	23	38	4.75	72	.284	.355	13	.308	1*	82	-6		-0.4
	Bro N	0	0	—	5	0	0	0	11.2	13	14	0	0	10	5	7.71	44	.271	.397	2	.500	0*		-7		-0.3
	Year	1	3	.250	23	3	1	0	64.2	73	43	1	0	33	43	5.29	65	.282	.363	15	.333	1	82	-13		-0.7
Total	2	1	3	.250	28	3	1	0	78.2	87	56	2	0	46	52	5.61	65	.279	.372	22	.273	1	78	-17		-0.9

SAYLOR, PHIL   Philip Andrew "Lefty"   B1.2.1871 Van Wert Co. OH   D7.23.1937 W.Alexandria OH   TL   d7.11   Col Ohio Wesleyan

YEAR	TM LG	W	L	PCT	G	GS	CG-SHO	SV-BS	IP	H	R	HR	HB	BB-IB	SO	ERA	AERA	OAV	OOB	AB-HR-SH	AVG	PB	SUP	APR	DL	PW
1891	Phi N	0	0	—		0	0	0	3	2	2	1	0	0	0	6.00	57	.182	.182	1	.000	-0		-1		0.0

SCANLAN, FRANK   Frank Aloysius   B4.28.1890 Syracuse NY   D4.9.1969 Brooklyn NY   BL/TL/6-1.5/175   d8.6   b-Doc   Col Notre Dame

YEAR	TM LG	W	L	PCT	G	GS	CG-SHO	SV-BS	IP	H	R	HR	HB	BB-IB	SO	ERA	AERA	OAV	OOB	AB-HR-SH	AVG	PB	SUP	APR	DL	PW
1909	Phi N	0	0	—	6	0	0	0	11	8	3	0	0	5	5	1.64	159	.211	.302	4	.000	-1		1		0.0

SCANLAN, BOB   Robert Guy   B8.9.1966 Los Angeles CA   BR/TR/6-8/210(200-215)   [PhiN84 25/636]   d5.7

YEAR	TM LG	W	L	PCT	G	GS	CG-SHO	SV-BS	IP	H	R	HR	HB	BB-IB	SO	ERA	AERA	OAV	OOB	AB-HR-SH	AVG	PB	SUP	APR	DL	PW
1991	Chi N	7	8	.467	40	13	0	1-1	111	114	60	5	3	40-3	44	3.89	100	.268		24-0-2	.042	-2	82	-3		-0.5
1992	Chi N	6	3	.333	69	0	0	14-4	87.1	76	32	4	1	30-6	42	2.89	126	.235	.301	4	.000	-0		7		0.9
1993	Chi N	4	5	.444	70	0	0	0-3	75.1	79	41	6	3	28-7	44	4.54	89	.278	.343	2-0-1	.500	-0		-4		0.9
1994	Mil A	2	6	.250	30	12	0	2-1	103	117	53	11	4	28-2	65	4.11	124	.288	.339	0	—	0	63	10		0.7
1995	Mil A	4	7	.364	17	14	0	0-0	83.1	101	66	9	7	44-3	29	6.59	76	.304	.391	0	—	0	102	-14	70	-1.4
1996	Det A	0	0	—	8	0	0	0-0	11	16	15	1	1	9-1	3	10.64	48	.348	.464	0	—	0		-7		-0.3
	KC A	0	1	.000	9	0	0	0-0	11.1	13	4	1	1	3-1	3	3.18	158	.295	.354	0	—	0		2		0.2
	Year	0	1	.000	17	0	0	0-1	22.1	29	19	2	2	12-2	6	6.85	74	.322	.413	0	—	0		-5		-0.1
1998	Hou N	0	1	.000	27	0	0	0-0	26.1	24	12	4	1	13-0	9	3.08	132	.245	.330	0	—	0		2		0.1
2000	Mil N	0	0	—	2	0	0	0-0	1.2	6	6	0	1	0-0	1	27.00	17	.600	.583	0	—	0		-4		-0.2
2001	Mon N	0	0	—	18	0	0	0-0	26.1	37	23	0	1	14-0	5	7.86	55	.339	.419	0	—	0		-10		-0.5
Total	9	20	34	.370	290	39	0	17-10	536.2	583	312	41	23	209-23	245	4.63	94	.287	.349	30-0-3	.067	-2	89	-21	70	-1.4

SCANLAN, DOC   William Dennis   B3.7.1881 Syracuse NY   D5.29.1949 Brooklyn NY   BL/TR/5-8/165   d9.24   b-Frank   Col Syracuse

YEAR	TM LG	W	L	PCT	G	GS	CG-SHO	SV-BS	IP	H	R	HR	HB	BB-IB	SO	ERA	AERA	OAV	OOB	AB-HR-SH	AVG	PB	SUP	APR	DL	PW
1903	Pit N	0	1	.000	7	1	1	0	9	5	7	0	0	6	0	4.00	81	.167	.306	2	.000	0	42	-1		-0.1
1904	Pit N	1	3	.250	4	3	1	0	22	21	18	0	2	20	10	4.91	56	.236	.387	6	.000	-1	109	-6		-1.0
	Bro N	6	6	.500	13	12	11-3	0	104	94	39	0	2	40	40	2.16	127	.242	.316	35-0-5	.143	-2	88	6		0.4
	Year	7	9	.438	17	15	12-3	0	126	115	57	0	4	60	50	2.64	104	.241	.331	41-0-5	.122	-2	92	1		-0.6
1905	Bro N	14	12	.538	33	28	22-2	0	249.2	220	119	4	8	104	135	2.92	99	.237	.339	96-0-3	.167	-2	103	-2		-0.5
1906	Bro N	18	13	.581	38	33	28-6	2	288	230	128	6	8	127	120	3.19	79	.214	.301	97-0-3	.186	3	109	-19		-2.1
1907	Bro N	6	8	.429	17	15	10-2	0	107	90	50	1	3	61	59	3.20	73	.239	.349	34	.265	5	93	-9		-0.7
1909	Bro N	8	7	.533	19	17	12-2	0	141.1	125	53	2	4	65	72	2.93	88	.252	.343	44-0-1	.273	5	87	-3		0.3
1910	Bro N	9	11	.450	34	25	14	2	217.1	175	76	1	5	116	103	2.61	116	.234	.341	69-0-2	.203	1	72	12		1.1
1911	Bro N	3	10	.231	22	15	3	1	113.2	101	67	2	6	69	45	3.64	92	.256	.374	33-0-2	.121	-2	66	-7		-1.0
Total	8	65	71	.478	181	149	102-15	5	1252	1061	557	15	36	608	584	3.00	93	.234	.330	416-0-16	.188	8	90	-29		-3.6

SCANTLEBURY, PAT   Patricio Athelstan   B11.11.1917 Gatun, Canal Zone   D5.24.1991 Glen Ridge NJ   BL/TL/6-1/180   d4.19   Negro Lg 1944-50

YEAR	TM LG	W	L	PCT	G	GS	CG-SHO	SV-BS	IP	H	R	HR	HB	BB-IB	SO	ERA	AERA	OAV	OOB	AB-HR-SH	AVG	PB	SUP	APR	DL	PW
1956	Cin N	0	1	.000	6	2	0	0	19	24	14	5	0	5-0	10	6.63	60	.293	.333	3-0-1	.000	-0*	144	-5		-0.3

SCARBERY, RANDY   Randy James   B6.22.1952 Fresno CA   BB/TR/6-1/185*   [OakA73 1/23]   d4.16   Col USC

YEAR	TM LG	W	L	PCT	G	GS	CG-SHO	SV-BS	IP	H	R	HR	HB	BB-IB	SO	ERA	AERA	OAV	OOB	AB-HR-SH	AVG	PB	SUP	APR	DL	PW
1979	Chi A	2	8	.200	45	5	0	4-0	101.1	102	56	9	3	34-3	45	4.62	92	.262	.323	0	—	0	43	-2		-0.2
1980	Chi A	1	2	.333	15	0	0	2-0	28.2	24	14	1	2	7-0	18	4.08	99	.238	.297	0	—	0		0		0.0
Total	2	3	10	.231	60	5	0	6-0	130	126	70	10	5	41-3	63	4.50	94	.257	.318	0	—	0	43	-2		-0.2

SCARBOROUGH, RAY   Ray Wilson (b Rae Wilson Scarborough)   B7.23.1917 Mt.Gilead NC   D7.1.1982 Mount Olive NC   BR/TR/6-0/185*   d6.26   Mil 1943-45   C1   Col Wake Forest

YEAR	TM LG	W	L	PCT	G	GS	CG-SHO	SV-BS	IP	H	R	HR	HB	BB-IB	SO	ERA	AERA	OAV	OOB	AB-HR-SH	AVG	PB	SUP	APR	DL	PW
1942	Was A	2	1	.667	17	5	1-1	0	63.1	68	32	2	0	32	16	4.12	89	.272	.355	21-0-1	.190	0	197	-2		-0.1
1943	Was A	4	4	.500	24	6	2	3	86	93	42	2	0	46	43	2.83	113	.273	.359	24-0-2	.333	2	171	0		0.2
1946	Was A	7	11	.389	32	20	6-1	1	155.2	176	85	8	1	74	46	4.05	83	.286	.364	50-0-4	.140	-2	83	-13		-1.4
1947	Was A	6	13	.316	33	18	8-2	0	161	165	74	5	1	67	63	3.41	109	.267	.339	50-0-3	.120	-3	58	3		0.0
1948	Was A	15	8	.652	31	26	9	1	185.1	166	71	0	3	72	74	2.82	154	.233	.307	64-0-6	.219	-0	98	29		3.4
1949	Was A	13	11	.542	34	27	11-1	0	199.2	204	115	10	7	88	81	4.60	93	.265	.346	67-0-7	.194	-0	94	-7		-0.7
1950	Was A	3	5	.375	8	8	4-2	0	58.1	62	30	2	2	22	24	4.01	112	.276	.345	20	.100	-1	63	3		0.3
	Chi A☆	10	13	.435	27	23	8-1	1	149.1	160	95	10	4	62	70	5.30	85	.274	.347	46-0-4	.174	-1	73	-12		-1.7
	Year	13	18	.419	35	31	12-3	1	207.2	222	125	12	6	84	94	4.94	91	.274	.346	66-0-4	.152	-3	71	-9		-1.4
1951	Bos A	12	9	.571	37	22	8	0	184	201	106	21	14	61	71	5.09	88	.275	.342	68-0-3	.191	-2	120	-7		-1.0
1952	Bos A	1	5	.167	28	8	1-1	4	76.2	79	47	8	4	35	29	4.81	90	.266	.351	18	.222	0	66	-7		-0.6
	†NY A	5	1	.833	9	4	1	0	34	27	11	4	1	15	13	2.91	114	.223	.314	14	.357	2	164	3		0.6
	Year	6	6	.500	37	12	2-1	4	110.2	106	58	12	5	50	42	4.23	89	.254	.340	32	.281	2	95	-5		0.0
1953	NY A	2	2	.500	25	1	0	2	54.2	52	23	4	4	26	20	3.29	112	.250	.345	12-1-1	.083	-0	144	2		0.2
	Det A	0	2	.000	13	0	0	2	20.2	34	24	3	1	11	12	8.27	49	.354	.436	2	.000	-0		-11		-1.2
	Year	2	4	.333	38	1	0	4	75.1	86	47	7	5	37	32	4.66	81	.283	.374	14-1-1	.071	-0	141	-10		-1.0
Total	10	80	85	.485	318	168	59-9	14	1428.2	1487	755	89	44	611	564	4.13	97	.267	.344	456-1-31	.186	-6	96	-19		-2.0

SCARCE, MAC   Guerrant McCurdy   B4.8.1949 Danville VA   BL/TL/6-3/193(180-200)   [PhiN71 8/177]   d7.10   Col Florida St.

YEAR	TM LG	W	L	PCT	G	GS	CG-SHO	SV-BS	IP	H	R	HR	HB	BB-IB	SO	ERA	AERA	OAV	OOB	AB-HR-SH	AVG	PB	SUP	APR	DL	PW
1972	Phi N	1	2	.333	31	0	0	4-0	36.2	30	14	6	2	20-2	40	3.44	105	.222	.331	6	.000	-1		1		0.1
1973	Phi N	1	8	.111	52	0	0	12-2	70.2	54	23	3	1	47-14	57	2.42	157	.220	.347	5-0-1	.000	-1		10		1.4
1974	Phi N	3	8	.273	58	0	0	5-1	70.1	72	40	6	2	35-7	50	4.99	76	.275	.359	6	.000	-1		-7		-1.3
1975	NY N	0	0	—	1	0	0	0-0	0	1	0	0	0	0-0	0	—		1.000	1.000	0	—	-1		0		0.0
1978	Min A	1	1	.500	17	0	0	0-1	32	35	19	5	3	15-0	17	3.94	98	.292	.381	0	—	0		-2		-0.1
Total	5	6	19	.240	159	0	0	21-4	209.2	192	96	20	8	117-23	164	3.69	102	.251	.354	17-0-1	.000	-2				0.1

SCHACHT, AL   Alexander   B11.11.1892 New York NY   D7.14.1984 Waterbury CT   BR/TR/5-11/142   d9.18   C12

YEAR	TM LG	W	L	PCT	G	GS	CG-SHO	SV-BS	IP	H	R	HR	HB	BB-IB	SO	ERA	AERA	OAV	OOB	AB-HR-SH	AVG	PB	SUP	APR	DL	PW
1919	Was A	2	0	1.000	2	2	1	0	15	14	5	0	0	4	4	2.40	134	.233	.281	3-0-2	.000	0	244	1		0.2
1920	Was A	6	4	.600	22	11	5-1	1	99.1	130	60	2	1	30	19	4.44	84	.319	.367	26-0-1	.192	1	165	-7		-0.4
1921	Was A	6	6	.500	29	5	2	1	82.2	110	59	2	2	27	15	4.90	84	.332	.386	22-0-1	.227	1	138	-9		-1.2
Total	3	14	10	.583	53	18	8-1	2	197	254	124	4	3	61	38	4.48	86	.318	.368	51-0-4	.196	2	163	-15		-1.4

SCHACHT, SID   Sidney   B2.3.1918 Bogota NJ   D3.30.1991 Ft.Lauderdale FL   BR/TR/5-11/170*   d4.23

YEAR	TM LG	W	L	PCT	G	GS	CG-SHO	SV-BS	IP	H	R	HR	HB	BB-IB	SO	ERA	AERA	OAV	OOB	AB-HR-SH	AVG	PB	SUP	APR	DL	PW
1950	StL A	0	0	—	8	1	0	1	10.2	24	22	5	0	14	7	16.03	31	.429	.543	2	.000	-0*	146	-12		-0.6
1951	StL A	0	0	—	6	0	0	1	6	14	15	1	0	5	4	21.00	21	.452	.528	0	—	0		-10		-0.5
	Bos N	0	2	.000	5	0	0	1	4.2	6	4	0	0	2	1	1.93	191	.300	.364	0	—	0		-1		-0.1
Total	2	0	2	.000	19	1	0	1	21.1	44	41	6	0	21	12	14.34	31	.411	.508	2	.000	-0	146	-22		-1.2

SCHACKER, HAL   Harold   B4.6.1925 Brooklyn NY   BR/TR/6-0/190   d5.9

YEAR	TM LG	W	L	PCT	G	GS	CG-SHO	SV-BS	IP	H	R	HR	HB	BB-IB	SO	ERA	AERA	OAV	OOB	AB-HR-SH	AVG	PB	SUP	APR	DL	PW
1945	Bos N	0	1	.000	6	0	0	0	15.1	14	12	2	0	9	6	5.28	73	.241	.343	2	.000	0		-3		-0.2

SCHAEFFER, HARRY   Harry Edward "Lefty"   B6.23.1924 Reading PA   BL/TL/6-2.5/175   d7.28   Col East Stroudsburg

YEAR	TM LG	W	L	PCT	G	GS	CG-SHO	SV-BS	IP	H	R	HR	HB	BB-IB	SO	ERA	AERA	OAV	OOB	AB-HR-SH	AVG	PB	SUP	APR	DL	PW
1952	NY A	0	0	—												5.29	63	.265	.419	3	.000	0	79	-5		-0.3

SCHAEFFER, MARK   Mark Philip   B6.5.1948 Santa Monica CA   BL/TL/6-5/215   [BosA66*2/22]   d4.18

YEAR	TM LG	W	L	PCT	G	GS	CG-SHO	SV-BS	IP	H	R	HR	HB	BB-IB	SO	ERA	AERA	OAV	OOB	AB-HR-SH	AVG	PB	SUP	APR	DL	PW
1972	SD N	2	0	1.000	41	0	0	1-0	41	52	21	3	2	28-2	25	4.61	72	.319	.418	0	—	0		-5		-0.3

SCHAFFERNOTH, JOE   Joseph Arthur   B8.6.1937 Trenton NJ   BR/TR/6-4.5/195*   d4.15

YEAR	TM LG	W	L	PCT	G	GS	CG-SHO	SV-BS	IP	H	R	HR	HB	BB-IB	SO	ERA	AERA	OAV	OOB	AB-HR-SH	AVG	PB	SUP	APR	DL	PW
1959	Chi N	1	0	1.000	5	1	0	0	7.2	11	7	1	0	4-0	3	8.22	48	.355	.429		.000	-0	158	-3	55	-0.4
1960	Chi N	2	3	.400	33	0	0	3	55	46	21	7	1	17-2	33	2.78	136	.235	.295	7-0-1	.286	-0		6		0.6
1961	Chi N	0	4	.000	20	2	0	0	38.1	43	29	7	1	18-2	23	6.34	66	.293	.373	5	.000	-1		-8		-0.8
	Cle A	0	1	.000	15	0	0	0	17	16	11	2	1	14-1	9	4.76	83	.242	.383	1	.000	-0		-2		-0.1
Total	3	3	8	.273	73	3	0	3	118	116	68	17	3	53-5	68	4.58	86	.264	.345	16-0-1	.125	-1	158	-8	55	-0.7

YEAR	TM LG	W	L	PCT	G	GS	CG-SHO	SV-BS	IP	H	R	HR	HB	BB-IB	SO	ERA	AERA	OAV	OOB	AB-HR-SH	AVG	PB	SUP	APR	DL	PW

SCHALLOCK, ART Arthur Lawrence B4.25.1924 Mill Valley CA BL/TL/5-9/160* d7.16 Col Marin (CA) CC

YEAR	TM LG	W	L	PCT	G	GS	CG-SHO	SV-BS	IP	H	R	HR	HB	BB-IB	SO	ERA	AERA	OAV	OOB	AB-HR-SH	AVG	PB	SUP	APR	DL	PW
1951	NY A	3	1	.750	11	6	1	0	46.1	50	20	3	1	20	19	3.88	99	.272	.346	17-0-1	.294	1	143	1		0.2
1952	NY A	0	0	—	2	0	0	0	2	3	2	0	0	2	1	9.00	37	.375	.500	0	—	0		-1		-0.1
1953	†NY A	0	0	—	7	1	0	1	21.1	30	12	2	1	15	13	2.95	125	.345	.447	6	.333	0	144	0		0.0
1954	NY A	0	1	.000	6	1	1	0	17.1	20	10	3	1	11	9	4.15	83	.282	.386	3	.000	-0	26	-2		-0.2
1955	NY A	0	0	—	2	0	0	0	3	4	2	1	0	1-0	2	6.00	62	.333	.385	0	—	0		-1		0.0
	Bal A	3	5	.375	30	6	1	0	80.1	92	52	2	2	42-3	33	4.15	92	.294	.378	19-0-3	.105	-1	58	-7		-0.7
	Year	3	5	.375	32	6	1	0	83.1	96	54	3	2	43-3	35	4.21	90	.295	.378	19-0-3	.105	-1	58	-8		-0.7
Total	5	6	7	.462	58	14	3	1	170.1	199	98	11	5	91-3	77	4.02	94	.295	.381	45-0-4	.200	1	100	-10		-0.8

SCHANZ, CHARLEY Charles Murrell B6.8.1919 Anacortes WA D5.28.1992 Sacramento CA BR/TR/6-3.5/215* d4.20

YEAR	TM LG	W	L	PCT	G	GS	CG-SHO	SV-BS	IP	H	R	HR	HB	BB-IB	SO	ERA	AERA	OAV	OOB	AB-HR-SH	AVG	PB	SUP	APR	DL	PW
1944	Phi N	13	16	.448	40	30	13-1	3	241.1	231	108	6	6	103	84	3.32	99	.254	.334	81-1-3	.148	-1	76	6		0.6
1945	Phi N	4	15	.211	35	21	5-1	5	144.2	165	99	9	4	87	56	4.35	88	.285	.387	39-0-5	.154	-0	66	-13		-3.1
1946	Phi N	6	6	.500	32	15	4	4	116.1	130	82	8	5	71	47	5.80	59	.286	.389	36-0-4	.083	-2	123	-28		-3.1
1947	Phi N	2	4	.333	34	6	1	2	101.2	107	59	7	3	47	42	4.16	96	.295	.380	27-0-1	.148	-1	84	-4		-1.4
1950	Bos A	3	2	.600	14	0	0	0	22.2	25	21	3	1	24	14	8.34	59	.281	.439	11	.091	-1		-7		-1.4
Total	5	28	43	.394	155	72	23-2	14	626.2	658	369	29	24	332	243	4.34	86	.275	.369	194-1-13	.134	-5	82	-46		-5.8

SCHAPPERT, JOHN John B Brooklyn NY D7.27.1917 Brooklyn NY BR/TR/5-10/170 d5.3

YEAR	TM LG	W	L	PCT	G	GS	CG-SHO	SV-BS	IP	H	R	HR	HB	BB-IB	SO	ERA	AERA	OAV	OOB	AB-HR-SH	AVG	PB	SUP	APR	DL	PW
1882	StL AA	8	7	.533	15	14	13	0	128	131	99	2	2	32	38	3.52	80	.248	.291	50	.180	0	135	-7		-0.8

SCHARDT, BILL Wilburt "Big Bill" B1.20.1886 Cleveland OH D7.20.1964 Vermilion OH BR/TR/6-4/210 d4.14

YEAR	TM LG	W	L	PCT	G	GS	CG-SHO	SV-BS	IP	H	R	HR	HB	BB-IB	SO	ERA	AERA	OAV	OOB	AB-HR-SH	AVG	PB	SUP	APR	DL	PW
1911	Bro N	5	15	.250	39	22	10-1	4	195.1	190	102	4	8	91	77	3.59	93	.266	.355	59-0-3	.169	-1		79	-7		-0.7
1912	Bro N	0	1	.000	7	0	0	1	20.2	25	13	1	2	6	7	4.35	77	.321	.384	6	.000	-1		-2		-0.1
Total	2	5	16	.238	46	22	10-1	5	216	215	115	5	10	97	84	3.67	91	.271	.358	65-0-3	.154	-1	79	-9		-0.8

SCHATTINGER, JEFF Jeffrey Charles B10.25.1955 Fresno CA BL/TR/6-5/200 [KCA79*S1/21] d9.21 Col USC

YEAR	TM LG	W	L	PCT	G	GS	CG-SHO	SV-BS	IP	H	R	HR	HB	BB-IB	SO	ERA	AERA	OAV	OOB	AB-HR-SH	AVG	PB	SUP	APR	DL	PW
1981	KC A	0	0	—	1	0	0	0-0	3	2	0	0	0	1-0	1	0.00	—	.182	.357	0	—	0		1		0.1

SCHATZEDER, DAN Daniel Ernest B12.1.1954 Elmhurst IL BL/TL/6-0/195(185-204) [MonN76 3/57] d9.4 Col Denver

YEAR	TM LG	W	L	PCT	G	GS	CG-SHO	SV-BS	IP	H	R	HR	HB	BB-IB	SO	ERA	AERA	OAV	OOB	AB-HR-SH	AVG	PB	SUP	APR	DL	PW
1977	Mon N	2	1	.667	3	3	1-1	0-0	21.2	16	6	0	0	13-0	14	2.49	155	.203	.312	6	.333	-0	77	4		0.5
1978	Mon N	7	7	.500	29	18	2	0-0	143.2	108	54	10	2	68-5	69	3.07	116	.213	.306	45-1-2	.222	3*	92	8		1.0
1979	Mon N	10	5	.667	32	21	3	1-0	162	136	57	17	1	59-2	106	2.83	131	.225	.294	51-1-1	.216	4	113	17	21	1.8
1980	Det A	11	13	.458	32	26	9-2	0-0	192.2	178	88	23	3	58-9	94	4.02	103	.246	.303	0	—	0	91	5		0.5
1981	Det A	6	8	.429	17	14	1	0-0	71.1	74	49	13	2	29-1	20	6.06	63	.265	.334	0	—	0	98	-17		-2.8
1982	SF N	1	4	.200	13	3	0	0-1	33.1	47	30	3	0	12-4	18	7.29	49	.333	.383	8	.125	-0	66	-13		-1.8
	Mon N	0	2	.000	26	1	0	0-0	36	37	16	1	2	12-5	15	3.50	106	.276	.340	5	.400	1	48	1		0.1
	Year	1	6	.143	39	4	0	0-1	69.1	84	46	4	2	24-9	33	5.32	68	.305	.362	13	.231	1	61	-13		-1.7
1983	Mon N	5	2	.714	58	2	0	2-2	87	88	34	3	5	25-6	48	3.21	113	.265	.324	10-0-1	.200	0	61	4		0.3
1984	Mon N	7	7	.500	36	14	1-1	1-0	136	112	44	13	2	36-1	89	2.71	128	.224	.276	35-0-5	.314	5*	78	12		1.7
1985	Mon N	3	5	.375	24	15	1	0-0	104.1	101	52	13	0	31-0	64	3.80	91	.259	.311	31-2-1	.194	3	96	-6	57	-0.1
1986	Mon N	3	2	.600	30	1	0	1-0	59	53	29	6	0	19-2	33	3.20	117	.240	.298	21-1-0	.429	6*	167	1		0.7
	Phi N	3	3	.500	25	0	0	1-0	29.1	28	14	3	0	16-7	14	3.38	116	.252	.344	5	.200	1		1		0.1
	Year	6	5	.545	55	1	0	2-0	88.1	81	43	9	0	35-9	47	3.26	117	.244	.314	26-1-0	.385	7	164	2		0.9
1987	Phi N	3	1	.750	26	0	0	0-0	37.2	40	21	4	0	14-7	28	4.06	106	.278	.333	12	.167	0		0		-0.8
	†Min A	3	1	.750	30	1	0	0-0	43.2	64	37	8	1	18-3	30	6.39	73	.342	.399	0	—	0	98	-10		-1.3
1988	Cle A	0	2	.000	15	0	0	3-1	16	26	19	6	1	2-0	10	9.56	43	.351	.377	0	—	0		-9		-1.3
	Min A	0	1	.000	10	0	0	0-0	10.1	8	2	1	1	5-1	7	1.74	235	.216	.326	0	—	0		3		0.1
	Year	0	3	.000	25	0	0	3-1	26.1	34	21	7	2	7-1	17	6.49	63	.306	.358	0	—	0		-7		-1.1
1989	Hou N	4	1	.800	36	0	0	1-1	56.2	64	33	2	3	28-6	46	4.45	77	.287	.374	9	.000	-1		-8	49	-0.8
1990	Hou N	1	3	.250	45	2	0	0-0	64	61	23	2	0	23-4	37	2.39	156	.261	.321	4	.250	0	73	8		0.1
	NY N	0	0	—	6	0	0	0-0	5.2	5	0	0	0	0-0	2	0.00	—	.263	.263	0	—	0		2		0.1
	Year	1	3	.250	51	2	0	0-0	69.2	66	23	2	0	23-4	39	2.20	170	.261	.317	4	.250	0	72	10		0.2
1991	KC A	0	0	—	8	0	0	0-0	6.2	11	9	0	1	7-1	4	9.45	44	.367	.486	0	—	0		-4		-0.2
Total	15	69	68	.504	504	121	18-4	10-5	1317	1257	617	128	23	475-64	748	3.74	100	.253	.319	242-5-10	.240	22	93	-1	127	-0.2

SCHAUER, RUBE Alexander John B3.19.1891 Kamenka, Russia D4.15.1957 Minneapolis MN BR/TR/6-2/192 d8.27

YEAR	TM LG	W	L	PCT	G	GS	CG-SHO	SV-BS	IP	H	R	HR	HB	BB-IB	SO	ERA	AERA	OAV	OOB	AB-HR-SH	AVG	PB	SUP	APR	DL	PW
1913	NY N	0	1	.000	3	1	1	0	12	14	11	0	0	9	7	7.50	42	.292	.404	3	.000	-0	24	-5		-0.4
1914	NY N	0	0	—	6	0	0	0	22.1	16	10	2	0	8	6	3.22	82	.205	.279	7	.143	-0		-1		-0.1
1915	NY N	2	8	.200	32	7	4	0	105.1	101	56	4	2	35	65	3.50	73	.258	.322	26	.077	-2	58	-13		-1.4
1916	NY N	1	4	.200	19	3	1	0	45.2	44	22	0	2	16	24	2.96	82	.257	.328	9	.222	0	61	-4		-0.4
1917	Phi A	7	16	.304	33	21	10	1	215	209	116	6	3	69	62	3.14	88	.263	.324	76-0-6	.145	-4	97	-13		-1.6
Total	5	10	29	.256	93	32	16	1	400.1	384	215	12	7	137	164	3.35	80	.259	.324	121-0-6	.132	-4	85	-36		-3.9

SCHEETZ, OWEN Owen Franklin B12.24.1913 New Bedford OH D9.28.1994 Kirkersville OH BR/TR/6-1/200 d4.22

YEAR	TM LG	W	L	PCT	G	GS	CG-SHO	SV-BS	IP	H	R	HR	HB	BB-IB	SO	ERA	AERA	OAV	OOB	AB-HR-SH	AVG	PB	SUP	APR	DL	PW
1943	Was A	0	0	—	4	0	0	0	9	7	4	0	0	4	5	7.00	46	.381	.435	2	.000	-0		-3		-0.2

SCHEFFER, AARON Aaron Alvin Marcus B10.15.1975 Ypsilanti MI BL/TR/6-2/165 d6.13

YEAR	TM LG	W	L	PCT	G	GS	CG-SHO	SV-BS	IP	H	R	HR	HB	BB-IB	SO	ERA	AERA	OAV	OOB	AB-HR-SH	AVG	PB	SUP	APR	DL	PW
1999	Sea A	0	0	—	4	0	0	0-0	4.2	6	5	0	1	3-0	4	1.93	248	.353	.417	0	—	0		0		0.0

SCHEGG, LEFTY Gilbert Eugene (b Gilbert Eugene Price) B8.29.1889 Leesville OH D2.27.1963 Niles OH BL/TL/5-11/180 d8.20

YEAR	TM LG	W	L	PCT	G	GS	CG-SHO	SV-BS	IP	H	R	HR	HB	BB-IB	SO	ERA	AERA	OAV	OOB	AB-HR-SH	AVG	PB	SUP	APR	DL	PW
1912	Was A	0	0	—	2	1	0	0	5.1	7	5	0	0	4	3	3.38	99	.333	.440	2	.000	-0	89	-1		-0.1

SCHEIB, CARL Carl Alvin B1.1.1927 Gratz PA BR/TR/6-1/192* d9.6 Mil 1945-46

YEAR	TM LG	W	L	PCT	G	GS	CG-SHO	SV-BS	IP	H	R	HR	HB	BB-IB	SO	ERA	AERA	OAV	OOB	AB-HR-SH	AVG	PB	SUP	APR	DL	PW
1943	Phi A	0	1	.000	6	0	0	0	18.2	24	14	4	1	3	3	4.34	78	.308	.341	5	.000	-1		-3		-0.3
1944	Phi A	0	0	—	15	0	0	0	36.1	36	18	1	4	11	13	4.21	83	.257	.329	10	.300	1		-2		0.1
1945	Phi A	0	0	—	4	0	0	0	8.2	6	3	0	0	4	2	3.12	110	.207	.303	2	.000	-0		0		0.1
1947	Phi A	4	6	.400	21	12	6-2	0	116	121	68	11	2	55	26	5.04	76	.274	.357	45	.133	-2*	81	-13		-1.4
1948	Phi A	14	8	.636	32	24	15-1	0	198.2	219	90	14	4	76	44	3.94	109	.286	.351	104-2-0	.298	7*	105	10		2.1
1949	Phi A	9	12	.429	38	23	11-2	0	182.2	191	117	16	2	118	43	5.12	80	.275	.382	72-0-2	.236	3*	103	-21		-1.9
1950	Phi A	3	10	.231	43	8	1	3	106	138	96	13	0	70	37	7.22	63	.317	.411	52-1-0	.250	2*	92	-32		-3.3
1951	Phi A	1	12	.077	46	11	3	10	143	132	78	7	8	71	49	4.47	96	.250	.347	53-2-0	.396	8*	74	-3		-0.6
1952	Phi A	11	7	.611	30	19	8-1	2	158	153	82	21	4	50	42	4.39	90	.253	.314	82-0-1	.220	-1*	131	-5		-0.6
1953	Phi A	3	7	.300	28	8	3-1	0	96	99	57	9	7	29	25	4.88	88	.261	.325	41	.195	-1*	80	-6	32	-0.7
1954	Phi A	0	1	.000	3	1	0	0	2	5	5	1	1	1	1	22.50	17	.500	.583	2	—	0	68	-4		-0.6
	StL N	0	1	.000	3	1	0	0	4.2	6	6	3	0	5	5	11.57	36	.300	.440	2	.000	-0	87	-3		-0.6
Total	11	45	65	.409	267	107	47-6	17	1070.2	1130	634	99	30	493	290	4.88	85	.274	.355	468-5-3	.250	16	100	-82	32	-6.4

SCHEIBECK, FRANK Frank S. B6.28.1865 Detroit MI D10.22.1956 Detroit MI BR/TR/5-7/145 d5.9 ▲

YEAR	TM LG	W	L	PCT	G	GS	CG-SHO	SV-BS	IP	H	R	HR	HB	BB-IB	SO	ERA	AERA	OAV	OOB	AB-HR-SH	AVG	PB	SUP	APR	DL	PW
1887	Cle AA	0	1	.000	1	1	1	0	9	17	18	1	4	3	3	12.00	36	.362	.423	9	.222	0*	29	-7		-0.5

SCHEIBLE, JACK John G. B2.16.1866 Youngstown OH D8.9.1897 Youngstown OH TL d9.8

YEAR	TM LG	W	L	PCT	G	GS	CG-SHO	SV-BS	IP	H	R	HR	HB	BB-IB	SO	ERA	AERA	OAV	OOB	AB-HR-SH	AVG	PB	SUP	APR	DL	PW
1893	Cle N	1	1	.500	2	2	2-1	0	18	15	9	0	0	11	1	2.00	244	.221	.329	7	.143	-0	64	5		0.4
1894	Phi N	0	1	.000	1	1	0	0	0.1	6	10	1	1	2	0	189.00	3	.857	.900	0	—	0	55	-7		-0.8
Total	2	1	2	.333	3	2-1	0	18.1	21	19	0	1	13	1	5.40	91	.280	.393	7	.143	-0	62	-2		-0.4

SCHEID, RICH Richard Paul B2.3.1965 Staten Island NY BL/TL/6-3/185(185-200) [NYA86 2/53] d9.11 Col Seton Hall

YEAR	TM LG	W	L	PCT	G	GS	CG-SHO	SV-BS	IP	H	R	HR	HB	BB-IB	SO	ERA	AERA	OAV	OOB	AB-HR-SH	AVG	PB	SUP	APR	DL	PW
1992	Hou N	1	0	1.000	7	1	0	0-0	12	14	8	2	0	6-1	8	6.00	57	.280	.357	1	.000	-0	80	-3		-0.3
1994	Fla N	1	3	.250	8	5	0	0-0	32.1	35	18	6	2	8-0	17	3.34	133	.269	.321	7-0-1	.000	-1	45	2		0.1
1995	Fla N	0	0	—	6	0	0	0-0	10.1	14	7	1	0	7-0	10	6.10	70	.341	.429	1	.000	-0		-2		-0.1
Total	3	1	4	.200	21	6	0	0-0	54.2	63	33	9	2	21-1	35	4.45	94	.285	.351	9-0-1	.000	-1	51	-3		-0.3

SCHELLE, JIM Gerard Anthony B4.13.1917 Baltimore MD D5.4.1990 Weymouth MA BR/TR/6-3/204 d7.23 Col Villanova

YEAR	TM LG	W	L	PCT	G	GS	CG-SHO	SV-BS	IP	H	R	HR	HB	BB-IB	SO	ERA	AERA	OAV	OOB	AB-HR-SH	AVG	PB	SUP	APR	DL	PW
1939	Phi A	0	0	—	1	0	0	0	4	8	3	0	1	3	0	∞	—	1.000	1.000	0	—	0		-3		-0.2

SCHEMANSKE, FRED Frederick George "Buck" B4.28.1903 Detroit MI D2.18.1960 Detroit MI BR/TR/6-2/190 d9.15

YEAR	TM LG	W	L	PCT	G	GS	CG-SHO	SV-BS	IP	H	R	HR	HB	BB-IB	SO	ERA	AERA	OAV	OOB	AB-HR-SH	AVG	PB	SUP	APR	DL	PW
1923	Was A	0	0	—	1	0	0	0	1	3	3	0	0	0	0	27.00	14	.600	.600	2	1.000	1*		-2		0.0

YEAR	TM LG	W	L	PCT	G	GS	CG-SHO	SV-BS	IP	H	R	HR	HB	BB-IB	SO	ERA	AERA	OAV	OOB	AB-HR-SH	AVG	PB	SUP	APR	DL	PW
SCHENCK, BILL	William G.	B7.1854 Brooklyn NY	D1.29.1934 Brooklyn NY	5-7/171	d5.29 ▲																				
1882	Lou AA	1	0	1.000	2	1	1	0	10	6	2	0		4		0.90	275	.162	.184	231	.260	0*	104	2		0.2
SCHENEBERG, JOHN	John Bluford	B11.20.1887 Guyandotte WV	D9.26.1950 Huntington WV	BB/TR/6-1/180	d9.23																				
1913	Pit N	0	1	.000	1	1	0	0	6	10	5	0	0	2	1	6.00	50	.400	.444	2	.500	0	25	-2		-0.2
1920	StL A	0	0	—	1	0	0	0	2	7	7	0	0	1	0	27.00	15	.583	.615	0	—	0		-5		-0.2
Total	2	0	1	.000	2	1	0	0	8	17	12	0	0	3	1	11.25	29	.459	.500	2	.500	0	25	-7		-0.4
SCHERMAN, FRED	Frederick John	B7.25.1944 Dayton OH	BL/TL/6-1/195*	d4.26	Col Ohio St.																				
1969	Det A	1	0	1.000	4	0	0-0		4	6	3	2	0	0-0	3	6.75	56	.333	.333	0	—	0		-1		-0.2
1970	Det A	4	4	.500	48	0	0	1-2	69.2	61	28	5	1	28-3	58	3.23	117	.237	.314	12	.167	-0		4		0.4
1971	Det A	11	6	.647	69	1	1	20-7	113	91	38	11	5	49-7	46	2.71	134	.226	.317	24-0-2	.208	-1	124	11		2.2
1972	†Det A	7	3	.700	57	3	0	12-6	94	91	43	5	5	53-9	53	3.64	87	.269	.371	22-0-1	.091	-1	56	-5		-0.8
1973	Det A	2	2	.500	34	0	0	1-1	61.2	59	30	6	3	30-4	28	4.23	97	.258	.350	0	—	0*		0		-0.1
1974	Hou N	2	5	.286	53	0	0	4-2	61.1	67	33	5	7	26-6	35	4.11	85	.284	.370	3	.000	-0		-5		-0.7
1975	Hou N	0	1	.000	16	0	0	0-1	16.1	21	11	4	1	4-1	13	4.96	68	.318	.361	1	.000	-0		-4		-0.2
	Mon N	4	3	.571	34	7	0	0-1	76.1	84	37	3	5	41-7	43	3.54	109	.283	.374	16	.063	-1	71	1		0.1
	Year	4	4	.500	50	7	0	0-2	92.2	105	48	7	6	45-8	56	3.79	100	.289	.371	17	.059	-1	73	-1		-0.1
1976	Mon N	2	2	.500	31	0	0	1-1	40	42	25	5	3	14-3	18	4.95	76	.261	.330	4-0-1	.250	0		-5		-0.5
Total	8	33	26	.559	346	11	1	39-21	536.1	522	248	46	30	245-40	297	3.66	100	.260	.347	82-0-4	.134	-1	73	-4		0.2
SCHERRER, BILL	William Joseph	B1.20.1958 Tonawanda NY	BL/TL/6-4/180(170-190)	[CinN77*S1/1]	d9.7																				
1982	Cin N	0	1	.000	5	2	0	0-0	17.1	17	7	1	0	10-1	7	2.60	142	.250	.250	2-0-1	.500	1*	84	1		0.1
1983	Cin N	2	3	.400	73	0	0	10-6	92	73	31	6	0	33-4	57	2.74	140	.225	.291	11-0-1	.091	-0		11		0.8
1984	Cin N	1	1	.500	36	0	0	1-1	52.1	64	31	6	0	15-3	35	4.99	76	.300	.342	3-0-1	.000	-0		-6	15	-0.3
	†Det A	1	0	1.000	18	0	0	0-0	19	14	4	1	0	8-1	16	1.89	209	.206	.289	0	—	-0		5		0.1
1985	Det A	3	2	.600	48	0	0	0-2	66	62	35	10	1	41-13	46	4.36	94	.248	.354	0	—	0		-2		-0.1
1986	Det A	0	1	.000	13	0	0	0-0	21	19	19	3	1	22-4	16	7.29	57	.244	.416	0	—	0		-7		-0.4
1987	Cin N	1	1	.500	23	0	0	0-0	33	43	17	3	0	16-4	24	4.36	97	.328	.393	1	.000	-0		0		0.0
1988	Bal A	0	1	.000	4	0	0	0-0	4	8	6	2	0	3-0	3	13.50	29	.400	.478	0	—	0		-4		-0.7
	Phi N	0	0	—	8	0	0	0-0	6.2	7	4	0	0	2-0	3	5.40	67	.269	.321	0	—	0		-1		-0.1
Total	7	8	10	.444	228	2	0	11-9	311.1	307	154	31	2	140-29	207	4.08	97	.260	.336	17-0-3	.118	-0	84	-3	15	-0.5
SCHESLER, DUTCH	Charles	B6.1.1900 Frankfurt, Germany	D11.19.1953 Harrisburg PA	BR/TR/6-2/185	d4.16																				
1931	Phi N	0	0	—	17	0	0	0	38.1	65	39	4	4	18	14	7.28	58	.385	.455	9	.111	-0		-13		-0.6
SCHETTLER, LOU	Louis Martin	B6.12.1886 Pittsburgh PA	D5.1.1960 Youngstown OH	BR/TR/5-11/160	d4.25																				
1910	Phi N	2	6	.250	27	7	3	1	107	96	53	2	2	51	62	3.20	98	.247	.337	41-0-1	.171	-1	92	-2		-0.3
SCHILLING, CURT	Curtis Montague	B11.14.1966 Anchorage AK	BR/TR/6-4/215(205-235)	[BosA86*2/39]	d9.7	Col Yavapai (AZ) JC																			
1988	Bal A	0	3	.000	4	4	0	0-0	14.2	22	19	3	1	10-1	4	9.82	40	.355	.434	0	—	0	52	-10		-1.6
1989	Bal A	0	1	.000	5	1	0	0-0	8.2	10	6	2	0	3-0	6	6.23	61	.286	.342	0	—	0	0	-2		-0.2
1990	Bal A	1	2	.333	35	0	0	3-6	46	38	13	1	0	19-0	32	2.54	150	.229	.302	0	—	0		7		0.5
1991	Hou N	3	5	.375	56	0	0	8-3	75.2	79	35	2	0	39-7	71	3.81	93	.271	.356	3	.333	0		-2		-0.3
1992	Phi N	14	11	.560	42	26	10-4	2-1	226.1	165	67	11	4	59-4	147	2.35	150	.201	.253	64-0-8	.156	-0	89	28		3.0
1993	†Phi N	16	7	.696	34	34	7-2	0-0	235.1	234	114	23	4	57-6	186	4.02	99	.259	.303	75-0-13	.147	-1	109	1		0.0
1994	Phi N	2	8	.200	13	13	1	0-0	82.1	87	42	10	3	28-3	58	4.48	96	.270	.333	28-0-1	.107	-1	85	0	69	-0.1
1995	Phi N	7	5	.583	17	17	1	0-0	116	96	52	12	3	26-2	114	3.57	118	.220	.267	40-0-5	.175	0	91	7	75	0.6
1996	Phi N	9	10	.474	26	26	8-2	0-0	183.1	149	69	16	3	50-5	182	3.19	135	.222	.278	63-0-7	.175	-0*	80	24	43	2.1
1997	Phi N★	17	11	.607	35	35	7-2	0-0	254.1	208	96	25	5	58-3	319	2.97	142	.224	.271	81-0-12	.173	0	88	33		3.5
1998	Phi N☆	15	14	.517	35	35	15-2	0-0	268.2	236	101	23	6	61-3	300	3.25	133	.236	.282	76-0-12	.132	-1	76	33		3.2
1999	Phi N★	15	6	.714	24	24	8-1	0-0	180.1	159	74	25	5	44-0	152	3.54	132	.237	.287	50-0-9	.100	0	111	23	26	2.4
2000	Phi N	6	6	.500	16	16	4-1	0-0	112.2	110	49	17	1	32-4	96	3.91	117	.253	.305	30-0-2	.167	0	101	10	26	1.4
	Ari N	5	6	.455	13	13	4-1	0-0	97.2	94	41	10	0	13-0	72	3.69	130	.257	.280	31-0-7	.258	2	83	13		1.4
	Year	11	12	.478	29	29	8-2	0-0	210.1	204	90	27	1	45-4	168	3.81	123	.255	.294	61-0-9	.213	2	93	22		2.3
2001	†Ari N☆	22	6	.786	35	35	6-1	0-0	256.2	237	86	37	1	39-0	293	2.98	156	.245	.273	83-0-14	.133	-3	96	47		4.4
2002	Ari N★	23	7	.767	36	35	5-1	0-0	259.1	218	95	29	3	33-1	316	3.23	139	.224	.251	86-0-8	.174	-1	112	35		3.6
2003	Ari N	8	9	.471	24	24	3-2	0-0	168	144	58	17	3	32-2	194	2.95	150	.230	.270	52-0-4	.058	-3	70	30	57	2.4
2004	†Bos A★	21	6	.778	32	32	3	0-0	226.2	206	84	23	5	35-0	203	3.26	150	.239	.271	7	.143	-0	133	43		4.5
2005	Bos A	8	8	.500	32	11	0	9-2	93.1	121	59	12	0	22-0	87	5.69	81	.314	.352	0	—	0	138	-9	90	-1.5
Total	18	192	131	.594	514	381	82-19	22-12	2906	2613	1160	298	47	660-41	2832	3.40	128	.239	.284	769-0-102	.150	-8	98	311	386	28.8
SCHILLINGS, RED	Elbert Isaiah	B3.29.1900 Deport TX	D1.7.1954 Oklahoma City OK	BR/TR/5-10/180	d9.11																				
1922	Phi A	0	0	—	4	0	0	0	8	10	6	1	0	11	4	6.75	63	.313	.488	2	.000	-0		-2		-0.1
SCHIRALDI, CALVIN	Calvin Drew	B6.16.1962 Houston TX	BR/TR/6-4/200(200-216)	[NYN83 1/27]	d9.1	Col Texas																			
1984	NY N	0	2	.000	5	3	0	0-0	17.1	20	13	3	0	10-0	16	5.71	63	.286	.375	3	.000	-0	82	-4		-0.5
1985	NY N	2	1	.667	10	4	0	0-2	26.1	43	27	4	3	11-0	21	8.89	39	.368	.435	8	.125	-0	120	-15	15	-1.5
1986	†Bos A	4	2	.667	25	0	0	9-3	51	36	8	5	1	15-2	55	1.41	298	.201	.265	0	—	0		16		2.3
1987	Bos A	8	5	.615	62	1	0	6-4	83.2	75	45	15	1	40-5	93	4.41	104	.240	.326	0	—	0	20	1		0.2
1988	Chi N	9	13	.409	29	27	2-1	1-0	166.1	166	87	13	2	63-7	140	4.38	83	.257	.323	60-0-4	.100	-2	105	-12	30	-1.8
1989	Chi N	3	6	.333	54	0	0	4-4	78.2	60	34	7	1	50-2	54	3.78	100	.209	.326	9-0-1	.000	-1		1		0.0
	SD N	3	1	.750	5	4	0	0-0	21.1	12	6	1	0	13-0	17	2.53	139	.162	.287	7-1-1	.143	1	126	3		0.6
	Year	6	7	.462	59	4	0	4-4	100	72	40	8	1	63-2	71	3.51	106	.199	.319	16-1-2	.063	0	119	4		0.6
1990	SD N	3	8	.273	42	8	0	1-1	104	105	59	11	1	60-6	74	4.41	87	.264	.360	21-1-1	.190	2	85	-7		-0.6
1991	Tex A	0	1	.000	3	0	0	0-0	4.2	5	6	3	0	5-0	1	11.57	35	.263	.417	0	—	0		-4		-0.6
Total	8	32	39	.451	235	47	2-1	21-14	553.1	522	285	62	9	267-22	471	4.28	91	.248	.334	108-2-7	.111	-1	96	-21	45	-1.9
SCHLITZER, BIFF	Victor Joseph	B12.4.1884 Rochester NY	D1.4.1948 Wellesley Hills MA	BR/TR/5-11/175	d4.17	Col Dayton																			
1908	Phi A	6	8	.429	24	18	11-2	0	131	110	56	1	2	45	57	3.16	81	.234	.303	46-0-1	.196	-1	80	-5		-0.8
1909	Phi A	0	3	.000	4	3	0	0	13.1	13	9	0	2	7	6	5.40	45	.245	.365	4	.250	0	88	-4		-0.7
	Bos A	4	4	.500	13	8	5	1	69.2	68	34	0	1	17	23	3.49	72	.234	.279	27-0-2	.185	0	109	-6		-0.7
	Year	4	7	.364	17	11	5	1	83	81	43	0	4	24	29	3.80	65	.236	.294	31-0-2	.194	1	103	-9		-1.4
1914	Buf F	0	0	—	3	0	0	0	3.1	7	8	3	0	2	1	16.20	18	.438	.500	1	1.000	1		-5		-0.2
Total	3	10	15	.400	44	29	16-2	1	217.1	198	107	4	6	71	87	3.60	71	.239	.303	78-0-3	.205	0	88	-20		-2.4
SCHMACK, BRIAN	Brian Robert	B12.7.1973 Chicago IL	BR/TR/6-2/190	d8.24	Col Northern Illinois																				
2003	Det A	1	0	1.000	11	0	0	0-0	13	14	6	1	1	4-0	4	3.46	127	.292	.345	—		0		1		0.1
SCHMELZ, AL	Alan George	B11.12.1943 Whittier CA	BR/TR/6-4/210	d9.7	Col Arizona St.																				
1967	NY N	0	0	—	2	0	0	0	3	4	1	0	0	1-0	2	3.00	113	.364	.417	0	—	0		0		0.0
SCHMIDT, CURT	Curtis Allen	B3.16.1970 Miles City MT	BR/TR/6-6/200	[MonN92 41/1135]	d4.28	Col Kansas																			
1995	Mon N	0	0	—	10.1								2	9-0	7	6.97	62	.357	.491	0		0		-3		-0.1
SCHMIDT, DAVE	David Joseph	B4.22.1957 Niles MI	BR/TR/6-1/185*	[TexA79 26/658]	d5.1	Col UCLA																			
1981	Tex A	0	1	.000	14	1	0	1-0	31.2	31	11	1	1	11-3	13	3.13	111	.258	.326	—		0	52	2		0.1
1982	Tex A	4	6	.400	33	8	0	6-2	109.2	118	45	5	5	25-5	69	3.20	121	.279	.325	—		0	79	8		0.7
1983	Tex A	3	5	.500	31	0	0	2-5	46.1	42	20	3	1	14-1	29	3.88	104	.241	.300	—		0		2	27	0.2
1984	Tex A	6	6	.500	43	0	0	12-4	70.1	69	30	3	0	20-9	46	2.56	163	.262	.311	—		0		9		1.8
1985	Tex A	7	6	.538	51	4	1-1	5-1	85.2	81	36	6	0	22-8	46	3.15	135	.246	.292	—		0	112	9		1.4
1986	Chi A	3	6	.333	49	1	0	8-3	92.1	94	37	10	0	27-7	67	3.31	131	.264	.322	—		0	42	10		1.0
1987	Bal A	10	5	.667	35	14	2-2	1-1	124	128	57	13	1	26-2	70	3.77	118	.263	.301	—		0	100	9		0.9
1988	Bal A	8	5	.615	41	9	0	2-1	129.2	129	59	14	3	38-5	67	3.40	116	.262	.317	—		0	106	6		0.6
1989	Bal A	10	13	.435	38	26	2	0-0	156.2	196	102	24	2	36-2	46	5.69	80	.310	.346	—		0	102	-31		-3.9
1990	Mon N	3	3	.500	34	0	0	13-4	48	58	26	3	0	13-5	22	4.31	85	.297	.340	3	.000	-0		-4	93	-0.7
1991	Mon N	0	1	.000	8	0	0	0-0	4.1	9	5	2	0	4-0	3	10.38	35	.429	.478	0	—	0		-3		-0.6

YEAR	TM LG	W	L	PCT	G	GS	CG-SHO	SV-BS	IP	H	R	HR	HB	BB-IB	SO	ERA	AERA	OAV	OOB	AB-HR-SH	AVG	PB	SUP	APR	DL	PW
1992	Sea A	0	0	—	3	0	0	0-0	3.1	7	7	1	0	3-0	1	18.90	21	.438	.526	0	—	0		-5		-0.3
Total	12	54	55	.495	376	63	5-3	50-21	902	962	434	85	18	237-47	479	3.88	104	.274	.321	3	.000	-0	97	12	120	1.2

SCHMIDT, FREDDY Frederick Albert B2.9.1916 Hartford CT BR/TR/6-1/185 d4.25 Mil 1945

YEAR	TM LG	W	L	PCT	G	GS	CG-SHO	SV-BS	IP	H	R	HR	HB	BB-IB	SO	ERA	AERA	OAV	OOB	AB-HR-SH	AVG	PB	SUP	APR	DL	PW
1944	†StL N	7	3	.700	37	9	3-2	5	114.1	94	48	5	1	58	58	3.15	112	.222	.317	34-0-1	.206	-0	119	4		0.3
1946	StL N	1	0	1.000	16	0	0	0	27.1	27	11	0	3	15	14	3.29	105	.276	.388	1	.000	-0		1		0.0
1947	StL N	0	0	—	2	0	0	0	4	5	2	1	0	1	2	2.25	184	.333	.375	0	—	0		0		0.0
	Phi N	5	8	.385	29	5	0	0	76.2	76	44	4	4	43	24	4.70	85	.285	.392	20	.050	-2	66	-5		-1.0
	Chi N	0	0	—	1	1	0	0	3	4	3	0	0	5	0	9.00	44	.333	.529	2	.000	-0	112	-1		-1.1
	Year	5	8	.385	32	6	0	0	83.2	85	49	5	4	49	26	4.73	85	.289	.398	22	.045	-2	73	-6		-0.8
Total	3	13	11	.542	85	15	3-2	5	225.1	206	108	10	8	122	98	3.75	98	.252	.355	57-0-1	.140	-2	101	-1		-0.8

SCHMIDT, BILL Frederick William B4.1861 New Orleans LA D5.28.1928 New Orleans LA TR/5-8/152 d7.6

YEAR	TM LG	W	L	PCT	G	GS	CG-SHO	SV-BS	IP	H	R	HR	HB	BB-IB	SO	ERA	AERA	OAV	OOB	AB-HR-SH	AVG	PB	SUP	APR	DL	PW
1886	Det N	5	4	.556	9	9	9	0	77	81	47	0	3	36	36	4.09	81	.259	.324	38	.184	-1*	147	-4		-0.5

SCHMIDT, PETE Friedrich Christoph Herman B7.23.1890 Lowden IA D3.11.1973 Pembroke ON, Can. BR/TR/5-11/175 d7.14

YEAR	TM LG	W	L	PCT	G	GS	CG-SHO	SV-BS	IP	H	R	HR	HB	BB-IB	SO	ERA	AERA	OAV	OOB	AB-HR-SH	AVG	PB	SUP	APR	DL	PW
1913	StL A	0	0	—	1	0	0	1	2	3	1	0	0	2	0	4.50	65	.333	.455	0	—	0		0		0.0

SCHMIDT, HENRY Henry Martin B6.26.1873 Brownsville TX D4.23.1926 Nashville TN BR/TR/5-11/170 d4.17

YEAR	TM LG	W	L	PCT	G	GS	CG-SHO	SV-BS	IP	H	R	HR	HB	BB-IB	SO	ERA	AERA	OAV	OOB	AB-HR-SH	AVG	PB	SUP	APR	DL	PW
1903	Bro N	22	13	.629	40	36	29-5	2	301	321	167	5	21	120	96	3.83	83	.280	.359	107-1-5	.196	3*	109	-15		-0.9

SCHMIDT, JASON Jason David B1.29.1973 Lewiston ID BR/TR/6-5/211(185-213) [AtlN91 8/205] d4.28

YEAR	TM LG	W	L	PCT	G	GS	CG-SHO	SV-BS	IP	H	R	HR	HB	BB-IB	SO	ERA	AERA	OAV	OOB	AB-HR-SH	AVG	PB	SUP	APR	DL	PW
1995	Atl N	2	2	.500	9	2	0	0-1	25	27	17	2	1	18-3	19	5.76	75	.287	.393	5-0-1	.200	0	52	-4		-0.5
1996	Atl N	3	4	.429	13	11	0	0-0	58.2	69	48	8	0	32-0	48	6.75	66	.296	.373	19-0-1	.000	-2	112	-14	46	-1.5
	Pit N	2	2	.500	6	6	1	0-0	37.2	39	19	2	2	21-0	26	4.06	108	.271	.365	12-0-1	.083	-1	130	1		0.0
	Year	5	6	.455	19	17	1	0-0	96.1	108	67	10	2	53-0	74	5.70	78	.286	.370	31-0-2	.032	-2	119	-13		-1.5
1997	Pit N	10	9	.526	32	32	2	0-0	187.2	193	106	16	9	76-2	136	4.60	93	.265	.341	56-0-9	.107	-1	94	-6		-0.8
1998	Pit N	11	14	.440	33	33	0	0-0	214.1	228	106	24	4	71-3	158	4.07	105	.285	.334	62-0-12	.097	-2	70	7		0.3
1999	Pit N	13	11	.542	33	33	2	0-0	212.2	219	110	24	3	85-4	148	4.19	110	.262	.330	60-0-12	.083	-2	88	10		0.6
2000	Pit N	2	5	.286	11	11	0	0-0	63.1	71	43	6	1	41-2	51	5.40	86	.284	.384	19-0-0	.000	-2	99	-6	129	-0.7
2001	Pit N	6	6	.500	14	14	1	0-0	84	81	46	11	7	28-2	77	4.61	97	.256	.328	23-1-5	.174	1	91	-1	40	0.0
	SF N	7	1	.875	11	11	0	0-0	66.1	57	29	2	0	33-1	65	3.39	121	.230	.319	26-1-1	.154	1	158	5		0.5
	Year	13	7	.650	25	25	1	0-0	150.1	138	75	13	7	61-3	142	4.07	106	.244	.324	49-2-6	.163	2	119	4		0.4
2002	†SF N	13	8	.619	29	29	2-2	0-0	185.1	148	78	15	2	73-1	196	3.45	115	.218	.294	56-0-4	.125	-1	110	10	24	1.8
2003	†SF N★	17	5	.773	29	29	5-3	0-0	207.2	152	56	14	5	46-1	208	**2.34**	**182**	**.200**	**.250**	61-0-15	.066	-4	107	**45**		4.0
2004	SF N☆	18	7	.720	32	32	4-3	0-0	225	165	84	18	3	77-3	251	3.20	135	.202	.272	66-2-13	.136	1	98	30	12	3.1
2005	SF N	12	7	.632	29	29	0	0-0	172	160	90	16	9	85-4	165	4.40	97	.246	.334	53-1-6	.094	-2	108	-3	16	-0.6
Total	11	116	81	.589	281	272	17-8	0-1	1739.2	1609	832	158	42	686-26	1548	3.95	109	.244	.318	518-5-82	.100	-14	99	74	267	5.2

SCHMIDT, JEFF Jeffrey Thomas B2.21.1971 Northfield MN BR/TR/6-5/205 [CalA92 1/29] d5.17 Col Minnesota [DL 1997 Ana A 12, 1998 Ana A 31]

YEAR	TM LG	W	L	PCT	G	GS	CG-SHO	SV-BS	IP	H	R	HR	HB	BB-IB	SO	ERA	AERA	OAV	OOB	AB-HR-SH	AVG	PB	SUP	APR	DL	PW
1996	Cal A	2	0	1.000	9	0	0	0-0	8	13	9	2	0	8-0	2	7.88	64	.394	.500	0	—	0		-3		-0.5

SCHMIDT, WILLARD Willard Raymond B5.29.1928 Hays KS BR/TR/6-1/187(180-193) d4.19

YEAR	TM LG	W	L	PCT	G	GS	CG-SHO	SV-BS	IP	H	R	HR	HB	BB-IB	SO	ERA	AERA	OAV	OOB	AB-HR-SH	AVG	PB	SUP	APR	DL	PW
1952	StL N	2	3	.400	18	3	0	1	34.2	36	20	6	2	18	30	5.19	72	.267	.361	8	.125	-0	64	-5		-0.6
1953	StL N	0	2	.000	6	2	0	0	17.2	21	20	1	1	13	11	9.17	46	.288	.402	4	.000	-1	52	-10		-0.9
1955	StL N	7	6	.538	20	15	8-1	0	129.2	89	40	7	3	57-7	86	2.78	146	.197	.289	42-0-2	.119	-3	88	20		1.6
1956	StL N	6	8	.429	33	21	2	1	147.2	131	69	18	1	78-7	52	3.84	99	.246	.341	43-0-3	.233	1	104	0		0.3
1957	StL N	10	3	.769	40	8	1	0	116.2	146	67	13	2	49-6	41	4.78	83	.312	.377	33-0-4	.212	-0	158	-9		-0.9
1958	Cin N	3	5	.375	41	2	0	0	69.1	60	29	4	1	33-7	41	2.86	145	.235	.320	11-0-1	.091	-1	152	7		0.8
1959	Cin N	3	2	.600	36	4	0	0	70.2	80	36	4	1	30-4	40	3.95	103	.296	.366	12-0-1	.083	-0	116	0		0.1
Total	7	31	29	.517	194	55	11-2	2	586.1	563	281	57	11	278-31	323	3.93	101	.258	.342	153-0-11	.163	-2	105	3		0.4

SCHMIT, CRAZY Frederick M. "Germany" B2.13.1866 Chicago IL D10.5.1940 Chicago IL BL/TL/5-10.5/165 d4.21

YEAR	TM LG	W	L	PCT	G	GS	CG-SHO	SV-BS	IP	H	R	HR	HB	BB-IB	SO	ERA	AERA	OAV	OOB	AB-HR-SH	AVG	PB	SUP	APR	DL	PW
1890	Pit N	1	9	.100	11	10	9-1	0	83.1	108	98	3	8	42	35	5.83	57	.304	.390	33	.061	-3	69	-30		-2.7
1892	Bal N	1	4	.200	6	6	6	0	47.1	37	26	0	0	26	17	3.23	106	.207	.307	19	.105	-1*	55	-2		0.1
1893	Bal N	3	2	.600	9	6	4	0	49	67	51	1	2	22	10	6.61	72	.316	.386	21	.238	-0	145	-10		-0.7
	NY N	0	2	.000	4	4	1	0	20.2	30	25	0	2	17	5	7.40	63	.330	.445	9	.444	1	146	-6		-0.3
	Year	3	4	.429	13	10	5	0	69.2	97	76	1	4	39	15	6.85	69	.320	.405	30	.300	1	145	-14		-1.0
1899	Cle N	2	17	.105	20	19	16	0*	138.1	197	138	3	14	62	24	5.86	68	.334	.410	70-0-1	.157	-2*	61	-39		-4.1
1901	Bal A	0	2	.000	4	3	1	0	22.2	25	20	0	0	16	2	1.99	195	.278	.387	9	.222	0	116	1		0.1
Total	5	7	36	.163	54	48	37-1	0	361.1	464	358	7	26	185	93	5.45	69	.306	.391	161-0-1	.161	-4	87	-82		-7.6

SCHMITZ, JOHNNY John Albert "Bear Tracks" B11.27.1920 Wausau WI BR/TL/6-0/170* d9.6 Mil 1943-45

YEAR	TM LG	W	L	PCT	G	GS	CG-SHO	SV-BS	IP	H	R	HR	HB	BB-IB	SO	ERA	AERA	OAV	OOB	AB-HR-SH	AVG	PB	SUP	APR	DL	PW
1941	Chi N	2	0	1.000	5	3	1	0	20.2	12	5	0	1	9	11	1.31	269	.182	.289	7-0-1	.571	2*	137	5		0.7
1942	Chi N	3	7	.300	23	10	1	2	86.2	70	41	3	3	45	51	3.43	93	.230	.335	26-0-2	.154	-1	113	-3		-0.2
1946	Chi N☆	11	11	.500	41	31	14-2	2	224.1	184	77	6	2	94	**135**	2.61	127	**.221**	.302	70-1-6	.129	-2*	92	17		1.6
1947	Chi N	13	18	.419	38	28	10-3	4	207	209	91	8	2	80	97	3.22	123	.262	.330	68-0-6	.132	-2	76	16		-0.7
1948	Chi N★	18	13	.581	34	30	18-2	1	242	186	92	11	2	97	100	2.64	148	**.215**	.295	84-0-7	.131	-1	73	31		3.8
1949	Chi N	11	13	.458	36	31	9-3	3	207	227	117	11	2	92	75	4.35	93	.284	.363	70-0-3	.143	1	85	-9		-0.7
1950	Chi N	10	16	.385	39	27	8-3	0	193	217	122	23	4	91	75	4.99	84	.284	.363	67-0-2	.119	-3	97	-15		-1.7
1951	Chi N	1	2	.333	8	3	0	0	18	22	16	1	0	15	16	8.00	51	.301	.420	6	.167	-0	43	-7		-0.9
	Bro N	1	4	.200	16	7	0	0	55.2	55	37	4	2	28	20	5.34	74	.259	.351	18-1-0	.222	2	125	-9		-1.4
	Year	2	6	.250	24	10	0	0	73.2	77	53	5	2	43	26	5.99	66	.270	.370	24-1-0	.208	1	100	-15		-1.4
1952	Bro N	1	1	.500	10	3	1	0	33.1	29	16	3	1	18	11	4.32	84	.238	.340	8-0-2	.125	-2	220	-2		-0.1
	NY A	1	1	.500	5	2	1	1	15	15	7	0	1	9	3	3.60	92	.263	.373	5	.600	2	105	-1		0.1
	Cin N	1	0	1.000	3	0	0	0	5	3	0	0	0	3	3	0.00	—	.188	.316	0	—	0		2		0.4
1953	NY A	0	0	—	3	0	0	0	4.1	2	1	1	0	3	2	2.08	178	.143	.294	0-0-1	—	1		1		0.1
	Was A	2	7	.222	24	13	5	4	107.2	118	52	9	4	37	39	3.68	106	.286	.351	34-0-3	.059	-4	86	1		-0.2
	Year	2	7	.222	27	13	5	4	112	120	53	10	4	40	39	3.62	108	.282	.349	34-0-4	.059	-4	86	2		-0.1
1954	Was A	11	8	.579	29	23	12-2	1	185.1	176	66	9	8	64	56	2.91	122	.255	.318	60-0-6	.117	-3	99	15		1.3
1955	Was A	7	10	.412	32	21	6-1	1	165	187	76	8	7	54-4	49	3.71	103	.291	.349	54-0-3	.185	0	96	3		0.1
1956	Bos A	0	0	—	2	0	0	0	4.1	5	2	0	0	4-0	1	0.00	—	.278	.409	1	.000	-0		1		0.1
	Bal A	0	3	.000	18	3	0	0	38.1	49	23	3	1	14-1	15	3.99	98	.318	.379	9-0-1	.000	-1	53	-2		-0.2
	Year	0	3	.000	20	3	0	0	42.2	54	25	3	1	18-1	15	3.59	111	.314	.382	10-0-1	.000	-2	52	-1		-0.2
Total	13	93	114	.449	366	235	86-16	19	1812.2	1766	841	97	35	757-5	746	3.55	107	.258	.335	587-2-43	.141	-14	91	44		1.4

SCHMOLL, STEVE Stephen John B2.4.1980 Silver Spring MD BR/TR/6-2/200 d4.6 Col Maryland

YEAR	TM LG	W	L	PCT	G	GS	CG-SHO	SV-BS	IP	H	R	HR	HB	BB-IB	SO	ERA	AERA	OAV	OOB	AB-HR-SH	AVG	PB	SUP	APR	DL	PW
2005	LA N	2	2	.500	48	0	0	3-1	46.2	47	26	4	3	22-2	29	5.01	82	.275	.360	1	.000	-0		-5		-0.5

SCHMUTZ, CHARLIE Charles Otto "King" B1.1.1892 San Diego CA D6.27.1962 Seattle WA BR/TR/6-1.5/195 d5.13

YEAR	TM LG	W	L	PCT	G	GS	CG-SHO	SV-BS	IP	H	R	HR	HB	BB-IB	SO	ERA	AERA	OAV	OOB	AB-HR-SH	AVG	PB	SUP	APR	DL	PW
1914	Bro N	1	3	.250	18	5	1	0	57.1	57	29	1	1	13	21	3.30	87	.265	.310	16	.188	1	65	-2		-0.1
1915	Bro N	0	0	—	1	0	0	0	4	7	5	0	1	1	1	6.75	41	.438	.471	1	.000	-0		-2		-0.2
Total	2	1	3	.250	19	5	1	0	61.1	64	34	1	1	14	22	3.52	81	.277	.321	17	.176	0	65	-4		-0.2

SCHNEIBERG, FRANK Frank Fred B3.12.1880 Milwaukee WI D5.18.1948 Milwaukee WI TR/6-1/165 d6.8

YEAR	TM LG	W	L	PCT	G	GS	CG-SHO	SV-BS	IP	H	R	HR	HB	BB-IB	SO	ERA	AERA	OAV	OOB	AB-HR-SH	AVG	PB	SUP	APR	DL	PW
1910	Bro N	0	0	—	1	1	0	0	1	5	8	0	0	4	0	63.00	5	.625	.750	0	—	0		-6		-0.3

SCHNEIDER, DAN Daniel Louis B8.29.1942 Evansville IN BL/TL/6-3/170* d5.12 Col Arizona

YEAR	TM LG	W	L	PCT	G	GS	CG-SHO	SV-BS	IP	H	R	HR	HB	BB-IB	SO	ERA	AERA	OAV	OOB	AB-HR-SH	AVG	PB	SUP	APR	DL	PW
1963	Mil N	1	0	1.000	30	3	0	0	43.2	36	20	2	0	20-5	19	3.09	104	.225	.309	7	.000	-1	116	-1		-0.2
1964	Mil N	1	2	.333	13	5	0	0	36.1	38	25	6	0	13-2	14	5.45	65	.270	.329	8-0-1	.000	-1*	165	-8	47	-0.6
1966	Atl N	0	0	—	14	0	0	0	26.1	35	13	1	1	5-0	11	3.42	106	.324	.360	8	.500	1		0		0.1
1967	Hou N	0	2	.000	54	0	0	0	52.2	60	33	5	2	25-8	39	4.96	67	.296	.377	5	.200	0*		-10		-0.6
1969	Hou N	0	1	.000	6	0	0	0-0	7.1	16	12	2	0	5-2	3	13.50	26	.485	.553	1	.000	-0		-8		-0.9
Total	5	2	5	.286	117	8	0	2-0	166.1	185	103	16	3	70-17	86	4.71	72	.287	.356	29-0-1	.172	-0	148	-27	47	-2.2

SCHNEIDER, JEFF Jeffrey Theodore B12.6.1952 Bremerton WA BB/TL/6-3/195 d8.12 Col Iowa St.

YEAR	TM LG	W	L	PCT	G	GS	CG-SHO	SV-BS	IP	H	R	HR	HB	BB-IB	SO	ERA	AERA	OAV	OOB	AB-HR-SH	AVG	PB	SUP	APR	DL	PW
1981	Bal A	0	0	—	11	0	0	1-0	24	27	15	4	1	12-1	17	4.88	75	.290	.377	0	—	0		-3		-0.2

YEAR	TM LG	W	L	PCT	G	GS	CG-SHO	SV-BS	IP	H	R	HR	HB	BB-IB	SO	ERA	AERA	OAV	OOB	AB-HR-SH	AVG	PB	SUP	APR	DL	PW

SCHNEIDER, PETE Peter Joseph B8.20.1895 Los Angeles CA D6.1.1957 Los Angeles CA BR/TR/6-1/194 d6.20

1914	Cin N	5	13	.278	29	15	11-1	1	144.1	143	71	1	7	56	62	2.81	104	.269	.347	45-1-1	.178	1*	54	0		0.0
1915	Cin N	14	19	.424	48	35	16-5	2	275.2	254	110	4	7	104	108	2.48	115	.251	.325	94-2-6	.245	5	74	7		1.4
1916	Cin N	10	19	.345	44	31	16-2	1	274.1	259	112	4	13	82	117	2.69	96	.255	.319	89-0-4	.236	2*	88	-6		-0.5
1917	Cin N	20	19	.513	46	42	24	0	333.2	311	128	4	11	117	138	2.10	124	.255	.326	114-1-2	.167	0*	97	14		1.5
1918	Cin N	10	15	.400	33	30	17-2	0	217	213	106	2	11	117	51	3.53	76	.272	.374	83-1-3	.289	6*	115	-20		-1.7
1919	NY N	0	1	.000	7	4	0	0	29	19	14	1	3	22	11	3.41	94	.192	.355	9	.111	-1	92	-1		-0.2
Total	6	59	86	.407	207	157	84-10	4	1274	1199	541	16	52	498	487	2.66	102	.257	.336	434-5-16	.221	14	89	-6		0.5

SCHNELL, KARL Karl Otto B9.20.1899 Los Angeles CA D5.31.1992 Palo Alto CA BR/TR/6-1/176 d4.24 Col St. Marys (CA)

1922	Cin N	0	0	—	10	0	0	0	20	21	10	0	0	18	5	2.70	148	.300	.443	4	.250	0		2		0.1
1923	Cin N	0	0	—	1	0	0	0	1	2	4	0	0	2	0	36.00	11	.667	.800	0	—	0		-3		-0.1
Total	2	0	0	—	11	0	0	0	21	23	14	0	0	20	5	4.29	93	.315	.462	4	.250	0		-1		-0.1

SCHOEN, GERRY Gerald Thomas B1.15.1947 New Orleans LA BR/TR/6-3/215 [TexA66 25/486] d9.14 Col Loyola-New Orleans

1968	Was A	0	1	.000	1	1	0	0	3.2	6	3	1	0	1-0	1	7.36	40	.400	.438	1	.000	-0	30	-2		-0.3

SCHOENEWEIS, SCOTT Scott David B10.2.1973 Long Branch NJ BL/TL/6-0/185* [AnaA96 3/85] d4.7 Col Duke

1999	Ana A	1	1	.500	31	0	0	0-0	39.1	47	27	4	0	14-1	22	5.49	89	.294	.349	0	—	0		-1		-0.1
2000	Ana A	7	10	.412	27	27	1-1	0-0	170	183	112	21	6	67-2	78	5.45	95	.276	.346	3	.333	0	92	-6	38	-0.5
2001	Ana A	10	11	.476	32	32	1	0-0	205.1	227	122	21	14	77-2	104	5.08	92	.281	.351	0	—	1	90	-8		-0.5
2002	†Ana A	9	8	.529	54	15	0	1-3	118	119	68	17	5	49-4	65	4.88	92	.264	.340	2	.000	-0	117	-5		-0.6
2003	Ana A	1	1	.500	39	0	0	0-1	38.2	37	19	2	3	10-3	29	3.96	111	.250	.309	0	—	0		2		0.1
	Chi A	2	1	.667	20	0	0	0-1	26	26	16	1	1	9-2	27	4.50	102	.255	.321	0	—	0		-1		-0.1
	Year	3	2	.600	59	0	0	0-2	64.2	63	35	3	4	19-5	56	4.18	107	.252	.314	0	—	0		1		0.0
2004	Chi A	6	9	.400	20	19	0	0-0	112.2	129	74	17	3	49-0	69	5.59	84	.291	.364	2	.500	1	88	-11	71	-1.0
2005	Tor A	3	4	.429	80	0	0	1-3	57	54	23	2	4	25-5	43	3.32	140	.245	.333	0	—	0		8		1.0
Total	7	39	45	.464	303	93	2-1	2-8	767	822	461	85	36	300-19	437	5.02	94	.275	.346	7	.286	1	95	-24	109	-1.6

SCHOOLER, MIKE Michael Ralph B8.10.1962 Anaheim CA BR/TR/6-3/220* [SeaA85 2/35] d6.10 Col Cal St.-Fullerton

1988	Sea A	5	8	.385	40	0	0	15-6	48.1	45	21	4	1	24-4	54	3.54	118	.245	.330	0	—	0		3		0.7
1989	Sea A	1	7	.125	67	0	0	33-7	77	81	27	2	2	19-3	69	2.81	144	.266	.313	0	—	0		10		1.8
1990	Sea A	1	4	.200	49	0	0	30-4	56	47	18	5	1	16-5	45	2.25	177	.227	.283	1	.000	-0		10	40	1.7
1991	Sea A	3	3	.500	34	0	0	7-3	34.1	25	14	2	0	10-0	31	3.67	113	.198	.255	0	—	0		2	91	0.4
1992	Sea A	2	7	.222	53	0	0	13-5	51.2	55	29	7	1	24-6	33	4.70	85	.272	.351	0	—	0		-4	37	-0.7
1993	Tex A	3	0	1.000	17	0	0	0-0	24.1	30	17	3	0	10-1	16	5.55	76	.303	.367	0	—	0		-4		-0.4
Total	6	15	29	.341	260	0	0	98-25	291.2	283	126	23	5	103-19	248	3.49	117	.253	.316	1	.000	-0		17	168	3.5

SCHORR, ED Edward Walter B2.14.1891 Bremen OH D9.12.1969 Atlantic City NJ BR/TR/6-2.5/180 d4.26

1915	Chi N	0	0	—	2	0	0	0	6	9	5	0	0	5	3	7.50	37	.409	.519	2	.500	0		-3		-0.1

SCHOTT, GENE Arthur Eugene B7.14.1913 Batavia OH D11.16.1992 Sun City Center FL BR/TR/6-2/185 d4.16

1935	Cin N	8	11	.421	33	19	9-1	0	159	153	84	5	1	64	49	3.91	102	.253	.326	60	.200	1*	92	1		0.3
1936	Cin N	11	11	.500	31	22	8	1	180	184	93	7	4	73	65	3.80	101	.262	.335	60-1-1	.300	7*	90	-1		0.7
1937	Cin N	4	13	.235	37	16	7-2	1	154.1	150	69	2	1	48	56	2.97	125	.253	.310	49-0-2	.143	-1*	58	10		0.9
1938	Cin N	5	5	.500	31	4	0	2	83	89	47	8	1	32	21	4.45	82	.279	.347	24	.125	-1	116	-7		-0.9
	Phi N	0	1	.000	4	0	0	0	11	14	7	0	2	5	1	4.91	82	.326	.420	6	.333	1*		-1		0.0
Total	5	28	41	.406	136	61	24-3	4	587.1	590	300	22	9	222	192	3.72	103	.261	.329	199-1-3	.211	6	85	2		1.0

SCHOUREK, PETE Peter Alan B5.10.1969 Austin TX BL/TL/6-5/205(195-220) [NYN87 2/56] d4.9

1991	NY N	5	4	.556	35	8	1-1	2-1	86.1	82	49	7	2	43-4	67	4.27	86	.248	.334	22	.136	0	129	-7		-0.6
1992	NY N	6	8	.429	22	21	0	0-0	136	137	60	9	2	44-6	60	3.64	96	.261	.319	42-0-2	.048	-3*	82	-2		-0.6
1993	NY N	5	12	.294	41	18	0	0-1	128.1	168	90	13	3	45-7	72	5.96	67	.319	.370	32-0-3	.219	2	102	-25		-2.7
1994	Cin N	7	2	.778	22	10	0	0-0	81.1	90	39	11	3	29-4	69	4.09	102	.287	.351	23-1-1	.174	1	96	2		0.3
1995	†Cin N	18	7	.720	29	29	2	0-0	190.1	158	72	17	8	45-3	160	3.22	130	.228	.281	59-0-12	.220	1	110	21		2.7
1996	Cin N	4	5	.444	12	12	0	0-0	67.1	79	48	7	3	24-1	54	6.01	71	.293	.352	19-0-5	.263	1*	109	-12	111	-1.2
1997	Cin N	5	8	.385	18	17	0	0-0	84.2	78	59	11	4	38-0	59	5.42	79	.241	.327	24-1-6	.167	1*	87	-12	67	-1.6
1998	Hou N	7	6	.538	15	15	0	0-0	80	82	43	10	4	36-0	59	4.50	90	.269	.350	19-0-5	.211	1	107	-4		-0.5
	†Bos A	1	3	.250	10	8	0	0-0	44	45	21	7	1	14-1	36	4.30	110	.273	.328	0	—	0	93	3		0.2
1999	Pit N	4	7	.364	30	17	0	0-0	113	120	75	20	5	49-5	94	5.34	86	.287	.358	25-0-3	.000	-2	65	-9	15	-0.9
2000	Bos A	3	10	.231	21	21	0	0-0	107.1	116	67	17	3	38-2	63	5.11	98	.278	.341	4	.500	1*	80	-1	53	0.0
2001	Bos A	5	1	.167	33	0	0	0-1	30.1	35	19	4	1	15-3	20	4.45	100	.292	.375	0	—	0		-1	18	-0.2
Total	8	66	77	.462	288	176	3-1	2-3	1149	1166	642	140	39	420-36	813	4.59	91	.270	.335	269-2-37	.164	2	95	-47	264	-5.1

SCHREIBER, BARNEY David Henry B5.8.1882 Waverly OH D10.6.1964 Chillicothe OH BL/TL/6-0/185 d5.15

1911	Cin N	0	0	—	3	0	0	1	10	19	11	2	0	2	5	5.40	61	.413	.438	3	.000	-0		-3		-0.2

SCHREIBER, PAUL Paul Frederick "Von" B10.8.1902 Jacksonville FL D1.28.1982 Sarasota FL BR/TR/6-2/180 d9.2 C13

1922	Bro N	0	0	—	1	0	0	0	1	2	0	0	0	0	0	0.00	—	.500	.500	0	—	0		0		0.0
1923	Bro N	0	0	—	9	0	0	1	15	16	9	1	2	8	4	4.20	92	.276	.382	2	.000	-0		-1		-0.1
1945	NY A	0	0	—	2	0	0	0	4.1	4	2	0	0	2	1	4.15	83	.267	.353	1	.000	-0		0		-0.1
Total	3	0	0	—	12	0	0	1	20.1	22	11	1	2	10	5	3.98	96	.286	.382	3	.000	-0		-1		-0.1

SCHRENK, STEVE Steven Wayne B11.20.1968 Chicago IL BR/TR/6-3/185(185-215) [ChiA87 4/89] d7.3

1999	Phi N	1	3	.250	32	2	0	1-0	50.1	41	24	6	7	14-4	36	4.29	109	.223	.301	3-0-1	.000	-0	148	3		0.2
2000	Phi N	2	3	.400	20	0	0	0-0	23.1	25	20	3	1	13-0	19	7.33	63	.269	.361	0	—	0		-7		-1.2
Total	2	3	6	.333	52	2	0	1-0	73.2	66	44	9	8	27-4	55	5.25	88	.238	.322	3-0-1	.000	-0	148	-4		-1.0

SCHROLL, AL Albert Bringhurst "Bull" B3.22.1932 New Orleans LA D11.30.1999 Alexandria LA BR/TR/6-2/210* d4.20 Col Tulane

1958	Bos A	0	0	—	3	0	0	0	10	6	5	1	0	4-0	5	4.50	89	.176	.263	1	1.000	0		0		0.0
1959	Phi N	1	1	.500	3	0	0	1	9.1	12	9	1	0	6-0	4	8.68	47	.353	.439	4	.250	0		-4		-0.7
	Bos A	1	4	.200	14	5	1	0	46	47	29	3	1	22-1	26	4.70	86	.269	.350	9-0-2	.111	-0	70	-4		-0.4
1960	Chi N	0	0	—	2	0	0	0	2.2	3	3	1	0	5-0	2	10.13	37	.273	.500	1	1.000	0		-2		-0.2
1961	Min A	4	4	.500	11	8	2	0	50	53	36	5	2	27-1	24	5.22	81	.266	.360	18-1-0	.278	2	104	-6		-0.7
Total	6	9	6	.400	35	13	3	1	118	121	82	11	3	64-2	61	5.34	77	.267	.359	33-1-2	.273	4	92	-16		-1.8

SCHROM, KEN Kenneth Marvin B11.23.1954 Grangeville ID BR/TR/6-2/195* [AnaA76 17/390] d8.8 Col Idaho [DL 1988 Cle A 81]

1980	Tor A	1	0	1.000	17	0	0	1-0	31	32	18	2	0	19-3	15	5.23	83	.274	.372	0	—	0*		-2		-0.1
1982	Tor A	1	0	1.000	6	0	0	0-0	15.1	13	11	3	0	15-3	8	5.87	77	.232	.394	0	—	0*		-2		-0.1
1983	Min A	15	8	.652	33	28	6-1	0-0	196.1	196	92	14	9	80-3	80	3.71	115	.266	.341	0	—	0*	92	11		1.0
1984	Min A	5	11	.313	25	21	3	0-0	137	156	75	15	1	41-2	49	4.47	95	.285	.333	0	—	0	82	-4	50	-0.5
1985	Min A	9	12	.429	29	26	6	0-0	160.2	164	95	28	4	59-2	74	4.99	89	.272	.333	0	—	0	82	-8		-0.9
1986	Cle A☆	14	7	.667	34	33	3-1	0-0	206	217	118	34	12	49-3	87	4.54	92	.271	.318	0	—	0	113	-8		-0.9
1987	Cle A	6	13	.316	32	29	4-1	0-0	153.2	185	126	29	3	57-1	61	6.50	70	.298	.357	0	—	0	91	-32		-3.3
Total	7	51	51	.500	176	137	22-3	1-0	900	963	535	125	25	320-17	372	4.81	90	.276	.338	0	—	0	93	-45	131	-4.8

SCHUELER, RON Ronald Richard B4.18.1948 Catharine KS BR/TR/6-4/205(185-205) [AtlN67*S3/43] d4.16 C7

1972	Atl N	5	8	.385	37	18	3	2-1	144.2	122	68	16	2	60-3	96	3.67	104	.227	.304	42-0-2	.190	0	71	0		0.1
1973	Atl N	8	7	.533	39	20	4-2	2-2	186	179	91	24	0	66-11	124	3.87	102	.255	.317	62-0-7	.177	-1	110	1		0.0
1974	Phi N	11	16	.407	44	27	5	1-0	203.1	202	91	17	4	98-18	109	3.72	102	.264	.350	51-0-7	.118	-2	77	3		0.0
1975	Phi N	4	4	.500	46	6	1	0-0	92.2	88	55	6	1	40-4	69	5.24	72	.258	.336	14-0-0	.154	-0	117	-12		-1.0
1976	Phi N	1	0	1.000	35	0	0	3-0	49.2	44	18	4	2	16-2	43	2.90	123	.243	.307	2-0-1	.000	-0		4		0.1
1977	Min A	8	7	.533	52	2	0	3-1	134.2	131	74	16	6	61-5	77	4.41	90	.260	.343	0	—	0	168	-7		-0.7
1978	Chi A	3	5	.375	30	7	0	0-2	81.2	76	50	10	7	39-2	39	4.30	88	.251	.341	0	—	0*	94	-8		-0.7
1979	Chi A	0	1	.000	8	1	0	0-0	19.2	19	16	3	2	13-1	6	7.32	58	.264	.382	0	—	0	64	-6	83	-0.3
Total	8	40	48	.455	291	86	13-2	11-6	912.1	861	463	96	24	393-46	563	4.08	95	.253	.331	170-0-18	.159	-3	95	-24	83	-2.5

SCHULER, DAVE David Paul B10.4.1953 Framingham MA BR/TL/6-4/210* [CleA75 10/223] d9.17 Col New Haven

YEAR	TM LG	W	L	PCT	G	GS	CG-SHO	SV-BS	IP	H	R	HR	HB	BB-IB	SO	ERA	AERA	OAV	OOB	AB-HR-SH	AVG	PB	SUP	APR	DL	PW
1979	Cal A	0	0	—	1	0	0	0-0	1.2	2	2	1	0	0-0	0	10.80	38	.333	.286	0	—	0		-1		-0.1
1980	Cal A	0	1	.000	8	0	0	0-0	12.2	13	5	3	0	2-1	7	3.55	111	.271	.288	0	—	0		1		0.0
1985	Atl N	0	0	—	9	0	0	0-0	10.2	19	8	4	0	3-0	10	6.75	57	.404	.440	0	—	0		-3		-0.2
Total	3	0	1	.000	18	0	0	0-0	25	34	15	8	0	5-1	17	5.40	73	.337	.358	0	—	0		-3		-0.3

SCHULLSTROM, ERIK Erik Paul B3.25.1969 San Diego CA BR/TR/6-5/220(220-235) [BalA90 2/60] d7.18 Col Cal St.-Fresno

YEAR	TM LG	W	L	PCT	G	GS	CG-SHO	SV-BS	IP	H	R	HR	HB	BB-IB	SO	ERA	AERA	OAV	OOB	AB-HR-SH	AVG	PB	SUP	APR	DL	PW
1994	Min A	0	0	—	9	0	0	1-1	13	13	7	0	1	5-0	13	2.77	178	.260	.339	0	—	0		2		0.1
1995	Min A	0	0	—	37	0	0	0-1	47	66	36	8	1	22-1	21	6.89	100	.332	.399	0	—	0		-9		-0.4
Total	2	0	0	—	46	0	0	1-2	60	79	43	8	2	27-1	34	6.00	81	.317	.387	0	—	0		-7		-0.3

SCHULTZ, BUDDY Charles Budd B9.19.1950 Cleveland OH BR/TL/6-0/175* [ChiN72 6/135] d9.3 Col Miami-Ohio

YEAR	TM LG	W	L	PCT	G	GS	CG-SHO	SV-BS	IP	H	R	HR	HB	BB-IB	SO	ERA	AERA	OAV	OOB	AB-HR-SH	AVG	PB	SUP	APR	DL	PW
1975	Chi N	2	0	1.000	6	0	0	0-0	5.2	11	6	4	0	5-1	4	6.35	61	.367	.457	0-0-1	—			-2		-0.4
1976	Chi N	1	1	.500	29	0	0	2-4	23.2	37	19	3	0	9-1	15	6.08	64	.356	.400	4	.000	-0		-6		-0.6
1977	StL N	6	1	.857	40	3	0	1-1	85.1	76	26	5	0	24-0	66	2.32	168	.245	.298	12-0-2	.167	0*	137	14	21	1.2
1978	StL N	2	4	.333	62	0	0	6-2	83	68	36	6	0	36-6	70	3.80	94	.226	.305	5-0-2	.200	1		0		0.0
1979	StL N	4	3	.571	31	0	0	3-1	42.1	40	21	7	0	14-5	38	4.46	85	.256	.312	4	.000	-0		-2	66	-0.4
Total	5	15	9	.625	168	3	0	12-8	240	232	108	21	0	88-13	193	3.68	103	.257	.320	25-0-5	.120	0	137	4	87	-0.2

SCHULTZ, BARNEY George Warren B8.15.1926 Beverly NJ BR/TR/6-2/200 d4.12 C6

YEAR	TM LG	W	L	PCT	G	GS	CG-SHO	SV-BS	IP	H	R	HR	HB	BB-IB	SO	ERA	AERA	OAV	OOB	AB-HR-SH	AVG	PB	SUP	APR	DL	PW
1955	StL N	1	2	.333	19	0	0	4	29.2	28	27	5	4	15-3	19	7.89	52	.259	.370	4	.000	-1		-12		-1.4
1959	Det A	1	1	.333	13	0	0	0	18.1	17	12	1	1	14-1	17	4.42	92	.254	.390	2	1.000	1		-1		-0.1
1961	Chi N	7	6	.538	41	0	0	7	66.2	57	32	6	4	25-4	59	2.70	155	.228	.307	10-0-2	.100	-1		7		1.3
1962	Chi N	5	5	.500	51	0	0	5	77.2	66	36	8	4	23-6	58	3.82	108	.231	.296	5-0-2	.000	-0		3		0.4
1963	Chi N	1	0	1.000	15	0	0	2	27.1	25	11	5	0	9-2	18	3.62	97	.263	.327	4	.000	-0		0		0.0
	StL N	2	0	1.000	24	0	0	1	35.1	36	15	5	2	8-2	26	3.57	99	.263	.311	0-0-1	—	-0		1		0.0
	Year	3	0	1.000	39	0	0	3	62.2	61	26	10	2	17-4	44	3.59	98	.263	.317	4-0-1	.000	-0		1		0.0
1964	†StL N	1	3	.250	30	0	0	14	49.1	35	14	1	0	11-3	29	1.64	232	.201	.246	6-0-1	.167	-0		10		1.4
1965	StL N	2	2	.500	34	0	0	2	42.1	39	22	8	0	11-3	30	3.83	100	.242	.289	2	.000	-0		-1		-0.1
Total	7	20	20	.500	227	0	0	35	346.2	303	169	39	15	116-24	264	3.63	109	.237	.307	33-0-6	.121	-1		6		1.5

SCHULTZ, BOB Robert Duffy B11.27.1923 Louisville KY D3.31.1979 Nashville TN BR/TL/6-3/200* d4.20

YEAR	TM LG	W	L	PCT	G	GS	CG-SHO	SV-BS	IP	H	R	HR	HB	BB-IB	SO	ERA	AERA	OAV	OOB	AB-HR-SH	AVG	PB	SUP	APR	DL	PW
1951	Chi N	3	6	.333	17	10	2	0	77.1	75	51	9	2	51	27	5.24	78	.251	.364	29-0-1	.138	-1	101	-10		-1.2
1952	Chi N	6	3	.667	29	5	1	0	74	63	34	3	2	51	31	4.01	96	.232	.357	18	.222	0	51	0		0.0
1953	Chi N	0	2	.000	7	2	0	0	11.2	13	10	2	1	11	4	5.40	82	.289	.439	3	.000	-0	100	-2		-0.4
	Pit N	0	2	.000	11	2	0	0	18.2	26	19	3	2	10	5	8.20	55	.321	.409	2-0-1	.000	-0	30	-7		-0.7
	Year	0	4	.000	18	4	0	0	30.1	39	29	5	3	21	9	7.12	63	.310	.420	5-0-1	.000	-0	65	-10		-1.1
1955	Det A	0	0	—	1	0	0	0	1.1	2	3	0	0	2-0	0	20.25	19	.333	.500	0	—	-0		-2		-0.1
Total	4	9	13	.409	65	19	3	0	183	179	117	17	7	125-0	67	5.16	79	.254	.372	52-0-2	.154	-1	82	-21		-2.4

SCHULTZ, WEBB Wilbert Carl B1.31.1898 Wautoma WI D7.26.1986 Delavan WI BR/TR/5-11/172 d8.3 Col Wisconsin-La Crosse

YEAR	TM LG	W	L	PCT	G	GS	CG-SHO	SV-BS	IP	H	R	HR	HB	BB-IB	SO	ERA	AERA	OAV	OOB	AB-HR-SH	AVG	PB	SUP	APR	DL	PW
1924	Chi N	0	0	—	1	0	0	0	1	1	1	0	0	1-0	0	9.00	46	.250	.250	0	—	0		0		0.0

SCHULTZ, MIKE William Michael B12.17.1920 Syracuse NY D8.2.2004 East Syracuse NY BL/TL/6-1/175 d4.20

YEAR	TM LG	W	L	PCT	G	GS	CG-SHO	SV-BS	IP	H	R	HR	HB	BB-IB	SO	ERA	AERA	OAV	OOB	AB-HR-SH	AVG	PB	SUP	APR	DL	PW
1947	Cin N	0	0	—	1	0	0		2	4	2	0	0	2	0	4.50	91	.444	.545	0	—	0		0		0.0

SCHULTZE, JOHN John F. B Burlington NJ 6-0.5/165 d5.6

YEAR	TM LG	W	L	PCT	G	GS	CG-SHO	SV-BS	IP	H	R	HR	HB	BB-IB	SO	ERA	AERA	OAV	OOB	AB-HR-SH	AVG	PB	SUP	APR	DL	PW
1891	Phi N	0	1	.000	6	1	0	0	15	18	15	1	0	11	4	6.60	52	.286	.392	6	.167	-0	18	-5		-0.

SCHULZ, AL Albert Christopher B5.12.1889 Toledo OH D12.13.1931 Gallipolis OH BR/TL/6-0/182 d9.25

YEAR	TM LG	W	L	PCT	G	GS	CG-SHO	SV-BS	IP	H	R	HR	HB	BB-IB	SO	ERA	AERA	OAV	OOB	AB-HR-SH	AVG	PB	SUP	APR	DL	PW
1912	NY A	1	1	.500	3	1	1	0	16.1	11	8	0	0	11	8	2.20	163	.183	.310	5	.000	-0	0	2		0.
1913	NY A	7	14	.333	38	22	9	0	193	197	110	4	5	69	77	3.73	80	.269	.336	63-0-2	.175	-0	92	-16		-1.
1914	NY A	1	3	.250	6	4	1	0	28.1	27	17	0	2	10	18	4.76	58	.237	.310	7	.000	-0	79	-6		-1.
	Buf F	9	12	.429	27	23	10	2	171	160	80	3	2	77	87	3.37	88	.259	.343	56-1-2	.179	-1	92	-8		-1.
1915	Buf F	21	14	.600	42	38	25-5	2	309.2	264	125	8	6	149	160	3.08	91	.238	.332	109-0-3	.165	-4	106	-7		-2.
1916	Cin N	8	19	.296	44	22	10	2	215	208	100	4	5	93	95	3.14	83	.268	.350	64-0-1	.125	-3	65	-15		-2.
Total	5	47	63	.427	160	110	56-5	4	933.1	867	440	19	20	409	445	3.32	85	.254	.338	304-1-8	.155	-9	91	-50		-6.

SCHULZ, WALT Walter Frederick B4.16.1900 St.Louis MO D2.27.1928 Prescott AZ BR/TR/6-0/170 d7.8

YEAR	TM LG	W	L	PCT	G	GS	CG-SHO	SV-BS	IP	H	R	HR	HB	BB-IB	SO	ERA	AERA	OAV	OOB	AB-HR-SH	AVG	PB	SUP	APR	DL	PW
1920	StL N	0	0	—	2	0	0	0	6	10	5	0	2	6	3	6.00	50	.370	.414	2	.000	-0		-2		-0.

SCHULZE, DON Donald Arthur B9.27.1962 Roselle IL BR/TR/6-3/225(215-230) [ChiN80 1/11] d9.13

YEAR	TM LG	W	L	PCT	G	GS	CG-SHO	SV-BS	IP	H	R	HR	HB	BB-IB	SO	ERA	AERA	OAV	OOB	AB-HR-SH	AVG	PB	SUP	APR	DL	PW
1983	Chi N	0	1	.000	4	3	0	0-0	14	19	11	1	1	7-0	8	7.07	54	.322	.403	1-0-1	.000	0	116	-4		-0.
1984	Chi N	0	0	—	4	3	0	0	3	8	4	0	0	1-0	2	12.00	33	.571	.563	0	—	.0	136	-2		-0.
	Cle A	3	6	.333	19	14	2	0	85.2	105	53	9	0	27-0	39	4.83	85	.302	.349	0	—	.0	121	-8		-0.
1985	Cle A	4	10	.286	19	18	1	0	94.1	128	75	9	4	19-2	37	6.01	69	.322	.357	0	—	0	97	-22	41	-2.
1986	Cle A	4	4	.500	19	13	1	0	84.2	88	48	9	5	34-0	33	5.00	84	.266	.342	0	—	.0	102	-5		-0.
1987	NY N	1	2	.333	5	4	0	0	21.2	24	15	4	1	6-0	6	6.23	62	.296	.344	2-0-1	.000	0	118	-5		-0.
1989	NY A	1	1	.500	2	2	0	0	11	12	5	1	1	5-0	5	4.09	95	.300	.375	0	—	0	70	0		0.
	SD N	2	1	.667	4	4	0	0	24.1	38	20	6	0	6-0	15	5.55	63	.352	.379	4-0-1	.000	-0	196	-7		-0.
Total	6	15	25	.375	76	59	4	0-0	338.2	422	231	40	12	105-2	144	5.47	74	.306	.357	7-0-3	.000	0	112	-53	41	-5.

SCHUMACHER, HAL Harold Henry "Prince Hal" B11.23.1910 Hinckley NY D4.21.1993 Cooperstown NY BR/TR/6-0/190 d4.15 Mil 1943-45 Col St. Lawrence

YEAR	TM LG	W	L	PCT	G	GS	CG-SHO	SV-BS	IP	H	R	HR	HB	BB-IB	SO	ERA	AERA	OAV	OOB	AB-HR-SH	AVG	PB	SUP	APR	DL	PW
1931	NY N	1	1	.500	8	2	1	1	18.1	31	23	0	0	14	11	10.80	34	.387	.409	7	.143	-0	255	-14		-1.
1932	NY N	6	4	.455	27	13	2-1	0	101.1	119	60	3	2	39	38	3.55	104	.288	.352	31-0-1	.226	1*	110	-3		-0.
1933	†NY N☆	19	12	.613	35	33	21-7	1	258.2	199	71	9	1	84	96	2.16	149	.214	.280	98-0-2	.214	1*	115	33		4.
1934	NY N	23	10	.697	41	36	18-2	0	297	299	131	16	2	89	112	3.18	120	.259	.313	117-6-2	.239	10*	125	22		3.
1935	NY N★	19	9	.679	33	33	19-3	0	261.2	235	100	11	5	70	79	2.89	133	.238	.292	107-2-3	.196	2*	125	27		3.
1936	†NY N	11	13	.458	35	30	9-2	1	215.1	234	103	15	1	69	75	3.47	112	.280	.336	74-1-0	.216	2*	102	8		1.
1937	†NY N	13	12	.520	38	29	10-1	1	217.2	222	100	12	0	89	100	3.60	108	.264	.335	81-2-1	.222	3*	98	7		1.
1938	NY N	13	8	.619	28	28	12-3	0	185	178	81	12	2	50	54	3.50	108	.248	.299	67-2-1	.239	4*	100	7		1.
1939	NY N	13	10	.565	29	27	8	0	181.2	199	106	14	1	89	58	4.81	82	.276	.338	69-0-4	.203	1*	127	-15		-1.
1940	NY N	13	13	.500	34	30	12-1	1	227	218	93	14	0	96	123	3.25	119	.251	.325	78-1-3	.192	2*	92	16		1.
1941	NY N	12	10	.545	30	26	12-3	0	206	187	81	11	5	79	63	3.36	110	.243	.317	66-0-4	.152	-1*	90	11		1.
1942	NY N	12	13	.480	29	29	12-3	1	216	208	81	12	3	82	49	3.04	111	.255	.321	75-1-5	.173	1*	112	10		1.
1946	NY N	4	4	.500	24	13	2	1	96.2	95	50	8	0	52	48	3.91	88	.255	.347	26-0-2	.038	-2	111	-5		-1.
Total	13	158	121	.566	391	329	138-26	7	2482.1	2424	1080	140	24	902	906	3.36	111	.255	.321	896-15-28	.202	24	110	104		15

SCHUMANN, HACK Carl J. B8.13.1884 Buffalo NY D3.25.1946 Millgrove NY TR/6-2/230 d9.19

YEAR	TM LG	W	L	PCT	G	GS	CG-SHO	SV-BS	IP	H	R	HR	HB	BB-IB	SO	ERA	AERA	OAV	OOB	AB-HR-SH	AVG	PB	SUP	APR	DL	PW
1906	Phi A	0	2	.000	4	2	1	0	18	21	13	0	2	8	8	9.00	68	.296	.383	6	.000	-1	66	-3		-0.

SCHUPP, FERDIE Ferdinand Maurice B1.16.1891 Louisville KY D12.16.1971 Los Angeles CA BR/TL/5-10/150 d4.19

YEAR	TM LG	W	L	PCT	G	GS	CG-SHO	SV-BS	IP	H	R	HR	HB	BB-IB	SO	ERA	AERA	OAV	OOB	AB-HR-SH	AVG	PB	SUP	APR	DL	PW
1913	NY N	0	0	—	5	1	0	0	12	10	3	0	3	2	2	0.75	416	.244	.295	3	.333	1	96	3		0.
1914	NY N	0	0	—	8	1	0	1	17	19	11	0	2	9	9	5.82	46	.306	.411	2	.000	-0		-5		-0.
1915	NY N	1	0	1.000	23	1	0	0	54.2	57	37	1	3	29	28	5.10	50	.281	.379	10	.200	0	203	-15		-0.
1916	NY N	9	3	.750	30	11	8-4	0	140.1	79	22	1	6	37	86	0.90	271	.167	.235	41	.098	-2	87	24		3.
1917	†NY N	21	7	.750	36	32	25-6	0	272	202	69	7	4	70	147	1.95	131	.209	.287	93-0-1	.161	1	142	21		2.
1918	NY N	0	1	.000	10	2	1	0	33.1	42	34	1	3	27	22	7.56	35	.328	.456	9	.111	-0	173	-19		-1.
1919	NY N	1	3	.250	9	4	0	0	32	32	24	2	0	18	11	5.63	50	.269	.365	6-0-2	.333	0	113	-10		-1.
	StL N	4	4	.500	10	10	6	0	69.2	55	31	2	1	30	37	3.75	75	.221	.307	20-1-1	.050	-0	88	-5		-0.
	Year	5	7	.417	19	14	6	0	101.2	87	55	4	1	48	54	4.34	64	.236	.326	26-1-3	.115	-0	95	-15		-1.
1920	StL N	16	13	.552	38	37	17	0	250.2	246	118	9	5	127	119	3.52	85	.265	.358	86-0-4	.256	6*	139	-14		-1.
1921	StL N	2	0	1.000	9	4	1	1	37.1	42	26	5	2	21	22	4.10	89	.276	.371	14-0-1	.286	0	185	-4		-0.
	Bro N	3	4	.429	20	7	1	2	61	75	34	2	2	27	26	4.57	85	.310	.384	12-0-1	.083	-1	76	-3		-0.
	Year	5	4	.556	29	11	2	3	98.1	117	60	7	4	48	48	4.39	87	.297	.379	26-0-2	.192	-0	114	-8		-0.
1922	Chi A	4	4	.500	18	12	3-1	6	74	79	61	4	2	66	38	6.08	67	.284	.425	23	.217	1	120	-19		-1.
Total	10	61	39	.610	216	121	62-11	6	1054	938	470	30	33	464	553	3.32	87	.244	.331	319-1-10	.182	5	129	-46		0

YEAR	TM LG	W	L	PCT	G	GS	CG-SHO	SV-BS	IP	H	R	HR	HB	BB-IB	SO	ERA	AERA	OAV	OOB	AB-HR-SH	AVG	PB	SUP	APR	DL	PW

SCHURR, WAYNE　Wayne Allen　B8.6.1937 Garrett IN　BR/TR/6-4/185　d4.15　Col Hillsdale

| 1964 | Chi N | 0 | 0 | — | 26 | 0 | 0 | 0 | 48.1 | 57 | 22 | 3 | 0 | 11-1 | 29 | 3.72 | 100 | .298 | .333 | 5 | .000 | -0 | | 0 | | 0.0 |

SCHUTZ, CARL　Carl James　B8.22.1971 Hammond LA　BL/TL/5-11/208　[AtlN93 3/96]　d9.3　Col Southeastern Louisiana

| 1996 | Atl N | 0 | 0 | — | 3 | 0 | 0 | 0-0 | 3.1 | 3 | 1 | 0 | 0 | 2-1 | 5 | 2.70 | 165 | .273 | .385 | 0 | — | 0 | | 1 | | 0.0 |

SCHWABE, MIKE　Michael Scott　B7.12.1964 Ft.Dodge IA　BR/TR/6-4/200*　[DetA87 21/547]　d5.27　Col Arizona St.

1989	Det A	2	4	.333	13	4	0	0-0	44.2	58	33	6	1	16-5	13	6.04	63	.307	.359	0	—	0	71	-11		-1.2
1990	Det A	0	0	—	1	0	0	0-0	3.2	5	1	0	0	0-0	1	2.45	162	.357	.357	0	—	0		1		0.1
Total 2		2	4	.333	14	4	0	0-0	48.1	63	34	6	1	16-5	14	5.77	67	.310	.359	0	—	0	71	-10		-1.1

SCHWALL, DON　Donald Bernard　B3.2.1936 Wilkes-Barre PA　BR/TR/6-6/200*　d5.21　Col Oklahoma

1961	Bos A★	15	7	.682	25	25	10-2	0	178.2	167	76	8	6	110-1	91	3.22	129	.255	.366	61-0-11	.180	-0*	121	17		1.9
1962	Bos A	9	15	.375	33	32	5-1	0	182.1	180	118	18	10	121-1	89	4.94	84	.260	.377	66-0-5	.136	-2*	105	-18		-2.3
1963	Pit N	6	12	.333	33	24	3-2	0	167.2	158	72	13	6	74-13	86	3.33	99	.255	.338	50	.160	-0	87	0		0.1
1964	Pit N	4	3	.571	15	9	0	0	49.2	53	28	1	0	15-1	36	4.35	81	.269	.321	19	.263	2*	136	-5		-0.5
1965	Pit N	9	6	.600	43	1	0	4	77	77	37	5	2	30-4	55	2.92	120	.269	.341	15	.000	-0	75	2		0.3
1966	Pit N	3	2	.600	11	4	0	0	41.2	31	13	3	1	21-2	24	2.16	165	.209	.312	10-0-1	.100	-2	86	6		0.7
	Atl N	3	3	.500	11	8	0	0	45.1	44	23	2	2	19-2	27	4.37	83	.256	.333	13	.000	-2	106	-3		-0.5
	Year	6	5	.545	22	12	0	0	87	75	36	5	3	40-4	51	3.31	109	.234	.323	23-0-1	.043	-2	100	2		0.2
1967	Atl N	1	0	0	1	0	0	0	0.2	0	0	0	0	1-1	0	0.00	—	.000	.500	0	—	0		0		0.0
Total 7		49	48	.505	172	103	18-5	4	743	710	367	50	27	391-25	408	3.72	102	.257	.352	234-0-17	.145	-5	108	-1		-0.3

SCHWAMB, BLACKIE　Ralph Richard　B8.6.1926 Lancaster CA　D12.21.1989 Los Angeles CA　BR/TR/6-5.5/198　d7.25

| 1948 | StL A | 1 | 1 | .500 | 12 | 5 | 0 | 0 | 31.2 | 44 | 34 | 3 | 0 | 21 | 7 | 8.53 | 53 | .331 | .422 | 10 | .300 | 1 | 131 | -13 | | -0.6 |

SCHWARZ, JEFF　Jeffrey William　B5.20.1964 Fort Pierce FL　BR/TR/6-5/190*　[ChiN82 24/597]　d4.24

1993	Chi A	2	2	.500	41	0	0	0-0	51	35	21	1	3	38-2	41	3.71	114	.201	.349	0	—	0		4	15	0.2
1994	Chi A	0	0	—	9	0	0	0-0	11.1	9	10	0	0	16-0	14	6.35	74	.205	.417	0	—	0		-3		-0.1
	Cal A	0	0	—	4	0	0	0-0	6.2	5	3	0	0	6-0	4	4.05	121	.250	.407	0	—	0		1		0.0
	Year	0	0	—	13	0	0	0-0	18	14	13	0	0	22-0	18	5.50	87	.219	.414	0	—	0		-2		-0.1
Total 2		2	2	.500	54	0	0	0-0	69	49	34	1	3	60-2	59	4.17	104	.206	.367	0	—	0		2	15	0.1

SCHWENCK, RUDY　Rudolph Christian　B4.6.1884 Louisville KY　D11.27.1941 Anchorage KY　BL/TL/6-0/174　d9.23

| 1909 | Chi N | 1 | 1 | .500 | 3 | 2 | 0 | 0 | 14 | 16 | 7 | 0 | 1 | 3 | 3 | 3.86 | 66 | .308 | .357 | 4 | .250 | 0 | 83 | -2 | | -0.1 |

SCHWENK, HAL　Harold Edward　B8.23.1890 Schuylkill Haven PA　D9.3.1955 Kansas City MO　BL/TL/6-0/185　d9.4

| 1913 | StL A | 1 | 0 | 1.000 | 1 | 1 | 0 | 0 | 11 | 12 | 4 | 0 | 0 | 4-1 | 3 | 3.27 | 90 | .333 | .400 | 3 | .333 | 1 | 126 | 0 | | 0.1 |

SCOGGINS, JIM　Lynn J. "Lefty"　B7.19.1891 Killeen TX　D8.16.1923 Columbia SC　BL/TL/5-11/165　d8.26

| 1913 | Chi A | 0 | 1 | .000 | 1 | 1 | 0 | 0 | 0 | 0 | 0 | 0 | 1 | 0 | 1 | — | — | .000 | .500 | 0 | — | 0 | 76 | 0 | | 0.0 |

SCORE, HERB　Herbert Jude　B6.7.1933 Rosedale NY　BL/TL/6-2/185*　d4.15

1955	Cle A☆	16	10	.615	33	32	11-2	0	227.1	158	85	18	1	154-1	**245**	2.85	140	.194	.322	84-0-8	.119	-4	106	28		2.3
1956	Cle A★	20	9	.690	35	33	16-5	0	249.1	162	82	18	2	129-2	**263**	2.53	**166**	**.186**	.290	87-1-4	.184	-1	98	45		4.9
1957	Cle A	2	1	.667	5	5	3-1	0	36	18	9	0	1	26-2	39	2.00	186	.149	.304	11	.091	-0	86	7	118	0.6
1958	Cle A	2	3	.400	12	5	2-1	3	41	29	19	1	0	34-1	48	3.95	92	.197	.346	11	.091	-0	74	-1	36	-0.2
1959	Cle A	9	11	.450	30	25	9-1	0	160.2	123	93	28	0	115-0	147	4.71	78	**.210**	.339	52	.096	-3	119	-19		-2.5
1960	Chi A	5	10	.333	23	22	5-1	0	113.2	91	54	10	2	87-0	78	3.72	102	.226	.363	30-0-2	.100	-0	84	0		-0.1
1961	Chi A	1	2	.333	8	5	1	0	24.1	22	19	3	0	24-1	14	6.66	59	.259	.411	6-0-1	.000	-1	77	-7		-0.8
1962	Chi A	0	0	—	4	0	0	0	6	6	3	1	0	4-0	3	4.50	87	.261	.370	0	—	0	0	0		0.0
Total 8		55	46	.545	150	127	47-11	3	858.1	609	364	79	7	573-7	837	3.36	117	.200	.326	281-1-15	.128	-8	99	53	154	4.2

SCOTT, DICK　Amos Richard　B2.5.1883 Bethel OH　D1.18.1911 Chicago IL　BR/TR/6-0/180　d6.26

| 1901 | Cin N | 0 | 2 | .000 | 3 | 2 | 2 | 0 | 21 | 26 | 15 | 2 | 3 | 9 | 7 | 5.14 | 62 | .302 | .388 | 9 | .000 | -1 | 55 | -4 | | -0.5 |

SCOTT, DARRYL　Darryl Nelson　B8.6.1968 Fresno CA　BR/TR/6-1/185　d5.31　Col Loyola Marymount

| 1993 | Cal A | 1 | 2 | .333 | 16 | 0 | 0 | 0-0 | 20 | 19 | 13 | 1 | 1 | 11-1 | 13 | 5.85 | 78 | .250 | .344 | 0 | | 0 | | -2 | | -0.3 |

SCOTT, GEORGE　George Wilson　B11.17.1895 Appanoose Co. IA　D12.3.1962 Philomath OR　BR/TR/6-1/175　d8.17

| 1920 | StL N | 0 | 0 | — | 2 | 0 | 0 | 0 | 6 | 4 | 3 | 0 | 0 | 3 | 1 | 4.50 | 66 | .200 | .304 | 1 | .000 | -0 | | -1 | | -0.1 |

SCOTT, JIM　James "Death Valley Jim"　B4.23.1888 Deadwood SD　D4.7.1957 Jacumba CA　BR/TR/6-1/235　d4.25　Mil 1917-18　U2　Col Nebraska Wesleyan

1909	Chi A	12	12	.500	36	29	20-4	0	250.1	194	86	0	16	93	135	2.30	102	.223	.310	85-0-2	.106	-1	104	3		0.0
1910	Chi A	8	18	.308	41	23	14-2	1	229.2	182	99	5	4	86	135	2.43	94	.226	.303	74-0-2	.203	2	77	-3		0.0
1911	Chi A	14	11	.560	39	26	13-3	0	222	195	83	3	4	81	128	2.39	135	.240	.311	71-0-5	.155	-2	89	21		1.7
1912	Chi A	2	2	.500	6	4	2-1	0	37.2	36	16	0	1	15	23	2.15	149	.265	.342	12	.000	-2	52	3		0.1
1913	Chi A	20	21	.488	48	38	25-4	1	312.1	252	96	2	9	86	158	1.90	154	.223	.283	97-1-8	.072	-7	72	35		3.8
1914	Chi A	14	18	.438	43	33	12-2	1	253.1	228	109	5	5	75	138	2.84	94	.246	.306	86-0-2	.163	-0	89	-2		-0.2
1915	Chi A	24	11	.686	48	35	23-7	2	296.1	256	98	3	5	78	120	2.03	146	.238	.292	95-0-6	.126	-5	97	28		2.9
1916	Chi A	7	14	.333	32	21	8-1	3	165.1	155	63	3	3	53	71	2.72	101	.258	.321	52-0-6	.115	-3	85	2		-0.1
1917	Chi A	6	7	.462	24	17	6-2	1	125	126	37	0	6	42	37	1.87	142	.272	.341	42	.119	-2	91	10		0.9
Total 9		107	114	.484	317	226	123-26	9	1892	1624	686	21	53	609	945	2.30	120	.238	.305	614-1-29	.129	-21	87	97		9.1

SCOTT, JACK　John William　B4.18.1892 Ridgeway NC　D11.30.1959 Durham NC　BL/TR/6-2.5/199　d9.6

1916	Pit N	0	0	—	1	0	0	0	5	5	6	1	0	3	4	10.80	25	.278	.381	2	.000	0*		-4		-0.2
1917	Bos N	1	2	.333	7	3	3	0	39.2	36	12	0	3	5	21	1.82	141	.255	.295	16	.125	-1	39	3		0.1
1919	Bos N	6	6	.500	19	12	7	1	103.2	109	47	3	1	39	44	3.13	91	.275	.341	40-0-2	.175	-1*	116	-4		-0.7
1920	Bos N	10	21	.323	44	33	22-3	0	291	308	148	6	13	85	94	3.53	87	.277	.336	99-0-3	.212	-1	95	-19		-2.1
1921	Bos N	15	13	.536	47	28	16-2	3	233.2	258	108	9	7	57	83	3.70	99	.283	.330	88-1-1	.341	10*	121	0		1.0
1922	Cin N	0	0	—	1	0	0	0	1	2	1	0	0	0	0	9.00	44	.500	.600	1	.000	-0		0		0.0
†NY N		8	2	.800	17	10	5	2	79.2	83	42	7	2	23	37	4.41	91	.265	.320	30-0-1	.267	1	130	0		-0.1
Year		8	2	.800	18	10	5	2	80.2	85	43	7	2	23	37	4.46	90	.268	.324	31-0-1	.258	1	130	-2		-0.1
1923	†NY N	16	7	.696	40	25	9-3	0	220	223	104	15	4	65	79	3.89	98	.267	.323	79-1-2	.316	7	134	0		0.6
1925	NY N	14	15	.483	36	28	18-2	3	239.2	251	98	10	4	55	87	3.15	128	.269	.313	87-1-0	.241	6*	88	25		3.5
1926	NY N	13	15	.464	50	22	13	5	226	242	118	13	13	53	82	4.34	86	.276	.319	83-1-0	.337	9*	71	-10		-0.3
1927	Phi N	9	21	.300	48	25	17-1	1	233.1	304	154	15	4	69	69	5.09	81	.330	.379	114-1-3	.289	8*	71	-26		-2.1
1928	NY N	4	1	.800	16	3	3	1	50.1	59	22	3	2	11	17	3.58	109	.295	.338	15	.267	1	144	2		0.3
1929	NY N	7	6	.538	30	6	2	0	91.2	89	44	12	0	27	40	3.53	130	.260	.314	26	.308	3	105	10		1.6
Total 12		103	109	.486	356	195	115-11	19	1814.2	1969	904	94	43	493	657	3.85	96	.281	.332	680-5-12	.275	44	103	-24		1.6

SCOTT, LEFTY　Marshall　B7.15.1915 Roswell NM　D3.3.1964 Houston TX　BR/TL/6-0.5/165　d6.15

| 1945 | Phi N | 0 | 2 | .000 | 7 | 4 | 0 | 0 | 22.1 | 24 | 15 | 5 | 4 | 5 | 4.43 | 86 | .312 | .390 | 3-0-1 | .000 | -0 | 11 | -1 | | -0.2 |

SCOTT, MIKE　Michael Warren　B4.26.1955 Santa Monica CA　BR/TR/6-3/215*　[NYN76 2/37]　d4.18　Col Pepperdine

1979	NY N	1	3	.250	18	9	0	0-0	52.1	59	35	4	0	20-3	21	5.33	70	.289	.351	12-0-1	.000	-1	119	-10		-0.8
1980	NY N	1	1	.500	6	6	1-1	0-0	29.1	40	14	2	0	8-1	13	4.30	84	.331	.369	9	.111	0	120	-1		-0.1
1981	NY N	5	10	.333	23	23	1	0-0	136	130	65	11	1	34-1	54	3.90	91	.261	.306	41-0-1	.073	-2	72	-4		-0.4
1982	NY N	7	13	.350	37	22	1	3-2	147	185	100	13	2	60-3	63	5.14	71	.321	.381	48	.146	1	97	-25		-2.9
1983	Hou N	10	6	.625	24	24	2-2	0-0	145	143	67	8	5	46-0	73	3.72	92	.258	.318	48-0-8	.167	1	124	-4		-0.3
1984	Hou N	5	11	.313	31	29	0	0-0	154	179	96	7	3	43-4	83	4.68	72	.293	.343	47-0-6	.128	-0	108	-25	29	-2.4
1985	Hou N	18	8	.692	36	35	4-2	0-0	221.2	194	91	20	3	80-4	137	3.29	106	.235	.302	72-1-3	.153	-2	128	6		0.9
1986	†Hou N★	18	10	.643	37	37	7-5	0-0	275.1	182	73	17	2	72-6	**306**	2.22	162	**.186**	.242	95-0-10	.126	-2*	97	**45**		**4.5**
1987	Hou N★	16	13	.552	36	36	8-3	0-0	247.2	199	94	21	4	79-6	233	3.23	122	.217	.281	80-0-8	.125	-1	84	22		2.2
1988	Hou N	14	8	.636	32	32	8-5	0-0	218.2	162	74	19	8	53-6	190	2.92	114	.204	.260	71-0-7	.085	-3	113	13	21	1.0
1989	Hou N★	20	10	.667	33	32	9-2	0-0	229	180	73	20	1	62-12	172	3.10	110	.212	.267	75-1-9	.133	-1	122	8		0.9
1990	Hou N	9	13	.409	32	32	4-2	0-0	205.2	194	90	27	1	66-6	121	3.81	98	.246	.302	54-0-6	.130	-0	76	-4		-0.5

YEAR	TM LG	W	L	PCT	G	GS	CG-SHO	SV-BS	IP	H	R	HR	HB	BB-IB	SO	ERA	AERA	OAV	OOB	AB-HR-SH	AVG	PB	SUP	APR	DL	PW
1991	Hou N	0	2	.000	2	2	0	0-0	7	11	10	2	1	4-1	3	12.86	27	.367	.457	1	.000	-0	51	-7	176	-1.1
Total	13	124	108	.534	347	319	45-22	3-2	2068.2	1858	908	173	33	627-53	1469	3.54	101	.240	.297	653-2-59	.124	-6	102	14	226	1.0

SCOTT, ED Philip Edwin B8.12.1870 Walbridge OH D11.1.1933 Toledo OH BR/TR/6-3/? d4.19

YEAR	TM LG	W	L	PCT	G	GS	CG-SHO	SV-BS	IP	H	R	HR	HB	BB-IB	SO	ERA	AERA	OAV	OOB	AB-HR-SH	AVG	PB	SUP	APR	DL	PW
1900	Cin N	17	20	.459	42	35	31	1	315	370	192	10	14	65	87	3.86	95	.292	.334	123-1-2	.154	-5	88	-9		-0.9
1901	Cle A	6	6	.500	17	16	11	1	124.2	149	82	2	7	38	23	4.40	81	.293	.350	48-1-2	.208	1	96	-8		-0.5
Total	2	23	26	.469	59	51	42	2	439.2	519	274	12	21	103	110	4.01	91	.292	.338	171-2-4	.170	-4	90	-17		-1.4

SCOTT, MICKEY Ralph Robert B7.25.1947 Weimar, Germany BL/TL/6-1/165* [NYA65 11/335] d5.6

YEAR	TM LG	W	L	PCT	G	GS	CG-SHO	SV-BS	IP	H	R	HR	HB	BB-IB	SO	ERA	AERA	OAV	OOB	AB-HR-SH	AVG	PB	SUP	APR	DL	PW
1972	Bal A	0	1	.000	15	0	0	0-1	23	23	7	2	1	5-0	11	2.74	114	.277	.319	1	.000	0		1		0.1
1973	Bal A	0	0	—	1	0	0	0-0	1.2	2	1	1	0	2-0	2	5.40	70	.286	.444	0	—	0		0		0.0
	Mon N	1	2	.333	22	0	0	0-1	24	27	14	3	2	9-0	11	5.25	73	.287	.362	3	.000	-0		-3		-0.3
1975	Cal A	4	2	.667	50	0	0	1-4	68.1	59	34	8	1	18-5	31	3.29	109	.233	.282	0	—	0		0		0.0
1976	Cal A	3	0	1.000	33	0	0	3-1	39	47	17	3	0	12-4	10	3.23	104	.307	.355	0	—	0*		0	27	0.0
1977	Cal A	0	2	.000	16	0	0	0-0	16	19	16	1	0	4-2	5	5.63	70	.302	.343	0	—	0		-5		-0.5
Total	5	8	7	.533	133	0	0	4-7	172	177	89	18	4	50-11	70	3.72	95	.271	.323	4	.000	0		-7	27	-0.7

SCOTT, DICK Richard Lewis B3.15.1933 Portsmouth NH BR/TL/6-2/185(185-200) d5.8

YEAR	TM LG	W	L	PCT	G	GS	CG-SHO	SV-BS	IP	H	R	HR	HB	BB-IB	SO	ERA	AERA	OAV	OOB	AB-HR-SH	AVG	PB	SUP	APR	DL	PW
1963	LA N	0	0	—	9	0	0	2	12	17	10	6	0	3-0	6	6.75	45	.340	.370	0	—	0		-5		-0.3
1964	Chi N	0	0	—	3	0	0	0	4.1	10	6	2	0	1-0	1	12.46	30	.417	.440	0	—	0		-4		-0.2
Total	2	0	0	—	12	0	0	2	16.1	27	16	8	0	4-0	7	8.27	39	.365	.392	0	—	0		-9		-0.5

SCOTT, TIM Timothy Dale B11.16.1966 Hanford CA BR/TR/6-2/205(185-205) [LAN84 2/51] d6.25

YEAR	TM LG	W	L	PCT	G	GS	CG-SHO	SV-BS	IP	H	R	HR	HB	BB-IB	SO	ERA	AERA	OAV	OOB	AB-HR-SH	AVG	PB	SUP	APR	DL	PW
1991	SD N	0	0	—	2	0	0	0-0	1	1	1	0	0	0-0	—	9.00	42	.400	.400	0	—	-0		-1		0.0
1992	SD N	4	1	.800	34	0	0	0-1	37.2	39	24	4	1	21-6	30	5.26	68	.267	.361	0	—	-0		-7		-0.9
1993	SD N	2	0	1.000	24	0	0	0-2	37.2	38	13	1	4	15-0	30	2.39	173	.260	.341	2-0-1	.000	-0		6		0.3
	Mon N	5	2	.714	32	0	0	1-1	34	31	15	3	0	19-2	35	3.71	113	.242	.340	2	.000	-0		2		0.4
	Year	7	2	.778	56	0	0	1-3	71.2	69	28	4	4	34-2	65	3.01	138	.252	.341	4-0-1	.000	-0		8		0.7
1994	Mon N	5	2	.714	40	0	0	1-0	53.1	51	17	0	2	18-3	37	2.70	157	.251	.318	2	.000	-0		9	15	1.0
1995	Mon N	2	0	1.000	62	0	0	2-3	63.1	52	30	6	6	23-2	57	3.98	108	.222	.307	4	.250	-0		2		0.1
1996	Mon N	3	5	.375	45	0	0	1-2	46.1	41	18	3	2	21-2	37	3.11	139	.238	.325	4	.000	-0		6		0.9
	SF N	2	2	.500	20	0	0	0-2	19.2	24	18	5	1	9-0	10	8.24	50	.316	.391	1	.000	-0		-8		-1.4
	Year	5	7	.417	65	0	0	1-4	66	65	36	8	3	30-2	47	4.64	92	.262	.345	5	.000	-1		-2		-0.5
1997	SD N	1	1	.500	14	0	0	0-1	18.1	25	17	2	3	5-0	14	7.85	50	.321	.379	0	—	0		-8		-0.7
	Col N	0	0	—	3	0	0	0-0	2.2	5	3	0	0	2-0	2	10.13	51	.455	.538	0	—	0		-1		0.0
	Year	1	1	.500	17	0	0	0-1	21	30	20	2	3	7-0	16	8.14	50	.337	.400	0	—	0		-9		-0.7
Total	7	24	13	.649	276	0	0	5-12	314	308	157	24	19	133-15	253	4.13	101	.257	.338	15-0-1	.067	-1		0	15	-0.3

SCUDDER, SCOTT William Scott B2.14.1968 Paris TX BR/TR/6-2/185* d6.6

YEAR	TM LG	W	L	PCT	G	GS	CG-SHO	SV-BS	IP	H	R	HR	HB	BB-IB	SO	ERA	AERA	OAV	OOB	AB-HR-SH	AVG	PB	SUP	APR	DL	PW
1989	Cin N	4	9	.308	23	17	0	0-0	100.1	91	54	14	1	61-11	66	4.49	80	.239	.345	24-0-4	.167	1	91	-8		-1.0
1990	†Cin N	5	5	.500	21	10	0	0-0	71.2	74	41	12	3	30-4	42	4.90	81	.265	.342	18-0-1	.056	-1	105	-7	68	-1.0
1991	Cin N	6	9	.400	27	14	0	1-0	101.1	91	52	6	6	36-4	51	4.35	87	.246	.352	29-1-2	.103	-0	101	-5	49	-0.7
1992	Cle A	6	10	.375	23	22	0	0-0	109	134	80	10	2	55-0	66	5.28	75	.303	.380	0	—	0	90	-20	43	-2.6
1993	Cle A	0	1	.000	2	1	0	0-0	4	5	4	0	1	4-0	1	9.00	49	.333	.500	0	—	0	63	-2	43	-0.3
Total	5	21	34	.382	96	64	0	1-0	386.1	395	231	42	13	206-19	226	4.80	80	.266	.358	71-1-7	.113	-0	95	-42	160	-5.6

SCURRY, ROD Rodney Grant B3.17.1956 Sacramento CA D11.5.1992 Reno NV BL/TL/6-2/180(180-195) [PitN74 1/11] d4.17

YEAR	TM LG	W	L	PCT	G	GS	CG-SHO	SV-BS	IP	H	R	HR	HB	BB-IB	SO	ERA	AERA	OAV	OOB	AB-HR-SH	AVG	PB	SUP	APR	DL	PW
1980	Pit N	0	2	.000	20	0	0	0-0	37.2	23	12	2	2	17-3	28	2.15	172	.176	.280	4	.250	0		5		0.3
1981	Pit N	4	5	.444	27	7	0	7-2	74	74	33	6	3	40-2	65	3.77	97	.261	.357	19	.158	0	45	0		0.0
1982	Pit N	4	5	.444	76	0	0	14-6	103.2	79	26	3	4	64-7	94	1.74	216	.212	.331	21-0-1	.238	1	21			2.4
1983	Pit N	4	9	.308	61	0	0	7-8	68	63	45	6	4	53-7	67	5.56	67	.249	.382	5	.000	-1		-12		-2.5
1984	Pit N	5	6	.455	43	0	0	4-1	46.1	28	14	1	0	28-1	48	2.53	144	.175	.275	2	.000	-0		6	58	1.3
1985	Pit N	0	1	.000	30	0	0	2-1	47.2	42	22	4	0	28-1	43	3.21	113	.236	.337	4	.000	-0		1		0.1
	NY A	1	0	1.000	5	0	0	1-0	12.2	5	4	2	0	10-1	17	2.84	142	.125	.300	0	—	0		2	73	0.2
1986	NY A	1	2	.333	31	0	0	2-1	39.1	38	18	1	4	22-1	36	3.66	113	.252	.354	0	—	0		0		0.0
1988	Sea A	0	2	.000	39	0	0	2-1	31.1	32	16	6	4	18-4	33	4.02	104	.258	.365	0	—	0		0		0.0
Total	8	19	32	.373	332	7	0	39-19	460.2	384	190	31	19	274-29	431	3.24	116	.227	.339	55-0-1	.164	0	45	25	131	1.5

SEALE, JOHNNIE Johnny Ray "Durango Kid" B11.14.1938 Edgewater CO BL/TL/5-10/155* d9.20

YEAR	TM LG	W	L	PCT	G	GS	CG-SHO	SV-BS	IP	H	R	HR	HB	BB-IB	SO	ERA	AERA	OAV	OOB	AB-HR-SH	AVG	PB	SUP	APR	DL	PW
1964	Det A	1	0	1.000	4	0	0	0-0	10	6	4	1	0	4-0	5	3.60	102	.171	.256	1	.000	-0		-3		-0.1
1965	Det A	0	0	—	4	0	0	0	3	7	4	1	0	2-0	3	12.00	29	.500	.500	0	—	0		-3		-0.1
Total	2	1	0	1.000	8	0	0	0-0	13	13	8	2	0	6-0	8	5.54	65	.265	.333	1	.000	-0		-3		-0.1

SEAMAN, KIM Kim Michael B5.6.1957 Pascagoula MS BL/TL/6-4/205* [NYN76*S4/80] d9.28 Col Mississippi Gulf Coast CC

YEAR	TM LG	W	L	PCT	G	GS	CG-SHO	SV-BS	IP	H	R	HR	HB	BB-IB	SO	ERA	AERA	OAV	OOB	AB-HR-SH	AVG	PB	SUP	APR	DL	PW
1979	StL N	0	0	—	1	0	0	0-0	2	0	0	0	0	2-0	3	0.00	—	.000	.250	0	—	0		1		0.1
1980	StL N	3	2	.600	26	0	0	4-1	23.2	16	9	2	0	13-1	10	3.42	110	.188	.296	1	.000	-0		1		0.1
Total	2	3	2	.600	27	0	0	4-1	25.2	16	9	2	0	15-1	13	3.16	119	.176	.292	1	.000	-0		2		0.2

SEANEZ, RUDY Rudy Caballero B10.20.1968 Brawley CA BR/TR/5-10/185(170-205) [CleA86 4/83] d9.7 [DL 1992 LA N 182, 1993 Col N 102]

YEAR	TM LG	W	L	PCT	G	GS	CG-SHO	SV-BS	IP	H	R	HR	HB	BB-IB	SO	ERA	AERA	OAV	OOB	AB-HR-SH	AVG	PB	SUP	APR	DL	PW
1989	Cle A	0	0	—	5	0	0	0-0	5	1	2	0	0	4-1	5	3.60	111	.071	.250	0	—	0		-4		-0.4
1990	Cle A	2	1	.667	24	0	0	0-0	27.1	22	17	2	1	25-1	24	5.60	70	.220	.378	0	—	0		-7	52	-0.8
1991	Cle A	0	0	—	5	0	0	0-1	5	10	12	2	0	7-0	7	16.20	26	.385	.515	0	—	0		-4		-0.7
1993	SD N	0	0	—	3	0	0	0-0	3.1	8	6	1	0	2-0	1	13.50	31	.471	.526	0	—	0		-3		-0.4
1994	LA N	1	1	.500	17	0	0	0-1	23.2	24	7	1	1	9-1	18	2.66	150	.273	.340	1	.000	-0		4		0.2
1995	LA N	1	3	.250	37	0	0	3-1	34.2	39	27	5	1	18-3	29	6.75	57	.285	.372	1	.000	-0		-11	19	-1.5
1998	†Atl N	4	1	.800	34	0	0	2-2	36	25	13	2	1	16-0	50	2.75	151	.195	.286	1	.000	-0		5		0.5
1999	Atl N	6	1	.857	56	0	0	3-5	53.2	47	21	3	1	21-1	41	3.35	133	.234	.307	1	.000	-0		7	44	0.5
2000	Atl N	2	4	.333	23	0	0	2-1	21	15	11	3	1	9-1	20	4.29	105	.192	.284	0	—	0		2	132	0.1
2001	SD N	0	2	.000	26	0	0	1-2	24	15	8	3	1	15-0	24	2.63	158	.176	.304	0	—	0		4	15	0.3
	†Atl N	0	0	—	12	0	0	0-0	12	8	4	1	0	4-0	17	3.00	144	.182	.250	0	—	0		2		0.2
	Year	0	2	.000	38	0	0	1-2	36	23	12	4	1	19-0	41	2.75	153	.178	.287	0	—	0		6		0.5
2002	Tex A	1	3	.250	33	0	0	0-4	33	28	25	5	0	24-1	40	5.73	84	.230	.354	0	—	0		-4	95	-0.7
2003	Bos A	0	1	.000	9	0	0	0-1	8.2	11	7	2	0	6-1	9	6.23	75	.297	.386	0	—	0		-2		-0.3
2004	KC A	1	1	.500	16	0	0	0-0	23	21	10	0	0	11-2	21	3.91	119	.244	.320	0	—	0		4		0.2
	Fla N	3	1	.750	23	0	0	0-1	23	18	7	3	0	8-1	25	2.74	150	.212	.280	0	—	0		4	35	0.3
2005	†SD N	7	1	.875	57	0	0	0-2	60.1	49	19	4	2	22-4	84	2.69	144	.222	.297	0	.000	-0		9	676	1.2
Total	14	27	20	.574	380	0	0	11-22	393.2	341	196	38	9	201-17	417	4.12	102	.232	.325	4	.000	-0		6		0.2

SEARAGE, RAY Raymond Mark B5.1.1955 Freeport NY BL/TL/6-1/180(180-201) [StLN76 22/518] d6.11 Col West Liberty St.

YEAR	TM LG	W	L	PCT	G	GS	CG-SHO	SV-BS	IP	H	R	HR	HB	BB-IB	SO	ERA	AERA	OAV	OOB	AB-HR-SH	AVG	PB	SUP	APR	DL	PW
1981	NY N	1	0	1.000	26	0	0	1-0	36.2	34	16	2	0	17-3	16	3.68	96	.252	.331	1	1.000	0		0		0.0
1984	Mil A	2	1	.667	21	0	0	6-1	38.1	20	3	0	1	16-3	29	0.70	553	.155	.253	0	—	0		14		1.1
1985	Mil A	1	4	.200	33	0	0	1-2	38	54	27	2	0	24-4	36	5.92	71	.338	.422	0	—	0		-7		-0.9
1986	Mil A	0	1	.000	17	0	0	1-1	22	29	17	6	1	9-1	10	6.95	63	.315	.382	0	—	0		-5		-0.6
	Chi A	1	0	1.000	29	0	0	0-0	29	15	3	1	0	19-3	26	0.62	700	.156	.291	0	—	0		11		0.9
	Year	1	1	.500	46	0	0	1-1	51	44	20	7	1	28-4	36	3.35	130	.234	.333	0	—	0		6		0.3
1987	Chi A	2	3	.400	58	0	0	2-3	55.2	56	28	9	1	24-3	33	3.53	97	.225	.313	0	—	0		0	38	0.0
1989	LA N	3	4	.429	41	0	0	0-1	35.2	29	15	1	0	18-6	24	3.53	97	.225	.313	2	.000	-0		0	79	0.0
1990	LA N	1	0	1.000	29	0	0	0-0	32.1	30	11	1	0	10-0	19	2.78	132	.250	.299	0	—	0		4	79	0.3
Total	7	11	13	.458	254	0	0	11-8	287.2	267	120	22	3	137-23	193	3.50	115	.249	.332	3	.333	0		20	117	1.3

SEARCY, STEVE William Steven B6.4.1964 Knoxville TN BL/TL/6-1/185* [DetA85 3/80] d8.29 Col Tennessee

YEAR	TM LG	W	L	PCT	G	GS	CG-SHO	SV-BS	IP	H	R	HR	HB	BB-IB	SO	ERA	AERA	OAV	OOB	AB-HR-SH	AVG	PB	SUP	APR	DL	PW
1988	Det A	0	2	.000	2	2	0	0-0	8	8	5	3	0	5-0	6	5.63	68	.242	.324		—	0	59	-2		-0.2
1989	Det A	1	1	.500	8	2	0	0-1	22.1	27	16	3	0	12-1	11	6.04	63	.307	.390		—	0	189	-5	32	-0.6
1990	Det A	2	7	.222	16	12	1	0	75.1	76	44	9	0	51-3	66	4.66	85	.270	.375	0	—	0	55	-6		-0.7
1991	Det A	1	2	.333	16	5	0	0-0	40.2	52	40	8	0	30-0	32	8.41	50	.313	.412		—	0	101	-18		-1.8
	Phi N	2	1	.667	18	0	0	0-0	30.1	29	16	2	0	14-1	21	4.15	89	.252	.328	4	.000	-0		-2		-0.2

YEAR	TM LG	W	L	PCT	G	GS	CG-SHO	SV-BS	IP	H	R	HR	HB	BB-IB	SO	ERA	AERA	OAV	OOB	AB-HR-SH	AVG	PB	SUP	APR	DL	PW
1992	Phi N	0	0	—	10	0	0	0-0	10.1	13	9	0	0	8-0	5	6.10	58	.325	.429	0	—	0		-4		-0.2
Total	5	6	13	.316	70	21	1	0-1	187	205	131	25	0	119-5	140	5.68	69	.283	.379	4	.000	-0	80	-37	32	-3.0

SEATON, TOM Thomas Gordon B8.30.1887 Blair NE D4.10.1940 ElPaso TX BB/TR/6-0/175 d4.13

YEAR	TM LG	W	L	PCT	G	GS	CG-SHO	SV-BS	IP	H	R	HR	HB	BB-IB	SO	ERA	AERA	OAV	OOB	AB-HR-SH	AVG	PB	SUP	APR	DL	PW
1912	Phi N	16	12	.571	44	27	16-2	2	255	246	126	8	9	106	118	3.28	111	.261	.342	83-0-4	.217	-0	95	11		0.9
1913	Phi N	27	12	.692	52	35	21-5	1	322.1	262	117	6	10	136	168	2.60	128	.226	.313	110-1-3	.109	-5	114	25		2.3
1914	Bro F	25	14	.641	44	38	26-7	2	302.2	299	130	6	13	102	172	3.03	95	.259	.326	107-1-1	.206	2	100	-4		-0.2
1915	Bro F	11	11	.500	32	24	13	3	189.1	199	123	6	3	99	86	4.42	62	.273	.362	66-1-8	.242	3*	145	-36		-3.5
	New F	2	6	.250	12	10	7	1	75	61	26	1	2	21	28	2.28	112	.224	.285	26-1-0	.154	-0	98	3		0.3
	Year	13	17	.433	44	34	20	4	264.1	260	149	7	5	120	114	3.81	70	.260	.342	92-2-8	.217	3	132	-35		-3.2
1916	Chi N	6	6	.500	31	12	4	1	121	108	54	3	4	43	45	3.27	89	.246	.319	38-0-1	.184	0	122	-3		-0.3
1917	Chi N	5	4	.556	16	9	3-1	1	74.2	60	30	0	1	23	27	2.53	115	.227	.292	21-0-1	.238	1	92	3		0.5
Total	8	92	65	.586	231	155	90-15	11	1340	1235	606	30	42	530	644	3.12	99	.249	.327	451-4-18	.186	0	109	-1		-0.0

SEATS, TOM Thomas Edward B9.24.1910 Farmington NC D5.10.1992 San Ramon CA BR/TL(BB 1940)/5-11/190 d5.4

YEAR	TM LG	W	L	PCT	G	GS	CG-SHO	SV-BS	IP	H	R	HR	HB	BB-IB	SO	ERA	AERA	OAV	OOB	AB-HR-SH	AVG	PB	SUP	APR	DL	PW
1940	Det A	2	2	.500	26	2	0	1	55.2	67	43	4	0	21	25	4.69	101	.290	.349	12	.083	-1	129	-3		-0.3
1945	Bro N	10	7	.588	31	18	6-2	0	121.2	127	71	8	5	37	44	4.36	86	.261	.320	43-0-4	.209	0	135	-7		-0.8
Total	2	12	9	.571	57	20	6-2	1	177.1	194	114	12	5	58	69	4.47	91	.271	.329	55-0-4	.182	-1	129	-10		-1.1

SEAVER, TOM George Thomas "Tom Terrific" B11.17.1944 Fresno CA BR/TR/6-1/206(195-210) d4.13 HF1992 Col USC

YEAR	TM LG	W	L	PCT	G	GS	CG-SHO	SV-BS	IP	H	R	HR	HB	BB-IB	SO	ERA	AERA	OAV	OOB	AB-HR-SH	AVG	PB	SUP	APR	DL	PW
1967	NY N★	16	13	.552	35	34	18-2	0-0	251	224	85	19	2	78-6	170	2.76	123	.241	.301	77-0-6	.143	2*	94	18		2.4
1968	NY N★	16	12	.571	36	35	14-5	1	278	224	73	15	8	48-5	205	2.20	137	.222	.261	95-0-3	.158	0*	76	26		3.1
1969	†NY N☆	25	7	.781	36	35	18-5	0-0	273.1	202	75	24	7	82-9	208	2.21	166	.207	.272	91-0-4	.121	-0*	102	43		5.3
1970	NY N★	18	12	.600	37	36	19-2	0-0	290.2	230	103	21	4	83-8	283	2.82	144	.214	.272	95-1-7	.179	4*	87	40		4.4
1971	NY N☆	20	10	.667	36	35	21-4	0-1	286.1	210	61	18	4	61-2	289	1.76	195	.206	.252	92-1-11	.196	4*	103	55		6.7
1972	NY N☆	21	12	.636	35	35	13-3	0-0	262	215	92	23	5	77-2	249	2.92	126	.224	.284	89-3-6	.146	4*	80	16		2.5
1973	†NY N	19	10	.655	36	36	18-3	0-0	290	219	74	23	4	64-5	251	2.08	175	.206	.252	93-1-9	.161	2*	95	51		5.5
1974	NY N	11	11	.500	32	32	12-5	0-0	236	199	89	19	3	75-10	201	3.20	113	.230	.293	71-0-7	.099	-2	91	14		1.2
1975	NY N★	22	9	.710	36	36	15-5	0-0	280.1	217	81	11	4	88-6	243	2.38	148	.214	.279	90-0-7	.179	2*	104	38		4.6
1976	NY N★	14	11	.560	35	34	13-5	0-0	271	211	83	14	4	77-9	235	2.59	129	.213	.272	82-0-9	.085	-2	92	26		2.3
1977	NY N	7	3	.700	13	13	5-3	0-0	96	79	33	7	0	28-3	72	3.00	127	.221	.275	31-0-2	.161	-0	96	10		1.0
	Cin N★	14	3	.824	20	20	14-4	0-0	165.1	120	45	12	0	38-3	124	2.34	168	.201	.248	55-3-11	.218	4	113	30		3.4
	Year	21	6	.778	33	33	19-7	0-0	261.1	199	78	19	0	66-6	196	2.58	150	.209	.258	86-3-13	.198	4	106	40		4.4
1978	Cin N☆	16	14	.533	36	36	8-1	0-0	259.2	218	97	26	0	89-11	226	2.88	124	.227	.289	74-0-13	.122	-0	100	18		1.9
1979	†Cin N	16	6	.727	32	32	9-5	0-0	215	187	85	16	0	61-6	131	3.14	118	.236	.289	76-2-4	.158	2*	116	13		1.4
1980	Cin N	10	8	.556	26	26	5-1	0-0	168	140	74	24	1	59-3	101	3.64	97	.225	.290	40-1-6	.130	1	113	-3		-0.1
1981	Cin N★	14	2	.875	23	23	6-1	0-0	166.1	120	51	10	3	66-8	87	2.54	138	.205	.285	55-1-4	.200	4	127	18	34	2.2
1982	Cin N	5	13	.278	21	21	0	0-0	111.1	136	75	14	3	44-4	62	5.50	67	.302	.367	34-0-5	.176	1*	79	-22		-3.1
1983	NY N	9	14	.391	34	34	5-2	0-0	231	201	104	18	4	86-5	135	3.55	104	.235	.305	64-0-6	.156	2	87	3		0.5
1984	Chi A	15	11	.577	34	33	10-4	0-0	236.2	216	108	27	4	61-3	131	3.95	106	.240	.288	0	—	0	100	8		0.9
1985	Chi A	16	11	.593	35	33	6-1	0-0	238.2	223	103	22	8	69-6	134	3.17	137	.248	.304	0	—	0	85	25		2.8
1986	Chi A	2	6	.250	12	12	1	0-0	72	66	37	9	2	27-1	31	4.38	99	.242	.319	0	—	0	64	1	17	0.0
	Bos A	5	7	.417	16	16	1	0-0	104.1	114	46	8	2	29-1	72	3.80	111	.278	.326	0	—	0	88	6		0.6
	Year	7	13	.350	28	28	2	0-0	176.1	180	83	17	4	56-2	103	4.03	106	.264	.323	0	—	0	78	7		0.6
Total	20	311	205	.603	656	647	231-61	1-1	4783	3971	1674	380	76	1390-116	3640	2.86	128	.226	.283	1315-12-121	.154	27	96	434	51	49.5

SEAY, BOBBY Robert Michael B6.20.1978 Sarasota FL BL/TL/6-2/221(190-235) d8.14 [DL 2002 TB A 64]

YEAR	TM LG	W	L	PCT	G	GS	CG-SHO	SV-BS	IP	H	R	HR	HB	BB-IB	SO	ERA	AERA	OAV	OOB	AB-HR-SH	AVG	PB	SUP	APR	DL	PW
2001	TB A	1	1	.500	12	0	0	0-0	13	13	11	3	1	5-1	12	6.23	72	.260	.339	0	—	0		-3		-0.4
2003	TB A	0	0	—	12	0	0	0-1	9	7	3	0	0	6-0	5	3.00	153	.226	.333	0	—	0		2	40	0.1
2004	TB A	0	0	—	21	0	0	0-0	22.2	21	6	2	2	5-1	17	2.38	196	.239	.295	0	—	0		6		0.3
2005	Col N	0	0	—	17	0	0	0-1	11.2	18	11	3	0	8-1	11	8.49	56	.367	.456	0	—	0		-4	49	-0.2
Total	4	1	1	.500	62	0	0	0-2	56.1	59	31	8	3	24-3	45	4.63	100	.271	.348	0	—	0		1	153	-0.2

SEBRA, BOB Robert Bush B12.11.1961 Ridgewood NJ BR/TR/6-2/200(185-200) [TexA83 5/109] d6.26 Col Nebraska

YEAR	TM LG	W	L	PCT	G	GS	CG-SHO	SV-BS	IP	H	R	HR	HB	BB-IB	SO	ERA	AERA	OAV	OOB	AB-HR-SH	AVG	PB	SUP	APR	DL	PW
1985	Tex A	0	2	.000	7	4	0	0-0	20.1	26	17	4	1	14-2	13	7.52	57	.306	.402	0	—	0	48	-6		-0.6
1986	Mon N	5	5	.500	17	13	3-1	0-0	91.1	82	39	9	3	25-2	66	3.55	106	.239	.294	29	.207	1*	84	3		0.3
1987	Mon N	6	15	.286	36	27	4-1	0-0	177.1	184	99	15	3	67-0	156	4.42	97	.272	.337	51-0-4	.157	-0	71	-3		-0.3
1988	Phi N	1	2	.333	3	3	0	0-0	11.1	15	11	0	0	10-0	7	7.94	45	.333	.417	5	.000	-0	115	-5		-1.0
1989	Phi N	2	3	.400	6	5	0	0-0	34.1	41	20	6	4	10-2	21	4.46	81	.295	.357	10-0-1	.000	-0	79	-4		-0.5
	Cin N	0	0	—	15	0	0	1-0	21	24	16	2	3	18-1	14	6.43	56	.296	.433	1	.000	-0		-6		-0.3
	Year	2	3	.400	21	5	0	1-0	55.1	65	36	8	7	28-3	35	5.20	69	.295	.388	11-0-1	.000	-1	79	-10		-0.8
1990	Mil A	1	2	.333	10	0	0	0-0	11	20	10	1	1	5-1	4	8.18	48	.408	.456	0	—	0		-5		-0.9
Total	6	15	29	.341	94	52	7-2	1-0	366.2	392	212	37	15	149-8	281	4.71	85	.276	.347	96-0-5	.146	0	76	-26		-3.3

SECHRIST, DOC Theodore O'Hara B2.10.1876 Williamstown KY D4.2.1950 Louisville KY BR/TR/5-9/160 d4.28

YEAR	TM LG	W	L	PCT	G	GS	CG-SHO	SV-BS	IP	H	R	HR	HB	BB-IB	SO	ERA	AERA	OAV	OOB	AB-HR-SH	AVG	PB	SUP	APR	DL	PW
1899	NY N	0	0	—	2	0	0		2	0	0	0	1	2	0		—	—	1.000	0	—	0				0.0

SECRIST, DON Donald Laverne B2.26.1944 Seattle WA BL/TL/6-2/195* d4.11 Col Bradley

YEAR	TM LG	W	L	PCT	G	GS	CG-SHO	SV-BS	IP	H	R	HR	HB	BB-IB	SO	ERA	AERA	OAV	OOB	AB-HR-SH	AVG	PB	SUP	APR	DL	PW
1969	Chi A	0	1	.000	19	0	0	0-0	40	35	28	7	1	14-2	23	6.07	63	.227	.296	7	.143	0		-9	25	-0.4
1970	Chi A	0	0	—	9	0	0	0-0	14.2	19	9	2	0	12-0	9	5.52	70	.333	.437	0	—	0		-2		-0.1
Total	2	0	1	.000	28	0	0	0-0	54.2	54	37	9	1	26-2	32	5.93	65	.256	.338	7	.143	0		-11	25	-0.5

SEDGWICK, DUKE Henry Kenneth B6.1.1898 Martins Ferry OH D12.4.1982 Clearwater FL BR/TR/6-0/175 d7.12

YEAR	TM LG	W	L	PCT	G	GS	CG-SHO	SV-BS	IP	H	R	HR	HB	BB-IB	SO	ERA	AERA	OAV	OOB	AB-HR-SH	AVG	PB	SUP	APR	DL	PW
1921	Phi N	1	3	.250	16	5	1	0	71.1	81	48	3	4	32	21	4.92	86	.283	.363	24	.208	-1	82	-3		-0.3
1923	Was A	0	1	.000	5	2	1	0	16	27	17	1	0	6	4	7.88	48	.415	.465	5	.000	-1	99	-8		-0.4
Total	2	1	4	.200	21	7	2	0	87.1	108	65	4	4	38	25	5.46	76	.308	.382	29	.172	-2	85	-11		-0.7

SEDLACEK, SHAWN Shawn Patrick B6.29.1977 Cedar Rapids IA BR/TR/6-4/200 [KCA98 14/407] d6.18 Col Iowa St.

YEAR	TM LG	W	L	PCT	G	GS	CG-SHO	SV-BS	IP	H	R	HR	HB	BB-IB	SO	ERA	AERA	OAV	OOB	AB-HR-SH	AVG	PB	SUP	APR	DL	PW
2002	KC A	3	5	.375	16	14	0	0-0	84.1	99	64	16	6	36-2	52	6.72	74	.303	.375	6	.000	-1	90	-13		-1.1

SEELBACH, CHUCK Charles Frederick B3.20.1948 Lakewood OH BR/TR/6-0/180* [DetA70 S1/12] d6.29 Col Dartmouth

YEAR	TM LG	W	L	PCT	G	GS	CG-SHO	SV-BS	IP	H	R	HR	HB	BB-IB	SO	ERA	AERA	OAV	OOB	AB-HR-SH	AVG	PB	SUP	APR	DL	PW
1971	Det A	0	0	—	4	6	0	2	4	6	6	2	1	7-0	1	13.50	27	.375	.583	0	—	0		-4		-0.2
1972	†Det A	9	8	.529	61	3	0	14-3	112	96	39	6	3	39-4	76	2.89	110	.238	.308	21-0-1	.143	1	74	4		0.9
1973	Det A	1	0	1.000	5	0	0	0-0	7	7	3	1	0	2-1	2	3.86	106	.250	.300	0	—	0		0	53	0.1
1974	Det A	0	0	—	4	0	0	0-0	7.2	9	4	2	1	3-0	0	4.70	82	.300	.382	0	—	0		0		0.0
Total	4	10	8	.556	75	3	0	14-3	130.2	118	52	11	5	51-5	79	3.38	97	.247	.325	21-0-1	.143	1	74	0	53	0.8

SEELBACH, CHRIS Christopher Don B12.18.1972 Lufkin TX BR/TR/6-4/180* [AtlN91 4/101] d9.9

YEAR	TM LG	W	L	PCT	G	GS	CG-SHO	SV-BS	IP	H	R	HR	HB	BB-IB	SO	ERA	AERA	OAV	OOB	AB-HR-SH	AVG	PB	SUP	APR	DL	PW
2000	Atl N	0	1	.000	2	0	0	0-0	1.2	3	2	1	0	0-0	1	10.80	42	.500	.429	0	—	0		-1		-0.2
2001	Atl N	0	0	—	5	0	0	0-0	8	9	7	3	0	5-1	8	7.88	55	.273	.368	0	—	0		-3		-0.1
Total	2	0	1	.000	7	0	0	0-0	9.2	12	9	4	0	5-1	9	8.38	52	.308	.378	0	—	0		-4		-0.3

SEGELKE, HERMAN Herman Neils B4.24.1958 San Mateo CA BR/TR/6-4/200 [ChiN76 1/7] d4.7

YEAR	TM LG	W	L	PCT	G	GS	CG-SHO	SV-BS	IP	H	R	HR	HB	BB-IB	SO	ERA	AERA	OAV	OOB	AB-HR-SH	AVG	PB	SUP	APR	DL	PW
1982	Chi N	0	0	—	3	0	0	0-0	4.1	6	4	1	0	6-0	1	8.31	46	.316	.480	0	—	0		-2		-0.1

SEGUI, DIEGO Diego Pablo (Gonzalez) B8.17.1937 Holguin, Cuba BR/TR/6-0/190* d4.12 s-David

YEAR	TM LG	W	L	PCT	G	GS	CG-SHO	SV-BS	IP	H	R	HR	HB	BB-IB	SO	ERA	AERA	OAV	OOB	AB-HR-SH	AVG	PB	SUP	APR	DL	PW
1962	KC A	8	5	.615	37	13	2	6	116.2	89	53	16	1	46-2	71	3.86	109	.211	.288	34-1-1	.235	2	106	5		0.8
1963	KC A	9	6	.600	38	23	4-1	0	167	173	84	17	2	73-7	116	3.77	103	.267	.341	55-0-4	.218	1	95	0		0.1
1964	KC A	8	17	.320	40	35	5-2	0	217	219	118	30	1	94-3	155	4.56	84	.260	.333	71-1-3	.155	0	89	-16		-1.6
1965	KC A	5	15	.250	40	25	5-1	0	163	166	102	18	2	67-3	119	4.64	75	.261	.331	47-1-4	.191	2*	94	-24		-2.5
1966	Was A	3	7	.300	21	13	1-1	0	72	82	42	8	0	24-1	54	5.00	69	.291	.345	18	.111	-1	61	-11		-1.5
1967	KC A	3	4	.429	36	3	0	1	70	62	30	4	2	31-5	52	3.09	103	.238	.323	0	.000	-0	27	-1		-0.2
1968	Oak A	6	5	.545	52	0	0	6	83	51	25	7	0	32-8	72	2.39	118	.173	.254	9	.111	0		4		0.6
1969	Sea A	12	6	.667	66	8	0	12-3	142.1	127	62	14	2	61-9	113	3.35	109	.238	.331	27-0-3	.148	-0	106	4		0.5
1970	Oak A	10	10	.500	47	19	3-2	2-0	162	130	54	9	2	68-4	95	2.56	138	.222	.303	43-0-6	.116	-2	100	17		1.8
1971	†Oak A	10	8	.556	26	21	5	0-0	146.1	122	59	13	4	63-4	81	3.14	106	.229	.315	47-1-1	.085	-1	107	3		0.1
1972	Oak A	0	1	.000	7	3	0	0-0	22.2	25	10	2	0	7-1	11	3.57	80	.287	.340	7	.143	-0	155	-2		-0.2
	StL N	3	1	.750	33	0	0	9-2	55.2	47	21	3	0	32-10	54	3.07	112	.229	.332	7	.143	-0		2		0.2

YEAR	TM LG	W	L	PCT	G	GS	CG-SHO	SV-BS	IP	H	R	HR	HB	BB-IB	SO	ERA	AERA	OAV	OOB	AB-HR-SH	AVG	PB	SUP	APR	DL	PW
1973	StL N	7	6	.538	65	0	0	17-6	100.1	78	35	6	0	53-12	93	2.78	132	.211	.310	10	.000	-1		10		1.5
1974	Bos A	6	8	.429	58	0	0	10-6	108	106	54	9	1	49-10	76	4.00	96	.257	.334	0	—	0		-2		-0.4
1975	†Bos A	2	5	.286	33	1	1	6-1	71	71	41	10	0	43-3	45	4.82	84	.270	.373	0	—	0	0	-5		-0.6
1977	Sea A	0	7	.000	40	7	0	2-0	110.2	108	75	20	1	43-4	91	5.69	73	.251	.319	0	—	0	56	-18		-1.1
Total	15	92	111	.453	639	171	28-7	71-18	1807.2	1656	867	185	18	786-86	1298	3.81	96	.243	.322	384-4-22	.151	-1	92	-34		-2.5

SEGURA, JOSE Jose Altagracia (Mota) B1.26.1963 Fundacion, D.R. BR/TR/5-11/180* d4.10

YEAR	TM LG	W	L	PCT	G	GS	CG-SHO	SV-BS	IP	H	R	HR	HB	BB-IB	SO	ERA	AERA	OAV	OOB	AB-HR-SH	AVG	PB	SUP	APR	DL	PW
1988	Chi A	0	0	—	4	0	0	0-0	8.2	19	17	1	0	8-0	2	13.50	30	.432	.519	0	—	0		-10		-0.5
1989	Chi A	0	1	.000	7	0	0	0-1	6	13	11	2	0	3-1	4	15.00	26	.464	.500	0	—	0		-7		-1.0
1991	SF N	0	1	.000	11	0	0	0-1	16.1	20	11	1	0	5-0	10	4.41	82	.303	.352	0	—	0		-3		-0.2
Total	3	0	2	.000	22	0	0	0-2	31	52	39	4	0	16-1	16	9.00	42	.377	.439	0	—	0		-20		-1.7

SEIBEL, PHIL Philip Matthew B1.28.1979 Louisville KY BL/TL/6-1/195 [MonN00 8/225] d4.15 Col Texas

YEAR	TM LG	W	L	PCT	G	GS	CG-SHO	SV-BS	IP	H	R	HR	HB	BB-IB	SO	ERA	AERA	OAV	OOB	AB-HR-SH	AVG	PB	SUP	APR	DL	PW
2004	Bos A	0	0	—	2	0	0	0-0	3.2	0	0	0	0	5-0	1	0.00	—	.000	.333	0	—	0		2		0.1

SEIBOLD, SOCKS Harry B5.31.1896 Philadelphia PA D9.21.1965 Philadelphia PA BR/TR/5-8.5/162 d9.18.1915 Mil 1918 ▲

YEAR	TM LG	W	L	PCT	G	GS	CG-SHO	SV-BS	IP	H	R	HR	HB	BB-IB	SO	ERA	AERA	OAV	OOB	AB-HR-SH	AVG	PB	SUP	APR	DL	PW
1916	Phi A	1	1	.500	3	2	1-1	0	21.2	22	12	0	0	9	5	4.15	69	.272	.344	12	.167	-0*	106	-3		-0.2
1917	Phi A	4	16	.200	33	15	9-1	1	160	141	86	1	3	85	55	3.94	70	.243	.343	59-0-5	.220	2*	84	-16		-1.0
1919	Phi A	2	3	.400	14	4	1	0	45.2	58	34	2	4	26	19	5.32	64	.322	.419	13-0-2	.154	-1*	34	-9		-1.0
1929	Bos N	12	17	.414	33	27	16-1	1	205.2	228	119	17	2	80	54	4.73	99	.285	.352	70-0-2	.286	4	84	0		0.5
1930	Bos N	15	16	.484	36	33	20-1	2	251	288	135	16	2	85	70	4.12	120	.290	.348	90-1-1	.211	0	73	20		2.0
1931	Bos N	10	18	.357	33	29	10-3	0	206.1	226	122	12	3	65	50	4.67	81	.279	.335	70-0-6	.129	-4	73	-21		-2.8
1932	Bos N	3	10	.231	28	20	6-1	0	136.2	173	91	12	2	41	33	4.68	80	.309	.358	46-0-2	.152	-2	103	-17		-1.5
1933	Bos N	1	4	.200	11	5	1	0	36.2	43	18	0	0	14	10	3.68	83	.295	.356	9	.111	-0	87	-3		-0.4
Total	8	48	85	.361	191	135	64-8	5	1063.2	1179	617	60	16	405	296	4.43	91	.284	.350	369-1-18	.198	-0	81	-49		-5.3

SELE, AARON Aaron Helmer B6.25.1970 Golden Valley MN BR/TR/6-5/215(215-230) [BosA91 1/23] d6.23 Col Washington St.

YEAR	TM LG	W	L	PCT	G	GS	CG-SHO	SV-BS	IP	H	R	HR	HB	BB-IB	SO	ERA	AERA	OAV	OOB	AB-HR-SH	AVG	PB	SUP	APR	DL	PW
1993	Bos A	7	2	.778	18	18	0	0-0	111.2	100	42	5	7	48-2	93	2.74	169	.237	.322	0	—	0	94	21		1.4
1994	Bos A	8	7	.533	22	22	2	0-0	143.1	140	68	13	9	60-2	105	3.83	132	.261	.342	0	—	0	94	18		1.6
1995	Bos A	3	1	.750	6	6	0	0-0	32.1	32	14	3	3	14-0	21	3.06	159	.252	.338	0	—	0	100	4	131	0.5
1996	Bos A	7	11	.389	29	29	1	0-0	157.1	192	110	14	8	67-2	137	5.32	96	.303	.373	0	—	-0	100	-14	18	-1.6
1997	Bos A	13	12	.520	33	33	1	0-0	177.1	196	115	25	15	80-4	122	5.38	87	.279	.361	2	.000	-0	119	12		1.1
1998	†Tex ☆	19	11	.633	33	33	3-2	0-0	212.2	239	116	14	13	84-6	167	4.23	116	.283	.354	4	.250	0	112	9		1.0
1999	†Tex A	18	9	.667	33	33	2-2	0-0	205	244	116	21	12	70-3	186	4.79	108	.293	.355	4-0-1	.000	0	125	9		1.0
2000	†Sea A★	17	10	.630	34	34	2-2	0-0	211.2	221	110	17	5	74-7	137	4.51	107	.271	.332	3-0-1	.167	0	130	17		1.2
2001	†Sea A	15	5	.750	34	33	2-1	0-0	215	216	93	25	7	51-2	114	3.60	118	.261	.301	6-0-2	.167	0	106	-6	39	-0.7
2002	Ana A	8	9	.471	26	26	1-1	0-0	160	190	92	21	7	49-2	82	4.89	92	.299	.351	2	.500	0	98	-18	40	-2.2
2003	Ana A	7	11	.389	25	25	0	0-0	121.2	135	82	17	12	58-1	53	5.77	76	.284	.372	3	.333	0	119	-11	15	-1.1
2004	Ana A	9	4	.692	28	24	0	0-0	132	163	84	16	5	51-2	51	5.05	89	.310	.371	1	.000	-0	85	-19		-2.5
2005	Sea A	6	12	.333	21	21	1-1	0-0	116	147	76	18	5	41-2	53	5.66	74	.315	.370	3-0-1	.000	0	108	17	243	-0.3
Total	13	137	104	.568	342	337	15-9	0-0	1996	2215	1117	209	108	747-35	1321	4.59	102	.282	.349	28-0-5	.143	0	108	17	243	-0.3

SELL, EPP Lester Elwood B4.26.1897 Llewellyn PA D2.19.1961 Reading PA BR/TR/6-0/175 d9.1

YEAR	TM LG	W	L	PCT	G	GS	CG-SHO	SV-BS	IP	H	R	HR	HB	BB-IB	SO	ERA	AERA	OAV	OOB	AB-HR-SH	AVG	PB	SUP	APR	DL	PW
1922	StL N	4	2	.667	7	5	0	0	33	47	26	2	2	6	5	6.82	57	.338	.374	12-0-2	.333	1	139	-10		-1.2
1923	StL N	0	1	.000	5	1	0	0	15	16	10	1	0	8	2	6.00	65	.291	.381	7	.000	-1	189	-3		-0.3
Total	2	4	3	.571	12	6	0	0	48	63	36	3	2	14	7	6.56	59	.325	.376	19-0-2	.211	0	147	-13		-1.5

SELLERS, JEFF Jeffrey Doyle B5.11.1964 Compton CA BR/TR/6-1/175(175-195) [BosA82 8/202] d9.15

YEAR	TM LG	W	L	PCT	G	GS	CG-SHO	SV-BS	IP	H	R	HR	HB	BB-IB	SO	ERA	AERA	OAV	OOB	AB-HR-SH	AVG	PB	SUP	APR	DL	PW
1985	Bos A	2	0	1.000	4	4	1	0-0	22.1	24	10	1	0	7-1	6	3.63	119	.273	.323	0	—	0	121	2		0.1
1986	Bos A	3	7	.300	14	13	1	0-0	82	90	56	13	3	40-1	51	4.94	85	.282	.365	0	—	0	100	-9		-0.8
1987	Bos A	7	8	.467	25	22	4-2	0-0	139.2	161	85	10	3	61-0	99	5.28	87	.298	.368	0	—	0	68	-6	63	-0.9
1988	Bos A	1	7	.125	18	12	1	0-0	85.2	89	49	9	3	56-3	70	4.83	85	.268	.379	0	—	0	92	-22	63	-2.2
Total	4	13	22	.371	61	51	7-2	0-0	329.2	364	200	33	9	164-5	226	4.97	88	.285	.367	0	—	0	92	-22	63	-2.2

SELLMAN, FRANK Charles Francis (aka Frank C. Williams 1871-75) B1852 Baltimore MD D5.6.1907 Baltimore MD d5.4.1871 ▲

YEAR	TM LG	W	L	PCT	G	GS	CG-SHO	SV-BS	IP	H	R	HR	HB	BB-IB	SO	ERA	AERA	OAV	OOB	AB-HR-SH	AVG	PB	SUP	APR	DL	PW
1873	Mar NA	0	1	.000	1	1	1	0	9	21	26	0	0	0	0	8.00	40	.350	.350	3	.333	0	55	-5		-0.3

SELLS, DAVE David Wayne B9.18.1946 Vacaville CA BR/TR/5-11/175* d8.2 Col Solano (CA) CC

YEAR	TM LG	W	L	PCT	G	GS	CG-SHO	SV-BS	IP	H	R	HR	HB	BB-IB	SO	ERA	AERA	OAV	OOB	AB-HR-SH	AVG	PB	SUP	APR	DL	PW
1972	Cal A	2	0	1.000	10	0	0	0-0	16	11	6	0	0	5-1	—	2.81	104	.196	.258	0	—	0	0	0		0.0
1973	Cal A	7	2	.778	51	0	0	10-3	68	72	30	2	5	35-6	25	3.71	97	.277	.368	0	—	0	0	0		0.0
1974	Cal A	2	3	.400	20	0	0	2-0	39	48	19	3	3	16-0	14	3.69	94	.312	.383	0	—	0		-1		-0.1
1975	Cal A	0	0	—	4	0	0	0-1	8.1	9	10	3	0	8-1	7	8.64	41	.250	.386	0	—	0		-5		-0.1
	LA N	0	2	.000	5	0	0	0-1	7	6	3	2	0	3-0	1	3.86	89	.222	.300	1	1.000	1		0		0.0
Total	4	11	7	.611	90	0	0	12-5	138.1	146	68	10	8	67-8	49	3.90	89	.274	.359	1	1.000	1		-6		-0.1

SELMA, DICK Richard Jay B11.4.1943 Santa Ana CA D8.29.2001 Clovis CA BR/TR/5-11/175(162-185) d9.2 Col Fresno (CA) City

YEAR	TM LG	W	L	PCT	G	GS	CG-SHO	SV-BS	IP	H	R	HR	HB	BB-IB	SO	ERA	AERA	OAV	OOB	AB-HR-SH	AVG	PB	SUP	APR	DL	PW
1965	NY N	2	1	.667	4	4	1-1	0	26.2	22	11	2	1	9-0	26	3.71	95	.229	.302	9	.222	0*	105	0		0.1
1966	NY N	4	6	.400	30	7	0	1	80.2	84	47	11	3	39-5	58	4.24	86	.274	.358	14-0-1	.071	0*	80	-7		-0.7
1967	NY N	2	4	.333	38	4	0	2	81.1	71	29	3	2	36-6	52	2.77	122	.241	.326	22-0-1	.091	-1*	91	5		0.3
1968	NY N	9	10	.474	33	23	4-3	0	170.1	148	63	11	5	54-5	117	2.75	110	.233	.297	58-0-4	.207	2*	102	3		0.6
1969	SD N	2	2	.500	4	3	1	0-0	22	19	10	3	0	9-0	20	4.09	87	.229	.304	7-0-1	.286	-0	50	-1		-0.1
	Chi N	10	8	.556	36	25	4-2	1-1	168.2	137	74	13	3	72-7	161	3.63	111	.222	.305	52-0-7	.154	-0	127	8		0.7
	Year	12	10	.545	40	28	5-2	1-1	190.2	156	84	16	3	81-7	181	3.68	108	.223	.305	59-0-8	.169	-0	120	7		0.5
1970	Phi N	8	9	.471	73	0	0	22-11	134.1	108	42	8	4	59-9	153	2.75	147	.226	.315	20-0-1	.150	0		20		3.2
1971	Phi N	0	2	.000	17	0	0	1-0	24.2	21	9	2	2	8-0	15	3.28	108	.231	.307	1	1.000	0*	1		79	0.0
1972	Phi N	2	9	.182	46	10	1	3-0	98.2	91	67	13	5	73-9	58	5.56	65	.249	.375	20-0-1	.200	1*	59	-20		-2.2
1973	Phi N	1	1	.500	6	0	0	0-0	8	6	5	1	0	5-1	4	5.09	68	.240	.355	0	—	0		-3		-0.2
1974	Cal A	2	2	.500	18	0	0	1-3	23	22	13	2	1	17-2	15	5.09	68	.272	.404	0	—	0		-4		-0.2
	Mil A	0	0	—	2	0	0	0-0	2.1	5	5	0	1	0-0	2	19.29	19	.455	.462	0	—	0		-8		-0.7
	Year	2	2	.500	20	0	0	1-3	25.1	27	18	2	2	17-2	17	6.39	56	.293	.411	0	—	0				
Total	10	42	54	.438	307	76	11-6	31-15	840.2	734	375	69	27	381-44	681	3.62	100	.238	.325	203-0-16	.172	2	100	1	79	1.2

SEMBERA, CARROLL Carroll William B7.26.1941 Shiner TX D6.15.2005 Shiner TX BR/TR/6-0/155* d9.28 Col Trinity (TX)

YEAR	TM LG	W	L	PCT	G	GS	CG-SHO	SV-BS	IP	H	R	HR	HB	BB-IB	SO	ERA	AERA	OAV	OOB	AB-HR-SH	AVG	PB	SUP	APR	DL	PW
1965	Hou N	0	1	.000	7	1	0	0	7.1	3	2	0	0	3-0	4	3.68	91	.185	.267	1-0-1	.000	-0	52	0		0.0
1966	Hou N	1	2	.333	24	0	0	1	33	36	11	3	0	16-0	21	3.00	114	.288	.366	3	.000	-0		2		0.2
1967	Hou N	2	6	.250	45	0	0	3	59.2	66	39	7	1	19-4	48	4.83	69	.269	.323	7-0-1	.143	-0		-11	24	-1.5
1969	Mon N	0	2	.000	23	0	0	2-1	33	28	14	1	2	24-4	15	3.55	104	.246	.383	4	.250	-0		1		0.1
1970	Mon N	0	0	—	5	0	0	0-0	6.2	14	14	2	1	11-3	6	18.90	22	.424	.578	0	—	0		-10		-0.9
Total	5	3	11	.214	99	1	0	6-1	139.2	149	81	13	4	73-11	94	4.70	74	.274	.362	15-0-2	.133	-0	52	-18	24	-1.7

SEMINARA, FRANK Frank Peter B5.16.1967 Brooklyn NY BR/TR/6-2/205* [NYA88 12/313] d6.2 Col Columbia

YEAR	TM LG	W	L	PCT	G	GS	CG-SHO	SV-BS	IP	H	R	HR	HB	BB-IB	SO	ERA	AERA	OAV	OOB	AB-HR-SH	AVG	PB	SUP	APR	DL	PW
1992	SD N	9	4	.692	19	18	0	0-0	100.1	98	46	3	4	46-3	61	3.68	98	.257	.340	34-0-2	.118	-1	127	-1		-0.2
1993	SD N	3	3	.500	18	7	0	0-1	46.1	53	34	5	3	21-3	22	4.47	93	.294	.374	10-0-1	.200	0	112	-3		-0.4
1994	NY N	0	2	.000	10	1	0	0-0	17	20	12	2	0	8-0	7	5.82	72	.303	.373	3	.000	-0	109	-3		-0.4
Total	3	12	9	.571	47	26	0	0-1	163.2	171	88	12	6	75-6	90	4.12	92	.273	.353	47-0-3	.128	0	121	-7		-1.0

SEMPROCH, RAY Roman Anthony "Baby" B1.7.1931 Cleveland OH BR/TR/5-11/180(168-180) d4.15

YEAR	TM LG	W	L	PCT	G	GS	CG-SHO	SV-BS	IP	H	R	HR	HB	BB-IB	SO	ERA	AERA	OAV	OOB	AB-HR-SH	AVG	PB	SUP	APR	DL	PW
1958	Phi N	13	11	.542	36	30	12-2	0	204.1	211	105	25	6	58-1	92	3.92	101	.264	.318	74-0-2	.095	-5	116	-1		-0.6
1959	Phi N	3	10	.231	30	18	2	3	111.2	119	76	12	3	59-1	54	5.40	76	.277	.366	34-0-2	.176	-0	79	-16		-1.7
1960	Det A	3	0	1.000	17	0	0	0	27	29	17	2	0	16-0	9	4.00	99	.269	.363	4-0-1	.000	-0		-2		0.0
1961	LA A	0	0	—	2	0	0	0	1	1	2	0	0	3-0	1	9.00	50	.333	.571	0	—	0		-1		0.0
Total	4	19	21	.475	85	48	14-2	3	344	360	200	39	9	136-2	156	4.42	91	.269	.338	112-0-5	.116	-5	101	-20		-2.4

SENTENEY, STEVE Stephen Leonard B8.7.1955 Indianapolis IN D6.18.1989 Colusa CA BR/TR/6-2/205 d6.6 Col St. Marys (CA)

YEAR	TM LG	W	L	PCT	G	GS	CG-SHO	SV-BS	IP	H	R	HR	HB	BB-IB	SO	ERA	AERA	OAV	OOB	AB-HR-SH	AVG	PB	SUP	APR	DL	PW
1982	Tor A	0	0	—	11	0	0	0-0	22	23	16	5	0	6-1	20	4.91	92	.247	.290	0	—	0		-2		0.0

YEAR	TM	LG	W	L	PCT	G	GS	CG-SHO	SV-BS	IP	H	R	HR	HB	BB-IB	SO	ERA	AERA	OAV	OOB	AB-HR-SH	AVG	PB	SUP	APR	DL	PW

SEO, JAE Jae Weong B5.24.1977 Kwangju, South Korea BR/TR/6-1/215* d7.21

2002	NY	N	0	0	—	1	0	0	0-0	1	1	0	0	0	0-0	1	0.00	—	.000	.000	0		0*		0		0.0
2003	NY	N	9	12	.429	32	31	0	0-0	188.1	193	94	18	6	46-11	110	3.82	110	.260	.307	51-0-4	.098	-1*	94	4		0.3
2004	NY	N	5	10	.333	24	21	0	0-0	117.2	133	67	17	2	50-7	54	4.90	88	.299	.370	32-0-3	.156	-1	88	-6		-0.6
2005	NY	N	8	2	.800	14	14	1	0-0	90.1	84	26	9	1	16-0	59	2.59	161	.251	.285	29-0-2	.103	-0	118	17		1.8
Total	4		22	24	.478	71	66	1	0-0	397.1	410	187	44	9	112-18	224	3.85	109	.269	.321	112-0-9	.116	-1	97	15		1.5

SEOANE, MANNY Manuel Modesto B6.26.1955 Tampa FL BR/TR/6-3/187* [PhiN73 6/122] d9.18

1977	Phi	N	0	0	—	2	1	0	0-0	6	11	4	0	0	3-0	4	6.00	67	.407	.467	2	.500	0	110	-1		0.0
1978	Chi	N	1	0	1.000	7	1	0	0-0	8.1	11	6	0	0	6-2	5	5.40	75	.297	.395	0	—	0	89	-1		-0.2
Total	2		1	0	1.000	9	2	0	0-0	14.1	22	10	0	0	9-2	9	5.65	72	.344	.425	2	.500	0	99	-2		-0.2

SERAD, BILLY William I. B1863 Philadelphia PA D11.1.1925 Chester PA BR/TR/5-7/156 d5.5

1884	Buf	N	16	20	.444	37	37	34-2	0	308	373	285	21		111	150	4.27	74	.281	.336	137	.175	-7	105	-38		-4.0
1885	Buf	N	7	21	.250	30	29	27	0	241.1	299	194	5		80	90	4.10	73	.293	.344	104	.154	-6	72	-31		-3.5
1887	Cin	AA	10	11	.476	22	21	20-2	1	187.1	201	139	7	8	80	34	4.08	106	.266	.343	79	.177	-4	89	4		-0.1
1888	Cin	AA	2	3	.400	6	5	5	0	50.2	62	43	1	6	19	4	3.55	89	.291	.366	23	.130	-1	110	-5		-0.5
Total	4		35	55	.389	95	92	86-4	1	787.1	935	661	34	14	290	278	4.13	82	.282	.342	343	.166	-17	92	-70		-8.1

SERAFINI, DAN Daniel Joseph B1.25.1974 San Francisco CA BB/TL/6-1/191(180-195) [MinA92 1/26] d6.25

1996	Min	A	0	1	.000	1	1	0	0-0	4.1	7	5	1	1	2-0	1	10.38	49	.368	.435	0	—	0	36	-2		-0.4
1997	Min	A	2	1	.667	6	4	1	0-0	26.1	27	11	1	0	11-0	15	3.42	137	.273	.345	0	—	0	138	3		0.3
1998	Min	A	7	4	.636	28	9	0	0-0	75	95	58	10	1	29-1	46	6.48	74	.310	.365	1	.000	-0	103	-14		-1.7
1999	Chi	N	3	2	.600	42	4	0	1-0	62.1	86	51	9	1	32-3	17	6.93	66	.333	.405	12-0-1	.083	-0	136	-16		-1.1
2000	SD	N	0	0	—	3	0	0	0-0	3	9	6	2	0	2-0	3	18.00	25	.500	.550	0		0		-4		-0.2
	Pit	N	2	5	.286	11	11	0	0-0	62.1	70	35	9	4	26-1	32	4.91	95	.292	.368	24-0-3	.083	-2	95	-1		-0.2
	Year		2	5	.286	14	11	0	0-0	65.1	79	41	11	4	28-1	35	5.51	84	.306	.380	24-0-3	.083	-2	96	-6		-0.4
2003	Cin	N	1	3	.250	10	4	0	0-0	30	41	23	5	0	14-1	13	5.40	77	.336	.399	6-0-1	.000	-1*	56	-6		-0.7
Total	6		15	16	.484	101	33	1	1-0	263.1	335	189	37	7	116-6	127	5.98	77	.315	.382	43-0-5	.070	-2	102	-40		-4.0

SERRANO, JIMMY James B5.9.1976 Grand Junction CO BR/TR/5-10/170 [MonN98 18/534] d8.7 Col New Mexico

| 2004 | KC | A | 1 | 2 | .333 | 10 | 5 | 0 | 0-0 | 32.2 | 35 | 17 | 5 | 1 | 12-0 | 25 | 4.68 | 100 | .280 | .340 | 0 | — | 0 | 72 | 1 | | 0.1 |

SERRANO, WASCAR Wascar Radames B6.2.1978 Santo Domingo, D.R. BR/TR/6-2/178 d5.12

| 2001 | SD | N | 3 | 3 | .500 | 20 | 5 | 0 | 0-0 | 46.2 | 60 | 37 | 7 | 2 | 21-1 | 39 | 6.56 | 63 | .313 | .382 | 9-0-2 | .111 | -0 | 147 | -13 | | -1.4 |

SERUM, GARY Gary Wayne B10.24.1956 Fargo ND BR/TR/6-1/175(160-180) d7.22 Col St. Cloud St.

1977	Min	A	0	0	—	8	0	0	0-0	22.2	22	11	4	2	10-1	14	4.37	91	.268	.362	0	—	0	0			0.0
1978	Min	A	9	9	.500	34	23	6-1	1-0	184.1	188	88	14	3	44-2	80	4.10	94	.266	.308	0	—	0	107	-2		-0.2
1979	Min	A	1	3	.250	20	5	0	0-0	64	93	47	10	0	20-2	31	6.61	67	.354	.398	0	—	0	103	-13		-0.7
Total	3		10	12	.455	62	28	6-1	1-0	271	303	146	28	5	74-5	125	4.72	84	.288	.335	0	—	0	105	-15		-0.9

SERVICE, SCOTT Scott David B2.26.1967 Cincinnati OH BR/TR/6-6/226(225-250) d9.5

1988	Phi	N	0	0	—	5	0	0	0-0	5.1	7	1	0	1	1-0	6	1.69	214	.333	.391	0		0		1		0.1
1992	Mon	N	0	0	—	5	0	0	0-0	7	15	11	1	0	5-0	11	14.14	25	.417	.488	2	.000	-0		-8		-0.4
1993	Col	N	0	0	—	3	0	0	0-0	4.2	8	5	1	1	1-0	3	9.64	50	.400	.417	0	—	0		-2		-0.1
	Cin	N	2	2	.500	26	0	0	2-0	41.1	36	19	5	1	15-4	40	3.70	109	.235	.304	7	.143	-0*	1			0.1
	Year		2	2	.500	29	0	0	2-0	46	44	24	6	2	16-4	43	4.30	95	.254	.318	7	.143	-0		-1		0.0
1994	Cin	N	1	2	.333	6	0	0	0-0	7.1	8	9	2	0	3-0	5	7.36	57	.267	.333	0		0		-4		-0.7
1995	SF	N	3	1	.750	28	0	0	0-0	31	18	11	4	2	20-4	30	3.19	129	.176	.317	1	.000	-0		4		0.4
1996	Cin	N	1	0	1.000	34	1	0	0-0	48	51	21	7	6	18-4	46	3.94	109	.277	.359	5	.000	-1	105	3		0.1
1997	Cin	N	0	0	—	4	0	0	0-0	5.1	11	7	1	0	1-0	3	11.81	36	.458	.480	0		0		-2		-0.2
	KC	A	0	3	.000	12	0	0	0-1	17	17	9	1	0	5-0	19	4.76	100	.274	.324	0		0		0		0.0
1998	KC	A	4	6	.400	73	0	0	4-4	82.2	70	35	7	9	34-4	95	3.48	140	.231	.322	1	.000	-0		12		1.4
1999	KC	A	5	5	.500	68	0	0	8-7	75.1	87	51	13	3	42-8	68	6.09	83	.294	.379	0	—	0		-6		-0.8
2000	Oak	A	1	2	.333	20	0	0	1-0	36.2	45	31	5	1	19-1	35	6.38	76	.302	.380	0	—	0		-7		-0.5
2003	Ari	N	0	2	.000	18	0	0	1-0	18.1	21	10	1	0	2-1	18	4.91	94	.288	.303	0	—	0		0		0.0
	Tor	A	0	0	—	15	0	0	0-1	16	17	8	3	0	6-0	17	4.50	105	.274	.333	0		0*	1			0.0
2004	Ari	N	1	1	.500	21	0	0	0-2	20.1	24	17	5	2	10-2	17	7.08	64	.286	.371	1	.000	-0		-5	63	-0.4
Total	12		20	22	.476	338	1	0	16-15	416.1	435	245	56	26	182-28	413	4.99	92	.272	.351	17	.059	-1	105	-14	63	-1.0

SETTLEMIRE, MERLE Edgar Merle "Lefty" B1.19.1903 Santa Fe OH D6.12.1988 Russells Point OH BL/TL/5-9/156 d4.13

| 1928 | Bos | A | 0 | 6 | .000 | 30 | 9 | 0 | 0-0 | 82.1 | 116 | 62 | 2 | 6 | 34 | 12 | 5.47 | 75 | .345 | .415 | 17-0-3 | .176 | -1* | 78 | -14 | | -0.8 |

SEVERINSEN, AL Albert Henry B11.9.1944 Brooklyn NY BR/TR/6-3/220(205-227) d7.1 Col Wagner

1969	Bal	A	1	1	.500	12	0	0	0-0	19.2	14	6	2	0	10-2	13	2.29	157	.206	.304	3-0-1	.333	0		3		0.3
1971	SD	N	2	5	.286	59	0	0	8-6	70	77	30	4	2	30-10	31	3.47	96	.292	.365	1-0-1	.000	-0		0		0.0
1972	SD	N	0	1	.000	17	0	0	1-0	21.1	13	8	1	2	7-1	9	2.53	131	.173	.259	1	.000	-0		1		0.1
Total	3		3	7	.300	88	0	0	9-6	111	104	44	7	4	47-13	53	3.08	109	.256	.335	5-0-2	.200	0		4		0.4

SEWARD, ED Edward William (b Edward William Sourhardt) B6.29.1867 Cleveland OH D7.30.1947 Cleveland OH TR/5-7/175 d9.30 U1

1885	Pro	N	0	0	—	1	0	0	0	6	2	0	0		0	1	0.00	—	.100	.100	3	.000	-0		2		0.1
1887	Phi	AA	25	25	.500	55	52	52-3	0	470.2	445	293	7	24	140	155	4.13	104	.244	.306	266-5	.188	-4*	88	16		0.8
1888	Phi	AA	35	19	.648	57	57	57-6	0	518.2	388	203	4	22	127	272	2.01	149	.200	.258	225-2	.142	-4*	107	60		5.1
1889	Phi	AA	21	15	.583	39	38	35-3	0	320	353	212	8	13	101	102	3.97	95	.271	.330	143-2	.217	6*	109	1		0.5
1890	Phi	AA	6	12	.333	21	19	15-1	0	154	165	105	4	7	72	55	4.73	82	.266	.349	72	.139	-1*	102	-11		-1.1
1891	Cle	N	2	1	.667	3	3	0	0	16.1	16	10	0	0	11	4	3.86	90	.246	.355	19	.211	0*	80	0		0.0
Total	6		89	72	.553	176	169	159-13	0	1485.2	1369	823	23	66	451	589	3.40	108	.237	.300	728-9	.174	-4	100	68		5.4

SEWARD, FRANK Frank Martin B4.7.1921 Pennsauken NJ D4.12.2004 Elmira NY BR/TR/6-3/200 d9.28 Col Duke

1943	NY	N	0	1	.000	1	1	0	0	9	12	3	0	0	5	2	3.00	115	.324	.405	4	.000	-1	49	1		0.0
1944	NY	N	3	2	.600	25	7	2	0	78.1	98	51	8	2	32	16	5.40	68	.306	.373	24-0-1	.083	-2	128	-13		-1.0
Total	2		3	3	.500	26	8	3	0	87.1	110	54	8	2	37	18	5.15	71	.308	.376	28-0-1	.071	-2	118	-12		-1.0

SEWELL, RIP Truett Banks B5.11.1907 Decatur AL D9.3.1989 Plant City FL BL/TR/6-1/180 d6.14 C1 Col Vanderbilt

1932	Det	A	0	0	—	5	0	0	0	10.2	19	15	2	0	4	2	12.66	37	.388	.474	2	.500	-0		-8		-0.3
1938	Pit	N	0	1	.000	17	0	0	1	38.1	41	27	3	2	21	17	4.23	90	.275	.372	12	.083	-1		-4		-0.3
1939	Pit	N	10	9	.526	52	12	5-1	2	176.1	177	93	10	1	73	69	4.08	94	.265	.339	55-1-4	.200	1	110	-5		-0.3
1940	Pit	N	16	5	.762	33	23	14-2	1	189.2	169	71	6	1	67	60	2.80	136	.238	.307	73-1-1	.192	2*	144	20		2.5
1941	Pit	N	14	17	.452	39	32	18-2	2	249	225	126	18	3	84	76	3.72	97	.235	.299	92-1-4	.174	0*	109	-4		-0.3
1942	Pit	N	17	15	.531	40	33	18-5	2	248	259	117	13	2	72	69	3.41	99	.265	.317	87-0-1	.149	-2*	102	-4		-0.6
1943	Pit	N★	21	9	.700	35	31	25-2	3	265.1	267	94	6	2	75	65	2.54	137	.260	.312	105-0-1	.286	6*	121	27		3.9
1944	Pit	N★	21	12	.636	38	33	24-3	2	286	263	112	15	3	99	87	3.18	117	.240	.304	112-1-2	.223	3*	109	21		2.6
1945	Pit	N★	11	9	.550	33	24	9-1	1	188	212	116	9	2	91	60	4.07	97	.279	.357	64-0-1	.313	6*	125	-9		-0.1
1946	Pit	N★	8	12	.400	25	20	11-2	0	149.1	140	68	6	1	53	33	3.68	96	.245	.310	50-0-2	.180	0*	104	-1		0.5
1947	Pit	N	6	4	.600	14	12	4-1	0	121	121	58	11	3	36	36	3.57	118	.263	.321	40-1-0	.125	-1	94	7		1.1
1948	Pit	N	13	3	.813	21	17	7	0	121.2	126	51	9	1	37	36	3.48	117	.262	.317	42-1-1	.143	1	105	8		1.1
1949	Pit	N	6	1	.857	28	6	2-1	1	76	82	35	8	0	32	26	3.91	108	.280	.351	16-0-2	.063	-0	84	3		0.2
Total	13		143	97	.596	390	243	137-20	15	2119.1	2101	983	116	23	748	636	3.48	108	.257	.320	750-6-19	.203	16	112	51		8.6

SEXAUER, ELMER Elmer George B5.21.1926 St.Louis Co. MO BR/TR/6-4/220 d9.6 Col Wake Forest [DL 1949 Phi N 77]

| 1948 | Bro | N | 0 | 0 | — | 2 | 0 | 0 | 0 | 0.2 | 3 | 2 | 1 | 0 | 2 | 0 | 13.50 | 30 | .000 | .500 | 0 | — | 0 | | 0 | | 0.0 |

SEXTON, FRANK Frank Joseph B7.8.1872 Brockton MA D1.4.1938 Brighton MA ?/160 d6.21 Col Michigan

| 1895 | Bos | N | 1 | 5 | .167 | 7 | 5 | 4 | 0 | 49 | 59 | 39 | 2 | 2 | 22 | 14 | 5.69 | 89 | .294 | .369 | 26-0-1 | .269 | -1* | 45 | -1 | | -0.2 |

YEAR	TM LG	W	L	PCT	G	GS	CG-SHO	SV-BS	IP	H	R	HR	HB	BB-IB	SO	ERA	AERA	OAV	OOB	AB-HR-SH	AVG	PB	SUP	APR	DL	PW
SEYFRIED, GORDON							Gordon Clay B7.4.1937 Long Beach CA BR/TR/6-0/185* d9.13 Col Long Beach (CA) City																		
1963	Cle A	0	1	.000	3	1	0	0	7.1	9	2	0	0	3-1	1	1.23	295	.300	.364	2	.000	-0	25	2		0.2
1964	Cle A	0	0	—	2	0	0	0	2.1	4	0	0	0	0-0	0	0.00	—	.444	.400	0	—	0		1		0.0
Total	2	0	1	.000	5	1	0	0	9.2	13	2	0	0	3-1	1	0.93	388	.333	.372	2	.000	-0	25	3		0.2
SEYMOUR, JAKE							Jacob (b Jacob Semer) B1854 Pittsburgh PA D8.1.1897 Allegheny (now part of Pittsburgh) PA d9.23																		
1882	Pit AA	0	1	.000	1	1	1	0	8	16	13	0		2	2	7.88	33	.390	.419	4	.000	-1	59	-5		-0.4
SEYMOUR, CY							James Bentley B12.9.1872 Albany NY D9.20.1919 New York NY BL/TL/6-0/200 d4.22 ▲																		
1896	NY N	2	4	.333	11	8	4	0	70.1	75	75	8	3	51	33	6.40	66	.271	.390	32	.219	-1*	135	-19		-1.3
1897	NY N	18	14	.563	39	34	29-2	1	286.2	257	162	4	22	168	156	3.27	127	.238	.352	141-2-1	.241	1*	101	28		2.9
1898	NY N	25	19	.568	45	43	39-4	0	356.2	313	199	4	32	213	239	3.18	109	.234	.353	297-4-2	.276	7*	113	11		2.1
1899	NY N	14	18	.438	32	32	31	0	268.1	247	139	5	20	170	142	3.56	106	.245	.364	159-2-5	.327	8*	100	10		2.0
1900	NY N	2	1	.667	13	7	2	0	53	58	54	4	10	54	19	6.96	52	.278	.447	40	.300	1*	150	-17		-0.6
1902	Cin N	0	0	—	1	0	0	0	3	4	3	0	0	3	2	9.00	33	.308	.438	244-2-3	.340	0*		-1		-0.1
Total	6	61	56	.521	141	124	105-6	1	1038	954	632	25	87	659	591	3.73	102	.243	.364	913-10-11	.296	16	110	12		5.0
SHACKELFORD, BRIAN							Brian Wesley B8.30.1976 McAlester OK BL/TL/6-1/195 d6.26 Col Oklahoma																		
2005	Cin N	1	0	1.000	37	0	0	0-0	29.2	21	9	2	6	9-1	17	2.43	172	.204	.303	1	.000	-0		6		0.2
SHAFFER, JOHN							John W. "Cannon Ball" B2.18.1864 Lock Haven PA D11.21.1926 Endicott NY TR/5-10/? d9.13																		
1886	NY AA	5	3	.625	8	8	8-1	0	69	40	29	0	1	29	36	1.96	167	.164	.255	25	.240	1	93	9		1.0
1887	NY AA	2	11	.154	13	13	13	0	112	148	119	3	11	53	22	6.19	69	.310	.391	48	.167	-3	78	-24		-2.0
Total	2	7	14	.333	21	21	21-1	0	181	188	148	3	12	82	58	4.57	84	.260	.346	73	.192	-2	83	-15		-1.0
SHALLIX, GUS							August (b August Schallick) B3.29.1858 Paderborn, Germany D10.28.1937 Cincinnati OH d6.22																		
1884	Cin AA	11	10	.524	23	23	23	0	199.2	163	113	6	26	53	78	3.70	90	.212	.286	84	.036	-10	110	-7		-1.5
1885	Cin AA	6	4	.600	13	12	7	0	91.1	95	59	1	13	33	15	3.25	100	.265	.349	39	.128	-2	113	-2		-0.3
Total	2	17	14	.548	36	35	30	0	291	258	172	7	39	86	93	3.56	93	.229	.306	123	.065	-12	111	-9		-1.8
SHANAHAN, GREG							Paul Gregory B12.11.1947 Eureka CA BR/TR/6-2/190* d9.4 Col Humboldt St.																		
1973	LA N	0	0	—	7	0	0	1-0	15.2	14	6	2	0	4-0	11	3.45	101	.230	.277	1	.000	0		0		0.0
1974	LA N	0	0	—	4	0	0	0-0	7	7	3	1	0	5-0	2	3.86	89	.259	.364	0	—	0		0		0.0
Total	2	0	0	—	11	0	0	1-0	22.2	21	9	3	0	9-0	13	3.57	97	.239	.306	1	.000	0		0		0.0
SHANK, HARVEY							Harvey Tillman B7.29.1946 Toronto ON, Can. BR/TR/6-4/220 [AnaA68 10/216] d5.16 Col Stanford																		
1970	Cal A	0	0	—	3	0	0	0-0	3	2	0	0	0	2-0	1	0.00	—	.182	.308	0	—	0		1		0.1
SHANNER, BILL							Wilfred William B11.4.1894 Oakland City IN D12.18.1986 Evansville IN BL/TR d10.1																		
1920	Phi A	0	0	—	1	0	0	0	4	6	4	2	0	1	1	6.75	60	.353	.389	1	.000	-0		-1		-0.1
SHANTZ, BOBBY							Robert Clayton B9.26.1925 Pottstown PA BR/TL/5-6/142(138-154) d5.1 b-Billy																		
1949	Phi A	6	8	.429	33	7	4-1	2	127	100	50	9	3	74	58	3.40	121	.221	.334	37-0-3	.189	1	121	12		1.5
1950	Phi A	8	14	.364	36	23	6-1	0	214.2	251	122	18	7	85	93	4.61	99	.294	.362	66-1-6	.167	-0*	68	-1		0.0
1951	Phi A☆	18	10	.643	32	25	13-3	0	205.1	213	96	15	5	70	77	3.94	108	.270	.333	72-0-8	.250	2*	107	9		1.5
1952	Phi A★	24	7	.774	33	33	27-5	0	279.2	230	87	21	4	63	152	2.48	160	.225	.272	96-0-13	.198	2*	78	43		5.1
1953	Phi A	5	9	.357	16	16	6	0	105.2	107	52	10	0	26	58	4.09	105	.263	.307	38-0-1	.237	0*	135	-3	95	0.5
1954	Phi A	1	0	1.000	2	1	0	0	8	12	7	2	1	3	3	7.88	56	.364	.421	3	.333	0*	86	-5		-0.3
1955	KC A	5	10	.333	23	17	4-1	0	125	124	70	8	1	66-11	58	4.54	92	.264	.352	41-0-2	.146	-2*	62	1		0.1
1956	KC A	2	7	.222	45	2	1	9	101.1	95	51	12	3	37-4	67	4.35	99	.248	.319	22-0-2	.091	-1*	62	1		0.1
1957	†NY A☆	11	5	.688	30	21	9-1	5	173	157	58	15	6	40-1	72	2.45	147	.248	.296	56-0-1	.179	2*	116	21		2.7
1958	NY A	7	6	.538	33	13	3	0	126	127	52	8	2	35-7	80	3.36	105	.262	.312	35-0-1	.229	2	88	4		0.8
1959	NY A	7	3	.700	33	4	2-2	3	94.2	64	33	4	0	33-5	66	2.38	153	.189	.260	23-0-3	.217	2*	85	12		1.6
1960	†NY A	5	4	.556	42	0	0	11	67.2	57	24	5	2	24-4	54	2.79	128	.235	.302	10-0-2	.100	-0*		6		1.0
1961	Pit N	6	3	.667	43	6	2-1	2	89.1	91	38	5	4	26-6	61	3.32	120	.271	.328	16-0-1	.438	-1*	133	6		1.0
1962	Hou N	1	1	.500	3	3	1	0	20.2	15	4	1	0	5-0	14	1.31	286	.208	.256	8	.000	-0		10		1.5
	StL N	5	3	.625	28	0	0	4	57.2	45	22	7	1	20-2	47	2.18	195	.211	.282	13	.154	-0		5		0.5
	Year	6	4	.600	31	3	1	4	78.1	60	26	8	1	25-2	61	1.95	211	.211	.276	21	.095	-1	120	15		2.0
1963	StL N	6	4	.600	55	0	0	11	79.1	55	28	6	2	17-5	70	2.61	158	.192	.240	7-0-1	.143	0		7		0.4
1964	StL N	1	3	.250	16	0	0	0	17.1	14	6	2	0	7-3	12	3.12	122	.226	.300	0	—	0		-2		-0.2
	Chi N	0	1	.000	20	0	0	0	11.1	15	7	2	0	6-2	12	5.56	67	.319	.396	0	—	0		-2		-0.2
	Phi N	1	1	.500	14	0	0	1	32	23	10	1	0	6-3	18	2.25	154	.204	.244	5	.000	-0		4		0.5
	Year	2	5	.286	50	0	0	1	60.2	52	23	5	0	19-8	42	3.12	116	.234	.293	5	.000	-0		4		0.5
Total	16	119	99	.546	537	171	78-15	48	1935.2	1795	817	151	41	643-53	1072	3.38	119	.248	.312	548-1-44	.195	11	97	134	95	18.7
SHARROTT, GEORGE							George Oscar B11.2.1869 Staten Island NY D1.6.1932 Jamaica NY BL/TL/5-8/164 d7.27																		
1893	Bro N	4	6	.400	13	10	10	1	95	114	80	3	8	58	24	5.87	75	.289	.390	39-1	.231	0	74	-13		-1.0
1894	Bro N	0	1	.000	3	3	2	0	18	25	21	0	5	8	7	9.00	55	.325	.422	7	.429	1	43	-7		-0.2
Total	2	4	7	.364	16	13	12	1	113	139	101	3	13	66	31	6.37	71	.294	.396	46-1	.261	1	67	-20		-1.2
SHARROTT, JACK							John Henry B8.13.1869 Bangor ME D12.31.1927 Los Angeles CA BR/TR/5-9/165 d4.22 ▲																		
1890	NY N	11	10	.524	19	18	9	0	184	162	107	3	9	88	84	2.89	122	.229	.322	109	.202	-2*	96	11		0.9
1891	NY N	5	5	.500	10	9	6	0	69.1	47	32	2	4	35	41	2.60	123	.185	.294	30-1	.333	4	89	6		1.1
1892	NY N	0	0	—	1	0	0	0	2	2	1	0	0	1	1	4.50	72	.250	.333	4	.125	-0*		0		0.0
1893	Phi N	4	2	.667	12	4	2	0	56	53	43	1	4	33	11	4.50	102	.242	.352	152-1	.250	0*	118	-1		-0.1
Total	4	20	17	.541	48	32	26	0	311.1	264	183	6	17	157	137	3.12	116	.222	.321	299-2	.237	2	96	16		1.9
SHAUTE, JOE							Joseph Benjamin "Lefty" B8.1.1899 Peckville PA D2.21.1970 Scranton PA BL/TL/6-0/190 d7.6 Col Juniata																		
1922	Cle A	0	0	—	2	0	0	0	3.2	7	6	0	0	3	3	19.64	20	.389	.476	5	.000	-0*		-6		-0.3
1923	Cle A	10	8	.556	33	16	7	0	172	176	93	4	4	53	61	3.51	113	.275	.332	68-0-1	.162	-4	126	5		3.0
1924	Cle A	20	17	.541	46	34	21-2	2	283	317	138	8	6	83	68	3.75	114	.287	.340	107-1-3	.318	3*	96	-13		-1.2
1925	Cle A	4	12	.250	26	17	10-1	4	131	160	91	6	1	44	34	5.43	84	.304	.358	53	.302	3*	113	13		1.6
1926	Cle A	14	10	.583	34	25	15-1	1	206.2	215	92	9	3	65	47	3.53	115	.278	.337	73-0-7	.274	4	113	13		1.0
1927	Cle A	9	16	.360	45	28	14	2	230.1	255	140	9	2	75	63	4.22	100	.286	.343	83	.325	6	77	-5		0.4
1928	Cle A	13	17	.433	36	31	21-1	2	253.2	295	145	6	4	68	81	4.04	102	.299	.348	92-0-4	.228	3	107	0		0.4
1929	Cle A	8	8	.500	26	24	8	0	162	211	100	6	1	52	43	4.28	104	.320	.370	58-0-5	.293	3	94	0		-0.2
1930	Cle A	0	0	—	4	0	0	0	4.2	8	10	0	4	4	2	15.43	31	.333	.429	0	—	0		-5		-0.2
1931	Bro N	11	8	.579	25	19	6	0	128.2	162	87	9	1	32	50	4.83	79	.305	.346	45-0-1	.178	-0	123	-18		-1.4
1932	Bro N	7	7	.500	34	9	1	4	117	147	67	8	2	21	32	4.54	84	.301	.333	45-0-1	.200	1*	127	-9		-0.4
1933	Bro N	3	4	.429	41	4	0	2	108.1	125	63	4	1	31	26	3.49	98	.287	.336	27	.222	4	52	-9		-0.4
1934	Cin N	0	2	.000	8	0	0	1	17.1	19	10	1	0	3	2	4.15	98	.268	.297	4	.250	0	106	0		-0.2
Total	13	99	109	.476	360	208	103-5	18	1818.1	2097	1043	75	24	534	512	4.15	99	.293	.345	660-1-22	.258	25	105	-28		-0.2
SHAVER, JEFF							Jeffrey Thomas B7.30.1963 Beaver PA BR/TR/6-3/195 [OakA85 22/559] d7.6 Col Fredonia																		
1988	Oak A	0	0	—	1	0	0	0-0	3	3	0	0	0	1	0-0	0	0.00	—	.000	.333	0	—	0		0	0.0
SHAW, DON							Donald Wellington B2.23.1944 Pittsburgh PA BL/TL/6-0/185(180-191) [NYN65 21/752] d4.11 Mil 1967 Col San Diego St.																		
1967	NY N	4	5	.444	40	0	0	3	51.1	40	19	5	0	23-5	44	2.98	114	.219	.301	3-0-1	.000	0		2		0.5
1968	NY N	0	0	—	7	0	0	0	12	3	1	1	0	5-0	11	0.75	403	.086	.200	0	—	0		3		0.2
1969	Mon N	2	5	.286	35	1	0	1-1	65.2	61	43	9	2	37-5	45	5.21	71	.254	.356	10	.000	-0	48	-10		-1.1
1971	StL N	7	2	.778	45	0	0	2-2	51	45	19	1	1	31-6	19	2.65	137	.237	.342	1-0-1	.000	-0		4		0.0
1972	StL N	0	1	.000	8	0	0	0-3	3	5	3	1	0	3-0	1	9.00	38	.417	.500	1	.000	-0		-2		-0.1
	Oak A	0	1	.000	3	0	0	0-0	5.1	12	10	2	0	2-0	3	16.88	17	.500	.500	0	—	0		-2		-0.1
Total	5	13	14	.481	166	1	0	6-6	188.1	166	95	19	3	101-16	123	4.01	88	.243	.338	15-0-2	.000	-0	48	-11		-1.1
SHAW, DUPEE							Frederick Lander B5.31.1859 Charlestown MA D1.12.1938 Wakefield MA BL/TL/5-8/165 d6.18																		
1883	Det N	10	15	.400	26	25	23-1	0	227	238	135	3		44	73	2.50	124	.256	.290	141	.206	-3*	96	10		0.
1884	Det N	9	18	.333	28	28	25	0	227.2	219	153	6		72	142	3.04	95	.237	.292	136-1	.191	-1*	84	-4		0.

YEAR	TM LG	W	L	PCT	G	GS	CG-SHO	SV-BS	IP	H	R	HR	HB	BB-IB	SO	ERA	AERA	OAV	OOB	AB-HR-SH	AVG	PB	SUP	APR	DL	PW
1885	Bos U	21	15	.583	39	38	35-5	0	315.2	227	128	1		37	309	1.77	135	.188	.212	153	.242	-5*	93	20		1.3
1886	Pro N	23	26	.469	49	49	47-6	0	399.2	343	209	7		99	194	2.57	105	.209	.254	165	.133	-10	74	5		-0.5
1887	Was N	13	31	.295	45	44	43-1	0	385.2	384	224	12		91	177	3.34	97	.250	.291	148	.088	-10	75	-4		-1.3
1888	Was N	7	13	.350	21	20	20	0	181.1	263	177	8	3	46	47	6.45	62	.250	.366	70	.186	-2	85	-40		-3.3
1888	Was N	0	3	.000	3	3	3	0	25	36	24	2	0	7	8	6.48	43	.333	.374	10	.000	-1	37	-9		-1.0
Total 6		83	121	.407	211	207	196-13	0	1762	1710	1050	41	3	396	950	3.10	96	.239	.279	823-1	.170	-32	83	-22		-4.5

SHAW, JIM
James Aloysius "Grunting Jim" B8.19.1893 Pittsburgh PA D1.27.1962 Washington DC BR/TR/6-0/180 d9.15

YEAR	TM LG	W	L	PCT	G	GS	CG-SHO	SV-BS	IP	H	R	HR	HB	BB-IB	SO	ERA	AERA	OAV	OOB	AB-HR-SH	AVG	PB	SUP	APR	DL	PW
1913	Was A	0	1	.000	6				13	8	4	2	1		14	2.08	142	.216	.356	2	.000	-0	0	1		0.1
1914	Was A	15	17	.469	48	31	15-5	4	257	198	99	3	8	137	164	2.70	104	.216	.324	85-1-3	.118	-3	84	3		0.1
1915	Was A	6	11	.353	25	18	7-1	1	133	102	50	2	2	76	78	2.50	119	.220	.333	43-0-1	.233	1	68	7		1.0
1916	Was A	3	8	.273	26	9	5-2	1	106.1	86	36	1	2	50	44	2.62	106	.227	.320	32-0-2	.156	-0	78	3		1.0
1917	Was A	15	14	.517	42	31	15-2	1	266.1	233	118	1	1	123	118	3.21	82	.242	.328	91-0-3	.154	-2	85	-15		-2.0
1918	Was A	16	12	.571	41	30	14-4	1	241.1	201	88	2	1	90	129	2.42	113	.228	.300	83-0-3	.133	-5	102	9		0.3
1919	Was A	17	17	.500	45	37	23-3	5	306.2	274	118	5	5	101	128	2.73	118	.244	.309	106-3-6	.160	-1	100	19		1.6
1920	Was A	11	18	.379	38	32	17	1	236.1	285	127	12	4	87	88	4.27	87	.314	.376	74-0-3	.189	0	83	-9		-1.1
1921	Was A	1	0	1.000	15	5	0	3	40.1	59	37	2	0	17	4	7.36	56	.345	.404	12-0-1	.417	2	174	-14		-0.5
Total 9		84	98	.462	287	194	96-17	17	1600.1	1446	677	28	24	688	767	3.07	99	.247	.329	528-4-22	.163	-8	91	4		-0.3

SHAW, JEFF
Jeffrey Lee B7.7.1966 Washington Court House OH BR/TR/6-2/200(185-200) [CleA86*1/1] d4.30 Col Rio Grande

YEAR	TM LG	W	L	PCT	G	GS	CG-SHO	SV-BS	IP	H	R	HR	HB	BB-IB	SO	ERA	AERA	OAV	OOB	AB-HR-SH	AVG	PB	SUP	APR	DL	PW
1990	Cle A	3	4	.429	12	9	0	0-0	48.2	73	38	11	0	20-0	25	6.66	59	.356	.408	0	—	0	105	-14		-1.7
1991	Cle A	0	5	.000	29	1	0	1-3	72.1	72	34	6	4	27-5	31	3.36	124	.262	.332	0	—	0	5	5		0.3
1992	Cle A	0	1	.000	2	1	0	0-0	7.2	7	7	2	0	4-0	3	8.22	48	.259	.355	0	—	0	116	-3		-0.4
1993	Mon N	2	7	.222	55	8	0	0-1	95.2	91	47	12	7	32-2	50	4.14	91	.254	.326	15	.067	-1	54	3		0.1
1994	Mon N	5	2	.714	46	0	0	1-1	67.1	67	32	8	2	15-2	47	3.88	109	.254	.295	7-0-1	.286	1	3	3		0.4
1995	Mon N	1	6	.143	50	0	0	3-2	62.1	58	35	4	3	26-4	45	4.62	93	.250	.332	6	.000	-0		-2		-0.2
	Chi A	0	0	—	9	0	0	0-0	9.2	12	7	2	1	1-0	6	6.52	69	.316	.350	0	—	0		-2		-0.1
1996	Cin N	8	6	.571	78	0	0	4-7	104.2	99	34	8	2	29-11	69	2.49	172	.252	.303	5	.000	-0		20		2.5
1997	Cin N	4	2	.667	78	0	0	42-7	94.2	79	26	7	1	12-3	74	2.38	180	.227	.253	3-0-1	.000	-0		20		2.8
1998	Cin N	2	4	.333	39	0	0	23-5	49.2	40	11	2	1	12-4	29	1.81	237	.231	.282	2-0-1	.000	-0		13		2.6
	LA N★	1	4	.200	34	0	0	25-4	35.1	35	11	6	0	7-1	26	2.55	158	.252	.288	0	—	1		13		2.6
	Year	3	8	.273	73	0	0	48-9	85	75	22	8	1	19-5	55	2.12	197	.240	.284	2-0-1	.000	-0		6		1.3
1999	LA N	2	4	.333	64	0	0	34-5	68	64	25	6	1	15-1	43	2.78	157	.242	.283	0	—	0		12		1.9
2000	LA N	3	4	.429	60	0	0	27-7	57.1	61	29	7	1	16-3	39	4.24	105	.227	.316	0	—	0		2	15	0.4
2001	LA N★	3	5	.375	77	0	0	43-9	74.2	63	32	10	2	18-8	58	3.62	114	.227	.277	0	—	0		5		1.0
Total 12		34	54	.386	633	19	0	203-51	848	821	368	91	25	234-44	545	3.54	119	.255	.308	38-0-3	.079	-1	75	68	15	10.9

SHAW, BOB
Robert John B6.29.1933 Bronx NY BR/TR/6-2/195(180-195) d8.11 C1 Col St. Lawrence

YEAR	TM LG	W	L	PCT	G	GS	CG-SHO	SV-BS	IP	H	R	HR	HB	BB-IB	SO	ERA	AERA	OAV	OOB	AB-HR-SH	AVG	PB	SUP	APR	DL	PW
1957	Det A	0	1	.000	7	0	0	0	9.2	11	9	2	0	7-1	4	7.45	52	.289	.400	2	.000	-0		-4		-0.4
1958	Det A	1	2	.333	11	2	0	0	26.2	32	16	2	0	13-1	17	5.06	80	.302	.375	4	.375	1*	33	-3		-0.1
	Chi A	4	2	.667	29	3	0	1	64	67	33	8	2	28-3	18	4.64	78	.271	.346	14	.000	-0	156	-6		-0.5
	Year	5	4	.556	40	5	0	1	90.2	99	49	10	2	41-4	35	4.76	79	.280	.355	22	.136	-0	105	-8		-0.6
1959	†Chi A	18	6	.750	47	26	8-3	3	230.2	217	72	15	6	54-5	89	2.69	140	.249	.295	73-0-10	.123	-2	101	31		2.9
1960	Chi A	13	13	.500	36	32	7-1	0	192.2	221	97	16	3	62-3	46	4.06	93	.292	.345	58-0-7	.138	-0	101	-6		-0.8
1961	Chi A	3	4	.429	14	10	3	0	71.1	85	40	11	1	20-5	31	3.79	103	.302	.346	18-0-2	.000	-1	97	-2		-0.3
	KC A	9	10	.474	26	24	9	0	150.1	165	87	14	7	58-2	60	4.31	97	.281	.346	55-0-1	.200	-1*	93	-4		-0.5
	Year	12	14	.462	40	34	9	0	221.2	250	127	25	8	78-7	91	4.14	99	.288	.347	73-0-3	.151	-2	95	-7		-0.8
1962	Mil N★	15	9	.625	38	29	12-3	2	225	223	80	20	12	44-10	124	2.80	136	.260	.303	73-0-3	.137	1	102	26		2.6
1963	Mil N	7	11	.389	48	16	3-3	13	159	144	51	10	4	55-12	105	2.66	121	.243	.310	41-0-7	.122	-0	97	11		1.4
1964	SF N	7	6	.538	61	1	0	11	93.1	105	43	5	5	31-6	57	3.76	95	.286	.348	13	.000	-1	74	-2		-0.5
1965	SF N	16	9	.640	42	33	6-1	2	235	213	85	17	3	53-5	148	2.64	136	.236	.280	79-0-4	.101	-3	99	22		2.0
1966	SF N	4	4	.200	13	6	0	0	31.2	45	23	9	0	7-1	21	6.25	59	.324	.356	6-0-2	.000	-1	76	-8		-1.2
	NY N	11	10	.524	26	25	7-2	0	167.2	171	85	12	7	42-1	104	3.92	93	.261	.312	50-0-5	.260	3	86	-6		-0.3
	Year	12	14	.462	39	31	7-2	0	199.1	216	108	21	7	49-2	125	4.29	85	.272	.319	56-0-7	.232	2	84	-17		-1.5
1967	NY N	3	9	.250	23	13	3-1	0	98.2	105	54	9	2	28-9	49	4.29	79	.273	.325	25-0-1	.040	-2	70	-10		-1.4
	Chi N	0	2	.000	9	3	0	0	22.1	33	16	0	4	9-4	7	6.04	59	.351	.418	4	.250	0	99	-6		-0.5
	Year	3	11	.214	32	16	3-1	0	121	138	70	9	6	37-13	56	4.61	74	.289	.344	29-0-1	.069	-1	75	-15		-1.9
Total 11		108	98	.524	430	223	55-14	32	1778	1837	791	150	56	511-68	880	3.52	105	.267	.321	519-0-40	.133	-7	96	33		2.4

SHAW, SAM
Samuel E. B5.1864 Baltimore MD BR/TR/5-5/140 d5.3

YEAR	TM LG	W	L	PCT	G	GS	CG-SHO	SV-BS	IP	H	R	HR	HB	BB-IB	SO	ERA	AERA	OAV	OOB	AB-HR-SH	AVG	PB	SUP	APR	DL	PW
1888	Bal AA	2	4	.333	6	6	6	0	53	65	37	2	4	15	22	3.40	88	.291	.347	20	.150	-1	110	-5		-0.5
1893	Chi N	1	0	1.000	2	2	1	0	16	12	12	2	9	13	1	5.63	82	.203	.420	7	.286	-0	151	-1		-0.1
Total 2		3	4	.429	8	8	7	0	69	77	49	4	13	28	23	3.97	86	.273	.365	27	.185	-1	123	-6		-0.6

SHAWKEY, BOB
James Robert B12.4.1890 Sigel PA D12.31.1980 Syracuse NY BR/TR/5-11/168 d7.16 Mil 1918 M1/C1 Col Slippery Rock

YEAR	TM LG	W	L	PCT	G	GS	CG-SHO	SV-BS	IP	H	R	HR	HB	BB-IB	SO	ERA	AERA	OAV	OOB	AB-HR-SH	AVG	PB	SUP	APR	DL	PW
1913	Phi A	6	5	.545	18	15	8-1	0	111.1	92	41	2	3	50	52	2.34	118	.221	.309	44-0-2	.136	-2	116	3		0.2
1914	†Phi A	15	8	.652	38	31	18-5	2	237	223	88	4	2	75	89	2.73	96	.262	.323	83-0-4	.205	-2	122	-4		-0.2
1915	Phi A	6	6	.500	17	13	7-1	0	100	103	57	3	1	38	56	4.05	72	.278	.346	31-0-2	.129	-1	123	-11		-1.2
	NY A	4	7	.364	16	9	5-1	0	85.2	78	38	2	2	35	31	3.26	90	.265	.347	29	.241	1	61	-3		-0.2
	Year	10	13	.435	33	22	12-2	0	185.2	181	95	5	3	73	87	3.68	80	.272	.347	60-0-2	.183	1	97	-13		-1.4
1916	NY A	24	14	.632	53	27	21-4	8	276.2	204	78	4	6	81	122	2.21	131	.209	.273	93-0-4	.183	-1	102	24		3.4
1917	NY A	13	15	.464	32	26	16-2	0	236.1	207	81	2	6	72	97	2.44	110	.243	.306	84-0-4	.190	-0	99	8		1.2
1918	NY A	1	1	.500	3	2	1-1	0	16	7	2	0	0	10	9	1.13	251	.143	.288	4	.750	2	107	3		0.7
1919	NY A	20	11	.645	41	27	22-3	5	261.1	218	94	7	5	92	122	2.72	117	.231	.303	94-0-6	.234	2	104	16		1.8
1920	NY A	20	13	.606	38	31	20-5	2	267.2	246	88	10	1	86	126	2.45	156	.248	.308	100-0-1	.230	-0	98	41		4.6
1921	†NY A	18	12	.600	38	31	18-3	2	245	245	131	15	7	86	126	4.08	104	.263	.308	90-1-8	.300	4	125	6		0.8
1922	†NY A	20	12	.625	39	34	22-3	1	299.2	286	112	16	0	98	130	2.91	138	.256	.316	115-1-7	.183	-3	103	37		3.3
1923	†NY A	16	11	.593	36	31	17-1	1	258.2	232	114	17	4	102	125	3.51	112	.246	.322	90-0-3	.202	-3	115	12		0.8
1924	NY A	16	11	.593	38	25	10-1	0	207.2	226	107	11	3	74	114	4.12	101	.286	.350	69-1-4	.319	8	133	2		0.8
1925	NY A	6	14	.300	33	19	9-1	0	186	209	101	12	5	67	81	4.11	104	.294	.359	68	.147	-4	59	2		-0.3
1926	†NY A	8	7	.533	29	10	3-1	0	104.1	102	49	8	2	49	63	3.62	106	.263	.330	35-0-2	.257	2	125	4		0.6
1927	NY A	2	3	.400	19	2	0	0	43.2	44	19	1	1	16	23	2.89	134	.262	.330	11	.091	-1	130	4		0.4
Total 15		195	150	.565	488	333	197-33	28	2937	2722	1200	114	48	1018	1360	3.09	114	.252	.319	1049-3-48	.214	4	108	144		16.7

SHEA, SPEC
Francis Joseph "The Naugatuck Nugget" (b Francis Joseph O'shea) B10.2.1920 Naugatuck CT D7.19.2002 New Haven CT BR/TR/6-0/195* d4.19

YEAR	TM LG	W	L	PCT	G	GS	CG-SHO	SV-BS	IP	H	R	HR	HB	BB-IB	SO	ERA	AERA	OAV	OOB	AB-HR-SH	AVG	PB	SUP	APR	DL	PW
1947	†NY A★	14	5	.737	27	23	13-3	1	178.2	127	63	10	4	89	89	3.07	115	.200	.303	56-0-8	.196	2	128	11		1.2
1948	NY A	9	10	.474	28	22	8-3	1	155.2	117	66	10	2	87	91	3.41	120	.208	.316	47-0-5	.149	1	105	12		1.2
1949	NY A	1	1	.500	20	3	0	1	52.1	48	36	5	0	43	22	5.33	76	.250	.387	12	.250	1	81	-8		-0.3
1951	NY A	5	5	.500	25	11	2-2	0	95.2	112	59	11	4	50	38	4.33	88	.300	.389	28-1-1	.214	1	120	-9		-0.7
1952	Was A	11	7	.611	22	21	12-2	0	169	144	62	6	4	92	65	2.93	121	.231	.331	63-0-1	.238	2	135	-9		1.5
1953	Was A	12	7	.632	23	23	11-1	0	164.2	151	82	11	4	75	38	3.94	99	.244	.329	62-0-4	.177	-1	120	-1		-0.3
1954	Was A	2	9	.182	23	11	1	0	71.1	97	54	9	2	34	22	6.18	58	.340	.412	20	.050	-2	108	-21		-2.9
1955	Was A	2	2	.500	27	4	1-1	2	56.1	53	31	4	1	27	17	3.99	96	.251	.335	10	.400	2	93	-2		0.0
Total 8		56	46	.549	195	118	48-12	5	943.2	849	453	66	19	497-0	361	3.80	99	.243	.339	298-1-19	.195	2	114	-6		-0.3

SHEA, JOHN
John Michael Joseph "Lefty" B12.27.1904 Everett MA D11.30.1956 Malden MA BL/TL/5-10.5/171 d6.30 Col Boston College

YEAR	TM LG	W	L	PCT	G	GS	CG-SHO	SV-BS	IP	H	R	HR	HB	BB-IB	SO	ERA	AERA	OAV	OOB	AB-HR-SH	AVG	PB	SUP	APR	DL	PW
1928	Bos A	0	0	—	1	0	0	0	1	1	1	0	1	0		18.00	23	.250	.400	—		0		-1		-0.1

SHEA, MIKE
Michael Joseph B3.10.1867 New Orleans LA D8.22.1927 New Orleans LA TR/5-10/170 d4.20

YEAR	TM LG	W	L	PCT	G	GS	CG-SHO	SV-BS	IP	H	R	HR	HB	BB-IB	SO	ERA	AERA	OAV	OOB	AB-HR-SH	AVG	PB	SUP	APR	DL	PW
1887	Cin AA	1	1	.500	2	2	1	0	26	25	16	0		10	3	7.02	62	.333	.409	8	.250	0	147	-6		-0.5

SHEA, RED
Patrick Henry B11.29.1898 Ware MA D11.17.1981 Stafford CT BR/TR/6-0/165 d5.6

YEAR	TM LG	W	L	PCT	G	GS	CG-SHO	SV-BS	IP	H	R	HR	HB	BB-IB	SO	ERA	AERA	OAV	OOB	AB-HR-SH	AVG	PB	SUP	APR	DL	PW
1918	Phi A	0	0	—	1	0	0	0	9	14	8	0		2	2	4.00	73	.378	.410	3	.000	-0				-0.2
1920	NY N	5	2	.714	9	2	1	0	32	28	13	2	3	2	10	3.09	119	.239	.270	9	.111	-1	56	2		0.3
1922	NY N	0	3	.000	11	2	0	0	22	22	14	2	0	11	5	4.70	85	.256	.340	7	.000	-1	122	-2		-0.2
Total 3		5	5	.500	23	4	1	0	64	64	35	4	3	15	17	3.80	97	.267	.318	19	.053	-2	93	-2		-0.1

YEAR	TM LG	W	L	PCT	G	GS	CG-SHO	SV-BS	IP	H	R	HR	HB	BB-IB	SO	ERA	AERA	OAV	OOB	AB-HR-SH	AVG	PB	SUP	APR	DL	PW

SHEA, STEVE   Steven Francis   B12.5.1942 Worcester MA   BR/TR/6-3/215*   d7.14   Col Massachusetts

1968	Hou N	4	4	.500	30	0	0	6	34.2	27	14	0	3	11-0	15	3.38	88	.229	.306	6	.000	-1		-1		-0.3
1969	Mon N	0	0	—	10	0	0	6-0	15.2	18	8	2	0	8-2	11	2.87	129	.300	.371	0	—	0		0		0.0
Total	2	4	4	.500	40	0	0		50.1	45	22	2	3	19-2	26	3.22	99	.253	.328	6	.000	-1		-1		-0.3

SHEALY, AL   Albert Berley   B3.20.1900 Chapin SC   D3.7.1967 Hagerstown MD   BR/TR/5-11/175   d4.13   Col Newberry

1928	NY A	8	6	.571	23	12	3	2	96	124	64	4	1	42	39	5.06	74	.308	.375	38-1-2	.237	2	128	-15		-1.7
1930	Chi N	0	0	—	24	0	0		27	37	24	2	0	14	14	8.00	61	.327	.402	5	.600	1		-8		-0.2
Total	2	8	6	.571	47	12	3	2	123	161	88	6	1	56	53	5.71	70	.313	.381	43-1-2	.279	4	128	-23		-1.9

SHEARON, JOHN   John M.   B1870 Pittsburgh PA   D2.1.1923 Bradford PA   d7.28 ▲

1891	Cle N	1	3	.250	6	5	4		46	57	39	2	1	24	19	3.52	98	.292	.373	124	.242	-0*	79	-2		-0.1

SHEARS, GEORGE   George Penfield   B4.13.1890 Marshall MO   D11.12.1978 Loveland CO   BR/TL/6-3/180   d4.24

1912	NY A	0	0	—	4	0	0		15	24	18	0	0	11	9	5.40	67	.364	.455	6	.167	0		-5		-0.2

SHEEHAN, TOM   Thomas Clancy   B3.31.1894 Grand Ridge IL   D10.29.1982 Chillicothe OH   BR/TR/6-2.5/190   d7.14   M1/C5

1915	Phi A	4	9	.308	15	13	8-1	0	102	131	73	1	1	38	22	4.15	71	.335	.395	34-0-2	.118	-3	82	-17		-2.2
1916	Phi A	1	16	.059	38	17	8	0	188	197	111	2	2	94	54	3.69	78	.287	.374	56-0-1	.125	-2	70	-21		-1.8
1921	NY A	1	0	1.000	12	1	0	1	33	43	23	1	1	19	7	5.45	78	.326	.414	8-0-2	.625	1	217	-1		0.0
1924	Cin N	9	11	.450	39	14	8-2	1	166.2	170	72	5	1	54	52	3.24	116	.269	.328	58	.310	4*	79	10		1.4
1925	Cin N	1	0	1.000	10	3	1	1	29	37	31	3	0	12	5	8.07	51	.298	.360	5-0-2	.200	1	123	-13		-0.5
	Pit N	1	1	.500	23	0	0	2	57.1	63	25	3	0	13	13	2.67	167	.286	.326	20	.150	-1*		9		0.3
	Year	2	1	.667	33	3	1	3	86.1	100	56	6	0	25	18	4.48	97	.291	.336	25-0-2	.160	-0	117	-2		-0.2
1926	Pit N	0	2	.000	9	2	1	0	31	36	24	0	2	12	16	6.68	59	.298	.370	9-0-2	.111	-1	116	-8		-0.5
Total	6	17	39	.304	146	50	26-3	5	607	677	359	14	7	242	169	4.00	86	.294	.362	190-0-9	.205	0	82	-44		-3.3

SHEETS, BEN   Ben M.   B7.18.1978 Baton Rouge LA   BR/TR/6-1/195(195-220)   [MilN99 1/10]   d4.5   Col Louisiana-Monroe

2001	Mil N★	11	10	.524	25	25	1-1	0-0	151.1	166	89	23	5	48-6	94	4.76	90	.283	.340	42-0-2	.071	-2	105	-9	46	-1.2
2002	Mil N	11	16	.407	34	34	1	0-0	216.2	237	105	21	10	70-10	170	4.15	99	.281	.343	68-0-4	.088	-3	81	1		0.0
2003	Mil N	11	13	.458	34	34	1	0-0	220.2	232	122	29	4	43-2	157	4.45	97	.268	.305	66-0-5	.076	-4	103	-5		-1.0
2004	Mil N★	12	14	.462	34	34	5	0-0	237	201	85	25	4	32-1	264	2.70	163	.226	.255	67-0-9	.134	-1	76	41	71	4.1
2005	Mil N	10	9	.526	22	22	3	0-0	156.2	142	66	19	2	25-1	141	3.33	128	.237	.270	45-0-7	.022	-4	78	15	117	1.1
Total	5	55	62	.470	149	149	11-1	0-0	982.1	978	467	117	27	218-20	826	3.83	112	.258	.302	288-0-27	.083	-13	88	43	117	3.0

SHELDON, ROLLIE   Roland Frank   B12.17.1936 Putnam CT   BR/TR/6-4/190(190-201)   d4.23   Col Connecticut

1961	NY A	11	5	.688	35	21	6-2	0	162.2	149	70	17	2	55-2	84	3.60	103	.246	.310	56-0-2	.125	-2*	112	3		0.1
1962	NY A	7	8	.467	34	16	2	1	118	136	78	12	1	28-3	54	5.49	68	.289	.324	26-0-6	.077	0	115	-23		-2.6
1964	†NY A	5	2	.714	19	12	3	1	102.1	92	43	18	1	18-2	57	3.61	100	.243	.276	34-0-2	.088	-2	129	1		-0.1
1965	NY A	0	0	—	3	0	0	0	6.1	5	1	0	0	1-0	1	1.42	240	.238	.261	1	.000	-0		1		0.1
	KC A	10	8	.556	32	29	4-1	0	186.2	180	86	22	7	56-3	105	3.95	88	.251	.311	51-0-7	.078	-3	96	-7		-1.0
	Year	10	8	.556	35	29	4-1	0	193	185	87	22	7	57-3	112	3.87	90	.251	.309	52-0-7	.077	-3	96	-4		-0.9
1966	KC A	4	7	.364	14	13	1-1	0	69	73	31	3	1	26-3	26	3.13	109	.275	.337	23-0-2	.087	-1	82	0		-0.1
	Bos A	1	6	.143	23	10	1	0	79.2	106	49	15	2	23-4	38	4.97	77	.320	.367	18	.111	-1	76	-9		-0.8
	Year	5	13	.278	37	23	2-1	0	148.2	179	80	18	3	49-7	64	4.12	88	.300	.353	41-0-2	.098	-2	78	-8		-0.9
Total	5	38	36	.514	160	101	17-4	2	724.2	741	358	87	14	207-17	371	4.09	89	.266	.317	209-0-19	.096	-9	102	-34		-4.4

SHELLENBACK, FRANK   Frank Victor   B12.16.1898 Joplin MO   D8.17.1969 Newton MA   BR/TR/6-2/192   d5.8   C15   Col Santa Clara

1918	Chi A	9	12	.429	28	21	10-2	2	182.2	180	77	1	4	74	47	2.66	103	.262	.338	54-0-5	.130	-1*	109	-1		-0.5
1919	Chi A	1	3	.250	8	4	2	0	35	40	24	1	0	16	10	5.14	62	.303	.378	11	.091	-0	111	-7		-0.8
Total	2	10	15	.400	36	25	12-2	2	217.2	220	101	2	4	90	57	3.06	92	.269	.344	65-0-5	.123	-1	109	-8		-1.3

SHELLENBACK, JIM   James Philip   B11.18.1943 Riverside CA   BL/TL/6-2/200*   d9.15   C1

1966	Pit N	0	0	—	2	0	0	0	3	3	3	2	0	3-1	0	9.00	40	.300	.462	0	—	0		-2		-0.1
1967	Pit N	1	1	.500	6	2	1	0	23.1	23	12	1	0	12-1	11	2.70	125	.250	.343	6	.167	-0	65	0		0.0
1969	Pit N	0	0	—	8	0	0	0-0	16.2	14	8	1	0	4-0	7	3.24	107	.233	.277	1	.000	-0		0		0.1
	Was A	4	7	.364	30	11	2	1-1	84.2	87	43	8	1	48-3	50	4.04	87	.268	.362	27	.185	-0	108	-5		-0.5
1970	Was A	6	7	.462	39	14	2-1	0-0	117.1	107	57	6	0	51-4	57	3.53	96	.267	.338	30-0-4	.067	-2*	106	-2		-0.4
1971	Was A	3	11	.214	40	15	3-1	0-0	120	123	56	10	3	49-5	47	3.53	96	.267	.338	30-0-1	.167	0	71	-3		-0.3
1972	Tex A	2	4	.333	22	6	0	1-0	57	46	24	6	2	16-0	30	3.47	88	.221	.283	10-0-1	.100	-1	58	-2	63	0.0
1973	Tex A	0	0	—	2	0	0	0	1.2	0	0	0	0	0-0	3	0.00	—	.000	.000	0	—	0		1		0.0
1974	Tex A	0	0	—	11	0	0	0-0	24.2	30	18	5	1	12-0	14	5.84	61	.306	.384	0	—	0		-6	26	-0.2
1977	Min A	0	0	—	5	0	0	0-0	5.2	10	7	1	0	5-0	3	7.94	50	.385	.469	0	—	0		-3		-0.3
Total	9	16	30	.348	165	48	8-2	2-1	454	443	228	40	8	200-14	222	3.81	91	.258	.335	104-0-6	.135	-2	88	-22	89	-2.0

SHEPARD, BERT   Bert Robert   B6.28.1920 Dana IN   BL/TL/5-11/185   d8.4   C1

1945	Was A	0	0	—	1	0	0	0	5.1	3	1	0	1	1	2	1.69	184	.167	.250	3	.000	-0		1		0.0

SHEPHERD, KEITH   Keith Wayne   B1.21.1968 Wabash IN   BR/TR/6-2/205(197-215)   [PitN86 11/264]   d9.6

1992	Phi N	1	1	.500	12	0	0	2-4	22	19	10	0	0	6-1	10	3.27	107	.244	.287	0	—	0		0		0.0
1993	Col N	1	3	.250	14	1	0	1-1	19.1	26	16	4	1	4-0	7	6.98	69	.333	.369	2	.000	-0	113	-4		-0.7
1995	Bos A	0	0	—	2	0	0	0-0	1	4	4	0	0	2-0	0	36.00	14	.571	.667	0	—	0		-3	35	-0.5
1996	Bal A	0	1	.000	13	0	0	0-0	20.2	31	27	6	0	18-1	17	8.71	57	.341	.445	0	—	0		-11		-0.5
Total	4	2	5	.286	41	1	0	3-5	63	80	57	10	1	30-2	34	6.71	66	.315	.383	2	.000	-0	113	-18	35	-1.3

SHERDEL, BILL   William Henry "Wee Willie"   B8.15.1896 McSherrystown PA   D11.14.1968 McSherrystown PA   BL/TL/5-10/160   d4.22

1918	StL N	6	12	.333	35	16	9-1	0	182.1	174	78	3	3	49	40	2.71	100	.259	.313	62-1-2	.242	3	108	-2		0.2
1919	StL N	5	9	.357	36	11	7	1	137.1	137	66	3	2	42	52	3.47	80	.270	.328	48	.271	2*	101	-10		-0.7
1920	StL N	11	10	.524	43	7	4	6	170	183	72	1	11	40	74	3.28	91	.297	.350	63-1-2	.222	2*	94	-4		-0.2
1921	StL N	9	8	.529	38	8	5-1	1	144.1	137	62	7	3	38	57	3.18	115	.247	.299	44	.114	-2*	118	9		0.7
1922	StL N	17	13	.567	47	31	15-3	2	242	298	132	12	5	81	79	3.87	100	.303	.348	88-1-2	.193	1*	106	-9		-0.3
1923	StL N	15	13	.536	39	26	14	2	225	270	127	15	6	59	78	4.32	90	.296	.343	83-1-3	.337	9*	99	7		0.8
1924	StL N	8	9	.471	35	10	6	1	168.2	188	77	9	5	38	57	3.42	111	.291	.335	75-0-1	.200	2*	112	29		1.4
1925	StL N	15	6	**.714**	32	21	17-2	1	200	216	77	8	3	42	53	3.11	139	.277	.316	73-1-1	.205	2*	107	13		1.4
1926	†StL N	16	12	.571	34	29	17-3	0	234.2	255	103	15	4	49	59	3.49	112	.278	.318	90-1-3	.244	2*	109	12		1.3
1927	StL N	17	12	.586	39	28	18	6	232.1	241	109	17	3	56	59	3.53	112	.269	.308	84-1-10	.226	4	112	31		2.3
1928	†StL N	21	10	.677	38	27	20	5	248.2	251	96	17	2	56	72	2.86	140	.261	.303	70-1-6	.229	2	85	-26		-2.6
1929	StL N	10	15	.400	38	22	11-1	0	195.2	278	144	14	2	58	69	5.93	79	.337	.382	70-1-6	.105	-1	122	5		-0.2
1930	StL N	3	2	.600	13	7	1	0	64	86	34	5	1	13	29	4.64	108	.325	.358	42-0-2	.095	-4	105	1		-0.2
	Bos N	6	5	.545	21	14	7	1	119.1	131	73	10	2	30	26	4.75	104	.283	.329	61-0-8	.098	-5	110	6		-0.1
	Year	9	7	.563	34	21	8	1	183.1	217	107	15	3	43	55	4.25	89	.294	.337	46	.304	-1	66	-5		-0.2
1931	Bos N	6	10	.375	27	16	8	0	137.2	163	70	13	1	35	41	4.25	89	.294	.337	46	.304	-1	66	-5		-0.2
1932	Bos N	0	0	—	1	0	0	0	1.2	3	3	0	0	1	0	0.00	—	.375	.444	—		0		-1		0.0
	StL N	0	0	—	3	0	0	0	5.2	7	3	0	1	0	1	4.76	83	.304	.333	1	1.000	1		0		0.1
	Year	0	0	—	4	0	0	0	7.1	10	6	0	1	1	1	3.68	106	.323	.364	1	1.000	1		-1		0.1
Total	15	165	146	.531	514	273	159-11	26	2709.1	3018	1326	149	54	661	839	3.72	103	.285	.330	960-9-44	.223	27	107	47		6.8

SHERID, ROY   Royden Richard   B1.25.1907 Norristown PA   D2.28.1982 Parker Ford PA   BR/TR/6-2/185   d5.11   Col Albright

1929	NY A	6	6	.500	33	15	9	1	154.2	165	81	6	5	55	51	3.61	107	.277	.343	50-0-3	.180	-1	120	2		0.0
1930	NY A	12	13	.480	37	21	8	4	184	214	122	13	5	87	59	5.23	82	.289	.368	69-0-4	.101	-6	131	-17		-2.5
1931	NY A	5	5	.500	17	8	3	2	74.1	94	52	4	3	24	39	5.69	70	.306	.362	30-0-5	.333	2	149	-15		-1.5
Total	3	23	24	.489	87	44	20	7	413	473	255	23	13	166	149	4.71	87	.288	.358	149-0-12	.174	-5	131	-30		-4.0

SHERMAN, JOE   Joel Powers   B11.4.1890 Yarmouth MA   D12.21.1987 Cape Coral FL   BR/TR/6-0/165   d9.24   Col Massachusetts

1915	Phi A	1	0	1.000	1	1	0	0	15	15	4	2	1	6	2	2.40	122	.259	.295	6	.333	1	100	1		0.1

SHERMAN, DAN   Lester Daniel "Babe"   B5.9.1890 Hubbardsville NY   D9.16.1955 Highland Park MI   BR/TR/5-6/145   d6.4

1914	Chi F	0	1	.000	1	1	0	0	0.1	1	2	0	0	2	0	0.00	—	.000	.667	0	—	0	103	-1		-0.1

YEAR	TM LG	W	L	PCT	G	GS	CG-SHO	SV-BS	IP	H	R	HR	HB	BB-IB	SO	ERA	AERA	OAV	OOB	AB-HR-SH	AVG	PB	SUP	APR	DL	PW

SHERRILL, GEORGE George Friederich B4.19.1977 Memphis TN BL/TL/6-0/210* d7.16 Col Austin Peay

YEAR	TM LG	W	L	PCT	G	GS	CG-SHO	SV-BS	IP	H	R	HR	HB	BB-IB	SO	ERA	AERA	OAV	OOB	AB-HR-SH	AVG	PB	SUP	APR	DL	PW
2004	Sea A	2	1	.667	21	0	0	0-0	23.2	24	12	3	1	9-1	16	3.80	118	.258	.327	0	—	0		1		0.1
2005	Sea A	4	3	.571	29	0	0	0-0	19	13	12	3	1	7-2	24	5.21	81	.194	.276	0	—	0		-2		-0.4
Total	2	6	4	.600	50	0	0	0-0	42.2	37	24	6	2	16-3	40	4.43	98	.231	.306	0	—	0		-1		-0.3

SHERRILL, TIM Timothy Shawn B9.10.1965 Harrison AR BL/TL/5-11/170* [StLN87 18/462] d8.14 Col Arkansas-Monticello

YEAR	TM LG	W	L	PCT	G	GS	CG-SHO	SV-BS	IP	H	R	HR	HB	BB-IB	SO	ERA	AERA	OAV	OOB	AB-HR-SH	AVG	PB	SUP	APR	DL	PW
1990	StL N	0	0	—	8	0	0	0-0	4.1	10	5	0	0	3-0	3	6.23	62	.476	.542	0	—	0		-2		-0.1
1991	StL N	0	0	—	10	0	0	0-0	14.1	20	13	2	2	3-1	4	8.16	46	.339	.379	0	—	0		-6		-0.3
Total	2	0	0	—	18	0	0	0-0	18.2	30	18	2	2	6-1	7	7.71	49	.375	.422	0	—	0		-8		-0.4

SHERRY, FRED Fred Peter (b Fred Peter Schuerholz) B1.13.1889 Honesdale PA D7.27.1975 Honesdale PA BR/TR/6-0/170 d4.25 Col Villanova

YEAR	TM LG	W	L	PCT	G	GS	CG-SHO	SV-BS	IP	H	R	HR	HB	BB-IB	SO	ERA	AERA	OAV	OOB	AB-HR-SH	AVG	PB	SUP	APR	DL	PW
1911	Was A	0	4	.000	10	3	2	0	52.1	63	40	1	0	19	20	4.30	76	.310	.369	19	.158	-1	66	-7		-0.5

SHERRY, LARRY Lawrence B7.25.1935 Los Angeles CA BR/TR/6-2/204(180-204) d4.17 C4 b-Norm

YEAR	TM LG	W	L	PCT	G	GS	CG-SHO	SV-BS	IP	H	R	HR	HB	BB-IB	SO	ERA	AERA	OAV	OOB	AB-HR-SH	AVG	PB	SUP	APR	DL	PW
1958	LA N	0	0	—	2	0	0	0	4.1	10	7	0	1	7-1	2	12.46	33	.476	.621	0	—	0		-4		-0.2
1959	†LA N	7	2	.778	23	9	1-1	3	94.1	75	27	9	2	43-5	72	2.19	193	.218	.308	32-2-1	.219	2	101	19		2.1
1960	LA N	14	10	.583	57	3	1	7	142.1	125	65	14	6	82-15	114	3.79	105	.238	.346	37-1-3	.162	1	89	4		0.7
1961	LA N	4	4	.500	53	1	0	15	94.2	90	48	10	4	39-9	79	3.90	111	.252	.332	13	.154	-0	0	4		0.3
1962	LA N	7	3	.700	58	0	0	11	90	81	40	8	6	44-5	71	3.20	113	.241	.335	17-0-1	.118	-0		3		0.4
1963	LA N	6	2	.250	36	3	0	3	79.2	82	43	8	4	24-4	47	3.73	81	.265	.321	9-0-1	.111	1	67	-9		-0.8
1964	Det A	7	5	.583	38	0	0	11	66.1	52	29	7	3	37-2	58	3.66	100	.216	.325	14	.000	-2		0	59	-0.1
1965	Det A	4	6	.333	39	0	0	5	78.1	71	30	5	1	40-10	46	3.10	112	.254	.346	10-0-2	.300	2		3		0.6
1966	Det A	8	5	.615	55	0	0	20	77.2	66	38	8	3	36-2	63	3.82	91	.232	.320	10	.400	2		-3		-0.6
1967	Det A	0	1	.000	20	0	0	1	28	35	22	3	0	7-0	20	6.43	51	.289	.328	1	.000	-0		-10		-0.5
	Hou N	1	2	.333	29	0	0	6	40.2	53	26	4	1	13-2	32	4.87	68	.327	.374	5	.000	-1		-8		-0.8
1968	Cal A	0	0	—	3	0	0	0	3	7	2	2	0	2-0	2	6.00	49	.467	.529	0	—	-1		-1		-0.1
Total	11	53	44	.546	416	16	2-1	82	799.1	747	377	78	32	374-55	606	3.67	101	.249	.336	148-3-8	.169	4	92	-2	59	1.0

SHIELDS, BEN Benjamin Cowan "Big Ben","Lefty" B6.17.1903 Huntersville NC D1.24.1982 Woodruff SC BR/TL(BB 1930-31)/6-1.5/195 d4.17

YEAR	TM LG	W	L	PCT	G	GS	CG-SHO	SV-BS	IP	H	R	HR	HB	BB-IB	SO	ERA	AERA	OAV	OOB	AB-HR-SH	AVG	PB	SUP	APR	DL	PW
1924	NY A	0	0	—	2	0	0	0	2	6	6	0	0	2	3	27.00	15	.545	.615	0	—	0		-5		-0.2
1925	NY A	3	0	1.000	4	2	2	0	24	24	13	2	2	12	5	4.88	87	.267	.365	8	.125	-1	128	-1		-0.2
1930	Bos A	0	0	—	3	0	0	0	10	16	11	0	0	6	1	9.00	51	.400	.478	3	.000	-1		-5		-0.2
1931	Phi N	1	0	1.000	4	0	0	0	5.1	9	9	1	0	7	0	15.19	28	.391	.533	2	.000	-0		-5		-0.8
Total	4	4	0	1.000	13	2	2	0	41.1	55	39	3	2	27	9	8.27	53	.335	.435	13	.077	-2	128	-16		-1.4

SHIELDS, CHARLIE Charles Jessamine B12.10.1879 Jackson TN D8.27.1953 Memphis TN BL/TL d4.23

YEAR	TM LG	W	L	PCT	G	GS	CG-SHO	SV-BS	IP	H	R	HR	HB	BB-IB	SO	ERA	AERA	OAV	OOB	AB-HR-SH	AVG	PB	SUP	APR	DL	PW
1902	Bal A	4	11	.267	23	15	10-1	1	142.1	201	102	7	2	32	28	4.24	89	.333	.368	48-0-1	.167	-1*	92	-8		-1.0
	StL A	3	0	1.000	4	4	3	0	30	37	16	1	0	7	6	3.30	107	.303	.341	13-0-1	.462	2	163	0		0.2
	Year	7	11	.389	27	19	13-1	1	172.1	238	118	8	2	39	34	4.07	92	.328	.364	61-0-2	.230	1	106	-8		-0.8
1907	StL N	0	2	.000	3	2	0	0	6.2	12	11	0	2	7	1	9.45	26	.444	.583	2	.000	-0	100	-5		-1.0
Total	2	7	13	.350	30	21	13-1	1	179	250	129	8	4	46	35	4.27	86	.332	.374	63-0-2	.222	1	103	-13		-1.8

SHIELDS, SCOT Robert Scot B7.22.1975 Fort Lauderdale FL BR/TR/6-1/175* [AnaA97 38/1137] d5.26 Col Lincoln Memorial

YEAR	TM LG	W	L	PCT	G	GS	CG-SHO	SV-BS	IP	H	R	HR	HB	BB-IB	SO	ERA	AERA	OAV	OOB	AB-HR-SH	AVG	PB	SUP	APR	DL	PW
2001	Ana A	0	0	—	8	0	0	0-0	11	8	1	0	1	7-0	7	0.00	—	.200	.333	0	—	0		5		0.2
2002	†Ana A	5	3	.625	29	1	0	0-0	49	31	13	4	1	21-1	30	2.20	203	.188	.283	0	—	0	124	12		1.8
2003	Ana A	5	6	.455	44	13	0	1-0	148.1	138	56	12	5	38-6	111	2.85	153	.247	.299	0	—	0	74	24		1.7
2004	†Ana A	8	2	.800	60	0	0	4-3	105.1	97	42	6	3	40-5	109	3.33	134	.238	.310	1	.000	-0		14		1.2
2005	†LA A	10	11	.476	78	0	0	7-6	91.2	66	33	5	2	37-2	98	2.75	157	.201	.283	1	.000	-0		15		3.0
Total	5	28	22	.560	219	14	0	12-9	405.1	340	145	27	12	143-14	355	2.80	158	.227	.297	2	.000	-0	78	70		7.9

SHIELDS, STEVE Stephen Mack B11.30.1958 Gadsden AL BR/TR/6-5/230* [BosA77 10/247] d6.1

YEAR	TM LG	W	L	PCT	G	GS	CG-SHO	SV-BS	IP	H	R	HR	HB	BB-IB	SO	ERA	AERA	OAV	OOB	AB-HR-SH	AVG	PB	SUP	APR	DL	PW
1985	Atl N	1	2	.333	23	6	0	0-0	68	86	46	9	1	32-6	29	5.16	75	.320	.390	18	.111	-1	92	-10		-0.6
1986	Atl N	0	0	—	6	0	0	0-0	12.2	13	10	4	0	7-0	6	7.11	56	.271	.364	1	.000	-0		-4		-0.2
	KC A	0	0	—	3	0	0	0-1	8.2	3	3	1	0	4-1	2	2.08	206	.111	.212	0	—	0		2		0.1
1987	Sea A	2	0	1.000	20	0	0	3-1	30	43	25	7	0	12-1	22	6.60	72	.333	.382	0	—	0		-6	30	-0.5
1988	NY A	5	5	.500	39	0	0	0-2	82.1	96	44	8	2	30-4	55	4.37	91	.298	.360	0	—	0		-4		-0.4
1989	Min A	0	1	.000	11	0	0	0-1	17.1	28	18	3	0	6-1	12	7.79	53	.354	.400	0	—	0		-7	104	-0.4
Total	5	8	8	.500	102	6	0	3-5	219	269	146	32	3	91-13	126	5.26	77	.308	.371	19	.105	-1	92	-29	134	-2.0

SHIELDS, VINCE Vincent William B11.18.1900 Fredericton NB, Can. D10.17.1952 Plaster Rock NB, Can. BL/TR/5-11/185 d9.20

YEAR	TM LG	W	L	PCT	G	GS	CG-SHO	SV-BS	IP	H	R	HR	HB	BB-IB	SO	ERA	AERA	OAV	OOB	AB-HR-SH	AVG	PB	SUP	APR	DL	PW
1924	StL N	1	1	.500	2	1	0	0	12	10	5	1	3	3	4	3.00	126	.227	.320	5	.400	0*	67	1		0.2

SHIELL, JASON Jason Alexander B10.19.1976 Savannah GA BR/TR/6-0/180* d9.8 [DL 2004 Bos A 183]

YEAR	TM LG	W	L	PCT	G	GS	CG-SHO	SV-BS	IP	H	R	HR	HB	BB-IB	SO	ERA	AERA	OAV	OOB	AB-HR-SH	AVG	PB	SUP	APR	DL	PW
2002	SD N	0	0	—	3	0	0	0-0	1.1	7	4	0	0	3-0	1	27.00	14	.700	.769	0	—	0		-3		-0.2
2003	Bos A	2	0	1.000	17	0	0	1-1	23.1	23	13	4	0	17-2	23	4.63	101	.253	.382	0	—	0		0		0.0
Total	2	2	0	1.000	20	0	0	1-1	24.2	30	17	4	0	20-2	24	5.84	79	.297	.423	0	—	0		-3	183	-0.2

SHIFFLETT, GARLAND Garland Jessie "Duck" B3.28.1935 Elkton VA BR/TR/5-10.5/165* d4.22

YEAR	TM LG	W	L	PCT	G	GS	CG-SHO	SV-BS	IP	H	R	HR	HB	BB-IB	SO	ERA	AERA	OAV	OOB	AB-HR-SH	AVG	PB	SUP	APR	DL	PW
1957	Was A	0	0	—	6	1	0	0	8	6	9	0	2	10-0	2	10.13	38	.222	.421	0	—	0	160	-5		-0.3
1964	Min A	0	2	.000	10	0	0	1	17.2	22	9	1	1	7-0	8	4.58	78	.297	.366	4	.000	-0		-1		-0.2
Total	2	0	2	.000	16	1	0	1	25.2	28	18	1	1	17-0	10	6.31	58	.277	.383	4	.000	-0	160	-6		-0.5

SHIFFLETT, STEVE Stephen Earl B1.5.1966 Kansas City MO BR/TR/6-1/205 d7.3 Col Emporia St.

YEAR	TM LG	W	L	PCT	G	GS	CG-SHO	SV-BS	IP	H	R	HR	HB	BB-IB	SO	ERA	AERA	OAV	OOB	AB-HR-SH	AVG	PB	SUP	APR	DL	PW
1992	KC A	1	4	.200	34	0	0	0-2	52	55	15	6	2	17-8	25	2.60	157	.279	.341	0	—	0		9		0.8

SHINALL, ZAK Zakary Sebastien B10.14.1968 St.Louis MO BR/TR/6-3/215 [LAN87 29/742] d5.12 Col El Camino (CA) JC

YEAR	TM LG	W	L	PCT	G	GS	CG-SHO	SV-BS	IP	H	R	HR	HB	BB-IB	SO	ERA	AERA	OAV	OOB	AB-HR-SH	AVG	PB	SUP	APR	DL	PW
1993	Sea A	0	0	—	1	0	0	0-0	2.2	4	1	1	0	2-0	0	3.38	132	.333	.429	0	—	0		0		0.0

SHIPANOFF, DAVE David Noel B11.13.1959 Edmonton AL, Can. BR/TR/6-2/185 d8.10 Col Wabash Valley (IL) CC

YEAR	TM LG	W	L	PCT	G	GS	CG-SHO	SV-BS	IP	H	R	HR	HB	BB-IB	SO	ERA	AERA	OAV	OOB	AB-HR-SH	AVG	PB	SUP	APR	DL	PW
1985	Phi N	1	2	.333	26	0	0	3-0	36.1	33	15	3	1	16-3	26	3.22	115	.231	.309	3	.000	-0		2		0.1

SHIPLEY, JOE Joseph Clark "Moses" B5.9.1935 Morristown TN BR/TR/6-4/210(190-210) d7.14

YEAR	TM LG	W	L	PCT	G	GS	CG-SHO	SV-BS	IP	H	R	HR	HB	BB-IB	SO	ERA	AERA	OAV	OOB	AB-HR-SH	AVG	PB	SUP	APR	DL	PW
1958	SF N	0	0	—	1	0	0	0	1.1	1	2	0	0	3-0	0	33.75	11	.429	.667	0	—	0		-4		-0.2
1959	SF N	0	0	—	10	1	0	0	18	16	11	2	1	17-0	11	4.50	85	.239	.400	3	.000	-0	70	-2		-0.1
1960	SF N	0	0	—	15	0	0	0	20	20	13	2	3	9-1	9	5.40	64	.274	.372	0	—	0		-4		-0.2
1963	Chi N	0	1	.000	3	0	0	0	4.2	9	7	0	0	6-0	3	5.79	61	.409	.536	2	.000	-0		-3		-0.2
Total	4	0	1	.000	29	1	0	0	44	48	36	4	6	35-1	23	5.93	61	.284	.422	5	.000	-1	70	-13		-1.1

SHIREY, DUKE Clair Lee B6.20.1898 Jersey Shore PA D9.1.1962 Hagerstown MD BR/TR/6-1/175 d9.28

YEAR	TM LG	W	L	PCT	G	GS	CG-SHO	SV-BS	IP	H	R	HR	HB	BB-IB	SO	ERA	AERA	OAV	OOB	AB-HR-SH	AVG	PB	SUP	APR	DL	PW
1920	Was A	0	1	.000	4	0	0	0	4	5	3	0	0	2	2	6.75	55	.313	.421	1	.000	-0	128	-1		-0.3

SHIRLEY, TEX Alvis Newman B4.25.1918 Birthright TX D11.7.1993 DeSoto TX BB/TR(BR 1941-42)/6-1/175 d9.6

YEAR	TM LG	W	L	PCT	G	GS	CG-SHO	SV-BS	IP	H	R	HR	HB	BB-IB	SO	ERA	AERA	OAV	OOB	AB-HR-SH	AVG	PB	SUP	APR	DL	PW
1941	Phi A	0	1	.000	5	0	0	1	7.1	8	4	1	0	6	1	2.45	171	.286	.412	1	.000	-0		1		0.1
1942	Phi A	0	1	.000	15	1	0	1	35.2	37	30	0	2	22	10	5.30	71	.272	.381	6	.000	-1	136	-8		-0.5
1944	†StL A	5	4	.556	23	11	2-1	0	80.1	59	45	4	1	64	35	4.15	87	.203	.348	28	.143	-2*	101	-5		-0.8
1945	StL A	8	12	.400	32	24	10-2	0	183.2	191	79	8	1	93	77	3.63	97	.274	.360	70-0-2	.286	2*	98	0		0.2
1946	StL A	6	12	.333	27	18	7	0	139.2	148	89	7	1	105	45	4.96	75	.273	.391	51-0-1	.196	-0*	119	-18		-2.1
Total	5	19	30	.388	102	54	19-3	2	446.2	443	247	20	5	290	168	4.25	85	.261	.371	159-0-4	.214	-1	106	-30		-3.1

SHIRLEY, BOB Robert Charles B6.25.1954 Cushing OK BR/TL/5-11/185* [SDN76*S1/8] d4.10 Col Oklahoma

YEAR	TM LG	W	L	PCT	G	GS	CG-SHO	SV-BS	IP	H	R	HR	HB	BB-IB	SO	ERA	AERA	OAV	OOB	AB-HR-SH	AVG	PB	SUP	APR	DL	PW
1977	SD N	12	18	.400	39	35	1	0-0	214	215	107	22	4	100-14	146	3.70	97	.259	.339	74-0-4	.122	-2	92	-6		-0.9
1978	SD N	8	11	.421	50	20	2	5-2	166	164	75	10	3	61-11	102	3.69	91	.262	.328	40-0-7	.125	-0	102	-5		-0.5
1979	SD N	8	16	.333	49	25	4-1	0-1	205	196	89	15	6	59-8	117	3.38	104	.257	.313	55-0-5	.091	-2	106	3		-0.2
1980	SD N	11	12	.478	59	12	3	7-3	137	143	68	12	0	54-8	67	3.55	96	.276	.341	30-0-4	.033	-2	94	-1		-0.3
1981	StL N	6	4	.600	28	11	1	1-0	79.1	78	42	6	1	34-3	36	4.08	89	.260	.335	22-0-1	.136	-1	112	-5		-0.8
1982	Cin N	8	13	.381	41	20	1	0-0	152.2	138	74	17	3	73-13	89	3.60	102	.248	.335	42-0-5	.143	-1	64	-1		-0.2
1983	NY A	5	8	.385	25	17	1-1	0-0	108	122	71	10	0	36-3	53	5.08	78	.293	.345	0	—	0	106	-15		-1.6
1984	NY A	3	3	.500	41	7	1	0-1	114.1	119	47	8	0	38-2	48	3.38	113	.271	.331	0	—	0	77	6		0.3
1985	NY A	5	5	.500	48	8	2	2-2	109	103	34	5	0	26-2	55	2.64	153	.251	.293	0	—	0	90	18		1.6

YEAR	TM LG	W	L	PCT	G	GS	CG-SHO	SV-BS	IP	H	R	HR	HB	BB-IB	SO	ERA	AERA	OAV	OOB	AB-HR-SH	AVG	PB	SUP	APR	DL	PW
1986	NY A	0	4	.000	39	6	0	3-0	105.1	108	60	13	3	40-1	64	5.04	82	.271	.336	0	—	0	48	-8		-0.3
1987	NY A	1	0	1.000	12	1	0	0-0	34	36	20	4	0	16-0	12	4.50	99	.277	.342	0	—	0	82	-1		-0.1
	KC A	0	0	—	3	0	0	0-0	7.1	10	12	5	0	6-0	1	14.73	31	.323	.432	0	—	0		-7		-0.4
	Year	1	0	1.000	15	1	0	0-0	41.1	46	32	9	0	22-0	13	6.31	71	.286	.360	0	—	0	82	-9		-0.4
Total	11	67	94	.416	434	162	16-2	18-9	1432	1432	689	127	20	543-72	790	3.82	97	.264	.331	263-0-26	.110	-8	91	-22		-2.9

SHIRLEY, STEVE   Steven Brian   B10.12.1956 San Francisco CA   BL/TL/6-0/185   [LAN74 2/45]   d6.21

YEAR	TM LG	W	L	PCT	G	GS	CG-SHO	SV-BS	IP	H	R	HR	HB	BB-IB	SO	ERA	AERA	OAV	OOB	AB-HR-SH	AVG	PB	SUP	APR	DL	PW
1982	LA N	1	1	.500	11	0	0	0	12.2	15	6	0	0	7-2	8	4.26	81	.300	.386	1	1.000	0		-1		-0.1

SHOCKER, URBAN   Urban James (b Urbain Jacques Shockcor)   B9.22.1890 Cleveland OH   D9.9.1928 Denver CO   BR/TR/5-10/170   d4.24   Mil 1918

YEAR	TM LG	W	L	PCT	G	GS	CG-SHO	SV-BS	IP	H	R	HR	HB	BB-IB	SO	ERA	AERA	OAV	OOB	AB-HR-SH	AVG	PB	SUP	APR	DL	PW
1916	NY A	4	3	.571	12	9	4-1	0	82.1	67	25	2	6	32	43	2.62	110	.230	.319	21-0-2	.190	1	102	4		0.5
1917	NY A	8	5	.615	26	13	7	1	145	124	59	5	0	46	68	2.61	103	.241	.303	45-0-5	.178	-1	109	0		0.0
1918	StL A	6	5	.545	14	9	7	2	94.2	69	26	0	1	40	33	1.81	152	.209	.296	34	.324	4	61	10		1.8
1919	StL A	13	11	.542	30	25	14-5	0	211	193	75	6	4	55	86	2.69	123	.244	.296	58-0-2	.138	-0	83	17		1.7
1920	StL A	20	10	.667	38	28	22-5	5	245.2	224	97	10	4	70	107	2.71	145	.248	.305	80-0-5	.225	2	98	30		3.7
1921	StL A	27	12	.692	47	38	30-4	4	326.2	345	151	21	6	86	132	3.55	126	.270	.319	104-0-7	.260	5	105	33		4.2
1922	StL A	24	17	.585	48	38	29-2	3	348	365	141	22	4	57	**149**	2.97	139	.272	.304	115-1-6	.191	2	97	44		4.9
1923	StL A	20	12	.625	43	35	24-3	5	277.1	292	122	12	3	49	109	3.41	122	.272	.306	80-0-12	.200	5	93	24		2.6
1924	StL A	16	13	.552	40	33	17-4	1	246.1	270	128	11	3	52	88	4.20	107	.277	.315	67-0-9	.239	5	105	11		1.5
1925	NY A	12	12	.500	41	30	15-2	2	244.1	278	108	17	3	58	74	3.65	117	.294	.336	64-0-10	.172	5	104	20		2.1
1926	†NY A	19	11	.633	41	32	18	2	258.1	272	113	13	2	71	59	2.84	136	.268	.306	54-0-20	.241	3	127	20		2.3
1927	NY A	18	6	.750	31	27	13-2	0	200	207	86	8	1	41	35	3.18	114	.269	.318	54-0-20	.241	0		1		0.0
1928	NY A	0	0	—	1	0	0	0	2	1	1	0	0	0	0	0.00		.429	.429	0	—	0		1		0.0
Total	13	187	117	.615	412	317	200-28	25	2681.2	2709	1131	127	37	657	983	3.17	124	.265	.311	798-1-98	.209	28	103	230		27.0

SHOFFNER, MILT   Milburn James   B11.13.1905 Sherman TX   D1.19.1978 Madison OH   BL/TL/6-1.5/184   d7.20

YEAR	TM LG	W	L	PCT	G	GS	CG-SHO	SV-BS	IP	H	R	HR	HB	BB-IB	SO	ERA	AERA	OAV	OOB	AB-HR-SH	AVG	PB	SUP	APR	DL	PW
1929	Cle A	2	3	.400	11	3	1	0	44.2	46	28	4	3	22	15	5.04	88	.284	.380	15	.000	-2	38	-2		-0.4
1930	Cle A	3	4	.429	24	10	1	0	84.2	129	86	8	1	50	17	7.97	61	.362	.442	33-1-2	.212	1	114	-26		-1.6
1931	Cle A	2	3	.400	12	4	1	0	41	55	34	4	2	26	12	7.24	64	.320	.415	13	.077	1	96	-9		-1.0
1937	Bos N	3	1	.750	6	5	3-1	1	42.2	38	14	1	1	9	13	2.53	142	.239	.284	16-1-3	.125	1	144	5		0.6
1938	Bos N	8	7	.533	26	15	9-1	1	139.2	147	60	7	2	36	49	3.54	97	.270	.317	57	.211	3*	100	0		0.3
1939	Bos N	4	6	.400	25	11	7	1	132.1	133	56	7	1	42	51	3.13	118	.265	.324	44-0-2	.159	-0	92	8		0.6
	Cin N	2	2	.500	10	3	0	0	37.2	43	18	3	2	11	6	3.35	115	.289	.346	11-0-1	.091	-1	99	1		0.0
	Year	6	8	.429	35	14	7	1	170	176	74	7	3	53	57	3.18	117	.271	.329	55-0-3	.145	-1	94	9		0.6
1940	Cin N	1	0	1.000	20	0	0	0	54.1	56	35	3	0	18	7	5.63	67	.268	.326	16-0-1	.125	-1		-10		-0.6
Total	7	25	26	.490	134	51	22-2	3	577	647	331	34	12	214	180	4.59	85	.287	.352	205-2-9	.156	-0	102	-33		-2.1

SHORE, ERNIE   Ernest Grady   B3.24.1891 East Bend NC   D9.24.1980 Winston-Salem NC   BR/TR/6-4/220   d6.20   Mil 1918   Col Guilford

YEAR	TM LG	W	L	PCT	G	GS	CG-SHO	SV-BS	IP	H	R	HR	HB	BB-IB	SO	ERA	AERA	OAV	OOB	AB-HR-SH	AVG	PB	SUP	APR	DL	PW
1912	NY N	0	0	—	1	0	0	0	8	10	1	0	1	3	3	27.00	13	.667	.692	0	—	0		-5		-0.6
1914	Bos A	10	5	.667	20	16	10-1	1	139.2	103	45	1	5	34	51	2.00	135	.204	.261	49-0-1	.102	-3	88	10		0.9
1915	†Bos A	19	8	.704	38	32	17-4	0	247	207	75	3	4	66	102	1.64	169	.228	.283	79-0-5	.101	-3	90	27		2.8
1916	†Bos A	16	10	.615	38	28	10-3	1	225.2	221	83	1	4	49	62	2.63	105	.259	.302	77-0-4	.091	-5	93	3		0.1
1917	Bos A	13	10	.565	29	27	14-1	1	226.2	201	76	1	12	55	57	2.22	116	.240	.297	78-0-4	.167	-1	94	8		-1.2
1919	NY A	5	8	.385	22	13	3	0	95	105	50	4	1	44	24	4.17	77	.288	.366	28-0-2	.143	-2	70	-8		-1.2
1920	NY A	2	2	.500	14	5	2	1	44.1	61	31	1	1	21	12	4.87	78	.333	.405	11-0-2	.182	0	112	-6		-0.4
Total	7	65	43	.602	160	121	56-9	5	979.1	906	370	12	27	270	309	2.47	113	.247	.304	322-0-18	.121	-14	91	29		0.5

SHORE, RAY   Raymond Everett   B6.9.1921 Cincinnati OH   D8.13.1996 St.Louis MO   BR/TR/6-3/210   d9.21   C5

YEAR	TM LG	W	L	PCT	G	GS	CG-SHO	SV-BS	IP	H	R	HR	HB	BB-IB	SO	ERA	AERA	OAV	OOB	AB-HR-SH	AVG	PB	SUP	APR	DL	PW
1946	StL A	0	0	—	1	0	0	0	1	1	2	0	0	1	1	18.00	21	.500	.571	0	—	0		-1		-0.1
1948	StL A	1	2	.333	17	4	0	0	38	40	30	2	4	35	12	6.39	71	.270	.422	9	.000	-1	79	-7		-0.6
1949	StL A	0	1	.000	13	0	0	0	23.1	27	30	3	2	31	13	10.80	42	.297	.484	5	.000	-1		-14		-0.7
Total	3	1	3	.250	31	4	0	0	62.1	70	62	5	6	67	26	8.23	55	.286	.450	14	.000	-2	79	-22		-1.4

SHORES, BILL   William David   B5.26.1904 Abilene TX   D2.19.1984 Purcell OK   BR/TR/6-0/185   d4.11

YEAR	TM LG	W	L	PCT	G	GS	CG-SHO	SV-BS	IP	H	R	HR	HB	BB-IB	SO	ERA	AERA	OAV	OOB	AB-HR-SH	AVG	PB	SUP	APR	DL	PW
1928	Phi A	1	1	.500	3	2	1	0	14	13	7	0	0	7	5	3.21	125	.250	.339	5	.000	-1	53	1		0.4
1929	Phi A	11	6	.647	39	13	5-1	7	152.2	150	71	6	3	59	49	3.60	118	.262	.334	40-0-6	.125	-2	94	11		1.6
1930	†Phi A	12	4	.750	31	19	7-1	0	159	169	86	11	3	70	48	4.19	112	.276	.353	57-0-3	.193	-2	120	8		0.4
1931	Phi A	0	3	.000	6	2	0	0	16	26	18	3	0	10	2	5.06	89	.361	.439	3	.333	0	66	-4		-0.6
1933	NY N	2	1	.667	8	3	1	0	36.2	41	18	4	0	14	20	3.93	82	.291	.355	11	.273	1	121	-2		-0.1
1936	Chi A	0	0	—	9	0	0	0	17	26	18	4	0	8	5	9.53	55	.356	.420	5	.200	-0	7	7		0.0
Total	6	26	15	.634	96	39	14-2	7	395.1	425	218	28	6	168	129	4.17	105	.279	.353	121-0-9	.174	-4	106	7		0.4

SHORT, CHRIS   Christopher Joseph   B9.19.1937 Milford DE   D8.1.1991 Wilmington DE   BR/TL/6-4/205(195-218)   d4.19   Col Bordentown Mil. Inst. (NJ) [JC

YEAR	TM LG	W	L	PCT	G	GS	CG-SHO	SV-BS	IP	H	R	HR	HB	BB-IB	SO	ERA	AERA	OAV	OOB	AB-HR-SH	AVG	PB	SUP	APR	DL	PW
1959	Phi N	0	0	—	3	2	0	0	14.1	19	13	3	1	10-0	8	8.16	50	.317	.423	6	.000	-1	141	-6		-0.3
1960	Phi N	6	9	.400	42	10	2	3	107.1	101	53	9	4	52-5	54	3.94	99	.249	.335	25	.000	-3	80	-2		-0.3
1961	Phi N	6	12	.333	39	16	1	1	127.1	157	94	12	9	71-11	80	5.94	69	.304	.390	37-0-7	.162	-1*	97	-26		-3.2
1962	Phi N	11	9	.550	47	12	4	3	142	149	66	13	8	56-6	91	3.42	113	.272	.347	36-0-4	.222	1*	112	5		0.4
1963	Phi N	9	12	.429	38	27	6-3	0	198	185	77	12	3	69-6	160	2.95	109	.248	.314	46-0-6	.106	-1*	96	31		3.3
1964	Phi N★	17	9	.654	42	31	12-4	2	220.2	174	63	10	4	51-5	181	2.20	158	.217	.266	65-0-8	.108	-1*	96	31		3.3
1965	Phi N	18	11	.621	47	40	15-5	*2	297.1	260	102	18	5	89-8	237	2.82	123	.235	.294	99-0-8	.131	-2	92	24		2.4
1966	Phi N	20	10	.667	42	39	19-4	0	272	257	120	28	9	68-2	177	3.54	102	.250	.301	106-0-1	.208	1	122	1		0.1
1967	Phi N★	9	11	.450	29	26	8-2	1	199.1	163	55	9	4	74-7	142	2.39	142	.225	.300	79-0-8	.152	0*	102	2	34	2.2
1968	Phi N	19	13	.594	42	36	9-2	1	269.2	236	99	25	9	81-10	202	2.94	102	.236	.298	79-0-8	.152	0*	102	2		0.3
1969	Phi N	0	0	—	2	2	0	0-0	10	11	8	2	1	4-0	5	7.20	50	.282	.364	3	.000	-5	73	-5		-1.0
1970	Phi N	9	16	.360	36	34	7-2	1-0	199	211	100	13	6	66-3	133	4.30	94	.272	.330	61-0-7	.049	-1	82	-6		-0.5
1971	Phi N	7	14	.333	31	26	5-2	1-0	173	182	85	22	3	63-2	95	3.85	92	.274	.339	48-0-6	.083	-1	82	-6	96	-0.5
1972	Phi N	1	1	.500	7	2	0	1-1	23	24	12	3	0	8-2	20	3.91	92	.267	.320		—	0	107	-9		-0.5
1973	Mil A	3	5	.375	42	1	0	2-3	72	86	42	5	2	44-7	44	5.13	74	.299	.394	0	—	0	95	34	295	0.0
Total	15	135	132	.506	501	308	88-24	18-4	2325	2215	991	183	61	806-74	1629	3.43	104	.252	.318	697-0-57	.126	-17	95	34		0.7

SHORT, BILL   William Ross   B11.27.1937 Kingston NY   BL/TL/5-9/170*   d4.23

YEAR	TM LG	W	L	PCT	G	GS	CG-SHO	SV-BS	IP	H	R	HR	HB	BB-IB	SO	ERA	AERA	OAV	OOB	AB-HR-SH	AVG	PB	SUP	APR	DL	PW
1960	NY A	3	5	.375	10	10	2	0	47	49	25	5	1	30-1	14	4.79	75	.282	.390	15	.200	1	103	-5		-0.1
1962	Bal A	0	0	—	5	0	0	0	4	8	7	0	1	6-0	3	15.75	23	.381	.536	1	.000	-0		-5		-0.1
1966	Bal A	2	3	.400	6	6	1-1	0	37.2	34	15	2	0	10-0	27	2.87	116	.239	.286	11	.091	-1	48	1		0.1
	Bos A	0	0	—	8	0	0	0	8.1	10	6	1	0	2-0	2	4.32	88	.294	.333	1	.000	-0		-1		0.0
	Year	2	3	.400	14	6	1-1	0	46	44	21	3	0	12-0	29	3.13	109	.250	.295	12	.083	-1	47	0		0.1
1967	Pit N	0	0	—	6	0	0	1	2.1	1	1	0	0	1-0	1	3.86	87	.143	.250	2	.000	-0		-6		-0.0
1968	NY N	0	3	.000	34	0	0	1	29.2	24	17	0	1	14-1	24	4.85	62	.230	.307	2	.000	-0		-3		-0.1
1969	Cin N	0	0	—	4	0	0	0-0	2.1	4	4	0	0	1-0	0	15.43	24	.400	.455	0	—	-0		-4		-0.0
Total	6	5	11	.313	73	16	3-1	2-0	131.1	130	75	8	3	64-2	71	4.73	72	.262	.346	32	.125	-1	85	-19		-0.4

SHOUN, CLYDE   Clyde Mitchell "Hardrock"   B3.20.1912 Mountain City TN   D3.20.1968 Mountain Home TN   BL/TL/6-1/188   d8.7   Mil 1945

YEAR	TM LG	W	L	PCT	G	GS	CG-SHO	SV-BS	IP	H	R	HR	HB	BB-IB	SO	ERA	AERA	OAV	OOB	AB-HR-SH	AVG	PB	SUP	APR	DL	PW
1935	Chi N	1	0	1.000	5	1	0	0	12.2	14	4	2	0	5	5	2.84	138	.298	.365	3	.000	-0	43	2		-0.0
1936	Chi N	0	0	—	4	0	0	0	4.1	3	6	0	0	6	1	12.46	32	.200	.429	0	—	0		-4		-0.0
1937	Chi N	7	7	.500	37	9	2	0	93	118	65	9	0	45	43	5.61	71	.309	.382	29-0-1	.138	-1	111	-17		-2.0
1938	StL N	6	6	.500	40	12	3	1	117.1	130	58	8	1	43	37	4.14	96	.283	.345	31-0-2	.258	-0	102	1		0.1
1939	StL N	3	1	.750	**53**	2	0	**9**	103	98	51	4	2	42	50	3.76	109	.248	.323	26-0-2	.115	-1	117	**3**		0.1
1940	StL N	13	11	.542	**54**	19	13-1	5	197.1	193	96	13	2	46	82	3.92	102	.255	.299	63-0-2	.190	0	81	3		-0.1
1941	StL N	3	5	.375	26	6	0	0	70	98	48	9	0	20	34	5.66	67	.337	.379	22-0-3	.182	0	116	-13		-1.0
1942	StL N	0	0	—	2	0	0	0	1.2	1	0	0	0	1	0	0.00	—	.167	.167	0	—	0		1		0.0
	Cin N	1	3	.250	34	0	0	0	72.2	55	23	2	0	24	32	2.23	147	.216	.283	13	.308	1	8			0.9
	Year	1	3	.250	36	0	0	0	74.1	56	23	2	0	24	32	2.18	151	.215	.281	13	.308	1		9		0.9
1943	Cin N	14	5	.737	45	5	2	7	147	131	52	5	0	46	61	3.06	108	.241	.300	42-0-1	.310	4	82	6		1.0
1944	Cin N	13	10	.565	38	21	12-1	5	202.2	193	83	10	3	42	55	3.42	116	.248	.290	67-0-5	.224	1	88	9		0.0
1946	Cin N	1	6	.143	19	10	0	0	79	87	42	3	1	26	20	4.10	82	.292	.351	21-0-1	.095	-1	67	-7		-0.0
1947	Cin N	0	0	—	10	0	0	0	14.1	16	8	2	1	5	7	5.02	82	.320	.393	1	.000	-1		-4		-0.0

YEAR	TM LG	W	L	PCT	G	GS	CG-SHO	SV-BS	IP	H	R	HR	HB	BB-IB	SO	ERA	AERA	OAV	OOB	AB-HR-SH	AVG	PB	SUP	APR	DL	PW
	Bos N	5	3	.625	26	3	1-1	1	73.2	73	41	6	0	21	23	4.40	89	.254	.305	19-0-1	.158	-1	83	-4		-0.5
1948	Year	5	3	.625	36	3	1-1	1	88	89	49	8	1	26	30	4.50	87	.264	.319	19-0-1	.158	-1	82	-5		-0.2
1949	Bos N	5	1	.833	36	2	1	4	74	77	37	7	0	20	25	4.01	96	.267	.315	21-0-2	.190	0	139	-2		-0.2
	Chi A	1	1	.500	16	0	0	0	23.1	37	17	1	0	13	8	0.00	—	.250	.250	0	—	0	0	0		0.0
Total	14	73	59	.553	454	85	34-3	29	1287	1325	631	81	10	404	483	5.79	72	.370	.442	5	.200	1	94	-19		-2.4

SHOUSE, BRIAN   Brian Douglas B9.26.1968 Effingham IL   BL/TL/5-11/180(175-190)   [PitN90 13/349]   d7.31 Col Bradley   [DL 1999 Ari N 16]

YEAR	TM LG	W	L	PCT	G	GS	CG-SHO	SV-BS	IP	H	R	HR	HB	BB-IB	SO	ERA	AERA	OAV	OOB	AB-HR-SH	AVG	PB	SUP	APR	DL	PW
1993	Pit N	0	0	—	6	0	0	0-0	4	7	4	1	0	2-0	1	9.00	45	.368	.409		—	0	-2			-0.1
1998	Bos A	0	1	.000	7	0	0	0-0	8	9	5	2	0	4-0	5	5.63	84	.281	.361	0	—	0	-1			-0.1
2002	KC A	0	0	—	23	0	0	0-0	14.2	15	10	3	2	9-1	11	6.14	81	.259	.371	0	—	0	-1	15		0.0
2003	Tex A	0	1	.000	62	0	0	1-0	61	62	24	1	4	14-6	40	3.10	160	.267	.320	0	—	0	11			0.6
2004	Tex A	2	0	1.000	53	0	0	0-0	44.1	36	12	3	1	18-3	34	2.23	221	.224	.302	0	—	0	12	39		0.7
2005	Tex A	3	2	.600	64	0	0	0-2	53.1	55	37	7	3	18-4	35	5.23	88	.266	.329	0	—	0	-5			-0.3
Total	6	5	4	.556	215	0	0	1-2	185.1	184	92	17	10	65-14	128	3.98	121	.260	.327	0	—	0	14	70		0.8

SHOW, ERIC   Eric Vaughn B5.19.1956 Riverside CA D3.16.1994 Dulzura CA   BR/TR/6-1/185(179-190)   [SDN78 18/447]   d9.2 Col California-Riverside

YEAR	TM LG	W	L	PCT	G	GS	CG-SHO	SV-BS	IP	H	R	HR	HB	BB-IB	SO	ERA	AERA	OAV	OOB	AB-HR-SH	AVG	PB	SUP	APR	DL	PW
1981	SD N	1	3	.250	15	0	0	3-3	23	17	9	2	1	9-3	22	3.13	104	.213	.300	0	—	0	0			0.0
1982	SD N	10	6	.625	47	14	2-2	3-0	150	117	49	10	5	48-3	88	2.64	130	.217	.284	41-0-2	.146	-1	103	14		1.5
1983	SD N	15	12	.556	35	33	4-2	0-0	200.2	201	97	25	6	74-3	120	4.17	84	.263	.331	64-0-5	.172	5	90	4		1.1
1984	†SD N	15	9	.625	32	32	3-1	0-0	206.2	175	88	18	4	88-4	104	3.40	106	.234	.316	69-3-6	.246	6	107	-13		-1.6
1985	SD N	12	11	.522	35	35	5-2	0-0	233	212	95	27	4	87-7	141	3.09	115	.243	.314	79-1-7	.127	-1	95	10		0.7
1986	SD N	9	5	.643	24	22	2	0-0	136.1	109	47	11	4	69-4	94	2.97	123	.225	.326	43-0-3	.163	1	92	12	62	1.2
1987	SD N	8	16	.333	34	34	5-3	0-0	206.1	188	99	26	9	85-7	117	3.84	103	.241	.321	70-0-7	.071	-4	90	3		-0.2
1988	SD N	16	11	.593	32	32	13-1	0-0	234.2	201	86	22	6	53-5	144	3.26	104	.231	.279	81-0-5	.148	-0	94	7		0.6
1989	SD N	8	6	.571	16	16	1	0-0	106.1	113	59	9	2	39-3	66	4.23	83	.274	.336	34-0-4	.235	2*	104	-9	88	-1.0
1990	SD N	6	8	.429	39	12	0	1-0	106.1	131	74	16	4	41-9	55	5.76	67	.306	.369	25-0-1	.200	1	96	-21		-2.5
1991	Oak A	1	2	.333	23	5	0	0-0	51.2	62	36	5	0	17-1	20	5.92	65	.298	.345	0	—	0	114	-13	25	-0.7
Total	11	101	89	.532	332	235	35-11	7-3	1655	1526	739	171	46	610-49	971	3.66	98	.247	.317	506-4-40	.160	3	97	-6	175	-0.9

SHREVE, LEV   Leven Lawrence B1.14.1869 Louisville KY D10.18.1942 Detroit MI   BR/TR/5-11/150   d5.2

YEAR	TM LG	W	L	PCT	G	GS	CG-SHO	SV-BS	IP	H	R	HR	HB	BB-IB	SO	ERA	AERA	OAV	OOB	AB-HR-SH	AVG	PB	SUP	APR	DL	PW
1887	Bal AA	3	1	.750	5	5	4-1	0	38	33	26	0	1	19	13	3.79	108	.228	.321	24	.167	-1*	143	1		0.0
	Ind N	5	9	.357	14	14	14-1	0	122	141	100	5	4	65	22	4.72	88	.278	.365	49	.265	-0	73	-9		-0.7
1888	Ind N	11	24	.314	35	35	34-1	0	297.2	352	208	23	8	93	101	4.63	64	.288	.342	115	.183	-1*	74	-49		-4.8
1889	Ind N	0	3	.000	3	3	1	0	15.2	25	27	3	1	12	5	13.79	30	.352	.452	7	.000	-1	145	-14		-1.6
Total	3	19	37	.339	57	57	53-3	0	473.1	551	361	31	14	189	141	4.89	70	.283	.351	195	.195	-3	85	-71		-7.1

SHRIVER, HARRY   Harry Graydon "Pop" B9.2.1896 Wadestown WV D1.21.1970 Morgantown WV   BR/TR/6-2/180   d4.14 Col West Virginia Wesleyan

YEAR	TM LG	W	L	PCT	G	GS	CG-SHO	SV-BS	IP	H	R	HR	HB	BB-IB	SO	ERA	AERA	OAV	OOB	AB-HR-SH	AVG	PB	SUP	APR	DL	PW
1922	Bro N	4	6	.400	25	13	4-2	0	108.1	114	49	5	2	48	38	2.99	136	.287	.367	27-0-3	.037	-3	48	11		0.5
1923	Bro N	0	0	—	1	1	0	0	4	8	3	0	0	1	6.75	58	.444	.444	1	.000	-0	148	-1		-0.1
Total	2	4	6	.400	26	14	4-2	0	112.1	122	52	5	2	48	39	3.12	130	.294	.370	28-0-3	.036	-3	54	10		0.4

SHUEY, PAUL   Paul Kenneth B9.16.1970 Lima OH   BR/TR/6-3/215*   [CleA92 1/2]   d5.8 Col North Carolina-Asheville   [DL 2004 LA N 183]

YEAR	TM LG	W	L	PCT	G	GS	CG-SHO	SV-BS	IP	H	R	HR	HB	BB-IB	SO	ERA	AERA	OAV	OOB	AB-HR-SH	AVG	PB	SUP	APR	DL	PW
1994	Cle A	0	1	.000	14	0	0	5-0	11.2	14	11	1	0	12-1	16	8.49	56	.280	.419	0	—	0	-4	24		-0.6
1995	Cle A	0	2	.000	7	0	0	0-0	6.1	5	4	0	0	5-0	5	4.26	111	.238	.385	0	—	0	0	18		0.0
1996	†Cle A	5	2	.714	42	0	0	4-3	53.2	45	19	6	0	26-3	44	2.85	171	.231	.317	0	—	0	12			1.5
1997	Cle A	4	2	.667	40	0	0	2-1	45	52	31	5	1	28-3	46	6.20	76	.294	.389	1	.000	-0	-6	59		-0.7
1998	Cle A	5	4	.556	43	0	0	2-3	51	44	19	6	3	25-5	58	3.00	159	.229	.327	1	.000	-0	10	66		1.5
1999	†Cle A	8	5	.615	72	0	0	6-6	81.2	68	37	8	1	40-7	103	3.53	140	.224	.314	0	—	0	13	15		1.9
2000	Cle A	4	2	.667	32	0	0	0-5	63.2	51	29	5	4	30-3	69	3.39	148	.219	.312	0	—	0	11	36		0.9
2001	†Cle A	5	3	.625	47	0	0	2-3	54.1	53	25	1	1	26-5	70	2.82	163	.251	.333	0	—	0	8	74		1.0
2002	Cle A	3	0	1.000	39	0	0	0-2	37.1	31	11	1	0	10-1	39	2.41	184	.225	.275	0	—	0	-3			-0.5
	LA N	5	2	.714	28	0	1	1-2	30.2	25	18	2	1	21-1	24	4.40	89	.217	.341	0	—	0	8	15		0.6
2003	LA N	6	4	.600	62	0	0	0-1	69	50	24	6	4	33-3	60	3.00	137	.207	.312	2	.000	-0	9	22		1.3
Total	10	45	27	.625	451	0	1	22-26	504.1	438	224	40	14	256-32	534	3.57	131	.233	.327	7	.143	-0	58	512		6.9

SHULTZ, TOOTS   Wallace Luther B10.10.1888 Homestead PA D1.30.1959 McKeesport PA   BR/TR/5-10/175   d5.5 Col Penn

YEAR	TM LG	W	L	PCT	G	GS	CG-SHO	SV-BS	IP	H	R	HR	HB	BB-IB	SO	ERA	AERA	OAV	OOB	AB-HR-SH	AVG	PB	SUP	APR	DL	PW
1911	Phi N	0	3	.000	5	3	2	0	25	30	28	5	4	15	9	9.36	37	.300	.412	8-0-1	.250	0	73	-14		-1.3
1912	Phi N	1	4	.200	22	4	1	1	59	75	44	2	3	35	20	4.58	79	.333	.430	21	.238	0*	157	-7		-0.5
Total	2	1	7	.125	27	7	3	1	84	105	72	7	7	50	29	6.00	60	.323	.424	29-0-1	.241	0	121	-21		-1.8

SHUMAKER, ANTHONY   Anthony Warren B5.14.1973 Tucson AZ   BL/TL/6-5/225   [PhiN95 23/633]   d7.23 Col Cardinal Stritch

YEAR	TM LG	W	L	PCT	G	GS	CG-SHO	SV-BS	IP	H	R	HR	HB	BB-IB	SO	ERA	AERA	OAV	OOB	AB-HR-SH	AVG	PB	SUP	APR	DL	PW
1999	Phi N	0	3	.000	4	0	0	0-0	22.2	23	17	3	1	14-0	17	5.96	78	.261	.369	5	.200	0	93	-4		-0.4

SHUMAN, HARRY   Harry B3.5.1915 Philadelphia PA D10.25.1996 Philadelphia PA   BR/TR/6-2/195   d9.14 Col Temple

YEAR	TM LG	W	L	PCT	G	GS	CG-SHO	SV-BS	IP	H	R	HR	HB	BB-IB	SO	ERA	AERA	OAV	OOB	AB-HR-SH	AVG	PB	SUP	APR	DL	PW
1942	Pit N	0	0	—	1	0	0	0	2	0	0	0	0	1	1	0.00	—	.000	.167	0	—	0	1			0.0
1943	Pit N	0	0	—	11	0	0	0	22	30	20	0	2	8	5	5.32	65	.337	.404	2	.000	-0	-6			-0.3
1944	Phi N	0	0	—	18	0	0	0	26.2	26	15	1	0	11	4	4.05	89	.245	.316	1	.000	-0	-2			-0.1
Total	3	0	0	—	30	0	0	0	50.2	56	35	1	2	20	10	4.44	80	.280	.351	3	.000	-0	-7			-0.4

SIEBERT, PAUL   Paul Edward B6.5.1953 Minneapolis MN   BL/TL/6-2/205(185-205)   [HouN71 3/58]   d9.7 f-Dick

YEAR	TM LG	W	L	PCT	G	GS	CG-SHO	SV-BS	IP	H	R	HR	HB	BB-IB	SO	ERA	AERA	OAV	OOB	AB-HR-SH	AVG	PB	SUP	APR	DL	PW
1974	Hou N	1	1	.500	5	5	1-1	0-0	25.1	21	12	3	0	11-0	10	3.55	98	.236	.314	6-0-2	.000	-1	110	-1		-0.1
1975	Hou N	0	2	.000	7	2	0	2-0	18.1	20	7	0	1	6-1	6	2.95	115	.294	.360	3	.000	-0	26	1		0.1
1976	Hou N	0	2	.000	19	0	0	0-0	25.2	29	10	0	1	18-7	10	3.16	102	.296	.403	2	.000	-0	0			-0.1
1977	SD N	0	0	—	4	0	0	0-0	3.2	3	4	1	0	4-1	1	2.45	146	.214	.368	0	—	0	-1			-0.1
	NY N	2	1	.667	25	0	0	0-0	28	27	12	0	1	13-4	20	3.86	98	.257	.336	1	.000	0	0			0.0
	Year	2	1	.667	29	0	0	0-0	31.2	30	16	1	1	17-5	21	3.69	102	.252	.340	1	.000	0	0			-0.1
1978	NY N	0	2	.000	27	0	0	1-1	28	30	16	2	1	21-5	12	5.14	69	.283	.406	1	.000	-0	-4			-0.3
Total	5	3	8	.273	87	7	1-1	3-1	129	130	61	6	4	73-18	59	3.77	93	.271	.366	13-0-2	.000	-2	87	-5		-0.4

SIEBERT, SONNY   Wilfred Charles B1.14.1937 St.Marys MO   BR/TR/6-3/198(190-205)   d4.26 C2 Col Missouri

YEAR	TM LG	W	L	PCT	G	GS	CG-SHO	SV-BS	IP	H	R	HR	HB	BB-IB	SO	ERA	AERA	OAV	OOB	AB-HR-SH	AVG	PB	SUP	APR	DL	PW
1964	Cle A	7	9	.438	41	14	3-1	3	156	142	61	15	2	57-4	144	3.23	111	.243	.310	49-2-0	.265	5*	85	7		1.2
1965	Cle A	16	8	.667	39	27	4-1	1	188.2	139	58	14	5	62-3	191	2.43	143	.206	.259	66-1-1	.106	-2*	102	22		2.7
1966	Cle A★	16	8	**.667**	34	32	11-1	0	241	193	89	25	6	62-3	163	2.80	123	.221	.276	85-0-5	.129	-2	111	15		1.3
1967	Cle A	10	12	.455	34	26	7-1	4	185.1	136	59	17	6	54-2	136	2.38	137	.202	.266	52-1-5	.135	-1	80	17		2.2
1968	Cle A	12	10	.545	31	30	8-4	0	206	145	76	12	8	88-10	146	2.97	100	.198	.288	70-0-5	.157	1*	113	1		0.4
1969	Cle A	0	1	.000	6	6	0	0-0	14	10	5	1	0	8-0	6	3.21	118	.196	.305	4	.250	0	35	1		0.1
	Bos A	14	10	.583	43	22	2	5-3	163.1	151	93	21	4	68-1	127	3.80	101	.245	.321	53-1-4	.151	1	109	-5		-0.6
	Year	14	11	.560	45	24	2	5-3	177.1	161	98	22	4	76-1	133	3.76	102	.241	.320	57-1-4	.158	1	103	-4		-0.5
1970	Bos A	15	8	.652	33	33	7-2	0-0	222.2	207	98	29	6	60-2	142	3.44	116	.248	.302	77-0-4	.130	-2	102	13		1.1
1971	Bos A☆	16	10	.615	32	32	12-4	0-0	235.1	220	84	20	3	60-5	131	2.91	128	.245	.292	79-6-2	.266	9	103	19		3.3
1972	Bos A	12	12	.500	32	30	7-3	0-0	196.1	204	105	17	7	59-4	123	3.80	85	.264	.321	72-1-1	.236	6*	129	-16		-1.2
1973	Bos A	0	1	.000	2	0	0	0-1	2.1	5	2	1	0	0-1	4	5.71	52	.417	.462	0	—	0	-1			-0.2
	Tex A	7	11	.389	25	20	1-1	2-0	119.2	120	68	11	3	37-1	76	3.99	94	.258	.314	0	—	0	96	-6		-1.0
	Year	7	12	.368	27	20	1-1	2-1	122	125	70	12	3	38-1	81	4.06	93	.262	.318	0	—	0	96	-8		-1.0
1974	StL N	8	8	.500	28	20	1-1	5-3	133.2	150	66	8	3	51-14	68	3.84	94	.288	.353	44-0-2	.114	-2	98	-4	23	-0.7
1975	SD N	3	2	.600	6	6	0	0-0	26.2	37	15	2	1	10-4	10	4.39	80	.330	.387	8-0-1	.375	2*	80	-2		-0.2
	Oak A	4	4	.500	17	13	0	0-0	61	60	28	4	0	3-5	35	3.69	99	.252	.335	1	.000	-0	97	-0	40	-0.1
Total	12	140	114	.551	399	307	67-21	16-4	2152	1919	907	197	54	692-55	1512	3.21	110	.238	.301	660-12-35	.173	18	103	61	63	8.5

SIEBLER, DWIGHT   Dwight Leroy B8.5.1937 Columbus NE   BR/TR/6-2/184(184-195)   d8.26 Col Nebraska

YEAR	TM LG	W	L	PCT	G	GS	CG-SHO	SV-BS	IP	H	R	HR	HB	BB-IB	SO	ERA	AERA	OAV	OOB	AB-HR-SH	AVG	PB	SUP	APR	DL	PW
1963	Min A	2	1	.667	7	5	2	2	38.2	25	13	4	1	12-0	22	2.79	130	.182	.253	15	.133	-0	112	4		0.2
1964	Min A	0	0	—	9	0	0	0	11	10	6	1	6	11-0	10	4.91	73	.256	.356	0	—	0	-1			-0.1
1965	Min A	0	0	—	7	1	0	0	15	11	7	2	0	11-0	15	4.20	85	.193	.324	1	.000	-0	49	-1		-0.1
1966	Min A	2	0	.500	23	2	0	1	49.2	47	26	6	1	14-2	24	3.44	104	.253	.302	11	.000	-1	159	-1		-0.2
1967	Min A	0	2	.000	2	0	0	0	3	4	1	0	0	2-0	0	3.00	115	.364	.417	0	—	0	1			0.0
Total	5	4	3	.571	48	8	2	1	117.1	97	53	16	2	44-3	71	3.45	104	.226	.298	27	.074	-1	116	1		-0.1

YEAR	TM LG	W	L	PCT	G	GS	CG-SHO	SV-BS	IP	H	R	HR	HB	BB-IB	SO	ERA	AERA	OAV	OOB	AB-HR-SH	AVG	PB	SUP	APR	DL	PW
SIERRA, CANDY	Ulises (Pizarro) B3.27.1967 Rio Piedras, PR BR/TR/6-2/190 d4.6																									
1988	SD N	0	1	.000	15	0	0	0-1	23.2	36	15	2	0	11-2	20	5.70	60	.379	.439	3	.000	-0		-5		-0.3
	Cin N	0	0	—	1	0	0	0-0	4	5	2	0	0	1-0	4	4.50	79	.294	.333	1	.000	-0		-0		0.0
	Year	0	1	.000	16	0	0	0-1	27.2	41	17	2	0	12-2	24	5.53	62	.366	.424	4	.000	-0		-6		-0.3
SIEVER, ED	Edward Tilden B4.2.1877 Goddard KS D2.4.1920 Detroit MI BL/TL/5-11.5/190 d4.26																									
1901	Det A	18	14	.563	38	33	30-2	0	288.2	334	166	9	8	65	85	3.24	119	.286	.328	107-0-6	.168	-5	102	18		1.2
1902	Det A	8	11	.421	25	23	17-4	1	188.1	166	73	0	2	32	36	1.91	191	.237	.272	66-0-4	.152	-4	86	29		2.1
1903	StL A	13	14	.481	31	27	24-1	0	254	245	102	6	5	39	90	2.48	117	.253	.285	93-0-2	.140	-4	83	11		0.8
1904	StL A	10	15	.400	29	24	19-2	0	217	235	112	3	3	65	77	2.65	93	.277	.330	71	.155	-1*	86	-14		-1.7
1906	Det A	14	11	.560	30	25	20-1	0	222.2	240	95	5	10	45	71	2.71	102	.278	.321	77-0-7	.156	-3	93	-1		-0.6
1907	†Det A	18	11	.621	39	33	22-3	1	274.2	256	89	1	11	52	88	2.16	120	.249	.293	94-0-3	.160	-3	110	16		1.2
1908	Det A	2	6	.250	11	9	4-1	0	61.2	74	37	0	0	13	23	3.50	69	.302	.337	18-0-1	.167	-1	97	-8		-1.1
Total	7	83	82	.503	203	174	136-14	2	1507	1550	674	24	39	311	470	2.60	116	.266	.308	526-0-23	.156	-21	95	51		1.9
SIGNER, WALTER	Walter Donald Aloysius B10.12.1910 New York NY D7.23.1974 Greenwich CT BR/TR/6-0/185 d9.18 Col NYU																									
1943	Chi N	2	1	.667	4	2	1	0	25	24	8	0	4	5	2.88	116	.245	.275	8	.250	0	38	2		0.3
1945	Chi N	0	0	—	6	0	0	1	8	11	6	1	0	5	3.38	108	.256	.333	1	.000	-0		-1		-0.1
Total	2	2	1	.667	10	2	1	1	33	35	14	4	0	9	3.00	114	.248	.293	9	.222	0	38	1		0.2
SIGSBY, SETH	Seth De Witt (b Seth De Witt) B4.30.1874 Cobleskill NY D9.15.1953 Schenectady NY 6-0/175 d6.27																									
1893	NY N	0	0	—	1	0	0	0	3	4	0	1	4	2	9.00	52	.100	.400	1	.000	-0		-1		-0.1
SIKORSKI, BRIAN	Brian Patrick B7.27.1974 Detroit MI BR/TR/6-1/190 [HouN95 4/109] d8.16 Col Western Michigan																									
2000	Tex A	1	3	.250	10	5	0	0-0	37.2	46	31	9	1	25-1	32	5.73	89	.287	.385	0	—	0	111	-4		-0.4
SILVA, CARLOS	Carlos B4.23.1979 Bolivar, Venez BR/TR/6-4/225(225-250) d4.1																									
2002	Phi N	5	0	1.000	68	0	0	1-4	84	88	34	4	4	22-6	41	3.21	119	.282	.334	2	.000			5	18	0.4
2003	Phi N	3	1	.750	62	1	0	1-2	87.1	92	43	7	8	37-5	48	4.43	90	.280	.365	9-0-1	.222	1	236	-3		-0.1
2004	†Min A	14	8	.636	33	33	1-1	0-0	203	255	100	23	5	35-2	76	4.21	110	.310	.342	3	.000	-0	105	11		0.9
2005	Min A	9	8	.529	27	27	2	0-0	188.1	212	83	25	3	9-2	71	3.44	128	.290	.300	2	.000	-0	90	18	15	0.3
Total	4	31	17	.646	190	61	3-1	2-6	562.2	647	260	59	20	103-15	236	3.84	113	.295	.331	16-0-1	.125	0	105	31	33	2.6
SILVA, JOSE	Jose Leonel B12.19.1973 Tijuana, Baja California, Mexico BR/TR/6-5/227(210-235) [TorA91 6/172] d9.10																									
1996	Tor A	0	0	—	2	0	0	0-0	2	5	3	1	0	0-0	0	13.50	37	.455	.455	0	—			-2		-0.1
1997	Pit N	2	1	.667	11	4	0	0-0	36.1	52	26	4	1	16-3	30	5.94	72	.347	.406	7-0-3	.143	-0	108	-6		-0.1
1998	Pit N	6	7	.462	18	18	1	0-0	100.1	104	55	7	1	30-2	64	4.40	97	.271	.321	27-0-5	.037	-1	122	-12	18	-1.2
1999	Pit N	2	8	.200	34	12	0	4-1	97.1	108	70	10	3	39-0	77	5.73	80	.281	.349	20-0-2	.100	-1	122	-15		-1.9
2000	Pit N	11	9	.550	51	19	1	0-2	136	178	96	16	5	50-7	98	5.56	84	.317	.375	34-0-5	.176	-0	97	-15		-1.2
2001	Pit N	3	3	.500	26	0	0	0-2	32	35	24	6	0	9-1	23	6.75	66	.271	.319	2	.000			-7	126	-1.2
2002	Cin N	1	0	1.000	12	0	0	0-0	23.1	25	11	3	3	10-3	6	4.24	101	.294	.384	0-0-1	—		1	133	0.1	-0.1
Total	7	25	28	.472	154	53	2	4-5	427.1	507	285	47	13	154-16	298	5.41	83	.297	.357	90-0-16	.111	-3	99	-42	362	-5.0
SIMA, AL	Albert B10.7.1921 Mahwah NJ D8.17.1993 Suffern NY BR/TL/6-0/187* d6.28																									
1950	Was A	4	5	.444	17	9	1	0	77	89	49	9	1	26	23	4.79	94	.291	.348	26-0-1	.115	-2	78	-3		-0.6
1951	Was A	3	7	.300	18	8	1	0	77	79	51	5	0	41	26	4.79	85	.261	.349	17-1-5	.176	1	92	-8		0.1
1953	Was A	2	3	.400	31	5	1	1	68.1	63	31	7	3	31	25	3.42	114	.249	.338	17	.118	-1	82	3		0.1
1954	Chi A	0	1	.000	5	1	0	1	7	11	5	1	0	2	1	5.14	73	.393	.406	2	.000	-0	47	-1		-0.2
	Phi A	2	5	.286	29	7	1	2	79.1	101	51	9	0	32	36	5.22	75	.309	.368	20-0-2	.050	-2	58	-11		-1.2
	Year	2	6	.250	34	8	1	3	86.1	112	56	10	0	34	37	5.21	75	.315	.372	22-0-2	.045	-2	57	-12		-1.4
Total	4	11	21	.344	100	30	4	4	308.2	343	187	31	4	132	111	4.61	89	.282	.353	82-1-8	.110	-5	77	-20		-2.7
SIMAS, BILL	William Anthony B11.28.1971 Hanford CA BL/TR/6-3/220(200-235) [CalA92 6/160] d8.15 Col Fresno (CA) City [DL 2001 Chi A 190]																									
1995	Chi A	1	1	.500	14	0	0	0-0	14	15	5	1	1	10-2	16	2.57	174	.273	.394	0	—	0		3		0.3
1996	Chi A	2	8	.200	64	0	0	2-6	72.2	75	39	5	3	39-6	65	4.58	104	.265	.358	0	—	0		2		0.2
1997	Chi A	3	1	.750	40	0	0	1-1	41.1	46	23	6	2	24-3	38	4.14	107	.279	.375	0	—	0		0	61	0.0
1998	Chi A	4	3	.571	60	0	0	18-6	70.2	54	29	12	1	22-4	56	3.57	128	.206	.270	0	—	0		9		1.1
1999	Chi A	6	3	.667	70	0	0	2-3	72	73	36	6	4	32-6	41	3.75	132	.263	.347	0	—	0		8		0.9
2000	†Chi A	2	3	.400	60	0	0	0-5	67.2	69	27	9	1	22-6	49	3.46	146	.276	.332	0	—	0		13		0.8
Total	6	18	19	.486	308	0	0	23-21	332	159	30	14	149-27	265	3.83	124	.257	.337	0	—	0		35	251	3.3
SIMMONS, CURT	Curtis Thomas B5.19.1929 Egypt PA BL/TL/6-0/187(175-190) d9.28 Mil 1951																									
1947	Phi N	1	0	1.000	1	1	1	0	9	5	4	0	1	6	9	1.00	401	.161	.297	2-0-1	.500	0	66	3		0.4
1948	Phi N	7	13	.350	31	23	7	0	170	169	100	8	2	108	86	4.87	81	.266	.374	51-0-3	.137	-1	81	-18		-1.9
1949	Phi N	4	10	.286	38	14	2	1	131.1	133	72	7	1	55	83	4.59	86	.275	.350	41	.171	-1*	105	-9		-0.9
1950	Phi N	17	8	.680	31	27	11-2	1	214.2	178	93	19	2	88	146	3.40	119	.223	.302	77-0-3	.156	-1*	118	16		1.6
1952	Phi N★	14	8	.636	28	28	15-6	0	201.1	170	72	11	1	70	141	2.82	130	.227	.294	67-1-5	.164	2	100	20		2.2
1953	Phi N★	16	13	.552	32	30	19-4	0	238	211	102	17	3	82	138	3.21	131	.236	.302	93-0-4	.140	-3	95	29		2.8
1954	Phi N	14	15	.483	34	33	21-3	1	253	226	101	14	5	98	125	2.81	144	.239	.312	91-0-6	.176	-1*	99	-12		-1.4
1955	Phi N	8	8	.500	25	22	3	0	130	148	76	15	3	50-2	58	4.92	81	.290	.355	46-0-1	.174	-1*	99	-12		-1.4
1956	Phi N	15	10	.600	33	27	14	0	198	186	95	17	3	65-7	88	3.36	111	.248	.308	72-0-2	.236	3*	113	4		1.3
1957	Phi N★	12	11	.522	32	29	9-2	0	212	214	92	11	2	50-11	92	3.44	111	.264	.305	71-0-3	.239	4*	92	8		1.1
1958	Phi N	7	14	.333	29	27	7-1	1	168.1	196	92	11	3	40-4	78	4.38	90	.293	.332	59-0-3	.203	0*	87	-7		-0.3
1959	Phi N	0	0	—	7	0	0	0	10	16	5	2	1	0-0	4	4.50	91	.400	.415	0	—	0*		0	44	0.6
1960	Phi N	0	0	—	4	2	0	0	4	13	8	3	0	6-0	4	18.00	22	.542	.633	0	—	0	114	-6		-1.0
	StL N	7	4	.636	23	17	3-1	0	152	149	50	11	0	31-6	95	2.66	154	.257	.294	47-0-2	.213	1*	86	22		1.7
	Year	7	4	.636	27	19	3-1	0	156	162	58	14	0	37-6	67	3.06	134	.269	.309	47-0-2	.213	1	89	18		1.4
1961	StL N	9	10	.474	30	29	6-2	0	195.2	203	91	14	2	64-6	99	3.13	141	.269	.326	66-0-3	.303	5*	107	21		2.8
1962	StL N	10	10	.500	31	22	9-4	0	154	167	78	18	3	32-2	74	3.51	122	.280	.318	50-0-2	.160	0	112	8		2.2
1963	StL N	15	9	.625	32	32	11-6	0	232.2	209	82	13	6	48-3	127	2.48	143	.239	.288	81-0-3	.160	0	112	23		2.2
1964	†StL N	18	9	.667	34	34	12-3	0	244	233	106	24	5	49-1	104	3.43	111	.249	.288	64-0-3	.047	-5	82	-6		-1.1
1965	StL N	9	15	.375	34	32	5	0	203	229	104	19	4	54-8	96	4.08	94	.283	.330	64-0-3	.125	-4	78	-3		-0.5
1966	StL N	1	1	.500	10	5	1	0	33.1	35	17	3	0	14-2	14	4.59	78	.269	.338	8	.125	0	78	-3		-0.2
	Chi N	4	7	.364	19	10	3-1	0	77.1	79	39	7	1	21-3	24	4.07	90	.268	.317	18-0-1	.111	-0	77	-3		-0.2
	Year	5	8	.385	29	15	4-1	0	110.2	114	56	10	1	35-5	38	4.23	86	.268	.323	26-0-3	.115	-1	77	-7		-0.5
1967	Chi N	3	7	.300	17	14	3	0	82	100	54	10	2	23-4	31	4.94	72	.300	.342	28-0-1	.143	-1	112	-14		-1.1
	Cal A	2	1	.667	14	4	1	1	34.2	41	19	3	2	13-2	9	2.60	121	.321	.372	9-0-1	.222	1	118	2		0.2
Total	20	193	183	.513	569	462	163-36	5	3348.1	3313	1551	255	53	1063-62	1697	3.54	111	.259	.317	1135-1-57	.171	1	102	114	44	11.7
SIMMONS, PAT	Patrick Clement (b Patrick Clement Simoni) B11.29.1908 Watervliet NY D7.3.1968 Albany NY BR/TR/5-11/172 d4.18																									
1928	Bos A	0	2	.000	31	3	0	1	69	69	38	4	1	38	16	4.04	102	.271	.367	15	.133	-1	82	0		-0.7
1929	Bos A	0	0	—	2	0	0	1	7	6	0	0	0	3	2	0.00	—	.231	.310	1	.000	-0		3		0.0
Total	2	0	2	.000	33	3	0	2	76	75	38	4	1	41	18	3.67	112	.267	.362	16	.125	-1	82	3		-0.7
SIMONS, DOUG	Douglas Eugene B9.15.1966 Bakersfield CA BL/TL/6-0/170* [MinA88 9/233] d4.9 Col Pepperdine																									
1991	NY N	2	3	.400	42	1	0	1-0	60.2	55	40	4	2	19-5	38	5.19	71	.246	.305	3-0-1	.000	-0	123	-10		-0.7
1992	Mon N	0	0	—	7	0	0	0-0	5.1	15	14	4	1	2-1	6	23.63	16	.536	.529	0	—	0		-11		-1.0
Total	2	2	3	.400	49	1	0	1-0	66	70	54	8	3	21-5	44	6.68	55	.276	.332	3-0-1	.000	-0	123	-21		-1.7
SIMONTACCHI, JASON	Jason William B11.13.1973 Mountain View CA BR/TR/6-2/185* [KCA96 21/619] d5.4 Col Albertson Idaho																									
2002	StL N	11	5	.688	24	24	0	0-0	143.1	134	68	18	6	54-4	72	4.02	100	.253	.327	50-0-4	.240	2*	101	1		0.1
2003	StL N	9	5	.643	46	16	1	1-2	126.1	153	82	21	5	41-0	74	5.56	74	.299	.355	38	.132	-1*	151	-21		-2.0
2004	StL N	0	0	—	13	0	0	0-0	15.1	17	10	5	1	7-0	3	5.28	81	.304	.385	2	.500	0*		-2		-0.1
Total	3	20	10	.667	83	40	1	1-2	285	304	160	44	12	102-4	149	4.77	86	.277	.343	90-0-4	.200	2	121	-22		-2.0

YEAR	TM LG	W	L	PCT	G	GS	CG-SHO	SV-BS	IP	H	R	HR	HB	BB-IB	SO	ERA	AERA	OAV	OOB	AB-HR-SH	AVG	PB	SUP	APR	DL	PW

SIMPSON, ALLAN Larry Allan B8.26.1977 Springfield IL BR/TR/6-4/185(185-200) [SeaA97 8/253] d5.17 Col Taft (CA) JC

YEAR	TM LG	W	L	PCT	G	GS	CG-SHO	SV-BS	IP	H	R	HR	HB	BB-IB	SO	ERA	AERA	OAV	OOB	AB-HR-SH	AVG	PB	SUP	APR	DL	PW
2004	Col N	2	1	.667	32	0	0	0-1	39	44	26	4	4	20-0	46	5.08	94	.289	.378	1	.000	-0		-3		-0.2
2005	Cin N	0	1	.000	9	0	0	0-1	6.2	3	5	1	1	5-0	6	6.75	62	.136	.321	0	—	0		-2		-0.2
	Col N	0	0	—	2	0	0	0-0	0.2	3	5	0	0	3-0	0	67.50	7	.750	.750	0	—	0		-4		-0.2
	Year	0	1	.000	11	0	0	0-1	7.1	6	10	1	1	8-0	6	12.27	34	.231	.417	0	—	0		-6		-0.4
Total 2		2	2	.500	43	0	0	0-2	46.1	50	36	5	5	28-0	52	6.22	75	.281	.384	1	.000	-0		-9		-0.6

SIMPSON, STEVE Steven Edward B8.30.1948 St.Joseph MO D11.2.1989 Omaha NE BR/TR/6-3/200 d9.10 Col Washburn Topeka

YEAR	TM LG	W	L	PCT	G	GS	CG-SHO	SV-BS	IP	H	R	HR	HB	BB-IB	SO	ERA	AERA	OAV	OOB	AB-HR-SH	AVG	PB	SUP	APR	DL	PW
1972	SD N	0	2	.000	9	0	0	2-1	11.1	10	6	0	0	8-1	9	4.76	70	.238	.360	0		0		-2		-0.3

SIMPSON, DUKE Thomas Leo B9.15.1927 Columbus OH BR/TR/6-1.5/190 d5.6 Col Ohio St.

YEAR	TM LG	W	L	PCT	G	GS	CG-SHO	SV-BS	IP	H	R	HR	HB	BB-IB	SO	ERA	AERA	OAV	OOB	AB-HR-SH	AVG	PB	SUP	APR	DL	PW
1953	Chi N	1	2	.333	30	1	0	0	45	60	47	8	1	25	21	8.00	56	.314	.396	8	.250	0	20	-17		-1.0

SIMPSON, WAYNE Wayne Kirby B12.2.1948 Los Angeles CA BR/TR/6-3/210* [CinN67 1/8] d4.9

YEAR	TM LG	W	L	PCT	G	GS	CG-SHO	SV-BS	IP	H	R	HR	HB	BB-IB	SO	ERA	AERA	OAV	OOB	AB-HR-SH	AVG	PB	SUP	APR	DL	PW
1970	Cin N☆	14	3	.824	26	26	10-2	0-0	176	125	73	15	9	81-3	119	3.02	134	.198	.296	64-0-5	.094	-4*	134	18		1.3
1971	Cin N	4	7	.364	22	21	1	0-0	117.1	106	66	9	3	77-5	61	4.76	71	.244	.359	32-0-5	.031	-2	98	-18		-1.7
1972	Cin N	8	5	.615	24	22	1	0-0	130.1	124	63	17	2	49-4	70	4.14	78	.247	.316	48	.063	-3	135	-12		-1.6
1973	KC A	3	4	.429	16	10	1	0-0	59.2	66	39	1	1	35-0	29	5.73	72	.284	.375	0	—	0	113	-9		-0.9
1975	Phi N	1	0	1.000	7	5	0	0-0	30.2	31	11	1	1	11-0	19	3.23	117	.263	.328	9	.222	0	126	2		0.2
1977	Cal A	6	12	.333	27	23	0	0-0	122	154	90	14	7	62-3	55	5.83	67	.308	.389	0	—	0	94	-26		-3.3
Total 6		36	31	.537	122	107	13-2	0-0	636	606	342	57	23	315-15	353	4.37	85	.251	.340	153-0-10	.078	-8	116	-45		-6.0

SIMS, PETE Clarence B5.24.1891 Crown City OH D12.2.1968 Dallas TX BR/TR/5-11.5/165 d9.16

YEAR	TM LG	W	L	PCT	G	GS	CG-SHO	SV-BS	IP	H	R	HR	HB	BB-IB	SO	ERA	AERA	OAV	OOB	AB-HR-SH	AVG	PB	SUP	APR	DL	PW
1915	StL A	1	0	1.000	3	2	0	0	8.1	6	4	0	0	6	4	4.32	66	.214	.353	1-0-1	1.000	1	89	-1		0.0

SINCLAIR, STEVE Steven Scott B8.2.1971 Victoria BC, Can. BL/TL/6-2/190* [TorA91 28/744] d4.25

YEAR	TM LG	W	L	PCT	G	GS	CG-SHO	SV-BS	IP	H	R	HR	HB	BB-IB	SO	ERA	AERA	OAV	OOB	AB-HR-SH	AVG	PB	SUP	APR	DL	PW
1998	Tor A	0	2	.000	24	0	0	0-2	15	13	7	0	0	5-0	8	3.60	129	.232	.295	0	—	0		2		0.2
1999	Tor A	0	0	—	3	0	0	0-0	5.2	7	8	1	1	4-0	3	12.71	39	.304	.429	0	—	0		-5		-0.2
	Sea A	0	1	.000	18	0	0	0-0	13.2	15	8	1	1	10-2	15	3.95	121	.268	.388	0	—	0		1		0.0
	Year	0	1	.000	21	0	0	0-0	19.1	22	16	2	2	14-2	16	6.52	74	.278	.400	0	—	0		-4		-0.2
Total 2		0	3	.000	45	0	0	0-2	34.1	35	23	2	2	19-2	26	5.24	91	.259	.359	0	—	0		-2		0.0

SINCOCK, BERT Herbert Sylvester B9.8.1887 Barkerville BC, Can. D8.1.1946 Houghton MI BL/TL/5-10.5/165 d6.25 Col Michigan

YEAR	TM LG	W	L	PCT	G	GS	CG-SHO	SV-BS	IP	H	R	HR	HB	BB-IB	SO	ERA	AERA	OAV	OOB	AB-HR-SH	AVG	PB	SUP	APR	DL	PW
1908	Cin N	0	0	—	1	0	0	0	4.2	3	2	0	0	1	1	3.86	60	.176	.176	2	.000	-0		0		-0.1

SINGER, BILL William Robert "The Singer Throwing Machine" B4.24.1944 Los Angeles CA BR/TR/6-4/200* d9.24 [DL 1978 Tor A 155]

YEAR	TM LG	W	L	PCT	G	GS	CG-SHO	SV-BS	IP	H	R	HR	HB	BB-IB	SO	ERA	AERA	OAV	OOB	AB-HR-SH	AVG	PB	SUP	APR	DL	PW
1964	LA N	0	1	.000	2	2	0	0	14	11	5	0	0	12-1	3	3.21	101	.216	.365	6	.167	0	81	0		0.0
1965	LA N	0	0	—	2	0	0	0	1	2	1	0	0	2-0	1	0.00	—	.400	.571	0	—	0		0		0.0
1966	LA N	0	0	—	3	0	0	0	4	4	0	0	0	2-0	4	0.00	—	.286	.375	0	—	0		2		0.1
1967	LA N	12	8	.600	32	29	7-3	0	204.1	185	68	5	8	61-11	169	2.64	117	.239	.300	67-0-4	.090	-3*	92	11		0.8
1968	LA N	13	17	.433	37	36	12-6	0	256.1	227	97	14	5	78-10	227	2.88	96	.237	.295	81-0-3	.148	3	106	-4		0.0
1969	LA N★	20	12	.625	41	40	16-2	1-0	315.2	244	96	22	10	74-4	247	2.34	143	.210	.261	108-0-8	.102	-4	100	36		3.1
1970	LA N	8	5	.615	16	16	5-3	0-0	106.1	79	39	10	2	32-3	93	3.13	123	.203	.267	38-0-1	.132	-0	117	10		1.0
1971	LA N	10	17	.370	31	31	8-1	0-0	203.1	195	103	19	4	71-1	144	4.16	78	.252	.315	58-0-8	.103	-0	92	-21	80	-2.6
1972	LA N	6	16	.273	26	25	4-3	0-0	169.1	148	84	8	5	60-4	101	3.67	92	.237	.306	55-0-6	.073	-3	71	-6	21	-1.0
1973	Cal A★	20	14	.588	40	40	19-2	0-0	315.2	280	124	15	9	130-5	241	3.22	111	.235	.314	55-0-6	.073	0	102	16		1.5
1974	Cal A	7	4	.636	14	14	8	0-0	108.2	102	48	3	1	43-0	77	2.98	116	.250	.319	0	—	0	127	3	116	0.3
1975	Cal A	7	15	.318	29	27	8	1-0	179	171	107	18	6	81-5	78	4.98	72	.257	.340	0	—	0	86	-26		-2.9
1976	Tex A	4	1	.800	10	10	2-1	0-0	64.2	56	31	4	5	27-0	34	3.48	103	.239	.328	0	—	0	120	0		-0.2
	Min A	9	9	.500	26	26	5-3	0-0	172	177	88	9	6	69-4	63	3.77	95	.274	.345	0	—	0	109	-5		-0.6
	Year	13	10	.565	36	36	7-4	0-0	236.2	233	119	13	11	96-4	97	3.69	97	.264	.340	0	—	0	112	-7		-0.6
1977	Tor A	2	8	.200	13	12	0	0-0	59.2	71	54	5	2	39-2	33	6.79	63	.296	.392	0	—	0	81	-17	101	-2.4
Total 14		118	127	.482	322	308	94-24	2-0	2174	1952	944	132	63	781-50	1515	3.39	100	.240	.309	413-0-30	.109	-7	99	-1	473	-2.7

SINGLETON, ELMER Bert Elmer "Smoky" B6.26.1918 Ogden UT D1.5.1996 Ogden UT BR/TR(BB 1957-58)/6-2/174(174-190) d8.20

YEAR	TM LG	W	L	PCT	G	GS	CG-SHO	SV-BS	IP	H	R	HR	HB	BB-IB	SO	ERA	AERA	OAV	OOB	AB-HR-SH	AVG	PB	SUP	APR	DL	PW
1945	Bos N	1	4	.200	7	5	1	0	37.1	35	22	1	1	14	14	4.82	79	.248	.321	11	.000	-1	53	-4		-0.6
1946	Bos N	0	1	.000	15	2	0	1	33.2	27	20	3	1	21	17	3.74	92	.221	.340	4-0-1	.000	-1*	162	-3		-0.2
1947	Pit N	2	2	.500	36	3	0	1	67	70	49	9	2	39	24	6.31	67	.267	.366	13-0-1	.308	1*	104	-13		-0.6
1948	Pit N	4	6	.400	38	5	1	2	92.1	90	52	11	4	40	53	4.97	82	.253	.330	23-0-1	.087	-2	105	-7		-0.8
1950	Was A	1	3	.333	21	1	0	0	36.1	39	23	4	0	17	19	5.20	86	.291	.371	7-0-1	.429	1	261	-2		0.0
1957	Chi N	0	1	.000	5	2	0	0	13.1	20	11	3	0	4	6	6.75	57	.333	.355	3-0-1	.000	-0*	91	-4		-0.3
1958	Chi N	1	0	1.000	4	1	0	0	4.2	1	0	0	0	1-1	2	0.00	—	.071	.133	1	.000	0		2	88	0.4
1959	Chi N	2	1	.667	21	1	0	0	43	40	15	2	0	12-2	25	2.72	145	.252	.304	6	.000	-1	23	6		0.3
Total 8		11	17	.393	145	19	2	4	327.2	322	192	33	5	146-3	160	4.83	83	.258	.338	68-0-5	.132	-3	99	-25	88	-1.8

SINGLETON, JOHN John Edward "Sheriff" B11.27.1896 Gallipolis OH D10.23.1937 Dayton OH BR/TR/5-11/171 d6.8

YEAR	TM LG	W	L	PCT	G	GS	CG-SHO	SV-BS	IP	H	R	HR	HB	BB-IB	SO	ERA	AERA	OAV	OOB	AB-HR-SH	AVG	PB	SUP	APR	DL	PW
1922	Phi N	1	10	.091	22	9	3-1	0	93	127	80	6	5	38	27	5.90	79	.346	.415	36-0-1	.139	-2	97	-11		-1.4

SIROTKA, MIKE Michael Robert B5.13.1971 Houston TX BL/TL/6-1/200* [ChiA93 15/425] d7.19 Col Louisiana St. [DL 2001 Tor A 190, 2002 Tor A 183]

YEAR	TM LG	W	L	PCT	G	GS	CG-SHO	SV-BS	IP	H	R	HR	HB	BB-IB	SO	ERA	AERA	OAV	OOB	AB-HR-SH	AVG	PB	SUP	APR	DL	PW
1995	Chi A	1	2	.333	6	6	0	0-0	34.1	39	16	2	0	17-0	19	4.19	107	.298	.371	0	—	0	83	2		0.1
1996	Chi A	1	2	.333	15	4	0	0-0	26.1	34	27	3	0	12-0	11	7.18	66	.315	.377	0	—	0	117	-10		-0.9
1997	Chi A	3	0	1.000	7	4	0	0-0	32	36	9	4	1	5-1	24	2.25	196	.290	.323	1	.000	-0	120	8		0.6
1998	Chi A	14	15	.483	33	33	5	0-0	211.2	255	137	30	2	57-2	128	5.06	91	.300	.336	4	.000	-0	111	-14		-1.5
1999	Chi A	11	13	.458	32	32	3-1	0-0	209	236	108	24	3	57-2	125	4.00	123	.283	.327	8	.250	0	84	19		1.8
2000	†Chi A	15	10	.600	32	32	0	0-0	197	203	101	23	2	69-1	128	3.79	133	.269	.330	4	.000	0	109	23		2.5
Total 6		45	42	.517	125	111	9-1	0-0	710.1	803	398	86	7	207-4	435	4.31	112	.286	.334	17	.118	0	102	28	373	2.6

SISCO, ANDY Andrew Frank B1.13.1983 Steamboat Springs CO BL/TL/6-10/270 d4.4

YEAR	TM LG	W	L	PCT	G	GS	CG-SHO	SV-BS	IP	H	R	HR	HB	BB-IB	SO	ERA	AERA	OAV	OOB	AB-HR-SH	AVG	PB	SUP	APR	DL	PW
2005	KC A	2	5	.286	67	0	0	0-5	75.1	62	37	5	2	42-4	76	3.11	136	.243	.343	1	.000	-0		10		0.7

SISK, DOUG Douglas Randall B9.26.1957 Renton WA BR/TR/6-2/210* d9.6 Col Washington St.

YEAR	TM LG	W	L	PCT	G	GS	CG-SHO	SV-BS	IP	H	R	HR	HB	BB-IB	SO	ERA	AERA	OAV	OOB	AB-HR-SH	AVG	PB	SUP	APR	DL	PW
1982	NY N	0	1	.000	8	0	0	1-0	8.2	5	1	0	1	4-2	4	1.04	354	.172	.294	0	—	0		0		0.3
1983	NY N	5	4	.556	67	0	0	11-6	104.1	88	38	1	4	59-7	33	2.24	164	.235	.342	6-0-1	.500	1		13		1.4
1984	NY N	1	3	.250	50	0	0	15-3	77.2	57	24	1	3	54-5	32	2.09	171	.215	.354	11-0-2	.091	-0		12	20	1.0
1985	NY N	4	5	.444	42	0	0	2-2	73	86	48	3	2	40-2	26	5.30	66	.291	.379	12	.000	-1		-15		-1.9
1986	†NY N	4	2	.667	41	0	0	1-0	70.2	77	31	0	5	31-5	31	3.06	117	.282	.366	4	.000	-0		3		0.1
1987	NY N	3	1	.750	55	0	0	3-3	78	83	38	5	5	22-4	37	3.46	111	.270	.323	5	.000	-0		1		0.1
1988	Bal A	3	3	.500	52	0	0	0-2	94.1	109	43	3	2	45-6	26	3.72	106	.306	.385	0	—	0		2	25	0.1
1990	Atl N	0	0	—	3	0	0	0-0	2.1	1	1	0	0	4-0	1	3.86	105	.143	.385	0	—	0		0	31	0.1
1991	Atl N	2	1	.667	14	0	0	0-0	14.1	21	14	1	0	8-2	5	5.02	77	.333	.403	0	—	0		-4		-0.7
Total 9		22	20	.524	332	0	0	33-16	523.1	527	238	15	20	267-33	195	3.27	113	.268	.359	38-0-3	.105	-1	15	163		0.4

SISK, TOMMIE Tommie Wayne B4.12.1942 Ardmore OK BR/TR/6-3/195* d7.19

YEAR	TM LG	W	L	PCT	G	GS	CG-SHO	SV-BS	IP	H	R	HR	HB	BB-IB	SO	ERA	AERA	OAV	OOB	AB-HR-SH	AVG	PB	SUP	APR	DL	PW
1962	Pit N	0	2	.000	9	0	0	0	17.2	18	9	1	1	8-1	6	4.08	97	.257	.342	5	.200	0	74	0		0.0
1963	Pit N	1	3	.250	57	4	1	0	108	85	42	6	1	45-10	73	2.92	113	.222	.303	16-0-1	.063	-0	78	4		0.2
1964	Pit N	1	4	.200	42	1	0	0	61.1	91	47	4	3	29-5	35	6.16	57	.364	.432	8	.000	-1	150	-18		-1.4
1965	Pit N	7	3	.700	38	12	1-1	0	111.1	103	48	6	1	50-7	66	3.40	103	.248	.328	33-0-1	.061	-2*	93	2		-0.1
1966	Pit N	10	5	.667	34	23	4-1	0	150	146	74	4	4	52-6	60	4.14	86	.256	.321	51-0-2	.098	-1	138	-8		-0.9
1967	Pit N	13	13	.500	37	31	11-2	0	207.2	196	88	6	3	78-10	85	3.34	101	.253	.321	69-0-6	.101	-2	107	1		-0.2
1968	Pit N	5	5	.500	33	11	0	1	96	101	40	4	3	35-8	41	3.28	89	.282	.351	24-0-2	.083	-1	116	-3		-0.4
1969	SD N	2	13	.133	53	13	1	6-1	143	160	81	11	1	48-8	59	4.78	75	.285	.339	25-0-4	.120	-1	70	-18		-1.8
1970	Chi A	1	1	.500	17	1	0	0-1	33.1	37	28	6	0	13-5	16	5.40	72	.276	.338	4	.250	0	46	-8		-0.4
Total 9		40	49	.449	316	99	19-4	10-2	928.1	937	457	57	17	358-60	441	3.92	88	.266	.335	235-0-16	.094	-7	106	-48		-5.0

SISLER, DAVE David Michael B10.16.1931 St.Louis MO BR/TR/6-4/200* d4.21 b-Dick f-George Col Princeton

YEAR	TM LG	W	L	PCT	G	GS	CG-SHO	SV-BS	IP	H	R	HR	HB	BB-IB	SO	ERA	AERA	OAV	OOB	AB-HR-SH	AVG	PB	SUP	APR	DL	PW
1956	Bos A	9	8	.529	39	14	3	3	142.1	120	81	13	7	72-2	93	4.62	100	.227	.326	42-0-4	.119	-2	83	2		-0.1
1957	Bos A	7	8	.467	22	19	5	1	122.1	135	68	15	2	61-1	55	4.71	85	.280	.361	42-0-4	.167	0	104	-8		-0.9
1958	Bos A	8	9	.471	30	25	4-1	0	149.1	157	94	22	1	79-2	71	4.94	81	.276	.361	46-0-11	.196	0	102	-14		-1.5

YEAR	TM LG	W	L	PCT	G	GS	CG-SHO	SV-BS	IP	H	R	HR	HB	BB-IB	SO	ERA	AERA	OAV	OOB	AB-HR-SH	AVG	PB	SUP	APR	DL	PW
1959	Bos A	0	0	—	3	0	0	0	6.2	9	5	3	0	1-0	3	6.75	60	.310	.333	2	.500	0		-2		-0.1
	Det A	1	3	.250	32	0	0	7	51.2	46	28	4	1	36-1	29	4.01	101	.242	.362	5-0-1	.200	-0		0		-0.1
	Year	1	3	.250	35	0	0	7	58.1	55	33	7	1	37-1	32	4.32	94	.251	.359	7-0-1	.286	-0		-2		-0.2
1960	Det A	7	5	.583	41	0	0	6	80	56	23	3	2	45-1	47	2.47	160	.199	.311	16-0-1	.125	0		14		2.2
1961	Was A	2	8	.200	45	1	0	11	60.1	55	34	6	3	48-5	30	4.18	96	.251	.390	6	.000	0	22	-2		-0.3
1962	Cin N	4	3	.571	35	0	0	1	43.2	44	19	4	0	26-3	27	3.92	103	.270	.370	0	—	0		2		-0.6
Total 7		38	44	.463	247	59	12-1	29	656.1	622	352	70	16	368-15	355	4.33	95	.253	.351	159-0-21	.157	-2	96	-8		-0.6

SISLER, GEORGE George Harold "Georgeous George" B3.24.1893 Manchester OH D3.26.1973 Richmond Heights MO BL/TL/5-11/170 d6.28 M3/C1 HF1939 s-Dave s-Dick Col Michigan ▲

YEAR	TM LG	W	L	PCT	G	GS	CG-SHO	SV-BS	IP	H	R	HR	HB	BB-IB	SO	ERA	AERA	OAV	OOB	AB-HR-SH	AVG	PB	SUP	APR	DL	PW
1915	StL A	4	4	.500	15	8	6	0	70	62	26	0	4	38	41	2.83	101	.247	.355	274-3-12	.285	3*	73	2		0.5
1916	StL A	1	2	.333	3	3	3-1	0	27	18	4	0	1	6	12	1.00	275	.198	.255	580-4-19	.305	1*	9	5		0.9
1918	StL A	0	0	—	2	1	0	1	8	10	6	0	1	4	4	4.50	61	.286	.375	452-2-9	.341	1*	165	-2		0.0
1920	StL A	0	0	—	1	0	0	1	1	0	0	0	0	0	1	0.00	—	.000	.000	631-19-13	.407	1*		0		0.0
1925	StL A	0	0	—	1	0	0	0	2	1	0	0	0	1	1	0.00	—	.167	.286	649-12-12	.345	0*		1		0.1
1926	StL A	0	0	—	1	0	0	1	2	0	0	0	0	0	3	0.00	—	.000	.286	613-7-16	.290	0*		1		0.1
1928	Bos N	0	0	—	1	0	0	0	1	0	0	0	0	1	0	0.00	—	.000	.333	491-4-14	.340	0*		0		0.1
Total 7		5	6	.455	24	12	9-1	3	111	91	36	0	6	52	63	2.35	123	.231	.330	3690-51-95	.335	7	64	7		1.7

SITTON, CARL Charles Vetter B9.22.1881 Pendleton SC D9.11.1931 Valdosta GA BR/TR/5-10.5/170 d4.24 Col Clemson

YEAR	TM LG	W	L	PCT	G	GS	CG-SHO	SV-BS	IP	H	R	HR	HB	BB-IB	SO	ERA	AERA	OAV	OOB	AB-HR-SH	AVG	PB	SUP	APR	DL	PW
1909	Cle A	3	2	.600	14	5	3	0	50	50	22	1	2	16	16	2.88	89	.263	.327	13	.154	0	88	-1		-0.1

SIVESS, PETE Peter B9.23.1913 South River NJ D6.1.2003 Candler NC BR/TR/6-3.5/195 d6.13 Col Dickinson

YEAR	TM LG	W	L	PCT	G	GS	CG-SHO	SV-BS	IP	H	R	HR	HB	BB-IB	SO	ERA	AERA	OAV	OOB	AB-HR-SH	AVG	PB	SUP	APR	DL	PW
1936	Phi N	3	4	.429	17	6	2	0	65	84	44	6	1	36	22	4.57	99	.310	.393	25	.120	-2	65	0		-0.3
1937	Phi N	1	1	.500	6	2	1	0	23	30	18	5	0	11	4	7.04	62	.330	.402	6	.000	-1	60	-5		-0.5
1938	Phi N	3	6	.333	39	8	2	3	116	143	78	12	1	69	32	5.51	71	.306	.397	32-0-1	.188	-1	76	-19		-1.5
Total 3		7	11	.389	62	16	5	3	204	257	136	23	2	116	58	5.38	77	.310	.396	63-0-1	.143	-4	71	-24		-2.

SIWY, JIM James Gerard B9.20.1958 Central Falls RI BR/TR/6-4/200* [ChiA80*3/59] d8.20 Col Rhode Island

YEAR	TM LG	W	L	PCT	G	GS	CG-SHO	SV-BS	IP	H	R	HR	HB	BB-IB	SO	ERA	AERA	OAV	OOB	AB-HR-SH	AVG	PB	SUP	APR	DL	PW
1982	Chi A	0	0	—	2	1	0	0-0	7	10	9	1	0	5-0	3	10.29	40	.385	.469	0	—	0	89	-4		0.
1984	Chi A	0	0	—	1	0	0	0-0	4.1	3	1	0	0	2-0	1	2.08	201	.231	.313	0	—	0		1		0.
Total 2		0	0	—	3	1	0	0-0	11.1	13	9	1	0	7-0	4	7.15	58	.333	.417	0	—	0	89	-3		-0.

SKALSKI, JOE Joseph Douglas B9.26.1964 Burnham IL BR/TR/6-3/190 [CleA86 3/57] d4.10 Col St. Xavier

YEAR	TM LG	W	L	PCT	G	GS	CG-SHO	SV-BS	IP	H	R	HR	HB	BB-IB	SO	ERA	AERA	OAV	OOB	AB-HR-SH	AVG	PB	SUP	APR	DL	PW
1989	Cle A	0	2	.000	2	1	0	0-0	6.2	7	6	0	0	4-0	3	6.75	59	.259	.394	0	—	0	46	-2		-0.

SKAUGSTAD, DAVE David Wendell B1.10.1940 Algona IA BL/TL/6-1/179 d9.25

YEAR	TM LG	W	L	PCT	G	GS	CG-SHO	SV-BS	IP	H	R	HR	HB	BB-IB	SO	ERA	AERA	OAV	OOB	AB-HR-SH	AVG	PB	SUP	APR	DL	PW
1957	Cin N	0	0	—	2	0	0	0	5.2	4	1	0	0	6-0	4	1.59	259	.190	.370	1	.000	0		2		0.

SKEELS, DAVE David B12.29.1892 Addy WA D12.2.1926 Spokane WA BL/TR/6-1/187 d9.14 Col Gonzaga

YEAR	TM LG	W	L	PCT	G	GS	CG-SHO	SV-BS	IP	H	R	HR	HB	BB-IB	SO	ERA	AERA	OAV	OOB	AB-HR-SH	AVG	PB	SUP	APR	DL	PW
1910	Det A	0	0	—	1	1	0	0	6	9	8	0	1	4	2	12.00	22	.333	.438	3	.000	-0	229	-5		-0.

SKOK, CRAIG Craig Richard B9.1.1947 Dobbs Ferry NY BR/TL/6-0/190(175-190) d5.4 Col Florida St.

YEAR	TM LG	W	L	PCT	G	GS	CG-SHO	SV-BS	IP	H	R	HR	HB	BB-IB	SO	ERA	AERA	OAV	OOB	AB-HR-SH	AVG	PB	SUP	APR	DL	PW
1973	Bos A	0	1	.000	11	0	1-0	0	28.2	35	22	2	0	11-2	22	6.28	64	.304	.357	0	—	0		-7		-0.
1976	Tex A	0	1	.000	9	0	0-2	5	13	7	2	0		3-0	5	12.60	28	.481	.533	0	—	0		-4		-0.
1978	Atl N	3	2	.600	43	0	0	2-0	62	64	38	6	3	27-8	28	4.35	93	.266	.338	8	.250	-0		-3		0.
1979	Atl N	1	3	.250	44	0	0	2-2	54.1	58	26	7	3	17-2	30	3.98	101	.282	.341	3	.000	0		1		0.
Total 4		4	7	.364	107	0	0	5-4	150	170	93	19	3	58-12	85	4.86	83	.289	.352	11	.182	0		-13		-1.

SKOPEC, JOHN John S. "Buckshot" B5.8.1880 Chicago IL D10.20.1912 Chicago IL BR/TL/5-10/190 d4.25

YEAR	TM LG	W	L	PCT	G	GS	CG-SHO	SV-BS	IP	H	R	HR	HB	BB-IB	SO	ERA	AERA	OAV	OOB	AB-HR-SH	AVG	PB	SUP	APR	DL	PW
1901	Chi A	6	3	.667	9	9	6	0	68.1	62	39	1	8	45	24	3.16	110	.239	.369	30-1-0	.333	3	136	2		0.
1903	Det A	2	2	.500	6	5	3	0	39.1	46	22	0	2	13	14	3.43	85	.291	.353	13-0-2	.154	-0	79	-2		0.
Total 2		8	5	.615	15	14	9	0	107.2	108	61	1	10	58	38	3.26	101	.259	.363	43-1-2	.279	3	118	0		0.

SKRMETTA, MATT Matthew Leland B11.6.1972 Biloxi MS BB/TR/6-3/220 [DetA93 26/725] d6.6 Col Jacksonville

YEAR	TM LG	W	L	PCT	G	GS	CG-SHO	SV-BS	IP	H	R	HR	HB	BB-IB	SO	ERA	AERA	OAV	OOB	AB-HR-SH	AVG	PB	SUP	APR	DL	PW
2000	Mon N	0	0	—	6	0	0	0-0	5.1	6	10	1	0	6-0	4	15.19	31	.273	.414	0	—	0		-6		-1.
	Pit N	2	2	.500	8	0	0	0-0	9.1	13	12	2	1	3-0	7	9.64	48	.333	.395	2	.000	-0		-6		-1.
	Year	2	2	.500	14	0	0	0-0	14.2	19	22	3	1	9-0	11	11.66	40	.311	.403	2	.000	-0		-12		-1.

SLAGLE, JOHN John A. B Lawrence IN BL/TR/?/175 d4.30

YEAR	TM LG	W	L	PCT	G	GS	CG-SHO	SV-BS	IP	H	R	HR	HB	BB-IB	SO	ERA	AERA	OAV	OOB	AB-HR-SH	AVG	PB	SUP	APR	DL	PW
1891	Cin AA	0	0	—	1	0	0	1	1.1	3	0	0	0	1	1	0.00	—	.429	.500	1	.000	-0		1		0.

SLAGLE, ROGER Roger Lee B11.4.1953 Wichita KS BR/TR/6-3/190 [NYA76 S1/19] d9.7 Col Kansas

YEAR	TM LG	W	L	PCT	G	GS	CG-SHO	SV-BS	IP	H	R	HR	HB	BB-IB	SO	ERA	AERA	OAV	OOB	AB-HR-SH	AVG	PB	SUP	APR	DL	PW
1979	NY A	0	0	—	1	0	0								2	0.00	—	.000	.000		—	0		1		0.

SLAGLE, WALT Walter Jennings B12.15.1878 Kenton OH D6.14.1974 San Gabriel CA BB/TR/6-0/165 d5.4

YEAR	TM LG	W	L	PCT	G	GS	CG-SHO	SV-BS	IP	H	R	HR	HB	BB-IB	SO	ERA	AERA	OAV	OOB	AB-HR-SH	AVG	PB	SUP	APR	DL	PW
1910	Cin N	0	0	—	1	0	0	0	1	0	1	0	1	3		9.00	32	.000	.571			0		-1		0.

SLAPNICKA, CY Cyril Charles B3.23.1886 Cedar Rapids IA D10.20.1979 Cedar Rapids IA BB/TR/5-10/165 d9.26

YEAR	TM LG	W	L	PCT	G	GS	CG-SHO	SV-BS	IP	H	R	HR	HB	BB-IB	SO	ERA	AERA	OAV	OOB	AB-HR-SH	AVG	PB	SUP	APR	DL	PW
1911	Chi N	0	2	.000	3	2	1	0	24	21	12	0	3	7	10	3.38	98	.236	.313	9	.222	-0	91	0		-1
1918	Pit N	1	4	.200	7	6	4	1	49.1	50	34	2	5	22	3	4.74	61	.269	.362	14-0-2	.071	-1	101	-10		-1
Total 2		1	6	.143	10	8	5	1	73.1	71	46	2	8	29	13	4.30	70	.258	.346	23-0-2	.130	-1	97	-10		-1

SLAPPEY, JOHN John Henry B8.8.1898 Albany GA D6.10.1957 Marietta GA BL/TL/6-4/170 d8.23 Col Georgia

YEAR	TM LG	W	L	PCT	G	GS	CG-SHO	SV-BS	IP	H	R	HR	HB	BB-IB	SO	ERA	AERA	OAV	OOB	AB-HR-SH	AVG	PB	SUP	APR	DL	PW
1920	Phi A	0	1	1.000	3	1	0	0	6.1	15	12	0	0	4	1	7.11	57	.441	.500	2	.500	1	99	-4		-0

SLATON, JIM James Michael B6.19.1950 Long Beach CA BR/TR/6-0/185(180-192) [MilA69 15/355] d4.14 C1 Col Antelope Valley (CA) JC

YEAR	TM LG	W	L	PCT	G	GS	CG-SHO	SV-BS	IP	H	R	HR	HB	BB-IB	SO	ERA	AERA	OAV	OOB	AB-HR-SH	AVG	PB	SUP	APR	DL	PW
1971	Mil A	10	8	.556	26	23	5-4	0-0	147.2	140	67	16	1	71-9	63	3.78	92	.253	.338	46-0-4	.109	-1	98	-3		-0
1972	Mil A	1	6	.143	9	8	0	0-0	44	50	31	3	1	21-1	17	5.52	55	.287	.362	11-0-3	.091	-1	80	-12		-1
1973	Mil A	13	15	.464	38	38	13-3	0-0	276.1	266	127	30	1	99-4	134	3.71	103	.251	.314	0	—	0	95	4		-0
1974	Mil A	13	16	.448	40	35	10-3	0-0	250	255	117	22	3	102-6	126	3.92	93	.268	.339	0	—	0	101	-7		-0
1975	Mil A	11	18	.379	37	33	10-3	0-1	217	238	129	28	2	90-6	119	4.52	85	.276	.343	0	—	0	82	-17		-2
1976	Mil A	14	15	.483	38	38	12-2	0-0	292.2	287	126	14	6	94-12	138	3.44	102	.259	.317	0	—	0	99	2		0
1977	Mil A☆	10	14	.417	32	31	7-1	0-0	221	223	104	25	11	77-5	104	3.58	115	.266	.333	0	—	0	108	-5		-0
1978	Det A	17	11	.607	35	34	11-2	0-0	233.2	235	117	27	8	85-1	92	4.12	95	.263	.329	0	—	0	112	14		0
1979	Mil A	15	9	.625	32	31	12-3	0-0	213	229	95	15	2	54-1	80	3.63	116	.278	.321	0	—	0	168	-5	129	-0
1980	Mil A	1	1	.500	3	3	0	0-0	16.1	17	10	3	0	10-2	4	4.41	89	.270	.324	0	—	0	111	-12		-0
1981	†Mil A	5	7	.417	24	21	0	0-0	117.1	120	60	10	2	50-2	47	4.37	79	.273	.346	0	—	0	136	7	18	-0
1982	†Mil A	10	6	.625	39	7	0	6-2	117.2	117	48	14	1	41-3	59	3.29	117	.264	.326	0	—	0		-6		-1
1983	Mil A	14	6	.700	46	0	0	5-6	112.1	112	57	12	3	56-5	38	4.33	88	.272	.356	0	—	0	101	-16		-0
1984	Cal A	7	10	.412	32	22	5-1	1-0	163	192	95	22	2	56-5	67	4.97	80	.295	.350	0	—	0	87	-5		-0
1985	Cal A	6	10	.375	29	24	1	1-0	148.1	162	82	22	2	63-1	60	4.37	94	.284	.355	0	—	0	102	-13		-0
1986	Cal A	4	6	.400	14	12	0	0-0	73.1	84	52	9	2	29-1	31	5.65	73	.295	.357	0	—	0		1		0
	Det A	0	0	—	22	0	0	2-1	40	46	18	5	1	11-3	12	4.05	103	.287	.333	0	—	0	102	-11		-0
	Year	4	6	.400	36	12	0	2-1	113.1	130	70	14	3	40-4	43	5.08	82	.292	.349	0	—	0	100	-11		-0
Total 16		151	158	.489	496	360	86-22	14-10	2683.2	2773	1335	277	48	1004-65	1191	4.03	95	.270	.334	57-0-7	.105	-2	100	-59	147	

SLATTERY, PHIL Philip Ryan B2.25.1893 Harper IA D3.2.1968 Long Beach CA BR/TL/5-11/160 d9.16

YEAR	TM LG	W	L	PCT	G	GS	CG-SHO	SV-BS	IP	H	R	HR	HB	BB-IB	SO	ERA	AERA	OAV	OOB	AB-HR-SH	AVG	PB	SUP	APR	DL	PW
1915	Pit N	0	0	—	3	0	0	0	8	5	0	0	2	1	1	0.00	—	.185	.267	1	.000	-0		2		0.

SLAUGHTER, BARNEY Byron Atkins B10.6.1884 Smyrna DE D5.17.1961 Philadelphia PA BR/TR/5-11.5/165 d8.9

YEAR	TM LG	W	L	PCT	G	GS	CG-SHO	SV-BS	IP	H	R	HR	HB	BB-IB	SO	ERA	AERA	OAV	OOB	AB-HR-SH	AVG	PB	SUP	APR	DL	PW
1910	Phi N	0	1	.000	8	1	0	1	18	21	12	0	0	11	7	5.50	57	.318	.416	5	.200	0	167	-4		-0

SLAUGHTER, STERLING Sterling Feore B11.18.1941 Danville IL BR/TR/5-11/165 d4.19 Col Arizona St.

YEAR	TM LG	W	L	PCT	G	GS	CG-SHO	SV-BS	IP	H	R	HR	HB	BB-IB	SO	ERA	AERA	OAV	OOB	AB-HR-SH	AVG	PB	SUP	APR	DL	PW
1964	Chi N	2	4	.333	20	6	1	0	72	64	35	8	0	32-6	32	5.75	65	.305	.393	12	.083	-0	55	-10		

SLAYBACK, BILL William Grover B2.21.1948 Hollywood CA BR/TR/6-4/185(185-200) [DetA68*7/113] d6.26 Col Cal St.-Northridge

YEAR	TM LG	W	L	PCT	G	GS	CG-SHO	SV-BS	IP	H	R	HR	HB	BB-IB	SO	ERA	AERA	OAV	OOB	AB-HR-SH	AVG	PB	SUP	APR	DL	PW
1972	Det A	5	6	.455	23	13	3-1	0-0	81.2	74	36	4	1	25-1	65	3.20	99	.239	.297	23-0-2	.174	-0	92	-2		0
1973	Det A	0	0	—	3	0	0	0-0	2	5	1	0	0	1-0	1	4.50	91	.417	.462	0	—	0		-1		0
1974	Det A	1	3	.250	16	4	0	0-0	54.2	57	34	1	3	26-2	23	4.77	80	.273	.351	0	—	0	58	-6		-0
Total 3		6	9	.400	42	17	3-1	0-0	138.1	136	74	5	5	51-3	89	3.84	90	.256	.323	23-0-2	.174	-0	80	-9		

YEAR	TM LG	W	L	PCT	G	GS	CG-SHO	SV-BS	IP	H	R	HR	HB	BB-IB	SO	ERA	AERA	OAV	OOB	AB-HR-SH	AVG	PB	SUP	APR	DL	PW

SLAYTON, STEVE Foster Herbert B4.26.1902 Barre VT D12.20.1984 Manchester NH BR/TR/6-0/163 d7.21 Col New Hampshire

1928	Bos A	0	0	—	3	0	0	0	7	6	3	0	0	3	2	3.86	107	.240	.321	2	.000	-0		0		0.0

SLEATER, LOU Louis Mortimer B9.8.1926 St.Louis MO BL/TL/5-10/185* d4.25 Col Maryland-Baltimore Co.

1950	StL A	0	0	—	1	0	0	0	1	0	0	0	0	1	1	0.00	—	.000	.000	0	—	0		1		0.0
1951	StL A	1	9	.100	20	8	4	1	81	88	53	7	5	53	33	5.11	86	.271	.381	31	.226	0*	51	-7		-0.8
1952	StL A	0	1	.000	4	2	0	0	8.2	9	8	1	0	5	1	7.27	54	.265	.359	2	.000	-0	111	-3		-0.7
	Was A	4	2	.667	14	9	3-1	0	57	56	29	4	2	30	22	3.63	98	.260	.356	20-0-1	.050	-2*	106	-2		-0.5
	Year	4	3	.571	18	11	3-1	0	65.2	65	37	5	2	35	23	4.11	88	.261	.357	22-0-1	.045	-2	108	-5		-0.8
1955	KC A	1	1	.500	16	1	0	0	25.2	33	22	3	0	21-0	11	7.71	54	.324	.429	13	.154	-1*	21	-9		-0.7
1956	Mil N	2	2	.500	25	1	0	2	45.2	42	22	6	0	27-9	32	3.15	110	.240	.338	10	.500	2	254	0		0.3
1957	Det A	3	3	.500	41	0	0	2	69.1	61	33	9	1	28-7	43	3.76	102	.237	.313	20-3-1	.250	3	0			0.3
1958	Det A	0	0	—	4	0	0	0	5.1	3	4	2	0	6-0	4	6.75	60	.158	.360	1-1-0	1.000	1		-1		0.1
	Bal A	1	0	1.000	6	0	0	0	7	14	10	0	0	2-0	5	12.86	28	.438	.471	6	.000	-1*	-7		51	-0.9
	Year	1	0	1.000	10	0	0	0	12.1	17	14	2	0	8-0	9	10.22	37	.333	.424	7-1-0	.143	0		-8		-0.8
Total	7	12	18	.400	131	21	7-1	5	300.2	306	181	32	8	172-16	152	4.70	83	.263	.360	103-4-2	.204	3	86	-28	51	-2.5

SLOAT, LEFTY Dwain Clifford B12.1.1918 Nokomis IL D4.18.2003 St.Paul MN BR/TL/6-0/168 d4.24

1948	Bro N	0	1	.000	4	1	0	0	7.1	7	5	0	0	8	1	6.14	65	.280	.455	1-0-1	.000	0	0	-1		-0.2
1949	Chi N	0	0	—	5	1	0	0	9	14	7	0	0	3	3	7.00	58	.400	.447	0-0-1	—	0	87	-3		-0.1
Total	2	0	1	.000	9	2	0	0	16.1	21	12	0	0	11	4	6.61	61	.350	.451	1-0-2	.000	0	44	-4		-0.3

SLOCUMB, HEATHCLIFF Heath B6.7.1966 Jamaica NY BR/TR/6-3/220* d4.11

1991	Chi N	2	1	.667	52	0	0	1-2	62.2	53	29	3	3	30-6	34	3.45	113	.231	.321	1	.000	-0		0		0.1
1992	Chi N	0	3	.000	30	0	0	1-0	36	52	27	3	1	21-3	27	6.50	56	.351	.430	4	.000	-0		-10		-0.9
1993	Chi N	1	0	1.000	10	0	0	0-0	10.2	7	5	0	0	4-0	4	3.38	120	.189	.262	1	.000	-0		1		0.0
	Cle A	3	1	.750	20	0	0	0-2	27.1	28	14	3	0	16-2	18	4.28	102	.272	.364	0	—	0		0		0.0
1994	Phi N	5	1	.833	52	0	0	0-5	72.1	75	32	0	2	28-4	58	2.86	150	.262	.328	4-0-1	.250	-0		9		0.7
1995	Phi N★	5	6	.455	61	0	0	32-6	65.1	64	26	2	1	35-3	63	2.89	146	.257	.351	1	.000	-0		6		1.7
1996	Bos A	5	5	.500	75	0	0	31-8	83.1	68	31	2	3	55-5	88	3.02	169	.222	.343	0	—	-0		19		3.3
1997	Bos A	0	5	.000	49	0	0	17-5	46.2	58	32	4	3	34-4	36	5.79	80	.312	.422	0	—	-0		-5		-0.8
	†Sea A	0	4	.000	27	0	0	10-1	28.1	26	13	2	1	15-1	28	4.13	110	.241	.339	0	—	0		2		0.3
	Year	0	9	.000	76	0	0	27-6	75	84	45	6	4	49-5	64	5.16	89	.286	.393	0	—	-0		-4		-0.5
1998	Sea A	2	5	.286	57	0	0	3-1	67.2	72	40	5	1	44-1	51	5.32	88	.275	.379	0	—	-0		-3		-0.3
1999	Bal A	0	0	—	10	0	0	0-0	8.2	15	12	2	2	9-2	12	12.46	38	.395	.531	0	—	-0		-7		-0.3
	StL N	3	2	.600	40	0	0	2-1	53.1	49	16	3	1	30-5	48	2.36	195	.243	.342	0	—	0		13	23	1.1
2000	StL N	2	3	.400	43	0	0	1-0	49.2	50	32	9	1	24-1	34	5.44	85	.266	.349	1	.000	-0*		-4		-0.4
	SD N	0	1	.000	22	0	0	0-0	19	19	11	0	2	13-3	12	3.79	117	.264	.378	0	—	-0		-0		-0.4
	Year	2	4	.333	65	0	0	1-0	68.2	69	43	9	3	37-4	46	4.98	92	.265	.357	1	.000	-0		-4		-0.4
Total	10	28	37	.431	548	0	0	98-31	631	636	320	38	21	358-40	513	4.08	109	.263	.360	12-0-1	.083	-1	25	23	4.5

SLUSARSKI, JOE Joseph Andrew B12.19.1966 Indianapolis IN BR/TR/6-4/195* [OakA88 2/46] d4.11 Col New Orleans

1991	Oak A	5	7	.417	20	19	1	0-0	109.1	121	69	14	4	52-1	60	5.27	73	.283	.364	0	—	0	124	-19		-1.8
1992	Oak A	5	5	.500	15	14	0	0-0	76	85	52	15	6	27-0	38	5.45	69	.284	.350	0	—	0	143	-15		-1.7
1993	Oak A	0	0	—	2	1	0	0-0	8.2	9	5	1	0	11-3	1	5.19	80	.300	.488	0	—	0	-1			-0.1
1995	Mil A	1	1	.500	12	0	0	0-0	15	21	11	3	2	6-1	6	5.40	93	.333	.403	0	—	0	-1			-0.1
1999	Hou N	0	0	—	3	0	0	0-0	3.2	1	0	0	0	3-1	3	0.00	—	.083	.267	0	—	0	2	15		0.1
2000	Hou N	2	7	.222	54	0	0	3-1	77	80	36	8	3	22-3	54	4.21	117	.268	.323	9	.111	-0	7			0.7
2001	Atl N	0	0	—	4	0	0	0-0	6	9	6	2	0	1-0	5	9.00	48	.346	.370	0	—	0	-3	28		-0.1
	Hou N	0	1	.000	8	0	0	0-0	10	16	10	2	0	3-0	6	9.00	51	.364	.396	0	—	0	-4			-0.4
	Year	0	1	.000	12	0	0	0-0	16	25	16	4	0	4-0	11	9.00	50	.357	.387	0	—	0	-7			-0.5
Total	7	13	21	.382	118	34	1	3-1	305.2	342	189	45	15	125-9	173	5.18	81	.285	.357	9	.111	-0	119	-34	43	-3.3

SMALL, AARON Aaron James B11.23.1971 Oxnard CA BR/TR/6-5/208(200-235) [TorA89 22/575] d6.11

1994	Tor A	0	0	—	1	0	0	0-0	2	5	2	0	2	2-0	0	9.00	54	.500	.538	0	—	0	-1			0.0
1995	Fla N	1	0	1.000	7	0	0	0-0	6.1	7	2	1	0	6-0	5	1.42	302	.269	.406	0	—	0	2			0.2
1996	Oak A	1	3	.250	12	3	0	0-0	28.2	37	28	3	1	22-1	17	8.16	61	.308	.417	0	—	0	87	-10		-1.1
1997	Oak A	9	5	.643	71	0	0	4-2	96.2	109	50	6	3	40-6	57	4.28	107	.294	.362	1	.000	-0	3			0.4
1998	Oak A	1	1	.500	24	0	0	0-0	36	51	34	3	3	14-3	19	7.25	64	.333	.398	0	—	0	-11			-0.5
	Ari N	3	1	.750	23	0	0	0-2	31.2	32	14	5	1	8-1	14	3.69	116	.269	.320	0	—	0	2			0.2
2002	Atl N	0	0	—	1	0	0	0-0	0.1	2	1	0	0	2-0	1	27.00	15	.667	.800	0	—	0	-1			0.0
2004	Fla N	0	0	—	7	0	0	0-0	16.1	24	15	5	0	7-0	8	8.27	50	.343	.403	2	.000	-0	-7			-0.4
2005	†NY A	10	0	1.000	15	9	1-1	0-1	76	71	27	4	5	24-0	37	3.20	137	.250	.317	2	.000	-0	155	11		1.3
Total	8	25	10	.714	161	12	1-1	4-5	294	338	173	28	13	125-11	158	4.90	92	.292	.365	3	.000	-0	135	-12		0.1

SMALL, MARK Mark Allen B11.12.1967 Portland OR BR/TR/6-3/205 [HouN89 17/438] d4.5 Col Washington St. [DL 1997 Hou N 27]

| 1996 | Hou N | 0 | 1 | .000 | 16 | 0 | 0 | 0-0 | 24.1 | 23 | 14 | 1 | 1 | 13-3 | 16 | 5.92 | 66 | .308 | .388 | 1 | .000 | -0 | -8 | | | -0.4 |

SMALLWOOD, WALT Walter Clayton B4.24.1893 Dayton MD D4.29.1967 Baltimore MD BR/TR/6-2/190 d9.19 Mil 1918-19

1917	NY A	0	0	—	2	0	0	0	2	1	1	0	0	1	2	0.00	—	.167	.286	0	—	0	1			0.0
1919	NY A	0	0	—	6	0	0	0	21.2	20	12	1	2	9	6	4.98	64	.263	.356	5	.000	-1	-3			-0.3
Total	2	0	0	—	8	0	0	0	23.2	21	12	1	2	10	7	4.56	69	.256	.351	5	.000	-1	-2			-0.3

SMART, J.D. Jon David B11.12.1973 San Saba TX BR/TR/6-2/185* [MonN95 4/115] d4.6 Col Texas [DL 2000 Mon N 123]

1999	Mon N	0	1	.000	29	0	0	0-0	52	56	30	4	0	17-0	21	5.02	89	.276	.330	3	.000	-0	-2			-0.1
2001	Tex A	1	2	.333	15	0	0	0-2	15.1	19	11	3	0	4-0	10	6.46	74	.306	.338	0	—	0	-2	99		-0.4
Total	2	1	3	.250	44	0	0	0-2	67.1	75	41	7	0	21-0	31	5.35	85	.283	.332	3	.000	-0	-4	222		-0.5

SMILEY, JOHN John Patrick B3.17.1965 Phoenixville PA BL/TL/6-4/200(180-215) [PitN83 12/300] d9.1 [DL 1998 Cle A 181]

1986	Pit N	1	0	1.000	12	0	0	0-0	11.2	4	6	2	0	4-0	9	3.86	101	.105	.190	0	—	0	0			0.0
1987	Pit N	5	5	.500	63	0	0	4-2	75	69	49	7	0	50-8	58	5.76	72	.244	.354	1	.143	0	-11			-1.4
1988	Pit N	13	11	.542	34	32	5-1	0-0	205	185	81	15	3	46-4	129	3.25	106	.241	.284	63-0-7	.079	-2	89	5		0.4
1989	Pit N	12	8	.600	28	28	8-1	0-0	205.1	174	78	22	4	49-5	123	2.81	121	.226	.273	65-0-7	.138	1	100	11		1.1
1990	†Pit N	9	10	.474	26	25	2	0-0	149.1	161	83	15	2	36-1	86	4.64	79	.275	.317	49-0-3	.122	-0	92	-15	43	-1.7
1991	†Pit N★	20	8	.714	33	32	2-1	0-0	207.2	194	78	17	3	44-0	129	3.08	117	.251	.292	70-0-6	.100	-1	116	13		1.5
1992	Min A	16	9	.640	34	34	5-2	0-0	241	205	93	17	6	65-0	163	3.21	127	.231	.286	0	—	0	91	23		2.3
1993	Cin N	3	9	.250	18	18	2	0-0	105.2	117	69	15	2	31-0	60	5.62	72	.286	.337	32-0-5	.250	2	101	-17	93	-1.5
1994	Cin N	11	10	.524	24	24	1-1	0-0	158.2	169	80	18	4	37-3	112	3.86	108	.275	.320	55-0-5	.200	2	122	4		0.7
1995	†Cin N★	12	5	.706	28	27	1	0-0	176.2	173	72	11	4	39-3	124	3.46	121	.263	.306	55-2-6	.164	2	111	15		1.5
1996	Cin N	13	14	.481	35	34	2-2	0-1	217.1	207	100	20	4	54-5	171	3.64	118	.256	.304	68-0-4	.191	2	90	14		1.7
1997	Cin N	9	10	.474	20	20	0	0-0	117	139	76	17	6	31-3	94	5.23	82	.296	.346	40-0-2	.100	-2	86	-13	15	-2.1
	Cle A	2	4	.333	6	6	0	0-0	37.1	45	24	8	1	10-0	26	5.54	85	.304	.350	0	—	0	72	-2	8	-0.3
Total	12	126	103	.550	361	280	28-8	4-3	1907.2	1842	888	185	39	496-32	1284	3.80	105	.255	.305	504-2-45	.145	2	99	27	355	2.2

SMITH d6.5

| 1884 | Bal U | 0 | 0 | — | 1 | 1 | 0 | 0 | 6 | 12 | 11 | 0 | 0 | 2 | 2 | 9.00 | 30 | .387 | .424 | 5 | .200 | -1 | 192 | -4 | | -0.2 |

SMITH d5.31

| 1886 | Cin AA | 0 | 1 | .000 | 1 | 1 | 1 | 0 | 9 | 8 | 8 | 0 | 0 | 10 | 1 | 4.00 | 88 | .229 | .400 | 4 | .250 | -0 | 202 | -3 | | -0.1 |

SMITH, AL Alfred John B10.12.1907 Belleville IL D4.28.1977 Brownsville TX BL/TL/5-11/180 d5.5 C1

1934	NY N	3	5	.375	30	4	0	5	66.2	70	40	2	0	21	27	4.32	90	.266	.320	14-0-1	.286	1	84	-4		-0.5
1935	NY N	10	8	.556	40	10	4-1	5	124	125	50	6	7	32	44	3.41	113	.263	.319	34-1-2	.118	-0	101	8		1.0
1936	†NY N	14	13	.519	43	30	9-4	2	209.1	217	116	16	4	69	89	3.78	103	.274	.335	73-0-4	.137	-1	128	-3		-0.5
1937	†NY N	5	4	.556	33	9	2	0	85.2	91	45	8	0	30	41	4.20	93	.275	.339	25-0-1	.120	-2	121	-2		-0.4
1938	Phi N	1	4	.200	19	9	0	0	86	115	70	7	0	40	46	6.28	62	.320	.388	21	.000	-2	131	-23		-1.4
1939	Phi N	0	0	—	3	0	0	0	9	11	5	1	0	2	2	4.00	100	.314	.429	2	—	0	0			0.0

YEAR	TM LG	W	L	PCT	G	GS	CG-SHO	SV-BS	IP	H	R	HR	HB	BB-IB	SO	ERA	AERA	OAV	OOB	AB-HR-SH	AVG	PB	SUP	APR	DL	PW
1940	Cle A	15	7	.682	31	24	11-1	2	183	187	79	12	6	55	46	3.44	122	.270	.329	62-0-1	.306	7	99	17		2.6
1941	Cle A	12	13	.480	29	27	13-2	0	206.2	204	95	12	1	75	76	3.83	103	.256	.329	71-1-1	.155	2*	92	4		0.8
1942	Cle A	10	15	.400	30	24	7-1	0	168.1	163	96	9	5	71	66	3.96	87	.251	.329	60-0-2	.250	3	94	-14		-1.6
1943	Cle A☆	17	7	.708	29	27	14-3	1	208.1	186	74	7	0	72	72	2.55	122	.239	.303	68-0-4	.206	3*	111	12		1.8
1944	Cle A	7	13	.350	28	26	7-1	0	181.2	197	83	6	3	69	44	3.42	96	.275	.340	64-0-1	.156	-1	91	-3		-0.4
1945	Cle A	5	12	.294	21	19	8-3	1	133.2	141	74	8	2	48	34	3.84	85	.275	.340	41-0-2	.293	4*	84	-13		-1.0
Total	12	99	101	.495	356	201	75-16	17	1662.1	1707	827	94	32	587	587	3.72	99	.267	.332	535-2-19	.191	14	101	-21		0.4

SMITH, AL Alfred Kendricks B12.13.1903 Norristown PA D8.11.1995 San Diego CA BR/TR/6-0/170 d6.18 Col Villanova

YEAR	TM LG	W	L	PCT	G	GS	CG-SHO	SV-BS	IP	H	R	HR	HB	BB-IB	SO	ERA	AERA	OAV	OOB	AB-HR-SH	AVG	PB	SUP	APR	DL	PW
1926	NY N	0	0	—	1	0	0	0	2	4	2	0	0	2	0	9.00	42	.444	.545	0	—	0		-1		-0.1

SMITH, ART Arthur Laird B6.21.1906 Boston MA D11.22.1995 Norwalk CT BR/TR/6-0/175 d6.9 Col Columbia

| 1932 | Chi A | 0 | 1 | .000 | 3 | 2 | 0 | 0 | 7 | 17 | 13 | 1 | 0 | 4 | 1 | 11.57 | 37 | .500 | .553 | 1 | .000 | -0 | 118 | -7 | | -0.7 |

SMITH, BILLY Billy Lavern B9.13.1954 LaMarque TX BR/TR/6-7/225 [HouN77 14/352] d6.9 Col Sam Houston St.

| 1981 | †Hou N | 1 | 1 | .500 | 10 | 1 | 0 | 1-1 | 20.2 | 20 | 7 | 3 | 0 | 3-1 | 3 | 3.05 | 108 | .263 | .291 | 2 | .000 | -0 | 54 | 1 | | 0.1 |

SMITH, BRYN Bryn Nelson B8.11.1955 Marietta GA BR/TR/6-2/205* d9.8 Col Hancock (CA) JC

YEAR	TM LG	W	L	PCT	G	GS	CG-SHO	SV-BS	IP	H	R	HR	HB	BB-IB	SO	ERA	AERA	OAV	OOB	AB-HR-SH	AVG	PB	SUP	APR	DL	PW
1981	Mon N	1	0	1.000	7	0	0	0-0	13	14	4	1	0	3-0	9	2.77	128	.280	.321	1-0-2	.000	-0		1		0.1
1982	Mon N	2	4	.333	47	1	0	3-0	79.1	81	43	5	0	23-5	50	4.20	88	.264	.311	8-0-1	.000	-0	0	-5		-0.4
1983	Mon N	6	11	.353	49	12	5-3	3-1	155.1	142	51	13	5	43-6	101	2.49	146	.248	.305	30-0-7	.167	1	83	18		2.0
1984	Mon N	12	13	.480	28	28	4-2	0-0	179	178	72	15	3	51-7	101	3.32	104	.259	.312	53-0-7	.132	1	93	4		0.7
1985	Mon N	18	5	.783	32	32	4-2	0-0	222.1	193	85	12	1	41-3	127	2.91	118	.232	.268	72-1-11	.194	3	140	11		1.4
1986	Mon N	10	8	.556	30	30	1	0-0	187.1	182	101	15	6	63-6	105	3.94	95	.251	.315	58-1-5	.138	1	108	-8		-0.5
1987	Mon N	10	9	.526	26	26	2	0-0	150.1	164	81	16	2	31-4	94	4.37	98	.274	.310	44-0-7	.136	-0	110	-1	25	-0.1
1988	Mon N	12	10	.545	32	32	1	0-0	198	179	79	15	10	32-2	122	3.00	121	.243	.282	55-0-8	.109	-1	103	12		1.1
1989	Mon N	10	11	.476	33	32	3-1	0-0	215.2	177	76	16	4	54-4	129	2.84	126	.223	.274	62-0-10	.065	-2	109	17	40	1.5
1990	StL N	9	8	.529	26	25	0	0-0	141.1	160	81	11	4	30-1	78	4.27	90	.286	.324	39-1-11	.256	3	97	-9		-0.7
1991	StL N	12	9	.571	31	31	3	0-0	198.2	188	95	16	7	45-3	94	3.85	97	.251	.315	3-0-1	.000	-0	112	-3		-0.6
1992	StL N	4	2	.667	13	1	0	0-0	21.1	20	11	3	3	5-1	9	4.64	74	.247	.315	3-0-1	.000	-0	397	-3	145	-1.6
1993	Col N	4	4	.333	11	5	0	0-1	29.2	47	29	2	3	11-1	9	8.49	56	.362	.412	6	.000	-0	79	-9	16	-1.6
Total	13	108	94	.535	365	255	23-8	6-2	1791.1	1725	808	140	48	432-43	1028	3.53	105	.253	.300	496-3-77	.153	7	108	25	226	2.9

SMITH, CHUCK Charles Edward B10.21.1969 Memphis TN BR/TR/6-1/185* d6.13 Col Indiana St.

YEAR	TM LG	W	L	PCT	G	GS	CG-SHO	SV-BS	IP	H	R	HR	HB	BB-IB	SO	ERA	AERA	OAV	OOB	AB-HR-SH	AVG	PB	SUP	APR	DL	PW
2000	Fla N	6	6	.500	19	19	1	0-0	122.2	111	53	6	3	54-2	118	3.23	136	.248	.330	40-0-1	.100	-2*	95	14		1.0
2001	Fla N	5	5	.500	15	15	0	0-0	88	89	47	10	6	35-4	71	4.70	89	.265	.341	26-0-2	.192	1	114	-4	110	-0.4
Total	2	11	11	.500	34	34	1		210.2	200	100	16	9	89-6	189	3.84	112	.255	.335	66-0-3	.136	-2	103	10	110	0.6

SMITH, CHARLIE Charles Edwin B4.20.1880 Cleveland OH D1.3.1929 Wickliffe OH BR/TR/6-1/185 d8.6 b-Fred

YEAR	TM LG	W	L	PCT	G	GS	CG-SHO	SV-BS	IP	H	R	HR	HB	BB-IB	SO	ERA	AERA	OAV	OOB	AB-HR-SH	AVG	PB	SUP	APR	DL	PW
1902	Cle A	2	1	.667	3	3	2-1	0	20	23	9	0	5	5	5	4.05	85	.287	.329	8	.125	-0	111	0		0.0
1906	Was A	9	16	.360	33	22	17-2	0	235.1	250	113	2	8	75	105	2.91	91	.275	.336	87-1-1	.184	-1	86	-10		-1.2
1907	Was A	10	20	.333	36	31	21-3	0	258.2	254	103	0	1	51	119	2.61	93	.259	.297	84-0-5	.143	-3*	80	-3		-0.5
1908	Was A	9	13	.409	26	23	14-1	1	183	166	76	2	3	60	83	2.41	95	.247	.311	65-0-5	.123	-2*	92	-4		-0.8
1909	Was A	3	12	.200	23	15	7-1	0	145.2	140	73	4	5	37	72	3.27	74	.250	.303	45-0-1	.156	-1	60	-13		-1.4
	Bos A	3	0	1.000	3	3	2	0	25	23	6	2	1	11		2.16	116	.237	.260	10	.300	1	160	2		0.3
	Year	12	12	.333	26	18	9-1	0	170.2	163	79	6	6	39	83	3.11	78	.248	.297	55-0-1	.182	-0	77	-10		-1.1
1910	Bos A	11	6	.647	24	18	11	1	156.1	141	57	4	2	35	53	2.30	111	.248	.244	44-0-10	.114	-2	99	5		0.1
1911	Bos A	0	0	—	1	1	0	0	2	3	2	3	1	1	0	9.00	36	.250	.333	0	—	0	66	-1		0.0
	Chi N	3	2	.600	7	5	3-1	0	38	31	11	0	1	31	11	1.42	233	.228	.271	13-0-1	.077	-1	127	7		0.7
1912	Chi N	7	4	.636	20	5	1	1	94	92	56	2	3	31	47	4.21	79	.269	.335	35-0-2	.257	1*	88	-9		-0.8
1913	Chi N	7	9	.438	20	17	8-1	0	137.2	138	53	2	4	34	47	2.55	125	.274	.325	45-0-1	.089	-3	61	9		0.6
1914	Chi N	2	4	.333	16	5	1	0	53.2	49	27	3	1	15	17	3.86	72	.251	.308	11-0-1	.091	-1	57	-4		-0.5
Total	10	66	87	.431	212	148	87-10	3	1349.1	1309	587	22	29	353	570	2.81	94	.259	.311	447-1-27	.150	-13	84	-21		-3.5

SMITH, POP-BOY Clarence Ossie B5.23.1892 Newport TN D2.16.1924 Sweetwater TX BR/TR/6-1/176 d4.19

YEAR	TM LG	W	L	PCT	G	GS	CG-SHO	SV-BS	IP	H	R	HR	HB	BB-IB	SO	ERA	AERA	OAV	OOB	AB-HR-SH	AVG	PB	SUP	APR	DL	PW
1913	Chi A	0	1	.000	15	2	0	0	32	31	15	0	3	11	13	3.38	87	.263	.341	5	.000	-1	51	-1		-0.1
1916	Cle A	1	2	.333	5	3	0	1	25.2	25	15	1	1	11	4	3.86	78	.253	.333	7-0-1	.286	0	101	-2		-0.3
1917	Cle A	0	1	.000	6	0	0	0	8.2	14	11	0	1	4	3	8.31	34	.368	.442	1	.000	-0		-5		-0.2
Total	3	1	4	.200	26	5	0	1	66.1	70	41	1	5	26	20	4.21	70	.275	.353	13-0-1	.154	-1	81	-8		-0.9

SMITH, CLAY Clay Jamieson B9.11.1914 Cambridge KS D3.5.2002 Winfield KS BR/TR/6-2/190 d9.13 Col Southwestern (KS)

YEAR	TM LG	W	L	PCT	G	GS	CG-SHO	SV-BS	IP	H	R	HR	HB	BB-IB	SO	ERA	AERA	OAV	OOB	AB-HR-SH	AVG	PB	SUP	APR	DL	PW
1938	Cle A	0	0	—	4	0	0	0	11	18	10	1	0	2	3	6.55	71	.367	.392	4	.000	-0		-3		-0.1
1940	†Det A	1	1	.500	14	1	0	0	28.1	32	18	3	1	13	14	5.08	94	.283	.362	7	.000	-1	92	-1		-0.1
Total	2	1	1	.500	18	1	0	0	39.1	50	28	4	1	15	17	5.49	86	.309	.371	11	.000	-1	92	-4		-0.2

SMITH, DAN Daniel Charles B9.15.1975 Flemington NJ BR/TR/6-3/210* d6.8 [TexA93 7/199] [DL 2004 Mon N 183]

YEAR	TM LG	W	L	PCT	G	GS	CG-SHO	SV-BS	IP	H	R	HR	HB	BB-IB	SO	ERA	AERA	OAV	OOB	AB-HR-SH	AVG	PB	SUP	APR	DL	PW
1999	Mon N	4	9	.308	20	17	0	0-1	89.2	104	64	12	4	39-0	72	6.02	74	.293	.368	24-0-3	.083	-1	106	-14		-1.8
2000	Bos N	0	0	—	2	0	0	0-0	3.1	2	3	0	0	3-0	1	8.10	62	.250	.357	0	—	0		-1		-0.1
2002	Mon N	1	1	.500	33	0	0	2-0	46.2	34	18	6	1	21-0	34	3.47	126	.210	.301	3	.000	-0		5		0.2
2003	Mon N	2	2	.500	32	0	0	0-1	37.2	42	23	11	2	18-2	35	5.26	85	.280	.365	2	.000	-0		-3	95	0.2
Total	4	7	12	.368	87	17	0	2-2	177.1	182	108	29	7	81-2	142	5.23	85	.270	.351	29-0-3	.069	-1	106	-13	278	-2.0

SMITH, DAN Daniel Scott B4.20.1969 St.Paul MN BL/TL/6-5/190* [TexA90 1/16] d9.12 Col Creighton [DL 1993 Tex A 33, 1995 Tex A 160]

YEAR	TM LG	W	L	PCT	G	GS	CG-SHO	SV-BS	IP	H	R	HR	HB	BB-IB	SO	ERA	AERA	OAV	OOB	AB-HR-SH	AVG	PB	SUP	APR	DL	PW
1992	Tex A	0	3	.000	4	2	0	0-0	14.1	18	8	1	0	8-1	5	5.02	76	.321	.400	0	—	0	48	-1		-0.3
1994	Tex A	1	2	.333	13	0	0	0-1	14.2	18	11	2	0	12-0	9	4.30	113	.281	.395	0	—	0		-1	60	-0.1
Total	2	1	5	.167	17	2	0	0-1	29	36	19	3	0	20-1	14	4.66	93	.300	.397	0	—	0	48	-2	253	-0.4

SMITH, DARYL Daryl Clinton B7.29.1960 Baltimore MD BR/TR/6-4/185 [TexA80*6/141] d9.18 Col Essex (MD) CC

| 1990 | KC A | 0 | 1 | .000 | 2 | 1 | 0 | 0-0 | 6.2 | 5 | 3 | 0 | 1 | 6-1 | 4 | 4.05 | 95 | .238 | .333 | 0 | — | 0 | 47 | 0 | | 0.0 |

SMITH, DAVE David Merwin B12.17.1914 Sellers SC D4.1.1998 Whiteville NC BR/TR/5-10/170 d6.16 Col Duke

YEAR	TM LG	W	L	PCT	G	GS	CG-SHO	SV-BS	IP	H	R	HR	HB	BB-IB	SO	ERA	AERA	OAV	OOB	AB-HR-SH	AVG	PB	SUP	APR	DL	PW
1938	Phi A	2	1	.667	21	0	0	0	44.1	50	29	0	1	28	13	5.08	95	.284	.385	12	.000	-1		-1		-0.2
1939	Phi A	0	0	—	1	0	0	0	0	0	0	0	0	0	2	0	—	1.000	1.000	0	—	0		0		0.0
Total	2	2	1	.667	22	0	0	0	44.1	50	29	0	1	30	13	5.08	98	.288	.394	12	.000	-1		-1		-0.2

SMITH, DAVE David Stanley B1.21.1955 Richmond CA BR/TR/6-1/195* [HouN76 8/169] d4.11 C3 Col San Diego St.

YEAR	TM LG	W	L	PCT	G	GS	CG-SHO	SV-BS	IP	H	R	HR	HB	BB-IB	SO	ERA	AERA	OAV	OOB	AB-HR-SH	AVG	PB	SUP	APR	DL	PW
1980	†Hou N	7	5	.583	57	0	0	10-5	102.2	90	24	1	4	32-7	85	1.93	170	.237	.303	12-0-2	.000	-1		18		2.1
1981	†Hou N	5	3	.625	42	0	0	8-3	75	54	26	2	2	23-4	52	2.76	119	.198	.264	8	.250	0		5		0.6
1982	Hou N	5	4	.556	49	1	0	11-3	63.1	69	30	4	0	31-4	28	3.84	87	.285	.361	2	.000	-0	186	-4	21	-0.1
1983	Hou N	3	1	.750	42	0	0	6-1	72.2	72	32	2	0	36-4	41	3.10	111	.258	.338	5-0-1	.000	-0		1		-0.1
1984	Hou N	5	4	.556	53	0	0	5-3	77.1	60	22	5	1	20-3	45	2.21	154	.214	.268	4-0-1	.000	-0		10		1.3
1985	Hou N	9	5	.643	64	0	0	27-6	79.1	69	26	3	1	17-5	40	2.27	154	.235	.279	3-0-1	.000	-0		7		2.0
1986	†Hou N☆	4	7	.364	54	0	0	33-6	56	39	17	5	1	22-3	46	2.73	132	.200	.283	2	.000	1		15		1.4
1987	Hou N	2	3	.400	50	0	0	24-5	60	60	39	13	0	21-8	73	1.65	238	.182	.257	2	.500	1		15		0.2
1988	Hou N	4	5	.444	51	0	0	27-5	57.1	60	26	1	1	19-8	38	2.67	125	.268	.327	1	.000	-0		5		0.2
1989	Hou N	3	4	.429	52	0	0	25-4	58	49	20	1	0	19-7	31	2.64	129	.233	.299	1	.000	0		9		1.9
1990	Hou N★	6	6	.500	49	0	0	23-5	60.1	45	18	4	0	19-5	50	2.39	157	.210	.277	1	.000	-0		-6	40	-1.3
1991	Chi N	0	6	.000	35	0	0	17-6	33	39	22	6	1	19-5	16	6.00	65	.302	.396	1	.000	-0		2	118	0.1
1992	Chi N	0	0	—	11	0	0	1	14.1	15	14	4	0	4-2	3	2.51	145	.273	.317	0	—	0	186	74	179	0.1
Total	13	53	53	.500	609	1	0	216-52	809.1	700	280	34	13	283-64	548	2.67	130	.234	.302	44-0-5	.068	-2	186	74	179	10.7

SMITH, DAVE David Wayne B8.30.1957 Tomball TX BR/TR/6-1/190* [NYN79 27/668] d9.18 Col Lamar

YEAR	TM LG	W	L	PCT	G	GS	CG-SHO	SV-BS	IP	H	R	HR	HB	BB-IB	SO	ERA	AERA	OAV	OOB	AB-HR-SH	AVG	PB	SUP	APR	DL	PW
1984	Cal A	0	0	—	2	0	0	0-0	1	2	2	1	0	0-0	1	18.00	22	.571	.571	0	—	0		-1		-0.1
1985	Cal A	0	0	—	4	0	0	0-0	5	5	4	1	0	1-0	3	7.20	57	.278	.300	0	—	0		-2		-0.1
Total	2	0	0	—	6	0	0	0-0	6	9	6	2	0	1-0	3	9.00	46	.360	.370	0	—	0		-3		-0.2

SMITH, DOUG Douglass Weldon B5.25.1892 Millers Falls MA D9.18.1973 Greenfield MA BL/TL/5-10/168 d7.10

| 1912 | Bos A | 0 | 0 | — | 1 | 0 | 0 | 0 | 3 | 4 | 1 | 0 | 0 | 0 | 1 | 3.00 | 113 | .364 | .364 | 0 | — | 0 | | 0 | | 0.0 |

YEAR	TM LG	W	L	PCT	G	GS	CG-SHO	SV-BS	IP	H	R	HR	HB	BB-IB	SO	ERA	AERA	OAV	OOB	AB-HR-SH	AVG	PB	SUP	APR	DL	PW
SMITH, ED Ed d4.18																										
1884	Bal U	3	4	.429	9	8	5	0	62	86	61	2		17	13	3.48	77	.308	.348	34	.147	-4	114	-8		-1.0
SMITH, EDDIE Edgar B12.14.1913 Mansfield NJ D1.2.1994 Willingboro NJ BB/TL/5-10/174 d9.20 Mil 1944-45																										
1936	Phi A	1	1	.500	2	2	2	0	19	22	10	3	0	8	7	1.89	269	.275	.341	8	.125	-1	86	4		0.3
1937	Phi A	4	17	.190	38	23	14-1	5	196.2	178	100	8	4	90	79	3.94	120	.242	.327	73-0-2	.233	1*	59	17		1.8
1938	Phi A	3	10	.231	43	7	0	4	130.2	151	102	13	4	76	78	5.92	82	.287	.381	42-0-2	.286	3	89	-16		-1.1
1939	Phi A	1	0	1.000	3	0	0	0	3.2	7	4	0	0	2	3	9.82	48	.412	.474	0	—	0		-2		-0.3
	Chi A	9	11	.450	29	22	7-1	0	176.2	161	83	11	4	90	67	3.67	129	.247	.342	52-0-5	.115	-1	72	19		1.7
	Year	10	11	.476	32	22	7-1	0	180.1	168	87	11	4	92	70	3.79	125	.251	.346	52-0-5	.115	-1	72	18		1.4
1940	Chi A	14	9	.609	32	28	12	0	207.1	179	92	16	3	95	119	3.21	138	.228	.313	69-0-8	.217	2	89	25		2.7
1941	Chi A★	13	17	.433	34	33	21-1	1	263.1	243	107	13	5	114	111	3.18	129	.246	.328	88-0-4	.216	4	74	28		3.4
1942	Chi A☆	7	20	.259	29	28	18-2	1	215	223	112	17	4	86	78	3.98	90	.269	.341	73-0-3	.123	-2	61	-10		-1.2
1943	Chi A	11	11	.500	25	25	14-2	0	187.2	197	85	2	5	76	66	3.69	90	.269	.351	69-1-4	.159	-1	102	-4		-0.6
1946	Chi A	8	11	.421	24	21	3-1	1	145.1	135	71	9	4	60*	59	2.85	120	.246	.325	45	.178	0	84	4		0.5
1947	Chi A	1	3	.250	15	5	0	0	33.1	40	36	1	0	24	12	7.29	50	.299	.405	6	.167	-0	82	-15		-1.7
	Bos A	1	3	.250	8	3	0	0	17	18	14	3	0	18	15	7.41	52	.269	.424	6	.167	0	167	-6		-1.1
	Year	2	6	.250	23	8	0	0	50.1	58	50	4	0	42	27	7.33	51	.289	.412	12	.167	-0	116	-21		-2.8
Total 10		73	113	.392	282	197	91-8	12	1595.2	1554	816	106	33	739	694	3.82	108	.256	.340	531-1-28	.188	5	77	44		4.4
SMITH, EDGAR Edgar Eugene B6.12.1862 Providence RI D11.3.1892 Providence RI BR/TR/5-10/160 d5.25 ▲																										
1883	Phi N	0	1	.000	1	1	0	0	7	18	17	0		3	2	15.43	20	.409	.447	4	.750	1	69	-9		-0.7
1884	Was AA	0	2	.000	3	2	2	0	22	27	23	0	1	5	4	4.91	62	.276	.317	57	.088	-1*	60	-5		-0.4
1885	Pro N	1	0	1.000	1	1	1	0	9	9	3	0	0	1	1	1.00	269	.273	.273	4	.250	0	84	1		0.1
1890	Cle N	1	4	.200	6	6	5	0	44	42	24	1	1	10	11	4.30	84	.243	.288	24	.292	2*	82	1		0.1
Total 4		2	7	.222	11	10	8	0	82	96	67	1	2	18	18	5.05	65	.276	.315	89	.180	2	78	-14		-0.9
SMITH, ELMER Elmer Ellsworth B3.23.1868 Pittsburgh PA D11.3.1945 Pittsburgh PA BL/TL/5-11/178 d9.10 ▲																										
1886	Cin AA	4	4	.500	9	9	8	0	72.2	72	54	1	3	44	40	3.72	95	.211	.328	28	.286	4	125	-5		-0.2
1887	Cin AA	34	17	.667	52	52	49-3	0	447.1	400	224	5	9	126	176	2.94	148	.230	.286	186	.253	5	89	71		6.3
1888	Cin AA	22	17	.564	40	40	37-5	0	348.1	309	167	1	19	89	154	2.74	116	.229	.286	129	.225	4	93	19		2.0
1889	Cin AA	9	12	.429	29	22	16	0	203	253	171	11	7	101	104	4.88	80	.296	.375	83-2	.277	6	102	-21		-1.3
1892	Pit N	6	7	.462	17	13	12-1	0	134	140	94	2	1	58	51	3.63	91	.258	.331	511-4	.274	6*	128	-5		0.0
1894	Pit N	0	0	—	1	0	0	0	4	6	2	0	1	1	4.50	117	.333	.400	490-6-10	.357	0*		1		0.0
1898	Cin N	0	0	—	1	0	0	0	1	2	2	0	0	3	0	18.00	21	.400	.625	.342	0*		-1		-0.1
Total 7		75	57	.568	149	136	122-9	0	1210.1	1167	714	20	40	422	525	3.35	113	.244	.311	1913-13-16	.307	25	98	59		6.7
SMITH, FRANK Frank Elmer "Nig","Piano Mover" (b Frank Elmer Schmidt) B10.28.1879 Pittsburgh PA D11.3.1952 Pittsburgh PA BR/TR/5-10.5/194 d4.22 Col Grove City																										
1904	Chi A	16	9	.640	26	23	22-4	0	202.1	157	62	0	12	58	107	2.09	117	.215	.284	72-0-3	.250	4	115	9		1.6
1905	Chi A	19	13	.594	39	31	27-4	0	291.2	215	97	0	8	107	171	2.13	134	.208	.287	106-1-1	.226	7*	133	12		2.2
1906	Chi A	5	5	.500	20	13	8-1	1	122	124	58	3	5	37	53	3.39	75	.267	.327	41-0-2	.293	5	105	-10		-0.2
1907	Chi A	23	10	.697	41	37	29-3	0	310	280	105	3	2	111	139	2.47	97	.243	.311	92-0-6	.196	5*	119	2		0.9
1908	Chi A	16	17	.485	41	35	24-3	1	297.2	213	92	2	2	73	129	2.03	114	.203	.256	106-0-6	.189	2*	106	9		1.5
1909	Chi A	25	17	.595	51	40	37-7	1	365	278	104	1	6	70	177	1.80	130	.214	.257	127-0-5	.173	6*	90	23		4.1
1910	Chi A	4	9	.308	19	15	9-3	0	128.2	91	43	1	2	40	50	2.03	118	.204	.272	43-0-2	.186	2*	67	6		1.0
	Bos A	1	2	.333	4	3	2	0	28	22	19	0	1	11	8	4.82	53	.234	.321	9-0-1	.111	-0	79	-6		-0.6
	Year	5	11	.313	23	18	11-3	0	156.2	113	62	1	3	51	58	2.53	96	.209	.281	52-0-3	.173	2	69	-1		0.4
1911	Bos A	0	0	—	1	1	0	0	2.1	6	4	0	0	3	1	15.43	21	.500	.600	0	—	0	308	-2		-0.1
	Cin N	10	14	.417	34	18	10	1	176.1	198	112	1	3	55	67	3.98	83	.289	.345	56-0-5	.214	3*	119	-16		-1.4
1912	Cin N	1	1	.500	7	3	1	0	22.2	34	25	1	0	15	5	6.35	53	.370	.458	6	.000	-0	167	-9		-0.7
1914	Bal F	10	8	.556	39	22	9-1	2	174.2	180	86	8	0	47	83	2.99	101	.259	.306	59-0-3	.203	0*	107	-3		-0.2
1915	Bal F	4	4	.500	17	9	2	0	88.2	108	53	5	0	31	37	4.67	61	.312	.369	29-1-1	.172	0	100	-15		-1.2
	Bro F	5	2	.714	15	5	4-1	0	63	69	31	2	0	18	24	3.14	87	.290	.340	20-0-1	.200	0	82	-4		-0.3
	Year	9	6	.600	32	14	6-1	0	151.2	177	84	7	0	49	61	4.04	70	.303	.357	49-1-2	.184	1	94	-18		-1.5
Total 11		139	111	.556	354	255	184-27	6	2273	1975	891	27	41	676	1051	2.59	99	.237	.297	766-2-36	.204	35	109	-4		6.6
SMITH, FRANK Frank Thomas B4.4.1928 Pierrepont Manor NY D9.24.2005 Malone FL BR/TR/6-3/200* d4.18																										
1950	Cin N	2	7	.222	38	4	0	3	90.2	73	43	12	8	39	55	3.87	109	.216	.312	21	.095	-2	94	4		0.2
1951	Cin N	5	5	.500	50	0	0	11	76	65	33	7	4	22	34	3.20	128	.230	.295	10-0-1	.000	-1		7		0.9
1952	Cin N	12	11	.522	53	2	1	7	122.1	109	56	13	7	41	77	3.75	101	.242	.315	29-0-1	.172	0	83	0		-0.1
1953	Cin N	8	1	.889	50	1	0	2	83.2	89	64	15	3	25	42	5.49	79	.272	.330	13-0-2	.154	-1	144	-13		-1.3
1954	Cin N	5	8	.385	50	0	0	20	81	60	29	15	3	29	51	2.67	157	.211	.286	10-0-1	.100	1		12		2.6
1955	StL N	3	1	.750	28	0	0	1	39	27	18	3	5	23-3	17	3.23	126	.205	.337	4-0-1	.000	-1		2		0.2
1956	Cin N	0	0	—	2	0	0	0	3	3	4	2	0	2-0	1	12.00	33	.300	.385	0	—	-1		-2		0.2
Total 7		35	33	.515	271	7	1	44	495.2	426	247	67	30	181-3	277	3.81	107	.234	.311	87-0-7	.115	-3	99	10		2.4
SMITH, FRED Frederick B11.24.1878 New Diggings WI D2.4.1964 Los Angeles CA BL/TR/6-0/186 d6.14																										
1907	Cin N	3	7	.222	18	9	1	0	85.1	90	44	3	4	24	19	2.85	91	.274	.331	28-0-1	.107	-2	88	-4		-0.6
SMITH, FRED Frederick C. B3.25.1863 Greene NY D1.9.1941 Syracuse NY BL/TR/5-11/156 d4.18																										
1890	Tol AA	19	13	.594	35	34	31-2	0	286	273	155	13	13	90	116	3.27	121	.244	.307	126	.167	-2*	88	21		1.8
SMITH, GEORGE George Allen "Columbia George" B5.31.1892 Byram CT D1.7.1965 Greenwich CT BR/TR/6-2/163 d8.9 Col Columbia																										
1916	NY N	3	0	1.000	9	1	0	0	20.2	14	9	0	1	6	9	2.61	93	.197	.269	2-0-1	.000	-0	184	-1		-0.1
1917	NY N	0	3	.000	14	1	1	0	38	38	13	1	1	11	16	2.84	90	.270	.327	9	.000	-1	30	0		-0.2
1918	Cin N	2	3	.400	10	6	4-1	0	55.1	71	36	3	0	11	19	4.07	66	.329	.361	17-0-1	.000	-2	76	-10		-1.1
	NY N	2	3	.400	5	2	1	0	26.2	26	12	0	1	6	4	4.05	65	.255	.303	8-0-1	.250	0	58	-3		-0.6
	Bro N	4	1	.800	8	5	4	0	50	43	14	0	2	5	18	2.34	119	.249	.278	15-0-1	.200	0	81	4		0.5
	Year	8	7	.533	23	13	9-1	0	132	140	62	3	3	22	41	3.41	79	.285	.320	40-0-3	.125	-2	75	-10		-1.2
1919	NY N	0	2	.000	3	2	0	0	11	18	8	1	0	4	4	5.73	49	.383	.431	3	.000	-0	113	-3		-0.6
	Phi N	5	11	.313	31	19	11-1	0	184.2	194	94	7	3	46	42	3.22	100	.278	.326	60-0-2	.133	-3	92	-5		-1.4
	Year	5	13	.278	34	21	11-1	0	195.2	212	102	8	3	50	42	3.36	95	.285	.332	63-0-2	.127	-4	94	-7		-1.4
1920	Phi N	13	18	.419	43	28	10-1	2	250.2	265	115	10	6	51	51	3.45	99	.283	.324	72-0-8	.097	-6	77	2		-0.4
1921	Phi N	4	20	.167	39	28	12-1	1	221.1	303	166	12	3	52	45	4.76	89	.335	.373	71-0-1	.056	-8	69	-14		-2.1
1922	Phi N	5	14	.263	42	16	6-1	0	194	250	124	16	6	35	44	4.78	98	.316	.350	66	.076	-7	63	1		-0.7
1923	Bro N	3	6	.333	25	7	3	1	99	99	53	4	3	28	15	3.66	106	.278	.336	26-0-1	.192	-1	103	0		-0.2
Total 8		41	81	.336	229	115	52-5	4	1143.1	1321	643	54	26	255	263	3.89	94	.298	.340	349-0-16	.097	-29	78	-29		-6.3
SMITH, HEINIE George Henry B10.24.1871 Pittsburgh PA D6.25.1939 Buffalo NY BR/TR/5-9.5/160 d9.8.1897 M1 ▲																										
1901	NY N	0	1	.000	1	1	1	0	13.1	24	13	0	3	5	5	8.10	41	.387	.457	29-1-1	.207	0*	86	-6		-0.3
SMITH, GEORGE George Shelby B10.27.1901 Louisville KY D5.26.1981 Richmond VA BR/TR/6-1/175 d4.21																										
1926	Det A	1	2	.333	23	1	0	0	44	55	37	3	2	33	15	6.95	58	.318	.433	5-0-1	.000	-0	41	-12		-0.8
1927	Det A	4	1	.800	29	0	0	0	71.1	62	38	3	2	50	32	3.91	108	.240	.368	19-2-1	.368	3		3		0.4
1928	Det A	1	1	.500	39	2	0	3	106	103	55	3	0	50	54	4.42	93	.263	.346	27-0-1	.111	-2	103	0		-0.3
1929	Det A	3	2	.600	14	2	1	0	35.2	42	33	1	0	36	13	5.80	74	.307	.451	12	.417	2	128	-8		-0.7
1930	Bos A	1	2	.333	27	2	0	0	73.2	92	62	7	1	49	21	6.60	70	.317	.418	24	.333	2*	103	-16		-0.6
Total 5		10	8	.556	132	7	1	3	330.2	354	225	17	5	218	135	5.28	81	.283	.392	87-2-3	.264	4	102	-33		-2.0
SMITH, HAL Harold Laverne B6.30.1902 Creston IA D9.27.1992 Ft.Lauderdale FL BR/TR/6-3/195 d9.14 Col Creston (IA) JC																										
1932	Pit N	1	0	1.000	7	1	1-1	0	12	9	1	0	0	4	0.75	508	.209	.244	3-0-1	.000	-0	154	4		0.3
1933	Pit N	8	7	.533	28	19	8-2	1	145	149	66	5	5	31	40	2.86	116	.261	.305	47-0-2	.128	-2	107	4		0.1
1934	Pit N	3	4	.429	20	5	1	0	50	72	44	3	4	18	15	7.20	57	.343	.405	17	.059	-2	109	-16		-2.1
1935	Pit N	0	0	—	1	0	0	0	3	2	1	0	0	0	3.00	137	.200	.273	0	—	0		0		0.0
Total 4		12	11	.522	51	25	10-3	1	210	232	112	8	9	52	59	3.77	94	.279	.328	67-0-3	.104	-4	108	-8		-1.7

YEAR	TM LG	W	L	PCT	G	GS	CG-SHO	SV-BS	IP	H	R	HR	HB	BB-IB	SO	ERA	AERA	OAV	OOB	AB-HR-SH	AVG	PB	SUP	APR	DL	PW

SMITH, HARRY   Harrison Morton   B8.15.1889 Union NE   D7.26.1964 Dunbar NE   BR/TR/5-9/160   d10.6

YEAR	TM LG	W	L	PCT	G	GS	CG-SHO	SV-BS	IP	H	R	HR	HB	BB-IB	SO	ERA	AERA	OAV	OOB	AB-HR-SH	AVG	PB	SUP	APR	DL	PW
1912	Chi A	1	0	1.000	1	1	0	0	5	6	1	0	0	0	1	1.80	178	.333	.333	1-0-1	.000	-0	208	1		0.2

SMITH, JACK   Jack Hatfield   B11.15.1935 Pikeville KY   BR/TR/6-0/185*   d9.10

YEAR	TM LG	W	L	PCT	G	GS	CG-SHO	SV-BS	IP	H	R	HR	HB	BB-IB	SO	ERA	AERA	OAV	OOB	AB-HR-SH	AVG	PB	SUP	APR	DL	PW
1962	LA N	0	0	—	8	0	0	1	10	10	6	0	0	4-1	7	4.50	81	.263	.326	1	.000	-0		-1		-0.1
1963	LA N	0	0	—	4	0	0	0	8.1	10	7	2	2	2-0	5	7.56	40	.303	.368	2	.000	-0		-4		-0.2
1964	Mil N	2	2	.500	22	0	0	0	31	28	15	3	0	11-5	19	3.77	93	.237	.300	3	.333	0		-1		0.0
Total 3		2	2	.500	34	0	0	1	49.1	48	28	5	2	17-6	31	4.56	76	.254	.318	6	.167	-0		-6		-0.3

SMITH, JAKE   Jacob John (b Jacob Schmidt)   B6.10.1887 Dravosburg PA   D11.7.1948 E.McKeesport PA   BB/TL/6-5/200   d10.3

YEAR	TM LG	W	L	PCT	G	GS	CG-SHO	SV-BS	IP	H	R	HR	HB	BB-IB	SO	ERA	AERA	OAV	OOB	AB-HR-SH	AVG	PB	SUP	APR	DL	PW
1911	Phi N	0	0	—	1	0	0	0	5	3	0	0	2		1	0.00	—	.176	.263	3	.000	-0		2		0.1

SMITH, PHENOMENAL   John Francis (b John Francis Gammon)   B12.12.1864 Philadelphia PA   D4.3.1952 Manchester NH   BL/TL/5-6.5/161   d8.14

YEAR	TM LG	W	L	PCT	G	GS	CG-SHO	SV-BS	IP	H	R	HR	HB	BB-IB	SO	ERA	AERA	OAV	OOB	AB-HR-SH	AVG	PB	SUP	APR	DL	PW
1884	Phi AA	0	1	.000	1	1	1	0	9	14	6	0	0	1	3	4.00	85	.368	.385	4	.250	-0	89	-1		-0.1
	Pit AA	0	1	.000	1	1	1	0	8	11	10	0	1	2	4	9.00	37	.306	.359	4	.000	-1	91	-4		-0.4
	Year	0	2	.000	2	2	2	0	17	25	16	0	1	3	7	6.35	53	.338	.372	8	.125	-1	90	-4		-0.5
1885	Bro AA	0	1	.000	1	1	1	0	8	12	18	0	1	6	2	12.38	27	.300	.404	3	.333	-0	90	-8		-0.6
	Phi AA	0	1	.000	1	1	1	0	4	7	9	0	1	4	7	9.00	38	.368	.500	2	.200	-0	141	-11		-1.0
	Year	0	2	.000	2	2	1	0	12	19	27	0	2	10	9	11.25	30	.322	.437	5	.200	-0	141	-11		-1.0
1886	Det N	1	1	.500	3	3	3	0	25	16	9	0	0	8	15	2.16	154	.174	.240	9	.111	-1	37	3		0.1
1887	Bal AA	25	30	.455	58	55	54-1	0	491.1	526	369	7	14	176	206	3.79	108	.261	.325	205-1	.234	8*	95	8		1.3
1888	Bal AA	14	19	.424	35	32	31	0	292	249	170	5	24	137	152	3.61	83	.222	.320	109-1	.248	8	94	-18		-1.1
	Phi AA	2	1	.667	3	3	3	0	22	21	15	0	0	10	19	2.86	104	.241	.320	9	.333	1	123	0		0.1
	Year	16	20	.444	38	35	34	0	314	270	185	5	24	147	171	3.55	84	.224	.320	118-1	.254	9	97	-9		-1.0
1889	Phi AA	2	3	.400	5	5	5	0	43	53	31	2	3	25	12	4.40	86	.294	.389	16	.188	0	62	-2		-0.1
1890	Phi N	8	12	.400	24	20	19-1	0	204	209	125	5	8	89	81	4.28	86	.257	.336	86	.279	4*	93	-5		-0.1
	Pit N	1	3	.250	5	5	5	0	44	39	25	0	1	13	15	3.07	108	.229	.288	17	.412	2	96	1		0.3
	Year	9	15	.375	29	25	24-1	0	248	248	150	5	9	102	96	4.06	89	.252	.328	103	.301	6	93	-6		-0.1
1891	Phi N	1	1	.500	3	2	0	0	19	20	15	1	0	8	3	4.26	80	.260	.329	8	.375	1	105	-2		-0.1
Total 8		54	74	.422	140	129	123-2	0	1169.1	1177	802	20	53	479	519	3.89	93	.251	.327	472-2	.250	23	93	-31		-1.2

SMITH, CHICK   John William (b Jan Smadt)   B12.2.1892 Dayton KY   D10.11.1935 Dayton KY   BL/TL/5-8/165   d4.12

YEAR	TM LG	W	L	PCT	G	GS	CG-SHO	SV-BS	IP	H	R	HR	HB	BB-IB	SO	ERA	AERA	OAV	OOB	AB-HR-SH	AVG	PB	SUP	APR	DL	PW
1913	Cin N				5	1	0	0	17.2	15	8	1	0	11	11	3.57	91	.238	.351	4-0-1	.000	-1	23	0		-0.1

SMITH, LEE   Lee Arthur   B12.4.1957 Shreveport LA   BR/TR/6-6/225(220-269)   [ChiN75 2/28]   d9.1

YEAR	TM LG	W	L	PCT	G	GS	CG-SHO	SV-BS	IP	H	R	HR	HB	BB-IB	SO	ERA	AERA	OAV	OOB	AB-HR-SH	AVG	PB	SUP	APR	DL	PW
1980	Chi N	2	0	1.000	18	1	0	0-0	21.2	21	9	0	0	14-5	17	2.91	136	.259	.365	0	—	0		2		0.2
1981	Chi N	3	6	.333	40	1	0	1-3	66.2	57	31	2	1	31-8	50	3.51	107	.239	.327	9-0-1	.000	-1	24	1		0.0
1982	Chi N	2	5	.286	72	5	0	17-1	117	105	38	5	3	37-5	99	2.69	140	.245	.306	16-1-1	.063	-0	89	14		1.2
1983	Chi N★	4	10	.286	66	0	0	29-4	103.1	70	23	5	1	41-14	91	1.65	230	.194	.277	9-0-1	.111	-0		23		4.3
1984	†Chi N	9	7	.563	69	0	0	33-9	101	98	42	6	0	35-7	86	3.65	107	.255	.314	13-0-1	.077	-1		4		0.7
1985	Chi N	7	4	.636	65	0	0	33-9	97.2	87	35	9	1	32-6	112	3.04	132	.242	.305	0	.000	-0		10		1.7
1986	Chi N	9	9	.500	66	0	0	31-8	90.1	69	32	7	0	42-11	93	3.09	132	.215	.303	5	.000	-1		10	15	2.0
1987	Chi N★	4	10	.286	62	0	0	36-12	83.2	84	30	4	0	32-5	96	3.12	139	.259	.326	2	.000	-0*		11		1.5
1988	†Bos A	4	5	.444	64	0	0	29-8	83.2	72	34	7	1	37-6	96	2.80	148	.225	.306	0	—	0		9		0.7
1989	Bos A	6	1	.857	64	0	0	25-5	70.2	53	30	6	0	33-6	96	3.57	115	.209	.299	0	—	0		3		0.7
1990	Bos A	2	1	.667	11	0	0	4-1	14.1	13	4	0	0	9-2	17	1.88	218	.236	.344	0	—	0		12		2.0
	StL N	3	4	.429	53	0	0	27-5	68.2	58	39	3	0	20-5	70	2.10	184	.227	.281	2	.000	-0		12		2.0
1991	StL N☆	6	3	.667	67	0	0	47-6	73	70	19	5	0	13-5	67	2.34	160	.249	.281	0	—	0		3		0.5
1992	StL N☆	4	9	.308	70	0	0	43-8	75	62	28	4	0	26-4	60	4.50	110	.221	.286	0	—	0		-1		-0.3
1993	StL N☆	2	4	.333	55	0	0	43-7	50	49	25	11	0	9-1	49	4.50	90	.251	.282	2	.000	-0		4		0.1
	NY A	0	0	—	8	0	0	3-0	8	4	0	0	0	5-1	11	0.00	—	.148	.273	0	—	0		7		1.2
1994	Bal A★	1	4	.200	41	0	0	33-6	38.1	34	16	6	0	11-1	42	3.29	154	.239	.290	0	—	0		8		1.4
1995	Cal A☆	0	5	.000	52	0	0	37-4	49.1	42	19	3	1	25-4	43	3.47	136	.237	.330	0	—	0		3	20	0.1
1996	Cal A	0	0	—	11	0	0	0-2	11	8	4	0	0	3-0	6	2.45	206	.205	.250	0	—	0		2		0.3
	Cin N	3	4	.429	43	0	0	2-4	44.1	49	29	4	0	23-4	35	4.06	105	.277	.363	0	—	0		-4		-0.3
1997	Mon N	0	0	—	25	0	0	5-1	21.2	28	16	2	1	8-0	15	5.82	72	.308	.370	0	—	0		5		0.1
Total 18		71	92	.436	1022	6	0	478-103	1289.1	1133	475	89	10	486-100	1251	3.03	133	.237	.306	64-1-4	.047	-4	75	138	35	22.9

SMITH, ROY   Le Roy Purdy   B9.6.1961 Mt.Vernon NY   BR/TR/6-3/200(200-217)   [PhiN79 3/72]   d6.23   Col Fordham

YEAR	TM LG	W	L	PCT	G	GS	CG-SHO	SV-BS	IP	H	R	HR	HB	BB-IB	SO	ERA	AERA	OAV	OOB	AB-HR-SH	AVG	PB	SUP	APR	DL	PW
1984	Cle A	5	5	.500	22	14	0	0-0	86.1	91	49	14	1	40-5	55	4.59	90	.270	.346	0	—	0	108	-5		-0.5
1985	Cle A	1	4	.200	12	11	1	0-0	62.1	84	40	8	1	17-0	28	5.34	78	.321	.359	0	—	0	123	-8	29	-0.6
1986	Min A	0	2	.000	5	0	0	0-1	10.1	13	8	1	1	5-1	8	6.97	62	.295	.380	0	—	0		-3		-0.4
1987	Min A	1	0	1.000	7	1	0	0-1	16.1	20	10	3	2	6-0	8	4.96	94	.290	.359	0	—	0	275	-1		0.0
1988	Min A	3	0	1.000	9	4	0	0-0	37	29	12	3	1	12-1	17	2.68	153	.210	.276	0	—	0	134	6		0.2
1989	Min A	10	6	.625	32	26	2	1-0	172.1	180	82	22	5	51-5	92	3.92	106	.269	.324	0	—	0	105	-11		-1.1
1990	Min A	5	10	.333	32	23	1-1	0-0	153.1	191	91	20	0	47-4	87	4.81	87	.313	.356	0	—	0	110	-14		-1.4
1991	Bal A	5	4	.556	17	14	0	0-0	80.1	99	52	9	1	24-0	25	5.60	71	.311	.358	0	—	0	117	4		0.4
Total 8		30	31	.492	136	93	4-1	1-2	618.1	707	344	80	12	202-16	320	4.60	90	.289	.343	0	—	0	117	-32	29	-3.4

SMITH, MARK   Mark Christopher   B11.23.1955 Arlington VA   BR/TR/6-2/215   [BalA77 9/227]   d8.12   Col American

YEAR	TM LG	W	L	PCT	G	GS	CG-SHO	SV-BS	IP	H	R	HR	HB	BB-IB	SO	ERA	AERA	OAV	OOB	AB-HR-SH	AVG	PB	SUP	APR	DL	PW
1983	Oak A	0	1	.000	1	1	0	0-0	14.2	24	11	0	1	6-1	14	6.75	58	.387	.449	0	—	0	47	-4		-0.3

SMITH, MIKE   Michael Anthony   B2.23.1961 Jackson MS   BR/TR/6-1/195(170-195)   d4.6   Col Hinds (MS) CC

YEAR	TM LG	W	L	PCT	G	GS	CG-SHO	SV-BS	IP	H	R	HR	HB	BB-IB	SO	ERA	AERA	OAV	OOB	AB-HR-SH	AVG	PB	SUP	APR	DL	PW
1984	Cin N	1	0	1.000	8	0	0	0-0	10.1	12	6	1	0	5-0	7	5.23	73	.286	.362	0-0-1	—	0		-1		-0.1
1985	Cin N	0	0	—	2	0	0	0-0	3.1	2	2	2	0	1-0	2	5.40	70	.167	.231	0	—	0		0		-0.2
1986	Cin N	0	0	—	2	1	0	0-0	3.1	7	5	0	0	1-0	1	13.50	29	.412	.444	0	—	0	208	-3		-0.2
1988	Mon N	0	0	—	5	0	0	1-0	8.2	6	3	0	0	5-0	4	3.12	117	.207	.324	2	.000	-0		1		-0.1
1989	Pit N	0	1	.000	16	0	0	0-0	24	28	12	1	0	10-1	12	3.75	91	.301	.362	3	.000	-1	208	-4		-0.4
Total 5		1	1	.500	33	1	0	1-0	49.2	55	28	4	0	22-1	26	4.71	76	.285	.355	5-0-1	.000	-1	208	-4		-0.4

SMITH, MIKE   Michael Anthony   B10.31.1963 San Antonio TX   BR/TR/6-3/190*   [CinN84*5/110]   d6.30   Col Ranger (TX) JC

YEAR	TM LG	W	L	PCT	G	GS	CG-SHO	SV-BS	IP	H	R	HR	HB	BB-IB	SO	ERA	AERA	OAV	OOB	AB-HR-SH	AVG	PB	SUP	APR	DL	PW
1989	Bal A	2	0	1.000	13	1	0	0-0	20	25	19	3	0	14-2	12	7.65	50	.313	.411	0	—	0	142	-9		-0.8
1990	Bal A	0	0	—	2	0	0	0-0	3	4	4	2	0	1-0	2	12.00	32	.308	.357	0	—	0		-3		-0.1
Total 2		2	0	1.000	15	1	0	0-0	23	29	23	5	0	15-2	14	8.22	46	.312	.404	0	—	0	142	-12		-0.5

SMITH, MIKE   Michael Anthony   B9.19.1977 Norwood MA   BR/TR/5-11/195   [TorA00 5/148]   d4.26   Col Richmond

YEAR	TM LG	W	L	PCT	G	GS	CG-SHO	SV-BS	IP	H	R	HR	HB	BB-IB	SO	ERA	AERA	OAV	OOB	AB-HR-SH	AVG	PB	SUP	APR	DL	PW
2002	Tor A	0	3	.000	14	6	0	0-0	35.1	43	28	9	2	20-0	16	6.62	70	.301	.409	0	—	0	84	-8		-0.5

SMITH, PETE   Peter John   B2.27.1966 Abington MA   BR/TR/6-2/200(183-200)   [PhiN84 1/21]   d9.8

YEAR	TM LG	W	L	PCT	G	GS	CG-SHO	SV-BS	IP	H	R	HR	HB	BB-IB	SO	ERA	AERA	OAV	OOB	AB-HR-SH	AVG	PB	SUP	APR	DL	PW
1987	Atl N	1	2	.333	6	6	0	0-0	31.2	39	21	3	0	14-0	11	4.83	90	.307	.371	11-0-1	.091	-1	91	-2		-0.3
1988	Atl N	7	15	.318	32	32	5-3	0-0	195.1	183	89	15	1	88-3	124	3.69	99	.250	.330	53-0-8	.113	-1	73	0		-2.0
1989	Atl N	5	14	.263	28	27	1	0-0	142	144	83	13	0	57-2	115	4.75	77	.263	.330	41-0-5	.098	-0*	74	-15		-2.1
1990	Atl N	5	6	.455	13	13	0	0-0	77	77	45	11	0	24-2	56	4.79	84	.260	.313	23-0-4	.087	-1	105	-6	70	-0.8
1991	Atl N	1	3	.250	14	10	0	0-0	48	48	33	5	0	22-3	29	5.06	77	.262	.335	12-0-1	.167	0	109	-7	45	-0.4
1992	†Atl N	7	0	1.000	11	8	2-1	0-0	79	63	19	3	0	28-2	43	2.05	179	.217	.285	26-0-3	.222	-1	105	2	38	1.0
1993	Atl N	4	8	.333	20	14	0	0-0	90.2	92	45	15	2	36-3	53	4.37	93	.270	.339	37-0-6	.135	0	85	-19	19	-1.1
1994	NY N	4	10	.286	21	21	0	0-0	131.1	145	83	25	2	42-4	62	5.55	75	.285	.388	3	.000	0	206	-7		-0.8
1995	Cin N	1	2	.333	11	2	0	0-0	24.1	30	19	8	1	7-1	14	6.66	63	.319	.362	0	—	1*	103	-10		-0.6
1997	SD N	7	6	.538	37	15	0	1-0	118	120	66	16	1	52-2	68	4.81	82	.267	.343	30-0-6	.167	-0*	153	-3		-0.3
1998	SD N	3	2	.600	10	8	0	0-0	43.1	45	23	5	3	18-1	36	4.78	83	.266	.344	14-0-1	.071	-0*	87	-8		-0.4
	Bal A	2	3	.400	27	4	0	0-1	45	57	31	7	0	16-1	29	6.20	73	.311	.363	0	—	0	95	-8		-0.4
Total 11		47	71	.398	231	163	12-4	1-1	1025.2	1043	557	126	10	404-24	640	4.55	86	.266	.333	279-0-38	.118	-2	95	-63	172	-7.1

SMITH, PETE   Peter Luke   B3.19.1940 Natick MA   BR/TR/6-2/190*   d9.13   Mil 1963   Col Colgate   [DL 1964 Bos A 134]

YEAR	TM LG	W	L	PCT	G	GS	CG-SHO	SV-BS	IP	H	R	HR	HB	BB-IB	SO	ERA	AERA	OAV	OOB	AB-HR-SH	AVG	PB	SUP	APR	DL	PW
1962	Bos A	0	1	.000	1	1	0	0	3.2	7	8	3	0	2-0	1	19.64	21	.438	.474	1	.000	-0	130	-6		-0.2
1963	Bos A	0	0	—	6	1	0	0	15	11	6	2	0	6-2	6	3.60	105	.212	.293	2	.000	-0	117	1		0.1
Total 2		0	1	.000	7	2	0	0	18.2	18	14	5	0	8-2	7	6.75	57	.265	.338	3	.000	-0	127	-5	134	-0.1

YEAR	TM LG	W	L	PCT	G	GS	CG-SHO	SV-BS	IP	H	R	HR	HB	BB-IB	SO	ERA	AERA	OAV	OOB	AB-HR-SH	AVG	PB	SUP	APR	DL	PW

SMITH, BRIAN Randall Brian B7.19.1972 Salisbury NC BR/TR/5-11/190 [TorA94 27/763] d9.11 Col North Carolina-Wilmington

YEAR	TM LG	W	L	PCT	G	GS	CG-SHO	SV-BS	IP	H	R	HR	HB	BB-IB	SO	ERA	AERA	OAV	OOB	AB-HR-SH	AVG	PB	SUP	APR	DL	PW
2000	Pit N	0	0	—	3	0	0	0-0	4.1	6	5	1	0	2-0	3	10.38	45	.375	.421	0	—	0		-3		-0.1

SMITH, REX Rex (b Henry W. Schmidt) B1864 Louisville KY D6.21.1895 Louisville KY d7.11

YEAR	TM LG	W	L	PCT	G	GS	CG-SHO	SV-BS	IP	H	R	HR	HB	BB-IB	SO	ERA	AERA	OAV	OOB	AB-HR-SH	AVG	PB	SUP	APR	DL	PW
1886	Phi AA	0	1	1.000	1	1	1	0	9	15	13	0	0	5	4	7.00	50	.385	.455	4	.000	-1	68	-4		-0.3

SMITH, ED Rhesa Edward B2.21.1879 Mentone IN D3.20.1955 Tarpon Springs FL BR/TR/5-11/170 d4.27

YEAR	TM LG	W	L	PCT	G	GS	CG-SHO	SV-BS	IP	H	R	HR	HB	BB-IB	SO	ERA	AERA	OAV	OOB	AB-HR-SH	AVG	PB	SUP	APR	DL	PW
1906	StL A	8	11	.421	19	18	13	0	154.2	153	90	3	8	53	45	3.72	69	.261	.331	54-0-2	.204	2	115	-19		-1.9

SMITH, BUD Robert Allan B10.23.1979 Torrance CA BL/TL/6-0/170* [StLN98 4/108] d6.10 Col Los Angeles Harbor (CA) JC

YEAR	TM LG	W	L	PCT	G	GS	CG-SHO	SV-BS	IP	H	R	HR	HB	BB-IB	SO	ERA	AERA	OAV	OOB	AB-HR-SH	AVG	PB	SUP	APR	DL	PW
2001	†StL N	6	3	.667	16	14	1-1	0-0	84.2	79	40	12	1	24-5	59	3.83	113	.250	.304	25-0-2	.160	-0	113	4		0.4
2002	StL N	1	5	.167	11	10	0	0-0	48	67	39	4	3	22-2	22	6.94	58	.338	.405	14-0-3	.214	1	92	-15	15	-1.6
Total 2		7	8	.467	27	24	1-1	0-0	132.2	146	79	16	4	46-7	81	4.95	85	.284	.344	39-0-5	.179	1	104	-11	15	-1.2

SMITH, BOB Robert Ashley (aka Robert M. Brown in 1914) B7.20.1890 Woodbury VT D12.27.1965 West Los Angeles CA BR/TR/5-11/160 d4.19 Col Tufts

YEAR	TM LG	W	L	PCT	G	GS	CG-SHO	SV-BS	IP	H	R	HR	HB	BB-IB	SO	ERA	AERA	OAV	OOB	AB-HR-SH	AVG	PB	SUP	APR	DL	PW
1913	Chi A	0	0	—	1	0	0	0	3	3	3	0	0	3	1	13.50	22	.273	.429	0	—	0		-2		-0.1
1914	Buf F	0	0	—	15	1	0	3	36.2	39	16	3	2	16	13	3.44	86	.281	.363	9	.222	0	70	-1		0.0
1915	Buf F	0	0	—	1	0	0	0	1	1	2	0	1	2	0	18.00	16	.333	.667	0	—	0		-1		0.0
Total 3		0	0	—	17	1	0	3	39.2	43	21	3	3	21	14	4.31	69	.281	.379	9	.222	0	70	-4		-0.2

SMITH, BOB Robert Eldridge B4.22.1895 Rogersville TN D7.19.1987 Waycross GA BR/TR/5-10/175 d4.19.1923 ▲

YEAR	TM LG	W	L	PCT	G	GS	CG-SHO	SV-BS	IP	H	R	HR	HB	BB-IB	SO	ERA	AERA	OAV	OOB	AB-HR-SH	AVG	PB	SUP	APR	DL	PW
1925	Bos N	5	3	.625	13	10	6	0	92.2	110	51	6	0	36	19	4.47	90	.304	.367	174-0-2	.282	3*	97	-3		0.0
1926	Bos N	10	13	.435	33	23	14-4	1	201.1	199	91	10	0	75	44	3.75	94	.269	.336	84-0-1	.298	7*	95	-1		0.7
1927	Bos N	10	18	.357	41	31	16-1	3	260.2	297	132	9	2	75	81	3.76	99	.301	.351	109-1-1	.248	4*	106	-3		0.3
1928	Bos N	13	17	.433	38	26	14	2	244.1	274	138	11	2	74	59	3.87	101	.289	.342	92-1-6	.250	3*	96	-4		0.1
1929	Bos N	11	17	.393	34	29	19-1	3	231	256	135	20	1	71	65	4.68	100	.285	.338	99-1-3	.172	-1*	78	1		0.1
1930	Bos N	10	14	.417	38	24	14-2	5	219.2	247	115	25	3	85	84	4.26	116	.290	.357	81-0-3	.235	-1*	61	17		1.6
1931	Chi N	15	12	.556	36	29	18-2	2	240.1	239	101	10	1	62	63	3.22	120	.256	.303	87-0-5	.218	2	105	16		1.9
1932	†Chi N	4	3	.571	34	11	4-1	2	119	148	64	4	3	36	35	4.61	82	.303	.355	42	.238	2*	126	-8		-0.2
1933	Cin N	4	4	.500	16	6	4	0	73.2	75	27	3	0	11	18	2.20	154	.260	.287	25-0-1	.200	0*	78	1		0.9
	Bos N	4	3	.571	14	4	3-1	1	58.2	68	24	3	0	7	16	3.22	95	.296	.316	20	.200	1	88	-1		0.0
	Year	8	7	.533	30	10	7-1	1	132.1	143	51	6	0	18	34	2.65	123	.276	.300	45-0-1	.200	1	82	6		0.9
1934	Bos N	6	9	.400	39	5	3	5	121.2	133	69	9	0	36	26	4.66	82	.277	.328	36-0-2	.250	1*	99	-10		-1.1
1935	Bos N	8	18	.308	46	20	8-2	5	203.1	232	105	13	3	61	58	3.94	96	.285	.337	63-0-6	.270	2*	85	-4		-0.3
1936	Bos N	6	7	.462	35	11	5-2	8	136	142	65	3	1	35	36	3.77	102	.264	.311	45-0-2	.222	0	80	1		0.2
1937	Bos N	0	1	.000	18	0	0	3	44	52	22	6	2	6	14	4.09	88	.295	.326	10	.200	0*		-2		-0.1
Total 13		106	139	.433	435	229	128-16	40	2246.1	2472	1139	132	18	670	618	3.94	100	.283	.335	967-3-32	.244	23	91	7		4.0

SMITH, BOB Robert Gilchrist B2.1.1931 Woodsville NH BR/TL/6-1.5/190* d4.29

YEAR	TM LG	W	L	PCT	G	GS	CG-SHO	SV-BS	IP	H	R	HR	HB	BB-IB	SO	ERA	AERA	OAV	OOB	AB-HR-SH	AVG	PB	SUP	APR	DL	PW
1955	Bos N	0	0	—	1	0	0	0	1.2	1	0	0	0	1-0	1	0.00	—	.200	.333	0	—	0		1		0.0
1957	StL N	0	0	—	6	0	0	1	9.2	12	10	0	1	6-1	11	4.66	85	.267	.365	2	.000	-0		-3		-0.2
	Pit N	2	4	.333	20	4	2	0	55	48	23	3	1	25-3	35	3.11	122	.229	.314	13-0-1	.077	-1	81	4	30	0.3
	Year	2	4	.333	26	4	2	1	64.2	60	33	3	2	31-4	46	3.34	114	.235	.323	15-0-1	.067	-1	81	1		0.1
1958	Pit N	2	2	.500	35	4	0	1	61	61	39	6	2	31-7	24	4.43	87	.262	.352	11	.091	-1	110	-6		-0.4
1959	Pit N	0	0	—	20	0	0	0	28.1	32	16	1	0	17-0	12	3.49	111	.291	.383	2	.000	-0		0		-0.4
	Det A	0	3	.000	9	0	0	1	11	20	15	5	0	3-1	10	8.18	50	.417	.451	1	.000	-0		-6		-1.2
Total 4		4	9	.308	91	8	2	2	166.2	174	102	15	4	83-12	93	4.55	95	.267	.353	29-0-1	.069	-2	95	-10	30	-1.6

SMITH, BOB Robert Walkup "Riverboat" B5.13.1927 Clarence MO D6.23.2003 Clarence MO BR/TL(BB 1959)/6-0/180* d4.22 Col Missouri

YEAR	TM LG	W	L	PCT	G	GS	CG-SHO	SV-BS	IP	H	R	HR	HB	BB-IB	SO	ERA	AERA	OAV	OOB	AB-HR-SH	AVG	PB	SUP	APR	DL	PW
1958	Bos A	4	3	.571	17	7	1	0	66.2	61	32	4	0	45-2	43	3.78	106	.248	.362	19-0-1	.105	-1	109	2		0.1
1959	Chi N	0	0	—	1	0	0	0	0.2	5	6	0	0	2-1	0	81.00	5	.833	.875	0	—	0		-5		-0.2
	Cle A	0	1	.000	12	3	0	0	29.1	31	19	2	0	12-0	17	5.22	71	.282	.341	6	.000	-1	112	-5		-0.3
Total 2		4	4	.500	30	10	1	0	96.2	97	57	6	0	59-3	60	4.75	82	.268	.365	25-0-1	.080	-2	110	-4		-0.4

SMITH, RUFUS Rufus Frazier "Shirt" B1.24.1905 Guilford College NC D8.21.1984 Aiken SC BR/TL/5-8/165 d10.2 Col Guilford

YEAR	TM LG	W	L	PCT	G	GS	CG-SHO	SV-BS	IP	H	R	HR	HB	BB-IB	SO	ERA	AERA	OAV	OOB	AB-HR-SH	AVG	PB	SUP	APR	DL	PW
1927	Det A	0	0	—	1	1	0	0	8	8	4	0	1	3	2	3.38	125	.242	.324	3	.000	-1	99	1		0.0

SMITH, SHERRY Sherrod Malone B2.18.1891 Monticello GA D9.12.1949 Reidsville GA BR/TL/6-1/170 d5.11 Mil 1918

YEAR	TM LG	W	L	PCT	G	GS	CG-SHO	SV-BS	IP	H	R	HR	HB	BB-IB	SO	ERA	AERA	OAV	OOB	AB-HR-SH	AVG	PB	SUP	APR	DL	PW
1911	Pit N	0	0	—	1	0	0	0	0.2	4	5	0	0	1	0	54.00	6	.667	.714	0	—	0		-4		-0.1
1912	Pit N	0	0	—	3	0	0	0	4	6	3	0	0	1	3	6.75	48	.600	.636	0	—	0		-1		-0.1
1915	Bro N	14	8	.636	29	20	11-2	2	173.2	169	71	3	5	42	52	2.59	107	.264	.315	57-0-1	.246	3	74	2		0.6
1916	†Bro N	14	10	.583	36	25	15-4	1	219	193	76	5	3	45	67	2.34	114	.239	.282	77-0-3	.273	5*	121	9		1.7
1917	Bro N	12	12	.500	38	23	15	3	211.1	210	103	5	2	51	58	3.32	84	.265	.311	77-0-1	.195	2*	95	-14		-1.1
1919	Bro N	7	12	.368	30	19	13-2	1	173	181	63	3	4	29	40	2.24	133	.278	.313	54-0-4	.148	2	103	11		1.2
1920	†Bro N	11	9	.550	33	13	6-2	3	136.1	134	42	1	2	39	33	1.85	173	.264	.304	43	.233	2	60	18		3.2
1921	Bro N	7	11	.389	35	17	9	4	175.1	232	95	4	1	34	36	3.90	100	.319	.350	57-1-1	.228	1	83	-1		0.2
1922	Bro N	4	8	.333	28	8	3-1	2	108.2	128	71	6	7	35	15	4.56	89	.309	.373	35-1-0	.257	2	93	-8		-0.5
1923	Cle A	1	0	1.000	2	2	1	0	15.2	18	7	0	0	3	4	3.45	116	.295	.328	6	.333	1	106	1		0.1
1924	Cle A	9	6	.600	30	16	10-1	1	124	129	62	4	2	37	23	3.27	121	.269	.324	45-1-2	.244	1	121	7		1.0
1924	Cle A	12	14	.462	39	27	20-2	5	247.2	267	110	5	7	42	34	3.02	142	.277	.312	89-1-4	.202	-1*	88	31		2.9
1925	Cle A	11	14	.440	31	30	22-1	1	237	296	151	11	5	48	30	4.86	91	.306	.342	92-1-3	.304	7	120	-11		-0.3
1926	Cle A	11	10	.524	27	24	16-1	0	188.1	214	80	8	4	31	25	3.73	109	.292	.324	65-1-4	.215	2	85	12		1.5
1927	Cle A	1	4	.200	11	2	1	0	38	53	25	2	0	14	8	5.45	77	.342	.396	12	.167	-0	99	-4		-0.5
Total 14		114	118	.491	373	226	142-16	21	2052.2	2234	964	57	42	440	428	3.32	108	.282	.324	709-6-23	.233	22	97	48		9.7

SMITH, TOM Thomas Edward B12.5.1871 Boston MA D3.2.1929 Dorchester MA BR/TR/5-7.5/165 d6.6 Col Fordham

YEAR	TM LG	W	L	PCT	G	GS	CG-SHO	SV-BS	IP	H	R	HR	HB	BB-IB	SO	ERA	AERA	OAV	OOB	AB-HR-SH	AVG	PB	SUP	APR	DL	PW
1894	Bos N	0	0	—	2	0	0	1	6	8	14	2	4	6	2	15.00	38	.320	.514	2	.000	-0		-6		-0.2
1895	Phi N	2	3	.400	11	7	4	0	68	76	67	1	7	53	21	6.88	70	.278	.408	33	.242	-0	123	-15		-0.8
1896	Lou N	2	3	.400	11	5	4	0	55	73	55	2	4	25	14	5.40	80	.316	.392	39	.205	-0*	89	-8		-0.5
1898	StL N	0	1	.000	1	1	1	0	9	9	8	0	2	5	1	2.00	189	.257	.381	2	.500	1	94	0		0.1
Total 4		4	7	.364	25	13	9	1	138	166	144	5	17	89	38	6.33	72	.294	.406	76	.224	0	107	-29		-1.4

SMITH, TRAVIS Travis William B11.7.1972 Springfield OR BR/TR/5-10/170* [MilA95 19/516] d6.21 Col Texas Tech

YEAR	TM LG	W	L	PCT	G	GS	CG-SHO	SV-BS	IP	H	R	HR	HB	BB-IB	SO	ERA	AERA	OAV	OOB	AB-HR-SH	AVG	PB	SUP	APR	DL	PW
1998	Mil N	0	0	—	1	0	0	0-0	2	1	0	0	0	0-0	1	0.00	—	.143	.143	1	.000	-0		1	98	0.0
2002	StL N	4	2	.667	12	10	0	0-0	54	69	44	10	3	20-0	32	7.17	56	.322	.388	18-0-2	.167	-0	119	-18		-1.7
2004	Atl N	2	3	.400	16	4	0	0-0	40.2	48	28	12	1	12-2	26	6.20	70	.293	.345	8	.125	-0	43	-7		-0.8
2005	Fla N	0	0	—	12	0	0	0-0	10.2	17	8	1	0	5-1	9	6.75	59	.370	.423	0	—	0		-3		-0.2
Total 4		6	5	.545	41	14	0	0-0	107.1	135	80	23	4	37-3	68	6.62	62	.313	.372	27-0-2	.148	-1	96	-27	98	-2.7

SMITH, ROY Walter Roy B5.18.1976 St.Petersburg FL BR/TR/6-6/235(210-235) [SeaA94 13/357] d5.26

YEAR	TM LG	W	L	PCT	G	GS	CG-SHO	SV-BS	IP	H	R	HR	HB	BB-IB	SO	ERA	AERA	OAV	OOB	AB-HR-SH	AVG	PB	SUP	APR	DL	PW
2001	Cle A	0	0	—	9	0	0	0-0	16.1	16	14	3	2	13-1	17	6.06	76	.246	.387	0	—	0		-3		0.0
2002	Cle A	0	0	—	4	1	0	0-0	6	9	4	1	0	5-0	2	3.00	148	.310	.429	0	—	0	146	0		0.0
Total 2		0	0	—	13	1	0	0-0	22.1	25	18	4	3	18-1	19	5.24	87	.266	.400	0	—	0	146	-3		-0.2

SMITH, BILL William Garland B6.8.1934 Washington DC D3.30.1997 Clinton MD BL/TL/6-0/190* d9.13

YEAR	TM LG	W	L	PCT	G	GS	CG-SHO	SV-BS	IP	H	R	HR	HB	BB-IB	SO	ERA	AERA	OAV	OOB	AB-HR-SH	AVG	PB	SUP	APR	DL	PW
1958	StL N	0	1	.000	2	1	0	0	9.2	12	7	0	0	6-0	4	6.52	63	.324	.390	2	.000	-0	65	-2		-0.2
1959	StL N	0	0	—	6	0	0	1	8.1	11	3	0	0	4	4	1.08	393	.333	.389	1	.000	-0		2		0.1
1962	Phi N	1	5	.167	24	5	0	0	50.1	59	32	8	1	10-3	26	4.29	90	.295	.329	11	.182	1	77	-5		-0.4
Total 3		1	6	.143	32	6	0	1	68.1	82	42	8	1	17-4	34	4.21	94	.304	.345	14	.143	0	74	-5		-0.5

SMITH, WILLIE Willie B2.11.1939 Anniston AL BL/TL/6-0/190(178-190) d6.18 ▲

YEAR	TM LG	W	L	PCT	G	GS	CG-SHO	SV-BS	IP	H	R	HR	HB	BB-IB	SO	ERA	AERA	OAV	OOB	AB-HR-SH	AVG	PB	SUP	APR	DL	PW
1963	Det A	1	0	1.000	11	2	0	2	21.2	24	13	2	0	13-2	16	4.57	82	.300	.389	8	.125	-0*	142	-2		-0.2
1964	LA A	1	4	.200	15	1	0	0	31.2	34	13	5	1	10-1	20	2.84	116	.293	.344	359-11-1	.301	6*	81	1		0.4
1968	Cle A	0	0	—	2	0	0	0	5	2	0	0	0	1-0	1	0.00	—	.125	.176	42	.143	6*		2		0.1
	Chi N	0	0	—	1	0	0	0										.000	.000	142-5-1	.275	0*		1		0.1
Total 3		2	4	.333	29	3	0	2	61	60	26	7	1	24-3	39	3.10	110	.273	.339	551-16-2	.279	6	130	2		0.4

YEAR	TM LG	W	L	PCT	G	GS	CG-SHO	SV-BS	IP	H	R	HR	HB	BB-IB	SO	ERA	AERA	OAV	OOB	AB-HR-SH	AVG	PB	SUP	APR	DL	PW
SMITH, WILLIE	Willie Everett B8.27.1967 Savannah GA BR/TR/6-6/250 d4.25																									
1994	StL N	1	1	.500	8	0	0	0-1	7	9	7	4	0	3-0	7	9.00	47	.300	.364	0	—	0		-3		-0.7
SMITH, ZANE	Zane William B12.28.1960 Madison WI BL/TL/6-2/195(195-207) [AtlN82 3/63] d9.10 Col Indiana St.																									
1984	Atl N	1	0	1.000	3	3	0	0-0	20	16	7	1	0	13-2	16	2.25	171	.219	.337	9	.556	2	76	3		0.4
1985	Atl N	9	10	.474	42	18	2-2	0-0	147	135	70	4	3	80-5	85	3.80	102	.254	.354	37-0-6	.162	-0*	84	1	27	0.2
1986	Atl N	8	16	.333	38	32	3-1	1-0	204.2	209	109	8	5	105-6	139	4.05	98	.275	.364	59-0-9	.085	-3*	84	-4		-0.5
1987	Atl N	15	10	.600	36	**36**	9-3	0-0	242	245	130	19	5	91-6	130	4.09	106	.266	.333	76-0-14	.132	-1*	109	4		-0.6
1988	Atl N	5	10	.333	23	22	3	0-0	140.1	159	72	8	3	44-4	59	4.30	85	.292	.347	42-0-7	.167	0*	74	-8	39	-0.6
1989	Atl N	1	12	.077	17	17	0	0-0	99	102	65	5	2	33-3	58	4.45	82	.267	.325	28-0-4	.179	-0*	71	-12		-1.4
	Mon N	0	1	.000	31	0	0	2-1	48	39	11	2	1	19-4	35	1.50	238	.220	.299	4	.250	0*		10		0.6
	Year	1	13	.071	48	17	0	2-1	147	141	76	7	3	52-7	93	3.49	104	.252	.317	32-0-4	.188	0	72	-3		-0.8
1990	Mon N	6	7	.462	22	21	1	0-0	139.1	141	57	11	3	41-3	80	3.23	144	.266	.322	40-0-7	.175	1*	74	6		0.7
	†Pit N	6	2	.750	11	10	3-2	0-0	76	55	20	4	0	9-1	50	1.30	280	.203	.228	28-0-1	.143	0	82	17		1.9
	Year	12	9	.571	33	31	4-2	0-0	215.1	196	77	15	3	50-4	130	2.55	144	.245	.291	68-0-8	.162	1	76	24		2.6
1991	†Pit N	16	10	.615	35	35	6-3	0-0	228	234	95	15	2	29-3	120	3.20	113	.268	.268	71-0-13	.183	2*	114	9	62	1.3
1992	Pit N	8	8	.500	23	22	4-3	0-0	141	138	56	8	2	19-3	56	3.06	113	.261	.287	49-0-3	.122	-0*	100	4	96	-0.6
1993	Pit N	3	7	.300	14	14	1	0-0	83	97	43	7	0	22-3	32	4.55	90	.298	.343	25-0-4	.080	-2	83	-4		-0.3
1994	Pit N	10	8	.556	25	24	2-1	0-0	157	162	67	18	0	34-7	57	3.27	134	.270	.307	57-0-2	.211	1*	84	17		2.0
1995	†Bos A	8	8	.500	24	21	0	0-0	110.2	144	78	7	1	23-1	47	5.61	87	.316	.347	0	—	0	111	-10	38	-1.2
1996	.Pit N	4	6	.400	16	16	1-1	0-0	83.1	104	55	7	4	21-4	45	5.08	86	.309	.353	26-0-2	.154	-1	105	-6	15	-0.7
Total	13	100	115	.465	360	291	35-16	3-1	1919.1	1980	933	122	31	583-55	1011	3.74	106	.271	.326	551-0-72	.158	0	94	27	277	3.0
SMITHBERG, ROGER	Roger Craig B3.21.1966 Elgin IL BR/TR/6-3/210* [SDN87 2/42] d9.1 Col Bradley																									
1993	Oak A	1	2	.333	13	0	0	3-1	19.2	13	7	1	0	7-2	12	2.75	151	.197	.284	0		0		3		0.5
1994	Oak A	0	0	—	2	0	0	0-0	2.1	6	4	1	0	1-0	3	15.43	29	.500	.538	0		0		-3		-0.1
Total	2	1	2	.333	15	0	0	3-1	22	19	11	3	1	8-2	7	4.09	102	.244	.322	0		0		0		0.4
SMITHSON, MIKE	Billy Mike B1.21.1955 Centerville TN BL/TR/6-8/215(200-215) [BosA76 5/118] d8.27 Col Tennessee																									
1982	Tex A	3	4	.429	8	8	3	0-0	46.2	51	26	5	3	13-2	24	5.01	78	.282	.338	0		0	73	-5		-0.7
1983	Tex A	10	14	.417	33	33	10	0-0	223.1	233	102	14	8	71-2	135	3.91	104	.269	.327	0		0	90	7		0.7
1984	Min A	15	13	.536	36	**36**	10-1	0-0	252	246	113	35	8	54-7	144	3.68	115	.252	.296	0		0	86	15		1.5
1985	Min A	15	14	.517	37	**37**	8-3	0-0	257	264	134	25	15	78-1	127	4.34	102	.270	.331	0		0	90	3		0.3
1986	Min A	13	14	.481	34	33	8-1	0-0	198	234	123	26	14	57-4	114	4.77	91	.294	.349	0		0	103	-12		-1.2
1987	Min A	4	7	.364	21	20	0	0-0	109	126	76	17	9	38-3	53	5.94	69	.286	.351	0		0	118	-14	28	-1.2
1988	†Bos A	9	6	.600	31	18	1	0-0	126.2	149	87	25	6	37-1	73	5.97	69	.292	.345	0		0	125	-23		-2.4
1989	Bos A	5	14	.333	40	19	1-1	2-1	143.2	170	84	21	10	35-5	61	4.95	83	.297	.343	0		0	108	-10		-1.4
Total	8	76	86	.469	240	204	41-6	2-1	1356.1	1473	745	168	73	383-25	731	4.58	93	.277	.331	0		0	98	-39	28	-4.6
SMOLL, LEFTY	Clyde Hetrick B4.17.1914 Quakertown PA D8.31.1985 Quakertown PA BB/TL/5-10/175 d4.26																									
1940	Phi N	2	8	.200	33	9	0	0	109	145	77	6	4	36	31	5.37	73	.322	.378	31	.161	-1	59	-19		-1.7
SMOLTZ, JOHN	John Andrew B5.15.1967 Detroit MI BR/TR/6-3/210(185-220) [DetA85 22/574] d7.23 [DL 2000 Atl N 181]																									
1988	Atl N	2	7	.222	12	12	0	0-0	64	74	40	10	2	33-4	37	5.48	67	.285	.369	17-0-3	.118	-0	71	-11		-1.4
1989	Atl N★	12	11	.522	29	29	5	0-0	208	160	79	15	2	72-2	168	2.94	124	.212	.280	62-1-6	.113	1*	78	15		1.9
1990	Atl N	14	11	.560	34	34	6-2	0-0	231.1	206	109	20	1	90-3	170	3.85	105	.240	.310	74-0-7	.162	1*	102	5		0.7
1991	†Atl N	14	13	.519	36	36	5	0-0	229.2	206	101	16	3	77-1	148	3.80	102	.243	.305	65-0-8	.108	-1*	102	6		0.7
1992	†Atl N★	15	12	.556	35	**35**	9-3	0-0	246.2	206	90	17	5	80-5	**215**	2.85	129	.224	.287	75-1-10	.160	2*	99	20		2.4
1993	†Atl N★	15	11	.577	35	35	3-1	0-0	243.2	208	104	23	6	100-12	208	3.62	112	.230	.309	71-1-11	.183	3	103	13		1.6
1994	Atl N	6	10	.375	21	21	1	0-0	134.2	120	69	15	4	48-4	113	4.14	104	.239	.307	37-1-6	.162	2	83	2		0.3
1995	†Atl N★	12	7	.632	29	29	2-1	0-0	192.2	166	76	15	4	72-8	193	3.18	136	.232	.304	56-0-6	.107	-1	93	23		1.9
1996	†Atl N★	**24**	8	**.750**	35	35	6-2	0-0	253.2	199	93	19	2	55-3	**276**	2.94	151	.216	**.260**	78-1-15	.218	3	104	40		4.2
1997	†Atl N	15	12	.556	35	**35**	7-2	0-0	256	234	97	21	4	63-9	241	3.02	139	.242	.288	79-0-6	.228	6*	98	33		3.9
1998	†Atl N	17	3	**.850**	26	26	2-2	0-0	167.2	145	58	10	4	44-2	173	2.90	144	.231	.285	51-0-8	.196	3	122	25	42	3.2
1999	†Atl N	11	8	.579	29	29	1-1	0-0	186.1	168	70	14	4	40-2	156	3.19	140	.245	.288	62-1-4	.274	-0	104	29	34	0.8
2001	†Atl N	3	3	.500	36	5	0	10-1	59	53	24	7	2	10-2	57	3.36	128	.238	.274	7-0-2	.000	-0	120	7	88	0.8
2002	†Atl N★	3	2	.600	75	0	0	**55**-4	80.1	59	30	4	0	24-1	85	3.25	125	.206	.266	2	.000	-0		8		1.5
2003	†Atl N☆	0	2	.000	62	0	0	45-4	64.1	48	9	2	0	8-1	73	1.12	375	.204	.230	1	.000	-0		15		1.5
2004	†Atl N	0	1	.000	73	0	0	44-5	81.2	75	29	8	2	13-2	85	2.76	156	.245	.276	2	.000	-0	92	31	27	1.0
2005	†Atl N★	14	7	.667	33	33	3-1	0-0	229.2	210	83	18	1	53-7	169	3.06	141	.243	.287	68-0-12	.147	0	92	31		2.6
Total	17	177	128	.580	635	394	50-15	154-14	2929.1	2537	1157	234	41	882-68	2567	3.26	127	.233	.291	807-5-104	.170	25	99	283	372	33.7
SMYTH, STEVE	Steven Delton B6.3.1978 Brawley CA BL/TL/6-1/220 [ChiN99 4/140] d8.6 Col USC																									
2002	Chi N	1	3	.250	8	7	0	0-0	26	34	28	9	1	10-0	16	9.35	43	.321	.372	9-0-1	.222	0	140	-15		-1.8
SMYTHE, HARRY	William Henry B10.24.1904 Augusta GA D8.28.1980 Augusta GA BL/TL/5-10.5/179 d7.21																									
1929	Phi N	4	6	.400	19	9	2	1	68.2	94	47	3	1	15	12	5.24	99	.330	.365	26	.192	-1*	106	-1		-0.1
1930	Phi N	0	3	.000	25	3	0	2	49.2	84	60	3	3	31	9	7.79	70	.368	.450	14-0-1	.286	-0	112	-15		-0.9
1934	NY A	0	2	.000	8	0	0	1	15	24	16	1	0	8	7	7.80	52	.381	.451	5	.200	-0		-7		-0.3
	Bro N	1	1	.500	8	0	0	0	21.1	30	19	3	1	8	5	5.91	66	.337	.398	9-0-1	.333	1*		-6		-0.3
Total	3	5	12	.294	60	12	2	4	154.2	232	142	10	5	62	33	6.40	77	.349	.408	54-0-2	.241	0	114	-29		-2.1
SNARE, RYAN	Ryan Delbert B2.8.1979 Clearwater FL BL/TL/6-0/200 [CinN00 2/63] d8.6 Col North Carolina																									
2004	Tex A	0	0	—	1	0	0	0-0	3.1	5	5	3	0	2-0	0	10.80	46	.333	.412	0	—	0		-2		-0.1
SNELL, IAN	Ian Dante B10.30.1981 Dover DE BR/TR/5-11/170* [PitN00 26/779] d8.20																									
2004	Pit N	0	1	.000	3	1	0	0-0	12	14	10	2	0	9-0	9	7.50	58	.298	.411	2-0-1	.000	-0	85	-4		-0.3
2005	Pit N	1	2	.333	15	6	0	0-0	42	43	25	5	1	24-3	34	5.14	82	.267	.364	8	.000	-1	88	-4		-0.4
Total	2	1	3	.250	18	6	0	0-0	54	57	35	7	1	33-3	43	5.67	75	.274	.374	10-0-1	.000	-1	87	-8		-0.7
SNELL, NATE	Nathaniel B9.2.1952 Orangeburg SC BR/TR/6-4/190* d9.20 Col Tennessee St.																									
1984	Bal A	1	1	.500	5	0	0	0-0	7.2	8	2	1	0	1-0	7	2.35	167	.258	.273	0	—	0		1		0.3
1985	Bal A	3	2	.600	43	0	0	5-0	100.1	100	44	4	1	30-5	41	2.69	151	.260	.314	0	—	0		11	30	0.6
1986	Bal A	2	1	.667	34	0	0	0-1	72.1	69	36	9	1	22-4	29	3.86	108	.257	.313	0	—	0		2		0.1
1987	Det A	1	2	.333	22	2	0	0-0	38.2	39	20	5	0	19-3	19	3.96	108	.267	.349	0	—	0	64	1		0.0
Total	4	7	6	.538	104	2	0	5-1	219	216	102	19	2	72-12	96	3.29	126	.260	.319	0	—	0	64	15	30	1.0
SNOOK, FRANK	Frank Walter B3.28.1949 Somerville NJ BR/TR/6-2/185 [SDN71 7/148] d7.13 Col Grand Canyon																									
1973	SD N	0	2	.000	18	0	0	1-1	27.1	19	15	4	0	18-0	13	3.62	97	.200	.319	2	.000	-0		-1		-0.1
SNOVER, COLONEL	Colonel Lester "Bosco" B5.16.1895 Hallstead PA D4.30.1969 Rochester NY BL/TL/6-0.5/200 d9.18																									
1919	NY N	1	0	1.000	1	1	1	0	9	7	5	0	1	4	4	1.00	281	.212	.297	2	.000	0	113	0		0.0
SNYDER, BRIAN	Brian Robert B2.20.1958 Flemington NJ BL/TL/6-3/185* [SeaA79 7/157] d5.25 Col Clemson																									
1985	Sea A	1	2	.333	15	6	1-0	35.1	44	28	2	1	19-2	23	6.37	66	.306	.388	0	—	0	97	-8		-0.6	
1989	Oak A	0	0	—	2	0	0	1-0	0.2	2	2	1	0	2-0	1	27.00	14	.500	.667	0	—	0		-2		-0.1
Total	2	1	2	.333	17	6	0	1-0	36	46	30	3	1	21-2	24	6.75	62	.311	.398	0	—	0	97	-10		-0.7
SNYDER, GENE	Gene Walter B3.31.1931 York PA D6.2.1996 York PA BR/TL/5-11/175 d4.26																									
1959	LA N	1	1	.500	11	2	0	0-0	26.1	32	19	1	0	20-2	20	5.47	77	.299	.409	6-0-1	.000	0	85	-4		-0.3
SNYDER, GEORGE	George T. B8.1.1848 Philadelphia PA D8.2.1905 Philadelphia PA d9.30																									
1882	Phi AA	1	0	1.000	1	1	1	0	2			0	0	0	0	0.00	—	.125	.176	3	.333	0	110	2		0.2
SNYDER, JOHN	John Michael B8.16.1974 Southfield MI BR/TR/6-3/185(185-200) [CalA92 13/356] d6.30																									
1998	Chi A	7	2	.778	15	14	1	0-0	86.1	96	49	14	2	23-1	52	4.80	96	.286	.332	0	—	0	125	-1		-0.1
1999	Chi A	9	12	.429	25	25	1	0-0	129.1	167	103	27	6	49-0	67	6.68	74	.311	.371	0	—	0	100	-23		-3.0

YEAR	TM LG	W	L	PCT	G	GS	CG-SHO	SV-BS	IP	H	R	HR	HB	BB-IB	SO	ERA	AERA	OAV	OOB	AB-HR-SH	AVG	PB	SUP	APR	DL	PW
2000	Mil N	3	10	.231	23	23	0	0-0	127	147	95	8	9	77-10	69	6.17	75	.296	.395	38-0-1	.079	-1*	90	-22	46	-1.9
Total 3		19	24	.442	63	62	2	0-0	342.2	410	247	49	17	149-11	188	6.01	79	.299	.371	38-0-1	.079	-1	102	-46	46	-5.0

SNYDER, KYLE Kyle Ehren B9.9.1977 Houston TX BB/TR/6-8/220* [KCA99 1/7] d5.1 Col North Carolina [DL 2004 KC A 183]

YEAR	TM LG	W	L	PCT	G	GS	CG-SHO	SV-BS	IP	H	R	HR	HB	BB-IB	SO	ERA	AERA	OAV	OOB	AB-HR-SH	AVG	PB	SUP	APR	DL	PW
2003	KC A	1	6	.143	15	15	0	0-0	85.1	94	54	11	2	21-3	39	5.17	93	.283	.321	2	.000	-0	62	-3	74	-0.2
2005	KC A	1	3	.250	13	3	0	0-0	36	55	29	3	1	10-1	19	6.75	62	.353	.391	0	—	0	104	-11	64	-1.0
Total 2		2	9	.182	28	18	0	0-0	121.1	149	81	14	3	31-4	58	5.64	82	.305	.343	2	.000	-0	70	-14	321	-1.2

SNYDER, BILL William Nicholas B1.28.1898 Mansfield OH D10.8.1934 Vicksburg MI BR/TR d9.4

YEAR	TM LG	W	L	PCT	G	GS	CG-SHO	SV-BS	IP	H	R	HR	HB	BB-IB	SO	ERA	AERA	OAV	OOB	AB-HR-SH	AVG	PB	SUP	APR	DL	PW
1919	Was A	0	1	.000	2	1	0	0	8	6	4	0	0	3	5	1.13	285	.200	.273	2	.000	-0	73	1		0.1
1920	Was A	2	1	.667	16	4	1	1	54	59	33	1	6	28	17	4.17	90	.280	.380	19	.316	1	101	-3		-0.1
Total 2		2	2	.500	18	5	1	1	62	65	37	1	6	31	22	3.77	97	.270	.367	21	.286	1	95	-2		0.0

SOBKOWIAK, SCOTT Scott B10.26.1977 Woodstock IL BR/TR/6-5/230 [AtlN98 7/221] d10.7 Col Northern Iowa

YEAR	TM LG	W	L	PCT	G	GS	CG-SHO	SV-BS	IP	H	R	HR	HB	BB-IB	SO	ERA	AERA	OAV	OOB	AB-HR-SH	AVG	PB	SUP	APR	DL	PW
2001	Atl N	0	0	—	1	0	0	0	1	3	3	1	0	1	0	9.00	48	.400	.400	0	—	0		0	106	0.0

SODERSTROM, STEVE Stephen Andrew B4.3.1972 Turlock CA BR/TR/6-3/215 [SFN93 1/6] d9.17 Col Cal St.-Fresno

YEAR	TM LG	W	L	PCT	G	GS	CG-SHO	SV-BS	IP	H	R	HR	HB	BB-IB	SO	ERA	AERA	OAV	OOB	AB-HR-SH	AVG	PB	SUP	APR	DL	PW
1996	SF N	2	0	1.000	3	3	0	0-0	13.2	16	11	1	2	6-0	9	5.27	79	.302	.381	5	.000	-1	181	-3		-0.4

SODOWSKY, CLINT Clint Rea B7.13.1972 Ponca City OK BL/TR/6-4/200(180-200) [DetA91 9/244] d9.4 Col Connors St. (OK) JC

YEAR	TM LG	W	L	PCT	G	GS	CG-SHO	SV-BS	IP	H	R	HR	HB	BB-IB	SO	ERA	AERA	OAV	OOB	AB-HR-SH	AVG	PB	SUP	APR	DL	PW
1995	Det A	2	2	.500	6	6	0	0-0	23.1	24	15	4	0	18-0	14	5.01	96	.258	.378	0	—	0	68	-1		-0.2
1996	Det A	1	3	.250	7	7	0	0-0	24.1	40	34	5	3	20-0	9	11.84	43	.370	.481	0	—	0	117	-18		-2.0
1997	Pit N	2	2	.500	45	0	0	0-2	52	49	22	6	2	34-7	51	3.63	118	.249	.362	2	.500	0		4	15	0.3
1998	Ari N	3	6	.333	45	6	0	0-3	77.2	86	56	5	7	39-5	42	5.68	75	.283	.375	10-0-1	.300	1*	129	-13		-1.2
1999	StL N	0	1	.000	3	1	0	0-0	6.1	15	11	1	0	6-0	2	15.63	29	.455	.538	1	.000	-0	140	-7	33	-0.8
Total 5		8	14	.364	106	20	0	0-5	183.2	214	138	21	12	117-12	118	6.17	72	.291	.395	13-0-1	.308	1	113	-35	48	-3.9

SOFF, RAY Raymond John B10.31.1958 Adrian MI BR/TR/6-0/185* [ChiN79 11/272] d7.17 Col Central Michigan

YEAR	TM LG	W	L	PCT	G	GS	CG-SHO	SV-BS	IP	H	R	HR	HB	BB-IB	SO	ERA	AERA	OAV	OOB	AB-HR-SH	AVG	PB	SUP	APR	DL	PW
1986	StL N	4	2	.667	30	0	0	0-0	38.1	37	17	4	0	13-1	22	3.29	112	.255	.313	2-0-1	.000	-0		1		0.2
1987	StL N	1	0	1.000	12	0	0	0-0	15.1	18	11	3	1	5-1	9	6.46	65	.295	.353	1	.000	-0		-3		-0.2
Total 2		5	2	.714	42	0	0	0-0	53.2	55	28	7	1	18-2	31	4.19	92	.267	.325	3-0-1	.000	-0		-2		0.0

SOLANO, JULIO Julio Cesar B1.8.1960 Agua Blanca, D.R. BR/TR/6-1/160* d4.5

YEAR	TM LG	W	L	PCT	G	GS	CG-SHO	SV-BS	IP	H	R	HR	HB	BB-IB	SO	ERA	AERA	OAV	OOB	AB-HR-SH	AVG	PB	SUP	APR	DL	PW
1983	Hou N	0	2	.000	4	0	0	0-0	6	5	5	1	0	4-1	3	6.00	57	.217	.333	0	—	0		-2		-0.4
1984	Hou N	1	3	.250	31	0	0	0-2	50.2	31	13	3	0	18-1	33	1.95	171	.179	.253	3	.333	0		8		0.6
1985	Hou N	2	2	.500	20	0	0	0-0	33.2	34	13	3	0	13-2	17	3.48	100	.262	.329	2	.000	-0		1		0.0
1986	Hou N	3	1	.750	16	1	0	0-1	32	39	28	5	3	22-2	21	7.59	47	.310	.421	6-0-1	.000	-1	25	-14		-1.6
1987	Hou N	0	0	—	11	0	0	0-0	20	25	17	5	0	9-0	12	7.65	51	.298	.366	2	.000	-0		-8		-0.4
1988	Sea A	0	0	—	17	0	0	3-1	22	22	13	4	0	12-2	10	4.09	102	.268	.354	0	—	0		-1		0.0
1989	Sea A	0	0	—	7	0	0	0-0	9.2	6	8	1	1	4-0	6	5.59	72	.176	.282	0	—	0		-2		-0.1
Total 7		6	8	.429	106	1	0	3-4	174	162	97	23	4	82-8	102	4.55	80	.248	.333	13-0-1	.077	-1	25	-18		-1.9

SOLIS, MARCELINO Marcelino B7.19.1930 San Luis Potosi, San Luis Potosi, Mexico D6.15.2001 Monterrey, Nuevo Leon, Mexico BL/6-1/185 d7.16

YEAR	TM LG	W	L	PCT	G	GS	CG-SHO	SV-BS	IP	H	R	HR	HB	BB-IB	SO	ERA	AERA	OAV	OOB	AB-HR-SH	AVG	PB	SUP	APR	DL	PW
1958	Chi N	3	3	.500	15	4	0	0	52	74	41	5	4	20-1	15	6.06	65	.339	.405	20	.250	1	86	-13		-1.2

SOLOMON, EDDIE Eddie "Buddy" B2.9.1951 Perry GA D1.12.1986 Macon GA BR/TR/6-3/190* d9.2

YEAR	TM LG	W	L	PCT	G	GS	CG-SHO	SV-BS	IP	H	R	HR	HB	BB-IB	SO	ERA	AERA	OAV	OOB	AB-HR-SH	AVG	PB	SUP	APR	DL	PW
1973	LA N	0	0	—	4	0	0	0-0	6.1	10	5	3	1	4-0	6	7.11	49	.357	.455	1	.000	-0		-2		-0.1
1974	†LA N	0	0	—	4	0	0	1-0	6	5	1	1	0	2-0	1	1.50	229	.217	.280	0	—	0		1		0.1
1975	Chi N	0	0	—	6	0	0	0-0	6.2	7	6	1	0	6-2	3	1.35	287	.269	.406	0	—	0		0		0.0
1976	StL N	1	1	.500	26	2	0	0-0	37	45	24	2	1	16-1	19	4.86	74	.306	.369	5	.400	-1	172	-6		-0.1
1977	Atl N	6	6	.500	18	16	0	0-0	88.2	110	64	10	2	34-2	54	4.57	97	.305	.365	31-0-1	.129	-1	90	-6		-0.8
1978	Atl N	4	6	.400	37	8	0	2-2	106	98	52	12	2	50-11	64	4.08	99	.247	.334	29	.138	-1*	67	1	25	-0.1
1979	Atl N	7	14	.333	31	30	4	0-0	186	184	98	19	6	51-4	96	4.21	95	.253	.307	64-0-3	.203	1*	89	-2		-0.2
1980	Pit N	7	3	.700	26	12	2	0-0	100.1	96	44	8	4	37-5	35	2.69	137	.253	.322	32-0-3	.219	1*	97	6		0.7
1981	Pit N	8	6	.571	22	17	2	1-0	127	133	49	10	3	27-3	38	3.12	117	.278	.320	43-0-5	.163	-1*	119	8		0.7
1982	Pit N	2	6	.250	11	10	0	0-0	46.2	69	38	9	1	18-0	18	6.75	56	.347	.400	15-0-1	.133	-1*	111	-15		-2.2
	Chi A	1	0	1.000	6	0	0	0-0	7.1	7	5	1	0	2-0	2	3.68	111	.241	.290	0	—	0		0		-0.1
Total 10		36	42	.462	191	95	8	4-2	718	764	386	76	20	247-28	337	4.00	98	.274	.335	220-0-13	.177	-1	98	-15	25	-2.1

SOMMER, JOE Joseph John B11.20.1858 Covington KY D1.16.1938 Cincinnati OH BR/TR d7.8.1880 ▲

YEAR	TM LG	W	L	PCT	G	GS	CG-SHO	SV-BS	IP	H	R	HR	HB	BB-IB	SO	ERA	AERA	OAV	OOB	AB-HR-SH	AVG	PB	SUP	APR	DL	PW
1883	Cin AA	0	0	—				5	9	6	0		1		2	5.40	60	.360	.385	413-3	.278	0*		-1		-0.1
1885	Bal AA	0	0	—	2	0	0	1	3	6	3	0	0	1	2	9.00	36	.429	.429	471-1	.251	0*		-1		-0.1
1886	Bal AA	0	0	—	1	0	0	0	4	14	12	0	0	3	1	18.00	19	.519	.567	560-1	.209	-0*		-6		-0.2
1887	Bal AA	0	0	—	1	0	0	0	1	2	1	0	0	1	0	9.00	46	.333	.429	463	.266	0*		0		0.0
1890	Cle N	0	0	—	1	0	0	0	1	2	3	1	0	2	0	0.00	—	.400	.571	35	.229	-0*		-1		0.0
Total 5		0	0	—	6	0	0	1	14	33	25	1	0	7	3	9.64	35	.429	.476	1942-5	.248	1		-9		-0.4

SOMMERS, RUDY Rudolph B10.30.1886 Cincinnati OH D3.18.1949 Louisville KY BB/TL/5-11/165 d9.8

YEAR	TM LG	W	L	PCT	G	GS	CG-SHO	SV-BS	IP	H	R	HR	HB	BB-IB	SO	ERA	AERA	OAV	OOB	AB-HR-SH	AVG	PB	SUP	APR	DL	PW
1912	Chi A	0	1	.000	3	0	0	0	3	4	1	0	0	2	2	3.00	111	.333	.429	1	.000	0		0		0.1
1914	Bro F	2	7	.222	23	8	2	0	82	88	54	2	3	34	40	4.06	71	.282	.358	24	.250	2	89	-13		-1.2
1926	Bos A	0	0	—	3	0	0	0	2	3	6	0	3	3	2	13.50	30	.333	.500	0	—	0		-2		-0.1
1927	Bos A	0	0	—	7	0	0	2	14	18	15	2	0	14	2	8.36	51	.353	.492	2	.500	0		-6		-0.2
Total 4		2	8	.200	33	8	2	2	101	113	73	4	3	53	44	4.81	64	.294	.384	27	.259	2	89	-21		-1.4

SOMMERVILLE, ANDY Andrew Henry (b Henry Travers Summersgill) B2.6.1876 Brooklyn NY D6.16.1931 Richmond Hill NY d8.8 Col Virginia

YEAR	TM LG	W	L	PCT	G	GS	CG-SHO	SV-BS	IP	H	R	HR	HB	BB-IB	SO	ERA	AERA	OAV	OOB	AB-HR-SH	AVG	PB	SUP	APR	DL	PW
1894	Bro N	0	1	.000	1	1	0	0	0.1	1	6	0	0	5	0	162.00	3	.500	.857	0	—	0	71	-5		-0.6

SONGER, DON Donald C. B1.31.1900 Walnut KS D10.3.1962 Kansas City MO BL/TL/6-0/165 d9.21

YEAR	TM LG	W	L	PCT	G	GS	CG-SHO	SV-BS	IP	H	R	HR	HB	BB-IB	SO	ERA	AERA	OAV	OOB	AB-HR-SH	AVG	PB	SUP	APR	DL	PW
1924	Pit N	0	0	—	4	1	0	0	9.1	14	7	1	0	3	3	6.75	57	.333	.378	2	.000	-0	221	-3		-0.1
1925	Pit N	0	1	.000	8	0	0	0	11.2	14	7	0	0	8	4	2.31	193	.298	.400	2	.000	-0		1		0.1
1926	Pit N	7	8	.467	35	15	5-1	2	126.1	118	60	4	11	52	27	3.13	126	.252	.340	38	.105	-2	96	9		0.7
1927	Pit N	0	0	—	2	0	0	0	4.2	10	10	0	1	4	1	11.57	36	.526	.625	1	.000	-0		-5		-0.2
	NY N	3	5	.375	22	1	0	1	50.1	48	22	4	1	31	9	2.86	135	.267	.370	10	.300	1	44	4		0.8
	Year	3	5	.375	24	1	0	1	55	58	32	4	2	35	10	3.60	108	.286	.396	11	.273	1	44	-1		0.6
Total 4		10	14	.417	71	17	5-1	4	202.1	204	106	9	13	98	44	3.38	117	.268	.361	53	.132	-2	100	6		1.3

SORENSEN, LARY Lary Alan B10.4.1955 Detroit MI BR/TR/6-2/205* [MilA76 8/172] d6.7 Col Michigan

YEAR	TM LG	W	L	PCT	G	GS	CG-SHO	SV-BS	IP	H	R	HR	HB	BB-IB	SO	ERA	AERA	OAV	OOB	AB-HR-SH	AVG	PB	SUP	APR	DL	PW
1977	Mil A	7	10	.412	23	20	9	0-0	142.1	147	72	10	1	36-4	57	4.36	94	.270	.315	0	—	0	85	-2		-0.2
1978	Mil A★	18	12	.600	37	36	17-3	1-0	280.2	277	111	14	15	50-4	78	3.21	118	.259	.291	0	—	0	107	19		1.9
1979	Mil A	15	14	.517	34	34	16-2	0-0	235.1	250	113	30	4	42-3	63	3.98	106	.275	.309	0	—	0	98	7		0.8
1980	Mil A	12	10	.545	35	29	8-2	1-0	195.2	242	91	13	2	45-6	54	3.68	106	.311	.347	0	—	0	117	5		0.6
1981	StL N	7	7	.500	23	23	3-1	0-0	140.1	149	59	3	1	26-2	52	3.27	111	.271	.305	46-0-5	.065	-3	100	4		0.6
1982	Cle A	10	15	.400	32	30	6-1	0-0	189.1	251	130	19	3	55-6	62	5.61	74	.322	.365	0	—	0	102	-30		-3.4
1983	Cle A	12	11	.522	36	34	8-1	0-0	222.2	238	112	21	2	65-9	76	4.24	101	.276	.326	0	—	0	92	3		0.3
1984	Oak A	6	13	.316	46	21	2	1-1	183.1	240	117	21	6	44-4	63	4.91	97	.317	.356	0	—	0	98	-27		-2.6
1985	Chi A	3	7	.300	45	3	0	0-1	82.1	86	44	8	4	24-10	34	4.26	94	.274	.331	6-0-4	.000	-0	118	-3		-0.4
1987	Mon N	3	4	.429	23	5	0	1-0	47.2	56	32	7	3	12-1	21	4.72	90	.286	.333	8-0-2	.000	-1	76	-4		-0.6
1988	SF N	0	0	—	12	0	0	2-1	16.2	24	13	1	0	3-0	9	4.86	67	.329	.346	1-0-1	.000	-0		-4		-0.3
Total 11		93	103	.474	346	235	69-10	7-3	1736.1	1960	894	147	31	402-49	569	4.15	96	.287	.327	61-0-12	.049	-4	100	-32		-3.9

SORIANO, RAFAEL Rafael B12.19.1979 San Jose, D.R. BR/TR/6-1/175(175-220) d5.10

YEAR	TM LG	W	L	PCT	G	GS	CG-SHO	SV-BS	IP	H	R	HR	HB	BB-IB	SO	ERA	AERA	OAV	OOB	AB-HR-SH	AVG	PB	SUP	APR	DL	PW
2002	Sea A	0	3	.000	10	8	0	0-0	47.1	45	25	8	0	16-1	32	4.56	94	.243	.303	4	.000	-0*	67	-1	30	-0.1
2003	Sea A	3	0	1.000	40	0	0	1-1	53	30	9	2	3	12-1	68	1.53	283	.162	.224	0	—	0		18		0.9
2004	Sea A	0	3	.000	6	0	0	0-0	3.1	9	5	0	0	3-0	3	13.50	33	.450	.522	0	—	0		-4	147	-0.7
2005	Sea A	0	0	—	7	0	0	0-0	7.1	6	2	0	1	1-0	9	2.45	171	.222	.267	0	—	0		2	155	0.1
Total 4		3	6	.333	63	8	0	2-2	111	90	42	10	4	32-2	112	3.24	133	.216	.277	4	.000	-0	67	15	332	0.2

YEAR	TM LG	W	L	PCT	G	GS	CG-SHO	SV-BS	IP	H	R	HR	HB	BB-IB	SO	ERA	AERA	OAV	OOB	AB-HR-SH	AVG	PB	SUP	APR	DL	PW
SORRELL, VIC	Victor Garland B4.9.1901 Morrisville NC D5.4.1972 Raleigh NC BR/TR/5-10/180 d4.22 Col Wake Forest																								
1928	Det A	8	11	.421	29	23	8	0	171	182	106	9	5	83	67	4.79	86	.277	.363	55-0-6	.109	-5	107	-11		-1.6
1929	Det A	14	15	.483	36	31	13-1	0	226	270	152	15	2	106	81	5.18	83	.302	.377	83-0-4	.145	-6	109	-20		-2.7
1930	Det A	16	11	.593	35	30	14-2	1	233.1	245	116	13	0	106	97	3.86	124	.274	.351	80-0-4	.188	-3	101	24		2.0
1931	Det A	13	14	.481	35	32	19-1	1	245	267	131	8	1	114	99	4.15	110	.278	.355	88-0-4	.159	-4	81	12		0.8
1932	Det A	14	14	.500	32	31	13-1	0	234.1	234	124	11	3	77	84	4.03	117	.259	.319	76-0-5	.118	-4*	82	18		1.4
1933	Det A	11	15	.423	36	28	13-1	1	232.2	233	112	18	2	78	75	3.79	114	.260	.321	74-0-4	.149	-2	83	16		1.3
1934	Det A	6	9	.400	28	19	6-1	2	129.2	146	76	13	3	45	46	4.79	92	.283	.345	37-0-3	.108	-1	110	-5		-0.5
1935	Det A	4	3	.571	12	6	4	0	51.1	65	28	2	2	25	22	4.03	103	.319	.398	18	.000	-3	167	0		-0.3
1936	Det A	6	7	.462	30	14	5-1	3	131.1	153	86	9	2	64	37	5.28	94	.294	.373	39-0-4	.154	1	109	4		-0.1
1937	Det A	0	2	.000	7	2	0	1	17	25	18	3	0	8	11	9.00	52	.338	.402	3-0-1	.000	-0	75	-8		-0.8
Total	10	92	101	.477	280	216	95-8	10	1671.2	1820	949	101	20	706	619	4.43	102	.279	.351	553-0-35	.139	-27	97	22		-0.5
SOSA, ELIAS	Elias (Martinez) B6.10.1950 LaVega, D.R. BR/TR/6-2/190(185-205) d9.8																								
1972	SF N	0	1	.000	8	0	0	3-0	15.2	10	4	0	0	12-0	10	2.30	152	.189	.338	4	.000	-0		2		0.2
1973	SF N	10	4	.714	71	1	0	18-3	107	95	42	7	4	41-8	70	3.28	117	.241	.315	14-0-1	.071	-0	115	8		1.1
1974	SF N	9	7	.563	68	0	0	6-8	101	94	54	8	1	45-5	48	3.48	110	.252	.329	15-0-2	.067	-1		1		-0.1
1975	StL N	0	3	.000	14	1	0	0-1	27.1	22	14	3	1	14-2	15	3.95	96	.227	.319	8	.125	-0	46	0		-0.1
	Atl N	2	2	.500	43	0	0	2-2	62.1	70	35	3	3	29-7	31	4.48	85	.294	.376	7-0-1	.143	-0		-4		-0.3
	Year	2	5	.286	57	1	0	2-3	89.2	92	49	6	4	43-9	46	4.32	88	.275	.359	15-0-1	.133	-1	46	-4		-0.4
1976	Atl N	4	4	.500	21	0	0	3-4	35.1	41	26	3	1	13-2	32	5.35	71	.287	.346	7	.143	-0		-7		-1.4
	LA N	2	4	.333	24	0	0	1-0	33.2	30	16	0	0	12-4	20	3.48	98	.242	.304	0	—	0		-1		-0.2
	Year	6	8	.429	45	0	0	4-4	69	71	42	3	1	25-6	52	4.43	81	.266	.327	7-0-1	.143	-0		-8		-1.6
1977	†LA N	2	2	.500	44	0	0	1-0	63.2	42	15	7	1	12-3	47	1.98	195	.189	.233	4-0-1	.250	0*	14			0.8
1978	Oak A	8	2	.800	68	0	0	14-4	109	106	37	5	1	44-10	61	2.64	139	.264	.337	0	—	0		13		1.5
1979	Mon N	8	7	.533	62	0	0	18-7	96.2	77	24	2	2	37-11	59	1.96	190	.219	.297	13-0-1	.154	-1		19		3.5
1980	Mon N	9	6	.600	67	0	0	9-8	93.2	104	33	5	1	19-3	58	3.07	118	.286	.320	11-0-1	.091	-1		7		1.1
1981	†Mon N	1	2	.333	32	0	0	3-2	39.1	46	16	3	1	8-0	18	3.66	97	.297	.329	2	1.000	1		0		0.1
1982	Det A	3	3	.500	38	0	0	4-3	61	64	31	11	2	18-3	24	4.43	92	.270	.327	0	—	0		-1		-0.1
1983	SD N	1	4	.200	41	1	0	1-1	72.1	72	41	7	3	30-5	45	4.35	81	.268	.322	7	.143	-0	151	-8		-0.6
Total	12	59	51	.536	601	3	0	83-43	918	873	388	64	21	334-63	538	3.32	112	.255	.322	92-0-8	.130	-3	103	43		5.5
SOSA, JORGE	Jorge Bolivar B4.28.1977 Santo Domingo, D.R. BR/TR/6-2/180* d4.4																								
2002	TB A	2	7	.222	31	14	0	0-0	99.1	88	63	16	2	54-0	48	5.53	82	.236	.332	0	—	0	92	-10	30	-0.8
2003	TB A	5	12	.294	29	19	1-1	0-0	128.2	137	71	14	4	60-4	72	4.62	99	.278	.358	0	—	0	80	0		-0.1
2004	TB A	4	7	.364	43	8	0	1-0	99.1	100	67	17	1	54-3	94	5.53	85	.259	.348	0	—	0	85	-9		-0.9
2005	†Atl N	13	3	.813	44	20	0	0-0	134	122	42	12	0	46-8	85	2.55	168	.241	.325	31-0-3	.097	-1*	102	25		2.4
Total	4	24	29	.453	147	61	1-1	1-0	461.1	447	243	59	7	232-15	299	4.41	102	.254	.341	31-0-3	.097	-1	90	6	30	0.6
SOSA, JOSE	Jose Ynocencio (b Jose Ynocencio (Sosa)) B12.28.1952 Santo Domingo, D.R. BR/TR/5-11/158* d7.22																								
1975	Hou N	1	3	.250	25	2	0	1-1	47	51	21	5	1	23-4	31	4.02	84	.291	.371	9-1-0	.333	2*	104	-3		-0.1
1976	Hou N	0	0	—	9	0	0	0-0	11.2	16	9	0	3	6-2	5	6.94	46	.340	.439	0	—	0		-5		-0.2
Total	2	1	3	.250	34	2	0	1-1	58.2	67	30	5	4	29-6	36	4.60	73	.302	.386	9-1-0	.333	2	104	-8		-0.3
SOTHORON, ALLEN	Allen Sutton B4.27.1893 Bradford OH D6.17.1939 St.Louis MO BB/TR(BR 1924-26)/5-11/182 d9.17 M1/C4 Col Juniata																								
1914	StL A	0	0	—	1	0	0		6	6	4	0	0	3	3	6.00	45	.261	.370	2	.000	-0		-2		-0.1
1915	StL A	1	0	1.000	3	1	0	0	3.2	8	10	0	1	5	2	7.36	39	.400	.520	1	.000	-0	0	-4		-0.7
1917	StL A	14	19	.424	48	32	17-3	4	276.2	259	135	2	9	96	85	2.83	92	.251	.320	92-0-5	.217	3*	100	-13		-1.2
1918	StL A	12	12	.500	29	24	14-2	0	209	152	64	3	6	67	71	1.94	141	.205	.311	63-0-4	.159	-2	96	17		1.6
1919	StL A	20	12	.625	40	30	21-3	3	270	256	101	4	10	87	106	2.20	151	.246	.311	97-0-3	.175	-2	82	27		2.5
1920	StL A	8	15	.348	36	26	12-1	0	218.1	263	151	6	6	89	81	4.70	83	.307	.376	72-0-5	.222	-1	96	-22		-2.2
1921	StL A	1	2	.333	5	4	1	0	27.2	33	19	0	1	8	9	5.20	86	.314	.348	9-0-1	.111	-1	98	-2		-0.3
	Bos A	0	2	.000	2	2	0	0	6	15	10	0	0	5	2	13.50	31	.455	.526	2	.500	1	39	-6		-0.9
	Cle A	12	4	.750	22	16	10-2	0	144.2	146	60	0	7	58	61	3.24	132	.279	.358	58-0-3	.276	2	128	17		1.7
	Year	13	8	.619	29	22	11-2	0	178.1	194	89	0	8	71	72	3.89	111	.293	.368	69-0-4	.261	2	115	10		0.5
1922	Cle A	1	3	.250	6	4	2	0	25.1	26	22	1	2	14	8	6.39	63	.274	.378	9	.444	1	117	-7		-0.8
1924	StL N	10	16	.385	29	28	16-**4**	0	196.2	209	102	9	10	84	62	3.57	106	.275	.354	72-0-5	.194	-2	111	1		-0.3
1925	StL N	10	10	.500	28	22	8-2	0	155.2	173	86	7	6	63	67	4.05	107	.280	.353	56-0-2	.196	-1	106	3		0.0
1926	StL N	3	3	.500	15	4	1	0	42.2	37	22	2	0	16	19	4.22	93	.247	.319	13	.231	0	128	-1		-0.1
Total	11	91	99	.479	264	193	102-17	9	1582.1	1583	786	34	54	596	576	3.31	105	.264	.336	546-0-28	.207	-2	102	8		-0.8
SOTO, MARIO	Mario Melvin B7.12.1956 Bani, D.R. BR/TR/6-0/185(165-190) d7.21																								
1977	Cin N	2	6	.250	12	10	2-1	0-0	60.2	60	38	12	3	26-4	44	5.34	74	.258	.337	13-0-1	.077	-0	90	-9		-1.1
1978	Cin N	1	0	1.000	5	1	0	0-0	18	13	5	1	0	13-3	13	2.50	142	.197	.329	2-0-1	.000	-0	126	9		0.1
1979	†Cin N	3	2	.600	25	0	0	0-0	37.1	33	25	2	1	30-2	32	5.30	70	.243	.381	7	.571	2		-7		-0.7
1980	Cin N	10	8	.556	53	12	3-1	4-1	190.1	126	72	11	2	84-10	182	3.07	115	.187	.276	46-0-8	.043	-4*	114	9		0.4
1981	Cin N	12	9	.571	25	25	10-3	0-0	175	142	69	13	3	61-3	151	3.29	107	.220	.289	61-3	.068	-4	106	5		0.0
1982	Cin N★	14	13	.519	35	34	13-2	0-0	257.2	202	88	19	4	71-3	274	2.79	131	.215	.278	84-0-11	.167	1*	92	25		2.7
1983	Cin N★	17	13	.567	34	34	18-**3**	0-0	273.2	207	96	28	5	95-6	242	2.70	142	.208	.278	88-0-11	.125	-2*	83	30		3.0
1984	Cin N★	18	7	.720	33	33	**13**	0-0	237.1	181	102	26	5	87-6	185	3.53	108	.209	.284	87-1-4	.207	3	106	7		0.9
1985	Cin N	12	15	.444	36	36	9-1	0-0	256.2	196	109	30	2	104-3	214	3.58	106	.211	.290	83-0-6	.133	-2*	86	8		1.0
1986	Cin N	5	10	.333	19	19	1-1	0-0	105	113	61	15	1	46-6	67	4.71	82	.280	.352	27-0-6	.111	-1*	84	-9	94	-1.3
1987	Cin N	3	2	.600	6	6	0	0-0	31.2	34	18	7	0	12-1	11	5.12	83	.279	.343	12	.083	-1	143	-2	150	-0.4
1988	Cin N	3	7	.300	14	14	3-1	0-0	87	88	49	8	2	28-3	34	4.66	77	.267	.326	22-0-4	.045	-1	96	-10		-1.2
Total	12	100	92	.521	297	224	72-13	4-1	1730.1	1395	732	172	28	657-50	1449	3.47	107	.220	.294	530-1-58	.132	-10	96	49	244	2.9
SOUZA, MARK	Kenneth Mark B2.1.1955 Redwood City CA BL/TL/6-0/180 [KCA74*1/17] d4.22 Col San Mateo (CA) [JC]																								
1980	Oak A	0	0	—	5	0	0	0-1	7	9	6	0	0	5-0	2	7.71	49	.310	.412	0	—	0		-3		-0.1
SOWDERS, JOHN	John B12.10.1866 Louisville KY D7.29.1939 Indianapolis IN BR/TL/6-0/150 d6.28 b-Len b-Bill																								
1887	Ind N	0	0	—	1	0	0	0	3	11	13	0	0	9	0	21.00	20	.500	.593	2	.000	-0		-6		-0.3
1889	KC AA	6	16	.273	25	23	20	1	185	204	181	9	7	105	104	4.82	88	.271	.366	87	.218	-2*	78	-12		-1.3
1890	Bro P	19	16	.543	39	37	28-1	0	309	358	233	3	11	161	91	3.82	117	.278	.363	132-1	.189	-5*	95	19		1.1
Total	3	25	32	.439	65	60	48-1	1	497	573	427	12	18	271	195	4.29	102	.278	.366	221-1	.199	-7	88	1		-0.5
SOWDERS, BILL	William Jefferson "Little Bill" B11.29.1864 Louisville KY D2.2.1951 Indianapolis IN BR/TR/6-0/155 d4.24 b-John b-Len																								
1888	Bos N	19	15	.559	36	35	34-2	0	317	278	155	3	9	73	132	2.07	139	.226	.275	122	.148	-4	85	19		1.5
1889	Bos N	1	2	.333	7	4	3	3	42	53	35	3	2	23	10	5.14	81	.299	.386	17	.235	-0	89	-5		-0.3
	Pit N	6	5	.545	13	11	9	0	52.2	94	55	1	4	29	33	7.35	51	.376	.449	48	.271	2*	96	-20		-2.7
	Year	7	7	.500	20	15	12	3	94.2	147	90	4	6	52	43	6.37	62	.344	.423	65	.262	2	92	-23		-3.0
1890	Pit N	3	8	.273	15	11	9	0	106	117	77	1	2	24	30	4.42	75	.271	.312	50	.180	-2*	71	-13		-1.3
Total	3	29	30	.492	71	61	55-2	3	517.2	542	322	8	17	149	205	3.34	95	.260	.314	237	.186	-4	85	-19		-2.8
SPADE, BOB	Robert B1.4.1877 Akron OH D9.7.1924 Cincinnati OH BR/TR/5-10/190 d9.22																								
1907	Cin N	1	2	.333	3	3	3-1	0	27	21	5	0	1	9	7	1.00	260	.219	.292	7	.286	1	37	4		0.7
1908	Cin N	17	12	.586	35	28	22-2	1	249.1	230	111	2	5	85	74	2.74	84	.250	.317	87-0-3	.195	1	107	-12		-1.6
1909	Cin N	5	5	.500	14	13	8	0	98	91	38	0	4	39	31	2.85	91	.236	.313	34	.294	4	99	0		0.2
1910	Cin N	1	2	.333	3	3	1	0	17.1	35	19	1	1	9	1	6.75	43	.479	.542	5	.000	-1	136	-8		-1.1
	StL A	1	3	.250	7	5	2-1	0	34.2	34	24	1	1	17	8	4.41	56	.270	.361	11	.273	2	119	-7		-0.6
Total	4	25	24	.510	62	52	36-4	1	426.1	411	197	4	12	159	121	2.96	82	.257	.329	144-0-3	.222	7	104	-23		-2.4
SPAHN, WARREN	Warren Edward B4.23.1921 Buffalo NY D11.24.2003 Broken Arrow OK BL/TL/6-0/175* d4.19 Mil 1943-46 C3 HF1973																								
1942	Bos N	0	0	—	4	2	1	0	15.2	25	15	0	0	11	7	5.74	58	.368	.456	6	.167	-0	126	-6		-0.3
1946	Bos N	8	5	.615	24	16	8	1	125.2	107	46	6	1	36	67	2.94	117	.228	.285	43-0-2	.163	-1	105	9		0.6
1947	Bos N★	21	10	.677	40	35	22-**7**	3	**289.2**	245	87	15	1	84	123	**2.33**	**167**	.226	**.283**	98-0-8	.163	1*	91	**52**		**5.3**
1948	†Bos N	15	12	.556	36	35	16-3	1	257	237	115	20	1	77	114	3.71	103	.242	.298	90-1-7	.167	2*	113	5		0.7

YEAR	TM LG	W	L	PCT	G	GS	CG-SHO	SV-BS	IP	H	R	HR	HB	BB-IB	SO	ERA	AERA	OAV	OOB	AB-HR-SH	AVG	PB	SUP	APR	DL	PW
1949	Bos N★	21	14	.600	38	38	25-4	0	302.1	283	125	27	3	86	151	3.07	123	.245	.299	111-2-5	.162	-0*	110	23		2.3
1950	Bos N☆	21	17	.553	41	39	25-1	1	293	248	123	22	1	111	191	3.16	122	.227	.299	106-1-5	.217	4	108	22		3.1
1951	Bos N☆	22	14	.611	39	36	26-7	0	310.2	278	111	20	1	109	164	2.98	123	.238	.304	116-1-4	.190	5*	124	29		3.6
1952	Bos N☆	14	19	.424	40	35	19-5	3	290	263	109	19	6	73	183	2.98	121	.240	.291	112-2-2	.161	2*	94	20		2.6
1953	Mil N★	23	7	.767	35	32	24-5	3	265.2	211	75	14	1	70	148	2.10	187	.217	.270	105-2-5	.219	5*	111	57		7.0
1954	Mil N★	21	12	.636	39	34	23-1	3	283.1	262	107	24	1	86	136	3.14	118	.245	.300	101-1-3	.208	6*	103	22		3.2
1955	Mil N	17	14	.548	39	32	16-1	1	245.2	249	99	25	2	65-4	110	3.26	115	.265	.312	81-4-3	.210	5*	111	15		2.3
1956	Mil N★	20	11	.645	39	35	20-3	3	281.1	249	92	25	3	52-12	128	2.78	124	.238	.275	105-3-2	.210	6	108	28		3.7
1957	†Mil N☆	21	11	.656	39	35	18-4	3	271	241	94	23	2	78-4	111	2.69	130	.237	.291	94-2-3	.138	1	124	26		3.1
1958	†Mil N☆	22	11	.667	38	36	23-2	1	290	257	106	29	3	76-7	150	3.07	115	.237	.287	108-2-8	.333	18*	113	18		4.1
1959	Mil N☆	21	15	.583	40	36	21-4	0	292	282	106	21	1	70-9	143	2.96	120	.253	.297	104-2-1	.231	7	113	23		3.4
1960	Mil N	21	10	.677	40	33	18-4	2	267.2	254	114	24	4	74-9	154	3.50	98	.250	.302	95-3-2	.147	3	122	0		0.4
1961	Mil N	21	13	.618	38	34	21-4	0	262.2	236	96	24	4	64-1	115	3.02	124	.243	.291	94-4-2	.223	10*	100	23		4.1
1962	Mil N☆	18	14	.563	34	34	22	0	269.1	248	97	25	3	55-4	118	3.04	125	.246	.284	98-2-3	.184	4*	93	26		3.5
1963	Mil N	23	7	.767	33	33	22-7	0	259.2	241	85	23	0	49-4	102	2.60	124	.248	.282	90-2-4	.178	5	117	18		3.0
1964	Mil N	6	13	.316	38	25	4-1	4	173.2	204	110	23	2	52-4	71	5.29	67	.297	.345	59-1-1	.186	2*	115	-32		-3.2
1965	NY N	4	12	.250	20	19	5	0	126	140	70	18	2	35-1	56	4.36	81	.281	.329	35-0-2	.114	1*	76	-12		-1.2
	SF N	3	4	.429	16	11	3	0	71.2	70	34	8	1	21-1	34	3.39	106	.256	.308	21	.143	0	115	0		0.1
	Year	7	16	.304	36	30	8	0	197.2	210	104	26	3	56-2	90	4.01	89	.272	.321	56-0-2	.125	2	90	-12		-1.1
Total 21		363	245	.597	750	665	382-63	29	5243.2	4830	2016	434	42	1434-60	2583	3.09	118	.244	.296	1872-35-68	.194	88	108	365		51.4

SPALDING, AL Albert Goodwill B9.2.1850 Byron IL D9.9.1915 San Diego CA BR/TR/6-1/170 d5.5 M2 HF1939 ▲

YEAR	TM LG	W	L	PCT	G	GS	CG-SHO	SV-BS	IP	H	R	HR	HB	BB-IB	SO	ERA	AERA	OAV	OOB	AB-HR-SH	AVG	PB	SUP	APR	DL	PW
1871	Bos NA	19	10	.655	31	31	22-1	0	257.1	333	272	2	0	38	2	3.36	124	.268	.290	144-1	.271	2	123	22		1.6
1872	Bos NA	38	8	.826	48	48	41-3	0	404.2	417	224	0	0	27	28	1.85	198	.244	.255	237	.354	18	114	81		7.5
1873	Bos NA	41	14	.745	60	54	46-1	3	496.2	643	413	5	0	36	50	2.99	111	.284	.296	323-1	.328	19	131	26		3.4
1874	Bos NA	52	16	.765	71	69	65-4	0	617.1	755	402	2	0	19	31	1.92	113	.273	.278	362	.329	21	141	17		2.8
1875	Bos NA	54	5	.915	72	62	52-7	9	570.2	573	241	1	0	18	75	1.59	135	.245	.251	343	.312	22*	165	33		4.4
1876	Chi N	47	12	.797	61	60	53-8	6	528.2	542	226	0	0	26	39	1.75	139	.247	.256	292	.312	9*	153	39		4.3
1877	Chi N	1	0	1.000	4	1	0	1	11	17	12	0	0	0	2	3.27	91	.321	.321	254	.256	0	197	-1		-0.1
Total 5 NA		204	53	.794	282	264	226-16	12	2346.2	2721	1552	9	0	138	207	2.21	130	.264	.274	1409-2	.323	83	135	179		19.7
Total 2		48	12	.800	65	61	53-8	1	539.2	559	238	0	0	26	41	1.78	138	.249	.257	546	.286	9	153	38		4.2

SPANSWICK, BILL William Henry B7.8.1938 Springfield MA BL/TL/6-3/195 d4.18 Col Holy Cross

YEAR	TM LG	W	L	PCT	G	GS	CG-SHO	SV-BS	IP	H	R	HR	HB	BB-IB	SO	ERA	AERA	OAV	OOB	AB-HR-SH	AVG	PB	SUP	APR	DL	PW
1964	Bos A	2	3	.400	29	7	0	0	65.1	75	51	9	3	44-1	55	6.89	56	.306	.412	14	.286	1	128	-19		-1.2

SPARKS, JEFF James Jeffrey B4.4.1972 Houston TX BR/TR/6-3/220* [CinN95 24/671] d9.12 Col St. Marys (TX)

YEAR	TM LG	W	L	PCT	G	GS	CG-SHO	SV-BS	IP	H	R	HR	HB	BB-IB	SO	ERA	AERA	OAV	OOB	AB-HR-SH	AVG	PB	SUP	APR	DL	PW
1999	TB A	0	0	—	8	0	0	1-0	10	6	6	1	1	12-1	17	5.40	92	.171	.396	0	—	0		0		0.0
2000	TB A	0	1	.000	15	0	0	0-0	20.1	13	8	2	2	18-1	24	3.54	138	.186	.367	0	—	0		3		0.1
Total 2		0	1	.000	23	0	0	1-0	30.1	19	14	3	3	30-2	41	4.15	118	.181	.377	0	—	0		3		0.1

SPARKS, STEVE Stephen Lanier B3.28.1972 Mobile AL BR/TR/6-4/210 [PitN98 28/838] d7.19 Col South Alabama

YEAR	TM LG	W	L	PCT	G	GS	CG-SHO	SV-BS	IP	H	R	HR	HB	BB-IB	SO	ERA	AERA	OAV	OOB	AB-HR-SH	AVG	PB	SUP	APR	DL	PW
2000	Pit N	0	0	—	6	0	0	0-0	4	4	3	0	0	5-0	2	6.75	69	.267	.450	0	—	0		-1		0.0

SPARKS, STEVE Steven William B7.2.1965 Tulsa OK BR/TR/6-0/180(180-195) [MilA87 5/123] d4.28 Col Sam Houston St. [DL 1997 Mil A 181]

YEAR	TM LG	W	L	PCT	G	GS	CG-SHO	SV-BS	IP	H	R	HR	HB	BB-IB	SO	ERA	AERA	OAV	OOB	AB-HR-SH	AVG	PB	SUP	APR	DL	PW
1995	Mil A	9	11	.450	33	27	3	0-0	202	210	111	17	5	86-1	96	4.63	108	.274	.346	0	—	0	87	9		0.9
1996	Mil A	4	7	.364	20	13	1	0-0	88.2	103	66	19	3	52-0	21	6.60	79	.297	.392	0	—	0	96	-11		-1.0
1998	Ana A	9	4	.692	22	20	0	0-0	128.2	130	66	14	5	58-0	90	4.34	109	.263	.345	1-0-1	.000	0	96	6		0.7
1999	Ana A	5	11	.313	28	26	0	0-0	147.2	165	101	21	9	82-0	73	5.42	90	.281	.373	3	.333	1*	87	-11		-0.8
2000	Det A	7	5	.583	20	15	1	1-0	104	108	55	7	4	29-0	53	4.07	121	.263	.317	0	—	0	115	8		0.8
2001	Det A	14	9	.609	35	33	8-1	0-0	232	244	110	22	6	64-1	116	3.65	121	.271	.321	4	.000	-0*	98	17		1.6
2002	Det A	8	16	.333	32	30	3	0-0	189	238	134	23	12	67-3	98	5.52	79	.306	.366	2	.000	-0	88	-27		-2.7
2003	Det A	0	6	.000	42	0	0	2-2	89.2	95	57	11	3	34-4	49	4.72	93	.287	.343	0	—	0		-6		-0.4
	†Oak A	0	0	—	9	0	0	0-0	17.1	19	11	2	0	3-0	5	5.71	80	.271	.297	0	—	0		-2		-0.1
	Year	0	6	.000	51	0	0	2-2	107	114	68	13	3	37-4	54	4.88	90	.277	.336	0	—	0		-7		-0.5
2004	Ari N	3	7	.300	29	18	0	0-0	120.2	139	89	18	5	45-2	57	6.04	75	.287	.351	31-0-1	.129	-1	64	-18		-1.4
Total 9		59	76	.437	270	182	16-2	3-2	1319.2	1451	800	154	52	520-11	658	4.88	96	.280	.348	41-0-2	.122	-1	91	-35	181	-2.4

SPARKS, TULLY Thomas Frank B12.12.1874 Etna GA D7.15.1937 Anniston AL BR/TR/5-10/160 d9.15 Col Beloit

YEAR	TM LG	W	L	PCT	G	GS	CG-SHO	SV-BS	IP	H	R	HR	HB	BB-IB	SO	ERA	AERA	OAV	OOB	AB-HR-SH	AVG	PB	SUP	APR	DL	PW
1897	Phi N	0	1	.000	1	1	1	0	8	12	9	0	0	4	9	10.13	41	.343	.410	3	.000	-1	17	-4		-0.4
1899	Pit N	8	6	.571	28	17	8	0	170	189	101	1	10	82	53	3.86	99	.271	.360	62	.129	-2	98	-1		-0.2
1901	Mil A	7	17	.292	29	26	18	0	210	228	157	5	14	93	62	3.51	102	.273	.356	71-0-3	.169	-1	82	-9		-1.0
1902	NY N	4	9	.286	16	14	12	1	123	142	72	2	4	41	42	4.17	67	.289	.348	40-0-2	.150	-1	78	-14		-1.3
	Bos A	7	4	.438	17	15	15-1	0	142.2	151	83	4	7	40	37	3.47	103	.272	.329	52-0-1	.154	-1	67	0		-0.1
1903	Phi N	11	15	.423	28	28	27	0	248	248	109	3	8	56	88	2.72	120	.263	.310	92-0-3	.109	-5	78	13		0.6
1904	Phi N	7	16	.304	26	25	19-3	0	200.2	208	109	4	7	40	72	2.65	101	.260	.302	76	.105	-5	89	-5		-1.3
1905	Phi N	14	11	.560	34	26	20-3	1	259.2	217	86	2	9	73	98	2.18	134	.236	.298	94-0-3	.128	-2	139	22		1.5
1906	Phi N	19	16	.543	42	37	29-6	3	316.2	244	99	4	10	62	114	2.16	121	.211	.257	104-0-3	.154	0	87	20		2.1
1907	Phi N	22	8	.733	33	31	24-3	1	265	221	78	2	7	51	90	2.00	121	.228	.271	89-0-4	.034	-8	117	13		0.3
1908	Phi N	16	15	.516	33	31	24-2	2	263.1	251	98	3	8	51	85	2.60	93	.257	.300	77-0-11	.052	-5	94	-3		-1.1
1909	Phi N	6	11	.353	24	16	6-1	0	121.2	126	54	4	3	32	40	2.96	88	.280	.332	36-0-1	.139	-1	49	-5		-0.8
1910	Phi N	0	2	.000	3	3	0	0	15	22	12	2	2	2	4	6.00	52	.324	.361	5	.000	-1	95	-4		-0.5
Total 12		121	137	.469	314	270	203-19	8	2343.2	2250	1067	33	87	630	780	2.82	104	.254	.310	801-0-31	.115	-32	90	23		-2.2

SPARMA, JOE Joseph Blase B2.4.1942 Massillon OH D5.14.1986 Columbus OH BR/TR/6-0/195* d5.20 Col Ohio St.

YEAR	TM LG	W	L	PCT	G	GS	CG-SHO	SV-BS	IP	H	R	HR	HB	BB-IB	SO	ERA	AERA	OAV	OOB	AB-HR-SH	AVG	PB	SUP	APR	DL	PW
1964	Det A	5	6	.455	21	11	3-2	0	84	62	33	4	3	45-1	71	3.00	122	.207	.313	5	.160	1*	93	5		0.8
1965	Det A	13	8	.619	30	28	6	0	167	142	69	13	3	75-5	127	3.18	109	.228	.312	52-0-4	.135	-0	96	4		0.4
1966	Det A	2	7	.222	29	13	0	0	91.2	103	57	14	3	52-0	51	5.30	66	.248	.382	23-0-2	.217	1	109	-17		-1.6
1967	Det A	16	9	.640	37	37	11-5	0	217.2	186	103	20	8	85-2	153	3.76	87	.227	.305	74-0-13	.054	-5	132	-13		-2.1
1968	†Det A	10	10	.500	34	31	7-1	0	182.1	169	81	14	7	77-3	110	3.70	81	.246	.326	60-0-6	.133	-1	119	-13		-1.7
1969	Det A	6	8	.429	24	16	3-2	0-0	92.2	78	56	5	1	77-1	41	4.76	79	.231	.373	29-0-3	.138	-1	84	-10		-1.5
1970	Mon N	0	4	.000	9	6	1	0-0	29.1	34	25	7	2	25-3	23	7.06	59	.296	.421	6-0-1	.000	-0	47	-9		-1.1
Total 7		52	52	.500	183	142	31-10	0-0	864.2	774	423	77	27	436-15	586	3.94	86	.239	.332	269-0-29	.119	-6	107	-53		-6.8

SPECK, CLIFF Robert Clifford B8.8.1956 Portland OR BR/TR/6-4/196 [NYN74 1/17] d7.30 [DL 1985 Chi A 42]

YEAR	TM LG	W	L	PCT	G	GS	CG-SHO	SV-BS	IP	H	R	HR	HB	BB-IB	SO	ERA	AERA	OAV	OOB	AB-HR-SH	AVG	PB	SUP	APR	DL	PW
1986	Atl N	2	1	.667	12	1	0	0	28.1	25	13	1	2	11-4	24	4.13	96	.238	.336	3-0-1	.000	-0	68	0		0.0

SPEECE, BY Byron Franklin B1.6.1897 West Baden IN D9.29.1974 Elgin OR BR/TR/5-11/170 d4.21

YEAR	TM LG	W	L	PCT	G	GS	CG-SHO	SV-BS	IP	H	R	HR	HB	BB-IB	SO	ERA	AERA	OAV	OOB	AB-HR-SH	AVG	PB	SUP	APR	DL	PW
1924	†Was A	2	1	.667	21	1	0	0	54.1	60	30	0	2	27	15	2.65	152	.303	.392	20	.150	-1	21	4		0.2
1925	Cle A	3	5	.375	28	3	3	1	90.1	106	48	0	3	28	26	4.28	103	.297	.353	31	.161	-2	51	3		0.1
1926	Cle A	0	0	—	2	0	0	0	3	1	0	0	0	2	0	3.00	—	.125	.300	0	—	0		0		0.1
1930	Phi N	0	0	—	11	0	0	0	19.2	41	30	1	0	4	9	13.27	41	.432	.455	3	.333	0		-14		-0.6
Total 4		5	6	.455	62	4	3	1	167.1	208	109	1	5	61	51	4.73	93	.316	.378	54	.167	-2	43	-6		-0.2

SPEER, FLOYD Floyd Vernie B1.27.1913 Booneville AR D3.22.1969 Little Rock AR BR/TR/6-0/180 d4.25

YEAR	TM LG	W	L	PCT	G	GS	CG-SHO	SV-BS	IP	H	R	HR	HB	BB-IB	SO	ERA	AERA	OAV	OOB	AB-HR-SH	AVG	PB	SUP	APR	DL	PW
1943	Chi A	0	0	—	2	0	0	0	1.1	1	1	0	0	2	1	9.00	37	.250	.500	0	—	0		-1		0.0
1944	Chi A	0	0	—	2	0	0	0	2	4	2	0	0	2	1	9.00	38	.500	.500	0	—	0		-1		-0.1
Total 2		0	0	—	4	0	0	0	3	5	3	0	0	4	2	9.00	38	.417	.500	0	—	0		-2		-0.1

SPEER, KID George Nathan B6.16.1886 Corning MO D1.13.1946 Edmonton AL, Can. BL/TL/5-9/152 d4.24

YEAR	TM LG	W	L	PCT	G	GS	CG-SHO	SV-BS	IP	H	R	HR	HB	BB-IB	SO	ERA	AERA	OAV	OOB	AB-HR-SH	AVG	PB	SUP	APR	DL	PW
1909	Det A	4	4	.500	12	8	4	1	76.1	88	39	2	4	13	12	2.83	89	.293	.331	25	.120	-0*	133	-5		-0.5

SPEIER, JUSTIN Justin James B11.6.1973 Daly City CA BR/TR/6-4/205* [ChiN95 55/1452] d5.27 f-Chris Col Nicholls St.

YEAR	TM LG	W	L	PCT	G	GS	CG-SHO	SV-BS	IP	H	R	HR	HB	BB-IB	SO	ERA	AERA	OAV	OOB	AB-HR-SH	AVG	PB	SUP	APR	DL	PW
1998	Chi N	0	0	—	1	0	0	0-0	1.1	2	2	0	0	1-0	2	13.50	33	.333	.429	0	—	0		-1		-0.1
	Fla N	0	3	.000	18	0	0	0-1	19.1	25	18	7	0	12-1	15	8.38	48	.325	.411	0	—	0		-9		-1.2
	Year	0	3	.000	19	0	0	0-1	20.2	27	20	7	0	13-1	17	8.71	47	.325	.412	0	—	0		-10		-1.3
1999	Atl N	0	0	—	19	0	0	0-0	28.2	28	18	8	0	13-1	22	5.65	79	.248	.323	3	.333	0		-3		-0.1
2000	Cle A	5	2	.714	47	0	0	0-1	68.1	57	25	8	4	28-3	69	3.29	152	.226	.309	2	.500	0		12		1.1

YEAR	TM LG	W	L	PCT	G	GS	CG-SHO	SV-BS	IP	H	R	HR	HB	BB-IB	SO	ERA	AERA	OAV	OOB	AB-HR-SH	AVG	PB	SUP	APR	DL	PW
2001	Cle A	2	0	1.000	12	0	0	0-0	20.2	24	16	5	3	8-0	15	6.97	66	.293	.365	0	—	0		-5		-0.4
	Col N	4	3	.571	42	0	0	0-1	56	47	24	8	5	12-3	47	3.70	144	.229	.283	7	.000	-1		9		0.8
2002	Col N	5	1	.833	63	0	0	1-3	62.1	51	31	9	3	19-4	47	4.33	109	.216	.282	3	.333	0		3	36	0.2
2003	Col N	3	1	.750	72	0	0	9-3	73.1	73	37	11	7	23-6	66	4.05	121	.257	.324	1	.000	-0		5		0.3
2004	Tor A	3	8	.273	62	0	0	7-4	69	61	32	8	5	25-6	52	3.91	125	.239	.316	1	.000	0		7	28	1.0
2005	Tor A	3	2	.600	65	0	0	0-4	66.2	48	20	10	3	15-2	56	2.57	180	.198	.254	0	—	0		15		0.9
Total	8	25	20	.556	401	0	0	17-17	465.2	416	225	75	30	156-26	391	4.14	117	.237	.307	17	.176	-0		33	64	2.5

SPEIER, RYAN Ryan Andrew B7.24.1979 Frankfort KY BR/TR/6-7/200 d4.4 Col Radford

2005	Col N	2	1	.667	22	0	0	0-1	24.2	26	12	0	1	13-0	10	3.65	130	.277	.367	2	.000	-0		2		0.2

SPENCER, HACK Fred Calvin B4.25.1885 St.Cloud MN D2.5.1969 St.Anthony MN BR/TR/5-7/172 d4.18

1912	StL A	0	0	—	1	0	0	0	1.2	2	2	0	0	0	0	0.00	—	.286	.286	0	—	0		0		0.0

SPENCER, GEORGE George Elwell B7.7.1926 Columbus OH BR/TR/6-1/215* d8.17 Col Ohio St.

1950	NY N	1	0	1.000	10	1	1	0	25.1	12	7	3	0	7	5	2.49	165	.141	.207	4	.000	-1	108	5		0.2
1951	†NY N	10	4	.714	57	4	2	6	132	125	62	21	1	56	36	3.75	104	.254	.332	32-0-3	.125	-1	135	4		0.3
1952	NY N	3	5	.375	35	4	0	3	60	57	39	13	3	21	27	5.55	67	.251	.323	10	.200	0	138	-11		-1.4
1953	NY N	0	0	—	1	0	0	0	2.1	3	2	0	0	2	1	7.71	56	.300	.417	0	—	0		-1		0.0
1954	NY N	1	0	1.000	6	0	0	0	12.1	9	5	1	0	8	4	3.65	111	.209	.333	3	.000	-0		1		0.1
1955	NY N	0	0	—	1	0	0	0	1.2	1	1	1	0	3-0	1	5.40	75	.167	.444	0	—	0		0		0.0
1958	Det A	1	0	1.000	7	0	0	0	10	11	4	0	0	4-0	5	2.70	149	.289	.349	0	—	0		1		0.1
1960	Det A	0	1	.000	5	0	0	0	7.2	10	3	1	0	5-1	4	3.52	112	.323	.417	1	.000	-0		1		0.0
Total	8	16	10	.615	122	9	3	9	251.1	228	123	40	4	106-1	82	4.05	96	.245	.324	50-0-3	.120	-2	131			-0.7

SPENCER, GLENN Glenn Edward B9.11.1905 Corning NY D12.30.1958 Binghamton NY BR/TR/5-11/155 d4.11

1928	Pit N	0	0	—	2	0	0	0	5.2	4	2	0	0	3	2	1.59	256	.200	.304	1	.000	-0		1		0.0
1930	Pit N	8	9	.471	41	11	5	4	156.2	185	110	16	2	63	60	5.40	92	.305	.372	53-0-1	.113	-4	102	-7		-1.1
1931	Pit N	11	12	.478	38	18	11-1	5	186.2	180	83	6	5	65	51	3.42	112	.260	.328	52-0-10	.096	-3	73	10		0.9
1932	Pit N	4	8	.333	39	13	5-1	1	137.2	167	104	10	3	44	35	4.97	77	.288	.341	37-0-3	.162	-1	104	-22		-1.8
1933	NY N	0	2	.000	17	3	1	0	47.1	52	33	3	1	26	14	5.13	63	.284	.376	12	.167	-0	95	-11		-0.6
Total	5	23	31	.426	139	45	22-2	8	534	588	333	37	11	201	162	4.53	91	.282	.349	155-0-14	.123	-9	90	-29		-2.6

SPENCER, SEAN Sean James B5.29.1975 Seattle WA BL/TL/5-11/185* [SeaA96 40/1197] d5.6 Col Washington

1999	Sea A	0	0	—	2	0	0	0-0	1.2	5	4	3	0	3-0	2	21.60	22	.556	.667	0	—	0		-3		-0.1
2000	Mon N	0	0	—	8	0	0	0-0	6.2	7	4	2	0	3-0	6	5.40	87	.292	.357	0	—	0		0		0.0
Total	2	0	0	—	10	0	0	0-0	8.1	12	8	2	0	6-0	8	8.64	55	.364	.450	0	—	0		-3		-0.1

SPENCER, STAN Stanley Roger B8.2.1968 Vancouver WA BR/TR/6-4/205(205-223) [MonN90 1/35] d8.27 Col Stanford

1998	SD N	1	0	1.000	6	5	0	0-0	30.2	29	16	5	1	4-0	31	4.70	85	.244	.274	9-0-3	.111	-0	148	-2		-0.1
1999	SD N	0	7	.000	9	8	0	0-0	38.1	56	44	11	1	11-1	36	9.16	47	.335	.380	10-0-1	.000	-1	54	-23		-3.0
2000	SD N	2	2	.500	8	8	0	0-0	49.2	44	22	7	2	19-1	40	3.26	137	.239	.316	12-0-2	.333	1*	80	6	103	0.6
Total	3	3	9	.250	23	21	0	0-0	118.2	129	82	23	4	34-2	107	5.54	77	.274	.328	31-0-6	.161	1	85	-19	103	-2.5

SPICER, BOB Robert Oberton B4.11.1925 Richmond VA BL/TR/5-10/173* d4.17

1955	KC A	0	0	—	2	0	0	0	2.2	9	10	2	1	4-0	2	33.75	12	.529	.636	1	.000	-0		-8		-0.4
1956	KC A	0	0	—	2	0	0	0	2.1	6	5	1	1	1-0	0	19.29	22	.545	.615	0	—	0		-3		-0.2
Total	2	0	0	—	4	0	0	0	5	15	15	3	2	5-0	2	27.00	16	.536	.629	1	.000	-0		-11		-0.6

SPILLNER, DAN Daniel Ray B11.27.1951 Casper WY BR/TR/6-1/190* [SDN70 2/25] d5.21

1974	SD N	9	11	.450	30	25	5-2	0-0	148	153	78	15	0	70-4	95	4.01	89	.267	.344	43-0-5	.023	-4	79	-9		-1.6
1975	SD N	5	13	.278	37	25	3	1-0	166.2	194	93	14	2	63-7	104	4.27	82	.293	.353	45-0-6	.133	1	82	-14		-1.3
1976	SD N	2	11	.154	32	14	0	0-1	106.2	120	70	11	0	55-8	57	5.06	65	.291	.371	25	.040	-1*	78	-23	62	-2.6
1977	SD N	7	6	.538	76	0	0	6-5	123	130	61	12	1	60-13	74	3.73	96	.280	.359	17	.118	1		-3		-0.4
1978	SD N	1	0	1.000	17	0	0	0-1	25.2	32	15	2	0	7-1	16	4.56	74	.317	.368	0-0-1	—	0		-4		-0.2
	Cle A	3	1	.750	36	0	0	3-2	56.1	54	26	2	1	21-3	48	3.67	103	.254	.323	0	—	0		1		0.0
1979	Cle A	9	5	.643	49	13	3	1-2	157.2	153	82	16	3	64-4	97	4.62	93	.256	.327	0	—	0	117	-2		-0.2
1980	Cle A	16	11	.593	34	30	7-1	0-0	194.1	225	122	23	3	74-2	100	5.28	78	.288	.350	0	—	0	111	-23		-2.9
1981	Cle A	4	4	.500	32	5	1	7-1	97.1	86	41	3	0	39-3	59	3.14	117	.240	.309	0	—	0	97	4		0.4
1982	Cle A	12	10	.545	65	0	0	21-10	133.2	117	44	9	0	45-7	90	2.49	167	.235	.295	0	—	0		23		4.2
1983	Cle A	2	9	.182	60	0	0	8-5	92.1	117	54	7	2	38-9	48	5.07	84	.315	.376	0	—	0		-6		-0.8
1984	Cle A	0	5	.000	14	8	0	1-0	51	70	36	3	0	22-2	23	5.65	73	.332	.385	0	—	0	74	-8		-0.7
	Chi A	1	0	1.000	22	0	0	1-1	48.1	51	25	7	1	14-0	26	4.10	102	.276	.328	0	—	0*		0		0.0
	Year	1	5	.167	36	8	0	2-1	99.1	121	61	10	1	36-2	49	4.89	85	.306	.359	0	—	0*	73	-9		-0.7
1985	Chi A	4	3	.571	52	3	0	1-1	91.2	83	39	10	0	33-2	41	3.44	127	.245	.309	0	—	0*	112	9		0.5
Total	12	75	89	.457	556	123	19-3	50-29	1492.2	1585	786	134	13	605-65	878	4.21	92	.275	.342	130-0-12	.077	-3	92	-56	62	-5.6

SPINKS, SCIPIO Scipio Ronald B7.12.1947 Chicago IL BR/TR/6-1/185* d9.16 Col Kennedy-King (IL) JC

1969	Hou N	0	0	—	1	0	0	0-0	2	1	1	0	0	2	0	4.00	—	.143	.250	0	—	0		0		0.0
1970	Hou N	0	1	.000	5	2	0	0-0	13.2	17	15	5	0	9-0	6	9.88	39	.293	.388	3	.000	-0*	127	-9		-0.6
1971	Hou N	1	0	1.000	5	3	1	0-0	29.1	22	12	2	1	13-0	26	3.68	91	.210	.303	9	.222	0	132	0		0.0
1972	StL N	5	5	.500	16	16	6	0-0	118	96	39	5	2	59-2	93	2.67	128	.221	.317	42-0-2	.167	-1*	93	10	92	0.8
1973	StL N	1	5	.167	8	6	0	0-0	38.2	39	25	4	0	25-2	25	4.89	75	.269	.374	11-1-1	.182	1	66	-6	96	-0.6
Total	5	7	11	.389	35	29	7	0-0	201.2	175	92	16	3	107-4	154	3.70	94	.234	.345	65-1-3	.169	0	92	-5	188	-0.2

SPLITTORFF, PAUL Paul William B10.8.1946 Evansville IN BL/TL/6-3/210(195-210) [KCA68 25/575] d9.23 Col Morningside

1970	KC A	0	1	.000	2	1	0	0-0	8.2	16	9	1	0	5-0	10	7.27	51	.390	.457	2	.500	0	0	-4		-0.3
1971	KC A	8	9	.471	22	22	6-3	0-0	144.1	129	49	4	4	35-1	80	2.68	128	.243	.292	48-0-1	.104	-1	78	12		1.3
1972	KC A	12	12	.500	35	33	12-2	0-1	216	189	81	11	4	67-2	140	3.13	97	.241	.301	71-0-7	.225	4	132	-1		0.5
1973	KC A	20	11	.645	38	38	12-3	0-0	262	279	135	19	5	78-7	110	3.98	103	.272	.325	0	—	0	123	1		0.1
1974	KC A	13	19	.406	36	36	8-1	0-0	226	252	122	23	1	75-8	90	4.10	93	.285	.338	0	—	0*	78	-8		-1.0
1975	KC A	9	10	.474	35	23	6-3	1-0	159	156	75	10	1	56-10	76	3.17	122	.255	.316	0	—	0	90	7		1.0
1976	†KC A	11	8	.579	26	23	5-1	0-0	158.2	169	79	8	3	59-0	59	3.97	88	.277	.341	0	—	0	106	-7	38	-0.7
1977	†KC A	16	6	**.727**	37	37	6-2	0-0	229	243	104	11	2	83-2	99	3.69	109	.278	.340	0	—	0	122	10		0.9
1978	†KC A	19	13	.594	39	38	13-2	0-0	262	244	113	22	3	60-2	76	3.40	113	.247	.290	0	—	0	112	13		1.5
1979	KC A	15	17	.469	36	35	11	0-0	240	248	137	25	5	77-1	77	4.24	101	.268	.324	0	—	0	105	-3		0.0
1980	†KC A	14	11	.560	34	33	4	0-0	204	236	101	17	1	43-1	53	4.15	98	.296	.329	0	—	0	103	-1		0.0
1981	KC A	5	5	.500	21	15	1	0-0	99	111	48	12	1	23-4	48	4.36	83	.294	.331	0	—	0	116	-6		-0.5
1982	KC A	10	10	.500	29	28	0	0-0	162	166	83	14	3	51-0	74	4.28	96	.266	.328	0	—	0	111	-3		-0.3
1983	KC A	13	8	.619	27	27	4	0-0	156	159	77	9	1	52-2	61	3.63	113	.262	.319	0	—	0	98	5		0.7
1984	KC A	1	3	.250	12	3	0	0-0	28	47	30	3	0	10-0	4	7.71	52	.376	.413	0	—	0	74	-13		-1.5
Total	15	166	143	.537	429	392	88-17	1-1	2554.2	2644	1243	192	34	780-41	1057	3.81	101	.270	.323	121-0-8	.182	3	106	2	38	1.3

SPOLJARIC, PAUL Paul Nikola B9.24.1970 Kelowna BC, Can. BR/TL/6-3/210* d4.6

1994	Tor A	2	1	.000	2	1	0	0-0	2.1	5	10	3	0	9-1	2	38.57	13	.417	.667	0	—	0	75	-8		-1.1
1996	Tor A	2	2	.500	28	0	0	1-0	38	30	17	6	2	19-1	38	3.08	128	.214	.315	0	—	0		7	24	0.7
1997	Tor A	0	3	.000	37	0	0	3-0	48	37	17	3	2	21-4	43	3.19	144	.215	.305	1	.000	-0		8	17	0.3
	†Sea A	0	0	—	20	0	0	0-2	22.2	24	13	1	1	15-2	27	4.76	95	.276	.388	0	—	0		-1		0.0
	Year	0	3	.000	57	0	0	3-2	70.2	61	30	4	3	36-6	70	3.69	124	.236	.333	1	.000	-0		7		0.6
1998	Sea A	4	6	.400	53	6	0	0-2	83.1	85	67	14	1	55-3	89	6.48	72	.263	.369	0	—	0	83	-17		-1.7
1999	Phi N	0	3	.000	5	3	0	0-0	11.1	23	24	1	1	7-0	10	15.09	31	.426	.492	2-0-2	.000	0	72	-14		-2.2
	KC A	2	2	.500	37	2	0	0-1	62	62	41	9	2	32-2	63	4.65	106	.258	.347	0	—	0	76	-1		0.0
2000	KC A	0	0	—	13	0	0	0-0	9.2	9	7	4	0	5-0	6	6.52	80	.265	.359	0	—	0		-1	23	0.0
Total	6	8	17	.320	195	12	0	4-5	277.1	275	196	41	9	163-13	278	5.52	87	.259	.359	3-0-2	.000	-0	78	-27	64	-0.2

SPONGBERG, KARL Karl Gustave B5.21.1884 Idaho Falls ID D7.21.1938 Los Angeles CA BR/TR/6-2/208 d8.1

1908	Chi N	0	0	—	1	0	0	0	7	9	7	1	2	6	4	9.00	26	.321	.472	3	.667	1		-4		-0.1

YEAR	TM LG	W	L	PCT	G	GS	CG-SHO	SV-BS	IP	H	R	HR	HB	BB-IB	SO	ERA	AERA	OAV	OOB	AB-HR-SH	AVG	PB	SUP	APR	DL	PW

SPOONER, KARL
Karl Benjamin B6.23.1931 Oriskany Falls NY D4.10.1984 Vero Beach FL BR/TL/6-0/185* d9.22

YEAR	TM LG	W	L	PCT	G	GS	CG-SHO	SV-BS	IP	H	R	HR	HB	BB-IB	SO	ERA	AERA	OAV	OOB	AB-HR-SH	AVG	PB	SUP	APR	DL	PW
1954	Bro N	2	0	1.000	2	2	2-2	0	18	7	0	0	0	6	27	0.00	—	.113	.191	6	.167	0	44	8		1.1
1955	†Bro N	8	6	.571	29	14	2-1	2	98.2	79	50	5	5	41-1	78	3.65	111	.215	.300	28-0-2	.286	3	110	3		0.7
Total	2	10	6	.625	31	16	4-3	2	116.2	86	50	5	5	47-1	105	3.09		.200	.285	34-0-2	.265	3	101	11		1.8

SPOONEYBARGER, TIM
Timothy Floyd B10.21.1979 San Diego CA BR/TR/6-3/190* [AtlN98 29/881] d9.5 Col Okaloosa-Walton (FL) CC [DL 2004 Fla N 183, 2005 Fla N 183]

YEAR	TM LG	W	L	PCT	G	GS	CG-SHO	SV-BS	IP	H	R	HR	HB	BB-IB	SO	ERA	AERA	OAV	OOB	AB-HR-SH	AVG	PB	SUP	APR	DL	PW
2001	Atl N	0	1	.000	4	0	0	0-0	4	5	1	0	0		3	2.25	192	.313	.368	0		0		1		0.2
2002	Atl N	1	0	1.000	51	0	0	1-0	51.1	38	16	4	2	26-5	33	2.63	154	.207	.310	1		-0		8		0.4
2003	Fla N	1	2	.333	33	0	0	0-1	42	27	21	1	1	11-0	32	4.07	101	.190	.248	1	.000	-0		0		0.0
Total	3	2	3	.400	88	0	0	1-1	97.1	70	38	5	3	39-6	68	3.24	126	.205	.288	4	.000	-0		9	366	0.6

SPRADLIN, JERRY
Jerry Carl B6.14.1967 Fullerton CA BB/TR/6-7/240(230-260) [CinN88 19/488] d7.2 Col Fullerton (CA) JC

YEAR	TM LG	W	L	PCT	G	GS	CG-SHO	SV-BS	IP	H	R	HR	HB	BB-IB	SO	ERA	AERA	OAV	OOB	AB-HR-SH	AVG	PB	SUP	APR	DL	PW
1993	Cin N	2	1	.667	37	0	0	2-1	49	44	20	4	0	9-0	24	3.49	116	.249	.279	2	.000	-0		3		0.1
1994	Cin N	0	0	—	6	0	0	0-0	8	12	11	2	0	2-0	4	10.13	41	.353	.368	0	—	0		-6		-0.3
1996	Cin N	0	0	—	1	0	0	0-0	0.1	0	0	0	0	0-0	0	0.00	—	.000	.000	0	—	0		0		0.0
1997	Phi N	4	8	.333	76	0	0	1-4	81.2	86	45	9	1	27-3	67	4.74	86	.274	.331	1	.000	-0		-4		-0.6
1998	Phi N	4	4	.500	69	0	0	1-3	81.2	63	34	9	2	20-1	76	3.53	123	.216	.270	1	1.000	1		7		0.7
1999	Cle A	0	0	—	4	0	0	0-0	3	6	6	1	0	3-0	2	18.00	28	.400	.500	0	—	0		-4		-0.2
	SF N	3	1	.750	59	0	0	0-1	58	59	31	4	10	29-6	52	4.19	102	.259	.367	1	.000	-0		0		-0.1
2000	KC A	4	4	.500	50	0	0	7-4	75	81	49	9	3	27-2	54	5.52	95	.283	.350	0	—	0		-2		-0.3
	Chi N	0	0	1.000	8	0	0	0-0	15	20	15	2	1	5-1	13	8.40	54	.328	.377	1	.000	-0		-0		-0.4
Total	7	17	19	.472	310	1	0	11-13	371.2	371	211	40	17	122-13	292	4.75	94	.264	.327	6	.167	0	80	-13		-1.1

SPRAGINS, HOMER
Homer Franklin B11.9.1920 Grenada MS D12.10.2002 Minter City MS BR/TR/6-1/190 d9.13 Col Mississippi St.

YEAR	TM LG	W	L	PCT	G	GS	CG-SHO	SV-BS	IP	H	R	HR	HB	BB-IB	SO	ERA	AERA	OAV	OOB	AB-HR-SH	AVG	PB	SUP	APR	DL	PW
1947	Phi N	0	0	—	4	0	0	0-0	5.1	3	4	0	0	3-0	3	6.75	59	.158	.273	0	—			-1		-0.1

SPRAGUE, CHARLIE
Charles Wellington B10.10.1864 Cleveland OH D12.31.1912 Des Moines IA BL/TL/5-11/150 d9.17 ▲

YEAR	TM LG	W	L	PCT	G	GS	CG-SHO	SV-BS	IP	H	R	HR	HB	BB-IB	SO	ERA	AERA	OAV	OOB	AB-HR-SH	AVG	PB	SUP	APR	DL	PW
1887	Chi N	1	0	1.000	3	3	2	0	22	24	16	1	4	13	9	4.91	92	.276	.394	13	.154	-1	82	0		-0.1
1889	Cle N	2	2	.000	2	2	2	0	17	27	31	0	2	10	9	8.47	48	.351	.438	7	.143	-0	117	-11		-0.8
1890	Tol AA	9	5	.643	19	12	9	0	122.2	111	83	0	18	78	59	3.89	102	.234	.363	199-1	.236	3*	145	0		0.1
Total	3	10	7	.588	24	17	13	0	161.2	162	130	1	24	101	76	4.51	89	.254	.376	219-1	.228	1	130	-11		-0.8

SPRAGUE, ED
Edward Nelson Sr. B9.16.1945 Boston MA BR/TR/6-4/195* d4.10 s-Ed

YEAR	TM LG	W	L	PCT	G	GS	CG-SHO	SV-BS	IP	H	R	HR	HB	BB-IB	SO	ERA	AERA	OAV	OOB	AB-HR-SH	AVG	PB	SUP	APR	DL	PW
1968	Oak A	3	4	.429	47	0	0	4	68.2	51	29	5	2	34-5	34	3.28	86	.209	.309	7	.000	-1	62	-4		-0.5
1969	Oak A	1	1	.500	27	0	0	2-1	46.1	47	24	4	2	31-6	20	4.47	77	.267	.383	5-0-2	.200	0		-5		-0.1
1971	Cin N	1	0	1.000	7	0	0	0-1	11	8	2	0	0	1-0	7	0.00	—	.195	.209	1	.000	0		3		0.3
1972	Cin N	3	3	.500	33	1	0	0-0	56.2	55	33	6	3	26-3	25	4.13	79	.261	.347	7	.000	-1	82	-8		-0.9
1973	Cin N	1	3	.250	28	0	0	1-0	38.2	35	22	3	2	22-7	19	5.12	67	.246	.353	2-0-1	.000	-0		-7		-0.7
	StL N	0	0	—	8	0	0	0-1	8	8	2	1	0	4-0	2	2.25	163	.276	.353	0		0		1		0.1
	Year	1	3	.250	36	0	0	1-1	46.2	43	24	4	2	26-7	21	4.63	75	.251	.353	2-0-1	.000	0		-5		-0.6
	Mil A	1	0	1.000	7	0	0	0-0	9.2	13	11	0	2	14-5	3	9.31	41	.317	.492	0		0		-6		-0.7
1974	Mil A	7	2	.778	20	10	3	0-0	94	94	32	3	4	31-0	25	2.39	152	.266	.327	0		0	160	11	47	1.0
1975	Mil A	1	7	.125	18	11	0	0-0	67.1	81	46	5	2	40-3	21	4.68	82	.297	.389	0		0	87	-9	64	-1.0
1976	Mil A	0	0	—	3	0	0	0-0	7.2	14	7	0	0	3-0	5	7.04	50	.438	.472	0		0		-3	41	-0.6
Total	8	17	23	.425	198	23	3	9-5	408	406	208	27	17	206-30	188	3.84	89	.263	.353	22-0-3	.045	-1	126	-27	152	-3.1

SPRING, JACK
Jack Russell B3.11.1933 Spokane WA BR/TL/6-1/180(167-182) d4.16 Col Washington St.

YEAR	TM LG	W	L	PCT	G	GS	CG-SHO	SV-BS	IP	H	R	HR	HB	BB-IB	SO	ERA	AERA	OAV	OOB	AB-HR-SH	AVG	PB	SUP	APR	DL	PW
1955	Phi N	0	1	.000	2	0	0	0	2.2	2	2	2	0	1-0	2	6.75	59	.200	.273	1	.000	-0		-1		-0.2
1957	Bos A	0	0	—	1	0	0	0	1	1	0	0	0	0-0	2	0.00	—	.000	.000	0		0		0		0.0
1958	Was A	0	0	—	3	1	0	0	7	16	11	1	0	7-3	1	14.14	27	.457	.535	2	.000	-0	259	-8		-0.4
1961	LA A	3	0	1.000	18	4	0	0	38	35	19	4	3	15-2	27	4.26	106	.243	.323	8-0-3	.000	-1	123	2		-0.1
1962	LA A	4	2	.667	57	0	0	6	65	66	32	7	2	30-10	31	4.02	96	.270	.353	11-0-1	.091	-0		0		-0.1
1963	LA A	3	0	1.000	45	0	0	2	38.1	40	18	3	0	9-0	13	3.05	112	.268	.310	3	.333	-1		0		0.1
1964	LA A	1	0	1.000	6	0	0	0	3.1	3	1	1	0	3-1	0	2.70	122	.273	.429	0		0		0		0.1
	Chi N	0	0	—	7	0	0	0	6	4	0	0	0	2-0	1	6.00	62	.200	.261	0		0		-2		-0.1
	StL N	0	0	—	2	0	0	0	3	8	9	1	0	1-1	0	3.00	127	.471	.500	0		0		-3		-0.1
	Year	0	0	—	9	0	0	0	9	12	14	1	0	3-1	1	4.75	93	.324	.366	0		0		-5		-0.2
1965	Cle A	1	2	.333	14	0	0	0	21.2	21	9	2	0	10-1	9	3.74	93	.259	.337	3-0-1	.333	0		0		0.0
Total	8	12	5	.706	155	5	0	8	186	195	106	21	5	78-18	86	4.26	90	.273	.346	28-0-5	.107	-1	167	-12		-0.7

SPRINGER, BRAD
Bradford Louis B5.9.1904 Detroit MI D1.4.1970 Birmingham MI BL/TL/6-0/155 d5.1

YEAR	TM LG	W	L	PCT	G	GS	CG-SHO	SV-BS	IP	H	R	HR	HB	BB-IB	SO	ERA	AERA	OAV	OOB	AB-HR-SH	AVG	PB	SUP	APR	DL	PW
1925	StL N	0	0	—	2	0	0	0	3	1	2	0	0	7	0	3.00	156	.200	.667	0		0		0		0.0
1926	Cin N	0	0	—	1	0	0	0	1.1	2	3	0	1	2	1	6.75	55	.286	.500	1	.000	-0		-1		-0.1
Total	2	0	0	—	3	0	0	0	4.1	3	5	0	2	9	1	4.15	105	.250	.591	1	.000	-0		-1		-0.1

SPRINGER, DENNIS
Dennis Leroy B2.12.1965 Fresno CA BR/TR/5-10/185* [LAN87 21/534] d9.13 Col Cal St.-Fresno

YEAR	TM LG	W	L	PCT	G	GS	CG-SHO	SV-BS	IP	H	R	HR	HB	BB-IB	SO	ERA	AERA	OAV	OOB	AB-HR-SH	AVG	PB	SUP	APR	DL	PW
1995	Phi N	0	3	.000	4	4	0	0-0	22.1	21	15	3	1	9-1	15	4.84	87	.256	.337	8	.125	-0	75	-2		-0.3
1996	Cal A	5	6	.455	20	15	2-1	0-0	94.2	91	65	24	6	43-0	64	5.51	92	.251	.339	0	—	0	104	-5		-0.5
1997	Ana A	9	9	.500	32	28	3-1	0-0	194.2	199	118	32	10	73-0	75	5.18	89	.267	.335	3	.000	-0	97	-10		-0.9
1998	TB A	3	11	.214	29	17	1	0-0	115.2	120	77	21	12	60-1	46	5.45	88	.271	.372	1	.000	-0	59	-9		-1.0
1999	Fla N	6	16	.273	38	29	3-2	1-0	196.1	231	121	23	7	64-4	83	4.86	90	.303	.358	50-0-3	.120	-2	83	-13		-1.4
2000	NY N	0	0	—	2	2	0	0-0	11.1	20	11	2	1	5-0	5	8.74	50	.377	.441	4	.000	-0	84	-5		-0.4
2001	LA N	1	1	.500	4	3	0	0-0	19	19	7	3	3	2-0	7	3.32	124	.275	.324	6-0-1	.000	-1	119	2		0.1
2002	LA N	1	1	.500	1	0	0	0-0	4	4	3	0	1	0-0	1	6.75	58	.200	.429	0	—	0		0		-0.1
Total	8	24	48	.333	130	98	9-4	1-0	655.1	702	415	108	40	258-6	296	5.18	89	.278	.351	72-0-4	.097	-4	87	-42		-4.5

SPRINGER, ED
Edward H. B2.9.1861 CA D4.24.1926 Los Angeles Co. CA 6-2/187 d7.12

YEAR	TM LG	W	L	PCT	G	GS	CG-SHO	SV-BS	IP	H	R	HR	HB	BB-IB	SO	ERA	AERA	OAV	OOB	AB-HR-SH	AVG	PB	SUP	APR	DL	PW
1889	Lou AA	0	1	.000	1	1	1	0	5	8	8	0	2	2	1	9.00	43	.348	.444	2	.000	-0	16	-3		-0.4

SPRINGER, RUSS
Russell Paul B11.7.1968 Alexandria LA BR/TR/6-4/205(195-215) [NYA89 7/181] d4.17 Col Louisiana St.

YEAR	TM LG	W	L	PCT	G	GS	CG-SHO	SV-BS	IP	H	R	HR	HB	BB-IB	SO	ERA	AERA	OAV	OOB	AB-HR-SH	AVG	PB	SUP	APR	DL	PW
1992	NY A	0	0	—	14	0	0	0	16	18	11	0	1	10-0	12	6.19	64	.281	.387	0	—	0		-3		-0.2
1993	Cal A	1	6	.143	14	9	1	0-0	60	73	48	11	3	32-1	31	7.20	63	.303	.390	0	—	0	90	-15	63	-1.5
1994	Cal A	2	2	.500	18	5	0	2-1	45.2	53	28	9	0	14-0	28	5.52	89	.291	.340	0	—	0	124	-2		-0.2
1995	Cal A	1	2	.333	19	6	0	0-0	51.2	60	37	11	5	25-1	31	6.10	77	.290	.380	0	—	0	115	-8		-0.4
	Phi N	0	0	—	14	0	0	0-0	26.2	22	11	2	2	10-3	32	3.71	114	.227	.306	1-0-1	.000	-0		2		0.1
1996	Phi N	3	10	.231	51	7	0	0-0	96.2	106	60	12	1	38-6	94	4.66	93	.272	.336	17-0-2	.059	-1	78	-5		-0.8
1997	†Hou N	3	3	.500	54	0	0	3-4	55.1	48	28	4	4	27-2	74	4.23	95	.232	.329	1	.000	-0		-1	23	0.1
1998	Ari N	4	3	.571	26	0	0	0-3	32.2	29	16	4	1	14-1	37	4.13	104	.232	.314	1	.000	-0		1		0.1
	Atl N	1	1	.500	22	0	0	0-1	20	22	10	0	0	16-3	19	4.05	103	.301	.422	0	—	0		0	15	0.0
	Year	5	4	.556	48	0	0	0-4	52.2	51	26	4	1	30-4	56	4.10	103	.258	.357	1	—	0		1		0.1
1999	†Atl N	2	1	.667	49	0	0	1-0	47.1	31	20	2	2	22-2	49	3.42	131	.185	.284	0	—	0		6	42	0.3
2000	Ari N	2	4	.333	52	0	0	0-2	62	63	36	11	2	34-6	59	5.08	94	.261	.354	5	.200	-0		-1		-0.1
2001	Ari N	0	0	—	18	0	0	1-0	17.2	20	16	5	0	4-0	12	7.13	65	.274	.308	0	—	0		-5	138	-0.2
2003	StL N	1	1	.500	17	0	0	0-1	17.1	19	16	8	1	6-0	11	8.31	50	.271	.338	1-0-1	.000	-0		-8	121	-0.8
2004	†Hou N	1		1.000	16	0	0	0-0	13.2	15	4	1	1	6-0	9	2.63	166	.288	.355	0	—	0		3		0.2
2005	†Hou N	4	4	.500	62	0	0	0-3	59	49	34	9	3	21-3	54	4.73	89	.222	.298	0	—	0		-4		-0.5
Total	13	24	38	.387	446	27	1	8-19	621.2	628	375	95	26	279-28	559	5.08	87	.260	.341	26-0-4	.077	-2	103	-40	402	-4.1

SPROULL, CHARLIE
Charles William B1.9.1919 Taylorsville GA D1.13.1980 Rockford IL BR/TR/6-3/185 d4.19

YEAR	TM LG	W	L	PCT	G	GS	CG-SHO	SV-BS	IP	H	R	HR	HB	BB-IB	SO	ERA	AERA	OAV	OOB	AB-HR-SH	AVG	PB	SUP	APR	DL	PW
1945	Phi N	4	10	.286	34	19	2	0						80	47	5.94	65	.298	.390	35-0-3	.143	-1	92	-28		-2.8

SPROUT, BOB
Robert Samuel B12.5.1941 Florin PA BL/TL/6-0/165 d9.27

YEAR	TM LG	W	L	PCT	G	GS	CG-SHO	SV-BS	IP	H	R	HR	HB	BB-IB	SO	ERA	AERA	OAV	OOB	AB-HR-SH	AVG	PB	SUP	APR	DL	PW
1961	LA A	0	0	—	1	1	0	0	4	4	3	0	0	3-0	2	4.50	100	.267	.389	0-0-1		0	157	0		0.0

SPROWL, BOBBY
Robert John B4.14.1956 Sandusky OH BL/TL/6-2/190* [BosA77 2/39] d9.5 Col Alabama

YEAR	TM LG	W	L	PCT	G	GS	CG-SHO	SV-BS	IP	H	R	HR	HB	BB-IB	SO	ERA	AERA	OAV	OOB	AB-HR-SH	AVG	PB	SUP	APR	DL	PW
1978	Bos A	0	2	.000	3	3	0	0-0	12.2	12	10	3	0	10-0	10	6.39	64	.245	.373	0	—	0	73	-3		-0.4
1979	Hou N	0	0	—	3	0	0	0-0	4	1	0	0	0	3-0	3	0.00	—	.083	.214	0	—	0		2		0.1

YEAR	TM LG	W	L	PCT	G	GS	CG-SHO	SV-BS	IP	H	R	HR	HB	BB-IB	SO	ERA	AERA	OAV	OOB	AB-HR-SH	AVG	PB	SUP	APR	DL	PW
1980	Hou N	0	0	—	1	0	0	0-0	1	1	0	0	0	1-0	3	0.00	—	.250	.400		—	0	0	0		0.0
1981	Hou N	0	1	.000	15	1	0	0-0	28.2	40	20	1	0	14-1	18	5.97	55	.333	.397	6	.167	-0	162	-8		-0.5
Total	.4	0	3	.000	22	4	0	0-0	46.1	54	30	4	0	27-1	34	5.44	65	.292	.379	6	.167	-0	101	-9		-0.8

SPURGEON, JAY   Jay Aaron   B7.5.1976 West Covina CA   BR/TR/6-6/211   [BalA97 8/255]   d8.15   Col Hawaii-Manoa

YEAR	TM LG	W	L	PCT	G	GS	CG-SHO	SV-BS	IP	H	R	HR	HB	BB-IB	SO	ERA	AERA	OAV	OOB	AB-HR-SH	AVG	PB	SUP	APR	DL	PW
2000	Bal A	1	1	.500	7	4	0		24	26	16	5	2	15-0	11	6.00	78	.283	.394	0	—	0	115	-3		-0.2

SPURLING, CHRIS   Christopher Michael   B6.28.1977 Dayton OH   BR/TR/6-6/240*   [NYA97 41/1246]   d4.2   Col Miami-Ohio/Sinclair (OH) CC   [DL 2004 Det A 183]

YEAR	TM LG	W	L	PCT	G	GS	CG-SHO	SV-BS	IP	H	R	HR	HB	BB-IB	SO	ERA	AERA	OAV	OOB	AB-HR-SH	AVG	PB	SUP	APR	DL	PW
2003	Det A	1	3	.250	66	0	0	3-3	77	78	42	9	3	22-1	38	4.68	94	.266	.319	0	—	-2				-0.2
2005	Det A	3	4	.429	56	0	0	0-1	70.2	58	30	8	2	22-6	26	3.44	123	.230	.292	0	—	0	6			0.5
Total	2	4	7	.364	122	0	0	3-4	147.2	136	72	17	5	44-7	64	4.08	106	.250	.306	0	—	0	4	183		0.3

STABLEIN, GEORGE   George Charles   B10.29.1957 Inglewood CA   BR/TR/6-4/185   [SDN78 3/57]   d9.20   Col Cal St.-Dominguez Hills

YEAR	TM LG	W	L	PCT	G	GS	CG-SHO	SV-BS	IP	H	R	HR	HB	BB-IB	SO	ERA	AERA	OAV	OOB	AB-HR-SH	AVG	PB	SUP	APR	DL	PW
1980	SD N	0	1	.000	4	2	0	0	11.2	16	4	0	0	3-0	4	3.09	111	.340	.380	3	.000	-0	65	1		0.0

STACK, EDDIE   William Edward   B10.24.1887 Chicago IL   D8.28.1958 Chicago IL   BR/TR/6-0/175   d6.7

YEAR	TM LG	W	L	PCT	G	GS	CG-SHO	SV-BS	IP	H	R	HR	HB	BB-IB	SO	ERA	AERA	OAV	OOB	AB-HR-SH	AVG	PB	SUP	APR	DL	PW
1910	Phi N	6	7	.462	20	16	8-1	0	117	115	61	7	4	34	48	4.00	78	.266	.326	36-0-2	.083	-3	76	-8		-1.2
1911	Phi N	5	5	.500	13	10	5	0	77.2	67	48	3	6	41	36	3.59	96	.234	.342	24	.083	-2	85	-4		-0.6
1912	Bro N	7	5	.583	28	17	4	1	142	139	80	3	9	55	45	3.36	100	.264	.343	52-0-2	.135	-3	94	-3		-0.6
1913	Bro N	4	4	.500	23	9	4-1	0	87	79	30	0	1	32	34	2.38	138	.250	.321	25	.160	-1	97	8		0.5
	Chi N	4	2	.667	11	7	3-1	1	51	56	29	1	2	15	28	4.24	75	.280	.336	16-0-1	.063	-1	105	-5		-0.7
	Year	8	6	.571	34	16	7-2	1	138	135	59	1	3	47	62	3.07	106	.262	.327	41-0-1	.122	-2	100	5		-0.2
1914	Chi N	0	1	.000	7	1	0	0	16.1	13	11	0	0	11	9	4.96	56	.220	.343	4	.000	-0	0	-3		-0.2
Total	5	26	24	.520	102	60	24-3	2	491	469	259	14	22	188	200	3.52	93	.258	.334	157-0-5	.108	-10	88	-15		-2.8

STAFFORD, GENERAL   James Joseph "Jamsey"   B7.9.1868 Webster MA   D9.18.1923 Worcester MA   BR/TR/5-8/165   d8.27   b-John ▲

YEAR	TM LG	W	L	PCT	G	GS	CG-SHO	SV-BS	IP	H	R	HR	HB	BB-IB	SO	ERA	AERA	OAV	OOB	AB-HR-SH	AVG	PB	SUP	APR	DL	PW
1890	Buf P	3	9	.250	12	12	11	0	98	123	89	8	4	43	21	5.14	80	.294	.366	49	.143	-2*	89	-13		-1.2

STAFFORD, JOHN   John Henry "Doc"   B4.8.1870 Dudley MA   D7.3.1940 Worcester MA   BR/TR/5-10/170   d6.15   b-General   Col Holy Cross

YEAR	TM LG	W	L	PCT	G	GS	CG-SHO	SV-BS	IP	H	R	HR	HB	BB-IB	SO	ERA	AERA	OAV	OOB	AB-HR-SH	AVG	PB	SUP	APR	DL	PW
1893	Cle N	0	2	.000	2	0	0	0	7	12	15	1	0	7	4	14.14	35	.364	.475	4	.000	-1		-6		-0.6

STAFFORD, BILL   William Charles   B8.13.1939 Catskill NY   D9.19.2001 Wayne MI   BR/TR/6-2/193(185-198)   d8.17

YEAR	TM LG	W	L	PCT	G	GS	CG-SHO	SV-BS	IP	H	R	HR	HB	BB-IB	SO	ERA	AERA	OAV	OOB	AB-HR-SH	AVG	PB	SUP	APR	DL	PW
1960	†NY A	3	1	.750	11	8	2-1	0	60	50	17	3	1	18-0	36	2.25	159	.226	.286	22	.045	-2*	80	10		0.4
1961	†NY A	14	9	.609	36	25	8-3	2	195	168	65	13	5	59-4	101	2.68	139	.232	.294	67-0-3	.179	2	120	24		2.8
1962	†NY A	14	9	.609	35	33	7-2	0	213.1	188	95	23	4	77-6	109	3.67	102	.233	.301	78-0-4	.218	3	130	3		0.5
1963	NY A	4	8	.333	28	14	0	3	89.2	104	64	16	3	42-3	52	6.02	58	.287	.363	24-0-2	.292	3	117	-25		-2.9
1964	NY A	5	0	1.000	31	1	0	4	60.2	50	19	4	2	22-7	39	2.67	136	.231	.308	13	.077	-1	270	7		0.6
1965	NY A	3	8	.273	22	15	1	0	111.1	93	45	16	2	31-4	71	3.56	96	.229	.284	29-0-4	.000	-3	89	0	32	-0.3
1966	KC A	0	4	.000	9	8	0	0	39.2	42	28	2	2	12-1	31	4.99	68	.273	.327	11-0-2	.000	-1	68	-8		-0.9
1967	KC A	0	1	.000	14	0	0	0	16	12	4	0	0	9-2	10	1.69	189	.214	.321	1-0-1	.000	-0		2		0.1
Total	8	43	40	.518	186	104	18-6	9	785.2	707	337	77	19	270-27	449	3.52	103	.240	.306	245-0-16	.155	0	113	13	32	0.3

STALEY, GERRY   Gerald Lee   B8.21.1920 Brush Prairie WA   BR/TR/6-0/195*   d4.20

YEAR	TM LG	W	L	PCT	G	GS	CG-SHO	SV-BS	IP	H	R	HR	HB	BB-IB	SO	ERA	AERA	OAV	OOB	AB-HR-SH	AVG	PB	SUP	APR	DL	PW
1947	StL N	1	0	1.000	18	1	1	0	29.1	33	11	2	1	8	14	2.76	150	.287	.339	6	.000	-1	64	4		0.2
1948	StL N	4	4	.500	31	3	0	0	52	61	44	5	0	21	23	6.92	59	.288	.352	9-1-1	.222	1	123	-16		-2.0
1949	StL N	10	10	.500	45	17	5-2	6	171.1	154	65	6	3	41	55	2.73	152	**.238**	.286	41-0-6	.122	-0	73	24		2.9
1950	StL N	13	13	.500	42	22	7-1	3	169.2	201	101	14	7	61	62	4.99	86	.300	.365	55-0-4	.145	-1	73	-11		-1.4
1951	StL N	19	13	.594	42	30	10-4	3	227	244	108	14	8	74	67	3.81	104	.275	.337	81-0-4	.160	-1	81	3		0.3
1952	StL N☆	17	14	.548	35	33	15	0	239.2	238	101	21	7	52	93	3.27	114	.256	.301	85-0-7	.153	-2	121	11		1.3
1953	StL N☆	18	9	.667	40	32	10-1	4	230	243	118	31	17	54	88	3.99	107	.269	.322	78-0-7	.103	-5	105	4		0.0
1954	StL N	7	13	.350	48	20	3-1	0	155.2	198	107	21	6	47	50	5.26	78	.308	.357	36-0-4	.139	-0	126	-21		-2.3
1955	Cin N	5	8	.385	30	18	2	0	119.2	146	72	22	3	28-3	40	4.66	91	.309	.347	36-0-4	.056	-4	97	-6		-0.9
	NY A	0	0	—	2	0	0	0	2	5	5	1	0	1-0	1	13.50	28	.417	.462	0	—	-0		-3		-0.1
1956	NY A	0	0	—	1	0	0	0	0.1	4	4	0	0	0-0	1	108.00	4	.800	.800	1	.000	-0		-4		-0.2
	Chi A	8	3	.727	26	10	5	0	101.2	98	37	11	6	20-3	25	2.92	140	.251	.293	32-0-1	.094	-2	122	13		1.0
	Year	8	3	.727	27	10	5	0	102	102	41	11	6	20-3	26	3.26	126	.258	.303	33-0-1	.091	-3	122	10		0.8
1957	Chi A	5	1	.833	47	0	0	7	105	95	27	7	0	27-9	44	2.06	182	.244	.293	22-0-4	.045	-1		19		1.3
1958	Chi A	4	5	.444	50	0	0	8	85.1	81	36	10	0	24-3	27	3.16	115	.259	.307	11-0-1	.000	-1		3		0.4
1959	†Chi A	8	5	.615	67	0	0	14	116.1	111	39	5	0	25-9	54	2.24	167	.259	.298	13-0-4	.154	0		17		2.3
1960	Chi A★	13	8	.619	64	0	0	10	115.1	94	40	8	3	25-7	52	2.42	156	.227	.271	17-0-1	.235	1		15		**3.2**
1961	Chi A	0	3	.000	16	0	0	0	18	17	10	3	0	5-1	8	5.00	78	.246	.297	0	—	-0		-2		-0.2
	KC A	1	1	.500	23	0	0	2	30	32	15	4	2	10-1	16	3.60	116	.278	.341	1	.000	0		1		0.2
	Det A	1	1	.500	13	0	0	2	13.1	15	6	1	0	6-1	8	3.38	121	.288	.356	1	.000	-0		1		0.2
	Year	2	5	.286	52	0	0	4	61.1	64	31	8	2	21-3	32	3.96	103	.271	.332	2	.000	0		0		0.2
Total	15	134	111	.547	640	186	58-9	61	1981.2	2070	946	189	63	529-37	727	3.70	108	.270	.321	525-1-51	.126	-16	101	52		6.2

STALEY, HARRY   Henry Eli   B11.3.1866 Jacksonville IL   D1.12.1910 Battle Creek MI   BR/TR/5-10/175   d6.23

YEAR	TM LG	W	L	PCT	G	GS	CG-SHO	SV-BS	IP	H	R	HR	HB	BB-IB	SO	ERA	AERA	OAV	OOB	AB-HR-SH	AVG	PB	SUP	APR	DL	PW
1888	Pit N	12	12	.500	25	24	24-2	0	207.1	185	104	6	7	53	89	2.69	98	.235	.289	85	.129	-4	105	-3		-0.7
1889	Pit N	21	26	.447	49	47	46-1	1	420	433	254	11	8	116	159	3.51	107	.258	.309	186	.161	-7*	90	4		-0.1
1890	Pit P	21	25	.457	46	46	44-3	0	387.2	392	246	5	11	74	145	3.23	121	.251	**.290**	164-1	.207	1*	85	29		2.5
1891	Pit N	4	5	.444	9	7	6	0	71.2	77	49	4	2	11	25	2.89	114	.265	.296	31	.226	1	122	2		0.3
	Bos N	20	8	.714	31	30	26-1	1	252.1	236	111	12	4	69	114	2.50	146	.238	.290	102-1	.167	-2	99	32		2.8
	Year	24	13	.649	40	37	32-1	1	324	313	160	16	6	80	139	2.58	138	.244	.292	133-1	.180	-1	103	36		3.1
1892	†Bos N	22	10	.688	37	35	31-3	0	299.2	273	144	10	3	97	93	3.03	116	.233	.293	122-1	.131	-6*	106	18		1.0
1893	Bos N	18	10	.643	36	31	23	0	263	344	224	22	6	81	61	5.13	96	.307	.356	113-2	.265	3	132	-11		-0.7
1894	Bos N	12	10	.545	27	21	18	1	208.2	305	204	15	5	61	32	6.81	83	.337	.382	85-2-2	.235	0*	126	-18		-1.4
1895	.StL N	6	13	.316	23	16	13	0	158.2	223	136	4	2	39	28	5.22	93	.327	.365	67-0-2	.134	-6	96	-9		-1.4
Total	8	136	119	.533	283	257	231-10	2	2269	2468	1472	93	48	601	746	3.80	105	.269	.317	955-7-4	.182	-19	104	44		2.3

STALLARD, TRACY   Evan Tracy   B8.31.1937 Coeburn VA   BR/TR/6-5/205*   d9.24

YEAR	TM LG	W	L	PCT	G	GS	CG-SHO	SV-BS	IP	H	R	HR	HB	BB-IB	SO	ERA	AERA	OAV	OOB	AB-HR-SH	AVG	PB	SUP	APR	DL	PW
1960	Bos A	0	0	—	4	0	0	0	4	0	0	0	0	2-0	6	0.00	—	.000	.133	0	—	0		2		0.1
1961	Bos A	2	7	.222	43	14	1	2	132.2	110	75	9	1	96-2	109	4.88	85	.229	.354	36-0-4	.083	-2	91	-7		-0.8
1962	Bos A	0	0	—	2	0	0	0	0	0	0	0	0	0-0	0	—	—	.000	.000	0	—	0		0		0.0
1963	NY N	6	17	.261	39	23	5	1	154.2	156	89	23	1	77-6	110	4.71	74	.262	.344	48-0-2	.063	-3	89	-17		-2.8
1964	NY N	10	20	.333	36	34	11-2	0	225.2	213	111	20	6	73-3	118	3.79	94	.252	.314	79-0-1	.190	2	81	-6		-0.7
1965	StL N	11	8	.579	40	26	4-1	0	194.1	172	83	25	6	70-4	99	3.38	114	.235	.304	68-0-4	.088	-4	104	8		0.2
1966	StL N	1	5	.167	20	7	0	1	52.1	65	40	9	2	25-4	35	5.68	63	.305	.383	14	.000	-2	116	-13		-1.6
Total	7	30	57	.345	183	104	21-3	4	764.2	716	398	92	16	343-19	477	4.17	90	.248	.329	245-0-11	.110	-9	92	-33		-5.6

STANCEU, CHARLEY   Charles   B1.9.1916 Canton OH   D4.3.1969 Canton OH   BR/TR/6-2/190   d4.16   Mil 1942-45

YEAR	TM LG	W	L	PCT	G	GS	CG-SHO	SV-BS	IP	H	R	HR	HB	BB-IB	SO	ERA	AERA	OAV	OOB	AB-HR-SH	AVG	PB	SUP	APR	DL	PW
1941	NY A	3	3	.500	22	2	0	0	48	58	41	3	1	35	21	5.63	70	.296	.405	12	.000	-2	77	-12		-1.5
1946	NY A	0	0	—	3	0	0	0	4	6	4	0	0	5	3	9.00	38	.316	.458	-0	—	-0		-2		-0.1
	Phi N	2	4	.333	14	11	1	0	70.1	71	35	4	0	39	23	4.22	81	.270	.364	19-0-1	.000	-2	79	-5		-0.6
Total	2	5	7	.417	39	13	1	0	122.1	135	80	7	1	79	47	4.93	74	.282	.385	31-0-1	.000	-4	76	-19		-2.2

STANDRIDGE, PETE   Alfred Peter   B4.25.1891 Black Diamond WA   D8.2.1963 San Francisco CA   BR/TR/5-10.5/165   d9.19

YEAR	TM LG	W	L	PCT	G	GS	CG-SHO	SV-BS	IP	H	R	HR	HB	BB-IB	SO	ERA	AERA	OAV	OOB	AB-HR-SH	AVG	PB	SUP	APR	DL	PW
1911	StL N	0	0	—	2	0	0	0	4.2	10	10	0	1	4	3	9.64	35	.435	.536	1	.000	-0		-5		-0.2
1915	Chi N	4	1	.800	29	3	2	0	112.1	120	56	2	2	36	42	3.61	77	.274	.332	40-0-1	.225	3*	268	-10		-0.3
Total	2	4	1	.800	31	3	2	0	117	130	66	2	3	40	45	3.85	73	.282	.343	41-0-1	.220	3	268	-15		-0.5

STANDRIDGE, JASON   Jason Wayne   B11.9.1978 Birmingham AL   BR/TR/6-4/217(217-230)   [TBA97 1/31]   d7.29

YEAR	TM LG	W	L	PCT	G	GS	CG-SHO	SV-BS	IP	H	R	HR	HB	BB-IB	SO	ERA	AERA	OAV	OOB	AB-HR-SH	AVG	PB	SUP	APR	DL	PW
2001	TB A	0	0	—	9	1	0	0-0	19.1	19	10	5	0	14-1	9	4.66	97	.260	.379	0	—	0	62	0		0.0
2002	TB A	0	0	—	1	0	0	0-0	3	7	3	1	0	4-0	1	9.00	50	.500	.611	0	—	0		-1		-0.1
2003	TB A	0	5	.000	8	7	1	0-0	35.1	38	25	7	1	16-0	20	6.37	72	.275	.353	0	—	0	54	-6		-0.7
2004	TB A	0	0	—	3	1	0	0-0	10	14	10	5	0	4-0	7	9.00	50	.326	.375	0	—	0	100	-4	50	-0.2
2005	Tex A	0	0	—	2	0	0	0-0	2.1	7	3	0	0	1-1	2	11.57	40	.467	.500	0	—	0		-2		-0.1
	Cin N	2	2	.500	32	0	0	0-0	31	38	14	3	2	16-7	17	4.06	103	.314	.399	0	—	0	62	-12		0.1
Total	5	2	7	.222	55	9	1	0-0	101	123	65	21	3	55-9	56	5.79	77	.304	.389	0	—	0	62	-12	50	-1.0

YEAR	TM LG	W	L	PCT	G	GS	CG-SHO	SV-BS	IP	H	R	HR	HB	BB-IB	SO	ERA	AERA	OAV	OOB	AB-HR-SH	AVG	PB	SUP	APR	DL	PW

STANEK, AL Albert Wilfred "Lefty" B12.24.1943 Springfield MA BL/TL/5-11.5/190 d4.26

| 1963 | SF N | 0 | 0 | — | 11 | 0 | 0 | 0 | 13.1 | 10 | 7 | 1 | 0 | 12-2 | 5 | 4.73 | 68 | .217 | .379 | 1 | | .000 | -0 | | -2 | | -0.1 |

STANFIELD, KEVIN Kevin Bruce B12.19.1955 Huron SD BL/TL/6-0/195 [MinA76*7/126] d9.14 Col San Bernardino Valley (CA) JC

| 1979 | Min A | 0 | 0 | — | 3 | 0 | 0 | 0-0 | 3 | 2 | 2 | 0 | 0 | 0-0 | 0 | 6.00 | 73 | .200 | .200 | | — | | 0 | 0 | | | 0.0 |

STANFORD, JASON Jason John B1.23.1977 Tucson AZ BL/TL/6-2/200* d7.6 Col North Carolina-Charlotte [DL 2005 Cle A 120]

2003	Cle A	1	3	.250	13	8	0	0-0	50	48	20	5	1	16-1	30	3.60	123	.246	.305	0	—		0	67	6		0.4
2004	Cle A	0	1	.000	2	2	0	0-0	11	12	1	0	1	5-0	5	0.82	531	.279	.367	0	—		0	11	5	171	0.4
Total	2	1	4	.200	15	10	0	0-0	61	60	21	5	2	21-1	35	3.10	143	.252	.317	0	—		0	56	11	291	0.8

STANGE, LEE Albert Lee B10.27.1936 Chicago IL BR/TR/5-10/170* d4.15 C12 Col Drake

1961	Min A	1	0	1.000	7	0	0	0	12.1	15	6	1	0	10-1	10	2.92	145	.294	.410	1	.000	-0		1			0.1
1962	Min A	4	3	.571	44	6	1	3	95	98	57	14	1	39-3	70	4.45	92	.271	.342	17-0-2	.059	-1	160	-6		-0.5
1963	Min A	12	5	.706	32	20	7-2	0	164.2	145	53	21	0	43-1	100	2.62	139	.233	.283	52-0-3	.096	-1	130	19		1.8
1964	Min A	3	6	.333	14	11	2	0	79.2	78	45	13	0	19-3	54	4.74	75	.255	.297	25	.040	-1	133	-9		-1.0
	Cle A	4	8	.333	23	14	0	0	91.2	98	47	14	1	31-4	78	4.12	87*	.270	.329	25-0-2	.080	-1*	95	-5		-0.8
	Year	7	14	.333	37	25	2	0	171.1	176	92	27	1	50-7	132	4.41	81	.263	.314	50-0-2	.060	-2	112	-14		-1.8
1965	Cle A	8	4	.667	41	12	4-2	0	132	122	50	13	1	26-6	80	3.34	104	.247	.284	28-0-4	.107	1	99	5		0.4
1966	Cle A	1	0	1.000	8	2	1	0	16	17	5	1	1	3-0	8	2.81	122	.279	.318	4-0-1	.250	-0	64	1		0.1
	Bos A	7	9	.438	28	19	8-2	0	153.1	140	65	17	1	43-9	77	3.35	114	.246	.296	48-0-3	.063	-3	76	7		0.3
	Year	8	9	.471	36	21	9-2	0	169.1	157	70	18	2	46-9	85	3.30	114	.249	.298	52-0-4	.077	-3	75	9		0.4
1967	†Bos A	8	10	.444	35	24	6-2	1	181.2	171	64	14	2	32-7	101	2.77	126	.246	.281	49-0-6	.061	-3	99	13		0.9
1968	Bos A	5	5	.500	50	2	1	12	103	89	54	10	1	25-5	53	3.93	80	.237	.280	15-0-2	.133	0	83	-10		-1.3
1969	Bos A	6	9	.400	41	15	2	3-1	137	137	70	14	6	56-8	59	3.68	104	.256	.332	35-0-8	.086	-2	96	0		-0.3
1970	Bos A	2	2	.500	20	0	0	2-0	27.1	34	24	5	2	12-3	14	5.60	71	.301	.369	5-0-1	.000	-0		-6		-1.0
	Chi A	1	0	1.000	16	0	0	0-1	22.1	28	13	5	0	5-1	14	5.24	74	.295	.300	1	.000	-0		-2		-0.2
	Year	3	2	.600	36	0	0	2-1	49.2	62	37	10	2	17-4	28	5.44	72	.298	.352	6-0-1	.000	-0		-9		-1.2
Total	10	62	61	.504	359	125	32-8	21-2	1216	1172	553	142	16	344-51	718	3.56	102	.252	.304	305-0-32	.079	-11	105	8		-1.5

STANHOUSE, DON Donald Joseph B2.12.1951 DuQuoin IL BR/TR/6-2/195(185-198) [OakA69 1/9] d4.19

1972	Tex A	2	9	.182	24	16	1	0-0	104.2	83	48	8	1	73-5	78	3.78	81	.223	.347	31-0-2	.129	-0*	62	-7	31	-0.7
1973	Tex A	1	7	.125	21	5	1	1-1	70	70	41	5	2	44-3	42	4.76	79	.262	.368	0	—	0*	100	-7		-0.3
1974	Tex A	1	1	.500	18	0	0	0-0	31.1	38	20	4	2	17-0	26	4.88	73	.302	.390	0	—	0		-5		-0.3
1975	Mon N	0	0	—	4	3	0	0-0	13	19	12	1	0	11-2	5	8.31	47	.345	.448	3	.333	0	106	-5		-0.3
1976	Mon N	9	12	.429	34	26	8-1	1-0	184	182	84	7	4	92-10	92	3.77	100	.263	.351	52-0-4	.212	2	70	2		0.6
1977	Mon N	10	10	.500	47	16	1-1	10-2	158.1	147	72	12	4	84-9	89	3.41	113	.251	.346	47-1-4	.191	1	102	6		0.8
1978	Bal A	6	9	.400	56	0	0	24-7	74.2	60	24	4	0	52-6	42	2.89	122	.230	.348	0	—	0		5		1.1
1979	†Bal A☆	7	3	.700	52	0	0	21-6	72.2	49	24	4	1	51-7	34	2.85	142	.202	.333	0	—	0		11		2.1
1980	LA N	2	2	.500	21	0	0	7-5	25	30	14	4	0	16-3	5	5.04	69	.306	.400	2	.000	0		-4	92	-0.7
1982	Bal A	0	1	.000	17	0	0	0-0	26.2	29	16	3	2	15-1	3	5.40	75	.276	.377	0	—	0		-4	45	-0.2
Total	10	38	54	.413	294	66	11-2	64-21	760.1	707	359	48	16	455-46	408	3.84	96	.252	.355	135-1-10	.185	3	80	-8	168	1.7

STANIFER, ROB Robert Wayne B3.10.1972 Easley SC BR/TR/6-3/205* [FlaN94 12/320] d5.3 Col Anderson

1997	Fla N	1	2	.333	36	0	0	1-1	45	43	23	9	3	16-0	28	4.60	88	.261	.337	3	.667	2		-2		0.0
1998	Fla N	2	4	.333	38	0	0	1-2	48	54	33	5	0	22-2	30	5.63	72	.277	.345	5	.000	-1		-9		-1.1
2000	Bos A	0	0	—	8	0	0	0-0	13	22	19	3	0	4-1	3	7.62	66	.355	.394	0	—	0		-7		-0.3
Total	3	3	6	.333	82	0	0	2-3	106	119	75	17	3	42-3	61	5.43	77	.282	.349	8	.250	1		-18		-1.4

STANKA, JOE Joe Donald B7.23.1931 Hammon OK BR/TR/6-5/201 d9.2 Col Oklahoma St.

| 1959 | Chi A | 1 | 0 | 1.000 | 2 | 0 | 0 | 0 | 5.1 | 2 | 2 | 1 | 0 | 4-1 | 3 | 3.38 | 111 | .111 | .273 | 3 | .333 | 0 | | 0 | | 0.1 |

STANLEY, BUCK John Leonard B11.13.1889 Washington DC D8.13.1940 Norfolk VA BL/TL/5-10/160 d9.12 b-Joe

| 1911 | Phi N | 0 | 0 | — | 4 | 0 | 0 | 0 | 11.1 | 14 | 11 | 0 | 0 | 9 | 5 | 6.35 | 54 | .326 | .442 | 4 | .000 | -1 | | -4 | | -0.3 |

STANLEY, BOB Robert William B11.10.1954 Portland ME BR/TR/6-4/215(205-225) [BosA74*S1/7] d4.16

1977	Bos A	8	7	.533	41	13	3-1	3-2	151	176	74	10	3	43-5	44	3.99	112	.294	.343	0	—	0	103	7		0.8
1978	Bos A	15	2	.882	52	3	0	10-5	141.2	142	50	5	1	34-5	38	2.60	158	.266	.308	0	—	0	189	20		2.8
1979	Bos A★	16	12	.571	40	30	9-4	1-0	216.2	250	110	14	4	44-4	56	3.99	112	.294	.330	0	—	0	95	9		1.1
1980	Bos A	10	8	.556	52	17	5-1	14-3	175	186	75	11	7	52-8	71	3.39	126	.278	.335	0	—	0	105	15		1.8
1981	Bos A	10	8	.556	35	1	0	0-3	98.2	110	46	3	6	38-4	28	3.83	102	.294	.365	0	—	0	46	2		0.5
1982	Bos A	12	7	.632	48	0	0	14-2	168.1	161	60	11	4	50-6	83	3.10	140	.255	.312	0	—	0		23		3.1
1983	Bos A★	8	10	.444	64	0	0	33-14	145.1	145	56	7	3	38-12	65	2.85	154	.266	.315	0	—	0		21		3.4
1984	Bos A	9	10	.474	57	0	0	22-5	106.2	113	57	9	2	23-9	52	3.54	119	.267	.307	0	—	0		4		0.8
1985	Bos A	6	6	.500	48	0	0	10-8	87.2	76	30	7	2	30-10	46	2.87	150	.237	.303	0	—	0		14		2.0
1986	†Bos A	6	6	.500	66	1	0	16-5	82.1	109	48	9	0	22-8	54	4.37	96	.322	.360	0	—	0	108	-3		-0.5
1987	Bos A	4	15	.211	34	20	4-1	0	152.2	198	96	17	1	42-7	67	5.01	91	.321	.363	0	—	0	85	-9	18	-0.9
1988	†Bos A	6	4	.600	57	0	0	5-6	101.2	90	41	6	7	29-7	57	3.19	130	.242	.304	0	—	0		10	38	0.9
1989	Bos A	5	2	.714	43	0	0	4-0	79.1	102	54	4	1	26-2	32	4.88	84	.321	.366	0	—	0		-9		-0.7
Total	13	115	97	.542	637	85	21-7	132-55	1707	1858	797	113	41	471-87	693	3.64	118	.282	.331	0	—	0	101	104	56	15.1

STANTON, MIKE Michael Thomas B9.25.1952 St.Louis MO BB/TR/6-2/205* [HouN73*S1/5] d7.9 Col Miami-Dade Kendall (FL) CC

1975	Hou N	0	2	.000	7	2	0	1-0	17.1	20	14	1	0	20-0	16	7.27	47	.290	.449	4	.250	0	26	-7		-0.8
1980	Cle A	1	3	.250	51	0	0	5-1	85.2	98	58	5	3	44-1	54	5.46	76	.297	.382	0	—	0		-13		-0.7
1981	Cle A	3	3	.500	24	0	0	2-2	43.1	43	21	4	0	18-4	34	4.36	84	.262	.333	0	—	0		-2		-0.3
1982	Sea A	2	4	.333	56	1	0	7-3	71.1	70	37	6	0	21-3	49	4.16	103	.260	.312	0	—	0	64	1		0.1
1983	Sea A	2	3	.400	50	0	0	7-2	65	65	26	3	1	28-5	47	3.32	129	.273	.349	0	—	0		7		0.6
1984	Sea A	4	4	.500	54	0	0	8-5	61	55	24	8	3	22-4	55	3.54	113	.241	.312	0	—	0		3		0.4
1985	Sea A	1	2	.333	24	0	0	1-1	29	32	20	4	3	21-3	17	5.28	80	.278	.403	0	—	0		-4		-0.4
	Chi A	0	1	.000	11	0	0	0-2	11.2	15	14	2	0	8-0	12	9.26	47	.294	.383	0	—	0		-6		-0.5
	Year	1	3	.250	35	0	0	1-3	40.2	47	34	6	3	29-3	29	6.42	66	.283	.397	0	—	0		-10		-0.9
Total	7	13	22	.371	277	3	0	31-16	384.1	398	218	27	9	182-20	304	4.61	89	.272	.354	4	.250	0	37	-21		-1.6

STANTON, MIKE William Michael B6.2.1967 Houston TX BL/TL/6-1/190(190-215) [AtlN87 13/324] d8.24 Col Southwestern (TX)

1989	Atl N	0	1	.000	20	0	0	7-1	24	17	4	0	0	8-1	27	1.50	244	.207	.278	0	—	0		6		0.5
1990	Atl N	0	3	.000	7	0	0	2-1	7	16	16	1	1	4-2	7	18.00	22	.444	.512	0	—	0		-10	160	-1.8
1991	†Atl N	5	5	.500	74	0	0	7-3	78	62	27	6	1	21-6	54	2.88	134	.217	.273	6	.500	2		9		1.5
1992	†Atl N	5	4	.556	65	0	0	8-3	63.2	59	32	6	2	20-2	44	4.10	89	.247	.308	2	.500	0		-3		-0.4
1993	†Atl N	4	6	.400	63	0	0	27-6	52	51	35	4	0	29-7	43	4.67	87	.255	.346	0	—	0		-6		-1.2
1994	Atl N	3	1	.750	49	0	0	3-1	45.2	41	18	2	3	26-3	35	3.55	122	.248	.359	3-0-1	.667	1		5		0.5
1995	Atl N	1	1	.500	26	0	0	1-1	19.1	31	14	3	1	6-2	13	5.59	77	.369	.413	0	—	0		-3		-0.3
	†Bos A	1	0	1.000	22	0	0	0-1	21	17	9	3	0	8-0	10	3.00	162	.224	.298	0	—	0		4		0.2
1996	Bos A	4	3	.571	59	0	0	1-4	56.1	58	24	9	3	23-4	46	3.83	133	.275	.343	0	—	0		9		1.0
	†Tex A	0	1	.000	22	0	0	0-1	22.1	20	8	2	0	4-1	14	3.22	163	.241	.276	0	—	0		5		0.2
	Year	4	4	.500	81	0	0	1-5	78.2	78	32	11	3	27-5	60	3.66	141	.265	.325	0	—	0		14		1.2
1997	†NY A	6	1	.857	64	0	0	3-2	66.2	50	19	3	4	34-2	70	2.57	174	.205	.310	0	—	0		15		1.5
1998	†NY A	4	1	.800	67	0	0	6-4	79	71	51	13	4	26-1	69	5.47	80	.239	.307	1	.000	-0		-10		-0.7
1999	†NY A	2	2	.500	73	0	0	0-5	62.1	71	30	6	1	18-4	59	4.33	109	.289	.337	1	.000	-0	118	4		0.2
2000	†NY A	2	3	.400	69	0	0	0-1	68	68	32	5	3	24-2	75	4.10	116	.263	.325	1	1.000	0		6		0.4
2001	†NY A★	9	4	.692	76	0	0	0-1	80.1	80	25	4	4	29-9	79	2.58	172	.263	.332	0	—	0		17		2.4
2002	†NY A	7	1	.875	79	0	0	6-3	78	73	29	4	0	28-3	44	3.00	144	.256	.316	2	.000	-0		12		1.2
2003	NY N	2	7	.222	50	0	0	5-2	45.1	37	25	6	2	19-4	34	4.57	92	.219	.301	1	.000	-0		-2	46	-0.4
2004	NY N	2	6	.250	83	0	0	0-6	77	70	32	6	2	33-6	58	3.16	136	.237	.317	2	.500	0		9		0.7
2005	NY A	1	2	.333	28	0	0	0-0	14	17	11	1	0	6-0	12	7.07	62	.298	.359	0	—	0		-4		-0.7
	Was N	1	1	.667	28	0	0	0-1	27.2	31	13	2	0	9-4	14	3.58	113	.292	.348	1	.000	-0		1		0.1

YEAR	TM LG	W	L	PCT	G	GS	CG-SHO	SV-BS	IP	H	R	HR	HB	BB-IB	SO	ERA	AERA	OAV	OOB	AB-HR-SH	AVG	PB	SUP	APR	DL	PW
	Bos A	0	0	—	1	0	0	0-0	1	1	0	0	0	0-0	1	0.00	—	.333	.333	0	—	0		0		0.0
Total	17	60	53	.531	1027	1	0	76-50	988.2	941	454	85	26	375-63	807	3.80	115	.252	.323	20-0-1	.400	3	118	64	206	5.1

STAPLETON, DAVE David Earl B10.16.1961 Miami AZ BL/TL/6-1/185* d9.14 Col Grand Canyon

YEAR	TM LG	W	L	PCT	G	GS	CG-SHO	SV-BS	IP	H	R	HR	HB	BB-IB	SO	ERA	AERA	OAV	OOB	AB-HR-SH	AVG	PB	SUP	APR	DL	PW
1987	Mil A	2	0	1.000	4	0	0	0-0	14.2	13	3	0	0	3-0	14	1.84	251	.241	.281	0	—	0		4		0.6
1988	Mil A	0	0	—	6	0	0	0-0	13.2	20	9	1	1	9-1	6	5.93	68	.339	.435	0	—	0	-2	141	-0.1
Total	2	2	0	1.000	10	0	0	0-0	28.1	33	12	1	1	12-1	20	3.81	113	.292	.365	0	—	0	2	141		0.5

STARK, DENNY Dennis James B10.27.1974 Hicksville OH BR/TR/6-2/210* [SeaA96 4/117] d9.15 Col Toledo [DL 2000 Sea A 31]

YEAR	TM LG	W	L	PCT	G	GS	CG-SHO	SV-BS	IP	H	R	HR	HB	BB-IB	SO	ERA	AERA	OAV	OOB	AB-HR-SH	AVG	PB	SUP	APR	DL	PW
1999	Sea A	0	0	—	5	0	0	0-0	6.1	10	8	0	0	4-0	4	9.95	48	.370	.452	0	—	0	-4			-0.2
2001	Sea A	1	1	.500	4	3	0	0-0	14.2	21	15	5	0	4-0	12	9.20	46	.333	.368	0	—	0	58	-8		-0.8
2002	Col N	11	4	.733	32	20	0	0-1	128.1	108	69	25	5	64-4	64	4.00	118	.225	.321	41-1-3	.171	0*	122	6		0.7
2003	Col N	3	3	.500	17	13	0	0-0	78.2	98	57	12	3	33-2	30	5.83	84	.305	.368	22-0-1	.000	-1	126	-8	93	-0.7
2004	Col N	0	5	.000	6	6	0	0-0	26	53	43	9	0	18-3	10	11.42	42	.427	.486	8	.000	-1	110	-21	76	-1.3
Total	5	15	13	.536	64	42	0	0-1	254	290	192	51	8	123-9	120	5.78	83	.286	.363	71-1-4	.099	-2	117	-35	200	-3.8

STARKEL, CON Conrad B11.16.1880 Red Oak IA D1.19.1933 Tacoma WA BR/TR/6-0/200 d4.19

YEAR	TM LG	W	L	PCT	G	GS	CG-SHO	SV-BS	IP	H	R	HR	HB	BB-IB	SO	ERA	AERA	OAV	OOB	AB-HR-SH	AVG	PB	SUP	APR	DL	PW
1906	Was A	0	0	—	1	0	0	0	3	7	6	1	0	2	1	18.00	15	.467	.529	0	—	0	-4			-0.2

STARR, RAY Raymond Francis "Iron Man" B4.23.1906 Nowata OK D2.9.1963 Baylis IL BR/TR/6-1/178 d9.11

YEAR	TM LG	W	L	PCT	G	GS	CG-SHO	SV-BS	IP	H	R	HR	HB	BB-IB	SO	ERA	AERA	OAV	OOB	AB-HR-SH	AVG	PB	SUP	APR	DL	PW
1932	StL N	1	1	.500	3	2	1-1	0	20	19	7	2	1	10	6	2.70	146	.284	.385	4-0-1	.250	0	43	3		0.3
1933	NY N	0	1	.000	6	2	0	1	13.1	19	11	0	1	10	2	5.40	59	.339	.448	3	.000	-0	104	-4		-0.3
	Bos N	0	1	.000	9	1	0	0	28	32	15	4	1	9	15	3.86	79	.296	.356	7-0-1	.143	0	81	-3		-0.1
	Year	0	2	.000	15	3	0	1	41.1	51	26	4	2	19	17	4.35	71	.311	.389	10-0-1	.100	0	98	-8		-0.4
1941	Cin N	3	2	.600	7	4	3-2	0	34	28	10	1	1	6	11	2.65	136	.219	.259	11-0-4	.182	-0	100	4		0.6
1942	Cin N☆	15	13	.536	37	33	17-4	0	276.2	228	88	10	3	106	83	2.67	123	.226	.301	88-0-12	.091	-5	78	24		1.9
1943	Cin N	11	10	.524	36	33	9-2	1	217.1	201	93	9	5	91	42	3.64	91	.248	.328	74-0-6	.122	-4	120	-6		-1.0
1944	Pit N	6	5	.545	27	12	5	3	89.2	116	60	6	1	36	25	5.02	74	.314	.377	22	.136	1	135	-12		-1.4
1945	Pit N	0	2	.000	4	0	0	0	6.2	10	7	0	0	4	0	9.45	42	.370	.452	1	1.000	1		-3		-0.3
	Chi N	1	0	1.000	9	1	0	0	13.1	17	11	1	0	7	5	7.43	49	.298	.375	2-0-1	.500	0	255	-5		-0.3
	Year	1	2	.333	13	1	0	0	20	27	18	1	0	11	5	8.10	46	.321	.400	3-0-1	.667	1	248	-9		-0.8
Total	7	37	35	.514	138	88	35-9	4	699	670	302	33	13	279	189	3.53	96	.255	.329	212-0-25	.123	-7	105	-2		-0.8

STARR, DICK Richard Eugene B3.2.1921 Kittanning PA BR/TR/6-3/190* d9.5

YEAR	TM LG	W	L	PCT	G	GS	CG-SHO	SV-BS	IP	H	R	HR	HB	BB-IB	SO	ERA	AERA	OAV	OOB	AB-HR-SH	AVG	PB	SUP	APR	DL	PW
1947	NY A	1	0	1.000	4	1	0	0	12.1	12	4	1	0	8	1	1.46	242	.250	.357	3-0-1	.333	1	200	2		0.2
1948	NY A	0	0	—	1	0	0	0	2	1	1	0	0	2	1	4.50	91	.000	.250	0	—	0	0	0		0.0
1949	StL A	1	7	.125	30	8	1-1	0	83.1	96	46	6	1	48	44	4.32	105	.292	.384	23	.087	-1	74	2		0.0
1950	StL A	7	5	.583	32	16	4-1	2	123.2	140	83	11	7	74	30	5.02	99	.287	.389	36-0-4	.139	-3*	105	-2		-0.5
1951	StL A	2	5	.286	15	9	0	0	62	66	55	10	2	42	26	7.40	59	.273	.385	18-0-1	.222	0	92	-19		-1.7
	Was A	1	7	.125	11	11	1	0	61.1	76	41	12	0	17	17	5.58	73	.304	.365	17	.176	1	104	-9		-1.1
	Year	3	12	.200	26	20	1	0	123.1	142	96	22	2	66	43	6.49	65	.289	.375	35-0-1	.200	1	98	-28		-2.8
Total	5	12	24	.333	93	45	7-2	2	344.2	390	230	40	10	198	120	5.25	86	.286	.381	97-0-6	.155	-2	98	-26		-3.1

STARRETTE, HERMAN Herman Paul B11.20.1938 Statesville NC BR/TR/6-0/175* d7.1 C17 Col Lenoir-Rhyne

YEAR	TM LG	W	L	PCT	G	GS	CG-SHO	SV-BS	IP	H	R	HR	HB	BB-IB	SO	ERA	AERA	OAV	OOB	AB-HR-SH	AVG	PB	SUP	APR	DL	PW
1963	Bal A	0	1	.000	18	0	0	0	26	26	10	1	2	7-0	13	3.46	100	.271	.327	1-0-1	.000	1		1		0.1
1964	Bal A	1	0	1.000	5	0	0	0	11	9	3	0	0	6-0	5	1.64	218	.250	.349	3	.000	-0		2		0.1
1965	Bal A	0	0	—	4	0	0	0	9	8	3	0	0	3-0	3	1.00	347	.258	.324	1	.000	-0		2		0.1
Total	3	1	1	.500	27	0	0	0	46	43	16	1	2	16-0	21	2.54	137	.264	.332	5-0-1	.000	0		5		0.3

STAUFFER, ED Charles Edward B1.10.1898 Emsworth PA D7.2.1979 St.Petersburg FL BR/TR/5-11/185 d4.26

YEAR	TM LG	W	L	PCT	G	GS	CG-SHO	SV-BS	IP	H	R	HR	HB	BB-IB	SO	ERA	AERA	OAV	OOB	AB-HR-SH	AVG	PB	SUP	APR	DL	PW
1923	Chi N	0	0	—	1	0	0	0	2	5	3	0	0	1	1	13.50	30	.556	.600	0	—	0		-2		-0.1
1925	StL A	0	1	.000	20	1	0	0	30.1	34	21	1	0	21	13	5.34	87	.283	.390	4	.250	-0	108	-2		-0.1
Total	2	0	1	.000	21	1	0	0	32.1	39	24	1	0	22	13	5.85	79	.302	.404	4	.250	-0	108	-4		-0.2

STAUFFER, TIM Timothy James B6.2.1982 Portland ME BR/TR/6-1/215 d5.11 Col Richmond

YEAR	TM LG	W	L	PCT	G	GS	CG-SHO	SV-BS	IP	H	R	HR	HB	BB-IB	SO	ERA	AERA	OAV	OOB	AB-HR-SH	AVG	PB	SUP	APR	DL	PW
2005	SD N	3	6	.333	15	14	0	0-0	81	92	50	10	2	29-0	49	5.33	72	.286	.348	24-0-3	.125	-0	106	-13		-1.3

STEARNS, BILL William E. B3.20.1853 Washington DC D12.30.1898 Washington DC TR d6.26

YEAR	TM LG	W	L	PCT	G	GS	CG-SHO	SV-BS	IP	H	R	HR	HB	BB-IB	SO	ERA	AERA	OAV	OOB	AB-HR-SH	AVG	PB	SUP	APR	DL	PW
1871	Oly NA	2	0	1.000	2	2	2	0	18	10	11	0		8	0	2.50	167	.149	.240	9	.000	-1	138	3		0.1
1872	Nat NA	0	11	.000	11	11	11	0	99	193	190	2		3	2	6.18	75	.339	.343	45	.244	-3	60	-13		-1.1
1873	Was NA	7	25	.219	32	32	32	0	283	481	395	8		16	5	4.61	73	.332	.340	133	.180	-6	83	-37		-3.0
1874	Har NA	3	14	.176	22	18	14	0	158.2	237	194	0		15	14	2.95	78	.297	.310	132	.159	-5*	70	-12		-1.3
1875	Was NA	1	14	.067	17	16	14	0	141	246	211	3		4	3	4.02	59	.332	.336	78	.256	-0*	52	-25		-2.1
Total	5 NA	13	64	.169	84	79	73	0	699.2	1167	1001	13		46	24	4.28	72	.322	.331	397	.191	-16	73	-84		-7.4

STECHER, WILLIAM William Theodore B10.20.1869 Riverside NJ D12.26.1926 Riverside NJ d9.6

YEAR	TM LG	W	L	PCT	G	GS	CG-SHO	SV-BS	IP	H	R	HR	HB	BB-IB	SO	ERA	AERA	OAV	OOB	AB-HR-SH	AVG	PB	SUP	APR	DL	PW
1890	Phi AA	0	10	.000	10	10	9	0	68	111	110	1	14	60	18	10.32	38	.356	.479	29	.241	1	47	-48		-4.4

STECHSCHULTE, GENE Gene Urban B8.12.1973 Lima OH BR/TR/6-5/210* d4.20 Col Ashland [DL 2003 StL N 183]

YEAR	TM LG	W	L	PCT	G	GS	CG-SHO	SV-BS	IP	H	R	HR	HB	BB-IB	SO	ERA	AERA	OAV	OOB	AB-HR-SH	AVG	PB	SUP	APR	DL	PW
2000	StL N	1	0	1.000	20	0	0	0-1	25.2	24	22	6	0	17-1	12	6.31	74	.247	.353	0	—	0		-6		-0.3
2001	†StL N	1	5	.167	67	0	0	6-2	70	71	35	10	4	30-3	51	3.86	112	.273	.354	3-1-0	.667	2*		3		0.4
2002	StL N	6	2	.750	29	0	0	0-2	32	27	19	4	1	17-1	21	4.78	84	.235	.328	2	.000	-0		-3		-0.6
Total	3	8	7	.533	116	0	0	6-5	127.2	122	76	20	5	64-4	84	4.58	94	.258	.347	5-1-0	.400	2		-6	183	-0.6

STEELE, ELMER Elmer Rae B5.17.1886 Poughkeepsie NY D3.9.1966 Rhinebeck NY BB/TR/5-11/200 d9.12

YEAR	TM LG	W	L	PCT	G	GS	CG-SHO	SV-BS	IP	H	R	HR	HB	BB-IB	SO	ERA	AERA	OAV	OOB	AB-HR-SH	AVG	PB	SUP	APR	DL	PW
1907	Bos A	0	1	.000	4	1	0	0	11.1	11	7	0	0	1	10	1.59	162	.256	.273	4	.000	-1	0	0		-0.1
1908	Bos A	5	7	.417	16	13	9-1	0	118	85	34	1	3	13	37	1.83	134	.209	.239	39-0-1	.051	-4	77	8		0.4
1909	Bos A	4	4	.500	16	8	2	1	75.2	75	37	1	0	15	32	2.85	88	.255	.294	22-0-1	.227	1	148	-4		-0.3
1910	Pit N	0	3	.000	3	3	2	0	24	19	9	0	0	3	7	2.25	138	.221	.247	7	.000	-1	32	2		0.2
1911	Pit N	9	9	.500	31	16	7-2	2	166	153	65	6	4	31	52	2.60	132	.256	.297	61-0-1	.180	-0	142	14		1.4
	Bro N	0	0	—	5	2	0	0	23	24	10	0	0	5	9	3.13	107	.258	.296	9	.000	-0	146	1		0.0
	Year	9	9	.500	36	18	7-2	2	189	177	75	6	4	36	61	2.67	128	.257	.297	70-0-1	.157	-1	143	15		1.4
Total	5	18	24	.429	75	43	20-3	3	418	367	162	7	8	68	147	2.41	122	.241	.278	142-0-3	.127	-6	114	21		1.6

STEELE, BOB Robert Wesley B1.5.1894 Cassburn ON, Can. D1.27.1962 Ocala FL BB/TL/5-10.5/175 d4.17

YEAR	TM LG	W	L	PCT	G	GS	CG-SHO	SV-BS	IP	H	R	HR	HB	BB-IB	SO	ERA	AERA	OAV	OOB	AB-HR-SH	AVG	PB	SUP	APR	DL	PW
1916	StL N	5	15	.250	29	21	7-1	0	148	156	74	6	3	42	67	3.41	78	.285	.340	51	.196	-1	73	-12		-1.9
1917	StL N	1	3	.250	12	6	1	0	42	33	17	1	0	19	23	3.21	84	.223	.311	13	.385	2	70	-2		0.0
	Pit N	5	11	.313	27	19	13-1	1	179.2	158	71	0	5	53	82	2.76	103	.237	.298	76-0-1	.224	1*	73	1		0.0
	Year	6	14	.300	39	25	14-1	1	221.2	191	88	1	5	72	105	2.84	99	.235	.301	89-0-1	.247	2	72	-1		0.0
1918	Pit N	2	3	.400	10	4	2-1	1	49	44	25	2	2	17	21	3.31	87	.240	.312	16	.125	-0	79	-3		-0.1
	NY N	3	5	.375	12	7	5-1	1	66	56	29	3	1	11	24	2.59	101	.226	.267	21	.286	2	115	-2		-0.1
	Year	5	8	.385	22	11	7-2	2	115	100	54	5	3	28	45	2.90	94	.232	.287	37	.216	2	101	-5		-0.3
1919	NY N	0	1	.000	5	0	0	0	3	3	3	0	0	2	0	6.00	47	.250	.357	1	.000	-0		-1		-0.3
Total	4	16	38	.296	91	57	28-4	3	487.2	450	219	10	13	144	217	3.05	90	.249	.310	178-0-1	.225	3	78	-19		-2.6

STEELE, BILL William Mitchell "Big Bill" B10.5.1885 Milford PA D10.19.1949 Overland MO BR/TR/5-11/200 d9.10

YEAR	TM LG	W	L	PCT	G	GS	CG-SHO	SV-BS	IP	H	R	HR	HB	BB-IB	SO	ERA	AERA	OAV	OOB	AB-HR-SH	AVG	PB	SUP	APR	DL	PW
1910	StL N	4	4	.500	9	8	8	1	71.2	71	35	1	6	24	25	3.27	91	.264	.338	31	.258	1	119	-3		-0.2
1911	StL N	18	19	.486	43	34	23-1	3	287.1	287	153	8	10	113	115	3.73	91	.269	.345	101-0-3	.208	4	77	-11		-0.7
1912	StL N	9	13	.409	40	25	7	2	194	245	143	6	7	66	67	4.69	73	.322	.381	61-0-1	.180	1*	128	-7		-1.3
1913	StL N	4	4	.500	12	9	2	0	54	58	31	3	3	18	10	5.00	65	.286	.353	18-0-1	.056	-1	98	-9		-1.3
1914	StL N	1	2	.333	17	2	0	1	53.1	55	30	3	3	7	16	2.70	104	.274	.308	17-0-1	.294	2	90	-2		0.1
	Bro N	1	1	.500	8	1	0	0	16.1	17	16	1	0	7	3	5.51	52	.258	.329	3-0-1	.333	1	175	-5		-0.6
	Year	2	3	.400	25	3	0	1	69.2	72	46	4	3	14	19	3.36	84	.270	.313	20-0-2	.300	3	119	-6		-0.5
Total	5	37	43	.463	129	79	40-1	7	676.2	733	408	21	29	235	236	4.02	82	.286	.352	231-0-7	.203	8	102	-57		-5.0

STEEN, BILL William John B11.11.1887 Pittsburgh PA D3.13.1979 Signal Hill CA BR/TR/6-0.5/180 d4.15 Col Washington & Jefferson

YEAR	TM LG	W	L	PCT	G	GS	CG-SHO	SV-BS	IP	H	R	HR	HB	BB-IB	SO	ERA	AERA	OAV	OOB	AB-HR-SH	AVG	PB	SUP	APR	DL	PW
1912	Cle A	9	8	.529	26	16	6-1	2	143.1	163	75	3	1	45	61	3.77	90	.298	.352	48-0-1	.271	2	102	-3		-0.2
1913	Cle A	4	5	.444	22	13	7-2	1	128.1	113	52	3	4	49	57	2.45	124	.239	.316	41-0-4	.171	-0	107	6		0.4

YEAR	TM LG	W	L	PCT	G	GS	CG-SHO	SV-BS	IP	H	R	HR	HB	BB-IB	SO	ERA	AERA	OAV	OOB	AB-HR-SH	AVG	PB	SUP	APR	DL	PW
1914	Cle A	9	14	.391	30	22	13-1	0	200.2	201	74	0	4	68	97	2.60	111	.272	.337	70-0-3	.200	1	82	9		1.1
1915	Cle A	1	4	.200	10	7	2	0	45.1	51	30	1	2	15	22	4.96	61	.290	.352	16	.188	-0	85	-8		-0.7
	Det A	5	1	.833	20	7	3	4	79.1	83	35	0	1	22	28	2.72	111	.269	.319	28-0-1	.179	-1	168	1		0.1
	Year	6	5	.545	30	14	5	4	124.2	134	65	1	3	37	50	3.54	86	.276	.331	44-0-1	.182	-1	127	-7		-0.6
Total 4		28	32	.467	108	65	31-4	6	597	611	266	7	12	199	265	3.05	101	.273	.335	203-0-9	.207	1	102	5		0.7

STEENGRAFE, MILT Milton Henry B5.26.1900 San Francisco CA D6.2.1977 Oklahoma City OK BR/TR/6-0/170 d5.5

YEAR	TM LG	W	L	PCT	G	GS	CG-SHO	SV-BS	IP	H	R	HR	HB	BB-IB	SO	ERA	AERA	OAV	OOB	AB-HR-SH	AVG	PB	SUP	APR	DL	PW
1924	Chi A	0	0	—	3	0	0	0	5.2	15	8	0	0	4	3	12.71	32	.484	.543	1	.000	-0		-5		-0.2
1926	Chi A	1	1	.500	13	1	0	0	38.1	43	22	1	2	19	10	3.99	97	.295	.383	14-0-1	.000	-2	44	-2		-0.3
Total 2		1	1	.500	16	1	0	0	44	58	30	1	2	23	13	5.11	76	.328	.411	15-0-1	.000	-2	44	-7		-0.5

STEENSTRA, KENNIE Kenneth Gregory B10.13.1970 Springfield MO BR/TR/6-5/220 [ChiN92 12/331] d5.21 Col Wichita St.

YEAR	TM LG	W	L	PCT	G	GS	CG-SHO	SV-BS	IP	H	R	HR	HB	BB-IB	SO	ERA	AERA	OAV	OOB	AB-HR-SH	AVG	PB	SUP	APR	DL	PW
1998	Chi N	0	0	—	4	0	0	0-0	3.1	7	4	2	0	1-0	4	10.80	41	.412	.444	0	—	0		-2		-0.1

STEEVENS, MORRIE Morris Dale B10.7.1940 Salem IL BL/TL/6-2/175* d4.13

YEAR	TM LG	W	L	PCT	G	GS	CG-SHO	SV-BS	IP	H	R	HR	HB	BB-IB	SO	ERA	AERA	OAV	OOB	AB-HR-SH	AVG	PB	SUP	APR	DL	PW
1962	Chi N	0	1	.000	12	1	0	0	15	10	4	0	1	11-0	5	2.40	173	.196	.333	1	.000	-0	63	3		0.2
1964	Phi N	0	0	—	4	0	0	0	2.2	5	3	0	0	1-0	3	3.38	103	.385	.429	0	—	0		-1		0.0
1965	Phi N	0	1	.000	6	0	0	0	2.2	5	5	1	0	4-0	3	16.88	20	.417	.563	0	—	0		-4		-0.7
Total 3		0	2	.000	22	1	0	0	20.1	20	12	1	1	16-0	11	4.43	90	.263	.385	1	.000	0	63	-2		-0.5

STEIN, ED Edward F. B9.5.1869 Detroit MI D5.10.1928 Detroit MI BR/TR/5-11/170 d7.24

YEAR	TM LG	W	L	PCT	G	GS	CG-SHO	SV-BS	IP	H	R	HR	HB	BB-IB	SO	ERA	AERA	OAV	OOB	AB-HR-SH	AVG	PB	SUP	APR	DL	PW
1890	Chi N	12	6	.667	20	18	14-1	0	160.2	147	100	9	11	83	65	3.81	96	.236	.336	59	.153	-2	99	-1		-0.3
1891	Chi N	7	6	.538	14	10	9-1	0	101	99	68	7	2	57	38	3.74	89	.247	.343	43	.163	-1	104	-6		-0.6
1892	Bro N	27	16	.628	48	42	38-6	1	377.1	310	166	6	15	150	190	2.84	111	.215	.296	144	.215	4	110	16		2.0
1893	Bro N	19	15	.559	37	34	28-1	0	298.1	294	190	4	8	119	81	3.77	117	.250	.323	118	.212	-3	99	20		1.5
1894	Bro N	26	14	.650	44	40	37-2	1	350	388	261	10	14	170	84	4.63	107	.278	.362	143-4-2	.252	4*	116	11		1.2
1895	Bro N	15	13	.536	32	27	24-1	1	255.1	282	163	8	6	93	55	4.72	93	.276	.340	104-0-2	.250	2	95	-5		-0.2
1896	Bro N	3	6	.333	17	10	6	0	90.1	130	79	6	2	51	-16	4.88	84	.334	.414	39-0-1	.256	0	105	-12		-0.8
1898	Bro N	0	2	.000	3	2	0	0	23	39	21	0	0	9	6	5.48	65	.371	.421	10	.400	1	59	-5		-0.3
Total 8		109	78	.583	215	183	158-12	3	1656	1689	1048	50	58	732	535	3.97	103	.258	.338	660-2-7	.224	5	105	18		2.5

STEIN, IRV Irvin Michael B5.21.1911 Madisonville LA D1.7.1981 Covington LA BR/TR/6-2/170 d7.7

YEAR	TM LG	W	L	PCT	G	GS	CG-SHO	SV-BS	IP	H	R	HR	HB	BB-IB	SO	ERA	AERA	OAV	OOB	AB-HR-SH	AVG	PB	SUP	APR	DL	PW
1932	Phi A	0	0	—	1	0	0	0	3	7	4	2	0	1	0	12.00	38	.500	.533	1	.000	-0		-2		-0.1

STEIN, BLAKE William Blake B8.3.1973 McComb MS BR/TR/6-7/240(210-240) [StLN94 6/166] d5.10 Col Spring Hill

YEAR	TM LG	W	L	PCT	G	GS	CG-SHO	SV-BS	IP	H	R	HR	HB	BB-IB	SO	ERA	AERA	OAV	OOB	AB-HR-SH	AVG	PB	SUP	APR	DL	PW
1998	Oak A	5	9	.357	24	20	1-1	0-0	117.1	117	92	22	5	71-3	89	6.37	73	.255	.359	5-0-1	.000	0	102	-22		-2.2
1999	Oak A	0	0	—	1	1	0	0-0	2.2	6	5	1	0	6-0	1	16.88	28	.462	.632	0	—	0	217	-3		-0.2
	KC A	1	2	.333	12	11	0	0-0	70.1	59	33	10	7	41-1	43	4.09	124	.230	.350	0	—	0	75	8		0.3
	Year	1	2	.333	13	12	0	0-0	73	65	38	11	7	47-1	44	4.56	111	.241	.366	0	—	0	86	5		0.1
2000	KC A	8	5	.615	17	17	1	0-0	107.2	98	57	19	3	57-1	78	4.68	112	.247	.343	2	.000	-0	108	7	92	0.7
2001	KC A	7	8	.467	36	15	0	1-1	131	112	73	20	3	79-2	111	4.74	105	.233	.342	2	.000	0	90	4		0.3
2002	KC A	0	4	.000	27	2	0	1-1	46.2	59	41	6	3	27-1	42	7.91	63	.306	.394	0	—	0	84	-12	61	-1.0
Total 5		21	28	.429	117	66	2-1	2-2	475.2	451	301	78	21	281-8	369	5.41	92	.251	.356	9-0-1	.000	-1	97	-18	153	-2.1

STEIN, RANDY William Randolph B3.7.1953 Pomona CA BR/TR/6-4/210* [BalA71 1/23] d4.17

YEAR	TM LG	W	L	PCT	G	GS	CG-SHO	SV-BS	IP	H	R	HR	HB	BB-IB	SO	ERA	AERA	OAV	OOB	AB-HR-SH	AVG	PB	SUP	APR	DL	PW
1978	Mil A	3	2	.600	31	1	0	1-1	72.2	78	51	5	4	39-1	42	5.33	71	.280	.371	0	—	0	47	-14		-0.9
1979	Sea A	2	3	.400	23	1	0	0-3	41.1	48	29	7	1	27-4	39	5.88	74	.291	.390	0	—	0	21	-6		-0.7
1981	Sea A	0	1	.000	5	0	0	0-1	9.1	18	12	1	0	8-0	6	10.61	37	.429	.510	0	—	0		-6		-0.6
1982	Chi N	0	0	—	6	0	0	0-0	10.1	7	4	2	0	7-2	6	3.48	109	.200	.326	0	—	0				0.0
Total 4		5	6	.455	65	2	0	1-5	133.2	151	96	15	5	81-7	93	5.72	70	.290	.385	0	—	0	34	-25		-2.2

STEINEDER, RAY Raymond J. B11.13.1895 Salem NJ D8.25.1982 Vineland NJ BR/TR/6-0.5/160 d7.16

YEAR	TM LG	W	L	PCT	G	GS	CG-SHO	SV-BS	IP	H	R	HR	HB	BB-IB	SO	ERA	AERA	OAV	OOB	AB-HR-SH	AVG	PB	SUP	APR	DL	PW
1923	Pit N	2	0	1.000	15	2	1	0	55	58	30	3	2	18	23	4.75	85	.278	.341	15-0-1	.467	3	297	-3		0.1
1924	Pit N	0	1	.000	5	0	0	0	2.2	6	6	0	0	5	0	13.50	28	.400	.550	0	—	0		-3		-0.6
	Phi N	1	1	.500	9	0	0	0	28.2	31	15	1	0	16	11	4.40	101	.284	.376	10	.300	0		1		0.1
	Year	1	2	.333	14	0	0	0	31.1	37	21	1	0	21	11	5.17	85	.298	.400	10	.300	0		-2		-0.5
Total 2		3	2	.600	29	2	1	0	86.1	95	51	4	2	39	34	4.90	85	.285	.364	25-0-1	.400	3	297	-5		-0.4

STEIRER, RICK Ricky Francis B8.27.1956 Baltimore MD BR/TR/6-4/200* [AnaA77 5/111] d8.5

YEAR	TM LG	W	L	PCT	G	GS	CG-SHO	SV-BS	IP	H	R	HR	HB	BB-IB	SO	ERA	AERA	OAV	OOB	AB-HR-SH	AVG	PB	SUP	APR	DL	PW
1982	Cal A	1	0	1.000	10	1	0	0-1	26.1	25	14	2	1	11-0	14	3.76	109	.243	.322	0	—	0	156	0		0.0
1983	Cal A	3	2	.600	19	5	0	0-0	61.2	77	40	3	3	18-4	25	4.82	84	.302	.351	0	—	0	121	-7		-0.5
1984	Cal A	0	1	.000	1	1	0	0-0	2.2	6	5	0	0	2-1	2	16.88	24	.500	.571	0	—	0	90	-4		-0.5
Total 3		4	3	.571	30	7	0	0-1	90.2	108	59	5	4	31-5	41	4.86	83	.292	.350	0	—	0	122	-11		-1.0

STELLBERGER, BILL William F. B4.22.1865 Detroit MI D11.9.1936 Detroit MI BL/TL d10.1

YEAR	TM LG	W	L	PCT	G	GS	CG-SHO	SV-BS	IP	H	R	HR	HB	BB-IB	SO	ERA	AERA	OAV	OOB	AB-HR-SH	AVG	PB	SUP	APR	DL	PW
1885	Pro N	0	1	.000	1	1	1	0	8	14	10	0	1	0	0	7.88	34	.389	.450	4	.000	-1	126	-4		-0.4

STEMBER, JEFF Jeffrey Alan B3.2.1958 Elizabeth NJ BR/TR/6-5/220 [SFN76 26/596] d8.5

YEAR	TM LG	W	L	PCT	G	GS	CG-SHO	SV-BS	IP	H	R	HR	HB	BB-IB	SO	ERA	AERA	OAV	OOB	AB-HR-SH	AVG	PB	SUP	APR	DL	PW
1980	SF N	0	0	—	1	1	0	0	3	2	3	1	0	2-0	0	3.00	117	.167	.286	1	.000	-0	229	-1		-0.1

STEMLE, STEVE Stephen J. B5.20.1977 Louisville KY BR/TR/6-4/200 d5.26 Col Western Kentucky

YEAR	TM LG	W	L	PCT	G	GS	CG-SHO	SV-BS	IP	H	R	HR	HB	BB-IB	SO	ERA	AERA	OAV	OOB	AB-HR-SH	AVG	PB	SUP	APR	DL	PW
2005	KC A	0	0	—	6	0	0	0-0	10.2	10	6	0	0	4-0	9	5.06	83	.256	.326	0	—	0		-1	114	0.0

STEMMEYER, BILL William "Cannon Ball" B5.6.1865 Cleveland OH D5.3.1945 Cleveland OH BR/TR/6-2/190 d10.3

YEAR	TM LG	W	L	PCT	G	GS	CG-SHO	SV-BS	IP	H	R	HR	HB	BB-IB	SO	ERA	AERA	OAV	OOB	AB-HR-SH	AVG	PB	SUP	APR	DL	PW
1885	Bos N	1	1	.500	2	2	2-1	0	11	7	7	0	0	11	8	0.00	—	.194	.383	7	.429	1	200	1		0.4
1886	Bos N	22	18	.550	41	41	41	0	348.2	300	218	11	9	144	239	3.02	106	.218	.292	148	.277	9	115	5		1.1
1887	Bos N	6	8	.429	15	14	14	1	119.1	138	107	4	2	41	41	5.20	79	.274	.331	47-1	.255	2	80	-17		-1.4
1888	Cle AA	0	2	.000	2	2	2	0	16	37	42	0	1	9	7	9.00	34	.435	.495	10	.400	1*	94	-14		-1.1
Total 4		29	29	.500	60	59	59-1	1	495	482	374	15	3	205	295	3.67	93	.241	.312	212-1	.283	14	108	-25		-1.0

STENHOUSE, DAVE David Rotchford B9.12.1933 Westerly RI BR/TR/6-0/190* d4.18 s-Mike Col Rhode Island

YEAR	TM LG	W	L	PCT	G	GS	CG-SHO	SV-BS	IP	H	R	HR	HB	BB-IB	SO	ERA	AERA	OAV	OOB	AB-HR-SH	AVG	PB	SUP	APR	DL	PW
1962	Was A★	11	12	.478	34	26	9-2	0	197	169	84	24	2	90-9	123	3.65	110	.234	.319	58-0-6	.052	-5	89	10		0.7
1963	Was A	3	9	.250	16	16	2-1	0	87	90	46	12	1	45-2	47	4.55	82	.260	.345	25-0-1	.080	-1	72	-6	42	-0.9
1964	Was A	2	7	.222	26	14	1	1	88	80	54	12	1	39-1	44	4.81	77	.239	.320	20-0-3	.300	2	91	-10	37	-0.8
Total 3		16	28	.364	76	56	12-3	1	372	339	184	48	4	174-12	214	4.14	94	.241	.326	103-0-10	.107	-4	84	-6	79	-1.0

STEPHEN, BUZZ Louis Roberts B7.13.1944 Porterville CA BR/TR/6-4/205 [MinA66 S1/6] d9.20 Col Cal St.-Fresno

YEAR	TM LG	W	L	PCT	G	GS	CG-SHO	SV-BS	IP	H	R	HR	HB	BB-IB	SO	ERA	AERA	OAV	OOB	AB-HR-SH	AVG	PB	SUP	APR	DL	PW
1968	Min A	1	1	.500	2	2	0	0	11.1	11	7	2	0	3-0	7	4.76	65	.275	.388	3-0-1	.000	-0	85	-2		-0.4

STEPHENS, BRYAN Bryan Maris B7.14.1920 Fayetteville AR D11.21.1991 Santa Ana CA BR/TR/6-4/175 d5.15

YEAR	TM LG	W	L	PCT	G	GS	CG-SHO	SV-BS	IP	H	R	HR	HB	BB-IB	SO	ERA	AERA	OAV	OOB	AB-HR-SH	AVG	PB	SUP	APR	DL	PW
1947	Cle A	5	10	.333	31	5	1	1	92	79	46	6	2	39	34	4.01	87	.230	.312	27-0-1	.111	-2	102	-6		-1.2
1948	StL A	3	6	.333	43	12	2	3	122.2	141	94	14	4	67	35	6.02	76	.289	.379	32-0-2	.125	-1	119	-20		-1.4
Total 2		8	16	.333	74	17	3	4	214.2	220	140	20	6	106	69	5.16	79	.264	.352	59-0-3	.119	-3	119	-26		-2.6

STEPHENS, CLARENCE Clarence Wright B8.19.1863 Cincinnati OH D2.28.1945 Cincinnati OH TR d10.8

YEAR	TM LG	W	L	PCT	G	GS	CG-SHO	SV-BS	IP	H	R	HR	HB	BB-IB	SO	ERA	AERA	OAV	OOB	AB-HR-SH	AVG	PB	SUP	APR	DL	PW
1886	Cin AA	1	0	1.000	1	1	1	0	8	9	8	0	1	5	6	5.63	63	.273	.385	5	.600	1	236	-2		-0.1
1891	Cin N	0	1	.000	1	1	1	0	8	9	9	1	2	3	3	7.88	43	.273	.333	3	.000	-0	0	-3		-0.3
1892	Cin N	0	1	.000	1	1	0	0	7	12	3	0	0	4	1	1.29	254	.364	.432	2	.000	-0	39	1		0.1
Total 3		1	2	.333	3	3	2	0	23	30	20	1	1	12	10	5.09	67	.303	.384		.300	0	95	-4		-0.3

STEPHENS, BEN George Benjamin B9.28.1867 Romeo MI D8.5.1896 Armada MI TR/5-10.5/170 d8.5

YEAR	TM LG	W	L	PCT	G	GS	CG-SHO	SV-BS	IP	H	R	HR	HB	BB-IB	SO	ERA	AERA	OAV	OOB	AB-HR-SH	AVG	PB	SUP	APR	DL	PW
1892	Bal N	1	1	.500	5	2	1	0	29	37	22	2	1	9	13	2.79	123	.298	.351	13	.120	-2	120	0		-0.2
1893	Was N	0	6	.000	9	6	6	0	63.2	83	58	1	4	31	14	5.80	80	.306	.386	29	.103	-4	50	-8		-0.5
1894	Was N	0	0	—	3	1	1	0	11	19	16	1	1	8	1	4.91	108	.373	.467	4	.250	-0	67	-1		-0.1
Total 3		1	7	.125	17	10	9	0	103.2	139	96	4	6	48	28	4.86	90	.312	.386	46	.087	-5	67	-9		-1.1

STEPHENS, JOHN John M. B11.15.1979 Sydney, New South Wales, Australia BR/TR/6-1/200 d7.30

YEAR	TM LG	W	L	PCT	G	GS	CG-SHO	SV-BS	IP	H	R	HR	HB	BB-IB	SO	ERA	AERA	OAV	OOB	AB-HR-SH	AVG	PB	SUP	APR	DL	PW
2002	Bal A	2	5	.286	12	11	0	0	65	68	44	13	3	22-2	56	6.09	71	.271	.332	0	—	0	80	-11		-1.0

YEAR	TM LG	W	L	PCT	G	GS	CG-SHO	SV-BS	IP	H	R	HR	HB	BB-IB	SO	ERA	AERA	OAV	OOB	AB-HR-SH	AVG	PB	SUP	APR	DL	PW

STEPHENSON, EARL   Chester Earl   B7.31.1947 Benson NC   BL/TR/6-3/175*   [ChiN67*3/39]   d4.7   Col Campbell

YEAR	TM LG	W	L	PCT	G	GS	CG-SHO	SV-BS	IP	H	R	HR	HB	BB-IB	SO	ERA	AERA	OAV	OOB	AB-HR-SH	AVG	PB	SUP	APR	DL	PW
1971	Chi N	1	0	1.000	16	0	0	1-2	20.1	24	10	1	0	11-0	11	4.43	89	.316	.393	2	.000	-0		-1		0.0
1972	Mil A	3	5	.375	35	8	1	0-1	80.1	79	32	5	3	33-5	33	3.25	94	.262	.339	18	.000	-2	61	-2		-0.4
1977	Bal A	0	0	—	1	0	0	0-0	3	5	3	1	0	0-0	2	9.00	43	.357	.357	0	—	0		-1		-0.1
1978	Bal A	0	0	—	2	0	0	0-0	9.2	10	3	0	0	5-0	4	2.79	126	.294	.375	0	—	0		1		0.0
Total	4	4	5	.444	54	8	1	1-3	113.1	118	48	7	3	49-5	50	3.57	92	.277	.353	20	.000	-2	61	-4		-0.5

STEPHENSON, GARRETT   Garrett Charles   B1.2.1972 Takoma Park MD   BR/TR/6-5/208(185-208)   [BalA92 18/492]   d7.25   Col Brigham Young-Idaho [JC]   [DL 2001 StL N 190]

YEAR	TM LG	W	L	PCT	G	GS	CG-SHO	SV-BS	IP	H	R	HR	HB	BB-IB	SO	ERA	AERA	OAV	OOB	AB-HR-SH	AVG	PB	SUP	APR	DL	PW
1996	Bal A	1	0	1.000	3	0	0	0-0	6.1	13	9	1	1	3-1	3	12.79	39	.433	.500			-0		-5		-0.6
1997	Phi N	8	6	.571	20	18	2	0-0	117	104	45	11	3	38-0	81	3.15	134	.244	.307	32-0-5	.094	-1	80	14	32	1.4
1998	Phi N	0	2	.000	6	6	0	0-0	23	31	24	3	0	19-0	17	9.00	48	.316	.427	6-0-1	.167	0	124	-11		-0.8
1999	StL N	6	3	.667	18	12	0	0-0	85.1	90	43	11	5	29-1	59	4.22	109	.275	.339	27-0-3	.074	-2	105	4		0.2
2000	†StL N	16	9	.640	32	31	3-2	0-0	200.1	209	105	31	7	63-0	123	4.49	103	.270	.327	59-0-13	.051	-4	115	6		0.2
2002	StL N	2	5	.286	12	10	0	0-0	45	48	27	4	5	25-0	34	5.40	75	.282	.388	12-0-2	.000	-1	135	-6	119	-0.9
2003	StL N	7	13	.350	32	27	1	0-0	174.1	167	94	30	13	60-3	91	4.59	90	.255	.326	44-0-7	.205	-2	96	-9		-0.9
Total	7	39	39	.500	123	104	6-2	0-0	651.1	662	347	91	34	237-5	408	4.55	96	.267	.336	180-0-31	.100	-6	105	-7	341	-1.4

STEPHENSON, JERRY   Jerry Joseph   B10.6.1943 Detroit MI   BL/TR/6-2/185(175-200)   d4.14   f-Joe

YEAR	TM LG	W	L	PCT	G	GS	CG-SHO	SV-BS	IP	H	R	HR	HB	BB-IB	SO	ERA	AERA	OAV	OOB	AB-HR-SH	AVG	PB	SUP	APR	DL	PW
1963	Bos A	0	0	—	1	1	0	0	2.1	5	2	0	0	2-0	3	7.71	49	.556	.538	1	.000	-0	141	-1		-0.1
1965	Bos A	1	5	.167	15	8	1	0	52	62	41	7	1	33-0	49	6.23	60	.287	.382	13	.231	0	74	-13		-1.3
1966	Bos A	2	5	.286	15	11	1	0	66.1	68	51	6	1	44-1	50	5.83	65	.264	.370	17-0-2	.118	-1	112	-14	47	-1.5
1967	†Bos A	3	1	.750	8	6	0	1	39.2	32	18	4	1	16-2	24	3.86	90	.227	.308	16	.250	-0	92	-1		-0.4
1968	Bos A	0	8	.200	23	7	2	0	68.2	81	51	4	2	42-3	51	5.64	56	.295	.387	17	.353	2	87	-19		-2.4
1969	Sea A	0	0	—	2	0	0	0-0	2.2	6	4	0	1	3-0	1	10.13	36	.429	.556	0	—	0		-2		-0.1
1970	LA N	0	0	—	3	0	0	0-0	6.2	11	7	0	0	5-0	6	9.45	41	.379	.471	1	.000	-0		-4		-0.2
Total	7	8	19	.296	67	33	3	1-0	238.1	265	174	21	6	145-6	184	5.70	62	.281	.377	65-0-2	.231	2	96	-54	47	-5.7

STERLING, JOHN   John A.   B Philadelphia PA   6-1/172   d10.12

YEAR	TM LG	W	L	PCT	G	GS	CG-SHO	SV-BS	IP	H	R	HR	HB	BB-IB	SO	ERA	AERA	OAV	OOB	AB-HR-SH	AVG	PB	SUP	APR	DL	PW
1890	Phi AA	0	1	.000	1	1	1	0	5	16	12	1	4	4	1	21.60	18	.516	.583	2	.000	-0	35	-8		-0.9

STERLING, RANDY   Randall Wayne   B4.21.1951 Key West FL   BB/TR/6-2/195   d9.16

YEAR	TM LG	W	L	PCT	G	GS	CG-SHO	SV-BS	IP	H	R	HR	HB	BB-IB	SO	ERA	AERA	OAV	OOB	AB-HR-SH	AVG	PB	SUP	APR	DL	PW
1974	NY N	1	1	.500	3	2	0	0	9.1	13	8	0	1	3-0	2	4.82	75	.351	.405	2	.000	0	73	-2		-0.4

STEVENS, DAVE   David James   B3.4.1970 Fullerton CA   BR/TR/6-3/195(195-215)   [ChiN89 20/512]   d5.20   Col Fullerton (CA) JC

YEAR	TM LG	W	L	PCT	G	GS	CG-SHO	SV-BS	IP	H	R	HR	HB	BB-IB	SO	ERA	AERA	OAV	OOB	AB-HR-SH	AVG	PB	SUP	APR	DL	PW
1994	Min A	5	2	.714	24	0	0	0-0	45	55	35	6	1	23-2	24	6.80	73	.302	.383	0		0		-8		-1.1
1995	Min A	5	4	.556	56	0	0	10-2	65.2	74	40	14	1	32-1	47	5.07	95	.285	.359	0		0		-2		-0.2
1996	Min A	3	3	.500	49	0	0	11-5	58	58	31	12	0	25-2	29	4.66	110	.264	.335	0		0		3	41	0.4
1997	Min A	1	3	.250	6	6	0	0-0	23	41	23	8	0	17-0	16	9.00	52	.383	.468	0		0	121	-10		-1.3
	Chi N	0	2	.000	10	0	0	0-0	9.1	13	11	0	1	9-0	13	9.64	45	.333	.460	1	.000	0		-5		-1.0
1998	Chi N	1	2	.333	31	0	0	0-0	38	42	20	6	1	17-5	31	4.74	93	.288	.364	4	.250	0		-1		-0.1
1999	Cle A	0	0	—	5	0	0	0-0	9	10	10	1	0	8-1	6	10.00	51	.286	.409	0	—	0		-4		-0.2
2000	Atl N	0	0	—	2	0	0	0-0	3	5	4	2	0	1-0	4	12.00	38	.357	.400	1	.000	-0		-2		-0.1
Total	7	15	16	.484	183	6	0	21-7	251	298	174	49	4	132-11	170	6.02	80	.297	.377	6	.167	-0	121	-29	41	-3.6

STEVENS, JIM   James Arthur "Steve"   B8.25.1889 Williamsburg MD   D9.25.1966 Baltimore MD   BR/TR/5-11/180   d8.24

YEAR	TM LG	W	L	PCT	G	GS	CG-SHO	SV-BS	IP	H	R	HR	HB	BB-IB	SO	ERA	AERA	OAV	OOB	AB-HR-SH	AVG	PB	SUP	APR	DL	PW
1914	Was A	0	0	—	2	0	0	0	3	4	3	0	1	2	1	9.00	31	.364	.500	1	.000	-0		-2		-0.1

STEWART, DAVE   David Keith   B2.19.1957 Oakland CA   BR/TR/6-2/200(200-230)   [LAN75 16/384]   d9.22   C3

YEAR	TM LG	W	L	PCT	G	GS	CG-SHO	SV-BS	IP	H	R	HR	HB	BB-IB	SO	ERA	AERA	OAV	OOB	AB-HR-SH	AVG	PB	SUP	APR	DL	PW
1978	LA N	0	0	—	1	0	0	0	2	1	0	0	0	0-0	1	0.00	—	.167	.167	0		0		1		0.0
1981	†LA N	4	3	.571	32	0	0	6-2	43.1	40	13	3	0	14-5	29	2.49	132	.250	.305	5	.400	2	98	4		0.9
1982	LA N	9	8	.529	45	14	0	1-1	146.1	137	72	14	2	49-11	80	3.81	91	.249	.310	39-0-5	.179	1	98	-7		-0.7
1983	LA N	5	2	.714	46	1	0	8-4	76	67	28	4	2	33-7	54	2.96	122	.237	.318	7-0-1	.143	0	171	6		0.6
	Tex A	5	2	.714	8	8	2	0-0	59	50	15	2	2	17-0	24	2.14	190	.233	.294	0	—	0	62	13		1.5
1984	Tex A	7	14	.333	32	27	3	0-1	192.1	193	106	26	4	87-3	119	4.73	88	.258	.337	0	—	0	75	-7		-0.8
1985	Tex A	0	6	.000	42	5	0	4-3	81.1	86	53	13	2	37-5	64	5.42	79	.273	.351	0	—	0	51	-10		-0.7
	Phi N	0	0	—	4	0	0	0-0	4.1	5	4	0	0	4-0	2	6.23	60	.278	.409	0	—	0		-1		-0.1
1986	Phi N	0	0	—	8	0	0	0-0	12.1	15	9	1	0	4-0	9	6.57	59	.306	.339	0	—	0		-3		-0.2
	Oak A	9	5	.643	29	17	4-1	0-1	149.1	137	67	15	3	65-0	102	3.74	104	.241	.320	0	—	0	96	4		0.3
1987	Oak A	20	13	.606	37	37	8-1	0-0	261.1	224	121	24	6	105-2	205	3.68	113	.229	.306	0	—	0	104	14		1.4
1988	Oak A	21	12	.636	37	37	14-2	0-0	275.2	240	111	14	3	110-5	192	3.23	118	.234	.307	0	—	0	105	13		1.4
1989	†Oak A★	21	9	.700	36	36	8	0-0	257.2	260	105	23	6	69-0	155	3.32	112	.263	.313	0	—	0	113	37		1.7
1990	†Oak A	22	11	.667	36	36	11-4	0-0	267	226	84	16	5	83-1	166	2.56	146	.231	.291	0	—	0	114	17		1.7
1991	Oak A	11	11	.500	35	35	2-1	0-0	226	245	135	24	9	105-1	144	5.18	74	.278	.356	0	—	0	112	0	24	-3.0
1992	†Oak A	12	10	.545	31	31	2	0-0	199.1	175	96	23	8	79-1	130	3.66	103	.237	.315	0	—	0	108	0	38	-0.1
1993	†Tor A	12	8	.600	26	26	0	0-0	162	146	86	23	4	72-0	96	4.44	99	.242	.325	0	—	0	99	-12		-1.2
1994	Tor A	7	8	.467	22	22	1	0-0	133.1	151	89	26	4	62-4	111	5.87	83	.285	.362	0	—	0	102	-21		-2.1
1995	Oak A	3	7	.300	16	16	0	0-0	81	101	65	11	2	39-1	58	6.89	66	.305	.379	0	—	0	106	14	79	3.1
Total	16	168	129	.566	523	348	55-9	19-12	2629.2	2499	1259	264	62	1034-46	1741	3.95	100	.251	.322	51-0-6	.196	2	106	14	79	3.1

STEWART, FRANK   Frank "Stewy"   B9.8.1906 Minneapolis MN   D4.30.2001 Stillwater MN   BR/TR/6-1.5/180   d10.2

YEAR	TM LG	W	L	PCT	G	GS	CG-SHO	SV-BS	IP	H	R	HR	HB	BB-IB	SO	ERA	AERA	OAV	OOB	AB-HR-SH	AVG	PB	SUP	APR	DL	PW
1927	Chi A	0	1	.000	1	1	0	0	4	5	4	0	0	4	3	9.00	45	.357	.500	1	.000	-0	62	-2		-0.3

STEWART, JOE   Joseph Lawrence "Ace"   B3.11.1879 Monroe NC   D2.9.1913 Youngstown OH   TR/5-11/175   d6.9   Col Erskine

YEAR	TM LG	W	L	PCT	G	GS	CG-SHO	SV-BS	IP	H	R	HR	HB	BB-IB	SO	ERA	AERA	OAV	OOB	AB-HR-SH	AVG	PB	SUP	APR	DL	PW
1904	Bos N	0	0	—	2	0	0	0	9.1	12	11	0	1	4	1	9.64	29	.286	.362	5	.200	-0		-6		-0.3

STEWART, JOSH   Joshua Craig   B12.5.1978 Paducah KY   BL/TL/6-3/200*   [ChiA99 5/159]   d4.6   Col Memphis

YEAR	TM LG	W	L	PCT	G	GS	CG-SHO	SV-BS	IP	H	R	HR	HB	BB-IB	SO	ERA	AERA	OAV	OOB	AB-HR-SH	AVG	PB	SUP	APR	DL	PW
2003	Chi A	1	2	.333	5	5	0	0-0	25.2	28	18	4	0	16-0	13	5.96	77	.272	.367	0	—	0	124	-4	29	-0.3
2004	Chi A	0	1	.000	3	2	0	0-0	7.2	16	13	3	0	3-0	5	15.26	31	.444	.463	0	—	0	208	-8		-0.8
Total	2	1	3	.250	8	7	0	0-0	33.1	44	31	7	0	19-0	18	8.10	57	.317	.391	0	—	0	148	-12	29	-1.1

STEWART, SAMMY   Samuel Lee   B10.28.1954 Asheville NC   BR/TR/6-3/208(207-219)   d9.1   Col Montreat

YEAR	TM LG	W	L	PCT	G	GS	CG-SHO	SV-BS	IP	H	R	HR	HB	BB-IB	SO	ERA	AERA	OAV	OOB	AB-HR-SH	AVG	PB	SUP	APR	DL	PW
1978	Bal A	1	1	.500	2	2	0	0-0	11.1	10	5	0	0	3-0	11	3.18	111	.238	.289	0	—	0	140	0		0.0
1979	†Bal A	8	5	.615	31	3	1	1-1	117.2	96	47	11	5	71-4	71	3.52	115	.232	.349	0	—	0	127	9		1.0
1980	Bal A	7	7	.500	33	3	2	3-2	118.2	103	51	9	2	60-8	78	3.56	111	.235	.328	0	—	0	68	5		0.6
1981	Bal A	4	8	.333	29	3	0	4-1	112.1	89	33	8	3	57-4	57	2.32	157	.225	.325	0	—	0	33	17		1.9
1982	Bal A	10	9	.526	38	12	1-1	5-4	139	140	68	9	2	62-3	69	4.14	98	.263	.339	0	—	0*	108	-1	23	-0.2
1983	†Bal A	9	4	.692	58	1	0	7-2	144.1	138	60	7	1	67-4	95	3.62	111	.253	.364	0	—	0*	0	8		0.7
1984	Bal A	7	4	.636	60	0	0	13-3	93	81	42	7	1	47-7	56	3.29	119	.241	.332	0	—	0		5		0.7
1985	Bal A	5	7	.417	56	1	0	9-1	129.2	117	60	15	1	66-10	77	3.61	113	.246	.336	0	—	0	45	5		0.5
1986	Bos A	4	1	.800	27	0	0	0-0	63.2	64	33	7	0	48-2	47	4.38	96	.266	.381	0	—	0		-1	35	-0.8
1987	Cle A	4	2	.667	25	0	0	3-4	27	25	22	4	1	21-1	25	5.67	81	.234	.362	0	—	0		-4	21	-0.8
Total	10	59	48	.551	359	25	4-1	45-18	956.2	863	421	77	16	502-43	586	3.59	111	.245	.338	0	—	0	92	43	79	4.3

STEWART, SCOTT   Scott Edward   B8.14.1975 Stoughton MA   BR/TL/6-2/225*   [TexA94 20/561]   d4.5

YEAR	TM LG	W	L	PCT	G	GS	CG-SHO	SV-BS	IP	H	R	HR	HB	BB-IB	SO	ERA	AERA	OAV	OOB	AB-HR-SH	AVG	PB	SUP	APR	DL	PW
2001	Mon N	3	1	.750	62	0	0	3-1	47.2	43	20	5	3	13-0	39	3.78	114	.243	.299			0		4	22	0.4
2002	Mon N	4	2	.667	67	0	0	17-2	64	49	29	4	1	22-5	67	3.09	142	.207	.275	2	.000	-0		7		0.9
2003	Mon N	3	1	.750	51	0	0	0-1	43	52	22	5	1	13-4	29	3.98	112	.306	.357	2	.000	-0		2	53	-0.1
2004	Cle A	0	2	.000	28	0	0	0-2	13.2	23	14	2	0	6-2	18	7.24	60	.365	.414	0	—	0		-6		-0.7
	LA N	1	0	1.000	11	0	0	0-0	12.1	20	8	3	0	6-3	8	5.84	71	.392	.441			0		-2		-0.2
Total	4	11	6	.647	214	0	0	20-6	180.2	187	93	19	5	60-14	161	3.99	109	.268	.326	4	.000	-0		5	75	0.5

STEWART, BUNKY   Veston Goff   B1.7.1931 Jasper NC   BL/TL/6-0/155*   d5.4   Col East Carolina

YEAR	TM LG	W	L	PCT	G	GS	CG-SHO	SV-BS	IP	H	R	HR	HB	BB-IB	SO	ERA	AERA	OAV	OOB	AB-HR-SH	AVG	PB	SUP	APR	DL	PW
1952	Was A	0	0	—	2	0	0	0	1	1	2	0	0	1	1	18.00	20	.500	.600	0	—	0		-2		-0.1
1953	Was A	0	2	.000	2	1	0	0	15.1	17	9	1	1	11	3	4.70	83	.283	.403	5	.200	-0	57	-1		-0.2
1954	Was A	0	2	.000	29	2	1	0	50.2	67	53	4	2	27	27	7.64	48	.324	.410	3	.000	-0	99	-25		-1.2
1955	Was A	0	0	—	7	1	0	0	15.1	18	7	0	0	6-1	10	4.11	93	.295	.358	2	.000	0	93	0		0.0

YEAR	TM LG	W	L	PCT	G	GS	CG-SHO	SV-BS	IP	H	R	HR	HB	BB-IB	SO	ERA	AERA	OAV	OOB	AB-HR-SH	AVG	PB	SUP	APR	DL	PW
1956	Was A	5	7	.417	33	9	1	2	105	111	77	15	5	82-4	36	5.57	78	.276	.402	28-0-4	.250	-0*	71	-15		-1.5
Total	5	5	11	.313	72	14	2	3	187.1	215	147	19	10	127-5	77	6.01	67	.293	.402	38-0-4	.211	-0	75	-43		-3.0

STEWART, LEFTY Walter Cleveland B9.23.1900 Sparta TN D9.26.1974 Knoxville TN BR/TL/5-10/160 d4.20

YEAR	TM LG	W	L	PCT	G	GS	CG-SHO	SV-BS	IP	H	R	HR	HB	BB-IB	SO	ERA	AERA	OAV	OOB	AB-HR-SH	AVG	PB	SUP	APR	DL	PW
1921	Det A	0	0	—	5	0	0	1	9	20	12	0	0	5	4	12.00	36	.455	.510	1	.000	-0		-7		-0.3
1927	Stl A	8	11	.421	27	19	11	1	155.2	187	83	7	2	43	43	4.28	102	.310	.306	49-0-4	.306	3*	82	4		0.7
1928	Stl A	7	9	.438	29	17	7-1	3	142.1	173	81	5	2	32	25	4.67	90	.310	.350	51	.275	-4	113	-5		-0.2
1929	Stl A	9	6	.600	23	18	8-1	0	149.2	137	67	11	4	49	47	3.25	136	.246	.312	51-0-6	.118	-4	97	17		1.1
1930	Stl A	20	12	.625	35	33	23-1	0	271	281	119	21	1	70	79	3.45	141	.268	.315	90-0-5	.244	2	87	41		4.4
1931	Stl A	14	17	.452	36	33	20-1	0	258	287	155	17	3	85	89	4.40	105	.277	.334	88-0-3	.250	2	93	5		1.2
1932	Stl A	15	19	.441	41	32	18-2	1	259.2	269	148	22	3	99	86	4.61	105	.270	.338	82-0-6	.146	-2	79	10		0.9
1933	†Was A	15	6	.714	34	31	11-1	0	230.2	227	116	19	1	60	69	3.82	109	.256	.304	77-0-9	.143	1*	115	7		0.6
1934	Was A	7	11	.389	24	22	7-1	0	152	184	74	8	1	36	36	4.03	107	.303	.343	45-0-13	.156	-1*	72	6		0.5
1935	Was A	0	1	.000	1	1	0	0	2.2	8	9	1	0	2	1	13.50	32	.533	.588	1	.000	-0		-5		-0.7
	Cle A	6	6	.500	24	10	2	2	91	122	68	6	1	17	24	5.44	83	.312	.342	30-0-2	.200	-1	108	-11		-1.4
	Year	6	7	.462	25	11	2	2	93.2	130	77	7	1	19	25	5.67	79	.320	.352	31-0-2	.194	-1	98	-17		-2.1
Total	10	101	98	.508	279	216	107-8	8	1722	1895	932	117	18	498	503	4.19	108	.281	.332	565-0-49	.204	6	92	62		6.8

STEWART, MACK William Macklin B9.23.1914 Stevenson AL D3.21.1960 Macon GA BR/TR/6-0/167 d7.7

YEAR	TM LG	W	L	PCT	G	GS	CG-SHO	SV-BS	IP	H	R	HR	HB	BB-IB	SO	ERA	AERA	OAV	OOB	AB-HR-SH	AVG	PB	SUP	APR	DL	PW
1944	Chi N	0	0	—	8	0	0	0	12.1	11	2	1	0	4	3	1.46	242	.239	.300	1	.000	-0		3		0.1
1945	Chi N	0	1	.000	16	1	0	0	28.1	37	16	0	1	14	9	4.76	77	.322	.395	3	.333	0	70	-3		-0.1
Total	2	0	1	.000	24	1	0	0	40.2	48	18	1	1	18	12	3.76	96	.298	.369	4	.250	-0	70	0		0.0

STIDHAM, PHIL Phillip Wayne B11.18.1968 Tulsa OK BR/TR/6-0/180 [DetA91 15/400] d6.4 Col Arkansas-Monticello

YEAR	TM LG	W	L	PCT	G	GS	CG-SHO	SV-BS	IP	H	R	HR	HB	BB-IB	SO	ERA	AERA	OAV	OOB	AB-HR-SH	AVG	PB	SUP	APR	DL	PW
1994	Det A	0	0	—	5	0	0	0-0	4.1	12	12	3	0	4-1	4	24.92	20	.571	.615	0	—	0		-9		-0.4

STIEB, DAVE David Andrew B7.22.1957 Santa Ana CA BR/TR/6-1/195* [TorA78 5/106] d6.29 Col Southern Illinois

YEAR	TM LG	W	L	PCT	G	GS	CG-SHO	SV-BS	IP	H	R	HR	HB	BB-IB	SO	ERA	AERA	OAV	OOB	AB-HR-SH	AVG	PB	SUP	APR	DL	PW
1979	Tor A	8	8	.500	18	18	7-1	0-0	129.1	139	70	11	4	48-3	52	4.31	102	.276	.342	0		0*	94	1		0.2
1980	Tor A★	12	15	.444	34	32	14-4	0-0	242.2	232	108	12	6	83-6	108	3.71	116	.260	.324	1	.000	-0*	80	17		2.0
1981	Tor A★	11	10	.524	25	25	11-2	0-0	183.2	148	70	10	11	61-2	89	3.19	124	.223	.296	0		0*	63	17		2.0
1982	Tor A★	17	14	.548	38	38	**19-5**	0-0	**288.1**	271	116	27	3	75-4	141	3.25	139	.248	.298	0		0	79	36		3.9
1983	Tor A★	17	12	.586	36	36	14-4	0-0	278	223	105	21	14	93-6	187	3.04	143	.219	.291	0		0	94	37		3.7
1984	Tor A★	16	8	.667	35	35	11-2	0-0	267	215	87	19	11	88-1	198	2.83	146	.221	.292	0		0	91	40		3.5
1985	†Tor A	14	13	.519	36	36	11-2	0-0	265	206	89	22	9	96-3	167	**2.48**	**171**	**.213**	.290	0		0	95	47		**4.9**
1986	Tor A	7	12	.368	37	34	1-1	1-0	205	239	128	29	15	87-1	127	4.74	90	.297	.373	0		0*	101	-15		-1.2
1987	Tor A	13	9	.591	33	31	3-1	0-0	185	164	92	16	7	87-4	115	4.09	111	.239	.329	0		0*	120	9		0.9
1988	Tor A★	16	8	.667	32	31	8-4	0-0	207.1	157	76	15	13	79-0	147	3.04	130	.210	.295	0		0*	108	22		2.5
1989	†Tor A	17	8	.680	33	33	3-2	0-0	206.2	164	83	12	13	76-2	101	3.35	113	.219	.301	0		0	124	12		1.3
1990	Tor A	18	6	.750	33	33	2-2	0-0	208.2	179	73	11	10	64-0	125	2.93	135	.230	.296	0		0	104	23		2.7
1991	Tor A	4	3	.571	9	9	1	0-0	59.2	52	22	4	2	23-0	29	3.17	133	.243	.321	0		0	79	7	137	0.8
1992	Tor A	4	6	.400	21	14	1	0-0	96.1	98	58	9	4	43-3	45	5.04	81	.275	.355	0		0	92	-9	73	-0.8
1993	Chi A	1	3	.250	4	4	0	0-0	22.1	27	17	1	0	14-0	11	6.04	70	.300	.390	0		0	98	-5	23	-0.3
1998	Tor A	1	2	.333	19	3	0	2-0	50.1	31	6	5	1-7	27		4.83	97	.284	.351	1	.000	-0	140	-2		-0.1
Total	16	176	137	.562	443	412	103-30	3-0	2895.1	2572	1225	225	129	1034-36	1669	3.44	123	.239	.312	2	.000	-0	96	237	233	25.6

STIELY, FRED Fred Warren "Lefty" B6.1.1901 Pillow PA D1.6.1981 Valley View PA BL/TL/5-8/170 d10.6

YEAR	TM LG	W	L	PCT	G	GS	CG-SHO	SV-BS	IP	H	R	HR	HB	BB-IB	SO	ERA	AERA	OAV	OOB	AB-HR-SH	AVG	PB	SUP	APR	DL	PW
1929	StL A	1	0	1.000	4	1	1	0	9	11	2	0	1	3	2	0.00	—	.297	.366	3	.667	1	76	3		0.6
1930	StL A	0	1	.000	4	2	1	0	19	27	21	4	1	8	5	8.53	57	.346	.414	7	.429	1*	115	-8		-0.2
1931	StL A	0	0	—	4	0	0	0	6.2	7	5	0	1	3	2	6.75	69	.269	.367	0	—	0		-1		-0.1
Total	3	1	1	.500	9	3	2	0	34.2	45	28	4	3	14	9	5.97	79	.319	.392	10	.500	2	103	-6		0.3

STIGMAN, DICK Richard Lewis B1.24.1936 Nimrod MN BR/TL/6-3/200* d4.22

YEAR	TM LG	W	L	PCT	G	GS	CG-SHO	SV-BS	IP	H	R	HR	HB	BB-IB	SO	ERA	AERA	OAV	OOB	AB-HR-SH	AVG	PB	SUP	APR	DL	PW
1960	Cle A☆	5	11	.313	41	18	3	9	133.2	118	78	13	0	87-1	104	4.51	83	.238	.348	36-0-1	.222	2	79	-13		-1.4
1961	Cle A	2	5	.286	22	6	0	4	64.1	65	35	9	0	25-1	48	4.62	85	.264	.327	16	.125	-1	49	-5	56	-0.4
1962	Min A	12	5	.706	40	15	6	3	142.2	122	60	19	2	64-3	116	3.66	112	.233	.318	45	.044	-4	152	9		0.5
1963	Min A	15	15	.500	33	33	15-3	0	241	210	99	30	6	81-2	193	3.25	112	.231	.293	84-0-5	.107	-2	108	15		1.4
1964	Min A	6	15	.286	32	29	5-1	0	190	160	94	31	5	70-7	159	4.03	89	.225	.298	69	.101	-3	81	-8		-1.2
1965	Min A	4	2	.667	33	8	0	4	70	59	34	14	0	33-3	70	4.37	81	.227	.327	15-0-1	.133	-0	114	-4		-0.4
1966	Bos A	2	1	.667	34	10	1-1	0	81	85	51	15	1	46-5	65	5.44	70	.268	.361	17-0-2	.118	-1	79	-11		-0.7
Total	7	46	54	.460	235	119	30-5	16	922.2	819	442	133	6	406-22	755	4.03	93	.237	.316	282-0-9	.113	-8	97	-16	56	-2.2

STILES, ROLLIE Rolland Mays "Lena" B11.17.1906 Ratcliff AR BR/TR/6-1.5/180 d6.19 Col Southeastern Oklahoma

YEAR	TM LG	W	L	PCT	G	GS	CG-SHO	SV-BS	IP	H	R	HR	HB	BB-IB	SO	ERA	AERA	OAV	OOB	AB-HR-SH	AVG	PB	SUP	APR	DL	PW
1930	StL A	3	6	.333	20	7	3	0	102	136	73	10	1	41	25	5.91	82	.337	.399	37	.270	-0	98	-11		-0.8
1931	StL A	3	1	.750	34	2	0	0	81	112	72	2	2	60	32	7.22	64	.352	.458	22	.045	-2	100	-19		-1.1
1933	StL A	3	7	.300	31	9	6-1	1	115	154	83	4	2	47	29	5.01	93	.327	.390	33-0-2	.061	-3	95	-9		-1.0
Total	3	9	14	.391	85	18	9-1	1	298	402	232	16	5	148	86	5.92	80	.337	.412	92-0-2	.141	-5	97	-39		-2.9

STIMMEL, ARCHIE Archibald May "Lumbago" B5.30.1873 Woodsboro MD D8.18.1958 Frederick MD BR/TR/6-0/175 d7.3

YEAR	TM LG	W	L	PCT	G	GS	CG-SHO	SV-BS	IP	H	R	HR	HB	BB-IB	SO	ERA	AERA	OAV	OOB	AB-HR-SH	AVG	PB	SUP	APR	DL	PW
1900	Cin N	1	1	.500	2	1	1	0	13	18	11	1	0	4	2	6.92	53	.327	.373	5	.200	-0	0	-4		-0.5
1901	Cin N	4	14	.222	20	18	14-1	0	153.1	170	96	10	12	44	55	4.11	78	.279	.339	62-0-2	.081	-5*	66	-16		-2.1
1902	Cin N	0	4	.000	4	3	3	0	26	37	16	1	2	12	7	3.46	87	.333	.408	10	.200	-0	53	-1		-0.2
Total	3	5	19	.208	26	22	18-1	0	192.1	225	123	12	14	60	64	4.21	76	.290	.352	77-0-2	.104	-5	61	-21		-2.8

STIMSON, CARL Carl Remus B7.18.1894 Hamburg IA D11.9.1936 Omaha NE BB/TR/6-5/190 d6.6

YEAR	TM LG	W	L	PCT	G	GS	CG-SHO	SV-BS	IP	H	R	HR	HB	BB-IB	SO	ERA	AERA	OAV	OOB	AB-HR-SH	AVG	PB	SUP	APR	DL	PW
1923	Bos A	0	0	—	2	0	0	0	4	12	10	1	1	5	1	22.50	18	.750	.818	2	.000	-0		-7		-0.3

STINE, HARRY Harry C. B2.20.1864 Shenandoah PA D6.5.1924 Niagara Falls NY TL/5-6/150 d7.22

YEAR	TM LG	W	L	PCT	G	GS	CG-SHO	SV-BS	IP	H	R	HR	HB	BB-IB	SO	ERA	AERA	OAV	OOB	AB-HR-SH	AVG	PB	SUP	APR	DL	PW
1890	Phi AA	0	1	.000	1	1	1	0	8	17	9	0	4	4	1	9.00	43	.415	.467	3	.000	-0	52	-4		-0.3

STINE, LEE Lee Elbert B11.17.1913 Stillwater OK D5.6.2005 Hemet CA BR/TR/5-11/185 d4.17

YEAR	TM LG	W	L	PCT	G	GS	CG-SHO	SV-BS	IP	H	R	HR	HB	BB-IB	SO	ERA	AERA	OAV	OOB	AB-HR-SH	AVG	PB	SUP	APR	DL	PW
1934	Chi A	0	0	—	4	0	0	0	11	11	10	2	1*	10	8	8.18	58	.268	.423	1	.000	0		-3		-0.2
1935	Chi A	0	0	—	1	0	0	0	2	2	2	1	0	2	2	9.00	51	.286	.500	0	—	0		-1		0.0
1936	Cin N	3	8	.273	40	13	5-1	2	121.2	157	79	6	8	41	26	5.03	76	.318	.379	27-0-2	.296	3	107	-16		-1.0
1938	NY A	0	0	—	4	0	0	0	8.2	9	1	0	0	1	4	1.04	437	.333	.357	2	.500	0		4		0.2
Total	4	3	8	.273	49	13	5-1	2	143.1	179	92	9	9	55	39	5.09	78	.315	.384	30-0-2	.300	4	107	-16		-1.0

STIVETTS, JACK John Elmer "Happy Jack" B3.31.1868 Ashland PA D4.18.1930 Ashland PA BR/TR/6-2/185 d6.26 ▲

YEAR	TM LG	W	L	PCT	G	GS	CG-SHO	SV-BS	IP	H	R	HR	HB	BB-IB	SO	ERA	AERA	OAV	OOB	AB-HR-SH	AVG	PB	SUP	APR	DL	PW
1889	StL AA	12	7	.632	26	20	18-2	2	191.2	153	85	4	5	68	143	**2.25**	**188**	**.212**	**.285**	79	.228	-1*	72	36		2.8
1890	StL AA	27	21	.563	54	46	41-3	0	419.1	399	256	14	17	179	289	3.52	123	.243	.324	226-7	.288	14*	103	31		4.2
1891	StL AA	33	22	.600	64	56	40-3	1	440	357	237	15	18	232	259	2.86	147	.214	.317	302-7	.305	9*	95	**58**		**6.8**
1892	†Bos N	35	16	.686	54	48	45-3	1	415.2	346	223	12	10	171	180	3.03	116	.217	.297	240-3	.296	15*	109	18		3.3
1893	Bos N	20	12	.625	38	34	29-1	1	283.2	315	194	17	10	115	61	4.41	112	.273	.344	172-3	.297	7*	115	15		1.7
1894	Bos N	26	14	.650	45	39	30	0	338	429	278	27	13	127	76	4.90	106	.306	.369	244-8-3	.328	10*	121	22		2.5
1895	Bos N	17	17	.500	38	34	30	0	291	341	219	15	12	89	111	4.64	110	.284	.344	158-0-2	.190	7*	86	15		0.5
1896	Bos N	22	14	.611	42	36	31-2	0	329	353	219	19	7	99	71	4.10	111	.272	.327	222-3-4	.347	12*	111	20		2.6
1897	†Bos N	11	4	.733	18	15	10	0	129.1	147	75	5	5	43	27	3.41	131	.284	.345	199-2-1	.367	7*	141	12		1.8
1898	Bos N	1	0	1.000	2	1	1	0	12	17	12	2	0	7	1	8.25	45	.333	.414	111-2-4	.252	0*	58	-5		-0.3
1899	Cle N	0	4	.000	7	4	3	0	38	48	39	0	2	25	1	5.68	65	.308	.410	39	.205	-1*	49	-11		-0.8
Total	11	203	132	.606	388	333	278-14	5	2887.2	2905	1836	130	99	1155	1223	3.74	121	.255	.329	1992-35-14	.298	65	104	211		25.1

STOBBS, CHUCK Charles Klein B7.2.1929 Wheeling WV BL/TL/6-1/185(185-205) d9.15

YEAR	TM LG	W	L	PCT	G	GS	CG-SHO	SV-BS	IP	H	R	HR	HB	BB-IB	SO	ERA	AERA	OAV	OOB	AB-HR-SH	AVG	PB	SUP	APR	DL	PW
1947	Bos A	0	0	—	9	1	0	0	9	10	6	0	0	10	5	6.00	65	.294	.455	1	.000	-0	68	-5		-0.2
1948	Bos A	0	0	—	6	0	0	0	7	9	5	0	0	4	4	6.43	68	.321	.457	1	.000	-0		-1		-0.1
1949	Bos A	11	6	.647	26	19	10	0	152	145	72	10	2	75	70	4.03	108	.254	.343	53-0-6	.208	0	124	7		0.6
1950	Bos A	12	7	.632	32	21	6	1	169.1	158	104	17	5	88	78	5.10	96	.250	.346	57-0-4	.246	3	151	-3		-0.7
1951	Bos A	10	9	.526	34	25	6	0	170	180	100	16	5	74	75	4.76	94	.271	.349	61-0-5	.180	-2	111	-5		-0.7
1952	Chi A	7	12	.368	38	17	2	1	135	118	64	11	4	69	73	3.13	116	.237	.339	38-0-4	.079	-1	70	7		0.8
1953	Was A	11	9	.579	27	20	8	0	153	146	64	11	2	44	67	3.29	118	.246	.299	44-0-10	.227	-1	128	10		1.3

YEAR	TM LG	W	L	PCT	G	GS	CG-SHO	SV-BS	IP	H	R	HR	HB	BB-IB	SO	ERA	AERA	OAV	OOB	AB-HR-SH	AVG	PB	SUP	APR	DL	PW
1954	Was A	11	11	.500	31	24	10-3	0	182	189	87	6	1	67	67	4.10	87	.270	.330	51-0-9	.137	0	103	-8		-0.8
1955	Was A	4	14	.222	41	16	5-0	3	140.1	169	90	13	1	57-8	60	5.00	77	.302	.364	35-0-1	.171	2	73	-20		-2.0
1956	Was A	15	15	.500	37	33	15-1	1	240	264	115	29	1	54-4	97	3.60	120	.279	.316	77-16	.179	-2*	77	16		1.7
1957	Was A	8	20	.286	42	31	5-2	1	211.2	235	140	28	5	80-10	114	5.36	73	.279	.343	76-0-4	.211	1	76	-35		-4.1
1958	Was A	2	6	.250	19	8	0	0	56.2	87	44	7	2	16-0	23	6.04	63	.369	.405	12	.000	-2	77	-15		-2.0
	StL N	1	3	.250	17	0	0	1	39.2	40	16	4	0	14-1	25	3.63	114	.261	.323	4-0-1	.250	0		3		0.4
1959	Was A	1	8	.111	41	7	0	7	90.2	82	42	13	2	24-1	50	2.98	131	.238	.290	19-0-1	.105	-1	74	6		0.5
1960	Was A	12	7	.632	40	13	1-1	2	119.1	115	54	13	3	38-4	72	3.32	117	.252	.311	34-0-1	.088	-2	92	7		0.8
1961	Min A	2	3	.400	24	3	0	2	44.2	56	37	8	2	15-2	17	7.46	57	.311	.363	8	.375	1	49	-13		-1.3
Total	15	107	130	.451	459	238	65-7	19	1920.1	2003	1030	184	35	735-30	897	4.29	95	.269	.336	578-0-50	.176	-1	99	-46		-5.1

STOCK, WES Wesley Gay B4.10.1934 Longview WA BR/TR/6-2/188* d4.19 C16 Col Washington St.

YEAR	TM LG	W	L	PCT	G	GS	CG-SHO	SV-BS	IP	H	R	HR	HB	BB-IB	SO	ERA	AERA	OAV	OOB	AB-HR-SH	AVG	PB	SUP	APR	DL	PW
1959	Bal A	0	0	—	7	0	0	1	12.2	16	6	1	0	2-0	5	3.55	107	.302	.327	2	.000	-0		0		0.0
1960	Bal A	2	2	.500	17	0	0	2	34.1	26	11	2	1	14-1	23	2.88	132	.218	.306	6	.000	-1		4		0.5
1961	Bal A	5	0	1.000	35	1	0	3	71.2	58	24	3	2	27-2	47	3.01	128	.225	.300	11	.000	-1	0	8		0.9
1962	Bal A	3	2	.600	53	0	0	1	65	50	33	7	1	36-6	34	4.43	83	.217	.326	3	.000	-0		-4		-0.2
1963	Bal A	7	0	1.000	47	0	0	1	75.1	69	41	11	0	31-7	55	3.94	88	.246	.319	10	.000	-1		-6		-0.7
1964	Bal A	2	0	1.000	14	0	0	0	20.2	17	9	5	0	8-1	14	3.92	91	.233	.305	4	.000	-0		0		-0.1
	KC A	6	3	.667	50	0	0	5	93	69	21	10	4	34-7	101	1.94	197	.213	.292	15-0-3	.200	0		19		2.0
	Year	8	3	.727	64	0	0	5	113.2	86	30	15	4	42-8	115	2.30	164	.217	.295	19-0-3	.158	-0		19		1.9
1965	KC A	0	4	.000	62	2	0	4	99.2	96	62	18	4	40-2	52	5.24	67	.251	.326	6-0-2	.000	-1	113	-18		-0.9
1966	KC A	2	2	.500	35	0	0	3	44	30	15	3	3	21-3	31	2.66	128	.199	.307	2	.000	-0		4		0.3
1967	KC A	0	0	—	1	0	0	0	1	3	2	0	0	2-0	0	18.00	18	.500	.625	—	—	0		-2		-0.1
Total	9	27	13	.675	321	3	0	22	517.1	434	224	60	15	215-29	365	3.60	101	.231	.313	59-0-5	.051	-4	73	5		1.4

STOCKSDALE, OTIS Otis Hinkley "Old Gray Fox" B8.7.1871 Arcadia MD D3.15.1933 Pennsville NJ BL/TR/5-10.5/180 d7.24 Col Johns Hopkins

YEAR	TM LG	W	L	PCT	G	GS	CG-SHO	SV-BS	IP	H	R	HR	HB	BB-IB	SO	ERA	AERA	OAV	OOB	AB-HR-SH	AVG	PB	SUP	APR	DL	PW
1893	Was N	2	8	.200	11	11	7	0	69	111	82	4	5	32	12	8.22	56	.352	.420	40	.300	2*	85	-24		-2.2
1894	Was N	5	9	.357	18	14	11	0	117.1	176	115	10	14	42	10	5.06	104	.342	.407	71-0-1	.324	1*	95	1		0.2
1895	Was N	6	11	.353	20	17	11	1	136	199	143	7	8	52	23	6.09	79	.336	.397	74-0-1	.311	2*	99	-18		-1.4
	Bos N	2	2	.500	4	4	1	0	23	31	22	2	0	8	2	5.87	87	.316	.368	15	.267	-0*	133	-2		-0.3
	Year	8	13	.381	24	21	12	1	159	230	165	9	8	60	25	6.06	80	.333	.393	89-0-1	.303	1*	106	-25		-1.7
1896	Bal N	0	1	.000	1	0	0	0	1.2	4	4	0	1	2	1	16.20	26	.444	.583	3	.333	1*		-2		-0.3
Total	4	15	31	.326	54	46	30	1	347	521	366	23	28	136	48	6.20	80	.341	.405	203-0-2	.310	5	97	-45		-4.0

STODDARD, BOB Robert Lyle B3.8.1957 San Jose CA BR/TR/6-1/200* [SeaA78 10/240] d9.4 Col Cal St.-Fresno

YEAR	TM LG	W	L	PCT	G	GS	CG-SHO	SV-BS	IP	H	R	HR	HB	BB-IB	SO	ERA	AERA	OAV	OOB	AB-HR-SH	AVG	PB	SUP	APR	DL	PW
1981	Sea A	2	1	.667	5	5	1	0-0	34.2	35	10	3	1	9-0	22	2.60	150	.269	.321	0	—	0	97	5		0.4
1982	Sea A	3	3	.500	9	9	2-1	0-0	67.1	48	22	7	3	18-0	24	2.41	178	.205	.267	0	—	0	71	13		1.1
1983	Sea A	9	17	.346	35	23	2-1	0-0	175.2	182	95	29	4	58-0	87	4.41	94	.274	.334	0	—	0	60	-2		-0.1
1984	Sea A	2	3	.400	27	6	0	0-0	79	86	51	10	2	37-3	39	5.13	78	.278	.357	0	—	0	86	-10		-0.5
1985	Det A	0	0	—	8	0	0	1-0	13.1	16	11	3	0	5-0	11	6.75	61	.268	.328	0	—	0		-4		-0.2
1986	SD N	1	0	1.000	18	0	0	1-1	23.1	20	7	1	1	11-1	17	2.31	158	.227	.317	1	.000	-0		3		0.1
1987	KC A	1	3	.250	17	2	0	1-0	40	51	26	3	3	22-3	23	4.27	107	.313	.402	0	—	0	40	-1		0.0
Total	7	18	27	.400	119	45	5-2	3-1	433.1	437	222	56	14	160-6	223	4.03	104	.266	.334	1	.000	-0	69	4		0.9

STODDARD, TIM Timothy Paul B1.24.1953 E.Chicago IN BR/TR/6-7/250(235-253) [ChiA75*S2/44] d9.7 Col North Carolina St.

YEAR	TM LG	W	L	PCT	G	GS	CG-SHO	SV-BS	IP	H	R	HR	HB	BB-IB	SO	ERA	AERA	OAV	OOB	AB-HR-SH	AVG	PB	SUP	APR	DL	PW
1975	Chi A	0	0	—	1	0	0	0-0	1	4	3	0	0	1-0	1	9.00	43	.400	.400	0	—	0		-1		0.0
1978	Bal A	0	1	.000	8	0	0	0-0	18	22	17	3	2	8-1	14	6.00	59	.301	.386	0	—	0		-7		-0.4
1979	†Bal A	3	1	.750	29	0	0	3-3	58	44	12	3	0	19-2	47	1.71	237	.212	.278	0	—	0	16	42		1.6
1980	Bal A	5	3	.625	64	0	0	26-7	86	72	27	2	1	38-1	64	2.51	158	.233	.317	0	—	0	14			2.1
1981	Bal A	4	2	.667	31	0	0	7-4	37.1	38	16	6	2	18-0	32	3.86	95	.268	.358	0	—	0	0			0.0
1982	Bal A	3	4	.429	50	0	0	12-3	56	53	26	4	1	29-6	42	4.02	101	.249	.337	0	—	0	1	57		0.1
1983	†Chi N	4	3	.571	47	0	0	9-2	57.2	65	39	10	1	29-4	50	6.09	66	.293	.371	0	—	0	-12			-1.6
1984	†Chi N	10	6	.625	58	0	0	7-4	92	77	41	9	1	57-11	87	3.82	102	.236	.346	11-0-1	.091	-1	2			0.2
1985	SD N	1	6	.143	44	0	0	1-0	60	63	35	3	0	37-7	42	4.65	97	.269	.366	5-0-1	.000	-1	-7			-0.9
1986	SD N	1	3	.250	30	0	0	0-1	45.1	33	20	6	0	34-6	47	3.77	97	.200	.337	4-1-0	.250	1	0			0.1
	NY A	4	1	.800	24	0	0	0-1	49.1	41	23	6	0	23-3	34	3.83	108	.232	.317	0	—	0	2			0.2
1987	NY A	4	3	.571	57	0	0	8-1	92.2	83	38	13	0	30-2	78	3.50	127	.235	.293	0	—	0	10	9		0.8
1988	NY A	2	2	.500	28	0	0	3-0	55	62	41	5	2	27-1	33	6.38	62	.286	.361	0	—	0	-14	21		-1.0
1989	Cle A	0	0	—	14	0	0	0-0	21.1	25	7	1	0	7-1	12	2.95	135	.313	.356	0	—	0	3			0.1
Total	13	41	35	.539	485	0	0	76-26	729.2	680	343	72	10	356-45	582	3.95	101	.250	.335	20-1-2	.100	-1	7	129		0.9

STOKES, ART Arthur Milton B9.13.1896 Emmitsburg MD D6.3.1962 Titusville PA BR/TR/5-10.5/155 d5.5

YEAR	TM LG	W	L	PCT	G	GS	CG-SHO	SV-BS	IP	H	R	HR	HB	BB-IB	SO	ERA	AERA	OAV	OOB	AB-HR-SH	AVG	PB	SUP	APR	DL	PW
1925	Phi A	1	1	.500	12	0	0	0	24.1	24	15	0	2	10	7	4.07	114	.270	.356	4		0		1		0.1

STONE, DICK Charles Richard B12.5.1911 Oklahoma City OK D2.18.1980 Oklahoma City OK BL/TL/5-9/153 d8.26 Col Oklahoma City

YEAR	TM LG	W	L	PCT	G	GS	CG-SHO	SV-BS	IP	H	R	HR	HB	BB-IB	SO	ERA	AERA	OAV	OOB	AB-HR-SH	AVG	PB	SUP	APR	DL	PW
1945	Was A	0	0	—	3	0	0	0	5	6	0	0	2	2	0	0.00	—	.316	.381	0	—	0		2		0.1

STONE, DEAN Darrah Dean B9.1.1930 Moline IL BL/TL/6-4/205* d9.13

YEAR	TM LG	W	L	PCT	G	GS	CG-SHO	SV-BS	IP	H	R	HR	HB	BB-IB	SO	ERA	AERA	OAV	OOB	AB-HR-SH	AVG	PB	SUP	APR	DL	PW
1953	Was A	0	1	.000	3	1	0	0	8.2	13	8	0	0	5	5	8.31	47	.361	.439	2	.000	-0	46	-4		-0.4
1954	Was A★	12	10	.545	31	23	10-2	0	178.2	161	76	7	1	69	87	3.22	110	.240	.310	52-1-6	.096	-0	113	6		0.5
1955	Was A	6	13	.316	43	24	5-1	1	180	180	98	14	3	114-5	84	4.15	92	.267	.371	46-0-10	.043	-4	80	-8		-1.2
1956	Was A	5	7	.417	41	21	2	3	132	148	107	10	7	93-0	86	6.27	69	.282	.395	34-0-2	.088	-1*	109	-28		-2.5
1957	Was A	0	0	—	3	0	0	0	3.1	5	3	0	0	2-1	3	8.10	48	.357	.412	0	—	0		-1		-0.1
	Bos A	1	3	.250	17	8	0	1	51.1	56	42	5	0	35-0	32	5.08	78	.284	.386	14-0-1	.000	-1	101	-10		-0.8
	Year	1	3	.250	20	8	0	1	54.2	61	45	5	0	37-1	35	5.27	76	.289	.387	14-0-1	.000	-1	101	-12		-0.9
1959	StL N	0	1	.000	18	1	0	1	30	30	15	4	0	16-4	17	4.20	101	.273	.357	4	.000	0	0	0		0.0
1962	Hou N	3	2	.600	15	7	2-2	0	52.1	61	31	4	1	20-0	31	4.47	84	.295	.360	16-0-3	.250	1	107	-5		0.2
	Chi A	1	0	1.000	27	0	0	5	30.1	28	11	3	1	9-2	12	3.26	120	.255	.306	2	.500	1		3		0.2
1963	Bal A	1	2	.333	17	0	0	1	19.1	23	11	0	0	10-2	12	5.12	68	.307	.384	0	—	0		-3		-0.5
Total	8	29	39	.426	215	85	19-5	12	686	705	402	47	13	373-14	380	4.47	86	.269	.360	170-1-22	.088	-6	100	-50		-5.1

STONE, DWIGHT Dwight Ely B8.2.1886 Holt Co. NE D6.3.1976 Glendale CA BR/TR/6-1.5/170 d4.13

YEAR	TM LG	W	L	PCT	G	GS	CG-SHO	SV-BS	IP	H	R	HR	HB	BB-IB	SO	ERA	AERA	OAV	OOB	AB-HR-SH	AVG	PB	SUP	APR	DL	PW
1913	StL A	2	6	.250	18	7	4-1	0	91	94	45	0	7	46	37	3.56	82	.271	.368	33	.273	2	72	-5		-0.2
1914	KC F	8	14	.364	39	22	6	0	186.2	205	110	8	8	77	88	4.34	64	.281	.356	58-1-2	.121	-4	91	-30		-3.5
Total	2	10	20	.333	57	29	10-1	0	277.2	299	155	8	15	123	125	4.08	69	.278	.360	91-1-2	.176	-2	86	-35		-3.7

STONE, ARNIE Edwin Arnold B10.9.1892 North Creek NY D7.29.1948 Hudson Falls NY BR/TL/6-0/180 d7.30

YEAR	TM LG	W	L	PCT	G	GS	CG-SHO	SV-BS	IP	H	R	HR	HB	BB-IB	SO	ERA	AERA	OAV	OOB	AB-HR-SH	AVG	PB	SUP	APR	DL	PW
1923	Pit N	0	1	.000	9	0	0	0	12.1	19	12	0	0	4	2	8.03	50	.352	.397	1	.000	-0		-5		-0.4
1924	Pit N	4	2	.667	26	2	1	0	64	57	27	0	0	15	7	2.95	130	.259	.306	15	.133	-1	155	5		0.3
Total	2	4	3	.571	35	2	1	0	76.1	76	39	0	0	19	9	3.77	102	.277	.324	16	.125	-1	155	0		-0.1

STONE, GEORGE George Heard B7.9.1946 Ruston LA BL/TL/6-3/195* [AtlN66 5/91] d9.15 Col Louisiana Tech

YEAR	TM LG	W	L	PCT	G	GS	CG-SHO	SV-BS	IP	H	R	HR	HB	BB-IB	SO	ERA	AERA	OAV	OOB	AB-HR-SH	AVG	PB	SUP	APR	DL	PW
1967	Atl N	0	0	—	2	1	0	0	7.1	8	4	0	0	1-0	5	4.91	68	.267	.290	2	.000	-0	26	-1		-0.1
1968	Atl N	7	4	.636	17	10	2	0	75	63	27	9	0	19-4	52	2.76	108	.222	.271	27-0-1	.333	3	142	2		0.5
1969	†Atl N	13	10	.565	36	20	3	3-1	165.1	166	82	20	6	48-5	102	3.65	99	.260	.316	59-1-5	.186	1	119	-4		-0.4
1970	Atl N	11	11	.500	35	30	9-2	0-0	207.1	218	111	27	6	50-7	131	3.86	111	.267	.312	70-0-3	.236	4	113	4		1.0
1971	Atl N	6	8	.429	27	24	4-2	0-0	172.2	186	80	19	6	35-4	110	3.60	104	.274	.313	62-0-3	.177	-0*	89	2		0.5
1972	Atl N	6	11	.353	31	16	2-1	1-0	111	143	72	18	4	44-11	63	5.51	69	.315	.378	25-0-6	.200	1*	92	-18		-2.3
1973	†NY N	12	3	.800	27	21	2-1	1-0	148	157	53	16	0	31-3	77	2.80	130	.274	.308	48-0-3	.271	2*	111	13		1.8
1974	NY N	2	7	.222	15	13	1	0-0	77	103	57	10	0	21-4	29	5.03	72	.322	.362	26	.115	-1	93	-15	54	-1.7
1975	NY N	3	3	.500	13	11	1	0-0	57	75	38	3	0	21-3	21	5.05	70	.323	.378	18-0-2	.167	0	132	-11	81	-1.0
Total	9	60	57	.513	203	145	24-5	5-1	1020.2	1119	524	122	21	270-41	590	3.89	96	.278	.325	339-1-23	.212	10	108	-28	135	-2.4

STONE, ROCKY John Vernon B8.23.1918 Redding CA D11.12.1986 Fountain Valley CA BR/TR/6-0/200 d5.2

YEAR	TM LG	W	L	PCT	G	GS	CG-SHO	SV-BS	IP	H	R	HR	HB	BB-IB	SO	ERA	AERA	OAV	OOB	AB-HR-SH	AVG	PB	SUP	APR	DL	PW
1943	Cin N	0	1	.000	9	0	0	0	24.2	24	14	0	0	8	11	4.38	76	.237	.295	4	.250	0		-3		-0.2

YEAR	TM LG	W	L	PCT	G	GS	CG-SHO	SV-BS	IP	H	R	HR	HB	BB-IB	SO	ERA	AERA	OAV	OOB	AB-HR-SH	AVG	PB	SUP	APR	DL	PW
STONE, RICKY	Ricky L. B11.25.1975 Hamilton OH BR/TR/6-1/168(168-195) [LAN94 4/104] d9.21																								
2001	Hou N	0	0	—	6	0	0	0-0	7.2	8	3	1	0	2-1	4	2.35	196	.258	.303	0	—	.0		1		0.1
2002	Hou N	3	3	.500	78	0	0	1-1	77.1	78	36	9	1	34-3	63	3.61	120	.266	.342	4-0-1	.000	-0		5		0.3
2003	Hou N	6	4	.600	65	0	0	1-0	83	76	36	11	6	31-4	47	3.69	120	.247	.327	3	.000	-0		7		0.7
2004	Hou N	1	1	.500	16	0	0	0-0	19	26	12	5	3	7-3	16	5.68	77	.317	.391	0	—	-0		-2		-0.2
	SD N	1	1	.500	27	0	0	0-0	32.2	40	27	6	3	9-0	22	6.89	57	.301	.356	1	.000	-0		-12		-0.7
	Year	2	2	.500	43	0	0	0-0	51.2	66	39	11	6	16-3	38	6.45	64	.307	.370	1	.000	-0		-13		-0.9
2005	Cin N	0	0	—	23	0	0	0-0	30.2	48	24	8	2	7-2	15	6.75	62	.364	.399	2	.000	-0		-9		-0.5
Total	5	11	9	.550	215	0	0		218	276	138	40	15	90-13	167	4.57	94	.282	.350	10-0-1	.000	-1		-10		-0.3
STONE, STEVE	Steven Michael B7.14.1947 Euclid OH BR/TR/5-10/175* [SFN69*S4/89] d4.8 Col Kent St. [DL 1982 Bal A 182]																								
1971	SF N	5	9	.357	24	19	2-2	0-0	110.2	110	56	9	3	55-4	63	4.15	82	.259	.349	34-0-3	.000	-2	89	-7		-1.0
1972	SF N	6	8	.429	27	16	4-1	0-1	123.2	97	48	11	2	49-2	85	2.98	117	.218	.297	34-0-6	.118	-1	95	6		0.6
1973	Chi N	6	11	.353	36	22	3	1-0	176.1	163	87	11	7	82-0	138	4.24	93	.245	.334	0	—	0*	64	-2		-0.2
1974	Chi N	8	6	.571	38	23	1	0-0	169.2	185	92	19	4	64-4	90	4.14	93	.278	.343	58-0-5	.121	-3*	109	-5		-0.7
1975	Chi N	12	8	.600	33	32	6-1	0-0	214.1	198	103	24	5	80-3	139	3.95	98	.245	.314	72-0-7	.111	-2*	102	0		-0.2
1976	Chi N	3	6	.333	17	15	1-1	0-0	75	70	36	6	3	21-1	33	4.08	95	.250	.305	21-0-1	.143	-1	73	0	68	-0.2
1977	Chi A	15	12	.556	31	31	8	0-0	207.1	228	115	25	5	80-3	124	4.51	91	.281	.346	21-0-1	.143	-1	109	-9		-1.0
1978	Chi A	12	12	.500	30	30	6-1	0-0	212	196	110	19	3	84-1	118	4.37	87	.247	.319	0	—	0	98	-12		-1.2
1979	†Bal A	11	7	.611	32	32	3	0-0	186	173	91	31	1	73-1	96	3.77	107	.248	.320	0	—	0	107	4		0.4
1980	Bal A★	25	7	.781	37	37	9-1	0-0	250.2	224	103	22	6	101-3	149	3.23	123	.240	.318	0	—	0*	124	18		2.1
1981	Bal A	4	7	.364	15	12	0	0-0	62.2	63	39	7	1	27-0	30	4.60	79	.266	.342	0	—	0	88	-8	96	-1.2
Total	11	107	93	.535	320	269	43-7	1-1	1788.1	1707	880	184	40	716-22	1065	3.97	98	.253	.326	219-0-22	.100	-9	100	-15	346	-2.6
STONEMAN, BILL	William Hambly B4.7.1944 Oak Park IL BR/TR/5-10/170* [ChiN66 31/595] d7.16 Col Idaho																								
1967	Chi N	2	4	.333	28	2	0	4	63	51	24	7	0	22-4	52	3.29	108	.223	.289	13-0-3	.000	-1	99	2		0.1
1968	Chi N	0	1	.000	18	0	0	0	29.1	35	19	6	1	14-1	18	5.52	57	.310	.388	4	.000	-0		-7		-0.4
1969	Mon N	11	19	.367	42	36	8-5	0-0	235.2	233	133	26	12	123-4	185	4.39	84	.261	.356	73-0-8	.055	-3	93	-18		-2.4
1970	Mon N	7	15	.318	40	30	5-3	0-0	207.2	209	118	26	14	109-8	176	4.59	90	.263	.360	60-0-4	.100	-2*	77	-10		-1.2
1971	Mon N	17	16	.515	39	**39**	20-3	0-0	294.2	243	112	20	5	146-11	251	3.15	114	.225	.320	93-0-8	.129	-1*	94	15		1.5
1972	Mon N★	12	14	.462	36	35	13-4	0-0	250.2	213	93	15	3	102-12	171	2.98	119	.229	.305	75-0-13	.080	-4*	77	14		1.0
1973	Mon N	4	8	.333	29	17	0	1-0	96.2	120	77	12	6	55-6	48	6.80	56	.310	.400	20-0-2	.050	-1	110	-27	30	-3.1
1974	Cal A	1	8	.111	13	11	0	0-0	58.2	78	41	8	2	31-0	33	6.14	57	.322	.401	0	—	0	76	-16		-2.1
Total	8	54	85	.388	245	170	46-15	5-0	1236.1	1182	617	120	43	602-46	934	4.08	90	.253	.342	338-0-38	.086	-13	88	-47	30	-6.6
STONER, LIL	Ulysses Simpson Grant B2.28.1899 Bowie TX D6.26.1966 Enid OK BR/TR/5-9.5/180 d4.15																								
1922	Det A	4	4	.500	17	7	2	0	62.2	76	53	3	3	35	18	7.04	55	.315	.409	20-0-1	.100	-1	144	-20		-2.2
1924	Det A	11	11	.500	36	25	10-1	0	215.2	271	130	13	5	65	66	4.72	87	.316	.367	77-2-1	.195	1*	111	-11		-0.9
1925	Det A	10	9	.526	34	18	8	1	152	166	79	6	9	53	51	4.26	101	.283	.352	55-0-1	.291	4	132	3		0.6
1926	Det A	7	10	.412	32	22	7	0	159.2	179	115	11	3	63	57	5.47	74	.291	.359	53	.170	-2	109	-24		-2.3
1927	Det A	10	13	.435	38	24	13	5	215	251	118	9	3	77	63	3.98	106	.301	.362	74-0-4	.108	-6	94	6		-0.1
1928	Det A	5	8	.385	36	11	4	4	126.1	151	75	16	3	42	29	4.35	95	.296	.353	39-0-3	.179	-1	127	-4		-0.5
1929	Det A	3	3	.500	24	3	1	4	53	57	37	2	2	31	12	5.26	82	.288	.390	15	.067	-0	98	-5		-0.7
1930	Pit N	0	0	—	5	0	0	0	5.2	7	3	2	0	3	1	4.76	105	.318	.400	0	—	0		0		0.0
1931	Phi N	0	0	—	7	1	0	0	13.2	22	13	0	0	5	2	6.59	64	.373	.422	5	.000	-1	101	-4		-0.3
Total	9	50	58	.463	229	111	45-1	14	1003.2	1180	623	62	28	374	299	4.76	87	.301	.366	338-2-10	.172	-7	113	-59		-6.4
STOOPS, JIM	James Wellington B6.30.1972 Edison NJ BR/TR/6-2/180 d9.9 Col South Carolina-Aiken																								
1998	Col N	1	0	1.000	3	0	0	0-0	4	5	1	1	1	3-0	0	2.25	230	.385	.529	0	—	0		1		0.2
STOTTLEMYRE, MEL	Melvin Leon Jr. B12.28.1963 Prosser WA BR/TR/6-0/190 [HouN85*S1/3] d7.17 b-Todd f-Mel Col Nevada-Las Vegas																								
1990	KC A	0	1	.000	13	2	0	0-0	30	37	17	4	0	12-1	14	4.88	79	.280	.343	0	—	0	47	-3		-0.2
STOTTLEMYRE, MEL	Melvin Leon Sr. B11.13.1941 Hazleton MO BR/TR/6-2/190(170-192) d8.12 C22 s-Mel s-Todd Col Yakima Valley (WA) CC																								
1964	†NY A	9	3	.750	13	12	5-2	0	96	77	26	2	4	35-3	49	2.06	176	.219	.294	37-0-1	.243	2*	113	16		2.3
1965	NY A☆	20	9	.690	37	37	18-4	0	**291**	250	99	18	7	88-3	155	2.63	129	.233	.294	99-2-9	.131	1	109	24		2.8
1966	NY A★	12	20	.375	37	37	9-3	1	251	239	116	18	1	82-7	146	3.80	87	.253	.311	80-1-4	.138	1	98	-12		-1.1
1967	NY A	15	15	.500	36	36	10-4	0	255	235	96	20	2	88-11	151	2.96	105	.248	.311	82-0-6	.098	-3	96	6		0.6
1968	NY A	21	12	.636	36	36	19-6	0	278.2	243	86	21	3	65-7	140	2.45	119	.234	.280	91-0-3	.143	2	108	16		2.3
1969	NY A★	20	14	.588	39	39	24-3	0-0	303	267	105	19	6	97-11	113	2.82	125	.239	.301	101-1-4	.178	5	91	26		3.8
1970	NY A	15	13	.536	37	37	14	0-0	271	262	110	23	6	84-8	126	3.09	116	.255	.313	85-2-3	.188	8*	104	14		2.4
1971	NY A	16	12	.571	35	35	19-7	0-0	269.2	234	100	16	4	69-6	132	2.87	115	.233	.284	94-1-3	.170	2	113	13		1.7
1972	NY A	14	18	.438	36	36	9-7	0-0	260	250	99	13	4	85-13	110	3.22	93	.254	.314	80-0-9	.200	3*	89	-4		0.0
1973	NY A	16	16	.500	38	38	19-4	0-0	273	259	112	13	5	79-3	95	3.07	121	.253	.307	0	—	0	94	18		2.1
1974	NY A	6	7	.462	16	15	6	0-0	113	119	54	7	4	37-3	40	3.58	99	.272	.333	0	—	0*	83	-1	91	-0.2
Total	11	164	139	.541	360	356	152-40	1-0	2661.1	2435	1003	171	44	809-75	1257	2.97	113	.245	.303	749-7-42	.160	20	100	116	91	16.7
STOTTLEMYRE, TODD	Todd Vernon B5.20.1965 Sunnyside WA BL/TR/6-3/195(185-215) [TorA85 S1/3] d4.6 b-Mel f-Mel Col Nevada-Las Vegas [DL 2001 Ari N 190]																								
1988	Tor A	4	8	.333	28	16	0	0-1	98	109	70	15	4	46-5	67	5.69	70	.283	.363	0	—	0	102	-19		-2.1
1989	†Tor A	7	7	.500	27	18	0	0-0	127.2	137	56	11	5	44-4	63	3.88	98	.283	.343	0	—	0	80	1		0.0
1990	Tor A	13	17	.433	33	33	4	0-0	203	214	101	18	4	69-4	115	4.34	91	.274	.337	0	—	0	116	-7		-0.9
1991	†Tor A	15	8	.652	34	34	1	0-0	219	194	97	21	12	75-3	116	3.78	112	.235	.305	0	—	0	92	12		1.1
1992	†Tor A	12	11	.522	28	27	6-2	0-0	174	175	99	20	10	63-4	98	4.50	91	.262	.329	0	—	0	118	-9	23	-1.1
1993	†Tor A	11	12	.478	30	28	1-1	0-0	176.2	204	107	11	3	69-5	98	4.84	91	.292	.353	0	—	0	101	-10	21	-1.2
1994	Tor A	7	7	.500	26	19	3-1	1-2	140.2	149	67	19	7	48-2	105	4.22	116	.275	.339	0	—	0	79	12		1.0
1995	Oak A	14	7	.667	31	31	2	0-0	209.2	228	117	26	6	80-7	205	4.55	100	.276	.343	1	.000	-0	129	-2		-0.2
1996	†StL N	14	11	.560	34	33	5-2	0-0	223.1	191	100	30	4	93-8	194	3.87	110	.231	.309	66-0-9	.227	3	102	12		1.6
1997	StL N	12	9	.571	28	28	0	0-0	181	155	86	16	12	65-3	160	3.88	108	.231	.308	55-0-5	.236	6*	99	7		1.3
1998	StL N	9	9	.500	23	23	3	0-0	161.1	146	74	20	4	51-0	147	3.51	120	.240	.301	53-0-5	.226	2	96	11		1.4
	†Tex A	5	4	.556	10	10	0	0-0	60.1	68	33	5	0	30-1	57	4.33	113	.282	.358	0	—	0	139	3		0.4
1999	†Ari N	6	3	.667	17	17	0	0-0	101.1	106	51	12	6	40-1	74	4.09	113	.268	.343	32-0-3	.125	0	125	6	94	0.5
2000	Ari N	9	6	.600	18	18	0	0-0	95.1	98	55	18	2	36-2	76	4.91	98	.268	.336	31-1-3	.194	2	116	-1	81	0.2
2002	Ari N	0	2	.000	5	4	0	0-0	20.1	26	17	4	0	7-0	21	7.52	60	.313	.363	-0		-0	62	-6	158	-0.5
Total	14	138	121	.533	372	339	25-6	1-3	2191.2	2200	1130	246	83	816-49	1587	4.28	101	.262	.330	242-1-26	.207	14	106	10	567	1.5
STOUT, ALLYN	Allyn McClelland "Fish Hook" B10.31.1904 Peoria IL D12.22.1974 Sikeston MO BR/TR/5-10/167 d5.16																								
1931	StL N	6	0	1.000	30	3	1	3	72.2	87	40	2	1	34	40	4.21	93	.305	.381	19-0-2	.105	-1	189	-2		-0.3
1932	StL N	4	5	.444	36	1	1	0	73.2	87	40	5	4	28	32	4.40	89	.305	.375	20-0-1	.100	-1	64	-3		-0.4
1933	StL N	0	0	—	1	0	0	0	2	1	0	0	0	0	1	0.00	—	.167	.286	0	—	0		1		0.1
	Cin N	2	3	.400	23	5	2	0	71.1	85	36	3	0	26	29	3.79	90	.295	.354	22-0-1	.182	-0	113	-2		-0.2
	Year	2	3	.400	24	5	2	0	73.1	86	36	3	0	26	30	3.68	92	.293	.352	22-0-1	.182	-0	113	-3		-0.1
1934	Cin N	6	8	.429	41	16	4	1	140.2	170	85	10	4	47	51	4.86	84	.297	.354	43-0-2	.186	-0	111	-9		-0.8
1935	NY N	1	4	.200	14	1	0	0	88	99	58	7	4	37	29	4.91	79	.289	.365	15-1-0	.133	-0	132	-12		-0.8
1943	Bos N	1	0	1.000	9	0	0	1	9.1	17	12	1	0	4	3	6.75	51	.378	.429	.000		-0		-5		-0.6
Total	6	20	20	.500	180	29	8	11	457.2	546	271	28	13	177	185	4.54	85	.299	.365	121-1-6	.149	-3	117	-32		-3.0
STOVALL, JESSE	Jesse Cramer "Scout" B7.24.1875 Leeds MO D7.12.1955 San Diego CA BL/TR/6-0/175 d8.31 b-George																								
1903	Cle A	5	1	.833	6	6	6-2	0	57	44	17	3	3	21	12	2.05	139	.213	.294	22	.045	-2	100	6		0.4
1904	Det A	2	13	.133	22	17	13-1	0	146.2	170	97	3	16	45	41	4.42	84	.291	.358	56	.196	0*	69	-29		-2.8
Total	2	7	14	.333	28	23	19-3	0	203.2	214	114	3	19	66	53	3.76	70	.270	.341	78	.154	-2	78	-23		-2.4
STOVEY, HARRY	Harry Duffield (b Harry Duffield Stowe) B12.20.1856 Philadelphia PA D9.20.1937 New Bedford MA BR/TR/5-11.5/175 d5.1 M2 ▲																								
1880	Wor N	0	0	—	2	0	0	0	3	4	3	0	0	3	4.50	58	.308	.379	355-6	.265	0*		-1		0.0
1883	Phi AA	0	0	—	1	0	0	0	3	5	3	0	0	4	9.00	39	.357	.357	421-14	.304	0*		-1		0.0
1886	Phi AA	0	0	—	1	0	0	0	0.1	1	0	0	0	0	27.00	13	.667	.667	489-7	.294	0*		-1		0.0
Total	3	0	0	—	4	0	0	0	9.1	15	9	0	0	7	6.75	44	.349	.391	1265-27	.289	1		-3		0.0

YEAR	TM LG	W	L	PCT	G	GS	CG-SHO	SV-BS	IP	H	R	HR	HB	BB-IB	SO	ERA	AERA	OAV	OOB	AB-HR-SH	AVG	PB	SUP	APR	DL	PW

STOWE, HAL   Harold Rudolph   B8.29.1937 Gastonia NC   BL/TL/6-0/170   d9.30   Col Clemson

| 1960 | NY A | 0 | 0 | — | 1 | 0 | 0 | | 1 | 0 | 1 | 0 | 0 | 1-0 | 0 | 9.00 | 40 | .000 | .333 | 0 | — | 0 | | -1 | | 0.0 |

STRAHLER, MIKE   Michael Wayne   B3.14.1947 Chicago IL   BR/TR/6-4/180*   d9.12   Col Sacramento (CA) City

1970	LA N	1	1	.500	6	0	0	1-0	18.2	13	6	1	0	10-0	11	1.45	266	.194	.299	8	.250	0		4		0.5
1971	LA N	0	0	—	6	0	0	0-0	12.2	10	4	1	0	8-0	7	2.84	114	.217	.333	1	.000	-0		1		0.0
1972	LA N	1	2	.333	19	2	1	0-0	47	42	25	5	1	22-1	25	3.26	103	.237	.322	11	.182	1	105	-1		0.0
1973	Det A	4	5	.444	22	11	1	0-1	80.1	84	45	7	1	39-1	37	4.37	94	.273	.355	0	—	0	95	-4		-0.4
Total	4	6	8	.429	53	13	2	1-1	158.2	149	80	14	2	79-2	80	3.57	106	.249	.337	20	.200	1	102	-1		0.1

STRAHS, DICK   Richard Bernard   B12.4.1923 Evanston IL   D5.26.1988 Las Vegas NV   BL/TR/6-0/192   d7.24

| 1954 | Chi A | 0 | 0 | — | 9 | 0 | 0 | 1 | 14.1 | 16 | 10 | 0 | 0 | 8 | 8 | 5.65 | 66 | .271 | .358 | 1-0-1 | .000 | -0 | | -3 | | -0.2 |

STRAKER, LES   Lester Paul (Bolnalda)   B10.10.1959 Ciudad Bolivar, Venez   BR/TR/6-1/193*   d4.11

1987	†Min A	8	10	.444	31	26	1	0-0	154.1	150	79	24	2	59-6	76	4.37	106	.257	.325	0	—	0	86	6		0.5
1988	Min A	2	5	.286	16	14	1-1	0-0	82.2	86	39	8	0	25-1	23	3.92	104	.276	.326	0	—	0	97	1	95	0.1
Total	2	10	15	.400	47	40	2-1	1-0	237	236	118	32	2	84-7	99	4.22	106	.264	.325	0	—	0	90	7	95	0.6

STRAMPE, BOB   Robert Edwin   B6.13.1950 Janesville WI   BB/TR/6-1/185   [DetA68 18/414]   d5.10

| 1972 | Det A | 0 | 0 | — | 7 | 0 | 0 | 0 | 4.2 | 8 | 6 | 0 | 0 | 7-1 | 4 | 11.57 | 27 | .300 | .481 | 0 | | 0 | | -4 | | 0.0 |

STRAND, PAUL   Paul Edward   B12.19.1893 Carbonado WA   D7.2.1974 Salt Lake City UT   BR/TL/6-0.5/190   d5.15 ▲

1913	Bos N	0	0	—	7	0	0	0	17	22	9	1	0	12	6	2.12	155	.393	.500	6	.167	-0		1		0.0
1914	Bos N	6	2	.750	16	3	1	0	55.1	47	23	1	1	23	33	2.44	113	.235	.317	24	.333	2*	164	0		0.3
1915	Bos N	1	1	.500	6	2	2	1	22.2	26	12	0	0	3	13	2.38	109	.295	.319	22	.091	-0*	158	-1		-0.2
Total	3	7	3	.700	29	5	3	1	95	95	44	2	1	38	52	2.37	119	.276	.350	52	.212	2	156	0		0.1

STRANGE, PAT   Patrick Martin   B8.23.1980 Springfield MA   BR/TR/6-5/243*   d9.13

2002	NY N	0	0	—	5	0	0	0-0	8	6	1	0	0	1-1	4	1.13	352	.207	.233	0	—	0		3		0.1
2003	NY N	0	0	—	6	0	0	0-0	9	13	11	4	0	11-0	5	11.00	38	.351	.500	1	.000	-0		-7		-0.3
Total	2	0	0	—	11	0	0	0-0	17	19	12	4	0	12-1	9	6.35	64	.288	.397	1	.000	-0		-4		-0.2

STRATTON, SCOTT   Chilton Scott   B10.2.1869 Campbellsburg KY   D3.8.1939 Louisville KY   BL/TR/6-0/180   d4.21 ▲

1888	Lou AA	10	17	.370	33	28	28-2	0	269.2	287	196	7	15	53	97	3.64	85	.263	.306	249-1	.257	5*	102	-12		-0.5
1889	Lou AA	3	13	.188	19	17	13	1	133.2	157	126	6	17	42	42	3.23	119	.284	.342	229-4	.288	4*	82	-5		0.0
1890	†Lou AA	34	14	**.708**	50	49	44-4	0	431	398	186	3	13	61	207	**2.36**	**163**	.238	**.270**	189	.323	16*	124	**74**		**8.9**
1891	Pit N	0	2	.000	2	2	2	0	18.1	16	9	0	0	5	5	2.45	134	.225	.276	8	.125	-1	55	2		0.2
	Lou AA	6	13	.316	20	20	20-1	0	172	204	112	10	7	34	52	4.08	90	.285	.324	115	.235	1*	73	-6		-0.3
1892	Lou N	21	19	.525	42	40	39-2	0	351.2	342	188	1	9	70	93	2.92	105	.245	.285	219	.256	10*	90	5		1.6
1893	Lou N	12	23	.343	37	35	34-1	0	314.2	445	253	8	8	100	43	5.43	81	.323	.373	221	.226	3*	92	-39		-2.6
1894	Lou N	1	5	.167	7	5	4	0	43	72	50	3	3	13	3	8.37	61	.367	.415	37	.324	2*	58	-13		-1.0
	Chi N	8	5	.615	16	13	12	0	128.1	205	131	5	3	42	24	5.89	96	.357	.403	99-3-0	.374	7*	123	-6		0.2
	Year	9	10	.474	23	18	16	0	171.1	277	181	8	6	55	27	6.51	84	.359	.406	136-3-0	.360	9	106	-19		-0.8
1895	Chi N	2	3	.400	5	5	3	0	30	51	42	1	4	14	4	9.60	53	.370	.442	24-0-1	.292	1*	81	-13		-1.3
Total	8	97	114	.460	231	214	199-10	1	1892.1	2177	1293	44	69	434	570	3.87	99	.280	.323	1390-8-1	.274	48	99	-13		5.2

STRATTON, MONTY   Monty Franklin Pierce "Gander"   B5.21.1912 Wagner TX   D9.29.1982 Greenville TX   BR/TR/6-5/180   d6.2   C3

1934	Chi A	0	0	—	1	0	0	0	3.1	4	2	0	0	3	1	5.40	88	.333	.385	2	.000	-0		0		0.0
1935	Chi A	1	2	.333	5	5	2	0	38	40	17	0	2	9	8	4.03	115	.274	.325	14-0-1	.143	-1	75	3		0.2
1936	Chi A	5	7	.417	16	14	3	0	95	117	66	8	1	46	37	5.21	100	.305	.381	37-1-0	.216	1	109	-2		0.0
1937	Chi A*	15	5	.750	22	21	14-5	0	164.2	142	55	6	2	37	69	2.40	**191**	.234	**.280**	60-1-5	.200	-0	90	39		4.3
1938	Chi A	15	9	.625	26	22	17	2	186.1	186	95	18	7	56	82	4.01	122	.255	.315	79-2-2	.266	5*	133	19		2.7
Total	5	36	23	.610	70	62	36-5	2	487.1	489	235	32	12	149	196	3.71	130	.261	.319	192-4-8	.224	5	109	59		7.2

STRATTON, ED   William Edward   B Baltimore MD   d5.14

| 1873 | Mar NA | 0 | 3 | .000 | 3 | 3 | 3 | 0 | 27 | 75 | 75 | 1 | | 1 | 0 | 8.33 | 39 | .412 | .415 | 16 | .125 | -1* | 41 | -14 | | -1.0 |

STREET, HUSTON   Huston Lowell   B8.2.1983 Austin TX   BR/TR/6-0/190   d4.6   Col Texas

| 2005 | Oak A | 5 | 1 | .833 | 67 | 0 | 0 | 23-4 | 78.1 | 53 | 17 | 3 | 2 | 26-4 | 72 | 1.72 | 259 | .194 | .267 | 0 | — | 0 | | 23 | | 2.8 |

STREIT, OSCAR   Oscar William   B7.7.1873 Florence AL   D10.10.1935 Birmingham AL   BL/TL/6-5/190   d4.21

1899	Bos N	1	0	1.000	2	1	1	0	14.2	15	17	1	2	15	0	6.75	62	.263	.432	7	.000	-1	121	-5		-0.3
1902	Cle A	0	7	.000	8	7	4	0	51.2	72	54	3	3	25	10	5.23	66	.330	.407	19-0-1	.211	1	81	-14		-1.4
Total	2	1	7	.125	10	8	5	0	66.1	87	71	4	5	40	10	5.56	65	.316	.412	26-0-1	.154	-0	85	-19		-1.7

STRELECKI, ED   Edward Harold   B4.10.1905 Newark NJ   D1.9.1968 Newark NJ   BR/TR/5-11.5/180   d4.16

1928	StL A	0	2	.000	22	2	1	1	50.1	49	27	4	1	17	8	4.29	98	.269	.335	10-0-2	.200	0	71	0		0.0
1929	StL A	1	1	.500	7	0	0	0	11	12	8	1	1	6	2	4.91	90	.279	.380	2	.000	-0		-1		-0.2
1931	Cin N	0	0	—	13	0	0	0	24.1	37	25	2	3	9	3	9.25	40	.394	.462	5	.200	0		-13		-0.6
Total	3	1	3	.250	42	2	1	1	85.2	98	60	7	5	32	13	5.78	71	.307	.379	17-0-2	.176	0	71	-14		-0.8

STREMMEL, PHIL   Philip   B4.16.1880 Zanesville OH   D12.26.1947 Chicago IL   BR/TR/6-0/175   d9.16

1909	StL A	0	2	.000	2	2	2	0	18	20	9	0	1	4	6	4.50	54	.308	.357	6	.000	-1	44	-3		-0.4
1910	StL A	0	2	.000	5	2	2	0	29	31	19	0	0	16	7	3.72	66	.287	.379	8-0-1	.125	-0	54	-4		-0.2
Total	2	0	4	.000	7	4	4	0	47	51	28	0	1	20	13	4.02	61	.295	.371	14-0-1	.071	-1	49	-7		-0.6

STRICKER, CUB   John A. (b John A. Streaker)   B2.15.1860 Philadelphia PA   D11.19.1937 Philadelphia PA   BR/TR/5-3/138   d5.2   M1 ▲

1882	Phi AA	1	0	1.000	2	0	0	0	7	3	1	0	0	1	2	1.29	218	.120	.154	272	.217	0*		1		0.2
1884	Phi AA	0	0	—	1	0	0	0	3	6	2	0	0	1	1	6.00	56	.333	.368	399-1	.231	0*		-1		0.0
1887	Cle AA	0	0	—	3	0	0	1	5.2	5	5	0	0	7	2	3.18	137	.238	.429	534-2	.264	0*		0		0.0
1888	Cle AA	1	0	1.000	2	0	0	0	12	16	6	0	1	2	5	4.50	69	.308	.345	493-1	.233	0*		-1		0.2
Total	4	2	0	1.000	8	0	0	1	27.2	30	14	0	1	11	10	3.58	93	.259	.328	1698-4	.240	1		-1		0.2

STRICKLAND, JIM   James Michael   B6.12.1946 Los Angeles CA   BL/TL/6-0/175*   d5.19

1971	Min A	1	0	1.000	24	0	0	1-1	31.1	20	14	2	2	18-2	21	1.44	247	.183	.303	1	.000	0		3		0.2
1972	Min A	3	1	.750	25	0	0	3-1	36	28	16	7	0	19-2	30	2.50	129	.214	.313	3	.333	1		1		0.2
1973	Min A	0	1	.000	7	0	0	0-0	5.1	11	8	0	0	5-0	6	11.81	34	.440	.516	0	—	0		-4		-0.7
1975	Cle A	0	0	—	4	0	0	1-0	4.2	4	1	0	1	2-0	3	1.93	198	.222	.333	4	.250	1		1		0.0
Total	4	4	2	.667	60	0	0	5-2	77.1	63	39	9	3	44-4	60	2.68	128	.223	.329	4	.250	1		1		-0.3

STRICKLAND, SCOTT   Scott Michael   B4.26.1976 Houston TX   BR/TR/5-11/180(180-195)   [MonN97 10/316]   d8.14   Col New Mexico   [DL 2004 NY N 183]

1999	Mon N	1	0	1.000	17	0	0	1-0	18	15	10	3	0	11-0	23	4.50	99	.231	.342	0		0		0		0.0
2000	Mon N	4	3	.571	49	0	0	9-4	48	38	18	2	1	16-2	48	3.00	157	.215	.279	2	.000	-0		9	60	1.4
2001	Mon N	2	6	.250	77	0	0	9-3	81.1	67	36	9	4	41-5	85	3.21	135	.222	.322	3	.000	-0		8		0.8
2002	Mon N	0	0	—	1	0	0	0-0	1	0	0	0	0	0-0	2	0.00	—	.000	.000	0		0		0		0.0
	NY N	6	9	.400	68	0	0	2-4	67.2	61	29	7	2	33-9	67	3.59	110	.236	.325	0		0		3		0.7
	Year	6	9	.400	69	0	0	2-4	68.2	61	29	7	2	33-9	69	3.54	112	.234	.322	0		0		3		0.7
2003	NY N	2	0	1.000	19	0	0	0-1	20	16	11	0	1	10-1	16	2.25	186	.219	.321	1-0-1	.000	0		4	141	0.4
2005	Hou N	0	0	—	5	0	0	0-0	4	4	3	1	0	0-0	2	6.75	62	.250	.250	0		0		-1		0.0
Total	6	12	21	.364	236	0	0	20-12	240	201	102	25	8	111-17	243	3.34	129	.225	.314	6-0-1	.000	-1		23	384	3.3

STRICKLAND, BILL   William Goss   B3.29.1908 Ray City GA   D1.26.2000 Lakeland FL   BR/TR/6-2/170   d7.16   Col Georgia Tech

| 1937 | StL A | 0 | 0 | — | 9 | 0 | 0 | 0 | 21.1 | 28 | 18 | 2 | 2 | 15 | 6 | 5.91 | 82 | .341 | .455 | 6 | .167 | -0 | | -3 | | -0.2 |

STRICKLETT, ELMER   Elmer Griffin "Spitball"   B8.29.1876 Glasco KS   D6.7.1964 Santa Cruz CA   BR/TR/5-6/140   d4.22   Col Santa Clara

1904	Chi A	0	1	.000	1	1	0	0	7	12	10	0	0	2	3	10.29	24	.375	.412	3	.000	-0	58	-6		-0.6
1905	Bro N	9	18	.333	33	28	25-1	1	237.1	259	143	0	14	71	77	3.34	87	.282	.343	88-0-2	.148	-1	82	-19		-1.6
1906	Bro N	14	18	.438	41	35	28-5	5	291.2	273	128	2	5	77	88	2.72	93	.253	.306	97-0-3	.206	5	92	-11		-0.1

YEAR	TM LG	W	L	PCT	G	GS	CG-SHO	SV-BS	IP	H	R	HR	HB	BB-IB	SO	ERA	AERA	OAV	OOB	AB-HR-SH	AVG	PB	SUP	APR	DL	PW
1907	Bro N	12	14	.462	29	26	25-4	0	229.2	211	85	1	8	65	69	2.27	103	.255	.315	81-0-1	.148	1*	81	1		0.7
Total	4	35	51	.407	104	90	78-10	6	765.2	755	366	3	27	215	237	2.84	91	.264	.322	269-0-6	.167	4		85	-35		-1.6

STRIKE, JOHN John B1865 PA d9.24

| 1886 | Phi N | 1 | 1 | .500 | 2 | 2 | 1 | 0 | 15 | 19 | 10 | 1 | 1 | 7 | 11 | 4.80 | 69 | .311 | .382 | 7 | | .000 | -1 | 84 | -1 | | -0.2 |

STRIKER, JAKE Wilbur Scott B10.23.1933 New Washington OH BL/TL/6-2/200* d9.25 Col Heidelberg

1959	Cle A	1	0	1.000	1	1	0	0	6.2	8	2	0	0	4-0	5	2.70	136	.296	.375	1		.000	1	192	1		0.2
1960	Chi A	0	0	—	2	0	0	0	3.2	5	3	1	1	1-0	1	4.91	77	.357	.438	0		—	.0		-1		0.0
Total	2	1	0	1.000	3	1	0	0	10.1	13	5	1	1	5-0	6	3.48	107	.317	.396	1		.000	1	192	0		0.2

STRINCEVICH, NICK Nicholas "Jumbo" B3.1.1915 Gary IN BR/TR/6-1/180 d4.23

1940	Bos N	4	8	.333	32	14	5	0	128.2	142	89	17	8	63	54	5.53	67	.278	.367	43-0-2	.116	-2*	99	-27		-2.5
1941	Bos N	0	0	—	3	0	0	0	3.1	7	5	0	1	6	1	10.80	33	.412	.583	0		—	0		-3		-0.1
	Pit N	1	2	.333	12	3	0	0	31	35	23	4	1	13	12	5.23	69	.280	.353	7		.429	1	141	-6		-0.4
	Year	1	2	.333	15	3	0	0	34.1	42	28	4	2	19	13	5.77	63	.296	.387	7		.429	1	141	-9		-0.5
1942	Pit N	0	0	—	7	1	0	0	22.1	19	7	2	1	9	10	2.82	120	.229	.312	4-0-1		.000	-1	50	2		0.0
1944	Pit N	14	7	.667	40	26	11	2	190	190	86	5	4	37	47	3.08	121	.257	.296	57-0-5	.158	-1	109	11		1.3
1945	Pit N	16	10	.615	36	29	18-1	2	228.1	235	94	7	3	49	74	3.31	119	.260	.301	84-0-6	.202	-0	104	18		1.8
1946	Pit N	10	15	.400	32	22	11-3	1	176	185	77	7	4	44	49	3.58	98	.268	.316	52-0-4	.154	1	78	1		0.1
1947	Pit N	1	6	.143	32	7	1	0	89	111	59	9	2	37	22	5.26	80	.316	.385	21-0-1	.048	-2	84	-10		-0.8
1948	Pit N	0	0	—	3	0	0	0	4.1	8	4	0	0	2	1	8.31	49	.444	.500	0		—	0		-2		-0.1
	Phi N	0	1	.000	6	1	0	0	16.2	26	18	1	0	10	4	9.18	43	.347	.424	4		.000	-1	0	-9		-0.5
	Year	0	1	.000	9	1	0	0	21	34	22	1	0	12	5	9.00	44	.366	.438	4		.000	-1	0	-11		-0.6
Total	8	46	49	.484	203	103	46-4	6	889.2	958	462	52	24	270	274	4.05	93	.273	.329	272-0-19	.158	-4		98	-25		-1.2

STROHMAYER, JOHN John Emery B10.13.1946 Belle Fourche SD BR/TR/6-1/181* d4.29 Col Pacific (CA)

1970	Mon N	3	1	.750	42	0	0	0-2	76	85	48	7	2	39-3	74	4.86	86	.279	.364	6-0-1	.167	-0		-7		-0.4
1971	Mon N	7	5	.583	27	14	2	1-0	114	124	63	16	4	31-2	56	4.34	82	.281	.331	35-0-5	.229	-0	140	-10		-1.0
1972	Mon N	1	2	.333	48	0	0	3-0	76.2	73	32	6	1	31-3	50	3.52	101	.256	.328	4-0-1	.000	-0		1		0.1
1973	Mon N	0	1	.000	17	3	0	0-1	34.2	34	20	4	1	22-2	15	5.19	73	.260	.370	5		.200	1	116	-4		-0.2
	NY N	0	0	—	7	0	0	0-0	10	13	10	2	0	4-1	5	8.10	45	.310	.370	5		—	0.		-5		-0.2
	Year	0	1	.000	24	3	0	0-1	44.2	47	30	6	1	26-3	20	5.84	65	.272	.370	5		.200	1	117	-9		-0.4
1974	NY N	0	0	—	1	0	0	0-0	1	0	0	0	0	1-0	0	0.00	—	.000	.250	0		—	0		0		0.0
Total	5	11	9	.550	142	17	2	4-3	312.1	329	173	35	8	128-11	200	4.47	84	.272	.344	50-0-7	.200	0	131	-25		-1.7

STROM, BRENT Brent Terry B10.14.1948 San Diego CA BR/TL/6-3/190* [NYN70 S1/3] d7.31 C3 Col USC

1972	NY N	0	3	.000	11	5	0	0-0	30.1	34	25	7	0	15-1	20	6.82	50	.296	.374	6-0-1	.000	-1	104	-11		-1.1
1973	Cle A	2	10	.167	27	18	2	0-0	123	134	73	18	3	47-4	91	4.61	86	.278	.344	6-0		.000	-0	84	-10		-0.8
1975	SD N	8	8	.500	18	16	6-2	0-0	120.1	103	42	6	2	33-2	56	2.54	138	.233	.287	30-0-6	.100	-1	66	13		1.6
1976	SD N	12	16	.429	36	33	8-1	0-0	210.2	188	100	15	2	73-8	103	3.29	100	.239	.302	63-0-10	.063	-2*	92	-6		-0.9
1977	SD N	0	2	.000	8	3	0	0-0	16.2	23	25	5	0	12-2	8	12.42	29	.329	.417	3-0-1	.333	0	108	-17		-1.7
Total	5	22	39	.361	100	75	16-3	0-0	501	482	265	51	7	180-17	278	3.95	89	.254	.318	102-0-18	.078	-3	86	-31	24	-2.9

STROMME, FLOYD Floyd Marvin "Rock" B8.1.1916 Cooperstown ND D2.7.1993 Wenatchee WA BR/TR/5-11/170 d7.5 Col Northwestern

| 1939 | Cle A | 0 | 1 | .000 | 5 | 0 | 0 | 0 | 13 | 15 | 8 | 1 | 0 | 9 | 4 | 4.85 | 91 | .265 | .419 | 3 | | .333 | 0 | | -1 | | 0.0 |

STRONG, JOE Joseph Benjamin B9.9.1962 Fairfield CA BB/TR/6-0/200* [OakA84 15/376] d5.11 Col California-Riverside

2000	Fla N	1	1	.500	18	0	0	1-1	19.2	26	16	3	2	12-1	18	7.32	60	.325	.426	1		.000	-0		-6		-0.6
2001	Fla N	0	0	—	5	0	0	0-0	6.2	3	1	1	0	3-0	4	1.35	309	.136	.240	1		.000	-0		2		0.1
Total	2	1	1	.500	23	0	0	1-1	26.1	29	17	4	2	15-1	22	5.81	74	.284	.387	2		.000	-0		-4		-0.5

STROUD, SAILOR Ralph Vivian B5.15.1885 Ironia NJ D4.11.1970 Stockton CA BR/TR/6-0/160 d4.29

1910	Det A	5	9	.357	28	15	7-3	1	130.1	123	54	9	7	41	63	3.25	81	.257	.325	39		.026	-4	88	-5		-1.2
1915	NY N	12	9	.571	32	22	8	1	184	194	76	3	6	35	62	2.79	92	.281	.321	56-0-3	.161	-1	157	-6		-0.7
1916	NY N	3	2	.600	10	4	0	1	46.2	47	18	1	1	9	16	2.70	90	.266	.305	14-0-1	.071	-1	131	-2		-0.3
Total	3	20	20	.500	70	41	15-3	3	361	364	148	13	14	85	141	2.94	88	.271	.321	109-0-4	.101	-6	128	-13		-2.2

STRUSS, STEAMBOAT Clarence Herbert B2.24.1909 Riverdale IL D9.12.1985 Grand Rapids MI BR/TR/5-11/163 d9.30

| 1934 | Pit N | 1 | 0 | 1.000 | 1 | 0 | 0 | 0 | 4 | 4 | 3 | 0 | 0 | 2 | 1 | 6.43 | 64 | .250 | .382 | 3 | | .333 | 0 | 105 | -2 | | -0.2 |

STRYKER, DUTCH Sterling Alpa B7.29.1895 Atlantic Highlands NJ D11.5.1964 Red Bank NJ BR/TR/5-11.5/180 d4.16

1924	Bos N	3	8	.273	20	10	2	0	73.1	90	56	4	1	22	22	6.01	64	.314	.365	23		.217	-0	107	-18		-2.1
1926	Bro N	0	0	—	2	0	0	0	2	8	8	0	1	1	0	27.00	14	.571	.600	0		—	0		-5		-0.3
Total	2	3	8	.273	22	10	2	0	75.1	98	64	4	1	23	22	6.57	58	.326	.375	23		.217	-0	107	-23		-2.4

STUART, JOHNNY John Davis "Stud" B4.27.1901 Clinton TN D5.13.1970 Charleston WV BR/TR/5-11/170 d7.27 Col Ohio St.

1922	StL N	0	0	—	2	1	0	0	2	2	4	0	1	2	1	9.00	43	.222	.417	0		—	0	148	-2		-0.1
1923	StL N	9	5	.643	37	10	7-1	3	149.2	139	82	11	9	70	55	4.27	91	.252	.345	57		.246	1	122	-4		-0.4
1924	StL N	9	11	.450	28	22	13	0	159	167	100	12	5	60	54	4.75	80	.273	.343	54-0-1	.204	-1*	127	-18		-2.1
1925	StL N	2	2	.500	15	1	1	0	47	52	41	6	2	24	14	6.13	71	.278	.366	16		.250	1	78	-11		-0.7
Total	4	20	18	.526	82	34	21-1	3	357.2	360	227	29	17	156	124	4.76	82	.265	.348	127-0-1	.228	1	122	-35		-3.3

STUART, MARLIN Marlin Henry B8.8.1918 Paragould AR D6.16.1994 Paragould AR BL/TR/6-2/185* d4.26

1949	Det A	0	2	.000	14	2	0	0	29.2	39	33	3	0	35	14	9.10	46	.348	.503	6		.333	1*	118	-16		-0.9
1950	Det A	3	1	.750	19	1	0	2	43.2	59	32	6	1	22	19	5.56	84	.330	.406	12-0-1	.083	-1	96	-5		-0.5
1951	Det A	4	6	.400	29	15	5	1	124	119	60	9	7	71	46	3.77	111	.258	.365	43-1-1	.233	1	84	5		0.5
1952	Det A	3	2	.600	30	9	2	1	91.1	91	60	9	7	48	32	4.93	77	.265	.360	23-0-3	.087	-1	127	-13		-0.8
	StL A	1	2	.333	12	2	0	1	26	26	18	3	0	9	13	4.15	94	.260	.321	6		.000	-1	156	-2		-0.4
	Year	4	4	.500	42	11	2	2	117.1	117	78	11	7	57	45	4.76	81	.264	.352	29-0-3	.069	-2	132	-14		-1.2
1953	StL A	8	2	.800	60	2	0	7	114.1	136	62	6	1	44	46	3.94	107	.300	.363	26		.192	1	95	1		0.0
1954	Bal A	2	2	.333	22	0	0	2	38.1	46	23	2	2	15	13	4.46	80	.303	.371	3		.000	-0		-5		-0.4
	NY A	3	0	1.000	10	0	0	1	18.1	28	12	0	0	12	2	5.40	64	.350	.435	6		.333	0		-4		-0.5
	Year	4	2	.667	32	0	0	3	56.2	74	35	2	2	27	15	4.76	74	.319	.393	9		.222	0		-9		-1.0
Total	5	23	17	.575	196	31	7	15	485.2	544	300	37	17	256	185	4.65	87	.289	.378	125-1-5	.176	-1	104	-39		-3.1

STUELAND, GEORGE George Anton B3.2.1899 Algona IA D9.9.1964 Onawa IA BB/TR/6-1.5/174 d9.15

1921	Chi N	0	1	.000	2	0	0	0	11	11	7	0	0	4	3	5.73	67	.282	.391	3		.333	0	65	-2		-0.1
1922	Chi N	9	4	.692	35	11	4	0	113	129	81	9	5	49	44	5.81	72	.292	.369	31-0-1	.129	-2	129	-17		-1.9
1923	Chi N	0	1	.000	6	0	0	0	8	11	7	0	5	8	3	5.63	71	.314	.571	0		—	0		-2		-0.2
1925	Chi N	0	0	—	2	0	0	0	3	2	1	0	0	3	2	3.00	144	.182	.357	1		1.000	0		1		0.1
Total	4	9	6	.600	45	12	4	0	135	153	96	9	5	64	52	5.73	73	.297	.380	35-0-1	.171	-1	124	-20		-2.1

STUFFEL, PAUL Paul Harrington "Stu" B3.22.1927 Canton OH BR/TR/6-2/185* d9.16 Col Kent St.

1950	Phi N	0	0	—	3	0	0	0	5	4	1	0	1	3	3	1.80	225	.211	.286	0		—	0		1		0.1
1952	Phi N	1	0	1.000	2	1	0	0	6	5	3	0	0	7	3	3.00	122	.217	.400	2		.000	-0	171	0		0.0
1953	Phi N	0	0	—	2	0	0	0	0	0	4	0	0	2	0	∞	—	1.000		0		—	-0		-4		-0.3
Total	3	1	0	1.000	7	1	0	0	11	9	8	0	1	12	6	5.73	67	.214	.400	2		.000	-0	171	-3		-0.1

STULL, EVERETT Everett James B8.24.1971 Fort Riley KS BR/TR/6-3/200* [MonN92 3/71] d4.14 Col Tennessee St. [DL 1998 Bal A 118, 2001 Mil N 133]

1997	Mon N	0	1	.000	3	0	0	0-0	3.1	7	6	1	0	4-0	2	16.20	26	.438	.550	0-0-1			-0		-5		-0.8
1999	Atl N	0	0	—	5	0	0	0-0	0.2	2	3	0	0	4-0	1	13.50	33	.500	.571	0		—	-0		-2		-0.1
2000	Mil N	2	3	.400	20	4	0	0-0	43.1	41	30	7	4	30-3	33	5.82	79	.256	.381	9		.000	-1	65	-5		-0.6
2002	Mil N	0	1	.000	3	2	0	0-0	10	15	7	0	1	9-2	7	6.30	65	.357	.481	3		.333	0	112	-2		-0.1
Total	4	2	5	.286	26	6	0	0-0	57.1	65	47	8	5	45-5	42	6.59	68	.293	.417	12-0-1	.083	-0	78	-14	251	-1.6

STULTZ, GEORGE George Irvin B6.30.1873 Louisville KY D3.19.1955 Louisville KY 5-10/150 d9.22

| 1894 | Bos N | 1 | 0 | 1.000 | 1 | 1 | 0 | 0 | 9 | 4 | 2 | 0 | 0 | 5 | 1 | 0.00 | — | .133 | .257 | 3 | | .333 | -0 | 37 | 5 | | 0.5 |

YEAR	TM LG	W	L	PCT	G	GS	CG-SHO	SV-BS	IP	H	R	HR	HB	BB-IB	SO	ERA	AERA	OAV	OOB	AB-HR-SH	AVG	PB	SUP	APR	DL	PW
STUMP, JIM	James Gilbert B2.10.1932 Lansing MI BR/TR/6-0/188(175-188) d8.29																									
1957	Det A	1	0	1.000	6	0	0	0	13.1	11	4	0	0	8-0	2	2.03	190	.220	.328	2-0-1	.500	0		2		0.2
1959	Det A	0	0	—	5	0	0	0	11.1	12	3	1	0	4-0	6	2.38	170	.279	.340	1	1.000	1		2		0.2
Total	2	1	0	1.000	11	0	0	0	24.2	23	7	1	0	12-0	8	2.19	180	.247	.333	3-0-1	.667	1		4		0.4
STUPER, JOHN	John Anton B5.9.1957 Butler PA BR/TR/6-2/200* [PitN78 18/460] d6.1 Col Point Park																									
1982	†StL N	9	7	.563	23	21	2	0-0	136.2	137	55	8	0	55-5	53	3.36	110	.266	.336	42-0-4	.119	-1	83	5		0.3
1983	StL N	12	11	.522	40	30	6-1	1-0	198	202	95	15	2	71-3	81	3.68	99	.265	.327	59-0-7	.136	-1	109	-2		-0.3
1984	StL N	3	5	.375	15	12	0	0-0	61.1	73	39	4	2	20-2	19	5.28	66	.297	.351	16-0-3	.063	-1	86	-12		-1.5
1985	Cin N	8	5	.615	33	13	1	0-0	99	116	60	8	0	37-3	38	4.55	83	.303	.358	17-0-7	.059	-0	120	-10		-1.2
Total	4	32	28	.533	111	76	9-1	1-0	495	528	249	35	4	183-13	191	3.96	93	.277	.339	134-0-21	.112	-3	100	-19		-2.7
STURDIVANT, TOM	Thomas Virgil "Snake" B4.28.1930 Gordon KS BL/TR/6-1/186(170-186) d4.14																									
1955	†NY A	1	3	.250	33	1	0	0	68.1	48	24	6	2	42-1	48	3.16	118	.203	.329	12-0-1	.083	-1	24	6		0.2
1956	†NY A	16	8	.667	32	17	6-2	5	158.1	134	63	15	4	52-4	110	3.30	117	.224	.291	64-0-3	.313	4	141	12		2.0
1957	†NY A	16	6	**.727**	28	28	7-2	0	201.2	170	65	14	4	80-2	118	2.54	141	.232	.309	71-0-4	.183	1	106	25		2.6
1958	NY A	3	6	.333	15	10	0	0	70.2	77	37	6	3	38-0	41	4.20	84	.274	.364	21-0-1	.190	0	99	-5	30	-0.6
1959	NY A	0	2	.000	7	3	0	0	25.1	20	16	4	0	9-0	16	4.97	73	.222	.290	6	.000	-1	48	-4		-0.3
	KC A	2	6	.250	36	3	0	5	71.2	70	45	9	6	34-4	57	4.65	86	.258	.347	17-0-1	.059	-2*	95	-6		-0.8
	Year	2	8	.200	43	6	0	5	97	90	61	13	6	43-4	73	4.73	83	.249	.333	23-0-1	.043	-3	71	-10		-1.1
1960	Bos A	3	3	.500	40	3	0	1	101.1	106	58	16	2	45-5	62	4.97	81	.279	.353	22-0-1	.182	-1	94	-8		-0.5
1961	Was A	2	6	.250	15	10	1-1	0	80	67	42	6	3	40-3	39	4.61	87	.233	.328	26-0-4	.077	-1	90	-3		-0.4
	Pit N	5	2	.714	13	11	6-1	1	85.2	81	29	6	1	17-3	45	2.84	141	.249	.288	32-0-1	.250	1	121	12		0.9
1962	Pit N	9	5	.643	49	12	2-1	2	125.1	120	62	12	3	39-11	76	3.73	105	.260	.318	33-0-4	.182	0	87	2		0.2
1963	Pit N	0	0	—	3	0	0	0	8.1	8	6	1	0	4-0	6	6.48	51	.267	.353	2	.000	-0		-2		-0.1
	Det A	1	2	.333	28	0	0	2	55	43	26	7	1	24-2	36	3.76	99	.221	.304	9	.000	-1		0		-0.1
	KC A	1	2	.333	17	3	0	0	53	47	24	3	1	17-2	26	3.74	104	.237	.300	11-0-2	.000	-1	99	1		-0.1
	Year	2	4	.333	45	3	0	2	108	90	50	10	2	41-4	62	3.75	102	.229	.302	20-0-2	.000	-2	101	1		-0.2
1964	KC A	0	0	—	3	0	0	0	3.2	4	4	0	2	1-0	1	9.82	39	.308	.438	1	1.000	-0		-2		-0.1
	NY N	0	0	—	16	0	0	1	28.2	34	20	2	2	7-0	18	5.97	60	.306	.347	1	.000	-0		-7		-0.4
Total	10	59	51	.536	335	101	22-7	17	1137	1029	521	107	34	449-37	704	3.74	102	.244	.319	328-0-22	.183	-1	105	21	30	2.5
STURTZE, TANYON	Tanyon James B10.12.1970 Worcester MA BR/TR/6-5/205* [OakA90 23/636] d5.3 Col Quinsigamond (MA) CC																									
1995	Chi N	0	0	—	2	0	0	0-0	2	2	2	1	0	1-0	0	9.00	46	.250	.333	0	—	0		-1		-0.1
1996	Chi N	1	0	1.000	6	0	0	0-0	11	16	11	3	0	5-0	7	9.00	49	.348	.412	1-0-1	.000	0		-5		-0.4
1997	Tex A	1	1	.500	9	5	0	0-0	32.2	45	30	6	0	18-0	18	8.27	59	.338	.406	0	—	0	117	-10		-0.6
1999	Chi A	0	0	—	1	1	0	0-0	6	4	0	0	0	2-0	2	0.00	—	.182	.273	0	—	0	19	3		0.2
2000	Chi A	1	2	.333	10	1	0	0-0	15.2	25	23	4	2	15-0	6	12.06	42	.379	.494	0	—	0	37	-12		-1.7
	TB A	4	0	1.000	19	5	0	0-0	52.2	47	16	4	1	14-1	38	2.56	191	.236	.290	0	—	0	126	14	35	0.9
	Year	5	2	.714	29	6	0	0-0	68.1	72	39	8	3	29-1	44	4.74	104	.272	.348	0	—	0	111	2		-0.8
2001	TB A	11	12	.478	39	27	0	1-2	195.1	200	98	23	9	79-0	110	4.42	102	.271	.345	8	.125	-0	97	6		0.6
2002	TB A	4	18	.182	33	33	4	0-0	224	271	141	33	9	89-2	137	5.18	87	.302	.369	4-0-1	.000	-0	76	-17		-1.5
2003	Tor A	7	6	.538	40	8	0	0-0	89.1	107	67	14	7	43-3	54	5.94	80	.296	.380	0	—	0	109	-12		-1.5
2004	†NY A	6	2	.750	28	3	0	1-0	77.1	75	49	9	6	33-2	56	5.47	84	.254	.340	3	.000	-0	155	-7		-0.6
2005	†NY A	5	3	.625	64	1	0	1-5	78	76	43	10	6	27-1	45	4.73	92	.257	.329	0	—	0	279	-2	18	-0.2
Total	10	40	44	.476	251	84	4	3-7	784	868	480	107	40	326-9	473	5.18	89	.284	.358	16-0-2	.063	-1	96	-43	53	-4.9
SUCH, DICK	Richard Stanley B10.15.1944 Sanford NC BL/TR/6-4/190 [TexA66*S8/101] d4.6 C19 Col Elon																									
1970	Was A	1	5	.167	21	5	0	0-0	50	48	42	8	3	45-5	41	7.56	48	.258	.403	13	.231	1*	59	-20		-2.0
SUCHE, CHARLEY	Charles Morris B8.5.1915 Cranes Mill TX D2.11.1984 San Antonio TX BR/TL/6-2/190 d9.18																									
1938	Cle A	0	0	—	1	0	0	0	4	4	4	0	0	3	1	27.00	17	.571	.700	1	1.000	1		-3		-0.1
SUCHECKI, JIM	James Joseph B8.25.1926 Chicago IL D7.20.2000 Crofton MD BR/TR/5-11/185* d5.20																									
1950	Bos A	0	0	—	4	0	0	0	4	3	2	0	0	4	4	4.50	109	.231	.412	0	—	0		0		0.0
1951	StL A	0	6	.000	29	6	0	0	89.2	113	64	8	1	42	47	5.42	81	.299	.371	20-0-2	.100	-2	74	-11		-0.8
1952	Pit N	0	0	—	5	0	0	0	10	14	7	1	1	4	6	5.40	74	.326	.396	2	.000	0		-2		-0.1
Total	3	0	6	.000	38	6	0	0	103.2	130	73	9	2	50	56	5.38	81	.300	.374	22-0-2	.091	-2	74	-13		-0.9
SUDHOFF, WILLIE	John William "Wee Willie" B9.17.1874 St.Louis MO D5.25.1917 St.Louis MO BR/TR/5-7/165 d8.20																									
1897	StL N	2	7	.222	11	9	9	0	92.2	126	72	8	4	21	19	4.47	98	.321	.362	42-0-1	.238	-1	86	-3		-0.3
1898	StL N	11	27	.289	41	38	35	1	315	355	205	11	27	102	65	4.34	87	.282	.349	120-0-5	.158	-6	70	-17		-1.9
1899	Cle N	3	8	.273	11	10	8	0	86.1	131	85	9	7	25	10	6.98	53	.347	.399	31-0-2	.065	-2	88	-30		-2.8
	StL N	12	10	.545	25	23	16	0	178.1	193	109	6	15	62	29	4.04	99	.276	.347	64-0-5	.203	-0	97	2		0.4
	Year	15	18	.455	36	33	24	0	264.2	324	194	9	22	87	39	5.00	78	.301	.365	95-0-7	.158	-2	94	-24		-2.4
1900	StL N	6	8	.429	16	14	13-2	0	127	128	62	3	8	37	29	2.76	132	.261	.323	106-0-1	.189	-0*	100	11		1.0
1901	StL N	17	11	.607	38	26	25-1	2	276.1	281	142	4	18	92	78	3.52	90	.262	.331	108-1-2	.176	3	129	-10		-0.5
1902	StL A	12	12	.500	30	25	20	0	220	213	99	6	12	67	42	2.86	123	.254	.319	77-0-3	.169	-2*	73	14		1.3
1903	StL A	21	15	.583	38	35	30-5	0	293.2	262	100	4	9	56	104	2.27	128	.238	.281	110-0-3	.182	-1*	88	23		2.7
1904	StL A	8	15	.348	27	24	20-1	0	222.1	232	121	8	10	54	63	3.76	66	.269	.320	85-0-1	.165	0*	98	-31		-2.7
1905	StL A	10	20	.333	32	30	23-1	0	244	222	121	8	13	78	70	2.99	85	.244	.313	86	.186	2	77	-14		-1.3
1906	Was A	0	2	.000	9	5	0	0	19.2	30	25	1	2	9	7	9.15	29	.353	.427	7	.429	1	169	-14		-1.1
Total	10	102	135	.430	278	239	199-10	3	2075.1	2153	1047	62	125	603	516	3.60	91	.269	.329	836-1-23	.178	-7	90	-69		-5.2
SUGGS, GEORGE	George Franklin B7.7.1882 Kinston NC D4.4.1949 Kinston NC BR/TR/5-7.5/168 d4.21																									
1908	Det A	1	1	.500	6	1	1	1	27	32	8	0	2	4	8	1.67	145	.299	.312	10-0-1	.200	0	57	2		0.2
1909	Det A	1	3	.250	9	4	2	1	44.1	34	12	1	3	10	18	2.03	124	.228	.290	15-0-1	.067	-1	112	3		0.2
1910	Cin N	20	12	.625	35	30	23-2	3	266	248	96	6	14	48	91	2.40	121	.253	.297	85-0-2	.165	2	105	18		2.4
1911	Cin N	15	13	.536	36	29	17-1	0	260.2	258	110	9	10	79	91	3.00	110	.268	.330	90-0-2	.256	6	102	12		2.1
1912	Cin N	19	16	.543	42	36	25-5	3	303	320	132	6	11	56	104	2.94	114	.278	.318	106-1-5	.160	-1	96	16		1.6
1913	Cin N	8	15	.348	36	22	9-2	2	199	220	110	6	7	35	73	4.03	81	.292	.329	67-0-2	.254	2	81	-13		-1.1
1914	Bal F	24	14	.632	46	38	26-6	4	319.1	322	118	6	10	57	132	2.90	104	.266	.304	99-0-7	.212	2	100	10		1.7
1915	Bal F	11	17	.393	35	25	12	3	232.2	288	134	12	7	68	71	4.14	69	.318	.370	77-0-3	.221	0	90	-31		-3.3
Total	8	99	91	.521	245	185	115-16	17	1652	1722	720	40	62	355	588	3.11	100	.277	.322	549-1-23	.204	11	97	17		3.8
SUKLA, ED	Edward Anthony (b Edward Anthony Suckla) B3.3.1943 Long Beach CA BR/TR/5-11/170* d9.17 Col Orange Coast (CA) JC																									
1964	LA A	0	1	.000	2	0	0	0	2.2	2	2	1	0	1-0	3	6.75	49	.200	.273	—		0		-1		-0.2
1965	Cal A	2	3	.400	25	0	0	3	32	32	16	3	1	10-2	15	4.50	76	.264	.326	0	—	0		-3		-0.5
1966	Cal A	1	1	.500	12	0	0	1	16.2	18	12	4	0	6-0	8	6.48	52	.281	.343	1	.000	-0		-5		-0.7
Total	3	3	5	.375	39	0	0	4	51.1	52	30	8	1	17-2	26	5.26	64	.267	.329	1	.000	-0		-9		-1.4
SULLIVAN, CHARLIE	Charles Edward B5.23.1903 Yadkin Valley NC D5.28.1935 Maiden NC BL/TR/6-1/185 d4.21																									
1928	Det A	0	2	.000	3	2	0	0	12.1	18	12	1	0	6	2	6.57	63	.360	.429	4	.000	-1	72	-4		-0.5
1930	Det A	1	5	.167	40	3	2	5	93.2	112	72	9	1	53	38	6.53	73	.311	.401	24	.292	2	24	-14		-0.7
1931	Det A	3	2	.600	31	4	2	4	95	109	60	6	1	46	28	4.93	93	.288	.366	24	.167	-1	101	-3		-0.3
Total	4	9	368	.308	74	9	4	5	201	239	144	16	2	105	68	5.78	81	.303	.386	52	.212	-0	67	-21		-1.5
SULLIVAN, JIM	Daniel James B4.25.1857 Charlestown MA D11.29.1901 Roxbury MA BR/TR/5-10/155 d4.22																									
1891	Bos N	0	0	—	1	0	0	0	0.1	1	1	0	0	5	0	81.00	5	.667	.875	0	—	0		-2		-0.1
	Col AA	1	0	1.000	1	1	1	0	9	10	9	1	2	5	3	4.00	86	.270	.372	4	.000	-1	90	-2		-0.2
1895	Bos N	11	9	.550	21	19	16	0	178.1	231	133	10	16	58	45	4.74	107	.309	.371	85-0-1	.176	-6*	123	8		0.1
1896	Bos N	11	12	.478	31	26	21-1	1	225.1	268	148	13	6	68	33	4.03	113	.293	.346	88-1-2	.216	-2	97	15		0.8
1897	†Bos N	4	5	.444	13	9	8-1	2	89	91	56	1	2	26	17	3.94	113	.262	.317	33-0-1	.182	-3	80	4		0.1
1898	Bos N	0	1	.000	2	1	0	0	12	19	16	1	0	9	1	12.00	31	.358	.460	3	.333	0	77	-9		-0.6
Total	5	26	28	.481	70	57	46-2	3	514	621	366	26	26	171	97	4.50	104	.295	.356	213-1-4	.192	-11	103	14		0.1

YEAR	TM LG	W	L	PCT	G	GS	CG-SHO	SV-BS	IP	H	R	HR	HB	BB-IB	SO	ERA	AERA	OAV	OOB	AB-HR-SH	AVG	PB	SUP	APR	DL	PW
SULLIVAN, FLEURY Florence P. B1862 E.St.Louis IL D2.15.1897 E.St.Louis IL d5.3																									
1884	Pit AA	16	35	.314	51	51	51-2	0	441	496	328	15	20	96	189	4.20	79	.268	.311	189	.153	-9*	65	-44		-4.7
SULLIVAN, FRANK Franklin Leal B1.23.1930 Hollywood CA BR/TR/6-6.5/215* d7.31																									
1953	Bos A	1	1	.500	14	0	0	0	25.2	24	16	3	1	11	17	5.61	75	.264	.350	4	.250	-0		-3		-0.2
1954	Bos A	15	12	.556	36	26	11-3	1	206.1	185	81	19	6	66	124	3.14	131	.240	.304	68-0-3	.103	-3	106	21		2.5
1955	Bos A★	18	13	.581	35	35	16-3	0	260	235	103	23	7	100-5	129	2.91	147	.241	.313	89-0-12	.112	-4	101	34		3.4
1956	Bos A	14	7	.667	34	33	12-1	0	242	253	112	22	8	82-6	116	3.42	135	.268	.330	85-0-7	.141	-5	107	27		1.6
1957	Bos A	14	11	.560	31	30	14-3	0	240.2	206	76	16	7	48-4	127	2.73	146	.230	**.273**	79-0-6	.165	-2	86	**35**		**3.5**
1958	Bos A	13	9	.591	32	29	10-2	3	199.1	216	91	12	3	49-0	107	3.57	112	.278	.322	67-0-8	.164	-1	104	9		0.8
1959	Bos A	9	11	.450	30	26	5-2	1	177.2	172	86	17	7	67-2	107	3.95	103	.258	.331	60-0-7	.200	-1	94	2		0.1
1960	Bos A	6	16	.273	40	22	4	1	153.2	164	94	10	6	52-6	98	5.10	79	.269	.331	40-0-4	.125	-1	92	-16		-2.2
1961	Phi N	3	16	.158	49	18	1-1	6	159.1	161	93	19	5	55-5	114	4.29	95	.262	.326	33-0-3	.152	0	70	-7		-0.7
1962	Phi N	0	0	.000	19	0	0	0	23	38	21	2	2	12-2	12	6.26	62	.396	.460	0	—	0		-8		-0.6
	Min A	4	1	.800	21	0	0	1	33.1	33	17	3	0	13-0	10	3.24	126	.258	.324	4	.000	-0		2		0.2
1963	Min A	0	1	.000	10	0	0	1	11	15	7	1	0	4-1	2	5.73	64	.349	.404	0	—	0		-2		-0.2
Total 11		97	100	.492	351	219	73-15	18	1732	1702	797	149	52	559-31	959	3.60	116	.257	.319	529-0-50	.144	-17	97	94		8.2
SULLIVAN, HARRY Harry Andrew B4.22.1888 Rockford IL D9.22.1919 Rockford IL BL/TL d8.11 Col St.Louis																									
1909	StL N	0	0	—	2	1	0	0	4	6	5	0	2	1	1	36.00	7	.500	.600	1	.000	-0	138	-4		-0.2
SULLIVAN, JIM James Richard B4.5.1894 Mine Run VA D2.12.1972 Burtonsville MD BR/TR/5-11/165 d9.27																									
1921	Phi A	0	2	.000	2	2	2	0	17	20	13	0	0	7	8	3.18	140	.294	.360	6	.000	-1	37	0		-0.1
1922	Phi A	0	2	.000	20	2	1	0	51.1	76	43	3	1	25	15	5.44	78	.373	.443	11-0-1	.091	-1	30	-9		-0.5
1923	Cle A	0	1	.000	3	0	0	0	5	10	10	0	1	5	4	14.40	28	.476	.593	1	.000	-0		-6		-0.9
Total 3		0	5	.000	25	4	3	0	73.1	106	66	3	2	37	27	5.52	78	.362	.437	18-0-1	.056	-2	35	-15		-1.5
SULLIVAN, JOE Joe B9.26.1910 Mason City IL D4.8.1985 Sequim WA BL/TL/5-11/175 d4.20																									
1935	Det A	6	6	.500	25	12	5	0	125.2	119	66	4	3	71	53	3.51	119	.244	.344	43-0-1	.163	-1	106	5		0.3
1936	Det A	2	5	.286	26	4	1	1	79.2	111	70	4	2	40	32	6.78	73	.331	.406	28-0-1	.179	-1	98	-17		-1.3
1939	Bos N	6	9	.400	31	11	7	2	113.2	114	57	7	2	50	46	3.64	101	.266	.346	40-0-1	.300	3*	86	-1		0.3
1940	Bos N	10	14	.417	36	22	7	1	177.1	157	89	9	8	89	64	3.55	105	.240	.339	71-0-3	.197	-0	110	-1		-0.1
1941	Bos N	2	2	.500	16	2	0	0	52.1	60	26	3	2	26	11	4.13	86	.290	.374	15	.067	-1	107	-2		-0.2
	Pit N	4	1	.800	16	4	0	1	39.1	40	26	2	0	22	10	2.97	121	.258	.350	11	.364	1	100	-1		-0.1
	Year	6	3	.667	32	6	0	1	91.2	100	52	5	2	48	21	3.63	99	.276	.364	26	.192	-0	103	-5		-0.3
Total 5		30	37	.448	150	55	20	5	588	601	334	25	17	298	216	4.01	99	.265	.355	208-0-6	.207	1	101	-17		-1.1
SULLIVAN, JOHN John Jeremiah "Lefty" B5.31.1894 Chicago IL D7.7.1958 Chicago IL BL/TL/5-11/165 d7.18																									
1919	Chi A	0	1	.000	4	2	1	0	15	24	15	0	1	8	9	4.20	76	.364	.440	3	.000	-0	160	-4		-0.3
SULLIVAN, MIKE Michael Joseph "Big Mike" B10.23.1866 Boston MA D6.14.1906 Boston MA BL/TR/6-1/210 d6.17 Col Boston U.																									
1889	Was N	0	3	.000	9	3	3	0	41	47	47	2	3	32	15	7.24	54	.288	.404	19	.053	-2	108	-14		-0.9
1890	Chi N	5	6	.455	12	12	10	0	96	108	77	3	4	58	33	4.59	80	.275	.374	40	.125	-3	82	-10		-1.2
1891	Phi AA	0	2	.000	2	2	2	0	18	17	13	2	3	10	7	3.50	108	.239	.357	7	.000	-1	65	0		-0.2
	NY N	1	2	.333	3	3	3	0	24	24	19	0	1	8	11	3.38	95	.250	.314	10	.200	-0	81	-1		-0.2
1892	Cin N	12	4	.750	21	16	15	0	166.1	179	90	8	9	74	56	3.08	106	.264	.344	74	.176	-2	102	2		-0.2
1893	Cin N	8	11	.421	27	18	14	1	183.2	200	146	5	17	103	46	5.05	95	.269	.370	79-1	.203	-3	89	-7		-0.8
1894	Was N	2	10	.167	20	12	11	1	117.2	166	134	10	8	74	21	6.58	80	.329	.422	57-1-1	.158	-4	100	-15		-1.4
	Cle N	6	5	.545	13	11	9	0	90.2	128	82	4	3	47	19	6.35	86	.329	.405	44-0-1	.295	0	105	-5		-0.5
	Year	8	15	.348	33	23	20	1	208.1	294	216	14	11	121	40	6.48	83	.329	.415	101-1-2	.218	-4	103	-26		-1.9
1895	Cle N	1	2	.333	4	3	2	0	31	42	34	1	1	16	5	8.42	59	.318	.396	15	.133	-2	119	-9		-0.7
1896	NY N	10	13	.435	25	22	18	0	185.1	188	131	3	13	71	42	4.66	90	.261	.388	77-0-2	.208	-3	83	-8		-1.0
1897	NY N	8	7	.533	23	16	11-1	2	148.2	183	113	6	14	71	35	5.09	82	.300	.386	66	.273	0	101	-11		-0.9
1899	Bos N	1	0	1.000	1	1	1	0	9	10	6	1	1	4	1	5.00	83	.278	.366	3	.333	0	121	-1		0.0
Total 10		54	65	.454	160	119	99-1	4	1111.1	1292	892	45	77	568	285	5.04	85	.284	.373	491-2-4	.196	-21	94	-79		-8.0
SULLIVAN, LEFTY Paul Thomas B9.7.1916 Nashville TN D11.1.1988 Scottsdale AZ BL/TL/6-3/204 d5.6																									
1939	Cle A	0	1	.000	7	1	0	0	12.2	9	8	1	0	9	4	4.26	103	.214	.365	3	.000	-0	20	0		-0.1
SULLIVAN, TOM Thomas B3.1.1860 New York NY D4.12.1947 Cincinnati OH d9.27																									
1884	Col AA	2	2	.500	4	4	4	0	31	42	22	2	0	3	12	4.06	75	.318	.333	11	.091	-1	70	-4		-0.5
1886	Lou AA	2	7	.222	9	9	8	0	75	94	70	6	2	33	27	3.96	92	.305	.376	27	.111	-2	60	-4		-0.5
1888	KC AA	8	16	.333	24	24	24	0	214.2	227	146	2	24	68	84	3.40	101	.262	.332	92	.109	-6*	67	-3		-0.6
1889	KC AA	2	8	.200	10	10	10	0	87.1	111	88	2	7	48	24	5.67	75	.300	.391	33	.152	-1	86	-10		-0.9
Total 4		14	33	.298	47	47	46	0	408	474	326	12	33	152	147	4.04	90	.282	.354	163	.117	-9	70	-21		-2.5
SULLIVAN, TOM Thomas Augustin B10.18.1895 Boston MA D9.23.1962 Boston MA BL/TL/5-11/178 d5.15																									
1922	Phi N	0	0	—	3	0	0	0	8	16	11	0	1	5	2	11.25	41	.410	.489	4-1-0	.250	1		-4		-0.1
SULLIVAN, BILL William F. B12.1868 Providence RI D10.8.1905 Providence RI BR/TR d4.19																									
1890	Syr AA	4	4	.200	6	6	4	0	42	51	50	2	6	27	13	7.93	45	.291	.404		.091	-2	137	-22		-1.9
SULLIVAN, SCOTT William Scott B3.13.1971 Tuscaloosa AL BR/TR/6-3/210* [CinN93 2/62] d5.6 Col Auburn-Montgomery [DL 2005 KC A 183]																									
1995	Cin N	0	0	—	3	0	0	0	3.2	4	2	0	0	2-0	1	4.91	85	.286	.375	1	.000	-0		0		0.0
1996	Cin N	0	0	—	7	0	0	0-0	8	7	2	0	1	5-0	3	2.25	190	.250	.382	1	.000	-0		2		0.1
1997	Cin N	5	3	.625	59	0	0	1-1	97.1	79	36	12	7	30-8	96	3.24	132	.220	.291	7-0-2	.000	-1		12		0.8
1998	Cin N	5	5	.500	67	0	0	1-3	102	98	62	14	9	36-4	95	5.21	82	.253	.327	11-0-1	.091	-1		-10		-0.9
1999	Cin N	5	4	.556	79	0	0	3-2	113.2	88	41	10	8	47-4	78	3.01	156	.216	.307	15	.000	-2		21		1.3
2000	Cin N	3	6	.333	79	0	0	0-3	106.1	87	44	14	9	38-8	96	3.47	137	.226	.307	7	.286	0*		15		1.2
2001	Cin N	7	1	.875	79	0	0	0-3	103.1	94	44	10	8	36-8	82	3.31	139	.243	.317	3	.000	0		13		0.8
2002	Cin N	6	5	.545	71	0	0	1-2	78.2	93	60	15	5	31-11	78	6.06	70	.294	.363	3	.333	0		-15	15	-2.0
2003	Cin N	6	0	1.000	50	0	0	0-1	49.2	39	22	4	5	26-4	42	3.62	115	.211	.321	0	—	0		3	24	0.3
	Chi A	0	0	—	15	0	0	0-0	14.1	9	6	2	1	6-0	13	3.77	122	.184	.281	0	—	0		2		0.1
2004	KC A	3	4	.429	49	0	0	0-1	60.1	73	34	8	7	24-10	45	4.77	98	.308	.382	0	—	0		0	39	0.1
Total 10		40	28	.588	558	0	0	9-16	737.1	671	353	89	60	281-57	622	3.98	113	.244	.324	48-0-3	.083	-3	43	261		1.7
SUMMERS, ED Oron Edgar "Kickapoo Ed","Chief" B12.5.1884 Ladoga IN D5.12.1953 Indianapolis IN BB/TR/6-2/180 d4.16 Col Wabash																									
1908	†Det A	24	12	.667	40	32	23-5	1	301	271	112	3	20	55	103	1.64	147	.242	.290	113-0-4	.124	-6	116	15		1.1
1909	†Det A	19	9	.679	35	32	24-3	1	281.2	243	91	4	10	52	107	2.24	113	.227	.269	94-0-3	.106	-0	109	10		0.6
1910	Det A	13	12	.520	30	25	18-1	0	220.1	211	83	8	5	60	82	2.53	104	.254	.308	76-2-4	.184	-0	111	2		0.3
1911	Det A	11	11	.500	30	20	13	1	179.1	189	108	3	11	51	65	3.66	95	.274	.334	63-0-3	.254	1	122	-7		-0.7
1912	Det A	1	1	.500	3	3	1	0	16.2	16	10	1	0	3	5	4.86	67	.250	.284	6	.500	1	136	-2		-0.1
Total 5		68	45	.602	138	112	79-9	3	999	930	404	19	46	221	362	2.42	111	.246	.296	352-2-14	.162	-9	115	18		1.2
SUNDIN, GORDIE Gordon Vincent B10.10.1937 Minneapolis MN BR/TR/6-4/215 d9.19																									
1956	Bal A	0	0	—	1	0	0	0	0	1	2	0	0	2-0	0	∞	—	—	1.000	0	—	0		-1	137	-0.1
SUNDRA, STEVE Stephen Richard "Smokey" B3.27.1910 Luxor PA D3.23.1952 Cleveland OH BR/TR(BB 1936-40)/6-2/190 d4.17 Mil 1944-45																									
1936	NY A	0	0	—	1	0	0	0	1	1	0	0	0	2	1	0.00	—	.286	.444	1	.000	-0		1		0.0
1938	NY A	6	4	.600	25	8	3	0	93.2	107	61	7	0	43	33	4.80	94	.291	.365	33-1-2	.182	1	141	-4		-0.2
1939	†NY A	11	1	.917	24	11	8-1	0	120.2	110	43	7	0	56	27	2.76	158	.240	.323	49-0-2	.265	4	162	22		2.3
1940	NY A	4	6	.400	27	8	2	2	99.1	121	68	11	4	42	26	5.53	73	.299	.366	29-0-1	.138	-1	101	-17		-1.6
1941	Was A	9	13	.409	28	23	11	0	168.1	203	108	11	1	61	50	5.29	76	.294	.352	60-0-4	.217	2	105	-20		-2.0
1942	Was A	1	3	.250	6	4	2	0	33.2	43	24	1	1	15	7	5.61	65	.305	.376	12	.167	-0	99	-7		-0.2
	StL A	8	3	.727	20	13	6	0	110.2	122	56	2	0	29	26	3.82	97	.275	.319	40-1-3	.225	3	138	-2		0.1
	Year	9	6	.600	26	17	8	0	144.1	165	80	3	1	44	31	4.24	87	.282	.333	52-1-3	.212	2	129	-8		-0.6
1943	StL A	15	11	.577	32	29	13-3	0	208	212	89	10	0	66	44	3.25	103	.266	.322	73-0-4	.219	1	104	1		0.2
1944	StL A	2	0	1.000	3	3	2	0	19	15	3	1	0	2	1	1.42	253	.211	.253	5	.000	-0	85	5		0.5

YEAR	TM LG	W	L	PCT	G	GS	CG-SHO	SV-BS	IP	H	R	HR	HB	BB-IB	SO	ERA	AERA	OAV	OOB	AB-HR-SH	AVG	PB	SUP	APR	DL	PW
1946	StL A	0	0		2	0	0	0	4	9	9	0	0	3	1	11.25	33	.409	.480	0	—	0		-4		-0.2
Total	9	56	41	.577	168	99	47-4	2	859.1	944	461	50	3	321	214	4.17	94	.277	.340	302-2-16	.209	10	116	-25		-1.6

SUNKEL, TOM   Thomas Jacob "Lefty"   B8.9.1912 Paris IL   D4.6.2002 Paris IL   BL/TL/6-1/190   d8.26

YEAR	TM LG	W	L	PCT	G	GS	CG-SHO	SV-BS	IP	H	R	HR	HB	BB-IB	SO	ERA	AERA	OAV	OOB	AB-HR-SH	AVG	PB	SUP	APR	DL	PW
1937	StL N	0	0		9	1	0	1	29.1	24	11	0	0	11	9	2.76	144	.214	.285	.9	.111	-1	173	4		0.1
1939	StL N	4	4	.500	20	11	2-1	0	85.1	79	47	4	1	56	54	4.22	98	.242	.354	28-0-1	.321	2	98	-1		0.0
1941	NY N	1	1	.500	2	2	1-1	0	15.1	7	5	0	1	12	14	2.93	126	.140	.317	6	.333	0	34	2		0.2
1942	NY N	3	6	.333	19	11	3	0	63.2	65	40	5	0	41	29	4.81	70	.269	.375	19	.105	-1	80	-10		-1.5
1943	NY N	0	1	.000	1	1	0	0	2.2	4	3	1	0	3	0	10.13	34	.308	.438	0	—	0	0	-2		-0.3
1944	Bro N	1	3	.250	12	3	0	1	24	39	20	1	0	10	6	7.50	47	.368	.422	4-0-1	.000	-1	79	-9		-1.5
Total	6	9	15	.375	63	29	6-2	2	220.1	218	126	11	2	133	112	4.53	83	.256	.358	66-0-2	.212	0	84	-16		-3.0

SUPPAN, JEFF   Jeffrey Scot   B1.2.1975 Oklahoma City OK   BR/TR/6-2/210(203-220)   [BosA93 2/49]   d7.17

YEAR	TM LG	W	L	PCT	G	GS	CG-SHO	SV-BS	IP	H	R	HR	HB	BB-IB	SO	ERA	AERA	OAV	OOB	AB-HR-SH	AVG	PB	SUP	APR	DL	PW
1995	Bos A	1	2	.333	8	3	0	0-0	22.2	29	15	4	0	5-1	19	5.96	82	.312	.343	0	—	0	89	-2		-0.2
1996	Bos A	1	1	.500	8	4	0	0-0	22.2	29	19	3	1	13-0	13	7.54	68	.330	.406	0	—	0	123	-5	36	-0.4
1997	Bos A	7	3	.700	23	22	0	0-0	112.1	140	75	12	4	36-1	67	5.69	82	.305	.358	2	.000	-0	118	-11		-1.0
1998	Ari N	1	7	.125	13	13	1	0-0	66	82	55	12	1	21-1	39	6.68	64	.301	.351	22-0-1	.273	1	94	-18		-1.6
	KC A	0	0	—	4	1	0	0-0	12.2	9	1	1	0	1-0	12	0.71	684	.200	.217	0	—	0	6	6		0.3
1999	KC A	10	12	.455	32	32	4-1	0-0	208.2	222	113	28	3	62-4	103	4.53	112	.274	.326	5	.200	0	97	13		1.1
2000	KC A	10	9	.526	35	33	3-1	0-0	217	240	121	36	7	84-3	128	4.94	106	.284	.351	3	.000	0	94	9		0.5
2001	KC A	10	14	.417	34	34	1	0-0	218.1	227	120	26	12	74-3	120	4.37	114	.267	.333	5	.400	1	81	12		1.2
2002	KC A	9	16	.360	33	33	3-1	0-0	208	229	134	32	7	68-3	109	5.32	94	.279	.335	1-0-3	.000	0	83	-8		-0.8
2003	Pit N	10	7	.588	21	21	3-2	0-0	141	147	57	11	6	31-5	78	3.57	121	.268	.313	41-0-8	.293	-4	94	13		1.8
	Bos A	3	4	.429	11	10	0	0-0	63	70	41	12	2	20-0	32	5.57	84	.281	.335	2-0-1	.000	-0	111	-5		-0.5
2004	†StL N	16	9	.640	31	31	0	0-0	188	192	98	25	8	65-1	110	4.16	102	.265	.330	57-0-7	.070	-4	118	1		-0.3
2005	†StL N	16	10	.615	32	32	0	0-0	194.1	206	93	24	7	63-1	114	3.57	118	.275	.335	58-1-6	.207	3	103	11		1.0
Total	11	94	94	.500	285	269	15-5	0-0	1674.2	1822	942	206	58	543-23	944	4.66	102	.278	.336	196-1-26	.189	0	97	16	36	1.8

SURHOFF, RICH   Richard Clifford   B10.3.1962 Bronx NY   BR/TR/6-3/210   [PhiN82*20/321]   d9.8   b-B.J.   Col St. Johns River (FL) CC

YEAR	TM LG	W	L	PCT	G	GS	CG-SHO	SV-BS	IP	H	R	HR	HB	BB-IB	SO	ERA	AERA	OAV	OOB	AB-HR-SH	AVG	PB	SUP	APR	DL	PW
1985	Phi N	1	0	1.000	2	0	0	0-0	1	2	0	0	0	0-0	1	0.00	—	.500	.500	0	—	0	0	0		0.1
	Tex A	0	1	.000	7	0	0	2-1	8.1	12	7	2	0	3-0	8	7.56	56	.343	.395	0	—	0		-3		-0.4
Total	1	1	1	.500	9	0	0	2-1	9.1	14	7	2	0	3-0	9	6.75	62	.359	.405	0	—	0		-3		-0.3

SURKONT, MAX   Matthew Constantine   B6.16.1922 Central Falls RI   D10.8.1986 Largo FL   BR/TR/6-0/205*   d4.19

YEAR	TM LG	W	L	PCT	G	GS	CG-SHO	SV-BS	IP	H	R	HR	HB	BB-IB	SO	ERA	AERA	OAV	OOB	AB-HR-SH	AVG	PB	SUP	APR	DL	PW
1949	Chi A	3	5	.375	44	2	0	4	96	92	61	9	3	60	38	4.78	87	.255	.366	22	.045	-1	75	-8		-0.8
1950	Bos N	5	2	.714	9	6	2	0	55.2	63	29	5	2	20	21	3.23	119	.285	.350	23-1-0	.435	5	142	1		0.7
1951	Bos N	12	16	.429	37	33	11-2	1	237	230	119	21	7	89	110	3.99	92	.252	.323	73-0-8	.151	0	98	-8		-1.0
1952	Bos N	12	13	.480	31	29	12-3	0	215	201	95	19	3	76	125	3.77	96	.245	.331	63-0-7	.111	-1	86	-2		-0.3
1953	Mil N	11	5	.688	28	24	11-2	0	170	168	82	22	0	64	83	4.18	94	.255	.321	56-0-5	.286	7	121	-1		0.6
1954	Pit N	9	18	.333	33	29	11	0	208.1	216	124	24	4	78	78	4.41	95	.268	.333	60-0-9	.167	0	78	-8		-0.8
1955	Pit N	7	14	.333	35	22	5	2	166.1	194	109	23	3	78-4	84	5.57	74	.298	.354	50-0-4	.140	-1	87	-22		-2.7
1956	Pit N	0	0	—	1	0	0	0	2	2	1	0	0	3-0	1	4.50	84	.333	.500	0	—	0	0	0		0.0
	StL N	0	0	—	5	0	0	0	5.2	10	6	3	0	2-0	5	9.53	40	.417	.462	1	.000	-0		-3		-0.2
	NY N	2	2	.500	8	4	1	1	32	24	17	5	0	9-1	18	4.78	79	.202	.256	9-0-2	.111	-0	93	-3		-0.4
	Year	2	2	.500	14	4	1	1	39.2	36	24	8	0	14-1	24	5.45	69	.242	.303	10-0-2	.100	-0	93	-6		-0.6
1957	NY N	1	0	1.000	5	0	0	0	5.2	9	7	2	0	2-0	8	9.95	42	.321	.367	0	—	0		-4		-0.5
Total	9	61	76	.445	236	149	53-7	8	1194.1	1209	650	134	22	481-5	571	4.38	89	.262	.334	357-1-35	.176	8	94	-58		-5.4

SUSCE, GEORGE   George Daniel   B9.13.1931 Pittsburgh PA   BR/TR/6-1/180*   d4.15   f-George

YEAR	TM LG	W	L	PCT	G	GS	CG-SHO	SV-BS	IP	H	R	HR	HB	BB-IB	SO	ERA	AERA	OAV	OOB	AB-HR-SH	AVG	PB	SUP	APR	DL	PW
1955	Bos A	9	7	.563	29	15	6-1	1	144.1	123	54	12	8	49-4	60	3.06	140	.232	.305	49-0-3	.143	-2	80	19		1.8
1956	Bos A	2	4	.333	21	6	0	0	69.2	71	54	14	4	44-1	26	6.20	74	.262	.371	18	.222	1	103	-10		-0.7
1957	Bos A	7	3	.700	29	5	0	1	88.1	93	45	6	3	41-5	40	4.28	93	.274	.354	25-0-1	.120	-1	85	-2		-0.3
1958	Bos A	0	0	—	2	0	0	0	2	6	4	1	0	1-0	0	18.00	22	.600	.583	0	—	0		-3		-0.1
	Det A	4	3	.571	27	10	2	1	90.2	90	45	7	3	26-1	42	3.67	110	.259	.312	24-0-2	.125	-1	89	2		0.0
	Year	4	3	.571	29	10	2	1	92.2	96	49	8	3	27-1	42	3.98	101	.269	.321	24-0-2	.125	-1	89	-1		-0.1
1959	Det A	0	0	—	9	0	0	0	14.2	24	22	4	2	9-0	9	12.89	32	.358	.449	1	.000	-0		-13		-0.6
Total	5	22	17	.564	117	36	8-1	3	409.2	407	224	44	20	170-11	177	4.42	95	.260	.337	117-0-6	.145	-2	88	-7		0.1

SUTCLIFFE, RICK   Richard Lee   B6.21.1956 Independence MO   BL/TR/6-7/215(200-240)   [LAN74 1/21]   d9.29

YEAR	TM LG	W	L	PCT	G	GS	CG-SHO	SV-BS	IP	H	R	HR	HB	BB-IB	SO	ERA	AERA	OAV	OOB	AB-HR-SH	AVG	PB	SUP	APR	DL	PW
1976	LA N	0	0	—	1	1	0	0-0	5	2	0	0	0	1-0	3	0.00	—	.125	.176	1	.000	-0	26	2		0.1
1978	LA N	0	0	—	2	0	0	0-0	1.2	2	0	0	1	1-0	0	—	—	.286	.444	0	—	0		1		0.0
1979	LA N	17	10	.630	39	30	5-1	0-0	242	217	104	16	2	97-6	117	3.46	105	.243	.316	85-1-6	.247	5*	132	6		1.1
1980	LA N	3	9	.250	42	10	1-1	5-3	110	122	73	10	1	55-2	59	5.56	62	.285	.366	27-0-3	.148	-0*	129	-25		-2.8
1981	LA N	2	2	.500	14	6	0	0-0	47	41	24	5	2	20-2	16	4.02	82	.238	.321	11	.182	0	72	-5	22	-0.3
1982	Cle A	14	8	.636	34	27	6-1	1-0	216	174	81	14	4	98-2	142	**2.96**	140	**.226**	.314	0	—	0	99	27		2.7
1983	Cle A☆	17	11	.607	36	35	10-2	0-1	243.1	251	131	23	6	102-5	160	4.29	100	.268	.341	0	—	0	104	-2		-0.1
1984	Cle A	4	5	.444	15	15	2	0-0	94.1	111	60	7	2	46-3	58	5.15	84	.298	.375	0	—	0	115	-11		-0.9
	†Chi N	16	1	**.941**	20	20	7-3	0-0	150.1	123	53	9	1	39-0	155	2.69	145	.220	.271	56-0-5	.250	3	125	17		2.4
1985	Chi N	8	8	.500	20	20	6-3	0-0	130	119	51	12	3	44-3	102	3.18	126	.240	.304	43-1-2	.233	2	82	10	93	1.5
1986	Chi N	5	14	.263	28	27	4-1	0-0	176.2	166	92	18	1	96-8	122	4.64	88	.252	.347	53-1-4	.208	2*	71	-7	34	-0.5
1987	Chi N★	**18**	10	.643	34	34	6-1	0-0	237.1	223	106	24	4	106-14	174	3.68	118	.252	.332	81-0-11	.148	2*	113	16		2.3
1988	Chi N	13	14	.481	32	32	12-2	0-0	226	232	97	18	2	70-9	144	3.86	94	.269	.323	75-1-4	.160	3*	98	-1		0.3
1989	†Chi N★	16	11	.593	35	34	5-1	0-0	229	202	98	18	2	69-8	153	3.66	103	.240	.296	70-0-10	.143	1*	103	5		0.9
1990	Chi N	0	2	.000	5	5	0	0-0	21.1	25	14	2	0	12-0	7	5.91	69	.305	.385	5-0-1	.000	0	88	-3	142	-0.3
1991	Chi N	6	5	.545	19	18	0	0-0	96.2	96	52	4	0	45-2	52	4.10	95	.264	.338	32-0-5	.094	-1*	97	-3	68	-0.5
1992	Bal A	16	15	.516	36	**36**	5-2	0-0	237.1	251	123	20	7	74-4	109	4.47	91	.273	.328	0	—	0	91	-9		-1.1
1993	Bal A	10	10	.500	29	28	3	0-0	166	212	112	23	6	74-5	80	5.75	79	.314	.385	0	—	0	101	-21	19	-2.1
1994	StL N	6	4	.600	16	14	0	0-0	67.2	93	53	11	2	32-2	26	6.52	65	.331	.402	23-0-3	.130*	-1	107	-17	47	-2.1
Total	18	171	139	.552	457	392	72-18	6-4	2697.2	2662	1324	236	46	1081-75	1679	4.08	98	.260	.331	562-4-54	.181	17	103	-20	446	0.6

SUTER, HARRY   Harry Richard "Handsome Harry","Rube"   B9.15.1887 Independence MO   D7.24.1971 Topeka KS   BL/TL/5-10/190   d4.16

YEAR	TM LG	W	L	PCT	G	GS	CG-SHO	SV-BS	IP	H	R	HR	HB	BB-IB	SO	ERA	AERA	OAV	OOB	AB-HR-SH	AVG	PB	SUP	APR	DL	PW
1909	Chi A	2	3	.400	18	7	3-1		87.1	72	34	2	4	28	53	2.47	95	.199	.264	32-0-1	.094	-1	112	-1		-0.3

SUTHERLAND, DARRELL   Darrell Wayne   B11.14.1941 Glendale CA   BR/TR/6-4/169*   d6.28   b-Gary   Col Stanford

YEAR	TM LG	W	L	PCT	G	GS	CG-SHO	SV-BS	IP	H	R	HR	HB	BB-IB	SO	ERA	AERA	OAV	OOB	AB-HR-SH	AVG	PB	SUP	APR	DL	PW
1964	NY N	0	3	.000	10	4	0	0	26.2	32	26	1	2	12-0	9	7.76	46	.302	.377	5	.200	0	111	-12		-1.2
1965	NY N	3	1	.750	18	2	0	0	48	33	16	4	4	17-2	16	2.81	125	.199	.284	13	.154	0	111	4		0.5
1966	NY N	2	0	1.000	31	0	0	0	44.1	60	25	6	2	25-8	23	4.87	75	.339	.422	3	.667	0		-5		-0.1
1968	Cle A	0	0	—	3	0	0	0	3.1	6	3	0	0	4-1	2	8.10	37	.375	.500	0	—	0		-2		-0.1
Total	4	5	4	.556	62	6	0	0	122.1	131	70	11	8	58-11	50	4.78	75	.282	.366	21	.238	1	111	-15		-0.9

SUTHERLAND, SUDS   Harvey Scott   B2.20.1894 Beaverton OR   D5.11.1972 Portland OR   BR/TR/6-0/180   d4.14

YEAR	TM LG	W	L	PCT	G	GS	CG-SHO	SV-BS	IP	H	R	HR	HB	BB-IB	SO	ERA	AERA	OAV	OOB	AB-HR-SH	AVG	PB	SUP	APR	DL	PW
1921	Det A	6	2	.750	13	8	3	0	58	80	43	1	0	18	18	4.97	86	.328	.374	27	.407	2*	156	-6		-0.3

SUTHERLAND, DIZZY   Howard Alvin   B4.9.1922 Washington DC   D8.26.1979 Washington DC   BL/TL/6-0/200   d9.20

YEAR	TM LG	W	L	PCT	G	GS	CG-SHO	SV-BS	IP	H	R	HR	HB	BB-IB	SO	ERA	AERA	OAV	OOB	AB-HR-SH	AVG	PB	SUP	APR	DL	PW
1949	Was A	0	1	.000	1	1	0	0	1	2	5	0	0	6	0	45.00	9	.400	.727	0	—	0	126	-4		-0.6

SUTTER, BRUCE   Howard Bruce   B1.8.1953 Lancaster PA   BR/TR/6-2/190*   d5.9   HF2006   [DL 1987 Atl N 182, 1989 Atl N 182]

YEAR	TM LG	W	L	PCT	G	GS	CG-SHO	SV-BS	IP	H	R	HR	HB	BB-IB	SO	ERA	AERA	OAV	OOB	AB-HR-SH	AVG	PB	SUP	APR	DL	PW
1976	Chi N	6	3	.667	52	0	0	10-2	83.1	63	27	4	0	26-8	73	2.70	144	.209	.271	8	.000	-1		10		1.3
1977	Chi N★	7	3	.700	62	0	0	31-9	107.1	69	21	5	1	23-7	129	1.34	329	.183	.231	20	.150	-0		31	21	4.7
1978	Chi N★	8	10	.444	64	0	0	27-14	98.2	82	44	10	1	34-7	106	3.19	127	.220	.285	13-0-4	.077	-0		6		1.3
1979	Chi N★	6	6	.500	62	0	0	**37**-10	101.1	67	29	8	0	32-5	110	2.22	187	.186	.249	12-0-2	.250	-1		**19**		3.9
1980	Chi N★	5	8	.385	60	0	0	28-9	102.1	90	35	4	1	34-8	76	2.64	150	.242	.306	9-0-1	.111	-1		13		2.4
1981	StL N★	3	5	.375	48	0	0	25-7	82.1	64	24	5	1	24-8	57	2.62	138	.218	.276	9	.000	-0		10		1.4
1982	†StL N	9	8	.529	70	0	0	36-9	102.1	88	38	8	3	34-13	61	2.90	127	.235	.302	8-0-2	.125	-1		8		1.7
1983	StL N	9	10	.474	60	0	0	21-9	89.1	90	45	8	1	30-14	64	4.23	86	.262	.321	7-0-1	.000	-1		-4		-0.9
1984	StL N☆	5	7	.417	71	0	0	**45**-8	122.2	109	26	9	3	23-4	77	1.54	227	.245	.281	10	.000	-1		**26**		4.4
1985	Atl N	7	7	.500	58	0	0	23-12	88.1	91	46	8	3	29-4	52	4.48	86	.267	.328	4	.000	-0		-4		-0.9

YEAR	TM LG	W	L	PCT	G	GS	CG-SHO	SV-BS	IP	H	R	HR	HB	BB-IB	SO	ERA	AERA	OAV	OOB	AB-HR-SH	AVG	PB	SUP	APR	DL	PW
1986	Atl N	2	0	1.000	16	0	0	3-3	18.2	17	9	3	0	9-2	16	4.34	91	.243	.329	1	.000	-0	0	131		0.0
1988	Atl N	1	4	.200	38	0	0	14-9	45.1	49	26	4	1	11-3	40	4.76	77	.275	.321	1	.000	0	-5	26		-0.8
Total	12	68	71	.489	661	0	0	300-101	1042	879	370	77	13	309-83	861	2.83	137	.230	.288	102-0-10	.088	-5		110	542	18.5

SUTTHOFF, JACK John Gerhard "Sunny Jack" B6.29.1873 Cincinnati OH D8.3.1942 Cincinnati OH BL/TR/5-9/175 d9.15

YEAR	TM LG	W	L	PCT	G	GS	CG-SHO	SV-BS	IP	H	R	HR	HB	BB-IB	SO	ERA	AERA	OAV	OOB	AB-HR-SH	AVG	PB	SUP	APR	DL	PW
1898	Was N	0	0	—	2	1	0	0	8.1	16	13	1	0	8	3	12.96	28	.400	.500	3	.333	0	194	-7		-0.3
1899	StL N	1	2	.333	3	3	3	0	24	29	25	0	0	15	8	4.13	97	.299	.393	10	.100	-1	120	-3		-0.4
1901	Cin N	1	6	.143	10	4	4	0	70.1	82	55	2	2	39	12	5.50	58	.289	.378	28-0-1	.107	-2*	78	-17		-1.6
1903	Cin N	16	9	.640	30	27	21-3	0	224.2	207	104	2	16	79	76	2.80	127	.246	.323	84-0-2	.143	-3	107	19		1.4
1904	Cin N	5	6	.455	12	10	8	0	90	83	49	1	3	43	27	2.30	127	.255	.348	33-0-1	.182	-0	120	1		0.0
	Phi N	6	13	.316	19	18	17	0	163.2	172	90	2	9	71	46	3.68	73	.272	.354	61-0-2	.164	-0	98	-14		-1.6
	Year	11	19	.367	31	28	25	0	253.2	255	139	3	12	114	73	3.19	87	.266	.352	94-0-3	.170	-1	107	-14		-1.6
1905	Phi N	3	4	.429	13	6	4-1	0	77.2	82	46	2	4	36	26	3.82	76	.290	.378	25-0-1	.080	-1	82	-8		-0.7
Total	6	32	40	.444	89	69	57-4	0	658.2	671	382	10	34	291	198	3.54	87	.268	.352	244-0-11	.143	-7	107	-29		-3.2

SUTTON, DON Donald Howard B4.2.1945 Clio AL BR/TR/6-1/185* d4.14 HF1998 Col Gulf Coast (FL) CC

YEAR	TM LG	W	L	PCT	G	GS	CG-SHO	SV-BS	IP	H	R	HR	HB	BB-IB	SO	ERA	AERA	OAV	OOB	AB-HR-SH	AVG	PB	SUP	APR	DL	PW
1966	LA N	12	12	.500	37	35	6-2	0	225.2	192	89	19	3	52-6	209	2.99	110	.228	.274	82-0-2	.183	1*	95	10		1.2
1967	LA N	11	15	.423	37	34	11-3	1	232.2	223	106	18	6	57-9	169	3.95	79	.250	.299	75-0-7	.133	-0*	107	-19		-2.2
1968	LA N	11	15	.423	35	27	7-2	1	207.2	179	64	6	2	59-14	162	2.60	106	.232	.287	62-0-6	.177	1*	87	7		1.0
1969	LA N	17	18	.486	41	41	11-4	0-0	293.1	269	123	25	3	91-6	217	3.47	97	.242	.299	98-0-9	.153	-1	106	-2		-0.4
1970	LA N	15	13	.536	38	38	10-4	0-0	260.1	251	127	38	10	78-7	201	4.08	94	.249	.308	84-0-5	.155	3*	110	-5		-0.3
1971	LA N	17	12	.586	38	37	12-4	1-0	265.1	231	85	10	5	55-5	194	2.54	128	.238	.280	88-0-4	.216	3*	98	22		2.7
1972	LA N★	19	9	.679	33	33	18-9		272.2	186	78	13	4	63-1	207	2.08	161	.189	.240	91-0-11	.143	-1	105	39		4.0
1973	LA N★	18	10	.643	33	33	14-3		256.1	196	78	19	5	56-4	200	2.42	144	.209	.257	84-0-7	.119	-2	91	32		3.2
1974	†LA N	19	9	.679	40	40	10-5		276	241	111	23	6	80-2	179	3.23	106	.229	.287	98-0-9	.184	1	137	6		0.8
1975	LA N★	16	13	.552	35	35	11-4		254.1	202	87	17	3	62-5	175	2.87	119	.213	.263	80-0-12	.138	-1	87	18		1.9
1976	LA N	21	10	.677	35	34	15-4		267.2	231	98	22	3	82-6	161	3.06	111	.234	.293	84-0-9	.083	-3	100	12		0.8
1977	†LA N★	14	8	.636	33	33	9-3		240.1	207	93	23	3	69-2	150	3.18	121	.233	.289	73-0-10	.151	1	111	19		1.6
1978	†LA N	15	11	.577	34	34	12-2		238.1	228	109	29	5	54-7	154	3.55	99	.250	.294	72-0-14	.083	-3	115	-2		-0.7
1979	LA N	12	15	.444	33	32	6-1	1-0	226	201	109	21	1	61-6	146	3.82	95	.239	.288	77-0-8	.143	-2	106	-4		-0.7
1980	LA N	13	5	.722	32	31	4-2	1-0	212.1	163	56	20	2	47-5	128	2.20	158	.211	.257	64-0-8	.078	-4	87	32		2.2
1981	Hou N	11	9	.550	23	23	6-3	0-0	158.2	132	51	6	1	29-3	104	2.61	126	.230	.265	51-0-5	.137	-0	105	13		1.7
1982	Hou N	13	8	.619	27	27	4	0-0	195	169	75	10	1	46-2	139	3.00	111	.232	.277	68-0-4	.162	-0	98	7		0.6
	†Mil A	4	1	.800	7	7	2-1	0	54.2	55	21	8	0	18-0	36	3.29	117	.263	.322	0	—	0	200	4		0.4
1983	Mil A	8	13	.381	31	31	4	0	220.1	209	109	21	5	54-2	134	4.08	93	.246	.292	0	—	0	101	-9		-0.7
1984	Mil A	14	12	.538	33	33	1	0	212.2	224	103	24	3	51-2	143	3.77	103	.266	.306	0	—	0	89	2		0.1
1985	Oak A	13	8	.619	29	29	1-1	0	194.1	194	88	19	0	51-0	91	3.89	100	.256	.301	0	—	0	111	2		0.2
	Cal A	2	2	.500	5	5	0	0	31.2	27	13	6	0	8-0	16	3.69	112	.233	.282	0	—	0	97	2		0.2
	Year	15	10	.600	34	34	1-1	0	226	221	101	25	0	59-0	107	3.86	101	.253	.298	0	—	0	109	5		0.4
1986	†Cal A	15	11	.577	34	34	3-1	0	207	192	93	31	3	49-2	116	3.74	111	.242	.287	0	—	0	102	-0		1.0
1987	Cal A	11	11	.500	35	34	1	0	191.2	199	101	38	7	41-0	99	4.70	92	.269	.311	0	—	0	104	-3		-0.4
1988	LA N	3	6	.333	16	16	0	0	87.1	91	44	7	1	30-6	44	3.92	85	.270	.327	23-0-6	.087	-1	103	-6	41	-0.7
Total	23	324	256	.559	774	756	178-58	5-0	5282.1	4692	2104	472	82	1343-102	3574	3.26	108	.236	.286	1354-0-136	.144	-8	104	190	41	17.5

SUTTON, JOHN Johnny Ike B11.13.1952 Dallas TX BR/TR/5-11/185* [TexA74*3/48] d4.7 Col Plano (TX) JC

YEAR	TM LG	W	L	PCT	G	GS	CG-SHO	SV-BS	IP	H	R	HR	HB	BB-IB	SO	ERA	AERA	OAV	OOB	AB-HR-SH	AVG	PB	SUP	APR	DL	PW
1977	StL N	2	1	.667	14	0	0	0-1	24.1	28	10	1	0	9-1	9	2.59	151	.315	.370	1	.000	-0		3		0.3
1978	Min A	0	0	—	17	0	0	0-0	44.1	46	19	3	1	15-3	18	3.45	111	.264	.326	0	—	0		2		0.1
Total	2	2	1	.667	31	0	0	0-1	68.2	74	29	4	1	24-4	27	3.15	123	.281	.341	1	.000	-0		5		0.4

SUZUKI, MAC Makoto B5.31.1975 Kobe, Japan BR/TR/6-3/195* d7.7

YEAR	TM LG	W	L	PCT	G	GS	CG-SHO	SV-BS	IP	H	R	HR	HB	BB-IB	SO	ERA	AERA	OAV	OOB	AB-HR-SH	AVG	PB	SUP	APR	DL	PW
1996	Sea A	0	0	—	1	0	0	0-0	1.1	2	3	0	0	2-1	1	20.25	25	.333	.500	0	—	0		-2		-0.1
1998	Sea A	1	2	.333	6	5	0	0-0	26.1	34	23	3	0	15-0	19	7.18	65	.304	.386	0	—	0	75	-7		-0.7
1999	Sea A	0	2	.000	16	4	0	0-0	42	47	47	7	4	34-2	32	9.43	51	.283	.411	0	—	0	102	-22		-1.0
	KC A	2	3	.400	22	9	0	0-0	68	77	45	9	3	30-1	36	5.16	94	.287	.365	0	—	0	79	-2		-0.1
	Year	2	5	.286	38	13	0	0-0	110	124	92	16	7	64-3	68	6.79	73	.286	.384	0	—	0	87	-23		-1.1
2000	KC A	8	10	.444	32	29	1-1	0-0	188.2	195	100	26	3	94-6	135	4.34	120	.265	.349	5-0-1	.200	0	86	16		1.2
2001	KC A	2	5	.286	15	9	0	0-0	56	61	38	12	3	25-1	37	5.30	94	.277	.355	0	—	0	91	-3		-0.3
	Col N	0	2	.000	3	1	0	0-0	6.1	9	12	3	1	11-0	5	15.63	34	.333	.538	1-0-1	.000	-0	52	-6		-1.0
	Mil N	3	5	.375	15	9	0	0-0	56	52	37	5	4	37-3	47	5.30	81	.251	.355	17-0-2	.000	-2	100	-7		-1.0
	Year	3	7	.300	18	10	0	0-0	62.1	61	49	8	5	48-3	52	6.35	69	.261	.397	18-0-3	.000	-2	94	-14		-2.0
2002	KC A	2	0	1.000	7	1	0	0-0	21	24	21	2	0	17-2	15	9.00	55	.296	.414	2	.500	-0	56	-8		-0.6
Total	6	16	31	.340	117	67	1-1	0-0	465.2	501	326	67	18	265-16	327	5.72	87	.275	.370	25-0-4	.080	-1	87	-41		-3.6

SWAGGERTY, BILL William David B12.5.1956 Sanford FL BR/TR/6-2/186(186-200) [BalA79 26/660] d8.13 Col Stetson

YEAR	TM LG	W	L	PCT	G	GS	CG-SHO	SV-BS	IP	H	R	HR	HB	BB-IB	SO	ERA	AERA	OAV	OOB	AB-HR-SH	AVG	PB	SUP	APR	DL	PW
1983	Bal A	1	1	.500	7	2	0	0-0	21.2	23	8	1	0	6-0	7	2.91	138	.267	.315	0	—	0	136	3		0.3
1984	Bal A	3	2	.600	23	6	0	0-0	57	68	41	7	0	21-3	18	5.21	75	.302	.356	0	—	0*	104	-10		-0.8
1985	Bal A	0	0	—	1	0	0	0-0	1.2	3	1	0	0	2-1	2	5.40	75	.375	.500	0	—	0		-0		-0.1
1986	Bal A	0	0	—	1	0	0	0-0	1	6	2	0	0	1-1	1	18.00	23	.750	.778	0	—	0		-1		-0.1
Total	4	4	3	.571	32	8	0	0-0	81.1	100	52	8	0	30-5	28	4.76	83	.306	.360	0	—	0	112	-8		-0.6

SWAIM, CY John Hillary B3.11.1874 Cadwallader (now West Chester) OH D12.27.1945 Eustis FL 6-6/180 d5.3 Col Mount Union

YEAR	TM LG	W	L	PCT	G	GS	CG-SHO	SV-BS	IP	H	R	HR	HB	BB-IB	SO	ERA	AERA	OAV	OOB	AB-HR-SH	AVG	PB	SUP	APR	DL	PW
1897	Was N	9	11	.450	26	19	14	0	184	219	129	5	10	59	52	4.60	94	.293	.353	71-0-1	.225	-3	105	0		-0.4
1898	Was N	3	11	.214	16	13	9	1	101.1	119	77	4	4	28	30	4.26	86	.290	.342	35	.143	-3	69	-10		-1.4
Total	2	12	22	.353	42	32	23	1	285.1	338	206	9	14	87	82	4.48	92	.292	.349	106-0-1	.198	-6	91	-10		-1.8

SWAN, CRAIG Craig Steven B11.30.1950 Van Nuys CA BR/TR/6-3/215(210-225) [NYN72 3/61] d9.3 Col Arizona St.

YEAR	TM LG	W	L	PCT	G	GS	CG-SHO	SV-BS	IP	H	R	HR	HB	BB-IB	SO	ERA	AERA	OAV	OOB	AB-HR-SH	AVG	PB	SUP	APR	DL	PW
1973	NY N	0	1	.000	3	1	0	0-0	8.1	16	9	2	0	4-0	4	8.64	42	.432	.450	2	.000	-0	73	-5		-0.5
1974	NY N	1	3	.250	7	5	0	0-1	30.1	28	19	1	0	21-3	10	4.45	81	.255	.366	11	.364	1	116	-4	38	-0.3
1975	NY N	1	3	.250	6	6	0	0-0	31	38	22	4	1	13-2	19	6.39	55	.302	.366	7-0-2	.000	-1	71	-9		-1.1
1976	NY N	6	9	.400	23	22	2-1	0-0	132.1	129	64	11	5	44-3	89	3.54	95	.254	.316	39-0-6	.103	-1	100	-5		-0.7
1977	NY N	9	10	.474	24	24	2-1	0-0	146.2	153	76	10	1	56-3	71	4.23	90	.268	.332	48-0-6	.188	-0	99	-7		-1.0
1978	NY N	9	6	.600	29	28	5-1	0-0	207.1	164	62	12	2	58-8	125	2.43	146	.219	.275	65-0-8	.154	-0	96	26		1.8
1979	NY N	14	13	.519	35	35	10-3	0-0	251.1	241	102	20	2	57-9	145	3.29	113	.255	.296	81-0-4	.123	-1	82	12		1.1
1980	NY N	5	9	.357	21	21	4-1	0-0	128.1	117	59	20	0	30-3	79	3.58	101	.247	.289	32-0-7	.219	2	73	0	69	0.0
1981	NY N	0	2	.000	5	3	0	0-0	13.2	10	6	0	0	1-0	9	3.29	107	.204	.220	3	.000	-0	92	0	67	0.0
1982	NY N	11	7	.611	37	21	2	1-1	166.1	165	70	13	0	37-4	67	3.35	110	.256	.295	44-1-3	.182	3	86	7		1.0
1983	NY N	2	8	.200	27	18	0	1-0	96.1	112	63	14	0	42-3	43	5.51	67	.299	.366	26-0-1	.077	-2	90	-17		-1.9
1984	NY N	1	0	1.000	10	0	0	0-1	18.2	18	15	5	0	7-0	10	8.20	44	.247	.309	0-0-1	—	0		-8		-0.4
	Cal A	0	0	—	2	1	0	0-0	5	8	6	3	0	4-0	2	10.80	37	.348	.348	0	—	0	113	-4	117	-0.5
Total	12	59	72	.450	231	185	25-7	2-3	1235.2	1199	575	115	11	368-38	673	3.74	97	.256	.309	358-1-38	.151	-0	89	-14	291	-2.5

SWAN, DUCKY Harry Gordon B8.11.1887 Lancaster PA D5.8.1946 Pittsburgh PA BR/TR/5-10/165 d4.28

YEAR	TM LG	W	L	PCT	G	GS	CG-SHO	SV-BS	IP	H	R	HR	HB	BB-IB	SO	ERA	AERA	OAV	OOB	AB-HR-SH	AVG	PB	SUP	APR	DL	PW
1914	KC F	0	0	—	1	0	0	0	1	0	0	0	0	1-0	1	0.00	—	.000	.250	0	—	0		0		0.0

SWAN, RUSS Russell Howard B1.3.1964 Fremont CA BL/TL/6-4/215* [SFN86 9/214] d8.3 Col Texas A&M-Commerce

YEAR	TM LG	W	L	PCT	G	GS	CG-SHO	SV-BS	IP	H	R	HR	HB	BB-IB	SO	ERA	AERA	OAV	OOB	AB-HR-SH	AVG	PB	SUP	APR	DL	PW
1989	SF N	0	2	.000	2	2	0	0-0	6.2	11	10	4	0	4-0	2	10.80	31	.393	.469	2	.000	-0	92	-6		-1.0
1990	SF N	0	1	.000	2	1	0	0-0	2.1	6	4	0	0	4-0	1	3.86	95	.429	.556	1	.000	-0	74	-1		-0.3
	Sea A	2	3	.400	11	8	0	0-0	47	42	22	3	0	18-2	15	3.64	109	.244	.311	0	—	0	89	2	55	0.2
1991	Sea A	6	2	.750	63	0	0	2-3	78.2	81	35	8	0	28-7	33	3.43	121	.269	.330	0	—	0		15	15	0.5
1992	Sea A	3	10	.231	55	9	1	9-2	104.1	104	60	8	3	45-7	45	4.74	84	.262	.338	0	—	0	61	-8		-1.0
1993	Sea A	3	3	.500	23	0	0	1-0	19.2	25	20	2	2	18-1	10	9.15	49	.316	.455	0	—	0		-9	42	-1.7
1994	Cle A	0	1	.000	12	0	0	0-0	8	13	11	1	0	7-1	2	11.25	42	.382	.488	0	—	0		-6		-0.6
Total	6	14	22	.389	168	20	1	11-5	266.2	282	162	26	5	124-18	108	4.83	85	.275	.353	3	.000	-0	73	-23	112	-3.9

SWANSON, RED Arthur Leonard B10.15.1936 Baton Rouge LA BR/TR/6-1.5/175* d9.10 Col Louisiana St.

YEAR	TM LG	W	L	PCT	G	GS	CG-SHO	SV-BS	IP	H	R	HR	HB	BB-IB	SO	ERA	AERA	OAV	OOB	AB-HR-SH	AVG	PB	SUP	APR	DL	PW
1955	Pit N	0	0	—	1	0	0	0	2	4	4	1	0	3-0	1	18.00	23	.286	.500	0	—	0		-3		-0.1
1956	Pit N	0	0	—	9	0	0	0	11.2	21	13	1	0	8-1	5	10.03	38	.438	.492	0	—	0*		-7		-0.3

YEAR	TM LG	W	L	PCT	G	GS	CG-SHO	SV-BS	IP	H	R	HR	HB	BB-IB	SO	ERA	AERA	OAV	OOB	AB-HR-SH	AVG	PB	SUP	APR	DL	PW
1957	Pit N	3	3	.500	32	8	1	0	72.2	68	35	9	1	31-3	29	3.72	102	.248	.327	13	.000	-1	128	0		-0.1
Total	3	3	3	.500	42	8	1	0	86.1	91	52	11	1	42-4	34	4.90	77	.277	.357	13	.000	-1	128	-10		-0.5

SWARBACK, BILL William (b William Schwappach) B10.1867 New York NY D5.17.1949 Stamford CT d7.9

YEAR	TM LG	W	L	PCT	G	GS	CG-SHO	SV-BS	IP	H	R	HR	HB	BB-IB	SO	ERA	AERA	OAV	OOB	AB-HR-SH	AVG	PB	SUP	APR	DL	PW
1887	NY N	0	2	.000	2	2	2	0	16	27	23	1	1	6	6	5.06	74	.346	.400	7	.000	-1	172	-5		-0.5

SWARTZ, BUD Sherwin Merle B6.13.1929 Tulsa OK D6.24.1991 Los Angeles CA BL/TL/6-2.5/180 d7.12

YEAR	TM LG	W	L	PCT	G	GS	CG-SHO	SV-BS	IP	H	R	HR	HB	BB-IB	SO	ERA	AERA	OAV	OOB	AB-HR-SH	AVG	PB	SUP	APR	DL	PW
1947	StL A	0	0	—	5	1	0	0	5.1	9	6	1	0	7	5	6.75	57	.360	.500	1	1.000	0		-2		-0.1

SWARTZ, MONTY Vernon Monroe "Dazzy" B1.1.1897 Farmersville OH D1.13.1980 Germantown OH BR/TR/5-11/182 d10.3

YEAR	TM LG	W	L	PCT	G	GS	CG-SHO	SV-BS	IP	H	R	HR	HB	BB-IB	SO	ERA	AERA	OAV	OOB	AB-HR-SH	AVG	PB	SUP	APR	DL	PW
1920	Cin N	0	1	.000	1	1	1	0	12	17	6	0	0	2	2	4.50	68	.333	.358	4	.500	1	78	-1		0.0

SWARTZBAUGH, DAVE David Theodore B2.11.1968 Middletown OH BR/TR/6-2/195(195-210) [ChiN89 9/226] d9.3 Col Miami-Ohio

YEAR	TM LG	W	L	PCT	G	GS	CG-SHO	SV-BS	IP	H	R	HR	HB	BB-IB	SO	ERA	AERA	OAV	OOB	AB-HR-SH	AVG	PB	SUP	APR	DL	PW
1995	Chi N	0	0	—	7	0	0	0-0	7.1	5	2	0	0	3-1	5	0.00	—	.208	.296	0	—	0		3		0.1
1996	Chi N	0	2	.000	6	5	0	0-0	24	26	17	3	0	14-1	13	6.38	69	.277	.370	6	.000	-0	66	-4		-0.4
1997	Chi N	0	1	.000	2	2	0	0-0	8	12	8	1	1	7-0	4	9.00	48	.364	.476	4	.000	-0	64	-4		-0.4
Total	3	0	3	.000	15	7	0	0-0	39.1	43	27	4	1	24-2	22	5.72	76	.285	.384	10	.000	-1	66	-5		-0.6

SWARTZEL, PARK Park B. B11.21.1865 Knightstown IN D1.3.1940 Los Angeles CA BR/TR/5-10/? d4.17

YEAR	TM LG	W	L	PCT	G	GS	CG-SHO	SV-BS	IP	H	R	HR	HB	BB-IB	SO	ERA	AERA	OAV	OOB	AB-HR-SH	AVG	PB	SUP	APR	DL	PW
1889	KC AA	19	27	.413	48	47	45	1	410.1	481	334	21	23	117	147	4.32	98	.283	.338	174	.144	-9*	89	0		-0.3

SWEENEY, BRIAN Brian Edward B6.13.1974 Yonkers NY BR/TR/6-2/180(180-200) d8.16 Col Mercy (NY)

YEAR	TM LG	W	L	PCT	G	GS	CG-SHO	SV-BS	IP	H	R	HR	HB	BB-IB	SO	ERA	AERA	OAV	OOB	AB-HR-SH	AVG	PB	SUP	APR	DL	PW
2003	Sea A	0	0	—	5	0	0	0-0	9.1	7	2	0	1	1-0	7	1.93	225	.212	.257	0	—	0		3		0.1
2004	SD N	1	0	1.000	7	2	0	0-0	14.1	20	9	1	0	2-0	10	5.65	70	.328	.349	4	.000	-0	106	-3		-0.2
Total	2	1	0	1.000	12	2	0	0-0	23.2	27	11	1	1	3-0	17	4.18	98	.287	.316	4	.000	-0	106	-1		-0.1

SWEENEY, CHARLIE Charles J. B4.13.1863 San Francisco CA D4.4.1902 San Francisco CA BR/TR/5-10.5/181 d5.11.1882 ▲

YEAR	TM LG	W	L	PCT	G	GS	CG-SHO	SV-BS	IP	H	R	HR	HB	BB-IB	SO	ERA	AERA	OAV	OOB	AB-HR-SH	AVG	PB	SUP	APR	DL	PW
1883	Pro N	7	7	.500	20	18	14	0	146.2	142	94	3		28	48	3.13	98	.237	.272	87	.218	-1*	108	0		0.0
1884	Pro N	17	8	.680	27	24	22-4	1	221	153	70	4		29	145	1.55	184	.187	.215	168-1	.298	8*	95	36		4.4
	StL U	24	7	.774	33	32	31-2	0	271	207	112	2		13	192	1.83	131	.197	.207	171-1	.316	6*	110	16		2.1
1885	StL N	11	21	.344	35	35	32-2	0	275	276	175	6		50	84	3.93	70	.250	.282	267	.206	-0*	72	-30		-2.8
1886	StL N	5	6	.455	11	11	11	0	93	108	73	9		39	28	4.16	77	.285	.352	64	.250	1*	92	-9		-0.7
1887	Cle AA	0	3	.000	3	3	3	0	24	42	36	0	0	13	8	8.25	53	.372	.437	133	.226	0*	59	-10		-0.7
Total	5	64	52	.552	129	123	113-8	1	1030.2	928	560	24	0	172	505	2.87	97	.228	.260	890-2	.252	14	93	3		2.4

SWEENEY, BILL William J. B Philadelphia PA D8.2.1903 Philadelphia PA TR/5-11/160 d6.27

YEAR	TM LG	W	L	PCT	G	GS	CG-SHO	SV-BS	IP	H	R	HR	HB	BB-IB	SO	ERA	AERA	OAV	OOB	AB-HR-SH	AVG	PB	SUP	APR	DL	PW
1882	Phi AA	9	10	.474	20	20	18	0	170	178	119	4		48	48	2.91	96	.252	.294	88	.159	-2*	116	-8		-0.9
1884	Bal U	40	21	.656	62	60	58-4	0	538	522	294	13		74	374	2.59	103	.241	.263	296	.240	-16*	102	7		-0.6
Total	2	49	31	.613	82	80	76-4	0	708	700	413	17		122	422	2.67	101	.244	.270	384	.221	-18	105	-1		-1.5

SWEETLAND, LES Lester Leo (Born Leo Sweetland) B8.15.1901 St.Ignace MI D3.4.1974 Melbourne FL BR/TL(BB 1930-31)/5-11.5/155 d7.4

YEAR	TM LG	W	L	PCT	G	GS	CG-SHO	SV-BS	IP	H	R	HR	HB	BB-IB	SO	ERA	AERA	OAV	OOB	AB-HR-SH	AVG	PB	SUP	APR	DL	PW
1927	Phi N	2	10	.167	21	13	6	0	103.2	147	77	3	3	53	21	6.16	67	.348	.425	38-0-1	.316	3*	93	-21		-1.5
1928	Phi N	3	15	.167	37	18	5	2	135.1	163	111	16	15	97	23	6.58	65	.306	.426	47-0-1	.191	1*	86	-32		-3.4
1929	Phi N	13	11	.542	43	26	10-2	2	204.1	255	129	23	9	87	47	5.11	102	.316	.389	89-0-1	.292	3*	88	2		0.7
1930	Phi N	7	15	.318	34	25	8-1	0	167	271	164	24	6	60	36	7.71	71	.373	.425	57-0-4	.281	4*	100	-37		-3.2
1931	Chi N	8	7	.533	26	14	9	0	130.1	156	89	3	5	61	32	5.04	77	.297	.375	56-0-1	.268	5*	144	-19		-1.4
Total	5	33	58	.363	161	96	38-3	4	740.2	992	570	68	37	358	159	6.10	77	.329	.407	287-0-8	.272	16	100	-107		-8.8

SWETONIC, STEVE Stephen Albert B8.13.1903 Mt.Pleasant PA D4.22.1974 Canonsburg PA BR/TR/5-11/185 d4.17 Col Pittsburgh

YEAR	TM LG	W	L	PCT	G	GS	CG-SHO	SV-BS	IP	H	R	HR	HB	BB-IB	SO	ERA	AERA	OAV	OOB	AB-HR-SH	AVG	PB	SUP	APR	DL	PW
1929	Pit N	8	10	.444	41	12	3	0	143.2	172	87	6	5	50	35	4.82	99	.299	.360	48-0-1	.271	3*	107	0		0.4
1930	Pit N	6	6	.500	23	6	3-1	5	96.2	107	53	7	0	27	35	4.47	111	.276	.323	36	.111	-3	96	7		0.5
1931	Pit N	0	2	.000	14	0	0	1	27.2	28	12	0	0	16	8	3.90	99	.264	.361	7	.143	-0		1		0.0
1932	Pit N	11	6	.647	24	19	11-4	0	162.1	134	57	11	0	55	39	2.82	135	.221	.286	48-0-1	.093	-4	92	21		1.6
1933	Pit N	12	12	.500	31	21	8-3	0	164.2	166	78	10	2	64	37	3.50	95	.260	.330	55-0-6	.200	1	100	-3		0.0
Total	5	37	36	.507	133	58	25-8	11	595.1	607	287	34	7	212	154	3.81	107	.262	.326	200-0-9	.170	-3	96	26		2.1

SWIFT, BILL William Charles B10.27.1961 Portland ME BR/TR/6-0/180(170-197) [SeaA84 1/2] d6.7 Col Maine

YEAR	TM LG	W	L	PCT	G	GS	CG-SHO	SV-BS	IP	H	R	HR	HB	BB-IB	SO	ERA	AERA	OAV	OOB	AB-HR-SH	AVG	PB	SUP	APR	DL	PW
1985	Sea A	6	10	.375	23	21	0	0-0	120.2	131	71	8	5	48-5	55	4.77	89	.279	.350	0	—	0	87	-7		-0.9
1986	Sea A	2	9	.182	29	17	1	0-1	115.1	148	85	5	7	55-2	55	5.46	78	.319	.397	0	—	0	96	-18		-1.4
1988	Sea A	8	12	.400	38	24	6-1	0-1	174.2	199	99	10	8	65-3	47	4.59	91	.294	.362	0	—	0	102	-7		-0.6
1989	Sea A	7	3	.700	37	16	0	1-0	130	140	72	7	2	38-4	45	4.43	91	.278	.329	0	—	0	125	-5	24	-0.1
1990	Sea A	6	4	.600	55	8	0	6-1	128	135	46	4	7	21-6	42	2.39	167	.272	.309	0	—	0	109	19		1.4
1991	Sea A	1	2	.333	71	0	0	17-1	90.1	74	22	3	1	26-4	48	1.99	208	.224	.283	0	—	0	21	14		1.4
1992	SF N	10	4	.714	30	22	3-2	1-0	164.2	144	41	6	3	43-3	77	2.08	161	.239	.292	51-0-5	.157	1*	110	25	43	2.4
1993	SF N	21	8	.724	34	34	1-1	0-0	232.2	195	82	18	6	55-5	157	2.82	139	.226	.277	80-0-10	.262	6	115	28		4.1
1994	SF N	8	7	.533	17	17	0	0-0	109.1	109	49	10	1	31-6	62	3.38	120	.262	.313	32-0-5	.188	2*	86	7	46	1.0
1995	†Col N	9	3	.750	19	19	0	0-0	105.2	122	62	12	1	43-2	68	4.94	109	.296	.363	36-1-5	.194	0	116	5	56	0.0
1996	Col N	1	1	.500	7	3	0	2-0	18.1	23	12	1	0	5-0	5	5.40	97	.307	.346	6	.333	0	63	0	146	0.0
1997	Col N	4	6	.400	14	13	0	0-0	65.1	85	57	11	2	26-0	29	6.34	82	.317	.377	19-0-4	.211	1*	119	-10	59	-1.7
1998	Sea A	11	9	.550	29	26	0	0-0	144.2	183	103	21	10	51-2	77	5.85	80	.306	.369	5	.000	-1	131	-19		-2.1
Total	13	94	78	.547	403	220	11-4	27-4	1599.2	1688	801	116	53	507-42	767	3.95	106	.273	.332	229-1-29	.210	10	111	39	389	5.0

SWIFT, BILL William Vincent B6.19.1908 Elmira NY D2.23.1969 Bartow FL BR/TR/6-1.5/192 d4.12

YEAR	TM LG	W	L	PCT	G	GS	CG-SHO	SV-BS	IP	H	R	HR	HB	BB-IB	SO	ERA	AERA	OAV	OOB	AB-HR-SH	AVG	PB	SUP	APR	DL	PW
1932	Pit N	14	10	.583	39	23	11	4	214.1	205	97	15	2	26	64	3.61	106	.248	.272	78-0-3	.192	-1	105	9		0.6
1933	Pit N	14	10	.583	37	29	13-2	0	218.1	214	96	11	4	36	64	3.13	106	.251	.285	82	.244	3	124	4		0.6
1934	Pit N	11	13	.458	37	25	13-1	0	212.2	244	107	15	8	46	81	3.98	103	.284	.326	84-0-1	.214	2	115	-4		0.4
1935	Pit N	15	8	.652	39	22	11-3	1	203.2	193	76	6	1	37	74	2.70	152	.247	.282	78-0-1	.244	3	120	31		3.3
1936	Pit N	16	16	.500	45	31	17	2	262.1	275	132	18	5	64	92	4.01	101	.265	.310	105-2-1	.295	9	99	4		1.1
1937	Pit N	9	10	.474	36	17	9	3	164	160	79	14	3	34	84	3.95	98	.256	.297	54-0-2	.167	-1	79	1		-0.1
1938	Pit N	7	5	.583	36	9	2	4	150	155	65	9	4	40	77	3.24	117	.271	.323	50-1-2	.200	2	69	9		0.1
1939	Pit N	5	7	.417	36	8	2-1	6	129.2	150	60	6	3	28	56	3.89	99	.293	.333	42-0-2	.238	2	80	1		0.1
1940	Bos N	1	1	.500	4	0	0	1	9.1	12	7	0	0	7	7	2.89	129	.308	.413	3	.000	-0		1		0.1
1941	Bro N	3	0	1.000	9	0	0	1	22	26	9	4	0	7	9	3.27	112	.289	.340	5	.200	-0		1		0.1
1943	Chi A	0	2	.000	18	1	0	0	51.1	48	25	5	6	27	28	4.21	79	.246	.355	10	.100	0	25	-3		0.0
Total	11	95	82	.537	336	165	78-7	20	1637.2	1682	753	103	36	351	636	3.58	108	.263	.305	591-3-12	.227	18	104	60		6.4

SWIGART, OAD Oadis Vaughn B2.13.1915 Archie MO D8.8.1997 St.Joseph MO BL/TR/6-0/175 d9.14 Mil 1941-45

YEAR	TM LG	W	L	PCT	G	GS	CG-SHO	SV-BS	IP	H	R	HR	HB	BB-IB	SO	ERA	AERA	OAV	OOB	AB-HR-SH	AVG	PB	SUP	APR	DL	PW
1939	Pit N	1	1	.500	3	3	1-1	0	24.1	27	14	1	0	8	8	4.44	87	.293	.337	8-0-2	.250	-1	144	-2		-0.1
1940	Pit N	0	2	.000	7	2	0	0	22.1	27	14	1	0	10	9	4.43	86	.297	.366	5-0-1	.200	-0	57	-2		-0.2
Total	2	1	3	.250	10	5	1-1	0	46.2	54	28	2	0	16	17	4.44	86	.295	.352	13-0-3	.231	-1	109	-4		-0.3

SWIGLER, AD Adam William "Doc" B9.21.1895 Philadelphia PA D2.5.1975 Philadelphia PA BR/TR/5-10/180 d9.25 Col Penn

YEAR	TM LG	W	L	PCT	G	GS	CG-SHO	SV-BS	IP	H	R	HR	HB	BB-IB	SO	ERA	AERA	OAV	OOB	AB-HR-SH	AVG	PB	SUP	APR	DL	PW
1917	NY N	0	1	.000	1	1	0	0	6	7	4	0	0	8	4	6.00	43	.333	.517	2	.000	-0	89	-2		-0.3

SWINDELL, GREG Forest Gregory B1.2.1965 Fort Worth TX BR/TL/6-3/225(225-239) [CleA86 1/2] d8.21 Col Texas

YEAR	TM LG	W	L	PCT	G	GS	CG-SHO	SV-BS	IP	H	R	HR	HB	BB-IB	SO	ERA	AERA	OAV	OOB	AB-HR-SH	AVG	PB	SUP	APR	DL	PW
1986	Cle A	5	2	.714	9	9	1	0-0	61.2	57	35	9	1	15-0	46	4.23	99	.243	.290	0	—	0	140	-1		-0.1
1987	Cle A	3	8	.273	16	15	4-1	0-0	102.1	112	62	18	1	37-1	97	5.10	90	.283	.343	0	—	0	89	-4	97	-0.4
1988	Cle A	18	14	.563	33	33	12-4	0-0	242	234	97	18	1	45-3	180	3.20	129	.252	.286	0	—	0	89	23		2.9
1989	Cle A★	13	6	.684	28	28	5-2	0-0	184.1	170	71	16	0	51-1	129	3.37	118	.246	.297	0	—	0	91	15	35	1.4
1990	Cle A	12	9	.571	34	34	3	0-0	214.2	245	110	27	4	47-2	135	4.40	90	.288	.324	0	—	0	121	-9		-0.9
1991	Cle A	9	16	.360	33	33	7	0-0	238	241	112	21	3	31-1	169	3.48	120	.263	.287	0	—	0	95	14		1.3
1992	Cin N	12	8	.600	31	30	5-3	0-0	213.2	210	72	14	2	41-4	138	2.70	134	.260	.295	80-0-5	.125	-2	110	20	15	2.4
1993	Hou N	12	13	.480	31	30	1-1	0-0	190.1	215	98	24	1	40-3	124	4.16	93	.283	.318	60-0-10	.183	-0	98	-6	20	-0.6
1994	Hou N	8	9	.471	24	24	1	0-0	148.1	175	80	20	1	26-2	74	4.37	91	.302	.329	44-0-12	.250	3	109	-7		-0.7
1995	Hou N	10	9	.526	33	26	1-1	0-2	153	180	86	21	2	39-2	96	4.47	86	.297	.337	50-0-6	.240	4*	128	-11		-0.7
1996	Hou N	0	3	.000	8	4	0	0-2	23	35	26	5	1	11-0	15	7.83	50	.340	.405	6	.333	1	174	-12	32	-1.2
	Cle A	1	1	.500	13	2	0	0-0	28.2	31	21	8	0	8-0	21	6.59	74	.279	.325	0	—	0	228	-5	17	-0.2
1997	Min A	7	4	.636	65	1	0	1-6	115.2	102	46	12	2	25-3	75	3.58	130	.238	.282	0	—	0	79	15		1.3

YEAR	TM LG	W	L	PCT	G	GS	CG-SHO	SV-BS	IP	H	R	HR	HB	BB-IB	SO	ERA	AERA	OAV	OOB	AB-HR-SH	AVG	PB	SUP	APR	DL	PW
1998	Min A	3	3	.500	52	0	0	2-2	66.1	67	27	10	3	18-2	45	3.66	131	.263	.317	0	—	0	9			0.7
	†Bos A	2	3	.400	29	0	0	0-1	24	25	13	3	0	13-1	18	3.38	140	.278	.369	0	—	0	2			0.4
	Year	5	6	.455	81	0	0	2-3	90.1	92	40	13	3	31-3	63	3.59	133	.267	.331	0	—	0	11			1.1
1999	†Ari N	4	0	1.000	63	0	0	1-1	64.2	54	19	8	1	21-1	51	2.51	184	.230	.296	4-0-2	.000	-0	15		15	0.8
2000	Ari N	2	6	.250	64	0	0	1-0	76	71	29	7	1	20-5	64	3.20	150	.247	.295	1-0-1	.000	-0	13			1.2
2001	†Ari N	2	6	.250	64	0	0	2-3	53.2	51	27	12	0	8-2	42	4.53	102	.250	.277	0	—	0	2			0.2
2002	†Ari N	0	2	.000	34	0	0	0-1	33	38	23	9	0	5-1	23	6.27	72	.279	.301	0	—	0	-5		53	-0.3
Total	17	123	122	.502	664	269	40-12	7-18	2233.1	2313	1053	262	21	501-34	1542	3.86	107	.268	.308	245-0-36	.188	6	101	68	284	7.0

SWINDELL, JOSH Joshua Ernest B7.5.1883 Rose Hill KS D3.19.1969 Fruita CO BR/TR/6-0/180 d9.16

YEAR	TM LG	W	L	PCT	G	GS	CG-SHO	SV-BS	IP	H	R	HR	HB	BB-IB	SO	ERA	AERA	OAV	OOB	AB-HR-SH	AVG	PB	SUP	APR	DL	PW
1911	Cle A	0	1	.000	4	1	1	0	17.1	19	9	0	1	4	6	2.08	164	.257	.304	4	.250	-0	21	1		0.0

SWINGLE, PAUL Paul Christopher B12.21.1966 Inglewood CA BR/TR/6-0/185 [CalA89 29/747] d9.7 Col Grand Canyon [DL 1994 Cal A 131]

YEAR	TM LG	W	L	PCT	G	GS	CG-SHO	SV-BS	IP	H	R	HR	HB	BB-IB	SO	ERA	AERA	OAV	OOB	AB-HR-SH	AVG	PB	SUP	APR	DL	PW
1993	Cal A	0	1	.000	9	0	0	0-0	9.2	15	9	4	0	6-0	6	8.38	50	.341	.429	0	—	0		-4		-0.3

SWITZER, JON Jon Michael B8.13.1979 Bowling Green KY BL/TL/6-3/190* [TBA01 2/47] d8.2 Col Arizona St.

YEAR	TM LG	W	L	PCT	G	GS	CG-SHO	SV-BS	IP	H	R	HR	HB	BB-IB	SO	ERA	AERA	OAV	OOB	AB-HR-SH	AVG	PB	SUP	APR	DL	PW
2003	TB A	0	0	—	5	0	0	0-0	9.2	13	8	2	4	3-0	7	7.45	62	.342	.435	0	—	0	-3			-0.1
2005	TB A	0	0	—	2	0	0	0-0	4	5	4	0	0	7-0	5	6.75	65	.278	.480	0	—	0	-1			-0.1
Total	2	0	0	—	7	0	0	0-0	13.2	18	12	2	4	10-0	12	7.24	62	.321	.451	0	—	0	-4			-0.2

SWORMSTEDT, LEN Leonard Jordan B10.6.1878 Cincinnati OH D7.19.1964 Salem MA BR/TR/5-11.5/165 d9.29

YEAR	TM LG	W	L	PCT	G	GS	CG-SHO	SV-BS	IP	H	R	HR	HB	BB-IB	SO	ERA	AERA	OAV	OOB	AB-HR-SH	AVG	PB	SUP	APR	DL	PW
1901	Cin N	2	1	.667	3	3	3 0		26	19	8	2	5		13	1.73	185	.202	.257	9	.000	-1	52	4		0.3
1902	Cin N	0	2	.000	2	2	2 0		18	22	11	1	0		5	4.00	75	.301	.346	6	.000	-1	45	-1		-0.2
1906	Bos A	1	1	.500	3	2	2 0		21	17	6	1	0		6	1.29	214	.224	.234	8	.125	-1	79	3		0.2
Total	3	3	4	.429	8	7	7 0		65	58	25	3	3		10	22	2.22	136	.239	.277	23	.043	-3	57	6		0.3

SYKES, BOB Robert Joseph B12.11.1954 Neptune NJ BB/TL/6-2/200* [DetA74 19/440] d4.9 Col Miami-Dade North (FL) CC

YEAR	TM LG	W	L	PCT	G	GS	CG-SHO	SV-BS	IP	H	R	HR	HB	BB-IB	SO	ERA	AERA	OAV	OOB	AB-HR-SH	AVG	PB	SUP	APR	DL	PW
1977	Det A	5	7	.417	32	20	3	0-1	132.2	141	74	15	2	50-0	58	4.41	98	.271	.334	0	—	0	109	-2		-0.2
1978	Det A	6	6	.500	22	10	3-2	2-2	93.2	99	43	14	1	34-0	58	3.94	99	.275	.338	0	—	0	104	1		0.0
1979	StL N	4	3	.571	13	11		0-0	67	86	49	11	1	34-2	35	6.18	62	.315	.392	21-0-2	.095	-1	137	-16	45	-1.5
1980	StL N	6	10	.375	27	19	4-3	0-0	126	134	67	12	0	54-3	50	4.64	81	.277	.348	39-0-3	.103	-2	118	-9		-1.4
1981	StL N	2	0	1.000	22	1	0	0-0	37.1	37	20	2	1	18-1	14	4.58	79	.266	.354	2	.000	0	172	-3		-0.1
Total	5	23	26	.469	116	61	10-5	2-5	456.2	497	253	54	5	190-6	215	4.65	85	.280	.349	62-0-5	.097	-2	118	-29	45	-3.2

SYLVESTER, LOU Louis J. B2.14.1855 Springfield IL D5.5.1936 Brooklyn NY BR/TR/5-6/165 d4.18 ▲

YEAR	TM LG	W	L	PCT	G	GS	CG-SHO	SV-BS	IP	H	R	HR	HB	BB-IB	SO	ERA	AERA	OAV	OOB	AB-HR-SH	AVG	PB	SUP	APR	DL	PW
1884	Cin U	0	1	.000	6	1	1 1		32.2	32	27	0	6		7	3.58	71	.239	.271	33-3-2	.267	-0*	100	-4		-0.2

SZUMINSKI, JASON Jason Ernest B12.11.1978 San Diego CA BR/TR/6-4/220 [ChiN00 27/793] d4.11 Col MIT

YEAR	TM LG	W	L	PCT	G	GS	CG-SHO	SV-BS	IP	H	R	HR	HB	BB-IB	SO	ERA	AERA	OAV	OOB	AB-HR-SH	AVG	PB	SUP	APR	DL	PW
2004	SD N	0	0	—	7	0	0	0-0	10	12	9	3	2	11-2	5	7.20	55	.286	.455	1	.000	-0	-4			-0.2

TABAKA, JEFF Jeffrey Jon B1.17.1964 Barberton OH BR/TL/6-2/195* [MonN86 2/43] d4.19 Col Kent St. [DL 1999 Pit N 182]

YEAR	TM LG	W	L	PCT	G	GS	CG-SHO	SV-BS	IP	H	R	HR	HB	BB-IB	SO	ERA	AERA	OAV	OOB	AB-HR-SH	AVG	PB	SUP	APR	DL	PW
1994	Pit N	0	0	—	5	0	0	0-0	4	4	4	1	0	8-0	2	18.00	24	.250	.500	0	—	0	-5			-0.3
	SD N	3	1	.750	34	0	0	1-0	37	28	21	0	1	19-3	30	3.89	106	.209	.305	1	1.000	1	0			0.1
	Year	3	1	.750	39	0	0	1-0	41	32	29	1	0	27-3	32	5.27	79	.213	.331	1	1.000	1	-7			-0.2
1995	SD N	0	0	—	10	0	0	0-1	6.1	10	5	1	0	5-1	6	7.11	57	.370	.469	0	—	-0	-2			-0.1
	Hou N	1	0	1.000	24	0	0	0-0	24.1	17	6	1	0	12-0	19	2.22	174	.202	.302	1-0-1	.000	-0	5			0.2
	Year	1	0	1.000	34	0	0	0-1	30.2	27	11	2	0	17-1	25	3.23	121	.243	.344	1-0-1	.000	-0	3			0.1
1996	Hou N	0	2	.000	18	0	0	1-0	20.1	28	18	5	3	14-0	18	6.64	58	.322	.433	1	.000	-0	-7			-0.7
1997	Cin N	0	0	—	3	0	0	0-0	2	1	1	1	2	1-0	1	4.50	95	.143	.400	0	—	0	0			0.0
1998	Pit N	2	2	.500	37	0	0	0-0	50.2	37	19	6	5	22-4	40	3.02	142	.204	.305	1	.000	1	-7		39	0.5
2001	StL N	0	0	—	8	0	0	0-1	3.2	6	3	1	0	1-0	3	7.36	59	.375	.412	0	—	0	-1		78	-0.1
Total	6	6	5	.545	139	0	0	2-2	148.1	131	81	16	10	82-8	119	4.31	95	.237	.345	4-0-1	.250	1	-3		299	-0.3

TABER, LEFTY Edward Timothy B1.11.1900 Rock Island IL D11.5.1983 Lincoln NE BL/TL/6-0/180 d9.4 Col Georgetown

YEAR	TM LG	W	L	PCT	G	GS	CG-SHO	SV-BS	IP	H	R	HR	HB	BB-IB	SO	ERA	AERA	OAV	OOB	AB-HR-SH	AVG	PB	SUP	APR	DL	PW
1926	Phi N	0	0	—	6	0	0	0-0	8.1	7	2	0	2	5	0	7.56	55	.242	.375	1	.000	-0		-2		-0.1
1927	Phi N	0	1	.000	3	1	0	0-0	3.1	8	9	0	1	5	0	18.90	22	.533	.667	1	.000	-0	41	-6		-1.0
Total	2	0	1	.000	9	1	0	0-0	11.2	16	11	0	3	10	0	10.80	38	.333	.475	2	.000	-0	41	-8		-1.1

TABER, JOHN John Pardon B6.28.1868 Acushnet MA D2.21.1940 Boston MA BR/TR/5-8/? d4.30

YEAR	TM LG	W	L	PCT	G	GS	CG-SHO	SV-BS	IP	H	R	HR	HB	BB-IB	SO	ERA	AERA	OAV	OOB	AB-HR-SH	AVG	PB	SUP	APR	DL	PW
1890	Bos N	0	1	.000	2	1	1 1		13	11	8	0	0	8	3	4.15	90	.220	.328	6	.000	-1	118	0		-0.1

TADANO, KAZUHITO Kazuhito B4.25.1980 Tokyo, Japan BR/TR/6-0/180* d4.27 Col Rikkyo (Japan)

YEAR	TM LG	W	L	PCT	G	GS	CG-SHO	SV-BS	IP	H	R	HR	HB	BB-IB	SO	ERA	AERA	OAV	OOB	AB-HR-SH	AVG	PB	SUP	APR	DL	PW
2004	Cle A	1	1	.500	14	4	0	0-0	50.1	55	30	6	3	18-0	39	4.65	93	.272	.341	3	.333	0	160	-3		-0.1
2005	Cle A	0	0	—	1	0	0	0-0	4	4	1	0	0	0-0	1	2.25	182	.250	.250	0	—	0	1			0.0
Total	2	1	1	.500	15	4	0	0-0	54.1	59	31	6	3	18-0	40	4.47	97	.271	.335	3	.333	0	160	-2		-0.1

TAFF, JOHN John Gallatin B6.3.1890 Austin TX D5.15.1961 Houston TX BR/TR/6-0/170 d5.11

YEAR	TM LG	W	L	PCT	G	GS	CG-SHO	SV-BS	IP	H	R	HR	HB	BB-IB	SO	ERA	AERA	OAV	OOB	AB-HR-SH	AVG	PB	SUP	APR	DL	PW
1913	Phi A	0	1	.000	7	1	0	0	17.2	22	13	0	0	9	9	6.62	42	.306	.351	5	.200	-0	54	-7		-0.4

TAKATSU, SHINGO Shingo B11.25.1968 Hiroshima, Japan BR/TR/6-0/180* d4.9

YEAR	TM LG	W	L	PCT	G	GS	CG-SHO	SV-BS	IP	H	R	HR	HB	BB-IB	SO	ERA	AERA	OAV	OOB	AB-HR-SH	AVG	PB	SUP	APR	DL	PW
2004	Chi A	6	4	.600	59	0	0	19-1	62.1	40	17	6	2	21-3	50	2.31	204	.182	.259	0	—	0	16			3.2
2005	Chi A	1	2	.333	31	0	0	8-1	28.2	30	19	9	0	16-1	32	5.97	76	.270	.359	0	—	0	-4			-0.5
	NY N	1	0	1.000	9	0	0	0-2	7.2	11	2	2	0	3-1	6	2.35	177	.314	.368	0	—	0	2			0.2
Total	2	8	6	.571	99	0	0	27-4	98.2	81	38	17	2	40-5	88	3.38	137	.221	.301	0	—	0	14			2.9

TALBOT, FRED Frederick Lealand "Bubby" B6.28.1941 Washington DC BR/TR/6-2/195(195-212) d9.28

YEAR	TM LG	W	L	PCT	G	GS	CG-SHO	SV-BS	IP	H	R	HR	HB	BB-IB	SO	ERA	AERA	OAV	OOB	AB-HR-SH	AVG	PB	SUP	APR	DL	PW
1963	Chi A	0	0	—	1	0	0		3	2	1	0	0	4-0	2	3.00	117	.222	.462	1	.000	-0	0			0.0
1964	Chi A	4	5	.444	17	12	3-2	0	75.1	83	31	7	4	20-0	34	3.70	93	.288	.340	19-0-2	.263	3*	99	0		0.2
1965	KC A	10	12	.455	39	33	2-1	0	198	188	96	25	6	86-3	117	4.14	84	.251	.330	70-0-3	.200	3*	99	-12		-0.9
1966	KC A	4	4	.500	11	11	0	0	72	65	39	6	2	28-6	37	4.79	71	.248	.324	20-0-5	.150	0	78	-10		-1.0
	NY A	7	7	.500	23	19	3	0	124.1	123	59	16	3	45-3	48	4.13	81	.262	.329	35-0-4	.143	1	117	-9		-0.8
	Year	11	11	.500	34	30	3	0	192	188	98	22	5	73-9	85	4.36	77	.257	.327	55-0-9	.145	1	103	-18		-1.8
1967	NY A	6	8	.429	29	22	2	0	138.2	132	78	20	6	54-5	61	4.22	74	.252	.325	38-1-2	.158	3*	111	-13		-1.3
1968	NY A	1	9	.100	29	11	1	0	99	89	47	6	2	42-6	67	3.36	87	.241	.319	17-1-2	.118	1	63	-7		-0.6
1969	NY A	0	0	—	8	0	0	0-1	12.1	13	9	1	0	6-2	7	5.11	69	.283	.352	1-0-1	.000	-0	-3			-0.1
	Sea A	5	8	.385	25	16	1-1		114.2	125	58	12	4	41-6	67	4.16	88	.278	.342	37-2-2	.162	2*	100	-6		-0.4
	Oak A	1	2	.333	12	2	0	1-0	19	22	11	2	0	7-0	9	5.21	66	.297	.358	3	.333	0	141	-3		-0.5
	Year	6	10	.375	45	18	1-1	1-1	146	160	78	15	4	54-8	83	4.38	82	.281	.345	41-2-3	.171	2	105	-11		-1.0
1970	Oak A	0	1	.000	1	0	0	0	1.2	2	2	1	0	1-0	0	10.80	33	.286	.375	0	—	0	-1			-0.2
Total	8	38	56	.404	195	126	12-4	1-1	853.2	844	431	96	27	334-31	449	4.12	81	.260	.331	241-4-21	.174	13	100	-69		-5.6

TALCOTT, ROY Le Roy Everett B1.16.1920 Brookline MA D12.6.1999 Miami FL BR/TR/6-1.5/180 d6.24 Col Princeton

YEAR	TM LG	W	L	PCT	G	GS	CG-SHO	SV-BS	IP	H	R	HR	HB	BB-IB	SO	ERA	AERA	OAV	OOB	AB-HR-SH	AVG	PB	SUP	APR	DL	PW
1943	Bos N	0	0	—	1	0	0	0	0.2	1	2	0	0	2	0	27.00	13	.333	.600	0	—	0	-2			-0.1

TALLET, BRIAN Brian Curtis B9.21.1977 Midwest City OK BL/TL/6-7/208(208-220) [CleA00 2/55] d9.16 Col Louisiana St. [DL 2004 Cle A 113]

YEAR	TM LG	W	L	PCT	G	GS	CG-SHO	SV-BS	IP	H	R	HR	HB	BB-IB	SO	ERA	AERA	OAV	OOB	AB-HR-SH	AVG	PB	SUP	APR	DL	PW
2002	Cle A	1	0	1.000	2	2	0	0-0	12	9	3	0	1	4-0	9	1.50	296	.214	.298	0	—	0	125	4		0.3
2003	Cle A	0	2	.000	5	3	0	0-0	19	23	14	2	1	8-0	9	4.74	94	.303	.376	2	.000	-0	62	-2		-0.2
2005	Cle A	0	0	—	2	0	0	0-0	4.2	6	4	2	1	3-0	2	7.71	53	.300	.417	0	—	0	-2			-0.1
Total	3	1	2	.333	9	5	0	0-0	35.2	38	21	4	3	15-0	16	4.04	109	.275	.359	2	.000	-0	89	0	113	0.0

TAM, JEFF Jeffrey Eugene B8.19.1970 Fullerton CA BR/TR/6-1/202(202-214) d6.30 Col Florida St.

YEAR	TM LG	W	L	PCT	G	GS	CG-SHO	SV-BS	IP	H	R	HR	HB	BB-IB	SO	ERA	AERA	OAV	OOB	AB-HR-SH	AVG	PB	SUP	APR	DL	PW
1998	NY N	1	1	.500	15	0	0	0-1	14.1	13	10	2	2	4-1	8	6.28	66	.241	.317	1	.000	-0	-3			-0.4
1999	Cle A	0	0	—	1	0	0	0-0	0.1	2	3	0	0	1-1	0	81.00	6	1.000	1.000	0	—	0	-3			-0.1
	NY N	0	0	—	9	0	0	0-0	11.1	6	4	3	0	3-0	8	3.18	137	.150	.209	0	—	0	2		41	0.1
2000	†Oak A	3	3	.500		0	0	3-3	85.2	86	30	3	1	23-8	46	2.63	185	.268	.315	0	—	0	21			1.4
2001	†Oak A	2	4	.333	70	0	0	3-3	74.2	68	27	3	3	29-9	44	3.01	151	.250	.326	0	—	0	13			1.0
2002	Oak A	1	2	.333	40	0	0	0-4	40.1	56	26	2	2	13-5	14	5.13	87	.333	.384	0	—	0	-3			-0.2
2003	Tor A	0	4	.000		0	0	1-1	44.2	58	30	5	1	25-7	26	5.64	84	.314	.396	1	1.000	1	-4			-0.2
Total	6	7	14	.333	251	0	0	7-12	271.1	289	130	18	9	98-31	146	3.91	119	.277	.342	2	.500	1	23		41	1.6

YEAR	TM LG	W	L	PCT	G	GS	CG-SHO	SV-BS	IP	H	R	HR	HB	BB-IB	SO	ERA	AERA	OAV	OOB	AB-HR-SH	AVG	PB	SUP	APR	DL	PW

TAMULIS, VITO Vitautis Casimirus B7.11.1911 Cambridge MA D5.5.1974 Nashville TN BL/TL/5-9/170 d9.25

YEAR	TM LG	W	L	PCT	G	GS	CG-SHO	SV-BS	IP	H	R	HR	HB	BB-IB	SO	ERA	AERA	OAV	OOB	AB-HR-SH	AVG	PB	SUP	APR	DL	PW
1934	NY A	1	0	1.000	1	1	1-1		9	7	0	0	0	1	5	0.00	—	.219	.242	4	.250	0	107	4		0.6
1935	NY A	10	5	.667	30	19	9-3	1	160.2	178	80	7	2	55	57	4.09	99	.280	.339	57-1-3	.246	4	129	2		0.5
1938	StL N	0	3	.000	3	2	0	0	15.1	26	15	2	0	10	11	7.63	65	.366	.444	5	.400	1	80	-5		-0.6
	Bro N	12	6	.667	38	18	9	2	159.2	181	81	11	2	40	70	3.83	102	.288	.333	55-0-3	.127	-3*	118	1		-0.2
1939	Bro N	9	8	.529	39	17	8-1	4	158.2	177	81	10	8	45	83	4.37	92	.287	.343	55-0-3	.182	-1	92	-3		-0.4
1940	Bro N	8	5	.615	41	12	4-1	0	154.1	147	60	9	3	34	55	3.09	129	.244	.288	46-0-1	.130	-1*	96	15		1.0
1941	Phi N	0	1	.000	6	1	0	0	12	21	13	1	1	7	5	9.00	41	.382	.460	2	.000	-0	46	-7		-0.5
	Bro N	0	0	—	12	0	0	1	22	21	10	1	0	10	8	3.68	100	.244	.323	5		-1		0		-0.1
	Year	0	1	.000	18	1	0	1	34	42	23	2	1	17	13	5.56	66	.298	.377	7	.000	-1	46	-6		-0.6
Total	6	40	28	.588	170	70	31-6	10	691.2	758	340	37	16	202	294	3.97	101	.278	.331	229-1-10	.175	-1	109	7		0.3

TANANA, FRANK Frank Daryl B7.3.1953 Detroit MI BL/TL/6-3/195(185-200) [CalA71 1/13] d9.9

YEAR	TM LG	W	L	PCT	G	GS	CG-SHO	SV-BS	IP	H	R	HR	HB	BB-IB	SO	ERA	AERA	OAV	OOB	AB-HR-SH	AVG	PB	SUP	APR	DL	PW
1973	Cal A	2	2	.500	4	4	2-1	0-0	26.1	20	11	2	0	8-0	22	3.08	116	.200	.259	0	—	0	75	1		0.2
1974	Cal A	14	19	.424	39	35	12-4	0-1	268.2	262	104	27	8	77-4	180	3.12	111	.255	.311	0	—	0	83	13		1.6
1975	Cal A	16	9	.640	34	33	16-5	0-0	257.1	211	80	21	7	73-6	269	2.62	137	.226	.286	0	—	0	117	32		3.2
1976	Cal A★	19	10	.655	34	34	23-2	0-0	288.1	212	88	24	9	73-5	261	2.43	138	.203	.261	0	—	0*	100	31		3.3
1977	Cal A*	15	9	.625	31	31	20-7	0-0	241.1	201	72	19	12	61-2	205	2.54	155	.227	.284	0	—	0	110	42		4.1
1978	Cal A☆	18	12	.600	33	33	10-4	0-0	239	239	108	26	9	60-7	137	3.65	99	.258	.306	0	—	0	117	0		-0.1
1979	†Cal A	7	5	.583	18	17	2-1	0-0	90.1	93	44	9	2	25-0	46	3.89	105	.264	.315	0	—	0	108	2	57	0.2
1980	Cal A	11	12	.478	32	31	7	0-0	204	223	107	18	8	45-0	113	4.15	95	.277	.320	0	—	0	97	0		0.0
1981	Bos A	4	10	.286	24	23	5-2	0-0	141.1	142	70	17	4	43-4	78	4.01	98	.265	.322	0	—	0	99	-6		-0.6
1982	Tex A	7	18	.280	30	30	7	0-0	194.1	199	102	16	7	55-10	87	4.21	92	.264	.319	0	—	0	77	-9		-1.0
1983	Tex A	7	9	.438	29	22	3	0-0	159.1	144	70	14	7	49-5	108	3.16	128	.240	.303	0	—	0	79	13		1.4
1984	Tex A	15	15	.500	35	35	9-0	0-0	246.1	234	117	30	6	81-3	141	3.25	128	.245	.306	0	—	0	96	18		2.1
1985	Tex A	2	7	.222	13	13	0	0-0	77.2	89	53	15	1	23-2	52	5.91	72	.287	.334	0	—	0	74	-13		-1.2
	Det A	10	7	.588	20	20	4	0-0	137.1	131	59	13	2	34-6	107	3.34	123	.250	.296	0	—	0	104	11		1.3
	Year	12	14	.462	33	33	4	0-0	215	220	112	28	3	57-8	159	4.27	97	.264	.310	0	—	0	92	-2		0.1
1986	Det A	12	9	.571	32	31	3-1	0-0	188.1	196	95	23	3	65-9	119	4.16	100	.268	.328	0	—	0	104	1		0.1
1987	†Det A	15	10	.600	34	34	5-3	0-0	218.2	216	106	27	5	56-5	146	3.91	109	.256	.302	0	—	0	117	10		1.0
1988	Det A	14	11	.560	32	32	2	0-0	203	213	105	21	8	64-7	127	4.21	91	.267	.323	0	—	0	98	-9		-0.9
1989	Det A	10	14	.417	33	33	6-1	0-0	223.2	227	105	21	8	74-8	147	3.58	107	.265	.326	0	—	0	87	5		0.6
1990	Det A	9	8	.529	34	29	1	1-0	176.1	190	104	25	9	66-7	114	5.31	75	.280	.349	0	—	0	118	-22		-1.8
1991	Det A	13	12	.520	33	33	3-2	0-0	217.1	217	98	26	2	78-9	107	3.77	111	.265	.327	1	.000	-0	105	10		1.1
1992	Det A	13	11	.542	32	31	3	0-0	186.2	188	102	22	7	90-9	91	4.39	91	.267	.351	0	—	0	105	-10		-1.1
1993	NY N	7	15	.318	29	29	0	0-0	183	198	100	26	9	48-7	104	4.48	90	.278	.330	58-0-3	.155	0	93	-7		-0.7
	NY A	0	2	.000	3	3	0	0-0	19	18	10	2	0	7-1	12	3.20	131	.222	.284	0	—	0	95	1		0.1
Total	21	240	236	.504	638	616	143-34	1-1	4188.1	4063	1910	448	129	1255-116	2773	3.66	106	.254	.312	59-0-3	.153	0	101	114	57	12.8

TANKERSLEY, DENNIS Dennis Lee B2.24.1979 Troy MO BR/TR/6-2/185* [BosA98 38/1135] d5.10 Col St. Louis-Meramec (MO) CC

YEAR	TM LG	W	L	PCT	G	GS	CG-SHO	SV-BS	IP	H	R	HR	HB	BB-IB	SO	ERA	AERA	OAV	OOB	AB-HR-SH	AVG	PB	SUP	APR	DL	PW
2002	SD N	1	4	.200	17	9	0	0-0	51.1	59	46	10	6	40-3	39	8.06	48	.304	.434	13-1-0	.308	2	87	-23		-1.7
2003	SD N	0	1	.000	1	1	0	0-0	0	3	7	0	0	4-0	0	∞	—	1.000	1.000	0	—	0	258	-7		-0.5
2004	SD N	0	5	.000	9	6	0	0-0	35	35	25	3	1	17-3	29	5.14	77	.254	.340	8-0-1	.250	1	55	-7		-0.8
Total	3	1	10	.091	27	16	0	0-0	86.1	97	78	13	7	61-6	68	7.61	51	.290	.407	21-1-1	.286	3	86	-37		-3.0

TANNEHILL, JESSE Jesse Niles "Powder" B7.14.1874 Dayton KY D9.22.1956 Dayton KY BB/TL(BL 1903)/5-8/150 d6.17 C1 b-Lee ▲

YEAR	TM LG	W	L	PCT	G	GS	CG-SHO	SV-BS	IP	H	R	HR	HB	BB-IB	SO	ERA	AERA	OAV	OOB	AB-HR-SH	AVG	PB	SUP	APR	DL	PW
1894	Cin N	1	1	.500	5	2	1	1	29	37	30	1	1	16	7	7.14	78	.306	.391	11	.000	-2	89	-4		-0.4
1897	Pit N	9	9	.500	21	16	11-1	1	142	172	97	1	8	24	40	4.25	98	.297	.333	184	.266	3*	68	-3		0.1
1898	Pit N	25	13	.658	43	38	34-5	2	326.2	338	147	2	12	63	93	2.95	121	.265	.306	152-1-6	.289	7*	102	23		3.4
1899	Pit N	24	14	.632	41	36	33-3	1	322	361	139	4	14	52	65	2.82	135	.283	.318	136-0-4	.250	4*	114	36		4.3
1900	Pit N	20	6	.769	29	27	23-2	0	234	247	108	3	17	43	50	2.88	126	.271	.316	110-0-5	.336	8*	118	20		2.7
1901	Pit N	18	10	.643	32	30	25-4	1	252.1	240	94	1	10	36	118	2.18	150	.249	.283	135-1-3	.244	5*	106	30		3.3
1902	Pit N	20	6	.769	26	24	23-2	0	231	203	78	0	10	25	100	1.95	141	.236	.266	148-1-1	.291	7*	149	17		2.7
1903	NY A	15	15	.500	32	31	22-2	0	239.2	258	123	3	10	34	106	3.27	96	.274	.307	111-1-1	.234	5*	107	-4		0.2
1904	Bos A	21	11	.656	33	31	30-4	0	281.2	256	89	5	13	33	116	2.04	131	.243	.275	122-0-2	.197	3*	110	19		2.8
1905	Bos A	22	9	.710	37	32	27-6	0	271.2	238	91	7	13	59	113	2.48	109	.237	.288	93-1-2	.226	6	122	9		1.9
1906	Bos A	13	11	.542	27	26	18-2	0	196.1	207	91	9	10	39	82	3.16	87	.274	.318	79-0-1	.278	6*	113	-8		-0.3
1907	Bos A	6	7	.462	18	16	10-2	1	131	131	59	3	5	20	29	2.47	104	.263	.298	51-0-1	.196	1*	97	-1		0.1
1908	Bos A	0	0	—	1	1	0	0	5	4	2	0	1	4	2	3.60	68	.200	.304	2	.500	0	111	0		0.0
	Was A	2	4	.333	10	9	5	0	71.2	77	36	0	6	23	14	3.77	61	.278	.346	43	.256	2*	116	-9		-0.5
	Year	2	4	.333	11	10	5	0	76.2	81	38	0	6	26	16	3.76	61	.273	.343	45	.267	2	116	-10		-0.5
1909	Was A	1	1	.500	3	2	2-1	0	21	19	8	1	1	5	8	3.43	71	.268	.325	36	.167	0*	73	-1		-0.1
1911	Cin N	0	0	—	1	0	0	0	4.1	6	7	0	0	3	2	6.23	53	.316	.409	1	.000	-0		-3		0.0
Total	15	197	117	.627	359	321	264-34	7	2759.1	2794	1199	40	130	478	944	2.80	114	.263	.303	1414-5-26	.255	54	109	121		20.2

TANNER, BRUCE Bruce Matthew B12.9.1961 New Castle PA BL/TR/6-3/220 [ChiA83 4/97] d6.12 C5 f-Chuck Col Florida St.

YEAR	TM LG	W	L	PCT	G	GS	CG-SHO	SV-BS	IP	H	R	HR	HB	BB-IB	SO	ERA	AERA	OAV	OOB	AB-HR-SH	AVG	PB	SUP	APR	DL	PW
1985	Chi A	1	2	.333	10	4	0	0-0	27	34	17	1	2	13-3	9	5.33	82	.309	.389	0	—	0	78	-3		-0.2

TAPANI, KEVIN Kevin Ray B2.18.1964 Des Moines IA BR/TR/6-0/187(180-195) [OakA86 2/40] d7.4 Col Central Michigan

YEAR	TM LG	W	L	PCT	G	GS	CG-SHO	SV-BS	IP	H	R	HR	HB	BB-IB	SO	ERA	AERA	OAV	OOB	AB-HR-SH	AVG	PB	SUP	APR	DL	PW
1989	NY N	0	0	—	3	0	0	0-0	7.1	5	3	1	0	4-0	2	3.68	95	.192	.290	2	.000	-0		0		0.0
	Min A	2	2	.500	5	5	0	0-0	32.2	34	15	2	0	8-1	21	3.86	108	.266	.307	0	—	0	79	1		0.1
1990	Min A	12	8	.600	28	28	1-1	0-0	159.1	164	75	12	2	29-2	101	4.07	102	.264	.297	0	—	0	90	4	24	0.4
1991	†Min A	16	9	.640	34	34	4-1	0-0	244	225	84	23	2	40-0	135	2.99	143	.245	.277	0	—	0	104	36		3.5
1992	Min A	16	11	.593	34	34	4-1	0-0	220	226	103	17	5	48-2	138	3.97	103	.269	.309	0	—	0	120	4		0.4
1993	Min A	12	15	.444	36	35	3-1	0-0	225.2	243	123	21	6	57-1	150	4.43	100	.272	.318	0	—	0	85	-1		-0.1
1994	Min A	11	7	.611	24	24	4-1	0-0	156	181	86	13	4	39-0	91	4.62	107	.291	.334	0	—	0	94	6		0.6
1995	Min A	6	11	.353	20	20	3-1	0-0	133.2	155	79	21	4	34-2	88	4.92	98	.290	.335	0	—	0	89	-1		-0.2
	†LA N	4	2	.667	13	11	0	0-0	57	72	37	8	1	14-2	43	5.05	77	.306	.345	17-0-3	.176	0	166	-8		-0.7
1996	Chi A	13	10	.565	34	34	1	0-0	225.1	236	123	34	3	76-5	150	4.59	104	.268	.326	0	—	0	109	5		0.4
1997	Chi N	9	3	.750	13	13	1-1	0-0	85	77	33	7	2	23-2	55	3.39	128	.242	.296	22-0-4	.136	-0	103	9	112	1.2
1998	†Chi N	19	9	.679	35	34	2-2	0-0	219	244	120	30	4	62-4	136	4.85	91	.284	.333	75-1-5	.133	1	112	-7		-0.7
1999	Chi N	6	12	.333	23	23	0	0-0	136	151	81	12	4	33-2	73	4.83	95	.280	.322	39-0-5	.051	-2	85	-4	48	-0.7
2000	Chi N	8	12	.400	30	30	2	0-0	195.2	208	113	35	8	47-1	150	5.01	91	.271	.319	56-1-9	.179	2	98	13		-0.5
2001	Chi N	9	14	.391	29	29	0	0-0	168.1	186	93	24	7	40-6	149	4.49	93	.279	.325	50-0-7	.240	2	91	-7		-0.5
Total	13	143	125	.534	361	354	26-9	0-0	2265	2407	1168	260	53	554-30	1482	4.35	102	.272	.317	261-2-33	.153	3	100	29	197	3.0

TASCHNER, JACK Jack Gerard B4.21.1978 Milwaukee WI BL/TL/6-3/190 d6.11 Col Wisconsin-Oshkosh

YEAR	TM LG	W	L	PCT	G	GS	CG-SHO	SV-BS	IP	H	R	HR	HB	BB-IB	SO	ERA	AERA	OAV	OOB	AB-HR-SH	AVG	PB	SUP	APR	DL	PW
2005	SF N	0	0	—	24	0	0	0-1	13	10	3	1	0	13-0	19	1.59	268	.185	.295	0	—	0		6		0.5

TATE, RANDY Randall Lee B10.23.1952 Florence AL BR/TR/6-3/190 [NYN72*5/99] d4.14 Col Calhoun (AL) CC

YEAR	TM LG	W	L	PCT	G	GS	CG-SHO	SV-BS	IP	H	R	HR	HB	BB-IB	SO	ERA	AERA	OAV	OOB	AB-HR-SH	AVG	PB	SUP	APR	DL	PW
1975	NY N	5	13	.278	26	23	2	0-0	137.2	121	73	8	5	86-3	99	4.45	79	.240	.355	41-0-5	.000	-4	84	-13		-2.0

TATE, STU Stuart Douglas B6.17.1962 Huntsville AL BR/TR/6-3/205 [SFN84 8/193] d9.20 Col Auburn-Montgomery

YEAR	TM LG	W	L	PCT	G	GS	CG-SHO	SV-BS	IP	H	R	HR	HB	BB-IB	SO	ERA	AERA	OAV	OOB	AB-HR-SH	AVG	PB	SUP	APR	DL	PW
1989	SF N	0	0	—	2	0	0	0-0	2.2	3	3	0	0	4-0	4	3.38	100	.250	.250	0	—	0		-1		0.0

TATE, AL Walter Alvin B7.1.1918 Coleman OK D5.8.1993 Bountiful UT BR/TR/6-0/180 d9.27

YEAR	TM LG	W	L	PCT	G	GS	CG-SHO	SV-BS	IP	H	R	HR	HB	BB-IB	SO	ERA	AERA	OAV	OOB	AB-HR-SH	AVG	PB	SUP	APR	DL	PW
1946	Pit N	0	1	.000	4	1	0		9	8	5	0	0	7	2	5.00	70	.267	.405	3	.333	0	49	-1		-0.1

TATIS, RAMON Ramon Francisco (Medrano) B1.5.1973 Guayubin, D.R. BL/TL/6-2/195* d4.6

YEAR	TM LG	W	L	PCT	G	GS	CG-SHO	SV-BS	IP	H	R	HR	HB	BB-IB	SO	ERA	AERA	OAV	OOB	AB-HR-SH	AVG	PB	SUP	APR	DL	PW
1997	Chi N	1	1	.500	56	0	0	0-1	55.2	66	36	13	3	29-6	33	5.34	81	.308	.394	3	.000	-0		-6		-0.3
1998	TB A	0	0	—	22	0	0	0-0	11.2	23	19	2	1	16-1	5	13.89	35	.418	.556	0	—	0		-11	15	-0.5
Total	2	1	1	.500	78	0	0	0-1	67.1	89	55	15	4	45-7	38	6.82	65	.331	.430	3	.000	0		-17	15	-0.8

TATUM, KEN Kenneth Ray B4.25.1944 Alexandria LA BR/TR/6-2/205* d5.28 Col Mississippi St.

YEAR	TM LG	W	L	PCT	G	GS	CG-SHO	SV-BS	IP	H	R	HR	HB	BB-IB	SO	ERA	AERA	OAV	OOB	AB-HR-SH	AVG	PB	SUP	APR	DL	PW
1969	Cal A	7	2	.778	45	0	0	22-1	86.1	51	13	1	4	39-5	65	1.36	258	.172	.276	21-2-2	.286	4		22		4.1
1970	Cal A	7	4	.636	62	0	0	17-8	88.2	68	35	12	5	26-5	50	2.94	123	.208	.274	11-1-0	.300	1		6		1.0
1971	Bos A	2	4	.333	36	1	0	9-3	53.2	50	25	7	8	25-7	21	4.19	89	.255	.358	10-1-0	.182	2	72	-3	29	-0.1

YEAR	TM	LG	W	L	PCT	G	GS	CG-SHO	SV-BS	IP	H	R	HR	HB	BB-IB	SO	ERA	AERA	OAV	OOB	AB-HR-SH	AVG	PB	SUP	APR	DL	PW
1972	Bos	A	0	2	.000	22	0	0	4-2	29.1	32	12	3	2	15-3	15	3.07	106	.283	.377	2	.000	0		0	40	0.0
1973	Bos	A	0	0	—		1	0	0-0	4	6	4	2	0	3-0	0	9.00	45	.462	.529	0	—		-2			-0.1
1974	Chi	A	0	0	—	10	1	0	0-0	20.2	23	12	3	0	9-0	5	4.79	78	.274	.340	1	.000	-0	259	-2		-0.1
Total	6		16	12	.571	176	2	0	52-14	282.2	230	143	24	19	117-20	156	2.93	122	.224	.311	45-4-2	.244	7	174	21	69	4.8

TAUSCHER, WALT Walter Edward B11.22.1901 LaSalle IL D11.27.1992 Winter Park FL BR/TR/6-1/186 d4.19

YEAR	TM	LG	W	L	PCT	G	GS	CG-SHO	SV-BS	IP	H	R	HR	HB	BB-IB	SO	ERA	AERA	OAV	OOB	AB-HR-SH	AVG	PB	SUP	APR	DL	PW
1928	Pit	N			—	17	0	0	1	29.1	28	20	0	3	12	7	4.91	83	.280	.374	6	.167	-0		-3		-0.2
1931	Was	A	1	0	1.000	6	0	0	0	12	24	16	2	0	4	5	7.50	57	.429	.467	0-0-2	—	0		-6		-0.4
Total	2		1	0	1.000	23	0	0	1	41.1	52	36	2	3	16	12	5.66	73	.333	.406	6-0-2	.167	-0		-9		-0.6

TAVAREZ, JULIAN Julian (Carmen) B5.22.1973 Santiago, D.R. BL/TR/6-2/190(165-195) d8.7

YEAR	TM	LG	W	L	PCT	G	GS	CG-SHO	SV-BS	IP	H	R	HR	HB	BB-IB	SO	ERA	AERA	OAV	OOB	AB-HR-SH	AVG	PB	SUP	APR	DL	PW
1993	Cle	A	2	2	.500	8	7	0	0-0	37	53	29	7	2	13-2	19	6.57	67	.340	.395	0		0	153	-8		-0.8
1994	Cle	A	0	1	.000	1	1	0	0-0	1.2	6	8	1	0	1-1	0	21.60	22	.500	.500	0	—	0	97	-5		-0.6
1995	†Cle	A	10	2	.833	57	0	0	0-4	85	76	36	7	3	21-0	68	2.44	194	.235	.286	0	—	0	17			2.0
1996	†Cle	A	4	7	.364	51	4	0	0-0	80.2	101	49	9	1	22-5	46	5.36	91	.315	.356	0	—	0	85	-3		-0.3
1997	†SF	N	6	4	.600	89	0	0	0-3	88.1	91	43	6	4	34-5	38	3.87	106	.277	.344	1	.000	-0		2		0.2
1998	SF	N	5	3	.625	60	0	0	1-5	85.1	96	41	5	8	36-11	52	3.80	106	.298	.379	9-0-1	.111	-0	1	-5	25	-0.5
1999	SF	N	2	0	1.000	47	0	0	0-2	54.2	65	38	7	8	25-3	33	5.93	72	.295	.384	5	.200	-0	-10		31	-0.5
2000	Col	N	11	5	.688	51	12	1	1-0	120	124	68	11	7	53-9	62	4.43	131	.268	.349	35-0-3	.086	-3	96	13		1.3
2001	Chi	N	10	9	.526	34	28	0	0-0	161.1	172	89	13	11	69-4	107	4.52	93	.277	.358	41-0-11	.122	-0	112	-11		-1.0
2002	Fla	N	10	12	.455	29	27	0	0-1	153.2	188	100	9	15	74-7	67	5.39	73	.308	.395	40-0-5	.125	-1	93	-26	24	-3.2
2003	Pit	N	3	3	.500	64	0	0	11-3	83.2	75	37	1	5	27-8	39	3.66	118	.244	.314	4	.000	-0	6			0.6
2004	†StL	N	7	4	.636	77	0	0	4-2	64.1	57	21	4	6	19-0	48	2.38	179	.238	.309	0	—	0	12			2.1
2005	†StL	N	2	3	.400	74	0	0	4-2	65.2	68	28	6	8	19-4	47	3.43	122	.278	.345	0-0-1	—	0	6			0.4
Total	13		72	55	.567	642	79	1	21-22	1081.1	1172	596	83	78	413-59	626	4.33	102	.281	.354	135-0-21	.111	-5	105	-6	80	0.2

TAYLOR, AARON Aaron Wade B8.20.1977 Valdosta GA BR/TR/6-7/230(230-245) [AtlN96 11/332] d9.9

YEAR	TM	LG	W	L	PCT	G	GS	CG-SHO	SV-BS	IP	H	R	HR	HB	BB-IB	SO	ERA	AERA	OAV	OOB	AB-HR-SH	AVG	PB	SUP	APR	DL	PW
2002	Sea	A	0	0	—	5	0	0	0-1	5	7	5	1	0	3-0	6	9.00	48	.348	.348	0	—	0		-3		-0.1
2003	Sea	A	0	0	—	10	0	0	0-0	12.2	17	12	0	1	6-0	9	8.53	51	.315	.387	0	—	0		-6		-0.3
2004	Sea	A	0	0	—	5	0	0	0-0	3.2	5	4	3	0	3-0	4	9.82	46	.313	.421	0	—	0	-2	89		-0.1
Total	3		0	0	—	20	0	0	0-1	21.1	30	21	4	1	9-0	19	8.86	49	.323	.385	0	—	0		-11	89	-0.5

TAYLOR, ARLAS Arlas Walter "Lefty","Foxy" B3.16.1896 Warrick Co. IN D9.10.1958 Dade City FL BR/TL/5-11/? d9.15

YEAR	TM	LG	W	L	PCT	G	GS	CG-SHO	SV-BS	IP	H	R	HR	HB	BB-IB	SO	ERA	AERA	OAV	OOB	AB-HR-SH	AVG	PB	SUP	APR	DL	PW
1921	Phi	A	0	1	.000	1	1	0	0	2	7	5	1	0	2	1	22.50	20	.636	.692	0	—	0	56	-3		-0.5

TAYLOR, BEN Benjamin Harrison B4.2.1889 Paoli IN D11.3.1946 Martin Co. IN BR/TR/5-11/163 d6.28

YEAR	TM	LG	W	L	PCT	G	GS	CG-SHO	SV-BS	IP	H	R	HR	HB	BB-IB	SO	ERA	AERA	OAV	OOB	AB-HR-SH	AVG	PB	SUP	APR	DL	PW
1912	Cin	N	0	0	—	2	0	0		5.2	9	7	0	1	3	2	3.18	106	.360	.448	2	.000	-0		-1		-0.1

TAYLOR, BRUCE Bruce Bell B4.16.1953 Holden MA BR/TR/6-0/175* d8.5

YEAR	TM	LG	W	L	PCT	G	GS	CG-SHO	SV-BS	IP	H	R	HR	HB	BB-IB	SO	ERA	AERA	OAV	OOB	AB-HR-SH	AVG	PB	SUP	APR	DL	PW
1977	Det	A	1	0	1.000	19	0	0	2-1	29.1	23	11	2	1	10-3	19	3.38	128	.219	.293	0	—	0		3		0.2
1978	Det	A	0	0	—	1	0	0	0-0	1	0	0	0	0	0-0	0	0.00	—	.000	.000	0	—	0		0		0.0
1979	Det	A	1	2	.333	10	0	0	0-0	18.2	16	13	1	2	7-2	8	4.82	90	.242	.325	0	—	0		-2		-0.3
Total	3		2	2	.500	30	0	0	2-1	49	39	24	3	3	17-5	27	3.86	112	.224	.301	0	—	0		1		-0.1

TAYLOR, CHUCK Charles Gilbert B4.18.1942 Murfreesboro TN BR/TR/6-2/195(180-195) d5.27 Col Middle Tennessee

YEAR	TM	LG	W	L	PCT	G	GS	CG-SHO	SV-BS	IP	H	R	HR	HB	BB-IB	SO	ERA	AERA	OAV	OOB	AB-HR-SH	AVG	PB	SUP	APR	DL	PW
1969	StL	N	7	5	.583	27	13	5-1	0-0	126.2	108	39	8	3	30-5	62	2.56	140	.235	.285	39-0-2	.179	1	74	15		1.4
1970	StL	N	6	7	.462	56	7	1-1	8-3	124.1	116	47	5	2	31-10	64	3.11	133	.256	.303	26-0-3	.115	-1	83	15		1.5
1971	StL	N	3	1	.750	43	1	0	3-2	71.1	72	32	7	1	25-5	46	3.53	103	.267	.327	12	.167	0	146	0		0.0
1972	NY	N	0	0	—	20	0	0	2-0	31	44	19	2	1	8-1	9	5.52	61	.341	.386	3	.000	-0	-6			-0.3
	Mil	A	0	0	—	5	0	0	1-0	11.2	8	2	1	1	3-0	5	1.54	199	.200	.273	2	.500	-0	-2			0.1
1973	Mon	N	2	0	1.000	8	0	0	0-1	20.1	17	4	3	0	2-1	10	1.77	216	.230	.250	4-0-2	.000	-0	5			0.4
1974	Mon	N	6	2	.750	61	0	0	11-3	107.2	101	27	8	3	25-8	43	2.17	177	.256	.301	10-0-4	.300	1	20			2.0
1975	Mon	N	2	2	.500	54	0	0	6-4	74	72	32	6	1	24-5	29	3.53	110	.264	.321	2	.000	-0	3			0.2
1976	Mon	N	2	3	.400	31	0	0	0-0	40	38	20	4	0	13-4	14	4.50	84	.273	.333	3	.000	-0	-2			-0.3
Total	8		28	20	.583	305	21	6-2	31-13	607	576	222	43	12	162-41	282	3.07	123	.258	.309	101-0-11	.158	0	80	52		5.1

TAYLOR, DORN Donald Clyde B8.11.1958 Abington PA BR/TR/6-2/180* d4.30 Col Pfeiffer

YEAR	TM	LG	W	L	PCT	G	GS	CG-SHO	SV-BS	IP	H	R	HR	HB	BB-IB	SO	ERA	AERA	OAV	OOB	AB-HR-SH	AVG	PB	SUP	APR	DL	PW
1987	Pit	N	2	3	.400	14	6	0	0-0	53.1	48	35	10	1	28-1	37	5.74	73	.247	.342	18	.167	-0*	95	-8	27	-0.7
1989	Pit	N	1	1	.500	9	0	0	0-0	10.2	14	6	0	0	5-2	3	5.06	67	.333	.404	1	.000	-0*	-2			-0.3
1990	Bal	A	0	1	.000	4	0	0	0-0	3.2	4	3	0	0	2-0	4	2.45	156	.250	.333	0	—	0	0			0.0
Total	3		3	5	.375	27	8	0	0-0	67.2	66	44	10	1	35-3	44	5.45	74	.262	.352	19	.158	-0	95	-10	27	-1.1

TAYLOR, ED Edgar Ruben "Rube" B3.23.1877 Palestine TX D1.31.1912 Dallas TX TL d8.8

YEAR	TM	LG	W	L	PCT	G	GS	CG-SHO	SV-BS	IP	H	R	HR	HB	BB-IB	SO	ERA	AERA	OAV	OOB	AB-HR-SH	AVG	PB	SUP	APR	DL	PW
1903	StL	N	0	0	—	1	0	0	0	3	0	0	0	0	1	1	0.00	—	.000	.000	1	.000	-0	1			0.0

TAYLOR, GARY Gary William B10.19.1945 Detroit MI BR/TR/6-2/190 [DetA65 8/163] d9.2 Col Central Michigan

YEAR	TM	LG	W	L	PCT	G	GS	CG-SHO	SV-BS	IP	H	R	HR	HB	BB-IB	SO	ERA	AERA	OAV	OOB	AB-HR-SH	AVG	PB	SUP	APR	DL	PW
1969	Det	A	0	1	.000	7	0	0	0-0	10.1	10	6	2	0	6-0	3	5.23	72	.244	.340			0		-1		-0.1

TAYLOR, HARRY Harry Evans B12.2.1935 San Angelo TX BR/TR/6-0/185 d9.17 Col Texas

YEAR	TM	LG	W	L	PCT	G	GS	CG-SHO	SV-BS	IP	H	R	HR	HB	BB-IB	SO	ERA	AERA	OAV	OOB	AB-HR-SH	AVG	PB	SUP	APR	DL	PW
1957	KC	A	0	0	—	2	0	0	0	8.2	11	4	0	1	4-0	4	3.12	127	.314	.400	4	.250	0		0		0.0

TAYLOR, HARRY James Harry B5.20.1919 E.Glenn IN D11.5.2000 Terre Haute IN BR/TR/6-1/175(175-190) d9.22

YEAR	TM	LG	W	L	PCT	G	GS	CG-SHO	SV-BS	IP	H	R	HR	HB	BB-IB	SO	ERA	AERA	OAV	OOB	AB-HR-SH	AVG	PB	SUP	APR	DL	PW
1946	Bro	N	0	0	—	4	0	0	1	4.2	5	2	0	0	1	6	3.86	88	.313	.353	0	—	0		0		0.0
1947	†Bro	N	10	5	.667	33	20	10-2	1	162	130	63	10	5	83	58	3.11	133	.225	.327	62-0-2	.129	-2	112	19		1.4
1948	Bro	N	2	7	.222	17	13	2	0	80.2	90	55	8	3	61	32	5.36	75	.288	.408	22-0-2	.273	1	130	-12		-1.0
1950	Bos	A	2	0	1.000	3	2	2-1	0	19	13	3	0	0	8	6	1.42	345	.197	.284	7	.286	0	92	7		0.7
1951	Bos	A	4	9	.308	31	8	1	2	81.1	100	59	6	1	42	22	5.75	78	.307	.388	29-0-1	.103	-3	112	-11		-1.8
1952	Bos	A	1	0	1.000	2	1	1	0	10	6	2	1	1	6	1	1.80	219	.176	.317	4	.250	0	244	2		0.2
Total	6		19	21	.475	90	44	16-3	4	357.2	344	184	25	10	201	127	4.10	102	.258	.359	124-0-5	.161	-3	118	5		-0.5

TAYLOR, JACK John Budd "Brewery Jack" B5.23.1873 Sandy Hill (now Stockton) MD D2.7.1900 Staten Island NY BR/TR/6-1/190 d9.16 Col Manhattan

YEAR	TM	LG	W	L	PCT	G	GS	CG-SHO	SV-BS	IP	H	R	HR	HB	BB-IB	SO	ERA	AERA	OAV	OOB	AB-HR-SH	AVG	PB	SUP	APR	DL	PW
1891	NY	N	0	1	.000	1				8	4	2	1	0	4	1	1.13	285	.143	.226	2	.000	0	37	2		0.2
1892	Phi	N	1	0	1.000	3	3	2	0	26	28	19	2	0	10	7	1.38	234	.264	.328	12	.167	-0	169	1		0.0
1893	Phi	N	10	9	.526	25	16	14	1	170	187	113	8	10	77	41	4.24	108	.271	.353	93	.215	-2*	100	5		0.3
1894	Phi	N	23	13	.639	41	34	31-1	1	298	347	201	13	17	96	76	4.08	126	.288	.349	145	.338	9*	105	31		3.5
1895	Phi	N	26	14	.650	41	37	33-1	1	335	403	233	7	15	83	93	4.49	90	.293	.340	155-3-1	.290	7*	111	9		1.5
1896	Phi	N	20	21	.488	45	41	35-1	1	359	459	282	17	20	112	97	4.79	90	.308	.365	158-0-3	.185	-7*	114	-26		-2.6
1897	Phi	N	16	20	.444	40	37	35-2	2	317.1	376	204	9	24	78	88	4.23	99	.292	.345	139-1-2	.252	2*	96	-3		0.0
1898	StL	N	15	29	.341	50	47	42		397.1	465	259	14	25	83	89	3.90	97	.290	.335	157-1-5	.242	3*	84	-12		-0.3
1899	Cin	N	9	10	.474	25	19	16-2	2	180.1	207	110	7	11	43	35	4.09	96	.287	.337	71-0-3	.239	-1	81	-3		-0.4
Total	9		120	117	.506	271	235	209-7	9	2091	2476	1423	74	126	583	529	4.22	104	.291	.346	931-5-19	.252	12	100	4		2.2

TAYLOR, JACK John W. B1.14.1874 New Straitsville OH D3.4.1938 Columbus OH BR/TR/5-10/170 d9.25

YEAR	TM	LG	W	L	PCT	G	GS	CG-SHO	SV-BS	IP	H	R	HR	HB	BB-IB	SO	ERA	AERA	OAV	OOB	AB-HR-SH	AVG	PB	SUP	APR	DL	PW
1898	Chi	N	5	0	1.000	5	5	5	0	41	32	12	0	1	10	11	2.20	163	.213	.267	15	.200	1	95	8		1.0
1899	Chi	N	18	21	.462	41	39	39-1	0	354.2	380	223	6	22	84	67	3.76	100	.274	.325	139-0-1	.266	10*	120	1		1.0
1900	Chi	N	10	17	.370	28	29	25-2	1	222.1	226	130	4	8	58	57	2.55	141	.263	.316	81-1-3	.235	2	63	18		2.0
1901	Chi	N	13	19	.406	33	31	30	0	275.2	341	165	5	8	44	56	3.36	96	.302	.332	106-0-2	.217	2*	92	-7		-0.4
1902	Chi	N	23	11	.676	37	34	34-8	1	333.2	273	86	2	12	45	88	1.29	209	.224	.258	189-0-9	.233	3*	94	51		6.1
1903	StL	N	21	14	.600	37	33	33-1	1	312.1	277	137	2	5	57	83	2.45	128	.235	.273	126-0-3	.222	4*	109	23		2.8
1904	StL	N	20	19	.513	41	39	39-2	0	352	297	133	5	13	62	103	2.22	121	.224	.271	133-1-1	.211	4*	103	17		2.4
1905	StL	N	15	21	.417	37	34	34-3	1	309	302	155	10	11	85	102	3.44	87	.259	.315	121-0-2	.190	4*	75	-14		-1.2
1906	StL	N	8	9	.471	17	17	17-1	0	155	133	56	3	7	47	27	2.15	122	.227	.292	53-0-2	.208	3	86	8		1.3
	Chi	N	12	3	.800	17	16	15-2	0	147.1	116	42	1	6	39	34	1.83	144	.223	.285	53	.208	2	121	13		1.6
	Year		20	12	.625	34	33	32-3	0	302.1	249	92	4	13	86	61	1.99	132	.225	.289	106-0-2	.208	5	103	20		2.9
1907	Chi	N	7	5	.583	18	13	8	1	123	127	62	3	1	33	22	3.29	76	.268	.318	47	.191	0	101	-9		-0.9
Total	10		152	139	.522	311	287	279-20	5	2626	2504	1195	42	94	584	662	2.65	115	.250	.297	1063-2-23	.222	34	97	109		15.7

YEAR	TM LG	W	L	PCT	G	GS	CG-SHO	SV-BS	IP	H	R	HR	HB	BB-IB	SO	ERA	AERA	OAV	OOB	AB-HR-SH	AVG	PB	SUP	APR	DL	PW

TAYLOR, KERRY   Kerry Thomas   B1.25.1971 Bemidji MN   BR/TR/6-3/200*   d4.13   [DL 1995 SD N 31]

1993	SD N	0	5	.000	36	7	0	0-0	68.1	72	53	5	4	49-0	45	6.45	64	.277	.396	12-0-1	.000	-1	81	-16		-1.2
1994	SD N	0	0	—	1	1	0	0-0	4.1	9	4	1	1	1-0	3	8.31	50	.409	.458	2	.000	-0	88	-2		-0.1
Total	2	0	5	.000	37	8	0		72.2	81	57	6	5	50-0	48	6.56	63	.287	.400	14-0-1	.000	-2	82	-18	31	-1.3

TAYLOR, DUMMY   Luther Haden   B2.21.1875 Oskaloosa KS   D8.22.1958 Jacksonville IL   BR/TR/6-1/160   d8.27

1900	NY N	4	3	.571	11	7	6	0	62.1	74	31	0	5	24	16	2.45	147	.294	.367	22-0-1	.136	-1	98	7		0.4
1901	NY N	18	27	.400	**45**	**43**	37-4	0	353.1	377	193	8	16	112	136	3.18	104	.271	.333	136-0-1	.132	-8	70	-1		-0.8
1902	Cle A	1	3	.250	4	4	4-1	0	34	37	17	0	2	8	8	1.59	217	.278	.329	10	.100	-0	52	5		0.5
	NY N	7	15	.318	26	25	18	0	200.2	194	98	4	15	55	87	2.29	123	.254	.317	65-0-2	.092	-5	61	5		-0.1
1903	NY N	13	13	.500	33	31	18-1	0	244.2	306	143	6	4	89	94	4.23	79	.314	.374	82-0-6	.146	-2	116	-19		-1.9
1904	NY N	21	15	.583	37	36	29-5	0	296.1	231	100	6	9	75	138	2.34	117	.214	.270	102-0-6	.157	-1*	108	15		0.7
1905	NY N	16	9	.640	32	28	18-4	0	213.1	200	85	5	8	51	91	2.66	110	.247	.298	69-0-10	.130	-1	125	7		0.7
1906	NY N	17	9	.654	31	27	13-2	0	213	186	81	3	6	57	91	2.20	119	.233	.289	74-0-6	.184	0	127	6		0.7
1907	NY N	11	7	.611	28	21	11-3	0	171	145	66	1	3	46	56	2.42	102	.232	.288	48-0-5	.125	-1*	94	0		-0.2
1908	NY N	8	5	.615	27	15	6-1	2	127.2	127	56	5	4	34	50	2.33	104	.253	.306	35-0-5	.229	2	138	-3		-0.2
Total	9	116	106	.523	274	237	160-21	3	1916.1	1877	870	38	72	551	767	2.75	107	.256	.314	645-0-38	.144	-17	100	22		0.9

TAYLOR, WILEY   Philip Wiley   B3.18.1888 Wamego KS   D7.8.1954 Westmoreland KS   BR/TR/6-1/175   d9.6

1911	Det A	0	2	.000	3	2	1	0	19	18	11	0	1	10	9	3.79	91	.247	.345	6	.000	-1	0	-1		-0.2
1912	Chi A	0	1	.000	3	3	0	0	20	21	12	0	0	14	4	4.95	65	.309	.427	5	.000	-1	115	-3		-0.2
1913	StL A	0	2	.000	5	4	1	0	31.2	33	19	0	0	16	12	4.83	61	.284	.371	10	.000	-1	120	-5		-0.4
1914	StL A	2	5	.286	16	8	2-1	0	50	41	24	0	2	25	20	3.42	79	.209	.305	12	.167	-0	74	-3		-0.5
Total	4	2	10	.167	27	17	4-1	0	120.2	113	66	0	3	65	45	4.10	72	.249	.347	33	.061	-3	81	-12		-1.3

TAYLOR, SCOTT   Rodney Scott   B8.2.1967 Defiance OH   BL/TL/6-1/190*   [BosA88 28/719]   d9.17   Col Bowling Green

1992	Bos A	1	1	.500	4	1	0	0-0	14.2	13	8	0	0	4-0	7	4.91	87	.245	.298	0	—	0	64	-1		-0.1
1993	Bos A	0	1	.000	16	0	0	0-0	11	14	10	1	1	12-3	8	8.18	57	.311	.466	0	—	0		-3		-0.3
Total	2	1	2	.333	20	1	0		25.2	27	18	1	1	16-3	15	6.31	70	.276	.383	0	—	0	64	-4		-0.4

TAYLOR, RON   Ronald Wesley   B12.13.1937 Toronto ON, Can.   BR/TR/6-1/195(180-200)   d4.11

1962	Cle A	2	2	.500	8	4	1	0	33.1	36	23	6	1	13-4	15	5.94	65	.281	.347	11	.273	0	98	-7		-0.7
1963	StL N	9	7	.563	54	9	2	11	133.1	119	44	10	4	30-6	91	2.84	125	.243	.289	32-0-2	.031	-3	67	12		1.2
1964	†StL N	8	4	.667	63	2	0	7	101.1	109	56	15	1	33-7	69	4.62	82	.274	.329	15	.133	-0	58	-6		-0.1
1965	StL N	2	1	.667	25	0	0	1	43.2	43	24	6	1	15-4	26	4.53	85	.261	.321	5	.400	1		-3		-0.2
	Hou N	1	5	.167	32	1	0	4	57.2	68	42	5	5	16-6	37	6.40	52	.305	.359	13	.000	-1	104	-18		-2.2
	Year	3	6	.333	57	1	0	5	101.1	111	66	11	6	31-10	63	5.60	64	.286	.343	18	.111	-1	98	-21		-2.3
1966	Hou N	2	3	.400	36	1	0	0	64.2	89	47	5	5	10-4	29	5.71	60	.333	.364	12	.167	-1	77	-17	44	-1.3
1967	NY N	4	6	.400	50	0	0	8	73	60	21	1	5	23-14	46	2.34	145	.230	.290	7-0-1	.000	-1	9	26		1.3
1968	NY N	1	5	.167	58	0	0	13	76.2	64	24	4	1	18-9	49	2.70	112	.228	.275	9	.000	-1	3			1.4
1969	†NY N	9	4	.692	59	0	0	13-4	76	61	23	7	1	24-6	42	2.72	134	.228	.292	4	.250	-0	9			1.9
1970	NY N	5	4	.556	57	0	0	13-6	66.1	65	31	5	0	16-10	28	3.93	103	.265	.305	4-0-1	.000	-0	0			0.3
1971	NY N	2	2	.500	45	0	0	2-1	69	71	28	7	1	11-6	32	3.65	94	.269	.300	4	.250	-0	0			0.0
1972	SD N	0	0	—	4	0	0	0-0	5	8	7	2	0	2-0	2	12.60	26	.375	.375	0	—	0		-5		-0.3
Total	11	45	43	.511	491	17	3	72-11	800	794	370	76	21	209-76	464	3.93	91	.264	.312	116-0-4	.103	-5	78	-21	70	0.2

TAYLOR, SCOTT   Scott Michael   B10.3.1966 Topeka KS   BR/TR/6-3/200   [SeaA88 15/383]   d7.28   Col Kansas

| 1995 | Tex A | 1 | 2 | .333 | 3 | 3 | 0 | 0-0 | 15.1 | 25 | 16 | 6 | 0 | 5-0 | 10 | 9.39 | 52 | .379 | .423 | 0 | — | 0 | 58 | -7 | | -1.0 |

TAYLOR, TERRY   Terry Derrell   B7.28.1964 Crestview FL   BR/TR/6-1/180   [SeaA82 4/86]   d8.19   [DL 1989 Sea A 113]

| 1988 | Sea A | 0 | 1 | .000 | 5 | 5 | 0 | 0-0 | 23 | 26 | 17 | 2 | 0 | 11-1 | 9 | 6.26 | 67 | .295 | .370 | 0 | — | 0 | 118 | -5 | | -0.3 |

TAYLOR, PETE   Vernon Charles   B11.26.1927 Severn MD   D11.17.2003 Annapolis MD   BR/TR/6-1/170   d5.2

| 1952 | StL N | 0 | 0 | — | 1 | 0 | 0 | 0 | 2 | 4 | 3 | 0 | 2 | 3 | 0 | 13.50 | 29 | .500 | .636 | 0 | — | 0 | | -2 | | -0.1 |

TAYLOR, WADE   Wade Eric   B10.19.1965 Mobile AL   BR/TR/6-1/185   d6.2   Col Miami

| 1991 | NY A | 7 | 12 | .368 | 23 | 22 | 0 | 0-0 | 116.1 | 144 | 85 | 13 | 7 | 53-0 | 72 | 6.27 | 66 | .314 | .388 | 0 | — | 0 | 91 | -25 | | -3.4 |

TAYLOR, BILLY   William Henry "Bollicky Bill"   B1855 Washington DC   D5.14.1900 Jacksonville FL   BR/TR/5-11.5/204   d5.21 ▲

1881	Wor N	0	1	.000	1	1	1	0	8	15	13	0	0	6	0	7.88	38	.366	.447	28	.107	-0*	18	-4		-0.4
	Cle N	0	0	—	1	0	0	0	3	0	0	0	0	1	2	0.00	—	.000	.100	103	.243	-0*		1		0.0
	Year	0	1	.000	2	1	1	0	11	15	13	0	0	7	2	5.73	51	.300	.386	131	.214	-0	19	-3		-0.4
1882	Pit AA	0	1	.000	1	0	0	0	5	11	10	0	0	4	1	16.20	16	.407	.484	299-3	.281	0*		-4		-1.7
1883	Pit AA	4	7	.364	19	9	8	0	127	166	115	0	0	34	41	5.39	60	.296	.337	369-2	.260	3*	90	-28		-1.7
1884	StL U	25	4	.862	33	29	29-2	4	263	222	97	2	0	40	154	1.68	142	.213	.243	186-3	.366	13*	142	21		2.8
	Phi AA	18	12	.600	30	30	30-1	3	260	232	118	3	12	44	130	2.53	134	.239	.258	111	.252	3	89	21		2.5
1885	Phi AA	1	5	.167	8	6	6	0	52.1	68	35	0	1	9	11	3.27	105	.343	.375	21	.190	-1	63	1		0.0
1886	Bal AA	1	6	.143	8	8	8	0	72.1	87	63	1	2	20	37	5.72	60	.284	.332	39	.308	1*	113	-15		-1.0
1887	Phi AA	1	0	1.000	1	1	1	0	9	10	5	1	0	2	5	3.00	143	.286	.405	4	.250	-0	89	1		0.1
Total	7	50	36	.581	100	84	83-3	4	799.2	811	456	11	15	165	376	3.17	96	.248	.287	1160-8	.277	20	107	-8		1.6

TAYLOR, BILLY   William Howell   B10.16.1961 Monticello FL   BR/TR/6-8/230(200-240)   [TexA80*2/39]   d4.5   Col Abraham Baldwin (GA) JC   [DL 1995 Oak A 160]

1994	Oak A	1	3	.250	41	0	0	1-2	46.1	38	24	4	2	18-5	48	3.50	128	.220	.299	0	—	0	3	16		0.2
1996	Oak A	6	3	.667	55	0	0	17-2	60.1	52	30	5	4	25-4	67	4.33	115	.231	.315	0	—	0	5	28		0.3
1997	Oak A	3	4	.429	72	0	0	23-7	73	70	32	3	5	36-9	66	3.82	120	.254	.348	0	—	0	7			1.6
1998	Oak A	4	9	.308	70	0	0	33-4	73	71	37	7	3	22-4	58	3.58	129	.255	.312	0	—	0	7			1.3
1999	Oak A	1	5	.167	43	0	0	26-7	43	48	23	3	2	14-3	38	3.98	119	.287	.346	0	—	0	3			0.5
	NY N	0	1	.000	18	0	0	0-1	13.1	20	12	2	0	9-5	14	8.10	54	.345	.433	0	—	0		-6		-0.4
2000	TB A	1	3	.250	17	0	0	0-2	13.2	13	13	2	2	9-2	13	8.56	57	.255	.387	0	—	0		-5		-0.9
2001	Pit N	0	0	—	1	0	0	0-0	2	1	1	0	0	0-0	1	4.50	99	.250	.250	0	—	0		0		0.0
Total	7	16	28	.364	317	0	0	100-25	324.2	314	172	27	18	133-32	307	4.21	111	.254	.332	0	—	0		14	204	2.6

TEACHOUT, BUD   Arthur John   B2.27.1904 Los Angeles CA   D5.11.1985 Laguna Beach CA   BR/TL/6-2/183   d5.12   Col Occidental

1930	Chi N	11	4	.733	40	16	6	0	153	178	80	16	0	48	59	4.06	120	.296	.348	63-0-3	.270	3*	133	14		1.3
1931	Chi N	1	2	.333	27	3	1	0	61.1	79	40	6	1	28	14	5.72	67	.305	.375	21	.238	0*	96	-10		-0.5
1932	StL N	0	0	—	1	0	0	0	1	2	1	0	0	0	0	0.00	—	.400	.400	0	—	0		-0		0.0
Total	3	12	6	.667	68	19	7	0	215.1	259	121	22	1	76	73	4.51	102	.299	.356	84-0-3	.262	3	131	4		0.8

TEBEAU, GEORGE   George E. "White Wings"   B12.26.1861 St.Louis MO   D2.4.1923 Denver CO   BR/TR/5-9/175   d4.16   b-Patsy ▲

1887	Cin AA	0	1	.000	1	1	1	0	8	21	16	0	1	3	1	13.50	32	.488	.532	318-4	.296	0*	88	-7		-0.6
1890	Tol AA	0	0	—	1	0	0	0	5	9	8	0	0	5	4	9.00	44	.375	.483	381-1	.268	0*		-3		-0.2
Total	2	0	1	.000	2	1	1	0	13	30	24	0	1	8	5	11.77	36	.448	.513	699-5	.280	1	88	-10		-0.8

TEDROW, AL   Allen Seymour   B12.14.1891 Westerville OH   D1.23.1958 Westerville OH   BR/TL/6-0/180   d9.15

| 1914 | Cle A | 1 | 2 | .333 | 4 | 3 | 1 | 0 | 22.1 | 19 | 6 | 0 | 3 | 14 | 4 | 1.21 | 239 | .235 | .367 | 6 | .167 | 0 | 67 | 3 | | 0.1 |

TEJEDA, ROBINSON   Robinson Garcia   B3.24.1982 Bani, D.R.   BR/TR/6-3/190   d5.10

| 2005 | Phi N | 4 | 3 | .571 | 26 | 13 | 0 | 0-0 | 85.2 | 67 | 36 | 5 | 8 | 51-4 | 72 | 3.57 | 122 | .218 | .342 | 20-0-5 | .100 | -1 | 107 | 7 | | 0.7 |

TEJERA, MICHAEL   Michael   B10.18.1976 Havana, Cuba   BL/TL/5-9/175(175-190)   [FlaN95 6/149]   d9.8   [DL 2000 Fla N 181]

1999	Fla N	0	0	—	3	1	0	0-0	6.1	10	8	1	0	5-0	7	11.37	39	.385	.484	0	—	0	105	-5		-0.7
2002	Fla N	8	8	.500	47	18	0	1-2	139.1	144	71	17	6	60-3	95	4.45	88	.269	.347	37-1-2	.189	2*	84	-7		-0.8
2003	†Fla N	3	4	.429	50	6	0	2-0	81	82	44	6	1	36-3	58	4.67	88	.267	.345	15-0-1	.067	-1	84	-5		-0.3
2004	Fla N	0	0	—	2	2	0	0-0	4	6	8	0	1	6-0	7	18.00	23	.375	.565	0	—	0	56	-6		-0.3
	Tex A	0	0	—	6	0	0	0-0	5.1	9	6	1	1	3-0	7	10.13	49	.360	.448	0	—	0		-3		-0.1
2005	Tex A	0	1	.000	3	0	0	0-0	2	5	3	0	1	1-0	2	13.50	34	.455	.538	0	—	0		-2		-0.1
Total	5	11	13	.458	111	27	0	3-2	238.1	256	140	26	10	111-6	172	5.14	78	.278	.360	52-1-3	.154	1	82	-28	181	-2.2

YEAR	TM LG	W	L	PCT	G	GS	CG-SHO	SV-BS	IP	H	R	HR	HB	BB-IB	SO	ERA	AERA	OAV	OOB	AB-HR-SH	AVG	PB	SUP	APR	DL	PW

TEKULVE, KENT Kenton Charles B3.5.1947 Cincinnati OH BR/TR/6-4/180(160-190) d5.20 Col Marietta

YEAR	TM LG	W	L	PCT	G	GS	CG-SHO	SV-BS	IP	H	R	HR	HB	BB-IB	SO	ERA	AERA	OAV	OOB	AB-HR-SH	AVG	PB	SUP	APR	DL	PW
1974	Pit N	1	1	.500	8	0	0	0-2	9	12	6	1	1	5-2	6	6.00	58	.343	.419	0	—	0		-2		-0.4
1975	†Pit N	1	2	.333	34	0	0	5-0	56	43	20	2	1	23-6	28	2.25	159	.215	.296	11	.091	-0		7		0.6
1976	Pit N	5	3	.625	64	0	0	9-3	102.2	91	30	3	0	25-7	68	2.45	144	.241	.287	9-0-1		-1		13		1.2
1977	Pit N	10	1	.909	72	0	0	7-7	103	89	41	5	1	33-6	59	3.06	132	.236	.296	12	.250	-0		10		1.3
1978	Pit N	8	7	.533	91	0	0	31-9	135.1	115	44	5	2	55-18	77	2.33	160	.228	.304	21	.095	-1		19		3.1
1979	†Pit N	10	8	.556	94	0	0	31-6	134.1	109	46	5	2	49-20	75	2.75	143	.222	.295	15-0-1	.133	-0		17		3.0
1980	Pit N☆	8	12	.400	78	0	0	21-11	93	96	39	6	1	40-16	47	3.39	109	.267	.342	9	.000	-1		3		0.6
1981	Pit N	5	5	.500	45	0	0	3-5	65	61	19	1	1	17-5	34	2.49	146	.250	.299	2	.000	-0		9		1.4
1982	Pit N	12	8	.600	85	0	0	20-10	128.2	113	47	7	3	46-23	66	2.87	131	.237	.305	14-0-1	.071	-1		12		2.1
1983	Pit N	7	7	.583	76	0	0	18-6	99	78	27	1	0	36-12	52	1.64	229	.223	.293	8-0-1	.000	-1		20		2.9
1984	Pit N	3	9	.250	72	0	0	13-4	88	86	30	4	1	33-12	36	2.66	137	.262	.330	7	.000	-1		9		1.5
1985	Pit N	0	0	—	3	0	0	0-0	3.1	7	7	1	0	5-1	4	16.20	22	.467	.600	0	—	0		-5		-0.2
	Phi N	4	10	.286	58	0	0	14-8	72.1	67	28	4	2	25-9	36	2.99	124	.246	.312	3	.000	-0		5		1.1
	Year	4	10	.286	61	0	0	14-8	75.2	74	35	5	2	30-10	40	3.57	104	.251	.330	3	.000	-0		1		0.9
1986	Phi N	11	5	.688	73	0	0	4-2	110	99	35	2	0	25-10	57	2.54	154	.240	.281	5	.000	-0		16		2.3
1987	Phi N	6	4	.600	90	0	0	3-3	105	96	38	8	0	29-13	60	3.09	139	.243	.293	1-0-1	.000	-0		14		1.4
1988	Phi N	3	7	.300	70	0	0	4-3	80	87	34	3	2	22-11	43	3.60	100	.276	.326	2	.000	-0		1	19	0.1
1989	Cin N	0	3	.000	37	0	0	1-2	52	56	35	5	0	23-8	31	5.02	72	.272	.342	2	.500	0		-9		-0.5
Total 16		94	90	.511	1050	0	0	184-81	1436.2	1305	526	63	17	491-179	779	2.85	133	.244	.307	121-0-5	.083	-6		139	19	21.5

TELEMACO, AMAURY Amaury (Regalado) B1.19.1974 Higuey, D.R. BR/TR/6-3/225(210-235) d5.16

YEAR	TM LG	W	L	PCT	G	GS	CG-SHO	SV-BS	IP	H	R	HR	HB	BB-IB	SO	ERA	AERA	OAV	OOB	AB-HR-SH	AVG	PB	SUP	APR	DL	PW
1996	Chi N	5	7	.417	25	17	0	0-0	97.1	108	67	20	3	31-2	64	5.46	80	.281	.336	29-0-4	.103	-1	113	-12	15	-1.5
1997	Chi N	0	3	.000	10	5	0	0-0	38	47	26	4	0	11-0	29	6.16	70	.303	.347	9	.222	0	68	-7		-0.4
1998	Chi N	1	1	.500	14	0	0	0-0	27.2	23	12	5	0	13-0	18	3.90	113	.219	.305	6	.167	-0		2		0.1
	Ari N	6	9	.400	27	18	0	0-0	121	127	63	13	4	33-2	60	3.94	109	.271	.321	29-0-1	.069	-1	79	2		0.1
	Year	7	10	.412	41	18	0	0-0	148.2	150	75	18	4	46-2	78	3.93	109	.261	.318	35-0-1	.086	-1	78	4		0.2
1999	Ari N	1	0	1.000	5	0	0	0-0	6	7	5	2	0	6-1	2	7.50	62	.333	.481	0	—	0		-2	33	-0.2
	Phi N	3	0	1.000	44	0	0	0-1	47	45	29	8	2	20-3	41	5.55	84	.250	.330	0	—	0		-4		-0.2
	Year	4	0	1.000	49	0	0	0-1	53	52	34	10	2	26-4	43	5.77	81	.259	.348	0	—	0		-5		-0.4
2000	Phi N	1	3	.250	13	2	0	0-1	24.1	25	22	6	0	14-0	22	6.66	69	.275	.364	4	.000	-0	50	-7		-1.0
2001	Phi N	5	5	.500	24	14	1	0-0	89.1	93	59	15	9	32-3	59	5.54	74	.274	.350	21-0-2	.095	-0	119	-15		-1.5
2003	Phi N	1	4	.200	45	0	0	0-0	45.1	41	22	5	7	11-2	29	3.97	100	.238	.309	14-0-1	.286	2	89	0		0.2
2004	Phi N	0	2	.000	42	0	0	0-0	54.1	51	27	12	0	19-2	32	4.31	103	.249	.313	4	.000	-0		1	51	0.2
2005	Phi N	0	1	.000	7	0	0	0-0	10.2	5	5	2	0	4-0	8	4.22	103	.139	.220	0	—	0		0		0.0
Total 9		23	35	.397	219	64	1	0-2	561	572	337	92	25	194-15	364	4.94	87	.265	.330	116-0-8	.121	-1	94	-42	99	-4.4

TELFORD, ANTHONY Anthony Charles B3.6.1966 San Jose CA BR/TR/6-0/195(175-195) [BalA87 3/65] d8.19 Col San Jose St.

YEAR	TM LG	W	L	PCT	G	GS	CG-SHO	SV-BS	IP	H	R	HR	HB	BB-IB	SO	ERA	AERA	OAV	OOB	AB-HR-SH	AVG	PB	SUP	APR	DL	PW
1990	Bal A	3	3	.500	8	8	0	0-0	36.1	43	22	4	1	19-0	20	4.95	77	.295	.375	0	—	0	98	-5		-0.7
1991	Bal A	0	0	—	9	1	0	0-0	26.2	27	12	3	0	6-1	24	4.05	98	.265	.303	0	—	0	115	0		0.0
1993	Bal A	0	0	—	3	0	0	0-0	7.1	11	8	3	1	1-0	9	9.82	46	.344	.382	0	—	0		-4		-0.2
1997	Mon N	4	6	.400	65	0	0	1-4	89	77	34	11	5	33-4	61	3.24	129	.236	.315	15-0-1	.200	0		10		1.2
1998	Mon N	3	6	.333	77	0	0	1-4	91	85	45	9	4	36-1	69	3.86	109	.247	.322	4	.250	0		3		0.3
1999	Mon N	5	4	.556	79	0	0	2-7	96	112	52	3	3	38-3	69	3.94	113	.295	.359	2-0-0	.000	0		4		0.4
2000	Mon N	5	4	.556	64	0	0	3-2	78.1	76	38	10	5	23-1	68	3.79	124	.257	.317	2-0-1	.000	-0		7	14	0.7
2001	Mon N	0	1	.000	8	0	0	0-0	7	14	12	2	1	5-1	5	10.29	42	.412	.500	0	—	0		-6	24	-0.7
2002	Tex A	2	1	.667	20	0	0	1-1	23.2	30	18	3	4	15-2	19	6.46	74	.316	.422	0	—	0		-4		-0.5
Total 9		22	25	.468	333	9	0	8-18	455.1	475	241	48	24	176-13	331	4.17	104	.271	.342	23-0-4	.174	-0	90	5	38	0.5

TELGHEDER, DAVE David William B11.11.1966 Middletown NY BR/TR/6-3/212(211-223) [NYN89 31/814] d6.12 Col Massachusetts

YEAR	TM LG	W	L	PCT	G	GS	CG-SHO	SV-BS	IP	H	R	HR	HB	BB-IB	SO	ERA	AERA	OAV	OOB	AB-HR-SH	AVG	PB	SUP	APR	DL	PW
1993	NY N	6	2	.750	24	2	0	0-0	75.2	82	40	10	4	21-2	35	4.76	84	.276	.331	15-0-4	.067	-0	128	-4		-0.4
1994	NY N	0	1	.000	6	0	0	0-0	10	11	8	2	0	8-2	4	7.20	58	.282	.404	0	—	0		-3		-0.3
1995	NY N	1	2	.333	7	4	0	0-0	25.2	34	18	4	0	7-3	16	5.61	72	.318	.357	6-0-1	.333	1	95	-5		-0.4
1996	Oak A	4	7	.364	16	14	1-1	0-0	79.1	92	42	12	1	26-1	43	4.65	107	.292	.345	0	—	0	87	4		0.4
1997	Oak A	4	6	.400	20	19	0	0-0	101	134	71	15	2	35-1	55	6.06	76	.318	.373	2	.000	0	125	-15	76	-1.2
1998	Oak A	0	1	.000	8	2	0	0-0	20	19	12	4	2	6-0	15	3.60	129	.235	.303	0	—	0	70	1	117	0.0
Total 6		15	19	.441	81	46	1-1	0-0	311.2	372	191	47	9	103-9	158	5.23	86	.297	.351	23-0-5	.130	-0	110	-22	193	-1.9

TELLMANN, TOM Thomas John B3.29.1954 Warren PA BR/TR/6-3/185(184-195) [SDN76 11/245] d6.9 Col Grand Canyon

YEAR	TM LG	W	L	PCT	G	GS	CG-SHO	SV-BS	IP	H	R	HR	HB	BB-IB	SO	ERA	AERA	OAV	OOB	AB-HR-SH	AVG	PB	SUP	APR	DL	PW
1979	SD N	0	0	—	1	0	0	0-0	2.2	7	5	1	0	0-0	1	16.88	21	.467	.467	1	.000	-0		-0.2		
1980	SD N	3	0	1.000	6	2	2	1-0	22.1	23	5	0	0	8-0	9	1.61	212	.264	.326	8	.125	-0	131	4		0.6
1983	Mil A	9	4	.692	44	0	0	8-4	99.2	95	34	7	2	35-4	48	2.80	135	.259	.324	0	—	0		12		1.7
1984	Mil A	6	3	.667	50	0	0	4-3	81	82	28	6	1	31-10	28	2.78	140	.257	.338	0	—	0		10	21	1.2
1985	Oak A	0	0	—	11	0	0	0-0	21.1	33	12	3	1	9-1	8	5.06	77	.347	.406	0	—	0		-2	119	-0.1
Total 5		18	7	.720	112	2	2	13-7	227	240	84	17	4	83-15	94	3.05	124	.277	.341	9	.111	-0	131	20	140	3.2

TEMPLETON, CHUCK Charles Sherman B6.1.1932 Detroit MI D10.9.1997 Irving TX BR/TL/6-3/210* d9.9

YEAR	TM LG	W	L	PCT	G	GS	CG-SHO	SV-BS	IP	H	R	HR	HB	BB-IB	SO	ERA	AERA	OAV	OOB	AB-HR-SH	AVG	PB	SUP	APR	DL	PW
1955	Bro N	0	0	—	4	0	0	0-0	4.2	5	7	2	1	5-0	3	11.57	35	.294	.478	0	—	0		-4		-0.7
1956	Bro N	0	1	.000	6	2	0	0-0	16.1	20	13	2	0	10-0	8	6.61	60	.294	.380	3-0-1	.000	-0	111	-4		-0.3
Total 2		0	1	.000	10	2	0	0-0	21	25	20	4	1	15-0	11	7.71	52	.294	.402	3-0-1	.000	-0	111	-8		-1.0

TENER, JOHN John Kinley B7.25.1863 Co. Tyrone, Ireland D5.19.1946 Pittsburgh PA BR/TR/6-4/180 d6.8.1885

YEAR	TM LG	W	L	PCT	G	GS	CG-SHO	SV-BS	IP	H	R	HR	HB	BB-IB	SO	ERA	AERA	OAV	OOB	AB-HR-SH	AVG	PB	SUP	APR	DL	PW
1888	Chi N	7	5	.583	12	12	11-1	0	102	90	59	6	8	25	39	2.74	111	.228	.288	46	.196	-0	101	1		0.1
1889	Chi N	15	15	.500	35	30	28-1	0	287	302	192	16	7	105	105	3.64	114	.262	.328	150-1	.273	5*	112	14		1.7
1890	Pit P	3	11	.214	14	13	4	0	117	160	147	6	5	70	30	7.31	53	.312	.400	63-2	.190	2*	122	-43		-3.1
Total 3		25	31	.446	61	56	52-2	0	506	552	398	28	20	200	174	4.30	90	.268	.339	259-3	.239	6	112	-28		-1.3

TENNANT, JIM James McDonnell B3.3.1907 Shepherdstown WV D4.16.1967 Trumbull CT BR/TR/6-1/190 d9.28 Col George Washington

YEAR	TM LG	W	L	PCT	G	GS	CG-SHO	SV-BS	IP	H	R	HR	HB	BB-IB	SO	ERA	AERA	OAV	OOB	AB-HR-SH	AVG	PB	SUP	APR	DL	PW
1929	NY N	0	0	—	1	0	0	0	1	1	0	0	0	0	1	0.00	—	.333	.333	0	—	0		1		0.0

TENNEY, FRED Fred Clay B7.9.1859 Marlborough NH D6.15.1919 Fall River MA d4.28 Col Brown ▲

YEAR	TM LG	W	L	PCT	G	GS	CG-SHO	SV-BS	IP	H	R	HR	HB	BB-IB	SO	ERA	AERA	OAV	OOB	AB-HR-SH	AVG	PB	SUP	APR	DL	PW
1884	Bos U	3	1	.750	4	4	4	0	35	31	21	0		5	18	2.31	103	.221	.248	17	.118	-3	148	-1		-0.3
	Wil U	0	1	.000	1	1	1	0	8	6	5	0		4	10	1.13	238	.194	.286	3	.000	-1	64	1		0.0
	Year	3	2	.600	5	5	5	0	43	37	26	0		9	28	2.09	116	.216	.256	20	.100	-3	130	0		-0.3

TERLECKI, BOB Robert Joseph B2.14.1945 Trenton NJ BR/TR/5-8/185 d8.16

YEAR	TM LG	W	L	PCT	G	GS	CG-SHO	SV-BS	IP	H	R	HR	HB	BB-IB	SO	ERA	AERA	OAV	OOB	AB-HR-SH	AVG	PB	SUP	APR	DL	PW
1972	Phi N	0	0	—	9	0	0	0-0	13.1	16	9	2	0	10-0	5	4.73	76	.308	.406	0	—	0		-2		-0.1

TERLECKY, GREG Gregory John B3.20.1952 Culver City CA BR/TR/6-3/200 [StLN70 5/109] d6.12

YEAR	TM LG	W	L	PCT	G	GS	CG-SHO	SV-BS	IP	H	R	HR	HB	BB-IB	SO	ERA	AERA	OAV	OOB	AB-HR-SH	AVG	PB	SUP	APR	DL	PW
1975	StL N	0	1	.000	20	0	0	0-0	30.1	38	16	4	0	12-5	13	4.45	85	.306	.365	3	.333	0		-1		0.0

TERPKO, JEFF Jeffrey Michael B10.16.1950 Sayre PA [TexA68 5/92] d9.21

YEAR	TM LG	W	L	PCT	G	GS	CG-SHO	SV-BS	IP	H	R	HR	HB	BB-IB	SO	ERA	AERA	OAV	OOB	AB-HR-SH	AVG	PB	SUP	APR	DL	PW
1974	Tex A	0	0	—	3	0	0	0-0	7	6	1	0	0	4-0	3	1.29	279	.231	.333	0	—	0		2		0.1
1976	Tex A	3	3	.500	32	0	0	0-3	52.2	42	15	3	0	29-1	24	2.39	150	.223	.321	0	—	0		7		0.8
1977	Mon N	0	1	.000	13	0	0	0-0	20.2	28	13	2	0	15-1	14	5.66	68	.346	.448	1	.000	-0		-4		-0.2
Total 3		3	4	.429	48	0	0	0-3	80.1	76	29	5	0	48-2	41	3.14	117	.258	.357	1	.000	-0		5		0.7

TERRELL, WALT Charles Walter B5.11.1958 Jeffersonville IN BL/TR/6-2/205* [TexA80 33/764] d9.18 Col Morehead St.

YEAR	TM LG	W	L	PCT	G	GS	CG-SHO	SV-BS	IP	H	R	HR	HB	BB-IB	SO	ERA	AERA	OAV	OOB	AB-HR-SH	AVG	PB	SUP	APR	DL	PW
1982	NY N	0	3	.000	3	3	0	0-0	21	22	12	2	0	14-2	9	3.43	107	.268	.375	5-0-1	.400	1	32	-1		0.0
1983	NY N	8	8	.500	21	20	4-2	0-0	133.2	123	57	7	2	55-7	59	3.57	103	.251	.326	44-3-3	.182	3	77	3		0.7
1984	NY N	11	12	.478	33	33	3-1	0-0	215	232	99	16	4	80-1	114	3.52	102	.282	.345	75-0-1	.080	-4	106	1		-0.3
1985	Det A	15	10	.600	34	34	5-3	0-0	229	221	107	9	4	95-5	130	3.85	104	.255	.329	0	—	0	102	8		0.9
1986	Det A	15	12	.556	34	33	9-2	0-0	217.1	199	116	30	3	98-5	93	4.56	91	.245	.328	0	—	0	104	-7		-0.7
1987	†Det A	17	10	.630	35	35	10-1	0-0	244.2	254	123	30	3	94-7	143	4.05	100	.268	.333	0	—	0	115	7		0.6
1988	Det A	7	16	.304	29	29	11-1	0-0	206.1	199	101	20	2	78-8	84	3.97	97	.258	.326	0	—	0	92	-3	26	-0.3
1989	SD N	5	13	.278	19	19	4-1	0-0	123.1	134	65	14	0	26-1	63	4.01	87	.277	.313	40-0-1	.100	-0	73	-8		-0.9
	NY A	6	5	.545	13	13	1-1	0-0	83	102	52	9	2	24-0	30	5.20	75	.307	.356	0	—	0	122	-12		-1.3

YEAR	TM LG	W	L	PCT	G	GS	CG-SHO	SV-BS	IP	H	R	HR	HB	BB-IB	SO	ERA	AERA	OAV	OOB	AB-HR-SH	AVG	PB	SUP	APR	DL	PW
1990	Pit N	2	7	.222	16	16	0	0-0	82.2	98	59	13	4	33-1	34	5.88	62	.295	.364	28-0-1	.107	-1	118	-20		-2.0
	Det A	6	4	.600	13	12	0	0-0	75.1	86	39	7	8	24-3	30	4.54	88	.290	.358	0	—	0	107	-4		-0.5
1991	Det A	12	14	.462	35	33	8-2	0-0	218.2	257	115	16	2	79-10	80	4.24	99	.301	.358	0	—	0	103	-3		-0.3
1992	Det A	7	10	.412	36	14	1	0-1	136.2	163	86	14	3	48-10	61	5.20	77	.298	.354	0	—	0	116	-18		-2.0
Total	11	111	124	.472	321	294	56-14	0-1	1986.2	2090	1031	187	37	748-60	929	4.22	94	.274	.339	192-3-7	.120	-1	102	-57	26	-6.1

TERRY, JOHN   John Burchard B11.1.1879 Waterbury CT D4.27.1933 Kansas City MO d9.17

YEAR	TM LG	W	L	PCT	G	GS	CG-SHO	SV-BS	IP	H	R	HR	HB	BB-IB	SO	ERA	AERA	OAV	OOB	AB-HR-SH	AVG	PB	SUP	APR	DL	PW
1902	Det A	0	1	.000	1	1	1	0	5	8	3	0	0	1	0	3.60	101	.364	.391	2	.000	-0	20	0		-0.1
1903	StL A	1	1	.500	3	1	1	0	17.2	21	6	0	3	4	2	2.55	114	.296	.359	9	.000	-1	245	1		0.0
Total	2	1	2	.333	4	2	2	0	22.2	29	9	0	3	5	2	2.78	111	.312	.366	11	.000	-2	128	1		-0.1

TERRY, YANK   Lancelot Yank B2.11.1911 Bedford IN D11.4.1979 Bloomington IN BR/TR/6-1/180 d8.3

YEAR	TM LG	W	L	PCT	G	GS	CG-SHO	SV-BS	IP	H	R	HR	HB	BB-IB	SO	ERA	AERA	OAV	OOB	AB-HR-SH	AVG	PB	SUP	APR	DL	PW
1940	Bos A	1	0	1.000	14	1	0	0	19.1	24	19	2	0	11	9	8.84	51	.304	.389	8	.250	0	234	-8		-0.4
1942	Bos A	6	5	.545	20	11	3	1	85	82	48	5	2	43	37	3.92	95	.248	.339	27-0-1	.111	-1	125	-4		-0.6
1943	Bos A	7	9	.438	30	22	7	1	163.2	147	70	8	1	63	63	3.52	94	.242	.314	45-0-3	.067	-3	97	-3		-0.6
1944	Bos A	6	10	.375	27	17	3	0	132.2	142	72	10	3	65	30	4.21	81	.276	.361	47	.234	1	114	-13		-1.2
1945	Bos A	0	4	.000	12	4	1	0	56.2	68	29	8	0	14	28	4.13	82	.296	.336	18	.111	-2	69	-4		-0.4
Total	5	20	28	.417	93	55	14	2	457.1	463	238	33	6	196	167	4.09	85	.263	.339	145-0-4	.145	-4	109	-32		-3.2

TERRY, RALPH   Ralph Willard B1.9.1936 Big Cabin OK BR/TR/6-3/195(182-195) d8.6

YEAR	TM LG	W	L	PCT	G	GS	CG-SHO	SV-BS	IP	H	R	HR	HB	BB-IB	SO	ERA	AERA	OAV	OOB	AB-HR-SH	AVG	PB	SUP	APR	DL	PW
1956	NY A	1	2	.333	3	3	0	0	13.1	17	15	2	0	11-0	8	9.45	41	.347	.459	6	.167	-0	100	-8		-1.3
1957	NY A	1	1	.500	7	2	1-1	0	20.2	18	7	1	0	8-1	7	3.05	118	.240	.310	4	.250	0	100	2		0.2
	KC A	4	11	.267	21	19	3-1	0	130.2	119	63	15	4	47-2	80	3.38	117	.239	.309	42-0-2	.143	-2*	71	4		0.3
	Year	5	12	.294	28	21	4-2	0	151.1	137	70	16	4	55-3	87	3.33	117	.239	.309	46-0-2	.152	-2	74	5		0.5
1958	KC A	11	13	.458	40	33	8-3	0	216.2	217	111	29	2	61-4	134	4.24	92	.262	.313	71-0-3	.197	-0	114	-7		-0.9
1959	KC A	2	4	.333	9	7	2	0	46.1	56	29	9	1	19-1	35	5.24	76	.308	.374	17-0-1	.176	-1	113	-5		-0.6
	NY A	3	7	.300	24	16	5-1	0	127.1	130	55	7	2	30-5	55	3.39	107	.270	.312	41-0-2	.098	-3	86	4		0.0
	Year	5	11	.313	33	23	7-1	0	173.2	186	84	16	3	49-6	90	3.89	96	.281	.329	58-0-3	.121	-3	95	-3		-0.6
1960	†NY A	10	8	.556	35	23	7-3	1	166.2	149	78	15	4	52-3	92	3.40	105	.237	.299	49-0-7	.122	-2	96	1		-0.1
1961	†NY A	16	3	.842	31	27	9-2	0	188.1	162	74	19	1	42-0	86	3.15	118	.232	.275	66-0-5	.227	2	127	12		1.3
1962	†NY A☆	23	12	.657	43	39	14-3	1	298.2	257	123	40	3	57-1	176	3.19	117	.231	.268	106-0-11	.189	1	127	18		0.5
1963	†NY A	17	15	.531	40	37	18-3	1	268	246	103	29	4	39-1	114	3.22	109	.242	.271	87-0-9	.080	-6	103	10		0.3
1964	†NY A	7	11	.389	27	14	2-1	0	115	130	60	20	1	31-3	77	4.54	80	.283	.326	35-0-4	.200	1	103	-10		-1.4
1965	Cle A	11	6	.647	30	26	6-2	0	165.2	154	77	22	1	23-3	84	3.69	94	.242	.268	49-1-10	.143	2	116	-3		-0.3
1966	KC A	1	5	.167	15	10	0	0	64	65	35	7	1	15-3	33	3.80	89	.263	.305	14-0-1	.214	1	101	-5	24	-0.3
	NY N	0	1	.000	11	1	0	1	24.2	27	14	1	0	11-1	14	4.74	77	.293	.369	6	.167	-0	121	-3		-0.2
1967	NY N	0	0	—	2	0	0	0	3.1	1	0	0	0	0-0	5	0.00		.091	.091	0	—	0		1		0.1
Total	12	107	99	.519	338	257	75-20	11	1849.1	1748	844	216	24	446-28	1000	3.62	102	.249	.294	593-1-55	.160	-6	108	11	24	-0.9

TERRY, SCOTT   Scott Ray B11.21.1959 Hobbs NM BR/TR/5-11/195* [CinN80 12/305] d4.9 Col Southwestern (TX) [DL 1992 StL N 182]

YEAR	TM LG	W	L	PCT	G	GS	CG-SHO	SV-BS	IP	H	R	HR	HB	BB-IB	SO	ERA	AERA	OAV	OOB	AB-HR-SH	AVG	PB	SUP	APR	DL	PW
1986	Cin N	1	2	.333	28	3	0	0-0	55.2	66	40	8	0	32-3	32	6.14	63	.300	.387	4-0-1	.250	0*	139	-13		-0.6
1987	StL N	0	0	—	11	0	0	0-0	13.1	13	5	0	0	8-2	9	3.38	125	.260	.362	0	.000	0		1		0.1
1988	StL N	9	6	.600	51	11	1	3-4	129.1	119	48	5	0	34-6	65	2.92	121	.247	.295	28-0-5	.250	2	110	8	27	1.1
1989	StL N	8	10	.444	31	24	1	2-0	148.2	142	65	14	3	43-6	69	3.57	103	.253	.308	45-2-4	.156	2*	93	2	22	0.2
1990	StL N	2	6	.250	50	2	0	2-1	72	75	45	7	4	27-5	35	4.75	81	.264	.331	11-0-1	.455	2	82	-8		-0.6
1991	StL N	4	4	.500	65	0	0	1-2	80.1	76	31	1	0	32-14	52	2.80	134	.249	.320	7	.143	-0		7		0.7
Total	6	24	28	.462	236	40	2	8-7	499.1	491	234	35	7	176-36	262	3.73	99	.258	.321	97-2-11	.216	5	99	-3	231	0.2

TERRY, ADONIS   William H B8.7.1864 Westfield MA D2.24.1915 Milwaukee WI BR/TR/5-11.5/168 d5.1 U1 ▲

YEAR	TM LG	W	L	PCT	G	GS	CG-SHO	SV-BS	IP	H	R	HR	HB	BB-IB	SO	ERA	AERA	OAV	OOB	AB-HR-SH	AVG	PB	SUP	APR	DL	PW
1884	Bro AA	19	35	.352	56	55	54-2	0	476	486	308	10	8	72	230	3.55	93	.247	.276	236	.233	3*	66	-14		-1.2
1885	Bro AA	6	17	.261	25	23	23	1	209	213	147	9	4	42	96	4.26	77	.262	.301	264-1	.170	-3*	82	-16		-1.8
1886	Bro AA	18	16	.529	34	34	32-5	0	288.1	263	177	1	16	115	162	3.09	113	.231	.310	299-2	.237	2*	98	12		1.5
1887	Bro AA	16	16	.500	40	35	35-1	3	318	331	230	10	9	99	138	4.02	107	.262	.320	352-3	.293	7*	100	7		1.2
1888	Bro AA	13	8	.619	23	23	20-2	0	195	145	79	2	9	67	138	2.03	147	.199	.275	115	.252	3*	100	21		2.1
1889	†Bro AA	22	15	.595	41	39	35-2	0	326	285	189	6	16	126	186	3.29	113	.228	.307	160-2	.300	12*	101	10		2.1
1890	†Bro N	26	16	.619	46	44	38-1	0	370	362	200	3	15	133	185	2.94	117	.248	.317	363-4	.278	15*	102	19		2.2
1891	Bro N	6	16	.273	25	22	18-1	1	194	207	139	5	7	80	65	4.22	78	.263	.336	61	.209	3*	86	-18		-1.1
1892	Bal N	0	1	.000	1	1	1	0	9	7	7	0	0	7	3	4.00	86	.206	.341	4	.000	-1	18	-1		-0.1
	Pit N	18	7	.720	30	26	24-2	1	240	185	106	3	8	106	95	2.51	131	.204	.293	100-2	.160	1*	111	23		2.2
	Year	18	8	.692	31	27	25-2	1	249	192	113	3	8	113	98	2.57	129	.204	.295	104-2	.154	1	107	23		2.2
1893	Pit N	12	8	.600	26	19	14	0	170	177	121	5	11	99	52	4.45	102	.262	.363	71	.254	2	112	2		0.4
1894	Pit N	0	1	.000	1	1	0	0	0.2	5	5	0	0	4	0	67.50	8	.500	.750	0	—	0	68	-4		-0.5
	Chi N	5	11	.313	23	21	16	0	163.1	232	191	12	16	123	39	5.84	97	.330	.441	95	.347	4*	96	-15		-0.7
	Year	5	12	.294	24	22	16	0	164	234	196	12	16	127	39	6.09	93	.330	.444	95	.347	4	95	-20		-1.2
1895	Chi N	21	14	.600	38	34	31	0	311.1	346	228	4	17	131	88	4.80	106	.277	.354	137-1-5	.219	-6*	89	12		0.9
1896	Chi N	15	14	.517	30	28	25-1	0	235.2	273	166	6	10	88	75	4.43	102	.288	.354	99-0-3	.263	2	112	1		0.8
1897	Chi N	0	1	.000	1	1	1	0	8	11	10	0	2	6	1	10.13	44	.324	.452	3-0-1	.000	-1	64	-4		-0.1
Total	14	197	196	.501	440	406	367-17	6	3514.1	3525	2303	76	148	1298	1553	3.74	103	.252	.323	2389-15-9	.249	45	95	35		7.1

TERWILLIGER, DICK   Richard Martin B6.27.1906 Sand Lake MI D1.21.1969 Greenville MI BR/TR/5-11/178 d8.18

YEAR	TM LG	W	L	PCT	G	GS	CG-SHO	SV-BS	IP	H	R	HR	HB	BB-IB	SO	ERA	AERA	OAV	OOB	AB-HR-SH	AVG	PB	SUP	APR	DL	PW
1932	StL N	0	0	—	1	0	0	0	3	1	0	0	1	2	2	0.00		.143	.400	1	.000	-0		1		0.1

TESREAU, JEFF   Charles Monroe B3.5.1889 Silver Mine MO D9.24.1946 Hanover NH BR/TR/6-2/218 d4.12 Def 1918 C1

YEAR	TM LG	W	L	PCT	G	GS	CG-SHO	SV-BS	IP	H	R	HR	HB	BB-IB	SO	ERA	AERA	OAV	OOB	AB-HR-SH	AVG	PB	SUP	APR	DL	PW
1912	†NY N	17	7	.708	36	28	19-3	1	243	177	90	2	10	.106	119	1.96	172	.204	.298	82-0-2	.146	-2	91	34		2.1
1913	†NY N	22	13	.629	41	38	17-1	0	282	222	98	7	7	119	167	2.17	144	.220	.306	95-0-3	.221	2	109	28		3.6
1914	NY N	26	10	.722	42	41	26-8	1	322.1	238	104	8	7	128	189	2.37	112	.209	.293	117-0-4	.239	6	144	12		1.9
1915	NY N	19	16	.543	43	39	24-8	3	306	235	98	4	5	75	176	2.29	112	.215	.269	103-1-2	.233	6	113	11		-1.2
1916	NY N	14	14	.500	40	32	23-5	2	268.1	249	103	9	6	65	113	2.92	83	.250	.300	94-1-3	.191	2*	120	-13		-1.1
1917	†NY N	13	8	.619	33	20	11-1	2	183.2	168	71	6	3	58	85	3.09	83	.244	.312	61-0-3	.230	2	86	-8		-0.1
1918	NY N	4	4	.500	12	9	3-1	0	73.2	61	27	1	0	21	31	2.32	113	.227	.283	22-0-0	.318	2	106	1		-0.1
Total	7	115	72	.615	247	207	123-27	9	1679	1350	591	37	38	572	880	2.43	114	.223	.295	574-2-19	.216	17	113	65		8.0

TESSMER, JAY   Jay Weldon B12.26.1971 Meadville PA BR/TR/6-3/190* [NYA95 19/534] d8.27 Col Miami

YEAR	TM LG	W	L	PCT	G	GS	CG-SHO	SV-BS	IP	H	R	HR	HB	BB-IB	SO	ERA	AERA	OAV	OOB	AB-HR-SH	AVG	PB	SUP	APR	DL	PW
1998	NY A	1	0	1.000	7	0	0	0-0	8.2	4	3	1	0	4-0	6	3.12	141	.143	.242	0	—	0		1		0.0
1999	NY A	0	0	—	6	0	0	0-0	6.2	16	11	1	1	4-2	5	14.85	32	.444	.512	0	—	0		-7		-0.5
2000	NY A	0	0	—	7	0	0	0-0	6.2	9	6	3	0	1-1	5	6.75	71	.300	.323	0	—	0		-2		-0.1
2002	NY A	0	0	—	2	0	0	0-0	1.1	0	1	0	0	2-0	0	6.75	64	.000	.333	0	—	0		0		-0.1
Total	4	1	0	1.000	22	0	0	0-0	23.1	29	21	5	1	11-3	14	7.71	59	.296	.369	0	—	0		-8		-0.5

TEUT, NATE   Nathan Mark B3.11.1976 Newton IA BR/TL/6-7/220 [ChiN97 4/124] d5.4 Col Iowa St.

YEAR	TM LG	W	L	PCT	G	GS	CG-SHO	SV-BS	IP	H	R	HR	HB	BB-IB	SO	ERA	AERA	OAV	OOB	AB-HR-SH	AVG	PB	SUP	APR	DL	PW
2002	Fla N	0	1	.000	2	1	0	0-0	7.1	13	8	0	0	3-1	4	9.82	40	.394	.444	2	.000	-0	94	-5		-0.5

TEWKSBURY, BOB   Robert Alan B11.30.1960 Concord NH BR/TR/6-4/200(180-208) [NYA81 19/493] d4.11 Col St. Leo

YEAR	TM LG	W	L	PCT	G	GS	CG-SHO	SV-BS	IP	H	R	HR	HB	BB-IB	SO	ERA	AERA	OAV	OOB	AB-HR-SH	AVG	PB	SUP	APR	DL	PW
1986	NY A	9	5	.643	23	20	2	0-0	130.1	144	58	8	5	31-0	49	3.31	125	.282	.325	0	—	0	110	10		1.1
1987	NY A	1	4	.200	8	6	0	0-0	33.1	47	26	5	1	7-0	12	6.75	66	.338	.374	0	—	0	93	-8		-1.1
	Chi N	0	4	.000	7	3	0	0-1	18	32	15	1	0	13-3	10	6.50	67	.421	.500	5	.000	-1	49	-4	53	-0.2
1988	Chi N	0	0	—	1	1	0	0-0	3.1	11	7	0	0	2-0	1	8.10	45	.400	.444	2	.000	-0	268	-2	21	-0.3
1989	StL N	1	0	1.000	7	4	1-1	0-0	30	25	12	2	4	10-3	17	3.30	111	.225	.298	9	.111	-0	103	1		0.0
1990	StL N	10	9	.526	28	20	3-2	1-0	145.1	151	67	7	3	15-3	50	3.47	111	.267	.286	49-1-0	.171	1	83	4		0.0
1991	StL N	11	12	.478	30	30	3	0-0	191	206	86	13	5	38-2	75	3.25	115	.281	.317	58-0-7	.155	1	97	6		0.0
1992	StL N★	16	5	.762	33	32	5	0-0	233	217	63	15	3	20-0	91	2.16	158	.248	.265	70-0-6	.086	-2	107	32		2.2
1993	StL N	17	10	.630	32	32	2	0-0	213.2	258	99	15	6	20-2	97	3.83	105	.301	.318	69-0-7	.203	2*	108	6		1.3
1994	StL N	12	10	.545	24	24	4-1	0-0	155.2	190	97	19	3	22-1	79	5.32	80	.304	.328	54-0-4	.185	1	99	-18		-2.2
1995	Tex A	8	7	.533	21	21	4-1	0-0	129.2	169	75	8	3	20-4	53	4.58	106	.319	.346	1	.000	-0	108	2	34	-0.1
1996	SD N	10	10	.500	36	33	1	0-0	206.2	224	99	17	2	43-3	126	4.31	93	.275	.310	65-0-8	.031	-5	115	-10		0.2
1997	Min A	8	13	.381	26	26	5-2	0-0	168.2	200	83	12	1	31-1	92	4.22	111	.297	.325	5	.200	0	73	9	50	0.1

YEAR TM LG	W	L	PCT	G	GS	CG-SHO	SV-BS	IP	H	R	HR	HB	BB-IB	SO	ERA	AERA	OAV	OOB	AB-HR-SH	AVG	PB	SUP	APR	DL	PW
998 Min A	7	13	.350	26	25	1	0-0	148.1	174	82	19	6	20-1	60	4.79	100	.292	.318	1	.000	-0	69	1	53	0.2
otal 13	110	102	.519	302	277	31-7	1-1	1807	2043	884	142	41	292-22	812	3.92	105	.287	.316	380-0-41	.132	-3	98	29	211	2.9

THATCHER, GRANT Ulysses Grant B2.23.1877 Maytown PA D3.17.1936 Lancaster PA TR/5-10.5/180 d9.9

YEAR TM LG	W	L	PCT	G	GS	CG-SHO	SV-BS	IP	H	R	HR	HB	BB-IB	SO	ERA	AERA	OAV	OOB	AB-HR-SH	AVG	PB	SUP	APR	DL	PW
903 Bro N	3	1	.750	4	4	4	0	28	33	12	1	0	7	9	2.89	110	.292	.333	11	.182	0	106	1		0.2
904 Bro N	1	0	1.000	1	0	0	0	9	9	6	0	0	2	4	4.00	89	.281	.324		.250	0		-1		-0.1
otal 2	4	1	.800	5	4	4	0	37	42	18	1	0	9	13	3.16	98	.290	.331	15	.200	0	106	0		0.1

THAYER, GREG Gregory Allen B10.23.1949 Cedar Rapids IA BR/TR/5-11/182 [SFN71 32/700] d4.7 Col St. Cloud St.

YEAR TM LG	W	L	PCT	G	GS	CG-SHO	SV-BS	IP	H	R	HR	HB	BB-IB	SO	ERA	AERA	OAV	OOB	AB-HR-SH	AVG	PB	SUP	APR	DL	PW
978 Min A	1	1	.500	20	0	0	0-2	45	40	19	5	3	30-1	30	3.80	101	.258	.380	0	—	0		1		0.1

THEIS, JACK John Louis B7.23.1891 Georgetown OH D7.6.1941 Georgetown OH BR/TR/6-0/190 d7.5

YEAR TM LG	W	L	PCT	G	GS	CG-SHO	SV-BS	IP	H	R	HR	HB	BB-IB	SO	ERA	AERA	OAV	OOB	AB-HR-SH	AVG	PB	SUP	APR	DL	PW
920 Cin N	0	0	—	1	0	0	0	4	6	4	0	0	3	0	0.00	—	.143	.400	0	—	0		1		0.0

THEISS, DUANE Duane Charles B11.20.1953 Zanesville OH BR/TR/6-3/185* [AtlN75 12/282] d8.5 Col Marietta

YEAR TM LG	W	L	PCT	G	GS	CG-SHO	SV-BS	IP	H	R	HR	HB	BB-IB	SO	ERA	AERA	OAV	OOB	AB-HR-SH	AVG	PB	SUP	APR	DL	PW
977 Atl N	1	1	.500	17	0	0	0-0	20.2	26	16	1	1	16-5	7	6.53	68	.338	.439	1-0-1	.000	-0		-4		-0.3
978 Atl N	0	0	—	3	0	0	0-0	6.1	3	1	0	1	3-0	3	1.42	284	.158	.292	1	.000	-0		2		0.1
otal 2	1	1	.500	20	0	0	0-0	27	29	17	1	2	19-5	10	5.33	82	.302	.410	2-0-1	.000	-0		-2		-0.2

THESENGA, JUG Arnold Joseph B4.27.1914 Jefferson SD D12.3.2002 Wichita KS BR/TR/6-0/200 d9.1

YEAR TM LG	W	L	PCT	G	GS	CG-SHO	SV-BS	IP	H	R	HR	HB	BB-IB	SO	ERA	AERA	OAV	OOB	AB-HR-SH	AVG	PB	SUP	APR	DL	PW
944 Was A	0	0	—	5	1	0	0	12.1	18	9	0	0	12	5	5.11	64	.340	.462	2-0-1	.000	-0	257	-3		-0.2

THIEL, BERT Maynard Bert B5.4.1926 Marion WI BR/TR/5-10/185 d4.17

YEAR TM LG	W	L	PCT	G	GS	CG-SHO	SV-BS	IP	H	R	HR	HB	BB-IB	SO	ERA	AERA	OAV	OOB	AB-HR-SH	AVG	PB	SUP	APR	DL	PW
952 Bos N	1	1	.500	4	0	0	0	7	11	7	1	2	4	6	7.71	47	.344	.447	0	—	0		-3		-0.7

THIELMAN, HENRY Henry Joseph B10.3.1880 St.Cloud MN D9.2.1942 New York NY BR/TR/5-11/175 d4.17 b-Jake Col Manhattan

YEAR TM LG	W	L	PCT	G	GS	CG-SHO	SV-BS	IP	H	R	HR	HB	BB-IB	SO	ERA	AERA	OAV	OOB	AB-HR-SH	AVG	PB	SUP	APR	DL	PW
902 NY N	0	1	.000	2	2	0	0	6	8	10	0	0	6	6	1.50	187	.320	.452	9	.111	-0*	121	-2		-0.3
Cin N	9	15	.375	25	23	22	1	211	201	111	2	19	78	49	3.24	92	.251	.332	91-0-2	.132	-4*	90	-4		-0.8
Year	9	16	.360	27	25	22	1	217	209	121	2	19	84	54	3.19	94	.253	.336	100-0-2	.130	-4	92	-10		-1.1
903 Bro N	0	3	.000	4	3	3	0	29	31	20	3	2	14	10	4.66	69	.330	.427	23-1-0	.217	-1*	35	-4		-0.2
otal 2	9	19	.321	31	28	25	1	246	240	141	5	21	98	64	3.37	90	.261	.346	123-1-2	.146	-3	85	-10		-1.3

THIELMAN, JAKE John Peter B5.20.1879 St.Cloud MN D1.28.1928 Minneapolis MN BR/TR/5-11/175 d4.23 b-Henry Col Manhattan

YEAR TM LG	W	L	PCT	G	GS	CG-SHO	SV-BS	IP	H	R	HR	HB	BB-IB	SO	ERA	AERA	OAV	OOB	AB-HR-SH	AVG	PB	SUP	APR	DL	PW
905 StL N	15	16	.484	32	29	26	0	242	265	138	4	12	62	87	3.50	85	.281	.333	91-0-2	.231	8*	94	-18		-1.1
906 StL N	0	1	.000	1	1	0	0	5	5	6	0	0	2	0	3.60	73	.263	.333	2	.500	0	139	-2		-0.2
907 Cle A	11	8	.579	20	18	18-3	0	166	151	60	2	7	34	56	2.33	107	.245	.292	59-0-4	.203	1*	96	5		0.5
908 Cle A	4	3	.571	11	8	5	0	61.2	59	26	2	4	9	15	3.65	65	.260	.300	23-0-3	.348	4*	125	-5		-0.1
Bos A	0	0	—	1	0	0	0	0.2	3	4	1	0	0	0	40.50	6	.600	.600	0	—	0		-3		-0.1
Year	4	3	.571	12	8	5	0	62.1	62	30	3	4	9	15	4.04	59	.267	.306	23-0-3	.348	4	125	-8		-0.2
otal 4	30	28	.517	65	56	49-3	0	475.1	483	234	9	23	107	158	3.16	86	.267	.316	175-0-9	.240	13	100	-23		-1.1

THIES, DAVE David Robert B3.21.1937 Minneapolis MN BR/TR/6-4/205 d4.20 Col St. Marys (MN)

YEAR TM LG	W	L	PCT	G	GS	CG-SHO	SV-BS	IP	H	R	HR	HB	BB-IB	SO	ERA	AERA	OAV	OOB	AB-HR-SH	AVG	PB	SUP	APR	DL	PW
963 KC A	0	1	.000	9	2	0	0	25.1	26	15	2	2	12-0	9	4.62	84	.274	.364	6	.333	1	171	-2		0.0

THIES, JAKE Vernon Arthur B4.1.1926 St.Louis MO BR/TR/5-11/170* d4.24 Col Illinois

YEAR TM LG	W	L	PCT	G	GS	CG-SHO	SV-BS	IP	H	R	HR	HB	BB-IB	SO	ERA	AERA	OAV	OOB	AB-HR-SH	AVG	PB	SUP	APR	DL	PW
954 Pit N	3	9	.250	33	18	3-1	0	130.1	120	70	13	3	49	57	3.87	108	.244	.312	33-0-2	.030	-2	77	2		0.0
955 Pit N	0	1	.000	1	1	0	0	3.2	5	5	0	1	3-1	0	4.91	84	.357	.450	0	—	0	65	-1		-0.2
otal 2	3	10	.231	34	19	3-1	0	134	125	75	13	4	52-1	57	3.90	107	.248	.317	33-0-2	.030	-2	76	1		-0.2

THIGPEN, BOBBY Robert Thomas B7.17.1963 Tallahassee FL BR/TR/6-3/195(195-222) [ChiA85 4/85] d8.6 Col Mississippi St.

YEAR TM LG	W	L	PCT	G	GS	CG-SHO	SV-BS	IP	H	R	HR	HB	BB-IB	SO	ERA	AERA	OAV	OOB	AB-HR-SH	AVG	PB	SUP	APR	DL	PW
986 Chi A	2	0	1.000	20	0	0	7-4	35.2	26	7	1	1	12-0	20	1.77	246	.205	.277	0	—	0		10		0.9
987 Chi A	7	5	.583	51	0	0	16-3	89	86	30	10	3	24-5	52	2.73	170	.256	.311	0	—	0		18		2.8
988 Chi A	5	8	.385	68	0	0	34-9	90	96	38	6	4	33-3	62	3.30	121	.273	.338	0	—	0		7		1.4
989 Chi A	2	6	.250	61	0	0	34-9	79	62	34	10	1	40-3	47	3.76	102	.218	.311	0	—	0		2		0.3
990 Chi A★	4	6	.400	77	0	0	57-8	88.2	60	20	5	1	32-3	70	1.83	211	.195	.271	0	—	0		20		4.2
991 Chi A	7	5	.583	67	0	0	30-9	69.2	63	32	10	4	38-8	47	3.49	115	.245	.348	0	—	0		3		0.6
992 Chi A	1	3	.250	55	0	0	22-7	55	58	29	4	3	33-5	45	4.75	82	.275	.375	0	—	0		-4		-0.5
993 Chi A	0	0	—	25	0	0	1-1	34.2	51	25	5	5	12-0	19	5.71	74	.349	.410	0	—	0		-6		-0.3
†Phi N	3	1	.750	17	0	0	0-2	19.1	23	13	2	1	9-1	10	6.05	66	.307	.384	1	.000	-0		-4		-0.7
994 Sea A	2	2	.000	7	0	0	0-0	7.2	12	9	3	0	5-0	4	9.39	53	.353	.436	0	—	0		-4		-0.7
otal 9	31	36	.463	448	0	0	201-52	568.2	537	237	56	23	238-28	376	3.43	119	.252	.330	1	.000	-0		42		8.0

THOBE, J. J. John Joseph B11.19.1970 Covington KY BR/TR/6-2/220 [CleA92 7/182] d9.18 b-Tom Col Santa Ana (CA) JC

YEAR TM LG	W	L	PCT	G	GS	CG-SHO	SV-BS	IP	H	R	HR	HB	BB-IB	SO	ERA	AERA	OAV	OOB	AB-HR-SH	AVG	PB	SUP	APR	DL	PW
995 Mon N	0	0	—	4	0	0	0-0	4	6	4	0	0	3-0	3	9.00	48	.333	.429	0	—	0		-2		-0.1

THOBE, TOM Thomas Neal B9.3.1969 Covington KY BL/TL/6-6/195* [ChiN87 38/961] d9.12 b-J.J.

YEAR TM LG	W	L	PCT	G	GS	CG-SHO	SV-BS	IP	H	R	HR	HB	BB-IB	SO	ERA	AERA	OAV	OOB	AB-HR-SH	AVG	PB	SUP	APR	DL	PW
995 Atl N	0	0	—	3	0	0	0-0	3.1	7	4	0	0	0-0	2	10.80	40	.412	.412		—	0		-2		-0.1
996 Atl N	0	1	.000	4	0	0	0-0	6	5	2	1	0	0-0	1	1.50	297	.217	.208	1	.000	-0		1		0.2
otal 2	0	1	.000	7	0	0	0-0	9.1	12	6	1	0	0-0	3	4.82	91	.300	.293	1	.000	-0		-1		0.1

THOENEN, DICK Richard Crispin B1.9.1944 Mexico MO BR/TR/6-6/215 d9.16 Col Notre Dame

YEAR TM LG	W	L	PCT	G	GS	CG-SHO	SV-BS	IP	H	R	HR	HB	BB-IB	SO	ERA	AERA	OAV	OOB	AB-HR-SH	AVG	PB	SUP	APR	DL	PW
967 Phi N	0	0	—	1	0	0	0-0	1	3	1	0	0	0-0	0	9.00	38	.500	.500	0	—	0		-1		0.0

THOMAS, TOMMY Alphonse B12.23.1899 Baltimore MD D4.27.1988 Dallastown PA BR/TR/5-10/175 d4.17 Col CC of Baltimore (MD)

YEAR TM LG	W	L	PCT	G	GS	CG-SHO	SV-BS	IP	H	R	HR	HB	BB-IB	SO	ERA	AERA	OAV	OOB	AB-HR-SH	AVG	PB	SUP	APR	DL	PW
926 Chi A	15	12	.556	44	32	13-2	2	249	225	115	7	1	110	127	3.80	102	.244	.325	86-0-3	.186	-1	103	6		0.3
927 Chi A	19	16	.543	40	36	24-3	1	307.2	271	110	16	1	94	107	2.98	136	.244	.303	95-1-19	.147	-3	87	42		3.8
928 Chi A	17	16	.515	36	32	24-3	2	283	277	114	14	4	76	129	3.08	131	.259	.310	96-2-7	.219	4	93	31		3.5
929 Chi A	14	18	.438	36	31	24-2	1	259.2	270	127	17	0	60	62	3.19	134	.269	.310	98-0-1	.255	2*	75	24		2.7
930 Chi A	5	13	.278	34	27	7	0	169	229	125	13	1	44	58	5.22	89	.323	.364	56-0-4	.125	-4	91	-13		-1.4
931 Chi A	10	14	.417	43	36	11-2	2	245.1	298	166	17	5	69	72	4.73	90	.292	.340	87-0-5	.241	1	108	-18		-1.4
932 Chi A	3	5	.500	12	3	1	0	43.2	55	33	6	1	15	11	6.18	70	.307	.364	13-0-1	.077	-1	105	-8		-0.9
Was A	8	7	.533	18	14	7-1	0	117	114	48	5	0	46	36	3.54	122	.255	.325	42-0-1	.238	1	100	12		1.3
Year	11	10	.524	30	17	8-1	0	160.2	169	81	11	1	61	47	4.26	101	.270	.336	55-0-2	.200	0	101	6		0.4
933 †Was A	7	5	.500	35	14	2	3	135	149	87	9	2	49	35	4.80	87	.273	.336	42-0-6	.238	1	128	-12		-1.1
934 Was A	8	9	.471	33	18	7-1	1	133.1	154	87	9	3	58	42	5.47	79	.294	.368	38-0-7	.184	-0	88	-16		-1.8
935 Was A	0	0	—	1	0	0	0	0.1	3	2	0	0	0	0	54.00	8	.750	.750	0	—	0		-2		-0.1
Phi N	0	1	.000	4	1	0	0	12	15	9	2	0	5	3	5.25	86	.313	.377	3	.000	-0	56	-1		-0.1
936 StL A	11	9	.550	36	21	8-1	0	179.2	219	132	25	4	72	40	5.26	102	.297	.362	58-0-7	.138	-3	97	-3		-0.6
937 StL A	0	1	.000	17	2	0	0	30.2	46	26	2	1	10	10	7.04	69	.348	.399	4	.000	-1	117	-7		-0.4
Bos A	0	0	—	9	0	0	0	11	16	6	2	1	4	4	4.09	116	.340	.404	4	.250	-0		-4		0.1
Year	0	1	.000	26	2	0	0	41.2	62	32	4	2	14	14	6.26	77	.346	.400	8	.125	-1	118	-6		-0.3
al 12	117	128	.478	398	267	128-15	12	2176.1	2341	1185	144	24	712	736	4.11	104	.275	.333	722-3-61	.195	-5	95	36		3.9

THOMAS, BLAINE Blaine M. "Baldy" B8.1888 Glendora CA D8.21.1915 Glendora CA BR/TR/5-10/165 d8.25

YEAR TM LG	W	L	PCT	G	GS	CG-SHO	SV-BS	IP	H	R	HR	HB	BB-IB	SO	ERA	AERA	OAV	OOB	AB-HR-SH	AVG	PB	SUP	APR	DL	PW
911 Bos A	0	0	—	2	0	0	0	4.2	3	2	0	1	7	0	0.00	—	.273	.579	2	.500	0	99	1		0.1

THOMAS, BRAD Bradley Richard B10.22.1977 Sydney, New South Wales, Australia BL/TL/6-4/220(204-235) d5.26 [DL 2004 Bos A 164]

YEAR TM LG	W	L	PCT	G	GS	CG-SHO	SV-BS	IP	H	R	HR	HB	BB-IB	SO	ERA	AERA	OAV	OOB	AB-HR-SH	AVG	PB	SUP	APR	DL	PW
001 Min A	0	2	.000	5	5	0	0-0	16.1	20	17	6	1	14-0	6	9.37	50	.303	.432	0	—	0	79	-8		-0.7
003 Min A	0	1	.000	3	0	0	0-0	4.2	6	4	1	0	3-1	2	7.71	58	.316	.409	0	—	0		-2		-0.3
004 Min A	0	0	—	3	0	0	0-0	2.2	7	5	0	0	1-0	0	16.88	27	.500	.533	0	—	0		-3		-0.2
al 3	0	3	.000	11	5	0	0-0	23.2	33	26	7	1	18-1	8	9.89	47	.333	.441	0	—	0	79	-13	164	-1.2

THOMAS, CARL Carl Leslie B5.28.1932 Minneapolis MN BR/TR/6-5/245 d4.19 Col Arizona

YEAR TM LG	W	L	PCT	G	GS	CG-SHO	SV-BS	IP	H	R	HR	HB	BB-IB	SO	ERA	AERA	OAV	OOB	AB-HR-SH	AVG	PB	SUP	APR	DL	PW
960 Cle A	1	0	1.000	4	0	0	0	9.2	8	8	1	1	10-0	5	7.45	50	.229	.413	3-0-1	.333	1*		-4		-0.3

THOMAS, LEFTY Clarence Fletcher B10.4.1903 Glade Spring VA D3.21.1952 Charlottesville VA BL/TL/6-0/183 d9.26 Col Lynchburg

YEAR TM LG	W	L	PCT	G	GS	CG-SHO	SV-BS	IP	H	R	HR	HB	BB-IB	SO	ERA	AERA	OAV	OOB	AB-HR-SH	AVG	PB	SUP	APR	DL	PW
925 Was A	0	2	.000	2	1	1	0	13	13	8	0	0	7	10	2.08	204	.264	.350	5	.000	-1	80	1		0.1
926 Was A	0	0	—	6	0	0	0	8.2	8	7	0	0	10	3	5.19	74	.267	.450	2	.000	0		-2		-0.1
al 2	0	2	.000	8	1	1	0	21.2	22	15	0	0	17	13	3.32	123	.265	.390	7	.000	-1	80	-1		0.0

YEAR	TM LG	W	L	PCT	G	GS	CG-SHO	SV-BS	IP	H	R	HR	HB	BB-IB	SO	ERA	AERA	OAV	OOB	AB-HR-SH	AVG	PB	SUP	APR	DL	P

THOMAS, CLAUDE Claude Alfred "Lefty" B5.15.1890 Stanberry MO D3.6.1946 Sulphur OK BL/TL/6-1/180 d9.14

| 1916 | Was A | 1 | 2 | .333 | 7 | 4 | 1-1 | 2 | 28.1 | 27 | 14 | 1 | 2 | 12 | 9 | 4.13 | 68 | .265 | .353 | 10 | .100 | -1 | 102 | -3 | | -0 |

THOMAS, FAY Fay Wesley "Scow" B10.10.1903 Holyrood KS D8.12.1990 Chatsworth CA BR/TR/6-2/195 d6.27 Col USC

1927	NY N	0	0	—	9	0	0	0	16.1	19	10	3	1	4	11	3.31	117	.302	.353	2	.000	-0		0		-0
1931	Cle A	2	4	.333	16	2	1	0	48.2	63	34	2	1	32	25	5.18	89	.323	.421	13	.154	-1	64	-3		-0
1932	Bro N	1	0	1.000	7	2	0	0	17	22	15	0	0	8	9	7.41	51	.306	.375	3-0-1	.000	-0	88	-6		-0
1935	StL A	7	15	.318	49	19	4	1	147	165	95	11	3	89	67	4.78	100	.289	.388	38-0-4	.105	-3	51	-2		-0
Total	4	9	20	.310	81	23	5	1	229	269	154	16	5	133	112	4.95	93	.299	.392	56-0-5	.107	-4	54	-11		-1

THOMAS, FROSTY Forrest B5.23.1881 Faucett MO D3.18.1970 St.Joseph MO BR/TR/6-0/185 d5.1

| 1905 | Det A | 0 | 1 | .000 | 2 | 1 | 0 | 0 | 6 | 10 | 8 | 0 | 1 | 3 | 5 | 7.50 | 36 | .370 | .452 | 2 | .000 | 0 | 104 | -3 | | -0 |

THOMAS, LARRY Larry Wayne B10.25.1969 Miami FL BR/TL/6-1/195* [ChiA91 2/69] d8.11 Col Maine

1995	Chi A	0	0	—	17	0	0	0-0	13.2	8	2	1	0	6-1	12	1.32	340	.167	.259	0	—	0		5		
1996	Chi A	2	3	.400	57	0	0	0-2	30.2	32	11	1	3	14-2	20	3.23	147	.281	.374	0	—	0		6	20	
1997	Chi A	0	0	—	5	0	0	0-0	3.1	3	3	1	0	2-0	0	8.10	54	.250	.357	0	—	0		-1		
Total	3	2	3	.400	79	0	0	0-2	47.2	43	16	3	3	22-3	32	3.02	154	.247	.342	0	—	0		10	20	

THOMAS, BUD Luther Baxter B9.9.1910 Faber VA D5.20.2001 North Garden VA BR/TR/6-0/180 d9.13

1932	Was A	0	0	—	2	0	0	0	3	1	0	0	0	2	1	0.00	—	.100	.250	0	—	0		1		-C
1933	Was A	0	0	—	2	0	0	0	4	11	8	1	1	2	1	15.75	27	.550	.609	1	.000	-0		-5		-C
1937	Phi A	8	15	.348	35	26	6-1	0	169.2	208	108	15	1	52	54	4.99	95	.295	.344	47-1-7	.128	-1	73	-4		-C
1938	Phi A	9	14	.391	42	29	7-1	0	212.1	259	138	23	2	62	48	4.92	98	.299	.347	69-0-7	.130	-3	87	-2		-C
1939	Phi A	0	1	.000	2	2	0	0	4	8	8	2	0	4	0	15.75	30	.421	.450	3	.000	-0		-2		-C
	Was A	0	0	—	4	0	0	0	9	11	7	0	0	2	0	6.00	72	.306	.342	2	.000	-0		4		
	Det A	7	0	1.000	27	0	0	1	47.1	45	25	7	0	20	14	4.18	117	.254	.330	9-0-1	.111	-1		4		
	Year	7	1	.875	33	2	0	1	60.1	64	40	9	0	23	14	5.22	92	.276	.341	14-0-1	.071	-2	147	-3		
1940	Det A	0	1	.000	3	0	0	0	4	8	5	1	0	3	0	9.00	53	.421	.500		—	0		-2		
1941	Det A	1	3	.250	26	1	0	2	72.2	74	45	4	0	22	17	4.21	108	.260	.313	19-0-1	.105	-1	57	0		-C
Total	7	25	34	.424	143	58	13-2	3	526	625	344	53	4	166	135	4.96	96	.292	.345	150-1-16	.120	-7	83	-15		-C

THOMAS, MIKE Michael Steven B9.2.1969 Sacramento CA BL/TL/6-2/205 [NYN89 23/606] d7.12 Col Labette (KS) CC

| 1995 | Mil A | 0 | 0 | — | 1 | 0 | 0 | 0-0 | 1.1 | 2 | 0 | 0 | 0 | 1-0 | 0 | 0.00 | — | .333 | .429 | 0 | — | 0 | | 1 | 17 | |

THOMAS, MYLES Myles Lewis B10.22.1897 State College PA D12.12.1963 Toledo OH BR/TR/5-9.5/170 d4.18 Col Penn St.

1926	†NY A	6	6	.500	33	13	3	0	140.1	140	79	6	3	65	38	4.23	91	.271	.356	43-0-5	.116	-3	136	-6		
1927	NY A	7	4	.636	21	9	1	0	88.2	111	58	4	1	43	25	4.87	79	.322	.398	27-0-3	.333	2	130	-11		
1928	NY A	1	0	1.000	12	1	0	0	31.2	33	19	3	0	9	10	3.41	110	.277	.328	10	.400	1*	135	-1		
1929	NY A	0	2	.000	5	1	0	0	15	27	21	1	0	9	3	10.80	36	.409	.480	7	.143	-1	87	-12		
	Was A	7	8	.467	22	14	7	2	125.1	139	72	3	0	48	33	3.52	121	.288	.352	48-0-1	.292	2	99	4		
	Year	7	10	.412	27	15	7	2	140.1	166	93	4	0	57	36	4.30	98	.302	.368	55-0-1	.273	1	99	-7		
1930	Was A	2	2	.500	12	2	0	0	33.2	49	35	3	0	15	12	8.29	55	.358	.421	11	.182	-1*	56	-14		
Total	5	23	22	.511	105	40	11	2	434.2	499	284	20	4	189	121	4.64	87	.299	.372	146-0-9	.240	0	116	-40		

THOMAS, ROY Roy Justin B6.22.1953 Quantico VA BR/TR/6-6/200(190-215) [PhiN71 1/6] d9.21 [DL 1986 Sea A 182]

1977	Hou N	0	0	—	4	0	0	0-0	6.1	5	2	0	0	3-0	4	2.84	127	.208	.296	0	—	0		1		
1978	StL N	1	1	.500	16	1	0	3-0	28.1	21	14	0	0	16-3	16	3.81	94	.216	.316	4	.250	0	76	-1		
1979	StL N	3	4	.429	26	6	0	1-1	77	66	29	9	0	24-3	44	2.92	130	.237	.298	17-0-1	.059	-1	62	7		
1980	StL N	2	3	.400	24	5	0	0-1	55	59	32	3	3	25-5	22	4.75	79	.274	.352	13	.154	-0	124	-6		
1983	Sea A	3	1	.750	43	0	0	1-3	88.2	95	44	7	2	32-3	77	3.45	124	.275	.337	0	—	0	90	-7	22	
1984	Sea A	3	2	.600	21	0	0	1-0	49.2	52	33	8	4	37-1	42	5.26	76	.280	.399	0	—	0		9		
1985	Sea A	7	0	1.000	40	0	0	1-0	93.2	66	37	8	2	48-12	70	3.36	126	.202	.303	0	—	0		0		
1987	Sea A	1	0	1.000	8	0	0	0-0	20.2	23	12	2	1	11-0	14	5.23	91	.299	.380	0	—	0	84	8	204	
Total	8	20	11	.645	182	13	0	7-5	419.1	387	203	33	12	196-27	289	3.82	106	.250	.334	34-0-1	.118	-0	84	8	204	

THOMAS, STAN Stanley Brown B7.11.1949 Rumford ME BR/TR/6-2/185* [TexA71 27/616] d7.5 Col New Haven

1974	Tex A	0	0	—	12	0	0	0-0	13.2	22	10	1	0	6-2	6	6.59	54	.379	.431	0	—	0		-4		
1975	Tex A	4	4	.500	46	1	0	3-0	81.1	72	36	2	3	34-6	46	3.10	122	.239	.322	0	—	0	23	5		
1976	Cle A	4	4	.500	37	7	2	6-2	105.2	88	33	5	4	41-4	54	2.30	153	.229	.309	0	—	0	136	13		
1977	Sea A	2	6	.250	13	9	1	0-1	58.1	74	49	8	3	25-0	14	6.02	69	.310	.378	0	—	0	82	-14	22	
	NY A	1	0	1.000	3	0	0	0-0	6.1	7	7	0	0	4-0	1	7.11	56	.280	.367	0	—	0		-3		
	Year	3	6	.333	16	9	1	0-1	64.2	81	56	8	3	29-0	15	6.12	67	.307	.377	0	—	0	82	-17		
Total	4	11	14	.440	111	17	3	9-3	265.1	263	135	16	10	110-12	123	3.70	101	.261	.338	0	—	0	101	-3	22	

THOMAS, TOM Thomas R. "Savage Tom" B12.27.1873 Shawnee OH D9.23.1942 Shawnee OH BR/TR/6-4/195 d9.20

1894	Cle N	0	0	—	1	0	0	1	0.1	0	1	0	0	2	0	27.00	34	.000	.667	0	—	0		-1		
1899	StL N	1	1	.500	4	2	2	0	25	22	14	1	0	4	8	2.52	158	.237	.268	12	.250	0	90	9		
1900	StL N	2	2	.500	5	1	1	0	26.1	38	22	2	1	4	7	3.76	97	.336	.364	11-0-1	.091	-1	171	-2		
Total	3	3	3	.500	10	3	3	1	51.2	60	37	3	1	10	15	3.31	115	.290	.326	23-0-1	.174	0	117	0		

THOMASON, ERSKINE Melvin Erskine B8.13.1948 Laurens SC BR/TR/6-1/190 d9.18 Col Erskine

| 1974 | Phi N | 0 | 0 | — | 1 | 0 | 0 | 0-0 | 1 | 0 | 0 | 0 | 0 | 0-0 | 1 | 0.00 | — | .000 | .000 | 0 | — | 0 | | 0 | | |

THOMPSON, ART Arthur J. d6.17

| 1884 | Was U | 0 | 1 | .000 | 1 | 1 | 1 | 0 | 8 | 10 | 11 | 0 | 0 | 3 | 8 | 6.75 | 36 | .286 | .342 | 3 | .000 | -1 | 18 | -4 | | |

THOMPSON, BRAD Bradley Joseph B1.31.1982 Las Vegas NV BR/TR/6-1/190 d5.8 Col Dixie (UT) JC

| 2005 | †StL N | 4 | 0 | 1.000 | 40 | 0 | 0 | 1-0 | 55 | 46 | 22 | 5 | 4 | 15-2 | 29 | 2.95 | 142 | .227 | .293 | 6-0-1 | .167 | -0* | | 7 | | |

THOMPSON, FORREST David Forrest B3.3.1918 Mooresville NC D2.26.1979 Charlotte NC BL/TL/5-11/195 d4.26

1948	Was A	6	10	.375	46	7	0	4	131.1	134	71	9	1	54	40	3.84	113	.262	.334	35	.286	2	74	4		
1949	Was A	1	3	.250	9	1	1	0	16.1	22	11	1	1	9	8	4.41	97	.328	.416	5	.600	2*	21	-1		
Total	2	7	13	.350	55	8	1	4	147.2	156	82	10	2	63	48	3.90	111	.270	.344	40	.325	4	68	3		

THOMPSON, DEREK Derek Ryan B1.8.1981 Tampa FL BL/TL/6-2/180 d5.28

| 2005 | LA N | 0 | 0 | — | 4 | 3 | 0 | 0 | 18 | 16 | 7 | 0 | 0 | 10-1 | 13 | 3.50 | 117 | .258 | .356 | 4-0-1 | .000 | -0 | 106 | 2 | | |

THOMPSON, JUNIOR Eugene Earl B6.7.1917 Latham IL BR/TR/6-1/185 d4.26 Def 1943

1939	†Cin N	13	5	.722	42	11	5-3	2	152.1	130	51	6	3	55	87	2.54	151	.236	.309	48-0-3	.229	0	70	22		
1940	†Cin N	16	9	.640	33	31	17-3	0	225.1	197	90	10	2	96	103	3.32	114	.233	.313	79-0-8	.228	3	107	13		
1941	Cin N	6	6	.500	27	15	4	1	109	117	65	6	3	57	46	4.87	74	.272	.361	30-0-7	.233	1	105	-14		
1942	Cin N	4	7	.364	29	10	1	0	101.2	86	61	5	2	53	35	3.36	98	.226	.324	30-0-1	.267	2	107	-7		
1946	NY N	4	6	.400	39	1	0	6	62.2	36	18	5	0	40	31	1.29	266	.190	.332	7-0-1	.143	0	50	12		
1947	NY N	4	2	.667	15	0	0	0	35.2	36	20	3	1	27	13	4.29	95	.279	.408	6	.000	-1		-1		
Total	6	47	35	.573	185	68	27-6	7	686.2	602	305	35	11	328	315	3.26	113	.239	.329	200-0-20	.225	6	100	25		

THOMPSON, FULLER Fuller Weidner B5.1.1889 Los Angeles CA D2.19.1972 Los Angeles CA BR/TR/5-11.5/164 d8.19 Col Wittenberg

| 1911 | Bos N | 0 | 0 | — | 3 | 0 | 0 | 0 | 4.2 | 5 | 4 | 0 | 2 | 0 | 3.86 | 99 | .294 | .368 | 0 | — | 0 | | 0 | | |

THOMPSON, HARRY Harold B9.9.1889 Nanticoke PA D2.14.1951 Reno NV BL/TL/5-8/150 d4.24

1919	Was A	0	3	.000	12	2	0	1	43.1	48	21	0	2	8	10	3.53	91	.293	.333	32-0-2	.250	1*	37	-1		
	Phi A	0	1	.000	3	0	0	0	12	16	9	4	0	3	1	6.75	51	.327	.365	6	.000	-1*		-3		
	Year	0	4	.000	15	2	0	1	55.1	64	30	4	2	11	11	4.23	77	.300	.341	38-0-2	.211	0	36	-5		

THOMPSON, LEE John Dudley "Lefty" B2.26.1898 Smithfield UT D2.17.1963 Santa Barbara CA BL/TL/6-1/185 d9.4 Col Occidental

| 1921 | Chi A | 0 | 3 | .000 | 4 | 4 | 0 | 0 | 20.2 | 32 | 14 | 0 | 0 | 6 | 4 | 8.27 | 51 | .333 | .373 | 7-0-1 | .286 | 0 | 89 | -9 | | |

YEAR	TM LG	W	L	PCT	G	GS	CG-SHO	SV-BS	IP	H	R	HR	HB	BB-IB	SO	ERA	AERA	OAV	OOB	AB-HR-SH	AVG	PB	SUP	APR	DL	PW
THOMPSON, GUS John Gustav B6.22.1877 Humboldt IA D3.28.1958 Kalispell MT 6-2/185 d8.31 Col Grinnell																										
1903	†Pit N	2	2	.500	5	4	3	0	43	52	30	1	1	16	22	3.56	91	.295	.358	16	.250	0	109	-3		-0.2
1906	StL N	2	11	.154	17	12	8	0	103	111	61	2	5	25	36	4.28	61	.285	.336	34	.176	-1	60	-18		-2.1
Total	2	4	13	.235	22	16	11	0	146	163	91	3	6	41	58	4.07	69	.288	.343	50	.200	-0	74	-21		-2.3
THOMPSON, JOCKO John Samuel B1.17.1917 Beverly MA D2.3.1988 Olney MD BL/TL/6-0/185* d9.21 Col Northeastern																										
1948	Phi N	1	0	1.000	2	1	1	0	13	10	4	0	0	9	7	2.77	142	.233	.365	3	.000	0	135	2		0.2
1949	Phi N	1	3	.250	8	5	1	0	31.1	38	24	6	0	11	12	6.89	57	.314	.371	11	.182	-0*	67	-9		-1.0
1950	Phi N	0	0	—	2	0	0	0	4	1	1	0	0	4	2	0.00	—	.077	.294	0	—	-0		1		0.1
1951	Phi N	4	8	.333	29	14	3-2	1	119.1	102	55	12	2	59	60	3.85	100	.231	.325	39-0-1	.103	-1*	102	1		-0.1
Total	4	6	11	.353	41	21	5-2	1	167.2	151	84	18	2	83	81	4.24	91	.244	.336	53-0-1	.113	-1	96	-5		-0.8
THOMPSON, JUSTIN Justin Willard B3.8.1973 San Antonio TX BL/TL/6-4/215(175-215) [DetA91 1/32] d5.27 [DL 2000 Tex A 181, 2001 Tex A 190]																										
1996	Det A	1	6	.143	11	11	0	0-0	59	62	35	7	2	31-2	44	4.58	111	.267	.356	0		0	58	2	75	0.3
1997	Det A★	15	11	.577	32	32	4	0-0	223.1	188	82	20	2	66-1	151	3.02	153	.233	.289	2	.000	-0	90	39	15	4.1
1998	Det A	11	15	.423	34	34	5	0-0	222	227	114	20	2	79-4	149	4.05	117	.267	.329	7	.143	-0	97	15		1.5
1999	Det A	9	11	.450	24	24	0	0-0	142.2	152	85	24	4	59-1	83	5.11	98	.274	.344	5	.000	-1	81	-1	49	-0.2
2005	Tex A	0	0	—	2	0	0	0-0	1.2	4	4	2	0	0-0	1	21.60	21	.444	.444	0	—	0		-3		-0.1
Total	5	36	43	.456	103	101	9	0-0	648.2	633	320	73	10	235-8	428	4.02	119	.258	.322	14	.071	-1	87	52	510	5.6
THOMPSON, MARK Mark Radford B4.7.1971 Russellville KY BR/TR/6-2/205* [ColN92 2/65] d7.26 Col Kentucky																										
1994	Col N	1	1	.500	2	2	0	0-0	9	16	9	2	1	8-0	5	9.00	55	.400	.510	4-0-1	.000	0	91	-3		-0.6
1995	†Col N	2	3	.400	21	5	0	0-0	51	73	42	7	1	22-2	30	6.53	82	.349	.407	13-0-1	.385	1	94	-6		-0.4
1996	Col N	9	11	.450	34	28	3-1	0-1	169.2	189	109	25	13	74-1	99	5.30	98	.285	.367	58-0-5	.138	-2	99	-1		-0.4
1997	Col N	3	3	.500	6	6	0	0-0	29.2	40	27	8	4	13-0	9	7.89	65	.323	.399	11-1-2	.182	1	116	-7	144	-1.1
1998	Col N	1	2	.333	6	6	0	0-0	23.1	36	22	8	5	12-0	14	7.71	67	.379	.465	1	.143	-0	77	-6	144	-0.6
1999	StL N	1	3	.250	5	5	0	0-0	29.1	26	12	1	2	17-1	22	2.76	167	.241	.354	8-0-1	.000	-0	76	5		0.5
2000	StL N	1	1	.500	20	0	0	0-1	25	24	21	4	3	15-0	19	5.04	92	.250	.365	3	.000	-0		-4	66	-0.3
Total	7	18	24	.429	94	52	3-1	0-2	337	404	242	55	29	161-4	198	5.74	90	.303	.386	104-1-10	.154	-3	96	-22	354	-2.9
THOMPSON, MIKE Michael Wayne B9.6.1949 Denver CO BR/TR/6-3/190* [TexA67 3/45] d5.19																										
1971	Was A	1	6	.143	16	12	0	0-0	66.2	53	39	3	3	54-2	41	4.86	70	.222	.370	17	.118	0	84	-10		-1.0
1973	StL N	0	0	—	2	2	0	0-0	4	1	0	0	0	5-0	3	0.00	—	.077	.333	1	.000	-0	60	2		0.1
1974	StL N	0	3	.000	19	4	0	0-0	38.1	37	24	1	2	35-4	25	5.63	64	.274	.430	8	.000	-1	103	-7		-0.6
	Atl N	0	0	—	1	1	0	0-0	4	7	2	0	0	2-0	2	4.50	84	.412	.474	1	1.000	0	115	-0		0.0
	Year	0	3	.000	20	5	0	0-0	42.1	44	26	1	2	37-4	27	5.53	66	.289	.435	9	.111	-1	106	-7		-0.6
1975	Atl N	0	6	.000	16	10	0	0-0	51.2	60	32	2	0	37-0	18	4.70	80	.305	.397	14-0-2	.071	-1	81	-5	25	-0.6
Total	4	1	15	.063	54	29	0	0-0	164.2	158	97	6	5	128-6	113	4.86	74	.263	.394	41-0-2	.098	-2	85	-20	25	-2.1
THOMPSON, RICH Richard Neil B11.1.1958 New York NY BR/TR/6-3/225* [CleA80 8/192] d4.28 Col Amherst																										
1985	Cle A	3	8	.273	57	1	0	5-6	80	95	63	8	6	48-6	30	6.30	66	.303	.398	0	—	0		-19		-2.6
1989	Mon N	0	2	.000	19	1	0	0-0	33	27	11	2	2	11-2	15	2.18	164	.241	.315	2	.000	0	50	4		0.2
1990	Mon N	0	0	—	1	0	0	0-0	1	1	0	0	0	0-0	0	0.00	—	.250	.250	0	—	0		0		0.0
Total	3	3	10	.231	77	1	0	5-6	114	123	74	10	8	59-8	45	5.05	79	.286	.376	2	.000	0	50	-15		-2.4
THOMPSON, TOMMY Thomas Carl B11.7.1889 Spring City TN D1.16.1963 LaJolla CA BR/TR/5-9.5/170 d6.5 b-Homer Col Georgia																										
1912	NY A	2	2	.000	7	2	1	0	32.2	43	32	0	3	13	15	6.06	59	.341	.415	10-0-1	.300	1*	82	-9		-0.4
THOMPSON, WILL Will McLain B8.30.1870 Pittsburgh PA D6.9.1962 Pittsburgh PA BR/TR/5-11.5/190 d7.9 Col Penn																										
1892	Pit N	0	1	.000	1	1	0	0	3	5	3	0	1	5	0	3.00	110	.250	.500	0	—	0	96	-9		-0.1
THOMSON, JOHN John Carl B10.1.1973 Vicksburg MS BR/TR/6-3/187(175-220) [ColN93 7/212] d5.11 Col Blinn (TX) JC [DL 2000 Col N 181]																										
1997	Col N	7	9	.438	27	27	2-1	0-0	166.1	193	94	15	5	51-0	106	4.71	110	.296	.350	47-0-6	.213	-0	83	7		0.6
1998	Col N	8	11	.421	26	26	2	0-0	161	174	86	21	2	49-0	106	4.81	108	.282	.335	50-0-9	.120	-3	84	8	40	0.5
1999	Col N	1	10	.091	14	13	1	0-0	62.2	85	62	11	1	36-1	34	8.04	72	.324	.405	18	.167	-0	71	-13		-1.8
2001	Col N	4	5	.444	14	14	1-1	0-0	93.2	84	46	15	4	25-3	68	4.04	132	.239	.295	29-0-6	.241	0	98	11	80	1.0
2002	Col N	7	8	.467	21	21	0	0-0	127.1	136	77	21	2	27-6	76	4.88	97	.268	.304	34-0-3	.176	-0	99	-3		-0.2
	NY N	2	6	.250	9	9	0	0-0	54.1	65	39	7	0	17-3	31	4.31	92	.290	.336	18-0-3	.278	1	101	-7		-0.7
	Year	9	14	.391	30	30	0	0-0	181.2	201	116	28	2	44-9	107	4.71	96	.275	.314	52-0-6	.212	1	100	-9		-0.9
2003	Tex A	13	14	.481	35	35	3-1	0-0	217	234	125	27	4	49-2	136	4.85	102	.276	.316	1	.000	-0	97	3		0.4
2004	†Atl N	14	8	.636	33	33	0	0-0	198.1	210	93	20	6	52-5	133	3.72	116	.276	.326	66-0-10	.197	1	116	12		1.2
2005	†Atl N	4	6	.400	17	17	1	0-0	98.1	111	52	6	2	28-2	61	4.47	96	.284	.332	25-0-9	.200	1	92	-2	88	0.0
Total	8	60	77	.438	196	195	10-3	0-0	1179.1	1292	674	143	26	334-22	751	4.69	104	.280	.330	288-0-46	.191	0	94	16	389	1.0
HORMAHLEN, HANK Herbert Ehler "Lefty" B7.5.1896 Jersey City NJ D2.6.1955 Los Angeles CA BL/TL/6-0/180 d9.29																										
1917	NY A	0	1	.000	1	1	0	0	8	9	3	0	1	4	5	2.25	119	.281	.378	2	.000	-0	27	0		0.0
1918	NY A	7	3	.700	16	12	5-2	0	112.2	85	39	1	6	52	22	2.48	114	.217	.318	39-0-4	.077	-3	118	4		0.0
1919	NY A	12	8	.600	30	25	13-2	1	188.2	155	69	10	4	61	62	2.62	122	.228	.295	59-0-3	.186	-0	103	12		1.0
1920	NY A	9	6	.600	29	15	6	1	143.1	178	86	5	2	43	35	4.14	92	.312	.362	45-0-5	.222	1	116	-7		-0.5
1921	Bos A	1	7	.125	23	9	3	0	96.1	101	56	3	6	34	17	4.48	94	.277	.349	23-0-1	.174	-1	57	-3		-0.3
1925	Bro N	0	3	.000	5	2	0	0	16	22	14	0	2	9	7	3.94	106	.333	.429	5	.200	0	61	-2		-0.2
Total	6	29	28	.509	104	64	27-4	2	565	550	267	19	21	203	148	3.33	105	.261	.332	173-0-13	.168	-3	98	4		0.1
HORMODSGARD, PAUL Paul Gayton B11.10.1953 San Francisco CA BR/TR/6-2/190* d4.10																										
1977	Min A	11	15	.423	37	37	8-1	0-0	218	236	122	25	3	65-1	94	4.62	86	.280	.331	0	—	0	112	-15		-1.6
1978	Min A	1	6	.143	12	12	1	0-0	66	81	40	7	1	17-0	23	5.05	76	.308	.347	0	—	0	72	-8		-0.8
1979	Min A	0	0	—	1	0	0	0-0	1	3	1	1	0	0-0	1	9.00	49	.500	.500	0	—	0		0		0.0
Total	3	12	21	.364	50	49	9-1	0-0	285	320	163	33	4	82-1	118	4.74	84	.288	.336	0	—	0	102	-23		-2.4
HORNTON, JOHN John B1870 Washington DC BL/TR/5-10.5/175 d8.14																										
1889	Was N	0	1	.000	1	1	1	0	9	8	11	0	0	7	3	5.00	79	.229	.357	4	.000	-1	153	-2		-0.2
1891	Phi N	15	16	.484	37	32	23-1	2	269	268	161	3	10	115	52	3.68	93	.250	.328	123	.138	-7*	91	-6		-1.2
1892	Phi N	0	2	.000	3	2	1	0	12	16	19	1	0	17	2	12.75	28	.308	.478	13	.385	1*	127	-10		-1.1
Total	3	15	19	.441	41	35	25-1	2	290	292	191	4	10	139	57	4.10	83	.252	.337	140	.157	-7	95	-18		-2.5
HORNTON, MATT Matthew J. B9.15.1976 Three Rivers MI BL/TL/6-6/220* [SeaA98 1/22] d6.27 Col Grand Valley St. [DL 2003 Sea A 45]																										
2004	Sea A	1	2	.333	19	1	0	0-0	32.2	30	15	2	0	25-1	30	4.13	108	.250	.377	0	—	0	42	2		0.1
2005	Sea A	0	4	.000	55	0	0	0-1	57	54	33	13	0	42-2	57	5.21	81	.248	.368	0	—	0		-6		-0.4
Total	2	1	6	.143	74	1	0	0-1	89.2	84	48	15	0	67-3	87	4.82	89	.249	.371	0	—	0	42	-4	45	-0.3
HORNTON, WALTER Walter Miller B2.18.1875 Lewiston ME D7.14.1960 Los Angeles CA BL/TL/6-1/180 d7.1 Col Cornell ▲																										
1895	Chi N	2	0	1.000	7	2	1	1	40	58	50	3	5	31	13	6.07	84	.333	.448	22-1-0	.318	2*	196	-8		-0.2
1896	Chi N	2	1	.667	5	5	2	0	23.2	30	26	1	0	13	10	5.70	80	.306	.387	22	.364	2*	144	-5		-0.4
1897	Chi N	6	7	.462	16	16	15	0	130.1	164	91	4	6	51	55	4.70	95	.305	.371	265-0-4	.321	4*	107	0		0.4
1898	Chi N	13	10	.565	28	25	21-2	0	215.1	226	116	4	18	56	56	3.34	107	.268	.327	210-0-3	.295	6*	104	10		1.4
Total	4	23	18	.561	56	48	40-2	1	409.1	478	283	12	29	151	134	4.18	97	.289	.359	519-1-7	.312	13	114	-3		1.2
HORPE, BOB Robert Joseph B1.12.1935 San Diego CA D3.17.1960 San Diego CA BR/TR/6-1/170 d4.17																										
1955	Chi N	0	0	—	2	0	0	0-0	3	1	1	1	0	1	0	3.00	136	.333	.333	0	—	0		0		0.0
HROOP, GEORGE George Lynford B11.24.1950 Pasadena CA BR/TR/6-7/205* [KCA72 16/378] d9.7 Col Cal St.-Long Beach																										
1975	KC A	0	0	—	4	0	0	2-0	9	8	5	1	2	4-0	8	4.00	97	.250	.286	0	—	0		0		0.0
1977	KC A	0	0	—	4	0	0	1-0	5.1	5	2	1	0	4-0	3	3.38	120	.059	.238	0	—	0		1		0.1
1978	KC A	1	0	1.000	4	0	0	0-0	2	1	0	0	1	0-0	2	0.00	—	.222	.417	0	—	0		0		0.3
1979	KC A	0	0	—	4	0	0	0-0	2.2	7	4	0	0	5-2	1	13.50	32	.467	.600	0	—	0		-2		-0.1
	Hou N	1	0	1.000	14	0	0	0-0	22.1	23	10	4	1	11-0	15	3.22	109	.271	.357	3	.000	-0		1		0.0
Total	4	2	0	1.000	30	0	0	3-0	42.1	41	21	6	4	25-2	27	3.83	97	.259	.360	3	.000	-0		0		0.2

YEAR	TM LG	W	L	PCT	G	GS	CG-SHO	SV-BS	IP	H	R	HR	HB	BB-IB	SO	ERA	AERA	OAV	OOB	AB-HR-SH	AVG	PB	SUP	APR	DL	PW
THUMAN, LOU	Louis Charles Frank B12.13.1916 Baltimore MD D12.19.2000 Baltimore MD BR/TR/6-2/185 d9.8 Mil 1941-45																									
1939	Was A	0	0	—	3	0	0	0	4	5	6	0	0	2	1	9.00	48	.278	.350	0	—	0		-3		-0.1
1940	Was A	0	1	.000	2	0	0	0	5	10	11	0	0	7	0	14.40	29	.400	.531	2	.000	-0		-7		-0.9
Total	2	0	1	.000	5	0	0	0	9	15	17	0	0	9	1	12.00	35	.349	.462	2		0		-10		-1.0
THURMAN, COREY	Corey Lamar B11.5.1978 Augusta GA BR/TR/6-1/215* [KCA96 4/109] d4.5																									
2002	Tor A	2	3	.400	43	1	0	0-2	68	65	34	11	2	45-2	56	4.37	106	.248	.362	1-0-1	.000	-0	60	3		0.1
2003	Tor A	1	1	.500	6	3	0	0-0	15.1	21	11	3	0	9-1	11	6.46	74	.313	.395	0	—	0	97	-1		-0.3
Total	3	4	.429	49	4	0	0-2	83.1	86	45	14	2	54-3	67	4.75	98	.261	.369	1-0-1	.000	-0	90	1		-0.2
THURMAN, MIKE	Michael Richard B7.22.1973 Corvallis OR BR/TR/6-5/210* [MonN94 S1/31] d9.2 Col Oregon St.																									
1997	Mon N	1	0	1.000	5	2	0	0-0	11.2	9	7	3	0	3-1	8	5.40	77	.186	.271	2-0-1	.500	0	154	-2		-0.1
1998	Mon N	4	5	.444	14	13	0	0-0	67	60	38	7	3	26-2	32	4.70	89	.238	.312	23-0-2	.000	-2	119	-3		-0.6
1999	Mon N	7	11	.389	29	27	0	0-0	146.2	140	84	17	7	52-4	85	4.05	110	.251	.321	40-0-4	.025	-3	78	3		-0.1
2000	Mon N	4	9	.308	17	17	0	0-0	88.1	112	69	9	3	46-4	52	6.42	73	.315	.393	24-0-6	.042	-2	79	-16	94	-2.1
2001	Mon N	9	11	.450	28	26	0	0-0	147	172	90	21	6	50-7	96	5.33	81	.294	.351	42-0-3	.024	-3	102	-14	33	-0.2
2002	NY A	1	0	1.000	12	2	0	0-1	33	45	21	2	1	12-1	23	5.18	84	.328	.387	0	—	0	246	-3		-0.2
Total	6	26	36	.419	105	87	0	0-1	493.2	537	311	59	21	190-18	296	5.05	87	.278	.346	131-0-16	.031	-10	97	-35	127	-5.1
THURMOND, MARK	Mark Anthony B9.12.1956 Houston TX BL/TL/6-0/193(180-195) [SDN79 5/118] d5.14 Col Texas A&M-Commerce																									
1983	SD N	7	3	.700	21	18	2	0-0	115.1	104	40	7	2	33-2	49	2.65	132	.248	.304	37-0-6	.054	-2	113	10		0.7
1984	†SD N	14	8	.636	32	29	1-1	0-0	178.2	174	70	12	0	55-3	57	2.97	121	.256	.310	58-0-7	.190	1	104	11		1.5
1985	SD N	7	11	.389	36	23	1-1	2-1	138.1	154	70	9	3	44-5	57	3.97	90	.291	.347	34-0-9	.088	-2	89	-7		-1.0
1986	SD N	3	7	.300	17	15	2-1	0-0	70.2	96	58	7	0	27-5	32	6.50	56	.325	.380	24-0-2	.250	1*	93	-23		-2.6
	Det A	4	1	.800	25	4	0	3-1	51.2	44	13	7	0	17-2	17	1.92	217	.234	.296	0	—	0	93	13		1.2
1987	†Det A	0	1	1.000	48	0	0	5-2	61.2	83	32	5	0	24-4	21	4.23	101	.331	.384	0	—	0	1			-0.7
1988	Bal A	1	8	.111	43	6	0	3-0	74.2	80	43	10	2	27-3	29	4.58	86	.277	.339	0	—	0	58	-6		-0.1
1989	Bal A	2	4	.333	49	2	0	4-0	90	102	43	6	1	17-2	34	3.90	98	.288	.322	0	—	0	47	-1		-0.1
1990	SF N	2	3	.400	43	0	0	4-3	56.2	53	26	6	0	18-3	24	3.34	110	.257	.309	5	.000	-1	1			0.1
Total	8	40	46	.465	314	97	6-3	21-7	837.2	890	395	69	8	262-29	320	3.69	101	.277	.330	158-0-24	.139	-1	94	-1		-0.9
THURSTON, SLOPPY	Hollis John B6.2.1899 Fremont NE D9.14.1973 Los Angeles CA BR/TR/5-11/165 d4.19																									
1923	StL A	0	0	—	2	1	0	0	4	8	4	0	2	2	0	6.75	62	.421	.476	0	—	0	139	-1		-0.1
	Chi A	7	8	.467	44	12	8	4	191.2	223	70	11	1	36	55	3.05	130	.308	.341	79-0-1	.316	6*	85	22		2.2
	Year	7	8	.467	46	13	8	4	195.2	231	74	11	1	38	55	3.13	127	.310	.345	79-0-1	.316	6	90	22		2.1
1924	Chi A	20	14	.588	38	36	28-1	1	291	330	150	17	6	60	37	3.80	108	.290	.329	122-1-5	.254	4*	117	9		-3.3
1925	Chi A	10	14	.417	36	25	9	1	183	250	140	14	5	47	35	5.95	70	.335	.378	84-0-3	.286	7*	125	-38		-3.3
1926	Chi A	6	8	.429	31	13	6-1	3	134.1	164	85	10	1	36	35	5.02	77	.311	.356	61-0-1	.311	6*	99	-17		-1.2
1927	Was A	13	13	.500	29	28	13-2	0	205.1	254	118	16	2	60	38	4.47	91	.308	.356	92-2-4	.315	9*	98	-3		-0.1
1930	Bro N	6	4	.600	24	11	5-2	1	106	110	46	4	0	17	26	3.40	145	.266	.295	50-1-4	.200	-0*	74	19		1.6
1931	Bro N	9	9	.500	24	17	11	0	143	175	72	3	1	39	23	3.97	96	.301	.346	60-1-2	.217	2	138	-2		0.0
1932	Bro N	12	8	.600	28	19	10-2	0	153	174	81	14	1	38	35	4.06	94	.287	.330	56-0-2	.304	5*	134	-5		-1.6
1933	Bro N	6	8	.429	32	15	5	13	131.1	171	63	4	6	34	22	4.52	71	.319	.366	44-0-1	.159	-1	100	-16		-1.0
Total	9	89	86	.509	288	177	95-8	23	1542.2	1859	836	93	23	369	306	4.24	94	.304	.346	648-5-23	.270	38	111	-37		-4.0
TIANT, LUIS	Luis Clemente (Vega) B11.23.1940 Marianao, Cuba BR/TR/5-11/190(180-205) d7.19																									
1964	Cle A	10	4	.714	19	16	9-3	1	127	94	41	13	2	47-2	105	2.83	127	.207	.283	45-1-3	.111	-1	116	13		1.2
1965	Cle A	11	11	.500	41	30	10-2	5	196.1	166	88	30	5	66-3	152	3.53	99	.228	.293	68-1-4	.088	-2	115	-1		-0.3
1966	Cle A	12	11	.522	46	16	7-5	8	155	121	50	16	2	50-4	145	2.79	123	.213	.279	36-0-8	.111	-1	88	13		1.8
1967	Cle A	12	9	.571	33	29	9-1	2	213.2	177	76	24	1	67-2	219	2.74	119	.221	.282	71-1-3	.254	5	109	12		1.1
1968	Cle A★	21	9	.700	34	32	19-9	0-0	258.1	152	53	16	4	73-4	264	1.60	185	.168	.233	87-0-11	.080	-5	96	40		4.4
1969	Cle A	9	20	.310	38	37	9-1	0-0	249.2	229	123	37	8	129-11	156	3.71	102	.246	.340	81-2-4	.235	5	86	0		0.6
1970	†Min A	7	3	.700	18	17	2-1	0-0	92.2	84	36	12	4	41-0	50	3.40	109	.246	.328	32-0-3	.406	6	132	5	63	1.2
1971	Bos A	1	7	.125	21	10	1	0-0	72.1	73	42	8	1	32-1	59	4.85	77	.259	.333	19	.158	-0	87	-8		-1.0
1972	Bos A	15	6	.714	43	19	12-6	3-4	179	128	45	7	0	65-5	123	1.91	170	.202	.275	56-0-3	.107	-2	114	25		2.9
1973	Bos A	20	13	.606	35	35	23	0-0	272	217	105	32	7	78-3	206	3.34	121	.219	.278	0	—	0	89	23		2.6
1974	Bos A★	22	13	.629	38	38	25-7	0-0	311.1	281	106	21	4	82-3	176	2.92	132	.241	.291	0	—	0	95	32		2.6
1975	†Bos A	18	14	.563	35	35	18-2	0-0	260	262	126	25	4	72-0	142	4.02	101	.264	.315	1	.000	-0	104	3		0.0
1976	Bos A★	21	12	.636	38	38	19-3	0-0	279	274	107	25	3	64-2	131	3.06	127	.260	.303	1	.000	0	117	1		0.0
1977	Bos A	12	8	.600	32	32	3-3	0-0	188.2	210	98	26	2	51-3	124	4.53	99	.279	.325	0	—	0	105	21	13	1.9
1978	Bos A	13	8	.619	32	31	12-5	0-0	212.1	185	80	26	5	57-4	104	3.91	105	.251	.299	0	—	0	117	4		0.0
1979	NY A	13	8	.619	30	30	5-1	0-0	195.2	190	94	22	1	53-1	104	4.89	81	.265	.326	0	—	0	108	-12	22	-1.3
1980	NY A	8	9	.471	25	25	3	0-0	136.1	139	79	10	1	50-3	84	3.92	93	.243	.303	16-0-2	.188	0	84	-3		-0.6
1981	Pit N	2	5	.286	9	9	1	0-0	57.1	54	31	9	0	19-2	32	3.92	93	.243	.303	0	—	0	120	-5		-0.6
1982	Cal A	2	2	.500	6	5	0	0-0	29.2	39	20	3	0	8-0	30	5.76	71	.310	.351	0	—	0	105	-2		-0.5
Total	19	229	172	.571	573	484	187-49	15-4	3486.1	3075	1400	346	49	1104-53	2416	3.30	114	.236	.297	513-5-41	.164	5	105	187	98	21.8
TIBBS, JAY	Jay Lindsey B1.4.1962 Birmingham AL BR/TR/6-3/183* [NYN80 2/27] d7.15																									
1984	Cin N	6	2	.750	14	14	3-1	0-0	100.2	87	34	4	0	33-1	40	2.86	133	.238	.302	36-0-1	.139	-1	105	10		0.4
1985	Cin N	10	16	.385	35	34	5-2	0-0	218	216	111	14	0	83-10	98	3.92	97	.262	.326	65-0-6	.092	-3*	96	-5		-0.5
1986	Mon N	7	9	.438	35	31	3-2	0-0	190.1	181	96	12	3	70-3	117	3.97	94	.256	.324	54-0-4	.130	-0*	86	-6		-0.5
1987	Mon N	4	5	.444	19	12	0	0-0	83	95	55	10	0	34-2	54	4.99	85	.289	.354	25	.120	0	104	-8		-1.1
1988	Bal A	4	15	.211	30	24	1	0-0	158.1	184	103	18	3	63-2	82	5.39	73	.293	.356	0	—	0	82	-25		-2.6
1989	Bal A	5	0	1.000	10	8	1	0-0	54.1	62	17	2	0	20-0	30	2.82	136	.287	.345	0	—	0	160	7	91	0.4
1990	Bal A	2	7	.222	10	10	0	0-0	50.2	55	34	8	0	14-1	23	5.68	67	.279	.324	0	—	0	74	-11		-1.1
	Pit N	1	0	1.000	5	0	0	0-0	7	7	2	0	0	2-0	1	2.57	142	.269	.310	0	—	0	1			0.1
Total	7	39	54	.419	158	133	13-5	0-0	862.2	887	452	68	6	319-19	448	4.20	92	.269	.333	180-0-11	.117	-4	95	-37	91	-5.0
TIDROW, DICK	Richard William B5.14.1947 San Francisco CA BR/TR/6-4/213* [CleA67*S4/76] d4.18 Col Chabot (CA) JC																									
1972	Cle A	14	15	.483	39	34	10-3	0-0	237.1	200	83	21	6	70-13	123	2.77	118	.230	.289	70-0-13	.100	-3	81	12		0.1
1973	Cle A	14	16	.467	42	40	13-2	0-0	274.2	289	150	31	8	95-10	138	4.42	89	.270	.332	0	—	0	95	-14		-1.1
1974	Cle A	1	3	.250	4	4	0	0-0	19	21	17	4	2	13-1	8	7.11	51	.276	.387	0	—	0	85	-7		-1.1
	NY A	11	9	.550	33	25	5	1-0	190.2	205	99	14	4	53-7	100	3.87	92	.279	.327	0	—	0	117	-9		-0.6
	Year	12	12	.500	37	29	5	1-0	209.2	226	116	18	6	66-8	108	4.16	85	.279	.333	0	—	0	113	-20		-2.1
1975	NY A	6	3	.667	37	0	0	5-4	69.1	65	27	5	3	31-6	38	3.12	119	.256	.341	0	—	0	219	9	53	1.1
1976	†NY A	4	5	.444	47	2	0	10-3	92.1	80	29	5	1	24-1	65	2.63	130	.233	.282	0	—	0	162	15		1.3
1977	†NY A	11	4	.733	49	7	0	5-2	151	143	57	20	2	41-11	83	3.16	128	.252	.300	0	—	0	99	-3		-0.2
1978	†NY A	7	11	.389	31	25	4	0-0	185.1	191	87	19	6	53-3	73	3.84	95	.267	.320	0	—	0	115	-3		-0.2
1979	NY A	2	1	.667	14	0	0	2-1	22.2	38	20	5	0	4-0	7	7.94	52	.380	.409	0	—	0	-9			-1.1
	Chi N	11	5	.688	63	0	0	4-1	102.2	86	35	5	2	42-11	68	2.72	153	.231	.310	10-0-2	.200	-0	15			2.2
1980	Chi N	6	5	.545	84	0	0	6-6	116	97	44	9	0	53-16	97	2.79	142	.229	.319	4	.000	-0	13			1.5
1981	Chi N	3	10	.231	51	0	0	9-4	74.2	73	49	9	3	30-15	39	5.06	74	.256	.328	5-0-1	.000	-1	-9			-1.2
1982	Chi N	8	3	.727	65	0	0	6-1	103.2	106	45	6	3	29-10	66	3.39	112	.265	.318	6	.000	-1	4			0.1
1983	†Chi N	2	4	.333	50	1	0	7-2	91.2	86	50	13	1	34-8	66	4.22	100	.242	.308	0	—	0	108	-1		-0.5
1984	NY N	0	2	—	10	0	0	0-0	15.2	25	15	5	0	7-2	9	9.19	38	.347	.410	0	—	0	-10			-0.8
Total	13	100	94	.515	620	138	32-5	55-24	1746.2	1705	807	163	43	579-112	975	3.68	102	.257	.318	95-0-16	.095	-5	99	11	53	0.2
TIEFENAUER, BOBBY	Bobby Gene B10.10.1929 Desloge MO D6.13.2000 Desloge MO BR/TR/6-2/185* d7.14 C1 [DL 1959 Cle A 172]																									
1952	StL N	0	0	—	6	0	0		8	12	8	1	0	7	3	7.88	47	.343	.452	1	.000	-0		-4		-0.5
1955	StL N	1	4	.200	18	0	0	1	32.2	31	19	6	4	10-4	16	4.41	92	.261	.331	5-0-1	.000	-0		-2		-0.5
1960	Cle A	0	0	.000	3	0	0	0	9	8	2	0	0	3-0	2	2.00	187	.242	.306	1	.000	0		1		0.1
1961	StL N	0	0	—	9	0	0	0	13	17	9	2	0	3-0	6	6.23	71	.450	.542	0	—	0		-3		-0.4
1962	Hou N	0	2	.000	43	0	0	1	85	91	42	6	2	21-2	60	4.34	86	.277	.320	9	.111	0		0		0.2
1963	Mil N	1	1	.500	12	0	0	2	29.2	20	4	1	0	4-0	22	1.21	265	.194	.222	5-0-1	.000	0		7		0.7
1964	Mil N	4	6	.400	46	0	0	13	73	61	33	6	3	15-2	48	3.21	110	.225	.300	0	—	0		-3		-0.5
1965	Mil N	0	1	.000	6	0	0	0	7	8	7	1	1	3-1	5	7.71	46	.286	.364	0	—	0				

YEAR	TM LG	W	L	PCT	G	GS	CG-SHO	SV-BS	IP	H	R	HR	HB	BB-IB	SO	ERA	AERA	OAV	OOB	AB-HR-SH	AVG	PB	SUP	APR	DL	PW
	NY A	1	1	.500	10	0	0	2	20.1	19	10	3	1	5-1	15	3.54	96	.253	.301	2	.000	0		-1		-0.1
	Cle A	0	5	.000	15	0	0	4	22.1	24	17	3	1	10-3	13	4.84	72	.273	.354	1	.000	-0		-5		-1.0
	Year	1	6	.143	25	0	0	6	42.2	43	27	6	2	15-4	28	4.22	82	.264	.330	3	.000	-0		-5		-1.1
1967	Cle A	0	1	.000	5	0	0	0	11.1	9	3	0	0	3-1	6	0.79	411	.225	.279	0	—	0		2		0.2
1968	Chi N	0	1	.000	9	0	0	1	13.1	20	12	2	0	2-1	9	6.08	52	.351	.367	1	.000	-0		-5		-0.5
Total	10	9	25	.265	179	0	0	23	316	312	161	29	12	87-15	204	3.84	94	.260	.314	39-0-3	.026	-1		-12	172	-1.9

TIEFENTHALER, VERLE Verle Matthew B7.11.1937 Breda IA BL/TR/6-1/190 d8.19

| 1962 | Chi A | 0 | 0 | — | 3 | 0 | 0 | 0 | 3.2 | 6 | 4 | 1 | 0 | 7-0 | 1 | 9.82 | 40 | .353 | .542 | 0 | | 0 | | -2 | | -0.1 |

TIERNAN, MIKE Michael Joseph "Silent Mike" B1.21.1867 Trenton NJ D11.7.1918 New York NY BL/TL/5-11/165 d4.30 ▲

| 1887 | NY N | 1 | 2 | .333 | 5 | 0 | 0 | 1 | 19.2 | 33 | 25 | 2 | 1 | 7 | 3 | 8.69 | 43 | .398 | .451 | 407-10 | .287 | 2* | | -10 | | -1.1 |

TIETJE, LES Leslie William "Toots" B9.11.1911 Sumner IA D10.2.1996 Rochester MN BR/TR/6-0.5/178 d9.18

1933	Chi A	2	0	1.000	3	3	1	0	22.1	16	8	1	0	15	9	2.42	175	.203	.330	8-0-1	.125	0	100	4		0.4
1934	Chi A	5	14	.263	34	22	6-1	0	176	174	106	20	2	96	81	4.81	98	.257	.351	59-0-3	.017	-7	65	0		-0.6
1935	Chi A	9	15	.375	30	21	9-1	0	169.2	184	88	14	2	81	64	4.30	108	.277	.357	61-0-3	.197	-1	75	7		0.7
1936	Chi A	0	0	—	2	0	0	0	2.1	6	7	0	0	5	3	27.00	19	.462	.611	0	—	0		-5		-0.2
	StL A	3	5	.375	14	7	2	0	50.1	65	44	2	2	30	16	6.62	81	.310	.401	15-0-1	.067	-1*	87	-7		-1.0
	Year	3	5	.375	16	7	2	0	52.2	71	51	2	2	35	19	7.52	71	.318	.415	15-0-1	.067	-1*	87	-12		-1.2
1937	StL A	1	2	.333	5	4	2	0	30	32	15	0	0	17	5	4.20	115	.283	.377	10-0-1	.000	-2	50	2		0.0
1938	StL A	2	5	.286	17	8	2-1	0	62	83	55	8	0	38	15	7.55	66	.327	.414	18-0-3	.111	-1*	95	-16		-1.5
Total	6	22	41	.349	105	65	22-3	0	512.2	560	323	45	6	282	193	5.11	93	.279	.369	171-0-12	.099	-12	75	-15		-2.2

TIFT, RAY Raymond Frank B6.21.1884 Fitchburg MA D3.29.1945 Verona NJ TL/5-10.5/155 d8.7 Col Brown

| 1907 | NY A | 0 | 0 | — | 4 | 1 | 0 | 0 | 19 | 33 | 14 | 0 | 0 | 4 | 6 | 4.74 | 59 | .384 | .411 | 5 | .000 | -0 | 145 | -3 | | -0.3 |

TILLMAN, JOHNNY John Lawrence "Ducky" B10.6.1893 Bridgeport CT D4.7.1964 Harrisburg PA BB/TR/5-11/170 d9.20

| 1915 | StL A | 1 | 0 | 1.000 | 2 | 1 | 0 | 0 | 10 | 6 | 2 | 0 | 0 | 4 | 6 | 0.90 | 318 | .176 | .263 | 3 | .000 | -0 | 76 | 2 | | 0.2 |

TILLOTSON, THAD Thaddeus Asa B12.20.1940 Merced CA BR/TR/6-2.5/195* d4.14 Col Fresno (CA) City

1967	NY A	3	9	.250	43	5	1	2	98.1	99	52	9	2	39-3	62	4.03	78	.261	.331	16-0-1	.063	-0	56	-10		-1.3
1968	NY A	1	0	1.000	7	0	0	0	10.1	11	6	0	0	7-2	1	4.35	67	.282	.383	1	.000	-0		-2		-0.2
Total	2	4	9	.308	50	5	1	2	108.2	110	58	9	2	46-5	63	4.06	77	.263	.336	17-0-1	.059	-1	56	-12		-1.5

TIMBERLAKE, GARY Gary Dale B8.9.1948 Laconia IN BR/TL/6-2/205 [NYA66 2/30] d6.18 Mil 1969

| 1969 | Sea A | 0 | 0 | — | 2 | 0 | 0 | 0 | 6 | 7 | 6 | 0 | 0 | 9-0 | 4 | 7.50 | 49 | .269 | .457 | 1-0-1 | .000 | 0 | 121 | -3 | | -0.2 |

TIMLIN, MIKE Michael August B3.10.1966 Midland TX BR/TR/6-4/210* [TorA87 5/127] d4.8 Col Southwestern (TX)

1991	†Tor A	11	6	.647	63	3	0	3-5	108.1	94	43	6	1	50-11	85	3.16	134	.233	.317	0	—	0	43	12	15	1.8
1992	†Tor A	0	2	.000	26	0	0	1-0	43.2	45	23	0	1	20-5	35	4.12	100	.271	.351	0	—	0	-1		67	0.0
1993	†Tor A	4	2	.667	54	0	0	1-3	55.2	63	32	7	1	27-3	49	4.69	93	.284	.360	0	—	0	-2			-0.1
1994	Tor A	0	1	.000	34	0	0	2-2	40	41	25	5	2	20-0	38	5.17	94	.261	.352	0	—	0	-1		15	-0.1
1995	Tor A	4	3	.571	31	0	0	5-4	42	38	13	1	2	17-5	36	2.14	222	.242	.324	0	—	0	11		57	1.9
1996	Tor A	1	6	.143	59	0	0	31-7	56.2	47	25	4	2	18-4	52	3.65	137	.229	.294	0	—	0	9			1.6
1997	Tor A	3	2	.600	38	0	0	9-4	47	41	17	6	1	15-4	36	2.87	160	.243	.306	0	—	0	9			1.1
	†Sea A	3	2	.600	26	0	0	1-4	25.2	28	13	2	0	5-1	9	3.86	118	.280	.314	0	—	0	1			0.3
	Year	6	4	.600	64	0	0	10-8	72.2	69	30	8	1	20-5	45	3.22	142	.257	.309	0	—	0	10			1.4
1998	Sea A	3	3	.500	70	0	0	19-5	79.1	78	26	5	3	16-2	60	2.95	159	.264	.306	0	—	0	16			1.8
1999	Bal A	3	9	.250	62	0	0	27-9	63	51	30	9	5	23-3	50	3.57	132	.221	.304	0	—	0	7			1.2
2000	Bal A	2	3	.400	37	0	0	11-4	35	37	22	6	2	15-3	26	4.89	96	.276	.355	0	—	0	-2		13	-0.2
	†StL N	3	1	.750	25	0	0	1-2	29.2	30	11	2	2	20-3	26	3.34	139	.265	.382	0	—	0	5			0.6
2001	†StL N	4	5	.444	67	0	0	3-4	72.2	78	35	6	3	19-4	47	4.09	106	.277	.327	1	.000	-0*	2		22	0.3
2002	StL N	1	3	.250	42	1	0	0-2	61	48	19	9	4	7-2	35	2.51	161	.215	.252	6	.000	-1	23	10		0.6
	Phi N	3	3	.500	30	0	0	0-2	35.2	27	16	6	1	7-0	15	3.79	101	.206	.250	0	—	0		0		0.0
	Year	4	6	.400	72	1	0	0-4	96.2	75	35	15	5	14-2	50	2.98	133	.212	.251	6	.000	-1	23	11		0.6
2003	†Bos A	6	4	.600	72	0	0	2-4	83.2	77	37	11	4	9-3	65	3.55	131	.239	.268	0	—	0	10			1.1
2004	†Bos A	5	4	.556	76	0	0	1-3	76.1	75	35	8	5	19-3	56	4.13	118	.257	.312	0	—	0	8			0.8
2005	†Bos A	7	3	.700	81	0	0	13-7	80.1	86	23	2	2	20-5	59	2.24	205	.277	.319	0	—	0	19			2.7
Total	15	63	62	.504	893	4	0	130-71	1035.2	984	445	95	41	327-61	779	3.50	129	.251	.314	7	.000	-1	36	113	189	15.4

TIMMERMANN, TOM Thomas Henry B5.12.1940 Breese IL BR/TR/6-4/215* d6.18 Col Southern Illinois

1969	Det A	4	3	.571	31	1	1	1-1	55.2	50	22	1	2	26-4	42	2.75	137	.238	.326	9	.111	-0	94	5		0.5
1970	Det A	6	7	.462	61	0	0	27-5	85.1	90	44	3	2	34-11	49	4.11	92	.273	.337	16	.000	-2		-4		-0.9
1971	Det A	7	6	.538	52	2	0	4-6	84	82	36	6	3	37-3	55	3.86	94	.262	.345	19-0-2	.053	-1	136	-1		-0.2
1972	Det A	8	10	.444	34	25	3-2	0-0	149.2	121	57	12	5	41-1	88	2.89	110	.216	.276	44-0-2	.136	-0*	109	3		0.3
1973	Det A	1	1	.500	17	1	0	1-0	39	39	17	4	0	11-1	21	3.69	111	.258	.309	0		0	0	2		0.1
	Cle A	8	7	.533	29	15	4	2-1	124.1	117	73	15	3	54-7	62	4.92	80	.251	.330	0		0	110	-12		-1.3
	Year	9	8	.529	46	16	4	3-1	163.1	156	90	19	3	65-8	83	4.63	86	.252	.325	0		0	102	-10		-1.2
1974	Cle A	1	1	.500	4	0	0	0-0	10	9	6	1	0	5-0	2	5.40	67	.250	.341	0		0		-2		-0.3
Total	6	35	35	.500	228	44	8-2	35-13	548	508	255	42	15	208-27	315	3.78	97	.246	.317	88-0-4	.091	-4	103	-9		-1.8

TINCUP, BEN Austin Ben B12.14.1890 Adair OK D7.5.1980 Claremore OK BL/TR/6-1/180 d5.22 Mil 1918 C1

1914	Phi N	8	10	.444	28	17	9-3	0	155	165	71	0	4	62	108	2.61	113	.286	.359	53-0-2	.170	-1*	92	4		0.4
1915	Phi N	0	0	—	10	0	0	0	31	26	8	1	0	9	10	2.03	135	.263	.324	9	.000	-1*		3		0.1
1918	Phi N	0	1	.000	8	1	0	0	16.2	24	20	0	0	6	6	7.56	40	.329	.380	8	.125	-0*	50	-9		-0.5
1928	Chi N	0	0	—	2	0	0	0	9	14	7	0	0	1	3	7.00	55	.378	.395	3	.000	-0		-3		-0.2
Total	4	8	11	.421	48	18	9-3	0	211.2	229	106	1	4	78	127	3.10	95	.291	.358	73-0-2	.137	-3	90	-5		-0.2

TINNING, BUD Lyle Forrest B3.12.1906 Pilger NE D1.17.1961 Evansville IN BB/TR(BR 1934-35)/5-11/198 d4.20

1932	†Chi N	5	3	.625	24	7	2	0	93.1	93	34	3	2	24	30	2.80	135	.263	.313	23	.087	-1	77	10		0.7
1933	Chi N	13	6	.684	32	21	10-3	1	175.1	169	73	3	4	60	59	3.18	103	.255	.320	67-0-3	.209	1	135	3		0.2
1934	Chi N	4	6	.400	39	7	1-1	3	129.1	134	59	9	1	46	44	3.34	116	.269	.332	39-0-2	.179	-1	89	6		0.3
1935	StL N	0	0	—	4	0	0	0	7.2	9	6	1	1	5	2	5.87	70	.300	.417	1	.000	-0		4		0.0
Total	4	22	15	.595	99	35	13-4	4	405.2	405	172	16	8	135	135	3.19	113	.262	.325	130-0-5	.177	-1	109	-5		1.1

TIPPLE, DAN Daniel E. "Big Dan","Rusty" B2.13.1890 Rockford IL D3.26.1960 Omaha NE BR/TR/6-0/176 d9.18

| 1915 | NY A | 0 | 1 | .000 | 3 | 1 | 0 | 0 | 11 | 9 | 5 | 0 | 0 | 8 | 4 | 3.38 | 90 | .203 | .313 | 6 | .000 | -1 | 99 | 3 | | 0.1 |

TISING, JACK Johnnie Joseph B10.9.1903 High Point MO D9.5.1967 Leadville CO BL/TR/6-2/180 d4.24 Col Denver

| 1936 | Pit N | 1 | 3 | .250 | 10 | 6 | 1 | 0 | 47 | 52 | 26 | 5 | 0 | 24 | 27 | 4.21 | 96 | .272 | .353 | 11 | .273 | 0 | 77 | -1 | | -0.1 |

TITCOMB, CANNONBALL Ledell B8.21.1866 W.Baldwin ME D6.8.1950 Kingston NH BL/TL/5-6/157 d5.5

1886	Phi N	0	5	.000	5	5	5	0	41	43	45	1	0	24	24	3.73	88	.244	.335	16	.063	-2	45	-6		-0.7
1887	Phi AA	1	2	.333	3	3	3	0	24	31	30	1	0	19	16	6.75	64	.298	.407	10	.000	-1	89	-8		-0.8
	NY N	4	3	.571	9	9	9	0	72	68	50	3	1	37	37	3.88	97	.233	.321	29	.069	-4	78	-1		-0.4
1888	†NY N	14	8	.636	23	23	22-4	0	197	149	91	4	5	46	129	2.24	122	.201	.253	82	.122	-4	123	10		0.4
1889	NY N	2	3	.333	3	3	3	0	26	27	26	1	2	16	7	6.58	60	.260	.369	12	.083	-1	74	-6		-0.6
1890	Roc AA	10	9	.526	20	19	19-1	0	168.2	168	123	6	14	97	73	3.74	95	.251	.358	75	.107	-5*	122	-9		-1.4
Total	5	30	29	.508	63	62	61-5	0	528.2	486	365	16	22	239	286	3.47	96	.233	.318	224	.098	-18	104	-20		-3.5

TOBIK, DAVE David Vance B3.2.1953 Euclid OH BR/TR/6-1/195* [DetA75*S1/2] d8.26 Col Ohio U.

1978	Det A	0	0	—	5	0	0	0-0	12	12	5	1	0	3-0	11	3.75	104	.261	.306	0		0		0		0.0
1979	Det A	3	6	.375	37	0	0	3-5	68.2	59	34	12	0	25-5	48	4.33	101	.231	.295	0		0		1		0.1
1980	Det A	1	0	1.000	17	1	0	0-0	61	61	27	7	0	21-4	34	3.98	104	.266	.325	0		0	152	2		0.1
1981	Det A	2	5	.500	27	0	0	1-2	60.1	47	19	7	0	33-3	32	2.69	141	.215	.313	0		0		7		0.4
1982	Det A	4	9	.308	51	1	0	9-3	98.2	86	45	8	1	38-8	63	3.56	115	.241	.312	0		0	156	5		0.7
1983	Tex A	2	1	.667	27	0	0	9-0	44	36	18	4	0	13-3	30	3.68	110	.222	.278	0		0		3		0.3

YEAR	TM LG	W	L	PCT	G	GS	CG-SHO	SV-BS	IP	H	R	HR	HB	BB-IB	SO	ERA	AERA	OAV	OOB	AB-HR-SH	AVG	PB	SUP	APR	DL	PW
1984	Tex A	1	6	.143	24	0	0	5-3	42.1	44	20	5	1	17-6	30	3.61	116	.265	.337	0	—	0		2		0.4
1985	Sea A	1	0	1.000	8	0	0	1-1	9	10	8	2	0	3-0	8	6.00	70	.286	.325	0	—	0		-2		-0.3
Total	8	14	23	.378	196	2	0	28-14	396	355	176	44	2	153-29	256	3.70	111	.242	.310	0	—	0	154	18		1.7

TOBIN, JIM   James Anthony "Abba Dabba" B12.27.1912 Oakland CA D5.19.1969 Oakland CA BR/TR/6-0/185 b-Johnny

YEAR	TM LG	W	L	PCT	G	GS	CG-SHO	SV-BS	IP	H	R	HR	HB	BB-IB	SO	ERA	AERA	OAV	OOB	AB-HR-SH	AVG	PB	SUP	APR	DL	PW
1937	Pit N	6	3	.667	20	8	7	1	87	74	38	1	1	28	37	3.00	129	.226	.289	34	.441	7*	100	7		1.3
1938	Pit N	14	12	.538	40	33	14-2	0	241.1	254	109	17	6	66	70	3.47	109	.270	.321	103-0-1	.243	7*	99	9		1.5
1939	Pit N	9	9	.500	25	19	8	0	145.1	194	84	7	2	33	43	4.52	85	.319	.356	74-2-1	.243	5*	99	-11		-0.8
1940	Bos N	7	3	.700	15	11	9	0	96.1	102	41	8	0	24	29	3.83	97	.264	.307	43	.279	3*	132	1		0.4
1941	Bos N	12	12	.500	33	26	20-3	0	238	229	91	12	0	60	61	3.10	115	.253	.300	103	.184	3*	93	15		2.1
1942	Bos N	12	21	.364	37	33	28-1	0	287.2	283	145	20	6	96	71	3.97	84	.257	.320	114-6-0	.246	14*	86	-19		-0.3
1943	Bos N	14	14	.500	33	30	24-1	0	250	241	96	12	0	69	52	2.66	128	.251	.303	107-2-0	.280	6*	80	18		3.1
1944	Bos N★	18	19	.486	43	36	28-5	3	299.1	271	125	8	3	97	83	3.01	127	.240	.302	116-2-2	.190	5*	85	23		3.8
1945	Bos N	9	14	.391	27	25	16	0	196.2	220	101	10	5	56	38	3.84	100	.282	.334	77-3-0	.143	5*	110	-2		0.5
	†Det A	4	5	.444	14	6	2	1	58.1	61	31	2	4	28	14	3.55	99	.274	.365	25-2-1	.120	0*	69	-1		-0.2
Total	9	105	112	.484	287	227	156-12	5	1900	1929	861	107	29	557	498	3.44	106	.262	.316	796-17-5	.230	54	94	40		11.4

TOBIN, PAT   Marion Brooks B1.28.1916 Hermitage AR D1.21.1975 Shreveport LA BR/TR/6-1/198 d8.21

YEAR	TM LG	W	L	PCT	G	GS	CG-SHO	SV-BS	IP	H	R	HR	HB	BB-IB	SO	ERA	AERA	OAV	OOB	AB-HR-SH	AVG	PB	SUP	APR	DL	PW
1941	Phi A	0	0	—	1	0	0	0	4	5	4	0	0	2	0	36.00	12	.571	.667	0	—	0		-4		-0.2

TODD, FRANK   George Franklin B10.18.1869 Aberdeen MD D8.11.1919 Havre de Grace MD TL d7.14

YEAR	TM LG	W	L	PCT	G	GS	CG-SHO	SV-BS	IP	H	R	HR	HB	BB-IB	SO	ERA	AERA	OAV	OOB	AB-HR-SH	AVG	PB	SUP	APR	DL	PW
1898	Lou N	0	2	.000	4	2	0	0	11	23	21	0	2	8	5	13.91	26	.418	.508	5	.200	0	49	-12		-1.5

TODD, JACKSON   Jackson A B11.20.1951 Tulsa OK BR/TR/6-2/180* [NYN73 2/38] d5.5 Col Oklahoma

YEAR	TM LG	W	L	PCT	G	GS	CG-SHO	SV-BS	IP	H	R	HR	HB	BB-IB	SO	ERA	AERA	OAV	OOB	AB-HR-SH	AVG	PB	SUP	APR	DL	PW
1977	NY N	3	6	.333	19	10	0	0-0	71.2	78	41	8	2	20-5	39	4.77	80	.273	.325	17	.059	-1	91	-8		-1.0
1979	Tor A	0	1	.000	12	1	0	0-0	32.1	40	26	7	1	7-0	14	5.85	75	.299	.333	0	—	0	21	-6		-0.3
1980	Tor A	5	2	.714	12	12	4	0-0	85	90	40	14	2	30-1	44	4.02	107	.276	.340	0	—	0	97	4		0.3
1981	Tor A	2	7	.222	21	13	3	0-0	97.2	94	51	10	4	31-2	41	3.96	100	.251	.313	0	—	0	63	-1		0.0
Total	4	10	16	.385	64	36	7	0-0	286.2	302	158	39	9	88-8	138	4.40	93	.270	.326	17	.059	-1	81	-11		-1.0

TODD, JIM   James Richard B9.21.1947 Lancaster PA BL/TR/6-2/190(180-195) [ChiN69 10/230] d4.29 Col Millersville

YEAR	TM LG	W	L	PCT	G	GS	CG-SHO	SV-BS	IP	H	R	HR	HB	BB-IB	SO	ERA	AERA	OAV	OOB	AB-HR-SH	AVG	PB	SUP	APR	DL	PW
1974	Chi N	4	2	.667	43	6	0	3-1	88	82	45	7	3	41-3	42	3.89	99	.252	.338	16	.063	-1	72	-1		-0.2
1975	†Oak A	8	3	.727	58	0	0	12-2	122	104	40	4	3	33-4	50	2.29	160	.234	.290	0	—	0		17		2.0
1976	Oak A	7	8	.467	49	0	0	4-1	82.2	87	43	6	6	34-8	22	3.81	88	.276	.357	0	—	0		-6		-1.0
1977	Chi N	1	1	.500	20	0	0	0-1	30.2	47	37	1	2	19-2	17	9.10	48	.336	.422	1-0-1	.000	-0		-15		-0.9
1978	Sea A	3	4	.429	49	2	0	3-2	106.2	113	52	4	0	61-4	37	3.88	99	.280	.373	0	—	0	70	-1		-1.0
1979	Oak A	2	5	.286	51	0	0	2-3	81	108	66	12	2	51-10	26	6.56	62	.329	.415	0	—	0		-23		-1.8
Total	6	25	23	.521	270	8	0	24-10	511	541	283	34	16	239-31	194	4.23	90	.277	.357	17-0-1	.059	-2	73	-29		-1.9

TOENES, HAL   William Harrel B10.8.1917 Mobile AL D6.28.2004 Tampa FL BR/TR/5-11.5/175 d9.17

YEAR	TM LG	W	L	PCT	G	GS	CG-SHO	SV-BS	IP	H	R	HR	HB	BB-IB	SO	ERA	AERA	OAV	OOB	AB-HR-SH	AVG	PB	SUP	APR	DL	PW
1947	Was A	1	0	1.000	4	1	0		6.2	11	5	0	0	2	6	6.75	55	.379	.419	1-0-1	.000	0	48	-2		-0.3

TOLAR, KEVIN   Kevin Anthony B1.28.1971 Panama City FL BR/TL/6-3/225* [ChiA89 9/225] d9.11

YEAR	TM LG	W	L	PCT	G	GS	CG-SHO	SV-BS	IP	H	R	HR	HB	BB-IB	SO	ERA	AERA	OAV	OOB	AB-HR-SH	AVG	PB	SUP	APR	DL	PW
2000	Det A	0	0	—	5	0	0	0-0	3	3	1	0	0	1-0	3	3.00	164	.091	.167	0	—	0		1		0.0
2001	Det A	0	0	—	9	0	0	0-0	10.2	7	8	0	0	13-1	11	6.75	66	.189	.400	0	—	0		-2		-0.1
2003	Bos A	0	0	—	6	0	0	0-0	4	5	5	1	0	2-0	3	9.00	52	.313	.389	0	—	0		-2		-0.1
Total	3	0	0	—	20	0	0	0-0	17.2	13	14	1	0	16-1	17	6.62	69	.203	.363	0	—	0		-3		-0.2

TOLIVER, FREDDIE   Freddie Lee B2.3.1961 Natchez MS BR/TR/6-1/170* [NYA79 3/77] d9.15

YEAR	TM LG	W	L	PCT	G	GS	CG-SHO	SV-BS	IP	H	R	HR	HB	BB-IB	SO	ERA	AERA	OAV	OOB	AB-HR-SH	AVG	PB	SUP	APR	DL	PW
1984	Cin N	0	0	—	3	1	0	0-0	10	7	2	0	0	7-0	4	0.90	421	.206	.341	1-0-1	.000	0	47	3		0.1
1985	Phi N	0	4	.000	11	3	0	1-1	25	27	15	2	0	17-1	23	4.68	79	.273	.376	4	.500	1	40	-3		-0.4
1986	Phi N	0	2	.000	5	5	0	0-0	25.2	28	14	0	0	11-0	20	3.51	111	.286	.358	6	.000	-0	91	0	116	0.0
1987	Phi N	1	1	.500	10	4	0	0-0	30.1	34	19	2	1	17-3	25	5.64	76	.291	.380	5-0-2	.000	-1	148	-3		-0.2
1988	Min A	7	6	.538	21	19	0	0-0	114.2	116	57	8	1	52-1	69	4.24	97	.270	.349	0	—	0	101	-1		-0.1
1989	Min A	1	3	.250	7	5	0	0-0	29	39	26	2	1	15-0	11	7.76	53	.317	.396	0	—	0*	52	-10		-1.1
	SD N	0	0	—	9	0	0	0-0	14	17	14	5	1	9-0	14	7.07	50	.321	.422	0	—	0		-6		-0.3
1993	Pit N	1	0	1.000	12	0	0	0-0	21.2	20	10	2	2	8-0	14	3.74	109	.267	.341	2	.000	-0		1		0.0
Total	7	10	16	.385	78	37	0	1-1	270.1	288	157	21	6	136-5	180	4.73	85	.280	.365	18-0-3	.111	-0	93	-19	116	-2.0

TOLLBERG, BRIAN   Brian Patrick B9.16.1972 Tampa FL BR/TR/6-3/195* d6.20 Col North Florida

YEAR	TM LG	W	L	PCT	G	GS	CG-SHO	SV-BS	IP	H	R	HR	HB	BB-IB	SO	ERA	AERA	OAV	OOB	AB-HR-SH	AVG	PB	SUP	APR	DL	PW
2000	SD N	4	5	.444	19	19	1	0-0	118	126	58	13	5	35-4	76	3.58	124	.274	.332	32-0-6	.094	-2	81	9		0.4
2001	SD N	10	4	.714	19	19	0	0-0	117.1	133	58	15	2	25-3	71	4.30	97	.287	.321	40-0-5	.200	1	127	0	70	0.2
2002	SD N	1	5	.167	12	11	0	0-0	61.2	88	47	11	1	19-2	33	6.13	68	.342	.382	19-0-1	.158	1	93	-17	123	-1.3
2003	SD N	0	2	.000	3	3	0	0-0	10.1	9	11	1	0	4-0	2	6.97	58	.231	.295	2-0-1	.000	0	86	-5		-0.1
Total	4	15	16	.484	53	52	1	0-0	307.1	356	174	40	8	83-9	182	4.48	94	.292	.337	93-0-13	.151	0	100	-13	193	-1.4

TOMANEK, DICK   Richard Carl "Bones" B1.6.1931 Avon Lake OH BL/TL/6-1/175* d9.25

YEAR	TM LG	W	L	PCT	G	GS	CG-SHO	SV-BS	IP	H	R	HR	HB	BB-IB	SO	ERA	AERA	OAV	OOB	AB-HR-SH	AVG	PB	SUP	APR	DL	PW
1953	Cle A	1	0	1.000	1	1	1	0	9	6	3	1	1	6	6	2.00	188	.176	.317	5	.000	-1	284	2		0.1
1954	Cle A	0	0	—	1	0	0	0	1.2	1	1	1	0	1	0	5.40	68	.167	.286	0	—	0		0		0.0
1957	Cle A	2	1	.667	34	2	0	0	69.2	67	51	13	1	37-3	55	5.68	65	.248	.341	13	.231	0	132	-16		-0.7
1958	Cle A	2	3	.400	18	6	2	0	57.2	61	37	8	2	28-2	42	5.62	65	.276	.361	17-1-1	.118	0*	111	-12		-0.9
	KC A	5	5	.500	36	2	1	5	72.1	69	34	5	0	28-3	50	3.61	108	.252	.321	13	.231	1	103	1		0.1
	Year	7	8	.467	54	8	3	5	130	130	71	13	2	56-5	92	4.50	84	.263	.339	30-1-1	.167	1	107	-10		-0.6
1959	KC A	0	1	.000	16	0	0	2	20.2	27	15	6	2	12-1	13	6.53	61	.310	.406	2	.500	0		-5	71	-0.3
Total	5	10	10	.500	106	11	4	7	231	231	141	34	6	112-9	166	4.95	77	.259	.345	50-1-1	.180	1	127	-30	71	-1.4

TOMASIC, ANDY   Andrew John B12.10.1919 Hokendauqua PA BR/TR/6-0/175 d4.28 Col Temple

YEAR	TM LG	W	L	PCT	G	GS	CG-SHO	SV-BS	IP	H	R	HR	HB	BB-IB	SO	ERA	AERA	OAV	OOB	AB-HR-SH	AVG	PB	SUP	APR	DL	PW
1949	NY N	0	1	.000	2	0	0	0	5	9	10	2	0	5	2	18.00	22	.375	.483	1	.000	-0		-7		-1.0

TOMKO, BRETT   Brett Daniel B4.7.1973 Cleveland OH BR/TR/6-4/215* [CinN95 2/54] d5.27 Col Florida Southern

YEAR	TM LG	W	L	PCT	G	GS	CG-SHO	SV-BS	IP	H	R	HR	HB	BB-IB	SO	ERA	AERA	OAV	OOB	AB-HR-SH	AVG	PB	SUP	APR	DL	PW
1997	Cin N	11	7	.611	22	19	0	0-0	126	106	50	14	4	47-4	95	3.43	125	.233	.305	36-0-3	.139	-0*	86	12		1.5
1998	Cin N	13	12	.520	34	34	1	0-0	210.2	198	111	22	7	64-3	162	4.44	97	.247	.307	65-0-9	.108	-2*	98	-3		-0.1
1999	Cin N	5	7	.417	33	26	0	0-0	172	175	103	31	4	60-10	132	4.92	95	.263	.325	47-0-8	.213	2	102	-4		-0.1
2000	†Sea A	7	5	.583	32	8	0	1-1	92.1	92	53	12	3	40-4	59	4.68	103	.264	.341	0	—	0	169	-5		-0.5
2001	Sea A	3	1	.750	11	4	0	0-1	34.2	42	24	9	0	15-2	22	5.19	82	.288	.350	0	—	0	86	-3		-1.0
2002	SD N	10	10	.500	32	32	3	0-0	204.1	212	107	31	2	60-9	126	4.49	86	.267	.317	66-0-7	.182	1	130	-12		-1.0
2003	StL N	13	9	.591	33	32	2	0-0	202.2	252	126	35	5	57-2	114	5.28	78	.305	.352	63-0-11	.286	6*	130	-27		-2.1
2004	SF N	11	7	.611	32	31	2-1	0-0	194	196	98	19	0	64-3	108	4.04	107	.260	.318	62-0-13	.113	-2*	74	-4	16	0.1
2005	SF N	8	15	.348	33	30	3	1-0	190.2	205	99	20	7	57-11	114	4.48	95	.274	.329	51-0-16	.164	-0	74	-37	32	-3.2
Total	9	81	73	.526	262	216	12-1	2-2	1427.1	1478	771	193	32	464-48	932	4.52	95	.267	.325	394-0-61	.173	4	103	-37	32	-3.2

TOMLIN, DAVE   David Allen B6.22.1949 Maysville KY BL/TL/6-3/185(170-185) [CinN67 29/554] d9.2

YEAR	TM LG	W	L	PCT	G	GS	CG-SHO	SV-BS	IP	H	R	HR	HB	BB-IB	SO	ERA	AERA	OAV	OOB	AB-HR-SH	AVG	PB	SUP	APR	DL	PW
1972	Cin N	0	0	—	6	0	0	0-0	6	4	7	4	2	1-0	2	9.00	36	.412	.421	0	—	0		-3		-0.1
1973	†Cin N	1	2	.333	16	0	0	1-0	27.2	24	15	5	0	15-3	20	4.88	71	.238	.336	3	.000	-0		-4		-0.2
1974	SD N	2	0	1.000	47	0	0	2-0	58	59	29	4	2	30-10	29	4.34	83	.271	.360	4	.000	-0		-4		-0.2
1975	SD N	4	2	.667	67	0	0	1-1	83	87	38	6	2	31-9	48	3.25	108	.275	.340	5-0-2	.200	1		1		0.0
1976	SD N	0	1	.000	49	1	0	0-1	73	62	24	4	1	20-6	43	2.84	116	.235	.289	0	.000	-1	187	5		0.3
1977	SD N	4	4	.500	76	0	0	3-4	101.2	98	38	2	4	32-11	55	3.01	119	.259	.317	7-0-1	.286	0		8		0.7
1978	Cin N	9	1	.900	57	0	0	4-4	62.1	88	54	3	3	30-7	32	5.78	62	.326	.397	5	.200	0		-20		-3.2
1979	†Cin N	2	2	.500	59	0	0	1-1	58.1	57	29	3	1	18-5	30	2.62	141	.269	.325	2	.500	0		9		0.8
1980	Cin N	3	0	1.000	27	0	0	0-0	26	38	17	2	0	11-5	6	5.54	64	.355	.412	0	—	0		-6		0.0
1982	Mon N	0	0	—	1	0	0	0-0	2	1	1	0	1	1-0	2	4.50	82	.167	.286	0	—	0		-2		-0.1
1983	Pit N	0	0	—	1	0	0	0-0	4	4	4	0	0	1-0	1	0.00	—	.333	.500	0	—	0		-1		0.0
1985	Pit N	0	0	—	3	0	0	0-0	10.1	13	8	1	1	7-2	5	5.23	72	.317	.420	0	—	0		-2	21	-0.1
1986	Mon N	0	0	—	7	0	0	0-0	4	7	0	0	0	1-0	5	0.00	—			0	—	0		-2		0.0
Total	13	25	12	.676	409	1	0	12-11	511.1	543	261	32	12	198-58	278	3.82	93	.277	.344	34-0-3	.147	0	187	-24	21	-3.2

YEAR	TM LG	W	L	PCT	G	GS	CG-SHO	SV-BS	IP	H	R	HR	HB	BB-IB	SO	ERA	AERA	OAV	OOB	AB-HR-SH	AVG	PB	SUP	APR	DL	PW
TOMLIN, RANDY	Randy Leon B6.14.1966 Bainbridge MD BL/TL/5-11/170(170-182) [PitN88 18/460] d8.6 Col Liberty																								
1990	Pit N	4	4	.500	12	12	2	0-0	77.2	62	24	11	1	12-1	42	2.55	143	.221	.254	25-0-2	.040	-1	97	10		1.0
1991	†Pit N	8	7	.533	31	27	4-2	0-0	175	170	75	9	6	54-4	104	2.98	121	.254	.315	52-0-13	.192	1*	129	8		0.9
1992	†Pit N	14	9	.609	35	33	1-1	0-0	208.2	226	85	11	5	42-4	90	3.41	102	.282	.320	65-0-7	.138	-0	111	2		0.3
1993	Pit N	4	8	.333	18	18	1	0-0	98.1	109	57	11	5	15-0	44	4.85	84	.291	.320	33-0-2	.182	0	84	-9	80	-0.9
1994	Pit N	0	3	.000	10	4	0	0-1	20.2	23	9	1	0	10-0	17	3.92	112	.291	.371	6	.500	1	89	1		0.3
Total	5	30	31	.492	106	94	8-3	0-1	580.1	590	250	37	17	133-9	297	3.43	107	.268	.312	181-0-24	.160	1	108	12	80	1.6
TOMPKINS, CHUCK	Charles Herbert B9.1.1889 Prescott AR D9.20.1975 Prescott AR BR/TR/6-0/185 d6.25 Col Washington and Lee																								
1912	Cin N	0	0	—	1	0	0	0	3	5	1	0	0	1	0.00	—	.357	.357	1	1.000	0		1		0.1
TOMPKINS, RON	Ronald Everett "Stretch" B11.27.1944 San Diego CA BR/TR/6-4/198(195-220) d9.9																								
1965	KC A	0	0	—	5	1	0	0	10.1	9	4	0	1	3-0	4	3.48	100	.237	.310		.000	-0	50	0		0.0
1971	Chi N	0	2	.000	35	0	0	3-1	39.2	31	18	3	3	21-3	20	4.08	96	.214	.324	0-0-1		-0		0		0.1
Total	2	0	2	.000	40	1	0	3-1	50	40	22	3	4	24-3	24	3.96	97	.219	.321	1-0-1	.000	-0	50	0		0.1
TOMS, TOMMY	Thomas Howard B10.15.1951 Charlottesville VA BR/TR/6-4/190* [SFN73 6/126] d5.4 Col East Carolina																								
1975	SF N	0	1	.000	7	0	0	0-0	10.1	13	8	1	0	6-5	6	6.10	63	.317	.396	0	—	0		-3		-0.2
1976	SF N	0	1	.000	7	0	0	1-0	8.2	13	7	1	0	1-0	4	6.23	58	.351	.359	0	—	0		-2		-0.3
1977	SF N	0	1	.000	4	0	0	0-0	4.1	7	5	0	0	2-0	2	2.08	190	.333	.391	0	—	0		-1		-0.2
Total	3	0	3	.000	18	0	0	1-0	23.1	33	20	2	0	9-5	12	5.40	70	.333	.382	0	—	0		-6		-0.7
TONEY, FRED	Fred Alexandra B12.11.1888 Nashville TN D3.11.1953 Nashville TN BR/TR/6-1/195 d4.15																								
1911	Chi N	1	1	.500	18	4	1	0	67	55	36	2	5	35	27	2.42	137	.229	.339	18-0-2	.111	-1	91	2		0.0
1912	Chi N	1	2	.333	9	2	0	0	24	21	19	0	1	11	9	5.25	63	.247	.340	4	.000	-0	33	-6		-0.7
1913	Chi N	2	2	.500	7	5	2	0	39	52	29	1	1	22	12	6.00	53	.327	.412	12	.250	1	95	-10		-0.8
1915	Cin N	17	6	.739	36	23	18-6	2	222.2	160	46	1	3	73	108	1.58	181	.207	.278	74-0-4	.095	-5	84	32		3.0
1916	Cin N	14	17	.452	41	38	21-3	1	300	247	98	7	8	78	146	2.28	114	.231	.288	99-0-2	.121	-4	71	10		0.4
1917	Cin N	24	16	.600	43	42	31-7	1	339.2	300	119	4	6	77	123	2.20	119	.238	.286	116-0-9	.112	-6	110	17		1.1
1918	Cin N	6	10	.375	21	19	9-1	2	136.2	148	61	2	0	31	32	2.90	92	.282	.322	42-0-3	.214	0	106	-5		-0.5
	NY N	6	2	.750	11	9	7-1	1	85.1	55	19	1	2	7	19	1.69	156	.192	.216	32	.188	-1	83	10		0.9
	Year	12	12	.500	32	28	16-2	3	222	203	80	3	2	38	51	2.43	109	.250	.285	74-0-3	.203	0	99	4		0.4
1919	NY N	13	6	.684	24	20	14-4	1	181	157	47	6	2	35	40	1.84	152	.235	.276	66-0-5	.227	1	116	20		2.1
1920	NY N	21	11	.656	42	37	17-4	1	278.1	266	101	6	5	57	81	2.65	113	.259	.302	96-0-2	.240	3	111	11		1.5
1921	†NY N	18	11	.621	42	32	16-1	3	249.1	274	112	14	4	65	63	3.61	102	.289	.338	86-3-3	.209	2	110	4		0.5
1922	NY N	5	6	.455	13	12	6	0	86.1	91	44	5	2	31	10	4.17	96	.277	.343	30	.067	-3	95	0		-0.3
1923	StL N	11	12	.478	29	28	16-1	0	196.2	211	104	8	6	61	48	3.84	102	.282	.341	69-0-3	.116	-5	92	1		-0.3
Total	12	139	102	.577	336	271	158-28	12	2206	2037	835	59	46	583	718	2.69	113	.251	.305	744-3-31	.159	-18	98	86		6.9
TONKIN, DOC	Harry Glenville B8.11.1881 Concord NH D5.30.1959 Miami FL BL/TL/5-9/165 d8.19 Col Maryland-Baltimore Co.																								
1907	Was A	0	0	—	1	0	0	0	4	3	3	0	0	5	0	6.75	36	.462	.611	2	1.000	1		-1		0.1
TOOLE, STEVE	Stephen John B4.9.1859 New Orleans LA D3.28.1919 Pittsburgh PA BR/TL/6-0/170 d4.20 U1																								
1886	Bro AA	6	6	.500	13	12	11	0	104	100	92	0	8	64	48	4.41	79	.246	.359	57	.351	4*	106	-11		-0.6
1887	Bro AA	14	10	.583	24	24	22-1	0	194	186	133	1	12	106	48	4.31	100	.254	.358	103-1	.233	-1*	104	3		0.2
1888	KC AA	5	6	.455	12	10	10	0	91.2	124	99	4	5	50	35	6.68	51	.312	.395	48	.208	-0*	122	-26		-2.4
1890	Bro AA	2	4	.333	6	6	6	0	53.1	47	32	0	4	39	10	4.05	96	.229	.363	20	.300	2	66	1		0.3
Total	4	27	26	.509	55	52	49-1	0	443	457	356	5	29	259	141	4.79	81	.262	.367	228-1	.263	5	104	-33		-2.5
TOPPIN, RUPE	Ruperto B12.7.1941 Panama City, Pan BR/TR/6-0/185 d7.28																								
1962	KC A	0	0	—	2	0	0	0	2	3	3	0	0	5-0	1	13.50	31	.167	.545	1	1.000	0		-2		0.1
TORKELSON, RED	Chester Leroy B3.19.1894 Chicago IL D9.22.1964 Chicago IL BR/TR/6-0/175 d8.29 Mil 1918																								
1917	Cle A	2	1	.667	4	3	0	0	22.1	33	25	1	2	13	10	7.66	37	.333	.421	9	.222	-0	118	-11		-1.2
TORREALBA, PABLO	Pablo Arnoldo (Torrealba) B4.28.1948 Barquisimeto, Venez BL/TL/5-9/173(159-175) d4.9 s-Steve																								
1975	Atl N	1	0	1.000	6	0	0	0-0	6.2	7	2	0	0	3-0	5	1.35	280	.250	.323	1	1.000	0		1		0.1
1976	Atl N	0	2	.000	36	0	0	2-1	53	67	25	0	3	22-7	33	3.57	106	.315	.387	4	.000	-0		1	20	0.1
1977	Oak A	4	6	.400	41	10	3	2-0	116.2	127	45	5	2	38-2	51	2.62	154	.279	.335	0	—	0	58	16	25	1.4
1978	Chi A	2	4	.333	25	3	1-1	1-1	57.1	69	37	6	3	39-5	23	4.71	81	.301	.407	0	—	0	87	-7	47	-0.8
1979	Chi A	0	0	—	3	0	0	0-1	5.2	5	1	1	0	2-0	1	1.59	268	.250	.318	0	—	0		2		0.1
Total	5	6	13	.316	111	13	4-1	5-3	239.1	275	110	12	8	104-14	113	3.27	120	.291	.364	5	.200	-0	65	13	92	1.1
TORRES, ANGEL	Angel Rafael (Ruiz) B10.24.1952 Las Cienagas, D.R. BL/TL/5-11/168 d9.12																								
1977	Cin N	0	0	—	5	0	0	0-0	8.1	7	2	0	0	8-1	8	2.16	182	.233	.395	0	—	0		2		0.1
TORRES, DILSON	Dilson Dario B5.31.1970 Sur Edo Aragua, Venez BR/TR/6-3/200 d4.29																								
1995	KC A	1	2	.333	24	2	0	0-0	44.1	56	30	6	1	17-2	28	6.09	79	.311	.374	0	—	0	107	-5		-0.2
TORRES, GIL	Don Gilberto (Nunez) B8.23.1915 Regla, Cuba D1.10.1983 Regla, Cuba BR/TR/6-0/155 d4.25 f-Ricardo ▲																								
1940	Was A	0	0	—	2	0	0	0	2.2	3	1	0	0	0	1	0.00	—	.273	.273	0	—	0		1		0.0
1946	Was A	0	0	—	3	0	0	1	7	9	6	0	0	3	2	7.71	43	.310	.375	185-0-4	.254	1*		-3		-0.1
Total	2	0	0	—	5	0	0	1	9.2	12	7	0	0	3	3	5.59	64	.300	.349	185-0-4	.254	1		-2		-0.1
TORRES, SALOMON	Salomon (Ramirez) B3.11.1972 San Pedro de Macoris, D.R. BR/TR/5-11/165(150-215) d8.29																								
1993	SF N	3	5	.375	8	8	1	0-0	44.2	37	21	5	1	27-3	23	4.03	98	.231	.344	13-0-3	.231	0	63	0		0.0
1994	SF N	2	8	.200	16	14	1	0-0	84.1	95	55	10	1	34-2	42	5.44	75	.292	.364	26-0-3	.154	-1	74	-13		-1.4
1995	SF N	0	1	.000	4	1	0	0-0	8	13	8	4	0	7-0	2	9.00	46	.394	.500	1	.000	0	66	-4		-0.4
1996	Sea A	3	8	.273	16	13	1	0-0	72	87	53	12	2	42-3	45	6.00	80	.291	.382	0	—	0	90	-10		-1.2
1997	Sea A	3	3	.500	10	7	1-1	0-0	49	44	27	5	3	23-2	36	4.59	108	.242	.335	0	—	0	120	2		0.2
	Mon N	0	0	—	2	0	0	0-0	3.1	7	10	0	1	3-0	0	27.00	17	.412	.524	0	—	0		-8		-0.3
2002	Pit N	2	1	.667	5	0	0	0-0	30	28	10	2	3	13-1	12	7.25	58	.284	.379	6	.000	-1		-7		-0.4
2003	Pit N	7	5	.583	41	16	0	2-1	121	128	65	19	7	42-5	84	4.76	91	.276	.344	32-0-6	.063	-1*	121	-4	23	-0.4
2004	Pit N	7	7	.500	84	0	0	0-4	92	87	33	6	6	22-6	62	2.64	164	.256	.310	4	.500	1		16		2.2
2005	Pit N	5	5	.500	78	0	0	3-0	94.2	76	34	7	5	36-7	55	2.76	154	.222	.304	4	.500	1		14		1.5
Total	9	32	43	.427	276	64	3-1	5-5	621.1	627	335	72	37	261-29	372	4.48	97	.266	.346	97-0-12	.144	-0	98	-9	23	0.2
TORREZ, MIKE	Michael Augustine B8.28.1946 Topeka KS BR/TR/6-5/210* d9.10																								
1967	StL N	0	1	.000	3	1	0	0	5.2	5	2	0	1	1-0	5	3.18	103	.238	.304	1	.000	-0	134	0		0.0
1968	StL N	2	1	.667	5	3	1	0	19	20	7	1	1	12-0	6	2.84	102	.286	.388	7	.286	0	165	0		0.1
1969	StL N	10	4	.714	24	15	3	0-0	107.2	96	47	7	3	62-2	61	3.59	100	.240	.345	41-0-4	.073	-2	147	1		-0.1
1970	StL N	8	10	.444	30	28	5-1	0-0	179.1	168	96	12	4	103-10	100	4.22	98	.248	.348	63-0-2	.270	4	90	-2		0.2
1971	StL N	1	2	.333	9	6	0	0-0	36	41	27	2	1	30-3	8	6.00	61	.304	.431	7-0-1	.143	1	102	-9		-0.6
	Mon N	0	0	—	1	0	0	0	3	4	0	0	0	2	2	0.00	—	.308	.357	0	—	0		1		0.1
	Year	1	2	.333	10	6	0	0-0	39	45	27	2	1	31-3	10	5.54	66	.304	.425	7-0-1	.143	1	102	-8		-0.5
1972	Mon N	16	12	.571	34	33	13	0-0	243.1	215	97	15	6	103-5	112	3.33	107	.242	.323	85-0-4	.176	0	93	6		0.9
1973	Mon N	9	12	.429	35	34	3-1	0-0	208	207	116	17	4	115-11	90	4.46	86	.262	.357	69-0-6	.174	-1*	103	-12		-1.2
1974	Mon N	15	8	.652	32	30	6-1	0-0	186.1	184	90	10	3	84-3	92	3.57	108	.257	.336	64-0-3	.125	-3*	106	3		0.3
1975	Bal A	20	9	**.690**	36	36	16-2	0-0	270.2	238	103	15	5	133-5	119	3.06	116	.239	.331	0	—	0	121	14		1.4
1976	Oak A	16	12	.571	39	39	13-4	0-0	266.1	231	93	15	6	87-2	115	2.50	135	.235	.301	0	—	0	116	5		1.3
1977	Oak A	3	1	.750	4	4	2	0-0	26.1	23	14	3	1	11-0	12	4.44	91	.242	.318	0	—	0	106	23		2.3
	†NY A	14	12	.538	31	31	15-2	0-0	217	212	99	20	6	75-1	90	3.82	104	.259	.324	0	—	0	110	-1		-0.1
	Year	17	13	.567	35	35	17-2	0-0	243.1	235	113	23	7	86-1	102	3.88	102	.257	.323	0	—	0	110	5		0.4
1978	Bos A	16	13	.552	36	36	15-2	0-0	250	272	122	19	3	99-10	120	3.96	104	.281	.347	0	—	0	110	5		0.4
1979	Bos A	16	13	.552	36	36	12-1	0-0	252.1	254	144	20	5	121-8	125	4.49	99	.264	.346	0	—	0	123	-3		-0.3
1980	Bos A	9	16	.360	36	32	6-1	0-0	207.1	206	113	16	8	75-10	97	5.08	84	.313	.367	0	—	0	103	-16		-1.6
1981	Bos A	10	3	.769	22	22	2	0-0	127.1	130	61	16	10	51-2	54	3.68	107	.267	.336	0	—	0	121	3		0.2

YEAR	TM LG	W	L	PCT	G	GS	CG-SHO	SV-BS	IP	H	R	HR	HB	BB-IB	SO	ERA	AERA	OAV	OOB	AB-HR-SH	AVG	PB	SUP	APR	DL	PW
1982	Bos A	9	9	.500	31	31	1	0-0	175.2	196	107	20	6	74-1	84	5.23	83	.282	.353	0	—	0	120	-14		-1.4
1983	NY N	10	17	.370	39	34	5	0-0	222.1	227	120	16	1	113-11	94	4.37	84	.271	.356	65-0-8	.046	-5	80	-15		-2.2
1984	NY N	1	5	.167	9	8	0	0-0	37.2	55	25	3	2	18-0	16	5.02	71	.369	.434	10	.300	1	65	-6		-0.8
	Oak A	0	0	—	2	0	0	0-0	2.1	9	7	0	0	3-0	2	27.00	14	.563	.632	0				-6		-0.3
Total	18	185	160	.536	494	458	117-15	0-0	3043.2	3043	1501	223	59	1371-84	1404	3.96	98	.264	.343	412-0-28	.155	-4	108	-23		-2.2

TOST, LOU Louis Eugene B6.1.1911 Cumberland WA D2.21.1967 Santa Clara CA BL/TL/6-0/175 d4.20 Mil 1944-45

YEAR	TM LG	W	L	PCT	G	GS	CG-SHO	SV-BS	IP	H	R	HR	HB	BB-IB	SO	ERA	AERA	OAV	OOB	AB-HR-SH	AVG	PB	SUP	APR	DL	PW
1942	Bos N	10	10	.500	35	22	5-1	0	147.2	146	66	12	4	52	43	3.53	94	.256	.322	51-0-2	.176	0	104	-3		-0.4
1943	Bos N	0	1	.000	3	1	0	0	6.2	10	5	2	0	4	3	5.40	63	.357	.438	1	.000	-0	25	-2		-0.1
1947	Pit N	0	0	—	1	0	0	0	1	3	1	0	0	0	0	9.00	47	.600	.600	0	—	0		0		0.0
Total	3	10	11	.476	39	23	5-1	0	155.1	159	72	14	4	56	46	3.65	92	.263	.330	52-0-2	.173	-0	100	-5		-0.6

TOTH, PAUL Paul Louis B6.30.1935 McRoberts KY D3.20.1999 Anaheim CA BR/TR/6-1/175(175-190) d4.22

YEAR	TM LG	W	L	PCT	G	GS	CG-SHO	SV-BS	IP	H	R	HR	HB	BB-IB	SO	ERA	AERA	OAV	OOB	AB-HR-SH	AVG	PB	SUP	APR	DL	PW
1962	StL N	1	0	1.000	6	1	1	0	16.2	18	10	1	0	4-0	5	5.40	79	.295	.333	5	.400	0	144	-1		0.0
	Chi N	3	1	.750	6	4	1	0	34	29	17	2	2	10-1	11	4.24	98	.240	.306	11-0-1	.182	0	100	0		0.0
	Year	4	1	.800	12	5	2	0	50.2	47	27	3	2	14-1	16	4.62	91	.258	.315	16-0-1	.250	1	109	-1		0.0
1963	Chi N	5	9	.357	27	14	3-2	0	130.2	115	50	9	2	35-3	66	3.10	113	.240	.291	39-0-2	.026	-3	75	6		0.3
1964	Chi N	0	2	.000	4	2	0	0	10.2	15	10	2	0	5-0	1	8.44	44	.341	.408	3	.333	0	59	-5		-0.7
Total	3	9	12	.429	43	21	5-2	0	192	177	87	14	4	54-4	82	3.80	97	.251	.305	58-0-3	.103	-2	83	0		-0.4

TOUCHSTONE, CLAY Clayland Maffitt B1.24.1903 Moores (now Prospect Park) PA D4.28.1949 Beaumont TX BR/TR/5-9/175 d9.4

YEAR	TM LG	W	L	PCT	G	GS	CG-SHO	SV-BS	IP	H	R	HR	HB	BB-IB	SO	ERA	AERA	OAV	OOB	AB-HR-SH	AVG	PB	SUP	APR	DL	PW
1928	Bos N	0	0	—	5	0	0	0	8	15	8	1	0	2	1	4.50	87	.417	.462	1	.000	-0		-2		-0.1
1929	Bos N	0	0	—	1	0	0	0	2.2	6	5	1	0	0	1	16.88	28	.429	.429	1	1.000	0		-3		-0.1
1945	Chi A	0	0	—	6	0	0	0	10	14	10	1	1	6	4	5.40	61	.311	.404	1	.000	-0		-4		-0.1
Total	3	0	0	—	12	0	0	0	20.2	35	23	2	2	8	6	6.53	57	.368	.429	4	.250	-0		-9		-0.4

TOWERS, JOSH Joshua Eric B2.26.1977 Port Hueneme CA BR/TR/6-1/165(165-190) [BalA96 15/441] d5.2 Col Oxnard (CA) JC

YEAR	TM LG	W	L	PCT	G	GS	CG-SHO	SV-BS	IP	H	R	HR	HB	BB-IB	SO	ERA	AERA	OAV	OOB	AB-HR-SH	AVG	PB	SUP	APR	DL	PW
2001	Bal A	8	10	.444	24	20	1-1	0-0	140.1	165	74	21	6	16-0	58	4.49	96	.296	.321	2	.000	-0	99	-1	7	-0.2
2002	Bal A	0	3	.000	5	3	0	0-0	27.1	42	24	11	0	5-0	13	7.90	55	.362	.382	0	—	-0	21	-10		-0.8
2003	Tor A	8	1	.889	14	8	1	1-0	64.1	67	34	15	4	7-1	42	4.48	106	.266	.294	1	.000	-0	128	2		0.3
2004	Tor A	9	9	.500	21	21	0	0-0	116.1	148	70	16	9	26-4	51	5.11	96	.310	.355	1-0-2	.000	-0	87	-3		-0.4
2005	Tor A	13	12	.520	33	33	2-1	1-0	208.2	237	101	24	6	29-2	112	3.71	125	.285	.312	6	.000	-1	100	17		1.8
Total	5	38	35	.521	97	85	4-2	1-0	557	659	303	87	25	83-7	276	4.49	103	.295	.325	10-0-2	.000	-1	97	5	7	0.7

TOWNSEND, IRA Ira Dance "Pat" B1.9.1894 Weimar TX D7.21.1965 Schulenburg TX BR/TR/6-1/180 d8.25

YEAR	TM LG	W	L	PCT	G	GS	CG-SHO	SV-BS	IP	H	R	HR	HB	BB-IB	SO	ERA	AERA	OAV	OOB	AB-HR-SH	AVG	PB	SUP	APR	DL	PW
1920	Bos N	0	0	—	4	1	0	0	6.2	10	3	0	1	2	1	1.35	226	.370	.433	2	.000	-0	258	1		0.0
1921	Bos N	0	0	—	4	0	0	0	7.1	11	7	1	2	4	0	6.14	59	.344	.447	2	.000	-0		-3		-0.1
Total	2	0	0	—	8	1	0	0	14	21	10	1	3	6	1	3.86	87	.356	.441	4	.000	-0	258	-2		-0.1

TOWNSEND, HAPPY John B4.9.1879 Townsend DE D12.21.1963 Wilmington DE BR/TR/6-0/190 d4.19 Col Washington College

YEAR	TM LG	W	L	PCT	G	GS	CG-SHO	SV-BS	IP	H	R	HR	HB	BB-IB	SO	ERA	AERA	OAV	OOB	AB-HR-SH	AVG	PB	SUP	APR	DL	PW
1901	Phi N	9	6	.600	19	16	14-2	0	143.2	118	73	3	5	64	72	3.45	99	**.223**	.312	64	.109	-4	102	0		-0.5
1902	Was A	8	16	.333	27	26	22	0	220.1	233	157	12	13	89	71	4.45	83	.272	.349	87-0-3	.264	3	99	-21		-1.6
1903	Was A	2	11	.154	20	13	10	0	126.2	145	85	3	9	48	54	4.76	66	.287	.359	44	.045	-4	61	-20		-2.2
1904	Was A	5	26	.161	36	34	31-2	0	291.1	319	163	3	9	100	143	3.58	74	.279	.342	119-1-0	.168	-2*	61	-31		-3.4
1905	Was A	7	16	.304	34	24	22	0	263	247	117	2	15	84	102	2.63	100	.250	.318	83-0-4	.181	-1	86	-2		-0.5
1906	Cle A	3	7	.300	17	12	8-1	0	92.2	92	45	1	6	31	31	2.91	90	.262	.332	30-0-1	.133	-1	124	-3		-0.3
Total	6	34	82	.293	153	125	107-5	0	1137.2	1154	640	24	57	416	473	3.59	83	.264	.336	427-1-8	.166	-8	87	-77		-8.4

TOWNSEND, LEO Leo Alphonse "Lefty" B1.15.1891 Mobile AL D12.3.1976 Mobile AL BL/TL/5-10/160 d9.8

YEAR	TM LG	W	L	PCT	G	GS	CG-SHO	SV-BS	IP	H	R	HR	HB	BB-IB	SO	ERA	AERA	OAV	OOB	AB-HR-SH	AVG	PB	SUP	APR	DL	PW
1920	Bos N	2	2	.500	7	1	1	0	24.1	18	4	1	0	2	0	1.48	206	.220	.238	6-0-1	.167	0	26	5		0.8
1921	Bos N	0	1	.000	1	1	0	0	1.1	2	4	0	0	3	0	27.00	14	.400	.625	0	—	0	180	-3		-0.5
Total	2	2	3	.400	8	2	1	0	25.2	20	8	1	0	5	0	2.81	110	.230	.272	6-0-1	.167	0	115	2		0.2

TOZER, BILL William Louis B7.3.1882 St.Louis MO D2.23.1955 Belmont CA BR/TR/6-0/200 d4.16

YEAR	TM LG	W	L	PCT	G	GS	CG-SHO	SV-BS	IP	H	R	HR	HB	BB-IB	SO	ERA	AERA	OAV	OOB	AB-HR-SH	AVG	PB	SUP	APR	DL	PW
1908	Cin N	0	0	—	5	1	0	0	10.2	11	5	0	1	4	5	1.69	137	.268	.348	2	.000	-0		0		0.0

TRABER, BILLY William Henry B9.18.1979 Torrance CA BL/TL/6-5/200 [NYN00 1/16] d4.4 Col Loyola Marymount [DL 2004 Cle A 183]

YEAR	TM LG	W	L	PCT	G	GS	CG-SHO	SV-BS	IP	H	R	HR	HB	BB-IB	SO	ERA	AERA	OAV	OOB	AB-HR-SH	AVG	PB	SUP	APR	DL	PW
2003	Cle A	6	9	.400	33	18	1-1	0-0	111.2	132	67	15	5	40-4	88	5.24	85	.293	.355	0	.000	-0	93	-7		-0.8

TRACHSEL, STEVE Stephen Christopher B10.31.1970 Oxnard CA BR/TR/6-4/205(185-205) [ChiN91 8/215] d9.19 Col Cal St.-Long Beach

YEAR	TM LG	W	L	PCT	G	GS	CG-SHO	SV-BS	IP	H	R	HR	HB	BB-IB	SO	ERA	AERA	OAV	OOB	AB-HR-SH	AVG	PB	SUP	APR	DL	PW
1993	Chi N	0	2	.000	3	3	0	0-0	19.2	16	10	4	0	3-0	14	4.58	88	.219	.247	6	.167	0	74	-1		0.0
1994	Chi N	9	7	.563	22	22	1	0-0	146	133	57	19	3	54-4	108	3.21	132	.242	.312	43-0-8	.186	0	94	16	15	1.8
1995	Chi N	7	13	.350	30	29	2	0-0	160.2	174	104	25	0	76-8	117	5.15	81	.277	.352	49-0-6	.265	3	102	-18		-1.7
1996	Chi N★	13	9	.591	31	31	3-2	0-0	205	181	82	30	8	62-3	132	3.03	144	.235	.298	66-1-6	.106	-2	90	27		2.4
1997	Chi N	8	12	.400	34	34	0	0-0	201.1	225	110	32	5	69-6	160	4.51	96	.287	.344	60-0-11	.117	-0	89	-5		-0.4
1998	Chi N	15	8	.652	33	33	1	0-0	208	204	107	27	8	84-5	149	4.46	99	.260	.334	64-1-9	.266	6	109	0		0.8
1999	Chi N	8	18	.308	34	34	4	0-0	205.2	226	133	32	3	64-4	149	5.56	82	.280	.330	63-0-7	.111	-3	84	-20		-2.3
2000	TB A	6	10	.375	23	23	3-1	0-0	137.2	160	76	16	6	49-1	78	4.58	107	.294	.356	4	.250	0	76	5		0.6
	Tor A	2	5	.286	11	11	0	0-0	63	72	40	10	0	25-1	32	5.29	95	.293	.357	0	—	0	103	-1		-0.1
	Year	8	15	.348	34	34	3-1	0-0	200.2	232	116	26	6	74-2	110	4.80	103	.294	.356	4	.250	0	82	-7		-0.8
2001	NY N	11	13	.458	28	28	1-1	0-0	173.2	168	90	28	3	47-7	144	4.46	91	.254	.304	56-0-5	.161	-0	97	9	21	1.0
2002	NY N	11	11	.500	30	30	1-1	0-0	173.2	170	80	16	0	69-4	105	3.37	117	.258	.327	46-0-9	.109	-1*	101	10		1.0
2003	NY N	16	10	.615	33	33	2-2	0-0	204.2	204	90	26	3	65-9	111	3.78	111	.264	.320	58-0-11	.190	1*	101	5		0.7
2004	NY N	12	13	.480	33	33	0	0-0	202.2	203	104	25	6	83-9	117	4.00	108	.262	.334	59-0-11	.186	0*	101	5		0.7
2005	NY N	1	4	.200	6	6	0	0-0	37	37	20	6	1	12-0	24	4.14	101	.264	.323	15	.067	-1	74	-1	142	-0.2
Total	13	119	135	.469	351	350	18-7	0-0	2138.2	2173	1103	296	45	762-61	1440	4.23	102	.265	.328	589-2-83	.166	6	93	19	178	3.2

TRAUTMAN, FRED Frederick Orlando B3.24.1892 Bucyrus OH D2.15.1964 Bucyrus OH BR/TR/6-1/175 d4.27

YEAR	TM LG	W	L	PCT	G	GS	CG-SHO	SV-BS	IP	H	R	HR	HB	BB-IB	SO	ERA	AERA	OAV	OOB	AB-HR-SH	AVG	PB	SUP	APR	DL	PW
1915	New F	0	0	—	1	0	0	0	3	4	3	0	1	1	2	6.00	43	.364	.462	1	.000	-0		-1		-0.1

TRAUTWEIN, JOHN John Howard B8.7.1962 Lafayette Hill PA BR/TR/6-3/205 d4.7 Col Northwestern

YEAR	TM LG	W	L	PCT	G	GS	CG-SHO	SV-BS	IP	H	R	HR	HB	BB-IB	SO	ERA	AERA	OAV	OOB	AB-HR-SH	AVG	PB	SUP	APR	DL	PW
1988	Bos A	0	1	.000	9	0	0	0-0	16	26	17	2	1	9-0	8	9.00	46	.382	.462	0	—	0		-8		-0.9

TRAVERS, ALLAN Aloysius Joseph "Joe" B5.7.1892 Philadelphia PA D4.19.1968 Philadelphia PA BR/TR/6-1/180 d5.18

YEAR	TM LG	W	L	PCT	G	GS	CG-SHO	SV-BS	IP	H	R	HR	HB	BB-IB	SO	ERA	AERA	OAV	OOB	AB-HR-SH	AVG	PB	SUP	APR	DL	PW
1912	Det A	0	1	.000	1	1	1	0	8	26	24	0	0	7	1	15.75	21	.605	.660	3	.000	-0	45	-13		-0.9

TRAVERS, BILL William Edward B10.27.1952 Norwood MA BL/TL/6-6/200(185-210) [MilA70 6/127] d5.19 [DL 1982 Cal A 182]

YEAR	TM LG	W	L	PCT	G	GS	CG-SHO	SV-BS	IP	H	R	HR	HB	BB-IB	SO	ERA	AERA	OAV	OOB	AB-HR-SH	AVG	PB	SUP	APR	DL	PW
1974	Mil A	2	3	.400	23	6	0	0-0	53	59	29	6	1	30-5	31	4.92	74	.296	.386	0	—	0	194	-6		-0.4
1975	Mil A	6	11	.353	28	23	5	1-0	136.1	130	78	15	11	60-3	57	4.29	90	.251	.338	0	—	0	78	-8		-0.7
1976	Mil A☆	15	16	.484	34	34	15-3	0-0	240	211	92	21	8	95-5	120	2.81	125	.237	.315	0	—	0	62	-14	39	2.4
1977	Mil A	4	12	.250	19	19	2-1	0-0	121.2	140	75	13	7	57-5	49	5.25	78	.291	.370	0	—	0	131	-11	37	-1.1
1978	Mil A	12	11	.522	28	28	8-3	0-0	175.2	184	93	20	6	58-1	66	4.41	86	.268	.329	0	—	0	98	7		0.5
1979	Mil A	14	8	.636	30	27	9-2	0-0	187.1	196	89	33	3	45-0	74	3.89	108	.270	.313	0-0-1	—	0	127	0		0.5
1980	Mil A	12	6	.667	29	25	7-1	0-0	154.1	147	76	20	4	47-2	62	3.91	100	.249	.309	0	—	0	104	-5	148	0.3
1981	Cal A	1	0	1.000	4	4	0	0-0	9.2	14	11	2	0	4-0	5	8.38	44	.333	.391	0	—	0	80	-9	36	-0.6
1983	Cal A	0	3	.000	10	7	0	0-0	42.2	58	32	4	2	19-1	24	5.91	69	.331	.397	0	—	0	97	-9	442	-0.8
Total	9	65	71	.478	205	168	46-10	1-0	1120.2	1139	575	134	44	415-22	488	4.10	94	.264	.333	0-0-1	—	0	97	-31	442	0.3

TREKELL, HARRY Harry Roy B11.18.1892 Buda IL D11.4.1965 Spokane WA BR/TR/6-1.5/170 d8.16

YEAR	TM LG	W	L	PCT	G	GS	CG-SHO	SV-BS	IP	H	R	HR	HB	BB-IB	SO	ERA	AERA	OAV	OOB	AB-HR-SH	AVG	PB	SUP	APR	DL	PW
1913	StL N	0	1	.000	7	1	1	0	30	35	20	2	0	8	15	4.50	72	.221	.285	9	.111	-0	47	-5		-0.4

TREMEL, BILL William Leonard "Mumbles" B7.4.1929 Lilly PA BR/TR/5-11/180* d6.12

YEAR	TM LG	W	L	PCT	G	GS	CG-SHO	SV-BS	IP	H	R	HR	HB	BB-IB	SO	ERA	AERA	OAV	OOB	AB-HR-SH	AVG	PB	SUP	APR	DL	PW
1954	Chi N	1	2	.333	33	0	0	4	51.1	45	27	3	0	28	21	4.21	100	.243	.338	8	.250	0		0		0.0
1955	Chi N	3	0	1.000	23	0	0	2	38.2	33	18	2	0	18-2	13	3.72	110	.239	.323	7	.286	0		1		0.0
1956	Chi N	0	0	—	1	0	0	0	1	3	1	0	0	0-0	0	9.00	42	.600	.600	0	—	0		-1		0.0
Total	3	4	2	.667	57	0	0	6	91	81	46	5	0	46-2	34	4.05	102	.247	.335	15	.267	1		0		0.0

YEAR	TM LG	W	L	PCT	G	GS	CG-SHO	SV-BS	IP	H	R	HR	HB	BB-IB	SO	ERA	AERA	OAV	OOB	AB-HR-SH	AVG	PB	SUP	APR	DL	PW

TRICE, BOB Robert Lee B8.28.1926 Newton GA D9.16.1988 Weirton WV BR/TR/6-3/190* d9.13 Negro Lg 1946-48

1953	Phi A	2	1	.667	3	3	1	0	23	25	14	4	0	6	4	5.48	78	.275	.320	7	.143	0	180	-2		-0.2
1954	Phi A	7	8	.467	19	18	8-1	0	119	146	86	14	0	48	22	5.60	70	.305	.362	42-1-0	.286	4*	103	-23		-2.0
1955	KC A	0	0	—	4	0	0	0	10	14	13	4	0	6-0	2	9.00	46	.326	.400	3	.667	1		-6		-0.2
Total	3	9	9	.500	26	21	9-1	0	152	185	113	22	0	60-0	28	5.80	69	.302	.359	52-1-0	.288	5	114	-31		-2.4

TRIMBLE, JOE Joseph Gerard B10.12.1930 Providence RI BR/TR/6-1/190* d4.29

1955	Bos A	0	0	—	2	0	0	0	2	0	0	0	0	3-0	1	0.00	—	.000	.375	0	—	0		1		0.1
1957	Pit N	0	2	.000	5	4	0	0	19.2	23	19	7	1	13-1	9	8.24	46	.291	.398	7	.143	-0	116	-9	108	-0.8
Total	2	0	2	.000	7	4	0	0	21.2	23	19	7	1	16-1	10	7.48	51	.274	.396	7	.143	-0	116	-8	108	-0.7

TRINKLE, KEN Kenneth Wayne B12.15.1919 Paoli IN D5.10.1976 Paoli IN BR/TR/6-1.5/175 d4.25 Mil 1944-45

1943	NY N	1	5	.167	11	6	1	0	45.2	51	23	3	1	15	10	3.74	92	.276	.333	12	.250	1	74	-2		-0.1
1946	NY N	7	14	.333	48	13	2	2	151	146	77	8	2	74	49	3.87	89	.253	.340	38-0-2	.079	-2	124	-3		-1.3
1947	NY N	8	4	.667	62	0	0	10	93.2	100	47	3	1	48	37	3.75	109	.278	.364	16	.188	-0		2		0.4
1948	NY N	4	5	.444	53	0	0	7	70.2	66	28	6	3	41	20	3.18	124	.244	.350	8	.250	0		6		1.0
1949	Phi N	1	1	.500	42	0	0	2	74.1	79	37	3	3	30	14	4.00	99	.299	.377	6	.000	-0		-1		0.0
Total	5	21	29	.420	216	19	3	21	435.1	442	212	23	10	208	130	3.74	100	.267	.352	80-0-2	.138	-2	102	-3		0.0

TRLICEK, RICK Richard Alan B4.26.1969 Houston TX BR/TR/6-2/200* [PhiN87 4/104] d4.8

1992	Tor A	0	0	—	2	0	0	0-0	1.2	2	2	0	0	2-0	1	10.80	38	.286	.444	0	—	0		-1		-0.1
1993	LA N	1	2	.333	41	0	0	1-0	64	59	32	3	2	21-4	41	4.08	95	.244	.309	0	.250	0		-1		0.0
1994	Bos A	1	1	.500	12	1	0	0-1	22.1	32	21	5	0	16-2	7	8.06	63	.330	.425	0	—	0	36	-7		-0.5
1996	NY N	0	1	.000	5	0	0	0-0	5.1	3	2	0	1	3-1	3	3.38	119	.214	.389	0	—	0		1		0.1
1997	Bos A	3	4	.429	18	0	0	0-0	23.1	26	14	2	1	18-4	10	4.63	101	.289	.409	0	—	0		0		-0.1
	NY N	0	0	—	9	0	0	0-1	9	10	9	2	0	5-0	4	8.00	50	.303	.395	0	—	0		-4	109	-0.2
Total	5	5	8	.385	87	1	0	1-2	125.2	132	80	12	4	65-11	66	5.23	81	.273	.363	0	.250	0	36	-12	109	-0.8

TROEDSON, RICH Richard La Monte B5.1.1950 Palo Alto CA BL/TL/6-1/195(170-195) d4.9 Col Santa Clara

1973	SD N	7	9	.438	50	18	3	1-0	152.1	167	77	12	1	59-0	81	4.25	83	.284	.347	40-0-3	.175	-0	78	-10		-0.9
1974	SD N	1	1	.500	15	1	0	1-0	18.2	24	18	6	1	8-1	11	8.68	41	.300	.371	1	.000	-0	24	-10		-1.0
Total	2	8	10	.444	65	19	2	2-0	171	191	95	18	2	67-9	92	4.74	74	.286	.350	41-0-3	.171	-0	75	-20		-1.9

TROMBLEY, MIKE Michael Scott B4.14.1967 Springfield MA BR/TR/6-2/203* [MinA89 14/373] d8.19 Col Duke

1992	Min A	3	2	.600	10	7	0	0-0	46.1	43	20	5	1	17-0	38	3.30	124	.247	.318	0	—	0	96	3		0.3
1993	Min A	6	6	.500	44	10	0	2-3	114.1	131	72	15	3	41-4	85	4.88	90	.290	.348	0	—	0	94	-8		-0.7
1994	Min A	2	0	1.000	24	0	0	0-1	48.1	56	36	10	3	18-2	32	6.33	78	.287	.353	0	—	0		-7		-0.3
1995	Min A	4	8	.333	20	18	0	0-0	97.2	107	68	18	3	42-1	68	5.62	86	.273	.346	0	—	0	107	-9		-0.9
1996	Min A	5	1	.833	43	0	0	6-3	68.2	61	24	2	5	25-8	57	3.01	170	.236	.312	0	—	0		16		1.4
1997	Min A	2	3	.400	67	0	0	1-0	82.1	77	43	7	2	31-4	74	4.37	107	.248	.317	1	.000	-0		3		0.1
1998	Min A	6	5	.545	77	1	0	1-3	96.2	90	41	16	5	41-3	89	3.63	132	.247	.331	0	—	0	78	12		1.2
1999	Min A	2	8	.200	75	0	0	24-6	87.1	93	42	15	2	28-2	82	4.33	120	.272	.328	0	—	0		9		1.3
2000	Bal A	4	5	.444	75	0	0	4-7	72	67	34	15	4	38-8	72	4.13	114	.247	.346	1	.000	-0		5		0.6
2001	Bal A	3	4	.429	50	0	0	6-3	54.2	38	23	4	2	27-2	45	3.46	125	.200	.302	0	—	0		6		0.7
	LA N	0	4	.000	19	0	0	0-0	23.1	27	17	5	0	10-3	27	6.56	63	.290	.356	0	—	0		-6		-0.9
2002	Min A	1	1	.500	19	0	0	0-0	4	10	7	2	0	1-0	3	15.75	28	.455	.478	0	—	0		-5		-0.8
Total	11	37	47	.440	509	36	0	44-27	795.2	800	427	114	30	319-37	672	4.48	105	.261	.334	2	.000	-0	98	19		2.0

TROSKY, HAL Harold Arthur Jr. "Hoot" B9.29.1936 Cleveland OH BR/TR/6-3/205 d9.25 f-Hal

| 1958 | Chi A | 1 | 0 | 1.000 | 2 | 0 | 0 | 2-0 | 3 | 5 | 3 | 0 | 0 | 2-0 | 1 | 6.00 | 61 | .385 | .467 | 0 | — | 0 | | -1 | | -0.2 |

TROTTER, BILL William Felix B8.10.1908 Cisne IL D8.26.1984 Arlington MA BR/TR/6-2/195 d4.23

1937	StL A	2	9	.182	34	12	3	1	122.1	150	88	14	7	50	37	5.81	83	.304	.376	33-0-2	.030	-3	92	-12		-1.2
1938	StL A	0	1	.000	1	1	1	0	8	8	7	2	0	0	1	5.63	88	.242	.242	2-0-1	.000	-0	89	-1		-0.1
1939	StL A	6	13	.316	41	13	4	0	156.2	205	120	16	5	54	61	5.34	91	.318	.376	37-0-7	.108	-1	68	-14		-1.5
1940	StL A	7	6	.538	36	4	1	2	98	117	56	5	1	31	29	3.77	122	.300	.353	22-0-2	.045	-2	67	4		0.3
1941	StL A	4	2	.667	29	0	0	1	49.2	68	35	2	2	19	17	5.98	72	.332	.394	6-0-1	.000	-1		-8		-0.8
1942	StL A	0	1	.000	3	0	0	0	2	5	5	0	0	2	0	18.00	21	.385	.467	0	—	0		-3		-0.6
	Was A	3	1	.750	17	0	0	0	40.2	52	29	4	0	14	13	5.75	63	.304	.357	8-0-1	.000	-0		-9		-0.8
	Year	3	2	.600	20	0	0	0	42.2	57	34	4	0	16	13	6.33	58	.310	.365	8-0-1	.000	-0		-12		-1.4
1944	StL N	0	1	1.000	2	1	0	0	6	14	14	5	0	4	0	13.50	26	.467	.529	1	.000	-0	119	-8		-1.0
Total	7	22	34	.393	163	31	9	3	483.1	619	354	46	15	174	158	5.40	85	.313	.373	109-0-14	.055	-7	82	-51		-5.7

TROUT, DIZZY Paul Howard B6.29.1915 Sandcut IN D2.28.1972 Harvey IL BR/TR/6-2.5/195* d4.25 s-Steve

1939	Det A	9	10	.474	33	22	9	2	162	168	82	5	4	74	72	3.61	135	.270	.351	57-0-2	.211	-0*	91	19		1.9
1940	†Det A	3	7	.300	33	10	1	2	100.2	125	60	4	3	54	64	4.47	106	.307	.392	31	.129	-2	100	2		0.1
1941	Det A	9	9	.500	37	18	6-1	2	151.2	144	76	7	2	84	88	3.74	122	.252	.350	50	.180	0*	81	11		1.3
1942	Det A	12	18	.400	35	29	13-1	0	223	214	98	15	4	89	91	3.43	115	.249	.322	75-1-4	.213	2*	82	14		2.2
1943	Det A	20	12	.625	44	30	18-5	6	246.2	204	83	6	0	101	111	2.48	142	.227	.305	94-1-3	.220	2*	98	26		4.1
1944	Det A☆	27	14	.659	49	40	33-7	0	352.1	314	104	9	4	83	144	2.12	168	.237	.284	133-5-2	.271	12*	96	53		8.2
1945	†Det A	18	15	.545	41	31	18-4	0	246.1	252	108	8	0	79	97	3.14	112	.267	.324	102-2-0	.245	4*	127	9		1.7
1946	Det A	17	13	.567	38	32	23-5	3	276.1	244	85	11	3	97	151	2.34	156	.238	.306	103-3-4	.194	3*	95	37		4.7
1947	Det A☆	10	11	.476	32	26	9-2	2	186.1	186	85	6	3	65	74	3.48	108	.261	.324	68-3-1	.162	3*	115	5		1.1
1948	Det A	10	14	.417	32	23	11-2	2	183.2	193	87	6	2	73	91	3.43	127	.269	.338	69-1-2	.217	2	94	16		2.1
1949	Det A	3	6	.333	33	0	0	3	59.1	68	35	2	0	21	19	4.40	95	.292	.350	14-0-0	.143	0		-3		-0.3
1950	Det A	13	5	.722	34	20	11-1	4	184.2	190	84	13	5	64	88	3.75	125	.267	.332	63-1-3	.190	1	97	19		1.9
1951	Det A	9	14	.391	42	22	7	5	191.2	172	98	13	1	75	89	4.04	103	.240	.312	52-1-3	.269	5	85	2		1.0
1952	Det A	1	5	.167	10	2	0	1	27	30	16	4	0	19	20	5.33	71	.286	.395	9-0-1	.333	1	23	-4		-0.6
	Bos A	9	8	.529	26	17	2	1	133.2	133	62	3	3	68	57	3.64	108	.263	.354	44-1-0	.136	-1	95	4		0.4
	Year	10	13	.435	36	19	2	2	160.2	163	78	7	3	87	77	3.92	100	.267	.361	53-1-1	.170	-1	88	1		-0.2
1957	Bal A	0	0	—	2	0	0	0	0.1	4	3	0	0	0-0	0	81.00	4	.800	.800	0	—	0		-3		-0.1
Total	15	170	161	.514	521	322	158-28	35	2725.2	2641	1166	112	34	1046-0	1256	3.23	124	.255	.325	961-20-26	.213	31	96	207		29.7

TROUT, STEVE Steven Russell B7.30.1957 Detroit MI BL/TL/6-4/195* [ChiA76 1/8] d7.1 f-Dizzy

1978	Chi A	3	0	1.000	4	3	1	0-0	22.1	19	10	0	0	11	11	4.03	94	.229	.313	0	—	0	157	0		0.0
1979	Chi A	11	8	.579	34	18	6-2	4-3	155	165	77	10	5	59-5	76	3.89	109	.273	.341	0	—	0	111	7		0.8
1980	Chi A	9	16	.360	32	30	7-2	0-0	199.2	229	102	14	9	49-5	89	3.70	110	.290	.337	0	—	0	85	5		0.7
1981	Chi A	8	7	.533	20	18	3	0-0	124.2	122	53	7	4	38-0	54	3.47	104	.261	.320	0	—	0	106	3		0.4
1982	Chi A	6	9	.400	25	19	2	0-0	120.1	130	76	9	2	50-2	62	4.26	96	.273	.342	0	—	0	94	-7		-0.8
1983	Chi N	10	14	.417	34	32	1	0-0	180	217	105	13	2	59-9	80	4.65	82	.305	.357	62-0-8	.194	0	97	-17		-1.9
1984	†Chi N	13	7	.650	32	31	6-2	0-1	190	205	80	7	4	59-7	81	3.41	115	.285	.339	61-0-5	.131	-1	106	9		1.0
1985	Chi N	9	7	.563	24	24	3-1	0-0	140.2	142	57	8	1	63-7	44	3.39	118	.270	.347	46-0-9	.109	-2	106	9	31	1.0
1986	Chi N	5	7	.417	37	25	0	0-0	161	184	88	6	1	78-13	69	4.75	86	.298	.375	43-0-4	.209	1	115	-9		-0.5
1987	Chi N	6	3	.667	11	11	3-2	0-0	75	72	27	3	1	27-0	32	3.00	144	.260	.326	26-0-3	.154	1	105	11	43	1.2
	NY A	0	4	.000	14	9	0	0-0	46.1	51	36	4	1	37-0	25	6.60	67	.274	.397	0	—	0	85	-11		-0.8
1988	Sea A	4	7	.364	15	13	0	0-0	56.1	86	53	6	5	31-2	16	7.83	53	.361	.440	0	—	0	89	-21	65	-3.3
1989	Sea A	4	3	.571	19	3	0	0-2	30	43	27	3	0	17-2	17	6.60	61	.333	.408	0	—	0	135	-9		-1.7
Total	14	88	92	.489	301	236	32-9	4-9	1501.1	1665	791	90	33	578-48	656	4.18	96	.286	.351	238-0-29	.160	-2	103	-30	139	-3.9

TROWBRIDGE, BOB Robert B6.27.1930 Hudson NY D4.3.1980 Hudson NY BR/TR/6-1/190* d4.22

1956	Mil N	3	2	.600	19	4	1	0	50.2	38	15	4	2	34-2	40	2.66	130	.210	.339	7-0-1	.000	-1	146	6		0.5
1957	†Mil N	7	5	.583	32	16	3-1	1	126	118	57	9	1	52-5	75	3.64	96	.248	.321	39-0-1	.103	-2	138	-2		-0.4
1958	Mil N	1	3	.250	27	4	0	1	55	53	26	4	1	25-3	31	3.93	90	.252	.332	9-0-1	.111	-1	89	-3		-0.3
1959	Mil N	1	0	1.000	16	0	0	1	30.1	45	25	2	0	10-2	22	5.93	60	.344	.387	4	.000	-0		-10		-0.6
1960	KC A	1	3	.250	22	1	0	2	68.1	70	41	6	1	34-3	33	4.61	86	.281	.365	18	.056	-1	111	-5		-0.4
Total	5	13	13	.500	116	25	4-1	5	330.1	324	164	25	4	155-15	201	3.95	91	.260	.341	77-0-3	.078	-5	128	-14		-1.2

YEAR	TM LG	W	L	PCT	G	GS	CG-SHO	SV-BS	IP	H	R	HR	HB	BB-IB	SO	ERA	AERA	OAV	OOB	AB-HR-SH	AVG	PB	SUP	APR	DL	PW

TROY, BUN Robert B8.27.1888 Bad Wurzach, Germany D10.7.1918 Petit Maujouym, France BR/TR/6-4/195 d9.15

| 1912 | Det A | 0 | 1 | .000 | 1 | 1 | 0 | 0 | 6.2 | 9 | 4 | 0 | 1 | 3 | 1 | 5.40 | 60 | .346 | .433 | 2 | .000 | -0 | 68 | -1 | | -0.2 |

TRUCKS, VIRGIL Virgil Oliver "Fire" B4.26.1917 Birmingham AL BR/TR/5-11/198(190-210) d9.27 Mil 1944-45 C1

1941	Det A	0	0	—	1	0	0	0	2	4	2	0	0	0	3	9.00	50	.500	.500	0	—	0		-1		0.0
1942	Det A	14	8	.636	28	20	8-2	0	167.2	147	64	3	2	74	91	2.74	144	.231	.314	65-0-1	.123	-4	96	20		2.1
1943	Det A	16	10	.615	33	25	10-2	2	202.2	170	72	11	1	52	118	2.84	124	.225	.276	72	.181	-2	111	16		1.8
1945	†Det A	0	0	—	1	1	0	0	5.1	3	1	0	0	2	3	1.69	208	.176	.263	2	.000	-0	145	1		0.1
1946	Det A	14	9	.609	32	29	15-2	0	236.2	217	94	23	3	75	161	3.23	113	.241	.302	95-0-2	.179	-4	95	12		0.9
1947	Det A	10	12	.455	36	26	8-2	2	180.2	186	105	14	2	79	108	4.53	83	.263	.339	70	.271	2	132	-15		-1.5
1948	Det A	14	13	.519	43	26	7	2	211.2	190	97	14	2	85	123	3.78	115	.240	.315	79-0-2	.165	-3	91	16		1.4
1949	Det A★	19	11	.633	41	32	17-6	4	275	209	95	16	4	124	153	2.81	148	.211	.301	100-0-5	.120	-6	82	42		3.5
1950	Det A	3	1	.750	7	7	2-1	0	48.1	45	20	6	1	21	25	3.54	133	.243	.324	20	.150	-1	113	6		0.4
1951	Det A	13	8	.619	37	18	6-1	1	153.2	153	81	9	5	75	89	4.33	96	.262	.350	55-0-2	.236	-0	108	-2		-0.2
1952	Det A	5	19	.208	35	29	8-3	1	197	190	99	12	7	82	129	3.97	96	.251	.330	64-1-2	.188	-0	62	-4		-0.4
1953	StL A	5	4	.556	16	12	4-2	2	88	83	37	4	4	32	47	3.07	137	.249	.322	25-0-4	.160	-1	72	9		0.8
	Chi A	15	6	.714	24	21	13-3	1	176.1	151	60	14	3	67	102	2.86	141	.232	.306	63-1-9	.238	2	133	24		3.0
	Year	20	10	.667	40	33	17-5	3	264.1	234	97	18	7	99	149	2.93	139	.238	.312	88-1-13	.216	1	110	32		3.8
1954	Chi A★	19	12	.613	40	33	16-5	3	264.2	224	87	13	1	95	152	2.79	134	.228	.296	93-0-9	.183	-1	117	30		3.3
1955	Chi A	13	8	.619	32	26	7-3	0	175	176	78	19	2	61-5	91	3.96	106	.260	.322	64-0-7	.125	-3	116	2		-0.1
1956	Det A	6	5	.545	22	16	3-1	1	120	104	56	15	6	63-5	43	3.83	108	.239	.342	45-0-2	.244	1	111	5		0.4
1957	KC A	9	7	.563	48	7	0	7	116	106	45	12	2	62-8	55	3.03	131	.248	.345	28-0-1	.143	-1	52	11		1.4
1958	KC A	0	1	.000	16	0	0	1	22	18	7	2	0	15-1	15	2.05	191	.222	.340	1	.000	0		4		0.3
	NY A	2	1	.667	25	0	0	1	39.2	40	24	1	2	24-0	26	4.54	78	.265	.359	8	.250	0		-5		-0.4
	Year	2	2	.500	41	0	0	4	61.2	58	31	3	2	39-1	41	3.65	100	.250	.352	9	.222	0		-1		-0.1
Total	17	177	135	.567	517	328	124-33	30	2682.1	2416	1124	188	47	1088-19	1534	3.39	117	.240	.316	949-2-46	.180	-19	101	171		16.8

TRUJILLO, J.J. John B10.9.1975 Corpus Christi TX BR/TR/6-0/180 d6.11 Col Dallas Baptist

| 2002 | SD N | 0 | 1 | .000 | 4 | 0 | 0 | 0-0 | 2.2 | 4 | 3 | 1 | 1 | 6-0 | 3 | 10.13 | 38 | .364 | .611 | 0 | — | 0 | | -2 | | -0.4 |

TRUJILLO, MIKE Michael Andrew B1.12.1960 Denver CO BR/TR/6-1/180* [ChiA82 7/172] d4.14 Col Northern Colorado

1985	Bos A	4	4	.500	27	7	1	1-0	84	112	55	7	3	23-1	19	4.82	89	.320	.365	0	—	0	120	-7		-0.5
1986	Bos A	0	0	—	3	0	0	0-0	5.2	7	6	0	0	6-2	4	9.53	44	.304	.448	0	—	0		-3		-0.1
	Sea A	3	2	.600	11	4	1-1	1-0	41.1	32	11	5	0	15-1	19	2.40	178	.215	.285	0	—	0	80	9		1.1
	Year	3	2	.600	14	4	1-1	1-0	47	39	17	5	0	21-3	23	3.26	131	.227	.309	0	—	0	96	-8		-0.9
1987	Sea A	4	4	.500	28	7	0	1-1	65.2	70	46	12	2	26-0	36	6.17	77	.277	.346	0	—	0		-8		-0.5
1988	Det A	0	0	—	6	0	0	0-0	12.1	11	7	2	0	5-2	5	5.11	75	.234	.308	0	—	0	130	-5		-0.1
1989	Det A	1	2	.333	8	4	1	0-0	25.2	35	17	3	0	13-0	13	5.96	64	.333	.397	0	—	0	107	-15		-0.5
Total	5	12	12	.500	83	22	3-1	3-1	234.2	267	142	29	5	88-6	96	5.02	86	.288	.350	0	—	0				-1.53

TRUMBULL, ED Edward J. (b Edward J. Trembly) B11.3.1860 Chicopee MA D1.14.1937 Kingston PA d5.10 ▲

| 1884 | Was AA | 1 | 9 | .100 | 10 | 10 | 10 | 0 | 90 | 90 | 4 | 1 | 3 | 31 | 43 | 4.71 | 64 | .295 | .352 | 86 | .116 | -2* | 88 | -18 | | -1.8 |

TSAMIS, GEORGE George Alex B6.14.1967 Campbell CA BR/TL/6-2/190 [MinA89 15/399] d4.26 Col Stetson

| 1993 | Min A | 1 | 2 | .333 | 41 | 0 | 0 | 1-1 | 68.1 | 86 | 51 | 9 | 3 | 27-5 | 30 | 6.19 | 71 | .317 | .378 | 0 | — | 0 | | -13 | | -0.6 |

TSAO, CHIN-HUI Chin-Hui B6.2.1981 Hualien, Taiwan BR/TR/6-2/170(170-190) d7.25

2003	Col N	3	3	.500	9	8	0	0-0	43.1	48	30	11	4	20-1	29	6.02	81	.284	.373	13-0-2	.154	-0	84	-4	23	-0.5
2004	Col N	0	0	—	10	0	0	1-1	9.1	7	4	2	0	1-0	11	3.86	123	.200	.222	0	—	0		1		0.0
2005	Col N	1	0	1.000	10	0	0	3-1	11	16	8	3	1	5-1	4	6.55	73	.333	.400	0	—	0		-2	153	-0.2
Total	3	4	3	.571	29	8	0	4-2	63.2	71	42	16	5	26-2	44	5.80	84	.282	.359	13-0-2	.154	-0	84	-5	176	-0.7

TSITOURIS, JOHN John Philip B5.4.1936 Monroe NC BR/TR/6-0/175(175-188) d6.13

1957	Det A	1	0	1.000	2	0	0	0	3.1	3	3	0	0	2-0	2	8.10	48	.500	.556	1	.000	-0		-1		-0.3
1958	KC A	0	0	—	1	1	0	0	3	2	1	0	0	2-0	1	3.00	130	.182	.308	1	.000	-0	92	0		0.0
1959	KC A	4	3	.571	24	10	0	0	83.1	90	52	3	3	35-3	50	4.97	81	.271	.344	20-0-3	.150	-1	110	-8		-0.5
1960	KC A	0	2	.000	14	2	0	0	33	38	25	3	8	21-1	12	6.55	61	.297	.421	6-0-1	.000	-1	111	-8	64	0.3
1962	Cin N	1	0	1.000	4	2	1-1	0	21.1	13	2	0	3	7-0	7	0.84	477	.181	.280	5-0-1	.000	-1	87	7		0.3
1963	Cin N	12	8	.600	30	21	8-3	0	191	167	73	20	11	38-1	113	3.16	106	.232	.280	62-0-3	.081	-3	83	5		-0.1
1964	Cin N	9	13	.409	37	24	6-1	2	175.1	178	90	20	5	75-6	146	3.80	95	.263	.338	58-0-2	.190	2	96	-6		-0.6
1965	Cin N	6	9	.400	31	20	3	1	131	134	87	18	9	65-1	91	4.95	76	.265	.354	43-0-3	.070	-2	120	-19		-2.3
1966	Cin N	0	0	—	1	0	0	0	1	3	2	0	1	1-0	0	18.00	22	.750	.800	0-0-1	—	0		-1		-0.1
1967	Cin N	1	0	1.000	2	1	0	0	8	4	3	1	0	6-0	6	3.38	111	.154	.313	0-0-1	—	0	234	0		0.1
1968	Cin N	0	3	.000	3	3	0	0	12.2	16	10	6	1	8-0	6	7.11	44	.302	.403	2	.000	0	27	-5		-0.1
Total	11	34	38	.472	149	84	18-5	3	663	653	348	71	40	260-12	432	4.13	88	.257	.333	198-0-14	.111	-6	100	-36	64	-5.1

TUCKER, T.J. Thomas John B8.20.1978 Clearwater FL BR/TR/6-3/245(245-265) [MonN97 1/47] d6.3

2000	Mon N	0	1	.000	2	2	0	0-0	7	11	9	5	0	3-0	2	11.57	41	.344	.400	1	1.000	0	97	-5	113	-0.5
2002	Mon N	6	3	.667	57	0	0	4-3	61.1	69	32	5	0	31-9	42	4.11	107	.290	.369	4	.750	1*		1	19	0.3
2003	Mon N	2	3	.400	45	7	0	0-2	80	90	49	8	4	20-1	47	4.72	94	.278	.327	19-0-1	.263	1*	106	-3		-0.1
2004	Mon N	4	2	.667	54	1	0	0-2	67.2	73	28	5	4	17-6	44	3.72	123	.275	.326	12	.083	-1	81	7		-0.2
2005	Was N	1	0	1.000	13	0	0	0-0	12.2	20	9	4	0	2-0	5	6.39	63	.370	.386	0	—	0		-3	143	-0.2
Total	5	13	9	.591	171	10	0	4-7	228.2	263	127	27	8	73-16	140	4.57	98	.288	.344	36-0-1	.278	2	102	-3	275	0.0

TUCKEY, TOM Thomas Henry "Tabasco Tom" B10.7.1884 Union City CT D10.17.1950 New York NY TL/5-11.5/190 d8.11

1908	Bos N	3	3	.500	8	8	3-1	0	72	60	21	2	4	20	26	2.50	96	.265	.336	20-0-1	.050	-2	80	2		0.0
1909	Bos N	0	9	.000	17	10	4	0	90.2	104	59	1	3	22	16	4.27	66	.295	.342	29-0-2	.138	-1	82	-13		-1.3
Total	2	3	12	.200	25	18	7-1	0	162.2	164	80	3	7	42	42	3.49	76	.284	.340	49-0-3	.102	-3	81	-11		-1.3

TUDOR, JOHN John Thomas B2.2.1954 Schenectady NY BL/TL/6-0/185* [BosA76*S3/57] d8.16 Col Georgia Southern

1979	Bos A	1	2	.333	6	6	1	0-0	28	39	23	2	0	9-1	11	6.43	69	.345	.384	0	—	0	85	-6		-0.5
1980	Bos A	8	5	.615	16	13	5	0-0	92.1	81	35	4	3	31-1	45	3.02	141	.238	.304	0	—	0	98	12		1.7
1981	Bos A	4	3	.571	18	11	2	1-0	78.2	74	44	11	3	28-1	44	4.58	86	.252	.319	0	—	0	117	-5		-0.4
1982	Bos A	13	10	.565	32	30	6-1	0-0	195.2	215	90	20	8	59-3	146	3.63	120	.280	.336	0	—	0	94	13		1.6
1983	Bos A	13	12	.520	34	34	7-2	0-0	242	236	122	32	4	81-3	136	4.09	107	.255	.316	0	—	0	84	8		0.7
1984	Pit N	12	11	.522	32	32	6-1	0-0	212	200	81	19	1	56-2	117	3.27	114	.248	.295	76-0-4	.211	2*	82	11		1.6
1985	†StL N	21	8	.724	36	36	14-10	0-0	275	209	68	14	9	49-4	169	1.93	185	.209	**.249**	94-0-7	.138	1*	110	50		5.6
1986	StL N	13	7	.650	30	30	3	0-0	219	197	81	22	1	53-5	107	2.92	127	.244	.289	72-0-13	.153	-1	94	18		2.0
1987	†StL N	10	2	.833	16	16	0	0-0	96	100	43	11	1	32-1	54	3.84	109	.272	.331	35-0-3	.200	1*	107	4	101	0.3
1988	StL N	6	5	.545	21	21	4-1	0-0	145.1	131	44	5	1	31-7	55	2.29	154	.247	.287	46-0-5	.109	-1*	91	18	21	1.4
	†LA N	4	3	.571	9	9	1	0-0	52.1	58	16	5	0	10-0	32	2.41	139	.284	.318	13-0-2	.000	-1	94	6		0.7
	Year	10	8	.556	30	30	5-1	0-0	197.2	189	60	10	1	41-7	87	2.32	150	.257	.295	59-0-7	.085	-2	92	24		2.1
1989	LA N	0	0	—	6	3	0	0-0	14.1	17	5	1	0	6-0	9	3.14	109	.309	.377	2	.000	0	86	1	141	0.0
1990	StL N	12	4	.750	25	22	1-1	1-0	146.1	120	48	10	2	30-4	63	2.40	161	.225	.268	46-0-7	.152	0	110	21	22	2.5
Total	12	117	72	.619	281	263	50-16	1-0	1797	1677	700	156	29	475-32	988	3.12	125	.248	.299	384-0-41	.154	2	96	151	305	16.9

TUERO, OSCAR Oscar (Monzon) (b Oscar Tuero Monzon) B12.17.1898 , Can D10.21.1960 Houston TX BR/TR/5-8.5/158 d5.30

1918	StL N	1	2	.333	11	3	2	0	44.1	32	12	0	3	10	13	1.02	267	.208	.269	12	.250	0*	28	7		0.4
1919	StL N	5	7	.417	45	16	4	4	154.2	137	71	4	10	42	45	3.20	87	.242	.306	39-0-2	.205	1	100	-8		-0.6
1920	StL N	0	0	—	2	0	0	0	0.2	5	4	0	0	1	0	54.00	6	.833	.857	0	—	0		-4		-0.2
Total	3	6	9	.400	58	19	6	4	199.2	174	87	4	13	53	58	2.88	96	.240	.303	51-0-2	.216	1	88	-5		-0.4

TUFTS, BOB Robert Malcolm B11.2.1955 Medford MA BL/TL/6-5/215* [SFN77 12/296] d8.10 Col Princeton

1981	SF N	0	0	—	11	0	0	0-1	15.1	20	9	1	1	6-0	12	3.52	97	.308	.370	1	.000	-0		-1		0.0
1982	KC A	2	0	1.000	10	0	0	2-1	20	24	10	3	0	3-0	13	4.50	91	.293	.314	0	—	0		0		-0.1
1983	KC A	0	0	—	6	0	0	0-0	6.2	16	8	1	1	5-0	3	8.10	51	.444	.524	0	—	0		-3		-0.1
Total	3	2	0	1.000	27	0	0	2-2	42	60	27	5	2	14-0	28	4.71	81	.328	.378	1	.000	-0		-4		-0.3

YEAR	TM LG	W	L	PCT	G	GS	CG-SHO	SV-BS	IP	H	R	HR	HB	BB-IB	SO	ERA	AERA	OAV	OOB	AB-HR-SH	AVG	PB	SUP	APR	DL	PW

TUNNELL, LEE Byron Lee B10.30.1960 Tyler TX BR/TR/6-1/180* [PitN81 2/40] d9.4 Col Baylor [DL 1988 StL N 8]

YEAR	TM LG	W	L	PCT	G	GS	CG-SHO	SV-BS	IP	H	R	HR	HB	BB-IB	SO	ERA	AERA	OAV	OOB	AB-HR-SH	AVG	PB	SUP	APR	DL	PW
1982	Pit N	1	1	.500	5	3	0	0-0	18.1	17	8	1	2	5-0	4	3.93	95	.254	.324	4-0-1	.000	-0	126	0		0.0
1983	Pit N	11	6	.647	35	25	5-3	0-0	177.2	167	81	15	2	58-3	95	3.65	103	.252	.311	58-0-8	.121	-1	96	2		0.1
1984	Pit N	1	7	.125	26	6	0	1-4	68.1	81	44	6	0	40-6	51	5.27	69	.298	.387	12-0-3	.083	-1	93	-12	21	-1.3
1985	Pit N	4	10	.286	24	23	0	0-0	132.1	126	70	11	1	57-4	74	4.01	90	.251	.327	47	.085	-2	94	-8		-1.0
1987	†StL N	4	4	.500	32	9	0	0-0	74.1	90	45	9	1	34-7	49	4.84	87	.307	.377	17-0-3	.235	0*	141	-6	24	-0.5
1989	Min A	1	0	1.000	10	0	0	0-0	12	18	8	1	0	6-1	7	6.00	69	.340	.407	0	—	0		-2		-0.2
Total 6		22	28	.440	132	66	5-3	1-4	483	499	256	39	6	200-21	280	4.23	89	.270	.341	138-0-15	.116	-4	103	-26	53	-2.9

TURBEVILLE, GEORGE George Elkins B8.24.1914 Turbeville SC D10.5.1983 Salisbury NC BR/TL/6-1/175 d7.20

YEAR	TM LG	W	L	PCT	G	GS	CG-SHO	SV-BS	IP	H	R	HR	HB	BB-IB	SO	ERA	AERA	OAV	OOB	AB-HR-SH	AVG	PB	SUP	APR	DL	PW
1935	Phi A	0	3	.000	19	6	2	0	63.2	74	58	2	0	69	20	7.63	60	.312	.467	19-0-1	.105	-2	51	-20		-1.1
1936	Phi A	2	5	.286	12	6	2	0	43.2	42	36	6	6	32	10	6.39	80	.258	.398	14-0-1	.143	-1	60	-6		-0.9
1937	Phi A	0	4	.000	31	3	0	0	77.1	80	50	2	0	56	17	4.77	99	.266	.381	26	.231	-1	117	-1		-0.1
Total 3		2	12	.143	62	15	4	0	184.2	196	144	10	6	157	47	6.14	77	.280	.416	59-0-2	.169	-2	69	-27		-2.1

TURK, LUCAS Lucas Newton "Harlem","Chief" B5.2.1898 Homer GA D1.11.1994 Homer GA BR/TR/6-0/165 d6.7 Col Oglethorpe

YEAR	TM LG	W	L	PCT	G	GS	CG-SHO	SV-BS	IP	H	R	HR	HB	BB-IB	SO	ERA	AERA	OAV	OOB	AB-HR-SH	AVG	PB	SUP	APR	DL	PW
1922	Was A	0	0	—	5	0	0	0	11.2	16	11	0	0	5	1	6.94	56	.340	.404	4	.250	0				-0.2

TURLEY, BOB Robert Lee "Bullet Bob" B9.19.1930 Troy IL BR/TR/6-2/215* d9.29 Mil 1952-53 C1

YEAR	TM LG	W	L	PCT	G	GS	CG-SHO	SV-BS	IP	H	R	HR	HB	BB-IB	SO	ERA	AERA	OAV	OOB	AB-HR-SH	AVG	PB	SUP	APR	DL	PW
1951	StL A	0	1	.000	1	1	0	0	7.1	11	6	0	0	3	5	7.36	60	.355	.412	2	.000	-0	61	-2		-0.2
1953	StL A	2	6	.250	10	8	3-1	0	60.1	39	24	4	2	44	61	3.28	128	.184	.329	18-1-2	.278	1	39	6		0.9
1954	Bal A☆	14	15	.483	35	35	14	0	247.1	178	106	7	7	181	**185**	3.46	104	**.203**	.340	81-0-6	.136	-3	82	4		0.2
1955	†NY A☆	17	13	.567	36	34	13-6	1	246.2	168	92	16	7	177-4	210	3.06	122	**.193**	.331	82-0-8	.134	-3	118	22		2.4
1956	NY A	8	4	.667	27	21	5-1	1	132	138	76	13	4	103-0	91	5.05	77	.273	.398	46-0-3	.174	-0	152	-15		-1.3
1957	†NY A	13	6	.684	32	23	9-4	3	176.1	120	59	17	9	85-1	152	2.71	133	**.194**	.298	57-0-2	.088	-2	115	19		1.8
1958	†NY A★	**21**	7	**.750**	33	31	**19-6**	1	245.1	178	82	24	8	128-2	168	2.97	119	**.206**	.311	88-2-6	.136	-1	128	22		2.2
1959	NY A	8	11	.421	33	22	7-3	0	154.1	141	80	15	3	83-3	111	4.32	84	.248	.338	46-0-2	.087	-2	90	-10		-1.3
1960	†NY A	9	3	.750	34	24	4-1	5	173.1	138	67	14	5	87-3	87	3.27	110	.222	.319	55-0-2	.073	-1	139	9		0.2
1961	NY A	3	5	.375	15	12	1	0	72	74	47	11	4	51-0	48	5.75	65	.269	.390	21-0-3	.095	-1	103	-16	33	-1.6
1962	NY A	3	3	.500	24	8	0	1	69	68	45	8	4	47-2	42	4.57	82	.263	.379	12-0-3	.000	-1	110	-9		-0.9
1963	LA A	2	7	.222	19	12	3-2	0	87.1	71	41	5	2	51-6	70	3.30	104	.222	.331	25-1-0	.160	-1	73	0		0.0
	Bos A	1	4	.200	11	7	0	0	41.1	42	28	6	1	28-0	35	6.10	62	.256	.364	14	.214	0	77	-9		-1.0
	Year	3	11	.214	30	19	3-2	0	128.2	113	69	11	3	79-6	105	4.20	84	.233	.343	39-1-0	.179	1	75	-10		-1.0
Total 12		101	85	.543	310	237	78-24	12	1712.2	1366	753	140	56	1068-21	1265	3.64	101	.220	.337	547-4-37	.126	-12	109	21	33	1.4

TURNBOW, DERRICK Thomas Derrick B1.25.1978 Union City TN BR/TR/6-3/195(180-210) [PhiN97 5/146] d4.17

YEAR	TM LG	W	L	PCT	G	GS	CG-SHO	SV-BS	IP	H	R	HR	HB	BB-IB	SO	ERA	AERA	OAV	OOB	AB-HR-SH	AVG	PB	SUP	APR	DL	PW
2000	Ana A	0	0	—	24	1	0	0-0	38	36	21	7	2	36-0	25	4.74	109	.254	.409	0	—	0	273	2		0.0
2003	Ana A	2	0	1.000	11	0	0	0-0	15.1	7	1	0	0	3-0	15	0.59	746	.140	.189	0	—	0		7		0.8
2004	Ana A	0	0	—	4	0	0	0-0	6.1	2	0	0	0	7-0	3	0.00	—	.105	.346	1	.000	-0		3		0.2
2005	Mil N	7	1	.875	69	0	0	39-4	67.1	49	15	5	1	24-2	64	1.74	246	.199	.273	0	—	0		18		3.8
Total 4		9	1	.900	108	1	0	39-4	127	94	37	12	3	70-2	107	2.41	189	.206	.315	1	.000	0	273	30		4.8

TURNER, JIM James Riley "Milkman Jim" B8.6.1903 Antioch TN D11.29.1998 Nashville TN BL/TR/6-0/185 d4.30 C24

YEAR	TM LG	W	L	PCT	G	GS	CG-SHO	SV-BS	IP	H	R	HR	HB	BB-IB	SO	ERA	AERA	OAV	OOB	AB-HR-SH	AVG	PB	SUP	APR	DL	PW
1937	Bos N	20	11	.645	33	30	24-5	1	256.2	228	80	13	0	52	69	**2.38**	150	.235	**.274**	96-0-7	.250	4*	100	**36**		**4.8**
1938	Bos N☆	14	18	.438	34	34	22-3	0	268	267	123	21	5	54	71	3.46	99	.259	.299	96-0-4	.229	4	87	-2		0.5
1939	Bos N	4	11	.267	25	22	9	0	157.2	181	83	10	4	51	50	4.28	86	.293	.351	55-1-3	.236	2	96	-9		-0.4
1940	†Cin N	14	7	.667	24	23	11	0	187	187	70	9	0	32	53	2.89	131	.264	.296	75-0-1	.240	3*	95	17		2.1
1941	Cin N	6	4	.600	23	10	3	0	113	120	49	5	1	24	34	3.11	116	.277	.317	41-0-2	.146	-1	116	5		0.4
1942	Cin N	0	0	—	3	0	0	0	3.1	5	5	1	0	2	0	10.80	30	.333	.444	1	.000	-0		-3		-0.1
	†NY A	1	1	.500	5	0	0	0	7	4	1	0	0	1	2	1.29	268	.167	.200	1	.000	-0		2		0.4
1943	NY A	3	0	1.000	18	0	0	1	43.1	44	22	1	0	13	15	3.53	91	.260	.313	13	.077	-1		-2		-0.3
1944	NY A	4	4	.500	35	0	0	0	41.2	42	23	3	0	22	13	3.46	101	.264	.354	10	.200	0		-2		-0.3
1945	NY A	3	4	.429	30	0	0	10	54.1	45	26	4	0	31	22	3.64	95	.225	.329	11	.091	-1		-1		-0.3
Total 9		69	60	.535	231	119	69-8	20	1132	1123	482	67	10	283	329	3.22	111	.260	.307	399-1-17	.218	12	96	41		6.8

TURNER, KEN Kenneth Charles B8.17.1943 Framingham MA BR/TL/6-2/190 d6.11

YEAR	TM LG	W	L	PCT	G	GS	CG-SHO	SV-BS	IP	H	R	HR	HB	BB-IB	SO	ERA	AERA	OAV	OOB	AB-HR-SH	AVG	PB	SUP	APR	DL	PW
1967	Cal A	1	2	.333	13	1	0	0	17.1	16	9	4	1	4-0	6	4.15	76	.239	.292	4	.000	-0	28	-2		-0.3

TURNER, TED Theodore Holhot B5.4.1892 Lawrenceburg KY D2.4.1958 Lexington KY BR/TR/6-0/180 d4.20

YEAR	TM LG	W	L	PCT	G	GS	CG-SHO	SV-BS	IP	H	R	HR	HB	BB-IB	SO	ERA	AERA	OAV	OOB	AB-HR-SH	AVG	PB	SUP	APR	DL	PW
1920	Chi N	0	0	—	1	0	0	0	2	3	3	0	0	2	0	13.50	24	.400	.500	1	.000	-0		-1		-0.1

TURNER, TINK Thomas Lovatt B2.20.1890 Swarthmore PA D2.25.1962 Philadelphia PA BR/TR/6-1/190 d9.24 Col Penn

YEAR	TM LG	W	L	PCT	G	GS	CG-SHO	SV-BS	IP	H	R	HR	HB	BB-IB	SO	ERA	AERA	OAV	OOB	AB-HR-SH	AVG	PB	SUP	APR	DL	PW
1915	Phi A	0	1	.000	1	1	0	0	2	5	6	1	0	3	1	22.50	13	.500	.615	0	—	0	125	-4		-0.6

TURNER, MATT William Matthew B2.18.1967 Lexington KY BR/TR/6-5/215* d4.23 Col Middle Georgia JC

YEAR	TM LG	W	L	PCT	G	GS	CG-SHO	SV-BS	IP	H	R	HR	HB	BB-IB	SO	ERA	AERA	OAV	OOB	AB-HR-SH	AVG	PB	SUP	APR	DL	PW
1993	Fla N	4	5	.444	55	0	0	0-1	68	55	23	7	1	26-9	59	2.91	150	.227	.300	2	.000	-0		11		1.3
1994	Cle A	1	0	1.000	9	0	0	1-2	12.2	13	6	0	3	7-0	5	2.13	223	.241	.359	0	—	0		3	78	0.2
Total 2		5	5	.500	64	0	0	1-3	80.2	68	29	7	4	33-9	64	2.79	159	.230	.312	2	.000	-0		14	78	1.5

TUTWILER, ELMER Elmer Strange B11.19.1905 Carbon Hill AL D5.3.1976 Pensacola FL BR/TR/5-11/158 d8.20

YEAR	TM LG	W	L	PCT	G	GS	CG-SHO	SV-BS	IP	H	R	HR	HB	BB-IB	SO	ERA	AERA	OAV	OOB	AB-HR-SH	AVG	PB	SUP	APR	DL	PW
1928	Pit N	0	0	—	2	0	0	0	3.2	4	2	0	0	0	1	4.91	83	.267	.267	1	.000	-0		0		0.0

TWINING, TWINK Howard Earle "Doc" B5.30.1894 Horsham PA D6.14.1973 Lansdale PA BR/TR/6-0/168 d7.9 Col Swarthmore

YEAR	TM LG	W	L	PCT	G	GS	CG-SHO	SV-BS	IP	H	R	HR	HB	BB-IB	SO	ERA	AERA	OAV	OOB	AB-HR-SH	AVG	PB	SUP	APR	DL	PW
1916	Cin N	0	0	—	2	0	0	0	1.2	3	3	1	1	1	1	13.50	19	.444	.545	0	—	0		-2		-0.1

TWITCHELL, LARRY Lawrence Grant B2.18.1864 Cleveland OH D8.23.1930 Cleveland OH BR/TR/6-0/185 d4.30 ▲

YEAR	TM LG	W	L	PCT	G	GS	CG-SHO	SV-BS	IP	H	R	HR	HB	BB-IB	SO	ERA	AERA	OAV	OOB	AB-HR-SH	AVG	PB	SUP	APR	DL	PW
1886	Det N	0	2	.000	4	4	2	0	25	35	22	1		12	6	6.48	51	.347	.416	16	.063	-2	101	-7		-0.5
1887	†Det N	11	1	.917	15	12	11	**1**	112.1	120	74	3	10	36	24	4.33	94	.268	.336	264	.333	4*	144	-2		0.1
1888	Det N	0	0	—	2	0	0	0	4	6	3	1	0	3		6.75	41	.375	.375	524-5	.244	0*		-1		0.0
1889	Cle N	0	0	—	1	0	0	0	1	0	0	0	0	1		0.00	—	.000	.250	549-4	.275	0*				0.0
1890	Buf P	5	7	.417	13	12	12	0	104.1	112	77	3	15	72	29	4.57	90	.262	.387	172-2	.221	1*	77	-4		-0.1
1891	Col AA	1	1	.500	6	1	1	0	31	29	22	1	3	13	8	4.06	85	.240	.328	224-2	.277	2*	18	-2		0.0
1894	Lou N	0	0	—	1	0	0	0	3	5	2	1	0	1		6.00	85	.357	.400	210-2-9	.267	0*				0.0
Total 7		17	11	.607	42	29	26	2	280.2	307	200	10	28	135	70	4.62	85	.272	.363	1959-15-9	.267	6	107	-16		-0.5

TWITCHELL, WAYNE Wayne Lee B3.10.1948 Portland OR BR/TR/6-6/220* [HouN66 1/3] d9.7

YEAR	TM LG	W	L	PCT	G	GS	CG-SHO	SV-BS	IP	H	R	HR	HB	BB-IB	SO	ERA	AERA	OAV	OOB	AB-HR-SH	AVG	PB	SUP	APR	DL	PW
1970	Mil A	0	0	—	2	0	0	0-0	1.2	3	2	0	0	1-0	5	10.80	35	.333	.400	0	—	0		-1		-0.1
1971	Phi N	1	0	1.000	6	1	0	0-0	16	8	4	1	1	10-0	15	0.00	—	.145	.284	3	.000	-0	125	4		0.2
1972	Phi N	5	9	.357	49	15	1-1	1-1	139.2	138	72	6	2	56-6	112	4.06	89	.259	.329	28-0-1	.071	-2	54	-8		-1.0
1973	Phi N★	13	9	.591	34	28	10-5	0-2	223.1	172	71	16	10	99-9	169	2.50	152	.219	.312	72-0-7	.097	-4	80	31		2.3
1974	Phi N	6	9	.400	25	18	2	0-2	112.1	122	71	11	7	65-7	72	5.21	73	.276	.375	35-0-2	.171	-1	101	-16	49	-2.1
1975	Phi N	5	10	.333	26	20	0	0-0	134.1	132	82	10	1	78-3	101	4.42	85	.261	.358	34-0-3	.088	-2	106	-13		-1.6
1976	Phi N	3	1	.750	26	2	0	1-0	61.2	55	18	3	1	18-1	67	1.75	204	.241	.302	6	.167	-0	62	10		0.7
1977	Phi N	0	5	.000	12	8	0	0-0	45.2	50	27	3	0	25-1	37	4.53	89	.287	.377	11	.091	-0	72	-3		-0.3
	Mon N	6	5	.545	22	22	2	0-0	139	116	71	18	5	49-3	93	4.21	92	.260	.301	39-0-4	.205	2	96	-5		-0.1
	Year	6	10	.375	34	30	2	0-0	184.2	166	98	21	5	74-4	130	4.29	91	.244	.321	50-0-4	.180	2	90	-8		-0.4
1978	Mon N	4	12	.250	33	15	0	0-0	112	121	86	16	5	71-5	69	5.38	66	.286	.392	24-0-2	.083	-1	99	-20		-2.7
1979	NY N	5	3	.625	33	2	0	0-1	63.2	55	44	6	4	55-8	44	5.23	71	.243	.396	8-0-1	.375	-1	95	-12		-1.3
	Sea A	0	2	.000	4	2	0	0-0	13.2	11	11	2	2	10-0	5	5.27	83	.220	.365	0	—	0	62	-2		-1.0
Total 10		48	65	.425	302	133	15-6	2-5	1063	983	541	92	40	537-43	789	3.98	94	.250	.343	260-0-20	.127	-7	89	-35	49	-6.3

TWITTY, JEFF Jeffrey Dean B11.10.1957 Lancaster SC BL/TL/6-2/185 [KCA79 25/638] d7.5 Col South Carolina-Aiken

YEAR	TM LG	W	L	PCT	G	GS	CG-SHO	SV-BS	IP	H	R	HR	HB	BB-IB	SO	ERA	AERA	OAV	OOB	AB-HR-SH	AVG	PB	SUP	APR	DL	PW
1980	KC A	2	1	.667	13	0	0	0-0	19	22	14	2	0	7-3	9	6.04	67	.351	.392	0	—	0		-5		-0.6

TWOMBLY, CY Edwin Parker B6.15.1897 Groveland MA D12.3.1974 Savannah GA BR/TR/5-10.5/170 d6.25 Col Springfield

YEAR	TM LG	W	L	PCT	G	GS	CG-SHO	SV-BS	IP	H	R	HR	HB	BB-IB	SO	ERA	AERA	OAV	OOB	AB-HR-SH	AVG	PB	SUP	APR	DL	PW
1921	Chi A	1	2	.333	7	4	0	0	27.2	26	21	1	2	25	7	5.86	72	.283	.445	10	.000	-2	128	-5		-0.6

TYLER, LEFTY George Albert B12.14.1889 Derry NH D9.29.1953 Lowell MA BL/TL/6-0/175 d9.20 b-Fred

YEAR	TM LG	W	L	PCT	G	GS	CG-SHO	SV-BS	IP	H	R	HR	HB	BB-IB	SO	ERA	AERA	OAV	OOB	AB-HR-SH	AVG	PB	SUP	APR	DL	PW
1910	Bos N	0	0	—	2	0	0	0	11.1	11	3	1	0	6	6	2.38	140	.275	.370	4	.500	1		1		0.2
1911	Bos N	7	10	.412	28	20	10-1	0	165.1	150	118	11	10	109	90	5.06	76	.243	.365	61-0-2	.164	-1	97	-19		-1.6
1912	Bos N	12	22	.353	42	31	15-1	0	256.1	262	150	8	10	126	144	4.18	86	.276	.366	96-0-1	.198	-1	86	-13		-1.4
1913	Bos N	16	17	.485	39	34	28-4	2	290.1	245	131	4	11	108	143	2.79	118	.235	.313	102-0-5	.206	4*	94	14		2.4
1914	†Bos N	16	13	.552	38	34	21-5	0	271.1	247	113	7	14	101	140	2.69	103	.249	.327	94-0-6	.202	1	93	-2		-0.3
1915	Bos N	10	9	.526	32	24	15-1	0	204.2	182	87	6	5	84	89	2.86	91	.243	.327	88-1-3	.261	8*	116	-6		2.3
1916	Bos N	17	9	.654	34	28	21-6	1	249.1	200	79	6	3	58	117	2.02	123	.226	.276	93-3-4	.204	7*	107	11		2.3
1917	Bos N	14	12	.538	32	28	22-4	1	239	203	81	1	6	86	98	2.52	101	.240	.314	134-0-7	.231	4*	99	2		1.1
1918	†Chi N	19	8	.704	33	30	22-6	1	269.1	218	72	1	5	67	102	2.00	139	.226	.279	100-0-3	.210	1*	126	27		3.2
1919	Chi N	2	2	.500	6	5	3	0	30	20	8	0	0	13	9	2.10	137	.196	.287	7-0-1	.143	1	94	3		0.6
1920	Chi N	11	12	.478	27	27	18-2	0	193	193	83	6	3	57	57	3.31	90	.268	.324	65-0-2	.262	1*	105	0		0.7
1921	Chi N	3	2	.600	10	6	4	0	50	59	22	2	0	14	8	3.24	118	.294	.340	26-0-1	.231	1*	115	3		0.3
Total	12	127	116	.523	323	267	179-30	7	2230	1990	947	51	67	829	1003	2.95	101	.245	.320	870-4-35	.217	30	102	21		7.8

TYNG, JIM James Alexander B3.27.1856 Philadelphia PA D10.30.1931 New York NY 5-9/155 d9.23 Col Harvard

YEAR	TM LG	W	L	PCT	G	GS	CG-SHO	SV-BS	IP	H	R	HR	HB	BB-IB	SO	ERA	AERA	OAV	OOB	AB-HR-SH	AVG	PB	SUP	APR	DL	PW
1879	Bos N	1	2	.333	3	3	3	0	27	35	25	0		6	7	5.00	50	.292	.325	14	.357	1	106	-7		-0.5
1888	Phi N	0	0	—	1	0	0	0	4	8	4	0	1	2	2	4.50	66	.381	.458	1	.000	-0		-1		0.0
Total	2	1	2	.333	4	3	3	0	31	43	29	0	1	8	9	4.94	52	.305	.347	15	.333	1	106	-8		-0.5

TYRIVER, DAVE David Burton B10.31.1937 Oshkosh WI D10.28.1988 Oshkosh WI BR/TR/6-0/175 d8.21

YEAR	TM LG	W	L	PCT	G	GS	CG-SHO	SV-BS	IP	H	R	HR	HB	BB-IB	SO	ERA	AERA	OAV	OOB	AB-HR-SH	AVG	PB	SUP	APR	DL	PW
1962	Cle A	0	0	—	4	0	0	0	10.2	16	6	2	1	7-1	7	4.22	92	.250	.375	3	.000	-0		-1		-0.1

UCHRINSCKO, JIMMY James Emerson B10.20.1900 W.Newton PA D3.17.1995 Mt.Pleasant PA BL/TR/6-0/180 d7.20

YEAR	TM LG	W	L	PCT	G	GS	CG-SHO	SV-BS	IP	H	R	HR	HB	BB-IB	SO	ERA	AERA	OAV	OOB	AB-HR-SH	AVG	PB	SUP	APR	DL	PW
1926	Was A	0	0	—	3	0	0	0	8	13	9	0	0	8	0	10.13	38	.433	.553	2	.000	-0		-5		-0.3

UHL, BOB Robert Ellwood "Lefty" B9.17.1913 San Francisco CA D8.21.1990 Santa Rosa CA BB/TL/5-11/175 d5.8

YEAR	TM LG	W	L	PCT	G	GS	CG-SHO	SV-BS	IP	H	R	HR	HB	BB-IB	SO	ERA	AERA	OAV	OOB	AB-HR-SH	AVG	PB	SUP	APR	DL	PW
1938	Chi A	0	0	—	1	0	0	0	2	1	0	0	0	0	0	0.00	—	.167	.167	0	—	0		1		0.0
1940	Det A	0	0	—	1	0	0	0	0	4	5	0	0	2	0	∞	—	1.000	1.000	0	—	0		-4		-0.3
Total	2	0	0	—	2	0	0	0	2	5	5	0	0	2	0	18.00	27	.500	.583	0	—	0		-3		-0.3

UHLE, GEORGE George Ernest "The Bull" B9.18.1898 Cleveland OH D2.26.1985 Lakewood OH BR/TR/6-0/190 d4.30 C4 ▲

YEAR	TM LG	W	L	PCT	G	GS	CG-SHO	SV-BS	IP	H	R	HR	HB	BB-IB	SO	ERA	AERA	OAV	OOB	AB-HR-SH	AVG	PB	SUP	APR	DL	PW
1919	Cle A	10	5	.667	26	12	7-1	0	127	129	52	1	7	43	50	2.91	115	.261	.329	43-0-1	.302	3	127	7		1.0
1920	†Cle A	4	5	.444	27	6	2	1	84.2	98	52	3	8	29	27	5.21	73	.296	.367	32	.344	2	94	-10		-0.7
1921	Cle A	16	13	.552	41	28	13-2	2	238	288	132	9	4	63	63	4.01	98	.306	.352	94-1-1	.245	3*	119	4		0.6
1922	Cle A	22	16	.579	50	40	23-5	3	287.1	328	147	6	13	89	82	4.07	98	.290	.348	109-0-3	.266	9*	121	-1		0.6
1923	Cle A	26	16	.619	54	44	29-1	5	357.2	378	167	8	12	102	109	3.77	105	.271	.326	144-0-5	.361	16*	140	16		**3.4**
1924	Cle A	9	15	.375	28	25	15	1	196.1	238	134	6	13	75	57	4.77	90	.306	.376	107-1-0	.308	7*	92	-13		-0.7
1925	Cle A	13	11	.542	29	26	17-1	0	210.2	218	118	5	8	78	68	4.10	108	.268	.330	101-0-4	.287	6*	86	6		1.0
1926	Cle A	27	11	**.711**	39	36	32-3	0	318.1	300	109	7	13	118	159	2.83	143	.253	.328	132-1-4	.227	4*	100	45		**5.4**
1927	Cle A	8	9	.471	25	22	10-1	1	153.1	187	88	3	9	59	69	4.34	97	.310	.379	79-0-2	.266	4*	89	-2		0.1
1928	Cle A	12	17	.414	31	28	18-2	1	214.1	252	121	8	8	48	74	4.07	102	.300	.344	98-1-6	.286	7*	77	0		0.8
1929	Det A	15	11	.577	32	30	23-1	0	249	283	141	9	2	58	100	4.08	105	.287	.328	108-0-2	.343	8*	120	4		1.0
1930	Det A	12	12	.500	33	29	18-1	3	239	239	110	18	5	79	117	3.65	131	.264	.323	117-2-4	.308	8*	106	31		**2.9**
1931	Det A	11	12	.478	29	18	15-2	2	193	190	88	10	4	49	63	4.48	105	.266	.320	90-2-1	.244	5*	56	23		0.4
1932	Det A	6	6	.500	33	15	6-1	0	146.2	152	84	15	4	42	51	4.48	105	.266	.320	55-0-2	.182	1*	103	5		0.4
1933	Det A	0	0	—	1	0	0	0	0.2	2	2	1	0	0	1	27.00	16	.500	.500	0	.000	-0*		-2		-0.1
	NY N	1	1	.500	6	1	0	0	13.2	16	12	1	0	4	4	7.90	41	.302	.373	5	.000	-0*	26	-6		-0.8
	NY N	6	1	.857	12	6	4	0	61	63	42	4	3	20	26	5.16	75	.257	.321	20-0-1	.400	4	179	-10		-0.6
1934	NY A	2	4	.333	10	2	0	0	16.1	30	19	3	0	7	10	9.92	41	.400	.451	5	.600	2	107	-11		-1.7
1936	Cle A	0	1	.000	7	0	0	0	12.2	26	12	2	0	5	5	8.53	59	.419	.463	21-1-0	.381	4*		-4		0.0
Total	17	200	166	.546	513	368	232-21	25	3119.2	3417	1635	119	113	966	1135	3.99	105	.281	.340	1360-9-36	.289	92	106	82		15.9

UJDUR, JERRY Gerald Raymond B3.5.1957 Duluth MN BR/TR/6-1/195* [DetA78 4/90] d8.17 Col Minnesota

YEAR	TM LG	W	L	PCT	G	GS	CG-SHO	SV-BS	IP	H	R	HR	HB	BB-IB	SO	ERA	AERA	OAV	OOB	AB-HR-SH	AVG	PB	SUP	APR	DL	PW
1980	Det A	1	0	1.000	9	2	0	0-0	21.1	36	20	5	1	10-2	8	7.59	54	.383	.443	0	—	0	141	-8		-0.4
1981	Det A	0	0	—	4	4	0	0-0	14	19	12	2	0	5-0	5	6.43	59	.322	.369	0	—	0	113	-5		-0.2
1982	Det A	10	10	.500	25	25	7	0-0	178	150	76	29	3	69-4	86	3.69	111	.230	.304	0	—	0	93	10		1.0
1983	Det A	0	4	.000	11	6	0	0-0	34	41	33	6	1	20-1	13	7.15	55	.293	.385	0	—	0	80	-14		-1.4
1984	Cle A	1	2	.333	4	3	0	0-0	14.1	22	14	1	2	6-0	6	6.91	60	.355	.423	0	—	0	110	-5		-0.9
Total	5	12	16	.429	53	40	7	0-0	261.2	268	155	43	7	110-7	118	4.78	85	.266	.340	0	—	0	96	-22		-1.9

ULLRICH, SANDY Carlos Santiago (Castello) B7.25.1921 Havana, Cuba D4.21.2001 Miami FL BR/TR/6-1/180 d5.3

YEAR	TM LG	W	L	PCT	G	GS	CG-SHO	SV-BS	IP	H	R	HR	HB	BB-IB	SO	ERA	AERA	OAV	OOB	AB-HR-SH	AVG	PB	SUP	APR	DL	PW
1944	Was A	0	0	—	3	0	0	0	9.2	17	10	2	1	4	2	9.31	35	.386	.449	3	.333	0		-6		-0.3
1945	Was A	3	3	.500	28	6	0	1	81.1	91	45	3	0	34	26	4.54	68	.276	.343	22-0-1	.273	1	114	-12		-0.9
Total	2	3	3	.500	31	6	0	1	91	108	55	5	1	38	28	5.04	62	.289	.356	25-0-1	.280	1	114	-18		-0.9

ULRICH, DUTCH Frank W. B11.18.1899 Baltimore MD D2.11.1929 Baltimore MD BR/TR/6-2/195 d4.18

YEAR	TM LG	W	L	PCT	G	GS	CG-SHO	SV-BS	IP	H	R	HR	HB	BB-IB	SO	ERA	AERA	OAV	OOB	AB-HR-SH	AVG	PB	SUP	APR	DL	PW
1925	Phi N	3	3	.500	21	4	2-1	0	65	73	30	6	1	12	29	3.05	157	.285	.320	16	.125	-1	57	10		0.8
1926	Phi N	8	13	.381	45	16	8-1	1	147.2	178	85	9	1	37	52	4.08	101	.304	.347	49-0-2	.245	1	91	-1		0.1
1927	Phi N	8	11	.421	32	18	14-1	1	193.1	201	82	6	0	40	42	3.17	131	.271	.308	73-0-3	.123	-6	84	17		0.9
Total	3	19	27	.413	98	38	24-3	2	406	452	197	21	2	89	123	3.48	122	.286	.324	138-0-5	.167	-5	83	26		1.8

UMBACH, ARNOLD Arnold William B12.6.1942 Williamsburg VA BR/TR/6-1/180* d10.3

YEAR	TM LG	W	L	PCT	G	GS	CG-SHO	SV-BS	IP	H	R	HR	HB	BB-IB	SO	ERA	AERA	OAV	OOB	AB-HR-SH	AVG	PB	SUP	APR	DL	PW
1964	Mil N	1	0	1.000	8	1	0	0	8.1	11	5	0	0	4-0	7	3.24	109	.333	.395	3	.000	0	275	0		-0.1
1966	Atl N	0	2	.000	22	3	0	0	40.2	40	15	1	2	18-3	23	3.10	117	.256	.339	5-0-1	.200	0	73	3		0.2
Total	2	1	2	.333	23	4	0	0	49	51	20	1	2	22-3	30	3.12	116	.270	.349	8-0-1	.125	0	122	3		0.1

UMBARGER, JIM James Harold B2.17.1953 Burbank CA BL/TL/6-0/200* [TexA74 16/362] d4.8 Col Arizona St.

YEAR	TM LG	W	L	PCT	G	GS	CG-SHO	SV-BS	IP	H	R	HR	HB	BB-IB	SO	ERA	AERA	OAV	OOB	AB-HR-SH	AVG	PB	SUP	APR	DL	PW
1975	Tex A	8	7	.533	56	12	3-2	2-0	131	134	63	11	2	59-9	50	4.12	92	.276	.353	0	—	0	72	-2		-0.2
1976	Tex A	10	12	.455	30	30	10-3	0-0	197.1	208	86	12	2	54-4	105	3.15	114	.274	.321	0	—	0	107	7		0.7
1977	Oak A	1	5	.167	12	8	1	0-0	44	62	40	3	4	28-2	24	6.55	62	.354	.448	0	—	0	67	-14		-1.5
	Tex A	1	1	.500	3	2	0	0-0	13	14	8	2	0	4-0	5	5.54	74	.275	.321	0	—	0	176	-2		-0.2
	Year	2	6	.250	15	10	1	0-0	57	76	48	5	4	32-2	29	6.32	64	.336	.421	0	—	0	89	-16		-1.3
1978	Tex A	5	8	.385	32	9	1	1-2	97.2	116	58	9	2	36-4	60	4.88	77	.299	.358	0	—	0	85	-11		-1.3
Total	4	25	33	.431	133	61	15-5	3-2	483	534	255	37	10	181-19	244	4.14	90	.287	.350	0	—	0	94	-22		-2.5

UMBRICHT, JIM James B9.17.1930 Chicago IL D4.8.1964 Houston TX BR/TR/6-4/215* d9.26 Col Georgia

YEAR	TM LG	W	L	PCT	G	GS	CG-SHO	SV-BS	IP	H	R	HR	HB	BB-IB	SO	ERA	AERA	OAV	OOB	AB-HR-SH	AVG	PB	SUP	APR	DL	PW
1959	Pit N	0	0	—	1	1	0	0	7	7	5	3	0	4-0	3	6.43	60	.259	.355	3	.000	-0	139	-2		-0.1
1960	Pit N	1	2	.333	17	3	0	1	40.2	40	23	5	0	27-1	26	5.09	74	.270	.374	6	.333	0	118	-5		-0.4
1961	Pit N	0	0	—	1	0	0	0	3.1	5	2	0	0	2-1	1	2.70	148	.333	.412	1	1.000	0	0			-0.4
1962	Hou N	4	0	1.000	34	0	0	2	67	51	19	3	2	17-1	55	2.01	185	.213	.269	9-0-1	.111	-0		13		0.8
1963	Hou N	4	3	.571	35	0	0	3	76	52	23	6	1	21-2	48	2.61	121	.195	.253	9-0-3	.111	-0	9	6	30	0.8
Total	5	9	5	.643	88	7	0	3	194	155	72	17	3	71-5	133	3.06	115	.222	.294	28-0-4	.179	0	78	12	30	0.8

UNDERHILL, WILLIE Willie Vern B9.6.1904 Yowell TX D10.26.1970 Bay City TX BR/TR/6-2/185 d9.8

YEAR	TM LG	W	L	PCT	G	GS	CG-SHO	SV-BS	IP	H	R	HR	HB	BB-IB	SO	ERA	AERA	OAV	OOB	AB-HR-SH	AVG	PB	SUP	APR	DL	PW
1927	Cle A	0	2	.000	4	1	0	0	8.1	12	11	0	0	11	7	9.72	43	.375	.535	1-0-1	.000	-0	79	-5		-0.9
1928	Cle A	1	2	.333	11	3	1	0	28	33	23	0	1	20	16	4.50	92	.306	.419	11	.364	2	150	-4		-0.2
Total	2	1	4	.200	15	4	1	0	36.1	45	34	0	1	31	23	5.70	73	.321	.448	12-0-1	.333	1	132	-9		-1.1

UNDERWOOD, FRED Frederick Theodore B10.14.1868 St.Louis Co. MO D1.26.1906 Kansas City MO ?/170 d7.18

YEAR	TM LG	W	L	PCT	G	GS	CG-SHO	SV-BS	IP	H	R	HR	HB	BB-IB	SO	ERA	AERA	OAV	OOB	AB-HR-SH	AVG	PB	SUP	APR	DL	PW
1894	Bro N	2	4	.333	7	6	5	0	47	80	62	1	2	30	10	7.85	63	.372	.453	18	.389	2	90	-18		-1.7

UNDERWOOD, PAT Patrick John B2.9.1957 Kokomo IN BL/TL/6-0/175* [DetA76 1/2] d5.31 b-Tom

YEAR	TM LG	W	L	PCT	G	GS	CG-SHO	SV-BS	IP	H	R	HR	HB	BB-IB	SO	ERA	AERA	OAV	OOB	AB-HR-SH	AVG	PB	SUP	APR	DL	PW
1979	Det A	6	4	.600	27	15	1	0-0	121.2	126	64	17	2	29-1	83	4.59	95	.269	.312	0	—	0	110	-1		-0.1
1980	Det A	3	6	.333	49	7	0	5-0	112.2	121	56	13	2	35-7	60	3.59	115	.277	.333	0	—	0	118	6		0.5
1982	Det A	4	8	.333	33	12	2	3-2	99	108	66	19	0	22-2	43	4.73	87	.269	.305	0	—	0	97	-11		-1.2
1983	Det A	0	0	—	4	0	0	0-0	10.1	11	10	1	0	6-0	2	8.71	45	.289	.386	0	—	0		-5		-0.2
Total	4	13	18	.419	113	34	3	8-2	343.2	366	196	47	4	92-10	188	4.43	95	.272	.319	0	—	0	107	-11		-1.6

YEAR	TM LG	W	L	PCT	G	GS	CG-SHO	SV-BS	IP	H	R	HR	HB	BB-IB	SO	ERA	AERA	OAV	OOB	AB-HR-SH	AVG	PB	SUP	APR	DL	PW
UNDERWOOD, TOM					Thomas Gerald		B12.22.1953 Kokomo IN	BR/TL/5-11/170(170-185)			[PhiN72 2/27]		d8.19	b-Pat												
1974	Phi N	1	0	1.000	6	0	0	0-0	13	15	8	1	0	5-1	8	4.85	79	.313	.364	1	.000	-0		-2		-0.1
1975	Phi N	14	13	.519	35	35	7-2	0-0	219.1	221	110	12	6	84-5	123	4.14	91	.262	.331	74-0-7	.122	-2	97	-7		-1.2
1976	†Phi N	10	5	.667	33	25	3	2-0	155.2	154	63	9	1	63-0	94	3.53	101	.260	.331	46-0-3	.109	-1*	100	3		0.0
1977	Phi N	3	2	.600	14	0	0	1-0	33.1	44	21	2	0	18-2	20	5.13	79	.328	.403	3-0-1	.000	-0		-4		-0.6
	StL N	6	9	.400	19	17	1	0-0	100	104	61	7	1	57-4	66	4.95	79	.278	.372	30-0-2	.133	-0	84	-11		-1.5
	Year	9	11	.450	33	17	1	1-0	133.1	148	82	9	1	75-6	86	4.99	79	.291	.380	33-0-3	.121	-0	84	-16		-2.1
1978	Tor A	6	14	.300	31	30	7-1	0-0	197.2	201	105	23	2	87-4	139	4.10	97	.263	.339	0	—	0	100	-7		-0.7
1979	Tor A	9	16	.360	33	32	12-1	0-0	227	213	113	23	9	95-3	127	3.69	119	.253	.333	0	—	0	72	14		1.4
1980	†NY A	13	9	.591	38	27	2-2	2-1	187	163	85	15	4	66-4	116	3.66	108	.237	.306	0	—	0	126	7		0.8
1981	NY A	1	4	.200	9	6	0	0-0	32.2	32	17	2	0	13-1	29	4.41	82	.262	.333	0	—	0	87	-2		-0.4
	†Oak A	3	2	.600	16	5	1	1-1	51	37	21	4	2	25-1	46	3.18	111	.202	.305	0	—	0	122	2		0.2
	Year	4	6	.400	25	11	1	1-1	83.2	69	38	6	2	38-2	75	3.66	97	.226	.316	0	—	0	103	-1		-0.2
1982	Oak A	10	6	.625	56	10	2	7-6	153	136	66	11	1	68-4	79	3.29	120	.241	.321	0	—	0	104	10		0.9
1983	Oak A	9	7	.563	51	15	0	4-2	144.2	156	69	13	2	50-4	62	4.04	96	.277	.332	0	—	0	106	-1		-0.2
1984	Bal A	1	0	1.000	37	1	0	1-1	71.2	78	33	8	0	31-5	39	3.52	111	.282	.350	0	—	0	46	3		0.2
Total	11	86	87	.497	379	203	35-6	18-11	1586	1554	772	130	28	662-38	948	3.89	101	.259	.333	154-0-13	.117	-4	97	5		-1.2

UPCHURCH, WOODY					Jefferson Woodrow		B4.13.1911 Buies Creek NC	D10.23.1971 Buies Creek NC	BR/TL/6-0/180		d9.14 Col Campbell															
1935	Phi A	0	2	.000	3	3	1	0	21.1	23	13	3	0	12	2	5.06	90	.271	.361	7	.286	0	76	-1		0.0
1936	Phi A	0	2	.000	7	2	1	0	22.1	36	27	7	0	14	6	9.67	53	.353	.431	7	.143	-0	86	-11		-0.8
Total	2	0	4	.000	10	5	2	0	43.2	59	40	10	0	26	8	7.42	65	.316	.399	14	.214	-0	80	-12		-0.8

UPHAM, BILL					William Lawrence		B4.4.1888 Akron OH	D9.14.1959 Newark NJ	BB/TR/6-0/178		d4.10															
1915	Bro F	7	8	.467	33	11	4-2	4	121	129	61	0	0	40	46	3.35	81	.274	.331	36	.111	-2	94	-9		-1.3
1918	Bos N	1	1	.500	3	2	2	0	20.2	28	14	2	0	1	8	5.23	51	.326	.333	9	.222	0	141	-5		-0.4
Total	2	8	9	.471	36	13	6-2	4	141.2	157	75	2	0	41	54	3.62	75	.282	.332	45	.133	-2	100	-14		-1.7

| **UPP, JERRY** | | | | | George Henry | | B12.10.1883 Sandusky OH | D6.30.1937 Sandusky OH | TL | | d9.2 | | | | | | | | | | | | | | | |
| 1909 | Cle A | 2 | 1 | .667 | 7 | 4 | 2 | 0 | 26.2 | 26 | 10 | 0 | 0 | 12 | 13 | 1.69 | 152 | .260 | .339 | 9 | .222 | 0 | 90 | 2 | | 0.3 |

UPSHAW, CECIL					Cecil Lee		B10.22.1942 Spearsville LA	D2.7.1995 Lawrenceville GA	BR/TR/6-6/185(185-205)		d10.1 Col Centenary Louisiana		[DL 1970 Atl N 165]												
1966	Atl N	0	0	—	1	0	0	0	3	0	0	0	0	3-0	2	0.00	—	.000	.273	1	1.000	0		1		0.1
1967	Atl N	2	3	.400	30	0	0	8	45.1	42	14	4	4	8-4	31	2.58	129	.247	.295	6-0-2	.167	1		4		0.7
1968	Atl N	8	7	.533	52	0	0	13	116.2	98	41	6	4	24-7	74	2.47	121	.229	.275	23-0-6	.174	0		5		0.8
1969	†Atl N	6	4	.600	62	0	0	27-5	105.1	102	36	7	1	29-6	57	2.91	125	.259	.309	21-1-3	.238	2		9		1.6
1971	Atl N	11	6	.647	49	0	0	17-9	82	95	33	5	2	28-12	56	3.51	106	.292	.349	15-0-2	.000	-2		3		0.5
1972	Atl N	3	5	.375	42	0	0	13-2	53.2	50	22	5	1	19-9	23	3.69	103	.249	.315	7-0-1	.143	-0		2	22	0.3
1973	Atl N	0	1	.000	5	0	0	1-0	3.2	8	5	0	0	2-1	3	9.82	40	.444	.476	0	—	0		-2		-0.5
	Hou N	2	3	.400	35	0	0	1-0	38.1	38	21	3	1	15-4	21	4.46	82	.259	.331	2	.000	-0		-2		-0.4
	Year	2	4	.333	40	0	0	1-0	42	46	26	3	1	17-5	24	4.93	75	.279	.348	2	.000	-0		-4		-0.9
1974	Cle A	1	0	1.000	7	0	0	0-1	8	10	4	1	0	4-1	7	3.38	108	.345	.400	0	—	0		-6		0.0
	NY A	1	5	.167	36	0	0	6-3	59.2	53	25	1	3	24-3	27	3.02	118	.254	.339	0	—	0		3		0.4
	Year	2	5	.286	43	0	0	6-4	67.2	63	29	2	3	28-4	34	3.06	116	.265	.347	0	—	0		-3		0.4
1975	Chi A	1	1	.500	29	0	0	1-2	47.1	49	19	5	4	21-3	22	3.23	120	.271	.359	0	—	0		3		0.2
Total	9	34	36	.486	348	0	0	86-22	563	545	220	37	20	177-50	323	3.13	112	.258	.320	75-1-14	.160	1		24	187	3.7

| **UPTON, BILL** | | | | | William Ray | | B6.18.1929 Esther MO | D1.2.1987 San Diego CA | BR/TR/6-0/167 | | d4.13 b-Tom | | | | | | | | | | | | | | | |
| 1954 | Phi A | 0 | 0 | — | 2 | 0 | 0 | 0 | 1 | 5 | 6 | 1 | 1 | 0 | 1 | 2 | 1.80 | 217 | .300 | .333 | 0 | — | 0 | | 1 | | 0.1 |

URBAN, JACK					Jack Elmer		B12.5.1928 Omaha NE	BR/TR/5-8/155*		d6.13																
1957	KC A	7	4	.636	31	13	3	0	129.1	111	55	7	1	45-3	55	3.34	118	.237	.300	39-0-1	.282	2*	97	8		1.0
1958	KC A	8	11	.421	30	24	5-1	1	132	150	92	17	2	51-1	54	5.93	66	.286	.348	46	.152	-2*	87	-27		-3.6
1959	StL N	0	0	—	8	0	0	0	10.2	18	11	1	0	7-4	4	9.28	46	.409	.490	1	.000	-0		-5		-0.3
Total	3	15	15	.500	69	37	8-1	1	272	279	158	25	3	103-8	113	4.83	82	.269	.333	86-0-1	.209	0	90	-24		-2.9

URBANI, TOM					Thomas James		B1.21.1968 Santa Cruz CA	BL/TL/6-1/190(190-210)		[StLN90 13/357]		d4.21 Col Cal St.-Long Beach														
1993	StL N	1	3	.250	18	9	0	0-1	62	73	44	4	0	26-2	33	4.65	87	.296	.355	16-0-2	.188	1	114	-8		-0.4
1994	StL N	3	7	.300	20	10	0	0-0	80.1	98	48	12	3	21-0	43	5.15	82	.302	.348	24-0-3	.250	1	84	-8		-0.7
1995	StL N	3	5	.375	24	13	0	0-0	82.2	99	40	11	2	21-4	52	3.70	116	.305	.351	19-1-2	.316	3	65	5	22	0.8
1996	StL N	1	0	1.000	3	2	0	0-0	11.2	15	10	3	0	4-0	1	7.71	55	.319	.365	6	.167	-0*	117	-3		-0.3
	Det A	2	2	.500	16	2	0	0-0	23.2	31	22	7	1	14-0	20	8.37	61	.310	.402	0	—	0	127	-8		-1.0
Total	4	10	17	.370	81	36	0	0-1	260.1	316	164	38	7	86-6	149	4.98	86	.303	.357	65-1-7	.246	5	88	-23	22	-1.6

URBINA, UGUETH					Ugueth Urtain (Villarreal)		B2.15.1974 Caracas, Venez	BR/TR/6-2/205(185-205)		d5.9															
1995	Mon N	2	2	.500	7	4	0	0-0	23.1	26	17	6	0	14-1	15	6.17	70	.280	.374	6	.333	0	63	-5		-0.6
1996	Mon N	10	5	.667	33	17	0	0-1	114	102	54	18	1	44-4	108	3.71	117	.234	.304	29-0-3	.103	-1	80	7		0.6
1997	Mon N	5	8	.385	63	0	0	27-5	64.1	52	29	9	1	29-2	84	3.78	111	.214	.300	5	.000	-1		3		0.6
1998	Mon N★	6	3	.667	64	0	0	34-4	69.1	37	11	2	0	33-2	94	1.30	324	.157	.259	6	.000	-1		23		4.5
1999	Mon N	6	6	.500	71	0	0	41-9	75.2	59	35	6	0	36-6	100	3.69	121	.208	.295	5	.000	-1		7		1.2
2000	Mon N	1	0	1.000	13	0	0	9-1	13.1	11	6	1	0	5-0	22	4.05	116	.224	.296	1	.000	-0		1	145	0.2
2001	Mon N	2	1	.667	45	0	0	15-3	46.2	42	24	8	0	21-1	57	4.24	102	.236	.315	1	.000	-0		0		0.2
	Bos A	1	0	1.000	19	0	0	9-1	20	16	5	1	0	3-0	32	2.25	197	.219	.250		—	0		5		0.6
2002	Bos A★	1	6	.143	61	0	0	40-6	60	44	21	8	0	20-5	71	3.00	149	.202	.266	0	—	0		10		2.0
2003	Tex A	0	4	.000	39	0	0	26-4	38.2	33	19	6	0	18-2	41	4.19	119	.232	.313	0	—	0		3		0.6
	†Fla N	3	0	1.000	33	0	0	6-2	38.1	23	6	2	0	13-0	37	1.41	291	.174	.245	0-0-1	—	0		12		1.2
2004	Det A	4	6	.400	54	0	0	21-3	54	38	28	7	3	32-3	66	4.50	100	.194	.313	0	—	0		5		0.0
2005	Det A	1	3	.250	25	0	0	9-2	27.1	21	9	4	1	14-2	31	2.63	161	.208	.310	0	—	0		5		0.9
	Phi N	4	3	.571	56	0	0	1-6	52.1	35	25	8	0	25-2	66	4.13	105	.186	.280	0	—	0		2		0.2
Total	11	44	49	.473	583	21	0	237-48	697.1	539	289	86	6	307-30	814	3.45	127	.210	.294	53-0-4	.094	-2	77	73	145	12.0

| **URDANETA, LINO** | | | | | Lino | | B11.20.1979 Caracas, Venez | BR/TR/6-1/170 | | d9.9 | | | | | | | | | | | | | | | |
| 2004 | Det A | 0 | 0 | — | 1 | 0 | 0 | 0-0 | 0 | 5 | 6 | 0 | 0 | 1-0 | 0 | ∞ | — | 1.000 | 1.000 | 0 | — | 0 | | -6 | 150 | -0.4 |

URREA, JOHN					John Godoy		B2.9.1955 Los Angeles CA	BR/TR/6-3/205*		[StLN74*1/14]		d4.10 Col Rio Hondo (CA) JC														
1977	StL N	7	6	.538	41	12	2-1	4-2	139.2	126	56	13	0	35-3	81	3.16	124	.244	.291	29-0-3	.138	2	101	11		1.2
1978	StL N	4	9	.308	27	12	1	0-1	98.2	108	75	4	7	47-4	61	5.38	66	.284	.369	24-0-2	.125	-1	88	-23		-2.8
1979	StL N	0	0	—	3	2	0	0-0	11.1	13	7	0	0	9-0	5	3.97	96	.310	.431	4	.250	0	151	-1		0.0
1980	StL N	4	1	.800	30	1	0	3-0	64.2	57	28	2	2	41-9	36	3.48	108	.239	.352	13-0-2	.231	0	214	2		0.1
1981	SD N	2	2	.500	38	0	0	2-1	49	43	14	1	3	28-0	19	2.39	136	.239	.346	4	.250	0	6	-5		0.4
Total	5	17	18	.486	139	27	3-1	9-4	363.1	347	180	20	12	160-16	202	3.74	99	.256	.337	74-0-7	.162	1	105	-6		-1.1

| **VAIL, BOB** | | | | | Robert Garfield "Doc" | | B9.24.1881 Linneus ME | D3.22.1942 Philadelphia PA | BR/TR/5-10/165 | | d8.27 Col Davidson | | | | | | | | | | | | | | |
| 1908 | Pit N | 1 | 2 | .333 | 4 | 1 | 0 | 0 | 15 | 15 | 10 | 0 | 1 | 7 | 9 | 6.00 | 38 | .268 | .359 | 3 | .333 | 1 | 0 | -5 | | -0.9 |

VALDES, MARC					Marc Christopher		B12.20.1971 Dayton OH	BR/TR/6-0/187(170-188)		[FlaN93 1/27]		d8.28 Col Florida														
1995	Fla N	0	0	—	3	3	0	0-0	7	17	13	1	1	9-0	2	14.14	30	.459	.563	2	.000	-0	133	-8		-0.4
1996	Fla N	1	3	.250	11	8	0	0-1	48.2	63	32	5	1	23-0	13	4.81	86	.315	.383	14	.000	-1	74	-5		-0.5
1997	Mon N	4	4	.500	48	7	0	2-0	95	84	36	2	8	39-5	56	3.13	134	.240	.326	19	.105	-1	69	12		0.8
1998	Mon N	1	3	.250	20	4	0	0-0	36.1	41	34	6	1	21-2	28	7.43	57	.285	.375	5	.000	-1	44	-13	112	-1.1
2000	Hou N	5	5	.500	53	0	0	2-4	56.2	69	41	3	5	25-1	35	5.08	97	.301	.379	3	.400	-0		-4		-0.6
2001	Atl N	1	0	1.000	9	0	0	0-0	7	7	6	4	0	1-1	3	7.71	56	.259	.286	0	—	0		-2		-0.3
Total	6	12	15	.444	144	22	0	4-5	250.2	281	162	21	16	118-9	135	4.95	88	.285	.366	43	.093	-1	73	-20	112	-2.1

YEAR	TM LG	W	L	PCT	G	GS	CG-SHO	SV-BS	IP	H	R	HR	HB	BB-IB	SO	ERA	AERA	OAV	OOB	AB-HR-SH	AVG	PB	SUP	APR	DL	PV

VALDEZ, CARLOS Carlos Luis (Lorenzo) B12.26.1971 Nizao Bani, D.R. BR/TR/5-11/175(165-191) d7.18

1995	SF N	0	1	.000	11	0	0	0-0	14.2	19	10	1	1	8-1	7	6.14	67	.322	.406	1	.000	-0		-3		-0.2
1998	Bos A	1	0	1.000	4	0	0	0-0	3.1	1	0	0	0	5-0	4	0.00	—	.100	.375	0	—	0		2		0.
Total	2	1	1	.500	15	0	0	0-0	18	20	10	1	1	13-1	11	5.00	85	.290	.400	1	.000	-0		-1		0.

VALDEZ, EFRAIN Efrain Antonio B7.11.1966 Nizao Bani, D.R. BL/TL/5-11/170* d8.13

1990	Cle A	1	1	.500	13	0	0	0-0	23.2	20	10	2	0	14-3	13	3.04	130	.233	.330	0	—	0		2		0.
1991	Cle A	0	0	—	7	0	0	0-0	6	5	1	0	1	3-1	1	1.50	278	.238	.346	0	—	0		0		0.
1998	Ari N	0	0	—	6	0	0	0-0	4.1	7	2	2	0	1-0	2	4.15	103	.368	.400	0	—	0		4		0.
Total	3	1	1	.500	26	0	0	0-0	34	32	13	4	1	18-4	16	2.91	138	.254	.342	0	—	0				0.

VALDEZ, ISMAEL Ismael (Alvarez) B8.21.1973 Ciudad Victoria, Tamaulipas, Mexico BR/TR/6-3/215(183-230) d6.15

1994	LA N	3	1	.750	21	1	0	0-0	28.1	21	10	2	0	10-2	28	3.18	125	.206	.277	2	.000	-0	160	3		2.
1995	†LA N	13	11	.542	33	27	6-2	1-0	197.2	168	76	17	1	51-5	150	3.05	127	.228	.277	62-0-7	.097	-3	86	20		2.
1996	†LA N	15	7	.682	33	33	0	0-0	225	219	94	20	3	54-10	173	3.32	118	.251	.294	70-0-13	.143	-1	106	17		1.
1997	LA N	10	11	.476	30	30	0	0-0	196.2	171	68	16	3	47-1	140	2.65	147	.234	.282	57-0-7	.088	-2	81	27	22	2.
1998	LA N	11	10	.524	27	27	2-2	0-0	174	171	82	17	2	66-4	122	3.98	101	.256	.323	48-0-8	.167	1	96	3	36	0.
1999	LA N	9	14	.391	32	32	2-1	0-0	203.1	213	97	32	6	58-2	143	3.98	109	.270	.321	58-0-10	.086	-3	89	10		0.
2000	Chi N	2	4	.333	12	12	0	0-0	67	71	40	17	2	27-2	45	5.37	85	.273	.344	14-0-5	.286	2*	82	-5	36	-0.
	LA N	0	3	.000	9	8	0	0-0	40	53	29	5	1	13-0	29	6.07	73	.327	.376	11-1-2	.091	0	124	-7		-0.
	Year	2	7	.222	21	20	0	0-0	107	124	69	22	3	40-2	74	5.64	80	.294	.356	25-1-7	.200	2	98	-12		-0.
2001	Ana A	9	13	.409	27	27	1	0-0	163.2	177	82	20	8	50-3	100	4.45	104	.277	.338	5	.200	0	66	6	33	1.
2002	Tex A	6	9	.400	23	23	0	0-0	146.2	135	65	19	2	36-1	75	3.93	122	.242	.297	3-0-1	.000	-0	74	15		1.
	Sea A	2	3	.400	8	8	1	0-0	49.1	59	29	7	0	11-0	27	4.93	87	.299	.333	0	—	0	140	-4		0.
	Year	8	12	.400	31	31	1	0-0	196	194	94	26	2	47-1	102	4.18	112	.257	.306	3-0-1	.000	-0	90	13	52	1.
2003	Tex A	8	8	.500	22	22	0	0-0	115	148	83	23	5	29-0	47	6.10	81	.318	.359	4-0-2	.000	-0	90	-13		-1.
2004	SD N	9	6	.600	23	20	1-1	0-0	114	141	75	21	2	31-1	37	5.53	71	.303	.347	35-0-3	.171	2	120	-21		-0.
	Fla N	5	3	.625	11	11	0	0-0	56	61	30	12	0	18-2	30	4.50	91	.277	.329	17	.235	1	102	-3		-0.
	Year	14	9	.609	34	31	1-1	0-0	170	202	105	33	2	49-3	67	5.19	77	.294	.341	52-0-3	.192	3	114	-21		-2.
2005	Fla N	2	2	.500	14	7	0	0-0	50.2	64	32	6	5	22-6	27	5.33	75	.314	.391	13-0-3	.154	-0	90	-8	109	-0.
Total	12	104	105	.498	325	288	13-6	1-0	1827.1	1872	892	234	47	523-39	1173	4.09	103	.265	.317	399-1-61	.130	-4	92	40	288	4.

VALDEZ, MERKIN Merkin R. B11.10.1981 San Cristobal, D.R. BR/TR/6-5/210 d8.1

| 2004 | SF N | 0 | 0 | — | 2 | 0 | 0 | 0-0 | 1.2 | 4 | 5 | 1 | 0 | 3-0 | 2 | 27.00 | 16 | .444 | .583 | 0 | — | -0 | | -4 | | -0 |

VALDEZ, RAFAEL Rafael Emilio (Diaz) B12.17.1967 Nizao Bani, D.R. BR/TR/5-11/165 d4.18

| 1990 | SD N | 1 | 0 | 1.000 | 3 | 0 | 0 | 0-0 | 5.2 | 11 | 7 | 4 | 0 | 2-0 | 3 | 11.12 | 35 | .393 | .433 | 1 | .000 | -0 | | -4 | | -0 |

VALDEZ, RENE Rene Gutierrez (b Rene Gutierrez (Valdez)) B6.2.1929 Guanabacoa, Cuba BR/TR/6-3/175 d4.21

| 1957 | Bro N | 1 | 1 | .500 | 5 | 1 | 0 | 0-0 | 13 | 13 | 8 | 1 | 0 | 7-1 | 5 | 5.54 | 75 | .265 | .351 | 3 | .000 | 0 | 169 | -1 | | -0. |

VALDEZ, SERGIO Sergio Sanchez (b Sergio Sanchez (Valdez)) B9.7.1964 Elias Pina, D.R. BR/TR/6-1/190* d9.10 [DL 1996 SF N 182]

1986	Mon N	0	4	.000	5	5	0	0-0	25	39	20	2	1	11-0	20	6.84	55	.361	.425	8	.125	-0	52	-8		-1.
1989	Atl N	1	2	.333	19	1	0	0-0	32.2	31	24	4	0	17-3	26	6.06	60	.246	.336	1	1.000	0	48	-8		-0.
1990	Atl N	0	0	—	6	0	0	0-0	5.1	6	4	0	0	3-0	3	6.75	60	.273	.360	0	—	0		-1		-0.
	Cle A	6	6	.500	24	13	0	0-0	102.1	109	62	17	1	35-2	63	4.75	83	.276	.333	0	—	0	123	-11		-0.
1991	Cle A	1	0	1.000	6	0	0	0-0	16.1	15	11	3	0	5-1	11	5.51	76	.238	.290	3	.000	0		-2		-0.
1992	Mon N	0	2	.000	27	0	0	0-1	37.1	25	12	2	0	12-1	32	2.41	145	.185	.252	3	.000	-0	4			0.
1993	Mon N	0	0	—	4	0	0	0-0	3	4	4	1	0	1-0	2	9.00	46	.308	.357	0	—	0	73	-5		-0.
1994	Bos A	0	1	.000	12	1	0	0-0	14.1	25	14	4	0	8-1	4	8.16	62	.391	.458	0	—	0	92	-7		-0.
1995	SF N	4	5	.444	13	11	1	0-1	66.1	78	43	12	3	17-3	29	4.75	87	.298	.344	21-0-3	.095	-1	92	-7		-0.
Total	8	12	20	.375	116	31	1	0-1	302.2	332	194	46	5	109-11	190	5.06	78	.279	.340	33-0-3	.121	-1	98	-40	182	-0

VALENTINE, CORKY Harold Lewis B1.4.1929 Troy OH D1.21.2005 Roswell GA BR/TR/6-1/203* d4.17

1954	Cin N	12	11	.522	36	28	7-3	1	194.1	211	98	24	4	60		4.45	94	.282	.337	65-0-5	.138	-2	87	-1		-1
1955	Cin N	2	1	.667	10	5	0		26.2	29	23	5	1	16-2	14	7.43	57	.276	.368	7	.000	-1	118	-8		-0
Total	2	14	12	.538	46	33	7-3	1	221	240	121	29	5	76-2	87	4.81	87	.282	.341	72-0-5	.125	-3	92	-9		-1

VALENTINE, JOHN John Gill B11.21.1855 Brooklyn NY D10.10.1903 Central Islip NY d5.3

| 1883 | Col AA | 2 | 10 | .167 | 13 | 12 | 11 | | 102 | 130 | 80 | 0 | | 17 | 13 | 3.53 | 87 | .291 | .317 | 60 | .283 | 3* | 70 | -8 | | -0 |

VALENTINE, JOE Joseph John B12.24.1979 Las Vegas NV BR/TR/6-2/190(190-210) [ChiA99 26/789] d8.24 Col Jefferson Davis (AL) CC

2003	Cin N	0	0	—	2	0	0	0-0	2	5	4	1	0	1-0	1	18.00	23	.455	.500			0		-3		-0
2004	Cin N	2	3	.400	24	1	0	4-0	29.1	23	18	4	2	25-1	29	5.22	82	.211	.368	1	.000	-0	43	-3		-0
2005	Cin N	0	1	.000	16	0	0	0-1	14.1	18	15	4	2	11-0	9	8.16	51	.295	.413	0	—	0		-7		-0
Total	3	2	4	.333	42	1	0	4-1	45.2	46	37	9	4	37-1	39	6.70	64	.254	.390	1	.000	-0	43	-13		-0

VALENTINETTI, VITO Vito John B9.16.1928 W.New York NJ BR/TR/6-0/195* d6.20 Col Iona

1954	Chi A	0	0	—	1	0	0		1	4	6	1	0	4-0	1	54.00	7	.571	.667	0		0		-5		-0
1956	Chi N	6	4	.600	42	2	0	1	95.1	84	47	10	1	36-7	26	3.78	100	.243	.313	20-0-1	.100	-1	128	0		0
1957	Chi N	0	0	—	9	0	0	0	12	12	5	1	0	7-1	8	2.25	172	.255	.352	2	.000	0		1		0
	Cle A	2	2	.500	11	2	1	0	23.2	26	14	3	1	13-0	9	4.94	75	.289	.381	5	.200	0	96	-3		0
1958	Det A	2	0	1.000	15	0	0	2	18.2	18	7	4	1	5-0	10	3.38	120	.257	.316	0	—	0		2		0
	Was A	4	6	.400	23	10	2	0	95.2	106	54	16	2	49-7	33	5.08	75	.286	.372	28-0-2	.321	2	85	-11		-0
	Year	5	6	.455	38	10	2	2	114.1	124	61	20	3	54-7	43	4.80	80	.282	.363	28-0-2	.321	2	84	-9		-0
1959	Was A	0	2	.000	7	1	0	0	10.2	16	12	0	1	10-0	7	10.13	39	.356	.482	0	—	0	45	-6		-0
Total	5	13	14	.481	108	15	3	3	257	266	145	35	6	122-15	94	4.73	81	.273	.356	55-0-3	.218	1	89	-22		-2

VALENZUELA, FERNANDO Fernando (Anguamea) B11.1.1960 Navojoa, Sonora, Mexico BL/TL/5-11/195(168-202) d9.15

1980	LA N★	2	0	1.000	10	0	0	1-0	17.2	8	2	0	0	5-0	16	0.00	—	.136	.200	1	.000	-0		6		-0
1981	†LA N★	13	7	.650	25	25	11-8	0-0	192.1	140	55	11	1	61-4	180	2.48	133	.205	.270	64-0-6	.250	3	97	19		4.
1982	LA N★	19	13	.594	37	37	18-4	0-0	285	247	105	13	2	83-12	199	2.87	121	.236	.292	95-1-10	.168	1*	100	19		3.
1983	†LA N☆	15	10	.600	35	35	9-4	0-0	257	245	122	16	3	99-10	189	3.75	96	.255	.325	91-1-12	.187	2*	118	-1		1.
1984	LA N	12	17	.414	34	34	12-2	0-0	261	218	109	14	2	106-4	240	3.03	117	.229	.306	79-3-9	.190	4*	77	12		3.
1985	†LA N★	17	10	.630	35	35	14-5	0-0	272.1	211	92	14	1	101-5	208	2.45	143	.214	.286	97-1-5	.216	4	106	31		4.
1986	LA N★	21	11	.656	34	34	20-3	0-0	269.1	226	104	18	1	85-5	242	3.14	110	.226	.287	109-0-6	.220	5*	121	11		5.
1987	LA N	14	14	.500	34	34	12-1	0-0	251	254	120	25	4	124-4	190	3.98	100	.262	.348	92-1-8	.141	-1*	92	2		1.
1988	LA N	5	8	.385	23	22	3	1-0	142.1	142	71	11	0	76-4	64	4.24	79	.268	.350	44-0-7	.182	1	129	-12	57	-1.
1989	LA N	10	13	.435	31	31	3	0-0	196.2	185	89	11	2	98-6	116	3.43	100	.251	.337	66-0-7	.182	1	94	-2		-0.
1990	LA N	13	13	.500	33	33	5-2	0-0	204	223	112	19	0	77-4	115	4.59	80	.276	.337	69-1-7	.304	8*	123	-18		-1.
1991	Cal A	0	2	.000	2	2	0	0-0	6.2	14	10	3	0	3-0	5	12.15	34	.452	.486	0	—	0	0	-6	22	-0.
1993	Bal A	8	10	.444	32	31	5-2	0-0	178.2	179	104	16	4	79-2	78	4.94	92	.266	.343	12-0-4	.250	1	67	7		-0.
1994	Phi N	1	2	.333	8	7	0	0-0	45	42	16	8	0	7-1	19	3.00	143	.247	.274	10-0-1	.250	-0	108	-8		-0.
1995	SD N	8	3	.727	29	15	0	0-0	90.1	101	53	16	0	34-2	57	4.98	82	.289	.351	32-2-3	.250	-0	108	-13		-0.
1996	†SD N	13	8	.619	33	31	0	0-0	171.2	177	78	17	0	67-2	95	3.62	111	.269	.334	63-0-3	.143	-1*	105	7		-0.
1997	SD N	2	8	.200	13	13	1	0-0	66.1	84	42	10	4	32-0	51	4.75	83	.309	.387	17-0-4	.176	0*	67	-8		-0.
	StL N	0	4	.000	5	5	0	0-0	22.2	22	19	2	1	14-0	10	5.56	75	.253	.363	5-0-2	.200	0	92	-5		-0.
	Year	2	12	.143	18	18	1	0-0	89	106	61	12	5	46-0	61	4.96	81	.295	.381	22-0-6	.182	0	74	-13		-0.
Total	17	173	153	.531	453	424	113-31	2-0	2930	2718	1303	226	25	1151-65	2074	3.54	104	.248	.319	936-10-93	.200	32	102	47	79	

VALERA, JULIO Julio Enrique (Torres) B10.13.1968 Aguadilla, PR BR/TR/6-2/215(185-215) d9.1 [DL 1994 Cal A 99]

1990	NY N	1	1	.500	3	3	0	0-0	13	20	11	6	0	6-1	9	6.92	54	.351	.422	5	.200	0	136	-5		-0
1991	NY N	0	0	—	2	0	0	0-0	2	1	0	0	0	4-1	3	0.00	—	.143	.455	0	—	0	84	7		0
1992	Cal A	8	11	.421	30	28	4-2	0-0	188	188	82	15	2	64-5	113	3.73	108	.262	.323	0	—	0	134	-12	102	1
1993	Cal A	3	6	.333	19	5	0	4-3	53	77	44	7	2	15-2	28	6.62	69	.344	.388	0	—	0	83	-8		-0
1996	KC A	3	2	.600	31	2	0	1-0	61.1	75	44	7	2	27-3	31	6.46	78	.307	.375	5	.200	0	91	-17	201	-0
Total	5	15	20	.429	85	38	4-2	5-3	317.1	361	181	31	6	117-11	179	4.85	88	.289	.351	0	—	0	89			-0

YEAR	TM LG	W	L	PCT	G	GS	CG-SHO	SV-BS	IP	H	R	HR	HB	BB-IB	SO	ERA	AERA	OAV	OOB	AB-HR-SH	AVG	PB	SUP	APR	DL	PW

VALVERDE, JOSE   Jose Rafael B7.24.1979 San Pedro de Macoris, D.R.   BR/TR/6-4/220(220-255)   d6.1

2003	Ari N	2	1	.667	54	0	0	10-1	50.1	24	16	4	2	26-2	71	2.15	215	.137	.255	1	1.000	1		12		1.1
2004	Ari N	1	2	.333	29	0	0	8-2	29.2	23	17	7	1	17-4	38	4.25	107	.213	.320	0	—	0		0	112	0.1
2005	Ari N	3	4	.429	61	0	0	15-2	66.1	51	19	5	2	20-1	75	2.44	180	.211	.275	0	—	0		14	29	1.9
Total	3	6	7	.462	144	0	0	33-5	146.1	98	52	16	5	63-7	184	2.71	166	.187	.278	1	1.000	1		26	141	3.1

VAN ALSTYNE, CLAY   Clayton Emory "Spike" B5.24.1900 Stuyvesant NY D1.5.1960 Hudson NY   BR/TR/5-11/180   d8.20

1927	Was A	0	0	—	2	0	0	0	3	3	1	0	0	0	0	3.00	136	.250	.250	0	—	0		0		0.0
1928	Was A	0	0	—	4	0	0	0	21.1	26	14	0	1	13	5	5.48	73	.329	.430	8-1-0	.250	1		-3		0.0
Total	2	0	0	—	6	0	0	0	24.1	29	15	0	1	13	5	5.18	78	.319	.410	8-1-0	.250	1		-3		0.0

VAN ATTA, RUSS   Russell "Sheriff" B6.21.1906 Augusta NJ D10.10.1986 Andover NJ   BL/TL/6-0/184   d4:25 Col Penn St.

1933	NY A	12	4	.750	26	22	10-2	1	157	160	81	8	1	63	76	4.18	93	.262	.332	60-0-5	.283	4	149	-4		0.0
1934	NY A	3	5	.375	28	9	0	0	88	107	69	3	2	46	39	6.34	64	.307	.390	29-1-1	.207	1	100	-23		-1.6
1935	NY A	0	0	—	5	0	0	0	4.2	5	5	0	2	4	3	3.86	105	.263	.391	1	.000	-0		-1		-0.1
	StL A	9	16	.360	53	17	1	3	170.1	201	116	10	3	87	87	5.34	90	.292	.374	42-0-6	.214	-1	80	-9		-1.3
	Year	9	16	.360	58	17	1	3	175	206	121	10	3	91	90	5.30	90	.291	.375	43-0-6	.209	-1	80	-11		-1.4
1936	StL A	4	7	.364	52	9	2	2	122.2	164	101	9	2	68	59	6.60	81	.320	.401	29	.172	-1*	78	-15		-1.1
1937	StL A	1	2	.333	16	6	1	0	58.2	74	41	2	0	32	34	5.52	87	.307	.388	13-1-0	.462	3	78	-5		0.1
1938	StL A	4	7	.364	25	12	3-1	0	104	118	75	7	1	61	35	6.06	82	.289	.382	30-0-3	.133	-1	61	-11		-1.0
1939	StL A	0	0	—	2	1	0	0	7	9	10	0	1	7	6	11.57	42	.310	.459	2	.000	-0	127	-5		-0.2
Total	7	33	41	.446	207	76	17-3	6	712.1	838	498	39	10	368	339	5.60	82	.293	.376	206-2-15	.228	5	95	-73		-5.2

VAN BENSCHOTEN, JOHN   John Wesley B4.14.1980 San Diego CA   BR/TR/6-4/215   [PitN01 1/8]   d8.18 Col Kent St.   [DL 2005 Pit N 183]

2004	Pit N	1	3	.250	6	5	0	0-0	28.2	33	27	3	2	19-0	18	6.91	63	.300	.406	8-1-2	.125	1	94	-10		-1.0

VAN BRABANT, OZZIE   Camille Oscar B9.28.1926 Kingsville ON, Can.   BR/TR/6-1/165*   d4.13

1954	Phi A	0	2	.000	9	2	0	0	26.2	35	23	3	1	18	10	7.09	55	.347	.446	5	.200	0	34	-9		-0.5
1955	KC A	0	0	—	2	0	0	0	2	4	4	1	0	2-1	1	18.00	23	.400	.462	0	—	0		-3		-0.1
Total	2	0	2	.000	11	2	0	0	28.2	39	27	4	1	20-1	11	7.85	50	.351	.448	5	.200	0	34	-12		-0.6

VAN BUREN, JERMAINE   Jermaine Russell B7.2.1980 Laurel MS   BR/TR/6-1/220   d8.31

2005	Chi N	0	2	.000	6	0	0	0-0	6	2	2	0	0	9-2	3	3.00	146	.118	.423	0	—	0		1		0.2

VANCE, DAZZY   Clarence Arthur B3.4.1891 Orient IA D2.16.1961 Homosassa Springs FL   BR/TR/6-2/200   d4.16   HF1955

1915	Pit N	0	1	.000	1	1	0	0	2.2	3	3	0	1	5	0	10.13	27	.375	.643	1	.000	-0	54	-2		-0.3
	NY A	0	3	.000	8	3	1	0	28	23	14	1	2	16	18	3.54	83	.232	.350	3-0-1	.667	2	41	-2		0.0
1918	NY A	0	0	—	2	0	0	0	2.1	9	5	0	0	2	0	15.43	18	.692	.733	0	—	0		-3		-0.2
1922	Bro N	18	12	.600	36	31	16-5	0	245.2	259	122	9	8	94	134	3.70	110	.276	.347	89-0-6	.225	1	112	10		1.3
1923	Bro N	18	15	.545	37	35	21-3	0	280.1	263	127	10	11	100	197	3.50	111	.250	.322	83-1-7	.084	-3	95	17		1.5
1924	Bro N	28	6	.824	35	34	30-3	0	308.1	238	89	11	9	77	262	2.16	173	.213	.269	106-2-8	.151	-2	114	57		5.9
1925	Bro N	22	9	.710	31	31	26-4	0	265.1	247	115	8	10	66	221	3.53	118	.250	.304	98-3-2	.143	-0	115	24		2.5
1926	Bro N	9	10	.474	24	22	12	1	169	172	80	7	1	58	140	3.89	98	.271	.333	55-0-3	.182	-1	84	2		0.2
1927	Bro N	16	15	.516	34	32	25-2	1	273.1	242	98	12	6	69	184	2.70	147	.239	.291	90-0-6	.167	-2	82	38		3.9
1928	Bro N	22	10	.688	38	34	24-4	2	280.1	226	79	11	7	72	200	2.09	191	.221	.277	96-0-1	.177	2	85	60		7.2
1929	Bro N	14	13	.519	31	27	17-1	0	231.1	244	110	15	9	47	126	3.89	119	.274	.316	74-0-2	.135	-2	76	23		2.1
1930	Bro N	17	15	.531	35	31	20-4	0	258.2	241	97	15	5	55	173	2.61	188	.246	.289	89-0-3	.135	-5	83	64		6.4
1931	Bro N	11	13	.458	30	29	12-2	0	218.2	221	99	12	0	53	150	3.38	113	.261	.304	67-0-7	.134	-2	79	9		0.7
1932	Bro N	12	11	.522	27	24	9-1	1	175.2	171	90	10	1	57	103	4.20	91	.256	.315	56-0-5	.089	-2	79	-6		-1.1
1933	StL N	6	2	.750	28	11	2	3	99	105	42	3	1	28	67	3.55	98	.267	.318	28-0-3	.179	-1	98	1		0.0
1934	Cin N	0	2	.000	6	2	0	0	18	28	21	1	1	11	9	7.50	54	.350	.435	4	.250	0	63	-8		-0.7
†StL N	1	1	.500	19	4	1	2	59	62	26	4	2	14	33	3.66	115	.271	.318	15-1-1	.133	-0	61	4		0.2
Year	1	3	.250	25	6	1	1	77	90	47	5	3	25	42	4.56	92	.291	.350	19-1-1	.158	-0	62	-3		-0.5
1935	Bro N	3	2	.600	20	0	0	2	51	55	29	3	3	16	28	4.41	90	.268	.330	17	.059	-2		-2		-0.4
Total	16	197	140	.585	442	349	216-29	11	2966.2	2809	1246	132	77	840	2045	3.24	125	.251	.308	971-7-55	.150	-18	92	286		29.2

VANCE, CORY   Cory Wade B6.20.1979 Dayton OH   BL/TL/6-1/195*   [ColN00 4/107]   d9.21 Col Georgia Tech

2002	Col N	0	0	—	2	1	0	0-0	4	4	3	2	1	4-0	1	6.75	70	.267	.450	1	.000	-0	156	-1		0.0
2003	Col N	1	3	.250	9	3	0	0-1	27.1	31	19	6	1	10-0	12	5.60	87	.287	.347	7-0-2	.286	-0	45	-2		-0.2
Total	2	1	3	.250	11	4	0	0-1	31.1	35	22	8	2	14-0	13	5.74	85	.285	.362	8-0-2	.250	0	72	-3		-0.2

VANCE, SANDY   Gene Covington B1.5.1947 Lamar CO   BR/TR/6-2/180*   [LAN68 S2/33]   d4.26 Col Stanford

1970	LA N	7	7	.500	20	18	2	0-0	115	109	47	9	1	37-2	45	3.13	123	.248	.306	37-0-4	.189	1	101	8		0.9
1971	LA N	2	1	.667	10	3	0	0-1	26	38	21	1	0	9-0	11	6.92	47	.355	.398	5	.000	-0	136	-11		-1.1
Total	2	9	8	.529	30	21	2	0-1	141	147	68	10	1	46-2	56	3.83	98	.269	.324	42-0-4	.167	0	106	-3		-0.2

VANCE, JOE   Joseph Albert "Sandy" B9.16.1905 Devine TX D7.4.1978 San Antonio TX   BR/TR/6-1.5/190   d4.18 Col Southwest Texas

1935	Chi A	2	2	.500	10	0	0	0	31	36	26	1	0	21	12	6.68	90	.295	.399	11	.182	-1		-7		-0.7
1937	NY A	1	0	1.000	2	2	0	0	15	11	5	2	0	9	3	3.00	148	.204	.317	5	.000	-1	88	3		0.1
1938	NY A	0	0	—	3	1	0	0	11.1	20	9	2	0	4	2	7.15	63	.408	.453	4	.750	2*	136	-3		0.1
Total	3	3	2	.600	15	3	0	0	57.1	67	40	5	0	34	17	5.81	79	.298	.390	20	.250	1	102	-7		-0.5

VAN CUYK, CHRIS   Christian Gerald B1.3.1927 Kimberly WI D11.3.1992 Hudson FL   BL/TL/6-6/215*   d7.16 b-Johnny

1950	Bro N	1	3	.250	12	4	1	0	33.1	33	19	3	1	12	21	4.86	84	.266	.336	10-0-1	.100	-1	119	-3		-0.4
1951	Bro N	1	2	.333	9	6	0	0	29.1	33	22	4	4	11	16	5.52	71	.295	.378	8	.250	0	124	-6		-0.5
1952	Bro N	5	6	.455	23	16	4	1	97.2	104	58	12	5	40	66	5.16	71	.271	.347	33-0-3	.242	2	144	-15		-1.5
Total	3	7	11	.389	44	26	5	1	160.1	170	99	19	10	63	103	5.16	73	.274	.351	51-0-4	.216	1	134	-24		-2.4

VAN CUYK, JOHNNY   John Henry B7.7.1921 Little Chute WI   BL/TL/6-1/190   d9.18 b-Chris

1947	Bro N	0	0	—	2	0	0	0	3.1	5	2	0	0	1	2	5.40	77	.357	.400	0	—	0		0		0.0
1948	Bro N	0	0	—	3	0	0	0	5	4	3	1	0	1	1	3.60	111	.200	.238	0	—	0		0		0.0
1949	Bro N	0	0	—	2	0	0	0	2	3	2	0	1	0	3	9.00	46	.429	.500	0	—	0		-1		-0.1
Total	3	0	0	—	7	0	0	0	10.1	12	7	1	0	3	3	5.23	77	.286	.341	0	—	0		-1		-0.1

VANDE BERG, ED   Edward John B10.26.1958 Redlands CA   BR/TL/6-2/180*   [SeaA80 13/318]   d4.7 Col Arizona St.

1982	Sea A	9	4	.692	78	0	0	5-2	76	54	21	5	2	32-7	60	2.37	181	.207	.296	0	—	0		16		2.9
1983	Sea A	2	4	.333	68	0	0	5-4	64.1	59	32	6	1	22-6	49	3.36	128	.246	.308	0	—	0		4		0.4
1984	Sea A	8	12	.400	50	17	0	7-5	130.1	165	76	18	0	50-4	71	4.76	84	.313	.368	0	—	0*	78	-10		-1.5
1985	Sea A	2	1	.667	76	0	0	3-1	67.2	71	30	4	1	31-5	34	3.72	114	.274	.350	0	—	0		4		0.2
1986	LA N	1	5	.167	60	0	0	0-2	71.1	83	32	8	1	33-7	42	3.41	102	.290	.364	1	.000	0		-2		-0.1
1987	Cle A	1	0	1.000	55	0	0	0-1	72.1	96	42	9	4	21-2	40	5.10	90	.325	.364	0	—	0		0		0.0
1988	Tex A	2	2	.500	26	0	0	0	37	44	19	2	1	11-4	18	4.14	99	.308	.353	0	—	0		0		0.0
Total	7	25	28	.472	413	17	2	22-15	519	572	252	52	5	200-35	314	3.92	105	.285	.347	1	.000	-0	78	12		1.9

VANDENBERG, HY   Harold Harris B3.17.1906 Abilene KS D7.31.1994 Bloomington MN   BR/TR/6-4/220   d6.8

1935	Bos A	0	0	—	3	0	0	0	5.1	15	12	1	0	4	1	20.25	23	.500	.559	1	1.000	0		-8		-0.3
1937	NY N	0	1	.000	1	1	0	0	8	10	7	0	0	6	2	7.88	49	.313	.421	4	.000	-1	89	-3		-0.3
1938	NY N	0	1	.000	6	1	0	0	18	28	16	2	0	12	7	7.50	50	.368	.455	4	.000	-1	270	-7		-0.4
1939	NY N	0	0	—	2	1	0	0	6.1	10	5	0	0	3	5	5.68	69	.345	.457	2	.000	-1	134	-1		-0.1
1940	NY N	1	1	.500	13	3	1	0	32.1	27	15	2	1	16	17	3.90	100	.227	.324	8-0-1	.125	-0	172	0		0.0
1944	Chi N	7	4	.636	35	9	2	2	126.1	123	67	8	1	51	54	3.63	97	.255	.327	38-0-3	.237	1	119	-4		-0.3
1945	†Chi N	7	3	.700	30	7	3-1	2	95.1	91	44	4	4	33	35	3.49	105	.259	.330	32-0-1	.125	0	99	2		0.1
Total	7	15	10	.600	90	22	7-1	5	291.2	304	166	17	6	128	120	4.32	85	.271	.349	89-0-5	.169	-1	126	-21		-1.2

VANDER MEER, JOHNNY   John Samuel "Double No-Hit", "The Dutch Master" B11.2.1914 Prospect Park NJ D10.6.1997 Tampa FL   BB/TL/6-1/190*   d4.22 Mil 1944-45

1937	Cin N	3	5	.375	19	10	4	0	84.1	63	41	0	2	69	52	3.84	97	.209	.359	23-0-5	.217	1*	92	0		0.2
1938	Cin N☆	15	10	.600	32	29	16-3	0	225.1	177	89	12	3	103	125	3.12	117	.213	.302	83-0-5	.181	-2*	104	14		1.2
1939	Cin N☆	5	9	.357	30	21	8	0	129	128	76	7	2	95	102	4.67	82	.264	.387	36-0-7	.111	-1	110	-11		-1.3

VANDER MEER (continued)

YEAR	TM LG	W	L	PCT	G	GS	CG-SHO	SV-BS	IP	H	R	HR	HB	BB-IB	SO	ERA	AERA	OAV	OOB	AB-HR-SH	AVG	PB	SUP	APR	DL	PW
1940	†Cin N	3	1	.750	10	7	2	1	48	38	24	3	1	41	41	3.75	101	.211	.360	20	.300	2*	111	-1		0.2
1941	Cin N	16	13	.552	33	32	18-6	0	226.1	172	83	8	1	126	**202**	2.82	127	.214	.321	76-0-9	.132	-3*	84	19		2.1
1942	Cin N★	18	12	.600	33	33	21-4	0	244	188	78	6	1	102	**186**	2.43	135	.208	.290	75-0-8	.147	-1*	85	25		3.1
1943	Cin N★	15	16	.484	36	**36**	21-3	0	289	228	102	5	3	162	**174**	2.87	116	.224	.332	95-0-8	.137	-2*	85	15		1.5
1946	Cin N	10	12	.455	29	25	11-4	0	204.1	175	77	11	0	78	94	4.40	105	.233	.305	73-0-1	.247	2*	73	7		0.9
1947	Cin N	9	14	.391	30	29	9-3	0	186	186	104	11	3	87	79	4.40	93	.261	.343	57-0-9	.088	-3*	104	-7		-1.0
1948	Cin N	17	14	.548	33	33	14-3	0	232	204	97	15	1	124	120	3.41	115	.239	.336	78-1-4	.141	0*	82	14		1.8
1949	Cin N	5	10	.333	28	24	7-3	0	159.2	172	92	12	2	85	76	4.90	85	.281	.370	52-0-8	.077	-3*	99	-9		-1.0
1950	Chi N	3	4	.429	32	6	0	1	73.2	60	46	10	2	59	41	3.79	111	.221	.363	16	.125	-0*	63	-1		-0.1
1951	Cle A	0	1	.000	1	1	0	0	3	8	6	0	0	1	2	18.00	21	.500	.529	1	.000	-0	235	-5		-0.7
Total	13	119	121	.496	346	286	131-29	2	2104.2	1799	915	100	21	1132	1294	3.44	107	.232	.332	685-1-60	.152	-9	92	60		6.9

VAN DYKE, BEN Benjamin Harrison B8.15.1888 Clintonville PA D10.22.1973 Sarasota FL BR/TL/6-1/150 d5.11

YEAR	TM LG	W	L	PCT	G	GS	CG-SHO	SV-BS	IP	H	R	HR	HB	BB-IB	SO	ERA	AERA	OAV	OOB	AB-HR-SH	AVG	PB	SUP	APR	DL	PW
1909	Phi N	0	0	—	2	0	0	0	7.1	7	3	0	0	4	5	3.68	71	.269	.367	3	.000	-0		0		-0.1
1912	Bos A	0	0	—	3	1	0	0	14.1	13	10	0	1	7	8	3.14	108	.245	.344	4	.250	-0	325	-1		-0.1
Total	2	0	0	—	5	1	0	0	21.2	20	13	0	1	11	13	3.32	94	.253	.352	7	.143	-0	325	-1		-0.2

VAN EGMOND, TIM Timothy Layne B5.31.1969 Shreveport LA BR/TR/6-2/185* [BosA91 17/460] d6.26 Col Jacksonville St.

YEAR	TM LG	W	L	PCT	G	GS	CG-SHO	SV-BS	IP	H	R	HR	HB	BB-IB	SO	ERA	AERA	OAV	OOB	AB-HR-SH	AVG	PB	SUP	APR	DL	PW
1994	Bos A	2	3	.400	7	7	1	0-0	38.1	38	27	7	0	21-3	22	6.34	80	.255	.341	0	—	0	89	-4		-0.5
1995	Bos A	0	1	.000	4	1	0	0-0	6.2	9	7	2	0	6-0	5	9.45	51	.310	.429	0	—	0	57	-3	15	-0.4
1996	Mil A	3	5	.375	12	9	0	0-0	54.2	58	35	6	1	23-2	33	5.27	86	.274	.343	0	—	0	59	-1		-0.1
Total	3	5	9	.357	23	17	1		99.2	105	69	15	1	50-5	60	5.96	86	.269	.349	0	—	0	71	-8	15	-1.0

VANGILDER, ELAM Elam Russell B4.23.1896 Cape Girardeau MO D4.30.1977 Cape Girardeau MO BR/TR/6-1/192 d9.18

YEAR	TM LG	W	L	PCT	G	GS	CG-SHO	SV-BS	IP	H	R	HR	HB	BB-IB	SO	ERA	AERA	OAV	OOB	AB-HR-SH	AVG	PB	SUP	APR	DL	PW
1919	StL A	1	0	1.000	3	1	1	0	13	15	4	0	0	3	6	2.08	160	.306	.346	3	.667	1	71	2		0.2
1920	StL A	3	8	.273	24	13	4	0	104.2	131	83	7	3	40	25	5.50	71	.310	.373	30	.133	-2	94	-19		-1.9
1921	StL A	11	12	.478	31	21	10-1	0	180.1	196	98	10	2	67	48	3.94	114	.278	.342	65-1-2	.200	-2	82	9		0.7
1922	StL A	19	13	.594	43	30	19-3	4	245	248	109	13	6	48	63	3.42	121	.270	.310	93-2-9	.344	13*	141	21		3.8
1923	StL A	16	17	.485	41	35	20-4	1	282.1	276	129	11	6	120	74	3.06	136	.266	.345	110-1-1	.218	-0*	82	**28**		2.8
1924	StL A	5	10	.333	43	18	6	0	145.1	183	114	10	9	55	49	5.64	80	.317	.385	44-1-0	.295	3	114	-20		-1.4
1925	StL A	14	8	.636	52	16	4-1	6	193.1	225	127	11	6	92	61	4.70	99	.303	.385	71-0-3	.183	-3	102	-3		-0.5
1926	StL A	9	11	.450	42	19	8-1	1	181	196	121	12	2	98	40	5.17	83	.285	.376	58-0-4	.190	1	-89	-16		-1.8
1927	StL A	10	12	.455	44	23	12-3	1	203	235	136	13	5	102	62	4.79	91	.310	.392	68-1-4	.279	2	85	-11		-1.0
1928	Det A	11	10	.524	38	11	7	5	156.1	163	82	4	3	68	43	3.91	105	.273	.350	58-2-1	.259	2	94	4		0.6
1929	Det A	0	1	.000	6	0	0	0	11.1	16	11	1	0	7	3	6.35	68	.348	.434	1	.000	-0		-3		-0.2
Total	9	99	102	.493	367	187	90-13	19	1715.2	1894	1014	92	42	700	474	4.28	100	.288	.360	601-8-24	.243	15	98	-8		2.2

VAN HALTREN, GEORGE George Edward Martin "Rip" B3.30.1866 St.Louis MO D9.29.1945 Oakland CA BL/TL/5-11/170 d6.27 M1 ▲

YEAR	TM LG	W	L	PCT	G	GS	CG-SHO	SV-BS	IP	H	R	HR	HB	BB-IB	SO	ERA	AERA	OAV	OOB	AB-HR-SH	AVG	PB	SUP	APR	DL	PW
1887	Chi N	11	7	.611	20	18	18-1	**1**	161	177	113	8	16	66	76	3.86	117	.277	.359	172-3	.203	-2*	92	10		0.7
1888	Chi N	13	13	.500	30	24	24-4	1	245.2	263	149	15	13	60	139	3.52	86	.267	.318	318-4	.283	11*	104	-9		1.0
1890	Bro P	15	10	.600	28	25	23	2	223	272	190	8	21	89	48	4.28	104	.288	.362	376-5	.335	10*	109	2		1.0
1891	Bal AA	0	1	.000	6	1	0	0	23	38	34	1	4	10	7	5.09	73	.358	.433	566-9	.318	3*	316	-7		-0.2
1892	Bal N	0	0	—	4	0	0	0	14.2	28	17	1	0	7	5	9.20	37	.389	.443	556-7	.302	2*		-7		-0.2
1895	NY N	0	0	—	1	0	0	0	5	13	12	0	2	2	1	12.60	37	.481	.548	521-8-6	.340	0*		-5		-0.2
1896	NY N	1	0	1.000	2	0	0	0	8	5	2	1	0	3	3	2.25	187	.179	.207	562-5-4	.351	1*		2		0.
1900	NY N	0	0	—	1	0	0	0	3	1	0	0	0	3	0	0.00	—	.100	.308	571-1-13	.315	0*		1		-0.
1901	NY N	0	0	—	1	0	0	0	6	12	10	0	1	6	2	3.00	110	.414	.528	543-1-7	.335	0*		-2		-0.
Total	9	40	31	.563	93	68	65-5	4	689.1	809	527	34	57	244	281	4.05	96	.285	.353	4185-43-30	.319	25	107	-15		1.6

VAN HEKKEN, ANDY Andrew William B7.31.1979 Holland MI BR/TL/6-3/175 [SeaA98 3/95] d9.3

YEAR	TM LG	W	L	PCT	G	GS	CG-SHO	SV-BS	IP	H	R	HR	HB	BB-IB	SO	ERA	AERA	OAV	OOB	AB-HR-SH	AVG	PB	SUP	APR	DL	PW
2002	Det A	1	3	.250	5	5	1	1	30	38	13	2	0	6	5	3.00	146	.311	.341	0	—	0	51	4		0.

VAN LANDINGHAM, WILLIAM William Joseph B7.16.1970 Columbia TN BR/TR/6-2/210* [SFN91 5/141] d5.21 Col Kentucky

YEAR	TM LG	W	L	PCT	G	GS	CG-SHO	SV-BS	IP	H	R	HR	HB	BB-IB	SO	ERA	AERA	OAV	OOB	AB-HR-SH	AVG	PB	SUP	APR	DL	PW
1994	SF N	8	2	.800	16	14	0	0-0	84	70	37	4	2	43-4	56	3.54	115	.223	.319	31-0-4	.065	-2	120	5		0.
1995	SF N	6	3	.667	18	18	1	0-0	122.2	124	58	14	2	40-2	95	3.67	112	.264	.321	46-1-1	.152	0	118	5	42	0.
1996	SF N	9	14	.391	32	32	0	0-0	181.2	196	123	17	9	78-6	97	5.40	77	.276	.352	61-0-6	.131	-1	99	-25		-2.
1997	SF N	4	7	.364	18	17	0	0-0	89	80	56	11	0	59-3	52	4.96	83	.237	.345	26-0-2	.115	-0	84	-9		-1.
Total	4	27	26	.509	84	81	1	0-0	477.1	470	274	46	13	220-15	300	4.54	91	.257	.337	164-1-13	.122	-3	104	-24	42	-3.

VAN POPPEL, TODD Todd Matthew B12.9.1971 Hinsdale IL BR/TR/6-5/210(210-235) [OakA90 1/14] d9.11

YEAR	TM LG	W	L	PCT	G	GS	CG-SHO	SV-BS	IP	H	R	HR	HB	BB-IB	SO	ERA	AERA	OAV	OOB	AB-HR-SH	AVG	PB	SUP	APR	DL	PW
1991	Oak A	0	0	—	1	1	0	0-0	4.2	7	5	1	0	2-0	6	9.64	40	.368	.429	0	—	0	142	-3		-0.
1993	Oak A	6	6	.500	16	16	0	0-0	84	76	50	10	2	62-0	47	5.04	82	.243	.369	0	—	0	125	-9		-2.
1994	Oak A	7	10	.412	23	23	0	0-0	116.2	108	80	20	3	89-2	83	6.09	74	.250	.379	0	—	0	82	-4		-0.
1995	Oak A	4	8	.333	36	14	1	0-0	138.1	125	77	16	4	56-1	122	4.88	93	.244	.320	0	—	0	106	-18		-1.
1996	Oak A	1	5	.167	28	6	0	1-1	63	86	56	13	2	33-3	37	7.71	64	.333	.406	0	—	0	127	-25		-2.
	Det A	2	4	.333	9	9	1	1-1	36.1	53	51	11	1	29-0	16	11.39	45	.338	.439	0	—	0	119	-44		-4.
	Year	3	9	.250	37	15	1	1-1	99.1	139	107	24	3	62-3	53	9.06	55	.313	.389	2-0-2	.000	-0	95	-8		-4.
1998	Tex A	1	2	.333	4	4	0	0-0	19.1	26	20	5	1	10-0	10	8.84	55	.313	.389	2-0-2	.000	-0	111	-6		-0.
	Pit N	1	2	.333	18	7	0	0-0	47	53	32	4	0	18-3	32	5.36	80	.286	.346	12-0-1	.250	-1	110	8		0.
2000	Chi N	4	5	.444	51	2	0	2-3	86.1	80	38	10	2	48-2	77	3.75	122	.249	.348	9-0-2	.000	-1	110	8		0.
2001	Chi N	4	1	.800	59	0	0	0-0	75	63	22	9	0	38-4	90	2.52	166	.223	.316	7	.286	-0		15		0.
2002	Tex A	3	2	.600	50	0	0	1-1	72.2	80	44	14	0	29-1	85	5.45	88	.275	.346	0	.000	-0		-4		-0.
2003	Tex A	1	0	1.000	7	1	0	0-0	12.2	20	14	1	0	9-2	9	8.53	58	.345	.433	0	—	0	111	0	34	-0.
	Cin N	2	1	.667	9	4	0	0-0	35.2	31	18	7	1	6-0	25	4.54	92	.228	.266	9-0-1	.111	-0	90	-1		-0.
2004	Cin N	4	6	.400	48	11	0	0-1	115.1	136	80	23	3	32-3	72	6.09	71	.298	.345	17-0-5	.176	-0	108	-21		-1.
Total	11	40	52	.435	359	98	2-1	4-6	907	944	587	143	22	461-21	711	5.58	81	.269	.355	57-0-11	.158	-0	109-100			-9.

VAN RYN, BEN Benjamin Ashley B8.9.1971 Fort Wayne IN BL/TL/6-5/195* [MonN90 1/37] d5.9

YEAR	TM LG	W	L	PCT	G	GS	CG-SHO	SV-BS	IP	H	R	HR	HB	BB-IB	SO	ERA	AERA	OAV	OOB	AB-HR-SH	AVG	PB	SUP	APR	DL	PW
1996	Cal A	0	0	—	2	0	0	1-0	0	1	1	0	0	1-0	0	0.00	—	.250	.400	0	—	-0		1		0
1998	Chi N	0	0	—	9	0	0	0-0	8	9	3	0	1	6-0	6	3.38	131	.290	.410	1	.000	-0		1		0
	SD N	0	1	.000	6	0	0	0-1	2.2	3	3	1	0	4-0	1	10.13	39	.273	.500	0	—	-0		-2		-0
	Year	0	1	.000	15	0	0	0-1	10.2	12	6	1	2	10-0	7	5.06	85	.286	.436	1	.000	-0		-1		-0
	Tor A	0	1	.000	10	0	0	0-0	4	6	4	0	0	2-0	3	9.00	52	.400	.471	0	—	-0		-2		-0
Total	2	0	2	.000	26	0	0	0-1	15.2	19	10	2	2	13-0	10	5.74	77	.311	.442	1	.000	-0		-2		-0

VAN ZANDT, IKE Charles Isaac B2.1876 Brooklyn NY D9.14.1908 Nashua NH BL/TL d8.5 ▲

YEAR	TM LG	W	L	PCT	G	GS	CG-SHO	SV-BS	IP	H	R	HR	HB	BB-IB	SO	ERA	AERA	OAV	OOB	AB-HR-SH	AVG	PB	SUP	APR	DL	PW
1901	NY N	0	0	—	2	0	0	0	12.2	16	15	0	1	8	2	7.11	47	.308	.410	6	.167	-0*		-6		-0
1905	StL A	0	0	—	1	0	0	0	6.2	2	0	0	1	2	3	0.00	—	.095	.208	322-1-9	.233	0*		2		-0
Total	2	0	0	—	3	0	0	0	19.1	18	15	0	2	10	5	4.66	65	.247	.353	328-1-9	.232	-0		-4		-0

VARGA, ANDY Andrew William B12.11.1930 Chicago IL D11.4.1992 Orlando FL BR/TL/6-4/187* d9.9 Col Bradley

YEAR	TM LG	W	L	PCT	G	GS	CG-SHO	SV-BS	IP	H	R	HR	HB	BB-IB	SO	ERA	AERA	OAV	OOB	AB-HR-SH	AVG	PB	SUP	APR	DL	PW
1950	Chi N	0	0	—	1	0	0	0	1	0	0	0	0	0	0	0.00	—	.000	.333	—		0		0		-0
1951	Chi N	0	0	—	2	0	0	0	3	2	1	0	0	6	1	3.00	136	.200	.500	—		0		0		-0
Total	2	0	0	—	3	0	0	0	4	2	1	0	0	7	1	2.25	183	.167	.474	—		0		0		-0

VARGAS, CLAUDIO Claudio (Almonte) B6.19.1978 Mao, D.R. BR/TR/6-3/210(210-230) d4.26

YEAR	TM LG	W	L	PCT	G	GS	CG-SHO	SV-BS	IP	H	R	HR	HB	BB-IB	SO	ERA	AERA	OAV	OOB	AB-HR-SH	AVG	PB	SUP	APR	DL	PW
2003	Mon N	6	8	.429	23	20	0	0-0	114	111	59	16	7	41-5	62	4.34	102	.255	.326	30-0-4	.000	-3	77	2	40	-0
2004	Mon N	5	5	.500	45	14	0	0-0	118.1	120	75	26	7	64-7	89	5.25	88	.266	.363	22-0-7	.045	-2	99	-8		-0
2005	Was N	0	3	.000	4	4	0	0-0	12.2	22	15	4	0	7-2	5	9.24	44	.373	.439	2	.500	-2	46	-8	38	-1
	Ari N	9	6	.600	21	19	0	0-0	119.2	124	66	21	7	40-3	90	4.81	91	.266	.333	34-0-7	.088	-2	116	-4		-2
	Year	9	9	.500	25	23	0	0-0	132.1	146	81	25	7	47-5	95	5.24	83	.278	.345	36-0-7	.111	-1	104	-12		-2
Total	3	20	22	.476	93	57	0	0-0	364.2	377	215	67	21	152-17	246	4.96	90	.267	.345	88-0-18	.057	-6	93	-18	78	-2

VARGAS, JASON Jason Matthew B2.2.1983 Apple Valley CA BL/TL/6-0/215 d7.14 Col Cal St.-Long Beach

YEAR	TM LG	W	L	PCT	G	GS	CG-SHO	SV-BS	IP	H	R	HR	HB	BB-IB	SO	ERA	AERA	OAV	OOB	AB-HR-SH	AVG	PB	SUP	APR	DL	PW
2005	Fla N	5	5	.500	17	13	1	0-0	73.2	71	34	4	3	34-7	59	4.03	99	.249	.330	26	.308	3*	113	1		0

VARGAS, ROBERTO Roberto Enrique (Velez) B5.29.1929 Santurce, PR BL/TL/5-11/170 d4.17 Negro Lg 1948

YEAR	TM LG	W	L	PCT	G	GS	CG-SHO	SV-BS	IP	H	R	HR	HB	BB-IB	SO	ERA	AERA	OAV	OOB	AB-HR-SH	AVG	PB	SUP	APR	DL	PW
1955	Mil N	0	0	—	25	0	0	2	24.2	39	25	4	1	14-2	13	8.76	43	.355	.432	2	.500	0		-14		

VARGUS, BILL William Fay B11.11.1899 N.Scituate MA D2.12.1979 Hyannis MA BL/TL/6-0/165 d6.23 Col Boston College

YEAR	TM LG	W	L	PCT	G	GS	CG-SHO	SV-BS	IP	H	R	HR	HB	BB-IB	SO	ERA	AERA	OAV	OOB	AB-HR-SH	AVG	PB	SUP	APR	DL	PW
1925	Bos N	1	1	.500	11	2	1	0	36.1	45	24	1	2	13	5	3.96	101	.302	.366	12	.250	0	137	-2		-0.1
1926	Bos N	0	0	—	4	0	0	0	3	4	1	0	0	1	0	3.00	118	.333	.385		—	0		0		0.0
Total		1	1	.500	15	2	1	0	39.1	49	25	1	2	14	5	3.89	102	.304	.367	12	.250	0	137	-2		-0.1

VARNEY, DIKE Lawrence Delano (b Lawrence Delano De Varney) B8.9.1880 Dover NH D4.23.1950 Long Island City NY BL/TL/6-0/165 d7.3 Col Dartmouth

YEAR	TM LG	W	L	PCT	G	GS	CG-SHO	SV-BS	IP	H	R	HR	HB	BB-IB	SO	ERA	AERA	OAV	OOB	AB-HR-SH	AVG	PB	SUP	APR	DL	PW
1902	Cle A	1	1	.500	3	3	0	0	14.2	14	15	0	5	12	7	6.14	56	.250	.425	6	.167	-0	174	-4		-0.5

VASBINDER, CAL Moses Calhoun B7.19.1880 Scio OH D12.22.1950 Cadiz OH BR/TR/6-2/? d4.27

YEAR	TM LG	W	L	PCT	G	GS	CG-SHO	SV-BS	IP	H	R	HR	HB	BB-IB	SO	ERA	AERA	OAV	OOB	AB-HR-SH	AVG	PB	SUP	APR	DL	PW
1902	Cle A	0	0	—	2	0	0	0	5	5	5	1	0	8	2	9.00	38	.263	.481	2	.500	0		-2		-0.1

VASQUEZ, JORGE Jorge Luis B7.16.1978 Nagua, D.R. BR/TR/6-1/165* d8.13

YEAR	TM LG	W	L	PCT	G	GS	CG-SHO	SV-BS	IP	H	R	HR	HB	BB-IB	SO	ERA	AERA	OAV	OOB	AB-HR-SH	AVG	PB	SUP	APR	DL	PW
2004	KC A	0	0	—	2	0	0	0-0	3.1	4	4	1	1	1-0	4	8.10	58	.267	.353	0	—	0		-2		-0.1
2005	Atl N	1	0	1.000	7	0	0	0-0	9	11	4	2	0	5-0	9	3.00	143	.297	.381	1	.000	-0		1		0.1
Total 2		1	0	1.000	9	0	0	0-0	12.1	15	8	3	1	6-0	13	4.38	100	.288	.373	1	.000	-0		-1		0.0

VASQUEZ, RAFAEL Rafael B6.28.1958 LaRomana, D.R. BR/TR/6-0/162 d4.6

YEAR	TM LG	W	L	PCT	G	GS	CG-SHO	SV-BS	IP	H	R	HR	HB	BB-IB	SO	ERA	AERA	OAV	OOB	AB-HR-SH	AVG	PB	SUP	APR	DL	PW
1979	Sea A	1	0	1.000	16	0	0	0	39	34	9	4	1	6-1	9	5.06	86	.354	.411	0	—	0		-1		-0.1

VAUGHAN, PORTER Cecil Porter "Lefty" B5.11.1919 Stevensville VA BR/TL/6-1/178 d6.16 Mil 1942-45 Col Richmond

YEAR	TM LG	W	L	PCT	G	GS	CG-SHO	SV-BS	IP	H	R	HR	HB	BB-IB	SO	ERA	AERA	OAV	OOB	AB-HR-SH	AVG	PB	SUP	APR	DL	PW
1940	Phi A	2	9	.182	18	15	5	2	99.1	104	74	9	3	61	46	5.35	83	.264	.367	34-0-1	.235	0	95	-11		-1.1
1941	Phi A	0	2	.000	5	3	1	0	22.2	32	25	3	0	12	6	7.94	53	.327	.400	7	.143	-0	96	-10		-0.8
1946	Phi A	0	0	—	1	0	0	0	0	1	0	0	0	1	0	—	—	1.000	1.000	—	0	0				0.0
Total 3		2	11	.154	24	18	6	2	122	137	99	12	3	74	52	5.83	75	.278	.375	41-0-1	.220	-0	95	-21		-1.9

VAUGHAN, CHARLIE Charles Wayne B10.6.1947 Mercedes TX BR/TL/6-1.5/175(170-185) [AtlN65 4/64] d9.3

YEAR	TM LG	W	L	PCT	G	GS	CG-SHO	SV-BS	IP	H	R	HR	HB	BB-IB	SO	ERA	AERA	OAV	OOB	AB-HR-SH	AVG	PB	SUP	APR	DL	PW
1966	Atl N	1	0	1.000	1	1	0	0	7	8	2	0	0	3-0	5	2.57	141	.296	.355	4	.250	0	290	1		0.1
1969	Atl N	0	0	—	1	0	0	0-0	1	1	2	0	0	3-0	1	18.00	20	.250	.571	0	—	0		-1		-0.1
Total 2		1	0	1.000	2	1	0	0	8	9	4	0	0	6-0	7	4.50	81	.290	.395	4	.250	0	290	0		0.0

VAUGHN, ROY Clarence Leroy B9.4.1911 Sedalia MO D3.1.1937 Martinsville VA BB/TR/6-0.5/178 d7.1

YEAR	TM LG	W	L	PCT	G	GS	CG-SHO	SV-BS	IP	H	R	HR	HB	BB-IB	SO	ERA	AERA	OAV	OOB	AB-HR-SH	AVG	PB	SUP	APR	DL	PW
1934	Phi A	0	0	—	2	0	0	0	4.1	3	2	1	0	2-1	4	2.08	211	.176	.300	2	.000	-0		1		0.0

VAUGHN, DE WAYNE De Wayne Mathew B7.22.1959 Oklahoma City OK BR/TR/5-11/180 d4.17 Col Oklahoma

YEAR	TM LG	W	L	PCT	G	GS	CG-SHO	SV-BS	IP	H	R	HR	HB	BB-IB	SO	ERA	AERA	OAV	OOB	AB-HR-SH	AVG	PB	SUP	APR	DL	PW
1988	Tex A	0	0	—	8	0	0	0-0	15.1	24	15	4	0	4-0	8	7.63	54	.348	.373	0	—	0		-6		-0.3

VAUGHN, HIPPO James Leslie B4.9.1888 Weatherford TX D5.29.1966 Chicago IL BB/TL/6-4/215 d6.19

YEAR	TM LG	W	L	PCT	G	GS	CG-SHO	SV-BS	IP	H	R	HR	HB	BB-IB	SO	ERA	AERA	OAV	OOB	AB-HR-SH	AVG	PB	SUP	APR	DL	PW
1908	NY A	0	0	—	2	0	0	0	2.1	1	1	0	0	4	3	3.86	64	.167	.500	1	.000	-0		0		0.0
1910	NY A	13	11	.542	30	25	18-5	1	221.2	190	76	1	10	58	107	1.83	146	.237	.297	75	.133	-2	98	14		1.3
1911	NY A	8	10	.444	26	19	10	0	145.2	158	92	2	7	54	74	4.39	82	.284	.354	49-0-2	.143	-1	100	-11		-1.2
1912	NY A	2	8	.200	15	10	5-1	0	63	66	48	1	9	37	46	5.14	70	.264	.361	21	.095	-2	109	-9		-1.4
	Was A	4	3	.571	12	8	4	0	81	75	33	0	4	43	49	2.89	115	.253	.356	30	.200	-1	69	5		0.5
	Year	6	11	.353	27	18	9-1	0	144	141	81	1	5	80	95	3.88	89	.258	.358	51	.157	-2	93	-5		-0.9
1913	Chi N	5	1	.833	7	6	5-2	0	56	37	13	0	2	27	36	1.45	220	.182	.284	21	.190	-1	114	10		1.1
1914	Chi N	21	13	.618	42	35	23-4	1	293.2	236	119	1	8	109	165	2.05	135	.222	.299	97-1-4	.144	-0	104	18		2.1
1915	Chi N	20	12	.625	41	34	18-4	1	269.2	240	105	4	11	77	148	2.87	97	.238	.299	86-0-2	.163	1*	110	-1		0.0
1916	Chi N	17	15	.531	44	35	21-4	1	294	269	94	4	7	67	144	2.20	132	.250	.298	104-0-5	.135	-4	89	20		1.9
1917	Chi N	23	13	.639	41	38	27-5	0	295.2	255	97	3	9	91	195	2.01	144	.235	.300	100-0-2	.160	-1	98	25		3.4
1918	†Chi N	**22**	10	.688	35	**33**	27-8	0	**290.1**	216	75	4	7	76	**148**	**1.74**	**161**	**.208**	.266	96-0-4	.240	-1	95	**34**		**4.5**
1919	Chi N	21	14	.600	38	**37**	25-4	1	**306.2**	264	83	3	6	62	141	1.79	161	.234	.278	98-0-1	.173	-0	85	**36**		4.3
1920	Chi N	19	16	.543	40	38	24-4	0	301	301	113	4	9	81	131	2.54	126	.264	.318	102-1-2	.216	4	99	19		2.6
1921	Chi N	3	11	.214	17	14	7	0	109.1	153	90	8	5	31	30	6.01	64	.341	.390	41-1-1	.244	2	109	-29		-2.8
Total 13		178	137	.565	390	332	214-41	5	2730	2461	1039	39	85	817	1416	2.49	120	.244	.306	921-3-23	.173	-1	98	131		16.3

VAZQUEZ, JAVIER Javier Carlos B6.25.1976 Ponce, PR BR/TR/6-2/195(180-205) [MonN94 5/140] d4.3

YEAR	TM LG	W	L	PCT	G	GS	CG-SHO	SV-BS	IP	H	R	HR	HB	BB-IB	SO	ERA	AERA	OAV	OOB	AB-HR-SH	AVG	PB	SUP	APR	DL	PW
1998	Mon N	5	15	.250	33	32	0	0-0	172.1	196	121	31	11	68-2	139	6.06	69	.292	.364	52-0-6	.173	1	89	-31		-2.9
1999	Mon N	9	8	.529	26	26	3-1	0-0	154.2	154	98	20	4	52-4	113	5.00	89	.255	.316	42-0-8	.286	4	100	-10		-0.4
2000	Mon N	11	9	.550	33	33	2-1	0-0	217.2	247	104	24	5	61-10	196	4.05	116	.286	.335	65-0-13	.231	-2	77	18		1.7
2001	Mon N	16	11	.593	32	32	5-3	0-0	223.2	197	92	24	3	44-4	208	3.42	126	.235	.274	62-0-16	.258	4	98	23		3.1
2002	Mon N	10	13	.435	34	34	2	0-0	230.1	243	111	28	4	49-6	179	3.91	112	.271	.300	73-0-10	.178	-0	94	12		1.0
2003	Mon N	13	12	.520	34	34	4-1	0-0	230.2	198	93	28	4	57-5	241	3.24	137	.229	.278	65-0-12	.154	-0	79	30		3.0
2004	†NY A★	14	10	.583	32	32	0	0-0	198	195	114	33	11	60-3	150	4.91	94	.255	.315	4-0-1	.250	0	92	-6		-0.4
2005	Ari N	11	15	.423	33	33	3-1	0-0	215.2	223	112	35	6	46-4	192	4.42	99	.266	.308	63-1-6	.238	3	78	1		0.4
Total 8		89	93	.489	257	256	19-7	0-0	1643	1653	845	223	47	437-38	1418	4.28	104	.260	.311	426-1-72	.214	15	88	37		5.5

VEACH, AL Alvis Lindel B8.6.1909 Maylene AL D9.6.1990 Charlotte NC BR/TR/5-11/178 d9.22

YEAR	TM LG	W	L	PCT	G	GS	CG-SHO	SV-BS	IP	H	R	HR	HB	BB-IB	SO	ERA	AERA	OAV	OOB	AB-HR-SH	AVG	PB	SUP	APR	DL	PW
1935	Phi A	0	2	.000	2	1	2	0	20	15	1	0	9	3		11.70	39	.417	.509	4	.000	-1	10	-8		-1.1

VEACH, PEEK-A-BOO William Walter B6.15.1862 Indianapolis IN D11.12.1937 Indianapolis IN 6-0/175 d8.24 ▲

YEAR	TM LG	W	L	PCT	G	GS	CG-SHO	SV-BS	IP	H	R	HR	HB	BB-IB	SO	ERA	AERA	OAV	OOB	AB-HR-SH	AVG	PB	SUP	APR	DL	PW
1884	KC U	3	9	.250	12	12	12	0	104	95	57	1		10	62	2.42	92	.227	.245	82-1	.134	-3*	60	-3		-0.6
1887	Lou AA	0	1	.000	1	1	1	0	9	5	6	1	0	8	2	4.00	110	.172	.351	3	.000	-3*	58	1		0.0
Total		3	10	.231	13	13	13	0	113	100	63	2	0	18	64	2.55	94	.223	.253	85-1	.129	-4	60	-2		-0.6

VEALE, BOB Robert Andrew B10.28.1935 Birmingham AL BB/TL/6-6/212(210-226) d4.16 Col Benedictine

YEAR	TM LG	W	L	PCT	G	GS	CG-SHO	SV-BS	IP	H	R	HR	HB	BB-IB	SO	ERA	AERA	OAV	OOB	AB-HR-SH	AVG	PB	SUP	APR	DL	PW
1962	Pit N	2	2	.500	11	6	2	1	45.2	39	25	2	0	25-1	42	3.74	105	.235	.332	16	.250	1	97	0		0.0
1963	Pit N	5	2	.714	34	7	3-2	3	77.2	59	15	1	1	40-2	68	1.04	316	.215	.314	23	.087	-0*	93	18		1.8
1964	Pit N	18	12	.600	40	38	14-1	0	279.2	222	100	8	3	124-9	**250**	2.74	128	.217	.302	96-0-6	.156	-0*	110	22		2.3
1965	Pit N☆	17	12	.586	39	37	14-7	0	266	221	98	5	7	119-7	276	2.84	124	.225	.312	93-0-8	.086	-4	91	20		1.6
1966	Pit N☆	16	12	.571	38	37	12-3	0	268.1	228	99	18	5	102-6	229	3.02	118	.232	.306	94-0-3	.138	-2	104	17		1.4
1967	Pit N	16	8	.667	33	31	6-1	0	203	184	90	12	5	119-10	179	3.64	93	.245	.350	69-0-3	.043	-5	121	-4		-1.0
1968	Pit N	13	14	.481	36	33	13-4	0	245.1	187	67	13	24	94-5	171	2.05	142	.211	.287	82-0-2	.110	-2	82	24		2.5
1969	Pit N	13	14	.481	34	34	9-1	0-0	225.2	232	93	8	3	91-4	213	3.23	108	.267	.336	79-0-4	.051	-5	97	6		0.1
1970	Pit N	10	15	.400	34	32	5-1	0-0	202	189	99	9	4	93-11	168	3.92	101	.246	.329	67-0-1	.164	1	92	0		0.1
1971	†Pit N	6	0	1.000	37	0	0	2-0	46.1	59	38	5	0	24-2	40	6.99	49	.314	.388	9-0-1	.333	4	92	-18		-2.3
1972	Pit N	0	0	—	5	0	0	0-0	9	10	7	0	0	7-2	6	6.00	55	.313	.425	1	.000	-0		-3		-0.2
	Bos A	2	0	1.000	30	0	0	2-0	8	2	0	0	0	3-0	10	0.00	—	.083	.185	1	.000	-0		-3		0.7
1973	Bos A	2	3	.400	32	0	0	11-4	36.1	37	16	2	0	12-2	25	3.47	116	.268	.327	0	—	0		2		0.4
1974	Bos A	0	1	.000	18	0	0	2-2	13	15	8	2	0	4-1	16	5.54	69	.283	.328	0	—	0		-2		-0.2
Total 13		120	95	.558	397	255	78-20	21-6	1926	1684	755	91	29	858-62	1703	3.07	113	.236	.319	630-0-28	.114	-17	100	85		7.2

VEDDER, LOU Louis Edward B4.20.1897 Oakville MI D3.9.1990 Lake Placid FL BR/TR/5-10.5/175 d9.18

YEAR	TM LG	W	L	PCT	G	GS	CG-SHO	SV-BS	IP	H	R	HR	HB	BB-IB	SO	ERA	AERA	OAV	OOB	AB-HR-SH	AVG	PB	SUP	APR	DL	PW
1920	Det A	0	0	—	2	0	0	0	2	2	0	0	0	2	0	0.00	—	.000	.000	0	—	0		1		0.1

VEIGEL, AL Allen Francis B1.30.1917 Dover OH BR/TR/6-1/180 d9.21

YEAR	TM LG	W	L	PCT	G	GS	CG-SHO	SV-BS	IP	H	R	HR	HB	BB-IB	SO	ERA	AERA	OAV	OOB	AB-HR-SH	AVG	PB	SUP	APR	DL	PW
1939	Bos N	0	1	.000	2	2	0	0	2.2	3	6	0	0	5	1	6.75	55	.250	.471	1	.000	-0	106	-3		-0.5

VEIL, BUCKY Frederick William B8.2.1881 Tyrone PA D4.16.1931 Altoona PA BR/TR/5-10/165 d4.19 Col Bucknell

YEAR	TM LG	W	L	PCT	G	GS	CG-SHO	SV-BS	IP	H	R	HR	HB	BB-IB	SO	ERA	AERA	OAV	OOB	AB-HR-SH	AVG	PB	SUP	APR	DL	PW
1903	†Pit N	5	3	.625	12	6	4	0	70.2	70	35	1	2	36	20	3.82	85	.269	.362	29	.207	-0	97	-1		-0.2
1904	Pit N	0	0	—	1	1	0	0	4.2	4	3	0	1	4	1	5.79	47	.250	.429	1	1.000	0	150	-1		0.0
Total 2		5	3	.625	13	7	4	0	75.1	74	38	1	3	40	21	3.94	81	.268	.367	30	.233	-0	102	-2		-0.2

VELAZQUEZ, CARLOS Carlos (Quinones) B3.22.1948 Loiza, PR BR/TR/5-11/180 d7.20

YEAR	TM LG	W	L	PCT	G	GS	CG-SHO	SV-BS	IP	H	R	HR	HB	BB-IB	SO	ERA	AERA	OAV	OOB	AB-HR-SH	AVG	PB	SUP	APR	DL	PW
1973	Mil A	2	2	.500	18	0	0	2-1	39.1	39	11	5	0	10-1	12	2.58	147	.297	.337	0	—	0		4		0.5

VENAFRO, MIKE Michael Robert B8.2.1973 Takoma Park MD BL/TL/5-10/180* [TexA95 29/794] d4.24 Col James Madison

YEAR	TM LG	W	L	PCT	G	GS	CG-SHO	SV-BS	IP	H	R	HR	HB	BB-IB	SO	ERA	AERA	OAV	OOB	AB-HR-SH	AVG	PB	SUP	APR	DL	PW
1999	†Tex A	3	2	.600	65	0	0	0-1	68.1	63	29	4	3	22-0	33	3.29	157	.251	.317	0	—	0		12		0.7
2000	Tex A	3	1	.750	77	0	0	1-1	56.1	64	27	2	4	21-4	32	3.83	133	.295	.362	0	—	0		7		0.5
2001	Tex A	5	5	.500	70	0	0	4-4	60	54	35	2	7	28-4	29	4.80	100	.240	.337	0	—	0		0		0.0
2002	Oak A	2	2	.500	47	0	0	0-0	37	45	22	5	1	24-12	16	4.62	97	.308	.372	0	—	0		-1		0.0

YEAR	TM LG	W	L	PCT	G	GS	CG-SHO	SV-BS	IP	H	R	HR	HB	BB-IB	SO	ERA	AERA	OAV	OOB	AB-HR-SH	AVG	PB	SUP	APR	DL	PW
2003	TB A	1	0	1.000	24	0	0	0-0	19	24	10	1	3	3-0	9	4.74	97	.308	.353	0	—	0		0		0.0
2004	†LA N	0	0	—	17	0	0	0-0	9	11	5	1	2	3-1	6	4.00	104	.306	.390	0	—	0		0		0.0
Total	6	14	10	.583	300	0	0	5-6	249.2	261	128	15	21	91-11	129	4.11	119	.274	.346	0	—	0		17		1.3

VERAS, DARIO
Dario Antonio B3.13.1973 Santiago, D.R. BR/TR/6-2/155* d7.31

YEAR	TM LG	W	L	PCT	G	GS	CG-SHO	SV-BS	IP	H	R	HR	HB	BB-IB	SO	ERA	AERA	OAV	OOB	AB-HR-SH	AVG	PB	SUP	APR	DL	PW
1996	†SD N	3	1	.750	23	0	0	0-0	29	24	10	3	1	10-4	23	2.79	144	.231	.302	0	—	0		4		0.5
1997	SD N	2	1	.667	23	0	0	0-1	24.2	28	18	5	2	12-3	21	5.11	77	.280	.368	0	—	0		-5	91	-0.5
1998	Bos A	0	1	.000	7	0	0	0-0	8	12	9	0	1	7-0	2	10.13	47	.343	.465	0	—	0		-4		-0.5
Total	5	5	3	.625	53	0	0	0-1	61.2	64	37	8	4	29-7	46	4.67	87	.268	.355	0	—	0		-5	91	-0.5

VERBANIC, JOE
Joseph Michael B4.24.1943 Washington PA BR/TR/6-0/175(155-175) d7.22 [DL 1969 NY A 124]

YEAR	TM LG	W	L	PCT	G	GS	CG-SHO	SV-BS	IP	H	R	HR	HB	BB-IB	SO	ERA	AERA	OAV	OOB	AB-HR-SH	AVG	PB	SUP	APR	DL	PW
1966	Phi N	1	1	.500	17	0	0	0	14	12	9	2	0	10-3	7	5.14	70	.226	.344	0	—	-0		-2		-0.3
1967	NY A	4	3	.571	28	6	1-1	2	80.1	74	27	6	2	21-3	39	2.80	112	.249	.300	18-0-3	.111	-0	79	4		0.4
1968	NY A	6	7	.462	40	11	2-1	4	97	104	36	6	6	41-8	40	3.15	92	.284	.363	25-0-3	.080	-1	103	-1		-0.2
1970	NY A	1	0	1.000	7	0	0	0-0	15.2	20	9	1	1	12-0	8	4.60	78	.323	.440	3	.333	0		-2		0.0
Total	4	12	11	.522	92	17	3-2	6-0	207	210	81	15	9	84-14	94	3.26	95	.270	.345	46-0-6	.109	-1	91	-1	124	-0.1

VERDEL, AL
Albert Alfred "Stumpy" B6.10.1921 Punxsutawney PA D4.16.1991 Sarasota FL BR/TR/5-9.5/186 d4.20

YEAR	TM LG	W	L	PCT	G	GS	CG-SHO	SV-BS	IP	H	R	HR	HB	BB-IB	SO	ERA	AERA	OAV	OOB	AB-HR-SH	AVG	PB	SUP	APR	DL	PW
1944	Phi N	0	0	—	1	0	0	0	1	0	0	0	0	0-0	0	0.00	—	.000	.000	0	—	0		0		0.0

VEREKER, TOMMY
John James B12.2.1893 Baltimore MD D4.2.1974 Baltimore MD 5-10/185 d6.17

YEAR	TM LG	W	L	PCT	G	GS	CG-SHO	SV-BS	IP	H	R	HR	HB	BB-IB	SO	ERA	AERA	OAV	OOB	AB-HR-SH	AVG	PB	SUP	APR	DL	PW
1915	Bal F	0	0	—	2	0	0	0	3	3	5	1	1	2	1	15.00	19	.273	.429	0	—	0		-3		-0.2

VERES, DAVE
David Scott B10.19.1966 Montgomery AL BR/TR/6-2/195(195-220) [OakA86*4/89] d5.10 Col Mt. Hood (OR) CC

YEAR	TM LG	W	L	PCT	G	GS	CG-SHO	SV-BS	IP	H	R	HR	HB	BB-IB	SO	ERA	AERA	OAV	OOB	AB-HR-SH	AVG	PB	SUP	APR	DL	PW
1994	Hou N	3	3	.500	32	0	0	1-0	41	39	13	4	1	7-3	28	2.41	164	.247	.280	2-0-1	.500	1		7		1.0
1995	Hou N	5	1	.833	72	0	0	1-2	103.1	89	29	5	4	30-6	94	2.26	171	.241	.299	5-0-1	.000	-1		20		1.0
1996	Mon N	6	3	.667	68	0	0	4-2	77.2	85	39	10	6	32-2	81	4.17	104	.277	.353	8	.375	1		2		0.3
1997	Mon N	2	3	.400	53	0	0	1-3	62	68	28	5	2	27-3	47	3.48	120	.278	.353	1	1.000	-0		4	30	0.3
1998	Col N	3	1	.750	63	0	0	8-5	76.1	67	26	6	2	27-2	74	2.83	183	.233	.301	3	.333	0		16		1.1
1999	Col N	4	8	.333	73	0	0	31-8	77	88	46	14	2	37-7	71	5.14	113	.290	.369	1	.000	-0		5		0.9
2000	†StL N	3	5	.375	71	0	0	29-7	75.2	65	26	6	6	25-2	67	2.85	163	.239	.315	1	.000	-0		15		2.4
2001	†StL N	3	2	.600	71	0	0	15-4	65.2	57	29	12	2	28-1	61	3.70	117	.232	.300	3-0-1	.000	-0		5		0.5
2002	†StL N	5	8	.385	71	0	0	4-4	82.2	67	34	12	2	39-4	68	3.48	116	.224	.315	3	.333	0		6	95	0.8
2003	†Chi N	2	1	.667	31	0	0	1-1	32.2	36	17	4	1	5-0	26	4.68	93	.290	.313	0	—	0		0		-0.1
Total	10	36	35	.507	605	0	0	95-36	694	661	287	78	28	257-30	617	3.44	130	.253	.323	27-0-3	.259	2		80	125	8.2

VERES, RANDY
Randolph Ruhland B11.25.1965 Sacramento CA BR/TR/6-3/210(189-210) [MilA85*S1/2] d7.1 Col Sacramento (CA) City

YEAR	TM LG	W	L	PCT	G	GS	CG-SHO	SV-BS	IP	H	R	HR	HB	BB-IB	SO	ERA	AERA	OAV	OOB	AB-HR-SH	AVG	PB	SUP	APR	DL	PW
1989	Mil A	0	1	.000	3	1	0	1-0	8.1	9	5	0	0	4	8	4.32	89	.290	.361	0	—	0	23	-1		-0.1
1990	Mil A	0	3	.000	26	0	0	1-0	41.2	38	17	5	1	16-3	16	3.67	106	.247	.318	1	.000	0		2		0.2
1994	Chi N	1	1	.500	10	0	0	0-2	9.2	12	6	3	1	2-2	5	5.59	76	.308	.349	1	.000	-0		-1		-0.2
1995	Fla N	4	4	.500	47	0	0	1-1	48.2	46	25	6	1	22-7	31	3.88	111	.251	.329	3	.000	-0		1	15	0.1
1996	Det A	0	4	.000	25	0	0	0-2	30.1	38	29	6	2	23-4	28	8.31	61	.306	.414	0	—	0		-10		-1.1
1997	KC A	0	1	.000	24	0	0	1-2	35.1	36	17	4	3	7-1	28	3.31	143	.273	.313	0	—	0		4	61	-0.2
Total	6	9	13	.409	135	1	0	3-7	174	179	99	24	8	74-15	116	4.60	96	.270	.343	4	.000	-0	23	-5	76	-0.7

VERHOEVEN, JOHN
John C B7.3.1952 Long Beach CA BR/TR/6-5/200* [AnaA74 12/274] d7.6 Col La Verne

YEAR	TM LG	W	L	PCT	G	GS	CG-SHO	SV-BS	IP	H	R	HR	HB	BB-IB	SO	ERA	AERA	OAV	OOB	AB-HR-SH	AVG	PB	SUP	APR	DL	PW
1976	Cal A	0	2	.000	21	0	0	4-3	37.1	35	15	2	0	14-8	23	3.38	99	.252	.320	0	—	0		0		0.1
1977	Cal A	0	2	.000	3	0	0	0-1	4.2	4	3	0	1	4-1	3	3.86	102	.222	.391	0	—	0		0		0.0
	Chi A	0	0	—	6	0	0	0-0	10.1	9	3	0	0	2-0	6	2.61	156	.231	.268	0	—	0		2		0.1
	Year	0	2	.000	9	0	0	0-1	15	13	6	0	1	6-1	9	3.00	135	.228	.313	0	—	0		2		0.1
1980	Min A	3	4	.429	44	0	0	0-0	99.2	109	53	10	3	29-5	42	3.97	110	.289	.337	0	—	0		3		0.2
1981	Min A	0	0	—	25	0	0	0-1	52	57	27	4	2	14-4	16	3.98	99	.288	.335	0	—	0		-1		0.0
Total	4	3	8	.273	99	0	0	4-5	204	214	101	16	6	63-18	90	3.79	107	.278	.332	0	—	0		4		0.4

VERLANDER, JUSTIN
Justin B. B2.20.1983 Hagerstown MD BR/TR/6-5/200 d7.4 Col Old Dominion

YEAR	TM LG	W	L	PCT	G	GS	CG-SHO	SV-BS	IP	H	R	HR	HB	BB-IB	SO	ERA	AERA	OAV	OOB	AB-HR-SH	AVG	PB	SUP	APR	DL	PW
2005	Det A	0	2	.000	2	2	0	0-0	11.1	15	9	1	1	5-0	7	7.15	59	.313	.389	0	—	0	22	-3		-0.5

VERNON, JOE
Joseph Henry B11.25.1889 Mansfield MA D3.13.1955 Philadelphia PA BR/TR/5-11/160 d7.20 Col Amherst

YEAR	TM LG	W	L	PCT	G	GS	CG-SHO	SV-BS	IP	H	R	HR	HB	BB-IB	SO	ERA	AERA	OAV	OOB	AB-HR-SH	AVG	PB	SUP	APR	DL	PW
1912	Chi N	0	0	—	1	0	0	0	4	4	6	0	1	6	1	11.25	30	.286	.524	2	.000	-0		-3		-0.2
1914	Bro F	0	0	—	1	1	0	0	3.1	4	4	0	0	5	0	10.80	27	.308	.500	1	.000	-0	286	-2		-0.1
Total	2	0	0	—	2	1	0	0	7.1	8	10	0	1	11	1	11.05	28	.296	.513	3	.000	-0	286	-5		-0.3

VESELIC, BOB
Robert Michael B9.27.1955 Pittsburgh PA D12.26.1995 Los Angeles CA BR/TR/6-0/175* [MinA76*1/9] d9.18 Col Mt. San Antonio (CA) JC

YEAR	TM LG	W	L	PCT	G	GS	CG-SHO	SV-BS	IP	H	R	HR	HB	BB-IB	SO	ERA	AERA	OAV	OOB	AB-HR-SH	AVG	PB	SUP	APR	DL	PW
1980	Min A	0	0	—	1	0	0	0-0	4	3	2	1	0	1-0	2	4.50	97	.214	.267	0	—	0		0		0.0
1981	Min A	1	1	.500	5	0	0	0-1	22.2	22	8	1	0	12-2	13	3.18	124	.250	.337	0	—	0		2		0.2
Total	2	1	1	.500	6	0	0	0-1	26.2	25	10	2	0	13-2	15	3.38	119	.245	.328	0	—	0		2		0.2

VIAU, LEE
Leon A. B7.5.1866 Corinth VT D12.17.1947 Hopewell NJ BR/TR/5-4/160 d4.22 Col Dartmouth

YEAR	TM LG	W	L	PCT	G	GS	CG-SHO	SV-BS	IP	H	R	HR	HB	BB-IB	SO	ERA	AERA	OAV	OOB	AB-HR-SH	AVG	PB	SUP	APR	DL	PW
1888	Cin AA	27	14	.659	42	42	42-1	0	387.2	331	192	7	20	110	164	2.65	120	.222	.285	149	.087	-11*	100	21		0.7
1889	Cin AA	22	20	.524	47	42	38-1	1	373	379	224	8	19	136	152	3.79	103	.255	.322	147	.143	-9	92	13		0.2
1890	Cle N	7	5	.583	13	10	7-1	0	90	97	69	8	1	39	41	4.50	79	.266	.339	36	.139	-2	87	-7		-0.9
	Cle N	4	9	.308	13	13	13-1	0	107	101	65	4	5	42	30	3.36	107	.241	.318	43	.163	-2	54	1		-0.1
	Year	11	14	.440	26	23	20-2	0	197	198	134	12	6	81	71	3.88	92	.253	.328	79	.152	-4	68	-8		-1.0
1891	Cle N	18	17	.514	45	38	31	0	343.2	367	239	3	15	138	130	3.01	115	.263	.336	144	.160	-3	105	9		-0.4
1892	Cle N	0	1	.000	1	1	0	0	1	5	5	0	0	1	0	36.00	9	.625	.667	3	—	0	56	-3		-0.4
	Lou N	4	11	.267	16	15	14-1	0	130.2	156	86	7	0	56	36	3.99	77	.285	.351	66	.197	1*	78	-12		-0.9
	Bos N	1	0	1.000	1	1	1	0	9	5	1	0	0	4	1	0.00	—	.156	.250	3	.000	0	144	3		0.3
	Year	5	12	.294	18	17	15-1	0	140.2	166	92	7	0	61	37	3.97	78	.282	.350	69	.188	1	82	-10		-1.0
Total	5	83	77	.519	178	162	146-5	1	1442	1441	881	37	51	526	554	3.33	105	.251	.320	588	.139	-27	93	25		-0.6

VICKERS, RUBE
Harry Porter B5.17.1878 St.Marys ON, Can. D12.9.1958 Belleville MI BL/TR/6-2/225 d9.21

YEAR	TM LG	W	L	PCT	G	GS	CG-SHO	SV-BS	IP	H	R	HR	HB	BB-IB	SO	ERA	AERA	OAV	OOB	AB-HR-SH	AVG	PB	SUP	APR	DL	PW
1902	Cin N	0	3	.000	3	3	3	0	21	31	20	0	1	8	5	6.00	50	.341	.400	11	.364	1*	60	-6		-0.7
1903	Bro N	0	1	.000	4	1	1	0	14	27	24	0	1	9	5	10.93	29	.415	.493	10	.100	-1*	63	-12		-0.7
1907	Phi A	2	2	.500	10	4	3-1	0	50.1	44	27	1	1	12	21	3.40	77	.238	.288	20-0-1	.150	-1	78	-4		1.0
1908	Phi A	18	19	.486	53	34	21-6	1	317	264	114	0	11	71	156	2.21	116	.231	.282	106-0-4	.160	-1	88	10		1.8
1909	Phi A	2	2	.500	18	3	1	1	55.2	60	32	0	2	19	25	3.40	71	.274	.338	16-0-1	.063	-1	107	-7		-0.8
Total	5	22	27	.449	88	45	29-7	2	458	426	216	1	16	119	213	2.93	98	.250	.305	163-0-6	.160	-3	86	-19		-1.6

VICKERY, TOM
Thomas Gill "Vinegar Tom" B5.5.1867 Milford NJ D3.21.1921 Burlington NJ TR/6-0/170 d4.21

YEAR	TM LG	W	L	PCT	G	GS	CG-SHO	SV-BS	IP	H	R	HR	HB	BB-IB	SO	ERA	AERA	OAV	OOB	AB-HR-SH	AVG	PB	SUP	APR	DL	PW
1890	Phi N	24	22	.522	46	46	41-2	0	382	405	250	8	29	184	162	3.44	106	.263	.353	159	.208	-4	83	4		-0.1
1891	Chi N	6	5	.545	14	12	7	0	79.2	72	55	4	5	44	39	4.07	82	.232	.337	39	.179	-2	124	-6		-0.8
1892	Bal N	8	10	.444	24	21	17	0	176	189	134	3	10	87	49	3.53	97	.264	.351	74	.243	2	106	-8		-0.6
1893	Phi N	4	5	.444	13	11	7	0	80	100	65	1	6	37	15	5.40	85	.297	.376	35	.314	1*	90	-7		-0.7
Total	4	42	42	.500	97	90	72-2	0	717.2	766	504	16	50	352	265	3.75	98	.264	.353	307	.225	-3	94	-17		-1.9

VILLACIS, EDUARDO
Eduardo Enrique B8.29.1979 Caracas, Venez BR/TR/6-2/170 d5.1

YEAR	TM LG	W	L	PCT	G	GS	CG-SHO	SV-BS	IP	H	R	HR	HB	BB-IB	SO	ERA	AERA	OAV	OOB	AB-HR-SH	AVG	PB	SUP	APR	DL	PW
2004	KC A	0	1	.000	1	1	0	0-0	3.1	6	5	1	0	4-0	0	13.50	35	.375	.500	0	—	0	80	-3		-0.4

VILLAFUERTE, BRANDON
Brandon Paul B12.17.1975 Hilo HI BR/TR/5-11/180(165-195) [NYN94 66/1587] d5.23 Col West Valley (CA) CC

YEAR	TM LG	W	L	PCT	G	GS	CG-SHO	SV-BS	IP	H	R	HR	HB	BB-IB	SO	ERA	AERA	OAV	OOB	AB-HR-SH	AVG	PB	SUP	APR	DL	PW
2000	Det A	0	0	—	3	0	0	0-0	4.1	4	5	0	0	4-0	1	10.38	47	.250	.400	0	—	0		-2		-0.1
2001	Tex A	0	0	—	6	0	0	0-0	5.2	12	9	1	1	4-0	4	14.29	33	.414	.486	0	—	0		-5		-0.3
2002	SD N	1	2	.333	31	0	0	1-0	32	29	5	2	2	12-2	25	1.41	276	.248	.326	0	—	0		10		0.9
2003	SD N	0	2	.000	31	0	0	2-3	40.2	39	20	7	3	26-2	34	4.20	95	.252	.368	1	.000	-0		-1	25	0.2
2004	Ari N	0	2	.000	20	0	0	0-0	20	25	9	2	1	14-2	13	4.05	113	.313	.421	1	.000	-0		2		0.2
Total	5	1	7	.125	91	0	0	3-3	102.2	109	48	14	7	60-6	77	4.12	101	.275	.377	2	.000	-0		4	25	0.2

VILLARREAL, OSCAR
Oscar Eduardo B11.22.1981 San Nicolas de los Garza, Nuevo Leon, Mexico BL/TR/6-0/170(170-205) d3.31

YEAR	TM LG	W	L	PCT	G	GS	CG-SHO	SV-BS	IP	H	R	HR	HB	BB-IB	SO	ERA	AERA	OAV	OOB	AB-HR-SH	AVG	PB	SUP	APR	DL	PW
2003	Ari N	10	7	.588	86	1	0	0-4	98	80	40	6	3	46-10	80	2.57	180	.222	.312	3	.000	-0	61	17		2.6
2004	Ari N	0	2	.000	17	0	0	0-0	18	25	14	3	1	7-1	17	7.00	65	.342	.407					-4	147	-0.4

YEAR	TM LG	W	L	PCT	G	GS	CG-SHO	SV-BS	IP	H	R	HR	HB	BB-IB	SO	ERA	AERA	OAV	OOB	AB-HR-SH	AVG	PB	SUP	APR	DL	PW
2005	Ari N	2	0	1.000	11	0	0	0-2	13.2	11	8	2	1	6-2	5	5.27	83	.234	.327	0	—	0		-1	144	-0.1
Total 3		12	9	.571	114	1	0	0-6	129.2	116	62	11	5	59-13	102	3.47	132	.241	.328	3	.000	-0	61	12	291	2.1

VILLEGAS, ISMAEL Ismael (Diaz) B8.12.1976 Rio Piedras, PR BR/TR/6-1/188 [ChiN95 5/119] d7.3

YEAR	TM LG	W	L	PCT	G	GS	CG-SHO	SV-BS	IP	H	R	HR	HB	BB-IB	SO	ERA	AERA	OAV	OOB	AB-HR-SH	AVG	PB	SUP	APR	DL	PW
2000	Atl N	0	0	—	1	0	0	0-0	2.2	4	4	2	1	2-0	2	13.50	33	.333	.467	1	.000	-0		-3		-0.1

VILLONE, RON Ronald Thomas B1.16.1970 Englewood NJ BL/TL/6-3/237* [SeaA92 1/14] d4.28 Col Massachusetts

YEAR	TM LG	W	L	PCT	G	GS	CG-SHO	SV-BS	IP	H	R	HR	HB	BB-IB	SO	ERA	AERA	OAV	OOB	AB-HR-SH	AVG	PB	SUP	APR	DL	PW
1995	Sea A	0	2	.000	19	0	0	0-3	19.1	20	19	6	1	23-0	26	7.91	60	.270	.449	0	—	0		-7		-0.6
	SD N	2	1	.667	19	0	0	1-1	25.2	24	12	5	0	11-0	37	4.21	97	.242	.315	1	.000	0		0		0.0
1996	SD N	1	1	.500	21	0	0	0-1	18.1	17	6	2	1	7-0	19	2.95	137	.243	.321	0	—	0		3		0.3
	Mil A	0	0	—	23	0	0	2-0	24.2	14	9	4	4	18-0	19	3.28	158	.175	.346	0	—	0		5		0.2
1997	Mil A	1	0	1.000	50	0	0	0-2	52.2	54	23	4	1	36-2	40	3.42	136	.271	.386	1	.000	-0		7		0.3
1998	Cle A	0	0	—	25	0	0	0-0	27	30	18	3	2	22-0	15	6.00	80	.297	.425	0	—	0		-3	17	-0.1
1999	Cin N	9	7	.563	29	22	0	2-0	142.1	114	70	8	5	73-2	97	4.23	111	.286	.319	43-0-5	.070	-3	90	9		0.6
2000	Cin N	10	10	.500	35	23	2	0-0	141	154	95	22	9	78-3	77	5.43	88	.286	.381	43-0-2	.163	-1	107	-11		-1.4
2001	Col N	1	3	.250	22	6	0	0-0	46.2	56	35	6	1	29-4	48	6.36	84	.295	.389	9-0-2	.000	-1	92	-4		-0.4
	†Hou N	5	7	.417	31	6	0	0-0	68	77	46	12	4	24-1	65	5.56	83	.282	.349	13-0-2	.077	-1	60	-7		-1.1
	Year	6	10	.375	53	12	0	0-0	114.2	133	81	18	5	53-5	113	5.89	83	.287	.366	22-0-4	.045	-2	79	-11		-1.5
2002	Pit N	4	6	.400	45	7	0	0-1	93	95	63	8	5	34-3	55	5.81	72	.270	.340	16	.250	1	60	-15	17	-1.3
2003	Hou N	6	6	.500	19	19	0	0-0	106.2	91	51	16	5	48-1	91	4.13	107	.233	.323	42-1-1	.167	0	122	4		0.6
2004	Sea A	8	6	.571	56	10	0	0-1	117	102	64	12	4	64-3	86	4.08	110	.232	.343	0	—	0	116	2		0.2
2005	Sea A	2	3	.400	52	0	0	1-5	40.1	33	14	2	5	23-1	41	2.45	171	.236	.345	0	—	0		7		0.8
	Fla N	3	2	.600	27	0	0	0-3	23.2	24	20	2	2	12-1	29	6.85	58	.264	.355	1	.000	-0		-8		-1.5
Total 11		52	54	.491	473	93	2	6-17	946.2	905	545	112	57	502-21	745	4.75	96	.254	.353	169-1-12	.130	-4	101	-18	34	-3.4

VINES, BOB Robert Earl B2.25.1897 Waxahachie TX D10.18.1982 Orlando FL BR/TR/6-4/184 d9.3

YEAR	TM LG	W	L	PCT	G	GS	CG-SHO	SV-BS	IP	H	R	HR	HB	BB-IB	SO	ERA	AERA	OAV	OOB	AB-HR-SH	AVG	PB	SUP	APR	DL	PW
1924	StL N	0	0	—	2	0	0	0	10.2	23	13	1	0	6-0	0	9.28	41	.426	.426	4	.000	-1		-7		-0.4
1925	Phi N	0	0	—	3	0	0	0	4	9	10	0	0	3	0	11.25	42	.450	.522	0	—	0		-4		-0.2
Total 2		0	0	—	5	0	0	0	14.2	32	23	1	0	3	0	9.82	41	.432	.455	4	.000	-1		-11		-0.6

VINEYARD, DAVE David Kent B2.25.1941 Clay WV BR/TR/6-3/195 d7.18

YEAR	TM LG	W	L	PCT	G	GS	CG-SHO	SV-BS	IP	H	R	HR	HB	BB-IB	SO	ERA	AERA	OAV	OOB	AB-HR-SH	AVG	PB	SUP	APR	DL	PW
1964	Bal A	2	5	.286	19	6	1	0	54	57	34	5	0	27-2	50	4.17	86	.274	.354	12-0-2	.167	0	71	-7		-0.8

VINING, KEN Kenneth Edward B12.5.1974 Decatur GA BL/TL/6-0/180 [SFN96 4/102] d5.23 Col Clemson

YEAR	TM LG	W	L	PCT	G	GS	CG-SHO	SV-BS	IP	H	R	HR	HB	BB-IB	SO	ERA	AERA	OAV	OOB	AB-HR-SH	AVG	PB	SUP	APR	DL	PW
2001	Chi A	0	0	—	8	0	0	0-0	6.2	15	14	3	1	7-0	3	17.55	27	.441	.548	0	—	0		-9		-0.4

VINTON, BILL William Miller B4.27.1865 Winthrop MA D9.3.1893 Pawtucket RI BR/TR/6-1/160 d7.3 Col Yale

YEAR	TM LG	W	L	PCT	G	GS	CG-SHO	SV-BS	IP	H	R	HR	HB	BB-IB	SO	ERA	AERA	OAV	OOB	AB-HR-SH	AVG	PB	SUP	APR	DL	PW
1884	Phi N	10	10	.500	21	21	20	0	182	166	131	6		35	105	2.23	134	.220	.255	78	.115	-6	110	4		-0.1
1885	Phi N	3	6	.333	9	9	8	0	77	90	59	0	0	23	21	3.04	92	.269	.317	30	.067	-3	113	-4		-0.7
	Phi AA	4	3	.571	7	7	6-2	0	55	46	41	1	4	15	34	2.45	140	.200	.261	26	.154	-1	130	3		0.2
Total 2		17	19	.472	37	37	34-2	0	314	302	231	7	4	73	160	2.46	122	.229	.272	134	.112	-10	115	3		-0.6

VIOLA, FRANK Frank John B4.19.1960 Hempstead NY BL/TL/6-4/209(195-210) [MinA81 2/37] d6.6 Col St. Johns

YEAR	TM LG	W	L	PCT	G	GS	CG-SHO	SV-BS	IP	H	R	HR	HB	BB-IB	SO	ERA	AERA	OAV	OOB	AB-HR-SH	AVG	PB	SUP	APR	DL	PW
1982	Min A	4	10	.286	22	22	3-1	0-0	126	152	77	22	0	38-2	84	5.21	82	.302	.351	0	—	0	90	-12		-1.2
1983	Min A	7	15	.318	35	34	4	0-0	210	242	141	34	8	92-7	127	5.49	78	.287	.362	0	—	0	95	-27		-2.5
1984	Min A	18	12	.600	35	35	10-4	0-0	257.2	225	101	28	4	73-1	149	3.21	132	.233	.289	0	—	0	88	28		2.9
1985	Min A	18	14	.563	36	36	9	0-0	250.2	262	136	26	2	68-3	135	4.09	108	.268	.315	0	—	0	84	4		0.4
1986	Min A	16	13	.552	37	37	7-1	0-0	245.2	257	136	37	3	83-0	191	4.51	96	.268	.327	0	—	0	102	-5		-0.6
1987	†Min A	17	10	.630	36	36	7-1	0-0	251.2	230	91	29	6	66-1	197	2.90	160	.241	.293	0	—	0	85	46		4.5
1988	Min A★	24	7	.774	35	35	7-2	0-0	255.1	236	80	20	3	54-2	193	2.64	155	.245	.286	0	—	0	118	40		4.7
1989	Min A	8	12	.400	24	24	7-1	0-0	175.2	171	80	17	3	47-1	138	3.79	109	.256	.306	0	—	0	86	7		0.7
	NY N	5	5	.500	12	12	2-1	0-0	85.1	75	35	5	1	27-3	73	3.38	98	.236	.296	23-0-5	.130	-0	110	0		-0.1
1990	NY N★	20	12	.625	35	35	7-3	0-0	249.2	227	83	15	2	60-2	182	2.67	141	.242	.288	85-0-7	.153	-1	103	31		3.7
1991	NY N★	13	15	.464	35	35	3	0-0	231.1	259	112	25	1	54-4	132	3.97	92	.268	.325	71-0-10	.127	-1	83	-6		-0.8
1992	Bos A	13	12	.520	35	35	6-1	0-0	238	214	99	13	7	89-4	121	3.44	124	.242	.313	0	—	0	75	22		2.4
1993	Bos A	11	8	.579	29	29	2-1	0-0	183.2	180	76	12	4	72-5	91	3.14	148	.259	.331	0	—	0	87	27		2.6
1994	Bos A	1	1	.500	6	6	0	0-0	31	34	17	2	0	17-0	9	4.65	109	.296	.381	0	—	0	94	2	100	0.1
1995	Cin N	0	1	.000	3	3	0	0-0	14.1	20	11	3	0	3-1	4	6.28	67	.333	.359	6	.167	0	87	-3	10	0.1
1996	Tor A	1	3	.250	6	6	0	0-0	30.1	43	28	6	2	21-3	18	7.71	65	.350	.443	0	—	0	99	-9		-0.9
Total 15		176	150	.540	421	420	74-16	0-0	2836.1	2827	1303	294	48	864-39	1844	3.73	113	.260	.316	185-0-22	.141	-2	92	145	110	15.7

VITELLI, JOE Antonio Joseph B4.12.1908 McKees Rocks PA D2.7.1967 Pittsburgh PA BR/TR/6-1/195 d5.30

YEAR	TM LG	W	L	PCT	G	GS	CG-SHO	SV-BS	IP	H	R	HR	HB	BB-IB	SO	ERA	AERA	OAV	OOB	AB-HR-SH	AVG	PB	SUP	APR	DL	PW
1944	Pit N	0	0	—	4	0	0	0-0	7	5	6	1	1		7	2.57	145	.185	.371	3	.000	-0		-1		-0.1

VITKO, JOE Joseph John B2.1.1970 Somerville NJ BR/TR/6-8/210 [NYN89 24/632] d9.18 Col St. Francis (PA) [DL 1993 NY N 182]

YEAR	TM LG	W	L	PCT	G	GS	CG-SHO	SV-BS	IP	H	R	HR	HB	BB-IB	SO	ERA	AERA	OAV	OOB	AB-HR-SH	AVG	PB	SUP	APR	DL	PW
1992	NY N	0	1	.000	3	1	0	0-0	4.2	12	11	1	0	1-0	6	13.50	26	.444	.448	0	—	0	155	-7		-1.1

VIZCAINO, LUIS Luis (Arias) B8.6.1974 Bani, D.R. BR/TR/5-11/170(169-185) d7.23

YEAR	TM LG	W	L	PCT	G	GS	CG-SHO	SV-BS	IP	H	R	HR	HB	BB-IB	SO	ERA	AERA	OAV	OOB	AB-HR-SH	AVG	PB	SUP	APR	DL	PW
1999	Oak A	0	0	—	1	0	0	0-0	3.1	3	2	1	0	3-0	2	5.40	88	.231	.375	0	—	0		0		0.0
2000	Oak A	0	1	.000	12	0	0	0-0	19.1	25	17	2	2	11-0	18	7.45	65	.305	.396	0	—	0		-5		-0.2
2001	Oak A	2	1	.667	36	0	0	1-0	36.2	38	19	8	0	12-1	31	4.66	98	.266	.321	0	—	0		0		0.0
2002	Mil N	5	3	.625	76	0	0	5-1	81.1	55	27	6	3	30-4	79	2.99	138	.192	.272	2	.000	-0		11		1.1
2003	Mil N	4	3	.571	75	0	0	0-6	62	64	45	16	1	25-3	61	6.39	68	.263	.333	0	—	0		-13		-1.3
2004	Mil N	4	4	.500	73	0	0	1-4	72	41	35	12	1	24-3	63	3.75	117	.228	.290	0	—	0		4		0.4
2005	Chi A	6	5	.545	65	0	0	0-3	70	74	30	8	2	29-6	43	3.73	121	.275	.349	0	—	0		7		0.9
Total 7		21	17	.553	338	0	0	7-14	344.2	320	175	53	9	134-17	297	4.36	101	.245	.317	2	.000	-0		4		0.9

VOGELSONG, RYAN Ryan Andrew B7.22.1977 Charlotte NC BR/TR/6-3/195(195-215) [SFN98 5/158] d9.2 Col Kutztown [DL 2002 Pit N 123]

YEAR	TM LG	W	L	PCT	G	GS	CG-SHO	SV-BS	IP	H	R	HR	HB	BB-IB	SO	ERA	AERA	OAV	OOB	AB-HR-SH	AVG	PB	SUP	APR	DL	PW
2000	SF N	0	0	—	4	0	0	0-0	6	4	0	0	2	2-0	6	0.00	—	.182	.250	0	—	0		3		0.1
2001	SF N	0	3	.000	13	0	0	0-0	28.2	29	21	5	2	14-0	17	5.65	65	.257	.346	0	—	0		-6		-0.5
	Pit N	0	2	.000	2	0	0	0-0	6	10	10	1	0	6-1	7	12.00	37	.357	.471	2	.000	-0		-6		-0.9
	Year	0	5	.000	15	2	0	0-0	34.2	39	31	6	2	20-1	24	6.75	62	.277	.372	2	.000	-0	103	-12		-1.4
2003	Pit N	2	2	.500	6	5	0	0-0	22	30	19	1	2	9-3	15	6.55	66	.323	.390	6-0-2	.167	-0	113	-6		-0.9
2004	Pit N	6	13	.316	34	26	0	0-0	133	148	97	22	10	67-7	92	6.50	67	.285	.374	31-0-10	.226	2*	88	-28		-3.3
2005	Pit N	2	2	.500	44	0	0	0-1	81.1	82	43	5	8	29-6	52	4.43	96	.259	.353	9	.111	0		-1		-0.1
Total 5		10	22	.313	100	33	0	0-1	277	303	190	34	22	138-12	189	5.78	74	.278	.367	56-0-12	.179	2	94	-44	123	-5.6

VOIGT, OLLIE Olen Edward "Ode" B1.29.1900 Wheaton IL D4.7.1970 Scottsdale AZ BL/TR/6-1/170 d4.19 Col Illinois

YEAR	TM LG	W	L	PCT	G	GS	CG-SHO	SV-BS	IP	H	R	HR	HB	BB-IB	SO	ERA	AERA	OAV	OOB	AB-HR-SH	AVG	PB	SUP	APR	DL	PW
1924	StL N	0	1	.000	8	1	0	0-0	16.1	21	13	1	0	13	4	5.51	82	.356	.472	4	.250	1	131	-2		0.0

VOISELLE, BILL William Symmes "Big Bill","Ninety-Six" B1.29.1919 Greenwood SC D1.31.2005 Greenwood SC BR/TR/6-4/200* d9.1

YEAR	TM LG	W	L	PCT	G	GS	CG-SHO	SV-BS	IP	H	R	HR	HB	BB-IB	SO	ERA	AERA	OAV	OOB	AB-HR-SH	AVG	PB	SUP	APR	DL	PW
1942	NY N	0	1	.000	2	1	0	0-0	9	6	4	1	0	4	5	2.00	168	.176	.263	2	.000	0	50	1		0.1
1943	NY N	1	2	.333	4	4	3	0-0	31	18	10	1	0	14	19	2.03	170	.154	.244	9-0-3	.111	-1	62	4		0.3
1944	NY N☆	21	16	.568	43	41	25-1	0	312.2	276	138	31	4	118	161	3.02	121	.232	.303	105-0-9	.210	3*	103	17		2.0
1945	NY N	14	14	.500	41	35	14-4	0	232.1	249	128	15	4	97	115	4.49	87	.273	.345				105	-13		-1.7
1946	NY N	9	15	.375	36	25	10-2	0	178	171	88	14	0	85	89	3.74	92	.248	.330	55-0-7	.164	-1	114	-7		-1.0
1947	NY N	1	4	.200	11	5	1	0	42.2	44	26	4	1	22	20	4.64	88	.284	.376	16	.133	-1	100	-3		-0.4
	Bos N	8	7	.533	22	20	7	0	131.1	146	66	10	1	51	59	4.32	90	.280	.345	53-0-3	.170	-1	118	-4		-0.4
	Year	9	11	.450	33	25	8	0	174	190	92	14	2	73	79	4.40	90	.281	.352	68-0-3	.162	-1	114	-7		-0.8
1948	†Bos N	13	13	.500	37	30	9-2	0	215.2	226	93	18	3	90	89	3.63	106	.272	.345	72-0-7	.097	-4	89	7		0.3
1949	Bos N	7	8	.467	30	22	5-4	1	169.1	170	84	14	1	78	63	4.04	94	.263	.343	61	.115	-2	109	-3		-0.7
1950	Chi N	0	4	.000	6	3	0	1	51.1	59	37	7	1	29	25	5.79	73	.303	.390	13	.077	-10	90	-4		-0.7
Total 9		74	84	.468	245	190	74-13	3	1373.1	1370	676	115	15	588	645	3.83	98	.258	.334	464-0-36	.147	-10	103	-10		-1.9

VOLQUEZ, EDISON Edison B7.3.1983 LaSegunda, D.R. BR/TR/6-1/190 d8.30

YEAR	TM LG	W	L	PCT	G	GS	CG-SHO	SV-BS	IP	H	R	HR	HB	BB-IB	SO	ERA	AERA	OAV	OOB	AB-HR-SH	AVG	PB	SUP	APR	DL	PW
2005	Tex A	0	4	.000	6	6	0	0-0	12.2	25	22	3	2	10-0	11	14.21	32	.403	.493	0	—	0	68	-13		-2.1

YEAR	TM LG	W	L	PCT	G	GS	CG-SHO	SV-BS	IP	H	R	HR	HB	BB-IB	SO	ERA	AERA	OAV	OOB	AB-HR-SH	AVG	PB	SUP	APR	DL	PW

VOLZ, JAKE   Jacob Phillip "Silent Jake"   B4.4.1878 San Antonio TX   D8.11.1962 San Antonio TX   BR/TR/5-10/175   d9.28

1901	Bos A	1	0	1.000	1	1	1	0	7	6	9	2	0	9	5	9.00	39	.231	.429	4	.000	-1	191	-4		-0.4
1905	Bos N	0	1	.000	3	2	0	0	8.2	12	11	0	1	8	1	10.38	30	.364	.500	2	.000	-0	47	-6		-1.1
1908	Cin N	1	2	.333	7	4	1	0	22.2	16	9	1	2	12	6	3.57	65	.195	.313	4	.250	-0	76	-2		-0.3
Total	3	2	4	.333	11	7	2	0	38.1	34	29	3	3	29	12	6.10	44	.241	.382	10	.100	-1	89	-12		-1.8

Von FRICKEN, TONY   Anthony   B5.30.1869 Brooklyn NY   D3.22.1947 Troy NY   BB/TR/5-11.5/160   d5.9

| 1890 | Bos N | 0 | 1 | .000 | 1 | 1 | 1 | 0 | 8 | 23 | 16 | 0 | 0 | 8 | 2 | 10.13 | 37 | .489 | .564 | 3 | .000 | -1 | 50 | -6 | | -0.5 |

Von HOFF, BRUCE   Bruce Frederick   B11.17.1943 Oakland CA   BR/TR/6-0/187*   d9.28   Col Northern Illinois

1965	Hou N	0	0	—	3	0	0	0	3	3	3	0	0	2-0	1	9.00	37	.250	.357	0	—	0		-2		-0.1
1967	Hou N	0	3	.000	10	10	0	0	50.1	52	29	3	0	28-1	22	4.83	69	.268	.356	15-0-1	.067	-1	90	-8		-0.6
Total	2	0	3	.000	13	10	0	0	53.1	55	32	3	0	30-1	23	5.06	65	.267	.356	15-0-1	.067	-1	90	-10		-0.7

Von OHLEN, DAVE   David   B10.25.1958 Flushing NY   BL/TL/6-2/200*   [NYN76 17/397]   d5.13

1983	StL N	3	2	.600	46	0	0	2-2	68.1	71	27	3	3	25-8	21	3.29	111	.280	.345	7-0-1	.143	0		3		0.3
1984	StL N	1	0	1.000	27	0	0	1-1	34.2	39	13	0	0	8-3	19	3.12	112	.300	.341	1	1.000	0		2		0.2
1985	Cle A	3	2	.600	26	0	0	0-1	43.1	47	20	3	0	20-6	12	2.91	143	.288	.358	0	—	0		4	18	0.1
1986	Oak A	0	3	.000	24	0	0	1-1	15.1	18	7	0	0	7-2	4	3.52	111	.300	.373	0	—	0		1		0.1
1987	Oak A	0	0	—	4	0	0	0-0	6	10	5	1	0	1-0	3	7.50	55	.400	.407	0	—	0		-2		-0.1
Total	5	7	7	.500	127	0	0	4-5	167.2	185	72	7	3	61-19	59	3.33	114	.293	.353	8-0-1	.250	1		8	18	0.6

VORHEES, CY   Henry Bert   B9.30.1874 Lodi OH   D2.8.1910 Perry OH   TR/6-3/200   d4.17   Col Syracuse

1902	Phi N	3	3	.500	10	5	3-1	0	53.2	63	33	1	1	20	24	3.86	73	.292	.354	20	.350	2	121	-7		-0.5
	Was A	0	1	.000	1	1	1	0	8	10	6	0	0	2	1	4.50	82	.303	.343	3	.667	1	39	-1		0.0
Total	1	3	4	.429	11	6	4-1	0	61.2	73	39	1	1	22	25	3.94	74	.293	.353	23	.391	3	103	-8		-0.5

VOSBERG, ED   Edward John   B9.28.1961 Tucson AZ   BL/TL/6-1/190(190-210)   [SDN83 3/64]   d9.17   Col Arizona   [DL 1998 SD N 181]

1986	SD N	0	1	.000	5	3	0	0-0	13.2	17	11	1	0	9-1	8	6.59	56	.304	.400	2	.000	-0	106	-4		-0.3
1990	SF N	1	1	.500	18	0	0	0-0	24.1	21	16	3	0	12-2	12	5.55	66	.233	.324	0	—	0		-5		-0.1
1994	Oak A	0	2	.000	16	0	0	0-1	13.2	16	7	2	0	5-0	12	3.95	114	.320	.382	0	—	0		1		0.1
1995	Tex A	5	5	.500	44	0	0	4-4	36	32	15	3	0	16-1	36	3.00	161	.241	.316	0	—	0		6		1.2
1996	†Tex A	1	1	.500	52	0	0	8-1	44	51	17	4	0	21-4	32	3.27	161	.298	.373	0	—	0		9		0.7
1997	Tex A	1	2	.333	42	0	0	0-1	41	44	23	3	2	15-6	29	4.61	105	.277	.341	0	—	0		1		0.1
	†Fla N	1	1	.500	17	0	0	1-1	12	15	7	0	3	6-0	15	3.75	108	.313	.414	0	—	0		-6		-0.2
1999	SD N	0	0	—	15	0	0	0-2	8.1	16	11	1	2	3-0	6	9.72	44	.421	.467	0	—	0		-6	19	-0.3
	Ari N	0	1	.000	4	0	0	0-0	2.2	6	1	0	0	0-0	2	3.38	137	.462	.462	0	—	0		1		0.1
	Year	0	1	.000	19	0	0	0-2	11	22	12	1	2	3-0	8	8.18	53	.431	.466	0	—	0		-5		-0.2
2000	Phi N	1	1	.500	31	0	0	0-0	24	21	14	2	0	18-0	23	4.13	111	.241	.371	0	—	0		2		0.2
2001	Phi N	0	0	—	18	0	0	0-0	12.2	8	4	0	0	3-0	11	2.84	145	.186	.239	0	—	0		2		0.1
2002	Mon N	0	0	—	4	0	0	0-0	1	3	3	1	0	1-0	0	18.00	24	.429	.500	0	—	0		-2		-0.1
Total	10	10	15	.400	266	3	0	13-10	233.1	250	126	22	7	109-14	179	4.32	106	.279	.358	2	.000	-0	106	4	200	1.3

VOSS, ALEX   Alexander   B5.16.1858 Roswell GA   D8.31.1906 Cincinnati OH   BR/TR/6-1/180   d4.17   ▲

1884	Was U	5	14	.263	27	20	18	0	186.1	206	136	2	2	32	112	3.57	67	.262	.291	245	.192	-9*	91	-24		-2.4
	KC U	0	6	.000	7	6	6	0	53	74	45	2	2	7	17	4.25	53	.310	.329	45	.089	-4*	41	-12		-1.3
	Year	5	20	.200	34	26	24	0	239.1	280	181	4	2	39	129	3.72	63	.273	.300	290	.176	-13	80	-36		-3.7

VOWINKEL, RIP   John Henry   B11.18.1884 Oswego NY   D7.13.1966 Oswego NY   BR/TR/5-10/195   d9.5

| 1905 | Cin N | 3 | 3 | .500 | 9 | 4 | 4 | 0 | 45.1 | 52 | 31 | 2 | 1 | 10 | 7 | 4.17 | 79 | .302 | .344 | 14-0-2 | .071 | -0 | 116 | -4 | | -0.6 |

VOYLES, BRAD   Bradley Roy   B12.30.1976 Green Bay WI   BR/TR/6-1/195*   [AtlN98 45/1348]   d9.8   Col Lincoln Memorial   [DL 2001 Atl N 68]

2001	KC A	0	0	—	7	0	0	0-0	9.1	5	4	1	0	8-0	6	3.86	129	.161	.350	—		0		1		0.0
2002	KC A	0	2	.000	22	0	0	1-1	27.2	31	21	5	2	18-1	26	6.51	77	.284	.395	0	—	0		-4		-0.3
2003	KC A	0	2	.000	11	3	0	0-0	31.1	47	29	6	1	18-1	24	7.18	67	.348	.423	1	.000	-0	95	-9		-0.5
Total	3	0	4	.000	40	3	0	1-1	68.1	83	54	12	4	44-2	56	6.45	76	.302	.403	1	.000	-0	95	-12	68	-0.8

VUCKOVICH, PETE   Peter Dennis   B10.27.1952 Johnstown PA   BR/TR/6-4/220(200-225)   [ChiA74 3/56]   d8.3   C4   Col Clarion   [DL 1984 Mil A 182]

1975	Chi A	0	1	.000	4	2	0	0-0	10.1	17	15	0	0	7-1	5	13.06	30	.386	.471	0	—	0	193	-10		-0.8
1976	Chi A	7	4	.636	33	7	1	0-0	110.1	122	59	3	4	60-4	62	4.65	77	.287	.375	0	—	0	102	-12		-1.1
1977	Tor A	7	7	.500	53	8	3-1	8-4	148	143	64	13	5	59-5	123	3.47	123	.257	.329	0	—	0	87	13		1.2
1978	StL N	12	12	.500	45	23	6-2	1-3	198.1	187	65	9	2	59-5	149	2.54	140	.253	.308	58-0-7	.138	-1	77	22		2.6
1979	StL N	15	10	.600	34	32	9	0-0	233	229	108	22	3	64-4	145	3.59	106	.260	.310	79-0-8	.152	-2	115	4		0.1
1980	StL N	12	9	.571	32	30	7-3	1-0	222.1	203	96	18	2	68-5	132	3.40	110	.247	.304	71-0-9	.183	1	106	8		0.0
1981	†Mil A	14	4	.778	24	23	2-1	0-1	149.2	137	61	9	4	57-1	84	3.55	98	.249	.323	0	—	0	124	11		1.1
1982	†Mil A	18	6	.750	30	30	9-1	0-0	223.2	234	105	22	5	102-1	105	3.34	115	.275	.354	0	—	0	88	-2	140	-0.3
1983	Mil A	0	2	.000	3	3	0	0-0	14.2	15	9	0	1	10-1	10	4.91	77	.259	.377	0	—	0	99	-14	24	-1.8
1985	Mil A	6	10	.375	22	22	1	0-0	112.2	134	74	16	2	48-2	55	5.51	76	.298	.374	0	—	0	42	2		0.4
1986	Mil A	2	4	.333	6	6	0	0-0	32.1	33	18	3	2	11-0	12	3.06	142	.273	.336	0	—	0	72	5		0.5
Total	11	93	69	.574	286	186	38-8	10-8	1455.1	1454	665	107	35	545-29	882	3.66	104	.264	.332	208-0-24	.159	-2	106	22	346	2.0

WACHTEL, PAUL   Paul Horine   B4.30.1888 Myersville MD   D12.15.1964 San Antonio TX   BR/TR/5-11/175   d9.18

| 1917 | Bro N | 0 | 0 | — | 2 | 0 | 0 | 0 | 6 | 9 | 7 | 0 | 0 | 4 | 3 | 10.50 | 27 | .375 | .464 | 3 | .333 | 0 | | -4 | | -0.2 |

WACKER, CHARLIE   Charles James   B12.8.1883 Jeffersonville IN   D8.7.1948 Evansville IN   BL/TL/5-9/?   d4.28

| 1909 | Pit N | 0 | 0 | — | 1 | 0 | 0 | 0 | 2 | 2 | 2 | 0 | 1 | 0 | 0 | 0.00 | — | .400 | .500 | 0 | — | 0 | | 0 | | 0.0 |

WADDELL, RUBE   George Edward   B10.13.1876 Bradford PA   D4.1.1914 San Antonio TX   BR/TL/6-1.5/196   d9.8   HF1946

1897	Lou N	0	1	.000	2	1	1	0	14	17	6	0	1	6	5	3.21	133	.298	.375	6	.000	-1	17	2		0.0
1899	Lou N	7	2	.778	10	9	9-1	1	79	69	38	4	8	14	44	3.08	125	.235	.288	34	.235	-0	89	8		0.7
1900	†Pit N	8	13	.381	29	22	16-2	0	208.2	176	96	3	13	55	130	**2.37**	153	**.229**	.291	81	.173	-2*	105	24		1.9
1901	Pit N	0	2	.000	2	2	0	0	7.2	10	12	0	1	9	4	9.39	50	.313	.476	3	.000	-0	76	-5		-0.9
	Chi N	14	14	.500	29	28	26	0	243.2	239	123	6	9	66	168	2.81	115	.255	.310	98-2-0	.255	6*	102	9		1.8
	Year	14	16	.467	31	30	26	0	251.1	249	135	5	10	75	172	3.01	108	.257	.317	101-2-0	.248	6	101	3		0.9
1902	Phi A	24	7	.774	33	27	26-3	0	276.1	224	90	7	10	64	210	2.05	179	.222	.276	112-1-1	.286	7*	95	48		5.8
1903	Phi A	21	16	.568	39	38	**34**-4	0	324	274	109	3	8	85	302	2.44	125	.229	.284	115-0-5	.122	-6	83	23		1.8
1904	Phi A	25	19	.568	46	46	39-8	0	383	307	109	5	14	91	349	1.62	**165**	.221	.275	139-0-1	.122	-7	97	40		4.1
1905	Phi A	**27**	10	**.730**	46	34	27-7	0	328.2	231	86	5	10	90	287	**1.48**	**180**	**.200**	.263	116-0-6	.172	-1	106	**40**		**4.5**
1906	Phi A	15	17	.469	43	34	22-8	0	272.2	221	89	1	10	92	196	2.21	123	.225	.297	86-0-5	.163	-0	74	17		1.9
1907	Phi A	19	13	.594	44	33	20-7	0	284.2	234	115	2	15	73	232	2.15	121	.227	.287	101-0-2	.119	-5	100	8		1.5
1908	StL A	19	14	.576	43	36	25-5	3	285.2	223	93	0	8	90	232	1.89	127	.218	.281	91-1-3	.110	-1	101	14		1.5
1909	StL A	11	14	.440	31	28	16-5	0	220.1	204	78	1	7	57	141	2.37	102	.267	.323	75	.067	-5	78	1		-0.5
1910	StL A	3	1	.750	10	2	1	1	33	31	19	1	1	11	16	3.55	70	.242	.307	9	.111	-0	108	-4		-0.2
Total	13	193	143	.574	407	340	261-50	5	2961.1	2460	1063	37	115	803	2316	2.16	135	.228	.288	1066-4-23	.161	-17	93	225		22.2

WADDELL, TOM   Thomas David   B9.17.1958 Dundee, Scotland   BR/TR/6-1/190*   d4.15   Col Manhattan   [DL 1986 Cle A 182]

1984	Cle A	7	4	.636	58	0	0	6-4	97	68	35	12	1	37-4	59	3.06	135	.202	.276	0	—	0		12		1.3
1985	Cle A	8	6	.571	49	9	1	9-4	112.2	104	61	20	1	39-8	53	4.87	85	.246	.309	0	—	0	133	-6		-0.7
1987	Cle A	0	1	.000	6	0	0	0-0	5.2	7	10	1	1	7-0	6	14.29	32	.292	.469	0	—	0		-6		-0.2
Total	3	15	11	.577	113	9	1	15-8	215.1	179	106	33	3	83-12	118	4.30	97	.229	.300	0	—	0	133	0	182	-0.2

WADE, BEN   Benjamin Styron   B11.26.1922 Morehead City NC   D12.2.2002 Los Angeles CA   BR/TR/6-3/205*   d4.30   b-Jake

1948	Chi N	0	1	.000	2	0	0	0	5	4	4	0	0	4	1	7.20	54	.211	.348	2	.000	-0		-2		-0.
1952	Bro N	11	9	.550	37	24	5-1	3	180	166	81	19	2	94	118	3.60	101	.246	.340	60-3-2	.117	1	100	0		0.6
1953	†Bro N	7	5	.583	32	0	0	0	90.1	79	40	15	4	33	65	3.79	113	.232	.308	24-1-3	.167	0		6		0.6
1954	Bro N	1	1	.500	23	0	0	0	45	62	46	9	2	25	19	8.20	50	.339	.393	5-0-1	.000	-1		-21		-0.2
	StL N	0	0	—	13	0	0	3	23	27	15	3	0	11	25	5.48	75	.303	.411	3	.000	-0		-3		-0.2
	Year	1	1	.500	36	0	0	3	68	89	61	12	2	36	44	7.28	56	.327	.399	8-0-1	.000	-1		-24		-1.

YEAR	TM LG	W	L	PCT	G	GS	CG-SHO	SV-BS	IP	H	R	HR	HB	BB-IB	SO	ERA	AERA	OAV	OOB	AB-HR-SH	AVG	PB	SUP	APR	DL	PW
1955	Pit N	0	1	.000	11	1	0	1	28	26	12	3	1	14-4	7	3.21	128	.252	.339	4	.000	-0	151	3		0.1
Total 5		19	17	.528	118	25	5-1	10	371.1	364	198	49	9	181-4	235	4.34	90	.259	.344	98-4-6	.112	-0	96	-17		-1.0

WADE, TERRELL Hawatha Terrell B1.25.1973 Rembert SC BL/TL/6-3/205* d9.12

YEAR	TM LG	W	L	PCT	G	GS	CG-SHO	SV-BS	IP	H	R	HR	HB	BB-IB	SO	ERA	AERA	OAV	OOB	AB-HR-SH	AVG	PB	SUP	APR	DL	PW
1995	Atl N	0	1	.000	3	0	0	0	4	3	2	1	0	4-0	3	4.50	96	.214	.389	0	—	0	0			0.0
1996	†Atl N	5	0	1.000	44	8	0	1-1	69.2	57	28	9	1	47-6	79	2.97	150	.227	.350	0	—	0	124	10		0.7
1997	Atl N	2	3	.400	12	9	0	0-0	42	60	31	6	2	16-1	35	5.36	78	.349	.400	12-0-1	.250	1	112	-7	114	-0.6
1998	TB A	1	1	.500	2	2	0	0-0	10.2	14	6	3	0	2-0	8	5.06	95	.318	.348	0	—	0	87	0	170	0.0
Total 4		8	5	.615	61	19	0	1-1	126.1	134	67	19	3	69-7	125	3.99	110	.279	.369	25-0-3	.200	1	113	3	284	0.1

WADE, JAKE Jacob Fields "Whistling Jake" B4.1.1912 Morehead City NC BL/TL/6-2/175 d4.22 Mil 1945 b-Ben Col North Carolina St.

YEAR	TM LG	W	L	PCT	G	GS	CG-SHO	SV-BS	IP	H	R	HR	HB	BB-IB	SO	ERA	AERA	OAV	OOB	AB-HR-SH	AVG	PB	SUP	APR	DL	PW
1936	Det A	4	5	.444	13	11	4-1	0	78.1	93	60	7	1	52	30	5.29	94	.296	.398	29	.172	-0	95	-6		-0.6
1937	Det A	7	10	.412	33	25	7-1	0	165.1	160	106	13	3	107	69	5.39	87	.257	.368	59-0-1	.186	-1	95	-10		-1.0
1938	'Det A	3	2	.600	27	2	0	0	70	73	56	9	0	48	23	6.56	76	.268	.378	21	.048	-2	53	-11		-0.9
1939	Bos A	1	4	.200	20	6	1	0	47.2	68	34	1	0	37	21	6.23	76	.358	.463	12	.000	-2	81	-6		-0.7
	StL A	0	2	.000	4	2	1	0	16.1	26	25	1	0	19	9	11.02	44	.356	.489	5	.000	-1	36	-12		-1.1
	Year	1	6	.143	24	8	2	0	64	94	59	2	0	56	30	7.45	64	.357	.470	17	.000	-3	69	-18		-1.8
1942	Chi A	5	5	.500	15	10	3	0	85.2	84	45	2	0	56	32	4.10	88	.255	.363	29	.241	1	93	-5		-0.3
1943	Chi A	3	7	.300	21	9	3-1	0	83.2	66	34	3	4	54	41	3.01	111	.222	.349	27-0-1	.148	0	62	3		0.3
1944	Chi A	2	4	.333	19	5	1	2	74.2	75	46	3	0	41	35	4.82	71	.261	.354	24	.292	1	112	-11		-0.8
1946	NY A	1	1	.667	13	1	0	1	35.1	33	9	2	1	14	22	2.29	151	.250	.327	9	.111	-0	0	5		0.5
	Was A	0	0	—	6	0	0	0	11.1	12	6	1	0	12	9	4.76	70	.279	.436	1	.000	-0		-1		-0.1
	Year	2	1	.667	19	1	0	1	46.2	45	15	3	1	26	31	2.89	118	.257	.356	10	.100	-0	0	4		0.4
Total 8		27	40	.403	171	71	20-3	3	668.1	690	421	42	9	440	291	5.00	84	.269	.378	216-0-2	.167	-5	89	-54		-4.7

WADSWORTH, JACK John L. B12.17.1867 Wellington OH D7.8.1941 Elyria OH BL/TR/?/180 d5.1

YEAR	TM LG	W	L	PCT	G	GS	CG-SHO	SV-BS	IP	H	R	HR	HB	BB-IB	SO	ERA	AERA	OAV	OOB	AB-HR-SH	AVG	PB	SUP	APR	DL	PW
1890	Cle N	2	16	.111	20	19	19	0	169.2	202	139	6	6	81	26	5.20	69	.286	.364	68	.176	-3	68	-27		-2.4
1893	Bal N	0	3	.000	3	3	0	0	16	37	30	0	0	8	2	11.25	42	.440	.489	7	.429	1	118	-12		-1.3
1894	Lou N	4	18	.182	22	22	20	0	173	261	204	10	4	103	57	7.60	67	.344	.425	74-0-1	.257	0	79	-45		-3.6
1895	Lou N	0	1	.000	2	0	0	0	9	24	20	0	0	7	2	16.00	34	.480	.544	4-0-1	.250	-0		-10		-0.7
Total 4		6	38	.136	47	44	39	0	367.2	524	393	16	10	199	87	6.85	64	.328	.405	153-0-2	.229	-2	78	-94		-8.0

WAECHTER, DOUG Douglas Michael B1.28.1981 St.Petersburg FL BR/TR/6-4/200* [TBA99 3/85] d8.27

YEAR	TM LG	W	L	PCT	G	GS	CG-SHO	SV-BS	IP	H	R	HR	HB	BB-IB	SO	ERA	AERA	OAV	OOB	AB-HR-SH	AVG	PB	SUP	APR	DL	PW
2003	TB A	3	2	.600	6	5	1-1	0-0	35.1	29	13	4	1	15-0	29	3.31	138	.225	.310	0	—	0	108	5		0.7
2004	TB A	5	7	.417	14	14	0	0-0	70.1	68	54	20	4	33-1	36	6.01	78	.252	.340	0	—	0	95	-11	89	-1.6
2005	TB A	5	12	.294	29	25	0	0-0	157	191	109	29	3	38-5	87	5.62	78	.297	.337	2-0-1	.000	-0	110	-22	26	-2.2
Total 3		13	21	.382	49	44	1-1	0-0	262.2	288	176	53	8	86-6	152	5.41	83	.276	.335	2-0-1	.000	-0	105	-28	115	-3.1

WAGNER, CHARLIE Charles Thomas "Broadway" B12.3.1912 Reading PA BR/TR/5-11/170 d4.19 Mil 1943-45 C1

YEAR	TM LG	W	L	PCT	G	GS	CG-SHO	SV-BS	IP	H	R	HR	HB	BB-IB	SO	ERA	AERA	OAV	OOB	AB-HR-SH	AVG	PB	SUP	APR	DL	PW
1938	Bos A	1	3	.250	13	6	1	0	36.2	47	36	5	1	24	14	8.35	59	.309	.407	12	.167	-1	113	-12		-1.1
1939	Bos A	3	1	.750	9	5	0	0	38.1	49	19	3	0	14	13	4.23	112	.320	.377	14	.071	-2*	123	3		0.1
1940	Bos A	1	0	1.000	12	1	0	0	29.1	45	22	5	0	8	13	5.52	81	.344	.381	5	.200	-0*	234	-4		-0.2
1941	Bos A	12	8	.600	29	25	12-3	0	187.1	175	76	14	1	85	51	3.07	136	.245	.326	63-0-10	.159	-1	120	22		2.0
1942	Bos A	14	11	.560	29	26	17-2	0	205.1	184	87	5	0	95	52	3.29	113	.247	.336	65-0-11	.077	-5	98	9		0.6
1946	Bos A	1	0	1.000	8	4	0	0	30.2	32	21	6	0	19	14	5.87	62	.276	.378	11-0-2	.091	-1	187	-6		-0.4
Total 6		32	23	.582	100	67	30-5	0	527.2	532	261	38	7	245	157	3.91	104	.264	.346	170-0-23	.118	-9	117	12		1.0

WAGNER, GARY Gary Edward B6.28.1940 Bridgeport IL BR/TR/6-4/191* d4.18 Col Eastern Illinois

YEAR	TM LG	W	L	PCT	G	GS	CG-SHO	SV-BS	IP	H	R	HR	HB	BB-IB	SO	ERA	AERA	OAV	OOB	AB-HR-SH	AVG	PB	SUP	APR	DL	PW
1965	Phi N	7	7	.500	59	0	0	7	105	87	43	6	2	49-8	91	3.00	115	.233	.323	13-0-1	.077	-0		4		0.6
1966	Phi N	0	1	.000	5	1	0	0	6.1	8	6	1	0	5-0	2	8.53	42	.333	.433	0	—	0	171	-3		-0.5
1967	Phi N	0	0	—	1	0	0	0	2	1	0	0	0	0-0	1	0.00	—	.167	.167	0	—	0		1		0.0
1968	Phi N	4	4	.500	44	0	0	8	78	69	27	0	5	31-6	43	3.00	100	.243	.326	12	.083	-1		1		0.1
1969	Phi N	0	3	.000	9	2	0	0-1	19.1	31	22	3	0	7-1	8	7.91	45	.365	.404	3	.000	-0	50	-11		-1.5
	Bos A	1	3	.250	6	1	0	0-0	16.1	18	11	1	0	15-0	9	6.06	63	.300	.440	3-0-1	.000	-0	0	-3		-0.7
1970	Bos A	3	1	.750	38	0	0	7-1	40.1	36	21	3	2	19-1	20	3.35	119	.232	.320	6	.167	-0		1		0.1
Total 6		15	19	.441	162	4	0	22-2	267.1	250	130	14	9	126-16	174	3.70	93	.253	.340	37-0-2	.081	-2	70	-10		-1.9

WAGNER, HECTOR Hector Raul Guerrero (b Hector Raul Guerrero (Wagner)) B11.26.1968 San Juan, D.R. BR/TR/6-3/185(185-200) d9.10

YEAR	TM LG	W	L	PCT	G	GS	CG-SHO	SV-BS	IP	H	R	HR	HB	BB-IB	SO	ERA	AERA	OAV	OOB	AB-HR-SH	AVG	PB	SUP	APR	DL	PW
1990	KC A	0	2	.000	5	5	0	0-0	23.1	32	24	4	0	11-1	14	8.10	48	.323	.384		—	0	108	-11		-0.8
1991	KC A	1	1	.500	2	2	0	0-0	10	16	10	2	0	3-0	5	7.20	58	.348	.388	0	—	0	210	-4		-0.6
Total 2		1	3	.250	7	7	0	0-0	33.1	48	34	6	0	14-1	19	7.83	50	.331	.385	0	—	0	139	-15		-1.4

WAGNER, MATT Matthew William B4.4.1972 Cedar Falls IA BR/TR/6-5/215 [SeaA94 3/77] d6.5 Col Iowa St. [DL 1997 Mon N 181]

YEAR	TM LG	W	L	PCT	G	GS	CG-SHO	SV-BS	IP	H	R	HR	HB	BB-IB	SO	ERA	AERA	OAV	OOB	AB-HR-SH	AVG	PB	SUP	APR	DL	PW
1996	Sea A	3	5	.375	15	14	1	0-0	80	91	62	15	3	38-2	41	6.86	72	.285	.363	0	—	0	121	-15		-1.2

WAGNER, PAUL Paul Alan B11.14.1967 Milwaukee WI BR/TR/6-1/202(185-211) [PitN89 12/314] d7.26 Col Illinois St.

YEAR	TM LG	W	L	PCT	G	GS	CG-SHO	SV-BS	IP	H	R	HR	HB	BB-IB	SO	ERA	AERA	OAV	OOB	AB-HR-SH	AVG	PB	SUP	APR	DL	PW
1992	Pit N	2	0	1.000	6	1	0	0-0	13	9	1	0	0	5-0	5	0.69	501	.191	.269	3	.333	10	130	4		0.7
1993	Pit N	8	8	.500	44	17	1-1	2-3	141.1	143	72	15	1	42-2	114	4.27	96	.263	.314	42-0-4	.190	0	93	-3	16	-0.4
1994	Pit N	7	8	.467	29	17	1	0-0	119.2	136	69	7	8	50-4	86	4.59	95	.293	.369	37-0-2	.162	-1	76	-3		-0.3
1995	Pit N	5	16	.238	32	25	3-1	1-0	165	174	96	18	7	72-7	120	4.80	91	.273	.352	42-0-6	.214	2*	68	-7	18	-0.2
1996	Pit N	4	8	.333	16	15	1	0-0	81.2	86	49	10	3	39-2	81	5.40	81	.275	.360	25-0-3	.040	-2*	68	-7	97	-0.9
1997	Pit N	0	0	—	14	0	0	0-1	16	17	7	3	0	13-3	9	3.94	109	.274	.395	1	.000	-2*	85	-6	108	0.0
	Mil A	1	0	1.000	2	0	0	0-0	2	3	2	1	0	4-0	1	9.00	51	.375	.375	0	—	0		-1		-0.2
1998	Mil N	1	5	.167	13	9	0	0-0	55.2	67	49	10	1	31-1	37	7.11	61	.302	.387	19-0-1	.158	0	66	-17	47	-1.6
1999	Cle A	0	1	.000	3	0	0	0-0	4.1	5	4	2	0	1-1	6	4.15	122	.263	.417	0	—	0		0		-0.1
Total 8		29	45	.392	160	84	6-2	3-4	598.2	640	349	64	22	255-19	452	4.83	89	.276	.351	169-0-16	.166	-1	78	-32	286	-3.4

WAGNER, RYAN Ryan Scott B7.15.1982 Yoakum TX BR/TR/6-4/210(210-225) d7.19 Col Houston

YEAR	TM LG	W	L	PCT	G	GS	CG-SHO	SV-BS	IP	H	R	HR	HB	BB-IB	SO	ERA	AERA	OAV	OOB	AB-HR-SH	AVG	PB	SUP	APR	DL	PW
2003	Cin N	2	0	1.000	17	0	0	0-1	21.2	13	4	2	0	12-1	25	1.66	251	.173	.284	0	—	0		6		0.5
2004	Cin N	3	2	.600	49	0	0	0-3	51.2	59	31	7	2	27-2	37	4.70	91	.284	.367	0	—	0		-3		-0.3
2005	Cin N	3	2	.600	42	0	0	0-1	45.2	56	33	4	4	17-1	39	6.11	68	.303	.368	1-0-1	.000	-0		-10	87	-1.0
Total 3		8	4	.667	108	0	0	0-5	119	128	68	13	6	56-4	101	4.69	90	.274	.354	1-0-1	.000	-0		-7	87	-0.8

WAGNER, BILLY William Edward B7.25.1971 Tannersville VA BL/TL/5-11/180(180-195) [HouN93 1/12] d9.13 Col Ferrum

YEAR	TM LG	W	L	PCT	G	GS	CG-SHO	SV-BS	IP	H	R	HR	HB	BB-IB	SO	ERA	AERA	OAV	OOB	AB-HR-SH	AVG	PB	SUP	APR	DL	PW
1995	Hou N	0	0	—	1	0	0	0-0	0.1	0	0	0	0	0-0	0	0.00	—	.000	.000	0	—	0		0		0.0
1996	Hou N	2	2	.500	37	0	0	9-4	51.2	28	16	6	3	30-2	67	2.44	159	.165	.298	5	.000	-1		9	15	0.8
1997	†Hou N	7	8	.467	62	0	0	23-6	66.1	49	23	5	3	30-1	106	2.85	141	.204	.299	1	.000	-0		9		1.8
1998	†Hou N	4	3	.571	58	0	0	30-5	60	46	19	6	0	25-1	97	2.70	150	.211	.292	3	.333	-0		10	22	1.9
1999	†Hou N★	4	1	.800	66	0	0	39-3	74.2	35	14	5	1	23-1	124	1.57	282	.135	.208	3	—	0		25		3.7
2000	Hou N	2	4	.333	28	0	0	6-9	27.2	28	19	6	1	18-0	28	6.18	79	.255	.364	2	.000	-0		-3	105	-0.6
2001	†Hou N★	2	5	.286	64	0	0	39-2	62.2	44	19	5	1	20-0	79	2.73	168	.198	.278	2	—	0		15		2.6
2002	Hou N	4	2	.667	70	0	0	35-6	75	51	21	7	2	22-5	88	2.52	172	.196	.261	2	.000	-0		15		2.4
2003	Hou N★	1	4	.200	78	0	0	44-3	86	52	18	8	3	23-5	105	1.78	248	.169	.234	2	.000	0		25		3.6
2004	Phi N	4	0	1.000	45	0	0	21-4	48.1	31	16	6	2	6-1	59	2.42	183	.181	.218	2	.000	-0*		10	75	1.4
2005	Phi N☆	4	3	.571	75	0	0	38-3	77.2	45	17	5	2	20-2	87	1.51	288	.165	.229	3	.333	-0		**23**		3.9
Total 11		34	32	.515	584	0	0	284-45	630.1	409	182	59	23	217-18	840	2.40	180	.183	.262	20	.100	-1	136	232		21.5

WAGNER, BULL William George B12.25.1887 Lilley MI D10.2.1967 Muskegon MI BR/TR/6-0.5/225 d6.2

YEAR	TM LG	W	L	PCT	G	GS	CG-SHO	SV-BS	IP	H	R	HR	HB	BB-IB	SO	ERA	AERA	OAV	OOB	AB-HR-SH	AVG	PB	SUP	APR	DL	PW
1913	Bro N	4	2	.667	18	1	0	0	70.2	77	49	5	3	30	11	5.48	60	.285	.363	26	.231	0	251	-14		-1.1
1914	Bro N	0	1	.000	6	0	0	0	12.1	14	11	0	1	12	4	6.57	44	.311	.466	1	.000	-0		-4		-0.3
Total 2		4	3	.571	24	1	0	0	83	91	60	5	4	42	15	5.64	57	.289	.380	27	.222	-0	251	-18		-1.4

WAINHOUSE, DAVE David Paul B11.7.1967 Toronto ON, Can. BL/TR/6-2/185(185-196) [MonN88 1/19] d8.3 Col Washington St.

YEAR	TM LG	W	L	PCT	G	GS	CG-SHO	SV-BS	IP	H	R	HR	HB	BB-IB	SO	ERA	AERA	OAV	OOB	AB-HR-SH	AVG	PB	SUP	APR	DL	PW
1991	Mon N	0	1	.000	2				2.2	2	2	0	0	4-0	1	6.75	54	.222	.429	0	—	0		-1		-0.2
1993	Sea A	0	0	—	3	0	0	0-0	3.1	7	7	1	1	5-0	1	27.00	17	.500	.650	0	—	0		-5		-0.3
1996	Pit N	1	0	1.000	17	0	0	0-0	23.2	22	16	3	0	10-1	16	5.70	77	.250	.320	1	.000	-0		-3		-0.1
1997	Pit N	1	0	1.000	25	0	0	0-0	28	34	28	2	3	17-0	21	8.04	53	.301	.403	2	.000	-0		-12		-0.6
1998	Col N	1	0	1.000	10	0	0	0-1	11	15	6	1	4	5-0	9	4.91	105	.341	.431	1	.000	-0		0		0.1

YEAR	TM LG	W	L	PCT	G	GS	CG-SHO	SV-BS	IP	H	R	HR	HB	BB-IB	SO	ERA	AERA	OAV	OOB	AB-HR-SH	AVG	PB	SUP	APR	DL	PW
1999	Col N	0	0	—	19	0	0	0-0	28.2	37	22	6	0	16-0	18	6.91	84	.330	.405	1	.000	-0		-2		-0.1
2000	StL N	0	1	.000	9	0	0	0-0	8.2	13	10	2	2	4-1	5	9.35	50	.351	.442	0	—		-5	88		-0.4
Total	7	2	3	.400	85	0	0	0-1	105	130	91	15	8	61-2	66	7.37	65	.312	.404	5	.000	-1	-28	88		-1.6

WAINWRIGHT, ADAM Adam Parrish B8.30.1981 Brunswick GA BR/TR/6-7/205 d9.11

YEAR	TM LG	W	L	PCT	G	GS	CG-SHO	SV-BS	IP	H	R	HR	HB	BB-IB	SO	ERA	AERA	OAV	OOB	AB-HR-SH	AVG	PB	SUP	APR	DL	PW
2005	StL N	0	0	—	2	0	0	0-0						1-0	0	13.50	31	.250	.333	0	—	0	-2			-0.1

WAITS, RICK Michael Richard B5.15.1952 Atlanta GA BL/TL/6-3/195* [TexA70 5/112] d9.17 C2

YEAR	TM LG	W	L	PCT	G	GS	CG-SHO	SV-BS	IP	H	R	HR	HB	BB-IB	SO	ERA	AERA	OAV	OOB	AB-HR-SH	AVG	PB	SUP	APR	DL	PW
1973	Tex A	0	0	—	1	0	0	1-0	1	1	0	0	0	1-0	0	9.00	42	.333	.500	0	—	0		-1		-0.1
1975	Cle A	6	2	.750	16	7	3	1-0	70.1	57	25	3	1	25-5	34	2.94	130	.221	.292	0	—	0	102	7		0.8
1976	Cle A	7	9	.438	26	22	4-2	0-0	123.2	143	60	7	0	54-1	65	4.00	88	.297	.368	0	—	0*	83	-6	29	-0.8
1977	Cle A	9	7	.563	37	16	1	2-3	135.1	132	67	8	1	64-7	62	3.99	100	.262	.346	0	—	0*	98	0		0.0
1978	Cle A	13	15	.464	34	33	15-2	0-0	230.1	206	97	16	2	86-0	97	3.20	118	.240	.309	0	—	0*	96	12		1.6
1979	Cle A	16	13	.552	34	34	8-3	0-0	231	230	123	26	4	91-1	91	4.44	97	.264	.334	0	—	0	99	-2		-0.2
1980	Cle A	13	14	.481	33	33	9-2	0-0	224.1	231	118	18	1	82-6	109	4.45	93	.270	.332	0	—	0	95	-7		-0.7
1981	Cle A	8	10	.444	22	21	5-1	0-0	126.1	173	74	7	1	44-1	51	4.92	75	.330	.380	0	—	0	93	-16		-2.0
1982	Cle A	2	13	.133	25	21	2	0-1	115	128	74	13	1	57-2	44	5.40	77	.290	.370	0	—	0	85	-14		-1.6
1983	Cle A	0	1	.000	8	0	0	0-1	19.2	23	13	1	0	9-2	13	4.58	93	.307	.364	0	—	0		-1		-0.1
	Mil A	0	2	.000	10	2	0	0-0	30	39	20	1	0	11-1	20	5.10	74	.320	.373	0	—	0	132	-5	52	-0.3
	Year	0	3	.000	18	2	0	0-1	49.2	62	33	2	0	20-3	33	4.89	81	.315	.369	0	—	0	125	-6		-0.4
1984	Mil A	2	4	.333	47	1	0	3-1	73	84	32	7	0	24-3	49	3.58	109	.297	.348	0	—	0	70	3	18	0.3
1985	Mil A	3	2	.600	24	0	0	1-1	47	67	37	3	0	20-5	24	6.51	64	.340	.399	1	.000	-0		-11		-1.1
Total	12	79	92	.462	317	190	47-10	8-7	1427	1514	741	110	11	568-34	659	4.25	93	.277	.344	1	.000	0	94	-41	99	-4.2

WAKEFIELD, TIM Timothy Stephen B8.2.1966 Melbourne FL BR/TR/6-2/206(195-215) [PitN88 8/200] d7.31 Col Florida Tech

YEAR	TM LG	W	L	PCT	G	GS	CG-SHO	SV-BS	IP	H	R	HR	HB	BB-IB	SO	ERA	AERA	OAV	OOB	AB-HR-SH	AVG	PB	SUP	APR	DL	PW
1992	†Pit N	8	1	.889	13	13	4-1	0-0	92	76	26	3	1	35-1	51	2.15	161	.232	.305	28-0-4	.071	-1*	106	13		1.2
1993	Pit N	6	11	.353	24	20	3-2	0-0	128.1	145	83	14	9	75-2	59	5.61	73	.291	.389	43-1-4	.163	1	86	-21		-2.3
1995	†Bos A	16	8	.667	27	27	6-1	0-0	195.1	163	76	22	8	68-0	119	2.95	165	.227	.300	0	—	0	92	38		4.2
1996	Bos A	14	13	.519	32	32	6	0-0	211.2	238	151	38	12	90-0	140	5.14	99	.280	.353	1	.000	0	90	-7		-0.8
1997	Bos A	12	15	.444	35	29	4-2	0-0	201.1	193	109	24	16	87-5	151	4.25	110	.256	.343	1	.000	0	96	7	21	0.7
1998	†Bos A	17	8	.680	36	33	2	0-0	216	211	123	30	14	79-1	146	4.58	103	.252	.324	2-0-2	.000	0*	129	2		0.1
1999	†Bos A	6	11	.353	49	17	0	15-3	140	146	93	29	5	72-2	104	5.08	98	.266	.332	3	.000	-0*	88	-3		-0.5
2000	Bos A	6	10	.375	51	17	0	0-1	159.1	170	107	31	4	65-3	102	5.48	92	.272	.340	2-0-1	.000	-0*	118	-9		-0.8
2001	Bos A	9	12	.429	45	17	0	3-2	168.2	156	84	13	18	73-5	148	3.90	114	.248	.339	3-0-1	.333	0	91	9		1.0
2002	Bos A	11	5	.688	45	15	0	3-2	163.1	121	57	15	9	51-2	134	2.81	159	.204	.276	0	—	0	111	30		2.6
2003	†Bos A	11	7	.611	35	33	0	1-0	202.1	193	106	23	12	71-0	169	4.09	114	.246	.317	0	—	0	110	-2		-0.2
2004	†Bos A	12	10	.545	32	30	0	0-0	188.1	197	121	29	16	63-3	116	4.87	100	.264	.333	2	.000	0	98	10		1.1
2005	†Bos A	16	12	.571	33	33	2	0-0	225.1	210	113	35	11	68-4	151	4.15	111	.245	.307	8-0-1	.250	0	98	10		1.1
Total	13	144	162	.539	457	316	28-6	22-8	2292	2219	1249	296	136	897-28	1590	4.28	109	.253	.329	92-1-13	.130	-0	103	78	21	7.1

WAKEFIELD, BILL William Sumner B5.24.1941 Kansas City MO BR/TR/6-0/175 d4.18

YEAR	TM LG	W	L	PCT	G	GS	CG-SHO	SV-BS	IP	H	R	HR	HB	BB-IB	SO	ERA	AERA	OAV	OOB	AB-HR-SH	AVG	PB	SUP	APR	DL	PW
1964	NY N	3	5	.375	62	4	0	0-0	119.2	103	57	10	9	61-6	61	3.61	99	.235	.337	24-0-3	.167	-0	98	-1		-0.1

WALBERG, RUBE George Elvin B7.27.1896 Pine City MN D10.27.1978 Tempe AZ BL/TL/6-1.5/190 d4.29

YEAR	TM LG	W	L	PCT	G	GS	CG-SHO	SV-BS	IP	H	R	HR	HB	BB-IB	SO	ERA	AERA	OAV	OOB	AB-HR-SH	AVG	PB	SUP	APR	DL	PW
1923	NY N	0	0	—	2	0	0	0	5	4	2	0	0	1	1	1.80	212	.211	.250	1	.000	-0		1		0.0
	Phi A	4	8	.333	26	10	4	0	115	122	77	10	2	66-5	38	5.32	77	.280	.369	41-0-3	.317	3	121	-12		-0.2
1924	Phi A	0	0	—	6	2	0	0	7	10	10	0	0	10	3	12.86	33	.345	.513	2	.500	0	89	-6		-0.2
1925	Phi A	8	14	.364	53	20	7	7	191.2	197	99	11	2	77	82	3.99	117	.269	.340	64	.156	-4	80	14		1.2
1926	Phi A	12	10	.545	40	19	5-2	2	151	168	67	4	6	60	72	2.80	149	.292	.365	46-0-5	.152	-2	83	19		2.3
1927	Phi A	16	12	.571	46	33	14	4	249.1	257	139	18	4	91	136	3.93	108	.271	.337	87-2-2	.207	3*	120	5		0.8
1928	Phi A	17	12	.586	38	30	15-3	1	235.2	236	111	19	3	64	112	3.55	113	.265	.337	86-1-3	.209	1	112	12		1.5
1929	†Phi A	18	11	.621	40	33	20-3	1	267.2	256	115	22	0	99	94	3.60	118	.254	.320	103-1-6	.223	0	108	24		2.2
1930	Phi A	13	12	.520	38	30	12-2	1	205.1	207	121	26	2	85	100	4.69	100	.262	.335	105-0-4	.164	-3	95	1		-0.3
1931	†Phi A	20	12	.625	44	35	19-1	3	291	298	133	16	0	109	106	3.74	120	.266	.331	105-0-4	.124	-6*	92	28		2.0
1932	Phi A	17	10	.630	41	34	19-3	1	272	305	159	16	0	103	96	4.73	96	.282	.344	94-0-9	.170	-1*	120	-7		-0.9
1933	Phi A	9	13	.409	40	20	10-1	4	201	224	132	12	1	95	68	4.88	88	.278	.354	68-0-7	.132	-1*	86	-14		-1.5
1934	Bos A	6	7	.462	30	10	2	1	104.2	118	62	5	1	41	38	4.04	119	.284	.350	32-0-1	.188	-1	98	6		0.6
1935	Bos A	5	9	.357	44	10	4	3	142.1	152	71	10	2	54	44	3.91	121	.273	.340	37-0-3	.162	-2	64	13		1.0
1936	Bos A	5	5	.556	34	9	5	0	100.1	98	53	7	1	36	49	4.40	121	.257	.323	37-0-3	.156	-1	72	11		0.7
1937	Bos A	5	7	.417	32	11	3	1	104.2	143	72	7	3	46	46	5.59	85	.332	.400	34-0-3	.147	-1	85	-9		-1.0
Total	15	155	141	.524	544	306	139-15	32	2644	2795	1423	163	27	1031	1085	4.16	107	.273	.341	905-4-52	.179	-18	99	86		7.6

WALDBAUER, DOC Albert Charles B2.22.1892 Richmond VA D7.16.1969 Yakima WA BR/TR/6-0/172 d9.24

YEAR	TM LG	W	L	PCT	G	GS	CG-SHO	SV-BS	IP	H	R	HR	HB	BB-IB	SO	ERA	AERA	OAV	OOB	AB-HR-SH	AVG	PB	SUP	APR	DL	PW
1917	Was A	0	0	—	2	0	0	1	5	10	4	0	0	2	2	7.20	36	.476	.522	1	.000	-0		-2		-0.1

WALK, BOB Robert Vernon B11.26.1956 Van Nuys CA BR/TR/6-4/208(195-217) [PhiN76 S3/52] d5.26 Col Canyons (CA) [JC]

YEAR	TM LG	W	L	PCT	G	GS	CG-SHO	SV-BS	IP	H	R	HR	HB	BB-IB	SO	ERA	AERA	OAV	OOB	AB-HR-SH	AVG	PB	SUP	APR	DL	PW
1980	†Phi N	11	7	.611	27	27	2	0-0	151.2	163	82	8	2	71-2	94	4.57	84	.276	.353	50-0-7	.140	-0	113	-10		-1.2
1981	Atl N	1	4	.200	12	8	0	0-0	43.1	41	25	6	0	23-0	16	4.57	77	.250	.342	7-0-3	.143	-0	120	-5	75	-0.6
1982	†Atl N	11	9	.550	32	27	3-1	0-0	164.1	179	101	19	6	59-2	84	4.87	76	.280	.344	51-0-6	.196	2	121	-21		-2.3
1983	Atl N	0	0	—	1	1	0	0-0	3.2	7	3	0	0	2-0	4	7.36	53	.412	.474	1	.000	0	137	-1		-0.1
1984	Pit N	1	1	.500	2	2	0	0-0	10.1	8	5	1	0	4-1	10	2.61	139	.200	.273	3	.000	-0	97	9	71	0.0
1985	Pit N	2	3	.400	9	9	1-1	0-0	58.2	60	27	3	0	18-2	40	3.68	99	.265	.318	17-0-4	.000	-2	114	-1		-0.3
1986	Pit N	7	8	.467	44	15	1-1	2-2	141.2	129	66	14	3	64-7	78	3.75	104	.251	.334	39-0-1	.154	0	83	2		0.3
1987	Pit N	8	2	.800	39	12	1-1	1-0	117	107	52	11	3	51-2	78	3.31	126	.245	.327	26-0-1	.231	1	118	9		0.8
1988	Pit N★	12	10	.545	32	32	1-1	0-0	212.2	183	75	6	2	65-5	81	2.71	127	.230	.288	69-0-3	.087	-2*	93	16		1.4
1989	Pit N	13	10	.565	33	31	2	0-1	196	208	106	15	4	65-1	83	4.41	77	.271	.330	70-0-5	.186	1	122	0	43	0.0
1990	†Pit N	7	5	.583	26	24	1-1	1-0	129.2	136	59	17	4	36-2	73	3.75	97	.270	.322	37-0-10	.162	1	122	-10	65	-2.1
1991	Pit N	9	2	.818	25	20	0	0-1	115	104	53	10	5	35-2	67	3.60	100	.240	.302	39-1-2	.205	0	134	0		0.3
1992	†Pit N	10	6	.625	36	19	1	2-1	135	132	54	10	6	43-5	60	3.20	108	.258	.322	43-0-1	.093	-2	132	3	38	0.3
1993	Pit N	13	14	.481	32	32	3	0-0	187	214	121	23	5	70-5	80	5.68	72	.294	.356	58-0-7	.121	-2	103	-31		-4.0
Total	14	105	81	.565	350	259	16-6	5-5	1666	1671	829	163	40	606-36	848	4.03	92	.263	.329	510-1-50	.145	1	114	-61	307	-7.7

WALKER, ED Edward Harrison B8.11.1874 Cambois, England D9.29.1947 Akron OH BL/TL/6-5/242 d9.26

YEAR	TM LG	W	L	PCT	G	GS	CG-SHO	SV-BS	IP	H	R	HR	HB	BB-IB	SO	ERA	AERA	OAV	OOB	AB-HR-SH	AVG	PB	SUP	APR	DL	PW
1902	Cle A	0	1	.000	1	1	1	0	8	11	4	0	0	3	1	3.38	102	.324	.378	3	.333	0	42	0		0.0
1903	Cle A	0	1	.000	3	3	0	0	12	13	12	0	0	10	4	5.25	54	.277	.404	3	.000	-0	159	-4		-0.3
Total	2	0	2	.000	4	4	1	0	20	24	16	0	0	13	5	4.50	69	.296	.394	6	.167	0	122	-4		-0.3

WALKER, DIXIE Ewart Gladstone B6.1.1887 Brownsville PA D11.14.1965 Leeds AL BL/TR/6-0/192 d9.17 b-Ernie s-Dixie s-Harry

YEAR	TM LG	W	L	PCT	G	GS	CG-SHO	SV-BS	IP	H	R	HR	HB	BB-IB	SO	ERA	AERA	OAV	OOB	AB-HR-SH	AVG	PB	SUP	APR	DL	PW
1909	Was A	3	1	.750	4	4	4	0	36	31	12	0	0	25	25	2.50	97	.217	.248	13	.154	-0	138	0		0.0
1910	Was A	11	11	.500	29	26	16-3	0	199.1	177	83	2	8	68	84	3.30	76	.245	.317	69-0-1	.130	-3	80	-10		-1.4
1911	Was A	8	13	.381	32	24	15-2	0	185.2	205	103	2	8	65	65	3.39	97	.286	.339	66	.303	4*	102	-3		-1.1
1912	Was A	3	6	.333	9	8	5	0	60	72	40	2	4	18	29	5.25	64	.300	.359	16	.125	1	100	-9		-1.1
Total	4	25	31	.446	74	62	40-5	0	481	485	238	6	20	142	203	3.52	82	.266	.326	164-0-1	.201	0	96	-22		

WALKER, MYSTERIOUS Frederick Mitchell B3.21.1884 Utica NE D2.1.1958 Oak Park IL BR/TR/5-10.5/185 d6.28 Col Chicago

YEAR	TM LG	W	L	PCT	G	GS	CG-SHO	SV-BS	IP	H	R	HR	HB	BB-IB	SO	ERA	AERA	OAV	OOB	AB-HR-SH	AVG	PB	SUP	APR	DL	PW
1910	Cin N	0	0	—	1	0	0	0	3	4	2	0	0	1	0	3.00	97	.333	.500		.000	-0		0		0.0
1912	Cle A	0	0	—	1	0	0	0	1	1	0	0	0	1	0	0.00	—	.000	.200	0	—	-0		0		0.1
1913	Bro N	1	3	.250	11	8	3	0	58.1	44	26	3	5	35	35	3.55	93	.233	.367	18-0-1	.167	-0	80	0		0.1
1914	Pit F	4	16	.200	35	21	12	0	169.1	197	108	3	4	74	79	4.31	67	.294	.367	53-0-2	.113	-3*	88	-29		-3.2
1915	Bro F	2	4	.333	13	7	2	1	65.2	61	37	3	0	22	28	3.70	73	.242	.303	27	.222	0	151	-8		-0.7
Total	5	7	23	.233	61	36	17	1	297.1	300	173	9	8	136	143	4.00	73	.272	.354	99-0-3	.152	-3	98	-37		-3.7

WALKER, GEORGE George A. B1863 Hamilton ON, Can. TR/5-9/184 d8.1

YEAR	TM LG	W	L	PCT	G	GS	CG-SHO	SV-BS	IP	H	R	HR	HB	BB-IB	SO	ERA	AERA	OAV	OOB	AB-HR-SH	AVG	PB	SUP	APR	DL	PW
1888	Bal AA	1	3	.250	4	4	4-1	0	35	36	31	2	0	14	18	5.91	50	.257	.325	13	.077	-1	68	-10		-1.0

YEAR	TM LG	W	L	PCT	G	GS	CG-SHO	SV-BS	IP	H	R	HR	HB	BB-IB	SO	ERA	AERA	OAV	OOB	AB-HR-SH	AVG	PB	SUP	APR	DL	PW

WALKER, LUKE James Luke B9.2.1943 DeKalb TX BL/TL/6-1.5/192* d9.7 Col Paris (TX) JC

YEAR	TM LG	W	L	PCT	G	GS	CG-SHO	SV-BS	IP	H	R	HR	HB	BB-IB	SO	ERA	AERA	OAV	OOB	AB-HR-SH	AVG	PB	SUP	APR	DL	PW
1965	Pit N	0	0	—	2	0	0		5	2	0	0	0	1-0	5	0.00	—	.118	.167	0	—	0		2		0.1
1966	Pit N	0	1	.000	10	1	0	0	10	8	9	0	1	15-2	7	4.50	79	.205	.436	2	.000	-0	98	-3		-0.3
1968	Pit N	0	3	.000	39	2	0	3	62.1	42	18	1	1	39-0	66	2.02	145	.190	.314	8-0-1	.000	-1	89	6		0.3
1969	Pit N	4	6	.400	31	15	3-1	0-0	118.2	98	51	5	2	57-3	96	3.64	96	.226	.318	32-0-3	.000	-0	115	-1		-0.3
1970	†Pit N	15	6	.714	42	19	5-3	3-1	163	129	56	6	1	89-8	124	3.04	130	.219	.322	46-0-8	.130	-1	117	19		2.3
1971	†Pit N	10	8	.556	28	24	4-2	0-0	159.2	157	69	9	2	53-2	86	3.55	96	.262	.321	46-0-2	.022	-0	116	-2		-0.6
1972	†Pit N	4	6	.400	26	12	2	2-0	92.2	98	41	4	0	34-4	48	3.40	98	.278	.338	24-0-1	.083	-1	100	-1		-0.3
1973	Pit N	7	12	.368	37	18	2-1	1-1	122	129	75	9	1	66-8	74	4.65	76	.270	.338	30-0-3	.067	-2	99	-17		-2.7
1974	Det A	5	5	.500	28	9	0	0-0	92	100	56	9	2	54-1	52	4.99	77	.278	.374	0	—	0	120	-10	24	-1.1
Total	9	45	47	.489	243	100	16-7	9-2	825.1	763	375	43	10	408-28	558	3.64	97	.247	.335	188-0-18	.059	-11	111	-7	24	-2.6

WALKER, JAMIE James Ross B7.1.1971 McMinnville TN BL/TL/6-2/190* [HouN92 10/265] d4.2 Col Austin Peay

YEAR	TM LG	W	L	PCT	G	GS	CG-SHO	SV-BS	IP	H	R	HR	HB	BB-IB	SO	ERA	AERA	OAV	OOB	AB-HR-SH	AVG	PB	SUP	APR	DL	PW
1997	KC A	3	3	.500	50	0	0	0-1	43	46	28	6	3	20-3	24	5.44	87	.271	.354	0	—	0		-3	19	-0.3
1998	KC A	0	1	.000	6	2	0		17.1	30	20	5	2	3-0	15	9.87	49	.380	.412	0	—	0	96	-9	106	-0.4
2002	Det A	1	1	.500	57	0	0	1-3	43.2	32	19	9	4	9-1	40	3.71	118	.199	.257	0	—	0		4		0.2
2003	Det A	4	3	.571	78	0	0	3-4	65	61	30	9	2	17-1	45	3.32	132	.247	.299	0	—	0		6		0.7
2004	Det A	3	4	.429	70	0	0	1-6	64.2	69	28	8	1	12-3	53	3.20	140	.263	.297	0	—	0		8		0.7
2005	Det A	4	3	.571	66	0	0	0-2	48.2	49	22	5	2	13-3	30	3.70	114	.257	.309	0	—	0		3		0.4
Total	6	15	15	.500	327	2	0	5-16	282.1	287	147	42	14	74-11	207	4.14	108	.259	.311	0	—	0	96	9	125	1.3

WALKER, ROY James Roy "Dixie" B4.13.1893 Lawrenceburg TN D2.10.1962 New Orleans LA BR/TR(BB 1918, 22)/6-1.5/180 d9.16

YEAR	TM LG	W	L	PCT	G	GS	CG-SHO	SV-BS	IP	H	R	HR	HB	BB-IB	SO	ERA	AERA	OAV	OOB	AB-HR-SH	AVG	PB	SUP	APR	DL	PW
1912	Cle A	0	0	—	1	0	0		2	0	0	0	0	2	1	0.00	—	.000	.250	0	—	0		1		0.0
1915	Cle A	4	9	.308	25	15	4	1	131	122	73	1	7	65	57	3.98	77	.261	.360	38-0-3	.132	-2	86	-10		-1.4
1917	Chi N	0	1	.000	2	1	0		7	8	5	0	0	5	4	3.86	75	.286	.394	1	.000	-0	26	-1		-0.2
1918	Chi N	1	3	.250	13	7	2	1	43.1	50	27	1	1	15	20	2.70	103	.298	.359	11-0-1	.000	-1	112	-3		-0.4
1921	StL N	11	12	.478	38	23	11	3	170.2	194	93	10	1	53	52	4.22	87	.293	.347	54-0-4	.204	-0	100	-9		-1.1
1922	StL N	1	2	.333	12	2	0		32	34	20	1	0	15	14	4.78	81	.293	.374	7-0-1	.143	-0	84	-3		-0.4
Total	6	17	27	.386	91	48	17	5	386	408	218	13	9	155	148	3.99	85	.282	.355	111-0-9	.153	-4	94	-25		-3.5

WALKER, JERRY Jerry Allen B2.12.1939 Ada OK BB/TR/6-1/195* d7.6 C5

YEAR	TM LG	W	L	PCT	G	GS	CG-SHO	SV-BS	IP	H	R	HR	HB	BB-IB	SO	ERA	AERA	OAV	OOB	AB-HR-SH	AVG	PB	SUP	APR	DL	PW
1957	Bal A	1	0	1.000	13	1	1-1	1	27.2	24	9	1	0	14-1	13	2.93	123	.245	.336	5	.000	-1	99	3		0.1
1958	Bal A	0	0	—	6	0	0		10.1	16	8	2	0	5-0	6	6.97	52	.340	.404	2	.000	-0		-4		-0.2
1959	Bal A★	11	10	.524	30	22	7-2	4	182	160	68	13	3	52-9	100	2.92	130	.240	.295	65-1-3	.169	-1*	92	17		1.9
1960	Bal A	3	4	.429	29	18	1	5	118	107	53	15	3	56-0	48	3.74	102	.247	.335	38-0-1	.368	5*	107	2		0.7
1961	KC A	8	14	.364	36	24	4	2	168	161	100	23	10	96-2	56	4.82	87	.253	.356	64-0-1	.250	3*	90	-10		-0.9
1962	KC A	8	9	.471	31	21	3-1	0	143.1	165	101	27	7	78-4	57	5.90	72	.288	.377	57-3-2	.263	5*	126	-24		-2.0
1963	Cle A	6	6	.500	39	2	0	1	88	92	53	15	2	36-6	41	4.91	74	.265	.334	19	.105	-2	25	-12		-1.6
1964	Cle A	0	1	.000	6	0	0		9.2	9	5	1	0	4-0	5	4.66	77	.257	.333	2	.000	-0		-1		-0.1
Total	8	37	44	.457	190	90	16-4	13	747	734	397	97	25	341-22	326	4.36	90	.259	.340	252-4-7	.230	10	103	-29		-2.1

WALKER, KEVIN Kevin Michael B9.20.1976 Irving TX BL/TL/6-4/190(190-215) [SDN95 6/145] d4.14

YEAR	TM LG	W	L	PCT	G	GS	CG-SHO	SV-BS	IP	H	R	HR	HB	BB-IB	SO	ERA	AERA	OAV	OOB	AB-HR-SH	AVG	PB	SUP	APR	DL	PW
2000	SD N	7	1	.875	70	0	0	0-0	66.2	49	35	5	5	38-6	56	4.18	106	.206	.325	4	.250	0		2		0.2
2001	SD N	0	0	—	16	0	0	0-1	12	5	4	0	0	8-2	11	3.00	138	.122	.265	0	—	0		2	157	0.1
2002	SD N	0	1	.000	11	0	0	0-1	8	12	6	2	0	5-1	11	5.63	69	.333	.415	0	—	0		-2	150	-0.2
2003	SD N	0	0	—	11	0	0	0-0	6.2	5	4	1	0	5-0	5	5.40	74	.200	.333	0	—	0		-1	71	0.0
2004	SF N	0	0	—	5	0	0	0-0	1.2	3	3	1	1	2-0	1	16.20	27	.429	.600	0	—	0		-2		-0.1
2005	Chi A	0	1	.000	9	0	0	0-1	7	10	7	1	0	5-1	11	9.00	50	.333	.429	0	—	0		-3		-0.4
Total	6	7	3	.700	122	0	0	0-3	102	84	59	10	6	63-10	95	4.76	91	.223	.342	4	.250	0		-4	378	-0.4

WALKER, MARTY Martin Van Buren "Buddy" B3.27.1899 Philadelphia PA D4.24.1978 Philadelphia PA BL/TL/6-0/170 d9.30

YEAR	TM LG	W	L	PCT	G	GS	CG-SHO	SV-BS	IP	H	R	HR	HB	BB-IB	SO	ERA	AERA	OAV	OOB	AB-HR-SH	AVG	PB	SUP	APR	DL	PW
1928	Phi N	0	1	.000	1	1	0		4	4	4	0	3	2	0	∞	—	1.000	1.000	0	—	0	20	-3		-0.2

WALKER, MIKE Michael Aaron B6.23.1965 Houston TX BR/TR/6-3/205 [PitN86 2/29] d6.16 Col Houston

YEAR	TM LG	W	L	PCT	G	GS	CG-SHO	SV-BS	IP	H	R	HR	HB	BB-IB	SO	ERA	AERA	OAV	OOB	AB-HR-SH	AVG	PB	SUP	APR	DL	PW
1992	Sea A	0	3	.000	5	3	0	0-0	14.2	21	14	4	0	9-3	5	7.36	54	.333	.411	0	—	0	76	-6		-1.0

WALKER, MIKE Michael Charles B10.4.1966 Chicago IL BR/TR/6-1/195(175-205) [CleA86*2/27] d9.9 Col Seminole (FL) CC

YEAR	TM LG	W	L	PCT	G	GS	CG-SHO	SV-BS	IP	H	R	HR	HB	BB-IB	SO	ERA	AERA	OAV	OOB	AB-HR-SH	AVG	PB	SUP	APR	DL	PW
1988	Cle A	0	1	.000	3	1	0	0-0	8.2	8	7	0	0	10-0	1	7.27	57	.258	.439	0	—	0	0	-3		-0.2
1990	Cle A	2	6	.250	18	11	0	0-0	75.2	82	49	6	0	42-4	34	4.88	81	.277	.376	0	—	0	71	-10		-0.9
1991	Cle A	0	1	.000	5	0	0	0-0	4.1	6	1	0	1	2-1	2	2.08	201	.316	.409	0	—	0		1		0.2
1995	Chi N	1	3	.250	42	0	0	1-2	44.2	45	22	2	0	24-3	26	3.22	129	.259	.342	3	.000	-0		3		0.2
1996	Det A	0	0	—	20	0	0	1-1	27.2	40	26	10	1	17-1	13	8.46	60	.351	.433	0	—	0		-9		-0.4
Total	5	3	11	.214	88	12	0	2-3	161	181	105	18	8	95-9	76	5.09	83	.285	.381	3	.000	-0	61	-18		-1.1

WALKER, PETE Peter Brian B4.8.1969 Beverly MA BR/TR/6-2/195* [NYN90 7/199] d6.7 Col Connecticut

YEAR	TM LG	W	L	PCT	G	GS	CG-SHO	SV-BS	IP	H	R	HR	HB	BB-IB	SO	ERA	AERA	OAV	OOB	AB-HR-SH	AVG	PB	SUP	APR	DL	PW
1995	NY N	1	0	1.000	13	0	0	0-0	17.2	24	9	3	0	5-0	9	4.58	88	.329	.367	0	—	0		-1		0.0
1996	SD N	0	0	—	3	0	0	0-0	0.2	0	0	0	0	3-0	1	0.00	—	.000	.600	0	—	0		0		0.0
2000	Col N	0	0	—	2	0	0	0-0	4.2	10	9	1	0	4-0	2	17.36	33	.435	.519	0	—	0		-5		-0.2
2001	NY N	0	0	—	2	0	0	0-0	6.2	6	2	0	0	0-0	4	2.70	150	.240	.240	1-0-1	.000	-0		1		0.0
2002	NY N	0	0	—	1	0	0	0-0	1	2	1	0	0	0-0	1	9.00	44	.400	.400	0	—	0		-1		0.0
	Tor A	10	5	.667	37	20	0	1-0	139.1	143	72	18	3	51-5	80	4.33	107	.270	.334	0	—	0	102	5		0.5
2003	Tor A	2	2	.500	23	7	0	0-0	55.1	59	31	11	2	24-2	29	4.88	97	.277	.354	0	—	0	119	0	100	0.0
2005	Tor A	6	6	.500	41	4	0	2-3	84	81	33	10	2	33-0	43	3.54	131	.254	.324	0	—	0	66	11		1.4
Total	7	19	13	.594	121	31	0	3-3	309.1	325	157	43	7	120-7	164	4.39	105	.273	.340	1-0-1	.000	-0	103	10	100	1.7

WALKER, TOM Robert Thomas B11.7.1948 Tampa FL BR/TR/6-1/188(188-200) [BalA68*1/9] d4.23 Col Brevard (FL) CC

YEAR	TM LG	W	L	PCT	G	GS	CG-SHO	SV-BS	IP	H	R	HR	HB	BB-IB	SO	ERA	AERA	OAV	OOB	AB-HR-SH	AVG	PB	SUP	APR	DL	PW
1972	Mon N	2	2	.500	46	0	0	2-0	74.2	71	27	4	1	22-2	42	2.89	123	.248	.304	3	.000	-0		5		0.2
1973	Mon N	7	5	.583	54	0	0	4-2	91.2	95	52	7	3	42-12	68	3.63	105	.274	.349	7-0-1	.000	-1		-2		-0.3
1974	Mon N	4	5	.444	33	8	1	2-0	91.2	96	45	7	2	28-5	70	3.83	100	.266	.321	16-0-1	.188	-0	102	0		0.0
1975	Det A	3	8	.273	36	9	1	0-0	115.1	116	69	16	5	40-3	60	4.45	91	.261	.325	0	—	0	61	-6		-0.6
1976	StL N	1	2	.333	10	0	0	3-1	19.2	22	10	2	0	3-1	11	4.12	87	.265	.291	5	.400	1		-1		-0.2
1977	Mon N	1	1	.500	11	0	0	0-0	19	15	10	2	0	7-0	10	4.74	81	.221	.293	2-0-2	.000	-1		-1		-0.2
	Cal A	0	0	—	1	0	0	0-0	2	3	2	2	0	0-0	1	9.00	44	.375	.375	0	—	0		-1		-0.1
Total	6	18	23	.439	191	17	2	11-3	414	418	215	40	11	142-23	262	3.87	99	.262	.323	33-0-4	.152	-0	83	-6		-1.2

WALKER, TOM Thomas William B8.1.1881 Philadelphia PA D7.10.1944 Woodbury Heights NJ BR/TR/5-11/170 d9.27

YEAR	TM LG	W	L	PCT	G	GS	CG-SHO	SV-BS	IP	H	R	HR	HB	BB-IB	SO	ERA	AERA	OAV	OOB	AB-HR-SH	AVG	PB	SUP	APR	DL	PW
1902	Phi A	0	1	.000	1	1	1		8	10	7	0	0	2	2	5.63	65	.303	.324	4	.250	-0	98	-2		-0.1
1904	Cin N	15	8	.652	34	24	22-2	0	217	196	76	2	18	53	64	2.24	131	.238	.299	77-0-2	.117	-4	85	17		1.2
1905	Cin N	9	7	.563	23	19	12-1	0	144.2	171	71	3	6	44	28	3.24	102	.305	.362	51-0-2	.137	-1	105	3		0.2
Total	3	24	16	.600	48	44	35-3	0	369.2	377	154	5	25	97	94	2.70	114	.266	.325	132-0-6	.129	-6	94	18		1.3

WALKER, TYLER Tyler Lanier B5.15.1976 San Francisco CA BR/TR/6-3/225* [NYN97 2/58] d7.2 Col California-Davis

YEAR	TM LG	W	L	PCT	G	GS	CG-SHO	SV-BS	IP	H	R	HR	HB	BB-IB	SO	ERA	AERA	OAV	OOB	AB-HR-SH	AVG	PB	SUP	APR	DL	PW
2002	NY N	1	0	1.000	5	1	0	0-0	10.2	11	7	3	0	5-1	7	5.91	67	.250	.327	2	.000	-0	117	-2		-0.2
2004	SF N	5	1	.833	52	0	0	1-0	63.2	69	31	8	1	24-1	48	4.24	102	.287	.346	7	.000	-1		2		0.0
2005	SF N	6	4	.600	67	0	0	23-5	61.2	68	31	9	3	27-6	54	4.23	101	.280	.358	1	.000	-0		0	18	0.0
Total	3	12	5	.706	124	1	0	24-5	136	148	69	20	4	56-8	109	4.37	98	.281	.350	10	.000	-1	117	0	18	-0.2

WALKER, BILL William Henry B10.7.1903 E.St.Louis IL D6.14.1966 E.St.Louis IL BR/TL/6-0/175 d9.13

YEAR	TM LG	W	L	PCT	G	GS	CG-SHO	SV-BS	IP	H	R	HR	HB	BB-IB	SO	ERA	AERA	OAV	OOB	AB-HR-SH	AVG	PB	SUP	APR	DL	PW
1927	NY N	0	0	—	3	0	0		4	6	6	0	0	4	2	9.00	43	.429	.579	0	—	0		-3		-0.1
1928	NY N	3	6	.333	22	8	1	0	76.1	79	43	9	1	31	39	4.72	83	.275	.348	22-0-2	.091	-2	108	-6		-0.8
1929	NY N	14	7	.667	29	23	13-1	0	177.2	188	71	11	4	57	65	3.09	148	.274	.334	61-1-7	.115	-3	110	30		2.6
1930	NY N	17	15	.531	39	34	13-2	1	245.1	258	133	19	7	88	105	3.93	121	.268	.334	86-2-5	.186	-1*	96	19		1.9
1931	NY N	16	9	.640	37	28	19-6	3	239.1	212	78	6	3	64	121	2.26	164	.231	.283	77-0-3	.065	-6	102	37		2.9
1932	NY N	8	12	.400	31	22	9	1	163	177	95	23	5	55	74	4.14	90	.274	.334	52-0-1	.135	-2	111	-10		-1.2
1933	StL N	9	10	.474	29	20	6-2	0	158	168	71	8	1	67	41	3.42	102	.273	.346	53-1-3	.132	-2	90	1		-0.1
1934	†StL N	12	4	.750	24	19	10-1	0	153	160	59	11	2	66	76	3.12	136	.270	.345	54-0-3	.093	-4	90	19		1.3
1935	StL N★	13	8	.619	37	25	8-2	1	193.1	222	93	7	5	78	79	3.82	107	.288	.357	59-0-7	.102	-4*	95	7		0.2

YEAR	TM LG	W	L	PCT	G	GS	CG-SHO	SV-BS	IP	H	R	HR	HB	BB-IB	SO	ERA	AERA	OAV	OOB	AB-HR-SH	AVG	PB	SUP	APR	DL	PW
1936	StL N	5	6	.455	21	13	4-1	1	79.2	106	62	5	2	27	22	5.87	67	.318	.373	25-0-2	.280	2*	127	-19		-2.0
Total	10	97	77	.557	272	192	83-15	8	1489.2	1576	711	99	28	538	626	3.59	114	.271	.335	489-4-33	.127	-23	102	75		4.7

WALKUP, JIM James Elton B12.14.1909 Havana AR D2.7.1997 Danville AR BR/TR/6-1/170 d9.22 Col Arkansas-Monticello

YEAR	TM LG	W	L	PCT	G	GS	CG-SHO	SV-BS	IP	H	R	HR	HB	BB-IB	SO	ERA	AERA	OAV	OOB	AB-HR-SH	AVG	PB	SUP	APR	DL	PW
1934	StL A	0	0		3	0	0	0	8.1	6	4	0	0	5	6	2.16	231	.200	.314	3	.333	0		2		0.1
1935	StL A	6	9	.400	55	20	4-1	0	181.1	226	139	17	2	104	44	6.25	77	.305	.392	47-0-4	.128	-3	95	-25		-2.0
1936	StL A	0	3	.000	5	2	0	0	15.2	20	17	0	0	6	5	8.04	67	.308	.366	4	.000	-1	41	-5		-0.7
1937	StL A	9	12	.429	27	18	6	0	150.1	218	127	16	0	83	46	7.36	66	.347	.423	58-0-3	.241	-1	111	-36		-3.8
1938	StL A	1	12	.077	18	13	1	0	94	127	83	13	3	53	28	6.80	73	.329	.414	29-0-3	.138	-2	67	-20		-2.3
1939	StL A	0	1	.000	1	0	0	0	0.2	2	1	0	0	1	0	0.00	—	.500	.600	0	—	0		0		0.0
	Det A	0	1	.000	7	0	0	0	12	15	10	3	0	8	5	7.50	65	.319	.418	2	.500	0		-3		-0.2
	Year	0	2	.000	8	0	0	0	12.2	17	11	3	0	9	5	7.11	69	.333	.433	2	.500	0		-3		-0.2
Total	6	16	38	.296	116	53	11-1	0	462.1	614	381	49	5	260	134	6.74	72	.323	.406	143-0-10	.182	-6	91	-87		-8.9

WALKUP, JIM James Huey B11.3.1895 Havana AR D6.12.1990 Duncan OK BR/TL/5-8/150 d4.30

1927	Det A	0	0		2	0	0	0	1.2	3	1	0	0	0	0	5.40	78	.429	.429	1	.000	-0		0		0.0

WALL, DONNE Donnell Lee B7.11.1967 Potosi MO BR/TR/6-1/180(180-205) [HouN89 18/464] d9.2 Col Louisiana-Lafayette

1995	Hou N	3	1	.750	6	5	0	0-0	24.1	33	19	5	0	5-0	16	5.55	70	.320	.345	5-0-3	.000	-1	150	-6		-0.9
1996	Hou N	9	8	.529	26	23	2-1	0-0	150	170	84	17	6	34-3	99	4.56	85	.286	.329	44-0-8	.205	2	106	-12		-1.0
1997	Hou N	2	5	.286	8	8	0	0-0	41.2	53	31	8	2	16-0	25	6.26	64	.315	.382	10-0-1	.100	-0	72	-10		-1.4
1998	†SD N	5	4	.556	46	1	0	1-3	70.1	50	20	6	1	32-2	56	2.43	163	.202	.293	7	.286	-0	69	13		1.6
1999	SD N	7	4	.636	55	0	0	0-6	70.1	58	31	11	0	23-3	53	3.07	139	.219	.280	1	.000	-0		8		1.1
2000	SD N	5	2	.714	44	0	0	1-4	53.2	36	20	4	0	21-1	29	3.35	133	.193	.274	1-0-1	.000	-0		8	29	0.9
2001	NY N	0	4	.000	32	0	0	0-0	42.2	51	24	8	1	17-6	31	4.85	83	.300	.363	0	—	0*		-4	38	-0.3
2002	Ana A	0	0	—	17	0	0	0-0	21	17	15	3	1	7-1	13	6.43	70	.221	.291	0	—	0		-4	21	-0.2
Total	8	31	28	.525	234	37	2-1	2-13	468	244	62	11	155-16	322	4.20	97	.258	.318	68-0-13	.176	1	100	-7	88	-0.2

WALL, MURRAY Murray Wesley B9.19.1926 Dallas TX D10.8.1971 Lone Oak TX BR/TR/6-3/185(185-205) d7.4 Col Texas

1950	Bos A	0	0		1	0	0	0	2	2	2	0	0	2	2	9.00	43	.333	.400	1	.000	-0		-3		-0.1
1957	Bos A	3	0	1.000	11	0	0	1	24.1	21	11	3	0	2-0	13	3.33	120	.233	.247	6	.333	-0		1		0.3
1958	Bos A	8	9	.471	52	1	0	10	114.1	109	51	14	5	33-4	53	3.62	111	.255	.313	28	.107	-2	67	5		0.8
1959	Bos A	1	4	.200	15	0	0	3	31.2	31	21	5	0	15-2	22	5.40	75	.267	.348	7	.000	-1		-5		-0.8
	Was A	0	0	—	1	0	0	0	1	3	1	1	0	0-0	0	6.75	58	.600	.600	1	.000	-0		0		0.0
	Bos A	1	1	.500	11	0	0	0	17.1	26	11	2	1	11-4	6	5.71	71	.371	.458	3	.000	-0		-3		-0.3
	Year	2	5	.286	27	0	0	3	50.1	60	33	8	1	26-6	14	5.54	73	.314	.395	11	.000	-1		-7		-1.1
Total	4	13	14	.481	91	1	0	14	193	196	100	25	6	63-10	82	4.20	96	.270	.330	46	.109	-3	67	-5		-0.1

WALL, STAN Stanley Arthur B6.16.1951 Butler MO BL/TL/6-1/175* [LAN69 6/126] d7.19

1975	LA N	0	1	.000	10	0	0	0-0	16	12	6	0	1	7-0	6	1.69	203	.222	.308	0	—	0		2		0.1
1976	LA N	2	2	.500	31	0	0	1-1	50	50	21	5	2	15-2	27	3.60	95	.269	.325	4	.000	-0		-1		-0.1
1977	LA N	2	3	.400	25	0	0	0-0	32	36	20	3	1	13-2	22	5.34	72	.279	.350	1-0-1	.000	-0		-5		-0.7
Total	3	4	6	.400	66	0	0	1-1	98	98	47	8	4	35-4	55	3.86	92	.266	.331	5-0-1	.000	-1		-4		-0.7

WALLACE, DAVE David William B9.7.1947 Waterbury CT BR/TR/5-10/185* d7.18 C8 Col New Haven

1973	Phi N	0	0	—	4	0	0	0-0	3.2	13	9	1	0	2-0	2	22.09	17	.591	.625	0	—	0		-7		-0.3
1974	Phi N	0	1	.000	3	0	0	0-0	3	4	4	2	0	3-1	5	9.00	42	.308	.438	0	—	0		-2		-0.4
1978	Tor A	0	0	—	6	0	0	0-0	14	12	6	1	0	11-0	7	3.86	103	.245	.371	0	—	0		0		0.0
Total	3	0	1	.000	13	0	0	0-0	20.2	29	19	4	0	16-1	12	7.84	50	.345	.441	0	—	0		-9		-0.7

WALLACE, DEREK Derek Robert B9.1.1971 Van Nuys CA BR/TR/6-3/200(185-215) [ChiN92 1/11] d8.13 Col Pepperdine [DL 1997 NY N 181]

1996	NY N	2	3	.400	19	0	0	3-0	24.2	29	12	2	0	14-2	15	4.01	100	.290	.377	0	—	0		0		0.1
1999	KC A	0	1	.000	8	0	0	0-0	8.1	7	4	2	0	5-0	5	3.24	157	.259	.364	0	—	0		1		0.1
Total	2	2	4	.333	27	0	0	3-0	33	36	16	4	0	19-2	20	3.82	112	.283	.374	0	—	0		1	181	0.2

WALLACE, HUCK Harry Clinton "Lefty" B7.27.1882 Richmond IN D7.6.1951 Cleveland OH BL/TL/5-6/160 d6.5

1912	Phi N	0	0	—	4	0	0	0-0	4.2	7	5	0	0	4	4	0.00	—	.350	.458	0	—	0		0		0.0

WALLACE, LEFTY James Harold B8.12.1921 Evansville IN D7.28.1982 Evansville IN BL/TL/5-11/160 d5.5 Mil 1943-44

1942	Bos N	1	3	.250	19	3	1	0	49.1	39	21	3	2	24	20	3.83	87	.217	.316	14	.143	-0	109	-1		-0.2
1945	Bos N	1	0	1.000	5	3	1	0	20	18	11	1	1	9	4	4.50	85	.240	.329	6-0-1	.000	-1*	96	-1		-0.1
1946	Bos N	3	3	.500	27	8	2	0	75.1	76	41	5	1	31	27	4.18	82	.253	.325	18	.056	-1	94	-6		-0.5
Total	3	5	6	.455	51	14	4	0	144.2	133	73	9	4	64	51	4.11	84	.240	.323	38-0-1	.079	-2	98	-8		-0.8

WALLACE, JEFF Jeffrey Allen B4.12.1976 Wheeling WV BL/TL/6-2/240(228-240) [KCA95 25/694] d8.21 [DL 1998 Pit N 181, 2002 Bos A 114]

1997	Pit N	0	0	—	11	0	0	0-1	12	3	1	0	1	8-1	14	0.75	571	.200	.327	0	—	0		4		0.2
1999	Pit N	1	0	1.000	41	0	0	0-1	39	26	17	2	1	38-1	41	3.69	125	.195	.372	0	—	0		4	47	0.2
2000	Pit N	2	0	1.000	38	0	0	0-0	35.2	42	32	5	4	34-1	27	7.07	66	.290	.432	1	.000	-0		-10		-0.5
2001	TB A	0	3	.000	29	1	0	0-0	50.1	43	26	4	1	37-0	38	3.40	133	.232	.363	0	—	0	41	4	25	0.2
Total	4	3	3	.500	119	1	0	0-2	137	119	77	11	5	117-3	120	4.20	108	.237	.383	1	.000	0	41	2	367	0.1

WALLACE, MIKE Michael Sherman B2.3.1951 Gastonia NC BL/TL/6-2/204(185-204) [PhiN69 4/76] d6.27

1973	Phi N	1	1	.500	20	3	1	1-1	33.1	38	16	1	0	15-4	20	3.78	101	.304	.373	4	.000	-0	131	0		0.0
1974	Phi N	1	0	1.000	8	0	0	0-0	8.1	12	6	0	0	2-0	1	5.40	70	.324	.359	0	—	0		-2		-0.2
	NY A	6	0	1.000	23	1	0	0-0	52.1	42	18	3	0	35-3	34	2.41	147	.222	.339	0	—	0	75	6		0.6
1975	NY A	0	0	—	3	0	0	0-0	4.1	11	7	1	0	1-0	2	14.54	26	.458	.480	0	—	0		-5		-0.2
	StL N	0	0	—	9	0	0	0-0	8.2	9	2	0	0	5-2	6	2.08	183	.281	.378	0	—	0		2		0.1
1976	StL N	3	2	.600	49	0	0	2-2	66.1	66	34	3	0	39-2	40	4.07	88	.264	.358	3	.333	0		-3		-0.2
1977	Tex A	0	0	—	5	0	0	0-0	8.1	10	7	1	0	10-0	2	7.56	54	.323	.488	0	—	0		-3		-0.1
Total	5	11	3	.786	117	4	1	3-3	181.2	188	90	9	0	107-11	105	3.91	94	.273	.367	7	.143	0	120	-5		0.0

WALLACE, BOBBY Rhoderick John B11.4.1873 Pittsburgh PA D11.3.1960 Torrance CA BR/TR/5-8/170 d9.15 M3/C1/U1 HF1953 ▲

1894	Cle N	2	1	.667	4	3	2	0	26	28	25	1	1	20	10	5.19	106	.272	.395	13	.154	-1	103	0		-0.1
1895	Cle N	12	14	.462	30	28	22-1	1	228.2	271	166	3	8	87	63	4.09	122	.290	.356	98-0-6	.214	-3	112	17		1.3
1896	†Cle N	10	7	.588	22	16	13-2	0	145.1	167	75	2	4	49	46	3.34	136	.286	.345	149-1-4	.235	0*	93	19		1.8
1902	StL A	0	0	—	1	1	0	0	2	3	2	0	0	1	1	0.00	—	.333	.333	494-1-6	.285	0*	82	0		0.0
Total	4	24	22	.522	57	48	37-3	1	402	469	268	6	13	156	120	3.87	125	.288	.355	754-2-16	.264	-3	104	36		3.0

WALLER, RED John Francis B6.16.1883 Washington DC D2.9.1915 Secaucus NJ BR/TR/6-0/175 d4.27

1909	NY N	0	0	—	1	0	0	0	3	3	2	0	1	0	0	—	.429	.500	—	—	0		0		0.0

WALROND, LES Leslie Dale B11.7.1976 Muskogee OK BL/TL/6-0/190 [StLN98 13/378] d6.8 Col Kansas

2003	KC A	0	2	.000	7	0	0	0-0	8	11	9	2	0	7-1	6	10.13	48	.324	.439	0	—	0		-4		-0.7

WALSH, AUGIE August Sothley B8.17.1904 Wilmington DE D11.12.1985 San Rafael CA BR/TR/6-0/175 d10.2

1927	Phi N	0	1	.000	1	1	1	0	10	12	5	3	0	5	0	4.50	92	.333	.415	4	.250	-0	82	0		0.0
1928	Phi N	4	9	.308	38	11	2	2	122.1	160	92	13	5	40	38	6.18	69	.321	.388	39-1-1	.256	2*	83	-23		-2.0
Total	2	4	10	.286	39	12	3	2	132.1	172	97	16	5	45	38	6.05	70	.322	.380	43-1-1	.256	2	83	-23		-2.0

WALSH, CONNIE Cornelius R. B4.23.1882 St.Louis MO D4.5.1953 St.Louis MO TR d9.16

1907	Pit N	0	0	—	1	0	0	0	4	5	1	1	0	0	1	0	9.00	27	.250	.400	—	—	0		-1		0.0

WALSH, DAVE David Peter B9.25.1960 Arlington MA BL/TL/6-1/185 [TorA82 9/212] d8.13 Col California-Santa Barbara

1990	LA N	0	0	—	14	0	0	0-1	16.1	15	12	1	0	6-1	15	3.86	96	.242	.304	0	—	0		-2		-0.1

WALSH, ED Edward Arthur B2.11.1905 Meriden CT D10.31.1937 Meriden CT BR/TR/6-1/180 d7.4 f-Ed Col Notre Dame

1928	Chi A	4	7	.364	14	10	3	0	78	86	45	2	5	42	32	4.96	82	.290	.387	27-0-1	.111	-2	86	-5		-0.8
1929	Chi A	6	11	.353	24	20	7	0	129	156	94	9	4	64	31	5.65	76	.312	.394	43-0-1	.233	2*	81	-19		-1.8
1930	Chi A	1	4	.200	37	4	0	0	103.2	131	67	8	4	50	37	5.38	86	.316	.367	34-0-1	.265	1*	93	-5		-0.1

YEAR	TM LG	W	L	PCT	G	GS	CG-SHO	SV-BS	IP	H	R	HR	HB	BB-IB	SO	ERA	AERA	OAV	OOB	AB-HR-SH	AVG	PB	SUP	APR	DL	PW
1932	Chi A	0	2	.000	4	4	1	0	20.1	26	22	3	0	13	7	8.41	51	.299	.390	7	.286	0	98	-9		-0.7
Total	4	11	24	.314	79	38	11	0	331	399	228	22	13	149	107	5.57	78	.307	.384	111-0-3	.216	1	84	-38		-3.4

WALSH, ED   Edward Augustine "Big Ed"   B5.14.1881 Plains PA   D5.26.1959 Pompano Beach FL   BR/TR/6-1/193   d5.7   M1/C6/U1   HF1946   s-Ed   Col Fordham

YEAR	TM LG	W	L	PCT	G	GS	CG-SHO	SV-BS	IP	H	R	HR	HB	BB-IB	SO	ERA	AERA	OAV	OOB	AB-HR-SH	AVG	PB	SUP	APR	DL	PW
1904	Chi A	6	3	.667	18	8	6-1	1	110.2	90	45	1	3	32	57	2.60	94	.223	.285	41-1-1	.220	3	120	-2		0.1
1905	Chi A	8	3	.727	22	13	9-1	0	136.2	121	53	0	3	29	71	2.17	113	.239	.284	58-0-1	.155	-0*	121	3		0.2
1906	†Chi A	17	13	.567	41	31	24-10	2	278.1	215	83	1	7	58	171	1.88	135	.217	.265	99-0-3	.141	-2*	90	21		2.6
1907	Chi A	24	18	.571	56	46	37-5	4	422.1	341	120	3	8	87	206	1.60	150	.223	.269	154-1-1	.162	-1*	100	33		4.6
1908	Chi A	40	15	.727	66	49	42-11	6	464	343	111	2	9	56	269	1.42	163	.203	.232	157-1-8	.172	2	98	43		6.8
1909	Chi A	15	11	.577	31	28	20-8	2	230.1	166	52	0	4	50	127	1.41	166	.203	.253	84-0-1	.214	4*	111	25		4.1
1910	Chi A	18	20	.474	45	36	33-7	5	369.2	242	87	5	4	61	258	1.27	189	.187	.226	138-0-5	.217	4*	71	45		6.3
1911	Chi A	27	18	.600	56	37	33-5	4	368.2	327	125	4	7	72	255	2.22	145	.239	.280	155-0-3	.219	-1*	117	42		5.5
1912	Chi A	27	17	.614	62	41	32-6	10	393	332	125	6	1	94	254	2.15	149	.231	.279	136-0-4	.243	6	94	49		6.5
1913	Chi A	8	3	.727	16	14	7-1	1	97.2	91	37	1	4	39	34	2.58	113	.245	.324	32-0-1	.156	-1*	96	5		0.5
1914	Chi A	2	3	.400	8	5	3-1	0	44.2	33	19	0	1	20	15	2.82	95	.212	.305	16-0-1	.063	-1*	60	0		-0.1
1915	Chi A	3	0	1.000	3	3	3-1	0	27	19	4	0	0	7	12	1.33	223	.202	.257	11-0-1	.364	1*	147	5		0.7
1916	Chi A	0	1	.000	2	1	0	0	3.1	4	3	0	0	3	3	2.70	102	.286	.412	0	—	0	55	-1		-0.1
1917	Bos N	0	1	.000	4	3	1	0	18	22	9	0	1	9	4	3.50	73	.314	.400	4	.250	1	108	-2		0.0
Total	14	195	126	.607	430	315	250-57	35	2964.1	2346	873	23	52	617	1736	1.82	145	.218	.264	1085-3-30	.194	15	99	266		37.7

WALSH, JUNIOR   James Gerald   B3.7.1919 Newark NJ   D11.12.1990 Olyphant PA   BR/TR/5-11/185*   d9.14

YEAR	TM LG	W	L	PCT	G	GS	CG-SHO	SV-BS	IP	H	R	HR	HB	BB-IB	SO	ERA	AERA	OAV	OOB	AB-HR-SH	AVG	PB	SUP	APR	DL	PW
1946	Pit N	0	1	.000	4	2	0	0	10.1	9	6	0	1	10	2	5.23	67	.237	.408	4	.000	-1	182	-1		-0.2
1948	Pit N	1	0	1.000	2	0	0	0	4.1	4	5	1	0	5	0	10.38	39	.235	.409	2	.000	-0		-3		-0.5
1949	Pit N	1	4	.200	9	7	1-1	0	42.2	40	27	5	0	16	24	5.06	83	.244	.311	12	.000	-1	60	-4		-0.6
1950	Pit N	1	1	.500	38	2	0	2	62.1	56	36	6	1	34	33	5.05	87	.246	.346	6	.167	1	201	-3		0.0
1951	Pit N	1	4	.200	36	1	0	0	73.1	92	66	9	1	46	32	6.87	61	.304	.397	7	.143	-1	21	-21		-1.2
Total	5	4	10	.286	89	12	1-1	2	193	201	140	21	3	111	91	5.88	72	.268	.365	31	.065	-1	97	-32		-2.5

WALSH, JIM   James Thomas   B7.10.1894 Roxbury MA   D5.13.1967 Boston MA   BL/TL/5-11/175   d8.25

YEAR	TM LG	W	L	PCT	G	GS	CG-SHO	SV-BS	IP	H	R	HR	HB	BB-IB	SO	ERA	AERA	OAV	OOB	AB-HR-SH	AVG	PB	SUP	APR	DL	PW
1921	Det A	0	0	—	3	0	0	0	4	2	1	0	0	1	3	2.25	190	.125	.176	0	—	0		1		0.0

WALTER, GENE   Gene Winston   B11.22.1960 Chicago IL   BL/TL/6-4/200*   [SDN82 29/720]   d8.9   Col Eastern Kentucky   [DL 1989 Sea A 182]

YEAR	TM LG	W	L	PCT	G	GS	CG-SHO	SV-BS	IP	H	R	HR	HB	BB-IB	SO	ERA	AERA	OAV	OOB	AB-HR-SH	AVG	PB	SUP	APR	DL	PW
1985	SD N	0	2	.000	15	0	0	3-0	22	12	6	0	0	8-1	18	2.05	174	.158	.235	1	.000	0		4		0.4
1986	SD N	2	2	.500	57	0	0	1-1	98	89	47	7	4	49-7	84	3.86	95	.247	.341	10-0-2	.200	1		-2		0.0
1987	NY N	1	2	.333	21	0	0	0-2	19.2	18	10	1	1	13-3	11	3.20	120	.243	.360	1-0-1	.000	0		0		0.1
1988	NY N	0	1	.000	19	0	0	0-0	16.2	21	9	0	0	11-1	14	3.78	86	.309	.400	0	—	0		-1		-0.1
	Sea A	1	0	1.000	16	0	0	0-0	26.1	21	16	0	2	15-4	13	5.13	82	.216	.330	0	—	0		-2		-0.1
Total	4	4	7	.364	128	0	0	4-3	182.2	161	88	8	7	96-16	140	3.74	99	.238	.336	12-0-3	.167	1		-1	182	0.3

WALTER, BERNIE   James Bernard   B8.15.1908 Dover TN   D10.30.1988 Nashville TN   BR/TR/6-1/175   d8.16   Col Tennessee

YEAR	TM LG	W	L	PCT	G	GS	CG-SHO	SV-BS	IP	H	R	HR	HB	BB-IB	SO	ERA	AERA	OAV	OOB	AB-HR-SH	AVG	PB	SUP	APR	DL	PW
1930	Pit N	0	0	—	1	0	0	0	1	0	0	0	0	1	0	0.00	—	.000	.000	0	—	0		1		0.0

WALTERS, CHARLIE   Charles Leonard   B2.21.1947 Minneapolis MN   BR/TR/6-4/190   d4.11

YEAR	TM LG	W	L	PCT	G	GS	CG-SHO	SV-BS	IP	H	R	HR	HB	BB-IB	SO	ERA	AERA	OAV	OOB	AB-HR-SH	AVG	PB	SUP	APR	DL	PW
1969	Min A	0	0	—	6	0	0	0-0	6.2	6	4	1	1	3-0	2	5.40	67	.240	.345	0	—	0		-1		-0.1

WALTERS, MIKE   Michael Charles   B10.18.1957 St.Louis MO   BR/TR/6-5/203*   [AnaA77 S1/20]   d7.8   Col Chaffey (CA) JC

YEAR	TM LG	W	L	PCT	G	GS	CG-SHO	SV-BS	IP	H	R	HR	HB	BB-IB	SO	ERA	AERA	OAV	OOB	AB-HR-SH	AVG	PB	SUP	APR	DL	PW
1983	Min A	1	1	.500	23	0	0	2-0	59	52	31	4	2	20-4	21	4.12	104	.243	.311	0	—	0		0		0.0
1984	Min A	0	3	.000	23	0	0	2-2	29	31	14	1	1	14-4	10	3.72	114	.287	.368	0	—	0		1		0.1
Total	2	1	4	.200	46	0	0	4-2	88	83	45	5	3	34-8	31	3.99	107	.258	.331	0	—	0		1		0.1

WALTERS, BUCKY   William Henry   B4.19.1909 Philadelphia PA   D4.20.1991 Abington PA   BR/TR/6-1/180*   d9.18.1931   M2/C8   ▲

YEAR	TM LG	W	L	PCT	G	GS	CG-SHO	SV-BS	IP	H	R	HR	HB	BB-IB	SO	ERA	AERA	OAV	OOB	AB-HR-SH	AVG	PB	SUP	APR	DL	PW
1934	Phi N	0	0	—	2	1	0	0	7	8	3	1	1	2	7	1.29	367	.296	.367	300-4-3	.260	0*	73	2		0.1
1935	Phi N	9	9	.500	24	22	8-2	0	151	168	86	9	7	68	40	4.17	109	.289	.370	96-0-2	.250	1*	85	5		0.8
1936	Phi N	11	21	.344	40	33	15-4	0	258	284	146	11	5	115	66	4.26	107	.277	.353	121-1-3	.240	2*	79	9		1.9
1937	Phi N★	14	15	.483	37	34	15-3	0	246.1	292	148	14	3	86	87	4.75	91	.295	.353	137-1-2	.277	4*	101	-11		-0.4
1938	Phi N	4	8	.333	12	12	9-1	0	82.2	91	53	8	3	42	28	5.23	74	.276	.363	35-1-0	.286	3*	102	-11		-1.0
	Cin N	11	6	.647	27	22	11-2	1	168.1	168	81	6	2	66	65	3.69	99	.255	.324	64-0-2	.141	-0*	136	-1		0.0
	Year	15	14	.517	39	34	20-3	1	251	259	134	13	5	108	93	4.20	89	.262	.337	99-1-2	.192	3	124	-11		-1.0
1939	†Cin N☆	27	11	.711	39	36	31-2	0	319	250	98	15	6	109	137	2.29	168	.220	.291	120-1-5	.325	13*	110	54		8.2
1940	†Cin N★	22	10	.688	36	36	29-3	0	305	241	95	19	5	92	115	2.48	153	.220	.283	117-1-6	.205	2*	117	44		4.7
1941	Cin N★	19	15	.559	37	35	27-5	2	302	292	108	10	2	88	129	2.83	127	.255	.309	106-0-4	.189	2*	88	27		3.3
1942	Cin N★	15	14	.517	34	32	21-3	0	253.2	223	101	8	5	73	109	2.66	123	.231	.289	99-2-2	.242	6*	97	14		2.5
1943	Cin N	15	15	.500	34	34	21-5	0	246.1	244	105	8	1	109	80	3.54	94	.264	.342	90-1-5	.267	8*	88	-5		0.3
1944	Cin N★	23	8	.742	34	32	27-6	0	285	233	92	10	4	87	77	2.40	145	.219	.281	107-0-5	.280	8*	97	34		4.7
1945	Cin N	10	10	.500	22	22	12-3	0	168	166	62	6	2	51	45	2.68	140	.259	.316	61-3-3	.230	5*	69	18		2.6
1946	Cin N	10	7	.588	22	22	10-2	0	151.1	146	55	9	2	64	60	2.56	131	.258	.336	55-0-4	.127	-1*	111	12		1.3
1947	Cin N	8	8	.500	20	20	5-2	0	122	137	83	15	3	69	43	5.75	71	.278	.347	45-0-2	.267	3	109	-20		-2.0
1948	Cin N	0	3	.000	7	5	1	0	35	42	25	6	0	18	19	4.63	84	.316	.397	15	.267	0	113	-5	60	-0.3
1950	Bos N	0	0	—	1	0	0	0	4	5	2	0	0	2	0	4.50	46	.313	.389	2	—	-0		0		0.0
Total	16	198	160	.553	428	398	242-42	4	3104.2	2990	1343	154	51	1121	1107	3.30	115	.253	.321	1570-15-48	.246	57	99	166	60	26.7

WALTON, BRUCE   Bruce Kenneth   B12.25.1962 Bakersfield CA   BR/TR/6-2/195*   [OakA85 16/403]   d5.11   C4   Col Hawaii-Manoa

YEAR	TM LG	W	L	PCT	G	GS	CG-SHO	SV-BS	IP	H	R	HR	HB	BB-IB	SO	ERA	AERA	OAV	OOB	AB-HR-SH	AVG	PB	SUP	APR	DL	PW
1991	Oak A	1	0	1.000	12	0	0	0-1	13	14	9	3	1	6-0	10	6.23	62	.269	.321	0	—	0		-3		-0.2
1992	Oak A	0	0	—	7	0	0	0-0	10	17	11	1	0	3-0	7	9.90	38	.378	.408	0	—	0		-6		-0.3
1993	Mon N	0	0	—	4	0	0	0-0	5.2	11	6	1	0	3-0	0	9.53	44	.407	.467	1	.000	0		-3		-0.1
1994	Col N	1	0	1.000	4	0	0	0-0	5.1	6	5	1	0	3-1	1	8.44	59	.273	.360	0	—	0		-2		-0.3
Total	4	2	0	1.000	27	0	0	0-1	34	45	31	6	1	15-1	18	8.21	49	.317	.381	1	.000	0		-14		-0.9

WANG, CHIEN-MING   Chien-Ming   B3.31.1980 Tainan City, Taiwan   BR/TR/6-3/200   d4.30   Col Tapei College of PE

YEAR	TM LG	W	L	PCT	G	GS	CG-SHO	SV-BS	IP	H	R	HR	HB	BB-IB	SO	ERA	AERA	OAV	OOB	AB-HR-SH	AVG	PB	SUP	APR	DL	PW
2005	†NY A	8	5	.615	18	17	0	0-0	116.1	113	58	9	6	32-3	47	4.02	109	.256	.313	1	.000	-0	94	4	59	0.6

WANTZ, DICK   Richard Carter   B4.11.1940 South Gate CA   D5.13.1965 Inglewood CA   BR/TR/6-5/175   d4.13   Col Cal St.-Los Angeles

YEAR	TM LG	W	L	PCT	G	GS	CG-SHO	SV-BS	IP	H	R	HR	HB	BB-IB	SO	ERA	AERA	OAV	OOB	AB-HR-SH	AVG	PB	SUP	APR	DL	PW
1965	Cal A	0	0	—	1	0	0	3	2	0	0	0	0	.500	.500	0	—	0		-2		-0.1

WAPNICK, STEVE   Steven Lee   B9.25.1965 Los Angeles CA   BR/TR/6-2/200*   [TorA87 30/777]   d4.14   Col Cal St.-Fresno

YEAR	TM LG	W	L	PCT	G	GS	CG-SHO	SV-BS	IP	H	R	HR	HB	BB-IB	SO	ERA	AERA	OAV	OOB	AB-HR-SH	AVG	PB	SUP	APR	DL	PW
1990	Det A	0	0	—	6	0	0	0-0	7	8	5	0	0	10-0	6	6.43	62	.296	.486	0	—	0		-2		-0.1
1991	Chi A	0	1	.000	4	0	0	0-0	5	2	1	0	0	4-0	1	1.80	222	.111	.273	0	—	0		1		0.2
Total	2	0	1	.000	10	0	0	0-0	12	10	6	0	0	14-0	7	4.50	89	.222	.407	0	—	°0		-1		0.1

WARD, BRYAN   Bryan Matthew   B1.28.1972 Bristol PA   BL/TL/6-2/210*   [FlaN93 20/575]   d7.3   Col South Carolina-Aiken

YEAR	TM LG	W	L	PCT	G	GS	CG-SHO	SV-BS	IP	H	R	HR	HB	BB-IB	SO	ERA	AERA	OAV	OOB	AB-HR-SH	AVG	PB	SUP	APR	DL	PW
1998	Chi A	1	2	.333	28	0	0	1-3	27	30	13	4	0	7-0	17	3.33	137	.278	.319	0	—	0		3		0.3
1999	Chi A	0	1	.000	40	0	0	0-0	39.1	63	36	10	0	11-1	35	7.55	65	.368	.404	0	—	0		-11		-0.5
2000	Phi N	0	0	—	20	0	0	0-0	19.1	14	5	2	0	8-0	11	2.33	197	.206	.282	0	—	0		5		0.2
	Ana A	0	0	—	7	0	0	0-0	8	8	5	1	0	2-0	3	5.63	92	.235	.278	6	—	0		-1		0.0
Total	3	1	3	.250	95	0	0	1-3	93.2	115	60	17	0	28-1	66	5.09	94	.302	.346	6	—	0		-4		0.0

WARD, COLIN   Colin Norval   B11.22.1960 Los Angeles CA   BL/TL/6-3/190   [DetA82 3/74]   d9.21   Col UCLA

YEAR	TM LG	W	L	PCT	G	GS	CG-SHO	SV-BS	IP	H	R	HR	HB	BB-IB	SO	ERA	AERA	OAV	OOB	AB-HR-SH	AVG	PB	SUP	APR	DL	PW
1985	SF N	0	0	—	6	2	0	0-0	12.1	10	6	0	0	7-0	8	4.38	79	.233	.333	2	.000	-0	115	-1		-0.1

WARD, JOHNNY   John B East St.Louis IL   d9.19

YEAR	TM LG	W	L	PCT	G	GS	CG-SHO	SV-BS	IP	H	R	HR	HB	BB-IB	SO	ERA	AERA	OAV	OOB	AB-HR-SH	AVG	PB	SUP	APR	DL	PW
1885	Pro N	0	1	.000	1	1	1	0	8	10	7	0	1		3	4.50	60	.286	.306	3		-0	0	-2		-0.2

WARD, JOHN   John Montgomery   B3.3.1860 Bellefonte PA   D3.4.1925 Augusta GA   BL/TR(TL 1884p, BB 1888)/5-9/165   d7.15   M7   HF1964   Col Penn St.   ▲

YEAR	TM LG	W	L	PCT	G	GS	CG-SHO	SV-BS	IP	H	R	HR	HB	BB-IB	SO	ERA	AERA	OAV	OOB	AB-HR-SH	AVG	PB	SUP	APR	DL	PW
1878	Pro N	22	13	.629	37	37	37-6	0	334	308	151	3		34	116	1.51	146	.231	.251	138-1	.196	2	95	22		2.2
1879	Pro N	47	19	.712	70	60	58-2	1	587	571	270	5		36	239	2.15	110	.239	.250	364-2	.286	17*	144	13		2.7
1880	Pro N	39	24	.619	70	67	59-8	1	595	501	230	5		45	230	1.74	127	.217	.232	356	.228	1*	108	35		3.5
1881	Pro N	18	18	.500	39	35	32-3	0	330	326	183	2		53	119	2.13	125	.242	.271	357	.244	3*	94	16		1.9
1882	Pro N	19	13	.594	34	33	30-4	1	286	268	143	6		36	72	2.55	111	.232	.255	355-1	.245	1*	95	11		1.2
1883	NY N	16	13	.552	34	25	24-1	0	277	278	165	3		31	121	2.70	115	.246	.267	380-7	.255	6*	97	13		1.7

YEAR	TM LG	W	L	PCT	G	GS	CG-SHO	SV-BS	IP	H	R	HR	HB	BB-IB	SO	ERA	AERA	OAV	OOB	AB-HR-SH	AVG	PB	SUP	APR	DL	PW
1884	NY N	3	3	.500	9	5	5	0	60.2	72	43	2		18	23	3.41	87	.280	.327	482-2	.253	1*	160	-4		-0.2
Total	7	164	103	.614	293	262	245-24	3	2469.2	2324	1185	26		253	920	2.10	118	.234	.254	2432-13	.249	31	111	106		13.0

WARD, DICK Richard Ole B5.21.1909 Herrick SD D5.30.1966 Freeland WA BR/TR/6-1/198 d5.3 Col St. Martins

YEAR	TM LG	W	L	PCT	G	GS	CG-SHO	SV-BS	IP	H	R	HR	HB	BB-IB	SO	ERA	AERA	OAV	OOB	AB-HR-SH	AVG	PB	SUP	APR	DL	PW
1934	Chi N	0	0	—	3	0	0	0	6	9	6	0	0	2	1	3.00	129	.375	.423	1	.000	-0		-1		-0.1
1935	StL N	0	0	—	1	0	0	0	0	0	1	0	0	1	0	—	—	1.000		0	—	0		0		0.0
Total	2	0	0	—	4	0	0	0	6	9	7	0	0	3	1	3.00	129	.375	.444	1	.000	-0		-1		-0.1

WARD, COLBY Robert Colby B1.2.1964 Lansing MI BR/TR/6-2/185 [CalA86 11/285] d7.27 Col Brigham Young

YEAR	TM LG	W	L	PCT	G	GS	CG-SHO	SV-BS	IP	H	R	HR	HB	BB-IB	SO	ERA	AERA	OAV	OOB	AB-HR-SH	AVG	PB	SUP	APR	DL	PW
1990	Cle A	1	3	.250	22	0	0	1-1	36	31	17	3	1	21-4	23	4.25	93	.238	.344	0	—	0		-1		-0.1

WARD, DUANE Roy Duane B5.28.1964 Park View NM BR/TR/6-4/210(205-225) [AtlN82 1/9] d4.12 [DL 1994 Tor A 131]

YEAR	TM LG	W	L	PCT	G	GS	CG-SHO	SV-BS	IP	H	R	HR	HB	BB-IB	SO	ERA	AERA	OAV	OOB	AB-HR-SH	AVG	PB	SUP	APR	DL	PW
1986	Atl N	0	1	.000	10	0	0	0-0	16	22	13	2	0	8-0	8	7.31	54	.349	.423	1	.000	0		-5		-0.3
	Tor A	0	1	.000	2	1	0	0-0	2	3	4	0	1	4-0	1	13.50	31	.300	.533	0	—	0	64	-2		-0.4
1987	Tor A	1	0	1.000	12	1	0	0-0	11.2	14	9	0	0	12-2	10	6.94	60	.326	.464	0	—	0	201	-3		-0.2
1988	Tor A	9	3	.750	64	0	0	15-3	111.2	101	46	5	5	60-8	91	3.30	120	.245	.344	0	—	0		8		1.0
1989	†Tor A	4	10	.286	66	0	0	15-12	114.2	94	55	4	5	58-11	122	3.77	101	.230	.326	0	—	0		0		0.0
1990	Tor A	2	8	.200	73	0	0	11-7	127.2	101	51	9	1	42-10	112	3.45	115	.221	.287	0	—	0		8		0.7
1991	†Tor A	7	6	.538	81	0	0	23-4	107.1	80	36	3	2	33-3	132	2.77	153	.207	.271	0	—	0		17		2.5
1992	†Tor A	7	4	.636	79	0	0	12-4	101.1	76	27	5	1	39-3	103	1.95	210	.207	.282	0	—	0		22		2.7
1993	†Tor A★	2	3	.400	71	0	0	45-6	71.2	49	17	4	1	25-2	97	2.13	205	.193	.266	0	—	0		18		3.1
1995	Tor A	0	1	.000	4	0	0	0-0	2.2	11	10	0	1	5-0	3	27.00	18	.579	.680	0	—	0		-7	122	-1.1
Total	9	32	37	.464	462	2	0	121-36	666.2	551	268	32	17	286-39	679	3.28	124	.228	.310	1	.000	-0	146	56	253	8.0

WARDEN, JON Jonathan Edgar "Warbler" B10.1.1946 Columbus OH BB/TL/6-0/205 [DetA66*4/62] d4.11

YEAR	TM LG	W	L	PCT	G	GS	CG-SHO	SV-BS	IP	H	R	HR	HB	BB-IB	SO	ERA	AERA	OAV	OOB	AB-HR-SH	AVG	PB	SUP	APR	DL	PW
1968	Det A	4	1	.800	28	0	0	3-0	37.1	30	15	5	0	13-0	23	3.62	83	.217	.294	2	.000	-0		-2		-0.4

WARDLE, CURT Curtis Ray B11.16.1960 Downey CA BL/TL/6-5/220* [MinA81 3/56] d8.30 Col California-Riverside

YEAR	TM LG	W	L	PCT	G	GS	CG-SHO	SV-BS	IP	H	R	HR	HB	BB-IB	SO	ERA	AERA	OAV	OOB	AB-HR-SH	AVG	PB	SUP	APR	DL	PW
1984	Min A	0	0	—	2	0	0	0-0	4	3	2	2	0	0-0	5	4.50	94	.200	.200	0	—	0		0		0.0
1985	Min A	1	3	.250	35	0	0	1-4	49	49	32	9	1	28-0	47	5.51	80	.266	.364	0	—	0		-5		-0.3
	Cle A	7	6	.538	15	12	0	0-0	66	78	51	11	1	34-0	37	6.68	62	.297	.373	0	—	0	135	-17		-2.7
	Year	8	9	.471	50	12	0	1-4	115	127	83	20	2	62-0	84	6.18	69	.284	.369	0	—	0	131	-22		-3.0
Total	2	8	9	.471	52	12	0	1-4	119	130	85	22	2	62-0	89	6.13	70	.281	.365	0	—	0	131	-22		-3.0

WARE, JEFF Jeffrey Allan B11.11.1970 Norfolk VA BR/TR/6-3/190* [TorA91 1/35] d9.2 Col Old Dominion

YEAR	TM LG	W	L	PCT	G	GS	CG-SHO	SV-BS	IP	H	R	HR	HB	BB-IB	SO	ERA	AERA	OAV	OOB	AB-HR-SH	AVG	PB	SUP	APR	DL	PW
1995	Tor A	2	1	.667	5	5	0	0-0	26.1	28	18	2	1	21-0	18	5.47	87	.277	.407	0	—	0	98	-2		-0.2
1996	Tor A	1	5	.167	13	4	0	0-0	32.2	35	34	6	2	31-1	11	9.09	55	.271	.420	0	—	0	46	-14		-1.9
Total	2	3	6	.333	18	9	0	0-0	59	63	52	8	3	52-1	29	7.47	66	.274	.414	0	—	0	74	-16		-2.1

WARHOP, JACK John Milton "Chief","Crab" (b John Milton Wauhop) B7.4.1884 Hinton WV D10.4.1960 Freeport IL BR/TR/5-9.5/168 d9.19

YEAR	TM LG	W	L	PCT	G	GS	CG-SHO	SV-BS	IP	H	R	HR	HB	BB-IB	SO	ERA	AERA	OAV	OOB	AB-HR-SH	AVG	PB	SUP	APR	DL	PW
1908	NY A	1	2	.333	14	4	4	2	36.1	40	19	0	4	8	11	4.46	56	.292	.349	16	.063	-1*	62	-5		-0.5
1909	NY A	13	15	.464	36	23	21-3	2	243.1	197	84	2	26	81	95	2.40	105	.233	.319	86-0-2	.128	-2	101	7		0.6
1910	NY A	14	14	.500	37	27	20	2	243	219	108	1	18	79	75	3.00	89	.246	.320	79-0-4	.177	-1	104	-8		-1.2
1911	NY A	12	13	.480	31	25	17-1	0	209.2	239	118	6	15	44	71	4.16	86	.286	.333	77-0-2	.156	-4*	85	-8		-1.3
1912	NY A	10	19	.345	39	22	16	3	258	256	121	3	16	59	110	2.86	126	.266	.319	92-0-2	.207	-1	64	17		1.6
1913	NY A	4	5	.444	15	7	1	0	62.1	69	42	1	12	33	11	3.75	80	.297	.412	23	.130	-0	113	-8		-1.1
1914	NY A	8	15	.348	37	23	15	0	216.2	182	75	8	11	44	56	2.37	117	.235	.286	71-0-2	.141	-1*	83	8		0.7
1915	NY A	7	9	.438	21	19	12	0	143.1	164	74	7	12	52	34	3.96	74	.309	.384	51	.137	-2	103	-14		-1.7
Total	8	69	92	.429	221	150	105-4	7	1412.2	1366	641	28	114	400	463	3.12	96	.262	.328	495-0-12	.156	-12	89	-11		-2.9

WARMOTH, CY Wallace Walter B2.2.1893 Bone Gap IL D6.20.1957 Mt.Carmel IL BL/TL/5-11/158 d8.31

YEAR	TM LG	W	L	PCT	G	GS	CG-SHO	SV-BS	IP	H	R	HR	HB	BB-IB	SO	ERA	AERA	OAV	OOB	AB-HR-SH	AVG	PB	SUP	APR	DL	PW
1916	StL N	0	0	—	3	0	0	0	5	12	10	0	1	4	1	14.40	18	.500	.586	2	.000	-0		-6		-0.4
1922	Was A	1	0	1.000	5	1	0	0	19	15	6	0	0	9	8	1.42	272	.205	.293	7	.143	-0	132	4		0.2
1923	Was A	7	5	.583	21	13	3	0	105	103	64	4	1	76	45	4.29	88	.261	.381	36-0-2	.222	2	112	-8		-0.5
Total	8	8	5	.615	29	14	4	0	129	130	80	4	2	89	54	4.26	88	.264	.379	45-0-2	.200	1	114	-10		-0.7

WARNEKE, LON Lonnie "The Arkansas Hummingbird" B3.28.1909 Mt.Ida AR D6.23.1976 Hot Springs AR BR/TR/6-2/185 d4.18 Mil 1944 U7

YEAR	TM LG	W	L	PCT	G	GS	CG-SHO	SV-BS	IP	H	R	HR	HB	BB-IB	SO	ERA	AERA	OAV	OOB	AB-HR-SH	AVG	PB	SUP	APR	DL	PW
1930	Chi N	0	0	—	1	1	0	0	1.1	2	5	0	3	5	0	33.75	14	.400	.700			0		-4		-0.2
1931	Chi N	2	4	.333	20	7	3	0	64.1	67	33	1	3	37	27	3.22	120	.269	.370	19	.263	1	73	2		0.2
1932	†Chi N	22	6	.786	35	32	25-4	0	277	247	84	12	2	64	106	2.37	159	.237	.283	99-0-4	.192	-0	112	45		4.3
1933	Chi N★	18	13	.581	36	34	26-4	1	287.1	262	83	8	3	75	133	2.00	163	.244	.295	100-2-3	.300	10*	88	39		5.8
1934	Chi N★	22	10	.688	43	35	23-3	3	291.1	273	116	16	2	66	143	3.21	121	.244	.287	113-0-2	.195	-1*	115	23		2.2
1935	†Chi N	20	13	.606	42	30	20-1	4	261.2	257	102	19	3	50	120	3.06	128	.257	.294	91-0-7	.220	1*	111	27		3.3
1936	Chi N★	16	13	.552	40	29	13-4	1	240.1	246	108	10	4	76	113	3.45	116	.264	.322	84-1-10	.202	0	109	12		1.3
1937	StL N	18	11	.621	36	33	18-2	0	238.2	280	139	32	0	69	87	4.53	88	.287	.335	80-0-6	.262	4	114	-13		-1.0
1938	StL N	13	8	.619	31	26	12-4	0	197	199	102	14	2	64	89	3.97	100	.256	.314	71-0-3	.324	5	116	1		0.5
1939	StL N☆	13	7	.650	34	21	6-2	0	162	160	73	14	2	49	59	3.78	109	.259	.316	52-0-6	.192	1	126	8		1.0
1940	StL N	16	10	.615	33	31	17-1	0	232	235	103	17	3	47	85	3.14	127	.257	.296	86-1-7	.209	2	129	18		2.1
1941	StL N☆	17	9	.654	37	30	12-4	0	246	227	100	19	3	82	83	3.15	120	.249	.313	77-0-8	.117	-2	101	17		1.9
1942	StL N	6	4	.600	12	12	5	0	82	76	34	8	0	15	31	3.29	104	.238	.272	30-0-3	.333	3	155	2		0.5
	Chi N	5	7	.417	15	12	8-1	2	99	97	33	2	0	21	28	2.27	141	.259	.298	32-0-2	.188	-0	88	9		1.1
	Year	11	11	.500	27	24	13-1	2	181	173	67	10	0	36	59	2.73	121	.249	.286	62-0-5	.258	2	123	11		1.6
1943	Chi N	4	5	.444	21	10	4	0	88.1	82	40	3	0	18	30	3.16	106	.246	.285	26-0-1	.192	1	107	0		0.2
1945	Chi N	0	1	.000	9	1	0	0	14	16	9	0	0	1	6	3.86	95	.267	.279	2	.000	-0	116	-1		-0.1
Total	15	192	121	.613	445	343	192-30	13	2782.1	2726	1164	175	27	739	1140	3.18	119	.255	.304	962-4-62	.223	27	112	185		22.6

WARNER, ED Edward Emory B6.20.1889 Fitchburg MA D2.5.1954 New York NY BR/TL/5-10.5/165 d7.2 Col Brown

YEAR	TM LG	W	L	PCT	G	GS	CG-SHO	SV-BS	IP	H	R	HR	HB	BB-IB	SO	ERA	AERA	OAV	OOB	AB-HR-SH	AVG	PB	SUP	APR	DL	PW
1912	Pit N	1	1	.500	13	3	1	0	35	30	22	1	3	18	13	3.60	91	.242	.328	15	.133	-1	112	-1		-0.1

WARNER, JACK Jack Dyer B7.12.1940 Brandywine WV BR/TR/5-11/195* d4.10

YEAR	TM LG	W	L	PCT	G	GS	CG-SHO	SV-BS	IP	H	R	HR	HB	BB-IB	SO	ERA	AERA	OAV	OOB	AB-HR-SH	AVG	PB	SUP	APR	DL	PW
1962	Chi N	0	0	—	7	0	0	0-0	7	9	7	3	0	0-0	3	7.71	54	.321	.321	0	—	0		-3		-0.1
1963	Chi N	0	1	.000	8	0	0	0	22.2	21	7	1	0	8-2	7	2.78	126	.256	.319	4	.250	0		2		0.1
1964	Chi N	0	0	—	7	0	0	0	9.1	12	3	0	0	4-0	6	2.89	128	.333	.390	0	—	0		1		0.0
1965	Chi N	0	1	.000	11	0	0	0	15.2	22	16	1	0	9-1	7	8.62	43	.355	.431	1	.000	-0		-8		-0.5
Total	4	0	2	.000	33	0	0	0	54.2	64	33	5	0	21-3	23	5.10	72	.308	.366	5	.200	0		-8		-0.4

WARREN, MIKE Michael Bruce B3.26.1961 Inglewood CA BR/TR/6-1/175* [DetA79 12/299] d6.12

YEAR	TM LG	W	L	PCT	G	GS	CG-SHO	SV-BS	IP	H	R	HR	HB	BB-IB	SO	ERA	AERA	OAV	OOB	AB-HR-SH	AVG	PB	SUP	APR	DL	PW
1983	Oak A	5	3	.625	12	9	3-1	0-0	65.2	51	33	4	1	18-1	30	4.11	95	.215	.269	0	—	0	109	-2		-0.2
1984	Oak A	3	6	.333	24	12	0	0-0	90	104	52	11	3	44-1	61	4.90	77	.291	.370	0	—	0	104	-11		-1.0
1985	Oak A	1	4	.200	16	6	0	0-0	49	52	42	13	4	38-0	48	6.61	59	.261	.387	0	—	0	98	-17		-1.5
Total	3	9	13	.409	52	27	3-1	0-0	204.2	207	127	28	8	100-2	139	5.06	76	.261	.361	0	—	0	104	-30		-2.7

WARREN, TOMMY Thomas Gentry B7.5.1917 Tulsa OK D1.2.1968 Tulsa OK BB/TL/6-1/190 d4.18

YEAR	TM LG	W	L	PCT	G	GS	CG-SHO	SV-BS	IP	H	R	HR	HB	BB-IB	SO	ERA	AERA	OAV	OOB	AB-HR-SH	AVG	PB	SUP	APR	DL	PW
1944	Bro N	1	4	.200	22	4	2		68.2	74	52	4	0	40	18	4.98	71	.270	.363	43	.256	2*	100	-14		-0.8

WARTHEN, DAN Daniel Dean B12.1.1952 Omaha NE BB/TL/6-0/200(190-205) [MonN71 2/28] d5.18 C8

YEAR	TM LG	W	L	PCT	G	GS	CG-SHO	SV-BS	IP	H	R	HR	HB	BB-IB	SO	ERA	AERA	OAV	OOB	AB-HR-SH	AVG	PB	SUP	APR	DL	PW
1975	Mon N	8	6	.571	40	18	2	3-0	167.2	130	62	8	1	87-4	128	3.11	124	.217	.315	51-0-4	.118	-2	85	15		1.0
1976	Mon N	2	10	.167	23	16	2-1	0-0	90	76	59	8	2	66-2	67	5.30	71	.232	.361	27-0-1	.000	-3	82	-14		-2.0
1977	Mon N	2	3	.400	12	6	1	0-0	35	33	34	7	0	38-1	26	7.97	48	.262	.430	9-0-1	.111	-0	146	-16		-1.9
	Phi N	0	1	.000	3	0	0	0-0	3.2	4	3	0	0	5-0	1	0.00	—	.267	.450	0	—	0		0		0.0
	Year	2	4	.333	15	6	1	0-0	38.2	37	37	7	0	43-1	27	7.22	54	.262	.432	9-0-1	.111	-0	145	-16		-1.8
1978	Hou N	0	1	.000	5	1	0	0-1	10.2	10	5	3	0	2-0	2	4.22	79	.250	.279	2	.000	-0	27	-1		-0.1
Total	4	12	21	.364	83	41	5-1	3-1	307	253	163	26	3	198-7	224	4.31	89	.228	.344	89-0-6	.079	-6	91	-16		-2.9

WASDIN, JOHN John Truman B8.5.1972 Fort Belvoir VA BR/TR/6-2/193* [OakA93 1/25] d8.24 Col Florida St.

YEAR	TM LG	W	L	PCT	G	GS	CG-SHO	SV-BS	IP	H	R	HR	HB	BB-IB	SO	ERA	AERA	OAV	OOB	AB-HR-SH	AVG	PB	SUP	APR	DL	PW
1995	Oak A	1	1	.500	5	2	0	0-0	17.1	14	9	4	1	3-0	6	4.67	97	.215	.261	0	—	0	93	0		0.0
1996	Oak A	8	7	.533	25	21	1	0-1	131.1	145	96	24	4	50-5	75	5.96	83	.283	.348	0	—	0	104	-16		-1.5
1997	Bos A	4	6	.400	53	7	0	0-2	124.2	121	68	22	3	38-4	84	4.40	106	.251	.306	0	—	0	82	3		0.1

YEAR	TM LG	W	L	PCT	G	GS	CG-SHO	SV-BS	IP	H	R	HR	HB	BB-IB	SO	ERA	AERA	OAV	OOB	AB-HR-SH	AVG	PB	SUP	APR	DL	PW
1998	†Bos A	6	4	.600	47	8	0	0-1	96	111	57	14	2	27-8	59	5.25	90	.288	.333	0	—	0	96	-4		-0.3
1999	†Bos A	8	3	.727	45	0	0	2-3	74.1	66	38	14	0	18-0	57	4.12	121	.236	.280	0	—	0		7	19	0.9
2000	Bos A	1	3	.250	25	1	0	1-1	44.2	48	25	8	2	15-1	36	5.04	100	.273	.328	0	—	0	75	1		0.0
	Col N	0	3	.000	14	3	1	0-0	35.2	42	23	6	3	9-2	35	5.80	100	.302	.353	8-0-1	.250	0	37	1		0.0
2001	Col N	2	1	.667	18	0	0	0-3	24.1	32	19	7	1	8-2	17	7.03	76	.320	.373	3	.333	0		-3		-0.3
	Bal A	1	1	.500	26	0	0	0-2	49.2	54	25	4	5	16-4	47	4.17	103	.277	.341	0	—	0		1		0.0
2003	Tor A	0	1	.000	3	2	0	0-0	5	16	13	2	0	4-0	5	23.40	20	.533	.571	0	—	0	87	-9		-1.3
2004	Tex A	2	4	.333	15	10	0	0-0	65	83	52	18	3	23-2	36	6.78	73	.305	.363	3	.000	-0	117	-12		-1.0
2005	Tex A	3	2	.600	31	6	0	4-2	75.2	77	37	9	1	20-2	44	4.28	107	.261	.308	1	.000	-0	109	3		0.1
Total 10		36	36	.500	307	60	2	7-15	743.2	809	462	128	25	231-30	501	5.26	92	.276	.330	15-0-1	.200	0	98	-28	19	-3.3

WASHBURN, GEORGE
George Edward B10.6.1914 Solon ME D1.5.1979 Baton Rouge LA BL/TR/6-1/175 d5.4

YEAR	TM LG	W	L	PCT	G	GS	CG-SHO	SV-BS	IP	H	R	HR	HB	BB-IB	SO	ERA	AERA	OAV	OOB	AB-HR-SH	AVG	PB	SUP	APR	DL	PW
1941	.NY A	0	1	.000	1	1	0	0	2	4	4	0	0	5	1	13.50	29	.286	.583	1	.000	-0	22	-2		-0.4

WASHBURN, GREG
Gregory James B12.3.1946 Coal City IL BR/TR/6-0/190 [CalA67 S1/19] d6.7 Col Lewis

YEAR	TM LG	W	L	PCT	G	GS	CG-SHO	SV-BS	IP	H	R	HR	HB	BB-IB	SO	ERA	AERA	OAV	OOB	AB-HR-SH	AVG	PB	SUP	APR	DL	PW
1969	Cal A	0	2	.000	8	2	0	0-0	11.1	21	11	0	1	5-0	4	7.94	44	.404	.458	0	—	0	38	-6		-0.9

WASHBURN, JARROD
Jarrod Michael B8.13.1974 LaCrosse WI BL/TL/6-1/198(187-200) [CalA95 2/31] d6.2 Col Wisconsin-Oshkosh

YEAR	TM LG	W	L	PCT	G	GS	CG-SHO	SV-BS	IP	H	R	HR	HB	BB-IB	SO	ERA	AERA	OAV	OOB	AB-HR-SH	AVG	PB	SUP	APR	DL	PW
1998	Ana A	6	3	.667	15	11	0	0-0	74	70	40	11	3	27-1	48	4.62	103	.248	.317	1-0-2	.000	-0	146	2		0.1
1999	Ana A	4	5	.444	16	10	0	0-0	61.2	61	36	6	1	26-0	39	5.25	93	.261	.335	0	—	0	57	-1		-0.2
2000	Ana A	7	2	.778	14	14	0	0-0	84.1	64	38	16	1	37-0	49	3.74	138	.215	.301	3-0-2	.333	1	105	13	74	1.2
2001	Ana A	11	10	.524	30	30	1	0-0	193.1	196	89	25	7	54-4	126	3.77	123	.263	.318	5	.600	1	96	18	15	1.9
2002	†Ana A	18	6	.750	32	32	1	0-0	206	183	75	19	3	59-1	139	3.15	143	.235	.289	5	.200	0	95	32		3.3
2003	Ana A	10	15	.400	32	32	2	0-0	207.1	205	106	34	11	54-4	118	4.43	99	.256	.310	5	.200	0	88	1		0.0
2004	†Ana A	11	8	.579	25	25	1	1-1	149.1	159	81	20	4	40-1	86	4.64	96	.269	.318	5-0-2	.400	1	135	-3	43	-0.2
2005	†LA A	8	8	.500	29	29	1	1-1	177.1	184	66	19	8	51-0	94	3.20	135	.274	.300	4	.000	-0	89	23	18	1.8
Total 8		75	57	.568	193	183	6-2	0-0	1153.1	1122	531	150	38	348-11	699	3.93	116	.255	.313	28-0-6	.286	3	100	85	150	7.9

WASHBURN, LIBE
Libeus B6.16.1874 Lyme NH D3.22.1940 Malone NY BB/TL/5-10/180 d5.30.1902 Col Brown ▲

YEAR	TM LG	W	L	PCT	G	GS	CG-SHO	SV-BS	IP	H	R	HR	HB	BB-IB	SO	ERA	AERA	OAV	OOB	AB-HR-SH	AVG	PB	SUP	APR	DL	PW
1903	Phi N	0	4	.000	4	4	0	0	35	44	23	0	0	11	9	4.37	75	.326	.377	18	.167	-0*	62	-4		-0.4

WASHBURN, RAY
Ray Clark B5.31.1938 Pasco WA BR/TR/6-1/200* d9.20 Col Whitworth

YEAR	TM LG	W	L	PCT	G	GS	CG-SHO	SV-BS	IP	H	R	HR	HB	BB-IB	SO	ERA	AERA	OAV	OOB	AB-HR-SH	AVG	PB	SUP	APR	DL	PW
1961	StL N	1	1	.500	3	2	1	0	20.1	10	4	1	1	7-0	12	1.77	248	.152	.243	8	.125	-1	131	6		0.5
1962	StL N	12	9	.571	34	25	2-1	0	175.2	187	90	25	3	58-2	109	4.10	104	.273	.331	56-0-4	.179	1	102	4		0.5
1963	StL N	5	3	.625	11	11	4-2	0	64.1	50	25	5	1	14-0	47	3.08	115	.212	.259	19-0-4	.053	-1	93	3		0.3
1964	StL N	3	4	.429	15	10	0	2	60	60	29	7	5	17-2	28	4.05	94	.264	.325	15-0-3	.133	-0	67	0	41	0.0
1965	StL N	9	11	.450	28	16	1-1	2	119.1	114	57	15	1	28-7	67	3.62	106	.254	.298	33-0-3	.152	-0	77	1		0.1
1966	StL N	11	9	.550	27	26	4-1	0	170	183	75	15	1	44-5	98	3.76	95	.280	.324	54-1-4	.093	-1	100	-1		-0.2
1967	†StL N	10	7	.588	27	27	3-1	0	186.1	190	78	14	4	42-7	98	3.53	93	.265	.307	66-0-4	.091	-2	106	-3	22	-0.4
1968	†StL N	14	8	.636	31	30	8-4	0	215.1	191	67	9	1	47-7	124	2.26	128	.239	.282	60-0-11	.083	0	118	14		1.4
1969	StL N	3	8	.273	28	16	2	1-0	132.1	133	59	9	1	49-9	80	3.06	117	.261	.324	37-0-1	.081	-2	80	4		0.1
1970	†Cin N	4	4	.500	35	3	0	0-0	66.1	90	61	7	0	48-9	37	6.92	58	.324	.421	13-0-1	.000	-0	81	-22		-2.4
Total 6		72	64	.529	239	166	25-10	5	1210	1208	545	107	18	354-48	700	3.53	101	.261	.315	361-1-35	.105	-7	97	6	63	-0.1

WASHER, BUCK
William B10.11.1882 Akron OH D12.8.1955 Akron OH BR/TR/5-10/175 d4.25 Col West Virginia

YEAR	TM LG	W	L	PCT	G	GS	CG-SHO	SV-BS	IP	H	R	HR	HB	BB-IB	SO	ERA	AERA	OAV	OOB	AB-HR-SH	AVG	PB	SUP	APR	DL	PW
1905	Phi N	0	0	—	1	0	0	0	3	4	2	0	0	5	0	6.00	49	.333	.529	1	.000	-0		-1		-0.1

WASLEWSKI, GARY
Gary Lee B7.21.1941 Meriden CT BR/TR/6-4/195* d6.11 Col Connecticut

YEAR	TM LG	W	L	PCT	G	GS	CG-SHO	SV-BS	IP	H	R	HR	HB	BB-IB	SO	ERA	AERA	OAV	OOB	AB-HR-SH	AVG	PB	SUP	APR	DL	PW
1967	†Bos A	2	2	.500	12	8	0	0	42	34	18	3	1	20-2	20	3.21	108	.225	.314	11-0-1	.091	-1	94	1		0.0
1968	Bos A	4	7	.364	34	11	2	2	105.1	108	50	9	6	40-9	59	3.67	86	.269	.341	26-0-2	.038	-2*	83	-6		-0.8
1969	StL N	2	0	.000	12	0	0	1-0	20.2	19	9	3	1	8-4	16	3.92	91	.244	.318	1	.000	-0		0		0.0
	Mon N	3	7	.300	30	14	3-1	1-0	109.1	102	53	5	8	63-5	63	3.29	112	.252	.362	30	.033	-2	67	2		0.0
	Year	3	9	.250	42	14	3-1	2-0	130	121	62	8	9	71-9	79	3.39	108	.251	.355	31	.032	-2	67	1		0.0
1970	Mon N	0	2	.000	6	4	0	0-1	24.2	23	14	3	0	15-4	19	5.11	81	.247	.352	6-0-1	.000	-0	59	-2		-0.1
	NY A	2	2	.500	26	5	0	0-0	55	42	20	4	4	27-4	27	3.11	115	.219	.323	10-0-1	.100	-1	70	4		0.2
1971	NY A	0	1	.000	24	0	0	1-0	35.2	28	15	2	1	16-2	17	3.28	100	.214	.302	1	.000	-0		0	57	0.0
1972	Oak A	0	3	.000	8	0	0	0-0	17.2	12	5	3	0	8-1	8	2.04	140	.190	.282	3	.000	-0		1		0.2
Total 6		11	26	.297	152	42	5-1	5-1	410.1	368	184	32	21	197-31	229	3.44	101	.243	.336	88-0-5	.045	-6	77	0	57	-0.5

WATERBURY, STEVE
Steven Craig B4.6.1952 Carbondale IL BR/TR/6-5/190 d9.14

YEAR	TM LG	W	L	PCT	G	GS	CG-SHO	SV-BS	IP	H	R	HR	HB	BB-IB	SO	ERA	AERA	OAV	OOB	AB-HR-SH	AVG	PB	SUP	APR	DL	PW
1976	StL N	0	0	—	5	0	0	0	6	7	4	0	0	3-0	4	6.00	60	.304	.385	0		0		-1		-0.1

WATERS, FRED
Fred Warren B2.2.1927 Benton MS D8.28.1989 Pensacola FL BL/TL/5-11/185* d9.20 Col Southern Mississippi

YEAR	TM LG	W	L	PCT	G	GS	CG-SHO	SV-BS	IP	H	R	HR	HB	BB-IB	SO	ERA	AERA	OAV	OOB	AB-HR-SH	AVG	PB	SUP	APR	DL	PW
1955	Pit N	0	0	—	2	0	0	0	5	7	2	1	0	2-0	0	3.60	114	.318	.375	1	.000	-0		0		0.0
1956	Pit N	2	2	.500	23	5	1	0	51	48	18	3	1	30-1	14	2.82	134	.258	.357	20	.050	-1	112	5		0.2
Total 2		2	2	.500	25	5	1	0	56	55	20	4	1	32-1	14	2.89	131	.264	.359	21	.048	-1	112	5		0.2

WATKINS, BOB
Robert Cecil B3.12.1948 San Francisco CA BR/TR/6-1/170 [HouN66 22/423] d9.6

YEAR	TM LG	W	L	PCT	G	GS	CG-SHO	SV-BS	IP	H	R	HR	HB	BB-IB	SO	ERA	AERA	OAV	OOB	AB-HR-SH	AVG	PB	SUP	APR	DL	PW
1969	Hou N	0	0	—	5	0	0	0-0	15.2	13	9	1	0	13-0	11	5.17	69	.241	.382	2	.000	-0		-2		-0.2

WATKINS, SCOTT
Scott Allen B5.15.1970 Tulsa OK BL/TL/6-3/180 [MinA92 23/654] d8.1 Col Oklahoma St.

YEAR	TM LG	W	L	PCT	G	GS	CG-SHO	SV-BS	IP	H	R	HR	HB	BB-IB	SO	ERA	AERA	OAV	OOB	AB-HR-SH	AVG	PB	SUP	APR	DL	PW
1995	Min A	0	0	—	5	0	0	0-0	21.2	22	14	5	0	14-0	11	5.40	89	.278	.355	0	—	0		-1		-0.1

WATKINS, STEVE
Stephen Douglas B7.19.1978 Lubbock TX BR/TR/6-4/190 [SDN98 16/472] d8.21 Col Lubbock Christian/Texas Tech

YEAR	TM LG	W	L	PCT	G	GS	CG-SHO	SV-BS	IP	H	R	HR	HB	BB-IB	SO	ERA	AERA	OAV	OOB	AB-HR-SH	AVG	PB	SUP	APR	DL	PW
2004	SD N	0	0	—	11	0	0	0-0	14.1	17	10	3	2	4-0	7	6.28	63	.293	.359	0	—	0		-4		-0.2

WATSON, ALLEN
Allen Kenneth B11.18.1970 Jamaica NY BL/TL/6-3/195(190-212) [StLN91 1/21] d7.8 Col New York Tech [DL 2001 NY A 190]

YEAR	TM LG	W	L	PCT	G	GS	CG-SHO	SV-BS	IP	H	R	HR	HB	BB-IB	SO	ERA	AERA	OAV	OOB	AB-HR-SH	AVG	PB	SUP	APR	DL	PW
1993	StL N	6	7	.462	16	15	0	0-1	86	90	53	11	3	28-2	49	4.60	88	.271	.330	26-0-1	.231	2	119	-7		-0.8
1994	StL N	6	5	.545	22	22	0	0-0	115.2	130	73	15	8	53-0	74	5.52	77	.286	.370	38-0-7	.158	1	121	-15		-1.2
1995	StL N	7	9	.438	21	19	0	0-0	114.1	126	68	17	5	41-0	49	4.96	86	.285	.352	36-0-3	.417	6	78	-7	31	-1.3
1996	SF N	8	12	.400	29	29	2	0-0	185.2	189	105	28	5	69-2	128	4.61	90	.273	.339	65-0-2	.231	4*	90	-8	23	-0.4
1997	Ana A	12	12	.500	35	34	0	0-0	199	220	121	37	8	73-0	141	4.93	94	.279	.344	0	—	0	104	-8		-0.8
1998	Ana A	7	7	.462	28	14	1	0-0	92.1	122	67	20	3	34-0	64	6.04	79	.323	.378	0	—	0	87	-13	50	-1.5
1999	NY N	2	2	.500	14	4	0	1-0	39.2	36	18	5	1	22-3	32	4.08	106	.252	.347	10	.300	1	85	1		0.2
	Sea A	0	1	.000	3	0	0	0-0	3	6	9	5	0	3-0	2	12.00	40	.400	.474	0	—	0		-5		-0.8
	†NY A	4	0	1.000	21	0	0	0-1	34.1	33	11	9	0	10-0	30	2.10	225	.236	.292	0	—	0		11		1.1
	Year	4	1	.800	24	0	0	0-1	37.1	36	17	8	0	13-0	32	2.89	164	.254	.314	0	—	0		6		0.3
2000	NY A	0	0	—	17	0	0	0-0	22	30	25	6	2	18-0	29	10.23	47	.330	.442	0	—	0		-13	118	-0.6
Total 8		51	55	.481	206	137	3	1-2	892	979	547	139	35	351-7	589	5.03	87	.283	.352	175-0-13	.257	14	99	-64	412	-5.0

WATSON, DOC
Charles John B1.30.1885 Kensington OH D12.30.1949 San Diego CA BR/TL/6-0/170 d9.3

YEAR	TM LG	W	L	PCT	G	GS	CG-SHO	SV-BS	IP	H	R	HR	HB	BB-IB	SO	ERA	AERA	OAV	OOB	AB-HR-SH	AVG	PB	SUP	APR	DL	PW
1913	Chi N	1	0	1.000	7	0	0	0	9	8	2	0	1	6	1	1.00	318	.242	.375	2-0-1	.000	0	166	2		0.2
1914	Chi F	9	8	.529	26	18	10-3	1	172	145	50	2	4	49	69	2.04	130	.236	.295	54-0-6	.093	-5	95	14		0.7
	StL F	3	4	.429	9	7	4-2	0	56	41	18	1	4	24	18	1.93	158	.211	.311	16-0-1	.125	-1	42	6		0.5
	Year	12	12	.500	35	25	14-5	1	228	186	68	3	7	73	87	2.01	137	.230	.299	70-0-7	.100	-6	79	20		1.2
1915	StL F	9	9	.500	33	20	6	0	135.2	132	66	1	4	58	45	3.98	72	.273	.355	40-0-2	.125	-3	77	-13		-2.2
Total 3		22	21	.512	69	46	21-5	1	372.2	326	136	4	12	137	133	2.70	144	.246	.322	112-0-10	.107	-9	80	9		-0.8

WATSON, MULE
John Reeves B10.15.1896 Homer LA D8.25.1949 Shreveport LA BR/TR/6-1.5/185 d7.4 Col Baylor

YEAR	TM LG	W	L	PCT	G	GS	CG-SHO	SV-BS	IP	H	R	HR	HB	BB-IB	SO	ERA	AERA	OAV	OOB	AB-HR-SH	AVG	PB	SUP	APR	DL	PW
1918	Phi A	7	10	.412	21	19	11-3	0	141.2	139	74	0	2	44	33	3.37	87	.288	.350	47-0-1	.128	-3	104	-8		-1.4
1919	Phi A	0	1	.000	4	2	0	0	14.1	17	11	2	0	7	6	6.91	50	.309	.387	6	.000	-1	103	-4		-0.3
1920	Phi N	0	0	—	1	0	0	0	3	6	1	0	0	0	0	—	—	.000	.000			-0		-1		0.0
	Pit N	0	0	—	5	0	0	0	11.1	15	11	2	0	7	1	8.74	37	.326	.415	3	.000	-0		-6		-0.3
	Bos N	5	4	.556	12	10	4-2	0	71.2	79	33	0	1	17	16	3.77	81	.298	.343	23-0-1	.130	-1	67	-4		-0.7
	Year	5	4	.556	18	10	4-2	0	86	94	44	2	1	24	17	4.29	72	.294	.345	27-0-1	.111	-2	67	-9		-1.0
1921	Bos N	14	13	.519	44	31	15-1	2	259.1	269	128	11	7	57	48	3.85	95	.270	.314	87-0-6	.138	-4	105	-6		-1.0
1922	Bos N	8	14	.364	41	27	8-1	1	201	262	140	9	2	66	53	4.70	85	.317	.366	66-0-3	.197	-0	79	-20		-1.8
1923	Bos N	5	2	.333	11	4	1	0	31.1	42	26	2	2	9	10	5.17	77	.339	.431	8-0-1	.250	-0	103	-6		-0.5

YEAR	TM LG	W	L	PCT	G	GS	CG-SHO	SV-BS	IP	H	R	HR	HB	BB-IB	SO	ERA	AERA	OAV	OOB	AB-HR-SH	AVG	PB	SUP	APR	DL	PW
	†NY N	8	5	.615	17	15	8	0	108.1	117	43	11	1	21	26	3.41	112	.280	.316	46-0-1	.174	-1	92	7		0.6
	Year	9	7	.563	28	19	9	1	139.2	159	69	13	1	41	36	3.80	101	.293	.344	54-0-2	.185	-1	94	0		0.1
1924	†NY N	7	4	.636	22	16	6-1	0	99.2	122	54	7	1	24	18	3.79	97	.303	.343	35-2-0	.257	4	110	-4		-0.1
Total	7	50	53	.485	178	124	53-8	4	941.2	1062	520	44	17	256	208	4.03	89	.293	.342	322-2-13	.165	-8	95	-50		-5.5

WATSON, MARK Mark Bradford B1.23.1974 Atlanta GA BR/TL/6-4/215* d5.19 Col Georgia

YEAR	TM LG	W	L	PCT	G	GS	CG-SHO	SV-BS	IP	H	R	HR	HB	BB-IB	SO	ERA	AERA	OAV	OOB	AB-HR-SH	AVG	PB	SUP	APR	DL	PW
2000	Cle A	0	1	.000	6	0	0	0-0	6.1	12	7	1	1	2-0	4	8.53	59	.400	.455	0	—	0		-3		-0.4
2002	Sea A	1	0	1.000	3	0	0	0-0	4	8	8	1	0	4-0	1	18.00	24	.421	.500	0	—	0		-6		-1.0
2003	Cin N	0	0	—	2	0	0	0-0	2	2	1	0	0	1-0	2	4.50	93	.250	.333	0	—	0		0	38	0.0
Total	3	1	1	.500	11	0	0	0-0	12.1	22	16	1	1	7-0	7	10.95	42	.386	.455	0	—	0		-9	38	-1.4

WATSON, MILT Milton Wilson "Mule" B1.10.1890 Flovilla GA D4.10.1962 Pine Bluff AR BR/TR/6-1/180 d7.26

YEAR	TM LG	W	L	PCT	G	GS	CG-SHO	SV-BS	IP	H	R	HR	HB	BB-IB	SO	ERA	AERA	OAV	OOB	AB-HR-SH	AVG	PB	SUP	APR	DL	PW
1916	StL N	4	6	.400	18	13	5-2	0	103	109	51	3	4	33	27	3.06	86	.283	.346	32-0-1	.219	0	83	-6		-0.6
1917	StL N	10	13	.435	41	20	5-3	0	161.1	149	74	3	9	51	45	3.51	77	.252	.321	51	.098	-4	74	-14		-2.3
1918	Phi N	5	7	.417	23	11	6	0	112.2	126	51	2	3	36	29	3.43	87	.293	.350	40-0-1	.075	-4	99	-4		-0.9
1919	Phi N	2	4	.333	8	4	3	0	47	51	30	2	1	19	12	5.17	62	.282	.356	16	.063	-2	74	-8		-1.1
Total	4	21	30	.412	90	48	19-5	0	424	435	206	9	17	139	113	3.57	79	.274	.339	139-0-2	.115	-9	82	-32		-4.9

WATSON, MOTHER Walter L. B1.27.1865 Middleport OH D11.23.1898 Middleport OH 5-9/145 d5.19

YEAR	TM LG	W	L	PCT	G	GS	CG-SHO	SV-BS	IP	H	R	HR	HB	BB-IB	SO	ERA	AERA	OAV	OOB	AB-HR-SH	AVG	PB	SUP	APR	DL	PW
1887	Cin AA	0	1	.000	2	2	1	0	14	22	18	0	0	6	1	5.79	75	.328	.384	8	.125	-0	139	-3		-0.2

WATT, EDDIE Eddie Dean B4.4.1941 Lamoni IA BR/TR/5-10/197(185-197) d4.12 Col Northern Iowa

YEAR	TM LG	W	L	PCT	G	GS	CG-SHO	SV-BS	IP	H	R	HR	HB	BB-IB	SO	ERA	AERA	OAV	OOB	AB-HR-SH	AVG	PB	SUP	APR	DL	PW
1966	Bal A	9	7	.563	43	13	1	4	145.2	123	67	11	5	44-1	102	3.83	87	.230	.292	46-2-2	.304	6	126	-7		-0.3
1967	Bal A	3	5	.375	49	0	0	8	103.2	67	26	5	3	37-6	93	2.26	140	.183	.262	22-1-2	.182	2		12		1.3
1968	Bal A	5	5	.500	59	0	0	11	83.1	63	32	7	4	35-7	72	2.27	129	.209	.293	8	.000	-0		3		0.4
1969	†Bal A	5	2	.714	56	0	0	16-5	71	49	18	3	2	26-5	46	1.65	218	.194	.270	8	.000	-0		14		2.0
1970	†Bal A	7	7	.500	53	0	0	12-7	55.1	44	20	3	5	29-5	33	3.25	113	.239	.355	8	.125	-0		4		0.7
1971	†Bal A	3	1	.750	35	0	0	11-1	39.2	39	12	1	0	8-1	26	1.82	188	.260	.296	5	.000	-0		6	22	0.9
1972	Bal A	2	3	.400	38	0	0	7-3	45.2	30	12	2	2	20-6	23	2.17	144	.191	.286	2	.000	-0		5		0.7
1973	†Bal A	3	4	.429	30	0	0	5-2	71	62	26	8	2	21-5	38	3.30	115	.235	.296	0	—	-0		5		0.5
1974	Phi N	1	1	.500	42	0	0	6-0	38.1	39	20	3	0	26-8	23	3.99	95	.275	.385	1	.000	-0		-1		-0.1
1975	Chi N	0	1	.000	6	0	0	0-1	6	14	11	0	1	8-4	6	13.50	29	.452	.575	0	—	0		-6		-0.9
Total	10	38	36	.514	411	13	1	80-19	659.2	530	244	37	24	254-48	462	2.91	116	.222	.301	100-3-4	.190	6	126	35	22	5.2

WATT, FRANK Frank Marion "Kilo" B12.15.1902 Washington DC D8.31.1956 Washington DC BR/TR/6-1/205 d4.14 b-Allie

YEAR	TM LG	W	L	PCT	G	GS	CG-SHO	SV-BS	IP	H	R	HR	HB	BB-IB	SO	ERA	AERA	OAV	OOB	AB-HR-SH	AVG	PB	SUP	APR	DL	PW
1931	Phi N	5	5	.500	38	12	5	2	122.2	147	81	5	3	49	25	4.84	88	.296	.362	39	.205	0	101	-8		-0.7

WAUGH, JIM James Elden B11.25.1933 Lancaster OH BR/TR/6-3/185* d4.19

YEAR	TM LG	W	L	PCT	G	GS	CG-SHO	SV-BS	IP	H	R	HR	HB	BB-IB	SO	ERA	AERA	OAV	OOB	AB-HR-SH	AVG	PB	SUP	APR	DL	PW
1952	Pit N	1	6	.143	17	7	1	0	52.1	61	43	4	2	32	18	6.36	63	.285	.383	10-0-1	.100	-0	86	-13		-1.6
1953	Pit N	4	5	.444	29	11	1	0	90.1	108	70	21	0	56	23	6.48	69	.295	.389	22-0-1	.227	0	94	-18		-1.5
Total	2	5	11	.313	46	18	2	0	142.2	169	113	25	2	88	41	6.43	67	.291	.387	32-0-2	.188	0	91	-31		-3.1

WAYENBERG, FRANK Frank B8.27.1898 Franklin KS D4.16.1975 Zanesville OH BR/TR/6-0.5/172 d8.25

YEAR	TM LG	W	L	PCT	G	GS	CG-SHO	SV-BS	IP	H	R	HR	HB	BB-IB	SO	ERA	AERA	OAV	OOB	AB-HR-SH	AVG	PB	SUP	APR	DL	PW
1924	Cle A	0	0	—	2	1	0	0	6.2	7	4	0	1	5	3	5.40	79	.259	.394	2	.500	0	118	0		0.0

WAYNE, GARY Gary Anthony B11.30.1962 Dearborn MI BL/TL/6-3/192(185-200) [MonN84 4/93] d4.7 Col Michigan

YEAR	TM LG	W	L	PCT	G	GS	CG-SHO	SV-BS	IP	H	R	HR	HB	BB-IB	SO	ERA	AERA	OAV	OOB	AB-HR-SH	AVG	PB	SUP	APR	DL	PW
1989	Min A	3	4	.429	60	0	0	1-2	71	55	28	4	1	36-4	41	3.30	126	.212	.309	0	—	0		6		0.6
1990	Min A	1	1	.500	38	0	0	1-1	38.2	38	19	2	1	13-0	28	4.19	99	.255	.315	0	—	0		0		0.0
1991	Min A	1	0	1.000	8	0	0	1-0	12.1	11	7	1	1	4-0	7	5.11	84	.244	.314	0	—	0		-1		-0.1
1992	Min A	3	3	.500	41	0	0	0-3	48	46	18	2	3	19-5	29	2.63	156	.260	.337	0	—	0		6		0.8
1993	Col N	5	3	.625	65	0	0	1-2	62.1	68	40	8	1	26-8	49	5.05	95	.276	.339	1	1.000	0		-2		-0.2
1994	LA N	1	3	.250	19	0	0	0-2	17.1	19	13	2	3	6-2	10	4.67	85	.279	.359	1	.000	-0		-3		-0.6
Total	6	14	14	.500	231	0	0	4-10	249.2	237	125	22	10	104-19	164	3.93	109	.251	.327	2	.500	0		6		0.5

WAYNE, JUSTIN Justin Morgan B4.16.1979 Honolulu HI BR/TR/6-3/200* [MonN00 1/5] d9.3 Col Stanford

YEAR	TM LG	W	L	PCT	G	GS	CG-SHO	SV-BS	IP	H	R	HR	HB	BB-IB	SO	ERA	AERA	OAV	OOB	AB-HR-SH	AVG	PB	SUP	APR	DL	PW
2002	Fla N	2	3	.400	5	5	0	0-0	23.2	22	16	3	0	13-0	16	5.32	74	.244	.333	7-0-1	.000	-0	94	-4		-0.8
2003	Fla N	0	2	.000	2	2	0	0-0	5.1	9	7	1	1	5-0	1	11.81	35	.375	.484	2	.000	-0	34	-5	13	-0.7
2004	Fla N	3	3	.500	19	1	0	0-2	32.2	35	24	6	2	18-1	20	5.79	71	.282	.374	3-0-1	.000	-0	90	-7	15	-1.2
Total	3	5	8	.385	26	8	0	0-2	61.2	66	47	10	3	36-1	37	6.13	66	.277	.371	12-0-2	.000	-1	77	-16	28	-2.7

WEAFER, KEN Kenneth Albert "Al" B2.6.1913 Woburn MA D6.4.2005 Guilderland NY BR/TR/6-0.5/183 d5.29 Col Duke

YEAR	TM LG	W	L	PCT	G	GS	CG-SHO	SV-BS	IP	H	R	HR	HB	BB-IB	SO	ERA	AERA	OAV	OOB	AB-HR-SH	AVG	PB	SUP	APR	DL	PW
1936	Bos N	0	0	—	1	0	0	3	6	4	1	0	3	1	12.00	32	.375	.474	1	.000	-0		-3		-0.1

WEATHERS, DAVID John David B9.25.1969 Lawrenceburg TN BR/TR/6-3/220(205-233) [TorA88 3/82] d8.2 Col Motlow St. (TN) CC

YEAR	TM LG	W	L	PCT	G	GS	CG-SHO	SV-BS	IP	H	R	HR	HB	BB-IB	SO	ERA	AERA	OAV	OOB	AB-HR-SH	AVG	PB	SUP	APR	DL	PW
1991	Tor A	1	0	1.000	15	0	0	0-0	14.2	15	9	1	2	17-3	13	4.91	86	.263	.442	0	—	0		-1		-0.1
1992	Tor A	0	0	—	2	0	0	0-0	3.1	5	3	1	0	2-0	3	8.10	51	.385	.467	0	—	0		-1		-0.1
1993	Fla N	2	3	.400	14	6	0	0-0	45.2	57	26	3	1	13-1	34	5.12	85	.306	.355	10-0-3	.100	-1	55	-3		-0.3
1994	Fla N	8	12	.400	24	24	0	0-0	135	166	87	13	4	59-9	72	5.27	84	.306	.376	44-0-4	.068	-2*	86	-11		-1.6
1995	Fla N	4	5	.444	28	15	0	0-0	90.1	104	68	8	5	52-3	60	5.98	72	.295	.391	26-0-5	.154	-1	122	-17	17	-1.6
1996	Fla N	2	2	.500	31	8	0	0-0	71.1	85	41	7	4	28-4	40	4.54	91	.302	.373	19-1-0	.158	1*	120	-2		-0.1
	†NY A	0	2	.000	11	4	0	0-0	17.1	23	19	1	2	14-1	13	9.35	53	.315	.433	0	—	0	154	-9		-0.8
1997	NY A	0	1	.000	10	0	0	0-1	9	15	10	1	0	7-0	4	10.00	45	.375	.468	0	—	0	39	-5		-0.5
	Cle A	1	2	.333	9	1	0	0-1	16.2	23	14	2	1	8-0	14	7.56	62	.343	.416	0	—	0	40	-10		-0.7
	Year	1	3	.250	19	1	0	0-1	25.2	38	24	3	1	15-0	18	8.42	55	.355	.435	0	—	0				-1.2
1998	Cin N	4	3	.333	16	9	0	0-0	62.1	86	47	3	1	27-2	51	6.21	69	.330	.393	15-1-3	.067	0	117	-14		-1.1
	Mil N	2	2	.500	28	0	0	0-1	47.2	44	22	3	2	14-1	43	3.21	135	.246	.306	8-0-1	.125	-0		4		0.4
	Year	6	5	.545	44	9	0	0-1	110	130	69	6	3	41-3	94	4.91	88	.295	.358	23-1-4	.087	0	116	-9		-0.7
1999	Mil N	7	4	.636	63	0	0	2-4	93	102	49	14	2	38-3	74	4.65	99	.279	.346	7	.143	0		1		0.1
2000	Mil N	3	5	.375	69	0	0	1-6	76.1	73	29	7	2	32-8	50	3.07	151	.260	.339	1	.000	-0		13	19	1.1
2001	Mil N	3	4	.429	52	0	0	4-3	57.2	37	14	3	2	25-7	46	2.03	212	.188	.284	1	.000	0		15		1.8
	Chi N	1	1	.500	28	0	0	0-3	28.1	28	10	3	1	9-1	20	3.18	132	.269	.328	0	—	0		4		0.2
	Year	4	5	.444	80	0	0	4-6	86	65	24	6	3	34-8	66	2.41	177	.216	.299	1	.000	0		19		2.0
2002	NY N	6	3	.667	71	0	0	0-5	77.1	69	30	6	3	36-7	61	2.91	136	.245	.332	1	.000	-0		8		0.9
2003	NY N	1	6	.143	77	0	0	7-2	87.2	87	33	6	6	40-6	75	3.08	136	.264	.354	3	.000	-0		11		0.9
2004	NY N	5	3	.625	32	0	0	0-1	33.2	41	19	5	2	15-0	25	4.28	100	.304	.377	0	—	0		-1		-0.1
	Hou N	1	4	.200	26	0	0	0-3	32	31	20	5	3	13-1	26	4.78	91	.261	.348	0	—	0		-2		-0.4
	Fla N	1	0	1.000	8	2	0	0-0	16.2	13	5	2	0	7-1	10	2.70	152	.232	.317	3	.000	-0	79	-3		0.1
	Year	7	7	.500	66	2	0	0-4	82.1	85	44	12	5	35-2	61	4.15	103	.274	.355	3	.000	-0	76	1		-0.4
2005	Cin N	7	4	.636	73	0	0	15-4	77.2	71	36	7	2	29-2	61	3.94	106	.241	.312	0	—	0		2		0.3
Total	15	59	66	.472	687	69	0	29-33	1093.2	1175	591	101	45	485-60	795	4.43	98	.279	.357	138-2-16	.101	-3	104	-12	36	-1.1

WEAVER, FLOYD David Floyd B5.12.1941 Ben Franklin TX BR/TR/6-4/195* d9.30 Col Paris (TX) JC

YEAR	TM LG	W	L	PCT	G	GS	CG-SHO	SV-BS	IP	H	R	HR	HB	BB-IB	SO	ERA	AERA	OAV	OOB	AB-HR-SH	AVG	PB	SUP	APR	DL	PW
1962	Cle A	1	0	1.000	1	1	0	0	5	3	1	1	0	0-0	8	1.80	215	.167	.167	2	.500	0	138	1		0.3
1965	Cle A	2	2	.500	32	1	0	0	61.1	61	40	10	5	24-3	37	5.43	64	.265	.344	11	.091	0	277	-12		-0.8
1970	Chi A	1	2	.333	31	3	0	0-0	61.2	52	33	7	2	31-5	51	4.38	89	.233	.328	7-0-1	.000	-1	115	-3		-0.3
1971	Mil A	0	1	.000	21	0	0	0-0	27.1	33	22	3	1	18-6	12	7.24	48	.320	.416	0-0-1	—	0		-10		-0.5
Total	4	4	5	.444	85	5	0	1-0	155.1	149	96	21	8	73-14	108	5.21	70	.260	.346	20-0-3	.100	-1	155	-24		-1.3

WEAVER, HARRY Harry Abraham B2.26.1892 Clarendon PA D5.30.1983 Rochester NY BR/TR/5-11/160 d9.18 Mil 1918

YEAR	TM LG	W	L	PCT	G	GS	CG-SHO	SV-BS	IP	H	R	HR	HB	BB-IB	SO	ERA	AERA	OAV	OOB	AB-HR-SH	AVG	PB	SUP	APR	DL	PW
1915	Phi N	0	2	.000	2	2	2	0	18	18	10	1	1	10	1	3.00	98	.290	.397	6	.167	0	50	-1		0.0
1916	Phi N	0	0	—	3	0	0	0	8	14	10	0	0	5	2	10.13	28	.424	.500	2	.500	0		-6		-0.3
1917	Chi N	1	1	.500	4	2	1-1	0	19.2	17	10	0	0	7	8	2.75	106	.230	.296	5	.200	-0	39	0		0.0
1918	Chi N	2	2	.500	8	3	1-1	0	32.2	27	13	1	0	7	9	2.20	126	.227	.270	8	.250	0	90	1		0.2
1919	Chi N	0	1	.000	2	1	0	1	3.1	6	7	0	1	2	1	10.80	27	.375	.474	1	.000	-0	28	-4		-0.7
Total	5	3	6	.333	19	8	4-2	1	81.2	82	50	2	2	31	21	3.64	79	.270	.341	22	.227	0	59	-10		-0.8

YEAR	TM LG	W	L	PCT	G	GS	CG-SHO	SV-BS	IP	H	R	HR	HB	BB-IB	SO	ERA	AERA	OAV	OOB	AB-HR-SH	AVG	PB	SUP	APR	DL	PW

WEAVER, JIM James Brian "Fluff" B2.19.1939 Lancaster PA BL/TL/6-0/178* d8.13

1967	Cal A	3	0	1.000	13	2	0	0	30.1	26	11	2	1	9-2	20	2.67	118	.232	.293	6-0-1	.000	-1	83	1		0.2
1968	Cal A	0	1	.000	14	0	0	0	22.2	22	7	4	0	10-2	8	2.38	122	.259	.337	1	.000	-0		1		0.0
Total	2	3	1	.750	27	2	0	0	53	48	18	6	1	19-4	28	2.55	120	.244	.312	7-0-1	.000	-1	83	2		0.2

WEAVER, JIM James Dement "Big Jim" B11.25.1903 Obion Co. TN D12.12.1983 Lakeland FL BR/TR/6-6/230 d8.27 Col Western Kentucky

1928	Was A	0	0	—	3	0	0	0	6	7	2	1	1	6	2	1.50	267	.143	.429	1	.000	-0		1		0.0
1931	NY A	2	1	.667	17	5	2	0	57.2	66	37	1	1	29	28	5.31	75	.280	.361	20-0-4	.050	-3	256	-8		-0.6
1934	StL A	2	0	1.000	5	5	2	0	19.2	17	14	3	0	20	11	6.41	78	.236	.402	7	.143	-0	122	-2		-0.1
	Chi N	11	9	.550	27	20	8-1	0	159	163	77	5	4	54	98	3.91	99	.263	.326	52-0-4	.058	-5	94	0		-0.6
1935	Pit N	14	8	.636	33	22	11-4	0	176.1	177	85	9	2	58	87	3.42	120	.254	.313	56-0-7	.071	-4	100	13		1.0
1936	Pit N	14	8	.636	38	31	11-1	0	225.2	239	125	12	1	74	108	4.31	94	.272	.329	79-0-6	.101	-5	111	-5		-1.0
1937	Pit N	8	5	.615	32	9	2-1	0	109.2	106	49	2	0	31	44	3.20	121	.255	.307	27-0-2	.148	-5	99	7		0.7
1938	StL A	0	1	.000	1	1	0	0	7	9	7	0	0	9	4	9.00	55	.321	.486	2	.000	-0		-3		-0.3
	Cin N	6	4	.600	30	15	2	3	129.1	109	58	6	1	54	64	3.13	117	.227	.306	44-0-4	.205	0	114	5		0.4
1939	Cin N	0	0	—	3	0	0	0	3	3	1	0	1	1	3.00	128	.250	.308	1	.000	-0		0		0.0
Total	8	57	36	.613	189	108	38-7	3	893.1	891	455	38	10	336	449	3.88	102	.258	.326	289-0-27	.104	-17	112	8		-0.5

WEAVER, ERIC James Eric B8.4.1973 Springfield IL BR/TR/6-5/230* d5.30

1998	LA N	2	0	1.000	7	0	0	0-0	9.2	5	1	1	0	6-0	5	0.93	433	.179	.324	1	.000	-0		4		0.7
1999	Sea A	0	1	.000	8	0	0	0-1	9.1	14	12	2	0	8-1	14	10.61	45	.318	.423	0	—	0		-6	141	-0.5
2000	Ana A	0	2	.000	17	0	0	0-1	18.1	20	16	5	0	16-1	8	6.87	75	.267	.391	0	—	0		-4		-0.3
Total	3	2	3	.400	32	0	0	0-2	37.1	39	29	8	0	30-2	27	6.27	76	.265	.388	1	.000	-0		-6	141	-0.1

WEAVER, JEFF Jeffrey Charles B8.22.1976 Northridge CA BR/TR/6-5/200* [DetA98 1/14] d4.14 Col Cal St.-Fresno

1999	Det A	9	12	.429	30	29	0	0-0	163.2	176	104	27	17	56-2	114	5.55	90	.278	.350	4-0-1	.500	1*	90	-8		-0.8
2000	Det A	11	15	.423	31	30	2	0-0	200	205	102	26	15	52-2	136	4.32	114	.266	.322	3	.000	-0	80	14		1.6
2001	Det A	13	16	.448	33	33	5	0-0	229.1	235	116	19	14	68-4	152	4.08	108	.266	.326	5-0-1	.000	-0	92	8		0.9
2002	Det A	8	8	.429	17	17	3-3	0-0	121.2	112	50	4	8	33-1	75	3.18	138	.243	.304	7	.286		65	16		1.8
	†NY A	5	3	.625	15	8	0	2-0	78	81	38	12	3	15-3	57	4.04	107	.260	.300	0	—	0	134	3		0.3
	Year	11	11	.500	32	25	3-3	2-0	199.2	193	88	16	11	48-4	132	3.52	124	.250	.302	7	.286		87	18		2.1
2003	†NY A	7	9	.438	32	24	0	0-0	159.1	211	113	16	11	47-2	93	5.99	73	.320	.371	0	—	0	104	-28		-2.4
2004	†LA N	13	13	.500	34	34	0	0-0	220	219	103	19	14	67-9	153	4.01	103	.260	.323	70-0-7	.214	3*	106	4		0.6
2005	LA N	14	11	.560	34	34	3-2	0-0	224	220	111	35	18	43-1	157	4.22	97	.256	.305	70-0-6	.229	3*	101	-2		0.0
Total	7	78	87	.473	226	209	13-5	2-0	1396	1459	737	158	100	381-24	937	4.44	100	.269	.326	159-0-15	.220	7	94	7		2.0

WEAVER, MONTE Montie Morton "Prof" B6.15.1906 Helton NC D6.14.1994 Orlando FL BL/TR/6-0/170 d9.20 Col Emory & Henry

1931	Was A	1	0	1.000	3	1	0	0	10	11	6	0	0	6	4.50	95	.268	.362	3	.000	-0	118	0		0.0
1932	Was A	22	10	.688	43	30	13-1	2	234	236	126	9	0	112	83	4.08	106	.261	.287	94-0-2	.287	6*	124	3		0.8
1933	†Was A	10	5	.667	23	21	12-1	0	152.1	147	57	3	1	53	45	3.25	129	.257	.322	56-0-1	.125	-3	107	18		1.2
1934	Was A	11	15	.423	31	31	11	0	204.2	255	127	16	0	63	51	4.79	90	.306	.355	80-0-4	.162	-2	103	-13		-1.7
1935	Was A	1	1	.500	5	2	0	0	12	16	8	1	0	6	4	5.25	82	.320	.393	3	.333	1	100	-1		-0.2
1936	Was A	6	4	.600	26	5	3	1	91	92	57	3	0	38	35	4.35	110	.262	.334	25	.200	0	122	2		0.2
1937	Was A	12	9	.571	30	29	9	0	188.2	197	102	21	0	70	44	4.20	105	.266	.330	68-0-4	.206	1	89	6		0.6
1938	Was A	7	6	.538	31	18	7	0	139	157	93	9	3	74	43	5.24	86	.282	.370	45-0-2	.267	4	114	-11		-0.5
1939	Bos A	0	0	1.000	9	1	1	1	20.1	26	15	0	1	13	6	6.64	71	.321	.421	4	.000	-1	149	-3		-0.3
Total	9	71	50	.587	201	135	57-2	4	1052	1137	591	62	5	435	297	4.36	101	.276	.345	378-0-13	.209	5	108	1		0.1

WEAVER, ORLIE Orville Forest B6.4.1886 Newport KY D11.28.1970 New Orleans LA BR/TR/6-0/180 d9.14 Col Maryville

1910	Chi N	1	1	.500	7	2	2	0	32	34	17	2	1	15	22	3.66	79	.270	.352	13	.154	-1	90	-3		-0.3
1911	Chi N	2	2	.500	6	3	1-1	0	43.2	29	12	0	4	17	20	2.06	161	.196	.296	17-0-1	.059	-1	98	7		0.4
	Bos N	3	12	.200	27	17	4	0	121	140	102	9	7	84	50	6.47	59	.303	.418	41-0-1	.122	-2	84	-28		-3.2
	Year	5	14	.263	33	20	5-1	0	164.2	169	114	9	11	101	70	5.30	70	.293	.389	58-0-2	.103	-4	88	-23		-2.8
Total	2	6	15	.286	40	22	7-1	0	196.2	203	131	11	12	116	92	5.03	71	.276	.383	71-0-2	.113	-4	89	-24		-3.1

WEAVER, ROGER Roger Edward B10.6.1954 Amsterdam NY BR/TR/6-3/200 [DetA76 16/362] d6.6 Col Oneonta

| 1980 | Det A | 3 | 4 | .429 | 19 | 6 | 0 | 0 | 63.2 | 56 | 32 | 5 | 1 | 34-3 | 42 | 4.10 | 101 | .247 | .342 | 0 | | 0 | 87 | 0 | 21 | 0.0 |

WEAVER, SAM Samuel H. B7.10.1855 Philadelphia PA D2.1.1914 Philadelphia PA BR/TR/5-10/175 d10.25

1875	Phi NA	1	0	1.000	1	1	1	0	6	6	2	0		2	1.50	152	.240	.296	4	.250	0	263	1		0.1
1878	Mil N	12	31	.279	45	43	39-1	0	383	371	214	2		21	95	1.95	135	.237	.247	170	.200	-3*	66	23		2.1
1882	Phi AA	26	15	.634	42	41	41-2	0	371	374	182	6		35	104	2.74	102	.245	.262	155	.232	2*	96	8		0.9
1883	Lou AA	24	22	.522	46	46	45-4	0	400.2	451	261	0		35	105	3.71	81	.266	.281	193	.192	0*	110	-32		-2.9
1884	Phi U	5	10	.333	17	17	14	0	136	206	146	3		11	40	5.76	40	.328	.339	84	.214	-5*	116	-52		-4.4
1886	Phi AA	0	2	.000	2	2	1	0	11	30	29	0	1	2	2	14.73	24	.423	.446	7	.143	-1	25	-13		-1.4
Total	5	67	80	.456	152	149	140-7	0	1301.2	1432	832	14	1	104	346	3.22	87	.261	.275	609	.207	-6	92	-66		-5.7

WEBB, BRANDON Brandon Tyler B5.9.1979 Ashland KY BR/TR/6-3/190(190-230) [AriN00 8/249] d4.22 Col Kentucky

2003	Ari N	10	9	.526	29	28	1-1	0-0	180.2	140	65	12	13	68-4	172	2.84	163	.212	.298	50-0-7	.100	-2	94	32	15	3.0
2004	Ari N	7	16	.304	35	35	1	0-0	208	194	111	17	11	119-11	164	3.59	127	.248	.353	64-0-4	.094	-3	86	14		1.2
2005	Ari N	14	12	.538	33	33	1	0-0	229	229	98	21	2	59-4	172	3.54	124	.265	.311	62-0-13	.097	-3	81	21		2.0
Total	3	31	37	.456	97	96	3-1	0-0	617.2	563	274	50	26	246-19	508	3.35	135	.244	.322	176-0-24	.097	-8	87	67	15	6.2

WEBB, LEFTY Cleon Earl B3.1.1885 Mt.Gilead OH D1.12.1958 Circleville OH BB/TL/5-11/165 d5.23 Col Ohio Wesleyan

| 1910 | Pit N | 2 | 1 | .667 | 7 | 3 | 2 | 0 | 27 | 29 | 17 | 0 | 2 | 9 | 5.67 | 55 | .266 | .333 | 10 | .200 | -0 | 144 | -5 | | -0.6 |

WEBB, HANK Henry Gaylon Matthew B5.21.1950 Copiague NY BR/TR/6-3/175* [NYN68 10/205] d9.5

1972	NY N	0	0	—	6	2	0	0-0	18.1	18	9	1	0	9-1	15	4.42	77	.261	.342	5	.000	-1	104	-2		-0.1
1973	NY N	0	0	—	2	0	0	0-0	1.2	2	2	1	0	2-0	1	10.80	34	.286	.444	0	—	0		-1		-0.1
1974	NY N	0	2	.000	3	2	0	0-0	10	15	9	1	1	10-0	8	7.20	50	.341	.473	3	.000	0	85	-4		-0.7
1975	NY N	7	6	.538	29	15	3-1	0-0	115	102	58	12	1	62-4	38	4.07	86	.236	.331	31	.258	2*	85	-7		-0.6
1976	NY N	0	1	.000	8	0	0	0-1	16	19	9	2	2	7-4	7	4.50	74	.274	.366	1	.000	0		-2		-0.1
1977	LA N	0	0	—	5	0	0	0-0	8	5	2	1	1	1-0	2	2.25	171	.192	.250	0	—	0		2		0.1
Total	6	7	9	.438	53	19	3-1	0-1	169	159	89	18	5	91-5	71	4.31	81	.248	.345	40	.200	1	87	-14		-1.5

WEBB, JOHN John Floyd B5.23.1979 Pensacola FL BR/TR/6-3/220* [ChiN99 19/590] d8.2 Col Manatee (FL) CC

2004	TB A	0	0	—	4	0	0	0-0	9	12	7	2	1	7-0	9	7.00	67	.324	.444	0	—	0		-2		-0.1
2005	TB A	0	1	.000	1	1	0	0-0	4	6	8	1	1	4-0	2	18.00	24	.333	.478	0	—	0	215	-6		-0.7
Total	2	0	1	.000	5	1	0	0-0	13	18	15	3	2	11-0	11	10.38	44	.327	.456	0	—	0	215	-8		-0.8

WEBB, RED Samuel Henry B9.25.1924 Washington DC D2.7.1996 Hyattsville MD BL/TR/6-0/175 d9.15

1948	NY N	2	1	.667	5	3	2	0	28	27	12	2	1	10	9	3.21	122	.248	.317	9-0-2	.222	0	120	2		0.2
1949	NY N	1	1	.500	20	0	0	0	44.2	41	23	2	0	21	9	4.03	99	.248	.333	10	.400	2		0		0.3
Total	2	3	2	.600	25	3	2	0	72.2	68	35	4	1	31	18	3.72	107	.248	.327	19-0-2	.316	2	120	2		0.5

WEBB, BILL Willie Fred B12.12.1913 Atlanta GA D6.1.1994 Austell GA BR/TR/6-2/180 d5.15

| 1943 | Phi N | 0 | 0 | — | 1 | 0 | 0 | 0 | 1 | 1 | 1 | 1 | 0 | 1 | 0 | 9.00 | 37 | .333 | .500 | 0 | — | 0 | | -1 | | 0.0 |

WEBBER, LES Lester Elmer B5.6.1915 Kelseyville CA D11.13.1986 Santa Maria CA BR/TR/6-0.5/185 d5.17

1942	Bro N	3	2	.600	19	3	1	1	51.2	46	17	2	0	22	23	2.96	110	.230	.306	14-0-2	.071	-1	223	3		0.2
1943	Bro N	2	2	.500	54	0	0	10	115.2	112	54	6	5	69	24	3.81	88	.264	.373	25-0-1	.120	-1		-5		-0.3
1944	Bro N	7	8	.467	48	9	1	1	140.1	157	85	9	1	64	42	4.94	72	.282	.357	39-1-2	.205	-1	89	-20		-1.7
1945	Bro N	7	3	.700	17	5	1	0	75.1	69	37	3	1	25	30	3.58	105	.237	.300	22-0-6	.091	-1	148	2		0.1
1946	Bro N	3	3	.500	11	4	0	0	43	34	11	5	0	15	16	2.30	147	.225	.295	10-0-1	.100	-1	63	6		0.7
	Cle A	1	1	.500	4	0	0	0	5.1	13	14	0	0	5	5	23.63	14	.464	.545	1	.000	0	91	-12		-1.9
1948	Cle A	0	0	—	1	0	0	0	0.2	3	3	0	0	1	1	40.50	10	.750	.800	0	—	0		-3		-0.1
Total	6	23	19	.548	154	25	7	14	432	434	221	26	7	201	141	4.19	83	.262	.345	111-1-12	.135	-2	119	-29		-3.0

YEAR	TM LG	W	L	PCT	G	GS	CG-SHO	SV-BS	IP	H	R	HR	HB	BB-IB	SO	ERA	AERA	OAV	OOB	AB-HR-SH	AVG	PB	SUP	APR	DL	PW
WEBER, BEN	Benjamin Edward B11.17.1969 Port Arthur TX BR/TR/6-4/185(180-210) [TorA91 20/536] d4.3 Col Houston																									
2000	SF N	0	1	.000	9	0	0	0-2	8	16	13	0	0	4-0	6	14.63	30	.400	.455	0	—	0	-9		-0.9
	Ana A	1	0	1.000	10	0	0	0-0	14.2	12	6	0	0	2-1	8	1.84	281	.214	.237	0	—	0	4		0.2
2001	Ana A	6	2	.750	56	0	0	0-1	68.1	66	28	4	5	31-8	40	3.42	136	.251	.341	0	—	0	9		1.0
2002	†Ana A	7	2	.778	63	0	0	7-4	78	70	25	4	2	22-3	43	2.54	177	.249	.308	0	—	0	16		2.0
2003	Ana A	5	1	.833	62	0	0	0-2	80.1	84	26	4	0	22-7	46	2.69	163	.275	.323	0	—	0	16		1.1
2004	Ana A	0	2	.000	18	0	0	0-1	22.1	37	24	4	0	15-0	11	8.06	55	.363	.444	0	—	0	-11		-0.9
2005	Cin N	0	0	—	10	0	0	0-0	12.1	20	11	0	1	9-1	8	8.03	52	.364	.455	0	—	0	-5	96	-0.2
Total	6	19	8	.704	228	0	0	7-10	284	305	133	19	9	105-20	162	3.77	120	.277	.343	0	—	0	20	96	2.4
WEBER, CHARLIE	Charles P. "Count" B10.22.1868 Cincinnati OH D6.13.1914 Beaumont TX TR d7.30																									
1898	Was N	0	1	.000	1	1	0	0	4	9	9	0	2	1	0	15.75	23	.450	.522	2	.000	-0	58	-5		-0.7
WEBER, NEIL	Neil Aaron B12.6.1972 Newport Beach CA BL/TL/6-5/215 [MonN93 8/230] d9.11 Col Cuesta (CA) JC																									
1998	Ari N	0	0	—	4	0	0	0-0	2.1	5	3	0	0	3-0	4	11.57	37	.417	.533	0	—	0	-2		-0.1
WEGENER, MIKE	Michael Denis B10.8.1946 Denver CO BR/TR/6-4/205(197-215) d4.9																									
1969	Mon N	5	14	.263	32	26	4-1	0-1	165.2	150	92	10	4	96-6	124	4.40	84	.243	.347	54-0-3	.241	2	90	-12		-1.0
1970	Mon N	3	6	.333	25	16	1	0-0	104.1	100	70	16	4	56-3	35	5.26	79	.252	.349	34-0-1	.118	-2	85	-13	37	-1.2
Total	2	8	20	.286	57	42	5-1	0-1	270	250	162	26	8	152-9	159	4.73	82	.247	.347	88-0-4	.193	0	88	-25	37	-2.2
WEGMAN, BILL	William Edward B12.19.1962 Cincinnati OH BR/TR/6-5/220(200-238) [MilA81 5/124] d9.14																									
1985	Mil A	2	0	1.000	3	3	0	0-0	17.2	17	8	3	0	3-0	6	3.57	118	.246	.274	0	—	0	166	1		0.1
1986	Mil A	5	12	.294	35	32	2	0-0	198.1	217	120	32	7	43-2	82	5.13	85	.279	.321	0	—	0*	84	-12		-1.0
1987	Mil A	12	11	.522	34	33	7	0-1	225	229	113	31	6	53-2	102	4.24	109	.265	.310	0	—	0	100	10	15	0.9
1988	Mil A	13	13	.500	32	31	4-1	0-0	199	207	104	24	4	50-5	84	4.12	97	.265	.309	0	—	0*	91	-4	17	-0.1
1989	Mil A	2	6	.250	11	8	0	0-1	51	69	44	6	0	21-2	27	6.71	58	.321	.375	0	—	0	97	-17	123	-2.1
1990	Mil A	2	2	.500	8	5	1-1	0-0	29.2	37	21	6	0	6-1	20	4.85	80	.298	.328	0	—	0	122	-4	123	-0.5
1991	Mil A	15	7	.682	28	28	7-2	0-0	193.1	176	76	16	7	40-0	89	2.84	141	.242	.286	0	—	0	114	21	25	2.0
1992	Mil A	13	14	.481	35	35	7	0-0	261.2	251	104	28	9	55-3	127	3.20	121	.250	.294	0	—	0	101	19		2.0
1993	Mil A	4	14	.222	20	18	5	0-0	120.2	135	70	13	2	34-5	50	4.48	96	.291	.335	0	—	0	65	-4	69	-0.4
1994	Mil A	8	4	.667	19	19	0	0-0	115.2	140	64	14	2	26-0	59	4.51	112	.303	.339	0	—	0	114	7	26	0.7
1995	Mil A	5	7	.417	37	4	0	2-1	70.2	89	45	14	3	21-2	50	5.35	94	.312	.363	0	—	0*	56	-2		-0.4
Total	11	81	90	.474	262	216	33-4	2-3	1482.2	1567	769	187	40	352-22	696	4.16	103	.271	.315	0	—	0	97	15	398	1.2
WEHDE, BIGGS	Wilbur B11.23.1906 Holstein IA D9.21.1970 Sioux Falls SD BR/TR/5-10.5/180 d9.15																									
1930	Chi A	0	0	—	4	0	0	0	6.1	7	8	1	1	7	3	9.95	46	.304	.484	1	.000	-0		-3		-0.1
1931	Chi A	1	0	1.000	8	0	0	0	16	19	12	0	2	10	3	6.75	63	.333	.449	3	.000	-0		-4		-0.2
Total	2	1	0	1.000	12	0	0	0	22.1	26	20	1	3	17	6	7.66	57	.325	.460	4	.000	-1		-7		-0.3
WEHMEIER, HERM	Herman Ralph B2.18.1927 Cincinnati OH D5.21.1973 Dallas TX BR/TR/6-2/200* d9.7 [DL 1959 Det A 33]																									
1945	Cin N	0	1	.000	2	2	0	0	5	10	7	0	0	4	0	12.60	30	.435	.519	1	.000	-0*	124	-5		-0.7
1947	Cin N	0	0	—	1	0	0	0	0	0	0	0	0	0	0	0.00	—	.000	.000	0	—	0		0		0.0
1948	Cin N	11	8	.579	33	24	6	0	147.1	179	105	21	2	75	56	5.86	67	.299	.379	55-0-3	.091	-3*	113	-31		-3.7
1949	Cin N	11	12	.478	33	29	11-1	0	213.1	202	119	20	7	117	80	4.68	89	.253	.353	78-0-5	.256	2*	98	-8		-0.7
1950	Cin N	10	18	.357	41	32	12	4	230	255	157	27	4	135	121	5.67	75	.281	.376	92-0-1	.152	-3*	97	-33		-3.9
1951	Cin N	7	10	.412	39	22	10-2	0	184.2	167	82	15	4	89	93	3.70	110	.241	.330	59-0-2	.288	3*	79	10		1.1
1952	Cin N	9	11	.450	33	26	6-1	0	190.1	197	115	23	7	103	83	5.15	73	.269	.365	64-1-2	.188	2*	99	-27		-2.6
1953	Cin N	1	6	.143	28	10	0	0	81.2	100	71	20	0	47	32	7.16	61	.299	.385	20	.200	-0	82	-24		-1.8
1954	Cin N	0	3	.000	12	3	0	2	33.2	36	29	6	1	21	13	6.68	63	.271	.372	9-0-1	.000	-1*	57	-10		-0.9
	Phi N	10	8	.556	25	17	10-2	0	138	117	61	10	1	51	49	3.85	105	.231	.300	50-0-5	.120	-2	90	5		0.4
	Year	10	11	.476	37	20	10-2	2	171.2	153	90	16	2	72	62	4.40	92	.239	.316	59-0-6	.102	-3	84	-5		-0.5
1955	Phi N	10	12	.455	31	29	10-1	0	193.2	176	101	21	2	67-7	85	4.41	90	.241	.304	72-0-3	.278	4*	104	-7		-0.4
1956	Phi N	0	2	.000	3	3	0	0	20	18	9	2	0	11-0	8	4.05	92	.240	.333	8	.000	-1	39	0		-0.2
	StL N	12	9	.571	34	19	7-2	1	170.2	150	80	16	1	71-8	68	3.69	102	.240	.315	58-2-1	.224	4*	78	2		0.6
	Year	12	11	.522	37	22	7-2	1	190.2	168	89	18	1	82-8	76	3.73	101	.240	.317	66-2-1	.197	3	73	0		0.4
1957	StL N	10	7	.588	36	18	5	0	165	165	91	25	2	54-7	91	4.31	92	.253	.311	59	.203	0*	125	-7		-0.7
1958	StL N	0	1	.000	3	3	0	0	6	13	9	2	0	2-0	4	13.50	31	.448	.484	2	.500	1	102	-6		-0.7
	Det A	0	1	1.000	7	3	0	0	22.2	21	8	2	0	5-0	11	2.38	169	.241	.280	6	.000	-1	67	3	75	0.3
Total	13	92	108	.460	361	240	79-9	9	1803	1806	1044	210	31	852-22	794	4.80	84	.260	.343	633-3-23	.196	5	96	-138	108	-14.1
WEHRMEISTER, DAVE	David Thomas B11.9.1952 Berwyn IL BR/TR/6-4/195* [SDN73*1/3] d4.16 Col Truman St.																									
1976	SD N	0	4	.000	7	4	0	0-0	19.1	27	17	0	0	11-1	10	7.45	44	.333	.409	6	.000	-1	73	-9		-1.6
1977	SD N	1	3	.250	30	6	0	0-0	69.2	81	53	8	3	44-4	32	6.07	59	.293	.393	12-0-2	.167	0	162	-21		-1.0
1978	SD N	1	0	1.000	4	0	0	0-0	7.1	8	5	1	0	5-1	2	6.14	55	.276	.382	0-0-1	—	0		-2		-0.3
1981	NY A	0	0	—	5	0	0	0-0	7	6	4	0	0	7-2	7	5.14	70	.240	.394	0	—	0		-1		-0.1
1984	Phi N	0	0	—	7	0	0	0-0	15	18	12	1	4	7-2	13	7.20	51	.300	.371	2	.000	-0		-5		-0.3
1985	Chi A	2	2	.500	23	0	0	2-2	39.1	35	15	4	3	10-0	96	3.43	127	.241	.304	0	—	0		4		0.4
Total	6	4	9	.308	76	10	0	2-2	157.2	175	106	14	7	84-10	96	5.65	66	.284	.373	20-0-3	.100	-1	120	-34		-2.8
WEIK, DICK	Richard Henry "Legs" B11.17.1927 Waterloo IA D4.21.1991 Harvey IL BR/TR/6-3.5/184* d9.8 Mil 1951-52 Col Illinois																									
1948	Was A	1	3	.333	3	3	0	0	12.2	14	8	1	0	22	5	5.68	76	.311	.537	4	.750	2	69	-1		-0.1
1949	Was A	3	12	.200	27	14	2-2	1	95.1	78	61	5	0	103	58	5.38	79	.230	.410	28-0-2	.179	-1*	56	-10		-1.4
1950	Was A	1	3	.250	14	5	1	0	44	38	27	2	0	47	26	4.30	105	.236	.409	13	.154	-1	60	0		-0.1
	Cle A	1	3	.250	11	2	0	0	26	18	17	1	1	26	16	3.81	114	.205	.391	5	.200	-1	83	0		0.0
	Year	2	6	.250	25	7	1	0	70	56	44	3	1	73	42	4.11	108	.225	.402	18	.167	-1	67	-1		-0.1
1953	Det A	0	1	.000	12	1	0	0	19.1	32	30	3	0	23	6	13.97	29	.386	.519	2-0-1	.500	1	218	-19		-0.9
1954	Det A	0	1	.000	9	1	0	0	16.1	23	14	3	1	16	7	7.16	52	.354	.482	1	.000	-0	382	-6		-0.4
Total	5	6	22	.214	76	26	3-2	1	213.2	203	157	15	2	237	123	5.90	72	.260	.433	53-0-3	.226	1	78	-36		-2.9
WEILAND, ED	Edwin Nicholas B11.26.1914 Evanston IL D7.12.1971 Chicago IL BL/TR/5-11/180 d5.1 Mil 1943-45 b-Bob																									
1940	Chi A	0	0	—	5	0	0	0	14.1	15	15	5	0	7	3	8.79	50	.263	.344	5	.200	-0		-6		-0.3
1942	Chi A	0	0	—	5	0	0	0	9.2	18	11	0	0	3	4	7.45	48	.383	.420	2	.000	-0		-5		-0.3
Total	2	0	0	—	10	0	0	0	24	33	26	5	0	10	7	8.25	50	.317	.377	7	.143	-0		-11		-0.6
WEILAND, BOB	Robert George "Lefty" B12.14.1905 Chicago IL D11.9.1988 Chicago IL BL/TL/6-4/215 d9.30 b-Ed																									
1928	Chi A	1	0	1.000	1	1	1-1	0	9	7	0	1	5	9	0.00	—	.212	.333	3	.333	0	21	4		0.5
1929	Chi A	2	4	.333	15	9	1	1	62	62	42	3	3	43	25	5.81	74	.268	.390	18-0-1	.111	-1	101	-8		-0.8
1930	Chi A	0	4	.000	14	3	0	0	32.2	38	31	1	2	21	15	6.61	70	.297	.404	8	.000	-0	43	-9		-0.9
1931	Chi A	2	7	.222	15	8	3	0	75	75	55	4	4	46	38	5.16	83	.259	.368	22	.182	1	92	-9		-0.7
1932	Bos A	6	16	.273	43	27	7	1	195.2	231	125	11	6	97	63	4.51	100	.295	.377	61-0-2	.148	-1	75	-3		-0.2
1933	Bos A	8	14	.364	39	27	12	3	216.1	197	107	19	5	100	97	3.87	113	.244	.331	65-0-6	.108	-4	65	13		0.7
1934	Cle A	1	5	.167	11	7	2	0	55.2	63	41	4	0	27	29	5.50	87	.293	.372	19	.105	-1	88	-4		-0.1
	StL A	1	5	.167	16	7	2	0	70	71	41	5	0	30	42	4.11	111	.262	.336	24-1-1	.125	-0	57	2		0.1
	Year	2	10	.167	27	14	4	0	125.2	134	82	9	0	57	71	4.73	99	.276	.352	43-1-1	.116	-1	73	-4		-0.4
1935	StL A	0	2	.000	14	4	0	0	32	39	35	6	1	31	11	9.56	50	.298	.436	8-0-1	.000	-1	100	-14		-0.9
1937	StL N	15	14	.517	41	34	21-2	0	264.1	283	127	14	5	94	105	3.54	112	.276	.339	89-2-5	.169	-0	106	11		1.1
1938	StL N	16	11	.593	35	29	11-1	1	228.1	248	118	14	4	80	117	3.59	110	.272	.324	80-0-10	.138	-3	112	9		0.3
1939	StL N	10	12	.455	32	23	6-3	1	146.1	146	69	4	6	50	63	3.57	115	.264	.331	40-0-6	.065	-4	103	7		0.5
1940	StL N	0	0	—	1	0	0	0	1	3	3	1	0	0	0	27.00	15	.600	.600	0	—	0		-2		-0.1
Total	12	62	94	.397	277	179	66-7	0	1388.1	1463	794	85	37	611	614	4.24	100	.272	.350	443-3-32	.129	-16	90	-5		-0.8
WEILMAN, CARL	Carl Woolworth "Zeke" (b Carl Woolworth Weilenmann) B11.29.1889 Hamilton OH D5.25.1924 Hamilton OH BL/TL/6-5.5/187 d8.24																									
1912	StL A	2	4	.333	18	6	1	0	81.1	81	42	19	0	2	24	2.79	119	.227	.239	17-0-1	.118	-1*	100	3		0.4
1913	StL A	10	19	.345	39	28	17-2	0	251.2	262	122	2	4	60	79	3.40	86	.283	.330	82-0-2	.146	-3	82	-10		-1.4
1914	StL A	17	12	.586	44	36	20-3	1	299	260	96	6	11	84	119	2.08	130	.237	.298	101-0-2	.149	-1	92	21		2.0
1915	StL A	18	19	.486	47	31	19-3	4	295.2	240	110	6	3	83	125	2.34	122	.229	.287	100-0-3	.230	2	79	17		2.4

YEAR	TM LG	W	L	PCT	G	GS	CG-SHO	SV-BS	IP	H	R	HR	HB	BB-IB	SO	ERA	AERA	OAV	OOB	AB-HR-SH	AVG	PB	SUP	APR	DL	PW
1916	StL A	17	18	.486	46	31	19-1	2	276	237	90	3	8	76	91	2.15	128	.242	.301	91-0-4	.154	-1	106	17		2.0
1917	StL A	1	2	.333	5	3	0	0	19	19	9	1	0	6	9	1.89	137	.268	.325	4	.000	-1	74	0		0.0
1919	StL A	10	6	.625	20	20	12-3	0	148	133	51	3	3	45	44	2.07	160	.244	.305	47-0-4	.191	0	118	17		1.9
1920	StL A	9	13	.409	30	24	13-1	2	183.1	201	103	6	3	61	45	4.47	88	.291	.351	63-0-4	.175	-2	109	-7		-0.9
Total 8		84	93	.475	239	179	105-15	10	1521	1394	600	22	32	418	536	2.67	112	.251	.308	505-0-20	.170	-7	97	58		6.4

WEIMER, JAKE Jacob "Tornado Jake" B11.29.1873 Ottumwa IA D6.19.1928 Chicago IL BR/TL/5-11/175 d4.17

YEAR	TM LG	W	L	PCT	G	GS	CG-SHO	SV-BS	IP	H	R	HR	HB	BB-IB	SO	ERA	AERA	OAV	OOB	AB-HR-SH	AVG	PB	SUP	APR	DL	PW
1903	Chi N	20	8	.714	35	33	27-3	0	282	241	111	4	11	104	128	2.30	136	**.225**	.301	107-0-1	.196	2	116	28		2.6
1904	Chi N	20	14	.588	37	37	31-5	0	307	229	96	1	7	97	177	1.91	140	.204	.272	115-0-2	.183	-1	102	26		2.8
1905	Chi N	18	12	.600	33	30	26-2	1	250.1	212	84	1	12	80	107	2.26	132	.229	.299	92-0-1	.207	2	130	21		2.5
1906	Cin N	20	14	.588	41	39	31-6	1	304.2	263	105	0	13	99	141	2.22	124	.226	.306	108-0-2	.269	6	94	18		2.8
1907	Cin N	11	14	.440	29	26	19-3	0	209	165	73	6	23	63	67	2.41	108	.226	.308	72-1-4	.194	2*	88	6		1.1
1908	Cin N	8	7	.533	15	15	9-2	0	116.2	110	38	2	6	50	36	2.39	96	.255	.341	45-0-2	.244	2	136	1		0.5
1909	NY N	0	0	—	1	0	0	0	3	7	4	0	1	0	1	9.00	28	.467	.500		.000	-0				-0.1
Total 7		97	69	.584	191	180	143-21	2	1472.2	1227	511	14	73	493	657	2.23	125	.227	.300	540-1-12	.213	11	108	98		12.2

WEINERT, LEFTY Phillip Walter B4.21.1902 Philadelphia PA D4.17.1973 Rockledge FL BL/TL/6-1/195 d9.24

YEAR	TM LG	W	L	PCT	G	GS	CG-SHO	SV-BS	IP	H	R	HR	HB	BB-IB	SO	ERA	AERA	OAV	OOB	AB-HR-SH	AVG	PB	SUP	APR	DL	PW
1919	Phi N	0	0	—	1	0	0	0	4	11	9	0	0	2		18.00	18	.478	.520	2	1.000	1		-6		-0.2
1920	Phi N	1	1	.500	10	2	0	0	22	27	11	1	1	19	10	6.14	56	.333	.465	5	.000	-1	127	-5		-0.5
1921	Phi N	1	0	1.000	8	0	0	0	12.1	8	6	1	1	5	2	1.46	290	.216	.326	1	1.000	-1		2		0.2
1922	Phi N	8	11	.421	34	22	10	1	166.2	189	103	10	5	70	70	3.40	137	.289	.362	58-0-1	.241	-0	82	13		1.3
1923	Phi N	4	17	.190	38	20	8	1	156	207	131	10	8	81	46	5.42	85	.327	.410	59	.322	2	76	-18		-1.9
1924	Phi N	0	1	.000	8	1	0	0	14.2	10	7	0	0	11	7	2.45	182	.204	.350	4	.000	-1	38	2		0.1
1927	Chi N	1	1	.500	5	3	1	0	19.2	21	13	2	0	6	5	4.58	84	.259	.310	5	.200	-1	118	-2		-0.2
1928	Chi N	1	0	1.000	17	0	0	0	17	24	10	0	1	9	9	5.29	73	.393	.479	2	.000	-0	154	-2		-0.2
1931	NY A	2	2	.500	17	0	0	0	24.2	31	19	2	5	19	24	6.20	64	.316	.451	6	.000	-0		-6		-0.9
Total 9		18	33	.353	131	49	19	2	437	528	315	26	21	222	160	4.59	97	.308	.393	142-0-1	.261	2	85	-22		-2.3

WEIR, ROY William Franklin "Bill" B2.25.1911 Portland ME D9.30.1989 Anaheim CA BL/TL/5-8.5/170 d6.25 Col New Hampshire

YEAR	TM LG	W	L	PCT	G	GS	CG-SHO	SV-BS	IP	H	R	HR	HB	BB-IB	SO	ERA	AERA	OAV	OOB	AB-HR-SH	AVG	PB	SUP	APR	DL	PW
1936	Bos N	4	3	.571	12	7	3-2	0	71	53	23	0	0	24	29	2.83	136	.241	.316	18-0-1	.278	2*	63	6		0.9
1937	Bos N	1	1	.500	10	4	1	0	33	27	18	0	0	19	8	3.82	94	.237	.333	10	.000	-1	138	-2		-0.2
1938	Bos N	1	0	1.000	5	0	0	0	13.1	14	10	4	0	6	3	6.75	51	.269	.345	3	.333	-0		-5		-0.3
1939	Bos N	0	0	—	2	0	0	0	2.2	1	0	0	1	1	2	0.00	—	.125	.222	1	.000	-0		1		0.1
Total 4		6	4	.600	29	11	4-2	0	106.1	95	51	4	0	50	42	3.55	104	.238	.323	32-0-1	.188	1	90			0.5

WELCH, TED Floyd John B10.17.1892 Coyville KS D1.7.1943 Great Bend KS BL/TR/5-9.5/160 d5.15

YEAR	TM LG	W	L	PCT	G	GS	CG-SHO	SV-BS	IP	H	R	HR	HB	BB-IB	SO	ERA	AERA	OAV	OOB	AB-HR-SH	AVG	PB	SUP	APR	DL	PW
1914	StL F	0	0	—	3	0	0	0	6	6	4	0	3	3	2	6.00	51	.273	.429	1	.000	-0		-1		-0.1

WELCH, JOHNNY John Vernon B12.2.1906 Washington DC D9.2.1940 St.Louis MO BL/TR/6-3/184 d5.22

YEAR	TM LG	W	L	PCT	G	GS	CG-SHO	SV-BS	IP	H	R	HR	HB	BB-IB	SO	ERA	AERA	OAV	OOB	AB-HR-SH	AVG	PB	SUP	APR	DL	PW
1926	Chi N	0	0	—	3	0	0	0	4.1	5	2	0	0	1		2.08	185	.357	.400	1	1.000	0		1		0.1
1927	Chi N	0	0	—	1	0	0	0	1	0	1	0	0	3	1	9.00	43	.000	.500	0	—	0		0		0.0
1928	Chi N	0	0	—	3	0	0	0	4	13	7	0	0	0	2	15.75	24	.591	.591	0	—	0		-5		-0.2
1931	Chi N	2	1	.667	8	3	1	0	33.2	39	16	2	1	10	7	3.74	103	.291	.345	12	.417	2	148	1		0.2
1932	Bos A	4	6	.400	20	8	3-1	0	72.1	93	46	3	3	38	26	5.23	86	.312	.395	36-1-1	.250	2*	66	-4		-0.3
1933	Bos A	4	9	.308	47	7	1	3	129	142	81	6	2	67	68	4.60	95	.283	.370	37-0-2	.162	-1	97	-4		-0.5
1934	Bos A	13	15	.464	41	22	8-1	0	206.1	223	116	14	8	76	91	4.49	107	.274	.342	74-0-6	.203	-1	110	11		1.1
1935	Bos A	10	9	.526	31	19	10-1	2	143	155	82	4	4	53	48	4.47	106	.273	.339	50-0-2	.180	-0	96	5		0.6
1936	Bos A	2	1	.667	9	3	1	0	32.2	43	24	4	0	8	9	5.51	90	.305	.342	11	.273	1	127	-1		0.0
	Pit N	0	0	—	9	1	0	1	22	22	12	3	0	6	5	4.50	90	.265	.315	7	.286	1	146	-1		0.0
Total 9		35	41	.461	172	63	24-3	6	648.1	735	383	36	18	262	257	4.66	99	.285	.355	228-1-11	.219	3	103	2		1.0

WELCH, MICKEY Michael Francis "Smiling Mickey" (b Michael Francis Walsh) B7.4.1859 Brooklyn NY D7.30.1941 Concord NH BR/TR/5-8/160 d5.1 HF1973

YEAR	TM LG	W	L	PCT	G	GS	CG-SHO	SV-BS	IP	H	R	HR	HB	BB-IB	SO	ERA	AERA	OAV	OOB	AB-HR-SH	AVG	PB	SUP	APR	DL	PW
1880	Tro N	34	30	.531	65	64	64-4	0	574	575	321	7		80	123	2.54	99	.249	.274	251	.287	10*	96	-2		0.5
1881	Tro N	21	18	.538	40	40	40-4	0	368	371	186	7		78	104	2.67	111	.255	.293	148	.203	-4	86	10		0.3
1882	Tro N	14	16	.467	33	33	30-5	0	281	334	221	9		62	53	3.46	82	.280	.315	151-1	.245	1*	96	-22		-1.8
1883	NY N	25	23	.521	54	52	46-4	0	426	431	271	11		66	144	2.73	114	.244	.272	320-2	.234	3*	97	16		1.4
1884	NY N	39	21	.650	65	65	62-4	0	557.1	528	275	12		146	345	2.50	119	.237	.284	249-3	.241	4*	106	29		3.2
1885	NY N	44	11	**.800**	56	55	55-7	1	492	372	170	4		131	258	1.66	160	.203	.256	199-2	.206	5	127	60		6.0
1886	NY N	33	22	.600	59	59	56-1	0	500	514	279	13		163	272	2.99	107	.259	.315	213	.216	1	94	10		0.7
1887	NY N	22	15	.595	41	40	39-2	0	346	339	191	7	5	91	115	3.36	112	.253	.303	148-2	.243	4	94	23		2.1
1888	NY N	26	19	.578	47	47	47-5	0	425.1	328	156	12	14	108	167	1.93	142	.207	.263	169-2	.189	1	97	42		3.9
1889	NY N	27	12	.692	45	41	39-3	2	375	340	196	14	10	149	125	3.02	130	.234	.310	156	.192	-2	120	41		3.1
1890	NY N	17	14	.548	37	37	33-2	0	292.1	268	145	5	12	122	97	2.99	117	.236	.317	123	.179	-3	85	24		1.6
1891	NY N	5	9	.357	22	15	14	1	160	177	136	7	11	97	97	4.27	75	.270	.373	71	.141	-4	92	-20		-1.9
1892	NY N	0	0	—	1	1	0	0	5	11	9	0	0	4	1	14.40	22	.423	.500	3	.333	-4	177	-5		-0.2
Total 13		307	210	.594	565	549	525-41	4	4802	4588	2556	106	52	1297	1850	2.71	113	.242	.292	2201-12	.224	21	100	206		18.9

WELCH, MIKE Michael Paul B8.25.1972 Haverhill MA BL/TR/6-2/210 [NYN93 3/80] d7.17 Col Southern Maine

YEAR	TM LG	W	L	PCT	G	GS	CG-SHO	SV-BS	IP	H	R	HR	HB	BB-IB	SO	ERA	AERA	OAV	OOB	AB-HR-SH	AVG	PB	SUP	APR	DL	PW
1998	Phi N	0	2	.000	10	2	0	0-0	8.2	17	8	2	0	3	7	8.31	52	.310	.376	3	.000	-0	32	-8		-0.7

WELCH, BOB Robert Lynn B11.3.1956 Detroit MI BR/TR/6-3/190* [LAN77 1/20] d6.20 C1 Col Eastern Michigan

YEAR	TM LG	W	L	PCT	G	GS	CG-SHO	SV-BS	IP	H	R	HR	HB	BB-IB	SO	ERA	AERA	OAV	OOB	AB-HR-SH	AVG	PB	SUP	APR	DL	PW
1978	†LA N	7	4	.636	23	13	4-3	3-0	111.1	92	28	6	1	26-2	66	2.02	174	.229	.274	29-0-6	.172	0	102	19		1.9
1979	LA N	5	6	.455	25	12	1	5-4	81.1	82	42	7	3	32-4	64	3.98	91	.265	.339	19-0-3	.158	-0	90	-4		-0.5
1980	LA N★	14	9	.609	32	32	3-2	0-0	213.2	190	85	15	3	79-6	141	3.29	106	.242	.310	70-0-5	.243	3*	98	5		0.9
1981	†LA N	9	5	.643	23	23	2-1	0-0	141.1	141	56	11	3	41-0	88	3.44	96	.259	.313	45-0-7	.222	2	131	-1		0.0
1982	LA N	16	11	.593	36	36	9-3	0-0	235.2	199	94	9	5	81-5	176	3.36	103	.229	.297	85-0-7	.141	-1*	115	5		0.4
1983	LA N	15	12	.556	31	31	4-3	0-0	204	164	73	13	3	72-4	156	2.65	136	.222	.291	71-3-3	.096	-2	78	22		2.5
1984	LA N	13	13	.500	31	29	3-1	0-1	178.2	191	86	11	2	58-7	126	3.78	94	.273	.330	51-0-8	.078	-3*	92	-4		-0.7
1985	†LA N	14	4	.778	23	23	8-3	0-0	167.1	141	49	16	6	35-2	96	2.31	151	.245	.272	50-0-7	.180	1*	117	24	37	2.7
1986	LA N	7	13	.350	33	33	7-3	0-0	235.2	227	95	14	7	55-6	183	3.28	106	.251	.297	76-1-5	.105	-0*	84	6		0.3
1987	LA N	15	9	.625	35	35	6-4	0-0	251.2	204	94	17	4	86-6	196	3.22	124	.221	.289	83-0-8	.157	1*	107	25		2.4
1988	†Oak A	17	9	.654	36	36	4-2	0-0	244.2	237	107	22	10	81-1	158	3.64	104	.257	.321	0	—	0	111	5		0.5
1989	†Oak A	17	8	.680	33	33	1	0-0	209.2	191	82	13	6	78-3	137	3.00	123	.241	.312	0	—	0	112	16	17	1.8
1990	†Oak A★	**27**	6	**.818**	35	35	2-0	0-0	238	214	90	26	5	77-4	127	2.95	127	.242	.304	0	—	0	123	20		2.7
1991	Oak A	12	13	.480	35	35	7-1	0-0	220	220	124	25	11	91-3	101	4.58	84	.263	.341		0*	103	-22			-2.2
1992	†Oak A	11	7	.611	20	20		0-0	123.2	114	47	13	2	43-0	47	3.27	115	.247	.312	0	—	0	109	9	78	1.1
1993	Oak A	9	11	.450	30	30	0	0-0	166.2	208	102	25	7	56-5	63	5.29	78	.310	.368	0	—	0	83	-21	16	-2.1
1994	Oak A	3	6	.333	25	25	0	0-1	68.2	79	56	10	4	43-2	44	7.08	63	.290	.384	1	.000	-0*	110	-20		-2.1
Total 17		211	146	.591	506	462	61-28	8-6	3092	2894	1310	267	79	1034-60	1969	3.47	106	.249	.312	582-2-59	.151	2	104	84	148	9.6

WELCHEL, DON Donald Ray B2.3.1957 Atlanta TX BR/TR/6-4/205* [BalA78 7/178] d9.15 Col Sam Houston St.

YEAR	TM LG	W	L	PCT	G	GS	CG-SHO	SV-BS	IP	H	R	HR	HB	BB-IB	SO	ERA	AERA	OAV	OOB	AB-HR-SH	AVG	PB	SUP	APR	DL	PW
1982	Bal A	1	0	1.000	2	0		0-0	4.1	6	6	0	0	2-0	3	8.31	49	.300	.364	0	—	0		-3		-0.5
1983	Bal A	0	2	.000	11	0		0-0	26.2	33	18	1	0	10-1	16	5.40	74	.297	.352	0	—	0		-4		-0.3
Total 2		1	2	.333	13	0		0-0	31	39	24	1	0	12-1	19	5.81	69	.298	.354	0	—	0		-7		-0.8

WELLEMEYER, TODD Todd Allen B8.30.1978 Louisville KY BR/TR/6-3/200* [ChiN00 4/103] d5.15 Col Bellarmine (KY)

YEAR	TM LG	W	L	PCT	G	GS	CG-SHO	SV-BS	IP	H	R	HR	HB	BB-IB	SO	ERA	AERA	OAV	OOB	AB-HR-SH	AVG	PB	SUP	APR	DL	PW
2003	Chi N	1	1	.500	15	0		1-0	27.2	25	21	4	5	19-1	30	6.51	67	.245	.364	1-0-1	.000	0		-7		-0.4
2004	Chi N	2	1	.667	20	0		1-0	24.1	27	16	1	0	20-2	30	5.92	75	.287	.405	0	—	0		-3		-0.4
2005	Chi N	2	1	.667	22	0		1-0	32.1	32	23	7	0	22-1	32	6.12	72	.264	.375	4	.250	0		-6	55	-0.5
Total 3		5	3	.625	57	0		2-0	84.1	84	61	13	0	61-4	92	6.19	71	.265	.381	5-0-1	.200	0		-16	55	-1.3

WELLS, DAVID David Lee "Boomer" B5.20.1963 Torrance CA BL/TL/6-4/225(225-250) [TorA82 2/30] d6.30

YEAR	TM LG	W	L	PCT	G	GS	CG-SHO	SV-BS	IP	H	R	HR	HB	BB-IB	SO	ERA	AERA	OAV	OOB	AB-HR-SH	AVG	PB	SUP	APR	DL	PW
1987	Tor A	4	3	.571	18	2		1-1	29.1	37	14	0	0	12-0	32	3.99	114	.311	.374	0	—	0	10	2		0.4
1988	Tor A	3	5	.375	41	0		4-2	64.1	65	36	12	2	31-9	56	4.62	86	.269	.354	0	—	0		-4		-0.6
1989	†Tor A	7	4	.636	54	0		2-7	86.1	66	25	6	0	28-7	78	2.40	158	.207	.269	0	—	0		14		1.8
1990	Tor A	11	6	.647	43	25	3-0		189	165	72	14	2	45-3	115	3.14	126	.235	.283	0	—	0	109	16		1.5
1991	†Tor A	15	10	.600	40	28	2	1-1	198.1	188	88	24	2	49-10	106	3.72	114	.251	.297	0	—	0	94	12		1.4

YEAR	TM LG	W	L	PCT	G	GS	CG-SHO	SV-BS	IP	H	R	HR	HB	BB-IB	SO	ERA	AERA	OAV	OOB	AB-HR-SH	AVG	PB	SUP	APR	DL	PW
1992	†Tor A	7	9	.438	41	14	0	2-2	120	138	84	16	8	36-6	62	5.40	76	.289	.346	0	—	0	100	-19		-2.3
1993	Det A	11	9	.550	32	30	0	0-0	187	183	93	26	7	42-6	139	4.19	104	.254	.300	0	—	0	105	5	19	0.5
1994	Det A	5	7	.417	16	16	5-1	0-0	111.1	113	54	13	2	24-6	71	3.96	124	.260	.302	0	—	0	97	12	51	1.1
1995	Det A★	10	3	.769	18	18	3	0-0	130.1	120	54	17	2	37-5	83	3.04	158	.242	.297	0	—	0	94	22		2.0
	†Cin N	6	5	.545	11	11	3	0-0	72.2	74	34	6	0	16-4	50	3.59	116	.265	.304	28-0-1	.143	-1	102	3		0.3
1996	†Bal A	11	14	.440	34	34	3	0-0	224.1	247	132	32	7	51-7	130	5.14	96	.285	.325	0	—	0	100	-2		-0.1
1997	†NY A	16	10	.615	32	32	5-2	0-0	218	239	109	24	4	45-0	156	4.21	106	.278	.317	0	—	0	95	7		0.8
1998	†NY A★	18	4	.818	30	30	8-5	0-0	214.1	195	86	29	1	29-0	163	3.49	126	.239	.265	4	.250	0	142	24		2.1
1999	†Tor A	17	10	.630	34	34	7-1	0-0	231.2	246	132	32	6	62-2	169	4.82	102	.271	.320	6-0-1	.000	-1	112	4		0.4
2000	Tor A★	20	8	.714	35	35	9-1	0-0	229.2	266	115	23	8	31-0	166	4.11	122	.289	.316	6	.167	-0	109	23		2.3
2001	Chi A	5	7	.417	16	16	1	0-0	100.2	120	55	12	3	21-1	59	4.47	104	.297	.335	2	.000	-0	94	2	101	0.1
2002	†NY A	19	7	.731	31	31	2-1	0-0	206.1	210	100	21	5	45-2	137	3.75	116	.259	.300	4-0-1	.000	-0	138	12		1.2
2003	†NY A	15	7	.682	31	30	4-1	0-0	213	242	101	24	8	20-0	101	4.14	106	.286	.306	6	.167	-0	120	9		0.9
2004	SD N	12	8	.600	31	31	0	0-0	195.2	203	85	23	2	20-1	101	3.73	106	.266	.285	57-0-8	.105	-1	117	7	21	0.6
2005	†Bos A	15	7	.682	30	30	2	0-0	184	220	95	21	9	21-0	107	4.45	103	.296	.321	7	.143	-0	135	4	22	0.3
Total	19	227	143	.614	618	447	54-12	13-13	3206.1	3337	1564	374	80	665-60	2081	4.06	110	.267	.307	120-0-11	.117	-3	112	153	214	14.7

WELLS, ED Edwin Lee "Satchelfoot" B6.7.1900 Ashland OH D5.1.1986 Montgomery AL BL/TL/6-1.5/183 d6.16 Col Bethany

YEAR	TM LG	W	L	PCT	G	GS	CG-SHO	SV-BS	IP	H	R	HR	HB	BB-IB	SO	ERA	AERA	OAV	OOB	AB-HR-SH	AVG	PB	SUP	APR	DL	PW
1923	Det A	0	0	—	7	0	0	0	10	11	6	0	0	6	6	5.40	72	.306	.405	1	.000	-0		-1		-0.1
1924	Det A	6	8	.429	29	15	5	4	102	117	58	2	1	42	33	4.06	101	.291	.360	33-0-2	.212	-1	79	0		0.0
1925	Det A	6	9	.400	35	14	5	2	134.1	190	106	8	2	62	45	6.23	69	.345	.413	43-0-1	.279	3	103	-28		-2.4
1926	Det A	12	10	.545	36	26	9-4	0	178	201	101	7	2	76	58	4.15	98	.297	.370	73	.205	-0	114	-2		-0.4
1927	Det A	0	1	.000	8	1	0	1	20	28	16	3	0	5	5	6.75	62	.333	.371	7	.286	-0	40	-4		-0.2
1929	NY A	13	9	.591	31	23	10-3	0	193.1	179	102	19	1	81	78	4.33	89	.248	.324	74-0-3	.230	2	156	-6		-0.7
1930	NY A	12	3	.800	27	21	7	0	150.2	185	101	11	4	49	46	5.20	83	.302	.358	58-0-2	.259	0*	151	-14		-1.2
1931	NY A	9	5	.643	27	10	6	2	116.2	130	68	7	1	37	34	4.32	92	.286	.341	45-0-2	.222	1*	194	-7		-0.7
1932	NY A	3	3	.500	22	0	0	2	31.2	38	19	1	0	12	13	4.26	96	.302	.362	6-0-1	.000	-1*		-1		-0.3
1933	StL A	6	14	.300	36	22	10	1	203.2	230	113	13	1	63	58	4.20	111	.278	.330	71-0-4	.197	-1	95	7		0.4
1934	StL A	1	7	.125	33	8	2	1	92	108	60	7	0	35	27	4.79	104	.292	.353	22-0-1	.045	-2	89	1		0.0
Total	11	68	69	.496	291	140	54-7	13	1232.1	1417	750	78	12	468	403	4.65	91	.291	.355	433-0-16	.215	1	121	-55		-5.6

WELLS, JOHN John Frederick B11.25.1922 Junction City KS D10.23.1993 Olean NY BR/TR/5-11.5/180 d9.14

YEAR	TM LG	W	L	PCT	G	GS	CG-SHO	SV-BS	IP	H	R	HR	HB	BB-IB	SO	ERA	AERA	OAV	OOB	AB-HR-SH	AVG	PB	SUP	APR	DL	PW
1944	Bro N	0	2	.000	4	2	0	0	15	18	9	1	0	11	7	5.40	66	.316	.426	4	.250	0	71	-2		-0.3

WELLS, KIP Robert Kip B4.21.1977 Houston TX BR/TR/6-3/195* [ChiA98 1/16] d8.2 Col Baylor

YEAR	TM LG	W	L	PCT	G	GS	CG-SHO	SV-BS	IP	H	R	HR	HB	BB-IB	SO	ERA	AERA	OAV	OOB	AB-HR-SH	AVG	PB	SUP	APR	DL	PW
1999	Chi A	4	1	.800	7	7	0	0-0	35.2	33	17	2	3	15-0	29	4.04	122	.248	.333	0	—	0	97	4		0.4
2000	Chi A	6	9	.400	20	20	0	0-0	98.2	126	76	15	2	58-4	71	6.02	84	.312	.398	2	.000	-0	107	-11		-1.1
2001	Chi A	10	11	.476	40	20	0	0-2	133.1	145	80	14	12	61-5	99	4.79	97	.281	.366	6	.167	-0	84	-3		-0.4
2002	Pit N	12	14	.462	33	33	1-1	0-0	198.1	197	92	21	7	71-11	134	3.58	117	.261	.328	63-1-13	.190	1*	88	11		1.4
2003	Pit N	10	9	.526	31	31	1	0-0	197.1	171	77	24	7	76-7	147	3.28	132	.233	.310	68-1-4	.191	2*	89	23		2.2
2004	Pit N	5	7	.417	24	24	0	0-0	138.1	145	71	14	6	66-4	116	4.55	95	.270	.330	43-0-4	.186	2*	93	-1	22	0.2
2005	Pit N	8	18	.308	33	33	1-1	0-0	182	186	116	23	12	99-8	132	5.09	83	.266	.363	57-1-3	.158	0*	74	-19		-2.3
Total	7	55	69	.444	188	168	3-2	0-2	983.2	1003	529	113	49	446-39	728	4.36	101	.265	.348	239-3-24	.180	6	89	4	22	-0.1

WELLS, BOB Robert Lee B11.1.1966 Yakima WA BR/TR/6-0/190(180-200) d5.16 Col Spokane Falls (WA) CC

YEAR	TM LG	W	L	PCT	G	GS	CG-SHO	SV-BS	IP	H	R	HR	HB	BB-IB	SO	ERA	AERA	OAV	OOB	AB-HR-SH	AVG	PB	SUP	APR	DL	PW
1994	Phi N	1	0	1.000	6	0	0	0-0	5	5	1	0	1	3-0	3	1.80	238	.235	.381	0	—	0		1		0.2
	Sea A	1	0	1.000	1	0	0	0-0	4	4	1	0	0	1-0	3	2.25	219	.250	.294	0	—	0		1		0.2
1995	†Sea A	4	3	.571	30	4	0	0-1	76.2	88	51	11	3	39-3	38	5.75	83	.284	.364	0	—	0	68	-7		-0.6
1996	Sea A	12	7	.632	36	16	1-1	0-0	130.2	141	78	25	6	46-5	94	5.30	94	.274	.338	0	—	0	121	-2		-0.3
1997	†Sea A	2	0	1.000	46	1	0	2-2	67.1	88	49	11	3	18-1	51	5.75	79	.314	.360	0	—	0	203	-10		-0.5
1998	Sea A	2	2	.500	30	0	0	0-1	51.2	54	38	12	2	16-1	29	6.10	77	.261	.319	0	—	0		-8	33	-0.5
1999	Min A	8	3	.727	76	0	0	1-4	87.1	79	41	8	5	28-4	44	3.81	136	.245	.312	0	—	0		12		1.2
2000	Min A	0	7	.000	76	0	0	10-10	86.1	80	39	14	4	15-2	76	3.65	144	.247	.284	0	—	0		14		1.2
2001	Min A	8	5	.615	65	0	0	2-2	68.2	72	39	12	10	16-2	49	5.11	91	.273	.338	0	—	0		-2		-0.4
2002	†Min A	2	1	.667	48	0	0	0-0	58	78	41	8	1	16-1	30	5.90	76	.325	.367	0	—	0		-9	41	-0.5
Total	9	40	28	.588	414	21	1-1	15-20	635.2	688	378	101	35	200-19	417	5.03	97	.276	.335	0	—	0	116	-10	74	0.0

WELLS, TERRY Terry B9.10.1963 Kankakee IL BL/TL/6-3/205 [HouN85 8/196] d7.3 Col Illinois

YEAR	TM LG	W	L	PCT	G	GS	CG-SHO	SV-BS	IP	H	R	HR	HB	BB-IB	SO	ERA	AERA	OAV	OOB	AB-HR-SH	AVG	PB	SUP	APR	DL	PW
1990	LA N	1	2	.333	5	5	0	0-0	20.2	25	23	4	0	14-0	18	7.84	47	.287	.386	1	.000	-1	123	-11		-1.4

WELSH, CHRIS Christopher Charles B4.14.1955 Wilmington DE BL/TL/6-2/185* [NYA77 21/536] d4.12 Col South Florida

YEAR	TM LG	W	L	PCT	G	GS	CG-SHO	SV-BS	IP	H	R	HR	HB	BB-IB	SO	ERA	AERA	OAV	OOB	AB-HR-SH	AVG	PB	SUP	APR	DL	PW
1981	SD N	6	7	.462	22	19	4-2	0-0	123.2	122	55	9	1	41-4	51	3.78	86	.264	.323	41-0-3	.146	0	105	-7		-0.6
1982	SD N	8	8	.500	28	20	3-1	0-0	139.1	146	88	16	3	63-2	48	4.91	70	.268	.346	42-0-5	.262	4	108	-25	22	-2.1
1983	SD N	0	0	—	7	1	0	0-0	14.1	13	5	2	0	2-0	5	2.51	140	.236	.263	4	.000	0	25	1		0.0
	Mon N	0	0	.000	16	5	0	0-0	44.2	46	30	5	4	18-1	17	5.04	72	.267	.349	14	.286	-0	141	-8		-0.2
	Year	0	2	.000	23	6	0	0-0	59	59	35	7	4	20-1	22	4.42	81	.260	.329	18	.222	1	123	-7		-0.2
1985	Tex A	2	5	.286	25	6	0	0-0	76.1	101	40	11	4	25-3	31	4.13	103	.316	.371	0	—	0	71	0		0.0
1986	Cin N	6	9	.400	24	24	1	0-0	139.1	163	79	9	3	40-4	40	4.78	81	.301	.350	42-1-4	.119	0	112	-12	21	-1.1
Total	5	22	31	.415	122	75	8-3	0-0	537.2	591	297	52	15	189-14	192	4.45	81	.282	.344	143-1-12	.182	5	106	-51	43	-4.0

WELTEROTH, DICK Richard John B8.3.1927 Williamsport PA BR/TR/5-11/165* d5.16

YEAR	TM LG	W	L	PCT	G	GS	CG-SHO	SV-BS	IP	H	R	HR	HB	BB-IB	SO	ERA	AERA	OAV	OOB	AB-HR-SH	AVG	PB	SUP	APR	DL	PW
1948	Was A	2	1	.667	33	4	0	0	65.1	73	43	6	1	50	16	5.51	79	.286	.405	10	.100	-1	135	-7		-0.5
1949	Was A	2	5	.286	52	0	0	2	95.1	107	83	6	1	89	37	7.36	58	.296	.437	17-0-1	.059	-1	95	-30		-2.1
1950	Was A	0	0	—	5	0	0	0	6	5	5	0	0	6	2	3.00	150	.217	.379	0	—	0		0		0.0
Total	3	4	6	.400	90	4	0	3	166.2	185	131	12	2	145	55	6.48	66	.290	.422	27-0-1	.074	-2	115	-37		-2.6

WELZER, TONY Anton Frank B4.5.1899 , Germany D3.18.1971 Milwaukee WI BR/TR/5-11/160 d4.13

YEAR	TM LG	W	L	PCT	G	GS	CG-SHO	SV-BS	IP	H	R	HR	HB	BB-IB	SO	ERA	AERA	OAV	OOB	AB-HR-SH	AVG	PB	SUP	APR	DL	PW
1926	Bos A	4	3	.571	39	5	1-1	0	139	167	88	5	3	53	29	4.86	84	.308	.373	38	.211	2	83	-12		-0.2
1927	Bos A	6	11	.353	37	19	8	1	171.2	214	109	10	4	71	56	4.72	89	.318	.386	42-0-7	.095	-2	79	-10		-1.0
Total	2	10	14	.417	76	24	9-1	1	310.2	381	197	15	7	124	85	4.78	87	.313	.380	80-0-7	.150	-0	81	-22		-1.2

WENDELL, TURK Steven John B5.19.1967 Pittsfield MA BB/TR/6-2/205(180-205) [AtlN88 5/112] d6.17 Col Quinnipiac [DL 2002 Phi N 183]

YEAR	TM LG	W	L	PCT	G	GS	CG-SHO	SV-BS	IP	H	R	HR	HB	BB-IB	SO	ERA	AERA	OAV	OOB	AB-HR-SH	AVG	PB	SUP	APR	DL	PW
1993	Chi N	1	2	.333	7	4	0	0-0	22.2	24	13	0	0	8-1	15	4.37	92	.273	.333	7	.143	-0	112	-1		-0.2
1994	Chi N	0	1	.000	6	2	0	0-0	14.1	22	20	3	0	10-1	9	11.93	35	.349	.432	2	.000	0	86	-12		-0.7
1995	Chi N	3	1	.750	43	0	0	0-0	60.1	71	35	11	2	24-4	50	4.92	85	.298	.363	7	.000	-0		-4	32	-0.2
1996	Chi N	4	5	.444	70	0	0	18-3	79.1	58	26	8	3	44-4	75	2.84	154	.201	.313	2-0-1	.500	.1		14		2.0
1997	Chi N	3	5	.375	52	0	0	4-1	60	53	32	4	1	39-5	54	4.20	103	.238	.350	3	.000	-0		0		0.0
	NY N	0	0	—	13	0	0	1-1	16.1	15	10	3	1	14-1	10	4.96	81	.250	.400	2	.000	-0		-2		-0.1
	Year	3	5	.375	65	0	0	5-2	76.1	68	42	7	2	53-6	64	4.36	98	.240	.361	5	.000	-0		-2		-0.1
1998	NY N	5	1	.833	66	0	0	4-4	76.2	62	25	4	2	33-9	58	2.93	140	.221	.306	4	.000	-0		11		0.8
1999	†NY N	5	4	.556	80	0	0	3-3	85.2	80	31	9	2	37-8	77	3.05	143	.245	.324	6	.000	-0		12		1.1
2000	†NY N	8	6	.571	77	0	0	1-4	82.2	60	35	9	4	41-7	73	3.59	121	.206	.312	4	.250	-0		8		1.2
2001	NY N	4	3	.571	49	0	0	1-2	51.1	42	23	8	3	22-6	41	3.51	115	.223	.310	2	.000	-0		3		0.3
	Phi N	0	2	.000	21	0	0	0-0	15.2	21	13	4	1	12-3	15	7.47	55	.323	.430	0	—	-0		-6		-0.6
	Year	4	5	.444	70	0	0	1-2	67	63	36	12	4	34-9	56	4.43	92	.249	.342	2	.000	-0		-3		-0.3
2003	Phi N	3	3	.500	56	0	0	1-4	64	54	24	6	6	28-5	27	3.38	118	.235	.330	2	.000	-0		15		-0.2
2004	Col N	0	0	—	12	0	0	0-1	16.2	21	14	4	2	12-1	11	7.02	68	.328	.438	2	.000	-0		-4	68	-0.2
Total	11	36	33	.522	552	6	0	33-23	645.2	583	301	73	28	324-55	515	3.93	108	.242	.336	43-0-1	.070	-2	101	24	298	3.8

WENGERT, DON Donald Paul B11.6.1969 Sioux City IA BR/TR/6-2/212* [OakA92 4/116] d4.30 Col Iowa St.

YEAR	TM LG	W	L	PCT	G	GS	CG-SHO	SV-BS	IP	H	R	HR	HB	BB-IB	SO	ERA	AERA	OAV	OOB	AB-HR-SH	AVG	PB	SUP	APR	DL	PW
1995	Oak A	1	1	.500	19	0	0	0-0	29.2	30	14	3	1	7-2	13	3.34	136	.263	.336	0	—	0		3	19	0.1
1996	Oak A	7	11	.389	36	25	1-1	0-0	161.1	200	102	29	6	60-5	75	5.58	89	.307	.368	0	—	0	95	-9	15	-0.9
1997	Oak A	5	11	.313	49	12	1	2-1	134	177	96	21	8	41-4	68	6.04	76	.321	.372	0	—	0	83	-21		-2.2
1998	SD N	0	0	—	10	0	0	1-0	13.2	21	9	2	0	5-0	5	5.93	67	.356	.406	3	.000	-0		-3		-0.2
	Chi N	1	5	.167	21	6	0	0-0	49.2	55	29	8	4	23-0	41	5.07	87	.279	.363	13-0-1	.000	-1*	104	-3		-0.5
	Year	1	5	.167	31	6	0	1-0	63.1	76	38	10	4	28-0	46	5.26	82	.297	.373	16-0-1	.000	-1	107	-6		-0.7
1999	KC A	0	1	.000	11	1	0	0-3	24.1	41	26	6	0	5-0	10	9.25	55	.376	.397	0	—	0	92	-10		-0.5

YEAR	TM LG	W	L	PCT	G	GS	CG-SHO	SV-BS	IP	H	R	HR	HB	BB-IB	SO	ERA	AERA	OAV	OOB	AB-HR-SH	AVG	PB	SUP	APR	DL	PW
2000	Atl N	0	1	.000	10	0	0	0-0	10	12	9	2	0	5-0	7	7.20	63	.286	.362	0	—	0		-3		-0.3
2001	Pit N	0	2	.000	4	4	0	0-0	16	33	22	2	0	6-2	9	12.38	36	.429	.470	3-0-1	.000	-0	119	-13		-1.2
Total	7	14	32	.304	160	48	2-1	3-4	438.2	569	307	73	18	157-13	226	6.01	78	.316	.374	19-0-2	.000	-2	96	-59	34	-5.7

WENSLOFF, BUTCH Charles William B12.3.1915 Sausalito CA D2.18.2001 San Rafael CA BR/TR/5-11/185 d5.2 Def 1944

YEAR	TM LG	W	L	PCT	G	GS	CG-SHO	SV-BS	IP	H	R	HR	HB	BB-IB	SO	ERA	AERA	OAV	OOB	AB-HR-SH	AVG	PB	SUP	APR	DL	PW
1943	NY A	13	11	.542	29	27	18-1	1	223.1	179	80	7	1	70	105	2.54	127	.219	.282	79-0-3	.177	-0	96	15		1.5
1947	†NY A	3	1	.750	11	5	1	0	51.2	41	17	3	0	22	18	2.61	135	.217	.299	19-0-1	.263	1	155	5		0.4
1948	Cle A	0	1	.000	1	0	0	0	1.2	2	2	1	0	3	2	10.80	38	.286	.500	0	—	0		-1		-0.2
Total	3	16	13	.552	41	32	19-1	1	276.2	222	99	11	1	95	125	2.60	126	.219	.287	98-0-4	.194	0	105	19		1.7

WENZ, FRED Frederick Charles "Fireball" B8.26.1941 Bound Brook NJ BR/TR/6-3/214* d6.4

YEAR	TM LG	W	L	PCT	G	GS	CG-SHO	SV-BS	IP	H	R	HR	HB	BB-IB	SO	ERA	AERA	OAV	OOB	AB-HR-SH	AVG	PB	SUP	APR	DL	PW
1968	Bos A	0	0	—	1	0	0	0	1	0	0	0	0	2-0	3	0.00	—	.000	.400	0		0		0		0.0
1969	Bos A	1	0	1.000	8	0	0	0-0	11	9	7	0	0	10-3	11	5.73	67	.225	.380	0	—	0		-2		-0.1
1970	Phi N	2	0	1.000	22	0	0	1-0	30.1	27	16	2	1	13-0	24	4.45	90	.237	.313	5	.000	-1		-1		-0.2
Total	3	3	0	1.000	31	0	0	1-0	42.1	36	23	2	1	25-3	38	4.68	85	.229	.333	5	.000	-0		-3		-0.3

WERDEN, PERRY Percival Wheritt B7.21.1865 St.Louis MO D1.9.1934 Minneapolis MN BR/TR/6-2/220 d4.24 ▲

YEAR	TM LG	W	L	PCT	G	GS	CG-SHO	SV-BS	IP	H	R	HR	HB	BB-IB	SO	ERA	AERA	OAV	OOB	AB-HR-SH	AVG	PB	SUP	APR	DL	PW
1884	StL U	12	1	.923	16	16	12-1	0	141.1	113	61	1		22	51	1.97	121	.204	.235	76		.237	-4*	153	7		0.2

WERLE, BILL William George "Bugs" B12.21.1920 Oakland CA BL/TL/6-2.5/182* d4.22 C1 Col California-Davis

YEAR	TM LG	W	L	PCT	G	GS	CG-SHO	SV-BS	IP	H	R	HR	HB	BB-IB	SO	ERA	AERA	OAV	OOB	AB-HR-SH	AVG	PB	SUP	APR	DL	PW
1949	Pit N	12	13	.480	35	29	10-2	1	221	243	117	23	8	51	106	4.24	99	.278	.324	77-0-2	.117	-3	93	-2		-0.4
1950	Pit N	8	16	.333	48	22	6	8	215.1	249	127	25	6	65	78	4.60	95	.290	.344	67-0-2	.194	1	81	-6		-0.3
1951	Pit N	8	6	.571	59	5	2	6	149.2	181	102	20	6	51	57	5.65	75	.304	.364	40-0-1	.300	3	116	-20		-1.3
1952	Pit N	0	0	—	5	0	0	0	4	9	5	1	0	1	1	9.00	44	.429	.455	0	—	-0		-2		-0.1
	StL N	1	2	.333	19	0	1	0	39	40	23	6	1	15	23	4.85	77	.268	.339	9	.111	-0		-5	65	-0.3
	Year	1	2	.333	24	0	1	0	43	49	28	7	1	16	24	5.23	71	.288	.353	9	.111	-0		-7		-0.4
1953	Bos A	0	1	.000	5	0	0	1	11.2	7	3	1	0	1	4	1.54	273	.179	.200	2	.000	-0		3		0.3
1954	Bos A	0	1	.000	14	0	0	0	24.2	41	13	5	2	10	14	4.38	94	.376	.434	4	.000	-0		0		0.0
Total	6	29	39	.426	185	60	18-2	15	665.1	770	390	81	23	194	283	4.69	90	.291	.345	199-0-5	.176	1	92	-32	65	-2.1

WERLEY, GEORGE George William B9.8.1938 St.Louis MO BR/TR/6-2/196 d9.29

YEAR	TM LG	W	L	PCT	G	GS	CG-SHO	SV-BS	IP	H	R	HR	HB	BB-IB	SO	ERA	AERA	OAV	OOB	AB-HR-SH	AVG	PB	SUP	APR	DL	PW
1956	Bal A	0	0	—	1	1	0	0	1	1	1	0	0	2-0	1	9.00	44	.250	.500		—	-0		-1		0.0

WERTS, JOHNNY Henry Levi B4.20.1898 Pomaria SC D9.24.1990 Newberry SC BR/TR/5-10/180 d4.14

YEAR	TM LG	W	L	PCT	G	GS	CG-SHO	SV-BS	IP	H	R	HR	HB	BB-IB	SO	ERA	AERA	OAV	OOB	AB-HR-SH	AVG	PB	SUP	APR	DL	PW
1926	Bos N	11	9	.550	32	23	7-1	0	189.1	212	85	6	10	47	65	3.28	108	.287	.338	64-1-3	.266	4	82	1		1.0
1927	Bos N	4	10	.286	42	15	4	1	164.1	204	95	5	4	52	39	4.55	82	.315	.369	43-0-2	.163	-0	84	-15		-1.2
1928	Bos N	0	2	.000	10	2	0	0	18.1	31	22	2	0	8	5	10.31	38	.369	.424	3	.333	1	87	-12		-1.1
1929	Bos N	0	0	—	4	0	0	1	6	13	8	1	0	4	2	10.50	45	.433	.500	1	1.000	0		-4		-0.1
Total	4	15	21	.417	88	40	11-1	2	378	460	210	14	14	111	111	4.29	85	.307	.360	111-1-5	.234	4	82	-27		-1.4

WERTZ, BILL William Charles B1.15.1967 Cleveland OH BR/TR/6-6/220* [CleA89 31/801] d5.22 Col Ohio St.

YEAR	TM LG	W	L	PCT	G	GS	CG-SHO	SV-BS	IP	H	R	HR	HB	BB-IB	SO	ERA	AERA	OAV	OOB	AB-HR-SH	AVG	PB	SUP	APR	DL	PW
1993	Cle A	2	3	.400	34	0	0	0-2	59.2	54	28	5	1	32-2	53	3.62	121	.238	.333	0	—	-0		4		0.2
1994	Cle A	0	0	—	1	0	0	0-0	4.1	9	5	0	0	1-0	1	10.38	46	.409	.435	0	—	-0		-2		-0.1
Total	2	2	3	.400	35	0	0	0-2	64	63	33	5	1	33-2	54	4.08	108	.253	.342	0		0		2		0.1

WEST, DAVID David Lee B9.1.1964 Memphis TN BL/TL/6-6/230(207-255) [NYN83 4/84] d9.24

YEAR	TM LG	W	L	PCT	G	GS	CG-SHO	SV-BS	IP	H	R	HR	HB	BB-IB	SO	ERA	AERA	OAV	OOB	AB-HR-SH	AVG	PB	SUP	APR	DL	PW
1988	NY N	1	0	1.000	2	1	0	0-0	6	6	2	0	0	3-0	3	3.00	109	.273	.360	2	1.000	1	381	0		0.2
1989	NY N	0	2	.000	11	2	0	0-0	24.1	25	20	4	1	14-2	19	7.40	45	.260	.357	5	.200	0	67	-11		-0.8
	Min A	3	2	.600	10	5	0	0-1	39.1	48	29	5	2	19-1	31	6.41	65	.306	.383	0	—	0	96	-9		-1.0
1990	Min A	7	9	.438	29	27	2	0-0	146.1	142	88	21	4	78-1	92	5.10	82	.256	.350	0	—	0	97	-13	27	-1.3
1991	†Min A	4	4	.500	15	12	0	0-0	71.1	66	37	13	4	28-0	52	4.54	94	.244	.314	0	—	0	91	-1	85	-0.1
1992	Min A	1	3	.250	9	3	0	0-0	28.1	32	24	3	1	20-0	19	6.99	58	.276	.381	0	—	0	30	-9		-1.1
1993	†Phi N	6	4	.600	76	0	0	3-6	86.1	60	37	6	5	51-4	87	2.92	136	.194	.316	5	.400	1		8		0.9
1994	Phi N	4	10	.286	31	14	0	0-2	99	74	44	7	1	61-2	83	3.55	121	.205	.320	28-0-1	.071	-2	73	8		0.7
1995	Phi N	3	2	.600	8	8	0	0-0	38	34	17	5	1	19-0	25	3.79	111	.241	.335	8-1-6	.125	1	96	2	120	0.3
1996	Phi N	2	2	.500	7	6	0	0-0	28.1	31	17	0	0	11-0	22	4.76	91	.272	.336	7-0-2	.286	1	70	-2	141	-0.1
1998	NY N	0	0	—	6	0	0	0-0	2	6	6	1	0	7-0	2	27.00	18	.538	.700	0	—	0		-5		-0.2
Total	10	31	38	.449	204	78	2	3-9	569.1	525	321	65	16	311-10	437	4.66	90	.244	.341	55-1-9	.182	2	90	-32	373	-2.5

WEST, HI James Hiram B8.8.1884 Roseville IL D5.24.1963 Los Angeles CA BR/TR/6-0/185 d9.8 Col Knox

YEAR	TM LG	W	L	PCT	G	GS	CG-SHO	SV-BS	IP	H	R	HR	HB	BB-IB	SO	ERA	AERA	OAV	OOB	AB-HR-SH	AVG	PB	SUP	APR	DL	PW
1905	Cle A	2	2	.500	6	4	4-1	0	33	43	23	0	3	10	15	4.09	64	.316	.376	13	.077	-1	40	-6		-0.9
1911	Cle A	3	4	.429	13	8	3	1	64.2	84	35	1	3	18	17	3.76	91	.343	.395	23	.130	-2	95	-2		-0.4
Total	2	5	6	.455	19	12	7-1	1	97.2	127	58	1	6	28	32	3.87	81	.333	.388	36	.111	-3	80	-8		-1.3

WEST, FRANK John Franklin B1.21.1873 Johnstown PA D9.6.1932 Wilmerding PA ?/180 d7.11

YEAR	TM LG	W	L	PCT	G	GS	CG-SHO	SV-BS	IP	H	R	HR	HB	BB-IB	SO	ERA	AERA	OAV	OOB	AB-HR-SH	AVG	PB	SUP	APR	DL	PW
1894	Bos N	0	0	—	1	0	0	0	3	5	5	0	0	2	1	9.00	63	.357	.438	1	.000	-0		-1		-0.1

WEST, LEFTY Weldon Edison B9.3.1915 Gibsonville NC D7.23.1979 Hendersonville NC BR/TL/6-0/165 d4.30

YEAR	TM LG	W	L	PCT	G	GS	CG-SHO	SV-BS	IP	H	R	HR	HB	BB-IB	SO	ERA	AERA	OAV	OOB	AB-HR-SH	AVG	PB	SUP	APR	DL	PW
1944	StL A	0	0	—	11	0	0	0	24.1	34	18	1	1	19	11	6.29	57	.366	.478	7	.143	-0		-6		-0.4
1945	StL A	3	4	.429	24	8	1	0	74.1	71	37	2	0	31	38	3.63	97	.245	.318	27-0-1	.074	-3	73	-2		-0.6
Total	2	3	4	.429	35	8	1	0	98.2	105	55	3	1	50	49	4.29	83	.274	.359	34-0-1	.088	-3	73	-8		-1.0

WESTBROOK, JAKE Jacob Cauthen B9.29.1977 Athens GA BR/TR/6-3/190(185-215) [ColN96 1/21] d6.17 [DL 2000 Cle A 30]

YEAR	TM LG	W	L	PCT	G	GS	CG-SHO	SV-BS	IP	H	R	HR	HB	BB-IB	SO	ERA	AERA	OAV	OOB	AB-HR-SH	AVG	PB	SUP	APR	DL	PW
2000	NY A	0	2	.000	3	2	0	0-0	6.2	15	10	1	0	4-1	0	13.50	35	.469	.500	0	—	0	108	-6		-1.0
2001	Cle A	4	4	.500	23	6	0	0-0	64.2	79	43	6	4	22-4	48	5.85	79	.306	.363	1-0-1	.000	-0	91	-7		-0.7
2002	Cle A	1	3	.250	11	4	0	0-2	41.2	50	30	6	1	12-1	20	5.83	76	.296	.344	0	—	0	63	-7	137	-0.6
2003	Cle A	7	10	.412	34	22	1	0	133	142	70	9	12	56-1	116	4.33	102	.281	.365	0	—	0	94	3		0.4
2004	Cle A☆	14	9	.609	33	30	5-1	0-0	215.2	208	95	19	5	61-3	116	3.38	129	.255	.308	3-0-1	.000	-0	133	21		2.2
2005	Cle A	15	15	.500	34	34	2	0-0	210.2	218	121	19	7	56-3	119	4.49	91	.265	.316	2	.000	-0	106	-12		-1.2
Total	6	41	43	.488	138	98	8-1	0-2	672.1	712	369	60	29	211-13	362	4.40	98	.273	.332	6-0-2	.000	-0	108	-8	167	-0.9

WESTERVELT, HUYLER Huyler B10.1.1869 Tenafly NJ D10.14.1949 Pelham Manor NY TR/5-9/170 d4.21

YEAR	TM LG	W	L	PCT	G	GS	CG-SHO	SV-BS	IP	H	R	HR	HB	BB-IB	SO	ERA	AERA	OAV	OOB	AB-HR-SH	AVG	PB	SUP	APR	DL	PW
1894	NY N	7	10	.412	23	18	11-1	0	141	170	118	4	5	76	35	5.04	104	.295	.382	56-0-2	.143	-5	92	4		0.0

WESTON, MICKEY Michael Lee B3.26.1961 Flint MI BR/TR/6-1/187* [NYN82 12/293] d6.18 Col Eastern Michigan

YEAR	TM LG	W	L	PCT	G	GS	CG-SHO	SV-BS	IP	H	R	HR	HB	BB-IB	SO	ERA	AERA	OAV	OOB	AB-HR-SH	AVG	PB	SUP	APR	DL	PW
1989	Bal A	1	0	1.000	7	0	0	1-0	13	18	8	1	1	2-0	7	5.54	69	.346	.382	0	—	0		-2	60	-0.2
1990	Bal A	0	1	.000	9	2	0	0-0	21	28	20	6	0	6-1	9	7.71	50	.322	.366	0	—	0	95	-10		-0.5
1991	Tor A	0	0	—	2	0	0	0-0	2	1	0	0	0	1-1	1	0.00	—	.143	.250	0	—	0	1	0		0.0
1992	Phi N	0	1	.000	1	1	0	0-0	3.2	7	5	1	1	1-0	0	12.27	29	.412	.474	2	.000	-0	26	-3		-0.5
1993	NY N	0	0	—	4	0	0	0-0	5.2	11	5	0	1	2-0	2	7.94	51	.393	.433	0	—	0		-2		-0.1
Total	5	1	2	.333	23	3	0	1-0	45.1	65	38	8	3	11-2	19	7.15	54	.340	.385	2	.000	-0	71	-16	60	-1.3

WETTELAND, JOHN John Karl B8.21.1966 San Mateo CA BR/TR/6-2/195(195-215) [LAN85*S2/39] d5.31 Col San Mateo (CA) [JC]

YEAR	TM LG	W	L	PCT	G	GS	CG-SHO	SV-BS	IP	H	R	HR	HB	BB-IB	SO	ERA	AERA	OAV	OOB	AB-HR-SH	AVG	PB	SUP	APR	DL	PW
1989	LA N	5	8	.385	31	12	0	1-1	102.2	81	46	9	0	34-4	96	3.77	91	.218	.283	21-0-5	.143	-0	95	-3		-0.4
1990	LA N	2	4	.333	22	5	0	0-1	43	44	28	6	4	17-3	36	4.81	77	.263	.344	7-1-1	.143	1	123	-6		-0.8
1991	LA N	1	0	1.000	6	0	0	0-0	9	5	2	0	0	3-0	9	0.00	—	.161	.250	0	—	0		3		0.3
1992	Mon N	4	4	.500	67	0	0	37-9	83.1	64	27	6	4	36-3	99	2.92	120	.213	.304	5-0-1	.200	0		6		1.1
1993	Mon N	9	3	.750	70	0	0	43-6	85.1	58	17	3	1	28-3	113	1.37	305	.188	.260	4-0-1	.000	-0		25	18	5.1
1994	Mon N	4	6	.400	52	0	0	25-10	63.2	46	22	5	3	21-4	68	2.83	150	.202	.273	4-0-1	.250	0		10	16	2.0
1995	†NY A	1	5	.167	60	0	0	31-6	61.1	40	22	6	0	14-2	66	2.93	158	.185	.233	0		0		11		1.9
1996	†NY A☆	2	3	.400	62	0	0	43-4	63.2	54	23	9	0	21-4	69	2.83	175	.224	.284	0		0		14	24	2.6
1997	Tex A	7	2	.778	61	0	0	31-6	65	43	18	5	0	21-3	63	1.94	251	.182	.248	1	1.000	1		19		3.7
1998	†Tex A★	3	1	.750	63	0	0	42-5	62	47	17	6	0	14-1	72	2.03	241	.203	.247	0	—	0		18		3.0
1999	†Tex A★	4	4	.500	62	0	0	43-7	66	67	30	9	0	19-1	65	3.68	141	.262	.307	0	—	0		10		1.8
2000	Tex A	6	5	.545	62	0	0	34-9	60	67	35	10	2	24-2	53	4.20	121	.285	.351	0	—	0		4		0.7
Total	12	48	45	.516	618	17	0	330-63	765	616	318	78	16	248-33	804	2.93	148	.218	.284	42-1-9	.167	1	86	111	58	21.0

WETZEL, BUZZ Charles Edward B8.25.1894 Jay OK D3.7.1941 Globe AZ BR/TR/6-1/162 d7.25

YEAR	TM LG	W	L	PCT	G	GS	CG-SHO	SV-BS	IP	H	R	HR	HB	BB-IB	SO	ERA	AERA	OAV	OOB	AB-HR-SH	AVG	PB	SUP	APR	DL	PW
1927	Phi A	0	0	—	2	1	0	0	4.2	5	4	0	0	3	0	7.71	55	.400	.520	1	1.000	0	117	-2		0.0

YEAR	TM LG	W	L	PCT	G	GS	CG-SHO	SV-BS	IP	H	R	HR	HB	BB-IB	SO	ERA	AERA	OAV	OOB	AB-HR-SH	AVG	PB	SUP	APR	DL	PW

WETZEL, SHORTY George William B1868 Philadelphia PA D2.25.1899 Dayton OH d8.26

1885	Bal AA	0	2	.000	2	2	1	0	17	27	26	0	3	9	6	8.47	38	.333	.419	7	.000	-1	45	-10		-0.8

WEVER, STEFAN Stefan Matthew B4.22.1958 Marburg, W.Germany BR/TR/6-8/245 [NYA79 6/155] d9.17 Col California-Santa Barbara

| 1982 | NY A | 0 | 1 | .000 | 1 | 1 | 0 | 0 | 2.2 | 6 | 9 | 1 | 0 | 3-0 | 2 | 27.00 | 15 | .429 | .500 | 0 | — | 0 | 0 | -7 | | -0.9 |

WEYHING, GUS August "Cannonball" B9.29.1866 Louisville KY D9.4.1955 Louisville KY BR/TR/5-10/145 d5.2 b-John

1887	Phi AA	26	28	.481	55	55	53-2	0	466.1	465	342	12	37	167	193	4.27	101	.253	.328	209	.201	-9*	94	-5		-1.2
1888	Phi AA	28	18	.609	47	47	45-3	0	404	314	198	4	42	111	204	2.25	133	.207	.279	184-1	.217	4*	124	30		3.3
1889	Phi AA	30	21	.588	54	53	50-4	0	449	382	271	15	34	212	213	2.95	128	.223	.321	191	.131	-15	98	35		1.6
1890	Bro P	30	16	.652	49	46	38-3	0	390	419	250	10	17	179	177	3.60	124	.263	.343	165-1	.164	-6	104	40		2.5
1891	Phi AA	31	20	.608	52	51	51-3	0	450	428	231	12	31	161	219	3.18	119	.242	.316	198	.111	-16*	91	29		1.0
1892	Phi N	32	21	.604	59	49	46-6	3	469.2	411	213	9	18	168	202	2.66	122	.226	.298	214	.136	-10*	104	31		1.6
1893	Phi N	23	16	.590	42	40	33-2	0	345.1	399	235	10	20	145	101	4.74	97	.281	.356	147	.150	-9*	117	-2		-1.0
1894	Phi N	16	14	.533	40	36	26-2	1	279	379	224	12	16	120	83	5.71	90	.321	.391	121-0-8	.174	-9	104	-11		-1.7
1895	Phi N	0	2	.000	2	2	0	0	9	23	22	0	0	13	5	20.00	24	.469	.581	4	.000	-1	104	-13		-1.6
	Pit N	1	0	1.000	1	1	1	0	9	10	7	0	0	5	3	1.00	451	.278	.366	4	.250	0	158	2		0.2
	Lou N	7	19	.269	28	25	22-1	0	213	285	205	9	8	66	53	5.41	80	.316	.368	89-1-0	.225	-1	77	-24		-2.1
	Year	8	21	.276	31	28	23-1	0	231	318	234	9	8	84	61	5.81	82	.322	.380	97-1-0	.216	-1	82	-38		-3.5
1896	Lou N	2	3	.400	5	5	4	0	42	62	46	6	2	15	9	6.64	65	.339	.395	15	.133	-1	105	-10		-0.9
1898	Was N	15	26	.366	45	42	39	0	361	428	232	10	16	84	92	4.51	81	.292	.338	141-0-7	.177	-5*	85	-25		-2.8
1899	Was N	17	21	.447	43	38	34-2	0	334.2	414	223	8	28	76	96	4.54	86	.303	.352	126-0-6	.206	-1	96	-20		-2.2
1900	StL N	3	2	.600	7	5	3	0	46.2	60	44	2	1	21	6	4.63	79	.311	.381	21	.095	-2	118	-8		-0.9
	Bro N	3	4	.429	8	8	3	0	48	66	33	1	2	20	8	4.31	89	.325	.391	18	.222	-3	146	-3		-0.3
	Year	6	6	.500	15	13	6	0	94.2	126	77	3	3	41	14	4.47	84	.318	.386	39	.154	-3	137	-10		-1.3
1901	Cle A	0	0	—	2	1	0	0	11.1	20	11	0	4	5	0	7.94	45	.377	.468	5	.000	-1	228	-4		-0.2
	Cin N	0	1	.000	1	1	1	0	9	11	9	0	2	2	3	3.00	107	.297	.366	3	.000	-0	22	-2		-0.2
Total	14	264	232	.532	540	505	449-28	4	4337	4576	2796	120	278	1570	1667	3.88	102	.264	.335	1855-3-21	.166	-83	102	40		-5.1

WEYHING, JOHN John B6.24.1869 Louisville KY D6.20.1890 Louisville KY BL/TL/6-2/185 d7.13 b-Gus

1888	Cin AA	3	4	.429	8	8	7	0	65.2	52	26	0	1	17	30	1.23	257	.210	.263	23	.130	-2	66	10		0.8
1889	Col AA	0	0	—	1	0	0	0	1	1	3	0	0	4	0	27.00	13	.250	.625	0	—	0		-2		-0.1
Total	2	3	4	.429	9	8	7	0	66.2	53	29	0	1	21	30	1.62	196	.210	.274	23	.130	-2	66	8		0.7

WHEAT, LEE Leroy William B9.15.1929 Edwardsville IL BR/TR/6-4/200* d4.21 Col Truman St.

1954	Phi A	0	2	.000	8	1	0	0	28.1	38	18	1	1	9	7	5.72	68	.304	.350	8	.125	-0	68	-5		-0.4
1955	KC A	0	0	—	3	0	0	0	2	8	7	1	0	3-2	1	22.50	19	.533	.611	0	—	0		-4		-0.2
Total*	2	0	2	.000	11	1	0	0	30.1	46	25	2	1	12-2	8	6.82	57	.329	.381	8	.125	-0	68	-9		-0.6

WHEATLEY, CHARLIE Charles B6.27.1893 Rosedale KS D12.10.1982 Tulsa OK BR/TR/5-11/174 d9.6

| 1912 | Det A | 1 | 4 | .200 | 5 | 5 | 2 | 0 | 35 | 45 | 27 | 1 | 2 | 17 | 14 | 6.17 | 53 | .331 | .413 | 12 | .000 | -2 | 68 | -9 | | -1.2 |

WHEATON, WOODY Elwood Pierce B10.3.1914 Philadelphia PA D12.11.1995 Lancaster PA BL/TL/5-8.5/160 d9.28.1943 ▲

| 1944 | Phi A | 0 | 1 | .000 | 11 | 1 | 1 | 0 | 38 | 36 | 17 | 1 | 1 | 20 | 15 | 3.55 | 98 | .255 | .352 | 59-0-1 | .186 | 0* | 0 | 0 | | 0.0 |

WHEELER, DAN Daniel Michael B12.10.1977 Providence RI BR/TR/6-3/220* [TBA96 34/1024] d9.1 Col Central Arizona JC

1999	TB A	0	4	.000	6	6	0	0-0	30.2	35	20	7	0	13-1	32	5.87	85	.287	.356	0	—	0	78	-2		-0.2
2000	TB A	1	1	.500	11	2	0	0-1	23	29	14	2	2	11-2	17	5.48	89	.302	.382	0	—	0	77	-1		-0.1
2001	TB A	1	0	1.000	13	0	0	0-0	17.2	30	17	3	0	5-0	12	8.66	52	.375	.402	0	—	0		-7		-0.3
2003	NY N	1	3	.250	35	0	0	2-1	51	49	23	6	1	17-4	35	3.71	113	.253	.312	2	.000	-0		3		0.1
2004	NY N	3	1	.750	32	1	0	0-0	50.2	65	29	9	0	17-2	46	4.80	90	.307	.357	5-0-1	.200	0	172	-2		-0.2
	†Hou N	0	0	—	14	0	0	0-0	14.1	11	4	1	1	3-0	9	2.51	174	.216	.273	0	—	0		3		0.1
	Year	3	1	.750	46	1	0	0-0	65	76	33	10	1	20-2	55	4.29	101	.289	.340	5-0-1	.200	-0	172	1		-0.1
2005	†Hou N	2	3	.400	71	0	0	3-2	73.1	53	18	7	3	19-3	69	2.21	190	.204	.265	0	—	0		17		1.2
Total	6	8	12	.400	182	9	0	5-4	260.2	272	125	35	7	85-12	210	4.18	105	.268	.326	7-0-1	.143	-0	97	11		0.6

WHEELER, RIP Floyd Clark B3.2.1898 Marion KY D9.18.1968 Marion KY BR/TR/6-0/180 d9.30

1921	Pit N	0	0	—	1	0	0	0	3	6	4	0	1	0	0	9.00	43	.500	.571	1	.000	-0		-2		-0.1
1922	Pit N	0	0	—	1	0	0	0	1	1	0	0	0	2	0	0.00	—	.333	.600	0	—	0		0		0.0
1923	Chi N	1	2	.333	3	3	1	0	24	28	14	2	3	5	5	4.88	82	.298	.353	9	.111	-1	82	-2		-0.2
1924	Chi N	3	6	.333	29	4	0	0	101.1	103	53	8	0	21	16	3.91	100	.265	.303	32	.219	-1	82	0		-0.1
Total	4	4	8	.333	34	7	1	0	129.1	138	71	10	4	28	21	4.94	90	.278	.323	42	.190	-2	83	-4		-0.4

WHEELER, GEORGE George Louis (b George Louis Heroux) B7.30.1869 Methuen MA D3.21.1946 Santa Ana CA BB/TR/5-9/180 d9.18

1896	Phi N	1	1	.500	3	2	2	0	16.1	18	11	0	2	5	2	3.86	112	.277	.347	9	.111	-1	124	0		-0.1
1897	Phi N	11	10	.524	26	19	17	0	191	229	114	0	3	62	35	3.96	106	.295	.349	79-0-1	.203	-1	91	4		0.4
1898	Phi N	6	8	.429	15	13	10	0	112.1	155	94	1	6	36	20	4.17	82	.325	.380	43-0-3	.186	-1	98	-16		-1.5
1899	Phi N	3	1	.750	6	5	3	0	39	44	30	1	3	13	3	6.00	61	.284	.351	17-1-1	.235	1	164	-8		-0.5
Total	4	21	20	.512	50	39	32	0	358.2	446	249	5	14	116	60	4.24	92	.303	.359	148-1-5	.196	-2	103	-20		-1.7

WHEELER, HARRY Harry Eugene B3.3.1858 Versailles IN D10.9.1900 Cincinnati OH BR/TR/5-11/165 d6.19 M1 ▲

1878	Pro N	6	1	.857	7	6	6	0	62	70	40	1		25	25	3.48	63	.275	.339	27	.148	-1	191	-6		-0.7
1879	Cin N	0	1	.000	1	1	0	0	1	6	10	0		4	0	81.00	3	.667	.769	3	.000	-0	20	-7		-0.8
1882	Cin AA	1	2	.333	4	1	1	0	21.2	21	17	0		12	10	5.40	49	.239	.330	344-1	.250	1*	156	-4		-0.3
1883	Col AA	0	1	.000	1	1	0	0	5	13	7	0		2	0	7.20	48	.448	.484	371	.226	0*	56	-2		-0.3
1884	KC U	0	1	.000	1	1	1	0	8	7	6	0		0	6	1.13	199	.219	.219	62	.258	-0*	38	0		0.0
Total	5	7	6	.538	14	10	8	0	97.2	117	80	1		43	41	4.70	50	.283	.351	807-1	.235	-1	141	-19		-2.3

WHEELOCK, GARY Gary Richard B11.29.1951 Bakersfield CA BR/TR/6-3/200* [AnaA74 6/130] d9.17 Col California-Irvine

1976	Cal A	0	0	—	2	0	0	0-0	2	6	6	0	1	1-0	0	27.00	12	.500	.571	0	—	0		-5		-0.3
1977	Sea A	6	9	.400	17	17	2	0-0	88.1	94	58	16	2	26-0	47	4.89	85	.268	.321	0	—	0	85	-9	88	-1.4
1980	Sea A	0	0	—	1	1	0	0-0	3	4	2	0	0	1-0	1	6.00	69	.333	.385	0	—	0	64	0		-0.1
Total	3	6	9	.400	20	18	2	0-0	93.1	104	66	16	3	28-0	50	5.40	76	.277	.332	0	—	0	85	-14	88	-1.7

WHILLOCK, JACK Jack Franklin B11.4.1942 Clinton AR BR/TR/6-3/195 d8.29 Col Arkansas-Monticello

| 1971 | Det A | 0 | 2 | .000 | 7 | 0 | 0 | 1-1 | 8 | 10 | 5 | 0 | 0 | 2-0 | 6 | 5.63 | 64 | .323 | .364 | 0 | .000 | -0 | | -2 | | -0.3 |

WHISENANT, MATT Matthew Michael B6.8.1971 Los Angeles CA BR/TL/6-3/215* [PhiN89 18/456] d7.4 Col Glendale (CA) CC

1997	Fla N	0	0	—	4	0	0	0-0	2.2	4	6	0	0	6-0	4	16.88	24	.333	.556	0	—	0*		-4	94	-0.2
	KC A	1	0	1.000	24	0	0	0-0	19	15	7	0	3	12-0	16	2.84	167	.211	.349	0	—	0		4		0.2
1998	KC A	2	1	.667	70	0	0	2-3	60.2	61	37	3	3	33-2	45	4.90	99	.271	.365	0	—	0		-1		-0.0
1999	KC A	4	4	.500	48	0	0	1-3	39.2	40	28	4	7	26-1	27	6.35	80	.267	.399	0	—	0		-4		-0.7
	SD N	0	1	.000	19	0	0	0-1	14.2	10	6	1	0	10-1	10	3.68	116	.200	.333	0	—	0		1		0.1
2000	SD N	2	2	.500	24	0	0	0-3	21.1	16	12	1	0	17-1	12	3.80	117	.213	.351	0	—	0		1		0.1
Total	4	9	8	.529	189	0	0	3-10	158	146	96	8	13	104-5	114	4.96	96	.250	.372	0	—	0		-3	94	-0.5

WHITAKER, PAT William H. B11.1864 St.Louis MO D7.15.1902 St.Louis MO TR d10.11

1888	Bal AA	1	1	.500	2	2	2	0	14	13	12	0	0	6	5	5.14	58	.236	.333	6	.000	-1	68	-3		-0.4
1889	Bal AA	1	0	1.000	1	1	1	0	9	10	4	0	0	4	1	2.00	197	.270	.341	4	.250	-0	126	2		0.2
Total	2	2	1	.667	3	3	3	0	23	23	16	0	0	10	6	3.91	86	.250	.337	10	.100	-1	89	-1		-0.2

WHITBY, BILL William Edward B7.29.1943 Crewe VA BR/TR/6-1/190 d6.17

| 1964 | Min A | 0 | 0 | — | 4 | 0 | 0 | 0 | 3 | 3 | 0 | 0 | 0 | 1-0 | 2 | 8.53 | 42 | .308 | .333 | 1 | .000 | -0 | | -2 | | -0.2 |

WHITCHER, BOB Robert Arthur B4.29.1917 Berlin NH D5.8.1997 Akron OH BL/TL/5-8/165 d8.20

| 1945 | Bos N | 0 | 2 | .000 | 6 | 3 | 0 | 0 | 15.2 | 12 | 6 | 1 | 0 | 12 | 6 | 2.87 | 133 | .235 | .381 | 3 | .333 | 0* | 37 | 2 | | 0.2 |

WHITE, ABE Adel B5.16.1904 Winder GA D10.1.1978 Atlanta GA BR/TL/6-0/185 d7.10

| 1937 | StL N | 0 | 1 | .000 | 5 | 0 | 0 | 0 | 9.1 | 14 | 7 | 1 | 0 | 3 | 2 | 6.75 | 59 | .341 | .386 | 1 | 1.000 | 0 | | -2 | | -0.2 |

YEAR	TM	LG	W	L	PCT	G	GS	CG-SHO	SV-BS	IP	H	R	HR	HB	BB-IB	SO	ERA	AERA	OAV	OOB	AB-HR-SH	AVG	PB	SUP	APR	DL	PW

WHITE, ERNIE Ernest Daniel B9.5.1916 Pacolet Mills SC D5.22.1974 Augusta GA BR/TL/5-11.5/175 d5.9 Mil 1944-45 C3

YEAR	TM	LG	W	L	PCT	G	GS	CG-SHO	SV-BS	IP	H	R	HR	HB	BB-IB	SO	ERA	AERA	OAV	OOB	AB-HR-SH	AVG	PB	SUP	APR	DL	PW
1940	StL	N	1	1	.500	8	1	0	0	21.2	29	13	0	1	14	15	4.15	96	.315	.411	7	.429	1*	0	-1		0.1
1941	StL	N	17	7	.708	32	25	12-3	2	210	169	72	6	7	70	117	2.40	157	.217	.287	79-0-3	.190	0*	113	28		3.0
1942	†StL	N	7	5	.583	26	19	7-1	2	128.1	113	57	11	2	41	67	2.52	136	.232	.294	41-0-5	.195	0*	123	7		0.5
1943	†StL	N	5	5	.500	14	10	5-1	0	78.2	78	38	4	1	33	28	3.78	89	.257	.332	28-0-2	.214	0*	124	-3		-0.5
1946	Bos	N	0	1	.000	12	1	0	0	23.2	22	11	1	0	12	8	4.18	82	.256	.347	4	.250	0*	150	-1		-0.1
1947	Bos	N	0	0	—	1	1	0	0	4	1	0	0	0	1	1	0.00	—	.083	.154	1	1.000	0	68	2		0.1
1948	Bos	N	0	2	.000	15	0	0	2	23	13	5	1	0	17	8	1.96	196	.167	.316	3	.000	-0*		4		0.3
Total 7			30	21	.588	108	57	24-5	6	489.1	425	198	28	10	188	244	2.78	130	.231	.306	163-0-10	.209	2	115	36		3.4

WHITE, GABE Gabriel Allen B11.20.1971 Sebring FL BL/TL/6-2/200* [MonN90 1/28] d5.27 [DL 1996 Cin N 13]

YEAR	TM	LG	W	L	PCT	G	GS	CG-SHO	SV-BS	IP	H	R	HR	HB	BB-IB	SO	ERA	AERA	OAV	OOB	AB-HR-SH	AVG	PB	SUP	APR	DL	PW
1994	Mon	N	1	1	.500	7	5	0	1-0	23.2	24	16	4	1	11-0	17	6.08	70	.261	.343	4-0-1	.000	-0	108	-4		-0.4
1995	Mon	N	1	2	.333	19	1	0	0-0	25.2	26	21	7	1	9-0	25	7.01	61	.260	.319	3-0-1	.000	-0	63	-7		-0.8
1997	Cin	N	2	2	.500	12	6	0	1-0	41	39	20	6	1	8-1	25	4.39	98	.253	.291	9-0-2	.111	-0	108	0		-0.1
1998	Cin	N	5	5	.500	69	3	0	9-4	98.2	86	46	17	3	27-6	83	4.01	107	.231	.284	6-0-4	.167	-0	50	3		0.3
1999	Cin	N	1	2	.333	50	0	0	0-1	61	68	31	13	2	14-1	61	4.43	106	.281	.324	0	—	0		3		0.1
2000	Cin	N	0	0	—	1	0	0	0-0	1	2	2	1	0	1-0	2	18.00	26	.400	.500	0	—	0		-1		-0.1
	Col	N	11	2	.846	67	0	0	5-4	83	62	21	5	3	14-2	82	2.17	267	.208	.246	9-1-1	.222	1		27		4.0
	Year		11	2	.846	68	0	0	5-4	84	64	23	6	3	15-2	84	2.36	245	.211	.251	9-1-1	.222	1		26		3.9
2001	Col	N	1	7	.125	69	0	0	0-2	67.2	70	47	18	1	26-5	47	6.25	85	.270	.337	3	.000	-0		-4		-0.5
2002	Cin	N	6	1	.857	62	0	0	0-1	54.1	49	19	3	2	10-2	41	2.98	143	.238	.280	2-0-1	.000	-0		8	51	0.9
2003	Cin	N	3	0	1.000	34	0	0	0-1	34.1	36	15	5	1	6-3	23	3.93	106	.275	.307	2	.000	-0		2	40	0.1
	†NY	A	2	1	.667	12	0	0	0-1	12.1	8	7	2	1	2-1	6	4.38	100	.182	.229	0	—	0		0	26	0.0
2004	NY	A	0	1	.000	24	0	0	0-2	20.2	33	19	2	2	7-4	8	8.27	56	.355	.408	0	—	0		-8		-0.4
	Cin	N	1	2	.333	40	0	0	1-2	39	39	27	12	0	5-0	35	6.23	69	.257	.277	0	—	0		-7		-0.6
2005	StL	N	0	0	—	6	0	0	0-0	8.1	14	2	1	0	1-1	1	2.16	194	.378	.395	0	—	0		2		0.1
Total 11			34	26	.567	472	15	0	17-18	570.2	556	293	96	16	141-26	454	4.51	104	.254	.301	38-1-10	.105	-1	86	14	130	2.6

WHITE, DEKE George Frederick B9.8.1872 Albany NY D11.5.1957 Ilion NY BB/TL d9.14

YEAR	TM	LG	W	L	PCT	G	GS	CG-SHO	SV-BS	IP	H	R	HR	HB	BB-IB	SO	ERA	AERA	OAV	OOB	AB-HR-SH	AVG	PB	SUP	APR	DL	PW
1895	Phi	N	1	0	1.000	3	1	1	1	17.1	17	23	1	2	13	6	9.87	48	.254	.390	8-0-1	.125	-1	134	-9		-0.5

WHITE, DOC Guy Harris B4.9.1879 Washington DC D2.19.1969 Silver Spring MD BL/TL/6-1/150 d4.22 Col Georgetown ▲

YEAR	TM	LG	W	L	PCT	G	GS	CG-SHO	SV-BS	IP	H	R	HR	HB	BB-IB	SO	ERA	AERA	OAV	OOB	AB-HR-SH	AVG	PB	SUP	APR	DL	PW
1901	Phi	N	14	13	.519	31	27	22	0	236.2	241	122	2	14	56	132	3.19	106	.262	.314	98-1-7	.276	5	118	3		0.9
1902	Phi	N	16	20	.444	36	35	34-3	1	306	277	126	3	13	72	185	2.53	111	.241	.294	179-1-9	.263	4*	78	7		1.5
1903	Chi	A	17	16	.515	37	36	29-3	0	300	258	119	4	14	69	114	2.13	132	.232	.285	99-0-2	.202	6*	95	19		2.8
1904	Chi	A	16	12	.571	30	30	23-7	0	228	201	82	6	9	68	115	1.78	138	.238	.301	76-0-2	.158	0*	94	10		1.4
1905	Chi	A	17	13	.567	36	33	25-4	0	260.1	204	67	2	9	58	120	1.76	140	.218	.270	90-0-4	.167	0*	86	24		2.9
1906	†Chi	A	18	6	.750	28	24	20-7	0	219.1	160	47	2	5	38	95	1.52	167	.207	.249	65-0-7	.185	4*	120	28		3.9
1907	Chi	A	27	13	.675	46	35	24-6	1	291	270	93	2	9	38	141	2.26	106	.248	.278	90-0-12	.222	4*	118	7		1.7
1908	Chi	A	18	13	.581	41	37	24-5	0	296	262	94	3	9	69	126	2.55	91	.240	.291	100-0-9	.229	4*	104	-1		0.8
1909	Chi	A	11	9	.550	24	21	14-3	0	177.2	149	56	1	7	31	77	1.72	136	.226	.269	192-0-13	.234	6*	80	10		1.9
1910	Chi	A	15	13	.536	33	29	20-2	1	236.2	219	84	2	12	50	111	2.66	90	.243	.291	126-0-12	.198	2*	106	0		0.4
1911	Chi	A	10	14	.417	34	29	16-4	2	214.1	219	91	2	9	35	72	2.98	108	.271	.309	78-0-4	.256	3*	109	8		1.1
1912	Chi	A	8	10	.444	32	19	9-1	0	172	172	81	1	8	47	57	3.24	99	.267	.325	56-0-2	.125	-1	91	1		-0.2
1913	Chi	A	2	4	.333	19	8	2	0	103	106	52	5	5	39	39	3.50	84	.281	.356	25-0-2	.120	-1*	73	-6		-0.3
Total 13			189	156	.548	427	363	262-45	5	3041	2738	1118	33	120	670	1384	2.39	112	.242	.292	1283-2-85	.217	37	100	110		18.8

WHITE, HAL Harold George B3.18.1919 Utica NY D4.21.2001 Venice FL BR/TR/5-10/170* d4.22 Mil 1944-45

YEAR	TM	LG	W	L	PCT	G	GS	CG-SHO	SV-BS	IP	H	R	HR	HB	BB-IB	SO	ERA	AERA	OAV	OOB	AB-HR-SH	AVG	PB	SUP	APR	DL	PW
1941	Det	A	0	0	—	4	0	0	0	9	11	6	0	0	6	2	6.00	76	.306	.405	2	.000	-0		-1		-0.1
1942	Det	A	12	12	.500	34	25	12-4	1	216.2	212	80	6	5	82	93	2.91	136	.252	.323	77-0-3	.169	-1	109	25		2.5
1943	Det	A	7	12	.368	32	24	7-2	2	177.2	150	84	6	1	71	58	3.39	104	.228	.304	57-0-2	.140	-1	105	1		0.0
1946	Det	A	1	1	.500	11	1	1	0	27.1	34	20	5	0	15	12	5.60	65	.312	.395	7-0-2	.000	-1	164	-6		-0.5
1947	Det	A	4	5	.444	35	5	0	2	84.2	91	43	5	2	47	34	3.61	104	.273	.373	18-0-1	.167	0	61	0		0.1
1948	Det	A	2	1	.667	27	0	0	1	42.2	46	31	2	1	26	17	6.12	71	.272	.372	13	.154	0		-7		-0.5
1949	Det	A	1	0	1.000	9	0	0	2	12	5	0	0	0	4	4	0.00	—	.125	.205	3	.333	0*		6		0.7
1950	Det	A	9	6	.600	42	8	3-1	1	111	96	59	7	1	65	53	4.54	103	.239	.347	33-0-2	.121	-2	103	3		0.2
1951	Det	A	3	4	.429	38	4	0	4	76	74	45	7	2	49	23	4.74	88	.264	.378	16	.250	0	48	-5		-0.4
1952	Det	A	1	8	.111	41	4	0	5	63.1	53	29	1	0	39	18	3.69	103	.237	.350	11	.182	-0		1		0.2
1953	StL	A	0	0	—	10	0	0	0	10.1	8	3	1	1	3	2	2.61	161	.205	.279	1	.000	0		2		0.1
	StL	N	6	5	.545	49	0	0	7	84.2	84	32	5	0	39	32	2.98	143	.272	.353	16	.000	-2		12		1.4
1954	StL	N	0	0	—	4	0	0	0	5	11	11	2	1	4	2	19.80	21	.440	.533	1	.000	-0		-8		-0.4
Total 12			46	54	.460	336	67	23-7	25	920.1	875	443	47	14	450	349	3.78	106	.253	.342	255-0-10	.145	-7	99	23		3.3

WHITE, DEACON James Laurie B12.7.1847 Caton NY D7.7.1939 Aurora IL BL/TR/5-11/175 d5.4.1871 M2 b-Will ▲

YEAR	TM	LG	W	L	PCT	G	GS	CG-SHO	SV-BS	IP	H	R	HR	HB	BB-IB	SO	ERA	AERA	OAV	OOB	AB-HR-SH	AVG	PB	SUP	APR	DL	PW
1876	Chi	N	0	0	—	1	0	0	1	2	1	0	0	0		3	0.00	—	.143	.143	303-1	.343	0*		1		0.1
1890	Buf	P	0	0	—	1	0	0	0	8	18	15	0	0	2		9.00	46	.429	.455	439	.260	0*		-5		-0.2
Total 2			0	0	—	2	0	0	1	10	19	15	0	0	2	3	7.20	53	.388	.412	742-1	.294	1		-4		-0.1

WHITE, LARRY Larry David B9.25.1958 San Fernando CA BR/TR/6-5/190* [CleA79 31/756] d9.20 Col San Francisco St.

YEAR	TM	LG	W	L	PCT	G	GS	CG-SHO	SV-BS	IP	H	R	HR	HB	BB-IB	SO	ERA	AERA	OAV	OOB	AB-HR-SH	AVG	PB	SUP	APR	DL	PW
1983	LA	N	0	0	—	4	0	0	0-0	7	4	1	0	0	3-0	5	1.29	281	.174	.269	0	—	0		2		0.1
1984	LA	N	0	1	.000	7	1	0	0-0	12	9	5	2	0	6-2	10	3.00	119	.209	.300	1	.000	-0	99	1		0.0
Total 2			0	1	.000	11	1	0	0-0	19	13	6	2	0	9-2	15	2.37	151	.197	.289	1	.000	0	99	3		0.1

WHITE, MATT Matthew Joseph B8.19.1977 Pittsfield MA BR/TL/6-0/205(180-205) [CleA98 15/453] d5.27 Col Clemson

YEAR	TM	LG	W	L	PCT	G	GS	CG-SHO	SV-BS	IP	H	R	HR	HB	BB-IB	SO	ERA	AERA	OAV	OOB	AB-HR-SH	AVG	PB	SUP	APR	DL	PW
2003	Bos	A	0	1	.000	3	0	0	0-0	3.2	10	11	1	0	3-0	1	27.00	17	.526	.565	0	—	0		-8	57	-1.3
	Sea	A	0	0	—	3	0	0	0-0	2	3	3	2	0	2-0	0	13.50	32	.375	.500	0	—	0		-2		-0.1
	Year		0	1	.000	6	0	0	0-0	5.2	13	14	3	0	5-0	1	22.24	20	.481	.545	0	—	0		-10		-1.4
2005	Was	N	0	1	.000	1	1	0	0-0	4	4	4	0	1	3-0	3	9.00	45	.267	.400	1	.000	-0	0	-2		-0.4
Total 2			0	2	.000	7	1	0	0-0	9.2	17	18	3	1	8-0	4	16.76	24	.405	.491	1	.000	-0	0	-12	57	-1.8

WHITE, KIRBY Oliver Kirby "Red","Buck" B1.3.1884 Hillsboro OH D4.22.1943 Hillsboro OH BL/TR/6-0/190 d5.4

YEAR	TM	LG	W	L	PCT	G	GS	CG-SHO	SV-BS	IP	H	R	HR	HB	BB-IB	SO	ERA	AERA	OAV	OOB	AB-HR-SH	AVG	PB	SUP	APR	DL	PW
1909	Bos	N	6	13	.316	23	19	11-1	0	148.1	134	73	5	1	80	53	3.22	88	.245	.343	50-0-3	.160	-1	69	-6		-0.9
1910	Bos	N	1	2	.333	3	3	0	0	26	15	7	2	3	12	6	1.38	240	.188	.316	6-0-1	.333	1	45	5		0.7
	Pit	N	10	9	.526	30	21	7-3	2	153.1	142	73	2	5	75	42	3.46	90	.258	.352	46-0-2	.261	3	106	-4		-0.3
	Year		11	11	.500	33	24	10-3	2	179.1	157	80	4	8	87	48	3.16	99	.249	.347	52-0-3	.269	4	98	0		0.4
1911	Pit	N	0	1	.000	2	1	0	0	3	3	4	1	0	1	1	9.00	38	.250	.308	1	.000	-0	0	-2		-0.4
Total 3			17	25	.405	58	44	21-4	2	330.2	294	157	10	9	168	102	3.24	93	.247	.345	103-0-6	.214	3	83	-7		-0.9

WHITE, RICK Richard Allen B12.23.1968 Springfield OH BR/TR/6-4/215(215-230) [PitN90 15/403] d4.6 Col Paducah (KY) CC

YEAR	TM	LG	W	L	PCT	G	GS	CG-SHO	SV-BS	IP	H	R	HR	HB	BB-IB	SO	ERA	AERA	OAV	OOB	AB-HR-SH	AVG	PB	SUP	APR	DL	PW
1994	Pit	N	4	5	.444	43	5	0	6-3	75.1	79	35	9	6	17-3	38	3.82	114	.280	.329	13	.077	-1	104	5		0.5
1995	Pit	N	2	3	.400	15	9	0	0-0	55	56	33	3	2	18-0	29	4.75	92	.299	.352	15-0-2	.067	-1	104	-3	22	-0.3
1998	TB	A	2	6	.250	38	9	0	0-0	68.2	66	32	8	2	23-2	39	3.80	126	.253	.315	3	.333	0	65	7		0.7
1999	TB	A	5	3	.625	63	1	0	0-2	108	132	56	8	1	38-5	81	4.08	122	.304	.358	0	—	0	75	10		0.6
2000	TB	A	3	6	.333	44	0	0	2-3	71.1	57	30	7	5	26-3	44	3.41	144	.220	.301	0	—	0		12		1.3
	†NY	N	2	3	.400	22	0	0	1-1	28.1	26	14	2	2	12-2	20	3.81	114	.232	.315	5	.200	0*		1		0.2
2001	NY	N	4	5	.444	55	0	0	2-2	69.2	71	38	7	2	17-4	51	3.88	104	.257	.303	3	.000	-0		-1	36	-0.2
2002	Col	N	2	6	.250	41	0	0	0-1	40.2	49	30	4	1	18-4	27	6.20	76	.310	.376	0	—	0		-6	22	-1.0
	†StL	N	3	1	.750	20	0	0	0-0	22	13	3	0	0	3-1	14	0.82	493	.169	.200	1	.000	-0		8		1.3
	Year		5	7	.417	61	0	0	0-1	62.2	62	33	4	1	21-5	41	4.31	104	.264	.322	1	.000	-0		1		0.3
2003	Chi	A	1	2	.333	34	0	0	1-0	47.2	56	39	11	1	13-2	37	6.61	70	.295	.340	0	—	0		-11		-0.6
	Hou	N	0	0	—	15	0	0	0-0	19.1	18	9	2	3	8-0	17	3.72	119	.243	.341	0	—	0		1		0.1
2004	Cle	A	5	5	.500	58	0	0	1-2	78.1	88	35	6	3	29-7	44	5.29	82	.293	.356	0	—	0		-10		-1.0
2005	Pit	N	4	7	.364	71	0	0	2-1	75	90	39	3	4	29-10	40	3.72	114	.308	.374	2	.000	-0		2		-0.3
Total 10			37	52	.416	520	18	0	15-15	759.1	811	410	79	31	251-43	484	4.24	107	.276	.336	42-0-2	.095	-2	95	15	80	1.8

YEAR	TM LG	W	L	PCT	G	GS	CG-SHO	SV-BS	IP	H	R	HR	HB	BB-IB	SO	ERA	AERA	OAV	OOB	AB-HR-SH	AVG	PB	SUP	APR	DL	PW

WHITE, STEVE Stephen Vincent B12.21.1884 Dorchester MA D1.29.1975 Braintree MA BR/TR/5-10/160 d5.29 Col Princeton

1912	Was A	0	0	—	1	0	0	0	0.2	2	2	1	0	0	1	0.00	—	.667	.667	0	—	0		0		0.0
	Bos N	0	0	—	3	0	0	0	6	9	5	0	1	5	2	6.00	60	.429	.556	3	.000	-0		-1		-0.1
Total	1	0	0	—	4	0	0	0	6.2	11	7	1	1	5	3	5.40	66	.458	.567	3	.000	-0		-1		-0.1

WHITE, WILL William Henry "Whoop-La" B10.11.1854 Caton NY D8.31.1911 Port Carling ON, Can. BB/TR/5-9.5/175 d7.20 M1 b-Deacon

1877	Bos N	2	1	.667	3	3	3-1	0	27	27	15	0		2	7	3.00	94	.243	.257	15	.200	-1	197	0		-0.1
1878	Cin N	30	21	.588	52	52	52-5	0	468	477	249			45	169	1.79	119	.252	.269	197	.142	-8	111	16		0.6
1879	Cin N	43	31	.581	76	75	75-4	0	680	676	404	10		68	232	1.99	117	.238	.256	294	.136	-17	122	22		0.1
1880	Cin N	18	42	.300	62	62	58-3	0	517.1	550	323	9		56	161	2.14	116	.255	.273	207	.169	-9	73	14		0.3
1881	Det N	0	2	.000	2	2	2	0	18	24	18	0		2	5	5.00	58	.296	.313	7	.000	-1	46	-4		-0.4
1882	Cin AA	40	12	.769	54	54	52-8	0	480	411	164	3		71	122	1.54	172	.216	.244	207	.266	6	117	60		6.7
1883	Cin AA	43	22	.662	65	64	64-6	0	577	473	255	16		104	141	2.09	155	.209	.244	240	.225	3	119	75		6.9
1884	Cin AA	34	18	.654	52	52	52-7	0	456	479	224	16	35	74	118	3.32	101	.255	.296	184-1	.190	-2	116	5		-0.1
1885	Cin AA	18	15	.545	34	34	33-2	0	293.1	295	169	9	27	64	80	3.53	92	.255	.309	118	.169	-3	97	-5		-0.8
1886	Cin AA	1	2	.333	3	3	3	0	26	28	23	1	6	10	6	4.15	85	.280	.379	9	.111	-1	107	-3		-0.4
Total	10	229	166	.580	403	401	394-36	0	3542.2	3440	1844	65	68	496	1041	2.28	120	.239	.268	1478-1	.183	-33	109	180		12.8

WHITEHEAD, JOHN John Henderson "Silent John" B4.27.1909 Coleman TX D10.20.1964 Bonham TX BR/TR/6-2/195 d4.19

1935	Chi A	13	13	.500	28	27	18-1	0	222.1	209	101	17	2	101	72	3.72	124	.250	.332	82-0-4	.146	-5	90	23		1.9
1936	Chi A	13	13	.500	34	32	15-1	1	230.2	254	137	9	5	98	45	4.64	112	.276	.349	87-0-7	.241	1	104	13		1.4
1937	Chi A	11	8	.579	26	24	8-4	0	165.2	191	84	14	5	56	45	4.07	113	.294	.354	58-0-4	.224	1	104	11		1.1
1938	Chi A	10	11	.476	32	24	10-2	2	183.1	218	108	12	4	80	38	4.76	103	.299	.370	60-0-5	.100	-4	71	5		0.1
1939	Chi A	0	3	.000	7	4	0	0	32	60	30	4	0	5	9	8.16	58	.408	.428	9	.000	-1	70	-11		-0.9
	StL A	1	3	.250	26	4	0	1	66	88	49	10	2	17	9	5.86	83	.321	.365	17	.059	-1	118	-7		-0.5
	Year	1	6	.143	33	8	0	1	98	148	79	14	2	22	18	6.61	73	.352	.387	26	.038	-3	94	-18		-1.4
1940	StL A	1	3	.250	15	4	1-1	0	40	46	25	3	0	14	11	5.40	85	.286	.343	12	.167	-1	72	-3		-0.3
1942	StL A	0	0	—	4	0	0	0	4	8	3	0	1	1	0	6.75	55	.421	.476	0	—	0		-1		0.0
Total	7	49	54	.476	172	119	52-9	4	944	1074	537	69	18	372	254	4.60	105	.287	.355	325-0-20	.169	-11	93	30		2.8

WHITEHILL, EARL Earl Oliver B2.7.1899 Cedar Rapids IA D10.22.1954 Omaha NE BL/TL/5-9.5/174 d9.15 C2

1923	Det A	2	0	1.000	8	3	1	0	33	22	14	2	3	15	19	2.73	142	.188	.296	11-0-1	.364	1	143	3		0.3
1924	Det A	17	9	.654	35	32	16-2	0	233	260	125	8	13	79	65	3.86	106	.288	.353	89-0-1	.213	1*	130	6		0.6
1925	Det A	11	11	.500	35	33	15-1	2	239.1	267	135	13	10	88	83	4.66	92	.293	.361	87-0-3	.218	0*	105	-5		-0.5
1926	Det A	16	13	.552	36	34	13	0	252.1	271	136	7	8	79	109	3.99	102	.277	.336	91-0-3	.253	4	98	2		0.5
1927	Det A	16	14	.533	41	31	17-3	3	236	238	110	4	9	105	95	3.36	125	.267	.350	78-0-6	.205	-0	93	22		2.4
1928	Det A	11	16	.407	31	30	12-1	0	196.1	214	131	8	1	78	93	4.31	95	.277	.344	67-0-3	.194	-1	95	-11		-1.4
1929	Det A	14	15	.483	38	28	18-1	1	245.1	267	147	16	3	96	103	4.62	93	.280	.348	90-3-4	.256	5	114	-7		-0.2
1930	Det A	17	13	.567	34	31	16	0	220.2	248	139	8	8	80	109	4.24	113	.285	.351	83-0-1	.193	-4	83	6		0.3
1931	Det A	13	16	.448	34	34	22	0	271.1	287	152	22	5	118	81	4.08	112	.274	.351	97-0-4	.155	-5	82	12		0.7
1932	Det A	16	12	.571	33	31	17-3	0	244	255	136	17	5	93	81	4.54	104	.269	.337	90-0-5	.244	1	112	9		1.0
1933	†Was A	22	8	.733	39	37	19-2	1	270	271	112	9	4	100	96	3.33	125	.262	.329	108-0-5	.222	2*	119	26		2.7
1934	Was A	14	11	.560	32	31	15	0	235	269	129	10	3	94	96	4.52	96	.290	.357	85-1-6	.200	4*	108	-4		0.0
1935	Was A	14	11	.519	34	34	19-1	0	279.1	318	149	16	7	104	102	4.29	101	.289	.354	104-0-4	.183	-1	113	1		0.1
1936	Was A	14	11	.560	28	28	14	0	212.1	252	124	17	2	89	63	4.87	98	.294	.362	77-0-5	.169	-0	101	2		0.2
1937	Cle A	8	8	.500	33	22	6-1	2	147	189	111	9	6	80	53	6.49	71	.322	.409	49-0-6	.224	1	120	-26		-2.2
1938	Cle A	9	8	.529	26	23	4	0	160.1	187	109	18	9	83	60	5.56	83	.289	.378	56	.125	-2	105	-15		-1.5
1939	Chi N	4	7	.364	24	11	2-1	1	89.1	102	59	8	5	50	42	5.14	77	.292	.389	29	.103	-2	83	-12		-1.5
Total	17	218	185	.541	541	473	226-16	11	3564.2	3917	2018	192	101	1431	1350	4.36	100	.282	.353	1291-4-57	.204	4	105	9		1.5

WHITEHOUSE, CHARLIE Charles Evis "Lefty" B1.25.1894 Charleston IL D7.19.1960 Indianapolis IN BB/TL/6-0/152 d8.29

1914	Ind F	2	0	1.000	8	2	2	0	26	34	14	0	1	5	10	4.85	64	.324	.360	8	.000	-1	143	-3		-0.4
1915	New F	2	2	.500	11	3	1	0	39.2	46	29	0	5	17	18	4.31	59	.299	.386	10-0-1	.000	-1	127	-9		-1.0
1919	Was A	1	1	.000	6	1	0	0	12	13	7	1	0	6	5	4.50	71	.283	.365	1	.000	-0	98	-1		-0.1
Total	3	4	3	.571	25	6	3	0	77.2	93	50	1	6	28	33	4.52	63	.305	.375	19-0-1	.000	-2	129	-13		-1.5

WHITEHOUSE, LEN Leonard Joseph B9.10.1957 Burlington VT BL/TL/5-11/175* d9.1

1981	Tex A	0	1	.000	2	1	0	0-0	3.1	8	7	1	0	2-0	2	16.20	21	.500	.526	0	—	0	52	-5		-0.9
1983	Min A	7	1	.875	60	0	0	2-1	73.2	70	34	6	2	44-11	44	4.15	103	.261	.365	0	—	0		3		0.2
1984	Min A	2	2	.500	30	0	0	1-3	31.1	29	11	3	2	17-3	18	3.16	134	.254	.361	0	—	0		4		0.5
1985	Min A	0	0	—	5	0	0	1-0	7.1	12	9	4	0	2-0	4	11.05	40	.353	.389	0	—	0		-5		-0.2
Total	4	9	4	.692	97	1	0	4-4	115.2	119	61	14	4	65-14	68	4.67	91	.275	.372	0	—	0	52	-3		-0.4

WHITEHURST, WALLY Walter Richard B4.11.1964 Shreveport LA BR/TR/6-3/195(180-200) [OakA85 3/65] d7.17 Col New Orleans

1989	NY N	0	1	.000	9	1	0	0-0	14	17	7	2	0	5-0	9	4.50	73	.293	.344	1-0-1	.000	0	81	-2		-0.1
1990	NY N	1	0	1.000	38	0	0	0-0	65.2	63	27	5	0	9-2	46	3.29	115	.251	.277	8-0-1	.250	0		3		0.2
1991	NY N	7	12	.368	36	20	0	1-0	133.1	142	67	12	4	25-3	87	4.18	88	.274	.311	33-0-5	.182	1	94	-6	15	-0.7
1992	NY N	3	9	.250	44	11	0	0-3	97	99	45	4	4	33-5	70	3.62	97	.264	.328	22-0-1	.182	1	87	-2		-0.2
1993	SD N	4	7	.364	21	19	0	0-0	105.2	109	47	11	3	30-5	57	3.83	108	.276	.326	24-0-10	.083	-2	79	5	88	0.4
1994	SD N	4	7	.364	13	13	0	0-0	64	84	37	8	1	26-4	43	4.92	84	.319	.383	19	.105	-2	80	-5	64	-0.7
1996	NY A	1	1	.500	2	2	0	0-0	8	11	6	1	0	2-0	1	6.75	73	.324	.361	0	—	0	75	-1		-0.2
Total	7	20	37	.351	163	66	0	3-3	487.2	525	236	43	12	130-19	313	4.02	95	.277	.325	107-0-18	.150	1	86	-3	167	-1.3

WHITESIDE, SEAN David Sean B4.19.1971 Lakeland FL BL/TL/6-4/190 [DetA92 11/308] d4.29 Col North Carolina-Charlotte

| 1995 | Det A | 0 | 0 | — | 2 | 0 | 0 | 0 | 3.2 | 7 | 6 | 1 | 0 | 4-1 | 2 | 14.73 | 33 | .438 | .500 | 0 | — | 0 | | -4 | | -0.2 |

WHITESIDE, MATT Matthew Christopher B8.8.1967 Charleston MO BR/TR/6-0/205(185-205) [TexA90 25/678] d8.5 Col Arkansas St.

1992	Tex A	1	1	.500	20	0	0	4-0	28	26	8	1	0	11-2	13	1.93	198	.245	.314	0	—	0		6		0.5
1993	Tex A	2	1	.667	60	0	0	1-4	73	78	37	7	1	23-6	39	4.32	97	.281	.337	0	—	0		0		0.0
1994	Tex A	2	2	.500	47	0	0	1-2	61	68	40	6	1	28-3	37	5.02	96	.286	.361	0	—	0		-2		-0.1
1995	Tex A	5	4	.556	40	0	0	3-1	53	48	24	5	1	19-2	46	4.08	119	.242	.308	0	—	0		5	16	0.8
1996	Tex A	0	1	.000	14	0	0	0-0	32.1	43	24	4	0	11-1	15	6.68	75	.321	.367	0	—	0		-4		-0.2
1997	Tex A	4	1	.800	42	1	0	0-4	72.2	85	45	4	3	26-3	44	5.08	96	.296	.355	0	—	0	132	0		0.0
1998	Phi N	1	1	.500	10	0	0	0-0	18	27	18	6	0	5-0	14	8.50	51	.338	.376	2	.000	-0		-8		-0.8
1999	SD N	1	0	1.000	10	0	0	0-0	11	19	17	1	0	5-0	9	13.91	31	.396	.444	0	—	0		-12		-0.9
2000	SD N	2	3	.400	28	0	0	0-0	37	32	21	6	1	17-3	27	4.14	108	.232	.318	0	—	0		0		0.1
2001	Atl N	0	1	.000	13	0	0	0-0	16.1	23	14	5	1	7-1	10	7.16	60	.319	.383	0	—	0		-5		-0.3
2005	Tor A	0	0	—	2	0	0	0-0	3.2	6	8	3	1	5-0	5	19.64	24	.353	.522	0	—	0		-5		-0.3
Total	11	18	15	.545	286	1	0	9-11	406	455	256	52	9	157-21	259	5.23	88	.285	.349	2	.000	-0	132	-27	16	-1.2

WHITING, JESSE Jesse W. B5.30.1879 Philadelphia PA D10.28.1937 Philadelphia PA TR/5-10/154 d9.27

1902	Phi N	0	1	.000	1	1	1	0	9	13	8	0	0	6		5.00	56	.333	.422	3	.333	0	48	-3		-0.2
1906	Bro N	1	1	.500	3	2	2-1	0	24.2	26	10	0	1	6	7	2.92	86	.286	.337	10	.300	1	72	-1		-0.0
1907	Bro N	0	0	—	1	0	0	0	3	3	4	0	0	3	2	12.00	20	.273	.429	2	.000	-0*		-3		-0.2
Total	3	1	2	.333	5	3	3-1	0	36.2	42	22	0	1	15		4.17	62	.298	.369	15	.267	0	65	-7		-0.4

WHITNEY, ART Arthur Wilson B1.16.1858 Brockton MA D8.15.1943 Lowell MA BR/TR/5-8/155 d5.1.1880 b-Frank ▲

1882	Det N	0	1	.000	3	2	1	0	18	31	17	1		8	11	6.00	49	.373	.429	115	.183	-1*	99	-5		-0.3
1886	Pit AA	0	0	—	1	0	0	0	6	7	4	0	0	4	2	3.00	113	.304	.385	511	.239	0*		0		0.0
1889	†NY N	0	0	—	1	0	0	0	4.1	1	3	0	0	4	3	2.08	190	.071	.278	473-1	.218	0*		0		0.0
Total	3	0	1	.000	5	2	1	0	28.1	39	24	1	0	15	16	4.76	67	.325	.400	1099-1	.224	-1	99	-5		-0.3

WHITNEY, JIM James Evans "Grasshopper Jim" B11.10.1857 Conklin NY D5.21.1891 Binghamton NY BL/TR/6-2/172 d5.2

1881	Bos N	31	33	.484	66	63	57-6	0	552.1	548	284	6		90	162	2.48	107	.248	.277	282	.255	11*	86	11		2.1
1882	Bos N	24	21	.533	48	48	46-3	0	420	404	229	3		41	180	2.64	109	.237	.255	251-5	.323	23*	110	7		2.8
1883	Bos N	37	21	.638	62	56	54-1	2	514	492	258	7		35	345	2.24	138	.238	.251	409-5	.281	20*	106	44		5.6
1884	Bos N	23	14	.622	38	37	35-6	0	336	272	140	7		27	270	2.09	138	.207	.223	270-3	.259	10*	100	27		3.6

YEAR	TM LG	W	L	PCT	G	GS	CG-SHO	SV-BS	IP	H	R	HR	HB	BB-IB	SO	ERA	AERA	OAV	OOB	AB-HR-SH	AVG	PB	SUP	APR	DL	PW
1885	Bos N	18	32	.360	51	50	50-2	0	441.1	503	286	14		37	200	2.98	90	.272	.286	290	.234	7*	95	-23		-1.3
1886	KC N	12	32	.273	46	44	42-3	0	393	465	292	9		55	167	4.49	84	.284	.308	247-2	.239	5*	64	-27		-1.4
1887	Was N	24	21	.533	47	47	46-2	0	404.2	430	253	16	16	42.	146	3.22	125	.259	.284	201-2	.264	10*	85	30		3.9
1888	Was N	18	21	.462	39	39	37-3	0	325	317	184	7	9	54	79	3.05	91	.245	.280	141-1	.170	-1*	92	-14		-1.6
1889	Ind N	2	7	.222	9	8	7	0	70	106	73	4	2	19	16	6.81	61	.339	.380	32	.375	5*	107	-19		-1.4
1890	Phi AA	2	2	.500	6	4	3	0	40	61	27	1	1	11	6	5.17	75	.341	.382	21	.238	-0*	109	-4		-0.3
Total 10		191	204	.484	413	396	377-26	2	3496.1	3598	2026	79	28	411	1571	2.97	104	.253	.275	2144-18	.261		89	93	32	12.0

WHITROCK, BILL William Franklin B3.4.1870 Cincinnati OH D7.26.1935 Derby CT TR/5-7.5/170 d5.3

YEAR	TM LG	W	L	PCT	G	GS	CG-SHO	SV-BS	IP	H	R	HR	HB	BB-IB	SO	ERA	AERA	OAV	OOB	AB-HR-SH	AVG	PB	SUP	APR	DL	PW
1890	StL AA	5	6	.455	16	11	10	1	105	104	62	2	7	40	39	3.51	123	.251	.327	48	.146	-3	68	8		0.5
1893	Lou N	2	5	.286	8	8	5	0	46.2	64	53	3	4	19	8	8.10	54	.317	.387	21	.286	1	88	-19		-1.8
1894	Lou N	0	1	.000	1	1	0	0	4	8	8	0	0	2	0	9.00	57	.400	.455	2	.000	-0	97	-2		-0.4
	Cin N	2	6	.250	11	9	9	0	79.1	121	88	7	9	46	10	6.24	89	.347	.436	65	.231	-2*	67	-9		-0.7
	Year	2	7	.222	12	10	9	0	83.1	129	96	7	9	48	10	6.37	87	.350	.437	67	.224	-3	69	-11		-1.1
1896	Phi N	0	1	.000	2	1	1	0	9	10	5	0	0	3	1	3.00	144	.278	.333	3	.000	-0	33	1		0.1
Total 4		9	19	.321	38	30	25	1	244	307	216	12	20	110	58	5.35	89	.300	.379	139	.201	-4	72	-21		-2.3

WHITSON, ED Eddie Lee B5.19.1955 Johnson City TN BR/TR/6-3/195(190-202) [PitN74 6/131] d9.4 [DL 1992 SD N 182]

YEAR	TM LG	W	L	PCT	G	GS	CG-SHO	SV-BS	IP	H	R	HR	HB	BB-IB	SO	ERA	AERA	OAV	OOB	AB-HR-SH	AVG	PB	SUP	APR	DL	PW
1977	Pit N	1	0	1.000	5	2	0	0-0	15.2	11	6	0	0	9-1	10	3.45	117	.204	.308	4	.000	-0	99	1		0.0
1978	Pit N	5	6	.455	43	0	0	4-3	74	66	31	5	2	37-5	64	3.28	114	.243	.333	11-0-1	.182	-0		4		0.5
1979	Pit N	2	3	.400	19	7	0	1-0	57.2	53	36	6	1	36-3	31	4.37	89	.238	.346	12-0-5	.000	-1	142	-5		-0.5
	SF N	5	8	.385	18	17	2	0-0	100.1	98	47	5	4	39-6	62	3.95	89	.254	.326	32-0-5	.156	-1	92	-4		-0.6
	Year	7	11	.389	37	24	2	1-0	158	151	83	11	5	75-9	93	4.10	89	.248	.334	45-0-9	.111	-2	107	-9		-1.1
1980	SF N☆	11	13	.458	34	34	6-2	0-0	211.2	222	88	7	4	56-7	90	3.10	113	.271	.318	66-0-9	.091	-4	79	8		0.3
1981	SF N	6	9	.400	22	22	2-1	0-0	123	130	61	10	2	47-5	65	4.02	85	.273	.339	33-0-9	.091	-1	96	-8		-1.1
1982	Cle A	4	2	.667	40	9	1-1	2-0	107.2	91	43	6	0	58-3	61	3.26	127	.231	.324	0	—	0	71	11		0.5
1983	SD N	5	7	.417	31	21	2	1-0	144.1	143	73	23	1	50-1	81	4.30	82	.256	.316	44-0-2	.182	1	101	-12	40	-1.0
1984	†SD N	14	8	.636	31	31	1	0-0	189	181	72	16	3	42-1	103	3.24	111	.255	.296	61-0-6	.049	-5*	104	9		0.6
1985	NY A	10	8	.556	30	30	2-2	0-0	158.2	201	100	19	2	43-0	89	4.88	83	.309	.350	0	—	0	133	-17		-1.7
1986	NY A	5	2	.714	14	4	0	0-0	37	54	37	5	0	23-1	27	7.54	55	.335	.412	0	—	0	154	-15	21	-2.3
	SD N	1	7	.125	17	12	0	0-0	75.2	85	48	8	0	37-0	46	5.59	66	.287	.364	18-0-2	.167	-0	91	-14		-1.3
1987	SD N	10	13	.435	36	34	3-1	0-0	205.2	197	113	36	3	64-3	135	4.73	84	.251	.309	65-0-10	.123	-1	101	-14		-1.6
1988	SD N	13	11	.542	34	33	3-1	0-0	205.1	202	93	17	1	45-1	118	3.77	90	.259	.298	66-0-9	.167	1	98	-8		-0.8
1989	SD N	16	11	.593	33	33	5-1	0-0	227	198	77	22	5	48-6	117	2.66	132	.235	.278	72-0-7	.139	1*	99	21		2.5
1990	SD N	14	9	.609	32	32	6-3	0-0	228.2	215	73	13	1	47-8	127	2.60	148	.251	.289	67-1-13	.149	1*	104	32		3.3
1991	SD N	4	6	.400	13	12	2	0-0	78.2	93	45	7	1	17-3	40	5.03	76	.299	.332	24-0-2	.125	-1	87	-9	115	-1.2
Total 15		126	123	.506	452	333	35-12		2240	2240	1045	201	29	869-54	1266	3.79	97	.261	.316	576-1-79	.125	-11	101	-20	358	-4.4

WHITTAKER, WALT Walter Elton "Doc" B6.11.1894 Chelsea MA D8.7.1965 Pembroke MA BL/TR/5-9.5/165 d7.6 Col Tufts

YEAR	TM LG	W	L	PCT	G	GS	CG-SHO	SV-BS	IP	H	R	HR	HB	BB-IB	SO	ERA	AERA	OAV	OOB	AB-HR-SH	AVG	PB	SUP	APR	DL	PW
1916	Phi A	0	0	—	1	0	0	0	2	3	1	0	0	2	0	4.50	63	.375	.500	0	—	0		0		0.0

WICKANDER, KEVIN Kevin Dean B1.4.1965 Fort Dodge IA BL/TL/6-2/202* [CleA86 2/30] d8.10 Col Grand Canyon

YEAR	TM LG	W	L	PCT	G	GS	CG-SHO	SV-BS	IP	H	R	HR	HB	BB-IB	SO	ERA	AERA	OAV	OOB	AB-HR-SH	AVG	PB	SUP	APR	DL	PW
1989	Cle A	0	0	—	2	0	0	0-0	2.2	6	1	0	0	2-1	0	3.38	118	.462	.533	0	—	0		0		0.0
1990	Cle A	0	1	.000	10	0	0	0-1	12.1	14	6	0	1	4-0	10	3.65	108	.304	.358	0	—	0		0	126	0.0
1992	Cle A	2	0	1.000	44	0	0	1-2	41	39	14	1	4	28-3	38	3.07	128	.258	.384	0	—	0		5		0.2
1993	Cle A	0	0	—	11	0	0	0-0	8.2	15	7	3	0	3-0	3	4.15	106	.366	.409	0	—	0		-1		-0.1
	Cin N	1	0	1.000	33	0	0	0-1	25.1	32	20	5	2	19-1	20	6.75	60	.308	.424	2	.000	-0		-7	35	-0.4
1995	Det A	0	0	—	21	0	0	1-2	17.1	18	6	1	0	9-4	9	2.60	185	.273	.364	0	—	0		4	21	0.2
	Mil A	0	0	—	8	0	0	0-0	6	1	0	0	0	3-1	2	0.00	—	.059	.190	0	—	0		3		0.1
	Year	0	0	—	29	0	0	1-2	23.1	19	6	1	1	12-5	11	1.93	252	.229	.327	0	—	0		7		0.3
1996	Mil A	2	0	1.000	21	0	0	0-2	25.1	26	16	2	0	17-2	19	4.97	104	.265	.368	0	—	0		0	45	-0.0
Total 5		1	.833		150	0	0	2-8	138.2	151	70	12	8	85-12	101	4.02	108	.282	.383	2	.000	-0		4	227	-0.0

WICKER, KEMP Kemp Caswell (b Kemp Caswell Whicker) B8.13.1906 Kernersville NC D6.11.1973 Kernersville NC BR/TL/5-11/182 d8.14 Col North Carolina St.

YEAR	TM LG	W	L	PCT	G	GS	CG-SHO	SV-BS	IP	H	R	HR	HB	BB-IB	SO	ERA	AERA	OAV	OOB	AB-HR-SH	AVG	PB	SUP	APR	DL	PW
1936	NY A	1	2	.333	7	0	0	0	20	31	18	2	0	11	5	7.65	61	.356	.429	7	.143	-0		-7		-0.8
1937	†NY A	7	3	.700	16	10	6-1	0	88	107	52	8	0	26	14	4.40	101	.296	.343	35-0-1	.114	-3	153	0		-0.4
1938	NY A	1	0	1.000	1	0	0	0	1	0	0	0	0	1	0	0.00	—	.000	.250	0	—	0		1		0.1
1941	Bro N	1	2	.333	16	2	0	1	32	30	14	3	0	14	8	3.66	100	.252	.331	4-0-3	.250	0	81	1		0.1
Total 4		10	7	.588	40	12	6-1	1	141	168	84	13	0	52	27	4.66	92	.294	.353	46-0-4	.130	-2	143	-5		-1.0

WICKER, BOB Robert Kitridge B5.25.1877 Bono IN D1.22.1955 Evanston IL BL/TR/5-11/210 d8.11

YEAR	TM LG	W	L	PCT	G	GS	CG-SHO	SV-BS	IP	H	R	HR	HB	BB-IB	SO	ERA	AERA	OAV	OOB	AB-HR-SH	AVG	PB	SUP	APR	DL	PW
1901	StL N	0	0	—	0	0	0	0	3	4	3	0	0	1	2	0.00	—	.308	.357	3	.333	0*		0		0.0
1902	StL N	5	12	.294	22	16	14-1	0	152.1	159	82	1	2	45	78	3.19	86	.269	.322	77-0-2	.234	1*	67	-9		-0.6
1903	StL N	0	0	—	5	4	1	0	5	4	1	0	0	3	3	0.00	—	.174	.269	2	.000	-0		2		0.1
	Chi N	20	9	.690	32	27	24-1	1	247	236	114	3	3	74	110	3.02	104	.253	.311	98-0-1	.245	6	119	8		1.2
	Year	20	9	.690	33	27	24-1	1	252	240	115	3	3	77	113	2.96	106	.252	.309	100-0-1	.240	6	119	5		1.3
1904	Chi N	17	9	.654	30	27	23-4	0	229	201	92	6	3	58	99	2.67	100	.232	.282	155-0-3	.219	1*	112	2		0.0
1905	Chi N	13	6	.684	22	22	17-4	0	178	139	46	3	1	47	86	2.02	147	.221	.276	72-0-3	.139	-2*	99	22		1.9
1906	Chi N	3	5	.375	10	8	5	0	72.1	70	36	0	0	19	25	2.99	88	.257	.306	20	.100	-1	97	-4		-0.6
	Cin N	6	11	.353	20	17	14	0	150	150	69	3	1	46	69	2.70	102	.263	.319	50-0-1	.180	2	76	-1		-0.1
	Year	9	16	.360	30	25	19	0	222.1	220	105	3	1	65	94	2.79	97	.261	.315	70-0-1	.157	1	83	-7		-0.7
Total 6		64	52	.552	138	117	97-10	1	1036.2	963	443	16	10	293	472	2.73	105	.247	.301	477-0-10	.205	6	99	20		1.9

WICKERSHAM, DAVE David Clifford B9.27.1935 Erie PA BR/TR/6-3/190* d9.18 Col Ohio U.

YEAR	TM LG	W	L	PCT	G	GS	CG-SHO	SV-BS	IP	H	R	HR	HB	BB-IB	SO	ERA	AERA	OAV	OOB	AB-HR-SH	AVG	PB	SUP	APR	DL	PW
1960	KC A	0	0	—	5	0	0	2	8.1	4	1	0	0	1-0	3	1.08	369	.148	.179	1	.000	-0		3		0.1
1961	KC A	2	1	.667	17	0	0	1	21	25	12	0	2	5-1	10	5.14	81	.309	.360	3	.667	1		-1		-0.1
1962	KC A	11	4	.733	39	9	1	1	110	105	53	13	8	43-1	61	4.17	101	.257	.337	35-0-2	.057	-3	106	2		0.0
1963	KC A	12	15	.444	38	34	4-1	1	237.2	244	116	21	9	79-2	118	4.09	95	.268	.330	80-0-4	.138	-3	86	-3		-0.6
1964	Det A	19	12	.613	40	36	11-1	1	254	224	108	28	12	81-3	164	3.44	106	.232	.299	82-0-12	.073	-5	96	5		-1.1
1965	Det A	9	14	.391	34	27	8-3	0	195.1	179	91	12	11	61-6	109	3.78	92	.241	.307	58-0-7	.069	-4	87	-6		-1.1
1966	Det A	8	3	.727	38	14	3	1	140.2	139	64	14	8	54-4	93	3.20	100	.261	.336	45-0-1	.044	-3	125	1		-0.2
1967	Det A	4	5	.444	36	4	0	4	85.1	72	30	6	4	33-2	44	2.74	119	.235	.315	15-0-1	.000	-2	60	4		0.4
1968	Pit N	1	0	1.000	11	0	0	1	20.2	21	12	0	0	13-3	9	3.48	84	.276	.362	3-0-1	.333	-0		-2		-0.1
1969	KC A	2	3	.400	34	0	0	5-2	50	58	27	6	2	14-2	27	3.96	93	.294	.346	2	.000	-0		-2		-0.2
Total 10		68	57	.544	283	124	29-5	18-2	1123	1071	514	100	56	384-24	638	3.66	100	.252	.320	324-0-28	.086	-18	94	1		-1.8

WICKMAN, BOB Robert Joe B2.6.1969 Green Bay WI BR/TR/6-1/212(207-242) [ChiA90 2/44] d8.24 Col Wisconsin-Whitewater [DL 2003 Cle A 183]

YEAR	TM LG	W	L	PCT	G	GS	CG-SHO	SV-BS	IP	H	R	HR	HB	BB-IB	SO	ERA	AERA	OAV	OOB	AB-HR-SH	AVG	PB	SUP	APR	DL	PW
1992	NY A	6	1	.857	8	8	0	0-0	50.1	51	25	2	2	20-0	21	4.11	96	.273	.344	0	—	0	144	-1		-0.1
1993	NY A	14	4	.778	41	19	1-1	4-4	140	156	82	13	5	69-7	70	4.63	90	.284	.368	0	—	0	160	-9		-1.0
1994	NY A	5	4	.556	53	0	0	6-4	70	54	26	3	4	27-3	56	3.09	149	.213	.287	0	—	0		12		1.5
1995	†NY A	2	4	.333	63	1	0	1-9	80	77	38	6	5	33-4	51	4.05	114	.253	.335	0	—	0	80	5		0.4
1996	NY A	4	1	.800	58	0	0	0-3	79	94	41	7	5	34-1	61	4.67	106	.299	.335	0	—	0		4		0.3
	Mil A	3	0	1.000	12	0	0	0-1	16.2	12	9	0	3	10-2	14	3.24	160	.200	.314	0	—	0		2		0.1
	Year	7	1	.875	70	0	0	0-4	95.2	106	50	7	8	44-3	75	4.42	113	.283	.363	0	—	0		6		0.6
1997	Mil A	7	6	.538	74	0	0	1-4	95.2	89	39	5	3	41-7	78	2.73	170	.252	.333	0	—	0		20		2.4
1998	Mil N	6	9	.400	72	0	0	25-7	82.1	79	38	5	4	39-2	71	3.72	117	.262	.352	1	.000	-0		5		1.0
1999	Mil N	3	8	.273	71	0	0	37-8	74.1	75	31	6	2	38-6	60	3.39	136	.262	.351	1	.000	-0		10		1.9
2000	Mil N★	2	2	.500	43	0	0	16-4	46	37	18	1	1	20-2	44	2.93	157	.215	.299	0	—	0		8		1.1
	Cle A	1	3	.250	26	0	0	14-3	26.2	27	12	0	0	12-3	11	3.38	148	.270	.348	0	—	0		4		0.8
2001	†Cle A	5	0	1.000	70	0	0	32-3	67.2	61	18	4	2	14-2	66	2.39	192	.240	.285	0	—	0		17		2.5
2002	Cle A	1	3	.250	36	0	0	20-2	34.1	42	22	3	1	10-0	36	4.46	100	.284	.333	0	—	0		-2	70	-0.4
2004	Cle A	0	0	—	30	0	0	13-1	29.2	33	14	4	2	10-0	26	4.25	102	.282	.349	0	—	0		1	93	0.1
2005	Cle A★	0	4	.000	64	0	0	45-5	62	57	17	9	1	21-3	41	2.47	166	.247	.310	0	—	0		13		2.3
Total 13		59	51	.536	721	28	1-1	214-58	954.2	944	423	74	34	398-41	706	3.62	124	.260	.337	2	.000	-0	141	89	346	13.1

YEAR	TM LG	W	L	PCT	G	GS	CG-SHO	SV-BS	IP	H	R	HR	HB	BB-IB	SO	ERA	AERA	OAV	OOB	AB-HR-SH	AVG	PB	SUP	APR	DL	PW
WIDMAR, AL	Albert Joseph								B3.20.1925 Cleveland OH				D10.15.2005 Tulsa OK			BR/TR/6-3/185*			d4.25 C17						
1947	Bos A	0	0	—	2	0	0		1.1	1	2	1	0		1	13.50	29	.200	.429	0	—	0		-1		-0.1
1948	StL A	2	6	.250	49	0	0	1	82.2	88	42	4	0	48	34	4.46	102	.275	.370	10	.300	1		2		0.4
1950	StL A	7	15	.318	36	26	8-1	4	194.2	211	115	16	3	74	78	4.76	104	.271	.337	67-0-2	.149	-3	72	6		0.3
1951	StL A	4	9	.308	26	16	4		107.2	157	84	19	2	52	28	6.52	67	.344	.414	30-0-6	.167	-1	92	-22		-2.3
1952	Chi N	0	0	—	1	0	0		2	4	1	1	0	0	2	4.50	81	.444	.444	0	—	0		0		0.0
Total	5	13	30	.302	114	42	12-1	5	388.1	461	244	41	5	176	143	5.21	90	.294	.367	107-0-8	.168	-4	80	-15		-1.7
WIDNER, WILD BILL	William Waterfield								B6.3.1867 Cincinnati OH				D12.10.1908 Cincinnati OH			BR/TR/6-0/180			d6.8						
1887	Cin AA	1	0	1.000	1	1	1		9	11	8	2	1	2	0	5.00	87	.275	.326	4	.250	-0	132	-1		-0.1
1888	Was N	5	7	.417	13	13	13		115	111	69	7	6	22	33	2.82	99	.247	.291	60	.200	-1*	89	-5		-0.5
1889	Col AA	12	20	.375	41	34	25-2	1	294	368	241	11	18	85	63	5.20	70	.297	.351	133-2	.211	-2	113	-46		-3.8
1890	Col AA	4	8	.333	13	10	8-1	0	96	103	52	3	3	24	14	3.28	109	.266	.314	41	.195	-1	86	4		0.4
1891	Cin AA	0	1	.000	1	1	1	0	8	13	7	0	2	4	0	7.88	52	.351	.442	4	.250	-0	61	-2		-0.2
Total	5	22	36	.379	69	59	48-3	1	522	606	377	23	30	137	110	4.36	79	.281	.333	242-2	.207	-3	104	-50		-4.2
WIEAND, TED	Franklin Delano Roosevelt								B4.4.1933 Walnutport PA				BR/TR/6-2/195*			d9.27									
1958	Cin N	0	0	—	1	0	0	0	2	4	2	1	0	0-0	2	9.00	46	.400	.400	0	—	0		-1		0.0
1960	Cin N	0	1	.000	5	0	0	0	4.1	4	5	2	0	5-1	3	10.38	37	.250	.429	0	—	0		-3		-0.5
Total	2	0	1	.000	6	0	0	0	6.1	8	7	3	0	5-1	5	9.95	39	.308	.419	0	—	0		-4		-0.5
WIEDEMEYER, CHARLIE	Charles John "Chick"								B1.31.1914 Chicago IL				D10.27.1979 Lake Geneva FL			BL/TL/6-3/180			d9.9						
1934	Chi N	0	0	—	4	1	0	0	6	4	6	1	0	4	2	9.72	46	.432	.500	1	.000	-0	156	-6		-0.3
WIEDMAN, STUMP	George Edward								B2.17.1861 Rochester NY				D3.2.1905 New York NY			BR/TR/5-7.5/165			d8.26 U1 ▲						
1880	Buf N	0	9	.000	17	13	13	0	113.2	141	77	0		9	25	3.40	72	.291	.304	78	.103	-5*	57	-10		-1.1
1881	Det N	8	5	.615	13	13	13-1	0	115	108	48	1		12	26	**1.80**	**162**	.238	**.258**	47	.255	0	101	13		1.2
1882	Det N	25	20	.556	46	45	43-4	0	411	391	204	10		39	161	2.63	112	.236	.253	193	.218	-5*	86	18		1.2
1883	Det N	20	24	.455	52	47	41-3	2	402.1	435	265	8		72	183	3.53	88	.257	.288	313-1	.185	-8*	90	-13		-1.6
1884	Det N	4	21	.160	26	26	24	0	212.2	257	179	9		57	96	3.72	78	.273	.314	300	.163	-4*	55	-21		-2.2
1885	Det N	14	24	.368	38	38	37-3	0	330	343	198	7		63	149	3.14	91	.252	.286	153-1	.157	-4*	90	-5		-1.0
1886	KC N	12	36	.250	51	51	48-1	0	427.2	549	323	11		112	168	4.52	83	.303	.344	179	.168	-10	63	-31		-3.4
1887	Det N	13	7	.650	21	21	20	0	183	221	132	9	9	60	56	5.36	76	.296	.356	82-1	.207	-2	117	-18		-1.6
	NY AA	4	8	.333	12	12	11-1	0	97	122	84	3	1	25	37	4.64	92	.292	.333	46	.152	-2*	60	-6		-0.6
	NY N	0	1	.000	1	1	1	0	8	10	6	0	0	2	4	1.13	335	.286	.324	3	.333	0	52	1		0.1
1888	NY N	1	1	.500	2	2	2	0	18	17	20	2	2	8	5	3.50	78	.230	.321	7	.000	-0	179	-4		-0.4
Total	9	101	156	.393	279	269	249-13	2	2318.1	2594	1536	61	12	459	910	3.61	89	.302	.302	1401-3	.177	-41	81	-76		-9.4
WIENEKE, JACK	John								B3.10.1894 Saltsburg PA				D3.16.1933 Pleasant Ridge MI			BR/TL/6-0/182			d7.4						
1921	Chi A	0	1	.000	10	3	0	0	25.1	39	24	4	1	17	10	8.17	52	.351	.442	9	.111	-1	66	-10		-0.5
WIESLER, BOB	Robert George								B8.13.1930 St.Louis MO				BB/TL/6-2/195*			d8.3 Mil 1951-52									
1951	NY A	0	2	.000	4	3	0	0	9.1	13	15	0	0	11	3	13.50	28	.361	.511	3	.000	-1	54	-10		-1.6
1954	NY A	3	2	.600	6	5	0	0	30.1	28	15	0	0	30	25	4.15	83	.259	.420	11-0-1	.273	1	97	-2		-0.3
1955	NY A	2	0	1.000	16	7	0	0	53	39	27	1	1	49-0	22	3.91	96	.212	.380	14	.143	-1	105	-1		-0.1
1956	Was A	3	12	.200	37	21	3	0	123	141	98	11	3	112-1	49	6.44	67	.300	.435	33-0-4	.091	-3*	88	-27		-3.0
1957	Was A	1	1	.500	3	2	1	0	16.1	15	8	2	1	11-0	9	4.41	88	.250	.375	6	.167	-0	126	-1		0.0
1958	Was A	0	2	—	4	0	0	0	9.1	14	8	2	1	5-0	5	6.75	56	.359	.435	2	.000	-0		-3		-0.2
Total	6	7	19	.269	70	38	4	0	241.1	250	171	16	6	218-1	113	5.74	70	.279	.421	69-0-5	.130	-3	92	-44		-5.2
WIGGINS, SCOTT	Scott Joseph								B3.24.1976 Fort Thomas KY				BL/TL/6-3/205			[NYA97 7/229] d9.11 Col Northern Kentucky									
2002	Tor A	0	0	—	3	0	0	0-0	2.2	5	1	1	0	1-0	1	3.38	137	.417	.462	0	—	0		0		0.0
WIGGS, JIMMY	James Alvin "Big Jim"								B9.1.1876 Trondheim, Norway				D1.20.1963 Xenia OH			BB/TR/6-4/200			d4.23						
1903	Cin N	1	0	1.000	2	1	0	0	5	12	7	0	1	2	2	5.40	66	.500	.556	1	—	-0	57	-2		-0.3
1905	Det A	3	3	.500	7	7	4	0	41.1	30	25	0	1	29	37	3.27	84	.205	.341	15	.133	-0	78	-4		-0.5
1906	Det A	0	0	—	4	1	0	0	10.1	11	9	1	2	7	7	5.23	53	.275	.408	3	.333	0	182	-3		-0.1
Total	3	4	.429	13	9	4	0	56.2	53	41	1	4	38	46	3.81	74	.252	.377	19	.158	-0	87	-9		-0.9
WIGHT, BILL	William Robert "Lefty"								B4.12.1922 Rio Vista CA				BL/TL/6-1/180*			d4.17									
1946	NY A	2	2	.500	14	4	1	1	40.1	44	22	1	1	30	11	4.46	77	.289	.410	9-0-2	.000	-1	124	-4		-0.5
1947	NY A	1	0	1.000	1	1	1	0	9	8	3	0	0	2	3	1.00	353	.242	.286	2-0-1	.000	0	125	2		0.2
1948	Chi A	9	20	.310	34	32	7-1	1	223.1	238	132	9	1	135	68	4.80	89	.278	.377	73-0-3	.082	-7	62	-13		-2.1
1949	Chi A	15	13	.536	35	33	14-3	1	245	254	106	9	0	96	78	3.31	126	.275	.343	85-0-9	.165	-1	96	22		2.2
1950	Chi A	10	16	.385	30	28	13-3	0	206	213	89	10	0	79	62	3.58	105	.270	.336	61-0-10	.000	-9	63	22		1.7
1951	Bos A	7	7	.500	34	17	4-2	0	118.1	128	77	5	0	63	38	5.10	85	.282	.369	41	.073	-4	95	-8		-1.2
1952	Bos A	2	1	.667	10	2	0	0	24.1	14	11	3	1	14	5	2.96	133	.169	.296	7	.143	-0	122	2		0.2
	Det A	5	9	.357	23	19	8-3	0	143.2	167	71	7	0	55	65	3.88	98	.291	.354	50-0-2	.220	1	93	-2		0.1
	Year	7	10	.412	33	21	8-3	0	168	181	82	10	1	69	70	3.75	102	.276	.346	57-0-2	.211	0	96	1		0.3
1953	Det A	0	3	.000	13	4	0	1	25.1	35	33	4	0	14	10	8.88	46	.333	.412	7	.429	-1	126	-16		-1.5
	Cle A	2	1	.667	20	0	0	0	26.2	29	12	1	0	16	14	3.71	101	.282	.378	5	.000	-1		0		0.0
	Year	2	4	.333	33	4	0	1	52	64	45	5	0	30	24	6.23	63	.308	.395	12	.250	0	131	-16		-1.5
1955	Cle A	0	0	—	17	0	0	1	24	24	8	0	0	9-1	9	2.63	152	.261	.327	0-0-1	—	0		4		0.3
	Bal A	6	8	.429	19	14	8-2	2	117.1	111	43	6	1	39-1	54	2.45	155	.252	.311	36-0-5	.083	-2	60	16		1.7
	Year	6	8	.429	36	14	8-2	3	141.1	135	51	6	1	48-2	63	2.48	155	.254	.315	36-0-6	.083	-2	59	19		2.0
1956	Bal A	9	12	.429	35	26	7-1	0	174.2	198	92	7	6	72-3	84	4.02	98	.289	.361	60-0-2	.200	-1	92	-5		-0.6
1957	Bal A	6	6	.500	27	17	2	0	121	122	53	4	4	54-1	50	3.64	99	.271	.351	34-0-4	.029	-3	92	-1		-0.4
1958	Cin N	3	0	1.000	7	0	0	0	6.2	7	4	1	0	4-0	5	4.05	102	.292	.393	0	—	0		0		0.0
	StL N	3	1	.750	28	1	1	2	57.1	64	35	7	0	32-1	18	5.02	82	.290	.375	10-0-1	.100	-0	109	-5		-0.3
	Year	3	1	.750	35	1	1	2	64	71	39	8	0	36-1	23	4.92	84	.290	.377	10-0-1	.100	-0	109	-5		-0.3
Total	12	77	99	.438	347	198	66-15	8	1563	1656	791	74	14	714-7	574	3.95	103	.277	.354	480-0-40	.115	-28	84	14		-0.2
WIGINGTON, FRED	Fred Thomas								B12.16.1897 Rogers NE				D5.8.1980 Mesa AZ			BR/TR/5-10/168			d4.20						
1923	StL N	0	0	—	4	0	0	0	8.1	11	4	0	0	5	2	3.24	121	.367	.457	1	.000	-0		0		0.0
WIHTOL, SANDY	Alexander Ames								B6.1.1955 Palo Alto CA				BR/TR/6-1/195*			[CleA74 S2/28] d9.7 Col De Anza (CA) JC									
1979	Cle A	0	0	—	5	0	0	0-0	10.2	10	4	0	0	3-0	6	3.38	127	.238	.289	0	—	0		1		0.1
1980	Cle A	1	0	1.000	17	0	0	1-1	35.1	35	18	2	2	14-2	20	3.57	116	.257	.333	0	—	0		1		0.0
1982	Cle A	0	0	—	6	0	0	0-0	11.2	9	6	1	1	7-0	8	4.63	90	.220	.340	0	—	0		0		0.0
Total	3	1	0	1.000	28	0	0	1-1	57.2	54	28	3	3	24-2	34	3.75	111	.247	.327	0	—	0		2		0.1
WILCOX, MILT	Milton Edward								B4.20.1950 Honolulu HI				BR/TR/6-2/185(185-220)			[CinN68 2/33] d9.5									
1970	†Cin N	3	1	.750	5	2	1	1-1	22.1	19	6	2	1	7-0	13	2.42	167	.229	.297	5-0-1	.200	0	133	4		0.8
1971	Cin N	2	2	.500	18	3	0	1-0	43.1	43	22	2	2	17-2	21	3.32	102	.269	.343	9	.000	-1	61	-2		-0.3
1972	Cle A	7	14	.333	32	27	4-2	0-0	156	145	67	18	5	72-11	90	3.40	96	.251	.336	45-0-4	.200	1	73	-3		-0.3
1973	Cle A	8	10	.444	26	19	4	0-0	134.1	143	90	14	8	68-9	82	5.83	68	.275	.366	0	—	-0	105	-24	22	-2.8
1974	Cle A	2	2	.500	41	2	1	4-1	71.1	74	42	10	4	24-4	33	4.67	78	.271	.339	0	—	0	133	-8		-0.5
1975	Chi N	1	0	1.000	25	0	0	0-0	38.1	50	27	4	1	17-2	21	5.63	69	.323	.389	3	.333			-7		-0.3
1977	Det A	6	2	.750	20	13	1	0-0	106.1	96	46	13	1	37-1	82	3.64	119	.241	.305	0	—	0	103	6		0.6
1978	Det A	13	12	.520	29	27	16-2	0-0	215.1	208	94	22	8	68-2	132	3.76	104	.255	.317	0	—	0	100	5		0.6
1979	Det A	12	10	.545	33	29	7	0-0	196.1	201	105	19	11	73-8	109	4.35	100	.267	.338	0	—	0	90	-1		0.1
1980	Det A	13	11	.542	32	31	13-1	0-1	198.2	201	112	24	6	68-5	97	4.48	92	.262	.325	0	—	0*	130	-10		-1.0
1981	Det A	12	9	.571	24	24	8	0-0	166.1	152	61	10	5	52-3	79	3.03	125	.247	.310	0	—	0	81	13		1.0
1982	Det A	12	10	.545	29	29	9-1	0-0	193.2	187	91	18	7	85-5	112	3.62	113	.257	.338	0	—	0*	111	8	21	1.0
1983	Det A	11	10	.524	26	26	9-2	0-0	186	164	89	24	4	74-6	101	3.97	100	.237	.313	0	—	0	110	0	31	0.1
1984	†Det A	17	8	.680	33	33	0	0-0	193.2	183	99	13	8	66-5	119	4.00	99	.252	.318	0	—	0	137	-2		0.2
1985	Det A	1	3	.250	8	8	0	0-0	39	51	24	9	1	14-2	20	4.85	85	.315	.369	0	—	0	100	-3	116	-0.2

YEAR	TM LG	W	L	PCT	G	GS	CG-SHO	SV-BS	IP	H	R	HR	HB	BB-IB	SO	ERA	AERA	OAV	OOB	AB-HR-SH	AVG	PB	SUP	APR	DL	PW
1986	Sea A	0	8	.000	13	10	0	0-0	55.2	74	38	11	1	28-1	26	5.50	78	.327	.399	0	—	0	57	-7		-0.9
Total	16	119	113	.513	394	283	73-10	6-2	2016.2	1991	1013	204	74	770-66	1137	4.07	97	.260	.331	62-0-5	.177	0	104	-29	190	-1.7

WILES, RANDY Randall E B9.10.1951 Fort Belvoir VA BL/TL/6-1/185 [StLN73 5/108] d8.7 Col Louisiana St.

YEAR	TM LG	W	L	PCT	G	GS	CG-SHO	SV-BS	IP	H	R	HR	HB	BB-IB	SO	ERA	AERA	OAV	OOB	AB-HR-SH	AVG	PB	SUP	APR	DL	PW
1977	Chi A	1	1	.500	5	0	0	0-0	2.2	5	3	1	0	3-1	0	10.13	40	.417	.533	0	—	0		-2		-0.3

WILEY, MARK Mark Eugene B2.28.1948 National City CA BR/TR/6-1/190* [MinA70 2/46] d6.17 C15 Col Cal Poly-Pomona

YEAR	TM LG	W	L	PCT	G	GS	CG-SHO	SV-BS	IP	H	R	HR	HB	BB-IB	SO	ERA	AERA	OAV	OOB	AB-HR-SH	AVG	PB	SUP	APR	DL	PW
1975	Min A	1	3	.250	15	3	1	2-1	38.2	50	30	4	1	13-1	15	6.05	63	.325	.374	0	—	0	115	-10		-1.0
1978	SD N	1	0	1.000	4	1	0	0-0	7.2	11	6	1	0	1-0	1	5.87	57	.324	.343	2	.000	-0	241	-2		-0.3
	Tor A	0	0		2	0	0	0-0	2.2	3	2	0	0	1-0	2	6.75	59	.273	.333	0	—	0		-1		0.0
Total	2	2	3	.400	21	4	1	2-1	49	64	38	5	1	15-1	18	6.06	62	.322	.367	2	.000	-0	141	-13		-1.3

WILHELM, HARRY Harry Lester B4.7.1874 Uniontown PA D2.20.1944 Republic PA BR/TR/5-7/155 d8.12 Col Westminster (PA)

YEAR	TM LG	W	L	PCT	G	GS	CG-SHO	SV-BS	IP	H	R	HR	HB	BB-IB	SO	ERA	AERA	OAV	OOB	AB-HR-SH	AVG	PB	SUP	APR	DL	PW
1899	Lou N	1	0	1.000	5	3	2	0	25	36	22	1	1	3	6	6.12	63	.336	.360	12-1-0	.250	2	131	-5		-0.1

WILHELM, KAISER Irvin Key B1.26.1874 Wooster OH D5.22.1936 Rochester NY BR/TR/6-0/162 d4.18 M2/C1/U1

YEAR	TM LG	W	L	PCT	G	GS	CG-SHO	SV-BS	IP	H	R	HR	HB	BB-IB	SO	ERA	AERA	OAV	OOB	AB-HR-SH	AVG	PB	SUP	APR	DL	PW
1903	Pit N	5	3	.625	12	9	7-1	0	86	88	51	0	3	25	20	3.24	100	.264	.321	34	.088	-2*	106	-2		-0.3
1904	Bos N	14	20	.412	39	36	30-3	0	288	316	150	8	7	74	73	3.69	75	.285	.333	100-0-5	.070	-8	88	-22		-3.2
1905	Bos N	3	23	.115	34	28	23	0	242.1	287	166	7	5	75	76	4.53	68	.295	.349	100-0-5	.160	-2*	64	-38		-3.7
1908	Bro N	16	22	.421	42	38	33-6	0	332	266	105	3	6	83	99	1.87	125	.217	.271	111-0-5	.108	-4	67	13		1.3
1909	Bro N	3	13	.188	22	17	14-1	0	163	176	92	6	2	59	45	3.26	80	.289	.353	57-0-2	.228	2	49	-18		-1.4
1910	Bro N	3	7	.300	15	5	0	0	68.1	88	45	3	1	18	17	4.74	64	.314	.358	19-0-2	.316	2	59	-13		-1.4
1914	Bal F	12	17	.414	47	27	11-1	5	243.2	263	141	10	0	81	113	4.03	75	.291	.349	84-0-4	.250	1*	82	-25		-2.6
1915	Bal F	0	0		1	0	0	0	1	0	0	0	0	0	0	0.00	—	.000	.000	0	—	0		0		0.0
1921	Phi N	0	0		4	0	0	0	8	11	3	0	0	3	1	3.38	125	.393	.452	2	.000	-0		-1		0.0
Total	9	56	105	.348	216	158	118-12	5	1432.1	1495	753	34	24	418	444	3.44	81	.274	.328	507-0-21	.154	-12	75	-104		-11.3

WILHELM, HOYT James Hoyt B7.26.1922 Huntersville NC D8.23.2002 Sarasota FL BR/TR/6-0/195* d4.18 HF1985

YEAR	TM LG	W	L	PCT	G	GS	CG-SHO	SV-BS	IP	H	R	HR	HB	BB-IB	SO	ERA	AERA	OAV	OOB	AB-HR-SH	AVG	PB	SUP	APR	DL	PW
1952	NY N	15	3	**.833**	**71**	0	0	11	159.1	127	60	12	5	57	108	**2.43**	152	.220	.296	38-1-3	.158	0		19		2.3
1953	NY N☆	7	8	.467	68	0	0	15	145	127	61	13	4	77	71	3.04	141	.238	.339	33-0-5	.152	1		**18**		2.1
1954	†NY N	12	4	.750	57	0	0	7	111.1	77	32	5	2	52	64	2.10	192	.198	.298	21-0-1	.048	-2		23		3.2
1955	NY N	4	1	.800	59	0	0	0	103	104	53	10	2	40-5	71	3.93	102	.266	.333	19-0-1	.158	-1		1		0.1
1956	NY N	4	9	.308	64	0	0	8	89.1	97	45	7	2	43-10	71	3.83	99	.280	.361	9	.222	0		-1		-0.1
1957	StL N	1	4	.200	40	0	0	11	55	52	28	7	3	21-1	29	4.25	93	.254	.332	6	.000	-1		-1		-0.3
	Cle A	1	0	1.000	2	0	0	1	3.2	2	1	1	1	1-0	0	2.45	154	.154	.267	0	—	0		1		0.1
1958	Cle A	2	7	.222	30	6	1	5	90.1	70	32	4	1	35-2	57	2.49	146	.215	.291	21-0-3	.095	-1	82	10		1.0
	Bal A	1	3	.250	9	4	3-1	0	40.2	25	9	2	1	10-2	35	1.99	180	.179	.238	11-0-1	.091	-1	44	8		0.7
	Year	3	10	.231	39	10	4-1	5	131	95	41	6	2	45-4	92	2.34	155	.204	.276	32-0-4	.094	-2	67	18		1.7
1959	Bal A★	15	11	.577	32	27	13-3	0	226	178	64	13	10	77-3	139	2.19	173	.224	.299	76-0-4	.053	-6	82	40		3.7
1960	Bal A	11	8	.579	41	11	3-1	7	147	125	69	13	1	39-0	107	3.31	115	.228	.279	42-0-3	.071	-3	74	5		0.3
1961	Bal A★	9	7	.563	51	0	0	18	109.2	89	35	5	4	41-5	87	2.30	167	.219	.296	20-0-2	.050	-1	92	18		3.0
1962	Bal A*	7	10	.412	52	0	0	15	93	64	28	5	3	34-2	90	1.94	191	.197	.276	16	.125	-0		17		3.5
1963	Chi A	5	8	.385	55	3	0	21	136.1	106	47	8	4	30-1	111	2.64	133	.215	.263	29-0-3	.069	-1	68	13		1.5
1964	Chi A	12	9	.571	73	0	0	27	131.1	94	35	7	2	30-1	95	1.99	174	.202	.252	21-0-2	.143	-0		21		4.2
1965	Chi A	7	7	.500	66	0	0	20	144	88	34	11	2	32-7	106	1.81	176	.177	.227	22-0-4	.000	-2		23		2.7
1966	Chi A	5	2	.714	46	0	0	6	81.1	50	21	6	1	17-2	61	1.66	191	.178	.226	8	.125	0	13	48		1.3
1967	Chi A	8	3	.727	49	0	0	12	89	58	21	2	4	34-4	76	1.31	236	.183	.270	13	.077	-1		16		2.4
1968	Chi A	4	4	.500	72	0	0	12	93.2	69	20	4	2	24-5	72	1.73	175	.205	.261	3-0-1	.000	-0		14		1.6
1969	Cal A	5	7	.417	44	0	0	10-3	65.2	45	21	4	3	18-4	53	2.47	142	.194	.260	8	.000	-1		8		1.5
	Atl N	2	0	1.000	8	0	0	4-1	12.1	5	1	0	1	4-0	14	0.73	496	.119	.213	1	.000	-0		4		0.9
1970	Atl N☆	6	4	.600	50	0	0	13-4	78.1	69	29	7	1	39-7	67	3.10	138	.234	.323	11	.091	-0		10		1.6
	Chi N	0	1	.000	3	0	0	0-0	3.2	4	4	1	0	3-0	1	9.82	46	.286	.412	0	—	0		-2		-0.3
	Year	6	5	.545	53	0	0	13-4	82	73	33	8	1	42-7	68	3.40	126	.236	.328	11	.091	-0		8		1.3
1971	Atl N	0	0		3	0	0	0-1	2.1	6	5	2	0	1-0	1	15.43	24	.500	.538	0	—	-0		-3	63	-0.1
	LA N	0	1	.000	9	0	0	3-0	17.2	6	2	1	0	4-0	15	1.02	319	.111	.169	3	.000	-0		5		0.4
	Year	0	1	.000	12	0	0	3-1	20	12	7	3	0	5-0	16	2.70	123	.182	.236	3	.000	-0		1		0.3
1972	LA·N	0	1	.000	16	0	0	1-0	25.1	20	16	0	0	15-0	9	4.62	73	.217	.315	1-0-1	.000	-0		-4		-0.2
Total	21	143	122	.540	1070	52	20-5	227-9	2254.1	1757	773	150	62	778-61	1610	2.52	146	.216	.288	432-1-34	.088	-21	78	276	111	37.1

WILKIE, LEFTY Aldon Jay B10.30.1914 Zealandia SK, Can. D8.5.1992 Tualatin OR BL/TL/5-11.5/175 d4.22 Mil 1943-45

YEAR	TM LG	W	L	PCT	G	GS	CG-SHO	SV-BS	IP	H	R	HR	HB	BB-IB	SO	ERA	AERA	OAV	OOB	AB-HR-SH	AVG	PB	SUP	APR	DL	PW
1941	Pit N	2	4	.333	26	6	2-1	2	79	90	42	1	1	40	16	4.56	79	.289	.372	24	.292	1	98	-6		-0.3
1942	Pit N	6	7	.462	35	6	3	1	107.1	112	53	4	1	37	18	4.19	81	.269	.330	38	.263	2*	99	-7		-0.5
1946	Pit N	0	0		7	0	0	0	7.2	13	9	1	0	3	3	10.57	33	.382	.432	0	—	0		-5		-0.3
Total	3	8	11	.421	68	12	5-1	3	194	215	104	5	2	80	37	4.59	76	.283	.352	62	.274	3	99	-18		-1.1

WILKINS, DEAN Dean Allan B8.24.1966 Blue Island IL BR/TR/6-1/170* [NYA86*2/51] d8.21 Col San Diego Mesa (CA) JC

YEAR	TM LG	W	L	PCT	G	GS	CG-SHO	SV-BS	IP	H	R	HR	HB	BB-IB	SO	ERA	AERA	OAV	OOB	AB-HR-SH	AVG	PB	SUP	APR	DL	PW
1989	Chi N	1	0	1.000	11	0	0	0-0	15.2	13	9	1	0	9-2	14	4.60	82	.228	.333	1-0-1	.000	-0		-1		-0.1
1990	Chi N	0	0		7	0	0	1-0	7.1	11	8	1	1	7-0	3	9.82	42	.333	.463	0	—	0		-4		-0.2
1991	Hou N	2	1	.667	7	0	0	1-1	8	16	14	0	0	10-2	4	11.25	31	.410	.531	1	.000	-0		-9		-1.6
Total	3	3	1	.750	25	0	0	2-1	31	40	31	3	1	26-4	21	7.55	50	.310	.429	2-0-1	.000	-0		-14		-1.9

WILKINS, ERIC Eric Lamoine B12.9.1956 St.Louis MO BR/TR/6-1/190 [CleA77 6/141] d4.11 Col Washington St.

YEAR	TM LG	W	L	PCT	G	GS	CG-SHO	SV-BS	IP	H	R	HR	HB	BB-IB	SO	ERA	AERA	OAV	OOB	AB-HR-SH	AVG	PB	SUP	APR	DL	PW
1979	Cle A	4	4	.333	16	14	0	0	69.2	77	41	4	4	38-1	52	4.39	98	.289	.384	0	—	0	89	-2	42	-0.2

WILKINS, MARC Marc Allen B10.21.1970 Mansfield OH BR/TR/5-11/207(200-221) [PitN92 47/1323] d5.11 Col Toledo

YEAR	TM LG	W	L	PCT	G	GS	CG-SHO	SV-BS	IP	H	R	HR	HB	BB-IB	SO	ERA	AERA	OAV	OOB	AB-HR-SH	AVG	PB	SUP	APR	DL	PW
1996	Pit N	4	3	.571	47	2	0	1-4	75	75	36	6	6	36-6	62	3.84	114	.266	.357	9	.222	0	123	4		0.4
1997	Pit N	9	5	.643	70	0	0	2-2	75.2	65	33	7	4	33-2	47	3.69	116	.242	.333	4-0-1	.000	-0		6		0.8
1998	Pit N	0	0		16	0	0	0-1	15.1	13	6	1	1	9-2	17	3.52	121	.236	.358	0	—	0	2	143		0.1
1999	Pit N	2	3	.400	46	0	0	0-0	51	49	28	3	4	26-1	44	4.24	109	.257	.354	1	.000	0	2	26		0.2
2000	Pit N	4	2	.667	52	0	0	0-0	60.1	54	34	4	6	43-3	37	5.07	92	.248	.376	6	.167	0		-1		-0.1
2001	Pit N	0	1	.000	14	0	0	0-0	17.1	22	13	2	1	8-1	11	6.75	66	.319	.397	0	—	0		-4		-0.2
Total	6	19	14	.576	245	2	0	3-7	294.2	278	150	23	23	155-15	218	4.28	104	.256	.357	20-0-1	.150	0	123	9	169	1.2

WILKINSON, ROY Roy Hamilton B5.8.1893 Canandaigua NY D7.2.1956 Louisville KY BR/TR/6-1/170 d4.29

YEAR	TM LG	W	L	PCT	G	GS	CG-SHO	SV-BS	IP	H	R	HR	HB	BB-IB	SO	ERA	AERA	OAV	OOB	AB-HR-SH	AVG	PB	SUP	APR	DL	PW
1918	Cle A	0	0		1	0	0	0	1	0	0	0	0	0	0	0.00	—	.000	.000	0	—	0		0		0.0
1919	†Chi A	1	1	.500	4	1	1-1	0	22	21	9	0	0	10	5	2.05	156	.266	.348	8	.375	2	172	2		0.4
1920	Chi A	7	9	.438	34	12	8	2	145	162	75	6	4	48	30	4.03	93	.297	.356	48-0-1	.146	-3	83	-3		-0.7
1921	Chi A	4	20	.167	38	23	11	3	198.1	259	135	4	4	78	50	5.13	83	.334	.397	65	.123	-4	57	-22		-2.4
1922	Chi A	0	1	.000	4	1	0	1	14.1	24	15	1	0	6	3	8.79	46	.393	.456	3	.000	0	0	-7		-0.6
Total	5	12	31	.279	79	37	20-1	6	380.2	466	234	11	7	142	88	4.66	86	.318	.381	124-0-1	.145	-5	67	-30		-3.3

WILKINSON, BILL William Carl B8.10.1964 Greybull WY BR/TL/5-10/160* [SeaA83 4/87] d6.13 ggf-Jim Bluejacket

YEAR	TM LG	W	L	PCT	G	GS	CG-SHO	SV-BS	IP	H	R	HR	HB	BB-IB	SO	ERA	AERA	OAV	OOB	AB-HR-SH	AVG	PB	SUP	APR	DL	PW
1985	Sea A	0	2	.000	2	2	0	0	6	8	9	2	0	6-1	5	13.50	31	.333	.467	0	—	0	86	-6		-0.9
1987	Sea A	3	4	.429	56	0	0	10-2	76.1	61	33	8	0	21-1	73	3.66	130	.223	.272	0	—	0		9	17	0.9
1988	Sea A	2	2	.500	30	0	0	2-1	31	28	14	3	0	15-0	25	3.48	120	.233	.316	0	—	0		2	39	0.2
Total	3	5	8	.385	88	2	0	12-3	113.1	97	56	13	0	42-2	103	4.13	110	.232	.298	0	—	0	86	5	56	0.2

WILKS, TED Theodore "Cork" B11.13.1915 Fulton NY D8.21.1989 Houston TX BR/TR/5-9.5/178(178-195) d4.25 C2

YEAR	TM LG	W	L	PCT	G	GS	CG-SHO	SV-BS	IP	H	R	HR	HB	BB-IB	SO	ERA	AERA	OAV	OOB	AB-HR-SH	AVG	PB	SUP	APR	DL	PW
1944	†StL N	17	4	**.810**	36	21	16-4	0	207.2	173	61	12	1	49	70	2.64	133	.227	**.275**	64-0-6	.141	-1	141	25		2.1
1945	StL N	4	7	.364	18	16	4-1	0	98.1	103	39	9	1	29	28	2.93	128	.270	.324	30-0-1	.133	-0	76	8		0.7
1946	†StL N	8	0	1.000	40	4	0	1	95	98	41	13	2	38	40	3.41	101	.248	.324	24	.208	0	112	1		0.0
1947	StL N	4	0	1.000	37	0	0	5	50.1	57	33	10	2	11	28	5.01	83	.279	.323	6	.167	0		-5		-0.5
1948	StL N	6	6	.500	57	2	1	13	130.2	113	43	6	0	39	71	2.62	156	.235	.293	30-0-3	.167	0	163	21		2.3
1949	StL N	10	3	.769	59	1	0	9	118.1	105	52	8	0	38	71	3.73	112	.240	.301	27-0-1	.037	-3		7		0.4
1950	StL N	2	0	1.000	18	0	0	0	24.1	27	18	4	1	9	15	6.66	65	.287	.356	4	.000	0		-5	42	-0.4
1951	StL N	0	0		17	0	0	1	18	19	7	1	0	6	4	3.00	132	.275	.329	1	.000	-0		0		0.0
	Pit N	3	5	.375	48	1	1	12	82.2	69	31	6	2	24	43	2.83	149	.231	.292	12-0-1	.083	-1	84	12		1.4

YEAR	TM LG	W	L	PCT	G	GS	CG-SHO	SV-BS	IP	H	R	HR	HB	BB-IB	SO	ERA	AERA	OAV	OOB	AB-HR-SH	AVG	PB	SUP	APR	DL	PW
	Year	3	5	.375	65	1	1	13	100.2	88	38	7	2	29	48	2.86	146	.240	.299	13-0-1	.077	-1	85	14		1.4
1952	Pit N	5	5	.500	44	0	0	4	72.1	65	32	9	2	31	24	3.61	111	.245	.329	8-0-1	.125	-0		3		0.4
	Cle A	0	0	—	7	0	0	1	11.2	8	6	0	0	7	6	3.86	87	.186	.300	0	—	0		-1		0.0
1953	Cle A	0	0	—	4	0	0	0	3.2	5	4	0	0	3	2	7.36	51	.278	.381	0	—	0		-2		-0.1
Total	10	59	30	.663	385	44	22-5	46	913	832	364	77	11	283	403	3.26	118	.244	.304	206-0-13	.131	-5	110	66	42	6.3

WILLETT, ED   Robert Edgar   B3.7.1884 Norfolk VA   D5.10.1934 Wellington KS   BR/TR/6-0/183   d9.5

YEAR	TM LG	W	L	PCT	G	GS	CG-SHO	SV-BS	IP	H	R	HR	HB	BB-IB	SO	ERA	AERA	OAV	OOB	AB-HR-SH	AVG	PB	SUP	APR	DL	PW
1906	Det A	0	3	.000	3	3	3	0	25	24	12	0	2	8	16	3.96	70	.255	.327	9	.000	-1	17	-2		-0.4
1907	Det A	1	5	.167	10	6	1	0	48.2	47	31	0	2	20	27	3.70	70	.255	.335	13	.077	-1	52	-6		-0.8
1908	Det A	15	8	.652	30	23	18-2	1	197.1	186	67	2	14	60	77	2.28	106	.261	.331	67-0-2	.164	-2	127	5		0.7
1909	†Det A	21	10	.677	41	34	25-3	1	292.2	239	112	5	15	76	89	2.34	108	.221	.281	112-0-3	.196	3*	134	3		0.6
1910	Det A	16	11	.593	37	25	18-4	0	224.1	175	85	2	17	74	65	2.37	111	.217	.296	83-0-2	.133	-2*	96	4		0.6
1911	Det A	13	14	.481	38	27	15-2	1	231.1	261	136	5	14	80	86	3.66	95	.295	.363	82-1-4	.268	7*	117	-8		-0.1
1912	Det A	17	15	.531	37	31	28-1	0	284.1	281	144	3	17	84	89	3.29	99	.262	.326	115-2-3	.165	-2	112	-2		-0.1
1913	Det A	13	14	.481	34	30	19	0	242	237	117	0	11	89	59	3.09	95	.263	.336	92-1-6	.283	7*	115	-5		0.4
1914	StL F	4	17	.190	27	22	14	0	175	208	102	5	10	56	73	4.27	71	.295	.355	64-1-2	.234	2*	73	-21		-1.9
1915	StL F	2	3	.400	17	2	1	2	52.2	61	36	2	3	18	19	4.61	62	.295	.360	15-0-1	.200	-0	170	-11		-1.0
Total	10	102	100	.505	274	203	142-12	5	1773.1	1719	842	24	105	565	600	3.08	94	.259	.326	652-5-23	.199	11	109	-43		-2.0

WILLEY, CARL   Carlton Francis   B6.6.1931 Cherryfield ME   BR/TR/6-0/175*   d4.30

YEAR	TM LG	W	L	PCT	G	GS	CG-SHO	SV-BS	IP	H	R	HR	HB	BB-IB	SO	ERA	AERA	OAV	OOB	AB-HR-SH	AVG	PB	SUP	APR	DL	PW
1958	†Mil N	9	7	.563	23	19	9-4	0	140	110	44	14	2	53-4	74	2.70	130	.215	.289	48-0-5	.104	-2	110	15		1.3
1959	Mil N	5	9	.357	26	15	5-2	0	117	126	60	12	2	31-4	51	4.15	85	.273	.319	39-0-1	.103	-1	103	-8		-1.0
1960	Mil N	6	7	.462	28	21	2-1	0	144.2	136	78	19	7	65-5	109	4.35	79	.248	.333	48-1-5	.146	1	104	-16		-1.2
1961	Mil N	6	12	.333	35	22	4	0	159.2	147	71	20	2	65-9	91	3.83	98	.247	.322	54-0-3	:019	-6	85	0		-0.5
1962	Mil N	2	5	.286	30	6	0	1	73.1	95	49	9	1	20-3	40	5.40	70	.319	.361	11-0-1	.273	1	96	-13		-1.0
1963	NY N	9	14	.391	30	28	7-4	0	183	149	74	24	4	69-2	101	3.10	113	.220	.294	54-1-6	.111	-1	82	8		0.9
1964	NY N	0	2	.000	14	3	0	0	30	37	19	5	1	8-2	14	3.60	99	.301	.343	4-0-1	.000	-0	65	-2	51	-0.3
1965	NY N	1	2	.333	13	1	0	0	28	30	13	2	2	15-1	13	4.18	84	.270	.364	5-0-2	.000	-1	58	-1		-0.2
Total	8	38	58	.396	199	117	28-11	1	875.2	830	408	105	21	326-30	493	3.76	95	.250	.318	263-2-24	.099	-9	93	-17	51	-2.0

WILLHITE, NICK   Jon Nicholas   B1.27.1941 Tulsa OK   BL/TL/6-2/195(175-195)   d6.16

YEAR	TM LG	W	L	PCT	G	GS	CG-SHO	SV-BS	IP	H	R	HR	HB	BB-IB	SO	ERA	AERA	OAV	OOB	AB-HR-SH	AVG	PB	SUP	APR	DL	PW
1963	LA N	2	3	.400	8	8	1-1	0	38	44	19	5	0	10-2	28	3.79	80	.286	.329	10-0-1	.300	1	89	-4		-0.4
1964	LA N	2	4	.333	10	7	2	0	43.2	43	19	4	0	13-2	24	3.71	87	.264	.315	11-0-1	.000	-0	81	-2		-0.2
1965	Was A	0	0	—	5	0	0	0	6.1	10	11	4	2	4-0	3	7.11	49	.345	.424	0	—	0		-5		-0.3
	LA N	2	2	.500	15	6	0	1	42	47	26	7	2	22-1	28	5.36	61	.288	.380	10	.400	3	103	-10		-0.6
1966	LA N	0	0	—	6	0	0	0	4.1	3	1	0	0	5-0	4	2.08	159	.214	.421	0	—	0		1		0.1
1967	Cal A	0	2	.000	10	7	0	0	39.1	39	20	8	0	16-0	22	4.35	72	.258	.329	10	.000	-1	55	-5		-0.4
	NY N	0	1	.000	4	1	0	0	8.1	9	8	1	0	5-0	9	8.64	39	.257	.350	2	.000	-0	259	-4		-0.5
Total	5	6	12	.333	58	29	3-1	1	182	195	104	27	2	75-5	118	4.55	70	.275	.345	43-0-2	.163	2	88	-29		-2.3

WILLIAMS, ALBERT   Albert Hamilton (De Souza)   B5.6.1954 Laguna de Perlas, Nicaragua   BR/TR/6-4/190*   d5.7

YEAR	TM LG	W	L	PCT	G	GS	CG-SHO	SV-BS	IP	H	R	HR	HB	BB-IB	SO	ERA	AERA	OAV	OOB	AB-HR-SH	AVG	PB	SUP	APR	DL	PW
1980	Min A	6	2	.750	18	9	3	1-0	77	73	33	9	0	30-1	35	3.51	125	.253	.323	0	—	0	125	7		0.7
1981	Min A	6	10	.375	23	22	4	0-0	150	160	72	11	1	52-4	76	4.08	97	.276	.334	0	—	0	97	0		-0.1
1982	Min A	9	7	.563	26	26	3	0-0	153.2	166	74	18	0	55-5	61	4.22	101	.276	.333	0	—	0	98	3		0.2
1983	Min A	11	14	.440	36	29	4-1	1-1	193.1	196	105	21	4	68-6	68	4.14	103	.262	.325	0	—	0	94	0		-0.1
1984	Min A	3	5	.375	17	11	1	0-0	68.2	75	46	9	7	22-1	22	5.77	73	.284	.351	0	—	0	81	-10	80	-1.0
Total	5	35	38	.479	120	97	15-1	2-1	642.2	670	330	68	12	227-17	262	4.24	99	.270	.332	0	—	0	97	0	80	-0.3

WILLIAMS, AL   Almon Edward   B5.11.1914 Valhermoso Springs AL   D7.19.1969 Groves TX   BR/TR/6-3/200   d4.19

YEAR	TM LG	W	L	PCT	G	GS	CG-SHO	SV-BS	IP	H	R	HR	HB	BB-IB	SO	ERA	AERA	OAV	OOB	AB-HR-SH	AVG	PB	SUP	APR	DL	PW
1937	Phi A	4	1	.800	16	8	2	1	75.1	88	51	0	4	49	27	5.38	88	.300	.402	24-0-3	.083	-2	132	-4		-0.4
1938	Phi A	0	7	.000	30	8	1	0	93.1	128	93	6	1	54	25	6.94	70	.324	.407	25-0-1	.040	-3	71	-25		-1.7
Total	2	4	8	.333	46	16	3	1	168.2	216	144	6	2	103	52	6.24	77	.314	.405	49-0-4	.061	-5	101	-29		-2.1

WILLIAMS, GUS   Augustine H.   B1870 New York NY   D10.14.1890 New York NY   5-11/170   d4.18

YEAR	TM LG	W	L	PCT	G	GS	CG-SHO	SV-BS	IP	H	R	HR	HB	BB-IB	SO	ERA	AERA	OAV	OOB	AB-HR-SH	AVG	PB	SUP	APR	DL	PW
1890	Bro AA	0	1	.000	2	2	1	0	12	13	15	0	0	12	2	7.50	52	.265	.410	4	.500	1	207	-4		-0.3

WILLIAMS, BRIAN   Brian O'Neal   B2.15.1969 Lancaster SC   BR/TR/6-2/195(195-230)   [HouN90 1/31]   d9.16   Col South Carolina-Aiken

YEAR	TM LG	W	L	PCT	G	GS	CG-SHO	SV-BS	IP	H	R	HR	HB	BB-IB	SO	ERA	AERA	OAV	OOB	AB-HR-SH	AVG	PB	SUP	APR	DL	PW
1991	Hou N	0	1	.000	2	2	0	0-0	12	11	5	2	1	4-0	4	3.75	94	.250	.327	3-0-2	.000	-0	102	0		0.0
1992	Hou N	7	6	.538	16	16	0	0-0	96.1	92	44	10	0	42-1	54	3.92	87	.255	.330	30-0-5	.133	-0*	108	-5		-0.6
1993	Hou N	4	4	.500	42	5	0	3-3	82	76	48	7	4	38-4	56	4.83	80	.248	.335	10-0-3	.200	1	116	-8	15	-0.6
1994	Hou N	6	5	.545	20	13	0	0-0	78.1	112	64	9	4	41-4	49	5.74	69	.343	.416	23-0-5	.261	1	138	-21	11	-2.3
1995	SD N	3	10	.231	44	6	0	0-2	72	79	54	3	8	38-4	75	6.00	68	.279	.379	14	.071	-1	126	-16		-2.5
1996	Det A	3	10	.231	40	17	2-1	2-2	121	145	107	21	6	85-2	72	6.77	75	.304	.411	0	—	0	88	-26		-2.3
1997	Bal A	0	0	—	13	0	0	0-1	24	20	8	0	0	18-0	14	3.00	147	.220	.345	0	—	0		4		0.2
1999	Hou N	2	1	.667	50	0	0	0-2	67.1	69	35	4	5	35-2	53	4.41	100	.272	.369	3	.333	1		0		0.1
2000	Chi N	1	1	.500	22	0	0	1-1	24.1	28	27	4	3	23-2	14	9.62	48	.304	.454	2	.500	1		-13		-1.0
	Cle A	0	0	—	7	0	0	0-0	18	23	9	2	1	8-1	6	4.00	125	.324	.395	0	—	0		2		0.1
Total	9	26	38	.406	256	59	2-1	6-11	595.1	655	401	62	32	332-20	397	5.37	78	.284	.378	85-0-15	.176	1	107	-83	26	-8.9

WILLIAMS, CHARLIE   Charles Prosek   B10.11.1947 Flushing NY   BR/TR/6-2/200*   [NYN68 7/133]   d4.23

YEAR	TM LG	W	L	PCT	G	GS	CG-SHO	SV-BS	IP	H	R	HR	HB	BB-IB	SO	ERA	AERA	OAV	OOB	AB-HR-SH	AVG	PB	SUP	APR	DL	PW
1971	NY N	5	6	.455	31	9	1	0-0	90.1	92	53	7	2	41-8	53	4.78	72	.267	.343	23-0-4	.087	-1	117	-13		-1.7
1972	SF N	0	2	.000	3	2	0	0-0	9.1	14	10	3	0	3-0	3	8.68	40	.333	.378	2	.000	-0	38	-5		-0.9
1973	SF N	3	0	1.000	12	2	0	0-0	23	32	19	2	0	7-2	11	6.65	58	.330	.371	3-0-1	.333	-1	229	-7		-0.7
1974	SF N	1	3	.250	39	7	0	0-1	100.1	93	38	6	2	31-6	48	2.78	137	.250	.308	22-0-2	.136	-1	85	11		0.6
1975	SF N	5	3	.625	55	2	0	3-2	98	94	41	2	4	66-14	45	3.49	109	.261	.378	16	.125	0	69	4		0.4
1976	SF N	2	0	1.000	48	2	0	1-1	85	80	33	4	2	39-2	34	2.96	123	.256	.340	8	.125	-0	157	6		0.4
1977	SF N	6	5	.545	55	8	1	0-0	119.1	116	62	9	3	60-16	41	4.00	99	.262	.352	18-0-1	.222	0	101	-1		-0.1
1978	SF N	1	3	.250	25	-1	0	0-0	48	60	31	5	1	28-6	22	5.44	64	.314	.401	5	.000	-1	26	-10		-0.9
Total	8	23	22	.511	268	33	2	4-5	573.1	581	287	38	14	275-54	257	3.97	94	.269	.352	97-0-8	.134	-2	105	-15		-2.9

WILLIAMS, LEFTY   Claude Preston   B3.9.1893 Aurora MO   D11.4.1959 Laguna Beach CA   BR/TL/5-9/160   d9.17   Def 1918

YEAR	TM LG	W	L	PCT	G	GS	CG-SHO	SV-BS	IP	H	R	HR	HB	BB-IB	SO	ERA	AERA	OAV	OOB	AB-HR-SH	AVG	PB	SUP	APR	DL	PW
1913	Det A	1	3	.250	5	4	3	1	29	34	18	0	1	4	9	4.97	59	.286	.315	10	.100	-0	82	-5		-0.8
1914	Det A	0	1	.000	1	1	0	1	3	3	5	0	0	2	0	0.00	—	.429	.556	0	—	0*	156	-1		-0.3
1916	Chi A	13	7	.650	43	26	10-2	1	224.1	220	99	5	8	65	138	2.89	96	.267	.327	74	.135	-0	124	-4		-0.7
1917	†Chi A	17	8	.680	45	29	8-1	1	230	221	94	3	9	81	85	2.97	89	.252	.321	67-0-6	.090	-3	121	-5		-1.1
1918	Chi A	6	4	.600	15	14	7-2	1	105.2	76	32	0	5	47	30	2.73	100	.209	.308	38-0-3	.132	-2	126	4		0.0
1919	†Chi A	23	11	.676	41	40	27-5	1	297	265	104	7	11	58	125	2.64	121	.244	.289	94-0-12	.181	1	127	20		2.0
1920	Chi A	22	14	.611	39	38	25	0	299	302	145	15	12	90	128	3.91	96	.271	.338	101-0-8	.218	0	95	0		-0.2
Total	7	82	48	.631	189	152	80-10	5	1186	1121	497	30	46	347	515	3.13	99	.255	.316	384-0-29	.159	-4	116	9		-1.1

WILLIAMS, DAVE   David Aaron   B3.12.1979 Anchorage AK   BL/TL/6-2/205(205-220)   [PitN98 17/508]   d6.6   Col Delaware Tech (DE) CC   [DL 2003 Pit N 65]

YEAR	TM LG	W	L	PCT	G	GS	CG-SHO	SV-BS	IP	H	R	HR	HB	BB-IB	SO	ERA	AERA	OAV	OOB	AB-HR-SH	AVG	PB	SUP	APR	DL	PW
2001	Pit N	3	7	.300	22	18	0	0-0	114	100	53	15	7	45-4	57	3.71	120	.244	.324	34-0-3	.118	-1	79	8		0.6
2002	Pit N	2	5	.286	9	9	0	0-0	43.1	38	26	9	4	24-2	33	4.98	84	.232	.333	16-1-0	.125	0*	51	-4	125	-0.4
2004	Pit N	2	3	.400	10	6	0	0-0	38.2	31	21	4	3	13-2	33	4.42	98	.215	.292	9	.111	-0	64	-1	18	-0.1
2005	Pit N	10	11	.476	25	25	1-1	0-0	138.2	137	74	20	8	58-5	88	4.41	96	.261	.342	42-0-6	.119	-1	107	-3		-0.4
Total	4	17	26	.395	66	58	1-1	0-0	334.2	306	174	48	22	140-13	211	4.25	102	.246	.331	101-1-9	.119	-2	85	0	208	-0.3

WILLIAMS, MUTT   David Carter   B7.31.1892 Ozark AR   D3.30.1962 Fayetteville AR   BR/TR/6-3.5/195   d10.4

YEAR	TM LG	W	L	PCT	G	GS	CG-SHO	SV-BS	IP	H	R	HR	HB	BB-IB	SO	ERA	AERA	OAV	OOB	AB-HR-SH	AVG	PB	SUP	APR	DL	PW
1913	Was A	1	0	1.000	1	1	0	0	4	4	3	1	0	2	1	4.50	66	.308	.400	2	.500	0*	251	-1		-0.1
1914	Was A	0	0	—	5	0	0	1	7	5	5	0	0	4	3	5.14	55	.227	.346	0	—	0		-2		-0.1
Total	2	1	0	1.000	6	1	0	1	11	9	8	1	0	6	4	4.91	58	.257	.366	2	.500	0	251	-3		-0.2

WILLIAMS, DAVE   David Owen   B2.7.1881 Scranton PA   D4.25.1918 Hot Springs AR   BR/TL/5-11.5/167   d7.2

YEAR	TM LG	W	L	PCT	G	GS	CG-SHO	SV-BS	IP	H	R	HR	HB	BB-IB	SO	ERA	AERA	OAV	OOB	AB-HR-SH	AVG	PB	SUP	APR	DL	PW
1902	Bos A	0	0	—	3	0	0	0	18.2	22	18	0	1	11	7	5.30	67	.293	.391	9	.333	1		-4		-0.2

WILLIAMS, DON   Donald Fred   B9.14.1931 Floyd VA   BR/TR/6-2/180*   d9.12   Col Tennessee

YEAR	TM LG	W	L	PCT	G	GS	CG-SHO	SV-BS	IP	H	R	HR	HB	BB-IB	SO	ERA	AERA	OAV	OOB	AB-HR-SH	AVG	PB	SUP	APR	DL	PW
1958	Pit N	0	0	—	2	0	0	0	4	6	3	1	0	1-0	3	6.75	57	.375	.412	0	—	0		-1		-0.1
1959	Pit N	0	0	—	6	0	0	0	12	17	9	1	0	3-1	3	6.75	57	.362	.377	3	.333	1		-3		-0.1

YEAR	TM LG	W	L	PCT	G	GS	CG-SHO	SV-BS	IP	H	R	HR	HB	BB-IB	SO	ERA	AERA	OAV	OOB	AB-HR-SH	AVG	PB	SUP	APR	DL	PW
1962	KC A	0	0	—	3	0	0	0	4	6	4	0	1	0-0	1	9.00	47	.353	.389	1	.000	-0		-2		-0.1
Total	3	0	0	—	11	0	0	0	20	29	16	2	1	4-1	7	7.20	55	.363	.386	4	.250	1		-6		-0.3

WILLIAMS, DON Donald Reid "Dino" B9.2.1935 Los Angeles CA D12.20.1991 LaJolla CA BR/TR/6-5/218 d8.4

1963	Min A	0	0	—	3	0	0	0	4.1	8	5	1	0	6-0	2	10.38	35	.381	.519	0	—	0		-3		-0.1

WILLIAMS, DALE Elisha Alphonso B10.6.1855 Ludlow KY D10.22.1939 Covington KY BR/TR/5-9/175 d8.12

1876	Cin N	1	8	.111	9			0	83	123	75	1		4	4	4.23	52	.339	.346	35	.200	-2	43	-15		-1.4

WILLIAMS, FRANK Frank Lee B2.13.1958 Seattle WA BR/TR/6-1/190(180-195) [SFN79 11/278] d4.5 Col Lewis-Clark St.

1984	SF N	9	4	.692	61	1	1-1	3-4	106.1	88	49	2	3	51-6	91	3.55	99	.226	.319	18	.222	1	175	-1		0.2
1985	SF N	2	4	.333	49	0	0	0-1	73	65	39	5	6	35-7	54	4.19	83	.242	.338	3-0-1	.000	-0		-6		-0.5
1986	SF N	3	1	.750	36	0	0	1-2	52.1	35	8	0	4	21-4	33	1.20	293	.212	.314	2-0-1	.500	0	14			1.2
1987	Cin N	4	0	1.000	85	0	0	2-5	105.2	101	37	5	2	39-9	60	2.30	184	.254	.322	5-0-1	.000	-1	19			0.9
1988	Cin N	3	2	.600	60	0	0	1-1	62.2	59	24	6	2	35-4	43	2.59	138	.252	.354	1	.000	-0	5			0.4
1989	Det A	3	3	.500	42	0	0	1-1	71.2	70	37	5	3	46-10	33	3.64	105	.254	.362	0	—	0	175	31	42	0.0
Total	6	24	14	.632	333	1	1-1	8-14	471.2	418	194	23	20	227-40	314	3.00	124	.242	.334	29-0-3	.172	1	175	31	42	2.2

WILLIAMS, WOODY Gregory Scott B8.19.1966 Houston TX BR/TR/6-0/190(180-200) [TorA88 28/732] d5.14 Col Houston

1993	Tor A	3	1	.750	30	0	0	0-2	37	40	18	2	1	22-3	24	4.38	100	.274	.371	0	—	0	1			0.1
1994	Tor A	1	3	.250	38	0	0	0-0	59.1	44	24	5	2	33-1	56	3.64	134	.205	.313	0	—	0	9			0.5
1995	Tor A	1	2	.333	23	3	0	0-1	53.2	44	23	6	2	28-1	41	3.69	129	.220	.322	0	—	0	131	7	77	0.3
1996	Tor A	4	5	.444	12	10	1	0-0	59	64	33	8	1	21-1	43	4.73	106	.278	.340	0	—	0	89	2	109	0.3
1997	Tor A	9	14	.391	31	31	0	0-0	194.2	201	98	31	5	66-3	124	4.35	106	.269	.329	2	.500	0	59	8		0.6
1998	Tor A	10	9	.526	32	32	1-1	0-0	209.2	196	112	39	2	81-3	151	4.46	104	.245	.314	6	.333	1	97	6		0.4
1999	SD N	12	12	.500	33	33	0	0-0	208.1	213	106	33	2	73-5	137	4.41	97	.268	.328	73-0-4	.178	2*	93	0		0.0
2000	SD N	10	8	.556	23	23	4	0-0	168	152	74	23	9	54-2	102	3.75	119	.239	.300	58-1-1	.259	6*	84	15	56	0.2
2001	SD N	8	8	.500	23	23	0	0-0	145	170	88	28	5	37-4	102	4.97	84	.296	.300	55-0-1	.164	2*	134	-13		-1.1
	†StL N	7	1	.875	11	11	3-1	0-0	75	54	22	7	3	19-1	52	2.28	190	.205	.267	27-0-1	.259	2	103	17		1.9
	Year	15	9	.625	34	34	3-1	0-0	220	224	110	35	8	56-5	154	4.05	104	.268	.317	82-0-2	.195	4	123	3		0.8
2002	†StL N	9	4	.692	17	17	1	0-0	103.1	84	30	10	4	25-2	76	2.53	160	.222	.276	29-1-5	.207	3*	93	18	92	2.6
2003	StL N★	18	9	.667	34	33	0	0-1	220.2	220	101	20	11	55-2	153	3.87	106	.256	.307	70-1-9	.243	7	141	6		1.4
2004	†StL N	11	8	.579	31	31	0	0-0	189.2	193	93	20	9	58-3	131	4.18	102	.262	.322	61-0-5	.180	2*	114	3		0.5
2005	†SD N	9	12	.429	28	28	0	0-0	159.2	174	92	24	3	51-1	106	4.85	80	.275	.330	46-0-8	.152	-1*	88	-18	34	-2.2
Total	13	112	96	.538	366	275	10-2	0-4	1883	1849	914	253	53	623-32	1307	4.12	105	.256	.318	427-3-34	.206	23	99	61	368	7.3

WILLIAMS, JEFF Jeffrey F. B6.6.1972 Canberra, Capital Territory, Australia BR/TL/6-0/185* d9.12 Col Southeastern Louisiana

1999	LA N	2	0	1.000	5	3	0	0-0	17.2	12	10	2	0	9-0	7	4.08	107	.190	.292	5-0-1	.200	0	197	0		0.0
2000	LA N	0	0	—	7	0	0	0-1	5.2	12	11	1	0	8-0	3	15.88	28	.462	.571	0	—	0		-7	67	-0.4
2001	LA N	2	1	.667	15	1	0	0-0	24.1	26	18	5	1	17-1	9	6.29	66	.295	.407	4	.000	-0	45	-6		-0.6
2002	LA N	0	0	—	10	0	0	0-0	10	15	13	2	1	7-0	11	11.70	33	.333	.426	2	.500	0		-9		-0.4
Total	4	4	1	.800	37	4	0	0-1	57.2	65	52	10	2	41-1	30	7.49	56	.293	.401	11-0-1	.182	0	165	-22	67	-1.4

WILLIAMS, JEROME Jerome Lee B12.4.1981 Honolulu HI BR/TR/6-3/180(180-245) [SFN99 1/39] d4.26

2003	†SF N	7	5	.583	21	21	2-1	0-0	131	116	54	10	7	49-3	88	3.30	129	.242	.319	37-0-6	.108	-1	86	13		0.9
2004	SF N	10	7	.588	22	22	0	0-0	129.1	123	69	14	17	44-1	80	4.24	102	.254	.332	36-0-6	.139	-1	99	0	47	-0.1
2005	SF N	0	2	.000	4	3	0	0-0	16.2	21	12	2	1	4-1	11	6.48	66	.313	.361	4	.000	-0	80	-4		-0.4
	Chi N	6	8	.429	18	17	0	0-0	106	98	50	12	9	45-0	59	3.91	112	.253	.339	30-0-6	.100	-1	80	5		0.5
	Year	6	10	.375	22	20	0	0-0	122.2	119	62	14	10	49-1	70	4.26	103	.262	.342	34-0-6	.088	-2	80	2		0.1
Total	3	23	22	.511	65	63	2-1	0-0	383	358	185	38	34	142-5	238	3.92	110	.252	.331	107-0-18	.112	-4	89	14	47	0.9

WILLIAMS, JOHNNIE John Brodie "Honolulu Johnnie" B7.16.1889 Honolulu HI D9.8.1963 Long Beach CA BR/TR/6-0/180 d4.21

1914	Det A	0	2	.000	4	3	1	0	11.1	17	12	0	0	5	4	6.35	44	.378	.440	3	.000	-0	95	-5		-0.8

WILLIAMS, LEON Leon Theo "Lefty" B12.2.1905 Macon GA D11.20.1984 Atlanta GA BL/TL/5-10.5/154 d6.2

1926	Bro N	0	0	—	8	0	0	0	8.1	16	6	2	0	3	1	5.40	71	.421	.450	2	.200	0*		-1		0.0

WILLIAMS, MARSH Marshall McDiarmid "Cap" B2.21.1893 Faison NC D2.22.1935 Tucson AZ BR/TR/6-0/180 d7.7 Col North Carolina-Asheville

1916	Phi A	0	6	.000	10	4	3	0	51.1	71	53	4	0	31	17	7.89	36	.350	.436	19	.105	-1	60	-26		-2.7

WILLIAMS, MATT Matthew Evan B7.25.1959 Houston TX BR/TR/6-1/200* [TorA81 1/5] d8.2 Col Rice

1983	Tor A	1	1	.500	4	3	0	0-0	8	13	13	5	1	7-0	5	14.63	30	.361	.467	0	—	0	174	-8		-1.3
1985	Tex A	2	1	.667	6	3	0	0-0	26	20	7	3	0	10-0	22	2.42	176	.211	.286	0	—	0	78	5		0.6
Total	2	3	2	.600	10	6	0	0-0	34	33	20	8	1	17-0	27	5.29	81	.252	.340	0	—	0	127	-3		-0.7

WILLIAMS, MATT Matthew Taylor B4.12.1971 Virginia Beach VA BB/TL/6-0/185 [CleA92 4/98] d4.5 Col Virginia Commonwealth

2000	Mil N	0	0	—	11	0	0	0-0	9	7	7	2	1	13-0	7	7.00	66	.219	.457	1	.000	-0		-2		-0.1

WILLIAMS, MIKE Michael Darren B7.29.1968 Radford VA BR/TR/6-2/195(190-209) [PhiN90 14/374] d6.30 Col VPI

1992	Phi N	1	1	.500	5	5	1	0-0	28.2	29	20	3	0	7-0	5	5.34	66	.259	.300	10-0-1	.400	1	155	-6		-0.3
1993	Phi N	1	3	.250	17	4	0	0-0	51	50	32	5	0	22-3	33	5.29	75	.253	.327	12-0-3	.083	-1	130	-7		-0.6
1994	Phi N	2	4	.333	12	8	0	0-0	50.1	61	31	7	0	20-3	29	5.01	86	.310	.368	12-0-5	.167	0	93	-4		-0.4
1995	Phi N	3	3	.500	33	8	0	0-0	87.2	78	37	10	3	29-2	57	3.29	128	.239	.304	16-0-7	.125	0	70	8		0.5
1996	Phi N	6	14	.300	32	29	0	0-0	167	188	107	25	6	67-6	103	5.44	79	.290	.360	51-0-6	.157	-1*	89	-18		-1.8
1997	KC A	0	2	.000	10	0	0	1-0	14	20	11	1	1	8-1	10	6.43	74	.333	.414	0	—	0		-3		-0.3
1998	Pit N	4	2	.667	37	1	0	0-1	51	39	14	0	0	16-4	59	1.94	220	.211	.271	3-0-2	.000	0	108	13		1.4
1999	Pit N	3	4	.429	58	0	0	23-5	58.1	63	36	9	1	37-7	76	5.09	90	.276	.378	2	.000	-0		-3	15	-0.4
2000	Pit N	3	4	.429	72	0	0	24-5	72	56	34	8	4	40-3	71	3.50	133	.218	.328	1	.000	-0	8			1.1
2001	Pit N	2	4	.333	40	0	0	22-2	41.2	39	18	6	0	21-2	43	3.67	122	.244	.331	0	—	-0	4			0.7
	†Hou N	4	0	1.000	25	0	0	0-1	22.1	21	10	3	0	14-1	16	4.03	114	.244	.347	0	—	0	2			0.3
	Year	6	4	.600	65	0	0	22-3	64	60	28	9	0	35-3	59	3.80	119	.244	.337	0	—	0	6			1.6
2002	Pit N★	2	6	.250	59	0	0	46-4	61.1	54	24	4	1	21-3	43	2.93	143	.233	.299	1	.000	1	7			1.6
2003	Pit N☆	1	3	.250	40	0	0	25-5	37.1	42	26	5	1	22-1	20	6.27	69	.282	.374	0	—	0	-7			-1.3
	Phi N	0	4	.000	28	0	0	3-2	25.2	24	18	0	3	19-5	19	5.96	67	.247	.387	0	—	0	-6			-0.9
	Year	1	7	.125	68	0	0	28-7	63	66	44	5	4	41-6	39	6.14	68	.268	.379	0	—	0	-13			-2.2
Total	12	32	54	.372	546	55	1	144-25	764	764	416	89	20	343-40	584	4.45	97	.260	.339	108-0-24	.157	-1	94	-12	15	-0.4

WILLIAMS, MITCH Mitchell Steven "Wild Thing" B11.17.1964 Santa Ana CA BL/TL/6-4/205* [SDN82 8/187] d4.9

1986	Tex A	8	6	.571	80	0	0	8-7	98	69	39	8	11	79-8	90	3.58	121	.202	.366	0	—	0	10			1.4
1987	Tex A	8	6	.571	85	1	0	6-1	108.2	63	47	9	7	94-7	129	3.23	140	.175	.353	0	—	0	121	14		1.8
1988	Tex A	2	7	.222	67	0	0	18-8	68	48	38	4	6	47-3	61	4.63	98	.203	.345	0	—	0	-3			-0.5
1989	†Chi N★	4	4	.500	76	0	0	36-11	81.2	71	27	6	8	52-4	67	2.76	137	.238	.361	5-1-0	.200	1	9			1.7
1990	Chi N	1	8	.111	59	2	0	16-4	66.1	60	38	4	1	50-6	55	3.93	104	.239	.364	5	.000	-1	66	-1	30	-0.3
1991	Phi N	12	5	.706	69	0	0	30-9	88.1	56	24	4	8	62-5	84	2.34	158	.182	.330	1	.000	0	14			2.9
1992	Phi N	5	8	.385	66	0	0	29-7	81	69	39	4	6	64-2	74	3.78	93	.240	.386	4	.250	1	-3			-0.7
1993	†Phi N	3	7	.300	65	0	0	43-6	62	56	30	3	2	44-1	60	3.34	119	.245	.368	1	1.000	1	2			0.8
1994	Hou N	1	4	.200	25	0	0	6-2	20	21	17	4	1	24-2	21	7.65	52	.269	.442	0	—	0	-8			-1.5
1995	Cal A	1	2	.333	20	0	0	0-1	10.2	13	10	1	2	21-0	9	6.75	70	.317	.554	0	—	0	-3			-0.6
1997	KC A	0	1	.000	7	0	0	0-0	6.2	11	8	2	0	7-1	10	10.80	44	.367	.474	0	—	0	-4			-0.5
Total	11	45	58	.437	619	3	0	192-56	691.1	537	317	49	52	544-39	660	3.65	111	.218	.367	16-1-0	.188	1	90	28	30	4.2

WILLIAMS, RANDY Randall Duane B9.18.1975 Harlingen TX BL/TL/6-3/195* [ChiN97 12/364] d9.11

2004	Sea A	0	0	—	6	0	0	0-0	4.2	3	3	0	0	6-0	4	5.79	77	.188	.409	0	—	0	-1			0.0
2005	SD N	1	0	1.000	2	0	0	0-0	4.1	7	6	1	1	4-0	2	12.46	31	.350	.480	1	.000	-0	-4			-0.7
	Col N	2	1	.667	30	0	0	0-2	22	26	15	4	0	9-3	19	5.73	83	.289	.350	0	—	0	-2			-0.3
	Year	3	1	.750	32	0	0	0-2	26.1	33	21	5	1	13-3	21	6.84	67	.300	.376	1	.000	-0	-6			-1.0
Total	2	3	1	.750	38	0	0	0-2	31	36	24	5	1	19-3	25	6.68	69	.286	.381	1	.000	-0	-7			-1.0

YEAR	TM LG	W	L	PCT	G	GS	CG-SHO	SV-BS	IP	H	R	HR	HB	BB-IB	SO	ERA	AERA	OAV	OOB	AB-HR-SH	AVG	PB	SUP	APR	DL	PW

WILLIAMS, STEAMBOAT   Rees Gephardt   B1.31.1892 Cascade MT   D6.29.1979 Deer River MN   BL/TR/5-11/170   d7.12

YEAR	TM LG	W	L	PCT	G	GS	CG-SHO	SV-BS	IP	H	R	HR	HB	BB-IB	SO	ERA	AERA	OAV	OOB	AB-HR-SH	AVG	PB	SUP	APR	DL	PW
1914	StL N	0	1	1.000	5	1	0	1	11	13	8	1	0	6	2	6.55	43	.295	.380	1	.000	-0	77	-3		-0.3
1916	StL N	6	7	.462	36	8	5	1	105	121	63	6	1	27	25	4.20	63	.291	.336	24	.208	1	92	-17		-2.0
Total	2	6	8	.429	41	9	5	1	116	134	71	7	1	33	27	4.42	60	.291	.340	25	.200	1	90	-20		-2.3

WILLIAMS, RICK   Richard Allen   B11.9.1952 Merced CA   BR/TR/6-1/180*   d6.12 Col Merced (CA) JC

YEAR	TM LG	W	L	PCT	G	GS	CG-SHO	SV-BS	IP	H	R	HR	HB	BB-IB	SO	ERA	AERA	OAV	OOB	AB-HR-SH	AVG	PB	SUP	APR	DL	PW
1978	Hou N	1	2	.333	17	1	0	0-0	34.2	43	19	2	0	10-2	17	4.67	71	.301	.342	5	.000	-1	54	-5		-0.5
1979	Hou N	4	7	.364	31	16	2-2	0-0	121.1	122	45	6	2	30-1	37	3.26	106	.261	.315	31-0-2	.258	3	58	6		0.8
Total	2	5	9	.357	48	17	2-2	0-0	156	165	64	8	2	40-3	54	3.58	97	.270	.315	36-0-2	.222	2	59	1		0.3

WILLIAMS, ACE   Robert Fulton   B3.18.1917 Montclair NJ   D9.16.1999 Fort Myers FL   BR/TL/6-2/174   d7.15 Mil 1943-45 Col Amherst

YEAR	TM LG	W	L	PCT	G	GS	CG-SHO	SV-BS	IP	H	R	HR	HB	BB-IB	SO	ERA	AERA	OAV	OOB	AB-HR-SH	AVG	PB	SUP	APR	DL	PW
1940	Bos N	0	0	—	5	0	0	0	9	21	17	0	1	12	5	16.00	23	.375	.493	2	.000	-0		-12		-0.6
1946	Bos N	0	0	—	1	0	0	0	0	1	0	0	0	1	0	—		1.000	1.000	0	—	0		0		0.0
Total	2	0	0	—	6	0	0	0	9	22	17	0	1	13	5	16.00	23	.386	.507	2	.000	-0		-12		-0.6

WILLIAMS, SHAD   Shad Clayton   B3.10.1971 Fresno CA   BR/TR/6-0/198(185-198)   [CalA91 17/454]   d5.18 Col Fresno (CA) City

YEAR	TM LG	W	L	PCT	G	GS	CG-SHO	SV-BS	IP	H	R	HR	HB	BB-IB	SO	ERA	AERA	OAV	OOB	AB-HR-SH	AVG	PB	SUP	APR	DL	PW
1996	Cal A	0	2	.000	13	2	0	0-0	28.1	42	34	7	2	21-4	26	8.89	57	.341	.442	0	—	0	55	-13		-0.8
1997	Ana A	0	0	—	1	0	0	0-0	1	1	0	0	0	1-0	0	0.00	—	.250	.400	0	—	0		1		0.0
Total	2	0	2	.000	14	2	0	0-0	29.1	43	34	7	2	22-4	26	8.59	59	.339	.441	0	—	0	55	-12		-0.8

WILLIAMS, STAN   Stanley Wilson   B9.14.1936 Enfield NH   BR/TR/6-5/230(200-230)   d5.17 C14

YEAR	TM LG	W	L	PCT	G	GS	CG-SHO	SV-BS	IP	H	R	HR	HB	BB-IB	SO	ERA	AERA	OAV	OOB	AB-HR-SH	AVG	PB	SUP	APR	DL	PW
1958	LA N	9	7	.563	27	21	3-2	0	119	99	58	10	7	65-1	80	4.01	102	.228	.336	40-1-3	.050	-3	92	2		-0.1
1959	†LA N	5	5	.500	35	15	2	0	124.2	102	64	12	9	86-7	89	3.97	106	.228	.359	36-0-1	.194	1	99	2		0.2
1960	LA N★	14	10	.583	38	30	9-2	1	207.1	162	84	26	5	72-1	175	3.00	133	.210	.280	64-2-7	.141	0	109	19		2.1
1961	LA N	15	12	.556	41	35	6-2	0	235.1	213	114	21	6	108-9	205	3.90	111	.242	.327	78-0-6	.167	-1	90	11		1.1
1962	LA N	14	12	.538	40	28	4-1	1	185.2	184	104	16	0	98-11	108	4.46	81	.253	.338	66-2-1	.076	-2	118	-17		-2.4
1963	†NY A	9	8	.529	29	21	6-1	0	146	137	59	7	4	57-1	98	3.21	110	.249	.325	49-0-1	.102	-1	126	4		0.4
1964	NY A	1	5	.167	21	10	1	0	82	76	39	7	0	38-2	54	3.84	94	.248	.329	21-0-1	.143	-0*	91	-2		-0.2
1965	Cle A	0	0	—	3	0	0	0	4.1	6	4	1	0	3-1	1	6.23	56	.353	.450	0	—	0		-2		-0.1
1967	Cle A	6	4	.600	16	8	2-1	1	79	64	26	6	1	24-2	75	2.62	125	.218	.277	22	.091	-1	73	6		0.5
1968	Cle A	13	11	.542	44	24	6-2	9	194.1	163	64	14	0	51-7	147	2.50	119	.225	.286	56-0-4	.161	1	81	10		1.5
1969	Cle A	6	14	.300	61	15	3	12-5	178.1	155	86	25	12	67-6	139	3.94	97	.235	.312	40-0-4	.100	-1	95	-1		-0.3
1970	†Min A	10	1	.909	68	0	0	15-4	113.1	85	34	8	5	32-6	76	1.99	186	.208	.272	19	.000	-2		20		2.0
1971	Min A	4	5	.444	46	1	0	4-3	78	63	44	7	8	44-7	47	4.15	85	.220	.336	10-0-1	.000	-1	127	-7		-1.0
	StL N	3	0	1.000	10	0	0	0-1	12.2	13	2	0	2	2-1	8	1.42	256	.265	.315	1	.000	-0		3		0.7
1972	Bos A	0	0	—	3	0	0	0	4.1	5	3	0	0	1-0	3	6.23	52	.294	.333	0	—	0		-1		-0.1
Total	14	109	94	.537	482	208	42-11	43-13	1764.1	1527	785	160	71	748-62	1305	3.48	108	.232	.315	502-5-29	.118	-10	101	47		4.3

WILLIAMS, TOM   Thomas C.   B8.19.1870 Minersville OH   D7.27.1940 Columbus OH   d5.1

YEAR	TM LG	W	L	PCT	G	GS	CG-SHO	SV-BS	IP	H	R	HR	HB	BB-IB	SO	ERA	AERA	OAV	OOB	AB-HR-SH	AVG	PB	SUP	APR	DL	PW
1892	Cle N	1	0	1.000	2	1	1	0	9	9	4	1	0	1	3	3.00	113	.250	.270	10	.100	-1*	205	1		0.0
1893	Cle N	1	1	.500	5	2	2	0	24	33	18	1	1	10	6	4.88	100	.317	.383	18	.278	0*	79	1		0.1
Total	2	2	1	.667	7	3	3	0	33	42	22	2	1	11	9	4.36	102	.300	.355	28	.214	-0	112	2		0.1

WILLIAMS, TODD   Todd Michael   B2.13.1971 Syracuse NY   BR/TR/6-3/185(185-220)   [LAN90 54/1333]   d4.29 Col Onondaga (NY) CC

YEAR	TM LG	W	L	PCT	G	GS	CG-SHO	SV-BS	IP	H	R	HR	HB	BB-IB	SO	ERA	AERA	OAV	OOB	AB-HR-SH	AVG	PB	SUP	APR	DL	PW
1995	LA N	2	2	.500	16	0	0	0-1	19.1	19	11	3	0	7-2	8	5.12	76	.264	.325	2	.500	0		-2		-0.3
1998	Cin N	0	1	.000	6	0	0	0-0	9.1	15	8	1	0	6-0	4	7.71	56	.341	.420	2	.000	-0		-3		-0.3
1999	Sea A	0	0	—	13	0	0	0-0	9.2	11	5	1	1	7-0	7	4.66	103	.289	.413	0	—	0		0		0.0
2001	NY A	1	0	1.000	15	0	0	0-0	15.1	22	8	1	2	9-2	13	4.70	95	.324	.402	0	—	0		-1	61	0.0
2004	Bal A	2	0	1.000	29	0	0	0-0	31.1	26	10	2	5	9-2	13	2.87	162	.232	.317	0	—	0		7		0.4
2005	Bal A	5	5	.500	72	0	0	1-2	76.1	72	34	5	3	26-4	38	3.30	134	.252	.317	0	—	0		8		0.9
Total	6	10	8	.556	151	0	0	1-3	161.1	165	77	13	11	64-8	83	3.90	113	.266	.341	4	.250	0		9	61	0.7

WILLIAMS, POP   Walter Merrill   B5.19.1874 Bowdoinham ME   D8.4.1959 Topsham ME   BR/TR/5-11/190   d9.14 Col Bowdoin

YEAR	TM LG	W	L	PCT	G	GS	CG-SHO	SV-BS	IP	H	R	HR	HB	BB-IB	SO	ERA	AERA	OAV	OOB	AB-HR-SH	AVG	PB	SUP	APR	DL	PW
1898	Was N	0	2	.000	2	2	2	0	17	32	18	0	0	7	3	8.47	43	.395	.443	8	.375	1	106	-7		-0.5
1902	Chi N	11	16	.407	32	32	27-1	0	263.1	267	112	1	10	63	99	2.49	108	.263	.312	120-0-3	.208	3*	100	8		1.3
1903	Chi N	0	1	.000	1	1	1	0	5	9	3	0	0	0	2	5.40	58	.409	.409	2	.000	0*	0	-1		-0.1
	Phi N	1	1	.500	2	2	2	0	18	21	11	0	1	6	8	3.00	109	.304	.368	7	.286	0	103	0		0.0
	Bos N	4	5	.444	10	10	9-1	0	83	97	60	3	9	37	20	4.12	78	.295	.381	42-0-1	.238	-0*	97	-9		-0.9
	Year	5	7	.417	13	13	12-1	0	106	127	74	3	10	43	30	3.99	81	.302	.381	51-0-1	.235	0	90	-13		-1.0
Total	3	16	25	.390	47	47	41-2	0	386.1	426	204	4	20	113	132	3.17	91	.281	.339	179-0-4	.223	5	97	-9		-0.2

WILLIAMSON, ED   Edward Nagle   B10.24.1857 Philadelphia PA   D3.3.1894 Mountain Valley Springs AR   BR/TR/5-11/210   d5.1.1878 ▲

YEAR	TM LG	W	L	PCT	G	GS	CG-SHO	SV-BS	IP	H	R	HR	HB	BB-IB	SO	ERA	AERA	OAV	OOB	AB-HR-SH	AVG	PB	SUP	APR	DL	PW
1881	Chi N	1	1	.500	3	1	1	0	18	14	9	0	0	0	2	2.00	137	.209	.209	343-1	.268	1*	118	1		0.1
1882	Chi N	0	0	—	1	0	0	0	3	9	8	1	0	1	0	6.00	48	.500	.526	348-3	.282	0*		-2		-0.1
1883	Chi N	0	0	—	1	0	0	0	1	1	1	0	0	1	1	9.00	37	.167	.286	402-2	.276	0*		-1		0.0
1884	Chi N	0	0	—	2	0	0	0	2	8	8	0	0	2	0	18.00	17	.500	.556	417-27	.278	1*		-3		-0.1
1885	†Chi N	0	0	—	2	0	0	2	6	2	0	0	0	0	3	0.00	—	.080	.080	407-3	.238	0*		2		0.2
1886	†Chi N	0	0	—	2	0	0	1	3	2	2	0	0	0	0	0.00	—	.143	.143	430-6	.216	0*		1		0.0
1887	Chi N	0	0	—	1	0	0	0	2	2	3	0	1	1	1	9.00	50	.222	.300	439-9	.267	0*		-1		0.0
Total	7	1	1	.500	12	1	1	3	35	38	31	1	0	5	7	3.34	90	.245	.269	2786-51	.260	3	118	-3		0.1

WILLIAMSON, MARK   Mark Alan   B7.21.1959 Corpus Christi TX   BR/TR/6-0/172(170-198)   [SDN82 4/83]   d4.8 Col San Diego St.

YEAR	TM LG	W	L	PCT	G	GS	CG-SHO	SV-BS	IP	H	R	HR	HB	BB-IB	SO	ERA	AERA	OAV	OOB	AB-HR-SH	AVG	PB	SUP	APR	DL	PW
1987	Bal A	8	9	.471	61	2	0	3-7	125	122	59	12	3	41-15	73	4.03	110	.261	.322	0	—	0	103	7		0.9
1988	Bal A	5	8	.385	37	10	2	2-1	117.2	125	70	14	2	40-8	69	4.90	80	.272	.332	0	—	0	65	-12		-1.3
1989	Bal A	10	5	.667	65	0	0	9-6	107.1	105	35	4	2	30-9	55	2.93	130	.261	.313	0	—	0		12		1.7
1990	Bal A	8	2	.800	49	0	0	1-4	85.1	65	25	8	0	28-2	60	2.21	172	.215	.276	0	—	0	14	59		1.7
1991	Bal A	5	5	.500	65	0	0	4-3	80.1	87	42	9	0	35-7	53	4.48	89	.275	.343	0	—	0	-4	18		-0.5
1992	Bal A	0	0	—	12	0	0	1-0	18.2	16	3	1	0	10-1	14	0.96	422	.239	.338	0	—	0	6	141		0.4
1993	Bal A	7	5	.583	48	1	0	0-2	88	106	54	5	0	25-8	45	4.91	92	.304	.345	0	—	0	61	-5		-0.6
1994	Bal A	3	1	.750	28	2	0	1-1	67.1	75	33	9	2	17-1	28	4.01	126	.278	.323	0	—	0	91	7		0.3
Total	8	46	35	.568	365	15	2	21-24	689.2	701	321	62	9	226-51	397	3.86	108	.266	.323	0	—	0	74	25	218	2.5

WILLIAMSON, SCOTT   Scott Ryan   B2.17.1976 Fort Polk LA   BR/TR/6-0/185*   [CinN97 9/278]   d4.5 Col Oklahoma St.

YEAR	TM LG	W	L	PCT	G	GS	CG-SHO	SV-BS	IP	H	R	HR	HB	BB-IB	SO	ERA	AERA	OAV	OOB	AB-HR-SH	AVG	PB	SUP	APR	DL	PW
1999	Cin N☆	12	7	.632	62	0	0	19-7	93.1	54	29	8	1	43-6	107	2.41	195	.171	.271	7-0-3	.000	-1		22		4.3
2000	Cin N	5	8	.385	48	10	0	6-2	112	92	45	7	3	75-7	136	3.29	145	.224	.346	16-0-4	.063	-1	77	18	13	1.9
2001	Cin N	0	0	—	2	0	0	0-0	0.2	1	0	0	1	2-0	0	0.00	—	.333	.667	0	—	0		0	187	0.0
2002	Cin N	3	4	.429	63	0	0	8-4	74	46	27	5	2	36-5	84	2.92	146	.181	.286	0	—	0		11		1.1
2003	Cin N	5	3	.625	42	0	0	21-5	42.1	34	15	6	1	25-4	53	3.19	131	.214	.324	0	—	0		5		1.0
	†Bos A	0	1	.000	24	0	0	0-2	20.1	20	15	1	0	9-2	21	6.20	75	.253	.326	0	—	0		-3		-0.1
2004	Bos A	0	0	—	28	0	0	1-1	28.2	11	6	0	3	18-1	28	1.26	389	.115	.267	0	—	0		10	93	0.2
2005	Chi N	0	0	—	17	0	0	0-0	14.1	15	15	3	2	6-0	23	5.65	78	.273	.365	0	—	0		-2	124	-0.1
Total	7	25	24	.510	286	10	0	55-21	385.2	273	146	30	13	214-25	452	3.08	149	.199	.311	23-0-7	.043	-1	77	61	417	8.6

WILLIAMSON, AL   Silas Albert   B2.20.1900 Buckville AR   D11.29.1978 Hot Springs AR   BR/TR/5-11/160   d4.27

YEAR	TM LG	W	L	PCT	G	GS	CG-SHO	SV-BS	IP	H	R	HR	HB	BB-IB	SO	ERA	AERA	OAV	OOB	AB-HR-SH	AVG	PB	SUP	APR	DL	PW
1928	Chi A	0	0	—	1	0	0	0	1	1	1	0	0	0	0	—		.167	.167	0	—	0		1		0.0

WILLIS, CARL   Carl Blake   B12.28.1960 Danville VA   BL/TR/6-4/213*   [DetA83 23/581]   d6.9 C3 Col North Carolina-Wilmington

YEAR	TM LG	W	L	PCT	G	GS	CG-SHO	SV-BS	IP	H	R	HR	HB	BB-IB	SO	ERA	AERA	OAV	OOB	AB-HR-SH	AVG	PB	SUP	APR	DL	PW
1984	Det A	0	2	.000	10	2	0	0-0	16	25	13	1	0	5-2	4	7.31	54	.362	.405	0	—	0	103	-5		-0.6
	Cin N	0	1	.000	7	0	0	1-0	9.2	8	4	1	0	2-0	3	3.72	102	.222	.263	0	—	0		0		0.0
1985	Cin N	1	0	1.000	11	0	0	1-0	13.2	21	18	3	0	5-0	6	9.22	41	.344	.382	1-0-1	.000	0		-9		-0.7
1986	Cin N	1	3	.250	29	0	0	0-1	52.1	54	29	4	1	32-9	24	4.47	86	.278	.382	3-0-1	.333	0		-3		-0.2
1988	Chi A	0	0	—	10	0	0	0-0	12	17	12	3	0	7-1	6	8.25	49	.362	.436	0	—	0		-5		-0.3
1991	†Min A	8	3	.727	40	0	0	2-1	89	76	31	4	1	19-1	53	2.63	163	.232	.273	0	—	0		15		1.7
1992	Min A	7	3	.700	59	0	0	1-2	79.1	73	25	4	0	11-1	45	2.72	150	.246	.276	0	—	0		12		1.4
1993	Min A	3	0	1.000	53	0	0	5-4	58	56	23	2	0	17-5	44	3.10	142	.259	.312	0	—	0		8	39	0.4
1994	Min A	2	4	.333	49	0	0	3-4	59.1	89	48	4	0	12-5	37	5.92	83	.335	.359	0	—	0		-9		-0.9

YEAR	TM LG	W	L	PCT	G	GS	CG-SHO	SV-BS	IP	H	R	HR	HB	BB-IB	SO	ERA	AERA	OAV	OOB	AB-HR-SH	AVG	PB	SUP	APR	DL	PW
1995	Min A	0	0	—	3	0	0	0-0	0.2	5	7	0	0	5-0	0	94.50	5	.833	.909	0	—	0		-6		-0.3
Total	9	22	16	.579	267	2	0	13-12	390	424	210	28	2	115-24	222	4.25	100	.279	.327	4-0-2	.250	0	103	-2	39	0.5

WILLIS, LEFTY Charles William B11.4.1905 Leetown WV D5.10.1962 Bethesda MD BL/TL/6-1/175 d10.3 Col Shepherd

YEAR	TM LG	W	L	PCT	G	GS	CG-SHO	SV-BS	IP	H	R	HR	HB	BB-IB	SO	ERA	AERA	OAV	OOB	AB-HR-SH	AVG	PB	SUP	APR	DL	PW
1925	Phi A	0	0	—	1	1	0	0	5	9	7	2	0	2	3	10.80	43	.409	.458	3	.000	-1	145	-3		-0.2
1926	Phi A	0	0	—	13	1	0	1	32.1	31	9	0	1	12	13	1.39	300	.270	.344	9	.222	-0	81	9		0.4
1927	Phi A	3	1	.750	15	2	1	0	27	32	18	2	0	11	7	5.67	75	.308	.374	6	.000	-1	88	-3		-0.4
Total	3	3	1	.750	29	4	1	1	64.1	72	34	4	1	25	23	3.92	108	.299	.367	18	.111	-1	104	3		-0.2

WILLIS, DALE Dale Jerome B5.29.1938 Calhoun GA BR/TR/5-11/165 d4.14 Col Florida

YEAR	TM LG	W	L	PCT	G	GS	CG-SHO	SV-BS	IP	H	R	HR	HB	BB-IB	SO	ERA	AERA	OAV	OOB	AB-HR-SH	AVG	PB	SUP	APR	DL	PW
1963	KC A	0	2	.000	25	0	0	1	44.2	46	28	3	4	25-3	47	5.04	77	.266	.369	6	.167	-0*		-5		-0.3

WILLIS, DONTRELLE Dontrelle Wayne B1.12.1982 Oakland CA BL/TL/6-4/200(200-240) [ChiN00 8/223] d5.9

YEAR	TM LG	W	L	PCT	G	GS	CG-SHO	SV-BS	IP	H	R	HR	HB	BB-IB	SO	ERA	AERA	OAV	OOB	AB-HR-SH	AVG	PB	SUP	APR	DL	PW
2003	†Fla N☆	14	6	.700	27	27	2-2	0-0	160.2	148	61	13	3	58-0	142	3.30	124	.245	.314	58-1-2	.241	5	104	16		2.2
2004	Fla N	10	11	.476	32	32	2	0-0	197	210	99	20	8	61-8	139	4.02	102	.273	.332	74-1-6	.263	4*	101	0		0.5
2005	Fla N★	22	10	.688	34	34	7-5	0-0	236.1	213	79	11	8	55-3	170	2.63	152	.243	.292	92-1-4	.261	8*	103	36		5.8
Total	3	46	27	.630	93	93	11-7	0-0	594	571	239	44	19	174-11	451	3.27	124	.254	.312	224-3-12	.237	17	103	52		8.5

WILLIS, JIM James Gladden B3.20.1927 Doyline LA BL/TR/6-3/175* d4.22 Col Northwestern Louisiana

YEAR	TM LG	W	L	PCT	G	GS	CG-SHO	SV-BS	IP	H	R	HR	HB	BB-IB	SO	ERA	AERA	OAV	OOB	AB-HR-SH	AVG	PB	SUP	APR	DL	PW
1953	Chi N	2	1	.667	13	3	2	0	43.1	37	15	1	3	17	15	3.12	143	.228	.313	9-0-1	.000	-1	94	7		0.4
1954	Chi N	0	1	.000	14	1	0	0	23	22	10	1	3	18	5	3.91	107	.256	.402	5	.000	-1	21	1		0.0
Total	2	2	2	.500	27	4	2	0	66.1	59	25	2	6	35	20	3.39	129	.238	.346	14-0-1	.000	-2	77	8		0.4

WILLIS, JOE Joseph Denk B4.9.1890 Coal Grove OH D12.4.1966 Ironton OH BR/TL/6-1/185 d5.3

YEAR	TM LG	W	L	PCT	G	GS	CG-SHO	SV-BS	IP	H	R	HR	HB	BB-IB	SO	ERA	AERA	OAV	OOB	AB-HR-SH	AVG	PB	SUP	APR	DL	PW
1911	StL A	0	1	.000	1	1	0	0	7	8	5	0	0	3	0	5.14	66	.308	.379	2	.000	0	43	-1		-0.1
	StL N	0	0	—	2	1	0	0	15	13	9	0	0	4	5	4.20	80	.232	.283	5	.000	-1	56	-1		-0.1
1912	StL N	4	9	.308	31	17	4	2	129.2	143	83	3	5	62	55	4.44	77	.288	.372	38-0-1	.158	-2	107	-12		-1.2
1913	StL N	0	0	—	7	0	0	1	9.2	9	9	0	0	11	6	7.45	43	.257	.435	3	.000	-0		-4		-0.3
Total	3	4	11	.267	41	20	5	3	161.1	173	106	3	5	80	66	4.63	74	.282	.369	48-0-1	.125	-2	99	-18		-1.7

WILLIS, LES Lester Evans "Wimpy","Lefty" B1.17.1908 Nacogdoches TX D1.22.1982 Jasper TX BL/TL/5-9.5/195 d4.28

YEAR	TM LG	W	L	PCT	G	GS	CG-SHO	SV-BS	IP	H	R	HR	HB	BB-IB	SO	ERA	AERA	OAV	OOB	AB-HR-SH	AVG	PB	SUP	APR	DL	PW
1947	Cle A	0	2	.000	22	2	0	1	44	58	26	3	0	24	10	3.48	100	.324	.404	11-0-1	.091	-1	89	-4		-0.3

WILLIS, MIKE Michael Henry B12.26.1950 Oklahoma City OK BL/TL/6-2/210* [BalA72 20/479] d4.13 Col Vanderbilt

YEAR	TM LG	W	L	PCT	G	GS	CG-SHO	SV-BS	IP	H	R	HR	HB	BB-IB	SO	ERA	AERA	OAV	OOB	AB-HR-SH	AVG	PB	SUP	APR	DL	PW
1977	Tor A	2	6	.250	43	3	0	5-4	107.1	105	48	15	0	38-6	59	3.94	108	.260	.321	0	—	0	78	6		0.5
1978	Tor A	3	7	.300	44	2	1	7-2	100.2	104	55	11	0	39-2	52	4.56	87	.271	.336	0	—	0	102	-6		-0.7
1979	Tor A	0	3	.000	17	1	0	0-0	26.2	35	27	1	1	16-2	8	8.44	52	.333	.419	0	—	0	41	-11		-1.0
1980	Tor A	2	1	.667	20	0	0	3-1	26.1	25	6	3	1	11-4	14	1.71	253	.248	.325	0	—	0		7		0.9
1981	Tor A	0	4	.000	20	0	0	0-1	35	43	25	6	1	20-1	16	5.91	67	.301	.386	0	—	0		-6		-0.7
Total	5	7	21	.250	144	6	1	15-8	296	312	161	36	3	124-15	149	4.59	90	.274	.344	0	—	0	80	-10		-1.0

WILLIS, RON Ronald Earl B7.12.1943 Willisville TN D11.21.1977 Memphis TN BR/TR/6-2/195(170-195) d9.20

YEAR	TM LG	W	L	PCT	G	GS	CG-SHO	SV-BS	IP	H	R	HR	HB	BB-IB	SO	ERA	AERA	OAV	OOB	AB-HR-SH	AVG	PB	SUP	APR	DL	PW
1966	StL N	0	0	—	4	0	0	1	3	1	0	0	0	1-1	2	0.00	—	.100	.182	0	—	0		1		0.1
1967	†StL N	6	5	.545	65	0	0	10	81	76	27	3	3	43-20	42	2.67	123	.257	.354	8	.375	1		6		1.2
1968	†StL N	2	3	.400	48	0	0	4	63.2	50	25	4	1	28-11	39	3.39	85	.213	.299	11	.000	-1		-2		-0.3
1969	StL N	1	2	.333	26	0	0	0-0	32.1	26	16	4	1	19-3	23	4.18	86	.224	.331	1	1.000	0		-2		-0.1
	Hou N	0	0	—	3	0	0	0-0	2.1	3	0	0	0	0-0	2	0.00	—	.300	.273	0	—	0		1		0.0
	Year	1	2	.333	29	0	0	0-0	34.2	29	16	4	1	19-3	25	3.89	92	.230	.327	1	1.000	0		-1		-0.1
1970	SD N	2	2	.500	42	0	0	4-2	56	53	33	4	4	28-5	20	4.02	100	.247	.340	5	.000	-1		-2		-0.2
Total	5	11	12	.478	188	0	0	19-2	238.1	209	101	15	9	119-40	128	3.32	102	.237	.330	25	.160	0		2		0.7

WILLIS, VIC Victor Gazaway B4.12.1876 Cecil Co. MD D8.3.1947 Elkton MD BR/TR/6-2/185 d4.20 HF1995 Col Delaware

YEAR	TM LG	W	L	PCT	G	GS	CG-SHO	SV-BS	IP	H	R	HR	HB	BB-IB	SO	ERA	AERA	OAV	OOB	AB-HR-SH	AVG	PB	SUP	APR	DL	PW
1898	Bos N	25	13	.658	41	38	29-1	0	311	264	143	5	29	148	160	2.84	130	.228	.331	117-0-2	.145	-6	100	26		2.2
1899	Bos N	27	8	.771	41	38	35-5	2	342.2	277	126	6	30	117	120	2.50	167	.221	.303	128-0-3	.216	-4	102	58		4.8
1900	Bos N	10	17	.370	32	29	22-2	0	236	258	157	11	12	106	53	4.19	98	.277	.359	88-0-3	.136	-6	94	-1		-0.7
1901	Bos N	20	17	.541	38	35	33-6	0	305.1	262	111	6	11	78	133	2.36	153	.230	.286	107-1-3	.187	-1	78	39		4.2
1902	Bos N	27	20	.574	51	46	45-4	3	410	372	142	6	14	101	225	2.20	129	.242	.295	150-0-1	.153	-6*	93	28		2.8
1903	Bos N	12	18	.400	33	32	29-2	0	278	256	121	3	10	88	125	2.98	108	.251	.317	128-0-2	.188	-1	72	14		1.3
1904	Bos N	18	25	.419	43	43	39-2	0	350	357	174	7	14	109	196	2.85	97	.266	.327	148-0-3	.182	1*	82	-8		-0.4
1905	Bos N	12	29	.293	41	41	36-4	0	342	340	174	7	13	107	149	3.21	97	.265	.328	131-0-2	.153	-3*	76	-8		-0.8
1906	Pit N	23	13	.639	41	36	32-6	1	322	295	84	0	5	76	124	1.73	154	.250	.298	115-0-3	.174	-1	111	34		4.3
1907	Pit N	21	11	.656	39	37	27-6	1	292.2	234	96	4	7	69	107	2.34	104	.219	.271	103-0-5	.136	-2	137	8		0.7
1908	Pit N	23	11	.676	41	37	25-7	0	304.2	239	95	2	6	69	97	2.07	111	.213	.262	103-0-6	.165	-1	122	9		0.9
1909	†Pit N	22	11	.667	39	35	24-4	1	289.2	243	84	3	4	83	95	2.24	122	.231	.289	103-0-6	.136	-2	120	20		2.1
1910	StL N	9	12	.429	33	23	12-1	0	212	224	113	6	1	61	67	3.35	89	.275	.326	66-0-4	.167	-2	84	-14		-1.4
Total	13	249	205	.548	513	471	388-50	11	3996	3621	1620	66	156	1212	1651	2.63	118	.243	.307	1493-1-41	.166	-33	97	205		20.0

WILLOUGHBY, CLAUDE Claude William "Flunky","Weeping Willie" B11.14.1898 Buffalo KS D8.14.1973 McPherson KS BR/TR/5-9.5/165 d9.18

YEAR	TM LG	W	L	PCT	G	GS	CG-SHO	SV-BS	IP	H	R	HR	HB	BB-IB	SO	ERA	AERA	OAV	OOB	AB-HR-SH	AVG	PB	SUP	APR	DL	PW
1925	Phi N	2	1	.667	3	3	1	1	23	26	7	0	1	11	9	1.96	244	.295	.380	8	.000	-1	71	6		0.6
1926	Phi N	8	12	.400	47	19	6	1	168	218	125	7	5	71	37	5.95	70	.327	.396	52-0-3	.212	-1	113	-28		-2.8
1927	Phi N	3	7	.300	35	6	1-1	2	97.2	126	83	7	2	53	14	6.54	63	.321	.404	26-0-1	.077	-2	106	-26		-2.6
1928	Phi N	6	5	.545	35	13	5-1	1	130.2	180	92	6	3	83	26	5.30	81	.340	.432	40-0-1	.150	-1	81	-16		-1.3
1929	Phi N	15	14	.517	49	35	14-1	4	243.1	288	156	15	5	108	50	4.99	104	.296	.370	91-0-1	.143	-5	99	3		0.1
1930	Phi N	4	17	.190	41	24	5-1	1	153	241	147	17	2	68	38	7.59	72	.349	.430	48	.104	-4	103	-31		-3.6
1931	Pit N	0	2	.000	9	2	1	0	25.2	32	21	4	0	12	4	6.31	61	.305	.376	7	.286	-0	178	-7		-0.4
Total	7	38	58	.396	219	102	33-4	9	841.1	1111	631	56	18	406	175	5.84	81	.326	.401	272-0-6	.143	-14	104	-99		-10.0

WILLOUGHBY, JIM James Arthur B1.31.1949 Salinas CA BR/TR/6-2/185(180-205) [SFN67 11/218] d9.5

YEAR	TM LG	W	L	PCT	G	GS	CG-SHO	SV-BS	IP	H	R	HR	HB	BB-IB	SO	ERA	AERA	OAV	OOB	AB-HR-SH	AVG	PB	SUP	APR	DL	PW
1971	SF N	0	1	.000	2	1	0	0-0	4	8	4	0	0	1-0	3	9.00	38	.400	.429	1	.000	-0	78	-2		-0.4
1972	SF N	6	4	.600	11	11	7	0-0	87.2	72	25	8	2	14-4	40	2.36	148	.222	.257	27-0-5	.185	0	96	11		1.4
1973	SF N	4	5	.444	39	12	1-1	1-0	123	138	74	21	3	37-4	60	4.68	82	.295	.347	28-1-3	.143	1*	105	-11		-0.7
1974	SF N	1	4	.200	18	4	0	0-0	40.2	51	27	7	0	9-1	12	4.65	82	.304	.339	10	.100	-0*	69	-4		-0.5
1975	†Bos A	5	2	.714	24	0	0	8-1	48.1	46	25	6	2	16-3	29	3.54	115	.247	.311	0	—			1		0.2
1976	Bos A	3	12	.200	54	0	0	10-3	99	94	38	4	8	31-12	37	2.82	138	.256	.324	1	.000	-0		10		1.7
1977	Bos A	6	2	.750	31	0	0	2-2	54.2	54	32	5	2	18-3	33	4.94	91	.258	.320	0	—	0		-2	68	-0.3
1978	Chi A	1	6	.143	59	0	0	13-2	93.1	95	41	6	4	19-2	36	3.86	99	.275	.319	0	—	0		1		0.6
Total	8	26	36	.419	238	35	8-1	34-8	550.2	558	266	57	21	145-29	250	3.79	102	.267	.319	67-1-8	.149	1	92	4	68	1.6

WILLS, FRANK Frank Lee B10.26.1958 New Orleans LA BR/TR/6-2/202(200-215) [KCA80 1/16] d7.31 Col Tulane

YEAR	TM LG	W	L	PCT	G	GS	CG-SHO	SV-BS	IP	H	R	HR	HB	BB-IB	SO	ERA	AERA	OAV	OOB	AB-HR-SH	AVG	PB	SUP	APR	DL	PW
1983	KC A	2	1	.667	6	4	0	0-0	34.2	35	17	2	0	15-0	23	4.15	99	.259	.329	0	—	0	105	0		0.0
1984	KC A	2	3	.400	10	5	0	0-0	37	39	21	3	0	13-0	21	5.11	79	.271	.323	0	—	0	89	-3	15	-0.4
1985	Sea A	5	11	.313	24	18	1	1-0	123	122	85	18	3	68-3	67	6.00	70	.266	.359	0	—	0	93	-21		-2.4
1986	Cle A	4	4	.500	26	0	0	4-2	40.1	43	23	6	0	16-4	32	4.91	85	.272	.335	0	—	0		-2		-0.5
1987	Cle A	0	1	.000	6	0	0	1-0	5.1	3	3	0	0	7-0	4	5.06	90	.176	.400	0	—	0		0		0.0
1988	Tor A	0	0	—	10	0	0	0-0	20.2	22	12	2	0	6-2	19	5.23	76	.272	.318	0	—	0		-2		-0.1
1989	Tor A	3	1	.750	24	4	0	0-0	71.1	65	31	4	1	30-2	41	3.66	104	.242	.319	0	—	0	119	2	17	0.1
1990	Tor A	6	4	.600	44	0	0	0-0	99	101	54	13	1	38-7	72	4.73	84	.266	.333	0	—	0	98	-8		-0.7
1991	Tor A	0	1	.000	4	0	0	0-0	4.1	8	8	2	1	5-0	2	16.62	25	.421	.560	0	—	0		-5		-0.9
Total	9	22	26	.458	154	35	1	6-2	435.2	438	254	50	6	198-18	281	5.06	80	.264	.341	0	—	0	99	-39	32	-4.9

WILLS, TED Theodore Carl B2.9.1934 Fresno CA BL/TL/6-2/200* d5.24 Col Cal St.-Fresno

YEAR	TM LG	W	L	PCT	G	GS	CG-SHO	SV-BS	IP	H	R	HR	HB	BB-IB	SO	ERA	AERA	OAV	OOB	AB-HR-SH	AVG	PB	SUP	APR	DL	PW
1959	Bos A	2	6	.250	9	8	2	0	56.1	68	35	9	1	24-2	24	5.27	77	.302	.369	16-0-2	.250	1	65	-7		-0.7
1960	Bos A	1	1	.500	15	6	1	0	30.1	38	26	4	3	16-1	28	7.42	55	.317	.404	8	.250	1*		-10		-0.6
1961	Bos A	3	2	.600	17	0	0	0	19.2	24	17	2	0	19-0	11	5.95	70	.304	.434	2	.000	-0		-5		-0.9
1962	Bos A	0	0	—	2	0	0	0	2	1	0	0	1	1-0	0	∞	—	1.000	1.000	0	—	0		-1		-0.1
	Cin N	0	2	.000	26	5	0	3	61	61	36	12	5	23-0	58	5.31	76	.266	.346	16	.313	1	148	-7		-0.2
1965	Chi A	2	0	1.000	14	0	0	2	19	17	9	1	1	14-2	12	2.84	112	.258	.386	2	.000	0		0		0.1
Total	5	8	11	.421	83	19	3	5	186.1	210	123	29	10	97-5	133	5.51	72	.291	.380	44-0-2	.250	3	99	-30		-2.4

YEAR	TM LG	W	L	PCT	G	GS	CG-SHO	SV-BS	IP	H	R	HR	HB	BB-IB	SO	ERA	AERA	OAV	OOB	AB-HR-SH	AVG	PB	SUP	APR	DL	PW

WILMET, PAUL Paul Richard B11.8.1958 Green Bay WI BR/TR/5-11/170 d7.25 Col Des Moines Area (IA) CC

| 1989 | Tex A | 3 | 4 | 0 | — | 1 | 0 | 0-0 | 2.1 | 5 | 4 | 0 | 0 | 2-1 | 1 | 15.43 | 26 | .417 | .500 | 0 | — | 0 | | -3 | | -0.1 |

WILSHERE, WHITEY Vernon Sprague B8.3.1912 Poplar Ridge NY D5.23.1985 Cooperstown NY BL/TL/6-0/180 d6.24 Col Indiana

1934	Phi A	0	1	.000	9	2	0	0	21.2	39	30	0	1	15	19	12.05	36	.394	.478	3	.000	-0	119	-18		-0.9
1935	Phi A	9	9	.500	27	18	7-3	1	142.1	136	69	8	10	78	80	4.05	112	.253	.358	43-0-5	.093	-4	90	10		0.7
1936	Phi A	1	2	.333	5	3	0	0	18.1	21	17	1	0	19	4	6.87	74	.288	.435	4	.000	-0	52	-4		-0.5
Total	3	10	12	.455	41	23	7-3	1	182.1	196	116	9	11	112	103	5.28	87	.276	.383	50-0-5	.080	-4	87	-12		-0.7

WILSHUSEN, TERRY Terry Wayne B3.22.1949 Atascadero CA D12.1.2000 Lomita CA BR/TR/6-2/210 d4.7 Col Los Angeles (CA) City

| 1973 | Cal A | 0 | 0 | — | 1 | 0 | 0 | 0-0 | 0.1 | 3 | 3 | 0 | 1 | 2-0 | 0 | 81.00 | 4 | .000 | .750 | 0 | — | 0 | | -3 | | -0.1 |

WILSON, C.J. Christopher John B11.18.1980 Newport Beach CA BL/TL/6-2/200 d6.10 Col Loyola Marymount

| 2005 | Tex A | 1 | 7 | .125 | 24 | 6 | 0 | 0 | 48 | 63 | 39 | 5 | 2 | 18-1 | 30 | 6.94 | 66 | .320 | .379 | 0 | — | 0 | 72 | -12 | | -1.6 |

WILSON, DON Donald Edward B2.12.1945 Monroe LA D1.5.1975 Houston TX BR/TR/6-3/205* d9.29 Col Compton (CA) CC

1966	Hou N	1	0	1.000	1	0	0	0	6	5	2	1	0	1-0	7	3.00	114	.238	.273	2	.500	1		0		0.2
1967	Hou N	10	9	.526	31	28	7-3	0	184	141	67	10	7	69-2	159	2.79	119	.209	.288	66-0-2	.091	-2	100	10		0.7
1968	Hou N	13	16	.448	33	30	9-3	0	208.2	187	85	9	4	70-5	175	3.28	90	.236	.300	70-1-6	.214	4*	89	-7		-0.7
1969	Hou N	16	12	.571	34	34	13-1	0-0	225	210	119	16	9	97-8	235	4.00	89	.245	.326	81-0-2	.099	-1	133	-12		-1.6
1970	Hou N	11	6	.647	29	27	3	0-0	184.1	188	92	15	7	66-4	94	3.91	100	.259	.325	69-0-3	.116	-2*	119	-2	17	-0.5
1971	Hou N★	16	10	.615	35	34	18-3	0-0	268	195	80	15	7	79-3	180	2.45	137	**.202**	.266	91-0-6	.154	-1	92	28		2.5
1972	Hou N	15	10	.600	33	33	13-3	0-0	228.1	196	79	16	2	66-2	172	2.68	125	.233	.289	76-0-8	.105	-2	116	16		1.5
1973	Hou N	11	16	.407	37	32	10-3	2-0	239.1	187	94	21	7	92-6	149	3.20	114	.213	.291	79-0-6	.177	1	76	12		1.2
1974	Hou N	11	13	.458	33	27	5-4	0-1	204.2	170	80	16	4	100-2	112	3.08	113	.227	.318	63-0-9	.206	2	81	9		1.2
Total	9	104	92	.531	266	245	78-20	2-1	1748.1	1479	698	119	47	640-32	1283	3.15	110	.228	.299	597-1-42	.146	-1	102	54	17	4.5

WILSON, DUANE Duane Lewis B6.29.1934 Wichita KS BL/TL/6-1/185 d7.3

| 1958 | Bos A | 0 | 0 | — | 2 | 2 | 0 | 0 | 6.1 | 5 | 5 | 0 | 0 | 7-1 | 3 | 5.68 | 70 | .400 | .515 | 1-0-1 | .000 | -0 | 112 | -1 | | -0.1 |

WILSON, FIN Finis Elbert B12.9.1889 East Fork KY D3.9.1959 Coral Gables FL BL/TL/6-1/194 d9.26

1914	Bro F	0	1	.000	2	1	1	0	7	7	7	0	0	11	4	7.71	37	.269	.486	2	.500	1	72	-3		-0.4
1915	Bro F	1	8	.111	18	11	5	0	102.1	85	56	2	4	53	47	3.78	72	.249	.356	35-0-1	.314	2*	87	-12		-0.7
Total	2	1	9	.100	20	12	6	0	109.1	92	63	2	4	64	51	4.03	68	.250	.367	37-0-1	.324	3	85	-15		-1.1

WILSON, ZEKE Frank Ealton B12.24.1869 Benton AL D4.26.1928 Montgomery AL BR/TR/5-10/165 d4.23

1895	Bos N	2	4	.333	6	6	4	0	45	54	48	1	0	27	5	5.20	98	.293	.384	19-1-0	.316	1	65	-4		-0.3
	Cle N	3	1	.750	9	8	4	0	52.2	75	38	4	4	24	20	4.27	117	.329	.402	22-0-2	.136	-3	87	3		0.0
	Year	5	5	.500	15	14	8	0	97.2	129	86	5	4	51	25	4.70	107	.313	.394	41-1-2	.220	-2	78	-1		-0.3
1896	Cle N	17	9	.654	33	29	20-1	1	240	265	150	9	8	81	56	4.01	113	.278	.339	100-0-2	.270	2	114	14		1.5
1897	Cle N	16	11	.593	34	30	26-1	0	263.2	323	171	9	9	83	69	4.16	108	.299	.354	116-0-3	.224	-3*	94	8		0.4
1898	Cle N	13	18	.419	33	31	28-1	0	254.2	307	141	4	7	51	45	3.60	100	.296	.333	118-0-7	.178	-3*	83	2		0.1
1899	StL N	1	1	.500	5	2	2	0	26	30	18	0	2	4	3	4.50	88	.288	.327	10	.000	-1	99	-1		-0.1
Total	5	52	44	.542	120	106	84-3	1	882	1054	566	27	30	270	198	4.03	106	.294	.348	385-1-14	.216	-8	95	22		1.6

WILSON, GARY Gary Morris B1.1.1970 Arcata CA BR/TR/6-3/190 [PitN92 18/511] d4.28 Col Cal St.-Sacramento

| 1995 | Pit N | 0 | 1 | .000 | 10 | 0 | 0 | 0 | 14.1 | 13 | 9 | 2 | 0 | 6-0 | 9 | 5.02 | 87 | .241 | .328 | 0-0-1 | — | 0 | | -1 | | 0.0 |

WILSON, GARY Gary Steven B11.21.1954 Camden AR BR/TR/6-2/185 [HouN76*1/2] d4.13 Col Southern Arkansas

| 1979 | Hou N | 0 | 0 | — | 6 | 0 | 0 | 0-0 | 7.1 | 15 | 11 | 2 | 0 | 6-0 | 6 | 12.27 | 29 | .441 | .500 | 0 | — | 0 | | -7 | | -0.4 |

WILSON, TEX Gomer Russell B7.8.1901 Trenton TX D9.15.1946 Sulphur Springs TX BR/TL/5-10/170 d9.2

| 1924 | Bro N | 0 | 0 | — | 2 | 0 | 0 | 0 | 3.2 | 7 | 6 | 0 | 1 | 2-1 | 1 | 14.73 | 25 | .412 | .444 | 1 | .000 | -0 | | -4 | | -0.2 |

WILSON, HIGHBALL Howard Paul B8.9.1878 Philadelphia PA D10.16.1934 Havre de Grace MD TR/5-9/164 d9.13

1899	Cle N	1	1	.000	1	1	1	0	7	12	8	0	5	1	5	9.00	41	.343	.425	3	.333	0	39	-4		-0.3
1902	Phi A	7	4	.636	13	10	8	0	96.1	103	44	1	9	19	18	2.43	151	.274	.324	35-0-1	.171	-1	108	11		0.9
1903	Was A	7	18	.280	30	28	25-1	0	242.1	269	123	7	10	43	56	3.31	95	.280	.318	85-0-2	.200	2*	70	-6		-0.5
1904	Was A	0	3	.000	3	3	3	0	25	33	17	0	2	6	11	4.68	87	.317	.355	9-0-1	.222	1*	36	-5		-0.5
Total	4	14	26	.350	47	42	37-1	0	371.2	417	192	8	21	71	86	3.29	99	.283	.325	132-0-4	.197	2	77	-4		-0.4

WILSON, JIM James Alger B2.20.1922 San Diego CA D9.2.1986 Newport Beach CA BR/TR/6-1.5/200* d4.18 Col San Diego St.

1945	Bos A	6	8	.429	23	21	8-2	0	144.1	121	61	7	1	88	50	3.30	103	.228	.338	53-0-2	.245	2*	89	2		0.2
1946	Bos A	0	0	—	1	0	0	0	0.2	2	2	1	0	0	0	27.00	14	.500	.500	0	—	0		-2		-0.1
1948	StL A	0	0	—	4	0	0	0	2.2	5	4	0	0	4	1	13.50	34	.417	.588	0	—	0		-2		-0.1
1949	Phi A	0	0	—	2	0	0	0	5	7	8	2	0	5	2*	14.40	29	.350	.480	1	.000	-0		-5		-0.3
1951	Bos N	7	7	.500	20	15	5	1	110	131	67	14	4	40	33	5.40	68	.294	.357	39-0-3	.179	-1	152	-19		-2.1
1952	Bos N	12	14	.462	33	33	14	0	234	234	114	19	4	90	104	4.23	85	.262	.333	86-0-3	.163	-0	101	-13		-1.4
1953	Mil N	4	9	.308	20	18	5	0	114	107	59	16	3	43	71	4.34	90	.243	.315	36-1-2	.167	1	94	-4		-0.2
1954	Mil N☆	8	2	.800	27	19	6-4	0	127.2	129	55	12	5	36	52	3.52	106	.266	.321	44-0-3	.159	-2	150	4		0.4
1955	Bal A☆	12	18	.400	34	31	14-4	0	235.1	200	104	17	4	87-5	96	3.44	111	.228	.297	89-0-2	.169	-2	78	10		1.0
1956	Bal A	4	2	.667	7	7	1	0	48.1	49	27	5	2	16-1	31	5.03	78	.268	.332	15	.267	2	91	-5		-0.3
	Chi A★	9	12	.429	28	21	6-3	0	159.2	149	82	15*	4	70-5	82	4.06	101	.248	.328	62-1-2	.306	4	105	0		0.3
	Year	13	14	.481	35	28	7-3	0	208	198	109	20	4	86-6	113	4.28	95	.253	.328	77-1-2	.299	6	102	-5		0.0
1957	Chi A	15	8	.652	30	29	12-5	0	201.2	189	85	22	3	65-8	100	3.48	107	.249	.309	68-0-4	.147	-0*	115	6		0.5
1958	Chi A	9	9	.500	28	23	4-1	1	155.2	156	75	21	1	63-8	70	4.10	89	.268	.337	51-0-4	.078	-3	125	-7		-1.1
Total	12	86	89	.491	257	216	75-19	2	1539	1479	743	161	29	608-27	692	4.01	93	.250	.326	546-2-24	.181	4	108	-35		-3.2

WILSON, JACK John Francis "Black Jack" B4.12.1912 Portland OR D4.19.1995 Edmonds WA BR/TR/5-11/210 d9.9 Col Portland

1934	Phi A	0	1	.000	7	0	0	0	9	15	12	0	0	9	2	12.00	37	.405	.522	3-0-1	.000	-0	119	-7		-0.6
1935	Bos A	3	4	.429	23	6	2	1	64	72	35	0	2	36	19	4.22	112	.290	.385	16-1-1	.313	2	70	4		0.6
1936	Bos A	6	8	.429	43	9	2	3	136.1	152	83	4	1	86	74	4.42	120	.284	.384	50-0-1	.220	-0*	63	10		0.8
1937	Bos A	16	10	.615	51	21	14-1	7	221.1	209	111	13	3	119	137	3.70	128	.248	.343	85-0-2	.165	-3	118	22		2.1
1938	Bos A	15	15	.500	37	27	11-3	0	194.2	200	108	16	2	91	96	4.30	116	.262	.342	68-0-6	.221	0	81	13		1.6
1939	Bos A	11	11	.500	36	22	6	2	177.1	198	109	10	1	75	80	4.67	101	.281	.351	63-0-5	.159	-4*	103	0		-0.4
1940	Bos A	12	6	.667	41	16	9	5	157.2	170	104	17	3	87	102	5.08	89	.270	.362	66-2-0	.273	4	144	-13		-1.0
1941	Bos A	4	13	.235	27	12	4-1	1	116.1	140	82	7	5	70	55	5.03	83	.300	.397	44-0-2	.159	-1	90	-13		-1.7
1942	Was A	1	4	.200	12	6	1	0	42	57	34	2	1	23	18	6.64	55	.322	.403	17-0-1	.118	-1	125	-13		-1.4
	Det A	0	0	—	9	0	0	0	13	20	8	0	2	5	7	4.85	81	.351	.403	1	.000	-0		-1		-0.1
	Year	1	4	.200	21	6	1	0	55	77	42	5	1	28	25	6.22	60	.329	.403	18-0-1	.111	-1	122	-14		-1.5
Total	9	68	72	.486	281	121	50-5	20	1131.2	1233	686	73	18	601	590	4.59	102	.276	.364	413-3-19	.199	-3	100	2		-0.1

WILSON, JOHN John Nicodemus B6.15.1890 Boonsboro MD D9.23.1954 Annapolis MD BR/TL/6-1/185 d6.11

| 1913 | Was A | 0 | 0 | — | 3 | 0 | 0 | 0 | 4 | 4 | 2 | 0 | 0 | 3 | 1 | 4.50 | 66 | .286 | .412 | 0 | — | 0 | | 0 | | 0.0 |

WILSON, JOHN John Samuel B4.25.1903 Coal City AL D8.27.1980 Chattanooga TN BR/TR/6-2/164 d5.9

1927	Bos A	0	2	.000	5	2	2	0	25.1	31	19	1	0	13	8	3.55	119	.326	.407	9	.111	-1	30	-1		-0.2
1928	Bos A	0	0	—	2	0	0	0	5	6	5	0	0	6	1	9.00	46	.333	.500	1	.000	-0		-2		-0.1
Total	2	0	2	.000	7	2	2	0	30.1	37	24	1	0	19	9	4.45	94	.327	.424	10	.100	-1	30	-3		-0.3

WILSON, KRIS Kristopher Kyle B8.6.1976 Washington DC BR/TR/6-4/225* [KCA97 9/271] d7.28 Col Georgia Tech

2000	KC A	0	1	.000	20	0	0	0-1	34.1	38	16	3	0	11-3	17	4.19	125	.288	.340	—		0		4		0.2
2001	KC A	6	5	.545	29	15	0	1-0	109.1	132	78	26	7	32-0	67	5.19	96	.297	.352	3	.333	0	87	-6		-0.5
2002	KC A	2	0	1.000	12	0	0	0-2	18.2	29	18	7	2	5-0	10	8.20	61	.354	.396	0	—	0		-6	56	-0.6
2003	KC A	6	3	.667	29	4	0	0-1	72.2	92	49	13	6	16-3	42	5.33	91	.305	.348	0	—	0	81	-5	56	-0.5
Total	4	14	9	.609	90	19	0	1-4	235	291	161	49	15	64-6	136	5.32	93	.303	.353	3	.333	0	86	-13	56	-1.4

YEAR	TM LG	W	L	PCT	G	GS	CG-SHO	SV-BS	IP	H	R	HR	HB	BB-IB	SO	ERA	AERA	OAV	OOB	AB-HR-SH	AVG	PB	SUP	APR	DL	PW

WILSON, MAX   Max B6.3.1916 Haw River NC D1.2.1977 Greensboro NC BL/TL/5-7/160 d9.10 Mil 1942-45

1940	Phi N	0	0		3	0	0	0			16	13	1	0	2	3	12.86	30	.444	.474	2	.000	-0		-8	-0.4
1946	Was A	0	1	.000	9	0	0	0		12.2	16	12	1	0	9	8	7.11	47	.320	.424	2	.000	0		-5	-0.4
Total	2	0	1	.000	12	0	0	0		19.2	32	25	2	0	11	11	9.15	39	.372	.443	4	.000	-0		-13	-0.8

WILSON, PAUL   Paul Anthony B3.28.1973 Orlando FL BR/TR/6-5/235(210-235) [NYN94 1/1] d4.4 Col Florida St. [DL 1998 NY N 181]

1996	NY N	5	12	.294	26	26	1	0-0	149	157	102	15	10	71-11	109	5.38	75	.268	.355	50-1-4	.080	-2	99	-23	40	-2.4
2000	TB A	1	4	.200	11	7	0	0-0	51	38	20	1	4	16-2	40	3.35	146	.209	.284	0	—	0	41	9		0.7
2001	TB A	8	9	.471	37	24	0	0-1	151.1	165	94	21	13	52-2	111	4.88	92	.278	.343	0		0	95	-7		-0.7
2002	TB A	6	12	.333	30	30	1	0-0	193.2	219	113	29	13	67-2	111	4.83	94	.287	.352	5-0-1	.000	-1	89	-7		-0.6
2003	Cin N	8	10	.444	28	28	0	0-0	166.2	190	97	24	7	50-5	93	4.64	90	.285	.342	52-0-4	.115	-1*	101	-11		-1.2
2004	Cin N	11	6	.647	29	29	1	0-0	183.2	192	93	26	8	63-5	117	4.36	99	.271	.334	60-0-7	.100	2	112	0	18	-0.2
2005	Cin N	1	5	.167	9	9	0	0-0	46.1	68	41	10	4	17-1	30	7.77	54	.343	.401	17-0-2	.176	-0	96	-18	139	-1.9
Total	7	40	58	.408	170	153	3	0-1	941.2	1029	560	126	59	336-28	619	4.86	89	.278	.345	184-1-18	.103	-5	96	-57	378	-6.3

WILSON, PETE   Peter Alex B10.9.1885 Springfield MA D6.5.1957 St.Petersburg FL TL d9.15

1908	NY A	3	3	.500	6	6	4-1	0	39	27	16	0	1	33	28	3.46	72	.191	.349	14-0-1	.071	-1*	55	-2		-0.4
1909	NY A	6	5	.545	14	13	7-1	0	93.2	82	55	2	4	43	44	3.17	80	.230	.320	34-0-1	.118	-1	114	-9		-1.1
Total	2	9	8	.529	20	19	11-2	0	132.2	109	71	2	5	76	72	3.26	77	.219	.329	48-0-2	.104	-2	94	-11		-1.5

WILSON, EARL   Robert Earl (Name Changed From Wilson, Earl Lawrence) B10.2.1934 Ponchatoula LA D4.23.2005 Southfield MI BR/TR/6-3/216* d7.28

1959	Bos A	1	1	.500	9	4	0	0	23.2	21	17	2	0	31-0	17	6.08	67	.241	.441	8	.500	2	201	-5		-0.2
1960	Bos A	3	2	.600	13	9	2	0	65	61	36	4	0	48-1	40	4.71	86	.247	.367	23	.174	-0*	109	-4		-0.3
1962	Bos A	12	8	.600	31	28	4-1	0	191.1	163	86	21	6	111-2	137	3.90	106	.231	.338	69-3-1	.174	3*	107	8		1.0
1963	Bos A	11	16	.407	37	34	6-3	0	210.2	184	99	18	1	105-4	123	3.76	101	.234	.323	72-1-2	.208	5*	89	0		0.5
1964	Bos A	11	12	.478	33	31	5	0	202.1	213	121	37	2	73-3	166	4.69	86	.269	.328	73-5-1	.205	8*	117	-17		-0.9
1965	Bos A	13	14	.481	36	36	8-1	0	230.2	221	119	27	4	77-4	164	3.98	94	.250	.311	79-6-3	.177	8*	108	-6		0.2
1966	Bos A	5	5	.500	15	14	5-1	0	100.2	88	45	14	2	36-2	67	3.84	99	.235	.303	32-2-2	.250	3*	106	1		0.5
	Det A	13	6	.684	23	23	8-2	0	163.1	126	49	16	4	38-1	133	2.59	134	.213	.265	64-5-4	.234	9*	123	18		3.2
	Year	18	11	.621	38	37	13-3	0	264	214	94	30	6	74-3	200	3.07	117	.222	.280	96-7-6	.240	12	116	19		3.7
1967	Det A	22	11	.667	39	38	12	0	264	216	103	34	3	92-7	184	3.27	112	.224	.291	108-4-4	.185	7*	126	1		1.0
1968	†Det A	13	12	.520	34	33	10-3	0	224.1	192	77	20	0	65-4	168	2.85	106	.231	.287	88-7-1	.227	10*	96	4		1.7
1969	Det A	12	10	.545	35	35	5-1	0-0	214.2	209	93	23	4	69-4	150	3.31	114	.256	.315	76-0-2	.132	-0	101	8		0.9
1970	Det A	4	6	.400	18	16	4-1	0-0	96	87	53	15	2	32-1	74	4.41	86	.238	.303	31-1-2	.194	2	93	-7		-0.5
	SD N	1	6	.143	15	9	0	0-0	65	82	36	5	2	19-2	29	4.85	83	.309	.356	17-1-0	.059	-0	99	-5		-0.5
Total	11	121	109	.526	338	310	69-13	0-0	2051.2	1863	934	236	30	796-35	1452	3.69	99	.242	.313	740-35-22	.195	57	108	-4		6.6

WILSON, ROY   Roy Edward "Lefty" B9.13.1896 Foster IA D12.3.1969 Clarion IA BL/TL/6-0/175 d4.18

| 1928 | Chi A | 0 | 0 | | 1 | 0 | 0 | 0 | 3.1 | 2 | 0 | 0 | 3 | | 0.00 | — | .167 | .333 | 1 | .000 | -0 | | 1 | | 0.1 |

WILSON, STEVE   Stephen Douglas B12.13.1964 Victoria BC, Can. BL/TL/6-4/195(195-224) [TexA85 4/83] d9.16 Col Portland

1988	Tex A	0	0		3	0	0	0	7.2	7	5	1	0	4-1	1	5.87	70	.259	.355	0	—	0		-1		-0.1
1989	†Chi N	6	4	.600	53	8	0	2-1	85.2	83	43	6	1	31-5	65	4.20	90	.257	.320	16-0-1	.063	-1	97	-3		-0.4
1990	Chi N	4	9	.308	45	15	1	1-1	139	140	77	17	2	43-6	95	4.79	85	.259	.315	37-0-5	.162	0	97	-8		-0.7
1991	Chi N	0	0		8	0	0	0-0	12.1	13	7	1	0	5-1	9	4.38	89	.277	.340	1	.000	-0*		-1		-0.1
	LA N	0	0		11	0	0	2-0	8.1	1	0	0	0	4-0	5	0.00	—	.042	.179	1	.000	-0		3		0.2
	Year	0	0		19	0	0	2-0	20.2	14	7	1	0	9-1	14	2.61	145	.197	.284	2	.000	-0		2		0.1
1992	LA N	2	5	.286	60	0	0	0-4	66.2	74	37	6	1	29-7	54	4.18	83	.282	.351	3	.333	-0		-6		-0.6
1993	LA N	1	0	1.000	25	0	0	1-0	25.2	30	13	2	1	14-4	23	4.56	85	.288	.378	2	.000	-0		-1		-0.1
Total	6	13	18	.419	205	23	1	6-6	345.1	348	182	33	5	130-24	252	4.40	88	.262	.328	60-0-6	.133	-1	100	-17		-1.8

WILSON, TREVOR   Trevor Kirk B6.7.1966 Torrance CA BL/TL/6-0/195(175-204) [SFN85 8/186] d9.5 [DL 1994 SF N 131]

1988	SF N	0	2	.000	4	4	0	0-0	22	25	14	1	0	8-0	15	4.09	80	.298	.355	7-0-1	.286	1	88	-3		-0.3
1989	SF N	2	3	.400	14	4	0	0-0	39.1	28	20	2	4	24-0	22	4.35	78	.207	.341	8	.250	1	137	-4		-0.3
1990	SF N	8	7	.533	27	17	3-2	0-0	110.1	87	52	11	4	49-3	66	4.00	92	.218	.304	29-0-5	.138	0	89	-4	15	-0.4
1991	SF N	13	11	.542	44	29	2-1	0-1	202	173	87	13	5	77-4	139	3.56	101	.234	.308	51-1-8	.235	5*	97	0		0.7
1992	SF N	8	14	.364	26	26	1-1	0-0	154	152	82	18	6	64-5	88	4.21	79	.265	.342	39-0-7	.077	-1*	84	-17	12	-2.2
1993	SF N	7	5	.583	22	18	1	0-0	110	110	45	8	4	40-3	57	3.60	109	.275	.347	29-1-8	.138	1	84	5	75	0.2
1995	SF N	3	4	.429	17	17	0	0-0	82.2	82	42	8	4	38-1	38	3.92	105	.269	.355	30-0-3	.233	1*	91	1	77	0.2
1998	Ana A	0	0		15	0	0	0-2	7.2	8	4	0	1	5-2	6	3.52	135	.267	.378	0	—	0		1		0.0
Total	8	41	46	.471	169	115	7-4	0-3	728	665	346	61	27	305-18	431	3.87	94	.249	.330	193-2-32	.176	7	91	-21	310	-1.7

WILSON, WALTER   Walter Wood B11.24.1913 Glenn GA D4.17.1994 Bremen GA BL/TR/6-4/190 d4.17

| 1945 | Det A | 1 | 3 | .250 | 54 | 4 | 1 | 2 | 70.1 | 76 | 40 | 4 | 3 | 35 | 28 | 4.61 | 76 | .284 | .373 | 19-0-2 | .053 | -2 | 79 | -7 | | -0.5 |

WILSON, WILLY   William B1.7.1884 Columbus OH D10.28.1925 Seattle WA BR/TR d10.3

| 1906 | Was A | 0 | 1 | .000 | 1 | 1 | 1 | 0 | 7 | 3 | 2 | 0 | 1 | 2 | 1 | 2.57 | 102 | .130 | .231 | 2 | .000 | -0 | | 27 | 0 | | 0.0 |

WILSON, MUTT   William Clarence "Lank" B7.20.1896 Keyser (now Addor) NC D8.31.1962 Leesburg FL BR/TR/6-3/167 d9.11

| 1920 | Det A | 1 | 1 | .500 | 3 | 2 | 1 | 0 | 13 | 12 | 10 | 0 | 0 | 5 | 4 | 3.46 | 108 | .240 | .309 | 4-0-1 | .250 | -0 | 96 | -1 | | -0.2 |

WILSON, BILL   William Harlan B9.21.1942 Pomeroy OH D8.11.1993 Broken Arrow OK BR/TR/6-2/200* d4.8 Col Marshall

1969	Phi N	2	5	.286	37	0	0	6-3	62.1	53	26	6	1	36-8	48	3.32	107	.231	.336	6	.000	-0		2		0.1
1970	Phi N	1	0	1.000	37	0	0	0-1	58.1	57	35	5	0	33-0	41	4.78	84	.263	.357	4	.250	0		-6		-0.2
1971	Phi N	4	6	.400	38	0	0	7-2	58.2	39	20	4	1	22-4	40	3.07	116	.188	.266	10	.100	-1		4		0.8
1972	Phi N	1	1	.500	23	0	0	0-2	30	26	13	1	0	11-3	18	3.30	109	.234	.301	0	—	-0		1	103	0.1
1973	Phi N	1	3	.250	44	0	0	4-2	48.2	54	39	7	0	29-7	24	6.66	57	.293	.388	4	.000	-0		-14		-1.4
Total	5	9	15	.375	179	0	0	17-10	258	229	133	23	2	131-22	171	4.22	88	.241	.332	24	.083	-1		-13	103	-0.6

WILTSE, HOOKS   George Leroy B9.7.1879 Hamilton NY D1.21.1959 Long Beach NY BR/TL/6-0/185 d4.21 C1 b-Snake

1904	NY N	13	3	.813	24	16	14-2	5	164.2	150	66	8	5	61	105	2.84	96	.240	.313	67-1-2	.224	3*	169	0		0.5
1905	NY N	15	6	.714	32	19	18-1	3	197	158	71	2	4	61	120	2.47	119	.219	.284	72-0-2	.278	7*	114	12		2.3
1906	NY N	16	11	.593	38	26	21-4	6	249.1	227	92	3	3	58	125	2.27	115	.241	.288	94-0-4	.191	2*	102	7		1.0
1907	NY N	13	12	.520	33	21	14-3	2	190.1	171	63	0	4	48	79	2.18	114	.241	.294	67-0-1	.134	0	114	6		0.9
1908	NY N	23	14	.622	44	38	30-7	2	330	266	95	4	9	73	118	2.24	108	.224	.274	110-0-7	.236	6*	126	12		2.1
1909	NY N	20	11	.645	37	30	22-4	3	269.1	228	91	9	6	51	119	2.00	128	.233	.275	95-1-2	.200	2	133	16		2.0
1910	NY N	14	12	.538	36	30	18-2	2	235.1	232	96	4	2	52	88	2.72	109	.261	.303	74-0-5	.176	0	110	7		0.6
1911	†NY N	12	9	.571	30	24	11-4	0	187.1	177	83	7	2	39	92	3.27	103	.251	.292	69-0-2	.188	-1*	107	5		0.3
1912	NY N	9	6	.600	28	17	5	3	134	140	63	7	0	48	58	3.16	107	.273	.312	46-0-1	.326	4	129	5		0.9
1913	†NY N	0	0		17	2	0	3	57.2	53	24	1	1	18	25	1.56	200	.237	.266	24	.208	0*	133	6		0.4
1914	NY N	1	1	.500	11	2	0	0	38	41	21	2	0	12	19	2.84	93	.289	.344	3	.667	2*		-3		0.0
1915	Bro F	3	5	.375	18	3	1	5	59.1	49	22	1	2	7	17	2.28	126	.226	.257	22	.045	-3*	26	2		0.0
Total	12	139	90	.607	357	226	154-27	33	2112.1	1892	787	54	40	498	965	2.47	112	.241	.290	743-2-26	.210	22	120	75		11.0

WILTSE, HAL   Harold James "Whitey" B8.6.1903 Clay City IL D11.2.1983 Bunkie LA BL/TL/5-9/168 d4.13

1926	Bos A	8	15	.348	34	29	9-1	0	196.1	201	112	6	6	99	59	4.22	97	.273	.363	59-0-4	.085	-5	79	-5		-0.9
1927	Bos A	10	18	.357	36	29	13-1	1	219	276	146	6	4	76	47	5.10	83	.321	.379	77-0-2	.208	-2	72	-20		-2.2
1928	Bos A	0	2	.000	2	2	1	0	12	16	12	1	3	1	5	9.00	46	.314	.364	4	.000	-1	62	-6		-0.7
	StL A	2	5	.286	26	5	0	0	72	93	49	4	3	35	23	5.25	80	.316	.395	22-0-1	.227	-0	93	-8		-0.6
	Year	2	7	.222	28	7	1	0	84	109	61	5	6	36	28	5.79	72	.316	.390	26-0-1	.192	-1	84	-13		-1.3
1931	Phi N	0	0		1	0	0	0	1	3	1	0	0	0	0	9.00	47	.600	.600		—	-0		0		0.0
Total	4	20	40	.333	102	65	23-2	1	500.1	589	320	16	16	211	134	4.87	85	.303	.375	162-0-7	.160	-7	76	-39		-4.4

WILTSE, SNAKE   Lewis De Witt B12.5.1871 Bouckville NY D8.25.1928 Harrisburg PA BR/TL d5.5 b-Hooks

1901	Pit N	1	4	.200	7	5	3	0	44.1	57	28	2	5	13	10	4.26	77	.310	.371	19-0-1	.158	-1	82	-4		-0.4
	Phi A	13	5	.722	19	19	18-2	0	166	185	91	1	7	35	40	3.58	105	.279	.322	67-0-2	.373	8	122	4		1.2
1902	Phi A	8	8	.500	19	17	13	1	138	182	99	7	5	41	28	5.15	71	.318	.368	57	.175	-0*	113	-17		-1.8

YEAR	TM LG	W	L	PCT	G	GS	CG-SHO	SV-BS	IP	H	R	HR	HB	BB-IB	SO	ERA	AERA	OAV	OOB	AB-HR-SH	AVG	PB	SUP	APR	DL	PW
	Bal A	7	11	.389	19	18	18	0	164	215	127	4	8	51	37	5.10	74	.316	.371	132-2-2	.295	6*	122	-20		-1.3
	Year	15	19	.441	38	35	31	1	302	397	226	11	13	92	65	5.13	73	.317	.370	189-2-2	.259	5	118	-38		-3.1
1903	NY A	0	3	.000	4	3	2	1	25	35	17	1	1	6	6	5.40	58	.330	.372	9	.222	0	46	-5		-0.5
Total	3	29	31	.483	68	62	54-2	2	537.1	674	362	16	26	146	121	4.59	80	.305	.356	284-2-5	.278	13	113	-42		-2.8

WINCHELL, FRED Frederick Russell (b Frederick Cook) B1.23.1882 Arlington MA D8.8.1958 Toronto ON, Can. TR/5-8/? d9.16 Col Princeton

YEAR	TM LG	W	L	PCT	G	GS	CG-SHO	SV-BS	IP	H	R	HR	HB	BB-IB	SO	ERA	AERA	OAV	OOB	AB-HR-SH	AVG	PB	SUP	APR	DL	PW
1909	Cle A	0	3	.000	4	3	0	1	14.1	16	11	0	0	2	7	6.28	41	.296	.321	5	.200	0	74	-5		-0.9

WINCHESTER, SCOTT Scott Joseph B4.20.1973 Midland MI BR/TR/6-2/210* [CleA95 14/390] d9.8 Col Clemson [DL 1999 Cin N 183]

YEAR	TM LG	W	L	PCT	G	GS	CG-SHO	SV-BS	IP	H	R	HR	HB	BB-IB	SO	ERA	AERA	OAV	OOB	AB-HR-SH	AVG	PB	SUP	APR	DL	PW
1997	Cin N	0	0	—	5	0	0	0-0	6	9	5	1	1	2-0	3	6.00	71	.360	.429	0	—	0		-1		-0.1
1998	Cin N	3	6	.333	16	16	1	0-0	79	101	56	12	4	27-2	40	5.81	74	.312	.370	23-0-2	.130	-1	80	-14		-1.4
2000	Cin N	0	0	—	5	0	0	0-0	7.1	10	4	1	0	2-0	3	3.68	129	.313	.343	0	—	0		1		0.0
2001	Cin N	0	2	.000	12	1	0	0-0	24	29	19	7	3	4-3	9	4.50	102	.315	.353	.000	.000	-0	81	-2	31	-0.2
Total	4	3	8	.273	38	17	1	0-0	116.1	149	84	21	8	35-5	55	5.42	81	.315	.368	*26-0-2	.115	-1	79	-16	214	-1.7

WINEAPPLE, ED Edward "Lefty" B8.10.1905 Boston MA D7.23.1996 Delray Beach FL BL/TL/6-0/210 d9.15 Col Providence

YEAR	TM LG	W	L	PCT	G	GS	CG-SHO	SV-BS	IP	H	R	HR	HB	BB-IB	SO	ERA	AERA	OAV	OOB	AB-HR-SH	AVG	PB	SUP	APR	DL	PW
1929	Was A	0	0	—	1	0	0	0	4	7	4	0	0	3	1	4.50	94	.467	.556	2	.000	-0		-1		-0.1

WINEGARNER, RALPH Ralph Lee B10.29.1909 Benton KS D4.14.1988 Wichita KS BR/TR/6-0/182 d9.20.1930 C4 Col Southwestern (KS)

YEAR	TM LG	W	L	PCT	G	GS	CG-SHO	SV-BS	IP	H	R	HR	HB	BB-IB	SO	ERA	AERA	OAV	OOB	AB-HR-SH	AVG	PB	SUP	APR	DL	PW
1932	Cle A	1	0	1.000	5	1	1	0	17.1	7	4	0	0	13	5	1.04	457	.123	.286	7	.143	-0*	108	6		0.2
1934	Cle A	5	4	.556	22	6	4	0	78.1	91	55	1	2	39	32	5.51	82	.289	.371	51-1-0	.196	1*	108	-8		-0.6
1935	Cle A	2	2	.500	25	4	2	0	67.1	89	51	10	1	29	41	5.75	78	.313	.379	84-3-1	.310	4*	135	-10		0.0
1936	Cle A	0	0	—	9	0	0	0	14.2	18	9	0	0	6	3	4.91	103	.295	.358	16	.125	-1*		0		-0.1
1949	StL A	0	0	—	9	0	0	0	16.2	24	16	2	0	2	8	7.56	60	.329	.347	5-1-0	.400	2		-5		-0.1
Total	5	8	6	.571	70	11	7	0	194.1	229	135	13	3	89	89	5.33	86	.290	.364	163-5-1	.252	5	117	-17		-0.6

WINFORD, JIM James Head "Cowboy" B10.9.1909 Shelbyville TN D12.16.1970 Miami OK BR/TR/6-1/180 d9.10

YEAR	TM LG	W	L	PCT	G	GS	CG-SHO	SV-BS	IP	H	R	HR	HB	BB-IB	SO	ERA	AERA	OAV	OOB	AB-HR-SH	AVG	PB	SUP	APR	DL	PW
1932	StL N	1	1	.500	4	1	0	0	8.1	9	7	0	0	5	4	6.48	61	.273	.368	3	.667	1	86	-2		-0.3
1934	StL N	0	2	.000	5	1	0	0	12.2	17	13	0	2	6	3	7.82	54	.327	.417	1	.000	-1	41	-5		-0.6
1935	StL N	0	0	—	2	1	0	0	11.1	13	5	1	0	5	7	3.97	103	.283	.353	2-0-1	.000	-0	145	0		0.0
1936	StL N	11	10	.524	39	23	10-1	3	192	203	90	10	5	68	72	3.80	104	.269	.333	59	.085	-4	90	4		-0.9
1937	StL N	2	4	.333	16	4	0	0	46.1	56	31	2	0	27	17	5.83	68	.311	.401	8	.125	-1	70	-7		-0.7
1938	Bro N	0	1	.000	2	1	0	0	5.2	9	10	1	0	4	4	11.12	35	.346	.433	1	.000	0	87	-5		-0.7
Total	6	14	18	.438	68	31	10-1	3	276.1	307	156	14	7	115	107	4.56	87	.281	.353	74-0-1	.108	-3	87	-15		-2.7

WINGARD, ERNIE Ernest James "Jim" B10.17.1900 Prattville AL D1.17.1977 Prattville AL BL/TL/6-2/176 d5.1 Col Alabama

YEAR	TM LG	W	L	PCT	G	GS	CG-SHO	SV-BS	IP	H	R	HR	HB	BB-IB	SO	ERA	AERA	OAV	OOB	AB-HR-SH	AVG	PB	SUP	APR	DL	PW
1924	StL A	13	12	.520	36	26	14	1	218	215	103	6	3	85	23	3.51	129	.262	.334	77-3-4	.234	2*	76	22		2.2
1925	StL A	9	10	.474	32	18	8	0	145	183	111	10	3	77	20	5.52	85	.319	.403	52-1-4	.288	3*	114	-15		-1.1
1926	StL A	5	8	.385	39	16	7	3	169	188	86	9	5	76	30	3.57	120	.290	.369	61-0-1	.230	1*	93	10		1.0
1927	StL A	2	13	.133	38	17	7	0	156.1	213	132	7	2	79	28	6.56	66	.340	.415	56-3-0	.179	2*	90	-34		-2.5
Total	5	29	43	.403	145	77	36	4	688.1	799	432	32	13	317	101	4.64	96	.299	.377	246-7-9	.232	7	92	-17		-0.4

WINGFIELD, TED Frederick Davis B8.7.1899 Bedford VA D7.18.1975 Johnson City TN BR/TR/5-11/168 d9.23

YEAR	TM LG	W	L	PCT	G	GS	CG-SHO	SV-BS	IP	H	R	HR	HB	BB-IB	SO	ERA	AERA	OAV	OOB	AB-HR-SH	AVG	PB	SUP	APR	DL	PW
1923	Was A	0	0	—	1	0	0	0	1	0	0	0	0	0	1	0.00	—	.000	.000	0	—	0		0		0.0
1924	Was A	0	0	—	4	0	0	0	7	9	2	0	0	4	2	2.57	157	.300	.382	2	.000	-0		1		0.0
	Bos A	0	2	.000	4	3	2	0	25.2	23	12	0	0	8	4	2.45	178	.240	.298	9	.333	1	64	4		0.3
	Year	0	2	.000	8	3	2	0	32.2	32	14	0	0	12	6	2.48	173	.254	.319	11	.273	1	65	5		0.3
1925	Bos A	12	19	.387	41	27	18-2	2	254.1	267	149	11	8	92	30	3.96	115	.278	.346	94-1-5	.245	1	77	13		1.8
1926	Bos A	11	16	.407	43	20	9-1	3	190.2	220	119	11	2	50	30	4.44	92	.298	.344	69	.217	-0	64	-12		-1.4
1927	Bos A	1	7	.125	20	8	2	0	74.2	105	60	2	3	27	1	5.06	83	.357	.417	18	.222	0*	57	-11		-0.8
Total	5	24	44	.353	113	58	31-3	5	553.1	624	342	24	13	181	68	4.18	103	.294	.353	192-1-5	.234	1	70	-5		-0.1

WINHAM, LAVE Lafayette Sharkey "Lefty" B10.23.1881 Brooklyn NY D9.12.1951 Brooklyn NY BL/TL/5-11/200 d4.21

YEAR	TM LG	W	L	PCT	G	GS	CG-SHO	SV-BS	IP	H	R	HR	HB	BB-IB	SO	ERA	AERA	OAV	OOB	AB-HR-SH	AVG	PB	SUP	APR	DL	PW
1902	Bro N	0	0	—	1	0	0	0	3	4	2	0	0	2	1	—	.308	.400	2	.000	-0		-1		0.0
1903	Pit N	3	1	.750	5	4	3-1	0	36	33	20	0	0	21	22	2.25	144	.231	.329	14	.071	-1	120	2		0.0
Total	2	3	1	.750	9	4	3-1	0	39	37	22	0	0	23	23	2.08	154	.237	.335	16	.063	-2	120	2		0.0

WINKELSAS, JOE Joseph B9.14.1973 Buffalo NY BR/TR/6-3/188 d4.10 Col Elon

YEAR	TM LG	W	L	PCT	G	GS	CG-SHO	SV-BS	IP	H	R	HR	HB	BB-IB	SO	ERA	AERA	OAV	OOB	AB-HR-SH	AVG	PB	SUP	APR	DL	PW
1999	Atl N	0	0	—	1	0	0	0-0	0.1	1	2	0	0	1-1	0	54.00	8	1.000	1.000	0	—	0		-2		-0.1

WINN, GEORGE George Benjamin "Breezy","Lefty" B10.26.1897 Perry GA D11.1.1969 Roberta GA BL/TL/5-11/170 d4.29 Col Mercer

YEAR	TM LG	W	L	PCT	G	GS	CG-SHO	SV-BS	IP	H	R	HR	HB	BB-IB	SO	ERA	AERA	OAV	OOB	AB-HR-SH	AVG	PB	SUP	APR	DL	PW
1919	Bos A	0	0	—	3	0	0	0	4.2	6	4	0	0	1	0	7.71	39	.353	.389	1	.000	-0		-2		-0.1
1922	Cle A	1	2	.333	8	3	1	0	33.2	44	20	2	0	5	7	4.54	88	.317	.340	9	.333	1	78	-2		-0.1
1923	Cle A	0	0	—	1	0	0	0	2	0	0	0	0	1	0	0.00	—	.000	.143	0	—	0		1		0.0
Total	3	1	2	.333	12	3	1	0	40.1	50	24	2	0	7	7	4.69	83	.309	.337	10	.300	1	78	-3		-0.1

WINN, JIM James Francis B9.23.1959 Stockton CA BR/TR/6-3/210(190-219) [PitN81 1/14] d4.10 Col John Brown

YEAR	TM LG	W	L	PCT	G	GS	CG-SHO	SV-BS	IP	H	R	HR	HB	BB-IB	SO	ERA	AERA	OAV	OOB	AB-HR-SH	AVG	PB	SUP	APR	DL	PW
1983	Pit N	0	0	—	7	0	0	0-0	11	12	9	2	0	9-0	7	7.36	51	.267	.353	0	—	0		-4		-0.2
1984	Pit N	1	0	1.000	9	0	0	1-0	18.2	19	8	2	0	9-1	11	3.86	94	.264	.346	1	.000	-0		0		0.0
1985	Pit N	3	6	.333	30	7	0	0-1	75.2	77	45	4	2	31-2	22	5.23	69	.266	.340	18-0-2	.111	-0	66	-12		-1.2
1986	Pit N	3	5	.375	50	3	0	3-4	88	85	44	9	2	38-7	70	3.58	109	.258	.335	16-0-1	.063	-1	69	1		0.1
1987	Chi A	4	6	.400	56	0	0	6-6	94	95	54	10	4	62-5	44	4.79	97	.271	.390	0	—	0		-2		0.6
1988	Min A	1	0	1.000	9	0	0	0-0	21	33	15	4	2	10-1	5	6.00	68	.355	.417	0	—	0		-4	17	-0.2
Total	6	12	17	.414	161	10	0	10-11	308.1	321	175	31	10	156-16	159	4.67	87	.272	.361	35-0-3	.086	-1	62	-21	17	-1.5

WINSTON, DARRIN Darrin Alexander B7.6.1966 Passaic NJ BR/TL/6-0/195* [MonN88 18/466] d9.10 Col Rutgers

YEAR	TM LG	W	L	PCT	G	GS	CG-SHO	SV-BS	IP	H	R	HR	HB	BB-IB	SO	ERA	AERA	OAV	OOB	AB-HR-SH	AVG	PB	SUP	APR	DL	PW
1997	Phi N	2	0	1.000	7	1	0	0-0	12	8	8	4	2	3-1	8	5.25	80	.178	.260	2	.500	1	44	-2		-0.1
1998	Phi N	2	2	.500	27	0	0	1-1	25	31	18	7	2	6-0	11	6.12	71	.298	.348	1	.000	-0		-5		-0.7
Total	2	4	2	.667	34	1	0	1-1	37	39	26	11	4	9-1	19	5.84	73	.262	.321	3	.333	1	44	-7		-0.9

WINSTON, HANK Henry Rudolph B6.15.1904 Youngsville NC D2.4.1974 Jacksonville FL BL/TR/6-3.5/226 d9.30

YEAR	TM LG	W	L	PCT	G	GS	CG-SHO	SV-BS	IP	H	R	HR	HB	BB-IB	SO	ERA	AERA	OAV	OOB	AB-HR-SH	AVG	PB	SUP	APR	DL	PW
1933	Phi A	0	0	—	1	0	0	0	6.2	7	5	0	0	6	2	6.75	63	.280	.419	3	.000	-0		-1		-0.1
1936	Bro N	1	3	.250	14	0	0	0	32.1	40	27	2	1	16	8	6.12	67	.301	.380	11	.091	-1		-7		-0.4
Total	2	1	3	.250	15	0	0	0	39	47	32	2	1	22	10	6.23	67	.297	.387	14	.071	-1		-8		-0.5

WINTER, GEORGE George Lovington "Sassafras" B4.27.1878 New Providence PA D5.26.1951 Franklin Lakes NJ TR/5-8/155 d6.15 Col Gettysburg

YEAR	TM LG	W	L	PCT	G	GS	CG-SHO	SV-BS	IP	H	R	HR	HB	BB-IB	SO	ERA	AERA	OAV	OOB	AB-HR-SH	AVG	PB	SUP	APR	DL	PW
1901	Bos A	16	12	.571	28	28	26-1	0	241	234	127	4	4	66	63	2.80	126	.252	.304	100-1-0	.190	-4	101	15		1.4
1902	Bos A	11	9	.550	20	20	18	0	168.1	149	77	2	7	53	51	2.99	119	.238	.305	61	.164	-2	84	12		1.4
1903	Bos A	9	8	.529	24	19	14	0	178.1	182	92	4	7	37	64	3.08	99	.263	.307	66-0-2	.106	-4	117	-3		-0.4
1904	Bos A	8	4	.667	20	16	12-1	0	135.2	126	47	4	6	27	31	2.32	115	.247	.293	43-0-4	.116	-2*	133	6		0.7
1905	Bos A	16	17	.485	35	27	24-2	0	264.1	249	118	5	5	54	119	2.96	91	.251	.293	92	.261	-1	100	-9		-0.7
1906	Bos A	6	18	.250	29	22	18-1	2	207.2	215	118	6	5	38	72	4.12	67	.270	.308	69-0-2	.246	2	94	-27		-2.2
1907	Bos A	12	15	.444	35	27	21-4	1	256.2	198	91	2	3	61	88	2.07	124	.215	.267	94-0-1	.223	1	90	12		1.3
1908	Bos A	4	14	.222	22	17	8	0	147.2	150	71	4	8	34	55	3.05	81	.274	.321	49	.184	-1	72	-9		-1.2
	†Det A	1	5	.167	7	6	5	1	56.1	49	19	0	3	7	25	1.60	151	.240	.276	18-0-2	.111	-1	57	4		0.6
	Year	5	19	.208	29	23	13	1	204	199	90	4	11	41	80	2.65	93	.265	.309	67-0-2	.164	-2	68	-5		-0.5
Total	8	83	102	.449	220	182	146-9	4	1656	1552	760	32	44	377	568	2.87	101	.250	.297	592-1-11	.193	-8	97	1		-1.0

WINTERS, CLARENCE Clarence John B9.7.1898 Detroit MI D6.29.1945 Detroit MI TR d8.28

YEAR	TM LG	W	L	PCT	G	GS	CG-SHO	SV-BS	IP	H	R	HR	HB	BB-IB	SO	ERA	AERA	OAV	OOB	AB-HR-SH	AVG	PB	SUP	APR	DL	PW
1924	Bos A	0	1	.000	4	2	0	0	22	16	10	0	4	22	3	20.57	21	.512	.553	3	.333	0	145	-11		-1.1

WINTERS, JESSE Jesse Franklin "Buck", "T-Bone" B12.22.1893 Stephenville TX D6.5.1986 Abilene TX BR/TR/6-1/165 d5.3 Col Hardin-Simmons

YEAR	TM LG	W	L	PCT	G	GS	CG-SHO	SV-BS	IP	H	R	HR	HB	BB-IB	SO	ERA	AERA	OAV	OOB	AB-HR-SH	AVG	PB	SUP	APR	DL	PW
1919	NY N	1	2	.333	16	2	1	0	28	39	18	1	3	13	6	5.46	51	.339	.420	1	.000	-0	128	-7		-1.1
1920	NY N	0	0	—	21	0	0	0	46.1	37	19	1	4	28	14	3.50	86	.223	.361	7	.000	-1		-1		-0.1
1921	Phi N	5	10	.333	18	14	10	0	114	142	73	4	4	28	22	3.63	116	.310	.355	39-0-1	.128	-3	78	3		-0.1
1922	Phi N	6	6	.500	34	9	4	2	138.1	176	100	8	4	56	29	5.33	87	.319	.386	43-0-2	.256	0	85	-7		-0.1
1923	Phi N	1	6	.143	21	6	0	1	78.1	116	76	7	4	39	23	7.35	63	.348	.423	25-0-1	.160	-1	80	-20		-3.1
Total	5	13	24	.351	110	31	15	6	405	510	286	21	19	164	94	5.04	86	.316	.385	117-0-4	.171	-5	85	-32		-3.3

YEAR	TM LG	W	L	PCT	G	GS	CG-SHO	SV-BS	IP	H	R	HR	HB	BB-IB	SO	ERA	AERA	OAV	OOB	AB-HR-SH	AVG	PB	SUP	APR	DL	PW

WIRTH, ALAN Alan Lee B12.8.1956 Mesa AZ BR/TR/6-4/190* [SFN74 3/67] d4.9

YEAR	TM LG	W	L	PCT	G	GS	CG-SHO	SV-BS	IP	H	R	HR	HB	BB-IB	SO	ERA	AERA	OAV	OOB	AB-HR-SH	AVG	PB	SUP	APR	DL	PW
1978	Oak A	5	6	.455	16	14	2-1	0-0	81.1	72	39	6	3	34-0	31	3.43	107	.252	.333	0	—	0	61	1		0.1
1979	Oak A	1	0	1.000	5	1	0	0-0	12	14	8	2	1	8-0	7	6.00	68	.298	.404	0	—	0	112	-2		-0.2
1980	Oak A	0	0	—	2	0	0	0-0	2	3	1	0	0	0-0	1	4.50	85	.333	.333	0	—	0	0			0.0
Total	3	6	6	.500	23	15	2-1	0-0	95.1	89	48	8	4	42-0	39	3.78	98	.260	.344	0	—	0	65	-1		-0.1

WISE, ARCHIE Archibald Edwin B7.31.1912 Waxahachie TX D2.2.1978 Dallas TX BR/TR/6-0/165 d7.24

YEAR	TM LG	W	L	PCT	G	GS	CG-SHO	SV-BS	IP	H	R	HR	HB	BB-IB	SO	ERA	AERA	OAV	OOB	AB-HR-SH	AVG	PB	SUP	APR	DL	PW
1932	Chi A	0	0	—	2	0	0	0	7.1	8	5	1	1	5	2	4.91	88	.258	.378	4	.000	-1*		-1		-0.1

WISE, MATT Matthew John B11.18.1975 Montclair CA BR/TR/6-4/190* [AnaA97 6/177] d8.2 Col Cal St.-Fullerton [DL 2003 Ana A 183]

YEAR	TM LG	W	L	PCT	G	GS	CG-SHO	SV-BS	IP	H	R	HR	HB	BB-IB	SO	ERA	AERA	OAV	OOB	AB-HR-SH	AVG	PB	SUP	APR	DL	PW
2000	Ana A	3	3	.500	8	6	0	0-0	37.1	40	23	7	1	13-1	20	5.54	93	.272	.331	0	—	0	79	-1		-0.1
2001	Ana A	1	4	.200	11	9	0	0-0	49.1	47	27	11	2	18-1	50	4.38	106	.250	.321	0	—	0	71	1		0.0
2002	Ana A	0	0	—	7	0	0	0-0	8.1	7	3	0	1	1-0	6	3.24	138	.233	.281	0	—	0		1		0.0
2004	Mil N	1	2	.333	30	3	0	0-0	52.2	51	27	3	2	15-1	30	4.44	99	.252	.308	4-0-1	.000	-0	49	1		0.0
2005	Mil N	4	4	.500	49	0	0	1-2	64.1	37	25	6	3	25-5	62	3.36	127	.160	.249	1	1.000	0		7	23	0.8
Total	5	9	13	.409	105	18	0	1-2	212	182	105	27	9	72-8	168	4.25	107	.228	.297	5-0-1	.200	0	74	9	206	0.7

WISE, RICK Richard Charles B9.13.1945 Jackson MI BR/TR/6-2/195* d4.18

YEAR	TM LG	W	L	PCT	G	GS	CG-SHO	SV-BS	IP	H	R	HR	HB	BB-IB	SO	ERA	AERA	OAV	OOB	AB-HR-SH	AVG	PB	SUP	APR	DL	PW
1964	Phi N	5	3	.625	25	8	0	0	69	78	41	7	3	25-2	39	4.04	86	.277	.341	17-0-2	.294	2	136	-7		-0.6
1966	Phi N	5	6	.455	22	13	3	0	99.1	100	50	5	3	24-3	58	3.71	97	.262	.308	30-0-1	.000	-4*	100	-3		-0.8
1967	Phi N	11	11	.500	36	25	6-3	0	181.1	177	69	8	4	45-5	111	3.28	104	.259	.307	53-0-2	.208	3	79	6		1.0
1968	Phi N	9	15	.375	30	30	7-1	0	182.1	210	100	12	6	37-3	97	4.54	66	.292	.330	58-2-2	.241	7	79	-29		-2.9
1969	Phi N	15	13	.536	33	31	14-4	0-0	220	215	100	17	9	61-3	144	3.23	110	.257	.307	74-1-6	.270	7	114	3		1.2
1970	Phi N	13	14	.481	34	34	5-1	0-0	220.1	215	115	15	3	65-7	113	4.17	97	.287	.337	75-2-6	.200	4*	87	-6		-0.1
1971	Phi N☆	17	14	.548	38	37	17-4	0-0	272.1	261	110	20	4	70-5	155	2.88	124	.254	.301	97-6-4	.237	9*	78	15		2.8
1972	StL N	16	16	.500	35	35	20-2	0-0	269	250	98	16	1	71-13	142	3.11	110	.251	.299	93-1-6	.172	1	96	13		1.7
1973	StL N★	16	12	.571	35	34	14-5	0-0	259	259	113	18	3	59-12	144	4.37	109	.257	.300	88-3-6	.193	6	99	8		1.4
1974	Bos A	3	4	.429	9	9	1	0-0	49	47	23	2	1	16-1	25	3.86	100	.251	.308	0	—	0	97	0	25	0.0
1975	†Bos A	19	12	.613	35	35	17-1	0-0	255.1	262	126	34	4	72-1	141	3.95	103	.263	.313	0	—	0	117	3		0.2
1976	Bos A	14	11	.560	34	34	11-4	0-0	224.1	218	100	18	2	48-1	93	3.53	110	.255	.294	0	—	0	97	9		1.0
1977	Bos A	11	5	.688	26	20	4-2	0-0	128.1	151	68	19	4	28-1	85	4.77	94	.291	.332	0	—	0	107	-1		-0.1
1978	Cle A	9	19	.321	33	31	9-1	0-0	211.2	226	116	22	3	59-3	106	4.34	87	.275	.322	0	—	0	84	-14		-1.7
1979	Cle A	15	10	.600	34	34	9-2	0-0	231.2	229	111	24	5	68-9	108	3.73	115	.256	.307	0	—	0	94	12		1.4
1980	SD N	6	8	.429	27	27	1	0-0	154.1	172	69	14	0	37-10	59	3.67	93	.285	.325	58-0-2	.138	-1*	93	-5	26	-0.5
1981	SD N	4	8	.333	18	18	0	0-0	98	116	44	10	0	19-4	27	3.77	86	.296	.327	25-0-3	.040	-2	67	-6		-0.8
1982	SD N	0	0	—	1	0	0	0-0	2	3	2	0	0	0-0	0	9.00	38	.333	.333	0	—	0		-1		-0.1
Total	18	188	181	.509	506	455	138-30	0-0	3127.1	3227	1455	261	44	804-83	1647	3.69	101	.267	.313	668-15-40	.195	34	94	-3	51	3.1

WISE, OGDEN Roy Ogden B11.18.1925 Springfield IL BB/TR/6-2/170 d5.12 Col Illinois Wesleyan

YEAR	TM LG	W	L	PCT	G	GS	CG-SHO	SV-BS	IP	H	R	HR	HB	BB-IB	SO	ERA	AERA	OAV	OOB	AB-HR-SH	AVG	PB	SUP	APR	DL	PW
1944	Pit N	0	0	—	2	0	0	0	3	4	3	0	3	3	1	9.00	41	.333	.467	0	—	0		-1		-0.1

WISE, BILL William E. B3.15.1861 Washington DC D5.5.1940 Washington DC d5.2

YEAR	TM LG	W	L	PCT	G	GS	CG-SHO	SV-BS	IP	H	R	HR	HB	BB-IB	SO	ERA	AERA	OAV	OOB	AB-HR-SH	AVG	PB	SUP	APR	DL	PW
1882	Bal AA	1	2	.333	3	3	3	0	26	30	14	1		4	9	2.77	99	.270	.296	20	.100	-1*	50	0		-0.1
1884	Was U	23	18	.561	50	41	34-4	0	364.1	383	219	5		60	268	3.04	79	.252	.281	339-2	.233	-8*	94	-23		-2.3
1886	Was N	0	1	.000	1	1	0	0	3	6	6	0	0	2	0	9.00	36	.400	.471	3	.000	-0	19	-2		-0.4
Total	3	24	21	.533	54	45	37-4	0	393.1	419	239	6		66	277	3.07	79	.255	.284	362-2	.224	-9	90	-25		-2.8

WISNER, JACK John Henry B11.5.1899 Grand Rapids MI D12.15.1981 Jackson MI BR/TR/6-3/195 d9.12 Col Eastern Michigan

YEAR	TM LG	W	L	PCT	G	GS	CG-SHO	SV-BS	IP	H	R	HR	HB	BB-IB	SO	ERA	AERA	OAV	OOB	AB-HR-SH	AVG	PB	SUP	APR	DL	PW
1919	Pit N	1	0	1.000	4	1	1	0	18.2	12	3	0	1	7	4	0.96	313	.185	.274	7	.000	-1	158	4		0.1
1920	Pit N	1	3	.250	17	2	1	0	44.2	46	19	1	1	10	13	3.43	94	.274	.318	7	.000	-1	49	0		-0.1
1925	NY N	0	0	—	25	0	0	0	40.1	33	19	4	2	14	13	3.79	106	.228	.304	7	.000	-1		2		0.0
1926	NY N	2	2	.500	5	3	2	0	28	21	12	4	0	10	5	3.54	106	.208	.279	10	.200	-0	148	1		0.1
Total	4	4	5	.444	51	6	4	0	131.2	112	53	9	4	41	35	3.21	111	.234	.300	31	.065	-3	114	7		0.1

WISTERT, WHITEY Francis Michael B2.20.1912 Chicago IL D4.23.1985 Painesville OH BR/TR/6-4/210 d9.11 Col Michigan

YEAR	TM LG	W	L	PCT	G	GS	CG-SHO	SV-BS	IP	H	R	HR	HB	BB-IB	SO	ERA	AERA	OAV	OOB	AB-HR-SH	AVG	PB	SUP	APR	DL	PW
1934	Cin N	0	1	.000	2	1	0	0	8	5	1	1	0	5	1	1.13	363	.185	.313	3	.000	-0*	0	3		0.3

WITASICK, JAY Gerald Alphonse B8.28.1972 Baltimore MD BR/TR/6-4/233(205-240) [StLN93 2/58] d7.7 Col Maryland-Baltimore Co.

YEAR	TM LG	W	L	PCT	G	GS	CG-SHO	SV-BS	IP	H	R	HR	HB	BB-IB	SO	ERA	AERA	OAV	OOB	AB-HR-SH	AVG	PB	SUP	APR	DL	PW
1996	Oak A	1	1	.500	12	0	0	0-1	13	12	9	5	0	5-0	12	6.23	80	.245	.309	0	—	0		-2		-0.2
1997	Oak A	0	0	—	8	0	0	0-0	11	14	7	2	0	6-0	8	5.73	80	.304	.385	0	—	0		-1	74	-0.1
1998	Oak A	1	3	.250	7	3	0	0-0	27	36	24	9	0	15-1	29	6.33	73	.310	.389	0	—	0	80	-6		-0.8
1999	KC A	9	12	.429	32	28	1-1	0-0	158.1	191	108	23	8	83-1	102	5.57	91	.304	.387	5	.000	-1	99	-9		-1.1
2000	KC A	3	8	.273	22	14	2	0-0	89.1	109	65	15	4	38-0	67	5.94	88	.301	.371	4	.000	-0	118	-8		-0.9
	SD N	3	2	.600	11	11	0	0-0	60.2	69	42	9	3	35-5	54	5.64	79	.284	.379	22-0-2	.136	-0	99	-8		-0.6
2001	SD N	5	2	.714	31	0	0	1-2	38.2	31	14	3	4	15-3	53	1.86	223	.218	.311	1	.000	-0		8		1.3
	†NY A	3	0	1.000	32	0	0	0-1	40.1	47	27	6	4	18-1	53	4.69	95	.283	.356	0	—	0		-3		-0.2
2002	†SF N	3	0	1.000	44	0	0	0-0	68.1	58	19	3	4	21-3	54	2.37	167	.228	.303	5	.000	-1	13	20	0.5
2003	SD N	3	7	.300	46	0	0	2-5	45.2	42	24	6	1	25-4	42	4.53	88	.244	.342	0	—	0	-3	71	-0.5
2004	SD N	0	1	.000	44	0	0	1-2	61.2	57	28	8	1	26-2	57	3.21	123	.244	.319	5	.000	-1	4	33	0.1
2005	Col N	0	4	.000	32	0	0	0-1	35.2	27	11	2	3	12-3	40	2.52	189	.209	.292	0	—	0	8		0.8
	Oak A	0	1	.500	28	0	0	1-2	27.2	26	15	2	3	17-2	33	3.25	137	.239	.357	0	—	0	2		0.1
Total	10	30	41	.423	349	56	3-1	5-14	677.1	719	393	92	33	316-25	604	4.54	101	.272	.354	42-0-2	.071	-3	112	-5	198	-1.6

WITHEM, SHANNON Shannon Bolt B9.21.1972 Ann Arbor MI BR/TR/6-3/185 [DetA90 5/130] d9.18

YEAR	TM LG	W	L	PCT	G	GS	CG-SHO	SV-BS	IP	H	R	HR	HB	BB-IB	SO	ERA	AERA	OAV	OOB	AB-HR-SH	AVG	PB	SUP	APR	DL	PW
1998	Tor A	0	0	—	1	0	0	0-0	3	3	1	0	0	2-0	2	3.00	155	.250	.357	0	—	0		1		0.0

WITHEROW, CHARLES Charles Lafayette B4.1852 Washington DC D7.3.1948 Washington DC d7.1

YEAR	TM LG	W	L	PCT	G	GS	CG-SHO	SV-BS	IP	H	R	HR	HB	BB-IB	SO	ERA	AERA	OAV	OOB	AB-HR-SH	AVG	PB	SUP	APR	DL	PW
1875	Was NA	0	1	.000	1	1	0	0	1	4	5	0		0	0	18.00	13	.444	.444	1	.000	-0	30	-1		-0.2

WITHERUP, ROY Foster Leroy B7.26.1886 N.Washington PA D12.23.1941 New Bethlehem PA BR/TR/6-0/185 d5.14

YEAR	TM LG	W	L	PCT	G	GS	CG-SHO	SV-BS	IP	H	R	HR	HB	BB-IB	SO	ERA	AERA	OAV	OOB	AB-HR-SH	AVG	PB	SUP	APR	DL	PW
1906	Bos N	0	3	.000	8	3	3	0	46	59	37	2	1	19	14	6.26	43	.322	.389	15	.133	-1	63	-15		-1.0
1908	Was A	2	4	.333	6	6	4	0	48.1	51	21	0	1	8	31	2.98	77	.264	.297	18	.167	-1	115	-3		-0.4
1909	Was A	1	5	.167	12	8	5	0	68	79	41	1	0	20	26	4.24	57	.306	.356	19-0-1	.053	-2	65	-12		-1.3
Total	3	3	12	.200	26	17	12	0	162.1	189	99	3	2	47	71	4.44	55	.298	.348	52-0-1	.115	-3	81	-30		-2.7

WITT, GEORGE George Adrian "Red" B11.9.1933 Long Beach CA BR/TR/6-3/200(185-200) d9.21

YEAR	TM LG	W	L	PCT	G	GS	CG-SHO	SV-BS	IP	H	R	HR	HB	BB-IB	SO	ERA	AERA	OAV	OOB	AB-HR-SH	AVG	PB	SUP	APR	DL	PW
1957	Pit N	0	1	.000	2	0	0	0	1.1	4	6	1	0	5-0	1	40.50	9	.500	.692	0	—	0	116	-5		-0.7
1958	Pit N	9	2	.818	18	15	5-3	0	106	78	22	2	2	59-3	81	1.61	240	.209	.318	39-0-1	.154	-1	93	27		2.5
1959	Pit N	0	7	.000	15	11	0	0	50.2	58	43	7	1	33-2	30	6.93	56	.293	.394	12-0-2	.000	-1	78	-17	32	-2.1
1960	†Pit N	1	2	.333	10	6	0	0	30	33	18	3	0	12-0	15	4.20	89	.300	.363	9	.000	-1	110	-3		-0.4
1961	Pit N	0	1	.000	9	1	0	0	15.2	17	12	5	0	5-0	9	6.32	63	.274	.328	2-0-1	.500	1	44	-4	48	-0.2
1962	LA A	1	1	.500	5	2	0	0	10	15	12	4	0	5-0	10	8.10	48	.349	.408	0	.333	0	139	-5		-0.9
	Hou N	0	2	.000	8	2	0	0	15.1	20	14	2	1	9-0	10	7.04	53	.339	.423	4	.250	0	23	-6		-0.6
Total	6	11	16	.407	66	38	5-3	0	229	225	127	24	4	127-5	156	4.42	89	.263	.359	69-0-4	.130	-2	89	-13	80	-2.4

WITT, MIKE Michael Atwater B7.20.1960 Fullerton CA BR/TR/6-7/192(185-203) [CalA78 4/92] d4.11 [DL 1992 NY A 182]

YEAR	TM LG	W	L	PCT	G	GS	CG-SHO	SV-BS	IP	H	R	HR	HB	BB-IB	SO	ERA	AERA	OAV	OOB	AB-HR-SH	AVG	PB	SUP	APR	DL	PW
1981	Cal A	8	9	.471	22	21	7-1	0-0	129	123	60	9	11	47-4	75	3.28	112	.251	.328	0	—	0	111	3		0.3
1982	†Cal A	8	6	.571	33	26	5-1	0-0	179.2	177	77	8	7	47-2	85	3.51	117	.260	.312	0	—	0	105	11		0.8
1983	Cal A	7	14	.333	43	19	2	5-3	154	173	90	14	6	75-7	77	4.91	82	.293	.375	0	—	0	102	-14		-1.7
1984	Cal A	15	11	.577	34	34	9-2	0-0	246.2	227	103	17	5	84-3	196	3.47	115	.244	.308	0	—	0	93	15		1.4
1985	Cal A	15	9	.625	35	35	6-1	0-0	250	228	115	22	4	98-6	180	3.56	116	.243	.316	0	—	0	105	12		1.2
1986	†Cal A☆	18	10	.643	34	34	14-3	0-0	269	218	95	22	3	73-2	208	2.84	145	.221	.275	0	—	0	115	38		3.8
1987	Cal A☆	16	14	.533	36	36	10	0-0	247	252	128	34	4	84-4	192	4.01	108	.261	.321	0	—	0	93	7		0.7
1988	Cal A	13	16	.448	34	34	12-2	0-0	249.2	263	130	14	5	87-7	133	4.15	94	.272	.332	0	—	0	91	-9		-0.9
1989	Cal A	9	15	.375	33	33	5	0-0	220	252	119	26	2	48-1	123	4.54	84	.292	.326	0	—	0	99	-17		-1.5
1990	Cal A	0	3	.000	10	0	0	1-2	20.1	19	9	1	1	13-2	14	1.77	217	.250	.363	0	—	0		3		0.4
	NY A	5	6	.455	16	16	2-1	0-0	96.2	87	56	8	4	34-2	60	4.47	89	.240	.308	0	—	0	87	-5	59	-0.5

YEAR	TM LG	W	L	PCT	G	GS	CG-SHO	SV-BS	IP	H	R	HR	HB	BB-IB	SO	ERA	AERA	OAV	OOB	AB-HR-SH	AVG	PB	SUP	APR	DL	PW
	Year	5	9	.357	26	16	2-1	1-2	117	106	62	9	5	47-4	74	4.00	99	.241	.318	0	—	0	87	-1		-0.1
1991	NY A	0	1	.000	2	2	0	0-0	5.1	8	7	1	0	1-0	0	10.13	41	.320	.346	0	—	0	88	-4	175	-0.5
1993	NY A	3	2	.600	9	9	0	0-0	41	39	26	7	3	22-0	30	5.27	79	.248	.352	0	—	0	122	-5	144	-0.5
Total	12	117	116	.502	341	299	72-11	6-5	2108.1	2066	1012	183	55	713-40	1373	3.83	105	.257	.320	0	—	0	99	36	560	3.0

WITT, BOBBY Robert Andrew B5.11.1964 Arlington MA BR/TR/6-2/205(200-215) [TexA85 1/3] d4.10 Col Oklahoma

YEAR	TM LG	W	L	PCT	G	GS	CG-SHO	SV-BS	IP	H	R	HR	HB	BB-IB	SO	ERA	AERA	OAV	OOB	AB-HR-SH	AVG	PB	SUP	APR	DL	PW
1986	Tex A	11	9	.550	31	31	0	0-0	157.2	130	104	18	3	143-2	174	5.48	79	.223	.374	0	—	0	106	-18		-1.9
1987	Tex A	8	10	.444	26	25	1	0-0	143	114	82	10	3	140-1	160	4.91	92	.219	.385	1	.000	-0*	89	-3	30	-0.3
1988	Tex A	8	10	.444	22	22	13-2	0-0	174.1	134	83	13	1	101-2	148	3.92	105	.216	.324	0	—	0	83	5		0.4
1989	Tex A	12	13	.480	31	31	5-1	0-0	194.1	182	123	14	2	114-3	166	5.14	78	.248	.347	0	—	0	106	-23		-2.6
1990	Tex A	17	10	.630	33	32	7-1	0-0	222	197	98	12	4	110-3	221	3.36	117	.238	.328	0	—	0*	99	12		1.3
1991	Tex A	3	7	.300	17	16	1-1	0-0	88.2	84	66	4	1	74-1	82	6.09	67	.254	.388	0	—	0	120	-20	66	-2.0
1992	Tex A	9	13	.409	25	25	0	0-0	161.1	152	87	14	2	95-1	100	4.46	86	.254	.354	0	—	0	93	-10		-1.3
	†Oak A	1	1	.500	6	6	0	0-0	31.2	31	12	2	0	19-1	25	3.41	111	.265	.362	0	—	0	93	2		0.1
	Year	10	14	.417	31	31	0	0-0	193	183	99	16	2	114-2	125	4.29	89	.256	.356	0	—	0	93	-8		-1.2
1993	Oak A	14	13	.519	35	33	5-1	0-0	220	226	112	16	3	91-5	131	4.21	98	.269	.340	0	—	0	86	-3		-0.2
1994	Oak A	8	10	.444	24	24	5-3	0-0	135.2	151	88	22	5	70-4	111	5.04	89	.283	.367	0	—	0*	102	-11		-1.2
1995	Fla N	2	7	.222	19	19	1	0-0	110.2	104	52	6	2	47-1	95	3.90	110	.251	.328	32-0-4	.063	-2*	74	5		0.2
	Tex A	3	4	.429	10	10	1	0-0	61.1	81	35	4	1	21-1	46	4.55	106	.324	.376	0	—	0	67	1		-0.1
1996	†Tex A	16	12	.571	33	32	3	0-0	199.2	235	129	28	2	96-3	157	5.41	97	.295	.370	0	—	0	94	-3		-0.4
1997	Tex A	12	12	.500	34	32	3	0-0	209	245	118	30	2	74-4	121	4.82	101	.294	.350	6-1-0	.333	2*	93	3		0.4
1998	Tex A	5	4	.556	14	13	0	0-0	69.1	95	62	14	0	33-1	30	7.66	64	.328	.391	1	.000	-0*	142	-19		-2.0
	StL N	2	5	.286	17	5	0	0-0	47.1	55	32	7	2	20-1	28	4.94	85	.289	.362	10-0-1	.200	1	61	-5		-0.6
1999	TB A	7	15	.318	32	32	3-2	0-0	180.1	213	130	23	3	96-1	123	5.84	85	.304	.386	2	.000	-0	80	-16		-0.2
2000	Cle A	0	1	.000	7	2	0	0-0	15.1	28	13	4	0	6-1	6	7.63	66	.394	.442	0	—	0	112	-4		-0.2
2001	Ari N	4	1	.800	7	1	0	0-0	43.1	36	23	6	3	25-1	31	4.78	97	.222	.333	12-0-1	.250	0	108	0	120	0.3
Total	16	142	157	.475	430	397	47-11	0-0	2465	2493	1449	252	39	1375-37	1955	4.83	91	.265	.358	64-1-6	.141	0	95	-107	216	-11.8

WITTIG, JOHNNIE John Carl "Hans" B6.16.1914 Baltimore MD D2.24.1999 Nassawadox VA BR/TR/6-0/180 d8.4 Def 1944-45

YEAR	TM LG	W	L	PCT	G	GS	CG-SHO	SV-BS	IP	H	R	HR	HB	BB-IB	SO	ERA	AERA	OAV	OOB	AB-HR-SH	AVG	PB	SUP	APR	DL	PW
1938	NY N	2	3	.400	13	6	2	0	39.1	41	22	4	0	26	14	4.81	78	.263	.368	10-0-1	.000	-1	90	-3		-0.6
1939	NY N	0	2	.000	5	2	1	0	16.2	18	15	0	1	14	4	7.56	52	.281	.418	5	.000	-1	56	-6		-0.7
1941	NY N	3	5	.375	25	9	0	0	85.1	111	57	5	1	45	47	5.59	66	.319	.398	25-0-1	.200	0	61	-16		-1.4
1943	NY N	5	15	.250	40	22	4-1	4	164	172	85	14	0	76	56	4.23	82	.273	.352	51-0-2	.098	-3	81	-13		-2.1
1949	Bos A	0	0	—	1	0	0	0	2	2	2	0	0	2	0	9.00	48	.286	.444	0	—	0		-1		-0.1
Total	5	10	25	.286	84	39	7-1	4	307.1	344	181	23	2	163	121	4.89	73	.286	.372	91-0-4	.110	-6	76	-39		-4.8

WOHLERS, MARK Mark Edward B1.23.1970 Holyoke MA BR/TR/6-4/207* [AtlN88 8/190] d8.17 [DL 1999 Cin N 171, 2003 Cle A 183]

YEAR	TM LG	W	L	PCT	G	GS	CG-SHO	SV-BS	IP	H	R	HR	HB	BB-IB	SO	ERA	AERA	OAV	OOB	AB-HR-SH	AVG	PB	SUP	APR	DL	PW
1991	†Atl N	3	1	.750	17	0	0	2-2	19.2	17	7	1	2	13-3	13	3.20	121	.239	.368	1	.000	-0		2		0.4
1992	†Atl N	1	2	.333	32	0	0	4-2	35.1	28	11	0	1	14-4	17	2.55	144	.235	.319	2	.000	-0		4		0.4
1993	†Atl N	6	2	.750	46	0	0	0-0	48	37	25	2	1	22-3	45	4.50	90	.218	.309	2		-0		-2		-0.2
1994	Atl N	7	2	.778	51	0	0	1-1	51	51	35	1	0	33-9	58	4.59	94	.264	.362	1-0-1	1.000	0		-4		-0.6
1995	Atl N	7	3	.700	65	0	0	25-4	64.2	51	16	2	1	24-3	90	2.09	207	.211	.285	3	.000	-0		16		3.1
1996	†Atl N★	2	4	.333	77	0	0	39-5	77.1	71	30	8	2	21-3	100	3.03	147	.240	.293	3	.000	-0		11		1.7
1997	†Atl N	5	7	.417	71	0	0	33-7	69.1	57	29	4	0	38-0	92	3.50	120	.224	.321	2	.000	-0		6		1.1
1998	Atl N	0	1	.000	27	0	0	8-0	20.1	18	23	2	1	33-0	22	10.18	41	.231	.464	0	—			-13	59	-1.4
1999	Atl N	0	0	—	2	0	0	0-0	0.2	1	2	0	0	6-0	0	27.00	17	.333	.778	0	—	0		-2		-0.1
2000	Cin N	1	2	.333	20	0	0	0-0	28	19	14	3	0	17-0	20	4.50	106	.192	.308	0	—	0		1		0.0
2001	Cin N	3	1	.750	30	0	0	0-1	32	36	20	5	1	7-2	21	3.94	117	.286	.326	0	—	0		0		0.0
	†NY A	1	0	1.000	31	0	0	0-0	35.2	33	20	3	1	18-0	33	4.54	98	.241	.329	0	—	0		-1		0.0
2002	Cle A	3	4	.429	64	0	0	7-4	71.1	71	41	6	3	26-3	46	4.79	93	.261	.330	0	—	0		-3		-0.3
Total	12	39	29	.574	533	0	0	119-26	553.1	490	273	37	13	272-30	557	3.97	108	.238	.328	12-0-1	.083	-1		15	413	4.2

WOJCIECHOWSKI, STEVE Steven Joseph B7.29.1970 Blue Island IL BL/TL/6-2/195(185-202) [OakA91 4/125] d7.18 Col St. Xavier

YEAR	TM LG	W	L	PCT	G	GS	CG-SHO	SV-BS	IP	H	R	HR	HB	BB-IB	SO	ERA	AERA	OAV	OOB	AB-HR-SH	AVG	PB	SUP	APR	DL	PW
1995	Oak A	2	3	.400	14	7	0	0-0	48.2	51	28	7	1	28-1	13	5.18	87	.273	.367	0	—	0	106	-3		-0.2
1996	Oak A	5	5	.500	16	15	0	0-0	79.2	97	57	10	2	28-0	30	5.65	88	.300	.358	0	—	0*	117	-8		-0.8
1997	Oak A	0	2	.000	2	2	0	0-0	10.1	17	9	2	0	1-0	5	7.84	59	.386	.400	0	—	0	50	-3	72	-0.5
Total	3	7	10	.412	32	24	0	0-0	138.2	165	94	19	3	57-1	48	5.65	85	.298	.364	0	—	0	109	-14	72	-1.5

WOJEY, PETE Peter Paul B12.1.1919 Stowe PA D4.23.1991 Mobile AL BR/TR/5-11/185* d7.2

YEAR	TM LG	W	L	PCT	G	GS	CG-SHO	SV-BS	IP	H	R	HR	HB	BB-IB	SO	ERA	AERA	OAV	OOB	AB-HR-SH	AVG	PB	SUP	APR	DL	PW
1954	Bro N	1	1	.500	14	1	0	1	27.2	24	13	3	2	14	21	3.25	126	.242	.348	3-0-1	.000	-0	131	2		0.1
1956	Det A	0	0	—	2	0	0	0	4	2	1	0	0	1-0	1	2.25	183	.167	.231	0	—	0		1		0.1
1957	Det A	0	0	—	2	0	0	0	1.1	1	0	0	0	0-0	0	0.00	—	.200	.200	0	—	0		1		0.0
Total	3	1	1	.500	18	1	0	1	33	27	14	3	2	15-0	22	3.00	136	.233	.331	3-0-1	.000	-0	131	4		0.2

WOJNA, ED Edward David B8.20.1960 Bridgeport CT BR/TR/6-1/185* [PhiN80 S5/77] d6.16 Col Indian River (FL) CC

YEAR	TM LG	W	L	PCT	G	GS	CG-SHO	SV-BS	IP	H	R	HR	HB	BB-IB	SO	ERA	AERA	OAV	OOB	AB-HR-SH	AVG	PB	SUP	APR	DL	PW
1985	SD N	2	4	.333	15	7	0	0-0	42	53	35	6	3	19-0	18	5.79	61	.312	.385	12	.167	-0	110	-13		-1.6
1986	SD N	2	2	.500	7	7	1	0-0	39	42	19	2	1	16-3	19	3.23	113	.268	.339	14-0-2	.143	-0	118	0		0.0
1987	SD N	0	3	.000	5	3	0	0-0	18.1	25	12	2	1	6-0	13	5.89	67	.333	.386	5	.000	-1	23	-3		-0.5
1989	Cle A	0	1	.000	9	3	0	0-0	33	31	17	0	0	14-1	10	4.09	97	.254	.328	0	—	0	99	-1		-0.1
Total	4	4	10	.286	36	20	1	0-0	132.1	151	83	10	5	55-4	60	4.62	81	.288	.358	31-0-2	.129	-1	97	-17		-2.1

WOLCOTT, BOB Robert William B9.8.1973 Huntington Beach CA BR/TR/6-0/195* [SeaA92 2/52] d8.18

YEAR	TM LG	W	L	PCT	G	GS	CG-SHO	SV-BS	IP	H	R	HR	HB	BB-IB	SO	ERA	AERA	OAV	OOB	AB-HR-SH	AVG	PB	SUP	APR	DL	PW
1995	†Sea A	3	2	.600	7	6	0	0-0	36.2	43	18	6	2	14-0	19	4.42	108	.297	.360	0	—	0	107	2		0.2
1996	Sea A	7	10	.412	30	28	1	0-0	149.1	179	101	26	7	54-5	78	5.73	87	.297	.360	0	—	0	110	-12		-1.1
1997	Sea A	5	6	.455	19	18	0	0-0	100	129	71	22	5	29-2	58	6.03	75	.314	.365	1	.000	-0	125	-16		-1.5
1998	Ari N	1	3	.250	6	6	0	0-0	33	32	27	7	0	13-1	21	7.09	60	.252	.321	9	.222	0	72	-9		-0.9
1999	Bos A	0	0	—	4	0	0	0-0	6.2	8	6	1	1	3-0	2	8.10	62	.333	.414	0	—	0		-2		-0.1
Total	5	16	21	.432	66	58	1	0-0	325.2	391	223	62	15	113-8	178	5.86	81	.298	.359	10	.200	0	110	-37		-3.4

WOLF, ERNIE Ernest Adolph B2.2.1889 Newark NJ D5.23.1964 Atlantic Highlands NJ BR/TR/5-11/174 d9.10

YEAR	TM LG	W	L	PCT	G	GS	CG-SHO	SV-BS	IP	H	R	HR	HB	BB-IB	SO	ERA	AERA	OAV	OOB	AB-HR-SH	AVG	PB	SUP	APR	DL	PW
1912	Cle A	0	1	.000	8	1	0	0	5.2	8	6	0	0	3-0	2	6.35	54	.348	.444	2	.000	-0		-2		-0.1

WOLF, RANDY Randall Christopher B8.22.1976 Canoga Park CA BL/TL/6-0/194* [PhiN97 2/54] d6.11 Col Pepperdine

YEAR	TM LG	W	L	PCT	G	GS	CG-SHO	SV-BS	IP	H	R	HR	HB	BB-IB	SO	ERA	AERA	OAV	OOB	AB-HR-SH	AVG	PB	SUP	APR	DL	PW
1999	Phi N	6	9	.400	22	21	0	0-0	121.2	126	78	20	4	67-0	116	5.55	84	.266	.362	30-0-7	.233	1	99	-10		-0.9
2000	Phi N	11	9	.550	32	32	1	0-0	206.1	210	107	25	8	83-2	160	4.36	105	.269	.342	57-0-10	.193	2	86	6		0.6
2001	Phi N	10	11	.476	28	25	2	0-0	163	150	74	15	10	51-4	152	3.70	111	.248	.314	45-0-5	.178	1	91	7	30	0.3
2002	Phi N	11	9	.550	31	31	3-2	0-0	210.2	172	77	23	7	63-5	172	3.20	120	.223	.285	59-1-12	.136	2*	87	18	12	1.7
2003	Phi N★	16	10	.615	33	33	2-2	0-0	200	176	101	27	6	78-4	177	4.23	94	.233	.309	74-0-6	.200	5	130	-6		-0.2
2004	Phi N	5	6	.385	23	23	1-1	0-0	136.2	145	73	20	5	36-4	89	4.28	104	.271	.321	45-3-8	.267	5*	112	1	59	0.1
2005	Phi N	6	4	.600	13	13	0	0-0	80	87	46	14	6	26-2	61	4.39	99	.282	.348	26-0-1	.154	0*	102	1	113	0.1
Total	7	65	60	.520	182	178	11-7	0-0	1118.1	1066	550	144	47	404-21	927	4.14	102	.252	.322	332-4-49	.193	16	101	17	214	2.7

WOLF, WALLY Walter Beck B1.5.1942 Los Angeles CA BR/TR/6-0.5/191* d9.27 Col USC

YEAR	TM LG	W	L	PCT	G	GS	CG-SHO	SV-BS	IP	H	R	HR	HB	BB-IB	SO	ERA	AERA	OAV	OOB	AB-HR-SH	AVG	PB	SUP	APR	DL	PW
1969	Cal A	0	0	—	2	0	0	0	2.1	3	3	0	0	3-0	2	11.57	30	.333	.500	0	—	0		-2		-0.1
1970	Cal A	0	0	—	4	0	0	0	5.1	3	3	1	0	4-0	5	5.06	72	.176	.333	0	—	0		-1		0.0
Total	2	0	0	—	6	0	0	0	7.2	6	6	1	0	7-0	7	7.04	51	.231	.394	0	—	0		-3		-0.1

WOLF, LEFTY Walter Francis B6.10.1900 Hartford CT D9.25.1971 New Orleans LA BR/TL/5-10/163 d7.4 Col Lebanon Valley

YEAR	TM LG	W	L	PCT	G	GS	CG-SHO	SV-BS	IP	H	R	HR	HB	BB-IB	SO	ERA	AERA	OAV	OOB	AB-HR-SH	AVG	PB	SUP	APR	DL	PW
1921	Phi A	0	0	—	8	0	0	0	15	15	15	0	2	16	11	7.20	62	.273	.452	4	.250	-0		-4		-0.2

WOLF, JIMMY William Van Winkle "Chicken" B5.12.1862 Louisville KY D5.16.1903 Louisville KY BR/TR/5-9/190 d5.2 M1 ▲

YEAR	TM LG	W	L	PCT	G	GS	CG-SHO	SV-BS	IP	H	R	HR	HB	BB-IB	SO	ERA	AERA	OAV	OOB	AB-HR-SH	AVG	PB	SUP	APR	DL	PW
1882	Lou AA	0	0	—	1	0	1	0	6	11	11	0		3	1	9.00	28	.367	.424	318	.299	0*		-4		-0.2
1885	Lou AA	0	0	—	1	0	0	0	1	1	2	0	0	3	1	9.00	36	.200	.200	483-1	.292	0*		-1		0.0
1886	Lou AA	0	0	—	1	0	0	0	3	7	8	0	0	0	0	15.00	24	.350	.350	545-3	.272	0*		-3		-0.1
Total	3	0	0	—	3	0	1	0	10	19	21	0	0	6	2	10.80	27	.345	.379	1346-4	.285	1		-8		-0.2

WOLFE, CHUCK Charles Hunt B2.15.1897 Wolfsburg PA D11.27.1957 Schellsburg PA BL/TL/5-7/175 d8.2

YEAR	TM LG	W	L	PCT	G	GS	CG-SHO	SV-BS	IP	H	R	HR	HB	BB-IB	SO	ERA	AERA	OAV	OOB	AB-HR-SH	AVG	PB	SUP	APR	DL	PW
1923	Phi A	0	0	—	3	0	0	0	9.2	6	4	1	0	8	1	3.72	110	.194	.359	3	.333	0		1		0.0

YEAR	TM LG	W	L	PCT	G	GS	CG-SHO	SV-BS	IP	H	R	HR	HB	BB-IB	SO	ERA	AERA	OAV	OOB	AB-HR-SH	AVG	PB	SUP	APR	DL	PW

WOLFE, ED Edward Anthony B1.2.1928 Los Angeles CA BR/TR/6-3/185 d4.19

| 1952 | Pit N | 0 | 0 | — | 3 | 0 | 0 | 0 | 3.2 | 3 | 1 | 1 | 1 | 5 | 1 | 7.36 | 54 | .467 | .619 | 0 | — | 0 | | -1 | | 0.0 |

WOLFE, BARNEY Wilbert Otto B1.9.1876 Independence (now Allenport) PA D2.27.1953 N.Charleroi PA BR/TR/6-1/? d4.24

1903	NY A	6	9	.400	20	16	12-1	0	148.1	143	66	1	6	26	48	2.97	105	.253	.293	53-0-1	.075	-4	89	3		-0.2
1904	NY A	0	3	.000	7	3	2	0	33.2	31	18	1	2	4	8	3.21	85	.246	.280	10-0-1	.000	-1	44	-2		-0.3
	Was A	6	10	.375	17	16	13-2	0	126.2	131	64	0	11	22	44	3.27	81	.268	.314	42-0-2	.119	-2	82	-9		-1.3
	Year	6	13	.316	24	19	15-2	0	160.1	162	82	1	13	26	52	3.26	82	.263	.307	52-0-3	.096	-3	76	-10		-1.6
1905	Was A	9	14	.391	28	23	17-1	1	182	162	76	1	8	37	52	2.57	103	.240	.287	63-1-0	.127	-1	66	1		-0.2
1906	Was A	0	3	.000	4	3	2	0	20	17	11	0	2	10	8	4.05	65	.233	.341	7	.286	-0	55	-3		-0.3
Total	4	21	39	.350	76	61	46-4	1	510.2	484	235	3	29	99	160	2.96	94	.251	.298	175-1-4	.109	-8	75	-10		-2.3

WOLFE, BILL William B Jersey City NJ d9.10

| 1902 | Phi N | 0 | 1 | .000 | 1 | 1 | 1 | 0 | 9 | 11 | 5 | 0 | 1 | 4 | 3 | 4.00 | 70 | .297 | .381 | 3 | .333 | | 0 | 24 | -1 | | -0.1 |

WOLFF, ROGER Roger Francis B4.10.1911 Evansville IL D3.23.1994 Chester IL BR/TR/6-0.5/208 d9.20

1941	Phi A	0	2	.000	7	2	1	0	17	15	6	0	0	4	3	3.18	132	.231	.275	5	.200	-0	10	2		0.2
1942	Phi A	12	15	.444	32	25	15-2	3	214.1	206	99	16	3	69	94	3.32	114	.249	.309	68-0-4	.088	-3	72	8		0.7
1943	Phi A	10	15	.400	41	26	13-2	6	221	232	97	11	4	72	91	3.54	96	.274	.334	74-0-3	.122	-4	78	-2		-0.8
1944	Was A	4	15	.211	33	21	9	2	155	186	107	9	6	60	73	4.99	65	.295	.362	55-0-1	.218	1	101	-32		-3.4
1945	Was A	20	10	.667	33	29	21-4	2	250	200	68	7	1	53	108	2.12	146	.215	.258	84-0-5	.107	-5	101	31		3.3
1946	Was A	5	8	.385	21	17	6	0	122	115	51	2	5	30	50	2.58	130	.249	.302	39-0-2	.103	-1	113	7		0.6
1947	Cle A	0	0	—	7	2	0	0	16	15	7	1	2	10	5	3.94	88	.259	.386	3-0-2	.000	-0	102	-1		0.0
	Pit N	1	4	.200	13	6	1	0	30	49	33	4	1	18	7	8.70	43	.368	.447	9	.000	-1	129	-14		-2.0
Total	7	52	69	.430	182	128	63-8	13	1025.1	1018	468	56	22	316	430	3.41	100	.258	.316	337-0-17	.122	-13	92	-1		-1.4

WOLFGANG, MELLIE Meldon John "Red" B3.20.1890 Albany NY D6.30.1947 Albany NY BR/TR/5-9/160 d4.18

1914	Chi A	9	5	.643	24	11	9-2	0	119.1	96	42	0	0	32	50	1.89	142	.219	.272	40-0-2	.175	-0	79	9		1.3
1915	Chi A	2	2	.500	17	2	0	0	53.2	39	18	0	1	12	21	1.84	161	.211	.263	17-0-1	.118	-1	98	5		0.2
1916	Chi A	4	6	.400	27	14	6-1	0	127	103	39	2	2	42	36	1.98	139	.228	.296	40-0-2	.225	0*	90	11		0.9
1917	Chi A	0	0	—	5	0	0	0	17.2	18	10	1	1	6	3	5.09	52	.305	.379	4	.000	-1		-3		-0.3
1918	Chi A	0	1	.000	4	0	0	0	8.1	12	6	0	0	3	1	5.40	51	.333	.385	2	.500	0*		-2		-0.2
Total	5	15	14	.517	77	27	15-3	0	326	268	115	3	4	95	111	2.18	127	.229	.289	103-0-5	.184	-1	85	20		1.9

WOLTER, HARRY Harry Meiggs B7.11.1884 Monterey CA D7.6.1970 Palo Alto CA BL/TL/5-10/175 d5.14 Col Santa Clara ▲

1907	Pit N	0	0	—	2	0	0	0	2	3	2	0	0	2	0	4.50	54	.333	.455	1	.000	-0		-1		-0.1
	StL N	0	2	.000	3	3	1	0	23	27	13	1	2	18	8	4.30	58	.318	.448	47	.340	1*	104	-3		-0.2
	Year	0	2	.000	4	3	1	0	25	30	15	1	2	20	8	4.32	58	.319	.448	48	.333	1	105	0		-0.3
1909	Bos A	4	4	.500	11	6	0	0	59	66	33	0	4	30	21	3.51	71	.303	.397	121-2-5	.240	2*	94	-7		-0.8
Total	2	4	6	.400	15	9	1	0	84	96	48	1	6	50	29	3.75	67	.308	.413	169-2-5	.266	3	97	-11		-1.1

WOLTERS, RYNIE Reinder Albertus B3.17.1842 Schantz, Netherlands D1.3.1917 Newark NJ TR/6-0/165 d5.18

1871	Mut NA	16	16	.500	32	32	31-1	0	283	345	283	7		39	22	3.43	110	.263	.285	138	.370	20	97	12		2.0
1872	Cle NA	3	6	.333	12	8	5	0	75.1	115	106	3		7	4	6.09	58	.304	.317	69	.232	-0*	89	-23		-1.7
1873	Res NA	0	1	.000	1	1	1	0	9	13	23	0		1	1	0.00	—	.220	.233	4	.000	-1	53	1		0.0
Total	3 NA	19	23	.452	45	41	37-1	0	367.1	473	412	10		47	27	3.90	96	.271	.290	211	.318	19	94	-10		0.3

WOMACK, DOOLEY Horace Guy B8.25.1939 Columbia SC BL/TR/6-0/170* d4.14

1966	NY A	7	3	.700	42	0	0	4	75	52	25	6	3	23-3	50	2.64	126	.198	.270	5	.200	0	53	6		1.0
1967	NY A	5	6	.455	65	0	0	18	97	80	33	6	3	35-14	57*	2.41	130	.230	.300	14	.286	1		7		1.4
1968	NY A	3	7	.300	45	0	0	2	61.2	53	23	6	1	29-9	27	3.21	91	.244	.335	5	.200	0		-1		0.0
1969	Hou N	2	1	.667	30	0	0	0-1	51.1	49	21	1	3	20-5	32	3.51	101	.259	.338	6-0-1	.167	-0		1		0.2
	Sea N	2	1	.667	9	0	0	0-0	14.1	14	4	0	0	3-2	8	2.51	145	.273	.310	1	.000	-0		2		0.4
1970	Oak A	0	0	—	2	0	0	0-0	3	4	5	2	0	1-0	3	15.00	24	.308	.357	0	—	0		-4		-0.2
Total	5	19	18	.514	193	1	0	24-1	302.1	253	111	21	10	111-33	177	2.95	110	.233	.308	31-0-1	.226	1	53	11		2.8

WOOD, SPADES Charles Asher B1.13.1909 Spartanburg SC D5.18.1986 Wichita KS BL/TL/5-10.5/150 d8.16 Col Wofford

1930	Pit N	4	3	.571	9	7	4-2	0	58	61	34	4	0	32	23	5.12	97	.270	.360	20-0-2	.250	1	105	-1		0.1
1931	Pit N	2	6	.250	15	10	2	0	64	69	45	2	1	46	33	6.05	64	.273	.387	22-0-1	.227	1*	96	-13		-1.3
Total	2	6	9	.400	24	17	6-2	0	122	130	79	6	1	78	56	5.61	78	.271	.375	42-0-3	.238	1	99	-12		-1.2

WOOD, GEORGE George A. "Dandy" B11.9.1858 Boston MA D4.4.1924 Harrisburg PA BL/TR/5-10.5/175 d5.1.1880 M1/U1 ▲

1883	Det N	0	0	—	1	0	0	0	5	8	9	0		3	0	7.20	43	.348	.423	441-5	.302	0*		-3		-0.1
1885	Det N	0	0	—	1	0	0	0	4	5	2	0		1	1	0.00	—	.333	.375	362-5	.290	0*		1		0.0
1888	Phi N	0	0	—	2	0	0	2	2	3	3	0	0	1	0	4.50	66	.300	.364	433-6	.229	0*		-1		-0.1
1889	Phi N	0	0	—	1	0	0	0	1	2	2	0	0	0	2	18.00	24	.400	.400	422-5	.251	0*		-1		-0.0
Total	4	0	0	—	5	0	0	2	12	18	16	0	0	5	3	5.25	59	.340	.397	1658-21	.267	1		-4		-0.2

WOOD, JOE Joe "Smokey Joe" (b Howard Ellsworth Wood) B10.25.1889 Kansas City MO D7.27.1985 West Haven CT BR/TR/5-11/180 d8.24 s-Joe ▲

1908	Bos A	1	1	.500	6	2	1-1	0	22.2	14	12	0	1	16	11	2.38	104	.163	.298	7	.000	-1	125	-1		-0.2
1909	Bos A	11	7	.611	24	19	13-4	0	160.2	121	51	1	6	43	88	2.18	114	.209	.270	55-0-1	.164	-0	93	7		0.5
1910	Bos A	12	13	.480	35	17	14-3	0	196.2	155	81	3	10	56	145	1.69	151	.220	.287	69-1-3	.261	5	93	9		1.9
1911	Bos A	23	17	.575	44	33	25-5	3	275.2	226	113	2	11	76	231	2.02	162	.223	.284	88-2-6	.261	9	105	34		5.7
1912	†Bos A	34	5	.872	43	38	35-10	1	344	267	104	2	12	82	258	1.91	178	.216	.272	124-1-6	.290	11	122	53		7.6
1913	Bos A	11	5	.688	23	18	12-1	2	145.2	120	54	0	8	61	123	2.29	129	.232	.323	56-0-1	.268	4*	148	9		1.8
1914	Bos A	10	3	.769	18	14	11-1	0	113.1	94	38	1	0	34	67	2.62	103	.229	.288	43-0-1	.140	-0*	110	3		0.4
1915	Bos A	15	5	.750	25	16	10-3	2	157.1	120	32	1	1	44	63	1.49	187	.216	.275	54-1-5	.259	4*	116	25		3.9
1917	Cle A	0	1	.000	5	1	0	1	15.2	17	7	0	0	7	2	3.45	82	.309	.387	6	.000	-1*	76	-1		-0.1
1919	Cle A	0	0	—	1	0	0	0	0.2	1	0	0	0	0	0	0.00	—	.000	.000	192-0-9	.255	0*		0		0.1
1920	†Cle A	0	0	—	1	0	0	0	2	4	5	0	0	1	1	22.50	17	.444	.545	137-1-12	.270	0*		-4		-0.2
Total	11	117	57	.672	225	158	121-28	10	1434.1	1138	497	10	49	421	989	2.03	146	.220	.285	831-6-44	.249	31	114	134		21.4

WOOD, JOE Joe Frank B5.20.1916 Shohola PA D10.10.2002 Old Saybrook CT BR/TR/6-0/190 d5.1 f-Joe Col Yale

| 1944 | Bos A | 0 | 1 | .000 | 3 | 1 | 0 | 0 | 9.2 | 13 | 9 | 0 | 0 | 3 | 5 | 6.52 | 52 | .317 | .364 | 2 | .000 | 0 | 25 | -4 | | -0.4 |

WOOD, JOHN John B. B5.1872 Harrisburg PA D1.30.1929 Philadelphia PA 5-7/142 d5.9

| 1896 | StL N | 0 | 0 | — | 1 | 0 | 0 | 0 | 0 | 1 | 1 | 0 | 1 | 2 | 0 | ∞ | — | 1.000 | 1.000 | 0 | — | 0 | | -1 | | -0.1 |

WOOD, KERRY Kerry Lee B6.16.1977 Irving TX BR/TR/6-5/220* [ChiN95 1/4] d4.12 [DL 1999 Chi N 182]

1998	†Chi N	13	6	.684	26	26	1-1	0-0	166.2	117	69	14	11	85-1	233	3.40	129	.196	.306	54-2-8	.130	-0	111	17		1.7
2000	Chi N	8	7	.533	23	23	1	0-0	137	112	77	17	9	87-0	132	4.80	95	.226	.349	40-1-4	.250	3*	96	-3	55	0.0
2001	Chi N	12	6	.667	28	28	1-1	0-0	174.1	127	70	16	10	92-3	217	3.36	125	.202	.311	48-0-13	.188	1*	92	17	34	1.7
2002	Chi N	12	11	.522	33	33	4-1	0-0	213.2	169	92	22	16	97-5	217	3.66	111	.221	.300	72-1-6	.167	1	113	11		1.1
2003	†Chi N★	14	11	.560	32	32	4-2	0-0	211	152	77	24	21	100-2	266	3.20	136	.203	.312	61-2-8	.164	1	98	29		3.3
2004	Chi N	8	9	.471	22	22	0	0-0	140.1	127	62	16	11	51-0	144	3.72	119	.244	.321	45-1-5	.133	0	87	11	60	1.1
2005	Chi N	3	4	.429	21	10	0	0-0	66	52	32	14	2	26-0	77	4.23	104	.215	.295	18-0-2	.111	-0	100	2	108	0.1
Total	7	70	54	.565	185	174	11-5	0-0	1109	856	479	123	80	538-11	1286	3.67	118	.214	.317	338-7-46	.166	6	100	84	439	9.0

WOOD, MIKE Michael Burton B4.26.1980 West Palm Beach FL BR/TR/6-3/190(190-210) [OakA01 10/311] d8.21 Col North Florida

2003	Oak A	2	1	.667	7	1	0	0-0	13.2	24	17	1	2	7-2	15	10.54	44	.387	.465	0	—	0	60	-9		-1.4
2004	KC A	3	8	.273	17	17	0	0-0	100	112	67	16	6	28-3	54	5.94	79	.286	.342	2'	.000	0	77	-11		-1.0
2005	KC A	5	8	.385	47	10	0	2-0	115	129	66	18	8	52-5	60	4.46	94	.287	.367	0	—	0	103	-6		-0.6
Total	3	10	17	.370	71	28	0	2-0	228.2	265	150	35	16	87-10	129	5.47	81	.293	.363	2	.000	0	87	-26		-3.0

WOOD, PETE Peter Burke B2.1.1857 Dundas ON, Can. D3.15.1923 Chicago IL TR/5-7/185 d7.15 b-Fred

1885	Buf N	8	15	.348	24	22	21	0	198.2	235	170	8		66	38	4.44	67	.280	.332	104	.221	-1*	102	-32		-3.1
1889	Phi N	1	1	.500	3	2	2	0	19	28	15	0	0	3	8	5.21	83	.333	.356	8	.000	-1	147	-1		-0.2
Total	2	9	16	.360	27	24	23	0	217.2	263	185	8	0	69	46	4.51	69	.285	.334	112	.205	-2	106	-33		-3.3

YEAR	TM LG	W	L	PCT	G	GS	CG-SHO	SV-BS	IP	H	R	HR	HB	BB-IB	SO	ERA	AERA	OAV	OOB	AB-HR-SH	AVG	PB	SUP	APR	DL	PW
WOOD, WILBUR	Wilbur Forrester B10.22.1941 Cambridge MA BR/TL/6-0/180(180-200) d6.30																									
1961	Bos A	0	0	—	6	1	0	0	13	14	8	2	0	7-0	7	5.54	75	.269	.350	3	.000	-0	170	-1		-0.1
1962	Bos A	0	0	—	1	1	0	0	7.2	6	3	0	0	3-0	3	3.52	117	.214	.290	3	.000	-0	65	1		0.0
1963	Bos A	0	5	.000	25	6	0	0	64.2	67	35	4	3	13-1	28	3.76	101	.270	.311	12-0-1	.000	-1	78	-2		-0.3
1964	Bos A	0	0	—	4	0	0	0	5.2	13	11	1	0	3-2	5	17.47	22	.433	.485	1	.000	-0		-8		-0.4
	Pit N	0	2	.000	3	2	1	0	17.1	16	8	0	2	11-3	7	3.63	97	.246	.367	5-0-1	.000	-0	50	0		-0.1
1965	Pit N	1	1	.500	34	1	0	0	51.1	44	21	3	1	16-3	29	3.16	111	.237	.298	6	.000	-1	91	6		0.4
1967	Chi A	4	2	.667	51	0	0	4	95.1	95	34	2	1	28-4	47	1.87	162	.222	.266	16	.063	-0	173	**20**		3.8
1968	Chi A	13	12	.520	**88**	2	0	16	159	127	39	8	3	33-12	74	1.87	162	.222	.266	22-0-2	.091	-1		8		1.5
1969	Chi A	10	11	.476	**76**	0	0	15-7	119.2	113	48	13	3	40-15	73	3.01	128	.248	.311	15-0-2	.000	-1		8		2.3
1970	Chi A	9	13	.409	**77**	0	0	21-6	121.2	118	50	7	2	36-7	85	2.81	138	.258	.312	18-0-2	.111	-1		11		2.3
1971	Chi A☆	22	13	.629	44	42	22-7	1-0	334	272	95	21	7	62-2	210	1.91	**186**	.222	.263	96-0-17	.052	-5	92	**55**		**5.7**
1972	Chi A★	**24**	17	.585	49	**49**	20-8	0-0	**376.2**	325	119	28	7	74-5	193	2.51	125	.235	.276	125-0-13	.136	-2	103	25		2.8
1973	Chi A	**24**	20	.545	49	48	21-4	0-0	**359.1**	381	166	26	7	91-3	199	3.46	114	.270	.315	0	—	0	99	15		1.8
1974	Chi A☆	20	19	.513	42	**42**	22-1	0-0	320.1	305	143	27	9	80-8	169	3.60	104	.254	.303	0	—	0	98	-7		-0.7
1975	Chi A	16	20	.444	43	**43**	14-2	0-0	291.1	309	148	26	5	92-5	140	4.11	95	.272	.328	0	—	0	91	4	145	-0.2
1976	Chi A	4	3	.571	7	7	5-1	0-0	56.1	51	24	3	0	11-0	31	2.24	160	.242	.278	0	—	0	82	-12	22	-1.1
1977	Chi A	7	8	.467	24	18	5-1	0-0	122.2	139	75	10	10	50-0	42	4.99	82	.293	.371	0	—	0	106	-24		-2.4
1978	Chi A	10	10	.500	28	27	4	0-0	168	187	103	23	3	74-1	69	5.20	73	.285	.357	0	—	0	99	-13	167	-4.6
Total	17	164	156	.512	651	297	114-24	57-13	2684	2582	1130	209	63	724-71	1411	3.24	112	.254	.306	322-0-38	.084	-13	99	99	167	14.6
WOODALL, BRAD	David Bradley B6.25.1969 Atlanta GA BB/TL/6-0/175* d7.22 Col North Carolina-Asheville																									
1994	Atl N	0	1	.000	1	1	0	0	6	5	3	2	0	2-0	2	4.50	96	.227	.292	2	.500	0	42	0		0.1
1995	Atl N	1	1	.500	9	0	0	0	10.1	13	10	1	0	8-1	5	6.10	71	.310	.412	1	1.000	0		-3		-0.5
1996	Atl N	2	2	.500	8	3	0	0	19.2	28	19	4	0	4-0	20	7.32	61	.333	.356	5	.200	0	128	-6		-1.2
1998	Mil N	7	9	.438	31	20	0	0	138	145	81	25	6	47-4	85	4.96	88	.273	.337	38-1-5	.237	3*	114	-8		-0.8
1999	Chi N	0	1	.000	6	3	0	0	16	17	12	5	1	6-0	7	5.63	81	.270	.338	2	.500	1	114	-2		-0.1
Total	5	10	14	.417	55	27	0	0	190	208	125	37	7	67-5	119	5.31	82	.280	.343	48-1-5	.271	5	113	-19		-1.9
WOODARD, STEVE	Steven Larry B5.15.1975 Hartselle AL BL/TR/6-4/217(217-236) [MilA94 5/123] d7.28																									
1997	Mil A	3	3	.500	7	7	0	0-0	36.2	39	25	5	2	6-0	32	5.15	90	.269	.307	0	—	0	60	-3	32	-0.4
1998	Mil N	10	12	.455	34	26	0	0-0	165.2	170	83	19	9	33-4	135	4.18	104	.264	.307	50-0-2	.140	-1	64	3		-0.7
1999	Mil N	11	8	.579	31	29	2	0-0	185	219	101	23	6	36-7	119	4.52	102	.294	.330	53-0-10	.132	0	103	2	29	-1.2
2000	Mil N	1	7	.125	27	11	1	0-0	93.2	125	70	16	4	33-4	65	5.96	78	.325	.381	22-0-2	.045	-1	90	-15		-1.2
	Cle A	3	3	.500	13	11	0	0-0	54	57	35	10	5	11-1	35	5.67	88	.269	.310	0		0	126	-3	20	-0.3
2001	Cle A	3	3	.500	29	10	0	0-0	97	129	60	10	5	17-1	52	5.20	88	.325	.358	1	.000	-0	99	-6		-0.8
2002	Tex A	0	0	—	14	0	0	0-1	17.2	20	13	4	2	8-1	14	6.62	72	.274	.361	0	—	0		-3		-0.6
2003	Bos A	1	0	1.000	7	0	0	0-0	17.2	15	12	5	1	5-2	12	5.09	92	.311	.358	0	—	0	0			-0.2
Total	7	32	36	.471	162	94	3	0-1	667.1	782	397	90	31	149-20	464	4.94	93	.292	.335	126-0-14	.119	-2	90	-25	81	-2.6
WOODBURN, GENE	Eugene Stewart B8.20.1886 Bellaire OH D1.18.1961 Sandusky OH BR/TR/6-0/175 d7.27																									
1911	StL N	1	5	.167	11	6	1	0	38.1	22	32	0	6	40	23	5.40	63	.167	.382	6-0-1	.167	1	82	-10		-1.1
1912	StL N	1	4	.200	20	5	1	0	48.1	60	48	0	4	42	25	5.59	61	.306	.438	13	.000	-2	68	-13		-1.1
Total	2	2	9	.182	31	11	2	0	86.2	82	80	0	10	82	48	5.50	62	.250	.414	19-0-1	.053	-0	75	-23		-2.2
WOODCOCK, FRED	Fred Wayland B5.17.1868 Winchendon MA D8.11.1943 Ashburnham MA BL/TL/6-2/190 d5.17 Col Brown																									
1892	Pit N	1	2	.333	5	4	3	0	33	42	28	1	2	17	8	3.55	93	.298	.381	15	.200	0	110	-3		-0.3
WOODEND, GEORGE	George Anthony B12.9.1917 Hartford CT D2.6.1980 Hartford CT BR/TR/6-0/200 d4.22																									
1944	Bos N	0	0	—	3	0	0	0	4	7	6	0	1	4-0	0	13.50	28	.556	.714	0	—	0		-2		-0.2
WOODESHICK, HAL	Harold Joseph B8.24.1932 Wilkes-Barre PA BR/TL/6-3/200* d9.14																									
1956	Det A	0	2	.000	2	2	0	0	5.1	12	8	1	0	3-0	1	13.50	30	.444	.500	0	—	0	130	-5		-0.4
1958	Cle A	6	6	.500	14	9	3	0	71.2	71	32	4	6	25-0	21	3.64	100	.265	.341	24	.167	-1	99	0		-0.2
1959	Was A	4	4	.333	31	3	0	0	61	58	39	2	1	36-8	30	3.69	106	.253	.352	8	.000	-1*	38	-3		-0.2
1960	Was A	4	5	.444	41	14	1	4	115	131	67	7	3	60-3	46	4.70	83	.289	.375	29-0-6	.069	-2	126	-9		-0.8
1961	Was A	3	2	.600	7	6	1	0	40.1	38	19	3	3	24-0	24	4.02	100	.257	.369	16	.125	-1	99	1		0.1
	Det A	1	1	.500	12	2	0	0	18.1	25	17	3	0	17-1	13	7.85	52	.316	.438	4	.000	-0	65	-7		-0.8
	Year	4	3	.571	19	8	1	0	58.2	63	36	6	3	41-1	37	5.22	77	.278	.393	20	.100	-1	90	-7		-0.7
1962	Hou N	5	16	.238	31	26	2-1	0	139.1	161	84	3	5	54-1	80	4.39	85	.290	.352	37-0-3	.081	-1	72	-13		-1.4
1963	Hou N★	11	9	.550	55	0	0	10	114	75	29	3	6	42-6	94	1.97	160	.186	.269	23	.130	-0		16		1.3
1964	Hou N	2	9	.182	61	0	0	23	78.1	73	32	3	7	32-11	58	2.76	124	.249	.336	10-0-1	.000	-0		4		0.4
1965	Hou N	3	4	.429	27	0	0	3	32.1	27	13	3	0	18-5	22	3.06	110	.227	.328	6-0-1	.167	-0		1		0.1
	StL N	3	2	.600	51	0	0	15	59.2	47	14	1	2	27-11	37	1.81	212	.221	.314	8	.000	-1		12		1.1
	Year	6	6	.500	78	0	0	18	92	74	27	4	2	45-16	59	2.25	163	.223	.319	14-0-1	.071	-1		13		1.2
1966	StL N	2	1	.667	59	0	0	4	70.1	57	17	5	1	23-6	30	1.92	187	.224	.289	5	.200	-0		13		1.3
1967	†StL N	2	1	.667	36	0	0	2	41.2	41	29	2	3	28-9	20	5.18	63	.252	.367	4	.000	-0		-10		-0.9
Total	11	44	62	.415	427	62	7-1	61	847.1	816	400	40	35	389-61	484	3.56	102	.254	.339	174-0-11	.092	-7	95	0		-2.3
WOODMAN, DAN	Daniel Courtenay "Cocoa" B7.8.1893 Danvers MA D12.14.1962 Danvers MA BR/TR/5-8/160 d7.10																									
1914	Buf F	0	0	—	13	1	0	1	33.2	30	16	0	1	11	13	2.41	123	.246	.313	7	.143	-1		0		-0.0
1915	Buf F	0	0	—	5	0	0	1	15.1	14	9	0	0	9	1	4.11	68	.246	.348	4	.250	-0*	125	-2		-0.0
Total	2	0	0	—	18	1	0	1	49	44	25	0	1	20	14	2.94	99	.246	.325	11	.182	-1	125	-2		-0.0
WOODS, CLARENCE	Clarence Cofield B6.11.1892 Woods Ridge (Ohio Co.) IN D7.2.1969 Rising Sun IN BR/TR/6-5/230 d8.8																									
1914	Ind F	0	0	—	2	0	0	1	2	1	1	0	2	1	4.50	69	.167	.375	0	—	0		0		-0.0
WOODS, PINKY	George Rowland B5.22.1915 Waterbury CT D10.29.1982 Los Angeles CA BR/TR/6-5/225 d6.20 Col Holy Cross																									
1943	Bos A	5	6	.455	23	12	2	1	100.2	109	61	6	1	55	32	4.92	67	.284	.375	36	.222	-0	102	-18		C
1944	Bos A	4	8	.333	38	20	5-1	0	170.2	171	73	4	6	88	56	3.27	104	.266	.360	48-0-4	.146	-1	88	2		C
1945	Bos A	4	7	.364	24	12	3	2	107.1	108	56	3	1	63	36	4.19	81	.268	.368	42-0-1	.214	1	100	-9		C
Total	3	13	21	.382	85	44	10-1	3	378.2	388	190	13	8	206	124	3.97	85	.272	.366	126-0-5	.190	-1	95	-25		C
WOODS, JAKE	Jacob Thomas B9.3.1981 Fresno CA BL/TL/6-1/190 d4.8 Col Bakersfield (CA) JC																									
2005	LA A	4	4	.500	28	0	0	0	27.2	30	18	7	2	8-0	20	4.55	95	.270	.331	0		0		-2		C
WOODS, JOHN	John Fulton "Abe" B1.18.1898 Princeton WV D10.4.1946 Norfolk VA BR/TR/6-0/175 d9.16 Col West Virginia																									
1924	Bos A	0	0	—	1	0	0	0	1	0	0	0	0	3	0	0.00	—	.000	.500	0		0		0		C
WOODS, WALT	Walter Sydney B4.28.1875 Rye NH D10.30.1951 Portsmouth NH BR/TR/5-9.5/165 d4.20																									
1898	Chi N	9	13	.409	27	22	18-3	0	215	224	128	7	10	59	26	3.14	114	.266	.322	154-0-3	.175	-4*	98	8		C
1899	Lou N	9	13	.409	26	21	17	0	186.1	216	100	9	7	37	21	3.28	117	.290	.329	126-1-6	.151	-3*	119	12		C
1900	Pit N	0	0	—	1	0	0	0	3	9	7	0	0	1	1	21.00	19	.500	.526	1	.000	-0		-5		C
Total	3	18	26	.409	54	43	35-3	0	404.1	449	235	16	17	97	48	3.34	111	.280	.328	281-1-9	.164	-7	109	15		C
WOODSON, DICK	Richard Lee B3.30.1945 Oelwein IA BR/TR/6-5/207(190-207) d4.8																									
1969	†Min A	7	5	.583	44	10	2	1-1	110.1	99	49	11	3	49-3	66	3.67	99	.237	.322	27	.074	-1	146	1		C
1970	†Min A	1	2	.333	21	0	0	1-1	30.2	29	18	2	0	19-0	22	3.82	97	.244	.345	2	.000	-0	88	1		C
1972	Min A	14	14	.500	36	36	9-3	0-0	251.2	193	93	19	2	101-5	150	2.72	118	.211	.290	88-0-8	.080	-5	105	13	21	C
1973	Min A	10	8	.556	23	23	4-2	0-0	141.1	137	68	12	2	68-0	53	3.95	101	.254	.338	0	—	0	88	-2		C
1974	Min A	1	1	.500	5	4	0	0-0	27	30	16	5	1	4-0	18	4.33	86	.273	.364	0	—	0	75	-6		C
	NY A	1	2	.333	12	8	0	0-0	28	34	19	1	1	12-2	12	5.79	61	.301	.370	0	—	0	99	-3		C
	Year	2	3	.400	17	12	0	0-0	55	64	35	11	2	16-2	24	5.07	72	.287	.339	0	—	0	83	-9		C
Total	5	34	32	.515	137	76	15-5	2-2	589	522	263	55	9	253-10	315	3.47	102	.236	.316	117-0-8	.077	-7	100	5	21	C
WOODSON, KERRY	Walter Browne B5.18.1969 Jacksonville FL BR/TR/6-2/190 [SeaA88 29/747] d7.19 Col San Jose (CA) City [DL 1993 Sea A 182]																									
1992	Sea A	0	1	.000	8	1	0	0	13.2	12	7	0	2	11-0	6	3.29	122	.245	.403	0	—	0	68	0	44	C

YEAR	TM LG	W	L	PCT	G	GS	CG-SHO	SV-BS	IP	H	R	HR	HB	BB-IB	SO	ERA	AERA	OAV	OOB	AB-HR-SH	AVG	PB	SUP	APR	DL	PW

WOODWARD, FRANK   Frank Russell B5.17.1894 New Haven CT D6.11.1961 New Haven CT BR/TR/5-10/175 d4.17 Mil 1918

YEAR	TM LG	W	L	PCT	G	GS	CG-SHO	SV-BS	IP	H	R	HR	HB	BB-IB	SO	ERA	AERA	OAV	OOB	AB-HR-SH	AVG	PB	SUP	APR	DL	PW
1918	Phi N	0	0	—	2	0	0	0	6	6	4	0	0	4	4	6.00	50	.250	.357	3	.333	0		-1		-0.1
1919	Phi N	6	9	.400	17	12	6	0	100.2	109	63	5	5	35	27	4.74	68	.291	.359	29-0-4	.207	1	111	-15		-2.1
	StL N	3	5	.375	17	7	2	1	72	65	27	1	1	28	18	2.63	106	.248	.323	21-0-1	.048	-2	65	1		-0.1
	Year	9	14	.391	34	19	8	1	172.2	174	90	6	6	63	45	3.86	79	.273	.344	50-0-5	.140	-1	96	-14		-2.2
1921	Was A	0	0	—	3	1	0	0	10.2	11	7	0	0	3	4	5.91	70	.282	.333	3	.333	-1	142	-2		-0.1
1922	Was A	0	0	—	1	0	0	0	2.1	3	3	0	0	3	1	11.57	33	.375	.545	1	.000	-0		-2		-0.1
1923	Chi A	0	1	.000	2	1	0	0	2	5	3	0	0	1	0	13.50	29	.500	.545	0	—	0	63	-2		-0.3
Total	5	9	15	.375	42	21	8	1	193.2	199	107	6	6	74	55	4.23	74	.277	.350	57-0-5	.158	-1	97	-21		-2.8

WOODWARD, ROB   Robert John B9.28.1962 Hanover NH BR/TR/6-3/185(185-212) [BosA81 3/70] d9.5

YEAR	TM LG	W	L	PCT	G	GS	CG-SHO	SV-BS	IP	H	R	HR	HB	BB-IB	SO	ERA	AERA	OAV	OOB	AB-HR-SH	AVG	PB	SUP	APR	DL	PW
1985	Bos A	1	0	1.000	5	2	0	0-0	26.2	17	8	0	2	9-0	16	1.69	256	.168	.250	0	—	0	158	6		0.3
1986	Bos A	2	3	.400	9	6	0	0-0	35.2	46	26	8	1	11-0	14	5.30	79	.313	.360	0	—	0	79	-5		-0.6
1987	Bos A	1	1	.500	9	6	0	0-0	37	53	33	6	1	15-0	15	7.05	65	.338	.394	0	—	0	126	-11		-0.5
1988	Bos A	0	0	—	1	0	0	0-0	0.2	2	1	0	0	1-0	0	13.50	31	.500	.600	0	—	0		-1		0.0
Total	4	4	4	.500	24	14	0	0-0	100	118	68	10	4	36-0	45	5.04	87	.289	.349	0	—	0	112	-11		-0.8

WOODYARD, MARK   Mark Anthony B12.19.1978 Mobile AL BR/TR/6-2/195 d9.17 Col Bethune-Cookman

YEAR	TM LG	W	L	PCT	G	GS	CG-SHO	SV-BS	IP	H	R	HR	HB	BB-IB	SO	ERA	AERA	OAV	OOB	AB-HR-SH	AVG	PB	SUP	APR	DL	PW
2005	Det A	0	0	—	3	0	0	0	6	3	1	0	0	0	3	1.50	282	.182	.182	0	—	0	2			0.1

WOOLDRIDGE, FLOYD   Floyd Lewis B8.25.1928 Jerico Springs MO BR/TR/6-1/185 d5.1

YEAR	TM LG	W	L	PCT	G	GS	CG-SHO	SV-BS	IP	H	R	HR	HB	BB-IB	SO	ERA	AERA	OAV	OOB	AB-HR-SH	AVG	PB	SUP	APR	DL	PW
1955	StL N	2	4	.333	18	8	2	0	57.2	64	36	9	1	27-4	14	4.84	84	.281	.355	18-0-1	.222	0	110	-6		-0.6

WORDEN, FRED   Frederick Bamford B9.4.1894 St.Louis MO D11.9.1941 St.Louis MO BR/TR d9.28

YEAR	TM LG	W	L	PCT	G	GS	CG-SHO	SV-BS	IP	H	R	HR	HB	BB-IB	SO	ERA	AERA	OAV	OOB	AB-HR-SH	AVG	PB	SUP	APR	DL	PW
1914	Phi A	0	0	—	1	0	0	0	2	8	5	0	0	1	1	18.00	15	.615	.615	1	.000	-0		-4		-0.2

WORKMAN, HOGE   Harry Hallworth B9.25.1899 Huntington WV D5.20.1972 Ft.Myers FL BR/TR/5-11/170 d6.27 Col Ohio St.

YEAR	TM LG	W	L	PCT	G	GS	CG-SHO	SV-BS	IP	H	R	HR	HB	BB-IB	SO	ERA	AERA	OAV	OOB	AB-HR-SH	AVG	PB	SUP	APR	DL	PW
1924	Bos A	0	0	—	11	0	0	0	18	25	19	2	1	18	5	9.50	51	.325	.422	2	.000	-0		-7		-0.4

WORKS, RALPH   Ralph Talmadge "Judge" B3.16.1888 Payson IL D8.8.1941 Pasadena CA BL/TR/6-2.5/185 d5.1

YEAR	TM LG	W	L	PCT	G	GS	CG-SHO	SV-BS	IP	H	R	HR	HB	BB-IB	SO	ERA	AERA	OAV	OOB	AB-HR-SH	AVG	PB	SUP	APR	DL	PW
1909	†Det A	4	1	.800	16	4	2		64	62	19	0	1	17	31	1.97	128	.261	.313	17	.059	-2	140	4		0.1
1910	Det A	3	6	.333	18	10	5	1	85.2	73	47	1	4	39	36	3.57	74	.235	.328	30-0-1	.267	1	115	-9		-0.9
1911	Det A	11	5	.688	30	15	9-3	0	167.1	173	93	3	6	67	68	3.87	89	.268	.342	61	.148	-3	94	-6		-1.0
1912	Det A	5	10	.333	27	16	9-1	0	157	185	101	1	7	66	64	4.24	77	.308	.383	56-0-3	.143	-3	120	-17		-1.8
	Cin N	1	1	.500	3	1	1	0	9.2	4	5	0	1	5	5	2.79	120	.133	.278	5	.200	-0	262	0		0.0
1913	Cin N	0	1	.000	5	2	0	0	15	15	14	0	3	8	4	7.80	42	.242	.356	6	.167	-0	116	-6		-0.4
Total	5	24	24	.500	99	48	28-4	4	498.2	512	279	5	22	202	208	3.79	83	.271	.348	175-0-4	.160	-8	115	-34		-4.0

WORRELL, TIM   Timothy Howard B7.5.1967 Pasadena CA BR/TR/6-4/215(215-240) [SDN89 20/520] d6.25 b-Todd Col Biola

YEAR	TM LG	W	L	PCT	G	GS	CG-SHO	SV-BS	IP	H	R	HR	HB	BB-IB	SO	ERA	AERA	OAV	OOB	AB-HR-SH	AVG	PB	SUP	APR	DL	PW
1993	SD N	2	7	.222	21	16	0	0-0	100.2	104	63	11	0	43-5	52	4.92	84	.269	.338	31-0-2	.032	-3	109	-9		-1.0
1994	SD N	0	1	.000	3	3	0	0-0	14.2	9	7	0	0	5-0	14	3.68	112	.170	.237	2-0-1	.500	1	118	1	115	0.1
1995	SD N	1	0	1.000	9	0	0	0-0	13.1	16	7	2	1	6-0	13	4.73	86	.291	.371	1	.000	-0		-1	129	0.0
1996	†SD N	9	7	.563	50	11	0	1-1	121	109	45	9	6	39-1	99	3.05	132	.236	.304	20-0-6	.150	-0	73	14		1.6
1997	SD N	4	8	.333	60	10	0	3-4	106.1	116	67	14	7	50-2	81	5.16	76	.280	.363	15	.200	1	122	-15		-1.5
1998	Det A	2	6	.250	15	9	0	0-1	61.2	66	42	11	1	19-2	47	5.98	79	.270	.325	0	—	0	104	-7		-0.8
	Cle A	0	0	—	3	0	0	0-0	5.1	6	3	0	0	2-0	2	5.06	94	.300	.333	0	—	0		0		0.0
	Oak A	0	1	.000	25	0	0	0-2	36	34	17	5	6	8-1	33	4.00	116	.241	.282	0	—	0		3		0.1
	Year	2	7	.222	43	9	0	0-3	103	106	62	16	7	29-3	82	5.24	90	.262	.311	0	—	0	105	-4		-0.7
1999	Oak A	2	2	.500	53	0	0	0-5	69.1	69	38	6	3	34-1	62	4.15	114	.256	.344	0	—	0		3	19	-0.4
2000	Bal A	2	2	.500	5	0	0	0-0	7.1	12	6	3	0	5-3	5	7.36	64	.353	.436	0	—	0		-2		-0.4
	Chi N	3	4	.429	54	0	0	3-3	62	60	20	7	1	24-8	52	2.47	186	.252	.322	2	.000	-0	14			1.4
2001	SF N	2	5	.286	73	0	0	0-3	78.1	71	33	4	3	33-4	63	3.45	119	.240	.318	2-0-1	.000	-0		6	17	0.4
2002	†SF N	8	2	.800	80	0	0	0-1	72	55	21	3	0	30-2	55	2.25	176	.212	.290	3	.000	-0	13			1.7
2003	†SF N	4	4	.500	76	0	0	38-7	78.1	74	35	5	0	28-6	65	2.87	148	.246	.307	3	.000	-0	8			1.4
2004	Phi N	5	6	.455	77	0	0	19-8	78.1	75	36	10	2	21-4	64	3.68	121	.254	.303	0	—	0	6			1.0
2005	Phi N	0	1	.000	19	0	0	1-2	17	29	17	4	1	3-0	17	7.41	59	.377	.402	0	—	0	-6	59	-0.4
	Ari N	1	1	.500	32	0	0	0-1	31.2	30	13	4	4	9-2	22	2.27	193	.250	.299	1	.000	-0	5			0.3
	Year	1	2	.333	51	0	0	1-3	48.2	59	30	8	2	12-2	39	4.07	108	.299	.338	1	.000	-0	-1			-0.1
Total	13	45	57	.441	655	49	0	65-38	953.1	935	470	98	26	359-41	746	3.89	110	.255	.323	80-0-10	.100	-2	102	33	339	4.0

WORRELL, TODD   Todd Roland B9.28.1959 Arcadia CA BR/TR/6-5/222(200-230) [StLN82 1/21] d8.28 b-Tim Col Biola [DL 1991 StL N 182]

YEAR	TM LG	W	L	PCT	G	GS	CG-SHO	SV-BS	IP	H	R	HR	HB	BB-IB	SO	ERA	AERA	OAV	OOB	AB-HR-SH	AVG	PB	SUP	APR	DL	PW
1985	†StL N	3	0	1.000	17	0	0	5-2	21.2	17	7	2	0	7-2	17	2.91	123	.215	.273	1	.000	-0		2		0.3
1986	StL N	9	10	.474	74	0	0	36-10	103.2	86	29	9	1	41-16	73	2.08	177	.229	.303	7	.143	0		18		3.7
1987	†StL N	8	6	.571	75	0	0	33-10	94.2	86	29	8	0	34-11	92	2.66	158	.242	.307	10-0-1	.100	0		16		3.2
1988	StL N★	5	9	.357	68	0	0	32-9	90	69	32	7	1	34-14	78	3.00	117	.214	.287	6	.000	0		6		1.2
1989	StL N	3	5	.375	47	0	0	20-3	51.2	42	21	4	0	26-13	41	2.96	124	.222	.315	1-0-1	.000	0		6		1.2
1992	StL N	5	3	.625	67	0	0	3-4	64	45	15	4	1	25-5	64	2.11	162	.198	.281	0	—	0		10	24	1.3
1993	LA N	1	1	.500	35	0	0	5-3	38.2	46	28	6	0	11-1	31	6.05	64	.313	.348	0	—	0	-9	83	-0.6
1994	LA N	6	5	.545	38	0	0	11-8	42	37	21	4	1	12-1	44	4.29	93	.236	.291	0	—	0	-1	18	-0.2
1995	LA N★	4	1	.800	59	0	0	32-4	62.1	50	15	4	1	19-2	61	2.02	191	.221	.282	2	.000	-0	14		2.4
1996	†LA N★	4	6	.400	72	0	0	44-9	65.1	70	29	5	2	15-1	66	3.03	129	.265	.307	0	—	0	5		1.0
1997	LA N	2	6	.250	65	0	0	35-9	59.2	60	38	12	0	23-1	61	5.28	74	.250	.316	0	—	0	-10		-1.8
Total	11	50	52	.490	617	0	0	256-71	693.2	608	264	65	7	247-67	628	3.09	123	.235	.301	27-0-2	.074	-1	54	307		11.2

WORTHAM, RICH   Richard Cooper B10.22.1953 Odessa TX BR/TL/6-0/185* [ChiA76*S2/27] d5.3 Col Texas

YEAR	TM LG	W	L	PCT	G	GS	CG-SHO	SV-BS	IP	H	R	HR	HB	BB-IB	SO	ERA	AERA	OAV	OOB	AB-HR-SH	AVG	PB	SUP	APR	DL	PW
1978	Chi A	3	2	.600	8	8	2	0	59	59	24	1	0	23-0	25	3.05	125	.267	.333	0	—	0	100	4		0.3
1979	Chi A	14	14	.500	34	33	5	0-0	204	195	126	21	3	100-3	119	4.90	87	.255	.339	0	—	0	96	-13		-1.6
1980	Chi A	4	7	.364	41	10	0	1-2	92	102	73	4	3	58-5	45	5.97	68	.285	.383	0	—	0	84	-21		-2.2
1983	Oak A	0	0	—	1	0	0	0-0	0	3	1	0	0	1-0	0	∞	—	1.000	1.000	0	—	0		-1		-0.1
Total	4	21	23	.477	84	51	7	1-2	355	359	224	26	6	182-8	189	4.89	84	.266	.352	0	—	0	95	-31		-3.6

WORTHINGTON, AL   Allan Fulton "Red" B2.5.1929 Birmingham AL BR/TR/6-2/205* d7.6 C2 Col Alabama

YEAR	TM LG	W	L	PCT	G	GS	CG-SHO	SV-BS	IP	H	R	HR	HB	BB-IB	SO	ERA	AERA	OAV	OOB	AB-HR-SH	AVG	PB	SUP	APR	DL	PW
1953	NY N	4	8	.333	20	17	5	5-2	0	102	103	55	6	2	54	52	3.44	125	.258	.349	31-0-4	.065	-2	97	5	0.4
1954	NY N	0	2	.000	10	4	0	0	18	21	7	0	0	15	8	3.50	115	.333	.456	4	.000	-1	155	0	-0.1
1956	NY N	7	14	.333	28	24	4	0	165.2	158	83	20	4	74-6	95	3.97	95	.254	.335	51-1-6	.235	2	75	-3	-0.1
1957	NY N	8	11	.421	55	12	1-1	4	157.2	140	75	19	5	56-7	90	4.22	93	.237	.306	40-0-1	.100	-2	103	-1	-0.4
1958	SF N	11	7	.611	54	12	1	6	151.1	152	72	17	2	57-6	76	3.63	105	.255	.320	44-0-3	.182	0	110	2	0.3
1959	SF N	2	3	.400	42	3	0	2	73.1	68	34	8	5	37-4	45	3.68	103	.253	.347	13	.077	-1	133	1	0.0
1960	Bos A	0	1	.000	6	0	0	0	11.2	17	12	1	0	11-3	7	7.71	52	.340	.459	1	.000	-0	-5		-0.4
	Chi A	1	1	.500	6	0	0	0	5.1	3	2	0	0	4-0	1	3.38	112	.176	.318	2	1.000	0		0	0.2
	Year	1	2	.333	10	0	0	0	17	20	14	1	0	15-3	8	6.35	62	.299	.422	3	.667	1	-5		-0.2
1963	Cin N	4	4	.500	50	0	0	10	81.1	75	34	6	3	31-3	55	2.99	112	.248	.321	12-0-2	.083	-0	2		0.3
1964	Cin N	1	0	1.000	6	0	0	0	7	11	11	0	1	2-0	6	10.29	35	.400	.436	0	—	0	-6		-0.8
	Min A	5	6	.455	41	0	0	14	72.1	47	18	4	0	28-6	59	1.37	261	.183	.262	16-0-4	.063	-0	16		2.9
1965	†Min A	10	7	.588	62	0	0	21	80.1	57	25	4	3	41-2	59	2.13	167	.207	.312	10-0-2	.100	0	11		2.6
1966	Min A	6	3	.667	65	0	0	16	91.1	66	26	6	1	27-3	93	2.46	146	.199	.260	11	.273	-1	12		1.8
1967	Min A	8	9	.471	59	0	0	16	92	77	36	6	1	38-10	80	2.84	122	.229	.307	8	.000	-1	5		1.0
1968	Min A	4	5	.444	54	0	0	18	76.1	67	26	1	0	32-9	57	2.71	114	.238	.311	7-0-2	.000	-1	4		0.6
1969	†Min A	4	1	.800	46	0	0	3-1	61	65	31	7	0	20-2	51	4.57	80	.278	.333	5-0-1	.000	-0	-5		-0.5
Total	14	75	82	.478	602	69	11-3	110-1	1246.2	1130	546	105	27	527-61	834	3.39	110	.243	.320	255-1-25	.137	-5	100	41		8.0

WRIGHT, GENE   Clarence Eugene "Big Gene" B12.11.1878 Cleveland OH D10.29.1930 Barberton OH BR/TR/6-2/185 d10.5

YEAR	TM LG	W	L	PCT	G	GS	CG-SHO	SV-BS	IP	H	R	HR	HB	BB-IB	SO	ERA	AERA	OAV	OOB	AB-HR-SH	AVG	PB	SUP	APR	DL	PW
1901	Bro N	1	0	1.000	1	1	0		9	6	2	0	0	1	6	1.00	335	.188	.212	3	.333	0	85	2		0.2
1902	Cle A	7	10	.412	21	18	15-1		148	150	94	6	8	75	52	3.95	87	.263	.357	70-1-1	.143	-2*	132	-7		-1.0
1903	Cle A	3	10	.231	15	12	8	0	101.2	122	94	1	4	58	42	5.75	50	.296	.388	43-0-1	.209	-1	115	-32		-3.1
	StL N	3	5	.375	8	8	7-1	0	61	73	29	2	4	16	37	3.69	79	.296	.348	21	.143	-1	86	-3		-0.4
	Year	6	15	.286	23	20	15-1	0	162.2	195	123	3	8	74	79	4.98	58	.296	.374	64-0-1	.188	-2	103	-38		-3.5

YEAR	TM LG	W	L	PCT	G	GS	CG-SHO	SV-BS	IP	H	R	HR	HB	BB-IB	SO	ERA	AERA	OAV	OOB	AB-HR-SH	AVG	PB	SUP	APR	DL	PW
1904	StL A	0	1	.000	1	1	0	0	4	10	6	0	0	2	3	13.50	18	.476	.522	1	.000	-0	115	-4		-0.6
Total	4	14	26	.350	46	40	31-2	1	323.2	361	225	9	16	152	140	4.50	70	.282	.365	138-1-2	.167	-1	117	-44		-4.9

WRIGHT, CLYDE Clyde B2.20.1941 Jefferson City TN BR/TL/6-1/185(185-200) [AnaA65 6/107] d6.15 s-Jaret Col Carson-Newman

1966	Cal A	4	7	.364	20	13	3-1	0	91.1	92	39	11	1	25-4	37	3.74	90	.265	.314	29-0-3	.103	-1*	93	-2		-0.4
1967	Cal A	5	5	.500	20	11	1	0	77.1	76	33	5	1	24-2	35	3.26	96	.260	.316	22-0-3	.273	2*	78	-1		0.1
1968	Cal A	10	6	.625	41	13	2-1	3	125.2	123	58	13	2	44-6	71	3.94	74	.256	.319	37-0-2	.216	2*	92	-13		-1.5
1969	Cal A	1	8	.111	37	5	0	0-2	63.2	66	33	4	1	30-5	31	4.10	85	.278	.361	11	.182	0*	30	-4		-0.5
1970	Cal A★	22	12	.647	39	39	7-2	0-0	260.2	226	97	24	7	88-4	110	2.83	128	.232	.298	105-2-4	.171	3*	122	21		2.9
1971	Cal A	16	17	.485	37	37	10-2	0-0	276.2	225	105	17	3	82-10	135	2.99	99	.226	.283	91-0-9	.154	2*	79	8		1.4
1972	Cal A	18	11	.621	35	35	15-2	0-0	251	229	101	14	4	80-6	87	2.98	99	.246	.307	83-2-6	.217	7	118	-4		0.5
1973	Cal A	11	19	.367	37	36	13-1	0-0	257	273	120	26	3	76-0	65	3.68	97	.273	.324	0	—	0	96	-3		-0.1
1974	Mil A	9	20	.310	38	32	15	0-0	232	264	122	22	0	54-4	64	4.42	82	.284	.322	0	—	0	88	-19		-2.1
1975	Tex A	4	6	.400	25	14	1	0-0	93.1	105	56	7	1	47-3	32	4.44	85	.294	.370	0	—	0	110	-8		-0.7
Total	10	100	111	.474	329	235	67-9	3-2	1728.2	1679	764	143	23	550-44	667	3.50	97	.256	.314	378-4-27	.183	14	98	-25		-0.4

WRIGHT, DAVE David William B8.27.1875 Dennison OH D1.18.1946 Dennison OH BR/TR/6-0/185 d7.22

1895	Pit N	0	0	—	1	0	0	0	2	6	6	0	0	1	0	27.00	17	.500	.538	1	.000	-0		-4		-0.2
1897	Chi N	1	0	1.000	1	1	1	0	7	17	14	1	2	2	4	15.43	29	.459	.512	3	.333	0	224	-7		-0.6
Total	2	1	0	1.000	2	1	1	0	9	23	20	1	2	3	4	18.00	25	.469	.519	4	.250	0	224	-11		-0.8

WRIGHT, ED Henderson Edward B5.15.1919 Dyersburg TN D11.19.1995 Dyersburg TN BR/TR/6-1/180* d7.29

1945	Bos N	8	3	.727	15	12	7-1	0	111.1	104	35	7	0	33	24	2.51	153	.254	.310	39-0-2	.128	-2	107	17		1.3
1946	Bos N	12	9	.571	36	21	9-2	0	176.1	164	82	8	2	71	44	3.52	97	.250	.325	59-0-4	.305	6	114	-3		0.3
1947	Bos N	3	3	.500	23	6	1	0	64.2	80	52	9	2	35	14	6.40	61	.305	.391	23	.130	-0	113	-19		-1.5
1948	Bos N	0	0	—	3	0	0	0	4.2	9	3	0	0	2	2	1.93	199	.474	.524	0	—	0		0		0.0
1952	Phi A	2	1	.667	24	0	0	0	41.1	55	36	6	3	20	9	6.53	61	.320	.400	7	.143	-0		-12		-0.9
Total	5	25	16	.610	101	39	17-3	1	398.1	412	208	30	7	161	93	4.00	92	.271	.344	128-0-6	.211	3	110	-17		-0.8

WRIGHT, JIM James "Jiggs" B9.19.1900 Hyde, England D4.11.1963 Oakland CA BR/TR/6-2.5/195 d9.14

1927	StL A	1	0	1.000	2	1	1	0	12	8	6	0	0	4	4	4.50	97	.182	.250	4	.000	-0	172	0		0.0
1928	StL A	0	0	—	2	0	0	0	2	3	3	0	0	2	2	13.50	31	.375	.500	0	—	0		-2		-0.1
Total	2	1	0	1.000	4	1	1	0	14	11	9	0	0	6	6	5.79	75	.212	.293	4	.000	-0	172	-2		-0.1

WRIGHT, JIM James Clifton B12.21.1950 Reed City MI BR/TR/6-1/165* [BosA69 4/83] d4.15

1978	Bos A	8	4	.667	24	16	5-3	0-0	116	122	51	8	7	24-2	56	3.57	115	.276	.321	0	—	0	86	7		0.6
1979	Bos A	1	0	1.000	11	1	0	0-0	23	19	13	5	3	7-1	15	5.09	88	.226	.302	0	—	0	81	-1	102	-.1
Total	2	9	4	.692	35	17	5-3	0-0	139	141	64	13	10	31-3	71	3.82	109	.268	.318	0	—	0	85	6	102	0.4

WRIGHT, JIM James Leon B3.3.1955 St.Joseph MO BR/TR/6-5/220(205-220) [PhiN73 5/98] d4.22 C2 [DL 1979 Phi N 179]

1981	KC A	2	3	.400	17	4	0	0-0	52	57	21	5	2	21-7	27	3.46	104	.277	.348	0	—	0	75	1		0.1
1982	KC A	0	0	—	7	0	0	0-0	23.2	32	18	3	0	6-0	9	5.32	77	.320	.358	0	—	0		-4		-0.2
Total	2	2	3	.400	24	4	0	0-0	75.2	89	39	8	2	27-7	36	4.04	93	.291	.351	0	—	0	75	-3	179	-0.1

WRIGHT, RICKY James Richard B11.22.1958 Paris TX BL/TL/6-3/175* [LAN80*S1/2] d7.28 Col Texas

1982	LA N	2	1	.667	14	5	0	0-0	32.2	28	12	1	0	20-6	24	3.03	115	.233	.340	8	.125	0	137	2		0.2
1983	LA N	0	0	—	6	0	0	0-0	6.1	5	2	0	0	2-1	5	2.84	127	.227	.280	0	—	0		1		0.0
	Tex A	0	0	—	1	0	0	0-0	2	0	0	0	0	1-0	2	0.00	—	.000	.167	0	—	0		1		0.0
1984	Tex A	0	2	.000	8	1	0	0-1	14.2	20	10	3	0	11-0	6	6.14	68	.357	.463	0	—	0	43	-2		-0.3
1985	Tex A	0	0	—	5	0	0	0-0	7.2	5	4	0	0	5-1	7	4.70	91	.185	.313	0	—	0		0		0.0
1986	Tex A	1	0	1.000	21	1	0	0-0	39.1	44	22	1	0	21-0	23	5.03	86	.284	.369	0	—	0*	42	-2	61	-0.2
Total	5	3	3	.500	55	7	0	0-1	102.2	102	50	5	0	60-8	67	4.30	92	.265	.362	8	.125	0	100	0	61	-0.2

WRIGHT, JAMEY Jamey Alan B12.24.1974 Oklahoma City OK BR/TR/6-5/221(203-236) [ColN93 1/28] d7.3

1996	Col N	4	4	.500	16	15	0	0-0	91.1	105	60	8	7	41-1	45	4.93	106	.298	.381	26-0-5	.077	-1	100	0		0.0
1997	Col N	8	12	.400	26	26	1	0-0	149.2	198	113	19	11	71-3	59	6.25	83	.327	.406	48-0-3	.125	-2	91	-15	24	-1.9
1998	Col N	9	14	.391	34	34	1	0-0	206.1	235	143	24	11	95-3	86	5.67	91	.294	.374	57-1-8	.175	0	91	-11		-0.9
1999	Col N	4	3	.571	16	16	0	0-0	94.1	110	52	10	4	54-3	49	4.87	119	.307	.400	32-0-3	.125	-2	96	9		0.4
2000	Mil N	7	9	.438	26	25	0	0-0	164.2	157	81	12	18	88-5	96	4.10	113	.261	.368	46-0-4	.065	-3	81	10	49	0.5
2001	Mil N	11	12	.478	33	33	1-1	0-0	194.2	201	115	26	20	98-10	129	4.90	88	.270	.374	67-0-4	.194	2*	102	-13	20	-1.1
2002	Mil N	5	13	.278	19	19	1-1	0-0	114.1	115	72	15	11	63-8	69	5.35	77	.270	.374	33-0-6	.152	0	66	-15	49	-1.0
	StL N	2	0	1.000	4	3	0	0-0	15	15	8	2	0	12-1	8	4.80	84	.259	.386	5-0-1	.000	-1	221	-1		-0.2
	Year	7	13	.350	23	22	1-1	0-0	129.1	130	80	17	11	75-9	77	5.29	78	.269	.375	38-0-7	.132	-0	87	-16		-2.1
2003	KC A	1	2	.333	4	4	2-1	0-0	25.1	23	14	1	1	11-0	19	4.26	113	.245	.330	1	—	0	76	1		0.1
2004	Col N	2	3	.400	14	14	0	0-0	78.2	82	39	6	4	45-3	41	4.12	116	.266	.369	19-0-8	.053	-1	82	4		0.2
2005	Col N	8	16	.333	34	27	0	0-0	171.1	201	119	22	15	81-4	101	5.46	87	.296	.382	55-1-3	.134	-2*	81	-15	142	-6.9
Total	10	61	88	.409	226	216	6-3	0-0	1305.2	1442	816	147	104	659-41	702	5.13	94	.287	.379	388-1-45	.134	-9	90	-46	142	-6.5

WRIGHT, JARET Jaret Samuel B12.29.1975 Anaheim CA BR/TR/6-2/230* [CleA94 1/10] d6.24 f-Clyde

1997	†Cle A	8	3	.727	16	16	0	0-0	90.1	81	45	9	2	35-0	63	4.38	107	.238	.314	3-0-2	.314	-0	125	4		0.4
1998	†Cle A	12	10	.545	32	32	1-1	0-0	192.2	207	109	22	11	87-4	140	4.72	101	.277	.358	7	.429	1	108	1		-1.6
1999	†Cle A	8	10	.444	26	26	0	0-0	133.2	144	99	18	7	77-1	91	6.06	84	.277	.376	1	.000	-0	96	-14	47	0.2
2000	Cle A	3	4	.429	9	9	1-1	0-0	51.2	44	27	6	1	28-0	36	4.70	107	.235	.336	1-0-1	.000	-0	121	2	134	0.2
2001	Cle A	2	2	.500	7	7	0	0-0	29	36	22	2	0	22-0	18	6.52	70	.313	.420	0	—	0	112	-6	85	-3.5
2002	Cle A	2	3	.400	8	6	0	0-0	18.1	40	34	2	2	19-0	12	15.71	28	.435	.526	0	—	0	139	-23	111	-3.5
2003	SD N	1	5	.167	39	0	0	2-2	47.1	69	44	9	2	28-2	41	8.37	48	.348	.427	4-0-1	.250	1		-23		-2.5
	†Atl N	1	0	1.000	11	0	0	0-1	9	7	2	0	1	3-0	9	2.00	210	.226	.314	0	—	0		2		0.0
	Year	2	5	.286	50	0	0	2-3	56.1	76	46	9	3	31-2	50	7.35	55	.332	.412	4-0-1	.250	1	115	-20		-2.3
2004	†Atl N	15	8	.652	32	32	0	0-0	186.1	168	79	11	3	70-5	159	3.28	131	.242	.312	57-1-6	.105	-1	115	20	113	-1.8
2005	NY A	5	5	.500	13	13	0	0-0	63.2	81	51	8	6	32-1	34	6.08	72	.313	.394	0	—	0	139	-14	490	-6.5
Total	9	57	50	.533	193	141	2-2	2-3	822	877	512	88	38	401-13	603	5.17	90	.276	.360	75-1-10	.147	0	115	-51	490	-6.1

WRIGHT, DAN Jonathan Daniel B12.14.1977 Longview TX BR/TR/6-5/225(225-240) [ChiA99 2/64] d7.27 Col Arkansas-Monticello

2001	Chi A	5	3	.625	13	12	0	0-0	66.1	78	45	12	2	39-1	36	5.70	82	.300	.389	0	—	0	129	-7		-0.7
2002	Chi A	14	12	.538	33	33	1-1	0-0	196.1	200	124	32	6	71-1	136	5.18	87	.263	.327	4	.000	-0	110	-14		-1.6
2003	Chi A	1	7	.125	20	15	0	1-0	86.1	91	63	16	3	46-2	47	6.15	75	.277	.366	2	.000	-0	85	-14	36	-1.1
2004	Chi A	0	4	.000	4	4	0	0-0	17.2	24	17	5	2	11-1	6	8.15	58	.320	.420	0	—	0	54	-7		-1.1
Total	4	20	26	.435	70	64	1-1	1-0	366.2	393	249	65	13	167-5	225	5.65	81	.276	.353	6	.000	-1	104	-42	36	-4.4

WRIGHT, KEN Kenneth Warren B9.4.1946 Pensacola FL BR/TR/6-2/210* d4.10

1970	KC A	1	2	.333	47	0	0	3-1	53.1	49	33	2	7	29-0	30	5.23	71	.261	.374	4	.000	-0		-8		-0.4
1971	KC A	3	6	.333	21	12	1-1	1-0	78	66	34	6	3	47-0	56	3.69	93	.230	.344	22-0-1	.091	-1	82	-2	21	-0.4
1972	KC A	1	3	.333	17	0	0	4-1	18.1	15	10	0	1	15-1	18	4.91	62	.231	.378	2	.000	-0		-3		-0.2
1973	KC A	6	5	.545	25	12	1	0-1	80.2	60	48	6	0	82-0	75	4.91	84	.210	.383	0	—	0	81	-6	21	-0.4
1974	NY A	0	0	—	3	0	0	0-0	5.2	5	2	0	0	7-0	2	3.18	112	.227	.414	0	—	0		0		0.0
Total	5	11	15	.423	113	24	2-1	8-3	236	195	127	14	11	180-1	181	4.54	82	.230	.369	28-0-1	.071	-2	83	-19	42	-2.5

WRIGHT, MEL Melvin James B5.11.1928 Manila AR D5.16.1983 Houston TX BR/TR/6-3/210* d4.17 C14

1954	StL N	0	0	—	9	0	0	1	10.1	16	15	2	2	11	4	10.45	39	.348	.492	1	.000	-0		-8		-0.5
1955	StL N	2	2	.500	29	0	0	1	36.1	44	26	4	1	9-2	15	6.19	66	.308	.351	6	.000	-1		-8		-0.5
1960	Chi N	0	1	.000	17	0	0	2	16.1	17	9	1	0	3-1	9	4.96	76	.279	.299	2	.000	-0		-2		-0.1
1961	Chi N	0	1	1.000	3	0	0	0	21	19	9	3	0	4-0	8	10.71	39	.416	.438	2	.000	-0		-13		-0.8
Total	4	2	4	.333	58	0	0	3	84	119	76	10	3	27-3	36	7.61	53	.339	.387	11	.000	-2		-31		-2.5

WRIGHT, BOB Robert Cassius B12.13.1891 Decatur Co. IN D7.30.1993 Carmichael CA BR/TR/6-1.5/175 d9.21

| 1915 | Chi N | | 0 | — | 2 | 0 | 0 | 0 | 4 | 6 | 4 | 0 | 0 | 0 | 3 | 2.25 | 123 | .353 | .353 | 0 | — | 0 | | -1 | | -0.2 |

YEAR	TM LG	W	L	PCT	G	GS	CG-SHO	SV-BS	IP	H	R	HR	HB	BB-IB	SO	ERA	AERA	OAV	OOB	AB-HR-SH	AVG	PB	SUP	APR	DL	PW
WRIGHT, ROY	Roy Earl			B9.26.1933 Buchtel OH			BR/TR/6-2/170	d9.30																		
1956	NY N	0	1	.000	1	1	0	0	2.2	8	5	1	0	2-0	0	16.88	22	.533	.588	1	.000	-0	47	-4		-0.6
WRIGHT, RASTY	Wayne Bromley			B11.5.1895 Ceredo WV			D6.12.1948 Columbus OH	BR/TR/5-11/160	d6.22	Col Ohio St.																
1917	StL A	0	1	.000	16	1	0	0	39.2	48	31	0	1	10	5	5.45	48	.300	.345	10-0-1	.200	0	111	-12		-0.6
1918	StL A	8	2	.800	18	13	6-1	0	111.1	99	39	1	5	18	25	2.51	109	.244	.285	34-0-2	.294	3	106	4		0.6
1919	StL A	0	5	.000	24	5	2	0	63.1	79	44	1	1	20	14	5.54	60	.315	.368	12	.083	-1	66	-13		-1.0
1922	StL A	9	7	.563	31	16	5	5	154	148	64	7	8	50	44	2.92	142	.262	.331	50-0-4	.140	-2	113	19		1.8
1923	StL A	7	4	.636	20	8	4	0	82.2	107	64	6	5	34	26	6.42	65	.317	.387	27-0-3	.222	0	134	-17		-1.9
Total	5	24	19	.558	109	43	17-1	5	451	481	242	15	20	132	114	4.05	87	.280	.338	133-0-10	.195	1	111	-19		-1.1
WRIGHT, HARRY	William Henry			B1.10.1835 Sheffield, England			D10.3.1895 Atlantic City NJ	BR/TR/5-9.5/157	d5.5	M23	HF1953	b-George b-Sam ▲														
1871	Bos NA	1	0	1.000	9	0	0	3	18.2	34	31	0		4	0	6.27	66	.337	.362	147	.299	1*		-4		-0.2
1872	Bos NA	1	0	1.000	7	0	0	4	25.2	26	12	0		0	1	2.10	173	.239	.239	208	.255	0*		5		0.3
1873	Bos NA	2	2	.500	14	6	0	4	39.1	65	47	0		6	5	4.12	81	.328	.348	263-2	.259	2*	153	-3		-0.2
1874	Bos NA	0	2	.000	6	2	0	3	16.2	24	13	0		4	0	2.16	100	.324	.359	184-2	.315	2*	88	0		0.1
Total	4 NA	4	4	.500	36	8	0	14	100.1	149	103	0		14	6	3.68	92	.309	.329	802-4	.278	5	132	-2		0.0
WRIGHT, LUCKY	William Simmons "William the Red","Deacon"			B2.21.1880 Waterville OH			D7.7.1941 Tontogany OH	BR/TR/6-0/178	d4.18																
1909	Cle A	0	4	.000	5	4	3	0	28	21	16	0	0	7	5	3.21	80	.223	.277	7	.000	-1	55	-2		-0.4
WUERTZ, MICHAEL	Michael James			B12.15.1978 Austin MN			BR/TR/6-3/205*	[ChiN97 11/334]	d4.5																	
2004	Chi N	1	0	1.000	31	0	0	1-0	29	22	14	4	0	17-1	30	4.34	102	.218	.325	1	.000	-0		1		0.0
2005	Chi N	6	2	.750	75	0	0	0-3	75.2	60	36	6	0	40-7	89	3.81	115	.219	.316	2	.000	-0		4		0.3
Total	2	7	2	.778	106	0	0	1-3	104.2	82	50	10	0	57-8	119	3.96	111	.219	.319	3	.000	-0		5		0.3
WUNSCH, KELLY	Kelly Douglas			B7.12.1972 Houston TX			BL/TL/6-5/192(192-225)	[MilA93 1/26]	d4.3	Col Texas A&M-Commerce															
2000	†Chi A	6	3	.667	83	0	0	1-4	61.1	50	22	4	2	29-1	51	2.93	172	.221	.313	0	—	0		14		1.8
2001	Chi A	2	1	.667	33	0	0	0-2	22.1	21	19	4	6	9-1	16	7.66	61	.247	.353	0	—	0		-6	112	-0.7
2002	Chi A	2	1	.667	50	0	0	0-1	31.2	26	12	3	5	19-1	22	3.41	132	.230	.365	0	—	0		4	48	0.4
2003	Chi A	0	0	—	43	0	0	0-0	36	17	13	1	7	25-4	33	2.75	167	.139	.308	0	—	0		7	43	0.3
2004	Chi A	0	0	—	3	0	0	0-0	2	2	0	0	0	1-0	1	0.00	—	.286	.375	0	—	0		1	35	0.1
2005	LA N	1	1	.500	45	0	0	0-1	23.2	20	12	2	2	14-2	22	4.56	90	.227	.346	1	.000	-0*		-1	87	0.0
Total	6	11	6	.647	257	0	0	1-8	177	136	78	14	22	97-9	145	3.76	124	.212	.332	1	.000	-0		19	325	1.9
WURM, FRANK	Frank James			B4.27.1924 Cambridge NY			D9.19.1993 Glens Falls NY	BB/TL/6-1/175	d9.4																
1944	Bro N	0	0	—	1	1	0	0	0.1	1	4	0	0	5	1	108.00	3	.500	.857	0	—	0	142	-4		-0.2
WYATT, JOHN	John Thomas			B4.19.1935 Chicago IL			D4.6.1998 Omaha NE	BR/TR/5-11.5/200*	d9.8																
1961	KC A	0	0	—	5	0	0	1	7.1	7	2	1	1	4-0	6	2.45	170	.296	.394	0		0		1		0.1
1962	KC A	10	7	.588	59	9	0	11	125	121	66	12	5	80-5	106	4.46	95	.253	.363	29	.103	-2	101	-2		-0.5
1963	KC A	6	4	.600	63	0	0	21	92	83	37	12	0	43-2	81	3.13	125	.239	.321	9	.000	-1		7		0.9
1964	KC A★	9	8	.529	81	0	0	20	128	111	53	23	1	52-5	74	3.59	106	.236	.311	14-0-4	.000	-1		4		0.5
1965	KC A	2	6	.250	65	0	0	18	88.2	78	36	8	4	53-12	70	3.25	107	.241	.350	4-0-1	.000	-0		2		0.3
1966	KC A	0	3	.000	19	0	0	2	23.2	16	14	3	2	16-4	25	5.32	64	.213	.346	0	—	0		-4		-0.6
	Bos A	3	4	.429	42	0	0	8	71.2	59	27	3	4	27-3	63	3.14	121	.229	.308	11	.000	-1		5		0.4
	Year	3	7	.300	61	0	0	10	95.1	75	41	6	6	43-7	88	3.68	101	.225	.318	11	.000	-1		1		-0.2
1967	†Bos A	10	7	.588	60	0	0	20	93.1	71	30	6	2	39-5	68	2.60	134	.217	.303	12	.083	-0		9		1.9
1968	Bos A	1	2	.333	8	0	0	0	10.2	9	7	2	1	6-0	11	4.22	75	.231	.348	0	.000	-0		-2		-0.4
	NY A	2	0	—	7	0	0	0	8.1	7	3	1	0	9	6	2.16	135	.219	.381	1	.000	-0		0		0.1
	Det A	1	0	1.000	22	0	0	2	30.1	26	9	2	1	11-2	25	2.37	127	.236	.311	2	.000	-0		2		0.1
	Year	2	4	.333	37	0	0	2	49.1	42	19	5	2	26-2	42	2.74	111	.232	.333	3	.000	-0		1		0.2
1969	Oak A	0	1	.000	4	0	0	0-0	8.1	8	5	0	2	6-1	5	5.40	64	.250	.400	1	.000	-0		-2		-0.2
Total	9	42	44	.488	435	9	0	103-0	687.1	600	290	72	23	346-39	540	3.47	108	.237	.331	83-0-5	.048	-6	101	20		2.6
WYATT, WHIT	John Whitlow			B9.27.1907 Kensington GA			D7.16.1999 Carrollton GA	BR/TR/6-1/185	d9.16	Mil 1944	C13	Col Georgia Tech														
1929	Det A	0	1	.000	4	4	1	0	25.1	30	22	1	1	18	14	6.75	64	.309	.422	10	.100	-1	128	-6		-0.4
1930	Det A	4	5	.444	21	7	2	0	85.2	76	41	6	3	35	68	3.57	134	.239	.320	34-1-1	.353	3*	105	11		1.3
1931	Det A	0	2	.000	4	1	1	0	20.1	30	23	2	1	12	8	8.85	52	.361	.448	7	.286	-0	18	-9		-0.7
1932	Det A	9	13	.409	43	22	10	1	205.2	228	136	12	3	102	82	5.03	93	.286	.369	78-2-1	.192	-0	100	-6		-0.6
1933	Det A	0	1	.000	10	0	0	0	17	20	9	1	2	7	9	4.24	102	.299	.397	2	.000	-0		0		0.0
	Chi A	3	4	.429	26	7	2	1	87.2	91	51	7	2	45	31	4.62	92	.266	.355	28-0-1	.214	0	106	-2		-0.1
	Year	3	5	.375	36	7	2	1	104.2	111	60	8	4	54	40	4.56	93	.271	.362	30-0-1	.200	0	106	-2		-0.1
1934	Chi A	4	11	.267	23	6	2	2	67.2	83	59	10	1	37	36	7.18	66	.303	.388	26-0-1	.231	0	86	-16		-2.8
1935	Chi A	4	3	.571	30	1	0	5	52	65	41	6	2	25	22	6.75	68	.308	.387	13	.231		94	-11		-1.2
1936	Chi A	0	0	—	3	0	0	0	3	3	0	0	0	0	0	0.00	—	.273	.273	0		-0		2		0.1
1937	Cle A	2	3	.400	29	4	2	0	73	67	38	5	0	40	52	4.44	104	.244	.340	18-0-1	.389	3	80	3		0.4
1939	Bro N☆	8	3	.727	16	14	6-2	0	109	88	34	3	2	39	52	2.31	174	.224	.297	36	.167	-0	91	19		1.9
1940	Bro N★	15	14	.517	37	34	16-5	1	239.1	233	105	19	5	62	124	3.46	116	.254	.304	80-1-8	.175	-0	97	13		1.3
1941	†Bro N★	22	10	.688	38	35	23-7	1	288.1	223	89	10	2	82	176	2.34	157	**.212**	**.270**	109-3-8	.239	7*	114	**42**		5.3
1942	Bro N☆	19	7	.731	31	30	16-0	0	217.1	185	82	9	7	63	104	2.73	119	.225	.286	77-0-6	.182	1	121	11		1.2
1943	Bro N	14	5	.737	26	26	13-3	0	180.2	139	55	6	0	43	80	2.49	135	**.207**	**.255**	60-0-6	.283	4*	117	18		2.3
1944	Bro N	2	6	.250	9	9	1	0	37.2	51	37	1	2	16	4	7.17	50	.311	.379	13-0-1	.154	-0*	97	-16		-2.7
1945	Phi N	0	7	.000	10	10	2	0	51.1	72	38	5	3	14	10	5.26	73	.330	.371	16	.125	0	80	-8		-0.9
Total	16	106	95	.527	360	210	97-17	13	1761	1684	860	98	33	642	872	3.79	105	.251	.319	607-7-34	.219	18	102	45		4.4
WYCKOFF, WELDON	John Weldon			B2.19.1892 Williamsport PA			D5.8.1961 Sheboygan Falls WI	BR/TR/6-1/175	d4.19	Col Bucknell															
1913	Phi A	2	4	.333	17	7	4	0	61.2	56	44	1	3	46	31	4.38	63	.262	.399	21	.190	-0	134	-15		-1.3
1914	†Phi A	11	7	.611	32	20	11	2	185	153	82	2	4	103	86	3.02	87	.228	.334	75-1-1	.147	-0*	133	-17		-1.4
1915	Phi A	10	22	.313	43	34	20-1	0	276	238	139	1	5	165	157	3.52	83	.246	.359	96-0-3	.125	-4*	77	-15		-1.9
1916	Phi A	0	1	.000	7	2	1	0	21.1	20	16	1	1	20	4	5.48	52	.247	.402	8	.375	1*	172	-6		-0.2
	Bos A	0	0	—	8	0	0	1	22.2	19	13	0	0	18	18	4.76	58	.232	.370	6	.167	-0		-4		-0.3
	Year	0	1	.000	15	2	1	1	44	39	29	1	1	38	22	5.11	55	.239	.386	14	.286	1	175	-10		-0.5
1917	Bos A	0	0	—	1	0	0	0	5	4	3	0	1	4	1	1.80	143	.222	.391	0	.000	-0		-0		0.0
1918	Bos A	0	0	—	1	0	0	0	1	1	1	0	0	1	2	0.00	—	.400	.455	1	.000	-0		0		0.0
Total	6	23	34	.404	109	63	36-1	3	573.2	494	298	5	14	357	299	3.55	79	.242	.358	208-1-4	.149	-4	103	-52		-5.1
WYMAN, FRANK	Frank H.			B5.10.1862 Haverhill MA			D2.4.1916 Everett MA	d6.10 ▲																	
1884	KC U	0	1	.000	3	1	1	0	21	37	29	0		3	9	6.86	33	.363	.381	124	.218	-1*	95	-11		-0.5
WYNN, EARLY	Early "Gus"			B1.6.1920 Hartford AL			D4.4.1999 Venice FL	BB/TR/6-0/200(195-220)	d9.13	Mil 1944-46	C6	HF1972														
1939	Was A	0	2	.000	3	3	2	0	20.1	26	15	0	0	10	1	5.75	76	.313	.387	6-0-1	.167	0	108	-3		-0.3
1941	Was A	3	1	.750	5	5	4	0	40	35	14	1	0	10	15	1.57	257	.226	.273	15-0-1	.133	-0	111	9		0.8
1942	Was A	10	16	.385	30	28	10-1	0	190	246	129	6	3	73	58	5.12	71	.314	.374	69-0-2	.217	-2	103	-31		-3.5
1943	Was A	18	12	.600	37	33	12-3	0	256.2	232	97	15	1	83	89	2.91	110	.240	.301	90-1-0	.296	7*	108	10		1.9
1944	Was A	8	17	.320	33	25	19-2	2	207.2	221	97	3	2	67	65	3.38	96	.277	.334	92-1-0	.207	2*	85	-3		-0.3
1946	Was A	8	5	.615	17	12	9	0	107	112	45	8	3	33	36	3.11	108	.267	.325	47-1-0	.319	2*	81	3		1.1
1947	Was A☆	17	15	.531	33	31	22-2	0	247	251	114	13	5	90	73	3.64	102	.262	.329	120-2-0	.275	7*	91	5		0.9
1948	Was A	8	19	.296	33	31	15-1	0	198	236	144	16	1	94	49	5.82	65	.295	.370	106	.217	-0	80	-31		-3.3
1949	Cle A	11	7	.611	26	23	6	0	164.2	186	84	8	1	57	62	4.15	96	.282	.340	70-1-2	.143	-2*	109	-3		-0.4
1950	Cle A	18	8	.692	32	28	14-2	0	213.2	166	88	20	4	101	143	**3.20**	135	**.212**	**.305**	77-2-4	.234	7*	118	28		3.7
1951	Cle A	20	13	.606	37	34	21-3	1	**274.1**	227	102	18	3	107	133	3.02	126	.225	.301	108-1-3	.185	-2	103	27		3.1
1952	Cle A	23	12	.657	42	33	19-4	3	285.2	239	103	21	1	132	153	2.90	115	.231	.318	99-0-4	.222	5*	121	18		2.6
1953	Cle A	17	12	.586	36	34	16-1	0	251.2	234	121	19	4	107	138	3.93	95	.245	.324	91-3-6	.275	-1	118	-4		-0.4
1954	†Cle A	23	11	.676	40	36	20-3	2	270.2	225	93	21	0	83	155	2.73	135	.225	.283	93-0-5	.183	1	109	29		3.6
1955	Cle A★	17	11	.607	32	31	16-6	0	230	207	86	19	3	80-3	122	2.82	142	.240	.304	84-1-2	.179	1*	91	28		3.3
1956	Cle A★	20	9	.690	38	35	18-4	2	277.2	233	93	26	2	91-7	158	2.72	154	.228	.291	101-1-5	.228	3	105	**46**		5.1

YEAR	TM LG	W	L	PCT	G	GS	CG-SHO	SV-BS	IP	H	R	HR	HB	BB-IB	SO	ERA	AERA	OAV	OOB	AB-HR-SH	AVG	PB	SUP	APR	DL	PW
1957	Cle A★	14	17	.452	40	37	13-1	1	263	270	139	32	5	104-7	**184**	4.31	86	.265	.335	86-0-3	.116	-2	107	-15		-1.8
1958	Chi A★	14	16	.467	40	34	11-4	2	239.2	214	115	27	6	104-3	179	4.13	88	.242	.323	75-0-2	.200	3	105	-11		-1.1
1959	†Chi A★	**22**	10	.688	37	**37**	14-5	0	**255.2**	202	106	20	9	119-5	179	3.17	119	.216	.308	90-2-2	.244	9	122	15		2.7
1960	Chi A★	13	12	.520	36	35	13-**4**	1	237.1	220	105	20	4	112-2	158	3.49	108	.247	.332	75-1-6	.200	7	125	7		1.2
1961	Chi A	8	2	.800	17	16	5	0	110.1	88	43	11	4	47-0	64	3.51	112	.220	.302	37-0-1	.162	-0	127	7		0.5
1962	Chi A	7	15	.318	27	26	11-3	0	167.2	171	90	15	3	56-6	91	4.46	88	.264	.325	54-0-2	.130	0	81	-10		-1.3
1963	Cle A	1	2	.333	20	5	1	0	55.1	50	14	2	0	15-3	29	2.28	159	.250	.300	11	.273	1	88	9		0.6
Total	23	300	244	.551	691	612	290-49	15	4564	4291	2037	338	64	1775-36	2334	3.54	106	.248	.320	1704-17-52	.214	72	105	126		19.5

WYNNE, BILLY Billy Vernon B7.31.1943 Williamston NC BL/TR/6-5/206* d8.6 Col Pfeiffer

YEAR	TM LG	W	L	PCT	G	GS	CG-SHO	SV-BS	IP	H	R	HR	HB	BB-IB	SO	ERA	AERA	OAV	OOB	AB-HR-SH	AVG	PB	SUP	APR	DL	PW
1967	NY N	0	0	—	6	1	0	0	8.2	12	4	0	0	2-0	4	3.12	109	.324	.350	1	.000	-0	130	0		0.0
1968	Chi A	0	0	—	1	0	0	0	2	2	2	0	0	2-0	1	4.50	67	.250	.400	0	—	0		-1		0.0
1969	Chi A	7	7	.500	20	20	6-1	0-0	128.2	143	63	14	3	50-8	67	4.06	95	.283	.350	41-0-7	.122	-1	80	-3		-0.4
1970	Chi A	1	4	.200	12	9	0	0-0	44	54	30	8	1	22-2	19	5.32	73	.298	.374	13	.077	-1	105	-7		-0.7
1971	Cal A	0	0	—	3	0	0	0-0	3.2	6	2	0	0	2-0	6	4.91	66	.375	.444	0	—	0		-1		0.0
Total	5	8	11	.421	42	30	6-1	0-0	187	217	101	22	4	78-10	97	4.33	88	.290	.359	55-0-7	.109	-2	90	-12		-1.1

WYNNE, BILL William Andrew B3.27.1869 Neuse NC D8.7.1951 Raleigh NC BR/TR/5-11.5/161 d8.31 Col Wake Forest

| 1894 | Was N | 0 | 1 | .000 | 1 | 1 | 0 | 0 | 8 | 10 | 11 | 0 | 2 | 8 | 2 | 6.75 | 78 | .303 | .465 | 3 | .000 | -0 | 67 | -2 | | -0.2 |

WYSE, HANK Henry Washington "Hooks" B3.1.1918 Lunsford AR D10.22.2000 Pryor OK BR/TR/5-11.5/185* d9.7

YEAR	TM LG	W	L	PCT	G	GS	CG-SHO	SV-BS	IP	H	R	HR	HB	BB-IB	SO	ERA	AERA	OAV	OOB	AB-HR-SH	AVG	PB	SUP	APR	DL	PW
1942	Chi N	2	1	.667	4	4	1-1	0	28	33	10	1	0	6	8	1.93	166	.287	.322	8-0-2	.125	-0	171	3		0.3
1943	Chi N	9	7	.563	38	15	8-2	5	156	159	57	4	2	34	45	2.94	113	.264	.306	50-0-5	.080	-4*	117	8		0.7
1944	Chi N	16	15	.516	41	34	14-3	1	257.1	277	113	9	2	57	86	3.15	112	.278	.318	90-0-6	.178	-1	116	9		0.9
1945	†Chi N*	22	10	.688	38	34	23-2	0	278.1	272	95	17	5	55	77	2.68	136	.256	.296	101-0-8	.168	-2	102	32		3.3
1946	Chi N	14	12	.538	40	27	12-2	1	201.1	206	73	7	3	52	52	2.68	124	.265	.313	74-0-4	.243	-1	107	13		1.9
1947	Chi N	6	9	.400	37	19	5-1	1	142	158	84	12	6	64	53	4.31	92	.286	.363	45-0-4	.111	-1	73	-8		-2.9
1950	Phi A	9	14	.391	41	23	4	0	170.2	192	121	16	8	87	33	5.85	78	.287	.376	59-0-3	.153	-3	97	-24		-1.0
1951	Phi A	1	2	.333	9	1	0	0	14.2	24	14	0	0	8	5	7.98	54	.381	.451	4	.250	-0	83	-6		-0.4
	Was A	0	0	—	3	2	0	0	9.1	17	14	0	1	10	3	9.64	42	.378	.500	4	.000	-1	130	-7		-1.4
	Year	1	2	.333	12	3	0	0	24	41	28	0	1	18	8	8.63	49	.380	.472	8	.125	-1	113	-12		-1.8
Total	8	79	70	.530	251	159	67-11	8	1257.2	1338	581	66	24	373	362	3.52	105	.274	.329	435-0-32	.163	-11	104	20		2.0

WYSONG, BIFF Harlan B4.13.1905 Clarksville OH D8.8.1951 Xenia OH BL/TL/6-3/195 d8.10

1930	Cin N	0	1	.000	1	1	0	0	2.1	6	5	0	0	3	1	19.29	25	.545	.643	0	—	0	0	-4		-0.5
1931	Cin N	0	2	.000	12	2	0	0	21.2	25	22	2	0	23	5	7.89	47	.298	.449	4	.250	0	115	-10		-0.8
1932	Cin N	1	0	1.000	7	0	0	0	12.1	13	7	0	0	8	5	3.65	106	.277	.382	2	.000	-0	0	0		0.0
Total	3	1	3	.250	20	3	0	0	36.1	44	34	2	0	34	11	7.18	54	.310	.443	6	.167	0	74	-14		-1.3

YABU, KEIICHI Keiichi B9.28.1968 Mie, Japan BR/TR/6-0/200 d4.9

| 2005 | Oak A | 4 | 0 | 1.000 | 40 | 0 | 0 | 1-1 | 69.1 | 64 | 34 | 6 | 8 | 26-3 | 44 | 4.50 | 99 | .287 | .377 | 1 | .000 | -0 | | -1 | | -0.1 |

YAN, ESTEBAN Esteban Luis B6.22.1975 Campina, D.R. BR/TR/6-4/230(230-255) d5.20

YEAR	TM LG	W	L	PCT	G	GS	CG-SHO	SV-BS	IP	H	R	HR	HB	BB-IB	SO	ERA	AERA	OAV	OOB	AB-HR-SH	AVG	PB	SUP	APR	DL	PW
1996	Bal A	0	0	—	4	0	0	0-0	9.1	13	7	3	0	3-1	7	5.79	86	.333	.381	0	—	0		-1		-0.1
1997	Bal A	0	1	.000	3	2	0	0-0	9.2	20	18	3	2	7-0	4	15.83	28	.417	.500	0	—	0	83	-13		-1.0
1998	TB A	5	4	.556	64	0	0	1-4	88.2	78	41	11	5	41-2	77	3.86	124	.236	.326	0	—	0	131	-4	28	-0.4
1999	TB A	3	4	.429	50	1	0	0-3	61	77	41	8	9	32-4	46	5.90	84	.326	.421	0	—	0	111	-18		-1.5
2000	TB A	7	8	.467	43	20	0	0-2	137.2	158	98	26	11	42-0	111	6.21	79	.285	.344	1-1-1	1.000	1	3	0		-1.5
2001	TB A	4	6	.400	54	0	0	22-9	62.1	64	34	7	5	11-1	64	3.90	116	.262	.307	0	—	0	2	0		0.5
2002	TB A	7	8	.467	55	0	0	19-8	69	70	35	10	3	29-1	53	4.30	105	.259	.337	0	—	0	4	0	20	-0.2
2003	Tex A	0	1	.000	15	0	0	0-0	23.1	31	19	5	2	7-1	25	6.94	72	.307	.364	0	—	0		-5		-0.2
	StL N	2	0	1.000	39	0	0	1-0	43.1	53	29	5	6	16-4	28	6.02	68	.300	.376	1	1.000	0		-9		-0.4
2004	Det A	3	6	.333	69	0	0	7-10	87	92	43	8	4	32-5	69	3.83	117	.274	.341	0	—	0		5		0.5
2005	†LA A	1	1	.500	49	0	0	0-0	66.2	66	36	8	0	30-4	45	4.59	94	.258	.331	0	—	0		-2		-0.1
Total	10	32	39	.451	445	23	0	50-36	658	722	401	97	46	250-23	529	5.12	91	.279	.350	2-1-1	1.000	2	114	-33	48	-1.4

YARNALL, ED Harvey Edward B12.4.1975 Lima PA BL/TL/6-3/234* [NYN96 3/78] d7.15 Col Louisiana St.

1999	NY A	1	0	1.000	5	2	0	0-0	17	17	8	1	0	10-0	13	3.71	128	.254	.351	0	—	0	168	2		0.1
2000	NY A	0	0	—	2	1	0	0-0	3	5	5	1	1	3-0	1	15.00	32	.417	.563	0	—	0	255	-3		-0.2
Total	2	1	0	1.000	7	3	0	0-0	20	22	13	2	1	13-0	14	5.40	88	.278	.387	0	—	0	197	-1		-0.1

YARNALL, RUSTY Waldo Ward B10.22.1902 Chicago IL D10.9.1985 Lowell MA BR/TR/6-0/175 d6.30 Col Vermont

| 1926 | Phi N | 0 | 0 | 1.000 | 1 | 1 | 0 | 0 | 3 | 3 | 2 | 0 | 1 | 0 | 1 | 18.00 | 23 | .500 | .571 | 1 | .000 | -0 | | -1 | | -0.2 |

YARRISON, RUBE Byron Wardsworth B3.9.1896 Montgomery PA D4.22.1977 Williamsport PA BR/TR/5-11/165 d4.13 Col Gettysburg

1922	Phi A	1	2	.333	18	1	0	0	33.2	50	32	4	2	12	10	8.29	51	.362	.421	6	.167	-0	40	-12		-0.9
1924	Bro N	0	2	.000	3	2	0	0	11	12	10	0	1	3	2	6.55	57	.287	.327	2	.000	-0	79	-4		-0.6
Total	2	1	4	.200	21	3	0	0	44.2	62	42	4	3	15	12	7.86	53	.339	.398	8	.125	-0	62	-16		-1.5

YATES, TYLER Tyler Kali B8.7.1977 Lihue HI BR/TR/6-4/220 [OakA98 23/675] d4.9 Col Hawaii-Hilo [DL 2005 NY N 183]

| 2004 | NY N | 2 | 4 | .333 | 21 | 7 | 0 | 0-0 | 46.2 | 61 | 36 | 6 | 3 | 25-3 | 35 | 6.36 | 68 | .311 | .394 | 11-0-1 | .091 | -1 | 71 | -11 | | -1.2 |

YDE, EMIL Emil Ogden B1.28.1900 Great Lakes IL D12.4.1968 Leesburg FL BB/TL(BL 1925)/5-11/165 d4.21

1924	Pit N	16	3	**.842**	33	22	14-**4**	0	194	170	71	3	6	62	53	2.83	136	.244	.311	88-1-4	.239	2*	114	22		2.2
1925	†Pit N	17	9	.654	33	28	13	0	207	254	125	11	2	75	41	4.13	108	.309	.369	89-0-2	.191	-2*	109	4		0.2
1926	Pit N	8	7	.533	37	22	12-1	0	187.1	181	97	3	2	81	34	3.65	108	.260	.339	74-0-2	.230	3*	110	4		0.5
1927	†Pit N	1	3	.250	9	2	0	0	29.2	45	35	1	2	15	9	9.71	42	.375	.453	18	.167	-0*	73	-17		-1.8
1929	Det A	7	3	.700	29	6	4-1	0	86.2	100	60	8	0	63	23	5.30	81	.296	.406	48-0-1	.333	2*	183	-9		-0.5
Total	5	49	25	.662	141	80	43-6	0	704.2	751	387	26	12	296	160	4.02	102	.281	.355	317-1-9	.233	5	116	4		0.6

YEAGER, JOE Joseph F. "Little Joe" B8.28.1875 Philadelphia PA D7.2.1937 Detroit MI BR/TR/5-10/160 d4.22 ▲

1898	Bro N	12	22	.353	36	33	32	0	291.1	333	177	4	6	80	70	3.65	98	.285	.334	134-0-3	.172	-3*	84	-6		-0.7
1899	Bro N	2	2	.500	10	4	2-1	1	47.2	56	29	1	2	16	6	4.72	83	.292	.352	47-0-2	.191	1*	142	-2		-0.3
1900	Bro N	1	1	.500	2	2	2	0	17	21	13	1	0	5	5	6.88	56	.304	.351	9	.333	0*	90	-4		-0.3
1901	Det A	12	11	.522	26	25	22-2	1	199.2	209	105	4	8	46	38	2.61	147	.266	.313	125-2-2	.296	5*	85	22		2.9
1902	Det A	6	12	.333	19	15	14	0	140	171	90	5	5	41	28	4.82	76	.301	.353	161-1-1	.242	3*	95	-13		-1.0
1903	Det A	0	1	.000	1	1	1	0	9	15	7	0	0	0	1	4.00	73	.366	.366	402-0-9	.256	0*	74	-1		-0.1
Total	6	33	49	.402	94	80	73-3	2	704.2	805	421	15	21	188	145	3.74	99	.285	.334	878-3-17	.244	6	90	-4		-0.4

YEARGIN, AL James Almond B10.16.1901 Mauldin SC D5.8.1937 Greenville SC BR/TR/5-11/170 d10.1

1922	Bos N	0	1	.000	1	1	1	0	7	11	5	3	1	0	2	3	1.29	311	.192	.250	3	.000	-0	0	1		0.1
1924	Bos N	1	11	.083	32	12	6	0	141.1	162	90	7	3	42	34	5.09	75	.293	.346	42-0-2	.143	-2	65	-19		-1.4
Total	2	1	12	.077	33	13	7	0	148.1	167	93	8	3	44	35	4.91	78	.288	.342	45-0-2	.133	-2	60	-18		-1.3

YELLEN, LARRY Lawrence Alan B1.4.1943 Brooklyn NY BR/TR/5-11/190* d9.26 Col Hunter

1963	Hou N	0	0	—	1	1	0	0	5	7	4	0	0	1-0	3	3.60	88	.280	.296	2	.000	-0	137	-1		-0.1
1964	Hou N	0	0	—	13	1	0	0	21	27	19	4	0	10-1	9	6.86	50	.297	.363	3	.000	-0	129	-9		-0.5
Total	2	0	0	—	14	2	0	0	26	34	23	4	0	11-1	12	6.23	54	.293	.349	5	.000	-0	130	-10		-0.6

YELLOWHORSE, CHIEF Moses J. B1.28.1898 Pawnee OK D4.10.1964 Pawnee OK BR/TR/5-10/180 d4.15

1921	Pit N	5	3	.625	10	4	1	1	48.1	45	17	1	0	13	19	2.98	129	.254	.305	17	.000	-2	75	5		0.8
1922	Pit N	3	1	.750	28	4	2	0	77.2	92	48	0	2	20	24	4.52	90	.305	.352	19-0-2	.316	1	120	-4		-0.2
Total	2	8	4	.667	38	8	3	1	126	137	65	1	2	33	43	3.93	101	.286	.335	36-0-2	.167	-2	97	1		0.5

YERKES, CARROLL Charles Carroll "Lefty" B6.13.1903 McSherrystown PA D12.20.1950 Oakland CA BR/TL/5-11/180 d5.31

1927	Phi A	0	0	—	1	0	0	0	0.0	0	0	0	0	0	0	0.00	—	.000	.333	0	—	0	0	0		0.0
1928	Phi A	0	1	.000	2	1	0	0	8.2	7	2	0	1	2	1	2.08	193	.233	.281	3	.000	0	0	2		0.2
1929	Phi A	1	0	1.000	19	2	0	1	37.1	47	20	0	1	13	11	4.58	92	.329	.389	10	.000	-2	179	0		0.0
1932	Chi N	0	0	—	2	0	0	0	9	5	3	2	0	3	4	3.00	126	.167	.242	3	.333	0		1		0.0

YEAR	TM LG	W	L	PCT	G	GS	CG-SHO	SV-BS	IP	H	R	HR	HB	BB-IB	SO	ERA	AERA	OAV	OOB	AB-HR-SH	AVG	PB	SUP	APR	DL	PW
1933	Chi N	0	0	—	1	0	0	0	2	2	1	0	0	1	0	4.50	73	.286	.375	0	—	0	0			0.0
Total	5	1	1	.500	25	3	1	1	58	61	26	2	1	20	16	3.88	106	.288	.352	16	.063	-2	124	3		0.2

YERKES, STAN Stanley Lewis "Yank" B11.28.1874 Cheltenham PA D7.28.1940 Boston MA BR/TR/5-10/165 d5.3

YEAR	TM LG	W	L	PCT	G	GS	CG-SHO	SV-BS	IP	H	R	HR	HB	BB-IB	SO	ERA	AERA	OAV	OOB	AB-HR-SH	AVG	PB	SUP	APR	DL	PW
1901	Bal A	0	1	.000	1	1	1	0	8	12	9	0	0	2	4	6.75	57	.343	.378	3	.333	0	70	-2		-0.2
	StL N	3	1	.750	4	4	4	0	34	35	14	0	1	6	15	3.18	100	.265	.302	12-0-1	.083	-1	117	1		0.0
1902	StL N	12	21	.364	39	37	27-1	0	272.2	341	160	1	2	79	81	3.66	75	.306	.353	91	.132	-3	93	-28		-3.4
1903	StL N	0	1	.000	1	1	0	0	5	8	6	0	0	0	3	1.80	181	.333	.333	2	.000	-0	124	-1		-0.1
Total	3	15	24	.385	45	43	32-1	0	319.2	396	189	2	3	87	103	3.66	77	.303	.348	108-0-1	.130	-4	95	-30		-3.7

YETT, RICH Richard Martin B10.6.1962 Pomona CA BR/TR/6-2/187(170-187) [MinA80 26/650] d4.13

YEAR	TM LG	W	L	PCT	G	GS	CG-SHO	SV-BS	IP	H	R	HR	HB	BB-IB	SO	ERA	AERA	OAV	OOB	AB-HR-SH	AVG	PB	SUP	APR	DL	PW
1985	Min A	0	0	—	1	0	0	0-0	0.1	1	1	0	0	2-0	0	27.00	16	.333	.600	0	—	0	144	-1		0.0
1986	Cle A	5	3	.625	39	3	1-1	1-3	78.2	84	48	10	1	37-4	50	5.15	81	.275	.351	0	—	0	145	-7		-0.7
1987	Cle A	3	9	.250	37	11	2	1-2	97.2	96	63	21	3	49-3	59	5.25	87	.257	.346	0	—	0	98	-6		-0.7
1988	Cle A	9	6	.600	23	22	0	0-0	134.1	146	72	11	1	55-1	71	4.62	90	.275	.344	0	—	0	92	-5	34	-0.6
1989	Cle A	5	6	.455	32	12	1	0-0	99	111	56	10	2	47-1	47	5.00	80	.283	.360	0	—	0	110	-9		-1.0
1990	Min A	0	0	—	4	0	0	0-0	4.1	6	2	1	0	1-1	2	2.08	201	.353	.389	0	—	0		1		0.0
Total	6	22	24	.478	136	49	4-1	2-5	414.1	444	242	53	7	191-10	229	4.95	85	.274	.351	0	—	0	102	-27	34	-3.0

YINGLING, EARL Earl Hershey "Chink" B10.29.1888 Chillicothe OH D10.2.1962 Columbus OH BL/TL/5-11.5/180 d4.12 Mil 1918

YEAR	TM LG	W	L	PCT	G	GS	CG-SHO	SV-BS	IP	H	R	HR	HB	BB-IB	SO	ERA	AERA	OAV	OOB	AB-HR-SH	AVG	PB	SUP	APR	DL	PW
1911	Cle A	1	0	1.000	4	3	1	0	22.1	30	17	1	1	9	6	4.43	77	.326	.392	11	.273	0*	127	-3		-0.1
1912	Bro N	6	11	.353	25	16	12	0	163	186	90	0	1	56	51	3.59	93	.293	.351	64-0-1	.250	3	89	-5		-0.2
1913	Bro N	8	8	.500	26	13	8-2	0	146.2	158	56	2	2	10	40	2.58	128	.280	.295	60-0-2	.383	8*	97	10		2.0
1914	Cin N	9	13	.409	34	27	8-3	0	198	207	102	6	6	54	80	3.45	85	.274	.328	120-1-1	.192	1*	98	-9		-0.8
1918	Was A	1	2	.333	5	2	1	0	38	30	15	0	0	12	15	2.13	128	.238	.304	15	.467	3*	69	2		0.6
Total	5	25	34	.424	94	61	31-5	0	568	611	280	19	10	141	192	3.22	98	.281	.328	270-1-4	.267	16	96	-5		1.5

YINGLING, JOE Joseph B2.28.1867 Baltimore MD D10.22.1903 Baltimore MD BR/TL/5-7.5/145 d5.28 b-Charlie

YEAR	TM LG	W	L	PCT	G	GS	CG-SHO	SV-BS	IP	H	R	HR	HB	BB-IB	SO	ERA	AERA	OAV	OOB	AB-HR-SH	AVG	PB	SUP	APR	DL	PW
1886	Was N	0	1	.000	3	7	6	1	7					1	1	12.00	27	.412	.444	2	.000	-0		-3		-0.1

YOCHIM, LEN Leonard Joseph B10.16.1928 New Orleans LA BL/TL/6-2/200* d9.18 b-Ray

YEAR	TM LG	W	L	PCT	G	GS	CG-SHO	SV-BS	IP	H	R	HR	HB	BB-IB	SO	ERA	AERA	OAV	OOB	AB-HR-SH	AVG	PB	SUP	APR	DL	PW
1951	Pit N	1	1	.500	2	1	0	0	8.2	10	9	0	1	11	5	8.31	51	.278	.458	3-0-1	.000	-0	94	-4		-0.6
1954	Pit N	0	1	.000	10	1	0	0	19.2	30	17	2	0	8	7	7.32	57	.361	.409	2	.500	0	0	-6		-0.2
Total	2	1	2	.333	12	3	0	0	28.1	40	26	2	1	19	12	7.62	55	.336	.426	5-0-1	.200	-0	63	-10		-0.8

YOCHIM, RAY Raymond Austin Aloysius B7.19.1922 New Orleans LA D1.26.2002 New Orleans LA BR/TR/6-1/170 d5.2 b-Len

YEAR	TM LG	W	L	PCT	G	GS	CG-SHO	SV-BS	IP	H	R	HR	HB	BB-IB	SO	ERA	AERA	OAV	OOB	AB-HR-SH	AVG	PB	SUP	APR	DL	PW
1948	StL N	0	0	—	1	0	0	0	1	0	0	0	0	3	1	0.00	—	.000	.500	0	—	0		0		0.0
1949	StL N	0	0	—	3	0	0	0	2.1	3	4	1	0	4	3	15.43	27	.273	.467	0	—	0		-3		-0.1
Total	2	0	0	—	4	0	0	0	3.1	3	4	1	0	7	4	10.80	38	.214	.476	0	—	0		-3		-0.1

YORK, LEFTY James Edward B11.1.1892 West Fork AR D4.9.1961 York PA BL/TL/5-10/185 d9.12

YEAR	TM LG	W	L	PCT	G	GS	CG-SHO	SV-BS	IP	H	R	HR	HB	BB-IB	SO	ERA	AERA	OAV	OOB	AB-HR-SH	AVG	PB	SUP	APR	DL	PW
1919	Phi A	0	2	.000	2	2	0	0	4.1	13	13	0	0	5	2	24.92	14	.500	.581	1	.000	-0	114	-9		-1.3
1921	Chi N	5	9	.357	40	11	4-1	1	139	170	82	5	5	63	57	4.73	81	.308	.384	39-0-3	.128	-2	67	-13		-1.5
Total	2	5	11	.313	42	13	4-1	1	143.1	183	95	5	5	68	59	5.34	71	.317	.393	40-0-3	.125	-2	73	-22		-2.8

YORK, JIM James Harlan B8.27.1947 Maywood CA BR/TR/6-3/200* [KCA69 16/381] d9.21 Col UCLA

YEAR	TM LG	W	L	PCT	G	GS	CG-SHO	SV-BS	IP	H	R	HR	HB	BB-IB	SO	ERA	AERA	OAV	OOB	AB-HR-SH	AVG	PB	SUP	APR	DL	PW
1970	KC A	1	1	.500	4	0	0	0-1	8	5	3	2	0	2-0	6	3.38	111	.179	.226	2	.000	-0		1		0.1
1971	KC A	5	5	.500	53	0	0	3-2	93.1	70	32	7	3	44-7	103	2.89	119	.203	.297	17-1-0	.118	1		6		0.8
1972	Hou N	0	1	.000	26	0	0	0-0	36	45	21	3	1	18-3	25	5.25	64	.321	.398	1	.000	-0		-7		-0.4
1973	Hou N	3	4	.429	41	0	0	6-3	53	65	26	4	1	20-5	22	4.42	83	.305	.364	5-0-1	.000	-0		-3		-0.5
1974	Hou N	2	2	.500	28	0	0	1-0	38.1	48	20	1	1	19-6	15	3.29	106	.298	.374	4	.000	-1		-1		-0.2
1975	Hou N	4	4	.500	19	4	0	0-0	46.2	43	22	1	2	25-3	17	3.86	88	.251	.358	11	.091	-0	155	-3		-0.5
1976	NY A	1	0	1.000	3	0	0	0-0	9.2	14	7	1	1	4-0	6	5.59	61	.333	.404	0	—	0	155	-3		-0.2
Total	7	16	17	.485	174	4	0	10-6	285	290	131	19	12	132-24	194	3.79	92	.264	.346	40-1-1	.075	-1	155	-10		-0.9

YORK, MIKE Michael David B9.6.1964 Oak Park IL BR/TR/6-1/190* [NYA82 40/820] d8.17

YEAR	TM LG	W	L	PCT	G	GS	CG-SHO	SV-BS	IP	H	R	HR	HB	BB-IB	SO	ERA	AERA	OAV	OOB	AB-HR-SH	AVG	PB	SUP	APR	DL	PW
1990	Pit N	1	1	.500	7	1	0	0-0	12.2	13	5	0	1	5-0	4	2.84	128	.277	.352	3	.333	0	173	1		0.2
1991	Cle A	1	4	.200	14	4	0	0-0	34.2	45	29	2	2	19-3	19	6.75	62	.333	.412	0	—	0	148	-10	51	-1.2
Total	2	2	5	.286	18	5	0	0-0	47.1	58	34	2	3	24-3	23	5.70	71	.319	.397	3	.333	0	154	-9	51	-1.0

YOSHII, MASATO Masato B4.20.1965 Osaka, Japan BR/TR/6-2/210* d4.5

YEAR	TM LG	W	L	PCT	G	GS	CG-SHO	SV-BS	IP	H	R	HR	HB	BB-IB	SO	ERA	AERA	OAV	OOB	AB-HR-SH	AVG	PB	SUP	APR	DL	PW
1998	NY N	6	8	.429	29	29	1	0-0	171.2	166	79	22	6	53-5	117	3.93	105	.255	.315	48-0-8	.063	-2	85	4		0.0
1999	†NY N	12	8	.600	31	29	1	0-0	174	168	86	25	6	58-3	105	4.40	99	.260	.324	55-0-6	.164	-1	112	0		-0.3
2000	Col N	6	15	.286	29	29	0	0-0	167.1	201	112	32	2	53-6	88	5.86	99	.306	.357	50-1-12	.180	-1	83	1		0.0
2001	Mon N	4	7	.364	42	11	0	0-0	113	127	65	18	5	26-2	63	4.78	90	.279	.323	16-0-2	.125	-1	101	-6		-0.5
2002	Mon N	4	9	.308	31	20	1	0-0	131.1	143	66	15	4	32-2	74	4.11	107	.281	.326	35-0-5	.057	-1	100	4		0.2
Total	5	32	47	.405	162	118	3	0-0	757.1	805	408	112	23	222-18	447	4.62	100	.276	.329	204-1-33	.123	-5	95	3		-0.6

YOST, GUS August 6-5/? d6.12

YEAR	TM LG	W	L	PCT	G	GS	CG-SHO	SV-BS	IP	H	R	HR	HB	BB-IB	SO	ERA	AERA	OAV	OOB	AB-HR-SH	AVG	PB	SUP	APR	DL	PW
1893	Chi N	0	1	.000	1	1	0	0	2.2	3	4	0	0	8	1	13.50	34	.273	.579	1	.000	-0	91	-2		-0.3

YOUMANS, FLOYD Floyd Everett B5.11.1964 Tampa FL BR/TR/6-1/190(180-200) [NYN82 2/33] d7.1 [DL 1990 Phi N 178]

YEAR	TM LG	W	L	PCT	G	GS	CG-SHO	SV-BS	IP	H	R	HR	HB	BB-IB	SO	ERA	AERA	OAV	OOB	AB-HR-SH	AVG	PB	SUP	APR	DL	PW
1985	Mon N	4	3	.571	14	12	0	0-0	77	57	27	3	1	49-1	54	2.45	140	.206	.325	19-0-3	.053	-0	96	7		0.5
1986	Mon N	13	12	.520	33	32	6-2	0-0	219	145	93	14	4	118-4	202	3.53	106	.188	.297	75-1-2	.160	1	96	7		0.7
1987	Mon N	9	8	.529	23	23	3-3	0-0	116.1	112	63	13	1	47-2	94	4.64	92	.251	.321	40-1-1	.150	-0	82	-2	50	0.3
1988	Mon N	3	6	.333	14	13	1-1	0-0	84	64	35	8	2	41-1	54	3.21	113	.213	.307	26	.154	-0	88	4	20	0.3
1989	Phi N	1	5	.167	10	10	0	0-0	42.2	50	31	7	2	25-3	20	5.70	63	.299	.391	13-0-1	.077	-1	86	-10	126	-1.3
Total	5	30	34	.469	94	90	10-6	0-0	539	428	249	45	10	280-11	424	3.74	101	.218	.316	173-2-7	.139	1	90	6	374	-0.1

YOUNG, ANTHONY Anthony Wayne B1.19.1966 Houston TX BR/TR/6-2/210(200-220) [NYN87 38/978] d8.5 Col Houston

YEAR	TM LG	W	L	PCT	G	GS	CG-SHO	SV-BS	IP	H	R	HR	HB	BB-IB	SO	ERA	AERA	OAV	OOB	AB-HR-SH	AVG	PB	SUP	APR	DL	PW
1991	NY N	2	5	.286	10	8	0	0-0	49.1	48	24	4	1	12-1	20	3.10	118	.257	.303	14-0-1	.143	0	74	3		0.3
1992	NY N	2	14	.125	52	13	1	15-5	121	134	66	8	1	31-5	64	4.17	84	.285	.328	27-0-2	.111	-1	95	-11		-1.7
1993	NY N	1	16	.059	39	10	1	3-2	100.1	103	62	8	1	42-9	62	3.77	107	.265	.336	14-0-2	.143	-0	45	-3		-0.5
1994	Chi N	4	6	.400	20	19	0	0-0	114.2	103	57	12	0	46-2	65	3.92	108	.246	.318	34-0-5	.176	-0	103	2	32	0.2
1995	Chi N	3	4	.429	32	1	0	2-0	41.1	47	20	5	3	14-2	15	3.70	113	.288	.356	3	.667	1	108	2	77	0.3
1996	Hou N	3	3	.500	28	0	0	0-1	33.1	36	18	4	4	22-4	19	4.59	84	.279	.397	2	.000	-0		-2	19	-0.4
Total	6	15	48	.238	181	51	2	20-8	460	471	243	41	10	167-23	245	3.89	100	.268	.333	94-0-10	.160	-0	86	-9	128	-1.8

YOUNG, PETE Bryan Owen B3.19.1968 Meadville MS BR/TR/6-0/225* [MonN89 6/150] d6.5 Col Mississippi St.

YEAR	TM LG	W	L	PCT	G	GS	CG-SHO	SV-BS	IP	H	R	HR	HB	BB-IB	SO	ERA	AERA	OAV	OOB	AB-HR-SH	AVG	PB	SUP	APR	DL	PW
1992	Mon N	0	0	—	13	0	0	0-0	20.1	18	9	1	0	9-2	11	3.98	87	.247	.329	0	—	0		-1		-0.1
1993	Mon N	1	0	1.000	4	0	0	0-0	5.1	4	2	1	0	0-0	3	3.38	124	.211	.211	1	.000	-0		1		0.1
Total	2	1	0	1.000	17	0	0	0-0	25.2	22	11	1	0	9-2	14	3.86	94	.239	.308	1	.000	-0		0		0.0

YOUNG, CHARLIE Charles "Cy" B1.12.1893 Philadelphia PA D5.12.1952 Riverside NJ BB/TR/5-10.5/155 d9.5

YEAR	TM LG	W	L	PCT	G	GS	CG-SHO	SV-BS	IP	H	R	HR	HB	BB-IB	SO	ERA	AERA	OAV	OOB	AB-HR-SH	AVG	PB	SUP	APR	DL	PW
1915	Bal F	2	3	.400	9	5	1	0	35	39	32	0	4	21	13	5.91	49	.289	.400	9-0-1	.222	0	49	-12		-1.5

YOUNG, CHRIS Christopher Ryan B5.25.1979 Dallas TX BR/TR/6-10/250* [PitN00 3/89] d8.24 Col Princeton

YEAR	TM LG	W	L	PCT	G	GS	CG-SHO	SV-BS	IP	H	R	HR	HB	BB-IB	SO	ERA	AERA	OAV	OOB	AB-HR-SH	AVG	PB	SUP	APR	DL	PW
2004	Tex A	3	2	.600	7	7	0	0-0	36.1	36	21	7	2	10-0	27	4.71	105	.248	.306	0	—	0	92	1		0.1
2005	Tex A	12	7	.632	31	31	0	0-0	164.2	162	84	19	7	45-2	137	4.26	108	.254	.307	5	.000	-1	126	6		0.5
Total	2	15	9	.625	38	38	0	0-0	201	198	105	26	9	55-2	164	4.34	107	.252	.306	5	.000	-1	119	7		0.6

YOUNG, CLIFF Clifford Raphael B8.2.1964 Willis TX D11.4.1993 Montgomery Co. TX BL/TL/6-4/200* [MonN83 5/120] d7.14

YEAR	TM LG	W	L	PCT	G	GS	CG-SHO	SV-BS	IP	H	R	HR	HB	BB-IB	SO	ERA	AERA	OAV	OOB	AB-HR-SH	AVG	PB	SUP	APR	DL	PW
1990	Cal A	1	1	.500	17	0	0	0-2	30.2	40	14	2	1	7-1	19	3.52	109	.325	.356	0	—	0		1		0.1
1991	Cal A	0	0	—	11	0	0	0-0	12.2	12	6	3	0	3-1	6	4.26	97	.261	.306	0	—	0		0		0.0
1993	Cle A	3	3	.500	21	7	0	1-1	60.1	74	35	9	3	18-1	31	4.62	95	.298	.352	0	—	0	81	-2	70	-0.2
Total	3	4	5	.556	49	7	0	1-3	103.2	126	55	14	4	28-3	56	4.25	98	.302	.348	0	—	0	81	-1	70	-0.1

YEAR	TM LG	W	L	PCT	G	GS	CG-SHO	SV-BS	IP	H	R	HR	HB	BB-IB	SO	ERA	AERA	OAV	OOB	AB-HR-SH	AVG	PB	SUP	APR	DL	PW
YOUNG, CURT	Curtis Allen B4.16.1960 Saginaw MI BR/TL/6-1/180* [OakA81 4/92] d6.24 C2 Col Central Michigan																								
1983	Oak A	0	1	.000	8	2	0	0-0	9	17	17	1	1	5-0	5	16.00	24	.386	.460	0	—	0	152	-12		-1.1
1984	Oak A	9	4	.692	20	17	2-1	0-0	108.2	118	53	9	8	31-0	41	4.06	93	.274	.331	0	—	0	114	-17	63	-0.3
1985	Oak A	0	4	.000	19	7	0	0-0	46	57	38	15	1	22-0	19	7.24	54	.300	.374	0	—	0	98	9		-1.3
1986	Oak A	13	9	.591	29	27	5-2	0-0	198	176	88	19	7	57-1	116	3.45	113	.236	.293	0	—	0	89	-2		0.9
1987	Oak A	13	7	.650	31	31	6	0-0	203	194	102	38	3	44-0	124	4.08	102	.252	.293	1	.000	-0	121	2	20	0.2
1988	†Oak A	11	8	.579	26	26	1	0-0	156.1	162	77	23	4	50-3	69	4.14	92	.275	.333	0	—	0	103	-5		-0.6
1989	Oak A	5	9	.357	25	20	1	0-0	111	117	56	10	3	47-2	55	3.73	99	.264	.338	0	—	0	88	-2		-0.3
1990	†Oak A	9	6	.600	26	21	0	0-0	124.1	124	70	17	2	53-1	56	4.85	77	.266	.342	0	—	0*	120	-14		-1.4
1991	Oak A	4	2	.667	41	1	0	0-0	68.1	74	38	8	2	34-2	27	5.00	77	.278	.363	0	—	0	71	-8	15	-0.6
1992	KC A	1	2	.333	10	2	0	0-1	24.1	29	14	1	0	7-1	7	5.18	79	.293	.336	0	—	0	89	-2		-0.3
	NY A	3	0	1.000	13	5	0	0-1	43.1	51	21	1	2	10-1	13	3.32	119	.298	.341	0	—	0	134	1	27	0.1
	Year	4	2	.667	23	7	0	0-2	67.2	80	35	2	2	17-2	20	3.99	100	.296	.339	0	—	0	121	0		-0.2
1993	Oak A	1	1	.500	3	3	0	0-0	14.2	14	7	5	0	6-0	4	4.30	96	.241	.313	0	—	0	96	0	110	0.0
Total	11	69	53	.566	251	162	15-3	0-2	1107	1133	581	147	33	366-11	536	4.31	90	.265	.326	1	.000	-0	110	-51	235	-4.7
YOUNG, DANNY	Daniel Bracy B11.3.1971 Smyrna TN BR/TL/6-4/210 [HouN90 83/1473] d3.30																								
2000	Chi N	0	0	—	4	0	0	0-0	3	5	7	1	0	6-0	0	21.00	22	.357	.550	0	—	0		-5		-0.9
YOUNG, CY	Denton True "Cyclone" B3.29.1867 Gilmore OH D11.4.1955 Newcomerstown OH BR/TR/6-2/210 d8.6 M1 HF1937																								
1890	Cle N	9	7	.563	17	16	16	0	147.2	145	87	6	8	30	39	3.47	103	.249	.295	65	.123	-6	78	2		-0.3
1891	Cle N	27	22	.551	55	46	43	2	423.2	431	244	4	10	140	147	2.85	122	.254	.314	174-1	.167	-3	104	28		2.3
1892	†Cle N	**36**	12	**.750**	53	49	48-**9**	0	453	363	158	8	11	118	168	**1.93**	**176**	.211	**.266**	196-1	.158	-8	108	**74**		**6.4**
1893	Cle N	34	16	.680	53	46	42-1	1	422.2	442	201	10	10	103	102	3.36	145	.261	**.307**	187-1	.235	-6	102	74		6.5
1894	Cle N	26	21	.553	52	47	44-2	1	408.2	488	265	19	5	106	108	3.94	139	.293	.337	186-2-0	.215	-8	92	65		-5.0
1895	†Cle N	**35**	10	.778	47	40	36-**4**	0	369.2	363	177	10	8	75	121	3.26	153	.253	**.294**	140-0-2	.214	-4	84	**73**		6.9
1896	†Cle N	28	15	.651	51	46	42-**5**	3	414.1	477	214	7	11	62	**140**	3.24	140	.286	.316	180-3-2	.289	7*	96	56		**5.7**
1897	Cle N	21	19	.525	46	38	35-2	0	335.2	391	189	7	9	49	88	3.78	119	.289	.318	153-0-2	.222	-4*	89	27		2.3
1898	Cle N	25	13	.658	46	41	40-1	0	377.2	387	167	6	9	41	101	2.53	143	.263	.287	154-2-5	.253	5*	100	40		4.4
1899	StL N	26	16	.619	44	42	40-**4**	1	369.1	368	173	10	6	44	111	2.58	154	.260	**.285**	148-1-6	.216	-1	101	50		**5.1**
1900	StL N	19	19	.500	41	35	32-**4**	0	321.1	337	144	7	3	36	115	3.00	121	.269	.291	124-1-1	.177	-2	86	28		2.0
1901	Bos A	**33**	10	.767	43	41	38-**5**	0	371.1	324	112	6	7	37	**158**	**1.62**	**217**	.232	**.256**	153-0-3	.209	0*	110	**77**		**7.5**
1902	Bos A	**32**	11	.744	**45**	43	41-3	0	**384.2**	350	136	6	13	53	160	2.15	166	.243	.276	148-1-1	.230	-4	107	59		**6.6**
1903	†Bos A	28	9	**.757**	40	35	34-**7**	2	341.2	294	115	6	9	37	176	2.08	146	.232	.251	137-1-5	.321	12*	136	34		**4.8**
1904	Bos A	26	16	.619	43	41	40-**10**	1	380	327	104	6	4	29	200	1.97	136	.233	**.251**	148-1-1	.223	2	94	33		3.8
1905	Bos A	18	19	.486	38	33	31-4	0	320.2	248	99	3	8	30	210	1.82	148	.215	**.241**	120-2-2	.150	-2	77	25		2.7
1906	Bos A	13	21	.382	39	34	28	2	287.2	288	137	3	8	25	140	3.19	86	.263	.285	104-0-2	.154	-2*	74	-14		-1.1
1907	Bos A	21	15	.583	43	37	33-6	2	343.1	286	101	3	7	51	147	1.99	129	**.263**		115-0-2	.216	0*	86	25		4.2
1908	Bos A	21	11	.656	36	33	30-3	2	299	230	68	1	1	37	150	1.26	195	.213	.240	115-0-0	.226	1	110	36		4.
1909	Cle A	19	15	.559	35	34	30-3	0	294.1	267	110	4	4	59	109	2.26	113	.250	.294	107-0-6	.196	-0	110	9		0.5
1910	Cle A	7	10	.412	21	20	14-1	0	163.1	149	62	0	4	27	58	2.53	102	.252	.289	55-0-3	.145	0	74	2		-0.1
1911	Cle A	3	4	.429	7	7	4-1	0	46.1	54	28	2	1	13	20	3.88	88	.298	.349	16	.063	-2	60	-3		-0.1
	Bos N	4	5	.444	11	11	8-2	0	80	83	47	4	3	15	35	3.71	103	.268	.308	25-0-5	.080	-2	66	0		-0.1
Total	22	511	316	.618	906	815	749-76	17	7356	7092	3167	138	163	1217	2803	2.63	138	.252	.287	2960-18-50	.210	-22	97	800		77.
YOUNG, HARLEY	Harlan Edward "Cy the Third" B9.28.1883 Portland IN D3.26.1975 Jacksonville FL BR/TR/6-2/? d4.21																								
1908	Pit N	0	2	.000	8	3	0	0	48.1	40	21	0	5	10	17	2.23	103	.234	.296	12-0-1	.083	-1	61	-1		-0.
	Bos N	0	1	.000	6	2	1	0	27.1	29	19	0	3	4	12	3.29	73	.269	.313	10-0-1	.200	0	117	-4		-0.
	Year	0	3	.000	14	5	1	0	75.2	69	40	0	8	14	29	2.62	89	.247	.302	22-0-2	.136	-0	84	-6		-0.
YOUNG, IRV	Irving Melrose "Young Cy","Cy the Second" B7.21.1877 Columbia Falls ME D1.14.1935 Brewer ME BL/TL/5-10/170 d4.14																								
1905	Bos N	20	21	.488	43	**42**	41-**7**	0	**378**	337	146	6	8	71	156	2.90	107	.241	.282	136-0-1	.103	-8	59	14		-1.
1906	Bos N	16	25	.390	43	**41**	37-4	0	358.1	349	157	7	6	83	151	2.91	92	.254	.309	125-0-2	.096	-7	72	-7		-1.
1907	Bos N	10	23	.303	40	32	22-3	1	245.1	287	131	5	13	58	86	3.96	64	.306	.354	80-0-1	.162	-1	74	-33		-1.
1908	Bos N	4	9	.308	16	11	7-1	0	85	94	49	2	2	19	32	2.86	84	.289	.332	32-0-1	.156	-1	101	-8		-1.
	Pit N	4	3	.571	16	7	3-1	1	89.2	73	33	1	5	21	31	2.01	115	.225	.283	30	.200	1	100	1		0.
	Year	8	12	.400	32	18	10-2	1	174.2	167	82	3	7	40	63	2.42	97	.257	.307	62-0-1	.177	0	101	-9		-1.
1910	Chi A	4	8	.333	27	17	7-4	0	135.2	122	52	0	3	39	64	2.72	88	.247	.306	44-0-3	.114	-2	74	-2		-0
1911	Chi A	5	6	.455	24	11	3-1	2	92.2	99	61	2	0	35	40	4.37	74	.269	.339	28-0-1	.179	-0	85	-12		-7
Total	6	63	95	.399	209	161	120-21	4	1384.2	1361	629	23	37	316	560	3.11	88	.260	.307	475-0-9	.126	-18	73	-47		-7.
YOUNG, J. B.	J. B. B Mt.Carmel PA d6.10																								
1892	StL N	0	0	—	1	0	0	0	2	9	13	0	2	2	1	22.50	14	.600	.647	1	.000	-0		-6		-0.9
YOUNG, JASON	Jason Kariya B9.2.1979 Oakland CA BR/TR/6-5/210* [ColN00 2/47] d5.12 Col Stanford																								
2003	Col N	0	2	.000	8	3	0	0-0	21.1	34	22	8	1	9-0	18	8.44	58	.354	.411	7	.286	1	102	-8		-0.
2004	Col N	0	1	.000	2	2	0	0-0	8.1	15	12	3	0	5-1	7	12.96	37	.385	.455	2-0-2	.000	-0	136	-7	135	-0.
Total	2	0	3	.000	10	5	0	0-0	29.2	49	34	11	1	14-1	25	9.71	50	.363	.424	9-0-2	.222	1	116	-15	135	-0.
YOUNG, KIP	Kip Lane B10.29.1954 Georgetown OH BR/TR/5-11/175* [DetA76 23/529] d7.21 Col Bowling Green																								
1978	Det A	6	7	.462	14	13	7	0-0	105.2	94	34	9	2	30-1	49	2.81	139	.246	.303	0	—	0	92	13		0.
1979	Det A	2	2	.500	13	7	0	0-0	43.2	60	32	11	1	11-0	22	6.39	68	.323	.362	0	—	0	128	-9		-1.
Total	2	8	9	.471	27	20	7	0-0	149.1	154	66	20	3	41-1	71	3.86	105	.271	.322	0	—	0	106	4		-0.
YOUNG, MATT	Matthew John B8.9.1958 Pasadena CA BL/TL/6-3/205* [SeaA80 2/32] d4.6 Col UCLA [DL 1988 Oak A 182]																								
1983	Sea A★	11	15	.423	33	32	5-2	0-0	203.2	178	86	17	7	79-2	130	3.27	131	.236	.312	0	—	0	125	-22	25	-3.
1984	Sea A	6	8	.429	22	22	1	0-0	113.1	141	81	11	1	57-3	73	5.72	70	.304	.380	0	—	0	95	-18		-3.3
1985	Sea A	12	19	.387	37	35	5-2	1-0	218.1	242	135	23	7	76-3	136	4.91	86	.282	.344	0	—	0	106	5		-0.
1986	Sea A	8	6	.571	65	5	1	13-12	103.2	108	50	9	8	46-2	82	3.82	112	.272	.357	0	—	0		-3		0.
1987	LA N	5	8	.385	47	0	0	11-4	54.1	62	30	9	0	17-5	42	4.47	89	.288	.339	3	.000	-0	61	-13	71	-1.
1989	†Oak A	1	4	.200	26	4	0	0-1	37.1	42	31	2	0	31-2	27	6.75	55	.286	.408	0	—	0	85	9		-1
1990	Sea A	8	18	.308	34	33	7-1	0-0	225.1	198	106	15	6	107-7	176	3.51	113	.237	.325	0	—	0	83	-7	57	-0.
1991	Bos A	3	7	.300	19	16	0	0-0	88.2	92	55	4	2	53-2	69	5.18	84	.266	.365	0	—	0	73	-3	16	-0.
1992	Bos A	0	4	.000	28	8	1	0-0	70.2	69	42	7	3	42-2	57	4.58	93	.257	.360	0	—	0	81	-6		-0.
1993	Cle A	4	6	.143	22	8	0	0-0	74.1	75	45	8	3	57-0	65	5.21	84	.266	.394	0	—	0	88	-6		-0.
Total	10	55	95	.367	333	163	20-5	25-17	1189.2	1207	661	99	37	565-28	857	4.40	95	.265	.348	3	.000	0	88	-37	351	-8.
YOUNG, TIM	Timothy R. B10.15.1973 Gulfport MS BL/TL/5-9/170* [MonN96 19/550] d9.5 Col Alabama																								
1998	Mon N	0	0	—	10	0	0	0-0	6	6	4	0	0	4-0	7	6.00	70	.250	.357	0	—	0		-1		-0.
2000	Bos A	0	0	—	8	0	0	0-0	7	7	5	3	1	2-0	6	6.43	78	.269	.345	0	—	0		-1		-0.
Total	2	0	0	—	18	0	0	0-0	13	13	9	3	1	6-0	13	6.23	74	.260	.351	0	—	0		-2		-0.
YOUNGBLOOD, CHIEF	Albert Clyde B6.13.1900 Hillsboro TX D7.6.1968 Amarillo TX BL/TR/6-3/202 d7.16 Col Clarendon (TX) JC																								
1922	Was A	0	0	—	2	0	0	0	4.1	9	9	0	2	7	2	14.54	27	.429	.600	2	.000	-0		-6		-0
YOUNT, DUCKY	Herbert Macon "Hub" B12.7.1885 Iredell Co. NC D5.9.1970 Winston-Salem NC BR/TR/6-2/178 d5.20																								
1914	Bal F	1	1	.500	13	1	1	0	41.1	44	28	2	2	19	8	4.14	73	.280	.365	12-0-1	.083	-1*	0	-6		-0
YOUNT, LARRY	Lawrence King B2.15.1950 Houston TX BR/TR/6-2/185 [HouN68 5/87] d9.15 b-Robin																								
1971	Hou N	0	0	—	1	0	0	0-0												0	—	0		0		
YOWELL, CARL	Carl Columbus "Sundown" B12.20.1902 Madison VA D7.27.1985 Jacksonville TX BL/TL/6-4/180 d9.5																								
1924	Cle A	1	1	.500	4	2	2	0	27	37	21	1	0	13	8	6.67	64	.343	.413	11	.182	-1	148	-6		-0
1925	Cle A	2	3	.400	12	4	1	0	36.1	40	21	1	1	17	12	4.46	99	.310	.395	8-0-1	.125	-1	57	0		-0
Total	2	3	4	.429	16	6	3	0	63.1	77	42	2	1	30	20	5.40	81	.325	.403	19-0-1	.158	-1	87	-6		-0

YUHAS, EDDIE John Edward B8.5.1924 Youngstown OH D7.6.1986 Winston-Salem NC BR/TR/6-1/180(165-180) d4.17

YEAR	TM LG	W	L	PCT	G	GS	CG-SHO	SV-BS	IP	H	R	HR	HB	BB-IB	SO	ERA	AERA	OAV	OOB	AB-HR-SH	AVG	PB	SUP	APR	DL	PW
1952	StL N	12	2	.857	54	0	0	6	99.1	90	35	5	2	35	39	2.72	137	.243	.312	21-0-2	.190	1	72	11		1.6
1953	StL N	0	0	—	2	0	0	0	1	3	2	0	0	0	0	18.00	24	.500	.500	0	—	0		-1	140	-0.1
Total 2		12	2	.857	56	2	0	6	100.1	93	37	5	2	35	39	2.87	130	.247	.315	21-0-2	.190	1	72	10	-140	1.5

ZABALA, ADRIAN Adrian (Rodriguez) B8.26.1916 San Antonio de los Banos, Cuba D1.4.2002 Jacksonville FL BL/TL/5-11/165 d8.11

YEAR	TM LG	W	L	PCT	G	GS	CG-SHO	SV-BS	IP	H	R	HR	HB	BB-IB	SO	ERA	AERA	OAV	OOB	AB-HR-SH	AVG	PB	SUP	APR	DL	PW
1945	NY N	2	4	.333	11	5	1	0	43.1	46	25	2	0	20	14	4.78	82	.284	.363		.231	1	69	-4		-0.4
1949	NY N	2	3	.400	15	4	2-1	1	41	44	28	5	1	10	13	5.27	76	.278	.325	13	.077	-1	122	-6		-0.8
Total 2		4	7	.364	26	9	3-1	1	84.1	90	53	7	1	30	27	5.02	79	.281	.345	26	.154	-0	92	-10		-1.2

ZABEL, ZIP George Washington B2.18.1891 Wetmore KS D5.31.1970 Beloit WI BR/TR/6-1.5/185 d10.5 Col Baker

YEAR	TM LG	W	L	PCT	G	GS	CG-SHO	SV-BS	IP	H	R	HR	HB	BB-IB	SO	ERA	AERA	OAV	OOB	AB-HR-SH	AVG	PB	SUP	APR	DL	PW
1913	Chi N	1	0	1.000	1	1	0	0	5	3	0	0	0	1		0.00	—	.167	.211	2	.000	0	118	2		0.4
1914	Chi N	4	4	.500	29	7	2	3	128	104	45	5	2	45	50	2.18	128	.235	.309	38-0-2	.184	-1	114	9		0.5
1915	Chi N	7	10	.412	36	17	8-3	3	163	124	80	3	4	84	60	3.20	87	.218	.323	54-0-2	.074	-4*	105	-10		-1.2
Total 3		12	14	.462	66	25	10-3	3	296	231	125	8	6	130	110	2.71	103	.224	.315	94-0-4	.117	-4	108	1		-0.3

ZACHARY, CHINK Albert Myron (b Albert Myron Zarski) B10.19.1917 Brooklyn NY BR/TR/5-11/182 d4.30

YEAR	TM LG	W	L	PCT	G	GS	CG-SHO	SV-BS	IP	H	R	HR	HB	BB-IB	SO	ERA	AERA	OAV	OOB	AB-HR-SH	AVG	PB	SUP	APR	DL	PW
1944	Bro N	0	2	.000	4	2	0	0	10.1	10	11	2	1	7	3	9.58	37	.238	.360		.000	-0	94	-6		-1.0

ZACHARY, TOM Jonathan Thompson Walton (aka Zach Walton in 1918) B5.7.1896 Graham NC D1.24.1969 Burlington NC BL/TL/6-1/187 d7.11 Mil 1918-19 Col Guilford

YEAR	TM LG	W	L	PCT	G	GS	CG-SHO	SV-BS	IP	H	R	HR	HB	BB-IB	SO	ERA	AERA	OAV	OOB	AB-HR-SH	AVG	PB	SUP	APR	DL	PW
1918	Phi A	2	0	1.000	2	2	0	0	8	9	5	0	0	7	1	5.63	52	.321	.457	4	.500	1	231	-2		-0.3
1919	Was A	1	5	.167	17	7	0	0	61.2	68	29	0	1	20	9	2.92	110	.292	.350	15	.333	2	77	1		0.3
1920	Was A	15	16	.484	44	31	19-3	2	262.2	289	141	7	4	78	53	3.77	99	.285	.339	111	.261	6*	106	-2		0.3
1921	Was A	18	16	.529	39	30	17-2	1	250	314	130	10	6	59	53	3.96	104	.319	.361	90-0-3	.256	3	96	6		0.9
1922	Was A	15	10	.600	32	25	13-1	1	184.2	190	74	6	3	43	37	3.12	124	.275	.321	71-1-2	.296	5	106	18		2.8
1923	Was A	10	16	.385	35	29	10	0	204.1	270	117	9	4	63	40	4.49	84	.321	.372	78-0-4	.192	-0	95	-14		-1.6
1924	†Was A	15	9	.625	33	27	13-1	2	202.2	198	74	5	3	53	45	2.75	147	.264	.315	72-0-4	.306	4	104	30		3.7
1925	†Was A	12	15	.444	33	33	11-1	2	217.2	247	112	10	2	74	58	3.85	110	.296	.355	69-1-7	.174	-2	84	9		0.8
1926	StL A	14	15	.483	34	31	18-3	0	247.1	264	126	14	6	97	53	3.60	119	.288	.359	86-1-2	.267	4	81	14		2.1
1927	StL A	4	6	.400	13	12	6	0	78.1	110	48	4	0	27	13	4.37	100	.345	.396	28-0-2	.107	-2	94	-1		-0.3
	Was A	4	7	.364	15	14	5-1	0	102.2	116	54	2	2	30	13	3.94	103	.290	.343	36-0-2	.139	-2	95	1		-0.2
	Year	8	13	.381	28	26	11-1	0	181	226	102	6	2	57	26	4.13	102	.314	.366	64-0-4	.125	-4	95	0		-0.5
1928	Was A	6	9	.400	20	14	5-1	0	102.2	130	72	5	1	40	19	5.44	74	.322	.384	33-0-5	.303	1	92	-16		-1.8
	†NY A	3	3	.500	7	6	3	1	45.2	54	26	1	0	15	7	3.94	95	.320	.375	15-1-1	.133	-0	109	-2		-0.2
	Year	9	12	.429	27	20	8-1	1	148.1	184	98	6	1	55	26	4.98	79	.321	.382	48-1-6	.250	1	97	-18		-2.0
1929	NY A	12	0	1.000	26	11	7-2	2	119.2	131	43	5	2	30	35	2.48	155	.277	.323	42-0-5	.238	1	135	19		1.7
1930	NY A	1	1	.500	3	0	0	0	16.2	18	16	0	0	9	1	6.48	66	.269	.355	8	.250	1	126	-5		-0.4
	Bos N	11	5	.688	24	22	10-1	0	151.1	192	90	9	0	50	57	4.58	108	.317	.369	54-2-4	.241	2*	110	5		0.5
1931	Bos N	11	15	.423	33	28	16-3	2	229	243	87	8	1	53	64	3.10	122	.272	.314	84	.167	-1	82	19		2.0
1932	Bos N	12	11	.522	32	24	12-1	0	212	231	83	5	2	55	67	3.10	121	.280	.326	77	.273	5*	84	17		2.2
1933	Bos N	7	9	.438	26	20	6-2	0	125	134	64	1	0	35	22	3.53	87	.276	.325	42-0-3	.119	-2*	94	-11		-1.5
1934	Bos N	1	2	.333	5	4	2-1	0	24	27	9	1	0	8	4	3.38	113	.278	.333	8	.000	-1	34	2		0.1
	Bro N	5	6	.455	22	12	4	2	101.2	122	53	5	2	21	28	4.43	84	.301	.339	38	.184	1*	101	-4		-0.3
	Year	6	8	.429	27	16	6-1	2	125.2	149	62	6	2	29	32	4.23	92	.297	.338	46	.152	-0	85	-2		-0.2
1935	Bro N	7	12	.368	25	21	9-1	4	158	193	76	10	2	35	33	3.59	111	.297	.335	52-0-2	.135	-1	82	7		0.6
1936	Bro N	0	0	—	1	0	0	0	0.1	2	2	0	0	1	0	54.00	8	1.000	1.000	0	—	0		-2		-0.1
	Phi N	0	3	.000	7	2	0	1	20.1	28	20	2	0	11	8	7.97	57	.329	.406	9	.333	1*	112	-6		-0.7
	Year	0	3	.000	8	2	0	1	20.2	30	22	2	0	12	8	8.71	52	.345	.424	9	.333	1	112	-7		-0.8
Total 19		186	191	.493	533	408	186-24	22	3126.1	3580	1551	119	41	914	720	3.73	106	.294	.345	1122-6-46	.226	25	95	83		10.6

ZACHARY, CHRIS William Christopher B2.19.1944 Knoxville TN D4.19.2003 Knoxville TN BL/TR/6-2/200(190-203) d4.11

YEAR	TM LG	W	L	PCT	G	GS	CG-SHO	SV-BS	IP	H	R	HR	HB	BB-IB	SO	ERA	AERA	OAV	OOB	AB-HR-SH	AVG	PB	SUP	APR	DL	PW
1963	Hou N	2	2	.500	22	7	0	0	57	62	38	5	3	22-0	42	4.89	64	.272	.340	13-0-1	.000	-1	125	-12		-0.9
1964	Hou N	0	1	.000	1	1	0	0	4	6	5	1	0	1-0	2	9.00	38	.333	.368	1	.000	-0	77	-3		-0.4
1965	Hou N	0	2	.000	4	2	0	0	10.2	12	6	0	0	6-1	4	4.22	80	.273	.360	2	.000	-0	13	-1		-0.2
1966	Hou N	3	5	.375	10	8	0	0	55	44	22	1	1	32-2	37	3.44	100	.221	.330	18	.222	1	90	1		0.2
1967	Hou N	1	6	.143	9	7	0	0	36.1	42	27	5	2	12-1	18	5.70	58	.290	.352	10	.100	-0*	49	-10		-1.7
1969	KC A	0	1	.000	6	2	0	0-0	18.1	27	17	4	0	7-0	6	7.85	47	.346	.395	2	.500	1	60	-8		-0.4
1971	StL N	3	10	.231	23	12	1-1	0-1	89.2	114	58	3	4	26-7	48	5.32	68	.316	.364	33	.242	1*	116	-16		-2.0
1972	†Det A	1	1	.500	25	1	0	1-1	38.1	27	6	2	1	15-2	21	1.41	225	.201	.283	2	.500	1	56	8	21	0.5
1973	Pit N	0	0	—	6	0	0	1-0	12	10	4	1	0	1-0	6	3.00	117	.222	.234	2	.000	0		1		0.1
Total 9		10	29	.256	108	40	1-1	2-2	321.1	344	183	22	11	122-13	184	4.57	75	.275	.341	83-0-1	.181	1	91	-40	21	-4.8

ZACHRY, PAT Patrick Paul B4.24.1952 Richmond TX BR/TR/6-5/175(168-180) [CinN70 19/454] d4.11

YEAR	TM LG	W	L	PCT	G	GS	CG-SHO	SV-BS	IP	H	R	HR	HB	BB-IB	SO	ERA	AERA	OAV	OOB	AB-HR-SH	AVG	PB	SUP	APR	DL	PW
1976	†Cin N	14	7	.667	38	28	6-1	0-0	204	170	70	8	2	83-4	143	2.74	128	.228	.305	62-0-12	.113	-2	123	17		1.3
1977	Cin N	3	7	.300	12	12	3	0-0	75	78	45	7	1	29-1	36	5.04	78	.273	.338	22-0-4	.136	-1	87	-9		-1.0
	NY N	7	6	.538	19	19	2-1	0-0	119.2	129	59	14	3	48-4	63	3.76	101	.278	.347	42-0-1	.143	-2	83	-1		-0.4
	Year	10	13	.435	31	31	5-1	0-0	194.2	207	104	21	4	77-5	99	4.25	91	.276	.344	64-0-5	.141	-2	84	-10		-1.4
1978	NY N☆	10	6	.625	21	21	5-2	0-0	138	120	57	9	1	60-4	78	3.33	107	.236	.316	43-0-5	.070	-2	94	3	37	0.2
1979	NY N	5	1	.833	7	7	1	0-0	42.2	44	19	3	2	21-2	17	3.59	104	.267	.356	16	.125	-1	123	1	138	0.0
1980	NY N	6	10	.375	28	26	7-3	0-0	164.2	145	65	16	5	58-5	88	3.01	120	.240	.310	46-0-5	.043	-4	90	10	24	0.4
1981	NY N	7	14	.333	24	24	3	0-0	139	151	78	13	4	56-1	76	4.14	85	.282	.349	38-0-4	.158	0	78	-10		-1.4
1982	NY N	6	9	.400	36	16	2	1-2	137.2	149	69	10	0	57-5	69	4.05	91	.279	.346	38-0-3	.079	-2	98	-5		-0.7
1983	†LA N	6	1	.857	40	1	0	0-0	61.1	63	22	4	1	21-6	35	2.49	145	.278	.337	4	.500	1	49	7		0.8
1984	LA N	5	6	.455	58	0	0	2-2	82.2	84	38	3	2	51-13	55	3.81	93	.267	.367	6	.333	1		-1		-0.1
1985	Phi N	0	0	—	10	0	0	0-0	12.2	14	7	1	0	11-1	8	4.26	87	.280	.410	1	.000	-0		-1		0.0
Total 10		69	67	.507	293	154	29-7	3-4	1177.1	1147	529	88	21	495-46	669	3.52	103	.259	.333	318-0-33	.113	-11	95	11	199	-0.9

ZACKERT, GEORGE George Carl "Zeke" B12.24.1884 Horton VT D2.18.1977 Burlington IA BL/TL/6-0/177 d9.22

YEAR	TM LG	W	L	PCT	G	GS	CG-SHO	SV-BS	IP	H	R	HR	HB	BB-IB	SO	ERA	AERA	OAV	OOB	AB-HR-SH	AVG	PB	SUP	APR	DL	PW
1911	StL N	0	2	.000	4	1	0	0	7.1	17	13	0	0	6	6	11.05	31	.486	.561	1	.000	-0	89	-7		-1.2
1912	StL N	0	0	—	1	0	0	0	1	2	2	0	1	1	0	18.00	19	.667	.800	0	—	0*		-1		-0.1
Total 2		0	2	.000	5	1	0	0	8.1	19	15	0	1	7	6	11.88	28	.500	.587	1	.000	-0	89	-8		-1.3

ZAHN, GEOFF Geoffrey Clayton B12.19.1945 Baltimore MD BL/TL/6-1/180* [LAN68*S5/86] d9.2 Col Michigan

YEAR	TM LG	W	L	PCT	G	GS	CG-SHO	SV-BS	IP	H	R	HR	HB	BB-IB	SO	ERA	AERA	OAV	OOB	AB-HR-SH	AVG	PB	SUP	APR	DL	PW
1973	LA N	1	0	1.000	6	1	0	0-0	13.1	5	2	2	0	2-0	9	1.35	258	.116	.156	2	.000	-0	76	3		0.2
1974	LA N	3	5	.375	21	10	1	0-0	79.2	78	28	3	2	16-1	33	2.03	169	.254	.295	23-0-3	.174	-0	97	10		0.9
1975	LA N	0	1	.000	2	0	0	0-0	3	2	3	0	0	5-1	1	9.00	38	.222	.500	0	—	0		-2		-0.3
	Chi N	2	7	.222	16	10	0	1-0	62.2	67	37	2	0	26-3	21	4.45	87	.282	.348	15-0-7	.133	-1	70	-5	43	-0.6
	Year	2	8	.200	18	10	0	1-0	65.2	69	40	2	0	31-4	22	4.66	83	.279	.356	15-0-7	.133	-1	71	-6		-0.9
1976	Chi N	0	1	.000	3	2	0	0-0	8.1	16	10	0	1	2-0	4	10.80	36	.410	.492	3	.000	-0	159	-5		-0.6
1977	Min A	12	14	.462	34	32	7-1	0-0	198	234	116	20	5	66-4	88	4.68	85	.299	.355	0	—	-0	109	-17		-1.8
1978	Min A	14	14	.500	35	35	12-1	0-0	252.1	260	101	18	4	81-2	106	3.03	127	.274	.331	0	—	-0	94	20		2.1
1979	Min A	13	7	.650	26	24	4	0-0	169	181	74	13	0	41-1	58	3.57	123	.279	.319	0	—	-0	100	15	31	1.7
1980	Min A	14	18	.438	38	35	13-5	0-0	232.2	273	138	17	2	66-3	96	4.41	99	.302	.347	0	—	-0	92	-4		-0.5
1981	Cal A	10	11	.476	25	25	9	0-0	161.1	181	93	18	0	43-2	52	4.41	83	.285	.329	0	—	-0	136	-15		-1.7
1982	†Cal A	18	8	.692	34	34	12-4	0-0	229.1	225	100	18	4	65-5	81	3.73	110	.259	.313	0	—	-0	124	10		1.0
1983	Cal A	9	11	.450	29	28	11-3	0-0	203	212	90	22	0	51-2	75	3.33	122	.269	.311	0	—	-0	96	13	31	1.1
1984	Cal A	13	10	.565	28	27	9-5	0-0	199.1	200	78	11	1	48-4	61	3.12	128	.263	.306	0	—	-0	103	18	31	2.0
1985	Cal A	2	2	.500	7	7	1-1	0-0	37	44	19	5	0	14-0	14	4.38	94	.299	.358	0	—	-0	110	-1	147	0.0
Total 13		111	109	.505	304	270	79-20	1-0	1849	1909	889	149	19	526-28	705	3.74	107	.278	.327	43-0-10	.140	-2	105	40	283	3.5

ZAHNISER, PAUL Paul Vernon B9.6.1896 Sac City IA D9.26.1964 Klamath Falls OR BR/TR/5-10.5/170 d5.18

YEAR	TM LG	W	L	PCT	G	GS	CG-SHO	SV-BS	IP	H	R	HR	HB	BB-IB	SO	ERA	AERA	OAV	OOB	AB-HR-SH	AVG	PB	SUP	APR	DL	PW
1923	Was A	9	10	.474	33	21	10-1	0	177	201	103	9	3	76	52	3.86	97	.291	.364	52-0-3	.096	-1	121	-6		-0.8
1924	Was A	5	7	.417	24	14	5-1	0	92	98	52	2	4	49	28	4.40	92	.283	.378	31-0-1	.129	-2	90	-3		-0.6
1925	Bos A	5	12	.294	37	21	7-1	0	176.2	232	124	6	1	89	30	5.15	88	.327	.403	58-0-1	.138	-4	63	-10		-1.3
1926	Bos A	6	18	.250	30	24	7-1	0	172	213	106	5	3	69	35	4.97	82	.321	.387	49	.163	-1	59	-15		-1.7

YEAR	TM LG	W	L	PCT	G	GS	CG-SHO	SV-BS	IP	H	R	HR	HB	BB-IB	SO	ERA	AERA	OAV	OOB	AB-HR-SH	AVG	PB	SUP	APR	DL	PW
1929	Cin N	0	0	—	1	0	0	0	1	2	3	1	0	1	0	27.00	17	.400	.500	0	—	0		-2		-0.1
Total	5	25	47	.347	125	80	29-4	1	618.2	746	388	21	11	284	145	4.66	88	.309	.384	190-0-5	.132	-8	80	-36		-4.5

ZAMBRANO, CARLOS   Carlos Alberto   B6.1.1981 Carabobo, Venez   BB/TR/6-4/250*   d8.20

YEAR	TM LG	W	L	PCT	G	GS	CG-SHO	SV-BS	IP	H	R	HR	HB	BB-IB	SO	ERA	AERA	OAV	OOB	AB-HR-SH	AVG	PB	SUP	APR	DL	PW
2001	Chi N	1	2	.333	6	1	0	0-1	7.2	11	13	2	1	6-0	4	15.26	27	.355	.488	2	.000	-0	44	-9		-1.6
2002	Chi N	4	8	.333	32	16	0	0-0	108.1	94	53	9	4	63-2	93	3.66	111	.235	.344	30-0-2	.033	-2	80	3	28	0.2
2003	†Chi N	13	11	.542	32	32	3-1	0-0	214	188	88	9	10	94-12	168	3.11	140	.239	.326	75-2-4	.240	6	98	26		3.5
2004	Chi N★	16	8	.667	31	31	1-1	0-0	209.2	174	73	14	20	81-4	188	2.75	161	.225	.314	70-1-8	.229	3	120	36		4.3
2005	Chi N	14	6	.700	33	33	2	0-0	223.1	170	88	21	8	86-3	202	3.26	134	.212	.293	80-1-4	.300	8*	101	26		3.2
Total	5	48	35	.578	134	113	6-2	0-1	763	637	315	55	43	332-21	655	3.26	133	.228	.318	257-4-18	.230	15	102	82	28	9.6

ZAMBRANO, VICTOR   Victor Manuel   B8.6.1975 Los Teques, Venez   BR/TR/6-0/190(190-205)   d6.21

YEAR	TM LG	W	L	PCT	G	GS	CG-SHO	SV-BS	IP	H	R	HR	HB	BB-IB	SO	ERA	AERA	OAV	OOB	AB-HR-SH	AVG	PB	SUP	APR	DL	PW
2001	TB A	6	2	.750	36	0	0	2-4	51.1	38	21	6	3	18-0	58	3.16	143	.201	.281	0	—	0		7		1.1
2002	TB A	8	8	.500	42	11	0	1-2	114	120	77	15	4	68-5	73	5.53	82	.278	.375	1	.000	-0	95	-13		-1.6
2003	TB A	12	10	.545	34	28	1	0-0	188.1	165	97	21	20	106-2	132	4.21	109	.237	.349	3-0-2	.000	-0	103	7		0.6
2004	TB A	9	7	.563	23	22	0	0-0	128	107	68	13	16	96-2	109	4.43	105	.230	.372	5	.200	-0	106	4		0.5
	NY N	2	0	1.000	3	3	0	0-0	14	12	9	0	0	6-0	14	3.86	111	.218	.295	6-0-1	.167	-0	122	0	47	-0.1
2005	NY N	7	12	.368	31	27	0	0-0	166.1	170	85	12	15	77-2	112	4.17	100	.264	.353	53-0-5	.132	-1	98	-1		-0.2
Total	5	44	39	.530	169	91	1	3-6	662	612	357	67	58	371-11	498	4.38	102	.246	.353	68-0-8	.132	-1	102	4	47	0.3

ZAMLOCH, CARL   Carl Eugene   B10.6.1889 Oakland CA   D8.19.1963 Santa Barbara CA   BR/TR/6-1/176   d5.7

YEAR	TM LG	W	L	PCT	G	GS	CG-SHO	SV-BS	IP	H	R	HR	HB	BB-IB	SO	ERA	AERA	OAV	OOB	AB-HR-SH	AVG	PB	SUP	APR	DL	PW
1913	Det A	1	6	.143	17	5	3	1	69.2	66	31	1	3	23	28	2.45	119	.260	.329	22	.182	-1	76	2		0.1

ZAMORA, OSCAR   Oscar Jose (Sosa)   B9.23.1944 Camaguey, Cuba   BR/TR/5-10/178(160-178)   d6.18   Col Miami-Dade North (FL) CC

YEAR	TM LG	W	L	PCT	G	GS	CG-SHO	SV-BS	IP	H	R	HR	HB	BB-IB	SO	ERA	AERA	OAV	OOB	AB-HR-SH	AVG	PB	SUP	APR	DL	PW
1974	Chi N	3	9	.250	56	0	0	10-3	83.2	82	33	6	0	19-7	38	3.12	123	.264	.301	11-0-3	.182	-0		7		1.1
1975	Chi N	5	2	.714	52	0	0	10-1	71	84	42	17	0	15-5	28	5.07	77	.298	.326	6-0-4	.167	-0	91	-7	21	-1.0
1976	Chi N	5	3	.625	40	2	0	3-2	55	70	34	8	1	17-6	27	5.24	77	.317	.365	9	.000	-1	91	-7		-1.1
1978	Hou N	0	0	—	10	0	0	0-0	15	20	12	2	0	7-3	6	7.20	46	.328	.391	2	.000	-0		-6		-0.4
Total	4	13	14	.481	158	2	0	23-6	224.2	256	121	33	1	58-21	99	4.53	85	.293	.332	28-0-7	.107	-2	91	-13	21	-1.4

ZANNI, DOM   Dominick Thomas   B3.1.1932 Bronx NY   BR/TR/5-11/180*   d9.28

YEAR	TM LG	W	L	PCT	G	GS	CG-SHO	SV-BS	IP	H	R	HR	HB	BB-IB	SO	ERA	AERA	OAV	OOB	AB-HR-SH	AVG	PB	SUP	APR	DL	PW
1958	SF N	1	0	1.000	1	0	0	0	4	7	1	1	0	1-0	3	2.25	169	.412	.444	2	.000	-0		1		0.1
1959	SF N	0	0	—	9	0	0	0	11	12	10	2	1	8-0	11	6.55	58	.273	.389	0		0		-4		-0.1
1961	SF N	1	0	1.000	8	0	0	0	13.2	13	7	1	0	12-2	11	3.95	96	.277	.417	0		0		0		0.0
1962	Chi A	6	5	.545	44	2	0	5	86.1	67	42	12	1	31-3	66	3.75	104	.214	.285	18-0-2	.278	0	57	0		0.3
1963	Chi A	0	0	—	5	0	0	0	4.1	5	4	1	0	4-0	2	8.31	42	.294	.429	0		0		-2		-0.1
	Cin N	1	1	.500	31	1	0	5	43	39	22	4	2	21-3	40	4.19	80	.247	.346	3	.333	0	206	-4		-0.2
1965	Cin N	0	0	—	8	0	0	0	13.1	7	2	1	0	5-0	10	1.35	278	.159	.240	1	.000	-0		3		0.2
1966	Cin N	0	0	—	5	0	0	0	7.1	5	1	0	1	3-1	5	0.00	—	.192	.300	1	1.000	0		3		0.2
Total	7	9	6	.600	111	3	0	10	183	155	89	20	7	85-9	148	3.79	99	.233	.323	25-0-2	.280	2	102	-3		0.4

ZASKE, JEFF   Lloyd Jeffrey   B10.6.1960 Seattle WA   BR/TR/6-5/180   [PitN78 27/642]   d7.21

YEAR	TM LG	W	L	PCT	G	GS	CG-SHO	SV-BS	IP	H	R	HR	HB	BB-IB	SO	ERA	AERA	OAV	OOB	AB-HR-SH	AVG	PB	SUP	APR	DL	PW
1984	Pit N	0	0	—	3	0	0	0	4	4	0	0	0	1-0	2	0.00	—	.211	.250	0		0		2		0.1

ZAVARAS, CLINT   Clinton Wayne   B1.4.1967 Denver CO   BR/TR/6-1/175   [SeaA85 3/61]   d6.3   [DL 1990 Sea A 178]

YEAR	TM LG	W	L	PCT	G	GS	CG-SHO	SV-BS	IP	H	R	HR	HB	BB-IB	SO	ERA	AERA	OAV	OOB	AB-HR-SH	AVG	PB	SUP	APR	DL	PW
1989	Sea A	1	6	.143	10	10	0	0-0	52	49	34	4	2	30-1	31	5.19	78	.253	.357	0		0	70	-6		-0.7

ZAY, WILLIAM   William   d10.7

YEAR	TM LG	W	L	PCT	G	GS	CG-SHO	SV-BS	IP	H	R	HR	HB	BB-IB	SO	ERA	AERA	OAV	OOB	AB-HR-SH	AVG	PB	SUP	APR	DL	PW
1886	Bal AA	0	1	.000	1	1	0	0	2	4	4	0	0	4	2	9.00	38	.333	.500	1	.000	-0	121	-1		-0.2

ZEISER, MATT   Matthew J.   B9.25.1888 Chicago IL   D6.10.1942 Chicago IL   BR/TR/5-10/170   d4.27

YEAR	TM LG	W	L	PCT	G	GS	CG-SHO	SV-BS	IP	H	R	HR	HB	BB-IB	SO	ERA	AERA	OAV	OOB	AB-HR-SH	AVG	PB	SUP	APR	DL	PW
1914	Bos A	0	0	—	2	0	0	0	10	9	4	0	1	8	0	1.80	150	.281	.439	3	.000	-0		1		0.0

ZEPP, BILL   William Clinton   B7.22.1946 Detroit MI   BR/TR/6-2/185*   d8.12   Col Michigan

YEAR	TM LG	W	L	PCT	G	GS	CG-SHO	SV-BS	IP	H	R	HR	HB	BB-IB	SO	ERA	AERA	OAV	OOB	AB-HR-SH	AVG	PB	SUP	APR	DL	PW
1969	Min A	0	0	—	4	0	0	0-1	5.1	6	7	1	0	4-1	2	6.75	54	.286	.385	1	.000	-0		-3		-0.2
1970	†Min A	9	4	.692	43	20	1-1	2-2	151	154	63	9	9	51-4	64	3.22	115	.266	.334	44-0-2	.136	-1	102	8		0.4
1971	Det A	1	1	.500	16	4	0	2-1	31.2	41	20	2	3	17-3	15	5.12	71	.328	.412	4	.000	-0	93	-5		-0.4
Total	3	10	5	.667	63	24	1-1	4-4	188	201	90	12	12	72-8	81	3.64	101	.278	.350	49-0-2	.122	-2	101	0		-0.2

ZERBE, CHAD   William Chad   B4.27.1972 Findlay OH   BL/TL/6-0/190*   d9.18   Col Hillsborough (FL) CC

YEAR	TM LG	W	L	PCT	G	GS	CG-SHO	SV-BS	IP	H	R	HR	HB	BB-IB	SO	ERA	AERA	OAV	OOB	AB-HR-SH	AVG	PB	SUP	APR	DL	PW
2000	SF N	0	0	—	4	0	0	0-0	6	6	3	1	0	1-0	5	4.50	97	.273	.304		—	0		0		0.0
2001	SF N	3	0	1.000	27	1	0	0-0	39	41	21	3	1	10-0	22	3.92	104	.281	.327	9-0-2	.222	0	135	0		0.0
2002	†SF N	2	0	1.000	50	0	0	0-1	56.1	52	22	3	4	21-2	26	3.04	130	.248	.326	6-0-1	.167	-0		5	16	-0.1
2003	SF N	1	1	.500	33	1	0	0-1	49.2	60	26	3	1	14-2	17	4.71	90	.311	.349	5-0-1	.000	-1	66	-2	16	0.1
Total	4	6	1	.857	114	2	0	0-2	151	159	72	10	6	46-4	70	3.87	106	.278	.333	20-0-4	.150	-0	102	3	16	0.1

ZETTLEIN, GEORGE   George "Charmer"   B7.18.1844 Brooklyn NY   D5.23.1905 Patchogue NY   BR/TR/5-9/162   d5.8

YEAR	TM LG	W	L	PCT	G	GS	CG-SHO	SV-BS	IP	H	R	HR	HB	BB-IB	SO	ERA	AERA	OAV	OOB	AB-HR-SH	AVG	PB	SUP	APR	DL	PW
1871	Chi NA	18	9	.667	28	28	25	0	240.2	298	233	6		25	22	2.73	168	.267	**.283**	128	.250	-7	93	**45**		**2.6**
1872	Tro NA	14	8	.636	25	22	17-2	1	187.2	207	132	2		8	17	2.16	168	.250	.257	114	.254	0	118	31		2.4
	Eck NA	1	8	.111	9	9	8	0	75.1	106	62	1		6	8	3.58	95	.299	.314	34	.088	-4	56	2		-0.1
	Year	15	16	.484	34	31	25-2	1	263	313	194	3		14	25	2.57	139	.265	.273	148	.216	-4	101	30		2.3
1873	Phi NA	36	15	.706	51	51	49	0	460	594	368	3		41	29	2.86	115	.284	.298	241	.207	-8	108	30		1.7
1874	Chi NA	27	30	.474	57	57	57-3	0	515.2	640	439	3		43	26	2.43	92	.273	.286	244	.193	-9	94	-13		-1.7
1875	Chi NA	17	14	.548	31	31	29-6	0	282	266	142	0		6	18	1.28	178	.230	.234	133	.218	-3*	84	31		2.5
	Phi NA	12	8	.600	21	21	20-1	0	181.1	209	121	0		10	13	2.08	109	.264	.273	83	.181	-4	113	1		-0.3
	Year	29	22	.569	52	52	49-7	0	463.1	475	263	0		16	31	1.59	143	.244	.250	216	.204	-7	96	24		2.2
1876	Phi N	4	20	.167	28	25	23-1	2	234	358	212	2		6	10	3.88	62	.331	.334	128	.211	-5*	73	-25		-2.4
Total	5 NA	125	92	.576	222	219	205-12	1	1942.2	2320	1497	15		139	133	2.39	124	.267	.279	977	.210	-36	99	127		7.1

ZICK, BOB   Robert George   B4.26.1927 Chicago IL   BL/TR/6-0/168   d5.2

YEAR	TM LG	W	L	PCT	G	GS	CG-SHO	SV-BS	IP	H	R	HR	HB	BB-IB	SO	ERA	AERA	OAV	OOB	AB-HR-SH	AVG	PB	SUP	APR	DL	PW
1954	Chi N	0	0	—	8	0	0	0	16.1	23	15	1	0	7	9	8.27	51	.343	.405	4	.250	0*		-6		-0.3

ZIEGLER, GEORGE   George J.   B1872 Chicago IL   D7.22.1916 Kankakee IL   5-8/150   d6.19

YEAR	TM LG	W	L	PCT	G	GS	CG-SHO	SV-BS	IP	H	R	HR	HB	BB-IB	SO	ERA	AERA	OAV	OOB	AB-HR-SH	AVG	PB	SUP	APR	DL	PW
1890	Pit N	0	1	.000	1	1	0	0	6	12	7	0	0	0	1	10.50	31	.400	.400	2	.000	-0	19	-4		-0.4

ZIEM, STEVE   Stephen Graeling   B10.24.1961 Milwaukee WI   BR/TR/6-2/210   [AtlN83 8/204]   d4.30   Col Cal Poly-Pomona

YEAR	TM LG	W	L	PCT	G	GS	CG-SHO	SV-BS	IP	H	R	HR	HB	BB-IB	SO	ERA	AERA	OAV	OOB	AB-HR-SH	AVG	PB	SUP	APR	DL	PW
1987	Atl N	0	1	.000	2	0	0	0-0	2.1	4	3	0	0	1-0	1	7.71	56	.364	.417	0		0		-1		-0.2

ZIMMERMAN, JEFF   Jeffrey Ross   B8.9.1972 Kelowna BC, Can.   BR/TR/6-1/200*   d4.13   b-Jordan   Col TCU   [DL 2002 Tex A 183, 2003 Tex A 183, 2004 Tex A 183]

YEAR	TM LG	W	L	PCT	G	GS	CG-SHO	SV-BS	IP	H	R	HR	HB	BB-IB	SO	ERA	AERA	OAV	OOB	AB-HR-SH	AVG	PB	SUP	APR	DL	PW
1999	†Tex A★	9	3	.750	65	0	0	3-4	87.2	50	24	9	2	20-3	67	2.36	219	.166	.225	0	—	0		26		3.1
2000	Tex A	4	5	.444	65	0	0	1-2	69.2	80	45	10	2	34-3	74	5.30	96	.286	.361	0		0		-1		-0.2
2001	Tex A	4	4	.500	66	0	0	28-3	71.1	48	19	10	4	16-1	72	2.40	199	.192	.251	0		0	18	3.0
Total	3	17	12	.586	196	0	0	32-9	228.2	178	88	29	8	73-5	213	3.27	154	.214	.280	0		0	43	549	5.9

ZIMMERMAN, JORDAN   Jordan William   B4.28.1975 Kelowna BC, Can.   BR/TL/6-0/200   [SeaA94 32/889]   d5.17   b-Jeff   Col Blinn (TX) JC

YEAR	TM LG	W	L	PCT	G	GS	CG-SHO	SV-BS	IP	H	R	HR	HB	BB-IB	SO	ERA	AERA	OAV	OOB	AB-HR-SH	AVG	PB	SUP	APR	DL	PW
1999	Sea A	0	0	—	12	0	0	0-0	8	14	8	0	1	4-0	3	7.88	61	.389	.463	0		0		-3	33	-0.1

ZINK, WALTER   Walter Noble   B11.21.1898 Pittsfield MA   D6.12.1964 Quincy MA   BR/TR/6-0/165   d7.6   Col Amherst

YEAR	TM LG	W	L	PCT	G	GS	CG-SHO	SV-BS	IP	H	R	HR	HB	BB-IB	SO	ERA	AERA	OAV	OOB	AB-HR-SH	AVG	PB	SUP	APR	DL	PW
1921	NY N	0	0	—	2	0	0	0	4	4	1	0	0	3-0	1	2.25	163	.235	.350	1	.000	-0		0		0.0

ZINN, JIMMY   James Edward   B1.21.1895 Benton AR   D2.26.1991 Memphis TN   BL/TR(BL 1929)/6-0.5/195   d8.19

YEAR	TM LG	W	L	PCT	G	GS	CG-SHO	SV-BS	IP	H	R	HR	HB	BB-IB	SO	ERA	AERA	OAV	OOB	AB-HR-SH	AVG	PB	SUP	APR	DL	PW
1919	Phi A	1	3	.250	7	4	2	0	25.2	38	20	1	1	10	9	6.31	54	.365	.426	13-1-0	.308	2*	61	-7		-0.7
1920	Pit N	1	1	.500	6	3	2	0	31	32	14	2	1	5	18	3.48	92	.260	.295	15	.200	0*	98	-1		0.0
1921	Pit N	7	6	.538	32	9	5-1	4	127.1	159	63	3	2	30	49	3.68	104	.318	.359	49	.224	0*	112	2		0.1
1922	Pit N	0	0	—	5	0	0	0	9.2	11	4	1	0	2	3	1.86	219	.297	.333	1	.000	-0		2		0.1
1929	Cle A	4	6	.400	18	11	6-1	2	105.1	150	75	8	3	33	29	5.04	88	.340	.390	42-1-3	.381	7*	119	-8		-0.1
Total	5	13	16	.448	68	24	15-2	7	299	390	176	15	7	80	108	4.30	92	.324	.369	120-2-3	.283	9	109	-12		-0.5

ZINSER, BILL   William Francis   B1.6.1918 Astoria NY   D2.16.1993 Englewood FL   BR/TR/6-1/185   d8.19

YEAR	TM LG	W	L	PCT	G	GS	CG-SHO	SV-BS	IP	H	R	HR	HB	BB-IB	SO	ERA	AERA	OAV	OOB	AB-HR-SH	AVG	PB	SUP	APR	DL	PW
1944	Was A	0	0	—	1	0	0	0	0.2	1	2	0	0	5	1	27.00	12	.333	.750	0	—	0		-2		-0.1

YEAR	TM LG	W	L	PCT	G	GS	CG-SHO	SV-BS	IP	H	R	HR	HB	BB-IB	SO	ERA	AERA	OAV	OOB	AB-HR-SH	AVG	PB	SUP	APR	DL	PW
ZITO, BARRY	Barry William B5.13.1978 Las Vegas NV BL/TL/6-4/205* [OakA99 1/9] d7.22 Col USC																									
2000	†Oak A	7	4	.636	14	14	1-1	0-0	92.2	64	30	6	2	45-2	78	2.72	178	.195	.296	0	—	0	145	23		2.4
2001	†Oak A	17	8	.680	35	35	3-2	0-0	214.1	184	92	18	13	80-0	205	3.49	131	.230	.309	5	.000	-1	117	25		2.6
2002	†Oak A★	23	5	.821	35	35	1	0-0	229.1	182	79	24	9	78-2	182	2.75	163	.218	.289	4-0-2	.000	-0	120	43		4.9
2003	†Oak A✳	14	12	.538	35	35	4-1	0-0	231.2	186	98	19	6	88-3	146	3.30	139	.219	.295	6	.000	-1	82	31		3.1
2004	Oak A	11	11	.500	34	34	0	0-0	213	216	116	28	9	81-2	163	4.48	103	.263	.333	4	.000	-0	89	3		0.3
2005	Oak A	14	13	.519	35	35	0	0-0	228.1	185	106	26	13	89-0	171	3.86	116	.221	.304	7	.143	-0	103	16		1.8
Total	6	86	53	.619	188	188	9-4	0-0	1209.1	1017	521	121	52	461-9	945	3.50	131	.228	.305	26-0-2	.038	-2	105	141		15.1
ZMICH, ED	Edward Albert B10.1.1884 Cleveland OH D8.20.1950 Cleveland OH BL/TL/6-0/180 d7.23																									
1910	StL N	0	5	.000	9	6	2	0	36	38	27	0	3	29	19	6.25	48	.304	.446	13	.077	-1	67	-11		-1.5
1911	StL N	1	0	1.000	4	0	0	0	12.2	8	5	0	1	8	4	2.13	158	.182	.321	4	.000	-1	1	1		0.0
Total	2	1	5	.167	13	6	2	0	48.2	46	32	0	4	37	23	5.18	60	.272	.414	17	.059	-2	67	-10		-1.5
ZOLDAK, SAM	Samuel Walter "Sad Sam" B12.8.1918 Brooklyn NY D8.25.1966 New Hyde Park NY BL/TL/5-11.5/185* d5.13 Col Fordham																									
1944	StL A	0	0	—	18	0	0	0	38.2	49	22	1	0	19	15	3.72	97	.310	.384	6	.333	0		-2		0.0
1945	StL A	3	2	.600	26	1	1	0	69.2	74	32	3	0	18	19	3.36	105	.267	.312	20	.050	-2*	48	0		-0.3
1946	StL A	9	11	.450	35	21	9-2	2	170.1	166	71	11	1	57	51	3.43	109	.256	.317	52-0-3	.173	-0	72	7		0.8
1947	StL A	9	10	.474	35	19	6-1	1	171	162	76	7	0	76	36	3.47	112	.254	.334	58-0-1	.172	-1	90	7		0.8
1948	StL A	2	4	.333	11	9	0	0	54	64	30	4	1	19	13	4.67	98	.296	.356	22-0-1	.273	0	77			0.1
	Cle A	9	6	.600	23	12	4-1	0	105.2	104	37	6	0	24	17	2.81	144	.261	.303	36-0-2	.139	-2	95	16		1.9
	Year	11	10	.524	34	21	4-1	0	159.2	168	67	10	1	43	30	3.44	123	.274	.322	58-0-3	.190	-2	88	15		2.0
1949	Cle A	1	2	.333	27	0	0	0	53	60	30	4	0	18	11	4.25	94	.291	.348	8	.375	1		-3		0.1
1950	Cle A	4	2	.667	33	3	0	4	63.2	64	33	6	1	21	15	3.96	109	.259	.320	16	.188	0	97	2		0.2
1951	Phi A	6	10	.375	26	18	8-1	0	128	127	51	9	0	24	18	3.16	135	.257	.292	45-0-1	.156	-3	83	15		1.3
1952	Phi A	0	6	.000	16	10	2	1	75.1	86	41	3	0	25	12	4.06	97	.290	.345	23-0-1	.174	-1	68	-2		-0.1
Total	9	43	53	.448	250	93	30-5	8	929.1	956	423	54	3	301	207	3.54	112	.267	.325	286-0-9	.175	-7	82	40		4.8
ZUBER, BILL	William Henry "Goober" B3.26.1913 Middle Amana IA D11.2.1982 Cedar Rapids IA BR/TR/6-2/195 d9.16																									
1936	Cle A	1	1	.500	2	1	1	0	13.2	14	11	0	0	15	5	6.59	76	.269	.433	5	.200	-0	131	-2		-0.2
1938	Cle A	0	3	.000	15	0	0	1	28.2	33	18	0	0	20	14	5.02	92	.295	.402	7-0-1	.000	-1		-1		-0.2
1939	Cle A	2	0	1.000	16	1	0	0	31.2	41	24	2	1	19	16	5.97	74	.323	.415	5	.200	1	160	-6		-0.2
1940	Cle A	1	1	.500	17	0	0	0	24	25	17	3	0	14	12	5.63	75	.260	.355	3	.333	0		-4		-0.3
1941	Was A	6	4	.600	36	7	1	2	96.1	110	63	5	2	61	51	5.42	75	.291	.392	26-0-2	.000	-3	95	-13		-1.5
1942	Was A	9	9	.500	37	7	3-1	1	126.2	115	66	5	0	82	64	3.84	95	.243	.355	39-0-3	.154	0	74	-3		-0.5
1943	NY A	8	4	.667	20	13	7	1	118	100	54	3	0	74	57	3.89	83	.234	.347	38-0-5	.184	2	167	-6		-0.5
1944	NY A	5	7	.417	22	13	2-1	0	107	101	54	3	0	54	59	4.21	83	.255	.346	31-0-4	.129	-2	92	-6		-0.9
1945	NY A	5	11	.313	21	14	7	1	127	121	50	2	0	56	50	3.19	109	.259	.338	42-0-2	.167	-1	56	5		0.4
1946	NY A	0	1	.000	3	0	0	0	5.2	10	9	2	0	3	3	12.71	27	.385	.448	2	.000	-0		-6		-0.9
	†Bos A	5	1	.833	15	7	2-1	0	56.2	37	20	4	0	39	29	2.54	144	.187	.321	18-0-1	.111	-1	150	6		0.5
	Year	5	2	.714	18	7	2-1	0	62.1	47	29	6	0	42	32	3.47	105	.210	.335	20-0-1	.100	-1	151	0		-0.4
1947	Bos A	1	0	1.000	20	1	0	0	50.2	60	32	4	0	31	23	5.33	73	.311	.406	20-0-1	.154	-0	114	-7		-0.4
Total	11	43	42	.506	224	65	23-3	6	786	767	418	35	4	468	383	4.28	87	.260	.362	229-0-20	.135	-6	103	-43		-4.7
ZUVERINK, GEORGE	George B8.20.1924 Holland MI BR/TR/6-4/200(195-210) d4.21																									
1951	Cle A	0	0	—	16	0	0	0	25.1	24	17	2	1	13	14	5.33	71	.253	.349	0	—	0		-5		-0.2
1952	Cle A	0	0	—	1	0	0	0	1.1	1	0	0	0	0	1	0.00	—	.200	.200	0	—	0*		1		0.0
1954	Cin N	0	0	—	2	0	0	0	6	10	6	1	0	1	2	9.00	47	.385	.407	2	.500	0		-3		-0.1
	Det A	9	13	.409	35	25	9-2	4	203	201	93	22	8	62	70	3.59	103	.257	.317	64-0-9	.125	0	75	2		0.0
1955	Det A	0	5	.000	14	1	0	0	28.1	38	27	6	1	14-3	13	6.99	55	.309	.384	4	.000	-1	116	-11		-1.7
	Bal A	4	3	.571	28	5	0	4	86.1	80	28	5	4	17-1	31	2.19	174	.264	.309	23-0-1	.217	1	107	15		1.4
	Year	4	8	.333	42	6	0	4	114.2	118	55	11	5	31-4	44	3.38	113	.277	.331	27-0-1	.185	0	109	4		-0.3
1956	Bal A	7	6	.538	62	0	0	16	97.1	112	52	6	3	34-9	33	4.16	94	.294	.352	17-0-4	.118	-1		-4		-0.6
1957	Bal A	10	6	.625	56	0	0	9	112.2	105	39	4	4	39-13	36	2.48	145	.257	.325	23-0-2	.130	-0		13		2.0
1958	Bal A	2	2	.500	45	0	0	7	69	74	29	4	4	17-3	22	3.39	106	.286	.340	9	.222	1		2		0.3
1959	Bal A	0	1	.000	6	0	0	0	13	15	7	1	0	6-0	1	4.15	91	.306	.382	0	—	1		-1	83	0.0
Total	8	32	36	.471	265	31	9-2	40	642.1	660	296	56	27	203-29	223	3.54	105	.271	.332	142-0-16	.148	-2	82	9	83	1.1

THE MEN IN THE DUGOUT: THE MANAGERS

Vin Scully, on the flap of the dust jacket for Leonard Koppett's 1993 book *The Man in the Dugout,* praised the author by saying, "If there would be a degree in baseball, Leonard Koppett would be a professor."

True enough. The late, great Koppett was certainly a professor of the National Pastime, and he was writing about men who had hard-earned Ph.D.'s in the game. The men in the dugout are perhaps the least understood of the important "players" in the game today. Manager's roles have changed greatly in recent decades; partly because of the prominence of millionaire superstars, but mostly due to the increasingly visible intrusion of the business of baseball into the game on the field.

In the early days, baseball was not nearly as studied a tactical game as it would later become and, when players did get "scientific," it was usually in the heat of battle rather than in any planned fashion. At this time, a manager's job involved mostly keeping his players under contract, on-time, on the train, and out of the bars. Players generally knew their roles, particularly in the days where regulars, including pitchers, played nearly every game.

Many of the great early managers—such as Cap Anson, Harry Wright, John Ward, and Charlie Comiskey—were thought of not only as leaders of men but also as particularly brainy players and sharp businessmen.

As baseball became more specialized in the 1890s, different managerial skills came into vogue. Managers began to make more of the decisions to bunt, steal, and the like, instead of letting the players play as they thought best. Furthermore, while teams always had a need to find and evaluate talent, the reserve clause now forced clubs to look into the "minor" leagues for new players. Well-traveled players and former players, who knew many different leagues, became especially valuable. Many of them—such as Hughie Jennings, John McGraw, and Wilbert Robinson—ended up as longtime managers.

In the 1890s, approximately half of managers were playing managers. Their experience on the field also helped these men manage ballplayers. Even at this time, rarely could a skipper become "one of the boys." Managers have long been expected to keep a fair distance from their players, because—as Sparky Anderson would comment many years later—"You take a guy out for a pinch hitter, he ain't gonna be your friend."

Most of the best managers—Joe McCarthy, Casey Stengel, Ned Hanlon, Frank Selee, Connie Mack, John McGraw, Earl Weaver, Walter Alston, Bill McKechnie, and others—respected their players and tried to treat them fairly, even if they weren't necessarily nice people to be around. Many of the greatest managers, especially in the early days, were also great teachers who showed younger men how to play the game as well as how to conduct their lives.

True renegades (e.g., Leo Durocher, Billy Martin, and Paul Richards) were impetuous, conniving, and often devious or deceitful. While many of their players didn't like them, the results were often positive—at least in the short term.

By the 1910s, managers were required to be better tacticians, not just shepherds of hard-bitten players. Relief pitchers, pinch hitters, and even platooning had come into use. As managing became more involved, fewer players were thought to be able to simultaneously handle the increased responsibility.

When the power era began in the 1920s, many a manager found himself less able to influence the game through tactical decisions and instead had to configure his lineup and rotation to provide the best offense and the most reliable pitching. Moreover, most managers were no longer the locus of player procurement. Clubs were now using general managers and, as a result, much of the personnel decisions were now out of the field manager's hands. The field manager also didn't necessarily control the salaries or the contracts of his players, taking away much of his power.

Managers ever since have had to deal with open revolt, dissension, and disobedience while maintaining order amidst changing social mores. Player salaries began to rise in the 1930s and star players soon made as much as or more money than the manager. How, then, to keep the respect of the players? The more successful and famous managers of the 1940s—Lou Boudreau, Leo Durocher, and Billy Southworth, for example—would have expressed very different opinions.

Increasing expectations of success during the postwar boom also meant that managers were being fired more often. Some of the most successful managers of the 1950s—Casey Stengel, Chuck Dressen, Charlie Grimm, and Fred Haney—lost their jobs when things got rocky.

Stengel, Al Lopez, and Walter Alston were tremendous managers, and all had different ways of winning. Lopez was largely focused on power and starting pitching, while Stengel kept the entire roster involved and always had strong defensive teams. The unflappable Alston used one-run offensive strategies and depended heavily on pitching, defense and, later, Dodger Stadium to keep opponents from scoring.

The success of the quiet, dignified Lopez and Alston was not lost among managers of the 1960s, who generally became less confrontational (with exceptions like Durocher and Alvin Dark). Most of the top managers of that time—Alston, Red Schoendienst, Ralph Houk, Gil Hodges—met this standard. However, highly qualified "Nervous Nellies"—tough, involved guys like Gene Mauch, Harry Walker, Dick Williams, and Dave Bristol—also enjoyed success, usually when brought in to turn around underachieving teams with fire and brimstone.

Free agency in the late 1970s meant even more challenges for managers trying to keep their highly paid and mobile stars in line. The kindly old man in the dugout was largely a character of the past. Instead, tough little guys—firebrands like Williams, Sparky Anderson, Earl Weaver, Billy Martin, and Whitey Herzog—became the game's top skippers in the 1970s and early 1980s. Much of their success came from a lack of fear of using untested players. The successful skippers of the era were never big stars; some had never even reached the majors. Therefore, they knew—as did Joe McCarthy, John McGraw, and Connie Mack before them—that plenty of talent was trapped in the minor leagues, just waiting to be given a chance.

By the 1980s and 1990s, the best managers had learned that lesson as a new type of manager evolved. True; there were some tough guys, like in the 1970s, but they were also more "nice guys." The *personalities* of winners like Tony La Russa, Tommy Lasorda, Bobby Cox, Jim Leyland, and Dave Johnson were very different. What they had in common, though, was an ability to keep a lid on the clubhouse full of millionaire players and million-dollar egos.

Keeping clubhouse dissension and other 'private matters' out of the public eye became an important mark of most successful teams. Baseball people now saw the media as even more of an enemy, largely because the rise in salaries had caused a rift between the press and the players, and because the media was working harder to break juicy stories rather than just report the games. Modern managers were able to get their players to buy into the team concept. Different managers did this in various ways, either through enthusiastic positive reinforcement, a caring demeanor, or simply excellent personnel management. Many teams continued to hire the older "pepperpot" type of manager, though few of them were now successful.

Today's managers must balance the skills and egos of their players, the omnipresence of the media, and their relationship with the front office to succeed on the field—but they have to do it with a decreasing amount of perceived authority. The contemporary game's ever-changing finances mean that few managers can count on a consistently high payroll. It's a tough job to do, and the most successful managers of today—such as Cox, La Russa, Dusty Baker, Lou Piniella, and Joe Torre—do it through by earning respect and building consensus.

This Manager Register includes everyone who has ever managed a major league baseball team, from 1871 to the preent, from the National Association to the Federal League to the American League, from Bill Adair to Ted Turner to Don Zimmer. Identifying managers, however, has not always been so obvious as it would seem, so there are some important things to note about this section.

First, a quick tongue-twister: A manager has to have managed to be listed as a manager, but he doesn't have to have been called a manager to have managed. In the early days of baseball history, the term "team manager" did not mean what it does now. Then, the person called the manager was what would now be called a general manager or a vice president. If those official team manager's duties did not include traveling with the club, making out the lineups, deciding when to change pitchers, arguing with the umpires, and the like, then this register does not include him. The "real" field manager of the team back then may have been the team captain; if so, this register will show him as the manager regardless of his title. This is a record of those who did the job of a baseball manager, not those who had the title of manager.

Sometimes baseball managers have been referred to as coaches, as they are in other sports. The most famous recent example comes from P.K. Wrigley's rotating "College of Coaches" that ran the Cubs for five seasons during the 1960s. In that case, the coach referred to as head coach by the team is listed herein as the Cubs' manager for the period he was head coach.

Managers do not necessarily manage every single game in a season, of course. Managers are human beings, and they do occasionally miss a few games when they fall ill, get suspended, or attend to their families. In those cases, the coach left in charge does not become the manager in any real sense. Though the coach may make the moves, he is in most cases simply carrying out the manager's wishes.

When a long absence occurs, however, the situation gets muddier. This section uses a reasonable, though admittedly arbitrary, requirement of 30 consecutive days of managing the team in these cases for a substitute to qualify as the *de facto* manager.

When a manager is fired, however, the situation requires a different standard. When the manager's position is left vacant for any reason, the interim manager *is* definitely in charge. Thus, even if his managerial career lasts but one day, he is considered to have been a manager.

This register shows the date of birth for all managers, plus full biographical information for managers who were not major leaguer players (and are, therefore, not listed in the batter or pitcher registers). Managers who never played professional baseball are shown with a "DNP" code (Did Not Play). If a manager played in the minors but not in the majors, his primary position is showed in parentheses.

For each manager, the register shows the team(s) he managed in each season, along with that team's won-lost record and

winning percentage during when he was manager. A lowercase *e*, *w*, or *c* after the league code indicates the team's division (East, West, or Central, respectively) from 1969–present. Player-managers are indicated by boldface years in the first column. Further information is available under the following headings:

The **Mgr/Yr** column gives results for clubs with multiple managers in a single season. If the team had more than one manager in the season listed, two numbers are shown, separated by a slash. In these cases, the second number indicates how many managers the team employed that season, and the first number indicating which of these the listed manager was. For example, Jack McKeon is listed in 2003 as 2/2, because he was the second of two managers for the Florida Marlins.

The **Finish** column indicates how the team did under that manager. For managers who guided the team all season, the number gives the team's standing at year's end. If manager B took over from manager A *during* the season, the first number indicates the team's standing when manager B took over, and the second number the team's standing at the end of the season. Three or more managers in one season for a team would produce a three-number entry for the manager(s) in the middle: the team's standing before, during, and after said manager was running the club.

Symbols after the finish show if the team that finished first won any postseason series. A solid star (★) indicates the team won the World Series (including the NL-AA World Series in the nineteenth century). A solid diamond (◆) indicates the team won their LCS but lost the World Series (1969–present). A (●) solid bullet indicates a team won the NL championship in the 1890s (i.e., the 1892 series between the first- and second-place teams, the 1894–97 Temple Cup, or the 1900 *Chronicle-Telegraph* Cup). A hollow star (☆) indicates the team won a Division Series but lost in their LCS (1995–present). A cross (✛) indicates a Wild Card team. A solid triangle (▲) indicates the team was tied at the end of the regular season for first place or the Wild Card and played a one-game or three-game playoff. A *t* after the finish indicates a tie in the standings below first place (e.g., *4t* means the team tied for fourth place that year).

The plus/minus column (**+/−**) indicates how many games the team won compared to how many the team was projected to win based on its run production. In other words, a 6.5 rating for a manager for a season indicates that his team won 6½ games more than could have been expected. A rating below zero indicates a disappointing performance, worse than expected given the team's runs scored and allowed.

On the career line, the manager's lifetime won-lost record and winning percentage are shown along with the number of seasons he managed and how many games his teams won compared to their projections.

ADAIR, BILL Marion Danne B2.10.1913 Mobile, AL D6.17.2002 Bay Minette, AL BR/TR/5-8/190(2B)

YEAR	TM/LG	W	L	PCT	FINISH	MGR/YR	+/-
1970	Chi A w	4	6	.400	6-6-6	2/3	0.2

ADCOCK, JOE B10.30.1927

YEAR	TM/LG	W	L	PCT	FINISH	MGR/YR	+/-
1967	Cle A	75	87	.463	8		0.0

ADDY, BOB B2.1845

YEAR	TM/LG	W	L	PCT	FINISH	MGR/YR	+/-
1875	Phi NA	3	4	.429	4-5	2/2	-1.3
1877	Cin N	5	19	.208	6-6-6	2/3	-0.3
2		8	23	.258			-1.6

ALLEN, BOB B7.10.1867

YEAR	TM/LG	W	L	PCT	FINISH	MGR/YR	+/-
1890	Phi N	25	10	.714	3-2-3	4/5	4.8
1900	Cin N	62	77	.446	7		-3.5
2		87	87	.500			1.3

ALLISON, ANDY B1848

YEAR	TM/LG	W	L	PCT	FINISH	MGR/YR	+/-
1872	Eck NA	0	11	.000	10-9	1/3	1.2

ALLISON, DOUG B7.1845

YEAR	TM/LG	W	L	PCT	FINISH	MGR/YR	+/-
1873	Res NA	2	21	.087	8		5.0

ALOU, FELIPE B5.12.1935

YEAR	TM/LG	W	L	PCT	FINISH	MGR/YR	+/-
1992	Mon N e	70	55	.560	4-2	2/2	1.9
1993	Mon N e	94	68	.580	2		7.9
1994	Mon N e	74	40	.649	1		4.0
1995	Mon N e	66	78	.458	5		-4.3
1996	Mon N e	88	74	.543	2		-0.4
1997	Mon N e	78	84	.481	4		1.9
1998	Mon N e	65	97	.401	4		-1.9
1999	Mon N e	68	94	.420	4		0.0
2000	Mon N e	67	95	.414	4		1.5
2001	Mon N e	21	33	.389	5-5	1/2	-1.3
2003	SF N w	100	61	.621	1		7.6
2004	SF N w	91	71	.562	2		2.4
2005	SF N w	75	87	.463	3		3.8
13		957	937	.505			23.0

ALSTON, WALTER B12.1.1911

YEAR	TM/LG	W	L	PCT	FINISH	MGR/YR	+/-
1954	Bro N	92	62	.597	2		11.4
1955	Bro N	98	55	.641	1★		1.6
1956	Bro N	93	61	.604	1		3.8
1957	Bro N	84	70	.545	3		-3.3
1958	LA N	71	83	.461	7		3.2
1959	LA N	88	68	.564	1▲★		6.5
1960	LA N	82	72	.532	4		-2.3
1961	LA N	89	65	.578	2		8.3
1962	LA N	102	63	.618	2▲		5.3
1963	LA N	99	63	.611	1★		8.0
1964	LA N	80	82	.494	6t		-5.7
1965	LA N	97	65	.599	1★		6.1
1966	LA N	95	67	.586	1		0.6
1967	LA N	73	89	.451	8		0.7
1968	LA N	76	86	.469	7t		-0.2
1969	LA N w	85	77	.525	4		-5.2
1970	LA N w	87	74	.540	2		-0.0
1971	LA N w	89	73	.549	2		-0.2
1972	LA N w	85	70	.548	3		1.1
1973	LA N w	95	66	.590	2		2.6
1974	LA N w	102	60	.630	1♦		-3.6
1975	LA N w	88	74	.543	2		-5.7
1976	LA N w	90	68	.570	2-2	1/2	3.9
23		2040	1613	.558			36.8

ALTOBELLI, JOE B5.26.1932

YEAR	TM/LG	W	L	PCT	FINISH	MGR/YR	+/-
1977	SF N w	75	87	.463	4		-2.1
1978	SF N w	89	73	.549	3		5.9
1979	SF N w	61	79	.436	4-4	1/2	-2.1
1983	Bal A e	98	64	.605	1★		2.3
1984	Bal A e	85	77	.525	5		2.5
1985	Bal A e	29	26	.527	4-4	1/3	-0.3
1991	Chi N e	0	1	.000	4-5-4	2/3	-0.5
7		437	407	.518			5.8

AMALFITANO, JOEY B1.23.1934

YEAR	TM/LG	W	L	PCT	FINISH	MGR/YR	+/-
1979	Chi N e	2	5	.286	5-5	2/2	-1.5
1980	Chi N e	26	46	.361	6-6	2/2	-4.7
1981-1	Chi N e	15	37	.288	6		-1.5
1981-2	Chi N e	23	28	.451	5		-1.5
3		66	116	.363			-9.3

ANDERSON, SPARKY B2.22.1934

YEAR	TM/LG	W	L	PCT	FINISH	MGR/YR	+/-
1970	Cin N w	102	60	.630	1♦		11.6
1971	Cin N w	79	83	.488	4t		-2.6
1972	Cin N w	95	59	.617	1♦		2.3
1973	Cin N w	99	63	.611	1		5.6
1974	Cin N w	98	64	.605	2		2.2
1975	Cin N w	108	54	.667	1★		1.3
1976	Cin N w	102	60	.630	1★		-1.2
1977	Cin N w	88	74	.543	2		-0.5
1978	Cin N w	92	69	.571	2		9.3
1979	Det A e	56	50	.528	5-5	3/3	0.9
1980	Det A e	84	78	.519	5		-4.0
1981-1	Det A e	31	26	.544	4		3.0
1981-2	Det A e	29	23	.558	2t		3.0
1982	Det A e	83	79	.512	4		-2.5
1983	Det A e	92	70	.568	2		0.0
1984	Det A e	104	58	.642	1★		4.5
1985	Det A e	84	77	.522	3		-0.6
1986	Det A e	87	75	.537	3		-2.2
1987	Det A e	98	64	.605	1		1.8
1988	Det A e	88	74	.543	2		2.3
1989	Det A e	59	103	.364	7		-1.9
1990	Det A e	79	83	.488	3		-1.6
1991	Det A e	84	78	.519	2t		0.8
1992	Det A e	75	87	.463	6		-5.7
1993	Det A e	85	77	.525	3t		-1.7
1994	Det A e	53	62	.461	5		-2.8
1995	Det A e	60	84	.417	4		5.7
26		2194	1834	.545			26.9

ANSON, CAP B4.17.1852

YEAR	TM/LG	W	L	PCT	FINISH	MGR/YR	+/-
1875	Ath NA	4	2	.667	2-2	2/2	-0.9
1879	Chi N	41	21	.661	2-4	1/2	8.1
1880	Chi N	67	17	.798	1		4.0
1881	Chi N	56	28	.667	1		-1.3
1882	Chi N	55	29	.655	1		-9.3
1883	Chi N	59	39	.602	2		-1.8
1884	Chi N	62	50	.554	4t		-9.5
1885	Chi N	87	25	.777	1★		-1.1
1886	Chi N	90	34	.726	1		-2.5
1887	Chi N	71	50	.587	3		2.1
1888	Chi N	77	58	.570	2		2.5
1889	Chi N	67	65	.508	3		-3.5
1890	Chi N	84	53	.613	2		1.5
1891	Chi N	82	53	.607	2		5.4
1892-1	Chi N	31	39	.443	8		6.8
1892-2	Chi N	39	37	.513	7		6.8
1893	Chi N	56	71	.441	9		-3.8
1894	Chi N	57	75	.432	8		-7.2
1895	Chi N	72	58	.554	4		6.0
1896	Chi N	71	57	.555	5		6.1
1897	Chi N	59	73	.447	9		-1.7
1898	NY N	9	13	.409	6-7-7	2/3	-2.5
21		1296	947	.578			4.1

APPLING, LUKE B4.2.1907

YEAR	TM/LG	W	L	PCT	FINISH	MGR/YR	+/-
1967	KC A	10	30	.250	10-10	2/2	-6.5

ARMOUR, BILL William Reginald
B9.3.1869 Homestead, PA D12.2.1922 Minneapolis, MN (DNP)

YEAR	TM/LG	W	L	PCT	FINISH	MGR/YR	+/-
1902	Cle A	69	67	.507	5		-0.8
1903	Cle A	77	63	.550	3		0.9
1904	Cle A	86	65	.570	4		-7.8
1905	Det A	79	74	.516	3		12.8
1906	Det A	71	78	.477	6		5.3
5		382	347	.524			10.4

ASPROMONTE, KEN B9.22.1931

YEAR	TM/LG	W	L	PCT	FINISH	MGR/YR	+/-
1972	Cle A e	72	84	.462	5		-0.4
1973	Cle A e	71	91	.438	6		4.4
1974	Cle A e	77	85	.475	4		-0.7
3		220	260	.458			3.3

AUSTIN, JIMMY B12.8.1879

YEAR	TM/LG	W	L	PCT	FINISH	MGR/YR	+/-
1913	StL A	2	6	.250	7-7-8	2/3	-1.3
1918	StL A	7	9	.438	6-6-5	2/3	-0.7
1923	StL A	22	29	.431	3-5	2/2	-2.4
3		31	44	.413			-4.5

BAKER, DEL B5.3.1892

YEAR	TM/LG	W	L	PCT	FINISH	MGR/YR	+/-
1933	Det A	2	0	1.000	5-5	2/2	1.0
1936	Det A	18	16	.529	3-4-2	2/3	0.0
1937	Det A	34	20	.630	3-3-2	2/5	4.1
1937	Det A	7	3	.700	2-2-2	4/5	1.5
1938	Det A	37	19	.661	5-4	2/2	6.8
1939	Det A	81	73	.526	5		-4.1
1940	Det A	90	64	.584	1		-2.9
1941	Det A	75	79	.487	4t		3.6
1942	Det A	73	81	.474	5		-4.2
1960	Bos A	2	5	.286	8-8-7	2/3	-1.0
9		419	360	.538			4.7

BAKER, DUSTY B6.15.1949

YEAR	TM/LG	W	L	PCT	FINISH	MGR/YR	+/-
1993	SF N w	103	59	.636	2		4.7
1994	SF N w	55	60	.478	2		-2.9
1995	SF N w	67	77	.465	4		6.8
1996	SF N w	68	94	.420	4		-2.5
1997	SF N w	90	72	.556	1		9.9
1998	SF N w	89	74	.546	2▲		-2.7
1999	SF N w	86	76	.531	2		1.2
2000	SF N w	97	65	.599	1		-0.6
2001	SF N w	90	72	.556	2		4.0
2002	SF N w	95	66	.590	2♦❖		-2.6
2003	Chi N c	88	74	.543	1☆		2.8
2004	Chi N c	89	73	.549	3		-4.4
2005	Chi N c	79	83	.488	4		-0.9
13		1096	945	.537			12.8

BAMBERGER, GEORGE B8.1.1923

YEAR	TM/LG	W	L	PCT	FINISH	MGR/YR	+/-
1978	Mil A e	93	69	.574	3		-3.4
1979	Mil A e	95	66	.590	2		6.2
1980	Mil A e	47	45	.511	2-4-3	2/3	-6.2
1982	NY N e	65	97	.401	6		-4.1
1983	NY N e	16	30	.348	6-6	1/2	-3.8
1985	Mil A e	71	90	.441	6		1.5
1986	Mil A e	71	81	.467	6-6	1/2	1.4
7		458	478	.489			-8.3

BANCROFT, DAVE B4.20.1891

YEAR	TM/LG	W	L	PCT	FINISH	MGR/YR	+/-
1924	Bos N	27	38	.415	6-8	1/3	6.6
1924	Bos N	15	35	.300	8-8	3/3	-0.7
1925	Bos N	70	83	.458	5		2.5
1926	Bos N	66	86	.434	7		-0.4
1927	Bos N	60	94	.390	7		-5.1
4		238	336	.415			2.9

BANCROFT, FRANK Frank Carter
B5.9.1846 Lancaster, MA D3.30.1921 Cincinnati, OH (DNP)

YEAR	TM/LG	W	L	PCT	FINISH	MGR/YR	+/-
1880	Wor N	40	43	.482	5		-5.7
1881	Det N	41	43	.488	4		-2.0
1882	Det N	42	41	.506	6		8.0
1883	Cle N	55	42	.567	4		3.2
1884	Pro N	84	28	.750	1★		0.7
1885	Pro N	53	57	.482	4		7.0
1887	Phi AA	26	29	.473	6-5	1/2	-1.6
1889	Ind N	25	43	.368	7-7	1/2	-5.8
1902	Cin N	9	7	.563	6-6-4	2/3	0.2
9		375	333	.530			4.0

BARKLEY, SAM B5.24.1858

YEAR	TM/LG	W	L	PCT	FINISH	MGR/YR	+/-
1888	KC A	21	36	.368	8-8-8	2/3	4.8

BARNIE, BILLY B1.26.1853

YEAR	TM/LG	W	L	PCT	FINISH	MGR/YR	+/-
1883	Bal AA	28	68	.292	8		2.9
1884	Bal AA	63	43	.594	6		-1.1
1885	Bal AA	41	68	.376	8		-0.7
1886	Bal AA	48	83	.366	8		5.6
1887	Bal AA	77	58	.570	3		0.0
1888	Bal AA	57	80	.416	5		0.2
1889	Bal AA	70	65	.519	5		2.9
1890	Bal AA	15	19	.441	8		-1.0
1891	Bal AA	71	64	.526	3		-1.0
1892-1	Was N	0	2	.000	11t-7	1/2	-0.8
1893	Lou N	50	75	.400	11		2.4
1894	Lou N	36	94	.277	12		-2.4
1897	Bro N	61	71	.462	6t		-1.3
1898	Bro N	15	20	.429	9-10	1/3	1.5
14		632	810	.438			7.0

BARROW, ED Edward Grant "Cousin Ed"
B5.10.1868 Springfield, IL D12.15.1953 Port Chester, NY (DNP)

YEAR	TM/LG	W	L	PCT	FINISH	MGR/YR	+/-
1903	Det A	65	71	.478	5		-6.0
1904	Det A	32	46	.410	7-7	1/2	0.1
1918	Bos A	75	51	.595	1★		1.2
1919	Bos A	66	71	.482	6		-3.8
1920	Bos A	72	81	.471	5		0.4
5		310	320	.492			-8.1

BARRY, JACK B4.26.1887

YEAR	TM/LG	W	L	PCT	FINISH	MGR/YR	+/-
1917	Bos A	90	62	.592	2		2.2

BATTIN, JOE B11.11.1851

YEAR	TM/LG	W	L	PCT	FINISH	MGR/YR	+/-
1883	Pit AA	2	11	.154	7-7	3/3	-2.2
1884	Pit AA	6	7	.462	11-10-10	3/5	3.1
1884	CP U	1	5	.167	5-5	2/3	-1.7
3		9	23	.281			-0.9

BAUER, HANK B7.31.1922

YEAR	TM/LG	W	L	PCT	FINISH	MGR/YR	+/-
1961	KC A	35	67	.343	8-9t	2/2	-4.9
1962	KC A	72	90	.444	9		-0.2
1964	Bal A	97	65	.599	3		3.8
1965	Bal A	94	68	.580	3		6.1
1966	Bal A	97	63	.606	1★		1.1
1967	Bal A	76	85	.472	6t		-11.2
1968	Bal A	43	37	.538	3-2	1/2	-1.7
1969	Oak A w	80	69	.537	2-2	1/2	-0.3
8		594	544	.522			-6.6

BAYLOR, DON B6.28.1949

YEAR	TM/LG	W	L	PCT	FINISH	MGR/YR	+/-
1993	Col N w	67	95	.414	6		5.2
1994	Col N w	53	64	.453	3		0.6
1995	Col N w	77	67	.535	2❖		4.8
1996	Col N w	82	79	.509	3		2.3
1997	Col N w	83	79	.512	3		0.0
1998	Col N w	77	85	.475	4		-1.3
2000	Chi N c	65	97	.401	6		-2.9
2001	Chi N c	88	74	.543	3		-0.5
2002	Chi N c	39	49	.443	5-4	1/2	-2.1
9		631	689	.478			6.6

BELL, BUDDY B8.27.1951

YEAR	TM/LG	W	L	PCT	FINISH	MGR/YR	+/-
1996	Det A e	53	109	.327	5		0.1
1997	Det A e	79	83	.488	3		-1.4
1998	Det A c	52	85	.380	5-5	1/2	-5.1
2000	Col N w	82	80	.506	4		-5.3
2001	Col N w	73	89	.451	5		-9.5
2002	Col N w	6	16	.273	5-4	1/2	-3.5
2005	KC A c	43	69	.384	5-5	3/3	-5.6
7		388	531	.422			-22.3

BENSON, VERN B9.19.1924

YEAR	TM/LG	W	L	PCT	FINISH	MGR/YR	+/-
1977	Atl N w	1	0	1.000	6-6-6	3/4	0.6

BERRA, YOGI B5.12.1925

YEAR	TM/LG	W	L	PCT	FINISH	MGR/YR	+/-
1964	NY A	99	63	.611	1		1.7
1972	NY N e	83	73	.532	3		10.6
1973	NY N e	82	79	.509	1♦		-0.7
1974	NY N e	71	91	.438	5		-1.9
1975	NY N e	56	53	.514	3-3t	1/2	-0.6
1984	NY A e	87	75	.537	3		-2.0

YEAR	TM/LG	W	L	PCT	FINISH	MGR/YR	+/-
1985	NY A e	6	10	.375	7-2	1/2	-3.7
7		484	444	.522			4.0

BEVINGTON, TERRY Terry Paul
B7.7.1956 Akron, OH BR/TR/6-2/190(C)

1995	Chi A c	57	56	.504	4-3	2/2	0.7
1996	Chi A c	85	77	.525	2		-5.7
1997	Chi A c	80	81	.497	2		4.6
3		222	214	.509			-0.3

BEZDEK, HUGO Hugo Frank
B4.1.1884 Prague, Czechoslovakia D9.19.1952 Atlantic City, NJ (DNP)

1917	Pit N	30	59	.337	8-8	3/3	-5.8
1918	Pit N	65	60	.520	4		-3.6
1919	Pit N	71	68	.511	4		0.8
3		166	187	.470			-8.6

BICKERSON, (DNP)

| 1884 | Was AA | 0 | 1 | .000 | 12-12 | 2/2 | -0.2 |

BIRMINGHAM, JOE B8.6.1884

1912	Cle A	21	7	.750	6-5	2/2	7.1
1913	Cle A	86	66	.566	3		-0.6
1914	Cle A	51	102	.333	8		-7.3
1915	Cle A	12	16	.429	6-7	1/2	0.6
4		170	191	.471			-0.2

BISSONETTE, DEL B9.6.1899

| 1945 | Bos N | 25 | 34 | .424 | 7-6 | 2/2 | -4.2 |

BLACKBURNE, LENA B10.23.1886

1928	Chi A	40	40	.500	6-5	2/2	3.6
1929	Chi A	59	93	.388	7		-0.8
2		99	133	.427			2.8

BLADES, RAY B8.6.1896

1939	StL N	92	61	.601	2		1.0
1940	StL N	14	24	.368	6-3	1/3	-6.2
1948	Bro N	1	0	1.000	5-5-3	2/3	0.5
3		107	85	.557			-4.7

BLAIR, WALTER B10.13.1883

| 1915 | Buf F | 1 | 1 | .500 | 8-8-6 | 2/3 | 0.1 |

BLUEGE, OSSIE B10.24.1900

1943	Was A	84	69	.549	2		0.1
1944	Was A	64	90	.416	8		-5.4
1945	Was A	87	67	.565	2		3.5
1946	Was A	76	78	.494	4		9.1
1947	Was A	64	90	.416	7		6.5
5		375	394	.488			13.7

BOCHY, BRUCE B4.16.1955

1995	SD N w	70	74	.486	3		-1.6
1996	SD N w	91	71	.562	1		1.1
1997	SD N w	76	86	.469	4		3.9
1998	SD N w	98	64	.605	1◆		5.3
1999	SD N w	74	88	.457	4		0.0
2000	SD N w	76	86	.469	5		1.1
2001	SD N w	79	83	.488	4		0.2
2002	SD N w	66	96	.407	5		0.2
2003	SD N w	64	98	.395	5		-2.0
2004	SD N w	87	75	.537	3		-0.3
2005	SD N w	82	80	.506	1		5.3
11		863	901	.489			13.2

BOLES, JOHN John
B8.19.1948 Chicago, IL BL/TR/5-10/165(OF)

1996	Fla N e	40	35	.533	4-3	3/3	3.2
1999	Fla N e	64	98	.395	5		-1.3
2000	Fla N e	79	82	.491	3		4.9
2001	Fla N e	22	26	.458	3-4	1/2	-1.9
4		205	241	.460			4.8

BOND, TOMMY B4.2.1856

| 1882 | Wor N | 2 | 4 | .333 | 8-8-8 | 2/3 | 0.7 |

BOONE, BOB B11.19.1947

1995	KC A c	70	74	.486	2		4.1
1996	KC A c	75	86	.466	5		-1.6
1997	KC A c	36	46	.439	4-5	1/2	-1.4
2001	Cin N c	66	96	.407	5		-4.0
2002	Cin N c	78	84	.481	3		3.4
2003	Cin N c	46	58	.442	5-5	1/3	5.8
6		371	444	.455			6.4

BOROS, STEVE B9.3.1936

1983	Oak A w	74	88	.457	4		0.3
1984	Oak A w	20	24	.455	5-4	1/2	-0.5
1986	SD N w	74	88	.457	4		-0.1
3		168	200	.457			-0.3

BOTTOMLEY, JIM B4.23.1900

| 1937 | StL A | 21 | 56 | .273 | 7-8 | 2/2 | -3.7 |

BOUDREAU, LOU B7.17.1917

1942	Cle A	75	79	.487	4		5.3
1943	Cle A	82	71	.536	3		3.0
1944	Cle A	72	82	.468	5t		-1.5
1945	Cle A	73	72	.503	5		-0.5
1946	Cle A	68	86	.442	6		2.0
1947	Cle A	80	74	.519	4		-7.4
1948	Cle A	97	58	.626	1★		-7.7
1949	Cle A	89	65	.578	3		1.4
1950	Cle A	92	62	.597	4		0.1

YEAR	TM/LG	W	L	PCT	FINISH	MGR/YR	+/-
1952	Bos A	76	78	.494	6		-2.0
1953	Bos A	84	69	.549	4		5.0
1954	Bos A	69	85	.448	4		-5.2
1955	KC A	63	91	.409	6		11.9
1956	KC A	52	102	.338	8		-4.3
1957	KC A	36	67	.350	8-7	1/2	-5.2
1960	Chi N	54	83	.394	7-7	2/2	-1.9
16		1162	1224	.487			-6.9

BOWA, LARRY B12.6.1945

1987	SD N w	65	97	.401	6		-6.4
1988	SD N w	16	30	.348	5-3	1/2	-7.3
2001	Phi N e	86	76	.531	2		2.3
2002	Phi N e	80	81	.497	3		0.9
2003	Phi N e	86	76	.531	3		-4.3
2004	Phi N e	86	76	.531	2		-0.6
6		419	436	.490			-15.4

BOWERMAN, FRANK B12.5.1868

| 1909 | Bos N | 22 | 54 | .289 | 8-8 | | -2.2 |

BOYD, BILL B12.22.1852

| 1875 | Atl NA | 0 | 2 | .000 | 12-12 | 2/2 | 0.2 |

BOYER, KEN B5.20.1931

1978	StL N e	62	81	.434	6-5	3/3	-4.1
1979	StL N e	86	76	.531	3		1.1
1980	StL N e	18	33	.353	6-4	1/4	-8.4
3		166	190	.466			-11.3

BRADLEY, BILL B2.13.1878

1905	Cle A	20	21	.488	1t-2-5	2/3	0.2
1914	Bro F	77	77	.500	5		1.5
2		97	98	.497			1.7

BRAGAN, BOBBY B10.30.1917

1956	Pit N	66	88	.429	7		-4.1
1957	Pit N	36	67	.350	7-7t	1/2	-7.8
1958	Cle A	31	36	.463	6-4	1/2	-5.1
1963	Mil N	84	78	.519	6		-4.9
1964	Mil N	88	74	.543	5		1.3
1965	Mil N	86	76	.531	5		-2.8
1966	Atl N	52	59	.468	7-5	1/2	-10.3
7		443	478	.481			-33.8

BRENLY, BOB B2.25.1954

2001	Ari N w	92	70	.568	1★		-2.9
2002	Ari N w	98	64	.605	1		2.7
2003	Ari N w	84	78	.519	3		-0.3
2004	Ari N w	29	50	.367	5-5	1/2	3.1
4		303	262	.536			2.6

BRESNAHAN, ROGER B6.11.1879

1909	StL N	54	98	.355	7		-6.8
1910	StL N	63	90	.412	7		-5.5
1911	StL N	75	74	.503	5		7.9
1912	StL N	63	90	.412	6		2.9
1915	Chi N	73	80	.477	4		1.9
5		328	432	.432			0.5

BRISTOL, DAVE James David
B6.23.1933 Macon, GA BR/TR/5-11/175(2B)

1966	Cin N	39	38	.506	8-7	2/2	1.0
1967	Cin N	87	75	.537	4		1.4
1968	Cin N	83	79	.512	4		0.2
1969	Cin N w	89	73	.549	3		5.1
1970	Mil A w	65	97	.401	4t		-1.7
1971	Mil A w	69	92	.429	6		-3.1
1972	Mil A e	10	20	.333	6-6	1/3	-2.8
1976	Atl N w	70	92	.432	6		-2.6
1977	Atl N w	8	21	.276	6-6	1/4	-2.8
1977	Atl N w	52	79	.397	6-6	4/4	3.4
1979	SF N w	10	12	.455	4-4	4/2	0.1
1980	SF N w	75	86	.466	5		1.2
9		657	764	.462			-0.5

BROWN, FREEMAN Freeman
B1.31.1845 Hubbardston, MA D12.27.1916 Worcester, MA (DNP)

| 1882 | Wor N | 9 | 32 | .220 | 8-8 | 1/3 | -0.1 |

BROWN, MORDECAI B10.19.1876

| 1914 | StL F | 50 | 63 | .442 | 7-8 | 1/2 | 3.9 |

BROWN, TOM B9.21.1860

1897	Was N	52	46	.531	11-6t	2/2	3.8
1898	Was N	12	26	.316	11-11	1/4	-1.6
2		64	72	.471			2.2

BRUCKER, EARLE B5.6.1901

| 1952 | Cin N | 3 | 2 | .600 | 7-7-6 | 2/3 | 0.6 |

BUCKENBERGER, AL Albert C.
B1.31.1861 Detroit, MI D7.1.1917 Syracuse, NY (DNP)

1889	Col AA	60	78	.435	6		3.5
1890	Col AA	39	41	.488	5-2	1/3	-12.9
1892-1	Pit N	15	14	.517	7-6	1/2	0.4
1892-2	Pit N	38	27	.585	10-4	2/2	5.3
1893	Pit N	81	48	.628	2		-0.3
1894	Pit N	53	55	.491	7-7	1/2	0.0
1895	StL N	16	34	.320	11-11	1/4	-0.0
1902	Bos N	73	64	.533	3		-1.6
1903	Bos N	58	80	.420	6		1.0
1904	Bos N	55	98	.359	7		5.9
9		488	539	.475			1.2

YEAR	TM/LG	W	L	PCT	FINISH	MGR/YR	+/-

BUFFINTON, CHARLIE B6.14.1861

| 1890 | Phi P | 61 | 54 | .530 | 5-5 | 2/2 | -2.6 |

BURDOCK, JACK B4.1852

| 1883 | Bos N | 30 | 24 | .556 | 4-1 | 1/2 | -7.4 |

BURKE, JIMMY B10.12.1874

1905	StL N	34	56	.378	7-6-6	2/3	1.2
1918	StL A	29	31	.483	6-5	3/3	0.2
1919	StL A	67	72	.482	5		1.1
1920	StL A	76	77	.497	4		-3.4
4		206	236	.466			-0.9

BURNHAM, GEORGE George Walter "Watch"
B5.20.1860 Albion, MI D11.18.1902 Detroit, MI (DNP)

| 1887 | Ind N | 6 | 22 | .214 | 8-8 | 1/3 | -1.7 |

BURNS, TOM B3.30.1857

1892-1	Pit N	22	25	.468	7-6	2/2	-1.7
1892-2	Pit N	5	7	.417	10-4	1/2	-1.0
1898	Chi N	85	65	.567	4		-4.2
1899	Chi N	75	73	.507	8		-3.6
3		187	170	.524			-10.5

BURWELL, BILL B3.27.1895

| 1947 | Pit N | 1 | 0 | 1.000 | 8-7t | 2/2 | 0.5 |

BUSH, DONIE B10.8.1887

1923	Was A	75	78	.490	4		1.1
1927	Pit N	94	60	.610	1		1.6
1928	Pit N	85	67	.559	4		-3.5
1929	Pit N	67	51	.568	2-2	1/2	-0.7
1930	Chi A	62	92	.403	7		-0.6
1931	Chi A	56	97	.366	8		1.2
1933	Cin N	58	94	.382	8		-1.8
7		497	539	.480			-2.7

BUTLER, ORMOND Ormond Hook
B11.1854 WV D9.12.1915 Mt.Hope, MD (DNP)

| 1883 | Pit AA | 17 | 36 | .321 | 6-6-7 | 2/3 | -0.3 |

BYRNE, CHARLIE Charles H.
B9.1843 New York, NY D1.4.1898 New York, NY (DNP)

1885	Bro AA	38	37	.507	7-5t	2/2	2.0
1886	Bro AA	76	61	.555	3		7.5
1887	Bro AA	60	74	.448	6		-5.8
3		174	172	.503			3.7

CALLAHAN, NIXEY B3.18.1874

1903	Chi A	60	77	.438	7		1.7
1904	Chi A	23	18	.561	4-3	1/2	-1.1
1912	Chi A	78	76	.506	4		1.9
1913	Chi A	78	74	.513	5		3.2
1914	Chi A	70	84	.455	6t		1.5
1916	Pit N	65	89	.422	6		-0.3
1917	Pit N	20	40	.333	8-8	1/3	-4.1
7		394	458	.462			2.8

CAMPAU, COUNT B10.17.1863

| 1890 | StL AA | 27 | 14 | .659 | 5-2-3 | 4/6 | 2.9 |

CANTILLON, JOE Joseph D. "Pongo Joe"
B8.19.1861 Janesville, WI D1.31.1930 Hickman, KY (DNP)

1907	Was A	49	102	.325	8		-6.4
1908	Was A	67	85	.441	7		-2.0
1909	Was A	42	110	.276	8		-1.9
3		158	297	.347			-10.2

CAREY, MAX B1.11.1890

1932	Bro N	81	73	.526	3		3.5
1933	Bro N	65	88	.425	6		-3.4
2		146	161	.476			0.1

CAREY, TOM B1849

1873	Bal NA	14	9	.609	3-3	2/2	-2.9
1874	Mut NA	13	12	.520	3-2	1/2	-3.4
2		27	21	.563			-6.3

CARRIGAN, BILL B10.22.1883

1913	Bos A	40	30	.571	5-4	2/2	4.0
1914	Bos A	91	62	.595	2		5.5
1915	Bos A	101	50	.669	1★		6.9
1916	Bos A	91	63	.591	1★		5.8
1927	Bos A	51	103	.331	8		-0.7
1928	Bos A	57	96	.373	8		-1.2
1929	Bos A	58	96	.377	8		0.7
7		489	500	.494			21.0

CARUTHERS, BOB B1.5.1864

| 1892-2 | StL N | 16 | 32 | .333 | 12-11 | 3/3 | -1.5 |

CAVARRETTA, PHIL B7.19.1916

1951	Chi N	27	47	.365	7-8	2/2	-3.4
1952	Chi N	77	77	.500	5		0.3
1953	Chi N	65	89	.422	7		7.7
3		169	213	.442			4.6

CAYLOR, O.P. Oliver Perry
B12.17.1849 Near Dayton, OH D10.19.1897 Winona, MN (DNP)

1885	Cin N	63	49	.563	2		0.9
1886	Cin AA	65	73	.471	5		-5.5
1887	NY AA	35	60	.368	7-7	3/3	7.4
3		163	182	.472			2.7

CHANCE, FRANK B9.9.1877

YEAR	TM/LG	W	L	PCT	FINISH	MGR/YR	+/-
1905	Chi N	55	33	.625	4-3	2/2	-3.5
1906	Chi N	116	36	.763	1		3.4
1907	Chi N	107	45	.704	1★		8.9
1908	Chi N	99	55	.643	1★		3.3
1909	Chi N	104	49	.680	2		-1.1
1910	Chi N	104	50	.675	1		4.2
1911	Chi N	92	62	.597	2		-0.3
1912	Chi N	91	59	.607	3		7.4
1913	NY A	57	94	.377	7		-3.6
1914	NY A	60	74	.448	7-6t	1/2	-5.7
1923	Bos A	61	91	.401	8		7.4
11		946	648	.593			20.4

CHAPMAN, JACK B5.8.1843

YEAR	TM/LG	W	L	PCT	FINISH	MGR/YR	+/-
1876	Lou N	30	36	.455	5		3.4
1877	Lou N	35	25	.583	2		0.2
1878	Mil N	15	45	.250	6		-3.0
1882	Wor N	7	30	.189	8-8	3/3	-1.2
1883	Det N	40	58	.408	7		2.1
1884	Det N	28	84	.250	8		-0.9
1885	Buf N	31	57	.352	7-7	2/2	5.7
1889	Lou AA	1	6	.143	8-8	4/4	-0.5
1890	Lou AA	88	44	.667	1		0.5
1891	Lou AA	54	83	.394	7		1.1
1892-1	Lou N	21	33	.389	10-11	1/2	-0.6
11		350	501	.411			6.8

CHAPMAN, BEN B12.25.1908

YEAR	TM/LG	W	L	PCT	FINISH	MGR/YR	+/-
1945	Phi N	28	57	.329	8-8	2/2	2.8
1946	Phi N	69	85	.448	5		7.2
1947	Phi N	62	92	.403	7t		-4.8
1948	Phi N	37	42	.468	7-6	1/3	4.7
4		196	276	.415			10.0

CHASE, HAL B2.13.1883

YEAR	TM/LG	W	L	PCT	FINISH	MGR/YR	+/-
1910	NY A	10	4	.714	3-2		2.3
1911	NY A	76	76	.500	6		3.9
2		86	80	.518			6.2

CLAPP, JOHN B7.17.1851

YEAR	TM/LG	W	L	PCT	FINISH	MGR/YR	+/-
1872	Man NA	5	19	.208	8		0.9
1878	Ind N	24	36	.400	5		-2.7
1879	Buf N	46	32	.590	3		4.2
1880	Cin N	21	59	.262	8		-1.6
1881	Cle N	32	41	.438	6-7	2/2	-2.6
1883	NY N	46	50	.479	6		2.2
6		174	237	.423			0.3

CLARKE, FRED B10.3.1872

YEAR	TM/LG	W	L	PCT	FINISH	MGR/YR	+/-
1897	Lou N	35	54	.393	9-11	2/2	2.3
1898	Lou N	70	81	.464	9		4.4
1899	Lou N	75	76	.497	9		-5.3
1900	Pit N	79	60	.568	2		-2.2
1901	Pit N	90	49	.647	1		-3.2
1902	Pit N	103	36	.741	1		-0.9
1903	Pit N	91	49	.650	1		3.9
1904	Pit N	87	66	.569	4		1.8
1905	Pit N	96	57	.627	2		6.7
1906	Pit N	93	60	.608	3		-0.7
1907	Pit N	91	63	.591	2		0.2
1908	Pit N	98	56	.636	2t		7.5
1909	Pit N	110	42	.724	1★		6.3
1910	Pit N	86	67	.562	3		1.1
1911	Pit N	85	69	.552	3		-11.4
1912	Pit N	93	58	.616	2		-1.5
1913	Pit N	78	71	.523	4		-5.8
1914	Pit N	69	85	.448	7		-3.7
1915	Pit N	73	81	.474	5		-8.2
19		1602	1180	.576			-8.6

CLEMENTS, JACK B7.24.1864

YEAR	TM/LG	W	L	PCT	FINISH	MGR/YR	+/-
1890	Phi N	13	6	.684	1-2-3	2/5	2.0

COBB, TY B12.18.1886

YEAR	TM/LG	W	L	PCT	FINISH	MGR/YR	+/-
1921	Det A	71	82	.464	6		-8.3
1922	Det A	79	75	.513	3		-1.4
1923	Det A	83	71	.539	2		-2.5
1924	Det A	86	68	.558	3		4.1
1925	Det A	81	73	.526	4		-2.7
1926	Det A	79	75	.513	6		5.5
6		479	444	.519			-5.3

COCHRANE, MICKEY B4.6.1903

YEAR	TM/LG	W	L	PCT	FINISH	MGR/YR	+/-
1934	Det A	101	53	.656	1		1.2
1935	Det A	93	58	.616	1★		-6.1
1936	Det A	29	24	.547	3-2	1/3	1.0
1936	Det A	36	31	.537	4-2	3/3	0.6
1937	Det A	16	13	.552	3-2	1/5	-0.1
1937	Det A	26	20	.565	3-2-2	3/5	0.5
1938	Det A	47	51	.480	5-4	1/2	-5.9
5		348	250	.582			-8.8

COHEN, ANDY B10.25.1904

YEAR	TM/LG	W	L	PCT	FINISH	MGR/YR	+/-
1960	Phi N	1	0	1.000	6t-4t-8	2/3	0.6

COLEMAN, JERRY B9.14.1924

YEAR	TM/LG	W	L	PCT	FINISH	MGR/YR	+/-
1980	SD N w	73	89	.451	6		-1.2

COLEMAN, BOB B9.26.1890

YEAR	TM/LG	W	L	PCT	FINISH	MGR/YR	+/-
1943	Bos N	21	25	.457	6-6	1/2	3.0
1944	Bos N	65	89	.422	6		-3.5
1945	Bos N	42	51	.452	7-6	1/2	-4.1
3		128	165	.437			-4.6

COLLINS, EDDIE B5.2.1887

YEAR	TM/LG	W	L	PCT	FINISH	MGR/YR	+/-
1924	Chi A	14	13	.519	6	3/4	1.6
1925	Chi A	79	75	.513	5		-1.8
1926	Chi A	81	72	.529	5		-2.0
3		174	160	.521			-2.3

COLLINS, JIMMY B1.16.1870

YEAR	TM/LG	W	L	PCT	FINISH	MGR/YR	+/-
1901	Bos A	79	57	.581	2		-3.4
1902	Bos A	77	60	.562	3		2.2
1903	Bos A	91	47	.659	1★		1.1
1904	Bos A	95	59	.617	1		1.7
1905	Bos A	78	74	.513	4		0.5
1906	Bos A	35	79	.307	8-8	1/2	-2.3
6		455	376	.548			-0.3

COLLINS, SHANO B12.4.1885

YEAR	TM/LG	W	L	PCT	FINISH	MGR/YR	+/-
1931	Bos A	62	90	.408	6		3.2
1932	Bos A	11	44	.200	8-8	1/2	-4.4
2		73	134	.353			-1.2

COLLINS, TERRY Terry Lee
B5.27.1949 Midland, MI BL/TR/5-8/160(2B)

YEAR	TM/LG	W	L	PCT	FINISH	MGR/YR	+/-
1994	Hou N c	66	49	.574	2		-1.1
1995	Hou N c	76	68	.528	2		-3.0
1996	Hou N c	82	80	.506	2		4.8
1997	Ana A w	84	78	.519	2		-0.3
1998	Ana A w	85	77	.525	2		3.6
1999	Ana A w	51	82	.383	4-4	1/2	-6.3
6		444	434	.506			-2.3

COMISKEY, CHARLIE B8.15.1859

YEAR	TM/LG	W	L	PCT	FINISH	MGR/YR	+/-
1883	StL AA	12	7	.632	2-2	2/2	-0.1
1884	StL AA	16	7	.696	5-4	2/2	2.2
1885	StL AA	79	33	.705	1		2.7
1886	StL AA	93	46	.669	1★		-8.3
1887	StL AA	95	40	.704	1		-2.5
1888	StL AA	92	43	.681	1		-3.7
1889	StL AA	89	46	.659	2		-1.9
1890	Chi P	75	62	.547	4		-3.5
1891	StL AA	85	51	.625	2		-2.0
1892-1	Cin N	44	31	.587	4		3.6
1892-2	Cin N	38	37	.507	8		3.6
1893	Cin N	65	63	.508	6t		5.8
1894	Cin N	55	75	.423	10		3.2
12		838	541	.608			-0.9

CONNOR, ROGER B7.1.1857

YEAR	TM/LG	W	L	PCT	FINISH	MGR/YR	+/-
1896	StL N	8	37	.178	11-11-11	4/5	-4.3

COOKE, DUSTY B6.23.1907

YEAR	TM/LG	W	L	PCT	FINISH	MGR/YR	+/-
1948	Phi N	6	6	.500	7-6-6	2/3	1.1

COOMBS, JACK B11.18.1882

YEAR	TM/LG	W	L	PCT	FINISH	MGR/YR	+/-
1919	Phi N	18	44	.290	8-8	1/2	-4.3

COONEY, JOHNNY B3.18.1901

YEAR	TM/LG	W	L	PCT	FINISH	MGR/YR	+/-
1949	Bos N	20	25	.444	4-4	2/2	-2.1

CORRALES, PAT B3.20.1941

YEAR	TM/LG	W	L	PCT	FINISH	MGR/YR	+/-
1978	Tex A w	1	0	1.000	2t-2t	2/2	0.5
1979	Tex A w	83	79	.512	3		-3.2
1980	Tex A w	76	85	.472	4		-4.9
1982	Phi N e	89	73	.549	2		6.9
1983	Phi N e	43	42	.506	1-1◆	1/2	-2.9
1983	Cle A e	30	32	.484	7-7	2/2	2.1
1984	Cle A e	75	87	.463	6		-5.5
1985	Cle A e	60	102	.370	7		-8.4
1986	Cle A e	84	78	.519	5		3.9
1987	Cle A e	31	56	.356	7-7	1/2	-1.8
9		572	634	.474			-13.2

CORRIDEN, RED B9.4.1887

YEAR	TM/LG	W	L	PCT	FINISH	MGR/YR	+/-
1950	Phi N	52	72	.419	8-6	2/2	0.1

COTTIER, CHUCK B1.8.1936

YEAR	TM/LG	W	L	PCT	FINISH	MGR/YR	+/-
1984	Sea A w	15	12	.556	7-5t	2/2	3.0
1985	Sea A w	74	88	.457	6		2.6
1986	Sea A w	9	19	.321	6-7	1/3	-3.0
3		98	119	.452			2.6

COX, BOBBY B5.21.1941

YEAR	TM/LG	W	L	PCT	FINISH	MGR/YR	+/-
1978	Atl N w	69	93	.426	6		3.6
1979	Atl N w	66	94	.412	6		-4.6
1980	Atl N w	81	80	.503	4		3.7
1981-1	Atl N w	25	29	.463	4		-0.7
1981-2	Atl N w	25	27	.481	5		-0.7
1982	Tor A e	78	84	.481	6t		2.2
1983	Tor A e	89	73	.549	4		1.2
1984	Tor A e	89	73	.549	2		2.6
1985	Tor A e	99	62	.615	1		0.8
1990	Atl N w	40	57	.412	6-6	2/2	-0.3
1991	Atl N w	94	68	.580	1◆		2.3
1992	Atl N w	98	64	.605	1◆		4.8
1993	Atl N w	104	58	.642	1		1.2
1994	Atl N e	68	46	.596	2		1.4
1995	Atl N e	90	54	.625	1★		7.0
1996	Atl N e	96	66	.593	1◆		2.3
1997	Atl N e	101	61	.623	1		-1.7
1998	Atl N e	106	56	.654	1☆		0.1
1999	Atl N e	103	59	.636	1◆		4.4
2000	Atl N e	95	67	.586	1		4.6
2001	Atl N e	88	74	.543	1☆		-1.9
2002	Atl N e	101	59	.631	1		5.7
2003	Atl N e	101	61	.623	1		4.3
2004	Atl N e	96	66	.593	1		1.6
2005	Atl N e	90	72	.556	1		-0.6
24		2092	1603	.566			43.3

CRAFT, HARRY B4.19.1915

YEAR	TM/LG	W	L	PCT	FINISH	MGR/YR	+/-
1957	KC A	23	27	.460	8-7	2/2	3.0
1958	KC A	73	81	.474	7		3.2
1959	KC A	66	88	.429	7		-3.3
1961	Chi N	4	8	.333	6t-7-7	2/9	-1.2
1961	Chi N	3	1	.750	7-7-7	5/9	1.3
1962	Hou N	64	96	.400	8		-2.8
1963	Hou N	66	96	.407	9		5.2
1964	Hou N	61	88	.409	9-9	1/2	0.4
7		360	485	.426			6.0

CRAIG, ROGER B2.17.1930

YEAR	TM/LG	W	L	PCT	FINISH	MGR/YR	+/-
1978	SD N w	84	78	.519	4		3.8
1979	SD N w	68	93	.422	5		-4.2
1985	SF N w	6	12	.333	6-6	2/2	-1.6
1986	SF N w	83	79	.512	3		-6.4
1987	SF N w	90	72	.556	1		-2.4
1988	SF N w	83	79	.512	4		-2.7
1989	SF N w	92	70	.568	1◆		0.5
1990	SF N w	85	77	.525	3		3.1
1991	SF N w	75	87	.463	4		-1.0
1992	SF N w	72	90	.444	5		-1.0
10		738	737	.500			-11.9

CRANDALL, DEL B3.5.1930

YEAR	TM/LG	W	L	PCT	FINISH	MGR/YR	+/-
1972	Mil A e	54	70	.435	6-6	3/3	1.2
1973	Mil A e	74	88	.457	5		-4.7
1974	Mil A e	76	86	.469	5		-3.6
1975	Mil A e	67	94	.416	5-5	1/2	-1.9
1983	Sea A w	34	55	.382	7-7	2/2	0.1
1984	Sea A w	59	76	.437	7-5t	1/2	-0.8
6		364	469	.437			-9.7

CRANE, SAM B1.2.1854

YEAR	TM/LG	W	L	PCT	FINISH	MGR/YR	+/-
1880	Buf N	24	58	.293	7		-0.6
1884	Cin U	49	21	.700	5-3	2/2	-0.2
2		73	79	.480			-0.8

CRAVATH, GAVY B3.23.1881

YEAR	TM/LG	W	L	PCT	FINISH	MGR/YR	+/-
1919	Phi N	29	46	.387	8-8	2/2	2.0
1920	Phi N	62	91	.405	8		1.0
2		91	137	.399			2.9

CRAVER, BILL B6.1844

YEAR	TM/LG	W	L	PCT	FINISH	MGR/YR	+/-
1871	Tro NA	12	12	.500	7-6	2/2	0.9
1872	Bal NA	27	13	.675	2-2	1/2	-2.6
1875	Cen NA	2	12	.143	11		0.3
1876	NY N	21	35	.375	6		6.3
4		62	72	.463			4.6

CREAMER, GEORGE B1855

YEAR	TM/LG	W	L	PCT	FINISH	MGR/YR	+/-
1884	Pit AA	0	8	.000	10-10-10	4/5	-1.8

CRONIN, JOE B10.12.1906

YEAR	TM/LG	W	L	PCT	FINISH	MGR/YR	+/-
1933	Was A	99	53	.651	1		5.4
1934	Was A	66	86	.434	7		-2.7
1935	Bos A	78	75	.510	4		2.9
1936	Bos A	74	80	.481	6		-4.0
1937	Bos A	80	72	.526	5		-0.3
1938	Bos A	88	61	.591	2		-0.1
1939	Bos A	89	62	.589	2		4.9
1940	Bos A	82	72	.532	4t		-3.7
1941	Bos A	84	70	.545	2		-3.7
1942	Bos A	93	59	.612	2		0.2
1943	Bos A	68	84	.447	7		-3.2
1944	Bos A	77	77	.500	4		-6.3
1945	Bos A	71	83	.461	7		1.9
1946	Bos A	104	50	.675	1		7.1
1947	Bos A	83	71	.539	3		0.9
15		1236	1055	.540			3.7

CROOKS, JACK B11.9.1865

YEAR	TM/LG	W	L	PCT	FINISH	MGR/YR	+/-
1892-1	StL N	24	22	.522	11-9	3/3	7.2
1892-2	StL N	3	11	.214	12-11	1/3	-2.1

CROSS, LAVE B5.12.1866

YEAR	TM/LG	W	L	PCT	FINISH	MGR/YR	+/-
1899	Cle N	8	30	.211	12-12	1/2	4.1

CUBBAGE, MIKE B7.21.1950

YEAR	TM/LG	W	L	PCT	FINISH	MGR/YR	+/-
1991	NY N e	3	4	.429	3-5	2/2	-0.9

CURTIS, ED Edwin Russell
B8.29.1843 Hartford, CT D8.6.1914 Bath, NY (DNP)

YEAR	TM/LG	W	L	PCT	FINISH	MGR/YR	+/-
1884	Alt U	6	19	.240	6		4.

CUSHMAN, CHARLIE Charles H.
B5.25.1850 New York, NY D6.29.1909 Milwaukee, WI (DNP)

YEAR	TM/LG	W	L	PCT	FINISH	MGR/YR	+/-
1891	Mil AA	21	15	.583	5		3.

CUTHBERT, NED B6.20.1845

YEAR	TM/LG	W	L	PCT	FINISH	MGR/YR	+/-
1882	StL AA	37	43	.463	5		3.

DAHLEN, BILL B1.5.1870

YEAR	TM/LG	W	L	PCT	FINISH	MGR/YR	+/-
1910	Bro N	64	90	.416	6		-1.
1911	Bro N	64	86	.427	7		-0.
1912	Bro N	58	95	.379	7		4.

YEAR	TM/LG	W	L	PCT	FINISH	MGR/YR	+/-
1913	Bro N	65	84	.436	6		-7.6
4		251	355	.414			-13.8

DARK, ALVIN B1.7.1922

YEAR	TM/LG	W	L	PCT	FINISH	MGR/YR	+/-
1961	SF N	85	69	.552	3		-3.7
1962	SF N	103	62	.624	1▲		2.2
1963	SF N	88	74	.543	3		-1.7
1964	SF N	90	72	.556	4		1.5
1966	KC A	74	86	.463	7		3.2
1967	KC A	52	69	.430	10-10	1/2	2.0
1968	Cle A	86	75	.534	3		4.1
1969	Cle A e	62	99	.385	6		-3.2
1970	Cle A e	76	86	.469	5		-2.3
1971	Cle A e	42	61	.408	6-6	1/2	4.3
1974	Oak A w	90	72	.556	1★		-6.0
1975	Oak A w	98	64	.605	1		1.3
1977	SD N w	48	65	.425	4-5	3/3	1.2
13		994	954	.510			2.9

DAVENPORT, JIM B8.17.1933

YEAR	TM/LG	W	L	PCT	FINISH	MGR/YR	+/-
1985	SF N w	56	88	.389	6-6	1/2	-4.6

DAVIDSON, MORDECAI Mordecai H.
B11.30.1846 Port Washington, OH D9.6.1940 Louisville, KY (DNP)

YEAR	TM/LG	W	L	PCT	FINISH	MGR/YR	+/-
1888	Lou AA	1	2	.333	8-8-7	2/4	-0.1
1888	Lou AA	34	52	.395	8-7	4/4	1.3

DAVIS, GEORGE B8.23.1870

YEAR	TM/LG	W	L	PCT	FINISH	MGR/YR	+/-
1895	NY N	16	17	.485	8-9	1/3	-0.9
1900	NY N	39	37	.513	8-8	2/2	6.5
1901	NY N	52	85	.380	7		4.4
3		107	139	.435			10.0

DAVIS, HARRY B7.19.1873

YEAR	TM/LG	W	L	PCT	FINISH	MGR/YR	+/-
1912	Cle A	54	71	.432	6-5	1/2	-8.2

DAVIS, SPUD B12.20.1904

YEAR	TM/LG	W	L	PCT	FINISH	MGR/YR	+/-
1946	Pit N	1	2	.333	7-7	2/2	-0.3

DAY, JOHN John B.
B9.23.1847 Colchester, CT D1.25.1925 Cliffside, NJ (DNP)

YEAR	TM/LG	W	L	PCT	FINISH	MGR/YR	+/-
1899	NY N	29	35	.453	9-10	1/2	2.0

DEANE, HARRY B5.6.1846

YEAR	TM/LG	W	L	PCT	FINISH	MGR/YR	+/-
1871	Kek NA	2	3	.400	7-8	2/2	1.4

DENT, BUCKY B11.25.1951

YEAR	TM/LG	W	L	PCT	FINISH	MGR/YR	+/-
1989	NY A e	18	22	.450	6-5	2/2	0.3
1990	NY A e	18	31	.367	7-7	1/2	-1.9
2		36	53	.404			-1.6

DICKEY, BILL B6.6.1907

YEAR	TM/LG	W	L	PCT	FINISH	MGR/YR	+/-
1946	NY A	57	48	.543	2-3-3	2/3	-5.4

DIDDLEBOCK, HARRY Henry H.
B6.27.1854 Philadelphia, PA D2.5.1900 Philadelphia, PA (DNP)

YEAR	TM/LG	W	L	PCT	FINISH	MGR/YR	+/-
1896	StL N	7	10	.412	10-11	1/5	2.4

DIERKER, LARRY B9.22.1946

YEAR	TM/LG	W	L	PCT	FINISH	MGR/YR	+/-
1997	Hou N c	84	78	.519	1		-8.8
1998	Hou N c	102	60	.630	1		-4.1
1999	Hou N c	37	23	.617	1-1	1/3	1.6
1999	Hou N c	47	28	.627	1t-1	3/3	2.7
2000	Hou N c	72	90	.444	4		-8.5
2001	Hou N c	93	69	.574	1		4.6
5		435	348	.556			-12.4

DOBY, LARRY B12.13.1923

YEAR	TM/LG	W	L	PCT	FINISH	MGR/YR	+/-
1978	Chi A w	37	50	.425	5-5	2/2	-1.1

DONOVAN, PATSY B3.16.1865

YEAR	TM/LG	W	L	PCT	FINISH	MGR/YR	+/-
1897	Pit N	60	71	.458	8		8.8
1899	Pit N	69	58	.543	10-7	2/2	-0.1
1901	StL N	76	64	.543	4		-3.6
1902	StL N	56	78	.418	6		7.2
1903	StL N	43	94	.314	8		3.0
1904	Was A	37	97	.276	8-8	2/2	-0.3
1906	Bro N	66	86	.434	5		4.3
1907	Bro N	65	83	.439	5		0.1
1908	Bro N	53	101	.344	7		-6.4
1910	Bos A	81	72	.529	4		-3.9
1911	Bos A	78	75	.510	5		-2.3
11		684	879	.438			6.8

DONOVAN, BILL B10.13.1876

YEAR	TM/LG	W	L	PCT	FINISH	MGR/YR	+/-
1915	NY A	69	83	.454	5		-6.6
1916	NY A	80	74	.519	4		1.2
1917	NY A	71	82	.464	6		-1.6
1921	Phi N	25	62	.287	8-8	1/2	-2.3
4		245	301	.449			-9.3

DOOIN, RED B6.12.1879

YEAR	TM/LG	W	L	PCT	FINISH	MGR/YR	+/-
1910	Phi N	78	75	.510	4		-2.1
1911	Phi N	79	73	.520	4		4.1
1912	Phi N	73	79	.480	5		-1.2
1913	Phi N	88	63	.583	2		6.6
1914	Phi N	74	80	.481	6		0.7
5		392	370	.514			8.0

DORGAN, MIKE B10.2.1853

YEAR	TM/LG	W	L	PCT	FINISH	MGR/YR	+/-
1879	Syr N	17	26	.395	6-7	1/3	6.1
1880	Pro N	26	12	.684	3-2	3/3	1.3
1881	Wor N	24	32	.429	7-8	1/2	1.1
3		67	70	.489			8.6

DOWD, TOMMY B4.20.1869

YEAR	TM/LG	W	L	PCT	FINISH	MGR/YR	+/-
1896	StL N	25	38	.397	11-11	5/5	7.8
1897	StL N	6	22	.214	12-12	1/4	0.9
2		31	60	.341			8.8

DOYLE, JACK B10.25.1869

YEAR	TM/LG	W	L	PCT	FINISH	MGR/YR	+/-
1895	NY N	32	31	.508	8-9-9	2/3	-0.2
1898	Was N	8	9	.471	11-10-11	2/4	1.9
2		40	40	.500			1.7

DRESSEN, CHUCK B9.20.1898

YEAR	TM/LG	W	L	PCT	FINISH	MGR/YR	+/-
1934	Cin N	21	39	.350	8-8	3/3	-0.7
1935	Cin N	68	85	.444	6		4.0
1936	Cin N	74	80	.481	5		0.7
1937	Cin N	51	78	.395	8-8	1/2	-5.4
1951	Bro N	97	60	.618	2▲		0.8
1952	Bro N	96	57	.627	1		2.2
1953	Bro N	105	49	.682	1		3.5
1955	Was A	53	101	.344	8		-4.9
1956	Was A	59	95	.383	7		7.6
1957	Was A	4	16	.200	8-8	1/2	-3.4
1960	Mil N	88	66	.571	2		4.4
1961	Mil N	71	58	.550	3-4	1/2	1.8
1963	Det A	55	47	.539	9-5t		4.2
1964	Det A	85	77	.525	4		1.8
1965	Det A	65	55	.542	3-4	2/2	-1.2
1966	Det A	16	10	.615	3-3	1/3	2.7
16		1008	973	.509			18.1

DUFFY, HUGH B11.26.1866

YEAR	TM/LG	W	L	PCT	FINISH	MGR/YR	+/-
1901	Mil A	48	89	.350	8		-3.2
1904	Phi N	52	100	.342	8		-2.4
1905	Phi N	83	69	.546	4		-3.8
1906	Phi N	71	82	.464	4		-1.4
1910	Chi A	68	85	.444	6		-5.8
1911	Chi A	77	74	.510	4		-8.1
1921	Bos A	75	79	.487	5		0.8
1922	Bos A	61	93	.396	8		1.2
8		535	671	.444			-22.7

DUNLAP, FRED B5.21.1859

YEAR	TM/LG	W	L	PCT	FINISH	MGR/YR	+/-
1882	Cle N	42	36	.538	8-5	2/2	3.8
1884	StL U	66	16	.805	1-1	2/2	-4.3
1885	StL U	21	29	.420	5-8	1/3	5.5
1885	StL N	9	11	.450	8-8	3/3	2.8
1889	Pit N	7	10	.412	6-7-5	2/3	-0.6
4		145	102	.587			7.1

DUROCHER, LEO B7.27.1905

YEAR	TM/LG	W	L	PCT	FINISH	MGR/YR	+/-
1939	Bro N	84	69	.549	3		1.1
1940	Bro N	88	65	.575	2		3.7
1941	Bro N	100	54	.649	1		0.8
1942	Bro N	104	50	.675	2		2.7
1943	Bro N	81	72	.529	3		0.4
1944	Bro N	63	91	.409	7		-0.4
1945	Bro N	87	67	.565	3		3.2
1946	Bro N	96	60	.615	2▲		4.2
1948	Bro N	35	37	.486	5-3	1/3	-4.5
1948	NY N	41	38	.519	4-5	2/2	-2.3
1949	NY N	73	81	.474	5		-8.3
1950	NY N	86	68	.558	3		-0.2
1951	NY N	98	59	.624	1▲		5.5
1952	NY N	92	62	.597	2		6.6
1953	NY N	70	84	.455	5		-9.0
1954	NY N	97	57	.630	1★		1.1
1955	NY N	80	74	.519	3		0.1
1966	Chi N	59	103	.364	10		-5.5
1967	Chi N	87	74	.540	3		-1.7
1968	Chi N	84	78	.519	3		2.9
1969	Chi N e	92	70	.568	2		-0.4
1970	Chi N e	84	78	.519	2		-9.6
1971	Chi N e	83	79	.512	3t		3.2
1972	Chi N e	46	44	.511	4-2	1/2	-6.3
1972	Hou N w	16	15	.516	2-2	3/3	-1.0
1973	Hou N w	82	80	.506	4		0.1
24		2008	1709	.540			-13.6

DWYER, FRANK B3.25.1868

YEAR	TM/LG	W	L	PCT	FINISH	MGR/YR	+/-
1902	Det A	52	83	.385	7		-6.4

DYER, EDDIE B10.11.1899

YEAR	TM/LG	W	L	PCT	FINISH	MGR/YR	+/-
1946	StL N	98	58	.628	1▲★		2.3
1947	StL N	89	65	.578	2		-2.5
1948	StL N	85	69	.552	2		-1.6
1949	StL N	96	58	.623	2		3.8
1950	StL N	78	75	.510	5		-0.8
5		446	325	.578			1.2

DYKES, JIMMY B11.10.1896

YEAR	TM/LG	W	L	PCT	FINISH	MGR/YR	+/-
1934	Chi A	49	88	.358	8-8	2/2	0.4
1935	Chi A	74	78	.487	5		-0.8
1936	Chi A	81	70	.536	3		1.4
1937	Chi A	86	68	.558	3		4.2
1938	Chi A	65	83	.439	6		-4.9
1939	Chi A	85	69	.552	4		6.3
1940	Chi A	82	72	.532	4t		-1.3
1941	Chi A	77	77	.500	3		1.1
1942	Chi A	66	82	.446	6		-0.3
1943	Chi A	82	72	.532	4		7.3
1944	Chi A	71	83	.461	7		6.8

YEAR	TM/LG	W	L	PCT	FINISH	MGR/YR	+/-
1945	Chi A	71	78	.477	6		0.4
1946	Chi A	10	20	.333	7-5	1/2	-4.3
1951	Phi A	70	84	.455	6		-6.1
1952	Phi A	79	75	.513	4		7.9
1953	Phi A	59	95	.383	7		-1.4
1954	Bal A	54	100	.351	7		-2.7
1958	Cin N	24	17	.585	8-4	2/2	1.5
1959	Det A	74	63	.540	8-4	2/2	7.2
1960	Det A	44	52	.458	6-6	1/3	-3.3
1960	Cle A	26	32	.448	4-4	3/3	-2.0
1961	Cle A	77	83	.481	5-5	1/2	1.5
21		1406	1541	.477			15.7

EBBETS, CHARLIE Charles Hercules
B10.29.1859 New York, NY D4.18.1925 New York, NY (DNP)

YEAR	TM/LG	W	L	PCT	FINISH	MGR/YR	+/-
1898	Bro N	38	68	.358	9-10	3/3	-2.8

EDWARDS, DOC B12.10.1936

YEAR	TM/LG	W	L	PCT	FINISH	MGR/YR	+/-
1987	Cle A e	30	45	.400	7-7	2/2	1.7
1988	Cle A e	78	84	.481	6		3.6
1989	Cle A e	65	78	.455	6-6	1/2	-1.7
3		173	207	.455			3.6

ELBERFELD, KID B4.13.1875

YEAR	TM/LG	W	L	PCT	FINISH	MGR/YR	+/-
1908	NY A	27	71	.276	6-8	2/2	-4.4

ELIA, LEE B7.16.1937

YEAR	TM/LG	W	L	PCT	FINISH	MGR/YR	+/-
1982	Chi N e	73	89	.451	5		-4.6
1983	Chi N e	54	69	.439	5-5	1/2	-6.1
1987	Phi N e	51	50	.505	5-4t	2/2	3.4
1988	Phi N e	60	92	.395	6-6	1/2	-2.5
4		238	300	.442			-9.8

ELLICK, JOE B4.3.1854

YEAR	TM/LG	W	L	PCT	FINISH	MGR/YR	+/-
1884	CP U	6	6	.500	5-5	3/3	0.6

ELLIOTT, BOB B11.26.1916

YEAR	TM/LG	W	L	PCT	FINISH	MGR/YR	+/-
1960	KC A	58	96	.377	8		-4.8

ENS, JEWEL B8.24.1889

YEAR	TM/LG	W	L	PCT	FINISH	MGR/YR	+/-
1929	Pit N	21	14	.600	2-2	2/2	0.9
1930	Pit N	80	74	.519	5		6.2
1931	Pit N	75	79	.487	5		3.6
3		176	167	.513			10.8

ERMER, CAL B11.10.1923

YEAR	TM/LG	W	L	PCT	FINISH	MGR/YR	+/-
1967	Min A	66	46	.589	6-2t	2/2	3.9
1968	Min A	79	83	.488	7		-3.8
2		145	129	.529			0.1

ESSIAN, JIM B1.2.1951

YEAR	TM/LG	W	L	PCT	FINISH	MGR/YR	+/-
1991	Chi N e	59	63	.484	5-4	3/3	1.0

ESTERBROOK, DUDE B6.20.1857

YEAR	TM/LG	W	L	PCT	FINISH	MGR/YR	+/-
1889	Lou AA	2	8	.200	7-8	1/4	-0.2

EVERS, JOHNNY B7.21.1881

YEAR	TM/LG	W	L	PCT	FINISH	MGR/YR	+/-
1913	Chi N	88	65	.575	3		2.4
1921	Chi N	41	55	.427	6-7	1/2	-0.6
1924	Chi A	10	11	.476	6	1/4	0.3
1924	Chi A	41	61	.402	8	4/4	-6.0
3		180	192	.484			-3.9

EWING, BUCK B10.17.1859

YEAR	TM/LG	W	L	PCT	FINISH	MGR/YR	+/-
1890	NY P	74	57	.565	3		-2.8
1895	Cin N	66	64	.508	8		-3.0
1896	Cin N	77	50	.606	3		-1.3
1897	Cin N	76	56	.576	4		4.7
1898	Cin N	92	60	.605	3		7.4
1899	Cin N	83	67	.553	6		0.2
1900	NY N	21	41	.339	8-8	1/2	-5.5
7		489	395	.553			-0.3

FAATZ, JAY B10.24.1860

YEAR	TM/LG	W	L	PCT	FINISH	MGR/YR	+/-
1890	Buf P	9	24	.273	8-8-8	2/3	0.4

FALK, BIBB B1.27.1899

YEAR	TM/LG	W	L	PCT	FINISH	MGR/YR	+/-
1933	Cle A	1	0	1.000	5-5-4	2/3	0.5

FANNING, JIM B9.14.1927

YEAR	TM/LG	W	L	PCT	FINISH	MGR/YR	+/-
1981-2	Mon N e	16	11	.593	2-1☆	2/2	1.2
1982	Mon N e	86	76	.531	3		-3.5
1984	Mon N e	14	16	.467	5-5	2/2	-1.2
3		116	103	.530			-3.5

FARRELL, JACK B7.5.1857

YEAR	TM/LG	W	L	PCT	FINISH	MGR/YR	+/-
1881	Pro N	24	27	.471	4-2	1/2	-2.7

FARRELL, KERBY B9.3.1913

YEAR	TM/LG	W	L	PCT	FINISH	MGR/YR	+/-
1957	Cle A	76	77	.497	6		3.5

FELSKE, JOHN B5.30.1942

YEAR	TM/LG	W	L	PCT	FINISH	MGR/YR	+/-
1985	Phi N e	75	87	.463	5		-5.4
1986	Phi N e	86	75	.534	2		2.9
1987	Phi N e	29	32	.475	5-4t	1/2	0.3
3		190	194	.495			-2.2

FERGUSON, BOB B1.31.1845

YEAR	TM/LG	W	L	PCT	FINISH	MGR/YR	+/-
1871	Mut NA	16	17	.485	4		0.3
1872	Atl NA	9	28	.243	6		6.7
1873	Atl NA	17	37	.315	6		3.5
1874	Atl NA	22	33	.400	6		6.7
1875	Har NA	54	28	.659	3		-6.8
1876	Har N	47	21	.691	3		-2.9
1877	Har N	31	27	.534	3		-0.7
1878	Har N	30	30	.500	4		-3.5
1879	Tro N	7	22	.241	8-8	2/2	0.2

YEAR	TM/LG	W	L	PCT	FINISH	MGR/YR	+/-
1880	Tro N	41	42	.494	4		3.9
1881	Tro N	39	45	.464	5		-0.3
1882	Tro N	35	48	.422	7		1.7
1883	Phi N	4	13	.235	8-8	1/2	1.9
1884	Pit AA	11	31	.262	9-11-10	2/5	1.6
1886	NY AA	48	70	.407	8-7	2/2	0.3
1887	NY AA	6	24	.200	8-7	1/3	-2.7
	16	417	516	.447			9.7

FERRARO, MIKE B8.18.1944
YEAR	TM/LG	W	L	PCT	FINISH	MGR/YR	+/-
1983	Cle A e	40	60	.400	7-7	1/2	-5.1
1986	KC A w	36	38	.486	4-3t	2/2	-0.1
	2	76	98	.437			-5.1

FESSENDEN, WALLACE Wallace Clifton
B10.5.1860 Windham, NH D5.16.1935 Brooklyn, NY (DNP)
YEAR	TM/LG	W	L	PCT	FINISH	MGR/YR	+/-
1890	Syr AA	4	7	.364		2/3	-0.5

FITZSIMMONS, FREDDIE B7.28.1901
YEAR	TM/LG	W	L	PCT	FINISH	MGR/YR	+/-
1943	Phi N	26	38	.406	7-7	2/2	-1.4
1944	Phi N	61	92	.399	8		-2.7
1945	Phi N	18	51	.261	8-8	1/2	-2.4
	3	105	181	.367			-6.5

FLETCHER, ART B1.5.1885
YEAR	TM/LG	W	L	PCT	FINISH	MGR/YR	+/-
1923	Phi N	50	104	.325	8		-3.8
1924	Phi N	55	96	.364	7		-4.1
1925	Phi N	68	85	.444	6t		2.0
1926	Phi N	58	93	.384	8		2.3
1929	NY A	6	5	.545	2-2	2/2	-0.3
	5	237	383	.382			-4.0

FLINT, SILVER B8.3.1855
YEAR	TM/LG	W	L	PCT	FINISH	MGR/YR	+/-
1879	Chi N	5	12	.294	2-4	2/2	-4.0

FOGARTY, JIM B2.12.1864
YEAR	TM/LG	W	L	PCT	FINISH	MGR/YR	+/-
1890	Phi P	7	9	.438	5-5	1/2	-1.9

FOGEL, HORACE Horace S.
B3.2.1861 Macungie, PA D11.15.1928 Philadelphia, PA (DNP)
YEAR	TM/LG	W	L	PCT	FINISH	MGR/YR	+/-
1887	Ind N	20	49	.290	8-8	3/3	1.1
1902	NY N	18	23	.439	4-8	1/3	4.2
	2	38	72	.345			5.4

FOHL, LEE B11.28.1876
YEAR	TM/LG	W	L	PCT	FINISH	MGR/YR	+/-
1915	Cle A	45	79	.363	6-7	2/2	-5.6
1916	Cle A	77	77	.500	6		-3.0
1917	Cle A	88	66	.571	3		6.4
1918	Cle A	73	54	.575	2		3.2
1919	Cle A	44	34	.564	3-2	1/2	-0.7
1921	StL A	81	73	.526	3		4.9
1922	StL A	93	61	.604	2		-5.5
1923	StL A	52	49	.515	3-5	1/2	3.6
1924	Bos A	67	87	.435	7		-3.2
1925	Bos A	47	105	.309	8		-2.5
1926	Bos A	46	107	.301	8		-3.3
	11	713	792	.474			-5.6

FONSECA, LEW B1.21.1899
YEAR	TM/LG	W	L	PCT	FINISH	MGR/YR	+/-
1932	Chi A	49	102	.325	7		-5.0
1933	Chi A	67	83	.447	6		4.5
1934	Chi A	4	11	.267	8-8	1/2	-1.3
	3	120	196	.380			-1.8

FOUTZ, DAVE B9.7.1856
YEAR	TM/LG	W	L	PCT	FINISH	MGR/YR	+/-
1893	Bro N	65	63	.508	6t		6.9
1894	Bro N	70	61	.534	5		4.2
1895	Bro N	71	60	.542	5t		2.1
1896	Bro N	58	73	.443	9t		-1.0
	4	264	257	.507			12.2

FOX, CHARLIE B10.7.1921
YEAR	TM/LG	W	L	PCT	FINISH	MGR/YR	+/-
1970	SF N w	67	53	.558	4-3	2/2	6.7
1971	SF N w	90	72	.556	1		2.6
1972	SF N w	69	86	.445	5		-9.8
1973	SF N w	88	74	.543	3		3.3
1974	SF N w	34	42	.447	5-5	1/2	0.3
1976	Mon N e	12	22	.353	6-6	2/2	-0.4
1983	Chi N e	17	22	.436	5-5	2/2	-2.1
	7	377	371	.504			0.5

FRANCONA, TERRY B4.22.1959
YEAR	TM/LG	W	L	PCT	FINISH	MGR/YR	+/-
1997	Phi N e	68	94	.420	5		3.9
1998	Phi N e	75	87	.463	3		3.3
1999	Phi N e	77	85	.475	3		-3.5
2000	Phi N e	65	97	.401	5		-4.1
2004	Bos A e	98	64	.605	2★✿		0.3
2005	Bos A e	95	67	.586	2✿		4.3
	6	478	494	.492			4.2

FRANKS, HERMAN B1.4.1914
YEAR	TM/LG	W	L	PCT	FINISH	MGR/YR	+/-
1965	SF N	95	67	.586	2		4.5
1966	SF N	93	68	.578	2		7.3
1967	SF N	91	71	.562	2		-1.1
1968	SF N	88	74	.543	2		-1.0
1977	Chi N e	81	81	.500	4		4.7
1978	Chi N e	79	83	.488	3		4.2
1979	Chi N e	78	77	.503	5-5	1/2	0.6
	7	605	521	.537			19.2

FRAZER, GEORGE George Kasson
B1.7.1861 Syracuse, NY D2.5.1913 New York, NY (DNP)
YEAR	TM/LG	W	L	PCT	FINISH	MGR/YR	+/-
1890	Syr AA	31	40	.437	7-6	1/3	2.0
1890	Syr AA	20	25	.444	7-6	3/3	1.6

FRAZIER, JOE B10.6.1922
YEAR	TM/LG	W	L	PCT	FINISH	MGR/YR	+/-
1976	NY N e	86	76	.531	3		-3.7
1977	NY N e	15	30	.333	6-6	1/2	-5.2
	2	101	106	.488			-8.9

FREGOSI, JIM B4.4.1942
YEAR	TM/LG	W	L	PCT	FINISH	MGR/YR	+/-
1978	Cal A w	62	54	.534	3-2t	2/2	2.1
1979	Cal A w	88	74	.543	1		-2.3
1980	Cal A w	65	95	.406	6		-5.3
1981-1	Cal A w	22	25	.468	4-4	1/2	-2.5
1986	Chi A w	45	51	.469	5-5	3/3	0.4
1987	Chi A w	77	85	.475	5		-4.2
1988	Chi A w	71	90	.441	5		3.4
1991	Phi N e	74	75	.497	6-3	2/2	4.5
1992	Phi N e	70	92	.432	6		-7.8
1993	Phi N e	97	65	.599	1◆		3.0
1994	Phi N e	54	61	.470	4		-5.9
1995	Phi N e	69	75	.479	2t		1.3
1996	Phi N e	67	95	.414	5		0.1
1999	Tor A e	84	78	.519	3		1.1
2000	Tor A e	83	79	.512	3		6.3
	15	1028	1094	.484			-5.9

FREY, JIM James Gottfried
B5.26.1931 Cleveland, OH BL/TL/5-9/170(OF)
YEAR	TM/LG	W	L	PCT	FINISH	MGR/YR	+/-
1980	KC A w	97	65	.599	1◆		4.7
1981-1	KC A w	20	30	.400	5		-0.6
1981-2	KC A w	10	10	.500	2t-1	1/2	0.2
1984	Chi N e	96	65	.596	1		5.0
1985	Chi N e	77	84	.478	4		0.9
1986	Chi N e	23	33	.411	5-5	1/3	-1.5
	5	323	287	.530			8.6

FRISCH, FRANKIE B9.9.1898
YEAR	TM/LG	W	L	PCT	FINISH	MGR/YR	+/-
1933	StL N	36	26	.581	5-5	2/2	1.7
1934	StL N	95	58	.621	1★		4.5
1935	StL N	96	58	.623	2		-0.9
1936	StL N	87	67	.565	2t		9.9
1937	StL N	81	73	.526	4		-1.4
1938	StL N	63	72	.467	6-6	1/2	-4.8
1940	Pit N	78	76	.506	4		-1.4
1941	Pit N	81	73	.526	4		-0.8
1942	Pit N	66	81	.449	5		-2.6
1943	Pit N	80	74	.519	4		-3.7
1944	Pit N	90	63	.588	2		5.3
1945	Pit N	82	72	.532	4		-1.6
1946	Pit N	62	89	.411	7-7	1/2	-1.3
1949	Chi N	42	62	.404	7-8	2/2	2.2
1950	Chi N	64	89	.418	7		0.3
1951	Chi N	35	45	.438	7-8	1/2	2.1
	16	1138	1078	.514			7.4

FUCHS, JUDGE Emil Edwin
B4.17.1878 Hamburg, Germany D12.5.1961 Boston, MA (DNP)
YEAR	TM/LG	W	L	PCT	FINISH	MGR/YR	+/-
1929	Bos N	56	98	.364	8		-0.2

GAFFNEY, JOHN John H.
B6.29.1855 Roxbury, MA D8.8.1913 New York, NY (DNP)
YEAR	TM/LG	W	L	PCT	FINISH	MGR/YR	+/-
1886	Was N	15	25	.375	8	2/2	6.0
1887	Was N	46	76	.377	7		5.0
	2	61	101	.377			11.0

GALANTE, MATT Matthew Joseph
B3.22.1944 Brooklyn, NY BR/TR/5-6/175(2B)
YEAR	TM/LG	W	L	PCT	FINISH	MGR/YR	+/-
1999	Hou N c	13	14	.481	1t-1	2/3	-2.9

GALVIN, JIM B12.25.1856
YEAR	TM/LG	W	L	PCT	FINISH	MGR/YR	+/-
1885	Buf N	7	17	.292	7-7	1/2	0.1

GANZEL, JOHN B4.7.1874
YEAR	TM/LG	W	L	PCT	FINISH	MGR/YR	+/-
1908	Cin N	73	81	.474	5		2.4
1915	Bro F	17	18	.486	7-7	2/2	0.1
	2	90	99	.476			2.5

GARCIA, DAVE David
B9.15.1920 E.St.Louis, IL BR/TR/6-0/180(2B)
YEAR	TM/LG	W	L	PCT	FINISH	MGR/YR	+/-
1977	Cal A w	35	46	.432	5-5	2/2	-4.5
1978	Cal A w	25	21	.543	3-2t	1/2	1.3
1979	Cle A e	38	28	.576	6-6	2/2	6.8
1980	Cle A e	79	81	.494	6		5.7
1981-1	Cle A e	26	24	.520	6		1.6
1981-2	Cle A e	26	27	.491	5		1.6
1982	Cle A e	78	84	.481	6t		3.6
	6	307	311	.497			16.1

GARDENHIRE, RON B10.24.1957
YEAR	TM/LG	W	L	PCT	FINISH	MGR/YR	+/-
2002	Min A c	94	67	.584	1☆		8.0
2003	Min A c	90	72	.556	1		4.8
2004	Min A c	92	70	.568	1		4.6
2005	Min A c	83	79	.512	3		-0.7
	4	359	288	.555			16.7

GARDNER, BILLY B7.19.1927
YEAR	TM/LG	W	L	PCT	FINISH	MGR/YR	+/-
1981-1	Min A w	6	14	.300	6-7	2/2	-1.9
1981-2	Min A w	24	29	.453	4		-1.9
1982	Min A w	60	102	.370	7		-4.9
1983	Min A w	70	92	.432	5		0.0
1984	Min A w	81	81	.500	2		0.2
1985	Min A w	27	35	.435	6-4	1/2	-1.1
1987	KC A w	62	64	.492	4-2	1/2	-2.9
	6	330	417	.442			-12.5

GARNER, PHIL B4.30.1949
YEAR	TM/LG	W	L	PCT	FINISH	MGR/YR	+/-
1992	Mil A e	92	70	.568	2		-3.2
1993	Mil A e	69	93	.426	7		-6.2
1994	Mil A c	53	62	.461	5		-0.8
1995	Mil A c	65	79	.451	4		-6.3
1996	Mil A c	80	82	.494	3		-0.5
1997	Mil A c	78	83	.484	3		3.7
1998	Mil N c	74	88	.457	5		3.3
1999	Mil N c	52	60	.464	5-5	1/2	0.6
2000	Det A c	79	83	.488	3		-0.5
2001	Det A c	66	96	.407	4		-0.5
2002	Det A c	0	6	.000	5		-1.9
2004	Hou N c	48	26	.649	5-2☆✿	2/2	6.3
2005	Hou N c	89	73	.549	2✿◆		-0.9
	13	845	901	.484			-8.2

GASTON, CITO B3.17.1944
YEAR	TM/LG	W	L	PCT	FINISH	MGR/YR	+/-
1989	Tor A e	77	49	.611	6-1	2/2	7.6
1990	Tor A e	86	76	.531	2		-5.7
1991	Tor A e	66	54	.550	1-1	1/3	1.1
1991	Tor A e	6	3	.667	1-1	3/3	1.1
1992	Tor A e	96	66	.593	1★		5.2
1993	Tor A e	95	67	.586	1★		3.9
1994	Tor A e	55	60	.478	3		-1.3
1995	Tor A e	56	88	.389	5		-3.1
1996	Tor A e	74	88	.457	4		-2.9
1997	Tor A e	72	85	.459	5-5	1/2	-2.5
	9	683	636	.518			3.6

GERHARDT, JOE B2.14.1855
YEAR	TM/LG	W	L	PCT	FINISH	MGR/YR	+/-
1883	Lou AA	52	45	.536	5		3.3
1890	StL AA	20	16	.556	2-3	6/6	2.2
	2	72	61	.541			2.2

GESSLER, DOC B12.23.1880
YEAR	TM/LG	W	L	PCT	FINISH	MGR/YR	+/-
1914	Pit F	3	8	.273	8-7	1/2	-1.8

GIBBONS, JOHN B6.8.1962
YEAR	TM/LG	W	L	PCT	FINISH	MGR/YR	+/-
2004	Tor A e	20	20	.500	5-5	2/2	2.5
2005	Tor A e	80	82	.494	3		-7.9
	2	100	102	.495			-5.4

GIBSON, GEORGE B7.22.1880
YEAR	TM/LG	W	L	PCT	FINISH	MGR/YR	+/-
1920	Pit N	79	75	.513	4		4.5
1921	Pit N	90	63	.588	2		3.4
1922	Pit N	32	33	.492	5-3t	1/2	-5.6
1925	Chi N	12	14	.462	7-8	3/3	-5.6
1932	Pit N	86	68	.558	2		10.0
1933	Pit N	87	67	.565	2		5.0
1934	Pit N	27	24	.529	4-5	1/2	0.8
	7	413	344	.546			17.9

GIFFORD, JIM James H.
B10.18.1845 Warren, NY D12.19.1901 Columbus, OH (DNP)
YEAR	TM/LG	W	L	PCT	FINISH	MGR/YR	+/-
1884	Ind AA	25	60	.294	10-11	2/2	3.5
1885	NY AA	44	64	.407	7		4.5
1886	NY AA	5	12	.294	8-7	1/2	-1.9
	3	74	136	.352			6.1

GLASSCOCK, JACK B7.22.1857
YEAR	TM/LG	W	L	PCT	FINISH	MGR/YR	+/-
1889	Ind N	34	32	.515	7-7	2/2	4.1
1892-1	StL N	1	3	.250	10-9	1/3	-0.5
	2	35	35	.500			3.7

GLEASON, KID B10.26.1866
YEAR	TM/LG	W	L	PCT	FINISH	MGR/YR	+/-
1919	Chi A	88	52	.629	1		4.4
1920	Chi A	96	58	.623	2		6.4
1921	Chi A	62	92	.403	7		1.6
1922	Chi A	77	77	.500	5		0.0
1923	Chi A	69	85	.448	7		-3.1
	5	392	364	.519			9.3

GOMEZ, PRESTON B4.20.1923
YEAR	TM/LG	W	L	PCT	FINISH	MGR/YR	+/-
1969	SD N w	52	110	.321	6		1.5
1970	SD N w	63	99	.389	6		-7.3
1971	SD N w	61	100	.379	6		-5.2
1972	SD N w	4	7	.364	4-6	1/2	-0.1
1974	Hou N w	81	80	.500	4		-2.2
1975	Hou N w	47	80	.370	6-6	1/2	-12.7
1980	Chi N e	38	52	.422	6-6	1/2	-0.4
	7	346	528	.396			-26.5

GONZALEZ, MIKE B9.24.1890
YEAR	TM/LG	W	L	PCT	FINISH	MGR/YR	+/-
1938	StL N	8	8	.500	6-6	2/2	-0.0
1940	StL N	1	5	.167	6-7-3	2/3	-2.2
	2	9	13	.409			-2.2

GORDON, JOE B2.18.1915
YEAR	TM/LG	W	L	PCT	FINISH	MGR/YR	+/-
1958	Cle A	46	40	.535	6-4	2/2	-0.4
1959	Cle A	89	65	.578	2		2.1
1960	Cle A	49	46	.516	4-4	1/3	3.1
1960	Det A	26	31	.456	6-6	3/3	2.9
1961	KC A	26	33	.441	8-9t	1/2	2.9
1969	KC A w	69	93	.426	4		-1.1
	5	305	308	.498			4.6

GORE, GEORGE B5.3.1857
YEAR	TM/LG	W	L	PCT	FINISH	MGR/YR	+/-
1892-2	StL N	6	9	.400	12-12-11	2/3	0.5

GORYL, JOHNNY B10.21.1933
YEAR	TM/LG	W	L	PCT	FINISH	MGR/YR	+/-
1980	Min A w	23	13	.639	4-3	2/2	6.2
1981-1	Min A w	11	25	.306	6-7	1/2	-3.2
	2	34	38	.472			3.0

GOULD, CHARLIE B8.21.1847

YEAR	TM/LG	W	L	PCT	FINISH	MGR/YR	+/-
1875	NH NA	2	21	.087	11-8	1/3	0.1
1876	Cin N	9	56	.138	8		5.4
2		11	77	.125			5.5

GOWDY, HANK B8.24.1889

YEAR	TM/LG	W	L	PCT	FINISH	MGR/YR	+/-
1946	Cin N	3	1	.750	6-6	2/2	1.1

GRAFFEN, MASE Samuel Mason
B1845 Philadelphia, PA D11.18.1883 Silver City, NM (DNP)

YEAR	TM/LG	W	L	PCT	FINISH	MGR/YR	+/-
1876	StL N	39	17	.696	2-2	1/2	-2.3

GRAMMAS, ALEX B4.3.1926

YEAR	TM/LG	W	L	PCT	FINISH	MGR/YR	+/-
1969	Pit N e	4	1	.800	3-3	2/2	1.3
1976	Mil A e	66	95	.410	6		-5.3
1977	Mil A e	67	95	.414	6		-1.2
3		137	191	.418			-5.1

GREEN, DALLAS B8.4.1934

YEAR	TM/LG	W	L	PCT	FINISH	MGR/YR	+/-
1979	Phi N e	19	11	.633	5-4	2/2	4.7
1980	Phi N e	91	71	.562	1★		0.8
1981-1	Phi N e	34	21	.618	1		3.6
1981-2	Phi N e	25	27	.481	3		3.6
1989	NY N e	56	65	.463	6-5	1/2	2.5
1993	NY N e	46	78	.371	7-7	2/2	-10.4
1994	NY N e	55	58	.487	3		0.5
1995	NY N e	69	75	.479	2t		-6.9
1996	NY N e	59	72	.450	4-4	1/2	-3.9
8		454	478	.487			-5.6

GRIFFIN, MIKE B3.20.1865

YEAR	TM/LG	W	L	PCT	FINISH	MGR/YR	+/-
1898	Bro N	1	3	.250	9-9-10	2/3	-0.5

GRIFFIN, SANDY B10.24.1858

YEAR	TM/LG	W	L	PCT	FINISH	MGR/YR	+/-
1891	Was AA	2	4	.333	8-8	4/4	0.4

GRIFFITH, CLARK B11.20.1869

YEAR	TM/LG	W	L	PCT	FINISH	MGR/YR	+/-
1901	Chi A	83	53	.610	1		-2.3
1902	Chi A	74	60	.552	4		-0.2
1903	NY A	72	62	.537	4		4.4
1904	NY A	92	59	.609	2		8.5
1905	NY A	71	78	.477	6		0.2
1906	NY A	90	61	.596	2		4.0
1907	NY A	70	78	.473	5		2.4
1908	NY A	24	32	.429	6-8	1/2	6.0
1909	Cin N	77	76	.503	4		-0.3
1910	Cin N	75	79	.487	5		4.6
1911	Cin N	70	83	.458	6		-4.1
1912	Was A	91	61	.599	2		2.7
1913	Was A	90	64	.584	2		9.3
1914	Was A	81	73	.526	3		-2.1
1915	Was A	85	68	.556	4		-0.4
1916	Was A	76	77	.497	7		0.3
1917	Was A	74	79	.484	5		-0.0
1918	Was A	72	56	.563	3		2.3
1919	Was A	56	84	.400	7		-10.0
1920	Was A	68	84	.447	6		-0.5
20		1491	1367	.522			24.9

GRIMES, BURLEIGH B8.18.1893

YEAR	TM/LG	W	L	PCT	FINISH	MGR/YR	+/-
1937	Bro N	62	91	.405	6		1.1
1938	Bro N	69	80	.463	7		-4.9
2		131	171	.434			-3.8

GRIMM, CHARLIE B8.28.1898

YEAR	TM/LG	W	L	PCT	FINISH	MGR/YR	+/-
1932	Chi N	37	18	.673	2-1	2/2	6.4
1933	Chi N	86	68	.558	3		-2.9
1934	Chi N	86	65	.570	3		3.8
1935	Chi N	100	54	.649	1		-1.5
1936	Chi N	87	67	.565	2t		-5.4
1937	Chi N	93	61	.604	2		3.6
1938	Chi N	45	36	.556	3-1	1/2	-1.9
1944	Chi N	74	69	.517	8-4	3/3	-0.6
1945	Chi N	98	56	.636	1		-0.3
1946	Chi N	82	71	.536	3		0.7
1947	Chi N	69	85	.448	6		7.9
1948	Chi N	64	90	.416	8		-1.8
1949	Chi N	19	31	.380	7-8	1/2	-0.1
1952	Bos N	51	67	.432	7-7	2/2	-1.2
1953	Mil N	92	62	.597	2		-0.4
1954	Mil N	89	65	.578	3		-0.1
1955	Mil N	85	69	.552	2		0.6
1956	Mil N	24	22	.522	5-2	1/2	-3.4
1960	Chi N	6	11	.353	7-7	1/2	-0.9
19		1287	1067	.547			2.4

GROH, HEINIE B9.18.1889

YEAR	TM/LG	W	L	PCT	FINISH	MGR/YR	+/-
1918	Cin N	7	3	.700	4-3	2/2	1.7

GUILLEN, OZZIE B1.20.1964

YEAR	TM/LG	W	L	PCT	FINISH	MGR/YR	+/-
2004	Chi A c	83	79	.512	2		-1.2
2005	Chi A c	99	63	.611	1★		8.2
2		182	142	.562			7.0

GUTTERIDGE, DON B6.19.1912

YEAR	TM/LG	W	L	PCT	FINISH	MGR/YR	+/-
1969	Chi A w	60	85	.414	4-5	2/2	-3.4
1970	Chi A w	49	87	.360	6-6	1/3	-3.1
2		109	172	.388			-6.5

HAAS, EDDIE B5.26.1935

YEAR	TM/LG	W	L	PCT	FINISH	MGR/YR	+/-
1985	Atl N w	50	71	.413	5-5	1/2	0.8

HACK, STAN B12.6.1909

YEAR	TM/LG	W	L	PCT	FINISH	MGR/YR	+/-
1954	Chi N	64	90	.416	7		-6.6
1955	Chi N	72	81	.471	6		4.4
1956	Chi N	60	94	.390	8		-5.4
1958	StL N	3	7	.300	5-5t	2/2	-1.4
4		199	272	.423			-9.1

HACKETT, CHARLIE Charles Michael
B1855 Lee, MA D8.1.1898 Holyoke, MA (DNP)

YEAR	TM/LG	W	L	PCT	FINISH	MGR/YR	+/-
1884	Cle N	35	77	.313	7		3.0
1885	Bro AA	15	22	.405	7-5t	1/2	-2.7
2		50	99	.336			0.3

HALLMAN, BILL B3.31.1867

YEAR	TM/LG	W	L	PCT	FINISH	MGR/YR	+/-
1897	StL N	13	36	.265	12-12-12	3/4	4.2

HANEY, FRED B4.25.1898

YEAR	TM/LG	W	L	PCT	FINISH	MGR/YR	+/-
1939	StL A	43	111	.279	8		-7.1
1940	StL A	67	87	.435	6		1.6
1941	StL A	15	29	.341	7-6t	1/2	-5.4
1953	Pit N	50	104	.325	8		-1.6
1954	Pit N	53	101	.344	8		4.6
1955	Pit N	60	94	.390	8		4.2
1956	Mil N	68	40	.630	5-2	2/2	3.7
1957	Mil N	95	59	.617	1★		2.0
1958	Mil N	92	62	.597	2		0.7
1959	Mil N	86	70	.551	2▲		-2.3
10		629	757	.454			0.4

HANLON, NED B8.22.1857

YEAR	TM/LG	W	L	PCT	FINISH	MGR/YR	+/-
1889	Pit N	26	18	.591	7-5	3/3	6.2
1890	Pit P	60	68	.469	6		0.7
1891	Pit N	31	47	.397	8-8	1/2	-4.5
1892-1	Bal N	17	39	.304	12-12	3/3	-3.0
1892-2	Bal N	26	46	.361	10		-6.5
1893	Bal N	60	70	.462	8		1.0
1894	Bal N	89	39	.695	1		-1.9
1895	Bal N	87	43	.669	1		-8.8
1896	Bal N	90	39	.698	1●		-2.7
1897	Bal N	90	40	.692	2●		-0.1
1898	Bal N	96	53	.644	2		-7.8
1899	Bro N	100	47	.680	1		4.7
1900	Bro N	82	54	.603	1●		5.4
1901	Bro N	79	57	.581	3		-2.8
1902	Bro N	75	63	.543	2		1.1
1903	Bro N	70	66	.515	5		3.4
1904	Bro N	56	97	.366	6		-7.4
1905	Bro N	48	104	.316	8		3.0
1906	Cin N	64	87	.424	6		-2.5
1907	Cin N	66	87	.431	6		-11.3
19		1312	1164	.530			-37.1

HARDER, MEL B10.15.1909

YEAR	TM/LG	W	L	PCT	FINISH	MGR/YR	+/-
1961	Cle A	1	0	1.000	5-5	2/2	0.5
1962	Cle A	2	0	1.000	6-6	2/2	1.1
2		3	0	1.000			1.6

HARGROVE, MIKE B10.26.1949

YEAR	TM/LG	W	L	PCT	FINISH	MGR/YR	+/-
1991	Cle A e	32	53	.376	7-7	2/2	-0.5
1992	Cle A e	76	86	.469	4t		2.3
1993	Cle A e	76	86	.469	6		-2.8
1994	Cle A c	66	47	.584	2		-1.1
1995	Cle A c	100	44	.694	1◆		5.9
1996	Cle A c	99	62	.615	1		1.7
1997	Cle A c	86	75	.534	1◆		0.6
1998	Cle A c	89	73	.549	1☆		1.3
1999	Cle A c	97	65	.599	1		2.8
2000	Bal A e	74	88	.457	4		4.0
2001	Bal A e	63	98	.391	4		-3.6
2002	Bal A e	67	95	.414	4		-3.3
2003	Bal A e	71	91	.438	4		-2.5
2005	Sea A w	69	93	.426	4		-6.8
14		1065	1056	.502			-1.9

HARRAH, TOBY B10.26.1948

YEAR	TM/LG	W	L	PCT	FINISH	MGR/YR	+/-
1992	Tex A w	32	44	.421	3-4	2/2	-2.6

HARRELSON, BUD B6.6.1944

YEAR	TM/LG	W	L	PCT	FINISH	MGR/YR	+/-
1990	NY N e	71	49	.592	4-2	2/2	-1.3
1991	NY N e	74	80	.481	3-5	1/2	-2.4
2		145	129	.529			-3.7

HARRIS, LUM B1.17.1915

YEAR	TM/LG	W	L	PCT	FINISH	MGR/YR	+/-
1961	Bal A	17	10	.630	3-3	2/2	1.7
1964	Hou N	5	8	.385	9-9	2/2	-0.3
1965	Hou N	65	97	.401	9		-0.8
1968	Atl N	81	81	.500	5		4.1
1969	Atl N w	93	69	.574	1		5.7
1970	Atl N w	76	86	.469	5		-1.5
1971	Atl N w	82	80	.506	3		6.8
1972	Atl N w	47	57	.452	4-4	1/2	2.0
7		466	488	.488			17.7

HARRIS, BUCKY B11.8.1896

YEAR	TM/LG	W	L	PCT	FINISH	MGR/YR	+/-
1924	Was A	92	62	.597	1★		0.6
1925	Was A	96	55	.636	1		5.3
1926	Was A	81	69	.540	4		2.2
1927	Was A	85	69	.552	3		3.0
1928	Was A	75	79	.487	4		-3.3
1929	Det A	70	84	.455	6		-6.8
1930	Det A	75	79	.487	5		2.6
1931	Det A	61	93	.396	7		1.9
1932	Det A	76	75	.503	5		-0.6
1933	Det A	73	79	.480	5-5	1/2	-1.9
1934	Bos A	76	76	.500	4		-4.2
1935	Was A	67	86	.438	6		-2.3
1936	Was A	82	71	.536	4		-2.6
1937	Was A	73	80	.477	6		4.4
1938	Was A	75	76	.497	5		4.8
1939	Was A	65	87	.428	6		-1.9
1940	Was A	64	90	.416	7		1.1
1941	Was A	70	84	.455	6t		-0.3
1942	Was A	62	89	.411	7		2.3
1943	Phi N	38	52	.422	7-7	1/2	-0.5
1947	NY A	97	57	.630	1★		-2.9
1948	NY A	94	60	.610	3		-4.6
1950	Was A	67	87	.435	5		1.9
1951	Was A	62	92	.403	7		-6.0
1952	Was A	78	76	.506	5		2.1
1953	Was A	76	76	.500	5		-7.5
1954	Was A	66	88	.429	6		-6.1
1955	Det A	79	75	.513	5		-9.5
1956	Det A	82	72	.532	5		-3.7
29		2157	2218	.493			-32.5

HART, JIM James Aristotle
B7.10.1855 Fairview, PA D7.18.1919 Chicago, IL (DNP)

YEAR	TM/LG	W	L	PCT	FINISH	MGR/YR	+/-
1885	Lou AA	53	59	.473	5t		0.2
1886	Lou AA	66	70	.485	4		-4.4
1889	Bos N	83	45	.648	2		0.8
3		202	174	.537			-3.4

HART, JOHN John Henry (b John Henry Reen)
B7.21.1948 Tampa, FL BR/TR/6-1/180(C)

YEAR	TM/LG	W	L	PCT	FINISH	MGR/YR	+/-
1989	Cle A e	8	11	.421	6-6	2/2	-0.9

HARTNETT, GABBY B12.20.1900

YEAR	TM/LG	W	L	PCT	FINISH	MGR/YR	+/-
1938	Chi N	44	27	.620	3-1	2/2	2.9
1939	Chi N	84	70	.545	4		2.4
1940	Chi N	75	79	.487	5		-6.6
3		203	176	.536			-1.3

HARTSFIELD, ROY B10.25.1925

YEAR	TM/LG	W	L	PCT	FINISH	MGR/YR	+/-
1977	Tor A e	54	107	.335	7		-4.6
1978	Tor A e	59	102	.366	7		-2.4
1979	Tor A e	53	109	.327	7		-3.2
3		166	318	.343			-10.3

HASTINGS, SCOTT B8.10.1847

YEAR	TM/LG	W	L	PCT	FINISH	MGR/YR	+/-
1871	Rok NA	4	21	.160	9		-4.8
1872	Cle NA	6	14	.300	6-7	1/2	0.9
2		10	35	.222			-3.9

HATFIELD, JOHN B7.20.1847

YEAR	TM/LG	W	L	PCT	FINISH	MGR/YR	+/-
1872	Mut NA	24	14	.632	4-3	2/2	-3.6
1873	Mut NA	11	17	.393	5-4	1/2	-4.6
2		35	31	.530			-8.1

HATTON, GRADY B10.7.1922

YEAR	TM/LG	W	L	PCT	FINISH	MGR/YR	+/-
1966	Hou N	72	90	.444	8		-0.2
1967	Hou N	69	93	.426	9		-0.0
1968	Hou N	23	38	.377	10-10	1/2	-4.1
3		164	221	.426			-4.3

HECKER, GUY B4.3.1856

YEAR	TM/LG	W	L	PCT	FINISH	MGR/YR	+/-
1890	Pit N	23	113	.169	8		7.5

HEFFNER, DON B2.8.1911

YEAR	TM/LG	W	L	PCT	FINISH	MGR/YR	+/-
1966	Cin N	37	46	.446	8-7	1/2	-4.0

HEILBRONER, LOUIE Louis Wilbur
B7.4.1861 Ft.Wayne, IN D12.21.1933 Ft.Wayne, IN (DNP)

YEAR	TM/LG	W	L	PCT	FINISH	MGR/YR	+/-
1900	StL N	23	25	.479	7-5t	2/2	-0.9

HELMS, TOMMY B5.5.1941

YEAR	TM/LG	W	L	PCT	FINISH	MGR/YR	+/-
1988	Cin N w	12	15	.444	4-4-2	2/3	-2.3
1989	Cin N w	16	21	.432	4t-5(C)	2/2	-1.1
2		28	36	.438			-3.4

HEMUS, SOLLY B4.17.1923

YEAR	TM/LG	W	L	PCT	FINISH	MGR/YR	+/-
1959	StL N	71	83	.461	7		2.5
1960	StL N	86	68	.558	3		6.6
1961	StL N	33	41	.446	6-5	1/2	-5.7
3		190	192	.497			3.3

HENDERSON, BILL William C. (DNP)

YEAR	TM/LG	W	L	PCT	FINISH	MGR/YR	+/-
1884	Bal U	58	47	.552	4		2.5

HENDRICKS, JACK B4.9.1875

YEAR	TM/LG	W	L	PCT	FINISH	MGR/YR	+/-
1918	StL N	51	78	.395	8		-5.5
1924	Cin N	83	70	.542	4		-0.9
1925	Cin N	80	73	.523	3		-1.3
1926	Cin N	87	67	.565	2		0.3
1927	Cin N	75	78	.490	5		-0.5
1928	Cin N	78	74	.513	5		5.9
1929	Cin N	66	88	.429	7		-3.7
7		520	528	.496			-5.7

HENGLE, ED Edward Siegfried
B Chicago, IL D11.4.1927 Norwich, England (DNP)

YEAR	TM/LG	W	L	PCT	FINISH	MGR/YR	+/-
1884	CP U	34	39	.466	5	1/3	0.9

HERMAN, BILLY B7.7.1909

YEAR	TM/LG	W	L	PCT	FINISH	MGR/YR	+/-
1947	Pit N	61	92	.399	8-7t	1/2	-8.7
1964	Bos A	2	0	1.000	8-8	2/2	1.1
1965	Bos A	62	100	.383	9		-6.8

YEAR	TM/LG	W	L	PCT	FINISH	MGR/YR	+/-
1966	Bos A	64	82	.438	9-9	1/2	-2.0
4		189	274	.408			-16.4

HERZOG, BUCK B7.9.1885
YEAR	TM/LG	W	L	PCT	FINISH	MGR/YR	+/-
1914	Cin N	60	94	.390	8		-3.8
1915	Cin N	71	83	.461	7		1.9
1916	Cin N	34	49	.410	8-7t	1/3	-0.7
3		165	226	.422			-2.6

HERZOG, WHITEY B11.9.1931
YEAR	TM/LG	W	L	PCT	FINISH	MGR/YR	+/-
1973	Tex A w	47	91	.341	6-6	1/3	-2.9
1974	Cal A w	2	2	.500	6-6-6	2/3	0.1
1975	KC A w	41	25	.621	2-2	2/2	5.4
1976	KC A w	90	72	.556	1		-1.7
1977	KC A w	102	60	.630	1		4.0
1978	KC A w	92	70	.568	1		-0.2
1979	KC A w	85	77	.525	2		0.7
1980	StL N e	38	35	.521	6-5-4	3/4	0.2
1981-1	StL N e	30	20	.600	2		3.2
1981-2	StL N e	29	23	.558	2		3.2
1982	StL N e	92	70	.568	1★		2.9
1983	StL N e	79	83	.488	4		1.2
1984	StL N e	84	78	.519	3		2.3
1985	StL N e	101	61	.623	1◆		1.6
1986	StL N e	79	82	.491	3		-0.4
1987	StL N e	95	67	.586	1◆		3.6
1988	StL N e	76	86	.469	5		1.0
1989	StL N e	86	76	.531	3		2.4
1990	StL N e	33	47	.412	6-6	1/3	-1.8
18		1281	1125	.532			24.8

HEWETT, WALTER Walter F.
B1861 Washington, DC D10.7.1944 Washington, DC (DNP)
YEAR	TM/LG	W	L	PCT	FINISH	MGR/YR	+/-
1888	Was N	10	29	.256	8-8	1/2	-2.2

HICKS, NAT B4.19.1845
YEAR	TM/LG	W	L	PCT	FINISH	MGR/YR	+/-
1874	Phi NA	29	29	.500	4		-3.6
1875	Mut NA	30	38	.441	7		4.9
2		59	67	.468			1.3

HIGGINS, PINKY B5.27.1909
YEAR	TM/LG	W	L	PCT	FINISH	MGR/YR	+/-
1955	Bos A	84	70	.545	4		-3.2
1956	Bos A	84	70	.545	4		4.2
1957	Bos A	82	72	.532	3		-0.3
1958	Bos A	79	75	.513	3		1.4
1959	Bos A	31	42	.425	8-8	1/3	-6.9
1960	Bos A	48	57	.457	8-7	3/3	3.3
1961	Bos A	76	86	.469	6		1.2
1962	Bos A	76	84	.475	8		0.9
8		560	556	.502			0.6

HIGHAM, DICK B7.24.1851
YEAR	TM/LG	W	L	PCT	FINISH	MGR/YR	+/-
1874	Mut NA	29	11	.725	3-2	2/2	2.8

HIMSL, VEDIE Avitus Bernard
B4.2.1917 Plevna, MT D3.1.2004 Chicago, IL BR/TR/6-1/200(P)
YEAR	TM/LG	W	L	PCT	FINISH	MGR/YR	+/-
1961	Chi N	5	6	.455	6-6t	1/9	0.3
1961	Chi N	5	12	.294	7-7-7	3/9	-2.3
1961	Chi N	0	3	.000	7-7-7	6/9	-1.3

HITCHCOCK, BILLY B7.31.1916
YEAR	TM/LG	W	L	PCT	FINISH	MGR/YR	+/-
1960	Det A	1	0	1.000	6-6-6	2/3	0.5
1962	Bal A	77	85	.475	7		-1.1
1963	Bal A	86	76	.531	4		2.5
1966	Atl N	33	18	.647	7-5	2/2	4.4
1967	Atl N	77	82	.484	7-7	1/2	-1.6
5		274	261	.512			4.8

HOBSON, BUTCH B8.17.1951
YEAR	TM/LG	W	L	PCT	FINISH	MGR/YR	+/-
1992	Bos A e	73	89	.451	7		-0.5
1993	Bos A e	80	82	.494	5		0.2
1994	Bos A e	54	61	.470	4		3.0
3		207	232	.472			2.7

HODGES, GIL B4.4.1924
YEAR	TM/LG	W	L	PCT	FINISH	MGR/YR	+/-
1963	Was A	42	79	.347	10-10	3/3	-0.6
1964	Was A	62	100	.383	9		-2.7
1965	Was A	70	92	.432	8		2.7
1966	Was A	71	88	.447	8		2.6
1967	Was A	76	85	.472	6t		5.1
1968	NY N	73	89	.451	9		-4.8
1969	NY N e	100	62	.617	1★		8.9
1970	NY N e	83	79	.512	3		-4.8
1971	NY N e	83	79	.512	3t		-2.3
9		660	753	.467			4.1

HOEY, FRED Frederick Chamberlain
B1866 New York, NY D12.7.1933 Paris, France (DNP)
YEAR	TM/LG	W	L	PCT	FINISH	MGR/YR	+/-
1899	NY N	31	55	.360	9-10	2/2	-5.3

HOFFMAN, GLENN B7.7.1958
YEAR	TM/LG	W	L	PCT	FINISH	MGR/YR	+/-
1998	LA N w	47	41	.534	3-3	2/2	3.5

HOLBERT, BILL B3.14.1855
YEAR	TM/LG	W	L	PCT	FINISH	MGR/YR	+/-
1879	Syr N	0	1	.000	6-6-7	2/3	-0.3

HOLLINGSHEAD, HOLLY B1.17.1853
YEAR	TM/LG	W	L	PCT	FINISH	MGR/YR	+/-
1875	Was N	4	16	.200	8-10	1/2	6.4
1884	Was AA	12	50	.194	12-12	1/2	1.2
2		16	66	.195			7.6

HOLMES, TOMMY B3.29.1917
YEAR	TM/LG	W	L	PCT	FINISH	MGR/YR	+/-
1951	Bos N	48	47	.505	5-4	2/2	-3.3
1952	Bos N	13	22	.371	7-7	1/2	-2.5
2		61	69	.469			-5.8

HORNSBY, ROGERS B4.27.1896
YEAR	TM/LG	W	L	PCT	FINISH	MGR/YR	+/-
1925	StL N	64	51	.557	8-4	2/2	2.0
1926	StL N	89	65	.578	1★		-1.5
1927	NY N	22	10	.688	4-3	2/2	4.1
1928	Bos N	39	83	.320	7-7	2/2	-3.2
1930	Chi N	4	0	1.000	2-2	2/2	1.7
1931	Chi N	84	70	.545	3		-4.3
1932	Chi N	53	46	.535	2-1	1/2	-2.2
1933	StL A	19	33	.365	8-8	3/3	-2.0
1934	StL A	67	85	.441	6		3.2
1935	StL A	65	87	.428	7		8.5
1936	StL A	57	95	.375	7		3.5
1937	StL A	25	52	.325	7-8	1/2	0.3
1952	StL A	22	29	.431	8-7	1/2	0.9
1952	Cin N	27	24	.529	7-6	3/3	3.0
1953	Cin N	64	82	.438	6-6	1/2	-2.2
14		701	812	.463			11.9

HOUK, RALPH B8.9.1919
YEAR	TM/LG	W	L	PCT	FINISH	MGR/YR	+/-
1961	NY A	109	53	.673	1★		6.3
1962	NY A	96	66	.593	1★		1.5
1963	NY A	104	57	.646	1		5.6
1966	NY A	66	73	.475	10-10	2/2	-3.4
1967	NY A	72	90	.444	9		2.2
1968	NY A	83	79	.512	5		1.4
1969	NY A e	80	81	.497	5		2.3
1970	NY A e	93	69	.574	2		4.8
1971	NY A e	82	80	.506	4		0.3
1972	NY A e	79	76	.510	4		-1.9
1973	NY A e	80	82	.494	4		-4.3
1974	Det A e	72	90	.444	6		6.2
1975	Det A e	57	102	.358	6		-0.3
1976	Det A e	74	87	.460	5		4.0
1977	Det A e	74	88	.457	4		-3.3
1978	Det A e	86	76	.531	5		-1.3
1981-1	Bos A e	30	26	.536	5		1.3
1981-2	Bos A e	29	23	.558	2t		1.3
1982	Bos A e	89	73	.549	3		4.0
1983	Bos A e	78	84	.481	6		2.0
1984	Bos A e	86	76	.531	4		0.6
20		1619	1531	.514			29.0

HOWARD, FRANK B8.8.1936
YEAR	TM/LG	W	L	PCT	FINISH	MGR/YR	+/-
1981-1	SD N w	23	33	.411	6		-6.1
1981-2	SD N w	18	36	.333	6		-6.1
1983	NY N e	52	64	.448	6-6	2/2	2.1
2		93	133	.412			-10.0

HOWE, ART B12.15.1946
YEAR	TM/LG	W	L	PCT	FINISH	MGR/YR	+/-
1989	Hou N w	86	76	.531	—3		7.3
1990	Hou N w	75	87	.463	4t		3.0
1991	Hou N w	65	97	.401	6		-4.2
1992	Hou N w	81	81	.500	4		6.4
1993	Hou N w	85	77	.525	3		-5.0
1996	Oak A w	78	84	.481	3		0.5
1997	Oak A w	65	97	.401	4		0.8
1998	Oak A w	74	88	.457	4		-1.2
1999	Oak A w	87	75	.537	2		1.7
2000	Oak A w	91	70	.565	1		-1.7
2001	Oak A w	102	60	.630	2✤		-2.3
2002	Oak A w	103	59	.636	1		7.4
2003	NY N e	66	95	.410	5		-3.1
2004	NY N e	71	91	.438	4		-5.2
14		1129	1137	.498			4.5

HOWLEY, DAN B10.16.1885
YEAR	TM/LG	W	L	PCT	FINISH	MGR/YR	+/-
1927	StL A	59	94	.386	7		-0.8
1928	StL A	82	72	.532	3		2.1
1929	StL A	79	73	.520	4		1.0
1930	Cin N	59	95	.383	7		0.3
1931	Cin N	58	96	.377	8		-3.7
1932	Cin N	60	94	.390	8		-2.4
6		397	524	.431			-3.5

HOWSER, DICK B5.14.1936
YEAR	TM/LG	W	L	PCT	FINISH	MGR/YR	+/-
1978	NY A e	0	1	.000	3-4-1★▲	2/3	-0.6
1980	NY A e	103	59	.636	1★		6.3
1981-2	KC A w	20	13	.606	2t-1	2/2	3.8
1982	KC A w	90	72	.556	2		2.4
1983	KC A w	79	83	.488	2		5.1
1984	KC A w	84	78	.519	1		4.3
1985	KC A w	91	71	.562	1★		5.0
1986	KC A w	40	48	.455	4-3t	1/2	-2.9
8		507	425	.544			23.4

HUFF, GEORGE George A. "Gee"
B6.11.1872 Champaign, IL D10.1.1936 Champaign, IL (DNP)
YEAR	TM/LG	W	L	PCT	FINISH	MGR/YR	+/-
1907	Bos A	2	6	.250	4t-6-7	2/4	-1.4

HUGGINS, MILLER B3.27.1878
YEAR	TM/LG	W	L	PCT	FINISH	MGR/YR	+/-
1913	StL N	51	99	.340	8		-0.5
1914	StL N	81	72	.529	3		2.5
1915	StL N	72	81	.471	6		-3.3
1916	StL N	60	93	.392	7t		0.6
1917	StL N	82	70	.539	3		10.0

YEAR	TM/LG	W	L	PCT	FINISH	MGR/YR	+/-
1918	NY A	60	63	.488	4		-3.4
1919	NY A	80	59	.576	3		2.7
1920	NY A	95	59	.617	3		-2.3
1921	NY A	98	55	.641	1		-0.4
1922	NY A	94	60	.610	1		2.9
1923	NY A	98	54	.645	1★		2.4
1924	NY A	89	63	.586	2		0.3
1925	NY A	69	85	.448	7		-1.4
1926	NY A	91	63	.591	1		1.3
1927	NY A	110	44	.714	1★		-2.4
1928	NY A	101	53	.656	1★		4.4
1929	NY A	82	61	.573	2-2	1/2	0.0
17		1413	1134	.555			13.5

HUNTER, BILLY B6.4.1928
YEAR	TM/LG	W	L	PCT	FINISH	MGR/YR	+/-
1977	Tex A w	60	33	.645	5-2	4/4	7.1
1978	Tex A w	86	75	.534	2t-2t	1/2	-0.8
2		146	108	.575			6.4

HURDLE, CLINT B7.30.1957
YEAR	TM/LG	W	L	PCT	FINISH	MGR/YR	+/-
2002	Col N w	67	73	.479	5-4	2/2	6.7
2003	Col N w	74	88	.457	4		-3.4
2004	Col N w	68	94	.420	4		-4.8
2005	Col N w	67	95	.414	5		-2.4
4		276	350	.441			-3.9

HURST, TIM Timothy Carroll
B6.30.1865 Ashland, PA D6.4.1915 Pottsville, PA 5-5/(DNP)
YEAR	TM/LG	W	L	PCT	FINISH	MGR/YR	+/-
1898	StL N	39	111	.260	12		-1.6

HUTCHINSON, FRED B8.12.1919
YEAR	TM/LG	W	L	PCT	FINISH	MGR/YR	+/-
1952	Det A	27	55	.329	8-8	2/2	-4.0
1953	Det A	60	94	.390	6		4.4
1954	Det A	68	86	.442	5		-0.5
1956	StL N	76	78	.494	4		1.0
1957	StL N	87	67	.565	2		2.9
1958	StL N	69	75	.479	5-5t	1/2	5.1
1959	Cin N	39	35	.527	7-5t	2/2	0.8
1960	Cin N	67	87	.435	6		-0.9
1961	Cin N	93	61	.604	1		10.3
1962	Cin N	98	64	.605	3		5.4
1963	Cin N	86	76	.531	5		-0.9
1964	Cin N	54	45	.545	3-2t	1/4	-1.8
1964	Cin N	6	4	.600	4-3-2t	2/2	0.4
12		830	827	.501			18.5

IRWIN, ARTHUR B2.14.1858
YEAR	TM/LG	W	L	PCT	FINISH	MGR/YR	+/-
1889	Was N	28	45	.384	8-8	2/2	4.8
1891	Bos AA	93	42	.689	1		-4.8
1892-1	Was N	35	39	.473	11t-7	2/2	4.3
1892-2	Was N	11	21	.344	11-12	1/2	-2.3
1894	Phi N	71	57	.555	4		-6.6
1895	Phi N	78	53	.595	3		4.0
1896	NY N	36	53	.404	10-7	1/2	-9.0
1898	Was N	10	19	.345	11-11	4/4	-0.4
1899	Was N	54	98	.355	11		-0.4
8		416	427	.493			-10.4

JENNINGS, HUGHIE B4.2.1869
YEAR	TM/LG	W	L	PCT	FINISH	MGR/YR	+/-
1907	Det A	92	58	.613	1		-0.2
1908	Det A	90	63	.588	1		2.7
1909	Det A	98	54	.645	1		2.8
1910	Det A	86	68	.558	3		-1.0
1911	Det A	89	65	.578	2		7.0
1912	Det A	69	84	.451	6		-2.0
1913	Det A	66	87	.431	6		-1.3
1914	Det A	80	73	.523	4		3.8
1915	Det A	100	54	.649	2		4.7
1916	Det A	87	67	.565	3		2.2
1917	Det A	78	75	.510	4		-5.1
1918	Det A	55	71	.437	7		0.6
1919	Det A	80	60	.571	4		5.5
1920	Det A	61	93	.396	7		1.5
1924	NY N	32	12	.727	3-1-1	2/3	4.0
1925	NY N	21	11	.656	1-1-2	2/3	4.0
16		1184	995	.543			29.9

JOHNSON, DARRELL B8.25.1928
YEAR	TM/LG	W	L	PCT	FINISH	MGR/YR	+/-
1974	Bos A e	84	78	.519	3		-0.8
1975	Bos A e	95	65	.594	1◆		6.5
1976	Bos A e	41	45	.477	5-3	1/2	6.3
1977	Sea A w	64	98	.395	6		-2.0
1978	Sea A w	56	104	.350	7		-2.5
1979	Sea A w	67	95	.414	6		-2.1
1980	Sea A w	39	65	.375	6-7	1/2	-1.1
1982	Tex A w	26	40	.394	6-6	2/2	-0.2
8		472	590	.444			

JOHNSON, DAVEY B1.30.1943
YEAR	TM/LG	W	L	PCT	FINISH	MGR/YR	+/-
1984	NY N e	90	72	.556	2		11.0
1985	NY N e	98	64	.605	2		4.0
1986	NY N e	108	54	.667	1★		8.0
1987	NY N e	92	70	.568	2		-1.0
1988	NY N e	100	60	.625	1		1.0
1989	NY N e	87	75	.537	2		-1.0
1990	NY N e	20	22	.476	4-2	1/2	-5.0
1993	Cin N w	53	65	.449	5-5		-2.0
1994	Cin N c	66	48	.579	1		-1.0
1995	Cin N c	85	59	.590	1☆		-1.0
1996	Bal A e	88	74	.543	2☆✤		

The Men in the Dugout: The Managers

YEAR	TM/LG	W	L	PCT	FINISH	MGR/YR	+/-
1997	Bal A e	98	64	.605	1☆		4.1
1999	LA N w	77	85	.475	3		-4.6
2000	LA N w	86	76	.531	2		-1.7
	14	1148	888	.564			9.8

JOHNSON, ROY B10.1.1895

YEAR	TM/LG	W	L	PCT	FINISH	MGR/YR	+/-
1944	Chi N	0	1	.000	8-8-4	2/3	-0.5

JOHNSON, TIM B7.22.1949

| 1998 | Tor A e | 88 | 74 | .543 | 3 | | 2.4 |

JOHNSON, WALTER B11.6.1887

YEAR	TM/LG	W	L	PCT	FINISH	MGR/YR	+/-
1929	Was A	71	81	.467	5		-0.6
1930	Was A	94	60	.610	2		-2.0
1931	Was A	92	62	.597	3		0.4
1932	Was A	93	61	.604	3		4.3
1933	Cle A	48	51	.485	5-4	3/3	-0.5
1934	Cle A	85	69	.552	3		3.2
1935	Cle A	46	48	.489	5-3	1/2	-3.2
	7	529	432	.550			1.6

JONES, FIELDER B8.13.1871

YEAR	TM/LG	W	L	PCT	FINISH	MGR/YR	+/-
1904	Chi A	66	47	.584	4-3	2/2	-0.4
1905	Chi A	92	60	.605	2		-2.6
1906	Chi A	93	58	.616	1★		4.7
1907	Chi A	87	64	.576	3		-1.7
1908	Chi A	88	64	.579	3		4.1
1914	StL F	12	26	.316	7-8	2/2	-3.5
1915	StL F	87	67	.565	2		-1.9
1916	StL A	79	75	.513	5		-2.8
1917	StL A	57	97	.370	7		-0.9
1918	StL A	22	24	.478	6-5	1/3	-0.1
	10	683	582	.540			-5.0

JOOST, EDDIE B6.5.1916

| 1954 | Phi A | 51 | 103 | .331 | 8 | | 7.2 |

JORGENSEN, MIKE B8.16.1948

| 1995 | StL N c | 42 | 54 | .438 | 4-4 | 2/2 | 0.5 |

JOYCE, BILL B9.21.1865

YEAR	TM/LG	W	L	PCT	FINISH	MGR/YR	+/-
1896	NY N	28	14	.667	10-7	2/2	6.8
1897	NY N	83	48	.634	3		-0.6
1898	NY N	22	21	.512	6-7	1/3	-0.5
1898	NY N	46	39	.541	7-7	3/3	1.6
	3	179	122	.595			7.3

JURGES, BILLY B5.9.1908

YEAR	TM/LG	W	L	PCT	FINISH	MGR/YR	+/-
1959	Bos A	44	36	.550	8-5	3/3	2.5
1960	Bos A	15	27	.357	8-7	1/3	-2.9
	2	59	63	.484			-0.4

KASKO, EDDIE B6.27.1932

YEAR	TM/LG	W	L	PCT	FINISH	MGR/YR	+/-
1970	Bos A e	87	75	.537	3		-0.3
1971	Bos A e	85	77	.525	3		1.5
1972	Bos A e	85	70	.548	2		5.4
1973	Bos A e	88	73	.547	2-2	1/2	-1.8
	4	345	295	.539			4.8

KEANE, JOHNNY John Joseph B11.3.1911 St.Louis, MO
D1.6.1967 Houston, TX BR/TR/5-10/165(SS)

YEAR	TM/LG	W	L	PCT	FINISH	MGR/YR	+/-
1961	StL N	47	33	.587	6-5	2/2	5.2
1962	StL N	84	78	.519	6		-8.1
1963	StL N	93	69	.574	2		-0.3
1964	StL N	93	69	.574	1★		5.5
1965	NY A	77	85	.475	6		-4.8
1966	NY A	4	16	.200	10-10	1/2	-6.0
	6	398	350	.532			-8.5

KELLEY, JOE B12.9.1871

YEAR	TM/LG	W	L	PCT	FINISH	MGR/YR	+/-
1902	Cin N	34	26	.567	6-4	3/3	1.0
1903	Cin N	74	65	.532	4		-5.8
1904	Cin N	88	65	.575	3		-4.3
1905	Cin N	79	74	.516	5		-1.2
1908	Bos N	63	91	.409	6		-4.6
	5	338	321	.513			-14.9

KELLY, TOM B8.15.1950

YEAR	TM/LG	W	L	PCT	FINISH	MGR/YR	+/-
1986	Min A w	12	11	.522	7-6	2/2	1.8
1987	Min A w	85	77	.525	1★		5.9
1988	Min A w	91	71	.562	2		1.2
1989	Min A w	80	82	.494	5		-1.2
1990	Min A w	74	88	.457	7		-0.6
1991	Min A w	95	67	.586	1★		1.5
1992	Min A w	90	72	.556	2		-0.6
1993	Min A w	71	91	.438	5t		3.4
1994	Min A c	53	60	.469	4		4.9
1995	Min A c	56	88	.389	4		0.8
1996	Min A c	78	84	.481	4		-0.9
1997	Min A c	68	94	.420	4		-4.6
1998	Min A c	70	92	.432	4		-2.9
1999	Min A c	63	97	.394	5		-1.5
2000	Min A c	69	93	.426	5		0.5
2001	Min A c	85	77	.525	2		3.5
	16	1140	1244	.478			11.3

KELLY, KICK B10.31.1856

YEAR	TM/LG	W	L	PCT	FINISH	MGR/YR	+/-
1887	Lou AA	76	60	.559	4		-0.5
1888	Lou AA	10	29	.256	8-7	1/4	-4.8
	2	86	89	.491			-5.3

KELLY, KING B12.31.1857

YEAR	TM/LG	W	L	PCT	FINISH	MGR/YR	+/-
1887	Bos N	49	43	.533	5-5	1/2	0.3
1890	Bos P	81	48	.628	1		-1.9

KENNEDY, JIM James C.
B1867 New York, NY D4.20.1904 Brighton Beach, NY (DNP)

YEAR	TM/LG	W	L	PCT	FINISH	MGR/YR	+/-
1891	Cin AA	43	57	.430	6		1.3
	3	173	148	.539			-0.3
1890	Bro AA	26	73	.263	8		-2.3

KENNEDY, KEVIN Kevin Curtis
B9.26.1954 Los Angeles, CA BR/TR/6-3/220(C)

YEAR	TM/LG	W	L	PCT	FINISH	MGR/YR	+/-
1993	Tex A w	86	76	.531	2		-3.1
1994	Tex A w	52	62	.456	1		2.4
1995	Bos A e	86	58	.597	1		5.3
1996	Bos A e	85	77	.525	3		3.4
	4	309	273	.531			8.1

KENNEDY, BOB B8.18.1920

YEAR	TM/LG	W	L	PCT	FINISH	MGR/YR	+/-
1963	Chi N	82	80	.506	7		1.9
1964	Chi N	76	86	.469	8		2.7
1965	Chi N	24	32	.429	9-8		-0.8
1968	Oak A	82	80	.506	6		-1.9
	4	264	278	.487			1.9

KERINS, JOHN B7.15.1858

YEAR	TM/LG	W	L	PCT	FINISH	MGR/YR	+/-
1888	Lou AA	3	4	.429	8-8-7	3/4	0.3
1890	StL AA	9	8	.529	4-4-3	2/6	-1.0
	2	12	12	.500			-0.6

KERRIGAN, JOE B11.30.1954

| 2001 | Bos A e | 17 | 26 | .395 | 2-2 | | -5.2 |

KESSINGER, DON B7.17.1942

| 1979 | Chi A | 46 | 60 | .434 | 5-5 | 1/2 | -5.8 |

KILLEFER, BILL B10.10.1887

YEAR	TM/LG	W	L	PCT	FINISH	MGR/YR	+/-
1921	Chi N	23	34	.404	6-7	2/2	-1.7
1922	Chi N	80	74	.519	5		6.5
1923	Chi N	83	71	.539	4		0.9
1924	Chi N	81	72	.529	5		4.6
1925	Chi N	33	42	.440	7-8	1/3	-2.2
1930	StL A	64	90	.416	6		-0.6
1931	StL A	63	91	.409	5		-0.1
1932	StL A	63	91	.409	6		0.9
1933	StL A	34	57	.374	8-8	1/3	-2.7
	9	524	622	.457			5.7

KIMM, BRUCE B6.29.1951

| 2002 | Chi N c | 28 | 46 | .378 | 3-4 | 2/2 | -6.6 |

KING, CLYDE B5.23.1924

YEAR	TM/LG	W	L	PCT	FINISH	MGR/YR	+/-
1969	SF N w	90	72	.556	2		1.0
1970	SF N w	19	23	.452	4-3	1/2	-2.1
1974	Atl N w	38	25	.603	4-3	2/2	2.3
1975	Atl N w	58	76	.433	5-5	1/2	4.6
1982	NY A e	29	33	.468	5t-5	3/3	-1.7
	5	234	229	.505			4.1

KITTRIDGE, MALACHI B10.12.1869

| 1904 | Was A | 1 | 16 | .059 | 8-8 | 1/2 | -3.7 |

KLEIN, LOU B10.22.1918

YEAR	TM/LG	W	L	PCT	FINISH	MGR/YR	+/-
1961	Chi N	5	6	.455	7-7-7	8/9	0.3
1962	Chi N	12	18	.400	9-9-9	2/3	0.6
1965	Chi N	48	58	.453	8-8	2/2	1.0
	3	65	82	.442			1.9

KLING, JOHNNY B2.25.1875

| 1912 | Bos N | 52 | 101 | .340 | 8 | | -7.7 |

KNABE, OTTO B6.12.1884

YEAR	TM/LG	W	L	PCT	FINISH	MGR/YR	+/-
1914	Bal F	84	70	.545	3		5.2
1915	Bal F	47	107	.305	8		-8.4
	2	131	177	.425			-3.2

KNIGHT, LON B6.16.1853

YEAR	TM/LG	W	L	PCT	FINISH	MGR/YR	+/-
1883	Phi AA	66	32	.673	1		2.6
1884	Phi AA	61	46	.570	7		-6.1
	2	127	78	.620			-3.5

KNIGHT, RAY B12.28.1952

YEAR	TM/LG	W	L	PCT	FINISH	MGR/YR	+/-
1996	Cin N c	81	81	.500	3		-0.5
1997	Cin N c	43	56	.434	4-3	1/2	0.6
2003	Cin N c	1	0	1.000	5-5-5	2/3	0.6
	3	125	137	.477			0.6

KNOOP, BOBBY B10.18.1938

| 1994 | Cal A w | 1 | 1 | .500 | 3-2-4 | 2/3 | 0.2 |

KROL, JACK John Thomas B7.5.1936 Chicago, IL
D5.30.1994 Winston-Salem, NC BR/TR/5-11/175(2B)

YEAR	TM/LG	W	L	PCT	FINISH	MGR/YR	+/-
1978	StL N e	1	1	.500	6-6-5	2/3	0.1
1980	StL N e	0	1	.000	6-6-4	2/4	-0.5
	2	1	2	.333			-0.4

KUEHL, KARL Karl Otto
B9.5.1937 Monterey Park, CA BL/TL/5-11/175(1B)

| 1976 | Mon N e | 43 | 85 | .336 | 6-6 | 1/2 | -3.8 |

KUENN, HARVEY B12.4.1930

YEAR	TM/LG	W	L	PCT	FINISH	MGR/YR	+/-
1975	Mil A e	1	0	1.000	5-5	2/2	0.6
1982	Mil A e	72	43	.626	5-1◆	2/2	2.7
1983	Mil A e	87	75	.537	5		0.4
	3	160	118	.576			3.7

KUHEL, JOE B6.25.1906

YEAR	TM/LG	W	L	PCT	FINISH	MGR/YR	+/-
1948	Was A	56	97	.366	7		1.4
1949	Was A	50	104	.325	8		0.7
	2	106	201	.345			2.1

LACHEMANN, MARCEL B6.13.1941

YEAR	TM/LG	W	L	PCT	FINISH	MGR/YR	+/-
1994	Cal A w	30	44	.405	2-4	3/3	-0.0
1995	Cal A w	78	67	.538	2▲		-4.2
1996	Cal A w	52	59	.468	4	1/2	8.0
	3	160	170	.485			3.8

LACHEMANN, RENE B5.4.1945

YEAR	TM/LG	W	L	PCT	FINISH	MGR/YR	+/-
1981-1	Sea A w	15	18	.455	7-6	2/2	1.4
1981-2	Sea A w	23	29	.442	5		-0.8
1982	Sea A w	76	86	.469	4		1.3
1983	Sea A w	26	47	.356	7-7	1/2	-1.8
1984	Mil A e	67	94	.416	7		-4.0
1993	Fla N e	64	98	.395	6		-1.9
1994	Fla N e	51	54	.486	5		4.3
1995	Fla N e	67	76	.469	4		-4.5
1996	Fla N e	39	47	.453	4-3	1/3	-3.2
	8	428	549	.438			-9.1

LAJOIE, NAP B9.5.1874

YEAR	TM/LG	W	L	PCT	FINISH	MGR/YR	+/-
1905	Cle A	37	21	.638	1t-5	1/3	9.0
1905	Cle A	19	36	.345	2-5	3/3	-7.6
1906	Cle A	89	64	.582	3		-7.7
1907	Cle A	85	67	.559	4		8.3
1908	Cle A	90	64	.584	2		0.1
1909	Cle A	57	57	.500	4-6	1/2	3.4
	5	377	309	.550			5.4

LAKE, FRED B10.16.1866

YEAR	TM/LG	W	L	PCT	FINISH	MGR/YR	+/-
1908	Bos A	22	17	.564	6-5	2/2	1.0
1909	Bos A	88	63	.583	3		6.8
1910	Bos N	53	100	.346	8		-1.1
	3	163	180	.475			6.8

LAMONT, GENE B12.25.1946

YEAR	TM/LG	W	L	PCT	FINISH	MGR/YR	+/-
1992	Chi A w	86	76	.531	3		0.1
1993	Chi A w	94	68	.580	1		1.7
1994	Chi A c	67	46	.593	1		-2.3
1995	Chi A c	11	20	.355	4-3	1/2	-4.4
1997	Pit N c	79	83	.488	2		1.5
1998	Pit N c	69	93	.426	6		-5.0
1999	Pit N c	78	83	.484	3		-1.8
2000	Pit N c	69	93	.426	5		-3.2
	8	553	562	.496			-13.3

LANIER, HAL B7.4.1942

YEAR	TM/LG	W	L	PCT	FINISH	MGR/YR	+/-
1986	Hou N w	96	66	.593	1		5.7
1987	Hou N w	76	86	.469	3		-1.9
1988	Hou N w	82	80	.506	5		2.5
	3	254	232	.523			6.4

LARKIN, HENRY B1.12.1860

| 1890 | Cle P | 34 | 45 | .430 | 7-7 | 1/2 | 3.1 |

LaRUSSA, TONY B10.4.1944

YEAR	TM/LG	W	L	PCT	FINISH	MGR/YR	+/-
1979	Chi A w	27	27	.500	5-5	2/2	0.6
1980	Chi A w	70	90	.438	5		4.2
1981-1	Chi A w	31	22	.585	3		-4.5
1981-2	Chi A w	23	30	.434	6		-4.5
1982	Chi A w	87	75	.537	3		-1.5
1983	Chi A w	99	63	.611	1		3.0
1984	Chi A w	74	88	.457	5t		-1.2
1985	Chi A w	85	77	.525	3		2.4
1986	Chi A w	26	38	.406	6-5	1/3	-3.7
1986	Oak A w	45	34	.570	7-3t	3/3	6.9
1987	Oak A w	81	81	.500	3		-1.6
1988	Oak A w	104	58	.642	1◆		4.8
1989	Oak A w	99	63	.611	1◆		3.5
1990	Oak A w	103	59	.636	1◆		4.8
1991	Oak A w	84	78	.519	4		4.6
1992	Oak A w	96	66	.593	1		7.6
1993	Oak A w	68	94	.420	7		-0.3
1994	Oak A w	51	63	.447	2		-2.2
1995	Oak A w	67	77	.465	4		-2.1
1996	StL N c	88	74	.543	1☆		1.7
1997	StL N c	73	89	.451	4		-6.1
1998	StL N c	83	79	.512	3		-0.7
1999	StL N c	75	86	.466	4		-2.8
2000	StL N c	95	67	.586	1☆		3.1
2001	StL N c	93	69	.574	2◆		-0.8
2002	StL N c	97	65	.599	1☆		2.0
2003	StL N c	85	77	.525	3		-3.5
2004	StL N c	105	57	.648	1◆		4.8
2005	StL N c	100	62	.617	1☆		1.8
	27	2214	1908	.537			20.2

LASORDA, TOM B9.22.1927

YEAR	TM/LG	W	L	PCT	FINISH	MGR/YR	+/-
1976	LA N w	2	2	.500	2-2	2/2	-0.2
1977	LA N w	98	64	.605	1◆		-2.4
1978	LA N w	95	67	.586	1◆		-2.3
1979	LA N w	79	83	.488	3		-4.2
1980	LA N w	92	71	.564	2▲		2.7
1981-1	LA N w	36	21	.632	1★		-2.4
1981-2	LA N w	27	26	.509	4		-2.4
1982	LA N w	88	74	.543	2		-1.4
1983	LA N w	91	71	.562	1		5.1
1984	LA N w	79	83	.488	4		0.2
1985	LA N w	95	67	.586	1		2.9
1986	LA N w	73	89	.451	5		-3.7
1987	LA N w	73	89	.451	4		-3.8
1988	LA N w	94	67	.584	1★		4.1

YEAR	TM/LG	W	L	PCT	FINISH	MGR/YR	+/-
1989	LA N w	77	83	.481	4		-5.1
1990	LA N w	86	76	.531	2		0.6
1991	LA N w	93	69	.574	2		1.1
1992	LA N w	63	99	.389	6		-8.2
1993	LA N w	81	81	.500	4		-1.4
1994	LA N w	58	56	.509	1		-1.3
1995	LA N w	78	66	.542	1		3.4
1996	LA N w	41	35	.539	1-2	1/2	0.5
	21	1599	1439	.526			-17.9

LATHAM, JUICE B9.6.1852
1875	NH NA	4	14	.222	11-8-8	2/3	2.5
1882	Phi AA	41	34	.547	2		1.9
	2	45	48	.484			4.4

LATHAM, ARLIE B3.15.1860
1896	StL N	0	3	.000	10-10-11	2/5	-0.8

LAVAGETTO, COOKIE B12.1.1912
1957	Was A	51	83	.381	8-8	2/2	1.7
1958	Was A	61	93	.396	8		4.2
1959	Was A	63	91	.409	8		-5.6
1960	Was A	73	81	.474	5		-1.6
1961	Min A	19	30	.388	8-7	1/4	-3.4
1961	Min A	4	6	.400	9-9-7	3/4	-0.6
	5	271	384	.414			-5.3

LEADLEY, BOB Robert H.
B11.11.1858 Brooklyn, NY D5.19.1936 Los Angeles, CA (DNP)
1888	Det N	19	19	.500	3-5	2/2	-2.5
1890	Cle N	23	33	.411	7-7	2/2	2.8
1891	Cle N	34	34	.500	4-5	1/2	2.2
	3	76	86	.469			2.5

LEFEBVRE, JIM B1.7.1942
1989	Sea A w	73	89	.451	6		-4.6
1990	Sea A w	77	85	.475	5		0.2
1991	Sea A w	83	79	.512	5		-0.9
1992	Chi N e	78	84	.481	4		0.4
1993	Chi N e	84	78	.519	4		3.1
1999	Mil N c	22	27	.449	5-5	2/2	-0.5
	6	417	442	.485			-2.2

LEMON, JIM B3.23.1928
1968	Was A	65	96	.404	10		0.1

LEMON, BOB B9.22.1920
1970	KC A w	46	64	.418	5-4t	2/2	-2.3
1971	KC A w	85	76	.528	2		0.4
1972	KC A w	76	78	.494	4		-4.9
1977	Chi A w	90	72	.556	3		2.1
1978	Chi A w	34	40	.459	5-5	1/2	1.6
1978	NY A e	48	20	.706	4-1★▲	3/3	7.3
1979	NY A e	34	31	.523	4-4	1/2	-1.0
1981-2	NY A e	11	14	.440	4-6	2/2	-3.5
1982	NY A e	6	8	.429	4t-5	1/3	-0.9
	8	430	403	.516			-1.4

LENNON, BILL B1848
1871	Kek NA	5	9	.357	7-8	1/2	3.2

LEYLAND, JIM James Richard
B12.15.1944 Toledo, OH BR/TR/5-11/170(P)
1986	Pit N e	64	98	.395	6		-13.2
1987	Pit N e	80	82	.494	4t		1.1
1988	Pit N e	85	75	.531	2		1.3
1989	Pit N e	74	88	.457	5		-2.4
1990	Pit N e	95	67	.586	1		2.2
1991	Pit N e	98	64	.605	1		3.1
1992	Pit N e	96	66	.593	1		4.6
1993	Pit N e	75	87	.463	5		3.7
1994	Pit N c	53	61	.465	3t		7.3
1995	Pit N c	58	86	.403	5		-3.6
1996	Pit N c	73	89	.451	5		-2.6
1997	Fla N e	92	70	.568	2★✤		3.8
1998	Fla N e	54	108	.333	5		-2.5
1999	Col N w	72	90	.444	5		1.6
	14	1069	1131	.486			4.3

LEYVA, NICK Nicholas Tomas
B8.16.1953 Ontario, CA BR/TR/5-11/165(3B)
1989	Phi N e	67	95	.414	6		-3.0
1990	Phi N e	77	85	.475	4t		4.5
1991	Phi N e	4	9	.308	6-3	1/2	-2.1
	3	148	189	.439			-0.5

LILLIS, BOB B6.2.1930
1982	Hou N w	28	23	.549	5-5	2/2	4.3
1983	Hou N w	85	77	.525	3		4.3
1984	Hou N w	80	82	.494	2t		-7.6
1985	Hou N w	83	79	.512	3t		0.5
	4	276	261	.514			1.5

LIPON, JOHNNY B11.10.1922
1971	Cle A e	18	41	.305	6-6	2/2	-3.6

LITTLE, GRADY William Grady
B3.30.1950 Abilene, TX BR/TR/5-11/190(C)
2002	Bos A e	93	69	.574	2		-7.0
2003	Bos A e	95	67	.586	2☆✤		0.2
	2	188	136	.580			-6.8

YEAR	TM/LG	W	L	PCT	FINISH	MGR/YR	+/-

LOBERT, HANS B10.18.1881
1938	Phi N	0	2	.000	8-8	2/2	-0.6
1942	Phi N	42	109	.278	8		1.2
	2	42	111	.275			0.6

LOCKMAN, WHITEY B7.25.1926
1972	Chi N e	39	26	.600	4-2	2/2	1.3
1973	Chi N e	77	84	.478	5		0.9
1974	Chi N e	52	52	.441	5-6	1/2	3.4
	3	157	162	.492			5.5

LOFTUS, TOM B11.15.1856
1884	Mil U	8	4	.667	2		-0.1
1888	Cle AA	30	38	.441	8-6	2/2	4.7
1889	Cle N	61	72	.459	6		0.5
1890	Cin N	77	55	.583	4		-0.2
1891	Cin N	56	81	.409	7		0.9
1900	Chi N	65	75	.464	5t		6.3
1901	Chi N	53	86	.381	6		-4.5
1902	Was A	61	75	.449	6		0.6
1903	Was A	43	94	.314	8		1.3
	9	454	580	.439			9.6

LOPAT, ED B6.21.1918
1963	KC A	73	89	.451	8		1.4
1964	KC A	17	35	.327	10-10	1/2	-2.1
	2	90	124	.421			-0.7

LOPES, DAVEY B5.3.1945
2000	Mil N c	73	89	.451	3		0.3
2001	Mil N c	68	94	.420	4		-6.6
2002	Mil N c	3	12	.200	6-6	1/2	-2.7
	3	144	195	.425			-9.0

LOPEZ, AL B8.20.1908
1951	Cle A	93	61	.604	2		5.4
1952	Cle A	93	61	.604	2		0.2
1953	Cle A	92	62	.597	2		0.7
1954	Cle A	111	43	.721	1		8.3
1955	Cle A	93	61	.604	2		6.0
1956	Cle A	88	66	.571	2		-2.6
1957	Chi A	90	64	.584	2		-1.8
1958	Chi A	82	72	.532	2		3.0
1959	Chi A	94	60	.610	1		8.4
1960	Chi A	87	67	.565	3		-2.5
1961	Chi A	86	76	.531	4		1.1
1962	Chi A	85	77	.525	5		-1.1
1963	Chi A	94	68	.580	2		-2.2
1964	Chi A	98	64	.605	2		1.1
1965	Chi A	95	67	.586	2		3.9
1968	Chi A	6	5	.545	9-9-8t	3/5	1.0
1968	Chi A	15	21	.417	9-8t	5/5	-1.3
1969	Chi A w	8	9	.471	4-5	1/2	0.6
	17	1410	1004	.584			28.3

LORD, HARRY B3.8.1882
1915	Buf F	60	49	.550	8-6	3/3	10.1

LOWE, BOBBY B7.10.1865
1904	Det A	30	44	.405	7-7	2/2	-0.3

LUCCHESI, FRANK Frank Joseph
B4.24.1927 San Francisco, CA BR/TR/5-8/175(OF)
1970	Phi N e	73	88	.453	5		6.7
1971	Phi N e	67	95	.414	6		0.1
1972	Phi N e	26	50	.342	6-6	1/2	-4.9
1975	Tex A w	35	32	.522	4-3	2/2	2.3
1976	Tex A w	76	86	.469	4t		-1.1
1977	Tex A w	31	31	.500	3t-2	1/4	-4.3
1987	Chi N e	8	17	.320	5-6	2/2	-3.3
	7	316	399	.442			-4.4

LUMLEY, HARRY B9.29.1880
1909	Bro N	55	98	.359	6		-0.6

LYONS, TED B12.28.1900
1946	Chi A	64	60	.516	7-5	2/2	4.9
1947	Chi A	70	84	.455	6		4.6
1948	Chi A	51	101	.336	8		0.6
	3	185	245	.430			10.1

MACHA, KEN B9.29.1950
2003	Oak A w	96	66	.593	1		2.3
2004	Oak A w	91	71	.562	2		5.0
2005	Oak A w	88	74	.543	2		-4.5
	3	275	211	.566			2.8

MACK, CONNIE B12.22.1862
1894	Pit N	12	10	.545	7-7	2/2	1.2
1895	Pit N	71	61	.538	7		3.6
1896	Pit N	66	63	.512	6		-2.5
1901	Phi A	74	62	.544	4		2.0
1902	Phi A	83	53	.610	1		2.0
1903	Phi A	75	60	.556	2		-0.7
1904	Phi A	81	70	.536	5		-0.7
1905	Phi A	92	56	.622	1		3.0
1906	Phi A	78	67	.538	4		3.1
1907	Phi A	88	57	.607	2		7.4
1908	Phi A	68	85	.444	6		0.3
1909	Phi A	95	58	.621	2		-4.1
1910	Phi A	102	48	.680	1★		1.1
1911	Phi A	101	50	.669	1★		0.5
1912	Phi A	90	62	.592	3		2.2

YEAR	TM/LG	W	L	PCT	FINISH	MGR/YR	+/-
1913	Phi A	96	57	.627	1★		-0.6
1914	Phi A	99	53	.651	1		-0.2
1915	Phi A	43	109	.283	8		0.8
1916	Phi A	36	117	.235	8		-5.5
1917	Phi A	55	98	.359	8		-4.2
1918	Phi A	52	76	.406	8		2.0
1919	Phi A	36	104	.257	8		1.3
1920	Phi A	48	106	.312	8		-1.3
1921	Phi A	53	100	.346	8		-1.0
1922	Phi A	65	89	.422	7		-0.1
1923	Phi A	69	83	.454	6		2.8
1924	Phi A	71	81	.467	5		4.0
1925	Phi A	88	64	.579	2		0.9
1926	Phi A	83	67	.553	3		-3.1
1927	Phi A	91	63	.591	2		3.1
1928	Phi A	98	55	.641	2		0.6
1929	Phi A	104	46	.693	1★		1.9
1930	Phi A	102	52	.662	1★		7.0
1931	Phi A	107	45	.704	1		8.6
1932	Phi A	94	60	.610	2		-3.5
1933	Phi A	79	72	.523	3		1.5
1934	Phi A	68	82	.453	5		-0.1
1935	Phi A	58	91	.389	8		-1.8
1936	Phi A	53	100	.346	8		5.9
1937	Phi A	39	80	.328	7-7	1/2	-9.0
1938	Phi A	53	99	.349	8		-2.1
1939	Phi A	25	37	.403	6-7	1/2	5.3
1940	Phi A	54	100	.351	8		-1.9
1941	Phi A	64	90	.416	8		-1.0
1942	Phi A	55	99	.357	8		3.5
1943	Phi A	49	105	.318	8		-4.4
1944	Phi A	72	82	.468	5t		2.7
1945	Phi A	52	98	.347	8		-7.1
1946	Phi A	49	105	.318	8		-11.8
1947	Phi A	78	76	.506	5		-1.0
1948	Phi A	84	70	.545	4		7.6
1949	Phi A	81	73	.526	5		3.9
1950	Phi A	52	102	.338	8		-2.3
	53	3731	3948	.486			13.6

MACK, DENNY B1851
1882	Lou AA	42	38	.525	3		-6.7

MACK, EARLE B2.1.1890
1937	Phi A	15	17	.469	7-7	2/2	2.1
1939	Phi A	30	60	.333	6-7	2/2	1.4
	2	45	77	.369			3.5

MACKANIN, PETE B8.1.1951
2005	Pit N c	12	14	.462	6-6	2/2	0.4

MACULLAR, JIMMY B1.16.1855
1879	Syr N	5	21	.192	6-7	3/3	-1.6

MADDON, JOE Joseph John
B2.8.1954 Hazleton, PA BR/TR/5-11/190(C)
1999	Ana A w	19	10	.655	4-4	2/2	6.5

MAGEE, LEE B6.4.1889
1915	Bro F	53	64	.453	7-7	1/2	-3.5

MALONE, FERGY B1842
1873	Phi NA	36	27	.571	2		0.1
1874	Chi NA	18	18	.500	4-5	1/2	2.9
1884	Phi U	21	46	.313	7		-2.1
	3	75	91	.452			0.9

MANNING, JIMMY B1.31.1862
1901	Was A	61	72	.459	6		2.7

MANNING, JACK B12.20.1853
1877	Cin N	7	12	.368	6-6	3/3	2.8

MANUEL, CHARLIE B1.4.1944
2000	Cle A c	90	72	.556	2		-3.2
2001	Cle A c	91	71	.562	1		3.0
2002	Cle A c	39	48	.448	3-3	1/2	0.6
2005	Phi N e	88	74	.543	2		-0.9
	4	308	265	.538			-0.5

MANUEL, JERRY B12.23.1953
1998	Chi A c	80	82	.494	2		5.3
1999	Chi A c	75	86	.466	2		3.3
2000	Chi A c	95	67	.586	1		1.5
2001	Chi A c	83	79	.512	3		1.7
2002	Chi A c	81	81	.500	2		-5.4
2003	Chi A c	86	76	.531	2		-2.5
	6	500	471	.515			3.9

MARANVILLE, RABBIT B11.11.1891
1925	Chi N	23	30	.434	7-7-8	2/3	-1.8

MARION, MARTY B12.1.1917
1951	StL N	81	73	.526	3		2.8
1952	StL A	42	61	.408	8-7	2/2	-0.7
1953	StL A	54	100	.351	8		-0.3
1954	Chi A	3	6	.333	3-3	2/2	-2.7
1955	Chi A	91	63	.591	3		-3.5
1956	Chi A	85	69	.552	3		-6.1
	6	356	372	.489			-10.5

MARSHALL, JIM B5.25.1931
1974	Chi N e	25	44	.362	5-6	2/2	-2.9
1975	Chi N e	75	87	.463	5t		5.2

YEAR	TM/LG	W	L	PCT	FINISH	MGR/YR	+/-
1976	Chi N e	75	87	.463	4		6.2
1979	Oak A w	54	108	.333	7		2.0
4		229	326	.413			10.5

MARTIN, BILLY B5.16.1928

YEAR	TM/LG	W	L	PCT	FINISH	MGR/YR	+/-
1969	Min A w	97	65	.599	1		-1.5
1971	Det A e	91	71	.562	2		4.2
1972	Det A e	86	70	.551	1		3.0
1973	Det A e	71	63	.530	3-3	1/2	6.8
1973	Tex A w	9	14	.391	6-6	3/3	0.7
1974	Tex A w	84	76	.525	2		4.8
1975	Tex A w	44	51	.463	4-3	1/2	-2.4
1975	NY A e	30	26	.536	3-3	2/2	-1.5
1976	NY A e	97	62	.610	1◆		1.3
1977	NY A e	100	62	.617	1★		1.1
1978	NY A e	52	42	.553	3-1★▲	1/3	-4.3
1979	NY A e	55	40	.579	4-4	2/2	3.8
1980	Oak A w	83	79	.512	2		-2.6
1981-1	Oak A w	37	23	.617	1☆		3.6
1981-2	Oak A w	27	22	.551	2		3.6
1982	Oak A w	68	94	.420	5		-0.4
1983	NY A e	91	71	.562	3		3.3
1985	NY A e	91	54	.628	7-2	2/2	2.6
1988	NY A e	40	28	.588	2-5	1/2	5.0
16		1253	1013	.553			31.2

MARTIN, PHONNEY B8.4.1845

YEAR	TM/LG	W	L	PCT	FINISH	MGR/YR	+/-
1872	Eck NA	1	8	.111	10-9	3/3	2.0

MARTINEZ, BUCK B11.7.1948

YEAR	TM/LG	W	L	PCT	FINISH	MGR/YR	+/-
2001	Tor A e	80	82	.494	3		-2.4
2002	Tor A e	20	33	.377	4-3	1/2	-6.0
2		100	115	.465			-8.4

MARTINEZ, MARTY B8.23.1941

YEAR	TM/LG	W	L	PCT	FINISH	MGR/YR	+/-
1986	Sea A w	0	1	.000	6-6-7	2/3	-0.4

MASON, CHARLIE B6.25.1853

YEAR	TM/LG	W	L	PCT	FINISH	MGR/YR	+/-
1887	Phi AA	38	40	.487	6-5	2/2	-1.1

MATHEWS, EDDIE B10.13.1931

YEAR	TM/LG	W	L	PCT	FINISH	MGR/YR	+/-
1972	Atl N w	23	27	.460	4-4	2/2	1.4
1973	Atl N w	76	85	.472	5		-6.9
1974	Atl N w	50	49	.505	4-3	1/2	-6.1
3		149	161	.481			-11.6

MATHEWSON, CHRISTY B8.12.1880

YEAR	TM/LG	W	L	PCT	FINISH	MGR/YR	+/-
1916	Cin N	25	43	.368	8-7t	3/3	-3.4
1917	Cin N	78	76	.506	4		2.1
1918	Cin N	61	57	.517	4-3	1/2	-1.3
3		164	176	.482			-2.7

MATTICK, BOBBY B12.5.1915

YEAR	TM/LG	W	L	PCT	FINISH	MGR/YR	+/-
1980	Tor A e	67	95	.414	7		0.2
1981-1	Tor A e	16	42	.276	7		-1.0
1981-2	Tor A e	21	27	.438	7		-1.0
2		104	164	.388			-1.8

MAUCH, GENE B11.18.1925

YEAR	TM/LG	W	L	PCT	FINISH	MGR/YR	+/-
1960	Phi N	58	94	.382	4t-8	3/3	-2.8
1961	Phi N	47	107	.305	8		-8.7
1962	Phi N	81	80	.503	7		5.9
1963	Phi N	87	75	.537	4		-1.0
1964	Phi N	92	70	.568	2t		4.6
1965	Phi N	85	76	.528	6		5.9
1966	Phi N	87	75	.537	4		0.1
1967	Phi N	82	80	.506	5		-2.4
1968	Phi N	27	27	.500	6t-7t	1/3	2.7
1969	Mon N e	52	110	.321	6		-7.5
1970	Mon N e	73	89	.451	6		3.9
1971	Mon N e	71	90	.441	5		1.6
1972	Mon N e	70	86	.449	5		2.7
1973	Mon N e	79	83	.488	4		1.5
1974	Mon N e	79	82	.491	4		-2.0
1975	Mon N e	75	87	.463	5t		3.5
1976	Min A w	85	77	.525	3		0.1
1977	Min A w	84	77	.522	4		-5.0
1978	Min A w	73	89	.451	4		-6.8
1979	Min A w	82	80	.506	4		-2.9
1980	Min A w	54	71	.432	4-3	1/2	-4.2
1981-1	Cal A w	9	4	.692	4-4	2/2	2.2
1981-2	Cal A w	20	30	.400	7		-6.4
1982	Cal A w	93	69	.574	1		-2.3
1985	Cal A w	90	72	.556	2		6.1
1986	Cal A w	92	70	.568	1		0.8
1987	Cal A w	75	87	.463	6t		-2.8
26		1902	2037	.483			-13.2

MAZZILLI, LEE B3.25.1955

YEAR	TM/LG	W	L	PCT	FINISH	MGR/YR	+/-
2004	Bal A e	78	84	.481	3		-4.1
2005	Bal A e	51	56	.477	4-4	1/2	2.1
2		129	140	.480			-2.0

McALEER, JIMMY B7.10.1864

YEAR	TM/LG	W	L	PCT	FINISH	MGR/YR	+/-
1901	Cle A	54	82	.397	7		1.0
1902	StL A	78	58	.574	2		8.8
1903	StL A	65	74	.468	6		-1.7
1904	StL A	65	87	.428	6		3.0
1905	StL A	54	99	.353	8		-11.8
1906	StL A	76	73	.510	5		-5.5
1907	StL A	69	83	.454	6		-5.4
1908	StL A	83	69	.546	4		-0.1
1909	StL A	61	89	.407	7		1.7
1910	Was A	66	85	.437	7		-3.7
1911	Was A	64	90	.416	7		1.1
11		735	889	.453			-12.7

McBRIDE, GEORGE B11.20.1880

YEAR	TM/LG	W	L	PCT	FINISH	MGR/YR	+/-
1921	Was A	80	73	.523	4		6.8

McBRIDE, DICK B1845

YEAR	TM/LG	W	L	PCT	FINISH	MGR/YR	+/-
1871	Ath NA	21	7	.750	1		0.1
1872	Ath NA	30	14	.682	4		-5.1
1873	Ath NA	28	23	.549	5		-2.7
1874	Ath NA	33	23	.589	3		-2.2
1875	Ath NA	49	18	.731	2-2	1/2	-6.1
5		161	85	.654			-16.0

McCALLISTER, JACK John
B1.19.1879 Marietta, OH D10.18.1946 Columbus, OH (DNP)

YEAR	TM/LG	W	L	PCT	FINISH	MGR/YR	+/-
1927	Cle A	66	87	.431	6		-0.9

McCARTHY, JOE Joseph Vincent "Marse Joe"
B4.21.1887 Philadelphia, PA
D1.13.1978 Buffalo, NY BR/TR/5-8.5/190(2B)

YEAR	TM/LG	W	L	PCT	FINISH	MGR/YR	+/-
1926	Chi N	82	72	.532	4		-3.3
1927	Chi N	85	68	.556	4		-0.3
1928	Chi N	91	63	.591	3		3.9
1929	Chi N	98	54	.645	1		1.9
1930	Chi N	86	64	.573	2-2	1/2	0.2
1931	NY A	94	59	.614	2		-9.3
1932	NY A	107	47	.695	1★		4.9
1933	NY A	91	59	.607	2		1.7
1934	NY A	94	60	.610	2		0.4
1935	NY A	89	60	.597	2		-3.4
1936	NY A	102	51	.667	1★		-3.9
1937	NY A	102	52	.662	1★		-3.5
1938	NY A	99	53	.651	1★		-0.5
1939	NY A	106	45	.702	1★		-8.5
1940	NY A	88	66	.571	3		-3.1
1941	NY A	101	53	.656	1★		4.5
1942	NY A	103	51	.669	1		-4.3
1943	NY A	98	56	.636	1★		7.4
1944	NY A	83	71	.539	3		0.1
1945	NY A	81	71	.533	4		-2.2
1946	NY A	22	13	.629	2-3	1/3	1.2
1948	Bos A	96	59	.619	2▲		1.2
1949	Bos A	96	58	.623	2		-2.6
1950	Bos A	31	28	.525	4-3	1/2	-5.9
24		2125	1333	.615			-23.6

McCARTHY, TOMMY B7.24.1863

YEAR	TM/LG	W	L	PCT	FINISH	MGR/YR	+/-
1890	StL AA	11	11	.500	4-3	1/6	-1.9
1890	StL AA	4	1	.800	2-2-3	5/6	1.1

McCLENDON, LLOYD B1.11.1959

YEAR	TM/LG	W	L	PCT	FINISH	MGR/YR	+/-
2001	Pit N c	62	100	.383	6		0.7
2002	Pit N c	72	89	.447	4		0.7
2003	Pit N c	75	87	.463	4		-1.4
2004	Pit N c	72	89	.447	5		-2.0
2005	Pit N c	55	81	.404	6-6	1/2	-5.5
5		336	446	.430			-7.5

McCLOSKEY, JOHN John Joseph "Honest John"
B4.4.1862 Louisville, KY D11.17.1940 Louisville, KY (DNP)

YEAR	TM/LG	W	L	PCT	FINISH	MGR/YR	+/-
1895	Lou N	35	96	.267	12		1.6
1896	Lou N	2	17	.105	12-12	1/2	-3.2
1906	StL N	52	98	.347	7		-7.5
1907	StL N	52	101	.340	8		-2.3
1908	StL N	49	105	.318	8		1.9
5		190	417	.313			-9.4

McCORMICK, JIM B11.3.1856

YEAR	TM/LG	W	L	PCT	FINISH	MGR/YR	+/-
1879	Cle N	27	55	.329	6		-0.5
1880	Cle N	47	37	.560	3		-0.1
1882	Cle N	0	4	.000	8-5	1/2	-2.0
3		74	96	.435			-2.6

McGAHA, MEL Fred Melvin
B9.26.1926 Bastrop, LA D2.3.2002 Tulsa, OK BR/TR/6-2/210(OF)

YEAR	TM/LG	W	L	PCT	FINISH	MGR/YR	+/-
1962	Cle A	78	82	.488	6-6	1/2	4.3
1964	KC A	40	70	.364	10-10	2/2	-0.3
1965	KC A	5	21	.192	10-10	1/2	-5.2
3		123	173	.416			-1.2

McGEARY, MIKE B1851

YEAR	TM/LG	W	L	PCT	FINISH	MGR/YR	+/-
1875	Phi NA	34	27	.557	4-5	1/2	-3.8
1880	Pro N	8	7	.533	4-2	1/3	-1.7
1881	Cle N	4	7	.364	6-7	1/2	-1.2
3		46	41	.529			-6.7

McGRAW, JOHN B4.7.1873

YEAR	TM/LG	W	L	PCT	FINISH	MGR/YR	+/-
1899	Bal A	86	62	.581	4		-0.9
1901	Bal A	68	65	.511	5		0.6
1902	Bal A	26	31	.456	7-8	1/2	2.5
1902	NY N	25	38	.397	8-8	3/3	3.8
1903	NY N	84	55	.604	2		-1.6
1904	NY N	106	47	.693	1		0.3
1905	NY N	105	48	.686	1★		-0.2
1906	NY N	96	56	.632	2		7.2
1907	NY N	82	71	.536	4		-1.8
1908	NY N	98	56	.636	2t		-1.2
1909	NY N	92	61	.601	3		7.0
1910	NY N	91	63	.591	2		-1.4
1911	NY N	99	54	.647	1		0.4
1912	NY N	103	48	.682	1		2.4
1913	NY N	101	51	.664	1		6.7
1914	NY N	84	70	.545	2		-3.2
1915	NY N	69	83	.454	8		-2.1
1916	NY N	86	66	.566	4		-0.5
1917	NY N	98	56	.636	1		0.7
1918	NY N	71	53	.573	2		1.7
1919	NY N	87	53	.621	2		2.4
1920	NY N	86	68	.558	2		-5.8
1921	NY N	94	59	.614	1★		-2.1
1922	NY N	93	61	.604	1★		-2.7
1923	NY N	95	58	.621	1		1.9
1924	NY N	16	13	.552	3-1	1/3	-2.4
1924	NY N	45	35	.563	1-1	3/3	-5.9
1925	NY N	10	4	.714	1-2	1/3	2.7
1925	NY N	55	51	.519	1-2	3/3	-0.3
1926	NY N	74	77	.490	5		-1.0
1927	NY N	70	52	.574	4-3	1/2	1.7
1928	NY N	93	61	.604	2		0.9
1929	NY N	84	67	.556	3		-8.9
1930	NY N	87	67	.565	3		-2.8
1931	NY N	87	65	.572	2		-6.0
1932	NY N	17	23	.425	8-6t	1/2	-4.2
33		2763	1948	.586			-11.9

McGUIRE, DEACON B11.18.1863

YEAR	TM/LG	W	L	PCT	FINISH	MGR/YR	+/-
1898	Was N	21	47	.309	10-11-11	3/4	-3.3
1907	Bos A	45	61	.425	8-7	4/4	-0.4
1908	Bos A	53	62	.461	6-5	1/2	-8.8
1909	Cle A	14	25	.359	4-6	2/2	-4.3
1910	Cle A	71	81	.467	5		7.0
1911	Cle A	6	11	.353	7-3	1/2	-2.3
6		210	287	.423			-12.2

McGUNNIGLE, BILL B1.1.1855

YEAR	TM/LG	W	L	PCT	FINISH	MGR/YR	+/-
1888	Bro AA	88	52	.629	2		1.0
1889	Bro AA	93	44	.679	1		-0.4
1890	Bro N	86	43	.667	1★		-1.7
1891	Pit N	24	33	.421	8-8	2/2	-1.9
1896	Lou N	36	76	.321	12-12	2/2	5.1
5		327	248	.569			2.1

McINNIS, STUFFY B9.19.1890

YEAR	TM/LG	W	L	PCT	FINISH	MGR/YR	+/-
1927	Phi N	51	103	.331	8		-4.9

McKECHNIE, BILL B8.7.1886

YEAR	TM/LG	W	L	PCT	FINISH	MGR/YR	+/-
1915	New F	54	45	.545	6-5	2/2	2.8
1922	Pit N	53	36	.596	5-3t	2/2	1.5
1923	Pit N	87	67	.565	3		1.3
1924	Pit N	90	63	.588	3		-0.6
1925	Pit N	95	58	.621	1★		0.4
1926	Pit N	84	69	.549	3		-0.4
1928	StL N	95	59	.617	1		1.2
1929	StL N	34	29	.540	4-4	3/3	1.5
1930	Bos N	70	84	.455	6		6.5
1931	Bos N	64	90	.416	7		2.8
1932	Bos N	77	77	.500	5		0.6
1933	Bos N	83	71	.539	4		3.6
1934	Bos N	78	73	.517	4		5.6
1935	Bos N	38	115	.248	8		-11.3
1936	Bos N	71	83	.461	6		2.6
1937	Bos N	79	73	.520	5		0.5
1938	Cin N	82	68	.547	4		-1.9
1939	Cin N	97	57	.630	1		2.5
1940	Cin N	100	53	.654	1★		4.5
1941	Cin N	88	66	.571	3		5.4
1942	Cin N	76	76	.500	4		2.0
1943	Cin N	87	67	.565	2		2.8
1944	Cin N	89	65	.578	3		8.0
1945	Cin N	61	93	.396	7		0.8
1946	Cin N	64	86	.427	6-6	1/2	-5.8
25		1896	1723	.524			37.0

McKEON, JACK John Aloysius
B11.23.1930 South Amboy, NJ BR/TR/5-8/205(C)

YEAR	TM/LG	W	L	PCT	FINISH	MGR/YR	+/-
1973	KC A w	88	74	.543	2		6.7
1974	KC A w	77	85	.475	5		-4.5
1975	KC A w	50	46	.521	2-2	1/2	-1.7
1977	Oak A w	26	27	.491	5t-7	1/2	4.4
1978	Oak A w	45	78	.366	1-6	2/2	-3.4
1988	SD N w	67	48	.583	5-3	2/2	8.6
1989	SD N w	89	73	.549	2		6.3
1990	SD N w	37	43	.463	4-5	1/2	-3.0
1997	Cin N c	33	30	.524	4-3	2/2	6.0
1998	Cin N c	77	85	.475	4		-3.0
1999	Cin N c	96	67	.589	2▲		-0.4
2000	Cin N c	85	77	.525	2		-1.8
2003	Fla N e	74	49	.602	4-2★★	2/2	8.0
2004	Fla N e	83	79	.512	3		0.2
2005	Fla N e	83	79	.512	3t		3.5
15		1010	940	.518			25.9

McKINNON, ALEX B8.14.1856

YEAR	TM/LG	W	L	PCT	FINISH	MGR/YR	+/-
1885	StL N	6	32	.158	5-8-8	2/3	-5.8

McKNIGHT, DENNY Dennis Hamar
B1847 Pittsburgh, PA D5.5.1900 Pittsburgh, PA (DNP)

YEAR	TM/LG	W	L	PCT	FINISH	MGR/YR	+/-
1884	Pit AA	4	8	.333	9-10	1/5	1.3

McMANUS, GEORGE George
B6.28.1846 Ireland D10.2.1918 New York, NY (DNP)

YEAR	TM/LG	W	L	PCT	FINISH	MGR/YR	+/-
1876	StL N	6	2	.750	2-2	2/2	0.1
1877	StL N	28	32	.467	4		1.2
2		34	34	.500			1.3

McMANUS, MARTY B3.14.1900

YEAR	TM/LG	W	L	PCT	FINISH	MGR/YR	+/-
1932	Bos A	32	67	.323	8-8	2/2	4.2
1933	Bos A	63	86	.423	7		-5.9
2		95	153	.383			-1.7

McMILLAN, ROY B7.17.1929

YEAR	TM/LG	W	L	PCT	FINISH	MGR/YR	+/-
1972	Mil A e	1	1	.500	6-6-6	2/3	0.1
1975	NY N e	26	27	.491	3-3t	2/2	-1.2
2		27	28	.491			-1.1

McNAMARA, JOHN John Francis
B6.4.1932 Sacramento, CA BR/TR/5-10/175(C)

YEAR	TM/LG	W	L	PCT	FINISH	MGR/YR	+/-
1969	Oak A w	8	5	.615	2-2	2/2	1.0
1970	Oak A w	89	73	.549	2		-1.1
1974	SD N w	60	102	.370	6		8.8
1975	SD N w	71	91	.438	4		4.2
1976	SD N w	73	89	.451	5		2.0
1977	SD N w	20	28	.417	4-5	1/3	0.1
1979	Cin N w	90	71	.559	1		0.6
1980	Cin N w	89	73	.549	3		4.2
1981-1	Cin N w	35	21	.625	2		9.5
1981-2	Cin N w	31	21	.596	2		9.5
1982	Cin N w	34	58	.370	6-6	1/2	-4.8
1983	Cal A w	70	92	.432	5t		-5.4
1984	Cal A w	81	81	.500	2t		0.1
1985	Bos A e	81	81	.500	5		-7.9
1986	Bos A e	95	66	.590	1♦		4.8
1987	Bos A e	78	84	.481	5		-4.6
1988	Bos A e	43	42	.506	4-1	1/2	-5.9
1990	Cle A e	77	85	.475	4		-3.5
1991	Cle A e	25	52	.325	7-7	1/2	-4.4
1996	Cal A w	18	32	.360	4	2/2	-1.8
19		1168	1247	.484			5.5

McPHEE, BID B11.1.1859

YEAR	TM/LG	W	L	PCT	FINISH	MGR/YR	+/-
1901	Cin N	52	87	.374	8		7.2
1902	Cin N	27	37	.422	6-4	1/3	-8.2
2		79	124	.389			-0.9

McRAE, HAL B7.10.1945

YEAR	TM/LG	W	L	PCT	FINISH	MGR/YR	+/-
1991	KC A w	66	58	.532	7-6	3/3	3.6
1992	KC A w	72	90	.444	5t		-2.9
1993	KC A w	84	78	.519	3		5.0
1994	KC A c	64	51	.557	3		2.4
2001	TB A e	58	90	.392	5-5	2/2	3.0
2002	TB A e	55	106	.342	5		-2.1
6		399	473	.458			9.0

McVEY, CAL B8.30.1850

YEAR	TM/LG	W	L	PCT	FINISH	MGR/YR	+/-
1873	Bal NA	20	13	.606	3-3	1/2	-4.3
1878	Cin N	37	23	.617	2		2.1
1879	Cin N	34	28	.548	4-5	2/2	1.6
3		91	64	.587			-0.6

MELE, SAM B1.21.1923

YEAR	TM/LG	W	L	PCT	FINISH	MGR/YR	+/-
1961	Min A	2	5	.286	8-9-7	2/4	-1.2
1961	Min A	45	49	.479	9-7	4/4	2.1
1962	Min A	91	71	.562	2		1.6
1963	Min A	91	70	.565	3		-6.5
1964	Min A	79	83	.488	6t		-8.0
1965	Min A	102	60	.630	1		3.1
1966	Min A	89	73	.549	2		-0.9
1967	Min A	25	25	.500	6-2t	1/2	-2.7
7		524	436	.546			-12.4

MELILLO, SKI B8.4.1899

YEAR	TM/LG	W	L	PCT	FINISH	MGR/YR	+/-
1938	StL A	2	7	.222	7-7	2/2	-1.4

MELVIN, BOB B10.28.1961

YEAR	TM/LG	W	L	PCT	FINISH	MGR/YR	+/-
2003	Sea A w	93	69	.574	2		-3.9
2004	Sea A w	63	99	.389	4		-5.8
2005	Ari N w	77	85	.475	2		11.5
3		233	253	.479			1.8

MERRILL, STUMP Carl Harrison
B2.25.1944 Brunswick, ME BL/TR/5-8/190(C)

YEAR	TM/LG	W	L	PCT	FINISH	MGR/YR	+/-
1990	NY A e	49	64	.434	7-7	2/2	3.1
1991	NY A e	71	91	.438	5		0.3
2		120	155	.436			3.4

METRO, CHARLIE B4.28.1919

YEAR	TM/LG	W	L	PCT	FINISH	MGR/YR	+/-
1962	Chi N	43	69	.384	9-9	3/3	0.5
1970	KC A w	19	33	.365	5-4t	1/2	-3.8
2		62	102	.378			-3.3

MEYER, BILLY B1.14.1892

YEAR	TM/LG	W	L	PCT	FINISH	MGR/YR	+/-
1948	Pit N	83	71	.539	4		5.5
1949	Pit N	71	83	.461	6		1.7
1950	Pit N	57	96	.373	8		-2.8
1951	Pit N	64	90	.416	7		1.9
1952	Pit N	42	112	.273	8		-6.3
5		317	452	.412			0.0

MICHAEL, GENE B6.2.1938

YEAR	TM/LG	W	L	PCT	FINISH	MGR/YR	+/-
1981-1	NY A e	34	22	.607	1♦		-3.3
1981-2	NY A e	14	12	.538	4-6	1/2	-1.1
1982	NY A e	44	42	.512	4t-5t-5	2/3	1.4
1986	Chi N e	46	56	.451	5-5	3/3	1.4
1987	Chi N e	68	68	.500	5-6	1/2	6.7
4		206	200	.507			5.1

MILAN, CLYDE B3.25.1887

YEAR	TM/LG	W	L	PCT	FINISH	MGR/YR	+/-
1922	Was A	69	85	.448	6		-2.3

MILEY, DAVE David Allen
B4.3.1962 Tampa, FL BL/TR/6-3/220(C)

YEAR	TM/LG	W	L	PCT	FINISH	MGR/YR	+/-
2003	Cin N c	22	35	.386	5-5	3/3	-0.0
2004	Cin N c	76	86	.469	4		9.7
2005	Cin N c	27	43	.386	6	1/2	-5.2
3		125	164	.433			4.5

MILLER, DOGGIE B8.15.1864

YEAR	TM/LG	W	L	PCT	FINISH	MGR/YR	+/-
1894	StL N	56	76	.424	9		5.2

MILLER, RAY Raymond Roger
B4.30.1945 Takoma Park, MD BR/TR/6-3/215(P)

YEAR	TM/LG	W	L	PCT	FINISH	MGR/YR	+/-
1985	Min A w	50	50	.500	6-4	2/2	4.7
1986	Min A w	59	80	.424	7-6	1/2	-2.4
1998	Bal A e	79	83	.488	4		-5.1
1999	Bal A e	78	84	.481	4		-6.4
4		266	297	.472			-9.1

MILLS, BUSTER B9.16.1908

YEAR	TM/LG	W	L	PCT	FINISH	MGR/YR	+/-
1953	Cin N	4	4	.500	6-6	2/2	0.4

MILLS, EVERETT B1.20.1845

YEAR	TM/LG	W	L	PCT	FINISH	MGR/YR	+/-
1872	Bal NA	8	6	.571	2-2	2/2	-2.3

MITCHELL, FRED B6.5.1878

YEAR	TM/LG	W	L	PCT	FINISH	MGR/YR	+/-
1917	Chi N	74	80	.481	5		-1.3
1918	Chi N	84	45	.651	1		3.2
1919	Chi N	75	65	.536	3		-0.7
1920	Chi N	75	79	.487	5t		-0.3
1921	Bos N	79	74	.516	4		0.1
1922	Bos N	53	100	.346	8		-1.2
1923	Bos N	54	100	.351	7		-7.0
7		494	543	.476			-7.2

MIZEROCK, JOHN B12.8.1960

YEAR	TM/LG	W	L	PCT	FINISH	MGR/YR	+/-
2002	KC A c	5	8	.385	4-4-4	2/3	-0.3

MOORE, JACKIE B2.19.1939

YEAR	TM/LG	W	L	PCT	FINISH	MGR/YR	+/-
1984	Oak A w	57	61	.483	5-4	2/2	2.1
1985	Oak A w	77	85	.475	4t		-1.1
1986	Oak A w	29	44	.397	6t-3t	1/3	-6.2
3		163	190	.462			-5.2

MOORE, TERRY B5.27.1912

YEAR	TM/LG	W	L	PCT	FINISH	MGR/YR	+/-
1954	Phi N	35	42	.455	3-4	2/2	-5.8

MORAN, PAT B2.7.1876

YEAR	TM/LG	W	L	PCT	FINISH	MGR/YR	+/-
1915	Phi N	90	62	.592	1		-0.4
1916	Phi N	91	62	.595	2		4.0
1917	Phi N	87	65	.572	2		2.2
1918	Phi N	55	68	.447	6		1.9
1919	Cin N	96	44	.686	1★		6.0
1920	Cin N	82	71	.536	3		-2.0
1921	Cin N	70	83	.458	6		-3.3
1922	Cin N	86	68	.558	2		0.2
1923	Cin N	91	63	.591	2		6.0
9		748	586	.561			14.6

MORGAN, JOE B11.19.1930

YEAR	TM/LG	W	L	PCT	FINISH	MGR/YR	+/-
1988	Bos A e	46	31	.597	4-1	2/2	1.7
1989	Bos A e	83	79	.512	3		-1.8
1990	Bos A e	88	74	.543	1		3.4
1991	Bos A e	84	78	.519	2t		1.1
4		301	262	.535			4.3

MORIARTY, GEORGE B6.7.1884

YEAR	TM/LG	W	L	PCT	FINISH	MGR/YR	+/-
1927	Det A	82	71	.536	4		1.8
1928	Det A	68	86	.442	6		-3.3
2		150	157	.489			-1.5

MORRILL, JOHN B2.19.1855

YEAR	TM/LG	W	L	PCT	FINISH	MGR/YR	+/-
1882	Bos N	45	39	.536	3t		-2.4
1883	Bos N	33	11	.750	4-1	2/2	2.5
1884	Bos N	73	38	.658	2		-3.1
1885	Bos N	46	66	.411	5		-4.2
1886	Bos N	56	61	.479	5		-2.1
1887	Bos N	12	17	.414	5-5	2/2	-3.3
1888	Bos N	70	64	.522	4		-1.9
1889	Was N	13	38	.255	8-8	1/2	-3.2
8		348	334	.510			-17.7

MORTON, CHARLIE B10.12.1854

YEAR	TM/LG	W	L	PCT	FINISH	MGR/YR	+/-
1884	Tol AA	46	58	.442	8		4.6
1885	Det N	7	31	.184	8-6	1/2	-9.7
1890	Tol AA	68	64	.515	4		-2.6
3		121	153	.442			-7.8

MOSES, FELIX Felix Inglesby
B5.13.1853 Charleston, SC D5.5.1888 Sheffield, AL (DNP)

YEAR	TM/LG	W	L	PCT	FINISH	MGR/YR	+/-
1884	Ric AA	12	30	.286	12		0.2

MOSS, LES B5.14.1925

YEAR	TM/LG	W	L	PCT	FINISH	MGR/YR	+/-
1968	Chi A	0	2	.000	9-9-8t	2/5	-0.9
1968	Chi A	12	12	.353	9-9-8t	4/5	-3.4
1979	Det A e	27	26	.509	5-5	1/3	-0.5
2		39	50	.438			-4.8

MURNANE, TIM B6.4.1852

YEAR	TM/LG	W	L	PCT	FINISH	MGR/YR	+/-
1884	Bos U	58	51	.532	5		-3.6

MURRAY, BILLY William Jeremiah
B4.13.1864 Peabody, MA D3.25.1937 Youngstown, OH (DNP)

YEAR	TM/LG	W	L	PCT	FINISH	MGR/YR	+/-
1907	Phi N	83	64	.565	3		5.1
1908	Phi N	83	71	.539	4		-1.2
1909	Phi N	74	79	.484	5		-2.3
3		240	214	.529			1.7

MURTAUGH, DANNY B10.8.1917

YEAR	TM/LG	W	L	PCT	FINISH	MGR/YR	+/-
1957	Pit N	26	25	.510	7-7t	2/2	4.3
1958	Pit N	84	70	.545	2		1.3
1959	Pit N	78	76	.506	4		4.0
1960	Pit N	95	59	.617	1★		3.5
1961	Pit N	75	79	.487	6		-3.9
1962	Pit N	93	68	.578	4		4.2
1963	Pit N	74	88	.457	8		-3.9
1964	Pit N	80	82	.494	6t		-3.9
1967	Pit N	39	39	.500	6-6	2/2	0.7
1970	Pit N e	89	73	.549	1		-3.9
1971	Pit N e	97	65	.599	1★		-3.4
1973	Pit N e	13	13	.500	2-3	2/2	-0.2
1974	Pit N e	88	74	.543	1		-2.6
1975	Pit N e	92	69	.571	1		-4.2
1976	Pit N e	92	70	.568	2		2.9
15		1115	950	.540			0.2

MUSER, TONY B8.1.1947

YEAR	TM/LG	W	L	PCT	FINISH	MGR/YR	+/-
1997	KC A c	31	48	.392	4-5	2/2	-5.1
1998	KC A c	72	89	.447	3		9.0
1999	KC A c	64	97	.398	4		-10.6
2000	KC A c	77	85	.475	4		-3.6
2001	KC A c	65	97	.401	5		-3.6
2002	KC A c	8	15	.348	4-4	1/3	-1.4
6		317	431	.424			-11.1

MUTRIE, JIM James J. "Truthful Jim"
B6.13.1851 Chelsea, MA D1.24.1938 New York, NY (DNP)

YEAR	TM/LG	W	L	PCT	FINISH	MGR/YR	+/-
1883	NY AA	54	42	.563	4		-3.1
1884	NY AA	75	32	.701	1		-7.5
1885	NY N	85	27	.759	2		-2.3
1886	NY N	75	44	.630	3		2.8
1887	NY N	68	55	.553	4		-1.6
1888	NY N	84	47	.641	1★		-0.3
1889	NY N	83	43	.659	1★		0.8
1890	NY N	63	68	.481	6		-3.9
1891	NY N	71	61	.538	3		1.1
9		658	419	.611			-14.1

MYATT, GEORGE B6.14.1914

YEAR	TM/LG	W	L	PCT	FINISH	MGR/YR	+/-
1968	Phi N	1	0	1.000	6t-5-7t	2/3	0.5
1969	Phi N e	19	35	.352	5-5	2/2	-4.6
2		20	35	.364			-4.0

MYERS, HENRY B5.1858

YEAR	TM/LG	W	L	PCT	FINISH	MGR/YR	+/-
1882	Bal AA	19	54	.260	6		4.8

NARRON, JERRY B1.15.1956

YEAR	TM/LG	W	L	PCT	FINISH	MGR/YR	+/-
2001	Tex A w	62	72	.463	4-4	2/2	0.7
2002	Tex A w	72	90	.444	4-4		-5.4
2005	Cin N c	46	46	.500	5	2/2	-1.1
3		180	208	.464			-1.1

NASH, BILLY B6.24.1865

YEAR	TM/LG	W	L	PCT	FINISH	MGR/YR	+/-
1896	Phi N	62	68	.477	8		-2.9

NEUN, JOHNNY B10.28.1900

YEAR	TM/LG	W	L	PCT	FINISH	MGR/YR	+/-
1946	NY A	8	6	.571	3-3	3/3	-0.3
1947	Cin N	73	81	.474	5		3.3
1948	Cin N	44	56	.440	7-7	1/2	4.8
3		125	143	.466			-2.9

NEWMAN, JEFF B9.11.1948

YEAR	TM/LG	W	L	PCT	FINISH	MGR/YR	+/-
1986	Oak A w	2	8	.200	6t-7-3t	2/3	-2.8

NICHOLS, KID B9.14.1869

YEAR	TM/LG	W	L	PCT	FINISH	MGR/YR	+/-
1904	StL N	75	79	.487	5		-2.8
1905	StL N	5	9	.357	7-6	1/3	-0.1
2		80	88	.476			-2.9

NICOL, HUGH B1.1.1858

YEAR	TM/LG	W	L	PCT	FINISH	MGR/YR	+/-
1897	StL N	8	32	.200	12-12-12	2/4	0.8

NIXON, RUSS B2.19.1935

YEAR	TM/LG	W	L	PCT	FINISH	MGR/YR	+/-
1982	Cin N w	27	43	.386	6-6	2/2	-2.5
1983	Cin N w	74	88	.457	6		2.1
1988	Atl N w	42	79	.347	6-6	2/2	-3.7
1989	Atl N w	63	97	.394	6		-6.7
1990	Atl N w	25	40	.385	6-6	1/2	-2.0
5		231	347	.400			-12.8

NORMAN, BILL B7.16.1910

YEAR	TM/LG	W	L	PCT	FINISH	MGR/YR	+/-
1958	Det A	56	49	.533	8-5	2/2	-0.3
1959	Det A	2	15	.118	8-4	1/2	-6.3
2		58	64	.475			

OAKES, REBEL B12.17.1883

YEAR	TM/LG	W	L	PCT	FINISH	MGR/YR	+/-
1914	Pit F	61	78	.439	8-7	2/2	0.4
1915	Pit F	86	67	.562	3		1.9
2		147	145	.503			2.3

OATES, JOHNNY B1.21.1946

YEAR	TM/LG	W	L	PCT	FINISH	MGR/YR	+/-
1991	Bal A e	54	71	.432	7-6	2/2	-0.1
1992	Bal A e	89	73	.549	3		2.9
1993	Bal A e	85	77	.525	3t		-0.0
1994	Bal A e	63	49	.563	2		-1.9

YEAR	TM/LG	W	L	PCT	FINISH	MGR/YR	+/-
1995	Tex A w	74	70	.514	3		4.8
1996	Tex A w	90	72	.556	1		-2.9
1997	Tex A w	77	85	.475	3		-2.5
1998	Tex A w	88	74	.543	1		0.8
1999	Tex A w	95	67	.586	1		6.3
2000	Tex A w	71	91	.438	4		1.3
2001	Tex A w	11	17	.393	4	1/2	-1.8
11		797	746	.517			6.9

O'CONNOR, JACK B6.2.1869

YEAR	TM/LG	W	L	PCT	FINISH	MGR/YR	+/-
1910	StL A	47	107	.305	8		1.9

O'DAY, HANK B7.8.1862

1912	Cin N	75	78	.490	4		5.1
1914	Chi N	78	76	.506	4		4.5
2		153	154	.498			9.6

O'FARRELL, BOB B10.19.1896

1927	StL N	92	61	.601	2		6.7
1934	Cin N	30	60	.333	8-8	1/3	-2.5
2		122	121	.502			4.2

O'LEARY, DAN B10.22.1856

1884	Cin U	20	15	.571	5-3	1/2	-4.6

O'NEILL, STEVE B7.6.1891

1935	Cle A	36	23	.610	5-3	2/2	5.1
1936	Cle A	80	74	.519	5		-2.3
1937	Cle A	83	71	.539	4		1.4
1943	Det A	78	76	.506	5		-6.8
1944	Det A	88	66	.571	2		2.8
1945	Det A	88	65	.575	1★		4.2
1946	Det A	92	62	.597	2		0.6
1947	Det A	85	69	.552	2		0.6
1948	Det A	78	76	.506	5		3.6
1950	Bos A	63	32	.663	4-3	2/2	3.5
1951	Bos A	87	67	.565	3		2.5
1952	Phi N	59	32	.648	6-4	2/2	6.9
1953	Phi N	83	71	.539	3t		1.0
1954	Phi N	40	37	.519	3-4	1/2	-0.8
14		1040	821	.559			22.2

ONSLOW, JACK B10.13.1888

1949	Chi A	63	91	.409	6		-5.1
1950	Chi A	8	22	.267	8-6	1/2	-4.6
2		71	113	.386			-9.7

O'ROURKE, JIM B9.1.1850

1881	Buf N	45	38	.542	3		4.1
1882	Buf N	45	39	.536	3t		-0.5
1883	Buf N	52	45	.536	5		0.2
1884	Buf N	64	47	.577	3		2.0
1893	Was N	40	89	.310	12		0.8
5		246	258	.488			6.7

ORR, DAVE B9.29.1859

1887	NY AA	3	5	.375	8-7-7	2/3	0.7

OTT, MEL B3.2.1909

1942	NY N	85	67	.559	3		1.2
1943	NY N	55	98	.359	8		-5.2
1944	NY N	67	87	.435	5		-1.1
1945	NY N	78	74	.513	5		5.3
1946	NY N	61	93	.396	8		-8.5
1947	NY N	81	73	.526	4		-2.5
1948	NY N	37	38	.493	4-5	1/2	-4.1
7		464	530	.467			-14.8

OWENS, PAUL Paul Francis B2.7.1924 Salamanca, NY
D12.26.2003 Woodbury, NJ BR/TR/6-3/185(1B)

1972	Phi N e	33	47	.412	6-6	2/2	0.5
1983	Phi N e	47	30	.610	1-1◆	2/2	5.5
1984	Phi N e	81	81	.500	4		-3.1
3		161	158	.505			2.9

OZARK, DANNY Daniel Leonard
(b Daniel Leonard Orzechowski)
B11.26.1923 Buffalo, NY BR/TR/6-3/210(1B)

1973	Phi N e	71	91	.438	6		-2.2
1974	Phi N e	80	82	.494	3		1.6
1975	Phi N e	86	76	.531	2		0.9
1976	Phi N e	101	61	.623	1		-2.3
1977	Phi N e	101	61	.623	1		2.4
1978	Phi N e	90	72	.556	1		-4.0
1979	Phi N e	65	67	.492	5-4	1/2	1.9
1984	SF N w	24	32	.429	6-6	2/2	0.3
8		618	542	.533			-1.4

PABOR, CHARLIE B9.24.1846

1871	Cle N	10	19	.345	7		1.6
1875	Atl NA	2	40	.048	12-12	1/2	5.3
1875	NH NA	1	5	.167	8-8	3/3	0.5
2		13	64	.169			7.5

PARKER, SALTY B7.8.1912

1967	NY N	4	7	.364	10-10	2/2	-0.2
1972	Hou N w	1	0	1.000	2-2	2/3	0.5
2		5	7	.417			0.3

PARKS, BILL B6.4.1849

1875	Was NA	1	7	.125	8-10	2/2	2.0

PARRISH, LARRY B11.10.1953

1998	Det A c	13	12	.520	5-5	2/2	2.6
1999	Det A c	69	92	.429	3		1.2
2		82	104	.441			3.8

PEARCE, DICKEY B2.29.1836

1872	Mut NA	10	6	.625	4-3	1/2	-1.6
1875	StL NA	39	29	.574			3.4
2		49	35	.583			1.8

PECKINPAUGH, ROGER B2.5.1891

1914	NY A	10	10	.500	7-6t	2/2	0.2
1928	Cle A	62	92	.403	7		0.0
1929	Cle A	81	71	.533	3		6.8
1930	Cle A	81	73	.526	4		6.2
1931	Cle A	78	76	.506	4		-3.7
1932	Cle A	87	65	.572	4		1.9
1933	Cle A	26	25	.510	4	1/3	1.0
1941	Cle A	75	79	.487	4t		-2.9
8		500	491	.505			9.5

PEDRIQUE, AL B8.11.1960

2004	Ari N w	22	61	.265	5-5	1/2	-5.2

PENA, TONY B6.4.1957

2002	KC A c	49	77	.389	4-4	3/3	-2.7
2003	KC A c	83	79	.512	3		4.9
2004	KC A c	58	104	.358	5		-5.5
2005	KC A c	8	25	.242	5-5	1/3	-4.0
4		198	285	.410			-7.3

PEREZ, TONY B5.14.1942

1993	Cin N w	20	24	.455	5-5	1/2	-0.3
2001	Fla N e	54	60	.474	3-4	2/2	-2.9
2		74	84	.468			-3.2

PERKINS, CY B2.27.1896

1937	Det A	6	9	.400	2-2	5/5	-2.3

PERLOZZO, SAM B3.4.1951

2005	Bal A e	23	32	.418	4-4	2/2	-2.1

PESKY, JOHNNY B9.27.1919

1963	Bos A	76	85	.472	7		-0.6
1964	Bos A	70	90	.438	8-8	1/2	0.3
1980	Bos A e	1	4	.200	3-4	2/2	-1.5
3		147	179	.451			-1.8

PFEFFER, FRED B3.17.1860

1892-1	Lou N	9	14	.391	10-11	2/2	-0.2
1892-2	Lou N	33	42	.440	9		2.1

PHELAN, LOU Louis A.
B3.1864 St.Louis, MO D11.2.1933 Los Angeles, CA (DNP)

1895	StL N	11	30	.268	11-11	4/4	-2.1

PHILLIPS, LEFTY Harold Ross
B6.16.1919 Los Angeles, CA
D6.12.1972 Fullerton, CA BL/TL/5-11/192(P)

1969	Cal A w	60	63	.488	6-3	2/2	9.0
1970	Cal A w	86	76	.531	3		4.9
1971	Cal A w	76	86	.469	4		2.5
3		222	225	.497			16.4

PHILLIPS, HORACE Horace B.
B5.14.1853 Salem, OH (DNP)

1879	Tro N	12	34	.261	8-8	1/2	1.2
1883	Col AA	32	65	.330	6		-0.4
1884	Pit AA	9	24	.273	10-10	5/5	1.6
1885	Pit AA	56	55	.505	3		-0.3
1886	Pit AA	80	57	.584	2		-3.7
1887	Pit N	55	69	.444	6		4.7
1888	Pit N	66	68	.493	6		3.9
1889	Pit N	28	43	.394	6-5	1/3	-3.9
8		338	415	.449			3.1

PHILLIPS, BILL B11.9.1868

1914	Ind N	88	65	.575	1		-2.6
1915	New F	26	27	.491	6-5	1/2	-1.4
2		114	92	.553			-4.0

PIKE, LIP B5.25.1845

1871	Tro NA	1	3	.250	7-6	1/2	-0.9
1874	Har NA	16	37	.302	7		-3.0
1877	Cin N	3	11	.214	6-6	1/3	-0.1
3		20	51	.282			-4.0

PINIELLA, LOU B8.28.1943

1986	NY A e	90	72	.556	2		3.2
1987	NY A e	89	73	.549	4		5.1
1988	NY A e	45	48	.484	2-5	2/2	-2.9
1990	Cin N w	91	71	.562	1★		-0.2
1991	Cin N w	74	88	.457	5		-6.8
1992	Cin N w	90	72	.556	2		3.5
1993	Sea A w	82	80	.506	4		0.7
1994	Sea A w	49	63	.438	3		-2.7
1995	Sea A w	79	66	.545	1☆▲		-1.7
1996	Sea A w	85	76	.528	2		-4.1
1997	Sea A w	90	72	.556	1		0.6
1998	Sea A w	76	85	.472	3		-4.9
1999	Sea A w	79	83	.488	3		2.2
2000	Sea A w	91	71	.562	2☆✿		-1.8
2001	Sea A w	116	46	.716	1☆		5.9
2002	Sea A w	93	69	.574	3		0.7
2003	TB A e	63	99	.389	5		-4.8
2004	TB A e	70	91	.435	4		1.9
2005	TB A e	67	95	.414	5		3.3
19		1519	1420	.517			-2.6

PLUMMER, BILL B3.21.1947

1992	Sea A w	64	98	.395	7		-5.1

POPOWSKI, EDDIE Edward Joseph
B8.20.1913 Sayreville, NJ
D12.4.2001 Sayreville, NJ BR/TR/5-4.5/145(2B)

1969	Bos A e	5	4	.556	3-3	2/2	0.5
1973	Bos A e	1	0	1.000	2-2	2/2	0.4
2		6	4	.600			0.9

PORTER, MATTHEW B

1884	KC U	3	13	.188	8-8-8	2/3	0.5

POWERS, PAT Patrick Thomas
B6.27.1860 Trenton, NJ D8.29.1925 Belmar, NJ (DNP)

1890	Roc AA	63	63	.500	5		0.2
1892-1	NY N	31	43	.419	10		-3.1
1892-2	NY N	40	37	.519	6		-3.1
2		134	143	.484			-6.1

PRATT, AL B11.19.1848

1882	Pit AA	39	39	.500	4		-0.9
1883	Pit AA	12	20	.375	6-7	1/3	1.6
2		51	59	.464			0.6

PRICE, JIM James Lyman
B9.20.1847 New York, NY D10.24.1925 Oak Park, IL (DNP)

1884	NY N	56	42	.571	4-4t	1/2	1.5

PROTHRO, DOC B7.16.1893

1939	Phi N	45	106	.298	8		-0.6
1940	Phi N	50	103	.327	8		0.4
1941	Phi N	43	111	.279	8		-3.7
3		138	320	.301			-3.9

PUJOLS, LUIS B11.18.1955

2002	Det A c	55	100	.355	5-5	2/2	5.4

PURCELL, BLONDIE B

1883	Phi N	13	68	.160	8-8	2/2	3.0

QUEEN, MEL B3.26.1942

1997	Tor A e	4	1	.800	5-5	2/2	1.6

QUILICI, FRANK B5.11.1939

1972	Min A w	41	43	.488	3-3	2/2	-1.1
1973	Min A w	81	81	.500	3		-4.6
1974	Min A w	82	80	.506	3		0.6
1975	Min A w	76	83	.478	4		-2.3
4		280	287	.494			-7.5

QUINN, JOE B12.25.1864

1895	StL N	11	28	.282	11-11-11	3/4	-1.5
1899	Cle N	12	104	.103	12-12	2/2	2.0
2		23	132	.148			0.5

RADER, DOUG B7.30.1944

1983	Tex A w	77	85	.475	3		-7.3
1984	Tex A w	69	92	.429	7		-5.5
1985	Tex A w	9	23	.281	7-7	1/2	-3.6
1986	Chi A w	1	1	.500	6-5-5	2/3	0.1
1989	Cal A w	91	71	.562	3		0.2
1990	Cal A w	80	82	.494	4		0.6
1991	Cal A w	61	63	.492	7-7	1/2	-1.3
7		388	417	.482			-16.9

RANDOLPH, WILLIE B7.6.1954

2005	NY N e	83	79	.512	3t		-5.6

RAPP, VERN Vernon Fred
B5.11.1928 St.Louis, MO BR/TR/6-0/195(C)

1977	StL N e	83	79	.512	3		-3.0
1978	StL N e	6	11	.353	6-5	1/3	-1.9
1984	Cin N w	51	70	.421	5-5	1/2	-0.3
3		140	160	.467			-5.1

REACH, AL B5.25.1840

1890	Phi N	4	7	.364	2-3-3	3/5	-2.4

REGAN, PHIL B4.6.1937

1995	Bal A e	71	73	.493	3		-7.3

RICE, DEL B10.27.1922

1972	Cal A w	75	80	.484	5		6.9

RICHARDS, PAUL B11.21.1908

1951	Chi A	81	73	.526	4		-3.1
1952	Chi A	81	73	.526	3		-0.6
1953	Chi A	89	65	.578	3		-0.8
1954	Chi A	91	54	.628	3-3	1/2	-0.5
1955	Bal A	57	97	.370	7		2.3
1956	Bal A	69	85	.448	6		6.0
1957	Bal A	76	76	.500	5		-1.0
1958	Bal A	74	79	.484	6		3.6
1959	Bal A	74	80	.481	6		4.6
1960	Bal A	89	65	.578	2		4.1
1961	Bal A	78	57	.578	3-3	1/2	1.3
1976	Chi A w	64	97	.398	6		0.1
12		923	901	.506			15.9

RICHARDSON, DANNY B1.25.1863

1892-2	Was N	12	31	.279	11-12	2/2	-5.9

RICKEY, BRANCH B12.20.1881

YEAR	TM/LG	W	L	PCT	FINISH	MGR/YR	+/-
1913	StL A	5	6	.455	7-8	3/3	0.4
1914	StL A	71	82	.464	5		4.8
1915	StL A	63	91	.409	6		3.2
1919	StL N	54	83	.394	7		-4.7
1920	StL N	75	79	.487	5t		-1.3
1921	StL N	87	66	.569	3		-1.8
1922	StL N	85	69	.552	3t		4.0
1923	StL N	79	74	.516	5		1.1
1924	StL N	65	89	.422	6		-11.0
1925	StL N	13	25	.342	8-4	1/2	-7.5
	10	597	664	.473			-12.7

RIDDOCH, GREG Gregory Lee
B7.17.1945 Greeley, CO BR/TR/5-11/175(SS)

YEAR	TM/LG	W	L	PCT	FINISH	MGR/YR	+/-
1990	SD N w	38	44	.463	4-5	2/2	-3.0
1991	SD N w	84	78	.519	3		4.1
1992	SD N w	78	72	.520	3-3	1/2	4.9
	3	200	194	.508			6.0

RIGGLEMAN, JIM James David
B11.9.1952 Fort Dix, NJ BR/TR/5-11/175(3B)

YEAR	TM/LG	W	L	PCT	FINISH	MGR/YR	+/-
1992	SD N w	4	8	.333	3-3	2/2	-1.8
1993	SD N w	61	101	.377	7		-10.7
1994	SD N w	47	70	.402	4		-6.2
1995	Chi N c	73	71	.507	3		-1.1
1996	Chi N c	76	86	.469	4		-5.1
1997	Chi N c	68	94	.420	5		-5.8
1998	Chi N c	90	73	.552	2✣▲		4.8
1999	Chi N c	67	95	.414	6		2.2
	8	486	598	.448			-23.8

RIGNEY, BILL B1.29.1918

YEAR	TM/LG	W	L	PCT	FINISH	MGR/YR	+/-
1956	NY N	67	87	.435	6		1.9
1957	NY N	69	85	.448	6		-2.1
1958	SF N	80	74	.519	3		0.1
1959	SF N	83	71	.539	3		-3.4
1960	SF N	33	25	.569	2-5	1/2	2.4
1961	LA A	70	91	.435	8		-6.6
1962	LA A	86	76	.531	3		3.8
1963	LA A	70	91	.435	9		-3.7
1964	LA A	82	80	.506	5		1.8
1965	Cal A	75	87	.463	7		-1.2
1966	Cal A	80	82	.494	6		3.2
1967	Cal A	84	77	.522	5		5.7
1968	Cal A	67	95	.414	8		-0.6
1969	Cal A w	11	28	.282	6-3	1/2	-5.2
1970	Min A w	98	64	.605	1		2.5
1971	Min A w	74	86	.463	5		-4.3
1972	Min A w	36	34	.514	3-3	1/2	0.9
1976	SF N w	74	88	.457	4		2.7
	18	1239	1321	.484			-2.0

RIPKEN, CAL Calvin Edwin Sr. B12.17.1935 Aberdeen, MD
D3.25.1999 Baltimore, MD BR/TR/6-0/175(C)

YEAR	TM/LG	W	L	PCT	FINISH	MGR/YR	+/-
1985	Bal A e	1	0	1.000	4-4-4	2/3	0.5
1987	Bal A e	67	95	.414	6		0.4
1988	Bal A e	0	6	.000	7-7	1/2	-2.1
	3	68	101	.402			-1.2

ROBINSON, FRANK B8.31.1935

YEAR	TM/LG	W	L	PCT	FINISH	MGR/YR	+/-
1975	Cle A	79	80	.497	4		1.0
1976	Cle A	81	78	.509	4		1.5
1977	Cle A	26	31	.456	5-5	1/2	-0.2
1981-1	SF N w	27	32	.458	5		-0.9
1981-2	SF N w	29	23	.558	3		-0.9
1982	SF N w	87	75	.537	3		7.4
1983	SF N w	79	83	.488	5		-1.0
1984	SF N w	42	64	.396	6-6	1/2	-2.9
1988	Bal A e	54	101	.348	7-7	2/2	0.4
1989	Bal A e	87	75	.537	2		3.7
1990	Bal A e	76	85	.472	5		-1.5
1991	Bal A e	13	24	.351	7-6	1/2	-3.0
2002	Mon N e	83	79	.512	2		0.3
2003	Mon N e	83	79	.512	4		2.5
2004	Mon N e	67	95	.414	5		-0.3
	15	994	1085	.478			6.1

ROBINSON, WILBERT B6.29.1863

YEAR	TM/LG	W	L	PCT	FINISH	MGR/YR	+/-
1902	Bal A	24	57	.296	7-8	2/2	-9.5
1914	Bro N	75	79	.487	5		-2.4
1915	Bro N	80	72	.526	3		6.7
1916	Bro N	94	60	.610	1		3.9
1917	Bro N	70	81	.464	7		-0.0
1918	Bro N	57	69	.452	5		6.1
1919	Bro N	69	71	.493	5		-2.3
1920	Bro N	93	61	.604	1		1.7
1921	Bro N	77	75	.507	5		2.4
1922	Bro N	76	78	.494	6		0.1
1923	Bro N	76	78	.494	6		-2.1
1924	Bro N	92	62	.597	2		11.2
1925	Bro N	68	85	.444	6t		-1.2
1926	Bro N	71	82	.464	6		2.9
1927	Bro N	65	88	.425	6		-3.0
1928	Bro N	77	76	.503	6		-2.1
1929	Bro N	70	83	.458	6		5.7
1930	Bro N	86	68	.558	4		-3.3
1931	Bro N	79	73	.520	4		2.2
	19	1399	1398	.500			16.8

ROBISON, STAN Matthew Stanley
B3.30.1859 Pittsburgh, PA D3.24.1911 Cleveland, OH (DNP)

YEAR	TM/LG	W	L	PCT	FINISH	MGR/YR	+/-
1905	StL N	19	31	.380	6-6	3/3	0.8

RODGERS, BUCK B8.16.1938

YEAR	TM/LG	W	L	PCT	FINISH	MGR/YR	+/-
1980	Mil A e	26	21	.553	2-3	1/3	-1.2
1980	Mil A e	13	10	.565	4-3	3/3	-0.3
1981-1	Mil A e	31	25	.554	3		4.0
1981-2	Mil A e	31	22	.585	1		4.0
1982	Mil A e	23	24	.489	5-1◆	1/2	-5.3
1985	Mon N e	84	77	.522	3		3.8
1986	Mon N e	78	83	.484	4		2.8
1987	Mon N e	91	71	.562	3		7.9
1988	Mon N e	81	81	.500	3		-3.9
1989	Mon N e	81	81	.500	4		-0.2
1990	Mon N e	85	77	.525	3		-2.9
1991	Mon N e	20	29	.408	6-6	1/2	-2.0
1991	Cal A w	20	18	.526	7-7	2/2	0.9
1992	Cal A w	19	20	.487	5-5t	1/3	1.9
1992	Cal A w	14	20	.412	5-5t	3/3	-0.9
1993	Cal A w	71	91	.438	5t		-1.4
1994	Cal A w	16	23	.410	3-4	1/3	0.2
	13	784	773	.504			7.5

ROGERS, JIM B4.9.1872

YEAR	TM/LG	W	L	PCT	FINISH	MGR/YR	+/-
1897	Lou N	17	24	.415	9-11	1/2	1.9

ROJAS, COOKIE B3.6.1939

YEAR	TM/LG	W	L	PCT	FINISH	MGR/YR	+/-
1988	Cal A w	75	79	.487	4-4	1/2	3.4
1996	Fla N e	1	0	1.000	4-4-3	2/3	0.5
	2	76	79	.490			3.9

ROLFE, RED B10.17.1908

YEAR	TM/LG	W	L	PCT	FINISH	MGR/YR	+/-
1949	Det A	87	67	.565	4		0.4
1950	Det A	95	59	.617	2		6.2
1951	Det A	73	81	.474	5		1.5
1952	Det A	23	49	.319	8-8	1/2	-4.2
	4	278	256	.521			3.9

ROSE, PETE B4.14.1941

YEAR	TM/LG	W	L	PCT	FINISH	MGR/YR	+/-
1984	Cin N	19	22	.463	5-5	2/2	1.6
1985	Cin N	89	72	.553	2		7.4
1986	Cin N	86	76	.531	2		3.5
1987	Cin N w	84	78	.519	2		-0.0
1988	Cin N w	11	12	.478	4-2	1/3	-1.2
1988	Cin N w	64	47	.577	4-2	3/3	5.1
1989	Cin N w	59	66	.472	4t-5	1/2	1.3
	6	412	373	.525			17.7

ROSEMAN, CHIEF B1856

YEAR	TM/LG	W	L	PCT	FINISH	MGR/YR	+/-
1890	StL AA	7	8	.467	4-5-3	3/6	-1.8

ROTHSCHILD, LARRY B3.12.1954

YEAR	TM/LG	W	L	PCT	FINISH	MGR/YR	+/-
1998	TB A e	63	99	.389	5		-4.5
1999	TB A e	69	93	.426	5		1.1
2000	TB A e	69	92	.429	5		-1.0
2001	TB A e	4	10	.286	5-5	1/2	-1.2
	4	205	294	.411			-5.6

ROWE, DAVE B10.9.1854

YEAR	TM/LG	W	L	PCT	FINISH	MGR/YR	+/-
1886	KC N	30	91	.248	7		3.9
1888	KC AA	14	36	.280	8-8	1/3	-0.2
	2	44	127	.257			3.7

ROWE, JACK B12.8.1856

YEAR	TM/LG	W	L	PCT	FINISH	MGR/YR	+/-
1890	Buf P	22	58	.275	8-8	1/3	1.1
1890	Buf P	5	14	.263	8-8	3/3	0.0

ROWLAND, PANTS Clarence Henry
B2.12.1879 Platteville, WI D5.17.1969 Chicago, IL BR/TR/5-9/168(C)

YEAR	TM/LG	W	L	PCT	FINISH	MGR/YR	+/-
1915	Chi A	93	61	.604	3		-6.2
1916	Chi A	89	65	.578	2		0.3
1917	Chi A	100	54	.649	1★		1.5
1918	Chi A	57	67	.460	6		-6.2
	4	339	247	.578			-10.7

ROYSTER, JERRY B10.18.1952

YEAR	TM/LG	W	L	PCT	FINISH	MGR/YR	+/-
2002	Mil N c	53	94	.361	6-6	2/2	-2.8

RUDOLPH, DICK B8.25.1887

YEAR	TM/LG	W	L	PCT	FINISH	MGR/YR	+/-
1924	Bos N	11	27	.289	6-8-8	2/3	-0.9

RUEL, MUDDY B2.20.1896

YEAR	TM/LG	W	L	PCT	FINISH	MGR/YR	+/-
1947	StL A	59	95	.383	8		0.5

RUNNELLS, TOM B4.17.1955

YEAR	TM/LG	W	L	PCT	FINISH	MGR/YR	+/-
1991	Mon N e	51	61	.455	6-6	2/2	0.7
1992	Mon N e	17	20	.459	4-2	1/2	-3.2
	2	68	81	.456			-2.4

RUNNELS, PETE B1.28.1928

YEAR	TM/LG	W	L	PCT	FINISH	MGR/YR	+/-
1966	Bos A	8	8	.500	9-9	2/2	0.8

RUSSELL, BILL B10.21.1948

YEAR	TM/LG	W	L	PCT	FINISH	MGR/YR	+/-
1996	LA N w	49	37	.570	1-2✣		3.2
1997	LA N w	88	74	.543	2		-2.9
1998	LA N w	36	38	.486	3-3	1/2	-0.6
	3	173	149	.537			-0.3

RYAN, CONNIE B2.27.1920

YEAR	TM/LG	W	L	PCT	FINISH	MGR/YR	+/-
1975	Atl N w	9	18	.333	5-5	2/2	-1.8
1977	Tex A w	2	4	.333	3-5-2	3/4	-1.4
	2	11	22	.333			-3.2

SAWYER, EDDIE Edwin Milby B9.10.1910 Westerly, RI
D9.22.1997 Phoenixville, PA BR/TR/6-0/210(OF)

YEAR	TM/LG	W	L	PCT	FINISH	MGR/YR	+/-
1948	Phi N	23	40	.365	6-6	3/3	-2.7
1949	Phi N	81	73	.526	3		4.6
1950	Phi N	91	63	.591	1		4.0
1951	Phi N	73	81	.474	5		-4.4
1952	Phi N	28	35	.444	6-4	1/2	-8.1
1958	Phi N	30	40	.429	8-8	2/2	-0.6
1959	Phi N	64	90	.416	8		-0.1
1960	Phi N	0	1	.000	6t-8	1/3	-0.4
	8	390	423	.480			-7.8

SCANLON, MIKE Michael B.
B11.1843 Cork, Ireland D1.18.1929 Washington, DC (DNP)

YEAR	TM/LG	W	L	PCT	FINISH	MGR/YR	+/-
1884	Was U	47	65	.420	6		0.7
1886	Was N	13	67	.162	8-8	1/2	-5.0
	2	60	132	.313			-4.3

SCHAEFER, BOB Robert Walden
B5.22.1944 Putnam, CT BL/TR/5-11/180(SS)

YEAR	TM/LG	W	L	PCT	FINISH	MGR/YR	+/-
1991	KC A w	1	0	1.000	7-7-6	2/3	0.5
2005	KC A c	5	12	.294	5-5-5	2/3	-1.2
	2	6	12	.333			-0.7

SCHALK, RAY B8.12.1892

YEAR	TM/LG	W	L	PCT	FINISH	MGR/YR	+/-
1927	Chi A	70	83	.458	5		-1.9
1928	Chi A	32	42	.432	6-5	1/2	-1.7
	2	102	125	.449			-3.6

SCHEFFING, BOB B8.11.1913

YEAR	TM/LG	W	L	PCT	FINISH	MGR/YR	+/-
1957	Chi N	62	92	.403	7t		-5.4
1958	Chi N	72	82	.468	5t		-3.4
1959	Chi N	74	80	.481	5t		-1.5
1961	Det A	101	61	.623	2		3.3
1962	Det A	85	76	.528	4		-2.1
1963	Det A	24	36	.400	9-5t	1/2	-5.9
	4	418	427	.495			-15.1

SCHLAFLY, LARRY B9.19.1878

YEAR	TM/LG	W	L	PCT	FINISH	MGR/YR	+/-
1914	Buf F	80	71	.530	4		2.6
1915	Buf F	13	28	.317	8-6	1/3	-5.8
	2	93	99	.484			-3.2

SCHMELZ, GUS Gustavius Heinrich
B9.26.1850 Columbus, OH D10.13.1925 Columbus, OH (DNP)

YEAR	TM/LG	W	L	PCT	FINISH	MGR/YR	+/-
1884	Col AA	69	39	.639	2		2.7
1886	StL N	43	79	.352	6		-2.3
1887	Cin AA	81	54	.600	2		0.8
1888	Cin AA	80	54	.597	4		1.9
1889	Cin AA	76	63	.547	4		-4.7
1890	Cle N	21	55	.276	7-7	1/2	-6.4
1890	Col AA	38	13	.745	5-2	2/3	4.9
1891	Col AA	61	70	.445	6		-0.6
1894	Was N	45	87	.341	11		-2.5
1895	Was N	43	85	.336	10		-4.1
1896	Was N	58	73	.443	9t		1.0
1897	Was N	9	25	.265	11-6t	1/2	-7.7
	11	624	703	.470			-17.1

SCHOENDIENST, RED B2.2.1923

YEAR	TM/LG	W	L	PCT	FINISH	MGR/YR	+/-
1965	StL N	80	81	.497	7		-3.9
1966	StL N	83	79	.512	6		2.7
1967	StL N	101	60	.627	1★		5.7
1968	StL N	97	65	.599	1		2.9
1969	StL N e	87	75	.537	4		-0.2
1970	StL N e	76	86	.469	4		-4.7
1971	StL N e	90	72	.556	2		5.0
1972	StL N e	75	81	.481	4		0.5
1973	StL N e	81	81	.500	2		-4.3
1974	StL N e	86	75	.534	2		1.9
1975	StL N e	82	80	.506	3t		3.8
1976	StL N e	72	90	.444	5		-4.6
1980	StL N e	18	19	.486	5-4	4/4	-1.1
1990	StL N e	13	11	.542	6-6-6	2/3	2.6
	14	1041	955	.522			6.2

SCHULTZ, JOE B8.29.1918

YEAR	TM/LG	W	L	PCT	FINISH	MGR/YR	+/-
1969	Sea A w	64	98	.395	6		-0.8
1973	Det A e	14	14	.500	3-3	2/2	0.6
	2	78	112	.411			-0.3

SCIOSCIA, MIKE B11.27.1958

YEAR	TM/LG	W	L	PCT	FINISH	MGR/YR	+/-
2000	Ana A w	82	80	.506	3		1.5
2001	Ana A w	75	87	.463	3		-2.0
2002	Ana A w	99	63	.611	2★✣		-2.4
2003	Ana A w	77	85	.475	3		-3.3
2004	Ana A w	92	70	.568	1		1.2
2005	LA A w	95	67	.586	1☆		2.0
	6	520	452	.535			-3.2

SELEE, FRANK Frank Gibson
B10.26.1859 Amherst, NY D7.5.1909 Denver, CO (DNP)

YEAR	TM/LG	W	L	PCT	FINISH	MGR/YR	+/-
1890	Bos N	76	57	.571	5		-6.5
1891	Bos N	87	51	.630	1		0.7
1892-1	Bos N	52	22	.703	1		6.7
1892-2	Bos N	50	26	.658	2●		6.7
1893	Bos N	86	43	.667	1		4.3
1894	Bos N	83	49	.629	3		1.0
1895	Bos N	71	60	.542	5t		-1.3
1896	Bos N	74	57	.565	4		-0.4
1897	Bos N	93	39	.705	1		-3.5

YEAR	TM/LG	W	L	PCT	FINISH	MGR/YR	+/-
1898	Bos N	102	47	.685	1		2.7
1899	Bos N	95	57	.625	2		-1.4
1900	Bos N	66	72	.478	4		-6.6
1901	Bos N	69	69	.500	5		2.7
1902	Chi N	68	69	.496	5		-4.8
1903	Chi N	82	56	.594	3		3.6
1904	Chi N	93	60	.608	2		7.5
1905	Chi N	37	28	.569	4-3	1/2	-6.2
16		1284	862	.598			5.2
SEWELL, LUKE	B1.5.1901						
1941	StL A	55	55	.500	7-6t	2/2	3.9
1942	StL A	82	69	.543	3		-2.8
1943	StL A	72	80	.474	6		-3.1
1944	StL A	89	65	.578	1		1.9
1945	StL A	81	70	.536	3		0.1
1946	StL A	53	71	.427	7-7	1/2	-1.6
1949	Cin N	1	2	.333	7-7	2/2	-0.2
1950	Cin N	66	87	.431	6		-2.5
1951	Cin N	68	86	.442	6		2.5
1952	Cin N	39	59	.398	7-6	1/3	-7.1
10		606	644	.485			-9.0
SHANNON, DAN	B3.23.1865						
1889	Lou AA	10	46	.179	8-8-8	3/4	-2.1
1891	Was AA	15	34	.306	7-8-8	3/4	2.0
2		25	80	.238			-0.1
SHARSIG, BILL	William A.						
B1855 Philadelphia, PA D2.1.1902 Philadelphia, PA (DNP)							
1886	Phi AA	22	17	.564	6-6	2/2	6.7
1888	Phi AA	81	52	.609	3		-7.1
1889	Phi AA	75	58	.564	3		0.5
1890	Phi AA	54	78	.409	7		8.6
1891	Phi AA	6	11	.353	7-4	1/2	-2.8
5		238	216	.524			5.9
SHAWKEY, BOB	B12.4.1890						
1930	NY A	86	68	.558	3		-4.8
SHEEHAN, TOM	B3.31.1894						
1960	SF N	46	50	.479	2-5	2/2	-4.6
SHEPARD, LARRY	Lawrence William						
B4.3.1919 Lakewood, OH BR/TR/5-11/180(P)							
1968	Pit N	80	82	.494	6		-6.9
1969	Pit N e	84	73	.535	3-3	1/2	-1.8
2		164	155	.514			-8.6
SHERRY, NORM	B7.16.1931						
1976	Cal A w	37	29	.561	6-4t	2/2	7.7
1977	Cal A w	39	42	.481	5-5		-0.5
2		76	71	.517			7.2
SHETTSLINE, BILL	William Joseph						
B10.25.1863 Philadelphia, PA D2.22.1933 Philadelphia, PA (DNP)							
1898	Phi N	59	44	.573	8t-6	2/2	5.0
1899	Phi N	94	58	.618	3		2.2
1900	Phi N	75	63	.543	3		4.4
1901	Phi N	83	57	.593	2		0.2
1902	Phi N	56	81	.409	7		4.8
5		367	303	.548			16.6
SHOTTON, BURT	B10.18.1884						
1928	Phi N	43	109	.283	8		-5.7
1929	Phi N	71	82	.464	5		5.9
1930	Phi N	52	102	.338	8		-4.4
1931	Phi N	66	88	.429	6		2.8
1932	Phi N	78	76	.506	4		-3.4
1933	Phi N	60	92	.395	7		-0.7
1934	Phi N	1	0	1.000	8-8-8	2/3	6.3
1947	Bro N	92	60	.605	1t-1	2/2	5.6
1948	Bro N	48	33	.593	5-3	3/3	3.6
1949	Bro N	97	57	.630	1		-1.8
1950	Bro N	89	65	.578	2		0.4
11		697	764	.477			3.0
SHOWALTER, BUCK	William Nathaniel						
B5.23.1956 DeFuniak Springs, FL BL/TL/5-9/195(1B)							
1992	NY A e	76	86	.469	4t		-3.7
1993	NY A e	88	74	.543	2		1.2
1994	NY A e	70	43	.619	1		1.0
1995	NY A e	79	65	.549	2✣		1.2
1998	Ari N w	65	97	.401	5		-1.4
1999	Ari N w	100	62	.617	1		-3.3
2000	Ari N w	85	77	.525	3		0.3
2003	Tex A w	71	91	.438	4		2.9
2004	Tex A w	89	73	.549	3		1.8
2005	Tex A w	79	83	.488	3		-2.6
10		802	751	.516			-2.6
SILVESTRI, KEN	B5.3.1916						
1967	Atl N	0	3	.000	7-7	2/2	-1.5
SIMMONS, JOE	B6.13.1845						
1875	Wes NA	1	12	.077	13		-1.5
1884	Wil U	2	16	.111	8		1.2
2		3	28	.097			-0.2
SIMMONS, LEW	Lewis						
B8.27.1838 New Castle, PA D9.2.1911 Jamestown, PA (DNP)							
1886	Phi AA	41	55	.427	6-6	1/2	3.3

YEAR	TM/LG	W	L	PCT	FINISH	MGR/YR	+/-
SISLER, GEORGE	B3.24.1893						
1924	StL A	74	78	.487	4		1.6
1925	StL A	82	71	.536	3		6.0
1926	StL A	62	92	.403	7		0.6
3		218	241	.475			8.2
SISLER, DICK	B11.2.1920						
1964	Cin N	3	3	.500	3-4-2t	2/4	-0.4
1964	Cin N	29	18	.617	3-2t	4/4	2.5
1965	Cin N	89	73	.549	4		-3.8
2		121	94	.563			-1.7
SKAFF, FRANK	B9.30.1910						
1966	Det A	40	39	.506	2-3	3/3	-0.5
SKINNER, JOEL	B2.21.1961						
2002	Cle A c	35	41	.467	3-3	2/2	1.9
SKINNER, BOB	B10.3.1931						
1968	Phi N	48	59	.449	5-7t	3/3	-0.2
1969	Phi N e	44	64	.407	5-5	1/2	-3.2
1977	SD N w	1	0	1.000	4-4-5	2/3	0.6
3		93	123	.431			-2.7
SLATTERY, JACK	B1.6.1878						
1928	Bos N	11	20	.355	7-7	1/2	0.3
SMITH, MAYO	B1.17.1915						
1955	Phi N	77	77	.500	4		-0.9
1956	Phi N	71	83	.461	5		1.0
1957	Phi N	77	77	.500	5		3.5
1958	Phi N	39	45	.464	8-8	1/2	2.3
1959	Cin N	35	45	.438	7-5t	1/2	-6.3
1967	Det A	91	71	.562	2t		-0.3
1968	Det A	103	59	.636	1★		1.8
1969	Det A e	90	72	.556	2		-1.6
1970	Det A e	79	83	.488	4		4.6
9		662	612	.520			4.0
SMITH, HEINIE	B10.24.1871						
1902	NY N	5	27	.156	4-8-8	2/3	-5.7
SMITH, HARRY	B10.31.1874						
1909	Bos N	23	54	.299	8-8		-1.6
SMITH, BILL	B						
1873	Mar NA	0	6	.000	9		3.9
SNYDER, POP	B10.6.1854						
1882	Cin AA	55	25	.688	1		-6.6
1883	Cin AA	61	37	.622	3		-10.6
1884	Cin AA	24	14	.632	5-5	2/2	-2.5
1891	Was AA	23	46	.333	6-7-8	2/4	4.7
4		163	122	.572			-14.9
SNYDER, JIM	B8.15.1932						
1988	Sea A w	45	60	.429	6-7	2/2	-2.2
SOTHORON, ALLEN	B4.27.1893						
1933	StL A	2	6	.250	8-8-8	2/3	-1.2
SOUTHWORTH, BILLY	B3.9.1893						
1929	StL N	43	45	.489	4-4	1/3	-2.3
1940	StL N	69	40	.633	7-3	3/3	11.1
1941	StL N	97	56	.634	2		5.6
1942	StL N	106	48	.688	1★		-0.3
1943	StL N	105	49	.682	1		5.4
1944	StL N	105	49	.682	1★		-1.8
1945	StL N	95	59	.617	2		0.2
1946	Bos N	81	72	.529	4		0.5
1947	Bos N	86	68	.558	3		1.3
1948	Bos N	91	62	.595	1		-1.4
1949	Bos N	55	54	.505	4-4	1/2	1.4
1950	Bos N	83	71	.539	4		1.3
1951	Bos N	28	31	.475	5-4	1/2	-3.8
13		1044	704	.597			17.2
SPALDING, AL	B9.2.1850						
1876	Chi N	52	14	.788	1		-11.1
1877	Chi N	26	33	.441	5		-2.7
2		78	47	.624			-13.9
SPEAKER, TRIS	B4.4.1888						
1919	Cle A	40	21	.656	3-2	2/2	5.0
1920	Cle A	98	56	.636	1★		0.3
1921	Cle A	94	60	.610	2		-2.6
1922	Cle A	78	76	.506	4		5.6
1923	Cle A	82	71	.536	3		-7.5
1924	Cle A	67	86	.438	6		-4.0
1925	Cle A	70	84	.455	6		-3.7
1926	Cle A	88	66	.571	2		-1.8
8		617	520	.543			-8.7
SPENCE, HARRY	Harrison L.						
B2.2.1856 New York, NY D5.17.1900 Chicago, IL (DNP)							
1888	Ind N	50	85	.370	7		-5.2
STAHL, CHICK	B1.10.1873						
1906	Bos A	14	26	.350	8-8	2/2	0.9
STAHL, JAKE	B4.13.1879						
1905	Was A	64	87	.424	7		-4.6
1906	Was A	55	95	.367	7		-4.4
1912	Bos A	105	47	.691	1★		3.1
1913	Bos A	39	41	.488	5-4	1/2	-2.2
4		263	270	.493			-8.0

YEAR	TM/LG	W	L	PCT	FINISH	MGR/YR	+/-
STALLINGS, GEORGE	B11.17.1867						
1897	Phi N	55	77	.417	10		-7.5
1898	Phi N	19	27	.413	8t-6	1/2	-5.1
1901	Det A	74	61	.548	3		2.2
1909	NY A	74	77	.490	5		-1.7
1910	NY A	78	59	.569	3-2	1/2	2.7
1913	Bos N	69	82	.457	5		-1.5
1914	Bos N	94	59	.614	1★		5.7
1915	Bos N	83	69	.546	2		2.9
1916	Bos N	89	63	.586	3		2.4
1917	Bos N	72	81	.471	6		-2.7
1918	Bos N	53	71	.427	7		-4.0
1919	Bos N	57	82	.410	6		-1.6
1920	Bos N	62	90	.408	7		1.8
13		879	898	.495			-6.6
STANKY, EDDIE	B9.3.1916						
1952	StL N	88	66	.571	3		6.2
1953	StL N	83	71	.539	3t		0.6
1954	StL N	72	82	.468	6		-5.8
1955	StL N	17	19	.472	5-7	1/2	1.4
1966	Chi A	83	79	.512	4		-4.6
1967	Chi A	89	73	.549	4		3.2
1968	Chi A	34	45	.430	9-8	1/5	-1.7
1977	Tex A w	1	0	1.000	3t-3-2	2/4	0.4
8		467	435	.518			-0.3
START, JOE	B10.14.1842						
1873	Mut NA	18	7	.720	5-4	2/2	4.1
STENGEL, CASEY	B7.30.1890						
1934	Bro N	71	81	.467	6		-0.6
1935	Bro N	70	83	.458	5		-1.1
1936	Bro N	67	87	.435	7		-1.0
1938	Bos N	77	75	.507	5		7.2
1939	Bos N	63	88	.417	7		-3.3
1940	Bos N	65	87	.428	7		1.2
1941	Bos N	62	92	.403	7		-1.8
1942	Bos N	59	89	.399	7		-1.0
1943	Bos N	47	60	.439	6-6	2/2	5.1
1949	NY A	97	57	.630	1★		1.3
1950	NY A	98	56	.636	1★		0.2
1951	NY A	98	56	.636	1★		3.5
1952	NY A	95	59	.617	1★		0.3
1953	NY A	99	52	.656	1★		-2.0
1954	NY A	103	51	.669	2		1.6
1955	NY A	96	58	.623	1		-0.7
1956	NY A	97	57	.630	1★		-1.8
1957	NY A	98	56	.636	1		1.2
1958	NY A	92	62	.597	1★		-3.6
1959	NY A	79	75	.513	3		-2.1
1960	NY A	97	57	.630	1		8.0
1962	NY N	40	120	.250	10		-8.1
1963	NY N	51	111	.315	10		-0.8
1964	NY N	53	109	.327	10		-6.4
1965	NY N	31	64	.326	10-10	1/2	-0.1
25		1905	1842	.508			-4.8
STOVALL, GEORGE	B11.23.1877						
1911	Cle A	74	62	.544	7-3	2/2	7.7
1912	Cle A	41	74	.357	8-7	2/2	-0.1
1913	StL A	50	84	.373	7-8	1/3	-6.1
1914	KC F	67	84	.444	6		-4.5
1915	KC F	81	72	.529	4		4.9
5		313	376	.454			1.9
STOVEY, HARRY	B12.20.1856						
1881	Wor N	8	18	.308	7-8	2/2	-2.6
1885	Phi AA	55	57	.491	4		-7.1
2		63	75	.457			-9.7
STREET, GABBY	B9.30.1882						
1929	StL N	1	0	1.000	4-4-4	2/3	0.5
1930	StL N	92	62	.597	1		-4.4
1931	StL N	101	53	.656	1★		4.2
1932	StL N	72	82	.468	6t		-1.7
1933	StL N	46	45	.505	5-5	1/2	-4.3
1938	StL A	53	90	.371	7-7	1/2	-0.9
6		365	332	.524			-6.6
STRICKER, CUB	B2.15.1860						
1892-1	StL N	6	17	.261	10-11-9	2/3	-2.4
STRICKLAND, GEORGE	B1.10.1926						
1964	Cle A	33	39	.458	8-6t	1/2	-2.8
1966	Cle A	15	24	.385	3-5	2/2	-4.2
2		48	63	.432			-7.0
STUBING, MOOSE	B3.31.1938						
1988	Cal A w	0	8	.000	4-4	2/2	-3.7
SUKEFORTH, CLYDE	B11.30.1901						
1947	Bro N	2	0	1.000	1t-1	1/2	0.9
SULLIVAN, HAYWOOD	B12.15.1930						
1965	KC A	54	82	.397	10-10	2/2	0.9
SULLIVAN, PAT	Patrick Joseph						
B3.24.1854 Lewisburg, VA D2.26.1896 Columbus, OH (DNP)							
1890	Col AA	2	1	.667	5-5-2	3/3	0.1

SULLIVAN, TED B1851

YEAR	TM/LG	W	L	PCT	FINISH	MGR/YR	+/-
1883	StL AA	53	26	.671	2-2	1/2	2.7
1884	StL U	28	3	.903	1-1	1/2	1.4
1884	KC U	13	46	.220	8-8	3/3	3.9
1888	Was N	38	57	.400	8-8	2/2	8.2
3		132	132	.500			16.2

SULLIVAN, BILLY B2.1.1875

YEAR	TM/LG	W	L	PCT	FINISH	MGR/YR	+/-
1909	Chi A	78	74	.513	4		-1.4

SWEASY, CHARLIE B11.2.1847

YEAR	TM/LG	W	L	PCT	FINISH	MGR/YR	+/-
1875	RS NA	4	15	.211	9		3.4

SWIFT, BOB B3.6.1915

YEAR	TM/LG	W	L	PCT	FINISH	MGR/YR	+/-
1965	Det A	24	18	.571	3-4	1/2	0.8
1966	Det A	32	25	.561	3-2-3	2/3	2.8
2		56	43	.566			3.6

TANNER, CHUCK B7.4.1929

YEAR	TM/LG	W	L	PCT	FINISH	MGR/YR	+/-
1970	Chi A w	3	13	.188	6-6	3/3	-3.1
1971	Chi A w	79	83	.488	3		-4.2
1972	Chi A w	87	67	.565	2		6.9
1973	Chi A w	77	85	.475	5		1.5
1974	Chi A w	80	80	.500	4		3.8
1975	Chi A w	75	86	.466	5		-0.5
1976	Oak A w	87	74	.540	2		-2.8
1977	Pit N e	96	66	.593	2		8.0
1978	Pit N e	88	73	.547	2		2.6
1979	Pit N e	98	64	.605	1★		3.6
1980	Pit N e	83	79	.512	3		-0.1
1981-1	Pit N e	25	23	.521	4		-3.1
1981-2	Pit N e	21	33	.389	6		-3.1
1982	Pit N e	84	78	.519	4		0.2
1983	Pit N e	84	78	.519	2		1.8
1984	Pit N e	75	87	.463	6		-11.3
1985	Pit N e	57	104	.354	6		-8.6
1986	Atl N w	72	89	.447	6		2.3
1987	Atl N w	69	92	.429	5		-3.6
1988	Atl N w	12	27	.308	6-6	1/2	-2.7
19		1352	1381	.495			-12.7

TAPPE, EL B5.21.1927

YEAR	TM/LG	W	L	PCT	FINISH	MGR/YR	+/-
1961	Chi N	2	0	1.000	7-7-7	4/9	1.1
1961	Chi N	35	43	.449	7-7-7	7/9	1.5
1961	Chi N	5	11	.313	7-7	9/9	-1.9
1962	Chi N	4	16	.200	9-9	1/3	-3.6
2		46	70	.397			-2.9

TAYLOR, GEORGE George J.
B11.22.1852 NY D10.28.1911 New York, NY (DNP)

YEAR	TM/LG	W	L	PCT	FINISH	MGR/YR	+/-
1884	Bro AA	40	64	.385	9		3.7

TAYLOR, ZACK B7.27.1898

YEAR	TM/LG	W	L	PCT	FINISH	MGR/YR	+/-
1946	StL A	13	17	.433	7-7	2/2	-0.2
1948	StL A	59	94	.386	6		-0.4
1949	StL A	53	101	.344	7		-0.9
1950	StL A	58	96	.377	7		2.6
1951	StL A	52	102	.338	8		1.1
5		235	410	.364			2.2

TEBBETTS, BIRDIE B11.10.1912

YEAR	TM/LG	W	L	PCT	FINISH	MGR/YR	+/-
1954	Cin N	74	80	.481	5		0.3
1955	Cin N	75	79	.487	5		-9.5
1956	Cin N	91	63	.591	3		2.5
1957	Cin N	80	74	.519	4		6.2
1958	Cin N	52	61	.460	8-4	1/2	-10.1
1961	Mil N	12	13	.480	3-4	2/2	-1.4
1962	Mil N	86	76	.531	5		-1.6
1963	Cle A	79	83	.488	5t		5.0
1964	Cle A	46	44	.511	8-6t	2/2	1.2
1965	Cle A	87	75	.537	5		0.7
1966	Cle A	66	57	.537	3-5	1/2	5.5
11		748	705	.515			-1.3

TEBEAU, PATSY B12.5.1864

YEAR	TM/LG	W	L	PCT	FINISH	MGR/YR	+/-
1890	Cle P	21	30	.412	7-7	2/2	1.0
1891	Cle N	31	40	.437	4-5	2/2	-2.2
1892-1	Cle N	40	33	.548	5		-4.9
1892-2	Cle N	53	23	.697	1		-4.9
1893	Cle N	73	55	.570	3		-2.0
1894	Cle N	68	61	.527	6		0.6
1895	Cle N	84	46	.646	2●		2.3
1896	Cle N	80	48	.625	2		-1.2
1897	Cle N	69	62	.527	5		-4.9
1898	Cle N	81	68	.544	5		1.8
1899	StL N	84	67	.556	5		0.9
1900	StL N	42	50	.457	7-5t	1/2	-3.8
11		726	583	.555			-17.1

TENACE, GENE B10.10.1946

YEAR	TM/LG	W	L	PCT	FINISH	MGR/YR	+/-
1991	Tor A e	19	14	.576	1-1-1	2/3	1.2

TENNEY, FRED B11.26.1871

YEAR	TM/LG	W	L	PCT	FINISH	MGR/YR	+/-
1905	Bos N	51	103	.331	7		2.7
1906	Bos N	49	102	.325	8		0.9
1907	Bos N	58	90	.392	7		0.3
1911	Bos N	44	107	.291	8		-2.4
4		202	402	.334			1.5

TERRY, BILL B10.30.1898

YEAR	TM/LG	W	L	PCT	FINISH	MGR/YR	+/-
1932	NY N	55	59	.482	8-6t	2/2	-5.5
1933	NY N	91	61	.599	1★		1.6
1934	NY N	93	60	.608	2		-1.4
1935	NY N	91	62	.595	3		5.1
1936	NY N	92	62	.597	1		2.8
1937	NY N	95	57	.625	1		5.8
1938	NY N	83	67	.553	3		1.1
1939	NY N	77	74	.510	5		-0.3
1940	NY N	72	80	.474	6		-4.4
1941	NY N	74	79	.484	5		1.4
10		823	661	.555			6.3

THOMAS, FRED Frederick L. B IN (DNP)

YEAR	TM/LG	W	L	PCT	FINISH	MGR/YR	+/-
1887	Ind N	11	18	.379	8-8-8	2/3	3.1

THOMPSON, ANDREW Andrew M.
B11.9.1845 Seward, IL D2.17.1895 Pecatonica, IL (DNP)

YEAR	TM/LG	W	L	PCT	FINISH	MGR/YR	+/-
1884	Stp U	2	6	.250	7		1.3

TIGHE, JACK John Thomas B8.9.1913 Kearny, NJ
D8.1.2002 Pompano Beach, FL BR/TR/5-8/170(C)

YEAR	TM/LG	W	L	PCT	FINISH	MGR/YR	+/-
1957	Det A	78	76	.506	4		1.0
1958	Det A	21	28	.429	8-5	1/2	-5.3
2		99	104	.488			-4.3

TINKER, JOE B7.27.1880

YEAR	TM/LG	W	L	PCT	FINISH	MGR/YR	+/-
1913	Cin N	64	89	.418	7		-1.2
1914	Chi F	87	67	.565	2		-1.6
1915	Chi F	86	66	.566	1		-1.1
1916	Chi N	67	86	.438	5		-7.1
4		304	308	.497			-10.9

TORBORG, JEFF B11.26.1941

YEAR	TM/LG	W	L	PCT	FINISH	MGR/YR	+/-
1977	Cle A e	45	59	.433	5-5	2/2	-2.9
1978	Cle A e	69	90	.434	6		-4.8
1979	Cle A e	43	52	.453	6-6	1/2	-1.9
1989	Chi A w	69	92	.429	7		-5.8
1990	Chi A w	94	68	.580	2		7.8
1991	Chi A w	87	75	.537	2		-1.8
1992	NY N e	72	90	.444	5		-3.2
1993	NY N e	13	25	.342	7-7	1/2	-4.3
2001	Mon N e	47	61	.435	5-5	2/2	2.4
2002	Fla N e	79	83	.488	4		4.4
2003	Fla N e	17	22	.436	4-2●★	1/2	-3.9
11		635	717	.470			-13.9

TORRE, JOE B7.18.1940

YEAR	TM/LG	W	L	PCT	FINISH	MGR/YR	+/-
1977	NY N	49	68	.419	6-6	2/2	-3.6
1978	NY N e	66	96	.407	6		-6.2
1979	NY N e	63	99	.389	6		-6.0
1980	NY N e	67	95	.414	5		-4.4
1981-1	NY N e	17	34	.333	5		-1.3
1981-2	NY N e	24	28	.462	4		-1.3
1982	Atl N w	89	73	.549	1		4.3
1983	Atl N w	88	74	.543	2		-3.9
1984	Atl N w	80	82	.494	2t		1.4
1990	StL N e	24	34	.414	6-6	3/3	-1.2
1991	StL N e	84	78	.519	2		2.7
1992	StL N e	83	79	.512	3		-0.9
1993	StL N e	87	75	.537	3		3.6
1994	StL N c	53	61	.465	3t		4.1
1995	StL N c	20	27	.426	4-4	1/2	-0.3
1996	NY A e	92	70	.568	1★		3.1
1997	NY A e	96	66	.593	2●		-4.5
1998	NY A e	114	48	.704	1★		3.7
1999	NY A e	77	49	.611	1-1★	2/2	1.6
2000	NY A e	87	74	.540	1★		1.2
2001	NY A e	95	65	.594	1♦		6.1
2002	NY A e	103	58	.640	1		3.4
2003	NY A e	101	61	.623	1♦		4.5
2004	NY A e	101	61	.623	1☆		11.8
2005	NY A e	95	67	.586	1		4.9
24		1855	1622	.534			24.0

TOSCA, CARLOS Carlos
B9.29.1953 Pinar Del Rio, Cuba 5-7/158(DNP)

YEAR	TM/LG	W	L	PCT	FINISH	MGR/YR	+/-
2002	Tor A e	58	51	.532	4-3	2/2	4.5
2003	Tor A e	86	76	.531	3		-1.3
2004	Tor A e	47	74	.388	5-5	1/2	-5.9
3		191	201	.487			-2.7

TRACEWSKI, DICK B2.3.1935

YEAR	TM/LG	W	L	PCT	FINISH	MGR/YR	+/-
1979	Det A e	2	0	1.000	5-5-5	2/3	1.0

TRACY, JIM B12.31.1955

YEAR	TM/LG	W	L	PCT	FINISH	MGR/YR	+/-
2001	LA N w	86	76	.531	3		3.6
2002	LA N w	92	70	.568	3		3.7
2003	LA N w	85	77	.525	2		2.0
2004	LA N w	93	69	.574	1		4.3
2005	LA N w	71	91	.438	4		-3.0
5		427	383	.527			10.6

TRAMMELL, ALAN B2.21.1958

YEAR	TM/LG	W	L	PCT	FINISH	MGR/YR	+/-
2003	Det A c	43	119	.265	5		-5.0
2004	Det A c	72	90	.444	4		-7.4
2005	Det A c	71	91	.438	4		-3.7
3		186	300	.383			-16.1

TRAYNOR, PIE B11.11.1899

YEAR	TM/LG	W	L	PCT	FINISH	MGR/YR	+/-
1934	Pit N	47	52	.475	4-5	2/2	-3.9
1935	Pit N	86	67	.562	4		-0.1
1936	Pit N	84	70	.545	4		-1.3
1937	Pit N	86	68	.558	3		3.2
1938	Pit N	86	64	.573	2		3.2
1939	Pit N	68	85	.444	6		-3.0
6		457	406	.530			-1.8

TREBELHORN, TOM Thomas Lynn
B1.27.1948 Portland, OR BL/TR/5-11/178(C)

YEAR	TM/LG	W	L	PCT	FINISH	MGR/YR	+/-
1986	Mil A e	6	3	.667	6-6	2/2	1.9
1987	Mil A e	91	71	.562	3		5.8
1988	Mil A e	87	75	.537	3t		-1.0
1989	Mil A e	81	81	.500	4		-2.9
1990	Mil A e	74	88	.457	6		-4.2
1991	Mil A e	83	79	.512	3		-3.3
1994	Chi N c	49	64	.434	5		-2.7
7		471	461	.505			-6.4

TROTT, SAM B3.1859

YEAR	TM/LG	W	L	PCT	FINISH	MGR/YR	+/-
1891	Was AA	4	7	.364	6-9	1/4	1.1

TURNER, TED Robert Edward
B11.19.1938 Cincinnati, OH (DNP)

YEAR	TM/LG	W	L	PCT	FINISH	MGR/YR	+/-
1977	Atl N w	0	1	.000	6-6-6	2/4	-0.4

UNGLAUB, BOB B7.31.1881

YEAR	TM/LG	W	L	PCT	FINISH	MGR/YR	+/-
1907	Bos A	9	20	.310	6-8-7	3/4	-3.4

VALENTINE, BOBBY B5.13.1950

YEAR	TM/LG	W	L	PCT	FINISH	MGR/YR	+/-
1985	Tex A w	53	76	.411	7-7	2/2	2.2
1986	Tex A w	87	75	.537	2		3.3
1987	Tex A w	75	87	.463	6t		-3.6
1988	Tex A w	70	91	.435	6		-0.4
1989	Tex A w	83	79	.512	4		3.9
1990	Tex A w	83	79	.512	3		4.1
1991	Tex A w	85	77	.525	3		2.6
1992	Tex A w	45	41	.523	3-4	1/2	5.8
1996	NY N e	12	19	.387	4-4	2/2	-2.9
1997	NY N e	88	74	.543	3		0.7
1998	NY N e	88	74	.543	2		0.7
1999	NY N e	97	66	.595	2☆▲♦		1.7
2000	NY N e	94	68	.580	2♦♦		6.3
2001	NY N e	82	80	.506	3		8.4
2002	NY N e	75	86	.466	5		-4.2
15		1117	1072	.510			28.1

VanHALTREN, GEORGE B3.30.1866

YEAR	TM/LG	W	L	PCT	FINISH	MGR/YR	+/-
1892-1	Bal N	1	10	.091	12-12	1/3	-2.9

VERNON, MICKEY B4.22.1918

YEAR	TM/LG	W	L	PCT	FINISH	MGR/YR	+/-
1961	Was A	61	100	.379	9t		-3.4
1962	Was A	60	101	.373	10		-8.2
1963	Was A	14	26	.350	10-10	1/3	-0.1
3		135	227	.373			-11.7

VIRDON, BILL B6.9.1931

YEAR	TM/LG	W	L	PCT	FINISH	MGR/YR	+/-
1972	Pit N e	96	59	.619	1		-0.8
1973	Pit N e	67	69	.493	2-3	1/2	-1.9
1974	NY A e	89	73	.549	2		2.9
1975	NY A e	53	51	.510	3-3	1/2	-5.4
1975	Hou N w	17	17	.500	6-6	2/2	1.0
1976	Hou N w	80	82	.494	3		2.4
1977	Hou N w	81	80	.500	3		-3.1
1978	Hou N w	74	88	.457	5		-3.9
1979	Hou N w	89	73	.549	2		7.9
1980	Hou N w	93	70	.571	1▲		6.2
1981-1	Hou N w	28	29	.491	3		-1.4
1981-2	Hou N w	33	20	.623	1		-1.4
1982	Hou N w	49	62	.441	5-5	1/2	-2.6
1983	Mon N e	82	80	.506	3		-2.3
1984	Mon N e	64	67	.489	5-5	1/2	-2.2
13		995	921	.519			-1.9

VITT, OSSIE B1.4.1890

YEAR	TM/LG	W	L	PCT	FINISH	MGR/YR	+/-
1938	Cle A	86	66	.566	3		4.0
1939	Cle A	87	67	.565	3		0.7
1940	Cle A	89	65	.578	2		4.6
3		262	198	.570			9.3

VonDER AHE, CHRIS Christian Frederick Wilhelm
B10.7.1851 Hille, Prussia D6.5.1913 St.Louis, MO (DNP)

YEAR	TM/LG	W	L	PCT	FINISH	MGR/YR	+/-
1895	StL N	1	0	1.000	11-11-11	2/4	0.7
1896	StL N	0	0	.000	10-11-11	3/5	-0.5
1897	StL N	2	12	.143	12-12	4/4	-0.5
3		3	14	.176			-0.4

VUKOVICH, JOHN B7.31.1947

YEAR	TM/LG	W	L	PCT	FINISH	MGR/YR	+/-
1986	Chi N e	1	1	.500	5-5-5	2/3	0.1
1988	Phi N e	5	4	.556	6-6	2/2	1.3
2		6	5	.545			1.4

WAGNER, HEINIE B9.23.1880

YEAR	TM/LG	W	L	PCT	FINISH	MGR/YR	+/-
1930	Bos A	52	102	.338	8		-5.1

WAGNER, HONUS B2.24.1874

YEAR	TM/LG	W	L	PCT	FINISH	MGR/YR	+/-
1917	Pit N	1	4	.200	8-8-8	2/3	-1.0

WALKER, HARRY B10.22.1916

YEAR	TM/LG	W	L	PCT	FINISH	MGR/YR	+/-
1955	StL N	51	67	.432	5-7	2/2	-0.2
1965	Pit N	90	72	.556	3		-1.3
1966	Pit N	92	70	.568	3		-1.0
1967	Pit N	42	42	.500	6-6	1/2	0.8
1968	Hou N	49	52	.485	10-10	2/2	4.1
1969	Hou N w	81	81	.500	5		-0.1
1970	Hou N w	79	83	.488	4		-0.1
1971	Hou N w	79	83	.488	4t		-4.0
1972	Hou N w	67	54	.554	2-2	1/3	0.7
9		630	604	.511			-1.9

YEAR	TM/LG	W	L	PCT	FINISH	MGR/YR	+/-
WALLACE, BOBBY B11.4.1873							
1911	StL A	45	107	.296	8		-6.6
1912	StL A	12	27	.308	8-7	1/2	-1.9
1937	Cin N	5	20	.200	8-8	2/2	-5.9
3		62	154	.287			-14.5
WALSH, ED B5.14.1881							
1924	Chi A	1	2	.333	6	2/4	-0.4
WALSH, MIKE Michael John							
B4.29.1850 Ireland D2.2.1929 Louisville, KY (DNP)							
1884	Lou AA	68	40	.630	3		-0.7
WALTERS, BUCKY B4.19.1909							
1948	Cin N	20	33	.377	7-7	2/2	-0.8
1949	Cin N	61	90	.404	7-7	1/2	-0.4
2		81	123	.397			-1.2
WALTZ, JAMES James William							
B1.12.1860 MD D4.27.1931 Baltimore, MD (DNP)							
1892-1	Bal N	2	6	.250	12-12-12	2/3	-0.9
WARD, JOHN B3.3.1860							
1880	Pro N	18	13	.581	4-3-2	2/3	-2.1
1884	NY N	6	8	.429	4-4t	2/2	-1.8
1890	Bro P	76	56	.576	2		4.3
1891	Bro N	61	76	.445	6		-2.6
1892-1	Bro N	51	26	.662	2		-0.7
1892-2	Bro N	44	33	.571	3		-0.7
1893	NY N	68	64	.515	5		-5.9
1894	NY N	88	44	.667	2●		8.4
7		412	320	.563			-1.1
WATERMAN, FRED B12.1845							
1872	Oly NA	2	7	.222	10		3.1
WATHAN, JOHN B10.4.1949							
1987	KC A w	21	15	.583	4-2	2/2	2.5
1988	KC A w	84	77	.522	3		-2.3
1989	KC A w	92	70	.568	2		5.2
1990	KC A w	75	86	.466	6		-5.3
1991	KC A w	15	22	.405	7-6	1/3	-3.6
1992	Cal A w	39	50	.438	5-5-5t	2/3	-0.0
6		326	320	.505			-3.6
WATKINS, HARVEY Harvey L. (DNP)							
1895	NY N	18	17	.514	9-9	3/3	0.1
WATKINS, BILL B5.5.1858							
1884	Ind AA	4	18	.182	10-11	2/2	-1.6
1885	Det N	34	36	.486	8-6	2/2	3.2
1886	Det N	87	36	.707	2		-1.0
1887	Det N	79	45	.637	1★		-4.4
1888	Det N	49	44	.527	3-5	1/2	-3.7
1888	KC AA	8	17	.320	8-8	3/3	0.9
1889	KC AA	55	82	.401	7		1.1
1893	StL N	57	75	.432	10		-1.6
1898	Pit N	72	76	.486	8		4.1
1899	Pit N	7	15	.318	10-7	1/2	-5.0
9		452	444	.504			-8.0
WEAVER, EARL Earl Sidney							
B8.14.1930 St.Louis, MO BR/TR/5-7/180(2B)							
1968	Bal A	48	34	.585	3-2		2.2
1969	Bal A e	109	53	.673	1♦		0.2
1970	Bal A e	108	54	.667	1★		4.5
1971	Bal A e	101	57	.639	1♦		-0.4
1972	Bal A e	80	74	.519	3		-7.8
1973	Bal A e	97	65	.599	1		-4.3
1974	Bal A e	91	71	.562	1		5.0
1975	Bal A e	90	69	.566	2		-3.4
1976	Bal A e	88	74	.543	2		4.7
1977	Bal A e	97	64	.602	2t		9.7
1978	Bal A e	90	71	.559	4		6.7
1979	Bal A e	102	57	.642	1♦		4.4
1980	Bal A e	100	62	.617	2		2.4
1981-1	Bal A e	31	23	.574	2		7.3
1981-2	Bal A e	28	23	.549	4		7.3
1982	Bal A e	94	68	.580	2		4.3
1985	Bal A e	53	52	.505	4-4	3/3	-2.9
1986	Bal A e	73	89	.451	7		-2.8
17		1480	1060	.583			37.2
WEDGE, ERIC B1.27.1968							
2003	Cle A c	68	94	.420	4		-5.2
2004	Cle A c	80	82	.494	3		-1.1
2005	Cle A c	93	69	.574	2		-2.9
3		241	245	.496			-9.2
WESTRUM, WES B11.28.1922							
1965	NY N	19	48	.284	10-10	2/2	-2.9
1966	NY N	66	95	.410	9		3.5
1967	NY N	57	94	.377	10-10	1/2	-0.4
1974	SF N e	38	48	.442	5-5	2/2	-0.1
1975	SF N w	80	81	.497	3		0.8
5		260	366	.415			0.9
WHEELER, HARRY B3.3.1858							
1884	KC U	0	4	.000	8-8	1/3	-0.6
WHITE, DEACON B12.7.1847							
1872	Cle NA	0	2	.000	6-7	2/2	-0.5
1879	Cin N	9	9	.500	4-5	1/2	-0.4
2		9	11	.450			-0.9
WHITE, JO-JO B6.1.1909							
1960	Cle A	1	0	1.000	4-4-4	2/3	0.5
WHITE, WILL B10.11.1854							
1884	Cin AA	44	27	.620	5	1/2	-5.6
WHITE, WARREN B1844							
1872	Nat NA	0	11	.000	11		1.2
1874	Bal NA	9	38	.191	8		6.6
2		9	49	.155			7.8
WILBER, DEL B2.24.1919							
1973	Tex A w	1	0	1.000	6-6-6	2/3	0.6
WILHELM, KAISER B1.26.1874							
1921	Phi N	26	41	.388	8-8	2/2	5.0
1922	Phi N	57	96	.373	7		-2.9
2		83	137	.377			2.1
WILLIAMS, JIMMY James Andrew							
B1.4.1847 Catawba, OH D10.23.1918 Westbury, NY (DNP)							
1884	StL AA	51	33	.607	5-4		0.5
1887	Cle AA	39	92	.298	8		4.4
1888	Cle AA	20	44	.313	8-6	1/2	-3.8
3		110	169	.394			1.1
WILLIAMS, JIMY B10.4.1943							
1986	Tor A e	86	76	.531	4		-2.4
1987	Tor A e	96	66	.593	2		-3.7
1988	Tor A e	87	75	.537	3t		-2.3
1989	Tor A e	12	24	.333	6-1	1/2	-7.8
1997	Bos A e	78	84	.481	4		-2.4
1998	Bos A e	92	70	.568	2✤		-3.0
1999	Bos A e	94	68	.580	2✤✤		1.6
2000	Bos A e	85	77	.525	2		-0.6
2001	Bos A e	65	53	.551	2-2	1/2	4.1
2002	Hou N c	84	78	.519	2		-2.4
2003	Hou N c	87	75	.537	2		-6.7
2004	Hou N c	44	44	.500	5-2✩✤	1/2	-5.6
12		910	790	.535			-31.5
WILLIAMS, DICK B5.7.1929							
1967	Bos A	92	70	.568	1		-0.3
1968	Bos A	86	76	.531	4		4.7
1969	Bos A e	82	71	.536	3-3	1/2	4.8
1971	Oak A w	101	60	.627	1		6.9
1972	Oak A w	93	62	.600	1★		-1.4
1973	Oak A w	94	68	.580	1★		-1.7
1974	Cal A w	36	48	.429	6-6	3/3	-3.8
1975	Cal A w	72	89	.447	6		1.3
1976	Cal A w	39	57	.406	6-4t	1/2	-3.7
1977	Mon N e	75	87	.463	5		1.2
1978	Mon N e	76	86	.469	4		-7.4
1979	Mon N e	95	65	.594	2		2.3
1980	Mon N e	90	72	.556	2		2.2
1981-1	Mon N e	30	25	.545	3		0.7
1981-2	Mon N e	14	12	.538	2-1✩	1/2	-0.3
1982	SD N w	81	81	.500	4		-1.8
1983	SD N w	81	81	.500	4		0.0
1984	SD N w	92	70	.568	1♦		5.5
1985	SD N w	83	79	.512	3t		-1.0
1986	Sea A w	58	75	.436	6-7	3/3	0.8
1987	Sea A w	78	84	.481	4		1.0
1988	Sea A w	23	33	.411	6-7	1/2	-2.2
21		1571	1451	.520			8.0
WILLIAMS, TED B8.30.1918							
1969	Was A e	86	76	.531	4		-0.2
1970	Was A e	70	92	.432	6		-4.4
1971	Was A e	63	96	.396	5		-3.1
1972	Tex A w	54	100	.351	6		-4.2
4		273	364	.429			-11.8
WILLS, MAURY B10.2.1932							
1980	Sea A w	20	38	.345	6-7	2/2	-2.3
1981-1	Sea A w	6	18	.250	7-6	1/2	-3.9
2		26	56	.317			-6.2
WILSON, JIMMIE B7.23.1900							
1934	Phi N	56	93	.376	7		-7.1
1935	Phi N	64	89	.418	7		5.2
1936	Phi N	54	100	.351	8		-9.2
1937	Phi N	61	92	.399	7		-1.9
1938	Phi N	45	103	.304	8-8	1/2	-0.7
1941	Chi N	70	84	.455	6		-6.6
1942	Chi N	68	86	.442	6		-1.2
1943	Chi N	74	79	.484	5		-6.0
1944	Chi N	1	9	.100	8-4	1/3	-4.2
9		493	735	.401			-31.8
WINE, BOBBY B9.17.1938							
1985	Atl N w	16	25	.390	5-5	2/2	-0.7
WINGO, IVEY B7.8.1890							
1916	Cin N	1	1	.500	8-8-7t	2/3	0.2
WINKLES, BOBBY Bobby Brooks							
B3.11.1930 Tuckerman, AR BR/TR/5-9/170(SS)							
1973	Cal A w	79	83	.488	4		1.0
1974	Cal A w	30	44	.405	6-6	1/3	-5.1
1977	Oak A w	37	71	.343	5t-7	2/2	-7.0
1978	Oak A w	24	15	.615	1-6	1/2	8.7
4		170	213	.444			-2.5
WOLF, JIMMY B5.12.1862							
1889	Lou AA	14	51	.215	8-8-8	2/4	-0.0
WOLVERTON, HARRY B12.6.1873							
1912	NY A	50	102	.329	8		-5.5
WOOD, GEORGE B11.9.1858							
1891	Phi AA	67	55	.549	7-4	2/2	4.2
WOOD, JIMMY B12.1.1843							
1871	Chi NA	19	9	.679	2		0.8
1872	Tro NA	15	10	.600	5		-3.2
1872	Eck NA	2	7	.222	10-10-9	2/3	3.0
1874	Chi NA	10	13	.435	4-5	2/2	0.4
1875	Chi NA	30	37	.448	6		-0.2
4		76	76	.500			0.8
WRIGHT, AL Alfred Hector							
B3.30.1842 Cedar Grove, NJ D4.20.1905 New York, NY (DNP)							
1876	Phi N	14	45	.237	7		-3.5
WRIGHT, GEORGE B1.28.1847							
1879	Pro N	59	25	.702	1		-5.9
WRIGHT, HARRY B1.10.1835							
1871	Bos NA	20	10	.667	3		-1.2
1872	Bos NA	39	8	.830	1		-6.0
1873	Bos NA	43	16	.729	1		-5.2
1874	Bos NA	52	18	.743	1		-6.9
1875	Bos NA	71	8	.899	1		-7.2
1876	Bos N	39	31	.557	4		2.3
1877	Bos N	42	18	.700	1		-2.0
1878	Bos N	41	19	.683	1		5.3
1879	Bos N	54	30	.643	2		-7.5
1880	Bos N	40	44	.476	6		1.8
1881	Bos N	38	45	.458	6		2.8
1882	Pro N	52	32	.619	2		-0.3
1883	Pro N	58	40	.592	3		-9.1
1884	Phi N	39	73	.348	6		6.7
1885	Phi N	56	54	.509	3		0.8
1886	Phi N	71	43	.623	4		2.0
1887	Phi N	75	48	.610	2		-3.4
1888	Phi N	69	61	.531	3		1.2
1889	Phi N	63	64	.496	3		0.0
1890	Phi N	14	8	.636	1-3	1/5	1.3
1890	Phi N	22	23	.489	2-3	5/5	-4.0
1891	Phi N	68	69	.496	4		1.0
1892-1	Phi N	46	30	.605	3		-5.6
1892-2	Phi N	41	36	.532	5		-5.6
1893	Phi N	57	58	.496	6		-6.2
23		1225	885	.581			-45.1
YORK, RUDY B8.17.1913							
1959	Bos A	0	1	.000	8-8-5	2/3	-0.5
YORK, TOM B7.13.1851							
1878	Pro N	33	27	.550	3		1.6
1881	Pro N	23	10	.697	4-2	2/2	5.7
2		56	37	.602			7.3
YOST, NED B8.19.1954							
2003	Mil N c	68	94	.420	6		2.2
2004	Mil N c	67	94	.416	6		-0.9
2005	Mil N c	81	81	.500	3		-2.9
3		216	269	.445			-1.6
YOST, EDDIE B10.13.1926							
1963	Was A	0	1	.000	10-10-10	2/3	-0.4
YOUNG, CY B3.29.1867							
1907	Bos A	3	3	.500	4t-7	1/4	0.4
YOUNG, NICK Nicholas Ephraim							
B9.12.1840 Fort Johnson, NY D10.31.1916 Washington, DC (OF)							
1871	Oly NA	15	15	.500	5		-0.5
1873	Was NA	8	31	.205	7		2.2
2		23	46	.333			1.7
ZIMMER, CHIEF B11.23.1860							
1903	Phi N	49	86	.363	7		-6.9
ZIMMER, DON B1.17.1931							
1972	SD N w	54	88	.380	4-6	2/2	1.0
1973	SD N w	60	102	.370	6		2.4
1976	Bos A e	42	34	.553	5-3	2/2	1.3
1977	Bos A e	97	64	.602	2t		2.4
1978	Bos A e	99	64	.607	2▲		3.5
1979	Bos A e	91	69	.569	3		-1.5
1980	Bos A e	82	73	.529	3-4	1/2	5.4
1981-1	Tex A w	33	22	.600	2		-2.2
1981-2	Tex A w	24	26	.480	3		-2.2
1982	Tex A w	38	58	.396	6-6	1/2	-0.2
1988	Chi N e	77	85	.475	4		-0.5
1989	Chi N e	93	69	.574	1		3.7
1990	Chi N e	77	85	.475	4t		4.4
1991	Chi N e	18	19	.486	4-4	1/3	0.4
1999	NY A e	21	15	.583	1-1	1/2	-0.6
14		906	873	.509			17.4

HOMETOWN HEROES: TEAM ROSTERS

Nineteenth century baseball writers often referred to their local clubs as the "hometown nine." That was both accurate and appropriate in an era when teams had very few extra players, when top pitchers started half or more of their team's games (and played in the field when they weren't pitching), and when most managers were player-managers. Moreover, baseball had little competition for the hearts of the fans from other team sports back then.

Today, with twenty-five-player active rosters, plus well-used disabled lists, plus shuttles operating almost daily between top farm teams and their parent clubs, calling a major league team the "hometown thirty-five" would be more accurate, if hardly as appealing.

Almost all players who don the uniform of a major league team, however, are truly hometown heroes—a phrase with a double meaning: Big league ballplayers are heroes where they play—their team's hometown—as well as in their individual hometowns, whether they came from large cities or from small towns.

One of the foremost goals of any encyclopedia is to present information in an accessible manner. The player registers show year-by-year information for each player's career, and the Historical Record presents detailed annual information for each league. Another important component is this Team Rosters section, which features a chronological record of all regular players and pitchers plus important reserves on each team, season-by-season, for the whole 136-year span of professional baseball history.

Roster format. In this section rosters are grouped by league for each year, with the teams in each league shown in alphabetical order. This enables quick comparisons of the various teams in a pennant race without constantly flipping from page to page. Mortal enemies like the 1951 Giants and Dodgers will be found cheek-by-jowl; and all four teams that engaged in the down-to-the-wire 1967 AL pennant race will be at most a column or two away from each other.

These team rosters provide much more complete information than typical rosters do about how each team was put together and how it utilized its players in a given season. This is especially true in the past two decades, when teams have become much more reluctant to let young pitchers learn the ropes or to let struggling players work their way out of slumps. The increasing frequency of serious injuries has also resulted in less stable lineups.

The plethora of televised games and the omnipresent and instantaneous nature of the electronic media today put tremendous pressure on major league team owners, general managers, and managers to solve problems *right now*. Of course, the enormous amount of money at stake is also a huge factor in the decreasing amount of patience exhibited by teams at every level. Big league teams, managers, and players have lived under the microscope of the media throughout baseball history, but now that media microscope broadcasts full-color video accompanied by unabashedly critical commentary, 24-7.

This intense pressure has resulted in managers using scores of different lineups and having far fewer "set" positions than in the past. This roster-coding scheme may seem complex, but it gives a much more detailed understanding of whatever team is being examined. From 1990–2005, these rosters show almost 10,000 player-seasons, with more than three-quarters of the entries using the familiar single-position codes. Because of the way these codes are defined, however, even the standard codes like *SS* and *RF* now convey more information than in other sources.

Simpler rosters that showed pitching staffs composed simply of *SPs* and *RPs* would be far less useful than rosters showing that many pitchers spent part of the season in the rotation as well as the bullpen. Rosters that showed position players only by their primary positions, or that labeled all reserves simply as utility players, would also omit much useful information. The most common combination codes are, not surprisingly, *RS* and *SR*,

followed by several codes for utility players. Two-position combination codes normally show up only a few times for each team.

From top to bottom, rosters list starting pitchers first, then relief pitchers, then regular position players, then reserves. Non-playing managers are shown last. Regular players who are traded during the season will normally show up on the team where they spent the bulk of the year, though some will fail to play at least half of either team's games and, thus, not qualify for either team's roster.

Pitchers. The rosters list as many as five starting pitchers and four relief pitchers for each team. Pitcher codes are:
- *SP* – starting pitcher;
- *RP* – relief pitcher;
- *SR* – starter-reliever;
- *RS* – reliever-starter;
- *CL* – closer.

Starting pitchers qualify if they are among the top five pitchers on the team in innings pitched, provided that they have pitched at least 0.6 innings for each of their team's games played. Relief pitchers make the roster if they are among the top four pitchers on the team in innings pitched plus saves, provided that they pitched at least 0.3 innings per team game.

Pitchers are assigned codes according to the following rules:
If a starting pitcher has 0–9 games in relief, he is labeled as *SP*.

If a pitcher has 10 or more games in relief, and if at least one third of his appearances are games started, then he is labeled as *SR*.

If the pitcher has started at least 5 games and has 10 or more games in relief, he is labeled as *RS*—provided he started less than one third of the time.

If a relief pitcher has 0–4 games started, he is labeled as *RP*.

If a relief pitcher's saves total is equal to at least one third of his relief appearances, than he is labeled as *CL*.

Position Players. In order to include as clear a picture as possible of each team, every player who played in at least 50 percent of his team's games is shown, so no one who made a major impact during the regular season is missing. Position players who played in fewer than 60 percent of their team's games are marked by a dash after their position code.

Regular players are always listed in the order shown below. If a player played at least 75 percent of his team's games at one position, he is shown as the regular with the following codes:
- *C* – catcher
- *1B* – first base (*1* when combined with other positions)
- *2B* – second base (*2* when combined)
- *3B* – third base (*3* when combined)
- *SS* – shortstop (*S* when combined)
- *LF*– left fielder (*L* when combined)
- *CF*– center fielder (*M* when combined)
- *RF* – right fielder (*R* when combined)
- *DH* – designated hitter (*D* when combined)

If no one played at least 75 percent of a team's games at one position, the regular shown will be the player who played the most games at that position—unless a player happened to have played the most games at two positions. If so, that player will be shown where he played the most, and the player with the second-most games at the other position will be shown as the regular. For example, for Oakland in 2001, Johnny Damon played 67 games in left and 86 in center out of a total of 154 games in the outfield. He led the team in games at both positions. Terrence Long played 62 games in left, 74 in center, and 28 in right (162 total). Damon was listed as *ML*, since he played more than 50 percent of his games in center and more than 25 percent in left. Long was listed as the regular center fielder with an *UO* code because he did not play 50 percent of his games at any one position, but he did play all three outfield spots.

In the overwhelming majority of circumstances, the regular at each position will have the standard position code or a combination code that starts with the first letter of that position (e.g., *3S* for third base/shortstop; *L1* for left field/first base). However, when a team has several players shifting among different positions during the season, the regular shown at a particular position might not have the expected code. (This usually happens on bad teams that have no set lineup.) The lineups that "fit the best" with the players who played the most are always shown.

In these rare circumstances, the "regular" third baseman might be someone who played only 40 games there, but who still played third more than anyone else on that team who wasn't a regular at another position. For example, in 1918 Fred Thomas played only 41 games at third base for the pennant-winning Red Sox, but that was still more than anyone else, so Thomas is shown as the regular.

Aside from the position codes shown above, four other codes are used for players who have played less than 75 percent of their games at one position. Details on these codes are found below:

- *OF* – outfield (*O* when used in combination);
- *IF* – infield (*I* when used in combination);
- *UT* – utility player (*U* when used in combination);
- *P* – Pitcher (when used in combination with position codes).

Combination Position Codes. If a player played between 50 percent and 75 percent of his games at one position, his primary position will be signified by the *first* letter of the above codes. (Exception: To avoid confusion with catcher, we have revived the old newspaper box score code *M*—for "middle outfielder"—to indicate center field).

Players with at least half their games at one position, but less than three quarters of their games at that position, are also given a secondary position code. The secondary code assigned depends on how many games they played at other positions, of course, as well as the number of other positions they played. The rules for secondary position codes are:

If a player played at least 25 percent of his other games at a position other than his primary position, the secondary position will be shown as the second letter of his position code.

If the player did not play 25 percent of his other games at any single position, but he did play at least 25 percent of his additional (i.e., non-primary position) games in the infield, the second letter of his position code will be *I*. In 2003 Desi Relaford played 141 games for Kansas City: 89 at second base, 33 at third base, 20 in the outfield, and 6 at shortstop. His 89 games at second put him in 50–75 percent range for a two-character code, with *2* as the first character. His next highest position was less than 25 percent of his total games, so his secondary code is a utility code. With 39 games at third and short combined, his second character becomes *I* and his position code becomes *2I*.

If the player did not play 25 percent of his other games at a single position, but he did play at least 25 percent of his additional games in the outfield, the second letter of his position code will be *O*. In 2003 Dustan Mohr of Minnesota had 30 games in left, 11 in center, and 70 in right out of a total of 121 games. Thus he qualifies for an *RO* code, with 50–75 percent of his games in right, less than 25 percent at any other position, but a total of 41 in left and center.

If a player's games are scattered among so many positions that none of these conditions apply, his secondary code will be *U.*

If the player's secondary position was pitcher and he pitched in at least 10 games, his second letter will be *P.* Only a few position players since 1901—the most famous being Babe Ruth, of course—have pitched in 10 games in one year while also playing in half their team's games.

If the position player has 100 innings pitched in a season and a *P* wouldn't appear as his secondary position code under the preceding rules, the *P* will take precedence. This occurs exclusively in the nineteenth century. A lowercase *p* will be used to distinguish, for example, between a right fielder who also pitched (*Rp*) from a relief pitcher (*RP*), though the location of such players on the roster will usually make this clear.

Utility Codes. No two-letter coding scheme can account for all the ways that managers can use players during a season. Therefore, a few utility codes are used to cover versatile players who didn't play 50 percent of their games at any position. (Of course, complete data on games at position for every player can be found in the player registers.) Utility codes indicating specific positions are used only for catchers and those who also pitched a substantial amount (see paragraphs immediately above). Otherwise, utility codes are assigned by the following rules:

If the player played all three outfield positions but never played the infield, he will be labeled *UO* (utility outfielder). Quinton McCracken had 115 games in 2003: 10 in left, 16 in center, and 34 in right. Since he did not have 50 percent of his games at any one position, but did play all three outfield positions, he is labeled *UO*.

If the player played two outfield positions but never played the infield, he will be labeled *OF* (outfield). In 2003 Troy O'Leary of the Chicago Cubs had 28 games in left and 24 in right out of 93 games. He is an *OF*.

If the player played three or four infield positions but never played the outfield, he will be labeled as *UI* (utility infielder). In 2003 Carlos Baerga of Arizona had 19 games at first base, 15 at second base, and 5 at third base out of 105 games total, making him a *UI*.

If the player played two infield positions but never played the outfield, he will be labeled as *IF* (infielder). In 2001 Keith Lockhart of Atlanta had 47 games at second base and 4 games at third base out of 104 total. Since he played only two infield positions with no games in the outfield and no position with at least 50 percent of his games, he qualifies as an *IF*.

If the player played two or more Outfield positions as well as at least one infield position, and he played more games in the outfield than in the Infield, he will be labeled as *OI* (outfielder-infielder). In 2003 Brian Banks had 92 games total for Florida: 23 games in left, 12 at first, and 10 in right, qualifying him as *OI*.

If the player played two or more infield positions and at least one outfield position, and he played more games in the infield than in the outfield, he will be labeled as *IO* (infielder-outfielder). In 2003 Greg Norton of Colorado had 34 games at third, 9 at first, and 3 in right field (114 games total), giving him an *IO* code.

If a player's first or second position (in terms of number of games) is catcher, but he played less than 50 percent of his games there or at any other position, he will be labeled as *IC* (infielder/catcher) or *OC* (outfielder/catcher) depending on whether he played primarily in the infield or the outfield. If he played more games at catcher than elsewhere, and he did not play another defensive position in most of his other games (i.e., he was a DH or a pinch hitter), he will be labeled as *UC* (utility catcher). In 2001 Shawn Wooten played 79 games for Anaheim: 27 at DH, 25 at catcher, 21 at first, and 1 at third. Since his second position was catcher, but he played more there than in the infield or outfield, he is listed as *UC*.

If a player doesn't fit into any of these categories, he will be labeled as *UT* (utility). Matt Franco, who was mainly a pinch hitter for Atlanta in 2003, played 112 games: 3 games at first base, 2 in right, and 1 in left. Since he played the same number of games in the infield and outfield, he gets a *UT* code.

Managers. Managers are indicated by the code *M;* see the Manager Register introduction for an explanation of who qualifies as a manager. If a team had multiple managers in a season, the order in which these managers served is shown by the number after the *M* (i.e., the first manager will be *M1,* the second *M2,* etc.). Managers' names are italicized in the rosters. Player-managers are shown with standard position code(s) and located as a player; their italicization indicates managerial status. Non-playing managers are shown at the end of the team roster.

Most of the above rules apply only to a small fraction of the players and pitchers listed in the team rosters. More than three quarters of the 40,000-plus player and pitcher seasons in this section are shown with a primary position code. Most of the remaining players are shown with two-position codes.

BOS 1871 NA
SP A Spalding
C C McVey
1B C Gould
2S R Barnes
SS- G Wright
3B H Schafer
LF F Cone
CF H Wright
RF D Birdsall
LU- F Barrows
2B- S Jackson

CHI 1871 NA
SP G Zettlein
C3 C Hodes
1B B McAtee
2B J Wood
SS E Duffy
3B E Pinkham
LF F Treacey
MR T Foley
RM J Simmons
MC M King

CLE 1871 NA
SP A Pratt
C D White
1B J Carleton
2I G Kimball
SS J Bass
3B E Sutton
LF C Pabor
CF A Allison
RF- E White
2R- C Johnson

KEK 1871 NA
SP B Mathews
C B Lennon
1B J Foran
2B T Carey
S3 W Goldsmith
3B F Sellman
LF- E Mincher
CF B Armstrong
RF B Kelly
M2 H Deane

MUT 1871 NA
SP R Wolters
C C Mills
1B J Start
2R D Higham
SS D Pearce
32 B Ferguson
LI J Hatfield
CF D Eggler
RL D Patterson
3B- C Smith

ATH 1871 NA
SPD McBride
C F Malone
1B W Fisler
2B A Reach
SS J Radcliff
3B L Meyerle
LF N Cuthbert
CF C Sensenderfer
RF G Heubel
RU G Bechtel

ROK 1871 NA
SP C Fisher
C S Hastings
1B D Mack
2B B Addy
SS C Fulmer
3B C Anson
LF R Ham
CF G Bird
RF G Stires

TRO 1871 NA
SP J McMullin
C M McGeary
1R C Flynn
2U B Craver
SS D Flowers
3B S Bellan
LF S King
CF T York
R2 L Pike

OLY 1871 NA
SP A Brainard
C D Allison
1B E Mills
2L A Leonard
SS D Force
3B F Waterman
L2- H Berthrong
CF G Hall
RF J Glenn
M N Young

BAL 1872 NA
SP B Mathews
SP C Fisher
C B Craver
1B E Mills
2I T Carey
SS J Radcliff
3B- D Force
LF T York
CF G Hall
UT L Pike
CR D Higham

BOS 1872 NA
SP A Spalding
C C McVey
1B C Gould
2B R Barnes
SS G Wright
3B H Schafer
LF A Leonard
CF H Wright
RF F Rogers

ECK 1872 NA
SPP Martin
SP G Zettlein
SP J McDermott
C D Allison
1B A Allison
IO C Nelson
SS J Snyder
3B- F Fleet
LF C Gedney
CF- D Patterson
UT J Clinton
M2 J Wood

ATL 1872 NA
SP J Britt
C T Barlow
1B H Dehlman
2B- J Hall
SS J Burdock
3B B Ferguson
LF- A Thake
CF J Remsen
RF- J McDonald

CLE 1872 NA
SP A Pratt
SP R Wolters
C2 D White
1B J Simmons
2B- C Sweasy
SS J Holdsworth
3B E Sutton
LF C Pabor
CF A Allison
RF R Wolters
C2 S Hastings

MAN 1872 NA
SP C Bentley
SP F Buttery
C J Clapp
1B T Murnane
2B E Booth
SC J O'Rourke
3O G Fields
LF J Tipper
CF F McCarton
RF C Bentley
S3 H Allen

MUT 1872 NA
SP C Cummings
C N Hicks
1B J Start
2B J Hatfield
SS D Pearce
3B B Boyd
LF J McMullin
CF D Eggler
RL G Bechtel
3S C Fulmer

ATH 1872 NA
SPD McBride
C1 F Malone
1S D Mack
2B W Fisler
IC M McGeary
3B C Anson
LF N Cuthbert
CF F Treacey
RF- L Meyerle
RF- A Reach

TRO 1872 NA
SP G Zettlein
C D Allison
1B B McAtee
2B J Wood
IO S Bellan
3S D Force
LF S King
CF- C Gedney
RF P Martin

OLY 1872 NA
SP A Brainard
C F Sellman
1B C Flynn
2U T Beals
S2 W Goldsmith
3B F Waterman
LF J Glenn
CF- G Heubel
RF V Robinson

NAT 1872 NA
SP B Stearns
C B Lennon
1B P Hines
2B H Hollingshead
SS J Doyle
3B W White
LF E Mincher
CF- S Studley
RF O Bielaski
MI D Coughlin

MAR 1873 NA
SP E Stratton
SP Mc Doolan
SP F Sellman
MC B Smith
1B B Lennon
2B M Simpson
SR- L Say
3B H Kohler
LC- M Hooper
SL J Smith
IO B French

BAL 1873 NA
SP C Cummings
SP A Brainard
CI C McVey
1B E Mills
2B T Carey
3B B Ferguson
LF- A Thake
CF J Remsen
CF G Hall
RF L Pike
CS B Craver
CM-S Hastings

BOS 1873 NA
SP A Spalding
C D White
1R J O'Rourke
2B R Barnes
SS G Wright
3B H Schafer
LF A Leonard
CF H Wright
RF- B Addy
1B- J Manning

ATL 1873 NA
SP J Britt
C T Barlow
1B H Dehlman
2B J Burdock
SS D Pearce
3B B Ferguson
LF C Pabor
CF J Remsen
RF B Boyd

RES 1873 NA
SP H Campbell
C D Allison
1B M Campbell
2B- B Laughlin
SS- F Wordsworth
3B- A Nevin
LF E Booth
OI A Allison
MR H Austin
UI F Fleet

MUT 1873 NA
SP B Mathews
C - N Hicks
1B J Start
2B C Nelson
SS J Holdsworth
3B J Hatfield
LF C Gedney
CF D Eggler
RF- P Martin
OI D Higham

PHI 1873 NA
SP G Zettlein
C F Malone
1B D Mack
2B J Wood
SS C Fulmer
3B L Meyerle
LF N Cuthbert
CF F Treacey
RF G Bechtel
13- J Devlin

ATH 1873 NA
SPD McBride
C J Clapp
1I C Anson
2B W Fisler
SS M McGeary
3B E Sutton
LF J McMullin
MI T Murnane
RF C Fisher

WAS 1873 NA
SP B Stearns
SP J Greason
C P Snyder
1B J Glenn
2C T Beals
SS- J Gerhardt
3B W White
LF P Hines
CF H Hollingshead
RF O Bielaski
IO J Donnelly
M N Young

BAL 1874 NA
SP A Brainard
SP J Manning
C P Snyder
1B C Gould
2B J Manning
SS- L Say
3B W White
LF J Ryan
CF H Deane
RF O Bielaski

BOS 1874 NA
SP A Spalding
C D White
1B J O'Rourke
2B R Barnes
SS G Wright
3B H Schafer
LI A Leonard
RC McVey
RF O Bielaski
C2 D Higham
M J Wood

ATL 1874 NA
SP T Bond
C - J Knowdell
1B H Dehlman
C2- J Farrow
SS D Pearce
3B B Ferguson
LF E Booth
CF- B Clack
RF J Chapman

CHI 1874 NA
SP G Zettlein
C F Malone
1R J Glenn
23 L Meyerle
S2 J Peters
3S D Force
LF N Cuthbert
CF P Hines
RM-F Treacey
1R J Devlin
M2 J Wood

HAR 1874 NA
SP C Fisher
SP B Stearns
C S Hastings
1B E Mills
2B B Addy
SS T Barlow
3B- B Boyd
LF J Tipper
MS L Pike
CR B Barnie

MUT 1874 NA
SP B Mathews
CR D Higham
1B J Start
2B C Nelson
SS T Carey
3B J Burdock
LF J Hatfield
CF J Remsen
RC D Allison

PHI 1874 NA
SP C Cummings
C N Hicks
1B D Mack
2B B Craver
S3 C Fulmer
3S J Holdsworth
LF T York
CF D Eggler
RF- G Bechtel

ATH 1874 NA
SPD McBride
CS M McGeary
1B W Fisler
2B J Battin
3S E Sutton
IO C Anson
LF C Gedney
CF J McMullin
CR J Clapp

BOS 1875 NA
SR A Spalding
C D White
1O C McVey
2B R Barnes
SS G Wright
3B H Schafer
LF A Leonard
M3 J O'Rourke
Rp J Manning
MO-T Beals
M H Wright

ATL 1875 NA
SP J Cassidy
SP J Clinton
SP J O'Neill
C J Knowdell
1B- F Crane
IC- F Fleet
SO- H Kessler
3B A Nichols
LF C Pabor
CF- B Clack
IO B Boyd

CHI 1875 NA
SP G Zettlein
SP M Golden
CO S Hastings
1p J Devlin
2B- J Miller
SS J Peters
3B W White
L1 J Glenn
M2 H Hines
RF O Bielaski
C2 D Higham
M J Wood

RS 1875 NA
SP J Blong
C S Flint
1B C Hautz
2B C Sweasy
SS B Redmon
3L T McSorley
LM A Croft
OP D Morgan
RF T Oran

WAS 1875 NA
SP B Stearns
C - A Thompson
1B A Allison
2B S Brady
SI J Miller
3B H Doscher
Lp B Parks
MO H Hollingshead
R2 L Ressler

BOS 1876 NL
SP J Borden
SP F Bradley
C L Brown
1B T Murnane
2C J Morrill
SS G Wright
3B H Schafer
L2 A Leonard
CF J O'Rourke
Rp J Manning
LR- F Whitney
M H Wright

CHI 1876 NL
SPA Spalding
C D White
1B C McVey
2B R Barnes
SS J Peters
3B C Anson
LF J Glenn
CF P Hines
RF- O Bielaski

CEN 1875 NA
SP G Bechtel
C T McGinley
1B J Abadie
2B E Somerville
S3 B Craver
3B G Trenwith
LF F Treacey
CF F Warner
RL C Mason

PHI 1875 NA
SP C Fisher
SP G Zettlein
SP J Borden
C P Snyder
UT T Murnane
23 L Meyerle
SS C Fulmer
UT M McGeary
LF F Treacey
ML J McMullin
RF B Addy
1B- F Malone

ATH 1875 NA
SPD McBride
SP L Knight
C J Clapp
2B W Fisler
SS D Force
3B E Sutton
LF G Hall
CF D Eggler
RF- G Bechtel
UT C Anson
2O- J Richmond

STL 1875 NA
SP G Bradley
SP J Galvin
C T Miller
1B H Dehlman
2B J Battin
SS D Pearce
3B B Hague
LF N Cuthbert
CF L Pike
RF J Chapman
RF- C Waitt

HAR 1875 NA
SP C Cummings
SP T Bond
C D Allison
1B E Mills
2B J Burdock
SS T Carey
3B B Ferguson
LF T York
CF J Remsen
RF- A Allison
CI B Harbridge

WES 1875 NA
SP M Golden
C P Quinn
1B J Carbine
2B J Miller
SS J Hallinan
3B W Goldsmith
LF C Jones
MU J Simmons
RF B Riley
OC B Barnie

NH 1875 NA
SP T Nichols
C T McGinley
1B- C Gould
2B E Somerville
SS S Wright
3B H Luff
LF J Ryan
CF J Tipper
RF J McKelvey
UT B Geer
M2 J Latham
M3 C Pabor

MUT 1875 NA
SP B Mathews
C N Hicks
1B J Start
23 C Nelson
SS T Carey
3B J Burdock
LF J Gerhardt
CF P Hines
RF- O Bielaski

CIN 1876 NL
SP D Dean
SP C Fisher
SP D Williams
IC A Booth
1B C Gould
2B C Sweasy
SS H Kessler
3B W Foley
LF R Snyder
CF C Jones
CR D Pierson

HAR 1876 NL
SP T Bond
SP C Cummings
C D Allison
1B E Mills
2B J Burdock
SS T Carey
3B B Ferguson
LF F Treacey
CF J Remsen
RF D Higham

LOU 1876 NL
SP J Devlin
C P Snyder
1B J Gerhardt
2B E Somerville
SS C Fulmer
3B B Hague
LF J Ryan
CF S Hastings
R1- A Allison
M J Chapman

NY 1876 NL
SP B Mathews
C N Hicks
1B J Start
2B B Craver
SS D Force
3B A Nichols
LF F Treacey
CF J Holdsworth
RF E Booth

PHI 1876 NL
SP L Knight
SP G Zettlein
C - F Malone
12 E Sutton
UT W Fisler
SS D Force
3B L Meyerle
LF G Hall
CF D Eggler
RC W Coon
M A Wright

STL 1876 NL
SP G Bradley
C J Clapp
1B H Dehlman
2B M McGeary
SS D Mack
3B J Battin
LF N Cuthbert
CF L Pike
RF J Blong
M1 M Graffen
M2 G McManus

BOS 1877 NL
SP T Bond
C L Brown
1R D White
2B G Wright
S3 E Sutton
IO J Morrill
LS A Leonard
ML J O'Rourke
R3- H Schafer
MU-T Murnane
M H Wright

CHI 1877 NL
SP G Bradley
C3 C McVey
1B A Spalding
2B- R Barnes
SS J Peters
3C C Anson
L1 J Glenn
CF- D Eggler
OI P Hines

CIN 1877 NL
SP C Cummings
SP B Mathews
SP B Mitchell
C - S Hastings
1B- C Gould
2B- J Hallinan
UT J Manning
3B W White
LF J Ryan
CF P Hines
RF- O Bielaski
M2 L Pike
RF B Addy
IC A Booth
LC C Jones

HAR 1877 NL
SP T Larkin
C B Harbridge
1B J Start
2B J Burdock
SS T Carey
3B B Ferguson
LF T York
CF J Holdsworth
RF J Cassidy

LOU 1877 NL
SP J Devlin
C P Snyder
1B J Latham
2B J Gerhardt
SS B Craver
3B B Hague
LF G Hall
CF B Crowley
RF O Shafer
M J Chapman

STL 1877 NL
SP T Nichols
C J Clapp
1B- H Dehlman
23 M McGeary
SS D Force
32 J Battin
OP J Blong
CF- J Remsen
UT M Dorgan
1L A Croft
M G McManus

BOS 1878 NL
SP T Bond
C P Snyder
1B J Morrill
2B J Burdock
SS G Wright
3B E Sutton
LF A Leonard
CF J O'Rourke
RF J Manning
M H Wright

CHI 1878 NL
SP T Larkin
C B Harbridge
1B J Start
2B B McClellan
SS B Ferguson
3B F Hankinson
LF C Anson
CF J Remsen
RF J Cassidy

CIN 1878 NL
SP W White
SP B Mitchell
C D White
1B C Sullivan
2B J Gerhardt
SS B Geer
3B C McVey
LF C Jones
CF- L Pike
RF K Kelly

IND 1878 NL
SP T Nolan
SP J McCormick
SP T Healey
C S Flint
1B A Croft
2B J Quest
SS F Warner
3B E Williamson
LI J Clapp
CF R McKelvy
RF O Shafer

MIL 1878 NL
SP S Weaver
CM C Bennett
1B J Goodman
2S J Peters
SS B Redmon
3B W Foley
LF A Dalrymple
Mp M Golden
RC B Holbert
2M G Creamer
M J Chapman

PRO 1878 NL
SP J Ward
SP T Nichols
SP H Wheeler
C L Brown
1B T Murnane
2B C Sweasy
SS T Carey
3B B Hague
LF T York
CF P Hines
RF D Higham

BOS 1879 NL
SP T Bond
SP C Foley
C P Snyder
1B- E Cogswell
2B J Burdock

S3 E Sutton
31 J Morrill
LF C Jones
CF J O'Rourke
RS S Houck
M H Wright

BUF 1879 NL
SP J Galvin
SP B McGunnigle
C J Clapp
1B O Walker
2B C Fulmer
SS D Force
3B H Richardson
LF J Hornung
CF D Eggler
RU B Crowley

CHI 1879 NL
SP T Larkin
SP F Hankinson
C S Flint
1B C Anson
2B J Quest
SS J Peters
3B E Williamson
LF A Dalrymple
CF G Gore
RF K Kelly
M1- J Remsen

CIN 1879 NL
SP W White
C D White
1B C McVey
2I J Gerhardt
SS R Barnes
3R W Foley
LF B Dickerson
CF P Hotaling
UT K Kelly

CLE 1879 NL
SPJ McCormick
SP B Mitchell
C - D Kennedy
1B B Phillips
2B J Glasscock
SS T Carey
3O F Warner
LF- B Riley
CF G Strief
RF C Eden
CL B Gilligan

PRO 1879 NL
SR J Ward
SP B Mathews
C L Brown
1B J Start
2B M McGeary
SS G Wright
3B- B Hague
LF T York
CF P Hines
RI J O'Rourke

SYR 1879 NL
SP H McCormick
C B Holbert
13 H Carpenter
2B J Farrell
SM J Macullar
3B- R Woodhead
LF M Mansell
OI J Richmond
Rp B Purcell
IO M Dorgan

TRO 1879 NL
SP G Bradley
SP H Salisbury
SP F Goldsmith
C C Reilley
1B- D Brouthers
2B T Hawkes
SC E Caskin
3B H Doscher
LF- T Mansell
CF A Hall
RF J Evans
M1 H Phillips
M2 B Ferguson

BOS 1880 NL
SP T Bond
SP C Foley
C - P Powers
1B C Foley
2B J Burdock
S3 E Sutton
13 J Morrill
LF C Jones
CF Jo O'Rourke
UT Ji O'Rourke
M H Wright

BUF 1880 NL
SP J Galvin
SP S Wiedman
SP T Poorman
C J Rowe
1U D Esterbrook
2S D Force
SS- M Moynahan
3B H Richardson
LF J Hornung
RC B Crowley
RC- E Stearns
M S Crane

CHI 1880 NL
SP L Corcoran
SP F Goldsmith
C S Flint
1B C Anson
2B J Quest
SS T Burns
3B E Williamson
LF A Dalrymple
CF G Gore
RF K Kelly

CIN 1880 NL
SP W White
C J Clapp
1B J Reilly
2B P Smith
SS- L Say
3B H Carpenter
LF M Mansell
Mp B Purcell
RF- J Manning

CLE 1880 NL
SPJ McCormick
SP G Gardner
C D Kennedy
1B B Phillips
2B F Dunlap
SS J Glasscock
3B F Hankinson
LF N Hanlon
CF P Hotaling
RF O Shafer

PRO 1880 NL
SP J Ward
C E Gross
1B J Start
2B J Farrell
SS J Peters
3p G Bradley
LF T York
CF P Hines
RF M Dorgan
LF- S Houck
M1 M McGeary
M2 M Ward

TRO 1880 NL
SP M Welch
SP T Keefe
C B Holbert
1B- E Cogswell
2B B Ferguson
SS E Caskin
3B R Connor
LF P Gillespie
MR J Cassidy
RF- J Evans

WOR 1880 NL
SP L Richmond
SP F Corey
C - C Bennett
1B- C Sullivan
2B G Creamer
SS A Irwin
3B H Carpenter
LF B Dickerson
CF P Hotaling
RC E Rowen

BOS 1881 NL
SP J Whitney
SP J Fox
C P Snyder
1B J Morrill
2B J Burdock
SS R Barnes
3B E Sutton
LF J Hornung
MR B Crowley
RF- F Lewis
CU- P Deasley
M H Wright

BUF 1881 NL
SP J Galvin
SP J Lynch
CU J Rowe
L1 D Brouthers
2S D Force
SS J Peters
3U J O'Rourke
LF- B Purcell
CF H Richardson
R1 C Foley
UT D White

CHI 1881 NL
SP L Corcoran
SP F Goldsmith
C S Flint
1B C Anson
2B J Quest
SS T Burns
3B E Williamson
LF A Dalrymple
CF G Gore
RF K Kelly

CLE 1881 NL
SP J McCormick
SP T Nolan
CO J Clapp
1B B Phillips
2B F Dunlap
SS J Glasscock
3B G Bradley
LF- M Moynahan
CF- J Remsen
RF O Shafer
M1 M McGeary

DET 1881 NL
SP G Derby
SP S Wiedman
SP F Mountain
C C Bennett
1B M Powell
2B J Gerhardt
SS S Houck
3B A Whitney
LF G Wood
RF L Knight
M F Bancroft

PRO 1881 NL
SP C Radbourn
SP B Mathews
C - E Gross
1B- J Start
2B J Farrell
3B J Denny
LF T York
CF P Hines
OP J Ward
C - B Gilligan

TRO 1881 NL
SP T Keefe
SP M Welch
CS B Ewing
1B R Connor
2B B Ferguson
SS E Caskin
3B F Hankinson
LF P Gillespie
1O R Connor
RF C Roseman

WOR 1882 NL
SP L Richmond
SP F Mountain
C D Bushong
1L H Stovey
2B G Creamer
3S A Irwin
3B- F Mann
LF- J Clinton
MU J Hayes
RF J Evans
Sp F Corey
M1 F Brown
M2 T Bond
M3 J Chapman

BAL 1882 AA
SP D Landis
SP T Nichols
SP E Geis
C E Whiting
1B C Householder
2B- G Pierce
SS H Myers
32 J Shetzline
LF C Waitt
CF- M Cline
RF T Brown

CIN 1882 AA
SP W White
SP H McCormick
C P Snyder
1U E Stearns
2B B McPhee
SS C Fulmer
3B H Carpenter
LF J Sommer
CF J Macullar
RF H Wheeler

LOU 1882 AA
SP T Mullane
SP D Sullivan
1p H Hecker

CHI 1882 NL
SP F Goldsmith
SP L Corcoran
1B C Anson
2S T Burns
SR K Kelly
3B E Williamson
LF A Dalrymple
CF G Gore
RF- H Nicol
2B- J Quest

CLE 1882 NL
SPJ McCormick
SP G Bradley
C F Briody
1B B Phillips
2B F Dunlap
SS J Glasscock
3L M Muldoon
LF- D Esterbrook
CF- J Richmond
RF O Shafer

DET 1882 NL
SP S Wiedman
SP G Derby
C C Bennett
1B M Powell
2B- D Troy
SS- M McGeary
32 J Farrell
LF G Wood
CF N Hanlon
RF L Knight
M F Bancroft

PRO 1882 NL
SP C Radbourn
C B Gilligan
1B J Start
2B J Farrell
SS- G Wright
3B J Denny
LF T York
CF P Hines
Rp J Ward
M H Wright

TRO 1882 NL
SP T Keefe
SP M Welch
SP J Egan
C B Holbert
1B- J Smith
2B B Ferguson
SS F Pfeffer
3C B Ewing
LF P Gillespie
1O R Connor
RF C Roseman

BUF 1882 NL
SP J Galvin
SP H Daily
CS J Rowe
1B D Brouthers
2B H Richardson
SS D Force
3B D White
LF B Purcell
CF J O'Rourke
RF C Foley

2S P Browning
S2 D Mack
3B B Schenck
RF S Wiedman
LF L Maskrey
MU J Reccius
RF J Wolf

PHI 1882 AA
SP S Weaver
SP B Sweeney
CF G Mountain
RF- H Nicol
2B- J Quest
1B J Latham
2B C Stricker
SS L Say
3B- F Mann
LF J Birchall
CF- J Mansell
UT B Blakiston
CR- J Dorgan

PIT 1882 AA
SP H Salisbury
SP D Driscoll
SP H Arundel
IC B Taylor
1B C Lane
2B G Strief
SS J Peters
3B- J Battin
LF M Mansell
RM E Swartwood
3R J Leary
M A Pratt

STL 1882 AA
SP J McGinnis
SP J Schappert
C B Dorr
1B C Comiskey
2B J Farrell
SS B Gleason
3B J Denny
LF- C Carroll
CF O Walker
RU- G Seward

BOS 1883 NL
SP J Whitney
C M Hines
1B J Morrill
2B J Burdock
SS S Wise
3B E Sutton
LF J Hornung
CF- E Smith
RM P Radford
PR C Buffinton

BUF 1883 NL
SP J Galvin
SP G Derby
CL J Rowe
1B D Brouthers
2B H Richardson
SS D Force
3B D White
LC J O'Rourke
MO- J Lillie
3B- F Mann
RF O Shafer
RF P Corkhill
CF J O'Rourke
RF C Roseman
M J Mutrie

NY 1883 NL
SP M Welch
SP T O'Neill
CU B Ewing
1B R Connor
2B D Troy
SS E Caskin
3B F Hankinson
LF P Gillespie
Mp J Ward
RF M Dorgan
M J Clapp

PHI 1883 NL
SP J Coleman
SP A Hagan
SP J Neagle
C - E Gross
1B S Farrar
2B B Ferguson
3B- F Warner
UT B Harbridge
RF J Manning
CU F Ringo
M1 A Pratt
M2 O Butler

PRO 1883 NL
SP C Radbourn
SP C Sweeney
SP L Richmond
C B Gilligan
1B J Start
2B J Farrell
SS A Irwin
3B J Denny
CF P Hines
RF J Cassidy
M H Wright

BAL 1883 AA
SP H Henderson
SP B Emslie
SP J Fox
C - J Kelly
1B E Stearns
2B- T Manning
SS L Say
3B J McCormick
LF J Clinton
CF- D Eggler
RF D Rowe
M B Barnie

CIN 1883 AA
SP W White
SP R Deagle
SP H McCormick
C - P Snyder
1B J Reilly
2B B McPhee
SS C Fulmer
3B H Carpenter
LF J Sommer
CF C Jones
RF P Corkhill

COL 1883 AA
SP F Mountain
SP E Dundon
SP J Valentine
C R Kemmler
1B J Field
2B P Smith
SS J Richmond
3I B Kuehne
LF W Wheeler
CF F Mann
RF T Brown
M H Phillips

LOU 1883 AA
SP G Hecker
SP W Weaver
C - E Whiting
1B B Phillips
2B J Latham
3B M Muldoon
SS- J Leary
3B J Gleason
LF- W Murphy
OI L Maskrey
RF J Wolf

NY 1883 AA
SP T Keefe
SP J Lynch
C B Holbert
1B S Crane
SS C Nelson
3B D Esterbrook
LF E Kennedy

PHI 1883 AA
SP B Mathews
SP J Bakely
CM J O'Brien
1B H Stovey
2B C Stricker
SS M Moynahan
3p G Bradley
LF J Birchall
CF- B Blakiston
RF L Knight
3p F Corey
C - E Rowen

PIT 1883 AA
SP D Driscoll
SP B Barr
SP J Neagle
CU J Hayes
1B C Householder
SS B McClellan
3B- F Warner
RF J Manning
CU F Ringo
Cp B Taylor

STL 1883 AA
SP T Mullane
SP J McGinnis
C - P Deasley
1B C Comiskey
2B G Strief
SS B Gleason
3B A Latham
CO T Dolan
CF- F Lewis
RF H Nicol
M1 T Sullivan

BOS 1884 NL
SP C Buffinton
SP J Whitney
C M Hackett
1B J Morrill
2B J Burdock
SS S Wise
3B E Sutton
LF J Hornung
CF J Manning
RF B Crowley

BUF 1884 NL
SP J Galvin
SP B Serad
CO J Rowe
1B J Reilly
3B D White
LF J O'Rourke
CF- D Eggler
RF J Lillie
CO G Myers

CHI 1884 NL
SP L Corcoran
SP F Goldsmith
SP J Clarkson
C S Flint
1B C Anson
2B F Pfeffer
SS T Burns
3B E Williamson
LF A Dalrymple
CF G Gore
RC K Kelly

CLE 1884 NL
SP J Harkins
SP J McCormick
SP S Moffett
C - D Bushong
1B B Phillips
2S G Smith
SS J Glasscock
3B M Muldoon
LF- W Murphy
CF P Hotaling
RL J Evans
M C Hackett

DET 1884 NL
SP D Shaw
SP C Getzien
SP F Brill
C C Bennett
1B M Scott
2B B Geis
3B J Farrell
Sp F Meinke
3B J Farrell
LF G Wood
CF N Hanlon
Rp S Wiedman
M J Chapman

NY 1884 NL
SP M Welch
SP E Begley
C B Ewing
1B A McKinnon
2M R Connor
SS E Caskin
3B F Hankinson
LF P Gillespie
M2 J Ward
Rp M Dorgan
RS D Richardson
M1 J Price
M2 M Ward

PHI 1884 NL
SP C Ferguson
SP B Vinton
SP J Coleman
SP J McElroy
C - J Crowley
1B S Farrar
2B E Andrews
SS B McClellan
3B J Mulvey
LF B Purcell
MU J Fogarty
RF J Manning
M H Wright

PRO 1884 NL
SP C Radbourn
SP C Sweeney
SP E Conley
C B Gilligan
1B J Start
2B J Farrell
SS A Irwin
3B J Denny
LF C Carroll
CF P Hines
RF P Radford
M F Bancroft

BAL 1884 AA
SP B Emslie
SP H Henderson
C S Trott
1B E Stearns
2B T Manning
SS J Macullar
3B J Sommer
LF T York
ML J Clinton
RF- G Gardner
C - B Traffley
M B Barnie

BRO 1884 AA
SP A Terry
SP S Kimber
SP J Conway
CU- J Corcoran
1C C Householder
2B B Greenwood
SS B Geer
3B F Warner
LF- I Benners
ML J Remsen
RF J Cassidy
OI O Walker
M G Taylor

CIN 1884 AA
SPW White
SP B Mountjoy
SP G Shallix
C - P Snyder
1B J Reilly
2B B McPhee
SU- J Peoples
3B H Carpenter
LM- T Mansell
LM C Jones
RF P Corkhill

COL 1884 AA
SP E Morris
SP F Mountain
SP E Dundon
C - R Kemmler
1B J Field
2B P Smith
SS J Richmond
3B B Kuehne
LF- J Cahill
CF M Mann
RF T Brown
C F Carroll
M G Schmelz

IND 1884 AA
SP L McKeon
SP B Barr
SP J Aydelott
SP A McCauley
C J Keenan
1B J Kerins
2B- E Merrill
SS M Phillips
3B- P Callaghan
LF J Peltz
CF- J Morrison
RM-P Weihe
M1 J Gifford
M2 B Watkins

LOU 1884 AA
SP G Hecker
SP D Driscoll
SP R Deagle
C - D Sullivan
1B J Latham
2B J Gerhardt
SS T McLaughlin
3I P Browning
LF L Maskrey
CF M Cline
RF J Wolf
3p P Reccius
M M Walsh

NY 1884 AA
SP J Lynch
SP T Keefe
C - B Holbert
1B D Orr
2B D Troy
SS C Nelson
3B D Esterbrook
LF E Kennedy
CF C Roseman
RF S Brady
C - C Reipschlager
M J Mutrie

PHI 1884 AA
SP B Mathews
SP B Taylor
SP A Atkinson
C J Milligan
1B H Stovey
2B C Stricker
SS S Houck
3B F Corey
LF- J Birchall
ML H Larkin
RF L Knight

PIT 1884 AA
SP F Sullivan
SP J Neagle
C - E Colgan
1B- J Knowles
2B G Creamer
SS B White
3B- J Battin
LC D Miller
CF- L Taylor
RF E Swartwood
M1 D McKnight
M2 B Ferguson
M5 H Phillips

RIC 1884 AA
SP P Meegan
SP E Dugan
C - J Hanna
1B J Powell
2B T Larkin
SS B Schenck
3B B Nash
LF E Glenn
CF D Johnston
RF M Mansell
M F Moses

STL 1884 AA
SP J McGinnis
SP D Foutz
SP D Davis
SP B Caruthers
C P Deasley
1B C Comiskey
2B J Quest
SS B Gleason
3B A Latham
Lp T O'Neill
CF F Lewis
RF H Nicol
M1 J Williams

TOL 1884 AA
SP T Mullane
SP H O'Day
C - F Walker
1B- C Lane
2B S Barkley

SS J Miller
3B- E Brown
LF- F Olin
CF C Welch
RF T Poorman
1l- J Moffett
M C Morton

WAS 1884 AA
SP B Barr
SP J Hamill
CU J Humphries
1B W Prince
2B T Hawkes
SS F Fennelly
3B B Gladman
UT B Morgan
CF- H Mullin
OP- E Trumbull
M1 H Hollingshead
M2 Bickerson

ALT 1884 UA
SP J Murphy
SP J Leary
CR J Moore
1O H Farris
2O C Dougherty
SS G Smith
3B J McCormick
LI B Hoover
CF B Kienzle
RF J Flynn
OI J Shafer
PR J Brown
M E Curtis

BAL 1884 UA
SP B Sweeney
SP T Lee
SP A Atkinson
C E Fusselback
1B C Levis
2B D Phelan
SS L Say
3U Y Robinson
LF E Seery
CF- N Cuthbert
MR-B Graham
CO-R Sweeney
M B Henderson

BOS 1884 UA
SP J Burke
SP D Shaw
SP T Bond
C1 L Brown
1B- T Murnane
2B T O'Brien
SS W Hackett
3B J Irwin
LI K Butler
CF M Slattery
OC E Crane

CP 1884 UA
SP H Daily
SP A Atkinson
SP J Horan
CO B Krieg
1B J Schoeneck
2B- M Hengle
SS- S Matthias
3B- W Foley
IO C Householder
CF- H Wheeler
RS J Ellick
MI- C Briggs
UT- G Gardner
CS-T Suck
M1 E Hengle
M2 J Battin

CIN 1884 UA
SP G Bradley
SP J McCormick
C - J Kelly
1B- M Powell
2B S Crane
S2 J Jones
3B- C Barber
LR L Sylvester
MR B Harbridge
OI B Hawes
PM D Burns
SS- J Glasscock
1B- M McQuery
M1 D O'Leary

KC 1884 UA
SP E Hickman
SP B Black
SP P Veach
SP A Voss
C K Baldwin
1B- J Sweeney
2B- C Berry
SS- C Cross
3M- P Sullivan
UT- F Wyman

UT- B McLaughlin
RF- T Shafer
M1 H Wheeler
M2 M Porter
M3 T Sullivan

MIL 1884 UA
SP H Porter
SP E Cushman
CM C Broughton
1B T Griffin
2B A Myers
SS T Sexton
3B T Morrissey
LF S Behel
MP-L Baldwin
RF E Hogan
M T Loftus

PHI 1884 UA
SP J Bakely
SP S Weaver
SP Fisher
C - T Gillen
1B J McGuinness
2B E Peak
SS- H Easterday
3B J McCormick
LI B Hoover
CF B Kienzle
RF J Flynn
OC J Clements
M F Malone

STL 1884 UA
SP C Sweeney
SP B Taylor
SP P Werden
SP C Hodnett
C G Baker
1B J Quinn
2B F Dunlap
SS M Whitehead
3B J Gleason
Lp- H Boyle
CF D Rowe
RF O Shafer
CO- J Brennan
LF- B Dickerson
M1 T Sullivan

STP 1884 UA
SP J Brown
SP L Galvin
C C Ganzel
1B S Dunn
2B M Hengle
SS J Werrick
3B B O'Brien
LF J Tilley
CF B Barnes
RF S Carroll
M A Thompson

WAS 1884 UA
SP B Wise
SP A Voss
SP C Gagus
SP A Powell
CO-C Fulmer
1B- P Joy
2B T Evers
SS- J Halpin
3B- J McCormick
LF H Moore
UT P Baker
RF B Wise
CO- J Gunson
M M Scanlon

WIL 1884 UA
SP J Murphy
SP T Nolan
SP D Casey
SP J Bakely
CS T Cusick
1B R Snyder
2B C Bastian
SS- H Myers
3B J Say
CL T Lynch
CF-G Fisher
RF- J Munce
M J Simmons

BOS 1885 NL
SP J Whitney
SP C Buffinton
SP D Davis
C - T Gunning
1B J Morrill
2B- J Burdock
SU S Wise
3B E Sutton
LF- T McCarthy
CF J Manning
RF- T Poorman

BUF 1885 NL
SPJ Galvin
SP B Serad
SP P Conway
SP P Wood
C G Myers
1B D Brouthers
2S D Force
SU J Rowe
3B D White
LF B Crowley
2M H Richardson
RF J Lillie
M2 J Chapman

CHI 1885 NL
SP J Clarkson
SP J McCormick
SP T Kennedy
C S Flint
1B C Anson
2B F Pfeffer
SS T Burns
3B E Williamson
LF A Dalrymple
CF G Gore
RC K Kelly
Lp A Terry
M1 C Hackett
M2 C Byrne

DET 1885 NL
SP C Getzien
SP S Wiedman
SP L Baldwin
SP D Casey
CU C Bennett
1B M McQuery
2B S Crane
SS- M Phillips
3B- J Donnelly
LF G Wood
CF N Hanlon
RF- S Thompson
M1 C Morton
M2 B Watkins

NY 1885 NL
SP M Welch
SP T Keefe
SP D Richardson
C B Ewing
1B R Connor
2B J Gerhardt
SS J Ward
3B P Reccius
LF- L Maskrey
CF P Browning
RF J Wolf
M J Mutrie

PHI 1885 NL
SP E Daily
SP C Ferguson
SP B Vinton
C - J Clements
1B S Farrar
2B A Myers
SS C Bastian
3B J Mulvey
LF E Andrews
CF J Fogarty
RF J Manning
M H Wright

PRO 1885 NL
SP C Radbourn
SP D Shaw
C B Gilligan
1B J Start
2B J Farrell
SS- A Irwin
3B J Denny
LF C Carroll
CF P Hines
RF P Radford
UI C Bassett
C - C Daily
M F Bancroft

STL 1885 NL
SP H Boyle
SP J Kirby
SP J Daily
C - F Briody
1B A McKinnon
2B F Dunlap
SS J Glasscock
3B E Caskin
LF- E Seery
CF- F Lewis
RF O Shafer
OP C Sweeney
UT J Quinn
M3 F Dunlap

BAL 1885 AA
SP H Henderson
SP B Emslie
SP J Henry

C B Traffley
1B E Stearns
2B- T Manning
SS J Macullar
3B M Muldoon
LF J Sommer
CF- D Casey
Rp T Burns
MU-E Greer
M B Barnie

BRO 1885 AA
SP H Porter
SP J Harkins
C - J Hayes
1B B Phillips
23 G Pinkney
SS G Smith
32 B McClellan
UT E Swartwood
CF P Hotaling
RF- J Cassidy
Lp A Terry
M1 C Hackett
M2 C Byrne

CIN 1885 AA
SP W White
SP L McKeon
SP B Mountjoy
SP G Pechiney
SP G Shallix
C - P Snyder
1B J Reilly
2B B McPhee
SS F Fennelly
3B H Carpenter
LF C Jones
CF G Gore
OC K Kelly
UT J Ryan

LOU 1885 AA
SP G Hecker
SP N Baker
SP A Mays
SP T Ramsey
C - J Crotty
1B J Kerins
2B T McLaughlin
SS J Miller
3B P Reccius
LF- L Maskrey
CF P Browning
RF J Wolf
M J Hart

NY 1885 AA
SP J Lynch
SP E Cushman
SP D Crothers
SP E Begley
SP B Becannon
C C Reipschlager
1B D Orr
2B- T Forster
SS C Nelson
3B H Hankinson
LF E Kennedy
CF C Roseman
RF S Brady
CU-B Holbert
M J Gifford

PHI 1885 AA
SP B Mathews
SP T Lovett
SP E Knouff
SP E Cushman
C - J Milligan
1M H Stovey
2B C Stricker
SS S Houck
3B F Corey
LF- B Purcell
ML H Larkin
RF J Coleman
Cl- J O'Brien

PIT 1885 AA
SP E Morris
SP P Meegan
SP H O'Day
SP J Galvin
C F Carroll
1B- J Field
2B P Smith
SS A Whitney
3B B Kuehne
LF C Eden
CF F Mann
RF T Brown
M H Phillips

STL 1885 AA
SP B Caruthers
SP D Foutz
SP J McGinnis

C D Bushong
1B C Comiskey
2B S Barkley
SS B Gleason
3B A Latham
LI Y Robinson
CF C Welch
RF H Nicol

BOS 1886 NL
SP C Radbourn
SP B Stemmeyer
SP C Buffinton
C - C Daily
1I S Wise
2B- J Burdock
UI J Morrill
3B M Nash
LF J Hornung
CF D Johnston
RF T Poorman
UT E Sutton

CHI 1886 NL
SP J Clarkson
SP J McCormick
SP J Flynn
C - S Flint
1B C Anson
2B F Pfeffer
SS E Williamson
3B T Burns
LF A Dalrymple
CF G Gore
OC K Kelly
UT J Ryan

DET 1886 NL
SP L Baldwin
SP C Getzien
SP P Conway
SP B Schmidt
C - C Bennett
1B D Brouthers
2B- F Dunlap
SS J Rowe
3B D White
L2 H Richardson
CF N Hanlon
RF S Thompson
M B Watkins

KC 1886 NL
SP S Wiedman
SP J Whitney
SP P Conway
C - F Briody
1B M McQuery
2B A Myers
SS S Bassett
3B J Donnelly
LF L Lillie
CF D Rowe
RF P Radford
C - M Hackett

NY 1886 NL
SP T Keefe
SP M Welch
CO-B Ewing
1B R Connor
2B J Gerhardt
SS J Ward
3B D Esterbrook
LF P Gillespie
ML-D Richardson
RF M Dorgan
MC J O'Rourke
M J Mutrie

PHI 1886 NL
SP C Ferguson
SP D Casey
C - D McGuire
1B S Farrar
2B C Bastian
SS A Irwin
3B J Mulvey
LF G Wood
CF E Andrews
RF J Fogarty
Rp E Daily
M H Wright

STL 1886 NL
SP J Healy
SP J Kirby
SP H Boyle
SP J Sweeney
C G Myers
1B A McKinnon
2B- F Dunlap
SS J Glasscock
3B J Denny
LF E Seery
CF- J McGeachy
CF- E.Greer
RF J Coleman

MI- J Quinn
M G Schmelz

WAS 1886 NL
SP D Shaw
SP B Barr
SP T Madigan
SP F Gilmore
C - B Gilligan
1O P Baker
23 J Knowles
LF C Carroll
CF P Hines
RU E Crane
M1 M Scanlon
M2 J Gaffney

BAL 1886 AA
SP M Kilroy
SP J McGinnis
SP H Henderson
C - C Fulmer
1B M Scott
23 M Muldoon
SS J Macullar
3B- J Davis
LI J Sommer
CF- P O'Connell
RF J Manning
23- J Farrell
M B Barnie

BRO 1886 AA
SP H Porter
SP J Harkins
SP A Terry
SP H Henderson
SP S Toole
C J Peoples
1B B Phillips
2B B McClellan
SS G Smith
3B G Pinkney
LF E Burch
RF J McTamany
CF E Swartwood
CO-B Clark
M C Byrne

CIN 1886 AA
SP T Mullane
SP G Pechiney
SP L McKeon
C K Baldwin
1B J Reilly
2B B McPhee
SS F Fennelly
3B H Carpenter
LF C Jones
CF- F Lewis
RF- P Corkhill
M O Caylor

LOU 1886 AA
SP T Ramsey
SP G Hecker
C1- A Cross
C1 J Kerins
2B R Mack
SS B White
3B J Werrick
LF- J Strauss
ML P Browning
RF J Wolf
M J Hart

NY 1886 AA
SP J Lynch
SP A Mays
SP E Cushman
C - C Reipschlager
1B- D Orr
2B- T Forster
SM C Nelson
3B D Hankinson
LM C Roseman
ML- S Behel
RF S Brady
SS- T McLaughlin
UI J Burnham
M2 B Ferguson

PHI 1886 AA
SP A Atkinson
SP B Mathews
SP B Hart
SP T Kennedy
SP C Miller
C G Myers
1B A McKinnon
1M H Stovey
2B L Bierbauer
SS- C McGarr
3B- J Gleason
LF H Larkin
CF- E.Greer
RF J Coleman

IC J O'Brien
C1- J Milligan
M1 L Simmons
M2 B Sharsig

PIT 1886 AA
SP E Morris
SP J Galvin
SP J Handiboe
CU F Carroll
1B- O Schomberg
2B S Barkley
SS P Smith
3S A Whitney
LF- E Glenn
CF F Mann
RF T Brown
UT B Kuehne
CO-D Miller
M H Phillips

STL 1886 AA
SP D Foutz
SP B Caruthers
SP N Hudson
SP J McGinnis
C. D Bushong
1B C Comiskey
2B Y Robinson
SS B Gleason
3B A Latham
LF T O'Neill
CF C Welch
RF- H Nicol

BOS 1887 NL
SP C Radbourn
SP K Madden
SP D Conway
SP B Stemmeyer
C - P Tate
1B J Morrill
2B- J Burdock
SU S Wise
3B M Nash
LF J Hornung
CF D Johnston
R2 K Kelly
UT E Sutton

CHI 1887 NL
SP J Clarkson
SP M Baldwin
SP G Van Haltren
C - T Daly
1B C Anson
2B F Pfeffer
SS E Williamson
3B T Burns
LF M Sullivan
CF J Ryan
RM-B Sunday

DET 1887 NL
SP C Getzien
SP L Baldwin
SP S Wiedman
SP P Conway
SP L Twitchell
C - C Ganzel
1B D Brouthers
2B- F Dunlap
SS J Rowe
3B D White
2L H Richardson
CF N Hanlon
RF S Thompson
M B Watkins

IND 1887 NL
SP J Healy
SP H Boyle
SP L Shreve
CU-G Myers
1B O Schomberg
2B C Bassett
SS J Glasscock
3B J Denny
LF E Seery
CF J McGeachy
RF- J Cahill
M1 W Burnham
M2 F Thomas
M3 F Fogel

NY 1887 NL
SP T Keefe
SP M Welch
SP B George
C - W Brown
1B R Connor
2B D Richardson
SS J Ward
3U- B Ewing
LF- D Gillespie
CF G Gore
RL M Tiernan
IC J O'Rourke

RF- M Dorgan
M J Mutrie

PHI 1887 NL
SP D Casey
SP C Buffinton
SP C Ferguson
C - J Clements
1B S Farrar
2B- B McLaughlin
SS A Irwin
3B J Mulvey
LF G Wood
CF E Andrews
RF J Fogarty
M H Wright

PIT 1887 NL
SP J Galvin
SP J McCormick
SP E Morris
C D Miller
12 S Barkley
2S P Smith
SS B Kuehne
3B A Whitney
LA A Dalrymple
CF- T Brown
RF J Coleman
OC F Carroll
M H Phillips

WAS 1887 NL
SP J Whitney
SP H O'Day
SP F Gilmore
SP D Shaw
C C Mack
1B B O'Brien
2S A Myers
S2 J Farrell
3B J Donnelly
LF C Carroll
CF P Hines
RF E Daily
RU- G Shoch
M J Gaffney

BAL 1887 AA
SP M Kilroy
SP P Smith
C S Trott
1B T Tucker
2B B Greenwood
S3 T Burns
3S J Davis
LF J Sommer
CF M Griffin
RF B Purcell
M B Barnie

BRO 1887 AA
SP H Porter
SP J Harkins
SP S Toole
SP H Henderson
C - J Peoples
1B B Phillips
2B B McClellan
SS G Smith
3B G Pinkney
LF E Greer
CF J McTamany
RF E Swartwood
OP A Terry
M C Byrne

CIN 1887 AA
SP E Smith
SP T Mullane
SP B Serad
C K Baldwin
1B J Reilly
2B B McPhee
SS F Fennelly
3B H Carpenter
LF G Tebeau
CF P Corkhill
RF H Nicol
M G Schmelz

CLE 1887 AA
SP B Crowell
SP M Morrison
SP H Daily
SP B Gilks
SP G Pechiney
C - P Snyder
1B J Toy
2C C Ganzel
2B C Stricker
2B S McKean
3B- F Reccius
LR- F Mann
CF P Hotaling
LR M Allen
M J Williams

LOU 1887 AA
SP T Ramsey
SP E Chamberlain
C - P Cook
1C J Kerins
2B R Mack
SS B White
3B J Werrick
LF H Collins
CF P Browning
RF J Wolf
1p G Hecker
M J Kelly

NY 1887 AA
SP A Mays
SP- E Cushman
SP J Lynch
SP J Shaffer
SP S Wiedman
C - B Holbert
1B D Orr
2B J Gerhardt
SR P Radford
3B F Hankinson
LF D O'Brien
CF- C Jones
MO-C Roseman
M1 B Ferguson
M3 O Caylor

PHI 1887 AA
SP E Seward
SP G Weyhing
SP A Atkinson
C - W Robinson
1C J Milligan
2B L Bierbauer
SS C McGarr
3B J Lyons
LI H Larkin
OI H Stovey
RF T Poorman
M1 F Bancroft
M2 C Mason

STL 1887 AA
SP S King
C J Boyle
1B C Comiskey
2B Y Robinson
SS B Gleason
3B A Latham
LF T O'Neill
CF C Welch
Rp B Caruthers
Rp D Foutz

BOS 1888 NL
SP J Clarkson
SP B Sowders
SP C Radbourn
SP K Madden
CR K Kelly
1B J Morrill
2B- J Quinn
SS S Wise
3B B Nash
LF J Hornung
CF D Johnston
RF T Brown

CHI 1888 NL
SP G Krock
SP M Baldwin
SP G Van Haltren
SP J Tener
C - T Daly
1B C Anson
2B F Pfeffer
SS E Williamson
3B T Burns
LF- M Sullivan
CF J Ryan
RF- H Duffy
M C Anson

DET 1888 NL
SP C Getzien
SP P Conway
SP H Gruber
SP E Beatin
C - C Bennett
1B D Brouthers
2B- B Richardson
SS J Rowe
3B D White
LF L Twitchell
CF N Hanlon
RF- C Campau
2C C Ganzel
M1 B Watkins
M2 B Leadley

IND 1888 NL
SP H Boyle
SP J Healy
SP L Shreve

CIN 1888 AA
SP L Viau
SP T Mullane
SP E Smith
C J Keenan
1B J Reilly
2B B McPhee
SS F Fennelly
3B H Carpenter
LF G Tebeau
CF P Corkhill
RF H Nicol
M H Spence

NY 1888 NL
SP T Keefe
SP M Welch
SP C Titcomb
SP E Crane
C B Ewing
1B R Connor
2B D Richardson
SS J Ward
3B A Whitney
LU J O'Rourke
CF M Slattery
RF M Tiernan
M J Mutrie

PHI 1888 NL
SP C Buffinton
SP D Casey
SP B Sanders
SP K Gleason
C J Clements
1B S Farrar
2B C Bastian
SS A Irwin
3B J Mulvey
LF G Wood
CF E Andrews
RF J Fogarty
2B- E Delahanty
M H Wright

PIT 1888 NL
SP E Morris
SP J Galvin
SP H Staley
CO D Miller
1B- J Beckley
2B- F Dunlap
S2 P Smith
3S B Kuehne
LF- A Dalrymple
CF B Sunday
RF J Coleman
CL F Carroll
1R- A Maul
M H Phillips

WAS 1888 NL
SP H O'Day
SP J Whitney
SP W Widner
SP G Keefe
SP F Gilmore
C C Mack
1B B O'Brien
2B A Myers
SR G Shoch
3B J Donnelly
LF W Wilmot
CF D Hoy
RF E Daily
M1 W Hewett
M2 T Sullivan

BAL 1888 AA
SP B Cunningham
SP M Kilroy
SP P Smith
C - C Fulmer
1B T Tucker
2U B Greenwood
S2 J Farrell
3B B Shindle
LS- T Burns
CF M Griffin
RF B Purcell
UT- J Sommer
M B Barnie

BRO 1888 AA
SP M Hughes
SP A Terry
SP A Mays
C - D Bushong
1B D Orr
2B- B Burdock
SS G Smith
3B G Pinkney
LF D O'Brien
CF P Radford
Rp D Foutz
OP B Caruthers
2B- B McClellan
M B McGunnigle

CHI 1889 NL
SP B Hutchison
SP J Tener
SP F Dwyer
SP A Gumbert
C D Farrell
1B C Anson
2B F Pfeffer
SS- E Williamson
3B T Burns
LF G Van Haltren
CF J Ryan
RF H Duffy
M G Schmelz

CLE 1889 NL
SP D O'Brien
SP E Beatin
SP J Bakely
SP H Gruber
C C Zimmer
1B J Faatz
2B C Stricker
SS E McKean
3B P Tebeau
LF L Twitchell
CF J McAleer
RF P Radford
M T Loftus

IND 1889 NL
SP H Boyle
SP C Getzien
SR A Rusie
C - D Buckley
1B P Hines
2B C Bassett
SS J Glasscock
3B J Denny
LF E Seery
CF- M Sullivan
RF J McGeachy
M1 F Bancroft
M3 B Watkins

NY 1889 NL
SP M Welch
SP T Keefe
SP E Crane
C B Ewing
1B R Connor
2B D Richardson
SS J Ward
3B A Whitney
LF J O'Rourke
CF G Gore
RF M Tiernan
3B J Werrick
UT H Collins
CF P Browning
RS J Wolf
OC- J Kerins
M1 J Kelly
M2 M Davidson
M4 M Davidson

PHI 1889 NL
SP C Buffinton
SP B Sanders
SP K Gleason
SP D Casey
C J Clements
1B S Farrar
2B- A Myers
SS B Hallman
3B J Mulvey
LF G Wood
CF J Fogarty
RF S Thompson
M H Wright

PIT 1889 NL
SP H Staley
SP J Galvin
SP E Morris
CO D Miller
1B J Beckley
2B F Dunlap
SS- J Rowe
3B B Kuehne
LR- A Maul
CF N Hanlon
RF B Sunday
OC F Carroll
LU- J Fields
SS- P Smith
M1 H Phillips

WAS 1889 NL
SP A Ferson
SP G Haddock
SP G Keefe
SP H O'Day
SP J Healy
C - T Daly
1B- J Carney
2l S Wise
SS A Irwin
3B- J Irwin
LF W Wilmot
CF D Hoy
RF- E Beecher
OC C Mack
M1 J Hart

BAL 1889 AA
SP M Kilroy
SP F Foreman
SP B Cunningham
C - P Tate
1B T Tucker
2B R Mack
SS- J Farrell
3B B Shindle
LF J Hornung
CF M Griffin
RF J Sommer
M B Barnie

BRO 1889 AA
SP B Caruthers
SP A Terry
SP T Lovett
SP M Hughes
CR- J Visner
1B D Foutz
2B H Collins
SS G Smith
3B G Pinkney
LF D O'Brien
CF P Corkhill
RF T Burns
M B McGunnigle

CIN 1889 AA
SP J Duryea
SP L Viau
SP T Mullane
SP E Smith
C J Keenan
1B J Reilly
2B B McPhee
SS O Beard
3B H Carpenter
LF G Tebeau
CF B Holliday
RF H Nicol
M G Schmelz

COL 1889 AA
SP M Baldwin
SP W Widner
SP H Gastright
SP A Mays
C J O'Connor
1B D Orr
2B B Greenwood
SS H Easterday
UT L Marr
LF E Daily
CF J McTamany
R3 S Johnson
M A Buckenberger

KC 1889 AA
SP P Swartzel
SP J Conway
SP J Sowders
SP J McCarty
SP T Sullivan
C - C Hoover
1B C Stearns
2B- S Barkley
SS H Long
3B- J Davis
L2 J Manning
CF J Burns
RF B Hamilton
M B Watkins

LOU 1889 AA
SP R Ehret
SP J Ewing
SP T Ramsey
SP S Stratton
C - P Cook
1p- G Hecker
2B D Shannon
SS P Tomney
3B H Raymond
LF- P Browning
CF F Weaver
RI J Wolf
CU F Vaughn
M1 D Esterbrook
M2 C Wolf
M4 J Chapman

PHI 1889 AA
SP G Weyhing
SP E Seward
SP S McMahon
C - W Robinson
1B H Larkin
2B L Bierbauer
SS F Fennelly
3B D Lyons
LF H Stovey
CF C Welch
RF B Purcell
M B Sharsig

STL 1889 AA
SP S King
SP E Chamberlain
SP J Stivetts
1J J Boyle
1B C Comiskey
2B Y Robinson
SS S Fuller
3B A Latham
LF T O'Neill
CF C Duffee
RF M McCarthy
C - J Milligan

BOS 1890 NL
SP K Nichols
SP J Clarkson
SP C Getzien
C C Bennett
1B T Tucker
2B P Smith
SS H Long
3B C McGarr
LF M Sullivan
CF- P Hines
RF S Brodie
M F Selee

BRO 1890 NL
SP T Lovett
SP B Caruthers
C T Daly
1B D Foutz
2B H Collins
SS G Smith
3B G Pinkney
CF P Corkhill
RF T Burns
M B McGunnigle

CHI 1890 NL
SP B Hutchison
SP P Luby
SP E Stein
SP M Sullivan
SP R Coughlin
C M Kittridge
1B C Anson
2B- B Glenalvin
SS J Cooney
3B T Burns
LF C Carroll
RF- J Andrews
R2 H Earl

CIN 1890 NL
SP B Rhines
SP J Duryea
SP T Mullane
SP F Foreman
SP L Viau
C - J Harrington
1B J Reilly
2B B McPhee
SS O Beard
IO L Marr
LF J Knight
CF B Holliday
RF- H Nicol
M T Loftus

CLE 1890 NL
SP E Beatin
SP J Wadsworth
SP C Young
SP E Lincoln
SP L Viau
C C Zimmer
1B- P Veach
2B J Ardner
SS E McKean
3B W Smalley
LF B Gilks
CF G Davis
RF- V Dailey
M1 G Schmelz
M2 B Leadley

NY 1890 NL
SP A Rusie
SP M Welch
SP J Sharrott
C - D Buckley
1B- L Whistler
2B C Bassett
SS J Glasscock
3B J Denny
L1 J Hornung
CF M Tiernan
Rp J Burkett
OC A Clarke
M J Mutrie

PHI 1890 NL
SP K Gleason
SP T Vickery
SP P Smith
C J Clements
1B A McCauley
2B A Myers
SS B Allen
3B E Mayer
LF B Hamilton
CF E Burke
RF S Thompson
M1 H Wright
M3 A Reach
M5 H Wright

PIT 1890 NL
SP K Baker
SP D Anderson
SP B Sowders
SP C Schmit
CH D Decker
1p G Hecker
2S S LaRoque
SS- E Sales
3U D Miller
LF- J Kelty
MR B Sunday
UT T Berger
OC B Wilson

BAL 1890 AA
SP L German
SP S McMahon
SP M O'Rourke
SP M Morrison
C - G Townsend
12 T Power
2B R Mack
SS I Ray
3B P Gilbert
LF J Sommer
CF- D Long
RF B Johnson
M B Barnie

BRO 1890 AA
SP C McCullough
SP M Mattimore
SP B Murphy
C - J Toy
1B B O'Brien
2B J Gerhardt
SS- C Nelson
3B- J Davis
LF H Simon
CF J Peltz
Rp E Daily
OC F Bowes
C3 H Pitz
M J Kennedy

COL 1890 AA
SP H Gastright
SP F Knauss
SP J Easton
SP E Chamberlain
SP W Widner
C J O'Connor
1B M Lehane
2B J Crooks
SS- H Easterday
3B C Reilly
LR S Johnson
CF J McTamany
RF J Sneed
IC- J Doyle
M1 A Buckenberger
M2 G Schmelz
M3 J Sullivan

LOU 1890 AA
SP S Stratton
SP R Ehret
SP G Meakim
SP H Goodall
SP E Daily
C J Ryan
1B H Taylor
2B T Shinnick
SS P Tomney
3B H Raymond
LF C Hamburg
CF F Weaver
RF J Wolf
M J Chapman

PHI 1890 AA
SP S McMahon
SP E Green
SP E Seward
SP D Esper
C W Robinson
1B J O'Brien
2B- T Shafer
S2 B Conroy
3B D Lyons

LF B Purcell
CF C Welch
RF O Shafer
M   B Sharsig

ROC 1890 AA
SP B Barr
SP W Calihan
SP C Titcomb
SP B Miller
C   D McGuire
1B- T O'Brien
2B B Greenwood
SS- M Phillips
3B J Knowles
LF H Lyons
CF S Griffin
RF T Scheffler
C- D McKeough
M   P Powers

STL 1890 AA
SP J Stivetts
SP T Ramsey
SP B Hart
SP B Whitrock
C   J Munyan
1B- E Cartwright
2B- B Higgins
SS S Fuller
M3 C Duffee
LR- C Campau
M1- C Roseman
RF T McCarthy
M2 J Kerins
M5 T McCarthy
M6 J Gerhardt

SYR 1890 AA
SP D Casey
SP J Keefe
SP M Morrison
SP E Mars
CM G Briggs
1B M McQuery
2B C Childs
SS B McLaughlin
C- T O'Rourke
LS B Ely
CF R Wright
RF- P Friel
3B T O'Rourke
M1 G Frazer
M2 W Fessenden
M3 G Frazer

TOL 1890 AA
SP J Healy
SP E Cushman
SP F Smith
SP C Sprague
C   H Sage
1B P Werden
2B P Nicholson
SS F Scheibeck
3B B Alvord
LF B Van Dyke
CF G Tebeau
RF E Swartwood
M   C Morton

BOS 1890 PL
SP C Radbourn
SP A Gumbert
SP B Daley
SP M Kilroy
C- M Murphy
1B D Brouthers
2B J Quinn
SS A Irwin
3B B Nash
LF H Richardson
CF T Brown
RF H Stovey
CS K Kelly

BRO 1890 PL
SP G Weyhing
SP J Sowders
SP C Murphy
SP G Hemming
C- T Kinslow
1B D Orr
2B L Bierbauer
SS J Ward
3B B Joyce
LF E Seery
CF E Andrews
RM J McGeachy
Rp G Van Haltren
M   M Ward

BUF 1890 PL
SP G Haddock
SP B Cunningham
SP G Keefe
SP L Twitchell
SP G Stafford

C   C Mack
31 D White
2B S Wise
SS J Rowe
3B- J Irwin
LF E Beecher
CF D Hoy
RC- J Halligan
OC- S Clark
M2 J Faatz
M3 J Rowe

CHI 1890 PL
SP M Baldwin
SP S King
SP C Bartson
C   D Farrell
1B C Comiskey
2B F Pfeffer
SS- C Bastian
3S- E Williamson
LF T O'Neill
CF J Ryan
RF H Duffy
C3 J Boyle

CLE 1890 PL
SP H Gruber
SP J Bakely
SP D O'Brien
SP W McGill
C   S Sutcliffe
1B H Larkin
2B C Stricker
SU E Delahanty
3B P Tebeau
LF P Browning
CF J McAleer
UT P Radford
M1 T Larkin

NY 1890 PL
SP H O'Day
SP E Crane
SP J Ewing
SP T Keefe
C   B Ewing
1B R Connor
2B D Shannon
S2 D Richardson
3S A Whitney
LM G Gore
LM M Slattery
RF J O'Rourke
3S- G Hatfield
CF- D Johnston

PHI 1890 PL
SP B Sanders
SP P Knell
SP C Buffinton
SP B Husted
SP B Cunningham
C- J Milligan
1B S Farrar
2B J Pickett
SS B Shindle
3B J Mulvey
LF G Wood
CF M Griffin
RM J Fogarty
OC B Hallman

PIT 1890 PL
SP H Staley
SP A Maul
SP J Galvin
SP E Morris
SP J Tener
CL F Carroll
1B B Beckley
2B Y Robinson
SS T Corcoran
3B B Kuehne
LI J Fields
CF N Hanlon
RF J Visner

BOS 1891 NL
SP J Clarkson
SP K Nichols
SP H Staley
SP C Getzien
C- C Bennett
1B T Tucker
2B J Quinn
SS H Long
3B B Nash
LM B Lowe
CF S Brodie
RL H Stovey
C- C Ganzel
M   F Selee

BRO 1891 NL
SP T Lovett
SP B Caruthers
SP G Hemming

SP A Terry
SP B Inks
C- T Kinslow
1B D Foutz
2L H Collins
SS J Ward
3B G Pinkney
LF D O'Brien
OF M Griffin
RF T Burns
M   M Ward

CHI 1891 NL
SP B Hutchison
SP A Gumbert
SP P Luby
SP E Stein
C- M Kittridge
1B C Anson
2B F Pfeffer
3S J Cooney
3O B Dahlen
LM W Wilmot
ML J Ryan
RF C Carroll

CIN 1891 NL
SP T Mullane
SP B Rhines
SP C Radbourn
SP E Crane
C   J Harrington
1O J Reilly
2B B McPhee
SS G Smith
3B A Latham
LF- P Browning
ML B Holliday
RF- L Marr
1C- J Keenan
M   T Loftus

CLE 1891 NL
SP C Young
SP H Gruber
SP L Viau
C   C Zimmer
1B J Virtue
2B C Childs
SS E McKean
3B- P Tebeau
LF J McAleer
CF G Davis
RF- S Johnson
OC- J Doyle
M1 B Leadley

NY 1891 NL
SP A Rusie
SP J Ewing
SP M Welch
C- D Buckley
1B R Connor
2B D Richardson
SS J Glasscock
3B C Bassett
LF J O'Rourke
CF G Gore
RF M Tiernan
UT- L Whistler
M   J Mutrie

PHI 1891 NL
SP K Gleason
SP D Esper
SP J Thornton
C   J Clements
1B W Brown
2B A Myers
SS B Allen
3B B Shindle
LF B Hamilton
MU E Delahanty
RF S Thompson
M   H Wright

PIT 1891 NL
SP M Baldwin
SP S King
SP J Galvin
C- C Mack
1B B Beckley
2B L Bierbauer
SS- F Shugart
3B C Reilly
LF- P Browning
ML N Hanlon
RF F Carroll
IC D Miller
M2 B McGunnigle

BAL 1891 AA
SP S McMahon
SP B Cunningham
SP K Madden
SP J Healy
C   W Robinson
1B P Werden

2B S Wise
LS G Van Haltren
3B P Gilbert
UO B Johnson
CF C Welch
RS I Ray
M   B Barnie

BOS 1891 AA
SP G Haddock
SP C Buffinton
SR D O'Brien
SP B Daley
C   M Murphy
1B D Brouthers
2B C Stricker
SS P Radford
3C D Farrell
LF- H Richardson
CF T Brown
RF H Duffy
3B- B Joyce
M   A Irwin

CIN 1891 AA
SP F Dwyer
SP E Crane
SP W Mains
SP W McGill
C   K Kelly
1B J Carney
2B Y Robinson
SS J Canavan
3B A Whitney
CF D Johnston
RF E Seery

COL 1891 AA
SP P Knell
SP H Gastright
SP J Dolan
SP J Easton
C- J Donahue
1B M Lehane
2B J Crooks
SS B Wheelock
3B- B Kuehne
LM C Duffee
CF- J McTamany
RF J Sneed
M   G Schmelz

LOU 1891 AA
SP W Fitzgerald
SP R Ehret
SP J Meekin
SP S Stratton
SP J Doran
RP E Daily
CI- J Ryan
1B H Taylor
2B T Shinnick
SS H Jennings
3B- O Beard
LF P Donovan
CF F Weaver
RF J Wolf
IC T Cahill
M   J Chapman

MIL 1891 AA
SP G Davies
SP F Killen
SP F Dwyer
C   F Vaughn
1B J Carney
2S J Canavan
S3 G Shoch
3B- G Alberts
LF A Dalrymple
CF E Burke
RF H Earl
C3 J Grim
M   C Cushman

PHI 1891 AA
SP G Weyhing
SP E Chamberlain
SP B Sanders
SP W Callahan
C1 J Milligan
1B H Larkin
2B B Hallman
SS T Corcoran
3B J Mulvey
LF- P Browning
LF G Wood
CF- P Corkhill
OC L Cross
M1 B Sharsig

STL 1891 AA
SP J Stivetts
SP W McGill
SR G Griffith
SP J Neale
SP G Rettger
C   J Boyle

1B C Comiskey
2B- B Eagan
SS S Fuller
3B D Lyons
LF T O'Neill
CF D Hoy
RF M McCarthy

WAS 1891 AA
SP K Carsey
SP F Foreman
SP J Bakely
C   D McGuire
1B- M McQuery
2B T Dowd
SS G Hatfield
3B- B Alvord
LF- E Beecher
CF- P Hines
LR L Murphy
M1 S Trott
M2 P Snyder
M3 D Shannon
M4 S Griffin

BAL 1892 NL
SP S McMahon
SP G Cobb
SP T Vickery
SP C Buffinton
C- W Robinson
1B- S Sutcliffe
2B- C Stricker
SS- T O'Rourke
3B B Shindle
LF- H Stovey
CF- W Welch
UT G Van Haltren
C- J Gunson
UT- J McGraw
M2 J Waltz
M3 N Hanlon

BOS 1892 NL
SP K Nichols
SP J Stivetts
SP H Staley
SP J Clarkson
C- K Kelly
1B T Tucker
2B J Quinn
SS H Long
3B B Nash
LI B Lowe
CF H Duffy
RF T McCarthy
M   F Selee

BRO 1892 NL
SP G Haddock
SP E Stein
SP D Foutz
SP B Hart
SP B Kennedy
C- C Daily
1B D Brouthers
2B J Ward
SS T Corcoran
3B B Joyce
LF D O'Brien
CF M Griffin
RF T Burns
IC T Daly
M   M Ward

CHI 1892 NL
SP B Hutchison
SP A Gumbert
SP P Luby
C   P Schriver
1B C Anson
2B J Canavan
S3 B Dahlen
3B- J Parrott
LF W Wilmot
CF J Ryan
RL S Dungan
RF- G Decker

CIN 1892 NL
SP E Chamberlain
SP T Mullane
SP F Dwyer
SP M Sullivan
C- M Murphy
1B C Comiskey
2B B McPhee
SS G Smith
3B A Latham
LF T O'Neill
ML- P Browning
MR B Holliday
CU- F Vaughn

CLE 1892 NL
SP C Young
SP N Cuppy
SP J Clarkson
C   J Boyle

SP G Davies
C   C Zimmer
1B J Virtue
2B C Childs
SS E McKean
3R G Davis
LF J Burkett
CF J McAleer
RU J O'Connor
3B- P Tebeau

LOU 1892 NL
SP S Stratton
SP B Sanders
SP F Clausen
SP J Meekin
SP A Jones
RP L Viau
CU J Grim
1B- L Whistler
2B F Pfeffer
SS H Jennings
3B- B Kuehne
LF F Weaver
CF T Brown
UT H Taylor
3B- C Bassett
M1 J Chapman

NY 1892 NL
SP A Rusie
SP S King
SP E Crane
C1 J Boyle
1C B Ewing
2L- E Burke
SS S Fuller
3B D Lyons
LF J O'Rourke
CF H Lyons
RF M Tiernan
IC- J Doyle
M   P Powers

PHI 1892 NL
SR G Weyhing
SP K Carsey
SP T Keefe
SP D Esper
C   J Clements
1B R Connor
2B B Hallman
SS B Allen
3B- C Reilly
LF B Hamilton
CF E Delahanty
RF S Thompson
IC L Cross
M   H Wright

PIT 1892 NL
SP M Baldwin
SP R Ehret
SP A Terry
SP J Galvin
C   C Mack
1B B Beckley
2B L Bierbauer
SS F Shugart
3B D Farrell
Lp E Smith
OC D Miller
RF- P Donovan
M1 A Buckenberger
M2 T Burns
M3 A Buckenberger

STL 1892 NL
SP K Gleason
SP T Breitenstein
SP P Hawley
SP C Getzien
SP B Hawke
C   D Buckley
1B P Werden
2B J Crooks
SS J Glasscock
3B- G Pinkney
LF C Carroll
CF S Brodie
Rp B Caruthers
M2 C Stricker
M4 G Gore

WAS 1892 NL
SP F Killen
SP B Abbey
SP P Knell
SP J Duryea
SP J Meekin
C   D McGuire
1B H Larkin
2U T Dowd
S2 D Richardson
3B- Y Robinson
LR C Duffee
CF D Hoy

C   C Zimmer
1B J Virtue
2B C Childs
3R E McKean
LF J Burkett
CF J McAleer
RU J O'Connor
3B- P Tebeau

SP G Davies
C1- J Milligan
M1 B Barnie
M2 A Irwin

BAL 1893 NL
SP S McMahon
SP T Mullane
SP B Hawke
SP E McNabb
SP K Baker
C   W Robinson
1B H Taylor
2B H Reitz
SS J McGraw
3B B Shindle
LF- J Long
CF J Kelley
RF G Treadway
M   N Hanlon

BOS 1893 NL
SP K Nichols
SP J Stivetts
SP H Staley
SP H Gastright
C- C Bennett
1B T Tucker
2B B Lowe
SS H Long
3B B Nash
LF T McCarthy
CF H Duffy
RL C Carroll
CO- C Ganzel
M   F Selee

BRO 1893 NL
SP B Kennedy
SP E Stein
SP G Haddock
SP D Daub
SP T Lovett
RP S Sharrott
C   T Kinslow
1B- D Brouthers
2B- D Richardson
SS T Corcoran
23 T Daly
L1 D Foutz
CF M Griffin
RF T Burns
UT G Shoch

CHI 1893 NL
SP B Hutchison
SP W McGill
SP H Mauck
C- M Kittridge
1B C Anson
UT B Lange
SS B Dahlen
3B J Parrott
LF W Wilmot
CF J Ryan
RF S Dungan
UT G Decker

CIN 1893 NL
SP F Dwyer
SP E Chamberlain
SP M Sullivan
SP T Parrott
SP T Mullane
RP S King
CU F Vaughn
1B- C Comiskey
2B B McPhee
SS G Smith
3B A Latham
LF J Canavan
CF B Holliday
RF- J McCarthy

CLE 1893 NL
SP C Young
SP J Clarkson
SP N Cuppy
SP C Hastings
C- C Zimmer
1B J Virtue
2B C Childs
3B- C McGarr
LF J Burkett
CF J McAleer
RB B Ewing
CM J O'Connor
UI P Tebeau

LOU 1893 NL
SP G Hemming
SP S Stratton
SP B Rhodes
SP J Menefee
C   J Grim
LR W Brown
CF D Hoy
2B F Pfeffer

SO T O'Rourke
3B G Pinkney
LF- P Browning
CF T Brown
RU F Weaver
M   B Barnie

NY 1893 NL
SP A Rusie
SP M Baldwin
SP L German
CM J Doyle
1B R Connor
2B J Ward
SS S Fuller
3B G Davis
LF E Burke
CF- G Stafford
RF M Tiernan
M   M Ward

PHI 1893 NL
SP G Weyhing
SP K Carsey
SP T Keefe
SP J Taylor
C   J Clements
1B J Boyle
2B B Hallman
SS B Allen
3B C Reilly
LF E Delahanty
CF B Hamilton
RF S Thompson
IC L Cross
M   H Wright

PIT 1893 NL
SP F Killen
SP R Ehret
SP A Terry
SP A Gumbert
C- D Miller
1B J Beckley
2B L Bierbauer
SS- J Glasscock
3B D Lyons
LF E Smith
CF G Van Haltren
RF P Donovan
M   A Buckenberger

STL 1893 NL
SP T Breitenstein
SP K Gleason
SP P Hawley
SP D Clarkson
C   H Peitz
1B J Werden
2B J Quinn
SS- J Glasscock
3B J Crooks
LF- C Frank
CF S Brodie
OI T Dowd
M   B Watkins

WAS 1893 NL
SP D Esper
SP A Maul
SP J Meekin
SP J Duryea
C3 D Farrell
1B H Larkin
23 S Wise
SS J Sullivan
3B- J Mulvey
L1 J O'Rourke
CF D Hoy
RF P Radford

BAL 1894 NL
SP S McMahon
SP B Hawke
SP K Gleason
SP B Inks
SP T Mullane
RP D Esper
C   W Robinson
1B D Brouthers
2B H Reitz
SS H Jennings
3B J McGraw
LF J Kelley
CF S Brodie
RF W Keeler
M   N Hanlon

BOS 1894 NL
SP K Nichols
SP J Stivetts
SP H Staley
SP T Lovett
C- C Ganzel
1B T Tucker
2B B Lowe
SS H Long
3B B Nash

(continued — BOS 1894 NL)
LF T McCarthy
CF H Duffy
RF J Bannon
M F Selee

BRO 1894 NL
SP B Kennedy
SP E Stein
SP D Daub
SP H Gastright
C- T Kinslow
1B- D Foutz
2B T Daly
SS T Corcoran
3B B Shindle
LF G Treadway
CF M Griffin
RF T Burns
C- C Daily
1B- C LaChance

CHI 1894 NL
SP B Hutchison
SP C Griffith
SP W McGill
SP A Terry
SP S Stratton
RP B Abbey
C P Schriver
1B C Anson
2B J Parrott
S3 B Dahlen
3S C Irwin
LF W Wilmot
CF B Lange
RF J Ryan
1O G Decker

CIN 1894 NL
SP F Dwyer
SP T Parrott
SP E Chamberlain
SP C Fisher
C- M Murphy
1B- C Comiskey
2B B McPhee
SS G Smith
3B A Latham
LF B Holliday
CF D Hoy
RF J Canavan
C1- F Vaughn

CLE 1894 NL
SP C Young
SR N Cuppy
SP J Clarkson
SP M Sullivan
SP C Zimmer
1B P Tebeau
2B C Childs
SS E McKean
3B C McGarr
LF C Burkett
CF- J McAleer
RF- H Blake
CM J O'Connor

LOU 1894 NL
SP G Hemming
SP P Knell
SP J Menefee
SP J Wadsworth
CI J Grim
1B- L Lutenberg
2B F Pfeffer
SS D Richardson
3B- J Denny
LF- F Clarke
CF T Brown
RF- O Smith
M B Barnie

NY 1894 NL
SP A Rusie
SP J Meekin
SP L German
SP H Westervelt
C D Farrell
1B J Doyle
2B J Ward
SS S Fuller
3B G Davis
LF E Burke
CF G Van Haltren
RF M Tiernan
SR- Y Murphy
M M Ward

PHI 1894 NL
SP J Taylor
SP K Carsey
SP G Weyhing
SP G Harper
C- J Clements
1B J Boyle
2B B Hallman
SS- J Sullivan
3B L Cross
LI E Delahanty
CF B Hamilton
RF S Thompson
LR T Turner
M A Irwin

PIT 1894 NL
SP R Ehret
SP A Gumbert
SP F Killen
SP T Colcolough
SP J Menefee
C- C Mack
1B J Beckley
2B L Bierbauer
SS J Glasscock
3B- D Lyons
LF E Smith
CF J Stenzel
RF P Donovan
M1 A Buckenberger

STL 1894 NL
SP T Breitenstein
SR P Hawley
SP D Clarkson
IC D Miller
1B R Connor
2B J Quinn
SS B Ely
IC H Peitz
LF C Frank
CF F Shugart
RL T Dowd
M G Miller

WAS 1894 NL
SR W Mercer
SP A Maul
SP M Sullivan
SP O Stocksdale
SP D Esper
RP C Petty
C D McGuire
1B E Cartwright
2B P Ward
SS- F Scheibeck
3B B Joyce
OI K Selbach
ML C Abbey
R3 B Hassamaer
UT P Radford
M G Schmelz

BAL 1895 NL
SP B Hoffer
SP G Hemming
SP D Esper
SP D Clarkson
SP S McMahon
C- W Robinson
1B S Carey
2B K Gleason
SS H Jennings
3B J McGraw
LF J Kelley
CF S Brodie
RF W Keeler
C- B Clarke
23- H Reitz
M N Hanlon

BOS 1895 NL
SP K Nichols
SP J Stivetts
SP C Dolan
SP J Sullivan
C C Ganzel
1B T Tucker
2B B Lowe
SS H Long
3B B Nash
LF T McCarthy
CF H Duffy
RF J Bannon
M F Selee

BRO 1895 NL
SP B Kennedy
SP E Stein
SP A Gumbert
SP D Daub
SP C Lucid
C J Grim
1B C LaChance
2B T Daly
SS T Corcoran
3B B Shindle
LF- J Anderson
CF M Griffin
RF G Treadway
M D Foutz

CHI 1895 NL
SP C Griffith
SP A Terry
SP B Hutchison
C- T Donahue
1B C Anson
2B A Stewart
SS B Dahlen
3B B Everitt
LF W Wilmot
CF B Lange
RF J Ryan
UT- G Decker

CIN 1895 NL
SP F Dwyer
SP B Rhines
SR T Parrott
SP F Foreman
SP B Phillips
C F Vaughn
1B B Ewing
2B B McPhee
SS G Smith
3B A Latham
LM D Hoy
MO- G Hogriever
RF D Miller

CLE 1895 NL
SP C Young
SP N Cuppy
SP B Wallace
SP P Knell
C C Zimmer
RF- P Tebeau
2B C Childs
SS E McKean
3B C McGarr
LF J Burkett
CF J McAleer
RF H Blake
C1 J O'Connor
R1 G Tebeau

LOU 1895 NL
SP B Cunningham
SP G Weyhing
SP M McDermott
SP B Inks
C- J Warner
1C- H Spies
2B J O'Brien
SS F Shugart
3B J Collins
LF F Clarke
MR-J Wright
MR-T Gettinger
M J McCloskey

NY 1895 NL
SP A Rusie
SP D Clarke
SP J Meekin
SP L German
C3 D Farrell
1U J Doyle
2B G Stafford
SS S Fuller
3U G Davis
LF- E Burke
CF G Van Haltren
RF M Tiernan
C- P Wilson
M3 H Watkins

PHI 1895 NL
SP K Carsey
SP J Taylor
SP W McGill
SP A Orth
C J Clements
1B J Boyle
2B B Hallman
SS J Sullivan
3B L Cross
LF E Delahanty
CF B Hamilton
RF S Thompson
M A Irwin

PIT 1895 NL
SP P Hawley
SP J Hart
SP B Foreman
SP F Killen
SP J Gardner
C- B Merritt
1B J Beckley
2B L Bierbauer
SS M Cross
3B B Clingman
LF E Smith
CF J Stenzel
RF P Donovan
UT- F Genins
M C Mack

STL 1895 NL
SP T Breitenstein
SP R Ehret
SP H Staley
SR B Kissinger
SP D McDougal
C H Peitz
1B R Connor
2B J Quinn
SS B Ely
IC D Miller
LF D Cooley
CF T Brown
RM T Dowd
M1 A Buckenberger
M2 C Von Der Ahe
M4 L Phelan

WAS 1895 NL
SP W Mercer
SP V Anderson
SP O Stocksdale
SP A Maul
SR J Malarkey
RP J Boyd
C D McGuire
1B E Cartwright
2B J Crooks
SS- F Scheibeck
3B B Joyce
LF K Selbach
MO C Abbey
RF B Hassamaer
M G Schmelz

BAL 1896 NL
SP B Hoffer
SP A Pond
SP G Hemming
SP S McMahon
SP D Esper
C- W Robinson
1B J Doyle
2B H Reitz
SS H Jennings
3B J Donnelly
LF J Kelley
CF S Brodie
C B Clarke
M N Hanlon

BOS 1896 NL
SP K Nichols
SP J Stivetts
SP J Ryan
SP F Klobedanz
C- M Bergen
1B T Tucker
2B- B Lowe
SS H Long
3B J Collins
LF H Duffy
CF B Hamilton
RF J Bannon
RC F Tenney
M F Selee

BRO 1896 NL
SP B Kennedy
SP H Payne
SP D Daub
SP B Abbey
SP E Stein
RP G Harper
C J Grim
1B C LaChance
2B- T Daly
SS T Corcoran
3B B Shindle
LF T McCarthy
CF M Griffin
RF J Jones
OI J Anderson
2B- G Shoch
M D Foutz

CHI 1896 NL
SP C Griffith
SP D Friend
SP A Terry
SP B Briggs
C- M Kittridge
1B C Anson
2B F Pfeffer
SS B Dahlen
3O B Everitt
L1 G Decker
CF B Lange
RF J Ryan

CIN 1896 NL
SP F Dwyer
SP R Ehret
SP F Foreman
SR C Fisher
SP B Rhines
C- H Peitz
1B- B Ewing
2B B McPhee
SS G Smith
3B C Irwin
LF E Burke
CF D Hoy
RF D Miller
1C F Vaughn

CLE 1896 NL
SP C Young
SP N Cuppy
SP Z Wilson
SP B Wallace
C C Zimmer
1B P Tebeau
2B C Childs
SS E McKean
3B C McGarr
LF J Burkett
CF J McAleer
RF H Blake
C1- J O'Connor

LOU 1896 NL
SP C Fraser
SP B Hill
SP B Cunningham
SP A Herman
IC D Miller
1B- J Rogers
2B- J O'Brien
SS- J Dolan
3B B Clingman
LF F Clarke
CM C Dexter
RF T McCreery
M1 J McCloskey
M2 B McGunnigle

NY 1896 NL
SP D Clarke
SP J Meekin
SP M Sullivan
SP E Doheny
C- P Wilson
1B- W Clark
2B K Gleason
SL F Connaughton
3S G Davis
LF- G Stafford
CF G Van Haltren
RF M Tiernan
M1 A Irwin
M2 B Joyce

PHI 1896 NL
SP J Taylor
SP A Orth
SP K Carsey
SP H Keener
SP W McGill
C- M Grady
1B- D Hallman
2B B Hallman
SS B Hulen
3B- B Nash
LF E Delahanty
ML- D Cooley
RF S Thompson
3S L Cross

PIT 1896 NL
SP F Killen
SP P Hawley
SR J Hughey
SP C Hastings
C- J Sugden
1B- J Beckley
2B- D Padden
SS B Ely
3B D Lyons
LF E Smith
CF J Stenzel
RF P Donovan
C- B Merritt
M C Mack

STL 1896 NL
SP T Breitenstein
SP B Hart
SP R Donahue
SP B Kissinger
C E McFarland
1B R Connor
2M T Dowd
SS M Cross
3B B Myers
LF- J Sullivan
MO T Parrott
RL K Douglass
M1 H Diddlebock
M2 A Latham
M3 C Von Der Ahe

WAS 1896 NL
SP W Mercer
SP D McJames
SP L German
SP S King
C D McGuire
1B E Cartwright
2B- J O'Brien
SS De Montreville
32 B Joyce
LF K Selbach
CF T Brown
RU B Lush
RF- C Abbey
M G Schmelz

BAL 1897 NL
SP J Corbett
SP B Hoffer
SP A Pond
SP J Nops
C- B Clarke
1B J Doyle
2B H Reitz
SS H Jennings
3B J McGraw
LF J Kelley
CF J Stenzel
RF W Keeler
UT- J Quinn
M N Hanlon

BOS 1897 NL
SP K Nichols
SP F Klobedanz
SP T Lewis
SP J Stivetts
SP J Sullivan
C M Bergen
1B F Tenney
2B B Lowe
SS H Long
3B J Collins
LF H Duffy
CF B Hamilton
RF C Stahl
M F Selee

BRO 1897 NL
SP B Kennedy
SP H Payne
SP J Dunn
SP C Fisher
SP D Daub
C- J Grim
1B C LaChance
2B G Shoch
SS G Smith
3B B Shindle
LF- G Stafford
CF G Van Haltren
RF M Tiernan
M1 A Irwin
M2 B Joyce

PHI 1897 NL
SP J Taylor
SP A Orth
SP J Fifield
SP G Wheeler
C1- J Boyle
1B N Lajoie
32 L Cross
SS- S Gillen
3B B Nash
LF E Delahanty
CF D Cooley
RM T Dowd
UT P Geier
M G Stallings

CHI 1897 NL
SP C Griffith
SP D Friend
SP B Briggs
SP W Thornton
SP R Denzer
C- M Kittridge
1B C Anson
2B- J Connor
SS- B Dahlen
3B B Everitt
L1 G Decker
CF B Lange
RF J Ryan
2p N Callahan
3S B McCormick

CIN 1897 NL
SP T Breitenstein
SP B Rhines
SP F Dwyer
SR R Ehret
SP B Dammann
C- H Peitz
1B J Beckley
2B B McPhee
SU C Ritchey
3B C Irwin
LF E Smith
CF J Stenzel
RF D Miller
C- B Merritt
M B Ewing

CLE 1897 NL
SP C Young
SP Z Wilson
SP J Powell
SP N Cuppy
C C Zimmer
1B P Tebeau
2B C Childs
SS E McKean
3B B Wallace
LF J Burkett
OI J O'Connor
RF- C Sockalexis

LOU 1897 NL
SP C Fraser
SP B Cunningham
SP B Hill
SP B Magee
C B Wilson
1B P Werden
2B- J Rogers
SS G Stafford
3B B Clingman
LF F Clarke
CF- O Pickering
RF T McCreery
OC- C Dexter

NY 1897 NL
SP A Rusie
SP J Meekin
SP C Seymour
SP M Sullivan
SP E Doheny
C J Warner
1B W Clark
2B K Gleason
SS G Davis
3B B Joyce
LF- D Holmes
CF- G Van Haltren
RL M Tiernan

PIT 1897 NL
SP F Killen
SP P Hawley
SP J Hughey
SP J Tannehill
SP C Hastings
RP J Gardner
C J Sugden
13 H Davis
2B D Padden
SS- B Ely
3B- J Hoffmeister
LF E Smith
CF S Brodie
RF P Donovan
RU- S Mertes
M T Burns

STL 1897 NL
SP R Donahue
SP B Hart
SP K Carsey
SP W Sudhoff
OC K Douglass
1B M Grady
2B B Hallman
SS M Cross
3B F Hartman
LF D Lally
CF D Harley
RF T Turner
2O T Houseman
M1 T Dowd
M2 H Nicol
M4 C Von Der Ahe

WAS 1897 NL
SP W Mercer
SP D McJames
SP C Swaim
SP S King
RS L German
C D McGuire
1B T Tucker
2B J O'Brien
SU De Montreville
3B C Reilly
LF K Selbach
CF T Brown
RF- C Abbey
UT Z Wrigley
C- D Farrell
M1 G Schmelz

BAL 1898 NL
SP D McJames
SP J Hughes
SP A Maul
SP J Nops
SP F Kitson
C- W Robinson
1B D McGann
2B De Montreville
SS H Jennings
3B J McGraw
LF D Holmes
ML J Kelley
RF W Keeler
M N Hanlon

BOS 1898 NL
SP K Nichols
SP T Lewis
SP V Willis
SP F Klobedanz
C M Bergen
1B F Tenney
2B B Lowe
SS H Long
3B J Collins
LF H Duffy
CF B Hamilton
RF C Stahl
M F Selee

BRO 1898 NL
SP B Kennedy
SP J Dunn
SP J Yeager
SP R Miller
SP W McKenna
C- J Ryan
1S C LaChance
2B C Hallman
SS G Magoon
3B B Shindle
LF J Sheckard
CF M Griffin
RF F Jones
M1 B Barnie
M3 H Ebbets

CHI 1898 NL
SP C Griffith
SP N Callahan
SP W Thornton
SP W Woods
SP M Kilroy
C- T Donahue
1B E Everitt
2B J Connor
SS B Dahlen
3B B McCormick
LF J Ryan
CF B Lange
RU- S Mertes
M T Burns

CIN 1898 NL
SP P Hawley
SP T Breitenstein
SP B Hill
SP F Dwyer
SR B Dammann
C H Peitz
1B J Beckley
2B B McPhee
SS T Corcoran
3B C Irwin
LF E Smith
CF A McBride
RF D Miller
UT- H Steinfeldt
1C- F Vaughn
M B Ewing

CLE 1898 NL
SP C Young
SP J Powell
SP N Cuppy
C- L Criger
12 P Tebeau
2B C Childs
SS E McKean
3B B Wallace
LF J Burkett
CF J McAleer
RF H Blake
1C J O'Connor

LOU 1898 NL
SP B Cunningham
SP B Magee
SP B Dowling
SP C Fraser
C- M Kittridge
UI H Wagner
1B H Smith
S2 B Ritchey
3S B Clingman
LF- F Clarke
CF D Hoy
RF C Dexter

NY 1898 NL
SP C Seymour
SP J Meekin
SP A Rusie
SP E Doheny

SP C Gettig
C J Warner
1B B Joyce
2B K Gleason
SS G Davis
3B F Hartman
LF M Tiernan
CF G Van Haltren
UT- J Doyle
CO- M Grady
M2 C Anson
M3 B Joyce

PHI 1898 NL
SP W Piatt
SP R Donahue
SP A Orth
SP J Fifield
SP G Wheeler
C E McFarland
1B K Douglass
2B N Lajoie
SS M Cross
3B B Lauder
LF E Delahanty
CF D Cooley
RF E Flick
M1 G Stallings
M2 B Shettsline

PIT 1898 NL
SP J Tannehill
SP B Rhines
SP J Gardner
SP F Killen
SP C Hastings
RP R Hart
C P Schriver
1B- W Clark
2B D Padden
SS B Ely
3B B Gray
LF J McCarthy
MI T O'Brien
RF P Donovan
M B Watkins

STL 1898 NL
SP J Taylor
SP W Sudhoff
SP J Hughey
SP K Carsey
C J Clements
1B- G Decker
2B- J Crooks
SS- G Smith
3B L Cross
LF D Harley
CF J Stenzel
RM T Dowd
2S J Quinn
CU- J Sugden
M T Hurst

WAS 1898 NL
SP G Weyhing
SP W Mercer
SP B Dinneen
SP F Killen
SP C Swaim
C1 D McGuire
1B- J Doyle
2B H Reitz
SS Z Wrigley
3I- J Smith
LF K Selbach
MU J Anderson
RF J Gettman
C1 D Farrell
M1 T Brown
M4 A Irwin

BAL 1899 NL
SP J McGinnity
SP F Kitson
SP J Nops
SP H Howell
C W Robinson
1B C LaChance
2B- De Montreville
S2 B Keister
3B J McGraw
LF D Holmes
CF S Brodie
RF J Sheckard

BOS 1899 NL
SP V Willis
SP K Nichols
SP T Lewis
SP J Meekin
SP F Killen
C - M Bergen
1B- F Tenney
2B B Lowe
SS H Long
3B J Collins
LF H Duffy
CF- B Hamilton
RF C Stahl
M. F Selee

BRO 1899 NL
SP J Dunn
SP J Hughes
SP B Kennedy
SP D McJames
C - D Farrell
1B- D McGann
2B T Daly
SS B Dahlen
3B D Casey
LF J Kelley
CF F Jones
RF W Keeler
UT P Chiles
C - K Douglass
M B Shettsline

CHI 1899 NL
SP J Taylor
SP C Griffith
SP N Callahan
SP N Garvin
C T Donahue
1B B Everitt
2B B McCormick
SS- De Montreville
3B H Wolverton
LF J Ryan
UT S Mertes
RF D Green
CF B Lange
M T Burns

CIN 1899 NL
SP N Hahn
SP P Hawley
SP B Phillips
SP T Breitenstein
SP J Taylor
C - H Peitz
1B J Beckley
2B B McPhee
SS T Corcoran
3B- C Irwin
UO- E Smith
LM K Selbach
RF- D Miller
32 H Steinfeldt
M B Ewing

CLE 1899 NL
SP J Hughey
SP C Knepper
SP F Bates
SP C Schmit
SP H Colliflower
C - J Sugden
1B T Tucker
2B J Quinn
SS H Lochhead
3B S Sullivan
LF D Harley
CF T Dowd
RU S McAllister
M1 L Cross

LOU 1899 NL
SP B Cunningham
SP D Phillippe
SP P Dowling
SP W Woods
C - C Zimmer
1B- M Kelley
2B C Ritchey
SS B Clingman
3B T Leach
LF F Clarke
CF D Hoy
RF- C Dexter
3R H Wagner

NY 1899 NL
SP J McGinnity
SP E Doheny
SP C Seymour
SP J Meekin
C - J Warner
1B J Doyle
2B K Gleason
SS G Davis
3B- F Hartman
LF K Selbach
CF G Van Haltren
RF- P Foster
IC P Wilson
C3- M Grady
M1 J Day
M2 F Hoey

PHI 1899 NL
SP W Piatt
SP R Donahue
SP C Fraser

PIT 1899 NL
SP A Orth
SP B Bernhard
RP J Fifield
C E McFarland
1B D Cooley
2B- N Lajoie
SS M Cross
3B B Lauder
LF E Delahanty
CF R Thomas
RF E Flick
UT P Chiles
C - K Douglass
M B Shettsline

PIT 1899 NL
SR S Leever
SP J Tannehill
SR T Sparks
SP B Hoffer
SP J Chesbro
C1 F Bowerman
1B- W Clark
2B- J O'Brien
SS B Ely
3B J Williams
LF J McCarthy
CF G Beaumont
RF P Donovan
UT T McCreery
C - P Schriver
M1 B Watkins

STL 1899 NL
SP J Powell
SP C Young
SP W Sudhoff
SP N Cuppy
C - L Criger
1B- P Tebeau
2B C Childs
S3 B Wallace
3B L Cross
LF J Burkett
MU H Blake
RF E Heidrick
C1- J O'Connor

WAS 1899 NL
SP G Weyhing
SP B Dinneen
SP D McFarlan
C - D McGuire
1B- D McGann
2B- F Bonner
S2 D Padden
3B- C Atherton
LF J O'Brien
CF J Slagle
RF B Freeman
UT- S Barry
M A Irwin

BOS 1900 NL
SP B Dinneen
SP V Willis
SP K Nichols
SP T Lewis
SP T Pittinger
RP N Cuppy
C - B Clarke
1B F Tenney
2B B Lowe
SS H Long
3B J Collins
RL C Stahl
CF B Hamilton
RU B Freeman
UT- S Barry
C - B Sullivan
M F Selee

BRO 1900 NL
SP J McGinnity
SP B Kennedy
SR F Kitson
SR H Howell
C - D Farrell
1B H Jennings
2B T Daly
SS B Dahlen
3B L Cross
LF J Sheckard
CF F Jones
RF W Keeler
L1 J Kelley
C - D McGuire
M N Hanlon

CHI 1900 NL
SP N Callahan
SP C Griffith
SP N Garvin
SP J Taylor
SP J Menefee
C - T Donahue

CIN 1900 NL
1B- J Ganzel
2B C Childs
SS B McCormick
3B B Bradley
LF J McCarthy
MR D Green
RL J Ryan
M1 S Mertes
M T Loftus

CIN 1900 NL
SP E Scott
SP N Hahn
SP D Newton
SP B Phillips
SP T Breitenstein
C H Peitz
1B J Beckley
2B- J Quinn
SS T Corcoran
32 H Steinfeldt
LU S Crawford
CF J Barrett
RF A McBride
3U C Irwin
M B Allen

NY 1900 NL
SP B Carrick
SP P Hawley
SP W Mercer
SP E Doheny
C - F Bowerman
1B J Doyle
2B K Gleason
3B C Hickman
LF K Selbach
CF G Van Haltren
IC- M Grady
M1 B Ewing

PHI 1900 NL
SP A Orth
SP R Donahue
SP C Fraser
SP B Bernhard
SP W Piatt
C E McFarland
1B E Delahanty
2B N Lajoie
SS M Cross
3B H Wolverton
LF J Slagle
CF R Thomas
RF E Flick
UI- J Dolan
M B Shettsline

PIT 1900 NL
SP D Phillippe
SP J Tannehill
SP S Leever
SP J Chesbro
SP B Waddell
C - C Zimmer
1B- D Cooley
2B C Ritchey
SS B Ely
3B J Williams
LF F Clarke
CF G Beaumont
RF H Wagner
1U T O'Brien

STL 1900 NL
SP C Young
SP C Jones
SP J Powell
SP W Sudhoff
SP J Hughey
C - L Criger
1B D McGann
2B B Keister
SS B Wallace
3B J McGraw
LF J Burkett
CF E Heidrick
RF E Flick
OI- M Donlin
M1 P Tebeau
M2 L Heilbroner

BOS 1901 NL
SP K Nichols
SP B Dinneen
SP V Willis
SP T Pittinger
C M Kittridge
1B F Tenney
2B De Montreville
SS H Long
3B L Cross
LF J Sheckard
CF F Jones
RF W Keeler
L1 J Kelley
UT H Wagner

STL 1901 NL
SP J Powell
SP J Harper
SR W Sudhoff
SP E Murphy
C - J Ryan
1B D McGann
2B De Montreville
SS B Wallace
RF- J Slagle
M F Selee

BRO 1901 NL
SP B Donovan
SP F Kitson
SP J Hughes
SP D Newton
RP B Kennedy
CM A Nichols

BAL 1901 AL
SP J McGinnity
SP H Howell
SP F Foreman
SP J Nops
C R Bresnahan
1B- B Hart
2B J Williams
SS B Keister
3B- J McGraw
ML J Jackson
CF S Brodie
RF C Seymour
M N Hanlon
3U R Thomas

CHI 1901 NL
SP T Hughes
SP J Taylor
SP R Waddell
SP M Eason
SP J Menefee
C - J Kling
1B- J Doyle
2B- C Childs
SS B McCormick
3I F Raymer
LF T Hartsel
CF D Green
RU- F Chance
UT C Dexter
M T Loftus

BOS 1901 AL
SP C Young
SP T Lewis
SP G Winter
SP F Mitchell
SP N Cuppy
C O Schreckengost
1B B Freeman
2B H Ferris
SS F Parent
3B J Collins
LF T Dowd
CF C Stahl
RF C Hemphill
C - L Criger

CIN 1901 NL
SP N Hahn
SP B Phillips
SP D Newton
SP A Stimmel
C B Bergen
1B J Beckley
32 H Steinfeldt
SS G Magoon
3B- C Irwin
LF D Harley
CF J Dobbs
RF S Crawford
C2- H Peitz
M B McPhee

CHI 1901 AL
SP R Patterson
SP C Griffith
SP N Callahan
SP J Katoll
SP Z Harvey
C B Sullivan
1B F Isbell
2B S Mertes
SS F Shugart
3B F Hartman
LF -H McFarland
C2- H Hoy
RF F Jones
M B McPhee

NY 1901 NL
SP D Taylor
SP C Mathewson
SP B Phyle
C J Warner
1B J Ganzel
2B- R Nelson
SS G Davis
32 S Strang
LF K Selbach
CF G Van Haltren
RF- A McBride
UT C Hickman

CLE 1901 AL
SP D Dowling
SP P Moore
SP B Hart
SP E Scott
SP B Hoffer
RP J Bracken
RP H McNeal
C B Wood
1B L LaChance
2B B Beck
SS F Scheibeck
3B B Bradley
LF J McCarthy
CF O Pickering
RL J O'Brien
M J McAleer

PHI 1901 NL
SP R Donahue
SP B Duggleby
SP A Orth
SP D White
SP H Townsend
C - E McFarland
1B- H Jennings
23 M Hallman
SS M Cross
3B H Wolverton
L1 E Delahanty
CF R Thomas
RF E Flick
M B Shettsline

DET 1901 AL
SP R Miller
SP E Siever
SP J Cronin
SP J Yeager
C - F Buelow
1B- P Dillon
2B J Gleason
SS K Elberfeld
3B D Casey
LF D Nance
CF J Barrett
RF D Holmes
IC S McAllister
M S Stallings

PIT 1901 NL
SP D Phillippe
SP J Chesbro
SP J Tannehill
SP S Leever
C - C Zimmer
1B K Bransfield
2B C Ritchey
SS- B Ely
3B T Leach
LF F Clarke
CF G Beaumont
RF L Davis
UT H Wagner

MIL 1901 AL
SP B Reidy
SR N Garvin
SP B Husting
SP T Sparks
SP P Hawley
C B Maloney
1B J Anderson
2B B Gilbert
SS W Conroy
3B- J Burke
RL B Hallman
CF- H Duffy
RF- I Waldron
3O B Friel

PHI 1901 AL
SP C Fraser
SP E Plank
SP B Bernhard

STL 1901 NL
3B O Krueger
LF J Burkett
CF E Heidrick
RF P Donovan
CM A Nichols

WAS 1901 AL
SP S Wiltse
SP W Piatt
C D Powers
1B H Davis
2B N Lajoie
S3 J Dolan
3B L Cross
LF- M McIntyre
MU D Fultz
RU S Seybold
M C Mack

WAS 1901 AL
SP B Carrick
SP W Lee
SP C Patten
SP W Mercer
SP D Gear
C B Clarke
1C M Grady
2M J Farrell
SS B Clingman
3B B Coughlin
LF P Foster
CF- I Waldron
R1 S Dungan
M J Manning

BOS 1902 NL
SP V Willis
SP T Pittinger
SP M Eason
SP J Malarkey
C - M Kittridge
1B F Tenney
2B De Montreville
SS H Long
3B E Gremminger
LU D Cooley
CF B Lush
RF P Carney
C - P Moran
M A Buckenberger

BRO 1902 NL
SP B Donovan
SP F Kitson
SP D Newton
SP J Hughes
SP R Evans
C - H Hearne
1B T McCreery
2B T Flood
SS B Dahlen
3B C Irwin
LF J Sheckard
CF C Dolan
RF W Keeler
C1- D Farrell
M N Hanlon

CHI 1902 NL
SP J Taylor
SP P Williams
SP J Menefee
SP C Lundgren
SP B Rhoads
RP J St.Vrain
C - J Kling
1C- F Chance
2B B Lowe
SS J Tinker
3B- G Schaefer
LF J Slagle
CF- J Dobbs
MR-D Jones
31- C Dexter
M F Selee

CIN 1902 NL
SP N Hahn
SP B Phillips
SP H Thielman
SP E Poole
SP B Ewing
C - B Bergen
1B J Beckley
IC H Peitz
SS T Corcoran
3B H Steinfeldt
LF- J Dobbs
CF- D Hoy
RF S Crawford
M1 B McPhee
M2 F Bancroft
M3 J Kelley

NY 1902 NL
SP C Mathewson
SP D Taylor
SP J McGinnity
SP T Sparks
RP J Cronin
C F Bowerman
1B- D McGann
2B H Smith

SS J Bean
SS J Bean
3B B Lauder
LO- J Jones
CF S Brodie
UT J Dunn
LF- G Browne
M1 H Fogel
M3 J McGraw

PHI 1902 NL
SP D White
SP B Duggleby
SP H Iburg
SP C Fraser
C R Dooin
1B- H Jennings
2B P Childs
SS R Hulswitt
3B- B Hallman
LF- G Browne
CF R Thomas
RF S Barry
1C K Douglass
M B Shettsline

PIT 1902 NL
SP J Chesbro
SP D Phillippe
SP J Tannehill
SP S Leever
SP E Doheny
C - H Smith
1B K Bransfield
2B C Ritchey
SS W Conroy
3B T Leach
LF F Clarke
CF G Beaumont
UT H Wagner

STL 1902 NL
SP M O'Neill
SP S Yerkes
SP E Murphy
SP B Wicker
SP C Currie
C - J Ryan
1U R Brashear
2B J Farrell
SS O Krueger
3B F Hartman
LF G Barclay
CF H Smoot
RF P Donovan
1B- A Nichols

BAL 1902 AL
SP J McGinnity
SP H Howell
SP S Wiltse
SP C Shields
SP J Katoll
RP I Butler
RP T Hughes
C W Robinson
1B- D McGann
2B J Williams
SS B Gilbert
IC- R Bresnahan
LF K Selbach
CF- H McFarland
RF- C Seymour
M1 J McGraw

BOS 1902 AL
SP C Young
SP B Dinneen
SP G Winter
SP T Sparks
C L Criger
1B C LaChance
2B H Ferris
SS F Parent
3B J Collins
LF P Dougherty
CF C Stahl
RF B Freeman
UT- H Gleason

CHI 1902 AL
SP N Callahan
SP R Patterson
SP W Piatt
SP C Griffith
SP N Garvin
C - B Sullivan
1B F Isbell
2B F Daly
SS G Davis
3B S Strang
LF S Mertes
CF F Jones
RF G Green
C - E McFarland

CLE 1902 AL
SP E Moore
SP A Joss

SP B Bernhard
SP G Wright
C H Bemis
1B C Hickman
2B N Lajoie
SP J Gochnauer
3B J Bradley
LF J McCarthy
MO H Bay
RF E Flick
CF- O Pickering
CU- B Wood
M B Armour

DET 1902 AL
SP W Mercer
SP G Mullin
SP E Siever
RP R Miller
SP J Yeager
C - D McGuire
1B- P Dillon
2B K Gleason
SS K Elberfeld
3B D Casey
LF D Harley
CF J Barrett
RF D Holmes
M F Dwyer

PHI 1902 AL
SP E Plank
SP R Waddell
SP B Husting
SP S Wiltse
SP F Mitchell
RP H Wilson
C - O Schreckengost
1B H Davis
2B- D Murphy
SS M Cross
3B L Cross
LF T Hartsel
CF D Fultz
RF S Seybold
C - D Powers
M C Mack

STL 1902 AL
SP J Powell
SP R Donahue
SP J Harper
SP W Sudhoff
SP B Reidy
C - J Sugden
1B J Anderson
2B D Padden
SS B Wallace
3B B McCormick
LF J Burkett
CF E Heidrick
RM C Hemphill
UT- B Friel
M J McAleer

WAS 1902 AL
SP A Orth
SP C Patten
SP B Carrick
SP H Townsend
C B Clarke
1B S Carey
2B- J Doyle
SS B Ely
3S B Coughlin
LF E Delahanty
CF J Ryan
UO W Lee
UT B Keister
M T Loftus

BOS 1903 NL
SP T Pittinger
SP V Willis
SP J Malarkey
SP W Piatt
C P Moran
1B F Tenney
2B E Abbaticchio
SS H Aubrey
3B E Gremminger
LF D Cooley
MU C Dexter
RF P Carney
OI J Stanley
M A Buckenberger

BRO 1903 NL
SP O Jones
SP H Schmidt
SP N Garvin
SP R Evans
SP B Reidy
C - L Ritter
1B J Doyle
2B T Flood

SS B Dahlen
3B S Strang
LF J Sheckard
CF J Dobbs
RF- W McCredie
2U- D Jordan
M N Hanlon

CHI 1903 NL
SP J Taylor
SP J Weimer
SP B Wicker
SP C Lundgren
SP J Menefee
C J Kling
1B F Chance
2B J Evers
SS J Tinker
3B D Casey
LF J Slagle
MR D Jones
RF D Harley
M F Selee

CIN 1903 NL
SP N Hahn
SP B Ewing
SP J Sutthoff
SP E Poole
SP J Harper
RP B Phillips
CU H Peitz
1B J Beckley
2B- T Daly
SS T Corcoran
3B H Steinfeldt
LR M Donlin
CF C Seymour
RF C Dolan
LI J Kelley

NY 1903 NL
SP J McGinnity
SP C Mathewson
SP D Taylor
SP J Cronin
C J Warner
1B D McGann
2B B Gilbert
SS C Babb
3B B Lauder
LF S Mertes
MU R Bresnahan
RF G Browne
IO- J Dunn
CF- G Van Haltren
M J McGraw

PHI 1903 NL
SP B Duggleby
SP C Fraser
SP T Sparks
SP F Mitchell
SP J McFetridge
C - F Roth
1B K Douglass
2B K Gleason
SS R Hulswitt
3B H Wolverton
LF S Barry
CF R Thomas
RF B Keister
RL- J Titus
M C Zimmer

PIT 1903 NL
SP D Phillippe
SP S Leever
SP E Doheny
SP B Kennedy
SP K Wilhelm
C - E Phelps
1B K Bransfield
2B- C Ritchey
SS H Wagner
3B T Leach
CF G Beaumont
RF J Sebring
IO- O Krueger

STL 1903 NL
SP C McFarland
SP M Brown
SP C Currie
SP M O'Neill
SP B Rhoads
RP E Murphy
RP J Dunleavy
C - J O'Neill
1B J Hackett
2B J Farrell
S3 D Brain
3B J Burke
LF G Barclay
CF H Smoot
RF P Donovan

BOS 1903 AL
SP C Young
SP B Dinneen
SP T Hughes
SP N Gibson
SP G Winter
C L Criger
1B C LaChance
2B H Ferris
SS F Parent
3B J Collins
LF P Dougherty
CF- C Stahl
RF B Freeman
MU J O'Brien

CHI 1903 AL
SP D White
SP P Flaherty
SP R Patterson
SP F Owen
C - J Slattery
1B F Isbell
2B G Magoon
SS L Tannehill
3B N Callahan
LF D Holmes
CF F Jones
RF D Green
M J Callahan

CLE 1903 AL
SP A Joss
SP E Moore
SP B Bernhard
SP R Donahue
SP G Wright
C H Bemis
1B C Hickman
2B N Lajoie
SS J Gochnauer
3B B Bradley
LF J McCarthy
CF J Bay
RF E Flick
C - F Abbott
M B Armour

DET 1903 AL
SP G Mullin
SP B Donovan
SP F Kitson
SP R Kisinger
C - D McGuire
1B C Carr
2B H Smith
SU- S McAllister
3B J Yeager
LU B Lush
CF J Barrett
RL S Crawford
S2- H Long
M E Barrow

NY 1903 AL
SP J Chesbro
SP J Tannehill
SP C Griffith
SR H Howell
SP B Wolfe
C M Beville
1B J Ganzel
2B J Williams
SS K Elberfeld
3B W Conroy
LF L Davis
ML H McFarland
RF W Keeler
CF- D Fultz

PHI 1903 AL
SP E Plank
SP R Waddell
SP C Bender
SP W Henley
C - O Schreckengost
1B H Davis
2B D Murphy
SS M Cross
3B L Cross
LF T Hartsel
CF O Pickering
RF S Seybold
LR- D Hoffman
C - D Powers
M C Mack

STL 1903 AL
SP J Powell
SP W Sudhoff
SP E Siever
SP R Donahue
C - M Kahoe
1B J Anderson
2U B Friel
SS B Wallace

3B H Hill
LF J Burkett
CF E Heidrick
RF C Hemphill
C - J Sugden
M J McAleer

WAS 1903 AL
SP C Patten
SP A Orth
SP H Wilson
SP H Townsend
SP D Dunkle
C - M Kittridge
1C B Clarke
2B- B McCormick
SS C Moran
3B B Coughlin
LF K Selbach
CF J Ryan
Rp- W Lee
UT R Robinson
M T Loftus

BOS 1904 NL
SP V Willis
SP T Pittinger
SP K Wilhelm
SR T Fisher
SP E McNichol
C - T Needham
1B F Tenney
2B- F Raymer
SS E Abbaticchio
3B J Delahanty
LF D Cooley
CF P Geier
RO R Cannell
C3 P Moran
RF- P Carney
M A Buckenberger

BRO 1904 NL
SP O Jones
SP J Cronin
SP N Garvin
SP E Poole
SP D Scanlan
C B Bergen
1B P Dillon
2B- D Jordan
SS C Babb
3B M McCormick
LF J Sheckard
CF J Dobbs
RF H Lumley
MU D Gessler
M N Hanlon

CHI 1904 NL
SP J Weimer
SP B Briggs
SP C Lundgren
SP B Wicker
SP M Brown
RP F Corridon
C J Kling
1B F Chance
2B J Evers
SS J Tinker
3B D Casey
LF J Slagle
CF J McCarthy
RF D Jones
M F Selee

CIN 1904 NL
SP N Hahn
SP J Harper
SP W Kellum
SP T Walker
SP B Ewing
C A Schlei
1B J Kelley
2B M Huggins
SS T Corcoran
3B H Steinfeldt
LF F Odwell
CF C Seymour
RU C Dolan
C - H Peitz
3I- S Woodruff

NY 1904 NL
SP J McGinnity
SP C Mathewson
SP D Taylor
SP H Wiltse
SP R Ames
C - J Warner
1B D McGann
2B J Gilbert
SS B Dahlen
3B A Devlin
LF S Mertes
MU R Bresnahan
RF G Browne

C - F Bowerman
M J McGraw

PHI 1904 NL
SP C Fraser
SP B Duggleby
SP T Sparks
SP J Sutthoff
SP J McPherson
RP R Dooin
C R Dooin
1B- J Doyle
2B K Gleason
SS R Hulswitt
3B H Wolverton
LU J Titus
CF R Thomas
RF S Magee
1R J Lush
C - F Roth
M H Duffy

PIT 1904 NL
SP S Leever
SP P Flaherty
SP M Lynch
SP D Phillippe
SP C Case
RP R Miller
C E Phelps
1B K Bransfield
2B C Ritchey
SS H Wagner
3B T Leach
LF- F Clarke
CF G Beaumont
RF- J Sebring
UT- O Krueger

STL 1904 NL
SP J Taylor
SP K Nichols
SP C McFarland
SP M O'Neill
SP J Corbett
C M Grady
1B J Beckley
2B J Farrell
SS D Shay
3B J Burke
LF G Barclay
CF H Smoot
RF S Shannon
UT D Brain

BOS 1904 AL
SP C Young
SP B Dinneen
SP J Tannehill
SP N Gibson
SP G Winter
C L Criger
1B C LaChance
2B H Ferris
SS F Parent
3B J Collins
LF K Selbach
CF C Stahl
RF B Freeman

CHI 1904 AL
SP F Owen
SP N Altrock
SP D White
SP F Smith
SP R Patterson
RS E Walsh
C B Sullivan
1B J Donahue
2B J Dundon
SS G Davis
3B L Tannehill
LF N Callahan
CF F Jones
RF D Green
12 F Isbell
M1 J Callahan

CLE 1904 AL
SP B Bernhard
SP R Donahue
SP E Moore
SP A Joss
SP B Rhoads
RP O Hess
C - H Peitz
C - T Needham

DET 1904 AL
SP G Mullin
SP E Killian

SP B Donovan
SP F Kitson
SP J Stovall
C - L Drill
1B- C Carr
2B B Lowe
SS C O'Leary
3B- B Gremminger
LF M McIntyre
CF J Barrett
RF S Crawford
UT R Robinson
2B J Kling
M1 E Barrow

NY 1904 AL
SP J Chesbro
SP J Powell
SP A Orth
SP T Hughes
SP C Griffith
C D McGuire
1B J Ganzel
2B J Williams
SS K Elberfeld
3B W Conroy
LF P Dougherty
OI J Anderson
RF W Keeler
CF D Fultz

PHI 1904 AL
SP R Waddell
SP E Plank
SP W Henley
SP C Bender
C O Schreckengost
1B H Davis
2B D Murphy
SS M Cross
3B L Cross
LF T Hartsel
CF O Pickering
RF S Seybold
M C Mack

STL 1904 AL
SP B Pelty
SP H Howell
SP F Glade
SP W Sudhoff
SP E Siever
C J Sugden
1B T Jones
2B P Padden
SS B Wallace
3B- C Moran
LF J Burkett
CF E Heidrick
RO C Hemphill
M J McAleer

WAS 1904 AL
SP C Patten
SP H Townsend
SP B Jacobson
SP B Wolfe
SP T Hughes
C - M Kittridge
1B J Stahl
2B B McCormick
SU J Cassidy
3B- H Hill
LF- F Huelsman
CF B O'Neill
RF P Donovan
C1- B Clarke

BOS 1905 NL
SP I Young
SP V Willis
SP C Fraser
SP K Wilhelm
C - P Moran
1B F Tenney
2B F Raymer
SS E Abbaticchio
3B H Wolverton
LF J Delahanty
CF R Cannell
RF C Dolan
C - T Needham

BRO 1905 NL
SP H McIntire
SP D Scanlan
SP E Stricklett
SP M Eason
SP O Jones
RP F Mitchell
C - L Ritter
1B D Gessler
2U C Malay
SS P Lewis
3B E Batch
LF J Sheckard
CF J Dobbs

RF H Lumley
C - B Bergen
M N Hanlon

CHI 1905 NL
SP E Reulbach
SP J Weimer
SP M Brown
SP B Wicker
SP C Lundgren
RP B Briggs
RP B Pfeffer
1B F Chance
2B J Evers
SS J Tinker
3B D Casey
LF F Schulte
CF J Slagle
RF B Maloney
2U- S Hofman
M1 F Selee

CIN 1905 NL
SP O Overall
SP B Ewing
SR C Chech
SP J Harper
SP T Walker
C A Schlei
1B S Barry
2B M Huggins
SS T Corcoran
3B H Steinfeldt
LF- J Kelley
CF C Seymour
RL F Odwell
3U- A Bridwell

NY 1905 NL
SP C Mathewson
SP J McGinnity
SP R Ames
SP D Taylor
SR H Wiltse
C R Bresnahan
1B D McGann
2B B Gilbert
SS B Dahlen
3B A Devlin
RF G Browne
CU F Bowerman
UT S Strang
M J McGraw

PHI 1905 NL
SP T Pittinger
SP B Duggleby
SP T Sparks
SP F Corridon
SP K Nichols
C R Dooin
1B K Bransfield
2B K Gleason
SS M Doolan
3B E Courtney
LF S Magee
CF R Thomas
RF J Titus
M H Duffy

PIT 1905 NL
SP D Phillippe
SP S Leever
SP C Case
SR M Lynch
SP P Flaherty
RP C Robitaille
C - H Peitz
1U D Howard
2B C Ritchey
SS H Wagner
3B- D Brain
LF F Clarke
CF G Beaumont
RF O Clymer
UT T Leach

STL 1905 NL
SP J Taylor
SP C McFarland
SP J Thielman
SP B Brown
SP W Egan
CU M Grady
1B J Beckley
2B H Arndt
SS- G McBride
3B J Burke
LF S Shannon
CF H Smoot
RF J Dunleavy
2S- D Shay
M1 K Nichols
M3 S Robison

BOS 1905 AL
SP C Young
SP J Tannehill
SP B Winter
SP B Dinneen
SP N Gibson
C L Criger
1B- M Grimshaw
2B H Ferris
SS F Parent
3B J Collins
LF J Burkett
CF C Stahl
RF K Selbach
1R B Freeman

CHI 1905 AL
SP F Owen
SP N Altrock
SP F Smith
SP D White
SP E Walsh
C B Sullivan
1B J Donahue
2B G Dundon
SS G Davis
3B L Tannehill
LU N Callahan
CF F Jones
RF D Green
LF- D Holmes
UT- F Isbell
C - E McFarland

CLE 1905 AL
SP A Joss
SP E Moore
SP B Rhoads
SP O Hess
SP B Bernhard
RP R Donahue
C - F Buelow
1B- C Carr
2B- N Lajoie
SS T Turner
3B B Bradley
LF J Jackson
CF H Bay
RF E Flick
12 G Stovall
M3 N Lajoie

DET 1905 AL
SP G Mullin
SP E Killian
SP B Donovan
SP F Kitson
C - L Drill
1B- C Lindsay
2B G Schaefer
SS C O'Leary
3B B Coughlin
LF M McIntyre
CF D Cooley
R1 S Crawford
M B Armour

NY 1905 AL
SP A Orth
SP J Chesbro
SP B Hogg
SR J Powell
RS C Griffith
C - R Kleinow
1B H Chase
2B J Williams
SS K Elberfeld
3B J Yeager
LF P Dougherty
CF D Fultz
RF W Keeler
UT W Conroy

PHI 1905 AL
SP E Plank
SR W Waddell
SP A Coakley
SR C Bender
SP W Henley
C O Schreckengost
1B H Davis
2B D Murphy
SS- J Knight
3B L Cross
LF T Hartsel
CF D Hoffman
RF S Seybold
SS- M Cross
M C Mack

STL 1905 AL
SP H Howell
SP F Glade
SP B Pelty
SP W Sudhoff
SP J Buchanan
C - J Sugden

1B T Jones
2B I Rockenfield
SS B Wallace
3B H Gleason
LF G Stone
CF B Koehler
RF E Frisk
OI I Van Zandt
M J McAleer

WAS 1905 AL
SP C Patten
SP T Hughes
SR H Townsend
SP B Wolfe
SP B Jacobson
C - M Heydon
1B J Stahl
2B- C Hickman
SS J Cassidy
3B H Hill
LF F Huelsman
CF C Jones
RF J Anderson
32 R Nill
C - M Kittridge
RU- P Knoll

BOS 1906 NL
SP I Young
SP V Lindaman
SP B Pfeffer
SP G Dorner
C - T Needham
1B F Tenney
2B A Strobel
SS A Bridwell
3B D Brain
L2 D Howard
CF J Bates
RF C Dolan

BRO 1906 NL
SP E Stricklett
SP D Scanlan
SP H McIntire
SP M Eason
SP J Pastorius
C B Bergen
1B T Jordan
2B W Alperman
SS P Lewis
3B D Casey
LF- J McCarthy
CF B Maloney
RF H Lumley
2U J Hummel
M P Donovan

CHI 1906 NL
SP M Brown
SP J Pfiester
SP E Reulbach
SP C Lundgren
SP J Taylor
RP O Overall
C J Kling
1B F Chance
2B J Evers
SS J Tinker
3B H Steinfeldt
LF J Sheckard
CF J Slagle
RF F Schulte

CIN 1906 NL
SP J Weimer
SP B Ewing
SP C Fraser
SP B Wicker
SP C Hall
C A Schlei
1B S Deal
2B M Huggins
SS T Corcoran
3B J Delahanty
LF J Kelley
CF- C Seymour
RF- F Jude
IO- H Lobert
M N Hanlon

NY 1906 NL
SP J McGinnity
SP C Mathewson
SR H Wiltse
SP D Taylor
SP R Ames
RP G Ferguson
CM R Bresnahan
1B D McGann
2B B Gilbert
SS B Dahlen
3B A Devlin
LF- S Shannon
CF- C Seymour
RF G Browne

CU F Bowerman
2O S Strang
M J McGraw

PHI 1906 NL
SP T Sparks
SR B Duggleby
SP J Lush
SR L Richie
SP T Pittinger
C R Dooin
1B K Bransfield
2B K Gleason
SS M Doolan
3B E Courtney
LF S Magee
CF R Thomas
RF J Titus
M H Duffy

PIT 1906 NL
SP V Willis
SP S Leever
SP L Leifield
SP D Phillippe
SP M Lynch
C - G Gibson
1B J Nealon
2B C Ritchey
SS H Wagner
3B T Sheehan
LF F Clarke
CF- G Beaumont
RF B Ganley
UT T Leach
OI- D Meier

STL 1906 NL
SP B Brown
SP E Karger
SP F Beebe
SP J Taylor
SP C Druhot
RP G Thompson
C1 M Grady
1B- J Beckley
2B P Bennett
SS- G McBride
3B- H Arndt
LF- S Shannon
MR-H Smoot
MR-A Burch
3U A Hoelskoetter
M J McCloskey

BOS 1906 AL
SP C Young
SP J Harris
SP B Dinneen
SP G Winter
SP J Tannehill
RP R Glaze
C - C Armbruster
1B M Grimshaw
2B H Ferris
SS F Parent
3B- R Morgan
LF J Hoey
CF C Stahl
RF- J Hayden
R1 B Freeman
M1 J Collins

CHI 1906 AL
SP F Owen
SP N Altrock
SR E Walsh
SP D White
SP R Patterson
RP F Smith
C B Sullivan
1B J Donahue
2B F Isbell
SS G Davis
3B L Tannehill
RL E Hahn
CF F Jones
RF B O'Neill
3U- G Rohe

CLE 1906 AL
SP O Hess
SP B Rhoads
SP A Joss
SP B Bernhard
C - H Bemis
1B C Rossman
2B N Lajoie
SS T Turner
3B- B Bradley
LF J Jackson
MR E Flick
RF B Congalton
UI G Stovall

DET 1906 AL
SP G Mullin
SP R Donahue

SP E Siever
SP B Donovan
SP E Killian
RS J Eubank
C - B Schmidt
1B C Lindsay
2B G Schaefer
SS C O'Leary
3B B Coughlin
LF M McIntyre
MO T Cobb
RF S Crawford
CF- D Jones
M B Armour

NY 1906 AL
SP A Orth
SP J Chesbro
SP B Hogg
SR W Clarkson
SP D Newton
C R Kleinow
1B H Chase
2B J Williams
SS K Elberfeld
3B F LaPorte
UT W Conroy
CF D Hoffman
RF W Keeler
LF- F Delahanty
M C Griffith

PHI 1906 AL
SP R Waddell
SP C Bender
SR J Dygert
SP E Plank
SP J Coombs
RP A Coakley
C O Schreckengost
1B H Davis
2B D Murphy
SS M Cross
3B- J Knight
LF T Hartsel
CF B Lord
RF S Seybold
OF H Armbruster
M C Mack

STL 1906 AL
SP H Howell
SP F Glade
SP B Pelty
SP J Powell
SP- B Jacobson
RP E Smith
C - B Rickey
1B T Jones
2B P O'Brien
SS B Wallace
3B R Hartzell
LF G Stone
MR C Hemphill
RU H Niles
M J McAleer

WAS 1906 AL
SP C Falkenberg
SP C Patten
SR C Smith
SP T Hughes
SP F Kitson
C - H Wakefield
1B J Stahl
2B L Schlafly
SS D Altizer
3B L Cross
LF J Anderson
CF C Jones
RF C Hickman
IO- R Nill

BOS 1907 NL
SP G Dorner
SP V Lindaman
SP I Young
SP H Camnitz
SP P Flaherty
SP B Pfeffer
RS J Boultes
C - T Needham
1B F Tenney
2B C Ritchey
SS A Bridwell
3B D Brain
LF- N Randall
CF G Beaumont
RF J Bates

BRO 1907 NL
SP N Rucker
SP G Bell
SP E Stricklett
SP J Pastorius
SP H McIntire
RP D Scanlan

C L Ritter
1B T Jordan
2B W Alperman
SS P Lewis
3B D Casey
LU E Batch
CF B Maloney
RF H Lumley
UT J Hummel
M P Donovan

CHI 1907 NL
SP O Overall
SP M Brown
SP C Lundgren
SP J Pfiester
SP E Reulbach
RP C Fraser
C - L Criger
1B F Chance
2B J Evers
SS J Tinker
3B H Steinfeldt
LF J Sheckard
CF J Slagle
RF F Schulte
UT S Hofman

CIN 1907 NL
SP B Ewing
SP A Coakley
SP J Weimer
SP R Hitt
SP D Mason
C L McLean
1B J Ganzel
2B M Huggins
SS H Lobert
3B M Mowrey
LF F Odwell
ML A Kruger
RF M Mitchell
UT- J Kane
C - A Schlei
M N Hanlon

NY 1907 NL
SP C Mathewson
SR J McGinnity
SR R Ames
SR H Wiltse
SP D Taylor
C R Bresnahan
1B- D McGann
2B- L Doyle
SS B Dahlen
3B A Devlin
LF S Shannon
CF C Seymour
RF G Browne
C1 F Bowerman
UT S Strang
M J McGraw

PHI 1907 NL
SP F Corridon
SP T Sparks
SP L Moren
SP B Brown
SR L Richie
RP T Pittinger
C R Dooin
1B K Bransfield
2B O Knabe
SS M Doolan
31 E Courtney
LF S Magee
CF R Thomas
RF J Titus
M B Murray

PIT 1907 NL
SP V Willis
SP L Leifield
SP S Leever
SP D Phillippe
SR H Camnitz
C G Gibson
1B J Nealon
2B E Abbaticchio
SS H Wagner
3I A Storke
LF F Clarke
MI T Leach
RU G Anderson
UO-B Hallman

STL 1907 NL
SP S McGlynn
SP E Karger
SP F Beebe
SP A Fromme
SP J Lush
C - D Marshall
1B- E Konetchy
2B- P Bennett

SS E Holly
3B B Byrne
LF R Murray
CF- J Burnett
RF- S Barry
2U A Hoelskoetter
M J McCloskey

BOS 1907 AL
SPC Young
SP G Winter
SR R Glaze
SR T Pruiett
SP J Tannehill
RP C Morgan
C - L Criger
1B B Unglaub
2B H Ferris
SS H Wagner
3B J Knight
LF J Barrett
CF D Sullivan
RF B Congalton
UT F Parent
M2 G Huff
M4 D McGuire

CHI 1907 AL
SR E Walsh
SP F Smith
SR D White
SP N Altrock
SP R Patterson
C B Sullivan
1B J Donahue
2B F Isbell
SS G Davis
32 G Rohe
LF P Dougherty
CF F Jones
RF E Hahn

CLE 1907 AL
SP A Joss
SP G Liebhardt
SP B Rhoads
SP J Thielman
C N Clarke
1B G Stovall
2B N Lajoie
SS T Turner
3B B Bradley
LF B Hinchman
MU J Birmingham
RF E Flick

DET 1907 AL
SP G Mullin
SP E Killian
SP E Siever
SP B Donovan
C B Schmidt
1B C Rossman
2B R Downs
SS C O'Leary
3B B Coughlin
LF D Jones
CF S Crawford
RF T Cobb
2I G Schaefer
M H Jennings

NY 1907 AL
SP A Orth
SP J Chesbro
SP S Doyle
SP B Hogg
SP D Newton
C - R Kleinow
1B H Chase
2B J Williams
SS K Elberfeld
3U G Moriarty
LS W Conroy
CF D Hoffman
RF W Keeler
UT F LaPorte
C - I Thomas
M C Griffith

PHI 1907 AL
SP E Plank
SR R Waddell
SR J Dygert
SP C Bender
SP J Coombs
C O Schreckengost
1B H Davis
2B D Murphy
SI S Nicholls
3B J Collins
LF T Hartsel
CF R Oldring
RF S Seybold
SS- M Cross
M C Mack

STL 1907 AL
SP H Howell
SP B Pelty
SP J Powell
SP F Glade
SP B Dinneen
C - T Spencer
1B T Jones
2B H Niles
SS A Wallace
3U J Yeager
LF G Stone
CF C Hemphill
RF O Pickering
M J McAleer

WAS 1907 AL
SP C Smith
SP C Patten
SP C Falkenberg
SP T Hughes
SP W Johnson
RP O Graham
C - J Warner
1L- J Anderson
23 J Delahanty
S1 D Altizer
3B- B Shipke
OI- O Clymer
MU C Jones
RL B Ganley
M J Cantillon

BOS 1908 NL
SR V Lindaman
SP P Flaherty
SR G Dorner
SR G Ferguson
CU- F Bowerman
1B D McGann
2B C Ritchey
SS B Dahlen
3B B Sweeney
LF J Bates
CF G Beaumont
RF G Browne
UT- J Hannifin
M J Kelley

BRO 1908 NL
SP N Rucker
SP K Wilhelm
SP H McIntire
SP J Pastorius
SR G Bell
C B Bergen
1B T Jordan
2B- H Pattee
SS P Lewis
3B T Sheehan
UO A Burch
CF B Maloney
RF H Lumley
2S C Charles
M P Donovan

CHI 1908 NL
SR M Brown
SR E Reulbach
SR O Overall
SP C Fraser
RP C Lundgren
C J Kling
1B F Chance
2B J Evers
SS J Tinker
3B H Steinfeldt
LF J Sheckard
ML J Slagle
RF F Schulte
UT S Hofman
RM D Howard

CIN 1908 NL
SP B Ewing
SP B Spade
SP A Coakley
SR B Campbell
SP J Weimer
C - A Schlei
1B- J Donahue
2U G Davis
SS F Parent
3B L Tannehill
LF P Dougherty
CF F Jones
RO E Hahn
RU J Anderson
2U- J Atz
1B- F Isbell

NY 1908 NL
SR C Mathewson
SP H Wiltse
SP D Crandall
SP J McGinnity
SR D Taylor
RP R Ames

C R Bresnahan
1B F Tenney
2B L Doyle
SS A Bridwell
3B A Devlin
LF- S Shannon
CF C Seymour
RF M Donlin
M J McGraw

PHI 1908 NL
SP G McQuillan
SP T Sparks
SP F Corridon
SR L Richie
SR L Moren
RP B Foxen
C R Dooin
1B K Bransfield
2B O Knabe
SS M Doolan
3B E Grant
LF S Magee
CF F Osborn
RF J Titus
M B Murray

PIT 1908 NL
SP V Willis
SP N Maddox
SR H Camnitz
SP L Leifield
SR S Leever
C G Gibson
1B- H Swacina
2B E Abbaticchio
SS H Wagner
3B T Leach
LF F Clarke
CF F Thomas
RF C Wilson

STL 1908 NL
SR B Raymond
SP J Lush
SR F Beebe
SP E Karger
SR S Sallee
RP A Fromme
RP I Higginbotham
C - B Ludwig
1B E Konetchy
2B- B Gilbert
SS- P O'Rourke
3B B Byrne
LF J Delahanty
MU A Shaw
MR M Murray
2S C Charles
M J McCloskey

BOS 1908 AL
SP C Young
SR E Cicotte
SP C Morgan
SR F Burchell
SP G Winter
RP E Steele
C - L Criger
1B- J Stahl
2B A McConnell
SS H Wagner
3B H Lord
LF J Thoney
CF D Sullivan
RF G Gessler
LU G Cravath
M1 D McGuire
M2 F Lake

CHI 1908 AL
SR E Walsh
SP F Smith
SP D White
SR F Owen
SR N Altrock
C B Sullivan
1B- J Donahue
2U G Davis
SS F Parent
3B L Tannehill
LF P Dougherty
CF J Kane
RF M Mitchell
CU L McLean

CLE 1908 AL
SP A Joss
SP B Rhoads
SR G Liebhardt
SP H Berger
SP C Chech
C N Clarke
1B G Stovall
2B N Lajoie

S3- G Perring
3B B Bradley
LF J Clarke
CF J Birmingham
UT B Hinchman
C - H Bemis

DET 1908 AL
SP E Summers
SP G Mullin
SP B Donovan
SP E Willett
SP E Killian
C B Schmidt
1B C Rossman
2B- R Downs
UI G Schaefer
3B B Coughlin
LF M McIntyre
CF S Crawford
RF T Cobb
M H Jennings

NY 1908 AL
SR J Chesbro
SR J Lake
SR M Manning
SP B Hogg
SP A Orth
C R Kleinow
1B- H Chase
2B H Niles
SS N Ball
3B W Conroy
LF- J Stahl
CF C Hemphill
RF- W Keeler
13 G Moriarty
M1 C Griffith
M2 K Elberfeld

PHI 1908 AL
SR R Vickers
SP E Plank
SR J Dygert
SP J Coombs
SP C Bender
RP B Schlitzer
C - O Schreckengost
1B H Davis
UT E Collins
SS S Nicholls
3B J Collins
LF T Hartsel
CF R Oldring
UT D Murphy
M C Mack

STL 1908 AL
SP H Howell
SP R Waddell
SP J Powell
SR B Dinneen
SP B Pelty
RP B Grahame
RS B Bailey
C - T Spencer
1B T Jones
2B J Williams
SS B Wallace
3B H Ferris
LF G Stone
UO D Hoffman
RI R Hartzell
M J McAleer

WAS 1908 AL
SR T Hughes
SP W Johnson
SP C Smith
SR B Keeley
SP B Burns
RP E Cates
C G Street
1B J Freeman
2B- J Delahanty
SS G McBride
3B B Shipke
LF B Ganley
CF C Milan
RU O Pickering
RU O Clymer
M J Cantillon

BOS 1909 NL
SR A Mattern
SP G Ferguson
SP K White
SP L Richie
SP B Brown
C - P Graham
1B- F Stem
2B- D Shean
SS- J Coffey
3B B Sweeney
LF- R Thomas

```
CF  G Beaumont
RF  B Becker
OI  F Beck
M1  F Bowerman
M2  H Smith

BRO 1909 NL
SP  N Rucker
SP  G Bell
RP  H McIntire
SP  K Wilhelm
SP  D Scanlan
RP  G Hunter
C   B Bergen
1B  T Jordan
2B  W Alperman
SS  T McMillan
3B  E Lennox
LF- W Clement
ML  A Burch
RF- H Lumley
UT  J Hummel
UT- P McElveen

CHI 1909 NL
SR  M Brown
SP  O Overall
SP  E Reulbach
SP  J Pfiester
SP  R Kroh
C - J Archer
1B  F Chance
2B  J Evers
SS  J Tinker
3B  H Steinfeldt
LF  J Sheckard
CF  S Hofman
RF  F Schulte

CIN 1909 NL
SP  A Fromme
SR  H Gaspar
SR  J Rowan
SP  B Ewing
SR  B Campbell
RP  B Spade
C   L McLean
1B  D Hoblitzel
2B  D Egan
SS  T Downey
3B  H Lobert
LF  B Bescher
CF  R Oakes
RF  M Mitchell
OI  D Paskert
M   C Griffith

NY  1909 NL
SP  C Mathewson
SP  H Wiltse
SP  B Raymond
SP  R Ames
SP  R Marquard
RS  D Crandall
C - A Schlei
1B  F Tenney
2B  L Doyle
SS  A Bridwell
3B  A Devlin
LF  M McCormick
CF  B O'Hara
RF  R Murray
1B- F Merkle
CU- C Meyers
CF- C Seymour
M   J McGraw

PHI 1909 NL
SP  E Moore
SP  L Moren
SR  G McQuillan
SP  F Corridon
SP  H Coveleski
RP  T Sparks
C   R Dooin
1B  K Bransfield
2B  O Knabe
SS  M Doolan
3B  E Grant
LF  S Magee
CF- J Bates
RF  J Titus
M   B Murray

PIT 1909 NL
SP  V Willis
SR  H Camnitz
SP  N Maddox
SP  L Leifield
SR  B Adams
RP  D Phillippe
C   G Gibson
1B  B Abstein
2B  D Miller
SS  H Wagner
3B- J Barbeau
LF  F Clarke
CF  T Leach
RF  C Wilson

STL 1909 NL
SR  F Beebe
SP  J Lush
SP  S Sallee
SP  B Harmon
SP  L Backman
RP  S Melter
C   E Phelps
1B  E Konetchy
2S  C Charles
SS- R Hulswitt
3B  B Byrne
LF  R Ellis
CF  A Shaw
RF  S Evans
OI  J Delahanty
M   R Bresnahan

BOS 1909 AL
SR  F Arellanes
SR  E Cicotte
SP  J Wood
SP  C Chech
C   B Carrigan
1B  J Stahl
2B  A McConnell
SS  H Wagner
3B  H Lord
LO  H Niles
CF  T Speaker
RF  D Gessler
LF- H Hooper
M   F Lake

CHI 1909 AL
SR  F Smith
SP  J Scott
SP  E Walsh
SP  D White
SP  B Burns
C   B Sullivan
1B  F Isbell
2B  J Atz
SO  F Parent
3S  L Tannehill
OI  D Altizer
RF- E Hahn
32  B Purtell

CLE 1909 AL
SP  C Young
SP  H Berger
SP  A Joss
SP  C Falkenberg
SP  B Rhoads
C   T Easterly
1B  G Stovall
3B  B Bradley
LM  B Hinchman
CF  J Birmingham
RF  W Good
3B- G Perring
M2  D McGuire

DET 1909 AL
SP  G Mullin
SP  E Willett
SP  E Summers
SP  E Killian
SP  B Donovan
C - B Schmidt
1B- C Rossman
2B- G Schaefer
SS  D Bush
3B  G Moriarty
LF  M McIntyre
CF  S Crawford
RF  T Cobb
M   H Jennings

NY  1909 AL
SR  J Warhop
SP  J Lake
SP  R Manning
SP  L Brockett
SP  S Doyle
RP  T Hughes
RS  J Quinn
RP  P Wilson
C - R Kleinow
1B  H Chase
2B- F LaPorte
SI  J Knight
3B  J Austin
LF  C Engle
MR  R Demmitt
RF  W Keeler
UT  B Cree
S3  K Elberfeld
M   G Stallings

PHI 1909 AL
SP  E Plank
SP  C Bender
SP  C Morgan
SR  H Krause
SP  J Coombs
RS  J Dygert
C - I Thomas
1B  H Davis
2B  E Collins
SS  J Barry
3B  F Baker
LF- T Hartsel
ML- R Oldring
RF  D Murphy
CF- B Ganley
M   C Mack

STL 1909 AL
SP  J Powell
SP  R Waddell
SP  B Pelty
SR  B Bailey
SR  B Grahame
RP  B Dinneen
C - L Criger
1B  T Jones
2B  J Williams
SS  B Wallace
3B  H Ferris
LF- G Stone
CF  D Hoffman
RS  R Hartzell
UT  A Griggs
OI- J McAleese
C - J Stephens
M   J McAleer

WAS 1909 AL
SP  W Johnson
SR  B Groom
SR  D Gray
SP  C Smith
SP  T Hughes
C   G Street
1B- J Donahue
2B- J Delahanty
SS  G McBride
3B  W Conroy
UO- J Lelivelt
MU  C Milan
LR  G Browne
UT  B Unglaub
M   J Cantillon

BOS 1910 NL
SR  A Mattern
SR  B Brown
SR  S Frock
SP  C Curtis
SR  G Ferguson
C   P Graham
1B  B Sharpe
2B  D Shean
SI  B Sweeney
3B  B Herzog
LF  B Collins
CF  F Beck
RF  D Miller
M   F Lake

BRO 1910 NL
SP  N Rucker
SP  G Bell
SP  C Barger
SP  D Scanlan
SP  E Knetzer
RP  R Dessau
C - B Bergen
1B  J Daubert
2B  J Hummel
SS  T Smith
1B  E Konetchy
3B  E Lennox
LF  Z Wheat
CF  B Davidson
RF- J Dalton
OI  A Burch
C - T Erwin
M   B Dahlen

CHI 1910 NL
SR  M Brown
SP  K Cole
SP  H McIntire
SP  E Reulbach
SP  O Overall
RS  L Richie
RP  J Pfiester
C - J Kling
1B- F Chance
2B  J Evers
SS  J Tinker
3B  H Steinfeldt
LF  J Sheckard
CF  S Hofman
RF  F Schulte
C1  J Archer
IO  H Zimmerman
M   P Donovan

CIN 1910 NL
SR  H Gaspar
SP  G Suggs
SR  J Rowan
SP  F Beebe
SR  B Burns
C   L McLean
1B  D Hoblitzel
2B  D Egan
SS- T McMillan
3B- H Lobert
LF  B Bescher
CF  D Paskert
RF  M Mitchell
S3  T Downey
OF- W Miller
M   C Griffith

NY  1910 NL
SP  C Mathewson
SP  H Wiltse
SP  L Drucke
SR  D Crandall
SR  R Ames
RP  B Raymond
C   C Meyers
1B  F Merkle
2B  L Doyle
SS  A Bridwell
3B  A Devlin
LF  J Devore
ML  F Snodgrass
RF  R Murray
OI- B Becker
CF- C Seymour
M   J McGraw

PHI 1910 NL
SR  E Moore
SP  B Ewing
SP  L Moren
SP  B Donovan
SP  G McQuillan
SP  E Stack
RS  J Schettler
2B- J Delahanty
1B  K Bransfield
2B  O Knabe
SS  M Doolan
3B  E Grant
LF  S Magee
CF  J Bates
RF  J Titus
UT- J Walsh

PIT 1910 NL
SP  H Camnitz
SP  B Adams
SR  L Leifield
SP  K White
SR  D Phillippe
RS  S Leever
C   G Gibson
1B  J Flynn
2B  D Miller
SS  H Wagner
3B  B Byrne
LF  B Collins
CF  F Beck
RF  D Miller
LF  F Clarke
CF  T Leach
RF  C Wilson
UO  V Campbell

STL 1910 NL
SR  B Harmon
SR  J Lush
SR  V Willis
SR  F Corridon
SR  L Backman
RP  S Sallee
C   E Phelps
1B  E Konetchy
2B  M Huggins
SS  A Hauser
3B  M Mowrey
LF  R Ellis
CF  R Oakes
RF  S Evans
C - R Bresnahan

BOS 1910 AL
SP  E Cicotte
SP  R Collins
SR  J Wood
SR  C Hall
SP  E Karger
SP  C Smith
RP  F Arellanes
C   B Carrigan
1B  J Stahl
2B  L Gardner
SS  H Wagner
3B- H Lord
LF  D Lewis
CF  T Speaker
RF  H Hooper
UT  C Engle

CHI 1910 AL
SP  E Walsh
SP  D White
SR  J Scott
SR  F Olmstead
SR  I Young
RP  F Lange
RP  F Smith
C - F Payne
1B- C Gandil
2S  R Zeider
SS- L Blackburne
3B  B Purtell
LF  P Dougherty
MU- F Parent
OI  S Collins
M   H Duffy

CLE 1910 AL
SP  C Falkenberg
SR  W Mitchell
SP  C Young
SR  E Koestner
SR  E Harkness
RP- F Link
RP  A Joss
CR  T Easterly
1B  G Stovall
2B  N Lajoie
S3  T Turner
3B- B Bradley
UO  J Graney
CF  J Birmingham
RL- B Lord
M   D McGuire

DET 1910 AL
SP  G Mullin
SR  E Willett
SP  E Summers
SP  B Donovan
SR  S Stroud
C - O Stanage
1B  T Jones
2B  J Delahanty
SS  D Bush
3B  G Moriarty
LF  D Jones
CF  T Cobb
RF  S Crawford
LU- M McIntyre
M   H Jennings

NY  1910 AL
SP  R Ford
SR  J Warhop
SP  J Quinn
SP  H Vaughn
SP  T Hughes
C - E Sweeney
1B  H Chase
2U  F LaPorte
SI  J Knight
2B  D Miller
3B  J Austin
SS  H Wagner
3B  B Byrne
ML  B Cree
MR  C Hemphill
RF  H Wolter
LF  B Daniels
2B- E Gardner
M1  G Stallings

PHI 1910 AL
SP  J Coombs
SP  C Morgan
SP  E Plank
SP  C Bender
SP  H Krause
RS  J Dygert
C - J Lapp
1B  H Davis
2B  E Collins
SS  J Barry
3B  F Baker
LF- T Hartsel
CF  R Oldring
RF  D Murphy
M   C Mack

STL 1910 AL
SP  J Lake
SR  B Bailey
SP  B Pelty
SP  F Ray
SP  J Powell
C   J Stephens
1B  P Newnam
2B  F Truesdale
S3  B Wallace
3S  R Hartzell
LF  G Stone
CF  D Hoffman
RM  A Schweitzer
UT  A Griggs
M   J O'Connor

WAS 1910 AL
SP  W Johnson
SP  D Gray
SP  D Walker
SR  D Reisling
C - G Street
1B  B Unglaub
2B  R Killefer
SS  G McBride
3B  K Elberfeld
LU  J Lelivelt
CF  C Milan
RF  D Gessler
UT  W Conroy
M   J McAleer

BOS 1911 NL
SR  B Brown
SR  A Mattern
SP  L Tyler
SP  H Perdue
SR  O Weaver
SR  B Pfeffer
C - J Kling
1B- F Tenney
2B  B Sweeney
SS- B Herzog
UT  S Ingerton
LM- A Kaiser
LM- M Donlin
RF  D Miller

BRO 1911 NL
SR  N Rucker
SR  C Barger
SR  B Knetzer
SR  B Schardt
SP  D Scanlan
RP  G Bell
RS  P Ragan
C - B Gibson
1B  J Daubert
2B  M Huggins
SS  A Hauser
3B  M Mowrey
LF  R Ellis
CF  R Oakes
RF  S Evans
C - R Bresnahan
IO- W Smith

CHI 1911 NL
SR  M Brown
SP  L Richie
SP  E Reulbach
SP  K Cole
SP  H McIntire
RS  R Richter
C   J Archer
1B- V Saier
2B  H Zimmerman
SS  J Tinker
3B  J Doyle
LF  J Sheckard
M1  S Hofman
RF  F Schulte
M - F Chance

CIN 1911 NL
SP  G Suggs
SR  H Gaspar
SR  B Keefe
SR  A Fromme
SR  F Smith
C   L McLean
1B  D Hoblitzel
2B  D Egan
SS  T Downey
3B  E Grant
LF  B Bescher
CF  J Bates
RF  M Mitchell
C - T Clarke
M   C Griffith

NY  1911 NL
SP  C Mathewson
SR  R Marquard
SR  R Ames
SR  D Crandall
SP  H Wiltse
C   C Meyers
1B  F Merkle
2B  L Doyle
SS- A Bridwell
3B  A Devlin
LF  J Graney
CF  J Birmingham
RM  J Jackson
RU  T Easterly
IF- N Lajoie
RL  R Murray
SI  A Fletcher
UO- B Becker
M   J McGraw

PHI 1911 NL
SR  G Alexander
SP  E Moore
SR  G Chalmers
SP  B Burns
C - R Dooin
1B  F Luderus
2B  O Knabe
SS  M Doolan
3B  H Lobert
LF  S Magee
CF  D Paskert
RF- F Beck
UT  J Walsh

PIT 1911 NL
SP  L Leifield
SP  B Adams
SP  H Camnitz
SR  E Steele
SR  C Hendrix
C   G Gibson
1B- N Hunter
2B  D Miller
SS  H Wagner
3B  B Byrne
LF  F Clarke
RF  C Wilson
CF  T Leach
1I  B McKechnie

STL 1911 NL
SR  B Harmon
SP  B Steele
SS  S Sallee
SR  R Geyer
SP  R Golden
C   J Bliss
1B  E Konetchy
2B  M Huggins
SS  A Hauser
3B  M Mowrey
LF  R Ellis
CF  R Oakes
RF  S Evans
IO- W Smith

BOS 1911 AL
SR  J Wood
SR  E Cicotte
SP  R Collins
SP  L Pape
SP  E Karger
RS  C Hall
C - B Carrigan
UT  C Engle
2S- H Wagner
SS  S Yerkes
32  L Gardner
LF  D Lewis
CF  T Speaker
RF  H Hooper
1C  R Williams
M   P Donovan

CHI 1911 AL
SR  E Walsh
SR  J Scott
SP  D White
SP  F Lange
SR  F Olmstead
RS  I Young
RS  J Baker
C - B Sullivan
1B  S Collins
2B  A McConnell
SI  L Tannehill
3B  H Lord
LF  N Callahan
MU  P Bodie
RF  M McIntyre
M   H Duffy

CLE 1911 AL
SP  V Gregg
SP  G Krapp
SR  F Blanding
SP  W Mitchell
SR  G Kahler
RP  C Falkenberg
C - G Fisher
1B  G Stovall
2B  N Ball
SS  I Olson
3B  T Turner
LF  J Graney
CF  J Birmingham
RM  J Jackson
RU  T Easterly
IF- N Lajoie
M1  D McGuire

DET 1911 AL
SP  G Mullin
SR  E Willett
SR  E Summers
SP  E Lafitte
SP  B Donovan
RS  R Works
RP  J Lively
C   O Stanage
UI  J Delahanty
2B- C O'Leary
SS  D Bush
3B  G Moriarty
LF  D Jones
CF  T Cobb
RF  S Crawford
LF  D Drake
M   H Jennings

NY  1911 AL
SP  R Ford
SR  R Caldwell
SP  J Warhop
SP  J Quinn
SP  F Fisher
RP  H Vaughn
C - W Blair
1B  H Chase
2B  E Gardner
SI  J Knight
3B  R Hartzell
LF  B Cree
MO  B Daniels
RF  H Wolter
C - E Sweeney

PHI 1911 AL
SP  J Coombs
SR  E Plank
SP  C Morgan
SP  C Bender
SP  H Krause
C   I Thomas
1B  S McInnis
2B  E Collins
SS  J Barry
3B  F Baker
LF  B Lord
CF  R Oldring
RF  D Murphy
M   C Mack

STL 1911 AL
SP  J Lake
SP  J Powell
SP  B Pelty
SR  E Hamilton
SR  R Mitchell
RS  L George
C - N Clarke
1B- J Black
2B  F LaPorte
SS  B Wallace
3B  J Austin
LW  W Hogan
CF  B Shotton
RU- A Schweitzer

WAS 1911 AL
SP  W Johnson
SP  B Groom
SP  T Hughes
SP  D Walker
SR  D Gray
C - G Street
1B  G Schaefer
2B  B Cunningham
SS  G McBride
3B  W Conroy
LF  T Walker
CF  C Milan
RF  D Gessler
23  K Elberfeld
C1- J Henry
M   J McAleer

BOS 1912 NL
SR  L Tyler
SP  O Hess
SP  H Perdue
SR  W Dickson
SR  E Donnelly
RS  B Brown
C - J Kling
1B  B Houser
2B  B Sweeney
SS- F O'Rourke
3B  E McDonald
LF  G Jackson
CF  V Campbell
RF  J Titus
1I  A Devlin
LU  J Kirke
C - B Rariden

BRO 1912 NL
SR  N Rucker
SR  P Ragan
SP  E Yingling
SR  E Stack
SR  E Knetzer
RP  F Allen
RP  C Barger
```

(BRO 1912 NL, cont.)
RS M Kent
C O Miller
1B J Daubert
2B G Cutshaw
SS- B Tooley
3B R Smith
LF Z Wheat
MR H Moran
UO H Northen
IO J Hummel
SS- B Fisher
M B Dahlen

CHI 1912 NL
SP L Cheney
SR J Lavender
SR L Richie
SR E Reulbach
RS C Smith
C J Archer
1B V Saier
2B J Evers
SS J Tinker
3B H Zimmerman
LF J Sheckard
CF- T Leach
RF F Schulte
UO- W Miller
M F Chance

CIN 1912 NL
SP G Suggs
SR R Benton
SP A Fromme
SR B Humphries
C L McLean
1B D Hoblitzel
2B D Egan
SS- J Esmond
3B A Phelan
LF B Bescher
MU A Marsans
RF M Mitchell
SU E Grant
CF- J Bates
M H O'Day

NY 1912 NL
SP C Mathewson
SP R Marquard
SP J Tesreau
SR R Ames
SR H Wiltse
RS D Crandall
C C Meyers
1B F Merkle
2B L Doyle
SS A Fletcher
3B B Herzog
UT F Snodgrass
MU B Becker
RF R Murray
LU J Devore
UI- T Shafer
M J McGraw

PHI 1912 NL
SR G Alexander
SR T Seaton
SP E Moore
SP A Brennan
SP E Rixey
RP T Shultz
C - B Killefer
1B F Luderus
2B O Knabe
SS M Doolan
3B- H Lobert
LF S Magee
CF D Paskert
RO G Cravath
RU- M Donlin
M F Clarke

STL 1912 NL
SR S Sallee
SP B Harmon
SR B Steele
SR R Geyer
SR J Willis
RS G Woodburn
C I Wingo
1B E Konetchy
2B M Huggins
SS A Hauser
3B M Mowrey
LU L Magee
CF R Oakes
RF S Evans
LU R Ellis
M R Bresnahan

BOS 1912 AL
SP J Wood
SP B O'Brien
SR H Bedient
SP R Collins
SR C Hall
3B- C Carrigan
1B J Stahl
2B S Yerkes
SS H Wagner
3B L Gardner
LF D Lewis
CF T Speaker
RF H Hooper

CHI 1912 AL
SR E Walsh
SR J Benz
SR D White
SR F Lange
SP E Cicotte
RS R Peters
C - W Kuhn
13 R Zeider
2B M Rath
SS B Weaver
3O H Lord
LF N Callahan
MR P Bodie
R1 S Collins
MU- W Mattick
M J Callahan

CLE 1912 AL
SP V Gregg
SP F Blanding
SP G Kahler
SR W Mitchell
SR B Steen
RS J Baskette
C - S O'Neill
1B- A Griggs
2B N Lajoie
SS- R Peckinpaugh
3B T Turner
LR B Ryan
CF J Birmingham
RF J Jackson
IO I Olson
LF- J Graney
M1 H Davis

DET 1912 AL
SP E Willett
SR J Dubuc
SP G Mullin
SR J Lake
SR R Works
C O Stanage
13 G Moriarty
2I B Louden
SS D Bush
3B- C Deal
LU J Jones
CF T Cobb
RF S Crawford
2L- J Delahanty
M H Jennings

NY 1912 AL
SP R Ford
SR J Warhop
SP R Caldwell
SP G McConnell
SP J Quinn
C S Sweeney
1B H Chase
2B H Simmons
SS- J Martin
UT R Hartzell
LR B Daniels
UT- D Sterrett
RM G Zinn
M H Wolverton

PHI 1912 AL
SP J Coombs
SP E Plank
SR B Brown
SR B Houck
SP C Bender
RP C Morgan
RP H Pennock
C - J Lapp
1B S McInnis
2B E Collins
SS J Barry
3B F Baker
LM A Strunk
CF R Oldring
RF B Lord
M C Mack

STL 1912 AL
SR E Hamilton
SP J Powell
SP G Baumgardner
SR M Allison
SR E Brown
C - J Stephens
1B G Stovall
2B D Pratt
SS B Wallace
3B J Austin
LF W Hogan
CF B Shotton
RF- G Williams
OF P Compton
UT- F LaPorte

WAS 1912 AL
SR W Johnson
SP B Groom
SP T Hughes
SP C Cashion
C - J Henry
1B C Gandil
2B- R Morgan
SS G McBride
3B- E Foster
LF H Shanks
CF C Milan
RF D Moeller
M C Griffith

BOS 1913 NL
SP L Tyler
SR D Rudolph
SP O Hess
SP H Perdue
SR B James
RP W Dickson
C B Rariden
1B H Myers
2B B Sweeney
SS R Maranville
3B- A Devlin
LF J Connolly
CF L Mann
RF- J Titus
3I- F Smith
C - B Whaling
M G Stallings

BRO 1913 NL
SR P Ragan
SP N Rucker
SP F Allen
SR C Curtis
SR E Yingling
RP E Reulbach
C O Miller
1B J Daubert
2B G Cutshaw
SS B Fisher
3B R Smith
LF Z Wheat
CF C Stengel
RF H Moran
M B Dahlen

CHI 1913 NL
SR L Cheney
SR J Lavender
SP B Humphries
SP G Pierce
SP C Smith
C J Archer
1B V Saier
2B J Evers
SS H Wagner
3B H Zimmerman
LF- M Mitchell
CF T Leach
RF F Schulte
LU- W Miller
23- A Phelan

CIN 1913 NL
SR C Johnson
SR G Suggs
SR G Packard
SR R Ames
SR M Brown
RP B Benton
RP F Harter
C T Clarke
1B D Hoblitzel
2B H Groh
SS J Tinker
3B J Dodge
LF B Bescher
CF- W Mattick
RF S Collins
RU J Bates
C - J Kling

NY 1913 NL
SP C Mathewson
SP R Marquard
SP J Tesreau
SP A Demaree
SP A Fromme
RP D Crandall
C C Meyers
1B F Merkle
2B L Doyle
SS A Fletcher
3B B Herzog
LF G Burns
CF F Snodgrass
RF R Murray
3I T Shafer
M J McGraw

PHI 1913 NL
SR T Seaton
SR G Alexander
SR A Brennan
SR E Mayer
SR E Rixey
RS G Chalmers
C B Killefer
1B F Luderus
2B- R Morgan
SS M Doolan
3B H Lobert
LF S Magee
CF D Paskert
RF G Cravath
OI- B Becker
M R Dooin

PIT 1913 NL
SP B Adams
SR C Hendrix
SR H Robinson
SR H Camnitz
SR M O'Toole
RP G McQuillan
C - M Simon
1B D Miller
2B J Viox
SS H Wagner
3B B Byrne
LF M Carey
RF C Wilson
IO- A Butler
M F Clarke

STL 1913 NL
SR S Sallee
SR B Harmon
SP D Griner
SR P Perritt
SP B Doak
RP R Geyer
C I Wingo
1B E Konetchy
2B M Huggins
SS C O'Leary
3B M Mowrey
LF L Magee
CF R Oakes
RU S Evans
UT P Whitted

BOS 1913 AL
SR H Bedient
SR D Leonard
SP R Collins
SP J Wood
SP E Moseley
RP C Hall
C - B Carrigan
1B C Engle
2B S Yerkes
SS H Wagner
3B L Gardner
LF D Lewis
CF T Speaker
RF H Hooper
SI- H Janvrin
M1 J Stahl

CHI 1913 AL
SR R Russell
SR J Scott
SR E Cicotte
SR J Benz
SR D White
RP W Walsh
C R Schalk
1B H Chase
2B M Rath
SS B Weaver
3B H Lord
ML P Bodie
CF- W Mattick
RF S Collins
2B- J Berger
M J Callahan

CLE 1913 AL
SR V Gregg
SP C Falkenberg
SR W Mitchell
SR F Blanding
SP B Steen
RP G Kahler
RS N Cullop
C - S O'Neill
1B D Johnston
2B N Lajoie
SS R Chapman
3U I Olson
LF G Graney
MU N Leibold
RF J Jackson
3I T Turner
C - F Carisch
M J Birmingham

DET 1913 AL
SP J Dubuc
SP E Willett
SP H Dauss
SP M Hall
SR J Lake
RP F House
C - O Stanage
1B D Gainer
2B O Vitt
SS D Bush
3B G Moriarty
LF B Veach
CF T Cobb
RF S Crawford
UO- H High
M H Jennings

NY 1913 AL
SR R Fisher
SP R Ford
SR A Schulz
SR G McConnell
SR R Caldwell
RP R Keating
C E Sweeney
12- J Knight
2U H Hartzell
SS R Peckinpaugh
3B- E Midkiff
LF B Cree
CF H Wolter
RF B Daniels
M F Clarke

PHI 1913 AL
SR C Bender
SR E Plank
SP B Brown
SR J Bush
SP B Houck
RP B Shawkey
C - J Lapp
1B S McInnis
2B E Collins
SS J Barry
3B F Baker
LF B Oldring
CF R Oakes
RU S Evans
UO J Walsh
RF E Murphy
CF A Strunk
C - W Schang
M C Mack

STL 1913 AL
SR S Sallee
SR C Weilman
SP R Mitchell
SP E Hamilton
SP W Leverenz
C S Agnew
1B- G Stovall
2B D Pratt
LR G Burns
SS- M Balenti
3B J Austin
LF J Johnston
3I- E Grant
C - L McLean
1U- B Brief
M3 B Rickey

WAS 1913 AL
SR W Johnson
SP B Groom
SR J Boehling
SR J Engel
RS T Hughes
RP B Gallia
C J Henry
1B C Gandil
2B M Rath
SS B Weaver
3B H Lord
ML P Bodie
CF- W Mattick
RF S Collins
CF C Milan
RF D Moeller
C - E Ainsmith
3U- F LaPorte
M C Griffith

BOS 1914 NL
SP D Rudolph
SP B James
SP L Tyler
SR D Crutcher
C H Gowdy
1B B Schmidt
2B J Evers
SS R Maranville
3B- C Deal
LF J Connolly
CF L Mann
RU- L Gilbert
M G Stallings

BRO 1914 NL
SP J Pfeffer
SR E Reulbach
SR P Ragan
SR R Aitchison
SR F Allen
RP N Rucker
C - L McCarty
1B J Daubert
2B G Cutshaw
SS E Smith
3B- R Smith
LF Z Wheat
CF J Dalton
RF C Stengel
M W Robinson

CHI 1914 NL
SR L Cheney
SP H Vaughn
SP J Lavender
SP B Humphries
SR G Pierce
RS Z Zabel
RP C Hageman
C - B Bresnahan
1B V Saier
2B B Sweeney
SS R Corriden
3B H Zimmerman
LF F Schulte
CF T Leach
C - J Archer
M H O'Day

CIN 1914 NL
SR R Ames
SP R Benton
SR P Douglas
SP E Yingling
SR P Schneider
C T Clarke
1B- D Hoblitzel
2B H Groh
SS J Niehoff
3B B Niehoff
LF- G Twombly
RM- B Daniels
RF H Moran
C M Gonzalez
UO- D Miller

NY 1914 NL
SP J Tesreau
SP C Mathewson
SP R Marquard
SP A Demaree
RS A Fromme
C C Meyers
1B F Merkle
2B L Doyle
SS A Fletcher
3B M Stock
LR G Burns
CF B Bescher
UT F Snodgrass
3I- E Grant
C - L McLean
OF- R Murray
RU- D Robertson
M J McGraw

PHI 1914 NL
SR G Alexander
SR E Mayer
SR B Tincup
SR R Marshall
SR J Oeschger
RP E Rixey
C B Killefer
1B F Luderus
2B J Byrne
SS- J Martin
3B H Lobert
LO B Becker

PIT 1914 NL
SP B Adams
SP W Cooper
SR W McQuillan
SP B Harmon
RS J Conzelman
SR G Gibson
1B E Konetchy
2B J Viox
SS W Hagner
3B- M Mowrey
LF M Carey
OF- J Kelly
RF- M Mitchell
CF J Kelly
M F Clarke

STL 1914 NL
SR S Sallee
SP S Perritt
SP B Doak
SP G Griner
SP H Perdue
RS H Robinson
C F Snyder
1S D Miller
2B M Huggins
SS- A Butler
LU C Dolan
M1 L Magee
RF C Wilson
OF W Cruise
C - J Wingo

BOS 1914 AL
SP R Collins
SR D Leonard
SP R Foster
SR H Bedient
SP E Shore
RP J Wood
RP J Johnson
C - B Carrigan
1B- D Hoblitzel
2B- S Yerkes
SS E Scott
3B L Gardner
LF D Lewis
CF T Speaker
RF H Hooper
UI H Janvrin
OF- W Rehg

CHI 1914 AL
SR J Benz
SR E Cicotte
SR J Scott
SR R Faber
SR R Russell
RS M Wolfgang
RP B Lathrop
C R Schalk
1B J Fournier
2B L Blackburne
SS B Weaver
3B- J Breton
LF R Demmitt
CF P Bodie
RM S Collins
M J Callahan

CLE 1914 AL
SP W Mitchell
SP B Steen
SR R Hagerman
SR G Morton
SR F Blanding
RS A Collamore
RP V Gregg
C - S O'Neill
1B D Johnston
21 N Lajoie
S2 R Chapman
3B T Turner
LF J Graney
CF N Leibold
RM J Jackson
UT- I Olson
M J Birmingham

DET 1914 AL
SP H Coveleski
SP H Dauss
SP J Dubuc
SP J Cavet
SR A Main
SR R Reynolds
C O Stanage
1B G Burns
2B M Kavanagh
SS D Bush

NY 1914 AL
SR J Warhop
SP R Caldwell
SP R Fisher
SP K Keating
RS K Cole
RP B Brown
C - E Sweeney
1B- C Mullen
2B L Boone
SS R Peckinpaugh
3B J Maisel
LO R Hartzell
CF- B Cree
RF D Cook
C - L Nunamaker
M1 F Chance

PHI 1914 AL
SP B Shawkey
SR J Bush
SR E Plank
SR W Wyckoff
SP C Bender
RS- H Pennock
RS R Bressler
C W Schang
1B S McInnis
2B E Collins
SS J Barry
3B F Baker
LF R Oldring
CF A Strunk
RF E Murphy
M C Mack

STL 1914 AL
SP E Hamilton
SP C Weilman
SP B James
SR G Baumgardner
SR W Leverenz
RS R Mitchell
C S Agnew
1B J Leary
2B D Pratt
SS- D Lavan
3B J Austin
LF T Walker
CF B Shotton
RF G Williams
UT- I Howard
SS- B Wares
M B Rickey

WAS 1914 AL
SR W Johnson
SR D Ayers
SR J Shaw
SP J Boehling
SR J Bentley
RS J Engel
RP H Harper
C - J Henry
1B C Gandil
2B R Morgan
SS G McBride
3B E Foster
LM H Shanks
CF C Milan
RF D Moeller
CU- R Williams
M C Griffith

BAL 1914 FL
SP J Quinn
SP G Suggs
SP K Wilhelm
SR F Smith
SP B Bailey
RS S Conley
C F Jacklitsch
1B H Swacina
2B O Knabe
SS M Doolan
3B J Walsh
LI H Simmons
MO V Duncan
RF B Meyer
CU- H Russell

BRO 1914 FL
SP T Seaton
SP E Lafitte
SP H Finneran
C G Land
1B- H Myers
2U- H Hofman
SS- E Gagnier

(continued)
3B T Wisterzil
JO C Cooper
CF A Shaw
RO S Evans
LU G Anderson
SS- A Halt
M B Bradley

BUF 1914 FL
SP F Anderson
SP R Ford
SP G Krapp
SP E Moore
SR A Schulz
RS H Moran
C W Blair
1L J Agler
2B T Downey
SR B Louden
3B F Smith
LF- F Delahanty
RF- T McDonald
UO- D Young
M L Schlafly

CHI 1914 FL
SR C Hendrix
SR M Fiske
SR E Lange
SP D Watson
SR M Prendergast
RS T McGuire
RP R Johnson
A Wilson
1B F Beck
2B J Farrell
SS J Tinker
3B R Zeider
LF M Flack
CF D Zwilling
RF A Wickland

IND 1914 FL
SP C Falkenberg
SP E Moseley
SP G Kaiserling
SP G Mullin
SR H Billiard
C B Rariden
1B C Carr
2B J LaPorte
SS J Esmond
3B B McKechnie
UT A Scheer
MR V Campbell
UO B Kauff
M B Phillips

KC 1914 FL
SP G Packard
SP N Cullop
SP D Stone
SR B Harris
SP P Henning
RS D Adams
RP C Johnson
C T Easterly
1B G Stovall
2B B Kenworthy
S3 P Goodwin
31 G Perring
LF C Chadbourne
CF A Kruger
RF G Gilmore
OI- C Coles

PIT 1914 FL
SP E Knetzer
SP H Camnitz
SP W Dickson
SP C Barger
SR M Walker
RS G LeClair
C C Berry
1B H Bradley
2B J Lewis
SS E Holly
3B E Lennox
LF D Jones
CF R Oakes
RI J Savage
M1 D Gessler

STL 1914 FL
SP B Groom
SP D Davenport
SP H Keupper
SP M Brown
SP E Willett
RF E Herbert
C M Simon
1B H Miller
2p D Crandall
SS A Bridwell
3B A Boucher
LM W Miller

LM D Drake
RF J Tobin
2S J Misse
IC- G Hartley
M2 F Jones

BOS 1915 NL
SP D Rudolph
SR T Hughes
SP P Ragan
SP L Tyler
C H Gowdy
1B B Schmidt
2B- J Evers
SS R Maranville
3B R Smith
LF J Connolly
MU S Magee
RF H Moran
2O E Fitzpatrick
UT- D Egan
M G Stallings

BRO 1915 NL
SP J Pfeffer
SR W Dell
SP J Coombs
SP S Smith
SP N Rucker
RS E Appleton
RP P Douglas
C- O Miller
1B J Daubert
2B G Cutshaw
SS O O'Mara
3B G Getz
LF Z Wheat
CF H Myers
RF C Stengel
C- L McCarty
M W Robinson

CHI 1915 NL
SP H Vaughn
SR J Lavender
SR G Pierce
SP B Humphries
SR Z Zabel
RP L Cheney
RP P Standridge
RS K Adams
C J Archer
1B V Saier
23 H Zimmerman
SS B Fisher
3B A Phelan
LF F Schulte
CF C Williams
RF W Good
M R Bresnahan

CIN 1915 NL
SR G Dale
SR P Schneider
SR F Toney
SR B Benton
SR K Lear
RS L McKenry
C I Wingo
1B F Mollwitz
2B- B Rodgers
SS B Herzog
3B H Groh
LM R Killefer
CF T Leach
RF T Griffith
C T Clarke

NY 1915 NL
SP J Tesreau
SP P Perritt
SP- C Mathewson
SR S Stroud
SP R Marquard
RS R Schauer
RP H Ritter
RP F Schupp
C C Meyers
1B F Merkle
2B L Doyle
SS A Fletcher
3B H Lobert
LF G Burns
CF- F Snodgrass
RF D Robertson
IO- F Brainerd
UI- E Grant
M J McGraw

PHI 1915 NL
SP G Alexander
SR E Mayer
SP A Demaree
SP E Rixey
SP G Chalmers
RP S Baumgartner
SP B Killefer
1B F Luderus
2B N Niehoff
SS D Bancroft
3B B Byrne
LF B Becker
ML P Whitted
RF G Cravath
MU D Paskert
M P Moran

PIT 1915 NL
SP B Harmon
SP A Mamaux
SR B Adams
SR W Cooper
SR E Kantlehner
RS G McQuillan
RP J Conzelman
C G Gibson
1B D Johnston
2B J Viox
SS H Wagner
3B D Baird
LF M Carey
CF Z Collins
RF B Hinchman
M F Clarke

NY 1915 AL
SP R Caldwell
SP R Fisher
SP J Warhop
SP B Brown
SR C Pieh
C- L Nunamaker
1B W Pipp
2B L Boone
SS R Peckinpaugh
3B F Maisel
LF H Hartzell
ML H High
RF D Cook
M B Donovan

PHI 1915 AL
SP W Wyckoff
SR R Bressler
SP J Bush
SP T Sheehan
SP T Knowlson
RP B Shawkey
C J Lapp
SS M McInnis
2B N Lajoie
S3 L Kopf
IC W Schang
LF R Oldring
UT J Walsh
OI A Strunk
M C Mack

STL 1915 AL
SR C Weilman
SP G Lowdermilk
SP E Hamilton
SR J Wood
RS C Mays
RS R Collins
C- P Thomas
1B D Hoblitzel
2B- H Wagner
SS E Scott
3B L Gardner
LF D Lewis
CF T Speaker
RF H Hooper
SI H Janvrin
2B- J Barry
C- H Cady
1U- D Gainer
M B Carrigan

CHI 1915 AL
SR R Faber
SR J Scott
SR J Benz
SR R Russell
SR E Cicotte
C R Schalk
1L J Fournier
2B E Collins
SS B Weaver
3B L Blackburne
OI S Collins
ML H Felsch
RF- E Murphy
M P Rowland

CLE 1915 AL
SP G Morton
SP W Mitchell
SP R Hagerman
SR R Walker
SR F Coumbe
RS S Jones
RS O Harstad
C S O'Neill
1B- J Kirke
23 B Wambsganss
SS R Chapman
3B- W Barbare
LF- J Graney
CF- N Leibold
RU E Smith
R1- J Jackson
M1 J Birmingham
M2 L Fohl

DET 1915 AL
SR H Coveleski
SR H Dauss
SP J Dubuc
SR B Boland
C O Stanage
1B G Burns
2B R Young
SS D Bush
3B O Vitt
LF B Veach
CF T Cobb
RF S Crawford
IO M Kavanagh
M H Jennings

WAS 1915 AL
SP W Johnson
SR B Gallia
SP J Boehling
SP D Ayers
SP J Shaw
C J Henry
1B C Gandil
2B- R Morgan
SS G McBride
32 E Foster
L3 H Shanks
CF C Milan
RF D Moeller
IC- R Williams
M C Griffith

BAL 1915 FL
SR J Quinn
SR G Suggs
SR B Bailey
SR C Bender
SP J Johnson
C F Owens
1B- H Swacina
2B O Knabe
SS M Doolan
3B J Walsh
UT V Duncan
UO J McCandless
RF- S Evans
LU G Zinn

BRO 1915 FL
SR H Finneran
SP D Marion
SP T Seaton
SP J Bluejacket
SP E Lafitte
RS B Upham
RP F Wilson
C G Land
1B H Myers
SS F Smith
3S A Halt
LU C Cooper
CF B Kauff
RL G Anderson
M2 J Ganzel

BUF 1915 FL
SP A Schulz
SR H Bedient
SP F Anderson
SP G Krapp
SP R Ford
RP R Marshall
RP H Ehmke
C W Blair
1B H Chase
2I B Louden
SS R Roach
3B H Lord
LF B Meyer
MI C Engle
UO J Dalton
UT S Hofman
C- N Allen
23 T Downey
RU- T McDonald
M1 L Schlafly

CHI 1915 FL
SP G McConnell
SP C Hendrix
SR M Prendergast
SR M Brown
SR D Black
RP A Brennan
C A Wilson
1B F Beck
2I R Zeider
SS J Smith
3B- H Fritz
LO L Mann
CF D Zwilling
RL M Flack
C W Fischer
UO-C Hanford
M J Tinker

KC 1915 FL
SP N Cullop
SR G Packard
SR C Johnson
SP A Main
SR P Henning
C T Easterly
1B G Stovall
2B B Kenworthy
SS J Rawlings
3I G Perring
LF A Shaw
CF C Chadbourne
RF A Gilmore
C- D Johnston
S2- P Goodwin
UO-A Kruger
M J Tinker

NEW 1915 FL
SP E Reulbach
SP E Moseley
SR G Kaiserling
SR H Moran
SP C Falkenberg
C B Rariden
1B B Huhn
2B F LaPorte
SS J Esmond
3B B McKechnie
LF A Scheer
CF A Roush
RF V Campbell
M1 B Phillips

PIT 1915 FL
SP F Allen
SP E Knetzer
SP C Rogge
SR B Hearn
SR B Barger
1B- H Swacina
2B O Knabe
SS M Doolan
3B J Walsh
UT V Duncan
UO J McCandless
RF- S Evans
LU G Zinn

STL 1915 FL
SP D Davenport
SR D Crandall
SR E Plank
SR B Groom
SR D Watson
C G Hartley
1B B Borton
2B D Vaughn
SS E Johnson
3B- C Deal
LW W Miller
MR D Drake
RF J Tobin
M F Jones

BOS 1916 NL
SP D Rudolph
SP L Tyler
SP P Ragan
SP J Barnes
SP A Nehf
RS T Hughes
RP F Allen
C H Gowdy
1B E Konetchy
2B- J Evers
SS R Maranville
3B R Smith
LF S Magee
CF F Snodgrass
UO-Z Collins
2U- D Egan
2R- E Fitzpatrick
M G Stallings

BRO 1916 NL
SP J Pfeffer
SP L Cheney
SR S Smith
SR R Marquard
SP J Coombs
RS W Dell
C- C Meyers
1B J Daubert
2B G Cutshaw
SS I Olson
3B M Mowrey
LF Z Wheat
CF H Myers
RF C Stengel
UO J Johnston
M W Robinson

CHI 1916 NL
SP H Vaughn
SR C Hendrix
SR J Lavender
SP G McConnell
SR G Packard
RS M Prendergast
RS T Seaton
C- J Archer
1B V Saier
2B- O Knabe
SS- C Wortman
3B H Zimmerman
LO L Mann
CF C Williams
RF M Flack
32 R Zeider
M J Tinker

CIN 1916 NL
SP F Toney
SR P Schneider
SR A Schulz
SP C Mitchell
SR E Knetzer
RS E Moseley
C I Wingo
1U H Chase
3B B McKechnie
SS- B Herzog
3I H Groh
LM G Neale
CF- E Roush
RF T Griffith
CU- T Clarke
M3 C Mathewson

NY 1916 NL
SP J Tesreau
SR P Perritt
SR B Benton
SR F Anderson
SR F Schupp
RS S Sallee
C B Rariden
1B F Merkle
2B L Doyle
SS A Fletcher
3B- B McKechnie
LF A Wickland
CF R Kelly
2U- J Lewis

PHI 1916 NL
SP G Alexander
SP E Rixey
SP A Demaree
SR E Mayer
SR C Bender
RP G McQuillan
C- B Killefer
1B F Luderus
2B B Niehoff
SS D Bancroft
3B M Stock
LF P Whitted
CF D Paskert
RF G Cravath
C- E Burns
M P Moran

PIT 1916 NL
SP A Mamaux
SR W Cooper
SR F Miller
SR B Harmon
SR E Kantlehner
RS E Jacobs
C- W Schmidt
1B D Johnston
2O- J Farmer
SU H Wagner
3U D Baird
RL- F Schulte
CF M Carey
RU B Hinchman
M J Callahan

STL 1916 NL
SR L Meadows
SR R Ames
SP B Doak
SP B Steele
SR H Jasper
RS S Williams
RP M Watson
C M Gonzalez
12 D Miller
2B B Betzel
SS R Corhan
3S R Hornsby
LF B Bescher
RM C Wilson
RF T Long
C1 F Snyder
UT- A Butler
M M Huggins

PHI 1916 AL
SP E Myers
SP J Bush
SR J Nabors
SR T Sheehan
C- B Meyer
1B M McInnis
2B N Lajoie
SS W Witt
3B C Pick
LC W Schang
CF A Strunk
RF J Walsh
M C Mack

BOS 1916 AL
SP B Ruth
SR D Leonard
SR C Mays
SR E Shore
SR R Foster
C P Thomas
1B D Hoblitzel
2B J Barry
SS E Scott
3B L Gardner
LF D Lewis
CF T Walker
RF H Hooper
S2 H Janvrin
C- H Cady
IO- M McNally
M B Carrigan

CHI 1916 AL
SR R Russell
SR L Williams
SR R Faber
SR E Cicotte
SR J Scott
RS J Benz
RS M Wolfgang
C R Schalk
1B J Fournier
2B E Collins
SS Z Terry
3S B Weaver
LF J Jackson
CF H Felsch
RF S Collins
M P Rowland

CLE 1916 AL
SR J Bagby
SR S Coveleski
SP G Morton
SR E Klepfer
SR F Coumbe
RS A Gould
RP F Beebe
C S O'Neill
1B C Gandil
2B- I Howard
SS B Wambsganss
32 T Turner
LF J Graney
CF T Speaker
RF B Roth
UI R Chapman
RU- E Smith
M L Fohl

DET 1916 AL
SP H Coveleski
SR H Dauss
SR J Dubuc
SR B James
SR G Cunningham
RS B Boland
RP W Mitchell
C O Stanage
1B G Burns
2B R Young
SS D Bush
3B O Vitt
LF B Veach
CF T Cobb
RF S Crawford
UT H Heilmann
M H Jennings

NY 1916 AL
SR B Shawkey
SP G Mogridge
SR F Fisher
SR A Russell
SP N Cullop
RP R Caldwell
RP S Love
C- L Nunamaker
1B W Pipp
2B J Gedeon
SS R Peckinpaugh
3B H Baker
LF H High
CF L Magee
RF- F Gilhooley
UT- P Baumann
M B Donovan

STL 1916 AL
SR D Davenport
SR C Weilman
SR E Plank
SR B Groom
SR E Koob
C H Severeid
1B G Sisler
2B D Pratt
SS D Lavan
3B J Austin
LF B Shotton
CF A Marsans
RF W Miller
C- G Hartley
M F Jones

WAS 1916 AL
SR W Johnson
SR B Gallia
SR H Harper
SR D Ayers
SP J Boehling
RS J Shaw
C J Henry
1B J Judge
2B R Morgan
SS G McBride
32 E Foster
LI H Shanks
CF C Milan
RL- D Moeller
M C Griffith

BOS 1917 NL
SR J Barnes
SP D Rudolph
SP L Tyler
SR P Ragan
SR P Nehf
RS F Allen
C W Tragesser
1B E Konetchy
2B J Rawlings
3B R Maranville
3B R Smith
LF J Kelly
CF- R Powell

RF- W Rehg
M G Stallings

BRO 1917 NL
SP L Cadore
SP J Pfeffer
SP R Marquard
SR S Smith
SR L Cheney
RS J Coombs
C - O Miller
1B J Daubert
2B G Cutshaw
SS I Olson
3B- M Mowrey
LF Z Wheat
MO J Hickman
RF C Stengel
UT J Johnston
MI H Myers
M W Robinson

CHI 1917 NL
SP H Vaughn
SR P Douglas
SR C Hendrix
SP A Demaree
SR P Carter
RS V Aldridge
RS M Prendergast
C - A Wilson
1B F Merkle
2B L Doyle
SS- C Wortman
3B C Deal
LF L Mann
CF C Williams
RL M Flack
RF H Wolter
IO R Zeider
C - R Elliott
M F Mitchell

CIN 1917 NL
SP F Toney
SP P Schneider
SP M Regan
SR C Mitchell
RS H Eller
C I Wingo
1B H Chase
2B D Shean
SS L Kopf
3B H Groh
LO G Neale
CF E Roush
RF T Griffith
M C Mathewson

NY 1917 NL
SP F Schupp
SR S Sallee
SR R Benton
SP P Perritt
SR J Tesreau
RS F Anderson
C B Rariden
1B W Holke
2B H Herzog
SS A Fletcher
3B H Zimmerman
LF G Burns
CF B Kauff
RF D Robertson
M J McGraw

PHI 1917 NL
SP G Alexander
SP E Rixey
SR J Oeschger
SR E Mayer
SR J Lavender
RS C Bender
C B Killefer
1B F Luderus
2B B Niehoff
SS D Bancroft
3B M Stock
LF P Whitted
CF D Paskert
RF G Cravath
M P Moran

PIT 1917 NL
SP W Cooper
SR E Jacobs
SR F Miller
SR B Grimes
SP B Steele
RS H Carlson
CU W Fischer
1I- H Wagner
2B J Pitler
SS C Ward
3B- T Boeckel
LU C Bigbee
CF M Carey

RF L King
M1 J Callahan
M3 H Bezdek

STL 1917 NL
SP B Doak
SP L Meadows
SR R Ames
SR M Watson
RS G Packard
RS O Horstmann
C F Snyder
1B G Paulette
21 D Miller
SS R Hornsby
3B D Baird
ML W Cruise
UO J Smith
RF T Long
2U B Betzel
CU M Gonzalez
M M Huggins

BOS 1917 AL
SP B Ruth
SP D Leonard
SP C Mays
SP E Shore
SP R Foster
RS H Pennock
C - S Agnew
1B D Hoblitzel
2B J Barry
SS E Scott
3B L Gardner
LF D Lewis
CF T Walker
RF H Hooper
C - P Thomas

CHI 1917 AL
SR E Cicotte
SR R Faber
SR L Williams
SR R Russell
SP J Scott
RS D Danforth
RP J Benz
C R Schalk
1B C Gandil
2B E Collins
SS S Risberg
3B B Weaver
LF J Jackson
CF H Felsch
RF N Leibold
RF- S Collins
M P Rowland

DET 1917 AL
SP H Dauss
SR B Boland
SR H Ehmke
SR B James
SP W Mitchell
RS G Cunningham
C O Stanage
1B G Burns
2B R Young
SS D Bush
3B O Vitt
LF B Veach
CF T Cobb
RU H Heilmann
M H Jennings

NY 1917 AL
SP B Shawkey
SR R Caldwell
SP G Mogridge
SR N Cullop
SR U Shocker
RP R Fisher
RS S Love
RS A Russell
C L Nunamaker
1B W Pipp
2B F Maisel
SS R Peckinpaugh
3B F Baker

LF H High
UO E Miller
RU T Hendryx
M B Donovan

PHI 1917 AL
SP J Bush
SR R Schauer
SR E Myers
SR J Johnson
SP W Noyes
RS S Seibold
CU W Schang
1B S McInnis
2B R Grover
SS W Witt
3B R Bates
LF P Bodie
CF A Strunk
RF- C Jamieson
M C Mack

STL 1917 AL
SP D Davenport
SR A Sothoron
SR B Groom
SR E Koob
SP E Plank
RS T Rogers
C H Severeid
1B G Sisler
2B D Pratt
SS D Lavan
3B J Austin
LF B Shotton
RM B Jacobson
RU T Sloan
UI- E Johnson
OF- W Rumler
M F Jones

WAS 1917 AL
SR W Johnson
SR J Shaw
SR D Ayers
SR B Gallia
SR G Dumont
SR O Lambeth
RP H Harper
C E Ainsmith
1B J Judge
2B R Morgan
SU H Shanks
32 E Foster
LF M Menosky
CF C Milan
RF S Rice
3U J Leonard
M C Griffith

BOS 1918 NL
SP A Nehf
SP P Ragan
SP D Rudolph
SP B Hearn
SP D Fillingim
C A Wilson
1B E Konetchy
2B B Herzog
SU J Rawlings
3B R Smith
UT- R Massey
CF- R Powell
RF A Wickland
M G Stallings

BRO 1918 NL
SR B Grimes
SP R Marquard
SR L Cheney
SP J Coombs
SP D Robertson
C - O Miller
1B J Daubert
2B M Doolan
SS I Olson
3B O O'Mara
LF Z Wheat
CF H Myers
RU J Johnston
UT- B Betzel
M W Robinson

CHI 1918 NL
SP H Vaughn
SP L Tyler
SP C Hendrix
SP P Douglas
C B Killefer
1B F Merkle
2B R Zeider
SS C Hollocher
3B C Deal
LF L Mann
CF D Paskert
RF M Flack
M F Mitchell

CIN 1918 NL
SR H Eller
SP P Schneider
SP J Ring
SP F Toney
SR R Bressler
RP D Luque
RS M Regan
C I Wingo
1B- H Chase
2B L Magee
SS L Blackburne
3B H Groh
LU G Neale
CF E Roush
RF T Griffith
1L S Magee
M1 C Mathewson

NY 1918 NL
SP P Perritt
SR R Causey
SR A Demaree
SR S Sallee
SP F Toney
C L McCarty
1B W Holke
2B L Doyle
SS A Fletcher
3B H Zimmerman
LF G Burns
CF- B Kauff
RF R Youngs
C - B Rariden
MO-J Wilhoit
M J McGraw

PHI 1918 NL
SP M Prendergast
SP B Hogg
SP J Oeschger
SP E Jacobs
SR M Watson
RP E Mayer
RP D Davis
C B Adams
1B F Luderus
2B- P McGaffigan
SS D Bancroft
3B M Stock
LM I Meusel
CF C Williams
RF G Cravath
C - E Burns
LR- J Fitzgerald
M P Moran

PIT 1918 NL
SP W Cooper
SP F Miller
SR R Sanders
SP E Mayer
SP B Harmon
RP R Comstock
C W Schmidt
1B F Mollwitz
2B G Cutshaw
SS H Caton
3B B McKechnie
LF C Bigbee
CF M Carey
RF- B Southworth
M H Bezdek

STL 1918 NL
SP B Doak
SP R Ames
SP G Packard
SR B Sherdel
SP L Meadows
RS J May
C M Gonzalez
1B G Paulette
2B- B Fisher
SS R Hornsby
3B D Baird
LF A McHenry
CF C Heathcote
LU- W Cruise
UT- B Betzel
M J Hendricks

BOS 1918 AL
SP C Mays
SP J Bush
SP S Jones
SP D Leonard
C - S Agnew
1B S McInnis
2B D Shean
SS E Scott
3B- F Thomas
LF- G Whiteman
CF A Strunk
RF H Hooper
Lp B Ruth

CU W Schang
M E Barrow

CHI 1918 AL
SP E Cicotte
SP F Shellenback
SR J Benz
SP R Russell
SP L Williams
RS D Danforth
RP R Faber
C R Schalk
1B C Gandil
2B E Collins
SS B Weaver
3B- F McMullin
LF N Leibold
OI S Collins
RU E Murphy
IO S Risberg
M P Rowland

CLE 1918 AL
SP S Coveleski
SR J Bagby
SP G Morton
SR F Coumbe
SR J Enzmann
C S O'Neill
1B- D Johnston
2B B Wambsganss
SS R Chapman
3B J Evans
LU J Wood
CF T Speaker
RF B Roth
MO-J Wilhoit
M J McGraw

DET 1918 AL
SP H Dauss
SP B Boland
SP R Kallio
SP G Cunningham
SP B James
RP E Erickson
C - A Wilson
M G Stallings

NY 1918 AL
SR G Mogridge
SP S Love
SP R Caldwell
SP A Russell
SR H Finneran
RP H Thormahlen
C T Hannah
1B W Pipp
2B D Pratt
SS R Peckinpaugh
3B F Baker
LF P Bodie
CF- E Miller
RF F Gilhooley
C - R Walters
M M Huggins

PHI 1918 AL
SP S Perry
SP V Gregg
SR W Adams
SP M Watson
SP E Myers
RP B Geary
C W McAvoy
1B G Burns
2B- J Dykes
S2 J Dugan
3B L Gardner
LF M Kopp
CF T Walker
RF C Jamieson
C - C Perkins
S2- R Shannon
M C Mack

STL 1918 AL
SP A Sothoron
SP D Davenport
SR T Rogers
2B D Shean
SS E Scott
3B- F Thomas
SP B Gallia
SP W Wright
RP U Shocker
RP G Lowdermilk
RP B Houck
C L Nunamaker
1B S Sisler

2B J Gedeon
S3 J Austin
3B F Maisel
LM E Smith
ML J Tobin
RF R Demmitt
UO T Hendryx
M1 F Jones
M3 J Burke

WAS 1918 AL
SR W Johnson
SP H Harper
SR J Shaw
SR D Ayers
C E Ainsmith
1B J Judge
2B R Morgan
SS D Lavan
3B E Foster
LR B Shotton
CF C Milan
RU F Schulte
UT H Shanks
M C Griffith

BOS 1919 NL
SP D Rudolph
SR D Fillingim
SP A Nehf
SP R Keating
SR A Demaree
RP J Scott
C - H Gowdy
1B W Holke
2B- B Herzog
SS R Maranville
3B T Boeckel
UO- W Cruise
CF- J Riggert
RF R Powell
OI R Smith
2B- J Rawlings
C - A Wilson
M G Stallings

BRO 1919 NL
SP J Pfeffer
SP L Cadore
SP A Mamaux
SP B Grimes
SR S Smith
RS C Mitchell
C - E Krueger
1B E Konetchy
2U J Johnston
SS I Olson
3B- L Malone
LF Z Wheat
CF H Myers
RF T Griffith
M W Robinson

CHI 1919 NL
SP H Vaughn
SP G Alexander
SP C Hendrix
SR S Martin
SP P Douglas
RS P Carter
C B Killefer
1B F Merkle
2B- C Pick
SS C Hollocher
3B C Deal
LF- L Mann
CF D Paskert
RF M Flack
LU- T Barber
UT- L Magee
M F Mitchell

CIN 1919 NL
SP H Eller
SP D Ruether
SP S Sallee
SR J Ring
SP R Fisher
RS D Luque
C - I Wingo
1B J Daubert
2B M Rath
SS L Kopf
3B H Groh
LU- R Bressler
CF E Roush
RF N Neale
C - B Rariden
M P Moran

NY 1919 NL
SP J Barnes
SR B Benton
SP F Toney
SP R Causey
SP A Nehf
RS J Dubuc

CU L McCarty
1B H Chase
SS A Fletcher
3B H Zimmerman
LF G Burns
CF R Youngs
M J McGraw

PHI 1919 NL
SR G Smith
SP L Meadows
SP E Rixey
SP B Hogg
SP G Packard
RP E Jacobs
RP F Woodward
C - B Adams
1B F Luderus
2B- G Paulette
SS D Bancroft
3B- L Blackburne
UO I Meusel
CF C Williams
UO- L Callahan
RU G Cravath
L2- P Whitted
M1 J Coombs

PIT 1919 NL
SP W Cooper
SP B Adams
SP F Miller
SP H Hamilton
SP H Carlson
RP E Mayer
C V Schmidt
1B- F Mollwitz
2B G Cutshaw
SS Z Terry
3B W Barbare
LR B Southworth
ML C Bigbee
RF C Stengel
M H Bezdek

STL 1919 NL
SP B Doak
SR M Goodwin
SR O Tuero
SP J May
SR L Meadows
RS B Sherdel
RP E Jacobs
C V Clemons
12 D Miller
23 M Stock
SS D Lavan
3S R Hornsby
LO A McHenry
RM J Smith
RU J Schultz
LF B Shotton
M B Rickey

BOS 1919 AL
SP S Jones
SP H Pennock
SP C Mays
SR A Russell
SP W Hoyt
RP R Caldwell
C W Schang
1B S McInnis
2B- R Shannon
SS E Scott
3B O Vitt
Lp B Ruth
CF- B Roth
RF H Hooper
M E Barrow

CHI 1919 AL
SP E Cicotte
SP L Williams
SR D Kerr
SP R Faber
SP G Lowdermilk
RP D Danforth
C R Schalk
1B C Gandil
2B E Collins
SS S Risberg
3S B Weaver
LF J Jackson
CF H Felsch
RF N Leibold
M K Gleason

WAS 1919 AL
SP J Shaw
SR W Johnson
SP H Harper
SP E Erickson
C - V Picinich
1B J Judge
2B- H Janvrin
S2 H Shanks
3B E Foster
LF M Menosky
RF S Rice
CL H Gharrity
IO- J Leonard
MU-B Murphy
M C Griffith

RP T Phillips
C S O'Neill
1B D Johnston
2B B Wambsganss
SS R Chapman
3B L Gardner
LF J Graney
CF T Speaker
RF E Smith
RO-J Wood
M1 L Fohl

DET 1919 AL
SP H Dauss
SP H Ehmke
SP B Boland
SP D Leonard
SR S Love
RS D Ayers
RP G Cunningham
C E Ainsmith
1B H Heilmann
2B R Young
SS D Bush
3B B Jones
LF B Veach
CF T Cobb
RF I Flagstead
RU R Shorten
M H Jennings

NY 1919 AL
SP J Quinn
SR B Shawkey
SP H Thormahlen
SR G Mogridge
SP C Mays
RP E Shore
RS A Russell
C - M Ruel
1B W Pipp
2B D Pratt
SS R Peckinpaugh
3B F Baker
LF D Lewis
CF P Bodie
RF S Vick
UT- C Fewster
C - T Hannah
M M Huggins

PHI 1919 AL
SP R Naylor
SR W Kinney
SP J Johnson
SP S Perry
SP T Rogers
C C Perkins
1R G Burns
UT W Witt
SS J Dugan
3B F Thomas
LF- M Kopp
MU T Walker
RU-A Strunk
1U- D Burrus
M C Mack

STL 1919 AL
SR A Sothoron
SP B Gallia
SP U Shocker
SP C Weilman
SP D Davenport
RS L Leifield
RP E Koob
RS R Wright
C H Severeid
1B G Sisler
2B J Gedeon
SS W Gerber
3B J Austin
LF J Tobin
MO B Jacobson
RU E Smith
RU- R Demmitt
M J Burke

BOS 1920 NL
SP J Oeschger
SR J Scott
SP D Fillingim
SR H McQuillan
C M O'Neil
1B W Holke
2B C Pick
SS R Maranville
3B T Boeckel
LF L Mann
CF R Powell
RF- W Cruise
UO- E Eayrs
2I- H Ford
C - H Gowdy
RO- J Sullivan
M G Stallings

BRO 1920 NL
SP B Grimes
SP L Cadore
SP J Pfeffer
SR A Mamaux
SP R Marquard
RS S Smith
C - O Miller
1B E Konetchy
2B P Kilduff
SS I Olson
3B J Johnston
LF Z Wheat
CF H Myers
RF T Griffith
RU B Neis
M W Robinson

CHI 1920 NL
SP G Alexander
SP H Vaughn
SP C Hendrix
SP L Tyler
SR S Martin
RS P Carter
C B O'Farrell
1B- F Merkle
S2 Z Terry
SS- C Hollocher
3B C Deal
LF D Robertson
CF D Paskert
RF M Flack
1U T Barber
23- B Herzog
OI- B Twombly
M F Mitchell

CIN 1920 NL
SP D Ruether
SP J Ring
SR H Eller
SR D Luque
SR R Fisher
RP S Sallee
C I Wingo
1B J Daubert
2B M Rath
SS L Kopf
3B H Groh
LF P Duncan
CF E Roush
RF G Neale
M P Moran

NY 1920 NL
SP J Barnes
SP A Nehf
SP F Toney
SP R Douglas
SP R Benton
C - F Snyder
1B G Kelly
2B L Doyle
SS D Bancroft
3B F Frisch
LF G Burns
CF L King
RF R Youngs
C - E Smith
M J McGraw

PHI 1920 NL
SP E Rixey
SR G Smith
SP L Meadows
SP R Causey
SP B Hubbell
C - M Wheat
1B G Paulette
2B J Rawlings
SS A Fletcher
3B R Miller
LR I Meusel
RF C Williams
CF E Stengel
2I D Miller
LO- B LeBourveau
M G Cravath

PIT 1920 NL
SP W Cooper
SP B Adams
SP H Carlson
SR E Hamilton
SR E Ponder
C W Schmidt
1B C Grimm
2B G Cutshaw
SS H Caton
3B P Whitted
LF C Bigbee
CF M Carey
RF B Southworth
UO F Nicholson
M M Gibson

STL 1920 NL
SR J Haines
SP B Doak
SP F Schupp
SP M Goodwin
RS B Sherdel
C V Clemons
1B J Fournier
2B R Hornsby
SS D Lavan
3B M Stock
LM A McHenry
MO-J Smith
MR C Heathcote
RF J Schultz
UT- H Janvrin
M B Rickey

BOS 1920 AL
SP S Jones
SP J Bush
SP H Pennock
SP H Harper
SR W Hoyt
RP A Russell
RP E Myers
C - R Walters
1B S McInnis
2B M McNally
SS E Scott
3B E Foster
LF M Menosky
CF T Hendryx
RF H Hooper
CM W Schang
3U- O Vitt
M E Barrow

CHI 1920 AL
SP R Faber
SP E Cicotte
SP L Williams
SR D Kerr
SR R Wilkinson
C R Schalk
1B S Collins
2B E Collins
SS S Risberg
3B B Weaver
LF J Jackson
CF H Felsch
RF N Leibold
M K Gleason

CLE 1920 AL
SR J Bagby
SP S Coveleski
SP R Caldwell
SR G Morton
C S O'Neill
1B D Johnston
2B B Wambsganss
SS R Chapman
3B L Gardner
LF C Jamieson
CF T Speaker
RF E Smith

DET 1920 AL
SP H Ehmke
SP H Dauss
SR R Oldham
SP D Leonard
C - O Stanage
1B H Heilmann
2B R Young
SS D Bush
3U B Pinelli
LF B Veach
CF T Cobb
RM C Shorten
RU I Flagstead
3B- B Jones
M H Jennings

NY 1920 AL
SP C Mays
SP B Shawkey
SP J Quinn
SR R Collins
SR H Thormahlen
RS G Mogridge
C - M Ruel
1B W Pipp
2B D Pratt
SS R Peckinpaugh
3B A Ward
LF D Lewis
CF P Bodie
RL B Ruth
UT B Meusel
C - T Hannah
M M Huggins

PHI 1920 AL
SP S Perry
SP R Naylor
SP S Harriss
SR E Rommel
SR R Moore
RS D Keefe
C C Perkins
1B I Griffin
2B J Dykes
SS C Galloway
3B- F Thomas
LF T Walker
CF F Welch
RO- A Strunk
UI J Dugan
M C Mack

STL 1920 AL
SP D Davis
SR U Shocker
SR A Sothoron
SP C Weilman
SR E Vangilder
RP B Burwell
RP B Bayne
C H Severeid
1B G Sisler
2B J Gedeon
SS W Gerber
3B- J Austin
LU K Williams
CF B Jacobson
RF J Tobin
3U E Smith
M J Burke

WAS 1920 AL
SR T Zachary
SR E Erickson
SP J Shaw
SR H Courtney
SP W Johnson
RS A Schacht
C P Gharrity
1B J Judge
2B B Harris
SS- J O'Neill
3U F Ellerbe
LF C Milan
CF S Rice
RF B Roth
UT H Shanks
M C Griffith

BOS 1921 NL
SR J Oeschger
SR M Watson
SR H McQuillan
SR D Fillingim
SR J Scott
C M O'Neil
1B W Holke
2B H Ford
SS W Barbare
3B T Boeckel
LF W Cruise
CF R Powell
RF B Southworth
LU- F Nicholson
M F Mitchell

BRO 1921 NL
SP B Grimes
SP D Ruether
SP L Cadore
SR C Mitchell
SR S Smith
RS J Miljus
C - O Miller
1B R Schmandt
2B P Kilduff
SS I Olson
3B J Johnston
LF Z Wheat
CF H Myers
RF T Griffith
OI B Neis
M W Robinson

CHI 1921 NL
SP G Alexander
SP S Martin
SR B Freeman
SR V Cheeves
SP H Vaughn
RS L York
RP P Jones
C B O'Farrell
1B R Grimes
2B Z Terry
SS C Hollocher
3B C Deal
LO T Barber
CF G Maisel
RF M Flack
IO J Kelleher
UO- B Twombly
M1 J Evers
M2 B Killefer

CIN 1921 NL
SP D Luque
SP E Rixey
SP R Marquard
SR P Donohue
RS B Napier
C I Wingo
1B J Daubert
23 S Bohne
SS L Kopf
3B H Groh
LF P Duncan
CF E Roush
RU R Bressler
2U- L Fonseca
C B Hargrave
M P Moran

NY 1921 NL
SR J Barnes
SP A Nehf
SR F Toney
SP R Douglas
SR R Ryan
RP S Sallee
C F Snyder
1B G Kelly
2B J Rawlings
SS D Bancroft
32 F Frisch
LF- I Meusel
LM G Burns
RF R Youngs
C - E Smith
M J McGraw

PHI 1921 NL
SP J Ring
SP H Hubbell
SP G Smith
SP L Meadows
SP J Winters
RP H Betts
C F Bruggy
3U F Ellerbe
LF C Milan
CF S Rice
RF B Roth
UT R Wrightstone
RL- I Meusel
RL B LeBourveau
1R- C Lee
UI- D Miller
M1 B Donovan
M2 K Wilhelm

PIT 1921 NL
SP W Cooper
SR W Glazner
SP E Hamilton
SP B Adams
SP J Morrison
RS J Zinn
RS H Carlson
C W Schmidt
1B C Grimm
2B G Cutshaw
SS R Maranville
3B C Barnhart
LF C Bigbee
CF M Carey
RF P Whitted
23 C Tierney
M M Gibson

STL 1921 NL
SP J Haines
SP B Doak
SP B Pertica
SR B Walker
SP J Pfeffer
RS B Sherdel
RP L North
C V Clemons
1B J Fournier
2B R Hornsby
SS D Lavan
3B M Stock
LM A McHenry
MU J Mann
RU- J Smith
RU- J Schultz
M B Rickey

BOS 1921 AL
SP S Jones
SP J Bush
SP H Pennock
SR A Russell
SR E Myers
RS B Karr
RS H Thormahlen
C M Ruel
1B S McInnis
2B D Pratt
SS E Scott
3B E Foster
LF M Menosky
CF N Leibold
RF S Collins
M H Duffy

CHI 1921 AL
SP R Faber
SP D Kerr
SR R Wilkinson
RS H Hodge
RS D McWeeny
C R Schalk
1B E Sheely
2B E Collins
SS E Johnson
3B E Mulligan
LF B Falk
MR A Strunk
CF J Mostil
RF H Hooper
CF S Rice
UO C Milan
RU- F Brower
M G McBride

CLE 1921 AL
SP S Coveleski
SR G Uhle
SP D Mails
SR J Bagby
SP A Sothoron
RS R Caldwell
RS G Morton
C S O'Neill
1B D Johnston
2B B Wambsganss
SS J Sewell
3B L Gardner
LF C Jamieson
CF T Speaker
RF E Smith
M T Speaker

DET 1921 AL
SP D Leonard
SP H Dauss
SR R Oldham
SP H Ehmke
SR B Cole
RS C Holling
RS J Middleton
C J Bassler
1B L Blue
2B R Young
SS D Bush
3B B Jones
LF B Veach
CF T Cobb
RF H Heilmann
SU- I Flagstead
UO- C Shorten
M T Cobb

NY 1921 AL
SR C Mays
SR W Hoyt
SP B Shawkey
SR R Collins
SR J Quinn
C W Schang
1B W Pipp
2B A Ward
SS R Peckinpaugh
3B F Baker
LF B Meusel
RF B Ruth
RU B Griffith
M M Huggins

PHI 1921 AL
SR E Rommel
SR S Harriss
SR B Moore
SR B Hasty
SR B Naylor
RU B Friberg
OI- T Barber
M B Killefer

WAS 1921 AL
SP G Mogridge
SP W Johnson
SP T Zachary
SR E Erickson
SR H Courtney
RS J Acosta
RS A Schacht
C P Gharrity
1B J Judge
2B B Harris
SS F O'Rourke
3B H Shanks
LF B Miller
CF S Rice
UO C Milan
RU- F Brower
M G McBride

BOS 1922 NL
SR M Watson
SP F Miller
SR R Marquard
SR J Oeschger
SR H McQuillan
RS D Fillingim
RS T McNamara
RS G Braxton
C - M O'Neil
1B W Holke
2S L Kopf
SS H Ford
3B T Boeckel
LM- A Nixon
CF R Powell
RL W Cruise
UI W Barbare
C - H Gowdy
RL- F Nicholson
M F Mitchell

BRO 1922 NL
SP D Ruether
SP B Grimes
SP D Vance
SP L Cadore
SR H Shriver
RS S Smith
RS A Mamaux
C - H DeBerry
1B R Schmandt
2B R Young
SS D Bush
3B B Jones
LF B Veach
1B R Schmandt
2B R Young
M B Rickey

CHI 1922 NL
SP V Aldridge
SP G Alexander
SP T Osborne
SR V Cheeves
RS T Kaufmann
RS G Stueland
C B O'Farrell
1B R Grimes
2B Z Terry
SS C Hollocher
3B M Krug
UO J Schultz
MR I Smith
RF- M Flack
SS- D Lavan
MU- L Mann
M B Rickey

CIN 1922 NL
SP E Rixey
SR J Couch
SP P Donohue
SR C Keck
RP D Gillespie
C B Hargrave
1B J Daubert
2B S Bohne
SS I Caveney
3B B Pinelli
LF D Duncan
MR G Burns
RF G Harper
2B- L Fonseca
C - I Wingo
M P Moran

NY 1922 NL
SP A Nehf
SP J Barnes
SR R Ryan
SP P Douglas
RP C Jonnard
RP C Causey
RP V Barnes
C F Snyder
1B G Kelly
23 F Frisch
SS D Bancroft
3B H Groh
LF I Meusel
CF- C Stengel
RF R Youngs
CF- B Cunningham
2B- J Rawlings
C - E Smith
M J McGraw

PHI 1922 NL
SP, J Ring
SP L Meadows
SR G Smith
SP B Hubbell
SR L Weinert
RS J Winters
RS J Singleton
C B Henline
1B R Leslie
SR R Marquard
2B F Parkinson
SS A Fletcher
3B G Rapp
LU C Lee
CF C Williams
RF C Walker
UI R Wrightstone
M K Wilhelm

PIT 1922 NL
SP W Cooper
SR J Morrison
SP W Glazner
SP B Adams
SR E Hamilton
RS H Carlson
RP C Yellowhorse
C J Gooch
1B C Grimm
2B C Tierney
SS R Maranville
3B P Traynor
LF C Bigbee
RF- R Russell
M1 M Gibson
M2 B McKechnie

STL 1922 NL
SR J Pfeffer
SR B Sherdel
SP J Haines
SP B Doak
SR B Pertica
RS L North
RPC C Barfoot
C E Ainsmith
1B J Fournier
2B R Hornsby
SS S Toporcer
3B M Stock
UO J Schultz
MR I Smith
RF- M Flack
SS- D Lavan
MU- L Mann
M B Rickey

BOS 1922 AL
SP J Quinn
SP R Collins
SP H Pennock
SR A Ferguson
SR B Piercy
RS B Karr
RS A Russell
RP C Fullerton
C M Ruel
1B G Burns
2B D Pratt
SS- J Mitchell
3B- J Dugan
LU M Menosky
CF- N Leibold
OI S Collins
LU J Harris
M H Duffy

CHI 1922 AL
SP R Faber
SP C Robertson
SP D Leverett
SP T Blankenship
RS S Hodge
C R Schalk
1B E Sheely
2B E Collins
SS E Johnson
3B E Mulligan
LF B Falk
CF J Mostil
RF H Hooper
3B- H McClellan
MU-A Strunk
M K Gleason

CLE 1922 AL
SR G Uhle
SP S Coveleski
SR G Morton
SR D Mails
SR J Bagby
RS J Lindsey
C S O'Neill
1B S McInnis
2B B Wambsganss
SS J Sewell
3B L Gardner
LF C Jamieson
CF T Speaker
RF J Wood
UT- R Stephenson

DET 1922 AL
SR H Ehmke
SP H Pillette
SR H Dauss
SR R Oldham
SR O Olsen
RS S Johnson
C J Bassler
1B- L Blue
2B G Cutshaw
SS T Rigney
3B B Jones
LF B Veach
CF T Cobb
RF H Heilmann
IO- D Clark
3U- F Haney

NY 1922 AL
SP B Shawkey
SR S Jones
SP W Hoyt
SP J Bush
SP C Mays
RP G Murray
C W Schang
1B W Pipp
2B A Ward
SS E Scott
3B- J Dugan
LR B Ruth
CW W Witt
RL B Meusel
M M Huggins

PHI 1922 AL
SR E Rommel
SR S Harriss
SP B Hasty
SR F Heimach
SP R Naylor
RP J Sullivan
RPC C Eckert
C C Perkins
1B J Hauser
2B R Young
SS C Galloway
3B J Dykes
LF T Walker
MR B Miller
RF F Welch
MR B McGowan
M C Mack

STL 1922 AL
SR U Shocker
SR E Vangilder
SP D Davis
SR R Kolp
SR R Wright
RS H Pruett

RS B Bayne
C H Severeid
1B G Sisler
2B M McManus
SS W Gerber
3B- F Ellerbe
LF K Williams
CF B Jacobson
RF J Tobin
M L Fohl

WAS 1922 AL
SR W Johnson
SP G Mogridge
SR F Francis
SP T Zachary
SR E Erickson
RS J Brillheart
C P Gharrity
1B J Judge
2B B Harris
SS R Peckinpaugh
3B- B LaMotte
LF G Goslin
CF S Rice
RF F Brower
3L- H Shanks
M C Milan

BOS 1923 NL
SP R Marquard
SR J Genewich
SP J Barnes
SR J Oeschger
SR T McNamara
RS L Benton
RS D Fillingim
RS J Cooney
C M O'Neil
1B S McInnis
2B H Ford
SS B Smith
3B T Boeckel
LF G Felix
CF R Powell
RF B Southworth
MU-A Nixon
M F Mitchell

BRO 1923 NL
SP B Grimes
SP D Vance
SP D Ruether
SR L Dickerman
RS A Decatur
C Z Taylor
1B J Fournier
2B- I Olson
2S J Johnston
3S A High
LF Z Wheat
MU B Neis
RF T Griffith
OI G Bailey
C - H DeBerry
LU- B Griffith
M W Robinson

CHI 1923 NL
SP G Alexander
SP V Aldridge
SP T Kaufmann
SR T Osborne
SR V Keen
RS N Dumovich
RP F Fussell
C B O'Farrell
1B- R Grimes
2B G Grantham
SS S Adams
3B B Friberg
LF H Miller
CF J Statz
RF C Heathcote
IC- G Hartnett
M B Killefer

CIN 1923 NL
SP D Luque
SP E Rixey
SP P Donohue
SP R Benton
RS C Keck
C B Hargrave
1B J Daubert
23 S Bohne
SS I Caveney
3B B Pinelli
LF P Duncan
CF E Roush
RF G Burns
M P Moran

NY 1923 NL
SP H McQuillan
SR J Scott
SP A Nehf

SP J Bentley
SP M Watson
RS R Ryan
RP C Jonnard
RP V Barnes
C F Snyder
1B G Kelly
2B F Frisch
SS D Bancroft
3B H Groh
LF I Meusel
MU-B Cunningham
RF R Youngs
S3 T Jackson
MU-J O'Connell
M J McGraw

PHI 1923 NL
SP J Ring
SP W Glazner
SR L Weinert
SR C Mitchell
SR P Behan
RS R Head
RS B Hubbell
C B Henline
1B W Holke
2B C Tierney
SS H Sand
3I R Wrightstone
LU J Mokan
CF C Williams
RF C Walker
LR C Lee
C - J Wilson
M A Fletcher

PIT 1923 NL
SP J Morrison
SP W Cooper
SP L Meadows
SP B Adams
SR E Hamilton
C W Schmidt
1B C Grimm
2B J Rawlings
SS R Maranville
3B P Traynor
LF C Bigbee
CF M Carey
RF C Barnhart
RF R Russell
M B McKechnie

STL 1923 NL
SP J Haines
SR B Sherdel
SP F Toney
SP B Doak
SP J Pfeffer
RS J Stuart
RP C Barfoot
RP L North
C - E Ainsmith
1B J Bottomley
2B H Hornsby
SS H Freigau
3B M Stock
LO J Smith
CF H Myers
RF M Flack
LF R Blades
2S S Toporcer
CF-H Mueller
M B Rickey

BOS 1923 AL
SP H Ehmke
SR J Quinn
SP A Ferguson
SP B Piercy
SR G Murray
RS C Fullerton
RP L O'Doul
C - V Picinich
1B G Burns
2S- C Fewster
SS- J Mitchell
32 H Shanks
LF J Harris
MU D Reichle
RF I Flagstead
MR S Collins
32 N McMillan
UO-M Menosky
M F Chance

CHI 1923 AL
SP C Robertson
SP R Faber
SR M Cvengros
SR T Blankenship
SR D Leverett
RS S Thurston
C R Schalk
1B E Sheely
2B E Collins

SS H McClellan
3B W Kamm
LF- B Falk
CF J Mostil
RF H Hooper
LU- R Elsh
M K Gleason

CLE 1923 AL
SR G Uhle
SP S Coveleski
SR J Edwards
SR J Shaute
SR G Morton
RS S Smith
RS D Metivier
RP D Boone
C S O'Neill
1B F Brower
2B B Wambsganss
SS J Sewell
3B R Lutzke
LF C Jamieson
CF T Speaker
RF H Summa
C G Myatt
2U- R Stephenson

DET 1923 AL
SR H Dauss
SR H Pillette
SR K Holloway
SR S Johnson
RS B Cole
RS R Francis
C J Bassler
1B L Blue
UI F Haney
SS T Rigney
3B B Jones
UO B Veach
CF T Cobb
RF H Heilmann
UO B Fothergill
LU H Manush
2I D Pratt

NY 1923 AL
SP J Bush
SP B Shawkey
SR S Jones
SP H Pennock
SP W Hoyt
C - W Schang
1B W Pipp
2B A Ward
SS E Scott
3B J Dugan
LR B Meusel
CF W Witt
OI B Ruth
M M Huggins

PHI 1923 AL
SR E Rommel
SP B Hasty
SR S Harriss
SR F Heimach
SR R Naylor
RS R Walberg
RP C Ogden
C C Perkins
1B J Hauser
2B J Dykes
SS C Galloway
3B S Hale
LF B Miller
CF W Matthews
RF F Welch
UO B McGowan
M C Mack

STL 1923 AL
SP E Vangilder
SP U Shocker
SP D Danforth
SR R Kolp
SP D Davis
RS H Pruett
RP C Root
C H Severeid
1B D Schliebner
2B M McManus
SS W Gerber
3B- G Robertson
LF K Williams
CF B Jacobson
RF J Tobin
CU- P Collins
3B- H Ezzell
M1 L Fohl
M2 J Austin

WAS 1923 AL
SP W Johnson
SP G Mogridge
SP T Zachary

SR P Zahniser
SP C Warmoth
RS A Russell
C M Ruel
1B J Judge
2B B Harris
SS R Peckinpaugh
3B O Bluege
LF G Goslin
CF N Leibold
RF S Rice
MU J Evans
IC P Gharrity
M D Bush

BOS 1924 NL
SP J Barnes
SP J Genewich
SR J Cooney
SR T McNamara
SR A Yeargin
RS L Benton
C M O'Neil
1B S McInnis
2B C Tierney
SS B Smith
3B E Padgett
LF B Cunningham
MU-G Felix
RF C Stengel
SS- D Bancroft
CU-F Gibson
M2 R Rudolph
M3 D Bancroft

BRO 1924 NL
SP B Grimes
SP D Vance
SP D Ruether
SP B Doak
SP T Osborne
RS A Decatur
C Z Taylor
1B J Fournier
2B A High
SS- J Mitchell
3B M Stock
LF Z Wheat
CF E Brown
RF T Griffith
C - H DeBerry
SU- J Johnston
UO-B Neis
M W Robinson

CHI 1924 NL
SP V Aldridge
SR V Keen
SP T Kaufmann
SR E Jacobs
SP G Alexander
RS S Blake
RP R Wheeler
C G Hartnett
1B H Cotter
2B G Grantham
3B B Friberg
LF D Grigsby
CF J Statz
RF C Heathcote
M B Killefer

CIN 1924 NL
SP E Rixey
SR C Mays
SP P Donohue
SP D Luque
SR T Sheehan
RS R Benton
RP J May
C B Hargrave
1B J Daubert
2B H Critz
SS I Caveney
3B B Pinelli
LF P Duncan
CF E Roush
RF C Walker
UI S Bohne
UT N Bressler
RF G Burns
M J Hendricks

NY 1924 NL
SP V Barnes
SP J Bentley
SP H McQuillan
SR A Nehf
SP W Dean
RS R Ryan
RP M Watson
RP C Jonnard
C F Snyder
1B G Kelly
2B F Frisch
SS T Jackson

3B H Groh
LF I Meusel
CF H Wilson
RF R Youngs
MU B Southworth
UM-B Terry
M1 J McGraw
M2 H Jennings
M3 J McGraw

PHI 1924 NL
SP J Ring
SR H Carlson
SR B Hubbell
SP C Mitchell
SR W Glazner
RS H Betts
RS J Couch
CU B Henline
1B W Holke
2B H Ford
SS H Sand
3B R Wrightstone
LF J Mokan
CF C Williams
RF G Harper
C J Wilson
LR- J Schultz
M A Fletcher

PIT 1924 NL
SP W Cooper
SR R Kremer
SR J Morrison
SP L Meadows
SR E Yde
RP A Stone
C - J Gooch
1B C Grimm
2B R Maranville
SS G Wright
3B P Traynor
LR K Cuyler
CF M Carey
RF C Barnhart
LF- C Bigbee
M B McKechnie

STL 1924 NL
SP J Haines
SP A Sothoron
SP J Stuart
SR E Dyer
SP L Dickerman
RS B Sherdel
RS H Bell
C M Gonzalez
1B J Bottomley
2B R Hornsby
SS J Cooney
3B H Freigau
LF R Blades
CF- W Holm
RO J Smith
OI- H Mueller
M B Rickey

BOS 1924 AL
SP H Ehmke
SP A Ferguson
SR J Quinn
SR C Fullerton
SP B Piercy
RS G Murray
C S O'Neill
1B J Harris
2B B Wambsganss
SS- D Lee
3B D Clark
LF B Veach
CF J Flagstead
RF I Boone
OI- S Collins
3U- H Ezzell
M L Fohl

CHI 1924 AL
SP S Thurston
SR T Lyons
SP R Faber
SR T Blankenship
SR M Cvengros
RS S Connally
RS D Leverett
RP C Robertson
C B Crouse
1B E Sheely
2B E Collins
SU B Barrett
3B W Kamm
LF B Falk
CF J Mostil
RF H Hooper
CF M Archdeacon
M1 J Evers
M2 E Walsh

M3 Collins
M4 J Evers

CLE 1924 AL
SR J Shaute
SR S Smith
SP S Coveleski
SP G Uhle
RS D Metivier
C G Myatt
1B G Burns
2B C Fewster
SS J Sewell
3B R Lutzke
LF C Jamieson
CF T Speaker
RF H Summa
UO M McNulty

DET 1924 AL
SP E Whitehill
SP R Collins
SR L Stoner
SR B Cole
SR E Wells
RS K Holloway
RS H Dauss
RS S Johnson
C J Bassler
1B L Blue
21 D Pratt
SS T Rigney
3B B Jones
LF H Manush
CF T Cobb
RF H Heilmann
3U- F Haney
UO-A Wingo

NY 1924 AL
SP H Pennock
SP J Bush
SR W Hoyt
SR B Shawkey
SR S Jones
RP M Gaston
C W Schang
1B W Pipp
2B A Ward
SS E Scott
3B J Dugan
LR B Meusel
CF W Witt
RL B Ruth
M M Huggins

PHI 1924 AL
SP E Rommel
SR F Heimach
SR S Baumgartner
SR D Burns
SR D Gray
RS D Meeker
RS S Harriss
RP B Hasty
C C Perkins
1B J Hauser
2B- M Bishop
SS C Galloway
3B- H Riconda
LF- B Lamar
ML A Simmons
RU B Miller
2I J Dykes
RF F Welch
3U- S Hale
M C Mack

STL 1924 AL
SP U Shocker
SR D Danforth
SR E Wingard
SP D Davis
SR E Vangilder
RS R Kolp
RS G Lyons
RP H Pruett
RP B Bayne
C H Severeid
1B G Sisler
2B M McManus
SS W Gerber
SS W Robertson
LF K Williams
CF B Jacobson
RF J Tobin
UO- J Evans

WAS 1924 AL
SP W Johnson
SP G Mogridge
SP T Zachary
SP J Martina
SP C Ogden
RS F Marberry
RPA Russell
RP B Speece

C M Ruel
2B B Harris
SS R Peckinpaugh
3B O Bluege
1B J Judge
MU-N Leibold
RF S Rice

BOS 1925 NL
SP J Cooney
SP J Barnes
SR L Benton
SR J Genewich
SR S Graham
RS R Ryan
RP B Smith
RS R Marquard
RP I Kamp
C F Gibson
1B D Burrus
2B- D Gautreau
SS D Bancroft
3B W Marriott
LF D Harris
ML G Felix
RF J Welsh
MU B Neis
2I- E Padgett

BRO 1925 NL
SP D Vance
SP B Grimes
SR R Ehrhardt
SR T Osborne
SP J Petty
RS H Hubbell
C Z Taylor
1B J Fournier
2B M Stock
SS J Mitchell
3U J Johnston
LF Z Wheat
CF E Brown
RF D Cox
3U C Tierney
M W Robinson

CHI 1925 NL
SP G Alexander
SP S Blake
SP W Cooper
SP T Kaufmann
SR G Bush
RS P Jones
RS V Keen
C G Hartnett
1B C Grimm
2B S Adams
SS- R Maranville
3B H Freigau
LF- A Jahn
CF- M Brooks
RF C Heathcote
M1 B Killefer
M3 M Gibson

CIN 1925 NL
SP P Donohue
SP D Luque
SP E Rixey
SR R Benton
RS J May
RP H Biemiller
C - B Hargrave
1B- W Holke
2B H Critz
SS I Caveney
3B B Pinelli
LF B Zitzmann
CF E Roush
RF C Walker
1L R Bressler
LR E Smith
M J Hendricks

NY 1925 NL
SP J Scott
SP V Barnes
SP K Greenfield
SP J Bentley
SP A Nehf
RS W Dean
RP W Huntzinger
C F Snyder
1B B Terry
2U G Kelly
SS T Jackson
3B F Lindstrom
LF I Meusel
CF B Southworth
RF R Youngs
UI F Frisch
M1 J McGraw
M2 H Jennings
M3 J McGraw

PHI 1925 NL
SP J Ring
SP H Carlson
SP C Mitchell
SR A Decatur
RS J Knight
RS H Betts
RS J Couch
C J Wilson
1B C Hawks
2B- B Friberg
SS H Sand
3B C Huber
LF- G Burns
UO G Harper
RF C Williams
21 L Fonseca
CU B Henline
UT R Wrightstone
M A Fletcher

PIT 1925 NL
SP L Meadows
SR K Kremer
SR J Morrison
SP V Aldridge
SP E Yde
RS B Adams
RP T Sheehan
C E Smith
1B G Grantham
2B E Moore
SS G Wright
3B P Traynor
LF C Barnhart
CF M Carey
RF K Cuyler
C - J Gooch
M B McKechnie

STL 1925 NL
SP J Haines
SR B Sherdel
SP F Rhem
SP A Sothoron
SP A Reinhart
RS L Dickerman
RP D Mails
C B O'Farrell
1B J Bottomley
2B R Hornsby
SS- S Toporcer
3B L Bell
LF R Blades
MU-H Mueller
RL C Hafey
RU- M Flack
UO- J Smith
M1 B Rickey

BOS 1925 NL
SP H Ehmke
SR T Wingfield
SR R Ruffing
SP P Zahniser
SP J Quinn
RS B Ross
RS O Fuhr
C - V Picinich
1B P Todt
2B B Wambsganss
SS- D Lee
3B D Prothro
OF R Carlyle
CF I Flagstead
RF I Boone
OF T Vache
M L Fohl

CHI 1925 AL
SR T Lyons
SP R Faber
SR T Blankenship
SR S Thurston
SP C Robertson
RP S Connally
RS M Cvengros
C S Schalk
1B E Sheely
2B E Collins
SS I Davis
3B W Kamm
LF B Falk
CF J Mostil
RF H Hooper
2R- B Barrett
M Collins

CLE 1925 AL
SP S Smith
SP G Uhle
SR B Karr
SR J Miller
SR G Buckeye
RP J Shaute
C G Myatt
1B G Burns

2B C Fewster
SS J Sewell
3B- R Lutzke
LF C Jamieson
CF T Speaker
RO F Spurgeon
32 F Spurgeon
RU- C Lee

DET 1925 AL
SP E Whitehill
SP H Dauss
SR K Holloway
SR L Stoner
SP R Collins
RS E Wells
RP D Leonard
RP J Doyle
C J Bassler
1B L Blue
2B F O'Rourke
SS J Tavener
3B F Haney
LF A Wingo
CF T Cobb
RF H Heilmann
MU H Manush
2U- L Burke

NY 1925 AL
SR H Pennock
SR W Hoyt
SR S Jones
SR U Shocker
SR B Shawkey
RP H Johnson
RS A Ferguson
C B Bengough
1B L Gehrig
2B A Ward
SS P Wanninger
3B J Dugan
LR B Meusel
CF E Combs
RL B Ruth
UO-B Paschal
M M Huggins

PHI 1925 AL
SR E Rommel
SR S Harriss
SP D Gray
SR R Walberg
SR L Grove
RS S Baumgartner
RP J Quinn
C M Cochrane
1B J Poole
2B M Bishop
SS C Galloway
3B S Hale
LF B Lamar
CF A Simmons
RF B Miller
32 J Dykes
RU- F Welch
M C Mack

STL 1925 AL
SR M Gaston
SP J Bush
SR D Davis
SR D Danforth
SP J Giard
RS E Vangilder
RS E Wingard
C L Dixon
1B G Sisler
2B M McManus
SS B LaMotte
3B G Robertson
LF K Williams
CF B Jacobson
RU H Rice
UO H Bennett
OI- J Tobin

WAS 1925 AL
SP S Coveleski
SP W Johnson
SP D Ruether
SP T Zachary
RP F Marberry
RS V Gregg
RP A Russell
C M Ruel
1B J Judge
2B B Harris
SS R Peckinpaugh
3B O Bluege
LF G Goslin
CF E McNeely
RF S Rice
1R J Harris

BOS 1926 NL
SR L Benton
SR J Genewich
SR B Smith
SP J Werts
SR B Hearn
RS G Mogridge
RP H Goldsmith
C Z Taylor
1B D Burrus
2B- D Gautreau
SS D Bancroft
32 A High
ML E Brown
MO J Smith
RF J Welsh
3S E Taylor
LU- F Wilson

BRO 1926 NL
SP J Petty
SP B Grimes
SR D McWeeny
SR B McGraw
SP D Vance
RP J Barnes
RP R Ehrhardt
C- M O'Neil
1O B Herman
2B C Fewster
S3 J Butler
3B W Marriott
LF Z Wheat
ML G Felix
RF D Cox
UO M Jacobson
1U- J Fournier
C- C Hargreaves
SS- R Maranville
M W Robinson

CHI 1926 NL
SR C Root
SR S Blake
SP T Kaufmann
SR P Jones
SR G Bush
RS B Osborn
C G Hartnett
1B C Grimm
2B S Adams
SS J Cooney
3B H Freigau
LF- R Stephenson
CF H Wilson
RF C Heathcote
C- M Gonzalez
OI- P Scott
M J McCarthy

CIN 1926 NL
SR P Donohue
SP C Mays
SP D Luque
SP E Rixey
RS J May
RS R Lucas
C B Hargrave
1B W Pipp
2B H Critz
SS- F Emmer
3B C Dressen
LU C Christensen
CF E Roush
RF C Walker
LF- R Bressler
C- V Picinich
M J Hendricks

NY 1926 NL
SR J Scott
SR K Greenfield
SR F Fitzsimmons
SP V Barnes
SR J Ring
RS H McQuillan
RP C Davies
C- P Florence
1B G Kelly
2B F Frisch
SS T Jackson
3B F Lindstrom
LF I Meusel
CF T Tyson
RF R Youngs
UT B Terry
UO-H Mueller
M J McGraw

PHI 1926 NL
SP H Carlson
SP W Dean
SP C Mitchell
SR C Willoughby
SR D Ulrich
RS J Knight
RS R Pierce

RP E Baecht
C- J Wilson
1U- J Bentley
2B B Friberg
SS H Sand
3B C Huber
LR J Mokan
ML F Leach
RF C Williams
C B Henline
CF A Nixon
IO R Wrightstone
M A Fletcher

PIT 1926 NL
SR R Kremer
SP L Meadows
SP V Aldridge
SR E Yde
SR D Songer
RS J Morrison
RP J Bush
C E Smith
1B G Grantham
2S H Rhyne
SS G Wright
3B P Traynor
ML K Cuyler
CF- M Carey
RF P Waner
C- J Gooch
M B McKechnie

STL 1926 NL
SP F Rhem
SR B Sherdel
SR J Haines
SP V Keen
SP G Alexander
RS A Reinhart
RP B Hallahan
RS S Johnson
C B O'Farrell
1B J Bottomley
2B R Hornsby
SS T Thevenow
3B L Bell
LF R Blades
CF T Douthit
RF B Southworth
OF- C Hafey

BOS 1926 AL
SP H Wiltse
SR T Wingfield
SP Z Pahniser
SR R Ruffing
SP S Harriss
RS T Welzer
RP F Heimach
RS J Russell
RP H Ehmke
C A Gaston
1B P Todt
2B B Regan
SS T Rigney
3B F Haney
OF S Rosenthal
CF I Flagstead
MR B Jacobson
M L Fohl

CHI 1926 AL
SP T Lyons
SR T Thomas
SP T Blankenship
SP R Faber
SR J Edwards
RS S Thurston
RS S Connally
C- R Schalk
1B E Sheely
2B E Collins
SU B Hunnefield
3B W Kamm
LF B Falk
CF J Mostil
RF B Barrett
RU- S Harris
M Collins

CLE 1926 AL
SP G Uhle
SP D Levsen
SP J Shaute
SP S Smith
SR G Buckeye
RS B Karr
C L Sewell
1B G Burns
2B F Spurgeon
SS J Sewell
3B R Lutzke
LF C Jamieson
CF T Speaker
RF H Summa

DET 1926 AL
SP E Whitehill
SR S Gibson
SR E Wells
SR L Stoner
SR R Collins
RS K Holloway
RS H Dauss
RS A Johns
C- C Manion
1B L Blue
2B C Gehringer
SS J Tavener
3B J Warner
LO B Fothergill
CF H Manush
RF H Heilmann
1U J Neun
32 F O'Rourke
LU A Wingo
UO- T Cobb

NY 1926 AL
SP H Pennock
SR U Shocker
SR W Hoyt
SR S Jones
SR W Thomas
RS B Shawkey
RP G Braxton
C P Collins
1B L Gehrig
2B T Lazzeri
SS M Koenig
3B J Dugan
LR B Meusel
CF E Combs
LR B Ruth
UO B Paschal
M M Huggins

PHI 1926 AL
SR L Grove
SR E Rommel
SR J Quinn
SR R Walberg
SR D Gray
RP H Ehmke
RP J Pate
C M Cochrane
1B J Poole
2B M Bishop
SS C Galloway
32 J Dykes
LF B Lamar
CF A Simmons
RF W French
3U S Hale
1U J Hauser
M C Mack

STL 1926 AL
SP T Zachary
SP M Gaston
SR E Vangilder
SR E Wingard
RS W Ballou
C W Schang
1B G Sisler
2B S Melillo
SS W Gerber
32 M McManus
LF K Williams
RM H Rice
RL B Miller
UO-H Bennett
MU-C Durst
CU-P Hargrave
3U- G Robertson

WAS 1926 AL
SP W Johnson
SP S Coveleski
SP D Ruether
SP A Crowder
SR C Ogden
RS F Marberry
RP B Morrell
RP A Ferguson
C M Ruel
1B J Judge
2B B Harris
SS B Myer
3B O Bluege
LM E McNeely
LM G Goslin
RF S Rice
UT J Harris

BOS 1927 NL
SR B Smith
SP K Greenfield
SR J Genewich
SR J Werts
SP C Robertson
RP G Mogridge
SR S Hogan

1B J Fournier
2U- D Gautreau
SS D Bancroft
3B A High
LF E Brown
CF J Welsh
RF L Richbourg
S2 D Farrell
UT E Moore
UO-J Smith

BRO 1927 NL
SP D Vance
SP J Petty
SP J Elliott
SR D McWeeny
SP B Doak
RP R Ehrhardt
RP W Clark
C- H DeBerry
1B B Herman
2B J Partridge
S3 J Butler
3B B Barrett
LF G Felix
CF J Statz
RF M Carey
R1 H Hendrick
M W Robinson

CHI 1927 NL
SR C Root
SP S Blake
SR G Bush
SP H Carlson
SR J Brillheart
RS P Jones
RS B Osborn
C G Hartnett
1B C Grimm
2B C Beck
SS- W English
UI S Adams
LF R Stephenson
CF H Wilson
RF E Webb
RU- C Heathcote
M J McCarthy

CIN 1927 NL
SR R Lucas
SR J May
SP D Luque
SP E Rixey
SP P Donohue
C B Hargrave
1B W Pipp
2B H Critz
SS C Galloway
32 J Dykes
LF B Lamar
CF A Simmons
2B H Ford
3B C Dressen
LF R Bressler
MU E Allen
RF C Walker
UT- B Zitzmann
M J Hendricks

NY 1927 NL
SP B Grimes
SR F Fitzsimmons
SP V Barnes
SP L Benton
RS D Henry
RP D Songer
C - Z Taylor
1B B Terry
2B R Hornsby
SS T Jackson
3B F Lindstrom
LU- H Mueller
CF E Roush
RF G Harper
3U R Reese
OF- M Ott
M1 J McGraw

PHI 1927 NL
SR J Scott
SP A Ferguson
SR D Ulrich
SP H Pruett
SP L Sweetland
RS W Willoughby
RP C Mitchell
RP A Decatur
C J Wilson
1B R Wrightstone
2B F Thompson
S3 H Sand
3B F Friberg
LF D Spalding
CF F Leach
RF C Williams
M S McInnis

PIT 1927 NL
SP L Meadows
SR C Hill

SP V Aldridge
SP R Kremer
RP J Morrison
RP M Cvengros
C J Gooch
1B J Harris
2B G Grantham
SS G Wright
3B P Traynor
LF C Barnhart
ML L Waner
RF P Waner
MO-K Cuyler
M D Bush

NY 1927 AL
SP W Hoyt
SP H Pennock
SP U Shocker
SP D Ruether
SP G Pipgras
RS W Moore
C - P Collins
1B L Gehrig
2I T Lazzeri
SS M Koenig
3B J Dugan
LR B Meusel
CF E Combs
RL B Ruth
M M Huggins

PHI 1927 AL
SR L Grove
SR R Walberg
SP J Quinn
SP H Ehmke
SR E Rommel
RS D Gray
RP J Pate
C M Cochrane
1I J Dykes
2B M Bishop
SS J Boley
3B S Hale
LF- B Lamar
CF A Simmons
RM T Cobb
2U E Collins
RU W French
SS- C Galloway
LU- Z Wheat
M C Mack

STL 1927 AL
SP M Gaston
SR E Vangilder
SP S Jones
SP L Stewart
SR E Wingard
RS E Nevers
C W Schang
1B G Sisler
2B S Melillo
SS W Gerber
3B F O'Rourke
LF K Williams
UO B Miller
RM H Rice
23- S Adams
UO H Bennett
M D Howley

WAS 1927 AL
SP H Lisenbee
SP S Thurston
SP B Hadley
SP W Johnson
SP T Zachary
RP G Braxton
RS F Marberry
C M Ruel
1B J Judge
2B B Harris
SS B Reeves
3B O Bluege
LF G Goslin
CF T Speaker
RF S Rice

BOS 1928 NL
SR B Smith
SP E Brandt
SR A Delaney
SR K Greenfield
RP F Edwards
C Z Taylor
1B G Sisler
2B R Hornsby
SS D Farrell
3B L Bell
LM E Brown
UO J Smith
RF L Richbourg
M1 J Slattery

BRO 1928 NL
SP D Vance
SR D McWeeny
SP J Petty
SR W Clark
SR J Elliott
RS B Doak
RF M Ross

RP R Ehrhardt
C - H DeBerry
1B D Bissonette
2B J Flowers
SS D Bancroft
3U H Hendrick
LF R Bressler
MR M Carey
RF B Herman
2I- H Riconda
MU-J Statz
M W Robinson

CHI 1928 NL
SR P Malone
SP S Blake
SR C Root
SR G Bush
SR A Nehf
RS P Jones
RP H Carlson
C G Hartnett
1B C Grimm
2B F Maguire
SS W English
3S C Beck
LF R Stephenson
CF H Wilson
RF K Cuyler
M J McCarthy

CIN 1928 NL
SP E Rixey
SP D Luque
SR R Kolp
SR P Lucas
SP D Donohue
RP P Appleton
C V Picinich
1B G Kelly
2B H Critz
SS H Ford
3B C Dressen
OI B Zitzmann
CF E Allen
RF C Walker
1B W Pipp
LM- M Callaghan
M J Hendricks

NY 1928 NL
SP L Benton
SP F Fitzsimmons
SP J Genewich
SP C Hubbell
SP V Aldridge
RS J Faulkner
C S Hogan
1B B Terry
2B A Cohen
SS T Jackson
3B F Lindstrom
LF L O'Doul
CF J Welsh
RF M Ott
LI R Reese
RF- L Mann
M J McGraw

PHI 1928 NL
SR B Benge
SR J Ring
SR A Ferguson
SR L Sweetland
SR C Willoughby
RS A Walsh
RP B McGraw
RS R Miller
C W Lerian
1B D Hurst
2B F Thompson
SS H Sand
3B F Whitney
LU F Leach
CF D Sothern
UO C Williams
M B Shotton

PIT 1928 NL
SR B Grimes
SP C Hill
SR R Kremer
SP F Fussell
SR E Brame
RS J Dawson
C - C Hargreaves
1B G Grantham
2B S Adams
SS G Wright
3B P Traynor
LU- F Brickell
CF L Waner
RF P Waner
M D Bush

STL 1928 NL
SR B Sherdel
SP G Alexander
SP J Haines
SP F Rhem
SP C Mitchell
RS S Johnson
RP H Haid
C J Wilson
1B J Bottomley
2B F Frisch
SS R Maranville
3B W Holm
LF C Hafey
CF T Douthit
RF G Harper
3U A High
M B McKechnie

BOS 1928 AL
SP R Ruffing
SR E Morris
SP J Russell
SP D Mac Fayden
SR S Harriss
RS M Settlemire
RP P Simmons
C - F Hofmann
1B P Todt
2B B Regan
SS W Gerber
3B B Myer
LF K Williams
CF I Flagstead
RF D Taitt
SU B Rogell
UT J Rothrock
C - C Berry
C - J Heving
M B Carrigan

CHI 1928 AL
SP T Thomas
SR T Lyons
SP G Adkins
SP R Faber
SP T Blankenship
RS S Connally
C - B Crouse
1B B Clancy
2B B Hunnefield
SS B Cissell
3B W Kamm
LF B Falk
CF J Mostil
UO A Metzler
2S- B Redfern
RU- C Reynolds
M1 R Schalk
M2 L Blackburne

CLE 1928 AL
SP J Shaute
SR W Hudlin
SP G Uhle
SP J Miller
SR G Grant
RS B Bayne
RP M Harder
C L Sewell
1I- L Fonseca
2B C Lind
SS J Sewell
3B J Hodapp
LF C Jamieson
ML S Langford
RF H Summa
1U- G Burns
M R Peckinpaugh

DET 1928 AL
SP O Carroll
SP E Whitehill
SP V Sorrell
SR K Holloway
SP S Gibson
RS E Vangilder
RS L Stoner
RP J Billings
RP G Smith
CU P Hargrave
1B- B Sweeney
2B C Gehringer
SS J Tavener
31 M McManus
LU B Fothergill
CF H Rice
RF H Heilmann
UO- A Wingo
M G Moriarty

NY 1928 AL
SP G Pipgras
SR W Hoyt
SP H Pennock
SP H Johnson
SR A Shealy
RP W Moore
C - J Grabowski
1B L Gehrig
2B T Lazzeri
SS M Koenig
3B J Dugan
LR B Meusel
CF E Combs
RL B Ruth
2S L Durocher
3B- G Robertson
M M Huggins

PHI 1928 AL
SP L Grove
SP R Walberg
SP J Quinn
SP G Earnshaw
SP H Ehmke
RS E Rommel
RS O Orwoll
C. M Cochrane
1B J Hauser
2B M Bishop
SS J Boley
3B- S Hale
LF A Simmons
UO B Miller
RF T Cobb
31 J Foxx
IO- J Dykes
CF- M Haas
M C Mack

STL 1928 AL
SP D Gray
SR A Crowder
SP J Ogden
SR G Blaeholder
SR L Stewart
RS D Coffman
RS H Wiltse
RP E Strelecki
C - W Schang
1B L Blue
2B O Brannan
SS R Kress
3B F O'Rourke
LF H Manush
CF F Schulte
RF E McNeely
M D Howley

WAS 1928 AL
SP B Hadley
SP S Jones
SR G Braxton
SP M Gaston
SR L Brown
RS F Marberry
RP T Zachary
C M Ruel
1B J Judge
2B B Harris
SI B Reeves
3B O Bluege
LF G Goslin
UQ S West
RF S Rice
CF R Barnes

BOS 1929 NL
SP B Smith
SP S Seibold
SR P Jones
SP E Brandt
SP B Cantwell
RS D Leverett
C A Spohrer
1B G Sisler
2B F Maguire
SS R Maranville
3B L Bell
LF G Harper
CF- E Clark
RF L Richbourg
M J Fuchs

BRO 1929 NL
SP W Clark
SP D Vance
SR R Moss
SR C Dudley
SR D McWeeny
RS J Morrison
RP C Moore
RP W Ballou
C V Picinich
1B D Bissonette
2S E Moore
SS D Bancroft
3B W Gilbert
LF R Bressler
CF J Frederick
RF B Herman
UT H Hendrick
M W Robinson

CHI 1929 NL
SR G Bush
SR C Root
SR P Malone
SP S Blake
SR A Nehf
RS H Carlson
RP M Cvengros
C - Z Taylor
1B C Grimm
2B R Hornsby
SS W English
3B N McMillan
LF R Stephenson
CF H Wilson
RF K Cuyler
RU- C Heathcote
M J McCarthy

CIN 1929 NL
SP R Lucas
SR E Rixey
SR J May
SP P Donohue
SR D Luque
RS R Kolp
RS K Ash
RP R Ehrhardt
C - J Gooch
1B G Kelly
2B H Critz
S2 H Ford
3B C Dressen
LM E Swanson
CF E Allen
RF C Walker
SU- P Pittinger
OF- P Purdy
C - C Sukeforth
M J Hendricks

NY 1929 NL
SP C Hubbell
SP L Benton
SP F Fitzsimmons
SP B Walker
RS C Mays
RS D Henry
RP R Judd
C S Hogan
1B B Terry
2B A Cohen
SS T Jackson
3B F Lindstrom
LF F Leach
CF E Roush
RF M Ott
C - B O'Farrell
ML- C Fullis
M J McGraw

PHI 1929 NL
SR C Willoughby
SR L Sweetland
SR R Benge
RS P Collins
RS H Elliott
RP B McGraw
RP S Dailey
C W Lerian
1B D Hurst
2B F Thompson
SS- T Thevenow
3B P Whitney
LF L O'Doul
CF- D Sothern
RF C Klein
C S Davis
SO B Friberg
M B Shotton

PIT 1929 NL
SP B Grimes
SP E Brame
SP R Kremer
SR J Petty
SR L French
RS S Swetonic
RP H Meine
RP C Hill
C C Hargreaves
1B E Sheely
2U G Grantham
S2 D Bartell
3B P Traynor
LF A Comorosky
CF L Waner
RF P Waner
C - R Hemsley
M1 D Bush
M2 J Ens

STL 1929 NL
SR B Sherdel
SR S Johnson
SP J Haines
SP C Mitchell
SR H Haid
RS F Frankhouse
RP G Alexander
RP B Hallahan
C J Wilson
1B J Bottomley
2B F Frisch
SS C Gelbert
3B A High
LF C Hafey
CF T Douthit
RU E Orsatti
RF- W Roettger
M1 M Southworth
M2 G Street
M3 B McKechnie

BOS 1929 AL
SR M Gaston
SP R Ruffing
SP J Russell
SP D Mac Fayden
SP E Morris
RP E Carroll
C - C Berry
1B P Todt
2B B Regan
SS H Rhyne
3B B Reeves
LF R Scarritt
CF J Rothrock
3U- E Barrett
RU E Bigelow
S2 B Narleski
RF B Barrett
M B Carrigan

CHI 1929 AL
SP T Thomas
SP T Lyons
SP R Faber
SR G Adkins
SP E Walsh
RS H McKain
C M Berg
1B A Shires
2B J Kerr
SS B Cissell
3B W Kamm
LF A Metzler
MU D Hoffman
RO C Reynolds
1B B Clancy
MR-J Watwood
M L Blackburne

CLE 1929 AL
SP W Hudlin
SR W Ferrell
SP J Miller
SP J Shaute
SR J Miljus
RS K Holloway
RP J Zinn
C L Sewell
1B L Fonseca
2B- J Hodapp
SS J Tavener
3B J Sewell
LF C Jamieson
CF E Averill
OF B Falk
RF E Morgan
SS- R Gardner
M R Peckinpaugh

DET 1929 AL
SP G Uhle
SR E Whitehill
SP V Sorrell
SP O Carroll
RS A Prudhomme
RS E Yde
RP L Stoner
C - E Phillips
1B D Alexander
2B C Gehringer
SS- H Schuble
3B M McManus
LM R Johnson
RP C Hill
RF H Heilmann
OF B Fothergill
M B Harris

NY 1929 AL
SP G Pipgras
SP W Hoyt
SP E Wells
SP H Pennock
SR R Sherid
RS H Heimach
RS T Zachary
RP W Moore
C B Dickey
1B L Gehrig
2B T Lazzeri
SS L Durocher
3B- G Robertson
LR B Meusel
CF E Combs
RL B Ruth
S3 M Koenig
LO- C Durst
3U- L Lary
M1 M Huggins
M2 A Fletcher

PHI 1929 AL
SP L Grove
SP R Walberg
SR G Earnshaw
SR J Quinn
RS B Shores
RS E Rommel
C M Cochrane
1B J Foxx
2B M Bishop
SS J Boley
3B S Hale
LF A Simmons
CF M Haas
RF B Miller
S3 J Dykes
M C Mack

STL 1929 AL
SP D Gray
SP A Crowder
SR G Blaeholder
SR P Collins
SP L Stewart
RS J Ogden
RP C Kimsey
RP D Coffman
C W Schang
1B L Blue
2B S Melillo
SS R Kress
3B F O'Rourke
LF H Manush
CF F Schulte
RM B McGowan
M D Howley

WAS 1929 AL
SR F Marberry
SR B Hadley
SR G Braxton
SR L Brown
SP S Jones
RS B Burke
RP M Thomas
RS A Liska
C - B Tate
1B J Judge
23 B Myer
SS J Cronin
32 J Hayes
LF G Goslin
CF S West
RF S Rice
M W Johnson

BOS 1930 NL
SP S Seibold
SR B Smith
SR B Cantwell
SP T Zachary
SP B Sherdel
RS E Brandt
RS B Cunningham
C A Spohrer
1B G Sisler
2B F Maguire
SS B Maranville
3B B Chatham
LF W Berger
CF J Welsh
RF L Richbourg
UO- E Clark
OI- R Moore
1U- J Neun
M B McKechnie

BRO 1930 NL
SP D Vance
SR W Clark
SP D Luque
SR J Elliott
SR R Phelps
RS R Moss
RS S Thurston
C A Lopez
1B D Bissonette
2B- N Finn
SS G Wright
3B W Gilbert
LF R Bressler
CF J Frederick
RF B Herman
2U- J Flowers
M W Robinson

CHI 1930 NL
SR P Malone
SR G Bush
SR C Root
SR S Blake
RS B Osborn
RP L Nelson
C G Hartnett
1B C Grimm
2B R Hornsby
3S W English
3B- L Bell
LU R Stephenson
CF H Wilson
RF K Cuyler
S2- C Beck
M1 J McCarthy
M2 R Hornsby

CIN 1930 NL
SR B Frey
SP R Lucas
SR L Benton
SR H Rhyne
SR E Rixey
RP J May
RP S Johnson
RA A Campbell
C C Sukeforth
13 - J Stripp
S2 H Ford
SS L Durocher
3B T Cuccinello
LR C Walker
LM B Meusel
RU H Heilmann
MU E Swanson
OF- M Callaghan
C - J Gooch
M D Howley

NY 1930 NL
SP B Walker
SP C Hubbell
SR F Fitzsimmons
SP C Mitchell
RS H Pruett
RP J Heving
C S Hogan
1B B Terry
2B H Critz
SS T Jackson
3B F Lindstrom
LF F Leach
MO W Roettger
RF M Ott
CU B O'Farrell
SI- D Marshall
M J McGraw

PHI 1930 NL
SR P Collins
SP R Benge
SP L Sweetland
SR C Willoughby
SR H Collard
RS H Elliott
RP H Smythe
C S Davis
1B D Hurst
2B F Thompson
SS T Thevenow
3B P Whitney
LF L O'Doul
CF- D Sothern
RF C Klein
UT B Friberg
CU- H McCurdy
1B- M Sherlock
M B Shotton

PIT 1930 NL
SP L French
SP R Kremer
SP E Brame
SP H Meine
RS G Spencer
RS S Swetonic
C R Hemsley
1B G Suhr
2B G Grantham
SS D Bartell
3B P Traynor
LF A Comorosky
CF- L Waner
RF P Waner
C - A Bool
M J Ens

STL 1930 NL
SP B Hallahan
SP S Johnson
SP J Haines
SP B Grimes
SP F Rhem
RS B Bell
RS J Lindsey
RS A Grabowski
C J Wilson
1B J Bottomley
2B F Frisch
SS C Gelbert
3B S Adams
LF C Hafey
CF T Douthit
RU G Watkins
OF- S Fisher
M G Street

BOS 1930 AL
SP M Gaston
SP D Mac Fayden
SP H Lisenbee
SP J Russell
SR E Durham
RP G Smith
C - C Berry
1B P Todt
2B B Regan
SS H Rhyne
3U O Miller
LF R Scarritt
CF T Oliver
RF E Webb
OF C Durst
3I- B Reeves
1U- B Sweeney
M H Wagner

CHI 1930 AL
SP T Lyons
SR P Caraway
SP R Faber
SP T Thomas
SR D Henry
RP E Walsh
RS H McKain
C - B Tate
UT J Watwood
2B B Cissell
SS- G Mulleavy
3B W Kamm
RL S Jolley
CF- R Barnes
UO C Reynolds
M D Bush

CLE 1930 AL
SP W Ferrell
SP W Hudlin
SP C Brown
SR M Harder
RS P Appleton
C - L Sewell
1B E Morgan
2B J Hodapp
SS J Goldman
3B J Sewell
LF C Jamieson
CF E Averill
RF D Porter
OF- B Falk
C - G Myatt
LO- B Seeds
M R Peckinpaugh

DET 1930 AL
SP G Uhle
SP V Sorrell
SP E Whitehill
SR C Hogsett
SP W Hoyt
RP C Sullivan
C - R Hayworth
1B D Alexander
2B C Gehringer
SS- M Koenig
3B M McManus
LU J Stone
CF L Funk
RF R Johnson
S3- B Akers
M B Harris

NY 1930 AL
SR G Pipgras
SR R Ruffing
SR H Sherid
SR H Johnson
SP H Pennock
RP E Wells
RP L McEvoy
C B Dickey
1B L Gehrig
23 T Lazzeri
SS L Lary
32 B Chapman
UQ E Combs
CF H Rice
RL B Ruth
LR- S Byrd
UO- D Cooke
2U- J Reese
M B Shawkey

PHI 1930 AL
SR L Grove
SR G Earnshaw
SR R Walberg
SR B Shores
SR R Mahaffey
RS E Rommel
RS J Quinn
C M Cochrane
1B J Foxx
2B M Bishop
SS J Boley
3B J Dykes
LF A Simmons
CF M Haas
RF B Miller
IO- E McNair
M C Mack

STL 1930 AL
SP L Stewart
SP D Coffman
SR G Blaeholder
SR R Collins
SP D Gray
RP C Kimsey
RS R Stiles
RP H Holshouser
C R Ferrell
1B L Blue
2B S Melillo
SS R Kress
3U F O'Rourke
LF G Goslin
CF F Schulte
RF- T Gullic
UO-R Badgro
M B Killefer

WAS 1930 AL
SP B Hadley
SP A Crowder
SR L Brown
SR F Marberry
SP S Jones
RS A Liska
C S Spencer
1B J Judge
2B B Myer
SS J Cronin
3B O Bluege
LF- H Manush
CF S West
RF S Rice
M W Johnson

BOS 1931 NL
SP E Brandt
SP T Zachary
SP S Seibold
SR B Cantwell
SR B Sherdel
RS B Cunningham
RS F Frankhouse
RP H Haid
C A Spohrer
1B B Sheely
2B F Maguire
SS R Maranville
3B- R Urbanski
LF R Worthington
CF W Berger
RF W Schulmerich
RU L Richbourg
UT- R Moore
UL- J Neun
M B McKechnie

BRO 1931 NL
SP W Clark
SP D Vance
SP R Phelps
SP S Thurston
SP J Shaute
RS F Heimach
RP D Luque
CL J Quinn
RP C Moore
C A Lopez
1B D Bissonette
2B N Finn
SS- G Slade
3B W Gilbert
LF L O'Doul
CF J Frederick
RF B Herman
SS- G Wright
M W Robinson

CHI 1931 NL
SP C Root
SP B Smith
SP P Malone
SR G Bush

SR L Sweetland
RP J May
RP B Teachout
 G Hartnett
 C Grimm
23 R Hornsby
RS W English
3B- L Bell
JO-D Taylor
ML H Wilson
RM K Cuyler
?1- F Blair
?2- B Jurges
?F- R Stephenson

CIN 1931 NL
SP S Johnson
SP R Lucas
SR L Benton
SR B Frey
S E Rixey
RS R Kolp
RS O Carroll
C Sukeforth
SR H Hendrick
B T Cuccinello
SS L Durocher
B J Stripp
OF E Roush
 T Douthit
RU E Crabtree
SS- N Ford
RU- C Heathcote
M D Howley

NY 1931 NL
SP F Fitzsimmons
SP C Hubbell
SP B Walker
SP C Mitchell
SR J Berly
 S Hogan
B B Terry
B- B Hunnefield
S T Jackson
 J Vergez
F F Leach
O E Allen
M M Ott
MU-C Fullis
?F- F Lindstrom
- B O'Farrell
 J McGraw

PHI 1931 NL
R J Elliott
P R Benge
R P Collins
P C Dudley
 R S Bolen
S F Watt
B S Davis
B D Hurst
S L Mallon
B P Whitney
R C Klein
F E Brickell
 B Arlett
 B Friberg
M B Shotton

PIT 1931 NL
P H Meine
 L French
P R Kremer
P G Spencer
P E Brame
P B Osborn
 E Phillips
B- G Suhr
2 G Grantham
S T Thevenow
 P Traynor
F A Comorosky
F L Waner
M P Waner
 J Ens

STL 1931 NL
P B Hallahan
R P Derringer
P B Grimes
P F Rhem
 S Johnson
P J Haines
P J Lindsey
P A Stout
 J Wilson
 B Bottomley
 F Frisch
S C Gelbert
S S Adams
F C Hafey
F P Martin
F G Watkins
1B- R Collins
M G Street

BOS 1931 AL
SP J Russell
SP D Mac Fayden
SR E Durham
SR H Lisenbee
SR E Morris
RS W Moore
RP M Gaston
RS B Kline
C C Berry
1B B Sweeney
2S- R Warstler
SS H Rhyne
3U O Miller
LI J Rothrock
CF T Oliver
RF U Webb
3U U Pickering
LU A Van Camp
M S Collins

CHI 1931 AL
SR V Frasier
SP T Thomas
SR P Caraway
SR R Faber
SR T Lyons
RS H McKain
RP J Moore
RP G Braxton
C- B Tate
1B L Blue
2B J Kerr
SS B Cissell
3B- B Sullivan
LU L Fonseca
MU J Watwood
RF C Reynolds
SS L Appling
OF B Fothergill
C- F Grube
3B- I Jeffries
M D Bush

CLE 1931 AL
SP W Ferrell
SR W Hudlin
SP C Brown
SR M Harder
RP P Appleton
C L Sewell
1B E Morgan
2B J Hodapp
SS- E Montague
3B W Kamm
LF J Vosmik
CF E Averill
RF D Porter
S2 J Burnett
OF- B Falk
M R Peckinpaugh

DET 1931 AL
SP E Whitehill
SP V Sorrell
SR G Uhle
SR T Bridges
SR A Herring
RS C Hogsett
RP C Sullivan
C- R Hayworth
1B D Alexander
2B C Gehringer
SS- B Rogell
3U M McManus
LF J Stone
MU-H Walker
RF R Johnson
2S M Koenig
UI M Owen
M B Harris

NY 1931 AL
SR L Gomez
SP R Ruffing
SP W Johnson
SP H Pennock
SP G Pipgras
RS E Wells
C B Dickey
1B L Gehrig
23 T Lazzeri
SS L Lary
3B J Sewell
LR B Chapman
CF E Combs
RL B Ruth
UO S Byrd
M J McCarthy

PHI 1931 AL
SR L Grove
SP R Walberg
SR G Earnshaw
SR R Mahaffey
SR E Rommel
RP W Hoyt
C M Cochrane
1B J Foxx
2B M Bishop
SS-D Williams
3B J Dykes
LF A Simmons
CF M Haas
RF B Miller
3I- E McNair
M C Mack

STL 1931 AL
SP D Gray
SP L Stewart
SP G Blaeholder
SR D Coffman
SP R Collins
RS W Hebert
RP C Kimsey
RP R Stiles
C R Ferrell
1B J Burns
2B S Melillo
SS J Levey
3R K Kress
LF G Goslin
CF F Schulte
RU- T Jenkins
3B- L Storti
M B Killefer

WAS 1931 AL
SR L Brown
SR A Crowder
SR F Marberry
SR C Fischer
SP S Jones
RS B Hadley
RS B Burke
C R Spencer
1B J Kuhel
2B B Myer
SS J Cronin
3B O Bluege
LF H Manush
CF S West
RU S Rice
RU- D Harris
M W Johnson

BOS 1932 NL
SP E Brandt
SP H Betts
SP B Brown
SP T Zachary
SP S Seibold
RS B Cantwell
RS F Frankhouse
RP B Cunningham
C A Spohrer
1B- A Shires
2B R Maranville
SS B Urbanski
3B- F Knothe
LF R Worthington
CF W Berger
RF W Schulmerich
IO R Moore
C- P Hargrave
UO-F Leach
M B McKechnie

BRO 1932 NL
SP W Clark
SP V Mungo
SP D Vance
SR F Heimach
SP S Thurston
RS J Shaute
RP J Quinn
RP C Moore
C A Lopez
1B- G Kelly
2B T Cuccinello
SS G Wright
31 J Stripp
LF L O'Doul
CF D Taylor
RF H Wilson
UO J Frederick
S3- G Slade
M M Carey

CHI 1932 NL
SP L Warneke
SR G Bush
SP P Malone
SR C Root
SR B Grimes
RS B Smith
RP J May
C G Hartnett
1B C Grimm
2B B Herman
SS B Jurges
3S W English
LF N Stephenson
CF J Moore
RM K Cuyler
M1 R Hornsby

CIN 1932 NL
SP R Lucas
SR S Johnson
SP O Carroll
SR L Benton
SR R Kolp
RS B Frey
RS E Rixey
RP J Ogden
C E Lombardi
1B H Hendrick
2B G Grantham
SS L Durocher
3B W Gilbert
LF W Roettger
MU E Crabtree
RF B Herman
CF T Douthit
LF- C Hafey
3U- A High
S2- J Morrissey
M D Howley

NY 1932 NL
SP C Hubbell
SP F Fitzsimmons
SP B Walker
SR J Mooney
SR H Schumacher
RS H Bell
RS D Luque
RP W Hoyt
RS S Gibson
C S Hogan
1B B Terry
2B H Critz
SS-D Marshall
3B J Vergez
LF- J Moore
CF F Lindstrom
RF M Ott
OI C Fullis
U3- S Leslie
M1 J McGraw

PHI 1932 NL
SP E Holley
SR R Benge
SR S Hansen
SR P Collins
SP F Rhem
RS J Elliott
C S Davis
1B D Hurst
2B L Mallon
SS D Bartell
3B P Whitney
LF H Lee
CF K Davis
RF C Klein
M B Shotton

PIT 1932 NL
SR L French
SR B Swift
SP H Meine
SR B Harris
SP S Swetonic
RS G Spencer
RS L Chagnon
RP E Brame
C E Grace
1B G Suhr
2B T Piet
SS A Vaughan
3B P Traynor
LU A Comorosky
CF L Waner
RF P Waner
LF D Barbee
M M Gibson

STL 1932 NL
SR D Dean
SP P Derringer
SR T Carleton
SP B Hallahan
SR S Johnson
RS J Lindsey
RP A Stout
C G Mancuso
1R R Collins
2B- J Reese
SS G Gelbert
3B- J Flowers
ML E Orsatti
CF- P Martin
RU- R Blades
1B- J Bottomley
C - J Wilson
M G Street

BOS 1932 AL
SR B Weiland
SR E Durham
SR B Kline
SP I Andrews
RP W Moore
RS J Michaels
RS L Boerner
C - B Tate
1B D Alexander
2B M Olson
SS R Warstler
3B U Pickering
LF S Jolley
CF T Oliver
RO R Johnson
OI J Watwood
23 M McManus
UO-G Stumpf
M1 S Collins

CHI 1932 AL
SP T Lyons
SP S Jones
SP M Gaston
SP V Frasier
RS P Gregory
RS R Faber
C F Grube
RF B Campbell
M B Killefer

CLE 1932 AL
SP W Ferrell
SP C Brown
SP M Harder
SR W Hudlin
SR O Hildebrand
RS S Connally
RP J Russell
C - L Sewell
1B E Morgan
2B B Cissell
SS J Burnett
3B W Kamm
LF J Vosmik
CF E Averill
RF D Porter
C - G Myatt
M R Peckinpaugh

DET 1932 AL
SP E Whitehill
SP V Sorrell
SR W Wyatt
SP T Bridges
SR G Uhle
RS C Hogsett
C R Hayworth
1B H Davis
2B C Gehringer
SS B Rogell
3U H Schuble
LF J Stone
RF-E Webb
IO- B Rhiel
UO-J White
M B Harris

NY 1932 AL
SP L Gomez
SP R Ruffing
SP G Pipgras
SR J Allen
SP H Pennock
RP D Mac Fayden
RP J Brown
C B Dickey
1B L Gehrig
2B T Lazzeri
SS F Crosetti
3B J Sewell
LF- B Chapman
CF E Combs
RF B Ruth
UI- S Byrd
M M McCarthy

PHI 1932 AL
SP R Mahaffey
SP T Freitas
RP E Rommel
RP L Krausse
C M Cochrane
1B J Foxx
2B M Bishop
SS E McNair
3B J Dykes
LF A Simmons
CF M Haas
OF-D Cramer
RF B Miller
M C Mack

STL 1932 AL
SP L Stewart
SP G Blaeholder
SP B Hadley
SR D Gray
SR W Hebert
RS C Fischer
RP C Kimsey
C R Ferrell
1B J Burns
2B S Melillo
SS J Levey
3B- A Scharein
LF G Goslin
CF G Schulte
RF B Campbell
M B Killefer

WAS 1932 AL
SR A Crowder
SR M Weaver
SR L Brown
SP T Thomas
RS F Marberry
C R Spencer
1B J Kuhel
2B B Myer
SS J Cronin
3B O Bluege
LF H Manush
CF S West
RF C Reynolds
UO S Rice
UT R Kress
1U B Sullivan
M W Johnson

BOS 1933 NL
SP E Brandt
SR B Cantwell
SR F Frankhouse
SP H Betts
SP T Zachary
C S Hogan
1B J Jordan
2B R Maranville
SS B Urbanski
3B P Whitney
LF- H Lee
CF W Berger
RF R Moore
LU- J Mowry
M B McKechnie

BRO 1933 NL
SP B Beck
SR V Mungo
SR B Benge
SP O Carroll
SR S Thurston
RP J Shaute
RP R Ryan
C A Lopez
1B S Leslie
2B T Cuccinello
SU-G Wright
3B J Stripp
LU H Wilson
CF D Taylor
RU J Frederick
IO- J Flowers
CU- C Outen
M M Carey

CHI 1933 NL
SP L Warneke
SP G Bush
SP C Root
SP P Malone
SR B Tinning
C G Hartnett
1B C Grimm
2B Bi Herman
SS B Jurges
3B W English
LF N Stephenson
CF F Demaree
RF Ba Herman
UI- M Koenig

CIN 1933 NL
SP P Derringer
SP R Lucas
SP S Johnson
SR L Benton
SR R Kolp
RS B Frey
RP E Rixey
C E Lombardi
1B J Bottomley
2S J Morrissey
SS O Bluege
3B S Adams
LM J Moore
ML C Hafey
RF H Rice
2B- G Grantham
UO-W Roettger
M D Bush

NY 1933 NL
SR C Hubbell
SP H Schumacher
SP F Fitzsimmons
SP R Parmelee
RS H Bell
RP D Luque
RP G Spencer
C G Mancuso
1B B Terry
2B H Critz
SS B Ryan
3B J Vergez
LF J Moore
CF K Davis
RF M Ott
OF-L O'Doul
UO-H Peel

PHI 1933 NL
SP E Holley
SR S Hansen
SR J Elliott
SR C Moore
SP F Rhem
RS P Collins
RP A Liska
C S Davis
1B D Hurst
23 J Warner
SS D Bartell
3B- J McLeod
LF W Schulmerich
CF. C Fullis
RF C Klein
M B Shotton

PIT 1933 NL
SR L French
SP B Swift
SP H Meine
SR S Swetonic
SP H Smith
RS W Hoyt
RS L Chagnon
RP B Harris
C E Grace
1B D Jordan
2B R Maranville
SS B Urbanski
3B P Whitney
LF- H Lee
CF W Berger
RF R Moore
LU- J Mowry
M B McKechnie

STL 1933 NL
SR D Dean
SR T Carleton
SP B Hallahan
SP B Walker
SP D Vance
RS J Haines
RP S Johnson
C J Wilson
1B R Collins
2B F Frisch
SS L Durocher
3B P Martin
LF- J Medwick
CF E Orsatti
RF G Watkins
MU-E Allen
UI- P Crawford
M1 G Street

BOS 1933 AL
SP G Rhodes
SR B Weiland
SR L Brown
SR H Johnson
SR I Andrews
RS J Welch
RS B Kline
RP G Pipgras
C R Ferrell
1B D Alexander
2B J Hodapp
SS R Warstler
3I M McManus
LU S Jolley
ML D Cooke
RO R Johnson
S3 B Werber
CF T Oliver
1O- B Seeds

CHI 1933 AL
SP T Lyons
SP S Jones
SP M Gaston
SP E Durham
SR J Miller
RS J Heving
RP J Gregory
RP C Kimsey
RP R Faber
C - F Grube
1B R Kress
2B J Hayes
SS L Appling
3B J Dykes
LF A Simmons
CF M Haas
RF E Swanson
C - C Berry
M L Fonseca

CLE 1933 AL
SR M Harder
SP O Hildebrand
SP W Ferrell
SR C Brown
SR W Hudlin
RP M Pearson
RP S Connally
RP B Bean
C - S Spencer
1B H Boss
2U O Hale
SS- B Knickerbocker
3B W Kamm
LF J Vosmik
CF E Averill
RF D Porter
2S B Cissell
UI- J Burnett
C - F Pytlak
M1 R Peckinpaugh
M2 B Falk
M3 W Johnson

DET 1933 AL
SP F Marberry
SP T Bridges
SP V Sorrell
SR C Fischer
SP S Rowe
RP C Hogsett
RP V Frasier
RP A Herring
C R Hayworth
1B H Greenberg
2B C Gehringer
SS B Rogell
3B M Owen
LU G Walker
CF P Fox
RF J Stone
UO-J White
M1 B Harris
M2 D Baker

NY 1933 AL
SP R Ruffing
SP L Gomez
SP J Allen
SP R Van Atta
RP W Moore
RS H Pennock
C B Dickey
1B L Gehrig
2B T Lazzeri
SS F Crosetti
3B J Sewell
RL B Chapman
MU E Combs
RL B Ruth
MU D Walker
UO-S Byrd
M J McCarthy

PHI 1933 AL
SR L Grove
SP S Cain
SR R Walberg
SR R Mahaffey
SR R Earnshaw
RS J Peterson
C M Cochrane
1B J Foxx
2B M Bishop
S2 D Williams
3B P Higgins

(PHI 1933 AL, cont.)
LF B Johnson
CF D Cramer
RF E Coleman
S2- E McNair
M C Mack

STL 1933 AL
SP B Hadley
SP G Blaeholder
SR E Wells
RS D Gray
RS R Stiles
RS W Hebert
RS H McDonald
C M Shea
1B J Burns
2B S Melillo
SS J Levey
3B A Scharein
LF C Reynolds
CF S West
RF B Campbell
UT T Gullic
UO- D Garms
M1 B Killefer
M2 A Sothoron
M3 R Hornsby

WAS 1933 AL
SR A Crowder
SP E Whitehill
SP L Stewart
SP M Weaver
SR T Thomas
RP J Russell
RS B Burke
RP B McAfee
C L Sewell
1B J Kuhel
2B B Myer
SS J Cronin
3B O Bluege
LF H Manush
CF F Schulte
RF G Goslin
UT- D Harris

BOS 1934 NL
SR E Brandt
SP F Frankhouse
SR H Betts
SP F Rhem
SP B Cantwell
RS B Smith
RP L Mangum
C A Spohrer
1B B Jordan
23 M McManus
SS B Urbanski
3B P Whitney
LF H Lee
CF W Berger
RU T Thompson
C S Hogan
OI R Moore
M B McKechnie

BRO 1934 NL
SP V Mungo
SP R Benge
SR D Leonard
SP J Babich
SR T Zachary
RS L Munns
RS O Carroll
C A Lopez
1B S Leslie
23 T Cuccinello
SS L Frey
3B J Stripp
LU D Taylor
CF L Koenecke
RO B Boyle
RU J Frederick
S2 J Jordan
M C Stengel

CHI 1934 NL
SP L Warneke
SP B Lee
SR G Bush
SR P Malone
SP J Weaver
RS B Tinning
RS C Root
C G Hartnett
1B- C Grimm
2B Bi Herman
SS B Jurges
3B S Hack
LF C Klein
CF K Cuyler
RF Ba Herman
S3 W English
LO T Stainback

CIN 1934 NL
SR P Derringer
SP B Frey
SR S Johnson
SR T Freitas
SR A Stout
RS D Brennan
RP R Kolp
C E Lombardi
1B J Bottomley
IF T Piet
S2 G Slade
UI M Koenig
LF H Pool
CF C Hafey
RL A Comorosky
IF- S Adams
M1 B O'Farrell
M2 B Shotton
M3 C Dressen

NY 1934 NL
SR C Hubbell
SP H Schumacher
SP F Fitzsimmons
SP R Parmelee
RS J Bowman
RP A Smith
RP H Bell
C G Mancuso
1B B Terry
2B H Critz
SS T Jackson
3B J Vergez
LF J Moore
MU G Watkins
RF M Ott
3S B Ryan
OF- L O'Doul

PHI 1934 NL
SR C Davis
SP P Collins
SR C Moore
SP E Moore
RS S Hansen
RS J Johnson
RS R Grabowski
C A Todd
1B D Camilli
2U L Chiozza
SS D Bartell
3B- B Walters
LM E Allen
CF K Davis
RF J Moore
C J Wilson

PIT 1934 NL
SR L French
SR B Swift
SR R Birkofer
SR W Hoyt
SP R Lucas
RS H Meine
RP L Chagnon
RS H Smith
C E Grace
1B B Suhr
2B- C Lavagetto
SS A Vaughan
3B P Traynor
LF F Lindstrom
CF L Waner
RF P Waner
23 T Thevenow
LU- W Jensen
C - T Padden
M1 M Gibson

STL 1934 NL
SR D Dean
SP T Carleton
SR P Dean
SP B Hallahan
SP B Walker
RS J Haines
RS J Mooney
C S Davis
1B R Collins
2B F Frisch
SS L Durocher
3B P Martin
LF J Medwick
CF E Orsatti
RF J Rothrock
UI B Whitehead
C B DeLancey

BOS 1934 AL
SR G Rhodes
SR J Welch
SR F Ostermueller
SP W Ferrell
SR H Johnson
RS L Grove
RS R Walberg
RP H Pennock
1B E Morgan
2B B Cissell
SS L Lary
3B B Werber
LF R Johnson
MR C Reynolds
RF- D Porter
2U M Bishop
MR M Solters
M B Harris

CHI 1934 AL
SP G Earnshaw
SP T Lyons
SP M Gaston
SP S Jones
SR L Tietje
RS P Gallivan
RP J Heving
RS W Wyatt
RS - E Madjeski
1B Z Bonura
2B- J Hayes
SS L Appling
3I J Dykes
LF A Simmons
CF M Haas
RF E Swanson
2S- B Boken
M1 L Fonseca

CLE 1934 AL
SR M Harder
SP M Pearson
SP O Hildebrand
SR W Hudlin
SR L Brown
RP B Bean
RP C Brown
C - F Pytlak
1B H Trosky
2B O Hale
SS B Knickerbocker
3B W Kamm
LF J Vosmik
CF E Averill
RU S Rice
M W Johnson

DET 1934 AL
SP T Bridges
SR S Rowe
SR E Auker
SR F Marberry
SP V Sorrell
RP C Fischer
RP C Hogsett
C M Cochrane
1B H Greenberg
2B C Gehringer
SS B Rogell
3B M Owen
LF G Goslin
CF J White
RF P Fox
UO G Walker

NY 1934 AL
SP L Gomez
SP R Ruffing
SR J Murphy
SP J Broaca
SR J DeShong
RS D Mac Fayden
C B Dickey
1B L Gehrig
2U T Lazzeri
SS F Crosetti
3B J Saltzgaver
RL M Hoag
ML B Chapman
RL B Ruth
RL S Byrd
S3- R Rolfe
M J McCarthy

PHI 1934 AL
SP J Marcum
SP S Cain
SR B Dietrich
SR J Cascarella
SR A Benton
RS R Mahaffey
C C Berry
1B J Foxx
2B R Warstler
SS E McNair
3B P Higgins
LF B Johnson
CF D Cramer
RF E Coleman
OI L Finney
C F Hayes
RU- B Miller
M C Mack

STL 1934 AL
SR B Newsom
SP G Blaeholder
SP B Hadley
SR D Coffman
RS I Andrews
RS J Knott
RS E Wells
RP B McAfee
C R Hemsley
1B J Burns
2B S Melillo
SS A Strange
3B H Clift
LM R Pepper
CF S West
RF B Campbell
IO O Bejma
UO- D Garms
M R Hornsby

WAS 1934 AL
SP E Whitehill
SP M Weaver
SR B Burke
SP L Stewart
SR T Thomas
RS J Russell
RP A McColl
RS A Crowder
C - E Phillips
1B- J Kuhel
2B B Myer
SS J Cronin
3B C Travis
LF H Manush
CF F Schulte
RF J Stone
IO O Bluege
RU D Harris

BOS 1935 NL
SR F Frankhouse
SR B Cantwell
SR B Smith
SP E Brandt
SR H Betts
RP D Mac Fayden
RP L Benton
C A Spohrer
1U B Jordan
23 L Mallon
SS B Urbanski
32 P Whitney
LF H Lee
CF W Berger
RU T Thompson
RU R Moore
UI- J Coscarart
UO- J Mowry

BRO 1935 NL
SR V Mungo
SP W Clark
SP G Earnshaw
SP T Zachary
SR J Babich
RS D Leonard
RP R Benge
RS L Munns
RP D Vance
C A Lopez
1B S Leslie
23 T Cuccinello
SS L Frey
3B J Stripp
LF D Taylor
MO F Bordagaray
RF B Boyle
UT J Bucher
UI J Jordan
MU L Koenecke
M C Stengel

CHI 1935 NL
SR L Warneke
SP B Lee
SR L French
SR C Root
SP T Carleton
RS R Henshaw
RP F Kowalik
C G Hartnett
1B P Cavarretta
2B B Herman
SS B Jurges
3B S Hack
LF A Galan
MR F Demaree
RF C Klein
M3- F Lindstrom
M C Grimm

CIN 1935 NL
SR P Derringer
SR A Hollingsworth
SR G Schott
SR T Freitas
SR S Johnson
RS D Brennan
RS B Frey
RS L Herrmann
CU E Lombardi
1B J Bottomley
2B A Kampouris
SS B Myers
3B L Riggs
LF- B Herman
ML S Byrd
RF I Goodman
C - G Campbell
UI- B Sullivan
M C Dressen

NY 1935 NL
SP C Hubbell
SP H Schumacher
SP R Parmelee
SP S Castleman
RS A Smith
RP A Stout
RP F Gabler
C G Mancuso
1B B Terry
2I M Koenig
SS D Bartell
3B T Jackson
LF J Moore
CF H Leiber
RF M Ott

PHI 1935 NL
SR C Davis
SR O Jorgens
SR S Johnson
SR B Walters
SR J Bowman
RS J Bivin
RS P Pezzullo
RS R Prim
RS H Mulcahy
C A Todd
1B D Camilli
2B L Chiozza
SS M Haslin
3B J Vergez
LF G Watkins
CF E Allen
RF J Moore
C - J Wilson

PIT 1935 NL
SP C Blanton
SR G Bush
SR B Swift
SR J Weaver
SR B Birkofer
RS W Hoyt
RP R Lucas
C T Padden
1B G Suhr
2B P Young
SS A Vaughan
3U T Thevenow
LF W Jensen
CF L Waner
RF P Waner
C - E Grace
2U- C Lavagetto
M P Traynor

STL 1935 NL
SR D Dean
SR P Dean
SR B Walker
SR B Hallahan
RS J Haines
RS E Heusser
C B DeLancey
2B F Frisch
SS L Durocher
3B P Martin
LF J Medwick
CF T Moore
RF J Rothrock
C S Davis

BOS 1935 AL
SP W Ferrell
SP L Grove
SR G Rhodes
SR J Welch
SP F Ostermueller
RS R Walberg
RS J Wilson
RU L Finney
RP G Hockette
1B D Bahlgren
2B S Melillo
SS J Cronin
3B B Werber
LF R Johnson
CF M Almada
UO D Cooke
OF- B Miller
RF- C Reynolds

CHI 1935 AL
SP J Whitehead
SP V Kennedy
SP T Lyons
SP L Tietje
SP S Jones
RS R Phelps
RP W Wyatt
C L Sewell
1B Z Bonura
2B- J Hayes
SS L Appling
3B J Dykes
LF R Radcliff
CF A Simmons
RU M Haas
RU G Washington
2B- T Piet

CLE 1935 AL
SP M Harder
SP W Hudlin
SR T Lee
SP M Pearson
SR O Hildebrand
RS L Brown
RP R Winegarner
RS C Brown
C - E Phillips
1B H Trosky
2B B Myer
S3 O Bluege
3B C Travis
LF H Manush
CF J Powell
RU J Stone
SU- R Kress
UO- F Schulte
M B Harris

DET 1935 AL
SP S Rowe
SP T Bridges
SP A Crowder
SR E Auker
SR J Sullivan
RP C Hogsett
C M Cochrane
1B H Greenberg
2B C Gehringer
SS B Rogell
3B M Owen
LF G Goslin
CF J White
RF P Fox
UO G Walker

NY 1935 AL
SP L Gomez
SP R Ruffing
SP J Broaca
SP J Allen
SP V Tamulis
RS J Murphy
RP J DeShong
RP P Malone
C B Dickey
1B L Gehrig
2B T Lazzeri
SS- F Crosetti
3B R Rolfe
LF J Hill
CF B Selkirk
LU- E Combs
M J McCarthy

PHI 1935 AL
SR J Marcum
SR B Dietrich
SP G Blaeholder
SP W Wilshere
SR R Mahaffey
RP G Caster
RP D Lieber
C - P Richards
1B J Foxx
2B R Warstler
SS E McNair
3B P Higgins
LF B Johnson
CF D Cramer
RF- W Moses

STL 1935 AL
SR I Andrews
SR J Knott
SR J Walkup
SP S Cain
SP F Thomas
RS R Van Atta
RS D Coffman
C R Hemsley
1B J Burns
2B- T Carey
SS L Lary
3B H Clift
LF M Solters
CF S West
RF E Coleman
UT- B Bell
UO- R Pepper
M R Hornsby

WAS 1935 AL
SP E Whitehill
SP B Hadley
SP B Newsom
SR E Linke
RS J Russell
RS L Pettit
C C Bolton
1B J Kuhel
2B B Myer
S3 O Bluege
3B C Travis
LF H Manush
CF J Powell
RU J Stone
SU- R Kress
UO- F Schulte
M B Harris

BOS 1936 NL
SP D Mac Fayden
SP T Chaplin
SP J Lanning
SR B Cantwell
SP R Benge
RS B Smith
RS B Reis
C A Lopez
1B B Jordan
2B T Cuccinello
S3 B Urbanski
3B J Coscarart
LF H Lee
CF W Berger
RF G Moore
OI T Thompson
M B McKechnie

BRO 1936 NL
SP V Mungo
SP E Brandt
SR F Frankhouse
SR M Butcher
SR W Clark
RS G Jeffcoat
RS T Baker
C R Berres
1B B Hassett
2B J Jordan
SS L Frey
3B J Stripp
LU G Watkins
CF J Cooney
UT F Bordagaray
UT J Bucher
C B Phelps
M C Stengel

CHI 1936 NL
SR B Lee
SR L French
SR L Warneke
SP T Carleton
SP C Davis
RS R Henshaw
RP C Root
RP C Bryant
C G Hartnett
1B P Cavarretta
2B B Herman
SS B Jurges
3B S Hack
LF- E Allen
CF A Galan
RF F Demaree
CU- K O'Dea
M C Grimm

CIN 1936 NL
SR P Derringer
SP A Hollingsworth
SP G Schott
SP B Hallahan
SR P Davis
RS B Frey
RS D Brennan
C E Lombardi
1B L Scarsella
2B A Kampouris
SS B Myers
3B L Riggs
LF B Herman
MO K Cuyler
RF I Goodman
UT C Chapman
S2 T Thevenow
C - G Campbell
ML- H Walker
M C Dressen

NY 1936 NL
SP C Hubbell
SP H Schumacher
SR A Smith
SR F Fitzsimmons
SR H Gumbert
RS F Gabler
RS S Castleman
RP D Coffman
C G Mancuso
1B J Leslie
2B- T Carey
SS D Bartell
3B T Jackson
LF M Solters
CF H Leiber
RF M Ott
1U- B Terry

PHI 1936 NL
SP B Walters
SR C Passeau
SR J Bowman
SR O Jorgens
RS S Johnson
RS E Moore
C - E Grace
1B D Camilli
2S C Gomez
SS L Norris
3B P Whitney
LR J Moore
ML E Sulik
RF C Klein
MI L Chiozza
CU- J Wilson

PIT 1936 NL
SR B Swift
SR C Blanton
SP J Weaver
SP L Lucas
SR W Hoyt
RS M Brown
RS R Birkofer
C - T Padden
1B G Suhr
2B P Young
SS A Vaughan
3B B Brubaker
LF W Jensen
CF L Waner
RF P Waner
M P Traynor

STL 1936 NL
SR D Dean
SP P Parmelee
SR J Winford
SR J Haines
RP E Heusser
RS G Earnshaw
C S Davis
1B J Mize
2B- S Martin
SS L Durocher
3S C Gelbert
LF J Medwick
CF T Moore
RF P Martin
1U R Collins
C B Ogrodowski
2U F Frisch
UO- L King

BOS 1936 AL
SP W Ferrell
SP L Grove
SR F Ostermueller
SP J Marcum
SR R Walberg
RS J Wilson
C R Ferrell
1B J Foxx
2B S Melillo
S2 E McNair
3L B Werber
LF- H Manush
CF D Cramer
RU D Cooke
RU M Almada
S3- J Cronin
IO- J Kroner

CHI 1936 AL
SP V Kennedy
SP J Whitehead
SP S Cain
SP T Lyons
SP M Stratton
RP C Brown
RP R Evans
C L Sewell
1B Z Bonura
2B J Hayes
SS L Appling
3B J Dykes
LF R Radcliff
JO M Kreevich
RF M Haas
23 T Piet
CF- L Rosenthal
U2- E Coleman
M R Hornsby

CLE 1936 AL
SP J Allen
SP M Harder
SR O Hildebrand
SR D Galehouse
SP L Brown
RS G Blaeholder
RS T Lee
SR W Hudlin
C - B Sullivan
1B H Trosky
2B H Hughes
SS B Knickerbocker
3B O Hale
LF J Vosmik
CF E Averill
RF- R Weatherly
M S O'Neill

DET 1936 AL
SP T Bridges
SR S Rowe
SP E Auker
SR V Sorrell
RS R Lawson
RP C Kimsey
C - R Hayworth
1B J Burns
2B C Gehringer
SS B Rogell
3B M Owen
LF G Goslin
CF A Simmons
RF G Walker
M1 M Cochrane
M2 D Baker
M3 M Cochrane

NY 1936 AL
SP R Ruffing
SP M Pearson
SR J Broaca
SP L Gomez
SP B Hadley
RS P Malone
C B Dickey
1B L Gehrig
2B T Lazzeri
SS F Crosetti
3B R Rolfe
JO J DiMaggio
RF J Powell
RF G Selkirk
M J McCarthy

PHI 1936 AL
SP H Kelley
SP G Rhodes
3B B Ross
SR H Fink
RP R Gumpert
C F Hayes
JO L Finney
B- R Warstler
SS S Newsome
B P Higgins
B J Johnson
RF W Moses
RF G Puccinelli
U C Dean
M C Mack

TL 1936 AL
R C Hogsett
R J Knott
R I Andrews
R E Caldwell
R T Thomas
S R Van Atta
P G Liebhardt
R Hemsley
3B J Bottomley
B T Carey
S L Lary
B H Clift
F M Solters
F S West
F B Bell

WAS 1936 AL
SP B Newsom
SP J DeShong
SP E Whitehill
SR P Appleton
SP J Cascarella
RS J Russell
C - C Bolton
1B J Kuhel
2S- O Bluege
SR C Travis
3B B Lewis
LF J Stone
CF B Chapman
RF- C Reynolds
S2 R Kress
LU- J Hill
M B Harris

BOS 1937 NL
SP L Fette
SP J Turner
SP D Mac Fayden
SR G Bush
SR J Lanning
RS I Hutchinson
C A Lopez
1B E Fletcher
2B T Cuccinello
SS R Warstler
3B- G English
L3 D Garms
RF G Moore
LU- R Johnson
M B McKechnie

BRO 1937 NL
SR M Butcher
SR L Hamlin
SP F Frankhouse
SP W Hoyt
SP V Mungo
RS R Henshaw
RP G Jeffcoat
C B Phelps
1B B Hassett
23 C Lavagetto
SS W English
3U- J Stripp
LF T Winsett
CF J Cooney
RF H Manush
UO G Brack
UT J Bucher
M B Grimes

CHI 1937 NL
SP B Lee
SP T Carleton
SR L French
SR C Root
SR R Parmelee
RS C Bryant
RS C Davis
RS C Shoun
C G Hartnett
1B R Collins
2B B Herman
SS B Jurges
3B S Hack
LF A Galan
CF- J Marty
OI P Cavarretta
UT- L Frey
C - K O'Dea
M C Grimm

CIN 1937 NL
SR L Grissom
SR P Derringer
SR P Davis
SR A Hollingsworth
SR G Schott
C E Lombardi
1B B Jordan
2B A Kampouris
SS B Myers
3B L Riggs
UO K Cuyler
OF- C Hafey
RF I Goodman
1U L Scarsella
MU-H Walker
M1 C Dressen
M2 B Wallace

NY 1937 NL
SP C Hubbell
SR C Melton
SP H Schumacher
SR H Gumbert
SP S Castleman
RS A Smith
RP D Coffman
C H Danning
1B J McCarthy
2B B Whitehead
SS D Bartell
3B L Chiozza
LF J Moore
OF J Ripple
R3 M Ott
C - G Mancuso
M B Terry

PHI 1937 NL
SR C Passeau
SP B Walters
SR W LaMaster
SR H Mulcahy
SR S Johnson
RS O Jorgens
RP H Kelleher
C - B Atwood
1B D Camilli
2B D Young
SS G Scharein
3B P Whitney
LF M Arnovich
CF H Martin
RL C Klein
OI E Browne
UO J Moore
2I L Norris
C - E Grace
M J Wilson

PIT 1937 NL
SP C Blanton
SR R Bauers
SP E Brandt
SR B Swift
SR J Bowman
RP R Lucas
RP M Brown
RS J Weaver
C A Todd
1B G Suhr
2B L Handley
SS A Vaughan
3B B Brubaker
LM W Jensen
CF L Waner
RF P Waner
UI P Young
LU- J Dickshot
M P Traynor

STL 1937 NL
SP B Weiland
SP L Warneke
SP D Dean
SR S Johnson
SR H Harrell
RS M Ryba
C - B Ogrodowski
1B J Mize
2B J Brown
SS L Durocher
3B D Gutteridge
LF J Medwick
CF T Moore
RF D Padgett
3O F Bordagaray
OI P Martin
2U- S Martin
C - M Owen
M F Frisch

BOS 1937 AL
SP L Grove
SR J Wilson
SP B Newsom
SR J Marcum
SR A McKain
RS R Walberg
C G Desautels
1B J Foxx
2B E McNair
SS J Cronin
3B P Higgins
LF B Mills
CF D Cramer
RF B Chapman

CHI 1937 AL
SP V Kennedy
SP T Lee
SP T Lyons
SP J Whitehead
SP M Stratton
RP B Dietrich
RP C Brown
C L Sewell
1B Z Bonura
2B J Hayes
SS L Appling
3B H Clift
LF J Vosmik
CF S West
RF B Bell
MO E Allen
M1 R Hornsby
M2 J Bottomley

CLE 1937 AL
SP M Harder
SP D Galehouse
SR W Hudlin
SP J Allen
SP B Feller
RS E Whitehill
RP J Heving
RS L Brown
RP W Wyatt
C F Pytlak
1B H Trosky
2U- J Kroner
SS L Lary
32 O Hale
LF M Solters
CF E Averill
RF B Campbell
32 R Hughes
M S O'Neill

DET 1937 AL
SP E Auker
SP T Bridges
SP R Lawson
SP J Wade
SR B Poffenberger
RS G Gill
RS S Coffman
C3 R York
1B H Greenberg
2B C Gehringer
SS B Rogell
3B M Owen
LR G Walker
CF J White
RO P Fox
OI- G Goslin
M1 M Cochrane
M2 D Baker
M3 M Cochrane
M4 D Baker
M5 C Perkins

NY 1937 AL
SP L Gomez
SP R Ruffing
SP B Hadley
SP M Pearson
RP J Murphy
RP F Makosky
C B Dickey
1B L Gehrig
2B T Lazzeri
SS F Crosetti
3B R Rolfe
LF J Powell
CF J DiMaggio
RO M Hoag
RF- G Selkirk
M J McCarthy

PHI 1937 AL
SP C Caster
SR H Kelley
SR E Smith
SP B Thomas
SP B Ross
RP L Nelson
RP H Fink
RP G Turbeville
C E Brucker
1B C Dean
23 R Peters
SS C Newsome
3B B Werber
LF B Johnson
CF- J Hill
RF W Moses
1M- L Finney
MU-J Rothrock
M1 C Mack
M2 E Mack

STL 1937 AL
SP O Hildebrand
SR J Knott
SR C Hogsett
SP J Walkup
SR J Bonetti
RS B Trotter
RS L Koupal
C R Hemsley
1B H Davis
2S T Carey
SS B Knickerbocker
3B H Clift
LF J Vosmik
CF S West
RF B Bell
MO E Allen
M1 R Hornsby
M2 J Bottomley

WAS 1937 AL
SP J DeShong
SP W Ferrell
SP M Weaver
SR P Appleton
RS E Linke
RP S Cohen
C - R Ferrell
1B J Kuhel
2B B Myer
SS C Travis
3B B Lewis
LF A Simmons
CF M Almada
RL J Stone
RU- F Sington
M B Harris

BOS 1938 NL
SP J Turner
SP L Fette
SP D Mac Fayden
SR M Shoffner
SR J Lanning
RS I Hutchinson
RS D Errickson
C - R Mueller
1B E Fletcher
2B T Cuccinello
SS R Warstler
3B- J Stripp
LR M West
CF V DiMaggio
RO J Cooney
UT D Garms
M C Stengel

BRO 1938 NL
SR L Hamlin
SP F Fitzsimmons
SR T Pressnall
SR V Tamulis
SR B Posedel
RP V Mungo
RS F Frankhouse
C - B Phelps
1B D Camilli
2B J Hudson
SS L Durocher
3B C Lavagetto
LU B Hassett
OI E Koy
UO G Rosen
RO-K Cuyler
M B Grimes

CHI 1938 NL
SP B Lee
SR C Bryant
SR L French
SP T Carleton
RS C Root
RP J Russell
C - G Hartnett
1B R Collins
2B B Herman
SS B Jurges
3B S Hack
LF A Galan
ML C Reynolds
RF P Demaree
OI- P Cavarretta
CF- J Marty
C - K O'Dea
M1 C Grimm

CIN 1938 NL
SP P Derringer
SP J Vander Meer
SR P Davis
SP B Walters
SR J Weaver
RP G Schott
RP J Cascarella
C E Lombardi
1B F McCormick
2B L Frey
SS B Myers
3B L Riggs
LF W Berger
CF H Craft
RF I Goodman
RF H Steinbacher
1B J McCarthy
2B- A Kampouris
SS D Bartell

WAS 1937 AL (continued / WAS col)
3B M Ott
LF J Moore
CF H Leiber
RF J Ripple
U3- S Leslie
UO- B Seeds
M B Terry

PHI 1938 NL
SR H Mulcahy
SR C Passeau
SP A Hollingsworth
SP M Butcher
RS P Sivess
RP A Smith
C - B Atwood
1B P Weintraub
2B H Mueller
SS D Young
3U P Whitney
LF M Arnovich
RF C Klein
S2 G Scharein
3U- B Jordan
M1 J Wilson
M2 H Lobert

PIT 1938 NL
SP R Bauers
SP J Tobin
SP C Blanton
SP B Klinger
SR E Brandt
SS B Rogell
RP M Brown
C A Todd
1B G Suhr
2B P Young
SS A Vaughan
3B L Handley
LF J Rizzo
CF L Waner
RF P Waner
M P Traynor

STL 1938 NL
SP B Weiland
SR B McGee
SR L Warneke
SR C Davis
SR R Henshaw
RS M Macon
RS C Shoun
RP H Harrell
C M Owen
1B J Mize
2B S Martin
SS- L Myers
3S D Gutteridge
LF J Medwick
CF T Moore
RU E Slaughter
UI J Brown
RU D Padgett
OI- F Bordagaray
OI- P Martin
M1 F Frisch
M2 M Gonzalez

BOS 1938 AL
SR J Bagby
SR J Wilson
SR F Ostermueller
SR E Dickman
RS A McKain
RP J Marcum
C G Desautels
1B J Foxx
2B B Doerr
SS J Cronin
3B P Higgins
LF J Vosmik
CF D Cramer
RF B Chapman
OI- R Nonnenkamp

CHI 1938 AL
SP T Lee
SP T Lyons
SP M Stratton
SP J Whitehead
SP J Knott
RS J Rigney
C - L Sewell
1B J Kuhel
2B- J Hayes
SS- L Appling
3B M Owen
OF G Walker
CF M Kreevich
RF H Steinbacher
S2 B Berger
LF R Radcliff
M J Dykes

WAS 1938 AL
SP D Leonard
SR K Chase
SP W Ferrell
SR H Kelley
SR M Weaver
RS P Appleton
RS J DeShong

CLE 1938 AL
SP B Feller
SP M Harder
SP J Allen
SP E Whitehill
SR W Hudlin
RS D Galehouse
RS J Humphries
RS A Milnar
C F Pytlak
1B H Trosky
2B O Hale
SS L Lary
3B K Keltner
LF J Heath
CF E Averill
UO-R Weatherly
M O Vitt

DET 1938 AL
SP V Kennedy
SP G Gill
SP E Auker
SP T Bridges
SR H Lawson
RS H Eisenstat
RS B Poffenberger
RS S Coffman
RP A Benton
C R York
1B H Greenberg
2B C Gehringer
SS B Rogell
3B- D Ross
LU D Walker
CF- C Morgan
RF P Fox
3U M Christman
UO- J White
M1 M Cochrane
M2 D Baker

NY 1938 AL
SP R Ruffing
SP L Gomez
SP M Pearson
SP S Chandler
CL J Murphy
RP I Andrews
C B Dickey
1B L Gehrig
2B J Gordon
SS F Crosetti
3B R Rolfe
LF G Selkirk
CF J DiMaggio
RF T Henrich
UO-M Hoag
M J McCarthy

PHI 1938 AL
SP G Caster
SR B Thomas
SP L Nelson
SP B Ross
RS E Smith
RS N Potter
RS A Williams
C F Hayes
1O L Finney
2B D Lodigiani
SS W Ambler
3B B Werber
LF S Chapman
CF B Johnson
RF W Moses
M C Mack

STL 1938 AL
SP B Newsom
SP L Mills
SP O Hildebrand
SR R Van Atta
RS E Cole
RS B Cox
C B Sullivan
1B G McQuinn
2B D Heffner
SS R Kress
3B H Clift
LF B Mills
CF M Almada
RF B Bell
UO-M Mazzera
M1 G Street
M2 S Melillo

CLE 1938 AL (col 8)
RS J Krakauskas
RS C Hogsett
C R Ferrell
1B Z Bonura
2B B Myer
SC S Travis
3B B Lewis
LF A Simmons
CF S West
RF G Case
UO T Wright
M B Harris

BOS 1939 NL
SP B Posedel
SP D Mac Fayden
SP J Turner
SR M Shoffner
RS J Lanning
RS D Errickson
RS J Sullivan
C A Lopez
1B B Hassett
2B- T Cuccinello
SS- E Miller
3B H Majeski
UO M West
CF J Cooney
R3 D Garms
LF A Simmons
UI R Warstler
M C Stengel

BRO 1939 NL
SP L Hamlin
SR H Casey
SR V Tamulis
SR T Pressnall
SP F Fitzsimmons
RP W Wyatt
RP I Hutchinson
RS R Evans
C B Phelps
1B D Camilli
2B P Coscarart
SS L Durocher
3B C Lavagetto
LF E Koy
CF- D Walker
RF G Moore
UI J Hudson
C - A Todd

CHI 1939 NL
SP B Lee
SP C Passeau
SR L French
SR C Root
SR V Page
RP D Dean
RP J Russell
C G Hartnett
1B R Russell
2B B Herman
SS D Bartell
3B S Hack
LF A Galan
CF H Leiber
RU J Gleeson
C - G Mancuso
MU-C Reynolds

CIN 1939 NL
SP B Walters
SP P Derringer
SR W Moore
SR L Grissom
SP J Vander Meer
RS J Thompson
C E Lombardi
1B F McCormick
2B L Frey
SS B Myers
3B B Werber
LM W Berger
CF H Craft
RF I Goodman
M B McKechnie

NY 1939 NL
SP H Gumbert
SR C Melton
SR B Lohrman
SP H Schumacher
SR C Hubbell
RS M Salvo
RP J Brown
RP R Lynn
C H Danning
1B Z Bonura
2B B Whitehead
SS B Jurges
3B- T Hafey
LF J Moore
CF F Demaree

RF M Ott
M B Terry

PHI 1939 NL
SP H Mulcahy
SP K Higbe
SR B Beck
SR I Pearson
SP S Johnson
RP M Butcher
RS R Harrell
RP R Kerksieck
C - S Davis
1B- G Suhr
2B- R Hughes
SS G Scharein
3B P May
LF M Arnovich
MU H Martin
RU- L Scott
OI- G Brack
UT H Mueller
MO-J Marty
C - W Millies
SU- D Young
M D Prothro

PIT 1939 NL
SP B Klinger
SR M Brown
SR J Bowman
SP J Tobin
RS R Sewell
RS B Swift
C - R Mueller
1B E Fletcher
2B- P Young
SS A Vaughan
3B L Handley
LF J Rizzo
CF L Waner
RF P Waner
23 B Brubaker
MO-F Bell
C - R Berres
OF- C Klein
M P Traynor

STL 1939 NL
SR C Davis
SR M Cooper
SR L Warneke
SR B McGee
SP B Weiland
RS B Bowman
RP C Shoun
C M Owen
1B J Mize
2B S Martin
S2 J Brown
3B D Gutteridge
LF J Medwick
CF T Moore
RF E Slaughter
UO-L King
OI- P Martin
CU-D Padgett
M R Blades

BOS 1939 AL
SP L Grove
SR J Wilson
SR F Ostermueller
SP E Auker
SR D Galehouse
RP E Dickman
RS J Heving
RS J Wade
C J Peacock
1B J Foxx
2B B Doerr
SS J Cronin
3B J Tabor
LF J Vosmik
CF D Cramer
RF T Williams
UT L Finney

CHI 1939 AL
SP T Lee
SP J Rigney
SP E Smith
SP T Lyons
SP J Knott
RP C Brown
RP B Dietrich
C M Tresh
1B J Kuhel
2B- O Bejma
SS L Appling
3B E McNair
LF G Walker
CF M Kreevich
RU L Rosenthal
RU R Radcliff
M J Dykes

CLE 1939 AL
SP B Feller
SR A Milnar
SP M Harder
SP J Allen
SP W Hudlin
RS H Eisenstat
RP J Dobson
C R Hemsley
1B H Trosky
2U O Hale
SS- S Webb
3B K Keltner
LF J Heath
CF B Chapman
RF B Campbell
UI O Grimes
UO R Weatherly
M O Vitt

DET 1939 AL
SP B Newsom
SP T Bridges
SR D Trout
SP S Rowe
SR A Benton
RS A McKain
RP B Thomas
SP B Tebbetts
1B H Greenberg
2B C Gehringer
SS F Croucher
3B P Higgins
LF- E Averill
CF B McCosky
RF B Fox
CU R York
M D Baker

NY 1939 AL
SP R Ruffing
SP L Gomez
SP B Hadley
SP A Donald
SP M Pearson
RP O Hildebrand
RS S Sundra
RS M Russo
CL J Murphy
C B Dickey
1B B Dahlgren
2B J Gordon
SS F Crosetti
3B R Rolfe
LR G Selkirk
CF J DiMaggio
RL C Keller
RM T Henrich
M J McCarthy

PHI 1939 AL
SR L Nelson
SR N Potter
SP B Ross
SP B Beckmann
SR G Caster
RP C Dean
RP C Pippen
RS B Joyce
C F Hayes
1B D Siebert
2U J Gantenbein
SS S Newsome
3U D Lodigiani
LF B Johnson
CF S Chapman
RF W Moses
SS W Ambler
RU D Miles
23 B Nagel
M1 C Mack
M2 E Mack

STL 1939 AL
SP J Kramer
SP V Kennedy
SR R Lawson
SR L Mills
SR B Harris
RS B Trotter
RS G Gill
RP J Whitehead
C - J Glenn
1B G McQuinn
2B J Berardino
S2 D Heffner
3B H Clift
LF- J Gallagher
MU C Laabs
UO M Hoag
OI B Sullivan
SS- M Christman
M F Haney

WAS 1939 AL
SP D Leonard
SP K Chase
SR J Krakauskas
SP J Haynes
SR A Carrasquel
RP P Appleton
RS W Masterson
C - R Ferrell
1B- M Vernon
2B- J Bloodworth
SS C Travis
3B B Lewis
RL T Wright
OI S West
MR G Case
LF- B Estalella
2B- B Myer
M B Harris

BOS 1940 NL
SP D Errickson
SP B Posedel
SR J Sullivan
SP M Salvo
SR N Strincevich
RP J Tobin
RP A Javery
RP D Coffman
C - R Berres
1B B Hassett
2B B Rowell
SS E Miller
3B S Sisti
LF C Ross
CF J Cooney
OI M West
RF G Moore
M C Stengel

BRO 1940 NL
SP W Wyatt
SP L Hamlin
SR T Carleton
SP C Davis
SP F Fitzsimmons
RS V Tamulis
RS H Casey
RP T Pressnell
C B Phelps
1B D Camilli
2B P Coscarart
SS- P Reese
3B C Lavagetto
LF J Medwick
CF D Walker
UO J Vosmik
UI- J Hudson
RU- J Wasdell
M L Durocher

CHI 1940 NL
SR C Passeau
SP L French
SP B Lee
SR V Olsen
SP J Mooty
RS K Raffensberger
RS C Root
RP V Page
C A Todd
1B- P Cavarretta
2B B Herman
SS B Mattick
3B S Hack
RL B Nicholson
MO J Gleeson
OI H Leiber
LU D Dallessandro
M G Hartnett

CIN 1940 NL
SP B Walters
SP P Derringer
SP J Thompson
SP J Turner
SR W Moore
RP J Beggs
RP J Hutchings
RP M Shoffner
C E Lombardi
1B F McCormick
2B L Frey
SS- B Myers
3B B Werber
UO M McCormick
CF H Craft
RF I Goodman
SS- E Joost
M B McKechnie

NY 1940 NL
SP H Gumbert
SP H Schumacher
SP C Hubbell
SP B Lohrman
SR C Melton
RS P Dean
RP J Brown
RP R Joiner
C H Danning
1B B Young
23- T Cuccinello
S2 M Witek
32 B Whitehead
LF J Moore
MR F Demaree
R3 M Ott
MU-J Rucker
M B Terry

PHI 1940 NL
SP K Higbe
SP H Mulcahy
SP I Pearson
SR S Johnson
SR B Beck
RS L Smoll
C B Warren
1B A Mahan
2B M Schulte
SS B Bragan
3B P May
LO J Rizzo
CF J Marty
RF C Klein
UT H Mueller
C - A Atwood
M D Prothro

PIT 1940 NL
SR R Sewell
SP J Bowman
SR M Brown
SR K Heintzelman
SR B Klinger
RS M Butcher
RS J Lanning
RS D Lanahan
RS D Mac Fayden
C S Davis
1B E Fletcher
2B C Gehringer
SS D Bartell
3B P Higgins
LF- H Greenberg
CF B McCosky
RF P Fox
RU B Campbell
CF V DiMaggio
RF B Elliott
3U D Garms
RU- P Waner
M F Frisch

STL 1940 NL
SP M Cooper
SP L Warneke
SP B McGee
SR C Shoun
SR B Bowman
RS M Lanier
RP J Russell
C M Owen
1B J Mize
23 J Brown
SS M Marion
32 S Martin
LF- E Koy
CF T Moore
RF E Slaughter
UI J Brown
OI- J Hopp
OI- P Martin
C - D Padgett
M1 R Blades
M2 M Gonzalez
M3 B Southworth

BOS 1940 AL
SR J Bagby
SR J Wilson
SP L Grove
SR F Ostermueller
SR H Hash
RS J Heving
RP D Galehouse
RS E Dickman
C - G Desautels
1C J Foxx
2B B Doerr
SS J Cronin
3B J Tabor
LF T Williams
MO D DiMaggio
MO D Cramer
R1 L Finney

CHI 1940 AL
SP J Rigney
SP T Lee
SP E Smith
SP T Lyons
SP J Knott
RP B Dietrich
RP C Brown
RP P Appleton
C M Tresh
1B J Kuhel
2B- S Webb
SS L Appling
3B B Kennedy
LF M Solters
CF M Kreevich
RF T Wright
LU L Rosenthal
M J Dykes

CLE 1940 AL
SP B Feller
SP A Milnar
SP M Harder
SP A Smith
SR J Allen
RS J Dobson
RP H Eisenstat
C R Hemsley
1B H Trosky
2B R Mack
SS L Boudreau
3B K Keltner
UO B Chapman
CF R Weatherly
RF B Bell
LF J Heath
M O Vitt

DET 1940 AL
SP B Newsom
SP T Bridges
SP S Rowe
SP J Gorsica
SP H Newhouser
RS D Trout
CL A Benton
RP T Seats
RP A McKain
C B Tebbetts
1B R York
2B C Gehringer
SS B Sisti
3B P Higgins
LF- H Greenberg
CF B McCosky
RF P Fox
RU B Campbell
CU- B Sullivan
M D Baker

NY 1940 AL
SP R Ruffing
SP M Russo
SP S Chandler
SP M Breuer
SR A Donald
RP M Pearson
RS S Sundra
RP T Bonham
RP J Murphy
C B Dickey
1B B Dahlgren
2B J Gordon
SS F Crosetti
3B R Rolfe
LR G Selkirk
CF J DiMaggio
RL C Keller
RM-T Henrich
M J McCarthy

PHI 1940 AL
SP J Babich
SP N Potter
SR G Caster
SR C Dean
SP B Ross
RS B Beckmann
RS E Heusser
RP P Vaughan
C F Hayes
1B D Siebert
2B B McCoy
SU A Brancato
3B A Rubeling
LF B Johnson
CF S Chapman
RF W Moses
UO-D Miles
SS J Cronin
M C Mack

STL 1940 AL
SP E Auker
SP V Kennedy
SP B Harris
SP J Niggeling
SR E Bildilli
RP B Trotter
RP R Lawson
RP S Coffman
RS L Mills
C B Swift
1B G McQuinn
2B D Heffner
SS J Berardino
3B H Clift
LF R Radcliff
CF W Judnich

WAS 1940 AL
RU- R Cullenbine
UO C Laabs
RU- J Grace
M F Haney

SP D Leonard
SP K Chase
SP S Hudson
SR W Masterson
RS J Krakauskas
RS R Monteagudo
RS J Haynes
RP A Carrasquel
C R Ferrell
1B- Z Bonura
2B J Bloodworth
SS J Pofahl
3B C Travis
LF G Walker
CF J Case
RF B Lewis
CU- J Early
UO- J Welaj
M O Vitt

BOS 1941 NL
SP J Tobin
SP M Salvo
SR A Johnson
SP D Errickson
SR A Javery
SR T Earley
RS J Hutchings
RP F LaManna
C R Berres
1B B Hassett
2B B Rowell
SS E Miller
3B S Sisti
CF J Cooney
RU G Moore
RU P Waner
C - P Waner
M C Stengel

BRO 1941 NL
SP K Higbe
SP W Wyatt
SR H Casey
SR C Davis
SR L Hamlin
C M Owen
1B D Camilli
2B B Herman
SS P Reese
3B C Lavagetto
LF J Medwick
CF P Reiser
RO D Walker
OI- J Wasdell
M L Durocher

CHI 1941 NL
SP C Passeau
SR V Olsen
SP B Lee
SR J Mooty
SR P Erickson
RP L French
RP C Root
RP T Pressnell
RP V Page
C C McCullough
1B D Dahlgren
2B L Stringer
SS S Sturgeon
3B S Hack
OF D Dallessandro
OI P Cavarretta
RF B Nicholson
M J Wilson

CIN 1941 NL
SP B Walters
SP P Derringer
SP J Vander Meer
SR E Riddle
SR J Turner
RS J Thompson
RP J Beggs
RP W Moore
C E Lombardi
1B F McCormick
2B L Frey
SS E Joost
3B B Werber
LU M McCormick
CF H Craft
UO J Gleeson
M B McKechnie

NY 1941 NL
SP H Schumacher
SR C Melton
SP C Hubbell
SR B Lohrman
SR B Carpenter
RP B McGee
RS B Bowman
RP A Adams
RP J Brown
C H Danning
1B B Young
2B B Whitehead
SS B Jurges
3B D Bartell
LF J Moore
CF B Rucker
RF M Ott
LU- M Arnovich
M B Terry

PHI 1941 NL
SR J Podgajny
SR T Hughes
SR S Johnson
SP C Blanton
SR L Grissom
RS I Pearson
RS L Hoerst
RS B Beck
RS B Crouch
C B Warren
1B N Etten
2B- D Murtaugh
SS B Bragan
3B P May
LF D Litwhiler
CF J Marty
RU S Benjamin
CU M Livingston
RU J Rizzo
UT H Mueller
M D Prothro

PIT 1941 NL
SP R Sewell
SP M Butcher
SR K Heintzelman
SR J Lanning
RS B Klinger
RS D Dietz
C A Lopez
1B E Fletcher
2B F Gustine
SS- A Vaughan
3B L Handley
LF M Van Robays
CF V DiMaggio
RF B Elliott
UT- D Garms
2U- S Martin
M F Frisch

STL 1941 NL
SP L Warneke
SP E White
SP M Cooper
SR M Lanier
SR H Gumbert
RS H Krist
RS C Shoun
RP I Hutchinson
C G Mancuso
1B J Mize
2B C Crespi
SS M Marion
3B J Brown
OI J Hopp
CF T Moore
RF E Slaughter
LU D Padgett
M B Southworth

BOS 1941 AL
SP D Newsome
SR M Harris
SP C Wagner
SP L Grove
SP J Dobson
RP M Ryba
RS J Wilson
C F Pytlak
1B J Foxx
2B B Doerr
SS J Cronin
3B J Tabor
LF T Williams
CF D DiMaggio
RU L Finney
SU S Newsome
C - J Peacock
OI- S Spence

CHI 1941 AL
SP T Lee
SP E Smith
SP J Rigney
SP T Lyons
RS B Dietrich
RP B Ross
C M Tresh
1B J Kuhel
2B- B Knickerbocker
SS L Appling
3B- D Lodigiani
LU M Hoag
CF M Kreevich
RF T Wright
M J Dykes

CLE 1941 AL
SP B Feller
SP A Milnar
SP A Smith
SP J Bagby
RP C Brown
RP J Heving
C R Hemsley
1B- H Trosky
2B R Mack
SS L Boudreau
3B K Keltner
LF- G Walker
CF R Weatherly
RF J Heath
MU S Campbell
M R Peckinpaugh

DET 1941 AL
SP B Newsom
SR J Gorsica
SP H Newhouser
SR A Benton
SR D Trout
RP T Bridges
RS S Rowe
RP B Thomas
C B Tebbetts
1B R York
2B C Gehringer
SS F Croucher
3B P Higgins
LF R Radcliff
CF B McCosky
RF B Campbell
UO T Stainback
CU- B Sullivan
M D Baker

NY 1941 AL
SP M Russo
SP R Ruffing
SP S Chandler
SP A Donald
SP L Gomez
RP M Breuer
RP T Bonham
CL J Murphy
RP N Branch
C B Dickey
1B J Sturm
2B J Gordon
SS P Rizzuto
3B R Rolfe
LF C Keller
CF J DiMaggio
RF T Henrich
M J McCarthy

PHI 1941 AL
SP P Marchildon
SP J Knott
SP L McCrabb
SP B Beckmann
SR B Hadley
RS L Harris
RP T Ferrick
C F Hayes
1B D Siebert
2B B McCoy
SS A Brancato
3B- P Suder
LF B Johnson
CF S Chapman
RF W Moses
UO-E Collins
UO-D Miles
M C Mack

STL 1941 AL
SP E Auker
SR B Muncrief
SP D Galehouse
SP B Harris
SP J Niggeling
RS G Caster
RP J Kramer
RP B Trotter
C R Ferrell
1B G McQuinn
2B D Heffner
SS J Berardino
3B H Clift
LU R Cullenbine
CF W Judnich
RO C Laabs
RF J Grace
2U J Lucadello

M1 F Haney
M2 L Sewell

WAS 1941 AL
SP D Leonard
SP S Hudson
SP K Chase
SP S Sundra
RS R Anderson
RS A Carrasquel
RS B Zuber
SR W Masterson
C J Early
1B M Vernon
2B J Bloodworth
SS C Travis
3U G Archie
LF G Case
CF D Cramer
B Lewis
M B Harris

BOS 1942 NL
SP J Tobin
SP A Javery
SR L Tost
SR M Salvo
SP T Earley
RP J Sain
RS B Donovan
RP D Errickson
RP L Wallace
C E Lombardi
1L M West
2B S Sisti
SS E Miller
3L N Fernandez
LU- C Ross
CF T Holmes
RF P Waner
M Stengel

BRO 1942 NL
SP K Higbe
SP W Wyatt
SP C Davis
SR L French
SR E Head
RP H Casey
RS J Allen
RP L Webber
C M Owen
1B D Camilli
2B B Herman
SS P Reese
3B A Vaughan
LF J Medwick
CF P Reiser
RF D Walker
RF- J Rizzo
M L Durocher

CHI 1942 NL
SP C Passeau
SP B Lee
SR H Bithorn
SR V Olsen
SR B Fleming
RP L Warneke
C C McCullough
OI P Cavarretta
2B L Stringer
SS L Merullo
3B S Hack
LF L Novikoff
UO D Dallessandro
RF B Nicholson
IO R Russell
M J Wilson

CIN 1942 NL
SP R Starr
SP B Walters
SP V Vander Meer
SP P Derringer
SR E Riddle
RS J Thompson
RP J Beggs
RP C Shoun
C R Lamanno
1B F McCormick
1L B Frey
SS E Joost
3B B Haas
LM- E Tipton
MO G Walker
RL M Marshall
RU- I Goodman
M B McKechnie

NY 1942 NL
SP H Schumacher
SP B Carpenter
SP B Lohrman
SP C Hubbell
SP C Melton
RS H Feldman

RS B McGee
RP A Adams
C H Danning
1B J Mize
2B M Witek
SS B Jurges
3B B Werber
LF B Barna
LM W Marshall
RF M Ott
MU B Young
3S- D Bartell
MU-B Maynard

PHI 1942 NL
SP T Hughes
SR R Melton
SR S Johnson
SR J Podgajny
SR L Hoerst
RS I Pearson
RP S Nahem
RP E Naylor
RP B Beck
C - B Warren
1B N Etten
2B A Glossop
SU B Bragan
3B P May
LF D Litwhiler
ML E Koy
RF R Northey
UI D Murtaugh
MU L Waner
OI- S Benjamin
C - M Livingston
M H Lobert

PIT 1942 NL
SP R Sewell
SR B Klinger
SP M Butcher
SP K Heintzelman
SR H Gornicki
RS D Dietz
RS J Lanning
RP L Hamlin
RS L Wilkie
C A Lopez
1B E Fletcher
2B F Gustine
SS P Coscarart
3B B Elliott
RL J Wasdell
CF V DiMaggio
RU- J Barrett
C B Phelps
LF M Van Robays
UT- B Stewart
M F Frisch

STL 1942 NL
SP M Cooper
SR J Beazley
SR H Gumbert
SR M Lanier
SP E White
RS M Dickson
RS H Krist
RS H Pollet
C W Cooper
1B J Hopp
2B- C Crespi
SS M Marion
3B W Kurowski
LF S Musial
CF T Moore
RF- E Slaughter
23 J Brown
1B R Sanders
M B Southworth

BOS 1942 AL
SP T Hughson
SP C Wagner
SP J Dobson
SP D Newsome
SR O Judd
RS B Butland
RP M Brown
C - B Conroy
1B T Lupien
2B B Doerr
SS J Pesky
3B J Tabor
LF T Williams
CF D DiMaggio
RF L Finney
RF- P Fox
C - J Peacock
M J Cronin

CHI 1942 AL
SP J Humphries
SP E Smith
SP T Lyons
SP B Dietrich

SP B Ross
RP J Haynes
C - M Tresh
1B J Kuhel
2B D Kolloway
SS L Appling
3B B Kennedy
LF- T Wright
ML M Hoag
RF W Moses
M J Dykes

CLE 1942 AL
SP J Bagby
SP M Harder
SP C Dean
SP A Smith
SP A Milnar
RS V Kennedy
RP T Ferrick
RP H Eisenstat
C - O Denning
1B L Fleming
2B R Mack
SS L Boudreau
3B K Keltner
LF J Heath
CF R Weatherly
RF O Hockett
UO-B Mills

DET 1942 AL
SP A Benton
SP D Trout
SP H White
SR H Newhouser
SP T Bridges
RP V Trucks
RP R Henshaw
RP J Gorsica
C B Tebbetts
1B R York
2B J Bloodworth
SS- B Hitchcock
3B P Higgins
LF B McCosky
CF D Cramer
RF N Harris
OI- D Ross
M D Baker

NY 1942 AL
SP T Bonham
SP S Chandler
SP R Ruffing
SP H Borowy
SP M Breuer
RP A Donald
CL J Murphy
RP J Lindell
C - B Dickey
1B B Hassett
2B J Gordon
SS P Rizzuto
3B- F Crosetti
LF C Keller
CF J DiMaggio
RF T Henrich
M J McCarthy

PHI 1942 AL
SP P Marchildon
SP R Wolff
SP L Harris
SR R Christopher
SR D Fowler
RS H Besse
RP J Knott
C H Wagner
1B D Siebert
2B- B Knickerbocker
S3 P Suder
3B B Blair
LF B Johnson
CF M Kreevich
RF E Valo
UO D Miles
2S- C Davis
M C Mack

STL 1942 AL
SP E Auker
SP J Niggeling
SP D Galehouse
SR A Hollingsworth
SP B Muncrief
RP S Sundra
RP G Caster
C R Ferrell
1B G McQuinn
2B D Gutteridge
SS V Stephens
3B H Clift
LU G McQuillen
CF W Judnich
RL C Laabs

UO T Criscola
M L Sewell

WAS 1942 AL
SP H Hudson
SP B Newsom
SP E Wynn
SR A Carrasquel
SR W Masterson
RS B Zuber
C J Early
1B M Vernon
2B- E Clary
SS J Sullivan
3O B Estalella
LR G Case
CF S Spence
RU B Campbell
SI- J Pofahl
UI- B Repass
M B Harris

BOS 1943 NL
SP A Javery
SP N Andrews
SP R Barrett
SP J Tobin
SP M Salvo
RP D Odom
C - P Masi
1B- J McCarthy
2B C Ryan
SS W Wietelmann
32 B Joost
LF B Nieman
CF T Holmes
RF C Workman
LC C Ross
1B- K Farrell
M1 B Coleman
M2 C Stengel

BRO 1943 NL
SP K Higbe
SP W Wyatt
SR E Head
SR C Davis
SR B Newsom
RP L Webber
RS R Melton
C M Owen
1B D Camilli
2B B Herman
3B A Glossop
S3 A Vaughan
RL D Walker
MU A Galan
RU- P Waner
OI- F Bordagaray
M L Durocher

CHI 1943 NL
SP C Passeau
SP H Bithorn
SR P Derringer
SR H Wyse
SR E Hanyzewski
RS R Prim
C - C McCullough
1B P Cavarretta
2B E Stanky
SS L Merullo
3B S Hack
LF- L Novikoff
CF P Lowrey
RF B Nicholson
OF- D Dallessandro
LU- I Goodman
M J Wilson

CIN 1943 NL
SP J Vander Meer
SP E Riddle
SP B Walters
SP R Starr
RS C Shoun
RP J Beggs
C R Mueller
1B F McCormick
2B L Frey
SS E Miller
3B S Mesner
LF E Tipton
MO G Walker
RF M Marshall
UO E Crabtree
IO B Haas
M B McKechnie

NY 1943 NL
SP C Melton
SR J Wittig
SP R Fischer
SP K Chase
RS V Mungo
RP A Adams
RS H Feldman

RP B Sayles
C G Mancuso
1B- J Orengo
2B M Witek
SU B Jurges
3S D Bartell
LF- J Medwick
CF J Rucker
RF M Ott
IO S Gordon
CU E Lombardi
OI B Maynard

PHI 1943 NL
SP A Gerheauser
SP J Kraus
SP S Rowe
SP D Barrett
SP S Johnson
RS N Kimball
C - M Livingston
1L J Wasdell
2B D Murtaugh
SU G Stewart
3B P May
LF C Triplett
CF B Adams
RF R Northey
13 B Dahlgren
M1 B Harris
M2 F Fitzsimmons

PIT 1943 NL
SP R Sewell
SR M Butcher
SP B Klinger
SR W Hebert
SR H Gornicki
RS X Rescigno
RP B Brandt
C A Lopez
1B E Fletcher
2S P Coscarart
S2 F Gustine
3B B Elliott
LF J Russell
CF V DiMaggio
RU J Barrett
OI- T O'Brien
M F Frisch

STL 1943 NL
SP M Cooper
SP M Lanier
SR H Krist
SR H Brecheen
SP H Gumbert
RP H Pollet
RS M Dickson
RS M Munger
C W Cooper
1B R Sanders
2B L Klein
SS M Marion
3B W Kurowski
LF- D Litwhiler
CF H Walker
RO S Musial
UT- D Garms
OI- J Hopp
M B Southworth

BOS 1943 AL
SP T Hughson
SP Y Terry
SP J Dobson
SP O Judd
SP D Newsome
RS M Ryba
RP M Brown
RS P Woods
C R Partee
1B T Lupien
2B B Doerr
SS J Tabor
ML- L Culberson
MR-C Metkovich
RF P Fox
LU- J Lazor
M J Cronin

CHI 1943 AL
SP O Grove
SP J Humphries
SP E Smith
SP B Dietrich
SP B Ross
RP T Lee
RP G Maltzberger
RP J Haynes
RP B Swift
C - M Tresh
1B J Kuhel
2B- D Kolloway
SS L Appling
UT R Hodgin

LF G Curtright
CF T Tucker
RF W Moses
M J Dykes

CLE 1943 AL
SP J Bagby
SP A Smith
SR A Reynolds
SR V Kennedy
SP M Harder
RP J Heving
RP M Naymick
C B Rosar
1B R Rocco
2B R Mack
SS L Boudreau
3B K Keltner
LF J Heath
MO O Hockett
RF R Cullenbine
CF H Edwards
3I- R Peters

DET 1943 AL
SR D Trout
SP V Trucks
SR H Newhouser
SP T Bridges
SP H White
RS S Overmire
RP J Gorsica
RP R Henshaw
C P Richards
1B R York
2B J Bloodworth
SS J Hoover
3B P Higgins
LF D Wakefield
CF D Cramer
RF N Harris
UT- D Ross
M S O'Neill

NY 1943 AL
SP S Chandler
SP T Bonham
SP B Wensloff
SP H Borowy
SP B Zuber
RP A Donald
RS M Russo
RP J Murphy
C - B Dickey
1B N Etten
2B J Gordon
SS F Crosetti
3B B Johnson
LF C Keller
RM J Lindell
RF B Metheny
SS- S Stirnweiss
CF- R Weatherly
M J McCarthy

PHI 1943 AL
SP J Flores
SR R Wolff
SP L Harris
SP D Black
SR O Arntzen
RP R Christopher
C - H Wagner
1B D Siebert
2I P Suder
SS I Hall
3B E Mayo
LF B Estalella
CF J White
UO J Welaj
C - B Swift
RU- E Valo
M C Mack

STL 1943 AL
SP D Galehouse
SP S Sundra
SP B Muncrief
SR N Potter
SR A Hollingsworth
RP J Niggeling
RP G Caster
C - F Hayes
1B G McQuinn
2B D Gutteridge
SS V Stephens
3B H Clift
LF C Laabs
MO M Byrnes
RU M Chartak
UI M Christman
M L Sewell

WAS 1943 AL
SP E Wynn
SP D Leonard
SR M Haefner

SP M Candini
RS A Carrasquel
RS J Mertz
C J Early
1B M Vernon
2B J Priddy
SS J Sullivan
3B- E Clary
LF B Johnson
CF S Spence
RF G Case
OI G Moore
M O Bluege

BOS 1944 NL
SP J Tobin
SP N Andrews
SP A Javery
SR R Barrett
RS I Hutchinson
CU- P Masi
1B B Etchison
2B- C Ryan
SS W Wietelmann
3S D Phillips
LR B Nieman
CF T Holmes
RU C Workman
1U M Macon
CU- C Kluttz
M B Coleman

BRO 1944 NL
SP H Gregg
SP C Davis
SR R Melton
RS L Webber
C M Owen
1B H Schultz
2S- E Stanky
SC B Bragan
3B F Bordagaray
LF A Galan
MU-G Rosen
RF D Walker
UT L Olmo
OF- P Waner
M L Durocher

CHI 1944 NL
SP H Wyse
SP C Passeau
SR P Derringer
SR B Fleming
SP B Chipman
RS H Vandenberg
RS P Erickson
C - D Williams
1B P Cavarretta
2B D Johnson
SS- L Merullo
3B S Hack
LF D Dallessandro
CF A Pafko
RF B Nicholson
3S R Hughes
M1 J Wilson
M2 R Johnson
M3 C Grimm

CIN 1944 NL
SP B Walters
SR C Shoun
SP E Heusser
SR T DeLa Cruz
SP H Gumbert
RS A Carter
RP J Konstanty
C R Mueller
1B F McCormick
2B W Williams
SS E Miller
3B S Mesner
LF E Tipton
CF D Clay
RM G Walker
M B McKechnie

NY 1944 NL
SP B Voiselle
SR H Feldman
SR E Pyle
SR R Fischer
RP A Adams
RP A Hansen
C - E Lombardi
1B P Weintraub
2B G Hausmann
SS B Kerr
32 H Luby
LF J Medwick
CF J Rucker
RF M Ott
13 N Reyes
3U- N Jurges
C - G Mancuso

PHI 1944 NL
SP K Raffensberger
SR C Schanz
SP D Barrett
SP B Lee
SP A Gerheauser
RP A Karl
C B Finley
1B T Lupien
2B M Mullen
SS- R Hamrick
3S G Stewart
LF J Wasdell
CF B Adams
RF R Northey
UI C Letchas
3U- T Cieslak
C - J Peacock
UO-C Triplett
M F Fitzsimmons

PIT 1944 NL
SP R Sewell
SP F Ostermueller
SP M Butcher
SR N Strincevich
SR P Roe
RS X Rescigno
RPC Cuccurullo
C A Lopez
1B B Dahlgren
2B P Coscarart
SS F Gustine
3B B Elliott
LF J Russell
CF V DiMaggio
RM J Barrett
RU F Colman
OI- T O'Brien
UT- A Rubeling
SS- F Zak
M F Frisch

STL 1944 NL
SP M Cooper
SP M Lanier
SR T Wilks
SP H Brecheen
SR A Jurisich
RP H Munger
RS F Schmidt
RP B Donnelly
C W Cooper
1B R Sanders
2B E Verban
SS M Marion
3B W Kurowski
LF D Litwhiler
CF J Hopp
RF S Musial
OI- A Bergamo
C - K O'Dea
M B Southworth

BOS 1944 AL
SP T Hughson
SP P Woods
SP J Bowman
SP E O'Neill
SR C Hausmann
RS M Ryba
RS Y Terry
RP F Barrett
C - R Partee
1B- L Finney
3B D Doerr
SS S Newsome
3B J Tabor
LF B Johnson
M1 C Metkovich
RF P Fox
32- J Bucher
M J Cronin

CHI 1944 AL
SP B Dietrich
SP O Grove
SP E Lopat
SR J Humphries
SR J Haynes
RP T Lee
RP G Maltzberger
C M Tresh
1B H Trosky
2B R Schalk
SS S Webb
3L R Hodgin
OI E Carnett
CF T Tucker
RF W Moses
M J Dykes

CLE 1944 AL
SR S Gromek
SR M Harder
SR E Klieman
SP A Smith

SP A Reynolds
RP J Heving
RS R Poat
RP P Calvert
C B Rosar
1B M Rocco
2B- R Mack
SS L Boudreau
3B K Keltner
LU P Seerey
ML O Hockett
RF R Cullenbine
2U- R Peters

DET 1944 AL
SP D Trout
SR H Newhouser
SP R Gentry
SP S Overmire
SR J Gorsica
RP B Beck
C P Richards
1B R York
2B E Mayo
SS J Hoover
3B P Higgins
LF- D Wakefield
CF D Cramer
LR J Outlaw
RU- C Hostetler
C - B Swift
M S O'Neill

NY 1944 AL
SP H Borowy
SP M Dubiel
SP T Bonham
SR A Donald
SP B Zuber
RP J Page
C - M Garbark
1B N Etten
2B S Stirnweiss
SS M Milosevich
3B O Grimes
LF- H Martin
CF J Lindell
RF B Metheny
C - R Hemsley
M J McCarthy

PHI 1944 AL
SP B Newsom
SR R Christopher
SP L Hamlin
SP J Flores
RP L Harris
RP J Berry
C F Hayes
1B- B McGhee
2S I Hall
SS E Busch
3B G Kell
LF F Garrison
MU B Estalella
RU- J White
1L D Siebert
M C Mack

STL 1944 AL
SP J Kramer
SP N Potter
SP B Muncrief
SR S Jakucki
SP D Galehouse
RS- A Hollingsworth
RP G Caster
C - F Mancuso
1B B McQuinn
2B D Gutteridge
SS V Stephens
3B M Christman
UO M Byrnes
CF M Kreevich
RF G Moore
LU A Zarilla
C - R Hayworth
M L Sewell

WAS 1944 AL
SP M Haefner
SP D Leonard
SP E Wynn
SP J Niggeling
SR R Wolff
RS- A Carrasquel
RS M Candini
RP B Lefebvre
C R Ferrell
1B J Kuhel
2B G Myatt
SS J Sullivan
3B G Torres
LO G Case
CF S Spence
RF- R Ortiz

LR J Powell
M O Bluege

BOS 1945 NL
SP J Tobin
SP B Logan
SP N Andrews
SP E Wright
SP B Lee
RS J Hutchings
RP D Hendrickson
C P Masi
1B- V Shupe
2S W Wietelmann
SS D Culler
3B C Workman
OF B Nieman
CF C Gillenwater
RF T Holmes
OF- B Ramsey
M1 F Fitzsimmons
M2 B Chapman

BRO 1945 NL
SP H Gregg
SR V Lombardi
SP C Davis
SP A Herring
SR T Seats
RP C King
RP R Branca
RP C Buker
CS- M Sandlock
IO A Galan
2B E Stanky
SS E Basinski
3U F Bordagaray
LU L Olmo
CF G Rosen
RF D Walker
M L Durocher

CHI 1945 NL
SP H Wyse
SP C Passeau
SP P Derringer
SR R Prim
SP H Borowy
RS P Erickson
RS H Vandenberg
C - M Livingston
1B P Cavarretta
2B D Johnson
SS L Merullo
3B S Hack
LF P Lowrey
CF A Pafko
RF B Nicholson
M C Grimm

CIN 1945 NL
SP E Heusser
SP J Bowman
SP B Walters
SP V Kennedy
SP F Dasso
RS H Fox
RP H Lisenbee
C - A Lakeman
1B F McCormick
2B W Williams
SS E Miller
3B S Mesner
LF E Tipton
CF D Clay
RU A Libke
RU G Walker
OF- D Sipek
M B McKechnie

NY 1945 AL
SP B Voiselle
SP H Feldman
SP V Mungo
SP J Brewer
SR A Hansen
RP A Adams
RS S Emmerich
RP R Fischer
C E Lombardi
1B- P Weintraub
2B G Hausmann
SS B Kerr
3B N Reyes
LU D Gardella
CF J Rucker
RF M Ott
UO- R Treadway

PHI 1945 NL
SP D Barrett
SR C Schanz
SR C Sproull
SP D Mauney
RP A Karl
C - A Seminick
OI J Wasdell

2B- T Daniels
S2- B Mott
3B J Antonelli
LF C Triplett
CF V DiMaggio
OI V Dinges
OP R Monteagudo
UT- G Crawford
IF- J Foxx
M1 F Fitzsimmons
M2 B Chapman

PIT 1945 NL
SP P Roe
SP N Strincevich
SP R Sewell
SP M Butcher
SR A Gerheauser
RS K Gables
RP X Rescigno
RP C Cuccurullo
C - A Lopez
1B B Dahlgren
2B P Coscarart
SS F Gustine
3R B Elliott
LF J Russell
MU A Gionfriddo
MR J Barrett
3B L Handley
C B Salkeld
UT- F Colman
M F Frisch

STL 1945 NL
SP R Barrett
SR K Burkhart
SP B Donnelly
SP H Brecheen
SR G Dockins
RP T Wilks
RS B Byerly
RS A Jurisich
C K O'Dea
1B R Sanders
2B E Verban
SS M Marion
3B W Kurowski
LF R Schoendienst
CF B Adams
RU J Hopp
RU A Bergamo
C - D Rice
M B Southworth

BOS 1945 AL
SP D Ferriss
SP J Wilson
SP E O'Neill
SR C Hausmann
SP R Woods
RS M Ryba
RP R Heflin
RP F Barrett
C - B Garbark
1O C Metkovich
2S S Newsome
SS E Lake
3B- J Tobin
LF B Johnson
CF L Culberson
RU J Lazor
MO T McBride
2B- B Steiner
M J Cronin

CHI 1945 AL
SP T Lee
SP O Grove
SP E Lopat
SP J Humphries
SP B Dietrich
RS E Caldwell
RP J Haynes
RP J Johnson
C M Tresh
1B K Farrell
2B R Schalk
SS C Michaels
3B T Cuccinello
LF J Dickshot
CF O Hockett
RF W Moses
UO G Curtright
3U- F Baker
M J Dykes

CLE 1945 AL
SP S Gromek
SR A Reynolds
SP J Bagby
SP A Smith
RS E Klieman
RS P Center
RP J Salveson
C F Hayes
1B M Rocco

2B D Meyer
SS L Boudreau
3B D Ross
LF J Heath
CF F Mackiewicz
RL P Seerey
UI A Cihocki
RU- P O'Dea

DET 1945 AL
SP H Newhouser
SR D Trout
SP A Benton
SP S Overmire
SP L Mueller
RP W Wilson
RP G Caster
C B Swift
1B R York
2B E Mayo
SS S Webb
3B B Maier
LU J Outlaw
CF D Cramer
RF R Cullenbine
LF- H Greenberg
C - P Richards
M S O'Neill

NY 1945 AL
SP B Bevens
SP T Bonham
SR A Gettel
SP M Dubiel
SP H Borowy
RP B Zuber
RS J Page
RP J Turner
RP K Holcombe
C - M Garbark
1B N Etten
2B S Stirnweiss
SS F Crosetti
3B O Grimes
LF H Martin
CF T Stainback
RF B Metheny
MO- R Derry
M J McCarthy

PHI 1945 AL
SP B Newsom
SP R Christopher
SP J Flores
SR L Knerr
SP D Black
RP J Berry
RS C Gassaway
RS S Gerkin
C B Rosar
1B D Siebert
2B I Hall
SS E Busch
3B G Kell
UO- M Smith
CF B Estalella
RF H Peck
OI B McGhee
M C Mack

STL 1945 AL
SP N Potter
SP J Kramer
SP S Jakucki
SP T Shirley
SP A Hollingsworth
RS B Muncrief
RP S Zoldak
C - F Mancuso
1B G McQuinn
2B D Gutteridge
SS V Stephens
3B- M Christman
OI M Byrnes
CF- M Kreevich
RF G Moore
32 L Schulte
OF- P Gray
M L Sewell

WAS 1945 AL
SP R Wolff
SP M Haefner
SR M Pieretti
SP D Leonard
SP J Niggeling
RS A Carrasquel
RS S Ullrich
C - R Ferrell
1B J Kuhel
2U G Myatt
SS G Torres
3B H Clift
LO G Case
MO G Binks
1B M Rocco

2B- F Vaughn
M O Bluege

BOS 1946 NL
SP J Sain
SP M Cooper
SR E Wright
SP B Lee
SR S Johnson
RP W Spahn
RS L Wallace
C P Masi
1B- R Sanders
2B C Ryan
SS D Culler
3U N Fernandez
LU B Rowell
MU C Gillenwater
RF T Holmes
1M J Hopp
LF- D Litwhiler
M B Southworth

BRO 1946 NL
SR J Hatten
SR K Higbe
SR V Lombardi
SR H Gregg
SR R Melton
RS H Behrman
RP H Casey
RP A Herring
C - B Edwards
1B E Stevens
2B E Stanky
SS P Reese
3B- C Lavagetto
LU P Reiser
CF C Furillo
RF D Walker
LI A Galan
ML D Whitman
C - F Anderson
1B- H Schultz
M L Durocher

CHI 1946 NL
SR J Schmitz
SR H Wyse
SP H Borowy
SR P Erickson
SP C Passeau
RS E Kush
RS B Chipman
C C McCullough
1B B Waitkus
2B- D Johnson
SS- B Jurges
3B- S Hack
LO M Rickert
LM P Lowrey
R1 P Cavarretta
RF B Nicholson
SU B Sturgeon
2B- L Stringer
M C Grimm

CIN 1946 NL
SP J Vander Meer
SP E Blackwell
SP J Beggs
SP E Heusser
SP B Walters
RS J Hetki
RS C Shoun
RP B Malloy
C R Mueller
1B B Haas
2B B Adams
SS- E Miller
3B G Hatton
LU E Lukon
CF D Clay
RF A Libke
2O L Frey
SS- C Corbitt
CU- R Lamanno
OI- B Usher
23- B Zientara
M1 B McKechnie
M2 H Gowdy

NY 1946 NL
SP D Koslo
SR M Kennedy
SR B Voiselle
SR H Schumacher
RS K Trinkle
RS M Budnick
RP J Thompson
C - W Cooper
1B J Mize
2B B Blattner
SS B Kerr
3S B Rigney
LU S Gordon

UO W Marshall
RM G Rosen
RU J Graham
MU J Rucker
UT B Young
CU- E Lombardi
23- M Ott
M M Ott

PHI 1946 NL
SR K Raffensberger
SP O Judd
SP S Rowe
SR C Schanz
SR T Hughes
RP A Karl
RS D Mulligan
C A Seminick
1B F McCormick
2B E Verban
SS S Newsome
3B J Tabor
LF D Ennis
CF J Wyrostek
RF R Northey
RO- C Gilbert
UI- R Mueller
M B Chapman

PIT 1946 NL
SP F Ostermueller
SR N Strincevich
SP K Heintzelman
SP R Sewell
SR E Bahr
RS J Hallett
RS K Gables
RP A Gerheauser
C - A Lopez
1B E Fletcher
2B F Gustine
SS B Cox
3B L Handley
OI J Russell
ML R Kiner
R3 B Elliott
UI- J Brown
M1 F Frisch
M2 S Davis

STL 1946 NL
SP H Pollet
SP H Brecheen
SR M Dickson
SR A Brazle
SP J Beazley
RS K Burkhart
RP T Wilks
C - J Garagiola
1L S Musial
2B R Schoendienst
SS M Marion
3B W Kurowski
LU E Dusak
MU H Walker
RF E Slaughter
OF- B Adams
MU- T Moore
UT- D Sisler
M E Dyer

BOS 1946 AL
SP T Hughson
SP D Ferriss
SP M Harris
SP J Dobson
SR J Bagby
RS E Johnson
RP B Klinger
RP C Dreisewerd
C H Wagner
1B R York
2B B Doerr
SS J Pesky
3B- R Russell
LF T Williams
CF D DiMaggio
RF- C Metkovich
M J Cronin

CHI 1946 AL
SP E Lopat
SP O Grove
SP J Haynes
SP E Smith
SR F Papish
RP E Caldwell
RS R Hamner
RP A Hollingsworth
C - M Tresh
1B- H Trosky
23 D Kolloway
SS L Appling
3B- D Lodigiani
L3 B Kennedy
IF- J Lucadello
M1 L Sewell
M2 Z Taylor

LU- R Hodgin
2U- C Michaels
UO- W Platt
M1 J Dykes
M2 T Lyons

CLE 1946 AL
SP B Feller
SP R Embree
SP A Reynolds
SP S Gromek
RS B Lemon
RS J Krakauskas
C - J Hegan
1B L Fleming
2B- D Meyer
SS L Boudreau
3B K Keltner
LF G Case
UO P Seerey
RF H Edwards
CF- F Mackiewicz

DET 1946 AL
SP H Newhouser
SP D Trout
SP V Trucks
SP F Hutchinson
SR A Benton
RS S Overmire
C - B Tebbetts
1B H Greenberg
2B- J Bloodworth
SS E Lake
3B G Kell
LF D Wakefield
CF- H Evers
RU R Cullenbine
RF P Mullin
OI- J Outlaw
M S O'Neill

NY 1946 AL
SP S Chandler
SP B Bevens
SR J Page
SR B Gumpert
SP T Bonham
RS A Gettel
C - A Robinson
1B N Etten
2B J Gordon
SS P Rizzuto
32 S Stirnweiss
LF C Keller
CF J DiMaggio
R1 T Henrich
OI J Lindell
3B- B Johnson
M1 J McCarthy
M2 B Dickey
M3 J Neun

PHI 1946 AL
SP P Marchildon
SP D Fowler
SR B Savage
SR J Dyers
SP L Knerr
RS L Harris
RS R Christopher
C B Rosar
1B G McQuinn
2B- G Handley
S3 P Suder
3B- H Majeski
LM S Chapman
CF- B McCosky
RF E Valo
UO- T Stainback
M C Mack

STL 1946 AL
SP J Kramer
SP J Galehouse
SR S Zoldak
SP N Potter
SP T Shirley
RS B Muncrief
RS E Kinder
RS S Ferens
C - F Mancuso
1B C Stevens
2B J Berardino
SS V Stephens
3S M Christman
LF- J Heath
CF W Judnich
UO A Zarilla
3U- B Dillinger
RF- C Laabs
IF- J Lucadello
M1 L Sewell
M2 Z Taylor

WAS 1946 AL
SP M Haefner
SP B Newsom
SP D Leonard
SR Scarborough
SR S Hudson
RP R Wolff
RP M Pieretti
C - A Evans
1B M Vernon
2B J Priddy
S3 B Hitchcock
S3 C Travis
LF- J Grace
CF S Spence
RF B Lewis
M O Bluege

BOS 1947 NL
SP W Spahn
SP J Sain
SR B Barrett
SP B Voiselle
RS J Johnson
RP C Shoun
RP W Lanfranconi
RS E Wright
C P Masi
1B E Torgeson
2B C Ryan
SS- D Culler
3B B Elliott
LF B Rowell
CF J Hopp
RF T Holmes
SU- N Fernandez
LU- D Litwhiler
1U- F McCormick
ML- M McCormick
M B Southworth

BRO 1947 NL
SP R Branca
SR J Hatten
SR V Lombardi
SR H Taylor
SR H Gregg
RS H Behrman
CL H Casey
RS R Barney
C - B Edwards
1B J Robinson
2B E Stanky
SS P Reese
3B S Jorgensen
ML P Reiser
CF C Furillo
RF D Walker
LF- G Hermanski
M1 C Sukeforth
M2 B Shotton

CHI 1947 NL
SR J Schmitz
SP D Lade
SR H Borowy
SR P Erickson
SR H Wyse
RS B Chipman
RP E Kush
RP J Meers
C B Scheffing
1B E Waitkus
2B D Johnson
SS L Merullo
3B P Lowrey
LO P Cavarretta
CF A Pafko
RF B Nicholson
CU- C McCullough
S2- B Sturgeon
M C Grimm

CIN 1947 NL
SP E Blackwell
SP J Vander Meer
SR K Peterson
SR B Lively
SP B Walters
RS E Erautt
RP K Raffensberger
RP H Gumbert
RS J Hetki
C - R Lamanno
1B B Young
2B B Zientara
SS E Miller
3B G Hatton
LF A Galan
OI B Haas
RF F Baumholtz
2B- B Adams
OF- E Lukon
MU- C Vollmer
M J Neun

Hometown Heroes: Team Rosters

NY 1947 NL
SR L Jansen
SP D Koslo
SR M Kennedy
SP C Hartung
RP K Trinkle
RP J Beggs
C W Cooper
1B J Mize
23 B Rigney
SS B Kerr
3B J Lohrke
LF S Gordon
CF B Thomson
RF W Marshall
M M Ott

PHI 1947 NL
SP D Leonard
SP S Rowe
SR O Judd
SP K Heintzelman
SR T Hughes
RS B Donnelly
SR A Jurisich
RS C Schanz
RS F Schmidt
C A Seminick
1B H Schultz
2B E Verban
SS S Newsome
3B L Handley
LF D Ennis
CF H Walker
RF J Wyrostek
UO-C Gilbert
M B Chapman

PIT 1947 NL
SR K Higbe
SP F Ostermueller
SR T Bonham
SR P Roe
SR R Sewell
RS J Bagby
RS N Strincevich
RP E Singleton
C- D Howell
1B H Greenberg
2B- J Bloodworth
SS B Cox
3B F Gustine
LF R Kiner
CF J Russell
RF W Westlake
UO C Rikard
M1 Herman
M2 B Burwell

STL 1947 NL
SR M Dickson
SP R Munger
SP H Brecheen
SR H Pollet
SR A Brazle
RS J Hearn
RS K Burkhart
RP T Wilks
C D Rice
1B S Musial
2B R Schoendienst
SS M Marion
3B W Kurowski
LU E Slaughter
CF T Moore
RU R Northey
UO C Diering
OI B Dusak
M E Dyer

BOS 1947 AL
SP J Dobson
SP D Ferriss
SP T Hughson
SR E Johnson
SP D Galehouse
RS H Dorish
RP J Murphy
RP B Zuber
C- B Tebbetts
1B J Jones
2B B Doerr
SS J Pesky
3B- S Dente
LF T Williams
CF D DiMaggio
RO S Mele
RU- W Moses
M J Cronin

CHI 1947 AL
SP E Lopat
SR F Papish
SP J Haynes
SP O Grove
SP B Gillespie
SR E Harrist
RP P Gebrian
RP G Maltzberger
RP E Caldwell
C- M Tresh
1B R York
2B D Kolloway
SS L Appling
3B F Baker
RL T Wright
ML D Philley
RF B Kennedy
23 C Michaels
C- G Dickey
MU-T Tucker
IO- J Wallaesa
M T Lyons

WAS 1947 AL
SP W Masterson
SP E Wynn
SP M Haefner
SR R Scarborough
SP S Hudson
RP M Candini
RP T Ferrick
RP S Cary
C A Evans
1B M Vernon
2B J Priddy
SS M Christman
3B E Yost
LU- J Grace
CF S Spence
RF B Lewis
LU S Robertson
M O Bluege

CLE 1947 AL
SP B Feller
SP D Black
SR B Lemon
SP R Embree
SR A Gettel
RP E Klieman
RS B Stephens
RS S Gromek
C J Hegan
1B E Robinson
2B J Gordon
SS L Boudreau
3B K Keltner
LM D Mitchell
CF C Metkovich
RL H Edwards
1U L Fleming
RF H Peck
LU- P Seerey

DET 1947 AL
SP H Newhouser
SP F Hutchinson
SP D Trout
SR V Trucks
SR S Overmire
RS A Benton
RS A Houtteman
RS H White
RP J Gorsica
C B Swift
1B- R Cullenbine
2B E Mayo
SS E Lake
3B G Kell
LF D Wakefield
CF H Evers
RF P Mullin
UO V Wertz
M S O'Neill

NY 1947 AL
SP A Reynolds
SP S Shea
SP B Bevens
SP S Chandler
SP B Newsom
RP J Page
RP V Raschi
RS R Gumpert
C- A Robinson
1B G McQuinn
2B S Stirnweiss
SS P Rizzuto
3B B Johnson
LF J Lindell
CF J DiMaggio
RF T Henrich
CO-Y Berra
M B Harris

PHI 1947 AL
SP P Marchildon
SP D Fowler
SR B McCahan
SR J Coleman
SP J Flores
RS B Savage
RP C Scheib
RP R Christopher
C B Rosar
1B F Fain
2B P Suder
SS E Joost
3B H Majeski
LF B McCosky
CF S Chapman
RF E Valo
OI G Binks
M C Mack

STL 1947 AL
SP J Kramer
SP E Kinder
SR F Sanford
SP B Muncrief
SR S Zoldak
RP C Fannin
RS N Potter
RP G Moulder
C L Moss
1B W Judnich
2B- J Berardino
SS V Stephens
3B B Dillinger
LF J Heath
CF P Lehner
RO A Zarilla
RU R Coleman
C- J Early
2I- B Hitchcock
M M Ruel

NY 1948 NL
SP L Jansen
SR S Jones
SR R Poat
SR C Hartung
SR D Koslo
RP M Kennedy
RS A Hansen
RP K Trinkle
C- W Cooper
1B J Mize
2B B Rigney
SS B Kerr
3B S Gordon
UO B Thomson
ML W Lockman
RF W Marshall
32 J Lohrke
M1 M Ott
M2 L Durocher

PHI 1948 NL
SP D Leonard
SP C Simmons
SR M Dubiel
SR S Rowe
SP R Roberts
RP B Donnelly
RS K Heintzelman
RP E Heusser
RP S Nahem
C A Seminick
1B D Sisler
2S G Hamner
SS E Miller
3U P Caballero
LF J Blatnik
CF R Ashburn
RF D Ennis
31 B Haas
MU H Walker
UT- B Rowell
M1 B Chapman
M2 D Cooke
M3 E Sawyer

PIT 1948 NL
SP B Chesnes
SP E Riddle
SR V Lombardi
SP T Bonham
SP F Ostermueller
RS K Higbe
RP R Sewell
RS E Singleton
RS M Queen
C E Fitz Gerald
1B E Stevens
2B D Murtaugh
SS S Rojek
3B F Gustine
LF R Kiner
MR W Westlake
RF D Walker
MU J Hopp
C C Kluttz
UT- M West
M B Meyer

BOS 1948 NL
SP J Sain
SP W Spahn
SP B Voiselle
SR V Bickford
SR R Barrett
RP B Hogue
RP C Shoun
C P Masi
1B E Torgeson
2B- E Stanky
SS A Dark
3B B Elliott
LF J Heath
CF- J Russell
RF T Holmes
UO M McCormick
ML- C Conatser
C- B Salkeld
2S- S Sisti
M B Southworth

BRO 1948 NL
SR R Barney
SP R Branca
SR J Hatten
SR P Roe
RS E Palica
RP H Behrman
RP P Minner
RP W Ramsdell
C- R Campanella
1C G Hodges
2B J Robinson
SS P Reese
3B- B Cox
UO-M Rackley
CF C Furillo
RF G Hermanski
CU E Edwards
23- E Miksis
M1 L Durocher
M2 R Blades
M3 B Shotton

CHI 1948 NL
SP J Schmitz
SP R Meyer
SR D McCall
SR B Rush
SR H Borowy
RS R Hamner
RS C Chambers
RP J Dobernic
RP E Kush
C B Scheffing
1B E Waitkus
2B E Schenz
SS R Smalley
3B A Pafko
UT P Lowrey
CF H Jeffcoat
RF B Nicholson
UT P Cavarretta
LU- R Walker
CU- R Maddern
M C Grimm

STL 1948 NL
SR M Dickson
SP H Brecheen
SR H Pollet
SR R Munger
SR A Brazle
RP T Wilks
RP G Staley
C D Rice
1B N Jones
2B R Schoendienst
SS M Marion
3B D Lang
LR E Slaughter
CF- T Moore
OI S Musial
UT E Dusak
RU R Northey
3B- W Kurowski
2S- R LaPointe
M E Dyer

CIN 1948 NL
SP J Vander Meer
SR K Raffensberger
SR H Fox
SP H Wehmeier
SP E Blackwell
SP K Peterson
RP H Gumbert
RP W Cress
C R Lamanno
1B T Kluszewski
2U- B Adams
SS V Stallcup
3B G Hatton
LF H Sauer
CF J Wyrostek
RO F Baumholtz
RU D Litwhiler
2I- C Corbitt
M1 J Neun
M2 B Walters

PHI 1948 AL
SP P Marchildon
SP J Coleman
SP D Fowler
SP C Scheib
SR L Brissie
RP B Harris
RP B Savage
C- B Rosar
1B F Fain
2B P Suder
SS E Joost
3B H Majeski
LF B McCosky
CF S Chapman
RF E Valo
OI- D White
M C Mack

BOS 1948 AL
SP J Dobson
SP M Parnell
SP J Kramer
SP E Kinder
SR D Galehouse
RS D Ferriss
RP M Harris
RP E Johnson
C T Tebbetts
1B B Goodman
2B B Doerr
SS V Stephens
3B J Pesky
LF T Williams
CF D DiMaggio
RU S Spence
RU- W Moses
M J McCarthy

CHI 1948 AL
SP B Wight
SP J Haynes
SP A Gettel
SP M Pieretti
SR F Papish
RS H Judson
RP R Gumpert
RS G Moulder
RS B Gillespie
C A Robinson
1B T Lupien
2U D Kolloway
SS S Dente
3B L Appling
LF P Seerey
CF D Philley
RF T Wright
3U F Baker
UO R Hodgin
M T Lyons

WAS 1948 AL
SP E Wynn
SP W Masterson
SP R Scarborough
SR S Hudson
SP M Haefner
RS F Thompson
RM M Candini
RP T Ferrick
RP D Welteroth
C J Early
1B M Vernon
2B A Kozar
SS M Christman
3B E Yost
LF G Coan
MR-J Wooten
C A Evans
CF- C Gillenwater
CF-T McBride
MR L Doby
RL- A Clark
OI- W Judnich
M J Kuhel

STL 1948 AL
SP F Sanford
SP C Fannin
SR N Garver
SP B Kennedy
RS B Stephens
RP F Biscan
RP A Widmar
C L Moss
1B- C Stevens
2B J Priddy
SS E Pellagrini
3B D Dillinger
LF W Platt
CF P Lehner
UO A Zarilla
SS S Dente
C- R Partee
M Z Taylor

CLE 1948 AL
SP B Lemon
SP B Feller
SR G Bearden
SR S Gromek
RP E Klieman
RP E Klieman
CL R Christopher
C J Hegan
1B E Robinson
2B J Gordon
SS L Boudreau
3B E Yost
LF D Mitchell
1B E Robinson
2B J Gordon
SS L Boudreau
3B W Jones
LF D Ennis
CF R Ashburn
RF D Walker
UT- S Sisti
OI- P Reiser
UI- C Ryan
UO-E Sauer
M1 B Southworth
M2 J Cooney

DET 1948 AL
SP H Newhouser
SP F Hutchinson
SP D Trout
SR V Trucks
SR S Overmire
RP J Gorsica
RS B Pierce
C B Swift
1B G Vico
2B E Mayo
SS J Lipon
3B- G Kell
LR V Wertz
CF H Evers
RF P Mullin
LF D Wakefield
M S O'Neill

NY 1948 AL
SP A Reynolds
SP E Lopat
SP V Raschi
SP S Shea
SR T Byrne
RP J Page
RS F Hiller
C- G Niarhos
1B G McQuinn
2B S Stirnweiss
SS P Rizzuto
3B B Johnson
LF- J Lindell
CF D DiMaggio
R1 T Henrich
CR Y Berra
UT B Brown
UT- C Keller
M B Harris

CHI 1949 NL
SP J Schmitz
SP J Rush
SP D Leonard
SR M Dubiel
RS W Hacker
RS B Chipman
RS D Adkins
RP B Muncrief
C- M Owen
1B H Reich
2B E Verban
SS R Smalley
3U- F Gustine
LF H Sauer
M3 A Pafko
MR H Jeffcoat
1U P Cavarretta
M1 C Grimm
M2 F Frisch

CIN 1949 NL
SP K Raffensberger
SP H Fox
SP H Wehmeier
SP J Vander Meer
RS E Erautt
RS B Lively
RP E Blackwell
RS K Peterson
C- W Cooper
2U J Bloodworth
SS V Stallcup
3B G Hatton
LF- P Lowrey
CF L Merriman
RM J Wyrostek
2U B Adams
RU D Litwhiler
OI- H Walker
M1 B Walters
M2 L Sewell

NY 1949 NL
SP L Jansen
SP M Kennedy
SR D Koslo
SR S Jones
SP C Hartung
RP K Higbe
RP H Behrman
RP A Hansen
C- W Westrum
1B J Mize
2B- H Thompson
SS- B Kerr
3B S Gordon
LF W Lockman
CF B Thomson
RF W Marshall
SI B Rigney
M L Durocher

PHI 1949 NL
SP K Heintzelman
SR R Roberts
SP R Meyer
SP H Borowy
SR C Simmons
RP J Konstanty
RP K Trinkle
RS R Rowe
C A Seminick
1B D Sisler
2B- E Miller
SS G Hamner
3B W Jones
LF D Ennis
CF R Ashburn
RF K Kennedy
SS- R Boone
OF- T Tucker
M E Sawyer

PIT 1949 NL
SR M Dickson
SP B Werle
SR C Chambers
SP B Chesnes
SR V Lombardi
RS R Sewell
C- R McCullough
OI- J Hopp
2B M Basgall
SS S Rojek
3B P Castiglione
LF R Kiner
MU-D Restelli
RM W Westlake
3B- E Bockman
1B- J Hopp
UT- D Walker
M B Meyer

STL 1949 NL
SR H Pollet
SP H Brecheen
SR A Brazle
SR G Staley
RP T Wilks
C- D Rice
1B N Jones
2B R Schoendienst
SS M Marion
3B- E Kazak
LF E Slaughter
CF C Diering
RM S Musial
C- J Garagiola
3B- T Glaviano
1B- R Nelson
RF- R Northey
M E Dyer

BOS 1949 NL
SP W Spahn
SP J Sain
SP V Bickford
SR J Antonelli
RP N Potter
RP B Hogue
RS B Hall
C- B Salkeld
1B E Fletcher
2B E Stanky
3B B Elliott
LR M Rickert
MU J Russell
RF T Holmes
UT S Sisti
OI- P Reiser
UI- C Ryan
UO-E Sauer
M1 B Southworth
M2 J Cooney

BRO 1949 NL
SP D Newcombe
SP P Roe
SP J Hatten
SR R Branca
SR R Barney
RS J Banta
RP E Palica
RP P Minner
C R Campanella
1B G Hodges
2B J Robinson
SS P Reese
3B B Cox
LU-G Hermanski
CF D Snider
RF C Furillo
M B Shotton

BOS 1949 AL
SP M Parnell
SR E Kinder
SP J Dobson
SP C Stobbs
SP J Kramer
RP T Hughson
RP E Johnson
C B Tebbetts
1B B Goodman
2B B Doerr
SS V Stephens
3B J Pesky
LF T Williams
CF D DiMaggio
RF A Zarilla
M J McCarthy

CHI 1949 AL
SP B Wight
SP R Gumpert
SP B Pierce
SR B Kuzava
SR H Judson
RS M Pieretti
RP M Surkont
C- D Wheeler
1B C Kress
2B C Michaels
SS L Appling
3B F Baker
LU- G Zernial
CF C Metkovich
RF D Philley
UT- S Souchock
M J Onslow

CLE 1949 AL
SP B Lemon
SP B Feller
SR M Garcia
SP E Wynn
SR G Bearden
RS A Benton
RS S Zoldak
RP F Papish
RP S Zoldak
C J Hegan
1B M Vernon
2B J Gordon
S3 L Boudreau
3B- K Keltner
LF D Mitchell
CF L Doby
RF B Kennedy
SS- R Boone
OF- T Tucker

DET 1949 AL
SP H Newhouser
SP V Trucks
SP A Houtteman
SP T Gray
SP F Hutchinson
RP D Trout
C- A Robinson
1B- P Campbell
2B N Berry
SS J Lipon
3B G Kell
LM H Evers
CF J Groth
RF V Wertz
UI D Kolloway
UI E Lake
LU P Mullin
M R Rolfe

NY 1949 AL
SP V Raschi
SP E Lopat
SP A Reynolds
SP T Byrne
SR F Sanford
RP J Page
RP S Shea

NY 1949 AL (continued)
RP C Marshall
C Y Berra
R1 T Henrich
2B J Coleman
SS P Rizzuto
3B B Brown
LU G Woodling
MR C Mapes
RO H Bauer
3U B Johnson
LF- J Lindell
M C Stengel

PHI 1949 AL
SR A Kellner
SP J Coleman
SP L Brissie
SP D Fowler
SR C Scheib
RS B Shantz
RP B Harris
C M Guerra
1B F Fain
2B P Suder
SS E Joost
3B H Majeski
LF E Valo
CF S Chapman
RF W Moses
2B- N Fox
M C Mack

STL 1949 AL
SP N Garver
SR A Papai
SR H Fox
SP C Fannin
SP K Drews
SR R Embree
RS B Kennedy
RS J Ostrowski
RP T Ferrick
RS D Starr
C S Lollar
1B J Graham
2B J Priddy
SS- E Pellagrini
3B B Dillinger
ML R Sievers
OI S Spence
RF D Kokos
OI P Lehner
C L Moss
LU W Platt
SI J Sullivan
M Z Taylor

WAS 1949 AL
SR S Hudson
SP R Scarborough
SP M Harris
SR D Weik
RS L Hittle
RS J Haynes
RP D Welteroth
C A Evans
1B E Robinson
2B A Kozar
SS S Dente
3B E Yost
LO B Stewart
CF C Vollmer
RU B Lewis
LM G Coan
2U S Robertson
RM- S Mele
M J Kuhel

BOS 1950 NL
SP V Bickford
SP W Spahn
SP J Sain
SR B Chipman
RP B Hogue
RS J Antonelli
RP B Hall
C W Cooper
1B E Torgeson
2B R Hartsfield
SS B Kerr
3B B Elliott
LF S Gordon
CF S Jethroe
RF T Holmes
RU W Marshall
C- D Crandall
M B Southworth

BRO 1950 NL
SP D Newcombe
SP P Roe
SR E Palica
SR R Branca
SP C Erskine
RS D Bankhead
C R Campanella
1B G Hodges
2B J Robinson
SS P Reese
3B B Cox
LF G Hermanski
CF D Snider
RF C Furillo
LU- J Russell
M B Shotton

CHI 1950 NL
SP B Rush
SR P Minner
SR J Schmitz
SR F Hiller
SR D Lade
RS M Dubiel
RS J Klippstein
RP D Leonard
RS J Vander Meer
C- M Owen
1B- P Ward
2B W Terwilliger
SS R Smalley
3B B Serena
LF H Sauer
CF A Pafko
OI- B Borkowski
1B- P Cavarretta
M F Frisch

CIN 1950 NL
SP E Blackwell
SP K Raffensberger
SR H Fox
SP W Ramsdell
RP F Smith
RP E Erautt
C- D Howell
1B T Kluszewski
2B C Ryan
SS V Stallcup
3B G Hatton
LU J Adcock
CF B Usher
RF J Wyrostek
IF B Adams
CF L Merriman
LU- P Lowrey
M L Sewell

NY 1950 NL
SP L Jansen
SR S Maglie
SR S Jones
SR D Koslo
SP J Hearn
RS M Kennedy
RS J Kramer
RP A Hansen
C W Westrum
1B T Gilbert
2B E Stanky
SS A Dark
3B H Thompson
LF W Lockman
CF B Thomson
RF D Mueller
1R M Irvin
M L Durocher

PHI 1950 NL
SP R Roberts
SP C Simmons
SR B Miller
SP R Meyer
SR B Church
RP J Konstanty
RP K Heintzelman
C- A Seminick
1B E Waitkus
1B M Goliat
SS G Hamner
3B W Jones
LF D Sisler
CF R Ashburn
RF D Ennis
M E Sawyer

PIT 1950 NL
SP- C Chambers
SR M Dickson
SR B Werle
SR B Macdonald
SR V Law
RS M Queen
RP V Lombardi
RP J Walsh
C C McCullough
1U J Hopp
2B A Murtaugh
SS- S Rojek
3B- N Fernandez
LF R Kiner
MU W Westlake
RF G Bell
UI P Castiglione
SS- D O'Connell
M B Meyer

STL 1950 NL
SP H Pollet
SP M Lanier
SR G Staley
SP H Brecheen
SR R Munger
RS A Brazle
RS C Boyer
RP F Martin
C D Rice
1B- R Nelson
2B R Schoendienst
SS M Marion
3B T Glaviano
OI S Musial
UO B Howerton
RF E Slaughter
CF- C Diering
3U E Kazak
M E Dyer

BOS 1950 AL
SP M Parnell
SR E Kinder
SR J Dobson
SR C Stobbs
SR M McDermott
RS W Masterson
RP W Nixon
C- B Tebbetts
1B W Dropo
2B B Doerr
SS V Stephens
3B J Pesky
LF- T Williams
CF D DiMaggio
RF A Zarilla
IO B Goodman
M1 J McCarthy
M2 S O'Neill

CHI 1950 AL
SP B Pierce
SP B Wight
SR B Cain
SP R Gumpert
SP R Scarborough
RP H Judson
RP K Holcombe
RP L Aloma
C P Masi
1B E Robinson
2B N Fox
SS C Carrasquel
3B H Majeski
LF G Zernial
RM D Philley
RF- M Rickert
3U- F Baker
UT- G Goldsberry
M1 J Onslow
M2 R Corriden

CLE 1950 AL
SP B Lemon
SP B Feller
SP E Wynn
SP M Garcia
SR S Gromek
RP S Zoldak
RP A Benton
RP J Flores
RP M Pieretti
C J Hegan
1B L Easter
2B J Gordon
SS A Rosen
3B D Mitchell
CF L Doby
RF B Kennedy
2B- B Avila
SS- L Boudreau
M L Boudreau

DET 1950 AL
SP A Houtteman
SR F Hutchinson
SP H Newhouser
SR D Trout
SP T Gray
RS H White
RP P Calvert
C A Robinson
1B D Kolloway
2B J Priddy
SS J Lipon
3B G Kell
LF H Evers
CF J Groth
RF V Wertz
M R Rolfe

NY 1950 AL
SP V Raschi
SP A Reynolds
SP E Lopat
SP T Byrne
SP W Ford
RS F Sanford
CL J Page
RP T Ferrick
C Y Berra
1B J Collins
2B J Coleman
SS P Rizzuto
3B B Johnson
LF G Woodling
CF J DiMaggio
RL H Bauer
3B B Brown
RU C Mapes
1B- J Mize
M C Stengel

PHI 1950 AL
SR L Brissie
SR A Kellner
SR B Shantz
SR B Hooper
SR H Wyse
RS C Scheib
C- M Guerra
1B F Fain
2B B Hitchcock
SS E Joost
3B- B Dillinger
LU P Lehner
CF S Chapman
RL E Valo
RU- W Moses
3U- K Wahl
M C Mack

STL 1950 AL
SP N Garver
SR A Widmar
SR S Overmire
SR D Starr
SR H Dorish
RP C Fannin
RS D Johnson
RP C Marshall
C S Lollar
1L D Lenhardt
2B O Friend
SS T Upton
32- B Sommers
LR D Kokos
UO R Coleman
RU K Wood
1B H Arft
MU R Sievers
CU- L Moss
23 S Stirnweiss
M Z Taylor

WAS 1950 AL
SP S Hudson
SP B Kuzava
SP C Marrero
SP- S Consuegra
SR J Haynes
RP M Harris
RP J Pearce
C- A Evans
1B- M Vernon
2B C Michaels
SS S Dente
3B E Yost
RL B Stewart
CF I Noren
RO S Mele
LF G Coan
M B Harris

BOS 1951 NL
SP W Spahn
SP M Surkont
SP V Bickford
SP J Sain
SR C Nichols
RP J Wilson
RS D Cole
RP G Estock
RP B Chipman
C W Cooper
1B E Torgeson
2B R Hartsfield
SS- B Kerr
3B B Elliott
LU S Gordon
CF S Jethroe
RF W Marshall
IO S Sisti
UO- B Addis
M1 B Southworth
M2 T Holmes

BRO 1951 NL
SP D Newcombe
SP P Roe
SR B Branca
SR C Erskine
RP C King
RS B Podbielan
C R Campanella
1B G Hodges
2B J Robinson
SS P Reese
3B B Cox
LF- A Pafko
CF D Snider
RF C Furillo
LU- D Thompson
M C Dressen

CHI 1951 NL
SP B Rush
SP P Minner
SR C McLish
SP F Hiller
SR T Lown
RS J Klippstein
RS B Kelly
RP D Leonard
RP M Dubiel
CU S Burgess
1B- C Connors
2B E Miksis
SS- R Smalley
3B R Jackson
LF H Sauer
UO H Jeffcoat
UO F Baumholtz
1U- P Cavarretta
M1 F Frisch

CIN 1951 NL
SP K Raffensberger
SP E Blackwell
SR H Fox
SP W Ramsdell
SR H Wehmeier
RS H Perkowski
RP F Smith
RP B Byerly
C- D Howell
1B T Kluszewski
2B C Ryan
SS V Stallcup
3B G Hatton
LF J Adcock
ML L Merriman
RF J Wyrostek
IO B Adams
MU B Usher
SU- R McMillan
M L Sewell

NY 1951 NL
SP S Maglie
SP L Jansen
SP J Hearn
SR D Koslo
RP G Spencer
RS S Jones
RS M Kennedy
RP A Gettel
C W Westrum
1B W Lockman
2B E Stanky
SS A Dark
3B- H Thompson
L1 M Irvin
CF W Mays
RF D Mueller
OI B Thomson
M L Durocher

PHI 1951 NL
SP R Roberts
SP B Church
SP R Meyer
SR J Thompson
SR K Heintzelman
RP J Konstanty
RP K Johnson
C A Seminick
1B E Waitkus
2U- P Caballero
SS G Hamner
3B W Jones
LF D Sisler
CF R Ashburn
RF D Ennis
UT- T Brown
UL- B Nicholson
2U- E Pellagrini
C- D Wilber
M E Sawyer

PIT 1951 NL
SR M Dickson
SR M Queen
SR B Friend
SP H Pollet
SR V Law
RS B Werle
RP T Wilks
RP J Walsh
RS B Podbielan
C R Campanella
1B G Hodges
SS G Strickland
3B P Castiglione
L1 R Kiner
M1 C Metkovich
RF G Bell
OI- B Howerton
M B Meyer

STL 1951 NL
SR G Staley
SR T Poholsky
SP M Lanier
SP H Brecheen
SP C Chambers
RS A Brazle
RS R Munger
RP D Bokelmann
C D Rice
1B- N Jones
2B R Schoendienst
SS S Hemus
3B B Johnson
L1 S Musial
MU P Lowrey
RF E Slaughter
M M Marion

BOS 1951 AL
SP M Parnell
SR R Scarborough
SR M McDermott
SP C Stobbs
SR W Nixon
RP E Kinder
RS B Wight
RP L Kiely
RS H Taylor
C- L Moss
1B W Dropo
2B B Doerr
SS J Pesky
3B- H Majeski
LF T Williams
CF D DiMaggio
RF C Vollmer
UT B Goodman
SU- L Boudreau
3U- F Hatfield
M S O'Neill

CHI 1951 AL
SP B Pierce
SP B Rogovin
SP K Holcombe
SP J Dobson
SR R Gumpert
RP L Kretlow
RS H Judson
RP H Dorish
RP L Aloma
C- P Masi
1B E Robinson
2B N Fox
SS C Carrasquel
3B- B Dillinger
UT M Minoso
CF J Busby
RF A Zarilla
LU B Stewart
3U- F Baker
M P Richards

CLE 1951 AL
SP E Wynn
SP B Lemon
SR M Garcia
SP B Feller
RP L Brissie
RS S Gromek
C J Hegan
1B L Easter
2B B Avila
SS R Boone
3B A Rosen
LF D Mitchell
CF L Doby
RF B Kennedy
OI S Chapman
OI H Simpson
M A Lopez

DET 1951 AL
SP T Gray
SR D Trout
SR F Hutchinson
SR V Trucks
SR B Cain
RS M Stuart
RP G Bearden
RP H Newhouser
RP H White
C J Ginsberg
1B D Kryhoski
2B J Priddy
SS J Lipon
3B G Kell
LM H Evers
CF J Groth
RF V Wertz
LU P Mullin
1B- D Kolloway
UT- S Souchock
M R Rolfe

NY 1951 AL
SP V Raschi
SP E Lopat
SR A Reynolds
SR T Morgan
SR S Shea
RP J Ostrowski
C. Y Berra
1B J Collins
2B J Coleman
SS P Rizzuto
3B B Brown
LF G Woodling
CF J DiMaggio
RL H Bauer
RF M Mantle
32 G McDougald
1B J Mize
M C Stengel

PHI 1951 AL
SP A Kellner
SR B Shantz
SR B Hooper
SR M Martin
SP S Zoldak
RS C Scheib
RP D Fowler
RS J Coleman
RP J Kucab
C- J Tipton
1B F Fain
2B P Suder
SS E Joost
3B- H Majeski
LF G Zernial
CF D Philley
RF E Valo
1U L Limmer
32- B Hitchcock
M J Dykes

STL 1951 AL
SP N Garver
SR D Pillette
SP T Byrne
SR A Widmar
RP B Mahoney
RS S Paige
RS B Kennedy
C S Lollar
1B H Arft
2B B Young
SS- B Jennings
3B F Marsh
LR- R Coleman
CF J Delsing
RL K Wood
C- M Batts
M Z Taylor

WAS 1951 AL
SP C Marrero
SP D Johnson
SP S Hudson
SR J Moreno
SR B Porterfield
RS S Consuegra
RP M Harris
RP J Haynes
C- M Guerra
1B M Vernon
2B C Michaels
SS- P Runnels
3B E Yost
LF G Coan
CF I Noren
RU S Mele
SU- S Dente
UO- M McCormick
M B Harris

BOS 1952 NL
SP W Spahn
SP J Wilson
SP M Surkont
SP V Bickford
RS L Burdette
RP S Jones
C W Cooper
1B E Torgeson
2B J Dittmer
SS J Logan
3B E Mathews
LF S Gordon
CF S Jethroe
RU J Daniels
UT- S Sisti
RF- B Thorpe
M1 T Holmes
M2 C Grimm

BRO 1952 NL
SP C Erskine
SR B Loes
SR B Wade
SP P Roe
SR J Rutherford
RP J Black
RP C Van Cuyk
C R Campanella
1B G Hodges
2B J Robinson
SS P Reese
3B B Cox
LR A Pafko
CF D Snider
RF C Furillo
LU G Shuba
M C Dressen

CHI 1952 NL
SP B Rush
SR J Klippstein
SR W Hacker
SP P Minner
SR T Lown
RS B Kelly
RP D Leonard
RS B Schultz
C T Atwell
1B D Fondy
2S E Miksis
SS- R Smalley
3B R Jackson
LF H Sauer
CF H Jeffcoat
RM F Baumholtz
RU G Hermanski
IF B Serena
UO B Addis
M P Cavarretta

CIN 1952 NL
SP K Raffensberger
SP H Perkowski
SP H Wehmeier
SP B Church
SR F Hiller
RP F Smith
RP E Blackwell
RS J Nuxhall
C A Seminick
1B T Kluszewski
2B G Hatton
SS R McMillan
3B B Adams
LU J Adcock
MO B Borkowski
RF W Marshall
M1 L Sewell
M2 E Brucker
M3 R Hornsby

NY 1952 NL
SP J Hearn
SP S Maglie
SR D Koslo
SP L Jansen
SR M Lanier
RP H Wilhelm
RS M Kennedy
RP G Spencer
C W Westrum
1B W Lockman
2B D Williams
SS A Dark
3M B Thomson
LU B Elliott
UT H Thompson
RF D Mueller
M L Durocher

PHI 1952 NL
SP R Roberts
SP R Meyer
SP K Drews
SP C Simmons
SR S Ridzik
RP J Konstanty
RP A Hansen
C S Burgess
1B E Waitkus
2B C Ryan
SS G Hamner
3B W Jones
LF D Ennis
CF R Ashburn
RF J Wyrostek

(col. 1)

M1 E Sawyer
M2 S O'Neill

PIT 1952 NL
SP M Dickson
SP H Pollet
SR B Friend
RS W Main
RP T Wilks
RP P LaPalme
B J Garagiola
SB T Bartirome
UI J Merson
SS D Groat
B- P Castiglione
F R Kiner
CF B Del Greco
CF G Bell
CI C Koshorek
CO C Metkovich
M B Meyer

STL 1952 NL
SP G Staley
SP V Mizell
RJ J Presko
P C Boyer
RP H Brecheen
SA A Brazle
SP E Yuhas
RS C Chambers
D Rice
RB D Sisler
SR R Schoendienst
SS S Hemus
SB B Johnson
PI P Lowrey
1U S Musial
CF E Slaughter
F H Rice
U- T Glaviano
E Stanky

BOS 1952 AL
SP M Parnell
SP M McDermott
SP D Trout
SP S Hudson
SP D Brodowski
SW W Nixon
SE E Kinder
SJ J Delock
SR R Scarborough
S White
3B D Gernert
2B J B Goodman
SS- J Lipon
3- G Kell
H Evers
UF D DiMaggio
JF J Throneberry
3- T Lepcio
3- V Stephens
O-C Vollmer
L Boudreau

CHI 1952 AL
B Pierce
S Rogovin
J Dobson
M Grissom
RC Stobbs
H Dorish
B Kennedy
S Lollar
E Robinson
N Fox
C Carrasquel
H Rodriguez
TM Minoso
O-R Coleman
FS Mele
J- B Stewart
P Richards

CLE 1952 AL
B Lemon
M Garcia
E Wynn
B Feller
S Gromek
L Brissie
M Harris
J Hegan
L Easter
B Avila
R Boone
A Rosen
D Mitchell
L Doby
H Simpson
A Lopez

DET 1952 AL
T Gray
A Houtteman
V Trucks

(col. 2)

SP H Newhouser
SP B Wight
RS B Hoeft
RP H White
RP D Littlefield
C J Ginsberg
1B W Dropo
2B- J Priddy
SS- N Berry
3B F Hatfield
LU P Mullin
CF J Groth
RF- V Wertz
RO- C Mapes
UT- S Souchock
M1 R Rolfe
M2 F Hutchinson

NY 1952 AL
SP A Reynolds
SP V Raschi
SR J Sain
SP E Lopat
SR B Kuzava
RP T Morgan
RS J McDonald
RP B Hogue
C Y Berra
1B J Collins
2B J Martin
SS P Rizzuto
3B G McDougald
LF G Woodling
CF M Mantle
RF H Bauer
UR- J Mize
OI I Noren
M C Stengel

PHI 1952 AL
SP B Shantz
SP A Kellner
SP H Byrd
SR C Scheib
RS B Hooper
RP J Kucab
C J Astroth
1B F Fain
2B- S Kell
SS E Joost
3B B Hitchcock
LF G Zernial
CF D Philley
RF E Valo
M J Dykes

STL 1952 AL
SP D Pillette
SP T Byrne
SP B Cain
SR G Bearden
SP N Garver
RS S Paige
RS E Harrist
RP D Madison
C C Courtney
1B D Kryhoski
2B B Young
SS- J DeMaestri
3L J Dyck
UO J Delsing
CF J Rivera
RU B Nieman
1B- G Goldsberry
M1 R Hornsby
M2 M Marion

WAS 1952 AL
SP B Porterfield
SP C Marrero
SP S Shea
SP W Masterson
SP J Moreno
RP R Gumpert
RP S Consuegra
RS D Johnson
RP J Haynes
C M Grasso
1B W Vernon
2B- F Baker
SS P Runnels
3B E Yost
LF G Coan
CF J Busby
RF J Jensen
M B Harris

BRO 1953 NL
SP C Erskine
SP R Meyer
SP B Loes
SP P Roe
SR J Podres
RS B Milliken
RP J Hughes
RP B Wade

(col. 3)

C R Campanella
1B G Hodges
2B J Gilliam
SS P Reese
3B B Cox
LR D Thompson
CF D Snider
RF C Furillo
L3 J Robinson
M C Dressen

CHI 1953 NL
SP W Hacker
SP P Minner
SR J Klippstein
SP B Rush
SP H Pollet
RS T Lown
RS B Church
RP D Leonard
C- C McCullough
1B D Fondy
2S E Miksis
SS- R Smalley
3B R Jackson
LF R Kiner
MR F Baumholtz
RL H Sauer
CF H Jeffcoat
23 B Serena
M P Cavarretta

CIN 1953 NL
SP H Perkowski
SR B Podbielan
SP K Raffensberger
SR J Nuxhall
SP F Baczewski
RS J Collum
RP F Smith
RP C King
RS B Kelly
C A Seminick
1B T Kluszewski
2B R Bridges
SS R McMillan
3B B Adams
LF J Greengrass
CF G Bell
RF W Marshall
RU B Borkowski
UI- G Hatton
M1 R Hornsby
M2 B Mills

MIL 1953 NL
SP W Spahn
SP J Antonelli
SP M Surkont
SR B Buhl
SR D Liddle
RS L Burdette
RP J Wilson
RP E Johnson
C D Crandall
1B J Adcock
2B J Dittmer
SS J Logan
3B E Mathews
LF S Gordon
CF B Bruton
RF A Pafko
LO J Pendleton
M C Grimm

NY 1953 NL
SP R Gomez
SP J Hearn
SR L Jansen
SP S Maglie
SP A Worthington
RP H Wilhelm
RS D Koslo
RS A Corwin
C W Westrum
1B W Lockman
2B D Williams
SU A Dark
3B H Thompson
LF M Irvin
CF J Rivera
CF B Thomson
RF D Mueller
UI D Spencer
M L Durocher

PHI 1953 NL
SP R Roberts
SP C Simmons
SR K Drews
SR J Konstanty
SR B Miller
RS B Ridzik
RP A Hansen
C S Burgess
1B E Torgeson
2S G Hamner
SS T Kazanski

(col. 4)

3B W Jones
LF D Ennis
CF R Ashburn
RF J Wyrostek
C- S Lopata
2U- C Ryan
1U- E Waitkus
M S O'Neill

PIT 1953 NL
SR M Dickson
SR P LaPalme
SP J Lindell
SP B Friend
SR B Hall
RP J Hetki
RS R Face
RP B Bowman
C- M Sandlock
1B- P Ward
2B- J O'Brien
SS- E O'Brien
32 D O'Connell
LF- H Rice
CF F Thomas
RF C Abrams
SS D Cole
1U P Smith
MO C Bernier
UI- E Pellagrini
M F Haney

STL 1953 NL
SP H Haddix
SP G Staley
SP V Mizell
SP J Presko
SR S Miller
RP A Brazle
RP H White
RS C Chambers
C D Rice
1B S Bilko
2B R Schoendienst
SS S Hemus
3B R Jablonski
LF S Musial
CF R Repulski
RF E Slaughter
UT P Lowrey
M E Stanky

BOS 1953 AL
SP M Parnell
SP M McDermott
SP H Brown
SR S Hudson
SP W Nixon
RP E Kinder
RS B Flowers
RP I Delock
C S White
1B D Gernert
2B B Goodman
SS M Bolling
3B G Kell
LF H Evers
CF T Umphlett
RF J Piersall
IF- F Baker
LF- G Stephens
M L Boudreau

CHI 1953 AL
SP B Pierce
SP V Trucks
SR M Fornieles
SP S Rogovin
SR S Consuegra
RS H Dorish
RP J Dobson
RS B Keegan
RP G Bearden
C S Lollar
1B F Fain
2B N Fox
SS C Carrasquel
3B- B Elliott
LF M Minoso
CF J Rivera
RF S Mele
OF- T Wright
M P Richards

CLE 1953 AL
SP B Lemon
SP M Garcia
SP E Wynn
SP B Feller
SP A Houtteman
RS D Hoskins
RP B Hooper
C J Hegan
1B B Glynn
2B B Avila
SS G Strickland
3B A Rosen

(col. 5)

LF D Mitchell
CF L Doby
RL B Kennedy
RF- H Simpson
UO- W Westlake
M A Lopez

DET 1953 AL
SP B Hoeft
SP N Garver
SP T Gray
SP S Gromek
SP R Branca
RS D Marlowe
RP R Herbert
RP D Madison
1B W Dropo
2U J Pesky
SS M Kuenn
3B R Boone
LR B Nieman
CF J Delsing
RL D Lund
UI F Hatfield
OF- P Mullin
OI- S Souchock
3B- B Cox
M F Hutchinson

NY 1953 AL
SP W Ford
SR J Sain
SP V Raschi
SP E Lopat
SR A Reynolds
RP J McDonald
RS B Kuzava
RP T Gorman
C- J Garagiola
1B J Collins
2B B Martin
SS P Rizzuto
3B G McDougald
LF R Kiner
CF M Mantle
RF H Bauer
UO I Noren
UR- J Mize
M C Stengel

PHI 1953 AL
SP H Byrd
SR M Fricano
SP A Kellner
SR C Bishop
SP B Shantz
RS M Martin
RS C Scheib
RP F Fanovich
C- J Astroth
1B E Robinson
2B C Michaels
SS J DeMaestri
3B B Babe
LF G Zernial
CF E McGhee
RF D Philley
32 P Suder
C- R Murray
M J Dykes

STL 1953 AL
SR D Larsen
SP D Pillette
SR D Littlefield
SR H Brecheen
SR B Cain
RP S Paige
RP M Stuart
RS M Blyzka
C C Courtney
1B D Kryhoski
2B B Young
SS B Hunter
OI J Dyck
LU D Kokos
CF J Groth
RF V Wertz
LU D Lenhardt
C- L Moss
1B- R Sievers
M M Marion

WAS 1953 AL
SP B Porterfield
SP W Masterson
SP S Shea
SP C Stobbs
SP C Marrero
RS S Dixon
RS J Schmitz
RS J Sima
RP J Lane
C- E Fitz Gerald
1B M Vernon
2B W Terwilliger

(col. 6)

SS P Runnels
3B E Yost
LF C Vollmer
CF J Busby
RF J Jensen
M B Harris

BRO 1954 NL
SP C Erskine
SP R Meyer
SP J Podres
SP B Loes
SP D Newcombe
RP C Labine
CL J Hughes
RP E Palica
RP B Milliken
C R Campanella
1B G Hodges
2B J Gilliam
SS P Reese
3B- D Hoak
L3 J Robinson
CF D Snider
RF C Furillo
LF- S Amoros
3B- B Cox
M W Alston

CHI 1954 NL
SP B Rush
SP P Minner
SP W Hacker
SR J Klippstein
SP H Pollet
RS J Davis
RP H Jeffcoat
RP B Tremel
C- J Garagiola
1B D Fondy
2B G Baker
SS E Banks
3B R Jackson
LF R Kiner
CF B Talbot
RF H Sauer
MO- F Baumholtz
M S Hack

CIN 1954 NL
SR A Fowler
SP C Valentine
SP J Nuxhall
SP B Podbielan
SP F Baczewski
CL- F Smith
RS H Judson
RS- H Perkowski
RP J Collum
C- A Seminick
1B- T Kluszewski
2B J Temple
SS R McMillan
3B B Adams
LF R Repulski
CF W Moon
RF W Post
3U C Harmon
M B Tebbetts

MIL 1954 NL
SP W Spahn
SP L Burdette
SP G Conley
SP J Wilson
SR C Nichols
RP J Jolly
RS B Buhl
RP E Johnson
RP J Crone
C D Crandall
1B J Adcock
2I D O'Connell
SS J Logan
3B E Mathews
LF H Aaron
CF C Diering
RF C Abrams
OF G Coan
3U B Kennedy
1U D Kryhoski
M J Dykes

NY 1954 NL
SP J Antonelli
SP R Gomez
SP S Maglie
SR J Hearn
SP D Liddle
RP H Wilhelm
RP W McCall
C W Westrum
1B W Lockman
2B D Williams
SS A Dark
3B H Thompson
LF M Irvin
CF W Mays
RF D Mueller

(col. 7)

C- R Katt
UO- D Rhodes
M L Durocher

PHI 1954 NL
SP R Roberts
SP C Simmons
SP M Dickson
SR B Miller
SR H Wehmeier
RS S Ridzik
RP J Konstanty
C S Burgess
1B E Torgeson
2B G Hamner
SS W Morgan
3B W Jones
LU D Schell
CF R Ashburn
OI D Ennis
RL- M Clark
C- S Lopata
RU J Wyrostek
M1 S O'Neill
M2 T Moore

PIT 1954 NL
SP M Surkont
SR B Friend
SR V Law
SP D Littlefield
SR J Thies
RS B Purkey
RS P LaPalme
RP J Hetki
C T Atwell
1B B Skinner
2B C Roberts
SS G Allie
UI D Cole
UO D Hall
ML F Thomas
R3 S Gordon
UO J Lynch
IO P Ward
C- J Shepard
M F Haney

STL 1954 NL
SP M Haddix
SP V Raschi
SR B Lawrence
SR G Staley
SR T Poholsky
RP A Brazle
RP C Deal
RS J Presko
RP R Lint
C B Sarni
1B- J Cunningham
2B R Schoendienst
SS A Grammas
3B R Jablonski
LF R Repulski
CF W Moon
RS S Musial
SI S Hemus
OI- J Frazier
M E Stanky

BAL 1954 AL
SP B Turley
SP J Coleman
SP D Larsen
SP D Pillette
SR L Kretlow
RS B Chakales
RP M Blyzka
RP H Fox
C C Courtney
1B E Waitkus
2B B Young
SS B Hunter
3B B Stephens
LF- J Fridley
CF C Diering
RF C Abrams
OF G Coan
3U B Kennedy
1U D Kryhoski
M J Dykes

BOS 1954 AL
SR F Sullivan
SR W Nixon
SR T Brewer
SP L Kiely
SR B Henry
RP E Kinder
RS H Brown
RS S Hudson
C S White
1B W Agganis
2I T Lepcio
SS M Bolling
3B G Hatton
LF T Williams

(col. 8)

MR J Jensen
RU J Piersall
2I B Goodman
UO K Olson
SI- B Consolo
M L Boudreau

CHI 1954 AL
SP V Trucks
SP B Keegan
SR J Harshman
SR S Consuegra
RS D Johnson
RS H Dorish
RP M Martin
C- S Lollar
1B- F Fain
2B N Fox
SS C Carrasquel
3B C Michaels
LF M Minoso
CF J Groth
RF J Rivera
M1 P Richards
M2 M Marion

CLE 1954 AL
SP E Wynn
SR M Garcia
SP B Lemon
SP A Houtteman
SP B Feller
RP R Narleski
RS D Mossi
RP H Newhouser
C J Hegan
1B B Glynn
2B B Avila
SS G Strickland
31 A Rosen
LU A Smith
CF L Doby
RF D Philley
1B V Wertz
LO- W Westlake
M A Lopez

DET 1954 AL
SP S Gromek
SP N Garver
SR G Zuverink
SP B Hoeft
SR A Aber
RP D Marlowe
RP R Herbert
RP B Miller
C F House
1B W Dropo
2B F Bolling
SS H Kuenn
3B R Boone
LU J Delsing
CF B Tuttle
RF A Kaline
1B- W Belardi
2U- F Hatfield
LU- B Nieman
M F Hutchinson

NY 1954 AL
SP W Ford
SR B Grim
SP E Lopat
SR A Reynolds
SR T Morgan
RP H Byrd
CL J Sain
C- Y Berra
1B J Collins
23 G McDougald
SS P Rizzuto
3B A Carey
OI I Noren
CF M Mantle
RF H Bauer
2S J Coleman
LF G Woodling
SS- W Miranda
UR- E Robinson
1U- B Skowron
M C Stengel

PHI 1954 AL
SP A Portocarrero
SP A Kellner
SR M Fricano
SP B Trice
SP J Gray
RS S Dixon
RP M Burtschy
RP C Bishop
RS A Sima
C- J Astroth
1U L Limmer
2B S Jacobs
SS J DeMaestri

3B J Finigan
LF G Zernial
UT V Power
RF B Renna
1U D Bollweg
OF E Valo
CF B Wilson
M J Joost

WAS 1954 AL
SP B Porterfield
SP M McDermott
SP J Schmitz
SP C Stobbs
SP D Stone
RP C Pascual
RP G Keriazakos
RP B Stewart
C E Fitz Gerald
1B M Vernon
2B W Terwilliger
SS P Runnels
3B E Yost
LF R Sievers
CF J Busby
RF T Umphlett
M B Harris

BRO 1955 NL
SP D Newcombe
SP C Erskine
SP J Podres
SP B Loes
SR K Spooner
RS C Labine
RP E Roebuck
RP D Bessent
C R Campanella
1B G Hodges
2L J Gilliam
SS P Reese
3B J Robinson
LF S Amoros
CF D Snider
RF C Furillo
3B D Hoak
2I- D Zimmer
M W Alston

CHI 1955 NL
SP S Jones
SP B Rush
SP W Hacker
SP P Minner
SR J Davis
RP H Jeffcoat
RS H Pollet
RP D Hillman
RP H Perkowski
C H Chiti
1B D Fondy
2B G Baker
SS E Banks
3B R Jackson
LF- H Sauer
MR E Miksis
RU J King
OF F Baumholtz
LU B Speake
M S Hack

CIN 1955 NL
SR J Nuxhall
SR A Fowler
SR J Klippstein
SR J Collum
SR G Staley
RS R Minarcin
RS J Black
RP H Freeman
C S Burgess
1B T Kluszewski
2B J Temple
SS R McMillan
3S R Bridges
LU- S Palys
CF G Bell
RF W Post
UT C Harmon
UL- B Thurman
M B Tebbetts

MIL 1955 NL
SP W Spahn
SP L Burdette
SR B Buhl
SP G Conley
SR C Nichols
RS R Crone
RP E Johnson
RP D Jolly
C D Crandall
1B G Crowe
2B D O'Connell
SS J Logan
3B E Mathews
LF B Thomson

CF B Bruton
RU H Aaron
LU C Tanner
1B- J Adcock
RU- A Pafko
M C Grimm

NY 1955 NL
SP J Antonelli
SP J Hearn
SP R Gomez
SP S Maglie
SR D Liddle
RP H Wilhelm
RS W McCall
RP M Grissom
RS R Monzant
C R Katt
1B- G Harris
2B- W Terwilliger
SS A Dark
L1 W Lockman
CF W Mays
RF D Mueller
IC B Hofman
UL D Rhodes
2B- D Williams
M L Durocher

PHI 1955 NL
SP R Roberts
SP M Dickson
SP H Wehmeier
SP C Simmons
RS J Meyer
RP B Miller
C A Seminick
1U M Blaylock
2S B Morgan
SS- R Smalley
3B W Jones
LF D Ennis
CF R Ashburn
RF J Greengrass
2B G Hamner
CU S Lopata
RU- G Gorbous
M M Smith

PIT 1955 NL
SR B Friend
SR V Law
SR M Surkont
SR R Kline
SR D Littlefield
RS R Face
RS L Donoso
RP D Hall
C J Shepard
1B D Long
2B- J O'Brien
SS D Groat
IF G Freese
OF- J Lynch
LM F Thomas
RF R Clemente
UI- D Cole
1U- P Ward
M F Haney

STL 1955 NL
SP H Haddix
SR L Jackson
SR L Arroyo
SP T Poholsky
SP W Schmidt
RS B Lawrence
RP P LaPalme
C B Sarni
1O S Musial
2B R Schoendienst
SS A Grammas
3B- K Boyer
LU R Repulski
CF B Virdon
OI W Moon
UI S Hemus
M1 E Stanky
M2 H Walker

BAL 1955 AL
SP J Wilson
SP E Palica
SP B Wight
RS R Moore
RS A Schallock
RP H Dorish
RS D Johnson
C H Smith
1C G Triandos
2B- F Marsh
SS W Miranda
3B- W Causey
RL- D Philley
CF C Diering
OI C Abrams

UO- D Pope
M P Richards

BOS 1955 AL
SP F Sullivan
SP W Nixon
SP T Brewer
SR I Delock
SR G Susce
RP L Kiely
RP T Hurd
CL E Kinder
C S White
1B N Zauchin
2B B Goodman
SS B Klaus
3B G Hatton
LF T Williams
CF J Piersall
RF J Jensen
LU G Stephens
M P Higgins

CHI 1955 AL
SP B Pierce
SP D Donovan
SP J Harshman
SP V Trucks
SP C Johnson
RS S Consuegra
RP D Howell
RP M Martin
C S Lollar
1B W Dropo
2B N Fox
SS C Carrasquel
3B G Kell
LF M Minoso
CF J Busby
RF J Rivera
RL B Nieman
3U- B Kennedy
M M Marion

CLE 1955 AL
SP E Wynn
SP H Score
SP M Garcia
SP B Lemon
SR A Houtteman
RP R Narleski
RP D Mossi
C J Hegan
1B- V Wertz
2B B Avila
SS G Strickland
3B A Rosen
LF R Kiner
CF L Doby
R3 A Smith
LF- G Woodling
M A Lopez

DET 1955 AL
SP F Lary
SP N Garver
SP B Hoeft
SP S Gromek
RP A Aber
RP B Birrer
RP P Foytack
C F House
1B- E Torgeson
2B F Hatfield
SS H Kuenn
3B R Boone
LF J Delsing
CF B Tuttle
RF A Kaline
LU B Phillips
C - R Wilson
M B Harris

KC 1955 AL
SR A Ditmar
SP A Kellner
SP B Shantz
SR A Ceccarelli
SP A Portocarrero
RP T Gorman
RP V Raschi
RS C Boyer
RP B Harrington
C J Astroth
1B V Power
23 J Finigan
SS J DeMaestri
32 H Lopez
LF G Zernial
CF H Simpson
RU E Slaughter
RU B Renna
MO B Wilson
UO E Valo
C - B Shantz
M L Boudreau

NY 1955 AL
SP W Ford
SP B Turley
SP T Byrne
SR J Kucks
SD D Larsen
RP J Konstanty
RP T Morgan
RP T Sturdivant
C Y Berra
1U B Skowron
2B G McDougald
SS B Hunter
3B A Carey
CF M Mantle
RF H Bauer
1R J Collins
LU E Howard
SS- P Rizzuto
1U- E Robinson
M C Stengel

WAS 1955 AL
SR D Stone
SP B Porterfield
SR J Schmitz
SR M McDermott
SR C Stobbs
RS P Ramos
RS C Pascual
RS T Abernathy
RP S Shea
C - E Fitz Gerald
1B M Vernon
2B P Runnels
SS J Valdivielso
3B E Yost
LF R Sievers
MO T Umphlett
RU C Paula
OF E Oravetz
SS- B Kline
M C Dressen

BRO 1956 NL
SP D Newcombe
SP R Craig
SP S Maglie
SP C Erskine
SR D Drysdale
RP C Labine
RP E Roebuck
RP D Bessent
RP K Lehman
C R Campanella
1B G Hodges
2L J Gilliam
SS P Reese
3B R Jackson
LU S Amoros
CF D Snider
RF C Furillo
3I J Robinson
M W Alston

CHI 1956 NL
SP B Rush
SP S Jones
SR W Hacker
SP D Kaiser
RP T Lown
RS J Davis
RP V Valentinetti
RS J Brosnan
C H Landrith
1B D Fondy
2B G Baker
SS E Banks
3B D Hoak
LF M Irvin
CF P Whisenant
RF W Moryn
LU J King
UT E Miksis
M S Hack

CIN 1956 NL
SR B Lawrence
SR J Klippstein
SR J Nuxhall
SR A Fowler
SR H Jeffcoat
RP H Freeman
RS T Acker
RP J Black
C E Bailey
1B T Kluszewski
2B J Temple
SS R McMillan
3B R Jablonski
LF F Robinson
CF G Bell
RF W Post
CU- S Burgess
M B Tebbetts

OF- B Thurman
M B Tebbetts

MIL 1956 NL
SP W Spahn
SP L Burdette
SP B Buhl
SR R Crone
SR G Conley
RP E Johnson
RP B Trowbridge
C D Crandall
1B J Adcock
2B D O'Connell
SS J Logan
3B E Mathews
LF B Thomson
CF B Bruton
RF H Aaron
1B F Torre
M1 C Grimm
M2 F Haney

NY 1956 NL
SP J Antonelli
SP R Gomez
SP A Worthington
SR J Hearn
RS D Littlefield
RP H Wilhelm
RS R Ridzik
RP M Grissom
C - B Sarni
1B B White
2B- R Schoendienst
UI D Spencer
3B F Castleman
LF J Brandt
CF W Mays
RF D Mueller
LU D Rhodes
3U- H Thompson
M B Rigney

PHI 1956 NL
SP R Roberts
SP H Haddix
SP C Simmons
SP S Rogovin
SP S Miller
RS B Miller
RS J Meyer
RP R Negray
C1 S Lopata
1B W Dropo
2B N Fox
2B T Kazanski
SS S Hamner
3B W Jones
LF D Ennis
CF R Ashburn
RF E Valo
RU- J Greengrass
2U- S Hemus
M M Smith

PIT 1956 NL
SP B Friend
SP R Kline
SP V Law
SR R Munger
RP R Face
RP N King
RS F Waters
C J Shepard
1B D Long
2B- B Mazeroski
SS D Groat
3L F Thomas
LR L Walls
CF B Virdon
RO R Clemente
UT B Skinner
C - H Foiles
M B Bragan

STL 1956 NL
SP V Mizell
SP T Poholsky
SP M Dickson
SR H Wehmeier
SR W Schmidt
RS L McDaniel
RP L Jackson
RP J Collum
C - H Smith
1R S Musial
2S D Blasingame
SS A Dark
3B K Boyer
LF R Repulski
CF B Del Greco
R1 W Moon
M F Hutchinson

BAL 1956 AL
SP R Moore
SP C Johnson

SP B Wight
SR H Brown
SR E Palica
RP G Zuverink
RS M Fornieles
RS D Ferrarese
RS B Loes
C1 G Triandos
1B- B Boyd
2B B Gardner
SS W Miranda
C D Crandall
1B J Adcock
2B D O'Connell
SS J Logan
3B E Mathews
LF B Thomson
CF B Bruton
RF H Aaron
1B F Torre
C - H Smith
M P Richards

BOS 1956 AL
SP T Brewer
SP F Sullivan
SP W Nixon
SP M Parnell
RS I Delock
RP B Porterfield
RP T Hurd
C S White
1B M Vernon
2B B Goodman
SS D Buddin
3B B Klaus
LF T Williams
CF J Piersall
RF J Jensen
UT D Gernert
LU G Stephens
23- T Lepcio
M P Higgins

CHI 1956 AL
SP B Pierce
SP D Donovan
SP J Harshman
SP J Wilson
SP B Keegan
RS G Staley
RP D Howell
C S Lollar
1B W Dropo
2B N Fox
SS L Aparicio
3B F Hatfield
LF M Minoso
CF L Doby
RF J Rivera
3B- S Esposito
CF L Berberet
1O- D Philley
M M Marion

CLE 1956 AL
SP E Wynn
SP B Lemon
SP H Score
SP M Garcia
RP D Mossi
RP R Narleski
RP C McLish
RP A Houtteman
C J Hegan
1B V Wertz
2B B Avila
SS C Carrasquel
3B A Rosen
UT A Smith
CF J Busby
RF R Colavito
LF G Woodling
UI- G Strickland
1U- P Ward
M A Lopez

DET 1956 AL
SP F Lary
SP P Foytack
SP B Hoeft
SP V Trucks
SP S Gromek
RP A Aber
RS D Maas
RP W Masterson
C F House
1U E Torgeson
2B P Bolling
SS H Kuenn
3B R Boone
LF C Maxwell
CF B Tuttle
RF A Kaline
UT- W Belardi
C - R Wilson
M B Harris

KC 1956 AL
SR A Ditmar
SP W Burnette
SP L Kretlow
SR T Herriage
RS T Gorman
RS J Crimian
RP B Shantz
CU- T Thompson
12 V Power
23- J Finigan
SS J DeMaestri
3B H Lopez
LU- L Skizas
MO J Groth
RU H Simpson
LU G Zernial
UO- E Slaughter
M L Boudreau

NY 1956 AL
SP W Ford
SP J Kucks
SP D Larsen
SR T Sturdivant
SP T Byrne
RS T Morgan
RS B Grim
C Y Berra
1B B Skowron
2B B Martin
SS G McDougald
3B A Carey
LC E Howard
CF M Mantle
RF H Bauer
OI J Collins
2S- J Coleman
M C Stengel

WAS 1956 AL
SP C Stobbs
SR C Pascual
SR P Ramos
SR D Stone
SR B Wiesler
RS B Stewart
RP B Chakales
RS H Griggs
RP C Grob
C C Courtney
12 P Runnels
2U- H Plews
SS- J Valdivielso
3B E Yost
L1 R Sievers
MU W Herzog
RF J Lemon
CU L Berberet
CF K Olson
UO- E Oravetz
M C Dressen

BRO 1957 NL
SP D Drysdale
SP D Newcombe
SP J Podres
SP D McDevitt
SR R Craig
RP C Labine
RS K Koufax
RP E Roebuck
RP S Maglie
C R Campanella
1B G Hodges
2B J Gilliam
SS C Neal
3U P Reese
RF C Furillo
LU S Amoros
OF- E Valo
UI- D Zimmer
M W Alston

CHI 1957 NL
SP M Drabowsky
SP D Drott
SP B Rush
SR D Elston
SR D Hillman
RP T Lown
RS J Brosnan
RP D Littlefield
C C Neeman
1B D Long
2B B Morgan
SS- J Littrell
S3 E Banks
LO L Walls
RF W Moryn
OI J Bolger

LM C Tanner
M B Scheffing

CIN 1957 NL
SR B Lawrence
SP H Jeffcoat
SR J Nuxhall
SR D Gross
SR J Klippstein
RS T Acker
RP H Freeman
RS A Fowler
RP R Sanchez
C E Bailey
1B G Crowe
2B J Temple
SS R McMillan
3B D Hoak
LU F Robinson
CF G Bell
RF W Post
CU- S Burgess
M B Tebbetts

MIL 1957 NL
SP W Spahn
SP L Burdette
SP B Buhl
SR G Conley
SR B Trowbridge
RS J Pizarro
RS T Phillips
RP E Johnson
RP D McMahon
C D Crandall
1B F Torre
2B R Schoendienst
SS J Logan
3B E Mathews
LF W Covington
CF- B Bruton
RM H Aaron
UO- A Pafko
M F Haney

NY 1957 NL
SP R Gomez
SR J Antonelli
SP C Barclay
SR S Miller
SP R Crone
RS A Worthington
RP M Grissom
RP R Monzant
C - V Thomas
1B W Lockman
23 D O'Connell
SI D Spencer
3U J Jablonski
LF H Sauer
CF W Mays
RF D Mueller
3O O Virgil
1U- G Harris
OF- D Rhodes
LU- B Thomson
M B Rigney

PHI 1957 NL
SP R Roberts
SP J Sanford
SP C Simmons
SP H Haddix
SR D Cardwell
RP T Farrell
RP J Hearn
RP B Miller
RP S Morehead
C S Lopata
1B E Bouchee
2B G Hamner
SS C Fernandez
3B W Jones
LF H Anderson
CF R Ashburn
RL R Repulski
RF B Bowman
M M Smith

PIT 1957 NL
SP B Friend
SP R Kline
SP V Purkey
SP V Law
RS L Arroyo
RP R Face
RS R Swanson
RP B Smith
C H Foiles
1B D Fondy
2B B Mazeroski
SS D Groat
3U G Freese
LU B Skinner
CF B Virdon
RF R Clemente
3S G Baker

UT F Thomas
OI- P Smith
M1 B Bragan
M2 D Murtaugh

STL 1957 NL
SR L Jackson
SP L McDaniel
SP S Jones
SR H Wehmeier
SR V Mizell
RS W Schmidt
RP L Merritt
RP H Wilhelm
C H Smith
1B S Musial
2B D Blasingame
SS A Dark
3B E Kasko
LR W Moon
M3 K Boyer
LR D Ennis
UT J Cunningham
MU B Smith
M F Hutchinson

BAL 1957 AL
SP C Johnson
SP R Moore
SR B Loes
SP H Brown
SR B O'Dell
RP G Zuverink
RS B Wight
RP K Lehman
C G Triandos
1B B Boyd
2B B Gardner
SS W Miranda
3B G Kell
LF B Nieman
CF- J Busby
RA Pilarcik
RL T Francona
S- Brideweser
UO-J Durham
C - J Ginsberg
RP R Richards

BOS 1957 AL
SP F Sullivan
SP T Brewer
SP W Nixon
SP M Fornieles
SP D Sisler
RP I Delock
RS B Porterfield
C S White
1U D Gernert
2B- T Lepcio
SS B Klaus
3B F Malzone
LF T Williams
CF J Piersall
LU G Stephens
1U M Vernon
C- P Daley
M P Higgins

CHI 1957 AL
SP B Pierce
SP D Donovan
SP J Wilson
SP J Harshman
SR B Keegan
RS B Fischer
SP G Staley
RP D Howell
C- S Lollar
1B- E Torgeson
2B N Fox
SS L Aparicio
3B B Phillips
LF M Minoso
LO J Landis
OI S Esposito
RU J Rivera
1U W Dropo
M A Lopez

CLE 1957 AL
SP E Wynn
SR M Garcia
SR D Mossi
SR B Lemon
RS R Narleski
RS C McLish
RS B Daley
RP D Tomanek
C - J Hegan
1B V Wertz
SS C Carrasquel
M A Smith
1F G Woodling

CF R Maris
RF R Colavito
IO L Raines
1U- J Altobelli
2S- G Strickland
M K Farrell

DET 1957 AL
SR J Bunning
SP F Lary
SR D Maas
SR P Foytack
SP B Hoeft
RP- L Sleater
RP H Byrd
C F House
1B- R Boone
2B F Bolling
SS H Kuenn
3B R Bertoia
CF B Tuttle
RF A Kaline
M J Tighe

KC 1957 AL
SP N Garver
SP A Kellner
SP R Terry
SR J Urban
SR A Portocarrero
RS T Morgan
RS T Gorman
RS V Trucks
RS W Burnette
C H Smith
1B V Power
2S B Hunter
SS J DeMaestri
3B H Lopez
LF G Zernial
CF- W Held
R3 L Skizas
UO B Cerv
UT- I Noren
C - T Thompson
M1 L Boudreau
M2 H Craft

NY 1957 AL
SP T Sturdivant
SR J Kucks
SP B Turley
SP B Shantz
SP D Larsen
RS A Ditmar
RP W Ford
CL B Grim
RP T Byrne
C Y Berra
1B B Skowron
2B B Richardson
SS B McDougald
3B- A Carey
LC E Howard
CF M Mantle
RF H Bauer
UT T Kubek
LU E Slaughter
UT- J Collins
M C Stengel

WAS 1957 AL
SR P Ramos
SR C Stobbs
SP C Pascual
SR R Kemmerer
RS T Clevenger
RP D Hyde
RP B Byerly
C L Berberet
1I P Runnels
2B H Plews
SS R Bridges
3B E Yost
LF R Sievers
CF B Usher
RF J Lemon
U1 J Adcock
UT- F Mantilla
M F Haney

PHI 1958 NL
SP R Roberts
SP R Semproch
SR J Sanford
SP C Simmons
RP D Cardwell
RP T Farrell
RS J Meyer
RP J Hearn
C - S Lopata
1B- E Bouchee
2B S Hemus
SS C Fernandez
3B W Jones
L1 H Anderson
CF R Ashburn
RF W Post
2I T Kazanski
UO-B Bowman
UT- D Philley
OF- R Repulski
M1 M Smith
M2 E Sawyer

PIT 1958 NL
SP B Friend
SP R Kline
SP V Law
SR C Raydon

SS E Banks
3B A Dark
LF W Moryn
CF B Thomson
RF L Walls
UO-J Bolger
32- J Goryl
M B Scheffing

CIN 1958 NL
SP B Purkey
SR B Lawrence
SP H Haddix
SR J Nuxhall
SP D Newcombe
RS T Acker
RP H Jeffcoat
RP W Schmidt
C E Bailey
1B G Crowe
2B J Temple
SS R McMillan
3B D Hoak
LM F Robinson
CF G Bell
RF J Lynch
CU S Burgess
S3 A Grammas
OF B Thurman
UT- D Fondy
OI- P Whisenant
M1 B Tebbetts
M2 J Dykes

LA 1958 NL
SR D Drysdale
SP J Podres
SR S Koufax
SP S Williams
RP C Labine
RS F Kipp
RP J Klippstein
RS C Erskine
C J Roseboro
1B G Hodges
2B C Neal
SS D Zimmer
3B- D Gray
UT J Gilliam
ML G Cimoli
RF C Furillo
MU D Snider
OI N Larker
M W Alston

MIL 1958 NL
SP W Spahn
SP L Burdette
SP B Rush
SP C Willey
SP J Pizarro
RP J Jay
RS G Conley
RP D McMahon
RP B Trowbridge
C D Crandall
1B F Torre
2B R Schoendienst
SS J Logan
3B E Mathews
LF A Pafko
CF B Bruton
RF H Aaron
1U J Adcock
LF- W Covington
UT- F Mantilla
M F Haney

BAL 1958 AL
SP J Harshman
SR B O'Dell
SP A Portocarrero
SR M Pappas
SP C Johnson
RS B Loes
RP H Brown
RP G Zuverink
RP K Lehman
C G Triandos
1B B Boyd
2B B Gardner
SS W Miranda
3B B Robinson
RL G Woodling
CF J Busby
RO A Pilarcik
SS F Castleman
LF B Nieman
UT D Williams
1U- J Marshall
M P Richards

BOS 1958 AL
SP T Brewer
SP F Sullivan
SR I Delock
SP D Sisler
RP M Wall
RS M Fornieles
RP L Kiely
C S White
1B D Gernert
21 P Runnels
SS B Buddin
3B F Malzone
LF T Williams
CF J Piersall
RF J Jensen
LU G Stephens
M P Higgins

CHI 1958 AL
SP D Donovan
SP B Pierce
SP E Wynn
SP J Wilson

SP G Witt
CL R Face
RS B Porterfield
RP D Gross
RP R Blackburn
C H Foiles
1U T Kluszewski
2B B Mazeroski
SS D Groat
3B F Thomas
LF B Skinner
CF B Virdon
RF R Clemente
M D Murtaugh

STL 1958 NL
SP S Jones
SR L Jackson
SP V Mizell
SR J Brosnan
SR B Mabe
RP L McDaniel
RS B Muffett
RP P Paine
RP B Wight
C- H Smith
1B S Musial
2B D Blasingame
SU E Kasko
3B K Boyer
LF D Ennis
CF C Flood
RL W Moon
1R J Cunningham
RC G Green
LU I Noren
M1 F Hutchinson
M2 S Hack

SF 1958 NL
SP J Antonelli
SR R Gomez
SR S Miller
SR M McCormick
SR R Monzant
RS A Worthington
RP M Grissom
C B Schmidt
C R Wilson
1B O Cepeda
2B D O'Connell
SS D Spencer
3B J Davenport
LF- H Sauer
CF W Mays
RF W Kirkland
3U- R Jablonski
UT- W Lockman
M B Rigney

DET 1958 AL
SP F Lary
SP P Foytack
SP J Bunning
SR B Hoeft
SR H Moford
RP H Aguirre
RP T Morgan
C R Wilson
1B G Harris
2B F Bolling
S3 B Martin
3B- R Bertoia
LF C Maxwell
CF H Kuenn
RF A Kaline
LO- J Groth
M1 J Tighe
M2 B Norman

SR R Moore
RP G Staley
RP B Shaw
C S Lollar
1B E Torgeson
2B N Fox
SS L Aparicio
3B B Goodman
UO J Rivera
CF J Landis
LR A Smith
3U S Esposito
1B- R Boone
3O- B Phillips
M A Lopez

CLE 1958 AL
SP C McLish
SR M Grant
SR R Narleski
SR G Bell
SR D Ferrarese
RS D Mossi
RS H Wilhelm
C R Nixon
1B M Vernon
23 A Avila
SS- B Hunter
IO B Harrell
LF M Minoso
MU-L Doby
RF R Colavito
2S B Moran
OI- G Geiger
IO V Power
M1 B Bragan
M2 J Gordon

KC 1958 AL
SP R Terry
SP N Garver
SR R McMillan
SP J Urban
SR B Grim
RS M Dickson
RP T Gorman
RP D Tomanek
RS B Daley
C G Triandos
1B- V Power
2B- M Baxes
SS J DeMaestri
23 H Lew
LF B Cerv
MR B Tuttle
RF R Maris
UO B Martyn
IC H Smith
OI- W Herzog
1U- H Simpson
IO- P Ward
M H Craft

NY 1958 AL
SP B Turley
SP W Ford
SR A Ditmar
SR J Kucks
SR B Shantz
RP D Larsen
RP D Maas
CL R Duren
RS Z Monroe
CU Y Berra
1B B Skowron
2B G McDougald
SS T Kubek
3B A Carey
LF N Siebern
CF M Mantle
RF H Bauer
CU H Howard
3B- J Lumpe
OF- E Slaughter
M C Stengel

WAS 1958 AL
SP P Ramos
SR R Kemmerer
SP C Pascual
SR H Griggs
SR V Valentinetti
RP T Clevenger
RP D Hyde
C C Courtney
1B N Zauchin
2B- K Aspromonte
SS R Bridges
3B E Yost
LF R Sievers
CF A Pearson
RF J Lemon
OI N Chrisley
23 H Plews
SU- O Alvarez
UT- J Becquer
M C Lavagetto

CHI 1959 NL
SP B Anderson
SP G Hobbie
SR D Hillman
SP M Drabowsky
SP A Ceccarelli
RP B Henry
RP D Elston
RS J Buzhardt
C S Taylor
1B D Long
2B T Taylor
SS E Banks
3B A Dark
LM B Thomson
CF G Altman
RF L Walls
1U J Marshall
LF W Moryn
M B Scheffing

CIN 1959 NL
SP D Newcombe
SP B Purkey
SP J Nuxhall
SP J O'Toole
RS O Pena
RS B Lawrence
RP W Schmidt
RP T Acker
C E Bailey
1B F Robinson
2B J Temple
S3 E Kasko
3B- R Bertoia
LF C Maxwell
CF V Pinson
RF G Bell
3L T Thomas
SS- R McMillan
M1 M Smith
M2 F Hutchinson

LA 1959 NL
SP D Drysdale
SP J Podres
SR S Koufax
SR R Craig
SR D McDevitt
RS S Williams
RP C Labine
RP A Fowler
C J Roseboro
1B G Hodges
2B C Neal
SS D Zimmer
3B J Gilliam
LF W Moon
CF D Demeter
RM D Snider
RO R Fairly
1O N Larker
SS- M Wills
M W Alston

MIL 1959 NL
SP W Spahn
SP L Burdette
SP B Buhl
SR J Jay
SR C Willey
RS B Rush
RP B McMahon
C D Crandall
1B J Adcock
2I F Mantilla
SS J Logan
3B E Mathews
LF W Covington
CF B Bruton
RF H Aaron
1B F Torre
M F Haney

BAL 1959 AL
SP H Wilhelm
SP M Pappas
SR B O'Dell
SP J Walker
SR H Brown
CL B Loes
RP E Johnson
C G Triandos
1B B Boyd
2B B Gardner
SS C Carrasquel
3B- B Robinson
2I F Mantilla
SS J Logan
3B B Klaus
LF B Nieman
UO-A Pearson
M P Richards

BOS 1959 AL
SP T Brewer
SP J Casale
SP T Sullivan
SR B Monbouquette
SR I Delock
RS F Baumann
RP M Fornieles

PHI 1959 NL
SP R Roberts
SP J Owens
SP G Conley
SP D Cardwell
SR R Semproch
RP H Robinson
RP T Phillips
RP T Farrell
1B E Bouchee
2B S Anderson
SS J Koppe
3B G Freese
LF H Anderson
CF R Ashburn
RF W Post
UT D Philley
M E Sawyer

PIT 1959 NL
SP V Law
SP B Friend
SP H Haddix
SP R Kline
SR B Daniels
RP R Face
C S Burgess
1B D Stuart
2B B Mazeroski
SS D Groat
3B D Hoak
LF B Skinner
CF B Virdon
RF R Clemente
RO R Mejias
1U R Nelson
IO- D Schofield
M D Murtaugh

STL 1959 NL
SP L Jackson
SP V Mizell
SR E Broglio
SR G Blaylock
RS L McDaniel
RP M Bridges
C H Smith
1B S Musial
2B D Blasingame
SS A Grammas
3B K Boyer
UO G Cimoli
CF C Flood
RF J Cunningham
L1 B White
M S Hemus

SF 1959 NL
SP J Antonelli
SR S Jones
SR M McCormick
SP J Sanford
RS M Miller
RP A Worthington
C H Landrith
1B O Cepeda
2B D Spencer
SS E Bressoud
3B J Davenport
LF J Brandt
CF W Mays
RF W Kirkland
RU F Alou
UL- L Wagner
M B Rigney

KC 1959 AL
SR B Daley
SP N Garver
SR R Herbert
SR J Kucks
RS B Grim
RP T Sturdivant
RP M Dickson
C F House
1B K Hadley
2B- W Terwilliger
SS J DeMaestri
3I D Williams
LF B Cerv
CF B Tuttle
RF R Maris
2S J Lumpe
3U H Smith
M H Craft

NY 1959 AL
SP W Ford
SR A Ditmar
SR B Turley
SR D Maas
SP R Terry
RP J Coates
RP B Shantz
CL R Duren
C Y Berra

RP L Kiely
C S White
1U D Gernert
21 P Runnels
SS B Buddin
3B F Malzone
LO- G Stephens
ML G Geiger
RF J Jensen
MU M Keough
1U V Wertz
LU T Williams
M1 P Higgins
M2 R York
M3 B Jurges

CHI 1959 AL
SP E Wynn
SR B Shaw
SP B Pierce
SP D Donovan
SR B Latman
RP G Staley
RP T Lown
C S Lollar
1B E Torgeson
2B N Fox
SS L Aparicio
3B B Phillips
LR A Smith
CF J Landis
RL- J Rivera
3U B Goodman
M A Lopez

CLE 1959 AL
SR G Bell
SP C McLish
SR M Grant
SP H Score
RS J Perry
RS M Garcia
C- R Nixon
1B V Power
2B- B Martin
S3 W Held
3S G Strickland
LF M Minoso
CF J Piersall
RF R Colavito
M1 T Francona
23- J Baxes
M J Gordon

DET 1959 AL
SP J Bunning
SP P Foytack
SP D Mossi
SP F Lary
RS R Narleski
RP T Morgan
RP D Sisler
C L Berberet
1B G Harris
2B F Bolling
SS B Bridges
3B E Yost
LF C Maxwell
CF A Kaline
RF H Kuenn
1U- B Osborne
SS- C Veal
M1 B Norman
M2 J Dykes

1B- B Skowron
2B- B Richardson
SO T Kubek
3L H Lopez
LU N Siebern
CF M Mantle
RF H Bauer
IC E Howard
UI G McDougald
1U- M Throneberry
M C Stengel

WAS 1959 AL
SP C Pascual
SP P Ramos
SP R Kemmerer
SP B Fischer
RS T Clevenger
RS H Griggs
RS C Stobbs
RP H Woodeshick
C - N Naragon
1B R Sievers
2B- R Bertoia
SS- B Consolo
3B H Killebrew
LF J Lemon
CF B Allison
RU F Throneberry
U2 J Becquer
UO-L Green
S2- R Samford
M C Lavagetto

CHI 1960 NL
SR G Hobbie
SP B Anderson
SP D Cardwell
SP D Ellsworth
RP D Elston
RS S Morehead
RS M Freeman
RP J Schaffernoth
C - M Thacker
1B E Bouchee
2B- J Kindall
SS E Banks
3B R Santo
ML R Ashburn
OI G Altman
RF B Will
UT F Thomas
23 D Zimmer
M1 C Grimm
M2 L Boudreau

CIN 1960 NL
SP B Purkey
SP J Hook
SP J O'Toole
SR C McLish
RS J Nuxhall
RP J Brosnan
RP B Henry
RP C Osteen
C E Bailey
1L F Robinson
2B B Martin
SS R McMillan
32 E Kasko
LR- W Post
CF V Pinson
RL G Bell
OF J Lynch
3U- W Jones
M F Hutchinson

LA 1960 NL
SP D Drysdale
SP J Podres
SP S Williams
SR S Koufax
SP R Craig
RP L Sherry
RP E Roebuck
RS D McDevitt
C J Roseboro
1B N Larker
2B C Neal
SS M Wills
3B J Gilliam
LF W Moon
MO T Davis
RF F Howard
1B G Hodges
OF D Snider
M W Alston

MIL 1960 NL
SR L Burdette
SP W Spahn
SP B Buhl
SP C Willey
SR J Jay
RP J Pizarro
RP D McMahon
RP R Piche

C D Crandall
1B J Adcock
2B C Cottier
SS J Logan
3B E Mathews
LF A Spangler
CF B Bruton
RF H Aaron
LF W Covington
1U- M Dressen
M C Dressen

PHI 1960 NL
SP R Roberts
SP J Buzhardt
SP G Conley
SP J Owens
SR D Green
RP T Farrell
RS C Short
RP A Mahaffey
RP R Gomez
C - J Coker
1B P Herrera
2B T Taylor
SS- R Amaro
3B- A Dark
LU B Smith
CF B Del Greco
RF K Walters
LU T Curry
UO J Callison
CU- C Dalrymple
CF- T Gonzalez
UI- B Malkmus
M1 E Sawyer
M2 A Cohen
M3 G Mauch

PIT 1960 NL
SP B Friend
SP V Law
SP H Haddix
SP V Mizell
RP R Face
RP F Green
C S Burgess
1B D Stuart
2B B Mazeroski
SS D Groat
3B D Hoak
LF B Skinner
CF B Virdon
RF R Clemente
ML G Cimoli
1B R Nelson
C - H Smith
M D Murtaugh

STL 1960 NL
SP L Jackson
SR E Broglio
SP R Sadecki
SP C Simmons
SR R Kline
RP L McDaniel
C H Smith
1B B White
2B J Javier
SS D Spencer
3B K Boyer
OI S Musial
CF C Flood
RF J Cunningham
UI A Grammas
RL- W Moryn
LU- B Nieman
C - C Sawatski
M S Hemus

SF 1960 NL
SP M McCormick
SP S Jones
SP J Sanford
SR B O'Dell
RS J Antonelli
RP S Miller
RP G Maranda
C B Schmidt
1U W McCovey
2B D Blasingame
SS E Bressoud
3B J Davenport
LO F Alou
CF W Mays
RF W Kirkland
32 J Amalfitano
L1 O Cepeda
S3- A Rodgers
M1 B Rigney
M2 T Sheehan

BAL 1960 AL
SR C Estrada
SP M Pappas
SR J Fisher
SP S Barber
SR H Brown

RS H Wilhelm
RS J Walker
RP G Jones
C G Triandos
1B J Gentile
2B M Breeding
SS R Hansen
3B B Robinson
LF G Woodling
MR J Brandt
RL- G Stephens
RU A Pilarcik
CF- J Busby
CU- C Courtney
1B- W Dropo
M P Richards

BOS 1960 AL
SP B Monbouquette
SP T Brewer
SR F Sullivan
SP I Delock
SP B Muffett
RP M Fornieles
RP T Sturdivant
RS J Casale
RP T Borland
C - R Nixon
1B V Wertz
2B P Runnels
SS D Buddin
3B F Malzone
LF T Williams
CF W Tasby
RF L Clinton
2S P Green
RF- G Geiger
M1 B Jurges
M2 D Baker
M3 P Higgins

CHI 1960 AL
SP E Wynn
SP B Pierce
SP B Shaw
SR F Baumann
SP H Score
RP G Staley
RS R Kemmerer
RS D Donovan
RP T Lown
C S Lollar
1B R Sievers
2B N Fox
SS L Aparicio
3B G Freese
LF M Minoso
CF J Landis
SS J Valdivielso
U1- T Kluszewski
M A Lopez

CLE 1960 AL
SP J Perry
SR M Grant
SP G Bell
SR B Latman
SR D Stigman
RS B Locke
RP J Klippstein
RP D Newcombe
C J Romano
1B V Power
23 K Aspromonte
SS W Held
3B B Phillips
LF T Francona
CF J Piersall
RF H Kuenn
2B J Temple
M1 J Gordon
M2 J White
M3 J Dykes

DET 1960 AL
SP F Lary
SP J Bunning
SP D Mossi
SR B Bruce
SR P Burnside
RS H Aguirre
RS P Foytack
RP D Sisler
RS B Fischer
C - L Berberet
1B N Cash
2B P Bolling
SS C Fernandez
3B E Yost
LF C Maxwell
CF A Kaline
RF R Colavito
OI N Chrisley
1B- S Bilko
M1 J Dykes

M2 B Hitchcock
M3 J Gordon

KC 1960 AL
SP R Herbert
SP B Daley
SP D Hall
SR N Garver
SR J Kucks
RS K Johnson
RP M Kutyna
C - P Daley
1U M Throneberry
2B J Lumpe
SS K Hamlin
3B A Carey
L1 N Siebern
CF B Tuttle
UO R Snyder
RU H Bauer
IO D Williams
RL- W Herzog
M B Elliott

NY 1960 AL
SP A Ditmar
SP W Ford
SR B Turley
SR R Terry
SR J Coates
RP B Shantz
RP D Maas
RP R Duren
RP J Gabler
C E Howard
1B B Skowron
2B B Richardson
SS T Kubek
3B C Boyer
LU H Lopez
CF M Mantle
RF R Maris
CO Y Berra
32 G McDougald
LU- B Cerv
M C Stengel

WAS 1960 AL
SP P Ramos
SR D Lee
SP C Pascual
SR J Kralick
SR H Woodeshick
RS T Clevenger
RS C Stobbs
CL R Moore
C E Battey
1U J Becquer
2B B Gardner
SS J Valdivielso
3B R Bertoia
LF J Lemon
MU L Green
RF B Allison
SS B Consolo
MO D Dobbek
13 H Killebrew
UO-F Throneberry
M C Lavagetto

CHI 1961 NL
SP D Cardwell
SP G Hobbie
SP D Ellsworth
SP J Curtis
RS B Anderson
RP D Elston
RS D Drott
RS J Brewer
C - D Bertell
1B E Bouchee
2B D Zimmer
SS E Banks
3B R Santo
LF B Williams
CF A Heist
RF G Altman
MU R Ashburn
2S J Kindall
C - S Taylor
OI- B Will
M1 V Himsl
M2 H Craft
M3 V Himsl
M4 E Tappe
M5 H Craft
M6 V Himsl
M7 E Tappe
M8 J Klein
M9 E Tappe

CIN 1961 NL
SP J O'Toole
SP J Jay
SP B Purkey
SP K Hunt
M1 J Dykes

RP J Brosnan
CL B Henry
RS J Hook
RP S Jones
C - J Zimmerman
1B G Coleman
2B D Blasingame
SS E Kasko
3B G Freese
OF W Post
CF V Pinson
RL F Robinson
UO G Bell
OF J Lynch
M F Hutchinson

LA 1961 NL
SP S Koufax
SP D Drysdale
SP S Williams
SR J Podres
SR R Craig
RP L Sherry
RP T Farrell
RP R Perranoski
C J Roseboro
1B G Hodges
2B C Neal
SS M Wills
32 J Gilliam
LF W Moon
CF W Davis
OI T Davis
OI R Fairly
1B N Larker
RU- F Howard
RM-D Snider
M W Alston

MIL 1961 NL
SP L Burdette
SP W Spahn
SP B Buhl
SR C Willey
SP B Hendley
RS D Nottebart
RP D McMahon
C J Torre
1B J Adcock
2B F Bolling
SS R McMillan
3B E Mathews
LF F Thomas
RM H Aaron
RU L Maye
M1 C Dressen
M2 B Tebbetts

PHI 1961 NL
SP A Mahaffey
SR J Buzhardt
SR F Sullivan
SR C Short
SP R Roberts
RS D Ferrarese
RS D Green
RP J Owens
RP J Baldschun
C - C Dalrymple
1B P Herrera
2B T Taylor
SS R Amaro
3B C Smith
LR J Callison
RP K Walters
RU- K Walters
UI B Malkmus
OI D Demeter
UO- B Smith
UT- L Walls
M G Mauch

PIT 1961 NL
SP B Friend
SP J Gibbon
SP H Haddix
SP E Francis
SP V Mizell
RP R Face
RP C Labine
RS B Shantz
RP A McBean
C S Burgess
1B D Stuart
2B B Mazeroski
SS D Groat
3B D Hoak
LF B Skinner
CF B Virdon
RF R Clemente
M D Murtaugh

STL 1961 NL
SP R Sadecki
SP J Gibson
SP L Jackson
SP C Simmons

RF F Robinson
RP L McDaniel
RS B Miller
RS A Cicotte
C - J Schaffer
1B B White
2B J Javier
SU- A Grammas
3B K Boyer
LF S Musial
CF C Flood
RL C James
RF J Cunningham
UO D Taussig
CU- C Sawatski
M1 S Hemus
M2 J Keane

SF 1961 NL
SP M McCormick
SP J Sanford
SP J Marichal
SR S Jones
SP B Loes
RP S Miller
RS B O'Dell
RP J Duffalo
RP E Bolin
C E Bailey
1B W McCovey
2B J Amalfitano
SS J Pagan
3B J Davenport
LI H Kuenn
CF W Mays
SS C Fernandez
3B S Boros
1L O Cepeda
UO-M Alou
M A Dark

BAL 1961 AL
SP S Barber
SP C Estrada
SR J Fisher
SP M Pappas
SP H Brown
RS B Hoeft
RP H Wilhelm
RS D Hall
RP W Stock
C G Triandos
1B J Gentile
2B J Adair
SS R Hansen
3B B Robinson
LO R Snyder
CF J Brandt
RU W Herzog
CF- B Del Greco
UT- D Johnson
C - J Pignatano
M1 J Gordon
M2 H Bauer

BOS 1961 AL
SP B Monbouquette
SP G Conley
SP D Schwall
SP I Delock
RS T Stallard
RS B Muffett
RP D Hillman
C J Pagliaroni
1B P Runnels
2B C Schilling
SS D Buddin
3B F Malzone
LF C Yastrzemski
CF G Geiger
RF J Jensen
SU- P Green
UO- C Hardy
C - R Nixon
2S- R Bridges
1B V Wertz
M P Higgins

CHI 1961 AL
SR J Pizarro
SR F Baumann
SR B Pierce
SP C McLish
SP R Herbert
RP T Lown
RP E Wynn
RP R Kemmerer
RP D Larsen
C S Lollar
1B R Sievers
2B N Fox
SS L Aparicio
RF B Allison
M1 C Lavagetto
M2 S Mele

RF F Robinson
13 J Martin
M A Lopez

CLE 1961 AL
SP M Grant
SP G Bell
SP J Perry
SR B Latman
SP W Hawkins
RP F Funk
RP B Locke
RP B Allen
RS D Stigman
C J Romano
1B V Power
2B J Temple
SS W Held
3B B Phillips
LF T Francona
CF J Piersall
RF W Kirkland
M1 J Dykes
M2 M Harder

DET 1961 AL
SP F Lary
SP J Bunning
SP D Mossi
SR P Foytack
SR P Regan
RP T Fox
RP H Aguirre
C - D Brown
1B N Cash
2B J Wood
SS C Fernandez
3B S Boros
LF R Colavito
CF B Bruton
RF A Kaline
C - M Roarke
M B Scheffing

KC 1961 AL
SR J Archer
SR N Bass
SR J Walker
SR J Nuxhall
RS E Rakow
RP B Kunkel
RS A Ditmar
C H Sullivan
1L N Siebern
2B J Lumpe
SS D Howser
3B W Causey
LR L Posada
CF- B Del Greco
UT- D Johnson
C - J Pignatano
M1 J Gordon
M2 H Bauer

LA 1961 AL
SP K McBride
SR E Grba
SR T Bowsfield
SR R Moeller
SR R Kline
RS J Donohue
RP T Morgan
RS R Duren
RP A Fowler
C E Averill
1B S Bilko
2B- K Aspromonte
SS- J Koppe
3B- E Yost
LF L Wagner
MU K Hunt
RM A Pearson
1U- T Kluszewski
R1 L Thomas
2S- R Bridges
M B Rigney

MIN 1961 AL
SP P Ramos
SP C Pascual
SP J Kralick
SP J Kaat
RS D Lee
RP R Moore
RP B Pleis
C E Battey
1B H Killebrew
2B B Martin
SS Z Versalles
3B B Tuttle
LF J Lemon
CF L Green
RF B Allison
M1 C Lavagetto
M2 S Mele

M3 C Lavagetto
M4 S Mele

NY 1961 AL
SP W Ford
SR R Stafford
SR R Terry
SR R Sheldon
SP B Daley
RP L Arroyo
RS J Coates
C E Howard
1B B Skowron
2B B Richardson
SS T Kubek
3B C Boyer
LU Y Berra
CF M Mantle
RF R Maris
CU- J Blanchard
LU- H Lopez
M R Houk

WAS 1961 AL
SP J McClain
SP B Daniels
SP D Donovan
SP E Hobaugh
SP R Burnside
RS M Kutyna
RP J Klippstein
RP D Sisler
CU G Green
1B D Long
2B C Cottier
SS- C Veal
32 D O'Connell
OI M Keough
CF W Tasby
RU J Woodling
RU J King
LU C Hinton
3U- B Klaus
M M Vernon

CHI 1962 NL
SP B Buhl
SP D Ellsworth
SR D Cardwell
SR C Koonce
SR G Hobbie
RP B Anderson
RP B Schultz
RP D Elston
RP D Gerard
C - D Bertell
1B B Banks
2B K Hubbs
SS A Rodgers
3B R Santo
LF B Williams
CF L Brock
RF G Altman
UO-D Landrum
U1- B Will
M1 E Tappe
M2 L Klein
M3 C Metro

CIN 1962 NL
SP B Purkey
SP J Jay
SP J O'Toole
SP J Maloney
RS J Klippstein
RP J Brosnan
RS T Wills
1B J Edwards
1B G Coleman
2B D Blasingame
SS L Cardenas
3B E Kasko
LF W Post
CF V Pinson
RF F Robinson
OI M Keough
LU J Lynch
M F Hutchinson

HOU 1962 NL
SR T Farrell
SP K Johnson
SP B Bruce
SP J Golden
SP H Woodeshick
RP B Tiefenauer
RP D McMahon
RP R Kemmerer
C H Smith
1B N Larker
2B J Amalfitano
SS B Lillis
3B B Aspromonte
LU A Spangler
CF C Warwick
RF R Mejias

(HOU 1962 NL continued)
LU J Pendleton
UI- B Goodman
M H Craft

LA 1962 NL
SP D Drysdale
SP J Podres
SR S Williams
SP S Koufax
RP E Roebuck
RP R Perranoski
RP L Sherry
RP P Ortega
C J Roseboro
1B R Fairly
2B L Burright
SS M Wills
23 J Gilliam
LF T Davis
CF W Davis
RF F Howard
1U- T Harkness
OI- W Moon
M W Alston

MIL 1962 NL
SP W Spahn
SP B Shaw
SP B Hendley
SP L Burdette
SP T Cloninger
RS J Curtis
RS C Willey
RP D Nottebart
C D Crandall
1B J Adcock
RP F Bolling
SS R McMillan
3B E Mathews
ML L Maye
MR H Aaron
RF- M Jones
1B T Aaron
M B Tebbetts

NY 1962 NL
SP R Craig
SP A Jackson
SP J Hook
SP B Miller
RS C Anderson
RS B Moorhead
RP R Daviault
RP K Mac Kenzie
C - C Cannizzaro
1B M Throneberry
2S C Neal
SS E Chacon
3I F Mantilla
LF F Thomas
MO J Hickman
OI R Ashburn
UO J Christopher
UT R Kanehl
OF- G Woodling
M C Stengel

PHI 1962 NL
SP A Mahaffey
SP J Hamilton
SP D Bennett
SP C McLish
RS C Short
RS D Green
RP J Baldschun
RP B Smith
C C Dalrymple
1B R Sievers
2B T Taylor
SS B Wine
3M D Demeter
LU T Savage
CF T Gonzalez
RF J Callison
LF W Covington
SB K Blaus
1U F Torre
M G Mauch

PIT 1962 NL
SP B Friend
SP A McBean
SR E Francis
SP H Haddix
SP V Law
SS T Sturdivant
CL R Face
RP D Olivo
RP J Lamabe
C S Burgess
1B D Stuart
2B B Mazeroski
SS D Groat
3B D Hoak
LF B Skinner
CF B Virdon
RF R Clemente
LO- H Goss
M D Murtaugh

STL 1962 NL
SP L Jackson
SP B Gibson
SP E Broglio
SP R Washburn
SP C Simmons
RP L McDaniel
RP R Sadecki
RP B Shantz
RP D Ferrarese
C G Oliver
1B B White
2B J Javier
SS J Gotay
3B K Boyer
LU S Musial
CF C Flood
RF C James
C - C Sawatski
IF R Schoendienst
LU- B Smith
M J Keane

SF 1962 NL
SP B O'Dell
SP J Sanford
SP J Marichal
SP B Pierce
RP S Miller
RS B Bolin
RP D Larsen
C - T Haller
1B O Cepeda
2B C Hiller
SS J Pagan
3B J Davenport
LF H Kuenn
CF W Mays
RF F Alou
C - E Bailey
OI- W McCovey
M A Dark

BAL 1962 AL
SP C Estrada
SP M Pappas
SP R Roberts
SP J Fisher
SP S Barber
RS D Hall
RP B Hoeft
RP H Wilhelm
RP W Stock
C - G Triandos
1B J Gentile
2B- M Breeding
SS J Adair
3B R Robinson
LF B Powell
CF J Brandt
UO R Snyder
RU W Herzog
UO-D Nicholson
CU- C Lau
UT- D Williams
M B Hitchcock

BOS 1962 AL
SP G Conley
SP B Monbouquette
SP E Wilson
SP D Schwall
RP D Radatz
RP M Fornieles
RP A Earley
RP H Kolstad
C - J Pagliaroni
1B P Runnels
2B C Schilling
SS E Bressoud
3B F Malzone
CF C Yastrzemski
CF G Geiger
RM C Hardy
RF L Clinton
C - B Tillman
M P Higgins

CHI 1962 AL
SP R Herbert
SP J Pizarro
SP E Wynn
SP J Buzhardt
SP J Horlen
RS E Fisher
RS F Baumann
RP D Zanni
RP T Lown
C C Carreon
1B J Cunningham
2B N Fox
SS L Aparicio
3L A Smith
LR F Robinson
CF J Landis
RM M Hershberger
C - S Lollar
M A Lopez

CLE 1962 AL
SP D Donovan
SR P Ramos
SP J Perry
SR B Latman
SP M Grant
RS G Bell
RP F Funk
C J Romano
1B T Francona
2B J Kindall
SS W Held
3B B Phillips
LF C Essegian
CF T Cline
RF W Kirkland
LU- A Luplow
UO-D Dillard
M1 M McGaha
M2 M Harder

DET 1962 AL
SP J Bunning
SR H Aguirre
SP D Mossi
SR P Regan
SP P Foytack
RS S Jones
RP R Kline
CL T Fox
RP R Nischwitz
C D Brown
1B N Cash
2B J Wood
SS C Fernandez
3B S Boros
LF R Colavito
CF B Bruton
RF A Kaline
23 D McAuliffe
OI- B Morton
M B Scheffing

KC 1962 AL
SP E Rakow
SR D Pfister
SR J Walker
SR B Fischer
SR D Segui
RS J Wyatt
RS D Wickersham
RP D McDevitt
C - H Sullivan
1B N Siebern
2B J Lumpe
SS- D Howser
3B E Charles
LF M Jimenez
ML B Del Greco
RF G Cimoli
UI W Causey
CF J Tartabull
OI- G Alusik
M H Bauer

LA 1962 AL
SR D Chance
SP B Belinsky
SR E Grba
SP D Lee
SP K McBride
RP T Bowsfield
RP A Fowler
RP R Duren
RP J Spring
1R L Thomas
2B B Moran
SS J Koppe
3B F Torres
LR L Wagner
CF A Pearson
RF- G Thomas
LU- E Averill
UT- T Burgess
M B Rigney

MIN 1962 AL
SP J Kaat
SP C Pascual
SP J Kralick
SR J Stigman
SR J Bonikowski
RS L Stange
SR R Moore
RP G Maranda
C E Battey
1B V Power
2B B Allen
SS Z Versalles
3B R Rollins
LF H Killebrew
CF L Green
RF B Allison
RF B Tuttle
U2- D Mincher
12 P Runnels
23 J Temple
M S Mele

NY 1962 AL
SP R Terry
SP W Ford
SP B Stafford
SR J Bouton
SR R Sheldon
RS J Coates
RS B Daley
CL M Bridges
C E Howard
1B B Skowron
2B B Richardson
SL T Tresh
3B C Boyer
LU H Lopez
CF M Mantle
RM R Maris
OC- Y Berra
OC- J Blanchard
UO- J Reed
M R Houk

WAS 1962 AL
SP D Stenhouse
SR D Rudolph
SR T Cheney
SR B Daniels
SR P Burnside
RP C Osteen
RS S Hamilton
RP M Kutyna
RP J Hannan
C K Retzer
1B H Bright
2B C Cottier
SS K Hamlin
3S B Johnson
UT C Hinton
CF J Piersall
RU J King
UO J Hicks
IF- D O'Connell
3U- J Schaive
C - B Schmidt
M M Vernon

CHI 1963 NL
SP D Ellsworth
SP L Jackson
SP B Buhl
SP G Hobbie
SP P Toth
CL L McDaniel
RP D Elston
RP J Brewer
C D Bertell
1B E Banks
2B K Hubbs
SS A Rodgers
3B R Santo
LF B Williams
CF- E Burton
RF L Brock
MU-D Landrum
M B Kennedy

CIN 1963 NL
SP J Maloney
SP J O'Toole
SP J Nuxhall
SP J Tsitouris
SP J Jay
RP B Purkey
RP A Worthington
RP B Henry
C J Edwards
1B G Coleman
2B P Rose
SS L Cardenas
3B- G Freese
LF F Robinson
CF V Pinson
RU T Harper
UT- M Keough
M F Hutchinson

HOU 1963 NL
SP K Johnson
SP T Farrell
SP D Nottebart
SP B Bruce
SP H Brown
RP H Woodeshick
RP D McMahon
RP J Umbricht
RS C Zachary
C J Bateman
1B R Staub
2B E Fazio
SS B Lillis
3B B Aspromonte
LM A Spangler
CF H Goss
RF C Warwick
12 P Runnels
23 J Temple
M H Craft

LA 1963 NL
SP D Drysdale
SP S Koufax
SP J Podres
SR B Miller
RP R Perranoski
RP L Sherry
C J Roseboro
1B R Fairly
2B J Gilliam
SS M Wills
3B- K McMullen
LF T Davis
CF W Davis
RF F Howard
UQ W Moon
SS D Tracewski
1U- B Skowron
M W Alston

MIL 1963 NL
SP W Spahn
SR D Lemaster
SR B Hendley
SR T Cloninger
SP B Sadowski
RS B Shaw
RS H Fischer
RP R Raymond
RP R Piche
C1 J Torre
1L- G Oliver
2B F Bolling
SS R McMillan
3B E Mathews
ML L Maye
MU-M Jones
RF H Aaron
S3 D Menke
C - D Crandall
M B Bragan

NY 1963 NL
SR R Craig
SP A Jackson
SP C Willey
SR T Stallard
SR J Hook
RS G Cisco
RP L Bearnarth
RP K Mac Kenzie
RP D Rowe
C C Coleman
1B T Harkness
2B R Hunt
SS A Moran
3B- C Neal
LF F Thomas
OI J Hickman
UO D Snider
UT R Kanehl
RU- E Kranepool
M C Stengel

PHI 1963 NL
SP C McLish
SP R Culp
SR C Short
SP A Mahaffey
SR D Green
RP J Baldschun
RP D Bennett
RP J Klippstein
RS R Duren
C C Dalrymple
1B R Sievers
2B T Taylor
SS B Wine
3B D Hoak
ML T Gonzalez
M3 D Demeter
RF J Callison
S3 R Amaro
LF W Covington
1U- F Torre
M G Mauch

PIT 1963 NL
SP B Friend
SP D Cardwell
SP R Herbert
SP D Schwall
SR J Gibbon
RS A McBean
RP T Sisk
RS C Zachary
C - J Pagliaroni
1B D Clendenon
2B B Mazeroski
SS D Schofield
3B B Bailey
OI W Stargell
CF B Virdon
RF R Clemente
C - S Burgess
SU- J Logan
LU- J Lynch
UO-T Savage
M D Murtaugh

STL 1963 NL
SP B Gibson
SP E Broglio
SP C Simmons
SP R Sadecki
RS R Taylor
RP B Shantz
RP E Bauta
C T McCarver
1B B White
2B J Javier
SS D Groat
3B K Boyer
LU C James
CF C Flood
RF G Altman
LF S Musial
M J Keane

SF 1963 NL
SP J Marichal
SP J Sanford
SP B O'Dell
SR B Pierce
RS B Bolin
RS J Fisher
RP G Perry
RS J Duffalo
C E Bailey
1B O Cepeda
2B C Hiller
SS J Pagan
3B J Davenport
LF W McCovey
CF W Mays
RF F Alou
C T Haller
OI H Kuenn
UI- E Bowman
M A Dark

BAL 1963 AL
SP S Barber
SP R Roberts
SP M Pappas
SP M McCormick
SP D McNally
RS S Miller
RP D Hall
RP W Stock
C J Orsino
1B J Gentile
2B J Adair
SS L Aparicio
3B R Robinson
LF B Powell
MR J Brandt
MR R Snyder
MI B Saverine
RF A Smith
2U- B Johnson
M B Hitchcock

BOS 1963 AL
SP B Monbouquette
SP E Wilson
SP D Morehead
SP B Heffner
RP J Lamabe
RP D Radatz
RP A Earley
RS W Wood
C - B Tillman
1B D Stuart
2B C Schilling
SS E Bressoud
3B F Malzone
LF C Yastrzemski
MU G Geiger
RF L Clinton
LF F Wagner
C R Nixon
M J Pesky

CHI 1963 AL
SR G Peters
SP J Pizarro
SP J Buzhardt
SP J Horlen
RP H Wilhelm
RS E Fisher
RS J Brosnan
RP F Baumann
C J Martin
1B T McCraw
2B N Fox
SS R Hansen
3B P Ward
LF D Nicholson
CF J Landis
RF R Robinson
C C Carreon
MR M Hershberger
UI A Weis
M A Lopez

CLE 1963 AL
SP M Grant
SP D Donovan
SP J Kralick
SP R Ramos
SR B Latman
RS G Bell
RP J Walker
RP T Abernathy
RP B Allen
C - J Azcue
1B F Whitfield
2O W Held
S2- J Kindall
3B M Alvis
LF T Francona
CF- V Davalillo
MR W Kirkland
1B- J Adcock
RU A Luplow
C - J Romano
M B Tebbetts

DET 1963 AL
SP J Bunning
SP H Aguirre
SR P Regan
SR M Lolich
SP D Mossi
C E Bailey
RP F Lary
RP T Fox
RP B Anderson
RP T Sturdivant
C G Triandos
1B N Cash
2B- J Wood
SS D McAuliffe
3B B Phillips
LF R Colavito
CF B Bruton
RF A Kaline
CU B Freehan
M1 B Scheffing
M2 C Dressen

KC 1963 AL
SP D Wickersham
SP O Pena
SP M Drabowsky
SP E Rakow
SR D Segui
RS T Bowsfield
RP J Wyatt
RP B Fischer
C - D Edwards
1B N Siebern
2B J Lumpe
SS W Causey
3B E Charles
MU R Del Greco
CF- J Tartabull
RG G Cimoli
LU C Essegian
UO- G Alusik
M E Lopat

LA 1963 AL
SR D Chance
SP K McBride
SR D Osinski
SR D Lee
RP J Navarro
RP A Fowler
RS P Foytack
RP M Nelson
C B Rodgers
1R L Thomas
2B B Moran
SS J Fregosi
3B F Torres
LF F Wagner
CF A Pearson
UO- B Perry
UT- B Sadowski
M B Rigney

MIN 1963 AL
SP C Pascual
SP D Stigman
SP J Kaat
SR J Perry
SR L Stange
RP B Dailey
RP B Pleis
RP G Roggenburk
C E Battey
1B V Power
2B B Allen
SS Z Versalles
3B R Rollins
LF H Killebrew
ML J Hall
RF B Allison
CF L Green
1U- D Mincher
M S Mele

NY 1963 AL
SP W Ford
SP R Terry
SR J Bouton
SP A Downing
SP S Williams
CL H Reniff
RP S Hamilton
C E Howard
1B J Pepitone
2B B Richardson
SS T Kubek
3B C Boyer
LF H Lopez
ML T Tresh
UO J Reed
RF- R Maris
M R Houk

WAS 1963 AL
SR C Osteen
SR D Rudolph
SP T Cheney
SR J Duckworth
RP K Kline
RP P Burnside
RP E Roebuck
RP J Bronstad
C - K Retzer
1U B Osborne
2B C Cottier
SS E Brinkman
3B- D Zimmer
LR C Hinton
CF D Lock
RF J King
LU M Minoso
1U D Phillips
M1 M Vernon
M2 E Yost
M3 G Hodges

CHI 1964 NL
SP L Jackson
SP D Ellsworth
SP B Buhl
SR L Burdette
SP E Broglio
RP L McDaniel
RP D Elston
RS S Slaughter
C D Bertell
1B E Banks
2B A Amalfitano
SS A Rodgers
3B R Santo
LF B Williams
CF B Cowan
RU- L Gabrielson
IO J Stewart
M B Kennedy

CIN 1964 NL
SP J O'Toole
SP J Maloney
SP B Purkey
SR J Jay
SR J Tsitouris
RS J Nuxhall
RS S Ellis
RP B McCool
RP B Henry
C J Edwards
1B D Johnson
2B P Rose
SS L Cardenas
3B S Boros
LF T Harper
CF V Pinson
RL R Robinson
RU M Keough
1U- G Coleman
M1 F Hutchinson
M2 D Sisler
M3 F Hutchinson
M4 D Sisler

HOU 1964 NL
SP K Johnson
SP B Bruce
SP T Farrell
SP D Nottebart
SP H Brown
RS D Larsen
CL H Woodeshick

RP C Raymond
C J Grote
1R W Bond
2B N Fox
SS E Kasko
3B B Aspromonte
LF A Spangler
MU-M White
RF- J Gaines
UI B Lillis
1R- R Staub
M1 H Craft
M2 L Harris

LA 1964 NL
SP D Drysdale
SP S Koufax
SP P Ortega
SP J Moeller
RP B Miller
RP R Perranoski
RS J Brewer
C J Roseboro
1B R Fairly
2B N Oliver
SS M Wills
3U J Gilliam
LF T Davis
CF W Davis
RF F Howard
OI W Parker
23 D Tracewski
M W Alston

MIL 1964 NL
SP T Cloninger
SP D Lemaster
SR W Spahn
SR B Sadowski
SP H Fischer
RS W Blasingame
RP B Tiefenauer
RP B Hoeft
RP C Olivo
C1 J Torre
1B- G Oliver
2B F Bolling
SS D Menke
3B E Mathews
LF R Carty
ML L Maye
RF H Aaron
OI F Alou
OI T Cline
C - E Bailey
M B Bragan

NY 1964 NL
SP J Fisher
SP T Stallard
SP A Jackson
SR G Cisco
RP B Wakefield
RP L Bearnarth
RP B Hunter
CU J Gonder
1B E Kranepool
2B R Hunt
SS R McMillan
3S C Smith
LF G Altman
ML J Hickman
RF J Christopher
UT R Kanehl
OC-H Taylor
M C Stengel

PHI 1964 NL
SP J Bunning
SR C Short
SP D Bennett
SP A Mahaffey
SR R Culp
RP J Baldschun
RP E Roebuck
RS R Wise
RP J Boozer
C C Dalrymple
1L J Herrnstein
2B T Taylor
SS B Wine
3B D Allen
LF W Covington
CF T Gonzalez
RF J Callison
S1 R Amaro
UT C Rojas
M G Mauch

PIT 1964 NL
SP B Veale
SP B Friend
SP V Law
SP J Gibbon
SR S Blass
CL A McBean
RP R Face

RP T Butters
RP T Sisk
C - J Pagliaroni
1B D Clendenon
2B B Mazeroski
SS D Schofield
3O B Bailey
OI M Mota
CF B Virdon
RF R Clemente
3U G Freese
LU J Lynch
OI W Stargell
SS- G Alley
M D Murtaugh

STL 1964 NL
SP J Gibson
SP C Simmons
SR R Sadecki
SR R Craig
RP R Taylor
RS M Cuellar
CL B Schultz
C T McCarver
1B B White
2B J Javier
SS D Groat
3B K Boyer
LF L Brock
CF C Flood
RF- M Shannon
LU- C James
OF- C Warwick
M J Keane

SF 1964 NL
SP J Marichal
SR G Perry
SR B Bolin
SP B Hendley
SR R Herbel
RP J Sanford
RP B Shaw
RS B O'Dell
RP J Duffalo
C T Haller
1B O Cepeda
2B H Lanier
SS J Pagan
3B J Hart
LR H Kuenn
CF W Mays
RF J Alou
UO M Alou
S3 J Davenport
LU W McCovey
OF- D Snider
M A Dark

BAL 1964 AL
SP M Pappas
SP W Bunker
SP R Roberts
SP D McNally
SR S Barber
CL S Miller
RP H Haddix
RP D Hall
RS D Vineyard
C - D Brown
1B N Siebern
2B J Adair
SS L Aparicio
3B B Robinson
LF B Powell
CF J Brandt
RF S Bowens
IO- B Johnson
C - J Orsino
M H Bauer

BOS 1964 AL
SP B Monbouquette
SP E Wilson
SR J Lamabe
SP D Morehead
RP D Radatz
RS B Heffner
RS P Charton
RS B Spanswick
C B Tillman
1B- D Stuart
2U D Jones
SS E Bressoud
3B F Malzone
LU T Conigliaro
CF C Yastrzemski
RF L Thomas
UT F Mantilla
CU- R Nixon
M1 J Pesky
M2 Herman

CHI 1964 AL
SP G Peters
SP J Pizarro

SP J Horlen
SP J Buzhardt
SP R Herbert
RP H Wilhelm
RP E Fisher
C J Martin
1L T McCraw
2B A Weis
SS R Hansen
3B P Ward
RF R Robinson
CF J Landis
RM M Hershberger
23 D Buford
LF- D Nicholson
UO-G Stephens
M A Lopez

CLE 1964 AL
SP J Kralick
SP S McDowell
SP D Donovan
SR S Siebert
SR P Ramos
RP L Tiant
RP D McMahon
RP G Bell
RP T Abernathy
C J Romano
1R B Chance
2B L Brown
SS D Howser
3B M Alvis
LF L Wagner
CF V Davalillo
RU T Francona
UT W Held
1B F Whitfield
C - J Azcue
R2- C Salmon
M1 G Strickland
M2 B Tebbetts

DET 1964 AL
SP D Wickersham
SR M Lolich
SR H Aguirre
SR P Regan
SP D McLain
RS R Rakow
RP L Sherry
RP F Gladding
RP T Fox
C B Freehan
1B N Cash
2B J Lumpe
SS D McAuliffe
3B D Wert
LF G Brown
MO G Thomas
RF A Kaline
MU B Bruton
OI D Demeter
M C Dressen

KC 1964 AL
SP O Pena
SP D Segui
SP J O'Donoghue
SR M Drabowsky
RP J Wyatt
RS T Bowsfield
RP W Stock
RS J Santiago
C - D Edwards
1B J Gentile
2B D Green
SS W Causey
3B E Charles
UO J Tartabull
CF N Mathews
RF R Colavito
OI G Alusik
CU-B Bryan
OF- M Jimenez
M1 E Lopat
M2 M McGaha

LA 1964 AL
SR D Chance
SP F Newman
SR B Latman
SR B Belinsky
SP K McBride
RS J Tsitouris
RP D Osinski
RS D Lee
RP B Duliba
C B Rodgers
1B J Adcock
2B B Knoop
SS J Fregosi
3U T Torres
UO W Smith
LM- J Piersall
RF- L Clinton

UO A Pearson
UI T Satriano
M B Rigney

MIN 1964 AL
SP C Pascual
SP J Kaat
SP D Stigman
SP M Grant
RS G Arrigo
CL A Worthington
RP J Perry
RP B Pleis
C E Battey
1O B Allison
2B- B Allen
SS Z Versalles
3B R Rollins
LF H Killebrew
CF J Hall
RF T Oliva
1U D Mincher
M S Mele

NY 1964 AL
SP J Bouton
SP A Downing
SP W Ford
SR R Terry
SP R Sheldon
RP P Mikkelsen
RP H Reniff
RP B Stafford
RP S Hamilton
C E Howard
1B J Pepitone
2B B Richardson
SS T Kubek
3B C Boyer
LM T Tresh
MU R Mantle
RU R Maris
UT P Linz
LO H Lopez
M Y Berra

WAS 1964 AL
SP C Osteen
SP B Narum
SP B Daniels
SR A Koch
RS S Ridzik
RS J Hannan
RP R Kline
RS D Rudolph
C M Brumley
1B- B Skowron
2B D Blasingame
SS D Brinkman
3S J Kennedy
LF C Hinton
CF D Lock
RF J King
1U D Phillips
UO F Valentine
M G Hodges

CHI 1965 NL
SP L Jackson
SP D Ellsworth
SP B Buhl
SR C Koonce
RP T Abernathy
RP L McDaniel
RP B Humphreys
RP B Hoeft
C - V Roznovsky
1B E Banks
2B G Beckert
SS D Kessinger
3B R Santo
UO D Clemens
CF D Landrum
RO B Williams
OI J Stewart
OI- G Altman
M1 B Kennedy
M2 L Klein

CIN 1965 NL
SP S Ellis
SP J Maloney
SR J Jay
SR J Nuxhall
SP J Tsitouris
RP J O'Toole
RP B McCool
RP T Davidson
SR J Craig
C - J Edwards
1B T Perez
2B P Rose
SS L Cardenas
3B D Johnson
LF T Harper
CF V Pinson

RF F Robinson
1B G Coleman
M D Sisler

HOU 1965 NL
SP B Bruce
SP T Farrell
SP D Nottebart
SP L Dierker
SR D Giusti
RS C Raymond
RP J Owens
RP R Taylor
RP M Cuellar
C R Brand
1O W Bond
2B J Morgan
SS B Lillis
3B B Aspromonte
LF L Maye
CF J Wynn
RF R Staub
OF J Gaines
1B- J Gentile
M L Harris

LA 1965 NL
SP S Koufax
SP D Drysdale
SP C Osteen
SP J Podres
RP R Perranoski
RP B Miller
RS H Reed
RP J Brewer
C J Roseboro
1B W Parker
2B J Lefebvre
SS M Wills
3B J Kennedy
LF L Johnson
CF W Davis
RF R Fairly
3U J Gilliam
M W Alston

MIL 1965 NL
SP T Cloninger
SP W Blasingame
SP K Johnson
SP D Lemaster
SR B Sadowski
RP B O'Dell
RS H Fischer
RP D Osinski
RP P Niekro
C1 J Torre
UT F Alou
2B F Bolling
SS W Woodward
3B E Mathews
LF- R Carty
CF M Jones
RF H Aaron
C1 G Oliver
OI T Cline
S3- M DeLa Hoz
M B Bragan

NY 1965 NL
SP J Fisher
SP A Jackson
SP W Spahn
SR G Cisco
RS T McGraw
RS T Parsons
RP L Bearnarth
RS L Miller
C C Cannizzaro
1B E Kranepool
2B G Hiller
SS R McMillan
3B C Smith
LO R Swoboda
UT J Hickman
RM J Lewis
OF J Christopher
2I B Klaus
MU-B Cowan
M1 C Stengel
M2 W Westrum

PHI 1965 NL
SP C Short
SP J Bunning
SP R Culp
SP J Herbert
SR B Belinsky
RP G Wagner
RP J Baldschun
RP E Roebuck
C C Dalrymple
1B ...

ML T Gonzalez
RF J Callison
1S R Amaro
2M C Rojas
MU-J Briggs
M G Mauch

PIT 1965 NL
SP B Veale
SP D Cardwell
SP B Friend
SP V Law
SP J Gibbon
RP A McBean
RS T Sisk
RP D Schwall
RP W Wood
C J Pagliaroni
1B D Clendenon
2B B Mazeroski
S2 G Alley
3B B Bailey
LF W Stargell
CF B Virdon
RF R Clemente
UO M Mota
M H Walker

STL 1965 NL
SP B Gibson
SP C Simmons
SR T Stallard
SP B Sadecki
SR B Purkey
RS R Washburn
RP N Briles
RP H Woodeshick
RP D Dennis
C T McCarver
1B B White
2B- J Javier
SS D Groat
3B K Boyer
LF L Brock
CF C Flood
RU M Shannon
UT P Gagliano
OI- T Francona
M R Schoendienst

SF 1965 NL
SP J Marichal
SP B Shaw
SR G Perry
SR R Herbel
RS B Bolin
CL F Linzy
RP M Murakami
C T Haller
1B W McCovey
2B H Lanier
SS D Schofield
3B J Hart
LO M Alou
CF W Mays
RF J Alou
UI J Davenport
LF- L Gabrielson
M H Franks

BAL 1965 AL
SP S Barber
SP M Pappas
SP D McNally
SP W Bunker
SP R Roberts
RP S Miller
RP D Hall
RP D Larsen
C - D Brown
1L B Powell
2B J Adair
SS L Aparicio
3B B Robinson
RL C Blefary
CF J Blair
UO R Snyder
1U N Siebern
RU- S Bowens
UO- J Brandt
UI- B Johnson
M H Bauer

BOS 1965 AL
SP E Wilson
SP B Monbouquette
SP D Morehead
SP J Lonborg
SP B Bennett
RP D Radatz
RP A Earley
RP J Ritchie
RP B Duliba
C B Tillman
1B L Thomas
2B F Mantilla

SS R Petrocelli
3B F Malzone
LF C Yastrzemski
MU L Green
RF T Conigliaro
SS E Bressoud
3U D Jones
CF- R Gosger
M Herman

CAL 1965 AL
SP F Newman
SP D Chance
SP M Lopez
SR G Brunet
SR R May
RP B Lee
RP A Gatewood
RP B Rodgers
1B V Power
2B B Knoop
SS J Fregosi
3B P Schaal
LF W Smith
CF J Cardenal
RU A Pearson
1B J Adcock
RF- L Clinton
M B Rigney

CHI 1965 AL
SP J Horlen
SP J Buzhardt
SR T John
SP G Peters
SP B Howard
RP E Fisher
RP H Wilhelm
RP B Locker
C J Martin
1B B Skowron
2B D Buford
SS R Hansen
3B P Ward
LF D Cater
CF K Berry
RF- R Robinson
C J Romano
2U A Weis
M A Lopez

CLE 1965 AL
SP S McDowell
SR L Tiant
SR S Siebert
SP R Terry
RS L Stange
RP G Bell
RP D McMahon
RP F Weaver
C J Azcue
1B F Whitfield
2B P Gonzalez
SS L Brown
3B M Alvis
LF L Wagner
CF V Davalillo
RF R Colavito
UT C Hinton
SU D Howser
M B Tebbetts

DET 1965 AL
SP M Lolich
SP D McLain
SP H Aguirre
SP D Wickersham
SP J Sparma
RP T Fox
RP L Sherry
RP F Gladding
RP O Pena
C B Freehan
1B N Cash
2B J Lumpe
SS D McAuliffe
3B D Wert
LF W Horton
OI D Demeter
OI A Kaline
LU- G Brown
SU- R Oyler
M1 B Swift
M2 C Dressen

KC 1965 AL
SP F Talbot
SP R Sheldon
SP J O'Donoghue
SP D Segui
SR C Hunter
RP J Wyatt
RP W Stock
RP J Dickson
RP D Mossi
C B Bryan

1B K Harrelson
2B D Green
SS B Campaneris
3B E Charles
LF- T Reynolds
OI J Landis
RF M Hershberger
UI W Causey
C - R Lachemann
UT- S Rosario
M1 M McGaha
M2 H Sullivan

MIN 1965 AL
SP M Grant
SP J Kaat
SR J Perry
SP C Pascual
SR D Boswell
CL A Worthington
RP J Klippstein
RS D Stigman
RP M Nelson
C E Battey
1B D Mincher
2B J Kindall
SS Z Versalles
3B R Rollins
LF B Allison
CF J Hall
RF T Oliva
13 H Killebrew
OF S Valdespino
MU-J Nossek
C - J Zimmerman
M S Mele

NY 1965 AL
SP M Stottlemyre
SP W Ford
SP A Downing
SP J Bouton
SP B Stafford
RP P Ramos
RP H Reniff
RP P Mikkelsen
RP S Hamilton
C E Howard
1B J Pepitone
2B B Richardson
SS T Kubek
3B C Boyer
LF M Mantle
ML T Tresh
OI H Lopez
1U R Barker
SU P Linz
MR-R Moschitto
M J Keane

WAS 1965 AL
SP P Richert
SP P Ortega
SR B Narum
SR M McCormick
SR B Daniels
RP R Kline
RP R Koplitz
RS H Koplitz
RP M Bridges
C - M Brumley
1B- D Nen
2B D Blasingame
SS E Brinkman
3B K McMullen
LF F Howard
CF D Lock
UT W Held
2S K Hamlin
RU J King
RL W Kirkland
1U- J Cunningham
IC- D Zimmer
M G Hodges

ATL 1966 NL
SP T Cloninger
SP K Johnson
SP D Lemaster
RP C Carroll
RP C Olivo
RP T Abernathy
RP P Niekro
C J Torre
1L F Alou
2S W Woodward
SS D Menke
3B E Mathews
LF R Carty
CF M Jones
RF H Aaron
M1 B Bragan
M2 B Hitchcock

CHI 1966 NL
SP D Ellsworth
SP K Holtzman

SR B Hands
RS F Jenkins
RS C Koonce
RS B Hendley
C R Hundley
1B E Banks
2B G Beckert
SS D Kessinger
3B R Santo
LM B Browne
CF A Phillips
RF B Williams
OI- G Altman
M L Durocher

CIN 1966 NL
SP J Maloney
SP S Ellis
SP M Pappas
SP J O'Toole
SP J Nuxhall
RP B McCool
RP D Nottebart
RP T Davidson
RP J Baldschun
C J Edwards
1B T Perez
2B P Rose
SS L Cardenas
3B T Helms
L1 D Johnson
CF V Pinson
RL T Harper
1U- G Coleman
CU- D Pavletich
UT- C Ruiz
OF A Shamsky
RU- D Simpson
M1 D Heffner
M2 D Bristol

HOU 1966 NL
SR M Cuellar
SP D Giusti
SP L Dierker
SR T Farrell
SP B Bruce
RP C Raymond
RS B Latman
RP T Raylor
RP J Owens
C J Bateman
C H Harrison
2B J Morgan
SS J Jackson
3B B Aspromonte
LF L Maye
CF J Wynn
RL R Staub
RO D Nicholson
M G Hatton

LA 1966 NL
SP S Koufax
SP D Drysdale
SP C Osteen
SP D Sutton
RP P Regan
RP B Miller
RP R Perranoski
RS J Moeller
C J Roseboro
1B W Parker
2B J Lefebvre
SS M Wills
3I J Kennedy
LR L Johnson
CF W Davis
RF R Fairly
LF T Davis
3B- J Gilliam
M W Alston

NY 1966 NL
SP J Fisher
SP D Ribant
SP B Shaw
RP R Gardner
RS J Hamilton
RS D Selma
SP B Hepler
RP L Bearnarth
C J Grote
1B E Kranepool
2B R Hunt
3I E Bressoud
3B K Boyer
LF R Swoboda
CF C Jones
RO A Luplow
IO C Hiller
MU-B Murphy
M W Westrum

PHI 1966 NL
SP J Bunning
SP C Short

SP L Jackson
SR B Buhl
SR R Culp
RP D Knowles
RP R Wise
RP R Herbert
C C Dalrymple
2O C Rojas
1B B White
2O D Groat
3L D Allen
LM T Gonzalez
CF- J Briggs
RF J Callison
23 T Taylor
MO-J Brandt
UT- H Kuenn
M G Mauch

PIT 1966 NL
SP B Veale
SP W Fryman
SP V Law
SP S Blass
SR T Sisk
RP P Mikkelsen
RS D Cardwell
RP A McBean
RP R Face
C J Pagliaroni
1B D Clendenon
2B B Mazeroski
SS G Alley
3B B Bailey
LF W Stargell
CF M Alou
RF R Clemente
OI M Mota
3B J Pagan
M H Walker

STL 1966 NL
SP B Gibson
SP A Jackson
SP R Washburn
SR N Briles
SP L Jaster
RP J Hoerner
RP H Woodeshick
RP D Dennis
C T McCarver
1B O Cepeda
2B J Javier
SS D Maxvill
3B C Smith
LF L Brock
CF C Flood
RF M Shannon
UI J Buchek
UT- T Francona
IO- P Gagliano
M R Schoendienst

SF 1966 NL
SP J Marichal
SP G Perry
SP B Bolin
SR R Herbel
SP R Sadecki
RP L McDaniel
RP F Linzy
RP B Priddy
RS J Gibbon
C T Haller
1B W McCovey
2B H Lanier
S2 T Fuentes
3B J Hart
LR J Alou
CF W Mays
RF O Brown
S3 J Davenport
LU- L Gabrielson
LU- C Peterson
M H Franks

BAL 1966 AL
SP D McNally
SP J Palmer
SP W Bunker
SP S Barber
SP J Miller
RS E Watt
CL S Miller
RP M Drabowsky
RP E Fisher
C A Etchebarren
1B B Powell
2O D Johnson
SS L Aparicio
3B B Robinson
LF C Blefary
CF P Blair
RF F Robinson
ML R Snyder

UO-S Bowens
M H Bauer

BOS 1966 AL
SR J Lonborg
SP J Santiago
SR B Brandon
SP L Stange
SP E Wilson
RP D McMahon
RS D Stigman
RP J Wyatt
RP D Osinski
C M Ryan
1B G Scott
2B G Smith
SS R Petrocelli
3B J Foy
LF C Yastrzemski
CF- D Demeter
RF T Conigliaro
2U D Jones
OF- L Green
M1 Herman
M2 P Runnels

CAL 1966 AL
SP D Chance
SP G Brunet
SP M Lopez
SP F Newman
RP B Lee
RS J Sanford
RP M Rojas
RPI L Burdette
C B Rodgers
1B N Siebern
2B B Knoop
SS J Fregosi
3B P Schaal
LF- R Reichardt
CF J Cardenal
RU E Kirkpatrick
IC T Satriano
1B- J Adcock
UR- F Malzone
OF- W Smith
M B Rigney

CHI 1966 AL
SP T John
SP J Horlen
SP G Peters
SR J Buzhardt
SP B Howard
RS J Lamabe
RP B Locker
RP D Higgins
RS J Pizarro
C J Romano
1B T McCraw
2U A Weis
SS- L Elia
3B D Buford
LR K Berry
CF T Agee
RF F Robinson
S2 J Adair
1B B Skowron
LI- P Ward
M E Stanky

CLE 1966 AL
SP G Bell
SP S Siebert
SP S McDowell
SR S Hargan
SR L Tiant
RS J O'Donoghue
RP J Kralick
RP D Radatz
RP B Allen
C J Azcue
1B F Whitfield
2B P Gonzalez
SS L Brown
3B M Alvis
LF L Wagner
CF V Davalillo
RF R Colavito
UT C Hinton
UT C Salmon
UO-J Landis
M1 B Tebbetts
M2 G Strickland

DET 1966 AL
SP D McLain
SP M Lolich
SP E Wilson
SR D Wickersham
SR J Podres
RP O Pena
RS H Aguirre
RS B Monbouquette
CL L Sherry
C B Freehan

1B N Cash
2B J Lumpe
SS D McAuliffe
3B D Wert
LF W Horton
MR A Kaline
RF J Northrup
2U J Wood
U3- G Brown
CF- M Stanley
2B- D Tracewski
M1 C Dressen
M2 B Swift
M3 F Skaff

KC 1966 AL
SR L Krausse
SP C Hunter
SP J Nash
SP P Lindblad
RP J Aker
RP K Sanders
C R Roof
1B- K Harrelson
2B D Green
SS B Campaneris
3B E Charles
LU L Stahl
MU-J Nossek
RF M Hershberger
UT D Cater
OI R Repoz
UT- O Chavarria
LM- J Gosger
M A Dark

MIN 1966 AL
SP J Kaat
SP M Grant
SP J Perry
SP D Boswell
SR J Merritt
RP A Worthington
RP C Pascual
RP P Cimino
RP D Siebler
C E Battey
1B D Mincher
2B B Allen
SS Z Versalles
31 H Killebrew
LO J Hall
CF T Uhlaender
RF T Oliva
2U C Tovar
3U- R Rollins
M S Mele

NY 1966 AL
SP M Stottlemyre
SP F Peterson
SP A Downing
SP F Talbot
SP J Bouton
RP H Reniff
RP P Ramos
RP S Hamilton
RP D Womack
C E Howard
1B J Pepitone
2B B Richardson
SU H Clarke
3S C Boyer
OI T Tresh
CF M Mantle
RF R Maris
LU R White
M1 J Keane
M2 R Houk

WAS 1966 AL
SP P Richert
SP M McCormick
SP P Ortega
SR J Hannan
RP C Cox
RP B Humphreys
CL R Kline
RP D Lines
C P Casanova
1B- D Nen
2I B Saverine
SS E Brinkman
3B K McMullen
LF H Howard
CF D Lock
OI F Valentine
RU J King
OF W Kirkland
M G Hodges

ATL 1967 NL
SR P Niekro
SP D Lemaster
SP K Johnson
SP P Jarvis
RS D Kelley

RS C Carroll
C J Grote
RP J Ritchie
RP R Hernandez
C J Torre
1O F Alou
2B W Woodward
SS D Menke
3B E Boyer
LU R Carty
MU M Jones
RF H Aaron
1U- T Francona
M1 B Hitchcock
M2 K Silvestri

CHI 1967 NL
SP F Jenkins
SP R Nye
SR J Niekro
SP R Culp
RS B Hands
RP C Hartenstein
RP B Stoneman
RP C Koonce
C R Hundley
1B E Banks
2B G Beckert
SS D Kessinger
3B R Santo
LF B Williams
CF A Phillips
RU- T Savage
M L Durocher

CIN 1967 NL
SP G Nolan
SP M Pappas
SP J Maloney
SP M Queen
SP S Ellis
RP T Abernathy
RP D Nottebart
RS G Arrigo
C - J Edwards
1L L May
2S T Helms
SS L Cardenas
3B T Perez
LF P Rose
CF V Pinson
RF T Harper
1B D Johnson
2U C Ruiz
M D Bristol

HOU 1967 NL
SP M Cuellar
SP D Giusti
SP D Wilson
SP B Belinsky
SP L Dierker
RP B Latman
RP C Sembera
RP D Eilers
RP D Schneider
C - J Bateman
1B E Mathews
2B J Morgan
SS J Jackson
3B B Aspromonte
LU- R Davis
CF J Wynn
RF R Staub
C - R Brand
M G Hatton

LA 1967 NL
SP C Osteen
SP D Drysdale
SP D Sutton
SP B Singer
SR J Brewer
RP R Perranoski
RP P Regan
RP B Miller
C J Roseboro
1B W Parker
2B R Hunt
SS G Michael
32 J Lefebvre
LF L Johnson
CF W Davis
R1 R Fairly
3U B Bailey
RU A Ferrara
LR- L Gabrielson
SS- D Schofield
M W Alston

NY 1967 NL
SP T Seaver
SP J Fisher
SR D Cardwell
SR B Shaw
RP D Selma
RP R Taylor

RP D Shaw
C J Grote
1B E Kranepool
2B B Harrelson
3B E Charles
LF T Davis
MO C Jones
RF R Swoboda
OI T Reynolds
UI- B Johnson
M1 W Westrum
M2 S Parker

PHI 1967 NL
SP J Bunning
SP L Jackson
SP C Short
SR R Wise
SR D Ellsworth
RP T Farrell
RP D Hall
RP G Jackson
RS J Boozer
C C Dalrymple
1B B White
2B C Rojas
SS B Wine
3B D Allen
LO T Gonzalez
ML J Briggs
RF J Callison
CF D Lock
SU G Sutherland
UI T Taylor
C - G Oliver
M G Mauch

PIT 1967 NL
SP T Sisk
SP B Veale
SR D Ribant
SR S Blass
SR W Fryman
RSA A McBean
RS J Pizarro
RP R Face
RP P Mikkelsen
C J May
1B D Clendenon
2B B Mazeroski
SS G Alley
3B M Alou
CF M Alou
RF R Clemente
OI M Mota
IO- J Pagan
M1 H Walker
M2 D Murtaugh

STL 1967 NL
SR D Hughes
SP S Carlton
SP R Washburn
SP B Gibson
SR L Jaster
RS N Briles
RS A Jackson
RP R Willis
RP J Hoerner
C T McCarver
1B O Cepeda
2B J Javier
SS D Maxvill
3B M Shannon
LF L Brock
CF C Flood
RF R Maris
OI B Tolan
RU- A Johnson
M R Schoendienst

SF 1967 NL
SP G Perry
SP M McCormick
SP J Marichal
SR R Sadecki
SR B Bolin
RS R Herbel
RP F Linzy
RP L McDaniel
C T Haller
1B W McCovey
2B T Fuentes
SS H Lanier
3L J Hart
LR J Alou
CF W Mays
RF O Brown
3I J Davenport
M H Franks

BAL 1967 AL
SP T Phoebus
SP P Richert
SR B Dillman

SP D McNally
SP J Hardin
RP E Watt
RP M Drabowsky
RP E Fisher
RP S Miller
C A Etchebarren
1B B Powell
2B D Johnson
SS L Aparicio
L1 C Blefary
CF P Blair
RU F Robinson
UO R Snyder
M H Bauer

BOS 1967 AL
SP J Lonborg
SR L Stange
SP G Bell
SR B Brandon
RS J Santiago
RP J Wyatt
RP D Osinski
C - M Ryan
1B G Scott
2B M Andrews
SS R Petrocelli
3B J Foy
LF C Yastrzemski
CF R Smith
RF- T Conigliaro
UO J Tartabull
UI- J Adair
UI- D Jones
M D Williams

CAL 1967 AL
SP G Brunet
SP J McGlothlin
SP R Clark
SP J Hamilton
RP M Rojas
RP B Kelso
RP C Cimino
RP J Coates
C B Rodgers
1B D Mincher
2B B Knoop
SS J Fregosi
3B P Schaal
LF R Reichardt
ML J Cardenal
RF J Hall
IC- T Satriano
M B Rigney

CHI 1967 AL
SP G Peters
SP J Horlen
SP T John
SR B Howard
RP B Locker
RP H Wilhelm
RS W Wood
RP D McMahon
C J Martin
1B T McCraw
2B W Causey
SS R Hansen
3B D Buford
L1 P Ward
CF T Agee
RL K Berry
LU W Williams
M E Stanky

CLE 1967 AL
SP S McDowell
SP L Tiant
SP S Siebert
SP J O'Donoghue
RP O Pena
RP G Culver
RS B Bailey
RP B Allen
C - J Azcue
1B T Horton
2B- P Gonzalez
SS L Brown
3B M Alvis
LF L Wagner
CF V Davalillo
RM C Hinton
OI L Maye
1U F Whitfield
UT- C Salmon
C - D Sims
M J Adcock

DET 1967 AL
SP E Wilson
SP D McLain
SP J Sparma
SP M Lolich

RP F Gladding
RP D Wickersham
RP M Marshall
RS J Hiller
C - B Freehan
1B N Cash
2B D McAuliffe
SS D Oyler
3B D Wert
ML J Northrup
CF M Stanley
RF A Kaline
LF W Horton
2U- J Lumpe
M M Smith

KC 1967 AL
SP C Hunter
SP J Nash
SP C Dobson
SR L Krausse
SR B Odom
RS P Lindblad
RS T Pierce
RP J Aker
RP D Segui
C P Roof
1U R Webster
2B J Donaldson
SS B Campaneris
UI D Green
UO J Gosger
CF R Monday
RF M Hershberger
IO D Cater
OF- J Nossek
M1 A Dark
M2 L Appling

MIN 1967 AL
SP D Chance
SP J Kaat
SP J Merritt
SP D Boswell
RS J Perry
RP A Worthington
RP R Kline
C J Zimmerman
1B H Killebrew
2B R Carew
SS Z Versalles
3B R Rollins
CF T Uhlaender
RF T Oliva
UT C Tovar
UT- R Reese
LU S Valdespino
M1 S Mele
M2 C Ermer

NY 1967 AL
SP M Stottlemyre
SP A Downing
SP F Peterson
SP F Talbot
RS B Monbouquette
RP D Womack
RS T Tillotson
RS J Verbanic
C J Gibbs
1B M Mantle
2B H Clarke
SS R Amaro
3B C Smith
LF T Tresh
CF J Pepitone
RO S Whitaker
UO R Robinson
M R Houk

WAS 1967 AL
SP P Ortega
SP C Pascual
SP B Moore
SP J Coleman
RP D Knowles
RS B Priddy
RP B Humphreys
RP D Lines
C P Casanova
1B- M Epstein
2B- B Allen
SS E Brinkman
3B K McMullen
LF H Howard
UO F Valentine
RU C Peterson
ML H Allen
S2 T Cullen
1U D Nen
2U- B Saverine
CF- E Stroud
M G Hodges

ATL 1968 NL
SP P Niekro
SP P Jarvis
SP R Reed
SR K Johnson
SP M Pappas
RP C Upshaw
RS J Britton
RP C Raymond
C J Torre
1B D Johnson
2B F Millan
SS S Jackson
3B- C Boyer
LU M Lum
CF F Alou
RF H Aaron
L1 T Francona
UI M Martinez
L1 T Aaron
C- B Tillman
M L Harris

CHI 1968 NL
SP F Jenkins
SP B Hands
SP K Holtzman
SP J Niekro
SP R Nye
RP P Regan
RP J Lamabe
C R Hundley
1B E Banks
2B G Beckert
SS D Kessinger
3B R Santo
LF B Williams
CF A Phillips
RM-J Hickman
1U- D Nen
UO-A Spangler
M L Durocher

CIN 1968 NL
SP G Culver
SP J Maloney
SP G Arrigo
SP G Nolan
RP T Abernathy
RP C Carroll
RP B Lee
RP J Ritchie
C J Bench
1B L May
2B T Helms
SS L Cardenas
3B T Perez
LF A Johnson
CF V Pinson
RF P Rose
UO M Jones
UI- C Ruiz
US- F Whitfield
M D Bristol

HOU 1968 NL
SP D Giusti
SP L Dierker
SP D Lemaster
SP D Wilson
SP M Cuellar
RP J Buzhardt
RP J Ray
RP T Dukes
C J Bateman
1B R Staub
2B D Menke
SS H Torres
3B D Rader
ML J Wynn
CF- R Davis
RF- N Miller
3L B Aspromonte
OI- L Thomas
M1 G Hatton
M2 H Walker

LA 1968 NL
SP B Singer
SP C Osteen
SP D Drysdale
SP D Sutton
SP M Kekich
RP M Grant
RP J Brewer
RP J Billingham
RP J Purdin
C T Haller
1B W Parker
2S P Popovich
SS Z Versalles
3B B Bailey
LR L Gabrielson
CF W Davis
R1 R Fairly
UO J Fairey

IF- K Boyer
2U- J Lefebvre
M W Alston

NY 1968 NL
SP T Seaver
SP J Koosman
SP D Cardwell
SR D Selma
SP N Ryan
RP C Koonce
RP R Taylor
RP D Frisella
C J Grote
1B E Kranepool
2B- P Linz
SS B Harrelson
3B E Charles
LF C Jones
CF T Agee
RF R Swoboda
LU A Shamsky
S2- A Weis
M G Hodges

PHI 1968 NL
SP C Short
SP J Jackson
SP W Fryman
SP R Wise
SR J James
RP T Farrell
RP G Wagner
RP J Boozer
RS G Jackson
C - M Ryan
1B B White
2B C Rojas
SS R Pena
3B T Taylor
LF D Allen
CF T Gonzalez
RF J Callison
OI J Briggs
UO D Lock
C - C Dalrymple
M1 G Mauch
M2 G Myatt
M3 B Skinner

PIT 1968 NL
SP B Veale
SP S Blass
SP A McBean
SR B Moose
SP J Bunning
RP R Kline
RS D Ellis
RP R Face
RP L Walker
C J May
1B D Clendenon
2B B Mazeroski
SS G Alley
3B M Wills
LF W Stargell
CF M Alou
RF R Clemente
UT M Mota
M L Shepard

STL 1968 NL
SP B Gibson
SP N Briles
SP S Carlton
SP R Washburn
SR L Jaster
RS D Hughes
RP R Willis
CL J Hoerner
RP M Nelson
C T McCarver
1B O Cepeda
2B J Javier
SS D Maxvill
3B M Shannon
LF L Brock
CF C Flood
RF R Maris
CU- J Edwards
RU- B Tolan
M R Schoendienst

SF 1968 NL
SP J Marichal
SP G Perry
SP R Sadecki
SR M McCormick
SR B Bolin
RP F Linzy
C D Dietz
1B W McCovey
2B R Hunt
SS H Lanier
3U J Davenport
RL J Alou
CF W Mays

RF- B Bonds
OI T Cline
3L J Hart
CU- J Hiatt
M H Franks

BAL 1968 AL
SP D McNally
SP J Hardin
SP T Phoebus
SR G Brabender
SR D Leonhard
RP E Watt
RP M Drabowsky
RP- P Richert
C - A Etchebarren
1B B Powell
2B D Johnson
SS M Belanger
3B B Robinson
OI C Blefary
CF P Blair
RL F Robinson
UT D Buford
RU- D May
LU- C Motton
M1 H Bauer
M2 E Weaver

BOS 1968 AL
SP R Culp
SP G Bell
SP D Ellsworth
SP J Santiago
SP J Lonborg
RP L Stange
RP J Pizarro
RS G Waslewski
RP S Lyle
C - R Gibson
1B G Scott
2B M Andrews
SS R Petrocelli
3B R Foy
LF C Yastrzemski
CF R Smith
RF K Harrelson
1I D Jones
M D Williams

CAL 1968 AL
SP G Brunet
SP J McGlothlin
SR S Ellis
SP T Murphy
RS C Wright
RP M Pattin
RS A Messersmith
RP T Burgmeier
C - B Rodgers
1B D Mincher
2B B Knoop
SS J Fregosi
3B- A Rodriguez
LF R Reichardt
CF- V Davalillo
MR R Repoz
UT C Hinton
C T Satriano
OI- E Kirkpatrick
RU- B Morton
M B Rigney

CHI 1968 AL
SP J Horlen
SP J Fisher
SP T John
SP G Peters
SP C Carlos
RP W Wood
RS B Priddy
RP H Wilhelm
RP B Locker
C J Josephson
1B T McCraw
2I S Alomar
SS L Aparicio
3U P Ward
LF T Davis
CF K Berry
RL B Bradford
M1 E Stanky
M2 L Moss
M3 A Lopez
M4 L Moss
M5 A Lopez

CLE 1968 AL
SP S McDowell
SP L Tiant
SP S Siebert
SR S Williams
SP S Hargan
RP E Fisher
RS M Paul
RP V Romo
C J Azcue

1B T Horton
2B- V Fuller
SS L Brown
3B M Alvis
LU L Maye
CF J Cardenal
LR T Harper
UT C Salmon
C1 D Sims
2U- D Nelson
M A Dark

DET 1968 AL
SP D McLain
SP E Wilson
SP M Lolich
SP J Sparma
RS P Dobson
RS J Hiller
RP D Patterson
C B Freehan
1B N Cash
2B D McAuliffe
SS R Oyler
3B D Wert
LF W Horton
CF M Stanley
RM J Northrup
RU A Kaline
SI- D Tracewski
M M Smith

MIN 1968 AL
SP D Chance
SP J Merritt
SP J Kaat
SP D Boswell
SR J Perry
RP A Worthington
RP R Perranoski
RP B Miller
RP J Roland
C J Roseboro
1U R Reese
2B R Carew
SS- J Hernandez
UT C Tovar
LB B Allison
CF T Uhlaender
RF T Oliva
3S R Clark
1B H Killebrew
UI- F Quilici
3U- R Rollins
M C Ermer

NY 1968 AL
SP M Stottlemyre
SP S Bahnsen
SP F Peterson
SP S Barber
SR F Talbot
RS J Verbanic
RP D Womack
RP S Hamilton
CL L McDaniel
C J Gibbs
1B M Mantle
2B H Clarke
SS T Tresh
3B B Cox
LU R White
UO B Robinson
RU A Kosco
CF J Pepitone
UI- D Howser
M R Houk

OAK 1968 AL
SP C Hunter
SP B Dobson
SP J Nash
SP C Dobson
SR L Krausse
RP D Segui
RP J Aker
RP E Sprague
RP P Lindblad
C - D Duncan
1B D Cater
2B J Donaldson
SS B Campaneris
3B S Bando
LR J Alou
LR M Hershberger
CF R Monday
RF R Jackson
UO- J Gosger
M B Kennedy

WAS 1968 AL
SP J Coleman
SP C Pascual
SP J Hannan
SP F Bertaina
SR B Moore
RP P Mikkelsen
RP J Moeller
C T Haller
RP D Higgins
RP B Humphreys
C - P Casanova
1B M Epstein
2B B Allen
SS- R Hansen
3B K McMullen
L1 F Howard
CF D Unser
RO E Stroud
OF- C Peterson
M J Lemon

ATL 1969 NL
SP P Niekro
SP R Reed
SP P Jarvis
SR G Stone
SP M Pappas
RP C Upshaw
RP G Neibauer
C B Didier
1B O Cepeda
2B F Millan
SS S Jackson
3B C Boyer
ML- T Gonzalez
CF F Alou
RF H Aaron
UO M Lum
IO- B Aspromonte
SS- G Garrido
M L Harris

CHI 1969 NL
SP F Jenkins
SP B Hands
SP K Holtzman
SR D Selma
RP P Regan
RP T Abernathy
RS R Nye
C R Hundley
1B E Banks
2B G Beckert
SS D Kessinger
3B R Santo
LF B Williams
CF D Young
RF J Hickman
OI W Smith
RU- A Spangler
M L Durocher

CIN 1969 NL
SP J Merritt
SP T Cloninger
SP J Maloney
SR J Fisher
SP G Nolan
RP W Granger
RP C Carroll
RS G Culver
RP P Ramos
C J Bench
1B L May
2B T Helms
SS- W Woodward
3B T Perez
LF A Johnson
MR B Tolan
RM P Rose
UT J Stewart
SS- D Chaney
IO- C Ruiz
M D Bristol

HOU 1969 NL
SP L Dierker
SP D Lemaster
SP D Wilson
SP T Griffin
RS J Ray
CL F Gladding
RP J Billingham
RS W Blasingame
C J Edwards
1B C Blefary
2B J Morgan
SS D Menke
3B D Rader
LR J Alou
CF J Wynn
RF N Miller
LU- G Geiger
M H Walker

LA 1969 NL
SP C Osteen
SP B Singer
SP D Sutton
SP A Foster
CL J Brewer
RP P Mikkelsen
RP J Moeller
C T Haller
1B W Parker
2S M Wills
3B B Sudakis
UO W Crawford
CF W Davis
RL A Kosco
RO R Russell
OI- L Gabrielson
UI- J Lefebvre
LF- M Mota
M W Alston

MON 1969 NL
SP B Stoneman
SR J Robertson
SP M Wegener
SR G Waslewski
SR H Reed
RP D McGinn
RP S Renko
RP D Shaw
RP R Face
C B Brand
1B B Bailey
2B G Sutherland
SS B Wine
3B C Laboy
LF M Jones
CF- A Phillips
RF R Staub
OI T Cline
M G Mauch

SD 1969 NL
SP C Kirby
SP J Niekro
SP A Santorini
SP D Kelley
RS T Sisk
RS G Ross
RP F Reberger
RP J Baldschun
C C Cannizzaro
1B N Colbert
2S J Arcia
SS T Dean
3B E Spiezio
LU A Ferrara
CF C Gaston
RF O Brown
OI I Murrell
OI- L Stahl
M P Gomez

NY 1969 NL
SP T Seaver
SP J Koosman
SP G Gentry
SP D Cardwell
SP J McAndrew
RP T McGraw
RP R Taylor
RP J DiLauro
C J Grote
1B E Kranepool
2B K Boswell
SS B Harrelson
32 W Garrett
LF C Jones
CF T Agee
RU R Swoboda
RO R Gaspar
RU A Shamsky
S2 A Weis
M G Hodges

PHI 1969 NL
SP G Jackson
SP W Fryman
SP R Wise
SR J Johnson
SP B Champion
RP J Boozer
RP T Farrell
RP A Raffo
RP B Wilson
C M Ryan
1B D Allen
2B C Rojas
SS D Money
3U R Joseph
UO R Stone
UI- T Harmon
L3 D Johnson
M1 B Skinner
M2 G Myatt

PIT 1969 NL
SP B Veale
SP D Ellis
SP S Blass
SR B Moose
SP J Bunning
RS L Walker
RP C Hartenstein
RP B Dal Canton
RP J Gibbon
C M Sanguillen
1B A Oliver
2B- B Mazeroski
SS F Patek
3B R Hebner
LF W Stargell
CF M Alou
RF R Clemente
UT J Pagan
OI C Taylor
2S- G Alley
M1 L Shepard
M2 A Grammas

STL 1969 NL
SP B Gibson
SP S Carlton
SP N Briles
SR R Washburn
SR C Taylor
RS M Torrez
RS D Giusti
RP M Grant
RP J Hoerner
C T McCarver
1B J Torre
2B J Javier
SS D Maxvill
3B M Shannon
LF L Brock
CF C Flood
RF V Pinson
M R Schoendienst

SF 1969 NL
SP G Perry
SP J Marichal
SP M McCormick
SP B Bolin
SR R Sadecki
RP F Linzy
RP R Herbel
C - D Dietz
1B W McCovey
2B R Hunt
SS H Lanier
3B J Davenport
LR K Henderson
CF W Mays
RM B Bonds
UT- B Burda
LU D Marshall
UI D Mason
LU- J Hart
M C King

BAL 1969 AL
SP M Cuellar
SP D McNally
SP T Phoebus
SP J Palmer
SR J Hardin
RP D Leonhard
RP E Watt
RP D Hall
RP M Lopez
C E Hendricks
1B B Powell
2B D Johnson
SS M Belanger
3B B Robinson
LF D Buford
CF P Blair
RF F Robinson
UO-M Rettenmund
M E Weaver

BOS 1969 AL
SP R Culp
SP M Nagy
SR S Siebert
SP J Lonborg
SR L Stange
RS V Romo
RP S Lyle
RS R Jarvis
RS R Landis
C - R Gibson
1U D Jones
2B M Andrews
SS R Petrocelli
31 G Scott
LF C Yastrzemski
CF R Smith
RF T Conigliaro
OI J Lahoud
3I S O'Brien
UT- D Schofield

M1 D Williams
M2 E Popowski

CAL 1969 AL
SP A Messersmith
SP T Murphy
SP J McGlothlin
SR R May
SP G Brunet
CL K Tatum
RP E Fisher
RP H Wilhelm
RS C Wright
C - J Azcue
1B J Spencer
2B S Alomar
SS J Fregosi
3B A Rodriguez
LF R Reichardt
CF J Johnstone
RF B Voss
OI R Repoz
OI- B Morton
M1 B Rigney
M2 L Phillips

CHI 1969 AL
SP J Horlen
SP T John
SP G Peters
SP B Wynne
RP W Wood
RP D Osinski
RP C Carlos
C E Herrmann
1B G Hopkins
2B B Knoop
SS L Aparicio
3B B Melton
LF C May
CF K Berry
RL W Williams
UT P Ward
RM-B Bradford
UI- R Hansen
UT- T McCraw
M1 A Lopez
M2 D Gutteridge

CLE 1969 AL
SP S McDowell
SP L Tiant
SP S Hargan
SR D Ellsworth
RS S Williams
RS M Paul
RP J Pizarro
RP R Law
C D Sims
1B T Horton
2B V Fuller
SS L Brown
3B- M Alvis
UO- R Snyder
CF J Cardenal
RF K Harrelson
UO R Scheinblum
OI- C Hinton
3U- K Klimchock
M A Dark

DET 1969 AL
SP D McLain
SP M Lolich
SP E Wilson
SR M Kilkenny
RS P Dobson
RS J Hiller
RP T Timmermann
C - B Freehan
1B N Cash
2B- D McAuliffe
SS- T Tresh
3B D Wert
LF W Horton
MR J Northrup
RF A Kaline
MS M Stanley
23- T Matchick
M M Smith

KC 1969 AL
SP W Bunker
SR D Drago
SP B Butler
SP R Nelson
SP J Rooker
RS M Hedlund
RP M Drabowsky
RP D Wickersham
RP T Burgmeier
C - E Rodriguez
1B M Fiore
2B J Adair
SS J Hernandez
3B J Foy
LF L Piniella

UT B Oliver
RM P Kelly
UT E Kirkpatrick
2S- J Rios
M J Gordon

MIN 1969 AL
SR J Perry
SP D Boswell
SP J Kaat
SR T Hall
RP R Perranoski
RS B Miller
RS D Woodson
RP A Worthington
C J Roseboro
RP R Reese
2B R Carew
SS L Cardenas
31 H Killebrew
ML T Uhlaender
UT C Tovar
RF J Oliva
32 F Quilici
LU- B Allison
UO- C Manuel
LU- G Nettles
M B Martin

NY 1969 AL
SP M Stottlemyre
SP F Peterson
SP S Bahnsen
SP B Burbach
SR A Downing
RS M Kekich
RP L McDaniel
RP J Aker
RP S Hamilton
C - J Gibbs
1B J Pepitone
2B H Clarke
SG J Michael
3U J Kenney
LF R White
CF- R Woods
RU B Murcer
3U- B Cox
CU- F Fernandez
OI- B Robinson
M R Houk

OAK 1969 AL
SP C Hunter
SP C Dobson
SB B Odom
SR L Krausse
SP J Nash
RS R Fingers
RP P Lindblad
RP J Roland
C P Roof
1B D Green
2B D Green
SS B Campaneris
3B S Bando
LF T Reynolds
RF R Monday
RF R Jackson
IF- T Kubiak
M1 H Bauer
M2 J McNamara

SEA 1969 AL
SR G Brabender
SP M Pattin
SP F Talbot
RS D Segui
SP J Gelnar
RP J Bouton
RP B Locker
C J McNertney
1B D Mincher
2B J Donaldson
SS R Oyler
UT T Harper
LF T Davis
MR W Comer
RM-S Hovley
JI- G Gil
RU- M Hegan
M J Schultz

WAS 1969 AL
SP J Coleman
SP D Bosman
SP J Hannan
SP B Moore
RS C Cox
SP D Higgins
RP B Humphreys
C P Casanova
1B M Epstein
2B B Allen
SS E Brinkman
3B K McMullen

L1 F Howard
CF D Unser
UT H Allen
OI B Alyea
2B T Cullen
UO E Stroud
M T Williams

ATL 1970 NL
SP P Jarvis
SP P Niekro
SP J Nash
SP G Stone
SP R Reed
RP H Wilhelm
RP B Priddy
C - B Tillman
1B- O Cepeda
2B F Millan
SS S Jackson
3B C Boyer
LF R Carty
CF T Gonzalez
RF H Aaron
SS G Garrido
UO M Lum
CU- H King
M L Harris

CHI 1970 NL
SP F Jenkins
SP K Holtzman
SP B Hands
SP M Pappas
SP J Decker
RP J Regan
RS J Colborn
C - R Hundley
1B- E Banks
2B G Beckert
SS D Kessinger
3B R Santo
LF B Williams
OI J Hickman
RF J Callison
CF C James
UT- W Smith
M L Durocher

CIN 1970 NL
SP G Nolan
SP J Merritt
SP J McGlothlin
SP W Simpson
SR T Cloninger
RP C Carroll
CL W Granger
RP D Gullett
RP R Washburn
C J Bench
1B L May
2B T Helms
SS D Concepcion
3B T Perez
LF B Carbo
CF B Tolan
RF P Rose
UT J Stewart
SS W Woodward
M S Anderson

HOU 1970 NL
SP L Dierker
SR J Billingham
SP D Wilson
SR D Lemaster
SP T Griffin
RP J Ray
RP F Gladding
RS R Cook
RS J Bouton
C J Edwards
1B- B Watson
2B J Morgan
SS D Menke
3B D Rader
ML J Wynn
CF- C Cedeno
RF J Alou
RF- N Miller
M H Walker

LA 1970 NL
SP D Sutton
SP C Osteen
SP A Foster
SR J Moeller
SP S Vance
CL J Brewer
RP B Singer
RP F Norman
C T Haller
1B W Parker
2B- T Sizemore
SS M Wills
3S- B Grabarkewitz

LF M Mota
CF W Davis
RL W Crawford
2U J Lefebvre
RM-B Russell
IC- B Sudakis
M W Alston

MON 1970 NL
SP C Morton
SP S Renko
SR B Stoneman
SP D McGinn
SP M Wegener
CL C Raymond
RP H Reed
RP J Strohmayer
RS M Marshall
C J Bateman
1B R Fairly
2B G Sutherland
SS B Wine
3B C Laboy
LF M Jones
IO B Bailey
CF- A Phillips
RF B Staub
IO B Bailey
2B M Staehle
UO-J Fairey
MO-J Gosger
LO- D Hahn
M G Mauch

NY 1970 NL
SP T Seaver
SP J Koosman
SP G Gentry
SP J McAndrew
SP R Sadecki
RP N Ryan
RP T McGraw
RP R Taylor
RP D Frisella
C J Grote
1B D Clendenon
2B K Boswell
SS B Harrelson
3B J Foy
LF C Jones
CF T Agee
RF R Swoboda
32 W Garrett
OI A Shamsky
OF- D Marshall
M G Hodges

PHI 1970 NL
SP R Wise
SP J Bunning
SP C Short
SP G Jackson
SP W Fryman
RP D Selma
RS B Lersch
RS L Palmer
RP J Hoerner
C - M Ryan
1B D Johnson
2B D Doyle
SS L Bowa
3B D Money
LU J Briggs
MR L Hisle
OI R Stone
RO B Browne
IO T Taylor
MR-O Gamble
M F Lucchesi

PIT 1970 NL
SP D Ellis
SP B Veale
SP S Blass
SP B Moose
SR L Walker
RP D Giusti
RS B Dal Canton
C M Sanguillen
1B B Robertson
2B D Mazeroski
SS G Alley
3B R Hebner
LF W Stargell
CF M Alou
RF R Clemente
1R A Oliver
UO-J Jeter
3U- J Pagan
SS- F Patek
M D Murtaugh

STL 1970 NL
SP B Gibson
SP S Carlton
SP M Torrez
SP J Reuss
SR N Briles

RS Ch Taylor
RP F Linzy
RP S Campisi
C - T Simmons
1R J Hague
2B J Javier
SS D Maxvill
C3 J Torre
LF L Brock
CF J Cardenal
RU L Lee
13 D Allen
UO V Davalillo
UT Ca Taylor
M R Schoendienst

SD 1970 NL
SP D Dobson
SP C Kirby
SP D Coombs
SR D Roberts
SP M Corkins
RP R Herbel
RP T Dukes
RP G Ross
RP W Willis
C C Cannizzaro
1B N Colbert
2B D Campbell
SI J Arcia
3B E Spiezio
LU A Ferrara
CF C Gaston
RF O Brown
OI I Murrell
S3 S Huntz
UT- R Webster
M P Gomez

SF 1970 NL
SP G Perry
SP J Marichal
SR R Robertson
SR F Reberger
RP D McMahon
RS R Bryant
RP J Johnson
C D Dietz
1B W McCovey
2U R Hunt
SS H Lanier
3B A Gallagher
LF K Henderson
CF W Mays
RF B Bonds
2S T Fuentes
M1 C King
M2 C Fox

BAL 1970 AL
SP J Palmer
SP M Cuellar
SP D McNally
SR J Hardin
SP T Phoebus
RP P Richert
RP E Watt
RP D Hall
RP M Lopez
C E Hendricks
1B B Powell
2B D Johnson
SS M Belanger
3B B Robinson
LF D Buford
CF P Blair
RF F Robinson
UO M Rettenmund
OI- T Crowley
M E Weaver

BOS 1970 AL
SP R Culp
SP S Siebert
SP G Peters
SR K Brett
SP M Nagy
RS V Romo
RP S Lyle
C - J Moses
1L C Yastrzemski
2B M Andrews
SS R Petrocelli
31 G Scott
LO B Conigliaro
CF R Smith
RF T Conigliaro
M E Kasko

CAL 1970 AL
SP C Wright
SP T Murphy
SP A May
SR A Messersmith
RP E Fisher
RP K Tatum
RS G Garrett

RP M Queen
C J Azcue
1B J Spencer
2B S Alomar
SS J Fregosi
3B T Harper
LF D Walton
MU J Johnstone
OI R Repoz
M L Phillips

CHI 1970 AL
SP T John
SP J Janeski
SP J Horlen
RP W Wood
RS J Crider
RP D Murphy
RS B Moore
C - E Herrmann
1U D Hopkins
2B B Knoop
SS L Aparicio
R3 B Melton
LF C May
CF K Berry
RU W Williams
UT T McCraw
32 S O'Brien
C - D Josephson
M1 D Gutteridge
M2 B Adair
M3 C Tanner

CLE 1970 AL
SP S McDowell
SR R Hand
SR D Chance
SP S Hargan
RP D Higgins
RP P Hennigan
RS R Austin
RP F Lasher
C R Fosse
1B T Horton
2B E Leon
SS J Heidemann
3B G Nettles
LF R Foster
CF T Uhlaender
RF V Pinson
UT C Hinton
OC D Sims
M A Dark

DET 1970 AL
SP M Lolich
SP J Niekro
SP L Cain
SR M Kilkenny
CL T Timmermann
RS J Hiller
RP D Patterson
RF F Scherman
C B Freehan
1B N Cash
2B D McAuliffe
SS C Gutierrez
3B D Wert
LF- W Horton
CF M Stanley
RM J Northrup
R1 A Kaline
UT E Maddox
UI- D Jones
M M Smith

KC 1970 AL
SP D Drago
SR B Johnson
SP J Rooker
SP B Butler
SR D Morehead
RP W Bunker
RS A Fitzmorris
RP T Burgmeier
RP T Abernathy
CU E Kirkpatrick
13 B Oliver
2B C Rojas
SS- J Hernandez
3B P Schaal
LF L Piniella
CF A Otis
RF P Kelly
M1 C Metro
M2 B Lemon

MIL 1970 AL
SP M Pattin
SP L Krausse
SP S Lockwood
SR B Bolin
SP G Brabender
RP K Sanders
RP J Gelnar

C P Roof
1B M Hegan
2S T Kubiak
SS R Pena
3B T Harper
LF D Walton
CF D May
UO R Snyder
C J McNertney
OI T Savage
M D Bristol

MIN 1970 AL
SP J Perry
SR J Kaat
SP B Blyleven
SR B Zepp
RS T Hall
RP R Perranoski
RS S Williams
C G Mitterwald
1B R Reese
2B- D Thompson
SS L Cardenas
3B H Killebrew
LM J Holt
CF C Tovar
RF T Oliva
2I F Quilici
LF- B Alyea
UT- R Renick
M B Rigney

NY 1970 AL
SP M Stottlemyre
SP F Peterson
SP S Bahnsen
SP S Kline
SR M Kekich
RP L McDaniel
RP R Klimkowski
CL J Aker
RS G Waslewski
C T Munson
1B D Cater
2B H Clarke
SS G Michael
3B J Kenney
LF R White
CF B Murcer
RF C Blefary
RU- R Woods
M R Houk

OAK 1970 AL
SP- C Dobson
SP C Hunter
SR D Segui
SP B Odom
SR R Fingers
RP M Grant
RP M Lachemann
RP B Locker
C - F Fernandez
1B D Mincher
2B D Green
SS B Campaneris
3B S Bando
LR F Alou
RM J Wynn
C - D Duncan
M J McNamara

WAS 1970 AL
SP D Bosman
SR J Coleman
SP C Cox
SP J Hannan
SP G Brunet
RP D Knowles
RS J Shellenback
RP J Grzenda
RP H Pina
C P Casanova
1B M Epstein
2B T Cullen
SS E Brinkman
3B A Rodriguez
L1 F Howard
CF E Stroud
UO D Unser
2B B Allen
OI R Reichardt
RU- L Maye
M T Williams

ATL 1971 NL
SP P Niekro
SP R Reed
SP G Stone
SP P Jarvis
SP T Kelley
RS J Nash

CL C Upshaw
RS B Barber
RP B Priddy
IC E Williams
1R H Aaron
2B F Millan
SS M Perez
3B- D Evans
LF R Garr
CF S Jackson
RU-M Lum
CU-H King
M L Harris

CHI 1971 NL
SP F Jenkins
SP M Pappas
SP B Hands
SP K Holtzman
SP J Pizarro
RP P Regan
RP B Bonham
C - C Cannizzaro
1B J Pepitone
2B G Beckert
SS D Kessinger
3B R Santo
LF B Williams
CF B Davis
RF J Callison
R1 J Hickman
UI- P Popovich
M L Durocher

CIN 1971 NL
SP G Nolan
SP D Gullett
SP J McGlothlin
SP W Simpson
RP W Granger
RP C Carroll
RS J Merritt
RP J Gibbon
C J Bench
1B L May
2B T Helms
SS D Concepcion
3B T Perez
LM H McRae
CF G Foster
RF P Rose
LF B Carbo
S3 W Woodward
M S Anderson

HOU 1971 NL
SP D Wilson
SP J Billingham
SR K Forsch
SP L Dierker
RP G Culver
RP J Ray
RP F Gladding
RP D Lemaster
C J Edwards
1I D Menke
2B J Morgan
SS R Metzger
3B D Rader
RL J Alou
CF C Cedeno
RM J Wynn
L1 B Watson
LU- C Geronimo
M H Walker

LA 1971 NL
SP D Sutton
SP A Downing
SP C Osteen
SP B Singer
RP P Mikkelsen
RP J Moeller
C - D Sims
1B W Parker
2B J Lefebvre
SS M Wills
3B- S Garvey
IO D Allen
CF W Davis
RF B Buckner
LR W Crawford
UT B Valentine
C - T Haller
LR- M Mota
UT- R Russell
M W Alston

MON 1971 NL
SP B Stoneman
SP S Renko
SP C Morton
SP E McAnally
SR J Strohmayer

RP M Marshall
RS D McGinn
RP H Reed
RP C Raymond
1R B Bateman
1B R Fairly
2B R Hunt
SS B Wine
3B B Bailey
LU- J Fairey
CF B Day
RF R Staub
2S G Sutherland
M G Mauch

NY 1971 NL
SP T Seaver
SP G Gentry
SP J Koosman
SR R Sadecki
SP N Ryan
RP T McGraw
RP D Frisella
RS C Williams
RP R Taylor
C J Grote
1B E Kranepool
2B K Boswell
SS- B Harrelson
3B B Aspromonte
LF C Jones
CF T Agee
RU K Singleton
23- T Foli
CF D Hahn
OF- D Marshall
1B- D Clendenon
M G Hodges

PHI 1971 NL
SP R Wise
SP B Lersch
SP C Short
SR K Reynolds
SR W Fryman
RS J Bunning
RS B Champion
RP B Brandon
RP J Hoerner
C T McCarver
1B D Johnson
2B- D Doyle
SS L Bowa
3B- J Vukovich
LR- O Gamble
CF W Montanez
RF R Freed
3L D Money
OI- R Stone
M F Lucchesi

PIT 1971 NL
SP S Blass
SP D Ellis
SP B Johnson
SP L Walker
SR B Moose
RS N Briles
CL D Giusti
RP M Grant
C M Sanguillen
1B B Robertson
2B D Cash
SS G Alley
3B R Hebner
LF W Stargell
CF A Oliver
RF R Clemente
UO- G Clines
OI V Davalillo
SS- J Hernandez
M D Murtaugh

STL 1971 NL
SP S Carlton
SP G Gibson
SP R Cleveland
SP J Reuss
RP C Taylor
RP M Drabowsky
RP F Linzy
RP D Shaw
C T Simmons
1R J Hague
2S T Sizemore
SS D Maxvill
3B J Torre
LF L Brock
OI M Alou
RF- J Cardenal
CF- J Cruz
2B- J Javier
RO-L Melendez
M R Schoendienst

SD 1971 NL
SP D Roberts
SP C Kirby
SP S Arlin
SP T Phoebus
SP F Norman
RP A Severinsen
RP B Miller
RP D Kelley
C B Barton
1B N Colbert
2B D Mason
SS E Hernandez
3B E Spiezio
OI L Stahl
CF C Gaston
RF O Brown
23 D Campbell
LU I Murrell
M P Gomez

SF 1971 NL
SP G Perry
SP J Marichal
SR J Cumberland
SP R Bryant
SP S Stone
RP J Johnson
RP D McMahon
RS R Robertson
C D Dietz
1B W McCovey
2B T Fuentes
SS C Speier
3B A Gallagher
LF K Henderson
M1 W Mays
RF B Bonds
3B H Lanier
MU-J Rosario
M C Fox

BAL 1971 AL
SP M Cuellar
SP P Dobson
SP J Palmer
SP D McNally
RS G Jackson
C E Hendricks
1B B Powell
2B D Johnson
SS M Belanger
3B B Robinson
LF D Buford
CF P Blair
RL M Rettenmund
R1 F Robinson
M E Weaver

BOS 1971 AL
SP R Culp
SP S Siebert
SP G Peters
SP J Lonborg
RP B Lee
RP B Bolin
RP S Lyle
RP K Tatum
C - D Josephson
1B G Scott
2B D Griffin
SS L Aparicio
3B R Petrocelli
LF C Yastrzemski
CF B Conigliaro
MR R Smith
RU J Lahoud
M E Kasko

CAL 1971 AL
SP A Messersmith
SP C Wright
SP T Murphy
SP R May
RP E Fisher
RP L Allen
RP D LaRoche
RP M Queen
C J Stephenson
1B J Spencer
2B S Alomar
SU J Fregosi
3B K McMullen
LU T Gonzalez
CF K Berry
RO R Repoz
SU- S O'Brien
M L Phillips

CHI 1971 AL
SP W Wood
SP T Bradley
SP T John
SR J Horlen
RS B Johnson
RP S Kealey
RP V Romo

RP T Forster
C E Herrmann
1B C May
2U M Andrews
SU L Alvarado
3B B Melton
LF R Reichardt
MO J Johnstone
RL W Williams
2U R McKinney
C - T Egan
SI- R Morales
SS- L Richard
M C Tanner

CLE 1971 AL
SP S McDowell
SP S Dunning
SR A Foster
SR R Lamb
SR S Hargan
RS V Colbert
RP P Hennigan
RP E Farmer
RP S Mingori
C R Fosse
1B C Chambliss
2B E Leon
SS- J Heidemann
3B G Nettles
LO T Uhlaender
MR V Pinson
RL R Foster
UT- C Hinton
M1 A Dark
M2 J Lipon

DET 1971 AL
SP M Lolich
SP J Coleman
SP L Cain
SR J Niekro
RP F Scherman
RP T Timmermann
RP B Denehy
C B Freehan
1B N Cash
2B D McAuliffe
SS E Brinkman
3B A Rodriguez
LF W Horton
CF M Stanley
RF A Kaline
ML J Northrup
LU- G Brown
UT- D Jones
M B Martin

KC 1971 AL
SP D Drago
SP M Hedlund
SP P Splittorff
SP B Dal Canton
SR A Fitzmorris
RP T Burgmeier
CL T Abernathy
RP J York
C - J May
1B G Hopkins
2B C Rojas
SS F Patek
3B P Schaal
LF L Piniella
CF A Otis
RF J Keough
OC E Kirkpatrick
1R B Oliver
M B Lemon

MIL 1971 AL
SP M Pattin
SP B Parsons
SP S Lockwood
SR L Krausse
SP J Slaton
RP K Sanders
RP J Morris
C E Rodriguez
OI J Briggs
2B T Theobald
SS- R Auerbach
3B- T Matchick
L3 T Harper
MR D May
RU B Voss
UT A Kosco
UI R Pena
2S- T Kubiak
M D Bristol

MIN 1971 AL
SP B Blyleven
SP J Perry
SP J Kaat
RS T Corbin
RS T Hall
RP S Williams

C G Mitterwald
1B R Reese
2B R Carew
SS L Cardenas
3I S Braun
LR C Tovar
MU J Holt
RF T Oliva
13 H Killebrew
M B Rigney

NY 1971 AL
SP F Peterson
SP M Stottlemyre
SP S Bahnsen
SP S Kline
SR M Kekich
RP L McDaniel
RP J Aker
C T Munson
13 D Cater
2B H Clarke
SS G Michael
3B J Kenney
LF R White
CF B Murcer
OI F Alou
1B- J Ellis
M R Houk

OAK 1971 AL
SP V Blue
SP C Hunter
SP C Dobson
SP D Segui
SP B Odom
RS R Fingers
RP B Locker
RP D Knowles
C D Duncan
1B M Epstein
2B D Green
SS B Campaneris
3B S Bando
LF J Rudi
CF R Monday
RF R Jackson
MO-A Mangual
M D Williams

WAS 1971 AL
SP D Bosman
SP D McLain
SP P Broberg
SR B Gogolewski
SR J Shellenback
RS C Cox
RP P Lindblad
RP J Grzenda
RP D Riddleberger
C - P Casanova
1B D Mincher
2S T Cullen
SS T Harrah
3B- D Nelson
L1 F Howard
MU E Maddox
MR D Unser
IF B Allen
CO D Billings
OI T McCraw
M T Williams

ATL 1972 NL
SP P Niekro
SP R Reed
SR R Schueler
SR T Kelley
SR G Stone
RS P Jarvis
RP C Upshaw
C E Williams
1B H Aaron
2B F Millan
SS M Perez
3B D Evans
LF- R Carty
CF D Baker
LR R Garr
RO M Lum
M1 L Harris
M2 E Mathews

CHI 1972 NL
SP F Jenkins
SP B Hooton
SP M Pappas
SP B Hands
SR R Reuschel
RP T Phoebus
CL J Aker
RP D McGinn
C R Hundley
1U J Hickman
2B J Beckert
SS D Kessinger
3B R Santo

LF B Williams
CF R Monday
RF J Cardenal
IO- C Fanzone
M1 L Durocher
M2 W Lockman

CIN 1972 NL
SP J Billingham
SP R Grimsley
SP G Nolan
SR J McGlothlin
SR D Gullett
RP P Borbon
RP C Carroll
RS T Hall
RP W Simpson
C J Bench
1B T Perez
2B J Morgan
SS D Concepcion
3B D Menke
LF P Rose
CF B Tolan
RF C Geronimo
SS- D Chaney
M S Anderson

HOU 1972 NL
SP D Wilson
SP L Dierker
SP D Roberts
SP J Reuss
SP K Forsch
RP G Culver
RP J Ray
RS T Griffin
RP F Gladding
C J Edwards
1B L May
2B T Helms
SS R Metzger
3B D Rader
LF B Watson
CF C Cedeno
RF J Wynn
M1 H Walker
M2 S Parker
M3 L Durocher

LA 1972 NL
SP D Sutton
SP C Osteen
SP A Downing
SP T John
SP B Singer
RP J Brewer
RP P Mikkelsen
RP P Richert
RP M Strahler
C - C Cannizzaro
1B W Parker
2B- L Lacy
SS B Russell
3B S Garvey
LF M Mota
CF W Davis
RF F Robinson
OI B Buckner
LR W Crawford
UT B Valentine
M W Alston

MON 1972 NL
SP B Stoneman
SP M Torrez
SP C Morton
SP E McAnally
SP B Moore
RP M Marshall
RS S Renko
RP J Strohmayer
RP T Walker
C - J Boccabella
1U M Jorgensen
2B R Hunt
SS T Foli
3B B Bailey
LF K Singleton
CF B Day
UO- C Mashore
R1 R Fairly
MU R Woods
UO- J Fairey
2U- H Torres
M G Mauch

SD 1972 NL
SP S Arlin
SP C Kirby
SR F Norman
SR M Caldwell
SR B Greif
RS M Corkins
RP G Ross
RP E Acosta
C - F Kendall
1B N Colbert
2S D Thomas
SS E Hernandez
3B D Roberts
LF L Lee
CF J Jeter
RU C Gaston
OI J Morales
OI L Stahl
23 G Jestadt
M1 P Gomez
M2 D Zimmer

SF 1972 NL
SP R Bryant
SR J Barr
SR J Marichal
SP S McDowell
SR S Stone
RP F Reberger
RP J Johnson
RP R Moffitt

1B E Kranepool
2B K Boswell
SS B Harrelson
3B J Fregosi
LF J Milner
CF T Agee
RF- R Staub
3U W Garrett
UT T Martinez
LU C Jones
M Y Berra

PHI 1972 NL
SP S Carlton
SP K Reynolds
SP B Champion
SP W Fryman
RS W Twitchell
RS B Brandon
RS D Selma
RS B Lersch
C - J Bateman
1R T Hutton
2B D Doyle
SS L Bowa
3B D Money
LF G Luzinski
CF W Montanez
UO- B Robinson
1U D Johnson
M1 F Lucchesi
M2 P Owens

PIT 1972 NL
SP S Blass
SP S Moose
SP N Briles
SP D Ellis
SR B Kison
RS B Johnson
CL D Giusti
RP R Hernandez
RP B Miller
C M Sanguillen
1U W Stargell
2B D Cash
SS G Alley
3B R Hebner
LO V Davalillo
CF A Oliver
RF R Smith
RF R Clemente
OF B Oglivie
UO G Clines
1B B Robertson
UT R Stennett
M B Virdon

STL 1972 NL
SP B Gibson
SP R Wise
SP R Cleveland
SR A Santorini
SP S Spinks
RP D Segui
C T Simmons
1R M Alou
1B B Oliver
2B S Sizemore
SS D Maxvill
3B J Torre
LF L Brock
MU J Cruz
MR L Melendez
RF B Carbo
UI E Crosby
M R Schoendienst

RP D McMahon
C D Rader
1B- W McCovey
2B T Fuentes
SS C Speier
3B- A Gallagher
LU K Henderson
CF G Maddox
RF B Bonds
IO D Kingman
M C Fox

DET 1972 AL
SP M Lolich
SP J Coleman
SP T Timmermann
RP C Seelbach
RP F Scherman
C B Freehan
1B N Cash
2B D McAuliffe
SS E Brinkman
3B A Rodriguez
LF W Horton
CF M Stanley
RL J Northrup
LU G Brown
RF A Kaline
2B- T Taylor
M B Martin

KC 1972 AL
SP D Drago
SP P Splittorff
SR R Nelson
SR B Dal Canton
SR M Hedlund
RPA Fitzmorris
RP T Burgmeier
RP T Abernathy
C E Kirkpatrick
1B J Mayberry
2B C Rojas
SS F Patek
3B P Schaal
LF L Piniella
CF A Otis
RF R Scheinblum
UO S Hovley
M B Lemon

CAL 1972 AL
SP N Ryan
SP C Wright
SP A May
SP A Messersmith
SR R Clark
RP E Fisher
RP S Barber
C - A Kusnyer
1B B Oliver
2B S Alomar
SS L Cardenas
3B K McMullen
LF V Pinson
CF K Berry
RF L Stanton
UT- J Spencer
M D Rice

CHI 1972 AL
SP W Wood
SP T Bradley
SP S Bahnsen
SP D Lemonds
RP T Forster
RP R Gossage
RP S Kealey
RP V Romo
C E Herrmann
1B D Allen
2B M Andrews
SS M Morales
3B- E Spiezio
LF C May
CF J Johnstone
RF P Kelly
SS L Alvarado
CF R Reichardt
RU- W Williams
M C Tanner

CLE 1972 AL
SP G Perry
SP D Tidrow
SP M Wilcox
SR S Dunning
RS R Lamb
RP H Hennigan
RP E Farmer
RS S Mingori
C R Fosse
1B C Chambliss

2B J Brohamer
SS F Duffy
3B G Nettles
LF A Johnson
MO D Unser
OI B Bell
OI T McCraw
IF- E Leon
M K Aspromonte

BAL 1972 AL
SP J Palmer
SP P Dobson
SP M Cuellar
SP D McNally
RS D Alexander
RP R Harrison
C - J Oates
1B B Powell
2B D Johnson
SS M Belanger
3B B Robinson
CF P Blair
RF M Rettenmund
OI D Baylor
RU T Crowley
S2 B Grich
M E Weaver

BOS 1972 AL
SP M Pattin
SP S Siebert
SR L Tiant
SP J Curtis
SP L McGlothen
RP R Culp
RP B Lee
RP G Peters
RS L Krausse
C C Fisk
1B- D Cater
2B D Griffin
SS L Aparicio
3B R Petrocelli
L1 C Yastrzemski
CF T Harper
RF R Smith
OF B Oglivie
ML- R Miller
M E Kasko

MIL 1972 AL
SP J Lonborg
SP B Parsons
SP S Lockwood
SP K Brett
SP G Ryerson
RS J Colborn
RP K Sanders
RP F Linzy
RS E Stephenson
C E Rodriguez
1B G Scott
2B R Theobald
SS R Auerbach
3B M Ferraro
LU J Briggs
CF D May
RL B Heise
23 B Heise
UO-B Davis
M1 D Bristol
M2 R McMillan
M3 D Crandall

MIN 1972 AL
SP B Blyleven
SP D Woodson
SP J Perry
SR R Corbin
SP J Kaat
RP W Granger
RP D LaRoche
C - P Roof
1B H Killebrew
2B R Carew
SS D Thompson
3B S Soderholm
LU S Brye
MR B Darwin
RL C Tovar
3I S Braun
MU J Nettles
1U R Reese
RU- W Williams
M1 B Rigney
M2 F Quilici

NY 1972 AL
SP M Stottlemyre
SP F Peterson
SP S Kline
SP M Kekich
SP G Gardner
RP S Lyle
RP L McDaniel
RP F Beene
C T Munson
1B R Blomberg

2B H Clarke
SS G Michael
3B- C Sanchez
LF R White
CF B Murcer
RF- J Callison
1B F Alou
3U- B Allen
RF- R Torres
M R Houk

OAK 1972 AL
SP C Hunter
SP K Holtzman
SP B Odom
SP V Blue
SR D Hamilton
RP R Fingers
RP B Locker
RS J Horlen
RP D Knowles
C D Duncan
1B M Epstein
2B- T Cullen
SS B Campaneris
3B S Bando
LF J Rudi
MR R Jackson
RO-A Mangual
1U M Hegan
CU-G Tenace
M D Williams

TEX 1972 AL
SR P Broberg
SR D Bosman
SP R Paul
SR M Paul
SR B Gogolewski
RP P Lindblad
RP D Stanhouse
RP- J Panther
RP H Pina
CL D Billings
1U F Howard
2B- L Randle
SS T Harrah
3B D Nelson
OI L Biittner
MO J Lovitto
RF T Ford
MO E Maddox
M T Williams

ATL 1973 NL
SP C Morton
SR P Niekro
SR R Schueler
SR R Harrison
SP R Reed
RP T House
C - J Oates
1L M Lum
2B D Johnson
SS M Perez
3B D Evans
LU H Aaron
CF D Baker
RF R Garr
OI S Jackson
C - P Casanova
IC- D Dietz
M E Mathews

CHI 1973 NL
SP F Jenkins
SP B Hooton
SP R Reuschel
SP M Pappas
SP B Bonham
RP B Locker
RP J Aker
RP R Burris
RP D LaRoche
C R Hundley
1U- J Hickman
2B G Beckert
SS D Kessinger
3B R Santo
LF B Williams
CF R Monday
RF J Cardenal
UO G Hiser
2B P Popovich
M W Lockman

CIN 1973 NL
SP J Billingham
SP D Gullett
SR D Gullett
SP F Norman
RP P Borbon
RS T Hall
RS C Carroll
C J Bench
1B T Perez
2B J Morgan

SS- D Concepcion
3B D Menke
LF P Rose
MU C Geronimo
MR B Tolan
SU D Chaney
3B D Driessen
M S Anderson

HOU 1973 NL
SP J Reuss
SP D Roberts
SP D Wilson
SR K Forsch
SR T Griffin
RP J Crawford
RP J Ray
RP J York
C- S Jutze
1B L May
2B T Helms
SR R Metzger
3B D Rader
LF B Watson
CF C Cedeno
RF J Wynn
UO-T Agee
M L Durocher

LA 1973 NL
SP D Sutton
SP A Messersmith
SP C Osteen
SP T John
SP A Downing
CL J Brewer
RP C Hough
RP D Rau
RP P Richert
C- J Ferguson
1L B Buckner
2B D Lopes
SS B Russell
3B R Cey
LF- M Mota
CF W Davis
RF W Crawford
1U S Garvey
OI- T Paciorek
M W Alston

MON 1973 NL
SP S Renko
SP M Torrez
SP B Moore
SP E McAnally
SP S Rogers
RP M Marshall
RP T Walker
C- J Boccabella
1B M Jorgensen
2B R Hunt
SS T Foli
3B B Bailey
LF R Fairly
MU R Woods
RF K Singleton
1U H Breeden
UO B Day
IO P Frias
M G Mauch

NY 1973 NL
SP T Seaver
SP J Koosman
SP J Matlack
SP G Stone
SR R Sadecki
RP T McGraw
RS H Parker
C- J Grote
1U J Milner
2B F Millan
SS B Harrelson
3B W Garrett
LF- C Jones
CF- D Hahn
RF R Staub
1L E Kranepool
UT- T Martinez
M Y Berra

PHI 1973 NL
SP S Carlton
SP W Twitchell
SP K Brett
SP J Lonborg
SP D Ruthven
RP B Lersch
RP M Scarce
RP B Brandon
RP B Wilson
C- B Boone
1R W Montanez
2B D Doyle
SS L Bowa
3B M Schmidt
LF G Luzinski
CF D Unser
RM B Robinson
1U T Hutton
UT- C Tovar
RU- M Anderson
M D Ozark

PIT 1973 NL
SP N Briles
SP B Moose
SP D Ellis
SR J Rooker
SR L Walker
RP D Giusti
RP R Hernandez
RP B Johnson
CR M Sanguillen
1B B Robertson
2B D Cash
SS- D Maxvill
3B H Hebner
LF W Stargell
M1 A Oliver
RU R Zisk
UO G Clines
C M May
2S R Stennett
M1 B Virdon
M2 D Murtaugh

STL 1973 NL
SP R Wise
SP R Cleveland
SP A Foster
SP B Gibson
RP D Segui
RS R Folkers
RP O Pena
RP A Hrabosky
C T Simmons
1B J Torre
2B T Sizemore
SS M Tyson
3B K Reitz
LF L Brock
MO L Melendez
MR J Cruz
RF B Carbo
1U T McCarver
M R Schoendienst

SD 1973 NL
SP B Greif
SP C Kirby
SP S Arlin
SR R Troedson
SP R Jones
RS M Caldwell
RS M Corkins
RP V Romo
RP G Ross
C F Kendall
1B N Colbert
2B- R Morales
S2 D Thomas
3B D Roberts
LU L Lee
CF J Grubb
RF C Gaston
UO J Morales
OI- I Murrell
M D Zimmer

SF 1973 NL
SP B Bryant
SP J Barr
SP T Bradley
SP J Marichal
RP E Sosa
RS J Willoughby
RP R Moffitt
RP D Carrithers
C D Rader
1B W McCovey
2B T Fuentes
SS C Speier
3B E Goodson
LF G Matthews
CF G Maddox
RF B Bonds
31 D Kingman
UT G Thomasson
M C Fox

BAL 1973 AL
SP J Palmer
SP M Cuellar
SP D McNally
SP D Alexander
SP- J Jefferson
RP B Reynolds
RP G Jackson
RP E Watt
C1 E Williams
1B B Powell
2B B Grich
SS M Belanger
3B B Robinson
LF D Baylor
CF P Blair
RM R Coggins
DH T Davis
LR A Bumbry
RF- M Rettenmund
M E Weaver

BOS 1973 AL
SP B Lee
SP L Tiant
SP J Curtis
SP M Pattin
SR R Moret
CL B Bolin
C C Fisk
1U C Yastrzemski
2B D Griffin
SS L Aparicio
3B R Petrocelli
LF T Harper
UO R Miller
RF D Evans
DH O Cepeda
CF R Smith
M1 E Kasko
M2 E Popowski

CAL 1973 AL
SP N Ryan
SP B Singer
SP C Wright
SP E May
SR S Barber
RP D Sells
C J Torborg
1B- M Epstein
2B S Alomar
SS R Meoli
3B A Gallagher
LM V Pinson
CF K Berry
RL L Stanton
DH F Robinson
OI T McCraw
IO B Oliver
M B Winkles

CHI 1973 AL
SP W Wood
SP S Bahnsen
SR S Stone
SR E Fisher
RS T Forster
CL C Acosta
RP R Gossage
1B T Muser
2B J Orta
SS E Leon
3B B Melton
DL C May
UO- J Jeter
RF P Kelly
OF- K Henderson
M C Tanner

CLE 1973 AL
SP G Perry
SP D Tidrow
SP M Wilcox
SR T Timmermann
SP B Strom
RP T Hilgendorf
RP R Lamb
RP J Johnson
C- D Duncan
1B C Chambliss
2B J Brohamer
SS F Duffy
3B B Bell
LU C Spikes
CF G Hendrick
RM R Torres
DR O Gamble
CD J Ellis
UT J Lowenstein
LD W Williams
M K Aspromonte

DET 1973 AL
SP M Lolich
SP J Coleman
SP J Perry
SP W Fryman
RP J Hiller
RP F Scherman
RP L LaGrow
C B Freehan
1B N Cash
2B D McAuliffe
SS B Brinkman
3B A Rodriguez
LF W Horton
CF M Stanley
RL J Northrup
DH G Brown
DH- F Howard
R1- A Kaline
RF- D Sharon
2B- T Taylor
M1 B Martin
M2 J Schultz

KC 1973 AL
SP P Splittorff
SP S Busby
SP D Drago
RS G Garber
RP D Bird
RP S Mingori
C- F Healy
1B J Mayberry
2B C Rojas
SS F Patek
3B P Schaal
LF L Piniella
CF A Otis
RO E Kirkpatrick
RD H McRae
UT K Bevacqua
RO S Hovley
M J McKeon

MIL 1973 AL
SP J Colborn
SP J Slaton
SP J Bell
SR S Lockwood
RS B Champion
RS E Rodriguez
RP F Linzy
RS C Short
C J Torborg
C D Porter
1B G Scott
2B P Garcia
SS T Johnson
3B D Money
LF J Briggs
CF D May
RO B Coluccio
DH-O Brown
OF- J Lahoud
C- E Rodriguez
M D Crandall

MIN 1973 AL
SP B Blyleven
SP J Kaat
SP J Decker
SR B Hands
SP D Woodson
RS D Corbin
RS D Goltz
RS E Bane
RP B Campbell
C G Mitterwald
1B J Lis
2B R Carew
SS D Thompson
3B S Braun
L1 J Holt
ML L Hisle
RF B Darwin
DH T Oliva
SI J Terrell
CF- S Brye
M F Quilici

NY 1973 AL
SP M Stottlemyre
SP D Medich
SP F Peterson
SP P Dobson
RP L McDaniel
CL S Lyle
C T Munson
1U- F Alou
2B H Clarke
SS G Michael
3B G Nettles
LF R White
CF B Murcer
R1 M Alou
DH J Hart
D1 R Blomberg
LF- J Callison
M R Houk

OAK 1973 AL
SP K Holtzman
SP V Blue
SP C Hunter
SP B Odom
RP R Fingers
RS R Knowles
RP H Pina
RP P Lindblad
C R Fosse
1B G Tenace
2B D Green
SS B Campaneris
3B B Sando
LF J Rudi
CF B North
RF R Jackson
DH D Johnson
2B T Kubiak
M D Williams

TEX 1973 AL
SP J Bibby
SR J Merritt
SP S Siebert
RP B Gogolewski
RS M Paul
RP J Brown
RP S Foucault
C- K Suarez
1B J Spencer
2B D Nelson
SS- J Mason
S3 T Harrah
LD- R Carty
MI V Harris
RL J Burroughs
DL A Johnson
MO E Maddox
OI- L Biittner
C- D Billings
IO- B Sudakis
M1 W Herzog
M2 D Wilber
M3 B Martin

ATL 1974 NL
SP P Niekro
SP C Morton
SR B Capra
SP R Reed
SP R Harrison
RP T House
RP M Leon
RP L Krausse
C J Oates
12 D Johnson
2B M Perez
SS C Robinson
3B D Evans
LF H Aaron
RF D Baker
LR R Garr
CF R Office
1O M Lum
M1 E Mathews
M2 C King

CHI 1974 NL
SP B Bonham
SP R Reuschel
SR B Hooton
SR S Stone
RS K Frailing
RP D LaRoche
RP O Zamora
RS J Todd
C- S Swisher
1B A Thornton
2B- V Harris
SS D Kessinger
3B B Madlock
LR J Morales
CF R Monday
RF J Cardenal
1L B Williams
OI- C Ward
M1 W Lockman
M2 J Marshall

CIN 1974 NL
SP D Gullett
SP C Kirby
SP J Billingham
SP F Norman
RP P Borbon
RP C Carroll
RP T Hall
C J Bench
1B T Perez
2B J Morgan
SS D Concepcion
3B D Driessen
LF P Rose
CF G Geronimo
RM G Foster
32 D Chaney
OI- T Crowley
RF-K Griffey
M S Anderson

HOU 1974 NL
SP L Dierker
SP T Griffin
SP D Roberts
SP D Wilson
SP C Osteen
RP K Forsch
RP M Cosgrove
RP F Scherman
C M May
1B L May
2B T Helms
SS R Metzger
3B D Rader
LF B Watson
CF C Cedeno
RF G Gross
RU B Gallagher
2B L Milbourne
IC- C Johnson
M P Gomez

LA 1974 NL
SP A Messersmith
SP D Sutton
SP D Rau
SP T John
RP M Marshall
RP C Hough
RP J Joshua
C- S Yeager
1B S Garvey
2B D Lopes
SS B Russell
3B R Cey
LF B Buckner
CF J Wynn
RF W Crawford
CR J Ferguson
UO-V Joshua
LM- T Paciorek
M W Alston

MON 1974 NL
SP S Rogers
SP S Renko
SP M Torrez
SP D Blair
SP E McAnally
RP C Taylor
RS T Walker
RP J Montague
RP D Murray
C B Foote
1U J Jorgensen
2B- J Cox
SS T Foli
3B B Bailey
32 R Hunt
L3 B Bailey
CW W Davis
RF K Singleton
1U R Fairly
2S L Lintz
UO-R Woods
M G Mauch

NY 1974 NL
SP J Koosman
SP J Matlack
SP T Seaver
SR H Parker
RS B Apodaca
RS R Sadecki
RP T McGraw
RP B Miller
C - J Grote
1B J Milner
2B F Millan
SS B Harrelson
3B W Garrett
LF C Jones
CF D Hahn
RF R Staub
SU T Martinez
UT- K Boswell
OI- E Kranepool
MO-D Schneck
M Y Berra

PHI 1974 NL
SP S Carlton
SP J Lonborg
SP D Ruthven
SR R Schueler
SP W Twitchell
RP M Scarce
C B Boone
1B W Montanez
2B D Cash
SS L Bowa
3B M Schmidt
LF- G Luzinski
CF D Unser
RF M Anderson
UO R Robinson
UT- T Hutton
M D Ozark

PIT 1974 NL
SP J Rooker
SP J Reuss
SP K Brett
SP D Ellis
SR B Kison
RP D Giusti
RP R Hernandez
RP J Morlan
C M Sanguillen
1U- R Robertson
2B R Stennett
SS F Taveras
3B R Hebner
LF W Stargell
M1 A Oliver
RF R Zisk
UO G Clines
1U E Kirkpatrick
SS- M Mendoza
M D Murtaugh

STL 1974 NL
SP B Gibson
SP L McGlothen
SP J Curtis
SP A Foster
RP S Siebert
RP B Forsch
RP A Hrabosky
RP R Folkers
RP M Garman
C T Simmons
1B J Torre
2B T Sizemore
SS M Tyson
3B K Reitz
LF L Brock
CF B McBride
RF R Smith
OI J Cruz
OI- L Melendez
M R Schoendienst

SD 1974 NL
SP B Greif
SP D Freisleben
SP R Jones
SP D Spillner
RP L Hardy
RP V Romo
RP D Tomlin
RP M Corkins
C F Kendall
1B W McCovey
2U D Thomas
SS E Hernandez
3B D Roberts
LO D Winfield
CF J Grubb
RF- B Tolan
1L N Colbert
OF C Gaston
M J McNamara

SF 1974 NL
SR J Barr
SP J D'Acquisto
SP M Caldwell
SP T Bradley
SR R Bryant
RP R Moffitt
RP E Sosa
RS C Williams
C D Rader
1B D Kingman
2B T Fuentes
SS C Speier
3U S Ontiveros
LF G Matthews
CF G Maddox
RF B Bonds
1U E Goodson
UI M Phillips
OI G Thomasson
M1 C Fox
M2 W Westrum

BAL 1974 AL
SP R Grimsley
SP M Cuellar
SP D McNally
SP J Palmer
SP D Alexander
RP G Jackson
RP B Reynolds
RP D Hood
RP J Jefferson
C1 E Williams
1B B Powell
2B B Grich
SS M Belanger
3B B Robinson
LF D Baylor
CF P Blair
RF R Coggins
DH T Davis
LU- A Bumbry
M E Weaver

BOS 1974 AL
SP L Tiant
SP B Lee
SR R Cleveland
SR D Drago
SR R Moret
RP D Segui
1U- R Montgomery
1L C Yastrzemski
2B- D Griffin
SS- M Guerrero
3B R Petrocelli
OF B Darwin
CF J Beniquez
RF D Evans
LD T Harper
SS R Burleson
MU R Miller
1D C Cooper
23 D McAuliffe
M D Johnson

CAL 1974 AL
SP N Ryan
SP F Tanana
SP A Hassler
SP D Lange
SP B Singer
RS E Figueroa
RP S Lockwood
C- E Rodriguez
1B- J Doherty
2B D Doyle
S3 D Chalk
3B- P Schaal
LR J Lahoud
CF M Rivers
RF L Stanton
DH F Robinson
13 B Oliver
LS B Valentine
M1 B Winkles
M2 W Herzog
M3 D Williams

CHI 1974 AL
SP W Wood
SP J Kaat
SP S Bahnsen
SP B Johnson
RP T Forster
RS J Pitlock
RP R Gossage
C E Herrmann
1B D Allen
2B J Orta
SS B Dent
3B B Melton
LF C May
CF K Henderson
RF B Sharp
DR P Kelly
CR B Downing
1B T Muser
UI R Santo
M C Tanner

CLE 1974 AL
SP G Perry
SP J Perry
SP F Peterson
SP D Bosman
RP T Buskey
RP F Beene
RP M Wilcox
C D Duncan
1C J Ellis
2B J Brohamer
SS F Duffy
3B B Bell
LI J Lowenstein
CF J Hendrick
RF C Spikes
DH O Gamble
UO R Torres
M K Aspromonte

DET 1974 AL
SP M Lolich
SP J Coleman
SP L LaGrow
SP W Fryman
RP J Hiller
RP J Ray
C - J Moses
1C B Freehan
2B G Sutherland
SS E Brinkman
3B A Rodriguez
LF- W Horton
CF M Stanley
RF- J Northrup
DH A Kaline
LU- B Oglivie
M R Houk

KC 1974 AL
SP S Busby
SP P Splittorff
SP A Fitzmorris
SP D Dal Canton
SR M Pattin
RS L McDaniel

RP N Briles
RP D Bird
RP S Mingori
C F Healy
1B J Mayberry
2B C Rojas
SS F Patek
3B G Brett
LF J Wohlford
CF A Otis
RF V Pinson
DL H McRae
RO A Cowens
2S F White
1U- T Solaita
M J McKeon

MIL 1974 AL
SP J Slaton
SP C Wright
SP J Colborn
SR K Kobel
SP B Champion
RP T Murphy
RS E Rodriguez
RP B Travers
C D Porter
1B G Scott
2B P Garcia
SS R Yount
3B D Money
LF J Briggs
MO B Coluccio
RF D May
DO- B Mitchell
CF K Berry
UT- M Hegan
S2- T Johnson
M D Crandall

MIN 1974 AL
SP B Blyleven
SP J Decker
SP D Goltz
SR V Albury
SR R Corbin
RP B Campbell
RS B Hands
RS B Butler
RP T Burgmeier
C G Borgmann
1B- C Kusick
2B R Carew
SS- D Thompson
3B E Soderholm
LM L Hisle
CF S Brye
RF B Darwin
DH T Oliva
LF S Braun
UT H Killebrew
IO J Terrell
SS- L Gomez
M F Quilici

NY 1974 AL
SP P Dobson
SP D Medich
SP D Tidrow
SP R May
SP M Stottlemyre
RP S Lyle
RP C Upshaw
RP M Wallace
C T Munson
1B C Chambliss
2B- S Alomar
SS J Mason
3B G Nettles
LU L Piniella
CF E Maddox
RM B Murcer
DU- R Blomberg
UT R White
2S- G Michael
IF- B Sudakis
M B Virdon

OAK 1974 AL
SP C Hunter
SP V Blue
SP K Holtzman
SR D Hamilton
RP R Fingers
RP P Lindblad
RS B Odom
RP D Knowles
C - L Haney
1C G Tenace
2B D Green
SS B Campaneris
3B S Bando
LF J Rudi
CF B North
RF R Jackson
OF- J Alou

2I T Kubiak
OI A Mangual
LS- H Washington
M A Dark

TEX 1974 AL
SP F Jenkins
SP J Bibby
SP J Brown
SR S Hargan
SP D Clyde
RP S Foucault
C J Sundberg
1U M Hargrove
2B D Nelson
SS T Harrah
32 L Randle
ML C Tovar
CF J Lovitto
RF J Burroughs
1D J Spencer
LD A Johnson
OI- T Grieve
M B Martin

ATL 1975 NL
SP C Morton
SP P Niekro
RP M Leon
RP T House
RP M Beard
RS R Sadecki
C V Correll
1B E Williams
2B M Perez
SS L Blanks
3B D Evans
LF R Garr
CF R Office
RF D Baker
UT M Lum
2U- R Gilbreath
UO- D May
M1 C King
M2 C Ryan

CHI 1975 NL
SP B Burris
SP R Reuschel
SP B Bonham
SP S Stone
RP D Knowles
RS T Dettore
RP O Zamora
RP K Frailing
C - S Swisher
1B A Thornton
2B M Trillo
SS D Kessinger
3B B Madlock
LF J Cardenal
CF R Monday
RF J Morales
1U P LaCock
CU- G Mitterwald
M J Marshall

CIN 1975 NL
SP G Nolan
SP J Billingham
SP F Norman
SP D Gullett
SP P Darcy
RP P Borbon
CL R Eastwick
RP C Kirby
RP W McEnaney
C J Bench
1B T Perez
2B J Morgan
SS D Concepcion
3B P Rose
LO G Foster
CF C Geronimo
RF K Griffey
UT- D Driessen
UI- D Flynn
OI- M Rettenmund
M S Anderson

HOU 1975 NL
SP L Dierker
SP J Richard
SP D Roberts
SP D Konieczny
RS K Forsch
RP J Niekro
RP J Crawford
RP W Granger
C M May
1B B Watson
2B R Andrews
SS R Metzger
3B D Rader
UO W Howard
CF C Cedeno
OF G Gross

UT E Cabell
RU J Cruz
IC C Johnson
IF- K Boswell
M1 P Gomez
M2 B Virdon

LA 1975 NL
SP A Messersmith
SP D Rau
SP D Sutton
SP B Hooton
SR B Rhoden
RP M Marshall
RP C Hough
C S Yeager
1B S Garvey
2B D Lopes
SS- B Russell
3B R Cey
LF- B Buckner
CF J Wynn
RF W Crawford
UT L Lacy
SS- R Auerbach
M W Alston

MON 1975 NL
SP S Rogers
SP S Renko
SR D Warthen
SP D Blair
SR W Fryman
RP D Murray
RP D Carrithers
RP D DeMola
RP C Taylor
C B Foote
1B M Jorgensen
2B P Mackanin
SS T Foli
3B L Parrish
UO L Biittner
CF P Mangual
RC G Carter
LU B Bailey
UT- J Morales
UO- T Scott
M G Mauch

NY 1975 NL
SP T Seaver
SP J Koosman
SP J Matlack
SP R Tate
SR H Webb
RP R Baldwin
RP B Apodaca
RP T Hall
C J Grote
1B E Kranepool
2B F Millan
SS M Phillips
3B W Garrett
L1 D Kingman
CF D Unser
RF B Staub
3U J Torre
UO- G Clines
OI- J Milner
M1 Y Berra
M2 R McMillan

PHI 1975 NL
SP S Carlton
SP T Underwood
SP L Christenson
SP J Lonborg
SR W Twitchell
RP G Garber
RP T McGraw
RP T Hilgendorf
RS R Schueler
C - B Boone
1B D Allen
2B D Cash
SS L Bowa
3B M Schmidt
LF G Luzinski
CF G Maddox
RF M Anderson
1U T Hutton
RF J Johnstone
RL- O Brown
C - J Oates
M D Ozark

PIT 1975 NL
SP J Reuss
SP J Rooker
SP B Kison
SP D Ellis
SP J Candelaria
RS L Demery
RP K Brett
RP D Giusti
RP R Hernandez

C M Sanguillen
1B W Stargell
2B R Stennett
SS F Taveras
3B R Hebner
LF R Zisk
CF A Oliver
RF D Parker
UT- K Kirkpatrick
UO- B Robinson
M D Murtaugh

STL 1975 NL
SP L McGlothen
SP B Forsch
SP R Reed
SR J Curtis
SP J Denny
CL A Hrabosky
RP B Gibson
RP M Garman
C T Simmons
R1 R Smith
2B T Sizemore
SS M Tyson
3B K Reitz
LF L Brock
CF B McBride
RU W Davis
1U R Fairly
UO L Melendez
M R Schoendienst

SD 1975 NL
SP R Jones
SP J McIntosh
SP D Freisleben
SR D Spillner
SP B Strom
RS R Folkers
RP D Frisella
RP D Tomlin
RP B Greif
C F Kendall
1B W McCovey
2B T Fuentes
SS E Hernandez
3U- T Kubiak
LU B Tolan
CF J Grubb
RF D Winfield
13 M Ivie
LU G Locklear
S3 H Torres
UO- D Sharon
M J McNamara

SF 1975 NL
SP J Barr
SP J Montefusco
SP J Falcone
SR M Caldwell
SP E Halicki
RP G Lavelle
RP K Moffitt
RP D Heaverlo
C D Rader
1B W Montanez
2B D Thomas
SS C Speier
3B S Ontiveros
LF M Matthews
CF V Joshua
RF B Murcer
3I B Miller
OI G Thomasson
M W Westrum

BAL 1975 AL
SP J Palmer
SP M Torrez
SP M Cuellar
SP R Grimsley
SR D Alexander
RP W Garland
RP J Jackson
C D Duncan
1B L May
2B B Grich
SS M Belanger
3B B Robinson
LF D Baylor
CF P Blair
RF K Singleton
DH T Davis
OI A Bumbry
C - E Hendricks
1B- T Muser
MU- J Northrup
M E Weaver

BOS 1975 AL
SP B Lee
SP L Tiant
SP R Wise
SR R Cleveland

SR R Moret
CL D Drago
RP D Segui
RP J Willoughby
RP J Burton
C - C Fisk
1B C Yastrzemski
2B D Griffin
SS R Burleson
3B R Petrocelli
OF B Carbo
CF F Lynn
RF D Evans
LD J Rice
D1 C Cooper
2B- D Doyle
M D Johnson

CAL 1975 AL
SP F Tanana
SP E Figueroa
SP N Ryan
SP B Singer
SR A Hassler
RS D Lange
RP D Kirkwood
RP M Scott
C - E Rodriguez
1B B Bochte
2B J Remy
SS- M Miley
3B D Chalk
UO M Nettles
CF M Rivers
RF L Stanton
DU- T Harper
LF- D Collins
M D Williams

CHI 1975 AL
SP J Kaat
SP W Wood
SP C Osteen
SP J Jefferson
RP R Gossage
RP D Hamilton
RP O Osborn
RP B Gogolewski
C B Downing
UT C May
2B J Orta
SS B Dent
3B B Melton
LO N Nyman
CF K Henderson
RF P Kelly
D1 D Johnson
M C Tanner

CLE 1975 AL
SR D Eckersley
SP F Peterson
SR D Hood
SP R Harrison
SP G Perry
RS J Bibby
RP D LaRoche
RP T Buskey
RP J Brown
C - A Ashby
1B B Powell
2B- D Kuiper
SS F Duffy
3B B Bell
LU O Gamble
MR R Manning
MR G Hendrick
DU R Carty
RL C Spikes
C - J Ellis
UT- J Lowenstein
M F Robinson

DET 1975 AL
SP M Lolich
SP J Coleman
SP V Ruhle
SP L LaGrow
SP R Bare
RS T Walker
RS D Lemanczyk
CL J Hiller
C B Freehan
1B- J Pierce
2B G Sutherland
SS T Veryzer
3B A Rodriguez
LF B Oglivie
CF R LeFlore
RF L Roberts
DH W Horton
L1 D Meyer
M R Houk

KC 1975 AL
SP S Busby
SP A Fitzmorris

SR D Leonard
SR M Pattin
SR P Splittorff
RP D Bird
RP N Briles
RP L McDaniel
RS S Mingori
C - B Martinez
1B J Mayberry
2B C Rojas
SS F Patek
3B G Brett
LF H McRae
CF A Otis
RM A Cowens
DH H Killebrew
RU V Pinson
2S F White
RL J Wohlford
UT- T Solaita
M1 J McKeon
M2 W Herzog

TEX 1975 AL
SP F Jenkins
SP S Hargan
SP G Perry
SP S Hands
RS J Umbarger
SP S Foucault
RP S Thomas
C J Sundberg
1B J Spencer
2M L Randle
SS T Harrah
3B R Howell
L1 M Hargrove
CF- D Moates
RF J Burroughs
DO C Tovar
UO T Grieve
M1 B Martin
M2 F Lucchesi

MIL 1975 AL
SP P Broberg
SP J Slaton
SP J Colborn
SP B Travers
SR B Champion
RS T Hausman
RP E Rodriguez
CL T Murphy
C D Porter
1B G Scott
2B P Garcia
SS R Yount
3B D Money
ML B Sharp
CF G Thomas
RF S Lezcano
C - V Correll
DH H Aaron
32 K Bevacqua
OI- M Hegan
LF- B Mitchell
M1 D Crandall
M2 H Kuenn

MIN 1975 AL
SP B Blyleven
SP J Hughes
SP D Goltz
SR V Albury
RS B Campbell
RP T Burgmeier
C G Borgmann
1B- C Kusick
2B R Carew
SS D Thompson
3B E Soderholm
LF S Braun
CF D Ford
RM L Bostock
DH T Oliva
IO J Terrell
1O- J Briggs
RO- S Brye
SS- L Gomez
UO- L Hisle
M F Quilici

NY 1975 AL
SP C Hunter
SP D Medich
SP R May
SP P Dobson
SP L Gura
RP S Lyle
RP D Tidrow
C T Munson
1B C Chambliss
2B S Alomar
SS- J Mason
3B G Nettles
LF R White
CF- E Maddox
RM B Bonds
UC- E Herrmann
S2- F Stanley
OI- W Williams
M1 B Virdon
M2 B Martin

OAK 1975 AL
SP V Blue
SP K Holtzman
SP D Bosman
SR G Abbott
SP S Bahnsen
RP R Fingers
RP J Todd
RP P Lindblad
C G Tenace
1L J Rudi
2B P Garner
SS B Campaneris
3B S Bando

LF C Washington
CF B North
RF R Jackson
DH B Williams
1U J Holt
UO- D Hopkins
S2- T Martinez
M A Dark

ATL 1976 NL
SP P Niekro
SP D Ruthven
SP A Messersmith
SP C Morton
SP F LaCorte
RP A Devine
RP B Dal Canton
RP P Torrealba
C - V Correll
1B W Montanez
2B R Gilbreath
SS D Chaney
3B J Royster
LM J Wynn
CF R Office
RF K Henderson
OF D May
UT J Paciorek
M D Bristol

CHI 1976 NL
SP R Reuschel
SP B Burris
SP B Bonham
SP S Renko
RP B Sutter
RP P Reuschel
RP J Coleman
RP D Knowles
C S Swisher
1U P LaCock
2B M Trillo
SS M Kelleher
3B B Madlock
LF J Cardenal
MU R Monday
RF J Morales
CU G Mitterwald
MU J Wallis
SS- D Rosello
OI- C Summers
M J Marshall

CIN 1976 NL
SP G Nolan
SR P Zachry
SP F Norman
SP J Billingham
SP S Alcala
RP R Eastwick
RP P Borbon
RP D Gullett
RP W McEnaney
C J Bench
1B T Perez
2B J Morgan
SS D Concepcion
3B P Rose
LF G Foster
CF C Geronimo
RF K Griffey
UT D Driessen
2I- D Flynn
UO- M Lum
M S Anderson

HOU 1976 NL
SP J Richard
SP L Dierker
SP J Andujar
SR J Niekro
CL K Forsch
RP G Pentz
RP J Sambito
C - E Herrmann

1B B Watson
2B R Andrews
SS R Metzger
3B E Cabell
LO J Cruz
CF C Cedeno
RF E Gross
CU C Johnson
IO- K Boswell
OI- W Howard
LU- L Roberts
M B Virdon

LA 1976 NL
SP D Sutton
SP D Rau
SP B Hooton
SP T John
SP R Rhoden
RP C Hough
RP M Marshall
RS B Wall
C S Yeager
1B S Garvey
2B D Lopes
SS B Russell
3B R Cey
LF B Buckner
MU D Baker
RF- B Smith
IO- E Goodson
2B- T Sizemore
M1 W Alston
M2 T Lasorda

MON 1976 NL
SP S Rogers
SP W Fryman
SP D Stanhouse
SR D Carrithers
RP D Murray
RS D Dunning
RP C Lang
RP J Kerrigan
C - B Foote
1O M Jorgensen
2B P Mackanin
SS T Foli
3B L Parrish
UO- D Unser
MU J White
MR- E Valentine
IC J Morales
CR- G Carter
M1 K Kuehl
M2 C Fox

NY 1976 NL
SP T Seaver
SP J Matlack
SP J Koosman
SP M Lolich
SP C Swan
CL S Lockwood
RP B Apodaca
C J Grote
1O E Kranepool
2B F Millan
SS B Harrelson
3B- R Staiger
LF J Milner
CF- D Unser
RF D Kingman
1U J Torre
UO B Boisclair
SI- M Phillips
M J Frazier

PHI 1976 NL
SP S Carlton
SP J Kaat
SP J Lonborg
SP L Christenson
SP T Underwood
RP R Reed
RP T McGraw
RP G Garber
RP W Twitchell
C B Boone
1B- D Allen
2B D Cash
SS L Bowa
3B M Schmidt
LF G Luzinski
CF G Maddox
RF J Johnstone
LO J Martin
UT B Tolan
RF- O Brown
1B- T Hutton
IC- T McCarver
M D Ozark

PIT 1976 NL
SP J Candelaria
SP J Reuss
SP J Rooker

[PIT 1976 NL]
SP B Kison
SP D Medich
RS L Demery
RP K Tekulve
RP -B Moose
RP D Giusti
... M Sanguillen
B W Stargell
SR R Stennett
SS F Taveras
B R Hebner
F R Zisk
CF A Oliver
RF D Parker
MT R Robinson
MT- E Kirkpatrick
... D Murtaugh

STL 1976 NL
SP P Falcone
SP J Denny
SP L McGlothen
SP B Forsch
SR E Rasmussen
RS J Curtis
RP A Hrabosky
RPM W Wallace
RP B Greif
C T Simmons
... K Hernandez
3B- M Tyson
S D Kessinger
B H Cruz
F L Brock
MU J Mumphrey
MF W Crawford
MT- V Harris
DI- M Anderson
M R Schoendienst

SD 1976 NL
SP R Jones
... P B Strom
R D Freisleben
R D Spillner
... B Metzger
P D Tomlin
P R Folkers
... F Kendall
B M Ivie
... T Fuentes
S E Hernandez
... D Rader
... J Grubb
F W Davis
F D Winfield
... J Turner
... T Kubiak
O-M Rettenmund
... J McNamara

SF 1976 NL
... J Montefusco
J Barr
E Halicki
R Dressler
J D'Acquisto
G Lavelle
R Moffitt
S M Caldwell
C Williams
D Rader
3- D Evans
... M Perez
S C Speier
... K Reitz
G Matthews
F L Herndon
B Murcer
G Thomasson
3- D Thomas
B Rigney

BAL 1976 AL
... J Palmer
W Garland
R May
R Grimsley
M Cuellar
D Miller
D Duncan
T Muser
B Grich
M Belanger
D DeCinces
K Singleton
P Blair
R Jackson
L May
A Bumbry
E Weaver

BOS 1976 AL
L Tiant
R Wise
F Jenkins
R Cleveland

SR D Pole
RP J Willoughby
RS R Jones
RP T Murphy
C C Fisk
1L C Yastrzemski
2B D Doyle
SS R Burleson
3B- B Hobson
LD J Rice
CF F Lynn
RF D Evans
1D C Cooper
UO R Miller
3B- R Petrocelli
M1 D Johnson
M2 D Zimmer

CAL 1976 AL
SP F Tanana
SP N Ryan
SP G Ross
SR P Hartzell
SP D Kirkwood
RS S Monge
RP D Drago
C A Etchebarren
OI B Bochte
2B J Remy
S3 D Chalk
3B R Jackson
UO-L Stanton
CF R Torres
RF B Bonds
DH-T Davis
LU D Collins
IF B Melton
IF- M Guerrero
M1 D Williams
M2 N Sherry

CHI 1976 AL
SP R Gossage
SP B Johnson
SP K Brett
SP B Barrios
SR T Forster
RS P Vuckovich
RP D Hamilton
RP C Carroll
C B Downing
1B J Spencer
2B J Brohamer
SS B Dent
3B- K Bell
OI J Orta
CF C Lemon
UO R Garr
IO B Stein
UT- L Johnson
M P Richards

CLE 1976 AL
SP P Dobson
SP D Eckersley
SP J Brown
SR J Bibby
SP R Waits
RP J Kern
RP D LaRoche
RS S Thomas
RP T Buskey
C - A Ashby
1B- B Powell
2B D Kuiper
SS F Duffy
3B B Bell
LF G Hendrick
CF R Manning
RF C Spikes
DH R Carty
S2 L Blanks
C - R Fosse
OI- J Lowenstein
M F Robinson

DET 1976 AL
SP D Roberts
SP M Fidrych
SP V Ruhle
SP R Bare
RP J Hiller
RS J Crawford
RP S Grilli
C - B Kimm
1B J Thompson
2B- P Garcia
SS T Veryzer
3B A Rodriguez
LU A Johnson
CF R LeFlore
RF R Staub
DH W Horton
UT D Meyer
OI B Oglivie

UT- M Stanley
M R Houk

KC 1976 AL
SP D Leonard
SP A Fitzmorris
SR D Bird
SP P Splittorff
SR M Pattin
RP M Littell
RP A Hassler
RP S Mingori
C - B Martinez
1B J Mayberry
2B F White
SS F Patek
3B G Brett
LF T Poquette
CF A Otis
RF A Cowens
DH H McRae
LF J Wohlford
M W Herzog

MIL 1976 AL
SP J Slaton
SP B Travers
SP J Colborn
SR J Augustine
RS E Rodriguez
RP B Castro
RP D Frisella
C D Porter
1B G Scott
2B T Johnson
SS R Yount
3B D Money
UO S Lezcano
CF V Joshua
MR G Thomas
DH- H Aaron
CL- C Moore
M A Grammas

MIN 1976 AL
SP D Goltz
SR J Hughes
SP B Singer
SP P Redfern
RP B Campbell
RS S Luebber
RP T Burgmeier
RP V Albury
C B Wynegar
1B R Carew
2B B Randall
SS R Smalley
3B M Cubbage
LF L Hisle
CF L Bostock
RF D Ford
DU C Kusick
DO S Braun
MO-S Brye
UT- J Terrell
M G Mauch

NY 1976 AL
SP C Hunter
SP E Figueroa
SP D Ellis
SP K Holtzman
SP D Alexander
RP S Lyle
RP D Tidrow
RP G Jackson
C T Munson
1B C Chambliss
2B W Randolph
SS F Stanley
3B G Nettles
LF G White
CF M Rivers
RF O Gamble
DH-C May
OF L Piniella
SS- J Mason
M B Martin

OAK 1976 AL
SP V Blue
SP M Torrez
SR S Bahnsen
SP M Mitchell
SR D Bosman
RP R Fingers
RP P Lindblad
RP J Todd
C - L Haney
1C G Tenace
2B P Garner
SS B Campaneris
3B S Bando
LF J Rudi
CF B North
RF C Washington
DH B Williams

OI D Baylor
IO K McMullen
M C Tanner

TEX 1976 AL
SP G Perry
SP N Briles
SP B Blyleven
SP J Umbarger
RS S Hargan
RP M Bacsik
RP J Terpko
C J Sundberg
1B M Hargrove
2B L Randle
SS T Harrah
3B R Howell
LF G Clines
CF J Beniquez
RF J Burroughs
DL T Grieve
RF R Smith
UO-D Moates
M F Lucchesi

ATL 1977 NL
SP P Niekro
SP D Ruthven
SR B Capra
SP A Messersmith
RP D Campbell
RP R Camp
RS M Leon
RS D Collins
C B Pocoroba
1B W Montanez
2B R Gilbreath
SS- P Rockett
3B J Moore
LF G Matthews
CF R Office
RF J Burroughs
M3 B Bonnell
IO J Royster
UO-B Asselstine
M1 D Bristol
M2 T Turner
M3 V Benson
M4 D Bristol

CHI 1977 NL
SP R Reuschel
SP R Burris
SP B Bonham
SP M Krukow
RP B Sutter
RP W Hernandez
RP P Reuschel
RP D Moore
C - G Mitterwald
1B B Buckner
2B M Trillo
SS I DeJesus
3B S Ontiveros
LU J Cardenal
CF J Morales
RF B Murcer
1L L Biittner
UO G Gross
UO G Clines
M H Franks

CIN 1977 NL
SP F Norman
SP T Seaver
SR J Billingham
SP P Moskau
SP D Capilla
RP P Borbon
RP D Murray
C J Bench
1B D Driessen
2B J Morgan
SS D Concepcion
3B P Rose
LF G Foster
CF C Geronimo
RF K Griffey
OI- M Lum
M S Anderson

HOU 1977 NL
SP J Richard
SP M Lemongello
SP J Andujar
SP F Bannister
RS J Niekro
RP J Sambito
RS K Forsch
RS B McLaughlin
C J Ferguson
1B B Watson
2B A Howe
SS- R Metzger
3B E Cabell
LF- T Puhl
1L B Robinson
CF C Cedeno

RF J Cruz
S2 J Gonzalez
LU- W Howard
M B Virdon

LA 1977 NL
SP D Sutton
SP B Hooton
SP T John
SP R Rhoden
SP D Rau
RPC Hough
RP M Garman
RP E Sosa
C S Yeager
1B S Garvey
2B D Lopes
SS B Russell
3B R Cey
LF D Baker
CF R Monday
RF R Smith
CF- G Burke
M T Lasorda

MON 1977 NL
SP S Rogers
SR J Brown
SR D Stanhouse
SP W Twitchell
SP S Bahnsen
RS S Alcala
RP J Kerrigan
RP B Atkinson
RPW McEnaney
C G Carter
1B T Perez
2B D Cash
SS C Speier
3B L Parrish
LF W Cromartie
CF A Dawson
RF E Valentine
OI D Unser
M D Williams

NY 1977 NL
SP J Koosman
SP N Espinosa
SP J Matlack
SP C Swan
SP P Zachry
RP S Lockwood
RP B Apodaca
RP B Myrick
RP R Baldwin
C J Stearns
1U J Milner
2B- F Millan
SS B Harrelson
3B L Randle
LF S Henderson
CF L Mazzilli
RF M Vail
OI E Kranepool
OI B Boisclair
S2- D Flynn
M1 J Frazier
M2 J Torre

PHI 1977 NL
SP S Carlton
SP L Christenson
SP R Lerch
SP J Kaat
SP J Lonborg
RP R Reed
RP G Garber
RP T McGraw
RP W Brusstar
C B Boone
1B R Hebner
2B T Sizemore
SS L Bowa
3B M Schmidt
LF G Luzinski
CF G Maddox
RF J Johnstone
1U T Hutton
OI J Martin
RU- B McBride
IC- T McCarver
M D Ozark

PIT 1977 NL
SP J Candelaria
SP J Reuss
SP J Rooker
SR B Kison
RP R Gossage
RP K Tekulve
RP J Jackson
RS L Demery
C - D Dyer
1B B Robinson
2B R Stennett

SS F Taveras
32 P Garner
LF A Oliver
CF O Moreno
RF D Parker
C E Ott
M C Tanner

STL 1977 NL
SP E Rasmussen
SP B Forsch
SP J Denny
SP P Falcone
SP T Underwood
RS J Urrea
RP B Metzger
RP A Hrabosky
RPC Carroll
C T Simmons
1B K Hernandez
2B M Tyson
SS G Templeton
3B K Reitz
LF L Brock
UO J Mumphrey
RU H Cruz
RF-M Anderson
CF-T Scott
M V Rapp

SD 1977 NL
SP B Shirley
SP B Owchinko
SR T Griffin
SP R Jones
SR D Freisleben
RP R Fingers
RP D Spillner
RP D Tomlin
CI G Tenace
1B M Ivie
2B M Champion
SS B Almon
3B- T Ashford
OI G Richards
CF G Hendrick
RF D Winfield
OI M Rettenmund
LU J Turner
C - D Roberts
RU R Zisk
M1 J McNamara
M2 B Skinner
M3 A Dark

SF 1977 NL
SP E Halicki
SP J Barr
SP B Knepper
SP J Montefusco
RP G Lavelle
RS C Williams
RP D Heaverlo
RP R Moffitt
C M Hill
1B W McCovey
2B R Andrews
SS T Foli
3B B Madlock
OI G Thomasson
MI D Thomas
RF J Clark
L1 D Evans
UO T Whitfield
M J Altobelli

BAL 1977 AL
SP J Palmer
SP R May
SP M Flanagan
SP R Grimsley
RS D Martinez
RS S McGregor
RP T Martinez
C - R Dempsey
1D L May
2B B Smith
SS M Belanger
3B D DeCinces
LF P Kelly
CF A Bumbry
RF K Singleton
D1 E Murray
1U T Muser
2B- R Dauer
M E Weaver

BOS 1977 AL
SP F Jenkins
SP L Cleveland
SP L Tiant
SP R Wise
RP B Stanley
RS M Paxton
RP J Willoughby

C C Fisk
1B G Scott
2B D Doyle
SS R Burleson
3B B Hobson
LF C Yastrzemski
CF F Lynn
RM-R Miller
DO J Rice
RU- B Carbo
M D Zimmer

CAL 1977 AL
SP N Ryan
SP F Tanana
SR P Hartzell
SP K Brett
SP W Simpson
RP D Miller
RP D LaRoche
RP M Barlow
C T Humphrey
1B T Solaita
2B J Remy
SS- R Mulliniks
3B D Chalk
LF- J Rudi
UO G Flores
RF B Bonds
OI D Baylor
IO R Jackson
IF- M Guerrero
M1 N Sherry
M2 D Garcia

CHI 1977 AL
SP F Barrios
SP S Stone
SP K Kravec
SP C Knapp
SP W Wood
RP L LaGrow
RP D Hamilton
C J Essian
1B J Spencer
2B J Orta
SS A Bannister
3B E Soderholm
LF R Garr
CF C Lemon
RU R Zisk
DR O Gamble
D1 L Johnson
M B Lemon

CLE 1977 AL
SP W Garland
SP D Eckersley
SP J Bibby
SR R Waits
SP D Dobson
RP A Fitzmorris
RP J Kern
RS D Hood
C F Kendall
1B A Thornton
2B D Kuiper
SS F Duffy
3B B Bell
L1 B Bochte
MR J Norris
UT P Dade
DH R Carty
SI L Blanks
OI- J Lowenstein
M1 F Robinson
M2 J Torborg

DET 1977 AL
SP D Rozema
SR F Arroyo
SR F Sykes
SP D Roberts
SP M Wilcox
RS J Hiller
RS J Crawford
RP S Foucault
RP S Grilli
C M May
1B J Thompson
2B T Fuentes
SS T Veryzer
3B- A Rodriguez
LF S Kemp
CF R LeFlore
RF B Oglivie
DH R Staub
3B- P Mankowski
M R Houk

KC 1977 AL
SP D Leonard
SP J Colborn
SP P Splittorff
SP A Hassler
RS D Bird
RS M Pattin

RS M Littell
RS L Gura
C D Porter
1B J Mayberry
2B F White
SS F Patek
3B G Brett
LR T Poquette
CF A Otis
RF A Cowens
DL H McRae
LF J Zdeb
UT- P LaCock
M W Herzog

MIL 1977 AL
SP J Slaton
SP J Augustine
SP M Haas
SP L Sorensen
SP B Travers
RS E Rodriguez
RP B Castro
RP B McClure
RP S Hinds
C C Moore
1B C Cooper
2B D Money
SS R Yount
3B S Bando
LF J Wohlford
CF V Joshua
RF S Lezcano
DU- J Quirk
UO-S Brye
M A Grammas

MIN 1977 AL
SP D Goltz
SP P Thormodsgard
SP G Zahn
SP P Redfern
RP T Johnson
RS R Schueler
RP T Burgmeier
RS D Johnson
C B Wynegar
1B R Carew
2B B Randall
SS R Smalley
3B M Cubbage
UO L Hisle
ML L Bostock
RF D Ford
DU C Kusick
DU R Chiles
OF-G Adams
3U- J Terrell
M G Mauch

NY 1977 AL
SP E Figueroa
SP M Torrez
SP R Guidry
SP D Gullett
SP C Hunter
RS S Lyle
RS D Tidrow
RP K Clay
C T Munson
1B C Chambliss
2B W Randolph
SS B Dent
3B G Nettles
LF R White
CF M Rivers
RF R Jackson
DH-C May
OI L Piniella
MR-P Blair
M B Martin

OAK 1977 AL
SP V Blue
SP R Langford
SP D Medich
RS J Coleman
RP B Lacey
RS P Torrealba
RP D Bair
C - J Newman
1B- D Allen
2B M Perez
SS R Picciolo
3B W Gross
LF M Page
MR T Armas
RU- J Tyrone
CD M Sanguillen
2S R Scott
UC E Williams
UT- M Alexander
UT- R McKinney
OI- L Murray

M1 J McKeon
M2 B Winkles

SEA 1977 AL
SP G Abbott
SP D Pole
RS J Montague
RP E Romo
RS D Segui
RP M Kekich
C B Stinson
1B D Meyer
2B- J Baez
SS C Reynolds
3B B Stein
LU S Braun
CF R Jones
RU L Stanton
DI- J Bernhardt
LD D Collins
RF C Lopez
UI- L Milbourne
M D.Johnson

TEX 1977 AL
SP G Perry
SP D Alexander
SP B Blyleven
SP D Ellis
SR N Briles
RP A Devine
RP P Lindblad
RP D Knowles
C J Sundberg
1B M Hargrove
2B B Wills
SS B Campaneris
3B T Harrah
LM C Washington
CF J Beniquez
RF D May
DH W Horton
M1 F Lucchesi
M2 E Stanky
M3 C Ryan
M4 B Hunter

TOR 1977 AL
SP D Lemanczyk
SP J Garvin
SP J Jefferson
RS P Vuckovich
RP M Willis
RP J Johnson
RP T Murphy
C A Ashby
1B D Ault
2B- S Staggs
S2- H Torres
3B- R Howell
LF A Woods
OI B Bailor
RU O Velez
UT R Fairly
OI S Ewing
RM-S Bowling
UI- D McKay
IO- D Rader
M R Hartsfield

ATL 1978 NL
SP P Niekro
SP P Hanna
SR M Mahler
SP L McWilliams
RS E Solomon
CL G Garber
RS J Easterly
RP R Camp
C - B Pocoroba
1B D Murphy
2S J Royster
SS- D Chaney
3B- B Horner
LF J Burroughs
CF R Office
RF G Matthews
UT B Beall
OI B Bonnell
32 M Gilbreath
CU-J Nolan
M B Cox

CHI 1978 NL
SP R Reuschel
SP D Lamp
SP R Burris
SR D Roberts
SP M Krukow
RP B Sutter
RP D Moore
RP L McGlothen
RP W Hernandez
C D Rader
1B B Buckner
2B M Trillo
SS I DeJesus

3B- S Ontiveros
LF G Kingman
ML G Gross
RF B Murcer
1U L Biittner
UO G Clines
M H Franks

CIN 1978 NL
SP T Seaver
SP F Norman
SR T Hume
SP P Moskau
SP B Bonham
RP M Sarmiento
RP D Bair
RP P Borbon
RP D Tomlin
C J Bench
1B D Driessen
2B J Morgan
SS D Concepcion
3B P Rose
LF G Foster
CF C Geronimo
RF K Griffey
UO D Collins
2B- J Kennedy
3U- R Knight
OI- M Lum
M S Anderson

HOU 1978 NL
SP J Richard
SP M Lemongello
SP J Niekro
SR T Dixon
SR J Andujar
RS K Forsch
RS F Bannister
RP J Sambito
C - L Pujols
1B B Watson
2B A Howe
SU- J Sexton
3B E Cabell
LU D Walling
ML T Puhl
RF J Cruz
1L D Bergman
OI- W Howard
M B Virdon

LA 1978 NL
SP D Sutton
SP B Hooton
SP T John
SP D Rau
SP R Rhoden
RS B Welch
RP C Hough
CL T Forster
RP L Rautzhan
C - S Yeager
1B S Garvey
2B D Lopes
SS B Russell
3B R Cey
LF D Baker
CF B North
RF R Smith
UT L Lacy
MR R Monday
M T Lasorda

MON 1978 NL
SP R Grimsley
SP S Rogers
SP R May
SR D Schatzeder
SR W Twitchell
RS H Dues
RP S Bahnsen
RP D Knowles
RP M Garman
C G Carter
1B T Perez
2B D Cash
SS C Speier
3B L Parrish
LF W Cromartie
CF A Dawson
RF E Valentine
UT D Unser
M D Williams

NY 1978 NL
SP J Koosman
SP C Swan
SP N Espinosa
SP P Zachry
SP M Bruhert
RS K Kobel
RS S Lockwood
RP D Murray
C J Stearns
1B W Montanez

2B D Flynn
SS T Foli
3B L Randle
LF S Henderson
CF L Mazzilli
R3 E Maddox
RU B Boisclair
UT J Youngblood
M J Torre

PHI 1978 NL
SP S Carlton
SP L Christenson
SP R Lerch
SP D Ruthven
SP J Kaat
RP R Reed
RP J Lonborg
RP T McGraw
RP W Brusstar
C B Boone
1B R Hebner
2B T Sizemore
SS L Bowa
3B M Schmidt
LF G Luzinski
CF G Maddox
RF B McBride
UO J Martin
1U- J Cardenal
IC- T McCarver
M D Ozark

PIT 1978 NL
SP B Blyleven
SP D Robinson
SP J Candelaria
SP J Rooker
SR J Bibby
RP K Tekulve
RP G Jackson
RP E Whitson
C E Ott
1B W Stargell
2B R Stennett
SS F Taveras
23 P Garner
LF B Robinson
CF O Moreno
RF D Parker
L1 J Milner
IC- M Sanguillen
M C Tanner

STL 1978 NL
SP J Denny
SP J Forsch
SR P Vuckovich
SP S Martinez
SR J Urrea
RP M Littell
RP B Schultz
RP A Lopez
RP T Bruno
C T Simmons
1B K Hernandez
2B M Tyson
SS G Templeton
3B K Reitz
LF- L Brock
CF G Hendrick
RM J Morales
UO J Mumphrey
UO-T Scott
M1 V Rapp
M2 J Krol
M3 K Boyer

SD 1978 NL
SP G Perry
SP R Jones
SP B Owchinko
SR B Shirley
SP E Rasmussen
RP R Fingers
RP J D'Acquisto
RP M Lee
C - R Sweet
1C G Tenace
2B F Gonzalez
SS O Smith
3B B Almon
LU G Richards
RM D Winfield
RL O Gamble
M2 D Thomas
UO J Turner
M R Craig

SF 1978 NL
SP B Knepper
SP V Blue
SP J Montefusco
SP E Halicki
SP J Barr
RP G Lavelle
RP R Moffitt

RP J Curtis
C M Hill
1B W McCovey
2B B Madlock
SS J LeMaster
3B J Evans
LF T Whitfield
CF L Herndon
RF J Clark
1U M Ivie
M J Altobelli

BAL 1978 AL
SP J Palmer
SP M Flanagan
SP D Martinez
SP S McGregor
CL D Stanhouse
RP J Kerrigan
RP T Martinez
C R Dempsey
1B E Murray
23 R Dauer
SS M Belanger
3B D DeCinces
LU P Kelly
CF L Harlow
RF K Singleton
DH L May
RM C Lopez
2B- B Smith
M E Weaver

BOS 1978 AL
SP D Eckersley
SP M Torrez
SP L Tiant
SP B Lee
SP J Wright
RP B Stanley
RP D Drago
RP T Burgmeier
RP B Campbell
C C Fisk
1B G Scott
2B J Remy
SS R Burleson
3B B Hobson
OI C Yastrzemski
CF F Lynn
RF D Evans
LD J Rice
IF- J Brohamer
M D Zimmer

CAL 1978 AL
SP F Tanana
SP N Ryan
SP C Knapp
SP D Aase
RS P Hartzell
CL D LaRoche
RS K Brett
RP D Miller
C B Downing
1B- R Fairly
2B B Grich
SI D Chalk
3B C Lansford
LF J Rudi
MR R Miller
RM L Bostock
DU D Baylor
13 R Jackson
UO-K Landreaux
M1 D Garcia
M2 J Fregosi

CHI 1978 AL
SP S Stone
SP K Kravec
SP F Barrios
SP W Wood
SP J Willoughby
RP L LaGrow
RP R Hinton
RS R Schueler
C B Nahorodny
1B- M Squires
2B J Orta
SS D Kessinger
3B E Soderholm
LF R Garr
CF C Washington
RO- C Washington
1U L Johnson
UO B Molinaro
UI- G Pryor
M1 B Lemon
M2 L Doby

CLE 1978 AL
SP R Waits
SP R Wise
SP M Paxton
SR D Hood
RP M Clyde

RP J Kern
RP S Monge
RP D Spillner
CD- G Alexander
1B A Thornton
2B D Kuiper
SS T Veryzer
3B B Bell
LF J Grubb
CF R Manning
RF- P Dade
DH- B Carbo
OI J Norris
UT- T Cox
M J Torborg

DET 1978 AL
SP J Slaton
SP M Wilcox
SP D Rozema
SP J Billingham
SP K Young
RP J Hiller
RS J Morris
C M May
1B J Thompson
2B L Whitaker
SS A Trammell
3B A Rodriguez
LF S Kemp
CF R LeFlore
RF T Corcoran
DH R Staub
3B- P Mankowski
C - L Parrish
M R Houk

KC 1978 AL
SP D Leonard
SP P Splittorff
SP L Gura
SP R Gale
RS D Bird
CL M Hrabosky
RS M Pattin
RP S Mingori
C D Porter
1B P LaCock
2B F White
SS F Patek
3B G Brett
LM W Wilson
CF A Otis
RF A Cowens
DH H McRae
UT C Hurdle
M W Herzog

MIL 1978 AL
SP M Caldwell
SP L Sorensen
SP J Augustine
SP B Travers
SR A Replogle
RS E Rodriguez
RP B McClure
RP R Stein
RP B Castro
C - C Moore
1B C Cooper
2I P Molitor
SS R Yount
3B S Bando
LU B Oglivie
CF G Thomas
RF S Lezcano
UO L Hisle
UI D Money
C - B Martinez
M G Bamberger

MIN 1978 AL
SP R Erickson
SP G Zahn
SP D Goltz
SR G Serum
RP R Marshall
C B Wynegar
1B R Carew
2B R Randall
SS R Smalley
3B M Cubbage
LF W Norwood
CF D Ford
RF H Powell
DH G Adams
DH J Morales
RL R Rivera
LU- R Chiles
2B- R Wilfong
3B- L Wolfe
M G Mauch

NY 1978 AL
SP R Guidry
SP E Figueroa
SR D Hood
SP D Tidrow

SP J Beattie
SP C Hunter
RP R Gossage
RP S Lyle
RS K Clay
C . T Munson
1B C Chambliss
2B W Randolph
SS B Dent
3B G Nettles
LU L Piniella
CF M Rivers
RD R Jackson
DC- C Johnson
LU R White
SS- F Stanley
M1 B Martin
M2 D Howser
M3 B Lemon

OAK 1978 AL
SP M Keough
SP J Johnson
SR R Langford
SP P Broberg
SP S Renko
RP D Heaverlo
RP B Lacey
RP E Sosa
C J Essian
1B D Revering
2B M Edwards
SS M Guerrero
3B W Gross
LF M Page
OI M Dilone
RM-T Armas
DH- G Alexander
3B T Duncan
C1 J Newman
MR-J Wallis
M1 B Winkles
M2 J.McKeon

SEA 1978 AL
SP P Mitchell
SP G Abbott
SP R Honeycutt
SP J Colborn
RP B McLaughlin
RP E Romo
RS T House
RP S Rawley
RP J Todd
C B Stinson
1B D Meyer
2B J Cruz
SS C Reynolds
3B B Stein
LD B Bochte
CF R Jones
RF L Roberts
UO J Hale
UI- L Milbourne
DL- L Stanton
M D Johnson

TEX 1978 AL
SP J Matlack
SP F Jenkins
SP D Alexander
SP D Medich
SP D Ellis
RS S Comer
RP R Cleveland
RP L Barker
C J Sundberg
1B M Hargrove
2B B Wills
SS B Campaneris
3S T Harrah
LF A Oliver
CF J Beniquez
RF B Bonds
OF R Zisk
3U- K Bevacqua
1B- M Jorgensen
M1 B Hunter
M2 P Corrales

TOR 1978 AL
SP J Jefferson
SP T Underwood
SP J Clancy
SP J Garvin
SR B Moore
RP D Lemanczyk
RP M Willis
RP T Murphy
RP J Coleman
C - R Cerone
1B J Mayberry
2B D McKay
SS L Gomez
3B R Howell
OI- O Velez

CF R Bosetti
RU B Bailor
DH R Carty
C - A Ashby
OI- W Upshaw
M R Hartsfield

ATL 1979 NL
SP P Niekro
SP E Solomon
SP R Matula
SP T Brizzolara
SP M Mahler
RP G Garber
RP J McLaughlin
RP A Devine
RP C Skok
C - B Benedict
1C D Murphy
2B G Hubbard
SS P Frias
31 B Horner
LF J Burroughs
CF R Office
RF G Matthews
UT M Lum
32 J Royster
C - J Nolan
M B Cox

CHI 1979 NL
SP R Reuschel
SR L McGlothen
SP D Lamp
SP K Krukow
SP K Holtzman
RP B Sutter
RP D Tidrow
RP W Hernandez
RP D Moore
C B Foote
1B B Buckner
2B T Sizemore
SS I DeJesus
3B S Ontiveros
LF D Kingman
CF J Martin
RO S Thompson
OI L Biittner
2U- S Dillard
OI- M Vail
M1 H Franks
M2 J Amalfitano

CIN 1979 NL
SP T Seaver
SP M LaCoss
SP F Norman
SP B Bonham
SP P Moskau
RS T Hume
RP D Bair
RP D Tomlin
C J Bench
1B D Driessen
2B J Morgan
SS D Concepcion
3B R Knight
LF G Foster
CF C Geronimo
RF- K Griffey
OI- D Collins
M1 D Ozark
M2 D Green

HOU 1979 NL
SP J Richard
SP J Niekro
SR J Andujar
SP K Forsch
SR W Williams
CL J Sambito
RS R Niemann
C A Ashby
1M C Cedeno
2B R Landestoy
SS C Reynolds
3B E Cabell
LF J Cruz
MR T Puhl
RU J Leonard
23 A Howe
OF- D Walling
M B Virdon

LA 1979 NL
SP R Sutcliffe
SP D Sutton
SP B Hooton
SR J Reuss
RS C Hough
RP D Patterson
C S Yeager
1B S Garvey
2B D Lopes
SS B Russell

3B R Cey
LF D Baker
CF D Thomas
MR G Thomasson
CR J Ferguson
UO-V Joshua
UI- T Martinez
M T Lasorda

MON 1979 NL
SP S Rogers
SP B Lee
SR D Sanderson
SP D Schatzeder
SP J Grimsley
RS D Palmer
RP E Sosa
RP S Bahnsen
RS R May
C G Carter
1B T Perez
2S R Scott
SS C Speier
3B L Parrish
LF W Cromartie
CF A Dawson
RF E Valentine
UT- T Hutton
UO-J White
M D Williams

NY 1979 NL
SP C Swan
SP P Falcone
SP K Kobel
RS N Allen
RP D Murray
RS A Hassler
RP E Glynn
C J Stearns
1B W Montanez
2B D Flynn
SS F Taveras
3B R Hebner
LF S Henderson
CF L Mazzilli
RL J Youngblood
UT- E Kranepool
OI- E Maddox
M J Torre

PHI 1979 NL
SP S Carlton
SP R Lerch
SP N Espinosa
SP D Ruthven
SP L Christenson
RP R Reed
RP T McGraw
RP K Eastwick
RP K Saucier
C B Boone
1B P Rose
2B M Trillo
SS L Bowa
3B M Schmidt
LF G Luzinski
CF G Maddox
RF B McBride
UO G Gross
OI- D Unser
M1 D Ozark
M2 D Green

PIT 1979 NL
SP B Blyleven
SP J Candelaria
SP B Kison
SP D Robinson
SR J Bibby
RP K Tekulve
RP E Romo
RP J Rooker
RP G Jackson
C E Ott
1B W Stargell
2B R Stennett
SS T Foli
3B- B Madlock
LF B Robinson
CF O Moreno
RF D Parker
23 P Garner
L1 J Milner
UT- L.Lacy
M C Tanner

STL 1979 NL
SP P Vuckovich
SP J Forsch
SP S Martinez
SP J Denny
SP J Fulgham
RP M Littell
RS T Thomas
RP W McEnaney
RP D Knowles

[STL 1979 NL]
C T Simmons
1B K Hernandez
2B K Oberkfell
SS G Templeton
3B K Reitz
LF L Brock
CF T Scott
RF G Hendrick
LO J Mumphrey
M K Boyer

SD 1979 NL
SP R Jones
SP G Perry
SR G Shirley
SR E Rasmussen
RS J D'Acquisto
RP R Fingers
RS S Mura
RP M Lee
C- B Fahey
C1 G Tenace
2B F Gonzalez
SS O Smith
3B- P Dade
LF J Turner
MU G Richards
RF D Winfield
2S B Almon
3U K Bevacqua
UT D Briggs
M R Craig

SF 1979 NL
SP V Blue
SP B Knepper
SP J Montefusco
SR E Halicki
SP J Curtis
RP G Lavelle
RS P Nastu
RP E Whitson
RP T Griffin
C- D Littlejohn
1U M Ivie
2B- J Strain
SS J LeMaster
3B D Evans
ML L Herndon
CF B North
RF J Clark
1B W McCovey
LF T Whitfield
SS- R Metzger
M1 J Altobelli
M2 D Bristol

BAL 1979 AL
SP D Martinez
SP M Flanagan
SP S Stone
SP S McGregor
SP J Palmer
RP S Stewart
CL D Stanhouse
RP T Martinez
RP T Stoddard
C R Dempsey
1B E Murray
23 R Dauer
SS K Garcia
3B D DeCinces
F G Roenicke
RF K Singleton
DH L May
SS M Belanger
UT J Lowenstein
M E Weaver

BOS 1979 AL
SP M Torrez
SP D Eckersley
SR B Stanley
SP S Renko
SP C Rainey
RP D Drago
RP T Burgmeier
RP B Campbell
C G Allenson
D- B Watson
2B- J Remy
SB B Burleson
B B Hobson
F J Rice
CF F Lynn
RF D Evans
JC C Yastrzemski
JC- C Fisk
M D Zimmer

CAL 1979 AL
SP D Frost
SP N Ryan
SR J Barr
SP D Aase

RP M Clear
RP D LaRoche
RP M Barlow
C B Downing
1B R Carew
2B B Grich
SS- B Campaneris
3B C Lansford
LF- J Rudi
CF R Miller
RF D Ford
OI D Baylor
UT W Aikens
SS- J Anderson
M J Fregosi

CHI 1979 AL
SP K Kravec
SP R Wortham
SP R Baumgarten
SR S Trout
RS R Scarbery
RS M Proly
CL E Farmer
RS F Howard
C- M May
1B M Squires
UT A Bannister
SS G Pryor
3B- K Bell
UO- R Torres
CF C Lemon
RF C Washington
D2 J Orta
LU R Garr
1D L Johnson
LU- J Moore
M1 D Kessinger
M2 T LaRussa

CLE 1979 AL
SP R Wise
SP R Waits
SP M Paxton
SR L Barker
RS D Spillner
RP S Monge
RP V Cruz
C G Alexander
1B A Thornton
2B D Kuiper
SS T Veryzer
3B T Harrah
UO J Norris
CF R Manning
RF B Bonds
DH- C Johnson
L1 M Hargrove
M1 J Torborg
M2 D Garcia

DET 1979 AL
SP J Morris
SP M Wilcox
SR J Billingham
SR P Underwood
SP D Petry
RP A Lopez
RP D Rozema
RP J Hiller
RP D Tobik
C L Parrish
1B J Thompson
2B L Whitaker
SS A Trammell
3B A Rodriguez
LF S Kemp
CF R LeFlore
RO J Morales
DH-R Staub
UO- L Jones
RU- C Summers
IC- J Wockenfuss
M1 L Moss
M2 S Tracewski
M3 S Anderson

KC 1979 AL
SP P Splittorff
SP D Leonard
SP L Gura
SP R Gale
RP A Hrabosky
RP E Rodriguez
C D Porter
1B P LaCock
2B F White
SS F Patek
3B G Brett
LF W Wilson
CF A Otis
RF A Cowens
DH H McRae
UI U Washington
1C- J Wathan
M W Herzog

MIL 1979 AL
SP M Caldwell
SP L Sorensen
SP J Slaton
SP B Travers
SP M Haas
RP J Augustine
RP R Cleveland
RP B McClure
RP B Galasso
C C Moore
1B C Cooper
2B P Molitor
SS R Yount
3B B Bando
LU B Oglivie
CF G Thomas
RF S Lezcano
DL- D Davis
UI- D Money
M G Bamberger

MIN 1979 AL
SP J Koosman
SP D Goltz
SP G Zahn
SP P Hartzell
SP R Erickson
RP M Marshall
RS P Redfern
RP M Bacsik
C B Wynegar
1B R Jackson
2B R Wilfong
SS R Smalley
3B J Castino
LR B Rivera
ML K Landreaux
RF H Powell
DH- J Morales
OF G Adams
3U- M Cubbage
UO- D Edwards
OF- W Norwood
M G Mauch

NY 1979 AL
SP T John
SP R Guidry
SP L Tiant
SP E Figueroa
SP C Hunter
RP R Davis
RS K Clay
CL R Gossage
RS D Hood
C T Munson
1B C Chambliss
2B W Randolph
SS B Dent
3B G Nettles
LU L Piniella
CF- B Murcer
RF R Jackson
DU J Spencer
UT- R White
M1 B Lemon
M2 B Martin

OAK 1979 AL
SP R Langford
SP S McCatty
SP M Keough
SR M Norris
SC M Minetto
RP B Kingman
RP D Heaverlo
RS D Hamilton
RP J Todd
C1 J Newman
1B D Revering
2B M Edwards
SS R Picciolo
3B W Gross
LM- R Henderson
CF D Murphy
RO L Murray
DH M Page
CU J Essian
M J Marshall

SEA 1979 AL
SP M Parrott
SP R Honeycutt
SP F Bannister
SP O Jones
SP G Abbott
RS B McLaughlin
RP J Montague
RS R Dressler
RP S Rawley
C L Cox
1B B Bochte
2B J Cruz
SS M Mendoza
3U D Meyer

OF L Roberts
CF R Jones
RO J Simpson
DH W Horton
S2 L Milbourne
OI T Paciorek
3B- B Stein
2B- B Kennedy
C- B Stinson
M D Johnson

TEX 1979 AL
SP F Jenkins
SP S Comer
SR D Medich
SP D Alexander
RP J Kern
RP S Lyle
RP D Rajsich
C J Sundberg
1U P Putnam
2B B Wills
SS N Norman
3B N Bell
LU B Sample
ML A Oliver
RF R Zisk
D1 J Ellis
UO J Grubb
1U- M Jorgensen
M P Corrales

TOR 1979 AL
SP T Underwood
SP P Huffman
SP D Lemanczyk
SR B Moore
SP D Stieb
RS J Jefferson
RP D Freisleben
RP T Buskey
C R Cerone
1B J Mayberry
2B- D Ainge
SS A Griffin
3B R Howell
LF A Woods
CF R Bosetti
RF B Bailor
DH R Carty
OI O Velez
M R Hartsfield

ATL 1980 NL
SP P Niekro
SP D Alexander
SP T Boggs
SP R Matula
SP L McWilliams
RP R Camp
RP G Garber
RP P Hanna
RP A Hrabosky
C B Benedict
1B C Chambliss
2B G Hubbard
SS L Gomez
3B B Horner
LU J Burroughs
CF D Murphy
RF G Matthews
IO J Royster
UO-B Asselstine
S3- L Blanks
UT- M Lum
M B Cox

CHI 1980 NL
SP R Reuschel
SP M Krukow
SP D Lamp
SR L McGlothen
RP B Sutter
RP B Caudill
RP D Tidrow
RS W Hernandez
C T Blackwell
1L B Buckner
2B M Tyson
SS I DeJesus
3B I Randle
LF- D Kingman
MR J Martin
RU M Vail
UT L Biittner
32 S Dillard
UO J Figueroa
23 M Kelleher
RU S Thompson
M1 P Gomez
M2 J Amalfitano

CIN 1980 NL
SP F Pastore
SP C Leibrandt
SP M LaCoss
SP T Seaver
SR P Moskau

RS M Soto
RP T Hume
RS J Price
RP D Bair
C J Bench
1B D Driessen
2B J Kennedy
SS J Concepcion
3B R Knight
LF G Foster
CF D Collins
RF K Griffey
CF C Geronimo
2B R Oester
M J McNamara

HOU 1980 NL
SP J Niekro
SP N Ryan
SP K Forsch
SP V Ruhle
SR J Andujar
RP J Richard
RP D Smith
RP J Sambito
RP F LaCorte
C A Ashby
1I A Howe
2B J Morgan
SS C Reynolds
3B E Cabell
LF J Cruz
CF C Cedeno
RF T Puhl
2S R Landestoy
1U D Walling
1U- D Bergman
RU- J Leonard
M B Virdon

LA 1980 NL
SP J Reuss
SP B Welch
SP D Sutton
SP B Hooton
SP D Goltz
RS R Sutcliffe
RF B Castillo
RS S Howe
RP J Beckwith
C- S Yeager
1B S Garvey
2B D Lopes
SS B Russell
3B R Cey
LF D Baker
CF R Law
RF- R Smith
RU J Johnstone
UT D Thomas
UO- R Monday
M T Lasorda

MON 1980 NL
SP S Rogers
SP S Sanderson
SP B Gullickson
SP D Palmer
SP B Lee
RP C Lea
RP E Sosa
RS F Norman
RP W Fryman
C G Carter
1B W Cromartie
2B R Scott
SS C Speier
3B L Parrish
LF R LeFlore
CF A Dawson
RO R Office
LU J White
IF- T Bernazard
RF- E Valentine
M D Williams

NY 1980 NL
SP R Burris
SP P Zachry
SR M Bomback
SR P Falcone
SP C Swan
RP T Hausman
CL N Allen
RP J Reardon
RP E Glynn
C A Trevino
1M L Mazzilli
2B D Flynn
SS F Taveras
3B M Maddox
LF S Henderson
RM J Youngblood
RL- C Washington
1O M Jorgensen
MU-J Morales

C - J Stearns
M J Torre

PHI 1980 NL
SP S Carlton
SP D Ruthven
SP B Walk
SP R Lerch
CL T McGraw
RP R Reed
RP D Noles
RP K Saucier
C B Boone
1B P Rose
2B M Trillo
SS L Bowa
3B M Schmidt
LF G Luzinski
CF G Maddox
RF B McBride
OI G Gross
LO L Smith
UT- D Unser
M D Green

PIT 1980 NL
SP J Bibby
SP J Candelaria
SP B Blyleven
SP D Robinson
SP R Rhoden
RP E Romo
RP K Tekulve
RS E Solomon
RP G Jackson
C E Ott
1U J Milner
2B P Garner
SS T Foli
3B B Madlock
LR M Easler
CF O Moreno
RF D Parker
LF L Lacy
UT B Robinson
3S- D Berra
M C Tanner

STL 1980 NL
SP P Vuckovich
SP B Forsch
SP B Sykes
SP B Martinez
RS J Kaat
RS D Hood
RP J Littlefield
RP J Urrea
C T Simmons
1B K Hernandez
2B K Oberkfell
SS G Templeton
3B K Reitz
LU- B Bonds
CF T Scott
RF G Hendrick
UT D Iorg
OI- L Durham
OC- T Kennedy
M1 K Boyer
M2 J Krol
M3 W Herzog
M4 R Schoendienst

SD 1980 NL
SP J Curtis
SR S Mura
SP J Jones
SP R Wise
RS G Lucas
RS B Shirley
RP R Fingers
RS E Rasmussen
RP D Kinney
C G Tenace
1B W Montanez
2B D Cash
SS O Smith
3B- A Rodriguez
LF G Richards
CF J Mumphrey
RF D Winfield
C- B Fahey
23- T Flannery
OF- J Turner
M J Coleman

SF 1980 NL
SP V Blue
SP B Knepper
SP E Whitson
SP J Montefusco
SP A Ripley
RP G Minton
RP G Lavelle
RP T Griffin
RP A Holland
C M May

1B- M Ivie
SS J LeMaster
3B D Evans
UO L Herndon
CF B North
RF J Clark
LF T Whitfield
OI- J Wohlford
M D Bristol

BAL 1980 AL
SP S McGregor
SP M Flanagan
SP S Stone
SP J Palmer
SR D Martinez
RP S Stewart
CL T Stoddard
RP T Martinez
RP D Ford
C R Dempsey
1B E Murray
2B R Dauer
SS M Belanger
3B M DeCinces
LR G Roenicke
CF A Bumbry
DU-T Crowley
SS K Garcia
LF J Lowenstein
C- D Graham
OF- P Kelly
M E Weaver

BOS 1980 AL
SP M Torrez
SP D Eckersley
SP S Renko
RS R Stanley
RS D Drago
RP T Burgmeier
C C Fisk
1B T Perez
2B D Stapleton
SS R Burleson
3B G Hoffman
LF J Rice
CF F Lynn
RF D Evans
OI C Yastrzemski
OI- J Dwyer
3D- B Hobson
M1 D Zimmer
M2 J Pesky

CAL 1980 AL
SP F Tanana
SR D Aase
SP A Martinez
SR C Knapp
RS D LaRoche
RP M Clear
RP A Hassler
RP J Montague
C - T Donohue
1U R Carew
2B B Grich
SS- F Patek
3B C Lansford
LF J Rudi
CF R Miller
RM L Harlow
UT J Thompson
OF- D Baylor
M J Fregosi

CHI 1980 AL
SP B Burns
SP S Trout
SP R Dotson
SP R Baumgarten
SR L Hoyt
RP M Proly
RP E Farmer
RS R Wortham
C B Kimm
1B M Squires
2B J Morrison
SS- T Cruz
3B- K Bell
OF W Nordhagen
CF C Lemon
RF H Baines
1D L Johnson
UT B Molinaro
S3 G Pryor
M T LaRussa

CLE 1980 AL
SP L Barker
SP R Waits
SP D Spillner
SP W Garland
SR B Owchinko
RP J Denny

RP S Monge
RP V Cruz
C R Hassey
1B M Hargrove
2B- J Brohamer
SS T Veryzer
3B T Harrah
LO M Dilone
CF R Manning
RF J Orta
LD J Charboneau
S2 J Dybzinski
2R- A Bannister
M D Garcia

DET 1980 AL
SP J Morris
SP M Wilcox
SP D Schatzeder
SP D Petry
RS D Rozema
RP A Lopez
RS P Underwood
C L Parrish
13 R Hebner
2B L Whitaker
SS A Trammell
3B T Brookens
LD S Kemp
MU R Peters
RA A Cowens
DO C Summers
UT J Wockenfuss
1U- T Corcoran
M S Anderson

KC 1980 AL
SP L Gura
SP D Leonard
SP P Splittorff
SP R Gale
SR R Martin
RP D Quisenberry
RP M Pattin
CD D Porter
1B W Aikens
2B F White
SS U Washington
3B G Brett
LM W Wilson
CF A Otis
RF C Hurdle
DH H McRae
1B P LaCock
CO J Wathan
M J Frey

MIL 1980 AL
SP M Haas
SP M Caldwell
SP L Sorensen
SP B Travers
RS R Cleveland
RS B McClure
RP B Castro
RP J Augustine
C C Moore
1B C Cooper
2B P Molitor
SS R Yount
32 J Gantner
LF B Oglivie
CF G Thomas
RF S Lezcano
DR D Davis
3U- D Money
M1 B Rodgers
M2 G Bamberger
M3 B Rodgers

MIN 1980 AL
SP J Koosman
SP G Zahn
SP R Erickson
SP D Jackson
SP P Redfern
RP D Corbett
RP J Verhoeven
C B Wynegar
1B R Jackson
2B R Wilfong
SS R Smalley
3B J Castino
LM R Sofield
ML K Landreaux
RF H Powell
DH J Morales
DH G Adams
13 M Cubbage
2S M Mackanin
ML- D Edwards
M1 G Mauch
M2 J Goryl

NY 1980 AL
SP T John
SP R Guidry
SR T Underwood
SR R May
SP L Tiant
RP R Davis
RP R Gossage
RP D Bird
C R Cerone
1B B Watson
2B W Randolph
SS B Dent
3B- G Nettles
LF L Piniella
MO B Brown
RD R Jackson
D3- E Soderholm
OF B Murcer
1B- J Spencer
CF- R Jones
M D Howser

OAK 1980 AL
SP R Langford
SP M Norris
SP M Keough
SP S McCatty
SP B Kingman
RP B Lacey
C - J Essian
1B D Revering
23 D McKay
SS M Guerrero
3B W Gross
LF R Henderson
CF D Murphy
RF T Armas
DH M Page
IC J Newman
CD- M Heath
S2- R Picciolo
M B Martin

SEA 1980 AL
SP F Bannister
SP G Abbott
SP R Honeycutt
SP J Beattie
SR R Dressler
RP S Rawley
RP B McLaughlin
RP- D Heaverlo
RP D Roberts
C L Cox
1B B Bochte
2B J Cruz
SS M Mendoza
3B- T Cox
LF D Meyer
OI J Simpson
RO L Roberts
DH- W Horton
S3 J Anderson
UI L Milbourne
OI T Paciorek
M1 D Johnson
M2 M Wills

TEX 1980 AL
SP J Matlack
SP D Medich
SP F Jenkins
SP G Perry
RP D Darwin
RP S Lyle
RP J Kern
C J Sundberg
1B P Putnam
2B B Wills
SS P Frias
3B B Bell
LF A Oliver
CF M Rivers
OI J Norris
DR R Zisk
RU J Grubb
IO D Roberts
D1 R Staub
SS- B Harrelson
UO B Sample
M P Corrales

TOR 1980 AL
SP J Clancy
SP D Stieb
SR P Mirabella
SR J Jefferson
RS J McLaughlin
RP J Garvin
RP T Buskey
RP B Moore
C E Whitt
1B J Mayberry
2B D Garcia
SS A Griffin

3B R Howell
UT B Bailor
UO B Bonnell
RF L Moseby
DH O Velez
LF A Woods
C - B Davis
M B Mattick

ATL 1981 NL
SP G Perry
SP T Boggs
SP P Niekro
SR R Mahler
SR J Montefusco
RP R Camp
RP G Garber
RP P Hanna
RP A Hrabosky
C B Benedict
1B C Chambliss
2B G Hubbard
SS R Ramirez
3B B Horner
LF R Linares
CF D Murphy
RF C Washington
IF- J Royster
OF- B Asselstine
IC- B Pocoroba
UT T Wallach
M B Cox

CHI 1981 NL
SP M Krukow
SR R Martz
SP R Reuschel
SR K Kravec
SP D Bird
RP D Tidrow
RS B Caudill
RP L Smith
RS L McGlothen
C - J Davis
1B B Buckner
2U- M Tyson
SS I DeJesus
3B K Reitz
LF S Henderson
MO J Morales
RF L Durham
C - T Blackwell
OI- S Thompson
M J Amalfitano

CIN 1981 NL
SP M Soto
SP T Seaver
SP F Pastore
SP B Berenyi
SP M LaCoss
RP T Hume
RP J Price
RP P Moskau
RP D Bair
C J Nolan
1B D Driessen
2B G Oester
SS D Concepcion
3B R Knight
LF G Foster
CF K Griffey
RF D Collins
RU S Mejias
C - M O'Berry
M J McNamara

HOU 1981 NL
SP J Niekro
SP D Sutton
SP B Knepper
SP N Ryan
SP V Ruhle
RP D Smith
RP J Sambito
RP F LaCorte
C A Ashby
1M C Cedeno
2U- J Pittman
SS C Reynolds
3B A Howe
LF J Cruz
CF- T Scott
RU T Puhl
UT- D Walling
RU- G Woods
M B Virdon

LA 1981 NL
SP F Valenzuela
SP J Reuss
SP B Hooton
SP B Welch
RS D Goltz
RP S Howe
RP B Castillo
RP D Stewart
C M Scioscia

1B S Garvey
2B- D Lopes
SS B Russell
3B R Cey
LF D Baker
CF K Landreaux
RU P Guerrero
UT D Thomas
OI- J Johnstone
RU R Monday
M T Lasorda

MON 1981 NL
SP S Rogers
SP B Gullickson
SP S Sanderson
SP R Burris
RS B Lee
RP S Bahnsen
RP W Fryman
RP J Reardon
C G Carter
1R W Cromartie
2B R Scott
SS C Speier
3B L Parrish
LF T Raines
CF A Dawson
UO- J White
UT T Wallach
M1 D Williams
M2 J Fanning

NY 1981 NL
SP2 P Zachry
SP M Scott
SP E Lynch
SP G Harris
RS P Falcone
RP N Allen
RP D Miller
RP R Searage
C J Stearns
1L D Kingman
2B D Flynn
SS F Taveras
3B H Brooks
LM L Mazzilli
MU M Wilson
UT M Cubbage
UT M Jorgensen
1U R Staub
C - A Trevino
M J Torre

PHI 1981 NL
SP S Carlton
SP D Ruthven
SP L Christenson
SP N Espinosa
RP S Lyle
RP R Reed
RP M Proly
RP T McGraw
C B Boone
1B P Rose
2B M Trillo
SS L Bowa
3B M Schmidt
LF G Matthews
CF G Maddox
RF- B McBride
UO G Gross
C - K Moreland
UO-L Smith
UT- D Unser
M D Green

PIT 1981 NL
SP R Rhoden
SP E Solomon
SP J Bibby
SP P Perez
RS R Scurry
C A Ashby
RP K Tekulve
RP E Romo
RP D Robinson
C T Pena
1B J Thompson
2B- P Garner
SS T Foli
3B B Madlock
LF M Easler
CF O Moreno
RF D Parker
3S D Berra
OI L Lacy
C - S Nicosia
M C Tanner

STL 1981 NL
SP L Sorensen
SP B Forsch
SP J Martin
SP S Martinez
SR B Shirley

RP B Sutter
RP J Kaat
RP M Littell
RP B Sykes
C - D Porter
1B K Hernandez
2B T Herr
SS G Templeton
3B K Oberkfell
LU D Iorg
RM G Hendrick
OF S Lezcano
LR T Landrum
CU- G Tenace
M W Herzog

SD 1981 NL
SP J Eichelberger
SP J Mura
SP C Welsh
SP R Wise
SR T Lollar
RP G Lucas
RS- J Curtis
RP J Littlefield
RP D Boone
C T Kennedy
1B B Perkins
2B J Bonilla
SS O Smith
3B L Salazar
LF G Richards
CF R Jones
RF J Lefebvre
1U R Bass
RU- D Edwards
UI- B Evans
M F Howard

SF 1981 NL
SP D Alexander
SP T Griffin
SP V Blue
SP E Whitson
SP A Ripley
RP A Holland
RP G Minton
RP F Breining
RP G Lavelle
C M May
1U E Cabell
2B J Morgan
SS J LeMaster
3B D Evans
C - R Hassey
LF L Herndon
CF J Martin
RF J Clark
1U- D Bergman
M F Robinson

BAL 1981 AL
SP D Martinez
SP S McGregor
SP J Palmer
SP M Flanagan
RP S Stewart
RP T Martinez
RP T Stoddard
RP D Ford
C R Dempsey
1B E Murray
2B R Dauer
SS M Belanger
3B M DeCinces
LF J Lowenstein
CF A Bumbry
RL R Roenicke
DU T Crowley
LR J Dwyer
RD K Singleton
CU- D Graham
S2- L Sakata
M E Weaver

BOS 1981 AL
SP D Eckersley
SP F Tanana
SP M Torrez
SP J Tudor
RP B Ojeda
RP B Stanley
RP M Clear
RP T Burgmeier
RP B Campbell
C - R Gedman
1D T Perez
2B J Remy
SS G Hoffman
3B C Lansford
LF J Rice
CF R Miller
RF D Evans
D1 C Yastrzemski
UI D Stapleton
M R Houk

CAL 1981 AL
SP G Zahn
SP K Forsch
SP M Witt
SP S Renko
RP A Hassler
RS J Jefferson
RP D Aase
RP L Sanchez
C E Ott
1B R Carew
2B B Grich
SS R Burleson
3B D Hobson
LC B Downing
CF F Lynn
RF D Ford
DH D Baylor
ML- J Beniquez
3B- B Campaneris
M1 J Fregosi
M2 G Mauch

CHI 1981 AL
SP B Burns
SP R Dotson
SR D Lamp
SP S Trout
SP R Baumgarten
RP L Hoyt
RP E Farmer
RP K Hickey
C C Fisk
1B W Squires
2B T Bernazard
SS B Almon
3B J Morrison
LF R LeFlore
CF C Lemon
RF H Baines
DH G Luzinski
UO R Kuntz
RL W Nordhagen
M T LaRussa

CLE 1981 AL
SP B Blyleven
SP L Barker
SP J Denny
SP R Waits
RS D Spillner
RP S Monge
RP M Stanton
C - R Hassey
1B M Hargrove
2B D Kuiper
SS T Veryzer
3B T Harrah
LF M Dilone
CF R Manning
RF J Orta
DH A Thornton
UT A Bannister
C B Diaz
M D Garcia

DET 1981 AL
SP J Morris
SP M Wilcox
SP D Petry
SP D Schatzeder
RS D Rozema
RP A Lopez
RP J Saucier
RP D Tobik
C L Parrish
1B R Hebner
2B L Whitaker
SS A Trammell
3B T Brookens
LF S Kemp
CF A Cowens
UO K Gibson
D1 J Wockenfuss
RU L Jones
3I- M Kelleher
1R- R Leach
MD-R Peters
DR- C Summers
M S Anderson

KC 1981 AL
SP D Leonard
SP L Gura
SP R Gale
SP P Splittorff
SP M Jones
RP D Quisenberry
RP R Martin
RP K Brett
C J Wathan
CF W Aikens
2B F White
SS U Washington
3B G Brett
LF W Wilson

CF A Otis
RF- G Geronimo
DH H McRae
M1 J Frey
M2 D Howser

MIL 1981 AL
SP P Vuckovich
SP M Caldwell
SP M Haas
SP J Slaton
SP R Lerch
RP R Fingers
RP R Cleveland
RP J Easterly
RP C Simmons
1B C Cooper
2B J Gantner
SS R Yount
3B- D Money
LF B Oglivie
OF G Thomas
RF- M Brouhard
DH- L Hisle
3U R Howell
MD-P Molitor
M B Rodgers

MIN 1981 AL
SP A Williams
SP P Redfern
SP R Arroyo
SP J Koosman
SP R Erickson
RP D Corbett
RP B Havens
RP D Cooper
RP J Verhoeven
C - S Butera
1U- D Goodwin
2B R Wilfong
SD- R Smalley
3B J Castino
LU G Ward
CF M Hatcher
RF D Engle
DH G Adams
UI P Mackanin
RU H Powell
1U- R Jackson
M1 J Goryl
M2 B Gardner

NY 1981 AL
SP R May
SP T John
SP R Guidry
SP R Righetti
SP R Reuschel
RP R Davis
CL R Gossage
RP D LaRoche
C R Cerone
1B- B Watson
2B W Randolph
SS B Dent
3B G Nettles
LF D Winfield
CF J Mumphrey
RD R Jackson
DU- B Murcer
OF O Gamble
SI- L Milbourne
OF- L Piniella
M1 G Michael
M2 B Lemon

OAK 1981 AL
SP R Langford
SP S McCatty
SP M Norris
SP M Keough
SP B Kingman
RP J Jones
RP B Owchinko
C M Heath
1B- J Spencer
2B- S Babitt
SS R Picciolo
3B W Gross
LF R Henderson
CF D Murphy
RF T Armas
DH C Johnson
32 D McKay
C1 J Newman
SS F Stanley
M B Martin

SEA 1981 AL
SP G Abbott
SP F Bannister
SP K Clay
SR M Parrott
SP J Gleaton
RS B Clark

RP S Rawley
RP L Andersen
RP J Beattie
C J Narron
1B B Bochte
2B J Cruz
SS J Anderson
32 J Randle
LF T Paciorek
CF J Simpson
RF J Burroughs
DH R Zisk
UT G Gray
3U D Meyer
C - B Bulling
MR-D Henderson
M1 M Wills
M2 R Lachemann

TEX 1981 AL
SP D Darwin
SP D Medich
SP R Honeycutt
SP F Jenkins
SP J Matlack
RP S Comer
RS C Hough
RP D Schmidt
C J Sundberg
1B P Putnam
2B B Wills
SS M Mendoza
3B B Bell
LF B Sample
CF M Rivers
RL L Roberts
DH A Oliver
RF J Grubb
M D Zimmer

TOR 1981 AL
SP D Stieb
SR L Leal
SR J Clancy
SP J Todd
SP M Bomback
RP B Berenguer
RP J McLaughlin
RP R Jackson
RP J Garvin
C E Whitt
1B J Mayberry
2B D Garcia
SS A Griffin
3B D Ainge
LF A Woods
CF L Moseby
RM B Bonnell
DH O Velez
2I G Iorg
OF- G Bell
UT- W Upshaw
M B Mattick

ATL 1982 NL
SP P Niekro
SP R Mahler
SR R Camp
SP B Walk
RP S Bedrosian
RP G Garber
C B Benedict
1B C Chambliss
2B G Hubbard
SS R Ramirez
3B B Horner
LU- R Linares
ML D Murphy
RF C Washington
3U J Royster
CF- B Butler
OF- L Whisenton
M J Torre

CHI 1982 NL
SP F Jenkins
SP D Bird
SP D Noles
SP R Martz
SP A Ripley
RS L Smith
RP D Tidrow
RP B Campbell
RP W Hernandez
C J Davis
1B B Buckner
2B B Wills
SS L Bowa
3B R Sandberg
OC K Moreland
ML G Woods
RM L Durham
RL J Johnstone
2S J Kennedy
LF- S Henderson
M L Elia

CIN 1982 NL
SP M Soto
SP B Berenyi
SP F Pastore
SR B Shirley
SP T Seaver
RS C Leibrandt
RS G Harris
CL T Hume
RP J Kern
C A Trevino
1B D Driessen
2B R Oester
SS D Concepcion
3B J Bench
LR E Milner
CF C Cedeno
RF P Householder
OI- L Biittner
3U- W Krenchicki
UO-D Walker
M1 J McNamara
M2 R Nixon

HOU 1982 NL
SP J Niekro
SP N Ryan
SP D Sutton
SP B Knepper
SR V Ruhle
RS M LaCoss
RP F LaCorte
RP D Smith
C A Ashby
13 R Knight
2B P Garner
SS D Thon
31 A Howe
LF J Cruz
CF T Scott
RF T Puhl
OI- D Heep
OI- D Walling
M1 B Virdon
M2 B Lillis

LA 1982 NL
SP F Valenzuela
SP J Reuss
SP B Welch
SP B Hooton
RS D Stewart
RP S Howe
RP T Forster
RP T Niedenfuer
C M Scioscia
1B S Garvey
2B S Sax
SS B Russell
3B R Cey
LF D Baker
CF K Landreaux
RM P Guerrero
OI R Monday
UO R Roenicke
OF- J Orta
C - S Yeager
M T Lasorda

MON 1982 NL
SP S Rogers
SP B Gullickson
SP S Sanderson
SP C Lea
SR B Burris
RP J Reardon
RP W Fryman
RP B Smith
C G Carter
1B A Oliver
2B- D Flynn
SS C Speier
3B T Wallach
LF T Raines
CF A Dawson
RF W Cromartie
M J Fanning

NY 1982 NL
SR P Falcone
SR C Puleo
SR C Swan
SR M Scott
SR P Zachry
RS E Lynch
RP J Orosco
RP R Jones
CL N Allen
C J Stearns
1B D Kingman
2B- W Backman
SS R Gardenhire
3B H Brooks
LF G Foster
CF M Wilson
RU E Valentine

S2 B Bailor
UT M Jorgensen
OI R Staub
M G Bamberger

PHI 1982 NL
SP S Carlton
SP L Christenson
SP M Krukow
SP D Ruthven
RP R Reed
RP E Farmer
RP R Monge
C B Diaz
1B P Rose
2B M Trillo
SS I DeJesus
3B M Schmidt
LF G Matthews
CF G Maddox
RF G Vukovich
UO G Gross
MR B Dernier
M P Corrales

PIT 1982 NL
SP R Rhoden
SP D Robinson
SP J Candelaria
SR M Sarmiento
SP L McWilliams
RP K Tekulve
RP R Scurry
RP E Romo
C T Pena
1B J Thompson
2B J Ray
SS D Berra
3B B Madlock
LF M Easler
CF O Moreno
RL L Lacy
M C Tanner

STL 1982 NL
SP J Andujar
SP B Forsch
SP S Mura
SR D LaPoint
SP J Stuper
RP B Sutter
RP D Bair
RP J Kaat
RS J Martin
C D Porter
1B K Hernandez
2B T Herr
SS O Smith
3B K Oberkfell
LF L Smith
CF W McGee
RF G Hendrick
UT D Iorg
IO M Ramsey
M W Herzog

SD 1982 NL
SP T Lollar
SP J Montefusco
SP J Eichelberger
SP C Welsh
SP J Curtis
RS E Show
RP L DeLeon
RP G Lucas
RS D Dravecky
C T Kennedy
1B B Perkins
2B T Flannery
SS G Templeton
3B L Salazar
LF G Richards
CF R Jones
RF S Lezcano
UT J Lefebvre
M D Williams

SF 1982 NL
SP B Laskey
SP A Hammaker
SP R Gale
SP R Martin
RP G Minton
RS F Breining
RS A Holland
RS J Barr
C M May
1B R Smith
2B J Morgan
SS J LeMaster
31 D Evans
LU- J Leonard
CF C Davis
RF J Clark
1U D Bergman
U3 D Kuiper
LU- J Wohlford

3B- T O'Malley
M F Robinson

BAL 1982 AL
SP D Martinez
SP M Flanagan
SP J Palmer
SP S McGregor
RS S Stewart
RP T Martinez
RS S Davis
RP T Stoddard
C R Dempsey
1B E Murray
2B R Dauer
2S L Sakata
S3 C Ripken
LR G Roenicke
CF A Bumbry
RF D Ford
DH K Singleton
LF J Lowenstein
M E Weaver

BOS 1982 AL
SP D Eckersley
SP J Tudor
SP M Torrez
SP C Rainey
SP B Hurst
RP B Stanley
RP M Clear
RP T Burgmeier
RP L Aponte
C G Allenson
1I D Stapleton
2B J Remy
SS G Hoffman
3B C Lansford
LF J Rice
CF R Miller
RF D Evans
DH C Yastrzemski
IO W Boggs
C R Gedman
ML- R Nichols
M R Houk

CAL 1982 AL
SP G Zahn
SP K Forsch
SP M Witt
SP S Renko
SR B Kison
RP L Sanchez
RP A Hassler
RP D Corbett
RP D Aase
C B Boone
1B R Carew
2B B Grich
SS T Foli
3B D DeCinces
LF B Downing
CF F Lynn
RF R Jackson
DH D Baylor
UO J Beniquez
RO B Clark
M G Mauch

CHI 1982 AL
SP L Hoyt
SP R Dotson
SR D Lamp
SR J Koosman
SP B Burns
RP S Barojas
RP S Trout
RP K Hickey
RPC C Escarrega
C C Fisk
1B M Squires
2B T Bernazard
SS B Almon
3B A Rodriguez
LF S Kemp
MU R Law
RF H Baines
DH G Luzinski
S3 V Law
1B T Paciorek
UO- J Hairston
CF- R LeFlore
M T LaRussa

CLE 1982 AL
SP L Barker
SP R Sutcliffe
SP L Sorensen
SP J Denny
SP R Waits
RP D Spillner
RS E Whitson
RP E Glynn
C R Hassey
1B M Hargrove

2B- J Perconte
SS M Fischlin
3B T Harrah
LF M Dilone
CF R Manning
RF V Hayes
DH A Thornton
UT A Bannister
2B- L Milbourne
M D Garcia

DET 1982 AL
SP J Morris
SP D Petry
SP M Wilcox
SP J Ujdur
SR P Underwood
RP D Tobik
RP E Sosa
RP D Rucker
C L Parrish
13 E Cabell
2B L Whitaker
SS A Trammell
3B T Brookens
LF L Herndon
CF- G Wilson
RU C Lemon
DH- M Ivie
1U- R Leach
DU- J Turner
M S Anderson

KC 1982 AL
SP L Gura
SP V Blue
SP P Splittorff
SP D Leonard
RP D Quisenberry
RP M Armstrong
RP D Hood
C J Wathan
1B W Aikens
2B F White
SS U Washington
3B G Brett
LF W Wilson
CF A Otis
RF J Martin
DH H McRae
M D Howser

MIL 1982 AL
SP M Caldwell
SP P Vuckovich
SP M Haas
SP B McClure
SP R Lerch
RS J Slaton
CL R Fingers
RP D Bernard
C T Simmons
1B C Cooper
2B J Gantner
SS R Yount
3B P Molitor
LF B Oglivie
CF G Thomas
RF C Moore
DH R Howell
DI- D Money
M1 B Rodgers
M2 H Kuenn

MIN 1982 AL
SR B Castillo
SP B Havens
SP A Williams
SP J O'Connor
SP F Viola
RP R Davis
RS T Felton
RP J Pacella
RP P Boris
C T Laudner
1B K Hrbek
2B J Castino
SS R Washington
3B G Gaetti
LF G Ward
CF B Mitchell
RF T Brunansky
DH- R Johnson
SS- L Faedo
OI- M Hatcher
M B Gardner

NY 1982 AL
SP R Guidry
SP J John
SP D Righetti
SR S Rawley
SP M Morgan
CL R Gossage
RP G Frazier
C R Hassey
RS R May
RP D LaRoche

C - R Cerone
1B- J Mayberry
2B W Randolph
S3 R Smalley
3B G Nettles
LF D Winfield
CF J Mumphrey
RF K Griffey
DH O Gamble
DR O Collins
OI D Collins
DR L Piniella
M1 B Lemon
M2 G Michael
M3 C King

OAK 1982 AL
SP M Langford
SP M Keough
SP M Norris
SP S McCatty
SP B Kingman
RS T Underwood
RP B Owchinko
RP D Beard
C M Heath
UT D Meyer
2B D Lopes
SS F Stanley
3B W Gross
LF R Henderson
CF D Murphy
RF T Armas
DU- C Johnson
OF J Burroughs
M B Martin

SEA 1982 AL
SP F Bannister
SP G Perry
SP J Beattie
SP M Moore
SP G Nelson
CL B Caudill
RS B Clark
RP L Andersen
RP E Vande Berg
C - R Sweet
1B- G Gray
2B J Cruz
SS T Cruz
3B M Castillo
LU B Bochte
CF D Henderson
RF A Cowens
DH R Zisk
ML J Simpson
M R Lachemann

TEX 1982 AL
SP C Hough
SP F Tanana
SP R Honeycutt
SR J Matlack
SP D Medich
RS D Schmidt
RP S Comer
RP D Darwin
RP P Mirabella
C J Sundberg
1B J Hostetler
2B M Richardt
SS- M Wagner
3B B Bell
LF- B Sample
CF G Wright
RF L Parrish
DU L Johnson
OF J Grubb
2S- D Flynn
IO- B Stein
M1 D Zimmer
M2 D Johnson

TOR 1982 AL
SP D Stieb
SP J Clancy
SP L Leal
SP J Gott
RP J Murray
RP R Jackson
RP J McLaughlin
RP J Garvin
C E Whitt
1B W Upshaw
2B D Garcia
SS A Griffin
3B R Mulliniks
LB B Bonnell
CF L Moseby
RF J Barfield
DH- D Revering
3B G Iorg
RU H Powell
C - B Martinez
LF- A Woods
M B Cox

ATL 1983 NL
SP C McMurtry
SP P Perez
SP P Niekro
SP R Camp
SR P Falcone
RP S Bedrosian
RP K Dayley
RP T Forster
RP D Moore
C B Benedict
1B C Chambliss
2B G Hubbard
SS R Ramirez
3B B Horner
LM B Oberkfell
CF D Murphy
RF C Washington
3U- R Johnson
32- J Royster
M J Torre

CHI 1983 NL
SP C Rainey
SP S Trout
SP F Jenkins
SP D Ruthven
SP D Noles
RP L Smith
RP B Campbell
RS C Lefferts
RP M Proly
C J Davis
1B B Buckner
2B R Sandberg
SS L Bowa
3B R Cey
LM L Durham
CF M Hall
RF K Moreland
OF- J Johnstone
OI- G Woods
M1 L Elia
M2 C Fox

CIN 1983 NL
SP M Soto
SP B Berenyi
SP F Pastore
SP J Price
SP C Puleo
RS T Power
RP B Scherrer
RS R Gale
RP B Hayes
C D Bilardello
1B D Driessen
2B R Oester
SS D Concepcion
3B- N Esasky
LF G Redus
CF E Milner
RM P Householder
IO J Bench
RU C Cedeno
OF D Walker
M R Nixon

HOU 1983 NL
SP J Niekro
SP B Knepper
SP N Ryan
SP M Scott
SR M LaCoss
RS V Ruhle
RP B Dawley
CL F DiPino
RP D Smith
C - A Ashby
1B R Knight
2B B Doran
SS D Thon
3B P Garner
LF J Cruz
CF- O Moreno
RF T Puhl
UT D Walling
RU- K Bass
M B Lillis

LA 1983 NL
SP F Valenzuela
SP J Reuss
SP B Welch
SP A Pena
SP B Hooton
RP T Niedenfuer
CL S Howe
RP S Stewart
RP J Beckwith
C S Yeager
1B G Brock
2B S Sax
SS B Russell
3B P Guerrero
LF D Baker

CF K Landreaux
RF M Marshall
UT D Thomas
OI R Monday
RO- R Roenicke
M T Lasorda

MON 1983 NL
SP S Rogers
SP B Gullickson
SP C Lea
SR R Burris
RS B Smith
RP J Reardon
RP D Schatzeder
RP B James
C G Carter
1B A Oliver
2S D Flynn
SS- C Speier
3B T Wallach
LF T Raines
CF A Dawson
RF W Cromartie
OI T Francona
S2 B Little
RU- J Wohlford
M B Virdon

NY 1983 NL
SP T Seaver
SP M Torrez
SP W Terrell
RP J Orosco
RP D Sisk
RS S Holman
RPC C Diaz
C R Hodges
1B- K Hernandez
2B B Giles
SS J Oquendo
3B H Brooks
LF G Foster
CF M Wilson
RF D Strawberry
S2 B Bailor
OI D Heep
1U D Kingman
UT R Staub
M1 G Bamberger
M2 F Howard

PHI 1983 NL
SP S Carlton
SP J Denny
SP C Hudson
SP M Bystrom
CL A Holland
RP R Reed
RP W Hernandez
RP T McGraw
C B Diaz
1U P Rose
2B J Morgan
SS I DeJesus
3B M Schmidt
LF G Matthews
CF- G Maddox
RM V Hayes
LO G Gross
RU J Lefebvre
MR B Dernier
2S- K Garcia
1B- T Perez
M1 P Corrales
M2 P Owens

PIT 1983 NL
SP R Rhoden
SP L McWilliams
SP J Candelaria
SR L Tunnell
SP J DeLeon
RP K Tekulve
RP C Guante
RP M Sarmiento
RP R Scurry
C T Pena
1B J Thompson
2B J Ray
SS D Berra
3B B Madlock
LF M Easler
CF W Wynne
RF D Parker
LR L Lacy
OI L Mazzilli
M C Tanner

STL 1983 NL
SP J Andujar
SR J Stuper
SP D LaPoint
SP B Forsch
SP N Allen
CL B Sutter

RP J Lahti
RP D Von Ohlen
SS J Martin
C D Porter
1R G Hendrick
2B- T Herr
SS O Smith
3B K Oberkfell
LF L Smith
CF W McGee
RO D Green
2I- M Ramsey
UT A Van Slyke
M W Herzog

SD 1983 NL
SP E Show
SP D Dravecky
SP T Lollar
SR E Whitson
SP A Hawkins
RP L DeLeon
RP M Thurmond
RP S Monge
C T Kennedy
1B S Garvey
2B J Bonilla
SS G Templeton
3B L Salazar
OI A Wiggins
CF R Jones
RF- S Lezcano
3I- T Flannery
RL- T Gwynn
LU- G Richards
M D Williams

SF 1983 NL
SP F Breining
SP M Krukow
SP A Hammaker
SP B Laskey
SR A McGaffigan
RP G Minton
RP M Davis
CL G Lavelle
RP J Barr
C B Brenly
1B D Evans
2B- B Wellman
SS J LeMaster
3B T O'Malley
LF J Leonard
CF C Davis
RF J Clark
2U J Youngblood
1U- D Bergman
UO- M Venable
M F Robinson

BAL 1983 AL
SP S McGregor
SP S Davis
SP M Boddicker
SP D Martinez
SP M Flanagan
RS S Stewart
RP T Martinez
RP T Stoddard
C R Dempsey
1B E Murray
2B R Dauer
SS C Ripken
3B- T Cruz
LF J Lowenstein
CF J Shelby
RF D Ford
OI J Dwyer
CF A Bumbry
LO G Roenicke
DH K Singleton
M J Altobelli

BOS 1983 AL
SP J Tudor
SP B Hurst
SP D Eckersley
SP B Ojeda
SP M Brown
RP B Stanley
RP M Clear
RP O Boyd
RP L Aponte
C - G Allenson
1B D Stapleton
2B J Remy
SS G Hoffman
3B W Boggs
LF J Rice
CF T Armas
RF D Evans
DH C Yastrzemski
OI R Miller
OI R Nichols

C - R Gedman
M R Houk

CAL 1983 AL
SP T John
SP K Forsch
SP G Zahn
SR M Witt
SP B Kison
RP J Sanchez
RP J Curtis
C B Boone
1U R Carew
2B B Grich
SS- T Foli
3B- D DeCinces
LU B Downing
CF F Lynn
RF- E Valentine
DR Re Jackson
UT Ro Jackson
1D D Sconiers
UO- J Beniquez
M J McNamara

CHI 1983 AL
SP L Hoyt
SP R Dotson
SP F Bannister
SP B Burns
SR J Koosman
RS D Lamp
RP S Barojas
RP D Tidrow
C C Fisk
1B M Squires
2B J Cruz
SS J Dybzinski
3B V Law
LF R Kittle
CF R Law
RF H Baines
DH G Luzinski
SS S Fletcher
UO J Hairston
1L T Paciorek
1U G Walker
M T LaRussa

CLE 1983 AL
SP R Sutcliffe
SP L Sorensen
SP B Blyleven
SR N Heaton
SP L Barker
RS J Eichelberger
RP D Spillner
RP B Anderson
RP J Easterly
C R Hassey
1B M Hargrove
2B- M Trillo
SS J Franco
3B T Harrah
UT A Bannister
CF G Thomas
RF G Vukovich
DH A Thornton
LU P Tabler
2U- M Fischlin
M1 M Ferraro
M2 P Corrales

DET 1983 AL
SP J Morris
SP D Petry
SP M Wilcox
SR J Berenguer
SR D Rozema
RP A Lopez
RP H Bailey
RP D Bair
C L Parrish
1B E Cabell
2B L Whitaker
SS A Trammell
3I T Brookens
LF L Herndon
CF C Lemon
RF G Wilson
DO K Gibson
1U R Leach
UC- J Wockenfuss
M S Anderson

KC 1983 AL
SP L Gura
SP B Black
SP P Splittorff
SP S Renko
RP D Quisenberry
RP M Armstrong
C1 J Wathan
1B W Aikens
2B F White
SS U Washington
3B G Brett

ML W Wilson
MR A Otis
UO P Sheridan
DH H McRae
UO-L Roberts
1O- J Simpson
C - D Slaught
M D Howser

MIL 1983 AL
SP M Caldwell
SP D Sutton
SP M Haas
SP B McClure
SP C Porter
RP J Slaton
RP T Tellmann
RS B Gibson
CL P Ladd
C - N Yost
1B C Cooper
2B J Gantner
SS R Yount
3B P Molitor
LF B Oglivie
CF R Manning
RF C Moore
CD T Simmons
M H Kuenn

MIN 1983 AL
SP F Viola
SP K Schrom
SP A Williams
SP B Castillo
RP R Lysander
CL R Davis
RP L Whitehouse
RP M Walters
CU D Engle
1B K Hrbek
2B J Castino
SS R Washington
3B G Gaetti
LF G Ward
CF- D Brown
RF T Brunansky
DH R Bush
UT M Hatcher
M B Gardner

NY 1983 AL
SP R Guidry
SP S Rawley
SP D Righetti
SP B Shirley
RP G Frazier
CL R Gossage
RP D Murray
C - B Wynegar
1B K Griffey
2B W Randolph
SI R Smalley
3B G Nettles
LF D Winfield
CF- J Mumphrey
RF S Kemp
DH D Baylor
SS A Robertson
UT- D Mattingly
M B Martin

OAK 1983 AL
SP C Codiroli
SR S McCatty
SR T Conroy
SP B Krueger
RS T Underwood
RP T Burgmeier
RP K Atherton
RP D Beard
C B Kearney
13 W Gross
2B D Lopes
S2 T Phillips
3B- C Lansford
LF R Henderson
CF D Murphy
RF M Davis
DH J Burroughs
UT B Almon
OI G Hancock
C - M Heath
M S Boros

SEA 1983 AL
SP M Young
SP J Beattie
SR B Stoddard
SR B Clark
SP M Moore
RP G Perry
CL B Caudill
RP R Thomas
RP M Stanton
C - R Sweet
1B P Putnam

2B- T Bernazard
SS- S Owen
3B- J Allen
LF S Henderson
MR D Henderson
RD A Cowens
DH-R Zisk
3U- M Castillo
UO-J Moses
RL R Nelson
M1 R Lachemann
M2 D Crandall

TEX 1983 AL
SP C Hough
SP M Smithson
SP D Darwin
SP R Honeycutt
SP F Tanana
RS J Butcher
RP O Jones
C J Sundberg
1B P O'Brien
2B W Tolleson
SS B Dent
3B B Bell
LF B Sample
CF G Wright
RF L Parrish
DH- D Hostetler
DU- M Rivers
M D Rader

TOR 1983 AL
SP D Stieb
SP J Clancy
SP L Leal
SP J Gott
SP D Alexander
RS J Acker
RP R Jackson
RP J McLaughlin
RP R Moffitt
C E Whitt
1B W Upshaw
2B D Garcia
SS A Griffin
3B R Mulliniks
LR B Bonnell
CF L Moseby
RF J Barfield
DH C Johnson
LF D Collins
32 G Iorg
DU J Orta
C - B Martinez
M B Cox

ATL 1984 NL
SP R Mahler
SP P Perez
SP C McMurtry
SR R Camp
SP L Barker
RS P Falcone
RP G Garber
RP S Bedrosian
RP J Dedmon
C - B Benedict
1B C Chambliss
2B G Hubbard
SS R Ramirez
3B- R Johnson
RL- B Komminsk
CF D Murphy
RF C Washington
1L G Perry
LU- A Hall
IO- J Royster
M J Torre

CHI 1984 NL
SP S Trout
SP D Eckersley
SP R Sutcliffe
SP S Sanderson
SP D Ruthven
RP L Smith
RP T Stoddard
RS R Bordi
RP W Brusstar
C J Davis
1B L Durham
2B R Sandberg
SS L Bowa
3B R Cey
LF G Matthews
CF B Dernier
RI K Moreland
UO H Cotto
OI- G Woods
M J Frey

CIN 1984 NL
SP M Soto
SP J Russell
SP J Price

SP J Tibbs
RP T Power
RS T Hume
RP B Owchinko
RP J Franco
C B Gulden
1B- D Driessen
2B R Oester
S3 D Concepcion
3U N Esasky
LF G Redus
CF E Milner
RF D Parker
OI C Cedeno
SS T Foley
3U- W Krenchicki
LO- D Walker
M1 V Rapp
M2 P Rose

HOU 1984 NL
SP J Niekro
SP B Knepper
SP N Ryan
SP M Scott
SR M LaCoss
RP B Dawley
RS V Ruhle
RP F DiPino
RP D Smith
C M Bailey
1B E Cabell
2B B Doran
SS C Reynolds
32 P Garner
LF J Cruz
CF J Mumphrey
RF T Puhl
OF K Bass
31- R Knight
3U- D Walling
M B Lillis

LA 1984 NL
SP F Valenzuela
SP A Pena
SR O Hershiser
SP R Honeycutt
SP B Welch
RS B Hooton
RS J Reuss
RP P Zachry
RP K Howell
C M Scioscia
1B- G Brock
2B S Sax
SS D Anderson
3B- G Rivera
LF M Marshall
CF K Landreaux
RM C Maldonado
3R P Guerrero
SU- B Russell
1O- T Whitfield
M T Lasorda

MON 1984 NL
SP B Gullickson
SP C Lea
SP B Smith
SP S Rogers
SR D Schatzeder
CL J Reardon
RP B James
RP D Palmer
RP G Lucas
C G Carter
1B- T Francona
2S D Flynn
SS- A Salazar
3B T Wallach
OI- J Wohlford
CF T Raines
RF A Dawson
SL D Thomas
U1- M Dilone
2B- B Little
UT- P Rose
M1 B Virdon
M2 J Fanning

NY 1984 NL
SP D Gooden
SP W Terrell
SP R Darling
SP B Berenyi
RS E Lynch
CL J Orosco
RP D Sisk
RP B Gaff
C M Fitzgerald
1B K Hernandez
2B W Backman
SS- J Oquendo
3B H Brooks

LF G Foster
CF M Wilson
RF D Strawberry
OI D Heep
M D Johnson

PHI 1984 NL
SP S Carlton
SP J Koosman
SP C Hudson
SP J Denny
SP S Rawley
RS K Gross
RP A Holland
RP L Andersen
RP B Campbell
C O Virgil
1B L Matuszek
2B J Samuel
SS J DeJesus
3B M Schmidt
LU G Wilson
CF V Hayes
RF S Lezcano
1U T Corcoran
OI G Gross
IC- J Wockenfuss
M P Owens

PIT 1984 NL
SP R Rhoden
SP L McWilliams
SP J Tudor
SP J DeLeon
RP J Candelaria
RP D Robinson
RP K Tekulve
RS L Tunnell
C T Pena
1B J Thompson
2B J Ray
SS D Berra
3B B Madlock
RL L Lacy
CF M Wynne
RF D Frobel
LU L Mazzilli
32 J Morrison
M C Tanner

STL 1984 NL
SP J Andujar
SP J LaPoint
SP D Cox
SR R Horton
SP K Kepshire
RP B Sutter
RP N Allen
RP J Lahti
RP D Rucker
C D Porter
1B G Green
2B T Herr
SS O Smith
3B- T Pendleton
LF L Smith
CF W McGee
RF G Hendrick
LO T Landrum
UT A Van Slyke
OI- S Braun
31- A Howe
M W Herzog

SD 1984 NL
SP E Show
SP T Lollar
SP E Whitson
SP M Thurmond
SR A Hawkins
RS D Dravecky
RP R Gossage
RP C Lefferts
RP G Booker
C T Kennedy
1B S Garvey
2B A Wiggins
SS G Templeton
3B G Nettles
LF C Martinez
CF K McReynolds
RF T Gwynn
UO-B Brown
UI- T Flannery
3O- L Salazar
M D Williams

SF 1984 NL
SP B Laskey
SP M Krukow
SR M Davis
SP J Robinson
RP G Minton
RP G Lavelle
RP F Williams
RP R Lerch
3B H Brenly

1U S Thompson
2B M Trillo
SS J LeMaster
3B J Youngblood
LF J Leonard
CF- D Gladden
UO C Davis
OF D Baker
IF- D Kuiper
1B- A Oliver
UO- G Richards
2S- B Wellman
M1 F Robinson
M2 D Ozark

BAL 1984 AL
SP M Boddicker
SP M Flanagan
SP S Davis
SP S McGregor
SR D Martinez
RP T Martinez
RP S Stewart
RP T Underwood
RS B Swaggerty
C R Dempsey
1B E Murray
2B B Dauer
SS C Ripken
3B W Gross
LR G Roenicke
CF J Shelby
RL M Young
DH K Singleton
MU A Bumbry
LU J Lowenstein
3B- T Cruz
C - F Rayford
2B- L Sakata
M J Altobelli

BOS 1984 AL
SP B Hurst
SP B Ojeda
SP O Boyd
SP A Nipper
SP R Clemens
RP B Stanley
RP M Clear
RP J Johnson
RP S Crawford
C R Gedman
1B B Buckner
2B M Barrett
SS J Gutierrez
3B W Boggs
LF J Rice
CF T Armas
RF D Evans
DH M Easler
OI- R Miller
M R Houk

CAL 1984 AL
SP M Witt
SP R Romanick
SP G Zahn
SP T John
SP J Slaton
RP L Sanchez
RP D Corbett
RP S Kaufman
C B Boone
1B- R Carew
2B R Wilfong
SS D Schofield
3B D DeCinces
LF B Downing
CF G Pettis
RF F Lynn
DH R Jackson
LR J Beniquez
2B B Grich
SS- R Picciolo
M J McNamara

CHI 1984 AL
SP R Dotson
SP T Seaver
SP L Hoyt
SP F Bannister
SR B Burns
RP R Reed
RP J Agosto
C C Fisk
1U G Walker
2B J Cruz
SS S Fletcher
3B V Law
LF R Kittle
CF R Law
RF H Baines
DH G Luzinski
UO J Hairston
1O T Paciorek
1U M Squires

SS- J Dybzinski
M T LaRussa

CLE 1984 AL
SP B Blyleven
SP N Heaton
SP S Comer
SR S Farr
RP E Camacho
RP T Waddell
RP M Jeffcoat
RP J Easterly
C - J Willard
1B M Hargrove
2B T Bernazard
SS J Franco
3B B Jacoby
LF- M Hall
CF B Butler
RF G Vukovich
DH A Thornton
IO P Tabler
RF- C Castillo
2I- M Fischlin
M P Corrales

DET 1984 AL
SP J Morris
SP D Petry
SP M Wilcox
SP J Berenguer
SR D Rozema
RP W Hernandez
RP A Lopez
RP D Bair
C L Parrish
1B D Bergman
2B L Whitaker
SS A Trammell
3B H Johnson
LF L Herndon
CF C Lemon
RF K Gibson
IF D Evans
3I T Brookens
1U B Garbey
OF- J Grubb
UO-R Kuntz
M S Anderson

KC 1984 AL
SP B Black
SP M Gubicza
SP L Gura
SR B Saberhagen
SP C Leibrandt
RP D Quisenberry
RP J Beckwith
RP M Huismann
C D Slaught
1B S Balboni
2B F White
SS- O Concepcion
3B G Pryor
LR D Motley
CF W Wilson
RM P Sheridan
DH H McRae
3B G Brett
DU J Orta
C1- J Wathan
M D Howser

MIL 1984 AL
SP D Sutton
SP M Haas
SP J Cocanower
SR B McClure
SP M Caldwell
RP P Ladd
RP R Waits
RP R Tellmann
C - J Sundberg
1B C Cooper
2B J Gantner
SS R Yount
3S E Romero
LF B Oglivie
CF R Manning
RO D James
D1 T Simmons
M R Lachemann

MIN 1984 AL
SP F Viola
SP M Smithson
SP J Butcher
SP K Schrom
SR B Hodge
RS P Filson
CL R Davis
RP R Lysander
C D Engle
1B K Hrbek
2B T Teufel
SS H Jimenez
3B G Gaetti

LU M Hatcher
CF K Puckett
RF T Brunansky
DH R Bush
OF- D Brown
C - T Laudner
SS- R Washington
M B Gardner

NY 1984 AL
SP P Niekro
SP R Guidry
SR F Fontenot
SP D Rasmussen
CL D Righetti
RS B Shirley
RP J Howell
RS J Rijo
C B Wynegar
1B D Mattingly
2B W Randolph
SS B Meacham
3B- T Harrah
OI K Griffey
CF O Moreno
RF D Winfield
DH D Baylor
LF- S Kemp
M Y Berra

OAK 1984 AL
SR R Burris
SR L Sorensen
SP S McCatty
SP B Krueger
SP C Young
CL B Caudill
RP K Atherton
C M Heath
1B B Bochte
2B J Morgan
S2 T Phillips
3B C Lansford
LF R Henderson
CF D Murphy
RF M Davis
DH D Kingman
UT B Almon
SI- M Wagner
M S Anderson

SEA 1984 AL
SP M Langston
SP M Moore
SP J Beattie
SR E Vande Berg
SP M Young
RP D Beard
RS B Stoddard
RP E Nunez
RP P Mirabella
C B Kearney
1B A Davis
2B J Perconte
SS S Owen
3B- J Presley
ML P Bradley
CF D Henderson
RF A Cowens
DH K Phelps
LO B Bonnell
UT S Henderson
M1 D Crandall
M2 C Cottier

TEX 1984 AL
SP C Hough
SP F Tanana
SP D Darwin
SP D Stewart
SR M Mason
RP D Schmidt
RP O Jones
C - D Scott
1B P O'Brien
2B W Tolleson
SS C Wilkerson
3B B Bell
LM B Sample
MR G Wright
UO G Ward
RD L Parrish
UO M Rivers
M D Rader

TOR 1984 AL
SP D Stieb
SP D Alexander
SP L Leal
SP J Clancy
SR J Gott
RP R Jackson
RP D Lamp
RP J Acker
RP J Key
C E Whitt

1B W Upshaw
2B D Garcia
SS A Griffin
3B R Mulliniks
LF C Moseby
CF L Bell
DH C Johnson
RU J Barfield
3B G Iorg
C B Martinez
DH- W Aikens
SS- T Fernandez
M B Cox

ATL 1985 NL
SP R Mahler
SP R Bedrosian
SP Z Smith
RP R Camp
CL B Sutter
RP G Garber
RP J Dedmon
C - R Cerone
13 R Horner
2B G Hubbard
SS R Ramirez
3B K Oberkfell
LF T Harper
CF D Murphy
RF C Washington
UL C Chambliss
RL R Komminsk
1U G Perry
2S- P Zuvella
M1 E Haas
M2 B Wine

CHI 1985 NL
SP D Eckersley
SR R Fontenot
SP S Trout
SP R Sutcliffe
SP S Sanderson
RP L Smith
RP L Sorensen
RP W Brusstar
RP G Frazier
C J Davis
1B L Durham
2B R Sandberg
SS- S Dunston
3B R Cey
LF- G Matthews
CF B Dernier
RF K Moreland
UO T Bosley
UT D Lopes
S3 C Speier
IO- R Hebner
LU- G Woods
M J Frey

CIN 1985 NL
SP T Browning
SP M Soto
SP J Tibbs
SR R Robinson
SR J Stuper
RP J Franco
CL T Power
RP T Hume
RS J Price
C - D Van Gorder
1B P Rose
2B R Oester
SS D Concepcion
3B- B Bell
LM G Redus
CF E Milner
RF D Parker
IO N Esasky
L1- C Cedeno
3U- W Krenchicki

HOU 1985 NL
SP B Knepper
SP N Ryan
SP M Scott
SP J Niekro
CL D Smith
RP B Dawley
RP F DiPino
RP J Calhoun
C M Bailey
1B G Davis
2B B Doran
SS C Reynolds
3B P Garner
LF J Cruz
MR K Bass
RM J Mumphrey
UT D Walling
SS- D Thon
M B Lillis

LA 1985 NL
SP F Valenzuela
SP O Hershiser
SP J Reuss
SP B Welch
SP R Honeycutt
RP T Niedenfuer
RP K Howell
RP C Diaz
RS B Castillo
C M Scioscia
1B G Brock
2B S Sax
SS M Duncan
3S- D Anderson
UO C Maldonado
CF K Landreaux
RF M Marshall
L3 P Guerrero
M J Lasorda

MON 1985 NL
SP B Smith
SP B Gullickson
SP J Hesketh
SP D Palmer
SP D Schatzeder
CL J Reardon
RP T Burke
RP R Boberge
RP G Lucas
C M Fitzgerald
1B- D Driessen
2B V Law
SS H Brooks
3B T Wallach
LF T Raines
CF H Winningham
RF A Dawson
1O T Francona
M B Rodgers

NY 1985 NL
SP D Gooden
SP R Darling
SP E Lynch
SP S Fernandez
SP R Aguilera
RP R McDowell
RP J Orosco
RP D Sisk
RP T Leach
C G Carter
1B K Hernandez
2B W Backman
SS R Santana
3B H Johnson
LF G Foster
CF- M Wilson
RF D Strawberry
CF- L Dykstra
OI- D Heep
3B- R Knight
M D Johnson

PHI 1985 NL
SP J Denny
SP K Gross
SP S Rawley
SR C Hudson
SP J Koosman
RP D Carman
RP K Tekulve
RP D Rucker
RP L Andersen
C O Virgil
13 M Schmidt
2B J Samuel
SS- S Jeltz
3B R Schu
CF V Hayes
CF G Maddox
RF G Wilson
1U T Corcoran
SI- L Aguayo
OI- G Gross
LU- J Russell
LF- J Stone
M J Felske

PIT 1985 NL
SP R Rhoden
SP R Reuschel
SP J DeLeon
SP L Tunnell
SR L McWilliams
RP C Guante
RS D Robinson
RS J Winn
RP J Candelaria
C T Pena
1B J Thompson
2B J Ray
SS- S Khalifa
3B L Madlock
ML J Orsulak

CF M Wynne
RF- G Hendrick
UT- B Almon
LU- S Kemp
UT- L Mazzilli
3U- J Morrison
M C Tanner

STL 1985 NL
SP J Tudor
SP J Andujar
SP D Cox
SP K Kepshire
SR B Forsch
CL J Lahti
RP K Dayley
RP B Campbell
C - T Nieto
1B J Clark
2B T Herr
SS O Smith
3B T Pendleton
LF V Coleman
CF W McGee
RF A Van Slyke
RF- T Landrum
C - D Porter
M W Herzog

SD 1985 NL
SP E Show
SP A Hawkins
SP D Dravecky
SP L Hoyt
SR M Thurmond
CL R Gossage
RP C Lefferts
RP T Stoddard
C T Kennedy
1B S Garvey
2B T Flannery
SS G Templeton
3B G Nettles
LF C Martinez
CF K McReynolds
RF T Gwynn
23- J Royster
M D Williams

SF 1985 NL
SP D LaPoint
SP M Krukow
SP A Hammaker
SP J Gott
SR V Blue
RP M Davis
RS S Garrelts
RP B Laskey
RP G Minton
C B Brenly
1U D Green
2B M Trillo
SS J Uribe
3B C Brown
LF J Leonard
CF D Gladden
RM C Davis
M1 J Davenport
M2 R Craig

BAL 1985 AL
SP S McGregor
SP M Boddicker
SP D Martinez
SP S Davis
SR K Dixon
RP S Stewart
RP N Snell
RP D Aase
RP T Martinez
C R Dempsey
1B E Murray
2B- A Wiggins
SS C Ripken
3C F Rayford
LD M Young
CF F Lynn
RF L Lacy
DH L Sheets
OF J Dwyer
3U W Gross
LU G Roenicke
2B- R Dauer
M1 J Altobelli
M3 E Weaver

BOS 1985 AL
SP O Boyd
SP B Hurst
SP A Nipper
SR B Ojeda
RP S Crawford
RP B Stanley
RP M Clear
C R Gedman

1B B Buckner
2B M Barrett
SS J Gutierrez
3B W Boggs
LF J Rice
CF S Lyons
RF D Evans
DH M Easler
MU T Armas
SS- G Hoffman
M J McNamara

CAL 1985 AL
SP M Witt
SP R Romanick
SP K McCaskill
SP J Slaton
RP D Moore
RS S Cliburn
RP P Clements
RP L Sanchez
C B Boone
1B R Carew
2B B Grich
SS D Schofield
3B D DeCinces
LF B Downing
CF G Pettis
UO R Jones
RD R Jackson
UT J Beniquez
2B- R Wilfong
M G Mauch

CHI 1985 AL
SP T Seaver
SP B Burns
SP F Bannister
SR G Nelson
RP B James
RP D Spillner
RP J Agosto
C C Fisk
1B G Walker
2B- J Cruz
SS O Guillen
3B T Hulett
LF R Law
CF- D Boston
RF H Baines
UT R Kittle
UI S Fletcher
M3 L Salazar
UT- J Hairston
M T LaRussa

CLE 1985 AL
SP N Heaton
SP B Blyleven
SR V Ruhle
RS T Waddell
RS J Easterly
RP R Thompson
RS J Reed
C J Willard
1B P Tabler
2B T Bernazard
SS J Franco
3B B Jacoby
LF J Carter
CF B Butler
RF G Vukovich
DH A Thornton
1B M Hargrove
LM O Nixon
M P Corrales

DET 1985 AL
SP J Morris
SP D Petry
SP W Terrell
SP F Tanana
RP W Hernandez
RP A Lopez
RP B Scherrer
RP D Bair
C L Parrish
1U D Evans
2B L Whitaker
SS A Trammell
3B T Brookens
LF L Herndon
CF C Lemon
RF K Gibson
OF- J Grubb
UT- B Garbey
M S Anderson

KC 1985 AL
SP C Leibrandt
SP B Saberhagen
3B D Jackson
SP B Black
SP M Gubicza
RP D Quisenberry
RP J Beckwith
RP M Jones

C J Sundberg
1B S Balboni
2B F White
SS O Concepcion
3B G Brett
LF L Smith
CF W Wilson
RL D Motley
DH H McRae
LR L Jones
DH J Orta
SS- B Biancalana
M D Howser

MIL 1985 AL
SR D Darwin
SP T Higuera
SP B Burris
SP M Haas
SP J Cocanower
RP P Vuckovich
RP B Gibson
RP B McClure
CL R Fingers
C C Moore
1B C Cooper
2B J Gantner
SS E Riles
3B P Molitor
RL B Oglivie
LM R Yount
RM-P Householder
DU T Simmons
UT- E Romero
M G Bamberger

MIN 1985 AL
SP M Smithson
SP F Viola
SP J Butcher
SP K Schrom
RS P Filson
CL R Davis
RP F Eufemia
RP R Lysander
C M Salas
1B K Hrbek
2B T Teufel
SS G Gagne
3B G Gaetti
LF M Hatcher
CF K Puckett
RF T Brunansky
UI R Smalley
OI- R Bush
OI- M Stenhouse
M1 B Gardner
M2 R Miller

NY 1985 AL
SP R Guidry
SP P Niekro
SP J Cowley
SP E Whitson
SP D Rasmussen
RP D Righetti
RP B Fisher
RS B Shirley
RP R Bordi
C B Wynegar
1B D Mattingly
2B W Randolph
SS B Meacham
3B M Pagliarulo
LF K Griffey
CF R Henderson
RF D Winfield
DH- J Burroughs
C - R Hassey
M1 Y Berra
M2 B Martin

OAK 1985 AL
SP C Codiroli
SP D Sutton
SP B Krueger
SP T Birtsas
RP J Howell
RP K Atherton
RS S McCatty
RP S Ontiveros
C M Heath
1B B Bochte
2B D Hill
SS A Griffin
3B C Lansford
LF D Collins
CF D Murphy
RF M Davis
DH D Kingman
1L D Baker
LU- S Henderson
M, J Moore

SEA 1985 AL
SP M Moore
SP M Young
SP M Langston
SP F Wills
SP B Swift
RP R Nunez
RP R Thomas
RP R Vande Berg
C B Kearney
1B A Davis
2B J Percente
SS S Owen
3B J Presley
LF P Bradley
CF D Henderson
RF A Cowens
DH G Thomas
M C Cottier

TEX 1985 AL
SP C Hough
SP M Mason
SP B Hooton
SR D Noles
RP G Harris
RP D Rozema
RP D Schmidt
RS D Stewart
C D Slaught
1B P O'Brien
2B T Harrah
SS C Wilkerson
3B- B Bell
LF G Ward
CF O McDowell
RM G Wright
DH- C Johnson
SI W Tolleson
OI- B Jones
RU- L Parrish
M1 D Rader
M2 B Valentine

TOR 1985 AL
SP D Stieb
SP D Alexander
SP J Key
SP J Clancy
RP D Lamp
RP J Acker
RP B Caudill
RP G Lavelle
C E Whitt
1B W Upshaw
2B D Garcia
SS T Fernandez
3B R Mulliniks
LF G Bell
CF L Moseby
RF J Barfield
DH- J Burroughs
3B G Iorg
M B Cox

ATL 1986 NL
SP R Mahler
SP D Palmer
SP Z Smith
SP D Alexander
RP J Dedmon
CL G Garber
RS C McMurtry
RP P Assenmacher
C O Virgil
1B B Horner
2B G Hubbard
SS A Thomas
3B K Oberkfell
LU T Harper
CF D Murphy
RO O Moreno
U1 C Chambliss
S3 R Ramirez
RU- B Sample
M C Tanner

CHI 1986 NL
SP D Eckersley
SP R Sutcliffe
SP S Sanderson
SR S Trout
SR E Lynch
CL S Smith
RS G Hoffman
RP D Gumpert
RP J Baller
C J Davis
1B L Durham
2B R Sandberg
SS S Dunston
3B R Cey
LF G Matthews
CF B Dernier
RF K Moreland
ML J Mumphrey

UO- T Bosley
OI- T Francona
3I- C Speier
3U- M Trillo
M1 J Frey
M2 J Vukovich
M3 G Michael

CIN 1986 NL
SP B Gullickson
SP T Browning
SP J Denny
SP C Welsh
SP N Soto
RP R Robinson
RP J Franco
RS T Power
RP S Terry
C B Diaz
2B B Oester
SS K Stillwell
3B B Bell
LM E Davis
CF E Milner
RF D Parker
UO M Venable
SI- D Concepcion
M P Rose

HOU 1986 NL
SP M Scott
SP B Knepper
SP N Ryan
SP J Deshaies
RP C Kerfeld
CL D Smith
RP A Lopez
RP L Andersen
C A Ashby
1B G Davis
2B B Doran
SS D Thon
3B D Walling
LF J Cruz
ML B Hatcher
RF K Bass
3B P Garner
SS C Reynolds
RU- T Puhl
CF- T Walker
M H Lanier

LA 1986 NL
SP F Valenzuela
SP B Welch
SP O Hershiser
SP R Honeycutt
RP K Howell
RP T Niedenfuer
RP E Vande Berg
RS D Powell
C M Scioscia
1B G Brock
2B S Sax
SS M Duncan
3B B Madlock
MR F Williams
RF M Marshall
1U E Cabell
MU K Landreaux
UT B Russell
3S- D Anderson
OI- L Matuszek
CU- A Trevino
M T Lasorda

MON 1986 NL
SP F Youmans
SP J Tibbs
SP B Smith
SP D Martinez
RS A McGaffigan
CL J Reardon
RP T Burke
RP B McClure
C - D Bilardello
1B A Galarraga
2B V Law
SS- H Brooks
3B T Wallach
LF T Raines
CF M Webster
RF A Dawson
IO W Krenchicki
2U- A Newman
MU-H Winningham
M B Rodgers

NY 1986 NL
SP D Gooden
SP R Darling
SP B Ojeda
SP S Fernandez
SP R Aguilera
RP R McDowell

CL J Orosco
RP D Sisk
C G Carter
1B K Hernandez
2B W Backman
SS R Santana
3B R Knight
LM M Wilson
CF L Dykstra
RF D Strawberry
UT K Mitchell
LU- D Heep
3S- H Johnson
2B- T Teufel
M D Johnson

PHI 1986 NL
SP K Gross
SP S Rawley
SP B Ruffin
SR C Hudson
RS D Carman
CL S Bedrosian
RP K Tekulve
RP T Hume
C - J Russell
1B V Hayes
2B J Samuel
SS S Jeltz
3B M Schmidt
LF- G Redus
CF- M Thompson
RF G Wilson
MO R Roenicke
OI- G Gross
3U- R Schu
OF- J Stone
M J Felske

PIT 1986 NL
SP R Rhoden
SP R Reuschel
SP M Bielecki
SR B Walk
SP B Kipper
RS L McWilliams
RP J Winn
RP D Robinson
RP C Guante
C T Pena
1B S Bream
2B J Ray
SS R Belliard
3B J Morrison
LR R Reynolds
CF B Bonds
RM J Orsulak
L3 B Almon
UT- M Diaz
RF- M Brown
M J Leyland

STL 1986 NL
SP B Forsch
SP D Cox
SP J Tudor
SP G Mathews
SP T Conroy
RP T Worrell
RS R Horton
RP P Perry
C M LaValliere
1B- J Clark
2B T Herr
SS O Smith
3B T Pendleton
LF V Coleman
CF W McGee
RF A Van Slyke
R1 A Thomas
OF- C Ford
RU- T Landrum
M W Herzog

SD 1986 NL
SP A Hawkins
SP D Dravecky
SR L Hoyt
SP E Show
RS L McCullers
RP C Lefferts
RP G Walter
CL R Gossage
C T Kennedy
1B S Garvey
2B T Flannery
SS G Templeton
3B G Nettles
ML K McReynolds
CF M Wynne
RF T Gwynn
LU J Kruk
LU C Martinez
2B R Roberts
3I J Royster
IO- D Iorg
M S Boros

SF 1986 NL
SP M Krukow
SP M LaCoss
SR S Garrelts
SP V Blue
RP J Robinson
RP M Davis
RP J Berenguer
RP G Minton
C3 B Brenly
1B W Clark
2B R Thompson
SS J Uribe
3B C Brown
OI C Maldonado
CF D Gladden
RFC C Davis
UT- J Youngblood
UT- M Aldrete
LF- J Leonard
C - B Melvin
M R Craig

BAL 1986 AL
SP M Boddicker
SP S McGregor
SP K Dixon
SP M Flanagan
SP S Davis
CL D Aase
RP B Bordi
RP B Havens
RP N Snell
RP C Dempsey
1B E Murray
23 J Bonilla
SS C Ripken
3B- F Rayford
UO J Shelby
CF F Lynn
RF L Lacy
DO L Sheets
UT J Beniquez
LD M Young
OI- J Dwyer
M E Weaver

BOS 1986 AL
SP R Clemens
SP O Boyd
SP B Hurst
SP A Nipper
SP T Seaver
RP B Stanley
RP S Stewart
RP S Crawford
CL C Schiraldi
C R Gedman
1B B Buckner
2B M Barrett
SS S Romero
3B W Boggs
LF J Rice
CF T Armas
RF D Evans
DH D Baylor
M J McNamara

CAL 1986 AL
SP M Witt
SP K McCaskill
SP D Sutton
SP R Romanick
CL D Moore
RP D Corbett
C B Boone
1B W Joyner
2B- R Wilfong
SS D Schofield
3B- D DeCinces
LF B Downing
CF G Pettis
RF R Jones
DH R Jackson
2B B Grich
RF G Hendrick
UI- R Burleson
M G Mauch

CHI 1986 AL
SP R Dotson
SP F Bannister
SP J Cowley
SP N Allen
SP J Davis
RP R Nelson
RP B Dawley
RP B Schmidt
RP B James
CU C Fisk
1B- G Walker
2B- J Cruz
SS O Guillen
32 T Hulett
OI- R Nichols
MU J Cangelosi

RF H Baines
DU- R Kittle
UT J Hairston
3B- W Tolleson
M1 T LaRussa
M2 D Rader
M3 J Fregosi

CLE 1986 AL
SP T Candiotti
SP P Niekro
SP K Schrom
RS S Bailes
RP R Yett
CL E Camacho
RP B Oelkers
C A Allanson
1B P Tabler
2B T Bernazard
SS J Franco
3B B Jacoby
LF M Hall
CF B Butler
OI J Carter
DH A Thornton
LF O Nixon
RS C Snyder
C- C Bando
UT- C Castillo
M P Corrales

DET 1986 AL
SP J Morris
SP W Terrell
SP F Tanana
SR E King
SP D Petry
RS R O'Neal
CL W Hernandez
RP B Campbell
RP M Thurmond
C- L Parrish
1D D Evans
2B L Whitaker
SS A Trammell
3B D Coles
LU D Collins
CF C Lemon
RF K Gibson
DU- J Grubb
UT T Brookens
LF L Herndon
MR P Sheridan
M S Anderson

KC 1986 AL
SP C Leibrandt
SP D Leonard
SP D Jackson
SR M Gubicza
SP B Saberhagen
RP B Black
RP S Bankhead
RP S Farr
RP D Quisenberry
C J Sundberg
1B S Balboni
2B F White
SS A Salazar
3B G Brett
LF L Smith
CF W Wilson
LR- R Law
DH J Orta
SS B Biancalana
DU H McRae
M1 D Howser
M2 M Ferraro

MIL 1986 AL
SP T Higuera
SP B Wegman
SP T Leary
SP J Nieves
SR D Darwin
RP D Plesac
RP M Clear
RP B Clutterbuck
C- C Moore
1B- B Robidoux
2B J Gantner
SS E Riles
3B P Molitor
UO- R Manning
CF R Yount
RF R Deer
1D C Cooper
OF B Oglivie
3I- D Sveum
M1 G Bamberger
M2 T Trebelhorn

MIN 1986 AL
SP B Blyleven
SP F Viola
SP M Smithson
SP N Heaton

SR M Portugal
RP K Atherton
RP R Jackson
RP F Pastore
C- M Salas
1B K Hrbek
2B S Lombardozzi
SS G Gagne
3B G Gaetti
LU R Bush
CF K Puckett
RF T Brunansky
DH R Smalley
UT M Hatcher
M1 R Miller
M2 T Kelly

NY 1986 AL
SP D Rasmussen
SP R Guidry
SP D Drabek
SP J Niekro
RP D Righetti
RS B Shirley
RP B Fisher
RP T Stoddard
C- B Wynegar
1B D Mattingly
2B W Randolph
SS- W Tolleson
3B M Pagliarulo
LU D Pasqua
CF R Henderson
RF D Winfield
DH M Easler
M L Piniella

OAK 1986 AL
SP C Young
SR J Rijo
SP J Andujar
SP D Stewart
SR E Plunk
RS B Mooneyham
RP S Ontiveros
CL J Howell
C- M Tettleton
1B B Bochte
23 T Phillips
SS A Griffin
31 C Lansford
LF J Canseco
CF D Murphy
RF M Davis
DH D Kingman
23 D Hill
OI- D Baker
M1 J Moore
M2 J Newman
M3 T LaRussa

SEA 1986 AL
SP M Moore
SP M Langston
SP M Morgan
SR B Swift
RS M Young
RP M Huismann
RP P Ladd
RP L Guetterman
C- B Kearney
1U A Davis
2B H Reynolds
SS S Owen
3B J Presley
LF P Bradley
CF J Moses
RU D Tartabull
DH- G Thomas
OF D Henderson
UT K Phelps
M1 C Cottier
M2 M Martinez
M3 D Williams

TEX 1986 AL
SP C Hough
SP E Correa
SP J Guzman
SP B Witt
SP M Mason
RP G Harris
RP M Williams
RP D Mohorcic
RP J Russell
C- D Slaught
1B P O'Brien
2B- T Harrah
SS S Fletcher
3B S Buechele
RL R Sierra
CF O McDowell
RU P Incaviglia
DH L Parrish
LF G Ward

2S C Wilkerson
UT- T Paciorek
M B Valentine

TOR 1986 AL
SP J Key
SP J Clancy
SP D Stieb
SR J Cerutti
SP D Alexander
RP M Eichhorn
CL T Henke
RP D Lamp
RS J Acker
C E Whitt
1B W Upshaw
2B D Garcia
SS T Fernandez
3B B Mulliniks
LF G Bell
CF L Moseby
RF J Barfield
DH C Johnson
32 G Iorg
OI R Leach
UT- K Gruber
C- B Martinez
M J Williams

ATL 1987 NL
SP Z Smith
SR R Mahler
SP D Palmer
SR C Puleo
SP D Alexander
RP J Acker
RP J Dedmon
RP G Garber
RP P Assenmacher
C O Virgil
1B G Perry
2B D Hubbard
SS- A Thomas
3B K Oberkfell
LF W Griffey
MU D James
RF D Murphy
IF. G Nettles
MU-A Hall
M C Tanner

CHI 1987 NL
SP R Sutcliffe
SP J Moyer
SP G Maddux
SR S Sanderson
SP L Lancaster
CL L Smith
RS E Lynch
RP F DiPino
RP D Noles
C J Davis
1B L Durham
2B R Sandberg
SS- S Dunston
3B K Moreland
LU J Mumphrey
CF D Martinez
RF A Dawson
LU B Dayett
UI M Trillo
CF- B Dernier
LU- R Palmeiro
M1 G Michael
M2 F Lucchesi

CIN 1987 NL
SP T Power
SP T Browning
SP B Gullickson
SR G Hoffman
SR R Robinson
CL J Franco
RP F Williams
RP R Murphy
RP D Landrum
C B Diaz
1B N Esasky
2B- R Oester
SS B Larkin
3B B Bell
UO T Jones
CF E Davis
RF D Parker
21 D Concepcion
LF K Daniels
1U T Francona
UI K Stillwell
OI- P O'Neill
M P Rose

HOU 1987 NL
SP M Scott
SP N Ryan
SP D Darwin
SP B Knepper
SP J Deshaies

RP L Andersen
CL D Smith
RP D Meads
C A Ashby
1B G Davis
2B B Doran
SS C Reynolds
3U D Walling
LF J Cruz
ML B Hatcher
RF K Bass
UO- T Puhl
M H Lanier

LA 1987 NL
SP O Hershiser
SP B Welch
SP F Valenzuela
SP R Honeycutt
RS T Leary
CL A Pena
RP B Holton
RP M Young
C M Scioscia
1B F Stubbs
2B S Sax
SS- M Duncan
UT M Hatcher
L1 P Guerrero
CF J Shelby
RF M Marshall
S3 D Anderson
UO K Landreaux
M T Lasorda

MON 1987 NL
SP N Heaton
SP B Sebra
SP B Smith
SP D Martinez
SP F Youmans
RPA A McGaffigan
RP T Burke
RP R St.Claire
RP J Parrett
C M Fitzgerald
1B A Galarraga
2B V Law
SS H Brooks
3B T Wallach
LF T Raines
CF H Winningham
RF M Webster
UT C Candaele
UI T Foley
M B Rodgers

NY 1987 NL
SP R Darling
SP D Gooden
SP S Fernandez
SP R Aguilera
SP J Mitchell
RS T Leach
CL R McDowell
RP D Cone
RP J Orosco
C G Carter
1B K Hernandez
3B H Johnson
LF K McReynolds
CF L Dykstra
RF D Strawberry
MO M Wilson
2B- W Backman
3U- D Magadan
OI- L Mazzilli
M D Johnson

PHI 1987 NL
SP S Rawley
SP D Carman
SP B Ruffin
SP K Gross
CL S Bedrosian
RS M Jackson
RP K Tekulve
RS T Hume
C L Parrish
1B V Hayes
2B J Samuel
SS S Jeltz
3B M Schmidt
LF C James
CF M Thompson
RF G Wilson
OI G Gross
SS- L Aguayo
IF- R Schu
M1 J Felske
M2 L Elia

PIT 1987 NL
SR B Fisher
SP R Reuschel

SP D Drabek
SP M Dunne
SP B Kipper
RS B Walk
RP D Robinson
C M LaValliere
1B S Bream
2B J Ray
SS- A Pedrique
3O B Bonilla
LM B Bonds
MU A Van Slyke
RU R Reynolds
UO J Cangelosi
OI M Diaz
M J Leyland

STL 1987 NL
SP D Cox
SP G Mathews
SP B Forsch
SP J Magrane
RS R Horton
CL T Worrell
RP B Dawley
RS L Tunnell
C T Pena
1B J Clark
2B T Herr
SS O Smith
3B T Pendleton
LF V Coleman
CF W McGee
RU- C Ford
RU J Morris
UT J Oquendo
M W Herzog

SD 1987 NL
SP E Show
SP E Whitson
SP J Jones
SP A Hawkins
SP M Grant
RP L McCullers
RP G Booker
RP R Gossage
C B Santiago
1U J Kruk
2B T Flannery
SS G Templeton
IO R Ready
ML S Jefferson
CF S Mack
RF T Gwynn
L1 C Martinez
UO M Wynne
UT- L Salazar
M L Bowa

SF 1987 NL
SR K Downs
SR M LaCoss
SP A Hammaker
SP M Krukow
SP D Dravecky
RS S Garrelts
RP J Robinson
RP J Gott
C B Brenly
1B W Clark
2B R Thompson
SS- J Uribe
3B- K Mitchell
LF J Leonard
CF C Davis
RF C Maldonado
OI M Aldrete
CF E Milner
UI C Speier
C- B Melvin
IF- H Spilman
SS- M Williams
M R Craig

BAL 1987 AL
SP M Boddicker
SP E Bell
SR D Schmidt
SR J Habyan
SR K Dixon
RP M Williamson
RP T Niedenfuer
RP T Arnold
C T Kennedy
1B E Murray
2B- B Ripken
3B R Knight
LM- K Gerhart
CF F Lynn
LR L Sheets

OF M Young
OF- J Dwyer
D2- A Wiggins

BOS 1987 AL
SP R Clemens
SP B Hurst
SP A Nipper
SR B Stanley
SP J Sellers
RP W Gardner
RP C Schiraldi
RP S Crawford
RP T Bolton
C- M Sullivan
1R D Evans
2B M Barrett
SS S Owen
3B W Boggs
LF J Rice
CF E Burks
LU M Greenwell
DH D Baylor
UI- E Romero
M J McNamara

CAL 1987 AL
SP M Witt
SP D Sutton
SR W Fraser
SR J Lazorko
SP J Candelaria
RP D Buice
RP C Finley
RP G Minton
RP G Lucas
C B Boone
1B W Joyner
2B M McLemore
SS D Schofield
3B C DeCinces
L3 J Howell
CF C Pettis
RF J White
DH B Downing
LO- R Jones
M G Mauch

CHI 1987 AL
SP F Bannister
SP R Dotson
SP J DeLeon
SP B Long
RP B Thigpen
RP J Winn
RP B James
RP R Searage
C C Fisk
1B G Walker
2B F Manrique
3B- T Hulett
LO G Redus
CF K Williams
RF I Calderon
DH H Baines
OF D Boston
2B D Hill
M J Fregosi

CLE 1987 AL
SP T Candiotti
SP K Schrom
SR S Bailes
SP P Niekro
SP S Carlton
RP G Swindell
RP D Jones
RS R Yett
RP E Vande Berg
C- C Bando
1L J Carter
2B- T Bernazard
SS J Franco
3B B Jacoby
LF M Hall
CF B Butler
RF C Snyder
1D P Tabler
OF- C Castillo
M1 P Corrales
M2 D Edwards

DET 1987 AL
SP J Morris
SP W Terrell
SP F Tanana
SP D Petry
SP J Robinson
RP E King
RP M Henneman
RP M Thurmond
RP W Hernandez
C M Nokes
1D D Evans
2B L Whitaker

SS A Trammell
3B T Brookens
LF K Gibson
CF C Lemon
RF P Sheridan
D1- B Madlock
CO- M Heath
OF- L Herndon
M S Anderson

KC 1987 AL
SP B Saberhagen
SP M Gubicza
SP C Leibrandt
SP D Jackson
SR B Black
RP S Farr
RP D Quisenberry
RP J Gleaton
C J Quirk
1U G Brett
2B F White
SS A Salazar
3B K Seitzer
LF B Jackson
CF W Wilson
RF D Tartabull
UT S Balboni
M1 B Gardner
M2 J Wathan

MIL 1987 AL
SP T Higuera
SP B Wegman
SP J Nieves
SR C Bosio
RS C Crim
CL D Plesac
RP M Clear
RP J Aldrich
C- B Surhoff
1B G Brock
2B J Castillo
SS D Sveum
3B- E Riles
LU R Deer
CF R Yount
RF G Braggs
DH- C Cooper
LU M Felder
RO- R Manning
IF P Molitor
23- J Gantner
M T Trebelhorn

MIN 1987 AL
SP B Blyleven
SP F Viola
SP L Straker
SP M Smithson
RS J Berenguer
CL J Reardon
RP K Atherton
C T Laudner
1B K Hrbek
2B S Lombardozzi
SS G Gagne
3B G Gaetti
LF D Gladden
CF K Puckett
RL T Brunansky
DU R Smalley
RU R Bush
UO M Davidson
S2 A Newman
UT- G Larkin
M T Kelly

NY 1987 AL
SP T John
SP R Rhoden
SR C Hudson
SP D Rasmussen
SP R Guidry
CL D Righetti
RP T Stoddard
RP P Clements
C- R Cerone
1B D Mattingly
2B W Randolph
SS W Tolleson
3B M Pagliarulo
OI G Ward
MU C Washington
RF D Winfield
LU D Pasqua
OF- R Henderson
M L Piniella

OAK 1987 AL
SP D Stewart
SP C Young
SR S Ontiveros
SP D Eckersley
RS G Nelson

RS D Lamp
RP D Leiper
C T Steinbach
1B M McGwire
2B T Phillips
SS A Griffin
3B C Lansford
LF J Canseco
ML L Polonia
RF M Davis
DU R Jackson
MO-S Javier
CF- D Murphy
C- M Tettleton
M T LaRussa

SEA 1987 AL
SP M Langston
SP M Moore
SP M Morgan
SP S Bankhead
SP L Guetterman
RP J Reed
RP B Wilkinson
RS M Trujillo
C S Bradley
1B A Davis
2B H Reynolds
SS R Quinones
3B J Presley
LF P Bradley
CF J Moses
RF M Brantley
DH K Phelps
MR-M Brantley
C- D Valle
M D Williams

TEX 1987 AL
SP C Hough
SP J Guzman
SP B Witt
SR G Harris
RP D Mohorcic
RP M Williams
RP J Russell
RS M Loynd
C- D Slaught
1B P O'Brien
2B J Browne
SS S Fletcher
3B S Buechele
LF P Incaviglia
CF O McDowell
RF R Sierra
DH L Parrish
ML B Brower
CI G Petralli
UC- D Porter
UI- C Wilkerson
M B Valentine

TOR 1987 AL
SP J Key
SP J Clancy
SP D Stieb
SR J Cerutti
RP M Eichhorn
CL T Henke
RS J Nunez
RP J Musselman
C E Whitt
1B W Upshaw
2U G Iorg
SS T Fernandez
3B K Gruber
LF G Bell
CF L Moseby
RF J Barfield
DH F McGriff
OI R Leach
3B R Mulliniks
DU- C Fielder
M J Williams

ATL 1988 NL
SP R Mahler
SP T Glavine
SP P Smith
SP Z Smith
RP C Puleo
RP J Alvarez
RP P Assenmacher
C O Virgil
1B G Perry
2B R Gant
SS A Thomas
3B K Oberkfell
LM D James
MU-A Hall
RF D Murphy
C- B Benedict
M1 C Tanner
M2 R Nixon

CHI 1988 NL
SP G Maddux
SP R Sutcliffe
SP J Moyer
SP C Schiraldi
SP J Pico
RP F. DiPino
RP L Lancaster
C- D Berryhill
1B M Grace
2B R Sandberg
SS S Dunston
3B V Law
LF R Palmeiro
UO D Jackson
RF A Dawson
C- J Davis
M D Zimmer

CIN 1988 NL
SP D Jackson
SP T Browning
SR J Rijo
CL J France
RP R Murphy
RP T Birtsas
RP F Williams
C- B Diaz
1B N Esasky
3B J Treadway
SS B Larkin
3B C Sabo
LF K Daniels
CF E Davis
RF P O'Neill
OI D Collins
2I- D Concepcion
M1 P Rose
M2 T Helms
M3 P Rose

HOU 1988 NL
SP N Ryan
SP M Scott
SP J Deshaies
SR D Darwin
SP B Knepper
SP J Agosto
RP L Andersen
CL D Smith
C- A Trevino
1B G Davis
2B B Doran
SS R Ramirez
3B- B Bell
LF B Hatcher
CF G Young
RF K Bass
JO T Puhl
M H Lanier

LA 1988 NL
SP O Hershiser
SP T Leary
SP F Valenzuela
SP A Pena
RP B Holton
CL J Howell
RP T Crews
C- M Scioscia
1U F Stubbs
2B S Sax
SS- A Griffin
3B J Hamilton
LF K Gibson
R1 M Marshall
SU D Anderson
4B M Davis
JT- M Hatcher
OI- D Heep
M T Lasorda

MON 1988 NL
SP D Martinez
SP B Smith
SP P Perez
SP J Dopson
SP B Holman
RP T Burke
RP J Parrett
RP A McGaffigan
RP J Hesketh
C- N Santovenia
4B A Galarraga
2S T Foley
SS L Rivera
3B T Wallach
LF T Raines
ML- O Nixon
RF H Brooks
F- W Johnson
MO-M Webster
M B Rodgers

NY 1988 NL
SP D Gooden
SP R Darling
SP D Cone
SP B Ojeda
SP S Fernandez
RP R McDowell
RP T Leach
CL R Myers
C G Carter
1B- K Hernandez
2B W Backman
SS K Elster
3B H Johnson
CF L Dykstra
RF D Strawberry
13 D Magadan
MO M Wilson
2B- T Teufel
M D Johnson

PHI 1988 NL
SP K Gross
SP D Carman
SP S Rawley
SP D Palmer
RS B Ruffin
RP G Harris
CL S Bedrosian
C L Parrish
1B V Hayes
2B J Samuel
SS S Jeltz
3B M Schmidt
LF P Bradley
CF M Thompson
RU C James
OI G Gross
M1 L Elia
M2 J Vukovich

PIT 1988 NL
SP D Drabek
SP B Walk
SP J Smiley
SP M Dunne
SR B Fisher
RP J Robinson
CL J Gott
RP B Kipper
RP B Jones
C M LaValliere
1B S Bream
2B J Lind
SS R Belliard
3B B Bonilla
LF B Bonds
CF A Van Slyke
RU R Reynolds
M J Leyland

STL 1988 NL
SP D DeLeon
SP J Magrane
SP J Tudor
SR L McWilliams
SR B Forsch
RS S Terry
CL T Worrell
RP K Dayley
RP J Costello
C T Pena
1B- B Horner
2B- L Alicea
SS O Smith
3B T Pendleton
LF V Coleman
CF W McGee
RF T Brunansky
UT J Oquendo
OI- C Ford
IC- T Pagnozzi
M W Herzog

SD 1988 NL
SP E Show
SP A Hawkins
SP E Whitson
SP J Jones
SP D Rasmussen
RP M Davis
RP L McCullers
RS M Grant
RP G Booker
C B Santiago
1L K Moreland
2B R Alomar
SS G Templeton
3B- C Brown
OI C Martinez
ML M Wynne
RF T Gwynn
1O J Kruk
3U R Ready
SU- D Thon
M1 L Bowa
M2 J McKeon

SF 1988 NL
SP R Reuschel
SR D Robinson
SP K Downs
SR A Hammaker
SP M Krukow
RP M LaCoss
RP S Garrelts
RP C Lefferts
RP J Price
C- B Melvin
1B W Clark
2B R Thompson
SS J Uribe
3L K Mitchell
LR M Aldrete
CF B Butler
RF C Maldonado
23- C Speier
UO- J Youngblood
M R Craig

BAL 1988 AL
SP J Bautista
SP J Tibbs
SP J Ballard
SP M Boddicker
RS D Schmidt
RS M Williamson
RP D Sisk
RS M Thurmond
C- M Tettleton
1D J Traber
2B B Ripken
3B- R Gonzales
LF- P Stanicek
MU-F Lynn
RL J Orsulak
OI L Sheets
ML K Gerhart
C- T Kennedy
3B- R Schu
M2 F Robinson

BOS 1988 AL
SP R Clemens
SP B Hurst
SR W Gardner
SP O Boyd
SR M Smithson
CL L Smith
RP- B Stanley
RP D Lamp
C- R Gedman
1R T Benzinger
2B M Barrett
SS J Reed
3B W Boggs
LF M Greenwell
CF E Burks
R1 D Evans
DH J Rice
C- R Cerone
SS- S Owen
M1 J McNamara
M2 J Morgan

CAL 1988 AL
SP M Witt
SP W Fraser
SP- C Finley
SP K McCaskill
SP D Petry
CL B Harvey
RP G Minton
RP S Cliburn
C- B Boone
1B W Joyner
2L J Ray
SS D Schofield
3B J Howell
LM T Armas
CF D White
RF C Davis
DH B Downing
M1 C Rojas
M2 M Stubing

CHI 1988 AL
SP M Perez
SP J Reuss
SR B Long
SP D LaPoint
SP J McDowell
CL B Thigpen
RS R Horton
RP J Davis
RS J Bittiger
C- C Fisk
1B G Walker
2B F Manrique
SS O Guillen
3B S Lyons
UO D Boston
CF D Gallagher
LR D Pasqua
DH H Baines
2U- D Hill
M J Fregosi

CLE 1988 AL
SP G Swindell
SP T Candiotti
SP T Farrell
SR S Bailes
SP R Yett
CL D Jones
RP D Gordon
RP B Havens
C A Allanson
1B W Upshaw
2B J Franco
SS- J Bell
3B B Jacoby
LF M Hall
CF J Carter
RF C Snyder
DH-R Kittle
M D Edwards

DET 1988 AL
SP J Morris
SP D Alexander
SP W Terrell
SP F Tanana
SP J Robinson
CL M Henneman
RP P Gibson
RP W Hernandez
RS E King
C M Nokes
1U R Knight
2B L Whitaker
SS A Trammell
3B T Brookens
LU P Sheridan
CF G Pettis
RF C Lemon
D1 D Evans
1D D Bergman
UT L Salazar
C- M Heath
2U- J Walewander
M S Anderson

KC 1988 AL
SP M Gubicza
SP B Saberhagen
SP C Leibrandt
SP F Bannister
RP S Farr
RP J Montgomery
C- J Quirk
1B G Brett
2B F White
SS K Stillwell
3B K Seitzer
LF B Jackson
CF W Wilson
RF D Tartabull
UT- B Buckner
UO- J Eisenreich
RP J Reed
CL M Schooler
C S Bradley
UT- P Tabler
M J Wathan

MIL 1988 AL
SP T Higuera
SP- B Wegman
SR C Bosio
SP D August
SP M Birkbeck
RP C Crim
RS J Nieves
RP T Filer
RP O Jones
C B Surhoff
1B G Brock
2B J Gantner
SS S Sveum
3D P Molitor
LF- J Leonard
CF R Yount
RL R Deer
D1 J Meyer
M T Trebelhorn

MIN 1988 AL
SP F Viola
SP B Blyleven
SP A Anderson
SP C Lea
SP F Toliver
CL J Reardon
RP J Berenguer
RP K Atherton
RP M Portugal
C L Laudner
1D K Hrbek
2B S Lombardozzi
SS G Gagne
3B M Gaetti
LF D Gladden
CF K Puckett
RF R Bush
D1 G Larkin
RF M Davidson
UO J Moses
3S A Newman
2B- T Herr
M T Kelly

NY 1988 AL
SP R Rhoden
SP T John
SP R Dotson
SP J Candelaria
SR C Hudson
RP N Allen
CL D Righetti
RP C Guante
RP S Shields
C D Slaught
1B D Mattingly
2B W Randolph
SS R Santana
3B M Pagliarulo
LF R Henderson
CF C Washington
RF D Winfield
DU J Clark
C- J Skinner
UT- G Ward
M1 B Martin
M2 L Piniella

OAK 1988 AL
SP D Stewart
SP B Welch
SP S Davis
SP C Young
SP T Burns
CL D Eckersley
RP G Nelson
RP R Honeycutt
RP E Plunk
C R Hassey
1B M McGwire
2B G Hubbard
SS W Weiss
3B C Lansford
LM S Javier
CF D Henderson
RF J Canseco
DH- D Baylor
2S M Gallego
DL D Parker
C T Steinbach
LF- L Polonia
M T LaRussa

SEA 1988 AL
SP M Langston
SP M Moore
SR B Swift
SP S Bankhead
SP M Campbell
RP M Jackson
RP J Reed
CL M Schooler
C S Bradley
1B A Davis
2B H Reynolds
SS R Quinones
3B J Presley
LF M Brantley
CF H Cotto
RF- G Wilson
DH- K Phelps
D1 S Balboni
C- D Valle
M1 D Williams
M2 J Snyder

TEX 1988 AL
SP C Hough
SP J Guzman
SP P Kilgus
SR J Russell
SP B Witt
RP M Williams
RP C McMurtry
RP D Mohorcic
CU G Petralli
1B P O'Brien
2I W Wilkerson
SS S Fletcher
3B S Buechele
UT C Espy
CF O McDowell
RF M Sierra
DH- L Parrish
LF P Incaviglia
UO-B Brower
CU- M Stanley
M B Valentine

TOR 1988 AL
SP M Flanagan
SP D Stieb
SP J Clancy
SP J Key
RP D Ward
RS J Cerutti
CL T Henke
RP M Eichhorn
C E Whitt
1B F McGriff
2B M Lee
SS T Fernandez
3B K Gruber
LF G Bell
CF L Moseby
RF J Barfield
DH R Mulliniks
2B N Liriano
OI- R Leach
M J Williams

ATL 1989 NL
SP J Smoltz
SP T Glavine
SP D Lilliquist
SP P Smith
SP M Clary
RP J Boever
RP J Acker
RP Z Smith
RP M Eichhorn
C- J Davis
1B- G Perry
2B J Treadway
SS A Thomas
32 J Blauser
LF L Smith
CF- O McDowell
MR D Murphy
IF D Evans
OI T Gregg
OF- G Berroa
M R Nixon

CHI 1989 NL
SP G Maddux
SP R Sutcliffe
SP M Bielecki
SR P Kilgus
SR S Sanderson
CL M Williams
RS J Pico
RS S Wilson
RP C Schiraldi
C- D Berryhill
1B M Grace
2B R Sandberg
SS S Dunston
3B V Law
LR D Smith
CF J Walton
RF A Dawson

CIN 1989 NL
SP T Browning
SP R Mahler
SP D Jackson
SP J Rijo
SP S Scudder
CL J Franco
RP R Dibble
RP N Charlton
RP T Birtsas
C- J Reed
1B T Benzinger
2B R Oester
SS- B Larkin
3B- C Sabo
UO R Roomes
CF E Davis
RF P O'Neill
LU K Griffey
23- L Quinones
UO H Winningham
M1 P Rose
M2 T Helms

HOU 1989 NL
SP M Scott
SP J Deshaies
SP J Clancy
SP B Knepper
SP B Forsch
RP D Darwin
RP M Portugal
RP L Andersen
RP J Agosto
C- B Biggio
1B G Davis
2B B Doran
SS R Ramirez
3B K Caminiti
LF B Hatcher
CF G Young
RL T Puhl
IO C Reynolds
RL- K Bass
M A Howe

LA 1989 NL
SP O Hershiser
SP T Belcher
SP F Valenzuela
SR M Morgan
CL T Leary
RS J Wetteland
RP R Martinez
RP A Pena
C M Scioscia
1B E Murray
2B W Randolph
SS A Griffin
3B J Hamilton
LF- K Gibson
CF J Shelby
RF M Marshall
UI- D Anderson
MR-J Gonzalez
UT- M Hatcher
M T Lasorda

MON 1989 NL
SP De Martinez
SP B Smith
SP K Gross
SP P Perez
SP M Langston
CL T Burke
RP A McGaffigan
C- N Santovenia
1B A Galarraga
2B T Foley
SS S Owen
3B T Wallach
LF T Raines
CF Da Martinez
RF H Brooks
C M Fitzgerald
MU O Nixon
UT- R Hudler
US- W Johnson
M B Rodgers

NY 1989 NL
SP D Cone
SP S Fernandez
SP R Darling
SP B Ojeda
SP D Gooden
CL R Myers
RP R Aguilera
RP D Aase
C- B Lyons
1U D Magadan
2B G Jefferies
SS K Elster
3B H Johnson
LF K McReynolds
CF- J Samuel
RF D Strawberry
IF- T Teufel
M D Johnson

PHI 1989 NL
SP K Howell
SP D Carman
SP B Ruffin
SR L McWilliams
SP D Cook
RP J Parrett
RP T Mulholland
RP G Harris
CL R McDowell
C D Daulton
1B R Jordan
2B T Herr
SS D Thon
3B- C Hayes
LF- J Kruk
CF- L Dykstra
RF V Hayes
UT C Ford
S3 S Jeltz
UO B Dernier
UO D Murphy
M N Leyva

PIT 1989 NL
SP D Drabek
SP J Smiley
SP W Walk
SR N Heaton
SR J Robinson
RS R Kramer
CL B Landrum
RP B Kipper
RP D Bair
C- J Ortiz
1U- G Redus
2B J Lind
SS- J Bell
3B B Bonilla
LF B Bonds
CF A Van Slyke
RO R Reynolds
UO J Cangelosi
RF G Wilson
1U- B Distefano
M J Leyland

STL 1989 NL
SP J DeLeon
SP J Magrane
SP K Hill
SP S Terry
RP F DiPino
RP K Dayley
RP D Quisenberry
CL T Worrell
C T Pena
1B P Guerrero
2B J Oquendo
SS O Smith
3B T Pendleton
LF V Coleman
CF M Thompson
RF T Brunansky
UO- J Morris
M W Herzog

SD 1989 NL
SP B Hurst
SP E Whitson
SP D Rasmussen
SP W Terrell
SP E Show
RS G Harris
CL M Davis
C B Santiago
1B J Clark
2B R Alomar
SS G Templeton
3B- L Salazar
LR- C James
UO W Mynne
MR T Gwynn
L1 C Martinez
UT B Roberts
M J McKeon

SF 1989 NL
SP R Reuschel
SP D Robinson
SP S Garrelts
SR M LaCoss
RP C Lefferts
RP J Brantley
RS A Hammaker
CL S Bedrosian
C T Kennedy
1B W Clark
2B R Thompson
SS J Uribe
3U E Riles
LF K Mitchell
CF B Butler
RF C Maldonado
C- K Manwaring
UO-D Nixon
UI- K Oberkfell
3B- M Williams
M R Craig

BAL 1989 AL
SP B Milacki
SP J Ballard
SR D Schmidt
SP P Harnisch
RS B Holton
RP M Williamson
CL G Olson
RP M Thurmond
CD M Tettleton
1B R Milligan
2B B Ripken
SS C Ripken
3B- C Worthington
LF P Bradley
MR M Devereaux
RU J Orsulak
DH L Sheets
CF- B Anderson
RM-S Finley
C- B Melvin
1B- J Traber
M F Robinson

BOS 1989 AL
SP R Clemens
SP M Boddicker
SP J Dopson

SR M Smithson
RP D Lamp
RP R Murphy
CL L Smith
RP B Stanley
C R Cerone
1B N Esasky
2B- M Barrett
SS- L Rivera
3B W Boggs
LF M Greenwell
CF- E Burks
MR-K Romine
RD D Evans
RU D Heep
S2 J Reed
C - R Gedman
M J Morgan

CAL 1989 AL
SP B Blyleven
SP M Witt
SP K McCaskill
SP C Finley
SP J Abbott
RP G Minton
RP W Fraser
CL B Harvey
RP B McClure
C L Parrish
1B W Joyner
2B J Ray
SS- D Schofield
3B J Howell
LF C Davis
CF D White
RF C Washington
DH B Downing
SS- K Anderson
M D Rader

CHI 1989 AL
SP M Perez
SP E King
SR S Rosenberg
SP G Hibbard
SP J Reuss
RS S Hillegas
CL B Thigpen
RS B Long
RP R Dotson
C C Fisk
1D- G Walker
21 S Lyons
SS O Guillen
31 C Martinez
LU D Boston
CF D Gallagher
RU I Calderon
DR- H Baines
M J Torborg

CLE 1989 AL
SP B Black
SP J Farrell
SP T Candiotti
SP G Swindell
SR R Yett
RS S Bailes
CL D Jones
RP J Orosco
C A Allanson
1B P O'Brien
2B J Browne
SS F Fermin
3B B Jacoby
ML J Carter
CF- B Komminsk
RF C Snyder
DU D Clark
M1 D Edwards
M2 J Hart

DET 1989 AL
SP F Tanana
SP D Alexander
SP J Morris
RS P Gibson
RP M Henneman
RP F Williams
RP E Nunez
C M Heath
1B D Bergman
2B L Whitaker
SS A Trammell
3B R Schu
LD F Lynn
CF G Pettis
RF C Lemon
D1- K Moreland
OI G Ward
UT- M Brumley
CD- M Nokes
OI- K Williams
M S Anderson

KC 1989 AL
SP B Saberhagen
SP M Gubicza
SP C Leibrandt
SR L Aquino
RS T Gordon
RP J Montgomery
CL S Farr
RP T Leach
C B Boone
1B G Brett
2B F White
SS K Stillwell
3B K Seitzer
LF B Jackson
CF W Wilson
MR J Eisenreich
RD D Tartabull
UT P Tabler
2S B Wellman
M J Wathan

SEA 1989 AL
SP S Bankhead
SP B Holman
SP R Johnson
SR B Swift
SP E Hanson
CL M Schooler
RP M Jackson
RP J Reed
C - D Valle
1B A Davis
2B H Reynolds
SS O Vizquel
3B J Presley
LF G Briley
CF K Griffey
RI D Coles
CU S Bradley
LM H Cotto
DH J Leonard
M J Lefebvre

MIL 1989 AL
SP C Bosio
SP D August
SP T Higuera
SP J Navarro
RP C Crim
RS M Knudson
RS B Krueger
CL D Plesac
C B Surhoff
1B G Brock
2B J Gantner
SS B Spiers
3U P Molitor
LF G Braggs
CF R Yount
RF B Deer
D1- J Meyer
OI M Felder
1D- T Francona
SU- G Sheffield
M T Trebelhorn

MIN 1989 AL
SP A Anderson
SP F Viola
SP R Smith
SP S Rawley
RP J Berenguer
CL J Reardon
RP G Wayne
C B Harper
1B K Hrbek
23 A Newman
SS G Gagne
3B G Gaetti
LF G Gladden
CF K Puckett
RU R Bush
DH- J Dwyer
UT G Larkin
CU T Laudner
OI J Moses
2B- W Backman
RU- C Castillo
M T Kelly

NY 1989 AL
SP A Hawkins
SP C Parker
SP D LaPoint
SR C Cary
RP L Guetterman
CL D Righetti
RP L McCullers
RS E Plunk
C D Slaught
1B D Mattingly
2B S Sax
SS A Espinoza
3B- M Pagliarulo
OF M Hall
CF R Kelly
RF J Barfield
DU S Balboni
DU- K Phelps
M1 D Green
M2 B Dent

OAK 1989 AL
SP D Stewart
SP M Moore
SP B Welch
SP S Davis
SP C Young
RP T Burns
CL D Eckersley
RP R Honeycutt
RP G Nelson
C T Steinbach
1B M McGwire
23 T Phillips
S2 M Gallego
3B C Lansford

LF- R Henderson
CF D Henderson
RM S Javier
DH D Parker
C - R Hassey
SS- W Weiss
M T LaRussa

ATL 1990 NL
SP J Smoltz
SP T Glavine
SP C Leibrandt
SR M Clary
SP S Avery
RP J Castillo
RP M Grant
RP P Luecken
C G Olson
1R D Justice
2B J Treadway
SS J Blauser
3B J Presley
LF L Smith
ML R Gant
RF- D Murphy
UT T Gregg
UI M Lemke
MU O McDowell
SS- A Thomas
M1 R Nixon
M2 B Cox

CHI 1990 NL
SP G Maddux
SP M Harkey
SP M Bielecki
RS S Wilson
RS L Lancaster

RP P Assenmacher
RS J Pico
C J Girardi
1B M Grace
2B R Sandberg
SS S Dunston
3B L Salazar
LM D Dascenzo
CF J Walton
RF A Dawson
3U D Ramos
LU D Smith
UM-D Clark
MU-M Wynne
M D Zimmer

CIN 1990 NL
SP T Browning
SP J Rijo
SP J Armstrong
SR R Mahler
SP D Jackson
RS N Charlton
CL R Myers
RP B Dibble
CU S Bradley
LM H Cotto
DH J Leonard
C J Oliver
1B T Benzinger
2B M Duncan
SS B Larkin
3B C Sabo
LM B Hatcher
ML E Davis
RF P O'Neill
1U H Morris
UI- L Quinones
MU-H Winningham
M L Piniella

HOU 1990 NL
SP J Deshaies
SP M Scott
SP M Portugal
SP B Gullickson
SR D Darwin
RP J Agosto
CL D Smith
RP L Andersen
RS J Clancy
C C Biggio
1B- G Davis
2B B Doran
SS R Ramirez
3B K Caminiti
UT F Stubbs
MS E Yelding
RF G Wilson
UT C Candaele
RU- E Anthony
M A Howe

LA 1990 NL
SP R Martinez
SP M Morgan
SP F Valenzuela
SP T Belcher
RP T Crews
CL J Howell
RS M Hartley
RP J Gott
C M Scioscia
1B E Murray
2B J Samuel
SS A Griffin
3B M Sharperson
LF K Daniels
MU S Javier
RF H Brooks
UO J Gonzalez
UO M Gwynn
32 L Harris
CF- K Gibson
IO- M Hatcher
M T Lasorda

MON 1990 NL
SP De Martinez
SP O Boyd
SP K Gross
SP M Gardner
SP Z Smith
CL T Burke
RP B Sampen
RP S Frey
RP D Hall
C M Fitzgerald
1B A Galarraga
2B D DeShields
SS S Owen
3B T Wallach
LF T Raines
CF Da Martinez
RF L Walker
UO M Grissom
MU O Nixon
OI- W Aldrete

UT- J Noboa
M B Rodgers

NY 1990 NL
SP F Viola
SP D Gooden
SP D Cone
SP S Fernandez
SR R Darling
RS B Ojeda
CL J Franco
RP A Pena
RP W Whitehurst
C' M Sasser
1B D Magadan
2B G Jefferies
SS- K Elster
3S H Johnson
LF K McReynolds
CF D Boston
RF D Strawberry
UO-M Carreon
MU-K Miller
IF- T O'Malley
M1 D Johnson
M2 B Harrelson

PHI 1990 NL
SP P Combs
SP J Mulholland
SP B Ruffin
SP D DeJesus
SP K Howell
RS D Cook
RP R McDowell
RP D Akerfelds
RP D Carman
C D Daulton
1B- R Jordan
2B T Herr
SS D Thon
3B C Hayes
OI J Kruk
CF L Dykstra
RL V Hayes
UT R Ready
M N Leyva

PIT 1990 NL
SP D Drabek
SP J Smiley
SP N Heaton
SP B Walk
RS B Patterson
RP B Landrum
RP S Belinda
RP B Kipper
C - M LaValliere
1B S Bream
2B J Lind
SS J Bell
3B J King
LF B Bonds
CF A Van Slyke
RB B Bonilla
3U W Backman
1B- G Redus
UO-R Reynolds
C - D Slaught
RP J Reed
M J Leyland

STL 1990 NL
SP J Magrane
SP J DeLeon
SP B Tewksbury
SP J Tudor
SP B Smith
CL L Smith
RP F DiPino
RP K Dayley
RP S Terry
CU T Zeile
1B P Guerrero
2B J Oquendo
SS O Smith
3B T Pendleton
LF V Coleman
CF W McGee
RU M Thompson
UT D Collins
UT- R Hudler
M1 W Herzog
M2 R Schoendienst
M3 J Torre

SD 1990 NL
SP E Whitson
SP B Hurst
SP A Benes
SP D Rasmussen
RP G Harris
RS E Show
RS C Schiraldi
CL C Lefferts
C - B Santiago
1B J Clark
2B R Alomar

SS G Templeton
3B M Pagliarulo
L3 B Roberts
ML J Carter
RF T Gwynn
1U P Stephenson
UO-S Abner
UO-F Lynn
M1 J McKeon
M2 G Riddoch

SF 1990 NL
SP J Burkett
SP S Garrelts
SP D Robinson
SR T Wilson
CL J Brantley
RP S Bedrosian
RS A Hammaker
RP M Thurmond
C T Kennedy
1B W Clark
2B R Thompson
SS J Uribe
3B M Williams
LF K Mitchell
CF B Butler
RU M Kingery
C - G Carter
UT- G Litton
UI- E Riles
M R Craig

BAL 1990 AL
SP P Harnisch
SP D Johnson
SP B Milacki
SR J Ballard
SP B McDonald
RP J Mitchell
CL G Olson
RP M Williamson
RP J Price
CD M Tettleton
1B R Milligan
2B B Ripken
SS C Ripken
3B C Worthington
LF- P Bradley
CF M Devereaux
RM S Finley
DH- S Horn
RU J Orsulak
UO-B Anderson
C - B Melvin
M F Robinson

BOS 1990 AL
SP M Boddicker
SP R Clemens
SP G Harris
SP D Kiecker
SP T Bolton
RP D Lamp
RS W Gardner
CL J Reardon
RP R Murphy
C T Pena
1B C Quintana
2B J Reed
SS L Rivera
3B W Boggs
LF M Greenwell
CF E Burks
RF T Brunansky
DH D Evans
M J Morgan

CAL 1990 AL
SP C Finley
SP M Langston
SP J Abbott
SP K McCaskill
SP B Blyleven
RP M Eichhorn
CL B Harvey
RP W Fraser
RP M Fetters
C L Parrish
1B- W Joyner
2B J Ray
SS D Schofield
3B J Howell
UO D Bichette
CF D White
RF D Winfield
DH- B Downing
DL C Davis
2I D Hill
LU L Polonia
UO-M Venable
M D Rader

CHI 1990 AL
SP G Hibbard
SP J McDowell
SP M Perez

SP E King
CL B Thigpen
RS W Edwards
RP D Pall
RP B Jones
C B Fisk
1B- C Martinez
2B S Fletcher
SS O Guillen
3B R Ventura
LF I Calderon
CF L Johnson
RF S Sosa
DO G Pasqua
D1- R Kittle
1U- S Lyons
M J Torborg

CLE 1990 AL
SP G Swindell
SP T Candiotti
SP S Black
SR S Valdez
CL D Jones
RP S Olin
RP J Orosco
C S Alomar
31 B Jacoby
2B J Browne
SS F Fermin
UI C Baerga
LR C Maldonado
MU M Webster
RF C Snyder
DH C James
UT- D James
M J McNamara

DET 1990 AL
SP J Morris
SP F Tanana
SP D Petry
SP J Robinson
RP M Henneman
RP P Gibson
RP J Gleaton
RP E Nunez
C M Heath
1B C Fielder
2B L Whitaker
SS A Trammell
32 T Phillips
LU G Ward
CF L Moseby
RF C Lemon
D1 D Bergman
OF L Sheets
M S Anderson

KC 1990 AL
SP T Gordon
SP M Appier
SP B Saberhagen
SP S Davis
RS S Farr
RP J Montgomery
RP M Davis
C M Macfarlane
1U B Brett
2B- F White
SS K Stillwell
3B K Seitzer
UO W Wilson
ML B Jackson
RL J Eisenreich
D1 G Perry
2I- B Pecota
RD- D Tartabull
M J Wathan

MIL 1990 AL
SP T Higuera
SP M Knudson
SR J Navarro
SP R Robinson
SP C Bosio
RS B Krueger
RP C Crim
CL D Plesac
RS T Edens
C B Surhoff
1B G Brock
2B- J Gantner
SS B Spiers
3B G Sheffield
LR M Felder
CF R Yount
RF B Deer
DH D Parker
21 P Molitor
LF G Vaughn
SS- E Diaz
UO-D Hamilton
M T Trebelhorn

MIN 1990 AL
SP A Anderson
SP K Tapani
SP R Smith
SP D West
SP M Guthrie
RS K Erickson
RP J Berenguer
CL R Aguilera
RP T Drummond
C B Harper
1B K Hrbek
2S A Newman
SS G Gagne
3B G Gaetti
LF D Gladden
CF K Puckett
UO S Mack
UT G Larkin
OI J Moses
M T Kelly

NY 1990 AL
SP T Leary
SP A Hawkins
SP D LaPoint
SP C Cary
RS G Cadaret
RP L Guetterman
CL D Righetti
RP J Robinson
C B Geren
1B D Mattingly
2B S Sax
SS A Espinoza
3B- R Velarde
LU- O Azocar
CF R Kelly
RF J Barfield
DU S Balboni
OF M Hall
3B- J Leyritz
CD-M Nokes
M1 B Dent
M2 S Merrill

OAK 1990 AL
SP D Stewart
SP B Welch
SP S Sanderson
SP M Moore
SP C Young
CL D Eckersley
RP T Burns
RP G Nelson
RP R Honeycutt
CU T Steinbach
1B M McGwire
2B- W Randolph
SS W Weiss
3B C Lansford
LF R Henderson
CF D Henderson
RF J Jose
RD J Canseco
2S M Gallego
UT- L Blankenship
CU- R Hassey
M T LaRussa

SEA 1990 AL
SP E Hanson
SP M Young
SP R Johnson
SP B Holman
RS B Swift
CL M Schooler
RP M Jackson
RP K Comstock
C D Valle
1B P O'Brien
2B H Reynolds
SS- O Vizquel
3B E Martinez
RL G Briley
CF K Griffey
RL H Cotto
D1 A Davis
CU S Bradley
LD J Leonard
M J Lefebvre

TEX 1990 AL
SP B Witt
SP C Hough
SP N Ryan
SP K Brown
RS M Jeffcoat
RP K Rogers
RS J Moyer
RP B Arnsberg
C G Petralli
1B R Palmeiro
2B J Franco
SS J Huson
3B- S Buechele

.F P Incaviglia
CF G Pettis
RF R Sierra
DH H Baines
OI J Daugherty
SI J Kunkel
CU M B Valentine

TOR 1990 AL
SP D Stieb
SP T Stottlemyre
SR D Wells
SP J Key
SP J Cerutti
RP D Ward
CL T Henke
RP F Wills
RP J Acker
P Borders
1B F McGriff
2B M Lee
SS T Fernandez
3B K Gruber
OI G Bell
CF M Wilson
RF J Felix
J Olerud
JO G Hill
C G Myers
M C Gaston

ATL 1991 NL
SP T Glavine
SP C Leibrandt
SP J Smoltz
SP S Avery
SP M Stanton
CL J Berenguer
RP K Mercker
C G Olson
1B B Hunter
2B M Lemke
SS R Belliard
3B T Pendleton
JO O Nixon
CF R Gant
RF D Justice
SI J Blauser
LF L Smith
2B J Treadway
3B B Sream
M B Cox

CHI 1991 NL
SP G Maddux
SP M Bielecki
SP S Boskie
SP F Castillo
RP R Sutcliffe
RS L Lancaster
RP P Assenmacher
RS B Scanlan
RP C McElroy
C R Wilkins
1B M Grace
2B R Sandberg
SS D Dunston
3B L Salazar
OI G Bell
CF J Walton
RF A Dawson
ML D Dascenzo
JT C Walker
JO D Smith
SS J Vizcaino
M1 D Zimmer
M2 J Altobelli
M3 J Essian

CIN 1991 NL
SP T Browning
SP J Rijo
SP J Armstrong
SR S Scudder
C Hammond
RS R Myers
CL R Dibble
RS N Charlton
RP T Power
C J Oliver
2 H Morris
2B B Doran
SS B Larkin
3B C Sabo
LM B Hatcher
RF P O'Neill
RS M Duncan
JI L Quinones
MU H Winningham
R G Braggs
C J Reed
M L Piniella

HOU 1991 NL
SP P Harnisch
SP M Portugal
SP J Deshaies
SR D Kile
SP J Jones
RP A Osuna
RP C Schilling
RP J Corsi
RP D Henry
C C Biggio
1B J Bagwell
2U C Candaele
SS- E Yelding
3B K Caminiti
LF L Gonzalez
MU G Young
CF S Finley
UI R Ramirez
UO- M Davidson
M A Howe

LA 1991 NL
SP M Morgan
SP R Martinez
SP T Belcher
SP B Ojeda
SP O Hershiser
RS K Gross
RP T Crews
RP J Gott
CL J Howell
C M Scioscia
1B E Murray
2B J Samuel
SS A Griffin
3B L Harris
LF K Daniels
CF B Butler
RF D Strawberry
CU G Carter
OI S Javier
3I M Sharperson
UO- C Gwynn
M T Lasorda

MON 1991 NL
SP De Martinez
SP M Gardner
SP B Barnes
SP C Nabholz
SP O Boyd
RP B Jones
RS B Sampen
RP S Ruskin
RP J Fassero
C - G Reyes
1B A Galarraga
2B D DeShields
SS S Owen
3B T Wallach
LF I Calderon
CF M Grissom
UO Da Martinez
R1 L Walker
S1- T Foley
M1 B Rodgers
M2 T Runnells

NY 1991 NL
SP D Cone
SP F Viola
SP D Gooden
SR W Whitehurst
SP R Darling
RS P Schourek
CL J Franco
RP J Innis
RP A Pena
C - R Cerone
1B D Magadan
23 G Jefferies
SS K Elster
3U H Johnson
LF K McReynolds
MR D Boston
RF H Brooks
UO M Carreon
2O K Miller
OC- M Sasser
M1 B Harrelson
M2 M Cubbage

PHI 1991 NL
SP T Mulholland
SP T Greene
SP J DeJesus
SR B Ruffin
SP D Cox
CL M Williams
RP J Boever
RP R McDowell
RP D Akerfelds
C - D Daulton
1O J Kruk
2B M Morandini

SS D Thon
3B C Hayes
LF W Chamberlain
ML- V Hayes
RF D Murphy
1U R Jordan
IF- W Backman
UO- J Morris
M1 N Leyva
M2 J Fregosi

PIT 1991 NL
SP D Drabek
SP Z Smith
SP J Smiley
SP R Tomlin
SP B Walk
RP S Belinda
RP B Landrum
RS V Palacios
RP N Heaton
C M LaValliere
1B O Merced
2B J Lind
SS J Bell
R3 B Bonilla
LF B Bonds
CF A Van Slyke
OI G Varsho
UT J Redus
OI- L McClendon
UI- C Wilkerson
M J Leyland

STL 1991 NL
SP B Smith
SP B Tewksbury
SP K Hill
SP O Olivares
SP J DeLeon
CL L Smith
RP J Agosto
RP S Terry
RP C Carpenter
C T Pagnozzi
1B P Guerrero
2B J Oquendo
SS O Smith
3B T Zeile
LU M Thompson
CF R Lankford
RF F Jose
UT R Hudler
2B G Pena
1U G Perry
LF- B Gilkey
M J Torre

SD 1991 NL
SP A Benes
SP B Hurst
SP D Rasmussen
SP G Harris
RP M Maddux
CL C Lefferts
RP R Rodriguez
C B Santiago
1B F McGriff
2O B Roberts
SS T Fernandez
3B- J Howell
LU J Clark
MU D Jackson
RF T Gwynn
UO T Howard
23- T Teufel
M G Riddoch

SF 1991 NL
SP B Black
SP J Burkett
SR T Wilson
SR D Robinson
RS K Downs
RP J Brantley
CL D Righetti
RP F Oliveras
C - S Decker
1B W Clark
2B R Thompson
SS- J Uribe
3B M Williams
UT M Felder
MR W McGee
RU K Bass
SI D Anderson
LF K Mitchell
OI- M Kingery
M R Craig

BAL 1991 AL
SP B Milacki
SP B McDonald
SP J Ballard
SP J Mesa
SP J Robinson
CL G Olson

RP M Flanagan
RP T Frohwirth
RP M Williamson
C C Hoiles
1B R Milligan
2B B Ripken
SS C Ripken
3B L Gomez
LO B Anderson
CF M Devereaux
LR J Orsulak
DH S Horn
2B J Bell
RU D Evans
UT- D Segui
M1 F Robinson
M2 J Oates

BOS 1991 AL
SP R Clemens
SR G Harris
SR J Hesketh
SP M Gardiner
SP T Bolton
CL J Reardon
RP D Lamp
RP J Gray
RP T Fossas
C T Pena
1B C Quintana
2B J Reed
SS L Rivera
3B W Boggs
LF M Greenwell
CF E Burks
RF T Brunansky
DH J Clark
UT- S Lyons
M J Morgan

CAL 1991 AL
SP M Langston
SP J Abbott
SP C Finley
SP K McCaskill
CL B Harvey
RP M Eichhorn
RP J Robinson
RP S Bailes
C L Parrish
1B W Joyner
2B L Sojo
SS D Schofield
3B G Gaetti
LF L Polonia
MR- D Gallagher
RF D Winfield
DH D Parker
UO- M Venable
M1 D Rader
M2 B Rodgers

CHI 1991 AL
SP J McDowell
SP C Hough
SP G Hibbard
SP A Fernandez
RS M Perez
CL B Thigpen
RP S Radinsky
RP D Pall
C C Fisk
1R D Pasqua
2B- S Fletcher
SS O Guillen
3B V Ventura
LF T Raines
CF L Johnson
RF S Sosa
D1 F Thomas
2B J Cora
UI C Grebeck
M J Torborg

CLE 1991 AL
SP G Swindell
SP C Nagy
SP E King
SR N Nichols
SP T Candiotti
RP D Otto
RP S Hillegas
CL S Olin
RP J Shaw
C J Skinner
1B- B Jacoby
2S- M Lewis
SS F Fermin
32 C Baerga
LD A Belle
CF A Cole
RF- M Whiten
DO C James
1O J Browne
1U- M Aldrete

M1 J McNamara
M2 M Hargrove

DET 1991 AL
SP B Gullickson
SP W Terrell
SP F Tanana
SR M Leiter
CL M Henneman
RP P Gibson
RS J Cerutti
RP J Gleaton
C M Tettleton
1U- D Bergman
2B L Whitaker
SS A Trammell
3S T Fryman
LF- L Moseby
CF M Cuyler
RF R Deer
1B C Fielder
LD- P Incaviglia
UT T Phillips
M S Anderson

KC 1991 AL
SP K Appier
SP B Saberhagen
SP M Boddicker
SR L Aquino
SP M Gubicza
RS T Gordon
CL J Montgomery
RS S Davis
RS M Davis
C - B Mayne
1B- T Benzinger
2B T Shumpert
SS K Stillwell
3B B Pecota
OI J Eisenreich
CF B McRae
RF D Tartabull
DH G Brett
LU K Gibson
S2- D Howard
C - M Macfarlane
3B- K Seitzer
M1 J Wathan
M2 B Schaefer
M3 H McRae

MIL 1991 AL
SP J Navarro
SP C Bosio
SP B Wegman
SP D August
RS D Plesac
RP C Crim
RP J Machado
RP D Holmes
C B Surhoff
1B F Stubbs
2B W Randolph
SS B Spiers
32 J Gantner
LF G Vaughn
CF R Yount
RF D Bichette
D1 P Molitor
UO D Hamilton
S3- D Sveum
M T Trebelhorn

MIN 1991 AL
SP J Morris
SP K Tapani
SP S Erickson
SP A Anderson
CL R Aguilera
RS M Guthrie
RP C Willis
RS R Bedrosian
C B Harper
1B K Hrbek
2B C Knoblauch
SS G Gagne
3B M Pagliarulo
LF D Gladden
CF K Puckett
RL S Mack
DH C Davis
UT G Larkin
3U S Leius
IO A Newman
OI- R Bush
M T Kelly

NY 1991 AL
SP S Sanderson
SP J Johnson
SR J Leary
SP W Taylor
RS G Cadaret
RS E Plunk
RP L Sampson
CL S Farr

C M Nokes
1B D Mattingly
2B S Sax
SS A Espinoza
3B- P Kelly
ML R Kelly
CF- B Williams
UO M Hall
DU K Maas
RF- J Barfield
LU- H Meulens
M S Merrill

OAK 1991 AL
SP D Stewart
SP B Welch
SP M Moore
SP J Slusarski
CL D Eckersley
RP C Young
RP S Chitren
RP J Klink
C T Steinbach
1B M McGwire
2B M Gallego
SS- M Bordick
3I E Riles
LF R Henderson
CF D Henderson
RF J Canseco
DH H Baines
UO W Wilson
2O- L Blankenship
M T LaRussa

SEA 1991 AL
SP R Johnson
SP B Holman
SP R DeLucia
SP E Hanson
SR E Krueger
RP B Swift
RP M Jackson
RP R Swan
C D Valle
1B P O'Brien
2B H Reynolds
SS O Vizquel
3B E Martinez
LR G Briley
CF K Griffey
RF J Buhner
DH A Davis
C - S Bradley
S3- J Schaefer
M J Lefebvre

TEX 1991 AL
SP K Brown
SP N Ryan
SP J Guzman
RS K Rogers
CL J Russell
RS G Alexander
RS J Barfield
C - I Rodriguez
1B R Palmeiro
2B J Franco
SS J Huson
3B S Buechele
ML J Gonzalez
CF G Pettis
RF S Sierra
DH B Downing
OF M Reimer
SI- M Diaz
3L- D Palmer
C - G Petralli
CU- M Stanley
M B Valentine

TOR 1991 AL
SP T Stottlemyre
SP J Key
SP D Wells
SP J Guzman
SP T Candiotti
RP D Ward
RP M Timlin
RP J Acker
CL T Henke
CL G Myers
1B J Olerud
2B R Alomar
SS M Lee
3B K Gruber
LF- C Maldonado
CF D White
RL J Carter
DH- R Mulliniks
C P Borders
DU- P Tabler
OF- M Wilson
M1 C Gaston
M2 G Tenace
M3 C Gaston

ATL 1992 NL
SP J Smoltz
SP S Avery
SP T Glavine
SP C Leibrandt
RP K Mercker
RP M Stanton
RP M Freeman
C - G Olson
1B S Bream
2B M Lemke
SS R Belliard
3B T Pendleton
LF R Gant
CF O Nixon
RF D Justice
RP D Berryhill
SS J Blauser
1B B Hunter
MU- D Sanders
UM- L Smith
M B Cox

CHI 1992 NL
SP G Maddux
SP M Morgan
SP F Castillo
SP D Jackson
RP B Scanlan
RS J Bullinger
RP C McElroy
RS J Robinson
C - J Girardi
1B M Grace
2B R Sandberg
SS- R Sanchez
3B- S Buechele
LF D May
MO D Dascenzo
RF A Dawson
UT L Salazar
UO D Smith
S3- J Vizcaino
C - R Wilkins
M J Lefebvre

CIN 1992 NL
SP T Belcher
SP G Swindell
SP J Rijo
SP C Hammond
CL N Charlton
RP R Dibble
RP D Henry
RP S Bankhead
C J Oliver
1B H Morris
2B B Doran
SS B Larkin
3B- C Sabo
ML R Sanders
CF D Martinez
RF P O'Neill
UT B Roberts
LR- G Braggs
M L Piniella

HOU 1992 NL
SP P Harnisch
SP B Henry
SP J Jones
SP D Kile
SP M Portugal
RP D Jones
RP X Hernandez
RP J Boever
RS W Blair
C E Taubensee
1B J Bagwell
2B C Biggio
SS- A Cedeno
3B K Caminiti
LF L Gonzalez
CF S Finley
RF E Anthony
UT C Candaele
LR P Incaviglia
M A Howe

LA 1992 NL
SP O Hershiser
SP K Gross
SP T Candiotti
SP B Ojeda
SP R Martinez
RP R McDowell
RP J Gott
RP T Crews
RP S Wilson
C M Scioscia
1B E Karros
2I L Harris
SS J Offerman
3B D Hansen
LF- E Davis
CF B Butler

UO M Webster
OI T Benzinger
UI M Sharperson
M T Lasorda

MON 1992 NL
SP D Martinez
SP K Hill
SP C Nabholz
SP M Gardner
SP B Barnes
CL J Wetteland
RP M Rojas
RP J Fassero
RP B Sampen
C - G Carter
31 T Wallach
2B D DeShields
SS S Owen
3U B Barberie
LU M Alou
CF M Grissom
RF L Walker
LU J Vander Wal
1U- A Cianfrocco
C - D Fletcher
M1 T Runnells
M2 F Alou

NY 1992 NL
SP S Fernandez
SP D Cone
SP D Gooden
SP P Schourek
RS A Young
RS W Whitehurst
RP J Innis
RP G Gibson
C T Hundley
1B M Murray
2B- W Randolph
SS D Schofield
3B D Magadan
LU D Boston
CF H Johnson
RF B Bonilla
UO D Gallagher
UI B Pecota
UT C Walker
IC- M Sasser
M J Torborg

PHI 1992 NL
SP T Mulholland
SR C Schilling
SR K Abbott
SP B Rivera
CL M Williams
RS C Brantley
RP M Hartley
RP B Jones
C D Daulton
1B J Kruk
2B M Morandini
SS- J Bell
3B D Hollins
IO M Duncan
CF- L Dykstra
RO R Amaro
ML- S Javier
1U- R Jordan
M J Fregosi

PIT 1992 NL
SP D Drabek
SP T Tomlin
SP Z Smith
SR B Walk
RP R Mason
RP S Belinda
RS D Neagle
RP B Patterson
C - M LaValliere
1B O Merced
2B J Lind
SS J Bell
3B- S Buechele
LF B Bonds
CF A Van Slyke
RO C Espy
3I J King
UO G Varsho
RU- L McClendon
C - D Slaught
M J Leyland

STL 1992 NL
SP B Tewksbury
SP O Olivares
SP R Cormier
SP D Osborne
SP M Clark
CL L Smith
RS J DeLeon
RP M Perez
RP C Carpenter
C T Pagnozzi

1B- A Galarraga
2B- L Alicea
SS O Smith
3B T Zeile
LF B Gilkey
CF R Lankford
RF F Jose
UO M Thompson
UR-G Perry
M J Torre

SD 1992 NL
SP A Benes
SP B Hurst
SP C Lefferts
SP G Harris
SP F Seminara
CL R Myers
RP R Rodriguez
RP J Melendez
RP M Maddux
C B Santiago
1B F McGriff
2B K Stillwell
SS T Fernandez
3B G Sheffield
LF J Clark
CF D Jackson
RF T Gwynn
OF O Azocar
23 T Teufel
UO-K Ward
M1 G Riddoch
M2 J Riggleman

SF 1992 NL
SP J Burkett
SP B Black
SP B Swift
SP T Wilson
RP R Beck
RP J Brantley
RP B Hickerson
RP M Jackson
C K Manwaring
1B W Clark
2B R Thompson
SS R Clayton
3B M Williams
OI M Felder
CF D Lewis
RU W McGee
LU C James
UT C Snyder
LU- K Bass
M R Craig

BAL 1992 AL
SP M Mussina
SP R Sutcliffe
SP B McDonald
SP B Milacki
RP T Frohwirth
RP A Mills
CL G Olson
RP S Davis
C - C Hoiles
1B R Milligan
2B B Ripken
SS C Ripken
3B L Gomez
LF B Anderson
CF M Devereaux
RF J Orsulak
DH G Davis
2U M McLemore
1B D Segui
RU- C Martinez
M J Oates

BOS 1992 AL
SP R Clemens
SP F Viola
SP J Hesketh
SP J Dopson
SR M Gardiner
RS D Darwin
RP G Harris
RS M Young
RP P Quantrill
C T Pena
1B M Vaughn
2B J Reed
SS L Rivera
3B W Boggs
LF- B Hatcher
ML B Zupcic
RU T Brunansky
DH- J Clark
13 S Cooper
OF H Winningham
RU P Plantier
M B Hobson

CAL 1992 AL
SP M Langston
SP J Abbott
SP C Finley
SP J Valera
SP B Blyleven
CL J Grahe
RP C Crim
RP M Eichhorn
C - M Fitzgerald
1B L Stevens
2B L Sojo
SS G DiSarcina
31 G Gaetti
LD L Polonia
CF J Felix
UO C Curtis
DH-H Brooks
32 R Gonzales
RF- V Hayes
M1 B Rodgers
M2 J Wathan
M3 B Rodgers

CHI 1992 AL
SP J McDowell
SP K McCaskill
SP A Fernandez
SP G Hibbard
SP C Hough
RS W Alvarez
RP R Hernandez
CL B Thigpen
RP T Leach
C R Karkovice
1B F Thomas
2B S Sax
SS- C Grebeck
3B R Ventura
LF T Raines
CF L Johnson
RF- S Abner
DH G Bell
RF- D Pasqua
M G Lamont

CLE 1992 AL
SP C Nagy
SR J Armstrong
SP D Cook
SP S Scudder
CL S Olin
RS R Nichols
RP T Power
RP E Plunk
C - S Alomar
1B P Sorrento
2B C Baerga
SS M Lewis
3B B Jacoby
LO T Howard
CF K Lofton
RF M Whiten
DL A Belle
UO G Hill
C - J Ortiz
M M Hargrove

DET 1992 AL
SP B Gullickson
SP F Tanana
SR W Terrell
SR M Leiter
RS J Doherty
CL M Henneman
RP L Lancaster
RP- K Knudsen
CD M Tettleton
1U- D Bergman
2B L Whitaker
SS T Fryman
3B S Livingstone
LF D Gladden
CF- M Cuyler
RF D Deer
1D C Fielder
LU M Carreon
UT T Phillips
UT- S Barnes
M S Anderson

KC 1992 AL
SP K Appier
SP H Pichardo
SP M Gubicza
SP R Reed
CL J Montgomery
RS T Gordon
RP R Meacham
RS M Boddicker
C M Macfarlane
1B W Joyner
2B K Miller
SS- D Howard
3B L Jefferies
LF K McReynolds
CF B McRae
RU J Eisenreich
DH G Brett
S2 C Wilkerson
C - B Mayne
RU- G Thurman
M H McRae

MIL 1992 AL
SP B Wegman
SP J Navarro
SP C Bosio
SP R Bones
SP C Eldred
CL D Henry
RP D Plesac
RP M Fetters
RP J Austin
RP B Surhoff
1U- F Stubbs
2B S Fletcher
SS P Listach
3B K Seitzer
LF G Vaughn
CF R Yount
RM D Hamilton
D1 P Molitor
RF D Bichette
23 J Gantner
M P Garner

MIN 1992 AL
SP J Smiley
SP K Tapani
SP S Erickson
SP B Krueger
CL R Aguilera
RP C Willis
RP T Edens
C B Harper
1B K Hrbek
2B C Knoblauch
SS G Gagne
3B S Leius
LF S Mack
CF K Puckett
RF P Munoz
DH C Davis
OI R Bush
UT G Larkin
M T Kelly

NY 1992 AL
SP M Perez
SP S Sanderson
SP S Kamieniecki
RS G Cadaret
RP R Monteleone
CL S Farr
RP J Habyan
C M Nokes
1B D Mattingly
2B P Kelly
S2 A Stankiewicz
3B C Hayes
LU M Hall
ML M Kelly
RD D Tartabull
DU K Maas
SU R Velarde
M B Showalter

OAK 1992 AL
SP M Moore
SP R Darling
SP D Stewart
SP B Welch
CL D Eckersley
RP J Parrett
RS K Campbell
RP G Nelson
C T Steinbach
1B M McGwire
2S M Bordick
SS W Weiss
3B C Lansford
LF R Henderson
CF W Wilson
RF- J Canseco
DH H Baines
2O L Blankenship
3O J Browne
M T LaRussa

SEA 1992 AL
SP D Fleming
SP R Johnson
SP E Hanson
RS R Swan
RP J Nelson
RP M Schooler
RP C Jones
C D Valle
1D P O'Brien
2B H Reynolds
SS O Vizquel
3B E Martinez
LM H Cotto
CF K Griffey
RF J Buhner
1D T Martinez
LD K Mitchell
UT- G Briley
M B Plummer

TEX 1992 AL
SP K Brown
SP J Guzman
SP B Witt
SP N Ryan
RS T Burns
RP K Rogers
CL J Russell
C I Rodriguez
1B R Palmeiro
2I A Newman
SS-D Thon
3B D Palmer
LU K Reimer
CF J Gonzalez
RF J Sierra
DH B Downing
S2 J Huson
CU-G Petralli
23 J Gantner
M1 B Valentine
M2 T Harrah

TOR 1992 AL
SP J Morris
SP J Key
SP J Guzman
SP T Stottlemyre
SR D Wells
RP D Ward
CL T Henke
RP M Hentgen
C P Borders
1B J Olerud
2B R Alomar
SS M Lee
3B K Gruber
LF C Maldonado
CF D White
RF J Carter
DH D Winfield
M C Gaston

ATL 1993 NL
SP G Maddux
SP J Smoltz
SP T Glavine
SP S Avery
RP G McMichael
CL M Stanton
RS K Mercker
RP J Howell
C B Berryhill
1B S Bream
2B M Lemke
SS J Blauser
3B T Pendleton
LF R Gant
CF O Nixon
RF D Justice
S2- R Belliard
C - G Olson
MU-D Sanders
M B Cox

CHI 1993 NL
SP M Morgan
SP J Guzman
SP G Hibbard
SP M Harkey
SP F Castillo
CL R Myers
RS J Bautista
RP B Scanlan
RP S Boskie
C R Wilkins
1B M Grace
2B R Sandberg
SS R Sanchez
3B S Buechele
LF D May
UO D Smith
RM S Sosa
S3 J Vizcaino
CF W Wilson
M J Lefebvre

CIN 1993 NL
SP J Rijo
SP T Pugh
SP T Belcher
SP T Browning
SP J Smiley
RS B Ayala
RP J Reardon
RP J Spradlin
C J Oliver
1B H Morris
2U J Samuel
SS B Larkin
3B C Sabo
3B- K Mitchell
MO J Brumfield
RF R Sanders
UI J Branson
1U- R Milligan
CF M Grissom
2B- B Roberts
M1 T Perez
M2 D Johnson

COL 1993 NL
SP A Reynoso
SR W Blair
RS B Ruffin
CL D Holmes
RP S Reed
RS J Parrett
C - J Girardi
1B A Galarraga
2L E Young
SS V Castilla
3B C Hayes
L1 J Clark
MU A Cole
RF D Bichette
UO D Boston
MU-C Jones
C - D Sheaffer
UT- J Tatum
M D Baylor

FLA 1993 NL
SP C Hough
SP J Armstrong
SP C Hammond
SP R Bowen
SR L Aquino
CL B Harvey
RP R Lewis
RP M Turner
C B Santiago
1B O Destrade
2B B Barberie
SS W Weiss
3B- G Sheffield
LF J Conine
CF C Carr
RF- D Whitmore
UO G Briley
IO R Renteria
UI- A Arias
M R Lachemann

HOU 1993 NL
SP D Drabek
SP P Harnisch
SP M Portugal
SP G Swindell
SP D Kile
CL D Jones
RP X Hernandez
RS B Williams
RP T Edens
C - E Taubensee
1B J Bagwell
2B C Biggio
SS A Cedeno
3B K Caminiti
LF L Gonzalez
CF S Finley
RF E Anthony
UO K Bass
UI- C Donnels
C - S Servais
M A Howe

LA 1993 NL
SP O Hershiser
SP T Candiotti
SP R Martinez
SP K Gross
SP P Astacio
RP J Martinez
CL J Gott
RP R McDowell
RP R Trlicek
C M Piazza
1B E Karros
2B J Reed
SS J Offerman
3B T Wallach
LF E Davis
CF B Butler
RF C Snyder
IO L Harris
U2- D Hansen
UO-M Webster
M T Lasorda

MON 1993 NL
SP D Martinez
SP K Hill
SP C Nabholz
RS J Fassero
CL J Wetteland
RS B Barnes
RP M Rojas
C D Fletcher
1B- G Colbrunn
2B D DeShields
SS W Cordero
3B S Berry
LF M Alou
CF M Grissom
RF L Walker
UT L Frazier
3S M Lansing
UT J Vander Wal
13- F Bolick
M F Alou

NY 1993 NL
SP D Gooden
SP F Tanana
SP E Hillman
SP M Saberhagen
SR P Schourek
RP S Fernandez
RS A Young
RP J Innis
RP M Maddux
C T Hundley
1B E Murray
2B J Kent
SS- T Bogar
3B- H Johnson
LF- V Coleman
OI J Orsulak
R3 B Bonilla
OI D Gallagher
UI J McKnight
UT C Walker
RU- J Burnitz
M1 J Torborg
M2 D Green

PHI 1993 NL
SP C Schilling
SP D Jackson
SP T Greene
SP T Mulholland
SP B Rivera
CL M Williams
RP D West
RP L Andersen
RP M Williams
C D Daulton
1B J Kruk
2B M Morandini
SS- K Stocker
3B D Hollins
LF M Thompson
CF L Dykstra
RF J Eisenreich
2S M Duncan
LF P Incaviglia
RF- W Chamberlain
UM-R Jordan
M J Fregosi

PIT 1993 NL
SP S Cooke
SP B Walk
SP R Wagner
SP T Wakefield
RP B Minor
RS D Neagle
RS D Otto
RP J Johnston
C D Slaught
1B K Young
2B C Garcia
SS J Bell
3B J King
LM A Martin
CF- A Van Slyke
RF O Merced
OF D Clark
UI- T Foley
RU- L McClendon
LU- L Smith
M J Leyland

STL 1993 NL
SP B Tewksbury
SP R Arocha
SP O Osborne
SR R Cormier
SP J Magrane
RS O Olivares
CL L Smith
RP M Perez
RP R Murphy
C - T Pagnozzi
1B G Jefferies
2B L Alicea
SS O Smith
3B T Zeile
LF B Gilkey
CF R Lankford
RF M Whiten
OI R Brewer
C - E Pappas
UT- G Perry
M J Torre

SD 1993 NL
SP A Benes
SP Gr Harris
SP D Brocail
SP W Whitehurst
SP T Worrell
CL Ge Harris
RS K Taylor
RP T Hoffman
RP R Mason
C - K Higgins
1B- F McGriff
2B J Gardner
SS R Gutierrez
3B- G Sheffield
LF P Plantier
CF D Bell
RF T Gwynn
UT P Clark
UT C Shipley
OI- B Bean
3B- A Cianfrocco
2U- T Teufel
M J Riggleman

SF 1993 NL
SP B Swift
SP J Burkett
SP T Wilson
CL R Beck
RS B Hickerson
RS J Brantley
RS D Burba
C K Manwaring
1B W Clark
2B R Thompson
SS R Clayton
3B M Williams
LF B Bonds
CF D Lewis
RF W McGee
IO- T Benzinger
UO-D Martinez
M D Baker

BAL 1993 AL
SP B McDonald
SP F Valenzuela
SP M Mussina
SP R Sutcliffe
SP J Moyer
RP A Mills
RP T Frohwirth
RP M Williamson
RP J Poole
C C Hoiles
1B D Segui
2B H Reynolds
SS C Ripken
3B- T Hulett
LF B Anderson
CF M Devereaux
RF M McLemore
DH H Baines
M J Oates

BOS 1993 AL
SP D Darwin
SP R Clemens
SP F Viola
SP J Dopson
SP A Sele
RS P Quantrill
RP G Harris
RS B Bankhead
RS J Hesketh
C T Pena
1B M Vaughn
2B S Fletcher
SS J Valentin
3B S Cooper
LF M Greenwell
CF B Hatcher
UO B Zupcic
DH A Dawson
1R C Quintana
UI- E Riles
M B Hobson

CAL 1993 AL
SP M Langston
SP C Finley
SP S Sanderson
RP J Grahe
RP K Patterson
RS J Valera
RP G Nelson
C G Myers
1B J Snow
2B T Lovullo
SS G DiSarcina
31 R Gonzales
LF L Polonia
CF C Curtis
RF T Salmon
DH C Davis
UT- S Javier
M B Rodgers

CHI 1993 AL
SP J McDowell
SP A Fernandez
SP W Alvarez
SP J Bere
SR K McCaskill
CL R Hernandez
RP D Pall
RP S Radinsky
RP J Schwarz
C K Karkovice
1B F Thomas
2B J Cora
SS O Guillen
LF T Raines
CF L Johnson
RF E Burks
DH G Bell
OF- B Jackson
M G Lamont

CLE 1993 AL
SP J Mesa
SR T Kramer
SR M Clark
RP E Plunk
RP J Hernandez
RP D Lilliquist
RP J Dipoto
C - J Ortiz
1B P Sorrento
2B C Baerga
SS F Fermin
3B A Espinoza
LF A Belle
CF K Lofton
RF W Kirby
DH R Jefferson
IF- J Treadway
M M Hargrove

DET 1993 AL
SP M Moore
SP D Wells
SP J Doherty
SP B Gullickson
SR M Leiter
RS T Bolton
CL M Henneman
RS B Krueger
RP M Mac Donald
C C Kreuter
1B C Fielder
2B L Whitaker
S3 A Trammell
S3 T Fryman
UT T Phillips
CF- M Cuyler
RF- R Deer
DM K Gibson
3D S Livingstone
IC M Tettleton
UT- S Barnes
LF- D Gladden
M S Anderson

KC 1993 AL
SP D Cone
SP K Appier
SP H Pichardo
SP C Haney
RS T Gordon
CL J Montgomery
C M Gubicza
C M Macfarlane
1B W Joyner
2B J Lind
SS G Gagne
3B- G Gaetti
LF K McReynolds
CF B McRae
RF F Jose
DH G Brett
LU C Gwynn
3B- P Hiatt
M H McRae

MIL 1993 AL
SP C Eldred
SP J Navarro
SP R Bones
SP B Wegman
SP A Miranda
RP D Henry
RP J Orosco
RP G Lloyd
RP M Fetters
C D Nilsson
1B- J Jaha
2B B Spiers
SS P Listach
3B B Surhoff
LD G Vaughn

CF R Yount
RM D Hamilton
DO K Reimer
2S- J Bell
UI- D Thon
M P Garner

MIN 1993 AL
SP K Tapani
SP S Erickson
SP W Banks
SP J Deshaies
RS M Trombley
CL R Aguilera
RP M Hartley
RP G Tsamis
C B Harper
1B K Hrbek
2B C Knoblauch
SS P Meares
3B- M Pagliarulo
LR P Munoz
ML S Mack
MR K Puckett
DU D Winfield
OI D McCarty
S3 J Reboulet
M T Kelly

NY 1993 AL
SP J Key
SP J Abbott
SP M Perez
SR S Kamieniecki
SR B Wickman
RP R Monteleone
RP S Howe
C M Stanley
1B D Mattingly
2B P Kelly
SS S Owen
3B W Boggs
LF D James
CF B Williams
RL P O'Neill
DR D Tartabull
UI M Gallego
UT- J Leyritz
LS- R Velarde
M B Showalter

OAK 1993 AL
SP B Witt
SP R Darling
SP B Welch
RS K Downs
CL D Eckersley
RP J Boever
RP E Nunez
C T Steinbach
1U- M Aldrete
2B B Gates
SS M Bordick
3B C Paquette
LF- R Henderson
MD D Henderson
RF R Sierra
D1 T Neel
MI- L Blankenship
C - S Hemond
M T LaRussa

SEA 1993 AL
SP R Johnson
SP E Hanson
SP T Leary
SP D Fleming
SP C Bosio
RP J Nelson
RP D Henry
C D Valle
1B T Martinez
2I R Amaral
SS O Vizquel
3B M Blowers
LF M Felder
CF K Griffey
RF J Buhner
DU- P O'Brien
OI- M Sasser
M L Piniella

TEX 1993 AL
SP K Brown
SP K Rogers
SP R Pavlik
SP C Leibrandt
CL T Henke
RS B Bohanon
RS C Lefferts
RP M Whiteside
C I Rodriguez
1B R Palmeiro
2B D Strange
SS- M Lee
3B D Palmer
LF J Gonzalez

CF D Hulse
RF- J Canseco
DH J Franco
M K Kennedy

TOR 1993 AL
SP J Guzman
SP P Hentgen
SP T Stottlemyre
SP D Stewart
SP J Morris
CL D Ward
RS A Leiter
RP D Cox
RP M Eichhorn
C P Borders
1B J Olerud
2B R Alomar
SS- T Fernandez
3B E Sprague
OI- T Ward
CF D White
RL J Carter
DH P Molitor
M C Gaston

FLA 1994 NL
SP D Weathers
SP P Rapp
SP C Hough
SP M Gardner
SP C Hammond
CL R Nen
RP R Lewis
RP L Aquino
RP T Mathews
C B Santiago
1B- G Colbrunn
2B B Barberie
SS K Abbott
3O J Browne
LF J Conine
CF C Carr
RF G Sheffield
UO M Carrillo
3U J Magadan
IF- A Arias
M R Lachemann

HOU 1994 NL
SP D Drabek
SP D Kile
SP G Swindell
SR S Reynolds
SP P Harnisch
RP T Jones
RP B Williams
CL J Hudek
RP T Edens
C S Servais
1B J Bagwell
2B C Biggio
SS A Cedeno
3B K Caminiti
LF L Gonzalez
RF J Mouton
RU K Bass
UO- M Felder
M T Collins

LA 1994 NL
SP R Martinez
SP K Gross
SP T Candiotti
SP P Astacio
SP O Hershiser
RP T Worrell
RP R McDowell
RP J Gott
C M Piazza
1B E Karros
2B D DeShields
SS J Offerman
3B T Wallach
LF H Rodriguez
CF B Butler
RF R Mondesi
LI C Snyder
LU M Webster
OF- C Gwynn
M T Lasorda

MON 1994 NL
SP K Hill
SP P Martinez
SP J Fassero
SP B Henry
SP K Rueter
RP M Rojas
CL J Wetteland
RP G Heredia
RP J Shaw
C D Fletcher
1B C Floyd
2B M Lansing
SS W Cordero
3B S Berry
LR M Alou
CF M Grissom
R1 L Walker
UT L Frazier
C - L Webster
M F Alou

NY 1994 NL
SP B Saberhagen
SP B Jones
SP P Smith
SR M Gozzo
CL J Franco

C J Girardi
1B A Galarraga
2B N Liriano
SS W Weiss
3B C Hayes
LU H Johnson
MU M Kingery
RF D Bichette
UT J Vander Wal
LU E Young
M D Baylor

PHI 1994 NL
SP D Jackson
SP B Munoz
SR D West
SP S Boskie
SP C Schilling
CL D Jones
RP H Slocumb
C D Daulton
1B J Kruk
2B M Morandini
SS K Stocker
3B- D Hollins
LF M Thompson
CF L Dykstra
RF J Eisenreich
UI M Duncan
LF P Incaviglia
1U W Jordan
3S- K Batiste
OT T Longmire
M J Fregosi

PIT 1994 NL
SP Z Smith
SP D Neagle
SP S Cooke
SR P Wagner
SP J Lieber
RS R White
RP M Dewey
RP R Manzanillo
C D Slaught
1B B Hunter
2B C Garcia
SS J Bell
3B J King
LF A Martin
CF A Van Slyke
R1 O Merced
RU D Clark
UI- T Foley
OI- G Varsho
13- K Young
M J Leyland

STL 1994 NL
SP B Tewksbury
SR V Palacios
SP A Watson
SR T Urbani
SP O Olivares
RS R Arocha
RP B Eversgerd
RP R Rodriguez
RP J Habyan
C T Pagnozzi
1B G Jefferies
2U G Pena
SS O Smith
3B T Zeile
LF B Gilkey
CF R Lankford
RF M Whiten
2U L Alicea
U2- G Perry
M J Torre

SD 1994 NL
SP A Benes
SP A Ashby
SP S Sanders
SP J Hamilton
CL T Hoffman
RP P Martinez
RP T Mauser
RP A Sager
C B Ausmus
1B- E Williams
2B B Roberts
SS R Gutierrez
3I C Shipley
LF P Plantier
CF D Bell
RF T Gwynn
OI B Bean
S2 L Lopez
31- A Cianfrocco
UT- P Clark
3B- S Livingstone
M J Riggleman

RP R Mason
RP D Linton
RP J Manzanillo
C T Hundley
1B D Segui
2B J Kent
SS J Vizcaino
3B B Bonilla
UO- J Cangelosi
CF R Thompson
RO J Orsulak
IO F Vina
M D Green

SF 1994 NL
SP J Burkett
SP M Portugal
SP B Swift
SR B Hickerson
SP S Torres
RP Van Landingham
CL R Beck
RP D Burba
RP M Jackson
C K Manwaring
1B T Benzinger
2U J Patterson
SS R Clayton
3B M Williams
LF B Bonds
CF D Lewis
R1 D Martinez
M D Baker

BAL 1994 AL
SP M Mussina
SP B McDonald
SP J Moyer
SP S Fernandez
RP M Eichhorn
CL L Smith
RP M Williamson
RPA A Mills
C C Hoiles
1B R Palmeiro
2B M McLemore
SS C Ripken
3B L Gomez
LM B Anderson
CF M Devereaux
RF J Hammonds
DH H Baines
3O C Sabo
RL- J Voigt
M J Oates

BOS 1994 AL
SP R Clemens
SP A Sele
SP J Hesketh
SP D Darwin
RP K Ryan
RP G Harris
RP C Howard
RP S Bankhead
C D Berryhill
1B M Vaughn
SS J Valentin
3B S Cooper
LF M Greenwell
CF O Nixon
RL- T Brunansky
DH A Dawson
2I T Naehring
S2- T Rodriguez
UO L Tinsley
M B Hobson

CAL 1994 AL
SP C Finley
SP M Langston
SP P Leftwich
SP B Anderson
SP J Magrane
RS M Leiter
RS J Dopson
RP J Grahe
RS R Springer
C - C Turner
1B- J Snow
2B H Reynolds
2U G DiSarcina
SS S Owen
LO J Edmonds
CF C Curtis
RF T Salmon
DH C Davis
32 D Easley
LU B Jackson
31 K Seitzer
M1 B Rodgers
M2 B Knoop
M3 M Lachemann

CHI 1994 AL
SP J McDowell
SP A Fernandez
SP W Alvarez
SP J Bere
SP S Sanderson
RP J DeLeon
RP R Hernandez
RP K McCaskill
C R Karkovice
1B F Thomas
2B J Cora
SS O Guillen
3B R Ventura
LF T Raines

CF L Johnson
RF D Jackson
DH J Franco
C - M LaValliere
OF- W Newson
M G Lamont

CLE 1994 AL
SP D Martinez
SP C Nagy
SP J Morris
SP M Clark
SP J Grimsley
RP J Mesa
RP E Plunk
C S Alomar
1B P Sorrento
C B Baerga
SS O Vizquel
3B J Thome
LF A Belle
CF K Lofton
RF M Ramirez
DH E Murray
UI A Espinoza
RU W Kirby
M M Hargrove

DET 1994 AL
SP T Belcher
SP M Moore
SP B Gullickson
SP D Wells
SP J Doherty
RP J Boever
RP M Gardiner
RS J Davis
RP M Henneman
C - C Kreuter
1B C Fielder
2B L Whitaker
SS A Trammell
3B T Fryman
LF T Phillips
ML- M Cuyler
RF J Felix
DO K Gibson
S2 C Gomez
IC M Tettleton
UT- J Samuel
M S Anderson

KC 1994 AL
SP D Cone
SP K Appier
SP T Gordon
SP M Gubicza
CL J Montgomery
RP H Pichardo
RP R Meacham
RP S Belinda
C M Macfarlane
1B W Joyner
2B J Lind
SS G Gagne
3B G Gaetti
LF V Coleman
CF B McRae
RF F Jose
DU B Hamelin
23- T Shumpert
M H McRae

MIL 1994 AL
SP C Eldred
SP R Bones
SP B Wegman
SR B Scanlan
SR J Navarro
CL M Fetters
RP G Lloyd
RP J Orosco
CD D Nilsson
1B J Jaha
2B J Reed
SS J Valentin
LU B Jackson
31 K Seitzer
LF G Vaughn
ML T Ward
RF M Mieske
DC- B Harper
MR A Diaz
IO B Spiers
M P Garner

MIN 1994 AL
SP K Tapani
SP S Erickson
SP J Deshaies
SP P Mahomes
SP C Pulido
CL R Aguilera
RP R Willis
RP M Guthrie
RP M Trombley
C M Walbeck

1B K Hrbek
2B C Knoblauch
SS P Meares
3B S Leius
LF S Mack
CF A Cole
RF K Puckett
DH D Winfield
LR P Munoz
SI J Reboulet
IO- C Hale
M T Kelly

NY 1994 AL
SP J Key
SP J Abbott
SP M Perez
SP T Mulholland
SP S Kamieniecki
RP B Wickman
CL S Howe
RS J Hitchcock
RP X Hernandez
C M Stanley
1B D Mattingly
2B P Kelly
SS M Gallego
3B W Boggs
LF L Polonia
CF B Williams
RF P O'Neill
DH O Tartabull
IC J Leyritz
S3 R Velarde
UO- G Williams
M B Showalter

OAK 1994 AL
SP R Darling
SP B Witt
SP T Van Poppel
SR S Ontiveros
RS C Reyes
RS B Welch
CL D Eckersley
RP J Briscoe
C T Steinbach
1D T Neel
2B- B Gates
SS M Bordick
3B S Brosius
LF R Henderson
CF S Javier
RF R Sierra
OI G Berroa
OI M Aldrete
IC S Hemond
M T LaRussa

SEA 1994 AL
SP R Johnson
SP C Bosio
SP D Fleming
SP G Hibbard
CL B Ayala
RP B Risley
RP T Davis
RP R Gossage
C D Wilson
1B T Martinez
2U R Amaral
SS F Fermin
3D E Martinez
LF E Anthony
CF K Griffey
RF J Buhner
DU- R Jefferson
3U M Blowers
2S- L Sojo
M L Piniella

TEX 1994 AL
SP K Brown
SP K Rogers
SP H Fajardo
RP C Carpenter
RP M Whiteside
CL T Henke
RP D Oliver
C I Rodriguez
1B W Clark
2B- J Frye
SS M Lee
3B D Palmer
LF J Gonzalez
CF D Hulse
RM R Greer
DH J Canseco
2U D Strange
MR-O McDowell
M K Kennedy

TOR 1994 AL
SP P Hentgen
SP J Guzman
SP T Stottlemyre
SP D Stewart

SP A Leiter
RP T Castillo
RP W Williams
RP M Timlin
C P Borders
1B J Olerud
2B R Alomar
SS D Schofield
3B E Sprague
LO M Huff
CF D White
RF J Carter
DH P Molitor
M C Gaston

ATL 1995 NL
SP G Maddux
SP T Glavine
SP J Smoltz
SP S Avery
SP K Mercker
CL M Wohlers
RP G McMichael
RP B Clontz
C J Lopez
1B F McGriff
2B M Lemke
SS J Blauser
3B C Jones
LF K Klesko
CF M Grissom
RF D Justice
LO M Kelly
OF D Smith
S2- R Belliard
M B Cox

CHI 1995 NL
SP J Navarro
SP F Castillo
SP K Foster
SP S Trachsel
SP J Bullinger
CL R Myers
RP M Perez
RP T Wendell
RP M Walker
C - S Servais
1B M Grace
2B R Sanchez
SS S Dunston
3B- T Zeile
LF- L Gonzalez
CF B McRae
RF S Sosa
LU S Bullett
UI J Hernandez
IO H Johnson
LU- O Timmons
M J Riggleman

CIN 1995 NL
SP P Schourek
SP J Smiley
SR T Pugh
CL J Brantley
RP X Hernandez
RP H Carrasco
RP M Jackson
C - B Santiago
1B H Morris
2B B Boone
SS B Larkin
3B J Branson
LF R Gant
OI J Walton
RF R Sanders
UT L Harris
UO T Howard
3B- M Lewis
C - E Taubensee
M D Johnson

COL 1995 NL
SP K Ritz
SP B Swift
SP M Freeman
SP A Reynoso
RP C Leskanic
RP S Reed
RS R Bailey
RP D Holmes
C J Girardi
1B A Galarraga
2I J Bates
SS W Weiss
3B V Castilla
LF D Bichette
CF M Kingery
RF L Walker
MU E Burks
UT J Vander Wal
2U E Young
M D Baylor

ATL 1994 NL
SP G Maddux
SP T Glavine
SP S Avery
SP J Smoltz
SP K Mercker
CL G McMichael
RP M Wohlers
RP M Stanton
RP S Bedrosian
C J Lopez
1B F McGriff
2B M Lemke
SS J Blauser
3B T Pendleton
LF K Klesko
CF- R Kelly
RF D Justice
OF T Tarasco
LF D Gallagher
IO- B Pecota
M B Cox

CHI 1994 NL
SP S Trachsel
SP W Banks
SP A Young
SP K Foster
SP M Morgan
RS J Bullinger
RP J Bautista
RP C Crim
CL R Myers
C R Wilkins
1B M Grace
2B- R Sandberg
SS S Dunston
3B S Buechele
LF D May
UO G Hill
RF S Sosa
MU K Rhodes
2S R Sanchez
UT- E Zambrano
M T Trebelhorn

CIN 1994 NL
SP J Rijo
SP J Smiley
SP E Hanson
SP J Roper
SR P Schourek
RP J Brantley
RP J Ruffin
RP C McElroy
RP H Carrasco
C B Dorsett
1B H Morris
2B B Boone
SS B Larkin
3B T Fernandez
LF K Mitchell
CF- D Sanders
RF R Sanders
UI- J Branson
UO- J Brumfield
IO- L Harris
UO T Howard
C - E Taubensee
M D Johnson

COL 1994 NL
SR G Harris
SP D Nied
SP M Freeman
SR M Harkey
SP L Painter
RP W Blair
RP K Ritz
RP B Ruffin
RP S Reed

FLA 1995 NL
SP J Burkett
SP P Rapp
SP C Hammond
SP B Witt
SR D Weathers
RS M Gardner
CL R Nen
RP T Mathews
RP R Veres
C C Johnson
1B G Colbrunn
2B Q Veras
SS K Abbott
3B T Pendleton
LF J Conine
CF C Carr
RF- G Sheffield
UI A Arias
UT- J Browne
RU- A Dawson
OI- T Gregg
M R Lachemann

HOU 1995 NL
SP S Reynolds
SP D Drabek
SP G Swindell
SP M Hampton
SP D Kile
RP T Jones
RP D Veres
RS D Brocail
RP J Dougherty
C T Eusebio
1B J Bagwell
2B C Biggio
SS O Miller
3B D Magadan
UO J Mouton
CF- B Hunter
RM D Bell
UO J Cangelosi
3U- C Shipley
UO M Thompson
LU- D May
M T Collins

LA 1995 NL
SP R Martinez
SP I Valdes
SP H Nomo
SP T Candiotti
RS P Astacio
CL T Worrell
RP A Osuna
C M Piazza
1B E Karros
2B D DeShields
SS J Offerman
3B T Wallach
LF- B Ashley
LM R Kelly
RF R Mondesi
UT C Fonville
3U D Hansen
M T Lasorda

MON 1995 NL
SP P Martinez
SP J Fassero
SP C Perez
SP B Henry
SR G Heredia
CL M Rojas
RP T Scott
RP J Shaw
RP G Harris
C D Fletcher
1B D Segui
2B M Lansing
SS W Cordero
3B S Berry
LR M Alou
CF R White
RF T Tarasco
31- S Andrews
UI- M Grudzielanek
M F Alou

NY 1995 NL
SP B Jones
SP D Mlicki
SP B Pulsipher
SP P Harnisch
SP B Saberhagen
RP J Isringhausen
RP J Dipoto
CL J Franco
RP D Henry
C T Hundley
1B R Brogna
2B J Kent
SS J Vizcaino
32 E Alfonzo
LR J Orsulak
CF B Butler
RF- C Everett
IO- T Bogar
3L- B Bonilla
OI- C Jones
C - K Stinnett
MR- R Thompson
M D Green

PHI 1995 NL
SP P Quantrill
SP T Green
SR M Mimbs
SP C Schilling
CL H Slocumb
RP R Bottalico
RS M Williams
RP T Borland
C D Daulton
1B- D Hollins
2B M Morandini
SS K Stocker
3B C Hayes
CF- A Van Slyke
CF- L Dykstra
RL J Eisenreich
1L G Jefferies
OF- G Varsho
M J Fregosi

PIT 1995 NL
SP D Neagle
SP E Loaiza
SP P Wagner
SP J Ericks
CL D Miceli
RP M Dyer
RP D Plesac
RP J McCurry
C - M Parent
1B- M Johnson
2B C Garcia
SS J Bell
31 J King
LF A Martin
CF J Brumfield
RF O Merced
2U N Liriano
OF- D Clark
UO- S Pegues
M J Leyland

STL 1995 NL
SP M Petkovsek
SP A Watson
SP D Osborne
SP K Hill
SP M Morgan
RP D Jackson
CL T Henke
RP R DeLucia
RP J Parrett
C - D Sheaffer
1O J Mabry
2S J Oquendo
SS T Cromer
3B S Cooper
3L T Phillips
CF R Lankford
RB B Jordan
M1 J Torre
M2 M Jorgensen

SD 1995 NL
SP J Hamilton
SP A Ashby
SP A Benes
SP G Dishman
SP S Sanders
RS W Blair
RS F Valenzuela
CL T Hoffman
RS B Williams
C B Ausmus
1B E Williams
2B J Reed
SS A Acedeno
3B K Caminiti
LU M Nieves
CF S Finley
RF T Gwynn
UI S Livingstone
1U R Petagine
OI- P Clark
L2- B Roberts
M B Bochy

SF 1995 NL
SP M Leiter
SP T Mulholland
SP Van Landingham
SP M Portugal
RS M Bautista
CL R Beck
RP C Hook
RP S Barton
C K Manwaring
1U M Carreon
2B R Thompson
SS R Clayton
3B- M Williams
LF B Bonds
CF- D Lewis
RF G Hill
2U J Patterson
1B J Phillips
3I- S Scarsone
M D Baker

BAL 1995 AL
SP M Mussina
SP K Brown
SP J Moyer
SP S Erickson
CL D Jones
RP M Oquist
RP J Orosco
RP A Benitez
C C Hoiles
1B R Palmeiro
2B M Alexander
SS C Ripken
3B J Manto
LF B Anderson
CF C Goodwin
OF K Bass
DH H Baines
2B B Barberie
M P Regan

BOS 1995 AL
SP T Wakefield
SP E Hanson
SP R Clemens
SP Z Smith
RS R Cormier
RP M Maddux
RS S Belinda
RP J Hudson
C M Macfarlane
1B M Vaughn
2B L Alicea
SS J Valentin
3B T Naehring
LF M Greenwell
CF L Tinsley
RF T O'Leary
DH J Canseco
RF J Nunnally
M K Kennedy

CAL 1995 AL
SP C Finley
SP M Langston
SP S Boskie
SP B Anderson
CL L Smith
RP T Percival
RP M James
RP B Patterson
C - J Fabregas
1B J Snow
2B D Easley
SS G DiSarcina
3L T Phillips
LF G Anderson
CF J Edmonds
RF T Salmon
DH C Davis
2O- R Hudler
CU- G Myers
UI- S Owen
M M Lachemann

CHI 1995 AL
SP A Fernandez
SP W Alvarez
SP J Bere
SP J Abbott
SR B Keyser
CL R Hernandez
RP K McCaskill
RP J DeLeon
C R Karkovice
OI D Martinez
2B R Durham
SS O Guillen
3B R Ventura
LF T Raines
CF L Johnson
RF M Devereaux
1D F Thomas
UT- N Martin
M1 G Lamont
M2 T Bevington

CLE 1995 AL
SP D Martinez
SP C Nagy
SP O Hershiser
SP M Clark
SP C Ogea
CL J Mesa
RP J Tavarez
RP E Plunk
RP J Poole
C T Pena
1B P Sorrento
2B B Baerga
SS O Vizquel
3B J Thome
LF A Belle
CF K Lofton
RF M Ramirez
DH E Murray
UO W Kirby
M M Hargrove

DET 1995 AL
SR F Lira
SP S Bergman
SP M Moore
SP D Wells
RP J Doherty
RS B Bohanon
RP J Boever
RP M Christopher
C J Flaherty
1D C Fielder
2B- L Whitaker
SS C Gomez
3B T Fryman
RL T Higginson
CF C Curtis
RF D James
DH- K Gibson
IO- J Samuel
SS- A Trammell
M S Anderson

KC 1995 AL
SP M Gubicza
SP K Appier
SP T Gordon
CL J Montgomery
RP H Pichardo
RP R Meacham
RP B Brewer
C B Mayne
1B W Joyner
2U K Lockhart
SS G Gagne
3B G Gaetti
LF- V Coleman
ML T Goodwin
RF J Nunnally
DH- B Hamelin
UT D Howard
M B Boone

MIL 1995 AL
SP S Sparks
SP R Bones
SP S Karl
SP B Givens
RP B Wegman
RP M Kiefer
C J Oliver
1B J Jaha
2B F Vina
SS J Valentin
3B J Cirillo
LM D Hulse
CF D Hamilton
RF M Mieske
DH G Vaughn
2S P Listach
31 K Seitzer
OI B Surhoff
C - M Matheny
RU- D Nilsson
M P Garner

MIN 1995 AL
SP B Radke
SP K Tapani
SP M Trombley
SP F Rodriguez
SP S Erickson
RS P Mahomes
RS E Guardado
RP D Stevens
RP R Robertson
C M Walbeck
1U S Stahoviak
2B C Knoblauch
SS P Meares
3B S Leius
LF M Cordova
CF M Becker
RF K Puckett
DU P Munoz
CU- M Merullo
UI J Reboulet
M T Kelly

NY 1995 AL
SP J McDowell
SP A Pettitte
SP S Hitchcock
SP D Cone
SP S Kamieniecki
CL J Wetteland
RP B Wickman
RP S Howe
RP R Mac Donald
C M Stanley
1B D Mattingly
2B P Kelly
SS T Fernandez
3B W Boggs
LR G Williams
CF B Williams
RF P O'Neill
DH- R Sierra
2S R Velarde
OI- D James
CU- J Leyritz
M B Showalter

OAK 1995 AL
SP T Stottlemyre
SR T Van Poppel
SP S Ontiveros
SP P Darling
CL D Eckersley
RP C Reyes
RP M Acre
RP J Corsi
C T Steinbach
1B M McGwire
2B M Bordick
3U C Paquette
LF R Henderson
CF S Javier
RF- R Sierra
DR G Berroa
UT S Brosius
M T LaRussa

SEA 1995 AL
SP R Johnson
SP T Belcher
SP C Bosio
RP B Ayala
RP J Nelson
RP B Wells
CL N Charlton
C D Wilson
1B T Martinez
2B J Cora
SS L Sojo
3B M Blowers
UO T Howard
CF E Davis
RF J Buhner
DH E Martinez
S2- F Fermin
CF- K Griffey
3U- D Strange
M L Piniella

TEX 1995 AL
SP K Rogers
SP R Pavlik
SP K Gross
SP B Tewksbury
RP R McDowell
RP M Whiteside
RP D Cook
RP T Burrows
C I Rodriguez
1B W Clark
2B J Frye
SS B Gil
3B- M Pagliarulo
L2 M McLemore
CF O Nixon
RF R Greer
DH J Gonzalez
OI M Tettleton
M J Oates

TOR 1995 AL
SP P Hentgen
SP A Leiter
SP J Guzman
SP D Cone
RP T Castillo
RP W Williams
RP D Cox
C - L Parrish
1B J Olerud
2B R Alomar
SS A Gonzalez
3B E Sprague
LF J Carter
CF D White
RF S Green
DH P Molitor
M C Gaston

ATL 1996 NL
SP J Smoltz
SP G Maddux
SP T Glavine
SP S Avery
CL M Wohlers
RP G McMichael
RP B Clontz
RS M Bielecki
C J Lopez
1B F McGriff
2B M Lemke
SS- J Blauser
3B C Jones
LF R Klesko
CF M Grissom
RL J Dye
OF D Smith
SU- R Belliard
M B Cox

CHI 1996 NL
SP J Navarro
SP S Trachsel
SP F Castillo
SR J Bullinger
RP T Adams
RP T Wendell
RP R Myers
RP K Bottenfield
C S Servais
1B M Grace
2B R Sandberg
SS- R Sanchez
3B L Gomez
LF L Gonzalez
CF B McRae
RF S Sosa
UO S Bullett
S3 J Hernandez
M J Riggleman

CIN 1996 NL
SP J Smiley
SP D Burba
SP M Portugal
SP K Jarvis
SR R Salkeld
CL J Brantley
RP H Carrasco
RP J Ruffin
C J Oliver
1B H Morris
2B B Boone
SS B Larkin
3U W Greene
UO T Howard
CF E Davis
RF- R Sanders
UI J Branson
UT L Harris
C E Taubensee
LU- E Owens
M R Knight

COL 1996 NL
SP K Ritz
SP M Thompson
SP A Reynoso
SP M Freeman
CL B Ruffin
RP C Leskanic
RP D Holmes
RP S Reed
C J Reed
1B A Galarraga
2B E Young
SS W Weiss
3B V Castilla
LF E Burks
MU Q McCracken
RF D Bichette
OI J Vander Wal
UI- J Bates
MR- L Walker
M D Baylor

FLA 1996 NL
SP K Brown
SP A Leiter
SP P Rapp
SP J Burkett
CL R Nen
RS C Hammond
RP J Powell
RS D Weathers
C C Johnson
1B G Colbrunn
2B- Q Veras
SS E Renteria
3B T Pendleton
LF J Conine
CF D White
RF G Sheffield
UI K Abbott
3U A Arias
OI J Orsulak
UO J Tavarez
M1 R Lachemann
M2 C Rojas
M3 J Boles

HOU 1996 NL
SP S Reynolds
SP D Kile
SP D Drabek
SP M Hampton
SP D Wall
RP X Hernandez
RP T Jones
RP B Wagner
RP D Brocail
C - R Wilkins
1B J Bagwell
2B C Biggio
SS O Miller
3B S Berry
LO J Mouton
CF B Hunter
RF D Bell
OF J Cangelosi
LU D May
3U B Spiers
SS- R Gutierrez
M T Collins

LA 1996 NL
SP H Nomo
SP I Valdes
SP P Astacio
SP R Martinez
SP T Candiotti
RS C Park
CL T Worrell
RP A Osuna
RP M Guthrie
C M Piazza
1B E Karros
2B D DeShields
3B- M Blowers
LF T Hollandsworth
MO- R Cedeno
RF R Mondesi
UT C Fonville
M1 T Lasorda
M2 B Russell

MON 1996 NL
SP J Fassero
SP P Martinez
SP R Cormier
SR U Urbina
CL M Rojas
RS O Daal
RP B Manuel
RP D Veres
C D Fletcher
1B D Segui
2B M Lansing
SS M Grudzielanek
3B S Andrews
L1 H Rodriguez
MO F Santangelo
RF M Alou
LU C Floyd
RU- S Obando
3U- D Silvestri
CF- R White
M F Alou

NY 1996 NL
SP M Clark
SP B Jones
SP P Harnisch
SP J Isringhausen
SP P Wilson
RP D Mlicki
RP D Henry
CL J Franco
RP J Dipoto
C T Hundley
1R B Huskey
2B- J Vizcaino
SS R Ordonez
3B- J Kent
LF B Gilkey
CF L Johnson
RF- A Ochoa
23 E Alfonzo
UO C Everett
UI- T Bogar
OI- C Jones
M1 D Green
M2 B Valentine

PHI 1996 NL
SP C Schilling
SP M Williams
SP T Mulholland
SP M Mimbs
CL R Bottalico
RP K Ryan
RS R Springer
RP T Borland
C B Santiago
1L G Jefferies
2B M Morandini
SS K Stocker
3B T Zeile
LU P Incaviglia
CF R Otero
UO J Eisenreich
M J Fregosi

PIT 1996 NL
SP D Neagle
SP D Darwin
RS J Lieber
RS F Cordova
RS D Miceli
RP D Plesac
C J Kendall
1B M Johnson
2B C Garcia
SS J Bell
3B C Hayes
LF A Martin
MU M Kingery
RF O Merced
12 J King
UI N Liriano
OF- D Clark
UT- J Wehner
M J Leyland

STL 1996 NL
SP An Benes
SP T Stottlemyre
SP D Osborne
SP Al Benes
SP M Morgan
CL D Eckersley
RP T Mathews
RS M Petkovsek
RP C Bailey
C T Pagnozzi
1B J Mabry
2B L Alicea
SS R Clayton
3B G Gaetti
LF R Gant
CF R Lankford
RF B Jordan
OI- W McGee
OI M Sweeney
SU- O Smith
M T LaRussa

SD 1996 NL
SP J Hamilton
SP B Tewksbury
SP F Valenzuela
SP A Ashby
SR S Sanders
CL T Hoffman
RS T Worrell
RS S Bergman
RP W Blair
C - J Flaherty
1B W Joyner
2B J Reed
SS- C Gomez
3B K Caminiti
LF R Henderson
CF S Finley
RF T Gwynn
IF S Livingstone
OI- C Gwynn
C - B Johnson
OI- M Newfield
M B Bochy

SF 1996 NL
SP A Watson
SP Van Landingham
SP M Gardner
SP O Fernandez
SP M Leiter
CL R Beck
RP M Dewey
RP J Bautista
RP R DeLucia
C - T Lampkin
1B- M Carreon
2U S Scarsone
SS R Aurilia
3B M Williams
LF B Bonds
CF M Benard
RF G Hill
SS- S Dunston
1U- D McCarty
M D Baker

BAL 1996 AL
SP M Mussina
SP D Wells
SP S Erickson
SP S Coppinger
SP T Borland
CL R Myers
RP R McDowell

RP A Mills
RP J Orosco
C C Hoiles
C C Hoiles
1B R Palmeiro
2B R Alomar
SS C Ripken
3U B Surhoff
UO B Devereaux
CF B Anderson
RD B Bonilla
DH-E Murray
M D Johnson

BOS 1996 AL
SP R Clemens
SP T Gordon
SP T Wakefield
SP A Sele
CL H Slocumb
RS V Eshelman
RS M Maddux
RP M Stanton
SP M Stanley
1B M Vaughn
2B J Frye
SS J Valentin
3B T Naehring
LF-M Greenwell
CF-L Tinsley
RL T O'Leary
DH-J Canseco
UT R Jefferson
M K Kennedy

CAL 1996 AL
SP C Finley
SP S Boskie
SP J Abbott
SR J Grimsley
SP M Langston
CL T Percival
RP M James
C - J Fabregas
1B J Snow
2B R Velarde
SS G DiSarcina
3B-G Arias
LF G Anderson
CF J Edmonds
RF T Salmon
DH C Davis
2U-R Hudler
M1 M Lachemann
M2 J McNamara

CHI 1996 AL
SP A Fernandez
SP K Tapani
SP W Alvarez
SP J Baldwin
CL H Hernandez
RP B Simas
RP B Keyser
RP M Karchner
C R Karkovice
1B F Thomas
2B D Durham
SS O Guillen
3B R Ventura
LF T Phillips
CF D Lewis
RF D Tartabull
DH H Baines
MR D Martinez
OF-L Mouton
M T Bevington

CLE 1996 AL
SP C Nagy
SP O Hershiser
SP J McDowell
SP C Ogea
SP D Martinez
CL J Mesa
RP J Tavarez
RP E Plunk
RP P Shuey
C S Alomar
1B J Franco
2B C Baerga
SS O Vizquel
3B J Thome
LF A Belle
CF K Lofton
RF M Ramirez
DH-E Murray
M M Hargrove

DET 1996 AL
SP F Lira
SP O Olivares
SR B Williams
RP R Lewis
RP J Lima
RM M Myers
C - B Ausmus
1B T Clark

2B M Lewis
SS-A Cedeno
3B T Fryman
UO B Higginson
CF C Curtis
RU M Nieves
DU-E Williams
CF K Bartee
1D C Fielder
OF-C Pride
M B Bell

KC 1996 AL
SP T Belcher
SP C Haney
SP K Appier
SP M Gubicza
SP J Rosado
RP D Linton
CL J Montgomery
RP H Pichardo
RP J Valera
C M Macfarlane
12 J Offerman
23 K Lockhart
SS D Howard
3B J Randa
ML T Goodwin
MR J Damon
RL M Tucker
DH-J Vitiello
IO C Paquette
D1-B Hamelin
2U-B Roberts
M B Boone

MIL 1996 AL
SP B McDonald
SP S Karl
SP R Bones
RS A Miranda
CL M Fetters
RP R Garcia
RP G Lloyd
C M Matheny
IF K Seitzer
2B F Vina
SS J Valentin
3B J Cirillo
LF G Vaughn
CF-P Listach
RF M Mieske
1D J Jaha
C J Levis
OI D Nilsson
UO-D Hulse
M P Garner

MIN 1996 AL
SP B Radke
SP F Rodriguez
SP R Robertson
SP S Aldred
SP A Aguilera
RP E Guardado
RP G Hansell
RP M Trombley
RS J Parra
C - G Myers
1B S Stahoviak
2B C Knoblauch
SS P Meares
3B D Hollins
LF M Cordova
CF R Becker
RM R Kelly
DH P Molitor
UT J Reboulet
1U-R Coomer
IO-C Hale
M T Kelly

NY 1996 AL
SP A Pettitte
SP K Rogers
SP D Gooden
SP J Key
RP M Rivera
CL J Wetteland
RP B Wickman
RP J Nelson
C J Girardi
1B T Martinez
2B M Duncan
SS D Jeter
3B W Boggs
LU G Williams
CF B Williams
RF P O'Neill
DL-R Sierra
23 A Fox
CU-J Leyritz
M J Torre

OAK 1996 AL
SR D Wengert
SR D Johns

SP J Wasdin
SP A Prieto
RS C Reyes
RP M Mohler
RP B Groom
RP J Corsi
C T Steinbach
1B M McGwire
2S-R Bournigal
SS M Bordick
3B S Brosius
LF-P Plantier
CF E Young
RF J Herrera
DR G Berroa
UT J Giambi
M A Howe

SEA 1996 AL
SP S Hitchcock
SP B Wolcott
SR B Wells
RP N Charlton
RP R Carmona
RP M Jackson
RP B Ayala
C D Wilson
1B P Sorrento
2B J Cora
SS A Rodriguez
3B-R Davis
LO R Amaral
CF K Griffey
RF J Buhner
DH E Martinez
UT-D Strange
M L Piniella

TEX 1996 AL
SP K Hill
SP R Pavlik
SP B Witt
SP D Oliver
SP K Gross
RP G Heredia
RP D Cook
RP J Russell
C I Rodriguez
1B W Clark
2B M McLemore
SS K Elster
3B D Palmer
LF R Greer
CF D Hamilton
RF J Gonzalez
DH M Tettleton
UO-D Buford
RU-W Newson
M J Oates

TOR 1996 AL
SP P Hentgen
SP E Hanson
SP J Guzman
SR P Quantrill
CL M Timlin
RP T Castillo
RP T Crabtree
C C O'Brien
1B J Olerud
2B-T Perez
SS A Gonzalez
3B E Sprague
L1 J Carter
CF O Nixon
RF S Green
DH C Delgado
UO-J Brumfield
LR-R Perez
M C Gaston

ATL 1997 NL
SP J Smoltz
SP T Glavine
SP G Maddux
SP D Neagle
CL M Wohlers
RP M Bielecki
RP P Byrd
C J Lopez
1B F McGriff
2B M Lemke
SS J Blauser
3B C Jones
LF R Klesko
RM A Jones
RL M Tucker
2U T Graffanino
CF K Lofton
IF-K Lockhart
M B Cox

CHI 1997 NL
SP S Trachsel
SP T Mulholland
SP K Foster
SP J Gonzalez

RP T Adams
RP K Bottenfield
RP M Rojas
RP T Wendell
C S Servais
1B M Grace
2B R Sandberg
SS S Dunston
3B K Orie
LF D Glanville
CF B McRae
RF S Sosa
OF D Clark
IO I Hernandez
S2-R Sanchez
3U-D Hansen
M J Riggleman

CIN 1997 NL
SP M Morgan
SP D Burba
SP K Mercker
SP B Tomko
SP J Smiley
CL J Shaw
RS M Remlinger
RP S Belinda
RP S Sullivan
C J Oliver
1B-H Morris
2B B Boone
SS P Reese
3O W Greene
UO-C Goodwin
ML D Sanders
RF-R Sanders
UT L Harris
1U E Perez
CU E Taubensee
M1 R Knight
M2 J McKeon

COL 1997 NL
SP R Bailey
SP J Thomson
SP J Wright
SP K Ritz
RP J Dipoto
RS D Holmes
RP M DeJean
RP S Reed
C K Manwaring
1B A Galarraga
2B E Young
SS W Weiss
3B V Castilla
LF D Bichette
CF Q McCracken
RF L Walker
ML E Burks
S2-N Perez
C - J Reed
M D Baylor

FLA 1997 NL
SP K Brown
SP A Fernandez
SP A Leiter
SP T Saunders
SP P Rapp
CL R Nen
RP J Powell
RS R Helling
RP D Cook
C C Johnson
1B J Conine
2B-L Castillo
SS E Renteria
3B B Bonilla
LM M Alou
CF-D White
RF G Sheffield
UO J Cangelosi
OI J Eisenreich
2U-K Abbott
M J Leyland

HOU 1997 NL
SP D Kile
SP M Hampton
SP C Holt
SP S Reynolds
SR R Garcia
CL B Wagner
RP J Lima
RP T Martin
RP R Springer
C B Ausmus
1B J Bagwell
2B C Biggio
SS-T Bogar
3B-S Berry
LF L Gonzalez
UO T Howard
RM D Bell
SI R Gutierrez

3I B Spiers
UO-J Mouton
M L Dierker

LA 1997 NL
SP H Nomo
SP I Valdes
SP C Park
SP P Astacio
SR T Candiotti
RP R Martinez
CL T Worrell
RP M Guthrie
RP D Dreifort
C M Piazza
1B E Karros
2B W Guerrero
SS G Gagne
3B T Zeile
LF T Hollandsworth
OF B Butler
RF B Mondesi
M B Russell

MON 1997 NL
SP P Martinez
SP C Perez
SP D Hermanson
SR J Bullinger
SP J Juden
RS M Valdes
CL U Urbina
RP A Telford
RP D Veres
C - C Widger
1B D Segui
2B M Lansing
SS M Grudzielanek
3B D Strange
LF H Rodriguez
CF W White
UT F Santangelo
OI J Orsulak
C - D Fletcher
RF-V Guerrero
OI-R McGuire
M F Alou

NY 1997 NL
SP R Reed
SP D Mlicki
SP B Jones
SP M Clark
CL J Franco
RP G McMichael
RP C Lidle
C T Hundley
1B J Olerud
2B C Baerga
SS R Ordonez
3B E Alfonzo
LF B Gilkey
MR C Everett
RI B Huskey
IO M Franco
RU A Ochoa
M B Valentine

PHI 1997 NL
SP C Schilling
SP M Leiter
SP M Beech
SP G Stephenson
CL R Bottalico
RP J Spradlin
RP R Blazier
RP R Harris
C M Lieberthal
1B R Brogna
2B M Morandini
SS K Stocker
3B S Rolen
LF G Jefferies
OI R Amaro
RF-D Murray
UI-K Jordan
RU-D May
M T Francona

PIT 1997 NL
SP E Loaiza
SP J Lieber
SP J Schmidt
SP F Cordova
SP S Cooke
CL S Loiselle
RP M Wilkins
RP R Rincon
RP M Ruebel
C J Kendall
1B-K Young
2B T Womack
SS-K Polcovich
3B C Ripken
3B J Randa
LF A Martin
CF J Allensworth
RF J Guillen

UI D Sveum
UO-J Mouton
M G Lamont

STL 1997 NL
SP M Morris
SP T Stottlemyre
SP An Benes
RP M Petkovsek
CL D Eckersley
RP R Beltran
C - M Difelice
1U D Young
2B D DeShields
SS R Clayton
3B G Gaetti
LF R Gant
CF R Lankford
UO W McGee
C T Lampkin
R1 J Mabry
M T LaRussa

SD 1997 NL
SP A Ashby
SP J Hamilton
SP S Hitchcock
SR P Smith
CL T Hoffman
RS T Worrell
RS S Bergman
RS W Cunnane
C J Flaherty
1B W Joyner
2B Q Veras
SS C Gomez
3B K Caminiti
LF G Vaughn
CF S Finley
RF T Gwynn
IO-A Cianfrocco
LO-R Henderson
UO-C Jones
M B Bochy

SF 1997 NL
SP S Estes
SP K Rueter
SP M Gardner
CL R Beck
RP J Tavarez
RP D Henry
RP J Roa
C - R Wilkins
1B J Snow
2B J Kent
SS J Vizcaino
3B B Mueller
LF B Bonds
CF D Hamilton
RM S Javier
RF G Hill
3U M Lewis
UO-M Benard
M D Baker

ANA 1997 AL
SP J Dickson
SP A Watson
SP D Springer
SP C Finley
RS H Hasegawa
RP P Harris
CL T Percival
RP M James
C - C Kreuter
1B D Erstad
2B L Alicea
SS G DiSarcina
3B D Hollins
LF G Anderson
CF J Edmonds
RF T Salmon
DH-E Murray
UT T Phillips
CU-J Leyritz
M T Collins
M B Bell

BAL 1997 AL
SP M Mussina
SP S Erickson
SP J Key
SP S Kamieniecki
CL R Myers
RP A Rhodes
RP A Benitez
RS S Boskie
C L Webster
1B R Palmeiro
2B R Alomar
SS M Bordick
3B C Ripken
LF B Surhoff
CF B Anderson
UO J Hammonds
DR-G Berroa

C C Hoiles
2I J Reboulet
RU T Tarasco
M D Johnson

BOS 1997 AL
SP T Wakefield
SR T Gordon
SP A Sele
SP J Suppan
RS J Wasdin
RS B Henry
RS C Hammond
RP J Corsi
C S Hatteberg
1B M Vaughn
2U J Frye
SS N Garciaparra
3B-T Naehring
LF W Cordero
CF D Bragg
RF T O'Leary
DH R Jefferson
D1-M Stanley
23 J Valentin
M J Williams

CHI 1997 AL
SP J Navarro
SP J Baldwin
SP D Drabek
SP W Alvarez
SP D Darwin
RP M Karchner
RP C Castillo
RP T Castillo
RP C McElroy
C J Fabregas
1D F Thomas
2B R Durham
SS O Guillen
3B-C Snopek
LF A Belle
CF M Cameron
R1 D Martinez
DH-H Baines
CF-D Lewis
RU-L Mouton
M T Bevington

CLE 1997 AL
SP C Nagy
SP O Hershiser
SP C Ogea
RP J Mesa
RP M Jackson
RS A Lopez
RP E Plunk
C S Alomar
1B J Thome
2B T Fernandez
SS O Vizquel
3B M Williams
LO B Giles
CF M Grissom
RF M Ramirez
LD D Justice
M M Hargrove

DET 1997 AL
SP J Thompson
SP W Blair
SP B Moehler
SP O Olivares
CL T Jones
RP A Sager
RP D Miceli
RP D Brocail
C R Casanova
1B T Clark
2B D Easley
SS D Cruz
3B T Fryman
LR B Higginson
CF B Hunter
RF M Nieves
DH B Hamelin
UT-P Nevin
M B Bell

KC 1997 AL
SP K Appier
SP T Belcher
SP J Rosado
SP G Rusch
RP J Pittsley
RP J Montgomery
RP H Pichardo
C - M Macfarlane
1B J King
2B J Offerman
SS J Bell
3B-S Brosius
LF B Roberts
CF T Goodwin
UO J Damon
DH C Davis

C - M Sweeney
M1 B Boone
M2 T Muser

MIL 1997 AL
SP C Eldred
SP S Karl
SP J Mercedes
SP J D'Amico
SP B McDonald
CL D Jones
RP B Wickman
RS J Adamson
RP M Fetters
C M Matheny
UT D Nilsson
2B-F Vina
SS J Valentin
3B J Cirillo
RL-M Mieske
CF G Williams
RF J Burnitz
D1-J Franco
C J Levis
UI M Loretta
UT-J Hueson
M P Garner

MIN 1997 AL
SP B Radke
SP B Tewksbury
SP R Robertson
SR F Rodriguez
SP L Hawkins
RP G Swindell
CL R Aguilera
RP M Trombley
RP T Ritchie
C T Steinbach
1B-S Stahoviak
2B C Knoblauch
SS P Meares
3B R Coomer
LF M Cordova
CF R Becker
UO M Lawton
DH P Molitor
UT M Hocking
M T Kelly

NY 1997 AL
SP A Pettitte
SP D Wells
SP D Cone
SP K Rogers
SR M Mendoza
CL M Rivera
RP D Gooden
RP J Nelson
RP M Stanton
C J Girardi
1B T Martinez
2B-L Sojo
SS D Jeter
3B C Hayes
LM-C Curtis
CF B Williams
RF P O'Neill
DH C Fielder
3U W Boggs
M J Torre

OAK 1997 AL
SP S Karsay
SP A Prieto
SP M Oquist
SP D Telgheder
RS D Wengert
RS M Mohler
RP A Small
RP B Taylor
C - B Mayne
1B McGwire
2B S Spiezio
SS-R Bournigal
3B S Brosius
UT J Giambi
CF-D Mashore
OI M Stairs
CF-M McDonald
IF D Magadan
DR J Canseco
M A Howe

SEA 1997 AL
SP J Fassero
SP R Johnson
SP J Moyer
SP B Wolcott
RP N Charlton
RP B Wells
RS S Sanders
C D Wilson
1B P Sorrento
2B J Cora
SS A Rodriguez

3B	R Davis
LR-	R Ducey
CF	K Griffey
RF	J Buhner
DH	E Martinez
UT-	R Amaral
M	L Piniella

TEX 1997 AL

SP	B Witt
SP	D Oliver
SP	J Burkett
SP	K Hill
SR	J Santana
CL	J Wetteland
RP	M Whiteside
RP	D Patterson
RP	E Gunderson
C	I Rodriguez
1B	W Clark
2B-	M McLemore
SS	B Gil
3B-	D Palmer
LF	R Greer
CF	D Buford
RU-	W Newson
DR	J Gonzalez
2S	D Cedeno
UT	L Stevens
M	J Oates

TOR 1997 AL

SP	R Clemens
SP	P Hentgen
SP	W Williams
SP	R Person
RP	P Quantrill
RP	D Plesac
C-	B Santiago
1B	C Delgado
2B	C Garcia
SS	A Gonzalez
3B	E Sprague
OF	S Green
CF	O Nixon
RF	O Merced
OI	J Carter
M1	C Gaston
M2	M Queen

ARI 1998 NL

SP	A Benes
SP	B Anderson
SR	O Daal
SP	W Blair
SP	A Telemaco
CL	G Olson
RS	C Sodowsky
C-	K Stinnett
1B	T Lee
2B-	A Stankiewicz
SS	J Bell
3B	M Williams
LF	D Dellucci
CF	D White
RF	K Garcia
UI	T Batista
OI	B Brede
UT	A Fox
LU-	Y Benitez
M	B Showalter

ATL 1998 NL

SP	G Maddux
SP	T Glavine
SP	D Neagle
SP	K Millwood
SP	J Smoltz
CL	K Ligtenberg
RS	D Martinez
C	J Lopez
1B	A Galarraga
2B	K Lockhart
SS-	W Weiss
3B	C Jones
LF	R Klesko
CF	A Jones
UO	G Williams
2B	T Graffanino
RF	M Tucker
LU-	D Bautista
SS-	O Guillen
M	B Cox

CHI 1998 NL

SP	K Tapani
SP	M Clark
SP	S Trachsel
SP	K Wood
SP	J Gonzalez
CL	B Beck
RS	T Mulholland
RP	T Adams
RS	D Wengert
C	S Servais
1B	M Grace
2B	M Morandini

SS	J Blauser
UT	J Hernandez
LF	H Rodriguez
ML	B Brown
RF	S Sosa
IO	M Alexander
CU-	T Houston
CF-	L Johnson
M	J Riggleman

CIN 1998 NL

SP	B Tomko
SP	P Harnisch
SP	M Remlinger
SP	S Parris
RP	G White
RP	S Sullivan
RP	D Graves
CL	J Shaw
C	E Taubensee
1B-	S Casey
2B	B Boone
SS	B Larkin
3O	W Greene
L1	D Young
MR	R Sanders
RM-J	Nunnally
LI	C Stynes
OF-	M Nieves
1U-	E Perez
UO-P	Watkins
M	J McKeon

COL 1998 NL

SP	D Kile
SP	P Astacio
SP	J Wright
SP	J Thomson
SR	B Jones
RP	J Dipoto
RP	D Veres
RP	C Leskanic
RP	M DeJean
C	K Manwaring
1B	T Helton
2B	M Lansing
SS	N Perez
3B	V Castilla
LF	D Bichette
CF	E Burks
RF	L Walker
MU	G Goodwin
C	J Reed
OI-	J Vander Wal
M	D Baylor

FLA 1998 NL

SP	L Hernandez
SP	B Meadows
SP	J Sanchez
RS	K Ojala
RP	A Alfonseca
RP	V Darensbourg
RP	M Mantei
C	G Zaun
1B	D Lee
2B	C Counsell
SS	E Renteria
3B-	T Zeile
LF	C Floyd
CF	T Dunwoody
RM	M Kotsay
UO	J Cangelosi
UT	R Jackson
UI-	D Berg
M	J Leyland

HOU 1998 NL

SP	J Lima
SP	S Reynolds
SP	M Hampton
SP	S Bergman
CL	B Wagner
RP	D Henry
RP	C Nitkowski
RP	S Elarton
C	B Ausmus
1B	J Bagwell
2B	C Biggio
SS	R Gutierrez
3B	B Spiers
LF	M Alou
CF	C Everett
RF	D Bell
3B	S Berry
OF-	D Clark
M	L Dierker

LA 1998 NL

SP	C Park
SP	D Dreifort
SP	I Valdes
SP	D Mlicki
SP	R Martinez
RP	S Radinsky
RP	A Osuna
RP	M Guthrie

C	C Johnson
1B	E Karros
2B	E Young
SS-	J Vizcaino
3B-	A Beltre
OI-	T Hubbard
MR	R Mondesi
RF-	G Sheffield
UO	R Cedeno
S2-	J Castro
M1	B Russell
M2	G Hoffman

MIL 1998 NL

SP	S Karl
SP	S Woodard
SP	J Juden
SR	B Woodall
SP	C Eldred
CL	B Wickman
RP	B Patrick
RP	D Jones
RP	C Fox
C	M Matheny
1S	M Loretta
2B	F Vina
SS	J Valentin
3B	J Cirillo
UO	D Jackson
CF	M Grissom
RF	J Burnitz
UT	B Hamelin
UT	D Nilsson
C-	B Hughes
LF-	G Jenkins
LU-	M Newfield
M	P Garner

MON 1998 NL

SP	D Hermanson
SP	J Vazquez
SP	C Perez
SP-	C Pavano
RS	M Batista
CL	U Urbina
RP	S Bennett
RP	A Telford
C	C Widger
1B	B Fullmer
2U-	J Vidro
SS	M Grudzielanek
3B	S Andrews
L2	F Santangelo
CF-	R White
RF	V Guerrero
1L	R McGuire
LU-	D May
M	F Alou

NY 1998 NL

SP	R Reed
SP	B Jones
SP	A Leiter
SP	M Yoshii
CL	J Franco
RP	T Wendell
RP	D Cook
RP	M Rojas
C	M Piazza
1B	J Olerud
2B	C Baerga
SS	R Ordonez
3B	E Alfonzo
LF-	B Gilkey
CF	B McRae
RF	B Huskey
UT	M Franco
UT	L Lopez
M-	B Valentine

PHI 1998 NL

SP	C Schilling
SP	M Portugal
SP	T Green
SP	C Loewer
SP	M Beech
RP	M Leiter
RP	W Gomes
RP	J Spradlin
RP	Y Perez
C-	M Lieberthal
1B	R Brogna
2B	M Lewis
SS	D Relaford
3B	S Rolen
LF	G Jefferies
CF	D Glanville
RF	B Abreu
UI	K Jordan
UT	K Sefcik
UO-	R Amaro
M	T Francona

PIT 1998 NL

SP	F Cordova
SP	J Schmidt
SP	J Lieber

SR	C Peters
SP	J Silva
RP	R Rincon
RS	E Dessens
CL	R Loiselle
SP	J Christiansen
C	J Kendall
1B	K Young
2B	T Womack
SS	L Collier
3B-	A Ramirez
LF	A Martin
UO	T Ward
RF	J Guillen
SI-	K Polcovich
UI-	D Strange
M	G Lamont

STL 1998 NL

SP	K Mercker
SP	T Stottlemyre
SR	K Bottenfield
SP	M Morris
RS	J Acevedo
RS	M Petkovsek
RP	J Frascatore
RP	J Brantley
C-	E Marrero
1B	M McGwire
2B	D DeShields
SS-	R Clayton
3B-	G Gaetti
LF	R Gant
CF	R Lankford
RF	B Jordan
UT	J Mabry
OI	W McGee
CU-	T Lampkin
M	T LaRussa

SD 1998 NL

SP	K Brown
SP	A Ashby
SP	J Hamilton
SR	S Hitchcock
CL	T Hoffman
RP	B Boehringer
RP	D Miceli
RP	D Wall
C	C Hernandez
1B	W Joyner
2B	Q Veras
SS	C Gomez
3B	K Caminiti
LF	G Vaughn
CF	S Finley
RF	T Gwynn
OI	M Sweeney
UI-	E Giovanola
RF-	R Rivera
UI-	A Sheets
M	B Bochy

SF 1998 NL

SP	M Gardner
SP	O Hershiser
SP	K Rueter
SP	D Darwin
SP	S Estes
CL	R Nen
RP	J Johnstone
RP	J Tavarez
RP	R Rodriguez
C	B Johnson
1B	J Snow
2B	J Kent
SS	R Aurilia
3B	B Mueller
LF	B Bonds
CF-	D Hamilton
RO	S Javier
RU	M Benard
IF	C Hayes
S2	R Sanchez
C-	B Mayne
M	D Baker

ANA 1998 AL

SP	C Finley
SR	O Olivares
SP	S Sparks
SP	J Dickson
SP	K Hill
CL	T Percival
RS	S Hasegawa
SP	F Castillo
CL	T Jones
RP	R DeLucia
RP	P Harris
C	M Walbeck
1D	C Fielder
2B-	J Baughman
SS	G DiSarcina
1B	T Clark
3B	D Hollins
1L	D Erstad
CF	J Edmonds
RF	G Anderson

DH	T Salmon
M	T Collins

BAL 1998 AL

SP	S Erickson
SP	M Mussina
SR	S Ponson
SP	D Drabek
RP	A Benitez
RS	D Johns
RP	A Rhodes
RP	A Mills
C	L Webster
1B	R Palmeiro
2B	A Alomar
SS	M Bordick
3B	C Ripken
LF	B Surhoff
CF	B Anderson
OF	E Davis
DH	H Baines
C-	C Hoiles
RD-	J Carter
M	R Miller

BOS 1998 AL

SP	P Martinez
SP	T Wakefield
SP	B Saberhagen
SR	S Avery
RS	D Lowe
CL	T Gordon
RS	J Wasdin
RP	J Corsi
C	S Hatteberg
1B	M Vaughn
2I	M Benjamin
SS	N Garciaparra
3B	J Valentin
LF	T O'Leary
MR	D Lewis
RF	D Bragg
DH-	R Jefferson
CF-	D Buford
C-	J Varitek
M	J Williams

CHI 1998 AL

SP	M Sirotka
SR	J Navarro
SR	J Baldwin
SP	J Parque
SR	S Eyre
RP	C Castillo
RP	B Simas
RP	K Foulke
RP	B Howry
C-	C Kreuter
1B-	W Cordero
2B	M Durham
SS	M Caruso
3B	R Ventura
LF	A Belle
CF	M Cameron
RF	M Ordonez
DH	F Thomas
1B	G Norton
UO-	J Abbott
M	J Manuel

CLE 1998 AL

SP	C Nagy
SP	D Burba
SP	B Colon
SP	J Wright
SP	D Gooden
CL	M Jackson
RP	J Mesa
RP	P Shuey
C	S Alomar
1B	J Thome
2B	D Bell
SS	O Vizquel
3B	T Fryman
LF	B Giles
CF	K Lofton
RF	M Ramirez
DH	D Justice
UO-	M Whiten
M	M Hargrove

DET 1998 AL

SP	J Thompson
SP	B Moehler
SP	B Florie
SP	S Greisinger
SP	F Castillo
CL	T Jones
RP	D Bochtler
RP	D Brocail
RP	A Sager
C-	P Bako
1B	T Clark
2B	D Easley
SS	D Cruz
3B	J Randa
LF	L Gonzalez

CF	B Hunter
RF	B Higginson
DU-	G Berroa
UI-	F Catalanotto
M1	B Bell
M2	L Parrish

KC 1998 AL

SP	T Belcher
SP	P Rapp
SR	J Rosado
SP	G Rusch
SP	H Pichardo
RS	C Haney
CL	J Montgomery
RP	S Service
RP	J Pittsley
C-	M Sweeney
1B	R King
2B	J Offerman
SS-	M Lopez
3B	D Palmer
LR-	J Conine
CF	J Damon
OI	L Sutton
D3-	T Pendleton
UT	H Morris
SS-	S Halter
M	T Muser

MIN 1998 AL

SP	B Radke
SP	L Hawkins
SP	E Milton
SP	B Tewksbury
CL	R Aguilera
RP	M Trombley
RS	D Serafini
RP	G Swindell
C	T Steinbach
1B-	D Ortiz
2B	T Walker
SS	P Meares
3U	B Gates
LF	M Cordova
CF	O Nixon
RM	M Lawton
DH	P Molitor
31	R Coomer
UT	D Hocking
RO-A	Ochoa
M	T Kelly

NY 1998 AL

SP	A Pettitte
SP	D Wells
SP	D Cone
SP	H Irabu
SP	O Hernandez
RS	R Mendoza
CL	M Rivera
RP	M Stanton
RP	D Holmes
C	J Posada
1B	T Martinez
2B	C Knoblauch
SS	D Jeter
3B	S Brosius
LM	C Curtis
CF-	B Williams
RF	P O'Neill
DH	D Strawberry
DL	T Raines
M	J Torre

OAK 1998 AL

SP	K Rogers
SP	T Candiotti
SP	J Haynes
SP	M Oquist
SP	B Stein
CL	B Taylor
RP	T Mathews
RP	M Mohler
RP	B Groom
C	A Hinch
1B	J Giambi
2B	S Spiezio
SS	M Tejada
3B	M Blowers
LF	R Henderson
CF	R Christenson
RF	B Grieve
DH	M Stairs
2S-	R Bournigal
M	A Howe

SEA 1998 AL

SP	J Moyer
SP	J Fassero
SP	R Johnson
SP	K Cloude
SP	J Swift
RP	M Timlin
RP	B Ayala
RS	P Spoljaric
RP	H Slocumb

C-	D Wilson
1B	D Segui
2B	J Cora
SS	A Rodriguez
3B	R Davis
LF-	G Hill
CF	K Griffey
RO	R Ducey
DH	E Martinez
M	L Piniella

TB 1998 AL

SP	R Arrojo
SP	T Saunders
SP	W Alvarez
SR	J Santana
SR	D Springer
CL	R Hernandez
RP	E Yan
RP	J Mecir
RP	A Lopez
C-	J Flaherty
1B	F McGriff
2B	M Cairo
SS	K Stocker
3B	B Smith
ML	Q McCracken
MO	R Winn
OF	M Kelly
DU	P Sorrento
3D	W Boggs
C-	M Difelice
SI-	A Ledesma
RF-	D Martinez
M	L Rothschild

TEX 1998 AL

SP	R Helling
SP	A Sele
SP	J Burkett
SP	D Oliver
CL	J Wetteland
RP	T Crabtree
RP	E Gunderson
RP	D Patterson
C	I Rodriguez
1B	W Clark
2B	M McLemore
SS-	K Elster
3B-	F Tatis
LF	R Greer
CF	T Goodwin
RF	J Gonzalez
D1	L Stevens
IO	L Alicea
OI-	M Simms
M	J Oates

TOR 1998 AL

SP	R Clemens
SP	W Williams
SP	P Hentgen
SP	C Carpenter
SP	J Guzman
RP	P Quantrill
RP	B Risley
RP	D Plesac
RP	D Stieb
C	D Fletcher
1B	C Delgado
2B	C Grebeck
SS	A Gonzalez
3B	E Sprague
LF	S Stewart
CF	J Cruz
RF	S Green
DL	J Canseco
23	T Fernandez
DU	M Stanley
M	T Johnson

ARI 1999 NL

SP	R Johnson
SP	O Daal
SP	A Benes
SP	A Reynoso
SR	B Anderson
RP	T Stottlemyre
RP	G Olson
RP	G Swindell
RP	D Holmes
C-	K Stinnett
1B	T Lee
2B	J Bell
SS	A Fox
3B	M Williams
LF	L Gonzalez
CF	S Finley
RF	T Womack
OF-	B Gilkey
M	B Showalter

ATL 1999 NL

SP	T Glavine
SP	K Millwood
SP-	G Maddux

SP	J Smoltz
CL	J Rocker
RP	M Remlinger
RP	K McGlinchy
RP	R Seanez
C	E Perez
1B	B Hunter
2B	B Boone
SS	W Weiss
3B	C Jones
LF	G Williams
CF	A Jones
RF	B Jordan
1L	K Klesko
IF	K Lockhart
SU-	O Guillen
LU-	O Nixon
1B-	R Simon
M	B Cox

CHI 1999 NL

SP	S Trachsel
SP	J Lieber
SP	S Tapani
SP	K Farnsworth
SR	T Mulholland
RS	S Sanders
RP	T Adams
RP	R Myers
RP	D Serafini
C	B Santiago
1B	M Grace
2B	M Morandini
SS	J Hernandez
3U	G Gaetti
LF	H Rodriguez
CF-	L Johnson
RF	S Sosa
IO	J Blauser
OF	G Hill
3U	T Houston
IO-	M Alexander
OF-	G Goodwin
M	J Riggleman

CIN 1999 NL

SP	P Harnisch
SP	B Tomko
SP	R Villone
SP	S Parris
SP	D Neagle
RP	D Graves
RP	S Sullivan
RP	S Williamson
RP	D Reyes
C	E Taubensee
1B	S Casey
2B	P Reese
SS	B Larkin
3B	A Boone
LF	G Vaughn
CF	M Cameron
RF	M Tucker
UO	J Hammonds
RU	D Young
3U-	M Lewis
M	J McKeon

COL 1999 NL

SP	P Astacio
SP	B Bohanon
SP	D Kile
SR	B Jones
SP	D Veres
CL	J Dipoto
RP	C Leskanic
RP	M DeJean
C-	H Blanco
1B	T Helton
2U-	K Abbott
SS	N Perez
3B	V Castilla
LF	D Bichette
CF-	D Hamilton
RF	L Walker
OI	A Echevarria
UT-	L Harris
2U-	T Shumpert
M	J Leyland

FLA 1999 NL

SP	D Springer
SP	B Meadows
SP	R Dempster
SP	A Fernandez
SP	L Hernandez
RP	A Alfonseca
RP	B Edmondson
RP	B Looper
RS	J Sanchez
C-	M Redmond
1B	K Millar
2B	L Castillo
SS	A Gonzalez
3B-	M Lowell
LU-	B Aven

MO P Wilson
RF M Kotsay
IO D Berg
C - J Fabregas
M J Boles

HOU 1999 NL
SP J Lima
SP M Hampton
SP S Reynolds
SS C Holt
SR S Elarton
CL B Wagner
SP S Bergman
RP J Powell
RP B Williams
C T Eusebio
1B J Bagwell
2B C Biggio
SS T Bogar
3B- K Caminiti
LF R Hidalgo
CF C Everett
RF D Bell
3O B Spiers
MU-G Barker
SS- R Gutierrez
UI- R Johnson
M1 L Dierker
M2 M Galante
M3 L Dierker

LA 1999 NL
SP K Brown
SP I Valdes
SP C Park
SP D Dreifort
CL J Shaw
RP A Mills
RP J Arnold
RP O Masaoka
C T Hundley
1B E Karros
2B E Young
SS M Grudzielanek
3B A Beltre
LF G Sheffield
CF D White
RF R Mondesi
IO D Hansen
OI- T Hollandsworth
OI- T Hubbard
IO- J Vizcaino
M D Johnson

MIL 1999 NL
SP S Karl
SP S Woodard
SP H Nomo
CL B Wickman
RP D Weathers
RS R Roque
RP E Plunk
C D Nilsson
UI M Loretta
2B R Belliard
3B J Valentin
3B J Cirillo
LF G Jenkins
CF M Grissom
RF J Burnitz
IC B Banks
1U S Berry
UO A Ochoa
UO- R Becker
M1 P Garner
M2 J Lefebvre

MON 1999 NL
SP D Hermanson
SP J Vazquez
SP M Thurman
SR M Batista
SP C Pavano
CL U Urbina
RP A Telford
RP S Kline
RP B Ayala
C C Widger
1B B Fullmer
2B J Vidro
SS O Cabrera
3B S Andrews
LM R White
CF M Martinez
RF V Guerrero
3C M Barrett
UT W Guerrero
UI M Mordecai
1O- R McGuire
UT- O Merced
UO-J Mouton
M F Alou

NY 1999 NL
SP A Leiter
SP O Hershiser

SP M Yoshii
SP R Reed
RP A Benitez
RP T Wendell
RP D Cook
RP P Mahomes
C M Piazza
1B J Olerud
2B E Alfonzo
SS R Ordonez
3B R Ventura
LF R Henderson
CF- B McRae
RF R Cedeno
UO B Agbayani
UT M Franco
M B Valentine

PHI 1999 NL
SP P Byrd
SP C Schilling
SP C Ogea
SP R Person
SP R Wolf
RP W Gomes
RP S Montgomery
RS M Grace
RP S Schrenk
C M Lieberthal
1B R Brogna
2B M Anderson
SS A Arias
3B S Rolen
LF R Gant
CF D Glanville
RF B Abreu
2B D Doster
UO R Ducey
32 K Jordan
OI K Sefcik
M T Francona

PIT 1999 NL
SP J Schmidt
SP K Benson
SP T Ritchie
SP F Cordova
SR P Schourek
RS J Silva
CL M Williams
RP S Sauerbeck
RP B Clontz
C - J Kendall
1B K Young
2B W Morris
SS M Benjamin
3B E Sprague
LF A Martin
CF B Giles
RM A Brown
OI B Brown
SU- A Nunez
M G Lamont

STL 1999 NL
SP D Oliver
SP K Bottenfield
SP J Jimenez
SP K Mercker
RS J Acevedo
RP M Aybar
RP R Bottalico
RP R Croushore
C E Marrero
1B M McGwire
2O J McEwing
SS E Renteria
3B F Tatis
LF R Lankford
CF J Drew
OI W McGee
OF T Howard
UO-D Bragg
C - A Castillo
2B- P Polanco
M T LaRussa

SD 1999 NL
SP W Williams
SP A Ashby
SP S Hitchcock
SP M Clement
CL T Hoffman
RP C Reyes
RP D Miceli
RP D Wall
C - B Davis
1B W Joyner
2B Q Veras
SS D Jackson
3U P Nevin
UT E Owens
CF R Rivera
LR R Sanders
RF T Gwynn
IF D Magadan

OI J Vander Wal
M B Bochy

SF 1999 NL
SP R Ortiz
SP S Estes
SP K Rueter
SP M Gardner
SP C Brock
CL R Nen
RP J Johnstone
RP F Rodriguez
RP A Embree
C B Mayne
1B J Snow
2B J Kent
SS R Aurilia
3B B Mueller
LF B Bonds
CF M Benard
RF E Burks
UO S Javier
UT F Santangelo
3U- C Hayes
M D Baker

ANA 1999 AL
SP C Finley
SP S Sparks
SP T Belcher
SP O Olivares
SP K Hill
CL T Percival
RP A Levine
RP M Petkovsek
RS S Hasegawa
C M Walbeck
1L D Erstad
2B- R Velarde
SS- G DiSarcina
3B T Glaus
LR O Palmeiro
MU G Anderson
RF T Salmon
1D M Vaughn
OF- T Greene
IO- J Huson
SS- A Sheets
M1 T Collins
M2 J Maddon

BAL 1999 AL
SP S Erickson
SP S Ponson
SP M Mussina
SP J Guzman
SP J Johnson
CL M Timlin
RS D Johns
RP S Kamieniecki
RP A Rhodes
C C Johnson
1U J Conine
2B- D DeShields
SS M Bordick
3B- C Ripken
LF B Surhoff
CF B Anderson
RF A Belle
DH H Baines
32 J Reboulet
UT- R Amaral
M R Miller

BOS 1999 AL
SP P Martinez
SR T Wakefield
SP M Portugal
SR P Rapp
SP B Saberhagen
RP D Lowe
RP J Wasdin
RP R Cormier
C J Varitek
1B M Stanley
2B J Offerman
SS N Garciaparra
3B J Valentin
LF T O'Leary
MR D Lewis
RF T Nixon
DU- R Jefferson
1D B Daubach
CF- D Buford
M J Williams

CHI 1999 AL
SP M Sirotka
SP J Baldwin
SP J Parque
SP J Navarro
3U P Nevin
UT E Owens
CL B Howry
RP S Lowe
RP B Simas
C B Fordyce

NY 1999 AL
SP O Hernandez
SP D Cone
SP A Pettitte
SP R Clemens
SP H Irabu
RS R Mendoza

1D P Konerko
2B R Durham
SS M Caruso
3B G Norton
LF C Lee
CF C Singleton
RF C Ordonez
D1 F Thomas
3I C Wilson
M J Manuel

CLE 1999 AL
SP D Burba
SP B Colon
SP C Nagy
SP J Wright
SP D Gooden
CL M Jackson
RP P Shuey
RP S Karsay
RS M Langston
C E Diaz
UT R Sexson
2B R Alomar
SS O Vizquel
3B- T Fryman
LD D Justice
CF K Lofton
RF M Ramirez
1B J Thome
3S E Wilson
M M Hargrove

DET 1999 AL
SP B Moehler
SP D Mlicki
SP J Weaver
SP J Thompson
SR W Blair
CL T Jones
RP D Brocail
RS C Nitkowski
RS N Cruz
C B Ausmus
1B T Clark
2B D Easley
SS D Cruz
3B D Palmer
LF J Encarnacion
CF G Kapler
RF B Higginson
OF- L Polonia
UI F Catalanotto
RL- K Garcia
M L Parrish

KC 1999 AL
SP J Suppan
SP J Rosado
SP J Witasick
SP K Appier
RS S Service
RP J Montgomery
RP A Morman
C C Kreuter
UT M Sweeney
2B C Febles
SS R Sanchez
3B J Randa
LF J Damon
CF C Beltran
RF J Dye
D1- J Giambi
UO- S Pose
M T Muser

MIN 1999 AL
SP B Radke
SP E Milton
SP L Hawkins
SR J Mays
RP M Trombley
RP B Wells
RP B Sampson
RP H Carrasco
C T Steinbach
1B D Mientkiewicz
2U T Walker
SS C Guzman
3U C Koskie
LF C Allen
CF T Hunter
RF M Lawton
DO M Cordova
13 R Coomer
32 B Gates
UT D Hocking
CF- J Jones
M T Kelly

CL M Rivera
RP J Grimsley
RP M Stanton
C J Posada
1B T Martinez
2B C Knoblauch
SS D Jeter
3B S Brosius
LF- C Curtis
CF B Williams
RF P O'Neill
DH C Davis
LF- R Ledee
M1 D Zimmer
M2 J Torre

OAK 1999 AL
SP G Heredia
SP J Haynes
SP M Oquist
SP T Hudson
SP K Rogers
RP D Jones
RP T Worrell
RP B Mathews
RP B Rigby
C - M Macfarlane
1B J Giambi
2M T Phillips
SS M Tejada
3B E Chavez
LF B Grieve
CF R Christenson
RF M Stairs
DH J Jaha
ML J McDonald
31- O Saenz
UI- S Spiezio
M A Howe

SEA 1999 AL
SP J Moyer
SP F Garcia
SR J Halama
SP J Fassero
CL J Mesa
RP J Paniagua
RS F Rodriguez
RS P Abbott
C D Wilson
1B- D Segui
2B D Bell
SS A Rodriguez
3B R Davis
LF B Hunter
CF K Griffey
RF- J Buhner
LU B Bonilla
2U W Joyner
UT- J Mabry
M L Piniella

TB 1999 AL
SP B Witt
SP W Alvarez
SP R Rupe
SP R Arrojo
CL R Hernandez
RP R White
RP A Lopez
RP E Yan
C J Flaherty
1B F McGriff
2B M Cairo
SS- K Stocker
3B- W Boggs
LU- B Trammell
CF- R Winn
RM D Martinez
DH J Canseco
L1 P Sorrento
S3- A Ledesma
M L Rothschild

TEX 1999 AL
SP R Helling
SP A Sele
SP J Burkett
SP M Morgan
SR E Loaiza
CL J Wetteland
RP J Zimmerman
RP M Venafro
RP T Crabtree
C I Rodriguez
1B L Stevens
2B M McLemore
SS R Clayton
3B T Zeile
LF R Greer
CF T Goodwin
RF J Gonzalez
DH R Palmeiro
UO-R Kelly
M J Oates

TOR 1999 AL
SP D Wells
SP P Hentgen
SP K Escobar
SP C Carpenter
SR R Halladay
CL B Koch
RP G Lloyd
RP P Spoljaric
RP P Munro
C D Fletcher
1B C Delgado
2B H Bush
SS T Batista
3B T Fernandez
LF S Stewart
CF J Cruz
RF S Green
DU- W Greene
M J Fregosi

ARI 2000 NL
SP R Johnson
SP B Anderson
SP A Reynoso
RP M Morgan
RP B Kim
RP G Swindell
RP R Springer
C D Miller
1B G Colbrunn
2B J Bell
SS T Womack
3B- M Williams
LF L Gonzalez
CF S Finley
RF- D Bautista
M B Showalter

ATL 2000 NL
SP G Maddux
SP T Glavine
SP K Millwood
SR T Mulholland
SP J Burkett
RP M Remlinger
CL J Rocker
C J Lopez
1B A Galarraga
2B- Q Veras
SS R Furcal
3B C Jones
LR R Sanders
CF A Jones
RF B Jordan
LU B Bonilla
UT W Joyner
2U K Lockhart
M B Cox

CHI 2000 NL
SP J Lieber
SP K Tapani
SP K Wood
RP T Van Poppel
RS K Farnsworth
RS D Garibay
RP T Worrell
C J Girardi
1B M Grace
2B E Young
SS R Gutierrez
3B W Greene
LF- H Rodriguez
CF D Buford
RF S Sosa
UI- J Nieves
C - J Reed
M D Baylor

CIN 2000 NL
SP S Parris
SR E Dessens
SR R Villone
SP R Bell
SP P Harnisch
CL D Graves
RP D Neagle
RS S Williamson
RP P Sullivan
C - B Santiago
1B S Casey
2B P Reese
SS B Larkin
3B- A Boone
OI M Tucker
CF K Griffey
RF D Bichette
LR A Ochoa
3U C Stynes
LU D Young
S2- E Castro
C - E Taubensee
M J McKeon

COL 2000 NL
SP P Astacio
SP B Bohanon
SP M Yoshii
SP K Jarvis
SP R Arrojo
RS J Tavarez
RP J Jimenez
RP G White
RP M DeJean
C B Mayne
1B T Helton
2B- M Lansing
SS N Perez
3B J Cirillo
RL- L Walker
CF- T Goodwin
RL J Hammonds
IO T Shumpert
M B Bell

FLA 2000 NL
SP R Dempster
SP J Sanchez
SP R Cornelius
SP C Smith
SP B Penny
CL A Alfonseca
RP R Bones
RP B Looper
RP V Darensbourg
C - M Redmond
1B D Lee
2B L Castillo
SS A Gonzalez
3B M Lowell
LF C Floyd
CF P Wilson
RF M Kotsay
UT K Millar
OF M Smith
SI- D Berg
M J Boles

HOU 2000 NL
SP C Holt
SP J Lima
SP S Elarton
SP S Reynolds
SP W Miller
RS O Dotel
RP J Slusarski
RP J Cabrera
RP M Valdes
C M Meluskey
1B J Bagwell
2B C Biggio
SS T Bogar
3B- C Truby
RL M Alou
CF R Hidalgo
RL L Berkman
S2 J Lugo
UT B Spiers
OI D Ward
CF-G Barker
M L Dierker

LA 2000 NL
SP K Brown
SP C Park
SP D Dreifort
SP C Perez
SP E Gagne
RP M Herges
RP T Adams
CL J Shaw
RP A Osuna
C - T Hundley
1B E Karros
2B M Grudzielanek
SS A Cora
3B A Beltre
LF G Sheffield
CF- T Hollandsworth
RF S Green
IO D Hansen
OI- F Santangelo
M D Johnson

MIL 2000 NL
SP J Haynes
SP J Wright
SP J D'Amico
SP J Snyder
SP J Bere
RP C Leskanic
RP J Acevedo
RP D Weathers
RP V DeLos Santos
C - H Blanco
1B- R Sexson
2B M Belliard
SS- M Loretta
3B J Hernandez
LF G Jenkins

CF M Grissom
RF J Burnitz
IF C Hayes
IF T Houston
C - R Casanova
UO-J Mouton
M D Lopes

MON 2000 NL
SP J Vazquez
SP D Hermanson
RS F Lira
RS M Johnson
RP S Kline
RP A Telford
C - C Widger
1B L Stevens
2B J Vidro
SS O Cabrera
3I- M Mordecai
LO T Jones
CF P Bergeron
RF V Guerrero
UI G Blum
OI W Guerrero
3C- M Barrett
IF- A Tracy
M F Alou

NY 2000 NL
SP M Hampton
SP A Leiter
SP G Rusch
SP R Reed
SP B Jones
CL A Benitez
RS M Mahomes
RP T Wendell
RP D Cook
C M Piazza
1B T Zeile
2B E Alfonzo
SS- M Bordick
3B R Ventura
LF A Agbayani
CF J Payton
RF D Bell
IO M Franco
UT- J McEwing
M B Valentine

PHI 2000 NL
SP R Wolf
SP R Person
SP C Schilling
SP A Ashby
RS C Brock
RP W Gomes
C - J Brantley
C M Lieberthal
1L P Burrell
2B- M Morandini
SS- D Relaford
3B S Rolen
LF- R Gant
CF J Glanville
RF B Abreu
UI K Jordan
UO K Sefcik
UT- B Hunter
M T Francona

PIT 2000 NL
SP K Benson
UO- T Ritchie
SP J Anderson
SR J Silva
RP M Williams
RP S Sauerbeck
RP M Wilkins
RP J Manzanillo
C J Kendall
1B K Young
2B W Morris
SS P Meares
RU- A Ramirez
LF- W Cordero
MU A Brown
UO B Giles
OI J Vander Wal
UI- M Benjamin
M G Lamont

STL 2000 NL
SP D Kile
SP G Stephenson
SP P Hentgen
SP R Ankiel
SP A Benes
CL D Veres
RP M Morris
RP H Slocumb
RP M James
C M Matheny
1B- M McGwire
2B F Vina
SS E Renteria

3B- F Tatis
LF R Lankford
CF J Edmonds
RO J Drew
UT S Dunston
3I C Paquette
UI P Polanco
RF- E Davis
OI- T Howard
M T LaRussa

SD 2000 NL
SP M Clement
SP W Williams
SP A Eaton
SP B Meadows
SP B Tollberg
CL T Hoffman
RPC Almanzar
RP K Walker
RP D Wall
C- W Gonzalez
1B R Klesko
2B B Boone
S2 D Jackson
3B P Nevin
LF- A Martin
CF R Rivera
OI E Owens
RU- K DeHaan
UI- D Magadan
M B Bochy

SF 2000 NL
SP L Hernandez
SP R Ortiz
SP S Estes
SP K Rueter
SR M Gardner
CL R Nen
RP R Rodriguez
RP A Fultz
RP A Embree
C B Estalella
1B J Snow
2B J Kent
SS R Aurilia
3B B Mueller
LF B Bonds
CF M Benard
RF E Burks
CF C Murray
RU A Rios
UT- F Crespo
S2- R Martinez
C- D Mirabelli
M D Baker

ANA 2000 AL
SP S Schoeneweis
SP K Bottenfield
SP R Ortiz
RP S Hasegawa
RS A Levine
RP M Petkovsek
CL T Percival
C B Molina
1B M Vaughn
2B A Kennedy
SS B Gil
3B T Glaus
LU D Erstad
CF G Anderson
RF T Salmon
UT S Spiezio
UO O Palmeiro
M M Scioscia

BAL 2000 AL
SP M Mussina
SP S Ponson
SP P Rapp
SR J Mercedes
SR J Johnson
RP M Trombley
RP B Groom
RP C McElroy
C- C Johnson
1B- W Clark
2L D DeShields
SS M Bordick
3B- C Ripken
LF B Surhoff
MO B Anderson
RF A Belle
DH- H Baines
UT J Conine
M M Hargrove

BOS 2000 AL
SP P Martinez
SR J Fassero
SP R Martinez
SP P Schourek
RS T Wakefield
CL D Lowe
RP R Garces

RP R Cormier
C J Varitek
1D- M Stanley
21 J Offerman
SS N Garciaparra
3I M Alexander
LF T O'Leary
CF C Everett
RF T Nixon
1D B Daubach
UO- D Lewis
CU- S Hatteberg
M J Williams

CHI 2000 AL
SP M Sirotka
SP J Parque
SP J Baldwin
SP C Eldred
SP K Wells
CL K Foulke
RP B Howry
RS S Lowe
RP B Simas
C- M Johnson
1B P Konerko
2B J Durham
SS J Valentin
3B H Perry
LF C Lee
CF C Singleton
RF M Ordonez
DH F Thomas
M J Manuel

CLE 2000 AL
SP C Finley
SP D Burba
SP B Colon
RS S Karsay
RP J Speier
RP P Shuey
RP S Reed
C- S Alomar
1D- D Segui
2B R Alomar
SS O Vizquel
3B T Fryman
L1- R Sexson
CF K Lofton
RF M Ramirez
1D J Thome
UT J Cabrera
M C Manuel

DET 2000 AL
SP J Weaver
SP H Nomo
SP B Moehler
SR W Blair
RS C Nitkowski
CL T Jones
RP S Sparks
RP M Anderson
C- B Ausmus
1B- T Clark
2B D Easley
SS D Cruz
3B D Palmer
LF B Higginson
CF- J Encarnacion
RM- R Becker
RD J Gonzalez
31 S Halter
RO- W Magee
M P Garner

KC 2000 AL
SP J Suppan
SP M Suzuki
SR D Reichert
SP B Stein
RP R Bottalico
RP J Spradlin
RP J Santiago
C- G Zaun
1D M Sweeney
2B C Febles
SS R Sanchez
3B J Randa
OF J Damon
CF C Beltran
RF J Dye
LD M Quinn
1U D McCarty
M T Muser

MIN 2000 AL
SP B Radke
SP E Milton
SP J Mays
SP M Redman
RP L Hawkins
RP B Wells
RS J Santana
RP H Carrasco

C- M LeCroy
1B R Coomer
2B J Canizaro
SS C Guzman
3B C Koskie
LM J Jones
CF T Hunter
RL M Lawton
DU D Ortiz
UT D Hocking
M T Kelly

NY 2000 AL
SP A Pettitte
SP R Clemens
SP O Hernandez
SP D Cone
CL M Rivera
RP J Grimsley
RP J Nelson
RP M Stanton
C J Posada
1B T Martinez
2B C Knoblauch
SS D Jeter
3B S Brosius
LR- D Justice
CF B Williams
RF P O'Neill
OF- S Spencer
UT C Bellinger
M J Torre

OAK 2000 AL
SP T Hudson
SP G Heredia
SP K Appier
SP M Mulder
SP O Olivares
CL J Isringhausen
RP J Tam
RP D Jones
RP T Mathews
C R Hernandez
1B Ja Giambi
2B R Velarde
SS M Tejada
3B E Chavez
LF B Grieve
CF T Long
RD M Stairs
OI Je Giambi
LO R Christenson
M A Howe

SEA 2000 AL
SP A Sele
SP P Abbott
SP J Halama
SP J Moyer
SP F Garcia
CL K Sasaki
RS B Tomko
RP J Paniagua
RP J Mesa
C- D Wilson
1B J Olerud
2B M McLemore
SS A Rodriguez
32 D Bell
OI S Javier
CF M Cameron
RF J Buhner
DH E Martinez
3B- C Guillen
LF- R Henderson
OI- R Ibanez
M L Piniella

TB 2000 AL
SR A Lopez
SP B Rekar
SR E Yan
SP S Trachsel
SR C Lidle
CL R Hernandez
RP R White
RP D Creek
RS T Sturtze
C J Flaherty
1B F McGriff
2B M Cairo
SS F Martinez
3B- V Castilla
LD G Vaughn
RF J Guillen
DH- J Canseco
OI S Cox
M L Rothschild

TEX 2000 AL
SP K Rogers
SP R Helling
SP D Oliver
SP E Loaiza
SR M Perisho

RS D Davis
CL J Wetteland
RP T Crabtree
RP F Cordero
C- I Rodriguez
1D R Palmeiro
2B L Alicea
SS R Clayton
3B M Lamb
LF R Greer
MR G Kapler
OF C Curtis
D1- D Segui
IO T Catalanotto
M J Oates

TOR 2000 AL
SP D Wells
SR K Escobar
SP C Carpenter
SP F Castillo
CL B Koch
RP P Quantrill
RP J Frascatore
RP L Painter
C D Fletcher
1B C Delgado
2B- H Bush
SS A Gonzalez
3B T Batista
LF S Stewart
CF J Cruz
RF- R Mondesi
DH B Fullmer
M J Fregosi

ARI 2001 NL
SP C Schilling
SP R Johnson
SR M Batista
SP B Anderson
RP B Kim
RP G Swindell
RP E Sabel
RP T Brohawn
C D Miller
1B M Grace
23 J Bell
SS T Womack
3B M Williams
LF L Gonzalez
CF S Finley
RF R Sanders
UO D Bautista
UI C Counsell
UO D Dellucci
UT- E Durazo
M B Brenly

ATL 2001 NL
SP G Maddux
SP J Burkett
SP T Glavine
SR J Marquis
SP K Millwood
RP M Remlinger
RS J Smoltz
RP J Cabrera
RP K Ligtenberg
C J Lopez
1B W Helms
2B- Q Veras
SS- R Furcal
3B C Jones
LF B Surhoff
CF A Jones
RF B Jordan
IF K Lockhart
OI D Martinez
M B Cox

CHI 2001 NL
SP J Lieber
SP J Bere
SP K Wood
SP K Tapani
SP J Tavarez
RP J Fassero
RP K Farnsworth
RP T Van Poppel
C- J Girardi
1U M Stairs
2B M Cairo
2B E Young
SS R Gutierrez
31 R Coomer
LF- R White
CF G Matthews
RF S Sosa
M D Baylor

CIN 2001 NL
SP E Dessens
SP C Reitsma
SP L Davis
RS J Brower
CL D Graves
SP S Sullivan

RP H Mercado
C J LaRue
1B S Casey
2B- T Walker
S2 P Reese
3B A Boone
L1 D Young
CF K Griffey
RF- A Ochoa
MO R Rivera
UI- J Castro
UO- B Clark
UO- M Tucker
IO F Catalanotto
M B Boone

COL 2001 NL
SP M Hampton
SP D Neagle
SP S Chacon
SP J Astacio
RP K Davis
RP G White
RP J Speier
C- B Petrick
1B T Helton
2B- T Walker
SS- N Perez
3B J Cirillo
LR- A Ochoa
CF J Pierre
RF L Walker
UT G Norton
IO T Shumpert
M B Bell

FLA 2001 NL
SP R Dempster
SP B Penny
SP A Burnett
SP M Clement
RP V Nunez
CL A Alfonseca
RP B Looper
RP R Bones
C C Johnson
1B D Lee
2B L Castillo
SS A Gonzalez
3B M Lowell
LF C Floyd
RM E Owens
UT K Millar
UI- D Berg
OI- J Mabry
M1 J Boles
M2 T Perez

HOU 2001 NL
SP W Miller
SP S Reynolds
SP R Oswalt
SP S Elarton
CL B Wagner
RP N Cruz
RP M Jackson
C B Ausmus
1B J Bagwell
2B C Biggio
SS J Lugo
3B V Castilla
LF L Berkman
CF R Hidalgo
RF M Alou
UI J Vizcaino
UT- O Merced
OI- D Ward
M L Dierker

LA 2001 NL
SP C Park
SR T Adams
SP E Gagne
SP L Prokopec
SP K Brown
CL J Shaw
RP M Herges
RP G Carrara
C P LoDuca
1B K Karros
2B M Grudzielanek
SS A Cora
3B A Beltre
LF- R White
CF G Matthews
RF S Green
MU T Goodwin
IF- D Hansen
SI- J Reboulet
M J Tracy

MIL 2001 NL
SP J Wright
SP J Haynes
SP B Sheets

SR A Levrault
RP M DeJean
RP C Leskanic
RP C Fox
RP D Weathers
C H Blanco
1B R Sexson
2B R Belliard
SS J Hernandez
3B- T Houston
LF G Jenkins
MU D White
RF J Burnitz
23 M Loretta
3I- L Lopez
M D Lopes

MON 2001 NL
SP J Vazquez
SP T Armas
SP M Thurman
RS M Yoshii
RS B Reames
RS P Strickland
RP G Lloyd
C M Barrett
1B L Stevens
2B J Vidro
SS O Cabrera
IO G Blum
LU- M Smith
CF P Bergeron
RF V Guerrero
IO- M Mordecai
M1 F Alou
M2 J Torborg

NY 2001 NL
SP K Appier
SP A Leiter
SP G Rusch
SP S Trachsel
SR R Reed
CL A Benitez
RP R White
RP J Franco
RP T Wendell
C M Piazza
1B T Zeile
2B E Alfonzo
SS R Ordonez
3B V Ventura
LF- B Agbayani
CF J Payton
UO T Shinjo
UT L Harris
UT J McEwing
UI D Relaford
RU- T Perez
M B Valentine

PHI 2001 NL
SP R Person
SP O Daal
SP R Wolf
CL J Mesa
RP R Bottalico
RP J Santiago
RP R Cormier
C- J Estrada
1B T Lee
2B M Anderson
SS J Rollins
3B S Rolen
LF P Burrell
CF D Glanville
RF B Abreu
UO- B Hunter
M L Bowa

PIT 2001 NL
SP T Ritchie
SP J Anderson
SP J Beimel
SP D Williams
RS O Olivares
RP J Manzanillo
RP S Sauerbeck
C J Kendall
1B K Young
2B- P Meares
SS J Wilson
3B A Ramirez
LF B Giles
CF- E Brown
RU- J Vander Wal
IO A Nunez
UT- R Mackowiak
UT- C Wilson
M L McClendon

STL 2001 NL
SP D Kile
SP M Morris
SP D Hermanson
SP A Benes
RS M Matthews

RP S Kline
RP D Veres
RP G Stechschulte
C M Matheny
1B- M McGwire
2B F Vina
SS E Renteria
3S P Polanco
LF- R Lankford
CF J Edmonds
RF J Drew
UT C Paquette
UT A Pujols
UO K Robinson
UT- B Bonilla
C- E Marrero
M T LaRussa

SD 2001 NL
SP B Jones
SP K Jarvis
SP W Williams
SP A Eaton
SP B Tollberg
RS B Lawrence
CL T Hoffman
RP J Nunez
RP D Lee
C B Davis
1B R Klesko
2B D Jackson
SS- D Jimenez
3B P Nevin
LF R Henderson
CF M Kotsay
RU B Trammell
RM M Darr
UI- D Magadan
M B Bochy

SF 2001 NL
SP L Hernandez
SP R Ortiz
SP K Rueter
SP S Estes
CL R Nen
RP F Rodriguez
RP A Fultz
C B Santiago
1B J Snow
2B J Kent
SS R Aurilia
3B- P Feliz
LF B Bonds
CF C Murray
MR M Benard
32 R Martinez
OI- S Dunston
RF- A Rios
M D Baker

ANA 2001 AL
SP R Ortiz
SP S Schoeneweis
SP J Washburn
SP P Rapp
SP I Valdes
CL T Percival
RP L Pote
RP A Levine
RP B Weber
C- B Molina
1B S Spiezio
2B A Kennedy
SS D Eckstein
3B T Glaus
LF G Anderson
CF D Erstad
RF T Salmon
UC- S Wooten
IO B Gil
UO O Palmeiro
M M Scioscia

BAL 2001 AL
SP J Johnson
SP J Mercedes
SP J Towers
SP S Ponson
SR W Roberts
RP B Groom
RP M Trombley
RP B Ryan
RP J Wasdin
C- B Fordyce
1O J Conine
2B J Hairston
SS- M Bordick
3B C Ripken
RL B Anderson
MS M Mora
RM C Richard
IF- T Batista
1B- D Segui
M M Hargrove

BOS 2001 AL
SP H Nomo
SR T Wakefield
SP F Castillo
SP D Cone
SP P Martinez
CL D Lowe
RS R Arrojo
RP R Beck
RP R Garces
C- S Hatteberg
1B B Daubach
21 J Offerman
S2 M Lansing
3B S Hillenbrand
LR T O'Leary
CF C Everett
RM T Nixon
DL M Ramirez
OF D Lewis
IO- C Stynes
M1 J Williams
M2 J Kerrigan

CHI 2001 AL
SP- M Buehrle
SR K Wells
SP K Biddle
SR J Garland
SP D Wells
RS S Lowe
CL K Foulke
RS S Glover
RP B Howry
C- S Alomar
1B P Konerko
2B R Durham
SS R Clayton
3U- H Perry
LF C Lee
CF C Singleton
RF M Ordonez
DH- J Canseco
3S J Valentin
UT- J Liefer
M J Manuel

CLE 2001 AL
SP B Colon
SP C Sabathia
SP D Burba
SP C Finley
CL B Wickman
RS J Westbrook
RP R Rincon
RP P Shuey
C E Diaz
1B J Thome
2B R Alomar
SS O Vizquel
3B T Fryman
LO M Cordova
CF K Lofton
RF J Gonzalez
DH E Burks
3L R Branyan
UT J Cabrera
LU- W Cordero
M C Manuel

DET 2001 AL
SP S Sparks
SP J Weaver
SP C Holt
SP J Lima
CL M Anderson
RS V Santos
RP D Patterson
RP H Murray
C- B Inge
1D T Clark
2B D Easley
SS D Cruz
3U J Jones
LF B Higginson
MR R Cedeno
RM J Encarnacion
DH- D Palmer
CU R Fick
3S S Halter
UO- W Magee
1D- R Simon
M P Garner

KC 2001 AL
SP J Suppan
SP C Durbin
SR B Stein
SP D Reichert
SR K Wilson
CL R Hernandez
RP J Grimsley
RP D Henry
RP C Bailey
C- H Ortiz

[KC 2001 AL]
U D McCarty
B- C Febles
SS R Sanchez
?B J Randa
OF M Quinn
CF C Beltran
RF- J Dye
D M Sweeney
U L Alicea
U D Brown
JT R Ibanez
M T Muser

MIN 2001 AL
SP J Mays
SP B Radke
SP E Milton
RP E Guardado
CL L Hawkins
RP H Carrasco
RP B Wells
C A Pierzynski
1B D Mientkiewicz
2B L Rivas
SS C Guzman
3B C Koskie
LF J Jones
CF T Hunter
ML M Lawton
DH- D Ortiz
JT D Hocking
M T Kelly

NY 2001 AL
SP M Mussina
SP R Clemens
SP A Pettitte
SP T Lilly
CL M Rivera
RP R Mendoza
RP M Stanton
C J Posada
1B T Martinez
2B A Soriano
SS D Jeter
3B S Brosius
LF C Knoblauch
CF B Williams
RF P O'Neill
DH D Justice
M J Torre

OAK 2001 AL
SP T Hudson
SP M Mulder
SP B Zito
SP C Lidle
SP G Heredia
CL J Isringhausen
RP J Tam
RP J Mecir
RP M Magnante
C R Hernandez
1B J Giambi
2B F Menechino
SS M Tejada
3B E Chavez
ML J Damon
UO T Long
RF- J Dye
1B J Giambi
D1 O Saenz
OI J Giambi
M A Howe

SEA 2001 AL
SP F Garcia
SP A Sele
SP J Moyer
SP P Abbott
SR J Halama
CL K Sasaki
RP R Franklin
RP A Rhodes
RP J Nelson
C D Wilson
1B J Olerud
2B B Boone
SS C Guillen
3B D Bell
LO- S Javier
CF M Cameron
RF I Suzuki
DH E Martinez
LU A Martin
L3 M McLemore
UT- C Gipson
M L Piniella

TB 2001 AL
SR T Sturtze
SP P Wilson
SP R Rupe
SP B Rekar
SP A Lopez
RP J Kennedy
CL E Yan
RP T Phelps
RP D Creek
C - J Flaherty
1U S Cox
2B- B Abernathy
SS- F Martinez
RP J Fassero
C - J Girardi
LM J Tyner
UO R Winn
OF B Grieve
DL G Vaughn
UI- R Johnson
2O- D Rolls
M1 L Rothschild
M2 H McRae

TEX 2001 AL
SP R Helling
SP D Davis
SP D Oliver
SP K Rogers
SP R Bell
RP P Mahomes
CL J Zimmerman
RP M Petkovsek
RP M Venafro
C I Rodriguez
1D R Palmeiro
2B M Young
SS A Rodriguez
3B- M Lamb
LU F Catalanotto
CF G Kapler
RF- R Ledee
DR- R Sierra
M1 J Oates
M2 J Narron

TOR 2001 AL
SP C Carpenter
SP E Loaiza
SP J Hamilton
SP C Michalak
SP S Parris
RS K Escobar
RP R Halladay
CL B Koch
RP P Quantrill
C D Fletcher
1B C Delgado
2B- H Bush
SS A Gonzalez
3B- T Batista
LF S Stewart
CF J Cruz
RF R Mondesi
DH B Fullmer
M B Martinez

ARI 2002 NL
SP R Johnson
SP C Schilling
SP M Batista
SP R Helling
SR B Anderson
CL B Kim
RP M Koplove
C D Miller
1B M Grace
2B J Spivey
SS T Womack
3B C Counsell
LF L Gonzalez
CF S Finley
RM Q McCracken
UO- D Dellucci
M B Brenly

ATL 2002 NL
SP T Glavine
SP K Millwood
SP G Maddux
SP D Moss
SP J Marquis
CL J Smoltz
RP C Hammond
RP M Remlinger
RP K Ligtenberg
C J Lopez
1B J Franco
2U K Lockhart
SS R Furcal
3B V Castilla
LF C Jones
CF A Jones
RF G Sheffield
UO D Bragg
C - H Blanco
1U- M Franco
13- W Helms
M B Cox

CHI 2002 NL
SP K Wood
SP M Clement
SP J Lieber
SP M Prior
SR C Zambrano
RP J Borowski
RS J Cruz
RP A Alfonseca
RP J Fassero
C - J Girardi
1B F McGriff
2I M Bellhorn
SS A Gonzalez
3B B Mueller
LF M Alou
CF C Patterson
RF S Sosa
UO R Brown
IF C Stynes
C - T Hundley
M1 D Baylor
M2 B Kimm

CIN 2002 NL
SP J Haynes
SP E Dessens
SR C Reitsma
SR J Hamilton
RP D Graves
RP S Williamson
RP S Sullivan
RS J Rijo
C J LaRue
1B S Casey
2B T Walker
SS B Larkin
3B A Boone
L1 A Dunn
ML R Taylor
RF A Kearns
IO- R Branyan
MR- J Encarnacion
M B Boone

COL 2002 NL
SP J Jennings
SP M Hampton
SP D Neagle
SR D Stark
SP J Thomson
RS S Chacon
CL J Jimenez
RP T Jones
RP J Speier
C - G Bennett
1B T Helton
23 B Butler
SS J Uribe
3B T Zeile
LF- T Hollandsworth
CF J Pierre
RF L Walker
IO G Norton
2U T Shumpert
M1 B Bell
M2 C Hurdle

FLA 2002 NL
SP A Burnett
SP J Tavarez
SR M Tejera
SP B Penny
SP R Dempster
RP V Nunez
RP J Beckett
RP B Looper
C - C Johnson
1B D Lee
2B L Castillo
SS A Fox
3B M Lowell
LU K Millar
CF P Wilson
LR E Owens
UT T Raines
RU- C Floyd
C - M Redmond
M J Torborg

HOU 2002 NL
SP R Oswalt
SP W Miller
SP C Hernandez
CL B Wagner
RP O Dotel
RS N Cruz
RP R Stone
C B Ausmus
1B J Bagwell
2B C Biggio
SS- J Lugo
3B G Blum
LF D Ward
CF L Berkman
RF R Hidalgo
CF B Hunter
UT O Merced
UI J Vizcaino
M J Williams

LA 2002 NL
SP O Perez
SP H Nomo
SP A Ashby
SR O Daal
SP K Ishii
CL E Gagne
RP G Carrara
RP P Quantrill
RP G Mota
C P LoDuca
1B E Karros
2B M Grudzielanek
SS C Izturis
3B A Beltre
LF B Jordan
CF D Roberts
RF S Green
S2 A Cora
ML M Grissom
IF- D Hansen
M J Tracy

MIL 2002 NL
SP B Sheets
SP G Rusch
SP G Gomez
SP J Wright
RS J Cabrera
CL M DeJean
RP L Vizcaino
RP R King
C - P Bako
1B R Sexson
2B E Young
SS J Hernandez
3B- T Houston
LF- G Jenkins
CF A Sanchez
MR J Hammonds
IF R Belliard
IO L Harris
3U- M Loretta
RU- A Ochoa
M1 D Lopes
M2 J Royster

MON 2002 NL
SP J Vazquez
SP T Ohka
SP T Armas
SR M Yoshii
SP B Colon
RP S Stewart
RP M Herges
RS B Reames
RP T Tucker
C M Barrett
1B A Galarraga
2B J Vidro
SS O Cabrera
3B F Tatis
LU- T O'Leary
OI B Wilkerson
RF V Guerrero
MI- J Macias
M F Robinson

NY 2002 NL
SP A Leiter
SP J Astacio
SP S Trachsel
SP J D'Amico
SP S Estes
CL A Benitez
RP D Weathers
RP S Strickland
C M Piazza
1B M Vaughn
2B R Alomar
SS R Ordonez
3B E Alfonzo
LF R Cedeno
MO T Perez
RF J Burnitz
UT J McEwing
UI J Valentin
CF- J Payton
M B Valentine

PHI 2002 NL
SP R Wolf
SP V Padilla
SP B Duckworth
SR T Adams
CL J Mesa
RP C Silva
RS D Coggin
RP R Cormier
C M Lieberthal
1B T Lee
2B M Anderson
SS J Rollins
3B S Rolen
2B J Burrell
CF D Glanville
RF B Abreu
UT- J Giambi
UO- R Ledee
OI- J Michaels
2I- T Perez
M L Bowa

PIT 2002 NL
SP K Wells
SP J Fogg
SP J Anderson
RS R Villone
RS J Beimel
RP B Boehringer
C J Kendall
1B K Young
2B P Reese
SS J Wilson
3B A Ramirez
RM R Mackowiak
R1 C Wilson
3I M Benjamin
IF A Nunez
MU-A Brown
M L McClendon

STL 2002 NL
SP M Morris
SP J Simontacchi
SP W Williams
CL J Isringhausen
RP D Veres
RS L Hackman
RP S Kline
C M Matheny
1B T Martinez
2B F Vina
SS E Renteria
3B- P Polanco
L3 A Pujols
CF J Edmonds
RF J Drew
UT M Cairo
OC E Marrero
UO K Robinson
UT- E Perez
M T LaRussa

SD 2002 NL
SP B Lawrence
SP B Tomko
SP B Jones
CL T Hoffman
RP J Fikac
C T Lampkin
1B A Galarraga
2S R Vazquez
SS D Cruz
31 P Nevin
LF- T O'Leary
OI B Wilkerson
RF R Trammell
LF R Gant
UT- T Hubbard
23- D Jimenez
RL- E Kingsale
LU- R Lankford
M B Bochy

SF 2002 NL
SP L Hernandez
SP R Ortiz
SP K Rueter
SP J Schmidt
SP J Jensen
CL R Nen
RP J Worrell
RP F Rodriguez
RP J Witasick
C B Santiago
1B J Snow
2B J Kent
SS R Aurilia
3B D Bell
LF B Bonds
CF T Shinjo
RF R Sanders
1U- D Minor
M D Baker

ANA 2002 AL
SP R Ortiz
SP J Washburn
SP K Appier
SP A Sele
SP J Lackey
RS T Schoeneweis
CL T Percival
RP B Weber
RP A Levine
RP B Molina
C B Molina
1B S Spiezio
2B A Kennedy
SS D Eckstein
3B T Glaus
LF G Anderson
CF D Erstad
DU B Fullmer
UO O Palmeiro
M M Scioscia

BAL 2002 AL
SP R Lopez
SP S Ponson
SP S Erickson
SR T Driskill
SP J Johnson
CL J Julio
RP R Bauer
RP B Groom
C G Gil
1B J Conine
2B J Hairston
SS M Bordick
3B T Batista
UT M Mora
CF C Singleton
RO G Matthews
LD M Cordova
RU J Gibbons
M M Hargrove

BOS 2002 AL
SP D Lowe
SP P Martinez
SP J Burkett
SR F Castillo
RS T Wakefield
RS C Fossum
CL U Urbina
RS A Arrojo
C J Varitek
1B- T Clark
2B R Sanchez
SS N Garciaparra
3B S Hillenbrand
LU- R Henderson
CF J Damon
RF T Nixon
LD M Ramirez
UT B Daubach
2B- L Merloni
M G Little

CHI 2002 AL
SP M Buehrle
SP D Wright
SP J Garland
SR G Glover
SP T Ritchie
RP K Foulke
RS K Biddle
RP A Osuna
RP D Marte
C - M Johnson
1B P Konerko
2B- R Durham
SS R Clayton
3S J Valentin
LF C Lee
ML A Rowand
RF M Ordonez
DH F Thomas
CF- K Lofton
M J Manuel

CLE 2002 AL
SP C Sabathia
SR D Baez
SP D Drese
SP B Colon
SP C Finley
CL D Riske
C E Diaz
1B J Thome
2B- R Gutierrez
SS O Vizquel
3B T Fryman
LR- C Magruder
CF M Bradley
RU M Lawton
DH E Burks
2I- J McDonald
M1 C Manuel
M2 J Skinner

DET 2002 AL
SP M Redman
SP S Sparks
SP M Maroth
SP J Weber
SR A Bernero
CL J Acevedo
RP K Farnsworth
RP J Santana
C - B Inge
1B- C Pena
2B- D Easley
SI S Halter
3B- C Truby
LF B Higginson
CF W Magee
RF R Fick
D1 R Simon
2U- D Jackson
M1 P Garner
M2 L Pujols

KC 2002 AL
SP P Byrd
SP J Suppan
SP D May
SR M Asencio
RS J Affeldt
CL R Hernandez
RS D Reichert
C B Mayne
1B M Sweeney
2B C Febles
SS N Perez
3B J Randa
LF- C Knoblauch
CF C Beltran
UT M Tucker
OI R Ibanez
IO- L Alicea
M1 T Muser
M2 M Mizerock
M3 T Pena

MIN 2002 AL
SP R Reed
SP K Lohse
SP E Milton
SP B Radke
SR J Santana
CL E Guardado
RP T Fiore
RP J Romero
RP L Hawkins
C A Pierzynski
1B D Mientkiewicz
2B- L Rivas
SS C Guzman
3B C Koskie
LF J Jones
CF T Hunter
RF D Mohr
DH D Ortiz
2I D Hocking
OI B Kielty
M R Gardenhire

NY 2002 AL
SP M Mussina
SP D Wells
SP R Clemens
SP O Hernandez
SP A Pettitte
RP S Karsay
RP R Mendoza
RP M Stanton
C J Posada
1D N Johnson
2B A Soriano
SS D Jeter
3B R Ventura
LF R White
CF B Williams
RF M Ordonez
RL- S Spencer
1D J Giambi
RU- J Vander Wal
M J Torre

OAK 2002 AL
SP T Hudson
SP B Zito
SP M Mulder
SP C Lidle
CL B Koch
RP C Bradford
RP J Mecir
C R Hernandez
1D S Hatteberg
2B M Ellis
SS M Tejada
3B E Chavez
LO- E Byrnes
CF T Long
RF J Dye
DH- R Durham
OF D Justice
1L- J Mabry
M A Howe

SEA 2002 AL
SP J Moyer
SP F Garcia
SP J Pineiro
SP J Baldwin
RS R Franklin
RS J Halama
CL K Sasaki
RP A Rhodes
C D Wilson
1B J Olerud
2B B Boone
SS C Guillen
3B J Cirillo
M McLemore
CF M Cameron
RF I Suzuki
DH- E Martinez
UT D Relaford
OF R Sierra
M L Piniella

TB 2002 AL
SP T Sturtze
SP J Kennedy
SP P Wilson
SR J Sosa
RS V Zambrano
CL E Yan
RS T Harper
RP S Kent
C - T Hall
1U S Cox
2B B Abernathy
SS C Gomez
3B J Sandberg
LF- C Crawford
CF R Winn
RF B Grieve
IF A Huff
M H McRae

TEX 2002 AL
SP K Rogers
SP I Valdes
SP C Park
SP D Burba
RP J Van Poppel
RP J Powell
C I Rodriguez
UT M Lamb
2B M Young
SS A Rodriguez
3B H Perry
RL K Mench
CF- R Rivera
UO C Everett
1D R Palmeiro
M J Narron

TOR 2002 AL
SP R Halladay
SP E Loaiza
SR P Walker
SP J Miller
CL K Escobar
RP C Thurman
RP S Cassidy
RP S Eyre
C - K Huckaby
1B C Delgado
2B- O Hudson
SS- C Woodward
3B B Hinske
LD S Stewart
CF V Wells
UO J Cruz
DH- J Phelps
UT D Berg
SS- F Lopez
CU- T Wilson
M1 B Martinez
M2 C Tosca

ARI 2003 NL
SP M Batista
SP W Webb
SP E Dessens
SP C Schilling
SP R Johnson
SP O Villarreal
CL M Mantei
RP S Randolph
RP J Valverde
C - R Barajas
1B- L Overbay
2B J Spivey
SS A Cintron
3S- C Counsell
LF L Gonzalez
CF S Finley
RU- D Bautista
UI C Baerga
UO Q McCracken
13- S Hillenbrand
M B Brenly

ATL 2003 NL
SP G Maddux
SP R Ortiz
SP M Hampton
SP R Ramirez
SP S Reynolds
CL J Smoltz
RP T Hodges

RP R Hernandez
RP R King
C J Lopez
1B R Fick
2B M Giles
SS R Furcal
3B V Castilla
LF C Jones
CF A Jones
RF G Sheffield
UO D Bragg
IO M DeRosa
1U M Franco
UT M Franco
M B Cox

CHI 2003 NL
SP C Zambrano
SP M Prior
SP K Wood
SP M Clement
SP S Estes
CL J Borowski
RP K Farnsworth
RP M Remlinger
RP A Alfonseca
C D Miller
1B E Karros
2B M Grudzielanek
SS A Gonzalez
3B- A Ramirez
LF M Alou
CF- C Patterson
RF S Sosa
UI R Martinez
UO- T Goodwin
OF- T O'Leary
M D Baker

CIN 2003 NL
SP D Graves
SP P Wilson
SP R Dempster
RS J Riedling
RP C Reitsma
RP F Heredia
RP B Reith
C J LaRue
1B S Casey
2B- D Jimenez
SS- B Larkin
3B A Boone
LF A Dunn
RM-A Kearns
RO-J Guillen
UI J Castro
UO R Taylor
M1 B Boone
M2 R Knight
M3 D Miley

COL 2003 NL
SP J Jennings
SP D Oliver
SP S Chacon
SR A Cook
RS J Jimenez
RP J Speier
RP B Fuentes
RP S Reed
C C Johnson
1B T Helton
2B R Belliard
SS- J Uribe
3B C Stynes
LF J Payton
CF P Wilson
RF L Walker
IO G Norton
M C Hurdle

FLA 2003 NL
SP C Pavano
SP B Penny
SP M Redman
SP D Willis
SP J Beckett
CL B Looper
RS M Tejera
RS T Phelps
RP A Almanza
C I Rodriguez
1B D Lee
2B L Castillo
SS A Gonzalez
3B M Lowell
LU- T Hollandsworth
CF J Pierre
RF J Encarnacion
OI- B Banks
L3- M Cabrera
M1 J Torborg
M2 J McKeon

HOU 2003 NL
SP W Miller
SP T Redding

SP J Robertson
SP R Oswalt
SP R Villone
CL B Wagner
RP O Dotel
RP B Lidge
RP R Stone
C B Ausmus
1B J Bagwell
2B J Kent
SS A Everett
3B M Ensberg
LF L Berkman
CF C Biggio
RF R Hidalgo
3I G Blum
UT O Merced
UI- J Vizcaino
M J Williams

LA 2003 NL
SP H Nomo
SP K Brown
SP O Perez
SP K Ishii
CL E Gagne
RP G Mota
RP P Quantrill
RP P Shuey
C P LoDuca
1B- F McGriff
2B A Cora
SS C Izturis
3B A Beltre
LF- B Jordan
CF D Roberts
RF S Green
UT J Cabrera
UT- M Kinkade
M J Tracy

MIL 2003 NL
SP B Sheets
SP W Franklin
SP M Kinney
SR G Rusch
RP M DeJean
RP L Estrella
RP L Vizcaino
RP B Kieschnick
C E Perez
1B R Sexson
2B E Young
SS R Clayton
3B W Helms
LF G Jenkins
CF S Podsednik
RU B Clark
IO K Ginter
RU J Vander Wal
M N Yost

MON 2003 NL
SP L Hernandez
SP J Vazquez
SP T Ohka
SP Z Day
SP C Vargas
CL R Biddle
RS T Tucker
RP L Ayala
RP J Eischen
C B Schneider
1B W Cordero
2B J Vidro
SS O Cabrera
3U J Carroll
LM B Wilkerson
CF E Chavez
RF V Guerrero
UO R Calloway
UT J Macias
UT H Mateo
M F Robinson

NY 2003 NL
SP S Trachsel
SP J Seo
SP T Glavine
SP A Leiter
RP D Weathers
CL A Benitez
RP D Wheeler
C - V Wilson
1U J Phillips
2B- R Alomar
SS- J Reyes
3B T Wigginton
LF C Floyd
UO T Perez
RF R Cedeno
1U T Clark
UO R Gonzalez
UT J McEwing
M A Howe

PHI 2003 NL
SP K Millwood
SP V Padilla
SP R Wolf
SP B Myers
RP C Silva
RP R Cormier
CL J Mesa
RP T Adams
C M Lieberthal
1B J Thome
2B P Polanco
SS J Rollins
3B- D Bell
LF J Burrell
CF M Byrd
RF B Abreu
UO R Ledee
UI T Perez
M L Bowa

PIT 2003 NL
SP K Wells
SP J D'Amico
SP J Fogg
SP J Suppan
SR S Torres
RP K Benson
RP J Tavarez
RS B Meadows
RP J Beimel
C J Kendall
1B- R Simon
2B- J Reboulet
SS J Wilson
3B- A Ramirez
LF B Giles
CF- K Lofton
RL R Sanders
2U A Nunez
OI M Stairs
OI C Wilson
M L McClendon

STL 2003 NL
SP W Williams
SP B Tomko
SP G Stephenson
SP M Morris
SR J Simontacchi
RS J Fassero
RP C Eldred
RP S Kline
C M Matheny
1B T Martinez
2B- B Hart
SS E Renteria
3B S Rolen
L1 A Pujols
CF J Edmonds
UO O Palmeiro
RM J Drew
RU E Perez
UO K Robinson
UT- M Cairo
M T LaRussa

SD 2003 NL
SP B Lawrence
SP J Peavy
SP A Eaton
SP O Perez
RP L Hackman
RP M Matthews
RP S Linebrink
C - G Bennett
1B R Klesko
2B M Loretta
SS R Vazquez
3B S Burroughs
LF R White
CF M Kotsay
RF X Nady
OI D Hansen
UI D Hansen
UO G Matthews
M B Bochy

SF 2003 NL
SP J Schmidt
SP K Rueter
SP J Williams
SP D Moss
SP J Foppert
CL T Worrell
RS J Brower
RP J Nathan
RP F Rodriguez
C B Santiago
1B J Snow
2B R Durham
SS R Aurilia
3B E Alfonzo
LF B Bonds
CF M Grissom
RF J Cruz

1U A Galarraga
UI N Perez
3U- P Feliz
M F Alou

ANA 2003 AL
SP J Washburn
SP J Lackey
SP R Ortiz
SP A Sele
RS S Shields
RP F Rodriguez
CL T Percival
RP B Weber
C B Molina
13 S Spiezio
2B A Kennedy
SS D Eckstein
3B- T Glaus
UO E Owens
RM J DaVanon
RD T Salmon
IF S Wooten
M M Scioscia

BAL 2003 AL
SP J Johnson
SP P Hentgen
SP S Ponson
SP R Lopez
SP R Helling
CL J Julio
RP R Bauer
RP K Ligtenberg
RP B Ryan
C B Fordyce
1B J Conine
2B B Roberts
SS D Cruz
3B T Batista
LF- L Bigbie
CF L Matos
RF J Gibbons
DH-D Segui
LO- M Mora
OI- B Surhoff
M M Hargrove

BOS 2003 AL
SP D Lowe
SP T Wakefield
SP P Martinez
SP J Burkett
CL B Kim
RP M Timlin
RP B Lyon
RS R Mendoza
C J Varitek
1U K Millar
2B T Walker
SS N Garciaparra
3B B Mueller
LF M Ramirez
CF J Damon
RF T Nixon
D1 D Ortiz
UT J Jackson
M G Little

CHI 2003 AL
SP B Colon
SP M Buehrle
SP E Loaiza
SP J Garland
RP D Marte
RP T Gordon
RP B Koch
C M Olivo
1B P Konerko
2B- D Jimenez
SS J Valentin
3B J Crede
LF C Lee
ML- A Rowand
RF M Ordonez
DH F Thomas
UT- B Daubach
UI- T Graffanino
M J Manuel

CLE 2003 AL
SP C Sabathia
SP J Davis
SP B Anderson
SR J Westbrook
SR B Traber
CL C Baez
RP T Mulholland
RP D Riske
RP J Boyd
C - J Bard
1B B Broussard
2B R Phillips
SS- J Peralta
3B C Blake
ML C Crisp

CF M Bradley
UO J Gerut
DH- E Burks
LU M Lawton
UT- T Hafner
UI- J McDonald
M E Wedge

DET 2003 AL
SP N Cornejo
SP M Maroth
SP J Bonderman
SP A Bernero
CL T Percival
RP B Weber
RP S Sparks
RS W Ledezma
RP C Spurling
C B Inge
1B C Pena
2B- W Morris
S2 R Santiago
3B E Munson
LR C Monroe
CF A Sanchez
RF B Higginson
UT D Young
IO S Halter
IO- K Witt
M A Trammell

KC 2003 AL
SP D May
SR J Affeldt
CL M Mac Dougal
RP D Carrasco
RP J Grimsley
RP K Wilson
C B Mayne
1U K Harvey
2I D Relaford
SS A Berroa
3B J Randa
LF R Ibanez
CF C Beltran
RF A Guiel
D1 M Sweeney
UO M Tucker
M T Pena

MIN 2003 AL
SP B Radke
SP K Lohse
SP K Rogers
SR J Santana
SP R Reed
RS J Mays
CL E Guardado
RP J Rincon
RP L Hawkins
C A Pierzynski
1B D Mientkiewicz
2B L Rivas
SS C Guzman
3B C Koskie
LU J Jones
CF T Hunter
RO D Mohr
DU M LeCroy
UT- D Hocking
M R Gardenhire

NY 2003 AL
SP M Mussina
SP D Wells
SP R Clemens
SP A Pettitte
SP J Weaver
CL M Rivera
RP C Hammond
RP A Osuna
RP S Hitchcock
C J Posada
1B J Giambi
1D- N Johnson
2B A Soriano
SS D Jeter
3B- R Ventura
LM H Matsui
CF B Williams
RF M Mondesi
1D J Giambi
M J Torre

OAK 2003 AL
SP T Hudson
SP B Zito
SP M Mulder
SP T Lilly
SR J Halama
CL K Foulke
RP C Bradford
RP R Rincon
C R Hernandez
1B S Hatteberg
2B M Ellis
SS M Tejada
3B E Chavez
ML E Byrnes

CF C Singleton
LR T Long
DH E Durazo
M K Macha

SEA 2003 AL
SP J Moyer
SP R Franklin
SP J Pineiro
SP F Garcia
SP G Meche
RP S Hasegawa
RP J Mateo
RP A Rhodes
RP R Soriano
C - D Wilson
1B J Olerud
2B B Boone
S3 C Guillen
3B- J Cirillo
LF R Winn
CF M Cameron
RF I Suzuki
DH E Martinez
IO M McLemore
UT- W Bloomquist
M B Melvin

TB 2003 AL
SP V Zambrano
SR J Sosa
SP R Bell
CL L Carter
RP T Harper
RP J Colome
RP A Levine
C T Hall
1B T Lee
2B M Anderson
SS J Lugo
3R D Rolls
LF C Crawford
RF R Baldelli
RU A Huff
DU A Martin
M L Piniella

TEX 2003 AL
SP J Thomson
SP C Lewis
SR R Dickey
SP I Valdes
SP J Benoit
RP F Cordero
RP A Fultz
RP B Shouse
RP J Powell
C E Diaz
1B M Teixeira
2B M Young
SS A Rodriguez
3B H Blalock
LR- E Everett
CF- R Christenson
RD-J Gonzalez
D1 R Palmeiro
M B Showalter

TOR 2003 AL
SP R Halladay
SP C Lidle
SR K Escobar
SP M Hendrickson
RS T Sturtze
RP A Lopez
RP C Politte
RP T Miller
CU G Myers
1B C Delgado
2B O Hudson
SS C Woodward
3B E Hinske
OI F Catalanotto
CF V Wells
RL R Johnson
DH J Phelps
SI M Bordick
UT L Gonzalez
C - T Wilson
M C Tosca

ARI 2004 NL
SP R Johnson
SP B Webb
SP C Fossum
SR S Sparks
RP M Koplove
RS E Dessens
RS R Randolph
RP R Choate
C - J Brito
1B S Hillenbrand
2B S Hairston
SS A Cintron
3B R Tracy
LF L Gonzalez

CF S Finley
RF D Bautista
M B Brenly
M A Pedrique

ATL 2004 NL
SP R Ortiz
SP J Thomson
SP M Wright
SP M Hampton
SP B Byrd
CL J Smoltz
RP C Reitsma
RP A Alfonseca
RP J Cruz
C J Estrada
1B A LaRoche
2B M Giles
SS R Furcal
3U C Jones
LR- E Marrero
CF A Jones
RF J Drew
3U M DeRosa
1U J Franco
2B- N Green
LF- C Thomas
M B Cox

CHI 2004 NL
SP G Maddux
SP C Zambrano
SP M Clement
SP K Wood
SR G Rusch
RP M Prior
RP L Hawkins
RP K Farnsworth
RP K Mercker
C M Barrett
1B D Lee
2U T Walker
SI R Martinez
3B A Ramirez
LF M Alou
CF C Patterson
RF S Sosa
UT J Macias
2B- M Grudzielanek
M D Baker

CIN 2004 NL
SP P Wilson
SP A Harang
SR A Acevedo
SP C Lidle
RS T Van Poppel
CL D Graves
RP J Riedling
RP P Norton
C J LaRue
1B S Casey
2B D Jimenez
SS B Larkin
3S J Castro
LF A Dunn
UO W Pena
UT R Freel
OI- J Cruz
CF- K Griffey
CU- J Valentin
M D Miley

COL 2004 NL
SP S Estes
SP J Jennings
SP J Kennedy
RS J Fassero
CL S Chacon
RP S Reed
RP T Harikkala
C J Johnson
1B T Helton
2B A Miles
SS C Clayton
3B V Castilla
LF M Holliday
CF- P Wilson
RM J Burnitz
SI- T Wilson
UT L Gonzalez
OI M Sweeney
M C Hurdle

FLA 2004 NL
SP C Pavano
SP D Willis
SP J Beckett
SP B Penny
SP A Burnett
CL A Benitez
RP N Bump
C - M Redmond
1B- H Choi
2B L Castillo
SS A Gonzalez
3B M Lowell
L1 J Conine

CF J Pierre
RL M Cabrera
IO D Easley
M J McKeon

HOU 2004 NL
SP R Oswalt
SP R Clemens
SR T Redding
SP P Munro
CL B Lidge
RP D Miceli
RS B Backe
RP C Harville
C - B Ausmus
1B J Bagwell
2B J Kent
SS A Everett
3B M Ensberg
LM C Biggio
CF- C Beltran
RL L Berkman
3U M Lamb
OI J Lane
UO O Palmeiro
UI J Vizcaino
M J Williams
M P Garner

LA 2004 NL
SP J Weaver
SP O Perez
SP K Ishii
SP J Lima
SR W Alvarez
CL E Gagne
RP D Sanchez
RP G Mota
RP G Carrara
C - P LoDuca
1R S Green
2B A Cora
SS C Izturis
3B A Beltre
LU- J Werth
MO M Bradley
RF- J Encarnacion
OI J Grabowski
IF R Ventura
2I- J Hernandez
M J Tracy

MIL 2004 NL
SP B Sheets
SP D Davis
SP V Santos
SP W Obermueller
CL D Kolb
RP L Vizcaino
RP D Burba
RP J Bennett
C C Moeller
1B L Overbay
2B- J Spivey
SS C Counsell
3U- W Helms
LF G Jenkins
CF S Podsednik
RF B Clark
IO K Ginter
RU B Grieve
UI B Hall
M N Yost

MON 2004 NL
SP L Hernandez
SR S Kim
SP Z Day
RS C Vargas
RP C Cordero
RP L Ayala
RS R Biddle
C - B Schneider
1L B Wilkerson
1B J Vidro
SS O Cabrera
3B T Batista
LR T Sledge
CF E Chavez
RF J Rivera
2U J Carroll
M F Robinson

NY 2004 NL
SP T Glavine
SP S Trachsel
SP A Leiter
SP J Seo
CL B Looper
RP M Stanton
RP R Bottalico
RP D Wheeler
C1 J Phillips
1C M Piazza
2B- D Garcia
SS K Matsui
3B- D Wright

LF C Floyd
CF M Cameron
RF- R Hidalgo
OI E Valent
IF T Zeile
SP T Wigginton
M A Howe

PHI 2004 NL
SP E Milton
SP B Myers
SP K Millwood
SP R Wolf
SP V Padilla
RP T Worrell
RP R Cormier
RP R Madson
RP R Hernandez
C M Lieberthal
1B J Thome
2B P Polanco
SS J Rollins
3B D Bell
LF P Burrell
CF M Byrd
RF B Abreu
UO J Michaels
MU-D Glanville
UI- T Perez
2U- C Utley
M L Bowa

PIT 2004 NL
SP O Perez
SP J Fogg
SP K Wells
SP R Vogelsong
SP K Benson
CL J Mesa
RP S Torres
RP B Meadows
RP J Grabow
C J Kendall
1B- D Ward
2B J Castillo
SS J Wilson
3B- C Stynes
LF J Bay
CF T Redman
R3 R Mackowiak
IF B Hill
UI A Nunez
R1 C Wilson
M L McClendon

STL 2004 NL
SP M Morris
SP J Marquis
SP W Williams
SP J Suppan
SP C Carpenter
CL J Isringhausen
RP C Eldred
RP J Tavarez
RP R King
C M Matheny
1B A Pujols
2B T Womack
SS E Renteria
3B S Rolen
UO S Taguchi
CF J Edmonds
RL R Sanders
UT M Anderson
OF- R Cedeno
LU- R Lankford
UT- H Luna
UT- J Mabry
M T LaRussa

SD 2004 NL
SP B Lawrence
SP A Eaton
SP D Wells
SP J Peavy
SP I Valdez
CL T Hoffman
RP S Linebrink
RP A Otsuka
RP J Witasick
C R Hernandez
1B P Nevin
2B M Loretta
SS K Greene
3B S Burroughs
LF K Klesko
CF J Payton
RF B Giles
UO T Long
M B Bochy

SF 2004 NL
SP J Schmidt
SP B Tomko
SP K Rueter
SR D Hermanson
SP J Williams
RP J Brower
RP M Herges
RP T Walker
RP S Eyre
C A Pierzynski
1B J Snow
2B R Durham
SS D Cruz
3B E Alfonzo
LF B Bonds
CF M Grissom
RF M Tucker
UT P Feliz
UO D Mohr
S2 N Perez
M F Alou

ANA 2004 AL
SP B Colon
SP K Escobar
SP J Lackey
SP J Washburn
SP A Sele
RS R Ortiz
RS S Shields
RP F Rodriguez
RP K Gregg
C- B Molina
1B D Erstad
2B A Kennedy
SS D Eckstein
3M C Figgins
LF J Guillen
CF G Anderson
RF V Guerrero
DU- T Salmon
UO J DaVanon
M M Scioscia

BAL 2004 AL
SP S Ponson
SR R Lopez
SP D Cabrera
SP E Bedard
CL J Julio
RP B Ryan
RP J Parrish
RP R Bauer
C J Lopez
1B R Palmeiro
2B B Roberts
SS M Tejada
3B M Mora
LF L Bigbie
CF- L Matos
UT- D Newhan
RU- J Gibbons
UT- J Hairston
M L Mazzilli

BOS 2004 AL
SP C Schilling
SP P Martinez
SP T Wakefield
SP D Lowe
SP B Arroyo
CL K Foulke
RP M Timlin
RP A Embree
C J Varitek
OI K Millar
2B M Bellhorn
S2- P Reese
3B B Mueller
LF M Ramirez
CF J Damon
RO G Kapler
DH D Ortiz
1U- D McCarty
M T Francona

CHI 2004 AL
SP M Buehrle
SP J Garland
SP E Loaiza
SP S Schoeneweis
SP F Garcia
RS S Takatsu
RP D Marte
RP N Cotts
RP J Adkins
C- B Davis
1B P Konerko
2U W Harris
SS J Valentin
3B J Crede
LF C Lee
CF A Rowand
UO T Perez
DH-F Thomas
UT- R Gload
2S J Uribe
M O Guillen

CLE 2004 AL
SP J Westbrook
SP C Sabathia
SP C Lee
SP S Elarton
SP J Davis
RP D Riske
RP R White
RP R Betancourt
RP M Miller
C V Martinez
1B B Broussard
2B R Belliard
SS O Vizquel
3B C Blake
LF M Lawton
ML C Crisp
RF J Gerut
DH T Hafner
M E Wedge

DET 2004 AL
SP M Maroth
SP N Robertson
SP J Johnson
SP J Bonderman
SR G Knotts
RP E Yan
CL U Urbina
RP A Levine
RP J Walker
C I Rodriguez
1B C Pena
2U O Infante
SS C Guillen
3B E Munson
LR C Monroe
CF- A Sanchez
RF B Higginson
DI D Young
3C B Inge
LD R White
M A Trammell

KC 2004 AL
SP D May
SP B Anderson
SP J Gobble
SP Z Greinke
SP M Wood
RS D Reyes
CL J Affeldt
RP S Camp
RP S Sullivan
C- J Buck
1D K Harvey
2B- T Graffanino
SS A Berroa
3B J Randa
CF- D DeJesus
CF- C Beltran
OI M Stairs
1D M Sweeney
UT D Relaford
M T Pena

MIN 2004 AL
SP J Santana
SP B Radke
SP C Silva
SP K Lohse
SR T Mulholland
CL J Nathan
RP J Rincon
RP J Romero
RP J Roa
C H Blanco
1B- D Mientkiewicz
2B L Rivas
SS C Guzman
3B C Koskie
LM L Ford
CF T Hunter
RF J Jones
DU- J Offerman
UC- M LeCroy
LF- S Stewart
M R Gardenhire

NY 2004 AL
SP J Vazquez
SP J Lieber
SP M Mussina
SP K Brown
CL M Rivera
RP P Quantrill
RP T Gordon
RP T Sturtze
C J Posada
1B T Clark
2B M Cairo
SS D Jeter
3B A Rodriguez
LF H Matsui
MD B Williams
RF G Sheffield
DO R Sierra
CF-K Lofton
2B- E Wilson
M J Torre

OAK 2004 AL
SP M Mulder
SP B Zito
SP M Redman
SP R Harden
SP T Hudson
RP J Duchscherer
CL O Dotel
RP C Bradford
RP C Hammond
C D Miller
1B S Hatteberg
2B M Scutaro
SS B Crosby
3B E Chavez
LF E Byrnes
CF M Kotsay
RF J Dye
DH E Durazo
LR- B Kielty
M K Macha

SEA 2004 AL
SP J Moyer
SP R Franklin
SP J Pineiro
SP G Meche
SP F Garcia
RS R Villone
RP J Putz
RP S Hasegawa
RP J Mateo
C D Wilson
1B- J Olerud
2B B Boone
SS- R Aurilia
31 S Spiezio
LF R Ibanez
CF R Winn
RF I Suzuki
DH E Martinez
UT J Cabrera
UT- W Bloomquist
M B Melvin

TB 2004 AL
SP M Hendrickson
SP V Zambrano
SP R Bell
SP D Brazelton
SR J Halama
RS J Sosa
CL D Baez
RP L Carter
RP T Harper
C T Hall
1B T Martinez
2B- R Sanchez
SS J Lugo
32 G Blum
LF C Crawford
CF M Baldelli
RF J Cruz
3U A Huff
M L Piniella

TEX 2004 AL
SP K Rogers
SP R Drese
SR R Dickey
SR J Benoit
CL F Cordero
RP C Almanzar
RP R Mahay
RP R Brocail
C R Barajas
1B M Teixeira
2B A Soriano
SS M Young
3B H Blalock
LF D Dellucci
CF L Nix
UO M Mench
DH- B Fullmer
UT E Young
RF- G Matthews
M B Showalter

TOR 2004 AL
SP M Batista
SP T Lilly
SP R Halladay
SP J Towers
SP D Bush
RP J Frasor
RP J Speier
RP V Chulk
RP K Ligtenberg
C G Zaun
2B O Hudson
SU C Gomez
3B E Hinske
UO R Johnson
CF V Wells
RF A Rios
DH- J Phelps
M C Tosca
M J Gibbons

ARI 2005 NL
SP B Webb
SP J Vazquez
SP B Halsey
SP S Estes
SP C Vargas
RP R Ortiz
RP J Valverde
RP L Cormier
RP M Koplove
C C Snyder
1U T Clark
2B C Counsell
SS R Clayton
3B T Glaus
LF L Gonzalez
CF- L Terrero
RF S Green
UI A Cintron
UO Q McCracken
1R C Tracy
M B Melvin

ATL 2005 NL
SP J Smoltz
SP H Ramirez
SP T Hudson
SR J Sosa
SP J Thomson
RP C Reitsma
RP D Kolb
C J Estrada
1B A LaRoche
2B M Giles
SS R Furcal
3B C Jones
LF- K Johnson
CF A Jones
UO R Langerhans
3U W Betemit
1U J Franco
IO P Orr
M B Cox

CHI 2005 NL
SP G Maddux
SP C Zambrano
SP M Prior
SR G Rusch
SP J Williams
CL R Dempster
RP M Wuertz
C M Barrett
1B D Lee
2B T Walker
SS N Perez
3B A Ramirez
LF T Hollandsworth
CF C Patterson
RF J Burnitz
UT J Hairston
UT J Macias
M D Baker

CIN 2005 NL
SP A Harang
SP E Milton
SP R Ortiz
SP B Claussen
RP D Weathers
RS M Belisle
RP K Mercker
RP T Coffey
C J LaRue
1B S Casey
2S R Aurilia
SS F Lopez
3B- J Randa
LF A Dunn
CF K Griffey
RF A Kearns
OI J Cruz
UT R Freel
RM W Pena
M D Miley
M J Narron

COL 2005 NL
SP J Francis
SP J Wright
SR B Kim
SP J Jennings
CL B Fuentes
RS J Acevedo
RP D Cortes
RP M Carvajal
C- J Closser
1B T Helton
2I L Gonzalez
SS- C Barmes
3B G Atkins
LF M Holliday
MU C Sullivan
RF B Hawpe
2B A Miles
RO D Mohr
UT M Anderson
M C Hurdle

FLA 2005 NL
SP D Willis
SP A Burnett
SP J Beckett
SR B Moehler
CL T Jones
RP G Mota
C P LoDuca
1B C Delgado
2B L Castillo
SS A Gonzalez
3B M Lowell
LF M Cabrera
CF J Pierre
RF J Encarnacion
OI J Conine
UI D Easley
UT- L Harris
M J McKeon

HOU 2005 NL
SP R Oswalt
SP A Pettitte
SP R Clemens
SP B Backe
SP W Rodriguez
CL B Lidge
RP C Qualls
RP D Wheeler
RP R Springer
C B Ausmus
1L L Berkman
2B C Biggio
SS A Everett
3B M Ensberg
LF C Burke
CF W Taveras
RF J Lane
1U M Lamb
UO O Palmeiro
UI J Vizcaino
UT- E Bruntlett
M P Garner

LA 2005 NL
SP J Weaver
SP D Lowe
SP B Penny
SR D Houlton
SP O Perez
RP Y Brazoban
RP D Sanchez
RP G Carrara
RS E Dessens
C J Phillips
1U H Choi
2B J Kent
SS C Izturis
UI O Robles
LR J Werth
UO J Repko
RM-J Drew
LU R Ledee
IO A Perez
1U O Saenz
UT- M Edwards
M J Tracy

MIL 2005 NL
SP D Davis
SP C Capuano
SP B Sheets
SP V Santos
SP T Ohka
CL D Turnbow
RP M Wise
C D Miller
1B L Overbay
2B- R Weeks
SS J Hardy
UI B Hall
LF C Lee
RF G Jenkins
UO C Magruder
3U- R Branyan
IF- W Helms
M N Yost

NY 2005 NL
SP P Martinez
SP T Glavine
SP K Benson
SP V Zambrano
RS A Heilman
CL B Looper
RP R Hernandez
C M Piazza
1B- D Mientkiewicz
2B M Cairo
SS J Reyes
3B D Wright
LF C Floyd
CF M Beltran
RF- V Diaz
UT M Anderson
C R Castro
2B- K Matsui
UT- C Woodward
M W Randolph

PHI 2005 NL
SP J Lieber
SP B Myers
SP C Lidle
SP V Padilla
CL B Wagner
RP R Madson
RP A Fultz
RP G Geary
C M Lieberthal
1B- R Howard
2B C Utley
SS J Rollins
3B D Bell
LF P Burrell
CF K Lofton
RF B Abreu
MO J Michaels
UO-E Chavez
UI- T Perez
M C Manuel

PIT 2005 NL
SP K Wells
SP M Redman
SP J Fogg
SP D Williams
SP O Perez
RP S Torres
CL J Mesa
RP R Vogelsong
RP R White
C - H Cota
1B D Ward
2B J Castillo
SS J Wilson
UI F Sanchez
LF J Bay
MU T Redman
UT R Mackowiak
M L McClendon
M P Mackanin

STL 2005 NL
SP C Carpenter
SP J Marquis
SP M Mulder
SP J Suppan
SP M Morris
CL J Isringhausen
RP J Tavarez
RP A Reyes
RP B Thompson
C Y Molina
1B A Pujols
2B M Grudzielanek
SS D Eckstein
3I A Nunez
UO S Taguchi
CF J Edmonds
RF L Walker
UT J Mabry
LF- R Sanders
M T LaRussa

SD 2005 NL
SP J Peavy
SP B Lawrence
SP W Williams
SP A Eaton
CL T Hoffman
RP S Linebrink
RP A Otsuka
RP R Seanez
C R Hernandez
1B- P Nevin
2B M Loretta
SS K Greene
3B- S Burroughs
LF R Klesko
CF D Roberts
RF B Giles
UT D Jackson
UT X Nady
UT M Sweeney
IC- R Fick
M B Bochy

SF 2005 NL
SP N Lowry
SP B Tomko
SP J Schmidt
SP B Hennessey
SP K Rueter
RS J Fassero
CL T Walker
RP S Eyre
C M Matheny
1B J Snow
2B R Durham
SS O Vizquel
3B E Alfonzo
3L P Feliz
MO J Ellison
LR M Alou
1U L Niekro
RU M Tucker
UI- D Cruz
M F Alou

WAS 2005 NL
SP L Hernandez
SP E Loaiza
SP J Patterson
SP T Armas
CL C Cordero
RS H Carrasco
RP G Majewski
RP L Ayala
C B Schneider
1B N Johnson
2B- J Vidro
SS C Guzman
3B V Castilla
LO R Church
ML B Wilkerson
RF J Guillen
2S J Carroll
UI- C Baerga
M F Robinson

BAL 2005 AL
SP R Lopez
SP B Chen
SP D Cabrera
SP E Bedard
SP S Ponson
CL B Ryan
RP T Williams
RP J Julio
RP S Kline
CD J Lopez
1B R Palmeiro
2B B Roberts
SS M Tejada
3B M Mora
OI- D Newhan
CF L Matos
RD S Sosa
RD J Gibbons
UI- C Gomez
LU- B Surhoff
M L Mazzilli
M S Perlozzo

BOS 2005 AL
SP T Wakefield
SP B Arroyo
SP M Clement
SP D Wells
CL C Schilling
RP M Timlin
RP J Gonzalez
C J Varitek
1B K Millar
2B- M Bellhorn
SS E Renteria
3B B Mueller
LF M Ramirez
CF J Damon
RF T Nixon
DH D Ortiz
1B- J Olerud
M T Francona

CHI 2005 AL
SP M Buehrle
SP F Garcia
SP J Garland
SP J Contreras
SP O Hernandez
CL D Hermanson
RP L Vizcaino
RP C Politte
RP N Cotts
C A Pierzynski
1B P Konerko
2B T Iguchi
SS J Uribe
3B J Crede
LF S Podsednik
CF A Rowand
RF J Dye
DH C Everett
M O Guillen

CLE 2005 AL
SP J Westbrook
SP C Lee

SP	C Sabathia	SS-	C Guillen	
SP	K Millwood	3B	B Inge	
SP	S Elarton	RL	C Monroe	
CL	B Wickman	CF	N Logan	
RP	B Howry	RF-	M Ordonez	
RP	D Riske	DU	D Young	
RP	R Betancourt	2S	O Infante	
C	V Martinez	LD-	R White	
1B	B Broussard	M	A Trammell	
2B	R Belliard			
SS	J Peralta	**KC 2005 AL**		
3B	A Boone	SP	Z Greinke	
LF	C Crisp	SP	J Lima	
CF	G Sizemore	SP	R Hernandez	
RF	C Blake	SP	D Carrasco	
DH	T Hafner	RS	M Wood	
13-	J Hernandez	RP	M Mac Dougal	
M	E Wedge	RP	A Sisco	
		RP	A Burgos	
DET 2005 AL		1D	M Stairs	
SP	J Johnson	2B-	R Gotay	
SP	M Maroth	SS	A Berroa	
SP	N Robertson	3B	M Teahen	
SP	J Bonderman	LF	T Long	
RP	C Spurling	CF	D DeJesus	
RP	F German	RF	E Brown	
RP	J Walker	D1	M Sweeney	
C	I Rodriguez	UT-	J McEwing	
1B	C Shelton			
2B-	P Polanco			

M	T Pena
M	B Schaefer
M	B Bell

LA 2005 AL

SP	B Colon
SP	J Lackey
SP	P Byrd
SP	J Washburn
SP	E Santana
CL	F Rodriguez
RP	S Shields
RP	E Yan
RP	B Donnelly
C	B Molina
1B	D Erstad
2B	A Kennedy
SS	O Cabrera
3B-	D McPherson
UO	J Rivera
CF	S Finley
RF	V Guerrero
LD	G Anderson
UO	J DaVanon
UT	C Figgins
M	M Scioscia

MIN 2005 AL

SP	J Santana
SP	B Radke
SP	C Silva
SP	K Lohse
SP	J Mays
CL	J Nathan
RP	J Crain
RP	J Rincon
RP	M Guerrier
C	J Mauer
1B	J Morneau
2S	N Punto
SS-	J Castro
3B	M Cuddyer
LF	S Stewart
UO	L Ford
RF	J Jones
DU	M LeCroy
CF	T Hunter
M	R Gardenhire

NY 2005 AL

SP	R Johnson
SP	M Mussina
SP	C Wang
SP	C Pavano
CL	M Rivera
RP	T Gordon
RP	T Sturtze
C	J Posada
1B	T Martinez
2B	R Cano
SS	D Jeter
3B	A Rodriguez
LU	H Matsui
CF	B Williams
RF	G Sheffield
1D	J Giambi
OI	T Womack
M	J Torre

OAK 2005 AL

SP	B Zito
SP	D Haren
SP	J Blanton
SP	K Saarloos
SP	R Harden
CL	H Street
RP	J Duchscherer
RP	K Yabu
RP	K Calero
C	J Kendall
1B	D Johnson
2B	M Ellis
SS-	B Crosby
3B	E Chavez
LR	B Kielty
CF	M Kotsay
RF	N Swisher
D1	S Hatteberg
S2	M Scutaro
M	K Macha

SEA 2005 AL

SP	J Moyer
SP	R Franklin
SP	J Pineiro
SP	G Meche
SP	A Sele
CL	E Guardado
RP	J Mateo
RP	S Hasegawa
RP	J Putz
C -	M Olivo
1B	R Sexson
2B-	B Boone
SS-	M Morse
3B	A Beltre
LF	R Winn
CF	J Reed
RF	I Suzuki
DL	R Ibanez
UT-	W Bloomquist
M	M Hargrove

TB 2005 AL

SP	S Kazmir
SP	M Hendrickson
SR	C Fossum
SP	D Waechter
SR	S McClung
CL	D Baez

RP	H Nomo
RP	T Harper
RP	L Carter
C	T Hall
1B	T Lee
2B	N Green
SS	J Lugo
3B	A Gonzalez
LF	C Crawford
MR	D Hollins
RU	A Huff
OF	J Gomes
23	J Cantu
M	L Piniella

TEX 2005 AL

SP	K Rogers
SP	C Young
SP	C Park
CL	F Cordero
RS	K Loe
RS	J Benoit
RS	J Wasdin
1B	M Teixeira
2B	A Soriano
SS	M Young
3B	H Blalock
LF	K Mench
MU	G Matthews
RF-	R Hidalgo
DL	D Dellucci
M	B Showalter

TOR 2005 AL

SP	J Towers
SP	G Chacin
SP	R Halladay
SP	D Bush
SP	T Lilly
CL	M Batista
RP	P Walker
RP	J Frasor
RP	V Chulk
C	G Zaun
IF	S Hillenbrand
2B	O Hudson
SS	R Adams
3B-	C Koskie
LF	R Johnson
CF	V Wells
RF	A Rios
1D	E Hinske
LF	F Catalanotto
UI	A Hill
M	J Gibbons

THE LONG SEASON: THE HISTORICAL RECORD

Part of what makes baseball special is its long season. It's been said that baseball isn't a sprint, but a marathon, and the historical record bears this out. Having to play nearly every day for six months or more affects everything about the game. A manager's strategy can change completely between March and October, given injuries, trades, predictable and not-so-predictable changes in player performance, and the capricious nature of rookies. A season that, at times, seems endless works its charms and wreaks havoc concurrently in many different ways. The best teams of all time still lose series during the season, and even the worst teams fashion together some form of a winning streak.

The long season is a player's chance to make or break his career. It gives a manager the option of sticking with a declining veteran until he rebounds—or until his poor performance sinks the team. After more than 100 games and four months of play, a team can sometimes pull a pennant out of its cap by promoting an untested but promising rookie. The guy who hits .375 in April may hit .130 in May and end up back in the minors, or a Hurricane Hazle can hit .403 down the stretch to win a pennant—and never be seen again.

When pitcher Jim Brosnan penned his 1959 diary, *The Long Season*, one thing he communicated expertly was the way baseball's fortunes could turn 360 degrees within those six months: from despair to ecstasy, with a whole lot of excitement and some stultifying ennui in between. That's how baseball has been for every one of its long seasons dating back to the nineteenth century: a roller-coaster ride of great stories buried inside a simple yet puzzling game that seems, to outsiders and other unfortunates, almost impenetrable.

For those of us who don't get to play the game for half a year at a time, baseball's long season provides artistic, scientific, emotional, and even spiritual fulfillment, and its memories keep us warm through many a long winter. A distillation of more than a century of baseball seasons is presented in this section—to learn about, argue about, and to savor—from team records to top individual performances, using both traditional statistics and new methods of measurement.

Needless to say, condensing the events of a baseball season into a single page is a very difficult task. Nevertheless, the format of this Historical Record section attempts to do justice to each of the 254 pennant races since 1871 in a concise manner, from the erratic and incomplete campaigns of the National Association, the original professional league; to the ill-conceived single season of the ill-fated Union Association in 1884; to the 130-year span of the National League, now in its third century of competition.

The top part of each Historical Record page includes final standings for the league along with extensive team batting, baserunning, pitching, and fielding statistics. Alongside the standings are each team's home wins and losses, allowing an examination of how each club fared in its home park as well as on the road. Separate park factors are listed for both batters and pitchers, showing how much each team's home field helped or hurt offensively and defensively. Note that these park factors are not simply the inverse of each other, as the calculations for each are related but not exactly the same.

Most of the team stats categories are also represented in the Batter and Pitcher Registers, though a few different stats of relevance at a team level are also included (e.g., Games in Relief). Because the official records were not as extensive, some categories will be blank for part or all of the nineteenth century (e.g., Hit Batsmen and Sacrifice Hits); others will also be blank for part of the first half of the twentieth century (e.g., Caught Stealing).

Below the standings and team statistics are individual league-leaders in 35 categories of batting, pitching, and fielding stats. Each category lists the top five players (unless multiple tied players would lengthen the list past the top five). The first and last categories—Batter-Fielder Wins and Pitcher Wins—are in boldface to indicate their importance.

Among the batting and pitching leaders, the minimums for qualifying as a league leader for any average or rate statistics are normally the same as qualifying for the batting or ERA titles. However, the minimum for qualifying as a league leader in Base Runners per 9 Innings was deliberately set low enough to include relief pitchers (60 innings pitched). Relief pitchers are unlikely to qualify for the league-leaders in many other pitching categories, such as Opponents' Average and Opponents OBP, as a result of the higher innings pitched requirements. The relief pitching categories (starting with Games and ending with Relief Ranking) have been grouped together for ease of comparison.

One category of team pitching stats is completely new: WPB. This represents the sum of wild pitches and passed balls—at a team level, there is no difference between them.

At the bottom of each page is a 300–350 word essay that gives a snapshot of what it was like to be a baseball fan that season. Each page in the Historical Record includes a summary of the pennant race and the postseason, along with comments about the level of scoring and why it might have increased or decreased. If attendance went up or down substantially, it will also be noted. The effects of major off-field events like wars, strikes, and lockouts are also briefly summarized.

Each yearly essay notes the comings and goings of the greatest players in the game's history, as well as some of its lesser lights. The debut or rookie seasons for standout players who would influence the course of the game for a decade or more are also shown, along with the final years of those stalwarts headed into retirement. Untimely deaths are listed along with the passing of those ballplayers who defined their eras: When a man of the stature of Babe Ruth, Ty Cobb, Mickey Mantle, Joe DiMaggio, or Ted Williams passes from the scene, the game is changed in invisible—yet very real—ways.

The lists below show all abbreviations used in the Historical Record section. Those that have not been defined elsewhere are explained here. Further information about the formulas and computations used can also be found in the Glossary.

TEAM AND LEAGUE BATTING AND BASESTEALING

W: Wins

L: Losses

T: Ties. Ties only happen if the game has completed 5 or more full innings, the game was tied after the last completed inning, and no further runs have been scored unless the home team has gone ahead in the bottom of the current inning.

PCT: Winning Percentage. Calculated by dividing the number of wins by the number of wins and losses.

GB: Games Behind. The number of games behind first place. If the team in question finished 83-79 and the team in first place finished 95-66, the team in question finished 12.5 games behind.

HW: Home Wins.

HL: Home Losses.

R: Runs.

OR: Opponent Runs.

PA: Plate Appearances.

H: Hits.

2B: Doubles.

3B: Triples.

HR: Home Runs.

BB: Bases on Balls. Generally referred to today as walks.

SO: Strikeouts.

HB: Hit Batsmen.

SH: Sacrifice Hits. Sacrifice flies were counted as sacrifice hits from 1908–1930 and in 1939.

AVG: Batting Average. Hits divided by at bats.

OBP: On-Base Percentage. Hits plus walks plus hit-by-pitch divided by at-bats plus walks plus hit-by-pitch plus sacrifice flies: $(H+BB+HBP)/(AB+BB+HBP+SF)$. Sacrifice flies (SF) were not used in the OBP calculation for 1908–30 and 1939 since they were combined with sacrifice bunts in the official stats.

SLG: Slugging Average. Total bases divided by at bats.

OPS: On-Base Percentage plus Slugging Average. The figure is multiplied by 1000, so .320 plus .500 would be 820.

AOPS: Adjusted On-Base plus Slugging. On-base percentage and slugging average are added and normalized for the context of the offensive level of the league and the team's home park(s) and then converted to a scale in which 100 is average.

BR: Batting Runs. The number of runs the team should have scored compared to the average team based on the team's offensive production.

ABR: Adjusted Batting Runs. Batting runs adjusted for the home park and the league average offensive level but ignoring the offensive contributions of pitchers. The entire league average batting stats are used for teams, since teams either have pitcher batting or they don't, depending on the league rules. For individual batters, BR, ABR, and AOPS are calculated using league figures with pitcher batting subtracted. Thus the team definition is slightly different from the player definition.

PF: Hitters' Park Factor. This measure of how the team's home park affects offense is used to adjust the team's raw offensive performance in a way that takes into account the context of the team's home park. This also includes a correction for not having to face your own pitchers, which ends up being used in AOPS and ABR.

SB: Stolen Bases. Totals are available for all seasons in all leagues from 1886 on, as well as for all the seasons of the National Association.

CS: Caught Stealing. These totals are available for all American League teams in 1914–15 and from 1920 on; caught stealing totals are available for all National League teams in 1913, 1915, from 1920–26, and from 1951 on.

BSA: Basestealing Average. Stolen bases divided by stolen bases plus caught stealing; not possible unless caught stealing totals are available.

BSR: Basestealing Runs. The number of runs added by a team's basestealing attempts.

Team and League Pitching and Fielding.

CG: Complete Games.

SHO: Shutouts.

GR: Games in Relief. The total number of relief appearances made by the team's pitchers.

SV: Saves. Saves became an official statistic in 1969. Saves are calculated based on the official definition of saves at the time. Saves before 1969 are based on how many times a relief pitcher finished pitching a victory for his team without getting a win.

IP: Innings Pitched.

H: Hits Allowed.

HR: Home Runs Allowed.

BB: Bases on Balls Allowed.

SO: Strikeouts.

BR/9: Baserunners Allowed Per 9 Innings.

ERA: Earned Run Average. Calculated by dividing earned runs by innings pitched and multiplying by 9.

AERA: Adjusted Earned Run Average. Calculated by normalizing ERA for the context of the offensive level of the league and the team's home park(s) and converting to a scale in which 100 is average.

OAV: Opponents' Batting Average. Hits allowed divided by opponent at bats.

OOB: Opponents' On-Base Percentage.

PR: Pitching Runs. Indicates how many runs the team's pitcher allowed to score compared to the average pitcher.

APR: Adjusted Pitching Runs. Indicates how many runs the team's pitcher allowed to score compared to the average pitcher in the context of the team's home park(s) and the offensive level of the league.

PF: Pitchers' Park Factor. This measures how the team's home park affects pitching. It is used to adjust the team's raw pitching performance in a way that takes the context of the team's home park into account. Again, there is a correction for pitchers not having to face their own batters. Park factor is used in the APR and AERA calculation.

OSB: Opponents' Stolen Bases.

OCS: Opponents' Caught Stealing.

FA: Fielding Average. Assists plus putouts divided by assists plus putouts plus errors: (A+PO/A+PO+E).

E: Errors.

WPB: Wild Pitches plus Passed Balls.

DP: Double Plays.

FW: Fielding Wins. Total number of wins the team achieved through its fielding compared to the average team in the context of the offensive level of the league and the team's home park(s).

PW: Pitching Wins. Total number of wins the team achieved through its pitching compared to the average team in the context of the offensive level of the league and the team's home park(s).

BW: Batting Wins. The total number of wins the team achieved through its hitting compared to the average team in the context of the offensive level of the league and the team's home park(s).

BSW: Basestealing Wins. Total number of wins the team achieved through its basestealing compared to the average team in the context of the offensive level of the league and the team's home park(s).

DIF: Differential. This measures the difference between how many games the team was projected to win based on its hitting, pitching, fielding, and baserunning, and how many games the team actually won. It is measured in the same way as teams measure how many games in the standings they are behind another.

Leaderboards below are not shown among team statistics

BFW: Batter-Fielder Wins. The sum of a player's batting wins, basestealing wins, and fielding wins, this figure indicates how many games the player won or lost for his team compared to an average player.

Total Bases. Calculated by adding singles plus 2x doubles plus 3x triples plus 4x home runs.

RBI: Runs Batted In.

Fielding Runs Infield and Outfield. Fielding Runs measures how many runs the player saves or loses for his team in the field compared to an average fielder. The formula takes into account assists, putouts, errors, and double plays. All of these defensive statistics are adjusted for the context in several different ways. Defensive innings are based on play-by-play from 1969 forward; they are estimated for previous years.

Fewest Bases on Balls Per Game.

Games.

Adjusted Relief Runs. Adjusted Relief Runs indicates how many runs the pitcher allowed to score compared to the average pitcher in the context of the offensive level of the league and the pitcher's home park(s). Relief pitchers are identified as pitchers who averaged less than 3 innings per appearance.

Relief Ranking. Calculated by putting Adjusted Relief Runs into the context of the importance of the relief innings thrown by the relief pitcher while taking into account the number of saves and decisions assigned to the pitcher.

Adjusted Starter Runs. This indicates how many runs the pitcher allowed to score compared to the average pitcher in the context of the offensive level of the league and the pitcher's home park(s). Starting pitchers are identified as pitchers who average at least 3 innings per appearance.

Pitcher Wins. Individual pitcher wins are calculated by adding up pitching, batting, fielding, and basestealing wins for individual pitchers; different from team pitching wins.

2005 National League

TEAM	W	L	T	PCT	GB	HW	HL	R	OR	PA	H	2B	3B	HR	BB	SO	HB	SH	AVG	OBP	SLG	OPS	AOPS	BR	ABR	PF	SB	CS	BSA	BSR
EAST																														
ATL	90	72	0	.556		53	28	769	674	6186	1453	308	37	184	534	1084	45	75	.265	.333	.435	768	102	42	23	103	92	32	74	9
PHI	88	74	0	.543	2	46	35	807	726	6345	1494	282	35	167	639	1083	56	62	.270	.348	.423	771	104	69	44	103	116	27	81	16
FLA	83	79	0	.512	7	45	36	717	732	6213	1499	306	32	128	512	918	67	82	.272	.339	.409	748	107	17	61	94	96	38	72	8
NY	83	79	0	.512	7	48	33	722	648	6146	1421	279	32	175	486	1075	48	69	.258	.322	.416	738	99	-24	-7	98	153	40	79	20
WAS	81	81	0	.500	9	41	40	639	673	6142	1367	311	32	117	491	1090	89	91	.252	.322	.386	708	96	-69	-23	93	45	45	50	-6
CENTRAL																														
STL	100	62	0	.617		50	31	805	634	6246	1494	287	26	170	534	947	62	77	.270	.339	.432	762	102	37	21	102	83	36	70	6
HOU	89	73	1	.549	11	53	28	693	609	6139	1400	281	32	161	481	1037	72	82	.256	.322	.408	730	95	-34	-37	100	115	44	72	10
MIL	81	81	0	.500	19	46	35	726	697	6156	1413	327	19	175	531	1162	73	66	.259	.331	.423	754	102	20	17	100	79	34	70	5
CHI	79	83	0	.488	21	38	43	703	714	6159	1506	323	23	194	419	920	50	69	.270	.324	.440	764	101	25	1	103	65	39	63	1
CIN	73	89	1	.451	27	42	39	820	889	6320	1453	335	15	222	611	1303	62	43	.261	.339	.446	785	114	84	112	97	72	23	76	8
PIT	67	95	0	.414	33	34	47	680	769	6221	1445	292	38	139	471	1092	72	56	.259	.322	.400	722	94	-48	-44	99	73	30	71	6
WEST																														
SD	82	80	0	.506		46	35	684	726	6271	1416	269	39	130	600	977	49	72	.257	.333	.391	724	100	-31	5	95	99	44	69	6
ARI	77	85	0	.475	5	36	45	696	856	6327	1419	291	27	191	606	1094	55	71	.256	.332	.421	753	97	20	-12	104	67	26	72	6
SF	75	87	0	.463	7	37	44	649	745	6077	1427	299	26	128	431	901	49	91	.261	.319	.396	715	88	-65	-90	104	71	35	67	3
LA	71	91	0	.438	11	40	41	685	755	6131	1374	284	21	149	541	1094	67	57	.253	.326	.395	721	93	-43	-43	100	58	35	62	1
COL	67	95	0	.414	15	40	41	740	862	6237	1477	280	34	150	509	1103	64	48	.267	.333	.411	744	86	-1	-95	115	65	32	67	3
TOT	1297					695	601	11535		99316	23058	4754	468	2580	8396	16880	980	1151	.262	.330	.414	744					1349	560	71	101

TEAM	CG	SHO	GR	SV	IP	H	HR	BB	SO	BR/9	ERA	AERA	OAV	OOB	PR	APR	PF	OSB	OCS	FA	E	WPB	DP	FW	PW	BW	BSW	DIF
EAST																												
ATL	8	12	484	38	1443.2	1487	145	520	929	12.7	3.98	108	.268	.333	38	48	102	89	36	.986	86	50	170	.7	4.8	2.3	.3	.9
PHI	4	6	442	40	1435.0	1379	189	487	1159	12.2	4.21	103	.253	.320	1	18	103	82	26	.985	90	48	132	.5	1.8	4.4	1.0	-.7
FLA	14	15	449	42	1442.1	1459	116	563	1125	13.0	4.16	96	.266	.339	10	-30	94	118	38	.983	103	54	177	-.0	3.0	6.1	.2	-1.2
NY	8	11	392	38	1435.2	1390	135	491	1012	12.1	3.76	110	.255	.321	74	64	94	107	25	.983	106	37	146	-.2	6.4	-.7	1.4	-4.9
WAS	4	9	470	51	1458.0	1456	140	539	997	12.8	3.87	104	.262	.333	57	28	96	76	41	.985	92	56	156	.4	2.8	-2.3	-1.2	.3
CENTRAL																												
STL	15	14	436	48	1445.2	1399	153	443	974	11.8	3.49	120	.257	.318	118	113	99	32	33	.984	100	53	196	.0	11.3	2.1	-.0	5.6
HOU	6	11	434	45	1443.0	1336	155	440	1164	11.4	3.51	119	.246	.308	113	109	99	53	31	.985	89	44	146	.6	10.9	-3.7	.4	-.2
MIL	7	6	395	40	1438.0	1382	169	569	1173	12.5	3.97	107	.251	.324	39	47	101	86	34	.980	119	74	139	-.8	4.7	1.7	-.1	-5.5
CHI	8	10	457	39	1440.0	1357	186	576	1256	12.4	4.19	104	.250	.325	4	28	104	90	40	.983	101	63	136	-.0	2.8	-.0	-.5	-4.4
CIN	2	1	491	31	1433.0	1657	219	492	955	14.0	5.15	81	.290	.352	-148	-159	99	76	35	.983	104	62	133	-.0	-15.9	11.2	.2	-3.4
PIT	4	14	451	35	1436.0	1456	162	612	958	13.4	4.42	96	.267	.344	-33	-31	100	64	36	.981	117	69	193	-.7	-3.1	-4.4	-.0	-5.8
WEST																												
SD	4	8	456	45	1455.1	1452	146	503	1133	12.4	4.13	93	.259	.322	14	-49	91	64	25	.982	109	48	136	-.3	-4.9	.5	-.0	5.8
ARI	6	10	458	45	1456.1	1580	193	537	1080	13.5	4.84	93	.278	.345	-100	-72	104	78	28	.985	94	69	159	.3	-7.2	-1.2	-.0	4.1
SF	4	8	511	46	1444.1	1456	151	592	972	13.0	4.33	98	.263	.336	-18	-13	101	78	54	.985	90	43	146	.5	-1.3	-9.0	-.3	4.1
LA	6	9	458	40	1427.1	1434	182	471	1004	12.4	4.38	93	.263	.327	-26	-49	97	130	34	.983	106	45	141	-.2	-4.9	-4.3	-.5	-.0
COL	6	4	459	37	1418.2	1600	175	604	981	14.5	5.13	93	.287	.362	-143	-53	113	102	37	.981	118	79	158	-.7	-5.3	-9.5	-.3	1.9
TOT	104	148	7243	666	23052.1					12.8	4.22		.262	.330						.983	1624	894	2464					

Batter-Fielder Wins		Batting Average		On-Base Percentage		Slugging Average		On-Base Plus Slugging		Adjusted OPS		Adjusted Batter Runs	
Lee-Chi	6.3	Lee-Chi	335	Helton-Col	445	Lee-Chi	662	Lee-Chi	1080	Lee-Chi	173	Lee-Chi	65.3
Furcal-Atl	4.8	Pujols-StL	330	Pujols-StL	430	Pujols-StL	609	Pujols-StL	1039	Pujols-StL	166	Pujols-StL	60.6
Pujols-StL	4.6	Cabrera-Fla	323	Giles-SD	423	Delgado-Fla	582	Delgado-Fla	981	Delgado-Fla	163	Delgado-Fla	50.7
Ensberg-Hou	4.3	Helton-Col	320	Lee-Chi	418	Griffey-Cin	576	Helton-Col	979	Cabrera-Fla	154	Cabrera-Fla	47.8
Bay-Pit	4.2	Casey-Cin	312	Berkman-Hou	411	A.Jones-Atl	575	Bay-Pit	961	Bay-Pit	151	Bay-Pit	47.3

Runs		Hits		Doubles		Triples		Home Runs		Total Bases		Runs Batted In	
Pujols-StL	129	Lee-Chi	199	Lee-Chi	50	Reyes-NY	17	A.Jones-Atl	51	Lee-Chi	393	A.Jones-Atl	128
Lee-Chi	120	Cabrera-Fla	198	Helton-Col	45	Pierre-Fla	13	Lee-Chi	46	Pujols-StL	360	Pujols-StL	117
Rollins-Phi	115	Rollins-Phi	196	Giles-Atl	45	Rollins-Phi	11	Pujols-StL	41	Cabrera-Fla	344	Burrell-Phi	117
Bay-Pit	110	Pujols-StL	195	Bay-Pit	44	Furcal-Atl	11	Dunn-Cin	40	A.Jones-Atl	337	Cabrera-Fla	116
Dunn-Cin	107	Reyes-NY	190			Roberts-SD	10	Glaus-Ari	37	Bay-Pit	335	Delgado-Fla	115

Stolen Bases		Base Stealing Runs		Fielding Runs-Infield		Fielding Runs-Outfield		Wins		Winning Pct.		Complete Games	
Reyes-NY	60	Reyes-NY	7.9	Eckstein-StL	33.0	Jenkins-Mil	11.2	Willis-Fla	22	Carpenter-StL	808	Willis-Fla	7
Pierre-Fla	57	Rollins-Phi	6.9	Furcal-Atl	31.3	Clark-Mil	10.9	Carpenter-StL	21	Willis-Fla	688	Carpenter-StL	7
Furcal-Atl	46	Furcal-Atl	6.6	J.Wilson-Pit	26.6	Floyd-NY	8.4	Oswalt-Hou	20	Mulder-StL	667	Oswalt-Hou	4
Rollins-Phi	41	Pierre-Fla	6.6	Perez-Cin	25.0	Guillen-Was	6.5	Capuano-Mil	18	Pettitte-Hou	654	Martinez-NY	4
Freel-Cin	36	Freel-Cin	4.4	Counsell-Ari	21.6	Ellison-SF	5.0					Burnett-Fla	4

Strikeouts		Fewest BB/Game		Games		Saves		Base Runners/9		Adjusted Relief Runs		Relief Ranking	
Peavy-Chi	216	Maddux-Chi	1.44	Eyre-SF	86	C.Cordero-Was	47	Wagner-Phi	7.88	Wagner-Phi	22.5	Wagner-Phi	37.4
Carpenter-StL	213	Pettitte-Hou	1.66	Sanchez-LA	79	Hoffman-SD	43	Martinez-NY	8.71	Carrasco-Was	19.9	Turnbow-Mil	36.9
Myers-Phi	208	Lieber-Phi	1.69	Majewski-Was	79	Lidge-Hou	42	C.Cordero-Was	8.96	Turnbow-Mil	18.5	Lidge-Hou	28.7
Martinez-NY	208	Weaver-LA	1.73			Jones-Fla	40	A.Reyes-StL	9.05	Linebrink-SD	17.9	C.Cordero-Was	28.1
D.Davis-Mil	208	Morris-StL	1.73					Wise-Mil	9.09	Wheeler-Hou	17.0	Jones-Fla	27.2

Innings Pitched		Opponents' Avg.		Opponents' OBP		Earned Run Average		Adjusted ERA		Adjusted Starter Runs		Pitcher Wins	
Hernandez-Was	246.1	Clemens-Hou	198	Martinez-NY	252	Clemens-Hou	1.87	Clemens-Hou	224	Clemens-Hou	53.3	**Willis-Fla**	5.8
Oswalt-Hou	241.2	Martinez-NY	204	Clemens-Hou	261	Pettitte-Hou	2.39	Pettitte-Hou	176	Pettitte-Hou	43.9	**Clemens-Hou**	5.7
Carpenter-StL	241.2	Zambrano-Chi	212	Pettitte-Hou	268	Willis-Fla	2.63	Willis-Fla	152	Carpenter-StL	38.8	**Pettitte-Hou**	4.7
Willis-Fla	236.1	Peavy-SD	217	Peavy-SD	271	Martinez-NY	2.82	Carpenter-StL	148	Willis-Fla	36.1	**Oswalt-Hou**	4.4
Smoltz-Atl	229.2	Prior-Chi	227	Carpenter-StL	273	Carpenter-StL	2.83	Martinez-NY	147	Martinez-NY	34.8	**Wagner-Phi**	3.9

Astros Blast Off in Second Half, Then Flame Out in World Series

The Washington Nationals began play after MLB finally moved the orphaned franchise from Montreal. The former Expos were glad to have a permanent home after many years of rumor and uncertainty and after two years of splitting home games between Canada and Puerto Rico. The good feelings in the nation's capital lasted all summer as the reborn Nats stayed in contention most of the season despite having one of the worst offenses in the league. The Cardinals closed out their 40-year history in Busch Stadium with a championship series loss to the Astros. The Gateway City's new park, also to be called Busch Stadium, opens in April 2006.

Seemingly ageless at 43, Roger Clemens continued to amaze and delight baseball fans with incredible performances on the mound. Clemens posted a league-best 1.87 ERA (more than half a run better than anybody else in baseball) and helped Houston rebound from a 21-35 start all the way to their first-ever World Series. Houston's strong rotation, which included Andy Pettitte and Roy Oswalt, helped make the Astros the hottest team in the league in the second half. While they couldn't catch the Cardinals in the NL Central, they claimed the NL Wild Card and then beat NL East winner Atlanta in the NLDS. The Astros clinched their first-ever postseason series win with Chris Burke's home run in the bottom of the 18th inning of the fourth game. Clemens, who threw the last three innings in relief when the Astros ran out of pitchers, wound up the winning pitcher in the longest postseason game (in both innings and time) in baseball history. St. Louis swept San Diego, winner of the NL West but barely above .500 at 82-80, in the other Division Series, but Houston prevailed in the LCS in six games. NLCS MVP Oswalt allowed only two runs in 14 innings, winning both of his starts. The magic ended in the World Series, however, as the Astros were swept by the even hotter White Sox.

Pete Rose remained on the suspended list for betting on baseball and, as a result, wasn't on the Hall of Fame ballot released in November, thus ending his chances of being elected to the Hall by the baseball writers.

2005 American League

TEAM	W	L	T	PCT	GB	HW	HL	R	OR	PA	H	2B	3B	HR	BB	SO	HB	SH	AVG	OBP	SLG	OPS	AOPS	BR	ABR	PF	SB	CS	BSA	BSR
EAST																														
NY	95	67	0	.586		53	28	886	789	6405	1552	259	16	229	637	989	73	28	.276	.355	.450	805	112	117	110	101	84	27	76	9
BOS	95	67	0	.586		54	27	910	805	6403	1579	339	21	199	653	1044	47	14	.281	.357	.454	811	108	139	88	106	45	12	79	6
TOR	80	82	0	.494	15	43	38	775	705	6233	1480	307	39	136	486	955	89	21	.265	.331	.407	738	90	-25	-65	106	72	35	67	4
BAL	74	88	0	.457	21	36	45	729	800	6134	1492	296	27	189	447	902	54	40	.269	.327	.434	761	100	7	2	101	83	37	69	5
TB	67	95	0	.414	28	40	41	750	936	6118	1519	289	40	157	412	990	69	34	.274	.329	.425	754	102	-5	16	97	151	49	76	16
CENTRAL																														
CHI	99	63	0	.611		47	34	741	645	6145	1450	253	23	200	435	1002	79	53	.262	.322	.425	747	93	-23	-56	105	137	67	67	7
CLE	93	69	0	.574	6	43	38	790	642	6255	1522	337	30	207	503	1093	54	39	.271	.334	.453	787	111	65	96	96	62	36	63	1
MIN	83	79	0	.512	16	45	36	688	662	6192	1441	269	32	134	485	978	59	42	.259	.323	.391	714	87	-80	-97	103	102	44	70	7
DET	71	91	0	.438	28	39	42	723	787	6135	1521	283	45	168	384	1038	53	44	.272	.321	.428	749	99	-22	-3	98	66	28	70	5
KC	56	106	0	.346	43	34	47	701	935	6086	1445	289	34	126	424	1008	63	46	.263	.320	.396	716	95	-77	-34	94	53	33	62	0
WEST																														
LA	95	67	0	.586		49	32	761	643	6182	1520	278	30	147	447	848	29	43	.270	.325	.409	734	95	-46	-35	99	161	57	74	15
OAK	88	74	0	.543	7	45	36	772	658	6275	1476	310	20	155	537	819	52	19	.262	.330	.407	737	94	-28	-39	102	31	22	58	-1
TEX	79	83	0	.488	16	44	37	865	858	6300	1528	311	29	260	495	1112	48	9	.267	.329	.468	797	105	73	43	104	67	15	82	6
SEA	69	93	0	.426	26	39	42	699	751	6095	1408	289	34	130	466	986	48	37	.256	.317	.391	708	93	-94	-48	94	102	47	68	6
TOT	1134					611	523	10790		86958	20933	4109	420	2437	6811	13764	817	469	.268	.330	.424	755					1216	509	70	89

TEAM	CG	SHO	GR	SV	IP	H	HR	BB	SO	BR/9	ERA	AERA	OAV	OOB	PR	APR	PF	OSB	OCS	FA	E	WPB	DP	FW	PW	BW	BSW	DIF
EAST																												
NY	8	14	418	46	1430.2	1495	164	463	985	12.8	4.52	97	.269	.332	-26	-24	100	125	50	.984	95	48	151	.5	-2.3	10.6	.3	4.9
BOS	6	8	442	38	1429.0	1550	164	440	959	13.1	4.74	97	.276	.335	-61	-23	105	87	29	.982	109	69	135	-.4	-2.2	8.5	-.0	8.2
TOR	9	8	432	35	1474.0	1475	185	444	958	12.4	4.06	114	.264	.324	46	84	106	100	35	.985	95	45	154	.5	8.1	-6.3	-.2	-3.1
BAL	2	9	474	38	1427.2	1458	180	580	1052	13.2	4.56	97	.263	.336	-34	-22	102	115	34	.982	107	83	154	-.3	-2.1	.2	-.1	-4.6
TB	1	4	401	43	1421.2	1570	194	615	949	14.2	5.39	81	.280	.355	-164	-163	100	68	35	.979	124	66	139	-1.5	-15.8	1.5	.9	.8
CENTRAL																												
CHI	9	10	454	54	1475.2	1392	167	459	1040	11.6	3.61	125	.249	.310	121	142	104	103	25	.985	94	74	166	.6	13.7	-5.4	.0	9.0
CLE	6	10	409	51	1452.2	1363	157	413	1050	11.3	3.61	113	.247	.302	120	83	94	103	33	.983	106	32	156	-.2	8.0	9.3	-.5	-4.6
MIN	9	8	396	44	1464.1	1458	169	348	965	11.4	3.71	118	.261	.307	104	107	101	44	36	.984	102	44	171	.0	10.3	-9.4	.0	.9
DET	7	2	425	37	1435.2	1504	193	461	907	12.6	4.51	94	.272	.330	-25	-47	97	60	49	.982	110	57	171	-.5	-4.5	-.3	-.1	-4.5
KC	4	4	443	25	1413.1	1640	178	580	924	14.6	5.49	77	.291	.362	-179	-209	97	70	44	.979	125	74	163	-1.6	-20.2	-3.3	-.6	.7
WEST																												
LA	7	11	378	54	1464.1	1419	158	443	1126	11.7	3.68	117	.254	.312	110	103	99	68	42	.986	87	83	139	1.1	10.0	-3.4	.8	5.5
OAK	9	12	410	38	1450.1	1315	154	504	1075	11.7	3.69	121	.241	.311	107	121	102	109	25	.986	88	46	166	1.0	11.7	-3.8	-.7	-1.2
TEX	2	6	454	46	1440.0	1589	159	522	932	13.6	4.96	92	.279	.343	-98	-59	105	69	26	.982	108	55	149	-.4	-5.7	4.2	.3	-.3
SEA	6	7	433	39	1427.2	1483	179	496	892	12.8	4.49	94	.268	.332	-22	-48	97	89	43	.986	86	50	144	1.2	-4.6	-4.6	-.0	-3.8
TOT	85	113	5927	588	20180.0					12.6	4.35		.268	.330						.983	1436	826	2158					

Leaders

Batter-Fielder Wins
- A.Rodriguez-NY 5.8
- Tejada-Bal 4.8
- Roberts-Bal 4.8
- Hafner-Cle 4.4
- Jeter-NY 4.3

Batting Average
- M.Young-Tex 331
- A.Rodriguez-NY 321
- Guerrero-LA 317
- Damon-Bos 316
- Roberts-Bal 314

On-Base Percentage
- Giambi-NY 440
- A.Rodriguez-NY 421
- Hafner-Cle 408
- Ortiz-Bos 397
- Guerrero-LA 394

Slugging Average
- A.Rodriguez-NY 610
- Ortiz-Bos 604
- Hafner-Cle 595
- M.Ramirez-Bos.......594
- Teixeira-Tex 575

On-Base Plus Slugging
- A.Rodriguez-NY 1.031
- Hafner-Cle 1003
- Ortiz-Bos 1001
- M.Ramirez-Bos........982
- Giambi-NY..............975

Adjusted OPS
- Hafner-Cle.............169
- A.Rodriguez-NY ...169
- Giambi-NY............157
- Guerrero-LA 154
- Ortiz-Bos 154

Adjusted Batter Runs
- A.Rodriguez-NY 63.4
- Hafner-Cle............52.6
- Ortiz-Bos..............49.1
- Guerrero-LA.........41.9
- Giambi-NY............41.9

Runs
- A.Rodriguez-NY 124
- Jeter-NY 122
- Ortiz-Bos 119
- Damon-Bos............117
- M.Young-Tex 114

Hits
- M.Young-Tex 221
- Suzuki-Sea 206
- Jeter-NY 202
- Tejada-Bal 199
- Damon-Bos...........197

Doubles
- Tejada-Bal 50
- Roberts-Bal 45
- Matsui-NY 45
- Soriano-Tex 43

Triples
- Crawford-TB 15
- Suzuki-Sea 12
- Sizemore-Cle..........11
- Figgins-LA.............10
- Inge-Det..................9

Home Runs
- A.Rodriguez-NY 48
- Ortiz-Bos 47
- M.Ramirez-Bos 45
- Teixeira-Tex 43
- Konerko-Chi 40

Total Bases
- Teixeira-Tex 370
- A.Rodriguez-NY ...369
- Ortiz-Bos................363
- M.Young-Tex 343
- Tejada-Bal 337

Runs Batted In
- Ortiz-Bos 148
- Teixeira-Tex 144
- M.Ramirez-Bos 144
- A.Rodriguez-NY 130
- Sheffield-NY............123

Stolen Bases
- Figgins-LA............62
- Podsednik-Chi.......59
- Crawford-TB 46
- Lugo-TB 39
- Suzuki-Sea 33

Base Stealing Runs
- Figgins-LA 7.7
- Crawford-TB 7.3
- Soriano-Tex 5.9
- Podsednik-Chi........4.9
- Lugo-TB 4.7

Fielding Runs-Infield
- Hudson-Tor...........28.3
- Inge-Det................23.7
- Tejada-Bal 14.2
- Infante-Det...........12.0
- Millar-Bos.............10.1

Fielding Runs-Outfield
- Suzuki-Sea 12.8
- Crawford-TB 8.7
- Hollins-TB 8.4
- Reed-Sea 7.9
- Nixon-Bos...............7.6

Wins
- Colon-LA 21
- Lee-Cle 18
- Garland-Chi 18
- R.Johnson-NY 17

Winning Pct.
- Lee-Cle 783
- Colon-LA 724
- Santana-Min 696
- Wells-Bos...............682
- Contreras-Chi.........682

Complete Games
- Halladay-Tor 5
- R.Johnson-NY 4
- Bonderman-Det.........4

Strikeouts
- Santana-Min..........238
- R.Johnson-NY.........211
- Lackey-LA 199
- Kazmir-TB 174
- Zito-Oak 171

Fewest BB/Game
- Silva-Min 43
- Wells-Bos 1.03
- Radke-Min 1.03
- Byrd-LA 1.23
- Towers-Tor 1.25

Games
- Timlin-Bos 81
- Schoeneweis-Tor......80
- Howry-Cle 79
- Gordon-NY 79
- Shields-LA...............78

Saves
- Wickman-Cle...........45
- Rodriguez-LA..........45
- Rivera-NY 43
- Nathan-Min.............43
- Baez-TB...................41

Base Runners/9
- Howry-Cle 8.01
- Rivera-NY 8.27
- Nathan-Min.............8.74
- Santana-Min 8.78
- Politte-Chi...............8.82

Adjusted Relief Runs
- Rivera-NY...............23.8
- Street-Oak 23.1
- Duchscherer-Oak...20.2
- Timlin-Bos..............19.2
- Politte-Chi...............18.8

Relief Ranking
- Rivera-NY...............47.6
- Shields-LA 29.4
- Street-Oak...............27.8
- Hermanson-Chi.......27.7
- Crain-Min................27.1

Innings Pitched
- Buehrle-Chi 236.2
- Santana-Min.......231.2
- Zito-Oak 228.1
- Garcia-Chi...........228.0
- R.Johnson-NY 225.2

Opponents' Avg.
- Santana-Min 210
- Zito-Oak 221
- Contreras-Chi.........232
- Blanton-Oak 236
- R.Johnson-NY 243

Opponents' OBP
- Santana-Min 250
- R.Johnson-NY 291
- Colon-LA 291
- Buehrle-Chi 295
- Radke-Min 295

Earned Run Average
- Millwood-Cle 2.86
- Santana-Min 2.87
- Buehrle-Chi 3.12
- Washburn-LA 3.20
- Silva-Min 3.44

Adjusted ERA
- Santana-Min 153
- Buehrle-Chi 145
- Millwood-Cle 143
- Washburn-LA 135
- Rogers-Tex 133

Adjusted Starter Runs
- Santana-Min..........40.5
- Halladay-Tor 33.7
- Buehrle-Chi 31.3
- Millwood-Cle...........25.9
- Harden-Oak............25.9

Pitcher Wins
- Rivera-NY 4.9
- Halladay-Tor 3.7
- Santana-Min 3.7
- Buehrle-Chi 3.0
- Shields-LA 3.0

By Any Other Name

Prior to the season, the Angels announced that they would henceforth be known as the Los Angeles Angels of Anaheim in an effort to market the franchise better in Los Angeles. That decision brought a lawsuit by the Anaheim city government, claiming the club's lease called for them to be known as the Anaheim Angels. It also brought a scornful response from SoCal's other ballclub, who sold merchandise saying they were the "Los Angeles Dodgers of Los Angeles." Manny Ramirez, one of the heroes of Boston's 2004 World Series championship squad, alternated saying he wanted a trade and then saying he was happy playing for the Red Sox. This led one teammate to opine that it was just "Manny being Manny."

Cleveland, operating on a thrifty budget of $41 million, rallied from 15 games back in the AL Central in the last two months to come within 1½ games of the Central Division-leading White Sox, but the surprising Sox trounced the Indians in the last week of the season to sew up their postseason berth. At the other hand of the financial spectrum, a record $208 million payroll barely got the Yankees into October, as the Bronx Bombers spent much of the first half in third place before rallying past the Orioles and Red Sox to win their eighth straight AL East title. New York was then eliminated in five games by the Angels, who had beaten the pesky Athletics in the AL West in one ALDS. Chicago swept the Wild Card winner Boston in the other.

After losing the first game of what turned out to be an extremely controversial ALCS, Chicago rallied in the ninth inning to win the second game with the help of a disputed dropped third strike. The stunned Angels never recovered, losing the next three games. Chicago's starting pitching ultimately was the difference in the series, as the Sox hurlers threw four consecutive complete games, a first in LCS play. Chicago then claimed its first World Championship since 1917 with a four-game sweep of Houston. The Sox lost only one game in three postseason series, equaling the best postseason mark since the Wild Card and Division Series format was instituted in 1995.

2004 National League

TEAM	W	L	T	PCT	GB	HW	HL	R	OR	PA	H	2B	3B	HR	BB	SO	HB	SH	AVG	OBP	SLG	OPS	AOPS	BR	ABR	PF	SB	CS	BSA	BSR
EAST																														
ATL	96	66	0	.593	—	49	32	803	668	6339	1503	304	37	178	587	1158	59	75	.270	.343	.434	777	104	49	43	101	86	32	73	8
PHI	86	76	0	.531	10	42	39	840	781	6456	1505	303	23	215	645	1133	58	64	.267	.345	.443	788	105	75	49	103	100	27	79	13
FLA	83	79	0	.512	13	42	38	718	700	6160	1447	275	32	148	499	968	58	77	.264	.329	.406	735	99	-40	-4	95	96	43	69	6
NY	71	91	0	.438	25	38	43	684	731	6208	1376	289	20	185	512	1159	61	69	.249	.317	.409	726	93	-69	-53	98	107	23	**82**	15
MON	67	95	0	.414	29	35	45	635	769	6138	1361	276	27	151	496	925	35	**100**	.249	.313	.392	705	83	-110	-135	104	109	38	74	11
CENTRAL																														
STL	105	57	0	.648	—	**53**	28	**855**	**659**	6297	**1544**	319	24	214	548	1085	51	73	**.278**	.344	**.460**	804	110	**91**	101	111	47	70	8
HOU	92	70	0	.568	13	48	33	803	698	6269	1458	294	36	187	590	999	61	98	.267	.342	.436	778	102	50	24	103	89	30	75	9
CHI	89	73	0	.549	16	45	37	789	665	6281	1508	308	29	**235**	489	1080	38	78	.268	.328	.458	786	103	47	23	103	66	28	70	5
CIN	76	86	0	.469	29	40	41	750	907	6278	1380	287	28	194	599	1335	81	55	.250	.331	.418	749	100	-15	1	98	77	25	75	8
PIT	72	89	0	.447	32.5	39	41	680	744	6114	1428	267	**39**	142	415	1066	95	79	.260	.321	.401	722	91	-74	-74	100	63	40	61	0
MIL	67	94	0	.416	37.5	36	45	634	757	6187	1358	295	32	135	540	1312	68	56	.248	.321	.387	708	86	-94	-100	101	**138**	40	78	**16**
WEST																														
LA	93	69	0	.574	—	49	32	761	684	6244	1450	226	30	203	536	1092	62	69	.262	.332	.423	755	100	-9	1	99	102	41	71	8
SF	91	71	0	.562	2	47	35	850	770	6466	1500	314	33	183	**705**	874	72	92	.270	**.357**	.438	795	106	**103**	73	104	43	23	65	1
SD	87	75	0	.537	6	42	39	768	705	6313	1521	304	32	139	566	910	56	52	.273	.342	.414	756	105	15	55	95	52	25	68	3
COL	68	94	0	.420	25	38	43	833	923	6333	1531	**331**	34	202	568	1181	54	77	.275	.345	.455	800	98	91	-4	113	44	33	57	-2
ARI	51	111	0	.315	42	29	52	615	899	6113	1401	295	38	135	441	1022	35	56	.253	.310	.393	703	80	-120	-159	107	53	32	62	0
TOT	1295					672	623	12018		100196	23271	4687	494	2846	8736	17299	944	1190	.263	.333	.423	756					1336	527	72	109

TEAM	CG	SHO	GR	SV	IP	H	HR	BB	SO	BR/9	ERA	AERA	OAV	OOB	PR	APR	PF	OSB	OCS	FA	E	WPB	DP	FW	PW	BW	BSW	DIF
EAST																												
ATL	4	13	483	48	1450.0	1475	154	523	1025	12.6	**3.74**	115	.265	.329	90	90	100	91	29	.981	116	46	171	-.7	8.8	4.2	.1	2.5
PHI	4	5	476	43	1462.2	1488	214	502	1070	12.7	4.45	99	.264	.330	-25	-6	103	103	26	.987	81	47	142	1.3	-.6	4.8	.6	-1.1
FLA	6	**14**	404	53	1439.0	1395	166	513	1116	12.3	4.10	100	.256	.324	33	1	95	118	38	.986	86	46	153	1.0	.0	-.4	-.0	1.4
NY	2	6	474	31	1449.0	1452	156	592	977	13.0	4.09	105	.261	.335	35	32	100	100	39	.978	137	42	144	-1.9	3.1	-5.2	.8	-6.8
MON	**11**	11	462	31	1447.0	1477	191	582	1032	13.3	4.33	106	.266	.342	-4	38	107	58	41	.984	99	50	172	.3	3.7	-13.2	.4	-5.1
CENTRAL																												
STL	4	12	469	**57**	1453.2	1378	169	440	1041	**11.7**	3.75	114	.251	**.313**	90	83	99	53	29	.985	97	51	154	.4	8.1	**8.9**	.1	6.4
HOU	2	13	493	47	1443.0	1416	174	525	1282	12.5	4.05	108	.258	.328	40	49	101	101	39	.983	101	49	136	.1	4.8	2.4	.2	3.5
CHI	3	6	460	42	1465.1	**1363**	169	545	**1346**	12.2	3.81	**116**	**.247**	.321	80	**97**	103	108	39	.986	86	59	126	1.0	**9.5**	2.3	-.2	-4.6
CIN	5	8	497	47	1443.2	1595	236	572	992	13.8	5.19	83	.280	.348	-142	-144	100	67	29	.981	113	91	123	-.5	-14.1	.0	.1	9.5
PIT	3	8	464	46	1428.0	1451	**149**	576	1079	13.2	4.29	101	.267	.342	3	5	100	72	38	.983	103	47	**189**	.0	.5	-7.3	-.7	-1.1
MIL	6	10	423	42	1442.0	1440	164	476	1098	12.3	4.24	103	.259	.320	10	22	102	89	29	.981	117	66	132	-.8	2.2	-9.8	**.9**	-5.9
WEST																												
LA	2	6	459	51	1453.1	1386	178	521	1066	12.1	4.01	103	.254	.323	48	21	96	96	40	**.988**	73	58	145	**1.7**	2.1	.0	.1	8.0
SF	8	8	**521**	46	1457.0	1481	161	548	1002	12.8	4.29	101	.266	.332	2	5	101	72	24	.984	101	63	153	.1	.5	7.2	-.6	2.8
SD	3	8	437	44	1441.0	1460	184	**422**	1079	12.1	4.03	98	.263	.318	44	-17	91	69	25	.982	108	**36**	146	-.3	-1.7	5.4	-.4	2.9
COL	3	2	473	36	1435.1	1634	198	697	947	15.1	5.54	86	.290	.372	-197	-114	110	111	32	.986	89	81	161	.8	-11.2	-.4	-.9	-1.4
ARI	5	6	471	33	1436.0	1480	197	668	1153	13.9	4.98	91	.266	.350	-107	-65	106	97	**50**	.977	139	89	144	-2.0	-6.4	-15.6	-.7	-5.3
TOT	71	136	7466	697	23146.0					12.8	4.30		.263	.333						.983	1646	921	2391					

Batter-Fielder Wins
Bonds-SF ...10.6
Rolen-StL ...6.4
Helton-Col ...6.2
Beltre-LA ...5.9
Edmonds-StL ...5.1

Batting Average
Bonds-SF ...362
Helton-Col ...347
Loretta-SD ...335
Beltre-LA ...334
Pujols-StL ...331

On-Base Percentage
Bonds-SF ...609
Helton-Col ...469
Berkman-Hou ...450
J.Drew-Phi ...436
Abreu-Phi ...428

Slugging Average
Bonds-SF ...812
Pujols-StL ...657
Edmonds-StL ...643
Beltre-LA ...629
Helton-Col ...620

On-Base Plus Slugging
Bonds-SF ...1422
Helton-Col ...1088
Pujols-StL ...1072
Edmonds-StL ...1061
Beltre-LA ...1017

Adjusted OPS
Bonds-SF ...255
Pujols-StL ...171
Edmonds-StL ...168
Beltre-LA ...160
Helton-Col ...159

Adjusted Batter Runs
Bonds-SF ...118.5
Pujols-StL ...64.7
Helton-Col ...57.1
Edmonds-StL ...54.6
Berkman-Hou ...54.6

Runs
Pujols-StL ...133
Bonds-SF ...129
Rollins-Phi ...119
J.Drew-Atl ...118
Abreu-Phi ...118

Hits
Pierre-Fla ...221
Loretta-SD ...208
J.Wilson-Pit ...201
Beltre-LA ...200
Pujols-StL ...196

Doubles
Overbay-Mil ...53
Pujols-StL ...51
Helton-Col ...49

Triples
J.Wilson-Pit ...12
Rollins-Phi ...12
Pierre-Fla ...12
Izturis-LA ...9

Home Runs
Beltre-LA ...48
Pujols-StL ...46
Dunn-Cin ...46
Bonds-SF ...45

Total Bases
Pujols-StL ...389
Beltre-LA ...376
Helton-Col ...339
Alou-Chi ...335
Dunn-Cin ...323

Runs Batted In
Castilla-Col ...131
Rolen-StL ...124
Pujols-StL ...123
Beltre-LA ...121
Cabrera-Fla ...112

Stolen Bases
Podsednik-Mil ...70
Pierre-Fla ...45
Abreu-Phi ...40
Freel-Cin ...37
Roberts-LA ...33

Base Stealing Runs
Podsednik-Mil ...10.9
Abreu-Phi ...7.1
Roberts-LA ...6.9
Beltran-Hou ...6.2
Freel-Cin ...4.6

Fielding Runs-Infield
J.Wilson-Pit ...27.4
Rolen-StL ...22.3
Helton-Col ...20.2
Perez-SF-Chi ...14.8
Furcal-Atl ...14.5

Fielding Runs-Outfield
Payton-SD ...14.2
Clark-Mil ...10.2
J.Drew-Atl ...5.0
Hidalgo-Hou-NY ...4.9
Bradley-LA ...4.8

Wins
Oswalt-Hou ...20
Schmidt-SF ...18
Pavano-Fla ...18
Clemens-Hou ...18

Winning Pct.
Clemens-Hou ...818
Carpenter-StL ...750
Schmidt-SF ...720
Peavy-SD ...714
Pavano-Fla ...692

Complete Games
Hernandez-Mon ...9
Lidle-Cin-Phi ...5
Sheets-Mil ...5
Schmidt-SF ...4
Johnson-Ari ...4

Strikeouts
Johnson-Ari ...290
Sheets-Mil ...264
Schmidt-SF ...251
Perez-Pit ...239
Clemens-Hou ...218

Fewest BB/Game
Wells-SD ...92
Sheets-Mil ...1.22
Maddux-Chi ...1.40
Johnson-Ari ...1.61
Lima-LA ...1.80

Games
Brower-SF ...89
King-StL ...86
Torres-Pit ...84
Reitsma-Atl ...84
Cormier-Phi ...84

Saves
Isringhausen-StL ...47
Benitez-Fla ...47
Gagne-LA ...45
Smoltz-Atl ...44
Mesa-Pit ...43

Base Runners/9
Benitez-Fla ...7.36
Johnson-Ari ...8.46
Gagne-LA ...8.74
Lidge-Hou ...8.84
Sheets-Mil ...9.00

Adjusted Relief Runs
Lidge-Hou ...25.9
Benitez-Fla ...22.7
Otsuka-SD ...20.9
Linebrink-SD ...18.3
Ayala-Mon ...17.9

Relief Ranking
Lidge-Hou ...40.3
Benitez-Fla ...37.4
Gagne-LA ...34.5
Ayala-Mon ...32.7
Madson-Phi ...23.9

Innings Pitched
Hernandez-Mon ...255.0
Johnson-Ari ...245.2
Sheets-Mil ...237.0
Oswalt-Hou ...237.0
Schmidt-SF ...225.0

Opponents' Avg.
Johnson-Ari ...197
Schmidt-SF ...202
Perez-Pit ...207
Clemens-Hou ...217
Leiter-NY ...218

Opponents' OBP
Johnson-Ari ...241
Sheets-Mil ...255
Schmidt-SF ...272
Wells-SD ...285
Carpenter-StL ...291

Earned Run Average
Peavy-SD ...2.27
Johnson-Ari ...2.60
Sheets-Mil ...2.70
Zambrano-Chi ...2.75
Clemens-Hou ...2.98

Adjusted ERA
Johnson-Ari ...175
Peavy-SD ...174
Sheets-Mil ...163
Zambrano-Chi ...161
Clemens-Hou ...147

Adjusted Starter Runs
Johnson-Ari ...47.4
Sheets-Mil ...41.1
Zambrano-Chi ...36.1
Clemens-Hou ...32.8
Peavy-SD ...32.2

Pitcher Wins
Johnson-Ari ...5.3
Zambrano-Chi ...4.3
Sheets-Mil ...4.1
Peavy-SD ...4.1
Lidge-Hou ...4.0

Say It Ain't, Sosa

Two new parks opened on the opposite ends of the country as well as of the baseball spectrum. Citizens Bank Park in Philadelphia quickly became one of the best venues for hitters outside of Colorado, while many sluggers complained it was easier to hit one out of the Grand Canyon than San Diego's Petco Park.

Two 40-year-old pitchers dominated the league. Roger Clemens, after ending a brief retirement, signed with Houston and beat out Arizona's Randy Johnson to become the oldest Cy Young Award winner. Ray Boone, father of Bob and grandfather of Bret and Aaron, passed during the year, as did Ken Caminiti, the 1996 NL MVP, who died of a drug overdose.

The Braves surprised many by winning the East yet again, their 10th straight division title and 13th in 14 years. The Cardinals claimed the Central division, winning a major league best 105 games, while Los Angeles won the West despite trading popular catcher Paul Lo Duca late in the year. Houston overtook Chicago for the Wild Card berth as the Cubs collapsed in the final days of September after fighting with each other (and the team's television broadcasters) all season. Sammy Sosa didn't dress for the season's final game and left Wrigley Field in the early innings, earning himself an $87,400 fine.

The Cardinals quickly eliminated the Dodgers in four games in their Division Series, while the Astros outslugged the Braves in five games for the club's first postseason series win in the team's 43-year history. The Cardinals won the first two NLCS games at home before the Astros rallied to take the next three games to come tantalizingly close to their first World Series berth. But Jim Edmonds' 12th inning blast in Game 6 kept the Cardinals alive, and St. Louis then beat up on Roger Clemens in Game 7, with Scott Rolen providing the key blow with a two-run bomb. St. Louis offered little resistance to Boston in the World Series, quickly and quietly losing all four games.

2004 American League

TEAM	W	L	T	PCT	GB	HW	HL	R	OR	PA	H	2B	3B	HR	BB	SO	HB	SH	AVG	OBP	SLG	OPS	AOPS	BR	ABR	PF	SB	CS	BSA	BSR
EAST																														
NY	101	61	0	.623		**57**	24	897	808	6364	1483	281	20	**242**	670	982	80	37	.268	.353	.458	811	109	91	93	100	84	33	72	7
BOS	98	64	0	.605	3	55	26	**949**	768	6515	1613	373	25	222	659	1189	69	12	**.282**	**.360**	**.472**	**832**	109	**145**	90	106	68	30	69	4
BAL	78	84	0	.481	23	38	43	842	830	6429	**1614**	319	18	169	528	949	57	46	.281	.345	.432	777	102	20	30	99	101	41	71	8
TB	70	91	0	.435	30.5	41	39	714	842	6098	1416	278	46	145	469	944	55	35	.258	.320	.405	725	90	-99	-82	98	132	42	**76**	14
TOR	67	94	0	.416	33.5	40	41	719	823	6177	1438	290	34	145	513	1083	71	20	.260	.328	.403	731	84	-79	-117	106	58	31	65	2
CENTRAL																														
MIN	92	70	0	.568		49	32	780	**715**	6286	1494	310	24	191	513	982	64	46	.266	.332	.431	763	95	-21	-41	103	116	51	60	-1
CHI	83	79	0	.512	9	46	35	865	831	6196	1481	284	19	**242**	499	1030	63	**58**	.268	.333	.457	790	100	26	1	103	78	51	60	1
CLE	80	82	0	.494	12	44	37	858	857	6449	1565	345	29	184	606	1009	78	47	.276	.351	.444	795	103	63	**98**	96	94	55	63	1
DET	72	90	0	.444	20	38	43	827	844	6284	1531	284	54	201	518	1144	50	50	.272	.337	.449	786	107	21	55	96	86	50	63	1
KC	58	104	0	.358	34	33	47	720	905	6153	1432	261	29	150	461	1057	76	40	.259	.322	.397	719	86	-110	-108	100	67	48	58	-2
WEST																														
ANA	92	70	0	.568		45	36	836	734	6295	1603	272	37	162	450	**942**	73	56	**.282**	.341	.429	770	103	-5	31	96	**143**	46	**76**	**15**
OAK	91	71	0	.562	1	52	29	793	742	6459	1545	336	15	189	608	1061	55	25	.270	.343	.433	776	102	19	27	99	47	22	68	3
TEX	89	73	0	.549	3	51	30	860	794	6256	1492	323	34	227	500	1099	61	23	.266	.329	.457	786	98	19	-11	104	69	36	66	3
SEA	63	99	0	.389	29	38	44	698	823	6362	1544	276	20	136	492	1058	54	46	.270	.331	.396	727	94	-88	-50	95	110	42	72	10
TOT	1133					627	506	11358		88323	21251	4232	404	2605	7486	14529	906	541	.270	.338	.433	771					1253	573	69	75

TEAM	CG	SHO	GR	SV	IP	H	HR	BB	SO	BR/9	ERA	AERA	OAV	OOB	PR	APR	PF	OSB	OCS	FA	E	WPB	DP	FW	PW	BW	BSW	DIF
EAST																												
NY	1	5	436	**59**	1443.2	1532	182	445	1058	12.7	4.69	98	.271	.328	-9	-16	99	90	32	.984	99	70	148	.6	-1.5	8.8	.2	12.0
BOS	4	**12**	437	36	1451.1	**1430**	159	447	1132	12.2	4.18	117	**.255**	**.318**	73	**107**	105	123	31	.981	118	60	129	-.5	**10.1**	8.5	-.1	-1.0
BAL	8	10	452	27	1455.1	1488	159	687	1090	13.8	4.70	99	.264	.348	-11	-7	101	82	39	.982	110	83	161	-.0	-.7	2.8	.2	-5.4
TB	3	5	401	35	1417.0	1459	192	580	923	13.5	4.81	97	.265	.342	-28	-23	101	67	32	.980	119	63	139	-.6	-2.2	-7.7	.8	-.8
TOR	6	11	431	37	1421.0	1505	181	608	956	13.8	4.91	100	.273	.348	-44	-3	106	91	41	.985	91	71	150	1.0	-.3	-11.0	-.3	-2.9
CENTRAL																												
MIN	4	9	435	48	1476.0	1523	167	**431**	1123	**12.2**	**4.03**	115	.267	.323	**98**	97	100	73	44	.984	101	51	158	.5	9.2	-3.9	.3	4.9
CHI	8	8	399	34	1432.1	1505	224	527	1013	13.1	4.91	96	.272	.338	-45	-34	101	90	48	.984	100	57	167	.5	-3.2	.0	-.6	5.2
CLE	8	8	**479**	32	1466.2	1553	201	579	1115	13.5	4.91	90	.275	.342	-30	-82	94	117	40	.983	106	58	152	.2	-7.7	**9.3**	-.4	-2.3
DET	7	9	432	35	1439.2	1542	190	530	995	13.3	4.93	91	.275	.347	-47	-75	97	71	41	.977	144	81	160	-2.0	-7.1	5.2	-.4	-4.7
KC	6	3	409	25	1420.1	1638	208	518	887	14.0	5.15	90	.290	.352	-82	-78	101	84	35	.978	131	77	169	-1.3	-7.4	-10.2	-.7	-3.5
WEST																												
ANA	2	11	343	50	1454.1	1476	170	502	**1164**	12.5	4.28	104	.263	.326	56	30	96	87	44	.985	**90**	72	126	1.1	2.8	2.9	**.9**	3.2
OAK	**10**	8	414	35	1471.1	1466	164	544	1034	12.7	4.17	111	.262	.332	75	73	100	74	**49**	**.986**	91	53	**172**	1.1	6.9	2.5	-.2	4.1
TEX	5	9	468	52	1439.2	1536	182	547	979	13.5	4.53	109	.273	.344	17	60	106	71	39	.981	117	50	152	-.5	5.7	-1.0	-.2	4.1
SEA	7	7	414	28	1459.1	1498	212	575	1036	13.2	4.76	94	.265	.338	-21	-50	96	**64**	38	.983	103	56	140	.4	-4.7	-4.7	.4	-9.4
TOT	79	115	5950	533	20248.0					13.1	4.63		.270	.338						.982	1520	902	2123					

Batter-Fielder Wins		Batting Average		On-Base Percentage		Slugging Average		On-Base Plus Slugging		Adjusted OPS		Adjusted Batter Runs	
Tejada-Bal	6.6	Suzuki-Sea	372	Mora-Bal	.419	Ramirez-Bos	.613	Ramirez-Bos	1009	Hafner-Cle	162	Guerrero-Ana	54.3
Guillen-Det	5.6	Mora-Bal	.340	Suzuki-Sea	.414	Ortiz-Bos	.603	Hafner-Cle	.993	Guerrero-Ana	161	Hafner-Cle	47.9
Guerrero-Ana	5.2	Guerrero-Ana	.337	Hafner-Cle	.410	Guerrero-Ana	.598	Guerrero-Ana	.989	Mora-Bal	155	Mora-Bal	47.8
Mora-Bal	5.1	Rodriguez-Det	.334	Posada-NY	.400	Hafner-Cle	.583	Ortiz-Bos	.983	Ramirez-Bos	150	Ramirez-Bos	43.7
Chavez-Oak	3.9	Durazo-Oak	.321	Chavez-Oak	.397	Mora-Bal	.562	Mora-Bal	.981	Ortiz-Bos	143	Ortiz-Bos	37.8

Runs		Hits		Doubles		Triples		Home Runs		Total Bases		Runs Batted In	
Guerrero-Ana	124	Suzuki-Sea	262	Roberts-Bal	.50	Crawford-TB	.19	Ramirez-Bos	.43	Guerrero-Ana	366	Tejada-Bal	150
Damon-Bos	123	M.Young-Tex	216	Belliard-Cle	48	Figgins-Ana	.17	Ortiz-Bos	.41	Ortiz-Bos	351	Ortiz-Bos	139
Sheffield-NY	117	Guerrero-Ana	206	Ortiz-Bos	.47	Guillen-Det	.10	Konerko-Chi	.41	Tejada-Bal	349	Ramirez-Bos	130
M.Young-Tex	114	Tejada-Bal	203	Ramirez-Bos	.44	M.Young-Tex	.9	Guerrero-Ana	.39	Ramirez-Bos	348	Guerrero-Ana	126
Rodriguez-NY	112	Kotsay-Oak	190	Jeter-NY	.44	Infante-Det	.9	Teixeira-Tex	.38	M.Young-Tex	333	Sheffield-NY	121

Stolen Bases		Base Stealing Runs		Fielding Runs-Infield		Fielding Runs-Outfield		Wins		Winning Pct.		Complete Games	
Crawford-TB	59	Crawford-TB	7.7	Hudson-Tor	33.2	Baldelli-TB	10.0	Schilling-Bos	.21	Schilling-Bos	.778	Westbrook-Cle	5
Suzuki-Sea	36	Rodriguez-NY	4.8	Tejada-Bal	28.4	Crawford-TB	9.4	Santana-Min	.20	Santana-Min	.769	Ponson-Bal	5
Figgins-Ana	34	Suzuki-Sea	4.1	Uribe-Chi	19.6	Rogers-Tex	.18	Mulder-Oak	.18	Mulder-Oak	.680	Mulder-Oak	5
Roberts-Bal	29	Ford-Min	3.7	Guillen-Det	17.0	Guerrero-Ana	7.7	Colon-Ana	.18	Rogers-Tex	.667	Buehrle-Chi	5
Rodriguez-NY	28	Jeter-NY	3.7	Valentin-Chi	17.0	Ibanez-Sea	5.7	Mulder-Oak	.17	P.Martinez-Bos	.640		

Strikeouts		Fewest BB/Game		Games		Saves		Base Runners/9		Adjusted Relief Runs		Relief Ranking	
Santana-Min	265	Lieber-NY	.92	Quantrill-NY	.86	Rivera-NY	.53	Gordon-NY	8.03	Gordon-NY	24.3	Rivera-NY	47.4
P.Martinez-Bos	227	Radke-Min	1.07	Gordon-NY	.80	Cordero-Tex	.49	Santana-Min	8.64	Nathan-Min	24.3	Cordero-Tex	41.5
Schilling-Bos	203	Schilling-Bos	1.39	Rincon-Min	.77	Nathan-Min	.44	Nathan-Min	9.08	Rodriguez-Ana	24.2	Foulke-Bos	38.7
Escobar-Sea	191	Silva-Min	1.55	Timlin-Bos	.76	Percival-Ana	.33	Takatsu-Chi	9.10	Foulke-Bos	24.1	Nathan-Min	37.3
Garcia-Sea-Chi	184	Buehrle-Chi	1.87	Ryan-Bal	.76	Foulke-Bos	.32	Rodriguez-Ana	9.11	Rivera-NY	24.0	Rincon-Min	33.8

Innings Pitched		Opponents' Avg.		Opponents' OBP		Earned Run Average		Adjusted ERA		Adjusted Starter Runs		Pitcher Wins	
Buehrle-Chi	245.1	Santana-Min	192	Santana-Min	.249	Santana-Min	2.61	Santana-Min	178	Santana-Min	51.9	**Santana-Min**	5.6
Santana-Min	228.0	Lilly-Tor	.230	Schilling-Bos	.271	Schilling-Bos	3.26	Schilling-Bos	150	Schilling-Bos	42.7	**Rivera-NY**	4.9
Schilling-Bos	226.2	P.Martinez-Bos	.238	Radke-Min	.291	Westbrook-Cle	3.38	Radke-Min	133	Radke-Min	27.8	**Schilling-Bos**	4.5
Mulder-Oak	225.2	Schilling-Bos	.239	P.Martinez-Bos	.301	Radke-Min	3.48	Hudson-Oak	131	P.Martinez-Bos	25.8	**Cordero-Tex**	4.1
Radke-Min	219.2	Garcia-Sea-Chi	.241	Garcia-Sea-Chi	.302	Hudson-Oak	3.53	R.Lopez-Bal	130	Hudson-Oak	22.3	**Foulke-Bos**	3.8

"The Idiots" Finally Beat the "Evil Empire"

Not everything that happened in the world of baseball in 2004 involved the Red Sox or Yankees, though it often seemed that way. Seattle's Ichiro Suzuki quietly totaled 262 hits, breaking George Sisler's single-season record. Equally as impressive was Minnesota pitcher Johan Santana, who won 13 straight decisions in the second half and was AL's unanimous Cy Young Award winner.

Despite these feats, most observers were focused on the simmering feud between the Red Sox and Yankees from the start of spring training. The Yankees intensified the rivalry by trading in February for All-Star shortstop Alex Rodriguez, who had nearly been traded to Boston two months earlier. That deal helped the Yankees win the AL East title again, though Boston made it close and easily claimed the league's Wild Card berth. Neither team had any problems in the Division Series as the Red Sox swept Anaheim (who had survived a tough AL West race over the Athletics and the surprising Rangers) and the Yankees beat Minnesota in four.

The result was another epic ALCS clash. New York won the first three games and led by a run entering the bottom of the ninth of Game 4. Down to their last outs, the Sox rallied for a run in the ninth off Mariano Rivera, the premier postseason closer in history. Boston then won that game, as well as Game 5, on extra inning hits by David Ortiz. Curt Schilling won Game 6 for Boston despite needing innovative temporary surgery on his right ankle before the game. Boston then scored six runs in the first two innings of an easy Game 7 win, making the Sox the first team in baseball history to win a postseason series after losing the first three games.

The Red Sox, who dubbed themselves "The Idiots" during the season, had no trouble sweeping the Cardinals in the World Series for the franchise's first World Championship since 1918. Manny Ramirez, who ironically would have been dealt had the Sox acquired A-Rod before the season, was the Series MVP.

2003 National League

TEAM	W	L	T	PCT	GB	HW	HL	R	OR	PA	H	2B	3B	HR	BB	SO	HB	SH	AVG	OBP	SLG	OPS	AOPS	BR	ABR	PF	SB	CS	BSA	BSR
EAST																														
ATL	101	61	0	.623		55	26	**907**	740	6378	**1608**	321	31	**235**	545	**933**	49	65	**.284**	.349	**.475**	824	**119**	152	158	99	68	22	**76**	7
FLA	91	71	0	.562	10	53	28	751	692	6185	1459	292	44	157	515	978	57	82	.266	.333	.421	754	105	7	39	96	**150**	74	67	7
PHI	86	76	0	.531	15	49	32	791	697	6333	1448	325	27	166	**651**	1155	55	46	.261	.343	.419	762	111	39	104	93	72	29	71	6
MON	83	79	0	.512	18	52	29	711	716	6116	1404	294	25	144	522	990	45	72	.258	.326	.401	727	92	-43	-58	102	100	39	72	8
NY	66	95	0	.410	34.5	34	46	642	754	6007	1317	262	24	124	489	1035	54	78	.247	.314	.374	688	88	-120	-94	96	70	31	69	5
CENTRAL																														
CHI	88	74	0	.543		44	37	724	683	6187	1431	302	24	172	492	1158	50	80	.259	.323	.416	739	94	-25	-40	102	73	31	70	5
HOU	87	75	0	.537	1	48	33	805	677	6320	1466	308	30	191	557	1021	81	61	.263	.336	.431	767	99	38	-2	105	66	30	69	4
STL	85	77	0	.525	3	48	33	876	796	6466	1580	**342**	32	196	580	952	73	87	.279	**.350**	.454	804	115	122	133	99	82	32	72	7
PIT	75	87	0	.463	13	39	42	753	801	6314	1492	275	45	168	529	1049	87	79	.267	.338	.420	758	101	20	12	101	86	37	70	6
CIN	69	93	0	.426	19	35	46	694	886	6210	1349	239	21	182	524	1326	79	66	.245	.318	.395	713	95	-81	-47	95	80	34	70	6
MIL	68	94	0	.420	20	31	50	714	873	6268	1423	266	24	196	547	1221	71	62	.256	.329	.419	748	100	-6	-1	99	99	39	72	8
WEST																														
SF	100	61	0	.621		**57**	24	755	638	6204	1440	281	29	180	593	980	40	76	.264	.338	.425	763	102	32	22	101	53	37	59	-1
LA	85	77	0	.525	15.5	46	35	574	**556**	6036	1328	260	25	124	407	985	72	71	.243	.303	.368	671	81	-167	-151	97	80	36	69	5
ARI	84	78	0	.519	16.5	45	36	717	685	6261	1467	303	**47**	152	531	1006	47	63	.263	.330	.417	747	91	-7	-63	108	76	38	67	3
COL	74	88	0	.457	26.5	49	32	853	892	6282	1472	330	31	198	619	1134	52	55	.267	.344	.445	789	97	87	-13	114	63	37	63	1
SD	64	98	0	.395	36.5	35	46	678	831	6245	1442	257	32	128	565	1073	57	50	.261	.333	.388	721	102	-48	21	91	76	39	66	3
TOT	1295					720	575	11945		99812	23126	4657	491	2708	8666	16996	967	1093	.262	.332	.417	749					1294	585	69	80

TEAM	CG	SHO	GR	SV	IP	H	HR	BB	SO	BR/9	ERA	AERA	OAV	OOB	PR	APR	PF	OSB	OCS	FA	E	WPB	DP	FW	PW	BW	BSW	DIF
EAST																												
ATL	4	7	489	51	1456.1	1425	147	555	992	12.5	4.10	102	.257	.327	29	16	98	91	34	.981	121	60	**166**	-.8	1.6	**15.5**	.2	3.5
FLA	7	11	395	36	1445.1	1415	128	530	1132	12.4	4.04	101	.258	.325	39	10	96	70	25	**.987**	78	62	162	**1.6**	1.0	3.8	.2	3.4
PHI	9	13	437	33	1443.2	1386	142	536	1060	12.5	4.04	98	.253	.327	38	-13	93	112	24	.984	97	69	146	.5	-1.3	10.2	.0	-4.6
MON	**15**	10	437	42	1437.2	1467	181	**463**	1028	12.5	4.01	111	.264	.327	43	65	104	**40**	38	.983	102	82	152	.3	6.4	-5.7	**.3**	.8
NY	3	10	412	38	1413.1	1497	168	576	907	13.5	4.48	93	.273	.345	-32	-48	98	98	52	.980	118	50	158	-.7	-4.4	-9.2	.0	.1
CENTRAL																												
CHI	13	14	420	36	1456.1	1304	143	617	**1404**	12.3	3.83	113	.241	.324	73	81	101	70	42	.983	106	75	157	.0	8.0	-3.9	.0	2.9
HOU	1	5	**502**	36	1450.0	1350	161	565	1139	12.3	3.86	114	.248	.326	67	86	103	86	48	.985	95	**44**	149	.6	8.5	-.2	-.0	-2.8
STL	9	10	460	41	1463.2	1544	210	508	969	13.0	4.60	89	.271	.336	-52	-82	96	55	24	**.987**	77	60	138	1.6	-8.1	13.1	.2	-2.9
PIT	7	10	457	44	1444.1	1527	178	502	926	13.0	4.64	93	.272	.336	-57	-51	101	69	26	.980	123	60	159	-.9	-5.0	1.2	.0	-1.4
CIN	4	5	475	38	1446.1	1578	209	590	932	13.8	5.09	82	.278	.349	-130	-154	97	77	28	.977	141	55	152	-1.9	-15.1	-4.6	.0	9.6
MIL	5	3	460	44	1452.0	1590	219	575	1034	13.8	5.02	86	.279	.348	-120	-114	101	100	37	.981	114	71	142	-.4	-11.2	-.0	.3	-1.6
WEST																												
SF	7	10	461	43	1437.1	1349	136	546	1006	12.1	3.73	114	.250	.321	88	83	99	67	29	**.987**	80	76	163	1.4	8.2	2.2	-.6	8.3
LA	3	**17**	438	**58**	1457.2	**1254**	127	526	1289	**11.2**	**3.16**	**130**	**.234**	**.306**	**182**	162	96	117	**75**	.981	119	58	164	-.7	**15.9**	-14.9	.0	3.6
ARI	7	11	452	42	1455.0	1379	150	526	1291	12.2	3.84	120	.250	.332	71	116	108	84	38	.983	107	67	132	-.0	11.4	-6.2	-.2	-2.0
COL	3	4	500	34	1420.0	1629	200	552	866	14.4	5.20	94	.290	.359	-146	-44	114	73	42	.981	116	59	165	-.6	-4.3	-1.3	-.4	-.5
SD	10	10	473	31	1431.1	1458	208	611	1091	13.4	4.87	82	.264	.341	-94	-147	94	95	25	.983	102	79	141	.3	-14.5	2.1	-.2	-4.7
TOT	99	150	7268	661	23110.1					12.8	4.28		.262	.332						.983	1696	1027	2446					

Batter-Fielder Wins		Batting Average		On-Base Percentage		Slugging Average		On-Base Plus Slugging		Adjusted OPS		Adjusted Batter Runs	
Bonds-SF	8.2	Pujols-StL	359	Bonds-SF	529	Bonds-SF	749	Bonds-SF	1278	Bonds-SF	226	Bonds-SF	87.1
Pujols-StL	7.1	Helton-Col	358	Helton-Col	458	Pujols-StL	667	Pujols-StL	1106	Pujols-StL	186	Pujols-StL	78.3
Helton-Col	5.9	Bonds-SF	341	Pujols-StL	439	Helton-Col	630	Helton-Col	1088	Sheffield-Atl	165	Sheffield-Atl	58.1
Giles-Atl	5.7	Renteria-Atl	330	Giles-Pit-SD	427	Edmonds-StL	617	Sheffield-Atl	1023	Helton-Col	159	Helton-Col	57.3
Lopez-Atl	5.5	Sheffield-Atl	330	Walker-LA	422	Sheffield-Atl	604	Edmonds-StL	1002	Thome-Phi	158	Thome-Phi	51.2

Runs		Hits		Doubles		Triples		Home Runs		Total Bases		Runs Batted In	
Pujols-StL	137	Pujols-StL	212	Pujols-StL	51	Furcal-Atl	10	Thome-Phi	47	Pujols-StL	394	Wilson-Col	141
Helton-Col	135	Helton-Col	209	Rolen-StL	49	Finley-Ari	10	Sexson-Mil	45	Helton-Col	367	Sheffield-Atl	132
Furcal-Atl	130	Pierre-Fla	204	Helton-Col	49	Lofton-Pit-Chi	8	Bonds-SF	45	Sheffield-Atl	348	Thome-Phi	131
Sheffield-Atl	126	Renteria-StL	194	Green-LA	49	Podsednik-Mil	8	Pujols-StL	43	Sexson-Mil	332	Sexson-Mil	124
		Furcal-Atl	194	Giles-Atl	49			Lopez-Atl	43	Thome-Phi	331	Pujols-StL	124

Stolen Bases		Base Stealing Runs		Fielding Runs-Infield		Fielding Runs-Outfield		Wins		Winning Pct.		Complete Games	
Pierre-Fla	65	Pierre-Fla	7.3	Cora-LA	30.8	Cruz-SF	14.7	Ortiz-Atl	21	Schmidt-SF	773	Hernandez-Mon	8
Podsednik-Mil	43	Podsednik-Mil	6.0	Gonzalez-Chi	25.6	Hidalgo-Hou	14.3	Williams-StL	18	Prior-Chi	750	Schmidt-SF	5
Roberts-LA	40	Renteria-StL	5.0	Helton-Col	19.8	Kotsay-SD	13.7	Prior-Chi	18	Ortiz-Atl	750	Morris-StL	5
Renteria-StL	34	Furcal-Atl	4.8	Giles-Atl	18.3	Edmonds-StL	12.8	Schmidt-SF	17	Williams-StL	667	Millwood-Phi	5
Lofton-Pit-Chi	30	Cabrera-Mon	4.6	Izturis-LA	17.5	Encarnacion-Fla	5.7						

Strikeouts		Fewest BB/Game		Games		Saves		Base Runners/9		Adjusted Relief Runs		Relief Ranking	
Wood-Chi	266	Maddux-Atl	1.36	Quantrill-LA	89	Gagne-LA	55	Gagne-LA	6.56	Gagne-LA	27.8	Gagne-LA	48.1
Prior-Chi	245	Schilling-Ari	1.71	Villarreal-Ari	86	Smoltz-Atl	45	Smoltz-Atl	7.83	Mota-LA	27.1	Wagner-Hou	35.4
Vazquez-Mon	241	Sheets-Mil	1.75	Martin-LA	80	Wagner-Hou	44	Wagner-Hou	8.16	Wagner-Hou	24.7	Smoltz-Atl	34.2
Schmidt-SF	208	Schmidt-SF	1.99	King-Atl	80	Worrell-SF	38	Cormier-Phi	8.50	Cormier-Phi	22.6	Villarreal-Ari	26.3
Schilling-Ari	194	Ohka-Mon	2.04			Biddle-Mon	34	Schmidt-SF	8.80	Smoltz-Atl	22.4	Mantei-Ari	23.2

Innings Pitched		Opponents' Avg.		Opponents' OBP		Earned Run Average		Adjusted ERA		Adjusted Starter Runs		Pitcher Wins	
Hernandez-Mon	233.1	Schmidt-SF	200	Schmidt-SF	250	Schmidt-SF	2.34	Schmidt-SF	182	Schmidt-SF	45.4	**Prior-Chi**	5.1
Vazquez-Mon	230.2	Wood-Chi	203	Schilling-Ari	270	Brown-LA	2.39	Prior-Chi	179	Prior-Chi	42.5	**Gagne-LA**	4.9
Millwood-Phi	222.0	Webb-Ari	212	Vazquez-Mon	278	Prior-Chi	2.43	Brown-LA	173	Brown-LA	39.4	**Brown-LA**	4.2
Williams-StL	220.2	Ortiz-Atl	223	Prior-Chi	283	Webb-Ari	2.84	Webb-Ari	163	Webb-Ari	32.3	**Schmidt-SF**	4.0
Sheets-Mil	220.2	Nomo-LA	223	Brown-LA	290	Schilling-Ari	2.95	Schilling-Ari	157	Hernandez-Mon	31.2	**Wagner-Hou**	3.6

Reeling in the Prize Fish

The Hall of Fame canceled an anniversary retrospective on *Bull Durham*, one of the most popular baseball movies ever, because lead actors Susan Sarandon and Tim Robbins, both political activists, were critical of the U.S.-led war in Iraq. Sammy Sosa clubbed his 500th career homer during the season's first week, though his hitting prowess came under scrutiny in June when he was caught using a corked bat.

Cincinnati opened Great American Ball Park, which instantly became one of the homer-happiest parks, while the Expos played 22 "home" games in San Juan, Puerto Rico. Bobby Bonds, Barry's father, and Hall of Famer Warren Spahn died.

Florida was 16-22 when skipper Jeff Torborg was fired and replaced with 72-year-old Jack McKeon. That move, and the help of rookie midseason call-ups Dontrelle Willis and Miguel Cabrera, made Florida the best team after the All-Star break. Ivan Rodriguez drove in 6 runs and withstood a series-ending collision to lead the Marlins over the Giants in a four-game NLDS. Chicago eliminated Atlanta in a five-game Division Series.

The Cubs were just five outs away from their first World Series appearance since 1945 when disaster struck in Game 6 of the NLCS. A fan prevented left fielder Moises Alou from reaching into the stands for a foul ball, which, compounded by an error, opened the door for 8 runs. Chicago led 5-3 early in Game 7, but Florida came back again. The Marlins bested the Yankees in six games in the World Series, with Brad Penny winning twice and brash Josh Beckett tossing a complete-game shutout in the clincher.

2003 American League

TEAM	W	L	T	PCT	GB	HW	HL	R	OR	PA	H	2B	3B	HR	BB	SO	HB	SH	AVG	OBP	SLG	OPS	AOPS	BR	ABR	PF	SB	CS	BSA	BSR
EAST																														
NY	101	61	1	.623		50	32	877	716	6430	1518	304	14	230	**684**	1042	81	25	.271	.356	.453	809	113	116	128	99	98	33	75	10
BOS	95	67	0	.586	6	53	28	**961**	809	6530	**1667**	**371**	40	238	620	943	53	24	**.289**	**.360**	**.491**	**851**	117	**199**	**158**	104	88	35	72	7
TOR	86	76	0	.531	15	41	40	894	826	6364	1580	357	33	190	546	1081	**90**	11	.279	.349	.455	804	106	98	64	104	37	25	60	7
BAL	71	91	1	.438	30	40	40	743	820	6241	1516	277	24	152	431	902	54	51	.268	.323	.405	728	92	-73	-69	99	89	36	71	7
TB	63	99	0	.389	38	36	45	715	852	6212	1501	298	38	137	420	1030	56	32	.265	.320	.404	724	92	-82	-67	98	**142**	42	**77**	17
CENTRAL																														
MIN	90	72	0	.556		48	33	801	758	6324	1567	318	**45**	155	512	1027	48	42	.277	.341	.431	772	98	29	0	104	94	44	68	5
CHI	86	76	0	.531	4	51	30	791	715	6148	1445	303	19	220	519	916	58	43	.263	.331	.446	777	99	26	-6	104	77	29	73	9
KC	83	79	0	.512	7	40	40	836	867	6239	1526	288	39	162	476	926	75	63	.274	.336	.427	763	94	7	-44	107	120	42	74	12
CLE	68	94	0	.420	22	38	43	699	778	6187	1413	296	26	158	466	1062	62	46	.254	.316	.401	717	88	-96	-94	100	86	61	59	-2
DET	43	119	0	.265	47	23	58	591	928	6070	1312	201	39	153	443	1099	47	**65**	.240	.300	.375	675	81	-188	-161	96	98	63	61	-5
WEST																														
OAK	96	66	0	.593		**57**	24	768	643	6187	1398	317	24	176	556	898	59	22	.254	.327	.417	744	95	-33	-37	101	48	14	**77**	4
SEA	93	69	0	.574	3	50	31	795	**637**	6281	1509	290	33	139	586	989	53	35	.271	.344	.410	754	103	1	44	95	108	37	74	11
ANA	77	85	0	.475	19	45	37	736	743	6119	1473	276	33	150	476	**838**	56	50	.268	.330	.413	743	99	-35	-6	96	65	21	68	1
TEX	71	91	0	.438	25	43	38	826	969	6293	1506	274	36	**239**	488	1052	75	24	.266	.330	.454	784	97	32	-20	107	65	25	72	9
TOT	1135					615	519	11033		87625	20931	4170	443	2499	7223	13805	882	533	.267	.333	.428	761					1279	547	70	90

TEAM	CG	SHO	GR	SV	IP	H	HR	BB	SO	BR/9	ERA	AERA	OAV	OOB	PR	APR	PF	OSB	OCS	FA	E	WPB	DP	FW	PW	BW	BSW	DI
EAST																												
NY	8	12	367	**49**	1462.0	1512	145	375	1119	11.9	4.02	109	.265	.314	82	62	97	92	37	.981	114	**46**	126	-.4	5.9	12.3	.3	1.9
BOS	5	6	437	36	1464.2	1503	153	488	**1141**	12.7	4.48	104	.263	.327	-27	8	105	101	35	.981	113	64	130	-.4	2.7	**15.1**	.0	-3.4
TOR	14	6	443	36	1435.0	1560	184	485	984	13.2	4.69	101	.276	.337	-27	8	105	126	32	.981	117	66	161	-.7	.8	6.1	-.7	-.5
BAL	9	3	425	41	1449.2	1579	198	526	981	13.6	4.76	97	.278	.346	-38	-26	102	121	37	.983	105	54	164	.0	-2.5	-6.6	.0	-1.0
TB	7	7	372	30	1436.2	1454	196	639	877	13.7	4.93	93	.264	.347	-65	-55	101	65	41	.983	103	74	158	.1	-5.3	-6.4	**1.0**	-7.5
CENTRAL																												
MIN	7	8	399	45	1462.0	1526	187	402	997	12.2	4.41	102	.268	.319	19	14	99	70	27	.985	87	72	114	1.0	1.3	.0	-.1	6.8
CHI	12	4	361	36	1431.0	1364	162	518	1056	12.2	4.17	110	.253	.321	56	66	101	**58**	29	.984	93	52	154	.7	6.3	-.6	.0	-1.5
KC	7	10	407	36	1438.2	1569	190	566	865	13.8	5.05	95	.279	.348	-85	-36	106	95	42	.982	108	68	143	-.1	-3.4	-4.2	.5	9.1
CLE	5	7	428	34	1459.1	1477	179	501	943	12.6	4.21	105	.264	.329	52	36	98	84	43	.980	126	60	178	-1.2	3.4	-9.0	-.8	-5.1
DET	3	5	451	27	1438.2	1616	195	557	764	13.9	5.30	83	.264	.352	-124	-153	107	128	**54**	.978	138	63	**194**	-1.8	-14.6	-15.4	-.6	-5.5
WEST																												
OAK	**16**	14	364	48	1441.2	**1336**	140	499	1018	11.8	**3.63**	126	.246	.314	**143**	**150**	101	91	43	.983	107	50	145	-.0	**14.4**	-3.5	-.0	4.2
SEA	8	**15**	366	38	1441.0	1340	173	466	1001	**11.6**	3.76	115	.247	**.311**	122	95	96	62	32	**.989**	65	47	159	**2.3**	9.1	4.2	.4	-4.0
ANA	5	9	375	39	1431.1	1444	190	486	980	12.6	4.28	102	.261	.327	40	16	97	80	48	.982	105	64	138	.0	1.5	-.6	.0	-5.6
TEX	4	3	**494**	43	1433.1	1625	208	603	1009	14.4	5.67	88	.288	.360	-182	-103	110	96	49	.985	94	62	168	.6	-9.9	-1.9	-.0	1.2
TOT	110	109	5689	538	20225.0					12.9	4.52		.267	.333						.983	1475	842	2132					

Batter-Fielder Wins		Batting Average		On-Base Percentage		Slugging Average		On-Base Plus Slugging		Adjusted OPS		Adjusted Batter Runs	
Rodriguez-Tex	6.7	Mueller-Bos	326	Ramirez-Bos	427	Rodriguez-Tex	600	Delgado-Tor	1019	Delgado-Tor	160	Delgado-Tor	55.
Posada-NY	5.1	Ramirez-Bos	325	Delgado-Tor	426	Delgado-Tor	593	Ramirez-Bos	1014	Ramirez-Bos	158	Ramirez-Bos	52.
Chavez-Oak	4.2	Jeter-NY	324	Giambi-NY	412	Ortiz-Bos	592	Rodriguez-Tex	995	Rodriguez-Tex	148	Giambi-NY	45.
Ramirez-Bos	4.1	Wells-Tor	317	Martinez-Sea	406	Ramirez-Bos	587	Nixon-Bos	975	Giambi-NY	148	Rodriguez-Tex	44.
Delgado-Tor	4.0	Ordonez-Chi	317	Posada-NY	405	Nixon-Bos	578	Ortiz-Bos	961	Nixon-Bos	147	Huff-TB	39.

Runs		Hits		Doubles		Triples		Home Runs		Total Bases		Runs Batted In	
Rodriguez-Tex	124	Wells-Tor	215	Wells-Tor	49	Guzman-Min	14	Rodriguez-Tex	47	Wells-Tor	373	Delgado-Tor	14
Garciaparra-Bos	120	Suzuki-Sea	212	Anderson-Ana	49	Garciaparra-Bos	13	Thomas-Chi	42	Rodriguez-Tex	364	Rodriguez-Tex	11
Wells-Tor	118	Young-Tex	204	Huff-TB	47	Beltran-KC	10	Delgado-Tor	42	Soriano-NY	358	Wells-Tor	11
Ramirez-Bos	117	Anderson-Ana	201	Ordonez-Chi	46			Giambi-NY	41	Huff-TB	353	Boone-Sea	11
Delgado-Tor	117											Anderson-Ana	11

Stolen Bases		Base Stealing Runs		Fielding Runs-Infield		Fielding Runs-Outfield		Wins		Winning Pct.		Complete Games	
Crawford-TB	55	Crawford-TB	8.6	Hudson-Tor	44.6	Cameron-Sea	16.2	Halladay-Tor	22	Halladay-Tor	759	Mulder-Oak	
Sanchez-Det	44	Beltran-KC	7.6	Ellis-Oak	30.0	Anderson-Ana	13.3	Pettitte-NY	21	Moyer-Sea	750	Halladay-Tor	
Beltran-KC	41	Soriano-NY	4.9	Chavez-Oak	23.1	Crawford-TB	10.6	Moyer-Sea	21	Pettitte-NY	724	Colon-Chi	
Soriano-NY	35	Suzuki-Sea	4.7	B.Phillips-Cle	15.7	Baldelli-TB	10.3	Loaiza-Chi	21	Lowe-Bos	708		
Suzuki-Sea	34	Damon-Bos	4.5	Valentin-Chi	13.7	Suzuki-Sea	9.2			Loaiza-Chi	700		

Strikeouts		Fewest BB/Game		Games		Saves		Base Runners/9		Adjusted Relief Runs		Relief Ranking	
Loaiza-Chi	207	Wells-NY	85	Miller-Tor	79	Foulke-Oak	43	Foulke-Oak	8.72	Marte-Chi	25.9	Foulke-Oak	48
Martinez-Bos	206	Halladay-Tor	1.08	Walker-Det	78	Guardado-Min	41	Guardado-Min	8.82	Hasegawa-Sea	24.5	M.Rivera-NY	42
Halladay-Tor	204	Radke-Min	1.19	Ryan-Bal	76	M.Rivera-NY	40	Riske-Cle	9.04	Foulke-Oak	24.4	Hawkins-Min	30
Mussina-NY	195	Mussina-NY	1.68	Grimsley-KC	76	Julio-Bal	36	F.Rodriguez-Ana	9.10	Donnelly-Ana	23.9	Hasegawa-Sea	26
Clemens-NY	190	Mulder-Oak	1.93	Hawkins-Min	74	Percival-Ana	33	Mateo-Sea	9.14	M.Rivera-NY	21.8	Cordero-Tex	26

Innings Pitched		Opponents' Avg.		Opponents' OBP		Earned Run Average		Adjusted ERA		Adjusted Starter Runs		Pitcher Wins	
Halladay-Tor	266.0	Martinez-Bos	215	Martinez-Bos	272	Martinez-Bos	2.22	Martinez-Bos	210	Martinez-Bos	48.8	Loaiza-Chi	4
Colon-Chi	242.0	Zito-Oak	219	Mussina-NY	275	Hudson-Oak	2.70	Hudson-Oak	170	Hudson-Oak	47.7	**Foulke-Oak**	4
Hudson-Oak	240.0	Hudson-Oak	223	Halladay-Tor	275	Loaiza-Chi	2.90	Loaiza-Chi	158	Loaiza-Chi	43.6	**Hudson-Oak**	4
Zito-Oak	231.2	Loaiza-Chi	233	Hudson-Oak	280	Mulder-Oak	3.13	Mulder-Oak	146	Halladay-Tor	40.1	**Martinez-Bos**	4
Buehrle-Chi	230.1	Zambrano-TB	237	Loaiza-Chi	286	Halladay-Tor	3.25	Halladay-Tor	146	Mulder-Oak	32.4	**M.Rivera-NY**	4

When Push Came to Shove

Boston surprised traditionalists by adding 278 seats atop the Green Monster. They quickly became the hottest ticket in baseball. Baltimore pitcher Steve Bechler died in spring training after collapsing during a workout. An over-the-counter diet supplement containing ephedra was linked to his death. Larry Doby, the AL's first black player, also died.

The season-opening series in Tokyo between Seattle and Oakland was canceled because of security concerns related to the U.S.-led war in Iraq. Yankees hurler Roger Clemens won his 300th game and recorded his 4,000th strikeout on the same night against the Cardinals. Toronto's Roy Halladay won 15 straight decisions, a victory shy of the league record for one season. Rafael Palmeiro smacked career homer number 500 for Texas, which led the league in long balls hit as well as allowed.

The small-market Twins won the Central for the second straight year, but they were dispatched in four games in the ALDS by the Yankees. The Red Sox rallied to win Games 3, 4 and 5 to beat Oakland in the other Division Series. The ALCS was marred by a bench-clearing brawl in Game 3; New York bench coach Don Zimmer charged Pedro Martinez, Boston starting pitcher, who casually moved aside and pushed Zimmer to the ground. Two Yankees later were involved in a bullpen brawl between innings with a partisan groundskeeper. Aaron Boone's leadoff homer in the bottom of the 11th of Game 7 sent the Yankees to the World Series again. New York was shocked in the Fall Classic for the second time in three years as the Marlins won in six games.

2002 National League

TEAM	W	L	T	PCT	GB	HW	HL	R	OR	PA	H	2B	3B	HR	BB	SO	HB	SH	AVG	OBP	SLG	OPS	AOPS	BR	ABR	PF	SB	CS	BSA	BSR
EAST																														
ATL	101	59	1	.631		52	28	708	**565**	6223	1428	280	25	164	558	1028	54	67	.260	.331	.409	740	99	0	1	100	76	39	66	3
MON	83	79	0	.512	19	49	32	735	718	6250	1432	300	36	162	575	1104	46	**108**	.261	.334	.418	752	97	23	-15	105	118	64	65	4
PHI	80	81	0	.497	21.5	40	40	710	724	6322	1428	**325**	41	165	640	1095	53	67	.259	.339	.422	761	112	46	99	94	104	43	71	8
FLA	79	83	0	.488	23	46	35	699	763	6260	1433	280	32	146	595	1130	61	59	.261	.337	.403	740	103	5	34	96	**177**	73	71	13
NY	75	86	0	.466	26.5	38	43	690	703	6150	1409	238	22	160	486	1044	63	75	.256	.322	.395	717	99	-56	-17	94	87	42	67	4
CENTRAL																														
STL	97	65	0	.599		52	29	787	648	6246	1475	285	26	175	542	**927**	67	83	.268	.338	.425	763	104	45	40	101	86	42	67	4
HOU	84	78	0	.519	13	47	34	749	695	6252	1441	291	32	167	589	1120	59	64	.262	.338	.417	755	95	31	-24	108	71	27	72	6
CIN	78	84	0	.481	19	38	43	709	774	6254	1386	297	21	169	583	1188	66	95	.253	.330	.408	738	95	-3	-27	104	116	52	69	7
PIT	72	89	0	.447	24.5	38	42	641	730	6049	1300	263	20	142	537	1109	73	68	.244	.319	.381	700	87	-80	-92	102	86	49	64	2
CHI	67	95	0	.414	30	36	45	706	759	6242	1351	259	29	**200**	585	1269	44	78	.246	.321	.413	734	97	-24	-23	100	63	21	75	7
MIL	56	106	0	.346	41	31	50	627	821	6083	1369	269	29	139	500	1125	55	79	.253	.320	.390	710	92	-65	-60	99	94	50	65	3
WEST																														
ARI	98	64	0	.605		55	26	**819**	674	6316	1471	283	41	165	643	1016	50	62	.267	**.346**	.423	769	97	67	-6	110	92	46	67	4
SF	95	66	1	.590	2.5	50	31	783	616	6298	1465	300	35	198	616	961	65	68	.267	.344	**.442**	786	115	95	124	97	74	21	**78**	9
LA	92	70	0	.568	6	46	35	713	643	6146	1464	286	29	155	428	940	53	67	.264	.320	.409	729	102	-36	4	94	96	37	72	8
COL	73	89	0	.451	25	47	34	778	898	6164	**1508**	283	41	152	497	1043	56	49	**.274**	.337	.423	760	92	35	-54	114	103	53	66	4
SD	66	96	0	.407	32	41	40	662	815	6178	1393	243	29	136	547	1062	30	45	.253	.321	.381	702	97	-81	-21	91	71	44	62	0
TOT	1294					706	587	11516		99433	22753	4482	488	2595	8921	17161	895	1134	.259	.331	.410	741					1514	703	68	87

TEAM	CG	SHO	GR	SV	IP	H	HR	BB	SO	BR/9	ERA	AERA	OAV	OOB	PR	APR	PF	OSB	OCS	FA	E	WPB	DP	FW	PW	BW	BSW	DIF
EAST																												
ATL	3	**15**	469	57	1467.1	**1302**	123	554	1058	11.6	**3.13**	129	**.240**	.313	158	**149**	98	96	55	.982	114	52	170	-.3	**14.9**	.1	-.2	6.5
MON	9	3	437	39	1453.0	1475	165	508	1088	12.6	3.97	110	.265	.329	22	60	106	85	44	.978	139	63	160	-1.7	6.0	-1.5	-.1	-.7
PHI	5	9	450	47	1449.2	1381	153	570	1075	12.5	4.17	92	.252	.328	-10	-59	93	74	34	**.986**	88	80	156	1.2	-5.9	9.9	.3	-5.9
FLA	11	12	461	36	1456.1	1449	151	631	1104	13.2	4.36	90	.262	.341	-42	-75	96	93	**61**	.983	106	61	163	.2	-7.5	3.4	**.8**	1.2
NY	9	10	451	36	1442.2	1408	163	543	1107	12.5	3.89	101	.256	.327	34	9	96	151	53	.976	144	**33**	138	-2.0	.9	-1.7	-.1	-2.6
CENTRAL																												
STL	4	9	472	42	1446.1	1355	141	547	1009	12.2	3.70	109	.251	.323	65	53	98	86	34	.983	103	49	168	.4	5.3	4.0	-.1	6.5
HOU	2	11	480	43	1445.0	1423	151	546	1219	12.6	4.00	108	.260	.330	17	48	105	104	36	**.986**	**83**	43	149	**1.5**	4.8	-2.4	.0	-.9
CIN	2	8	462	42	1453.2	1502	173	550	980	13.1	4.27	100	.269	.338	-27	-2	104	**67**	42	.981	120	80	169	-.6	-.2	-2.7	.2	.4
PIT	2	7	458	47	1412.2	1447	163	572	920	13.2	4.23	99	.268	.342	-20	-7	102	94	44	.982	115	46	**177**	-.4	-.7	-9.2	-.3	2.1
CHI	11	9	390	23	1441.1	1373	167	606	**1333**	12.7	4.29	94	.253	.342	-30	-40	99	112	54	.981	114	59	144	-.3	-4.4	-2.3	.2	-7.6
MIL	7	4	446	32	1432.1	1468	199	666	1026	13.8	4.73	87	.268	.352	-99	-99	100	109	49	.983	103	76	154	.4	-9.9	-6.0	-.2	-3.2
WEST																												
ARI	**14**	10	422	40	1446.2	1361	170	**421**	1303	**11.4**	3.92	114	.247	**.305**	30	82	109	43	43	.985	89	61	116	1.1	8.2	-.6	-.1	8.4
SF	10	13	417	43	1437.1	1349	**116**	523	992	11.9	3.54	111	.251	.319	90	66	96	87	36	.985	90	43	166	1.1	6.6	**12.4**	.4	-6.0
LA	4	**15**	423	56	1457.2	1311	165	555	1132	11.8	3.69	105	.241	.315	67	33	95	110	53	.985	90	45	134	1.1	3.4	.3	.6	0.0
COL	1	8	**506**	40	1426.2	1554	225	582	920	13.9	5.20	91	.277	.349	-174	-67	115	87	23	.982	112	54	158	-.2	-6.7	-5.4	-.1	4.4
SD	5	10	459	40	1436.1	1522	177	582	1108	13.6	4.62	84	.274	.346	-82	-126	94	76	40	.979	128	65	162	-1.1	-12.6	-2.1	-.5	1.3
TOT	99	153	7203	666	23105.0					12.7	4.11		.259	.331						.982	1738	910	2484					

Batter-Fielder Wins		Batting Average		On-Base Percentage		Slugging Average		On-Base Plus Slugging		Adjusted OPS		Adjusted Batter Runs	
Bonds-SF	11.5	Bonds-SF	.370	Bonds-SF	.582	Bonds-SF	.799	Bonds-SF	1381	Bonds-SF	.269	Bonds-SF	126.2
Giles-Pit	5.5	Walker-Col	.338	Giles-Pit	.622	Giles-Pit	.622	Giles-Pit	1072	Giles-Pit	.176	Giles-Pit	63.5
Edmonds-StL	4.9	V.Guerrero-Mon	.336	V.Guerrero-Mon	.435	Walker-Col	.602	Walker-Col	1023	Sosa-Chi	.158	V.Guerrero-Mon	.51.3
Kent-SF	4.8	Helton-Col	.329	Helton-Col	.429	Sosa-Chi	.594	V.Guerrero-Mon	1010	Edmonds-StL	.156	Abreu-Phi	.51.2
Rolen-Phi-StL	4.4	C.Jones-Atl	.327	Walker-Col	.421	V.Guerrero-Mon	.593	Helton-Col	1006	C.Jones-Atl	.155	C.Jones-Atl	.50.2

Runs		Hits		Doubles		Triples		Home Runs		Total Bases		Runs Batted In	
Sosa-Chi	122	V.Guerrero-Mon	206	Abreu-Phi	50	Rollins-Phi	10	Sosa-Chi	49	V.Guerrero-Mon	364	Berkman-Hou	128
Pujols-StL	118	Kent-SF	195	Lowell-Fla	44	Rolen-Phi-StL	8	Bonds-SF	46	Kent-SF	352	Pujols-StL	127
Bonds-SF	117	Vidro-Mon	190	Vidro-Mon	43	Wilkerson-Mon	8	Green-LA	42	Berkman-Hou	334	Burrell-Phi	116
Green-LA	110	Pujols-StL	185	Cabrera-Mon	43	McCracken-Ari	8	Berkman-Hou	42	Pujols-StL	331	Green-LA	114
Helton-Col	107	Castillo-Fla	185			Furcal-Atl	8	V.Guerrero-Mon	39	Sosa-Chi	330	V.Guerrero-Mon	111

Stolen Bases		Base Stealing Runs		Fielding Runs-Infield		Fielding Runs-Outfield		Wins		Winning Pct.		Complete Games	
Castillo-Fla	48	Roberts-LA	6.4	Reese-Pit	27.8	Shinjo-SF	12.1	Johnson-Ari	24	Johnson-Ari	.828	Johnson-Ari	8
Pierre-Col	47	Pierre-Col	6.1	Uribe-Col	26.5	Sanders-SF	8.7	Schilling-Ari	23	Miller-Hou	.789	Burnett-Fla	7
Roberts-LA	45	Castillo-Fla	5.3	Cabrera-Mon	21.2	Owens-Fla	8.6	Oswalt-Hou	19	Schilling-Ari	.767	Schilling-Ari	5
V.Guerrero-Mon	40	Fox-Fla	4.4	Rolen-Phi-StL	20.2	Perez-NY	6.8	Millwood-Atl	18	Nomo-LA	.727	Hernandez-SF	5
Sanchez-Mil	37	Boone-Cin	4.2	J.Wilson-Pit	19.9	Edmonds-StL	5.5	Glavine-Atl	18	Maddux-Atl	.727		

Strikeouts		Fewest BB/Game		Games		Saves		Base Runners/9		Adjusted Relief Runs		Relief Ranking	
Johnson-Ari	334	Schilling-Ari	1.15	Quantrill-LA	86	Smoltz-Atl	55	Gagne-LA	7.98	Dotel-Hou	25.7	Kim-Ari	40.7
Schilling-Ari	316	Perez-LA	1.54	Dotel-Hou	83	Gagne-LA	52	Dotel-Hou	8.23	Hammond-Atl	23.8	Gagne-LA	31.9
Wood-Chi	217	Vazquez-Mon	1.91	Worrell-SF	80	M.Williams-Pit	46	Kim-Ari	8.75	Kim-Ari	21.1	Nen-SF	30.4
Clement-Chi	215	Maddux-Atl	2.03	Jones-Col	79	Mesa-Phi	45	Schilling-Ari	8.81	Gagne-LA	19.3	Dotel-Hou	26.6
Oswalt-Hou	208	Ohka-Mon	2.10			Nen-SF	43	Isringhausen-StL	8.95	Eischen-Mon	16.2	Hammond-Atl	25.3

Innings Pitched		Opponents' Avg.		Opponents' OBP		Earned Run Average		Adjusted ERA		Adjusted Starter Runs		Pitcher Wins	
Johnson-Ari	260.0	Johnson-Ari	.208	Schilling-Ari	.251	Johnson-Ari	2.32	Johnson-Ari	193	Johnson-Ari	54.6	**Johnson-Ari**	5.7
Schilling-Ari	259.1	Burnett-Fla	.209	Perez-LA	.262	Maddux-Atl	2.62	Maddux-Atl	154	Schilling-Ari	35.1	**Kim-Ari**	4.3
Oswalt-Hou	233.0	Clement-Chi	.215	Johnson-Ari	.273	Glavine-Atl	2.96	Oswalt-Hou	144	Oswalt-Hou	31.6	**Schilling-Ari**	3.6
Vazquez-Mon	230.1	Schmidt-SF	.218	Wolf-Phi	.285	Perez-LA	3.00	Dessens-Cin	141	Maddux-Atl	30.8	**Maddux-Atl**	3.6
Glavine-Atl	224.2	Moss-Atl	.221	Millwood-Atl	.292	Oswalt-Hou	3.01	Schilling-Ari	139	Schilling-Ari	26.0	**Oswalt-Hou**	3.5

Monty Hall Would Have Been Proud

In a transaction worthy of *Let's Make a Deal*, Florida owner John Henry bought the Red Sox and sold the Marlins to Montreal owner Jeffrey Loria. What was behind door number three? The Expos. The other 29 clubs took ownership of Montreal, rather than sell to an owner who would oppose contraction. Several Latin players were found to be older than previously thought. The discrepancies were discovered during increased background checks following the 2001 terrorist attacks.

The Rockies began treating baseballs in a Coors Field "humidor" in an attempt to decrease scoring. It seemed to work and helped league scoring drop to its lowest level since 1992, the last season BC: Before Colorado. Even so, Barry Bonds became only the fourth player to hit 600 home runs.

Tragedy claimed the life of two active players: San Diego outfielder Mike Darr was killed in a car wreck during spring training, and St. Louis pitcher Darryl Kile died of heart problems in midseason. Hall of Famer Enos Slaughter and legendary Cardinals broadcaster Jack Buck also passed.

St. Louis overpowered Randy Johnson in Game 1 of the NLDS and wound up sweeping their series with Arizona. Three Bonds homers helped San Francisco beat Atlanta in a five-game Division Series. Bonds homered only once in the NLCS, as he was walked 10 times, but the Giants beat St. Louis in five with clutch hitting by the rest of the lineup. San Francisco was a win away from a World Series title, but the Giants dropped two heartbreakers and lost to Anaheim in seven.

2002 American League

TEAM	W	L	T	PCT	GB	HW	HL	R	OR	PA	H	2B	3B	HR	BB	SO	HB	SH	AVG	OBP	SLG	OPS	AOPS	BR	ABR	PF	SB	CS	BSA	BSR
EAST																														
NY	103	58	0	.640		52	28	**897**	697	6377	1540	314	12	223	**640**	1171	72	23	.275	.354	.455	809	114	**124**	**132**	99	100	38	72	9
BOS	93	69	0	.574	10.5	42	39	859	665	6332	1560	**348**	33	177	545	944	72	22	.277	.345	.444	789	106	78	63	102	80	28	74	8
TOR	78	84	0	.481	25.5	42	39	813	828	6230	1457	305	38	187	522	1142	53	17	.261	.327	.430	757	95	-1	-29	104	71	18	**80**	9
BAL	67	95	0	.414	36.5	34	47	667	773	6096	1353	311	27	165	452	993	64	40	.246	.309	.403	712	93	-98	-61	95	110	48	70	7
TB	55	106	0	.342	48	30	51	673	918	6198	1418	297	35	133	456	1115	58	44	.253	.314	.390	704	88	-112	-98	98	102	45	69	7
CENTRAL																														
MIN	94	67	0	.584		**54**	27	768	712	6196	1518	**348**	36	167	472	1089	56	34	.272	.332	.437	769	99	26	0	103	79	62	56	-4
CHI	81	81	0	.500	13.5	47	34	856	798	6207	1475	289	29	217	555	952	49	48	.268	.338	.449	787	103	62	-31	104	75	31	71	6
CLE	74	88	0	.457	20.5	39	42	739	837	6099	1349	255	26	192	542	1000	56	49	.249	.321	.412	733	91	-51	-64	102	52	37	58	-2
KC	62	100	0	.383	32.5	37	44	737	891	6206	1415	285	42	140	524	921	52	30	.256	.323	.398	721	81	-68	-147	113	**140**	65	68	8
DET	55	106	0	.342	39	33	47	575	864	5920	1340	265	37	124	363	1035	64	30	.248	.300	.379	679	82	-163	-141	96	65	44	60	-1
WEST																														
OAK	103	59	0	.636		**54**	27	800	654	6291	1450	279	28	205	609	1008	68	20	.261	.339	.432	771	104	35	41	99	46	20	70	3
ANA	99	63	0	.611	4	54	27	851	**644**	6327	**1603**	333	32	152	462	**805**	74	49	**.282**	.341	.433	774	106	44	58	98	117	51	70	**10**
SEA	93	69	0	.574	10	48	33	814	699	6362	1531	285	31	152	629	1003	51	41	.275	.350	.419	769	108	49	78	97	137	58	70	7
TEX	72	90	0	.444	31	42	39	843	882	6332	1510	304	27	**230**	554	1055	62	48	.269	.338	**.455**	793	106	76	53	103	62	34	65	2
TOT	1132					608	524	10892			87173	20519	4218	433	2464	7325	14233	851	499	.264	.331	.424	755				1236	579	68	69

TEAM	CG	SHO	GR	SV	IP	H	HR	BB	SO	BR/9	ERA	AERA	OAV	OOB	PR	APR	PF	OSB	OCS	FA	E	WPB	DP	FW	PW	BW	BSW	DIF
EAST																												
NY	9	11	334	53	1452.0	1441	144	**403**	1135	11.7	3.87	112	.256	.309	94	75	97	92	39	.979	127	69	117	-1.2	7.2	**12.7**	.4	3.4
BOS	5	17	338	51	1446.0	**1339**	146	430	**1157**	11.5	3.75	119	**.246**	**.308**	.113	114	100	118	50	.983	104	51	140	.2	11.0	6.1	.3	-5.5
TOR	6	6	461	41	1438.1	1504	177	590	991	13.5	4.80	96	.269	.344	-55	-29	104	107	41	.982	107	75	159	-.2	-2.8	-2.8	.4	2.2
BAL	8	3	407	31	1450.2	1491	208	549	967	13.0	4.46	97	.266	.336	0	-21	97	103	44	.985	91	76	**173**	.9	-2.0	-5.9	.2	-7.2
TB	**12**	3	306	25	1440.1	1567	215	620	925	14.3	5.29	85	.279	.357	-133	-123	101	92	53	.979	126	75	168	-1.2	-11.8	-9.4	.2	-3.3
CENTRAL																												
MIN	8	9	435	47	1444.2	1454	184	439	1026	12.1	4.12	108	.261	.318	54	54	100	**57**	27	**.987**	**74**	67	124	**1.9**	5.2	.0	-.9	7.3
CHI	7	7	423	35	1423.0	1422	190	528	945	12.7	4.53	99	.260	.330	-11	-5	101	99	38	.984	97	63	157	.6	-.5	3.0	-.1	-3.2
CLE	9	4	421	34	1424.2	1508	142	603	1058	13.7	4.91	90	.274	.348	-71	-76	99	126	**59**	.981	113	67	161	-.4	-7.3	-6.2	-.7	-7.5
KC	**12**	6	421	30	1441.0	1587	212	572	909	13.8	5.21	96	.281	.349	-120	-33	112	90	36	.979	130	76	153	-1.4	-3.2	-14.1	.3	-6.6
DET	11	7	372	33	1414.0	1593	163	463	794	13.5	4.92	89	.285	.343	-73	-88	98	72	34	.977	142	82	148	-2.1	-8.5	-13.6	-.6	-7.0
WEST																												
OAK	9	**19**	408	48	1452.0	1391	**135**	474	1021	11.9	**3.68**	122	.252	.315	**126**	**128**	100	68	46	.984	102	**49**	144	.3	**12.3**	3.9	-.5	5.6
ANA	7	14	400	**54**	1452.1	1345	169	500	999	11.8	3.69	121	.247	.314	124	127	100	78	51	.986	87	59	151	1.2	12.2	5.6	.3	-1.3
SEA	8	12	343	43	1445.1	1422	178	441	1063	11.9	4.07	106	.257	.315	62	38	96	66	35	.985	88	**49**	134	1.1	3.7	7.5	**.5**	-1.3
TEX	4	4	**487**	33	1439.2	1528	194	669	1030	14.2	5.15	93	.272	.355	-111	-56	107	74	28	.984	99	95	152	.5	-5.4	5.1	-.3	-8.9
TOT	115	122	5556	558	20164.0					12.8	4.46		.264	.331						.982	1487	953	2081					

Batter-Fielder Wins	Batting Average	On-Base Percentage	Slugging Average	On-Base Plus Slugging	Adjusted OPS	Adjusted Batter Runs
A.Rodriguez-Tex .7.4	Ramirez-Bos 349	Ramirez-Bos 450	Thome-Cle 677	Thome-Cle 1122	Thome-Cle 190	Thome-Cle 68.3
Garciaparra-Bos .5.4	Sweeney-KC 340	Thome-Cle 445	Ramirez-Bos 647	Ramirez-Bos 1097	Ramirez-Bos 184	Giambi-NY 65.8
Thome-Cle 5.1	B.Williams-NY ...333	Giambi-NY 435	A.Rodriguez-Tex .623	Giambi-NY 1034	Giambi-NY 173	Ramirez-Bos 56.6
Ramirez-Bos ...4.6	Suzuki-Sea 321	Sweeney-KC 417	Giambi-NY 598	A.Rodriguez-Tex .1015	A.Rodriguez-Tex ..160	A.Rodriguez-Tex ...54.3
Giambi-NY 4.5	Ordonez-Chi 320	B.Williams-NY ...415	Ordonez-Chi 597	Sweeney-KC 979	Ordonez-Chi 149	Ordonez-Chi 42.0

Runs	Hits	Doubles	Triples	Home Runs	Total Bases	Runs Batted In
Soriano-NY 128	Soriano-NY 209	Garciaparra-Bos ..56	Damon-Bos 11	A.Rodriguez-Tex ..57	A.Rodriguez-Tex ...389	A.Rodriguez-Tex 142
A.Rodriguez-Tex ...125	Suzuki-Sea 208	Anderson-Ana 56	Winn-TB 9	Thome-Cle 52	Soriano-NY 381	Ordonez-Chi 135
Jeter-NY 124	B.Williams-NY ...204	Soriano-NY 51	Young-Tex 8	Palmeiro-Tex 43	Ordonez-Chi 352	Tejada-Oak 131
Giambi-NY 120	Tejada-Oak 204	Ordonez-Chi 47	Suzuki-Sea 8	Giambi-NY 41	Anderson-Ana 344	Anderson-Ana 123
Damon-Bos 118	Garciaparra-Bos .197	Beltran-KC 44	Beltran-KC 7	Soriano-NY 39	Tejada-Oak 336	Giambi-NY 122

Stolen Bases	Base Stealing Runs	Fielding Runs-Infield	Fielding Runs-Outfield	Wins	Winning Pct.	Complete Games
Soriano-NY 41	Jeter-NY 6.0	Bordick-Bal 26.2	Erstad-Ana 19.4	Zito-Oak 23	Martinez-Bos 833	Byrd-KC 7
Beltran-KC 35	Beltran-KC 5.3	Garciaparra-Bos ..18.8	Jones-Min 13.3	Lowe-Bos 21	Zito-Oak 821	Kennedy-TB 5
Jeter-NY 32	Damon-Bos 4.7	Young-Tex 13.9	Fick-Det 9.3	Martinez-Bos 20	Washburn-Ana 750	Buehrle-Chi 5
	Soriano-NY 4.5	Vizquel-Cle 12.7	Suzuki-Sea 6.7			
	Cameron-Sea 4.0	Chavez-Oak 12.2	Rowand-Chi 5.8			

Strikeouts	Fewest BB/Game	Games	Saves	Base Runners/9	Adjusted Relief Runs	Relief Ranking
Martinez-Bos 239	Reed-Min 1.24	Koch-Oak 84	Guardado-Min 45	Rhodes-Sea 7.49	Romero-Min 23.8	Percival-Ana 32.9
Clemens-NY 192	Byrd-KC 1.50	Romero-Min 81	Koch-Oak 44	Groom-Bal 8.42	Groom-Bal 19.8	Julio-Bal 31.0
Zito-Oak 182	Milton-Min 1.58	Stanton-NY 79	Urbina-Bos 40	Hawkins-Min 8.74	Hawkins-Min 19.7	Rhodes-Sea 30.7
Mussina-NY 182	Martinez-Bos 1.81	Karsay-NY 78	Percival-Ana 40	Martinez-Bos 8.98	Rhodes-Sea 16.5	Romero-Min 29.6
Garcia-Sea 181	Lidle-Oak 1.83	Escobar-Tor 56	Escobar-Tor 38	Lowe-Bos 9.26	Percival-Ana 16.5	Koch-Oak 24.6

Innings Pitched	Opponents' Avg.	Opponents' OBP	Earned Run Average	Adjusted ERA	Adjusted Starter Runs	Pitcher Wins
Halladay-Tor 239.1	Martinez-Bos 198	Martinez-Bos 254	Martinez-Bos 2.26	Martinez-Bos 198	Lowe-Bos 48.2	**Lowe-Bos** 6.2
Buehrle-Chi 239.0	Wakefield-Bos 204	Lowe-Bos 266	Lowe-Bos 2.58	Lowe-Bos 173	Martinez-Bos 45.9	**Martinez-Bos** 5.2
Hudson-Oak 238.1	Lowe-Bos 211	Wakefield-Bos 276	Zito-Oak 2.75	Zito-Oak 163	Zito-Oak 43.1	**Zito-Oak** 4.9
Moyer-Sea 230.2	Zito-Oak 218	Moyer-Sea 278	Wakefield-Bos 2.81	Wakefield-Bos 159	Hudson-Oak 39.4	**Halladay-Tor** ...4.0
Zito-Oak 229.1	Moyer-Sea 230	Reed-Min 288	Halladay-Tor 2.93	Halladay-Tor 158	Halladay-Tor 39.4	**Hudson-Oak** 3.8

(Labor) Peace of Mind

Major League Baseball endured a rocky season as the plan to contract two teams failed because of Minnesota state court rulings. Then, in the Midsummer Classic in Milwaukee's new Miller Park, the commissioner had to declare the All-Star Game a tie when both leagues ran out of pitchers after the 11th inning. After the rough start, however, things improved dramatically when a deadline deal averted a strike by the players.

Texas superstar Alex Rodriguez became the first shortstop with back-to-back 50 home runs seasons. Ted Williams, called by many—including himself—the greatest hitter ever, died.

The Twins, who would have been contracted if Selig had his way, won the Central. Many expected a quick exit, but the Twins survived a five-game ALDS against Oakland, which rode a league-record 20-game winning streak to the West title.

The A's had the tying run on base with two outs in the ninth, but Twins closer "Everyday" Eddie Guardado finally shut the door. Wild Card Anaheim pounded the Yankees in the other ALDS, batting .376 and scoring 31 runs in four games. The Angels' hitting continued in a five-game win over the Twins in the ALCS.

The Angels capped a magical season with a seven-game triumph over San Francisco in the World Series. Facing elimination, Anaheim rallied from a 5-0 deficit in Game 6, and then won the next night behind rookie starter John Lackey. Francisco Rodriguez, aka K-Rod, didn't make his big league debut until September 18, but he had 5 wins during Anaheim's unlikely October run and led an outstanding bullpen.

2001 National League

TEAM	W	L	T	PCT	GB	HW	HL	R	OR	PA	H	2B	3B	HR	BB	SO	HB	SH	AVG	OBP	SLG	OPS	AOPS	BR	ABR	PF	SB	CS	BSA	BSR
EAST																														
ATL	88	74	0	.543		40	41	729	643	6152	1432	263	24	174	493	1039	45	64	.260	.324	.412	736	93	-45	-51	101	85	46	65	3
PHI	86	76	0	.531	2	47	34	746	719	6219	1431	295	29	164	551	1125	43	67	.260	.329	.414	743	101	-22	15	95	153	47	77	17
NY	82	80	0	.506	6	44	37	642	713	6156	1361	273	18	147	545	1062	65	52	.249	.323	.387	710	95	-89	-38	93	66	43	58	-2
FLA	76	86	0	.469	12	46	34	742	744	6184	1461	325	30	166	470	1145	67	60	.264	.326	.423	749	100	-17	9	97	89	40	69	6
MON	68	94	0	.420	20	34	47	670	812	6026	1361	320	28	131	478	1071	60	64	.253	.319	.396	715	90	-81	-75	99	101	51	66	4
CENTRAL																														
HOU	93	69	0	.574		44	37	847	769	6325	1500	313	29	208	581	1119	89	71	.271	.347	.451	798	103	95	37	107	64	49	57	-3
STL	93	69	0	.574		54	28	814	684	6177	1469	274	32	199	529	1089	65	83	.270	.339	.441	780	103	47	31	102	91	35	72	8
CHI	88	74	0	.543	5	48	33	777	701	6219	1409	268	32	194	577	1077	66	117	.261	.336	.430	766	105	23	50	97	67	36	65	2
MIL	68	94	0	.420	25	36	45	740	806	6148	1378	273	30	209	488	1399	72	65	.251	.319	.426	745	98	-36	-19	98	66	36	65	2
CIN	66	96	0	.407	27	27	54	735	852	6222	1464	304	22	176	468	1172	65	66	.262	.324	.419	743	91	-31	-68	105	103	54	66	4
PIT	62	100	0	.383	31	38	43	657	858	6027	1333	256	25	161	467	1106	67	60	.247	.313	.393	706	84	-107	-122	103	93	73	56	-5
WEST																														
ARI	92	70	0	.568		48	33	818	677	6346	1494	284	35	208	587	1052	57	71	.267	.341	.442	783	99	55	3	107	71	38	65	2
SF	90	72	0	.556	2	49	32	799	748	6408	1493	304	40	235	625	1090	50	67	.266	.342	.460	802	118	95	152	94	57	42	58	-2
LA	86	76	0	.531	6	44	37	758	744	6169	1399	264	27	206	519	1062	56	57	.255	.323	.425	748	104	-25	24	94	89	42	68	5
SD	79	83	0	.488	13	35	46	789	812	6278	1379	273	26	161	678	1273	41	29	.252	.336	.399	735	103	-28	34	92	129	44	75	13
COL	73	89	0	.451	19	41	40	923	906	6393	1663	324	61	213	511	1027	61	81	.292	.354	.483	837	100	166	8	120	132	54	71	10
TOT	1296					675	621			12186	99449	23027	4613	488	2952	8567	17908	969	1074	.261	.331	.425	756				1456	735	66	63

TEAM	CG	SHO	GR	SV	IP	H	HR	BB	SO	BR/9	ERA	AERA	OAV	OOB	PR	APR	PF	OSB	OCS	FA	E	WPB	DP	FW	PW	BW	BSW	DIF
EAST																												
ATL	5	13	411	41	1447.1	1363	153	499	1133	11.8	3.59	120	.250	.314	123	115	99	102	50	.983	103	50	133	.4	11.2	-5.0	-.0	.4
PHI	8	7	473	47	1445.1	1417	170	527	1086	12.5	4.15	99	.259	.329	33	-8	94	57	32	.985	91	49	145	1.1	-.8	1.5	1.3	2.0
NY	6	14	397	48	1445.2	1418	186	438	1086	11.8	4.07	99	.257	.314	46	-6	93	131	40	.983	101	64	132	.5	-.6	-3.7	-.6	5.3
FLA	5	11	430	32	1438.0	1397	151	617	1119	13.0	4.32	96	.257	.338	5	-28	96	75	51	.983	103	50	174	.4	-2.7	.9	-.2	-3.8
MON	5	11	491	28	1431.1	1509	190	525	1103	13.2	4.68	92	.272	.339	-52	-60	97	128	33	.982	108	67	139	.1	-5.8	-7.3	-.0	-.0
CENTRAL																												
HOU	7	6	405	48	1454.2	1453	221	486	1228	12.4	4.37	105	.261	.325	-3	33	105	66	49	.982	110	46	138	.0	3.2	3.6	-.7	5.8
STL	8	11	484	38	1435.1	1389	196	526	1083	12.5	3.93	110	.256	.328	68	63	99	51	37	.982	110	52	156	.0	6.1	3.0	.4	2.4
CHI	8	6	452	41	1435.0	1357	164	550	1344	12.3	4.03	104	.249	.321	53	26	96	106	46	.982	109	61	113	.0	2.5	4.9	-.2	-.3
MIL	3	8	489	28	1436.1	1452	197	667	1057	13.7	4.64	92	.265	.350	-45	-57	98	93	47	.983	103	69	156	.4	-5.5	-1.8	-.2	-5.8
CIN	2	2	461	35	1442.2	1572	198	515	943	13.3	4.77	96	.279	.341	-67	-29	105	75	62	.978	138	74	136	-1.5	-2.8	-6.6	.0	-4.0
PIT	8	9	410	36	1416.1	1493	167	549	908	13.5	5.05	88	.272	.344	-108	-89	103	97	37	.978	133	58	168	-1.3	-8.7	-11.9	-.9	3.7
WEST																												
ARI	12	13	421	34	1459.2	1352	195	461	1297	11.5	3.87	120	.247	.311	79	117	106	107	55	.986	84	57	148	1.5	11.4	.3	-.2	-2.0
SF	3	8	439	47	1463.1	1437	145	579	1080	12.6	4.18	98	.258	.329	28	-17	94	86	45	.981	118	58	170	-.4	-1.7	14.8	-.6	-3.1
LA	3	5	408	46	1450.2	1387	184	524	1212	12.3	4.25	97	.252	.323	17	-23	95	82	51	.981	116	53	138	-.3	-2.2	2.3	.1	5.1
SD	5	6	422	46	1440.2	1519	219	476	1088	12.8	4.62	92	.269	.330	-27	-64	95	94	52	.976	145	61	127	-1.9	-6.2	3.3	.9	2.0
COL	8	8	476	26	1430.0	1522	239	598	1058	13.7	5.29	101	.275	.350	-149	4	122	100	36	.984	96	52	167	.8	.4	.8	.6	-10.6
TOT	96	138	7069	621	23074.1					12.7	4.36		261	.331						.982	1768	921	2340					

Batter-Fielder Wins		Batting Average		On-Base Percentage		Slugging Average		On-Base Plus Slugging		Adjusted OPS		Adjusted Batter Runs	
Bonds-SF	11.7	L.Walker-Col	.350	Bonds-SF	.515	Bonds-SF	.863	Bonds-SF	1379	Bonds-SF	263	Bonds-SF	132.8
Sosa-Chi	8.6	Helton-Col	.336	L.Walker-Col	.449	Sosa-Chi	.737	Sosa-Chi	1174	Sosa-Chi	204	Sosa-Chi	93.7
Gonzalez-Ari	5.8	Alou-Hou	.331	Sosa-Chi	.437	Gonzalez-Ari	.688	Gonzalez-Ari	1117	Gonzalez-Ari	171	Gonzalez-Ari	67.4
Nevin-SD	5.2	Berkman-Hou	.331	Helton-Col	.432	Helton-Col	.685	Helton-Col	1116	Sheffield-LA	166	C.Jones-Atl	56.3
Pujols-StL	5.0	C.Jones-Atl	.330	Berkman-Hou	.430	L.Walker-Col	.662	L.Walker-Col	1111	C.Jones-Atl	162	Sheffield-LA	54.3

Runs		Hits		Doubles		Triples		Home Runs		Total Bases		Runs Batted In	
Sosa-Chi	146	Aurilia-SF	206	Berkman-Hou	55	Rollins-Phi	12	Bonds-SF	73	Sosa-Chi	425	Sosa-Chi	160
Helton-Col	132	Pierre-Col	202	Helton-Col	54	Uribe-Col	11	Sosa-Chi	64	Gonzalez-Ari	419	Helton-Col	146
Bonds-SF	129	Gonzalez-Ari	198	Kent-SF	49	Pierre-Col	11	Gonzalez-Ari	57	Bonds-SF	411	Gonzalez-Ari	142
Gonzalez-Ari	128	Helton-Col	197	Abreu-Phi	48	Castillo-Fla	10	Helton-Col	49	Helton-Col	402	Bonds-SF	137
Bagwell-Hou	126	Pujols-StL	194	Pujols-StL	47			Green-LA	49	Green-LA	370		

Stolen Bases		Base Stealing Runs		Fielding Runs-Infield		Fielding Runs-Outfield		Wins		Winning Pct.		Complete Games	
Rollins-Phi	46	Rollins-Phi	7.3	Cabrera-Mon	29.0	Shinjo-NY	12.7	Schilling-Ari	22	Schilling-Ari	.786	Schilling-Ari	6
Pierre-Col	46	Pierre-Col	4.2	Polanco-StL	24.3	A.Jones-Atl	11.1	Morris-StL	22	Johnson-Ari	.778	Vazquez-Mon	5
Guerrero-Mon	37	Reese-Cin	4.1	Cirillo-Col	17.9	Jordan-Atl	10.2	Johnson-Ari	21	Lieber-Chi	.769	Lieber-Chi	5
Abreu-Phi	36	Glanville-Phi	4.1	Lugo-Hou	15.6	Glanville-Phi	6.3	Lieber-Chi	20	Morris-StL	.733		
Castillo-Fla	33	Womack-Ari	3.7	Bagwell-Hou	15.0	Sosa-Chi	5.9			Glavine-Atl	.696		

Strikeouts		Fewest BB/Game		Games		Saves		Base Runners/9		Adjusted Relief Runs		Relief Ranking	
Johnson-Ari	372	Maddux-Atl	1.04	Kline-StL	89	Nen-SF	45	Rodriguez-SF	9.07	Rodriguez-SF	23.2	Wagner-Hou	26.1
Schilling-Ari	293	Schilling-Ari	1.37	Lloyd-Mon	84	Shaw-LA	43	Reed-NY	9.16	Kline-StL	21.4	Rodriguez-SF	26.0
Park-LA	218	Lieber-Chi	1.59	King-Mil	82	Hoffman-SD	43	Nen-SF	9.39	Dotel-Hou	20.9	Kim-Ari	25.3
Wood-Chi	217	Jones-SD	1.75	Fassero-Chi	82	Benitez-NY	43	Schilling-Ari	9.71	Weathers-Mil-Chi	18.6	Batista-Ari	22.3
Vazquez-Mon	208	Vazquez-Mon	1.77			Mesa-Phi	42	Johnson-Ari	9.73	Kim-Ari	18.5	Dotel-Hou	22.2

Innings Pitched		Opponents' Avg.		Opponents' OBP		Earned Run Average		Adjusted ERA		Adjusted Starter Runs		Pitcher Wins	
Schilling-Ari	256.2	Wood-Chi	.202	Schilling-Ari	.273	Johnson-Ari	2.49	Johnson-Ari	186	Johnson-Ari	56.2	Johnson-Ari	5.4
Johnson-Ari	249.2	Johnson-Ari	.203	Johnson-Ari	.274	Schilling-Ari	2.98	Schilling-Ari	156	Schilling-Ari	46.8	Schilling-Ari	4.4
Park-LA	234.0	Park-LA	.216	Vazquez-Mon	.274	Burkett-Atl	3.04	Burkett-Atl	142	Maddux-Atl	33.8	Maddux-Atl	4.2
Maddux-Atl	233.0	Burkett-Atl	.230	Maddux-Atl	.278	Maddux-Atl	3.05	Maddux-Atl	141	Kile-StL	32.3	Kile-StL	3.6
Lieber-Chi	232.1	Burnett-Fla	.231	Lieber-Chi	.290	Kile-StL	3.09	Kile-StL	140	Burkett-Atl	31.1	Morris-StL	3.3

Bonds Is Best

New ballparks opened in Pittsburgh and Milwaukee. Compared to recent openings, attendance was good the first season, but the numbers for both also-rans dropped by one-quarter the following season—a new stadium was no longer a cure-all. Umpire Al Clark was fired following allegations he broke MLB rules: exchanging first-class plane tickets for economy class (and pocketing the difference) and soliciting players' autographs to sell as memorabilia.

Barry Bonds had one of the most impressive seasons ever, breaking Mark McGwire's record with 73 home runs, and setting single-season marks for walks (177) and slugging percentage (.863). Sammy Sosa became the first player with 60 or more homers in three seasons. McGwire retired after the season, fifth on the all-time home run list; Tony Gwynn also hung up the spikes. Hall of Famers Eddie Mathews and Willie Stargell died.

Arizona won the West for the second time in four years, behind the pitching duo of Randy Johnson and Curt Schilling. Johnson fanned 20 Reds in May, equaling the nine-inning record, but he was removed when the game went into extra innings. Schilling, who won 22 during the season, tossed a complete-game in Game 5 of the Division Series as the Diamondbacks beat St. Louis in the bottom of the ninth. Atlanta swept Houston in the other Division Series. Johnson won both his starts in the D-backs' five-game NLCS victory over the Braves. Arizona and the Yankees played a seven-game World Series thriller, with Johnson winning three times, including Game 7 in relief. It took a ninth-inning rally, capped by a broken-bat hit by Luis Gonzalez, to give Arizona the title.

2001 American League

TEAM	W	L	T	PCT	GB	HW	HL	R	OR	PA	H	2B	3B	HR	BB	SO	HB	SH	AVG	OBP	SLG	OPS	AOPS	BR	ABR	PF	SB	CS	BSA	BSR
EAST																														
NY	95	65	1	.594		51	28	804	713	6233	1488	289	20	203	519	1035	64	30	.267	.334	.435	769	100	12	4	101	161	53	75	17
BOS	82	79	0	.509	13.5	41	40	772	745	6264	1493	316	29	198	520	1131	70	28	.266	.334	.439	773	102	21	19	100	46	35	57	-2
TOR	80	82	0	.494	16	40	42	767	753	6284	1489	287	36	195	470	1094	74	34	.263	.325	.430	755	95	-25	-42	102	156	55	74	15
BAL	63	98	1	.391	32.5	30	50	687	829	6150	1359	262	24	136	514	989	77	38	.248	.319	.380	699	89	-123	-87	95	133	53	72	11
TB	62	100	0	.383	34	37	44	672	887	6104	1426	311	21	121	456	1116	54	45	.258	.320	.388	708	87	-111	-100	98	115	52	69	7
CENTRAL																														
CLE	91	71	0	.562		44	36	897	821	6357	1559	294	37	212	577	1076	69	49	.278	.350	.458	808	107	100	65	104	79	41	66	3
MIN	85	77	0	.525	6	47	34	771	766	6182	1514	328	38	164	495	1083	64	25	.272	.337	.433	770	96	17	-25	106	146	67	69	9
CHI	83	79	0	.512	8	46	35	798	795	6150	1463	300	29	214	520	998	52	63	.268	.334	.451	785	99	42	-6	106	123	59	68	6
DET	66	96	0	.407	25	37	44	724	876	6144	1439	291	60	158	466	972	51	41	.260	.320	.409	729	93	-72	-55	98	133	61	69	8
KC	65	97	0	.401	26	35	46	729	858	6176	1503	277	37	152	406	898	44	36	.266	.318	.409	727	82	-82	-147	110	100	42	70	7
WEST																														
SEA	116	46	0	.716		57	24	927	627	6474	1637	310	38	169	614	989	62	48	.288	.360	.445	805	117	112	164	95	174	42	81	24
OAK	102	60	0	.630	14	53	28	884	645	6385	1469	334	22	199	640	1021	88	25	.264	.345	.439	784	104	61	57	101	68	29	70	5
ANA	75	87	0	.463	41	39	42	691	730	6221	1447	275	26	158	494	1001	77	46	.261	.327	.405	732	90	-59	-73	102	116	52	69	7
TEX	73	89	0	.451	43	41	41	890	968	6388	1566	326	23	246	548	1093	75	25	.275	.344	.471	815	109	109	82	103	97	32	75	10
TOT	1133					598	534	11013		87512	20852	4200	440	2506	7239	14496	921	533	.267	.334	.428	762					1647	673	71	127

TEAM	CG	SHO	GR	SV	IP	H	HR	BB	SO	BR/9	ERA	AERA	OAV	OOB	PR	APR	PF	OSB	OCS	FA	E	WPB	DP	FW	PW	BW	BSW	DIF
EAST																												
NY	7	9	362	57	1451.1	1429	158	465	1266	12.1	4.02	110	.257	.318	72	67	99	146	45	.982	109	75	132	.3	6.4	.4	.8	7.2
BOS	3	9	424	48	1448.0	1412	146	544	1259	12.7	4.15	107	.254	.329	53	46	99	223	51	.981	113	77	129	.0	4.4	1.8	-1.1	-3.7
TOR	7	10	471	41	1462.2	1553	165	490	1041	13.0	4.28	107	.275	.339	31	47	102	112	47	.985	97	43	184	1.0	4.5	-4.0	.6	-3.1
BAL	10	6	392	31	1432.1	1504	194	528	938	13.2	4.67	92	.269	.337	-32	-61	96	157	51	.979	125	52	137	-.6	-5.8	-8.3	.2	-2.9
TB	1	6	370	30	1423.2	1513	207	569	1030	13.6	4.94	91	.273	.345	-73	-69	101	113	44	.977	139	83	144	-1.4	-6.6	-9.6	-.2	-1.2
CENTRAL																												
CLE	3	4	483	42	1446.2	1512	148	573	1218	13.3	4.64	99	.270	.341	-27	-9	102	128	60	.982	107	70	137	.4	-.9	6.2	-.6	4.8
MIN	12	8	402	45	1441.1	1494	192	445	965	12.5	4.51	103	.268	.325	-6	24	104	73	43	.982	108	62	118	.4	2.3	-2.4	.0	3.7
CHI	8	9	406	51	1433.1	1465	181	500	921	12.8	4.55	102	.266	.334	-13	15	104	107	40	.981	118	70	149	-.2	1.4	-.6	-.3	1.7
DET	16	2	391	34	1429.1	1624	180	553	859	14.2	5.01	88	.288	.357	-85	-95	99	104	50	.979	131	70	164	-1.0	-9.1	-5.3	-.1	.4
KC	5	1	396	30	1440.1	1537	209	576	911	14.6	4.87	102	.276	.348	-61	12	111	105	45	.981	117	83	204	.2	1.1	-14.1	-.2	-2.7
WEST																												
SEA	8	14	391	56	1465.0	1293	160	465	1051	11.2	3.54	120	.236	.301	152	122	95	73	29	.986	83	46	137	1.8	11.7	15.7	1.4	4.4
OAK	13	9	416	44	1463.1	1384	153	440	1117	11.5	3.59	127	.249	.308	144	154	102	124	55	.980	125	46	151	-.6	14.8	5.5	-.4	-6.0
ANA	6	1	384	43	1437.2	1452	168	525	947	12.8	4.20	111	.263	.331	44	68	104	109	59	.983	103	62	142	.7	6.5	-7.0	-.2	-6.0
TEX	4	3	410	37	1438.1	1670	222	596	951	14.6	5.71	83	.293	.362	-198	-142	107	79	66	.981	114	72	167	.0	-13.6	7.9	.0	-2.4
TOT	103	91	5698	589	20213.0					12.9	4.47		.267	.334						.981	1589	911	2095					

Batter-Fielder Wins		Batting Average		On-Base Percentage		Slugging Average		On-Base Plus Slugging		Adjusted OPS		Adjusted Batter Runs	
A.Rodriguez-Tex	6.9	Suzuki-Sea	350	J.Giambi-Oak	477	J.Giambi-Oak	660	J.Giambi-Oak	1137	J.Giambi-Oak	196	J.Giambi-Oak	84.2
J.Giambi-Oak	6.3	J.Giambi-Oak	342	Martinez-Sea	423	Thome-Cle	624	Thome-Cle	1040	Thome-Cle	163	A.Rodriguez-Tex	56.2
Alomar-Cle	5.6	Alomar-Cle	336	Thome-Cle	416	A.Rodriguez-Tex	622	A.Rodriguez-Tex	1021	Martinez-Sea	163	Thome-Cle	51.7
Martinez-Sea	4.1	Boone-Sea	331	Alomar-Cle	415	Ramirez-Bos	609	Ramirez-Bos	1014	Ramirez-Bos	162	Ramirez-Bos	50.0
Ramirez-Bos	3.8	Catalanotto-Tex	330	Delgado-Tor	408	Gonzalez-Cle	590	Martinez-Sea	966	A.Rodriguez-Tex	160	Martinez-Sea	49.9

Runs		Hits		Doubles		Triples		Home Runs		Total Bases		Runs Batted In	
A.Rodriguez-Tex	133	Suzuki-Sea	242	J.Giambi-Oak	47	Guzman-Min	14	A.Rodriguez-Tex	52	A.Rodriguez-Tex	393	Boone-Sea	141
Suzuki-Sea	127	Boone-Sea	206	Sweeney-KC	46	Beltran-KC	12	Thome-Cle	49	Boone-Sea	360	Gonzalez-Cle	140
Boone-Sea	118	Stewart-Tor	202	Stewart-Tor	44	Alomar-Cle	12	Palmeiro-Tex	47	J.Giambi-Oak	343	A.Rodriguez-Tex	135
Alomar-Cle	113	A.Rodriguez-Tex	201	Chavez-Oak	43	Cedeno-Det	11	Ramirez-Bos	41	Palmeiro-Tex	338	Ramirez-Bos	125
Jeter-NY	110	Anderson-Ana	194	Durham-Chi	42	Durham-Chi	10	Glaus-Ana	41	Thome-Cle	328	Thome-Cle	124

Stolen Bases		Base Stealing Runs		Fielding Runs-Infield		Fielding Runs-Outfield		Wins		Winning Pct.		Complete Games	
Suzuki-Sea	56	Suzuki-Sea	7.4	Gonzalez-Tex	33.3	Hunter-Min	18.6	Mulder-Oak	21	Clemens-NY	870	Sparks-Det	8
Cedeno-Det	55	Cedeno-Det	6.8	Menechino-Oak	17.6	Singleton-Chi	7.3	Moyer-Sea	20	Abbott-Sea	810	Radke-Min	6
Soriano-NY	43	Beltran-KC	6.5	Halter-Det	14.4	Suzuki-Sea	7.0	Clemens-NY	20	Sabathia-Cle	773	Mulder-Oak	6
McLemore-Sea	39	McLemore-Sea	6.1	Easley-Det	12.7	Higginson-Det	6.7	Hudson-Oak	18	Moyer-Sea	769	Weaver-Det	6
Knoblauch-NY	38	Cameron-Sea	5.7	Chavez-Oak	12.3	Salmon-Ana	6.2	Garcia-Sea	18				

Strikeouts		Fewest BB/Game		Games		Saves		Base Runners/9		Adjusted Relief Runs		Relief Ranking	
Nomo-Bos	220	Radke-Min	1.04	Quantrill-Tor	80	M.Rivera-NY	50	Rhodes-Sea	7.81	Foulke-Chi	21.0	Foulke-Chi	42.0
Mussina-NY	214	Mussina-NY	1.65	Stanton-NY	76	Sasaki-Sea	45	M.Rivera-NY	8.26	Rhodes-Sea	20.2	M.Rivera-NY	37.0
Clemens-NY	213	Pettitte-NY	1.84	Grimsley-KC	73	Foulke-Chi	42	Sasaki-Sea	8.51	M.Rivera-NY	18.5	Levine-Ana	33.9
Zito-Oak	205	Moyer-Sea	1.89	Foulke-Chi	72	Percival-Ana	39	Zimmerman-Tex	8.58	Zimmerman-Tex	18.2	Zimmerman-Tex	30.8
Colon-Cle	201	Loaiza-Tor	1.89			Koch-Tor	36	Pineiro-Sea	8.84	Levine-Ana	17.0	Wickman-Cle	25.1

Innings Pitched		Opponents' Avg.		Opponents' OBP		Earned Run Average		Adjusted ERA		Adjusted Starter Runs		Pitcher Wins	
Garcia-Sea	238.2	Garcia-Sea	225	Mussina-NY	274	Garcia-Sea	3.05	Mays-Min	148	Mays-Min	37.6	Mays-Min	4.4
Hudson-Oak	235.0	Sabathia-Cle	228	Buehrle-Chi	279	Mussina-NY	3.15	Buehrle-Chi	141	Garcia-Sea	33.6	Foulke-Chi	4.2
Mays-Min	233.2	Zito-Oak	230	Garcia-Sea	283	Mays-Min	3.16	Mussina-NY	141	Mussina-NY	33.4	M.Rivera-NY	3.8
Sparks-Det	232.0	Buehrle-Chi	230	Moyer-Sea	285	Buehrle-Chi	3.29	Garcia-Sea	135	Buehrle-Chi	32.2	Mussina-NY	3.8
		Nomo-Bos	231	Mays-Min	289	Hudson-Oak	3.37	Hudson-Oak	135	Mulder-Oak	29.9	Mulder-Oak	3.6

Tragedy Affects All

Baseball, like the rest of the world, was affected by the September 11 terrorist attacks in New York, Washington, D.C., and Pennsylvania. Games were postponed for six days while the nation evaluated its new travel procedures. No contests were lost, however, as the season was extended by a week. That meant a first-ever November finish for the World Series.

Texas and Toronto began the season in Puerto Rico, the third consecutive season opener outside the U.S. or Canada. Cal Ripken, Harold Baines, and Paul O'Neill retired; Lou Boudreau died.

Seattle's Ichiro Suzuki, a former Japanese superstar, finished the year with 242 hits, the highest total since 1930. The right fielder, known simply as Ichiro on two continents, helped the Mariners to a league-record 116 wins. Oakland, a distant second, won 102 games to take the Wild Card.

The Yankees, East champs again, looked in trouble against the A's in the Division Series. Oakland won the first two games, but New York came back, thanks to one of the most replayed defensive gems in postseason history. With the Yankees leading Game 3, 1-0, shortstop Derek Jeter ranged across the diamond to corral a throw from right field, and threw off balance to catcher Jorge Posada to nail Jeremy Giambi. Like New York, Seattle survived a five-game ALDS. Jamie Moyer and three relievers held Cleveland to 4 hits and 1 run in the deciding game. New York became the first club to win an LCS four straight times—spoiling a guarantee by Mariners manager Lou Piniella—but the Yankees were finally beaten in the World Series by Arizona.

2000 National League

TEAM	W	L	T	PCT	GB	HW	HL	R	OR	PA	H	2B	3B	HR	BB	SO	HB	SH	AVG	OBP	SLG	OPS	AOPS	BR	ABR	PF	SB	CS	BSA	BSR
EAST																														
ATL	95	67	0	.586		51	30	810	**714**	6275	1490	274	26	179	595	1010	59	87	.271	.346	.429	775	101	.7	17	99	148	56	73	13
NY	94	68	0	.580	1	**55**	26	807	738	6327	1445	281	20	198	675	1037	45	70	.263	.346	.430	776	106	13	63	94	66	46	59	-2
FLA	79	82	0	.491	15.5	43	38	731	797	6202	1441	274	29	160	540	1184	60	42	.262	.331	.409	740	96	-70	-29	95	**168**	55	75	**18**
MON	67	95	0	.414	28	37	44	738	902	6152	1475	-310	35	178	476	1048	29	78	.266	.326	.432	758	95	-49	-51	100	58	48	55	-4
PHI	65	97	0	.401	30	34	47	708	830	6273	1386	304	40	144	611	1117	44	70	.251	.329	.400	729	89	-92	-86	99	102	30	**77**	12
CENTRAL																														
STL	95	67	0	.586		50	31	887	771	6369	1481	259	25	235	675	1253	**84**	79	.270	.356	.455	811	107	84	68	102	87	51	63	1
CIN	85	77	1	.525	10	43	38	825	765	6372	1545	302	36	200	559	995	66	56	.274	.343	.447	790	100	32	10	103	100	38	72	9
MIL	73	89	1	.451	22	42	39	740	826	6354	1366	297	25	177	620	1245	61	61	.246	.325	.403	728	89	-95	-87	99	72	44	62	0
HOU	72	90	0	.444	23	39	42	938	944	6444	1547	289	36	**249**	673	1129	83	57	.278	.361	**838**	177	70	108	114	52	69	7	7
PIT	69	93	0	.426	26	37	44	793	888	6369	1506	**320**	31	168	564	1032	66	59	.267	.339	.424	763	97	-24	-23	100	86	40	68	5
CHI	65	97	0	.401	30	38	43	764	904	6397	1426	272	23	183	632	1120	54	**89**	.256	.335	.411	746	93	-56	-44	98	93	37	72	8
WEST																														
SF	97	65	0	.599		**55**	26	925	747	6418	1535	304	44	226	·709	1032	51	73	.278	**.362**	.472	834	**122**	133	**202**	93	79	39	67	4
LA	86	76	0	.531	11	44	37	798	729	6312	·1408	265	28	211	668	1083	51	66	.257	.341	.431	772	104	-4	39	95	95	42	69	6
ARI	85	77	0	.525	12	47	34	792	754	6240	1466	282	44	179	535	975	59	61	.265	.333	.429	762	93	-29	-54	103	97	44	69	6
COL	82	80	0	.506	15	48	33	**968**	897	6453	**1664**	**320**	**53**	161	601	**907**	42	75	**.294**	**.362**	.455	817	90	102	-72	123	131	61	68	7
SD	76	86	0	.469	21	41	40	752	815	6290	1413	279	37	157	602	1177	46	39	.254	.330	.402	732	95	-87	-37	94	131	53	71	10
TOT	1296					704	592	12976		101247	23594	4632	532	3005	9735	17344	898	1062	.266	.342	.432	773					1627	736	69	100

TEAM	CG	SHO	GR	SV	IP	H	HR	BB	SO	BR/9	ERA	AERA	OAV	OOB	PR	APR	PF	OSB	OCS	FA	E	WPB	DP	FW	PW	BW	BSW	DIF
EAST																												
ATL	13	9	376	**53**	1440.1	1428	165	**484**	1093	12.2	4.05	111	.258	**.319**	93	75	97	99	33	.979	129	**32**	138	-.6	**7.1**	1.6	.6	5.3
NY	8	10	411	49	1450.0	1398	164	574	1164	12.6	4.05	105	**.252**	.327	76	34	94	133	46	.980	118	42	121	-.0	3.2	5.9	-.8	4.7
FLA	5	4	429	48	1429.2	1477	169	650	1051	13.7	4.59	95	.269	.348	6	-36	95	104	55	.980	125	61	144	-.5	-3.4	-2.7	**1.1**	4.0
MON	4	7	452	39	1424.2	1575	181	579	1011	14.0	5.13	92	.282	.353	-79	-66	102	123	38	.978	132	74	151	-.8	-6.2	-4.8	-1.0	-1.2
PHI	8	6	414	34	1438.2	1458	201	640	1123	13.4	4.77	96	.265	.343	-23	-31	99	77	44	.983	100	58	136	1.0	-2.9	-8.1	.5	-6.5
CENTRAL																												
STL	10	7	386	37	1433.2	1403	196	606	1100	13.0	4.38	106	.259	.338	39	41	100	**70**	66	.981	111	57	148	.4	3.9	6.4	-.5	3.9
CIN	8	7	387	42	1456.1	1446	190	659	1015	13.3	4.33	110	.261	.341	49	68	103	81	33	.982	111	108	156	.4	6.4	-.9	.3	-4.0
MIL	2	7	433	29	1466.1	1501	174	728	967	14.1	4.63	100	.269	.357	-1	-4	100	86	58	.981	118	72	**187**	.0	-.4	-8.2	-.6	1.2
HOU	8	2	410	30	1437.2	1596	230	598	1064	14.1	5.42	90	.281	.352	-125	-78	106	111	32	.978	133	61	149	-.9	-7.4	6.6	.0	-7.5
PIT	5	7	466	27	1449.0	1554	163	711	1070	14.4	4.94	94	.277	.361	-50	-49	100	101	42	.979	132	79	169	-.8	-4.6	-2.2	-.1	-4.3
CHI	10	5	421	39	1454.2	1505	231	658	1143	13.8	5.25	87	.268	.348	-101	-112	99	94	54	.983	100	51	139	1.0	-10.6	-4.2	.2	-2.4
WEST																												
SF	9	**15**	384	47	1444.1	1452	**151**	623	1076	13.2	4.21	103	.266	.342	68	23	94	97	48	**.985**	93	58	173	**1.3**	2.2	**19.1**	-.2	-6.4
LA	9	11	371	36	1444.0	1452	176	600	1154	12.8	4.10	108	**.252**	.332	84	55	96	106	52	.978	135	75	151	-1.0	5.2	3.7	-.0	-2.9
ARI	**16**	8	390	38	1443.2	1441	190	500	**1220**	12.4	4.35	110	.262	.326	45	68	103	102	56	.982	107	34	138	.6	6.4	-5.1	-.0	2.1
COL	7	2	**479**	33	1430.0	1568	221	588	1001	14.0	5.26	110	.281	.354	-99	68	125	102	35	**.985**	94	55	176	**1.3**	6.4	-6.8	.0	.0
SD	5	4	443	46	1459.1	1443	191	649	1071	13.3	4.52	98	.258	.340	18	-13	96	106	50	.977	141	79	-155	-1.3	-1.2	-3.5	.4	.7
TOT	127	112	6652	627	23103.1					13.4	4.63		.266	.342						.981	1879	996	2431					

Batter-Fielder Wins		Batting Average		On-Base Percentage		Slugging Average		On-Base Plus Slugging		Adjusted OPS		Adjusted Batter Runs	
Bonds-SF	6.8	Helton-Col	.372	Helton-Col	.463	Helton-Col	.698	Helton-Col	1162	Bonds-SF	193	Bonds-SF	73.5
Kent-SF	6.4	Alou-Hou	.355	Bonds-SF	.440	Bonds-SF	.688	Bonds-SF	1127	Sheffield-LA	178	Sheffield-LA	63.9
Alfonzo-NY	5.6	V.Guerrero-Mon	.345	Sheffield-LA	.438	V.Guerrero-Mon	.664	Sheffield-LA	1081	Kent-SF	166	Kent-SF	63.3
Helton-Col	5.4	Hammonds-Col	.335	Giles-Pit	.432	Sheffield-LA	.643	V.Guerrero-Mon	1074	V.Guerrero-Mon	165	Sosa-Chi	57.2
Hidalgo-Hou	4.8	Castillo-Fla	.334	Alfonzo-NY	.425	Hidalgo-Hou	.636	Sosa-Chi	1040	Sosa-Chi	161	V.Guerrero-Mon	55.0

Runs		Hits		Doubles		Triples		Home Runs		Total Bases		Runs Batted In	
Bagwell-Hou	152	Helton-Col	216	Helton-Col	.59	Womack-Ari	14	Sosa-Chi	50	Helton-Col	405	Helton-Col	147
Helton-Col	138	Vidro-Mon	200	Cirillo-Col	.53	Perez-Col	11	Bonds-SF	49	Sosa-Chi	383	Sosa-Chi	138
Edmonds-StL	129	A.Jones-Atl	199	Vidro-Mon	.51	V.Guerrero-Mon	11	Bagwell-Hou	47	V.Guerrero-Mon	379	Bagwell-Hou	132
Bonds-SF	129	V.Guerrero-Mon	197	Gonzalez-Ari	.47	Abreu-Phi	10	Hidalgo-Hou	44	Bagwell-Hou	363	Kent-SF	125
A.Jones-Atl	122	Kent-SF	196	Green-LA	.44			V.Guerrero-Mon	44				

Stolen Bases		Base Stealing Runs		Fielding Runs-Infield		Fielding Runs-Outfield		Wins		Winning Pct.		Complete Games	
Castillo-Fla	62	E.Young-Chi	9.4	Perez-Col	36.5	Hidalgo-Hou	14.3	Glavine-Atl	21	Johnson-Ari	.731	Schilling-Phi-Ari	8
Goodwin-Col-LA	55	Goodwin-Col-LA	8.6	Meares-Pit	21.7	Kotsay-Fla	11.2	Kile-StL	20	Estes-SF	.714	Johnson-Ari	8
E.Young-Chi	54	Womack-Ari	6.1	Morris-Pit	19.3	Abreu-Phi	10.6	Maddux-Atl	19	Elarton-Hou	.708	Maddux-Atl	6
Womack-Ari	45	Castillo-Fla	5.9	Helton-Col	18.7	Jenkins-Mil	7.1	Johnson-Ari	19	Glavine-Atl	.700	Lieber-Chi	6
Furcal-Atl	40	Reese-Cin	5.3	Beltre-LA	16.9	Jordan-Atl	6.2	Park-LA	18	Kile-StL	.690		

Strikeouts		Fewest BB/Game		Games		Saves		Base Runners/9		Adjusted Relief Runs		Relief Ranking	
Johnson-Ari	347	Maddux-Atl	1.52	Kline-Mon	83	Alfonseca-Fla	.45	Nen-SF	7.91	White-Cin-Col	25.8	Nen-SF	41.8
Park-LA	217	Anderson-Ari	1.65	Sullivan-Cin	79	Hoffman-SD	.43	White-Cin-Col	8.79	Nen-SF	20.9	Graves-Cin	41.2
Brown-LA	216	Reed-NY	1.66	Myers-SF	78	Nen-SF	41	Hoffman-SD	8.96	Graves-Cin	20.6	White-Cin-Col	38.8
Dempster-Fla	209	Brown-LA	1.84	Wendell-NY	77	Benitez-NY	41	Benitez-NY	9.12	Leskanic-Mil	18.2	Benitez-NY	30.8
Leiter-NY	200	Schilling-Phi-Ari	1.93			Graves-Cin	30	Brown-LA	9.27	Williamson-Cin	17.7	Leskanic-Mil	30.7

Innings Pitched		Opponents' Avg.		Opponents' OBP		Earned Run Average		Adjusted ERA		Adjusted Starter Runs		Pitcher Wins	
Lieber-Chi	251.0	Brown-LA	.213	Brown-LA	.261	Brown-LA	2.58	Johnson-Ari	181	Johnson-Ari	52.9	Maddux-Atl	5.0
Maddux-Atl	249.1	Park-LA	.214	Maddux-Atl	.276	Johnson-Ari	2.64	D'Amico-Mil	174	Brown-LA	48.2	Johnson-Ari	5.0
Johnson-Ari	248.2	Ankiel-StL	.219	Johnson-Ari	.288	D'Amico-Mil	2.66	Brown-LA	172	Maddux-Atl	43.3	Graves-Cin	4.3
Glavine-Atl	241.0	Johnson-Ari	.224	Schilling-Phi-Ari	.294	Maddux-Atl	3.00	Maddux-Atl	151	D'Amico-Mil	34.3	Park-LA	4.1
Hernandez-SF	240.0	Leiter-NY	.228	Glavine-Atl	.296	Hampton-NY	3.14	Hampton-NY	139	Park-LA	30.2	Nen-SF	4.1

Rocking the Boat

Atlanta reliever John Rocker, who saved 38 games the previous season, was suspended for two weeks after making incendiary and racist comments in an interview with *Sports Illustrated*. Rocker instantly became the most hated player in baseball, and was booed vociferously in every road ballpark—especially in his least favorite city, New York.

The Reds pulled off the last "Deal of the Century," acquiring hometown legend Ken Griffey Jr., and sending Seattle four relatively unknown players. Griffey signed a long-term deal with Cincinnati at a below-market rate, and later became the youngest player to hit 400 homers. The Cubs and Mets opened the year in Tokyo, the first regular-season games played outside North America. Chicago's Sammy Sosa hit 50 homers for the third straight year and Todd Helton of the

Rockies hit the most doubles since 1936. Will Clark, Dwight Gooden, and Orel Hershiser retired.

Atlanta's vaunted pitching fell apart in the Division Series against the Cardinals, giving up 24 runs in the St. Louis sweep. The Cards won Game 1 despite starter Rick Ankiel's postseason-record 5 wild pitches in the third inning. The Wild Card Mets scraped by San Francisco in four games, clinching the NLDS with a complete-game, 1-hit shutout by unheralded Bobby Jones. Ankiel's control problems played a part in the Cardinals' five-game NLCS loss. He walked 3, threw 2 wild pitches, and allowed 2 runs in the first inning of Game 2, ultimately a 6-5 New York victory. Mets fans were ecstatic over their first pennant since 1986, but the club was dismissed in five games by the hated Yankees in the World Series.

2000 American League

TEAM	W	L	T	PCT	GB	HW	HL	R	OR	PA	H	2B	3B	HR	BB	SO	HB	SH	AVG	OBP	SLG	OPS	AOPS	BR	ABR	PF	SB	CS	BSA	BSR
EAST																														
NY	87	74	0	.540		44	36	871	814	6310	1541	294	25	205	631	1007	57	16	.277	.354	.450	804	103	28	40	99	99	48	67	5
BOS	85	77	0	.525	2.5	42	39	792	**745**	6371	1503	316	32	167	611	1019	42	40	.267	.341	.423	764	89	-59	-82	103	43	30	59	-1
TOR	83	79	0	.512	4.5	45	36	861	908	6326	1562	328	21	**244**	526	1026	**60**	29	.275	.341	.469	810	100	21	-8	103	89	34	72	5
BAL	74	88	0	.457	13.5	44	37	794	913	6237	1508	310	22	184	558	900	49	27	.272	.341	.435	776	100	-37	4	95	**126**	65	66	5
TB	69	92	0	.429	18	36	44	733	842	6206	1414	253	22	162	558	1022	51	52	.257	.329	.399	728	85	-138	-130	99	99	46	66	4
CENTRAL																														
CHI	95	67	0	.586		46	35	**978**	839	6406	1615	325	33	216	591	960	53	55	.286	.356	.470	826	103	70	37	104	119	42	74	11
CLE	90	72	0	.556	5	**48**	33	950	816	6512	1639	310	30	221	685	1057	51	41	**.288**	**.367**	.470	**837**	106	**105**	**72**	104	113	34	77	13
DET	79	83	0	.488	16	43	38	823	827	6340	1553	307	41	177	562	982	43	42	.275	.343	.438	781	97	-29	-22	99	83	38	69	5
KC	77	85	0	.475	18	42	39	879	930	6394	**1644**	281	27	150	511	840	48	56	**.288**	.348	.425	773	90	-36	-81	106	121	35	78	14
MIN	69	93	0	.426	26	36	45	748	880	6281	1516	325	**49**	116	556	1021	35	24	.270	.337	.407	744	82	-99	-147	107	90	45	67	4
WEST																														
OAK	91	70	0	.565		47	34	947	813	6432	1501	281	23	239	750	1159	52	26	.270	.360	.458	818	**107**	59	71	99	40	15	73	4
SEA	91	71	0	.562	0.5	47	34	907	780	6444	1481	300	26	198	**775**	1073	48	63	.269	.361	.442	803	104	41	56	98	122	56	69	2
ANA	82	80	0	.506	9.5	46	35	864	869	6373	1574	309	34	236	608	1024	47	47	.280	.352	**.472**	824	104	60	34	103	93	52	64	2
TEX	71	91	0	.438	20.5	42	39	848	974	6363	1601	**330**	35	173	580	922	39	48	.283	.352	.446	798	100	13	1	101	69	47	59	3
TOT	1132					608	524	11995			88995	21652	4269	420	2688	8502	14012	675	566	.276	.349	.443	792					1297	587	69	80

TEAM	CG	SHO	GR	SV	IP	H	HR	BB	SO	BR/9	ERA	AERA	OAV	OOB	PR	APR	PF	OSB	OCS	FA	E	WPB	DP	FW	PW	BW	BSW	DIF
EAST																												
NY	9	6	382	40	1424.1	1458	177	577	1040	13.2	4.76	100	.263	.336	24	1	97	91	37	.981	109	62	132	.2	.0	3.7	-.0	2.6
BOS	7	**12**	425	**46**	1452.2	**1433**	173	498	1121	12.3	**4.23**	118	**.257**	**.322**	110	**123**	102	159	47	.984	109	59	120	.2	**11.3**	-7.5	.2	.6
TOR	**15**	4	388	37	1437.1	1615	195	560	978	14.0	5.14	98	.285	.354	-37	-18	102	99	38	.984	100	**48**	176	.7	-1.6	-.7	.2	3.4
BAL	14	6	396	33	1433.1	1547	202	665	1017	14.1	5.37	87	.275	.352	-73	-113	96	104	31	.981	116	57	151	-.2	-10.4	.4	-.0	3.2
TB	10	8	401	38	1431.1	1553	198	533	955	13.5	4.86	101	.277	.345	8	4	100	114	46	.981	118	71	169	-.4	.4	-11.9	-.2	.6
CENTRAL																												
CHI	5	7	**466**	43	1450.1	1509	195	614	1037	13.5	4.66	108	.270	.346	41	61	103	79	**58**	.978	133	56	**190**	-1.2	5.6	3.4	.5	5.7
CLE	6	5	462	34	1442.1	1511	173	666	**1213**	13.8	4.84	103	.270	.350	12	26	102	109	42	**.988**	**72**	60	147	**2.4**	2.4	**6.6**	.7	-3.1
DET	6	6	429	44	1443.1	1583	177	**496**	978	13.3	4.71	104	.280	.340	33	30	100	55	42	.983	105	58	171	.5	2.7	-2.0	-.0	-3.1
KC	10	6	329	29	1439.1	1585	239	693	927	14.5	5.48	95	.282	.362	-90	-40	106	118	38	.983	102	84	185	.6	-3.7	-7.4	**.8**	5.7
MIN	6	4	412	35	1432.2	1634	212	516	1042	13.7	5.14	102	.287	.347	-37	16	107	64	33	.983	102	81	155	.6	1.5	-13.5	-.2	-.3
WEST																												
OAK	7	11	381	43	1435.1	1535	**158**	615	963	13.8	4.58	107	.274	.348	53	43	99	92	39	.978	134	54	164	-1.3	3.9	6.5	-.2	-1.5
SEA	4	10	383	44	1441.2	1442	167	634	998	13.2	4.49	107	.262	.339	67	51	98	82	38	.984	99	51	176	.8	4.7	5.1	.1	-.7
ANA	5	3	441	**46**	1448.0	1534	228	662	846	13.9	5.00	103	.273	.351	-15	23	105	101	56	.978	134	53	182	-1.2	2.1	3.1	-.3	-2.6
TEX	3	4	415	39	1429.0	1683	202	661	918	15.2	5.52	92	.294	.369	-96	-67	103	65	37	.978	135	48	162	-1.3	-6.1	-.0	-.6	-2.0
TOT	107	92	5710	551	20141.0					13.7	4.91		.276	.349						.982	1568	842	2280					

Batter-Fielder Wins		Batting Average		On-Base Percentage		Slugging Average		On-Base Plus Slugging		Adjusted OPS		Adjusted Batter Runs	
A.Rodriguez-Sea	6.6	Garciaparra-Bos	372	J.Giambi-Oak	476	M.Ramirez-Cle	697	M.Ramirez-Cle	1154	J.Giambi-Oak	185	Delgado-Tor	76.7
J.Giambi-Oak	5.1	Erstad-Ana	355	Delgado-Tor	470	Delgado-Tor	664	Delgado-Tor	1134	M.Ramirez-Cle	181	J.Giambi-Oak	76.6
Garciaparra-Bos	5.0	M.Ramirez-Cle	351	M.Ramirez-Cle	457	J.Giambi-Oak	647	J.Giambi-Oak	1123	Delgado-Tor	178	Thomas-Chi	58.4
Glaus-Ana	4.9	Delgado-Tor	344	Thomas-Chi	436	Thomas-Chi	625	Thomas-Chi	1061	A.Rodriguez-Sea	160	M.Ramirez-Cle	58.3
Delgado-Tor	4.7	Jeter-NY	339	Garciaparra-Bos	434	A.Rodriguez-Sea	606	Garciaparra-Bos	1033	Thomas-Chi	160	A.Rodriguez-Sea	54.7

Runs		Hits		Doubles		Triples		Home Runs		Total Bases		Runs Batted In	
Damon-KC	136	Erstad-Ana	240	Delgado-Tor	57	Guzman-Min	20	Glaus-Ana	47	Delgado-Tor	378	Martinez-Sea	145
A.Rodriguez-Sea	134	Damon-KC	214	Garciaparra-Bos	51	Kennedy-Ana	11	Thomas-Chi	43	Erstad-Ana	366	Sweeney-KC	144
Erstad-Ana	121	Sweeney-KC	206	D.Cruz-Det	46	Damon-KC	10	J.Giambi-Oak	43	Thomas-Chi	364	Thomas-Chi	143
Durham-Chi	121	Jeter-NY	201	Olerud-Sea	45	Durham-Chi	9			Glaus-Ana	340	J.Giambi-Oak	137
Glaus-Ana	120	Garciaparra-Bos	197							Dye-KC	337	Delgado-Tor	137

Stolen Bases		Base Stealing Runs		Fielding Runs-Infield		Fielding Runs-Outfield		Wins		Winning Pct.		Complete Games	
Damon-KC	46	R.Alomar-Cle	7.2	Velarde-Oak	22.0	Martinez-TB-Tx-Tor	11.5	D.Wells-Tor	20	Hudson-Oak	769	D.Wells-Tor	9
R.Alomar-Cle	39	Damon-KC	7.0	Sanchez-KC	19.1	Higginson-Det	9.7	Hudson-Oak	20	P.Martinez-Bos	750	P.Martinez-Bos	7
DeShields-Bal	37	DeShields-Bal	4.6	Valentin-Chi	17.9	Erstad-Ana	8.6	Pettitte-NY	19	Burba-Cle	727	Ponson-Bal	6
Henderson-Sea	31	Lofton-Cle	4.2	Olerud-Sea	14.5	Jones-Min	7.1	P.Martinez-Bos	18	D.Wells-Tor	714	Mussina-Bal	6
		Cairo-TB	3.7	R.Alomar-Cle	14.3	Salmon-Ana	5.8	Sele-Sea	17	Pettitte-NY	679		

Strikeouts		Fewest BB/Game		Games		Saves		Base Runners/9		Adjusted Relief Runs		Relief Ranking	
P.Martinez-Bos	284	D.Wells-Tor	1.21	Wunsch-Chi	83	Koch-Tor	42	P.Martinez-Bos	7.22	Lowe-Bos	25.0	Lowe-Bos	41.3
Colon-Cle	212	P.Martinez-Bos	1.33	Venafro-Tex	77	Jones-Det	42	Foulke-Chi	9.20	Tam-Oak	20.5	Koch-Tor	38.7
Mussina-Bal	210	Mussina-Bal	1.74	Wells-Min	76	Sasaki-Sea	37	Rivera-NY	9.87	Foulke-Chi	20.5	Rivera-NY	33.2
Finley-Cle	189	Milton-Min	1.98	Trombley-Bal	75	Rivera-NY	36	Wells-Min	10.32	Koch-Tor	19.3	Mecir-TB-Oak	27.2
Clemens-NY	188	Moehler-Det	2.02	Lowe-Bos	74			Rhodes-Sea	10.38	Mecir-TB-Oak	18.3	Nelson-NY	26.1

Innings Pitched		Opponents' Avg.		Opponents' OBP		Earned Run Average		Adjusted ERA		Adjusted Starter Runs		Pitcher Wins	
Mussina-Bal	237.2	P.Martinez-Bos	167	P.Martinez-Bos	213	P.Martinez-Bos	1.74	P.Martinez-Bos	288	P.Martinez-Bos	78.3	**P.Martinez-Bos**	8.4
D.Wells-Tor	229.2	Hudson-Oak	227	Mussina-Bal	291	Clemens-NY	3.70	Sirotka-Chi	133	Mussina-Bal	26.1	**Lowe-Bos**	3.9
Rogers-Tex	227.1	Colon-Cle	233	Hernandez-NY	298	Mussina-Bal	3.79	Colon-Cle	129	Sirotka-Chi	23.3	**Koch-Tor**	3.6
Radke-Min	226.2	Clemens-NY	236	Milton-Min	303	Sirotka-Chi	3.79	Clemens-NY	129	D.Wells-Tor	23.1	**Rivera-NY**	3.2
Ponson-Bal	222.0	Abbott-Sea	243	Hudson-Oak	306	Colon-Cle	3.88	Mussina-Bal	124	Colon-Cle	22.9	**Mecir-TB-Oak**	2.5

Three Times for Yankees

Umpires formed a new union to replace the one broken a year earlier in their botched mass resignation. One of its first duties was to agree to merge the league staffs, so arbiters could work games in both leagues. New parks opened in Detroit, San Francisco, and Houston, lifting average attendance to near pre-strike levels. Slugger Albert Belle had to retire because of a degenerative hip condition. Pitching sensations Mark Mulder and Barry Zito debuted with Oakland; Hall of Famer Bob Lemon died.

The Yankees had the worst record of any team in the postseason, but their veteran-laden squad held off upstart Oakland in the Division Series. While the A's defeated Roger Clemens twice, they did not win at home after the opener. Following an overnight trip to Oakland for Game 5, the Yankees scored 6 runs in the top of the first and then held on. Seattle, which didn't clinch the Wild Card until the season's final day, swept the White Sox in the other ALDS. The Yankees dispatched the Mariners in six games, including the first complete-game ALCS shutout in fifteen years—a 15-strikeout, 1-hit masterpiece by Clemens.

New York's first Subway Series since 1956 was big on talk, low on ratings, and just five games start to finish—although three games were decided in the eigth inning or later. The Mets broke the Yankees' 14-game World Series winning streak but little else as the Yanks claimed baseball's first "three-peat" since the 1972–74 A's. After the season Alex Rodriguez signed a 10-year, $252 million contract with Texas, the richest deal in American pro sports history.

1999 National League

TEAM	W	L	T	PCT	GB	HW	HL	R	OR	PA	H	2B	3B	HR	BB	SO	HB	SH	AVG	OBP	SLG	OPS	AOPS	BR	ABR	PF	SB	CS	BSA	BSR
EAST																														
ATL	103	59	0	.636		**56**	25	840	**661**	6351	1481	309	23	197	608	962	53	74	.266	.341	.436	777	101	11	18	99	148	66	69	9
NY	97	66	0	.595	6.5	49	32	853	711	6454	1553	297	14	181	717	994	48	63	.279	**.363**	.434	797	**111**	75	**118**	95	150	61	71	12
PHI	77	85	0	.475	26	41	40	841	846	6386	1539	302	44	161	631	1081	46	70	.275	.351	.431	782	101	27	17	101	125	35	**78**	15
MON	68	94	0	.420	35	35	46	718	853	6149	1473	**320**	47	163	438	939	53	71	.265	.323	.427	750	97	-63	-33	96	70	51	58	-2
FLA	64	98	0	.395	39	35	45	691	852	6216	1465	266	44	128	479	1145	59	44	.263	.325	.395	720	91	-114	-73	94	92	46	67	4
CENTRAL																														
HOU	97	65	0	.599		50	32	823	675	6402	1463	293	23	168	**728**	1138	52	79	.267	.355	.420	775	102	28	40	99	166	75	69	10
CIN	96	67	0	.589	1.5	45	36	865	711	6377	1536	312	37	209	569	1125	45	70	.272	.341	.451	792	101	34	9	103	164	54	75	17
PIT	78	83	0	.484	18.5	45	36	775	782	6233	1417	282	40	171	573	1197	**60**	87	.259	.334	.419	753	94	-43	-46	100	112	48	74	9
STL	75	86	0	.466	21.5	38	42	809	838	6353	1461	294	27	194	613	1202	51	75	.262	.338	.426	764	96	-18	-30	102	134	48	74	13
MIL	74	87	0	.460	22.5	32	48	815	886	6433	1524	299	30	165	658	1065	55	87	.273	.353	.426	779	102	27	24	100	81	33	71	6
CHI	67	95	0	.414	30	34	47	747	920	6201	1411	255	35	189	571	1170	39	65	.257	.329	.420	749	93	-55	-51	100	60	44	58	-2
WEST																														
ARI	100	62	0	.617		52	29	**908**	676	6415	1566	289	46	216	588	1045	48	61	.277	.347	.459	806	107	64	59	101	137	39	**78**	16
SF	86	76	0	.531	14	49	32	872	831	6448	1507	307	18	188	696	1028	**60**	87	.271	.356	.434	790	**111**	52	114	93	109	56	66	4
LA	77	85	0	.475	23	37	44	793	787	6338	1480	253	23	187	594	1030	52	74	.266	.339	.420	759	101	-25	16	95	167	68	71	13
SD	74	88	0	.457	26	46	35	710	781	6136	1360	256	22	153	631	1169	35	36	.252	.332	.393	725	95	-90	-34	93	**174**	67	72	15
COL	72	90	0	.444	28	39	42	906	1028	6368	**1644**	305	39	**223**	508	863	43	54	**.288**	.348	**.472**	820	88	**87**	-96	126	70	43	62	0
TOT	1295					683	612	12966		101260	23880	4619	512	2893	9602	17153	799	1097	.268	.342	.429	771					1959	830	70	140

TEAM	CG	SHO	GR	SV	IP	H	HR	BB	SO	BR/9	ERA	AERA	OAV	OOB	PR	APR	PF	OSB	OCS	FA	E	WPB	DP	FW	PW	BW	BSW	DIF
EAST																												
ATL	9	9	394	45	1471.0	1398	142	507	1197	11.8	3.63	**123**	.251	**.314**	152	**140**	98	108	45	.982	111	**44**	127	.6	**13.2**	1.7	.0	6.5
NY	5	7	439	49	1456.2	1372	167	617	1172	12.6	4.27	102	.252	.331	47	12	95	134	44	**.989**	68	48	147	3.3	1.1	**11.1**	.3	-.3
PHI	11	6	441	32	1438.1	1494	212	627	1030	13.6	4.92	95	.269	.347	-58	-41	102	94	35	.983	100	80	144	1.3	-3.9	1.6	.6	-3.6
MON	6	4	432	44	1434.1	1505	152	572	1043	13.4	4.69	95	.270	.342	-21	-40	98	157	47	.974	160	62	125	-2.4	-3.8	-3.1	-1.0	-2.7
FLA	6	5	453	33	1435.2	1560	171	655	943	14.2	4.90	89	.281	.359	-54	-87	96	94	67	.979	127	56	150	-.4	-8.2	-6.9	-.5	-1.0
CENTRAL																												
HOU	12	8	339	48	1458.2	1485	**128**	478	1204	12.4	3.83	116	.267	.326	119	99	97	94	43	.983	106	63	175	.9	9.4	3.8	.1	1.9
CIN	6	11	381	**55**	1462.0	**1309**	190	636	1081	12.3	3.94	118	**.241**	.324	94	111	103	124	34	.983	105	76	139	1.0	10.5	.9	**.8**	1.4
PIT	8	3	425	34	1433.1	1444	160	633	1083	13.4	4.33	106	.263	.343	37	42	101	99	50	.976	147	63	179	-1.7	-4.0	-4.3	.0	-.5
STL	5	3	**454**	38	1445.1	1519	161	667	1025	14.0	4.74	97	.273	.355	-29	-22	101	80	69	.978	132	68	163	-.8	-2.1	-2.8	.4	-.2
MIL	2	5	453	40	1442.2	1618	213	616	987	13.5	5.07	91	.284	.356	-82	-76	101	177	44	.979	127	77	146	-.4	-7.2	2.3	-.3	-.9
CHI	11	6	441	32	1430.2	1619	221	529	980	13.7	5.27	87	.286	.346	-112	-111	100	100	43	.977	139	73	135	-1.1	-10.5	-4.8	-1.0	3.5
WEST																												
ARI	**16**	9	382	42	1467.1	1387	176	543	1198	12.1	3.77	122	.249	.320	128	135	101	138	66	.983	104	56	132	1.0	12.8	5.6	.7	-1.0
SF	6	3	450	42	1456.1	1486	194	655	1076	13.5	4.71	91	.265	.345	-24	-76	94	129	53	.983	105	70	155	.9	-7.2	10.8	-.5	.9
LA	8	6	399	37	1453.0	1438	192	594	1077	13.0	4.45	98	.258	.334	18	-16	95	156	56	.978	137	66	137	-1.0	-1.5	1.5	.4	-3.4
SD	5	6	403	43	1420.1	1454	193	529	1078	12.8	4.47	95	.266	.332	15	-34	94	114	45	.979	129	88	151	-.5	-3.2	-3.2	.6	-.6
COL	12	2	420	33	1429.0	1700	237	737	1032	15.7	6.01	96	.301	.384	-231	-29	127	163	63	.981	118	79	**189**	.1	-2.7	-9.1	-.8	3.5
TOT	128	93	6706	647	23134.2					13.3	4.56		.268	.342						.980	1915	1069	2394					

Batter-Fielder Wins		Batting Average		On-Base Percentage		Slugging Average		On-Base Plus Slugging		Adjusted OPS		Adjusted Batter Runs	
Bagwell-Hou	5.3	Walker-Col	379	Walker-Col	458	Walker-Col	710	Walker-Col	1168	McGwire-StL	175	C.Jones-Atl	66.8
Ventura-NY	4.7	Gonzalez-Ari	336	Bagwell-Hou	454	McGwire-StL	697	McGwire-StL	1120	C.Jones-Atl	170	Bagwell-Hou	66.3
Biggio-Hou	4.3	Abreu-Phi	335	Abreu-Phi	446	Sosa-Chi	635	C.Jones-Atl	1074	Bagwell-Hou	165	McGwire-StL	62.7
McGwire-StL	4.1	Casey-Cin	332	C.Jones-Atl	441	C.Jones-Atl	633	Bagwell-Hou	1045	Giles-Pit	157	Giles-Pit	48.5
Sosa-Chi	4.1	Cirillo-Mil	326	Olerud-NY	427	Giles-Pit	614	Giles-Pit	1032	Walker-Col	152	Abreu-Phi	46.6

Runs		Hits		Doubles		Triples		Home Runs		Total Bases		Runs Batted In	
Bagwell-Hou	143	Gonzalez-Ari	206	Biggio-Hou	56	Perez-Col	11	McGwire-StL	65	Sosa-Chi	397	McGwire-StL	147
Bell-Ari	132	Glanville-Phi	204	Vidro-Mon	45	Abreu-Phi	11	Sosa-Chi	63	V.Guerrero-Mon	366	Williams-Ari	142
Biggio-Hou	123	Cirillo-Mil	198	Gonzalez-Ari	45	Womack-Ari	10	Vaughn-Cin	45	McGwire-StL	363	Sosa-Chi	141
Alfonzo-NY	123	Casey-Cin	197	Grace-Chi	44	Finley-Ari	10	C.Jones-Atl	45	C.Jones-Atl	359	Bichette-Col	133
				Jenkins-Mil	43					Helton-Col	339	V.Guerrero-Mon	131

Stolen Bases		Base Stealing Runs		Fielding Runs-Infield		Fielding Runs-Outfield		Wins		Winning Pct.		Complete Games	
Womack-Ari	72	Womack-Ari	11.3	Benjamin-Pit	34.8	A.Jones-Atl	17.3	Hampton-Hou	22	Hampton-Hou	846	Johnson-Ari	12
Cedeno-NY	66	Cedeno-NY	8.6	Perez-Col	26.7	Kotsay-Fla	12.4	Lima-Hou	21	Millwood-Atl	720	Schilling-Phi	8
Young-LA	51	Glanville-Phi	6.8	Ventura-NY	18.5	Jenkins-Mil	10.6	Maddux-Atl	19	Bottenfield-StL	720	Astacio-Col	7
Castillo-Fla	50	Reese-Cin	5.9	Biggio-Hou	17.7	Sosa-Chi	9.3			Schilling-Phi	714	Brown-LA	5
		Renteria-StL	5.3	Reese-Cin	16.9	Hidalgo-Hou	8.5			Maddux-Atl	679		

Strikeouts		Fewest BB/Game		Games		Saves		Base Runners/9		Adjusted Relief Runs		Relief Ranking	
Johnson-Ari	364	Reynolds-Hou	1.44	Kline-Mon	82	Urbina-Mon	41	Wagner-Hou	7.11	Wagner-Hou	24.5	Williamson-Cin	44.7
Brown-LA	221	Maddux-Atl	1.52	Wendell-NY	80	Hoffman-SD	40	Hoffman-SD	8.42	Benitez-NY	22.5	Wagner-Hou	38.0
Astacio-Col	210	Lima-Hou	1.61	Telford-Mon	79	Wagner-Hou	39	Millwood-Atl	9.12	Williamson-Cin	22.3	Graves-Cin	31.9
Millwood-Atl	205	Woodard-Mil	1.75	Sullivan-Cin	79	Rocker-Atl	38	Benitez-NY	9.35	Sullivan-Cin	21.0	Rocker-Atl	30.9
Reynolds-Hou	197	Smoltz-Atl	1.93	Benitez-NY	77			Williamson-Cin	9.45	Remlinger-Atl	20.2	Benitez-NY	29.7

Innings Pitched		Opponents' Avg.		Opponents' OBP		Earned Run Average		Adjusted ERA		Adjusted Starter Runs		Pitcher Wins	
Johnson-Ari	271.2	Millwood-Atl	202	Millwood-Atl	258	Johnson-Ari	2.48	Johnson-Ari	186	Johnson-Ari	62.1	**Hampton-Hou**	5.3
Brown-LA	252.1	Johnson-Ari	208	Johnson-Ari	266	Millwood-Atl	2.68	Millwood-Atl	167	Millwood-Atl	44.1	**Johnson-Ari**	5.1
Lima-Hou	246.1	Brown-LA	222	Brown-LA	273	Hampton-Hou	2.90	Hampton-Hou	153	Hampton-Hou	40.7	**Millwood-Atl**	4.3
Hampton-Hou	239.0	Daal-Ari	236	Schilling-Phi	287	Brown-LA	3.00	Brown-LA	145	Brown-LA	36.7	**Williamson-Cin**	4.3
Glavine-Atl	234.0	Schilling-Phi	237	Smoltz-Atl	288	Smoltz-Atl	3.19	Smoltz-Atl	140	Smoltz-Atl	28.6	**Wagner-Hou**	3.7

An All-Century Re-Pete

Under pressure from its corporate sponsor, Commissioner Bud Selig agreed to let Pete Rose participate in on-field ceremonies during the World Series for baseball's All-Century Team. Rose, in the 10th year of lifetime ban for "conduct relating to gambling," was overwhelmingly voted to the team by fans. Marge Schott, Cincinnati's twice-suspended owner, was forced to sell controlling interest to Carl Lindner, one of the team's limited partners.

Mark McGwire hit 65 homers and Sammy Sosa slammed 63 as they became the first players in history to belt 60 or more in two different seasons. Three workers were killed at the Miller Park construction site in Milwaukee when a crane collapsed. The accident ultimately delayed opening of the new park by a year. Dodgers star Pee Wee Reese died.

Arizona won 100 games and became the first team to make the postseason in its second year. Yet the Diamondbacks were surprised in four games by the Mets, who reached the NLDS by winning a one-game playoff with the Reds for the Wild Card. The Braves advanced to the NLCS for the fifth straight year with a four-game Division Series win against Houston. Atlanta defeated New York in six games, but the Braves had to work for it. After dropping the first three games, the Mets rallied for two wins; 15-inning, rain-drenched Game 5 ended on Robin Ventura's grand slam that changed to an RBI-single when one of the celebrating runners passed Ventura during his trot. The Braves won Game 6, and the series, in 11 innings, but Atlanta was swept by the Yankees in the World Series.

1999 American League

TEAM	W	L	T	PCT	GB	HW	HL	R	OR	PA	H	2B	3B	HR	BB	SO	HB	SH	AVG	OBP	SLG	OPS	AOPS	BR	ABR	PF	SB	CS	BSA	BSF
EAST																														
NY	98	64	0	.605		48	33	900	731	6416	1568	302	36	193	718	978	55	22	.282	.366	.453	819	**110**	84	**98**	99	104	57	65	
BOS	94	68	0	.580	4	49	32	836	**718**	6321	1551	334	42	176	597	928	55	34	.278	.350	.448	798	99	27	0	103	67	39	63	
TOR	84	78	0	.519	14	40	41	883	862	6369	1580	**337**	14	212	578	1077	76	28	.280	.352	.457	809	103	50	35	102	119	48	71	7
BAL	78	84	0	.481	20	41	40	851	815	6409	1572	299	21	203	615	890	61	41	.279	.353	.447	800	107	34	65	97	107	46	70	
TB	69	93	0	.426	29	33	48	772	913	6272	1531	272	29	145	544	1042	64	30	.274	.343	.411	754	91	-65	-77	102	73	49	60	
CENTRAL																														
CLE	97	65	0	.599		47	34	**1009**	860	6553	1629	309	32	209	743	1099	55	**54**	.289	**.373**	.467	**840**	107	**135**	85	105	**147**	50	75	15
CHI	75	86	1	.466	21.5	38	42	777	870	6262	1563	298	37	162	499	**810**	34	40	.277	.337	.429	766	92	-52	-65	102	110	50	69	
DET	69	92	0	.429	27.5	38	43	747	882	6095	1433	289	34	212	458	1049	**82**	35	.261	.326	.443	769	93	-60	-71	102	108	70	61	
KC	64	97	0	.398	32.5	33	47	856	921	6325	1584	294	**52**	151	535	932	64	46	.282	.348	.433	781	94	-12	-43	104	127	39	**77**	14
MIN	63	97	1	.394	33	31	50	686	845	6124	1450	285	30	105	500	978	49	24	.264	.328	.384	712	83	77	-151	-185	105	118	60	66
WEST																														
TEX	95	67	0	.586		51	30	945	859	6388	**1653**	304	29	230	611	937	29	35	**.293**	.361	**.479**	**840**	106	112	58	106	111	54	67	
OAK	87	75	0	.537	8	**52**	29	893	846	6440	1430	287	20	235	**770**	1129	71	39	.259	.355	.446	801	106	39	65	97	70	37	65	
SEA	79	83	0	.488	16	43	38	859	905	6310	1499	263	21	**244**	610	1095	42	38	.269	.343	.455	798	103	13	22	99	130	45	74	
ANA	70	92	0	.432	25	37	44	711	826	6131	1404	248	22	158	511	1022	43	41	.256	.322	.395	717	82	-154	-153	100	71	45	61	
TOT	1132					581	551	11725		88415	21447	4121	419	2635	8289	13966	780		507	.275	.347	.439	786				1462	689	68	8

TEAM	CG	SHO	GR	SV	IP	H	HR	BB	SO	BR/9	ERA	AERA	OAV	OOB	PR	APR	PF	OSB	OCS	FA	E	WPB	DP	FW	PW	BW	BSW	DI
EAST																												
NY	6	10	359	**50**	1439.2	1402	158	581	1111	12.8	4.13	114	.255	.330	116	95	97	131	48	.982	111	67	132	.2	8.8	**9.1**	-.3	-.8
BOS	6	**12**	412	**50**	1436.2	**1396**	160	**469**	1131	12.0	**4.00**	124	**.253**	**.315**	137	**151**	102	159	58	.979	127	59	132	-.6	**14.0**	.0	-.4	-.1
TOR	14	9	377	39	1439.0	1582	191	575	1009	13.8	4.92	100	.280	.349	-11	-2	101	124	53	.983	106	68	165	.4	-.2	3.2	.3	-9.2
BAL	**17**	11	393	33	1435.0	1468	198	647	982	13.8	4.77	98	.269	.348	14	-13	97	93	50	**.986**	**89**	60	191	1.3	-1.2	6.0	.1	-1.1
TB	6	5	453	45	1433.0	1606	172	695	1055	14.9	5.06	98	.286	.370	-32	-16	102	101	**69**	.978	135	64	**198**	-1.1	-1.5	-7.1	-.6	-1.1
CENTRAL																												
CLE	3	6	**466**	46	1450.1	1503	197	634	1120	13.6	4.89	104	.268	.346	-5	28	104	118	46	.983	106	62	154	.4	2.6	7.9	**.9**	4.2
CHI	6	3	409	39	1438.1	1608	210	596	968	14.2	4.92	100	.282	.353	-10	1	101	102	46	.982	136	74	149	-1.1	-.0	-6.0	.1	1.4
DET	4	6	421	33	1421.0	1528	209	583	976	13.8	5.17	96	.276	.349	-50	-30	103	81	44	.982	106	55	156	.4	-2.8	-6.6	-.5	-1.9
KC	11	3	416	29	1420.2	1607	202	643	831	14.7	5.35	95	.288	.365	-78	-42	104	111	49	.980	125	70	188	-.6	-3.9	-4.0	.8	-8.8
MIN	13	8	417	34	1423.1	1591	208	487	927	13.3	5.00	103	.283	.341	-23	24	106	73	37	.985	92	69	150	1.1	2.2	-17.1	-.0	-3.2
WEST																												
TEX	6	9	439	47	1436.1	1626	186	509	979	13.6	5.07	102	.286	.346	-34	13	106	**47**	52	.981	119	**52**	169	-.2	1.2	5.4	.0	7.1
OAK	6	5	406	48	1438.1	1537	160	569	967	13.5	4.69	101	.274	.344	26	4	97	110	51	.980	122	75	166	-.4	.4	6.0	-.3	2.2
SEA	7	6	346	40	1433.2	1613	191	684	980	14.9	5.24	91	.287	.368	-60	-75	98	107	50	.981	113	71	182	.0	-6.9	2.0	.7	2.1
ANA	4	7	400	37	1431.1	1472	177	624	877	13.5	4.79	102	.269	.346	10	13	100	103	62	.983	106	85	156	.4	1.2	-14.2	-.5	2.0
TOT	109	100	5714	570	20076.2					13.7	4.86		.275	.347						.981	1593	931	2288					

Batter-Fielder Wins
R.Alomar-Cle 5.1
Garciaparra-Bos 4.7
M.Ramirez-Cle 4.4
Williams-NY 4.3
Rodriguez-Tex 4.1

Batting Average
Garciaparra-Bos 357
Jeter-NY 349
Williams-NY 342
Martinez-Sea 337
M.Ramirez-Cle 333

On-Base Percentage
Martinez-Sea 447
M.Ramirez-Cle 442
Jeter-NY 438
Williams-NY 435
Fernandez-Tor 427

Slugging Average
M.Ramirez-Cle 663
Palmeiro-Tex 630
Garciaparra-Bos 603
Gonzalez-Tex 601
Green-Tor 588

On-Base Plus Slugging
M.Ramirez-Cle 1105
Palmeiro-Tex 1050
Garciaparra-Bos 1022
Martinez-Sea 1001
Jeter-NY 989

Adjusted OPS
M.Ramirez-Cle 170
Martinez-Sea 156
Palmeiro-Tex 155
Jeter-NY 154
Garciaparra-Bos 152

Adjusted Batter Runs
M.Ramirez-Cle .....59.
Jeter-NY .....55.
Giambi-Oak .....50.
Palmeiro-Tex .....49.
Martinez-Sea .....48.

Runs
R.Alomar-Cle 138
Jeter-NY 134
Green-Tor 134
M.Ramirez-Cle 131
Griffey-Sea 123

Hits
Jeter-NY 219
Surhoff-Bal 207
Williams-NY 202
Velarde-Ana-Oak 200
Rodriguez-Tex 199

Doubles
Green-Tor 45
Sweeney-KC 44
Dye-KC 44
Garciaparra-Bos 42

Triples
Offerman-Bos 11
Jeter-NY 9
Febles-KC 9
Damon-KC 9

Home Runs
Griffey-Sea 48
Palmeiro-Tex 47
M.Ramirez-Cle 44
Delgado-Tor 44

Total Bases
Green-Tor 361
Palmeiro-Tex 356
Griffey-Sea 349
M.Ramirez-Cle 346
Jeter-NY 346

Runs Batted In
M.Ramirez-Cle .....16_
Palmeiro-Tex .....14_
Griffey-Sea .....13_
Delgado-Tor .....13_
Gonzalez-Tex .....12_

Stolen Bases
Hunter-Det-Sea 44
Vizquel-Cle 42
Goodwin-Tex 39
Stewart-Tor 37
R.Alomar-Cle 37

Base Stealing Runs
Hunter-Det-Sea 6.9
Vizquel-Cle 6.1
R.Alomar-Cle 6.0
Damon-KC 5.8
Anderson-Bal 5.5

Fielding Runs-Infield
Bordick-Bal 35.1
Sanchez-KC 29.4
Cairo-TB 27.4
Valentin-Bos 12.4
Bush-Tex 10.1

Fielding Runs-Outfield
Dye-KC 14.3
Singleton-Chi 11.9
Hunter-Det-Sea 9.9
Ordonez-Chi 7.4
Surhoff-Bal 5.7

Wins
P.Martinez-Bos 23
Sele-Tex 18
Mussina-Bal 18
Colon-Cle 18

Winning Pct.
P.Martinez-Bos 852
Colon-Cle 783
Mussina-Bal 720
Garcia-Sea 680
Sele-Tex 667

Complete Games
D.Wells-Tor
Ponson-Bal
Erickson-Bal

Strikeouts
P.Martinez-Bos 313
Finley-Ana 200
Sele-Tex 186
Cone-NY 177
Burba-Cle 174

Fewest BB/Game
Heredia-Oak 1.53
P.Martinez-Bos 1.56
Radke-Min 1.81
Moyer-Sea 1.89
Mussina-Bal 2.30

Games
Wells-Min 76
Groom-Oak 76
Trombley-Min 75
Lowe-Bos 74
Lloyd-Tor 74

Saves
Rivera-NY 45
Wetteland-Tex 43
Hernandez-TB 43
Jackson-Cle 39
Mesa-Sea 33

Base Runners/9
Zimmerman-Tex 7.70
Foulke-Chi 8.20
Rivera-NY 8.35
P.Martinez-Bos 8.69
Lowe-Bos 9.30

Adjusted Relief Runs
Foulke-Chi 31.7
Lowe-Bos 28.3
Zimmerman-Tex 26.0
Rivera-NY 23.1
Brocail-Det 22.7

Relief Ranking
Rivera-NY .....46.
Zimmerman-Tex .....33.
Lowe-Bos .....27.
Hernandez-TB .....26.
Karsay-Cle

Innings Pitched
D.Wells-Tor 231.2
Erickson-Bal 230.1
Moyer-Sea 228.0
Burba-Cle 220.0
Helling-Tex 219.1

Opponents' Avg.
P.Martinez-Bos 205
Cone-NY 229
Hernandez-NY 233
Colon-Cle 242
Milton-Min 243

Opponents' OBP
P.Martinez-Bos 248
Milton-Min 299
Hernandez-NY 311
Moyer-Sea 311
Mussina-Bal 312

Earned Run Average
P.Martinez-Bos 2.07
Cone-NY 3.44
Mussina-Bal 3.50
Radke-Min 3.75
Rosado-KC 3.85

Adjusted ERA
P.Martinez-Bos 241
Radke-Min 138
Cone-NY 137
Mussina-Bal 134
Rosado-KC 132

Adjusted Starter Runs
P.Martinez-Bos 67.2
Radke-Min 32.6
Cone-NY 27.1
Saberhagen-Bos 26.7
Mussina-Bal 26.6

Pitcher Wins
P.Martinez-Bos .....8.
Rivera-NY .....4.
Radke-Min .....3.
Saberhagen-Bos .....3.
Mussina-Bal .....3.

The Umps Definitely Blew That Call

The Orioles traveled to Cuba for a spring exhibition game against the Cuban national team, the first game involving American pros there in forty years. The Mariners gleefully moved into Safeco Field in mid-July, while teary-eyed fans in Detroit said farewell to beloved Tiger Stadium. Yankees legend Joe DiMaggio died in March, while an awe-struck Ted Williams was lauded at the All-Star Game at Fenway Park.

In what was perhaps the game's worst negotiating tactic ever, most of baseball's umpires resigned en masse in July, attempting to get around a no-strike clause in their contract. Many resignations were accepted and twenty-two umps wound up losing their jobs.

Pedro Martinez averaged a record 13.2 strikeouts per game. Tampa Bay's 35-year-old reliever Jim Morris became the oldest rookie in nearly thirty years.

The Yankees were postseason juggernauts again. For the second straight year, they permitted Texas 1 run in a three-game Division Series sweep. After losing the first two games in the other ALDS, the Red Sox pummeled Cleveland pitchers in the final three games, including the greatest scoring display in postseason history: a 23-7 rout in Game 4. Aside from a lopsided Boston win in Game 3, it was all New York in the ALCS. In the other games the Yanks outscored the Red Sox, 22-8, in the first meeting between the long-time rivals in the postseason. The Yankees crushed Atlanta for their 25th world championship, an eighth by sweep. The Braves held eighth-inning leads in Game 1 and 3, but New York rallied to win both times.

1998 National League

TEAM	W	L	T	PCT	GB	HW	HL	R	OR	PA	H	2B	3B	HR	BB	SO	HB	SH	AVG	OBP	SLG	OPS	AOPS	BR	ABR	PF	SB	CS	BSA	BSR
EAST																														
ATL	106	56	0	.654		56	25	826	581	6215	1489	297	26	215	548	1062	61	76	.272	.342	.453	795	114	104	111	99	98	43	70	7
NY	88	74	0	.543	18	47	34	706	645	6255	1425	289	24	136	572	1049	37	88	.259	.330	.394	724	98	-29	-6	97	62	46	57	-2
PHI	75	87	0	.463	31	40	41	713	808	6300	1482	286	36	126	508	1080	45	65	.264	.326	.395	721	94	-38	-39	100	97	45	68	6
MON	65	97	0	.401	41	39	42	644	783	6041	1348	280	32	147	439	1058	60	87	.249	.310	.394	704	92	-86	-68	97	91	46	66	4
FLA	54	108	0	.333	52	31	50	667	923	6227	1381	277	36	114	525	1120	45	70	.248	.317	.373	690	92	-107	-66	94	115	57	67	5
CENTRAL																														
HOU	102	60	0	.630		55	26	874	620	6441	1578	326	28	166	621	1122	72	58	.280	.356	.436	792	116	121	146	97	155	51	75	16
CHI	90	73	0	.552	12.5	51	31	831	792	6393	1494	250	34	212	601	1223	39	67	.264	.337	.433	770	103	56	28	104	65	44	60	-1
STL	83	79	1	.512	19	48	34	810	782	6413	1444	292	30	223	676	1179	42	68	.258	.341	.441	782	111	84	89	99	133	41	76	15
CIN	77	85	0	.475	25	39	42	750	760	6268	1441	298	28	138	608	1107	37	78	.262	.337	.402	739	98	7	0	101	95	42	69	6
MIL	74	88	0	.457	28	38	43	707	812	6232	1439	266	17	152	532	1039	66	61	.260	.330	.396	726	94	-28	-40	102	81	59	58	-3
PIT	69	93	1	.426	33	40	40	650	718	6111	1395	271	35	107	393	1060	91	78	.254	.311	.374	685	83	-116	-120	91	159	51	76	17
WEST																														
SD	98	64	0	.605		54	27	749	635	6243	1390	292	30	167	604	1072	48	56	.253	.330	.409	739	106	-2	54	93	79	37	68	4
SF	89	74	0	.546	9.5	49	32	845	739	6484	1540	292	26	161	678	1040	44	81	.274	.353	.421	774	115	87	132	95	102	51	67	5
LA	83	79	0	.512	15	48	33	669	678	6076	1374	209	27	159	447	1056	36	91	.252	.310	.387	697	91	-102	-70	95	137	53	72	12
COL	77	85	0	.475	21	42	39	826	855	6277	1640	333	36	183	469	949	37	98	.291	.347	.461	808	96	132	-21	121	67	47	59	-2
ARI	65	97	0	.401	33	34	47	665	812	6116	1353	235	46	159	489	1239	64	45	.246	.314	.393	707	90	-83	-84	100	73	38	66	3
TOT	1298					711	586	11932		100092	23213	4493	491	2565	8710	17455	824	1167	.262	.331	.410	741					1609	751	68	91

TEAM	CG	SHO	GR	SV	IP	H	HR	BB	SO	BR/9	ERA	AERA	OAV	OOB	PR	APR	PF	OSB	OCS	FA	E	WPB	DP	FW	PW	BW	BSW	DIF
EAST																												
ATL	24	23	354	45	1438.2	1291	117	467	1232	11.2	3.25	128	.240	.303	156	147	98	85	40	.985	91	64	139	1.3	14.5	11.0	.1	-1.9
NY	9	16	399	46	1458.0	1381	152	532	1129	12.2	3.76	109	.253	.325	76	59	97	117	64	.984	101	51	151	.8	5.8	-.6	-.8	1.7
PHI	21	10	385	32	1463.0	1476	188	544	1176	12.8	4.64	93	.262	.331	-66	-52	102	87	33	.982	110	88	131	.3	-5.1	-3.8	.0	2.6
MON	4	5	443	39	1427.0	1448	156	533	1017	12.9	4.38	96	.264	.332	-24	-29	99	132	64	.975	155	68	127	-2.1	-9.4	-6.7	-.2	-4.1
FLA	11	3	420	24	1449.2	1617	182	715	1016	14.8	5.18	78	.287	.370	-153	-189	96	109	54	.979	129	80	177	-.7	-18.7	-6.5	-.0	-1.0
CENTRAL																												
HOU	12	11	340	44	1471.1	1435	147	465	1187	11.9	3.50	116	.256	.315	119	94	96	75	42	.983	108	59	144	.4	9.3	14.4	1.0	-4.1
CHI	7	7	449	56	1477.1	1528	180	575	1207	13.1	4.47	99	.266	.336	-39	-11	104	120	43	.984	101	55	107	.8	-1.1	2.8	-.7	6.7
STL	6	10	428	44	1469.2	1513	151	598	972	13.0	4.31	98	.268	.337	-12	-17	99	92	44	.978	142	48	160	-1.4	-1.7	8.8	.9	-4.6
CIN	6	8	366	42	1441.1	1400	170	573	1098	12.6	4.44	97	.256	.330	-34	-24	101	117	46	.980	122	70	142	-.3	-2.4	.0	.0	-1.3
MIL	2	2	416	39	1451.0	1538	188	550	1063	13.3	4.63	94	.275	.344	-64	-47	102	125	34	.982	110	62	192	.3	-4.6	-3.9	-.9	2.1
PIT	7	10	395	44	1449.0	1433	147	530	1112	12.4	3.91	109	.259	.324	58	58	101	95	39	.977	140	59	161	-1.3	5.7	-11.8	1.1	-5.7
WEST																												
SD	14	11	369	59	1454.2	1384	139	501	1217	12.0	3.63	109	.252	.318	97	57	94	94	40	.983	104	80	155	.6	5.6	5.3	-.2	5.6
SF	6	6	433	44	1477.0	1457	171	562	1089	12.6	4.18	96	.259	.330	8	-27	95	97	39	.984	101	71	157	.8	-2.7	13.0	-.0	-3.6
LA	16	10	342	47	1447.1	1332	135	587	1178	12.3	3.81	106	.246	.314	68	37	95	93	57	.978	134	54	154	-1.0	3.7	-6.9	.6	5.6
COL	9	5	406	36	1432.2	1583	174	562	951	13.9	4.99	104	.285	.355	-121	24	122	108	52	.984	102	56	193	.7	2.4	-2.1	-.8	-4.3
ARI	7	6	368	37	1432.1	1463	188	489	908	12.5	4.63	92	.266	.328	-64	-57	101	93	63	.984	100	58	125	.4	-5.6	-8.3	-.3	-2.7
TOT	161	143	6313	675	23240.0					12.7	4.23		.262	.331						.981	1850	1023	2415					

League Leaders

Batter-Fielder Wins
- McGwire-StL 7.1
- Bonds-SF 6.6
- Piazza-LA-Fla-NY 6.0
- Biggio-Hou 5.5
- Rolen-Phi 5.2

Batting Average
- Walker-Col 363
- Olerud-NY 354
- Bichette-Col 331
- Piazza-LA-Fla-NY 328
- Kendall-Pit 327

On-Base Percentage
- McGwire-StL 470
- Olerud-NY 447
- Walker-Col 445
- Bonds-SF 438
- Sheffield-Fla-LA 428

Slugging Average
- McGwire-StL 752
- Sosa-Chi 647
- Walker-Col 630
- Bonds-SF 609
- Vaughn-SD 597

On-Base Plus Slugging
- McGwire-StL 1222
- Walker-Col 1075
- Bonds-SF 1047
- Sosa-Chi 1024
- Olerud-NY 998

Adjusted OPS
- McGwire-StL 217
- Bonds-SF 182
- Olerud-NY 167
- Bagwell-Hou 161
- Alou-Hou 159

Adjusted Batter Runs
- McGwire-StL 96.3
- Bonds-SF 73.9
- Olerud-NY 60.7
- Bagwell-Hou 53.3
- Alou-Hou 51.6

Runs
- Sosa-Chi 134
- McGwire-StL 130
- Bagwell-Hou 124
- C.Jones-Atl 123
- Biggio-Hou 123

Hits
- Bichette-Col 219
- Biggio-Hou 210
- Castilla-Col 206
- V.Guerrero-Mon 202

Doubles
- Biggio-Hou 51
- Young-Cin 48
- Bichette-Col 48
- Walker-Col 46

Triples
- Dellucci-Ari 12
- B.Larkin-Cin 10
- W.Guerrero-LA-Mon 9
- Perez-Col 9

Home Runs
- McGwire-StL 70
- Sosa-Chi 66
- Vaughn-SD 50
- Castilla-Col 46
- Galarraga-Atl 44

Total Bases
- Sosa-Chi 416
- McGwire-StL 383
- Castilla-Col 380
- V.Guerrero-Mon 367
- Vaughn-SD 342

Runs Batted In
- Sosa-Chi 158
- McGwire-StL 147
- Castilla-Col 144
- Kent-SF 128
- Burnitz-Mil 125

Stolen Bases
- Womack-Pit 58
- Biggio-Hou 50
- Young-LA 42
- Renteria-Fla 41
- Bonds-SF 28

Base Stealing Runs
- Womack-Pit 10.0
- Biggio-Hou 8.2
- Young-LA 4.7
- B.Larkin-Cin 4.7
- A.Jones-Atl 4.5

Fielding Runs-Infield
- Perez-Col 29.4
- Vina-Mil 28.4
- Cirillo-Mil 21.7
- Veras-SD 20.3
- Andrews-Mon 18.2

Fielding Runs-Outfield
- A.Jones-Atl 20.0
- Kotsay-Fla 18.5
- Rodriguez-Chi 9.4
- Dunwoody-Fla 7.4
- Sosa-Chi 7.4

Wins
- Glavine-Atl 20
- Tapani-Chi 19
- Reynolds-Hou 19
- Maddux-Atl 18
- Brown-SD 18

Winning Pct.
- Smoltz-Atl 850
- Glavine-Atl 769
- Leiter-NY 739
- Brown-SD 720
- Reynolds-Hou 704

Complete Games
- Schilling-Phi 15
- Maddux-Atl 9
- Hernandez-Fla 9
- C.Perez-Mon-LA 7
- Brown-SD 7

Strikeouts
- Schilling-Phi 300
- Brown-SD 257
- Wood-Chi 233
- Reynolds-Hou 209
- Maddux-Atl 204

Fewest BB/Game
- Anderson-Ari 1.04
- Reed-NY 1.23
- Lima-Hou 1.23
- Maddux-Atl 1.61
- Brown-SD 1.72

Games
- Beck-Chi 81
- Nen-SF 78
- McElroy-Col 78
- Kline-Mon 78
- Telford-Mon 77

Saves
- Hoffman-SD 53
- Beck-Chi 51
- Shaw-Cin-LA 48
- Nen-SF 40
- J.Franco-NY 38

Base Runners/9
- Hoffman-SD 7.77
- Nen-SF 8.63
- Maddux-Atl 9.07
- Urbina-Mon 9.09
- R.Johnson-Mon 9.18

Adjusted Relief Runs
- Nen-SF 23.6
- Urbina-Mon 22.7
- Hoffman-SD 22.0
- Shaw-Cin-LA 19.5
- Acevedo-StL 18.6

Relief Ranking
- Nen-SF 47.2
- Urbina-Mon 45.4
- Hoffman-SD 43.9
- Shaw-Cin-LA 39.0
- Acevedo-StL 23.6

Innings Pitched
- Schilling-Phi 268.2
- Brown-SD 257.0
- Maddux-Atl 251.0
- C.Perez-Mon-Fla 241.0
- Hernandez-Fla 234.1

Opponents' Avg.
- Wood-Chi 196
- Leiter-NY 216
- Maddux-Atl 220
- Harnisch-Cin 228
- Smoltz-Atl 231

Opponents' OBP
- Maddux-Atl 260
- Brown-SD 279
- Schilling-Phi 282
- Smoltz-Atl 285
- Lima-Hou 285

Earned Run Average
- Maddux-Atl 2.22
- Brown-SD 2.38
- Leiter-NY 2.47
- Glavine-Atl 2.47
- Daal-Ari 2.88

Adjusted ERA
- Maddux-Atl 187
- Glavine-Atl 168
- Leiter-NY 167
- Brown-SD 167
- Daal-Ari 149

Adjusted Starter Runs
- Maddux-Atl 52.5
- Brown-SD 46.7
- Glavine-Atl 45.4
- Leiter-NY 36.9
- Schilling-Phi 32.7

Pitcher Wins
- Maddux-Atl 6.4
- Glavine-Atl 5.6
- Brown-SD 4.9
- Nen-SF 4.8
- Urbina-Mon 4.5

The Year They'll All Remember

Sluggers Mark McGwire and Sammy Sosa put on a season-long show. McGwire broke Roger Maris' record first, smashing his 62nd homer on September 8 against the Cubs. Sosa briefly took the league lead on the third-to-last day of the season when he smacked his 66th homer. Not to be outdone, McGwire tied Sosa that night and clubbed four more in the final two games to finish with 70. The "Mark & Sammy Power Tour" captivated the attention of hundreds of millions of fans and non-fans around the world, though McGwire's usage of the legal, over-the-counter supplement androstenedione generated some controversy.

The addition of two teams, the Diamondbacks and (surprise!) the Brewers, brought a record 2,565 homers to the sixteen-team NL, but scoring per game remained essentially unchanged. Chicago rookie Kerry Wood fanned 20 Astros in only his fifth start, tying the single-game record. Rupert Murdoch, head of the FOX media empire, bought the Dodgers from Peter O'Malley, whose family had controlled the franchise since 1950. Chicago lost two legendary broadcasters: Harry Caray died in February, while Jack Brickhouse passed in August.

Sosa's power helped the Cubs win the Wild Card after a one-game playoff with the Giants, who overtook the Mets in a furious final week. The Division Series saw Atlanta sweep Chicago, while San Diego, allowing 1 run in each of its victories, beat Houston in four. The Padres won the first three games of the NLCS and closed it out with a 5-0 shutout over the Braves in Game 6, only to be swept by the powerful Yankees in the Series.

1998 American League

TEAM	W	L	T	PCT	GB	HW	HL	R	OR	PA	H	2B	3B	HR	BB	SO	HB	SH	AVG	OBP	SLG	OPS	AOPS	BR	ABR	PF	SB	CS	BSA	BSR
EAST																														
NY	114	48	0	.704		**62**	19	**965**	**656**	6444	1625	290	31	207	**653**	1025	57	32	.288	**.364**	.460	824	118	**125**	167	96	153	63	71	
BOS	92	70	0	.568	22	51	30	876	729	6299	1568	**338**	35	205	541	1049	70	35	.280	.348	.463	811	107	79	60	102	72	39	65	
TOR	88	74	1	.543	26	51	30	816	768	6323	1482	316	19	221	564	1132	**87**	43	.266	.340	.448	788	103	31	28	100	**184**	81	69	
BAL	79	83	0	.488	35	42	39	817	785	6304	1520	303	11	214	593	**903**	58	44	.273	.347	.447	794	107	48	63	98	86	48	64	
TB	63	99	0	.389	51	33	48	620	751	6156	1450	267	**43**	111	473	1107	37	18	.266	.321	.385	706	81	-141	-157	100	120	73	62	
CENTRAL																														
CLE	89	73	0	.549		46	35	850	779	6376	1530	334	30	198	600	1061	41	30	.272	.347	.448	795	105	55	24	104	143	60	70	
CHI	80	82	1	.494	9	44	37	861	931	6280	1516	291	38	198	551	916	47	38	.271	.339	.444	783	104	17	31	98	127	46	73	
KC	72	89	0	.447	16.5	29	51	714	899	6191	1459	274	40	134	475	984	60	45	.263	.324	.399	723	84	-101	-128	104	135	50	73	
MIN	70	92	0	.432	19	35	46	734	818	6262	1499	285	32	115	506	915	45	18	.266	.328	.389	717	84	-111	-129	103	112	54	67	
DET	65	97	0	.401	24	32	49	722	863	6242	1494	306	29	165	455	1070	62	16	.264	.323	.415	738	89	-80	-89	101	122	62	66	
WEST																														
TEX	88	74	0	.543		48	33	940	871	6401	**1637**	314	32	201	595	1045	39	41	**.289**	.357	.462	819	105	104	56	106	82	47	64	
ANA	85	77	0	.525	3	42	39	787	783	6278	1530	314	27	147	510	1028	48	49	.272	.335	.415	750	92	-43	-57	102	93	45	67	
SEA	76	85	0	.472	11.5	42	39	859	855	6327	1553	321	28	**234**	558	1081	57	36	.276	.345	.468	813	108	78	71	101	115	39	**75**	
OAK	74	88	0	.457	14	39	42	804	866	6282	1413	295	13	149	633	1122	55	**58**	.257	.338	.397	735	92	-62	-54	99	131	47	74	
TOT	1134					596	537	11365		88165	21276	4248	408	2499	7737	14438	763	538	.271	.340	.432	771					1675	754	69	

TEAM	CG	SHO	GR	SV	IP	H	HR	BB	SO	BR/9	ERA	AERA	OAV	OOB	PR	APR	PF	OSB	OCS	FA	E	WPB	DP	FW	PW	BW	BSW	DP
EAST																												
NY	**22**	**16**	334	48	1456.2	**1357**	156	466	1080	11.7	3.82	114	.247	.312	133	95	94	102	51	.984	98	49	146	.9	**9.0**	**15.7**	.4	7.
BOS	5	8	432	**53**	1436.0	1406	168	504	1025	12.3	4.18	113	.255	.321	75	85	102	132	58	.983	105	97	128	.5	8.0	5.7	-.5	-2.
TOR	10	11	384	47	1465.0	1443	169	587	1154	12.7	4.24	109	.256	.329	60	60	100	149	47	.979	125	43	131	-.6	5.7	2.6	.4	-1.
BAL	16	10	402	37	1431.1	1505	169	535	1065	13.1	4.74	96	.272	.338	-15	-32	98	182	53	**.987**	81	63	144	**1.8**	-3.0	5.9	-.5	-6.
TB	7	7	410	28	1443.0	1425	171	643	1008	13.4	4.35	110	.261	.345	47	68	103	97	61	.985	94	62	**178**	1.1	6.4	-14.8	-.6	-10.
CENTRAL																												
CLE	9	4	423	47	1460.0	1552	171	563	1037	13.5	4.44	107	.274	.344	33	52	103	110	47	.982	110	**43**	146	.2	4.9	2.3	.2	
CHI	8	4	405	42	1438.2	1569	211	580	911	13.8	4.98	88	.278	.348	-92	-106	98	122	59	.977	140	67	161	-1.4	-10.0	2.9	.4	7.
KC	6	5	388	46	1436.1	1590	196	568	999	13.9	5.15	94	.281	.350	-80	-46	104	80	43	.980	125	83	172	-.7	-4.3	-12.1	.4	8.
MIN	7	8	432	42	1447.2	1622	180	**457**	952	13.2	4.75	101	.284	.338	-16	6	103	101	45	.982	108	66	135	.3	-6.2	-12	-.1	
DET	9	4	**446**	32	1446.1	1551	185	595	942	13.6	4.93	96	.277	.348	-45	-29	102	120	**69**	.982	115	74	164	-.0	-2.7	-8.4	-.2	-7.
WEST																												
TEX	10	4	402	46	1431.1	1624	164	519	994	13.8	4.99	98	.285	.346	-55	-16	105	**64**	55	.980	121	72	140	-.4	-1.5	5.3	-.5	5.
ANA	3	5	415	52	1444.0	1481	164	630	1091	13.5	4.49	106	.267	.344	26	39	102	156	65	.983	106	98	146	.4	3.7	-5.4	-.2	5.
SEA	17	7	368	31	1424.1	1530	196	528	**1156**	13.4	4.93	95	.273	.340	-45	-41	101	127	49	.979	141	81	155	-.7	-3.9	6.7	.4	4.
OAK	12	4	408	39	1434.0	1555	179	529	922	13.4	4.81	96	.276	.342	-25	-30	99	103	48	.977	141	81	155	-1.5	-2.8	-5.1	.4	2.
TOT	141	101	5649	590	20194.2					13.2	4.65		.271	.340						.981	1594	970	2085					

Batter-Fielder Wins		Batting Average		On-Base Percentage		Slugging Average		On-Base Plus Slugging		Adjusted OPS		Adjusted Batter Runs	
Belle-Chi	5.8	Williams-NY	339	Martinez-Sea	.429	Belle-Chi	.655	Belle-Chi	1055	Belle-Chi	173	Belle-Chi	66
Griffey-Sea	5.0	Vaughn-Bos	337	Williams-NY	.422	Gonzalez-Tex	.630	Thome-Cle	.997	Williams-NY	164	Martinez-Sea	51
Rodriguez-Sea	4.4	Belle-Chi	328	Thome-Cle	.413	Griffey-Sea	.611	Williams-NY	.997	Martinez-Sea	156	Williams-NY	49
Martinez-Sea	4.2	Davis-Bal	327	Salmon-Ana	.410	M.Ramirez-Cle	.599	Gonzalez-Tex	.997	Davis-Bal	152	Vaughn-Bos	46
Williams-NY	4.0	Jeter-NY	324	Offerman-KC	.403	Delgado-Tor	.592	Vaughn-Bos	.993	Vaughn-Bos	151	Griffey-Sea	42

Runs		Hits		Doubles		Triples		Home Runs		Total Bases		Runs Batted In	
Jeter-NY	127	Rodriguez-Sea	213	Gonzalez-Tex	50	Offerman-KC	13	Griffey-Sea	56	Belle-Chi	399	Gonzalez-Tex	15
Durham-Chi	126	Vaughn-Bos	205	Belle-Chi	48	Damon-KC	10	Belle-Chi	49	Griffey-Sea	387	Belle-Chi	15
Rodriguez-Sea	123	Jeter-NY	203	Martinez-Sea	46	Winn-TB	9	Canseco-Tor	46	Rodriguez-Sea	384	Griffey-Sea	14
Griffey-Sea	120	Belle-Chi	200	Valentin-Bos	44			M.Ramirez-Cle	45	Gonzalez-Tex	382	M.Ramirez-Cle	14
Knoblauch-NY	117	Garciaparra-Bos	195	Delgado-Tor	43			Gonzalez-Tex	45	Vaughn-Bos	360	Rodriguez-Sea	12

Stolen Bases		Base Stealing Runs		Fielding Runs-Infield		Fielding Runs-Outfield		Wins		Winning Pct.		Complete Games	
Henderson-Oak	66	Henderson-Oak	10.0	Easley-Det	25.7	Lawton-Min	14.3	Helling-Tex	20	Wells-NY	.818	Erickson-Bal	
Lofton-Cle	54	Lofton-Cle	8.4	Alomar-Bal	21.0	Griffey-Sea	7.6	Cone-NY	20	Clemens-Tor	.769	Wells-NY	
Stewart-Tor	51	Offerman-KC	5.7	Bordick-Bal	20.9	Anderson-Ana	5.3	Clemens-Tor	20	Helling-Tex	.741	Rogers-Oak	
Rodriguez-Sea	46	Nixon-Min	5.7	Valentin-Bos	18.2	Ordonez-Chi	4.6	Sele-Tex	19	Cone-NY	.741	Fassero-Sea	
Offerman-KC	45	Rodriguez-Sea	5.6	Segui-Sea	17.6	McCracken-TB	4.6	Martinez-Bos	19	Martinez-Bos	.731		

Strikeouts		Fewest BB/Game		Games		Saves		Base Runners/9		Adjusted Relief Runs		Relief Ranking	
Clemens-Tor	271	Wells-NY	1.22	Runyan-Det	88	Gordon-Bos	46	Jackson-Cle	8.44	Jackson-Cle	22.8	Gordon-Bos	36
Martinez-Bos	251	Saberhagen-Bos	1.49	Quantrill-Tor	82	Wetteland-Tex	42	Wetteland-Tex	8.85	Gordon-Bos	18.4	Wetteland-Tex	31
Johnson-Sea	213	Moyer-Sea	1.61	Swindell-Min-Bos	81	Percival-Ana	42	Gordon-Bos	9.08	Rivera-NY	18.3	Jackson-Cle	31
Finley-Ana	212	Mussina-Bal	1.79	Guardado-Min	79	Jackson-Cle	40	Wells-NY	9.45	Quantrill-Tor	18.1	Rivera-NY	31
Cone-NY	209	Radke-Min	1.81	Plesac-Tor	78	Aguilera-Min	38	Brocail-Det	9.48	Wetteland-Tex	18.0	Lopez-TB	3

Innings Pitched		Opponents' Avg.		Opponents' OBP		Earned Run Average		Adjusted ERA		Adjusted Starter Runs		Pitcher Wins	
Erickson-Bal	251.1	Clemens-Tor	197	Wells-NY	.265	Clemens-Tor	2.65	Clemens-Tor	176	Clemens-Tor	51.5	Clemens-Tor	
Rogers-Oak	238.2	Martinez-Bos	217	Clemens-Tor	.277	Martinez-Bos	2.89	Martinez-Bos	164	Martinez-Bos	46.9	**Martinez-Bos**	4
Clemens-Tor	234.2	Irabu-NY	233	Martinez-Bos	.278	Rogers-Oak	3.17	Rogers-Oak	146	Rogers-Oak	38.5	**Rogers-Oak**	3
Moyer-Sea	234.1	Cone-NY	237	Mussina-Bal	.282	Finley-Ana	3.39	Finley-Ana	140	Finley-Ana	30.5	Gordon-Bos	3
Belcher-KC	234.0	Wells-NY	239	Moyer-Sea	.295	Wells-NY	3.49	Arrojo-TB	135	Moyer-Sea	30.4	**Arrojo-TB**	3

Selig Not Acting Anymore

Expansion took place for the second time in five years with the addition of Tampa Bay and Arizona. Milwaukee agreed to move to the National League so the Devil Rays and Diamondbacks could be placed in different leagues, marking the first time an AL team had joined the NL. Brewers owner Bud Selig, acting commissioner since 1992, finally was given the title full time.

Chicago's Albert Belle smacked 99 extra-base hits (49 homers, 48 doubles and 2 triples), the second highest number of extra-base hits since 1949, behind Belle's own 103 in 1995. Baltimore's Cal Ripken voluntarily ended his consecutive games played streak at 2,632 when he took himself out of the starting lineup just before Baltimore's final home game of the season. Paul Molitor and Dennis Eckersley retired; Dan Quisenberry and Mark Belanger died a week apart.

The Yankees won 114 games, an AL record, and breeze through the postseason. Texas led the league in hitting an placed second in runs, but scored just once in a three-gam Division Series sweep by the Yankees. Cleveland rallied fo three straight wins over Boston to win the other ALDS in fou The Tribe won two of the first three against the Yankees, b New York blanked Cleveland, 4-0, in Game 4, and then wo the next two games to take the ALCS in six. New York cruise through San Diego in the World Series. Although the Padre took three-run leads into the seventh in Games 1 and 3, th Yankees won both times. The Series ended with a 3-0 shuto of the Padres in Game 4.

1997 National League

TEAM	W	L	T	PCT	GB	HW	HL	R	OR	PA	H	2B	3B	HR	BB	SO	HB	SH	AVG	OBP	SLG	OPS	AOPS	BR	ABR	PF	SB	CS	BSA	BSR
EAST																														
ATL	101	61	0	.623		50	31	791	**581**	6312	1490	268	37	174	597	1160	52	83	.270	.343	.426	769	105	56	46	101	108	58	65	3
FLA	92	70	0	.568	9	**52**	29	740	669	6299	1410	272	28	136	**686**	1074	61	71	.259	.346	.395	741	104	14	50	96	115	58	66	5
NY	88	74	0	.543	13	50	31	777	709	6248	1448	274	28	153	550	1029	57	58	.262	.332	.405	737	103	-11	27	95	97	74	57	-5
MON	78	84	0	.481	23	45	36	691	740	6131	1423	**339**	34	172	420	1084	73	72	.258	.316	.425	741	99	-22	-13	99	75	46	62	0
PHI	68	94	0	.420	33	38	43	668	840	6126	1390	290	35	116	420	1032	40	74	.255	.322	.385	707	91	-72	-62	99	92	56	62	1
CENTRAL																														
HOU	84	78	0	.519		46	35	777	660	6362	1427	314	40	133	633	1085	100	74	.259	.344	.404	737	104	25	52	97	171	74	70	12
PIT	79	83	0	.488	5	43	38	725	760	6200	1440	291	52	129	481	1161	45	77	.262	.329	.404	733	94	-25	-37	102	160	50	**76**	**18**
CIN	76	86	0	.469	8	40	41	651	764	6152	1386	269	27	142	518	1113	45	75	.253	.321	.389	710	88	-73	-84	102	**190**	67	74	**18**
STL	73	89	0	.451	11	41	40	689	708	6211	1409	269	39	144	543	1191	42	58	.255	.324	.396	720	93	-52	-53	100	164	60	73	15
CHI	68	94	0	.420	16	42	39	687	759	6095	1444	269	39	127	451	1003	34	83	.263	.321	.396	717	89	-64	-85	103	116	60	66	5
WEST																														
SF	90	72	0	.556		48	33	784	793	6296	1415	266	37	172	642	1120	46	64	.258	.337	.414	751	103	22	39	98	121	49	71	9
LA	88	74	0	.543	2	47	34	742	645	6216	1488	242	33	174	498	1079	33	105	.268	.330	.418	748	107	-1	51	94	131	64	67	6
COL	83	79	0	.512	7	47	34	**923**	908	6336	**1611**	269	40	**239**	562	1060	63	73	**.288**	**.357**	**.478**	835	100	**180**	8	123	137	65	68	7
SD	76	86	0	.469	14	39	42	795	891	6369	1519	275	16	152	604	1129	35	63	.271	.342	.407	749	108	22	**74**	94	140	60	70	10
TOT	1134					628	506	10440		87353	20300	3907	485	2163	7704	15320	773	1030	.263	.333	.410	744					1817	841	68	105

TEAM	CG	SHO	GR	SV	IP	H	HR	BB	SO	BR/9	ERA	AERA	OAV	OOB	PR	APR	PF	OSB	OCS	FA	E	WPB	DP	FW	PW	BW	BSW	DIF
EAST																												
ATL	21	**17**	374	37	1465.2	**1319**	111	450	1196	11.1	3.18	132	.241	.301	166	165	100	124	54	.982	114	49	136	.3	**16.3**	4.5	-.4	-.7
FLA	12	10	404	39	1446.2	1353	131	639	1188	12.8	3.83	106	.250	.334	60	37	96	95	70	.981	116	48	167	.2	3.6	4.9	-.2	2.5
NY	7	8	376	**49**	1459.1	1452	160	504	982	12.9	3.95	101	.262	.326	101	9	95	106	44	.981	120	57	165	-.0	.9	2.7	-1.2	4.7
MON	**27**	14	390	37	1447.0	1365	149	557	1138	12.3	4.14	101	.250	.325	10	6	99	192	42	.979	132	65	150	-.7	.6	-1.3	-.7	-.9
PHI	13	7	409	35	1420.1	1441	171	616	1209	13.4	4.85	87	.265	.342	-102	-101	100	107	57	.982	108	89	134	.7	-9.9	-6.1	-.6	3.0
CENTRAL																												
HOU	16	12	354	37	1459.0	1379	134	511	1138	12.0	3.66	109	.251	.319	87	57	95	**92**	57	.979	131	52	169	-.7	5.6	5.1	.4	-7.5
PIT	6	8	451	41	1436.0	1503	143	560	1080	13.3	4.28	100	.271	.342	-13	-1	102	109	66	.979	131	72	149	-.7	-.0	-3.6	**1.0**	1.4
CIN	5	8	423	**49**	1449.0	1408	173	558	1159	12.7	4.41	97	.255	.330	-34	-21	102	139	48	.982	**106**	77	129	.8	-2.1	-8.3	**1.0**	3.5
STL	5	3	399	39	1455.2	1422	124	536	1130	12.5	3.88	108	.259	.328	52	50	100	134	66	.980	123	66	156	-.2	4.9	-5.2	.7	-8.3
CHI	6	4	441	57	1429.0	1451	185	590	1072	13.4	4.44	97	.266	.339	-38	-19	103	146	59	.981	112	51	117	.5	-1.9	-8.4	-.2	-3.0
WEST																												
SF	5	9	**481**	45	1446.0	1494	160	578	1044	13.1	4.39	94	.270	.340	-31	-46	98	108	73	.980	125	57	157	-.3	-4.5	3.8	.1	9.8
LA	6	6	412	45	1459.1	1325	163	546	**1232**	11.8	3.62	108	**.241**	.313	94	49	93	118	58	.981	116	**47**	104	.2	4.8	5.0	-.2	-2.9
COL	9	5	426	38	1432.2	1697	196	566	870	14.6	5.25	98	.300	.367	-167	-12	123	130	54	**.983**	111	55	**202**	.5	-1.2	.8	-.0	1.9
SD	5	2	426	43	1450.0	1581	172	596	1059	13.9	4.98	79	.280	.352	-125	-182	93	171	**75**	.979	132	66	132	-.7	-17.9	**7.3**	.2	6.1
TOT	143	113	5766	571	20255.2					12.8	4.20		.263	.333						.981	1677	851	2067					

Batter-Fielder Wins		Batting Average		On-Base Percentage		Slugging Average		On-Base Plus Slugging		Adjusted OPS		Adjusted Batter Runs	
Biggio-Hou	8.2	Gwynn-SD	372	Walker-Col	452	Walker-Col	720	Walker-Col	1172	Piazza-LA	189	Piazza-LA	72.9
Piazza-LA	7.7	Walker-Col	366	Bonds-SF	446	Piazza-LA	638	Piazza-LA	1070	Bonds-SF	172	Bagwell-Hou	65.2
Bonds-SF	6.2	Piazza-LA	362	Piazza-LA	431	Bagwell-Hou	592	Bonds-SF	1031	Bagwell-Hou	170	Bonds-SF	64.8
Bagwell-Hou	6.0	Lofton-Atl	333	Bagwell-Hou	425	Galarraga-Col	585	Bagwell-Hou	1017	Walker-Col	164	Walker-Col	56.4
Caminiti-SD	5.0	Joyner-SD	327	Sheffield-Fla	424	Lankford-StL	585	Lankford-StL	996	Gwynn-SD	160	Gwynn-SD	52.2

Runs		Hits		Doubles		Triples		Home Runs		Total Bases		Runs Batted In	
Biggio-Hou	146	Gwynn-SD	220	Grudzielanek-Mon	54	DeShields-StL	14	Walker-Col	49	Walker-Col	409	Galarraga-Col	140
Walker-Col	143	Walker-Col	208	Gwynn-SD	49	Perez-Col	10	Bagwell-Hou	43	Piazza-LA	355	Bagwell-Hou	135
Bonds-SF	123	Piazza-LA	201	Walker-Col	46	Womack-Pit	9	Galarraga-Col	41	Galarraga-Col	351	Walker-Col	130
Galarraga-Col	120			Lansing-Mon	45	Randa-Pit	9			Castilla-Col	335	Piazza-LA	124
Bagwell-Hou	109			Mondesi-LA	42	Guerrero-LA	9			Bagwell-Hou	335	Kent-SF	121

Stolen Bases		Base Stealing Runs		Fielding Runs-Infield		Fielding Runs-Outfield		Wins		Winning Pct.		Complete Games	
Womack-Pit	60	Womack-Pit	10.8	Young-Col	25.5	A.Jones-Atl	17.3	Neagle-Atl	20	Maddux-Atl	826	Martinez-Mon	13
D.Sanders-Cin	56	D.Sanders-Cin	7.8	Biggio-Hou	25.4	Glanville-Chi	9.2	Maddux-Atl	19	Neagle-Atl	800	Perez-Mon	8
DeShields-StL	55	DeShields-StL	7.2	Weiss-Col	19.0	Mondesi-LA	8.6	Kile-Hou	19	Estes-SF	792	Smoltz-Atl	7
Biggio-Hou	47	Biggio-Hou	6.8	Randa-Pit	18.6	Sosa-Chi	7.4	Estes-SF	19	Kile-Hou	731	Schilling-Phi	7
Young-Col-LA	45	Bonds-SF	5.3	Rolen-Phi	18.5	Finley-SD	5.8			Martinez-Mon	680	Hampton-Hou	7

Strikeouts		Fewest BB/Game		Games		Saves		Base Runners/9		Adjusted Relief Runs		Relief Ranking	
Schilling-Phi	319	Maddux-Atl	.77	Tavarez-SF	89	Shaw-Cin	42	Martinez-Mon	8.73	Shaw-Cin	20.1	Shaw-Cin	27.5
Martinez-Mon	305	Reed-NY	1.34	Belinda-Cin	84	Hoffman-SD	37	Maddux-Atl	8.74	Frascatore-StL	15.2	Hoffman-SD	25.3
Smoltz-Atl	241	Neagle-Atl	1.89	Shaw-Cin	78	Beck-SF	37	Shaw-Cin	8.75	Osuna-LA	13.4	J.Franco-NY	21.1
Nomo-LA	233	Schilling-Phi	2.05	Rojas-Chi-NY	77	J.Franco-NY	36	Hoffman-SD	9.18	Martin-Hou	13.2	Wagner-Hou	18.2
		Perez-Mon	2.09			Eckersley-StL	36	Schilling-Phi	9.59	Hoffman-SD	13.1	McMichael-NY	18.1

Innings Pitched		Opponents' Avg.		Opponents' OBP		Earned Run Average		Adjusted ERA		Adjusted Starter Runs		Pitcher Wins	
Smoltz-Atl	256.0	Martinez-Mon	184	Martinez-Mon	249	Martinez-Mon	1.90	Martinez-Mon	220	Martinez-Mon	57.8	**Martinez-Mon**	5.8
Kile-Hou	255.2	Park-LA	213	Maddux-Atl	256	Maddux-Atl	2.20	Maddux-Atl	191	Maddux-Atl	54.3	**Maddux-Atl**	5.3
Schilling-Phi	254.1	Estes-SF	223	Schilling-Phi	271	Kile-Hou	2.57	Kile-Hou	156	Kile-Hou	40.0	**Kile-Hou**	4.0
Martinez-Mon	241.1	Schilling-Phi	224	Reed-NY	272	Valdez-LA	2.65	Brown-Fla	151	Brown-Fla	37.4	**Smoltz-Atl**	3.9
Glavine-Atl	240.0	Kile-Hou	225	Neagle-Atl	277	Brown-Fla	2.69	Valdez-LA	147	Glavine-Atl	34.3	**Brown-Fla**	3.8

Wild Things

On April 15, the 50th anniversary of Jackie Robinson's momentous debut, baseball permanently retired Robinson's uniform number 42 during a Dodgers-Mets game at Shea Stadium. Bud Selig's surprise announcement upstaged President Bill Clinton, who spoke during a break in the fifth inning.

The Braves opened Turner Field, the rebuilt former outdoor track stadium used in the 1996 Olympics. Outfielders Brett Butler and Eric Davis returned to action after cancer treatments, while pitcher Pete Harnisch recovered from clinical depression. Butler, Ryne Sandberg, and Fernando Valenzuela retired. Former Phillies star Richie Ashburn and Curt Flood, whose holdout ultimately led to players gaining free agent rights, died.

Atlanta had the best record in baseball and was expecting another trip to the Fall Classic following a dominating NLDS sweep of Houston. But the Marlins, who swept San Francisco in the other Division Series, pounded Greg Maddux for 5 runs early in NLCS opener and the Braves never really recovered. Livian Hernandez won once in relief and fanned 15 as a starter—aided by a liberal strike zone—as Florida, in just its fifth season of existence, headed to the World Series.

Six lackluster Series games were outshone by Game 7. Cleveland led by a run heading into the ninth, but Craig Counsell's sacrifice fly tied the game. Edgar Renteria singled with the bases loaded in the bottom of the 11th to make the Marlins the first Wild Card world champion. Victory celebrations would be short and sweet, however, as the Marlins quickly dismantled their expensive team simply to cut payroll.

1997 American League

TEAM	W	L	T	PCT	GB	HW	HL	R	OR	PA	H	2B	3B	HR	BB	SO	HB	SH	AVG	OBP	SLG	OPS	AOPS	BR	ABR	PF	SB	CS	BSA	BSR
EAST																														
BAL	98	64	0	.605		46	35	812	**681**	6340	1498	264	22	196	586	952	65	46	.268	.341	.429	770	103	5	30	97	63	26	71	5
NY	96	66	0	.593	2	**47**	33	891	688	6527	1636	325	23	161	**676**	954	37	34	.287	**.362**	.436	798	108	85	94	99	161	58	63	1
DET	79	83	0	.488	19	42	39	784	790	6189	1415	268	24	176	578	1164	49	34	.258	.332	.415	747	94	-48	-44	100	100	72	69	10
BOS	78	84	0	.481	20	39	42	851	857	6430	**1684**	373	32	147	514	1044	59	21	.291	.352	.463	815	109	100	81	102	68	48	59	-2
TOR	76	86	0	.469	22	42	39	654	694	6109	1333	275	41	147	487	1138	59	38	.244	.310	.389	699	81	-154	-156	100	134	50	73	12
CENTRAL																														
CLE	86	75	0	.534		44	37	868	815	6304	1589	301	22	220	617	955	37	47	.286	.358	.467	825	109	120	86	104	118	59	67	5
CHI	80	81	0	.497	6	45	36	779	833	6200	1498	260	28	158	569	**901**	33	48	.273	.341	.417	758	100	-17	10	97	106	52	67	3
MIL	78	83	0	.484	8	**47**	33	681	742	6096	1415	294	27	135	494	967	58	48	.270	.333	.409	742	91	-57	-69	102	151	52	74	**15**
MIN	68	94	0	.420	18.5	35	46	772	861	6265	1522	305	40	132	495	1121	60	20	.270	.333	.409	742	91	-57	-69	103	130	66	66	6
KC	67	94	0	.416	19	33	47	747	820	6295	1478	256	35	158	561	1061	42	51	.264	.333	.407	740	89	-62	-84	103	130	66	66	6
WEST																														
SEA	90	72	0	.556		45	36	**925**	833	6384	1574	312	21	**264**	626	1110	49	46	.280	.355	**.485**	840	117	143	146	100	89	40	69	6
ANA	84	78	0	.519	6	46	36	829	794	6387	1531	279	25	161	617	953	45	40	.272	.346	.416	762	98	-4	-6	100	126	72	64	3
TEX	77	85	0	.475	13	39	42	807	823	6265	1547	311	27	187	500	1116	34	28	.254	.334	.438	772	94	-4	-54	107	72	37	66	3
OAK	65	97	0	.401	25	35	46	764	946	6369	1451	274	23	197	642	1181	49	49	.260	.339	.423	762	98	-14	-12	100	71	36	66	
TOT	1132					585	547	11164		88160	21171	4097	398	2477	7962	14617	676	547	.271	.340	.428	768					1491	723	67	75

TEAM	CG	SHO	GR	SV	IP	H	HR	BB	SO	BR/9	ERA	AERA	OAV	OOB	PR	APR	PF	OSB	OCS	FA	E	WPB	DP	FW	PW	BW	BSW	DIF
EAST																												
BAL	8	10	400	**59**	1461.0	**1404**	164	563	1139	12.3	3.91	113	**.253**	.323	106	83	97	149	50	.984	97	**50**	148	.8	7.9	2.9	-.0	5.4
NY	11	10	368	51	1467.2	1463	**144**	532	1165	12.5	3.84	116	.260	.327	118	102	97	111	47	.983	104	81	156	.5	9.7	8.9	-.4	-3.7
DET	13	8	417	42	1445.2	1476	178	552	982	12.9	4.56	101	.266	.334	1	8	101	130	48	.985	92	62	146	1.1	.8	-4.2	.4	-.1
BOS	7	4	417	40	1451.2	1569	149	611	987	13.9	4.85	96	.277	.351	-46	-32	102	171	53	.978	135	87	179	-1.3	-3.0	7.7	-.7	-5.7
TOR	**19**	**16**	336	34	1442.2	1453	167	497	1150	12.4	3.92	117	.263	.326	104	106	100	77	64	.984	94	65	150	1.0	**10.1**	-14.8	.6	-1.9
CENTRAL																												
CLE	4	3	428	39	1425.2	1528	181	575	1036	13.6	4.73	99	.276	.347	-26	-5	103	126	54	.983	106	67	159	.3	-.5	8.2	-.0	-2.5
CHI	6	7	389	52	1422.1	1505	175	575	961	13.4	4.73	93	.271	.340	-27	-54	97	119	52	.978	127	87	131	-.9	-5.1	1.0	-.0	4.6
MIL	6	8	367	44	1427.1	1419	177	542	1016	12.7	4.22	110	.261	.333	55	63	101	106	52	.980	121	57	171	-.5	6.0	-9.6	-.2	1.9
MIN	10	4	390	30	1434.0	1596	187	**495**	908	13.3	5.00	93	.283	.342	-69	-52	102	85	46	.983	101	80	170	.6	-4.9	-6.6	**.9**	-3.0
KC	11	5	393	29	1443.0	1530	186	531	961	13.2	4.70	101	.274	.340	-21	6	104	72	42	.985	91	76	168	1.1	.6	-8.0	-.0	-7.3
WEST																												
SEA	9	8	392	38	1447.2	1500	192	598	**1207**	13.5	4.78	95	.267	.342	-35	-41	99	99	**66**	.979	126	60	143	-.8	-3.9	13.9	.0	-.3
ANA	9	5	400	39	1454.2	1506	202	605	1050	13.4	4.52	102	.269	.343	8	14	101	101	63	.980	123	76	140	-.6	1.3	-.6	-.2	3.1
TEX	8	9	382	33	1429.2	1598	169	541	925	13.7	4.69	103	.283	.342	-20	24	106	60	56	.980	121	61	155	-.5	2.3	-5.1	-.2	-.4
OAK	2	1	**480**	38	1445.1	1734	197	642	953	15.2	5.48	84	.301	.372	-147	-142	101	131	48	.980	122	56	170	-.6	-13.5	-1.1	-.2	-.6
TOT	123	98	5559	568	20198.1					13.3	4.56		.271	.340						.982	1560	965	2186					

Batter-Fielder Wins		Batting Average		On-Base Percentage		Slugging Average		On-Base Plus Slugging		Adjusted OPS		Adjusted Batter Runs	
Griffey-Sea	6.0	F.Thomas-Chi	.347	F.Thomas-Chi	.456	Griffey-Sea	.646	F.Thomas-Chi	1.067	F.Thomas-Chi	183	F.Thomas-Chi	71.9
F.Thomas-Chi	5.1	E.Martinez-Sea	.330	E.Martinez-Sea	.456	F.Thomas-Chi	.611	Griffey-Sea	1.028	Griffey-Sea	164	E.Martinez-Sea	59.7
E.Martinez-Sea	4.7	Justice-Cle	.329	Thome-Cle	.423	Justice-Cle	.596	Justice-Cle	1.013	E.Martinez-Sea	163	Griffey-Sea	56.3
Valentin-Bos	4.0	Williams-NY	.328	Vaughn-Bos	.420	Gonzalez-Tex	.589	E.Martinez-Sea	1.009	Justice-Cle	156	Thome-Cle	44.4
Rodriguez-Tex	3.9	Ramirez-Cle	.328	Justice-Cle	.418	Thome-Cle	.579	Thome-Cle	1.001	Thome-Cle	154	Justice-Cle	43.1

Runs		Hits		Doubles		Triples		Home Runs		Total Bases		Runs Batted In	
Griffey-Sea	125	Garciaparra-Bos	209	Valentin-Bos	47	Garciaparra-Bos	11	Griffey-Sea	56	Griffey-Sea	393	Griffey-Sea	147
Garciaparra-Bos	122	Greer-Tex	193	Cirillo-Mil	46	Knoblauch-Min	10	Martinez-NY	44	Garciaparra-Bos	365	Martinez-NY	141
Knoblauch-Min	117	Jeter-NY	190	Belle-Chi	45	Damon-KC	8	Gonzalez-Tex	42	Martinez-NY	343	Gonzalez-Tex	131
Jeter-NY	116	Anderson-Ana	189	Garciaparra-Bos	44	Burnitz-Mil	8	Thome-Cle	40	F.Thomas-Chi	324	Salmon-Ana	129
		Rodriguez-Tex	187					Buhner-Sea	40	Greer-Tex	319	F.Thomas-Chi	125

Stolen Bases		Base Stealing Runs		Fielding Runs-Infield		Fielding Runs-Outfield		Wins		Winning Pct.		Complete Games	
Hunter-Det	74	Knoblauch-Min	10.1	Cirillo-Mil	24.0	Cameron-Chi	13.0	Clemens-Tor	21	Johnson-Sea	.833	Hentgen-Tor	
Knoblauch-Min	62	Hunter-Det	10.0	King-KC	21.2	Salmon-Ana	10.1	Radke-Min	20	Moyer-Sea	.773	Clemens-Tor	
Goodwin-KC-Tex	50	Nixon-Tor	6.8	Brosius-Oak	18.8	Anderson-Ana	9.9	Johnson-Sea	20	Clemens-Tor	.750	Wells-NY	
Nixon-Tor	47	Goodwin-KC-Tex	5.4	Valentin-Bos	17.7	Higginson-Det	8.6	Pettitte-NY	18	Pettitte-NY	.720	Tewksbury-Min	
Vizquel-Cle	43	Vizquel-Cle	5.3	Meares-Min	14.7	Edmonds-Ana	7.4	Moyer-Sea	17	Erickson-Bal	.696	Johnson-Sea	

Strikeouts		Fewest BB/Game		Games		Saves		Base Runners/9		Adjusted Relief Runs		Relief Ranking	
Clemens-Tor	292	Burkett-Tex	1.43	Myers-Bal	88	Myers-Bal	45	Jones-Mil	8.29	Quantrill-Tor	23.9	Jones-Mil	46.0
Johnson-Sea	291	Tewksbury-Min	1.65	Groom-Oak	78	Rivera-NY	43	Wetteland-Tex	8.86	Jones-Mil	23.0	Rivera-NY	41.5
Cone-NY	222	Radke-Min	1.80	Quantrill-Tor	77	Jones-Mil	36	Clemens-Tor	9.68	Rivera-NY	20.8	Myers-Bal	38.7
Mussina-Bal	218	Wells-NY	1.86	Nelson-NY	77	Wetteland-Tex	31	Johnson-Sea	9.89	Wickman-Mil	20.0	Wetteland-Tex	37.5
Appier-KC	196	Moyer-Sea	2.05	Slocumb-Bos-Sea	76	Jones-Det	31	Rhodes-Bal	9.91	Myers-Bal	19.3	Quantrill-Tor	34.2

Innings Pitched		Opponents' Avg.		Opponents' OBP		Earned Run Average		Adjusted ERA		Adjusted Starter Runs		Pitcher Wins	
Hentgen-Tor	264.0	Johnson-Sea	.194	Clemens-Tor	.273	Clemens-Tor	2.05	Clemens-Tor	224	Clemens-Tor	74.8	**Clemens-Tor**	7.9
Clemens-Tor	264.0	Clemens-Tor	.213	Johnson-Sea	.277	Johnson-Sea	2.28	Johnson-Sea	199	Johnson-Sea	53.0	**Johnson-Sea**	5.6
Pettitte-NY	240.1	Cone-NY	.218	Mussina-Bal	.282	Cone-NY	2.82	Cone-NY	158	Pettitte-NY	42.3	Jones-Mil	4.
Radke-Min	239.2	Gordon-Bos	.226	Thompson-Det	.289	Pettitte-NY	2.88	Pettitte-NY	154	Thompson-Det	38.7	**Thompson-Det**	4.
Appier-KC	235.2	Thompson-Det	.233	Radke-Min	.293	Thompson-Det	3.02	Thompson-Det	153	Cone-NY	36.4	**Pettitte-NY**	4.

Interleague Affair

Interleague play began during the regular season for the first time in history. Pushed for by acting commissioner Bud Selig, it was decried by purists and led to some dramatic differences in the schedules of competing teams. New York and Chicago enthusiasts have sold out every Mets-Yankees and Cubs-White Sox game since. Acting Commissioner Bud Selig failed to pass his radical realignment plan. Several clubs were adamantly against the idea, which would have created divisions based solely on geographic location.

Before the season Cleveland outfielder Albert Belle jumped to a division rival and became the first eight-figure player. He signed as a free agent with the White Sox for $11 million per year (plus an escape clause if he did not remain among the top three MLB players in salary). A midseason trade sent Oakland slugger Mark McGwire to St. Louis. McGwire hit a combined 58 home runs, making him the second player to slug at least 50 in consecutive seasons after Babe Ruth in 1927–28; ironically McGwire did not lead either league in homers. Bartolo Colon, Magglio Ordonez, and Miguel Tejada all debuted.

Cleveland, Central champs for the third straight season, had a fierce battle with the Wild Card Yankees in the ALDS. Facing elimination in Game 4, Cleveland rallied for a run in the eighth and another in the ninth to survive. The Indians nearly blew an early four-run lead in Game 5, but held on to advance. Baltimore shut down Seattle's potent offense to win the other ALDS in four games. Though the O's blanked Cleveland in the ALCS opener, Cleveland scored the winning run in the eighth inning or later four times to take the series in six. The Indians came within two outs of winning their first World Series title since 1948, but dropped a heartbreaker to Florida in Game 7

1996 National League

TEAM	W	L	T	PCT	GB	HW	HL	R	OR	PA	H	2B	3B	HR	BB	SO	HB	SH	AVG	OBP	SLG	OPS	AOPS	BR	ABR	PF	SB	CS	BSA	BSR
EAST																														
ATL	96	66	0	.593		56	25	773	648	6290	1514	264	28	197	530	1032	27	69	.270	.333	.432	765	100	48	1	106	83	43	66	3
MON	88	74	0	.543	8	50	31	741	668	6170	1441	297	27	148	492	1077	58	79	.262	.327	.406	733	96	-28	102	108	34	76	12		
FLA	80	82	0	.494	16	52	29	688	703	6192	1413	240	30	150	553	1122	55	41	.257	.329	.393	722	98	-30	-10	.97	99	46	68	6
NY	71	91	0	.438	25	42	39	746	779	6220	1515	267	47	147	445	1069	33	75	.270	.324	.412	736	103	-14	25	95	97	48	67	5
PHI	67	95	0	.414	29	35	46	650	790	6171	1405	249	39	132	536	1092	45	54	.256	.325	.387	712	93	-54	-57	101	117	41	74	11
CENTRAL																														
STL	88	74	0	.543		48	33	759	706	6177	1468	281	31	142	495	1089	44	88	.267	.330	.407	737	99	-4	-6	100	149	58	72	12
HOU	82	80	0	.506	6	48	33	753	792	6269	1445	297	29	129	554	1057	84	68	.262	.336	.397	733	106	2	64	93	180	63	74	18
CIN	81	81	0	.500	7	46	35	778	773	6213	1398	259	36	191	604	1134	34	71	.256	.331	.422	753	101	29	17	102	171	63	73	16
CHI	76	86	0	.469	12	43	38	772	771	6229	1388	267	19	175	523	1090	61	66	.251	.320	.401	721	91	-39	-64	104	108	50	68	6
PIT	73	89	0	.451	15	36	44	776	833	6336	1509	319	33	138	510	989	40	72	.266	.329	.407	736	96	-4	-31	104	126	49	72	11
WEST																														
SD	91	71	0	.562		45	36	771	682	6417	1499	285	24	147	601	1014	50	59	.265	.338	.402	740	104	15	51	96	109	55	66	5
LA	90	72	0	.556	1	47	34	703	652	6185	1396	215	33	150	516	1190	22	74	.252	.316	.384	700	95	-85	-42	94	124	40	76	13
COL	83	79	0	.512	8	55	26	961	964	6332	1607	297	37	221	527	1108	82	81	.287	.355	.472	827	99	181	0	124	201	66	75	21
SF	68	94	0	.420	23	38	44	752	862	6316	1400	245	21	153	615	1189	48	77	.253	.331	.388	719	97	-32	-15	98	113	53	68	6
TOT	1134					641	493	10623		87517	20398	3782	434	2220	7501	15252	683	974	.262	.330	.408	738		1785	709	72	145			

TEAM	CG	SHO	GR	SV	IP	H	HR	BB	SO	BR/9	ERA	AERA	OAV	OOB	PR	APR	PF	OSB	OCS	FA	E	WPB	DP	FW	PW	BW	BSW	DIF
EAST																												
ATL	14	9	408	46	1469.0	1372	120	451	1245	11.3	3.52	126	.247	.304	113	142	105	116	44	.980	130	60	143	-.1	13.9	.0	-.7	1.9
MON	11	7	433	43	1441.1	1353	152	482	1206	11.8	3.78	114	.247	.312	70	85	103	156	48	.980	126	56	121	.0	8.3	-2.7	.2	1.2
FLA	8	13	417	41	1443.0	1386	113	598	1050	12.7	3.95	104	.256	.334	42	26	98	84	57	.982	111	61	187	1.0	8.3	-1.0	-.4	-3.2
NY	10	10	335	41	1440.0	1517	159	532	999	13.1	4.22	95	.272	.337	-1	-34	99	125	33	.974	159	70	163	-1.9	-3.3	2.4	-.5	-6.7
PHI	12	6	387	42	1423.1	1463	160	510	1044	12.7	4.48	96	.267	.331	-42	-27	102	88	44	.981	116	81	145	.7	-2.6	-5.6	.0	-6.6
CENTRAL																												
STL	13	11	413	43	1452.1	1380	173	539	1050	12.1	3.97	107	.251	.319	39	42	100	104	54	.980	125	51	139	.2	4.1	-.6	.2	3.2
HOU	13	4	371	35	1447.0	1541	154	539	1163	13.4	4.37	89	.274	.342	-24	-87	92	115	55	.978	130	79	130	-.6	-8.5	6.3	.8	3.1
CIN	6	8	425	52	1443.0	1447	167	591	1089	13.0	4.32	99	.263	.336	-16	-7	101	146	50	.978	121	73	145	.4	-.7	1.7	.6	-1.9
CHI	10	10	439	34	1456.1	1447	184	546	1044	12.7	4.36	100	.260	.330	-23	1	104	129	50	.983	104	61	147	1.4	.0	-6.3	-.4	.1
PIT	5	7	422	37	1453.1	1602	183	479	1044	13.2	4.61	95	.281	.339	-63	-36	104	185	57	.980	128	72	144	-.0	-3.5	-3.0	.0	-1.5
WEST																												
SD	5	11	411	47	1489.0	1395	138	506	1194	11.8	3.72	108	.248	.313	81	51	95	136	54	.981	118	73	136	.6	5.0	5.0	-.1	-.0
LA	6	9	383	50	1466.1	1378	125	534	1212	12.0	3.46	113	.249	.317	123	78	93	171	39	.980	125	54	143	.2	7.6	-4.1	.3	5.1
COL	5	4	447	34	1422.2	1597	198	624	932	14.5	5.59	93	.285	.361	-218	-50	124	122	55	.976	149	85	167	-1.3	-4.9	.0	1.0	7.2
SF	9	8	425	35	1442.1	1520	194	570	997	13.5	4.71	88	.273	.345	-80	-94	98	108	69	.978	136	71	165	-.5	-9.2	-1.5	-.4	-1.4
TOT	127	117	5716	580	20289.0					12.7	4.21		.262	.330						.979	1786	947	2075					

Batter-Fielder Wins		Batting Average		On-Base Percentage		Slugging Average		On-Base Plus Slugging		Adjusted OPS		Adjusted Batter Runs	
Bonds-SF	7.6	Gwynn-SD	353	Sheffield-Fla	465	Burks-Col	639	Sheffield-Fla	1090	Sheffield-Fla	190	Sheffield-Fla	79.3
Caminiti-SD	7.4	Burks-Col	344	Bonds-SF	461	Sheffield-Fla	624	Bonds-SF	1076	Bonds-SF	186	Bonds-SF	79.1
Bagwell-Hou	7.1	Piazza-LA	336	Bagwell-Hou	451	Caminiti-SD	621	Burks-Col	1047	Bagwell-Hou	182	Bagwell-Hou	75.0
Larkin-Cin	6.0	Johnson-NY	333	Piazza-LA	422	Bonds-SF	615	Caminiti-SD	1028	Caminiti-SD	176	Caminiti-SD	61.6
Gilkey-NY	5.9	Grace-Chi	331	Henderson-SD	410	Galarraga-Col	601	Bagwell-Hou	1021	Piazza-LA	167	Piazza-LA	55.2

Runs		Hits		Doubles		Triples		Home Runs		Total Bases		Runs Batted In	
Burks-Col	142	Johnson-NY	227	Bagwell-Hou	48	Johnson-NY	21	Galarraga-Col	47	Burks-Col	392	Galarraga-Col	150
Finley-SD	126	Burks-Col	211	Finley-SD	45	Howard-Cin	10	Sheffield-Fla	42	Galarraga-Col	376	Bichette-Col	141
Bonds-SF	122	Grissom-Atl	207	Burks-Col	45	Grissom-Atl	10	Bonds-SF	42	Finley-SD	348	Caminiti-SD	130
Galarraga-Col	119	Grudzielanek-Mon	201	Gilkey-NY	44	Finley-SD	9	Hundley-NY	41	Castilla-Col	345	Bonds-SF	129
Sheffield-Fla	118	Bichette-Col	198	Rodriguez-Mon	42					Caminiti-SD	339	Burks-Col	128

Stolen Bases		Base Stealing Runs		Fielding Runs-Infield		Fielding Runs-Outfield		Wins		Winning Pct.		Complete Games	
Young-NY	53	Johnson-NY	6.8	Castilla-Col	33.8	Gilkey-NY	17.5	Smoltz-Atl	24	Smoltz-Atl	750	Schilling-Phi	8
Johnson-NY	50	DeShields-LA	6.7	Young-Col	27.4	Jordan-StL	10.8	A.Benes-StL	18	Martinez-LA	714	Smoltz-Atl	6
DeShields-LA	48	Bonds-SF	6.3	Andrews-Mon	16.2	Merced-Pit	10.0	Ritz-Col	17	Valdez-LA	682		
Bonds-SF	40	Bell-Hou	5.3	Caminiti-SD	14.8	Santangelo-Mon	7.3	Brown-Fla	17	A.Benes-StL	643		
Martin-Pit	38	Lankford-StL	5.3	Gagne-LA	13.8	Mondesi-LA	6.9			Neagle-Pit-Atl	640		

Strikeouts		Fewest BB/Game		Games		Saves		Base Runners/9		Adjusted Relief Runs		Relief Ranking	
Smoltz-Atl	276	Maddux-Atl	1.03	Worrell-LA	81	Worrell-LA	44	Hoffman-SD	8.49	Nen-Fla	20.0	Hoffman-SD	37.7
Nomo-LA	234	Brown-Fla	1.27	Patterson-Chi	79	Brantley-Cin	44	Smoltz-Atl	9.08	Shaw-Cin	19.7	Nen-Fla	27.9
Martinez-Mon	222	Darwin-Pit-Hou	1.48	Shaw-Cin	78	Hoffman-SD	42	Brown-Fla	9.12	Hoffman-SD	18.8	J.Franco-NY	25.5
Fassero-Mon	222	Reynolds-Hou	1.66	Dewey-SF	78	Wohlers-Atl	39	Maddux-Atl	9.40	Ryan-Phi	15.9	Shaw-Cin	25.1
Kile-Hou	219	Tewksbury-SD	1.87	Wohlers-Atl	77	Rojas-Mon	36	Rojas-Mon	9.56	Adams-Chi	15.5	Brantley-Cin	21.5

Innings Pitched		Opponents' Avg.		Opponents' OBP		Earned Run Average		Adjusted ERA		Adjusted Starter Runs		Pitcher Wins	
Smoltz-Atl	253.2	Leiter-Fla	202	Smoltz-Atl	260	Brown-Fla	1.89	Brown-Fla	218	Brown-Fla	56.5	Brown-Fla	6.9
Maddux-Atl	245.0	Smoltz-Atl	216	Brown-Fla	262	Maddux-Atl	2.72	Maddux-Atl	164	Maddux-Atl	43.9	Smoltz-Atl	5.2
Reynolds-Hou	239.0	Nomo-LA	218	Maddux-Atl	264	Leiter-Fla	2.93	Smoltz-Atl	151	Smoltz-Atl	40.4	Maddux-Atl	4.8
Navarro-Chi	236.2	Brown-Fla	220	Schilling-Phi	278	Smoltz-Atl	2.94	Glavine-Atl	149	Glavine-Atl	35.0	Glavine-Atl	4.4
Glavine-Atl	235.1	Schilling-Phi	223	Reynolds-Hou	288	Glavine-Atl	2.98	Trachsel-Chi	144	Leiter-Fla	31.0	Hoffman-SD	3.7

Schott Herself in the Foot

Cincinnati owner Marge Schott was removed from day-to-day operations of the Reds for a second time after telling a reporter that Adolf Hitler was good at first, but then "went too far." Schott also looked petty after the tragic death of umpire John McSherry on Opening Day. McSherry, working the plate for Cincy's game against Montreal, collapsed behind home plate and died from a massive heart attack only minutes into the contest. Schott protested the cancellation of the game, saying, "I feel cheated."

In August the Mets and Padres played a regular-season series in Monterey, Mexico. They were the first big league games played outside the U.S. or Canada. It was the final season for Ozzie Smith, Andre Dawson, and longtime Dodgers skipper Tommy Lasorda. Scott Rolen, Vladimir Guerrero, and

Andruw Jones debuted. San Diego third baseman Ken Caminiti, who later admitted he took steroids regularly during the 1996 season, was the overwhelming choice for MVP.

Both Division Series ended quickly. The Braves easily swept the Dodgers, who won the Wild Card despite losing their final three regular-season games to the division-winning Padres. San Diego lost three straight to St. Louis to set up a classic NLCS. Atlanta won the first game, but allowed 5 runs in the seventh inning the next night and squandered leads in Games 3 and 4 to fall behind three games to one. However, Atlanta's bats and arms came alive at the same time as the Braves outscored St. Louis, 32-1, in the final three games. The Braves were denied a second straight World Series title, falling in six games to the Yankees.

1996 American League

TEAM	W	L	T	PCT	GB	HW	HL	R	OR	PA	H	2B	3B	HR	BB	SO	HB	SH	AVG	OBP	SLG	OPS	AOPS	BR	ABR	PF	SB	CS	BSA	BSR
EAST																														
NY	92	70	0	.568		49	31	871	787	6414	1621	293	28	162	632	909	41	41	.288	.360	.436	796	100	17	19	100	96	46	68	5
BAL	88	74	1	.543	4	43	38	949	903	6493	1557	299	29	**257**	645	915	61	31	.274	.350	.472	822	106	50	57	99	76	40	66	3
BOS	85	77	0	.525	7	47	34	928	921	6545	1631	308	31	209	642	1020	67	33	.283	.359	.457	816	102	48	32	102	91	44	67	5
TOR	74	88	0	.457	18	35	46	766	809	6295	1451	302	35	177	529	1105	92	38	.259	.331	.420	751	89	-103	-97	99	116	38	75	12
DET	53	109	0	.327	39	27	54	783	1103	6202	1413	257	21	204	546	1268	29	48	.256	.323	.420	743	86	-126	-127	100	87	50	64	2
CENTRAL																														
CLE	99	62	0	.615		**51**	29	952	769	6486	**1665**	335	23	218	671	844	43	34	.293	**.369**	.475	844	111	114	116	100	160	50	**76**	18
CHI	85	77	0	.525	14.5	44	37	898	794	6497	1586	284	33	195	**701**	927	34	56	.281	.360	.447	807	107	35	76	96	105	49	73	9
MIL	80	82	0	.494	19.5	38	43	894	899	6434	1578	304	40	178	624	986	53	45	.279	.353	.441	794	95	0	-34	104	101	48	68	5
MIN	78	84	0	.481	21.5	39	43	877	900	6397	1633	332	47	118	576	958	65	20	.288	.357	.425	782	95	-14	-27	102	143	53	73	13
KC	75	86	0	.466	24	37	43	746	786	6229	1477	286	38	123	529	943	43	**66**	.267	.332	.398	730	83	-136	-138	100	195	85	70	13
WEST																														
TEX	90	72	1	.556		50	31	928	799	6494	1622	323	32	221	660	1041	31	32	.284	.358	.469	827	101	69	13	106	83	26	**76**	9
SEA	85	76	0	.528	4.5	43	38	**993**	895	6517	1625	**343**	19	245	670	1052	75	46	.287	.366	**.484**	**850**	112	123	120	100	90	39	70	6
OAK	78	84	0	.481	12	40	41	861	900	6402	1492	283	21	243	640	1114	58	35	.276	.339	.431	770	92	-67	-76	101	58	35	62	1
CAL	70	91	0	.435	19.5	43	38	762	943	6320	1571	256	24	192	527	974	29	45	.276	.339	.431	770					53	39	58	-2
TOT	1133					586	546	12208		89725	21922	4205	421	2742	8592	14056	721	570	.277	.350	.445	795					1454	634	70	98

TEAM	CG	SHO	GR	SV	IP	H	HR	BB	SO	BR/9	ERA	AERA	OAV	OOB	PR	APR	PF	OSB	OCS	FA	E	WPB	DP	FW	PW	BW	BSW	DIF
EAST																												
NY	6	**9**	411	**52**	1440.0	**1469**	**143**	610	1139	13.3	4.65	106	**.265**	.341	55	48	99	120	42	.985	91	72	146	1.2	4.4	1.7	-.2	3.9
BAL	13	1	378	44	1468.2	1604	209	597	1047	13.7	5.14	96	.280	.349	-25	-33	99	135	37	.984	97	52	173	.9	-3.0	5.2	-.4	4.2
BOS	17	5	409	37	1458.0	1606	185	722	**1165**	14.7	4.98	102	.279	.360	1	17	102	147	36	.978	135	74	152	-1.2	1.5	2.9	-.2	1.0
TOR	**19**	7	303	35	1445.2	1476	187	610	1033	13.2	4.57	110	.266	.340	68	70	100	74	41	.982	110	77	187	.2	6.4	-8.8	.5	-5.2
DET	10	4	**426**	22	1432.2	1699	241	784	957	16.1	6.38	80	.296	.384	-221	-202	102	117	54	.978	137	89	157	-1.4	-18.4	-11.6	-.5	3.8
CENTRAL																												
CLE	13	**9**	382	46	1452.1	1530	173	484	1033	**12.7**	**4.34**	113	.271	**.331**	105	90	98	104	52	.980	124	60	156	-.7	8.2	10.6	**1.0**	-.6
CHI	7	4	391	43	1461.0	1529	174	616	1039	13.4	4.52	105	.270	.343	77	40	95	105	55	.982	109	67	145	.2	3.6	6.9	.2	-7.0
MIL	6	4	384	42	1447.1	1570	213	635	846	14.1	5.14	101	.278	.354	-23	8	104	96	40	.978	134	65	180	-1.2	.7	-3.1	-.2	2.7
MIN	13	5	387	31	1439.2	1561	233	581	959	13.6	5.28	97	.277	.346	-46	-23	103	84	42	.984	94	60	142	1.1	-2.1	-2.5	.5	-.0
KC	17	8	322	35	1450.0	1563	176	**460**	926	12.9	4.55	110	.277	.335	71	75	101	69	42	.982	111	67	184	.0	6.8	-12.6	.5	-.4
WEST																												
TEX	**19**	6	347	43	1449.1	1569	168	582	976	13.6	4.65	113	.278	.347	55	**92**	105	62	56	**.986**	87	48	150	1.5	8.4	1.2	-.2	-2.2
SEA	4	4	403	34	1431.2	1562	216	605	1000	14.0	5.21	95	.279	.353	-35	-39	105	78	42	.982	110	**45**	155	.1	-3.6	**10.9**	-.0	-2.9
OAK	7	5	418	34	1456.1	1638	205	644	884	14.4	5.20	96	.287	.362	-33	-38	100	117	41	.984	103	71	**195**	.6	-3.5	.2	-.5	.3
CAL	12	8	383	38	1439.0	1546	219	662	1052	14.3	5.30	95	.275	.357	-49	-40	101	146	54	.979	128	92	156	-.9	-3.6	-6.9	-.8	1.8
TOT	163	79	5344	536	20271.2					13.9	4.99		.277	.350						.982	1570	939	2278					

Batter-Fielder Wins		Batting Average		On-Base Percentage		Slugging Average		On-Base Plus Slugging		Adjusted OPS		Adjusted Batter Runs	
Alomar-Bal	6.0	Rodriguez-Sea	.358	McGwire-Oak	.467	McGwire-Oak	.730	McGwire-Oak	1198	McGwire-Oak	199	F.Thomas-Chi	71.5
Rodriguez-Sea	5.6	F.Thomas-Chi	.349	E.Martinez-Sea	.464	Gonzalez-Tex	.643	F.Thomas-Chi	1085	F.Thomas-Chi	180	McGwire-Oak	70.8
Thome-Cle	5.3	Molitor-Min	.341	F.Thomas-Chi	.459	Anderson-Bal	.637	Thome-Cle	1062	Thome-Cle	166	E.Martinez-Sea	60.7
McGwire-Oak	4.9	Knoblauch-Min	.341	Thome-Cle	.450	Rodriguez-Sea	.631	E.Martinez-Sea	1059	E.Martinez-Sea	165	Thome-Cle	57.3
F.Thomas-Chi	4.9	Greer-Tex	.332	Knoblauch-Min	.448	Griffey-Sea	.628	Rodriguez-Sea	1045	Rodriguez-Sea	160	Rodriguez-Sea	56.1

Runs		Hits		Doubles		Triples		Home Runs		Total Bases		Runs Batted In	
Rodriguez-Sea	141	Molitor-Min	225	Rodriguez-Sea	.54	Knoblauch-Min	14	McGwire-Oak	52	Rodriguez-Sea	379	Belle-Cle	148
Knoblauch-Min	140	Rodriguez-Sea	215	E.Martinez-Sea	.52	Vina-Mil	10	Anderson-Bal	50	Belle-Cle	375	Gonzalez-Tex	144
Lofton-Cle	132	Lofton-Cle	210	Rodriguez-Tex	.47			Griffey-Sea	49	Vaughn-Bos	370	Vaughn-Bos	143
Alomar-Bal	132	Vaughn-Bos	207	Cordova-Min	.46			Belle-Cle	48	Anderson-Bal	369	Palmeiro-Bal	142
Griffey-Sea	125	Knoblauch-Min	197	Cirillo-Mil	.46			Gonzalez-Tex	47	Gonzalez-Tex	348	Griffey-Sea	140

Stolen Bases		Base Stealing Runs		Fielding Runs-Infield		Fielding Runs-Outfield		Wins		Winning Pct.		Complete Games	
Lofton-Cle	75	Lofton-Cle	10.6	Gonzalez-Tor	28.4	Becker-Min	17.2	Pettitte-NY	21	Nagy-Cle	.773	Hentgen-Tor	10
Goodwin-KC	66	Nixon-Tor	7.3	McLemore-Tex	23.7	Phillips-Chi	9.4	Hentgen-Tor	20	Pettitte-NY	.724	Pavlik-Tex	
Nixon-Tor	54	Goodwin-KC	6.8	Fryman-Det	22.6	Green-Tor	7.8	Mussina-Bal	19	Hentgen-Tor	.667	Hill-Tex	
Knoblauch-Min	45	Durham-Chi	5.2	Alomar-Bal	22.0	Mieske-Mil	7.0	Nagy-Cle	17	Pavlik-Tex	.652		
Vizquel-Cle	35	Knoblauch-Min	5.0	Vina-Mil	18.2	Bragg-Sea-Bos	6.1			Mussina-Bal	.633		

Strikeouts		Fewest BB/Game		Games		Saves		Base Runners/9		Adjusted Relief Runs		Relief Ranking	
Clemens-Bos	257	Haney-KC	2.01	Myers-Det	83	Wetteland-NY	43	Percival-Cal	8.64	M.Rivera-NY	35.3	Hernandez-Chi	54.1
Finley-Cal	215	Wells-Bal	2.05	Guardado-Min	83	Mesa-Cle	39	M.Rivera-NY	9.11	Hernandez-Chi	27.4	M.Rivera-NY	35.1
Appier-KC	207	Radke-Min	2.21	Stanton-Bos-Tex	81	Hernandez-Chi	38	Guzman-Tor	10.45	Percival-Cal	22.8	Slocumb-Bos	34.3
Mussina-Bal	204	Nagy-Cle	2.47	Slocumb-Bos	75	Percival-Cal	36	Wetteland-NY	10.60	Plunk-Cle	22.6	Wetteland-NY	28.8
Fernandez-Chi	200	Fernandez-Chi	2.51			Fetters-Mil	32	Cone-NY	10.75	James-Cal	21.1	Percival-Cal	26.8

Innings Pitched		Opponents' Avg.		Opponents' OBP		Earned Run Average		Adjusted ERA		Adjusted Starter Runs		Pitcher Wins	
Hentgen-Tor	265.2	Guzman-Tor	.228	Guzman-Tor	.289	Guzman-Tor	2.93	Guzman-Tor	171	Hentgen-Tor	52.7	Hentgen-Tor	5.1
Fernandez-Chi	258.0	Clemens-Bos	.237	Radke-Min	.302	Hentgen-Tor	3.22	Hentgen-Tor	156	Guzman-Tor	43.0	**Hernandez-Chi**	5.1
Hill-Tex	250.2	Hentgen-Tor	.241	Nagy-Cle	.306	Nagy-Cle	3.41	Hill-Tex	145	Hill-Tex	42.3	**Hill-Tex**	3.4
Mussina-Bal	243.1	Appier-KC	.245	Fernandez-Chi	.307	Fernandez-Chi	3.45	Nagy-Cle	144	Clemens-Bos	41.1	**Guzman-Tor**	3.3
Clemens-Bos	242.2	Fernandez-Chi	.253	Hentgen-Tor	.308	Appier-KC	3.62	Clemens-Bos	140	Nagy-Cle	38.9	**Appier-KC**	3.3

The Yankees Ride Again

Home runs were hit at a record pace; the 2,742 long balls at the rate of 1.21 per team per game remain AL marks. Oakland's Mark McGwire and Baltimore's Brady Anderson, who never before or after surpassed 24 homers, each surpassed 50. It was the first season since 1961 that two players had reached that plateau.

Baltimore's Roberto Alomar spat in the face of umpire John Hirschbeck during a heated argument in the final series of the year. Although Alomar was suspended, umps were incensed that Alomar was allowed to play in the postseason. Mel Allen, the longtime radio voice of the Yankees, and narrator of *This Week in Baseball*, died, as did former A's owner Charlie Finley. Nomar Garciaparra made his debut.

Both Division Series were decided in four games. Despite owning the league's best record, Cleveland was thwarted by Orioles second baseman Roberto Alomar, who tied Game 4 in the ninth and won it with a homer in the 12th. Texas, playing in the postseason for the first time, won Game 1 of the other Division Series and got 5 home runs from Juan Gonzalez, but the Yankees took three close games. New York then cruised past Baltimore in five games in the ALCS.

The Yankees appeared dead after scoring only once against Atlanta in two World Series losses at Yankee Stadium. New York won Game 3, but fell behind 6-0 to the Braves in Game 4, and many conceded Atlanta its second straight world championship. The Yankees, however, mounted a fierce comeback, tying the game on a Jim Leyritz homer and winning in 10 innings. Momentum shifted, and the Yankees captured their first Series title since 1978.

1995 National League

TEAM	W	L	T	PCT	GB	HW	HL	R	OR	PA	H	2B	3B	HR	BB	SO	HB	SH	AVG	OBP	SLG	OPS	AOPS	BR	ABR	PF	SB	CS	BSA	BSR
EAST																														
ATL	90	54	0	.625		**44**	28	645	**540**	5464	**1202**	210	27	168	520	933	40	56	.250	.326	.409	735	94	-11	-40	105	73	43	63	1
NY	69	75	0	.479	21	40	32	657	618	5581	1323	218	34	125	446	994	42	**92**	.267	.330	.400	730	100	-17	6	97	58	39	60	-1
PHI	69	75	0	.479	21	35	37	615	658	5611	1296	263	30	94	497	884	46	77	.262	.332	.384	716	94	-31	-33	100	72	25	74	7
FLA	67	76	0	.469	22.5	37	34	673	673	5569	1278	214	29	144	517	916	44	69	.262	.335	.406	741	98	8	-3	102	131	53	71	10
MON	66	78	0	.458	24	31	41	621	638	5451	1268	265	24	118	400	901	56	58	.259	.320	.394	714	90	-48	-70	104	120	49	71	9
CENTRAL																														
CIN	85	59	0	.590		**44**	28	747	623	5574	1326	**277**	35	161	519	946	40	62	.270	.342	.440	782	109	80	72	101	**190**	68	74	**18**
HOU	76	68	0	.528	9	36	36	747	674	5857	1403	260	22	109	**566**	992	**69**	47		.353	.399	752	**111**	47	99	94	176	60	**75**	**18**
CHI	73	71	0	.507	12	34	38	693	671	5543	1315	267	39	158	440	953	34	71	.265	.327	.430	757	104	23	24	100	105	37	74	10
STL	62	81	0	.434	22.5	39	33	563	658	5349	1182	238	24	107	436	920	46	48	.247	.314	.374	688	84	-90	-100	102	79	46	63	1
PIT	58	86	0	.403	27	31	41	629	736	5501	1281	245	27	125	456	972	24	51	.259	.323	.396	719	92	-39	-53	102	84	55	60	-1
WEST																														
LA	78	66	0	.542		39	33	634	609	5543	1303	191	31	140	468	1023	30	68	.264	.329	.400	729	104	-23	26	93	127	45	74	12
COL	77	67	0	.535	1	**44**	28	**785**	783	5647	**1406**	259	**43**	**200**	484	943	56	82	**.282**	.350	**.471**	**821**	94	142	-39	128	125	59	68	7
SD	70	74	0	.486	8	40	32	668	672	5526	1345	231	20	116	447	**872**	56	56	.272	.334	.397	731	101	-12	7	97	124	46	73	11
SF	67	77	0	.465	11	37	35	652	776	5603	1256	229	33	152	472	1060	57	79	.253	.323	.404	727	98	-29	-14	98	138	46	**75**	14
TOT	1007					531	476	9329		77819	18184	3367	418	1917	6668	13309	624	947	.263	.331	.408	739					1602	671	70	118

TEAM	CG	SHO	GR	SV	IP	H	HR	BB	SO	BR/9	ERA	AERA	OAV	OOB	PR	APR	PF	OSB	OCS	FA	E	WPB	DP	FW	PW	BW	BSW	DIF
EAST																												
ATL	**18**	11	339	34	1291.2	**1184**	107	436	1087	11.5	3.44	126	.244	.309	**106**	**122**	103	132	37	.982	100	46	113	.6	**12.0**	-3.9	-.7	10.0
NY	9	9	298	36	1291.0	1296	133	**401**	901	12.1	3.88	104	.262	.319	44	24	97	127	40	.979	115	53	125	-.3	2.4	.6	-.9	-4.8
PHI	8	8	341	41	1290.1	1241	134	538	980	12.8	4.21	100	.254	.333	-4	1	101	137	38	.982	97	76	139	.8	.0	-3.2	-.1	-.5
FLA	12	7	400	29	1286.0	1299	139	562	994	13.3	4.27	100	.264	.343	-13	3	103	82	53	.979	115	**44**	143	-.3	.3	-.3	.2	-4.4
MON	7	9	396	42	1283.2	1286	128	416	950	12.3	4.11	105	.262	.325	10	26	103	145	56	.980	109	51	119	.1	2.6	-6.9	.0	-1.8
CENTRAL																												
CIN	8	10	330	38	1289.1	1270	131	424	903	12.0	4.03	103	.260	.320	21	20	100	92	30	**.986**	79	69	140	1.9	2.0	7.1	.9	1.1
HOU	6	8	394	32	1320.1	1357	118	460	1056	12.7	4.06	95	.266	.331	17	-32	92	120	49	.979	121	67	120	-.6	-3.1	9.7	.9	-2.9
CHI	6	**12**	414	**45**	1301.0	1313	162	518	926	12.9	4.13	101	.262	.333	7	6	100	123	56	.979	115	57	115	-.3	.6	2.4	.2	-1.8
STL	4	6	377	38	1265.2	1290	135	445	842	12.6	4.09	105	.268	.333	13	26	102	132	64	.980	113	60	156	-.2	2.6	-9.8	-.7	-1.3
PIT	11	7	391	29	1275.1	1407	130	477	871	13.7	4.70	93	.283	.350	-74	-48	104	125	61	.978	122	77	138	-.7	-4.7	-5.2	-.9	-2.5
WEST																												
LA	16	11	355	37	1295.0	1188	125	462	1060	11.7	3.66	106	**.243**	.311	76	32	92	108	45	.976	130	68	120	-1.2	3.1	2.6	.4	1.1
COL	1	1	**456**	43	1288.1	1443	160	512	891	13.9	4.97	108	.286	.355	-113	44	128	100	43	.981	107	72	146	.2	4.3	-3.8	-.1	4.4
SD	6	10	337	35	1284.2	1242	142	512	1047	12.6	4.13	98	.255	.331	7	-10	97	91	54	.980	108	68	130	.2	-1.0	.7	.3	-2.1
SF	12	5	381	34	1293.2	1368	173	505	801	13.4	4.86	85	.275	.345	-98	-108	99	88	45	.980	108	50	142	.2	-10.6	-1.4	.6	6.3
TOT	124	114	5209	513	18056.0					12.7	4.18		.263	.331						.980	1539	858	1846					

Batter-Fielder Wins
- Bonds-SF 5.6
- Piazza-LA 4.8
- Caminiti-SD 4.5
- Biggio-Hou 4.4
- R.Sanders-Cin 4.0

Batting Average
- Gwynn-SD .368
- Piazza-LA .346
- Bichette-Col .340
- Bell-Hou .334
- Grace-Chi .326

On-Base Percentage
- Bonds-SF .431
- Biggio-Hou .406
- Gwynn-SD .404
- Weiss-Col .403
- Piazza-LA .400

Slugging Average
- Bichette-Col .620
- Walker-Col .607
- Piazza-LA .606
- R.Sanders-Cin .579
- Bonds-SF .577

On-Base Plus Slugging
- Bonds-SF 1009
- Piazza-LA 1006
- Walker-Col .988
- Bichette-Col .984
- R.Sanders-Cin .975

Adjusted OPS
- Piazza-LA 173
- Bonds-SF 168
- R.Sanders-Cin 153
- Karros-LA 146
- Bagwell-Hou 145

Adjusted Batter Runs
- Bonds-SF 56.0
- Piazza-LA 44.2
- Biggio-Hou 40.2
- R.Sanders-Cin 38.7
- Karros-LA 35.8

Runs
- Biggio-Hou 123
- Bonds-SF 109
- Finley-SD 104
- Bichette-Col 102
- Larkin-Cin 98

Hits
- Gwynn-SD 197
- Bichette-Col 197
- Grace-Chi 180

Doubles
- Grace-Chi 51
- McRae-Chi 38
- Bichette-Col 38
- R.Sanders-Cin 36

Triples
- Butler-NY-LA 9
- Young-Col 9
- D.Sanders-Cin-SF 8
- Gonzalez-Hou-Chi 8
- Finley-SD 8

Home Runs
- Bichette-Col 40
- Walker-Col 36
- Sosa-Chi 36
- Bonds-SF 33

Total Bases
- Bichette-Col 359
- Walker-Col 300
- Castilla-Col 297
- Karros-LA 295
- Bonds-SF 292

Runs Batted In
- Bichette-Col 128
- Sosa-Chi 119
- Galarraga-Col 106
- Karros-LA 105
- Conine-Fla 105

Stolen Bases
- Veras-Fla 56
- Larkin-Cin 51
- DeShields-LA 39
- R.Sanders-Cin 36
- Finley-SD 36

Base Stealing Runs
- Larkin-Cin 9.5
- Sosa-Chi 5.0
- Veras-Fla 5.0
- Mondesi-LA 4.5
- Lansing-Mon 4.5

Fielding Runs-Infield
- Bagwell-Hou 17.7
- Reed-SD 17.7
- Vizcaino-NY 15.4
- Lansing-Mon 15.1
- Weiss-Col 13.9

Fielding Runs-Outfield
- Mondesi-LA 8.9
- Sosa-Chi 8.3
- Gonzalez-Hou-Chi 7.0
- Carr-Fla 6.4
- D.Lewis-SF-Cin 5.1

Wins
- Maddux-Atl 19
- Schourek-Cin 18
- Martinez-LA 17
- Glavine-Atl 16

Winning Pct.
- Maddux-Atl .905
- Schourek-Cin .720
- Martinez-LA .708
- Glavine-Atl .696

Complete Games
- Maddux-Atl 10
- Leiter-SF 7
- Valdez-LA 6
- Neagle-Pit 5

Strikeouts
- Nomo-LA 236
- Smoltz-Atl 193
- Maddux-Atl 181
- Reynolds-Hou 175
- Martinez-Mon 174

Fewest BB/Game
- Maddux-Atl .99
- Reynolds-Hou 1.76
- Neagle-Pit 1.93
- Saberhagen-NY-Col 1.94
- Smiley-Cin 1.99

Games
- Leskanic-Col 76
- Veres-Hou 72
- Reed-Col 71
- Perez-Fla 69

Saves
- Myers-Chi 38
- Henke-StL 36
- Beck-SF 33
- Worrell-LA 32
- Slocumb-Phi 32

Base Runners/9
- Maddux-Atl 7.47
- Reed-Col 8.89
- Brantley-Cin 9.47
- Schilling-Phi 9.70
- Nomo-LA 9.74

Adjusted Relief Runs
- Reed-Col 22.8
- Veres-Hou 20.1
- Leskanic-Col 17.7
- Bottalico-Phi 17.5
- Wohlers-Atl 15.7

Relief Ranking
- Wohlers-Atl 31.5
- Worrell-LA 23.4
- Henke-StL 22.8
- Reed-Col 18.5
- Leskanic-Col 17.8

Innings Pitched
- Neagle-Pit 209.2
- Maddux-Atl 209.2
- Martinez-LA 206.1
- Hamilton-SD 204.1
- Navarro-Chi 200.1

Opponents' Avg.
- Nomo-LA .182
- Maddux-Atl .197
- Martinez-Mon .227
- Valdez-LA .228
- Schourek-Cin .228

Opponents' OBP
- Maddux-Atl .224
- Nomo-LA .269
- Valdez-LA .277
- Schourek-Cin .281
- Reynolds-Hou .300

Earned Run Average
- Maddux-Atl 1.63
- Nomo-LA 2.54
- Ashby-SD 2.94
- Valdez-LA 3.05
- Glavine-Atl 3.08

Adjusted ERA
- Maddux-Atl 265
- Nomo-LA 152
- Glavine-Atl 140
- Ashby-SD 138
- Smoltz-Atl 136

Adjusted Starter Runs
- Maddux-Atl 61.8
- Nomo-LA 30.2
- Glavine-Atl 25.9
- Smoltz-Atl 23.1
- Ashby-SD 21.4

Pitcher Wins
- Maddux-Atl 6.5
- Glavine-Atl 3.3
- Wohlers-Atl 3.1
- Schourek-Cin 2.7
- Worrell-LA 2.4

Brave New World

Players' union head Donald Fehr claimed all 835 players without signed contracts were free agents because baseball imposed new work rules, including a salary cap. Owners, of course, said no. Baseball officials must have figured that with no players, they needed no umpires, and with players still on strike, locked out its arbiters. Replacements—umpires, that is—were used for a week once the players came to terms.

Suspended for sixty days for violating MLB's drug policy, Darryl Strawberry was released by the Giants, then pleaded guilty to tax evasion. The Dodgers had to forfeit a game to St. Louis in August after Los Angeles fans flung giveaway baseballs onto the field following a controversial call. Hideo Nomo, 13-6 and leading the league in strikeouts for those Dodgers, became the first Japanese player in thirty-one years to debut in the big leagues.

Former Reds outfielders Vada Pinson and Gus Bell died, but Cincinnati, sparked by MVP Barry Larkin, won the Central and swept Los Angeles in the Division Series. Colorado, in only its third season, had four 30-homer men at new Coors Field and claimed the Wild Card despite a league-worst 4.97 ERA. Atlanta, with 19-2 Greg Maddux, had the best record in the league and lost only once in reaching the World Series, besting the Rockies in the Division Series and sweeping the Reds in the NLCS.

Atlanta pitchers dominated the World Series, holding Cleveland's potent offense to a collective .179 average. Tom Glavine and Mark Wohlers combined on a 1-0, 1-hit shutout in Game 6, with Dave Justice's home run providing the difference. The win gave the Braves their first Series crown since 1957 and made them the first franchise to win world championships in three different cities.

1995 American League

TEAM	W	L	T	PCT	GB	HW	HL	R	OR	PA	H	2B	3B	HR	BB	SO	HB	SH	AVG	OBP	SLG	OPS	AOPS	BR	ABR	PF	SB	CS	BSA	BSR
EAST																														
BOS	86	58	0	.597		42	30	791	698	5716	1399	**286**	31	175	560	923	**65**	45	.280	.357	.455	812	106	79	55	103	99	44	69	6
NY	79	65	1	.549	7	46	26	749	688	5699	1365	280	34	122	**625**	851	39	20	.276	.357	.420	777	102	31	38	99	50	30	63	1
BAL	71	73	0	.493	15	36	36	704	640	5531	1267	229	27	173	574	803	39	40	.262	.342	.428	770	97	-4	-17	102	92	45	67	4
DET	60	84	0	.417	26	35	37	654	844	5535	1204	228	29	159	551	987	41	35	.247	.327	.404	731	89	-80	-80	100	73	36	67	11
TOR	56	88	0	.389	30	29	43	642	777	5650	1309	275	27	140	492	906	44	33	.260	.328	.409	737	90	-70	-71	100	75	16	**82**	11
CENTRAL																														
CLE	100	44	0	.694		**54**	18	**840**	**607**	5684	**1461**	279	23	**207**	542	**766**	35	31	**.291**	**.361**	**.479**	**840**	114	**125**	**108**	102	**132**	53	71	10
KC	70	74	0	.486	30	35	37	629	691	5526	1275	240	35	119	475	849	43	**66**	.260	.328	.396	724	85	-91	-104	102	120	53	69	8
CHI	68	76	1	.472	32	38	34	755	758	5770	1417	252	37	146	576	767	32	46	.280	.334	.431	765	107	32	65	96	110	39	74	11
MIL	65	79	1	.451	35	33	39	740	747	5631	1329	249	**42**	128	502	800	46	41	.266	.336	.409	745	88	-52	-90	106	105	40	72	9
MIN	56	88	0	.389	44	29	43	703	889	5588	1398	270	34	120	471	916	58	18	.279	.346	.419	765	97	-11	-15	101	105	57	65	3
WEST																														
SEA	79	66	0	.545		46	27	796	708	5670	1377	276	20	182	549	871	39	52	.276	.350	.448	798	105	47	38	101	110	41	73	10
CAL	78	67	0	.538	1	39	33	801	697	5690	1390	252	25	186	564	889	36	33	.277	.352	.448	800	107	52	59	99	58	39	60	-1
TEX	74	70	0	.514	4.5	41	31	691	720	5566	1304	247	24	138	526	877	33	49	.265	.338	.410	748	90	-43	-65	103	90	47	66	3
OAK	67	77	0	.465	11.5	38	34	730	761	5616	1296	228	18	169	565	911	45	32	.264	.341	.420	761	102	-15	21	95	112	46	71	5
TOT	1010					541	468	10225		78872	18791	3591	406	2164	7572	12116	595	541	.270	.344	.427	771					1331	586	69	88

TEAM	CG	SHO	GR	SV	IP	H	HR	BB	SO	BR/9	ERA	AERA	OAV	OOB	PR	APR	PF	OSB	OCS	FA	E	WPB	DP	FW	PW	BW	BSW	DIF
EAST																												
BOS	7	9	370	39	1292.2	1338	**127**	476	888	12.9	4.39	110	.268	.334	46	64	103	80	41	.978	120	86	151	-1.2	6.0	5.2	-.0	4.1
NY	18	5	302	35	1284.2	1286	159	535	908	13.0	4.56	101	.261	.334	22	9	98	117	40	**.986**	74	70	121	**1.4**	.8	3.6	-.5	1.7
BAL	**19**	**10**	336	29	1267.0	**1165**	149	523	930	12.3	4.31	111	**.245**	.322	56	64	101	98	43	**.986**	**72**	38	141	**1.4**	6.0	-1.6	-.2	-6.6
DET	5	3	366	38	1275.0	1509	170	536	729	14.8	5.49	88	.296	.365	-110	-95	102	102	38	.981	106	70	143	-.4	-8.9	-7.5	-.3	5.2
TOR	16	8	265	22	1292.2	1336	145	654	894	14.2	4.88	97	.267	.356	-24	-19	101	98	50	.982	97	104	131	.0	-1.8	-6.7	**.4**	-8.1
CENTRAL																												
CLE	10	**10**	335	**50**	1301.0	1261	135	**445**	926	**12.1**	**3.83**	123	.255	**.320**	127	128	100	117	38	.982	101	59	142	-.2	**12.0**	10.1	.2	5.7
KC	11	**10**	308	37	1288.0	1323	142	503	763	13.0	4.49	107	.268	.338	32	43	102	78	29	.984	90	56	168	-.4	-9.8	.2	.3	-4.6
CHI	12	4	**373**	36	1284.2	1374	164	617	892	14.2	4.85	92	.275	.356	-20	-58	95	106	**59**	.980	108	57	131	-.5	-5.4	6.1	**.4**	-.8
MIL	7	4	321	31	1286.0	1391	146	603	699	14.3	4.82	104	.280	.360	-16	25	106	110	36	.981	105	79	186	-.4	2.3	-8.4	.3	-1.8
MIN	7	2	336	27	1272.2	1450	210	533	790	14.3	5.76	83	.287	.356	-149	-132	102	102	25	.981	100	63	141	-.1	-12.4	-1.4	-.3	-1.8
WEST																												
SEA	9	9	324	39	1289.1	1343	149	591	**1068**	13.8	4.50	106	.268	.347	31	38	101	88	46	.980	104	63	108	-.3	3.6	3.6	**.4**	-.7
CAL	8	9	368	42	1284.1	1310	163	486	901	12.9	4.52	104	.265	.333	28	27	100	88	46	.982	95	55	120	.2	2.5	5.5	-.7	-2.1
TEX	14	4	310	34	1285.0	1385	152	514	838	13.6	4.66	104	.278	.346	8	25	103	**55**	44	.982	98	70	156	.0	2.3	-6.1	-.3	6.1
OAK	8	4	358	34	1273.0	1320	153	556	890	13.6	4.93	92	.269	.347	-31	-60	96	92	51	.981	102	60	151	-.2	-5.6	2.0	-.3	-1.4
TOT	151	90	4672	493	17976.0					13.5	4.71		.270	.344						.982	1372	930	1990					

Batter-Fielder Wins		Batting Average		On-Base Percentage		Slugging Average		On-Base Plus Slugging		Adjusted OPS		Adjusted Batter Runs	
E.Martinez-Sea	5.8	E.Martinez-Sea	.356	E.Martinez-Sea	.479	Belle-Cle	.690	E.Martinez-Sea	1107	E.Martinez-Sea	184	E.Martinez-Sea	73.4
Belle-Cle	5.0	Knoblauch-Min	.333	F.Thomas-Chi	.454	E.Martinez-Sea	.628	Belle-Cle	1091	F.Thomas-Chi	183	F.Thomas-Chi	70.2
Salmon-Cal	5.0	Salmon-Cal	.330	Thome-Cle	.438	F.Thomas-Chi	.606	F.Thomas-Chi	1061	Belle-Cle	174	Belle-Cle	60.1
Valentin-Bos	4.6	Boggs-NY	.324	Salmon-Cal	.429	Salmon-Cal	.594	Salmon-Cal	1024	Salmon-Cal	165	Salmon-Cal	55.3
F.Thomas-Chi	4.5	Murray-Cle	.323	Davis-Cal	.429	Palmeiro-Bal	.583	Thome-Cle	996	Thome-Cle	154	McGwire-Oak	51.3

Runs		Hits		Doubles		Triples		Home Runs		Total Bases		Runs Batted In	
E.Martinez-Sea	121	Johnson-Chi	186	E.Martinez-Sea	52	Lofton-Cle	13	Belle-Cle	50	Belle-Cle	377	Vaughn-Bos	126
Belle-Cle	121	E.Martinez-Sea	182	Belle-Cle	52	Johnson-Chi	12	F.Thomas-Chi	40	Palmeiro-Bal	323	Belle-Cle	126
Edmonds-Cal	120	Knoblauch-Min	179	Puckett-Min	39	Anderson-Bal	10	Buhner-Sea	40	E.Martinez-Sea	321	Buhner-Sea	121
Phillips-Cal	119	Salmon-Cal	177	Valentin-Bos	37	B.Williams-NY	9			Salmon-Cal	319	E.Martinez-Sea	113
Salmon-Cal	111	Baerga-Cle	175	T.Martinez-Sea	35	Knoblauch-Min	8			Vaughn-Bos	316		

Stolen Bases		Base Stealing Runs		Fielding Runs-Infield		Fielding Runs-Outfield		Wins		Winning Pct.		Complete Games	
Lofton-Cle	54	Johnson-Chi	6.7	Fryman-Det	27.3	Cordova-Min	13.8	Mussina-Bal	19	Johnson-Sea	.900	McDowell-NY	8
Nixon-Tex	50	Lofton-Cle	6.6	Gil-Tex	18.3	Edmonds-Cal	11.7	Cone-Tor-NY	18	Hanson-Bos	.750	Erickson-Min-Bal	7
Goodwin-KC	50	Javier-Oak	6.2	Alicea-Bos	14.9	Javier-Oak	8.6	Johnson-Sea	18	Nagy-Cle	.727	Mussina-Bal	7
Knoblauch-Min	46	Alomar-Tor	5.6	Gagne-KC	12.4	Becker-Min	7.4	Rogers-Tex	17	Hershiser-Cle	.727		
Coleman-KC-Sea	42	Goodwin-KC	4.7	Vina-Mil	12.2	Salmon-Cal	6.8			Rogers-Tex	.708		

Strikeouts		Fewest BB/Game		Games		Saves		Base Runners/9		Adjusted Relief Runs		Relief Ranking	
Johnson-Sea	294	Mussina-Bal	2.03	Orosco-Bal	65	Mesa-Cle	46	Percival-Cal	7.78	Mesa-Cle	25.5	Mesa-Cle	44.5
Stottlemyre-Oak	205	Martinez-Cle	2.21	McDowell-Tex	64	Smith-Cal	37	Wetteland-NY	7.92	Nelson-Sea	22.4	Aguilera-Min-Bos	27.7
Finley-Cal	195	Radke-Min	2.34	Wickman-NY	63	Aguilera-Min-Bos	32	Mesa-Cle	9.28	Percival-Cal	22.0	Nelson-Sea	26.6
Cone-Tor-NY	191	K.Brown-Bal	2.51	Belinda-Bos	63	Hernandez-Chi	32	Johnson-Sea	9.66	Tavarez-Cle	16.7	Tavarez-Cle	21.2
Appier-KC	185	Gubicza-KC	2.62	Ayala-Sea	63			Mussina-Bal	9.66	Plunk-Cle	15.4	Wetteland-NY	20.6

Innings Pitched		Opponents' Avg.		Opponents' OBP		Earned Run Average		Adjusted ERA		Adjusted Starter Runs		Pitcher Wins	
Cone-Tor-NY	229.1	Johnson-Sea	.201	Johnson-Sea	.266	Johnson-Sea	2.48	Johnson-Sea	193	Johnson-Sea	53.9	**Johnson-Sea**	4.8
Mussina-Bal	221.2	Appier-KC	.221	Mussina-Bal	.270	Wakefield-Bos	2.95	Wakefield-Bos	165	Wakefield-Bos	37.9	Mesa-Cle	4.2
McDowell-NY	217.2	Mussina-Bal	.226	Wakefield-Bos	.300	Martinez-Cle	3.08	Martinez-Cle	153	Mussina-Bal	36.0	**Wakefield-Bos**	4.2
Johnson-Sea	214.1	Wakefield-Bos	.227	K.Brown-Bal	.302	Mussina-Bal	3.29	Mussina-Bal	145	Martinez-Cle	33.7	**Mussina-Bal**	4.2
Gubicza-KC	213.1	Cone-Tor-NY	.228	Martinez-Cle	.302	Rogers-Tex	3.38	Rogers-Tex	143	Rogers-Tex	31.9	**Rogers-Tex**	3.4

Ripken and "The Streak" Pull Baseball Off the DL

Owners announced plans to use replacement players if a labor deal wasn't reached by Opening Day. Baltimore owner Peter Angelos refused to sign replacements players, thus the O's played no exhibition contests. His stated motive: preserving Cal Ripken's consecutive games streak. Angelos' stand led to his being virtually ostracized by other owners.

A March 31 injunction against MLB by U.S. District Court judge Sonia Sotomayor ended the strike. Fans were understandably bitter and jaded all summer, but the harsh feeling seemed to relent for one magical night at Camden Yards. On September 6, on national television, Ripken broke Lou Gehrig's record by playing in his 2,131st consecutive game.

Yankees great Mickey Mantle died in August, two months after receiving a liver transplant, while colorful umpire Ron Luciano committed suicide. Two Yankees greats retired—Dave Winfield and Don Mattingly—as Derek Jeter and Jason Giambi debuted. Eddie Murray collected his 3,000th hit.

Sparked by Albert Belle, the first player to hit 50 homers and 50 doubles in a season, Cleveland won the Central by an amazing 30 games and swept Boston to reach the ALCS. Seattle climaxed a furious comeback by winning a one-game playoff against California to reach the postseason for the first time. The Mariners then outlasted the Wild Card Yankees in the other inaugural AL Division Series. Game 5 ended with starters Randy Johnson and Jack McDowell pitching in relief. Edgar Martinez drove home the tying and winning runs in the home 11th, sending the Kingdome into a frenzy. Despite Jay Buhner's 3 homers for Seattle, Cleveland's outstanding starting pitching prevailed in a six-game ALCS. The Tribe, however, ran out of steam in the World Series, losing to Atlanta in six.

1994 National League

TEAM	W	L	T	PCT	GB	HW	HL	R	OR	PA	H	2B	3B	HR	BB	SO	HB	SH	AVG	OBP	SLG	OPS	AOPS	BR	ABR	PF	SB	CS	BSA	BSR
EAST																														
MON	74	40	0	.649		32	20	585	454	4514	1111	246	30	108	379	669	40	53	.278	.343	.435	778	106	51	46	101	**137**	36	79	18
ATL	68	46	0	.596	6	31	24	542	448	4349	1031	198	18	**137**	377	668	22	60	.267	.333	.434	767	100	26	6	104	48	31	61	0
NY	55	58	0	.487	18.5	23	30	506	526	4347	966	164	21	117	336	807	52	59	.250	.316	.394	710	90	-59	-53	99	25	26	49	-4
PHI	54	61	0	.470	20.5	34	26	521	497	4436	1028	208	28	80	396	711	31	51	.262	.332	.390	722	91	-30	-38	102	67	24	74	6
FLA	51	64	0	.443	23.5	25	34	468	576	4387	1043	180	24	94	349	746	40	42	.266	.330	.396	726	90	-31	-50	104	65	26	71	5
CENTRAL																														
CIN	66	48	1	.579		37	22	**609**	490	4511	**1142**	211	36	124	388	738	29	53	**.286**	**.350**	**.449**	**799**	113	79	80	100	119	51	70	8
HOU	66	49	1	.574	0.5	37	22	602	503	4500	1099	**252**	25	120	394	718	43	**73**	.278	.347	.445	792	117	71	**103**	95	124	44	74	12
STL	53	61	1	.465	13	23	33	535	621	4450	1026	213	27	108	**434**	686	33	44	.263	.339	.414	753	101	16	17	100	76	46	62	1
PIT	53	61	1	.465	13	32	29	466	580	4299	1001	198	23	80	349	725	22	36	.259	.322	.384	706	88	-57	-65	102	53	25	68	3
CHI	49	64	0	.434	16.5	20	39	500	549	4386	1015	189	26	109	364	750	27	54	.259	.325	.404	729	94	-30	-30	100	69	53	57	-3
WEST																														
LA	58	56	0	.509		33	23	532	509	4371	1055	160	29	115	366	687	19	51	.270	.333	.414	747	105	-2	28	95	74	37	67	3
SF	55	60	0	.478	3.5	29	31	504	500	4364	963	159	32	123	364	719	39	65	.249	.318	.402	720	96	-47	-28	96	114	40	74	11
COL	53	64	0	.453	6.5	25	32	573	638	4493	1098	206	39	125	378	761	23	50	.274	.337	.439	776	91	39	-43	117	91	53	63	1
SD	47	70	0	.402	12.5	26	31	479	531	4518	1117	200	19	92	319	762	31	67	.275	.330	.401	731	98	-25	-8	97	79	37	68	4
TOT	803					407	395	7422		61925	14695	2784	377	1532	5193	10147	451	758	.267	.333	.415	747					1141	529	68	66

TEAM	CG	SHO	GR	SV	IP	H	HR	BB	SO	BR/9	ERA	AERA	OAV	OOB	PR	APR	PF	OSB	OCS	FA	E	WPB	DP	FW	PW	BW	BSW	DIF
EAST																												
MON	4	8	259	**46**	1036.2	970	100	288	805	11.3	3.56	119	.247	**.302**	75	76	100	99	32	.979	94	**35**	90	-.5	7.5	4.5	**1.3**	4.2
ATL	**16**	8	244	26	1026.1	929	76	378	865	11.7	3.57	121	.242	.311	73	**82**	102	90	32	.982	81	46	85	.3	**8.1**	.6	-.5	2.5
NY	7	3	238	35	1023.0	1069	117	332	640	12.5	4.13	101	.271	.328	9	4	99	68	34	.980	89	36	112	-.2	.4	-5.2	-.9	4.4
PHI	7	6	243	30	1024.1	1028	98	377	699	12.6	3.85	111	.261	.328	41	48	102	87	30	.978	94	36	96	-.4	4.7	-3.7	.1	-4.2
FLA	5	7	300	30	1015.0	1069	120	428	649	13.6	4.50	99	.274	.349	-32	-6	106	59	52	.978	95	75	111	-.5	-.6	-4.9	.0	-.6
CENTRAL																												
CIN	6	6	261	27	1038.1	1037	117	339	799	12.2	3.78	110	.262	.322	50	46	99	78	39	.983	73	58	91	.8	4.5	7.9	.3	-4.5
HOU	9	6	268	29	1029.2	1043	102	367	739	12.6	3.97	100	.265	.331	28	-2	94	85	36	.983	76	51	110	.6	-2	**10.1**	.7	-2.8
STL	7	7	**330**	29	1018.0	1154	134	355	632	13.7	5.14	83	.289	.351	-105	-101	101	70	40	.982	80	46	119	.4	-9.9	1.7	-.4	4.2
PIT	8	2	285	24	1005.2	1094	117	370	650	13.5	4.64	94	.281	.347	-47	-29	104	78	31	.980	91	35	131	-.3	-2.9	-6.4	-.2	5.7
CHI	5	5	286	27	1023.2	1054	120	392	717	12.9	4.47	94	.268	.335	-29	-29	100	75	46	.982	81	51	110	.2	-2.9	-3.0	-.8	-1.2
WEST																												
LA	14	5	239		1014.0	1041	90	354	732	12.7	4.17	95	.267	.331	4	-23	99	90	33	.980	88	54	104	-.1	-2.3	2.8	-.2	.8
SF	2	4	288	33	1025.1	1014	122	372	655	12.5	3.99	102	.262	.330	26	8	96	76	35	**.985**	**68**	38	113	**1.1**	-2.8	-2.6	-.2	-2.2
COL	4	5	329	28	1031.0	1185	120	448	703	14.7	5.15	97	.292	.366	-108	-17	118	87	44	.981	84	55	117	.2	-1.7	-4.2	-.4	.5
SD	8	6	273	27	1045.2	1008	99	393	862	12.3	4.08	101	.252	.321	15	6	98	99	45	.975	111	59	82	-1.3	.6	-.8	-.0	-9.9
TOT	102	78	3843	411	14356.2					12.8	4.21		.267	.333						.980	1205	695	1471					

Batter-Fielder Wins
- **Bagwell-Hou** 7.7
- **Bonds-SF** 4.8
- **Gwynn-SD** 3.9
- **Mitchell-Cin** 3.8
- **Biggio-Hou** 3.7

Batting Average
- Gwynn-SD 394
- Bagwell-Hou 368
- Alou-Mon 339
- Morris-Cin 335
- Mitchell-Cin 326

On-Base Percentage
- Gwynn-SD 454
- Bagwell-Hou 451
- Mitchell-Cin 429
- Justice-Atl 427
- Bonds-SF 426

Slugging Average
- Bagwell-Hou 750
- Mitchell-Cin 681
- Bonds-SF 647
- McGriff-Atl 623
- Williams-SF 607

On-Base Plus Slugging
- Bagwell-Hou 1201
- Mitchell-Cin 1110
- Bonds-SF 1073
- Gwynn-SD 1022
- McGriff-Atl 1012

Adjusted OPS
- Bagwell-Hou 219
- Mitchell-Cin 186
- Bonds-SF 182
- Gwynn-SD 171
- Alou-Mon 153

Adjusted Batter Runs
- Bagwell-Hou 72.8
- Bonds-SF 49.9
- Gwynn-SD 47.0
- Mitchell-Cin 41.4
- Alou-Mon 33.1

Runs
- Bagwell-Hou 104
- Grissom-Mon 96
- Lankford-StL 89
- Bonds-SF 89
- Biggio-Hou 88

Hits
- Gwynn-SD 165
- Bichette-Col 147
- Bagwell-Hou 147
- Morris-Cin 146
- Conine-Fla 144

Doubles
- Walker-Mon 44
- Biggio-Hou 44
- Gwynn-SD 35
- Bell-Pit 35
- Bichette-Col 33

Triples
- Lewis-SF 9
- Butler-LA 9
- R.Sanders-Cin 8
- Mondesi-LA 8
- Kingery-Col 8

Home Runs
- Williams-SF 43
- Bagwell-Hou 39
- Bonds-SF 37
- McGriff-Atl 34
- Galarraga-Col 31

Total Bases
- Bagwell-Hou 300
- Williams-SF 270
- Bichette-Col 265
- McGriff-Atl 264
- Bonds-SF 253

Runs Batted In
- Bagwell-Hou 116
- Williams-SF 96
- Bichette-Col 95
- McGriff-Atl 94
- Piazza-LA 92

Stolen Bases
- Biggio-Hou 39
- D.Sanders-Atl-Cin 38
- Grissom-Mon 36
- Carr-Fla 32
- Lewis-SF 30

Base Stealing Runs
- Biggio-Hou 7.2
- Grissom-Mon 5.8
- Larkin-Cin 5.0
- Carr-Fla 4.2
- Clayton-SF 4.0

Fielding Runs-Infield
- Sanchez-Chi 20.4
- Garcia-Pit 18.0
- Bell-Pit 17.7
- Bagwell-Hou 15.4
- Karros-LA 13.3

Fielding Runs-Outfield
- Whiten-StL 11.2
- Grissom-Mon 9.0
- R.Sanders-Cin 6.4
- Carr-Fla 6.1
- Gonzalez-Hou 5.7

Wins
- Maddux-Atl 16
- Hill-Mon 16
- Saberhagen-NY 14
- Jackson-Phi 14
- Glavine-Atl 13

Winning Pct.
- Saberhagen-NY 778
- Hill-Mon 762
- Maddux-Atl 727
- Jackson-Phi 700
- Martinez-Mon 688

Complete Games
- Maddux-Atl 10
- Drabek-Hou 6
- Candiotti-LA 5

Strikeouts
- Benes-SD 189
- Rijo-Cin 171
- Maddux-Atl 156
- Saberhagen-NY 143
- Martinez-Mon 142

Fewest BB/Game
- Saberhagen-NY 66
- Tewksbury-StL 1.27
- Maddux-Atl 1.38
- Reynolds-Hou 1.52
- Swindell-Hou 1.58

Games
- Reed-Col 61
- Rojas-Mon 58
- Bautista-Chi 58
- Munoz-Col 57
- Burba-SF 57

Saves
- Franco-NY 30
- Beck-SF 28
- Jones-Phi 27
- Wetteland-Mon 25

Base Runners/9
- Maddux-Atl 8.33
- Saberhagen-NY 9.44
- Drabek-Hou 9.78
- Jones-Hou 9.78
- Wetteland-Mon 9.90

Adjusted Relief Runs
- Jones-Phi 12.8
- McElroy-Cin 12.7
- Brantley-Cin 12.6
- Jackson-Phi 12.4
- Carrasco-Cin 11.7

Relief Ranking
- Brantley-Cin 25.1
- Jones-Phi 24.1
- Carrasco-Cin 22.8
- Hoffman-SD 20.7
- Wetteland-Mon 19.9

Innings Pitched
- Maddux-Atl 202.0
- Jackson-Phi 179.1
- Saberhagen-NY 177.1
- Rijo-Cin 172.1
- Benes-SD 172.1

Opponents' Avg.
- Maddux-Atl 207
- Martinez-Mon 220
- Drabek-Hou 220
- Avery-Atl 227
- Fassero-Mon 229

Opponents' OBP
- Maddux-Atl 243
- Saberhagen-NY 271
- Drabek-Hou 275
- Ashby-SD 285
- Fassero-Mon 285

Earned Run Average
- Maddux-Atl 1.56
- Saberhagen-NY 2.74
- Drabek-Hou 2.84
- Fassero-Mon 2.99
- Reynolds-Hou 3.05

Adjusted ERA
- Maddux-Atl 277
- Saberhagen-NY 152
- Fassero-Mon 142
- Drabek-Hou 139
- Rijo-Cin 136

Adjusted Starter Runs
- Maddux-Atl 58.0
- Saberhagen-NY 29.6
- Freeman-Col 22.7
- Henry-Mon 22.3
- Drabek-Hou 21.6

Pitcher Wins
- **Maddux-Atl** 6.8
- **Saberhagen-NY** 3.1
- **Drabek-Hou** 2.7
- **Brantley-Cin** 2.6
- **Henry-Mon** 2.5

Summertime Strikeout

The 1994 season was like a wonderful outdoor party held under a black sky. Major league per-game attendance was even higher than 1993's record rate, San Diego's Tony Gwynn flirted with .400, San Francisco third baseman Matt Williams was on pace to possibly break Roger Maris' single-season home run record, Greg Maddux of Atlanta was enjoying his best season to that point, and Jeff Bagwell, hitting in the pitcher-dominant Astrodome, had 116 RBIs in 110 games. A broken hand ended Bagwell's season early; everyone else waited helplessly for the storm. It hit on August 12.

The strike ended Montreal's dream season, as les Expos owned the best record in baseball and had a 6-game lead in the East over the Braves, who held a slight advantage over the Astros in the new Wild Card standings. The star-crossed Expos seemed a lock to make the postseason for the first time since 1981. Felipe Alou's club, with All-Stars Moises Alou, Wil Cordero, Marquis Grissom, Darrin Fletcher, and 16-game winner Ken Hill, plus dominant seasons from Larry Walker and John Wetteland, would never look the same again.

Central leader Cincinnati and West frontrunner Los Angeles led tight races as of the strike, though Major League Baseball declined to officially name any division winners. The decision by owners to cancel the remainder of the season meant the first year with no World Series since 1904. In December owners declared an impasse in negotiations and implemented new rules, including a salary cap. Players appealed to the National Labor Relations Board, which also heard unfair labor practice claims by owners against players.

1994 American League

TEAM	W	L	T	PCT	GB	HW	HL	R	OR	PA	H	2B	3B	HR	BB	SO	HB	SH	AVG	OBP	SLG	OPS	AOPS	BR	ABR	PF	SB	CS	BSA	BSR
EAST																														
NY	70	43	0	.619	—	33	24	670	534	4611	1155	238	16	139	**530**	660	31	27	**.290**	**.374**	.462	**836**	118	102	**128**	97	55	40	58	-2
BAL	63	49	0	.563	6.5	28	27	589	**497**	4384	1047	185	20	139	438	655	39	16	.272	.349	.438	787	96	12	-20	106	69	13	**84**	11
TOR	55	60	0	.478	16	33	26	566	579	4461	1064	210	30	115	387	691	38	30	.269	.336	.424	760	93	-31	-38	101	79	26	75	8
BOS	54	61	0	.470	17	31	33	552	621	4446	1038	222	19	120	404	723	31	38	.263	.334	.421	755	89	-38	-63	105	81	38	68	5
DET	53	62	0	.461	18	34	24	652	671	4574	1048	216	25	161	520	897	34	17	.265	.352	.454	806	105	44	35	101	46	33	58	-1
CENTRAL																														
CHI	67	46	0	.593	—	34	19	633	498	4556	1133	175	39	121	497	568	20	**51**	.287	**.384**	.444	810	109	56	63	99	77	27	74	7
CLE	66	47	0	.584	1	**35**	16	**679**	562	4493	**1165**	**240**	20	**167**	382	629	18	33	**.290**	.351	**.484**	835	111	75	68	101	**140**	48	73	**12**
KC	64	51	0	.557	4	**35**	24	574	532	4390	1051	211	38	100	376	698	33	32	.269	.335	.419	754	89	-40	-66	105	94	30	76	10
MIN	53	60	0	.469	14	32	27	594	608	4408	1092	239	23	103	359	635	**41**	22	.276	.340	.427	767	95	-19	-23	101	94	30	76	10
MIL	53	62	0	.461	15	24	32	547	586	4494	1045	238	21	99	417	698	33	28	.263	.335	.408	743	86	-52	-79	105	59	37	61	0
WEST																														
TEX	52	62	0	.456	—	31	32	613	697	4531	1114	198	27	124	437	730	36	41	.280	.353	.436	789	101	19	12	101	82	35	70	6
OAK	51	63	0	.447	1	24	32	549	589	4395	1009	178	13	113	417	686	18	24	.260	.330	.399	729	94	-70	-27	92	91	39	70	6
SEA	49	63	0	.438	2	22	22	569	616	4361	1045	211	18	153	372	652	26	48	.269	.335	.451	786	98	-2	-15	102	65	54	55	-5
CAL	47	68	0	.409	5.5	23	40	543	660	4443	1042	178	16	120	402	715	27	40	.264	.334	.400	743	88	-56	-65	102	65	54	55	-5
TOT	797					419	378	8330		62547	15048	2939	325	1774	5938	9619	425	449	.273	.345	.434	779					1117	503	69	70

TEAM	CG	SHO	GR	SV	IP	H	HR	BB	SO	BR/9	ERA	AERA	OAV	OOB	PR	APR	PF	OSB	OCS	FA	E	WPB	DP	FW	PW	BW	BSW	DIF
EAST																												
NY	8	2	241	31	1019.2	1045	120	398	656	12.9	4.34	106	.267	.335	52	30	96	55	29	.982	80	56	122	.1	2.8	**11.8**	-.6	-.6
BAL	13	4	234	37	997.2	1005	131	**351**	666	12.5	4.31	117	.263	.327	54	78	105	61	28	**.986**	57	23	103	1.5	7.2	-1.8	.6	-.4
TOR	13	4	221	26	1025.0	1053	127	482	**832**	13.8	4.70	104	.266	.348	12	19	102	101	43	.981	81	68	105	.2	1.8	-3.5	.3	-1.2
BOS	6	3	**308**	30	1029.1	1104	120	450	729	13.9	4.93	102	.276	.351	-15	11	105	98	38	.981	81	62	124	.2	1.0	-5.8	.0	1.1
DET	15	1	246	20	1018.0	1139	148	449	560	14.3	5.38	91	.282	.356	-66	-51	103	94	36	.981	82	67	90	.1	-4.7	3.2	-.6	-2.6
CENTRAL																												
CHI	13	**9**	239	20	1011.1	**964**	115	377	754	**12.1**	**3.96**	118	**.250**	**.317**	94	84	98	81	30	.981	79	31	91	.2	7.8	5.8	.2	-3.5
CLE	**17**	5	222	21	1018.2	1097	**94**	404	666	13.6	4.36	109	.275	.346	49	44	99	75	33	.980	90	65	119	-.4	4.1	6.3	**.6**	-1.9
KC	5	6	247	**38**	1031.2	1018	95	392	717	12.6	4.23	**119**	.260	.328	65	**86**	105	91	30	.982	80	65	102	.2	**7.9**	-6.1	.4	4.0
MIN	6	4	272	29	1005.0	1197	153	388	602	14.5	5.68	87	.299	.361	-98	-82	103	85	**53**	.982	75	48	99	.4	-7.6	-2.1	-.5	5.3
MIL	11	3	252	23	1036.0	1071	127	421	577	13.2	4.62	110	.269	.340	20	49	106	117	28	.981	85	41	**130**	-.0	4.5	-7.3	-.5	-1.2
WEST																												
TEX	10	4	301	26	1023.0	1176	157	394	683	14.1	5.45	89	.288	.351	-75	-70	101	**47**	33	.976	106	59	106	-1.4	-6.5	1.1	.0	1.6
OAK	12	**9**	**308**	23	1003.1	979	128	510	732	13.7	4.80	93	.257	.347	0	-38	93	60	45	.979	88	47	105	-.3	-3.5	-2.5	.0	-3.9
SEA	13	7	252	21	984.0	1051	109	486	763	14.3	4.99	99	.274	.347	-21	-8	103	69	39	.977	95	49	102	-.8	-.7	-1.4	-.2	-3.9
CAL	11	4	257	21	1027.0	1149	150	436	682	14.3	5.42	91	.287	.360	-70	-57	102	83	38	.983	76	59	110	.5	-5.3	-6.0	-.9	1.2
TOT	153	65	3600	366	14229.2					13.5	4.80		.273	.345						.981	1155	740	1508					

Leaderboards

Batter-Fielder Wins
- Thomas-Chi ...5.2
- Belle-Cle ...4.5
- Griffey-Sea ...4.2
- O'Neill-NY ...3.9
- Lofton-Cle ...3.7

Batting Average
- O'Neill-NY ...359
- Belle-Cle ...357
- Thomas-Chi ...353
- Lofton-Cle ...349
- Boggs-NY ...342

On-Base Percentage
- Thomas-Chi ...487
- O'Neill-NY ...460
- Belle-Cle ...438
- Boggs-NY ...433
- Clark-Tex ...431

Slugging Average
- Thomas-Chi ...729
- Belle-Cle ...714
- Griffey-Sea ...674
- O'Neill-NY ...603
- Hamelin-KC ...599

On-Base Plus Slugging
- Thomas-Chi ...1217
- Belle-Cle ...1152
- Griffey-Sea ...1076
- O'Neill-NY ...1064
- Hamelin-KC ...987

Adjusted OPS
- Thomas-Chi ...212
- Belle-Cle ...190
- O'Neill-NY ...179
- Griffey-Sea ...167
- Davis-Cal ...146

Adjusted Batter Runs
- Thomas-Chi ...75.4
- Belle-Cle ...56.6
- O'Neill-NY ...47.9
- Griffey-Sea ...42.5
- Lofton-Cle ...30.0

Runs
- Thomas-Chi ...106
- Lofton-Cle ...105
- Griffey-Sea ...94
- Phillips-Det ...91
- Belle-Cle ...90

Hits
- Lofton-Cle ...160
- Molitor-Tor ...155
- Belle-Cle ...147
- Thomas-Chi ...141

Doubles
- Knoblauch-Min ...45
- Belle-Cle ...35
- Thomas-Chi ...34
- Fryman-Det ...34

Triples
- L.Johnson-Chi ...14
- Coleman-KC ...12
- Lofton-Cle ...9
- Diaz-Mil ...7

Home Runs
- Griffey-Sea ...40
- Thomas-Chi ...38
- Belle-Cle ...36
- Canseco-Tex ...31
- Fielder-Det ...28

Total Bases
- Belle-Cle ...294
- Griffey-Sea ...292
- Thomas-Chi ...291
- Lofton-Cle ...246
- Palmeiro-Bal ...240

Runs Batted In
- Puckett-Min ...112
- Carter-Tor ...103
- Thomas-Chi ...101
- Belle-Cle ...101
- Franco-Chi ...98

Stolen Bases
- Lofton-Cle ...60
- Coleman-KC ...50
- Nixon-Bos ...42
- Knoblauch-Min ...35
- Anderson-Bal ...31

Base Stealing Runs
- Lofton-Cle ...9.0
- Coleman-KC ...8.2
- Anderson-Bal ...6.5
- Nixon-Bos ...5.7
- Knoblauch-Min ...5.6

Fielding Runs-Infield
- Valentin-Mil ...21.3
- Espinoza-Cle ...15.8
- Gallego-NY ...15.7
- Fielder-Det ...15.5
- Gagne-KC ...13.4

Fielding Runs-Outfield
- Edmonds-Cal ...8.3
- Curtis-Cal ...7.3
- L.Johnson-Chi ...7.3
- Ward-Mil ...6.1
- Puckett-Min ...5.9

Wins
- Key-NY ...17
- Mussina-Bal ...16
- Cone-KC ...16
- McDonald-Bal ...14

Winning Pct.
- Bere-Chi ...857
- Key-NY ...810
- Clark-Cle ...786
- Mussina-Bal ...762
- Cone-KC ...762

Complete Games
- Johnson-Sea ...9
- Martinez-Cle ...8
- Finley-Cal ...8

Strikeouts
- Johnson-Sea ...204
- Clemens-Bos ...168
- Finley-Cal ...148
- Hentgen-Tor ...147
- Appier-KC ...145

Fewest BB/Game
- Gubicza-KC ...1.80
- Gullickson-Det ...1.95
- Wegman-Mil ...2.02
- Ontiveros-Oak ...2.03
- McDowell-Chi ...2.09

Games
- Wickman-NY ...53
- Mesa-Cle ...51
- Guthrie-Min ...50
- Brewer-KC ...50
- Willis-Min ...49

Saves
- L.Smith-Bal ...33
- Montgomery-KC ...27
- Aguilera-Min ...23
- Eckersley-Oak ...19
- Ayala-Sea ...18

Base Runners/9
- Ontiveros-Oak ...9.75
- Cone-KC ...10.01
- Clemens-Bos ...10.49
- Mussina-Bal ...10.51
- Wickman-NY ...10.54

Adjusted Relief Runs
- Eichhorn-Bal ...21.2
- Castillo-Tor ...16.9
- Plunk-Cle ...16.7
- Ryan-Bos ...13.4
- Howe-NY ...13.3

Relief Ranking
- Eichhorn-Bal ...30.1
- Plunk-Cle ...20.4
- Fetters-Mil ...19.6
- Ryan-Bos ...19.6
- Risley-Sea ...19.1

Innings Pitched
- Finley-Cal ...183.1
- McDowell-Chi ...181.0
- Eldred-Mil ...179.0
- Martinez-Cle ...176.2
- Mussina-Bal ...176.1

Opponents' Avg.
- Clemens-Bos ...203
- Cone-KC ...209
- Johnson-Sea ...216
- Ontiveros-Oak ...217
- Bere-Chi ...229

Opponents' OBP
- Ontiveros-Oak ...271
- Cone-KC ...277
- Clemens-Bos ...288
- Mussina-Bal ...291
- Martinez-Cle ...298

Earned Run Average
- Ontiveros-Oak ...2.65
- Clemens-Bos ...2.85
- Cone-KC ...2.94
- Mussina-Bal ...3.06
- Johnson-Sea ...3.19

Adjusted ERA
- Clemens-Bos ...177
- Cone-KC ...171
- Ontiveros-Oak ...169
- Mussina-Bal ...165
- Johnson-Sea ...155

Adjusted Starter Runs
- Cone-KC ...38.7
- Clemens-Bos ...38.5
- Mussina-Bal ...36.9
- Johnson-Sea ...34.0
- Bones-Mil ...27.7

Pitcher Wins
- Cone-KC ...4.3
- Mussina-Bal ...4.0
- Johnson-Sea ...3.5
- Clemens-Bos ...3.2
- Eichhorn-Bal ...3.0

Crossing the Rubicon

The high-velocity rhetoric started flying early in the year as owners tried to link revenue sharing to a salary cap in labor negotiations. Players steadfastly refused a cap, however. Milwaukee owner Bud Selig, now interim commissioner, was given total control over negotiations. Talks were fruitless, and the players went on strike on August 12. The season, including the post-season, was officially pronounced kaput on September 14.

Before the catastrophe, two new ballparks opened: Jacobs Field in Cleveland and the Ballpark in Arlington in Texas. Also new was baseball's revamped postseason format, which included three divisions in each league for the first time and a Wild Card postseason berth for the second place team with the best record.

Cleveland slugger Albert Belle was caught using a corked bat. Basketball superstar Michael Jordan, in what proved to be a temporary retirement from basketball, signed a minor league contract with White Sox. The glory of the NBA spent the summer struggling at Double-A, hitting only .202 and slugging .266 in his lone season in baseball. Goose Gossage, Kent Hrbek, Bo Jackson, and Jack Morris retired. Eighteen-year-old shortstop Alex Rodriguez debuted for Seattle.

Seattle's Ken Griffey Jr. led the league with 40 home runs and was close to a pace needed to break Roger Maris' revered record. Chicago's Frank Thomas (38) and Belle (36) were right behind Griffey. For all the immense damage it wrought, the strike saved baseball the embarrassment of a division champion 10 games under .500: the Rangers, who led the four-team West. Baseball's decision not to officially declare division champions robbed deserving AL leaders Chicago (Central) and New York (East) of titles. Cleveland, which had not reached the postseason since 1954, was the leading Wild Card team.

1993 National League

TEAM	W	L	T	PCT	GB	HW	HL	R	OR	PA	H	2B	3B	HR	BB	SO	HB	SH	AVG	OBP	SLG	OPS	AOPS	BR	ABR	PF	SB	CS	BSA	BSR
EAST																														
PHI	97	65	0	.599		52	29	877	740	6527	**1555**	297	51	156	**665**	1049	42	84	.274	**.351**	.426	777	115	121	**135**	98	91	32	74	9
MON	94	68	1	.580	3	**55**	26	732	682	6233	1410	270	36	122	542	860	48	100	.257	.326	.386	712	92	-23	-53	104	228	56	**80**	31
STL	87	75	0	.537	10	49	32	758	744	6279	1508	262	34	118	588	882	27	59	.272	.341	.395	736	103	35	40	99	153	72	68	8
CHI	84	78	1	.519	13	43	38	738	739	6216	1521	259	32	161	446	923	34	67	.270	.325	.414	739	103	17	23	99	100	43	70	7
PIT	75	87	0	.463	22	40	41	707	806	6268	1482	267	50	110	536	972	55	76	.267	.335	.393	728	100	17	23	99	92	55	63	1
FLA	64	98	0	.395	33	35	46	581	724	6125	1356	197	31	94	498	1054	51	58	.248	.314	.346	660	77	-128	-161	106	117	56	68	6
NY	59	103	0	.364	38	28	53	672	744	6056	1350	228	37	158	448	879	24	89	.248	.305	.390	695	91	-76	-67	99	79	50	61	0
WEST																														
ATL	104	58	0	.642		51	30	767	**559**	6234	1444	239	29	**169**	560	946	36	73	.262	.331	.408	739	101	27	10	102	125	48	72	11
SF	103	59	0	.636	1	50	31	808	636	6271	1534	269	33	168	516	930	46	102	.276	.340	**.427**	767	114	83	110	97	120	65	65	4
HOU	85	77	0	.525	19	44	37	716	630	6130	1459	288	37	138	497	911	40	82	.267	.340	.409	739	107	26	51	97	103	60	63	2
LA	81	81	0	.500	23	41	40	675	662	6261	1458	234	28	130	492	937	27	**107**	.261	.321	.383	704	98	-47	-8	95	126	61	67	6
CIN	73	89	0	.451	31	41	40	722	785	6163	1457	261	28	137	485	1025	32	63	.264	.324	.396	720	97	-12	-16	101	142	59	71	11
COL	67	95	0	.414	37	39	42	758	967	6073	1507	278	**59**	142	388	944	46	70	.273	.323	.422	745	89	26	-79	117	146	90	62	1
SD	61	101	0	.377	43	34	47	679	772	6135	1386	239	28	153	443	1046	**59**	80	.252	.312	.389	701	91	-60	-65	101	92	41	69	6
TOT	1135					602	532	10190		86971	20427	3588	513	1956	7104	13358	567	1110	.264	.327	.399	726					1714	788	69	101

TEAM	CG	SHO	GR	SV	IP	H	HR	BB	SO	BR/9	ERA	AERA	OAV	OOB	PR	APR	PF	OSB	OCS	FA	E	WPB	DP	FW	PW	BW	BSW	DIF
EAST																												
PHI	**24**	11	350	46	1472.2	1419	129	573	**1117**	12.4	3.95	100	.251	.322	14	1	98	101	49	.977	141	86	123	-.4	.0	**13.5**	.2	2.7
MON	8	7	385	**61**	1456.2	1369	119	521	934	12.0	3.55	118	.249	.317	80	98	103	172	51	.975	159	60	144	-1.4	9.8	-5.3	**2.4**	7.5
STL	5	7	423	54	1453.0	1553	152	**383**	775	12.3	4.09	98	.276	.324	-8	-10	100	112	54	.975	159	54	157	-1.4	-1.0	4.0	.0	4.4
CHI	8	5	422	56	1449.2	1514	153	470	905	12.6	4.18	96	.273	.332	-22	-24	100	84	69	.982	115	57	162	1.1	-2.4	2.3	-.0	2.0
PIT	12	5	384	34	1445.2	1557	153	485	832	13.0	4.77	86	.280	.339	-117	-110	101	148	51	.983	105	74	161	1.7	-11.0	1.4	-.6	2.5
FLA	4	5	409	48	1440.1	1437	135	598	945	12.9	4.13	106	.261	.334	-14	34	108	118	51	.980	125	114	130	.5	3.4	-16.1	-.1	-4.7
NY	16	8	297	22	1438.0	1483	139	434	867	12.3	4.05	99	.269	.324	-2	-7	99	143	56	.975	156	**36**	143	-1.3	-.7	-6.7	-.7	-12.6
WEST																												
ATL	18	**16**	353	46	1455.0	**1297**	101	480	1036	11.1	3.14	129	.240	.303	146	147	100	121	53	.983	108	59	146	1.5	**14.7**	1.0	.4	5.5
SF	4	9	414	50	1456.2	1385	168	442	982	11.6	3.61	109	.253	.313	69	52	97	**81**	66	**.984**	101	48	**169**	1.9	5.2	11.0	-.3	4.3
HOU	18	14	324	42	1441.1	1363	117	476	1056	11.7	3.49	111	.251	.313	88	63	96	110	42	.979	126	67	141	.5	6.3	5.1	-.5	-7.3
LA	17	9	346	36	1472.2	1406	103	567	1043	12.3	3.50	110	.254	.324	88	61	96	129	66	.979	133	64	141	.0	6.1	-.8	-.1	-5.2
CIN	11	8	375	37	1434.0	1510	158	508	996	12.9	4.51	89	.272	.336	-74	-77	100	134	56	.980	121	59	133	.8	-7.7	-1.6	.4	.2
COL	9	0	**453**	35	1431.1	1664	181	609	913	14.6	5.41	88	.294	.362	-218	-85	118	119	56	.973	167	93	149	-1.9	-8.5	-7.9	-.6	4.9
SD	8	6	397	32	1437.2	1470	148	558	957	12.9	4.23	98	.266	.334	-30	-15	102	142	68	.974	160	77	129	-1.5	-1.5	-6.5	-.1	-10.4
TOT	162	110	5332	599	20284.2					12.5	4.04		.264	.327						.978	1876	946	2028					

Batter-Fielder Wins		Batting Average		On-Base Percentage		Slugging Average		On-Base Plus Slugging		Adjusted OPS		Adjusted Batter Runs	
Bonds-SF	8.0	Galarraga-Col	.370	Bonds-SF	.458	Bonds-SF	.677	Bonds-SF	1136	Bonds-SF	207	Bonds-SF	89.9
Dykstra-Phi	5.6	Gwynn-SD	.358	Kruk-Phi	.430	Galarraga-Col	.602	Galarraga-Col	1005	Piazza-LA	155	Dykstra-Phi	47.8
Bell-Pit	5.4	Jefferies-StL	.342	Dykstra-Phi	.420	Williams-SF	.561	Piazza-LA	.932	Bagwell-Hou	146	Kruk-Phi	41.7
Wilkins-Chi	5.3	Bonds-SF	.336	Merced-Pit	.414	Piazza-LA	.561	McGriff-SD-Atl	.924	Kruk-Phi	145	Piazza-LA	40.2
Piazza-LA	5.3	Grace-Chi	.325	Jefferies-StL	.408	McGriff-SD-Atl	.549	Kruk-Phi	.905	Dykstra-Phi	144	Bagwell-Hou	36.3

Runs		Hits		Doubles		Triples		Home Runs		Total Bases		Runs Batted In	
Dykstra-Phi	143	Dykstra-Phi	194	Hayes-Col	45	Finley-Hou	13	Bonds-SF	46	Bonds-SF	365	Bonds-SF	123
Bonds-SF	129	Grace-Chi	193	Dykstra-Phi	44	Butler-LA	10	Justice-Atl	40	Williams-SF	325	Justice-Atl	120
Gant-Atl	113	Grissom-Mon	188	Bichette-Col	43	Morandini-Phi	9	Williams-SF	38	Gant-Atl	309	Gant-Atl	117
McGriff-SD-Atl	111	Bell-Pit	187	Gwynn-SD	41	Bell-Pit	9	McGriff-SD-Atl	37	Piazza-LA	307	Piazza-LA	112
Blauser-Atl	110	Jefferies-StL	186	Biggio-Hou	41			Gant-Atl	36	Dykstra-Phi	307	Williams-SF	110

Stolen Bases		Base Stealing Runs		Fielding Runs-Infield		Fielding Runs-Outfield		Wins		Winning Pct.		Complete Games	
Carr-Fla	58	Grissom-Mon	8.2	O.Smith-StL	23.4	Gonzalez-Hou	14.9	Glavine-Atl	22	Portugal-Hou	.818	Maddux-Atl	8
Grissom-Mon	53	Jefferies-StL	7.0	Bell-Pit	21.5	Plantier-SD	9.9	Burkett-SF	22	Greene-Phi	.800		
Nixon-Atl	47	DeShields-Mon	6.0	Lemke-Atl	18.4	Bichette-Col	9.1	Swift-SF	21	Glavine-Atl	.786		
Lewis-SF	46	Nixon-Atl	5.8	Thompson-SF	16.8	Merced-Pit	8.8	Maddux-Atl	20	Burkett-SF	.759		
Jefferies-StL	46	Davis-LA	5.5	Vizcaino-Chi	15.2	Carr-Fla	7.1			Avery-Atl	.750		

Strikeouts		Fewest BB/Game		Games		Saves		Base Runners/9		Adjusted Relief Runs		Relief Ranking	
Rijo-Cin	227	Tewksbury-StL	.84	Jackson-SF	81	Myers-SF	53	Harvey-Fla	7.57	Fassero-Mon	28.5	Wetteland-Mon	50.3
Smoltz-Atl	208	Arocha-StL	1.48	West-Phi	76	Beck-SF	48	Beck-SF	8.28	Wetteland-Mon	25.1	Harvey-Fla	36.1
Maddux-Atl	197	Burkett-SF	1.55	Beck-SF	76	Harvey-Fla	45	S.Fernandez-NY	9.10	McMichael-Atl	20.8	Fassero-Mon	29.4
Schilling-Phi	186	Avery-Atl	1.73	McMichael-Atl	74			Wetteland-Mon	9.28	Harvey-Fla	19.0	Gott-LA	27.2
Harnisch-Hou	185	Maddux-Atl	1.75					McMichael-Atl	9.52	P.Martinez-LA	16.5	Beck-SF	24.3

Innings Pitched		Opponents' Avg.		Opponents' OBP		Earned Run Average		Adjusted ERA		Adjusted Starter Runs		Pitcher Wins	
Maddux-Atl	267.0	Harnisch-Hou	.214	Maddux-Atl	.273	Maddux-Atl	2.36	Maddux-Atl	172	Maddux-Atl	46.6	**Maddux-Atl**	5.3
Rijo-Cin	257.1	Swift-SF	.226	Swift-SF	.277	Rijo-Cin	2.48	Rijo-Cin	162	Rijo-Cin	45.1	**Wetteland-Mon**	5.1
Smoltz-Atl	243.2	Rijo-Cin	.230	Rijo-Cin	.278	Portugal-Hou	2.77	Portugal-Hou	140	Swift-SF	28.1	**Rijo-Cin**	4.8
Glavine-Atl	239.1	Smoltz-Atl	.230	Mulholland-Phi	.282	Swift-SF	2.82	Swift-SF	139	Avery-Atl	27.3	**Swift-SF**	4.1
Drabek-Hou	237.2	Maddux-Atl	.232	Harnisch-Hou	.289	Avery-Atl	2.94	Avery-Atl	138	Portugal-Hou	25.4	**Harvey-Fla**	3.7

A Race for the Ages

The NL expanded for the first time since 1969, adding the Colorado Rockies and Florida Marlins. More than 80,000 watched Colorado's opener in Denver's Mile High Stadium as the Rockies went on to draw more than 4.4 million fans, shattering the individual club record. The Marlins also surpassed three million, propelling MLB to a new all-time record. Aided substantially by Denver's thin air, NL offense increased tremendously. Runs per game jumped 16 percent, and home runs per game were up 33 percent. Conspiracy theorists blamed their favorite chimera, a "juiced ball."

Cincinnati's problems continued as owner Marge Schott was suspended from daily activities for a year because of racist comments, and new Reds skipper Tony Perez was fired after only 44 games. Houston hired Bob Watson as baseball's second African-American general manager. Mets hurler Anthony Young lost 16 straight decisions and a record 27 straight over two years.

Dodgers stars Roy Campanella and Don Drysdale died, as did Johnny Mize. Dale Murphy retired in Colorado; Trevor Hoffman debuted in Florida.

In the last year before the Wild Card, the NL West experienced one of the greatest races ever. The Braves and Giants battled all season, both winning more than 100 games, and the clubs were tied going into the final day. The Braves beat the Rockies, meaning that the Giants knew as their game with the Dodgers began they had to beat their bitter rivals to force a one-game playoff. But Los Angeles overpowered San Francisco, 12-1, spoiling what had been a magical season for the Bay Area. Philadelphia edged out Montreal in the East, then upset the mighty Braves in six games in the NLCS. However, the fightin' Phils' mojo evaporated ten days later, north of the border, in the World Series against Toronto.

1993 American League

TEAM	W	L	T	PCT	GB	HW	HL	R	OR	PA	H	2B	3B	HR	BB	SO	HB	SH	AVG	OBP	SLG	OPS	AOPS	BR	ABR	PF	SB	CS	BSA	BSR
EAST																														
TOR	95	67	0	.586		48	33	847	742	6319	1556	317	42	159	588	861	52	46	**.279**	.350	**.436**	786	108	88	73	102	170	49	78	20
NY	88	74	0	.543	7	**50**	31	821	761	6359	**1568**	294	24	178	629	910	43	22	**.279**	.353	.435	788	**113**	96	120	97	39	35	53	
BAL	85	77	0	.525	10	48	33	786	745	6309	1470	287	24	157	655	930	41	49	.267	.346	.413	759	98	39	2	105	73	54	57	
DET	85	77	0	.525	10	44	37	**899**	837	6505	1546	282	38	178	**765**	1122	35	33	.275	**.362**	.434	**796**	113	124	123	100	104	63	62	
BOS	80	82	0	.494	15	43	38	686	698	6195	**1451**	319	29	114	508	871	**62**	80	.264	.330	.409	725	88	-39	-82	106	73	38	66	
CLE	76	86	0	.469	19	46	35	790	813	6267	1547	264	31	141	488	843	49	39	.275	.335	.409	744	99	-7	-9	100	159	55	74	11
MIL	69	93	0	.426	26	38	43	733	792	6222	1426	240	25	125	555	932	40	57	.258	.328	.378	706	90	-80	-73	99	138	93	60	
WEST																														
CHI	94	68	0	.580		45	36	776	**664**	6253	1454	228	**44**	162	604	**834**	33	72	.265	.338	.411	749	102	7	20	98	106	57	65	
TEX	86	76	0	.531	8	**50**	31	835	751	6166	1472	284	39	**181**	428	984	40	69	.267	.329	.431	760	105	15	40	97	113	67	63	
KC	84	78	0	.519	10	43	38	675	694	6101	1455	294	35	125	428	936	52	48	.263	.331	.397	717	85	-69	-112	107	100	75	57	
SEA	82	80	0	.506	12	46	35	734	731	6288	1429	272	24	161	624	901	56	63	.260	.339	.406	745	97	4	-12	102	91	68	57	
CAL	71	91	0	.438	23	44	37	684	770	6089	1399	259	24	114	564	930	38	50	.260	.331	.380	711	88	-63	-85	103	169	100	63	
MIN	71	91	0	.438	23	36	45	693	830	6209	1480	261	27	121	493	850	51	27	.264	.327	.385	712	90	-72	-79	101	83	59	58	
OAK	68	94	0	.420	26	38	43	715	846	6293	1408	260	21	158	622	1048	33	46	.254	.330	.394	724	99	-43	-3	95	131	59	69	30
TOT	1134					619	515	10674		87575	20661	3861	427	2074	8006	12952	633	701	.267	.337	.408	745					1549	872	64	

TEAM	CG	SHO	GR	SV	IP	H	HR	BB	SO	BR/9	ERA	AERA	OAV	OOB	PR	APR	PF	OSB	OCS	FA	E	WPB	DP	FW	PW	BW	BSW	DIP
EAST																												
TOR	11	11	344	**50**	1441.1	1441	134	620	1023	13.1	4.21	104	.261	.336	18	25	101	136	64	.982	107	89	144	.5	2.4	7.1	**1.7**	2.
NY	11	**13**	332	38	1438.1	1467	170	552	899	12.8	4.35	96	.266	.333	-5	-29	97	115	47	.983	105	**40**	166	.6	-2.8	11.7	-.6	-1.
BAL	21	10	329	42	1442.2	1591	162	579	900	12.8	4.31	105	.261	.333	2	30	104	96	64	.984	100	47	171	.9	2.9	.2	-.5	-2.
DET	11	7	375	36	1436.2	1547	188	542	828	13.4	4.65	93	.276	.342	-52	-49	101	102	57	.979	132	53	148	-1.0	-4.8	**12.0**	-.2	-2.
BOS	9	11	389	44	1452.1	**1379**	127	552	997	**12.3**	3.77	**122**	**.252**	**.322**	88	**128**	107	92	44	.980	122	53	155	-.4	**12.5**	-8.0	.0	-5.
CLE	7	8	410	45	1445.2	1591	182	591	888	13.8	4.58	95	.281	.351	-41	-33	101	113	68	.976	148	50	174	-1.9	-3.2	-.9	-1.3	-.
MIL	**26**	6	353	29	1447.0	1511	153	522	810	13.0	4.45	97	.271	.336	-21	-24	100	115	51	.979	131	57	148	-.9	-2.3	-7.1	-.4	-1.
WEST																												
CHI	16	11	322	48	1454.0	1398	125	566	974	12.4	**3.70**	114	.255	.328	100	83	97	**82**	**82**	.982	112	66	153	.2	8.1	1.9	.0	2.
TEX	20	6	359	45	1438.1	1476	144	562	957	13.0	4.28	98	.267	.337	6	-16	97	95	67	.979	132	70	145	-1.0	-1.6	3.9	-.2	3.
KC	16	6	303	48	1445.1	**1379**	**105**	571	985	12.4	4.04	114	.254	.327	45	84	107	119	71	.984	97	91	150	1.0	8.2	**-10.9**	-.6	5.
SEA	22	10	353	41	1453.2	1421	135	605	**1083**	13.1	4.20	106	.259	.337	20	40	103	105	68	**.985**	120	65	161	**1.5**	3.9	-1.2	-.6	-4.
CAL	**26**	6	320	41	1430.1	1482	153	550	843	13.1	4.34	104	.270	.339	-3	28	105	122	52	.984	100	64	160	.4	-4.8	-7.7	-.4	2.
MIN	5	3	356	44	1444.1	1591	148	**514**	901	13.4	4.71	93	.283	.344	-63	-49	102	137	66	.984	100	64	169	-.7	-8.3	-.0	-.4	1.
OAK	8	2	**424**	42	1452.1	1551	157	680	864	14.1	4.90	84	.276	.356	-94	-131	96	120	71	.982	111	54	161	.2	-12.7	-.3	.5	-.
TOT	209	110	4969	593	20222.1					13.0	4.32		.267	.337						.981	1607	892	2209					

Batter-Fielder Wins		Batting Average		On-Base Percentage		Slugging Average		On-Base Plus Slugging		Adjusted OPS		Adjusted Batter Runs	
Olerud-Tor	5.7	Olerud-Tor	.363	Olerud-Tor	.473	Gonzalez-Tex	.632	Olerud-Tor	1072	Olerud-Tor	184	Olerud-Tor	.75..
Hoiles-Bal	5.3	Molitor-Tor	.332	Phillips-Det	.443	Griffey-Sea	.617	Thomas-Chi	1033	Thomas-Chi	179	Thomas-Chi	.66..
Griffey-Sea	5.1	Alomar-Tor	.326	Henderson-Oak-Tor	.432	Thomas-Chi	.607	Griffey-Sea	1025	Griffey-Sea	169	Griffey-Sea	.58..
Palmeiro-Tex	4.8	Lofton-Cle	.325	Thomas-Chi	.426	Olerud-Tor	.599	Hoiles-Bal	1001	Gonzalez-Tex	169	Gonzalez-Tex	48
Henderson-Oak-Tor	4.5	Baerga-Cle	.321	Hoiles-Bal	.416	Hoiles-Bal	.585	Gonzalez-Tex	1000	Hoiles-Bal	159	Palmeiro-Tex	.43..

Runs		Hits		Doubles		Triples		Home Runs		Total Bases		Runs Batted In	
Palmeiro-Tex	124	Molitor-Tor	211	Olerud-Tor	54	Johnson-Chi	14	Gonzalez-Tex	46	Griffey-Sea	359	Belle-Cle	12.
Molitor-Tor	121	Olerud-Tor	200	White-Tor	42	Cora-Chi	13	Griffey-Sea	45	Gonzalez-Tex	339	Thomas-Chi	12.
White-Tor	116	Baerga-Cle	200	Valentin-Bos	40	Hulse-Tex	10	Thomas-Chi	41	Thomas-Chi	333	Carter-Tor	12.
Lofton-Cle	116	Alomar-Tor	192	Palmeiro-Tex	40	McRae-KC	9	Belle-Cle	38	Palmeiro-Tex	331	Gonzalez-Tex	11.
Henderson-Oak-Tor	114	Lofton-Cle	185	Puckett-Min	39	Fernandez-Tor	9	Palmeiro-Tex	37	Olerud-Tor	330	Fielder-Det	11.

Stolen Bases		Base Stealing Runs		Fielding Runs-Infield		Fielding Runs-Outfield		Wins		Winning Pct.		Complete Games	
Lofton-Cle	70	Lofton-Cle	10.5	Gallego-NY	26.2	Kirby-Cle	14.1	McDowell-Chi	22	Key-NY	.750	Finley-Cal	1.
Polonia-Cal	55	Henderson-Oak-Tor	8.9	Boggs-NY	21.3	Hamilton-Mil	10.7	Johnson-Sea	19	Johnson-Sea	.704	Brown-Tex	1.
Alomar-Tor	55	Alomar-Tor	6.8	Vizquel-Sea	19.7	Belle-Cle	10.6	Hentgen-Tor	19	Appier-KC	.692	McDowell-Chi	..
Henderson-Oak-Tor	53	White-Tor	6.1	Joyner-KC	19.2	McLemore-Bal	9.0			McDowell-Chi	.688	Johnson-Sea	..
Curtis-Cal	48	Johnson-Chi	5.3	Whitaker-Det	18.3	Mack-Min	8.9			Hentgen-Tor	.679	Eldred-Mil	..

Strikeouts		Fewest BB/Game		Games		Saves		Base Runners/9		Adjusted Relief Runs		Relief Ranking	
Johnson-Sea	308	Key-NY	1.64	Harris-Bos	80	Montgomery-KC	45	Montgomery-KC	9.27	Montgomery-KC	22.1	Montgomery-KC	44
Langston-Cal	196	Darwin-Bos	1.92	Radinsky-Chi	73	Montgomery-KC	45	Aguilera-Min	9.33	D.Ward-Tor	18.5	D.Ward-Tor	31
Guzman-Tor	194	Wells-Det	2.02	D.Ward-Tor	71	Henke-Tex	40	D.Ward-Tor	9.42	Hernandez-Chi	17.8	Hernandez-Chi	29
Cone-KC	191	Tapani-Min	2.27	Nelson-Sea	71	Hernandez-Chi	38	Darwin-Bos	9.73	Lilliquist-Cle	14.0	Henke-Tex	23
Finley-Cal	187	Doherty-Det	2.34	Fossas-Bos	71	Eckersley-Oak	36	Hernandez-Chi	9.84	Mills-Bal	13.7	Lilliquist-Cle	..

Innings Pitched		Opponents' Avg.		Opponents' OBP		Earned Run Average		Adjusted ERA		Adjusted Starter Runs		Pitcher Wins	
Eldred-Mil	258.0	Johnson-Sea	.203	Darwin-Bos	.272	Appier-KC	2.56	Appier-KC	180	Appier-KC	50.6	**Appier-KC**	5.
McDowell-Chi	256.2	Appier-KC	.212	Appier-KC	.279	Alvarez-Chi	2.95	Viola-Bos	148	Langston-Cal	37.0	**Montgomery-KC**	..
Langston-Cal	256.1	Cone-KC	.223	Key-NY	.279	Key-NY	3.00	Finley-Cal	144	Johnson-Sea	34.7	**Langston-Cal**	3.
Johnson-Sea	255.1	McDonald-Bal	.228	Johnson-Sea	.290	Fernandez-Chi	3.13	Alvarez-Chi	143	Cone-KC	33.4	**Finley-Cal**	3.
Cone-KC	254.0	Bosio-Sea	.229	Langston-Cal	.295	Viola-Bos	3.14	Darwin-Bos	142	Darwin-Bos	33.4	**Darwin-Bos**	3.

Walk-Off to the North

Tragedy struck in spring training as Cleveland pitchers Tim Crews and Steve Olin were killed in a boating accident. Indians hurler Bob Ojeda also was badly hurt in the crash. Cliff Young, another Cleveland pitcher, died in a truck accident in November. Also passing were second baseman Charlie Gehringer and catcher Bill Dickey, both Hall of Famers, and Royals owner Ewing Kauffman. It was the last season for George Brett, Robin Yount, Carlton Fisk and Nolan Ryan, all future Hall of Famers.

On the bright side, Bo Jackson made a remarkable comeback from hip replacement surgery, hitting 16 homers for the White Sox. Minnesota's Dave Winfield collected his 3,000th hit. Toronto first baseman John Olerud carried a .400 batting average into August; Olerud, Paul Molitor, and Roberto Alomar finished 1-2-3 in the batting race, a first for teammates. Outfielders Shawn Green (Blue Jays) and Jim Edmonds (Angels) began their careers.

Toronto in the East and Chicago in the West were runaway division winners. The visiting team won the first four games of the ALCS before Toronto finally won at home in Game 5. The Jays then won their second straight AL pennant by scoring runs in the top of the ninth inning of Game 6. Alomar and Molitor were the hitting stars in an offensively-charged World Series against the Phillies, but it was Joe Carter's dramatic walk-off home run against "Wild Thing" Mitch Williams in the bottom of the ninth inning in Game 6 that gave the Jays their second consecutive world championship.

Ominously, Congress considered legislation that would take away baseball's exemption from antitrust laws as dark storm clouds gathered on the labor front. The silver lining was that the exciting 1993 season was played to completion in front of a record number of fans.

1992 National League

TEAM	W	L	T	PCT	GB	HW	HL	R	OR	PA	H	2B	3B	HR	BB	SO	HB	SH	AVG	OBP	SLG	OPS	AOPS	BR	ABR	PF	SB	CS	BSA	BSR
EAST																														
PIT	96	66	0	.593		**53**	28	**693**	595	6266	1409	272	**54**	106	569	872	25	89	.255	.324	.381	705	105	50	**53**	100	110	53	67	6
MON	87	75	0	.537	9	43	38	648	581	6120	1381	263	37	102	463	976	43	82	.252	.313	.370	683	100	-3	1	99	196	63	76	21
STL	83	79	0	.512	12	45	36	631	604	6230	**1464**	263	44	94	495	996	32	68	**.262**	.323	.375	698	107	30	46	98	**208**	118	64	4
CHI	78	84	0	.481	18	43	38	593	624	6156	1420	221	41	104	417	**816**	31	78	.254	.307	.364	671	92	-35	-52	103	77	51	60	-1
NY	72	90	0	.444	24	41	40	599	653	6059	1254	259	17	93	**572**	956	28	74	.235	.310	.342	652	91	-50	-45	99	129	52	71	10
PHI	70	92	0	.432	26	41	40	686	717	6171	1392	255	36	118	509	1059	52	64	.253	.320	.377	697	103	28	28	100	127	31	**80**	17
WEST																														
ATL	98	64	0	.605		51	30	682	**569**	6142	1391	223	48	**138**	493	924	26	93	.254	.316	**.388**	704	99	32	-7	106	126	60	68	7
CIN	90	72	0	.556	8	**53**	28	660	609	6162	1418	**281**	44	99	563	888	21	66	.260	**.328**	.382	**710**	104	**61**	43	103	125	65	66	5
SD	82	80	0	.506	16	45	36	617	636	6074	1396	255	30	135	453	864	26	78	.255	.313	.386	699	101	23	12	102	69	52	57	-3
HOU	81	81	0	.500	17	47	34	608	668	6162	1350	255	38	96	506	1025	48	88	.254	.313	.359	672	100	-19	6	96	139	54	72	12
SF	72	90	0	.444	26	42	39	574	647	6070	1330	220	36	105	435	1067	39	101	.244	.302	.355	657	96	-60	-30	95	112	64	64	2
LA	63	99	0	.389	35	37	44	548	636	6037	1333	201	34	72	503	899	24	**102**	.248	.313	.339	652	92	-57	-51	99	142	78	65	4
TOT	972					541	431	7539		73649	16538	2967	459	1262	5978	11342	395	983	.252	.315	.368	684					1560	741	68	84

TEAM	CG	SHO	GR	SV	IP	H	HR	BB	SO	BR/9	ERA	AERA	OAV	OOB	PR	APR	PF	OSB	OCS	FA	E	WPB	DP	FW	PW	BW	BSW	DIF
EAST																												
PIT	20	20	354	43	1479.2	1410	101	455	844	11.5	3.35	103	.254	.312	25	19	99	124	73	.984	101	63	144	.9	2.0	**5.7**	-.1	6.5
MON	11	14	349	49	1468.0	**1296**	92	525	1014	11.5	3.25	107	**.238**	.309	41	38	99	199	68	.980	124	57	113	-.4	4.1	.1	**1.5**	.7
STL	10	9	**424**	47	1480.0	1405	118	**400**	842	**11.2**	3.38	101	.252	**.303**	20	6	98	124	39	**.985**	94	49	146	**1.3**	.6	5.0	-.3	-4.6
CHI	16	11	372	37	1469.0	1337	107	575	901	12.0	3.39	107	.246	.320	18	36	103	116	72	.982	114	82	142	.2	3.9	-5.6	-.9	-.6
NY	17	13	333	34	1446.2	1404	98	482	1025	12.0	3.66	96	.256	.318	-25	-26	100	148	67	.981	116	44	134	.0	-2.8	-4.8	.3	-1.7
PHI	**27**	7	323	34	1428.0	1387	113	549	851	12.4	4.11	85	.257	.325	-96	-96	100	111	53	.978	131	56	128	-.8	-10.3	3.0	1.1	-4.0
WEST																												
ATL	26	**24**	338	41	1460.0	1321	89	489	948	11.3	**3.14**	**116**	.242	.305	58	**80**	104	149	66	.982	109	71	121	.4	**8.6**	-.8	.0	8.7
CIN	9	11	357	**55**	1449.2	1362	109	470	**1060**	11.5	3.46	104	.251	.312	6	21	103	104	54	.984	96	62	128	1.2	2.3	4.6	-.2	1.2
SD	9	11	363	46	1461.1	1444	111	439	971	11.7	3.56	101	.261	.315	-9	4	102	141	69	.982	115	27	127	.0	.4	1.3	-1.1	.3
HOU	5	12	422	45	1459.1	1386	114	539	978	12.1	3.72	91	.252	.310	-35	-56	97	129	54	.981	114	58	125	.2	-6.0	.6	.5	4.7
SF	9	12	386	30	1461.0	1385	128	502	927	11.8	3.61	92	.253	.318	-17	-48	95	74	64	.982	113	50	174	.2	-5.2	-3.2	-.5	-.3
LA	18	13	353	29	1438.0	1401	**82**	553	981	12.4	3.41	102	.257	.326	15	9	99	141	62	.972	174	84	136	-3.2	1.0	-5.5	-.3	-9.9
TOT	177	157	4374	490	17500.2					11.8	3.50		.252	.315						.981	1401	703	1618					

Batter-Fielder Wins		Batting Average		On-Base Percentage		Slugging Average		On-Base Plus Slugging		Adjusted OPS		Adjusted Batter Runs	
Bonds-Pit	7.9	Sheffield-SD	.330	Bonds-Pit	.456	Bonds-Pit	.624	Bonds-Pit	1080	Bonds-Pit	205	Bonds-Pit	75.1
Sheffield-SD	6.0	VanSlyke-Pit	.324	Kruk-Phi	.423	Sheffield-SD	.580	Sheffield-SD	.965	Sheffield-SD	168	Sheffield-SD	49.0
Sandberg-Chi	5.6	Kruk-Phi	.323	Butler-LA	.413	McGriff-SD	.556	McGriff-SD	.950	McGriff-SD	164	McGriff-SD	47.4
Larkin-Cin	5.5	Roberts-Cin	.323	McGriff-SD	.394	Daulton-Phi	.524	Daulton-Phi	.908	Daulton-Phi	156	VanSlyke-Pit	41.5
Daulton-Phi	4.8	Gwynn-SD	.317	Roberts-Cin	.393	Sandberg-Chi	.510	VanSlyke-Pit	.886	Clark-SF	152	Kruk-Phi	40.0

Runs		Hits		Doubles		Triples		Home Runs		Total Bases		Runs Batted In	
Bonds-Pit	109	VanSlyke-Pit	199	VanSlyke-Pit	45	Sanders-Atl	14	McGriff-SD	35	Sheffield-SD	323	Daulton-Phi	109
Hollins-Phi	104	Pendleton-Atl	199	Lankford-StL	40	Finley-Hou	13	Bonds-Pit	34	Sandberg-Chi	312	Pendleton-Atl	105
VanSlyke-Pit	103	Sandberg-Chi	186	Duncan-Phi	40	VanSlyke-Pit	12	Sheffield-SD	33	VanSlyke-Pit	310	McGriff-SD	104
Sandberg-Chi	100	Grace-Chi	185	Clark-SF	40	Butler-LA	11	Hollins-Phi	27	Pendleton-Atl	303	Bonds-Pit	103
Grissom-Mon	99	Sheffield-SD	184			Alicea-StL	11	Daulton-Phi	27			Sheffield-SD	100

Stolen Bases		Base Stealing Runs		Fielding Runs-Infield		Fielding Runs-Outfield		Wins		Winning Pct.		Complete Games	
Grissom-Mon	78	Grissom-Mon	12.6	Thompson-SF	25.5	Jackson-SD	14.4	Maddux-Chi	20	Tewksbury-StL	.762	Mulholland-Phi	12
DeShields-Mon	46	Finley-Hou	6.5	Wallach-Mon	18.7	Gonzalez-Hou	13.5	Glavine-Atl	20	Glavine-Atl	.714	Schilling-Phi	10
Roberts-Cin	44	O.Smith-StL	6.3	Sharperson-LA	18.2	Sanders-Cin	10.7			Leibrandt-Atl	.682	Drabek-Pit	10
Finley-Hou	44	Bonds-Pit	5.8	Harris-LA	15.8	Nixon-Atl	9.5			Morgan-Chi	.667	Smoltz-Atl	9
O.Smith-StL	43	DeShields-Mon	4.9	O.Smith-StL	15.8	O'Neill-Cin	9.2			Maddux-Chi	.645	Maddux-Chi	9

Strikeouts		Fewest BB/Game		Games		Saves		Base Runners/9		Adjusted Relief Runs		Relief Ranking	
Smoltz-Atl	215	Tewksbury-StL	1.77	Boever-Hou	81	L.Smith-StL	43	Beck-SF	7.73	Rojas-Mon	23.4	D.Jones-Hou	36.1
Cone-NY	214	Cormier-StL	1.60	D.Jones-Hou	80	Myers-SD	38	Schilling-Phi	8.95	D.Jones-Hou	18.0	Rojas-Mon	20.9
Maddux-Chi	199	Swindell-Cin	1.73	Perez-StL	77	Wetteland-Mon	37	Tewksbury-StL	9.27	Beck-SF	16.9	Perez-StL	18.2
Fernandez-NY	193	Mulholland-Phi	1.81	Hernandez-Hou	77	D.Jones-Hou	36	D.Jones-Hou	9.51	Perez-StL	15.7	Beck-SF	15.5
Drabek-Pit	177	Tomlin-Pit	1.81	Innis-NY	76	M.Williams-Phi	29	Rojas-Mon	9.57	Hernandez-Hou	15.3	Hernandez-Hou	14.1

Innings Pitched		Opponents' Avg.		Opponents' OBP		Earned Run Average		Adjusted ERA		Adjusted Starter Runs		Pitcher Wins	
Maddux-Chi	268.0	Schilling-Phi	.201	Schilling-Phi	.253	Swift-SF	2.08	Maddux-Chi	166	Maddux-Chi	43.9	**Maddux-Chi**	6.0
Drabek-Pit	256.2	Maddux-Chi	.210	Tewksbury-StL	.265	Tewksbury-StL	2.16	Swift-SF	160	Tewksbury-StL	32.4	**D.Jones-Hou**	3.9
Smoltz-Atl	246.2	Fernandez-NY	.210	Martinez-Mon	.271	Maddux-Chi	2.18	Tewksbury-StL	158	Schilling-Phi	28.2	**Schilling-Phi**	3.0
Morgan-Chi	240.0	Martinez-Mon	.211	Maddux-Chi	.272	Schilling-Phi	2.35	Schilling-Phi	150	Morgan-Chi	26.3	**Glavine-Atl**	3.0
Avery-Atl	233.2	Cone-NY	.223	Fernandez-NY	.273	Martinez-Mon	2.47	Morgan-Chi	142	Swift-SF	24.7	**Rijo-Cin**	3.0

Pirates Leave Their Heart with Francisco

Commissioner Fay Vincent announced his plan to realign the divisions, which would have put Atlanta and Cincinnati in the East and St. Louis and Chicago in the West, making the layout geographical. The Reds and Cubs vehemently opposed the move, which was later blocked by a U.S. District Court judge. That debacle, combined with an inability to break the union, sealed the commish's fate as owners voted 18-9 to fire Vincent, who finally resigned in September. One of Vincent's most outspoken critics was Milwaukee owner Bud Selig, who effectively became commissioner as chair of the owners' Executive Council. Owners also prevented the Giants from moving to Tampa-St. Petersburg.

The Reds were in turmoil again, with skipper Lou Piniella and reliever Rob Dibble fighting in the clubhouse, and owner Marge Schott accused of making anti-Semitic remarks. Pedro Martinez and Mike Piazza, debuted for the Dodgers in September, while Gary Carter, Jack Clark and Pedro Guerrero called it a career. Hall of Fame second baseman Billy Herman passed away. Philadelphia's Mickey Morandini turned the league's first unassisted triple play since 1927.

Barry Bonds won his second MVP award and led the Pirates and an unheralded mound staff to a third consecutive East title. Atlanta, with strong starters and a mix-and-match bullpen, took its second straight West crown. The Braves again eliminated Pittsburgh in a thrilling seven-game NLCS. The Braves were down 2-0 in the last of the ninth of Game 7. But the Pirates fell apart on the hill and in the field, and Sid Bream slid in with the winning run with two outs on pinch hitter Francisco Cabrera's two-run single. After this emotional peak, however, Atlanta lost the World Series again, this time to Toronto in six games.

1992 American League

TEAM	W	L	T	PCT	GB	HW	HL	R	OR	PA	H	2B	3B	HR	BB	SO	HB	SH	AVG	OBP	SLG	OPS	AOPS	BR	ABR	PF	SB	CS	BSA	BSR
EAST																														
TOR	96	66	0	.593		53	28	780	682	6224	1458	265	40	163	561	933	47	26	.263	.333	**.414**	747	103	63	27	105	129	39	77	15
MIL	92	70	0	.568	4	53	28	740	604	6181	1477	272	35	82	511	779	33	61	.268	.330	.375	705	98	-11	-1	99	256	115	69	16
BAL	89	73	0	.549	7	43	38	705	656	6292	1423	243	36	148	647	827	51	50	.259	.340	.398	738	103	56	32	103	89	48	65	3
NY	76	86	0	.469	20	41	40	733	746	6252	1462	281	18	163	536	903	42	26	.261	.328	.406	734	104	35	36	100	78	37	68	4
CLE	76	86	0	.469	20	41	40	674	746	6199	1495	227	24	127	448	885	45	42	.266	.323	.383	706	99	-27	-19	99	144	67	68	8
DET	75	87	0	.463	21	38	42	791	794	6310	1411	256	16	182	675	1055	24	43	.256	.337	.407	744	106	65	54	101	66	45	59	-1
BOS	73	89	0	.451	23	44	37	599	669	6186	1343	259	21	84	591	865	31	60	.246	.321	.347	668	81	-83	-125	107	44	48	48	-7
WEST																														
OAK	96	66	0	.593		51	30	745	672	6274	1389	219	24	142	707	831	49	72	.258	**.346**	.386	732	110	55	93	95	143	59	71	11
MIN	90	72	0	.556	6	48	33	747	653	6267	1544	275	27	104	527	834	53	46	.277	.341	.391	732	101	47	19	104	123	74	62	1
CHI	86	76	0	.531	10	50	32	738	690	6267	1434	269	36	110	622	784	31	56	.261	.336	.383	719	102	21	26	99	160	57	74	15
TEX	77	85	0	.475	19	36	45	682	753	6238	1387	266	23	159	550	1036	50	56	.250	.321	.393	714	102	-5	17	97	81	44	65	2
KC	72	90	0	.444	24	44	37	610	667	6082	1411	284	42	75	439	741	51	45	.256	.315	.364	679	87	-74	-94	103	131	71	65	4
CAL	72	90	0	.444	24	41	40	579	671	5916	1306	202	20	88	416	882	40	56	.243	.301	.338	639	78	-158	-164	101	160	101	61	0
SEA	64	98	0	.395	32	38	43	679	799	6179	1466	278	24	149	474	841	38	52	.263	.323	.402	725	101	13	5	101	100	55	65	3
TOT	1134					621	513	9802		86867	20006	3596	386	1776	7704	12196	585	682	.259	.328	.385	713					1704	860	66	74

TEAM	CG	SHO	GR	SV	IP	H	HR	BB	SO	BR/9	ERA	AERA	OAV	OOB	PR	APR	PF	OSB	OCS	FA	E	WPB	DP	FW	PW	BW	BSW	DIF
EAST																												
TOR	18	14	284	49	1440.2	1346	124	541	954	12.1	3.91	105	.248	.318	5	29	104	144	63	.985	93	81	109	1.4	3.0	2.7	1.0	6.9
MIL	19	14	338	39	1457.0	**1344**	127	**435**	793	**11.3**	**3.43**	113	**.246**	.316	82	71	98	96	53	**.986**	89	42	146	1.6	7.2	-.1	**1.1**	1.2
BAL	20	**16**	290	48	1464.0	1419	124	518	846	12.1	3.79	107	.256	.322	25	43	103	131	44	.985	93	60	168	1.4	4.4	3.3	-.2	-.8
NY	20	9	308	44	1452.2	1453	129	612	851	13.0	4.21	94	.263	.338	-43	-42	100	164	62	.982	114	68	165	.2	-4.3	3.7	-.1	-4.5
CLE	13	7	379	46	1470.0	1507	159	566	890	12.9	4.11	96	.268	.336	-28	-29	100	109	64	.978	141	62	176	.1	-3.0	-1.9	.3	-.9
DET	10	4	355	36	1435.2	1534	155	564	693	13.3	4.60	87	.277	.343	-105	-96	101	102	65	.981	116	65	164	.1	-9.8	5.5	-.6	-1.2
BOS	22	13	328	39	1448.2	1403	107	535	943	12.3	3.58	118	.255	.323	57	98	108	114	51	.978	139	58	170	-1.2	10.0	-12.7	-1.3	-2.9
WEST																												
OAK	8	9	**400**	**58**	1447.0	1396	129	601	843	12.7	3.73	101	.256	.331	34	7	96	118	76	.979	125	75	158	-.4	.7	9.5	.6	4.6
MIN	16	13	323	50	1453.0	1391	121	479	923	11.8	3.70	110	.254	.316	38	58	104	152	60	.985	95	66	155	1.3	5.9	1.9	-.4	.3
CHI	21	5	292	52	1461.2	1400	123	550	810	12.3	3.82	107	.251	.323	19	9	98	120	57	.979	129	48	134	-.6	.9	2.6	1.0	1.2
TEX	19	3	359	42	1460.1	1471	113	598	**1034**	13.0	4.09	93	.264	.337	-24	-45	97	**87**	**84**	.975	154	91	153	-2.0	-4.6	1.7	-.3	1.2
KC	9	12	340	44	1447.1	1426	**106**	512	834	12.3	3.81	107	.259	.323	21	41	104	107	52	.980	122	56	164	-.2	4.2	-9.6	-.1	-3.3
CAL	**26**	13	297	42	1446.0	1449	130	532	888	12.6	3.84	104	.264	.331	16	27	102	120	70	.979	134	47	172	-.9	2.7	-16.7	-.5	6.4
SEA	21	9	372	30	1445.0	1467	129	661	894	13.6	4.55	88	.266	.348	-97	-87	102	140	62	.982	112	70	170	.3	-8.9	.5	-.2	-8.8
TOT	242	141	4665	619	20329.0					12.5	3.94		.259	.328						.981	1656	889	2204					

Batter-Fielder Wins		Batting Average		On-Base Percentage		Slugging Average		On-Base Plus Slugging		Adjusted OPS		Adjusted Batter Runs	
Ventura-Chi	5.1	E.Martinez-Sea	343	Thomas-Chi	439	McGwire-Oak	585	Thomas-Chi	975	McGwire-Oak	178	Thomas-Chi	66.4
E.Martinez-Sea	4.9	Puckett-Min	329	Tartabull-NY	409	E.Martinez-Sea	544	McGwire-Oak	970	Thomas-Chi	175	McGwire-Oak	51.0
R.Henderson-Oak	4.5	Thomas-Chi	323	Alomar-Tor	405	Thomas-Chi	536	E.Martinez-Sea	948	E.Martinez-Sea	162	E.Martinez-Sea	45.4
Thomas-Chi	4.4	Molitor-Mil	320	E.Martinez-Sea	404	Griffey-Sea	535	Tartabull-NY	898	Tartabull-NY	151	R.Henderson-Oak	36.4
Baerga-Cle	3.7	Mack-Min	315	Mack-Min	394	Gonzalez-Tex	529	Griffey-Sea	896	Griffey-Sea	147	Molitor-Mil	35.7

Runs		Hits		Doubles		Triples		Home Runs		Total Bases		Runs Batted In	
Phillips-Det	114	Puckett-Min	210	Thomas-Chi	46	Johnson-Chi	12	Gonzalez-Tex	43	Puckett-Min	313	Fielder-Det	124
Thomas-Chi	108	Baerga-Cle	205	E.Martinez-Sea	46	Devereaux-Bal	11	McGwire-Oak	42	Carter-Tor	310	Carter-Tor	119
Alomar-Tor	105	Molitor-Mil	195	Yount-Mil	40	Anderson-Bal	10	Fielder-Det	35	Gonzalez-Tex	309	Thomas-Chi	115
Puckett-Min	104	Mack-Min	189	Mattingly-NY	40	Raines-Chi	9	Carter-Tor	34	Thomas-Chi	307	Belle-Cle	112
Knoblauch-Min	104	Thomas-Chi	185	Griffey-Sea	39			Belle-Cle	34	Devereaux-Bal	303	Bell-Chi	112

Stolen Bases		Base Stealing Runs		Fielding Runs-Infield		Fielding Runs-Outfield		Wins		Winning Pct.		Complete Games	
Lofton-Cle	66	Lofton-Cle	10.3	Reed-Bos	30.4	Raines-Chi	9.6	Morris-Tor	21	Mussina-Bal	783	McDowell-Chi	13
Listach-Mil	54	Raines-Chi	7.8	Ventura-Chi	26.1	Wilson-Oak	8.1	Brown-Tex	21	Morris-Tor	778	Clemens-Bos	11
Anderson-Bal	53	Alomar-Tor	7.6	Gagne-Min	19.3	White-Tor	7.3	McDowell-Chi	20	Guzman-Tor	762	Brown-Tex	11
Polonia-Cal	51	White-Tor	6.7	Sojo-Cal	14.4	Lofton-Cle	7.0	Mussina-Bal	18	Bosio-Mil	727	Perez-NY	11
Alomar-Tor	49	R.Henderson-Oak	6.7	Gaetti-Cal	13.7	Anderson-Bal	5.4	Clemens-Bos	18	McDowell-Chi	667	Nagy-Cle	10

Strikeouts		Fewest BB/Game		Games		Saves		Base Runners/9		Adjusted Relief Runs		Relief Ranking	
Johnson-Sea	241	Bosio-Mil	1.71	Rogers-Tex	81	Eckersley-Oak	51	Eckersley-Oak	8.32	D.Ward-Tor	22.0	Eckersley-Oak	35.7
Perez-NY	218	Mussina-Bal	1.79	D.Ward-Tor	79	Aguilera-Min	41	Lilliquist-Cle	8.61	Eckersley-Oak	18.3	Olin-Cle	29.8
Clemens-Bos	208	Wegman-Mil	1.89	Olin-Cle	72	Montgomery-KC	39	Hernandez-Chi	8.75	Harris-Bos	17.9	J.Russell-Tex-Oak	28.1
Guzman-Tex	179	Tapani-Min	1.96	Lilliquist-Cle	71	Olson-Bal	36	Eldred-Mil	9.06	Hernandez-Chi	17.7	Hernandez-Chi	27.3
McDowell-Chi	178	Gullickson-Det	2.03	Harris-Bos	70	Henke-Tor	34	Willis-Min	9.53	Frohwirth-Bal	17.4	D.Ward-Tor	25.8

Innings Pitched		Opponents' Avg.		Opponents' OBP		Earned Run Average		Adjusted ERA		Adjusted Starter Runs		Pitcher Wins	
Brown-Tex	265.2	Johnson-Sea	206	Mussina-Bal	278	Clemens-Bos	2.41	Clemens-Bos	177	Clemens-Bos	45.1	Clemens-Bos	5.3
Wegman-Mil	261.2	Guzman-Tor	207	Clemens-Bos	278	Appier-KC	2.46	Appier-KC	166	Mussina-Bal	40.9	Appier-KC	4.1
McDowell-Chi	260.2	Appier-KC	217	Appier-KC	281	Mussina-Bal	2.54	Mussina-Bal	160	Appier-KC	37.7	Mussina-Bal	3.8
Nagy-Cle	252.0	Clemens-Bos	224	Smiley-Min	286	Guzman-Tor	2.64	Guzman-Tor.	156	Guzman-Tor	29.1	Eckersley-Oak	3.8
Perez-NY	247.2	Smiley-Min	231	Guzman-Tor	286	Abbott-Cal	2.77	Abbott-Cal	145	Nagy-Cle	27.9	Guzman-Tor	3.2

A Special on Canadian Club

Oriole Park at Camden Yards opened in April, making several other parks instantly obsolete. It started a craze for ballparks designed with idiosyncrasies, asymmetrical dimensions, and memorable features, like the Baltimore & Ohio Warehouse beyond right field. Camden Yards drew three million people for every non-strike season through 2001.

In August Bret Boone debuted with Seattle. Following grandfather Ray and dad Bob, Bret became the first third-generation player in big league history. Rookie Jeff Kent was part of the year's biggest trading deadline deal, going from Toronto to the Mets for David Cone. It was the final season for Bert Blyleven, Brian Downing, and Willie Randolph. Jean Yawkey, Red Sox owner since 1976, died without an heir, leaving the club out of family control for the first time since 1933.

Milwaukee's Robin Yount and Kansas City's George Brett each surpassed 3,000 career hits. Texas' Juan Gonzalez hammered 43 long balls to become, at 22, the youngest home run champ ever. Oakland reliever Dennis Eckersley won both the MVP and Cy Young awards.

Bolstered by Mark McGwire's 42 homers, Oakland, which traded Jose Canseco to Texas at midseason, again won the West. The A's were denied a fourth straight World Series appearance by Toronto, winners in the East by just 4 games over surprising Milwaukee.

The Blue Jays were sparked by a great season from second sacker Roberto Alomar and won four of the last five ALCS contests, slugging 10 home runs and hitting Eckersley hard. Toronto capped its magic season by beating the Braves in six games in the World Series. Pat Borders' timely hitting and some excellent bullpen work helped the Jays win a low-scoring series, bringing the World Series trophy north of the border for the first time.

1991 National League

TEAM	W	L	T	PCT	GB	HW	HL	R	OR	PA	H	2B	3B	HR	BB	SO	HB	SH	AVG	OBP	SLG	OPS	AOPS	BR	ABR	PF	SB	CS	BSA	BSR
EAST																														
PIT	98	64	0	.605		52	32	**768**	632	6269	**1433**	**259**	50	126	620	901	35	99	**.263**	.338	.398	**736**	114	**107**	115	99	124	46	73	11
STL	84	78	0	.519	14	52	32	651	648	6020	1366	239	**53**	68	532	857	21	58	.255	.322	.357	679	96	-13	-20	101	202	110	65	6
PHI	78	84	0	.481	20	47	36	629	680	6133	1332	248	33	111	490	1026	21	52	.241	.303	.358	661	92	-60	-54	99	92	30	**75**	10
CHI	77	83	0	.481	20	46	37	695	734	6130	1395	232	26	159	442	879	36	75	.253	.309	.390	699	97	9	-21	105	123	64	66	5
NY	77	84	0	.478	20.5	40	42	640	646	6076	1305	250	24	117	578	**789**	27	60	.244	.317	.365	682	97	-6	-3	100	153	70	69	9
MON	71	90	0	.441	26.5	33	35	579	655	6035	1329	236	42	95	484	1056	28	64	.246	.308	.357	665	93	-48	-41	99	**221**	100	69	**14**
WEST																														
ATL	94	68	0	.580		48	33	749	644	6182	1407	255	30	141	563	906	32	86	.258	.328	.393	721	102	68	28	106	165	76	68	10
LA	93	69	0	.574	1	**54**	27	665	**565**	6159	1366	191	29	108	583	957	28	94	.253	.326	.359	685	100	0	12	98	126	68	65	4
SD	84	78	0	.519	10	42	39	636	646	6057	1321	204	36	121	578	1069	32	78	.244	.310	.362	672	91	-38	-57	103	101	64	61	0
SF	75	87	0	.463	19	43	38	649	697	6097	1345	215	48	141	471	973	**40**	80	.246	.309	.381	690	102	-12	7	97	95	57	63	1
CIN	74	88	0	.457	20	39	42	689	691	6134	1419	250	27	**164**	488	1006	32	72	.258	.320	**.403**	723	104	58	30	104	124	56	69	8
HOU	65	97	0	.401	29	37	44	605	717	6147	1345	240	43	79	502	1027	35	63	.244	.309	.347	656	95	-65	-31	95	125	68	65	4
TOT	970					533	437	7955		73439	16363	2819	441	1430	6254	11446	367	891	.250	.317	.373	689					1651	809	67	80

TEAM	CG	SHO	GR	SV	IP	H	HR	BB	SO	BR/9	ERA	AERA	OAV	OOB	PR	APR	PF	OSB	OCS	FA	E	WPB	DP	FW	PW	BW	BSW	DIF
EAST																												
PIT	**18**	11	353	**51**	1456.2	1411	117	**401**	919	11.4	3.44	104	.256	.308	39	26	98	142	73	.981	120	49	134	.4	2.7	**12.0**	.5	1.5
STL	9	5	**369**	51	1435.1	1367	114	454	822	11.7	3.69	102	.255	.315	0	10	102	121	81	**.982**	107	41	133	**1.1**	1.0	-2.1	-.0	3.0
PHI	16	11	321	35	1463.0	1346	114	670	988	12.7	3.86	96	.246	.329	-29	-27	100	151	47	.981	119	90	111	.4	-2.8	-5.6	.3	4.7
CHI	12	4	360	40	1456.2	1415	117	542	927	12.3	4.03	97	.257	.324	-57	-21	106	139	64	.982	113	67	120	.7	-2.2	-2.2	-.2	.9
NY	12	11	314	39	1437.1	1403	108	410	1028	11.5	3.56	103	.257	.309	20	18	100	134	75	.977	143	71	112	-1.0	1.9	-.3	.2	-4.3
MON	12	**14**	367	39	1440.1	**1304**	111	584	909	12.0	3.64	100	.244	.320	7	0	99	149	81	.979	133	73	128	-.4	.0	-4.3	**.8**	-5.5
WEST																												
ATL	**18**	7	345	48	1452.2	**1304**	118	481	969	**11.2**	3.49	111	**.240**	**.303**	32	60	105	149	59	.978	138	80	122	-.7	6.3	2.9	.3	4.1
LA	15	**14**	367	40	1458.0	1312	**96**	500	1028	11.4	**3.06**	118	.241	.306	101	90	98	145	60	.980	123	56	126	.2	**9.4**	1.3	-.3	1.4
SD	14	11	334	47	1452.2	1385	139	457	921	11.5	3.57	106	.252	.308	18	36	103	**109**	65	.982	113	58	130	.8	3.8	-6.0	-.7	5.1
SF	10	10	334	45	1442.0	1397	143	544	965	12.3	4.03	89	.257	.326	-56	-72	98	129	**83**	.982	109	53	151	1.0	-7.5	.7	-.6	.4
CIN	7	11	354	43	1440.0	1372	127	560	997	12.3	3.83	99	.253	.323	-24	-4	103	140	60	.979	125	80	131	.0	-.4	3.1	-.1	-9.9
HOU	7	13	365	36	1453.0	1347	129	651	**1033**	12.6	4.00	88	.247	.328	-51	-80	96	143	61	.974	161	62	129	-2.0	-8.4	-3.2	-.3	-2.1
TOT	150	122	4183	514	17387.2					11.9	3.68		.250	.317						.980	1504	780	1527					

Batter-Fielder Wins
Larkin-Cin 6.2
Bonds-Pit 5.6
Pendleton-Atl 5.1
Bonilla-Pit 4.3
Thompson-SF 3.6

Batting Average
Pendleton-Atl 319
Morris-Cin 318
Gwynn-SD 317
McGee-SF 312
Jose-StL 305

On-Base Percentage
Bonds-Pit 410
Butler-LA 401
McGriff-SD 396
Bonilla-Pit 391
Bagwell-Hou 387

Slugging Average
Clark-SF 536
Johnson-NY 535
Pendleton-Atl 517
Bonds-Pit 514
Larkin-Cin 506

On-Base Plus Slugging
Bonds-Pit 924
Clark-SF 895
McGriff-SD 890
Larkin-Cin 884
Bonilla-Pit 883

Adjusted OPS
Bonds-Pit 162
Clark-SF 153
Bonilla-Pit 150
Johnson-NY 146
McGriff-SD 145

Adjusted Batter Runs
Bonds-Pit 48.2
Bonilla-Pit 42.6
Clark-SF 38.1
McGriff-SD 36.0
Johnson-NY 34.1

Runs
Butler-LA 112
Johnson-NY 108
Sandberg-Chi 104
Bonilla-Pit 102
Gant-Atl 101

Hits
Pendleton-Atl 187
Butler-LA 182
Sabo-Cin 175
Bonilla-Pit 174
Jose-StL 173

Doubles
Bonilla-Pit 44
Jose-StL 40
Zeile-StL 36
O'Neill-Cin 36

Triples
Lankford-StL 15
Gwynn-SD 11
Finley-Hou 10
Grissom-Mon 9
Gonzalez-Hou 9

Home Runs
Johnson-NY 38
Williams-SF 34
Gant-Atl 32
McGriff-SD 31
Dawson-Chi 31

Total Bases
Pendleton-Atl 303
Clark-SF 303
Johnson-NY 302
Williams-SF 294
Sabo-Cin 294

Runs Batted In
Johnson-NY 117
Clark-SF 116
Bonds-Pit 116
McGriff-SD 106
Gant-Atl 105

Stolen Bases
Grissom-Mon 76
Nixon-Atl 72
DeShields-Mon 56
Lankford-StL 44
Bonds-Pit 43

Base Stealing Runs
Grissom-Mon 10.8
Nixon-Atl 8.5
Bonds-Pit 4.9
O.Smith-StL 4.6
DeShields-Mon 4.3

Fielding Runs-Infield
Lind-Pit 25.8
Larkin-Cin 22.9
Griffin-LA 20.8
Pendleton-Atl 19.6
Grace-Chi 16.8

Fielding Runs-Outfield
Gonzalez-Hou 8.9
O'Neill-Cin 8.8
Grissom-Mon 8.2
Bonds-Pit 6.4
Gwynn-SD 4.7

Wins
Smiley-Pit 20
Glavine-Atl 20
Avery-Atl 18
Martinez-LA 17

Winning Pct.
Smiley-Pit 714
Rijo-Cin 714
Avery-Atl 692
Hurst-SD 652
Glavine-Atl 645

Complete Games
D.Martinez-Mon 9
Glavine-Atl 9
Mulholland-Phi 8
Maddux-Chi 7

Strikeouts
Cone-NY 241
Maddux-Chi 198
Glavine-Atl 192
Rijo-Cin 172
Harnisch-Hou 172

Fewest BB/Game
Smith-Pit 1.14
Tewksbury-StL 1.79
Mulholland-Phi 1.90
Smiley-Pit 1.91
B.Smith-StL 2.04

Games
Jones-NY 77
Assenmacher-Chi 75
Stanton-Atl 74
Burke-Mon-NY 72
Agosto-StL 72

Saves
L.Smith-StL 47
Dibble-Cin 31
Williams-Phi 30
Franco-NY 30
Righetti-SF 24

Base Runners/9
Berenguer-Atl 9.23
Innis-NY 9.46
Maddux-SD 9.67
Stanton-Atl 9.69
Harris-SD 9.74

Adjusted Relief Runs
McElroy-Chi 17.2
Maddux-SD 14.4
Williams-Phi 13.7
Brantley-SF 12.9
Pena-NY-Atl 12.5

Relief Ranking
Williams-Phi 27.4
L.Smith-StL 24.2
Pena-NY-Atl 16.1
McElroy-Chi 13.1
Maddux-SD 13.0

Innings Pitched
Maddux-Chi 263.0
Glavine-Atl 246.2
Morgan-LA 236.1
Drabek-Pit 234.2
Cone-NY 232.2

Opponents' Avg.
Harnisch-Hou 212
Rijo-Cin 219
Glavine-Atl 222
Hill-StL 224
DeJesus-Phi 224

Opponents' OBP
Rijo-Cin 272
Glavine-Atl 278
Morgan-LA 278
D.Martinez-Mon 282
Benes-SD 285

Earned Run Average
D.Martinez-Mon 2.39
Rijo-Cin 2.51
Glavine-Atl 2.55
Belcher-LA 2.62
Harnisch-Hou 2.70

Adjusted ERA
D.Martinez-Mon 152
Glavine-Atl 152
Rijo-Cin 152
DeLeon-StL 138
Belcher-LA 138

Adjusted Starter Runs
Glavine-Atl 33.2
D.Martinez-Mon 29.6
Rijo-Cin 26.4
Benes-SD 22.2
Harnisch-Hou 21.5

Pitcher Wins
Glavine-Atl 4.9
D.Martinez-Mon 3.6
Williams-Phi 2.9
Rijo-Cin 2.8
L.Smith-StL 2.5

Pete Rose Just Won't Go Away

On New Year's Day Pete Rose was released from federal prison after serving five months for income tax evasion. The Hall of Fame caused much controversy less than two weeks later by announcing a change in eligibility rules. No player on the permanently ineligible list, as Rose had been for eighteen months, could now be listed on the annual ballot. In more pleasant news, especially for fans in Denver and Miami, the NL announced that those cities would receive expansion franchises for the 1993 season.

Baseball lost one of its most colorful characters when Leo Durocher passed away the day before the postseason began. Durocher, who won more than 2,000 games as a big league skipper, titled his autobiography, *Nice Guys Finish Last*. Meanwhile, Houston rookie Jeff Bagwell began his journey to 400-plus home runs. Mark Wohlers also made his debut later in the year. It was the last season for Dave Parker, Rick Reuschel, and Ken Griffey Sr., the first major leaguer to play alongside his son.

The Pirates, with Barry Bonds, Andy Van Slyke, and Bobby Bonilla spearheading the league's best offense, had no trouble repeating as NL champs, finishing 14 games ahead of St. Louis. Atlanta, which finished last in the West in 1990, battled Los Angeles all season and didn't eliminate the Dodgers until the next to last game. The Braves had great seasons from outfielder Ron Gant, MVP Terry Pendleton, and a devastating young pitching trio of Tom Glavine, Steve Avery, and John Smoltz.

Those hurlers, especially Avery, made the difference in a thrilling NLCS, hurling 3 shutouts, including back-to-back blankings in Games 6 and 7 in Pittsburgh. The Braves lost a heartbreaking World Series to Minnesota, dropping the final two games in extra innings.

1991 American League

TEAM	W	L	T	PCT	GB	HW	HL	R	OR	PA	H	2B	3B	HR	BB	SO	HB	SH	AVG	OBP	SLG	OPS	AOPS	BR	ABR	PF	SB	CS	BSA	BSR
EAST																														
TOR	91	71	0	.562		46	35	684	**622**	6167	1412	295	45	133	499	1043	**58**	56	.257	.322	.400	722	94	-6	-33	104	148	53	74	**14**
DET	84	78	0	.519	7	49	32	817	794	6359	1372	259	26	**209**	**699**	1185	31	38	.247	.333	.416	749	104	52	37	102	109	47	70	8
BOS	84	78	0	.519	7	43	38	731	712	6256	1486	**305**	25	126	593	820	32	50	.269	.340	.401	741	99	47	7	106	59	39	60	-1
MIL	83	79	0	.512	8	43	37	799	744	6308	1523	247	**53**	116	556	802	23	52	.271	.336	.396	732	104	21	36	98	106	68	**75**	0
NY	71	91	0	.438	20	42	49	674	777	6140	1418	249	19	147	473	861	39	35	.256	.316	.387	703	92	-49	-54	101	109	36	**75**	11
BAL	67	95	0	.414	24	33	48	686	796	6257	1421	256	29	170	528	974	33	47	.254	.319	.401	720	102	-18	9	96	50	33	60	-1
CLE	57	105	0	.352	34	30	52	576	759	6070	1390	236	26	79	449	888	43	62	.254	.313	.350	663	82	-122	-127	101	84	58	59	-2
WEST																														
MIN	95	67	0	.586		**51**	30	776	652	6215	**1557**	270	42	140	526	**747**	40	44	**.280**	**.344**	.420	764	105	82	45	105	107	68	61	0
CHI	87	75	0	.537	8	46	35	758	681	6358	1464	226	39	139	610	896	37	76	.262	.336	.391	727	102	10	25	98	134	74	64	4
TEX	85	77	0	.525	10	46	35	**829**	814	6441	1539	288	31	177	596	1039	42	59	.270	.341	**.424**	765	112	87	101	98	102	50	67	5
OAK	84	78	0	.519	11	47	34	760	776	6192	1342	246	19	159	642	981	50	41	.248	.331	.389	720	103	0	40	95	**151**	64	70	11
SEA	83	79	0	.512	12	45	36	702	674	6236	1400	268	29	126	588	811	37	55	.255	.328	.381	711	96	-19	-22	100	97	44	69	6
KC	82	80	0	.506	13	40	41	727	722	6242	1475	290	41	117	523	969	35	53	.264	.328	.394	722	98	-4	-10	101	119	68	64	2
CAL	81	81	0	.500	14	40	41	653	649	6050	1396	245	29	115	448	928	38	63	.255	.314	.374	688	89	-81	-82	100	94	56	63	1
TOT	1134					598	536	10172		87291	20195	3680	453	1953	7730	12944	538	733	.260	.329	.395	724					1469	758	66	58

TEAM	CG	SHO	GR	SV	IP	H	HR	BB	SO	BR/9	ERA	AERA	OAV	OOB	PR	APR	PF	OSB	OCS	FA	E	WPB	DP	FW	PW	BW	BSW	DIF
EAST																												
TOR	10	**16**	347	60	1462.2	**1301**	121	523	971	11.5	3.50	120	.238	.307	**96**	113	103	118	53	.980	127	76	115	-.6	**11.3**	-3.3	**1.0**	1.6
DET	18	8	326	38	1450.1	1570	148	593	739	13.6	4.51	93	.280	.348	-66	-53	102	88	56	.983	104	62	171	.7	-5.3	3.7	.4	3.5
BOS	15	-13	328	45	1439.2	1405	147	530	999	12.3	4.01	108	.257	.323	13	47	106	97	53	.981	116	**53**	165	.0	4.7	.7	-.5	-1.9
MIL	23	11	341	41	1463.2	1498	147	527	859	12.7	4.14	96	.266	.332	-8	-26	97	115	47	.981	118	69	176	-.0	-2.6	3.6	-.4	1.5
NY	3	11	377	37	1444.0	1510	152	506	936	12.8	4.42	84	.271	.334	-52	-41	102	134	51	.979	133	66	181	-.9	-4.1	-5.4	.7	-2.2
BAL	8	8	372	42	1457.2	1534	147	504	868	12.8	4.59	86	.273	.333	-80	-104	97	111	51	**.985**	**91**	57	172	**1.4**	-10.4	.9	-.5	-5.4
CLE	22	8	289	33	1441.1	1551	110	**441**	862	12.7	4.23	98	.276	.329	-22	-10	102	102	47	.976	149	67	150	-1.8	-1.0	-12.7	-.6	-7.9
WEST																												
MIN	21	12	291	53	1449.1	1402	139	488	876	11.9	3.69	116	.255	.317	64	89	104	118	43	**.985**	95	69	161	1.2	8.9	4.5	-.4	-.2
CHI	**28**	8	338	40	1478.0	1302	154	601	923	11.8	3.79	105	.239	.315	50	34	97	96	67	.982	116	64	151	.0	3.4	2.5	-.0	.0
TEX	9	10	386	41	1479.0	1486	151	662	**1022**	13.3	4.47	91	.262	.341	-61	-70	99	107	58	.979	134	92	138	-1.0	-7.0	**10.1**	-.0	1.8
OAK	14	10	**397**	49	1444.1	1425	155	655	892	13.3	4.57	84	.260	.342	-77	-124	94	116	60	.982	107	68	150	.5	-12.4	4.0	.7	10.2
SEA	10	13	383	48	1464.1	1387	136	628	1003	12.7	3.79	106	.253	.332	50	56	101	84	44	.983	110	106	187	.3	5.6	-2.2	.2	-1.9
KC	17	12	295	41	1466.0	1473	105	529	1004	12.6	3.92	106	.261	.327	28	35	101	94	56	.980	125	58	141	-.5	3.5	-1.0	-.2	-.3
CAL	18	10	310	50	1441.2	1351	141	543	990	12.1	3.69	112	.250	.321	65	68	101	89	72	.984	102	72	156	.8	6.8	-8.2	-.3	.9
TOT	216	150	4780	618	20382.0					12.6	4.09		.260	.329						.981	1627	979	2214					

Batter-Fielder Wins	Batting Average	On-Base Percentage	Slugging Average	On-Base Plus Slugging	Adjusted OPS	Adjusted Batter Runs
C.Ripken-Bal 8.5	Franco-Tex 341	Thomas-Chi 453	Tartabull-KC 593	Thomas-Chi...........1006	Thomas-Chi...........181	Thomas-Chi...........71.1
Thomas-Chi 5.8	Boggs-Bos 332	Randolph-Mil 424	C.Ripken-Bal 566	Tartabull-KC 990	Tartabull-KC 170	C.Ripken-Bal 54.5
K.Griffey-Sea 4.6	Randolph-Mil 327	Boggs-Bos 421	Canseco-Oak 556	C.Ripken-Bal 940	C.Ripken-Bal 163	Palmeiro-Tex.........49.5
Phillips-Det 4.1	K.Griffey-Sea 327	Franco-Tex 408	Thomas-Chi 553	K.Griffey-Sea 926	Canseco-Oak 159	Tartabull-KC..........46.8
Boggs-Bos 3.8	Molitor-Mil 325	E.Martinez-Sea 405	Palmeiro-Tex..........532	Palmeiro-Tex 922	Palmeiro-Tex..........156	Canseco-Oak.........45.6
Runs	**Hits**	**Doubles**	**Triples**	**Home Runs**	**Total Bases**	**Runs Batted In**
Molitor-Mil 133	Molitor-Mil 216	Palmeiro-Tex.........49	Molitor-Mil 13	Fielder-Det.............44	C.Ripken-Bal 368	Fielder-Det............133
Palmeiro-Tex 115	C.Ripken-Bal 210	C.Ripken-Bal 46	Johnson-Chi 13	Canseco-Oak 44	Palmeiro-Tex 336	Canseco-Oak........122
Canseco-Oak 115	Sierra-Tex 203	Sierra-Tex 44	Alomar-Tor 11	C.Ripken-Bal 34	Sierra-Tex 332	Sierra-Tex 116
White-Tor 110	Palmeiro-Tex 203		White-Tor 10	Carter-Tor 33	Molitor-Mil 325	C.Ripken-Bal 114
Sierra-Tex 110	Franco-Tex............201		Devereaux-Bal.......10	Thomas-Chi............32	Carter-Tor 321	Thomas-Chi...........109
Stolen Bases	**Base Stealing Runs**	**Fielding Runs-Infield**	**Fielding Runs-Outfield**	**Wins**	**Winning Pct.**	**Complete Games**
R.Henderson-Oak 58	Alomar-Tor 7.8	Sojo-Cal 26.6	Orsulak-Bal 17.2	Gullickson-Det........20	Erickson-Min 714	McDowell-Chi 15
Alomar-Tor.............53	R.Henderson-Oak ..6.5	Vizquel-Sea 26.1	Whiten-Tor-Cle 10.4	Erickson-Min 20	Langston-Cal 704	Clemens-Bos..........11
Raines-Chi 51	Raines-Chi 6.0	Espinoza-NY 21.0	Bichette-Mil 8.9	Langston-Cal 19	Gullickson-Det 690	Navarro-Mil 10
Polonia-Cal 48	Cuyler-Det 5.5	C.Ripken-Bal 19.5	Buhner-Sea 7.2		Wegman-Min 682	Morris-Min 10
Cuyler-Det 41	Franco-Tex 4.8	Baerga-Cle 16.5	R.Henderson-Oak ..6.5		Moore-Oak 680	Terrell-Det 8
Strikeouts	**Fewest BB/Game**	**Games**	**Saves**	**Base Runners/9**	**Adjusted Relief Runs**	**Relief Ranking**
Clemens-Bos 241	Swindell-Cle 1.17	D.Ward-Tor 81	Harvey-Cal 46	Gray-Bos 7.30	Frohwirth-Bal 22.0	Harvey-Cal 32.8
Johnson-Sea 228	Sanderson-NY 1.25	Olson-Bal 72	Eckersley-Oak 43	Harvey-Cal 7.89	Swift-Sea 21.3	Aguilera-Min 28.2
Ryan-Tex 203	Tapani-Min 1.48	Jackson-Sea 72	Aguilera-Min 42	Eckersley-Oak 8.29	Harvey-Cal 19.8	Farr-NY 27.4
McDowell-Chi 191	Gullickson-Det 1.75	Swift-Sea 71	Reardon-Bos 40	Eichhorn-Cal 8.60	Eichhorn-Cal 18.8	D.Ward-Tor 24.4
Langston-Cal 183	Wegman-Mil 1.86		Montgomery-KC 33	Frohwirth-Bal 8.78	Flanagan-Bal 18.4	Radinsky-Chi 22.9
Innings Pitched	**Opponents' Avg.**	**Opponents' OBP**	**Earned Run Average**	**Adjusted ERA**	**Adjusted Starter Runs**	**Pitcher Wins**
Clemens-Bos 271.1	Ryan-Tex 172	Ryan-Tex 263	Clemens-Bos 2.62	Clemens-Bos 165	Clemens-Bos 46.5	**Clemens-Bos** 4.7
McDowell-Chi 253.2	Johnson-Sea 213	Clemens-Bos 270	Candiotti-Cle-Tor ..2.65	Candiotti-Cle-Tor ...159	Candiotti-Cle-Tor ...38.9	Candiotti-Cle-Tor 4.1
Morris-Min 246.2	Langston-Cal 215	Tapani-Min 277	Wegman-Mil 2.84	Tapani-Min.............143	Tapani-Min 35.7	**J.Abbott-Cal** 4.0
Langston-Cal 246.1	Clemens-Bos 221	Sanderson-NY 279	J.Abbott-Cal 2.89	J.Abbott-Cal...........143	J.Abbott-Cal 33.4	**Tapani-Min** 3.5
Tapani-Min 244.0	Candiotti-Cle-Tor ...228	Saberhagen-KC 280	Ryan-Tex 2.91	Wegman-Mil............141	Langston-Cal 31.2	**Harvey-Cal** 3.4

Morris Dance

The year began sadly as Hall of Fame shortstop Luke Appling passed away two days after New Year's Day at age 83, then three days later, 32-year-old Alan Wiggins died of AIDS complications. Also passing was Hall of Fame outfielder James "Cool Papa" Bell, a Negro Leagues superstar. The terrible run of bad luck off the field continued in July when respected umpire Steve Palermo, was partially paralyzed when shot in the back during a restaurant robbery.

Baltimore hurler Jim Palmer, already elected to the Hall of Fame, attempted a brief and unsuccessful comeback during spring training. Chicago's "New" Comiskey Park opened to trumpet fanfare, though the stadium would be horribly outdated within a few years as more fashionable "retro" ballparks opened.

May 1 was a historic night. In Texas Nolan Ryan extended his own record by throwing a seventh no-hitter, and in Oakland Rickey Henderson copped Lou Brock's all-time stolen base record. As Dwight Evans was concluding his memorable twenty-year career, future postseason heroes Mike Mussina, Ivan Rodriguez, and Bernie Williams were making their first appearances.

Minnesota, last-place finishers the year before, and Toronto had easy times winning their respective division titles. The Twins, buffed up by free agent Jack Morris and rookie Chuck Knoblauch, had three strong starters and a solid all-around club, while the Blue Jays sported a spectacular three-man bullpen in Tom Henke, Duane Ward, and Mike Timlin.

Behind Kirby Puckett's bat and Jack Morris' arm, Minnesota cruised past the Blue Jays in five games in the ALCS, then beat Atlanta in one of the game's most memorable World Series. Both the Twins and Braves had heroes galore, but Morris' 10-inning, complete-game shutout in Game 7 took the cake.

1990 National League

TEAM	W	L	T	PCT	GB	HW	HL	R	OR	PA	H	2B	3B	HR	BB	SO	HB	SH	AVG	OBP	SLG	OPS	AOPS	BR	ABR	PF	SB	CS	BSA	BSR
EAST																														
PIT	95	67	0	.586		49	32	733	619	6156	1395	**288**	42	138	582	914	24	**96**	.259	**.330**	.405	**735**	**112**	**68**	**93**	97	137	52	72	12
NY	91	71	0	.562	4	**52**	29	**775**	613	6182	1410	278	21	172	536	851	32	54	.256	.323	**.408**	731	106	52	51	100	110	33	**77**	13
MON	85	77	0	.525	10	47	34	662	598	6189	1363	227	**43**	114	576	1024	26	87	.250	.322	.370	692	99	-19	5	97	**235**	99	70	17
PHI	77	85	0	.475	18	41	40	646	729	6245	1410	237	27	103	**582**	915	30	59	.255	.327	.363	690	96	-18	-17	100	108	35	76	12
CHI	77	85	0	.475	18	39	42	690	774	6148	**1474**	240	36	136	406	869	30	61	.263	.314	.392	706	93	-10	-54	107	151	50	75	16
STL	70	92	0	.432	25	34	47	599	698	6127	1398	255	41	73	517	**844**	21	77	.256	.320	.358	678	91	-46	-50	101	221	74	75	**23**
WEST																														
CIN	91	71	0	.562		46	35	693	**597**	6163	1466	284	40	125	466	913	**42**	88	**.265**	.325	.399	724	101	37	9	104	166	66	72	13
LA	86	76	0	.531	5	47	34	728	685	6179	1436	222	27	129	538	952	31	71	.262	.328	.382	710	103	17	33	98	141	65	68	8
SF	85	77	0	.525	6	49	32	719	710	6215	1459	221	35	152	488	973	33	76	.262	.323	.396	719	107	22	46	97	109	56	66	4
SD	75	87	0	.463	16	37	44	673	673	6218	1429	243	35	123	509	902	28	79	.257	.320	.380	700	97	-9	-16	101	138	59	70	10
HOU	75	87	0	.463	16	49	32	573	656	6075	1301	209	32	94	548	997	28	79	.242	.313	.345	658	89	-85	-69	97	179	83	68	10
ATL	65	97	0	.401	26	37	44	682	821	6084	1376	263	26	162	473	1010	27	49	.250	.311	.396	707	94	-8	-43	106	92	55	63	1
TOT	972					527	445	8173		73981	16917	2967	405	1521	6221	11164	352	876	.256	.321	.383	704					1787	727	71	139

TEAM	CG	SHO	GR	SV	IP	H	HR	BB	SO	BR/9	ERA	AERA	OAV	OOB	PR	APR	PF	OSB	OCS	FA	E	WPB	DP	FW	PW	BW	BSW	DIF
EAST																												
PIT	18	8	364	43	1447.0	1367	135	**413**	848	11.3	3.40	107	.251	.305	63	41	96	135	68	.979	134	51	125	-.4	4.2	**9.6**	.0	.6
NY	18	**14**	268	41	1440.0	1339	119	444	**1217**	11.3	3.42	110	.246	**.304**	59	54	99	201	71	.978	132	71	107	-.3	5.6	5.3	.1	-.6
MON	18	11	341	**50**	1473.1	1349	127	510	991	11.6	**3.37**	109	**.245**	.311	70	51	97	194	45	.982	110	**48**	134	.9	5.3	.5	.6	-3.3
PHI	18	7	**374**	35	1449.0	1381	124	651	840	12.8	4.07	95	.253	.333	-45	-35	102	104	56	.981	117	77	**150**	.5	-3.6	-1.8	.0	.8
CHI	13	7	346	42	1442.2	1510	121	572	877	13.2	4.34	94	.271	.340	-87	-38	108	**98**	56	.980	124	86	136	.1	-3.9	-5.6	.5	4.9
STL	8	13	364	39	1443.1	1432	**98**	475	833	12.1	3.87	99	.261	.320	-13	-4	101	144	**76**	.979	130	56	114	-.2	-.4	-5.2	**1.2**	-6.4
WEST																												
CIN	14	12	316	**50**	1456.1	**1338**	124	543	1029	11.8	3.39	**116**	.246	.316	64	86	104	135	60	**.983**	102	67	126	1.4	**8.9**	.9	.1	-1.4
LA	**29**	12	339	29	1442.0	1364	137	478	1021	11.7	3.72	99	.249	.310	11	-7	97	134	59	.979	130	73	123	-.2	-.7	3.4	-.4	2.9
SF	14	6	335	45	1446.1	1477	131	553	788	12.8	4.08	90	.267	.333	-46	-71	96	147	53	**.983**	107	**48**	148	1.1	-7.3	4.7	-.8	6.2
SD	21	6	288	35	1461.2	1437	147	507	928	12.1	3.68	104	.258	.320	19	25	101	132	60	.977	141	**48**	141	-.8	2.6	-1.6	-.2	-5.9
HOU	12	6	348	37	1450.0	1396	130	496	854	12.0	3.61	103	.255	.318	30	20	98	182	61	.978	131	54	124	-.3	2.1	-7.1	-.2	-.5
ATL	17	8	346	30	1429.2	1527	128	579	938	13.4	4.58	88	.275	.343	-125	-82	106	181	62	.974	158	76	133	-1.8	-8.5	-4.4	-1.1	-.2
TOT	200	116	4029	476	17381.1					12.2	3.79		.256	.321						.980	1516	755	1561					

Batter-Fielder Wins		Batting Average		On-Base Percentage		Slugging Average		On-Base Plus Slugging		Adjusted OPS		Adjusted Batter Runs	
Bonds-Pit	6.4	McGee-StL	.335	Dykstra-Phi	.418	Bonds-Pit	.565	Bonds-Pit	.970	Bonds-Pit	171	Bonds-Pit	53.6
Dykstra-Phi	4.8	Murray-LA	.330	Magadan-NY	.417	Sandberg-Chi	.559	Murray-LA	.934	Murray-LA	160	Murray-LA	47.9
Sandberg-Chi	4.3	Magadan-NY	.328	Murray-LA	.414	Mitchell-SF	.544	Daniels-LA	.920	Daniels-LA	155	J.Clark-SD	36.9
Larkin-Cin	4.2	Dykstra-Phi	.325	Bonds-Pit	.406	Gant-Atl	.539	Sandberg-Chi	.913	Mitchell-SF	151	Dykstra-Phi	35.9
Murray-LA	3.9	Dawson-Chi	.310	Butler-SF	.397	Justice-Atl	.535	Justice-Atl	.908	Magadan-NY	142	Daniels-LA	35.3

Runs		Hits		Doubles		Triples		Home Runs		Total Bases		Runs Batted In	
Sandberg-Chi	116	Dykstra-Phi	192	Jefferies-NY	40	Duncan-Cin	11	Sandberg-Chi	40	Sandberg-Chi	344	Williams-SF	122
Bonilla-Pit	112	Butler-SF	192	Bonilla-Pit	39	Gwynn-SD	10	Strawberry-NY	37	Bonilla-Pit	324	Bonilla-Pit	120
Butler-SF	108	Sandberg-Chi	188	Sabo-Cin	38	L.Smith-Atl	9	Mitchell-SF	35	Gant-Atl	310	Carter-SD	115
Gant-Atl	107	Wallach-Mon	185	Wallach-Mon	37	Coleman-StL	9	Williams-SF	33	Williams-SF	301	Bonds-Pit	114
Dykstra-Phi	106	Larkin-Cin	185	Johnson-NY	37	Butler-SF	9	Bonds-Pit	33	Wallach-Mon	295	Strawberry-NY	108

Stolen Bases		Base Stealing Runs		Fielding Runs-Infield		Fielding Runs-Outfield		Wins		Winning Pct.		Complete Games	
Coleman-StL	77	Coleman-StL	11.0	Grace-Cin	25.3	Wilson-Hou	10.0	Drabek-Pit	22	Drabek-Pit	.786	Martinez-LA	12
Yelding-Hou	64	Bonds-Pit	6.9	Treadway-Atl	23.9	Bonds-Pit	7.8	Viola-NY	20	Martinez-LA	.769	Hurst-SD	9
Bonds-Pit	52	Nixon-Mon	6.4	Larkin-Cin	21.0	Hatcher-Cin	7.4	Martinez-LA	20	Gooden-NY	.731	Drabek-Pit	9
Butler-SF	51	Roberts-SD	5.9	Thompson-SF	20.1	Dykstra-Phi	6.8	Gooden-NY	19	Viola-NY	.625	Maddux-Chi	8
Nixon-Mon	50	Dykstra-Phi	5.5	Lind-Pit	19.8	Walker-Mon	6.4			Browning-Cin	.625		

Strikeouts		Fewest BB/Game		Games		Saves		Base Runners/9		Adjusted Relief Runs		Relief Ranking	
Cone-NY	233	Darwin-Hou	1.72	Agosto-Hou	82	Franco-NY	33	Tomlin-NY	8.69	Dibble-Cin	22.5	Myers-Cin	27.7
Martinez-LA	223	Whitson-SD	1.85	Assenmacher-Chi	74	Myers-Cin	31	Dibble-Cin	8.91	Brantley-SF	20.2	Dibble-Cin	27.4
Gooden-NY	223	Leibrandt-Atl	1.94	Harris-SD	73	L.Smith-StL	27	Tudor-StL	9.35	Harris-SD	19.3	Harris-SD	26.4
Viola-NY	182	D.Martinez-Mon	1.95	McDowell-Phi	72	Smith-Hou	23	Darwin-Hou	9.46	Charlton-Cin	19.1	Brantley-SF	24.9
Fernandez-NY	181	Browning-Cin	2.06	Akerfelds-Phi	71	Lefferts-SD	23	Drabek-Pit	9.69	Myers-Cin	16.3	Charlton-Cin	23.8

Innings Pitched		Opponents' Avg.		Opponents' OBP		Earned Run Average		Adjusted ERA		Adjusted Starter Runs		Pitcher Wins	
Viola-NY	249.2	Fernandez-NY	.200	Darwin-Hou	.266	Darwin-Hou	2.21	Darwin-Hou	169	Whitson-SD	31.8	**Viola-NY**	3.7
Maddux-Chi	237.0	Rijo-Cin	.212	Drabek-Pit	.274	Smith-Mon-Pit	2.55	Whitson-SD	148	Viola-NY	30.6	**Drabek-Pit**	3.6
Martinez-LA	234.1	Martinez-LA	.220	D.Martinez-Mon	.274	Whitson-SD	2.60	Rijo-Cin	147	Darwin-Hou	29.3	**Whitson-SD**	3.3
Gooden-NY	232.2	Drabek-Pit	.225	Fernandez-NY	.277	Viola-NY	2.67	Smith-Mon-Pit	144	Rijo-Cin	26.0	**Myers-Cin**	3.0
		Darwin-Hou	.225	Martinez-LA	.278	Rijo-Cin	2.70	Viola-NY	141	Drabek-Pit	24.9	**Rijo-Cin**	2.9

Hunt for a Reds October

The season began a week late as players scrambled to get in condition after the owners ended their lockout of spring training camps. By adding doubleheaders and extending the season three days, all teams played a full 162-game schedule. The NL announced in June that it would expand to fourteen teams, the same number as the AL, for 1993. The finalist cities were Buffalo, Denver, Miami, Orlando, Tampa-St. Petersburg, and Washington, D.C.

The decline and fall of Pete Rose continued, as the former superstar pled guilty to filing false income tax returns and was sentenced to five months in federal prison. Moises Alou, Felipe's son, debuted in June, while Luis Gonzalez made his first appearance in September. Keith Hernandez hung up the spikes after seventeen seasons. Bo Diaz, former catcher for the Phillies and Reds, died one year after retiring when he was crushed by a satellite dish he was installing.

Cincinnati led the West wire-to-wire, sparked by the Nasty Boys bullpen trio of Randy Myers, Rob Dibble and Norm Charlton. Pittsburgh, behind Barry Bonds' MVP performance (his first of a record six), won 10 of 11 games late in the season to hold off the Mets in the East. Doug Drabek, enjoying a career year with 22 wins and the Cy Young Award, led a pedestrian Pirates staff.

While the Reds dropped the first game of the NLCS to Pittsburgh, they rallied to take four of the next five. Cincinnati then brought back memories of the Big Red Machine by sweeping heavily favored Oakland in the World Series. Series MVP Jose Rijo dominated Oakland hitters, winning Games 1 and 4, while Billy Hatcher set offensive records by getting hits in seven consecutive at bats and batting .750 (9-for-12).

1990 American League

TEAM	W	L	T	PCT	GB	HW	HL	R	OR	PA	H	2B	3B	HR	BB	SO	HB	SH	AVG	OBP	SLG	OPS	AOPS	BR	ABR	PF	SB	CS	BSA	BSR
EAST																														
BOS	88	74	0	.543		51	30	699	664	6234	1502	298	31	106	598	795	28	48	.272	.344	.395	739	101	61	24	105	53	52	50	-7
TOR	86	76	0	.531	2	44	37	767	661	6223	1479	263	50	167	526	970	28	18	.265	.328	.419	747	105	54	38	102	111	52	68	6
DET	79	83	0	.488	9	39	42	750	754	6224	1418	241	32	172	634	952	34	36	.259	.337	.409	746	107	63	54	101	82	57	59	-2
CLE	77	85	0	.475	11	41	40	732	737	6087	1465	266	41	110	458	836	29	54	.267	.324	.391	715	99	-7	-6	100	107	52	67	5
BAL	76	85	0	.472	11.5	40	40	669	698	6223	1328	234	22	132	660	962	40	72	.245	.330	.370	700	98	-20	-2	97	94	52	64	7
MIL	74	88	0	.457	14	39	42	732	760	6185	1408	247	36	128	519	821	33	59	.256	.320	.384	704	96	-26	-23	100	164	72	69	11
NY	67	95	0	.414	21	37	44	603	749	6036	1322	208	19	147	427	1027	53	37	.241	.300	.366	666	84	-114	-119	101	119	45	73	10
WEST																														
OAK	103	59	0	.636		51	30	733	570	6238	1379	209	22	164	651	992	46	65	.254	.336	.391	727	107	31	58	96	141	54	72	12
CHI	94	68	0	.580	9	49	31	682	633	6038	1393	251	44	106	478	903	36	75	.258	.320	.379	699	97	-37	-24	98	140	90	61	-1
TEX	83	79	0	.512	20	47	35	676	696	6176	1416	257	27	110	575	1054	34	54	.259	.331	.376	707	97	-10	-13	100	115	48	71	0
CAL	80	82	0	.494	23	42	39	690	706	6267	1448	237	27	147	566	1000	28	58	.260	.329	.391	720	103	9	21	98	69	43	62	0
SEA	77	85	0	.475	26	38	43	640	680	6205	1419	251	26	107	596	749	40	41	.259	.333	.373	706	96	-5	-14	101	105	51	67	5
KC	75	86	0	.466	27.5	45	36	707	709	6098	1465	316	44	100	498	879	27	31	.267	.328	.395	723	102	16	25	99	107	62	63	2
MIN	74	88	0	.457	29	41	40	666	729	6086	1458	281	39	100	445	749	53	40	.265	.324	.385	709	91	-17	-57	106	96	53	64	3
TOT	1133					604	529	9746		86320	19900	3559	460	1796	7631	12689	509	683	.259	.327	.388	715					1503	783	66	57

TEAM	CG	SHO	GR	SV	IP	H	HR	BB	SO	BR/9	ERA	AERA	OAV	OOB	PR	APR	PF	OSB	OCS	FA	E	WPB	DP	FW	PW	BW	BSW	DIF
EAST																												
BOS	15	13	323	44	1442.0	1439	92	519	997	12.5	3.72	110	.261	.327	30	56	105	127	58	.980	123	70	154	-.2	5.7	2.4	-1.1	.2
TOR	6	9	317	48	1454.0	1434	143	445	892	11.9	3.84	103	.260	.311	11	18	101	95	67	.986	86	57	144	2.0	1.8	3.9	.2	-2.9
DET	15	12	300	45	1430.1	1401	154	661	856	13.3	4.39	90	.259	.341	-76	-65	102	136	59	.979	131	91	178	-.7	-6.6	5.5	-.6	.4
CLE	12	10	301	47	1427.1	1491	163	518	860	12.9	4.26	92	.270	.334	-57	-53	101	97	53	.981	117	64	146	.2	-5.4	-.6	.0	1.7
BAL	10	5	357	43	1435.1	1445	161	537	776	12.5	4.04	94	.264	.328	-21	-38	98	103	44	.985	93	39	151	1.6	-3.9	-.2	-.2	-1.8
MIL	23	13	340	42	1445.0	1558	121	469	771	12.9	4.08	95	.275	.331	-28	-33	99	111	45	.976	149	58	152	-1.8	-3.4	-2.3	.7	-.2
NY	15	6	342	41	1444.2	1430	144	618	909	12.9	4.21	95	.261	.336	-49	-36	102	106	83	.980	126	110	164	-.4	-3.7	-12.1	.6	1.6
WEST																												
OAK	18	16	303	64	1456.0	1287	123	494	831	11.2	3.18	117	.238	.302	118	93	95	73	44	.986	87	64	152	2.0	9.5	5.9	.8	3.9
CHI	17	10	367	68	1449.1	1313	106	548	914	11.8	3.61	106	.244	.316	48	37	98	89	60	.980	124	48	169	-.3	3.8	-2.4	-.5	12.5
TEX	25	9	302	36	1444.2	1343	113	623	997	12.5	3.83	102	.248	.327	12	15	101	131	52	.979	133	96	161	-.8	1.5	-1.3	.5	2.1
CAL	21	13	269	42	1454.0	1482	106	544	944	12.8	3.79	101	.267	.334	18	6	99	91	69	.978	142	65	186	-1.4	.6	2.1	-.4	-2.0
SEA	21	7	312	41	1443.1	1319	120	606	1064	12.3	3.69	107	.243	.321	34	44	102	120	56	.979	130	87	152	-.6	4.5	-1.4	.0	-6.3
KC	18	8	312	33	1420.2	1449	116	560	1006	13.0	3.93	98	.264	.334	-5	-13	99	115	28	.980	122	72	161	-.2	-1.3	2.5	-.2	-6.3
MIN	13	13	310	43	1435.2	1509	134	489	872	12.7	4.12	101	.273	.332	-35	4	106	109	65	.983	101	66	161	1.1	.4	-5.8	-.1	-2.6
TOT	229	144	4455	637	20182.1					12.5	3.91		.259	.327						.981	1664	987	2231					

Batter-Fielder Wins		Batting Average		On-Base Percentage		Slugging Average		On-Base Plus Slugging		Adjusted OPS		Adjusted Batter Runs	
R.Henderson-Oak	7.7	Brett-KC	.329	R.Henderson-Oak	.439	Fielder-Det	.592	R.Henderson-Oak	1016	R.Henderson-Oak	189	R.Henderson-Oak	64.2
Fielder-Det	4.4	R.Henderson-Oak	.325	McGriff-Tor	.400	R.Henderson-Oak	.577	Fielder-Det	969	Fielder-Det	166	Fielder-Det	50.6
McGriff-Tor	4.3	Palmeiro-Tex	.319	E.Martinez-Sea	.397	J.Canseco-Oak	.543	McGriff-Tor	930	J.Canseco-Oak	159	McGriff-Tor	43.7
Fisk-Chi	4.1	Trammell-Det	.304	Brett-KC	.387	McGriff-Tor	.530	J.Canseco-Oak	914	McGriff-Tor	155	Brett-KC	39.7
Parrish-Cal	3.8	Boggs-Bos	.302	Davis-Sea	.387	Brett-KC	.515	Brett-KC	902	Brett-KC	153	J.Canseco-Oak	38.0

Runs		Hits		Doubles		Triples		Home Runs		Total Bases		Runs Batted In	
R.Henderson-Oak	119	Palmeiro-Tex	191	J.Reed-Bos	45	Fernandez-Tor	17	Fielder-Det	51	Fielder-Det	339	Fielder-Det	132
Fielder-Det	104	Boggs-Bos	187	Brett-KC	45	Sosa-Chi	10	McGwire-Oak	39	Gruber-Tor	303	Gruber-Tor	118
Reynolds-Sea	100	Kelly-NY	183	Calderon-Chi	44	Polonia-NY-Cal	9	J.Canseco-Oak	37	McGriff-Tor	295	McGwire-Oak	108
Yount-Mil	98	Greenwell-Bos	181	Boggs-Bos	44	Liriano-Tor-Min	9	McGriff-Tor	35	K.Griffey-Sea	287	J.Canseco-Oak	101
Phillips-Det	97			Harper-Min	42	Johnson-Chi	9	Gruber-Tor	31	Burks-Bos	286	Sierra-Tex	96

Stolen Bases		Base Stealing Runs		Fielding Runs-Infield		Fielding Runs-Outfield		Wins		Winning Pct.		Complete Games	
R.Henderson-Oak	65	R.Henderson-Oak	10.8	Espinoza-NY	22.9	Orsulak-Bal	8.9	Welch-Oak	27	Welch-Oak	.818	Stewart-Oak	11
Sax-NY	43	Sax-NY	6.3	Reynolds-Sea	20.1	Deer-Mil	8.5	Stewart-Oak	22	Clemens-Bos	.778	Morris-Det	11
Kelly-NY	42	Cole-Cle	5.7	Whitaker-Det	17.7	Gladden-Min	8.5	Clemens-Bos	21	Stieb-Tor	.750		
Cole-Cle	40	Wilson-Tor	3.7	Phillips-Det	15.4	Webster-Cle	8.0			Boddicker-Bos	.680		
Pettis-Tex	38	Cotto-Sea	3.6	Quintana-Bos	13.2	Mack-Min	8.0						

Strikeouts		Fewest BB/Game		Games		Saves		Base Runners/9		Adjusted Relief Runs		Relief Ranking	
Ryan-Tex	232	Anderson-Min	1.86	Thigpen-Chi	77	Thigpen-Chi	57	Eckersley-Oak	5.52	Farr-KC	26.9	Eckersley-Oak	44.7
Witt-Tex	221	Swindell-Cle	1.97	Ward-Tor	73	Eckersley-Oak	48	Nelson-Oak	9.04	Eckersley-Oak	25.0	Thigpen-Chi	40.1
Hanson-Sea	211	Clemens-Bos	2.13	Montgomery-KC	73	Jones-Cle	43	McDonald-Bal	9.33	Thigpen-Chi	20.1	Farr-KC	38.4
Clemens-Bos	209	Knudson-Mil	2.14	Rogers-Tex	69	Olson-Bal	37	Henke-Tor	9.40	Swift-Sea	19.1	Olson-Bal	25.1
Langston-Cal	195	Wells-Tor	2.14	Henneman-Det	69	Righetti-NY	36	Thigpen-Chi	9.44	Nelson-Oak	19.1	Jones-Chi	24.3

Innings Pitched		Opponents' Avg.		Opponents' OBP		Earned Run Average		Adjusted ERA		Adjusted Starter Runs		Pitcher Wins	
Stewart-Oak	267.0	Ryan-Tex	188	Ryan-Tex	.267	Clemens-Bos	1.93	Clemens-Bos	212	Clemens-Bos	50.6	**Clemens-Bos**	6.2
Morris-Det	249.2	Johnson-Sea	216	Clemens-Bos	.278	Finley-Cal	2.40	Finley-Cal	160	Stewart-Oak	36.7	**Eckersley-Oak**	4.7
Welch-Oak	238.0	Clemens-Bos	228	Wells-Tor	.283	Stewart-Oak	2.56	Stewart-Oak	146	Finley-Cal	36.4	**Stewart-Oak**	4.3
Hanson-Sea	236.0	Stieb-Tor	287	Hanson-Sea	.287	Appier-KC	2.76	Appier-KC	140	Stieb-Tor	33.3	**Thigpen-Chi**	4.2
Finley-Cal	236.0	Stewart-Oak	231	Black-Cle-Tor	.290	Stieb-Tor	2.93	Stieb-Tor	135	Hanson-Sea	22.9	**Farr-KC**	4.1

March Comes In Like a Lion; A's Go Out Like Lambs

Although a spring lockout by the owners delayed the start of the regular season by a week, a full 162-game schedule was played after Commissioner Fay Vincent ordered the opening of the training camps. This angered many owners who believed that the formerly solid Players Association was about to crack, with several star players reportedly on the verge of crossing the "picket lines."

Toronto led the East by 1 game in late September, but lost six of its last eight and fell to Boston. Roger Clemens was again outstanding for the Red Sox, leading the league in ERA while pitching in Fenway Park. The Jays had a more impressive club than Boston but suffered from a lack of lefty relief and inconsistent starting pitching (David Wells shuttled between both roles and won 11 games). Behemoth first baseman Cecil Fielder of Detroit, signed after playing in Japan, hit 51 homers.

Oakland's Rickey Henderson shattered Ty Cobb's career AL steals record. Teammate Bob Welch won the Cy Young with 27 victories, the AL's most since 1968, although Clemens probably deserved the award. With Mark McGwire and Jose Canseco combining for 76 homers, the A's had little trouble in the West. Texas' 43-year-old Nolan Ryan won his 300th game and pitched his sixth no-hitter. The second-place White Sox, in their final season at venerable Comiskey Park, won 90 games for the first time since 1983. Chicago was led by Bobby Thigpen's record 57-save season plus rookie slugger Frank Thomas.

The AL West's top clubs of the 1980s, California and Kansas City, lost two players each to retirement: Bob Boone, Fred Lynn, Dan Quisenberry, and Frank White all sat down. The A's swept Boston in the ALCS, allowing just 4 runs, but they were in turn broomed out by the Reds in the World Series.

1989 National League

TEAM	W	L	T	PCT	GB	HW	HL	R	OR	PA	H	2B	3B	HR	BB	SO	HB	SH	AVG	OBP	SLG	OPS	AOPS	BR	ABR	PF	SB	CS	BSA	BSR
EAST																														
CHI	93	69	0	.574		48	33	**702**	623	6141	**1438**	235	45	124	472	921	26	80	.261	.319	.387	**706**	100	52	7	107	136	57	70	10
NY	87	75	0	.537	6	51	30	683	595	6130	1351	**280**	21	**147**	504	934	33	56	.246	.311	.385	696	108	33	62	96	158	53	**75**	**16**
STL	86	76	2	.531	7	46	35	632	608	6141	1418	263	47	73	507	848	21	78	.258	**.321**	.363	684	98	17	-5	103	155	54	74	15
MON	81	81	0	.500	12	44	37	632	630	6206	1353	267	30	100	**572**	958	35	71	.247	.319	.361	680	98	16	4	102	**160**	70	70	11
PIT	74	88	2	.457	19	39	42	637	680	6260	1334	263	**53**	95	563	914	24	83	.241	.311	.359	670	100	-12	9	97	155	69	69	10
PHI	67	95	1	.414	26	38	42	629	735	6126	1324	215	36	123	558	926	22	57	.243	.314	.364	678	99	0	0	100	106	50	68	6
WEST																														
SF	92	70	0	.568		**53**	28	699	600	6138	1365	241	52	141	508	1071	**40**	82	.250	.316	**.390**	**706**	**110**	49	**68**	97	87	54	62	0
SD	89	73	0	.549	3	46	35	642	626	6119	1360	215	32	120	552	1013	9	**95**	.251	.319	.369	688	102	21	20	100	136	67	67	6
HOU	86	76	0	.531	6	47	35	647	669	6200	1316	239	28	97	530	860	27	83	.239	.306	.345	651	95	-50	-29	97	144	62	70	10
LA	77	83	0	.481	14	44	37	554	**536**	6123	1313	241	17	89	507	885	27	83	.240	.306	.339	645	91	-60	-52	99	81	54	60	-1
CIN	75	87	0	.463	17	38	43	632	691	6158	1362	243	28	128	493	1028	30	66	.247	.309	.370	679	96	1	-19	103	128	71	64	3
ATL	63	97	1	.394	28	33	46	584	680	6079	1281	201	22	128	485	996	24	65	.234	.298	.350	648	89	-67	-79	102	83	54	61	-1
TOT	.973					527	443	7673		73821	16215	2903	411	1365	6251	11354	318	899	.246	.312	.365	678					1529	715	68	86

TEAM	CG	SHO	GR	SV	IP	H	HR	BB	SO	BR/9	ERA	AERA	OAV	OOB	PR	APR	PF	OSB	OCS	FA	E	WPB	DP	FW	PW	BW	BSW	DIF
EAST																												
CHI	18	10	338	**55**	1460.1	1369	106	532	918	11.9	3.43	110	.250	.316	11	52	108	87	56	.980	124	56	130	.6	5.6	.7	.3	4.8
NY	24	12	274	38	1454.1	**1260**	115	532	**1108**	11.3	3.29	100	**.231**	**.301**	33	0	94	158	57	.976	144	61	110	-.6	.0	6.6	**.9**	-1.0
STL	18	18	**358**	43	1461.0	1330	**84**	482	844	11.3	3.36	100	.243	.306	21	46	105	133	55	**.982**	**112**	52	134	1.4	4.9	-.5	.8	-1.6
MON	20	13	287	35	1468.1	1344	120	519	1059	11.6	3.48	102	.245	.312	3	14	102	166	70	.979	136	51	126	-.1	1.5	.4	.4	-2.2
PIT	20	9	325	40	1487.2	1394	121	539	827	11.9	3.64	93	.248	.314	-24	-43	97	190	56	.975	160	74	130	-1.4	-4.6	1.0	.3	-2.3
PHI	10	10	348	33	1433.1	1408	127	613	899	12.9	4.04	89	.259	.335	-87	-72	103	113	66	.979	133	97	136	.1	-7.7	.0	-.1	-6.3
WEST																												
SF	12	16	318	47	1457.0	1320	120	471	802	11.2	3.30	102	.243	.304	31	12	97	96	56	**.982**	114	48	135	1.2	1.3	**7.3**	-.8	2.1
SD	21	11	245	52	1457.1	1359	133	481	933	11.5	3.38	104	.249	.310	19	20	100	68	44	.976	154	56	147	-1.1	2.1	2.1	-.1	5.0
HOU	19	12	346	38	1479.1	1379	105	551	965	11.9	3.44	93	.247	.311	-25	-41	97	170	40	.977	142	64	121	-.4	-4.4	-3.1	.3	12.6
LA	25	19	285	36	1463.1	1278	95	504	1052	**11.1**	**2.95**	116	.237	.304	89	80	98	99	72	.981	118	63	153	.8	**8.6**	-5.6	-.6	-6.0
CIN	16	9	339	37	1464.1	1404	125	559	981	12.3	3.73	96	.253	.323	-38	-21	103	141	65	.980	121	**47**	108	.8	-2.2	-2.0	-.4	-2.0
ATL	15	8	340	33	1447.2	1370	114	**468**	966	11.5	3.70	99	.250	.309	-33	-7	105	108	**78**	.976	152	62	124	-1.1	-.7	-8.4	-.9	-5.9
TOT	218	147	3803	487	17534.0					11.7	3.49		.246	.312						.978	1610	731	1554					

Batter-Fielder Wins
Mitchell-SF	6.2
Clark-SF	5.1
L.Smith-Atl	4.8
Oquendo-StL	4.3
Bonilla-Pit	4.2

Batting Average
Gwynn-SD	.336
Clark-SF	.333
L.Smith-Atl	.315
Grace-Chi	.314
Guerrero-StL	.311

On-Base Percentage
L.Smith-Atl	.415
J.Clark-SD	.410
Clark-SF	.407
Grace-Chi	.405
Raines-Mon	.395

Slugging Average
Mitchell-SF	.635
Johnson-NY	.559
Clark-SF	.546
Davis-Cin	.541
L.Smith-Atl	.533

On-Base Plus Slugging
Mitchell-SF	1023
Clark-SF	.953
L.Smith-Atl	.948
Johnson-NY	.928
Davis-Cin	.908

Adjusted OPS
Mitchell-SF	194
Clark-SF	176
Johnson-NY	170
L.Smith-Atl	167
Davis-Cin	154

Adjusted Batter Runs
Mitchell-SF	67.0
Clark-SF	60.2
Johnson-NY	52.3
L.Smith-Atl	46.4
J.Clark-SD	37.4

Runs
Sandberg-Chi	104
Johnson-NY	104
Clark-SF	104
Mitchell-SF	100
Butler-SF	100

Hits
Gwynn-SD	203
Clark-SF	196
R.Alomar-SD	184
Guerrero-StL	177
Sandberg-Chi	176

Doubles
Wallach-StL	42
Guerrero-StL	42
Johnson-NY	41
Clark-SF	38
Bonilla-Pit	37

Triples
Thompson-SF	11
Bonilla-Pit	10
VanSlyke-Pit	9
Coleman-StL	9
Clark-SF	9

Home Runs
Mitchell-SF	47
Johnson-NY	36
Davis-Hou	34
Davis-Cin	34
Sandberg-Chi	30

Total Bases
Mitchell-SF	345
Clark-SF	321
Johnson-NY	319
Bonilla-Pit	302
Sandberg-Chi	301

Runs Batted In
Mitchell-SF	125
Guerrero-StL	117
Clark-SF	111
Johnson-NY	101
Davis-Cin	101

Stolen Bases
Coleman-StL	65
Samuel-Phi-NY	42
R.Alomar-SD	42
Raines-Mon	41
Johnson-NY	41

Base Stealing Runs
Coleman-StL	10.8
Johnson-NY	6.2
Raines-Mon	5.9
Samuel-Phi-NY	5.0
Nixon-Mon	3.9

Fielding Runs-Infield
Pendleton-StL	34.9
Oquendo-StL	24.9
Thon-Phi	19.6
Uribe-SF	17.3
Foley-Mon	15.5

Fielding Runs-Outfield
Young-Hou	14.2
Bonds-Pit	12.2
McReynolds-NY	7.6
Strawberry-NY	4.9
Dykstra-NY-Phi	4.3

Wins
Scott-Hou	20
Maddux-Chi	19
Magrane-StL	18
Bielecki-Chi	18
Reuschel-SF	17

Winning Pct.
Bielecki-Chi	.720
D.Martinez-Mon	.696
Reuschel-SF	.680
Scott-Hou	.667
Magrane-StL	.667

Complete Games
Hurst-SD	10
Belcher-LA	10
Scott-Hou	9
Magrane-StL	9
Browning-Cin	9

Strikeouts
DeLeon-StL	201
Belcher-LA	200
Fernandez-NY	198
Cone-NY	190
Hurst-SD	179

Fewest BB/Game
Robinson-SF	1.69
Lilliquist-Atl	1.85
D.Martinez-Mon	1.90
Whitson-SD	1.90
Glavine-Atl	1.94

Games
Williams-Chi	76
Dibble-Cin	74
Parrett-Phi	72
Dayley-StL	71
Agosto-Hou	71

Saves
Davis-SD	44
Williams-Chi	36
Franco-Cin	32
Howell-LA	28
Burke-Mon	28

Base Runners/9
Andersen-Hou	8.93
Garrelts-SF	9.08
Howell-LA	9.26
Lancaster-Chi	9.29
Darwin-Hou	9.37

Adjusted Relief Runs
Lancaster-Chi	18.2
Andersen-Hou	17.6
Dibble-Cin	17.5
Davis-SD	17.4
Howell-LA	17.0

Relief Ranking
Davis-SD	26.6
Howell-LA	26.1
Dibble-Cin	24.5
Burke-Mon	19.7
Darwin-Hou	18.5

Innings Pitched
Hershiser-LA	256.2
Browning-Cin	249.2
Hurst-SD	244.2
DeLeon-StL	244.2
Drabek-Pit	244.1

Opponents' Avg.
DeLeon-StL	.197
Fernandez-NY	.198
Smoltz-Atl	.212
Garrelts-SF	.212
Scott-Hou	.212

Opponents' OBP
Garrelts-SF	.258
Scott-Hou	.267
DeLeon-StL	.268
Fernandez-NY	.271
Smiley-Pit	.273

Earned Run Average
Garrelts-SF	2.28
Hershiser-LA	2.31
Langston-Mon	2.39
Whitson-SD	2.66
Hurst-SD	2.69

Adjusted ERA
Langston-Mon	149
Hershiser-LA	148
Garrelts-SF	148
Whitson-SD	132
Hurst-SD	131

Adjusted Starter Runs
Hershiser-LA	32.1
Garrelts-SF	23.1
Hurst-SD	22.1
Whitson-SD	21.3
Langston-Mon	20.5

Pitcher Wins
Hershiser-LA	4.4
Maddux-Chi	2.9
Howell-LA	2.8
Davis-SD	2.7
Whitson-SD	2.5

Shaken to the Core

Just before Opening Day, NL President Bart Giamatti was appointed commissioner, and Bill White became the first African American league president. Giamatti immediately was presented with serious allegations against Pete Rose, accused of gambling on baseball games in which he was involved. Despite being Cincinnati's manager since 1984, Rose's shady dealings made him appear guilty to many.

In late August Rose—with no other option—signed an agreement banning him for life from the game, even though he denied gambling on baseball. Nine days later, Giamatti died of a heart attack, and Fay Vincent became the new commissioner.

Horror also visited the playing field. Giants pitcher Dave Dravecky suffered a broken arm while pitching, ending his career. He eventually lost the arm. Darrell Evans, Mike Schmidt, and Kent Tekulve also called it quits. Late in the season, Montreal debuted Larry Walker and Marquis Grissom, but the Expos goofed by trading Randy Johnson for Mark Langston, who soon departed via free agency.

San Francisco won again, with a veteran pitching staff and Kevin Mitchell's MVP season; Will Clark finished second in the voting. Despite Tony Gwynn's fourth batting title and reliever Mark Davis' Cy Young, the Padres fell just short.

Chicago, in another potentially earth-shaking event, captured the East despite a string of injuries. Outfielders Jerome Walton was Rookie of the Year, but Ryne Sandberg and Greg Maddux did most of the heavy lifting.

The Giants beat Chicago in a five-game NLCS. First basemen Clark and Mark Grace put on hitting shows, but San Francisco won three straight squeakers at home to wrap things up. The Bay Area was struck by an earthquake in the middle of a four-game A's World Series sweep of the Giants. Baseball's core had been shaken, and it would get worse.

1989 American League

TEAM	W	L	T	PCT	GB	HW	HL	R	OR	PA	H	2B	3B	HR	BB	SO	HB	SH	AVG	OBP	SLG	OPS	AOPS	BR	ABR	PF	SB	CS	BSA	BSR
EAST																														
TOR	89	73	0	.549		46	35	731	651	6216	1449	265	40	142	521	923	31	30	.260	.323	.398	721	103	19	29	99	144	58	71	11
BAL	87	75	0	.537	2	47	34	708	686	6173	1369	238	33	129	593	957	30	63	.252	.326	.379	705	101	-5	13	97	118	55	68	5
BOS	83	79	0	.512	6	46	35	**774**	735	6455	**1571**	**326**	30	108	**643**	755	36	52	**.277**	**.351**	**.403**	754	105	**114**	63	106	56	35	62	0
MIL	81	81	0	.500	8	45	36	707	679	6083	1415	235	32	126	455	791	**50**	51	.259	.318	.382	700	97	-23	-19	99	**165**	62	73	15
NY	74	87	0	.460	14.5	41	40	698	792	6094	1470	229	23	130	502	831	27	58	.269	.331	.391	722	104	25	30	99	137	60	70	9
CLE	73	89	0	.451	16	41	40	604	654	6110	1340	221	26	127	499	934	35	72	.245	.310	.365	675	88	-74	-86	102	74	51	59	-2
DET	59	103	0	.364	30	38	43	617	816	6132	1315	198	24	116	585	899	37	35	.242	.318	.351	669	90	-75	-62	98	103	50	67	5
WEST																														
OAK	99	63	0	.611		54	27	712	**576**	6110	1414	220	25	127	562	865	34	36	.261	.331	.381	712	103	12	35	97	157	55	74	15
KC	92	70	0	.568	7	**55**	26	690	635	6150	1428	227	41	101	554	897	29	42	.261	.329	.373	702	97	-10	-9	100	154	51	**75**	**16**
CAL	91	71	0	.562	8	52	29	669	578	6102	1422	208	37	**145**	429	1011	28	54	.256	.311	.386	697	97	-43	-32	98	89	40	69	6
TEX	83	79	0	.512	16	45	36	695	714	6098	1433	260	**46**	122	503	989	34	63	.263	.326	.394	720	100	18	5	102	101	49	67	5
MIN	80	82	0	.494	19	45	36	740	738	6207	1542	278	35	117	478	**743**	39	35	.257	.324	.402	726	99	55	8	107	111	53	68	6
SEA	73	89	0	.451	26	40	41	694	728	6133	1417	237	29	134	489	838	45	35	.257	.322	.384	704	95	-16	-37	103	81	55	60	-1
CHI	69	92	0	.429	29.5	35	45	693	750	6132	1493	262	36	94	464	873	28	**85**	.271	.328	.383	711	102	4	17	98	97	52	65	3
TOT	1133					630	503	9732		86195	20078	3404	457	1718	7277	12296	483	727	.261	.326	.384	709					1587	726	69	95

TEAM	CG	SHO	GR	SV	IP	H	HR	BB	SO	BR/9	ERA	AERA	OAV	OOB	PR	APR	PF	OSB	OCS	FA	E	WPB	DP	FW	PW	BW	BSW	DIF
EAST																												
TOR	12	12	277	38	1467.0	1408	99	478	849	11.8	3.58	106	.255	.317	49	34	98	115	54	.980	127	74	164	-.1	3.5	3.0	.4	1.3
BAL	16	7	312	44	1448.1	1518	134	486	676	12.6	4.00	93	.272	.331	-19	-31	98	114	51	**.986**	**87**	46	163	**2.3**	-3.2	1.3	.0	5.5
BOS	14	9	297	42	1460.1	1448	131	548	1054	12.5	4.01	102	.261	.328	-20	15	106	161	58	.980	127	51	162	-.1	1.5	**6.4**	-.7	-5.1
MIL	16	8	291	45	1432.1	1463	129	457	812	12.2	3.80	101	.265	.321	14	8	99	113	46	.975	155	46	164	-1.8	.8	-1.9	.8	2.1
NY	15	9	278	44	1414.2	1550	150	521	787	13.4	4.50	86	.281	.344	-98	-98	100	81	51	.980	122	49	**183**	.1	-10.0	3.1	.2	0.0
CLE	23	13	287	38	1453.0	1423	107	**452**	844	11.8	3.65	109	.257	.313	38	51	102	126	50	.981	118	60	126	.4	5.2	-8.8	-.9	-4.0
DET	24	4	252	26	1427.1	1514	150	652	831	13.9	4.53	84	.274	.352	-103	-114	99	126	**65**	.979	130	60	153	-.3	-11.6	-6.3	-.2	-3.6
WEST																												
OAK	17	**20**	317	**57**	1448.1	1287	103	510	930	**11.3**	**3.09**	120	**.238**	**.305**	128	102	95	89	48	.979	129	84	159	-.2	**10.4**	3.6	.8	3.4
KC	27	13	264	38	1451.2	1415	**86**	455	978	11.7	3.55	109	.257	.314	54	52	100	**79**	56	.982	114	68	139	.7	5.3	-.9	**.9**	5.0
CAL	**32**	20	252	38	1454.1	1384	113	465	897	11.6	3.28	116	.253	.312	97	89	98	111	42	.985	96	65	173	1.7	9.1	-3.3	-.0	2.2
TEX	26	7	321	44	1434.1	**1279**	119	654	**1112**	12.4	3.91	102	.239	.324	-4	11	103	140	51	.978	136	107	137	-.6	1.1	.5	-.2	1.2
MIN	19	8	297	38	1429.1	1495	139	500	851	12.8	4.28	97	.269	.332	-63	-21	107	115	49	.982	107	54	141	1.1	-2.1	.8	-.0	-.7
SEA	15	10	**330**	44	1438.0	1422	116	560	897	12.7	4.00	101	.259	.330	-19	5	104	115	52	.977	143	57	168	-1.1	.5	-3.8	-.8	-2.9
CHI	9	5	321	46	1422.0	1472	144	539	778	12.9	4.23	91	.269	.335	-54	-63	99	102	53	.975	151	71	176	-1.6	-6.4	1.7	-.4	-4.8
TOT	265	145	4096	582	20181.0					12.4	3.88		.261	.326						.980	1742	892	2208					

Batter-Fielder Wins		Batting Average		On-Base Percentage		Slugging Average		On-Base Plus Slugging		Adjusted OPS		Adjusted Batter Runs	
R.Henderson-NY-Oak	4.6	Puckett-Min	.339	Boggs-Bos	.430	Sierra-Tex	.543	McGriff-Tor	.924	McGriff-Tor	161	McGriff-Tor	50.1
Boggs-Bos	**4.3**	Lansford-Oak	.336	Davis-Sea	.424	McGriff-Tor	.525	Davis-Sea	.920	Davis-Sea	155	Davis-Sea	42.6
Molitor-Mil	**4.1**	Boggs-Bos	.330	R.Henderson-NY-Oak	.411	Yount-Mil	.511	Yount-Mil	.896	Yount-Mil	152	Yount-Mil	42.6
McGriff-Tor	**4.0**	Yount-Mil	.318	McGriff-Tor	.399	Esasky-Bos	.500	Sierra-Tex	.889	Sierra-Tex	146	Boggs-Bos	41.3
Yount-Mil	**4.0**	Franco-Tex	.316	Lansford-Oak	.398	Davis-Sea	.496	Boggs-Bos	.879	Baines-Chi-Tex	143	Sierra-Tex	34.8

Runs		Hits		Doubles		Triples		Home Runs		Total Bases		Runs Batted In	
R.Henderson-NY-Oak	113	Puckett-Min	215	Boggs-Bos	51	Sierra-Tex	14	McGriff-Tor	36	Sierra-Tex	344	Sierra-Tex	119
Boggs-Bos	113	Sax-NY	205	Puckett-Min	45	White-Cal	13	Carter-Cle	35	Yount-Mil	314	Mattingly-NY	113
Yount-Mil	101	Boggs-Bos	205	Reed-Bos	42	Bradley-Bal	10	McGwire-Oak	33	Carter-Cle	303	Esasky-Bos	108
Sierra-Tex	101	Yount-Mil	195	Bell-Tor	41			Jackson-KC	32	Mattingly-NY	301	Jackson-KC	105
McGriff-Tor	98			Yount-Mil	38			Esasky-Bos	30	Puckett-Min	295	Carter-Cle	105

Stolen Bases		Base Stealing Runs		Fielding Runs-Infield		Fielding Runs-Outfield		Wins		Winning Pct.		Complete Games	
R.Henderson-NY-Oak	77	R.Henderson-NY-Oak	12.0	Reynolds-Sea	24.6	Snyder-Cle	12.9	Saberhagen-KG	23	Saberhagen-KC	793	Saberhagen-KC	12
Espy-Tex	45	Pettis-Det	4.2	Howell-Cal	24.1	Puckett-Min	10.7	Stewart-Oak	21	Blyleven-Cal	773	Morris-Det	10
White-Cal	44	White-Cal	4.1	Buechele-Tex	18.8	Barfield-Tor-NY	9.9	Moore-Oak	19	Davis-Oak	731	Finley-Cal	9
Sax-NY	43	Felder-Mil	4.0	Espinoza-NY	18.5	Polonia-Oak-NY	8.8	Davis-Oak	19	Stewart-Oak	700		
Pettis-Det	43	Franco-Tex	3.6	Gantner-Mil	17.8	Orsulak-Bal	6.0	Ballard-Bal	18	Ballard-Bal	692		

Strikeouts		Fewest BB/Game		Games		Saves		Base Runners/9		Adjusted Relief Runs		Relief Ranking	
Ryan-Tex	301	Key-Tor	1.13	Crim-Mil	76	Russell-Tex	38	Saberhagen-KC	8.71	Montgomery-KC	25.5	Montgomery-KC	33.7
Clemens-Bos	230	Saberhagen-KC	1.48	Murphy-Bos	74	Thigpen-Chi	34	Burns-Oak	8.88	Olson-Bal	20.5	Henke-Tor	29.4
Saberhagen-KC	193	Blyleven-Cal	1.64	Rogers-Tex	73	Schooler-Sea	33	Russell-Tex	8.92	Henke-Tor	19.5	Russell-Tex	29.3
Gubicza-KC	173	Bosio-Mil	1.84	Russell-Tex	71	Plesac-Mil	33	Montgomery-KC	9.10	Lamp-Bos	19.4	Jones-Cle	27.2
Bosio-Mil	173	Witt-Cal	1.96	Guetterman-NY	70	Eckersley-Oak	33	Plesac-Mil	9.39	Minton-Cal	17.5	Olson-Bal	26.6

Innings Pitched		Opponents' Avg.		Opponents' OBP		Earned Run Average		Adjusted ERA		Adjusted Starter Runs		Pitcher Wins	
Saberhagen-KC	262.1	Ryan-Tex	187	Saberhagen-KC	251	Saberhagen-KC	2.16	Saberhagen-KC	179	Saberhagen-KC	48.4	**Saberhagen-KC**	**5.3**
Stewart-Oak	257.2	Gordon-KC	210	Ryan-Tex	275	Finley-Cal	2.57	Finley-Cal	149	Blyleven-Cal	31.7	**Moore-Oak**	**3.7**
Gubicza-KC	255.0	Saberhagen-KC	217	Moore-Oak	286	Moore-Oak	2.61	Moore-Oak	142	Moore-Oak	30.0	**Montgomery-KC**	**3.2**
Clemens-Bos	253.1	Stieb-Tor	219	Blyleven-Cal	287	Blyleven-Cal	2.73	Blyleven-Cal	140	Finley-Cal	27.6	**Finley-Cal**	**3.2**
Milacki-Bal	243.0	Moore-Oak	219	Bosio-Mil	289	McCaskill-Cal	2.93	Clemens-Bos	132	Clemens-Bos	25.7	**Russell-Tex**	**3.1**

Get Outta My Nest, It's Starting to Rumble

Baltimore, last-place finishers the year before, led the East for most of the summer on Jeff Ballard's 18-8 surprise season and a balanced lineup. Toronto, after a 12-24 start, hired Cito Gaston as manager. While the Orioles came to earth, the Blue Jays stayed hot and pulled into a first-place tie on August 31. Through the final month, both teams played well, and Toronto won the title by taking two thrilling contests from Baltimore at SkyDome on the season's last weekend.

In their new domed stadium, Toronto—featuring sluggers Fred McGriff and George Bell—topped three million fans, an AL first. Robin Yount won his second MVP for Milwaukee. Tommy John retired at 46, and Jim Rice quit with elbow problems. Former Angels hurler Donnie Moore was a suicide, and on Christmas, Billy Martin perished in a car crash.

Despite another Cy Young for Kansas City's Bret Saberhagen, Tony LaRussa's A's easily won the West. Dave Stewart enjoyed his third straight 20-win season, and Dennis Eckersley was dominating in relief. A thrill for third-place California was the rookie season of lefty Jim Abbott, born without a right hand. Seattle debuted two rookies, Omar Vizquel and Ken Griffey Jr., on Opening Day. Texas gave cups of coffee to kid outfielders Juan Gonzalez and Sammy Sosa.

Rickey Henderson, back in the A's fold after a midseason deal, went to town in the ALCS: Henderson reached base 15 times, stole 8 bases, scored 8 runs, and even hit 2 homers. While Oakland beat Toronto in five, the final two were nail-biters.

The A's-Giants World Series was longer and more earth-shaking than anyone would have guessed. Prior to Game 3, with Oakland up two games to none, a deadly earthquake hit the Bay Area. After a ten-day hiatus, the series resumed. The Athletics twice more wiped the floor with the Giants to sweep the Series, outscoring the NL champs, 32-14.

1988 National League

TEAM	W	L	T	PCT	GB	HW	HL	R	OR	PA	H	2B	3B	HR	BB	SO	HB	SH	AVG	OBP	SLG	OPS	AOPS	BR	ABR	PF	SB	CS	BSA	BSR
EAST
NY	100	60	0	.625		56	24	**703**	532	6105	1387	251	24	**152**	544	842	32	65	.256	**.325**	**.396**	**721**	118	**99**	129	96	140	51	73	13
PIT	85	75	0	.531	15	43	38	651	616	6090	1327	240	45	110	**553**	947	32	66	.247	.317	.369	686	104	34	40	99	119	60	66	5
MON	81	81	1	.500	20	43	38	628	592	6169	1400	260	**48**	107	454	1053	32	66	.251	.309	.373	682	97	12	-19	105	189	89	68	10
CHI	77	85	1	.475	24	39	42	660	694	6202	**1481**	262	46	113	403	910	21	57	**.261**	.310	.383	693	100	30	0	105	120	46	72	10
STL	76	86	0	.469	25	41	40	578	633	6177	1373	207	33	71	484	**827**	22	66	.249	.309	.337	646	90	-49	-59	102	**234**	64	**79**	**29**
PHI	65	96	1	.404	35.5	38	42	597	734	6054	1294	246	31	106	489	981	**47**	67	.239	.306	.355	661	94	-21	-35	102	112	49	70	7
WEST
LA	94	67	1	.584		45	36	628	544	6045	1346	217	25	99	437	947	32	95	.248	.305	.352	657	98	-33	-16	97	131	46	74	13
CIN	87	74	0	.540	7	45	35	641	596	6062	1334	246	25	122	479	922	37	69	.246	.309	.368	677	97	7	-14	104	207	56	**79**	26
SD	83	78	0	.516	11	47	34	594	583	6032	1325	205	35	94	494	892	21	91	.247	.310	.351	661	98	-9	98	123	50	71	10
SF	83	79	0	.512	11.5	45	36	670	626	6175	-1353	227	44	113	550	1023	33	91	.248	.318	.368	686	108	32	61	96	121	78	61	-1
HOU	82	80	0	.506	12.5	44	37	617	617	6127	1338	239	31	96	474	840	38	77	.244	.306	.350	657	99	-32	-8	96	198	71	74	19
ATL	54	106	0	.338	39.5	28	51	555	741	6013	1319	228	28	96	432	848	21	74	.242	.298	.348	646	87	-57	-79	104	95	69	58	-3
TOT	969					514	453	7522		73251	16277	2828	415	1279	5793	11032	368	938	.248	.310	.363	673					1789	729	71	138

TEAM	CG	SHO	GR	SV	IP	H	HR	BB	SO	BR/9	ERA	AERA	OAV	OOB	PR	APR	PF	OSB	OCS	FA	E	WPB	DP	FW	PW	BW	BSW	DIF
EAST
NY	31	22	241	46	1439.0	**1253**	78	**404**	1100	10.6	2.91	112	**.235**	**.291**	86	59	95	204	52	**.981**	115	56	127	.9	6.4	**13.9**	.2	-1.3
PIT	12	11	313	46	1440.2	1349	108	469	790	11.6	3.47	99	.250	.311	-3	-4	100	142	58	.980	125	74	128	.3	-.4	4.3	-.7	1.5
MON	18	12	307	43	1482.2	1310	122	476	923	11.1	3.08	118	.238	.301	60	**86**	105	194	58	.978	142	53	145	-.5	9.3	-2.0	-.2	-6.6
CHI	30	10	290	29	1464.1	1494	115	490	897	12.4	3.84	95	.265	.325	-64	-32	106	139	77	.980	125	71	128	.5	-3.4	.0	-.2	-.8
STL	17	14	333	42	1470.2	1387	91	486	881	11.6	3.47	101	.252	.312	-4	7	102	118	62	**.981**	121	69	131	.6	.8	-6.4	**1.9**	-1.9
PHI	16	6	336	36	1433.0	1447	118	628	859	13.3	4.14	87	.265	.341	-110	-82	105	185	66	.976	145	70	139	-.7	-8.8	-3.8	-.5	-1.7
WEST
LA	**32**	**24**	295	49	1463.1	1291	84	473	1029	11.0	2.96	113	.237	.299	78	63	97	126	74	.977	142	50	126	-.5	6.8	-1.7	.2	8.8
CIN	24	13	**343**	43	1455.0	1271	121	504	934	11.1	3.35	107	.237	.303	16	34	103	129	72	.980	125	46	131	.4	3.7	-1.5	1.6	2.4
SD	30	9	238	39	1449.0	1332	112	439	885	11.1	3.38	104	.247	.304	27	19	99	**74**	56	**.981**	120	52	**147**	.6	2.0	-1.0	-.2	.9
SF	25	13	290	42	1462.1	1323	99	422	875	10.9	3.39	96	.242	.298	10	-22	95	119	44	.980	129	63	145	.2	-2.4	6.6	-1.4	-1.0
HOU	21	15	284	40	1474.2	1339	123	478	1049	11.3	3.41	98	.242	.304	7	-14	96	211	47	.978	138	**39**	124	-.3	-1.5	-.9	.8	2.9
ATL	14	4	318	25	1446.0	1481	108	524	810	12.7	4.09	89	.268	.334	-103	-65	106	148	62	.976	151	57	138	-1.1	-7.0	-8.5	-1.6	-7.8
TOT	270	153	3588	480	17480.2					11.6	3.45		.248	.310						.979	1578	700	1609					

Batter-Fielder Wins	Batting Average	On-Base Percentage	Slugging Average	On-Base Plus Slugging	Adjusted OPS	Adjusted Batter Runs
Strawberry-NY ...4.9	Gwynn-SD 313	Daniels-Cin............397	Strawberry-NY 545	Strawberry-NY 911	Strawberry-NY 166	Clark-SF 50.6
Smith-StL 4.6	Palmeiro-Chi.........307	Butler-SF 393	Galarraga-Mon 540	Clark-SF 894	Clark-SF 163	Strawberry-NY 47.5
Gibson-LA 4.4	Dawson-Chi 303	Clark-SF 386	Clark-SF 508	Galarraga-Mon 893	Gibson-LA 151	Gibson-LA 37.8
Larkin-Cin 4.3	Galarraga-Mon 302	Gibson-LA 377	VanSlyke-Pit 506	Gibson-LA 860	Bonds-Cin 146	Galarraga-Mon ...34.7
VanSlyke-Pit 4.1	Perry-Atl 300	Gwynn-SD 373	Dawson-Chi 504	Daniels-Cin 860	Galarraga-Mon 146	Bonilla-Pit 34.0

Runs	Hits	Doubles	Triples	Home Runs	Total Bases	Runs Batted In
Butler-SF 109	Galarraga-Mon 184	Galarraga-Mon 42	VanSlyke-Pit 15	Strawberry-NY 39	Galarraga-Mon ...329	Clark-SF 109
Gibson-LA 106	Dawson-Chi 179	Palmeiro-Chi 41	Coleman-StL 10	Davis-Hou 30	Dawson-Chi..........298	Strawberry-NY 101
Clark-SF 102	Palmeiro-Chi 178	Sabo-Cin 40	Young-Hou 9	Galarraga-Mon 29	VanSlyke-Pit 297	VanSlyke-Pit 100
VanSlyke-Pit 101	Sax-LA 175	Bream-Pit 37	Samuel-Phi 9	Clark-SF 29	Strawberry-NY 296	Bonilla-Pit 100
Strawberry-NY 101	Larkin-Cin 174		Butler-SF 9	McReynolds-NY 27	Clark-SF 292	

Stolen Bases	Base Stealing Runs	Fielding Runs-Infield	Fielding Runs-Outfield	Wins	Winning Pct.	Complete Games
Coleman-StL 81	Smith-StL 9.4	Smith-StL 21.0	Murphy-Atl 10.6	Jackson-Cin...........23	Cone-NY 870	Jackson-Cin...........15
Young-Hou 65	Coleman-StL 8.4	Wallach-Mon 19.3	Thompson-Phi 6.9	Hershiser-LA 23	Browning-Cin 783	Hershiser-LA 15
Smith-StL 57	McGee-StL 6.9	Bream-Pit 19.0	James-Phi 6.1	Cone-NY 20	Jackson-Cin 742	Show-SD 13
Sabo-Cin 46	Davis-Cin 6.7	R.Alomar-SD 15.5	McReynolds-NY 5.5	Reuschel-SF 19	Hershiser-LA 742	Sutcliffe-Chi...........12
Nixon-Mon 46	Larkin-Cin 6.3	Dunston-Chi 13.6	Bradley-Phi 5.3		Maddux-Chi 692	Gooden-NY 10

Strikeouts	Fewest BB/Game	Games	Saves	Base Runners/9	Adjusted Relief Runs	Relief Ranking
Ryan-Hou 228	B.Smith-Mon 1.45	Murphy-Cin 76	Franco-Cin............39	Myers-NY 8.47	Franco-Cin 17.9	Franco-Cin 35.7
Cone-NY 213	Mahler-Atl............1.52	Robinson-Pit 75	Gott-Pit 34	Perez-Mon 8.81	Holton-LA 15.6	Davis-SD 29.4
DeLeon-StL 208	Reuschel-SF..........1.54	Agosto-Hou 75	Worrell-StL 32	Franco-Cin 9.10	Davis-SD 15.5	Myers-NY 24.6
Scott-Hou 190	Ojeda-NY 1.56	Tekulve-Phi 70	Davis-SD 28	J.Howell-LA 9.14	Harris-Phi 13.0	Pena-LA 18.6
Fernandez-NY 189	Tudor-StL-LA 1.87	Franco-Cin.............70	Bedrosian-Phi 28	Scott-Hou 9.18	Pena-LA 12.6	Parrett-Mon 17.8

Innings Pitched	Opponents' Avg.	Opponents' OBP	Earned Run Average	Adjusted ERA	Adjusted Starter Runs	Pitcher Wins
Hershiser-LA 267.0	Fernandez-NY 191	Perez-Mon 252	Magrane-StL 2.18	Magrane-StL 162	Hershiser-LA 34.5	**Hershiser-LA** 4.5
Jackson-Cin 260.2	Perez-Mon 196	Scott-Hou 260	Cone-NY 2.22	Tudor-StL-LA 150	Cone-NY 27.6	**Franco-Cin** 4.0
Browning-Cin 250.2	Scott-Hou 204	Ojeda-NY 261	Hershiser-LA 2.26	Rijo-Cin 150	Tudor-StL-LA 24.2	**Davis-SD** 3.6
Mahler-Atl 249.0	Rijo-Cin 209	Hershiser-LA 269	Tudor-StL-LA 2.32	Perez-Mon 149	Jackson-Cin 24.1	Jackson-Cin 3.0
Maddux-Chi 249.0	Cone-NY 213	Fernandez-NY 271	Rijo-Cin 2.39	Hershiser-LA 148	Perez-Mon 23.8	**Cone-NY** 2.8

"I Don't Believe What I Just Saw"

Despite an undermanned offense and several pitching injuries, Los Angeles clung to the West Division lead. Free agent signing Kirk Gibson was MVP, while Orel Hershiser's record 59 scoreless innings won him a unanimous Cy Young. John Tudor's late-season acquisition buffed up the rotation.

The Mets, meanwhile, easily wrapped up the East. Darryl Strawberry enjoyed another spectacular season, as did Kevin McReynolds. Five Mets starters won in double figures. Manager Davey Johnson effectively platooned Mookie Wilson and Lenny Dykstra and found a position for late-season sensation Gregg Jefferies.

New York led in attendance, while second-place Pittsburgh's gate increased 61 percent. Wrigley Field saw its first night game on August 9; lights were difficult for many fans to accept. Cincinnati's Chris Sabo was Rookie of the Year, but several players not as impressive as freshmen had longer careers: Mark Grace, Roberto Alomar, Tom Glavine, Craig Biggio, and John Smoltz.

Owners were found guilty of collusion against 1987 free agents. This greased the path for Peter Ueberroth's resignation.

Several "new-look" free agents were also granted their freedom and the owners paid hundreds of millions in damages.

Scoring dropped 14 percent to 3.88 runs per game, the lowest since 1968, and homers fell 30 percent. Both Los Angeles and New York played in great pitchers' parks. Injuries ended Bruce Sutter's career, while Steve Carlton, Dave Concepcion, Ted Simmons, and Don Sutton retired. Giants 1930s ace Carl Hubbell passed away at 85.

Nobody expected the Dodgers to win the NLCS, but Tommy Lasorda's boys hung in, winning a 12-inning Game 4 to knot the series. In Game 7 Hershiser threw yet another complete-game shutout—he had eight during the season and added a final one in the World Series. Los Angeles then shocked prohibitive favorite Oakland in the World Series. An injured Gibson limped off the bench and ripped Dennis Eckersley for a magical game-winning homer in the opener, sparking the five-game upset. Most games were close, and Los Angeles pitchers held the A's to just 11 runs.

1988 American League

TEAM	W	L	T	PCT	GB	HW	HL	R	OR	PA	H	2B	3B	HR	BB	SO	HB	SH	AVG	OBP	SLG	OPS	AOPS	BR	ABR	PF	SB	CS	BSA	BSR
EAST																														
BOS	89	73	0	.549		53	28	**813**	689	6334	**1569**	310	39	124	**623**	728	45	66	**.283**	**.357**	.420	777	112	**146**	108	105	65	36	64	2
DET	88	74	0	.543	1	50	31	703	658	6153	1358	213	28	143	588	841	29	66	.250	.324	.378	702	99	-21	3	97	87	42	67	4
TOR	87	75	0	.537	2	45	36	763	680	6193	1491	271	**47**	158	521	935	31	34	.268	.332	.419	751	108	69	62	101	107	36	75	11
MIL	87	75	0	.537	2	47	34	682	**616**	6064	1409	258	26	113	439	911	37	59	.257	.314	.375	689	91	-57	-65	101	**159**	55	74	16
NY	85	76	0	.528	3.5	46	34	772	748	6297	1469	272	12	148	588	935	30	36	.263	.333	.395	728	103	37	40	100	146	39	**79**	18
CLE	78	84	0	.481	11	44	37	666	731	6045	1435	235	28	134	416	866	37	36	.261	.314	.387	701	92	-38	-57	103	97	50	66	4
BAL	54	107	0	.335	34.5	34	46	550	789	5979	1275	199	20	137	504	869	32	40	.238	.305	.359	664	87	-105	-91	98	69	44	61	0
WEST																														
OAK	104	58	0	.642		**54**	27	800	620	6356	1474	251	22	156	580	926	**65**	54	.263	.336	.399	735	108	51	76	97	129	54	70	9
MIN	91	71	0	.562	13	47	34	759	672	6180	1508	294	31	151	528	832	55	37	.274	.340	**.421**	761	109	97	73	103	107	63	63	1
KC	84	77	0	.522	19.5	44	36	704	648	6085	1419	275	40	121	486	944	33	46	.259	.321	.391	712	97	-9	-18	101	137	54	72	11
CAL	75	87	0	.463	29	35	46	714	771	6215	1458	258	31	124	469	819	49	63	.261	.321	.385	706	99	-19	-2	98	86	52	62	1
CHI	71	90	0	.441	32.5	40	41	631	757	6039	1327	224	35	132	446	908	34	**67**	.244	.303	.370	673	87	-96	-95	100	98	46	68	5
TEX	70	91	0	.435	33.5	38	43	637	735	6157	1378	227	39	112	542	1022	35	48	.252	.310	.368	688	90	-50	-67	103	130	57	70	9
SEA	68	93	0	.422	35.5	37	44	664	744	6017	1397	271	27	148	461	787	38	40	.257	.317	.398	715	95	-6	-37	105	95	61	61	0
TOT	1131					614	517	9858		86114	19967	3558	425	1901	7191	12323	550	692	.259	.324	.391	715					1512	689	69	91

TEAM	CG	SHO	GR	SV	IP	H	HR	BB	SO	BR/9	ERA	AERA	OAV	OOB	PR	APR	PF	OSB	OCS	FA	E	WPB	DP	FW	PW	BW	BSW	DIF
EAST																												
BOS	26	14	250	37	1426.1	1415	143	493	**1085**	12.3	3.97	104	.259	.322	-1	23	104	107	48	.984	93	59	123	1.6	2.3	**10.9**	-.5	-6.4
DET	34	8	220	36	1445.2	1361	150	497	890	11.8	3.71	103	.248	.312	41	21	97	**80**	43	.982	109	65	129	.6	2.1	.3	-.3	4.2
TOR	16	**17**	294	47	1449.0	1404	143	528	904	12.4	3.80	104	.256	.326	27	26	100	120	55	.982	110	60	170	.6	2.6	6.3	.5	-3.9
MIL	30	8	252	51	1449.1	1355	125	**437**	832	**11.2**	3.45	116	.248	**.303**	84	**88**	100	91	45	.981	120	46	146	-.0	**8.9**	-6.6	1.0	2.7
NY	16	5	**304**	43	1456.0	1512	157	487	861	12.7	4.26	93	.267	.328	-48	-48	100	85	29	.978	134	**41**	161	-.9	-4.9	4.0	**1.2**	5.0
CLE	35	10	230	46	1434.0	1501	144	442	812	12.4	4.16	99	.270	.326	-31	-5	104	99	53	.980	124	46	131	-.3	-.5	-5.8	-.3	3.8
BAL	20	7	287	26	1416.0	1506	153	523	709	13.2	4.54	87	.274	.340	-90	-97	99	136	56	.980	119	60	172	.0	-9.8	-9.2	-.7	-6.8
WEST																												
OAK	22	9	290	**64**	1489.1	1376	116	553	983	11.8	**3.44**	110	.247	.316	87	62	96	93	56	.983	105	75	151	.6	8.3	7.7	.2	7.9
MIN	18	9	265	52	1431.2	1457	146	453	897	12.3	3.93	104	.266	.325	6	23	103	112	41	**.986**	**84**	56	155	**2.1**	2.3	7.4	-.6	-1.2
KC	29	12	253	32	1428.1	1415	102	465	886	12.1	3.65	109	.258	.318	49	54	101	117	42	.980	124	67	147	-.3	5.5	-1.8	.5	3.0
CAL	26	9	262	33	1455.2	1503	135	508	817	13.1	4.32	90	.270	.338	-57	-73	98	98	**64**	.979	135	81	175	-.9	-7.4	-.2	-.6	3.0
CHI	11	9	293	43	1439.0	1467	138	533	754	12.7	4.12	97	.266	.331	-25	-20	101	108	53	.976	154	71	**177**	-2.1	-2.0	-9.6	-.2	-4.3
TEX	**41**	11	251	31	1438.2	**1310**	129	654	912	12.6	4.05	101	**.244**	.329	-13	7	103	145	52	.979	131	108	145	-.7	.7	-6.8	.2	-4.0
SEA	28	11	292	28	1428.1	1385	144	558	981	12.5	4.15	101	.256	.327	-30	3	105	117	52	.980	123	66	168	-.2	.3	-3.7	-.7	-8.2
TOT	352	139	3743	569	20187.0					12.4	3.97		.259	.324						.981	1665	901	2150					

Batter-Fielder Wins		Batting Average		On-Base Percentage		Slugging Average		On-Base Plus Slugging		Adjusted OPS		Adjusted Batter Runs	
Boggs-Bos	6.4	Boggs-Bos	366	Boggs-Bos	476	Canseco-Oak	569	Boggs-Bos	965	Canseco-Oak	171	Boggs-Bos	62.2
Canseco-Oak	5.9	Puckett-Min	356	Greenwell-Bos	416	McGriff-Tor	552	Canseco-Oak	959	Boggs-Bos	165	Canseco-Oak	59.9
Puckett-Min	4.9	Greenwell-Bos	325	Davis-Sea	412	Gaetti-Min	551	Greenwell-Bos	946	Winfield-NY	158	Greenwell-Bos	49.1
Greenwell-Bos	4.7	Winfield-NY	322	Winfield-NY	398	Puckett-Min	545	McGriff-Tor	928	Greenwell-Bos	157	Winfield-NY	45.3
C.Ripken-Bal	4.2	Molitor-Mil	312	Henderson-NY	394	Greenwell-Bos	531	Winfield-NY	927	McGriff-Tor	156	Puckett-Min	42.1

Runs		Hits		Doubles		Triples		Home Runs		Total Bases		Runs Batted In	
Boggs-Bos	128	Puckett-Min	234	Boggs-Bos	45	Yount-Mil	11	Canseco-Oak	42	Puckett-Min	358	Canseco-Oak	124
Canseco-Oak	120	Boggs-Bos	214	Ray-Cal	42	Wilson-KC	11	McGriff-Tor	34	Canseco-Oak	347	Puckett-Min	121
Henderson-NY	118	Greenwell-Bos	192	Puckett-Min	42	Reynolds-Sea	11	McGwire-Oak	32	Greenwell-Bos	313	Greenwell-Bos	119
Molitor-Mil	115	Yount-Mil	190	Brett-KC	42	Greenwell-Bos	8	Murray-Bal	28	Brett-KC	300	Evans-Bos	107
Puckett-Min	109	Molitor-Mil	190	Fernandez-Tor	41			Gaetti-Min	28	Carter-Cle	297	Winfield-NY	107

Stolen Bases		Base Stealing Runs		Fielding Runs-Infield		Fielding Runs-Outfield		Wins		Winning Pct.		Complete Games	
Henderson-NY	93	Henderson-NY	15.9	Guillen-Chi	40.8	Barfield-Tor	13.1	Viola-Min	24	Viola-Min	774	Stewart-Oak	14
Pettis-Det	44	Pettis-Det	6.2	Gruber-Tor	26.4	Gladden-Min	12.1	Stewart-Oak	21	Hurst-Bos	750	Clemens-Bos	14
Molitor-Mil	41	Molitor-Mil	5.5	Schofield-Cal	21.7	Snyder-Cle	9.6	Gubicza-KC	20	Gubicza-KC	714	Witt-Tex	13
Canseco-Oak	40	Wilson-KC	5.3	White-KC	20.9	Puckett-Min	9.3			Davis-Oak	696	Witt-Cal	12
		Redus-Chi	5.0	Randolph-NY	13.9	White-Cal	8.5			Stieb-Tor	667	Swindell-Cle	12

Strikeouts		Fewest BB/Game		Games		Saves		Base Runners/9		Adjusted Relief Runs		Relief Ranking	
Clemens-Bos	291	Anderson-Min	1.65	Crim-Mil	70	Eckersley-Oak	45	Eckersley-Oak	7.93	Henneman-Det	19.7	Henneman-Det	37.7
Langston-Sea	235	Swindell-Cle	1.67	Thigpen-Chi	68	Reardon-Min	42	Higuera-Mil	9.22	Mirabella-Mil	15.7	Harvey-Cal	25.8
Viola-Min	193	Alexander-Det	1.81	Williams-Tex	67	Jones-Cle	37	McMurtry-Tex	9.30	Jones-Cle	15.3	Jones-Cle	23.8
Stewart-Oak	192	Bosio-Mil	1.88	Henneman-Det	65	Thigpen-Chi	34	Jones-Cle	9.40	Jackson-Sea	14.4	Eckersley-Oak	23.3
Higuera-Mil	192	Viola-Min	1.90			Plesac-Mil	30	Harvey-Cal	9.47	Harvey-Cal	14.2	Reardon-Min	23.0

Innings Pitched		Opponents' Avg.		Opponents' OBP		Earned Run Average		Adjusted ERA		Adjusted Starter Runs		Pitcher Wins	
Stewart-Oak	275.2	Robinson-Det	197	Higuera-Mil	263	Anderson-Min	2.45	Anderson-Min	167	Higuera-Mil	40.2	**Viola-Min**	4.7
Gubicza-KC	269.2	Higuera-Mil	207	Clemens-Bos	270	Higuera-Mil	2.45	Higuera-Mil	163	Viola-Min	40.1	**Higuera-Mil**	4.4
Clemens-Bos	264.0	Stieb-Tor	210	Robinson-Det	282	Viola-Min	2.64	Viola-Min	155	Gubicza-KC	37.3	**Gubicza-KC**	3.9
Langston-Sea	261.1	Witt-Tex	216	Viola-Min	286	Gubicza-KC	2.70	Gubicza-KC	148	Clemens-Bos	34.3	**Henneman-Det**	3.9
Saberhagen-KC	260.2	Clemens-Bos	220	Swindell-Cle	286	Clemens-Bos	2.93	Clemens-Bos	141	Anderson-Min	31.0	**Anderson-Min**	3.8

Oakland Surprise

Some years, it's better just to stay home. The Baltimore Orioles lost their first 21 games of the season and finished a deep last. As scoring dropped 11 percent to its lowest full-season total since 1978, several big names from that time retired: Don Baylor, Chris Chambliss, Ron Guidry, Graig Nettles, and Joe Niekro.

The balance of power in the AL switched from East to West in the late 1980s; the league's best teams were now Oakland and Minnesota. The A's had a veteran staff led by 21-game winner Dave Stewart, who survived a record 16 balks called by umpires trying to enforce a short-lived edict from the commissioner's office. "Bash Brothers" Mark McGwire and MVP Jose Canseco (the first player with 40 homers and 40 steals in the same year), plowed up enough runs for 104 wins, the franchise's highest total since Connie Mack's Philadelphia juggernaut of 1931. The Twins actually won six more games than their world championship team of '87, but Oakland kept them at arm's length. Cy Young winner Frank Viola couldn't make up for lineup gaps and a lack of quality pitching.

Early in the schedule, the Yankees and Tigers paced the East. Slumping Boston fired manager John McNamara, and got hot under new skipper Joe Morgan. With Wade Boggs claiming his fifth batting title in six years, and Dwight Evans, Ellis Burks, and Mike Greenwell fashioning the league's top outfield, Boston won even though the team didn't have a dependable *third* starter until Mike Boddicker's arrival in July. Detroit, Milwaukee, Toronto, and New York all finished within 5 games. A second-place finish was the end of the road for the Tigers, the oldest team in the league and about to collapse.

Oakland took care of business in the ALCS, sweeping Boston in four with excellent pitching and Canseco's 3 homers. The World Series against the Dodgers, however, was anything but businesslike. After Kirk Gibson's pinch-homer sunk the A's in Game 1, Oakland fell in five.

1987 National League

TEAM	W	L	T	PCT	GB	HW	HL	R	OR	PA	H	2B	3B	HR	BB	SO	HB	SH	AVG	OBP	SLG	OPS	AOPS	BR	ABR	PF	SB	CS	BSA	BSR
EAST																														
STL	95	67	0	.586		**49**	32	798	693	6297	1449	252	49	94	**644**	933	18	84	.263	**.340**	.378	718	95	-9	-28	103	248	72	78	29
NY	92	70	0	.568	3	**49**	32	823	698	6333	**1499**	287	34	192	592	1012	31	70	**.268**	.339	**.434**	773	115	84	119	96	159	49	76	18
MON	91	71	0	.562	4	48	33	741	720	6162	1467	**310**	39	120	501	918	35	57	.265	.328	.401	729	95	-4	-30	104	166	74	69	11
PIT	80	82	0	.494	15	47	34	723	744	6222	1464	282	45	131	535	914	29	71	.264	.330	.403	733	99	4	-5	101	140	58	71	11
PHI	80	82	0	.494	15	43	38	702	749	6190	1390	248	**51**	169	587	1109	25	63	.254	.327	.410	737	98	7	-18	104	111	49	69	7
CHI	76	85	0	.472	18.5	40	40	720	801	6197	1475	244	33	**209**	504	1064	21	59	.264	.326	.432	758	102	38	8	104	109	48	69	7
WEST																														
SF	90	72	0	.556		46	35	783	**669**	6248	1458	274	32	205	511	1094	**39**	55	.260	.324	.430	754	110	33	71	95	126	97	57	-6
CIN	84	78	0	.519	6	42	39	783	752	6196	1478	262	29	192	514	928	31	56	.264	.330	.427	757	102	42	14	104	169	46	**79**	21
HOU	76	86	0	.469	14	47	34	648	678	6143	1386	238	28	122	526	936	24	58	.253	.318	.373	691	92	-79	-54	96	162	46	78	20
LA	73	89	0	.451	17	40	41	635	611	6114	1389	236	23	125	445	923	31	82	.252	.309	.371	680	87	-111	-95	98	128	59	68	8
ATL	69	92	0	.429	20.5	42	39	747	829	6227	1401	284	24	152	641	**834**	38	**86**	.258	.339	.403	742	98	33	4	104	135	68	67	6
SD	65	97	0	.401	25	37	44	668	763	6177	1419	209	48	113	577	992	21	81	.260	.332	.378	710	98	-37	-10	96	198	91	69	12
TOT	971					530	441	8771		74506	17275	3126	435	1824	6577	11657	349	823	.261	.328	.404	732					1851	757	71	142

TEAM	CG	SHO	GR	SV	IP	H	HR	BB	SO	BR/9	ERA	AERA	OAV	OOB	PR	APR	PF	OSB	OCS	FA	E	WPB	DP	FW	PW	BW	BSW	DIF
EAST																												
STL	10	7	362	48	1466.0	1484	**129**	533	873	12.5	3.91	107	.265	.331	28	46	103	**100**	49	**.982**	116	62	172	.9	4.6	-2.8	**1.7**	9.6
NY	16	7	308	**51**	1454.0	1407	135	510	1032	12.1	3.84	100	.254	.319	38	-3	94	161	57	.978	137	51	137	-.3	-.3	**11.8**	.6	-.8
MON	16	8	335	50	1450.1	1428	145	**446**	1012	**11.8**	3.92	109	.257	.312	26	**52**	104	202	46	.976	147	55	122	-.9	**5.2**	-3.0	-.0	8.8
PIT	25	**13**	313	39	1445.0	1377	164	562	914	12.2	4.20	99	.253	.323	19	-6	102	134	84	.980	123	70	147	.5	-.6	-.5	-.0	-.3
PHI	13	7	389	48	1448.1	1453	167	587	877	12.9	4.18	102	.263	.335	-16	16	105	184	63	.980	121	52	137	.6	1.6	-1.8	-.5	-.9
CHI	11	5	327	48	1434.2	1524	159	628	1024	13.7	4.55	95	.275	.349	-76	-36	106	169	69	.979	130	71	154	.0	-3.6	.8	-.5	-1.3
WEST																												
SF	19	10	348	38	1471.0	1407	146	547	1038	12.1	**3.68**	105	.255	.323	66	29	94	132	**87**	.980	129	74	**183**	.1	2.9	7.1	-1.8	.7
CIN	7	6	**392**	44	1452.1	1486	170	485	919	12.4	4.24	99	.267	.326	-27	-4	103	139	75	.979	130	**46**	137	.0	-.4	1.4	.9	1.0
HOU	13	**13**	316	33	1441.1	**1363**	141	525	**1137**	12.0	3.84	102	**.250**	.317	38	14	96	199	54	.981	116	50	113	.9	1.4	-5.4	.8	-2.7
LA	**29**	8	281	32	1455.0	1415	130	565	1097	12.4	3.72	107	.255	.325	59	43	98	120	65	.975	155	62	144	-1.3	4.3	-9.5	-.4	-1.1
ATL	16	4	324	32	1427.2	1529	163	587	837	13.6	4.63	93	.276	.347	-87	-45	106	185	57	**.982**	116	53	170	.8	-4.5	.4	-.6	-7.7
SD	14	10	335	33	1433.1	1402	175	602	897	12.8	4.27	93	.256	.332	-30	-51	97	126	51	.976	147	77	135	-.9	-5.1	-1.0	.0	-9.1
TOT	189	98	4030	496	17379.0					12.5	4.08		.261	.328						.979	1567	723	1751					

Batter-Fielder Wins		Batting Average		On-Base Percentage		Slugging Average		On-Base Plus Slugging		Adjusted OPS		Adjusted Batter Runs	
Davis-Cin	5.9	Gwynn-SD	370	Clark-StL	459	Clark-StL	597	Clark-StL	1055	Clark-StL	173	Gwynn-SD	55.3
Gwynn-SD	5.8	Guerrero-LA	338	Gwynn-SD	447	Davis-Cin	593	Murphy-Atl	997	Strawberry-NY	163	Clark-StL	53.3
Raines-Mon	4.9	Raines-Mon	330	Raines-Mon	429	Strawberry-NY	583	Davis-Cin	991	Gwynn-SD	160	Strawberry-NY	51.2
Murphy-Atl	4.6	Kruk-SD	313	Murphy-Atl	417	Clark-SF	580	Strawberry-NY	981	Guerrero-LA	156	Murphy-Atl	49.7
Smith-StL	4.3	James-Atl	312	Guerrero-LA	416	Murphy-Atl	580	Gwynn-SD	958	Murphy-Atl	155	Guerrero-LA	46.3

Runs		Hits		Doubles		Triples		Home Runs		Total Bases		Runs Batted In	
Raines-Mon	123	Gwynn-SD	218	Wallach-Mon	42	Samuel-Phi	15	Dawson-Chi	49	Dawson-Chi	353	Dawson-Chi	137
Coleman-StL	121	Guerrero-LA	184	Smith-StL	40	Gwynn-SD	13	Murphy-Atl	44	Samuel-Phi	329	Wallach-Mon	123
Davis-Cin	120	Smith-StL	182	Galarraga-Mon	40	VanSlyke-Pit	11	Strawberry-NY	39	Murphy-Atl	328	Schmidt-Phi	113
Gwynn-SD	119	Coleman-StL	180			McGee-StL	11	Davis-Cin	37	Strawberry-NY	310	Clark-StL	106
Murphy-Atl	115					Coleman-StL	10	Johnson-NY	36	Clark-SF	307		

Stolen Bases		Base Stealing Runs		Fielding Runs-Infield		Fielding Runs-Outfield		Wins		Winning Pct.		Complete Games	
Coleman-StL	109	Coleman-StL	16.3	Hubbard-Atl	28.3	Bonds-Pit	16.4	Sutcliffe-Chi	18	Gooden-NY	682	Reuschel-Pit-SF	12
Gwynn-SD	56	Raines-Mon	9.3	Hernandez-NY	16.3	Davis-Cin	15.5	Rawley-Phi	17	Sutcliffe-Chi	643	Valenzuela-LA	12
Hatcher-Hou	53	Davis-Cin	8.9	Templeton-SD	13.4	Wilson-Phi	9.9	Scott-Hou	16	Welch-LA	625	Hershiser-LA	10
Raines-Mon	50	Hatcher-Hou	8.5	Santana-NY	12.6	Raines-Mon	6.9	Hershiser-LA	16	Rawley-Phi	607	Z.Smith-Atl	9
Davis-Cin	50	Gwynn-SD	8.1	Smith-StL	11.8	Hatcher-Hou	5.1			Z.Smith-Atl	600	Scott-Hou	8

Strikeouts		Fewest BB/Game		Games		Saves		Base Runners/9		Adjusted Relief Runs		Relief Ranking	
Ryan-Hou	270	Reuschel-Pit-SF	1.67	Tekulve-Phi	90	Bedrosian-Phi	40	Burke-Mon	8.01	Burke-Mon	28.0	Worrell-StL	31.8
Scott-Hou	233	Heaton-Mon	1.72	Murphy-Cin	87	Smith-Chi	36	Perez-Mon	8.83	McGaffigan-Mon	23.3	Franco-Cin	29.3
Welch-LA	196	Gullickson-Cin	2.13	Williams-Cin	85	Worrell-StL	33	Smith-Hou	9.15	Williams-Cin	18.6	Burke-Mon	29.1
Valenzuela-LA	190	Forsch-StL	2.26	J.Robinson-SF-Pit	81	Franco-Cin	32	Perry-StL-Cin	9.78	Worrell-StL	16.4	Smith-Chi	22.8
Hershiser-LA	190	Drabek-Pit	2.35	McCullers-SD	78	McDowell-NY	25	Reuschel-Pit-SF	10.19	J.Robinson-SF-Pit	15.8	J.Robinson-SF-Pit	22.7

Innings Pitched		Opponents' Avg.		Opponents' OBP		Earned Run Average		Adjusted ERA		Adjusted Starter Runs		Pitcher Wins	
Hershiser-LA	264.2	Ryan-Hou	199	Scott-Hou	281	Ryan-Hou	2.76	Ryan-Hou	142	Ryan-Hou	26.9	**Hershiser-LA**	3.5
Welch-LA	251.2	Scott-Hou	217	Reuschel-Pit-SF	282	Dunne-Pit	3.03	Dunne-Pit	138	Hershiser-LA	26.1	**Worrell-StL**	3.2
Valenzuela-LA	251.0	Welch-LA	221	Ryan-Hou	284	Hershiser-LA	3.06	Reuschel-Pit-SF	132	Welch-LA	25.2	**Franco-Cin**	2.9
Scott-Hou	247.2	Darling-NY	233	Welch-LA	289	Reuschel-Pit-SF	3.09	Hershiser-LA	130	Reuschel-Pit-SF	23.9	**Burke-Mon**	2.9
Z.Smith-Atl	242.0	Dunne-Pit	240	Drabek-Pit	294	Gooden-NY	3.21	Welch-LA	124	Scott-Hou	21.8	**Ryan-Hou**	2.5

Hum-Birds

Prior to the season, some very attractive free agents found surprisingly little interest. "Unwanted" Andre Dawson gave the Cubs a blank contract, then for a relatively small salary hit 49 homers and captured MVP honors. He couldn't carry Chicago out of last place, however. St. Louis jumped to an early lead, and then held off the Mets to win Whitey Herzog's last title.

Vince Coleman cleared 100 steals for the third time, Jack Clark led the NL in slugging and on-base percentage, and Ozzie Smith finished second in MVP voting. No St. Louis pitcher won more than 11, but eight won at least eight. The Cardinals—along with the Mets—became the first besides Los Angeles to draw three million; league attendance increased 10 percent.

Mets sluggers Darryl Strawberry and Howard Johnson did their best, but Dwight Gooden was suspended for drug possession and several hurlers suffered injuries. Philadelphia's Steve Bedrosian won an extraordinarily close Cy Young vote over Ricks Sutcliffe and Reuschel.

Last in 1985, Roger Craig's "Hum Baby" Giants acquired Reuschel, Kevin Mitchell, Dave Dravecky, and Don Robinson in midseason deals and won the West Division. Will Clark led the attack. The remarkable Eric Davis couldn't quite carry Cincinnati to the division crown; the Reds lacked pitching. Padres receiver Benito Santiago took Rookie of the Year. Houston's Nolan Ryan was 8-16 but fanned a record 11.48 hitters per game.

The .261 league average was the decade's highest, as was the scoring rate. Homers also increased 19 percent. Former Dodgers infielders Ron Cey, Steve Garvey, and Davey Lopes all retired, as did 48-year-old Phil Niekro.

San Francisco went up three games to two in the NLCS on timely hitting and veteran pitching, but John Tudor and Danny Cox shut out the Giants in Games 6 and 7 at Busch Stadium. St. Louis couldn't win the World Series, however, falling in seven to Minnesota.

1987 American League

TEAM	W	L	T	PCT	GB	HW	HL	R	OR	PA	H	2B	3B	HR	BB	SO	HB	SH	AVG	OBP	SLG	OPS	AOPS	BR	ABR	PF	SB	CS	BSA	BSR
EAST																														
DET	98	64	0	.605		54	27	896	735	6443	1535	274	32	**225**	653	913	46	39	.272	.349	.451	800	114	94	131	96	106	50	68	6
TOR	96	66	0	.593	2	52	29	845	**655**	6293	1514	277	38	215	555	970	38	30	.269	.336	.446	782	103	43	23	102	126	50	72	10
MIL	91	71	0	.562	7	48	33	862	817	6368	1552	272	46	163	598	1040	32	63	.276	.346	.428	774	101	41	15	103	**176**	74	70	**13**
NY	89	73	0	.549	9	51	30	788	758	6219	1445	239	16	196	604	949	28	38	.262	.336	.418	754	99	-5	1	99	105	43	71	3
BOS	78	84	0	.481	20	50	30	842	825	6359	**1554**	273	26	174	606	**825**	**57**	52	**.278**	**.352**	.430	782	103	64	40	103	77	45	63	1
BAL	67	95	0	.414	31	31	51	729	880	6185	1437	219	20	211	524	939	22	31	.258	.322	.418	740	96	-50	-32	98	69	45	61	2
CLE	61	101	0	.377	37	35	46	742	957	6212	1476	267	30	187	489	977	31	44	.263	.324	.422	746	95	-36	-43	101	140	54	72	12
WEST																														
MIN	85	77	0	.525		**56**	25	786	806	6088	1422	258	35	196	523	898	38	47	.261	.328	.430	758	95	-8	-36	104	113	65	63	2
KC	83	79	0	.512	2	46	35	715	691	6128	1443	239	40	168	523	1034	30	34	.262	.328	.412	740	91	-42	-62	103	125	43	**74**	12
OAK	81	81	0	.500	4	42	39	806	789	6238	1432	263	33	199	593	1056	36	50	.260	.333	.428	761	107	5	60	94	140	63	69	7
SEA	78	84	0	.481	7	40	41	760	801	6139	1499	282	**48**	161	500	863	43	38	.272	.335	.428	763	95	9	-30	105	174	73	70	**13**
CHI	77	85	0	.475	8	38	43	748	746	6164	1427	**283**	36	173	487	971	33	54	.258	.319	.415	734	90	-57	-77	103	138	52	73	12
TEX	75	87	0	.463	10	43	38	823	849	6248	1478	264	35	194	567	1081	24	42	.266	.333	.430	763	99	9	4	101	120	71	63	2
CAL	75	87	0	.463	10	38	43	770	803	6301	1406	257	26	172	590	926	35	70	.252	.326	.401	727	94	-64	-40	97	125	44	**74**	12
TOT	1134					624	510	11112		87385	20620	3667	461	2634	7812	13442	493	632	.265	.333	.425	759					1734	772	69	111

TEAM	CG	SHO	GR	SV	IP	H	HR	BB	SO	BR/9	ERA	AERA	OAV	OOB	PR	APR	PF	OSB	OCS	FA	E	WPB	DP	FW	PW	BW	BSW	DIF
EAST																												
DET	33	10	247	31	1456.0	1430	180	563	976	12.5	4.02	106	.256	.325	70	38	95	118	43	.980	122	85	147	.1	3.6	**12.5**	-.2	1.0
TOR	18	8	**336**	43	1454.0	**1323**	158	567	1064	11.8	3.74	121	.244	.316	115	123	101	123	59	.982	111	69	148	.8	**11.7**	2.2	.2	.1
MIL	28	6	282	45	1464.0	1548	169	529	1039	12.9	4.62	99	.271	.333	-27	-5	103	119	58	.976	145	58	155	-1.3	-.5	1.4	.0	5.6
NY	19	10	278	**47**	1446.1	1475	179	542	900	12.8	4.36	101	.266	.332	16	10	99	114	63	.983	102	83	155	1.3	1.0	.0	.0	-3.7
BOS	**47**	**13**	236	16	1439.2	1584	190	517	1034	13.4	4.77	95	.282	.344	-50	-34	102	109	60	.982	110	67	158	.8	-3.2	3.8	-.7	-3.7
BAL	17	6	294	30	1439.2	1555	226	547	870	13.3	5.01	88	.276	.341	-88	-94	99	145	57	.982	111	57	**174**	.8	-9.0	-3.1	-.9	-1.9
CLE	24	8	308	25	1422.2	1566	219	606	849	14.1	5.28	86	.278	.351	-131	-113	102	111	51	.975	153	90	128	-1.8	-10.8	-4.1	.4	-3.7
WEST																												
MIN	16	4	289	39	1427.1	1465	210	564	990	13.1	4.63	100	.266	.337	-27	0	104	168	46	**.984**	**98**	83	147	**1.6**	.0	-3.4	-.6	6.4
KC	44	11	225	26	1424.0	1424	**128**	548	923	12.7	3.86	119	.261	.330	95	111	103	124	**66**	.979	131	71	151	-.5	10.6	-5.9	.4	-2.6
OAK	18	6	328	40	1445.2	1442	176	531	1042	12.5	4.32	96	.258	.324	22	-30	93	117	54	.977	142	70	122	-1.1	-2.9	5.7	.1	-1.8
SEA	39	10	251	33	1430.2	1503	199	**497**	919	12.8	4.49	105	.272	.332	-5	36	106	111	50	.980	122	51	150	.1	3.4	-2.9	**.5**	-4.2
CHI	29	12	270	37	1447.2	1436	189	537	792	12.5	4.30	107	.259	.327	26	49	104	98	51	.981	116	**46**	174	.5	4.7	-7.3	.4	-2.2
TEX	20	3	329	27	1444.1	1388	199	760	**1103**	13.7	4.63	97	.253	.347	-28	-21	101	205	56	.976	151	134	148	-1.7	-2.0	.4	-.6	-2.1
CAL	20	7	244	36	1457.1	1481	212	504	941	12.5	4.38	99	.264	.327	13	-11	97	**72**	58	.981	117	65	162	.4	-1.0	-3.8	.4	-1.9
TOT	372	114	3917	475	20195.2					12.9	4.46		.265	.333						.980	1731	1029	2119					

Leaderboards

Batter-Fielder Wins		Batting Average		On-Base Percentage		Slugging Average		On-Base Plus Slugging		Adjusted OPS		Adjusted Batter Runs	
Boggs-Bos	6.5	Boggs-Bos	363	Boggs-Bos	461	McGwire-Oak	618	Boggs-Bos	1049	Boggs-Bos	172	Boggs-Bos	64.5
Trammell-Det	6.1	Molitor-Mil	353	Molitor-Mil	438	Bell-Tor	605	Molitor-Mil	1003	McGwire-Oak	167	McGwire-Oak	53.5
Fernandez-Tor	4.1	Trammell-Det	343	Evans-Bos	417	Boggs-Bos	588	McGwire-Oak	987	Molitor-Mil	159	Trammell-Det	49.7
Molitor-Mil	3.9	Puckett-Min	332	Randolph-NY	411	Evans-Bos	569	Evans-Bos	986	Trammell-Det	157	Evans-Bos	48.0
McGwire-Oak	3.5	Mattingly-NY	327	Trammell-Det	402	Molitor-Mil	566	Bell-Tor	957	Evans-Bos	155	Molitor-Mil	43.3

Runs		Hits		Doubles		Triples		Home Runs		Total Bases		Runs Batted In	
Molitor-Mil	114	Seitzer-KC	207	Molitor-Mil	41	Wilson-KC	15	McGwire-Oak	49	Bell-Tor	369	Bell-Tor	134
Bell-Tor	111	Puckett-Min	207	Boggs-Bos	40	Polonia-Oak	10	Bell-Tor	47	McGwire-Oak	344	Evans-Bos	123
Whitaker-Det	110	Trammell-Det	205			P.Bradley-Sea	10			Puckett-Min	333	McGwire-Oak	118
Downing-Cal	110	Boggs-Bos	200			Yount-Mil	9			Trammell-Det	329	Joyner-Cal	117
		Yount-Mil	198							Boggs-Bos	324	Mattingly-NY	115

Stolen Bases		Base Stealing Runs		Fielding Runs-Infield		Fielding Runs-Outfield		Wins		Winning Pct.		Complete Games	
Reynolds-Sea	60	Wilson-KC	9.1	Barrett-Bos	32.6	White-Cal	17.6	Stewart-Oak	20	Clemens-Bos	690	Clemens-Bos	18
Wilson-KC	59	Redus-Chi	7.6	Reynolds-Sea	24.0	Kingery-Sea	13.6	Clemens-Bos	20	Key-Tor	680	Saberhagen-KC	15
Redus-Chi	52	Molitor-Mil	6.4	White-KC	22.1	Barfield-Tor	13.4	Langston-Sea	19	Saberhagen-KC	643	Hurst-Bos	15
Molitor-Mil	45	Henderson-NY	6.2	Salazar-KC	20.3	Braggs-Mil	10.2			Higuera-Mil	643	Langston-Sea	14
Henderson-NY	41	Reynolds-Sea	6.2	Gagne-Min	19.3	Gladden-Min	7.1					Higuera-Mil	14

Strikeouts		Fewest BB/Game		Games		Saves		Base Runners/9		Adjusted Relief Runs		Relief Ranking	
Langston-Sea	262	Long-Chi	1.49	Eichhorn-Tor	89	Henke-Tor	34	Henke-Tor	8.33	Henke-Tor	21.6	Henke-Tor	29.2
Clemens-Bos	256	Saberhagen-KC	1.86	Williams-Tex	85	Righetti-NY	31	Alexander-Det	9.07	Eichhorn-Tor	19.8	Thigpen-Chi	28.4
Higuera-Mil	240	Sutton-Cal	1.93	Mohorcic-Tex	74	Reardon-Min	31	Eckersley-Oak	9.26	Mohorcic-Tex	18.3	Mohorcic-Tex	27.9
Hough-Tex	223	Bannister-Chi	1.93	Henke-Tor	72	Plesac-Mil	23	Key-Tor	9.59	Thigpen-Chi	17.8	Plesac-Mil	27.8
Morris-Det	208	Young-Oak	1.95	Musselman-Tex	68	Buice-Cal	17	Wilkinson-Sea	9.67	Eckersley-Oak	16.8	Eichhorn-Tor	23.7

Innings Pitched		Opponents' Avg.		Opponents' OBP		Earned Run Average		Adjusted ERA		Adjusted Starter Runs		Pitcher Wins	
Hough-Tex	285.1	Key-Tor	221	Key-Tor	272	Key-Tor	2.76	Key-Tor	164	Clemens-Bos	49.2	**Clemens-Bos**	4.5
Clemens-Bos	281.2	Hough-Tex	223	Bannister-Chi	285	Viola-Min	2.90	Viola-Min	160	Key-Tor	47.9	**Viola-Min**	4.5
Langston-Sea	272.0	Morris-Det	228	Morris-Det	293	Clemens-Bos	2.97	Clemens-Bos	154	Viola-Min	45.9	Key-Tor	4.3
Blyleven-Min	267.0	Stewart-Oak	229	Young-Oak	293	Saberhagen-KC	3.36	Saberhagen-KC	137	Saberhagen-KC	38.3	**Saberhagen-KC**	3.8
Morris-Det	266.0	DeLeon-Chi	230	Viola-Min	293	Morris-Det	3.38	Leibrandt-KC	135	Leibrandt-KC	30.3	**Leibrandt-KC**	3.3

Twinkies in a Box

Milwaukee won 13 straight to start the season, but the Brewers fell off the pace despite Paul Molitor's 39-game hitting streak. Boston didn't win despite Roger Clemens' second consecutive Cy Young. The real race was at the border.

The Tigers and Blue Jays hung close into September. Toronto's George Bell was MVP, while Doyle Alexander went 9-0 for Detroit when acquired from Atlanta in August (for farmhand John Smoltz). Detroit was old; only one regular and one starter were under 29. Toronto, meanwhile, struggled to find starting pitching. From September 24-26, the Jays swept the Tigers to build a lead of 3½; from that point, Toronto lost four straight while Detroit perked up. In a thrilling Jays-Tigers set on the final weekend at Detroit, the Tigers won to move into a tie on Friday, moved ahead with a comeback victory Saturday, and clinched on Frank Tanana's 1-0 shutout on Sunday.

Hitters bashed a record 2,634 homers; Rookie of the Year Mark McGwire led the league with 49. Strikeouts also rose to their highest levels since 1968; Nolan Ryan established a big league mark for whiffs per game. Reggie Jackson retired from Oakland. Hal McRae hung it up for Kansas City, which also lost manager Dick Howser to cancer.

The A's and Royals struck around in the race until the end, but the title went to Minnesota, 29-52 on the road but great in the Metrodome. Minnesota was carried by four position players—Kirby Puckett, Tom Brunansky, Kent Hrbek, and Gary Gaetti—and starting pitchers Bert Blyleven and Frank Viola. Others helped in limited roles, and the Twins ground out a title.

Then Minnesota surprised Detroit in five for the league title as Brunansky hit .412 with 9 RBIs. Few expected the "Twinkies" to beat the Cardinals in the World Series, but—true to form—the Twins lost all three on the road but won their four in the dome. Viola, Blyleven, and reliever Jeff Reardon were magnificent.

1986 National League

TEAM	W	L	T	PCT	GB	HW	HL	R	OR	PA	H	2B	3B	HR	BB	SO	HB	SH	AVG	OBP	SLG	OPS	AOPS	BR	ABR	PF	SB	CS	BSA	BSR
EAST																														
NY	108	54	0	.667		55	26	783	578	6348	1462	261	31	148	631	968	31	75	.263	.339	.401	740	112	87	103	98	118	48	71	9
PHI	86	75	0	.534	21.5	49	31	739	713	6229	1386	266	39	154	589	1154	40	66	.253	.327	.400	727	102	52	26	104	153	59	72	13
STL	79	82	0	.491	28.5	42	39	601	611	6120	1270	216	48	58	568	905	20	108	.236	.309	.327	636	81	-123	-122	100	262	78	77	30
MON	78	83	0	.484	29.5	36	44	637	688	6173	1401	255	50	110	537	1016	33	53	.254	.322	.379	701	99	-2	1	100	193	95	67	9
CHI	70	90	0	.438	37	42	38	680	781	6127	1409	258	27	155	508	966	15	54	.256	.318	.398	716	96	21	-27	108	132	62	68	7
PIT	64	98	0	.395	44	31	50	663	700	6157	1366	273	33	111	569	929	20	68	.250	.321	.374	695	96	-10	-27	103	152	84	64	4
WEST																														
HOU	96	66	0	.593		55	29	654	569	6095	1388	244	32	125	536	916	24	53	.255	.322	.381	703	103	2	21	97	163	75	68	10
CIN	86	76	0	.531	10	43	38	732	717	6246	1404	237	35	144	586	920	18	65	.254	.325	.387	712	98	20	-6	104	177	53	77	20
SF	83	79	0	.512	13	46	35	698	618	6209	1394	269	29	114	536	1087	37	101	.253	.322	.375	697	103	-7	27	95	148	93	61	0
SD	74	88	0	.457	22	43	38	656	723	6118	1442	239	25	136	484	917	18	66	.261	.321	.388	709	103	8	23	98	96	68	59	-3
LA	73	89	0	.451	23	46	35	638	679	6101	1373	232	14	130	478	966	32	81	.251	.313	.370	683	101	-43	2	93	155	67	70	11
ATL	72	89	0	.447	23.5	41	40	615	719	6067	1348	241	24	138	538	904	24	79	.250	.319	.381	700	95	-5	-34	105	93	76	55	-6
TOT	969					526	443	8096		73990	16643	2991	387		1523	6560	11648	312	869	.253	.322	.380	702				1842	858	68	105

TEAM	CG	SHO	GR	SV	IP	H	HR	BB	SO	BR/9	ERA	AERA	OAV	OOB	PR	APR	PF	OSB	OCS	FA	E	WPB	DP	FW	PW	BW	BSW	DIF
EAST																												
NY	27	11	252	46	1484.0	1304	103	509	1083	11.2	3.11	115	.236	.302	100	80	96	159	55	.978	138	48	145	.1	8.3	10.7	.0	7.9
PHI	22	11	321	39	1451.2	1473	130	553	874	12.7	3.85	101	.265	.331	-22	6	105	216	70	.978	137	68	157	.1	.6	2.7	.4	1.6
STL	17	4	287	46	1466.1	1364	135	485	761	11.5	3.37	109	.250	.311	56	51	99	91	60	.981	123	47	178	.9	5.3	-12.7	2.2	2.8
MON	15	9	326	50	1466.1	1350	119	566	1051	12.0	3.78	99	.246	.318	-11	-7	101	200	54	.979	133	70	132	.3	-.2	.1	.0	-2.2
CHI	11	6	346	42	1445.0	1546	143	557	962	13.2	4.49	91	.279	.344	-124	-62	109	132	102	.980	124	72	147	.8	-6.4	-2.8	-.2	-1.4
PIT	17	9	356	30	1450.2	1397	138	570	924	12.4	3.90	99	.255	.327	-30	-3	104	137	80	.978	143	68	134	-.2	-.3	-2.8	-.5	-13.2
WEST																												
HOU	18	19	299	51	1456.1	1203	116	523	1160	10.8	3.15	114	.225	.295	92	76	97	176	62	.979	130	59	108	.6	7.9	2.2	.1	4.2
CIN	14	8	313	45	1460.0	1465	136	524	924	12.3	3.91	98	.264	.326	-32	-11	103	135	69	.978	140	52	160	.0	-1.1	-.6	1.2	5.6
SF	18	10	346	35	1460.1	1264	121	591	992	11.6	3.33	106	.236	.313	62	32	95	137	88	.977	143	70	149	-.2	3.3	-.8	-.9	-3.1
SD	13	7	350	32	1443.1	1406	150	607	934	12.7	3.99	92	.258	.333	-44	-55	98	159	65	.978	137	52	135	.2	-5.7	2.4	-1.2	-2.6
LA	35	14	280	25	1454.1	1428	115	499	1051	12.1	3.76	92	.255	.319	-7	-53	93	123	73	.978	181	62	118	-2.2	-5.5	.2	.2	-.7
ATL	17	5	309	39	1424.2	1443	117	576	932	12.9	3.97	99	.266	.338	-41	-3	106	177	80	.978	141	55	181	-.1	-.3	-3.5	-1.5	-3.0
TOT	224	113	3785	480	17471.0					12.1	3.72		.253	.322						.978	1670	723	1744					

Batter-Fielder Wins		Batting Average		On-Base Percentage		Slugging Average		On-Base Plus Slugging		Adjusted OPS		Adjusted Batter Runs	
Sax-LA	4.9	Raines-Mon	334	Raines-Mon	413	Schmidt-Phi	547	Schmidt-Phi	937	Schmidt-Phi	151	Schmidt-Phi	41.0
Raines-Mon	4.8	Sax-LA	332	Hernandez-NY	413	Strawberry-NY	507	Raines-Mon	889	Raines-Mon	146	Raines-Mon	39.2
Hernandez-NY	4.6	Gwynn-SD	329	Sax-LA	390	McReynolds-SD	504	Strawberry-NY	865	Strawberry-NY	140	Hernandez-NY	36.1
Gwynn-SD	4.2	Bass-Hou	311	Schmidt-Phi	390	Davis-Hou	493	McReynolds-SD	862	Hernandez-NY	140	Sax-LA	34.6
Hubbard-Atl	3.7	Hernandez-NY	310	Gwynn-SD	381	Bass-Hou	486	Hayes-Phi	859	McReynolds-SD	140	Gwynn-SD	30.7

Runs		Hits		Doubles		Triples		Home Runs		Total Bases		Runs Batted In	
Hayes-Phi	107	Gwynn-SD	211	Hayes-Phi	46	Webster-Mon	13	Schmidt-Phi	37	Parker-Cin	304	Schmidt-Phi	119
Gwynn-SD	107	Sax-LA	210	Sax-LA	43	Samuel-Phi	12	Parker-Cin	31	Schmidt-Phi	302	Parker-Cin	116
Schmidt-Phi	97	Raines-Mon	194	Dunston-Chi	37	Raines-Mon	10	Davis-Hou	31	Gwynn-SD	300	Carter-NY	105
Davis-Cin	97	Hayes-Phi	186	Bream-Pit	37	Coleman-StL	8	Murphy-Atl	29	Murphy-Atl	293	Davis-Hou	101
		Bass-Hou	184	Samuel-Phi	36					Hayes-Phi	293	Hayes-Phi	98

Stolen Bases		Base Stealing Runs		Fielding Runs-Infield		Fielding Runs-Outfield		Wins		Winning Pct.		Complete Games	
Coleman-StL	107	Coleman-StL	18.6	Hubbard-Atl	39.6	Wilson-Phi	14.8	Valenzuela-LA	21	Ojeda-NY	783	Valenzuela-LA	20
Davis-Cin	80	Davis-Cin	13.8	Ramirez-Atl	22.9	Gwynn-SD	14.3	Krukow-SF	20	Gooden-NY	739	Rhoden-Pit	12
Raines-Mon	70	Raines-Mon	12.3	Bream-Pit	21.4	Wilson-NY	9.0	Scott-Hou	18	Fernandez-NY	727	Gooden-NY	12
Duncan-LA	48	Duncan-LA	6.0	Dunston-Chi	21.2	VanSlyke-StL	5.5	Ojeda-NY	18	Darling-NY	714	Krukow-SF	10
		Bonds-Pit	5.5	Pendleton-StL	19.0	Dykstra-NY	4.0			Krukow-SF	690		

Strikeouts		Fewest BB/Game		Games		Saves		Base Runners/9		Adjusted Relief Runs		Relief Ranking	
Scott-Hou	306	Eckersley-Chi	1.93	Lefferts-SD	83	Worrell-StL	36	Scott-Hou	8.37	Worrell-StL	17.6	Worrell-StL	35.2
Valenzuela-LA	242	Sanderson-Chi	1.96	McDowell-NY	75	Reardon-Mon	35	Horton-StL	9.33	Horton-StL	17.5	Orosco-NY	24.1
Youmans-Mon	202	Krukow-SF	2.02	Worrell-StL	74	Smith-Hou	33	Krukow-SF	9.66	McGaffigan-Mon	16.4	Tekulve-Phi	22.1
Gooden-NY	200	Welch-LA	2.10	Franco-Cin	74	Smith-Chi	31	Ojeda-NY	9.90	Tekulve-Phi	16.1	Garber-Atl	21.3
Fernandez-NY	200	Ojeda-NY	2.15	Tekulve-Phi	73			Gooden-NY	10.12	McCullers-SD	14.2	McCullers-SD	19.7

Innings Pitched		Opponents' Avg.		Opponents' OBP		Earned Run Average		Adjusted ERA		Adjusted Starter Runs		Pitcher Wins	
Scott-Hou	275.1	Scott-Hou	186	Scott-Hou	242	Scott-Hou	2.22	Scott-Hou	162	Scott-Hou	45.1	Scott-Hou	4.5
Valenzuela-LA	269.1	Ryan-Hou	188	Krukow-SF	269	Ojeda-NY	2.57	Ojeda-NY	140	Rhoden-Pit	31.4	Rhoden-Pit	4.4
Knepper-Hou	258.0	Youmans-Mon	188	Ojeda-NY	278	Darling-NY	2.81	Rhoden-Pit	137	Ojeda-NY	24.6	Worrell-StL	3.7
Rhoden-Pit	253.2	Gooden-NY	215	Gooden-NY	278	Rhoden-Pit	2.84	Darling-NY	128	Darling-NY	21.0	Orosco-NY	2.6
Gooden-NY	250.0	Fernandez-NY	216	Ryan-Hou	283	Gooden-NY	2.84	Cox-StL	127	Gooden-NY	20.1	Tekulve-Phi	2.3

Fast Forward to October

Mike Schmidt won his third MVP, eighth homer crown, and 10th Gold Glove. The Giants debuted rookies Will Clark and Robby Thompson on the same day, while Pittsburgh welcomed Barry Bonds. Other future stars taking bows included Rookie of the Year Todd Worrell, Reds shortstop Barry Larkin, and Chicago's Greg Maddux and Rafael Palmeiro. Veterans Pete Rose, Tony Perez, and Cesar Cedeno all retired. But the whole season seemed like window dressing for the titanic clashes of October.

New York, which captured the East by 21½ games, the league's biggest margin since 1902, faced Houston in the NLCS. The Astros also won the West going away, as Cy Young winner Mike Scott no-hit the Giants to clinch the division title.

Despite Scott's two victories, the Mets took the NLCS, winning three times in their last at bat. Houston blew a 4-0 lead and lost Game 3 on Lenny Dykstra's two-run homer in the home ninth. The Mets won Game 5 in the 12th, 2-1. In Game 6—perhaps the best LCS game ever—Houston led 3-0 in the ninth when New York tied the score. Both teams tallied in the 14th. The Mets scored three in the top of the 16th; Houston rebounded with two. Finally, Jesse Orosco fanned Kevin Bass with two on, sending the Mets to the World Series.

After Boston won the first two World Series games in New York, the Mets snagged a pair at Fenway Park. Boston won a tight Game 5, and led 2-0, 3-2, and 5-3 (with two out in the 10th) in quest of the Series-clinching victory, but the Mets kept coming back, and won miraculously to force Game 7. The Red Sox leapt in front 3-0, but the Mets battered five Red Sox pitchers over the last three innings to win the clincher, 8-5.

1986 American League

TEAM	W	L	T	PCT	GB	HW	HL	R	OR	PA	H	2B	3B	HR	BB	SO	HB	SH	AVG	OBP	SLG	OPS	AOPS	BR	ABR	PF	SB	CS	BSA	BSR
EAST																														
BOS	95	66	0	.590		51	30	794	696	6255	1488	**320**	21	144	595	**707**	66	44	.271	.346	.415	761	105	67	62	101	41	34	55	-3
NY	90	72	0	.556	5.5	41	39	797	738	6325	1512	275	23	188	645	911	28	36	.271	**.347**	**.430**	777	**111**	**93**	**98**	99	139	48	**74**	14
DET	87	75	0	.537	8.5	49	32	798	714	6269	1447	234	30	**198**	496	885	43	52	.263	.338	.424	762	106	53	51	100	138	58	70	4
TOR	86	76	1	.531	9.5	42	39	809	733	6318	1540	285	35	181	496	848	33	24	.269	.329	.427	756	101	30	9	103	110	59	65	4
CLE	84	78	1	.519	11.5	45	35	831	841	6287	**1620**	270	45	157	456	944	24	56	**.284**	.337	.430	767	109	55	67	99	**141**	54	72	12
MIL	77	84	0	.478	18	41	39	667	734	6124	1393	255	38	127	530	986	27	53	.255	.321	.385	706	88	-60	-82	103	100	50	67	5
BAL	73	89	0	.451	22.5	37	42	708	760	6202	1425	223	13	169	563	862	31	33	.258	.327	.395	722	96	-28	-20	99	64	34	65	2
WEST																														
CAL	92	70	0	.568		50	32	786	684	6296	1387	236	36	167	**671**	860	40	**91**	.255	.338	.404	742	102	23	31	99	109	42	72	9
TEX	87	75	0	.537	5	**51**	30	771	743	6148	1479	248	43	184	511	1088	35	31	.267	.331	.428	759	102	35	14	103	103	85	55	-7
KC	76	86	0	.469	16	45	36	654	**673**	6128	1403	264	45	137	474	919	36	24	.252	.313	.390	703	88	-79	-93	102	97	46	68	5
OAK	76	86	0	.469	16	47	36	731	760	6127	1370	213	25	163	553	983	32	56	.252	.322	.390	712	100	-50	3	93	139	61	70	9
CHI	72	90	0	.444	20	41	40	644	699	6030	1335	197	34	121	487	940	34	50	.247	.310	.363	673	79	-130	-151	104	115	54	68	6
MIN	71	91	0	.438	21	43	38	741	839	6151	1446	257	39	196	501	977	37	44	.261	.325	.428	753	100	20	-2	103	81	61	57	-4
SEA	67	95	0	.414	25	41	41	718	835	6185	1392	243	41	158	572	1148	34	52	.253	.326	.399	725	95	-29	-37	101	93	76	55	-6
TOT	1134					624	509	10449		86845	20237	3520	468	2290	7667	13058	500	646	.262	.330	.408	737					1470	762	66	57

TEAM	CG	SHO	GR	SV	IP	H	HR	BB	SO	BR/9	ERA	AERA	OAV	OOB	PR	APR	PF	OSB	OCS	FA	E	WPB	DP	FW	PW	BW	BSW	DIF
EAST																												
BOS	36	6	254	41	1429.2	1469	167	**474**	1033	12.4	3.93	107	.266	.325	38	41	100	79	62	.979	129	71	146	-.2	4.0	6.1	-.7	5.2
NY	13	8	289	**58**	1443.1	1461	175	492	878	12.3	4.11	100	.263	.323	11	3	99	95	45	.979	127	57	153	.0	.3	**9.6**	**1.0**	-1.9
DET	33	12	239	38	1443.2	1374	183	571	880	12.3	4.02	103	.251	.323	25	22	100	87	49	.982	108	62	163	1.1	2.2	5.0	.6	-2.9
TOR	16	12	290	44	1476.0	1467	164	487	1002	12.2	4.08	104	.261	.322	16	26	102	95	46	**.984**	100	**47**	150	**1.7**	2.6	.9	.0	-.0
CLE	31	7	290	34	1447.3	1548	167	605	744	13.7	4.58	91	.273	.346	-64	-64	100	113	41	.975	157	83	148	-1.7	-6.3	6.6	.8	3.7
MIL	29	12	237	32	1431.2	1478	158	494	952	12.6	4.01	108	.267	.328	26	52	104	95	**75**	.976	146	72	146	-1.2	5.1	-8.1	.0	.5
BAL	17	6	262	39	1436.2	1451	177	535	954	12.6	4.30	97	.263	.328	-20	-23	100	123	56	.978	135	59	163	-.5	-2.3	-2.0	-.2	-3.1
WEST																												
CAL	29	12	246	40	1456.0	1356	153	478	955	**11.5**	3.84	107	.248	**.309**	54	47	99	**61**	56	.983	107	56	156	1.2	4.6	3.0	.5	1.6
TEX	15	8	**328**	41	1450.1	1356	145	736	**1059**	13.2	4.11	105	.249	.340	11	33	103	165	51	.980	122	119	160	.3	3.2	1.4	-1.1	2.2
KC	24	**13**	230	31	1440.2	1413	121	479	888	12.1	**3.82**	112	.258	.319	56	69	102	85	66	.980	123	59	153	.2	**6.8**	-9.1	.0	-3.0
OAK	22	8	286	37	1433.0	**1334**	166	667	937	12.8	4.31	90	**.247**	.330	-21	-72	93	139	53	.979	135	78	120	-.5	-7.1	.3	.5	1.8
CHI	18	8	297	38	1442.1	1361	143	561	895	12.2	3.93	110	.251	.323	39	62	104	116	56	.981	117	69	142	.6	6.1	-14.8	.2	-1.0
MIN	**39**	6	240	24	1432.2	1579	200	503	937	13.4	4.77	91	.281	.342	-94	-67	104	111	44	.980	118	70	168	.5	-6.6	-.2	-.8	-3.0
SEA	33	5	281	27	1439.2	1590	171	585	944	13.9	4.65	92	.283	.353	-76	-62	102	106	62	.975	156	63	**191**	-1.7	-6.1	-3.6	-1.0	-1.6
TOT	355	123	3769	524	20203.1					12.7	4.18		.262	.330						.979	1780	965	2159					

Batter-Fielder Wins
Boggs-Bos ...5.4
Ripken-Bal ...4.6
Trammell-Det ...4.5
Mattingly-NY ...4.5
Barfield-Tor ...4.3

Batting Average
Boggs-Bos ...357
Mattingly-NY ...352
Puckett-Min ...328
Tabler-Cle ...326
Rice-Bos ...324

On-Base Percentage
Boggs-Bos ...453
P.Bradley-Sea ...405
Brett-KC ...401
Murray-Bal ...396
Mattingly-NY ...394

Slugging Average
Mattingly-NY ...573
Barfield-Tor ...559
Puckett-Min ...537
Bell-Tor ...532
Gaetti-Min ...518

On-Base Plus Slugging
Mattingly-NY ...967
Boggs-Bos ...939
Barfield-Tor ...927
Puckett-Min ...903
Brett-KC ...881

Adjusted OPS
Mattingly-NY ...162
Boggs-Bos ...155
Barfield-Tor ...145
Puckett-Min ...138
Rice-Bos ...136

Adjusted Batter Runs
Mattingly-NY ...58.2
Boggs-Bos ...53.5
Barfield-Tor ...36.9
Puckett-Min ...33.5
Rice-Bos ...33.1

Runs
Henderson-NY ...130
Puckett-Min ...119
Mattingly-NY ...117
Carter-Cle ...108

Hits
Mattingly-NY ...238
Puckett-Min ...223
Fernandez-Tor ...213
Boggs-Bos ...207

Doubles
Mattingly-NY ...53
Boggs-Bos ...47
Rice-Bos ...39
Buckner-Bos ...39
Barrett-Bos ...39

Triples
Butler-Cle ...14
Sierra-Tex ...10
Fernandez-Tor ...9
Carter-Cle ...9

Home Runs
Barfield-Tor ...40
Kingman-Oak ...35
Gaetti-Min ...34
Deer-Mil ...33
Canseco-Oak ...33

Total Bases
Mattingly-NY ...388
Puckett-Min ...365
Carter-Cle ...341
Bell-Tor ...341
Barfield-Tor ...329

Runs Batted In
Carter-Cle ...121
Canseco-Oak ...117
Mattingly-NY ...113
Rice-Bos ...110

Stolen Bases
Henderson-NY ...87
Pettis-Cal ...50
Cangelosi-Chi ...50
Wilson-KC ...34
Gibson-Det ...34

Base Stealing Runs
Henderson-NY ...12.8
Pettis-Cal ...6.4
Gibson-Det ...5.4
Cangelosi-Chi ...5.1
Wilson-KC ...4.7

Fielding Runs-Infield
Owen-Sea-Bos ...35.8
Reynolds-Sea ...30.2
Buckner-Bos ...19.5
Guillen-Chi ...18.3
Gaetti-Min ...17.0

Fielding Runs-Outfield
Barfield-Tor ...16.0
Pettis-Cal ...10.5
Rice-Bos ...8.4
Henderson-Sea-Bos ...7.8
Baines-Chi ...7.5

Wins
Clemens-Bos ...24
Morris-Det ...21
Higuera-Mil ...20
Witt-Cal ...18
Rasmussen-NY ...18

Winning Pct.
Clemens-Bos ...857
Rasmussen-NY ...750
Morris-Det ...724
Higuera-Mil ...645
Witt-Cal ...643

Complete Games
Candiotti-Cle ...17
Blyleven-Min ...16
Morris-Det ...15
Higuera-Mil ...15
Witt-Cal ...14

Strikeouts
Langston-Sea ...245
Clemens-Bos ...238
Morris-Det ...223
Blyleven-Min ...215
Witt-Cal ...208

Fewest BB/Game
Guidry-NY ...1.78
Boyd-Bos ...1.89
Blyleven-Min ...1.92
Wegman-Mil ...1.95
Sutton-Cal ...2.13

Games
Williams-Tex ...80
Righetti-NY ...74
Harris-Tex ...73
Eichhorn-Tor ...69

Saves
Righetti-NY ...46
Aase-Bal ...34
Henke-Tor ...27
Hernandez-Det ...24
Moore-Oak ...21

Base Runners/9
Clemens-Bos ...8.86
Eichhorn-Tor ...9.00
Henke-Tor ...9.46
Candelaria-Cal ...9.52
Haas-Oak ...9.71

Adjusted Relief Runs
Eichhorn-Tor ...43.9
Righetti-NY ...20.9
Harris-Tex ...17.6
Clear-Mil ...16.0
Mohorcic-Tex ...15.3

Relief Ranking
Eichhorn-Tor ...55.7
Righetti-NY ...41.9
Harris-Tex ...31.8
Plesac-Mil ...27.1
Clear-Mil ...26.3

Innings Pitched
Blyleven-Min ...271.2
Witt-Cal ...269.0
Morris-Det ...267.0
Moore-Sea ...266.0
Clemens-Bos ...254.0

Opponents' Avg.
Clemens-Bos ...195
Rasmussen-NY ...217
Witt-Cal ...221
Hough-Tex ...221
Correa-Tex ...223

Opponents' OBP
Clemens-Bos ...252
Witt-Cal ...275
Morris-Det ...287
Sutton-Cal ...287
Rasmussen-NY ...289

Earned Run Average
Clemens-Bos ...2.48
Higuera-Mil ...2.79
Witt-Cal ...2.84
Hurst-Bos ...2.99
D.Jackson-KC ...3.20

Adjusted ERA
Clemens-Bos ...169
Higuera-Mil ...156
Witt-Cal ...145
Hurst-Bos ...140
D.Jackson-KC ...134

Adjusted Starter Runs
Clemens-Bos ...48.8
Higuera-Mil ...43.3
Witt-Cal ...38.4
Morris-Det ...27.8
Hurst-Bos ...24.0

Pitcher Wins
Eichhorn-Tor ...5.8
Higuera-Mil ...5.1
Clemens-Bos ...5.1
Righetti-NY ...4.2
Witt-Cal ...3.8

Sorrow in Beantown

Despite Dave Righetti's record 46 saves and amazing seasons from Don Mattingly and Rickey Henderson, it wasn't the Yankees' year. The AL East went to Boston. Roger Clemens, who primed Hub hysteria in April with the major leagues' first 20-K nine-inning game, was both MVP and Cy Young. Wade Boggs led the league in both batting and on-base percentage for the third time; four Red Sox drove in 90 or more runs. Boston wrapped it up with an 11-game win streak starting August 30.

Kansas City collapsed in the West, and the Angels easily stepped into the breach. Rookie first baseman Wally Joyner was a surprise, leavening an old team with a young bat. Four California regulars were 35 or older, and the bench and bullpen were stocked with graybeards as well. Rookies also sparked second-place Texas; Ruben Sierra impressed with power and speed, while Pete Incaviglia slugged 30 homers but fanned an AL-record 185 times. The Rookie of the Year, however, was Jose Canseco of third-place Oakland. Others making their first major league appearances included Mark McGwire, Jamie Moyer, Kevin Brown, Fred McGriff, and Chuck Finley. Minnesota's Bert Blyleven allowed 50 home runs, a new record, but ended 17-14; his team finished 20 games under .500.

Each LCS again went seven games. Each team blew out the other, and then the Angels took the next two in Anaheim with dramatic late-inning rallies. California couldn't pull the trigger. Boston, trailing 5-2 in the ninth in Game 5, took the lead on Dave Henderson's home run; the Angels tied it, but the Red Sox won in the 11th. Back at Fenway, the Red Sox twice blasted the Angels to reach the World Series. The Fall Classic, however, was painful for Boston fans. Just one strike away from winning, the Red Sox found a way to lose Game 6 to the Mets; another lead slipped away in Game 7.

Two Tigers first basemen, Hank Greenberg and Norm Cash, passed on. Following the season, Bobby Grich and Tom Seaver retired.

1985 National League

TEAM	W	L	T	PCT	GB	HW	HL	R	OR	PA	H	2B	3B	HR	BB	SO	HB	SH	AVG	OBP	SLG	OPS	AOPS	BR	ABR	PF	SB	CS	BSA	BSR
EAST																														
STL	101	61	0	.623		**54**	27	**747**	572	6182	1446	245	**59**	87	586	853	18	70	**.264**	**.335**	.379	714	107	52	56	99	**314**	96	77	**35**
NY	98	64	0	.605	3	51	30	695	**568**	6248	1425	239	35	134	546	872	20	89	.257	.323	.385	708	106	32	46	98	117	53	69	7
MON	84	77	0	.522	16.5	44	37	633	636	6053	1342	242	49	118	492	880	26	61	.247	.310	.375	685	103	-20	16	95	169	77	69	10
CHI	77	84	1	.478	23.5	41	39	686	729	6177	1397	239	28	**150**	562	937	18	66	.254	.324	**.390**	714	95	42	-22	110	182	49	**79**	23
PHI	75	87	0	.463	26	41	40	667	673	6122	1343	238	47	141	527	1095	25	49	.245	.312	.383	695	98	-1	-17	103	122	51	71	9
PIT	57	104	0	.354	43.5	35	45	568	708	6099	1340	251	28	80	514	842	14	91	.247	.311	.347	658	91	-63	-58	99	110	60	65	3
WEST																														
LA	95	67	0	.586		48	33	682	579	6222	1434	226	28	129	539	846	31	**104**	.261	.328	.382	710	106	38	54	98	136	58	70	10
CIN	89	72	1	.553	5.5	47	34	677	666	6143	1385	249	34	114	576	856	23	72	.255	.327	.376	703	98	28	-5	105	159	70	69	10
SD	83	79	0	.512	12	44	37	650	622	6150	1405	241	28	109	513	**809**	23	75	.255	.320	.368	688	99	-8	-2	99	60	39	61	0
HOU	83	79	0	.512	12	44	37	706	691	6192	**1457**	**261**	42	121	477	873	23	66	.261	.319	.388	707	105	25	41	98	96	56	63	2
ATL	66	96	0	.407	29	32	49	632	781	6207	1359	213	28	126	553	849	22	65	.246	.315	.363	678	90	-29	-64	106	72	52	58	-2
SF	62	100	0	.383	33	38	43	556	674	6063	1263	217	31	115	488	962	**37**	93	.233	.299	.348	647	90	-95	-70	96	99	55	64	3
TOT	971					519	451	7899		73858	16596	2861	437	1424	6373	10674	280	901	.252	.319	.374	692					1636	716	70	109

TEAM	CG	SHO	GR	SV	IP	H	HR	BB	SO	BR/9	ERA	AERA	OAV	OOB	PR	APR	PF	OSB	OCS	FA	E	WPB	DP	FW	PW	BW	BSW	DIF
EAST																												
STL	**37**	20	296	44	1464.0	1343	**98**	453	798	11.2	3.10	115	.246	.305	79	75	99	104	37	**.983**	108	48	166	**1.7**	7.9	**5.9**	**2.7**	1.8
NY	32	19	243	37	1488.0	1306	111	515	**1039**	11.1	3.11	112	.237	.302	80	65	97	122	65	.982	115	50	138	1.3	6.8	4.8	-.2	4.3
MON	13	13	323	**53**	1457.0	1346	99	509	870	11.6	3.55	97	.247	.312	7	-19	96	189	45	.981	121	62	152	.8	-2.0	1.7	.0	2.9
CHI	20	8	313	42	1442.1	1492	156	519	820	12.7	4.16	96	.271	.333	-91	-24	111	137	**82**	.979	134	48	150	.1	-2.5	-2.3	1.5	-.2
PHI	24	9	315	30	1447.0	1424	115	596	899	12.7	3.68	101	.259	.331	-15	4	103	164	55	.978	139	49	142	-.2	.4	-1.8	-.0	-4.4
PIT	15	6	297	29	1445.1	1406	107	584	962	12.6	3.97	91	.255	.329	-61	-56	101	105	72	.979	133	54	127	.1	-5.9	-6.1	-.6	-11.0
WEST																												
LA	37	**21**	250	36	1465.0	**1280**	102	462	979	10.8	2.96	118	.234	.295	102	89	97	99	67	.974	166	49	131	-1.8	**9.4**	5.7	.0	.7
CIN	24	11	287	45	1451.1	1347	131	535	910	11.8	3.71	102	.248	.315	-19	11	105	133	57	.980	122	52	142	.8	1.2	-.5	.0	6.9
SD	26	19	283	44	1451.1	1399	127	**443**	727	11.6	3.40	104	.250	.313	30	23	99	138	65	.980	124	**29**	158	.7	2.4	-2.0	-1.0	.0
HOU	17	9	282	42	1458.0	1393	119	543	909	12.1	3.66	95	.254	.321	-11	-31	97	144	59	.976	152	105	159	-1.0	-3.3	4.3	-.7	2.7
ATL	9	9	**351**	29	1457.1	1512	134	642	776	13.5	4.19	92	.271	.347	-98	-53	107	158	59	.976	159	43	**197**	-1.4	-5.6	-6.7	-1.2	-.1
SF	13	5	321	24	1448.0	1348	125	572	985	12.1	3.61	96	.247	.319	-3	-26	96	143	53	.976	148	77	134	-.7	-2.7	-7.4	-.6	-7.5
TOT	267	149	3561	455	17474.2					12.0	3.59		.252	.319						.979	1621	666	1796					

Batter-Fielder Wins		Batting Average		On-Base Percentage		Slugging Average		On-Base Plus Slugging		Adjusted OPS		Adjusted Batter Runs	
Guerrero-LA	5.8	McGee-StL	.353	Guerrero-LA	.422	Guerrero-LA	.577	Guerrero-LA	.999	Guerrero-LA	182	Guerrero-LA	56.4
Hubbard-Atl	5.6	Guerrero-LA	.320	Scioscia-LA	.407	Parker-Cin	.551	Murphy-Atl	.927	Raines-Mon	154	Raines-Mon	44.1
Sandberg-Chi	5.4	Raines-Mon	.320	Raines-Mon	.405	Murphy-Atl	.539	Parker-Cin	.916	Clark-StL	151	Murphy-Atl	41.8
Raines-Mon	5.3	Gwynn-SD	.317	Rose-Cin	.395	Schmidt-Phi	.532	Schmidt-Phi	.907	Murphy-Atl	149	Parker-Cin	37.8
Carter-NY	4.5	Parker-Cin	.312	Clark-StL	.393	Marshall-LA	.515	Clark-StL	.895	Schmidt-Phi	148	Schmidt-Phi	37.0

Runs		Hits		Doubles		Triples		Home Runs		Total Bases		Runs Batted In	
Murphy-Atl	118	McGee-StL	216	Parker-Cin	42	McGee-StL	18	Murphy-Atl	37	Parker-Cin	350	Parker-Cin	125
Raines-Mon	115	Parker-Cin	198	Wilson-Phi	39	Samuel-Phi	13	Parker-Cin	34	Murphy-Atl	332	Murphy-Atl	111
McGee-StL	114	Gwynn-SD	197	Herr-StL	38	Raines-Mon	13	Schmidt-Phi	33	McGee-StL	308	Herr-StL	110
Sandberg-Chi	113	Sandberg-Chi	186	Wallach-Mon	36	Garner-Hou	10	Guerrero-LA	33	Sandberg-Chi	307	Moreland-Chi	106
Coleman-StL	107	Murphy-Atl	185			Coleman-StL	10	Carter-NY	32	Schmidt-Phi	292	Wilson-Phi	102

Stolen Bases		Base Stealing Runs		Fielding Runs-Infield		Fielding Runs-Outfield		Wins		Winning Pct.		Complete Games	
Coleman-StL	110	Coleman-StL	15.4	Hubbard-Atl	59.9	Wilson-Phi	15.8	Gooden-NY	24	Hershiser-LA	.864	Gooden-NY	16
Raines-Mon	70	Raines-Mon	12.3	Wallach-Mon	35.8	Milner-Cin	14.3	Tudor-StL	21	Gooden-NY	.857	Valenzuela-LA	14
McGee-StL	56	Lopes-Chi	8.9	Pendleton-StL	25.9	Gwynn-SD	10.6	Andujar-StL	21	Smith-NY	.783	Tudor-StL	14
Sandberg-Chi	54	Sandberg-Chi	8.0	O.Smith-StL	18.1	McReynolds-SD	8.8	Browning-Cin	20	Darling-NY	.727	Cox-StL	10
Samuel-Phi	53	McGee-StL	6.7	Ramirez-Atl	15.0	Hayes-Phi	7.8	Hershiser-LA	19	Tudor-StL	.724	Andujar-StL	10

Strikeouts		Fewest BB/Game		Games		Saves		Base Runners/9		Adjusted Relief Runs		Relief Ranking	
Gooden-NY	268	Hoyt-SD	.86	Burke-Mon	78	Reardon-Mon	41	Tudor-StL	8.61	Franco-Cin	16.7	Franco-Cin	26.6
Soto-Cin	214	Eckersley-Chi	1.01	M.Davis-SF	77	Smith-Chi	33	Gooden-NY	8.75	Burke-Mon	16.3	Gossage-SD	21.7
Ryan-Hou	209	Lynch-NY	1.27	Garrelts-SF	74	Smith-Hou	27	Eckersley-Chi	8.88	Carman-Phi	14.2	Carman-Phi	21.4
Valenzuela-LA	208	Tudor-StL	1.60	Carman-Phi	71	Power-Cin	27	Gossage-SD	9.34	Gossage-SD	14.1	Niedenfuer-LA	20.7
Fernandez-NY	180	Smith-Mon	1.66	Minton-SF	68	Gossage-SD	26	Niedenfuer-LA	9.39	Lahti-StL	13.6	Lahti-StL	19.8

Innings Pitched		Opponents' Avg.		Opponents' OBP		Earned Run Average		Adjusted ERA		Adjusted Starter Runs		Pitcher Wins	
Gooden-NY	276.2	Fernandez-NY	.181	Tudor-StL	.249	Gooden-NY	1.53	Gooden-NY	229	Gooden-NY	62.7	**Gooden-NY**	7.6
Tudor-StL	275.0	Gooden-NY	.201	Eckersley-Chi	.254	Tudor-StL	1.93	Tudor-StL	185	Tudor-StL	50.0	**Tudor-StL**	5.6
Valenzuela-LA	272.1	Hershiser-LA	.206	Gooden-NY	.254	Hershiser-LA	2.03	Hershiser-LA	173	Hershiser-LA	36.8	**Hershiser-LA**	3.8
Andujar-StL	269.2	Tudor-StL	.209	Hershiser-LA	.267	Reuschel-Pit	2.27	Reuschel-Pit	160	Valenzuela-LA	30.9	**Reuschel-Pit**	3.6
Mahler-Atl	266.2	Soto-Cin	.211	Smith-Mon	.268	Welch-LA	2.31	Welch-LA	151	Reuschel-Pit	27.3	**Valenzuela-LA**	3.6

Cardinal Numbers

After sliding in 1983–84, did the Cardinals have anything left? Yes. The NL East was a two-horse race after early August, and the Redbirds outran the Mets. The pundits said it was all about speed, but Cardinals baseball was multi-faceted. While Rookie of the Year Vince Coleman swiped 110 bases, and the team combined for 314 (most in the NL since 1912), MVP Willie McGee's .353 average, Jack Clark's power, and Tommy Herr and Ozzie Smith's on-base skills proved just as important. John Tudor and Joaquin Andujar each won 20 games with a good bullpen in reserve.

Again the Mets were bridesmaids, and New York waved goodbye to 23-year vet Rusty Staub, but attendance rose another 50 percent. Dwight Gooden, 24-4 with a 1.53 ERA, was a unanimous Cy Young. Chicago's pitching crumbled, and the club released Larry Bowa in favor of rookie Shawon Dunston. Montreal began building a roof over Olympic Stadium in September.

Los Angeles, with an excellent offense despite a big ballpark, had few problems after July as the Padres fell apart. Four excellent Dodgers starters benefited from Pedro Guerrero's bat. Cincinnati improved to second on Dave Parker's comeback season. The club's most emotional moment came September 11, when Pete Rose became "hit king," collecting safety No. 4,192 against the Padres.

The Dodgers won the first two NLCS games at home on fine pitching; however, the Cardinals bats evened the series. Smith won Game 5 with a ninth-inning blast off Tom Niedenfuer (the Wizard's first career home run batting left-handed). In Game 6 Los Angeles lost a 4-1 lead, moved ahead in the eighth, but lost in the ninth. Clark's three-run homer (also off Niedenfuer) gave St. Louis a 7-5 win and the pennant. The Cardinals blew a three-to-one lead in games to the Royals and lost the World Series, but the franchise had reasserted itself.

1985 American League

TEAM	W	L	T	PCT	GB	HW	HL	R	OR	PA	H	2B	3B	HR	BB	SO	HB	SH	AVG	OBP	SLG	OPS	AOPS	BR	ABR	PF	SB	CS	BSA	BSR
EAST																														
TOR	99	62	0	.615		54	26	759	**588**	6106	1482	281	**53**	158	503	807	30	21	.269	.331	.425	756	102	44	22	103	144	77	65	5
NY	97	64	0	.602	2	**58**	22	**839**	660	6236	1458	272	31	176	620	771	**50**	48	.267	.344	.425	769	**111**	86	**100**	98	**155**	53	**75**	**16**
DET	84	77	0	.522	15	44	37	729	688	6221	1413	254	45	202	526	926	27	40	.253	.318	.424	742	101	7	9	100	75	41	65	2
BAL	83	78	0	.516	16	45	36	818	764	6211	1451	234	22	**214**	604	908	19	31	.263	.336	**.430**	766	110	65	82	98	69	43	62	0
BOS	81	81	1	.500	18.5	43	37	800	720	6419	**1615**	**292**	31	162	562	816	30	50	**.282**	**.347**	.429	776	106	**100**	63	104	66	27	71	5
MIL	71	90	0	.441	28	40	40	690	802	6158	1467	250	44	101	462	**746**	19	54	.263	.319	.379	698	90	-71	-70	100	69	34	67	3
CLE	60	102	0	.370	39.5	38	43	729	861	6120	1465	254	31	116	462	817	15	38	.265	.324	.385	709	93	-44	-41	100	132	72	65	4
WEST																														
KC	91	71	0	.562		50	32	687	639	6094	1384	261	49	154	473	840	36	44	.252	.313	.401	714	99	-49	-54	101	128	48	73	11
CAL	90	72	0	.556	1	49	30	732	703	6263	1364	215	31	153	**648**	902	39	**99**	.251	.333	.386	719	96	-17	-16	100	106	51	68	5
CHI	85	77	1	.525	6	45	36	736	720	6088	1386	247	37	146	471	843	43	59	.253	.315	.392	707	88	-56	-85	105	108	56	66	4
MIN	77	85	0	.475	14	49	35	705	782	6128	1453	282	41	141	502	779	31	39	.264	.320	.407	733	93	0	-43	106	68	44	61	0
OAK	77	85	0	.475	14	43	36	757	787	6215	1475	230	34	155	508	861	16	63	.264	.325	.401	726	104	-17	36	93	117	58	67	5
SEA	74	88	0	.457	17	42	41	719	818	6185	1410	277	38	171	564	942	31	28	.255	.326	.412	738	99	9	2	101	94	35	73	4
TEX	62	99	0	.385	28.5	37	43	617	785	6003	1359	213	41	129	530	819	33	34	.253	.322	.381	703	90	-57	-70	102	130	76	63	2
TOT	1132					637	494	10317		86447	20182	3562	528	2178	7465	11777	419	648	.261	.327	.406	733					1461	715	67	71

TEAM	CG	SHO	GR	SV	IP	H	HR	BB	SO	BR/9	ERA	AERA	OAV	OOB	PR	APR	PF	OSB	OCS	FA	E	WPB	DP	FW	PW	BW	BSW	DIF
EAST																												
TOR	18	9	316	47	1448.0	**1312**	147	484	823	**11.3**	**3.31**	128	.243	**.306**	**135**	147	102	83	44	.980	125	39	164	.2	**14.5**	2.2	.0	1.6
NY	25	9	271	**49**	1440.1	1373	157	518	907	11.9	3.69	110	.251	.316	74	59	98	107	46	.979	126	52	172	.2	5.8	**9.9**	1.1	-.5
DET	31	**11**	250	40	1456.0	1313	141	556	943	11.7	3.78	109	**.240**	.311	59	53	99	93	53	.977	143	72	152	-.8	5.2	.9	-.3	-1.5
BAL	32	6	238	33	1427.1	1480	160	568	793	13.1	4.38	93	.270	.338	-36	-51	98	130	37	.979	129	**36**	168	-.0	-5.0	8.1	-.5	-.0
BOS	35	8	202	29	1461.1	1487	130	540	913	12.7	4.06	106	.265	.331	14	40	104	94	**62**	.977	145	48	161	-.8	4.0	6.2	.0	-9.4
MIL	34	5	248	37	1437.0	1510	175	499	777	12.8	4.39	96	.271	.331	-39	-31	101	109	56	.977	142	63	153	-.7	-3.1	-6.9	-.2	1.4
CLE	24	7	306	28	1421.0	1556	170	547	702	13.6	4.91	85	.281	.346	-121	-118	100	134	53	.977	141	59	161	-.6	-11.7	-4.1	-.1	-4.5
WEST																												
KC	27	**11**	216	41	1461.0	1433	**103**	463	846	11.9	3.49	120	.257	.315	107	111	101	92	50	.980	127	52	160	.1	11.0	-5.3	.6	3.6
CAL	22	8	250	41	1457.1	1453	171	544	767	12.3	3.91	105	.263	.326	38	35	99	79	56	**.982**	112	53	**202**	1.0	3.5	-1.6	.0	6.1
CHI	20	8	305	39	1451.2	1411	161	569	**1023**	12.5	4.07	107	.256	.327	13	43	105	112	55	**.982**	111	65	152	1.1	4.3	-8.4	-.1	7.2
MIN	**41**	7	237	34	1426.1	1468	164	**462**	767	12.4	4.48	99	.268	.326	-53	-8	107	100	54	.980	120	64	139	.5	-.8	-4.3	-.5	1.0
OAK	10	6	299	41	1453.0	1451	172	607	785	12.9	4.41	88	.259	.331	-43	-92	94	104	51	.977	140	67	137	-.6	-9.1	3.6	.0	2.1
SEA	23	8	**335**	30	1432.0	1456	154	637	868	13.4	4.68	90	.265	.343	-84	-70	102	105	57	.980	122	83	156	.4	-6.9	.2	.3	-1.0
TEX	18	5	264	33	1411.2	1479	173	501	863	12.9	4.56	93	.269	.331	-65	-46	103	119	41	.980	120	66	145	.5	-4.5	-6.9	-.3	-7.2
TOT	360	108	3737	522	20184.0					12.5	4.15		.261	.327						.979	1803	819	2222					

Batter-Fielder Wins
- **Henderson-NY** ...6.9
- **Brett-KC** ...6.6
- **Boggs-Bos** ...5.6
- **Ripken-Bal** ...4.5
- **Murray-Bal** ...4.4

Batting Average
- Boggs-Bos ...368
- Brett-KC ...335
- Mattingly-NY ...324
- Henderson-NY ...314
- Butler-Cle ...311

On-Base Percentage
- Boggs-Bos ...450
- Brett-KC ...436
- Harrah-Tex ...432
- Henderson-NY ...419
- Murray-Bal ...383

Slugging Average
- Brett-KC ...585
- Mattingly-NY ...567
- Barfield-Tor ...536
- Murray-Bal ...523
- Evans-Det ...519

On-Base Plus Slugging
- Brett-KC ...1022
- Mattingly-NY ...939
- Henderson-NY ...934
- Boggs-Bos ...928
- Murray-Bal ...906

Adjusted OPS
- Brett-KC ...177
- Henderson-NY ...158
- Mattingly-NY ...158
- Murray-Bal ...150
- Boggs-Bos ...148

Adjusted Batter Runs
- Brett-KC ...64.4
- Mattingly-NY ...51.3
- Boggs-Bos ...50.6
- Henderson-NY ...48.8
- Murray-Bal ...42.5

Runs
- Henderson-NY ...146
- Ripken-Bal ...116
- Murray-Bal ...111
- Evans-Bos ...110
- Brett-KC ...108

Hits
- Boggs-Bos ...240
- Mattingly-NY ...211
- Buckner-Bos ...201
- Puckett-Min ...199
- Baines-Chi ...198

Doubles
- Mattingly-NY ...48
- Buckner-Bos ...46
- Boggs-Bos ...42
- Cooper-Mil ...39

Triples
- Wilson-KC ...21
- Butler-Cle ...14
- Puckett-Min ...13
- Fernandez-Tor ...10

Home Runs
- Evans-Det ...40
- Fisk-Chi ...37
- Balboni-KC ...36
- Mattingly-NY ...35
- G.Thomas-Sea ...32

Total Bases
- Mattingly-NY ...370
- Brett-KC ...322
- Bradley-Sea ...319
- Murray-Bal ...312
- Murray-Bal ...305

Runs Batted In
- Mattingly-NY ...145
- Murray-Bal ...124
- Winfield-NY ...114
- Baines-Chi ...113
- Brett-KC ...112

Stolen Bases
- Henderson-NY ...80
- Pettis-Cal ...56
- Butler-Cle ...47
- Wilson-KC ...43
- Smith-KC ...40

Base Stealing Runs
- Henderson-NY ...14.1
- Pettis-Cal ...9.2
- Smith-KC ...6.3
- Perconte-Sea ...6.1
- Wilson-KC ...5.6

Fielding Runs-Infield
- Buckner-Bos ...25.4
- Owen-Sea ...24.6
- White-KC ...22.5
- Gaetti-Min ...17.5
- Barrett-Bos ...16.3

Fielding Runs-Outfield
- Barfield-Tor ...15.1
- Butler-Cle ...13.9
- Henderson-NY ...10.0
- Puckett-Min ...9.8
- Pettis-Cal ...8.8

Wins
- Guidry-NY ...22
- Saberhagen-KC ...20
- Viola-Min ...18
- Burns-Chi ...18

Winning Pct.
- Guidry-NY ...786
- Saberhagen-KC ...769
- Leibrandt-KC ...654
- Higuera-Mil ...652

Complete Games
- Blyleven-Cle-Min ...24
- Moore-Sea ...14
- Hough-Tex ...14
- Morris-Det ...13
- Boyd-Bos ...13

Strikeouts
- Blyleven-Cle-Min ...206
- Bannister-Chi ...198
- Morris-Det ...191
- Hurst-Bos ...189
- Witt-Cal ...180

Fewest BB/Game
- Haas-Mil ...1.39
- Saberhagen-KC ...1.45
- Guidry-NY ...1.46
- Butcher-Min ...1.86
- Key-Tor ...2.12

Games
- Quisenberry-KC ...84
- VandeBerg-Sea ...76
- Hernandez-Det ...74
- Nunez-Sea ...70

Saves
- Quisenberry-KC ...37
- James-Chi ...32
- Moore-Cal ...31
- Hernandez-Det ...31

Base Runners/9
- Ontiveros-Oak ...7.96
- Hernandez-Det ...8.18
- James-Chi ...9.41
- Saberhagen-KC ...9.56
- Fisher-NY ...9.70

Adjusted Relief Runs
- James-Chi ...24.8
- Quisenberry-KC ...24.6
- Moore-Cal ...23.7
- Cliburn-Cal ...22.7
- Harris-Tex ...21.5

Relief Ranking
- Moore-Cal ...47.1
- James-Chi ...44.6
- Quisenberry-KC ...42.9
- Righetti-NY ...31.8
- Hernandez-Det ...31.8

Innings Pitched
- Blyleven-Cle-Min ...293.2
- Boyd-Bos ...272.1
- Stieb-Tor ...265.0
- Alexander-Tor ...260.2
- Guidry-NY ...259.0

Opponents' Avg.
- Stieb-Tor ...213
- Hough-Tex ...215
- Petry-Det ...217
- Morris-Det ...225
- Higuera-Mil ...235

Opponents' OBP
- Saberhagen-KC ...271
- Guidry-NY ...277
- Key-Tor ...282
- Hough-Tex ...283
- Petry-Det ...285

Earned Run Average
- Stieb-Tor ...2.48
- Leibrandt-KC ...2.69
- Saberhagen-KC ...2.87
- Key-Tor ...3.00
- Blyleven-Cle-Min ...3.16

Adjusted ERA
- Stieb-Tor ...171
- Leibrandt-KC ...155
- Saberhagen-KC ...146
- Key-Tor ...141
- Seaver-Chi ...137

Adjusted Starter Runs
- Stieb-Tor ...47.1
- Saberhagen-KC ...36.5
- Leibrandt-KC ...36.5
- Blyleven-Cle-Min ...32.4
- Key-Tor ...29.2

Pitcher Wins
- **Stieb-Tor** ...4.9
- **Moore-Cal** ...4.8
- **James-Chi** ...4.5
- **Quisenberry-KC** ...4.4
- **Leibrandt-KC** ...4.0

Cards Get Royal Flush

California, with Rod Carew collecting his 3,000th hit in his final season, led the West in early September, but Kansas City took 12 of 13 to forge ahead, then three of four from the Angels in the final week to clinch. The Royals essentially won with a six-man staff: five starters (including 21-year-old Cy Young winner Bret Saberhagen) and Dan Quisenberry. George Brett had another great year, while Steve Balboni provided unexpected power.

Toronto used three big streaks to motor ahead of the Yankees, clinching on the penultimate day with a home win over New York. (The following day, Yankees hurler Phil Niekro won his 300th game.) Yankee Don Mattingly was MVP, but the Blue Jays' outfield of Jesse Barfield, Lloyd Moseby, and George Bell defeated all comers. Despite cold weather and a bad ballpark, Toronto boasted the league's second-best attendance.

Tom Seaver won his 300th game in New York—at Yankee Stadium as a member of the White Sox. A rotator cuff tear ended Rollie Fingers' career, while declining production finished Al Oliver's. Smokey Joe Wood passed on at 95 and cancer-stricken Roger Maris died at just 51.

In the first year of a best-of-seven League Championship Series, the Jays and Royals went the limit. Big rallies gave Toronto three wins in the first four games, which would have ended the series a year earlier. The opportunistic Royals took full advantage, winning Games 5 and 6 with good pitching. Kansas City blew out the home Jays with a four-run sixth in the decisive game. Brett hit .348 with 3 homers.

In the "I-70" World Series Kansas City again fell behind three games to one as St. Louis won three close contests. Unfazed, Danny Jackson won 6-1 in Game 5 to send the Series back to Kansas City. Trailing 1-0 in the ninth of Game 6, the Royals rallied—with the help of a controversial call—and Dane Iorg's two-run single sent the Series to a seventh game. Kansas City, with momentum, big bats, and Saberhagen, captured its first championship, 11-0.

1984 National League

TEAM	W	L	T	PCT	GB	HW	HL	R	OR	PA	H	2B	3B	HR	BB	SO	HB	SH	AVG	OBP	SLG	OPS	AOPS	BR	ABR	PF	SB	CS	BSA	BSR
EAST																														
CHI	96	65	0	.596		51	29	762	658	6143	1415	240	47	136	567	967	29	59	.260	.331	.397	728	102	80	23	108	154	66	70	11
NY	90	72	0	.556	6.5	48	33	652	676	6066	1400	235	25	107	500	1001	20	59	.257	.320	.369	689	100	2	10	99	149	54	73	14
STL	84	78	0	.519	12.5	44	37	652	645	6086	1369	225	44	75	516	924	23	68	.252	.317	.351	668	96	-36	-22	98	220	71	76	24
PHI	81	81	0	.500	15.5	39	42	720	690	6283	1494	248	51	147	555	1084	29	39	.266	.333	.407	740	112	103	91	102	186	60	76	20
MON	78	83	0	.484	18	39	42	593	585	6042	1367	242	36	96	470	782	25	74	.251	.312	.362	674	99	-32	-6	96	131	38	78	16
PIT	75	87	0	.463	21.5	41	40	615	567	6119	1412	237	33	98	438	841	19	81	.255	.310	.363	673	95	-38	-39	100	96	62	61	-1
WEST																														
SD	92	70	0	.568		48	33	686	634	6119	1425	207	42	109	472	810	24	64	.259	.317	.371	688	99	-4	-7	101	152	68	69	10
HOU	80	82	0	.494	12	43	38	693	630	6201	1465	222	67	79	494	837	17	87	.264	.323	.371	694	108	11	56	94	105	61	63	2
ATL	80	82	0	.494	12	38	43	632	655	6106	1338	234	27	111	555	896	20	64	.247	.317	.361	678	90	-16	-59	107	140	85	62	1
LA	79	83	0	.488	13	40	41	580	600	6041	1316	213	23	102	488	829	14	92	.244	.306	.348	654	89	-69	-68	100	109	69	61	0
CIN	70	92	0	.432	22	39	42	627	747	6200	1342	238	30	106	566	978	12	71	.244	.313	.356	669	90	-33	-61	105	106	63	72	13
SF	66	96	0	.407	26	35	46	682	807	6290	1499	229	26	112	528	980	17	51	.265	.328	.375	703	107	31	51	97	126	76	62	1
TOT	971					505	466	7894		73696	16842	2770	451	1278	6149	10929	249	809	.255	.319	.369	688					1728	773	69	110

TEAM	CG	SHO	GR	SV	IP	H	HR	BB	SO	BR/9	ERA	AERA	OAV	OOB	PR	APR	PF	OSB	OCS	FA	E	WPB	DP	FW	PW	BW	BSW	DIF
EAST																												
CHI	19	8	271	50	1434.0	1458	99	442	879	12.1	3.75	104	.267	.321	-26	22	109	134	69	.981	121	50	137	1.1	2.3	2.4	.2	9.5
NY	12	15	278	50	1442.2	1371	104	573	1028	12.3	3.60	99	.252	.324	-2	-5	99	150	64	.979	129	55	154	.7	-.5	1.1	.5	7.3
STL	19	12	313	51	1449.0	1427	94	494	808	12.1	3.58	98	.262	.324	1	-14	98	125	65	.982	118	64	184	1.3	-1.5	-2.3	1.6	3.9
PHI	11	6	287	35	1458.1	1416	101	448	904	11.6	3.62	101	.253	.308	-5	6	102	145	50	.975	161	51	112	-1.2	.6	9.6	1.1	-10.1
MON	19	10	272	48	1431.0	1333	114	474	861	11.5	3.31	104	.249	.310	45	24	96	138	67	.978	132	48	147	.4	2.5	-.6	.7	-5.6
PIT	27	13	246	34	1470.0	1344	102	502	995	11.4	3.11	117	.246	.308	78	84	101	115	71	.980	128	49	142	.7	8.8	-4.1	-1.1	-10.4
WEST																												
SD	13	17	285	44	1460.1	1327	122	563	812	11.8	3.48	103	.244	.315	17	17	100	125	46	.978	138	56	144	.1	1.8	-.7	.0	9.7
HOU	24	13	312	29	1449.1	1350	91	502	950	11.6	3.32	101	.248	.311	44	4	93	188	68	.979	133	83	160	.4	.4	5.9	-.7	-7.0
ATL	17	7	278	49	1447.0	1401	122	525	859	12.1	3.57	108	.257	.322	3	42	107	155	63	.978	139	44	153	.0	4.4	-6.2	-.9	1.6
LA	39	16	259	27	1460.2	1381	76	499	1033	11.7	3.17	112	.250	.313	68	63	99	132	74	.975	163	52	146	-1.3	6.6	-7.1	-1.0	.8
CIN	25	6	327	25	1461.1	1445	128	578	946	12.6	4.16	91	.259	.348	-92	-57	106	149	70	.977	139	51	116	.0	-6.0	-6.4	.4	.9
SF	9	7	359		1461.0	1589	125	549	854	13.4	4.39	80	.278	.342	-131	-142	98	172	66	.973	173	76	134	-1.9	-14.9	5.4	-.9	-2.6
TOT	234	130	3487	480	17424.2					12.0	3.59		.255	.319						.978	1674	679	1729					

Batter-Fielder Wins		Batting Average		On-Base Percentage		Slugging Average		On-Base Plus Slugging		Adjusted OPS		Adjusted Batter Runs	
Sandberg-Chi	6.6	Gwynn-SD	351	Matthews-Chi	410	Murphy-Atl	547	Schmidt-Phi	919	Schmidt-Phi	155	Schmidt-Phi	40.4
O.Smith-StL	5.0	Lacy-Pit	321	Gwynn-SD	410	Schmidt-Phi	536	Murphy-Atl	919	C.Davis-SF	148	Hernandez-NY	38.5
Raines-Mon	4.8	C.Davis-SF	315	Hernandez-NY	409	Sandberg-Chi	520	Sandberg-Chi	887	Cruz-Hou	147	Cruz-Hou	37.6
Schmidt-Phi	4.7	Sandberg-Chi	314	Raines-Mon	393	C.Davis-SF	507	C.Davis-SF	875	Murphy-Atl	145	Murphy-Atl	36.4
Hernandez-NY	4.6	Ray-Pit	312	Schmidt-Phi	383	Durham-Chi	505	Durham-Chi	874	Hernandez-NY	144	Raines-Mon	36.2

Runs		Hits		Doubles		Triples		Home Runs		Total Bases		Runs Batted In	
Sandberg-Chi	114	Gwynn-SD	213	Ray-Pit	38	Sandberg-Chi	19	Schmidt-Phi	36	Murphy-Atl	332	Schmidt-Phi	106
Wiggins-SD	106	Sandberg-Chi	200	Raines-Mon	38	Samuel-Phi	19	Murphy-Atl	36	Sandberg-Chi	331	Carter-Mon	106
Raines-Mon	106	Raines-Mon	192	Sandberg-Chi	36	Cruz-Hou	13	Carter-Mon	27	Samuel-Phi	310	Murphy-Atl	100
Samuel-Phi	105	Samuel-Phi	191	Samuel-Phi	36			Strawberry-NY	26	Carter-Mon	290	Strawberry-NY	97
Matthews-Chi	101	Cruz-Hou	187					Cey-Chi	25	Schmidt-Phi	283	Cey-Chi	97

Stolen Bases		Base Stealing Runs		Fielding Runs-Infield		Fielding Runs-Outfield		Wins		Winning Pct.		Complete Games	
Raines-Mon	75	Raines-Mon	13.0	O.Smith-StL	31.5	Milner-Cin	13.8	Andujar-StL	20	Sutcliffe-Chi	941	Soto-Cin	13
Samuel-Phi	72	Samuel-Phi	10.6	Reynolds-Hou	24.1	Lacy-Pit	13.7	Soto-Cin	18	Soto-Cin	720	Valenzuela-LA	12
Wiggins-SD	70	Wiggins-SD	8.1	Sax-LA	22.9	Martinez-SD	11.0	Gooden-NY	17	Gooden-NY	654	Andujar-StL	12
L.Smith-StL	50	Wilson-NY	7.0	Wallach-Mon	22.4	McReynolds-SD	9.9	Sutcliffe-Chi	16	Show-SD	625	Knepper-Hou	11
		Redus-Cin	6.7	Sandberg-Chi	22.3	Wilson-NY	9.5	Niekro-Hou	16			Mahler-Atl	9

Strikeouts		Fewest BB/Game		Games		Saves		Base Runners/9		Adjusted Relief Runs		Relief Ranking	
Gooden-NY	276	Gullickson-Mon	1.47	Power-Cin	78	Sutter-StL	45	Denny-Phi	9.04	Sutter-StL	26.3	Sutter-StL	40.7
Valenzuela-LA	240	Candelaria-Pit	1.65	Lavelle-SF	77	Smith-Chi	33	Smith-Hou	9.43	Dawley-Hou	16.9	Bedrosian-Atl	25.5
Ryan-Hou	197	Whitson-SD	2.00	Minton-SF	74	Orosco-NY	31	Lefferts-SD	9.62	Lefferts-SD	16.7	Dawley-Hou	24.8
Soto-Cin	185	Pena-LA	2.08	Tekulve-Pit	72	Holland-Phi	29	Orosco-NY	9.72	Bedrosian-Atl	13.8	Orosco-NY	19.2
Carlton-Phi	163	Knepper-Hou	2.12	Sutter-StL	71	Gossage-SD	25	Gooden-NY	9.74	Sisk-NY	11.6	Power-Cin	17.2

Innings Pitched		Opponents' Avg.		Opponents' OBP		Earned Run Average		Adjusted ERA		Adjusted Starter Runs		Pitcher Wins	
Andujar-StL	261.1	Gooden-NY	202	Gooden-NY	269	Pena-LA	2.48	Pena-LA	143	Gooden-NY	24.2	**Sutter-StL**	4.4
Valenzuela-LA	261.0	Soto-Cin	209	Hershiser-LA	278	Gooden-NY	2.60	Gooden-NY	137	Rhoden-Pit	23.7	**Rhoden-Pit**	3.5
Niekro-Hou	248.1	Ryan-Hou	211	Andujar-StL	284	Hershiser-LA	2.66	Hershiser-LA	134	Pena-LA	22.8	**Gooden-NY**	3.0
Rhoden-Pit	238.1	DeLeon-Pit	214	Soto-Cin	284	Rhoden-Pit	2.72	Rhoden-Pit	134	Hershiser-LA	19.3	**Dawley-Hou**	2.8
Soto-Cin	237.1	Hershiser-LA	225	Ryan-Hou	286	Candelaria-Pit	2.72	Candelaria-Pit	134	Denny-Phi	18.9	**Bedrosian-Atl**	2.6

Padres Castigate Cubs

In the thirty-nine years since the Cubs had won, television, rock music, computers, and black voting rights had come along. It was about time for Chicago, and they pulled away from the surprising Mets in August. MVP second baseman Ryne Sandberg starred in all facets and was ably supported by a veteran Cubs lineup. Midseason trades brought in Dennis Eckersley, still a dependable starter, and Rick Sutcliffe, who went 16-1 for the Cubs and took home the Cy Young.

Mets hurler Dwight Gooden, just 19, was Rookie of the Year and finished second in Cy Young balloting. First baseman Keith Hernandez was outstanding, and rookie manager Davey Johnson eagerly inserted talented youngsters into New York's lineup and rotation.

Cubs attendance rose 42 percent, while Mets crowds increased 66 percent. League attendance, however, decreased in eight cities and fell 3.6 percent. Peter Ueberroth was tabbed as the new commissioner to bring financial sensibility to the game,

and he *did* help baseball garner more television money. Terry Pendleton debuted for St. Louis, while the Reds welcomed Jose Rijo and Eric Davis. It was the end, though, for Joe Morgan and Tug McGraw.

San Diego, strong defensively and deep in decent pitchers, won the West by July. Tony Gwynn nailed down his first batting crown. Manager Dick Williams moved outfielder Alan Wiggins to second base, creating an instant leadoff man.

Chicago easily won the first two NLCS games at Wrigley Field, winning by a combined score of 17-2. Back in San Diego, the Padres walloped the Cubs in Game 3, and then won a seesaw Game 4 on Steve Garvey's ninth-inning homer. Chicago led the deciding game, 3-2, until Cubs errors and big hits gave San Diego a four-run seventh and their first pennant. It almost didn't matter that the Padres lost to the Tigers in the World Series. San Diego fans had no expectations of glory.

1984 American League

TEAM	W	L	T	PCT	GB	HW	HL	R	OR	PA	H	2B	3B	HR	BB	SO	HB	SH	AVG	OBP	SLG	OPS	AOPS	BR	ABR	PF	SB	CS	BSA	BSR
EAST																														
DET	104	58	0	.642		53	29	**829**	**643**	6373	1529	254	46	**187**	602	941	34	48	.271	**.342**	.432	774	113	105	**106**	100	106	68	61	0
TOR	89	73	1	.549	15	49	32	750	696	6283	1555	**275**	**68**	143	460	816	**52**	35	.273	.331	.421	752	102	51	21	104	**193**	67	**74**	19
NY	87	75	0	.537	17	51	30	758	679	6356	1560	**275**	32	130	534	**673**	38	64	.276	.339	.404	743	109	50	77	97	62	38	62	0
BOS	86	76	0	.531	18	41	40	810	764	6250	**1598**	259	45	181	500	842	20	36	**.283**	.341	**.441**	**782**	110	113	73	105	38	25	60	0
BAL	85	77	0	.525	19	44	37	681	667	6186	1374	234	23	160	**620**	884	22	45	.252	.328	.391	719	100	-2	10	98	51	36	59	-1
CLE	75	87	1	.463	29	41	39	761	766	6374	1498	222	39	123	600	815	27	37	.265	.335	.384	719	96	4	-11	102	126	77	62	1
MIL	67	94	0	.416	36.5	38	43	641	734	6057	1446	232	36	96	432	673	26	42	.262	.317	.370	687	92	-77	-54	97	52	57	48	-9
WEST																														
KC	84	78	0	.519		44	37	673	686	6063	1487	269	52	117	400	832	24	41	.268	.317	.399	716	96	-25	-33	101	106	64	62	1
CAL	81	81	0	.500	3	37	44	696	697	6166	1363	211	30	150	556	928	29	65	.249	.319	.381	700	93	-47	-46	100	80	51	61	0
MIN	81	81	0	.500	3	47	34	673	675	6107	1473	259	33	114	437	735	24	26	.265	.318	.385	703	88	-45	-78	105	39	30	57	-2
OAK	77	85	0	.475	7	44	37	738	796	6161	1415	257	29	158	568	871	22	37	.259	.327	.404	731	107	21	68	94	145	64	69	10
SEA	74	88	0	.457	10	42	39	682	774	6211	1429	244	34	129	519	871	42	**66**	.258	.324	.384	708	96	-31	-27	99	116	62	65	4
CHI	74	88	0	.457	10	43	38	679	736	6156	1360	225	38	172	523	883	39	37	.247	.314	.395	709	90	-38	-71	105	109	49	69	7
TEX	69	92	0	.429	14.5	34	46	656	714	6099	1452	227	29	120	420	807	20	47	.261	.313	.377	690	87	-78	-101	104	81	50	62	0
TOT	1134					608	525	10027		86842	20539	3443	534	1980	7171	11571	419	626	.264	.326	.398	724					1304	738	64	29

TEAM	CG	SHO	GR	SV	IP	H	HR	BB	SO	BR/9	ERA	AERA	OAV	OOB	PR	APR	PF	OSB	OCS	FA	E	WPB	DP	FW	PW	BW	BSW	DIF
EAST																												
DET	19	8	268	**51**	1464.0	**1358**	130	489	914	**11.5**	3.49	113	**.246**	.308	81	76	99	68	52	.979	127	63	162	.3	**7.6**	**10.7**	-.2	4.6
TOR	34	10	257	33	1464.0	1433	140	528	875	12.3	3.86	107	.257	.323	21	42	103	75	40	.980	123	51	166	.6	4.2	2.1	**1.7**	-.6
NY	15	12	287	43	1465.1	1485	**120**	518	**992**	12.4	3.78	101	.264	.325	35	9	96	88	60	.977	142	41	**177**	-.5	.9	7.7	-.2	-1.9
BOS	40	12	201	32	1442.0	1524	141	517	927	12.9	4.18	100	.270	.332	-29	3	105	111	67	.977	143	47	128	-.6	.3	7.3	-.2	-.4
BAL	**48**	**13**	208	32	1439.1	1393	137	512	714	12.1	3.71	105	.256	.320	44	32	98	99	48	**.981**	123	67	166	.5	3.2	1.0	-.3	-.4
CLE	21	7	**308**	35	1467.2	1523	141	545	803	12.8	4.26	97	.269	.332	-43	-22	103	100	47	.977	146	60	163	-.7	-2.2	-1.1	-.1	-1.9
MIL	13	7	283	41	1433.0	1532	137	480	785	12.8	4.06	96	.274	.331	-10	-28	97	96	59	.978	136	53	156	-.3	-2.8	-5.4	-1.1	-3.9
WEST																												
KC	18	9	214	50	1444.0	1426	136	**433**	724	11.8	3.92	103	.258	.312	11	19	101	94	51	.979	131	**34**	157	.0	1.9	-3.3	-.1	4.4
CAL	36	12	203	26	1458.0	1526	143	474	754	12.5	3.96	101	.271	.328	6	5	100	71	49	.980	128	48	170	.2	.5	-4.6	-.2	4.1
MIN	32	9	249	38	1437.2	1429	159	463	713	12.1	3.85	110	.260	.319	23	57	106	92	58	.980	**120**	42	134	**.7**	5.7	-7.8	-.4	1.8
OAK	15	6	282	44	1430.0	1554	155	592	695	13.7	4.48	84	.278	.348	-78	-120	94	94	**67**	.975	146	56	159	-.8	-12.1	6.8	.8	1.2
SEA	26	4	292	35	1442.0	1497	138	619	972	13.5	4.31	93	.270	.345	-50	-47	101	88	58	.979	128	64	143	.2	-4.7	-2.7	.2	
CHI	43	9	238	32	1454.1	1416	155	483	840	12.0	4.13	101	.256	.317	-23	6	105	100	41	**.981**	122	43	160	.6	.6	-7.1	.5	-1.5
TEX	38	6	190	21	1438.2	1443	148	518	863	12.5	3.91	107	.260	.325	13	39	104	128	41	.977	138	95	138	-.4	3.9	-10.2	-.2	-4.7
TOT	398	124	3480	513	20280.0					12.5	3.99		.264	.326						.979	1853	764	2179					

League Leaders

Batter-Fielder Wins
- Ripken-Bal 9.4
- Mattingly-NY 5.3
- Yount-Mil 5.2
- Murray-Bal 5.1
- Henderson-Oak 4.6

Batting Average
- Mattingly-NY .343
- Winfield-NY .340
- Boggs-Bos .325
- Bell-Tex .315
- Trammell-Det .314

On-Base Percentage
- Murray-Bal .410
- Boggs-Bos .407
- Henderson-Oak .399
- Winfield-NY .393
- Davis-Sea .391

Slugging Average
- Baines-Chi .541
- Mattingly-NY .537
- Evans-Bos .532
- Armas-Bos .531
- Hrbek-Min .522

On-Base Plus Slugging
- Evans-Bos .920
- Murray-Bal .918
- Mattingly-NY .918
- Winfield-NY .908
- Hrbek-Min .906

Adjusted OPS
- Mattingly-NY 158
- Murray-Bal 157
- Winfield-NY 155
- Davis-Sea 146
- Henderson-Oak 146

Adjusted Batter Runs
- Murray-Bal 50.3
- Mattingly-NY 46.7
- Winfield-NY 43.1
- Evans-Bos 41.5
- Davis-Sea 40.0

Runs
- Evans-Bos 121
- Henderson-Oak 113
- Boggs-Bos 109
- Butler-Cle 108
- Armas-Bos 107

Hits
- Mattingly-NY 207
- Boggs-Bos 203
- Ripken-Bal 195
- Winfield-NY 193

Doubles
- Mattingly-NY 44
- Parrish-Tex 42
- Bell-Tor 39
- Ripken-Bal 37
- Evans-Bos 37

Triples
- Moseby-Tor 15
- Collins-Tor 15
- Gibson-Det 10
- Baines-Chi 10

Home Runs
- Armas-Bos 43
- Kingman-Oak 35
- Thornton-Cle 33
- Parrish-Det 33
- Murphy-Oak 33

Total Bases
- Armas-Bos 339
- Evans-Bos 335
- Ripken-Bal 327
- Mattingly-NY 324
- Easler-Bos 310

Runs Batted In
- Armas-Bos 123
- Rice-Bos 122
- Kingman-Oak 118
- Davis-Sea 116

Stolen Bases
- Henderson-Oak 66
- Collins-Tor 60
- Butler-Cle 52
- Pettis-Cal 48
- Wilson-KC 47

Base Stealing Runs
- Wilson-KC 8.6
- Collins-Tor 8.3
- Henderson-Oak 8.2
- Garcia-Tor 5.9
- Moseby-Tor 5.4

Fielding Runs-Infield
- Ripken-Bal 39.3
- White-KC 29.0
- Bell-Tex 23.8
- Cruz-Chi 23.6
- Boggs-Bos 22.3

Fielding Runs-Outfield
- Vukovich-Cle 18.8
- Puckett-Min 17.8
- Murphy-Oak 11.0
- Henderson-Oak 7.7
- Davis-Sea 6.7

Wins
- Boddicker-Bal 20
- Morris-Det 19
- Blyleven-Cle 19
- Viola-Min 18
- Petry-Det 18

Winning Pct.
- Alexander-Tor .739
- Blyleven-Cle .731
- Petry-Det .692
- Wilcox-Det .680

Complete Games
- Hough-Tex 17
- Boddicker-Bal 16
- Dotson-Chi 14
- Blyleven-Cle 12
- Beattie-Sea 12

Strikeouts
- Langston-Sea 204
- Stieb-Tor 198
- Witt-Cal 196
- Blyleven-Cle 170
- Hough-Tex 164

Fewest BB/Game
- Hoyt-Chi 1.64
- Smithson-Min 1.93
- Guidry-NY 2.02
- Alexander-Tor 2.03
- Haas-Mil 2.04

Games
- Hernandez-Det 80
- Quisenberry-KC 72
- Lopez-Det 71
- Camacho-Cle 69
- Caudill-Oak 68

Saves
- Quisenberry-KC 44
- Caudill-Oak 36
- Hernandez-Det 32
- Righetti-NY 31
- Davis-Min 29

Base Runners/9
- Hernandez-Det 8.72
- Quisenberry-KC 9.26
- Waddell-Cle 9.84
- Saberhagen-KC 10.05
- Caudill-Oak 10.09

Adjusted Relief Runs
- Hernandez-Det 33.8
- Quisenberry-KC 21.0
- Camacho-Cle 17.7
- Corbett-Cal 17.6
- Righetti-NY 16.0

Relief Ranking
- Hernandez-Det 41.3
- Camacho-Cle 30.4
- Quisenberry-KC 27.4
- Righetti-NY 26.7
- Caudill-Oak 26.4

Innings Pitched
- Stieb-Tor 267.0
- Hough-Tex 266.0
- Alexander-Tor 261.2
- Boddicker-Bal 261.1
- Viola-Min 257.2

Opponents' Avg.
- Stieb-Tor .221
- Blyleven-Cle .224
- Boddicker-Bal .228
- Langston-Sea .230
- Berenguer-Det .232

Opponents' OBP
- Black-KC .283
- Alexander-Tor .284
- Blyleven-Cle .285
- Mason-Tex .285
- Seaver-Chi .288

Earned Run Average
- Boddicker-Bal 2.79
- Stieb-Tor 2.83
- Blyleven-Cle 2.87
- Niekro-NY 3.09
- Zahn-Cal 3.12

Adjusted ERA
- Stieb-Tor 146
- Blyleven-Cle 144
- Boddicker-Bal 140
- Alexander-Tor 132
- Viola-Min 132

Adjusted Starter Runs
- Stieb-Tor 39.9
- Blyleven-Cle 33.2
- Boddicker-Bal 31.5
- Alexander-Tor 28.9
- Viola-Min 27.5

Pitcher Wins
- Hernandez-Det 4.3
- Boddicker-Bal 3.5
- Stieb-Tor 3.5
- Blyleven-Cle 3.4
- Camacho-Cle 3.1

Runaway Tigers

Riding a 35-5 start, the Detroit Tigers dominated the league. Drawing league-leading crowds to the corner of Michigan and Trumbull, the Tigers led the league in scoring and ERA. Under Sparky Anderson, Detroit won 104 games with a great middle infield of Lou Whitaker and Alan Trammell, star right fielder Kirk Gibson, and slugging catcher Lance Parrish. Three strong starters were supplemented by reliever Willie Hernandez, who won the Cy Young and MVP trophies. Lefty Hernandez and righty Aurelio Lopez appeared in a combined 151 games.

On-base percentage became an official statistic, and the AL's first declared leader was Eddie Murray of the Orioles. While stolen bases dipped to their lowest level since 1973, strikeouts were their highest since the inception of the DH. Seattle rookie Mark Langston paced the league in whiffs and walks. Toronto rose to second in the East, using speed and power while debuting southpaw Jimmy Key as a co-closer. Shoulder miseries forced Jim Palmer to retire from the Orioles, but AL hitters found an equally annoying successor in Boston's 21-year-old rookie Roger Clemens.

The Angels contended with four 20-homer hitters, but again lacked a solid bullpen. The Twins, showing improvement in their third year in the Metrodome, welcomed rookie center fielder Kirby Puckett. Chicago crumbled to fifth. Kansas City was the West's only team over .500. The Royals, riding a hot September, made their sixth postseason appearance since 1976 despite losing Willie Wilson to a drug suspension; George Brett playing just 104 games due to injury; using rookie starters Bret Saberhagen, Mark Gubicza, and Danny Jackson; and allowing more runs than they scored. Dan Quisenberry was again a late-inning savior.

Detroit swept the Royals easily in the ALCS. In the World Series Jack Morris twice went the distance in victories, and Trammell and Gibson were the hitting stars. The five-game win against the Padres sparked celebrations and rioting all over the Motor City.

1983 National League

TEAM	W	L	T	PCT	GB	HW	HL	R	OR	PA	H	2B	3B	HR	BB	SO	HB	SH	AVG	OBP	SLG	OPS	AOPS	BR	ABR	PF	SB	CS	BSA	BSR
EAST																														
PHI	90	72	1	.556		50	31	696	635	6218	1352	209	45	125	640	906	26	80	.249	.329	.373	702	102	17	23	99	143	75	66	5
PIT	84	78	0	.519	6	41	40	659	648	6169	1460	238	29	121	497	873	19	84	.264	.325	.383	708	99	18	-2	103	124	77	62	0
MON	82	80	1	.506	8	46	35	677	646	6293	1482	297	41	102	509	733	38	78	.264	.326	.386	712	103	34	34	100	138	44	76	15
STL	79	83	0	.488	11	44	37	679	710	6238	1496	262	63	83	543	879	24	72	.270	.335	.384	719	104	48	44	101	207	89	70	14
CHI	71	91	0	.438	19	43	38	701	719	6132	1436	272	42	140	470	868	29	71	.261	.319	.401	720	100	37	5	105	84	40	68	4
NY	68	94	0	.420	22	41	41	575	680	6009	1314	172	26	112	436	1031	31	66	.241	.300	.344	644	85	-118	-115	99	141	64	69	9
WEST																														
LA	91	71	1	.562		48	32	609	6129	1358	197	34	146	541	925	22	86	.250	.318	.379	697	99	-7	-7	100	166	76	69	10
ATL	88	74	0	.543	3	46	34	746	640	6195	1489	218	45	130	582	847	17	78	.272	.341	.400	741	104	91	40	107	146	88	62	1
HOU	85	77	0	.525	6	46	36	643	646	6173	1412	239	60	97	517	869	19	81	.257	.320	.375	695	104	-8	30	95	164	95	63	3
SD	81	81	1	.500	10	47	34	653	653	6163	1384	207	34	93	482	822	20	89	.250	.311	.351	662	92	-77	-59	97	179	67	73	16
SF	79	83	0	.488	12	43	38	687	697	6126	1324	206	30	142	619	990	25	64	.247	.325	.375	700	103	12	32	97	140	78	64	4
CIN	74	88	0	.457	17	36	45	623	710	6057	1274	236	35	107	588	1006	19	72	.239	.314	.356	670	89	-47	-68	104	154	77	67	7
TOT	974					531	441	7993		73902	16781	2753	484	1398	6424	10749	292	921	.255	.322	.376	698					1786	870	67	88

TEAM	CG	SHO	GR	SV	IP	H	HR	BB	SO	BR/9	ERA	AERA	OAV	OOB	PR	APR	PF	OSB	OCS	FA	E	WPB	DP	FW	PW	BW	BSW	DIF
EAST																												
PHI	20	10	300	41	1461.2	1429	111	464	1092	11.8	3.34	108	.256	.314	47	42	99	167	79	.976	152	57	117	-.7	4.4	2.4	-.2	3.2
PIT	25	14	290	41	1462.1	1378	109	563	1061	12.1	3.55	105	.252	.321	12	29	103	126	64	.982	115	61	165	1.4	3.0	-.2	-.8	-.5
MON	38	15	252	34	1471.0	1406	120	479	899	11.7	3.58	101	.254	.315	8	6	100	115	86	.981	116	46	130	1.4	.6	3.6	.8	-5.4
STL	22	10	327	27	1460.2	1479	115	525	709	12.5	3.79	96	.266	.330	-26	-23	101	110	64	.976	152	74	173	-.8	-2.4	4.6	.7	-4.1
CHI	9	10	369	42	1428.2	1496	117	498	807	12.7	4.08	93	.274	.335	-71	-41	105	152	66	.982	115	67	164	1.4	-4.3	.5	-.4	-7.3
NY	18	7	274	33	1451.0	1384	97	615	717	12.5	3.68	100	.256	.331	-8	-2	101	194	73	.976	151	58	171	-.7	-.2	-12.0	.2	-.2
WEST																												
LA	27	12	278	40	1464.0	1336	97	495	1000	11.4	3.10	116	.244	.307	85	81	99	114	88	.974	168	58	132	-1.7	8.5	-.7	.3	3.7
ATL	18	4	305	48	1440.2	1412	132	540	895	12.3	3.67	105	.260	.327	-7	28	106	172	68	.978	137	40	176	.1	2.9	4.2	-.7	.4
HOU	22	14	261	48	1466.1	1276	94	570	904	11.5	3.45	99	.236	.309	29	-5	94	182	54	.977	147	84	165	-.5	-.5	3.1	-.5	2.3
SD	23	5	294	44	1467.2	1389	144	528	850	11.9	3.62	97	.253	.320	1	-20	97	152	74	.979	129	42	135	.6	-2.1	-6.2	.9	6.7
SF	20	9	276	47	1445.2	1431	127	520	881	12.3	3.70	96	.259	.323	-11	-26	98	167	73	.973	171	64	109	-1.9	-2.7	3.3	-.4	-.4
CIN	34	5	271	29	1441.1	1365	135	627	934	12.6	3.98	96	.253	.330	-57	-26	105	135	81	.981	114	43	121	1.5	-2.7	-7.1	-.0	1.4
TOT	276	115	3497	474	17461.0					12.1	3.63		.255	.322						.978	1667	694	1758					

Batter-Fielder Wins		Batting Average		On-Base Percentage		Slugging Average		On-Base Plus Slugging		Adjusted OPS		Adjusted Batter Runs	
Schmidt-Phi	6.4	Madlock-Pit	323	Schmidt-Phi	.399	Murphy-Atl	540	Murphy-Atl	933	Schmidt-Phi	156	Schmidt-Phi	45.1
Thon-Hou	6.2	L.Smith-StL	321	Hernandez-StL-NY	.396	Dawson-Mon	539	Schmidt-Phi	923	Evans-SF	150	Murphy-Atl	38.7
Raines-Mon	4.6	Cruz-Hou	318	Murphy-Atl	.393	Guerrero-LA	531	Guerrero-LA	904	Guerrero-LA	149	Guerrero-LA	38.2
Carter-Mon	4.3	Hendrick-StL	318	Raines-Mon	.393	Schmidt-Phi	524	Evans-SF	894	Murphy-Atl	147	Evans-SF	37.1
Sandberg-Chi	4.2	Knight-Hou	304	Madlock-Pit	.386	Evans-SF	516	Dawson-Mon	877	Cruz-Hou	142	Cruz-Hou	34.2

Runs		Hits		Doubles		Triples		Home Runs		Total Bases		Runs Batted In	
Raines-Mon	133	Dawson-Mon	189	Ray-Pit	38	Butler-Atl	13	Schmidt-Phi	40	Dawson-Mon	341	Murphy-Atl	121
Murphy-Atl	131	Cruz-Hou	189	Oliver-Mon	38	Moreno-Hou	11	Murphy-Atl	36	Murphy-Atl	318	Dawson-Mon	113
Schmidt-Phi	104	Ramirez-Atl	185	Buckner-Chi	38	Green-StL	10	Guerrero-LA	32	Guerrero-LA	310	Guerrero-LA	109
Dawson-Mon	104	Oliver-Mon	184	Carter-Mon	37	Dawson-Mon	10	Dawson-Mon	32	Thon-Hou	283	Guerrero-LA	103
		Raines-Mon	183					Evans-SF	30	Schmidt-Phi	280	Kennedy-SD	98

Stolen Bases		Base Stealing Runs		Fielding Runs-Infield		Fielding Runs-Outfield		Wins		Winning Pct.		Complete Games	
Raines-Mon	90	Raines-Mon	14.9	Sandberg-Chi	44.3	Milner-Cin	12.8	Denny-Phi	19	Denny-Phi	.760	Soto-Cin	18
Wiggins-SD	66	Wiggins-SD	10.0	Bowa-Chi	25.6	Raines-Mon	9.4	Soto-Cin	17	Perez-Atl	.652	Rogers-Mon	13
S.Sax-LA	56	Wilson-NY	6.3	Hubbard-Atl	24.9	Butler-Atl	5.7	Rogers-Mon	17	McWilliams-Pit	.652	Gullickson-Mon	10
Wilson-NY	54	McGee-StL	5.8	Buckner-Chi	21.8	Clark-SF	5.5	Gullickson-Mon	17	Candelaria-Pit	.652	
L.Smith-StL	43	Dernier-Phi	5.3	Schmidt-Phi	21.7	Leonard-SF	4.2	Lea-Mon	16	McMurtry-Atl	.625	

Strikeouts		Fewest BB/Game		Games		Saves		Base Runners/9		Adjusted Relief Runs		Relief Ranking	
Carlton-Phi	275	Hammaker-SF	1.67	Campbell-Chi	82	Smith-Chi	29	Niedenfuer-LA	8.08	Orosco-NY	23.9	Orosco-NY	45.9
Soto-Cin	242	Ruthven-Phi-Chi	1.87	Holland-Phi	76	Holland-Phi	25	Dawley-Hou	8.36	Smith-Chi	22.8	Smith-Chi	39.7
McWilliams-Pit	199	Denny-Phi	1.97	Hernandez-Chi-Phi	74	Minton-SF	22	Howe-LA	8.91	Tekulve-Pit	19.6	Howe-LA	30.7
Valenzuela-LA	189	Reuss-LA	2.01	Scherrer-Cin	73	Sutter-StL	21	Holland-Phi	9.13	Niedenfuer-LA	19.0	Tekulve-Pit	27.9
Ryan-Hou	183	Candelaria-Pit	2.05	Minton-SF	73	Reardon-Mon	21	DiPino-Hou	9.21	Howe-LA	15.9	Niedenfuer-LA	23.9

Innings Pitched		Opponents' Avg.		Opponents' OBP		Earned Run Average		Adjusted ERA		Adjusted Starter Runs		Pitcher Wins	
Carlton-Phi	283.2	Ryan-Hou	195	Hammaker-SF	.266	Hammaker-SF	2.25	Hammaker-SF	158	Denny-Phi	32.5	**Orosco-NY**	5.2
Soto-Cin	273.2	Soto-Cin	208	Soto-Cin	.278	Denny-Phi	2.37	Denny-Phi	152	Soto-Cin	30.3	**Smith-Chi**	4.3
Rogers-Mon	273.0	Welch-LA	222	Pena-LA	.283	Welch-LA	2.65	Soto-Cin	142	Hammaker-SF	22.5	**Denny-Phi**	3.4
Niekro-Hou	263.2	Hammaker-SF	228	Welch-LA	.291	Soto-Cin	2.70	Welch-LA	136	Welch-LA	21.7	**Howe-LA**	3.4
Valenzuela-LA	257.0	Pena-LA	229	Denny-Phi	.293	Pena-LA	2.75	Pena-LA	132	Smith-Mon	18.0	**Soto-Cin**	3.0

One More for Cincinnati East

With the departure of Joe Morgan, Tony Perez, Pete Rose, and others, the Reds had declined. In 1982 they had crashed into the basement. Following the 1983 season, Johnny Bench, shifted uncomfortably to third base, retired at 35. The Big Red Machine was dead.

But it lived, one last time, in Philadelphia. With a hot September under new manager Paul Owens, the Phillies squeezed out one last division title as Cincinnati East. Morgan, Rose, and Perez all played key roles for the Phillies. Von Hayes was the only young regular, and the pitching depended heavily on graybeards and reliever Al Holland.

For the first time (excluding 1981) since 1931, the NL had no 20-game winner. As a result, Phillies right-hander John Denny was voted the Cy Young winner. His career was effectively destroyed by elbow problems the next season. Thirty-nine-year-old Fergie Jenkins had the second-best ERA among Cubs starters, but chose to retire. Mets right field prospect Darryl Strawberry lived up to the hype, winning Rookie of the Year honors.

The Dodgers edged Atlanta in the West, getting hot in August just as the Braves cooled. Dale Murphy won his second straight MVP for the Braves, but the late-season acquisition of Len Barker backfired in Atlanta; the club was demoralized when news leaked that Brett Butler was the player to be named going to Cleveland.

Pedro Guerrero was the main cog in Los Angeles' offense. Fernando Valenzuela was not as sharp as he was in his first two seasons, although he remained among the leaders in strikeouts and innings; Bob Welch and Alejandro Pena provided solid rotation support. In the postseason, though, the Dodgers didn't get much hitting or pitching—Valenzuela won their lone game against Philadelphia. Los Angeles dropped the last two games by 7-2 tallies. Steve Carlton was excellent in two starts, and he also pitched well in the World Series. Unfortunately for the Phillies, the offense was out to lunch, and they lost to the Orioles in five games.

1983 American League

TEAM	W	L	T	PCT	GB	HW	HL	R	OR	PA	H	2B	3B	HR	BB	SO	HB	SH	AVG	OBP	SLG	OPS	AOPS	BR	ABR	PF	SB	CS	BSA	BSR
EAST																														
BAL	98	64	0	.605	—	50	31	799	652	6272	1492	283	27	**168**	601	800	23	46	.269	**.340**	.421	761	109	74	85	99	61	33	65	2
DET	92	70	0	.568	6	48	33	789	679	6246	1530	283	53	156	508	831	39	48	.274	.335	.427	762	110	68	86	98	93	53	64	2
NY	91	71	0	.562	7	51	30	770	703	6279	1535	269	40	153	533	686	37	37	.273	.337	.416	753	109	53	77	97	84	42	67	4
TOR	89	73	0	.549	9	48	33	795	726	6213	1546	268	**58**	167	510	810	32	36	**.277**	.338	**.436**	774	104	**88**	37	107	131	72	65	4
MIL	87	75	0	.537	11	52	29	764	708	6240	**1556**	281	57	132	475	**665**	27	61	**.277**	.333	.418	751	**113**	43	**100**	93	101	49	67	5
BOS	78	84	0	.481	20	38	43	724	775	6251	1512	**287**	32	142	536	758	28	49	.270	.335	.409	744	97	37	-17	108	30	26	54	-2
CLE	70	92	0	.432	28	36	45	704	785	6222	1451	249	31	86	**605**	691	29	48	.265	.338	.369	707	90	-21	-48	104	109	71	61	4
WEST																														
CHI	99	63	0	.611	—	**55**	26	**800**	650	6163	1439	270	42	157	527	888	**43**	53	.262	.329	.413	742	99	27	-4	104	165	50	77	19
KC	79	83	1	.488	20	45	36	696	767	6083	1515	273	54	109	397	722	23	32	.271	.320	.397	717	95	-34	-39	101	182	47	**79**	**24**
TEX	77	85	1	.475	22	44	37	639	**609**	6161	1429	242	33	106	442	767	29	38	.255	.310	.366	676	86	-111	-104	99	119	60	66	5
OAK	74	88	0	.457	25	42	39	708	782	6188	1447	237	28	121	524	872	31	55	.262	.326	.381	707	99	-35	4	95	**235**	98	71	4
CAL	70	92	0	.432	29	35	46	722	779	6294	1467	241	22	154	509	835	31	**68**	.260	.322	.393	715	96	-30	-28	100	41	39	51	-5
MIN	70	92	0	.432	29	37	44	709	822	6171	1463	280	41	141	467	802	29	29	.261	.319	.401	720	93	-23	-51	104	44	29	60	0
SEA	60	102	0	.370	39	30	51	558	740	5905	1280	247	31	111	460	840	24	40	.240	.301	.360	661	78	-137	-159	104	144	80	64	4
TOT	1135					611	523	10177		86688	20662	3710	549	1903	7094	10967	425	640	.266	.328	.401	728					1539	749	67	76

TEAM	CG	SHO	GR	SV	IP	H	HR	BB	SO	BR/9	ERA	AERA	OAV	OOB	PR	APR	PF	OSB	OCS	FA	E	WPB	DP	FW	PW	BW	BSW	DIF
EAST																												
BAL	36	**15**	225	38	1452.1	1451	130	452	774	11.9	3.63	110	.261	.316	70	60	98	98	47	.981	121	41	159	.5	6.0	8.5	-.3	2.3
DET	42	9	205	28	1451.0	**1318**	170	522	875	11.6	3.80	103	**.242**	.309	42	22	97	80	63	.980	125	71	142	.3	2.2	8.6	-.3	.2
NY	**47**	12	202	32	1456.2	1449	116	455	892	11.9	3.86	102	.260	.315	33	13	97	110	52	.978	139	42	157	-.5	1.3	7.7	-.1	1.6
TOR	43	8	257	32	1445.1	1434	145	517	835	12.4	4.12	105	.259	.325	-10	32	107	83	47	.981	115	**32**	148	.9	3.2	3.7	-.1	.4
MIL	35	10	211	43	1454.0	1513	133	491	689	12.6	4.02	94	.270	.329	6	-43	93	157	47	**.982**	**113**	37	162	1.0	-4.3	**10.0**	-.0	.4
BOS	29	7	201	42	1446.1	1572	158	493	767	13.0	4.34	101	.279	.337	-44	6	108	155	53	.979	130	36	168	.0	.6	-1.7	-.7	-1.2
CLE	34	8	226	25	1441.2	1531	120	529	794	13.1	4.43	96	.275	.339	-60	-26	105	101	56	.980	122	70	174	.5	-2.6	-4.8	-.6	-3.5
WEST																												
CHI	35	12	243	48	1445.1	1355	128	**447**	877	**11.4**	3.67	115	.248	**.307**	63	84	104	99	45	.981	120	50	158	.6	8.4	-.4	1.4	8.1
KC	19	8	229	**49**	1437.2	1535	133	471	593	12.7	4.25	96	.274	.330	-30	-25	101	109	53	.974	165	44	178	-1.9	-2.5	-3.9	**1.9**	4.4
TEX	43	11	190	32	1466.2	1392	**97**	471	826	11.7	**3.31**	122	.252	.313	122	119	99	101	63	**.982**	113	50	151	1.0	**11.9**	-10.4	-.0	-6.5
OAK	22	12	**287**	33	1454.1	1462	135	626	719	13.1	4.34	89	.263	.337	-46	-46	95	95	50	.974	157	57	157	-1.5	-8.0	.4	1.2	.9
CAL	39	7	237	23	1474.0	1636	130	496	668	13.2	4.31	94	.284	.341	-41	-46	99	83	61	.977	154	57	**190**	-1.3	-4.6	-2.8	-1.0	-1.3
MIN	20	5	268	39	1437.1	1559	163	580	748	13.6	4.66	91	.280	.348	-96	-60	105	136	57	.980	121	52	170	.5	-6.0	-5.1	-.5	-7.0
SEA	25	9	282	39	1418.1	1455	145	544	**910**	12.9	4.12	104	.268	.337	-9	23	105	132	55	.978	136	64	159	-.3	2.3	-15.9	-.1	-7.0
TOT	469	133	3263	503	20281.0					12.5	4.06		.266	.328						.979	1831	703	2273					

Batter-Fielder Wins		Batting Average		On-Base Percentage		Slugging Average		On-Base Plus Slugging		Adjusted OPS		Adjusted Batter Runs	
Ripken-Bal	7.0	Boggs-Bos	361	Boggs-Bos	444	Brett-KC	563	Brett-KC	947	Murray-Bal	157	Murray-Bal	47.6
Yount-Mil	5.6	Carew-Cal	339	Henderson-Oak	414	Rice-Bos	550	Boggs-Bos	931	Brett-KC	156	Yount-Mil	44.3
Henderson-Oak	5.1	Whitaker-Det	320	Carew-Cal	409	Murray-Bal	538	Murray-Bal	930	Yount-Mil	153	Boggs-Bos	43.2
Grich-Cal	4.9	Trammell-Det	319	Singleton-Bal	393	Fisk-Chi	518	Rice-Bos	911	Boggs-Bos	146	Ripken-Bal	40.1
Boggs-Bos	4.4	Ripken-Bal	318	Murray-Bal	393	Ripken-Bal	517	Ripken-Bal	888	Ripken-Bal	144	Brett-KC	37.1

Runs		Hits		Doubles		Triples		Home Runs		Total Bases		Runs Batted In	
Ripken-Bal	121	Ripken-Bal	211	Ripken-Bal	47	Yount-Mil	10	Rice-Bos	39	Rice-Bos	344	Rice-Bos	126
Murray-Bal	115	Boggs-Bos	210	Boggs-Bos	44	Herndon-Det	9	Armas-Bos	36	Ripken-Bal	343	Cooper-Mil	126
Cooper-Mil	106	Whitaker-Det	206	Yount-Mil	42	Griffin-Tor	9	Kittle-Chi	35	Cooper-Mil	336	Winfield-NY	116
Henderson-Oak	105	Cooper-Mil	203	Parrish-Det	42	Gibson-Det	9	Murray-Bal	33	Murray-Bal	313	Parrish-Det	114
Moseby-Tor	104	Rice-Bos	191							Winfield-NY	307	Murray-Bal	111

Stolen Bases		Base Stealing Runs		Fielding Runs-Infield		Fielding Runs-Outfield		Wins		Winning Pct.		Complete Games	
Henderson-Oak	108	Henderson-Oak	17.1	T.Cruz-Sea-Bal	24.2	Ward-Min	18.5	Hoyt-Chi	24	Dotson-Chi	759	Guidry-NY	21
R.Law-Chi	77	R.Law-Chi	12.7	Fletcher-Chi	22.9	Brunansky-Min	13.4	Dotson-Chi	22	McGregor-Bal	720	Morris-Det	20
Wilson-KC	59	Wilson-KC	10.2	White-KC	22.2	Davis-Oak	10.8	Guidry-NY	21	Hoyt-Chi	706	Stieb-Tor	15
J.Cruz-Sea-Chi	57	J.Cruz-Sea-Chi	8.3	J.Cruz-Sea-Chi	18.5	Collins-Tor	9.9	Morris-Det	20	Guidry-NY	700	Rawley-NY	13
Sample-Tex	44	Sample-Tex	6.9	Grich-Cal	17.8	Rice-Bos	9.7	Petry-Det	19	Boddicker-Bal	667	McGregor-Bal	12

Strikeouts		Fewest BB/Game		Games		Saves		Base Runners/9		Adjusted Relief Runs		Relief Ranking	
Morris-Det	232	Hoyt-Chi	1.07	Quisenberry-KC	69	Quisenberry-KC	45	Quisenberry-KC	8.35	Quisenberry-KC	32.7	Quisenberry-KC	38.4
Bannister-Chi	193	McGregor-Bal	1.56	VandeBerg-Sea	68	Stanley-Bos	33	Hoyt-Chi	9.25	Stanley-Bos	21.1	Stanley-Bos	33.2
Stieb-Tor	187	John-Cal	1.88	Davis-Min	66	Davis-Min	30	Warren-Oak	9.59	T.Martinez-Bal	19.3	Gossage-NY	31.4
Righetti-NY	169	Honeycutt-Tex	1.91	T.Martinez-Bal	65	Caudill-Sea	26	Boddicker-Bal	9.70	Barojas-Det	17.4	T.Martinez-Bal	28.1
Sutcliffe-Cle	160	Eckersley-Bos	1.99	Stanley-Bos	64	Ladd-Mil	25	T.Martinez-Bal	9.84	Lopez-Det	16.8	Lopez-Det	27.6

Innings Pitched		Opponents' Avg.		Opponents' OBP		Earned Run Average		Adjusted ERA		Adjusted Starter Runs		Pitcher Wins	
Morris-Det	293.2	Boddicker-Bal	216	Hoyt-Chi	260	Honeycutt-Tex	2.42	Honeycutt-Tex	167	Stieb-Tor	37.1	**Quisenberry-KC**	4.0
Stieb-Tor	278.0	Stieb-Tor	219	Boddicker-Bal	273	Boddicker-Bal	2.77	Boddicker-Bal	145	Honeycutt-Tex	29.1	**Honeycutt-Tex**	3.7
Petry-Det	266.1	Conroy-Oak	232	Morris-Det	287	Stieb-Tor	3.04	Stieb-Tor	143	Dotson-Chi	26.7	**Stieb-Tor**	3.7
Hoyt-Chi	260.2	Bannister-Chi	233	Guidry-NY	288	Hough-Tex	3.18	Young-Sea	131	Hough-Tex	26.5	**Stanley-Bos**	3.4
McGregor-Bal	260.0	Morris-Det	233	Stieb-Tor	289	McGregor-Bal	3.18	Dotson-Chi	131	McGregor-Bal	24.5	**Dotson-Chi**	3.2

Ripken the Best Bird

This was the year of the great shortstop parade. Greg Gagne, Tony Fernandez, Spike Owen, and Dick Schofield all made their major league debuts. For the first time, five AL clubs drew more than two million fans—and two other clubs barely missed the mark.

Five teams clustered atop the AL East in August. While the Blue Jays and Brewers slid from contention, the Orioles turned it on and had no competition in September. Joe Altobelli struck it rich in his first season as Orioles manager. Cal Ripken, setting a new standard for shortstops, was a deserving MVP, and Eddie Murray could have been. When Jim Palmer came up lame, 21-year-old Storm Davis stepped into the rotation.

The White Sox routed the West; their 20-game winning margin was the largest in league history. But it was a war of attrition; Texas and California had shots at the top in June, but tanked as Chicago began winning. The White Sox, who reached the postseason for the first time since 1959, were the only division club to clear .500. Dan Quisenberry saved 45 games for the second-place Royals, establishing a new record and voiding the preconception that relief aces were sideburned, fire-tossing behemoths.

In his final season, Boston's Carl Yastrzemski set the all-time games played record—he still holds the AL mark. Gaylord Perry retired after winning his 300th game; Jim Kaat called it quits at 44; and Bert Campaneris and Bobby Murcer closed it out with the Yankees.

Baltimore beat Chicago in the ALCS, holding the White Sox to 4 runs and taking the deciding Game 4 in 10 innings on a Tito Landrum homer. The Orioles took that momentum into the World Series. After losing the opener, 2-1, Baltimore roared back to take three close games before blowing out the Phillies, 5-0, clinching its first title since 1970. Scott McGregor and Mike Boddicker combined to allow just 2 runs in 26 innings for the Orioles.

1982 National League

TEAM	W	L	T	PCT	GB	HW	HL	R	OR	PA	H	2B	3B	HR	BB	SO	HB	SH	AVG	OBP	SLG	OPS	AOPS	BR	ABR	PF	SB	CS	BSA	BSR
EAST																														
STL	92	70	0	.568		46	35	685	**609**	6196	1439	239	**52**	67	569	805	30	87	.264	**.334**	.364	698	98	25	6	103	**200**	91	69	12
PHI	89	73	0	.549	3	**51**	30	664	654	6107	1417	245	25	112	506	831	24	85	.260	.323	.376	699	98	16	-5	103	128	76	63	2
MON	86	76	0	.531	6	40	41	697	616	6221	1454	270	38	133	503	816	**35**	85	.262	.325	.396	721	103	55	30	104	156	56	**74**	15
PIT	84	78	0	.519	8	42	39	724	696	6234	**1535**	**272**	40	134	447	862	28	78	**.273**	.327	**.408**	**735**	106	**81**	48	105	161	75	68	9
CHI	73	89	0	.451	19	38	43	676	709	6141	1436	239	46	102	460	869	25	76	.260	.317	.375	692	95	-5	-29	104	132	70	65	5
NY	65	97	0	.401	27	33	48	609	723	6108	1361	227	26	97	456	1005	25	64	.247	.305	.350	655	89	-76	-78	100	137	58	70	10
WEST																														
ATL	89	73	0	.549		42	39	**739**	702	6229	1411	215	22	**146**	554	869	29	96	.256	.325	.383	708	102	34	20	102	151	77	66	6
LA	88	74	0	.543	1	43	38	691	612	6361	1487	222	32	138	528	**804**	30	**106**	.264	.327	.388	715	**109**	47	**69**	97	151	56	73	14
SF	87	75	0	.537	2	45	36	673	687	6227	1393	213	30	133	**607**	915	17	59	.253	.327	.376	703	103	28	35	99	130	56	70	9
SD	81	81	0	.500	8	43	38	675	658	6159	1435	217	**52**	81	429	877	22	86	.257	.311	.359	670	99	-53	-14	94	165	77	68	9
HOU	77	85	0	.475	12	43	38	569	620	6008	1342	236	48	74	435	830	19	68	.247	.302	.349	651	94	-87	-40	92	140	61	70	9
CIN	61	101	0	.377	28	33	48	545	661	6099	1375	228	34	82	470	817	21	88	.251	.310	.350	660	90	-64	-66	100	131	69	66	5
TOT	972					499	473	7947		74090	17085	2823	445	1299	5964	10300	305	978	.258	.319	.373	692		1782	822	68	104			

TEAM	CG	SHO	GR	SV	IP	H	HR	BB	SO	BR/9	ERA	AERA	OAV	OOB	PR	APR	PF	OSB	OCS	FA	E	WPB	DP	FW	PW	BW	BSW	DIF
EAST																												
STL	25	10	318	47	1465.1	1420	94	502	689	11.9	3.37	109	.258	.320	37	48	102	149	64	**.981**	124	60	169	.9	5.0	.6	.3	4.0
PHI	**38**	13	287	33	1456.1	1395	86	472	**1002**	11.7	3.61	102	.255	.314	-1	12	102	154	64	**.981**	**121**	60	138	**1.1**	1.3	-.5	-.7	6.8
MON	34	10	250	43	1460.2	1371	110	**448**	936	11.3	3.31	**111**	.250	.306	46	**60**	103	121	75	.980	122	55	117	**1.1**	6.3	3.2	**.7**	-6.2
PIT	19	7	280	39	1466.2	1434	118	521	933	12.2	3.81	98	.257	.321	-34	-11	104	**108**	72	.977	145	71	133	-.3	-1.2	5.0	.0	-.6
CHI	9	7	**354**	43	1447.1	1510	125	452	764	12.4	3.92	96	.272	.327	-51	-22	105	156	76	.979	132	45	110	.5	-2.3	-3.0	-.4	-2.7
NY	15	5	278	37	1447.1	1508	119	582	759	13.1	3.88	94	.273	.341	-45	-34	102	153	86	.972	175	**38**	134	-2.0	-3.6	-8.2	.1	-2.4
WEST																												
ATL	15	11	314	**51**	1463.0	1484	126	502	813	12.4	3.82	96	.267	.328	-36	-22	102	167	67	.979	137	50	**186**	.2	-2.3	2.1	-.3	8.3
LA	37	**16**	295	28	1488.1	1356	91	468	933	**11.2**	**3.26**	106	**.244**	**.303**	**56**	35	96	127	69	.979	139	51	131	.0	3.7	**7.2**	.6	-4.6
SF	18	4	323	45	1465.1	1507	109	466	810	12.3	3.64	98	.270	.326	-6	-10	99	185	**96**	.973	173	40	125	-1.9	-1.1	3.7	.0	5.2
SD	20	11	277	41	1476.0	1348	139	502	.765	11.4	3.52	97	**.244**	.307	13	-18	95	136	43	.976	152	39	142	-.7	-1.9	-1.5	.0	4.0
HOU	37	**16**	244	31	1446.2	**1338**	87	479	899	11.5	3.42	97	.247	.310	30	-17	92	177	57	.978	136	93	154	.3	-1.8	-4.2	.0	1.7
CIN	22	7	293	31	1460.1	1414	105	570	998	12.4	3.66	100	.258	.328	-10	1	102	149	53	.980	128	62	158	.7	.1	-6.9	-.4	-13.5
TOT	289	117	3513	469	17543.1					12.0	3.60		.258	.319						.978	1684	664	1697					

Batter-Fielder Wins		Batting Average		On-Base Percentage		Slugging Average		On-Base-Plus Slugging		Adjusted OPS		Adjusted Batter Runs	
Carter-Mon	6.7	Oliver-Mon	.331	Schmidt-Phi	.403	Schmidt-Phi	.547	Schmidt-Phi	.949	Schmidt-Phi	159	Schmidt-Phi	45.1
Schmidt-Phi	6.3	Madlock-Pit	.319	Morgan-SF	.400	Guerrero-LA	.536	Guerrero-LA	.914	Guerrero-LA	158	Guerrero-LA	44.0
O.Smith-StL	4.7	Durham-Chi	.312	Hernandez-StL	.397	Durham-Chi	.521	Durham-Chi	.909	Lezcano-SD	150	Oliver-Mon	40.2
Guerrero-LA	4.3	L.Smith-StL	.307	Oliver-Mon	.392	Oliver-Mon	.514	Oliver-Mon	.906	Oliver-Mon	147	Thompson-Pit	37.5
Thon-Hou	4.3	Buckner-Chi	.306	Thompson-Pit	.391	Thompson-Pit	.511	Thompson-Pit	.902	Durham-Chi	147	Murphy-Atl	36.2

Runs		Hits		Doubles		Triples		Home Runs		Total Bases		Runs Batted In	
L.Smith-StL	120	Oliver-Mon	204	Oliver-Mon	43	Thon-Hou	10	Kingman-NY	37	Oliver-Mon	317	Oliver-Mon	109
Murphy-Atl	113	Buckner-Chi	201	Kennedy-SD	42	Wilson-NY	9	Murphy-Atl	36	Guerrero-LA	308	Murphy-Atl	109
Schmidt-Phi	108	Dawson-Mon	183	Dawson-Mon	37	Puhl-Hou	9	Schmidt-Phi	35	Murphy-Atl	303	Buckner-Chi	105
Dawson-Mon	107	L.Smith-StL	182	Knight-Hou	36	Moreno-Pit	9	Horner-Atl	32	Dawson-Mon	303	Hendrick-StL	104
Sandberg-Chi	103	Ray-Pit	182					Guerrero-LA	32	Buckner-Chi	290	Clark-SF	103

Stolen Bases		Base Stealing Runs		Fielding Runs-Infield		Fielding Runs-Outfield		Wins		Winning Pct.		Complete Games	
Raines-Mon	78	Raines-Mon	11.6	O.Smith-StL	35.5	Lezcano-SD	9.4	Carlton-Phi	23	Niekro-Atl	.810	Carlton-Phi	19
L.Smith-StL	68	Wilson-NY	7.2	Concepcion-Cin	18.8	Dawson-Mon	8.2	Valenzuela-LA	19	Rogers-Mon	.704	Valenzuela-LA	18
Moreno-Pit	60	L.Smith-StL	5.9	Hubbard-Atl	18.5	Dernier-Phi	7.9	Rogers-Mon	19	Carlton-Phi	.676	Niekro-Hou	16
Wilson-NY	58	Thon-Hou	5.3	Schmidt-Phi	18.5	Householder-Cin	7.9	Reuss-LA	18	Lollar-SD	.640	Rogers-Mon	14
S.Sax-LA	49	Wiggins-SD	5.2	Thon-Hou	18.4	Wilson-NY	7.7			Forsch-StL	.625	Soto-Cin	13

Strikeouts		Fewest BB/Game		Games		Saves		Base Runners/9		Adjusted Relief Runs		Relief Ranking	
Carlton-Phi	286	Bird-Chi	1.41	Tekulve-Pit	85	Sutter-StL	36	DeLeon-SD	8.29	Minton-SF	24.0	Minton-SF	35.6
Soto-Cin	274	Hammaker-SF	1.44	Minton-SF	78	Minton-SF	30	Howe-LA	9.42	Scurry-Pit	20.7	Garber-Atl	28.1
Ryan-Hou	245	Andujar-StL	1.69	Scurry-Pit	76	Garber-Atl	30	Soto-Cin	9.68	Bedrosian-Atl	20.2	Reardon-Mon	26.4
Valenzuela-LA	199	Reuss-LA	1.77	Reardon-Mon	75	Reardon-Mon	26	Niekro-Hou	9.77	Reardon-Mon	19.5	DeLeon-SD	26.0
Rogers-Mon	179	Candelaria-Pit	1.91	Hernandez-StL	75	Tekulve-Pit	20	Andujar-StL	9.96	DeLeon-SD	17.2	Bedrosian-Atl	21.5

Innings Pitched		Opponents' Avg.		Opponents' OBP		Earned Run Average		Adjusted ERA		Adjusted Starter Runs		Pitcher Wins	
Carlton-Phi	295.2	Ryan-Hou	.213	Soto-Cin	.271	Rogers-Mon	2.40	Rogers-Mon	154	Rogers-Mon	39.0	**Minton-SF**	3.9
Valenzuela-LA	285.0	Soto-Cin	.215	Sutton-Hou	.277	Niekro-Hou	2.47	Andujar-StL	149	Andujar-StL	33.2	**Rogers-Mon**	3.8
Rogers-Mon	277.0	Lea-Mon	.222	Reuss-LA	.277	Andujar-StL	2.47	Niekro-Hou	135	Niekro-Hou	30.1	Garber-Atl	3.2
Niekro-Hou	270.0	Lollar-SD	.224	Niekro-Hou	.278	Soto-Cin	2.79	Soto-Cin	131	Soto-Cin	25.1	**Andujar-StL**	3.0
Andujar-StL	265.2	Niekro-Hou	.229	Andujar-StL	.281	Valenzuela-LA	2.87	Candelaria-Pit	128	Carlton-Phi	19.0	DeLeon-SD	2.9

My Beer's Better Than Yours

The NL West was nothing if not streaky. Atlanta, featuring Bob Horner and MVP Dale Murphy, won its first 13 games of the season under new manager Joe Torre. The Braves then fell apart in late July, losing 19 of 21 to sag below the streaking Dodgers. Meanwhile, San Francisco, featuring veterans Reggie Smith (in his last season), Joe Morgan, and Jack Clark plus rookie Chili Davis, won 10 straight in August, and then 18 of 21 in September.

With the title in sight, Los Angeles lost eight straight; on September 26, one game separated the Braves, Giants, and Dodgers. Atlanta won five of their final seven to capture the division as Los Angeles and San Francisco knocked each other out.

Steve Sax was the fourth successive Dodger to be Rookie of the Year. A superior crew of freshmen became regulars in '82, including Davis, Ryne Sandberg, Willie McGee, and Tony Gwynn. Willie Stargell ended his career as a pinch hitter for Pittsburgh, a team ready for collapse amid shady characters and an aging lineup. The Mets, hoping for a quick fix, traded for George Foster and then made him the first $2 million player. He didn't help.

Whitey Herzog's Cardinals battled the Phillies starting in July, and then pulled away in September. Lonnie Smith sparked the offense, and Bruce Sutter led the NL in saves for the fourth consecutive time. Steve Carlton won his fourth Cy Young for the Phillies, but Mike Schmidt aside, Philadelphia's lineup couldn't deliver.

St. Louis easily swept Atlanta in the NLCS. The Cardinals then played a rollicking, entertaining seven-game World Series against Milwaukee. The final contest between beer towns was a seesaw affair; St. Louis came back in the late innings to win. This was the NL's fourth straight Series victory.

NL owners worked to bounce Bowie Kuhn from the commissioner's chair, feeling that he was too weak in negotiations and had no long-term vision. The game had no full-time commissioner until 1984.

1982 American League

TEAM	W	L	T	PCT	GB	HW	HL	R	OR	PA	H	2B	3B	HR	BB	SO	HB	SH	AVG	OBP	SLG	OPS	AOPS	BR	ABR	PF	SB	CS	BSA	BSR
EAST																														
MIL	95	67	1	.586		48	34	**891**	717	6337	1599	277	41	216	484	714	18	56	.279	.335	**.455**	790	120	109	154	95	84	52	62	
BAL	94	68		.580	1	53	28	774	687	6325	1478	259	27	179	634	796	25	57	.266	.341	.419	760	108	71	77	99	49	38	56	-3
BOS	89	73	0	.549	6	49	32	753	713	6262	1536	271	31	136	547	736	28	53	.274	.340	.407	747	98	42	-2	106	42	39	52	-4
DET	83	79	0	.512	12	47	34	729	685	6166	1489	237	40	177	470	807	26	41	.266	.324	.418	742	101	13	9	101	93	66	58	-3
NY	79	83	0	.488	16	42	39	709	716	6244	1417	225	37	161	590	719	24	55	.256	.328	.398	726	99	-5	5	99	69	45	61	-3
TOR	78	84	0	.481	17	44	37	651	701	6067	1447	262	45	106	415	749	28	48	.262	.314	.383	697	83	-72	-124	109	118	81	59	-2
CLE	78	84	0	.481	17	41	40	683	748	6359	1458	225	32	109	**651**	625	35	74	.262	.341	.373	714	96	-11	-15	101	151	68	69	9
WEST																														
CAL	93	69	0	.574		52	29	814	670	6350	1518	268	26	186	613	760	35	114	.274	.347	.433	780	112	**113**	104	101	55	53	51	-6
KC	90	72	0	.556	3	**56**	25	784	717	6177	**1603**	295	58	132	442	758	25	32	**.285**	.337	.428	765	107	68	62	101	133	48	**73**	12
CHI	87	75	0	.537	6	49	31	786	710	6242	1523	266	52	136	533	866	30	54	.273	.337	.413	750	104	44	40	101	136	58	70	10
SEA	76	86	0	.469	17	42	39	651	712	6181	1431	259	33	130	456	806	22	42	.254	.311	.381	692	86	-85	-107	104	131	82	62	0
OAK	68	94	0	.420	25	36	45	691	819	6154	1286	211	27	149	582	948	20	50	.236	.309	.367	676	88	-107	-87	97	**232**	87	**73**	**21**
TEX	64	98	0	.395	29	38	43	590	749	6020	1354	204	26	115	447	750	32	64	.249	.308	.359	667	86	-131	-105	96	63	45	58	-2
MIN	60	102	0	.370	33	37	44	657	819	6115	1427	234	44	148	474	887	24	22	.257	.316	.396	712	91	-46	-67	103	38	33	54	-3
TOT	1135					634	500	10163		86999	20566	3493	519	2080	7338	10921	372	762	.264	.328	.402	730					1394	795	64	28

TEAM	CG	SHO	GR	SV	IP	H	HR	BB	SO	BR/9	ERA	AERA	OAV	OOB	PR	APR	PF	OSB	OCS	FA	E	WPB	DP	FW	PW	BW	BSW	DIF
EAST																												
MIL	34	6	213	**47**	1467.1	1514	152	511	717	12.5	3.98	96	.270	.330	15	-26	94	121	62	.980	125	56	**185**	.1	-2.6	**15.4**	-.2	1.3
BAL	38	8	231	34	1462.1	1436	147	488	719	12.0	3.99	102	.257	**.317**	14	11	100	98	51	**.984**	101	42	140	**1.4**	1.1	7.7	-.5	3.3
BOS	23	11	214	33	1453.0	1557	155	478	816	12.8	4.03	108	.276	.334	7	47	107	101	55	.981	121	40	172	.3	4.7	-.2	-.6	2.8
DET	**45**	5	228	27	1451.0	**1371**	172	554	740	12.1	3.80	107	.251	.321	44	45	100	84	63	.981	117	68	165	.5	4.5	.9	-.5	-3.4
NY	24	8	251	39	1459.0	1471	113	491	939	12.2	3.99	101	.264	.323	13	5	99	98	44	.979	128	56	158	-.0	.5	.5	-.3	-2.6
TOR	41	**13**	220	25	1443.2	1428	147	493	776	12.1	3.95	114	.257	.319	20	**80**	110	78	46	.978	136	45	146	-.5	**8.0**	-12.4	-.4	2.3
CLE	31	9	221	30	1468.1	1433	122	589	882	12.5	4.11	101	.257	.327	-5	6	102	125	60	.980	123	62	129	.2	.6	-1.5	.7	-3.0
WEST																												
CAL	40	10	248	27	1464.0	1436	124	482	728	**12.0**	3.82	107	.259	.321	42	43	100	**66**	**77**	.983	108	40	171	1.0	4.3	10.4	-.8	-2.9
KC	16	12	228	45	1431.0	1443	163	471	650	12.2	4.08	100	.262	.320	-1	-1	100	85	53	.979	127	49	140	-.0	-.1	6.2	1.0	1.8
CHI	30	10	258	41	1439.0	1502	**99**	460	753	12.4	3.87	105	.270	.326	33	32	100	102	60	.976	154	41	173	-1.5	3.2	4.0	.8	-.5
SEA	23	11	**303**	39	1476.1	1431	173	547	**1002**	12.3	3.88	110	.256	.324	32	62	105	118	51	.978	139	57	158	-.7	6.2	-10.7	-.2	.4
OAK	42	6	239	22	1456.0	1506	177	648	697	13.5	4.54	87	.268	.343	-76	-100	97	97	58	.974	160	66	140	-1.8	-10.0	-8.7	**1.9**	5.6
TEX	32	5	214	24	1431.0	1554	128	483	690	13.1	4.28	91	.280	.339	-33	-68	95	93	59	.981	121	53	169	.3	-6.8	-10.5	-.4	.4
MIN	26	7	244	30	1433.0	1484	208	643	812	13.4	4.72	90	.269	.344	-103	-70	105	128	57	.982	108	51	162	1.0	-7.0	-6.7	-.5	-7.8
TOT	445	121	3312	463	20335.0					12.5	4.07		.264	.328						.980	1768	726	2208					

Batter-Fielder Wins		Batting Average		On-Base Percentage		Slugging Average		On-Base Plus Slugging		Adjusted OPS		Adjusted Batter Runs	
Yount-Mil	7.1	Wilson-KC	.332	Evans-Bos	.402	Yount-Mil	.578	Yount-Mil	.957	Yount-Mil	168	Yount-Mil	58.1
DeCinces-Cal	5.7	Yount-Mil	.331	Harrah-Cle	.398	Winfield-NY	.560	Murray-Bal	.940	Murray-Bal	157	Murray-Bal	44.4
Bell-Tex	5.6	Carew-Cal	.319	Henderson-Oak	.398	Murray-Bal	.549	Evans-Bos	.936	DeCinces-Cal	148	Evans-Bos	42.4
Grich-Cal	4.2	Murray-Bal	.316	Carew-Cal	.396	DeCinces-Cal	.548	DeCinces-Cal	.916	Evans-Bos	146	Harrah-Cle	38.4
Bernazard-Chi	4.2	Cooper-Mil	.313	Murray-Bal	.391	McRae-KC	.542	McRae-KC	.910	McRae-KC	145	DeCinces-Cal	38.3

Runs		Hits		Doubles		Triples		Home Runs		Total Bases		Runs Batted In	
Molitor-Mil	136	Yount-Mil	210	Yount-Mil	46	Wilson-KC	15	Thomas-Mil	39	Yount-Mil	367	McRae-KC	133
Yount-Mil	129	Cooper-Mil	205	McRae-KC	46	Herndon-Det	13	R.Jackson-Cal	39	Cooper-Mil	345	Cooper-Mil	121
Evans-Bos	122	Molitor-Mil	201	White-KC	45	Yount-Mil	12	McRae-KC	37	McRae-KC	332	Thornton-Cle	116
Henderson-Oak	119	Wilson-KC	194	DeCinces-Cal	42	Mumphrey-NY	10	Winfield-NY	37	Evans-Bos	325	Yount-Mil	114
Downing-Cal	109	McRae-KC	189	Cowens-Sea	39			Oglivie-Mil	34	DeCinces-Cal	315	Thomas-Mil	112

Stolen Bases		Base Stealing Runs		Fielding Runs-Infield		Fielding Runs-Outfield		Wins		Winning Pct.		Complete Games	
Henderson-Oak	130	Henderson-Oak	13.9	Bell-Tex	37.7	Brunansky-Min	11.3	Hoyt-Chi	19	Vuckovich-Mil	.750	Stieb-Tor	19
Garcia-Tor	54	Molitor-Mil	5.9	Bernazard-Chi	31.1	Wilson-KC	11.0	Zahn-Cal	18	Palmer-Bal	.750	Morris-Det	17
J.Cruz-Sea	46	J.Cruz-Sea	5.6	DeCinces-Cal	22.8	Mitchell-Min	10.6	Vuckovich-Mil	18	Zahn-Cal	.692	Langford-Oak	15
Molitor-Mil	41	Dilone-Cle	5.5	Almon-Chi	19.7	Ward-Min	10.6	Gura-KC	18	Petry-Det	.625	Hoyt-Chi	14
Wilson-KC	37	Garcia-Tor	4.9	Grich-Cal	16.6	Murphy-Oak	9.9			Gura-KC	.600		

Strikeouts		Fewest BB/Game		Games		Saves		Base Runners/9		Adjusted Relief Runs		Relief Ranking	
Bannister-Sea	209	John-NY/Cal	1.58	VandeBerg-Sea	78	Quisenberry-KC	35	Gossage-NY	8.81	Stanley-Bos	23.5	Spillner-Cle	42.0
Barker-Cle	187	Eckersley-Bos	1.73	T.Martinez-Bal	76	Gossage-NY	30	Quisenberry-KC	9.09	Quisenberry-KC	23.1	Caudill-Sea	41.5
Righetti-NY	163	Hoyt-Chi	1.80	Quisenberry-KC	72	Fingers-Mil	29	Stoddard-Sea	9.22	Spillner-Cle	23.0	Quisenberry-KC	37.3
Guidry-NY	162	Haas-Mil	1.82	Caudill-Sea	70	Caudill-Sea	26	Fingers-Mil	9.49	Burgmeier-Bos	21.4	Gossage-NY	31.7
Tudor-Bos	146	Langford-Oak	1.86	Spillner-Cle	65	Davis-Min	22	Caudill-Sea	9.50	Caudill-Sea	20.8	Clear-Bos	29.0

Innings Pitched		Opponents' Avg.		Opponents' OBP		Earned Run Average		Adjusted ERA		Adjusted Starter Runs		Pitcher Wins	
Stieb-Tor	288.1	Sutcliffe-Cle	226	Palmer-Bal	286	Sutcliffe-Cle	2.96	Stanley-Bos	140	Stieb-Tor	36.2	**Caudill-Sea**	4.2
Clancy-Tor	266.2	Righetti-NY	229	Eckersley-Bos	296	Stanley-Bos	3.10	Sutcliffe-Cle	140	Sutcliffe-Cle	27.3	**Spillner-Cle**	4.2
Morris-Det	266.1	Ujdur-Det	230	Stieb-Tor	298	Palmer-Bal	3.13	Stieb-Tor	139	Petry-Det	23.8	**Quisenberry-KC**	4.2
Caldwell-Mil	258.0	Palmer-Bal	231	Barker-Cle	299	Petry-Det	3.22	Palmer-Bal	130	Palmer-Bal	23.0	**Stieb-Tor**	3.9
D.Martinez-Bal	252.0	Barker-Cle	232	Hoyt-Chi	301	Stieb-Tor	3.25	Beattie-Sea	128	Clancy-Tor	21.2	**Gossage-NY**	3.2

Harvey's Wallbangers

With Rotisserie® baseball gaining popularity, and *The Bill James Baseball Abstract* first printed by a major publisher, interest in the analytical side of the game began to grow. But there was no accounting for streaks.

In early September, the white-hot Royals seemed poised to win, but they cooled while the Angels caught fire. California, featuring a veteran lineup acquired through trades and free agency, led the league in attendance, almost doubling their 1981 total, and setting a new league mark. Newest Angel Reggie Jackson led the league in homers, and set the career record for strikeouts, which he still holds. Manager Gene Mauch seemed to keep together his shaky pitching staff with duct tape and bailing wire.

Oakland began to crumble, falling to fifth despite Rickey Henderson's record 130 steals. In their last season at Metropolitan Stadium, the Twins were terrible, but rookies Gary Gaetti, Tom Brunansky, and Kent Hrbek developed camaraderie amidst the rebuilding. In Boston, Wade Boggs debuted at .349; Don Mattingly got in his first swings for the Yankees.

MVP Robin Yount headed the Brewers' bruising offense, and the pitching was barely good enough. Milwaukee got hot in June shortly after Harvey Kuenn was named manager; the Brewers took over the East in mid-July. Baltimore, riding Eddie Murray and top rookie Cal Ripken, took three from the Brewers on the last weekend to tie the race. On the season's last day, Milwaukee stretch pickup Don Sutton defeated Jim Palmer.

California took the first two ALCS contests with complete games from Tommy John and Bruce Kison. Their pitching collapsed in Milwaukee as the Brewers won the next two games with big innings. In the deciding tilt, California took a 3-1 lead, but Cecil Cooper's seventh-inning, bases-loaded single gave Milwaukee a 4-3 win. The Brewers went to their first—and to date, only—World Series and played valiantly, but they lost to the Cardinals in seven.

1981 National League

TEAM	W	L	T	PCT	GB	HW	HL	R	OR	PA	H	2B	3B	HR	BB	SO	HB	SH	AVG	OBP	SLG	OPS	AOPS	BR	ABR	PF	SB	CS	BSA	BSR
EAST	*Split Season: First-half Winner PHI (34-21); Second-half Winner MON (30-23)*																													
STL	59	43	1	.578		32	21	464	417	4013	936	158	**45**	50	379	495	16	46	.265	.336	.377	713	103	43	23	105	88	45	66	4
MON	60	48	0	.556	2	**38**	18	443	394	4068	883	146	28	81	368	498	16	63	.246	.316	.370	686	97	2	-11	103	**138**	40	**78**	**16**
PHI	59	48	0	.551	2.5	36	19	**491**	472	4141	**1002**	165	25	69	372	**432**	23	44	**.273**	**.341**	**.389**	730	107	68	42	106	103	46	69	7
PIT	46	56	1	.451	13	22	28	407	425	3959	920	176	30	55	278	494	15	54	.257	.311	.369	680	93	-9	-28	105	122	52	70	9
NY	41	62	2	.398	18.5	24	27	348	432	3885	868	136	35	57	304	603	13	41	.248	.308	.356	664	94	-28	-27	100	103	42	71	8
CHI	38	65	3	.369	21.5	27	30	370	483	3984	838	138	29	57	342	611	13	53	.236	.303	.340	643	83	-53	-73	106	72	41	64	1
WEST	*Split Season: First-half Winner LA (36-21); Second-half Winner HOU (33-20)*																													
CIN	66	42	0	.611		32	22	464	440	4123	972	**190**	24	64	375	553	18	53	.267	.335	.385	720	**111**	57	**59**	100	58	37	61	0
LA	63	47	0	.573	4	33	23	450	356	4188	984	133	20	**82**	331	550	17	62	.262	.323	.374	697	108	15	35	96	73	46	61	0
HOU	61	49	0	.555	6	31	26	394	**331**	4155	948	160	35	45	340	488	18	**79**	.257	.318	.356	674	103	-13	12	94	81	43	65	3
SF	56	55	0	.505	11.5	29	24	427	414	4258	941	161	26	63	**386**	543	14	65	.250	.320	.357	677	101	-7	7	97	89	50	64	2
ATL	50	56	1	.472	15	22	27	395	416	4055	886	148	22	64	321	540	18	56	.243	.306	.349	655	91	-42	-43	100	98	39	72	8
SD	41	69	0	.373	26	20	35	382	455	4184	963	170	35	32	311	525	14	72	.256	.313	.346	659	100	-34	-2	92	83	62	57	-3
TOT	644					346	294	5035		49013	11141	1881	354	719	4107	6332	185	688	.255	.319	.364	683					1108	543	67	54

TEAM	CG	SHO	GR	SV	IP	H	HR	BB	SO	BR/9	ERA	AERA	OAV	OOB	PR	APR	PF	OSB	OCS	FA	E	WPB	DP	FW	PW	BW	BSW	DIF
STL	11	5	219	**33**	943.0	902	52	290	388	11.5	3.63	100	.255	.312	-14	-1	104	94	40	**.981**	82	**27**	108	.6	-.1	2.5	-.0	5.1
MON	20	12	183	23	975.0	902	58	**268**	520	11.0	3.30	108	.247	.300	21	28	102	**65**	48	.980	81	33	88	.9	3.0	-1.2	**1.2**	2.0
PHI	19	5	184	23	960.1	967	72	347	580	12.4	4.05	90	.267	.329	-60	-40	105	124	41	.980	86	34	90	.6	-4.3	4.5	.3	4.4
PIT	11	5	201	29	942.0	953	60	346	492	12.6	3.56	102	.266	.331	-8	8	104	**65**	34	.979	86	39	106	.4	.9	-3.0	.5	-3.8
NY	7	3	234	24	926.1	906	74	336	490	12.2	3.55	100	.259	.323	-6	-1	101	68	39	.968	130	31	89	-1.6	-.1	-2.9	.4	-6.2
CHI	6	2	263	20	956.2	983	59	388	532	13.1	4.01	93	.270	.340	-55	-26	107	109	55	.974	113	48	103	-.8	-2.8	-7.8	-.4	-1.7
WEST																												
CIN	25	14	182	20	965.2	863	67	393	593	11.8	3.73	94	.241	.315	-26	-24	100	107	35	**.981**	80	30	99	**1.0**	-2.6	**6.3**	-.5	7.8
LA	**26**	**19**	187	24	997.0	904	54	302	603	11.0	3.01	110	.245	.302	54	34	95	80	45	.980	87	32	101	.7	3.7	3.8	-.5	.4
HOU	23	**19**	164	25	990.0	**842**	40	300	610	10.5	**2.66**	123	**.231**	**.289**	91	72	94	86	52	.980	87	44	81	.7	**7.7**	1.3	-.2	-3.6
SF	8	9	211	**33**	1009.1	970	57	393	561	12.4	3.28	104	.256	.327	23	14	98	117	47	.977	102	43	102	.0	1.5	.8	-.3	-1.5
ATL	11	4	215	24	968.0	936	62	330	471	11.9	3.45	102	.257	.318	4	8	101	98	58	.976	102	35	93	-.2	.9	-4.6	.4	.6
SD	9	6	239	23	1002.0	1013	64	414	492	13.0	3.72	87	.268	.341	-25	-57	93	95	53	.977	102	35	**117**	-.0	-6.1	.2	-.8	-7.2
TOT	176	103	2482	301	11635.1					11.9	3.49		.255	.319						.978	1138	431	1177					

Batter-Fielder Wins		Batting Average		On-Base Percentage		Slugging Average		On-Base Plus Slugging		Adjusted OPS		Adjusted Batter Runs	
Schmidt-Phi	7.1	Madlock-Pit	.341	Schmidt-Phi	.435	Schmidt-Phi	.644	Schmidt-Phi	1080	Schmidt-Phi	193	Schmidt-Phi	46.3
Dawson-Mon	4.4	Rose-Phi	.325	Madlock-Pit	.412	Dawson-Mon	.553	Dawson-Mon	.918	Dawson-Mon	154	Foster-Cin	28.8
Concepcion-Cin	3.2	Baker-LA	.320	Hernandez-StL	.401	Foster-Cin	.519	Foster-Cin	.907	Foster-Cin	153	Dawson-Mon	26.9
Foster-Cin	2.9	Schmidt-Phi	.316	Matthews-Phi	.398	Madlock-Pit	.495	Madlock-Pit	.892	Madlock-Pit	150	Hernandez-StL	22.7
Trillo-Phi	2.6	Buckner-Chi	.311	Rose-Phi	.391	Hendrick-StL	.485	Hernandez-StL	.864	Cey-LA	146	Madlock-Pit	20.5

Runs		Hits		Doubles		Triples		Home Runs		Total Bases		Runs Batted In	
Schmidt-Phi	78	Rose-Phi	140	Buckner-Chi	35	Richards-SD	12	Schmidt-Phi	31	Schmidt-Phi	228	Schmidt-Phi	91
Rose-Phi	73	Buckner-Chi	131	Jones-SD	34	Reynolds-Hou	12	Dawson-Mon	24	Dawson-Mon	218	Foster-Cin	90
Dawson-Mon	71	Concepcion-Cin	129	Concepcion-Cin	28	Herr-StL	9	Kingman-NY	22	Foster-Cin	215	Buckner-Chi	75
Hendrick-StL	67	Baker-LA	128	Hernandez-StL	27			Foster-Cin	22	Buckner-Chi	202	Carter-Mon	68
		Griffey-Cin	123	Chambliss-Atl	25			Hendrick-StL	18	Hendrick-StL	191		

Stolen Bases		Base Stealing Runs		Fielding Runs-Infield		Fielding Runs-Outfield		Wins		Winning Pct.		Complete Games	
Raines-Mon	71	Raines-Mon	11.8	Schmidt-Phi	22.8	Dawson-Mon	12.0	Seaver-Cin	14	Seaver-Cin	.875	Valenzuela-LA	11
Moreno-Pit	39	Dawson-Mon	4.3	Smith-SD	22.2	Maddox-Phi	7.6	Valenzuela-LA	13	Carlton-Phi	.765	Soto-Cin	10
Scott-Mon	30	Lacy-Pit	4.2	Trillo-Phi	18.1	Easler-Pit	6.4	Carlton-Phi	13	Ryan-Hou	.688	Carlton-Phi	10
		Scott-Mon	4.2	Flynn-NY	14.0	Wilson-NY	5.0			Valenzuela-LA	.650	Reuss-LA	8
		Lopes-LA	3.7	Templeton-StL	10.6	Griffey-Cin	5.0			Hooton-LA	.647	Rogers-Mon	7

Strikeouts		Fewest BB/Game		Games		Saves		Base Runners/9		Adjusted Relief Runs		Relief Ranking	
Valenzuela-LA	180	Perry-Atl	1.43	Lucas-SD	57	Sutter-StL	25	Reardon-NY-Mon	9.09	Camp-Atl	14.6	Camp-Atl	26.9
Carlton-Phi	179	Reuss-LA	1.59	Minton-SF	55	Minton-SF	21	Sutter-StL	9.19	Reardon-NY-Mon	11.9	Lucas-SD	19.1
Soto-Cin	151	Sutton-Hou	1.64	Tidrow-Chi	51	Allen-NY	18	Valenzuela-LA	9.45	Lucas-SD	11.4	Sambito-Hou	16.7
Ryan-Hou	140	Sorensen-StL	1.67	Hume-Cin	51	Camp-Atl	17	Sambito-Hou	9.47	Holland-SF	11.1	Sutter-StL	14.3
Gullickson-Mon	115	Solomon-SF	1.91	Sambito-Hou	49			D.Smith-Hou	9.48	Falcone-NY	10.3	Holland-SF	13.4

Innings Pitched		Opponents' Avg.		Opponents' OBP		Earned Run Average		Adjusted ERA		Adjusted Starter Runs		Pitcher Wins	
Valenzuela-LA	192.1	Ryan-Hou	.188	Sutton-Hou	.265	Ryan-Hou	1.69	Ryan-Hou	194	Ryan-Hou	26.9	**Ryan-Hou**	3.4
Carlton-Phi	190.0	Valenzuela-LA	.205	Valenzuela-LA	.270	Knepper-Hou	2.18	Carlton-Phi	151	Carlton-Phi	23.6	**Camp-Atl**	2.9
Soto-Cin	175.0	Seaver-Cin	.205	Knepper-Hou	.278	Hooton-LA	2.28	Knepper-Hou	150	Knepper-Hou	21.2	**Valenzuela-LA**	2.5
Seaver-Cin	166.1	Berenyi-Cin	.211	Sanderson-Mon	.278	Reuss-LA	2.30	Hooton-LA	145	Valenzuela-LA	19.4	**Seaver-Cin**	2.2
Niekro-Hou	166.0	Blue-SF	.217	Ryan-Hou	.280	Carlton-Phi	2.42	Reuss-LA	144	Seaver-Cin	18.0	**Hooton-LA**	2.1

One Strike Away

Pushed by the owners on the free-agent compensation issue, the players went on strike in June and the game didn't resume until August. As a result, the owners instituted a "split season" with the winners in each half declared division co-champs, with a five-game Division Series to decide who advanced to the LCS. Unfortunately, the worst came to pass: Cincinnati and St. Louis posted the best overall division records but didn't "win" either half. The flawed system did, however, provide Montreal with its only postseason appearance to date.

Portly rookie southpaw Fernando Valenzuela of the Dodgers went a long way toward erasing the game's black eye. "Fernandomania" struck parks all over the league, giving fans a new idol—and the Dodgers a great pitcher who won Cy Young and Rookie of the Year honors. Philadelphia's 40-year-old Pete Rose shattered Stan Musial's NL hit record, but this time Charlie Hustle broke a record as a first baseman with little power rather than as a second baseman, third baseman, left fielder, or right fielder.

Los Angeles, first-half winners by a smidgen, scraped by Houston, sparked by Nolan Ryan and Don Sutton, in five games in the West. The Expos, with Andre Dawson and rookie Tim Raines providing the stickwork, defeated Philadelphia in the East. Mike Schmidt won another MVP; Carlton was great during the season, but 0-2 in the postseason.

The Montreal-Los Angeles NLCS went the full five. In the deciding contest, Ray Burris—a shutout winner in Game 2—went eight innings for Montreal against Valenzuela. With the game tied in the ninth, 1-1, Expos manager Jim Fanning brought in starter Steve Rogers on two days' rest, even though he had a rested bullpen. Rogers promptly allowed Rick Monday's pinch-homer that won the series.

The Yankees took the first two World Series games in New York, but the Dodgers roared back with three consecutive one-run victories. In Game 6 they walloped Tommy John and five relievers, 9-2, earning the Dodgers their first title since 1965.

1981 American League

TEAM	W	L	T	PCT	GB	HW	HL	R	OR	PA	H	2B	3B	HR	BB	SO	HB	SH	AVG	OBP	SLG	OPS	AOPS	BR	ABR	PF	SB	CS	BSA	BSR
EAST	*Split Season: First-half Winner NY (34-22); Second-half Winner MIL (31-22)*																													
MIL	62	47	0	.569		28	21	493	459	4152	961	173	20	96	300	461	29	35	.257	.313	.391	704	106	9	29	96	39	36	52	-4
BAL	59	46	0	.562	1	33	22	429	437	3985	883	165	11	88	**404**	454	15	26	.251	.329	.379	708	104	25	27	100	41	34	55	-3
NY	59	48	0	.551	2	32	19	421	**343**	3994	889	148	22	100	391	434	7	40	.252	.325	.391	716	106	30	35	99	47	30	61	0
DET	60	49	0	.550	2	32	23	427	404	4109	922	148	29	65	404	500	18	50	.256	.331	.368	699	97	15	-2	104	61	37	62	0
BOS	59	49	0	.546	2.5	30	23	**519**	481	4281	**1052**	168	17	90	378	520	13	37	**.275**	**.340**	**.399**	739	105	67	35	107	32	31	51	-4
CLE	52	51	0	.505	7	25	29	431	442	3952	922	150	21	39	343	**379**	13	46	.263	.327	.351	678	96	11	-9	99	**119**	37	**76**	**13**
TOR	37	69	0	.349	23.5	17	36	329	466	3887	797	137	23	61	284	556	20	44	.226	.286	.330	616	73	-106	-124	106	66	57	54	-5
WEST	*Split Season: First-half Winner OAK (37-23); Second-half Winner KC (30-23)*																													
OAK	64	45	0	.587		**35**	21	458	403	4113	910	119	26	**104**	342	647	16	36	.247	.312	.379	691	102	-11	5	96	98	47	68	5
TEX	57	48	0	.543	5	32	24	452	389	3972	968	**178**	15	49	295	396	21	36	.270	.326	.369	695	105	7	28	95	46	41	53	-4
CHI	54	52	0	.509	8.5	25	24	476	423	4064	982	135	27	76	322	518	43	48	.272	.335	.387	722	**110**	40	**47**	99	86	44	66	4
KC	50	53	0	.485	11	19	28	397	405	3941	952	169	29	61	301	419	17	28	.267	.325	.383	708	103	17	17	100	100	53	65	3
CAL	51	59	0	.464	13.5	26	28	476	453	4191	944	134	16	97	393	571	29	**51**	.256	.330	.380	710	103	26	-22	101	44	33	57	-2
SEA	44	65	1	.404	20	20	37	426	521	4201	950	148	13	89	329	553	27	41	.251	.314	.368	682	92	-19	-38	105	100	50	67	5
MIN	41	68	1	.376	23	24	36	378	486	4025	884	147	**36**	47	275	497	11	36	.240	.293	.338	631	76	-90	-110	105	34	27	56	-2
TOT	750					378	371	6112		56867	13016	2119	305	1062	4761	6905	279	564	.256	.321	.373	693				913	557	62	6

TEAM	CG	SHO	GR	SV	IP	H	HR	BB	SO	BR/9	ERA	AERA	OAV	OOB	PR	APR	PF	OSB	OCS	FA	E	WPB	DP	FW	PW	BW	BSW	DIF
MIL	11	4	**199**	35	986.0	994	72	352	448	12.4	3.91	89	.266	.328	-27	-51	95	70	40	.982	79	40	**135**	.3	-5.4	3.0	-.5	9.9
BAL	25	10	133	23	940.0	923	83	347	489	12.3	3.70	99	.260	.326	-4	-6	100	50	41	.983	68	40	114	.8	-.6	2.8	-.4	3.9
NY	16	**13**	161	30	948.0	**827**	64	287	**606**	10.7	**2.90**	125	.235	.293	80	76	99	70	35	.982	72	30	100	.7	**8.0**	3.7	-.0	-6.8
DET	33	**13**	146	22	969.1	840	83	373	476	11.5	3.53	107	.236	.310	14	26	103	58	40	**.984**	**67**	32	109	**1.0**	2.7	-.2	-.0	2.0
BOS	19	4	157	24	987.1	983	90	354	536	12.4	3.81	103	.262	.328	-17	-11	107	93	35	.979	91	27	108	-.4	1.2	3.7	-.5	1.0
CLE	33	10	111	13	931.0	989	67	311	569	12.7	3.88	95	.274	.330	-23	-20	101	**48**	46	.978	87	38	91	-.4	-2.1	-.9	**1.3**	2.6
TOR	20	4	189	18	953.1	908	72	377	451	12.5	3.81	104	.252	.326	-17	14	108	55	36	.975	105	45	102	-1.3	1.5	-13.0	-.6	-2.6
WEST																												
OAK	**60**	11	112	10	993.0	883	80	370	505	11.6	3.30	107	.240	.311	40	25	96	50	45	.980	81	32	74	.2	2.6	.5	.5	5.6
TEX	23	**13**	142	18	940.1	851	67	322	488	11.4	3.40	102	.243	.308	27	8	95	50	38	**.984**	69	28	102	.7	.8	2.9	-.5	-.5
CHI	20	8	173	23	940.2	891	73	336	529	12.0	3.47	104	.252	.319	19	15	99	74	37	.979	87	26	113	-.3	1.6	**4.9**	.4	-5.6
KC	24	8	127	24	922.1	909	75	**273**	404	11.7	3.56	101	.260	.313	10	5	99	72	26	.982	72	**20**	94	.5	.5	1.8	.3	-4.6
CAL	27	8	155	19	971.1	958	81	323	426	12.1	3.70	99	.261	.321	-4	-3	100	73	49	.977	101	24	120	-.9	-.3	2.3	-.3	-4.9
SEA	10	5	**199**	23	997.1	1039	76	360	478	12.8	4.23	92	.271	.334	-64	-37	106	85	35	.979	91	49	122	-.3	-3.9	-4.0	.5	-2.9
MIN	13	6	165	22	979.2	1021	79	376	500	13.0	3.98	99	.272	.338	-35	-3	108	65	**53**	.978	96	22	103	-.6	-.3	-11.5	-.3	-.8
TOT	334	117	2169	304	13459.2					12.1	3.66		.256	.321						.980	1166	453	1487					

Batter-Fielder Wins	Batting Average	On-Base Percentage	Slugging Average	On-Base Plus Slugging	Adjusted OPS	Adjusted Batter Runs
Grich-Cal 5.2	Lansford-Bos 336	Hargrove-Cle 424	Grich-Cal 543	Evans-Bos 937	Grich-Cal 162	Evans-Bos 35.1
Bell-Tex 5.1	Paciorek-Sea 326	Evans-Bos 415	Murray-Bal 534	Grich-Cal 921	Evans-Bos 159	Henderson-Oak ...30.3
Yount-Mil 4.7	Cooper-Mil 320	Henderson-Oak ...408	Evans-Bos 522	Murray-Bal 895	Murray-Bal 156	Cooper-Mil 28.0
Henderson-Oak ..4.6	Henderson-Oak ...319	Kemp-Det 389	Paciorek-Sea 509	Paciorek-Sea 888	Lemon-Chi 154	Grich-Cal 27.9
Burleson-Cal 4.5	Hargrove-Cle 317	Lansford-Bos 389	Cooper-Mil 495	Lemon-Chi 874	Cooper-Mil 153	Murray-Bal 26.8

Runs	Hits	Doubles	Triples	Home Runs	Total Bases	Runs Batted In
Henderson-Oak 89	Henderson-Oak ...135	Cooper-Mil 35	Castino-Min 9	Murray-Bal 22	Evans-Bos 215	Murray-Bal 78
Evans-Bos 84	Lansford-Bos 134	Oliver-Tex 29	Wilson-KC 7	Grich-Cal 22	Armas-Oak 211	Armas-Oak 76
Cooper-Mil 70	Wilson-KC 133	Paciorek-Sea 28	Henderson-Oak 7	Evans-Bos 22	Paciorek-Sea 206	Oglivie-Mil 76
Harrah-Cle 64	Cooper-Mil 133	Dauer-Bal 27	G.Brett-KC 7	Armas-Oak 22	Cooper-Mil 206	Evans-Bos 71
Rivers-Tex 62	Paciorek-Sea 132	G.Brett-KC 27	Baines-Chi 7		Murray-Bal 202	Winfield-NY 68

Stolen Bases	Base Stealing Runs	Fielding Runs-Infield	Fielding Runs-Outfield	Wins	Winning Pct.	Complete Games
Henderson-Oak 56	Cruz-Sea 6.7	Bell-Tex 34.3	Wilson-KC 17.6	Vuckovich-Mil 14	Vuckovich-Mil 778	Langford-Oak 18
Cruz-Sea 43	Wilson-KC 4.7	Yount-Mil 30.0	Henderson-Oak ...14.8	Morris-Det 14	D.Martinez-Bal ...737	McCatty-Oak 16
LeFlore-Chi 36	Henderson-Oak ...4.6	Burleson-Cal 27.4	Manning-Cle 7.8	McCatty-Oak 14	McGregor-Bal 722	Morris-Det 16
Wilson-KC 34	Manning-Cle 4.4	Grich-Cal 18.3	Evans-Bos 6.1	D.Martinez-Bal 14	Guidry-NY 688	Norris-Oak 12
Dilone-Cle 29	LeFlore-Chi 4.1	Castino-Min 17.3	Roenicke-Mil 4.6			Gura-KC 12

Strikeouts	Fewest BB/Game	Games	Saves	Base Runners/9	Adjusted Relief Runs	Relief Ranking
Barker-Cle 127	Honeycutt-Tex 1.20	Corbett-Min 54	Fingers-Mil 28	Fingers-Mil 7.96	Fingers-Mil 22.6	Fingers-Mil 41.4
Burns-Chi 108	Forsch-Cal 1.69	Fingers-Mil 47	Gossage-NY 20	Davis-NY 8.88	Gossage-NY 14.3	Gossage-NY 27.3
Leonard-KC 107	Gura-KC 1.83	Rawley-Sea 46	Quisenberry-KC ...18	Guidry-NY 9.00	Corbett-Min 12.1	Saucier-Det 17.9
Blyleven-Cle 107	Leonard-KC 1.83	Easterly-Mil 44	Corbett-Min 17	Gura-KC 9.30	Quisenberry-KC ...12.0	Quisenberry-KC ..16.3
Guidry-NY 104	Guidry-NY 1.84		Saucier-Det 13	Righetti-NY 9.66	Aase-Cal 10.6	Aase-Cal 15.7

Innings Pitched	Opponents' Avg.	Opponents' OBP	Earned Run Average	Adjusted ERA	Adjusted Starter Runs	Pitcher Wins
Leonard-KC 201.2	McCatty-Oak 211	Guidry-NY 256	McCatty-Oak 2.33	Stewart-Bal 157	McCatty-Oak 27.1	**Fingers-Mil** 4.6
Morris-Det 198.0	Guidry-NY 214	Gura-KC 265	Stewart-Bal 2.32	McCatty-Oak 151	Righetti-NY 19.5	**McCatty-Oak** 3.1
Langford-Oak 195.1	Darwin-Tex 218	Honeycutt-Tex 272	Lamp-Chi 2.41	Lamp-Chi 150	Burns-Chi 17.7	**Gossage-NY** 3.0
McCatty-Oak 185.2	Morris-Det 218	McCatty-Oak 277	John-NY 2.63	John-NY 137	Morris-Det 16.7	**Righetti-NY** 2.2
Stieb-Tor 183.2	Lamp-Chi 222	Forsch-Cal 286	Burns-Chi 2.64	Burns-Chi 137	Stieb-Tor 16.7	**Stieb-Tor** 2.0

Shattered Season

On June 12 players called the first in-season strike in baseball history. Owners provoked the action by trying to force free-agent compensation onto the bargaining table through the courts. Once the owners' strike insurance ran out, they compromised, and the season resumed August 10. To revive interest in the destroyed season, the owners instituted a "split" format—the standings before the strike would stand, with the leading clubs declared first-half winners. The rest of the schedule would produce its own "winners."

The folly of the "split season" was palpable—why expect a team to push if it had *already clinched* a postseason berth? All four divisions had "split" championships. The ad hoc 1981 Division Series—a format institutionalized in the mid-1990s—helped the owners and NBC turn the strike into extra profits. Attendance was down almost everywhere, of course. Oakland's attendance had been so bad that their gate went up 55 percent *despite* the strike.

The league's biggest surprise was Toronto, which played at a .276 pre-strike clip. In the second half, playing sophomore Lloyd Moseby and rookies George Bell and Jesse Barfield, the Jays went 21-27; they would no longer be patsies.

Oakland, the West's first-half winner, had homer and steal leaders in Tony Armas and Rickey Henderson. They swept the Royals in three games in the West Division Series.

The Brewers and Yankees won the East, with Milwaukee's Rollie Fingers winning Cy Young and MVP honors. New York, however, won the East playoff, in five hotly-contested games. The Yankees defeated Oakland in four for the AL title before falling to the Dodgers in the World Series.

Postseason excitement aside, this was a disaster of historic proportions for baseball. With football and college sports taking over media and public consciousness, the last thing the major leagues needed was a crippling strike when it should have been the only game in town. Forgiveness came hard, and some people never returned to baseball.

1980 National League

TEAM	W	L	T	PCT	GB	HW	HL	R	OR	PA	H	2B	3B	HR	BB	SO	HB	SH	AVG	OBP	SLG	OPS	AOPS	BR	ABR	PF	SB	CS	BSA	BSR
EAST																														
PHI	91	71	0	.562		49	32	728	639	6265	1517	272	54	117	472	708	33	77	.270	.327	**.400**	727	101	62	17	107	140	62	69	9
MON	90	72	0	.556	1	51	29	694	629	6164	1407	250	61	114	547	865	20	76	.257	.324	.388	712	102	36	22	102	237	82	74	23
PIT	83	79	0	.512	8	47	34	666	646	6125	1469	249	38	116	452	760	25	75	.266	.322	.388	710	100	27	4	104	209	102	67	10
STL	74	88	0	.457	17	41	40	**738**	710	6202	**1541**	**300**	49	101	451	781	21	73	**.275**	**.328**	**.400**	**728**	66	33	105	117	54	68	7
NY	67	95	0	.414	24	38	44	611	702	6130	1407	218	41	61	501	840	15	73	.257	.319	.345	664	92	-53	-45	99	158	99	61	0
CHI	64	98	0	.395	27	37	44	614	728	6217	1411	251	35	107	471	912	18	69	.251	.309	.365	674	86	-47	-94	108	93	64	59	-2
WEST																														
HOU	93	70	0	.571		**55**	26	637	**589**	6253	1455	231	**67**	75	540	755	13	89	.261	.326	.367	693	**108**	0	**59**	92	194	74	72	17
LA	92	71	0	.564	1	**55**	27	663	591	6221	1462	209	24	**148**	492	846	24	96	.263	.323	.388	711	107	29	48	97	123	72	63	2
CIN	89	73	1	.549	3.5	44	37	707	670	6208	1445	256	45	113	537	852	23	78	.262	.327	.386	713	106	41	55	98	156	43	**78**	19
ATL	81	80	0	.503	11	50	30	630	660	5958	1352	226	22	144	434	899	20	69	.250	.307	.380	687	96	-27	-33	101	73	52	58	-2
SF	75	86	0	.466	17	44	37	573	634	6045	1310	199	44	80	509	840	14	**100**	.244	.308	.342	650	90	-84	-64	97	100	58	63	2
SD	73	89	1	.451	19.5	45	36	591	654	6254	1410	195	43	67	**563**	791	21	92	.255	.324	.342	666	99	-50	-6	93	**239**	73	77	**27**
TOT	973					556	416	7852		74042	17186	2856	523	1243	5969	9849	257	967	.259	.320	.374	695					1839	835	69	112

TEAM	CG	SHO	GR	SV	IP	H	HR	BB	SO	BR/9	ERA	AERA	OAV	OOB	PR	APR	PF	OSB	OCS	FA	E	WPB	DP	FW	PW	BW	BSW	DIF
EAST																												
PHI	25	8	277	40	1480.0	1419	87	530	889	12.0	3.43	**111**	.255	.319	28	**60**	106	166	79	.979	136	59	136	.2	**6.3**	1.8	-.0	1.7
MON	33	15	280	36	1456.2	1447	100	460	823	11.9	3.48	104	.261	.317	20	23	101	**116**	71	.977	144	44	126	-.2	2.4	2.3	1.4	3.0
PIT	25	8	271	**43**	1458.1	1422	110	**451**	832	11.7	3.58	103	.259	.316	4	17	102	125	64	.978	137	**34**	154	.2	1.8	.4	.0	-.5
STL	**34**	9	297	27	1447.0	1454	90	495	664	12.3	3.93	95	.265	.326	-53	-29	104	169	68	.981	122	51	**174**	1.0	-3.1	3.5	-.2	-8.2
NY	17	9	324	33	1451.1	1473	140	510	886	12.4	3.85	94	.267	.328	-40	-40	100	132	80	.975	154	40	132	-.7	-4.2	-4.8	-1.0	-3.3
CHI	13	6	**344**	35	1479.0	1525	109	589	923	13.0	3.89	102	.272	.340	-47	10	110	154	**105**	.974	174	51	149	-1.7	1.1	-9.9	-1.2	-5.2
WEST																												
HOU	31	18	246	41	1482.2	1367	**69**	466	**929**	11.3	**3.10**	106	**.246**	**.305**	82	31	91	157	47	.978	140	62	145	.0	3.3	**6.2**	.8	1.1
LA	24	**19**	266	42	1472.2	**1358**	105	480	835	**11.3**	3.25	107	.247	.306	58	38	96	168	51	.981	123	44	149	1.0	4.0	5.1	-.8	1.2
CIN	30	12	262	37	1459.1	1404	113	506	833	11.9	3.25	91	.255	.317	-40	-55	98	187	57	**.983**	**106**	47	144	**1.9**	-.5	5.8	1.0	5.1
ATL	29	9	289	37	1428.0	1397	131	454	696	11.8	3.77	98	.258	.316	-27	-14	102	144	64	.975	162	50	156	-1.2	-1.5	-3.5	-1.2	7.8
SF	27	10	288	35	1448.1	1446	92	492	811	12.2	3.46	101	.261	.323	24	8	97	156	74	.975	159	38	124	-1.0	.8	-6.8	-.8	2.2
SD	19	9	296	39	1466.1	1474	97	536	728	12.4	3.65	93	.267	.331	-8	-41	95	165	75	.980	132	45	157	.5	-4.3	-.6	**1.9**	-5.4
TOT	307	132	3440	445	17529.2					12.0	3.60		.259	.320						.978	1689	565	1746					

Batter-Fielder Wins
Schmidt-Phi 6.8
Templeton-StL 5.3
Carter-Mon 5.0
Smith-SD 4.2
Dawson-Mon 3.8

Batting Average
Buckner-Chi 324
Hernandez-StL 321
Templeton-StL 319
McBride-Phi 309
Cedeno-Hou 309

On-Base Percentage
Hernandez-StL 408
Cedeno-Hou 389
Clark-SF 382
Schmidt-Phi 380
Driessen-Cin 377

Slugging Average
Schmidt-Phi 624
Clark-SF 517
Murphy-Atl 510
Simmons-StL 505
Baker-LA 503

On-Base Plus Slugging
Schmidt-Phi 1004
Hernandez-StL 902
Clark-SF 900
Simmons-StL 880
Murphy-Atl 858

Adjusted OPS
Schmidt-Phi 167
Clark-SF 156
Cedeno-Hou 150
Hernandez-StL 144
Simmons-StL 138

Adjusted Batter Runs
Schmidt-Phi 49.3
Hernandez-StL 39.4
Cedeno-Hou 35.3
Easler-Pit 35.3
Clark-SF 34.6

Runs
Hernandez-StL 111
Schmidt-Phi 104
Murphy-Atl 98
Dawson-Mon 96

Hits
Garvey-LA 200
Richards-SD 193
Hernandez-StL 191
Buckner-Chi 187

Doubles
Rose-Phi 42
Dawson-Mon 41
Buckner-Chi 41
Knight-Cin 39
Hernandez-StL 39

Triples
Scott-Mon 13
Moreno-Pit 13
LeFlore-Mon 11
Herndon-SF 11

Home Runs
Schmidt-Phi 48
Horner-Atl 35
Murphy-Atl 33
Carter-Mon 29
Baker-LA 29

Total Bases
Schmidt-Phi 342
Garvey-LA 307
Hernandez-StL 294
Baker-LA 291
Murphy-Atl 290

Runs Batted In
Schmidt-Phi 121
Hendrick-StL 109
Garvey-LA 106
Carter-Mon 101
Hernandez-StL 99

Stolen Bases
LeFlore-Mon 97
Moreno-Pit 96
Collins-Cin 79
Scott-Mon 63
Richards-SD 61

Base Stealing Runs
LeFlore-Mon 14.7
Collins-Cin 10.0
Mumphrey-SD 9.7
Moreno-Pit 9.6
Scott-Mon 9.3

Fielding Runs-Infield
Smith-SD 38.5
Templeton-StL 35.5
Trillo-Phi 24.3
Hubbard-Atl 21.2
Schmidt-Phi 18.5

Fielding Runs-Outfield
Youngblood-NY 19.4
Moreno-Pit 11.3
Puhl-Hou 9.5
Dawson-Mon 7.3
Richards-SD 6.9

Wins
Carlton-Phi 24
Niekro-Hou 20
Bibby-Pit 19
Reuss-LA 18
Ruthven-Phi 17

Winning Pct.
Bibby-Pit 760
Reuss-LA 750
Carlton-Phi 727
Ruthven-Phi 630
Niekro-Hou 625

Complete Games
Rogers-Mon 14
Carlton-Phi 13
Niekro-Atl 11
Niekro-Hou 11

Strikeouts
Carlton-Phi 286
Ryan-Hou 200
Soto-Cin 182
Niekro-Atl 176
Blyleven-Pit 168

Fewest BB/Game
Forsch-StL 1.38
Reuss-LA 1.57
Forsch-Hou 1.66
Candelaria-Pit 1.93
Sutton-LA 1.99

Games
Tidrow-Chi 84
Tekulve-Pit 78
Hume-Cin 78
Camp-Atl 77
Romo-Pit 77

Saves
Sutter-Chi 28
Hume-Cin 25
Fingers-SD 23
Camp-Atl 22
Allen-NY 22

Base Runners/9
Richard-Hou 8.31
McGraw-Phi 8.48
Sambito-Hou 8.87
Sutton-LA 8.99
Reuss-LA 9.14

Adjusted Relief Runs
McGraw-Phi 23.2
Caudill-Chi 22.3
Camp-Atl 20.6
Smith-Hou 17.6
Holland-SF 15.3

Relief Ranking
McGraw-Phi 30.3
Camp-Atl 25.4
Sutter-Chi 22.5
Hume-Cin 22.5
Smith-Hou 21.9

Innings Pitched
Carlton-Phi 304.0
Rogers-Mon 281.0
Niekro-Atl 275.0
Reuschel-Chi 257.0
Niekro-Hou 256.0

Opponents' Avg.
Soto-Cin 187
Sutton-LA 211
Carlton-Phi 218
Seaver-Cin 225
Reuss-LA 227

Opponents' OBP
Sutton-LA 257
Reuss-LA 260
Pastore-Cin 275
Carlton-Phi 276
Soto-Cin 276

Earned Run Average
Sutton-LA 2.20
Carlton-Phi 2.34
Reuss-LA 2.51
Blue-SF 2.97
Rogers-Mon 2.98

Adjusted ERA
Carlton-Phi 163
Sutton-LA 158
Reuss-LA 138
Rogers-Mon 122
Zachry-NY 120

Adjusted Starter Runs
Carlton-Phi 48.0
Sutton-LA 31.9
Reuss-LA 24.0
Rogers-Mon 21.5
Richard-Hou 17.6

Pitcher Wins
Carlton-Phi 5.2
McGraw-Phi 3.3
Camp-Atl 2.9
Hume-Cin 2.6
Reuss-LA 2.5

Finally, Philly

Defending world champion Pittsburgh, leading the East in late August, suddenly dropped 13 of 15 to fall from contention. The Phillies and Expos took the mantle, and the season went down to the last three games of the year—in Montreal. Philly captured the first two to clinch. Mike Schmidt, whose homer won the division-clinching game, was MVP, while Steve Carlton won his third Cy Young. Montreal's Gary Carter finished second in MVP voting.

Houston gave free agent Nolan Ryan the first $1 million annual salary. As it turned out, they really needed Ryan; fireballer J.R. Richard suffered a career-ending stroke on July 30. The Astros and Dodgers traded the West lead from June onward, spending six straight days tied in mid-September. Los Angeles lost five straight late in the month, but then swept a season-ending home series (with three one-run games) against Houston to force a playoff, also at Dodger Stadium. The Astros won, 7-1, behind Joe Niekro, for their first title.

The Dodgers, who led the NL league in attendance each year until 1986, had the Rookie of the Year in Steve Howe. Giants mainstay Willie McCovey retired. Game-winning RBI became an official statistic and would remain so through 1988.

Houston and Philadelphia hooked up in a wild five-game NLCS, with the last four contests decided in extra innings. After the Phillies' Game 1 win, the Astros won the next two. Philadelphia staved off elimination in Game 4 with three in the eighth and two in the 10th. In Game 5 Houston scored three in the seventh to go up, 5-2, but Philadelphia plated five in the eighth, and the Astros scored twice to tie it. The Phillies won in the 10th when Garry Maddox doubled home Del Unser.

The Phillies finally won their first World Series ever with a six-game triumph over Kansas City. Every game was close, with late-inning magic on both sides, but Carlton's two wins and great relief from Tug McGraw cinched it for the Phils.

1980 American League

TEAM	W	L	T	PCT	GB	HW	HL	R	OR	PA	H	2B	3B	HR	BB	SO	HB	SH	AVG	OBP	SLG	OPS	AOPS	BR	ABR	PF	SB	CS	BSA	BSR
EAST																														
NY	103	59	0	.636		**53**	28	820	662	6329	1484	239	34	189	643	739	28	51	.267	.343	.425	768	111	81	94	99	86	36	70	6
BAL	100	62	0	.617	3	50	31	805	**640**	6281	1523	258	29	156	587	766	21	42	.273	.342	.413	755	108	55	67	99	111	38	74	11
MIL	86	76	0	.531	17	40	42	811	682	6242	1555	**298**	36	**203**	455	745	25	58	.275	.329	**.448**	**777**	114	80	**100**	98	131	56	70	9
BOS	83	77	0	.519	19	36	45	757	767	6200	1588	297	36	162	475	720	32	40	.283	.340	.436	776	105	**89**	47	105	79	48	62	1
DET	84	78	1	.519	19	43	38	**830**	757	6444	1543	232	53	143	**645**	844	33	63	.273	.348	.409	757	104	66	46	103	75	68	52	-7
CLE	79	81	0	.494	23	44	35	738	807	6258	1517	221	40	89	617	625	37	60	.277	**.350**	.381	731	99	27	19	101	118	58	67	6
TOR	67	95	0	.414	36	35	46	624	762	6149	1398	249	53	126	448	813	33	63	.251	.309	.383	692	85	-95	-120	104	67	72	48	-10
WEST																														
KC	97	65	0	.599		49	32	809	694	6357	**1633**	266	**59**	115	508	709	38	34	**.286**	.345	.413	758	105	62	50	102	**185**	43	**81**	**26**
OAK	83	79	0	.512	14	46	35	686	642	6160	1424	212	35	137	.506	824	19	99	.259	.322	.385	707	99	-54	-12	94	175	82	68	10
MIN	77	84	0	.478	19.5	44	36	670	724	6130	1468	252	46	99	436	703	21	92	.265	.319	.381	700	85	-67	-111	107	62	46	57	2
TEX	76	85	2	.472	20.5	39	41	756	752	6319	1616	263	27	124	480	**589**	23	70	.284	.339	.405	744	106	31	52	97	91	49	65	3
CHI	70	90	2	.438	26	37	42	587	722	6000	1408	255	38	91	399	670	**39**	67	.259	.311	.370	681	86	-105	-104	100	68	54	56	-4
CAL	65	95	0	.406	31	30	51	698	797	6134	1442	236	32	106	539	889	32	71	.265	.332	.378	710	95	-32	-22	99	91	63	59	-2
SEA	59	103	1	.364	38	36	45	610	793	6141	1359	211	35	104	483	727	19	**106**	.248	.308	.356	664	80	-139	-148	102	116	62	65	4
TOT	1132					582	547	10201		87144	20958	3489	553	1844	7221	10363	**400**	916	.269	.331	.399	731					1455	775	65	49

TEAM	CG	SHO	GR	SV	IP	H	HR	BB	SO	BR/9	ERA	AERA	OAV	OOB	PR	APR	PF	OSB	OCS	FA	E	WPB	DP	FW	PW	BW	BSW	DIF
EAST																												
NY	29	**15**	210	**50**	1464.1	1433	**102**	463	845	11.8	3.58	110	.259	.316	73	61	98	**64**	69	.978	138	61	160	.0	6.1	9.4	.3	6.3
BAL	42	10	190	41	1460.0	1438	134	507	789	12.1	3.64	109	.261	.323	63	52	98	93	-67	**.985**	95	54	178	**2.4**	5.2	6.7	.7	3.9
MIL	48	14	231	30	1450.0	1530	137	**420**	575	12.3	3.71	105	.273	.323	53	33	97	81	46	.977	147	39	189	-.5	3.3	**10.0**	.6	-8.3
BOS	30	8	238	43	1441.1	1557	129	481	696	12.9	4.38	97	.279	.337	-55	-18	106	107	45	.977	149	34	206	-.7	-1.8	4.7	-.1	1.1
DET	40	9	210	30	1467.1	1505	152	558	741	12.8	4.25	97	.267	.334	-35	-21	102	102	45	.979	133	78	165	.3	-2.1	4.6	-1.0	3.7
CLE	35	8	225	32	1428.0	1519	137	552	843	13.3	4.68	88	.275	.341	-103	-86	102	124	56	.983	105	69	143	1.8	-8.6	1.9	.3	3.7
TOR	39	9	**286**	23	1466.0	1523	135	635	705	13.4	4.19	103	.274	.348	-26	18	107	115	53	.979	133	49	**206**	.3	1.8	-12.0	-1.3	-2.8
WEST																												
KC	37	10	201	42	1459.1	1496	129	465	614	12.2	3.83	106	.267	.323	33	34	100	109	56	.978	141	50	150	-.2	3.4	5.0	**2.2**	5.5
OAK	**94**	9	146	13	1471.2	**1347**	142	521	769	11.6	**3.46**	110	**.244**	**.310**	94	59	94	87	66	.979	130	60	115	.5	5.9	-1.2	.6	-3.8
MIN	35	9	213	30	1451.0	1502	120	468	744	12.4	3.93	**111**	.272	.328	16	**64**	108	76	59	.977	148	40	192	-.6	**6.4**	-11.1	-.5	-6.8
TEX	35	6	256	25	1451.2	1561	119	519	**890**	13.1	4.02	96	.277	.339	2	-24	96	112	60	.977	147	79	169	-.5	2.1	-10.4	-.7	-.9
CHI	32	12	236	42	1435.1	1434	108	563	724	12.8	3.92	103	.263	.333	18	21	100	124	58	.973	171	61	162	-1.9	2.1	-10.4	-.7	.2
CAL	22	6	268	30	1428.1	1548	141	529	725	13.3	4.52	87	.278	.342	-77	-92	98	147	41	.978	134	42	144	.1	-9.2	-2.2	-.5	-3.2
SEA	31	7	236	26	1457.1	1565	159	540	703	13.2	4.38	95	.278	.341	-56	-35	103	114	54	.977	149	44	189	-.6	-3.5	-14.8	.0	-3.2
TOT	549	132	3146	457	20331.2					12.7	4.03		.269	.331						.978	1920	760	2368					

Batter-Fielder Wins		Batting Average		On-Base Percentage		Slugging Average		On-Base Plus Slugging		Adjusted OPS		Adjusted Batter Runs	
G.Brett-KC	6.5	G.Brett-KC	.390	G.Brett-KC	.454	G.Brett-KC	.664	G.Brett-KC	1118	G.Brett-KC	201	G.Brett-KC	64.0
Henderson-Oak	5.5	Cooper-Mil	.352	Randolph-NY	.427	Jackson-NY	.597	Jackson-NY	.995	Jackson-NY	172	Jackson-NY	51.6
Bell-Tex	5.1	Dilone-Cle	.341	Henderson-Oak	.420	Oglivie-Mil	.563	Cooper-Mil	.926	Cooper-Mil	156	Cooper-Mil	46.2
Randolph-NY	5.0	Rivers-Tex	.333	Hargrove-Cle	.415	Cooper-Mil	.539	Oglivie-Mil	.925	Oglivie-Mil	154	Oglivie-Mil	42.3
Oglivie-Mil	4.7	Carew-Cal	.331	Thompson-Det-Cal	.398	Yount-Mil	.519	Singleton-Bal	.882	Singleton-Bal	143	Singleton-Bal	38.2

Runs		Hits		Doubles		Triples		Home Runs		Total Bases		Runs Batted In	
Wilson-KC	133	Wilson-KC	230	Yount-Mil	49	Wilson-KC	15	Oglivie-Mil	41	Cooper-Mil	335	Cooper-Mil	122
Yount-Mil	121	Cooper-Mil	219	Oliver-Tex	43	Griffin-Tor	15	Jackson-NY	41	Oglivie-Mil	333	Oglivie-Mil	118
Bumbry-Bal	118	Rivers-Tex	210	Morrison-Chi	40	Washington-KC	11	Thomas-Mil	38	Murray-Bal	322	G.Brett-KC	118
Henderson-Oak	111	Oliver-Tex	209	McRae-KC	39	Landreaux-Min	11	Armas-Oak	35	Yount-Mil	317	Oliver-Tex	117
Trammell-Det	107	Bumbry-Bal	205	Evans-Bos	37	Yount-Mil	10	Murray-Bal	32	Oliver-Tex	315	Murray-Bal	116

Stolen Bases		Base Stealing Runs		Fielding Runs-Infield		Fielding Runs-Outfield		Wins		Winning Pct.		Complete Games	
Henderson-Oak	100	Wilson-KC	13.9	Burleson-Bos	31.2	Wilson-KC	13.9	Stone-Bal	25	Stone-Bal	.781	Langford-Oak	28
Wilson-KC	79	Henderson-Oak	12.9	Bell-Tex	26.6	Henderson-Oak	13.9	Norris-Oak	22	May-NY	.750	Norris-Oak	24
Dilone-Cle	61	Cruz-Sea	7.4	Smalley-Min	26.2	Oglivie-Mil	12.9	John-NY	22	McGregor-Bal	.714	Keough-Oak	20
Cruz-Sea	45	Dilone-Cle	7.1	DeCinces-Bal	26.1	Murphy-Oak	11.9	McGregor-Bal	20	Norris-Oak	.710	John-NY	16
Bumbry-Bal	44	Bumbry-Bal	5.8	Castino-Min	21.4	Armas-Oak	10.6	Leonard-KC	20	John-NY	.710	Gura-KC	16

Strikeouts		Fewest BB/Game		Games		Saves		Base Runners/9		Adjusted Relief Runs		Relief Ranking	
Barker-Cle	187	Matlack-Tex	1.84	Quisenberry-KC	75	Quisenberry-KC	33	May-NY	9.39	Corbett-Min	34.8	Corbett-Min	45.2
Norris-Oak	180	Splittorff-KC	1.90	Corbett-Min	73	Gossage-NY	33	Corbett-Min	9.57	Burgmeier-Bos	21.0	Burgmeier-Bos	28.5
Guidry-NY	166	John-NY	1.90	Monge-Cle	67	Farmer-Chi	30	Norris-Oak	9.62	Gossage-NY	18.7	Quisenberry-KC	27.9
Leonard-KC	155	Tanana-Cal	1.99	Lopez-Det	67	Stoddard-Bal	26	Burgmeier-Bos	9.91	Garvin-Tor	17.6	Gossage-NY	27.4
Bannister-Sea	155	Langford-Oak	1.99			Burgmeier-Bos	24	Lacey-Oak	10.17	Darwin-Tex	16.0	Garvin-Tor	24.9

Innings Pitched		Opponents' Avg.		Opponents' OBP		Earned Run Average		Adjusted ERA		Adjusted Starter Runs		Pitcher Wins	
Langford-Oak	290.0	Norris-Oak	.209	May-NY	.268	May-NY	2.46	May-NY	161	Norris-Oak	43.8	**Corbett-Min**	4.8
Norris-Oak	284.1	May-NY	.224	Norris-Oak	.270	Norris-Oak	2.53	Norris-Oak	151	Burns-Chi	33.8	**Norris-Oak**	4.8
Gura-KC	283.1	Clancy-Tor	.233	Eckersley-Bos	.289	Burns-Chi	2.84	Burns-Chi	143	Gura-KC	32.9	**Burns-Chi**	3.8
Leonard-KC	280.1	Keough-Oak	.236	Burns-Chi	.293	Keough-Oak	2.92	Gura-KC	137	May-NY	29.1	May-NY	3.2
John-NY	265.1	Underwood-NY	.237	Langford-Oak	.294	Gura-KC	2.95	Erickson-Min	135	Keough-Oak	25.0	**Gura-KC**	3.1

.390

Kansas City's George Brett *looked* like a .400 hitter, with quick wrists, strong power, and in a good ballpark for his stroke. And despite various injuries, he was over .400 in early September, though a late slump brought him to .390—still the highest mark in the majors over a full season since 1941. An easy MVP, Brett helped the Royals destroy the West Division.

Prior to the season, Charlie Finley sold the A's. The new owners hired Billy Martin to pump up the team and the gate. With Rickey Henderson stealing 100 bases, the A's improved 29 games to second, and their attendance skyrocketed. Part of Martin's "win now" regimen involved his best pitchers doing all the work; his staff completed 94 games, most of any AL team since 1946. Most of the team's top pitchers soon came up lame.

The White Sox brought up rookie Harold Baines, and used 57-year-old Minnie Minoso for 2 at bats. While Reggie Jackson got the acclaim for the Yankees' division title, Willie Randolph, Tommy John, and Rich Gossage were also key performers. New York lost a member of its family as Elston Howard succumbed to cancer.

The Orioles were the league's first second-place 100-game winner since 1961. Steve Stone won 14 in a row and captured the Cy Young. The next year, he was finished by arm problems. Three big-name Tigers retired: Mark Fidrych with shoulder trouble and John Hiller and Willie Horton due to age.

Kansas City avenged their three ALCS defeats at New York's hands by sweeping the Yankees in three. The Royals supplemented their booming bats with excellent starting pitching and help from submarining reliever Dan Quisenberry. The World Series, however, went Philadelphia's way as they defeated Kansas City in six.

1979 National League

TEAM	W	L	T	PCT	GB	HW	HL	R	OR	PA	H	2B	3B	HR	BB	SO	HB	SH	AVG	OBP	SLG	OPS	AOPS	BR	ABR	PF	SB	CS	BSA	BSR
EAST																														
PIT	98	64	1	.605		48	33	**775**	643	6330	1541	264	52	148	483	855	32	98	.272	.330	**.416**	**746**	103	**68**	27	106	180	66	**73**	**17**
MON	95	65	1	.594	2	**56**	25	701	581	6029	1445	273	42	143	432	890	27	67	.264	.319	.408	727	104	24	22	100	121	56	68	7
STL	86	76	1	.531	12	42	39	731	693	6347	**1594**	**279**	**63**	100	460	838	27	63	**.278**	.331	.401	732	103	46	32	102	116	69	63	1
PHI	84	78	1	.519	14	43	38	683	718	6219	1453	250	53	119	602	764	**37**	60	.266	**.340**	.396	736	102	65	33	104	128	76	63	2
CHI	80	82	0	.494	18	45	36	706	707	6182	1494	250	43	135	478	762	35	77	.269	.329	.403	732	96	40	-25	**110**	73	52	58	-2
NY	63	99	1	.389	35	28	53	593	706	6230	1399	255	41	74	498	817	35	66	.250	.313	.350	663	89	-90	-75	98	135	79	63	2
WEST																														
CIN	90	71	0	.559		48	32	731	644	6218	1445	266	31	132	**614**	902	19	62	.264	.338	.396	734	106	60	61	100	99	47	68	5
HOU	89	73	0	.549	1.5	52	39	583	582	6029	1382	224	52	49	461	**745**	22	109	.256	.315	.344	659	91	-96	-61	94	**190**	95	67	9
LA	79	83	0	.488	11.5	46	35	739	717	6188	1443	220	24	**183**	504	834	23	83	.263	.331	.412	743	**110**	63	77	98	106	46	70	7
SF	71	91	0	.438	19.5	38	43	672	751	6131	1328	192	36	125	580	925	20	89	.246	.319	.365	684	99	-47	0	93	140	73	66	5
SD	68	93	1	.422	22	39	42	603	681	6168	1316	193	53	93	534	770	32	**113**	.242	.311	.348	659	92	-101	-63	94	100	58	63	2
ATL	66	94	1	.413	23.5	34	45	669	763	6035	1389	220	28	126	490	818	23	62	.256	.318	.377	695	90	-31	-67	106	98	50	66	4
TOT	971					519	450	8186		74106	17229	2886	518	1427	6188	9920	332	949	.261	.325	.385	709					1486	767	66	58

TEAM	CG	SHO	GR	SV	IP	H	HR	BB	SO	BR/9	ERA	AERA	OAV	OOB	PR	APR	PF	OSB	OCS	FA	E	WPB	DP	FW	PW	BW	BSW	DIF
EAST																												
PIT	24	7	326	**52**	1493.1	1424	125	504	904	11.8	3.41	115	.254	.316	53	79	105	82	52	.979	134	62	163	.4	8.2	2.8	**1.3**	4.4
MON	33	18	260	39	1447.1	1379	116	**450**	813	11.5	**3.14**	**118**	.253	.310	95	**92**	99	103	77	.979	131	**32**	123	.4	**9.5**	2.3	.2	2.6
STL	38	10	275	25	1486.2	1449	127	501	788	11.9	3.72	102	.258	.318	1	13	102	134	52	.980	132	61	166	.5	1.3	3.3	-.4	.2
PHI	33	14	261	44	1441.1	1455	135	477	787	12.2	4.16	93	.266	.325	-69	-45	104	**95**	68	**.983**	**106**	41	148	**2.1**	-4.6	3.4	-.3	2.5
CHI	20	11	287	44	1446.2	1500	127	521	**933**	12.8	3.88	107	.270	.335	-24	38	111	123	67	.975	159	48	163	-1.1	3.9	-2.6	-.7	-.5
NY	16	10	**328**	36	1440.2	1486	120	607	819	12.9	3.84	96	.266	.338	-18	-23	99	136	**82**	.978	140	60	**168**	.0	-2.4	-7.7	-.3	-7.6
WEST																												
CIN	27	10	281	40	1440.1	1415	103	485	773	12.0	3.58	103	.260	.319	24	19	99	110	55	.980	124	39	152	.9	2.0	6.3	.0	.3
HOU	**55**	**19**	237	31	1447.2	**1278**	**90**	504	854	**11.2**	3.20	110	**.237**	**.304**	86	53	94	127	50	.978	138	73	146	.1	5.5	-6.3	.4	8.3
LA	30	6	240	34	1444.0	1425	101	555	811	12.5	3.83	94	.260	.329	-15	-36	97	118	63	.981	118	65	123	1.3	-3.7	7.9	.2	-7.8
SF	25	6	302	34	1436.0	1484	143	577	880	13.1	4.16	84	.269	.338	-69	-116	93	144	76	.974	163	67	138	-1.4	-12.0	.0	.0	3.3
SD	29	7	279	25	1453.0	1438	108	513	779	12.3	3.69	95	.263	.325	6	-29	94	107	76	.978	141	35	154	-.1	-3.0	-6.5	-.3	-2.6
ATL	32	3	283	34	1407.2	1496	132	494	779	13.0	4.18	96	.272	.335	-70	-25	107	181	48	.970	183	70	139	-2.7	-2.6	-6.9	-.0	-1.8
TOT	362	121	3359	423	17426.2					12.3	3.73		.261	.325						.978	1669	653	1783					

Batter-Fielder Wins		Batting Average		On-Base Percentage		Slugging Average		On-Base Plus Slugging		Adjusted OPS		Adjusted Batter Runs	
Schmidt-Phi	5.6	Hernandez-StL	344	Rose-Phi	418	Kingman-Chi	613	Kingman-Chi	956	Winfield-SD	168	Winfield-SD	55.8
Hernandez-StL	5.3	Rose-Phi	331	Hernandez-StL	417	Schmidt-Phi	564	Winfield-SD	953	Foster-Cin	156	Hernandez-StL	46.4
Winfield-SD	5.2	Knight-Cin	318	Tenace-SD	403	Foster-Cin	561	Schmidt-Phi	950	Schmidt-Phi	151	Schmidt-Phi	41.1
Templeton-StL	4.9	Garvey-LA	315	Mazzilli-NY	395	Winfield-SD	558	Foster-Cin	948	Hernandez-StL	151	Parker-Pit	34.3
Concepcion-Cin	4.5	Horner-Atl	314	Winfield-SD	395	Horner-Atl	552	Hernandez-StL	930	Parrish-Mon	144	Foster-Cin	34.1

Runs		Hits		Doubles		Triples		Home Runs		Total Bases		Runs Batted In	
Hernandez-StL	116	Templeton-StL	211	Hernandez-StL	48	Templeton-StL	19	Kingman-Chi	48	Winfield-SD	333	Winfield-SD	118
Moreno-Pit	110	Hernandez-StL	210	Cromartie-Mon	46	Moreno-Pit	12	Schmidt-Phi	45	Parker-Pit	327	Kingman-Chi	115
Schmidt-Phi	109	Rose-Phi	208	Parker-Pit	45	McBride-Phi	12	Winfield-SD	34	Kingman-Chi	326	Schmidt-Phi	114
Parker-Pit	109	Garvey-LA	204	Reitz-StL	41	Dawson-Mon	12	Horner-Atl	33	Garvey-LA	322	Garvey-LA	110
Lopes-LA	109	Moreno-Pit	196	Rose-Phi	40			Stargell-Pit	32	Matthews-Atl	317	Hernandez-StL	105

Stolen Bases		Base Stealing Runs		Fielding Runs-Infield		Fielding Runs-Outfield		Wins		Winning Pct.		Complete Games	
Moreno-Pit	77	Moreno-Pit	9.6	Royster-Atl	29.3	Maddox-Phi	17.2	Niekro-Atl	21	Seaver-Cin	727	Niekro-Atl	23
North-SF	58	Lopes-LA	8.3	Templeton-StL	24.2	McBride-Phi	13.1	Niekro-Hou	21	Niekro-Hou	656	Richard-Hou	19
Taveras-Pit-NY	44	Royster-Atl	4.9	Concepcion-Cin	20.1	Youngblood-NY	10.3	Richard-Hou	18	Martinez-StL	652	Rogers-Mon	13
Lopes-LA	44	Scott-Mon	4.4	Smith-SD	19.5	Cromartie-Mon	9.8	Reuschel-Chi	18	Sutcliffe-LA	630	Carlton-Phi	13
Scott-Mon	39	North-SF	4.4	Trillo-Phi	18.3	Geronimo-Cin	6.3	Carlton-Phi	18	Carlton-Phi	621	Hooton-LA	12

Strikeouts		Fewest BB/Game		Games		Saves		Base Runners/9		Adjusted Relief Runs		Relief Ranking	
Richard-Hou	313	Forsch-Hou	1.77	Tekulve-Pit	94	Sutter-Chi	37	Sutter-Chi	8.79	Sutter-Chi	19.3	Sambito-Hou	37.5
Carlton-Phi	213	Candelaria-Pit	1.78	Romo-Pit	84	Tekulve-Pit	31	Fulgham-StL	9.37	Sosa-Mon	19.1	Sutter-Chi	35.1
Niekro-Atl	208	Hume-Cin	1.82	Jackson-Pit	72	Garber-Atl	25	Forsch-Hou	9.62	Sambito-Hou	19.0	Sosa-Mon	34.0
Blyleven-Pit	172	Lee-Mon	1.86	Lavelle-SF	70	Sambito-Hou	22	Richard-Hou	9.88	Hume-Cin	18.2	Tekulve-Pit	28.4
McGlothen-Chi	147	Swan-NY	2.04	Garber-Atl	68	Lavelle-SF	20	Minton-SF	9.94	Tekulve-Pit	16.9	Littell-StL	25.8

Innings Pitched		Opponents' Avg.		Opponents' OBP		Earned Run Average		Adjusted ERA		Adjusted Starter Runs		Pitcher Wins	
Niekro-Atl	342.0	Richard-Hou	209	Forsch-Hou	273	Richard-Hou	2.71	Hume-Cin	134	Richard-Hou	28.6	**Sambito-Hou**	4.3
Richard-Hou	292.1	Carlton-Phi	219	Richard-Hou	276	Hume-Cin	2.76	Schatzeder-Mon	131	Fulgham-StL	20.0	**Sutter-Chi**	3.9
Niekro-Hou	263.2	Schatzeder-Mon	225	Sutton-LA	288	Schatzeder-Mon	2.83	Richard-Hou	130	Rogers-Mon	19.2	**Sosa-Mon**	3.5
Jones-SD	263.0	Niekro-Hou	228	Seaver-Cin	289	Hooton-LA	2.97	Rogers-Mon	124	Niekro-Atl	18.2	**Tekulve-Pit**	3.0
Swan-NY	251.1	Andujar-Hou	233	Candelaria-Pit	290	Niekro-Hou	3.00	Kison-Pit	123	Schatzeder-Mon	16.8	**Richard-Hou**	2.8

Family Affair

After ten years, Montreal began to grow up. Under Dick Williams, the young Expos featured catcher Gary Carter and one of baseball's best outfields: Warren Cromartie, Andrew Dawson, and Ellis Valentine. The Pirates—adopting Sister Sledge's dance anthem "We Are Family"—led the division most of the season. In a crazy two-week stretch, the Bucs defeated the Expos five of six and took the NL East by two games.

Aging Cincinnati squeezed out one last title, with George Foster and Tom Seaver the stars. Relievers Doug Bair and Tom Hume did yeoman work as the Reds surged ahead of the Astros in September. Houston contended by playing 'little ball'; their 49 homers were the NL's fewest since 1946. Outfielders Jeffrey Leonard, Jose Cruz, and Terry Puhl provided line drives, steals, and on-base ability. Poor second-line pitching was Houston's downfall.

There were just two 20-game winners—ironically, brothers Phil (at 40!) and Joe Niekro. Dominating Cubs reliever Bruce Sutter won Cy Young honors. Houston's J.R. Richard led in ERA and strikeouts.

Cardinals left fielder Lou Brock sprinted into the sunset, ending his career shortly after collecting his 3,000th hit. The NL's superior leadoff man of the 1980s, Montreal's Tim Raines, debuted. Another rookie was skinny 22-year-old Mets reliever Jesse Orosco.

The Pirates eliminated the Reds in three straight, but the Orioles appeared to have the World Series in hand, winning three of the first four. However, Pittsburgh pitchers suddenly became stingy, permitting Baltimore to score but twice over the final three games. The Pirates got the key hits, including Willie Stargell's Series winner, a two-run homer in Game 7 at Baltimore. Kent Tekulve, who pitched 94 times during the season, racked up 3 saves for the "Fam-i-lee."

Stargell was elected league co-MVP with Cardinals first baseman and batting champion Keith Hernandez. Voting "Pops" as the league's best player in '79 was a sentimental selection; few would argue, though, about his choice as NLCS and World Series MVP. He batted .455 against Cincinnati and hit .400 with all 3 Pirates home runs against Baltimore.

1979 American League

TEAM	W	L	T	PCT	GB	HW	HL	R	OR	PA	H	2B	3B	HR	BB	SO	HB	SH	AVG	OBP	SLG	OPS	AOPS	BR	ABR	PF	SB	CS	BSA	BSR
EAST																														
BAL	102	57	0	.642		55	24	757	582	6106	1401	258	24	181	608	847	31	42	.261	.336	.419	755	106	28	56	97	99	49	67	5
MIL	95	66	0	.590	8	52	29	807	722	6227	1552	291	41	185	549	745	20	72	.280	.345	.448	793	112	98	96	100	100	53	65	3
BOS	91	69	0	.569	11.5	51	29	841	711	6184	1567	310	34	194	512	708	33	42	.283	.344	.456	800	108	112	67	106	60	43	58	-2
NY	89	71	0	.556	13.5	51	30	734	672	6061	1443	226	40	150	509	814	18	56	.269	.328	.406	734	99	23	-1	103	176	86	67	9
DET	85	76	0	.528	18	46	34	770	738	6080	1446	221	35	164	575	814	22	56	.269	.339	.415	754	99	23	-1	103	176	86	67	9
CLE	81	80	0	.503	22	47	34	760	805	6205	1388	206	29	138	657	786	42	70	.258	.340	.384	724	95	-20	-22	100	143	90	61	
TOR	53	109	0	.327	50.5	32	49	613	862	6010	1362	253	34	95	448	663	36	65	.251	.311	.363	674	80	-143	-150	101	75	56	57	-1
WEST																														
CAL	88	74	0	.543		49	32	866	768	6311	1563	242	43	164	589	843	37	79	.282	.351	.429	780	112	84	110	97	100	53	65	3
KC	85	77	0	.525	3	46	35	851	816	6349	1596	286	79	116	528	675	35	57	.282	.343	.422	765	103	51	32	102	207	76	73	19
TEX	83	79	0	.512	5	44	37	750	698	6193	1549	252	26	140	461	607	33	78	.278	.334	.409	743	96	-1	-25	99	79	51	61	
MIN	82	80	0	.506	6	39	42	764	725	6296	1544	256	46	112	526	693	31	142	.275	.333	.410	743	96	7	-25	100	66	45	59	-1
CHI	73	87	0	.456	14	33	46	730	748	6056	1505	290	33	127	454	668	36	61	.269	.331	.404	735	95	-19	-34	102	126	52	71	10
SEA	67	95	0	.414	21	36	45	711	820	6202	1490	250	52	132	515	725	28	61	.269	.331	.404	735	95	-19	-34	102	126	52	71	10
OAK	54	108	0	.333	34	31	50	573	860	5971	1276	188	32	108	482	751	20	75	.239	.302	.346	648	78	-195	-167	95	104	69	60	-1
TOT	1128					612	516	10527			86251	20682	3529	548	2006	7413	10115	422	947	.270	.334	.408	743				1497	831	64	38

TEAM	CG	SHO	GR	SV	IP	H	HR	BB	SO	BR/9	ERA	AERA	OAV	OOB	PR	APR	PF	OSB	OCS	FA	E	WPB	DP	FW	PW	BW	BSW	DIF
EAST																												
BAL	52	12	167	30	1434.1	1279	133	467	786	11.0	3.26	124	.241	.301	152	129	96	88	58	.980	125	46	161	.8	12.6	5.5	.2	3.5
MIL	61	12	204	23	1439.2	1563	162	381	580	12.3	4.03	104	.279	.324	29	25	99	97	60	.977	142	51	166	-.2	6.1	6.5	-.5	-1.0
BOS	47	11	198	29	1431.1	1487	133	463	731	12.5	4.03	110	.270	.328	29	62	105	116	41	.977	142	53	153	.7	2.4	9.4	.0	1.9
NY	43	10	217	37	1432.1	1446	123	455	731	12.0	3.83	107	.268	.323	61	45	97	83	55	.981	122	60	183	1.0	4.4	-1.1	-.5	5.2
DET	25	5	221	37	1423.1	1429	167	547	802	12.8	4.27	102	.265	.335	-9	10	103	97	65	.980	134	60	184	1.1	1.0	-.0	.6	1.9
CLE	28	7	241	32	1431.2	1502	138	570	781	13.2	4.57	94	.272	.339	-56	-45	102	146	47	.978	134	60	149	-.3	-4.4	-2.1	-.3	7.0
TOR	44	7	195	11	1417.0	1537	165	594	613	13.8	4.82	91	.281	.353	-95	-67	104	85	56	.975	159	72	187	-1.0	-6.5	-14.6	-.6	-5.2
WEST																												
CAL	46	9	209	33	1436.0	1463	131	573	820	13.0	4.34	94	.267	.336	-19	-44	97	138	51	.978	135	65	172	.3	-4.3	10.7	.0	.2
KC	42	7	239	27	1448.1	1477	165	536	640	12.7	4.45	96	.267	.331	-38	-31	101	75	59	.977	146	55	160	-.3	-3.0	3.1	1.6	2.6
TEX	26	10	217	42	1437.0	1371	135	532	773	12.1	3.86	107	.253	.331	56	44	98	90	58	.979	130	45	151	.4	4.3	.5	-.3	-3.1
MIN	31	6	214	33	1444.1	1590	128	452	721	12.8	4.13	106	.285	.338	14	39	104	77	71	.979	134	44	203	.4	3.8	-2.4	-.4	-.4
CHI	28	9	236	37	1409.0	1365	114	618	675	12.9	4.10	104	.256	.334	18	22	101	135	66	.972	173	67	142	-1.9	2.1	-.5	-.3	-6.5
SEA	37	7	217	26	1438.0	1567	165	571	736	13.6	4.58	95	.281	.348	-57	-33	104	152	58	.978	141	50	170	.0	-3.2	-3.3	.7	-8.2
OAK	41	4	243	20	1429.1	1606	147	654	726	14.5	4.75	85	.288	.363	-84	-117	96	117	86	.972	174	87	137	-1.9	-11.4	-16.3	-.4	2.9
TOT	551	116	3018	417	20051.2					12.8	4.22		.270	.334						.978	1962	835	2318					

Batter-Fielder Wins		Batting Average		On-Base Percentage		Slugging Average		On-Base Plus Slugging		Adjusted OPS		Adjusted Batter Runs	
Smalley-Min	5.6	Lynn-Bos	.333	Lynn-Bos	.423	Lynn-Bos	.637	Lynn-Bos	1059	Lynn-Bos	173	Lynn-Bos	57.?
Lynn-Bos	5.3	Brett-KC	.329	Porter-KC	.421	Rice-Bos	.596	Lezcano-Mil	.987	Lezcano-Mil	164	Singleton-Bal	50.?
Porter-KC	5.0	Downing-Cal	.326	Downing-Cal	.418	Lezcano-Mil	.573	Rice-Bos	.977	Singleton-Bal	157	Lezcano-Mil	45.
Brett-KC	4.9	Rice-Bos	.325	Lezcano-Mil	.414	Brett-KC	.563	Kemp-Det	.941	Rice-Bos	152	Rice-Bos	44.?
Grich-Cal	3.9	Oliver-Tex	.323	Singleton-Bal	.405	Jackson-NY	.544	Brett-KC	.939	Jackson-NY	150	Baylor-Cal	41.

Runs		Hits		Doubles		Triples		Home Runs		Total Bases		Runs Batted In	
Baylor-Cal	120	Brett-KC	212	Lemon-Chi	.44	Brett-KC	20	Thomas-Mil	45	Rice-Bos	369	Baylor-Cal	139
Brett-KC	119	Rice-Bos	201	Cooper-Mil	.44	Molitor-Mil	16	Rice-Bos	39	Brett-KC	363	Rice-Bos	130
Rice-Bos	117	Bell-Tex	200	Lynn-Bos	.42	Wilson-KC	13	Lynn-Bos	39	Lynn-Bos	338	Thomas-Mil	12?
Lynn-Bos	116	Molitor-Mil	188	Brett-KC	.42	Randolph-NY	13	Baylor-Cal	36	Baylor-Cal	333	Lynn-Bos	12?
Lansford-Cal	114	Lansford-Cal	188	Bell-Tex	.42			Singleton-Bal	35	Singleton-Bal	304	Porter-KC	11?

Stolen Bases		Base Stealing Runs		Fielding Runs-Infield		Fielding Runs-Outfield		Wins		Winning Pct.		Complete Games	
Wilson-KC	83	Wilson-KC	14.1	Smalley-Min	32.6	Wilson-KC	13.1	Flanagan-Bal	23	Caldwell-Mil	.727	D.Martinez-Bal	1?
LeFlore-Det	78	LeFlore-Det	12.3	Dent-NY	31.8	Bosetti-Tor	9.2	John-NY	21	Flanagan-Bal	.719	Ryan-Cal	1?
Cruz-Sea	49	Cruz-Sea	7.6	Burleson-Bos	30.2	R.Miller-Cal	8.0	Koosman-Min	20	Morris-Det	.708	John-NY	1?
Bumbry-Bal	37	Otis-KC	4.8	Bell-Tex	28.4	Bonds-Cle	7.0	Guidry-NY	18	John-NY	.700	Eckersley-Bos	1?
Wills-Tex	35	Bumbry-Bal	3.9	Cruz-Sea	19.9	Manning-Cle	6.9			Guidry-NY	.692		

Strikeouts		Fewest BB/Game		Games		Saves		Base Runners/9		Adjusted Relief Runs		Relief Ranking	
Ryan-Cal	223	McGregor-Bal	1.19	Marshall-Min	90	Marshall-Min	32	McGregor-Bal	9.79	Kern-Tex	38.7	Kern-Tex	61.?
Guidry-NY	201	Caldwell-Mil	1.49	Monge-Cle	76	Kern-Tex	29	Darwin-Tex	9.81	Monge-Cle	27.9	Marshall-Min	52.?
Flanagan-Bal	190	Sorensen-Mil	1.61	Kern-Tex	71	Stanhouse-Bal	21	Lyle-Tex	10.04	Lopez-Det	26.7	Monge-Cle	51.?
Jenkins-Tex	164	Stanley-Bos	1.83	Lyle-Tex	67	Lopez-Det	21	Kern-Tex	10.26	Marshall-Min	26.1	Lopez-Det	26.?
Koosman-Min	157	John-NY	2.12	Heaverlo-Oak	62	Monge-Cle	19	Guidry-NY	10.43	Stoddard-Bal	15.9	Drago-Bos	26.

Innings Pitched		Opponents' Avg.		Opponents' OBP		Earned Run Average		Adjusted ERA		Adjusted Starter Runs		Pitcher Wins	
D.Martinez-Bal	292.1	Ryan-Cal	.212	McGregor-Bal	.273	Guidry-NY	2.78	Eckersley-Bos	149	Eckersley-Bos	38.9	**Kern-Tex**	5?
John-NY	276.1	Kravec-Chi	.233	Guidry-NY	.292	John-NY	2.96	Guidry-NY	148	Guidry-NY	34.8	**Marshall-Min**	5.
Flanagan-Bal	265.2	Guidry-NY	.236	Flanagan-Bal	.296	Eckersley-Bos	2.99	John-NY	139	John-NY	32.1	**Monge-Cle**	5.
Koosman-Min	263.2	Baumgarten-Chi	.243	Eckersley-Bos	.297	Flanagan-Bal	3.08	Morris-Det	133	Koosman-Min	28.6	**Eckersley-Bos**	4.
Jenkins-Tex	259.0	Morris-Det	.244	Leonard-KC	.297	Morris-Det	3.28	Flanagan-Bal	131	Flanagan-Bal	27.2	**Lopez-Det**	3.

Gimme an "O"

As scoring reached its highest level since 1950, four teams—Boston, New York, Kansas City, and California—attracted two million fans. Last-place Oakland, on the other hand, drew just over 300,000 fans. No team had drawn that few fans since, well, the A's—in 1954, their last year in Philadelphia. There was only one reason to watch these A's: rookie outfielder Rickey Henderson.

Although six clubs in the AL East finished over .500, the Orioles had no serious challenge after July. Underrated Ken Singleton had a superb season at bat and was ably supported by a mix of youngsters and veterans. Lefty Mike Flanagan took Cy Young honors; he came up big when Jim Palmer went down with elbow problems. The Brewers, led by home run champ Gorman Thomas, won 95 games, but finished 8 games back.

Toronto, miserable in its first two seasons, was even worse in year three. The Blue Jays ended 50½ out, the deepest last-place finish since 1954; rookie Dave Stieb was an impressive 8-8. Ron Guidry led the AL in ERA for the second straight time, but the Yankees' season ended when Thurman Munson was killed in an airplane crash on August 2. Catfish Hunter retired after the season.

California won a poor AL West; their record would have placed them fifth in the East. The Angels, fortified by trades that brought Rod Carew and Dan Ford, led the league in runs. MVP Don Baylor, Carney Lansford, and Ford each scored more than 100 times. California pitching was very thin, but it was good enough. The pitching-poor Royals couldn't turn it on early enough, the Rangers didn't hit, and the Twins just didn't have the horses, although reliever Mike Marshall pitched an AL-record 90 times.

Baltimore defeated the Angels in four games, three of them close, to win the ALCS. The Orioles lost the World Series in seven despite being up three games to one; just like 1971, the O's dropped Game 7 to the Pirates at home. It was Earl Weaver's last trip to the Fall Classic.

1978 National League

TEAM	W	L	T	PCT	GB	HW	HL	R	OR	PA	H	2B	3B	HR	BB	SO	HB	SH	AVG	OBP	SLG	OPS	AOPS	BR	ABR	PF	SB	CS	BSA	BSR
EAST																														
PHI	90	72	0	.556		54	28	708	586	6152	1404	248	32	133	552	866	42	61	.258	.328	.388	716	104	51	39	102	152	58	72	13
PIT	88	73	0	.547	1.5	55	26	684	637	6038	1390	239	54	115	480	874	42	64	.257	.320	.385	705	98	20	-12	105	213	90	70	15
CHI	79	83	0	.488	11	44	38	664	724	6258	1461	224	48	72	562	746	21	84	.264	.331	.385	692	89	10	-62	112	110	58	65	4
MON	76	86	0	.469	14	41	39	633	611	6063	1404	269	31	121	396	881	35	62	.254	.306	.379	685	97	-27	-25	100	80	42	66	3
STL	69	93	0	.426	21	37	44	600	657	5965	1351	263	44	79	420	713	22	55	.249	.303	.358	661	90	-67	-64	100	97	42	70	7
NY	66	96	0	.407	24	33	47	607	690	6132	1332	227	47	86	549	829	24	71	.245	.314	.352	666	95	-48	-31	97	100	77	56	-5
WEST																														
LA	95	67	0	.586		54	27	727	573	6225	1435	251	27	149	610	818	20	111	.264	.338	.402	740	113	102	100	100	137	52	72	12
CIN	92	69	0	.571	2.5	49	31	710	688	6192	1378	270	32	136	636	899	26	84	.256	.334	.393	727	109	80	77	100	137	58	70	10
SF	89	73	0	.549	6	50	31	613	594	6102	1331	240	41	117	554	814	17	127	.248	.318	.374	692	102	-1	21	97	87	54	62	0
SD	84	78	0	.519	11	50	31	591	598	6081	1349	208	42	75	536	848	32	114	.252	.321	.348	669	100	-38	9	93	152	70	68	9
HOU	74	88	0	.457	21	50	31	605	634	6034	1408	231	45	70	434	743	22	76	.258	.313	.355	668	99	-52	-11	94	178	59	75	19
ATL	69	93	0	.426	26	39	42	600	750	6066	1313	191	39	123	550	874	27	61	.244	.315	.363	678	86	-30	-88	111	90	65	58	-3
TOT	971					556	415	7742		73308	16556	2861	482	1276	6279	9905	330	970	.254	.320	.372	692					1533	725	68	84

TEAM	CG	SHO	GR	SV	IP	H	HR	BB	SO	BR/9	ERA	AERA	OAV	OOB	PR	APR	PF	OSB	OCS	FA	E	WPB	DP	FW	PW	BW	BSW	DIF
EAST																												
PHI	38	9	234	29	1436.1	1343	118	393	813	11.0	3.33	108	.251	.303	39	43	101	91	56	.983	104	35	156	2.0	4.5	4.1	.6	-2.3
PIT	30	13	272	44	1444.2	1366	103	499	880	11.8	3.41	109	.249	.313	26	48	104	138	47	.973	167	53	133	-1.4	5.1	-1.3	.9	4.3
CHI	24	7	327	38	1455.1	1475	125	539	768	12.7	4.05	100	.265	.331	-77	-2	113	118	62	.978	144	62	154	-.2	-.2	-6.6	-.3	5.2
MON	42	13	267	32	1446.0	1332	117	572	740	12.0	3.42	104	.249	.323	24	22	100	108	61	.979	134	43	150	.4	2.3	-2.6	-.4	-4.6
STL	32	13	258	22	1437.2	1300	94	600	859	12.1	3.58	99	.245	.323	-1	-3	100	162	78	.978	136	72	155	.3	-.3	-6.8	.0	-5.2
NY	21	7	270	26	1455.1	1447	114	531	775	12.4	3.87	91	.265	.330	-48	-54	99	111	69	.979	132	49	160	.5	-5.7	-3.3	-1.3	-5.2
WEST																												
LA	46	16	198	38	1440.1	1362	107	440	800	11.4	3.12	112	.250	.307	73	63	98	105	56	.978	140	45	138	.0	6.7	10.6	.5	-3.8
CIN	16	10	299	46	1448.1	1437	122	567	908	12.6	3.81	93	.261	.329	-38	-43	99	106	60	.978	134	53	120	.3	-4.5	8.1	.3	7.2
SF	42	17	239	29	1455.0	1377	84	453	840	11.5	3.30	105	.252	.309	44	26	97	159	54	.977	146	38	118	-.3	2.8	2.2	-.7	4.0
SD	21	10	265	55	1433.2	1385	74	483	744	11.8	3.30	102	.257	.317	47	12	94	102	65	.975	160	44	171	-1.0	1.3	1.0	.2	1.6
HOU	48	17	218	23	1440.1	1328	86	578	930	12.1	3.63	92	.247	.320	-9	-52	93	167	59	.978	133	69	109	.4	-5.5	-1.2	1.3	-2.0
ATL	29	12	293	32	1440.1	1404	132	624	848	12.9	4.08	99	.257	.335	-81	-8	113	166	57	.975	153	99	126	-.6	-.8	-9.3	-1.1	-.1
TOT	389	144	3140	414	17333.1					12.0	3.57		.254	.320						.978	1683	662	1690					

Batter-Fielder Wins		Batting Average		On-Base Percentage		Slugging Average		On-Base Plus Slugging		Adjusted OPS		Adjusted Batter Runs	
Parker-Pit	4.4	Parker-Pit	334	Burroughs-Atl	432	Parker-Pit	585	Parker-Pit	979	Smith-LA	163	Parker-Pit	47.1
Lopes-LA	4.3	Garvey-LA	316	Parker-Pit	394	Smith-LA	559	Burroughs-Atl	961	Parker-Pit	162	Burroughs-Atl	40.8
Templeton-StL	4.2	Cruz-Hou	315	Tenace-SD	392	Foster-Cin	546	Smith-LA	942	Clark-SF	154	Luzinski-Phi	40.7
Clark-SF	4.1	Madlock-SF	309	Luzinski-Phi	388	Clark-SF	537	Luzinski-Phi	914	Burroughs-Atl	152	Clark-SF	40.5
Simmons-StL	4.0	Winfield-SD	308	Smith-LA	382	Burroughs-Atl	529	Foster-Cin	906	Winfield-SD	152	Foster-Cin	38.8

Runs		Hits		Doubles		Triples		Home Runs		Total Bases		Runs Batted In	
DeJesus-Chi	104	Garvey-LA	202	Rose-Cin	51	Templeton-StL	13	Foster-Cin	40	Parker-Pit	340	Foster-Cin	120
Rose-Cin	103	Rose-Cin	198	Clark-SF	46	Richards-SD	12	Luzinski-Phi	35	Foster-Cin	330	Parker-Pit	117
Parker-Pit	102	Cabell-Hou	195	Simmons-StL	40	Parker-Pit	12	Parker-Pit	30	Garvey-LA	319	Garvey-LA	113
Foster-Cin	97	Parker-Pit	194	Parrish-Mon	39			Smith-LA	29	Clark-SF	318	Luzinski-Phi	101
Moreno-Pit	95	Bowa-Phi	192	Perez-Mon	38					Winfield-SD	293	Clark-SF	98

Stolen Bases		Base Stealing Runs		Fielding Runs-Infield		Fielding Runs-Outfield		Wins		Winning Pct.		Complete Games	
Moreno-Pit	71	Lopes-LA	8.5	Templeton-StL	32.6	Cromartie-Mon	17.6	Perry-SD	21	Perry-SD	778	Niekro-Atl	22
Taveras-Pit	46	Moreno-Pit	7.9	Smith-SD	29.7	Valentine-Mon	10.6	Grimsley-Mon	20	Hooton-LA	655	Grimsley-Mon	19
Lopes-LA	45	McBride-Phi	5.1	Trillo-Chi	29.4	S.Henderson-NY	7.9	Niekro-Atl	19	Grimsley-Mon	645	Richard-Hou	16
DeJesus-Chi	41	Cruz-Hou	5.0	Russell-LA	21.4	Clark-SF	7.7	Hooton-LA	19	Blue-SF	643	Knepper-SF	16
Smith-SD	40	DeJesus-Chi	4.8	DeJesus-Chi	15.3	Puhl-Hou	6.6			John-LA	630		

Strikeouts		Fewest BB/Game		Games		Saves		Base Runners/9		Adjusted Relief Runs		Relief Ranking	
Richard-Hou	303	Christenson-Phi	1.86	Tekulve-Pit	91	Fingers-SD	37	Garber-Phi-Atl	8.69	Garber-Phi-Atl	20.2	Bair-Cin	32.4
Niekro-Atl	248	Barr-SF	1.93	Littell-StL	72	Tekulve-Pit	31	Reed-Phi	9.52	Tekulve-Pit	18.9	Tekulve-Pit	27.9
Seaver-Cin	226	R.Reuschel-Chi	2.00	Moore-Cin	71	Bair-Cin	28	Fingers-SD	9.56	Bair-Cin	18.5	Garber-Phi-Atl	26.1
Blyleven-Pit	182	Halicki-SF	2.04	Moffitt-SF	70	Sutter-Chi	27	Welch-LA	9.62	Reed-Phi	15.4	Fingers-SD	22.5
Montefusco-SF	177	Sutton-LA	2.04	Bair-Cin	70	Garber-Phi-Atl	25	Swan-NY	9.72	D'Acquisto-SD	14.0	Forster-LA	20.3

Innings Pitched		Opponents' Avg.		Opponents' OBP		Earned Run Average		Adjusted ERA		Adjusted Starter Runs		Pitcher Wins	
Niekro-Atl	334.1	Richard-Hou	196	Halicki-SF	270	Swan-NY	2.43	Swan-NY	146	Niekro-Atl	35.3	Niekro-Atl	4.5
Richard-Hou	275.1	Swan-NY	219	Swan-NY	275	Rogers-Mon	2.47	Rogers-Mon	145	Rogers-Mon	28.1	Bair-Cin	3.4
Grimsley-Mon	263.0	Halicki-SF	221	Hooton-LA	275	Vuckovich-StL	2.54	Vuckovich-StL	140	Swan-NY	25.8	Hooton-LA	3.1
Perry-SD	260.2	Hooton-LA	226	Christenson-Phi	282	Knepper-SF	2.63	Niekro-Atl	140	Hooton-LA	24.8	Tekulve-Pit	3.1
Knepper-SF	260.0	Seaver-Cin	227	D.Robinson-Pit	283	Hooton-LA	2.71	Knepper-SF	132	Knepper-SF	24.7	Carlton-Phi	3.1

Coming into Los Angeles

The Dodgers, who lost coach Jim Gilliam to cancer, became the first team in history to draw more than three million fans. While the AL surpassed the NL in overall attendance, thanks to the addition of two extra teams in 1977, the average Senior Circuit team drew approximately 200,000 more than their counterparts in the other league in '78.

The NL East compressed to a 24-game first-to-last gap, with the Phillies barely holding off the Pirates, who rose from fourth place with a torrid August stretch. Pittsburgh's Dave Parker was MVP, but the Bucs lacked the starting pitching or power to win. Amazingly, the Cubs had just one player—Dave Kingman—to hit more than 9 homers, ranking 11th in the league in long balls despite playing 81 games in the cozy confines of Wrigley Field.

Deep pitching and big power won the Dodgers another crown. Los Angeles didn't take the division lead until late August, but the Reds had just one top starter (Tom Seaver) and suffered poor performances from key regulars. Pete Rose did make the news, however, collecting his 3,000th hit and fashioning a 44-game hitting streak.

Last-place Atlanta showcased Rookie of the Year Bob Horner and catcher Dale Murphy, playing his first full season. Phil Niekro, at 39, was 19-18 for a team that won just 69 games. Another 39-year-old, San Diego's Gaylord Perry, became the first pitcher to win a Cy Young in each league, and teammate Rollie Fingers paced the NL in saves for the second straight season. The surprising Padres also broke in rookie Ozzie Smith at shortstop.

The NLCS was another breeze for the Dodgers, who hit Phillies starters very hard; only the fourth and final NLCS game was close. Once again, though, Los Angeles couldn't solve the Yankees in the World Series. After winning the first two, the Dodgers were outscored 28-8 as they dropped the last four.

1978 American League

TEAM	W	L	T	PCT	GB	HW	HL	R	OR	PA	H	2B	3B	HR	BB	SO	HB	SH	AVG	OBP	SLG	OPS	AOPS	BR	ABR	PF	SB	CS	BSA	BSR
EAST																														
NY	100	63	0	.613		55	26	735	582	6219	1489	228	38	125	505	695	42	37	.267	.329	.388	717	103	13	26	98	98	42	70	7
BOS	99	64	0	.607	1	**59**	23	796	657	6316	1493	270	46	132	582	835	24	65	.267	.336	.424	760	101	98	23	110	74	51	59	-2
MIL	93	69	0	.574	6.5	54	27	**804**	650	6227	**1530**	265	38	**173**	520	805	32	89	**.276**	**.339**	.432	771	114	**116**	**111**	101	95	53	64	2
BAL	90	71	0	.559	9	51	30	659	633	6079	1397	248	19	154	552	864	22	41	.258	.326	.396	722	108	21	63	94	75	61	55	-5
DET	86	76	0	.531	13.5	47	34	714	653	6299	1520	218	34	106	563	695	31	57	.261	.323	.379	702	98	-21	-15	99	64	63	50	-8
CLE	69	90	0	.434	29	42	36	639	694	6011	1400	223	45	106	488	698	26	92	.255	.316	.371	687	102	44	22	103	90	38	70	7
TOR	59	102	0	.366	40	37	44	590	775	6015	1358	217	39	98	448	645	23	77	.250	.308	.359	667	85	-97	-108	102	28	52	35	-12
WEST																														
KC	92	70	0	.568		56	25	743	634	6129	1469	**305**	**59**	98	498	644	30	55	.268	.329	.399	728	101	37	16	103	**216**	84	**72**	18
TEX	87	75	0	.537	5	52	30	692	632	6141	1353	216	36	132	**624**	779	32	83	.253	.332	.381	713	99	12	8	101	196	91	68	11
CAL	87	75	0	.537	5	50	31	691	666	6206	1417	226	28	108	539	682	**67**	72	.259	.330	.370	700	99	-13	9	97	86	69	55	-5
MIN	73	89	0	.451	19	38	43	666	678	6323	1472	259	47	82	604	684	33	**109**	.267	**.339**	.375	714	99	23	5	103	99	56	64	2
CHI	71	90	0	.441	20.5	38	42	634	731	5955	1423	221	41	106	409	**625**	33	63	.264	.317	.379	696	94	-38	-45	101	83	68	55	-5
OAK	69	93	0	.426	23	38	42	532	690	5914	1304	200	31	100	433	800	25	108	.245	.303	.351	654	87	-121	-94	95	144	117	55	-9
SEA	56	104	0	.350	35	32	49	614	834	6023	1327	229	37	97	522	702	22	68	.248	.314	.359	673	89	-74	-73	100	123	47	**72**	11
TOT	1131					649	482	9509		85857	19952	3325	538	1680	7287	10153	442	1016	.261	.326	.385	711					1471	892	62	11

TEAM	CG	SHO	GR	SV	IP	H	HR	BB	SO	BR/9	ERA	AERA	OAV	OOB	PR	APR	PF	OSB	OCS	FA	E	WPB	DP	FW	PW	BW	BSW	DIF
EAST																												
NY	39	16	188	**36**	1460.2	**1321**	111	478	817	11.3	3.18	115	**.243**	.306	95	78	97	83	61	**.982**	113	54	134	1.5	8.0	2.7	.6	5.6
BOS	57	15	178	26	1472.2	1530	137	464	706	12.4	3.54	**116**	.270	.327	37	**85**	109	114	55	.977	146	24	171	-.3	8.8	2.4	-.3	7.0
MIL	62	**19**	173	24	1436.0	1442	109	398	577	11.8	3.65	104	.262	.313	17	20	94	81	68	**.982**	150	38	144	-.6	2.1	**11.4**	.1	-1.0
BAL	**65**	16	161	33	1429.0	1340	107	509	754	11.7	3.56	99	.251	.316	32	-8	94	81	68	**.982**	110	51	**177**	**1.6**	-.8	6.5	-.6	2.8
DET	60	12	157	21	1455.2	1441	135	503	684	12.2	3.64	107	.263	.325	20	38	103	85	59	.981	118	58	142	1.2	3.9	2.3	.6	-3.0
CLE	36	6	214	28	1407.1	1397	**100**	568	739	12.7	3.97	95	.261	.332	-33	-31	100	129	59	.980	123	71	163	.4	-3.2	-1.5	-.9	-5.6
TOR	35	5	213	23	1429.1	1529	149	614	758	13.6	4.54	87	.279	.351	-123	-90	105	101	66	.979	131	63	163	.4	-9.3	-11.1	-1.3	-.2
WEST																												
KC	53	14	208	33	1439.0	1350	108	478	657	11.6	3.44	111	.251	.313	52	59	101	90	52	.976	150	48	153	-.6	6.1	1.6	**1.8**	2.1
TEX	54	12	170	25	1456.1	1431	108	421	776	11.6	3.36	111	.259	.312	66	62	99	84	75	.976	153	47	140	-.8	6.4	.8	1.0	-1.5
CAL	44	13	193	33	1455.2	1382	125	599	**892**	12.4	3.65	99	.253	.327	19	-5	96	154	**80**	.977	136	41	136	.2	-.5	.9	-.6	6.0
MIN	48	9	176	26	1459.2	1468	102	520	703	12.5	3.69	104	.266	.330	11	21	102	91	76	.977	146	58	130	-.4	2.2	.5	.1	-10.4
CHI	38	9	200	33	1409.1	1380	128	586	710	12.8	4.21	90	.259	.334	-71	-66	97	110	**80**	.971	179	47	145	-2.3	.4	-9.7	-1.0	.6
OAK	26	11	**271**	26	1433.1	1401	106	582	750	12.6	3.62	101	.259	.330	22	4	97	110	**80**	.971	141	37	174	-.2	-13.4	-7.5	1.0	-3.9
SEA	28	4	249	20	1419.1	1540	155	567	630	13.6	4.67	82	.280	.348	-144	-130	102	140	55	.978								
TOT	645	161	2751	390	20163.1					12.4	3.76		.261	.326						.978	1935	688	2146					

Batter-Fielder Wins
Smalley-Min 5.1 · DeCinces-Bal 4.2 · Rice-Bos 4.2 · Yount-Mil 4.0 · Fisk-Bos 3.9

Batting Average
Carew-Min .333 · Oliver-Tex .324 · Rice-Bos .315 · Piniella-NY .314 · Oglivie-Mil .303

On-Base Percentage
Carew-Min .411 · Singleton-Bal .409 · Hargrove-Tex .388 · Randolph-NY .381 · Lynn-Bos .380

Slugging Average
Rice-Bos .600 · Hisle-Mil .533 · DeCinces-Bal .526 · Otis-KC .525 · Thornton-Cle .516

On-Base Plus Slugging
Rice-Bos .970 · Hisle-Mil .906 · Otis-KC .905 · Thornton-Cle .893 · Roberts-Sea .879

Adjusted OPS
Singleton-Bal 154 · Rice-Bos 153 · Hisle-Mil 152 · Thornton-Cle 152 · DeCinces-Bal 151

Adjusted Batter Runs
Rice-Bos 44.5 · Singleton-Bal 41.3 · Thornton-Cle 37.4 · Hisle-Mil 36.5 · Murray-Bal 34.2

Runs
LeFlore-Det 126 · Rice-Bos 121 · Baylor-Cal 103 · Thornton-Cle 97 · Hisle-Mil 96

Hits
Rice-Bos 213 · LeFlore-Det 198 · Carew-Min 188 · Munson-NY 183 · Staub-Det 175

Doubles
Brett-KC 45 · McRae-KC 39 · Fisk-Bos 39 · DeCinces-Bal 37 · Ford-Min 36

Triples
Rice-Bos 15 · Ford-Min 10 · Carew-Min 10 · Yount-Mil 9 · Garr-Chi 9

Home Runs
Rice-Bos 46 · Hisle-Mil 34 · Baylor-Cal 34 · Thornton-Cle 33 · Thomas-Mil 32

Total Bases
Rice-Bos 406 · Murray-Bal 293 · Staub-Det 279 · Baylor-Cal 279 · Thompson-Det 278

Runs Batted In
Rice-Bos 139 · Staub-Det 12_ · Hisle-Mil 115 · Thornton-Cle 105

Stolen Bases
LeFlore-Det 68 · Cruz-Sea 59 · Wills-Tex 52 · Dilone-Oak 50 · Wilson-KC 46

Base Stealing Runs
Cruz-Sea 9.5 · LeFlore-Det 9.4 · Wills-Tex 6.5 · Wilson-KC 5.9 · Randolph-NY 5.5

Fielding Runs-Infield
Belanger-Bal 30.3 · Bell-Cle 26.5 · Wills-Tex 21.7 · Yount-Mil 20.6 · Whitaker-Det 20.0

Fielding Runs-Outfield
Bosetti-Tor 14.4 · Bailor-Tor 9.7 · R.Miller-Cal 8.0 · Wilson-KC 7.1 · Roberts-Sea 6.1

Wins
Guidry-NY 25 · Caldwell-Mil 22 · Palmer-Bal 21 · Leonard-KC 21

Winning Pct.
Guidry-NY .893 · Stanley-Bos .882 · Gura-KC .800 · Eckersley-Bos .714 · Caldwell-Mil .710

Complete Games
Caldwell-Mil 2_ · Leonard-KC 2_ · Palmer-Bal 2_ · Matlack-Tex 1_

Strikeouts
Ryan-Cal 260 · Guidry-NY 248 · Leonard-KC 183 · Flanagan-Bal 167 · Eckersley-Bos 162

Fewest BB/Game
Jenkins-Tex 1.48 · Sorensen-Mil 1.60 · Caldwell-Mil 1.66 · Matlack-Tex 1.70 · Rozema-Det 1.76

Games
Lacey-Oak 74 · Heaverlo-Oak 69 · Sosa-Oak 68 · Gossage-NY 63

Saves
Gossage-NY 27 · LaRoche-Cal 25 · Stanhouse-Bal 24 · Marshall-Min 21 · Hrabosky-KC 20

Base Runners/9
Guidry-NY 8.55 · Hiller-Det 9.65 · Caldwell-Mil 9.79 · Jenkins-Tex 9.83 · Gossage-NY 9.92

Adjusted Relief Runs
Gossage-NY 22.1 · Stanley-Bos 20.5 · Hiller-Det 15.2 · Marshall-Min 14.8 · Sosa-Oak 13.3

Relief Ranking
Gossage-NY 41._ · Marshall-Min 29._ · Stanley-Bos 25._ · Hiller-Det 24._ · Hrabosky-KC 18._

Innings Pitched
Palmer-Bal 296.0 · Leonard-KC 294.2 · Caldwell-Mil 293.1 · Flanagan-Bal 281.1 · Sorensen-Mil 280.2

Opponents' Avg.
Guidry-NY .193 · Ryan-Cal .220 · Palmer-Bal .227 · Gura-KC .229 · Tiant-Bos .234

Opponents' OBP
Guidry-NY .249 · Caldwell-Mil .273 · Jenkins-Tex .278 · Matlack-Tex .283 · Gura-KC .283

Earned Run Average
Guidry-NY 1.74 · Matlack-Tex 2.27 · Caldwell-Mil 2.36 · Palmer-Bal 2.46 · Goltz-Min 2.49

Adjusted ERA
Guidry-NY 210 · Matlack-Tex 165 · Caldwell-Mil 161 · Goltz-Min 154 · Palmer-Bal 143

Adjusted Starter Runs
Guidry-NY 59.6 · Caldwell-Mil 44.7 · Matlack-Tex 38.0 · Palmer-Bal 36.0 · Eckersley-Bos 31.9

Pitcher Wins
Guidry-NY 6._ · Caldwell-Mil 4._ · Gossage-NY 4._ · Palmer-Bal 4._ · Matlack-Tex 4._

The Boston Massacre

Hoping to wipe out the past once and for all, Boston surged to a 14½-game lead by July 19. But when Bob Lemon replaced Billy Martin as New York's manager on July 24, the Yankees began winning. In just 12 days, they cut Boston's lead to 6½, where it remained until early September. With a four-game sweep of the Red Sox at Fenway (dubbed "The Boston Massacre"; no game was close), New York eventually plowed to a 3½-game advantage over the demoralized Sox.

Boston turned it on during the last week, though, winning their final eight to force a tie on the season's last day. In a classic one-game playoff, the Yankees overcame a 2-0 seventh-inning deficit on homers by Bucky Dent and Reggie Jackson to win, 5-4.

Ron Guidry—a remarkable 25-3 with a 1.74 ERA—won the Cy Young for the mostly veteran Yankees. Jim Rice took MVP honors for Boston. Lou Whitaker of Detroit was Rookie of the Year over impressive Milwaukee freshman Paul Molitor. Lost in all the Yankees-Red Sox hysteria was a 93-win season by the Brewers.

The slumping Royals and overachieving Angels were clos[e] heading into September, but Kansas City was great in the las[t] month while California went 7-11 in a critical stretch. The Ang[els] were devastated on September 24 when outfielder Lyma[n] Bostock was murdered near Chicago. California finished tie[d] with Texas for second. Jim Fregosi, the last original activ[e] Angel, retired as a player on June 1 to take California's man[aging] job, and guided the club to a 62-54 mark.

The ALCS was tight; the last two games were one-ru[n] affairs, with the Yankees beating the Royals in four. The secon[d] straight Yankees-Dodgers World Series featured another Ne[w] York comeback. After Los Angeles took the first two at hom[e], New York took the next four. The clincher was a blowout [of] Don Sutton at Dodger Stadium. Dent and fill-in second base[-]man Brian Doyle both batted over .400; Reggie Jackson to[r]mented the Dodgers with 2 more homers and drove in 8 runs[.]

1977 National League

TEAM	W	L	T	PCT	GB	HW	HL	R	OR	PA	H	2B	3B	HR	BB	SO	HB	SH	AVG	OBP	SLG	OPS	AOPS	BR	ABR	PF	SB	CS	BSA	BSR
EAST																														
PHI	101	61	0	.623		60	21	847	668	6290	1548	266	56	186	573	806	38	59	**.279**	.346	.448	794	112	145	102	105	135	68	67	6
PIT	96	66	0	.593	5	58	23	734	665	6262	**1550**	278	57	133	474	878	34	49	.274	.331	.413	744	100	36	11	104	**260**	120	68	15
STL	83	79	0	.512	18	52	31	737	688	6136	1490	252	56	96	489	823	25	66	.270	.330	.388	718	99	-14	-9	99	134	112	54	-10
CHI	81	81	0	.500	20	46	35	692	739	6286	1489	271	37	111	534	**796**	27	69	.266	.330	.387	717	88	-10	-81	111	98	50	64	-2
MON	75	87	0	.463	26	38	43	665	736	6282	1474	**294**	50	138	478	877	21	69	.260	.318	.402	720	100	-20	-6	98	88	50	64	2
NY	64	98	0	.395	37	35	44	587	663	6069	1319	227	30	88	529	887	30	63	.244	.313	.346	659	85	-126	-105	97	98	81	55	-7
WEST																														
LA	98	64	0	.605		51	30	769	**582**	6327	1484	223	28	**191**	588	896	23	83	.266	.336	.418	754	106	58	54	101	114	62	65	3
CIN	88	74	0	.543	10	48	33	802	725	6261	1513	269	42	181	600	911	25	62	.274	.345	.436	781	**112**	118	100	102	170	64	73	15
HOU	81	81	0	.500	17	46	35	680	650	6200	1405	263	**60**	114	515	839	**40**	76	.254	.320	.385	705	102	-42	14	92	187	72	72	**16**
SF	75	87	0	.463	23	35	43	673	711	6215	1392	227	41	134	568	842	21	78	.253	.323	.383	706	94	-37	-38	100	90	59	60	-1
SD	69	93	0	.426	29	35	46	692	834	6353	1397	245	49	120	**602**	1057	19	90	.249	.324	.375	699	103	-49	25	90	133	57	70	9
ATL	61	101	0	.377	37	40	41	678	895	6205	1404	218	20	139	537	876	17	83	.254	.320	.376	696	83	-60	-125	111	82	53	61	-1
TOT	972					547	425	8556		74886	17465	3033	526	1631	6487	10488	330	847	.262	.328	.396	724				1555	843	65	47

TEAM	CG	SHO	GR	SV	IP	H	HR	BB	SO	BR/9	ERA	AERA	OAV	OOB	PR	APR	PF	OSB	OCS	FA	E	WPB	DP	FW	PW	BW	BSW	DIF
EAST																												
PHI	31	7	246	**47**	1455.2	1451	134	482	856	12.1	3.71	108	.263	.323	32	49	103	119	62	.981	120	48	168	1.3	5.0	**10.3**	.2	3.2
PIT	25	**15**	278	39	1481.2	1406	149	485	890	11.6	3.61	111	.252	.311	50	66	103	102	63	.977	145	57	137	-.0	6.7	1.1	1.1	6.2
STL	26	10	305	31	1446.0	1420	139	532	768	12.3	3.81	102	.260	.326	16	14	100	117	62	.978	139	53	174	.3	1.4	-.9	-1.4	2.6
CHI	16	10	319	44	1468.0	1500	128	489	**942**	12.3	4.01	110	.266	.325	-16	57	113	134	63	.977	153	63	147	-.5	5.8	-8.2	-.6	3.5
MON	31	11	307	33	1481.0	1426	135	579	856	12.3	4.01	96	.255	.325	-17	-26	99	135	63	.980	129	62	128	.8	-2.6	-.6	-.2	-3.4
NY	27	12	248	28	1433.2	**1378**	118	490	911	11.9	3.77	100	.254	.317	22	3	97	127	70	.978	134	**36**	132	.5	.3	-10.6	-1.1	-6.1
WEST																												
LA	34	13	238	39	1475.1	1393	119	**438**	930	11.3	3.22	120	.251	.308	113	105	99	108	59	.981	124	48	160	1.1	**10.6**	5.5	-.0	-.0
CIN	33	12	261	32	1437.1	1469	156	544	868	12.8	4.21	93	.267	.334	-49	-45	101	**87**	54	**.984**	**95**	61	154	2.7	-4.6	10.1	1.1	-2.4
HOU	**37**	11	234	28	1465.2	1384	110	545	871	12.8	3.54	102	.251	.319	61	13	92	143	80	.978	142	70	136	.0	1.3	1.4	**1.2**	-4.0
SF	27	10	312	33	1459.0	1501	114	529	854	12.7	3.75	105	.267	.331	26	30	101	158	75	.972	179	43	136	-2.0	3.0	-3.8	-.5	-2.7
SD	6	5	**382**	44	1466.1	1556	160	673	827	13.8	4.43	81	.276	.353	-85	-153	91	120	**87**	.971	189	67	142	-2.5	-15.5	2.5	.5	3.0
ATL	28	5	327	31	1445.1	1581	169	701	915	14.5	4.85	92	.279	.360	-151	-58	114	205	83	.972	175	98	127	-1.7	-5.9	-12.6	-.5	.8
TOT	321	121	3457	429	17515.0					12.5	3.91		.262	.328						.977	1724	706	1741					

Batter-Fielder Wins		Batting Average		On-Base Percentage		Slugging Average		On-Base Plus Slugging		Adjusted OPS		Adjusted Batter Runs	
Schmidt-Phi	6.4	Parker-Pit	338	Smith-LA	427	Foster-Cin	631	Foster-Cin	1013	Smith-LA	167	Foster-Cin	53.7
Foster-Cin	5.8	Templeton-StL	322	Morgan-Cin	417	Luzinski-Phi	594	Smith-LA	1003	Foster-Cin	164	Smith-LA	51.2
Parker-Pit	5.0	Foster-Cin	320	Tenace-SD	415	Smith-LA	576	Luzinski-Phi	988	Luzinski-Phi	154	Luzinski-Phi	43.7
Morgan-Cin	4.6	Griffey-Cin	318	Simmons-StL	408	Schmidt-Phi	574	Schmidt-Phi	967	Schmidt-Phi	149	Schmidt-Phi	40.3
DeJesus-Chi	4.2	Simmons-StL	318	Parker-Pit	397	Bench-Cin	540	Parker-Pit	927	Hendrick-SD	147	Parker-Pit	38.8

Runs		Hits		Doubles		Triples		Home Runs		Total Bases		Runs Batted In	
Foster-Cin	124	Parker-Pit	215	Parker-Pit	44	Templeton-StL	18	Foster-Cin	52	Foster-Cin	388	Foster-Cin	149
Griffey-Cin	117	Rose-Cin	204	Cash-Mon	42	Schmidt-Phi	11	Burroughs-Atl	41	Parker-Pit	338	Luzinski-Phi	130
Schmidt-Phi	114	Templeton-StL	200	Hernandez-StL	41	Richards-SD	11	Luzinski-Phi	39	Luzinski-Phi	329	Garvey-LA	115
Morgan-Cin	113	Foster-Cin	197	Cromartie-Mon	41	Almon-SD	11	Schmidt-Phi	38	Garvey-LA	322	Burroughs-Atl	114
Parker-Pit	107	Garvey-LA	192					Garvey-LA	33	Schmidt-Phi	312		

Stolen Bases		Base Stealing Runs		Fielding Runs-Infield		Fielding Runs-Outfield		Wins		Winning Pct.		Complete Games	
Taveras-Pit	70	Taveras-Pit	9.1	DeJesus-Chi	45.5	Parker-Pit	23.2	Carlton-Phi	23	Candelaria-Pit	800	Niekro-Atl	20
Cedeno-Hou	61	Cedeno-Hou	8.5	Trillo-Chi	30.1	Winfield-SD	11.6	Seaver-NY-Cin	21	Seaver-NY-Cin	778	Seaver-NY-Cin	19
Richards-SD	56	Richards-SD	8.1	Schmidt-Phi	26.6	Foster-Cin	10.9			Christenson-Phi	760	Rogers-Mon	17
Moreno-Pit	53	Morgan-Cin	7.3	Tyson-StL	23.9	Hendrick-SD	7.9			John-LA	741	Carlton-Phi	17
Morgan-Cin	49	Lopes-LA	6.1	Russell-LA	16.7	Geronimo-Cin	6.6			Forsch-StL	741	Richard-Hou	13

Strikeouts		Fewest BB/Game		Games		Saves		Base Runners/9		Adjusted Relief Runs		Relief Ranking	
Niekro-Atl	262	Candelaria-Pit	1.95	Fingers-SD	78	Fingers-SD	35	Sosa-LA	7.77	Gossage-Pit	34.4	Gossage-Pit	60.3
Richard-Hou	214	John-LA	2.04	Tomlin-SD	76	Sutter-Chi	31	Sutter-Chi	7.80	Sutter-Chi	31.3	Sutter-Chi	44.7
Rogers-Mon	206	Rau-LA	2.08	Spillner-SD	76	Gossage-Pit	26	Gossage-Pit	8.73	Lavelle-SF	23.2	Lavelle-SF	32.7
Carlton-Phi	198	Barr-SF	2.15	Metzger-SD-StL	75	Hough-LA	22	Seaver-NY-Cin	9.13	Garber-Phi	18.7	Garber-Phi	29.9
Seaver-NY-Cin	196	Lemongello-Hou	2.18					Garber-Phi	9.32	Reed-Phi	17.7	Reed-Phi	19.7

Innings Pitched		Opponents' Avg.		Opponents' OBP		Earned Run Average		Adjusted ERA		Adjusted Starter Runs		Pitcher Wins	
Niekro-Atl	330.1	Seaver-NY-Cin	209	Seaver-NY-Cin	258	Candelaria-Pit	2.34	Candelaria-Pit	172	Candelaria-Pit	43.3	**Gossage-Pit**	6.4
Rogers-Mon	301.2	Richard-Hou	218	Candelaria-Pit	274	Seaver-NY-Cin	2.58	R.Reuschel-Chi	158	R.Reuschel-Chi	41.9	**Carlton-Phi**	5.5
Carlton-Phi	283.0	Carlton-Phi	223	Hooton-LA	279	Hooton-LA	2.62	Carlton-Phi	153	Seaver-NY-Cin	40.2	**R.Reuschel-Chi**	5.3
Richard-Hou	267.0	Hooton-LA	225	Carlton-Phi	286	Carlton-Phi	2.64	Seaver-NY-Cin	150	Carlton-Phi	39.5	**Candelaria-Pit**	5.0
Seaver-NY-Cin	261.1	Koosman-NY	232	Sutton-LA	289	John-LA	2.78	Hooton-LA	147	Hooton-LA	30.1	**Sutter-Chi**	4.7

Runs, Runs, Runs

Scoring leapt to its highest since 1970, and although the Astros and Cardinals both pushed their outfield fences out, homers rose 27 percent. More homers were hit in every NL park except Wrigley Field. Stolen bases also rose again, reaching their highest per-game total since 1919.

Larry Dierker, Al Downing, Doug Rader, Ray Sadecki, Joe Torre, and Jimmy Wynn hung 'em up. All had been reduced to part-time status. And with great teams came terrible ones: the last-place Mets, managed by Torre, and Braves, managed for one night by maverick owner Ted Turner, both finished 37 games out of first.

The Expos moved from cozy Jarry Park to Olympic Stadium, a smaller field but with far more seats; attendance more than doubled for Montreal, which showed signs of life under Dick Williams. Outfielder Andre Dawson was Rookie of the Year.

Lou Brock shattered Ty Cobb's career steals mark, but the champ speed demons were the second-place Pirates, whose 260 swipes were the highest NL total since 1913. Despite the thievery, the Bucs scored 113 runs fewer than the division champion Phillies, who boasted seven players with double-figure home runs; Mike Schmidt (who became the first $500,000-a-year player) and Greg Luzinski combined for 77. Steve Carlton won his second Cy Young. Chicago led until August, but crumbled when Bruce Sutter went down with a shoulder injury and Philadelphia won 19 of 20.

While MVP George Foster of Cincinnati was spectacular, the Dodgers were better. Under rookie manager Tommy Lasorda, Los Angeles led by 11½ on May 15, and the Reds never got much closer. Steve Garvey, Ron Cey, Reggie Smith, and Dusty Baker each hit 30 homers, and the superb infield of Garvey, Davey Lopes, Bill Russell, and Cey could not be matched.

While the Dodgers convincingly beat the Phillies in a four-game NLCS, the World Series went to the Yankees in six despite Smith's 3 homers. A different Reggie hit 3 homers in Game 6.

1977 American League

TEAM	W	L	T	PCT	GB	HW	HL	R	OR	PA	H	2B	3B	HR	BB	SO	HB	SH	AVG	OBP	SLG	OPS	AOPS	BR	ABR	PF	SB	CS	BSA	BSR
EAST																														
NY	100	62	0	.617		**55**	26	831	**651**	6260	1576	267	47	184	533	681	28	46	.281	.344	.444	788	114	106	**111**	99	93	57	62	1
BAL	97	64	0	.602	2.5	54	27	719	653	6173	1433	231	25	148	560	945	24	48	.261	.329	.393	722	102	-22	20	94	90	51	64	2
BOS	97	64	0	.602	2.5	51	29	859	712	6184	1551	258	56	**213**	528	905	42	45	.281	.345	**.465**	810	106	**145**	56	111	66	47	58	-2
DET	74	88	0	.457	26	39	42	714	751	6177	1480	228	45	166	452	764	20	45	.264	.318	.410	728	92	-28	-63	105	60	46	57	-3
CLE	71	90	0	.441	28.5	37	44	676	739	6204	1476	221	46	100	531	688	34	94	.269	.334	.380	714	97	-32	-12	97	87	87	50	-11
MIL	67	95	0	.414	33	37	44	639	765	6087	1425	255	46	125	443	862	22	60	.258	.314	.389	703	90	-74	-75	100	85	67	56	-5
TOR	54	107	0	.335	45.5	25	55	605	822	6055	1367	230	41	100	499	819	23	81	.252	.316	.365	681	84	-107	-115	101	65	55	54	-5
WEST																														
KC	102	60	0	.630		**55**	26	822	**651**	6268	1549	299	**77**	146	522	687	45	49	.277	.340	.436	776	109	84	75	101	170	87	**66**	7
TEX	94	68	0	.580	8	44	37	767	657	6342	1568	267	39	135	**596**	904	39	**116**	.278	.344	.405	747	102	38	28	101	154	85	64	4
CHI	90	72	0	.556	12	48	33	844	771	6322	1568	254	52	192	559	**666**	34	33	.278	.344	.444	788	113	108	108	100	42	65	62	0
MIN	84	77	0	.522	17.5	48	32	**867**	776	6382	**1588**	273	60	123	563	754	43	81	**.282**	**.348**	.417	765	108	73	82	99	105	65	62	0
CAL	74	88	0	.457	28	39	42	675	695	6113	1380	233	40	131	542	880	36	74	.255	.324	.386	710	96	-47	-22	97	159	89	64	4
SEA	64	98	0	.395	38	29	52	624	855	6044	1398	218	33	133	426	769	35	81	.256	.312	.381	693	88	-94	-91	100	110	67	62	5
OAK	63	98	0	.391	38.5	35	46	605	749	6020	1284	176	37	117	516	910	36	64	.240	.308	.352	660	80	-149	-142	99	**176**	89	**66**	**8**
TOT	1131					596	535	10247		86631	20572	3408	644	2013	7270	11234	461	917	.266	.330	.405	735					1462	936	61	1

TEAM	CG	SHO	GR	SV	IP	H	HR	BB	SO	BR/9	ERA	AERA	OAV	OOB	PR	APR	PF	OSB	OCS	FA	E	WPB	DP	FW	PW	BW	BSW	DIF
EAST																												
NY	52	16	154	34	1449.1	1395	139	486	758	11.8	3.61	110	.254	**.315**	73	57	97	89	60	.979	132	52	151	.6	5.7	**11.0**	.1	1.6
BAL	**65**	11	169	23	1451.0	1414	124	494	737	12.0	3.74	102	.260	.322	51	14	94	77	72	**.983**	**106**	37	**189**	2.0	1.4	2.0	.2	10.9
BOS	40	13	209	40	1428.0	1555	158	378	758	12.3	4.11	109	.278	.325	-8	52	110	**69**	54	.978	133	**19**	162	.5	5.2	5.6	-.2	5.4
DET	44	3	198	-23	1457.0	1526	162	470	784	12.5	4.13	104	.271	.327	-11	26	106	90	69	.978	142	43	153	.0	2.6	-6.3	-.3	-6.0
CLE	45	8	230	30	1452.1	1441	136	550	876	12.5	4.10	97	.261	.329	-6	-19	98	158	64	.978	139	61	165	-.2	-3.6	-7.5	-.5	-2.7
MIL	38	6	215	25	1431.0	1461	136	566	719	13.0	4.32	95	.268	.337	-42	-36	101	105	75	.978	154	69	133	-1.2	-5.1	-11.4	-.5	-8.3
TOR	40	3	187	20	1428.1	1538	152	623	771	13.7	4.57	93	.278	.350	-81	-51	104	85	75	.974	164	69	133	-1.2	-5.1	-11.4	-.5	-8.3
WEST																												
KC	41	15	219	**42**	1460.2	**1377**	110	499	850	11.8	**3.52**	114	**.251**	.315	88	82	99	84	51	.978	137	69	145	.3	**8.1**	7.5	.7	4.3
TEX	49	**17**	200	31	1472.1	1412	134	471	864	**11.7**	3.56	114	.255	.315	81	81	100	**69**	60	.982	117	49	156	1.5	8.0	2.8	.4	3.3
CHI	34	3	221	40	1444.2	1557	136	516	842	13.2	4.25	96	.277	.339	-31	-29	100	130	77	.978	159	50	125	-.9	-2.9	10.7	-.6	2.6
MIN	35	4	242	25	1442.0	1546	151	507	737	13.0	4.36	91	.278	.340	-48	-63	98	107	67	.978	143	58	184	-.0	-6.3	8.1	.0	-8.3
CAL	53	13	185	26	1437.2	1383	136	572	**965**	12.5	3.72	105	.256	.330	54	33	97	129	78	.976	147	64	162	-.2	-10.8	-9.0	.1	-8.3
SEA	18	5	**280**	14	1433.0	1508	194	578	785	13.5	4.83	86	.272	.344	-123	-109	102	146	60	.976	147	64	162	-.2	-.3	-14.1	.8	-1.2
OAK	32	4	249	26	1436.4	1459	145	560	788	12.8	4.04	100	.265	.333	3	-3	99	123	**91**	.970	190	67	136	-2.7	-.3	-14.1	.8	-1.2
TOT	586	117	2958	416	20224.0					12.6	4.06		.266	.330						.977	1986	754	2143					

Batter-Fielder Wins		Batting Average		On-Base Percentage		Slugging Average		On-Base Plus Slugging		Adjusted OPS		Adjusted Batter Runs	
Carew-Min	6.5	Carew-Min	388	Carew-Min	449	Rice-Bos	593	Carew-Min	1019	Carew-Min	178	Carew-Min	69.
Fisk-Bos	4.6	Bostock-Min	336	Singleton-Bal	438	Carew-Min	570	Rice-Bos	969	Singleton-Bal	167	Singleton-Bal	57.
Brett-KC	4.6	Singleton-Bal	328	Hargrove-Tex	420	Jackson-NY	550	Singleton-Bal	945	Page-Oak	153	Page-Oak	39.8
Singleton-Bal	4.6	Rivers-NY	326	Page-Oak	405	Hisle-Min	533	Page-Oak	926	Jackson-NY	150	Jackson-NY	38.
Page-Oak	4.5	LeFlore-Det	325	Fisk-Bos	402	Brett-KC	532	Jackson-NY	925	Thornton-Cle	148	Hargrove-Tex	37.

Runs		Hits		Doubles		Triples		Home Runs		Total Bases		Runs Batted In	
Carew-Min	128	Carew-Min	239	McRae-KC	54	Carew-Min	16	Rice-Bos	39	Rice-Bos	382	Hisle-Min	119
Fisk-Bos	106	LeFlore-Det	212	Jackson-NY	39	Rice-Bos	15	Nettles-NY	37	Carew-Min	351	Bonds-Cal	115
Brett-KC	105	Rice-Bos	206	Lemon-Chi	38	Cowens-KC	14	Bonds-Cal	37	McRae-KC	330	Rice-Bos	11
		Bostock-Min	199	Carew-Min	38	Brett-KC	13	Scott-Bos	33	Cowens-KC	318	Hobson-Bos	11
		Burleson-Bos	194			Bostock-Min	12	Jackson-NY	32	LeFlore-Det	310	Cowens-KC	11

Stolen Bases		Base Stealing Runs		Fielding Runs-Infield		Fielding Runs-Outfield		Wins		Winning Pct.		Complete Games	
Patek-KC	53	Page-Oak	7.5	Campaneris-Tex	26.1	Lemon-Chi	23.1	Palmer-Bal	20	Splittorff-KC	727	Ryan-Cal	2.
Page-Oak	42	Patek-KC	7.1	Burleson-Bos	20.1	Yastrzemski-Bos	9.7	Leonard-KC	20	T.Johnson-Min	696	Palmer-Bal	2
Remy-Cal	41	Harrah-Tex	4.2	Smalley-Min	19.7	R.Jones-Sea	9.4	Goltz-Min	20	Guidry-NY	696	Leonard-KC	2
Bonds-Cal	41	White-KC	3.3	Belanger-Bal	18.9	Armas-Oak	8.8	Ryan-Cal	19	Rozema-Det	682	Garland-Cle	2
LeFlore-Det	39	Remy-Cal	3.1	Brett-KC	18.0	Lezcano-Mil	8.6					Tanana-Cal	2

Strikeouts		Fewest BB/Game		Games		Saves		Base Runners/9		Adjusted Relief Runs		Relief Ranking	
Ryan-Cal	341	Rozema-Det	1.40	Lyle-NY	72	Campbell-Bos	31	Foucault-Det	9.81	Lyle-NY	26.2	Campbell-Bos	42.
Leonard-KC	244	Jenkins-Bos	1.68	T.Johnson-Min	71	Lyle-NY	26	Blyleven-Tex	9.86	Campbell-Bos	22.3	Lyle-NY	28.
Tanana-Cal	205	Hartzell-Cal	1.81	Campbell-Bos	69	LaGrow-Chi	25	Eckersley-Cle	10.01	LaGrow-Chi	17.1	Romo-Sea	28.
Palmer-Bal	193	Eckersley-Cle	1.96	McClure-Mil	68	Kern-Cle	17	Guidry-NY	10.21	Romo-Sea	16.3	LaGrow-Chi	25.
Eckersley-Cle	191	Cleveland-Bos	2.03	LaGrow-Chi	66	LaRoche-Cle-Cal	17	Tanana-Cal	10.22	Torrealba-Oak	16.0	T.Johnson-Min	24.

Innings Pitched		Opponents' Avg.		Opponents' OBP		Earned Run Average		Adjusted ERA		Adjusted Starter Runs		Pitcher Wins	
Palmer-Bal	319.0	Ryan-Cal	193	Eckersley-Cle	276	Tanana-Cal	2.54	Tanana-Cal	155	Tanana-Cal	41.8	Campbell-Bos	4.
Goltz-Min	303.0	Blyleven-Tex	214	Blyleven-Tex	278	Blyleven-Tex	2.72	Blyleven-Tex	150	Ryan-Cal	38.4	**Lyle-NY**	4.
Ryan-Cal	299.0	Guidry-NY	224	Leonard-KC	283	Ryan-Cal	2.77	Ryan-Cal	142	Palmer-Bal	37.7	**Ryan-Cal**	4.
Leonard-KC	292.2	Tanana-Cal	227	Guidry-NY	283	Guidry-NY	2.82	Guidry-NY	141	Blyleven-Tex	34.8	**Tanana-Cal**	4.
Garland-Cle	282.2	Leonard-KC	227	Tanana-Cal	284	Palmer-Bal	2.91	Rozema-Det	140	Leonard-KC	30.3	**Blyleven-Tex**	4.

Room for Two More

The AL expanded to 14 teams, adding Seattle and Toronto. Runs per team per game rose 13 percent to its highest rate since 1961—not so coincidentally, another expansion year. League attendance was up five million, and two AL teams—the Yankees and Red Sox—drew two million fans in the same year for the first time since 1949.

With free agents Reggie Jackson and Don Gullett, plus holdovers Graig Nettles, Thurman Munson, and Sparky Lyle (the first AL reliever to win a Cy Young), the Yankees leapt from third place in August to win the division. As Boog Powell and Brooks Robinson retired, Baltimore finished second. First baseman Eddie Murray was the league's top rookie, but the Birds' lineup was mediocre. Third-place Boston had an ordinary offense away from Fenway Park. Meanwhile, the awful Tigers debuted Alan Trammell, Lou Whitaker, Lance Parrish, and Jack Morris.

Bill Veeck's ramshackle White Sox led the West for much of the year, but slumped just as the other contenders turned hot. Texas won 14 straight, but Kansas City captured 17 in a row to take the division. The Royals had six players with double-digit homers, excellent defense, and a very deep bullpen. Rod Carew's .388 was the highest batting average since 1941. Nolan Ryan fanned 341 but walked 204, the most since Bob Feller in 1938. With their key players gone, Oakland finished last below the expansion Mariners, and their attendance was the league's lowest since 1970.

The Yanks and Royals traded booming hits, and wins, in the first four ALCS games. The Royals led the decisive fifth contest at Kansas City, 3-1, after seven. A Yankees run in the eighth tightened the game, and in the ninth, New York scored three times off three pitchers (handing Sparky Lyle his second victory) to move to the World Series.

New York then took it to the Dodgers, winning in six games. Jackson hit 3 home runs in the deciding game, but just as important to the Yankees were pitchers Lyle, Mike Torrez, and Ron Guidry.

1976 National League

TEAM	W	L	T	PCT	GB	HW	HL	R	OR	PA	H	2B	3B	HR	BB	SO	HB	SH	AVG	OBP	SLG	OPS	AOPS	BR	ABR	PF	SB	CS	BSA	BSR
EAST																														
PHI	101	61	0	.623		53	28	770	557	6236	1505	259	45	110	542	793	40	59	.272	.338	.395	733	110	110	81	104	127	70	64	3
PIT	92	70	0	.568	9	47	34	708	630	6177	1499	249	56	110	433	807	29	61	.267	.321	.391	712	106	49	37	102	130	45	74	13
NY	86	76	0	.531	15	45	37	615	538	6129	1334	198	34	102	561	797	28	92	.246	.319	.352	671	101	-20	9	96	66	58	53	-6
CHI	75	87	0	.463	26	42	39	611	728	6155	1386	216	24	105	490	834	30	75	.251	.313	.356	669	88	-27	-78	109	74	74	50	-10
STL	72	90	0	.444	29	37	44	629	671	6181	1432	224	57	63	512	860	22	86	.260	.323	.359	682	98	1	-11	102	123	55	69	8
MON	55	107	0	.340	46	27	53	531	734	5992	1275	224	32	94	433	841	16	75	.235	.291	.340	631	80	-110	-134	105	86	44	66	4
WEST																														
CIN	102	60	0	.630		49	32	857	633	6538	1599	271	63	141	681	902	28	67	.280	.357	.424	781	125	219	195	103	210	57	79	26
LA	92	70	0	.568	10	49	32	608	543	6125	1371	200	34	91	486	744	29	91	.251	.313	.349	662	95	-41	-35	99	144	55	72	12
HOU	80	82	0	.494	22	46	36	625	657	6111	1401	195	50	66	530	719	21	57	.256	.322	.347	669	104	-22	32	92	150	57	72	13
SF	74	88	0	.457	28	40	41	595	686	6123	1340	211	35	87	518	778	25	80	.246	.312	.345	657	89	-49	-67	103	88	55	62	0
SD	73	89	0	.451	29	42	38	570	662	6047	1327	216	37	64	488	716	23	125	.247	.310	.337	647	97	-66	-18	92	92	46	67	4
ATL	70	92	0	.432	32	34	47	620	700	6107	1309	170	30	82	589	811	19	107	.245	.320	.334	654	87	-45	-78	106	74	61	55	-5
TOT	972					511	461	7739		73921	16778	2652	499	1113	6263	9602	310	975	.255	.320	.361	681					1364	677	67	63

TEAM	CG	SHO	GR	SV	IP	H	HR	BB	SO	BR/9	ERA	AERA	OAV	OOB	PR	APR	PF	OSB	OCS	FA	E	WPB	DP	FW	PW	BW	BSW	DIF
EAST																												
PHI	34	9	247	44	1459.0	1377	98	397	918	11.1	3.08	116	.250	.301	69	78	102	103	38	.981	115	44	148	1.7	8.3	8.6	-.2	1.6
PIT	45	12	237	35	1466.1	1402	95	460	762	11.5	3.36	105	.253	.310	22	25	101	94	66	.975	163	39	142	-1.0	2.7	3.9	.8	4.6
NY	53	18	183	25	1449.0	1248	97	419	1025	10.5	2.94	114	.233	.290	91	68	96	103	66	.975	131	51	116	.8	7.2	1.0	-1.2	-2.8
CHI	27	12	329	33	1471.1	1511	123	490	850	12.4	3.93	99	.268	.327	-71	-8	111	112	59	.978	140	49	145	.3	-.8	-8.3	-1.6	4.5
STL	35	15	298	26	1453.2	1416	91	581	731	12.5	3.60	99	.258	.329	-16	-4	102	87	72	.973	174	77	163	-1.7	-.4	-1.2	.3	-6.0
MON	26	10	309	21	1440.0	1442	89	659	783	13.4	3.99	94	.260	.347	-79	-36	107	113	69	.976	155	74	179	-.6	-3.8	-14.2	-.1	-7.2
WEST																												
CIN	33	12	274	45	1471.0	1436	100	491	790	11.9	3.51	100	.258	.318	-1	-2	100	94	51	.984	102	49	157	2.5	-.2	20.7	2.2	-4.2
LA	47	17	182	28	1470.2	1330	97	479	747	11.2	3.02	113	.243	.305	79	64	97	114	55	.980	128	46	154	1.0	6.8	-3.7	.7	6.2
HOU	42	17	235	29	1444.1	1349	82	662	780	12.7	3.56	91	.250	.332	-9	-59	92	166	59	.978	140	89	155	.3	-6.3	3.4	.8	.7
SF	27	18	304	31	1461.2	1464	68	746	746	12.3	3.53	103	.263	.325	-4	17	104	136	46	.971	186	62	153	-2.4	1.8	-7.1	-.6	1.2
SD	47	11	258	18	1432.1	1368	87	543	652	12.1	3.65	90	.253	.321	-24	-61	94	104	53	.978	141	57	148	.2	-6.5	-1.9	-.1	.3
ATL	33	13	264	27	1438.0	1435	86	564	818	12.8	3.86	98	.261	.332	-58	-11	108	138	51	.973	167	98	151	-1.3	-1.2	-8.3	-1.1	.8
TOT	449	164	3120	362	17457.1					12.0	3.50		.255	.320						.977	1742	735	1811					

Batter-Fielder Wins		Batting Average		On-Base Percentage		Slugging Average		On-Base Plus Slugging		Adjusted OPS		Adjusted Batter Runs	
Morgan-Cin	6.7	Madlock-Chi	339	Morgan-Cin	444	Morgan-Cin	576	Morgan-Cin	1020	Morgan-Cin	186	Morgan-Cin	60.2
Schmidt-Phi	5.9	Griffey-Cin	336	Madlock-Chi	412	Foster-Cin	530	Madlock-Chi	912	Watson-Hou	150	Schmidt-Phi	39.7
Concepcion-Cin	4.2	Maddox-Phi	330	Rose-Cin	404	Schmidt-Phi	524	Schmidt-Phi	900	Foster-Cin	149	Watson-Hou	38.8
Cey-LA	3.9	Rose-Cin	323	Griffey-Cin	401	Monday-Chi	507	Foster-Cin	894	Schmidt-Phi	149	Rose-Cin	38.1
Maddox-Phi	3.7	Morgan-Cin	320	Cey-LA	386	Kingman-NY	506	Rose-Cin	854	Madlock-Chi	146	Madlock-Chi	33.8

Runs		Hits		Doubles		Triples		Home Runs		Total Bases		Runs Batted In	
Rose-Cin	130	Rose-Cin	215	Rose-Cin	42	Cash-Phi	12	Schmidt-Phi	38	Schmidt-Phi	306	Foster-Cin	121
Morgan-Cin	113	Montanez-SF-Atl	206	Johnstone-Phi	38	Geronimo-Cin	11	Kingman-NY	37	Rose-Cin	299	Morgan-Cin	111
Schmidt-Phi	112	Garvey-LA	200	Maddox-Phi	37	Parker-Pit	10	Monday-Chi	32	Foster-Cin	298	Schmidt-Phi	107
Griffey-Cin	111	Buckner-LA	193	Garvey-LA	37	W.Davis-SD	10	Foster-Cin	29	Garvey-LA	284	Watson-Hou	102
Monday-Chi	107							Morgan-Cin	27			Luzinski-Phi	95

Stolen Bases		Base Stealing Runs		Fielding Runs-Infield		Fielding Runs-Outfield		Wins		Winning Pct.		Complete Games	
Lopes-LA	63	Lopes-LA	10.4	Royster-Atl	25.0	Maddox-Phi	14.1	Jones-SD	22	Carlton-Phi	741	Jones-SD	25
Morgan-Cin	60	Morgan-Cin	10.1	Stennett-Pit	23.8	Johnstone-Phi	8.9	Sutton-LA	21	Candelaria-Pit	696	Koosman-NY	17
Taveras-Pit	58	Taveras-Pit	8.9	Schmidt-Phi	18.1	Winfield-SD	7.6	Koosman-NY	21	Sutton-LA	677	Matlack-NY	16
Cedeno-Hou	58	Cedeno-Hou	7.5	Foli-Mon	16.9	Cruz-Hou	7.1	Richard-Hou	20	Koosman-NY	677	Sutton-LA	15
Brock-StL	56	Brock-StL	5.7	Concepcion-Cin	16.8	Wynn-Atl	7.1	Carlton-Phi	20	Rooker-Pit	652	Richard-Hou	14

Strikeouts		Fewest BB/Game		Games		Saves		Base Runners/9		Adjusted Relief Runs		Relief Ranking	
Seaver-NY	235	Nolan-Cin	1.02	Murray-Mon	81	Eastwick-Cin	26	Reed-Phi	8.58	Hough-LA	17.4	Eastwick-Cin	29.7
Richard-Hou	214	Kaat-Phi	1.27	Metzger-SD	77	Lockwood-NY	19	Lockwood-NY	9.35	Eastwick-Cin	15.8	Hough-LA	27.0
Koosman-NY	200	Jones-SD	1.43	Hough-LA	77	Forsch-Hou	19	Jones-SD	9.36	Reed-Phi	15.4	Reed-Phi	20.1
Carlton-Phi	195	Matlack-NY	1.96	Eastwick-Cin	71	Hough-LA	18	Sutter-Chi	9.61	Moffitt-SF	13.1	Lavelle-SF	18.9
Niekro-Atl	173	Lonborg-Phi	2.03	Borbon-Cin	69	Metzger-SD	16	Candelaria-Pit	9.61	Tekulve-Pit	13.1	Moffitt-SF	17.8

Innings Pitched		Opponents' Avg.		Opponents' OBP		Earned Run Average		Adjusted ERA		Adjusted Starter Runs		Pitcher Wins	
Jones-SD	315.1	Richard-Hou	212	Jones-SD	265	Denny-StL	2.52	Denny-StL	142	Seaver-NY	26.4	Hough-LA	3.1
Richard-Hou	291.0	Seaver-NY	213	Candelaria-Pit	271	Rau-LA	2.57	Rau-LA	132	Montefusco-SF	24.0	Eastwick-Cin	2.9
Seaver-NY	271.0	Candelaria-Pit	216	Seaver-NY	272	Seaver-NY	2.59	Seaver-NY	129	Rau-LA	22.8	Koosman-NY	2.9
Niekro-Atl	270.2	Messersmith-Atl	219	Nolan-Cin	275	Koosman-NY	2.69	Montefusco-SF	128	Denny-StL	22.1	Rau-LA	2.9
Sutton-LA	267.2	Falcone-StL	222	Koosman-NY	278	Zachry-Cin	2.74	Zachry-Cin	128	Jones-SD	20.9	Denny-StL	2.4

Red Moon Rising

There were no pennant races in the NL's centennial season; the Phillies and Reds ran away with their respective divisions. This was the Phillies' first title of any kind in more than a quarter-century, and they did it convincingly. An extraordinary bullpen supported a lefty-loaded rotation, while Mike Schmidt won his third straight homer crown and a .300-hitting outfield Jay Johnstone, Garry Maddox, and Greg Luzinski chipped in. Philadelphia was also defensively strong where it counted.

Cincinnati easily outclassed the Dodgers again in the West as Joe Morgan was a repeat MVP. Pete Rose enjoyed another terrific season, and George Foster began to blossom into a fine power hitter. Walter Alston retired from second-place Los Angeles in September following twenty-three seasons as the franchise's manager.

At midseason of otherwise bad campaigns, the Cubs and Cardinals brought up rookies Bruce Sutter and Garry Templeton. Stolen bases continue to rise as homers fell to their lowest level since 1968. The Cardinals hit just 63 homers, fewest for an NL club since 1963. It was especially tough to homer in Busch Stadium, the Astrodome, or San Diego Stadium.

San Diego's finesse lefty Randy Jones won Cy Young honors, and Houston's hard-throwing starter J.R. Richard blossomed at age 26. Former Cub Billy Williams ended his career in Oakland as the A's dynasty ground to a halt.

The postseason was all Reds. Cincy swept the NLCS in three, and then blew out the Yankees in four to win back-to-back World Series crowns. Foster hit 2 homers in the NLCS, while Johnny Bench homered twice in Game 4 to clinch the World Series sweep.

The Pirates were hit hard after the season. Hurler Bob Moose was killed in an auto crash on October 9, while manager Danny Murtaugh, who had just retired after fifteen seasons, died less than two months later.

1976 American League

TEAM	W	L	T	PCT	GB	HW	HL	R	OR	PA	H	2B	3B	HR	BB	SO	HB	SH	AVG	OBP	SLG	OPS	AOPS	BR	ABR	PF	SB	CS	BSA	BSR
EAST																														
NY	97	62	0	.610		45	35	730	575	6156	1496	231	36	120	470	**616**	35	50	.269	.328	.389	717	**110**	65	**69**	100	163	65	71	13
BAL	88	74	0	.543	10.5	42	39	619	598	6091	1326	213	28	119	519	883	23	57	.243	.310	.358	668	101	-33	2	95	150	61	71	12
BOS	83	79	0	.512	15.5	46	35	716	660	6154	1448	257	53	**134**	500	832	29	65	.263	.324	**.402**	**726**	100	**81**	5	112	95	70	58	-4
CLE	81	78	0	.509	16	44	35	615	615	6029	1423	189	38	85	479	631	11	46	.257	.321	.359	680	100	-4	0	99	75	69	52	3
DET	74	87	0	.460	24	36	44	609	709	6018	1401	207	38	101	450	730	31	46	.257	.315	.365	680	95	-9	-34	104	107	59	64	3
MIL	66	95	0	.410	32	36	45	570	655	6056	1326	170	38	88	511	909	23	78	.246	.311	.340	651	93	-60	-49	98	62	61	50	-8
WEST																														
KC	90	72	0	.556		49	32	713	611	6197	1490	**259**	**57**	65	484	650	31	71	.269	.327	.371	698	103	39	34	101	218	106	67	11
OAK	87	74	0	.540	2.5	**51**	30	686	598	6106	1319	208	33	113	**592**	818	**45**	58	.246	.323	.361	684	104	15	42	96	**341**	123	**73**	**32**
MIN	85	77	0	.525	5	44	37	**743**	704	6307	**1526**	222	51	81	550	714	41	72	.250	.321	.341	662	92	-31	-43	102	87	45	66	6
TEX	76	86	0	.469	14	39	42	616	652	6269	1390	213	26	80	568	809	29	72	.250	.306	.318	624	88	-104	-69	94	126	80	61	7
CAL	76	86	0	.469	14	38	43	550	631	6101	1265	210	23	63	534	812	42	92	.235	.306	.318	624	88	-104	-69	94	126	80	61	8
CHI	64	97	0	.398	25.5	35	45	586	745	6171	1410	209	46	73	471	739	34	79	.255	.314	.349	663	93	-38	-42	101	120	53	69	8
TOT	967					505	462	7753		73655	16820	2588	467	1122	6128	9143	374	818	.256	.320	.361	681					1690	867	66	68

TEAM	CG	SHO	GR	SV	IP	H	HR	BB	SO	BR/9	ERA	AERA	OAV	OOB	PR	APR	PF	OSB	OCS	FA	E	WPB	DP	FW	PW	BW	BSW	DIF
EAST																												
NY	62	15	156	37	1455.0	**1300**	97	448	674	**10.9**	**3.19**	107	**.241**	**.298**	53	37	97	110	67	.980	126	55	141	.9	3.9	**7.3**	.8	4.6
BAL	59	16	171	23	1468.2	1396	**80**	489	678	11.7	3.32	99	.255	.315	33	-4	94	127	65	**.982**	**118**	44	157	**1.5**	-.4	.2	.7	5.1
BOS	49	13	195	27	1458.0	1495	109	**409**	673	12.0	3.52	110	.267	.318	-1	**52**	110	115	60	.978	141	41	148	.2	**5.5**	.5	-1.0	-3.2
CLE	30	**17**	237	**46**	1432.0	1361	80	533	928	12.1	3.47	101	.255	.324	8	7	100	163	72	.980	121	51	159	1.2	.7	.0	-1.5	1.2
DET	55	12	164	20	1431.1	1426	101	550	738	12.6	3.87	96	.263	.331	-56	-22	106	140	71	.974	168	52	161	-1.4	-2.3	-3.6	-.3	1.2
MIL	45	10	202	27	1435.1	1406	99	567	677	12.6	3.64	96	.260	.331	-20	-21	100	144	69	.975	152	70	160	-.5	-2.2	-5.2	-1.5	-5.1
WEST																												
KC	41	12	**248**	35	1472.1	1356	83	493	735	11.5	3.21	109	.247	.309	51	48	100	146	66	.978	139	**38**	147	.3	5.1	3.6	.6	-.6
OAK	39	15	233	29	1459.1	1412	96	475	711	11.5	3.26	103	.255	.308	42	18	96	126	63	.977	144	51	130	-.0	1.9	4.5	**2.8**	-2.6
MIN	29	11	221	23	1459.0	1421	89	610	762	12.8	3.69	97	.259	.335	-29	-20	101	157	81	.973	172	72	**182**	-1.6	-2.1	7.0	.0	.7
TEX	63	15	196	15	1472.0	1464	106	461	773	12.0	3.45	104	.262	.320	10	21	102	120	82	.976	156	57	142	-.7	2.2	-4.6	-.3	-1.7
CAL	**64**	15	177	17	1477.1	1323	95	553	**992**	11.7	3.36	100	**.241**	.313	26	-2	95	191	**88**	.977	150	42	139	-.3	-.2	-7.3	-.6	3.5
CHI	54	10	166	22	1448.0	1460	87	600	802	13.0	4.25	84	.266	.338	-118	-109	101	151	82	.979	130	45	155	.7	-11.6	-4.5	.2	-1.5
TOT	590	161	2366	321	17468.1					12.0	3.52		.256	.320						.977	1717	618	1821					

Batter-Fielder Wins		Batting Average		On-Base Percentage		Slugging Average		On-Base Plus Slugging		Adjusted OPS		Adjusted Batter Runs	
Grich-Bal	4.8	Brett-KC	.333	McRae-KC	.407	R.Jackson-Bal	.502	McRae-KC	.868	R.Jackson-Bal	157	McRae-KC	39.5
Nettles-NY	4.2	McRae-KC	.332	Hargrove-Tex	.397	Rice-Bos	.482	Carew-Min	.858	McRae-KC	154	Carew-Min	38.2
Brett-KC	4.1	Carew-Min	.331	Carew-Min	.395	Nettles-NY	.475	R.Jackson-Bal	.853	Tenace-Oak	149	Brett-KC	35.3
Belanger-Bal	3.7	Bostock-Min	.323	Staub-Det	.386	Lynn-Bos	.467	Brett-KC	.839	Carew-Min	149	R.Jackson-Bal	34.8
McRae-KC	3.7	LeFlore-Det	.316	Carty-Cle	.379	Carew-Min	.463	Lynn-Bos	.835	Nettles-NY	145	Carty-Cle	31.9

Runs		Hits		Doubles		Triples		Home Runs		Total Bases		Runs Batted In	
White-NY	104	Brett-KC	215	Otis-KC	40	Brett-KC	14	Nettles-NY	32	Brett-KC	298	L.May-Bal	109
Carew-Min	97	Carew-Min	200	McRae-KC	34	Garner-Oak	12	R.Jackson-Bal	27	Chambliss-NY	283	Munson-NY	105
Rivers-NY	95	Chambliss-NY	188	Evans-Bos	34	Carew-Min	12	Bando-Oak	27	Rice-Bos	280	Yastrzemski-Bos	102
Brett-KC	94	Munson-NY	186	Carty-Cle	34	Poquette-KC	10			Carew-Min	280		
		Rivers-NY	184	Brett-KC	34	Bostock-Min	9			Nettles-NY	277		

Stolen Bases		Base Stealing Runs		Fielding Runs-Infield		Fielding Runs-Outfield		Wins		Winning Pct.		Complete Games	
North-Oak	75	Campaneris-Oak	7.7	Remy-Cal	19.2	Beniquez-Tex	12.9	Palmer-Bal	22	Campbell-Min	.773	Fidrych-Det	24
LeFlore-Det	58	Baylor-Oak	7.2	White-NY	18.2	Hisle-Min	10.9	Tiant-Bos	21	Garland-Bal	.741	Tanana-Cal	23
Campaneris-Oak	54	Rivers-NY	7.0	Nettles-NY	16.9	Lemon-Chi	7.5	Garland-Bal	20	Ellis-NY	.680	Palmer-Bal	23
Baylor-Oak	52	North-Oak	6.3	Kuiper-Cle	16.8	Evans-Bos	7.2			Fidrych-Det	.679		
Patek-KC	51	Patek-KC	6.0	Belanger-Bal	16.3	Lezcano-Mil	5.8						

Strikeouts		Fewest BB/Game		Games		Saves		Base Runners/9		Adjusted Relief Runs		Relief Ranking	
Ryan-Cal	327	Bird-KC	1.41	Campbell-Min	78	Lyle-NY	23	Tanana-Cal	9.18	Littell-KC	17.4	Hiller-Det	29.5
Tanana-Cal	261	Jenkins-Bos	1.85	Fingers-Oak	70	LaRoche-Cle	21	Gura-KC	9.77	Hiller-Det	17.0	Fingers-Oak	28.8
Blyleven-Min-Tex	219	Perry-Tex	1.87	Lindblad-Oak	65	Fingers-Oak	20	G.Jackson-Bal-NY	9.81	Fingers-Oak	14.9	Littell-KC	24.1
Eckersley-Cle	200	Blue-Oak	1.90	Lyle-NY	64	Campbell-Min	20	Fidrych-Det	9.81	LaRoche-Cle	14.4	Lyle-NY	21.5
Hunter-NY	173	Fidrych-Det	1.91	LaRoche-Cle	61	Littell-KC	16	Burgmeier-Min	9.83	Burgmeier-Min	14.2	Kern-Cal	21.2

Innings Pitched		Opponents' Avg.		Opponents' OBP		Earned Run Average		Adjusted ERA		Adjusted Starter Runs		Pitcher Wins	
Palmer-Bal	315.0	Ryan-Cal	.195	Tanana-Cal	.261	Fidrych-Det	2.34	Fidrych-Det	159	Fidrych-Det	36.1	**Fidrych-Det**	4.5
Hunter-NY	298.2	Tanana-Cal	.203	Fidrych-Det	.277	Blue-Oak	2.35	Blue-Oak	143	Blue-Oak	34.4	**Blue-Oak**	3.5
Blue-Oak	298.1	Eckersley-Cle	.214	Palmer-Bal	.278	Tanana-Cal	2.43	Tanana-Cal	138	Tanana-Cal	31.4	**Tanana-Cal**	3.3
Blyleven-Min-Tex	297.2	Palmer-Bal	.224	Blue-Oak	.279	Torrez-Oak	2.50	Torrez-Oak	135	Palmer-Bal	27.5	**Fingers-Oak**	3.2
Slaton-Mil	292.2	Brett-NY-Chi	.233	Bird-KC	.279	Palmer-Bal	2.51	Palmer-Bal	131	Tiant-Bos	24.2	**Hiller-Det**	3.2

New York State of Mind

Prior to the season, Oakland owner Charlie Finley traded Reggie Jackson and Ken Holtzman to Baltimore. During the year, he tried to sell Vida Blue, Rollie Fingers, and Joe Rudi, but Bowie Kuhn blocked the sales—thus forcing the stubborn Finley, unwilling to pay high salaries, to watch his players test free agency.

Free agency came at a time when the AL set a new attendance record, which invalidated the poormouth cries of many successful owners. Detroit's fortunes were temporarily improved by Mark "The Bird" Fidrych, whose baffling deliveries made him Rookie of the Year and one of the league's best attractions. Tigers attendance increased 38 percent and tickets for his starts were hard to find. But as the economics changed, more stars of the 1960s retired, including Hank Aaron, Bill Freehan, Tony Oliva, and Frank Robinson.

In renovated Yankee Stadium, East champ New York led the league in attendance for the first time since 1964, and did so the remainder of the decade. Thurman Munson was MVP and in-season acquisitions Holtzman, Grant Jackson, and Doyle Alexander bolstered the staff.

The three-time bridesmaid Royals won the West. George Brett won his first batting title, and Whitey Herzog's Royals used a line-drive and speed-based attack. But the real runners were the A's, who swiped an all-time record 341 bases, with eight players in double figures. Bill North, Bert Campaneris, and Don Baylor all topped 50. For all that, the team didn't score much and had just three solid pitchers.

Come-from-behind victories and seesawing leads defined the ALCS. In Game 5 at Yankee Stadium, John Mayberry's two-run homer put Kansas City in front, but New York rallied for a 6-3 lead. Brett's dramatic three-run homer tied the score in the eighth. Yankees first baseman Chris Chambliss ended the series with a homer in the last of the ninth. The momentum didn't carry, as the Yankees lost in four to the overpowering Reds, but the swagger was back.

Texas infielder Danny Thompson died of leukemia after the season.

1975 National League

TEAM	W	L	T	PCT	GB	HW	HL	R	OR	PA	H	2B	3B	HR	BB	SO	HB	SH	AVG	OBP	SLG	OPS	AOPS	BR	ABR	PF	SB	CS	BSA	BSR
EAST																														
PIT	92	69	0	.571		52	28	712	565	6111	1444	255	47	**138**	468	832	**38**	76	.263	.323	**.402**	725	106	43	40	101	49	28	64	1
PHI	86	76	0	.531	6.5	51	30	735	694	6363	1506	**283**	42	125	610	960	31	88	.269	.342	**.402**	744	108	102	65	105	126	57	69	8
NY	82	80	0	.506	10.5	42	39	646	625	6237	1430	217	34	101	501	805	37	75	.256	.319	.361	680	97	-38	-18	97	32	26	55	-2
STL	82	80	1	.506	10.5	45	36	662	689	6207	**1527**	239	46	81	444	649	29	92	**.273**	.327	.375	702	97	5	-24	105	116	49	70	8
MON	75	87	0	.463	17.5	39	42	601	690	6272	1346	216	31	98	579	954	27	110	.244	.317	.348	665	87	-64	-93	105	108	58	65	3
CHI	75	87	0	.463	17.5	42	39	712	827	6323	1419	229	41	95	650	802	30	107	.259	.338	.368	706	97	34	1	105	67	55	55	-5
WEST																														
CIN	108	54	0	.667		64	17	**840**	586	6418	1515	278	37	124	691	916	35	66	.271	**.353**	.401	754	114	134	123	101	168	36	**82**	24
LA	88	74	0	.543	20	49	32	648	**534**	6246	1355	217	31	118	611	825	31	104	.248	.325	.365	690	102	-9	19	96	138	52	73	12
SF	80	81	0	.497	27.5	46	35	659	671	6186	1412	235	45	84	604	775	22	62	.259	.333	.365	698	97	11	-11	103	99	47	68	5
SD	71	91	0	.438	37	38	43	552	683	6151	1324	215	22	78	506	754	37	**133**	.244	.310	.335	645	91	-101	-62	93	85	50	63	1
ATL	67	94	0	.416	40.5	37	43	583	739	6092	1323	179	28	107	543	759	16	72	.244	.313	.346	659	86	-78	-95	103	55	38	59	-1
HOU	64	97	1	.398	43.5	37	44	664	711	6211	1401	218	**54**	84	523	762	32	97	.254	.320	.359	679	101	-39	9	93	133	62	68	8
TOT	971					542	428	8014		74817	17002	2781	458	1233	6730	9793	367	1082	.257	.327	.369	696					1176	558	68	63

TEAM	CG	SHO	GR	SV	IP	H	HR	BB	SO	BR/9	ERA	AERA	OAV	OOB	PR	APR	PF	OSB	OCS	FA	E	WPB	DP	FW	PW	BW	BSW	DIF
EAST																												
PIT	43	14	226	31	1437.1	1302	**79**	551	768	11.7	3.01	119	.243	.313	98	**92**	99	81	35	.976	151	56	147	.2	**9.6**	4.2	-.4	-2.0
PHI	33	11	283	30	1455.0	1353	111	546	897	11.9	3.82	98	.249	.317	-33	-11	104	69	52	.976	152	60	156	.2	-1.1	6.8	.3	-1.1
NY	40	14	229	31	1466.0	1344	99	580	**989**	12.0	3.39	103	.246	.319	38	19	97	116	63	.976	151	56	144	.3	2.0	-1.9	-.8	1.4
STL	33	13	272	36	1454.2	1452	98	571	824	12.7	3.57	106	.260	.328	8	34	105	110	39	.973	171	86	140	-.8	3.5	-2.5	.3	.5
MON	30	12	271	25	1480.0	1448	102	665	831	13.1	3.72	104	.259	.339	-17	21	107	78	46	.973	180	85	**179**	-1.3	2.2	-9.7	-.2	3.1
CHI	27	8	**298**	33	1444.1	1587	130	551	850	13.6	4.49	86	.281	.347	-140	-94	107	93	54	.972	179	**50**	152	-1.3	-9.8	.1	-1.1	6.1
WEST																												
CIN	22	8	277	**50**	1459.0	1422	112	487	663	12.0	3.37	106	.257	.319	41	33	99	**61**	29	**.984**	**102**	52	173	**3.0**	3.4	**12.8**	**2.0**	5.8
LA	**51**	**18**	169	21	1469.2	**1215**	104	**448**	894	**10.4**	**2.92**	117	**.225**	**.285**	114	85	94	68	33	.979	127	51	106	1.6	8.9	2.0	.7	-6.2
SF	37	9	259	24	1432.2	1406	92	612	856	12.9	3.74	102	.259	.336	-19	9	105	114	47	.976	146	64	164	.5	.9	-1.1	-.0	-.8
SD	40	12	290	20	1463.1	1494	99	521	713	12.5	3.48	100	.266	.329	23	1	96	118	51	.971	188	51	163	-1.8	.1	-6.5	-.4	-1.4
ATL	32	4	267	24	1430.0	1543	101	519	669	13.3	3.91	96	.278	.341	-47	-22	104	147	44	.972	175	90	147	-1.1	-2.3	-9.9	-.7	.5
HOU	39	6	265	25	1458.1	1436	106	679	839	13.3	4.04	84	.262	.343	-67	-113	94	125	**65**	.979	137	113	166	1.1	-11.8	.9	-3.0	-7.0
TOT	427	129	3106	350	17450.1					12.4	3.62		.257	.327						.976	1859	814	1837		.9	-3.0		

Batter-Fielder Wins		Batting Average		On-Base Percentage		Slugging Average		On-Base Plus Slugging		Adjusted OPS		Adjusted Batter Runs	
Morgan-Cin	8.1	Madlock-Chi	354	Morgan-Cin	466	Parker-Pit	541	Morgan-Cin	974	Morgan-Cin	169	Morgan-Cin	57.4
Bench-Cin	5.5	Simmons-StL	332	Rose-Cin	406	Luzinski-Phi	540	Luzinski-Phi	934	Watson-Hou	152	Luzinski-Phi	43.0
Schmidt-Phi	5.2	Sanguillen-Pit	328	Wynn-LA	403	Schmidt-Phi	523	Parker-Pit	898	Luzinski-Phi	151	Rose-Cin	33.3
Evans-Atl	4.4	Morgan-Cin	327	Madlock-Chi	402	Bench-Cin	519	Stargell-Pit	891	Parker-Pit	146	Thornton-Chi	32.7
Speier-SF	3.5	Watson-Hou	324	Cardenal-Chi	397	Foster-Cin	518	Schmidt-Phi	890	Stargell-Pit	145	Watson-Hou	32.4

Runs		Hits		Doubles		Triples		Home Runs		Total Bases		Runs Batted In	
Rose-Cin	112	Cash-Phi	213	Rose-Cin	47	Garr-Atl	11	Schmidt-Phi	38	Luzinski-Phi	322	Luzinski-Phi	120
Cash-Phi	111	Rose-Cin	210	Cash-Phi	40	Parker-Pit	10	Kingman-NY	36	Garvey-LA	314	Bench-Cin	110
Lopes-LA	108	Garvey-LA	210	Oliver-Pit	39	Kessinger-Chi	10	Luzinski-Phi	34	Parker-Pit	302	Perez-Cin	109
Morgan-Cin	107	Simmons-StL	193	Bench-Cin	39	Joshua-SF	10	Bench-Cin	28	Schmidt-Phi	294	Staub-NY	105
Thomas-SF	99	Millan-NY	191	Garvey-LA	38	Gross-Hou	10			Rose-Cin	286		

Stolen Bases		Base Stealing Runs		Fielding Runs-Infield		Fielding Runs-Outfield		Wins		Winning Pct.		Complete Games	
Lopes-LA	77	Lopes-LA	12.7	Evans-Atl	31.3	Maddox-SF-Phi	14.5	Seaver-NY	22	Gullett-Cin	789	Messersmith-LA	19
Morgan-Cin	60	Morgan-Cin	11.2	Stennett-Pit	25.7	Geronimo-Cin	11.4	Jones-SD	20	Seaver-NY	710	Jones-SD	18
Brock-StL	56	Brock-StL	6.7	Schmidt-Phi	18.7	Foster-Cin	9.6	Messersmith-LA	19	Hooton-Chi-LA	667	Seaver-NY	15
Cedeno-Hou	50	Concepcion-Cin	5.2	Trillo-Chi	18.0	Cardenal-Chi	9.3	Hooton-Chi-LA	18	Murray-Mon	652	Reuss-Pit	15
Cardenal-Chi	34	Cedeno-Hou	5.1	Cash-Phi	17.6	Unser-NY	8.6	Reuss-Pit	18				

Strikeouts		Fewest BB/Game		Games		Saves		Base Runners/9		Adjusted Relief Runs		Relief Ranking	
Seaver-NY	243	Nolan-Cin	1.24	Garber-Phi	71	Hrabosky-StL	22	Jones-SD	9.41	Hrabosky-StL	19.9	Hrabosky-StL	39.5
Montefusco-SF	215	Jones-SD	1.77	McEnaney-Cin	70	Eastwick-Cin	22	Sutton-LA	9.45	Apodaca-NY	18.7	Apodaca-NY	20.4
Messersmith-LA	213	Reed-Atl-StL	1.91	Tomlin-SD	67	Giusti-Pit	17	Messersmith-LA	9.65	Hilgendorf-Phi	14.2	Eastwick-Cin	14.7
Carlton-Phi	192	Rau-LA	2.13	Borbon-Cin	67	McEnaney-Cin	15	Hrabosky-StL	9.80	Eastwick-Cin	10.9	Garman-StL	14.5
Richard-Hou	176	Barr-SF	2.14	Garman-StL	66	Knowles-Chi	15	Hooton-Chi-LA	9.89	C.Carroll-Cin	10.5	McGraw-NY	14.2

Innings Pitched		Opponents' Avg.		Opponents' OBP		Earned Run Average		Adjusted ERA		Adjusted Starter Runs		Pitcher Wins	
Messersmith-LA	321.2	Messersmith-LA	213	Sutton-LA	263	Jones-SD	2.24	Jones-SD	156	Messersmith-LA	42.7	**Seaver-NY**	4.6
Jones-SD	285.0	Sutton-LA	213	Jones-SD	269	Messersmith-LA	2.29	Messersmith-LA	149	Seaver-NY	37.9	**Messersmith-LA**	4.5
Seaver-NY	280.1	Seaver-NY	214	Hooton-Chi-LA	274	Seaver-NY	2.38	Seaver-NY	148	Jones-SD	37.4	**Jones-SD**	4.5
Morton-Atl	277.2	Warthen-Mon	217	Messersmith-LA	275	Reuss-Pit	2.54	Reuss-Pit	141	Reuss-Pit	30.3	**Hrabosky-StL**	4.2
Niekro-Atl	275.2	Hooton-Chi-LA	219	Nolan-Cin	275	Forsch-StL	2.86	Forsch-StL	133	Montefusco-SF	25.3	**Reuss-Pit**	4.1

Free and Clear

The Reds cruised in a lopsided pennant "race." Joe Morgan was an easy MVP, enjoying one of the greatest seasons ever for a second baseman. Everyone in Cincinnati's lineup contributed offensively and defensively, and the deep pitching featured left-right relief combo Will McEnaney and Rawly Eastwick.

The NL East was again tightly packed, with just 17½ games separating first from last. Pittsburgh used six strong starting pitchers, including rookie John Candelaria, to withstand Philadelphia's challenge to win its fourth crown in five years. The Pirates favored power and boasted little speed. Philadelphia stole 126 bases, but could hit the long ball, too; third baseman Mike Schmidt won the second of his eight NL home run crowns.

The Cardinals lost 1930s star Joe Medwick, who passed away, and Bob Gibson, who hung up the spikes. Claude Osteen and Vada Pinson also retired. Astros pitcher Don Wilson died in his car of carbon monoxide poisoning.

Pirates second baseman Rennie Stennett had one of the great afternoons of all time, going 7-for-7 in a 22-0 massacre at Wrigley Field to tie Wilbert Robinson's 1892 mark. Giants mainstay Juan Marichal retired, while the club welcomed Jack Clark and Rookie of the Year John Montefusco.

The Pirates were no match for the Reds, who took the NLCS in three games. But the 1975 World Series was different; packed with drama, controversy, great plays, and unexpected heroes, five of the seven games were one-run affairs. The Reds won Games 2, 3, and 7 with dramatic rallies in their last at bats; the Red Sox won two games with big innings and took a nail-biting, 12-inning, Game 6 on Carlton Fisk's barely-fair homer. The next night Morgan's ninth-inning single plated Pete Rose with the Series-winning run.

The biggest change of the year came December 23, when federal arbitrator Peter Seitz ruled baseball's reserve clause invalid, opening the door for free agency, distribution of talent, and increased salaries. Litigant Andy Messersmith (and the newly retired Dave McNally) first benefited from the ruling, but the doors soon blew out and nearly every club entered the market.

1975 American League

TEAM	W	L	T	PCT	GB	HW	HL	R	OR	PA	H	2B	3B	HR	BB	SO	HB	SH	AVG	OBP	SLG	OPS	AOPS	BR	ABR	PF	SB	CS	BSA	BSR
EAST																														
BOS	95	65	0	.594		47	34	**796**	709	6175	**1500**	284	44	134	565	741	34	75	**.275**	**.344**	**.417**	761	105	**112**	50	108	66	58	53	-6
BAL	90	69	0	.566	4.5	44	33	682	553	6211	1382	224	33	124	580	834	38	73	.252	.326	.373	699	103	-13	28	94	104	55	65	4
NY	83	77	0	.519	12	43	35	681	588	6038	1430	230	39	110	486	710	30	54	.264	.325	.382	707	100	-3	4	99	102	59	63	2
CLE	79	80	0	.497	15.5	41	39	688	703	6057	1409	201	25	153	525	667	24	64	.261	.327	.392	719	102	16	14	100	106	89	54	-8
MIL	68	94	0	.420	28	36	45	675	792	6081	1343	242	34	146	553	922	28	73	.250	.320	.389	709	99	-1	-5	101	65	64	50	-8
DET	57	102	0	.358	37.5	31	49	570	786	5852	1338	171	39	125	383	872	28	37	.249	.301	.366	667	84	-101	-124	104	63	57	53	-6
WEST																														
OAK	98	64	0	.605		**54**	27	758	606	6184	1376	220	33	151	609	846	51	74	.254	.333	.391	724	**106**	35	50	98	183	82	**69**	**12**
KC	91	71	0	.562	7	51	30	710	649	6230	1431	263	**58**	118	591	675	29	68	.261	.333	.394	727	102	42	24	103	155	75	67	8
TEX	79	83	0	.488	19	39	41	714	733	6342	1431	208	17	134	**613**	863	25	64	.256	.330	.371	701	99	-9	-2	99	102	62	62	1
MIN	76	83	0	.478	20.5	39	43	724	736	6243	1497	215	28	121	563	746	40	62	.271	.341	.386	727	104	47	40	101	81	48	63	3
CHI	75	86	0	.466	22.5	42	39	655	703	6243	1400	209	38	94	611	800	40	**97**	.255	.331	.358	689	94	-24	-32	101	101	54	65	3
CAL	72	89	0	.447	25.5	35	46	628	723	6141	1324	195	41	55	593	811	27	97	.246	.322	.328	650	90	-100	-57	93	**220**	108	67	11
TOT	963					502	461	8281		73779	16861	2662	429	1465	6672	9487	394	791	.258	.328	.379	707				1348	811	62	18

TEAM	CG	SHO	GR	SV	IP	H	HR	BB	SO	BR/9	ERA	AERA	OAV	OOB	PR	APR	PF	OSB	OCS	FA	E	WPB	DP	FW	PW	BW	BSW	DIF
EAST																												
BOS	62	11	167	31	1436.2	1463	145	**490**	720	12.4	3.98	102	.265	.325	-33	11	107	111	60	.977	139	**37**	142	.9	1.1	**5.1**	-.7	8.6
BAL	**70**	**19**	149	21	1451.0	1285	110	500	717	**11.1**	**3.17**	112	.242	**.306**	98	63	94	93	62	**.983**	**107**	47	**175**	2.6	6.4	2.9	.3	-1.7
NY	**70**	11	147	20	1424.0	1325	104	502	809	11.7	3.29	**113**	.249	.314	78	**67**	98	**80**	71	.978	135	48	148	1.1	-.7	1.4	-.9	-5.4
CLE	37	6	218	33	1435.1	1395	136	599	800	12.7	3.84	99	.258	.333	-10	-7	101	121	74	.978	134	66	156	1.1	-.7	1.4	-.9	-2.3
MIL	36	10	223	34	1431.2	1496	133	624	643	13.7	4.34	89	.271	.348	-89	-77	102	118	73	.971	180	85	162	-1.4	-7.9	-.5	-.9	-2.3
DET	52	10	155	17	1396.0	1496	137	533	787	13.3	4.27	94	.275	.340	-77	-36	107	123	68	.972	173	59	141	-1.1	-3.7	-12.7	-.7	-4.3
WEST																												
OAK	36	10	**245**	44	1448.2	**1267**	**102**	523	784	11.4	3.27	111	**.236**	**.306**	82	62	96	110	50	.977	143	60	140	.7	6.5	**5.1**	**1.1**	3.7
KC	52	11	204	25	1456.2	1422	108	498	815	12.0	3.47	111	.258	.320	50	61	102	119	64	.976	155	53	151	.0	6.2	2.5	.7	1.8
TEX	60	16	224	17	1465.2	1456	123	518	792	12.4	3.86	97	.261	.327	-14	-16	100	96	71	.971	191	60	173	-2.0	-1.6	-.2	.0	1.8
MIN	57	7	163	22	1423.0	1381	137	617	846	12.9	4.05	94	.257	.335	-43	-36	101	119	79	.978	140	38	155	-.9	-.8	-3.3	.2	-2.5
CHI	34	7	209	39	1452.1	1489	107	655	799	13.5	3.93	99	.268	.347	-24	-8	103	109	**80**	.978	184	74	164	-1.6	-5.5	-5.8	1.0	3.5
CAL	59	**19**	192	16	1453.1	1386	123	613	**975**	12.9	3.89	92	.253	.330	-18	-54	95	150	65	.971	184	74	164					
TOT	625	137	2296	319	17273.2					12.5	3.78		.258	.328						.975	1851	685	1854					

Batter-Fielder Wins
- Harrah-Tex 6.9
- Carew-Min 6.7
- Grich-Bal 6.5
- Mayberry-KC 4.5
- Munson-NY 4.4

Batting Average
- Carew-Min 359
- Lynn-Bos 331
- Munson-NY 318
- Rice-Bos 309
- C.Washington-Oak .308

On-Base Percentage
- Carew-Min 421
- Mayberry-KC 416
- Singleton-Bal 415
- Harrah-Tex 403
- Lynn-Bos 401

Slugging Average
- Lynn-Bos 566
- Mayberry-KC 547
- Powell-Cle 524
- Scott-Mil 515
- Bonds-NY 512

On-Base Plus Slugging
- Lynn-Bos 967
- Mayberry-KC 963
- Carew-Min 919
- Powell-Cle 901
- Bonds-NY 888

Adjusted OPS
- Mayberry-KC 167
- Carew-Min 159
- Lynn-Bos 159
- Singleton-Bal 155
- Powell-Cle 153

Adjusted Batter Runs
- Mayberry-KC 55.5
- Singleton-Bal 50.8
- Carew-Min 43.9
- Lynn-Bos ....42.
- Bonds-NY 37.5

Runs
- Lynn-Bos 103
- Mayberry-KC 95
- Bonds-NY 93
- Rice-Bos 92

Hits
- Brett-KC 195
- Carew-Min 192
- Munson-NY 190
- C.Washington-Oak 182

Doubles
- Lynn-Bos 47
- Jackson-Oak 39
- McRae-KC 38
- Mayberry-KC 38
- Chambliss-NY 38

Triples
- Rivers-Cal 13
- Brett-KC 13
- Orta-Chi 10
- Cowens-KC 8

Home Runs
- Scott-Mil 36
- Jackson-Oak 36
- Mayberry-KC 34
- Bonds-NY 32

Total Bases
- Scott-Mil 318
- Mayberry-KC 303
- Jackson-Oak 303
- Lynn-Bos 299
- Brett-KC 289

Runs Batted In
- Scott-Mil 10
- Mayberry-KC 10
- Lynn-Bos 10
- Jackson-Oak 10

Stolen Bases
- Rivers-Cal 70
- C.Washington-Oak 40
- Otis-KC 39
- Carew-Min 35
- Remy-Cal 34

Base Stealing Runs
- Rivers-Cal 10.5
- Otis-KC 4.7
- Patek-KC 4.6
- Carew-Min 4.6
- Alomar-NY 4.1

Fielding Runs-Infield
- Belanger-Bal 29.5
- Rodriguez-Det 26.5
- Grich-Bal 26.3
- Dent-Chi 18.2
- Harrah-Tex 16.5

Fielding Runs-Outfield
- Evans-Bos 18.7
- North-Oak 11.4
- Sharp-Chi-Mil 11.1
- Manning-Cle 10.2
- White-NY 8.1

Wins
- Palmer-Bal 23
- Hunter-NY 23
- Blue-Oak 22
- Torrez-Bal 20
- Kaat-Chi 20

Winning Pct.
- Torrez-Bal 690
- Leonard-KC 682
- Palmer-Bal 676
- Blue-Oak 667
- Lee-Bos 654

Complete Games
- Hunter-NY 3
- G.Perry-Cle-Tex 2
- Palmer-Bal 2
- Jenkins-Tex 2
- Blyleven-Min 2

Strikeouts
- Tanana-Cal 269
- G.Perry-Cle-Tex 233
- Blyleven-Min 233
- Palmer-Bal 193
- Blue-Oak 189

Fewest BB/Game
- Jenkins-Tex 1.87
- G.Perry-Cle-Tex 2.06
- Grimsley-Bal 2.15
- Palmer-Bal 2.23
- Hunter-NY 2.28

Games
- Fingers-Oak 75
- Lindblad-Oak 68
- Gossage-Chi 62
- LaRoche-Cle 61
- Foucault-Tex 59

Saves
- Gossage-Chi 26
- Fingers-Oak 24
- Murphy-Mil 20
- LaRoche-Cle 17
- Drago-Bos 15

Base Runners/9
- Hunter-NY 9.22
- Palmer-Bal 9.33
- Fingers-Oak 9.52
- Blyleven-Min 10.02
- Tanana-Cal 10.18

Adjusted Relief Runs
- Gossage-Chi 31.4
- Todd-Oak 17.1
- Hiller-Det 13.8
- LaRoche-Cle 13.5
- Lindblad-Oak 12.3

Relief Ranking
- Gossage-Chi ....46.
- Fingers-Oak ....18.
- LaRoche-Cle ....18.
- Todd-Oak ....17.
- Hiller-Det ....

Innings Pitched
- Hunter-NY 328.0
- Palmer-Bal 323.0
- G.Perry-Cle-Tex 305.2
- Kaat-Chi 303.2
- Wood-Chi 291.1

Opponents' Avg.
- Hunter-NY 208
- Ryan-Cal 213
- Eckersley-Cle 215
- Palmer-Bal 216
- Blyleven-Min 219

Opponents' OBP
- Hunter-NY 261
- Palmer-Bal 266
- Blyleven-Min 281
- G.Perry-Cle-Tex 284
- Tanana-Cal 286

Earned Run Average
- Palmer-Bal 2.09
- Hunter-NY 2.58
- Eckersley-Cle 2.60
- Tanana-Cal 2.62
- Figueroa-Cal 2.91

Adjusted ERA
- Palmer-Bal 170
- Eckersley-Cle 146
- Hunter-NY 144
- Tanana-Cal 137
- Blyleven-Min 128

Adjusted Starter Runs
- Palmer-Bal 53.0
- Hunter-NY 41.7
- Tanana-Cal 31.9
- Blyleven-Min 25.6
- Eckersley-Cle 25.3

Pitcher Wins
- **Palmer-Bal** ....5.
- **Gossage-Chi** ....5.
- **Hunter-NY** ....4.
- **Tanana-Cal** ....3.
- **Busby-KC** ....

The Red and the Black

Boston had no trouble after June, pulling away while the Brewers and Yankees sagged, and the Orioles didn't get going until it was too late. Red Sox center fielder Fred Lynn was an immediate sensation, winning Rookie of the Year as well as MVP honors. Fellow freshman Jim Rice was nearly as good.

It was a fine season all around for rookies. Dennis Eckersley, Jerry Remy, and Lyman Bostock all played well, and Butch Hobson and Willie Randolph also made their first appearances. It was the end, however, for Harmon Killebrew, who hit .199 in Kansas City.

New York owner George Steinbrenner came out with a huge contract for free agent Catfish Hunter, but his 23 wins couldn't carry a mediocre staff. Cleveland made Frank Robinson the game's first African American manager; Robby also served as a part-time DH and homered in his first at bat Opening Day.

Kansas City's John Mayberry, Hal McRae, and George Brett blossomed, but the Royals couldn't deter the A's from their fifth straight division title. A 13-of-14 stretch in June put Oakland well ahead. Despite playing in a pitcher's park, the offense was superb, boasting power, speed, and on-base ability. Alvin Dark used seven starters 10 or more times, and Vida Blue won 20 games for the third time. Nolan Ryan went down with elbow problems, allowing his Angels teammate, 21-year-old Frank Tanana, to lead the AL in strikeouts.

Boston easily crushed the A's to win the league pennant, but the World Series was another Hub disappointment. Indelible moments—Luis Tiant's twisting, Bernie Carbo's swinging, Dwight Evans' leaping, Carlton Fisk's gesturing—made the seven-game loss to Cincinnati even tougher to swallow.

Lefty Grove and Casey Stengel died, and the Oakland dynasty also came to an end. A's owner Charlie Finley—not unlike franchise predecessor Connie Mack—would be forced to trade or sell his stars. Many of Finley's "mustache gang" eventually walked away as free agents, happily moving to greener, calmer, but less storied pastures.

1974 National League

TEAM	W	L	T	PCT	GB	HW	HL	R	OR	PA	H	2B	3B	HR	BB	SO	HB	SH	AVG	OBP	SLG	OPS	AOPS	BR	ABR	PF	SB	CS	BSA	BSR
EAST																														
PIT	88	74	0	.543		52	29	751	657	6361	**1560**	238	46	114	514	828	38	54	**.274**	.335	.391	726	112	65	85	97	55	31	64	1
STL	86	75	0	.534	1.5	44	37	677	643	6318	1492	216	46	83	531	752	**44**	68	.265	.331	.365	696	100	7	7	100	**172**	62	74	**16**
PHI	80	82	0	.494	8	46	35	676	701	6117	1434	233	**50**	95	469	822	26	84	.261	.320	.373	693	95	-9	-38	105	115	58	66	5
MON	79	82	0	.491	8.5	42	38	662	657	6190	1355	201	29	86	652	812	33	106	.254	.335	.350	685	92	3	-33	106	124	49	72	10
NY	71	91	0	.438	17	36	45	572	646	6226	1286	183	22	96	597	**735**	29	87	.235	.311	.329	640	85	-100	-97	99	43	23	65	1
CHI	66	96	0	.407	22	32	49	669	826	6344	1397	221	42	110	621	857	29	80	.251	.327	.365	692	95	0	-28	104	78	73	52	-8
WEST																														
LA	102	60	0	.630		52	29	**798**	**561**	6332	1511	231	34	**139**	597	820	28	86	.272	.342	**.401**	**743**	118	105	**134**	96	149	75	67	7
CIN	98	64	1	.605	4	50	31	776	631	6372	1437	**271**	35	135	**693**	940	30	68	.260	**.343**	.394	737	114	101	113	99	146	49	**75**	15
ATL	88	74	1	.543	14	46	35	661	563	6279	1375	202	37	120	571	772	24	**109**	.249	.319	.363	682	93	-25	-48	104	72	44	62	0
HOU	81	81	0	.500	21	46	35	653	632	6120	1441	222	41	110	471	864	29	83	.263	.322	.346	700	106	4	35	96	108	65	62	1
SF	72	90	0	.444	30	37	44	634	723	6159	1380	228	38	93	548	869	30	75	.252	.322	.358	680	92	-28	-54	104	107	51	68	6
SD	60	102	0	.370	42	36	45	541	830	6117	1239	196	27	99	564	900	20	83	.229	.302	.330	632	86	-124	-97	95	85	45	65	3
TOT	972					519	452	8070		74935	16907	2642	447	1280	6828	9971	360	983	.255	.326	.367	693					1254	625	67	57

TEAM	CG	SHO	GR	SV	IP	H	HR	BB	SO	BR/9	ERA	AERA	OAV	OOB	PR	APR	PF	OSB	OCS	FA	E	WPB	DP	FW	PW	BW	BSW	DIF
EAST																												
PIT	**51**	9	229	17	1466.0	1428	93	543	721	12.3	3.49	99	.256	.323	21	-3	96	85	54	.975	162	58	154	-.5	-.3	8.8	-.4	-.7
STL	37	13	293	20	1473.1	1399	97	616	794	12.5	3.48	103	.254	.329	22	19	100	119	57	.977	147	57	**192**	.4	2.0	.7	**1.2**	1.3
PHI	46	4	283	19	1447.1	1394	111	682	892	13.1	3.91	97	.257	.341	-47	-18	105	122	52	.976	148	75	168	.4	-1.9	-4.0	.0	4.5
MON	35	8	223	**27**	1429.0	1340	99	544	822	12.0	3.60	107	.249	.319	3	36	106	89	64	.976	153	74	157	.0	3.7	-3.4	.5	-2.4
NY	46	15	212	14	1470.1	1433	99	504	908	12.0	3.42	105	.257	.320	33	30	99	113	48	.975	158	52	150	-.2	3.1	-10.1	-.4	-2.4
CHI	23	6	347	26	1466.1	1593	122	576	895	13.6	4.28	89	.277	.344	-108	-70	106	126	54	.969	199	81	141	-2.6	-7.3	-2.9	-1.3	-.8
WEST																												
LA	33	19	209	23	1465.1	**1272**	112	464	943	10.8	2.97	115	**.233**	**.294**	105	77	95	76	47	.975	157	55	122	-.2	8.0	**14.0**	.2	-1.0
CIN	34	11	256	**27**	1466.1	1364	126	536	875	11.8	3.41	102	.247	.314	33	13	96	**56**	41	.979	134	59	151	1.2	1.4	11.8	1.1	1.6
ATL	46	**21**	215	22	1474.1	1343	97	488	772	11.3	3.05	**124**	.244	.307	93	**115**	105	107	50	.979	132	64	161	1.3	**12.0**	-5.0	-.5	-.8
HOU	36	18	272	18	1450.2	1396	**84**	601	738	12.6	3.46	100	.255	.331	25	2	96	123	56	**.982**	**113**	65	161	2.4	.2	3.6	-.4	-5.9
SF	27	11	292	25	1439.0	1409	116	559	756	12.5	3.78	101	.257	.325	-26	4	105	107	36	.972	175	51	126	-1.2	-.4	-5.6	.1	-2.7
SD	25	7	**352**	19	1445.2	1536	124	715	855	14.3	4.58	78	.275	.359	-155	-163	99	131	**65**	.973	170	71	126	-.9	-17.0	-10.1	-.2	7.2
TOT	439	142	3183	257	17493.2					12.4	3.62		.255	.326						.976	1848	762	1836					7.2

Batter-Fielder Wins		Batting Average		On-Base Percentage		Slugging Average		On-Base Plus Slugging		Adjusted OPS		Adjusted Batter Runs	
Schmidt-Phi	7.3	Garr-Atl	353	Morgan-Cin	427	Schmidt-Phi	546	Stargell-Pit	944	Stargell-Pit	168	Stargell-Pit	49.3
Morgan-Cin	7.0	Oliver-Pit	321	Stargell-Pit	407	Stargell-Pit	537	Schmidt-Phi	941	Morgan-Cin	160	Morgan-Cin	49.1
Bench-Cin	5.7	Gross-Hou	314	Bailey-Mon	396	Smith-StL	528	Morgan-Cin	921	Smith-StL	156	Schmidt-Phi	44.0
Evans-Atl	4.7	Buckner-LA	314	Schmidt-Phi	395	Bench-Cin	507	Smith-StL	917	Schmidt-Phi	155	Wynn-LA	41.0
Cash-Chi	4.4	Madlock-Chi	313	Gross-Hou	393	Garr-Atl	503	Garr-Atl	886	Wynn-LA	153	Smith-StL	38.9

Runs		Hits		Doubles		Triples		Home Runs		Total Bases		Runs Batted In	
Rose-Cin	110	Garr-Atl	214	Rose-Cin	45	Garr-Atl	17	Schmidt-Phi	36	Bench-Cin	315	Bench-Cin	129
Schmidt-Phi	108	Cash-Phi	206	Oliver-Pit	38	Oliver-Pit	12	Bench-Cin	33	Schmidt-Phi	310	Schmidt-Phi	116
Bench-Cin	108	Garvey-LA	200	Bench-Cin	38	Cash-Phi	11	Wynn-LA	32	Garr-Atl	305	Garvey-LA	111
Morgan-Cin	107	Oliver-Pit	198	Stargell-Pit	37	Metzger-Hou	10	Perez-Cin	28	Garvey-LA	301	Wynn-LA	108
Brock-StL	105	Stennett-Pit	196			Bowa-Phi	10	Cedeno-Hou	26	Oliver-Pit	293	Simmons-StL	103

Stolen Bases		Base Stealing Runs		Fielding Runs-Infield		Fielding Runs-Outfield		Wins		Winning Pct.		Complete Games	
Brock-StL	118	Brock-StL	14.4	Foli-Mon	34.8	Geronimo-Cin	10.5	P.Niekro-Atl	20	Messersmith-LA	769	P.Niekro-Atl	18
Lopes-LA	59	Morgan-Cin	8.6	Cash-Phi	30.7	Anderson-Phi	9.8	Messersmith-LA	20	Sutton-LA	679	Carlton-Phi	17
Morgan-Cin	58	Lintz-Mon	8.6	Schmidt-Phi	28.3	Rose-Cin	9.3	Sutton-LA	19	Capra-Atl	667	Lonborg-Phi	16
Cedeno-Hou	57	Concepcion-Cin	6.9	Evans-Atl	26.6	Zisk-Pit	6.9	Capra-Atl	19	Torrez-Mon	652	Rooker-Pit	15
Lintz-Mon	50	Lopes-LA	6.7	Stennett-Pit	20.9	Cedeno-Hou	6.4	Billingham-Cin	19	Billingham-Cin	633		

Strikeouts		Fewest BB/Game		Games		Saves		Base Runners/9		Adjusted Relief Runs		Relief Ranking	
Carlton-Phi	240	Barr-SF	1.76	Marshall-LA	106	Marshall-LA	21	Murray-Mon	8.91	Marshall-LA	24.2	Marshall-LA	33.7
Messersmith-LA	221	Reed-Atl	1.98	Hardy-SD	76	Moffitt-SF	15	House-Atl	9.12	Taylor-Mon	20.1	C.Carroll-Cin	26.1
Seaver-NY	201	Ellis-Pit	2.09	Borbon-Cin	73	Borbon-Cin	14	Leon-Atl	9.96	House-Atl	19.8	House-Atl	18.7
P.Niekro-Atl	195	Lonborg-Phi	2.23	Forsch-Hou	70	Giusti-Pit	12	Messersmith-LA	9.97	Murray-Mon	19.4	Taylor-Mon	18.1
Matlack-NY	195	Marshall-LA	2.42	Sosa-SF	68			P.Niekro-Atl	10.21	C.Carroll-Cin	15.8	Leon-Atl	14.6

Innings Pitched		Opponents' Avg.		Opponents' OBP		Earned Run Average		Adjusted ERA		Adjusted Starter Runs		Pitcher Wins	
P.Niekro-Atl	302.1	Capra-Atl	208	Messersmith-LA	277	Capra-Atl	2.28	Capra-Atl	166	P.Niekro-Atl	45.0	**P.Niekro-Atl**	5.0
Messersmith-LA	292.1	Messersmith-LA	212	Matlack-NY	283	P.Niekro-Atl	2.38	P.Niekro-Atl	159	Matlack-NY	35.7	**Messersmith-LA**	3.8
Carlton-Phi	291.0	Gullett-Cin	222	P.Niekro-Atl	284	Matlack-NY	2.41	Matlack-NY	150	Capra-Atl	32.7	**Marshall-LA**	3.7
Lonborg-Phi	283.0	P.Niekro-Atl	225	Reed-Atl	285	Marshall-LA	2.42	Marshall-LA	142	Messersmith-LA	30.9	**Capra-Atl**	3.5
Sutton-LA	276.0	Matlack-NY	226	Capra-Atl	286	Messersmith-LA	2.59	Barr-SF	139	Barr-SF	29.5	**Rooker-Pit**	3.3

Records, Records, Records

Henry Aaron, boosted by a mid-career move to hitter-friendly Fulton County Stadium, had slowly closed in on Babe Ruth's all-time home run record. Despite the media pressure, the hate mail, and the nagging injuries, the 40-year-old Aaron tied the record on Opening Day in Cincinnati and then broke it in Atlanta against Los Angeles on April 8.

The Braves finished third with surprising pitching, but Atlanta never contended. Cincinnati was excellent, but the Dodgers were even better. Los Angeles, led from start to finish. The Dodgers shored up a mediocre bullpen by acquiring Mike Marshall from Montreal, and the muttonchopped screwballer set a big-league mark with 106 appearances and became the first reliever to win the Cy Young. The Dodgers also got big production from center fielder Jimmy Wynn and first baseman Steve Garvey, an All-Star write-in starter and eventual MVP.

With Willies Mays and McCovey departed, the Giants sank to fifth. Their attendance, just 50 percent of their 1971 total, was the league's lowest figure of the decade. Both Felipe and Matty Alou ended their major league careers. Catastrophic control problems forced Pirates hurler Steve Blass from the game, while Orlando Cepeda and Ron Santo's careers ground to disappointing halts in the AL. Former Cardinals pitching great—and beloved TV announcer—Dizzy Dean passed away, and Kent Tekulve, Keith Hernandez, and Gary Carter made their major league bows.

Lou Brock of St. Louis used his 35-year-old legs to steal 118 bases, shattering Maury Wills's record, and his club almost took the NL East crown. But the Cardinals didn't hit enough, and Willie Stargell's Pirates, sometimes known as the Pittsburgh Lumber Company, led the league in batting average and took a see-saw race.

A four-game NLCS went easily to the Dodgers; Pirates reliever Dave Giusti allowed 13 hits in 3.1 innings of "relief." The World Series, however, was no celebration as the Oakland A's beat Los Angeles in five. Four of the games were decided by 3-2 scores.

1974 American League

TEAM	W	L	T	PCT	GB	HW	HL	R	OR	PA	H	2B	3B	HR	BB	SO	HB	SH	AVG	OBP	SLG	OPS	AOPS	BR	ABR	PF	SB	CS	BSA	BS
EAST																														
BAL	91	71	0	.562		46	35	659	612	6230	1418	226	27	116	509	770	58	72	.256	.322	.370	692	101	-1	16	98	145	58	**71**	**1**
NY	89	73	0	.549	2	47	34	671	623	6181	1451	220	30	101	515	**690**	21	49	.263	.324	.368	692	100	1	8	99	53	35	60	
BOS	84	78	0	.519	7	46	35	**696**	661	6214	1449	**236**	31	109	**569**	811	33	64	.264	.333	.377	710	97	42	-5	107	104	58	64	
CLE	77	85	0	.475	14	40	41	662	694	6019	1395	201	19	131	432	756	26	56	.255	.311	.370	681	96	-38	-34	99	79	68	54	
MIL	76	86	0	.469	15	40	41	647	660	6090	1335	228	**49**	120	500	909	27	56	.244	.309	.369	678	94	-42	-40	100	106	75	59	
DET	72	90	0	.444	19	36	45	620	768	6106	1375	200	35	131	436	784	24	41	.247	.303	.366	669	89	-68	-89	104	67	38	64	
WEST																														
OAK	90	72	0	.556		49	32	689	**551**	6048	1315	205	37	132	568	876	38	60	.247	.321	.373	694	105	2	42	94	**164**	93	64	
TEX	84	76	1	.525	5	42	38	690	698	6123	1482	198	39	99	508	710	38	81	**.272**	**.336**	.377	713	**108**	41	**58**	98	113	80	59	
MIN	82	80	1	.506	8	48	33	673	669	6302	**1530**	190	37	111	508	791	46	64	**.272**	**.336**	.378	714	102	42	20	103	74	45	62	
CHI	80	80	0	.500	7	46	34	684	721	6235	1492	225	23	**135**	519	858	26	70	.268	.330	**.389**	**719**	103	50	32	103	64	53	55	
KC	77	85	0	.475	13	40	41	667	662	6263	1448	232	42	89	500	768	32	56	.259	.327	.364	691	94	-1	-37	106	146	76	66	
CAL	68	94	1	.420	22	36	45	618	657	6085	1372	203	31	95	509	801	45	**82**	.254	.321	.356	677	100	-30	4	95	119	79	60	
TOT	973					516	454	7976		73896	17062	2564	400	1369	6135	9524	414	751	.258	.323	.371	694					1234	758	62	

TEAM	CG	SHO	GR	SV	IP	H	HR	BB	SO	BR/9	ERA	AERA	OAV	OOB	PR	APR	PF	OSB	OCS	FA	E	WPB	DP	FW	PW	BW	BSW	D
EAST																												
BAL	57	**16**	185	25	1474.0	1393	101	480	701	11.6	3.27	106	.253	.314	56	35	96	91	58	**.980**	128	50	174	1.0	3.7	1.7	**1.2**	2
NY	53	13	182	24	1455.1	1402	104	528	829	12.1	3.31	107	.256	.323	50	38	98	**80**	55	.977	142	54	158	.2	4.0	.8	-.2	3
BOS	**71**	12	139	18	1455.1	1462	126	463	751	12.1	3.72	103	.262	.320	-16	18	106	108	60	.977	145	51	156	.0	1.9	-.5	.3	1
CLE	45	9	214	27	1445.2	1419	138	479	650	12.0	3.80	96	.260	.320	-30	-27	101	92	48	.977	146	**30**	157	-.0	-2.8	-3.6	-.7	3
MIL	43	11	189	24	1457.2	1476	126	493	621	12.3	3.76	97	.266	.326	-23	-20	101	103	56	**.980**	**127**	62	168	1.1	-2.1	-4.2	-.4	
DET	54	7	154	15	1455.2	1443	148	621	869	13.0	4.16	92	.262	.338	-88	-52	106	134	79	.975	158	75	155	-.7	-5.4	-9.3	.0	6
WEST																												
OAK	49	12	**216**	28	1439.2	**1322**	90	430	755	**11.1**	**2.95**	113	**.246**	**.302**	107	67	92	83	59	.977	141	37	154	.3	**7.0**	4.4	.4	-3
TEX	62	**16**	189	12	1433.2	1423	126	449	871	12.0	3.82	94	.260	.318	-33	-39	99	99	60	.974	163	59	164	-1.1	-4.1	**6.1**	-.4	3
MIN	43	11	189	**29**	1455.1	1436	115	513	934	12.3	3.94	102	.260	.325	-4	14	103	119	**86**	.976	151	43	164	-.3	1.5	2.1	.0	-2
CHI	55	11	201	**29**	1465.2	1470	103	548	826	12.7	3.94	95	.263	.332	-52	-30	104	111	69	.977	147	60	**188**	-.0	-3.1	3.3	-.5	
KC	54	13	209	17	1471.2	1477	91	482	731	12.2	3.51	109	.263	.322	17	47	106	115	55	.976	152	71	166	-.4	4.9	-3.9	.6	-5
CAL	64	13	190	12	1439.0	1339	101	649	**986**	12.7	3.52	98	.248	.332	15	-9	96	98	72	.976	147	73	150	-.0	-.9	.4	-.2	-12
TOT	650	144	2257	260	17448.2					12.2	3.62		.258	.323						.977	1747	665	1954					

Batter-Fielder Wins
- Carew-Min 6.9
- Grich-Bal 6.0
- Jackson-Oak 5.3
- Harrah-Tex 3.3
- Burroughs-Tex 3.0

Batting Average
- Carew-Min .364
- Orta-Chi .316
- McRae-KC .310
- Piniella-NY .305
- Maddox-NY .303

On-Base Percentage
- Carew-Min .433
- Yastrzemski-Bos .414
- Burroughs-Tex .397
- Maddox-NY .395
- Jackson-Oak .391

Slugging Average
- D.Allen-Chi .563
- Jackson-Oak .514
- Burroughs-Tex .504
- Rudi-Oak .484
- Freehan-Det .479

On-Base Plus Slugging
- D.Allen-Chi .938
- Jackson-Oak .905
- Burroughs-Tex .901
- Carew-Min .879
- Yastrzemski-Bos .859

Adjusted OPS
- Jackson-Oak 170
- Burroughs-Tex 164
- D.Allen-Chi 164
- Carew-Min 149
- Robinson-Cal-Cle 143

Adjusted Batter Runs
- Burroughs-Tex
- Jackson-Oak
- Carew-Min
- D.Allen-Chi
- Yastrzemski-Bos

Runs
- Yastrzemski-Bos 93
- Grich-Bal 92
- Jackson-Oak 90
- Otis-KC 87
- Carew-Min 86

Hits
- Carew-Min 218
- Davis-Bal 181
- Money-Mil 178
- K.Henderson-Chi 176
- Rudi-Oak 174

Doubles
- Rudi-Oak 39
- Scott-Mil 36
- McRae-KC 36
- K.Henderson-Chi 35
- Burroughs-Tex 33

Triples
- Rivers-Cal 11
- Otis-KC 9

Home Runs
- D.Allen-Chi 32
- Jackson-Oak 29
- Tenace-Oak 26
- Darwin-Min 25
- Burroughs-Tex 25

Total Bases
- Rudi-Oak 287
- K.Henderson-Chi 281
- Burroughs-Tex 279
- Carew-Min 267

Runs Batted In
- Burroughs-Tex
- Bando-Oak
- Rudi-Oak
- K.Henderson-Chi
- Darwin-Min

Stolen Bases
- North-Oak 54
- Carew-Min 38
- Lowenstein-Cle 36
- Campaneris-Oak 34
- Patek-KC 33

Base Stealing Runs
- Jackson-Oak 3.8
- Coggins-Bal 3.6
- Pinson-KC 2.9
- Blair-Bal 2.8
- North-Oak 2.8

Fielding Runs-Infield
- Nettles-NY 20.3
- Doyle-Cal 17.8
- Grich-Bal 15.6
- Rodriguez-Det 15.0
- Bell-Cle 14.5

Fielding Runs-Outfield
- Evans-Bos 11.6
- North-Oak 11.4
- Maddox-NY 10.0
- Piniella-NY 9.3
- Jackson-Oak 6.2

Wins
- Jenkins-Tex 25
- Hunter-Oak 25

Winning Pct.
- Cuellar-Bal .688
- Jenkins-Tex .676
- Hunter-Oak .676
- Tiant-Bos .629

Complete Games
- Jenkins-Tex
- G.Perry-Cle
- Lolich-Det
- Ryan-Cal
- Tiant-Bos

Strikeouts
- Ryan-Cal 367
- Blyleven-Min 249
- Jenkins-Tex 225
- G.Perry-Cle 216
- Lolich-Det 202

Fewest BB/Game
- Jenkins-Tex 1.23
- Hunter-Oak 1.30
- Holtzman-Oak 1.80
- Kaat-Chi 2.04
- Wright-Mil 2.09

Games
- Fingers-Oak 76
- Murphy-Mil 70
- Foucault-Tex 69
- Lyle-NY 66
- Campbell-Min 63

Saves
- Forster-Chi 24
- Murphy-Mil 20
- Campbell-Min 19
- Buskey-NY-Cle 18
- Fingers-Oak 18

Base Runners/9
- Hunter-Oak 8.99
- Jenkins-Tex 9.29
- G.Perry-Cle 9.35
- Jackson-Bal 9.59
- Garland-Bal 9.59

Adjusted Relief Runs
- Murphy-Mil 24.2
- Lyle-NY 22.0
- Hiller-Det 18.4
- Foucault-Tex 17.4
- Campbell-Min 15.7

Relief Ranking
- Murphy-Mil
- Hiller-Det
- Lyle-NY
- Campbell-Min
- Foucault-Tex

Innings Pitched
- Ryan-Cal 332.2
- Jenkins-Tex 328.1
- G.Perry-Cle 322.1
- Wood-Chi 320.1
- Hunter-Oak 318.1

Opponents' Avg.
- Ryan-Cal .190
- G.Perry-Cle .204
- DalCanton-KC .211
- Hassler-Cal .225
- Hunter-Oak .229

Opponents' OBP
- Hunter-Oak .258
- Jenkins-Tex .262
- G.Perry-Cle .270
- Blyleven-Min .290
- Tiant-Bos .291

Earned Run Average
- Hunter-Oak 2.49
- G.Perry-Cle 2.51
- Hassler-Cal 2.61
- Blyleven-Min 2.66
- Fitzmorris-KC 2.79

Adjusted ERA
- G.Perry-Cle 145
- Blyleven-Min 141
- Fitzmorris-KC 137
- Hunter-Oak 134
- Hassler-Cal 133

Adjusted Starter Runs
- G.Perry-Cle 41.9
- Hunter-Oak 35.4
- Tiant-Bos 32.4
- Blyleven-Min 30.7
- Jenkins-Tex 28.4

Pitcher Wins
- **Murphy-Mil**
- **G.Perry-Cle**
- **Hiller-Det**
- **Hunter-Oak**
- **Blyleven-Min**

Sprinting to a Dynasty

Following the 1973 World Series, A's manager Dick Williams quit, unable to stomach capricious owner Charlie Finley. Under Alvin Dark, who'd worked for Finley back in the 1960s, the A's won their fourth consecutive AL West title. Catfish Hunter led an extraordinary staff and earned Cy Young honors. Four Oakland batters hit 20 or more homers. Oakland also brought Finley's long-standing speed obsession to fruition, using former Olympic sprinter Herb Washington 92 times as a pinch runner—he never batted or took the field.

Under new skipper Billy Martin, the Rangers leapt from last to second as Fergie Jenkins won 25 games and Jeff Burroughs was MVP. Nolan Ryan fanned 367 hitters for the last-place Angels, but he walked 202.

The Red Sox, leading by 8 games near the end of August, crumbled. Cozy Fenway Park disguised a mediocre offense, and Luis Tiant's heroics weren't enough. Meanwhile, Baltimore caught fire the last two weeks, rising from fourth at the beginning of September to win; the Birds captured 16 of their final 18. Mik[e] Cuellar and Dave McNally were a combined 10-0 with a su[b] 2.00 ERA in September.

New York finished second on strong pitching, althoug[h] shoulder troubles ended Mel Stottlemyre's career. Due to st[a]dium renovations, the Yankees played at Shea Stadium [in] 1974-75; the Yankees drew more people than they had in [a] decade. Milwaukee gave a job to 18-year-old rookie shortsto[p] Robin Yount, who stayed in the lineup until 1993. Detroi[t's] great era ended as Norm Cash and Al Kaline, who garnered h[is] 3,000th hit, retired.

Oakland wrapped up the ALCS in four, then edged L[os] Angeles in a competitive five-game World Series. Four of t[he] A's-Dodgers contests were decided by one run. It was Oaklan[d's] third straight Series crown, a feat unmatched since the 1951–[?] Yankees. Over the winter, though, Finley "forgot" a payment [on] Hunter's contract, and the pitcher was ruled a free agent.

1973 National League

TEAM	W	L	T	PCT	GB	HW	HL	R	OR	PA	H	2B	3B	HR	BB	SO	HB	SH	AVG	OBP	SLG	OPS	AOPS	BR	ABR	PF	SB	CS	BSA	BSR
EAST																														
NY	82	79	0	.509		43	38	608	588	6164	1345	198	24	85	540	805	23	108	.246	.315	.338	653	88	-82	-78	99	27	22	55	-2
STL	81	81	0	.500	1.5	43	38	643	603	6177	1418	240	35	75	531	796	29	89	.259	.325	.357	682	95	-23	-26	101	100	46	68	6
PIT	80	82	0	.494	2.5	41	40	704	693	6167	1465	257	44	154	432	842	27	60	.261	.315	.405	720	107	29	43	98	23	30	43	-5
MON	79	83	0	.488	3.5	43	38	668	702	6251	1345	190	23	125	695	777	44	115	.251	.340	.364	704	98	32	7	104	77	68	53	-7
CHI	77	84	0	.478	5	41	39	614	655	6070	1322	201	21	117	575	855	20	75	.247	.320	.357	677	87	-35	-79	108	65	68	53	-6
PHI	71	91	0	.438	11.5	38	43	642	717	6156	1381	218	29	134	476	979	33	56	.249	.310	.371	681	91	-41	-58	103	51	47	52	-5
WEST																														
CIN	99	63	0	.611		50	31	741	621	6304	1398	232	34	137	639	947	31	78	.254	.332	.383	715	109	46	78	96	148	55	73	13
LA	95	66	1	.590	3.5	50	31	675	565	6267	1473	219	29	110	497	795	28	81	.263	.323	.371	694	101	-6	17	97	109	50	69	6
SF	88	74	0	.543	11	47	34	739	702	6274	1452	219	52	161	590	913	35	75	.262	.335	.407	742	107	87	55	104	112	52	64	6
HOU	82	80	0	.506	17	41	40	681	672	6153	1391	216	35	134	469	962	33	83	.251	.312	.376	688	97	-30	-25	99	92	48	66	3
ATL	76	85	1	.472	22.5	40	40	799	774	6384	1497	216	29	206	608	870	34	65	.266	.339	.427	766	110	136	78	108	84	40	68	4
SD	60	102	0	.370	39	31	50	548	770	5985	1330	198	26	112	401	966	21	73	.244	.296	.351	647	92	-114	-67	92	88	36	71	7
TOT	971					508	462	8062		74352	16817	2600	386	1550	6453	10507	358	958	.254	.322	.376	698					976	552	64	22

TEAM	CG	SHO	GR	SV	IP	H	HR	BB	SO	BR/9	ERA	AERA	OAV	OOB	PR	APR	PF	OSB	OCS	FA	E	WPB	DP	FW	PW	BW	BSW	DIF
EAST																												
NY	47	15	194	40	1465.0	1345	127	490	1027	11.4	3.26	112	.245	.307	65	62	99	67	43	.980	126	46	140	1.1	6.5	-8.1	-.4	2.5
STL	42	14	264	36	1460.2	1366	105	486	867	11.6	3.25	113	.248	.310	66	67	100	74	53	.975	159	72	149	-.7	7.0	-2.7	.4	-4.0
PIT	26	11	284	44	1450.2	1426	110	564	839	12.6	3.73	94	.258	.329	-12	-37	96	84	39	.976	151	51	156	-.3	-3.9	4.5	-.7	-.7
MON	26	6	272	38	1451.2	1356	128	681	866	12.8	3.71	103	.250	.334	-9	15	104	76	50	.974	163	83	156	-.9	1.6	.7	-.9	-2.4
CHI	27	13	249	40	1437.2	1471	128	438	885	12.1	3.66	108	.267	.322	1	42	108	78	53	.975	157	54	155	-.7	4.4	-8.2	-.8	1.8
PHI	49	11	257	22	1447.1	1435	131	632	919	13.1	3.99	95	.263	.341	-53	-30	104	85	60	.979	134	80	179	.7	-3.1	-6.0	-.7	-.8
WEST																												
CIN	39	17	267	43	1473.0	1389	135	518	801	11.8	3.40	101	.252	.318	42	7	94	43	33	.982	115	49	162	1.8	.7	8.1	1.2	6.2
LA	45	15	212	38	1491.0	1270	129	461	961	10.6	3.00	116	.231	.292	109	83	95	74	36	.981	125	71	166	1.2	8.6	1.8	.4	2.4
SF	33	8	252	44	1452.1	1442	145	485	787	12.1	3.79	101	.257	.318	-21	8	105	103	34	.974	163	73	138	-.9	.8	5.7	.4	.9
HOU	45	14	268	26	1460.2	1389	111	575	907	12.3	3.75	97	.252	.323	-14	-18	99	102	43	.974	116	67	140	1.7	-1.9	-2.6	.1	3.6
ATL	34	9	287	35	1462.0	1467	144	575	803	12.7	4.25	93	.263	.332	-95	-44	108	119	60	.974	166	75	142	-1.1	-4.6	8.1	.2	-7.2
SD	34	10	269	23	1430.0	1461	157	548	845	12.8	4.16	84	.267	.334	-79	-108	96	84	44	.973	170	67	152	-1.3	-11.2	-7.0	.5	-2.0
TOT	447	143	3075	429	17482.0					12.2	3.66		.254	.322						.977	1745	788	1835					

Leaders

Batter-Fielder Wins		Batting Average		On-Base Percentage	
Morgan-Cin	7.4	Rose-Cin	338	Singleton-Mon	425
Evans-Atl	6.3	Cedeno-Hou	320	Fairly-Mon	422
Stargell-Pit	5.7	Maddox-SF	319	Morgan-Cin	406
Cedeno-Hou	4.6	Perez-Cin	314	Watson-Hou	403
Ferguson-LA	3.9	Watson-Hou	312	Evans-Atl	403

Slugging Average		On-Base Plus Slugging		Adjusted OPS		Adjusted Batter Runs	
Stargell-Pit	646	Stargell-Pit	1038	Stargell-Pit	187	Stargell-Pit	62.5
Evans-Atl	556	Evans-Atl	959	Perez-Cin	160	Morgan-Cin	48.9
Johnson-Atl	546	Perez-Cin	919	Morgan-Cin	155	Perez-Cin	47.5
Cedeno-Hou	537	Johnson-Atl	916	Evans-Atl	153	Evans-Atl	46.4
Bonds-SF	530	Cedeno-Hou	913	Cedeno-Hou	152	Singleton-Mon	42.2

Runs		Hits		Doubles		Triples		Home Runs		Total Bases		Runs Batted In	
Bonds-SF	131	Rose-Cin	230	Stargell-Pit	43	Metzger-Hou	14	Stargell-Pit	44	Bonds-SF	341	Stargell-Pit	119
Morgan-Cin	116	Garr-Atl	200	Oliver-Pit	38	Matthews-SF	10	Johnson-Atl	43	Stargell-Pit	337	May-Hou	105
Rose-Cin	115	Brock-StL	193	Staub-NY	36	Maddox-SF	10	Evans-Atl	41	Evans-Atl	331	Bench-Cin	104
Evans-Atl	114	Simmons-StL	192	Simmons-StL	36	Davis-LA	9	Aaron-Atl	40	Johnson-Atl	305	Evans-Atl	104
Brock-StL	110	Oliver-Pit	191	Rose-Cin	36			Bonds-SF	39	Oliver-Pit	303	Singleton-Mon	103

Stolen Bases		Base Stealing Runs		Fielding Runs-Infield		Fielding Runs-Outfield		Wins		Winning Pct.		Complete Games	
Brock-StL	70	Morgan-Cin	9.5	Kessinger-Chi	26.7	Unser-Phi	14.3	Bryant-SF	24	John-LA	696	Seaver-NY	18
Morgan-Cin	67	Brock-StL	8.4	Foli-Mon	18.3	Rose-Cin	7.6	Seaver-NY	19	Gullett-Cin	692	Carlton-Phi	18
Cedeno-Hou	56	Cedeno-Hou	7.1	Schmidt-Phi	18.1	Williams-Chi	6.3	Billingham-Cin	19	Bryant-SF	667	Billingham-Cin	16
Bonds-SF	43	Baker-Atl	4.2	Evans-Atl	17.2	Bonds-SF	5.9	Sutton-LA	18	Seaver-NY	655		
Lopes-LA	36	Garr-Atl	3.8	Stennett-Pit	16.5	Cedeno-Hou	5.5	Gullett-Cin	18	Billingham-Cin	655		

Strikeouts		Fewest BB/Game		Games		Saves		Base Runners/9		Adjusted Relief Runs		Relief Ranking	
Seaver-NY	251	Marichal-SF	1.61	Marshall-Mon	92	Marshall-Mon	31	Seaver-NY	8.91	Marshall-Mon	22.0	Marshall-Mon	35.4
Carlton-Phi	223	Jenkins-Chi	1.89	Borbon-Cin	80	McGraw-NY	25	Sutton-LA	9.02	Borbon-Cin	18.0	Borbon-Cin	24.4
Matlack-NY	205	Barr-SF	1.91	Sosa-SF	71	Giusti-Pit	20	Rogers-Mon	9.60	Moffitt-SF	15.6	Locker-Chi	21.8
Sutton-LA	200	Sutton-LA	1.97	Giusti-Pit	67	Brewer-LA	20	R.Hernandez-Pit	10.04	Locker-Chi	12.8	Giusti-Pit	17.9
		Seaver-NY	1.99	Segui-StL	65			Messersmith-LA	10.06	Giusti-Pit	12.6	Moffitt-SF	15.6

Innings Pitched		Opponents' Avg.		Opponents' OBP		Earned Run Average		Adjusted ERA		Adjusted Starter Runs		Pitcher Wins	
Carlton-Phi	293.1	Seaver-NY	206	Seaver-NY	252	Seaver-NY	2.08	Seaver-NY	175	Seaver-NY	50.8	Seaver-NY	5.5
Billingham-Cin	293.1	Sutton-LA	209	Sutton-LA	257	Sutton-LA	2.42	Twitchell-Phi	152	Rogers-Mon	32.1	Marshall-Mon	4.1
Seaver-NY	290.0	Wilson-Mon	213	Messersmith-LA	278	Twitchell-Phi	2.50	Sutton-LA	144	Sutton-LA	32.0	Rogers-Mon	3.8
Reuss-Hou	279.1	Messersmith-LA	214	Gibson-StL	281	Marshall-Mon	2.66	Marshall-Mon	143	Twitchell-Phi	30.5	Renko-Mon	3.5
Jenkins-Chi	271.0	Renko-Mon	218	Briles-Pit	287	Messersmith-LA	2.70	Renko-Mon	136	Renko-Mon	25.6	Sutton-LA	3.2

Power of Belief

The Dodgers cruised along atop the NL West through August, but they picked the wrong time to slump. Cincinnati, barely over .500 through June, had two separate seven-game September win streaks as Los Angeles' pitching rusted down the stretch. The Reds scraped out the division title with just four good hitters; MVP Pete Rose and Joe Morgan again did the heavy lifting.

Dave Winfield joined the Padres without visiting the minors, while Dave Parker debuted in Pittsburgh and Ken Griffey with Cincinnati. The Expos' Mike Marshall was the league's most discussed pitcher, setting a new record with 92 appearances, winning 14, and saving 31. But the biggest number of the year was 713—Henry Aaron's end-of-season career home run total.

The NL East had a nutty race. As no team seemed to be able to clear .500, everyone but Philadelphia had a chance to win in the last week. The Cubs blew a big lead in July; the Cardinals surged ahead in August but fell back. New York sputtered until late August when they won 19 of 26, moving from last to first in 27 days. On September 23 just 2½ separated the front-running Mets from the fifth-place Cubs.

Despite challenges from St. Louis and Pittsburgh, the Mets clinched the day after the season's scheduled ending—thanks to a rainout—as Tom Seaver won in Chicago. New York finished with the lowest winning percentage ever for a champion (.509). Seaver took his second Cy Young in a close vote, while Rusty Staub headed a mediocre offense.

The underdog Mets (slogan: "Ya Gotta Believe!") then took out the favored Reds in a five-game NLCS. Cincinnati won 2-1 twice, but New York won three blowouts, two behind Seaver—shortstop Bud Harrelson did lose a one-sided brawl with Rose. In the World Series, New York fell in seven, with Willie Mays, now a Mets reserve, playing for the last time in the major leagues.

1973 American League

TEAM	W	L	T	PCT	GB	HW	HL	R	OR	PA	H	2B	3B	HR	BB	SO	HB	SH	AVG	OBP	SLG	OPS	AOPS	BR	ABR	PF	SB	CS	BSA	BSR
EAST																														
BAL	97	65	0	.599		**50**	31	754	**561**	6335	1474	229	48	119	648	752	43	58	.266	**.345**	.389	734	105	**63**	59	101	**146**	64	70	10
BOS	89	73	0	.549	8	48	33	738	647	6223	1472	235	30	147	581	799	31	54	.267	.338	**.401**	739	101	60	17	106	114	45	**72**	9
DET	85	77	0	.525	12	47	34	642	674	6135	1400	213	32	157	509	722	39	48	.254	.320	.390	710	93	-10	-51	107	28	30	48	-4
NY	80	82	0	.494	17	**50**	31	641	610	6064	1435	212	17	131	489	**680**	22	27	.261	.322	.378	700	99	-25	-10	98	47	43	52	-5
MIL	74	88	0	.457	23	40	41	708	731	6227	1399	229	40	145	563	977	42	61	.253	.325	.388	713	101	2	11	99	110	66	63	1
CLE	71	91	0	.438	26	34	47	680	826	6178	1429	205	29	**158**	471	793	32	40	.256	.315	.387	702	95	-30	-44	102	60	68	47	-11
WEST																														
OAK	94	68	0	.580		**50**	31	**758**	615	6257	1431	216	28	147	595	919	35	**67**	.260	.333	.389	722	**108**	29	**63**	96	**128**	57	69	8
KC	88	74	0	.543	6	48	33	755	752	6274	1440	239	40	114	644	696	26	34	**.270**	.342	.393	735	102	58	26	104	87	46	65	3
MIN	81	81	0	.500	13	37	44	738	692	6331	**1521**	**240**	14	120	598	954	34	34	.270	.342	.388	722	100	6	5	93	59	47	56	-3
CAL	79	83	0	.488	15	43	38	629	657	6153	1395	183	29	93	509	816	34	60	.253	.318	.348	666	93	-87	-43	93	83	73	53	-7
CHI	77	85	0	.475	17	40	41	652	705	6135	1400	228	38	111	537	952	32	45	.255	.318	.361	679	94	-28	-51	96	91	53	63	-7
TEX	57	105	0	.352	37	35	46	619	844	6113	1397	195	29	110	503	791	27	45	.259	.328	.381	710		-65	-42	96				
TOT	972					522	450	8314		74425	17193	2624	404	1552	6647	9851	397	592	.259	.328	.381	710					1058	661	62	1

TEAM	CG	SHO	GR	SV	IP	H	HR	BB	SO	BR/9	ERA	AERA	OAV	OOB	PR	APR	PF	OSB	OCS	FA	E	WPB	DP	FW	PW	BW	BSW	DIF
EAST																												
BAL	67	14	140	26	1461.2	**1297**	124	475	715	11.0	3.07	123	.240	.302	122	116	99	70	54	.981	119	43	184	1.3	**11.9**	6.0	**1.0**	-4.2
BOS	67	10	144	33	1440.1	1417	158	499	808	12.2	3.65	110	.259	.323	27	57	105	72	45	.979	127	30	162	.8	5.8	-5.2	-.4	5.0
DET	39	11	211	**46**	1447.2	1468	154	493	911	12.4	3.90	105	.265	.326	-13	29	107	107	71	.982	112	58	144	1.7	3.0	-1.0	-.5	4.7
NY	47	16	143	39	1427.2	1379	109	**457**	708	11.7	3.34	111	.254	.313	75	59	97	61	52	.976	145	66	167	-.2	-3.0	1.1	.0	-5.1
MIL	50	11	217	28	1454.0	1476	119	623	671	13.2	3.98	95	.265	.340	-27	-29	100	81	**73**	.977	139	114	174	.2	-10.2	-4.5	-1.1	5.7
CLE	55	9	206	21	1464.2	1532	172	602	883	13.4	4.58	86	.271	.343	-125	-100	104	109	47	.978	156	54	172	-.8	6.0	-1.0	-.5	5.7
WEST																												
OAK	46	16	203	41	1457.1	1311	143	494	797	11.3	3.29	108	.241	.305	86	47	93	**54**	60	.978	137	61	170	.3	4.8	**6.4**	.8	.7
KC	40	7	213	41	1449.1	1521	114	617	790	13.5	4.19	98	.273	.346	-60	-13	108	86	49	.974	167	51	**192**	-1.4	-1.3	-1.8	-.1	11.7
MIN	48	**18**	190	34	1451.2	1443	115	519	879	12.4	3.77	105	.259	.324	7	30	104	93	54	.978	139	80	147	.2	3.1	2.7	.3	-6.2
CAL	**72**	13	164	19	1456.1	1351	**104**	614	**1010**	12.4	3.53	101	.246	.324	46	8	94	105	40	.975	156	72	153	-.8	.8	-4.4	-.3	2.7
CHI	48	15	176	35	1456.0	1484	110	574	848	13.0	3.86	102	.266	.336	-8	13	104	110	57	.977	161	70	164	-1.1	-14.6	-4.3	-.7	-4.1
TEX	35	10	**241**	27	1430.0	1514	130	680	831	14.1	4.64	81	.273	.353	-131	-143	98	109	58	.974	144	71	165	-.1	1.3	-5.2	-.7	.7
TOT	614	150	2248	390	17396.2					12.5	3.82		.259	.328						.977	1702	770	1994					

Leaders

Batter-Fielder Wins
Carew-Min 5.8
Grich-Bal 5.4
Munson-NY 4.9
Jackson-Oak 4.1
Patek-KC 4.1

Batting Average
Carew-Min 350
Scott-Mil 306
Davis-Bal 306
Murcer-NY 304
May-Mil 303

On-Base Percentage
Mayberry-KC 417
Carew-Min 411
Yastrzemski-Bos ..407
Tenace-Oak 387
Jackson-Oak 383

Slugging Average
Jackson-Oak 531
Bando-Oak 498
Robinson-Cal 489
Scott-Mil 488
Munson-NY 487

On-Base Plus Slugging
Jackson-Oak 914
Mayberry-KC 895
Carew-Min 881
Bando-Oak 873
Yastrzemski-Bos ..870

Adjusted OPS
Jackson-Oak 164
Robinson-Cal 152
Bando-Oak 152
Carew-Min 143
Scott-Mil 142

Adjusted Batter Runs
Jackson-Oak 46.9
Bando-Oak 41.9
Robinson-Cal 39.2
Mayberry-KC 34.5
Carew-Min 34.4

Runs
Jackson-Oak 99
Scott-Mil 98
North-Oak 98
Carew-Min 98
Bando-Oak 97

Hits
Carew-Min 203
May-Mil 189
Murcer-NY 187
Scott-Mil 185
Johnson-Tex 179

Doubles
Garcia-Mil 32
Bando-Oak 32
Scott-Mil 30
Chambliss-Cle 30
Carew-Min 30

Triples
Carew-Min 11
Bumbry-Bal 11
Orta-Chi 10
Coggins-Bal 9
Coluccio-Mil 8

Home Runs
Jackson-Oak 32
Robinson-Cal 30
Burroughs-Tex 30
Bando-Oak 29

Total Bases
Scott-Mil 295
May-Mil 295
Bando-Oak 295
Murcer-NY 286
Jackson-Oak 286

Runs Batted In
Jackson-Oak 117
Scott-Mil 107
Mayberry-KC 100
Bando-Oak 98
Robinson-Cal 97

Stolen Bases
Harper-Bos 54
North-Oak 53
Nelson-Tex 43
Carew-Min 41
Patek-KC 36

Base Stealing Runs
Harper-Bos 7.0
North-Oak 4.7
Campaneris-Oak ...4.0
Baylor-Bal 3.9
Nelson-Tex 3.9

Fielding Runs-Infield
Patek-KC 39.8
Nettles-NY 32.7
Bell-Cle 27.2
Grich-Bal 26.8
Clarke-NY 16.2

Fielding Runs-Outfield
North-Oak 15.4
Burroughs-Tex 9.7
Coluccio-Mil 8.4
Blair-Bal 5.6
Stanley-Det 4.9

Wins
Wood-Chi 24
Coleman-Det 23
Palmer-Bal 22

Winning Pct.
Hunter-Oak 808
Palmer-Bal 710
Blue-Oak 690
Splittorff-KC 645
Colborn-Mil 625

Complete Games
Perry-Cle 26
Ryan-Cal 26
Blyleven-Min 25
Tiant-Bos 25
Colborn-Mil 22

Strikeouts
Ryan-Cal 383
Blyleven-Min 258
Singer-Cal 241
Perry-Cle 238
Lolich-Det 214

Fewest BB/Game
Kaat-Min-Chi 1.73
Blyleven-Min 1.86
Holtzman-Oak 2.00
Wood-Chi 2.28
Lolich-Det 2.30

Games
Hiller-Det 65
Fingers-Oak 62
Bird-KC 54
Knowles-Oak 52

Saves
Hiller-Det 38
Lyle-NY 27
Fingers-Oak 22
Bird-KC 20
Acosta-Chi 18

Base Runners/9
Jackson-Bal 8.74
Lyle-NY 9.18
Hiller-Det 9.19
Beene-NY 9.40
Reynolds-Bal 9.65

Earned Run Average
Palmer-Bal 2.40
Blyleven-Min 2.52
Lee-Bos 2.75
Ryan-Cal 2.87
Medich-NY 2.95

Adjusted ERA
Blyleven-Min 158
Palmer-Bal 157
Lee-Bos 146
Medich-NY 126
Ryan-Cal 125

Adjusted Relief Runs
Hiller-Det 34.8
Reynolds-Bal 22.8
Fingers-Oak 20.3
Jackson-Bal 17.4
Acosta-Chi 16.8

Relief Ranking
Hiller-Det 61.1
Acosta-Chi 31.9
Fingers-Oak 29.5
Reynolds-Bal 26.3
Jackson-Bal 19.9

Innings Pitched
Wood-Chi 359.1
Perry-Cle 344.0
Ryan-Cal 326.0
Blyleven-Min 325.0
Singer-Cal 315.2

Opponents' Avg.
Bibby-Tex 192
Ryan-Cal 203
Palmer-Bal 211
Tiant-Bos 219
Blue-Oak 224

Opponents' OBP
Tiant-Bos 278
Hunter-Oak 282
Blyleven-Min 284
Holtzman-Oak 286
Palmer-Bal 288

Adjusted Starter Runs
Blyleven-Min 48.2
Palmer-Bal 47.0
Lee-Bos 36.7
Ryan-Cal 30.0
Holtzman-Oak 23.1

Pitcher Wins
Hiller-Det 6.7
Blyleven-Min 5.3
Palmer-Bal 4.8
Lee-Bos 3.6
Acosta-Chi 3.3

All A's Again

With the AL adopting the designated hitter, scoring increased 23 percent, the biggest rise since 1911. Perhaps not coincidentally, attendance leapt to a new all-time high. Oakland took the AL West lead in July. When the Royals made a run in August, the A's responded, winning 13 of 14. Reggie Jackson won his only MVP, and four teammates scored 89 or more runs while three starters won 20.

Kansas City's new stadium sported artificial turf and a much smaller outfield, which helped center fielder Amos Otis develop. In addition, the Royals debuted George Brett and Frank White. California's Nolan Ryan, an overpowering pitcher in a great pitcher's park, threw his first two no-hitters and set an all-time mark with 383 strikeouts.

With an offense that appeared unprepossessing but was quite effective, Baltimore won 14 straight in August to break open a tough AL East race with Boston and Detroit. Jim Palmer was the Cy Young winner, as again Earl Weaver let hi[s] starters finish their business. Detroit's John Hiller saved 38, setting a record that lasted until 1983, but the aging Tigers were slowing up. Boston and Luis Aparicio parted ways in a post season salary dispute, ending the 39-year-old's career.

Four of the five ALCS games were close, but Catfish Hunter came through with a Game 5 shutout (his second win of the series) to send Oakland to the World Series. Despite being outhit, outscored, and outpitched by the Mets, Oakland won the Series in seven. Two games went extra innings and there was much human drama. New York's Rusty Staub played right field with a dead arm, Oakland owner Charlie Finley forced Mike Andrews off the roster after 2 errors, and Willie Mays ended his career. Darold Knowles, the only pitcher to appear in seven games, and Rollie Fingers pitched 20 innings of relief between them, allowing the Mets 1 run.

1972 National League

TEAM	W	L	T	PCT	GB	HW	HL	R	OR	PA	H	2B	3B	HR	BB	SO	HB	SH	AVG	OBP	SLG	OPS	AOPS	BR	ABR	PF	SB	CS	BSA	BSR
EAST																														
PIT	96	59	0	.619		49	29	691	512	6021	1505	251	47	110	404	871	25	52	.274	.324	.397	721	113	75	85	99	49	30	62	0
CHI	85	70	1	.548	11	46	31	685	567	5950	1346	206	40	133	565	815	28	67	.257	.330	.387	717	99	76	9	111	69	47	59	-1
NY	83	73	0	.532	13.5	41	37	528	578	5883	1154	175	31	105	589	990	34	86	.225	.307	.332	639	89	-67	-58	98	41	41	50	-5
STL	75	81	0	.481	21.5	40	37	568	600	5884	1383	214	42	70	437	793	27	58	.260	.317	.355	672	98	-14	-10	99	104	48	68	6
MON	70	86	0	.449	26.5	35	43	513	609	5817	1205	156	22	91	474	828	49	69	.234	.303	.344	646	88	-94	-103	102	68	66	51	-8
PHI	59	97	0	.378	37.5	28	51	503	635	5862	1240	200	36	98	487	930	22	69	.236	.302	.344	646	88	-66	-80	103	42	50	46	-8
WEST																														
CIN	95	59	0	.617		42	34	707	557	6003	1317	214	44	124	606	914	37	65	.251	.330	.380	710	113	70	105	95	140	63	69	9
HOU	84	69	0	.549	10.5	41	34	708	636	5936	1359	233	38	134	524	907	32	62	.258	.326	.393	719	114	78	99	97	111	56	66	5
LA	85	70	0	.548	10.5	41	34	584	527	5903	1349	178	39	98	480	786	24	89	.256	.319	.360	679	101	-1	8	99	82	39	68	4
ATL	70	84	1	.455	25	36	41	628	730	5938	1363	186	17	144	532	770	35	55	.258	.328	.382	710	99	62	8	109	47	35	57	-2
SF	69	86	0	.445	26.5	34	43	662	649	5858	1281	211	36	150	484	964	30	64	.244	.309	.384	693	101	18	8	102	123	45	73	11
SD	58	95	0	.379	36.5	26	54	488	665	5750	1181	168	38	102	407	976	15	90	.227	.283	.332	615	86	-135	-100	93	78	46	63	1
TOT	930					459	470	7265		70805	15683	2392	430	1359	5985	10544	358	865	.248	.315	.365	680					954	566	63	12

TEAM	CG	SHO	GR	SV	IP	H	HR	BB	SO	BR/9	ERA	AERA	OAV	OOB	PR	APR	PF	OSB	OCS	FA	E	WPB	DP	FW	PW	BW	BSW	DIF
EAST																												
PIT	39	15	205	48	1414.1	1282	90	433	838	11.1	2.81	118	.243	.302	102	84	96	54	41	.978	136	40	171	-.0	9.0	9.1	-.1	.5
CHI	54	19	197	32	1398.2	1329	112	421	824	11.5	3.22	118	.251	.309	37	83	110	95	46	.979	132	44	148	.2	8.9	1.0	-.2	-2.4
NY	32	12	207	41	1414.2	1263	118	486	1059	11.3	3.26	104	.240	.306	30	19	98	60	61	.980	116	60	122	1.1	2.0	-6.2	-.6	8.8
STL	64	13	216	13	1399.2	1290	87	531	912	11.8	3.42	100	.247	.317	5	1	99	91	55	.977	141	71	146	-.3	.1	-1.1	.5	-2.3
MON	39	11	217	23	1401.1	1281	103	579	888	12.1	3.59	99	.245	.321	-21	-5	103	73	67	.978	134	58	141	.0	-.5	-11.1	-1.0	4.5
PHI	43	13	263	15	1400.0	1318	117	536	927	12.1	3.66	98	.251	.321	-33	-9	104	87	45	.981	116	66	142	1.1	-1.0	-8.6	-1.0	-9.5
WEST																												
CIN	25	15	239	60	1412.2	1313	129	435	806	11.3	3.21	101	.247	.305	38	5	94	31	40	.982	110	47	143	1.3	.5	11.3	.4	4.0
HOU	38	14	245	31	1385.1	1340	114	498	971	12.2	3.77	89	.256	.323	-48	-65	97	99	37	.980	116	75	151	.9	-7.0	10.6	.4	2.5
LA	50	23	176	29	1403.0	1196	83	429	856	10.6	2.78	120	.230	.291	104	91	97	79	37	.974	162	55	145	-1.5	9.8	.9	.3	-2.0
ATL	40	4	220	27	1377.0	1412	155	512	732	12.7	4.27	89	.266	.331	-126	-66	110	96	37	.974	162	105	130	-1.1	-7.1	.9	-.3	.7
SF	44	8	219	23	1386.1	1309	130	507	771	12.0	3.69	95	.250	.318	-37	-30	101	87	53	.974	156	105	130	-1.1	-3.2	.9	1.1	-6.1
SD	39	17	270	19	1403.2	1350	121	618	960	12.9	3.78	88	.255	.334	-50	-76	96	98	46	.976	144	75	146	-.6	-8.2	-10.8	.0	1.0
TOT	507	164	2674	361	16796.2					11.8	3.45		.248	.315						.978	1619	759	1706					
										11.8	3.45		.248	.315						.978								

Batter-Fielder Wins
Bench-Cin 6.5
Morgan-Cin 5.8
Cedeno-Hou 5.3
Santo-Chi 3.9
Williams-Chi 3.8

Batting Average
Williams-Chi 333
Garr-Atl 325
Baker-Atl 321
Cedeno-Hou 320
Watson-Hou 312

On-Base Percentage
Morgan-Cin 417
Williams-Chi 398
Santo-Chi 391
Aaron-Atl 390
Wynn-Hou 389

Slugging Average
Williams-Chi 606
Stargell-Pit 558
Bench-Cin 541
Cedeno-Hou 537
Aaron-Atl 514

On-Base Plus Slugging
Williams-Chi 1005
Stargell-Pit 930
Cedeno-Hou 921
Bench-Cin 920
Aaron-Atl 904

Adjusted OPS
Bench-Cin 169
Williams-Chi 165
Cedeno-Hou 165
Stargell-Pit 165
Hebner-Pit 153

Adjusted Batter Runs
Bench-Cin 50.8
Williams-Chi 49.6
Cedeno-Hou 47.3
Morgan-Cin 44.1
Stargell-Pit 42.1

Runs
Morgan-Cin 122
Bonds-SF 118
Wynn-Hou 117
Rose-Cin 107
Cedeno-Hou 103

Hits
Rose-Cin 198
Brock-StL 193
Williams-Chi 191
Simmons-StL 180
Garr-Atl 180

Doubles
Montanez-Phi 39
Cedeno-Hou 39
Simmons-StL 36
Williams-Chi 34

Triples
Bowa-Phi 13
Rose-Cin 11
Sanguillen-Pit 8
Cedeno-Hou 8
Brock-StL 8

Home Runs
Bench-Cin 40
Colbert-SD 38
Williams-Chi 37
Aaron-Atl 34
Stargell-Pit 33

Total Bases
Williams-Chi 348
Cedeno-Hou 300
Bench-Cin 291
May-Hou 290
Colbert-SD 286

Runs Batted In
Bench-Cin 125
Williams-Chi 122
Stargell-Pit 112
Colbert-SD 111
May-Hou 98

Stolen Bases
Brock-StL 63
Morgan-Cin 58
Cedeno-Hou 55
Bonds-SF 44
Tolan-Cin 42

Base Stealing Runs
Bonds-SF 7.6
Brock-StL 7.6
Morgan-Cin 6.8
Cedeno-Hou 4.8
Hernandez-SD 4.2

Fielding Runs-Infield
Helms-Hou 28.8
Foli-Mon 18.4
Rader-Hou 16.7
Kessinger-Chi 16.7
Santo-Chi 14.6

Fielding Runs-Outfield
Baker-Atl 12.3
Rose-Cin 9.9
Henderson-SF 8.5
Montanez-Phi 8.1
Lum-Atl 5.6

Wins
Carlton-Phi 27
Seaver-NY 21
Osteen-LA 20
Jenkins-Chi 20

Winning Pct.
Nolan-Cin 750
Carlton-Phi 730
Pappas-Chi 708
Blass-Pit 704
Ellis-Pit 682

Complete Games
Carlton-Phi 30
Jenkins-Chi 23
Gibson-StL 23
Wise-StL 20
Sutton-LA 18

Strikeouts
Carlton-Phi 310
Seaver-NY 249
Gibson-StL 208
Sutton-LA 207
Jenkins-Chi 184

Fewest BB/Game
Pappas-Chi 1.34
Nolan-Cin 1.53
Niekro-Atl 1.69
Ellis-Pit 1.82
Moose-Pit 1.87

Games
Marshall-Mon 65
Carroll-Cin 65
Borbon-Cin 62
Ross-SD 60

Saves
Carroll 37
McGraw-NY 27
Giusti-Pit 22
Marshall-Mon 18

Base Runners/9
Brewer-LA 7.81
Sutton-LA 8.35
Carlton-Phi 8.97
Willoughby-SF 9.03
Nolan-Cin 9.10

Adjusted Relief Runs
Marshall-Mon 21.8
McGraw-NY 18.7
Brewer-LA 17.6
R.Hernandez-Pit 13.8
Giusti-Pit 12.3

Relief Ranking
Marshall-Mon 43.6
Brewer-LA 35.3
McGraw-NY 33.0
Giusti-Pit 24.4
Carroll-Cin 19.9

Innings Pitched
Carlton-Phi 346.1
Jenkins-Chi 289.1
Niekro-Atl 282.1
Gibson-StL 278.0
Sutton-LA 272.2

Opponents' Avg.
Sutton-LA 189
Carlton-Phi 206
Gibson-StL 224
Seaver-NY 224
Bryant-SF 224

Opponents' OBP
Sutton-LA 240
Carlton-Phi 257
Nolan-Cin 259
Niekro-Atl 274
McAndrew-NY 276

Earned Run Average
Carlton-Phi 1.97
Nolan-Cin 1.99
Sutton-LA 2.08
Matlack-NY 2.32
Gibson-StL 2.46

Adjusted ERA
Carlton-Phi 183
Nolan-Cin 163
Sutton-LA 161
Matlack-NY 146
Gibson-StL 139

Adjusted Starter Runs
Carlton-Phi 60.4
Sutton-LA 39.2
Gibson-StL 31.3
Matlack-NY 25.7
Blass-Pit 24.1

Pitcher Wins
Carlton-Phi 7.4
Marshall-Mon 4.9
Gibson-StL 4.4
Osteen-LA 4.2
Brewer-LA 4.1

Best Pitcher on the Worst Team

Prior to the season, the penny-pinching Cardinals sent Steve Carlton to the Phillies for Rick Wise. In addition to completing St. Louis' post-1968 destruction, the deal also helped Philadelphia build a powerhouse. Carlton was 27-10 for a horrible Phillies club in 1972, earning Cy Young honors and finishing fifth in MVP voting. Future Phils debuting around Lefty included Bob Boone and Mike Schmidt; Greg Luzinski hit 18 homers in his first year as a regular.

There was doubt, however, that the season would begin. For the first time, players went on strike, wiping out the first 12 days of the season. Mets manager Gil Hodges died of a heart attack during spring training; Yogi Berra took charge of the club. Chicago's Billy Williams finished second in MVP voting in both 1970 and 1972, but the Cubs couldn't catch the Pirates either year. The '72 Bucs boasted deep pitching and seven regulars who hit at least .280.

The Reds pulled away from surprising Houston in July and coasted to a division crown. Johnny Bench again was MVP, with Clay Carroll saving an all-time record 37. Pete Rose and new acquisition Joe Morgan set the table like perhaps no other combination in history.

Pittsburgh and Cincinnati traded wins through the first four NLCS contests. In Game 5, with Cincinnati down 3-2 in the last of the ninth, Bench led off with a game-tying homer; two outs and two singles later, Bob Moose's wild pitch gave the game—and pennant—to the Reds. Cincinnati was denied again in the World Series, however, as Oakland won a tight Series in seven.

Following the season, Bill Mazeroski, Hoyt Wilhelm, and Maury Wills retired. Pie Traynor, Jackie Robinson, and Gabby Hartnett passed away. The most shocking death of the year, however, was that of Roberto Clemente, lost in a December 31 air crash en route to earthquake-torn Nicaragua. Clemente had collected his 3,000th and final hit on September 30.

1972 American League

TEAM	W	L	T	PCT	GB	HW	HL	R	OR	PA	H	2B	3B	HR	BB	SO	HB	SH	AVG	OBP	SLG	OPS	AOPS	BR	ABR	PF	SB	CS	BSA	BSR
EAST																														
DET	86	70	0	.551		44	34	558	514	5721	1206	179	32	122	483	793	31	74	.237	.305	.356	661	99	17	-2	104	17	21	45	-4
BOS	85	70	0	.548	0.5	52	26	**640**	620	5871	1289	**229**	34	124	522	858	37	56	.248	.318	.376	**694**	107	**86**	51	106	66	30	**69**	4
BAL	80	74	0	.519	5	38	39	519	**430**	5676	1153	193	29	100	507	935	36	65	.229	.302	.339	641	93	-11	-31	104	78	41	66	3
NY	79	76	0	.510	6.5	46	31	557	527	5793	1288	201	24	103	491	**689**	29	74	.249	.316	.357	673	109	47	60	98	71	42	63	1
CLE	72	84	0	.462	14	43	34	472	519	5769	1220	187	18	91	420	762	26	83	.234	.293	.330	623	88	-55	-72	104	49	53	48	-8
MIL	65	91	0	.417	21	37	42	493	595	5733	1204	167	22	88	472	868	29	78	.235	.302	.328	630	96	-36	-27	98	64	57	53	-6
WEST																														
OAK	93	62	0	.600		48	29	604	457	5846	1248	195	29	**134**	463	886	**47**	**100**	.240	.306	.366	672	**111**	37	66	95	87	48	64	**2**
CHI	87	67	0	.565	5.5	**55**	23	566	538	5721	1208	170	28	108	511	991	34	68	.238	.310	.346	656	100	14	3	102	100	52	66	**4**
MIN	77	77	0	.500	15.5	42	32	537	535	5848	1277	182	31	93	478	905	35	73	.244	.310	.344	654	96	8	-18	105	53	41	56	-3
KC	76	78	0	.494	16.5	44	33	580	545	5845	1249	220	26	78	**534**	711	34	72	**.255**	**.327**	.353	680	110	68	**71**	100	85	44	66	3
CAL	75	80	0	.484	18	44	36	454	533	5639	1249	171	26	78	358	850	25	66	.242	.293	.330	623	96	-59	-33	95	57	37	61	0
TEX	54	100	0	.351	38.5	31	46	461	628	5680	1092	166	17	56	503	926	30	84	.217	.290	.290	580	82	-115	-101	97	**126**	73	63	2
TOT	929					524	405	6441		69142	14751	2260	316	1175	5742	10174	393	893	.239	.306	.343	649					853	539	61	-1

TEAM	CG	SHO	GR	SV	IP	H	HR	BB	SO	BR/9	ERA	AERA	OAV	OOB	PR	APR	PF	OSB	OCS	FA	E	WPB	DP	FW	PW	BW	BSW	DIF
EAST																												
DET	46	11	248	33	1388.1	1212	101	465	952	11.2	2.96	107	.236	.304	15	30	103	87	46	**.984**	96	55	137	**1.9**	3.4	-.2	-.4	3.3
BOS	48	20	216	25	1382.2	1309	101	512	918	12.1	3.47	93	.251	.321	-63	-35	106	66	40	.978	130	42	141	-.0	-4.0	5.8	**.5**	5.3
BAL	**62**	20	167	21	1371.2	1116	**85**	395	788	10.0	**2.53**	123	.224	**.282**	81	86	102	44	44	.983	100	41	150	1.6	**9.8**	-3.5	.1	-5.2
NY	35	19	188	39	1373.1	1306	87	419	625	11.5	3.05	98	.252	.310	2	-10	97	**42**	34	.978	134	57	**179**	-.3	-1.1	6.8	.1	-4.0
CLE	47	13	255	25	1410.0	1232	123	534	846	11.5	2.92	111	.237	.311	23	49	106	66	43	.981	116	59	157	.8	5.6	-8.2	-.9	-3.3
MIL	37	14	216	32	1391.2	1289	116	486	740	11.7	3.45	88	.247	.312	-61	-62	100	65	43	.977	139	51	145	-.5	-7.0	-3.1	-.7	-1.7
WEST																												
OAK	42	**23**	236	**43**	1417.2	1170	96	418	862	10.2	2.58	110	.226	.284	76	45	93	72	38	.979	130	42	146	-.0	5.1	7.5	.2	2.7
CHI	36	14	248	42	1385.1	1269	94	431	936	11.2	3.12	100	.245	.305	-9	-1	102	75	**60**	.977	135	70	136	-.4	-.1	.3	**.5**	9.4
MIN	37	17	203	34	1399.1	1188	105	444	838	10.7	2.84	113	.230	.294	35	54	105	69	48	.974	159	**33**	146	-1.8	6.1	-2.0	-.3	-2.0
KC	44	16	242	28	1381.1	1293	85	405	801	11.3	3.24	94	.251	.307	-27	-32	99	86	42	.981	116	54	164	.7	-3.6	**8.1**	.4	-6.5
CAL	57	18	192	16	1377.2	**1109**	90	620	**1000**	11.5	3.06	96	**.222**	.310	0	-22	96	102	44	.981	114	70	135	.8	-2.5	-3.8	.0	2.9
TEX	11	8	**324**	34	1374.2	1258	92	613	868	12.6	3.53	86	.246	.329	-71	-75	99	77	56	.972	166	58	147	-2.2	-8.5	-11.5	.2	-1.0
TOT	502	193	2735	372	16653.2					11.3	3.06		.239	.306						.979	1535	632	1770					

Batter-Fielder Wins	Batting Average	On-Base Percentage	Slugging Average	On-Base Plus Slugging	Adjusted OPS	Adjusted Batter Runs
D.Allen-Chi 5.8	Carew-Min .318	D.Allen-Chi .420	D.Allen-Chi .603	D.Allen-Chi 1023	D.Allen-Chi 198	D.Allen-Chi 65.1
Fisk-Bos 5.1	Piniella-KC .312	May-Chi .405	Fisk-Bos .538	Fisk-Bos .909	Murcer-NY 169	Murcer-NY 47.7
Murcer-NY 4.3	D.Allen-Chi .308	Mayberry-KC .394	Murcer-NY .537	Mayberry-KC .900	Mayberry-KC 168	Mayberry-KC 44.5
Patek-KC 4.2	May-Chi .308	White-NY .384	Mayberry-KC .507	Murcer-NY .898	Epstein-Oak 165	Epstein-Oak 38.1
Mayberry-KC 3.5	Rudi-Oak .305	Scheinblum-KC .383	Epstein-Oak .490	Epstein-Oak .866	Fisk-Bos 159	May-Chi 36.0

Runs	Hits	Doubles	Triples	Home Runs	Total Bases	Runs Batted In
Murcer-NY 102	Rudi-Oak 181	Piniella-KC 33	Rudi-Oak 9	D.Allen-Chi 37	Murcer-NY 314	D.Allen-Chi 113
Rudi-Oak 94	Piniella-KC 179	Rudi-Oak 32	Fisk-Bos 9	Murcer-NY 33	D.Allen-Chi 305	Mayberry-KC 100
Harper-Bos 92	Murcer-NY 171	Murcer-NY 30	Blair-Bal 8	Killebrew-Min 26	Rudi-Oak 288	Murcer-NY 96
D.Allen-Chi 90	Carew-Min 170	White-NY 29	Murcer-NY 7	Epstein-Oak 26	Mayberry-KC 255	Scott-Mil 84
Tovar-Min 86	May-Chi 161	Harper-Bos 29	Kelly-Chi 7		Piniella-KC 253	Powell-Bal 81

Stolen Bases	Base Stealing Runs	Fielding Runs-Infield	Fielding Runs-Outfield	Wins	Winning Pct.	Complete Games
Campaneris-Oak 52	Campaneris-Oak 6.5	Patek-KC 37.7	Berry-Cal 8.0	Wood-Chi 24	Hunter-Oak .750	Perry-Cle 29
Nelson-Tex 51	Nelson-Tex 5.3	Michael-NY 24.0	Ford-Tex 7.4	Perry-Cle 24	Tiant-Bos .714	Lolich-Det 23
Patek-KC 33	Patek-KC 4.8	Rodriguez-Det 20.2	Blair-Bal 5.3	Lolich-Det 22	Odom-Oak .714	Wood-Chi 20
Kelly-Chi 32	Baylor-Bal 4.6	Clarke-NY 15.3	May-Mil 5.2		Palmer-Bal .677	Ryan-Cal 20
Otis-KC 28	Kelly-Chi 3.9	Killebrew-Min 10.9	Unser-Cle 4.4		Kline-NY .640	Palmer-Bal 1

Strikeouts	Fewest BB/Game	Games	Saves	Base Runners/9	Adjusted Relief Runs	Relief Ranking
Ryan-Cal 329	Peterson-NY 1.58	Lindblad-Tex 66	Lyle-NY 35	Nelson-KC 7.89	Lyle-NY 13.6	Lyle-NY 25.
Lolich-Det 250	Nelson-KC 1.61	Fingers-Oak 65	Forster-Chi 29	Hunter-Oak 8.32	Knowles-Oak 11.3	Knowles-Oak 13.
Perry-Cle 234	Kline-NY 1.68	Granger-Min 63	Fingers-Oak 21	Kaat-Min 9.05	Bell-Mil 10.8	Forster-Chi 13.
Blyleven-Min 228	Holtzman-Oak 1.76		Granger-Min 19	Perry-Cle 9.11	Harrison-Bal 9.6	Abernathy-KC 9.
Coleman-Det 222	Wood-Chi 1.77		Sanders-Mil 17	Alexander-Bal 9.23	Forster-Chi 8.2	Fingers-Oak 9.

Innings Pitched	Opponents' Avg.	Opponents' OBP	Earned Run Average	Adjusted ERA	Adjusted Starter Runs	Pitcher Wins
Wood-Chi 376.2	Ryan-Cal .171	Nelson-KC .234	Tiant-Bos 1.91	Perry-Cle .170	Perry-Cle 49.2	**Perry-Cle** 6.
Perry-Cle 342.2	Hunter-Oak .189	Hunter-Oak .241	Perry-Cle 1.92	Tiant-Bos .170	Palmer-Bal 30.2	**Palmer-Bal** 4.
Lolich-Det 327.1	Nelson-KC .196	Perry-Cle .261	Hunter-Oak 2.04	Palmer-Bal .151	Hunter-Oak 29.2	**Hunter-Oak** 3.
Hunter-Oak 295.1	Tiant-Bos .202	Palmer-Bal .268	Palmer-Bal 2.07	Nelson-Bal .147	Wood-Chi 24.7	**Lyle-NY** 3.
Blyleven-Min 287.1	Perry-Cle .205	Tiant-Bos .275	Nelson-KC 2.08	Paul-Tex .140	Lolich-Det 24.6	**Ryan-Cal** 2.

First Strike

Players went on strike in spring training, canceling the first 13 days of action. Once the strike ended, the AL East saw its first close race. New York, Baltimore, Boston, and Detroit bunched together in August, with the division lead switching seemingly every hour through Labor Day. The Yankees and Orioles faded while the Red Sox and Tigers split four in mid-September at Fenway and met three times to close the schedule at Detroit. The Tigers took the first two to win by a mere half-game.

The West again went to Oakland, although the resurgent White Sox—with knuckleballer Wilbur Wood, who made 49 starts, and MVP Dick Allen—made a run in August. Nolan Ryan, in his first year as an Angel, set a new record for fewest hits allowed per game; he also recorded his first of six 300-strikeout seasons. Minnesota's Rod Carew won his first of six batting titles in the decade. Moving from Washington to Texas, the Rangers had an attendance bump...of just 6,000.

With labor strife taking games off the schedule as well as a continued scoring reduction—only Bobby Murcer cleared 100 runs—attendance dipped for the third straight year. The Yankees failed to draw one million for the first time since 1945. Boston, second to Detroit in attendance and the standings boasted Rookie of the Year Carlton Fisk plus Sparky Lyle whose 35 saves set a league record.

In a thrilling ALCS, each team came back once in the bottom of the 10th to win. Oakland prevailed, winning the first two on the coast, then losing two and taking the deciding game in Detroit as Blue Moon Odom and Vida Blue held off the Tigers 2-1. However, Reggie Jackson injured his knee and missed the World Series.

Six of the seven games in the see-saw Reds-A's Series were one-run affairs. Each team had dramatic come-from-behind wins and good pitching; the unlikely hero was Oakland's Gene Tenace who hit 4 homers, including long balls in his first 2 at bats. Catfish Hunter won Game 7 in relief, holding off the Reds, 3-2.

1971 National League

TEAM	W	L	T	PCT	GB	HW	HL	R	OR	PA	H	2B	3B	HR	BB	SO	HB	SH	AVG	OBP	SLG	OPS	AOPS	BR	ABR	PF	SB	CS	BSA	BSR
EAST																														
PIT	97	65	0	.599		52	28	788	599	6283	1555	223	61	154	469	919	29	62	.274	.330	.416	746	116	120	115	101	65	31	68	3
STL	90	72	1	.556	7	45	36	739	699	6300	1542	225	54	95	543	757	25	63	.275	.338	.385	723	106	92	58	105	124	53	70	9
NY	83	79	0	.512	14	44	37	588	550	6178	1365	203	29	98	547	958	28	91	.249	.319	.351	670	96	-20	-19	100	89	43	67	5
CHI	83	79	0	.512	14	44	37	637	648	6131	1401	202	34	128	527	772	34	92	.258	.325	.378	703	91	42	-45	115	44	32	58	-2
MON	71	90	1	.441	25.5	36	44	622	729	6098	1312	197	29	88	543	800	78	102	.246	.322	.343	665	94	-18	-26	101	51	43	54	-4
PHI	67	95	0	.414	30	34	47	558	688	6171	1289	209	35	123	499	1031	34	55	.233	.298	.350	648	89	-75	-77	100	63	39	62	0
WEST																														
SF	90	72	0	.556		51	30	706	644	6258	1348	224	36	140	654	1042	37	69	.247	.329	.378	707	107	61	70	99	101	36	74	10
LA	89	73	0	.549	1	42	39	663	587	6155	1469	213	38	95	489	755	21	72	.266	.325	.370	695	108	28	63	95	76	40	66	3
ATL	82	80	0	.506	8	43	39	643	699	6172	1434	192	30	153	434	747	28	91	.257	.312	.385	697	97	16	-24	107	57	46	55	-4
HOU	79	83	0	.488	11	39	42	585	567	6105	1319	230	52	71	478	888	29	65	.240	.302	.340	642	91	-81	-64	97	101	51	66	4
CIN	79	83	0	.488	11	46	35	586	581	5973	1306	203	28	138	438	907	27	69	.241	.300	.366	666	95	-46	-40	99	59	33	64	1
SD	61	100	0	.379	28.5	33	48	486	610	5935	1250	184	31	96	438	966	25	87	.233	.293	.332	625	89	-120	-86	94	70	45	61	0
TOT	972					509	462	7601		73759	16590	2505	457	1379	6059	10542	395	918	.252	.316	.366	683					900	492	65	26

TEAM	CG	SHO	GR	SV	IP	H	HR	BB	SO	BR/9	ERA	AERA	OAV	OOB	PR	APR	PF	OSB	OCS	FA	E	WPB	DP	FW	PW	BW	BSW	DIF
EAST																												
PIT	43	15	229	48	1461.0	1426	108	470	813	11.9	3.31	103	.257	.316	26	15	98	42	45	.979	133	54	164	.0	1.6	12.3	.0	1.9
STL	56	14	274	22	1467.0	1482	104	576	911	12.9	3.85	94	.263	.333	-63	-35	105	54	36	.978	142	80	155	-.4	-3.8	6.2	.7	6.2
NY	42	13	211	22	1466.1	1227	100	529	1157	11.0	2.99	115	.227	.299	78	73	99	78	28	.981	114	54	135	1.2	7.8	-2.0	.3	-5.3
CHI	75	17	202	13	1444.0	1458	132	411	829	11.3	4.12	87	.260	.341	-104	-85	103	87	43	.976	150	74	164	-.9	-9.1	-2.8	-.7	4.0
MON	49	8	215	25	1434.1	1418	133	658	838	12.0	3.71	96	.254	.320	-41	-26	102	110	60	.981	122	80	158	.7	-2.8	-8.3	-.2	-3.4
PHI	31	10	253	25	1470.2	1396	132	525																				
WEST																												
SF	45	14	252	30	1454.2	1324	128	471	831	11.3	3.32	103	.242	.303	24	15	98	74	23	.972	179	65	153	-2.6	1.6	7.5	.8	1.6
LA	48	18	187	33	1449.2	1363	110	399	853	11.1	3.23	100	.250	.301	37	2	94	77	42	.979	131	56	159	.2	.2	6.8	.0	.7
ATL	40	11	224	31	1474.2	1529	152	485	823	12.5	3.75	99	.269	.328	-46	-4	107	84	33	.977	146	89	180	-.7	-.4	-2.6	-.7	5.3
HOU	43	10	245	25	1471.1	1318	75	475	914	11.3	3.13	107	.241	.307	55	39	97	68	44	.983	106	82	152	1.6	4.2	-6.9	.2	-1.2
CIN	27	11	255	38	1444.0	1298	140	501	750	11.4	3.35	101	.243	.310	18	3	97	50	32	.984	103	44	174	1.8	.3	-4.3	-.1	.3
SD	47	10	237	17	1438.0	1351	112	501	923	12.1	3.22	103	.249	.321	39	16	96	54	54	.974	161	70	144	-1.6	1.7	-9.2	-.2	-10.2
TOT	546	151	2784	329	17475.2					11.9	3.47		.252	.316						.979	1613	804	1888					

Leader categories

Batter-Fielder Wins		Batting Average		On-Base Percentage		Slugging Average		On-Base Plus Slugging		Adjusted OPS		Adjusted Batter Runs	
Stargell-Pit	4.9	Torre-StL	.363	Mays-SF	.425	H.Aaron-Atl	.669	H.Aaron-Atl	1079	H.Aaron-Atl	190	Stargell-Pit	59.4
H.Aaron-Atl	4.2	Garr-Atl	.343	Torre-StL	.421	Stargell-Pit	.628	Stargell-Pit	1026	Stargell-Pit	186	H.Aaron-Atl	58.5
Mays-SF	3.7	Beckert-Chi	.342	H.Aaron-Atl	.410	Torre-StL	.555	Torre-StL	.976	Torre-StL	167	Torre-StL	57.0
Torre-StL	3.7	Clemente-Pit	.341	Hunt-Mon	.402	May-Cin	.532	Mays-SF	.907	Mays-SF	159	Allen-LA	41.5
Bonds-SF	3.5	H.Aaron-Atl	.327	Stargell-Pit	.398	Bonds-SF	.512	Williams-Chi	.888	Allen-LA	152	Mays-SF	40.6

Runs		Hits		Doubles		Triples		Home Runs		Total Bases		Runs Batted In	
Brock-StL	126	Torre-StL	230	Cedeno-Hou	40	Morgan-Hou	11	Stargell-Pit	48	Torre-StL	352	Torre-StL	137
Bonds-SF	110	Garr-Atl	219	Brock-StL	37	Metzger-Hou	11	H.Aaron-Atl	47	H.Aaron-Atl	331	Stargell-Pit	125
Stargell-Pit	104	Brock-StL	200	Torre-StL	34	Davis-LA	10	May-Cin	39	Stargell-Pit	321	H.Aaron-Atl	118
Garr-Atl	101	Davis-LA	198	Staub-Mon	34	Gaston-SD	9	Johnson-Phi	34	Bonds-SF	317	Bonds-SF	102
Torre-StL	97			Davis-LA	33					Williams-Chi	300	Montanez-Phi	99

Stolen Bases		Base Stealing Runs		Fielding Runs-Infield		Fielding Runs-Outfield		Wins		Winning Pct.		Complete Games	
Brock-StL	64	Brock-StL	7.4	Helms-Cin	26.1	Lum-Atl	8.7	Jenkins-Chi	24	Gullett-Cin	.727	Jenkins-Chi	30
Morgan-Hou	40	Morgan-Hou	6.0	Sizemore-StL	17.6	Garr-Atl	8.5	Seaver-NY	20	Downing-LA	.690	Seaver-NY	21
Garr-Atl	30	Agee-NY	4.1	Harrelson-NY	14.7	Alou-Hou	7.7	Downing-LA	20	Carlton-StL	.690	Stoneman-Mon	20
		Mays-SF	4.0	Robertson-Pit	13.7	Clemente-Pit	7.3	Carlton-StL	20	Ellis-Pit	.679	Gibson-StL	20
		Harrelson-NY	3.7	Kessinger-Chi	11.3	Day-Mon	7.2	Ellis-Pit	19	Seaver-NY	.667		

Strikeouts		Fewest BB/Game		Games		Saves		Base Runners/9		Adjusted Relief Runs		Relief Ranking	
Seaver-NY	289	Jenkins-Chi	1.02	Granger-Cin	70	Giusti-Pit	30	Seaver-NY	8.64	McGraw-NY	22.4	McGraw-NY	30.8
Jenkins-Chi	263	Marichal-SF	1.81	J.Johnson-SF	67	Marshall-Mon	23	Brewer-LA	8.74	Miller-Chi-SD-Pit	17.8	Brewer-LA	26.0
Stoneman-Mon	251	Stone-Atl	1.82	Marshall-Mon	66	Brewer-LA	22	Wilson-Hou	9.44	Brewer-LA	14.2	Miller-Chi-SD-Pit	25.2
Kirby-SD	231	Hands-Chi	1.86	McMahon-SF	61	J.Johnson-SF	18	McGraw-NY	9.49	Ray-Hou	13.2	Frisella-NY	19.6
Sutton-LA	194	Sutton-LA	1.87	Carroll-Cin	61	Upshaw-Atl	17	Jenkins-Chi	9.58	Frisella-NY	12.3	Ray-Hou	18.0

Innings Pitched		Opponents' Avg.		Opponents' OBP		Earned Run Average		Adjusted ERA		Adjusted Starter Runs		Pitcher Wins	
Jenkins-Chi	325.0	Wilson-Hou	.202	Seaver-NY	.252	Seaver-NY	1.76	Seaver-NY	195	Seaver-NY	54.8	Seaver-NY	6.7
Stoneman-Mon	294.2	Seaver-NY	.206	Wilson-Hou	.266	Roberts-SD	2.10	Roberts-SD	158	Jenkins-Chi	36.3	Jenkins-Chi	5.6
Seaver-NY	286.1	Kirby-SD	.216	Jenkins-Chi	.269	Wilson-Hou	2.45	Jenkins-Chi	142	Roberts-SD	36.2	Roberts-SD	4.7
Perry-SF	280.0	Cumberland-SF	.223	Marichal-SF	.273	Forsch-Hou	2.53	Wilson-Hou	137	Wilson-Hou	28.5	McGraw-NY	3.6
Marichal-SF	279.0	Gentry-NY	.224	Nolan-Cin	.277	Sutton-LA	2.54	Forsch-Hou	133	Sutton-LA	22.0	Brewer-LA	3.0

Pittsburgh's Glory

San Francisco looked like a shoo-in for NL West honors, leading by 8½ in early September, but a late slide and a furious Los Angeles rally closed the gap. But the Dodgers could get no closer as the Giants held a 1-game lead over the final five days. Willie Mays and Willie McCovey were declining and injured, respectively, but Bobby Bonds, Ken Henderson, and Dick Dietz provided the hitting; Juan Marichal headed a very thin rotation.

An 11-game July winning streak put the Bucs over the top in the East. Seven Pittsburgh pitchers made at least 13 starts, and Willie Stargell was the league's dominant power hitter. On the other side of the state, and the standings, the Phillies opened Veterans Stadium, another bowl-shaped artificial turf stadium; their attendance more than doubled. The league reached a new all-time attendance high, with everyone but San Diego clearing a million.

MVP Joe Torre of the Cardinals hit .363, the NL's highest since 1948. Atlanta's Earl Williams was Rookie of the Year. Fergie

Jenkins captured the Cy Young, but the Cubs lacked the offense to win. Ernie Banks and Jim Bunning retired, neither ever appearing in a World Series.

The Pirates disposed of the Giants in four games—the first League Championship Series in six tries that did not end in a sweep. Bucs first baseman Bob Robertson hit 4 homers in the NLCS, including 3 long balls at Candlestick in Game 2. Pittsburgh lost the first two World Series games at Baltimore as the Orioles tallied 16 runs. The Pirates, however, won the next three with pitching and big rallies (Game 4 was the first World Series game played at night).

The Orioles came back from a 2-0 deficit to win a 10-inning thriller in Game 6. Roberto Clemente, who hit .414 in the Series and played astounding defense, clubbed a homer the next day in the deciding 2-1 victory. Steve Blass, who allowed just 7 hits—and 4 walks—in 18 innings, racked up his second complete-game victory of the Series.

1971 American League

TEAM	W	L	T	PCT	GB	HW	HL	R	OR	PA	H	2B	3B	HR	BB	SO	HB	SH	AVG	OBP	SLG	OPS	AOPS	BR	ABR	PF	SB	CS	BSA	BSR
EAST																														
BAL	101	57	0	.639		53	24	**742**	530	6143	1382	207	25	158	**672**	844	46	85	**.261**	**.347**	.398	745	117	**137**	132	101	66	38	63	1
DET.	91	71	0	.562	12	**54**	27	701	645	6196	1399	214	38	**179**	540	854	55	62	.254	.325	**.405**	730	108	88	58	104	35	43	45	-7
BOS	85	77	0	.525	18	47	33	691	667	6107	1360	**246**	28	161	552	871	32	75	.252	.322	.397	719	102	72	24	107	51	34	60	-1
NY	82	80	0	.506	21	44	37	648	641	6164	1377	195	**43**	97	581	**717**	37	77	.254	.328	.360	688	107	22	54	95	75	55	58	-3
WAS	63	96	0	.396	38.5	35	46	537	660	5986	1219	189	30	86	575	956	28	58	.230	.307	.326	633	90	-86	-61	95	68	45	60	-1
CLE	60	102	0	.370	43	29	52	543	747	6061	1303	200	20	109	467	868	31	67	.238	.300	.342	642	80	-85	-131	110	57	37	61	0
WEST																														
OAK	101	60	0	.627		46	35	691	564	6191	1383	195	25	160	542	1018	37	80	.252	.321	.384	705	108	41	54	98	**130**	46	74	13
KC	85	76	0	.528	16	44	37	603	566	5914	1323	225	40	80	490	819	25	45	.250	.313	.353	666	96	-28	-23	99	93	52	53	-4
CHI	79	83	0	.488	22.5	39	42	617	597	6114	1346	185	30	138	562	870	51	81	.250	.325	.373	698	101	33	16	103	83	72	68	-4
CAL	76	86	0	.469	25.5	35	46	511	576	6079	1271	213	18	96	441	827	29	83	.231	.290	.329	619	87	-132	-95	103	66	44	60	-1
MIN	74	86	0	.463	26.5	37	42	654	670	6072	**1406**	197	31	116	512	846	25	64	.260	.323	.372	695	100	27	9	103	66	40	60	-1
MIL	69	92	0	.429	32	34	48	534	609	5904	1188	160	23	104	543	924	30	**107**	.229	.304	.329	633	86	-90	-85	99		865	547	61	-1
TOT	966					497	469	7472		72931	15957	2426	351	1484	6477	10414	426	884	.247	.317	.364	681					865	547	61	

TEAM	CG	SHO	GR	SV	IP	H	HR	BB	SO	BR/9	ERA	AERA	OAV	OOB	PR	APR	PF	OSB	OCS	FA	E	WPB	DP	FW	PW	BW	BSW	DIF
EAST																												
BAL	**71**	15	177	22	1415.1	1257	125	**416**	793	10.8	2.99	114	.239	**.295**	74	66	98	56	51	.981	112	53	148	.7	7.1	**14.2**	.1	-.0
DET	53	11	265	32	1468.1	1355	126	609	**1000**	12.3	3.63	100	.247	.325	-28	-3	105	81	41	**.983**	**106**	52	156	1.2	-.3	6.2	-.7	3.6
BOS	44	11	247	35	1443.0	1424	136	535	871	12.5	3.80	98	.259	.327	-55	-13	107	78	31	.981	116	55	149	.6	-1.4	2.6	-.0	2.3
NY	67	15	189	12	1452.0	1382	126	423	707	11.3	3.43	96	.252	.306	4	-26	95	**38**	40	.981	125	58	159	.1	-2.8	5.8	-.3	-1.8
WAS	30	10	315	26	1418.2	1376	132	554	762	12.5	3.70	91	.258	.331	-37	-53	97	84	45	.977	141	66	170	-1.0	-5.7	-6.6	-.0	-3.2
CLE	21	7	**325**	32	1440.0	1352	154	770	937	13.6	4.28	90	.252	.348	-130	-59	112	73	52	.981	116	84	159	.6	-6.3	-14.1	.1	-1.2
WEST																												
OAK	57	18	227	36	1469.1	**1229**	131	501	999	10.8	3.05	109	**.228**	.296	67	46	96	72	33	.981	117	54	157	.5	4.9	5.8	-.0	9.3
KC	34	15	264	**44**	1420.1	1301	**84**	496	775	11.6	3.25	106	.247	.314	33	30	99	68	43	.979	132	52	**178**	-.4	3.2	-2.5	**1.4**	2.7
CHI	46	19	259	32	1450.1	1348	100	468	976	11.4	3.12	114	.247	.307	55	**68**	103	102	48	.975	160	75	128	-1.9	**7.3**	1.7	-.4	-8.7
CAL	39	11	243	32	1481.0	1246	101	607	904	11.5	3.10	105	.230	.310	60	25	94	85	49	.980	131	85	159	-.2	2.7	-10.2	-.4	2.3
MIN	43	9	252	25	1416.2	1384	139	520	895	12.4	3.81	93	.257	.326	-55	-43	102	73	44	.980	118	54	134	.4	-4.6	1.0	-.0	-2.7
MIL	32	**23**	238	32	1416.1	1303	130	569	795	12.1	3.38	103	.247	.321	13	16	101	55	**70**	.977	138	**41**	152	-.7	1.7	-9.1	-.0	-3.3
TOT	537	164	3001	360	17291.1					11.9	3.46		.247	.317						.980	1512	729	1849					

Batter-Fielder Wins
Nettles-Cle 5.9
Melton-Chi 4.9
Murcer-NY 4.5
Patek-KC 4.3
White-NY 3.8

Batting Average
Oliva-Min 337
Murcer-NY 331
Rettenmund-Bal 318
Tovar-Min 311
Carew-Min 307

On-Base Percentage
Murcer-NY 427
Rettenmund-Bal 422
Kaline-Det 416
Buford-Bal 413
White-NY 388

Slugging Average
Oliva-Min 546
Murcer-NY 543
Cash-Det 531
F.Robinson-Bal 510
Jackson-Oak 508

On-Base Plus Slugging
Murcer-NY 969
Oliva-Min 915
Cash-Det 903
F.Robinson-Bal 894
Buford-Bal 890

Adjusted OPS
Murcer-NY 182
Oliva-Min 153
White-NY 152
F.Robinson-Bal 152
Buford-Bal 151

Adjusted Batter Runs
Murcer-NY 60.5
White-NY 39.2
Rettenmund-Bal 35.2
Buford-Bal 34.8
F.Robinson-Bal 33.8

Runs
Buford-Bal 99
Tovar-Min 94
Murcer-NY 94
Carew-Min 88
Jackson-Oak 87

Hits
Tovar-Min 204
Alomar-Cal 179
Carew-Min 177
Smith-Bos 175
Murcer-NY 175

Doubles
Smith-Bos 33
Schaal-KC 31
Rodriguez-Det 30
Oliva-Min 30

Triples
Patek-KC 11
Carew-Min 10
Blair-Bal 8

Home Runs
Melton-Chi 33
Jackson-Oak 32
Cash-Det 32
Smith-Bos 30

Total Bases
Smith-Bos 302
Jackson-Oak 288
Murcer-NY 287
Melton-Chi 267
Oliva-Min 266

Runs Batted In
Killebrew-Min 119
F.Robinson-Bal 99
Smith-Bos 96
Murcer-NY 94
Bando-Oak 94

Stolen Bases
Otis-KC 52
Patek-KC 49
Alomar-Cal 39
Campaneris-Oak 34

Base Stealing Runs
Otis-KC 8.6
Patek-KC 5.9
Alomar-Cal 5.1
Campaneris-Oak 5.0
Harper-Mil 4.4

Fielding Runs-Infield
Nettles-Cle 46.1
Michael-NY 24.6
Melton-Chi 23.7
Alomar-Cal 22.8
Patek-KC 21.6

Fielding Runs-Outfield
Tovar-Min 14.1
Yastrzemski-Bos ...10.7
Unser-Was 9.6
Stanley-Det 9.3
Otis-KC 8.2

Wins
Lolich-Det 25
Blue-Oak 24
Wood-Chi 22
McNally-Bal 21
Hunter-Oak 21

Winning Pct.
McNally-Bal 808
Dobson-Oak 750
Blue-Oak 750
Dobson-Bal 714

Complete Games
Lolich-Det 29
Blue-Oak 24
Wood-Chi 22
Cuellar-Bal 21
Palmer-Bal 20

Strikeouts
Lolich-Det 308
Blue-Oak 301
Coleman-Det 236
Blyleven-Min 224
Wood-Chi 210

Fewest BB/Game
Peterson-NY 1.38
Kline-NY 1.50
Kaat-Min 1.62
Wood-Chi 1.67
Drago-KC 1.72

Games
Sanders-Mil 83
Scherman-Det 69
Burgmeier-KC 67
Abernathy-KC 63

Saves
Sanders-Mil 31
Abernathy-KC 23
Scherman-Det 20
Fingers-Oak 17
Burgmeier-KC 17

Base Runners/9
Blue-Oak 8.68
Fingers-Oak 9.19
Wood-Chi 9.19
Grzenda-Was 9.21
Sanders-Mil 9.84

Adjusted Relief Runs
Sanders-Mil 22.9
Burgmeier-KC 15.0
Mingori-Cle 13.7
Grzenda-Was 10.8
Scherman-Det 10.6

Relief Ranking
Sanders-Mil ....40.
Burgmeier-KC ....30.
Scherman-Det ....18.
Abernathy-KC ....12.
Grzenda-Was ....11.

Innings Pitched
Lolich-Det 376.0
Wood-Chi 334.0
Blue-Oak 312.0
Cuellar-Bal 292.1
Coleman-Det 286.0

Opponents' Avg.
Blue-Oak 189
McDowell-Cle 207
May-Cal 213
Messersmith-Cal 218
Palmer-Bal 221

Opponents' OBP
Blue-Oak 251
Wood-Chi 263
Kline-NY 275
Dobson-Bal 278
Hunter-Oak 281

Earned Run Average
Blue-Oak 1.82
Wood-Chi 1.91
Palmer-Bal 2.68
Hedlund-KC 2.71
Blyleven-Min 2.81

Adjusted ERA
Wood-Chi 186
Blue-Oak 183
Siebert-Bos 128
Palmer-Bal 127
Hedlund-KC 127

Adjusted Starter Runs
Wood-Chi 55.1
Blue-Oak 53.6
Lolich-Det 28.0
Palmer-Bal 23.3
Blyleven-Min 22.9

Pitcher Wins
Wood-Chi ....5.
Blue-Oak ....5.
Sanders-Mil ....4.
Burgmeier-KC ....3.
Siebert-Bos ....3.

The Beltway Bandit

After missing the 1970 season as his case against baseball's reserve clause went to Federal Court, Curt Flood joined Washington but retired after 13 games. Those Senators were a sad bunch. As manager Ted Williams fumed, owner Bob Short hauled in problems and rejects like Denny McLain, Don Wert, Jerry Janeski, and Joe Foy; things worked out as well as could be expected. The Senators lost 96 games, but Cleveland kept them out of the basement.

Boston made an early run at the AL East title, but the Orioles again improved as the weather got hotter, clearing 100 wins for the third consecutive season. Earl Weaver's club again paced in runs and fewest allowed, with four 20-game winners in his rotation and Don Buford and Merv Rettenmund ranking among the league's top four in on-base percentage.

With Aurelio Rodriguez, Ed Brinkman, and Joe Coleman heisted from Washington, the Tigers improved under Billy Martin. Yankees center fielder Bobby Murcer enjoyed a breakout season.

Oakland won the franchise's first crown since 1931 on the left arm of MVP and Cy Young winner Vida Blue, who led the AL in ERA and shutouts. Only Reggie Jackson starred on offense, but everyone in Dick Williams' lineup made a solid contribution. Defending champion Minnesota collapsed to fifth, declining 23 games amidst poor pitching; Tony Oliva won the batting title but tore up his knee. Kansas City finished second but never contended.

Baltimore swept the A's in the ALCS, then lost a painful seven-game World Series to the Pirates.

Following the season, the carpetbagging Short—refusing to pay his rent bills and citing poor attendance—moved the Senators to Dallas for 1972 and renamed them the Texas Rangers. As Short left the nation's capital without a major league team for the first time since 1900, it was fitting, then, that two great Senators of years past, Goose Goslin and Heinie Manush, died.

1970 National League

TEAM	W	L	T	PCT	GB	HW	HL	R	OR	PA	H	2B	3B	HR	BB	SO	HB	SH	AVG	OBP	SLG	OPS	AOPS	BR	ABR	PF	SB	CS	BSA	BSR
EAST																														
PIT	89	73	0	.549		50	32	729	664	6231	**1522**	235	70	130	444	871	44	53	.270	.325	.406	731	102	8	10	100	66	34	66	3
CHI	84	78	0	.519	5	46	34	806	679	6229	1424	228	44	179	607	844	20	75	.259	.333	.415	748	94	50	-35	112	39	16	71	3
NY	83	79	0	.512	6	44	38	695	**630**	6275	1358	211	42	120	684	1062	26	74	.249	.333	.370	703	94	-21	-29	101	118	54	69	7
STL	76	86	0	.469	13	34	47	744	747	6376	1497	218	51	113	569	961	26	52	.263	.331	.379	710	94	-22	-42	103	117	47	71	9
PHI	73	88	0	.453	15.5	40	40	594	730	6099	1299	224	58	101	519	1066	25	62	.238	.305	.356	661	85	-127	-113	98	72	64	53	-7
MON	73	89	0	.451	16	39	41	687	807	6251	1284	211	35	136	659	972	39	**107**	.237	.323	.365	688	91	-61	-62	100	65	45	59	-1
WEST																														
CIN	102	60	0	.630		57	24	775	681	6222	1498	253	45	**191**	547	984	29	58	.270	.336	**.436**	**772**	**112**	115	90	101	115	52	69	7
LA	87	74	0	.540	14.5	39	42	749	684	6293	1515	233	67	87	541	841	24	72	.270	.334	.382	716	102	-6	22	96	**138**	57	71	10
SF	86	76	0	.531	16	48	33	**831**	826	6469	1460	257	35	165	**729**	1005	56	66	.262	**.351**	.409	760	111	98	**107**	99	83	27	**75**	9
HOU	79	83	0	.488	23	44	37	744	763	6305	1446	250	47	129	598	911	27	63	.259	.332	.391	723	104	6	36	96	114	41	74	**11**
ATL	76	86	0	.469	26	42	39	736	772	6202	1495	215	24	160	522	736	38	54	.270	.334	.404	738	98	32	-9	106	58	34	63	1
SD	63	99	0	.389	39	31	50	681	788	6145	1353	208	36	172	500	1164	39	83	.246	.312	.391	703	98	-51	-26	96	60	45	57	-3
TOT	971					514	457	8771		75097	17151	2743	554	1683	6919	11417	393	819	.258	.329	.392	721		1045			516	67		49

TEAM	CG	SHO	GR	SV	IP	H	HR	BB	SO	BR/9	ERA	AERA	OAV	OOB	PR	APR	PF	OSB	OCS	FA	E	WPB	DP	FW	PW	BW	BSW	DIF
EAST																												
PIT	36	13	288	43	1453.2	1386	106	625	990	12.7	3.70	107	.255	.334	56	42	98	64	56	.979	137	55	**195**	.3	4.2	1.0	-.1	2.6
CHI	**59**	9	205	25	1435.0	1402	143	**475**	1000	11.9	3.76	**120**	.256	.316	46	**106**	111	71	48	.978	137	59	146	.3	**10.6**	-3.5	-.1	-4.3
NY	47	10	228	32	1459.2	1402	135	575	**1260**	11.5	**3.45**	118	**.233**	**.307**	97	98	100	64	42	.978	124	54	136	1.0	9.8	-2.9	.3	-6.2
STL	51	11	278	20	1475.2	1483	**102**	632	960	13.0	4.06	102	.263	.337	-2	13	102	86	45	.977	150	86	159	-.4	-4.2	-.5	.3	-2.2
PHI	24	8	277	36	1461.0	1483	132	538	1047	12.7	4.17	96	.265	.330	-20	-25	99	122	47	**.981**	114	71	134	1.5	-2.5	-11.3	-1.1	5.8
MON	29	10	285	32	1438.2	1434	162	716	914	13.8	4.50	92	.261	.349	-73	-56	103	78	45	.977	141	61	193	.0	-5.6	-6.2	-.5	4.2
WEST																												
CIN	32	15	252	**60**	1444.2	1370	118	592	843	12.4	3.69	109	.251	.325	57	56	100	46	38	.976	151	53	173	-.5	5.6	9.0	.3	6.6
LA	37	**17**	227	42	1458.2	1394	164	496	880	11.9	3.82	101	.250	.314	37	4	95	106	28	.978	135	66	135	.4	4.2	2.2	.6	3.0
SF	50	7	253	30	1457.2	1514	156	604	931	13.3	4.50	88	.267	.339	-74	-88	98	114	31	.973	135	106	135	.4	2.2	.6	.6	3.0
HOU	36	6	**302**	35	1456.0	1491	131	577	942	13.0	4.23	92	.265	.339	-30	-58	96	78	**58**	.973	140	103	153	-1.5	-8.8	**10.7**	.5	4.1
ATL	45	9	204	24	1430.2	1451	185	478	960	13.3	4.33	99	.261	.320	-45	-7	106	123	32	.977	141	74	118	.0	-.7	-.9	-.3	-.6
SD	24	9	279	32	1440.1	1483	149	611	886	13.3	4.36	92	.267	.341	-50	-57	99	93	46	.975	158	42	159	-.9	-.7	-.9	-.3	-3.2
TOT	470	124	3078	411	17411.2					12.6	4.05		.258	.329						.977	1698	830	1845		-5.7	-2.6	-.7	-8.2

Batter-Fielder Wins		Batting Average		On-Base Percentage		Slugging Average		On-Base Plus Slugging		Adjusted OPS		Adjusted Batter Runs	
McCovey-SF	6.5	Carty-Atl	.366	Carty-Atl	.454	McCovey-SF	.612	McCovey-SF	1056	McCovey-SF	182	McCovey-SF	66.5
Bench-Cin	5.9	Torre-StL	.325	McCovey-SF	.444	Perez-Cin	.589	Carty-Atl	1037	Carty-Atl	167	Perez-Cin	52.0
Perez-Cin	4.6	Sanguillen-Pit	.325	Dietz-SF	.426	Bench-Cin	.587	Hickman-Chi	1001	Perez-Cin	162	Carty-Atl	48.8
Carty-Atl	4.0	Williams-Chi	.322	Hickman-Chi	.419	Williams-Chi	.586	Perez-Cin	990	Dietz-SF	153	Dietz-SF	44.4
Morgan-Hou	3.9	Parker-LA	.319	Perez-Cin	.401	Carty-Atl	.584	Williams-Chi	977	Hickman-Chi	148	Carbo-Cin	41.3

Runs		Hits		Doubles		Triples		Home Runs		Total Bases		Runs Batted In	
Williams-Chi	137	Williams-Chi	205	Parker-LA	47	Davis-LA	16	Bench-Cin	45	Williams-Chi	373	Bench-Cin	148
Bonds-SF	134	Rose-Cin	205	McCovey-SF	39	Kessinger-Chi	14	Williams-Chi	42	Bench-Cin	355	Williams-Chi	129
Rose-Cin	120	Torre-StL	203	Rose-Cin	37	Clemente-Pit	10	Perez-Cin	40	Perez-Cin	346	Perez-Cin	129
Brock-StL	114	Brock-StL	202	Dietz-SF	36	Bonds-SF	10	McCovey-SF	39	Bonds-SF	334	McCovey-SF	126
Tolan-Cin	112	Alou-Pit	201	Bonds-SF	36					Gaston-SD	317	H.Aaron-Atl	118

Stolen Bases		Base Stealing Runs		Fielding Runs-Infield		Fielding Runs-Outfield		Wins		Winning Pct.		Complete Games	
Tolan-Cin	57	Bonds-SF	7.1	Alley-Pit	31.4	Staub-Mon	6.3	Perry-SF	23	Gibson-StL	.767	Jenkins-Chi	24
Brock-StL	51	Brock-StL	6.0	Maxvill-StL	27.6	Bonds-SF	5.8	Gibson-StL	23	Nolan-Cin	.720	Perry-SF	23
Bonds-SF	48	Tolan-Cin	5.5	Rader-Hou	25.3	Jones-NY	5.8	Jenkins-Chi	22	Walker-Pit	.714	Gibson-StL	23
Morgan-Hou	42	Morgan-Hou	4.7	Wine-Mon	18.7	Davis-LA	5.7	Merritt-Cin	20	Perry-SF	.639	Seaver-NY	19
Davis-LA	38	Harrelson-NY	3.7	Santo-Chi	18.3	Henderson-SF	3.9			Merritt-Cin	.625	Dierker-Hou	17

Strikeouts		Fewest BB/Game		Games		Saves		Base Runners/9		Adjusted Relief Runs		Relief Ranking	
Seaver-NY	283	Jenkins-Chi	1.73	Herbel-SD-NY	76	Granger-Cin	35	Jenkins-Chi	9.55	Selma-Phi	20.3	Selma-Phi	30.1
Jenkins-Chi	274	Marichal-SF	1.78	Selma-Phi	73	Giusti-Pit	26	Singer-LA	9.56	Carroll-Cin	15.3	Granger-Cin	22.3
Gibson-StL	274	Osteen-LA	1.81	Linzy-SF-StL	67	Brewer-LA	24	Seaver-NY	9.82	C.Taylor-StL	14.5	Carroll-Cin	22.2
Perry-SF	214	McAndrew-NY	1.86	Granger-Cin	67	Raymond-Mon	23	Brewer-LA	10.01	Gullett-Cin	14.4	McMahon-SF	21.7
Holtzman-Chi	202	Merritt-Cin	2.04	Giusti-Pit	66	Selma-Phi	22	McAndrew-NY	10.06	McMahon-SF	12.3	Giusti-Pit	17.3

Innings Pitched		Opponents' Avg.		Opponents' OBP		Earned Run Average		Adjusted ERA		Adjusted Starter Runs		Pitcher Wins	
Perry-SF	328.2	Simpson-Cin	.198	Jenkins-Chi	.264	Seaver-NY	2.82	Seaver-NY	144	Seaver-NY	39.8	**Gibson-StL**	4.5
Jenkins-Chi	313.0	Seaver-NY	.214	Seaver-NY	.272	Simpson-Cin	3.02	Simpson-Cin	134	Jenkins-Chi	37.1	**Seaver-NY**	4.4
Gibson-StL	294.0	Walker-Pit	.219	McAndrew-NY	.279	Walker-Pit	3.04	Pappas-Atl-Chi	134	Gibson-StL	34.3	**Jenkins-Chi**	3.9
Seaver-NY	290.2	Jenkins-Chi	.224	Perry-SF	.289	Gibson-StL	3.12	Holtzman-Chi	133	Holtzman-Chi	31.4	**Selma-Phi**	3.2
Holtzman-Chi	287.2	Gentry-NY	.224	Gibson-StL	.293	Koosman-NY	3.14	Jenkins-Chi	133	Perry-SF	26.3	**Holtzman-Chi**	3.0

The Times They Are A-Changin'

Veteran outfielder Curt Flood sat out the season, refusing a trade from St. Louis to Philadelphia. Instead he filed suit to challenge baseball's reserve clause, which bound him to the team that first signed him. Flood lost, but he laid the groundwork for free agency.

Two rust-belt clubs built new "cereal bowl" artificial turf parks in midseason: the Reds opened Riverfront Stadium and the Pirates debuting Three Rivers Stadium. In April 1970 only one NL team used turf; by 1979 half did. Great crowds in New York and the new parks helped spike NL attendance. Scoring rose nearly a half-run per game, with homers an all-time high until 1987. But it wasn't just slugging; speed was also back, with steals per game the highest since 1929.

The top NL shortstops of the decade debuted on consecutive days: Dave Concepcion and Larry Bowa. Twenty-year-old Houston outfielder Cesar Cedeno was an immediate sensation.

In a closely bunched NL East, the Pirates pulled away from the Cubs and Mets in September. Last-place Montreal improved 21 games and finished just 16 out. Willie Stargell and Roberto Clemente's bats, and deep pitching, won for Pittsburgh.

Cincinnati, finally showing its tremendous talent, led from opening day and was never challenged. Johnny Bench was the MVP for his awesome power and fine defense, and Tony Perez and Lee May also dented the fences. Wayne Granger's 35 saves established a new mark. The Reds won the NLCS in three nail-biters, allowing just 3 runs to the vaunted Pirates.

During the postseason, umpires in both leagues briefly went on strike—the first-ever arbiter walkout. A few days later, the Reds hosted the first World Series game on plastic, but the Baltimore Orioles won the Fall Classic in five games, including three one-run affairs.

1970 American League

TEAM	W	L	T	PCT	GB	HW	HL	R	OR	PA	H	2B	3B	HR	BB	SO	HB	SH	AVG	OBP	SLG	OPS	AOPS	BR	ABR	PF	SB	CS	BSA	BSR
EAST																														
BAL	108	54	0	.667		59	22	792	574	6416	1424	213	25	179	717	952	44	64	.257	**.344**	.401	745	**110**	105	92	102	84	39	68	5
NY	93	69	1	.574	15	53	28	680	612	6211	1381	208	41	111	588	**808**	25	60	.251	.324	.365	689	100	-18	12	96	105	61	63	2
BOS	87	75	0	.537	21	52	29	786	722	6250	**1450**	**252**	28	**203**	594	855	40	34	**.262**	.335	**.428**	763	109	123	72	107	50	48	51	-6
DET	79	83	0	.488	29	42	39	666	731	6199	1282	207	38	148	656	825	34	83	.238	.322	.374	696	97	-3	-9	101	29	30	49	-4
CLE	76	86	0	.469	32	43	38	649	675	6124	1358	197	23	183	503	909	37	44	.238	.314	.394	708	96	1	-30	105	25	36	41	1
WAS	70	92	0	.432	38	40	41	626	689	6223	1302	184	28	138	635	989	**46**	44	.238	.321	.358	679	97	-36	-6	96	72	42	63	1
WEST																														
MIN	98	64	0	.605		51	30	744	605	6143	1438	230	**41**	153	501	905	42	79	**.262**	.327	.403	730	105	50	39	102	57	52	52	-6
OAK	89	73	0	.549	9	49	32	678	593	6105	1338	208	24	171	584	977	36	73	.249	.325	.392	717	107	30	52	97	**131**	66	66	5
CAL	86	76	0	.531	12	43	38	631	630	6114	1391	197	40	114	447	922	29	69	.251	.309	.363	672	94	-68	-49	97	69	27	**72**	-6
MIL	65	97	1	.401	33	38	42	613	751	6170	1305	202	24	126	592	985	36	**115**	.242	.319	.358	677	93	-41	-41	100	91	73	55	-6
KC	65	97	0	.401	33	35	44	611	705	6128	1341	202	**41**	97	514	958	21	63	.244	.309	.348	657	87	-91	-93	100	97	53	65	3
CHI	56	106	0	.346	42	31	53	633	822	6132	1394	192	20	123	477	872	42	51	.253	.315	.362	677	90	-52	-73	104				-7
TOT	973					536	436	8109		74215	16404	2492	373	1746	6808	10957	432		.250		.322	.379	701				863	562	61	

TEAM	CG	SHO	GR	SV	IP	H	HR	BB	SO	BR/9	ERA	AERA	OAV	OOB	PR	APR	PF	OSB	OCS	FA	E	WPB	DP	FW	PW	BW	BSW	DIF
EAST																												
BAL	**60**	12	228	31	1478.2	1317	139	469	941	**11.0**	**3.15**	117	.240	**.300**	93	88	99	55	43	.981	117	56	148	**1.1**	**9.1**	**9.5**	.6	6.7
NY	36	6	239	49	1471.2	1386	**130**	**451**	777	11.4	3.24	110	.249	.306	77	56	96	40	41	.980	130	**44**	146	.4	5.8	1.2	.3	4.3
BOS	38	8	284	44	1446.1	1391	156	594	1003	12.6	3.87	103	.251	.327	-25	17	107	73	34	.974	156	83	131	-1.2	1.8	7.5	-.6	-1.5
DET	33	9	288	39	1447.1	1443	153	623	1045	13.1	4.09	92	.260	.336	-31	-52	101	68	54	.978	133	76	168	.2	1.6	-3.1	-.7	-2.9
CLE	34	8	312	35	1451.1	1333	163	689	**1076**	12.8	3.91	102	.247	.335	-13	-32	97	56	49	**.982**	116	63	173	**1.1**	-3.3	-.6	.2	-8.4
WAS	20	11	**316**	40	1457.2	1375	139	611	823	12.4	3.80	95	.252	.328	-13	-32	97	56	49	.982	116	63	173	1.1	-3.3	-.6	.2	-8.4
WEST																												
MIN	26	12	269	**58**	1448.1	1329	**130**	486	940	11.5	3.23	114	.244	.308	78	76	100	55	49	.980	123	49	130	.7	7.9	4.0	-.6	4.9
OAK	33	**15**	309	40	1442.2	**1253**	134	542	858	11.4	3.30	107	**.234**	.307	66	38	95	70	39	.977	141	68	152	-.3	3.9	5.4	.6	-1.6
CAL	21	10	314	49	1462.1	1280	154	559	922	11.6	3.48	104	.237	.312	37	23	98	77	41	.980	127	79	169	.5	2.4	-5.1	**.7**	-6.5
MIL	31	2	283	27	1446.2	1397	146	587	895	12.6	4.21	90	.255	.330	-79	-68	102	106	51	.978	136	55	142	.0	-7.1	-4.3	-.6	-4.2
KC	30	11	268	25	1463.2	1346	138	641	915	12.4	3.78	99	.247	.328	-11	-8	101	100	**62**	.976	152	72	162	-.9	-.8	-9.6	.4	-5.0
CHI	20	6	280	30	1430.1	1554	164	556	762	13.6	4.54	85	.280	.347	-132	-101	104	106	45	.975	165	90	**187**	-1.7	-10.5	-7.6	-.1	-5.3
TOT	382	110	3390	467	17447.0					12.2	3.71		.250	.322						.978	1629	806	1850					

Batter-Fielder Wins		Batting Average		On-Base Percentage		Slugging Average		On-Base Plus Slugging		Adjusted OPS		Adjusted Batter Runs	
Harper-Mil	5.6	Johnson-Cal	.329	Yastrzemski-Bos	.452	Yastrzemski-Bos	.592	Yastrzemski-Bos	1.044	Yastrzemski-Bos	.174	Yastrzemski-Bos	64.5
Yastrzemski-Bos	5.5	Yastrzemski-Bos	.329	Howard-Was	.416	Powell-Bal	.549	Howard-Was	.962	Howard-Was	.172	Howard-Was	61.3
Aparicio-Chi	5.3	Oliva-Min	.325	Powell-Bal	.412	Killebrew-Min	.546	Powell-Bal	.962	Powell-Bal	.162	Killebrew-Min	49.2
Fregosi-Cal	4.6	Aparicio-Chi	.313	Killebrew-Min	.411	Howard-Was	.546	Killebrew-Min	.957	Killebrew-Min	.161	Powell-Bal	49.0
Howard-Was	4.3	F.Robinson-Bal	.306	Bando-Oak	.407	Harper-Mil	.522	F.Robinson-Bal	.918	F.Robinson-Bal	.150	Harper-Mil	38.6

Runs		Hits		Doubles		Triples		Home Runs		Total Bases		Runs Batted In	
Yastrzemski-Bos	125	Oliva-Min	204	Tovar-Min	36	Tovar-Min	13	Howard-Was	44	Yastrzemski-Bos	335	Howard-Was	126
Tovar-Min	120	Johnson-Cal	202	Otis-KC	36	Stanley-Det	11	Killebrew-Min	41	Oliva-Min	323	T.Conigliaro-Bos	116
White-NY	109	Tovar-Min	195	Oliva-Min	36	Otis-KC	9	Yastrzemski-Bos	40	Harper-Mil	315	Powell-Bal	114
Smith-Bos	109	Yastrzemski-Bos	186	Harper-Mil	35			T.Conigliaro-Bos	36	Howard-Was	309	Killebrew-Min	113
Harper-Mil	104	White-NY	180	Cardenas-Min	34			Powell-Bal	35	Powell-Bal	289	Oliva-Min	107

Stolen Bases		Base Stealing Runs		Fielding Runs-Infield		Fielding Runs-Outfield		Wins		Winning Pct.		Complete Games	
Campaneris-Oak	42	Otis-KC	6.6	Brinkman-Was	31.4	Oliva-Min	13.3	Perry-Min	24	Cuellar-Bal	.750	Cuellar-Bal	21
Harper-Mil	38	Campaneris-Oak	5.7	Knoop-Chi	27.3	Blair-Bal	12.1	McNally-Bal	24	McNally-Bal	.727	McDowell-Cle	19
Alomar-Cal	35	Stroud-Was	3.6	Nettles-Cle	26.0	Alou-Oak	7.8	Cuellar-Bal	24	Perry-Min	.667	Palmer-Bal	17
Kelly-KC	34	Alomar-Cal	3.5	Aparicio-Chi	25.3	Tovar-Min	7.5	Wright-Cal	22	Palmer-Bal	.667	McNally-Bal	15
Otis-KC	33	Johnson-Cal	3.3	Leon-Cle	16.8	Smith-Bos	6.8			Siebert-Bos	.652	Culp-Bos	15

Strikeouts		Fewest BB/Game		Games		Saves		Base Runners/9		Adjusted Relief Runs		Relief Ranking	
McDowell-Cle	304	Peterson-NY	1.38	Wood-Chi	77	Perranoski-Min	34	Grant-Oak	8.36	Grant-Oak	25.6	McDaniel-NY	32.4
Lolich-Det	230	Perry-Min	1.84	Grant-Oak	72	McDaniel-NY	29	McDaniel-NY	8.95	Hall-Min	22.2	Knowles-Was	30.7
Johnson-KC	206	Cox-Was	2.06	Knowles-Was	71	Timmermann-Det	27	Sanders-Mil	9.06	Sanders-Mil	20.9	Perranoski-Min	25.8
Palmer-Bal	199	Cuellar-Bal	2.09	Williams-Min	68	Knowles-Was	27	Hall-Min	9.39	McDaniel-NY	20.0	Grant-Oak	24.2
Culp-Bos	197	Horlen-Chi	2.14			Grant-Oak	24	Williams-Min	9.69	Williams-Min	19.6	Hall-Min	23.0

Innings Pitched		Opponents' Avg.		Opponents' OBP		Earned Run Average		Adjusted ERA		Adjusted Starter Runs		Pitcher Wins	
Palmer-Bal	305.0	Messersmith-Cal	.205	Peterson-NY	.279	Segui-Oak	2.56	Segui-Oak	138	Palmer-Bal	35.0	**McDaniel-NY**	3.8
McDowell-Cle	305.0	McDowell-Cle	.213	Cuellar-Bal	.284	Palmer-Bal	2.71	McDowell-Cle	137	McDowell-Cle	33.3	**Knowles-Was**	3.2
Cuellar-Bal	297.2	Segui-Oak	.222	Perry-Min	.286	Wright-Cal	2.83	Palmer-Bal	136	Culp-Bos	22.1	**Palmer-Bal**	3.1
McNally-Bal	296.0	Culp-Bos	.224	Blyleven-Min	.288	Peterson-NY	2.90	Culp-Bos	131	Wright-Cal	20.9	**Perry-Min**	3.1
Perry-Min	278.2	Johnson-KC	.228	Messersmith-Cal	.289	McDowell-Cle	2.92	Wright-Cal	128	Perry-Min	19.6	**McDowell-Cle**	2.9

This One's for the Birds

As spring training adjourned, the expansion Seattle Pilots—the subject of pitcher Jim Bouton's controversial book *Ball Four*—were sold to car salesman Bud Selig, moved to Milwaukee, and rechristened the Brewers.

Once again, Baltimore was the class of the league, pacing the East from May on. The Yankees had a brief flurry in June, but the Orioles pulled away as the Senators and Tigers declined 16 and 17 games apiece. Baltimore boasted no league leaders in the hitting categories, but with MVP Boog Powell and Frank Robinson, they topped the loop in scoring. The Birds had a deep rotation and a solid bullpen that garnered few saves; the starters completed 60 games, the AL's most in a decade. The rich got richer as the Orioles also welcomed rookies Bobby Grich and Don Baylor. The league's top freshman, however, was Yankees catcher Thurman Munson.

Sparked by the arms of Cy Young winner Jim Perry and 19-year-old Bert Blyleven, Minnesota won its second straight West title. California made a brief run in July but fell back, and the Athletics came on too late. Chicago fell into the basement for the first time since 1948.

Baltimore swept the Twins in the ALCS, then stomped the Reds in a five-game World Series. Brooks Robinson grabbed the headlines with several great defensive plays, but the key was that the Orioles battered Cincinnati pitching and came back from deficits of three or more runs in three of their victories.

Neither division champ escaped tragedy, however. The Twins lost two outfielders, veteran Bob Allison to retirement and rookie Herm Hill to a drowning in Venezuela during winter ball. Former Orioles catcher Dick Brown, forced from the game in 1966 with a brain tumor, also died.

1969 National League

TEAM	W	L	T	PCT	GB	HW	HL	R	OR	PA	H	2B	3B	HR	BB	SO	HB	SH	AVG	OBP	SLG	OPS	AOPS	BR	ABR	PF	SB	CS	BSA	BSR
EAST																														
NY	100	62	0	.617	—	**52**	30	632	541	6102	1311	184	41	109	527	1089	33	82	.242	.311	.351	662	90	-53	-68	103	66	43	61	-1
CHI	92	70	1	.568	8	49	32	720	611	6243	1400	215	40	142	559	928	36	72	.253	.323	.384	707	93	38	-42	113	30	32	48	-5
PIT	88	74	0	.543	12	47	34	725	652	6235	1557	220	**52**	119	454	944	46	73	**.277**	.334	.398	732	**115**	83	**100**	98	74	34	**69**	**4**
STL	87	75	0	.537	13	42	38	595	**540**	6152	1403	**228**	44	90	503	876	23	57	.253	.316	.359	675	95	-25	-30	101	87	49	64	2
PHI	63	99	0	.389	37	30	51	645	745	6080	1304	227	35	137	549	1130	26	61	.241	.312	.372	684	100	-10	6	98	73	49	60	-1
MON	52	110	0	.321	48	24	57	582	791	6073	1300	202	33	125	529	962	38	57	.240	.310	.359	669	94	-40	-43	101	52	52	50	-7
WEST																														
ATL	93	69	0	.574	—	50	31	691	631	6098	1411	195	22	141	485	**665**	32	81	.258	.321	.380	701	102	20	15	101	59	48	55	-4
SF	90	72	0	.556	3	**52**	29	713	636	6375	1325	187	28	136	**711**	1054	**66**	82	.242	.334	.361	695	103	35	44	99	71	32	**69**	**4**
CIN	89	73	1	.549	4	50	31	**798**	768	6301	**1558**	224	42	**171**	474	1042	46	**100**	**.277**	**.335**	**.422**	**757**	113	**133**	93	105	79	56	59	-2
LA	85	77	0	.525	8	50	31	645	561	6166	1405	185	**52**	97	484	823	21	96	.254	.315	.359	674	101	-35	6	94	80	51	61	0
HOU	81	81	0	.500	12	**52**	29	676	668	6196	1284	208	40	104	699	972	41	68	.240	.330	.352	682	99	-1	20	99	**101**	58	64	2
SD	52	110	0	.321	41	28	53	468	746	5891	1203	180	42	99	423	1143	35	56	.225	.285	.329	614	81	-158	-142	97	45	44	51	-5
TOT	973					526	446	7890		73912	16461	2455	471	1470	6397	11628	443	891	.250	.319	.369	688					817	548	60	-12

TEAM	CG	SHO	GR	SV	IP	H	HR	BB	SO	BR/9	ERA	AERA	OAV	OOB	PR	APR	PF	OSB	OCS	FA	E	WPB	DP	FW	PW	BW	BSW	DIF
EAST																												
NY	51	**28**	203	35	1468.1	**1217**	119	517	1012	10.8	2.99	**123**	**.227**	**.296**	99	**108**	102	55	48	.980	122	63	146	1.4	**11.3**	-7.1	.0	13.4
CHI	58	22	245	27	1454.1	1366	118	475	1017	11.6	3.34	120	.248	.310	-41	97	112	59	54	.979	136	**50**	149	.6	10.2	-4.4	-.4	5.0
PIT	39	9	267	33	1445.2	1348	**96**	553	1124	12.1	3.61	96	.248	.320	-3	-22	97	62	50	.975	155	**50**	169	-.5	-2.3	**10.5**	**.5**	-1.2
STL	63	12	183	26	1460.1	1289	99	511	1004	11.3	**2.94**	122	.237	.305	106	105	100	77	40	.978	138	60	144	.5	11.0	-3.1	.3	-4.3
PHI	47	14	236	21	1434.0	1494	134	570	921	13.2	4.14	86	.270	.340	-88	-94	99	68	47	.978	137	76	157	.5	-9.9	.6	.0	-9.3
MON	26	8	299	21	1426.0	1429	145	702	973	13.8	4.33	85	.263	.350	-117	-99	103	92	49	.971	184	87	**179**	-2.1	-10.4	-4.5	-.6	-11.3
WEST																												
ATL	38	7	221	42	1445.0	1334	144	438	893	11.2	3.53	103	.245	.302	11	14	101	78	27	**.981**	**115**	71	114	**1.8**	1.5	1.6	-.3	7.5
SF	**71**	15	174	17	1473.2	1381	120	461	906	11.5	3.26	108	.248	.307	55	43	98	64	43	.974	169	73	155	-1.3	4.5	4.6	**.5**	.6
CIN	23	11	307	**44**	1465.0	1478	149	611	818	13.2	4.11	91	.262	.338	-84	-55	105	42	43	.974	167	93	158	-1.1	-5.8	9.8	-.1	5.2
LA	47	20	190	31	1457.0	1324	122	**420**	975	11.0	3.08	109	.242	.299	83	46	93	80	43	.980	126	68	130	1.2	4.8	.6	.1	-2.7
HOU	52	11	256	34	1435.2	1347	111	547	**1221**	12.1	3.60	99	.247	.318	-1	-7	99	66	**55**	.975	153	88	136	-.4	-.7	2.1	.3	-1.3
SD	16	9	**322**	25	1422.1	1454	113	592	764	13.2	4.24	84	.267	.341	-102	-106	100	74	49	.975	156	86	140	-.5	-11.1	-14.9	-.4	-2.0
TOT	531	166	2903	356	17387.1					12.1	3.59		.250	.319						.977	1758	865	1777					

Batter-Fielder Wins		Batting Average		On-Base Percentage		Slugging Average		On-Base Plus Slugging		Adjusted OPS		Adjusted Batter Runs	
McCovey-SF	6.5	Rose-Cin	.348	McCovey-SF	.453	McCovey-SF	.656	McCovey-SF	1108	McCovey-SF	211	McCovey-SF	80.2
Wynn-Hou	5.8	Clemente-Pit	.345	Wynn-Hou	.436	H.Aaron-Atl	.607	H.Aaron-Atl	1003	H.Aaron-Atl	176	H.Aaron-Atl	56.7
H.Aaron-Atl	5.1	Jones-NY	.340	Rose-Cin	.428	Allen-Phi	.573	Clemente-Pit	.955	Clemente-Pit	170	Wynn-Hou	54.7
Staub-Mon	4.8	Alou-Pit	.331	Staub-Mon	.426	Stargell-Pit	.556	Staub-Mon	.952	Allen-Phi	167	Staub-Mon	53.6
Clemente-Pit	4.8	McCovey-SF	.320	Jones-NY	.422	Clemente-Pit	.544	Allen-Phi	.949	Wynn-Hou	167	Rose-Cin	50.3

Runs		Hits		Doubles		Triples		Home Runs		Total Bases		Runs Batted In	
Rose-Cin	120	Alou-Pit	231	Alou-Pit	41	Clemente-Pit	12	McCovey-SF	45	H.Aaron-Atl	332	McCovey-SF	126
Bonds-SF	120	Rose-Cin	218	Kessinger-Chi	38	Rose-Cin	11	H.Aaron-Atl	44	Perez-Cin	331	Santo-Chi	123
Wynn-Hou	113	Brock-StL	195	Williams-Chi	33	Williams-Chi	10	May-Cin	38	McCovey-SF	322	Perez-Cin	122
Kessinger-Chi	109	Tolan-Cin	194	Rose-Cin	33	Tolan-Cin	10	Perez-Cin	37	Rose-Cin	321	May-Cin	110
Alou-Pit	105	Williams-Chi	188	Brock-StL	33	Brock-StL	10	Wynn-Hou	33	May-Cin	321	Banks-Chi	106

Stolen Bases		Base Stealing Runs		Fielding Runs-Infield		Fielding Runs-Outfield		Wins		Winning Pct.		Complete Games	
Brock-StL	53	Bonds-SF	8.5	Kessinger-Chi	24.8	Callison-Phi	11.9	Seaver-NY	25	Seaver-NY	.781	Gibson-StL	28
Morgan-Hou	49	Brock-StL	6.8	Lanier-SF	23.6	Flood-StL	7.0	Niekro-Atl	23	Marichal-SF	.656	Marichal-SF	27
Bonds-SF	45	Morgan-Hou	5.9	Wine-Mon	19.6	Hisle-Phi	6.9	Marichal-SF	21	Merritt-Cin	.654	Perry-SF	26
Wills-Mon-LA	40	Wynn-Hou	2.6	Money-Phi	17.6	Clemente-Pit	5.7	Jenkins-Chi	21	Koosman-NY	.654	Jenkins-Chi	23
Tolan-Cin	26	Alou-Pit	2.0	Maxvill-StL	14.3	Jones-NY	4.6			Reed-Atl	.643	Niekro-Atl	21

Strikeouts		Fewest BB/Game		Games		Saves		Base Runners/9		Adjusted Relief Runs		Relief Ranking	
Jenkins-Chi	273	Marichal-SF	1.62	Granger-Cin	90	Gladding-Hou	29	Marichal-SF	9.13	McGraw-NY	14.1	McGraw-NY	19.0
Gibson-StL	269	Niekro-Atl	1.80	McGinn-Mon	74	Upshaw-Atl	27	Dierker-Hou	9.23	Granger-Cin	9.5	Taylor-NY	17.2
Singer-LA	247	Jenkins-Chi	2.05	Regan-Chi	71	Granger-Cin	27	Singer-LA	9.35	Upshaw-Atl	9.1	Brewer-LA	13.9
Wilson-Hou	235	Niekro-Chi-SD	2.07	Carroll-Cin	71	Brewer-LA	20	Niekro-Atl	9.40	Taylor-NY	8.9	Upshaw-Atl	13.1
Perry-SF	233	Osteen-LA	2.07	Reberger-SD	67	Regan-Chi	17	Seaver-NY	9.58	DiLauro-NY	8.7	Granger-Cin	12.9

Innings Pitched		Opponents' Avg.		Opponents' OBP		Earned Run Average		Adjusted ERA		Adjusted Starter Runs		Pitcher Wins	
Perry-SF	325.1	Seaver-NY	.207	Dierker-Hou	.261	Marichal-SF	2.10	Marichal-SF	167	Gibson-StL	50.2	**Gibson-StL**	6.3
Osteen-LA	321.0	Maloney-Cin	.208	Marichal-SF	.261	Carlton-StL	2.17	Seaver-NY	166	Marichal-SF	45.3	**Seaver-NY**	5.3
Singer-LA	315.2	Singer-LA	.210	Singer-LA	.261	Gibson-StL	2.18	Carlton-StL	165	Seaver-NY	43.2	**Marichal-SF**	5.0
Gibson-StL	314.0	Dierker-Hou	.214	Niekro-Atl	.264	Seaver-NY	2.21	Gibson-StL	165	Hands-Chi	42.4	**Carlton-StL**	5.0
Jenkins-Chi	311.1	Carlton-StL	.216	Seaver-NY	.272	Koosman-NY	2.28	Hands-Chi	161	Dierker-Hou	40.0	**Niekro-Atl**	4.6

Magical Mystery Mets

The wackiest decade in American history reached an appropriate end as the New York Mets, of all teams, rallied in September to win the NL East, the NLCS, and the World Series. The Mets made a run at the Cubs in July, but sagged as Chicago—with four fine starters and strong hitters in Ron Santo and Billy Williams—built a 9½ game lead in late August. But the Cubs lost 10 of 11 down the stretch as the Mets rallied furiously. With Tom Seaver winning nine times in the last five weeks, the pitching-rich Mets won going away.

Five teams in the NL West, meanwhile, stood poised to win. In fact, on September 10, first-place San Francisco and fifth-place Houston were separated by just 2 games. By September 22, though, only the Giants and Braves remained, but San Francisco lost four to the brutal Padres as Atlanta won 10 straight to clinch. This was the Giants' fifth consecutive second-place finish.

Seaver was a near-unanimous Cy Young and finished a close second in MVP voting behind the Giants' Willie McCovey.

Bobby Bonds fanned a new record 187 times, and Jimmy Wynn walked 148 times, also setting an NL mark. Pitcher Wayne Granger made history with his 90 appearances. For the first time, saves were an official statistic. Macmillan published the first edition of its ground-breaking *Baseball Encyclopedia*, setting the standard for sports reference for 20 years.

A sore arm forced Don Drysdale to retire, and Ken Boyer was released. It was also goodbye to former top relievers Roy Face, Dick Radatz, and John Wyatt. Gene Mauch reappeared in a new country with a new team: the Montreal Expos. Almost eight years of experience in Philly prepared him for the 110 losses.

The first National League Championship Series packed surprising power as New York swept the Braves. The World Series was another shock; after Baltimore took Game 1, the Mets roared back to win the next four. Great catches by Tommie Agee and Ron Swoboda, clutch homers from Donn Clendenon and Al Weis, and excellent pitching buried the Orioles.

1969 American League

TEAM	W	L	T	PCT	GB	HW	HL	R	OR	PA	H	2B	3B	HR	BB	SO	HB	SH	AVG	OBP	SLG	OPS	AOPS	BR	ABR	PF	SB	CS	BSA	BSR
EAST																														
BAL	109	53	0	.673		**60**	21	779	517	6328	1465	234	29	175	634	806	43	74	.265	**.343**	.414	**757**	117	**139**	**131**	101	82	45	65	2
DET	90	72	0	.556	19	46	35	701	601	6155	1316	188	29	182	578	922	30	63	.242	.316	.387	703	99	17	-10	104	35	28	56	-7
BOS	87	75	0	.537	22	46	35	743	736	6294	1381	234	37	**197**	**658**	923	32	67	.251	.333	**.415**	748	110	113	78	105	41	47	47	-3
WAS	86	76	0	.531	23	47	34	694	644	6196	1365	171	40	148	630	900	32	51	.251	.330	.378	708	110	36	74	95	52	40	57	-3
NY	80	81	1	.497	28.5	48	32	562	587	5990	1247	210	44	94	565	840	14	63	.235	.308	.344	652	91	-74	-53	97	119	74	62	0
CLE	62	99	0	.385	46.5	33	48	573	717	6014	1272	173	24	119	535	906	24	47	.237	.307	.345	652	85	-79	-95	103	85	37	70	6
WEST																														
MIN	97	65	0	.599		57	24	**790**	618	6424	**1520**	**246**	32	163	599	906	43	65	**.268**	.340	.408	748	113	121	100	103	115	70	62	3
OAK	88	74	0	.543	9	49	32	740	678	6403	1400	210	28	148	617	953	**63**	74	.249	.329	.376	705	108	33	61	96	100	39	72	8
CAL	71	91	1	.438	26	43	38	528	652	5980	1221	151	29	88	516	929	32	**75**	.240	.319	.338	619	83	-142	-119	96	54	39	58	-2
KC	69	93	1	.426	28	36	45	586	688	6122	1311	179	32	98	522	901	43	57	.240	.309	.338	647	86	-87	-94	101	129	70	65	4
CHI	68	94	0	.420	29	41	40	625	723	6158	1346	210	27	112	552	844	49	70	.247	.320	.357	677	92	-24	-53	105	54	22	71	4
SEA	64	98	1	.395	33	34	47	639	799	6205	1276	179	27	125	626	1015	34	72	.234	.316	.346	662	92	-54	-49	99	**167**	59	**74**	16
TOT	973					540	431	7960		74269	16120	2385	378	1649	7032	10845	439	778	.246	.321	.369	690					1033	570	64	28

TEAM	CG	SHO	GR	SV	IP	H	HR	BB	SO	BR/9	ERA	AERA	OAV	OOB	PR	APR	PF	OSB	OCS	FA	E	WPB	DP	FW	PW	BW	BSW	DIF
EAST																												
BAL	50	**20**	235	36	1473.2	**1194**	**117**	498	897	10.5	2.83	127	**.223**	**.290**	130	125	99	48	51	**.984**	101	48	145	2.2	**13.1**	**13.7**	-.0	-1.0
DET	**55**	**20**	251	28	1455.1	1250	128	586	**1032**	11.6	3.31	113	.232	.310	50	69	104	109	44	.979	130	60	130	.5	7.2	-1.0	-.5	2.7
BOS	30	7	298	41	1466.2	1423	155	685	935	13.2	3.92	97	.256	.341	-49	-16	105	84	51	.975	157	82	178	-1.0	-1.7	8.2	-1.1	1.5
WAS	28	10	311	41	1447.1	1310	135	656	835	12.4	3.49	100	.244	.328	22	2	97	84	58	.978	140	70	159	-.0	.2	7.8	-.6	-2.4
NY	53	13	199	20	1440.2	1258	118	522	801	11.2	3.23	109	.236	.304	63	47	97	76	43	.979	131	65	158	.5	4.9	-5.6	-.2	-.1
CLE	35	7	294	22	1437.0	1330	134	681	1000	12.9	3.94	96	.248	.335	-51	-22	105	87	53	.976	145	71	153	-.4	-2.3	-10.0	-.4	-6.2
WEST																												
MIN	41	8	302	**43**	1497.2	1388	119	524	906	11.7	3.24	112	.246	.313	64	66	100	70	35	.977	150	66	177	-.6	6.9	10.5	-.1	-.7
OAK	42	14	276	36	1480.2	1356	163	586	887	12.0	3.71	93	.245	.320	-15	-48	95	84	48	.979	136	81	162	.2	-5.0	6.4	.6	4.8
CAL	25	9	285	39	1438.1	1294	126	517	885	11.7	3.54	99	.242	.313	13	-8	96	89	56	.978	136	94	164	.2	-.8	-12.5	-.5	3.5
KC	42	10	249	25	1464.2	1357	136	560	894	11.9	3.72	99	.246	.313	-15	-4	102	75	43	.975	157	69	114	-1.0	-.4	-9.9	.2	-9
CHI	29	10	265	25	1437.2	1470	146	564	810	12.9	4.21	91	.267	.337	-93	-55	106	109	47	.981	122	95	163	1.0	-5.8	-5.6	.2	-2.8
SEA	21	6	**357**	33	1463.2	1490	172	653	963	13.5	4.35	84	.264	.343	-118	-115	100	117	46	.974	167	82	149	-1.5	-12.1	-5.1	**1.4**	.3
TOT	451	134	3322	389	17503.1					12.1	3.62		.246	.321						.978	1672	883	1852					

Batter-Fielder Wins	Batting Average	On-Base Percentage	Slugging Average	On-Base Plus Slugging	Adjusted OPS	Adjusted Batter Runs
Petrocelli-Bos 7.6	Carew-Min 332	Killebrew-Min 427	Jackson-Oak 608	Jackson-Oak 1018	Jackson-Oak 189	Jackson-Oak 69.6
Jackson-Oak 6.3	Smith-Bos..............309	F.Robinson-Bal 415	Petrocelli-Bos 589	Killebrew-Min 1011	Howard-Was 180	Howard-Was.........64.5
Aparicio-Chi 5.4	Oliva-Min 309	Jackson-Oak 410	Killebrew-Min 584	Petrocelli-Bos 992	Killebrew-Min........176	Killebrew-Min.......63.6
Cardenas-Min 4.9	F.Robinson-Bal 308	Petrocelli-Bos 403	Howard-Was 574	Howard-Was 976	Petrocelli-Bos 168	Petrocelli-Bos 50.9
Killebrew-Min ...4.6	Powell-Bal.............304	Howard-Was 402	Powell-Bal..............559	F.Robinson-Bal 955	F.Robinson-Bal 164	F.Robinson-Bal 49.4

Runs	Hits	Doubles	Triples	Home Runs	Total Bases	Runs Batted In
Jackson-Oak 123	Oliva-Min 197	Oliva-Min 39	Unser-Was...............8	Killebrew-Min..........49	Howard-Was 340	Killebrew-Min..........140
F.Robinson-Bal 111	Clarke-NY 183	Jackson-Oak 36	Smith-Bos.................7	Howard-Was 48	Jackson-Oak 334	Powell-Bal................119
Howard-Was 111	Blair-Bal 178	Johnson-Bal 34	Clarke-NY................7	Jackson-Oak 47	Killebrew-Min 324	Jackson-Oak 118
Killebrew-Min ...106	Howard-Was 175	Petrocelli-Bos 32		Yastrzemski-Bos 40	Oliva-Min 316	Bando-Oak 113
Bando-Oak 106	Horton-Cle.............174	Blair-Bal 32		Petrocelli-Bos 40	Petrocelli-Bos 315	

Stolen Bases	Base Stealing Runs	Fielding Runs-Infield	Fielding Runs-Outfield	Wins	Winning Pct.	Complete Games
Harper-Sea 73	Campaneris-Oak ...10.8	Knoop-Cal-Chi 32.5	Blair-Bal 11.7	McLain-Det 24	Palmer-Bal 800	Stottlemyre-NY 24
Campaneris-Oak ...62	Harper-Sea 9.8	Aparicio-Chi 32.5	Piniella-KC 10.1	Cuellar-Bal.............23	Perry-Min 769	McLain-Det 18
Tovar-Min 45	Cardenal-Cle 5.8	Cardenas-Min......23.2	Tovar-Min 9.4		McNally-Bal 741	McDowell-Cle 18
Kelly-KC..............40	Tovar-Min 5.7	McMullen-Was 21.4	Comer-Sea 7.3		McLain-Det 727	Cuellar-Bal........18
Foy-KC................37	Kelly-KC.................4.3	Brinkman-Was 19.7	Voss-Cal 7.1		Odom-Oak 714	Peterson-NY 16

Strikeouts	Fewest BB/Game	Games	Saves	Base Runners/9	Adjusted Relief Runs	Relief Ranking
McDowell-Cle 279	Peterson-NY 1.42	Wood-Chi 76	Perranoski-Min 31	Hall-Bal.................8.09	K.Tatum-Cal 22.2	Perranoski-Min 40.7
Lolich-Det 271	Bosman-Was 1.82	Perranoski-Min 75	K.Tatum-Cal 22	Wilhelm-Cal 9.05	Perranoski-Min 20.3	K.Tatum-Cal 33.5
Messersmith-Cal ...211	McLain-Det 1.86	Lyle-Bos 71	Lyle-Bos 17	Peterson-NY 9.07	Lyle-Bos 14.0	Watt-Bal ....19.
Boswell-Min 190	Perry-Min 2.27	Locker-Chi-Sea 68	Watt-Bal 16	Cuellar-Bal 9.07	Watt-Bal 13.9	Drabowsky-KC ...19.
	Cuellar-Bal 2.45	Segui-Sea 66	Higgins-Was 16	Drabowsky-KC 9.18	Hall-Bal 13.1	Lyle-Bos 18.7

Innings Pitched	Opponents' Avg.	Opponents' OBP	Earned Run Average	Adjusted ERA	Adjusted Starter Runs	Pitcher Wins
McLain-Det..........325.0	Messersmith-Cal ...190	Cuellar-Bal 260	Bosman-Was 2.19	Bosman-Was 160	McLain-Det 37.2	Perranoski-Min ....4.
Stottlemyre-NY ...303.0	Palmer-Bal 200	Bosman-Was 260	Palmer-Bal 2.34	Palmer-Bal 154	Cuellar-Bal 35.7	**K.Tatum-Cal** .....4.
Cuellar-Bal 290.2	Cuellar-Bal 204	Peterson-NY 261	Cuellar-Bal 2.38	Cuellar-Bal 151	Messersmith-Cal ...27.9	**Stottlemyre-NY** ...3.
McDowell-Cle 285.0	Lolich-Det 210	Palmer-Bal 272	Messersmith-Cal 2.52	Messersmith-Cal 139	Palmer-Bal 27.5	**Cuellar-Bal** ....3.
Lolich-Det 280.2	McDowell-Cle 213	Messersmith-Cal ...274	Peterson-NY 2.38	Peterson-NY 138	Peterson-NY 26.9	**Peterson-NY** .....3.

A Whole New Game

In less than a decade, the league had expanded by a third, added divisions, and instituted a new set of league championship series. It was a shock to the system. Responding to pressure from fans, hitters, and the media, the leagues shrunk the strike zone, which now ranged from the armpits to the top of the knees. AL scoring per game increased 20 percent.

Reggie Jackson of Oakland was on a record home run pace, but settled for "just" 47, third best in the AL. For the first time, five men hit 40 or more homers. Sam McDowell of Cleveland took his fourth strikeout crown, and Lou Piniella was Rookie of the Year for expansion Kansas City, which finished ahead of Chicago and fellow expansion team Seattle in the West.

Three future catching mainstays debuted: Thurman Munson, Carlton Fisk, and Rick Dempsey. Meanwhile, pitcher Paul Edmondson of Chicago perished in an accident traveling to 1970 spring training.

Minnesota's Rod Carew won the first of his seven batting titles, and under the tutelage of rookie manager Billy Martin,

Carew stole home seven times. Tony Oliva led the AL in hits, Harmon Killebrew was MVP, and the Twins won the West. They were no match, however, for the Orioles, who took the inaugural American League Championship Series in three straight. Neither division race was close.

Feisty Earl Weaver, in his first full season as manager in Baltimore, knew how to structure a lineup. His club led the East in runs and its pitching was the league's best. Mike Cuellar (co-Cy Young winner with Denny McLain) and Dave McNally each earned 20 wins. However, the Orioles were a surprise World Series loser as the Cinderella New York Mets won in five. The Orioles tallied just 9 runs.

With two new clubs added, AL attendance again reached an all-time high. But most clubs' attendance fell, with seven clubs drawing fewer than a million, as football—busily merging the AFL and NFL—made further inroads on the American psyche.

1968 National League

TEAM	W	L	T	PCT	GB	HW	HL	R	OR	PA	H	2B	3B	HR	BB	SO	HB	SH	AVG	OBP	SLG	OPS	AOPS	BR	ABR	PF	SB	CS	BSA	BSR
STL	97	65	0	.599		47	34	583	472	6080	1383	227	48	73	378	897	32	67	.249	.298	.346	644	101	2	9	99	110	45	71	8
SF	88	74	1	.543	9	42	39	599	529	6132	1301	162	33	108	508	904	47	92	.239	.307	.341	648	102	20	20	100	50	37	57	-2
CHI	84	78	1	.519	13	47	34	612	611	6020	1319	203	43	130	415	854	36	74	.242	.298	.366	664	99	36	0	107	50	41	58	-1
CIN	83	79	1	.512	14	40	41	690	673	6286	1573	281	36	106	379	938	37	64	.273	.320	.389	709	113	134	0	107	106	59	55	-6
ATL	81	81	1	.500	16	41	40	514	549	6118	1399	179	31	80	414	782	36	86	.252	.307	.339	646	101	8	6	100	83	44	65	3
PIT	80	82	1	.494	17	40	41	583	532	6163	1404	180	44	80	422	953	33	96	.252	.306	.343	649	104	-16	25	99	130	59	69	8
PHI	76	86	0	.469	21	38	43	543	615	5966	1253	178	30	100	462	1003	22	64	.233	.294	.330	627	95	-24	-23	100	58	51	53	-5
LA	76	86	0	.469	21	41	40	470	509	5935	1234	202	36	67	439	980	18	79	.230	.289	.319	608	96	-61	-23	93	57	43	57	-3
NY	73	89	1	.451	24	32	49	473	499	6027	1252	178	30	81	379	1203	43	75	.228	.281	.315	596	84	-93	-96	101	72	45	62	0
HOU	72	90	1	.444	25	42	39	510	588	5994	1233	205	28	66	479	988	48	97	.231	.298	.317	615	94	-38	-28	98	44	51	46	-8
TOT	813					410	400	5577		60721	13351	1995	359	891	4275	9502	352	794	.243	.300	.341	641					704	460	60	-6

TEAM	CG	SHO	GR	SV	IP	H	HR	BB	SO	BR/9	ERA	AERA	OAV	OOB	PR	APR	PF	OSB	OCS	FA	E	WPB	DP	FW	PW	BW	BSW	DIF
STL	63	30	196	32	1479.1	1282	82	375	971	10.3	2.49	116	.234	.285	82	69	97	50	36	.978	140	40	135	-.0	7.9	1.0	1.0	6.1
SF	77	20	167	16	1469.0	1302	86	344	942	10.2	2.71	109	.236	.282	45	39	99	93	47	.975	162	79	125	-1.3	4.5	2.3	-.2	1.7
CHI	46	12	221	32	1453.2	1399	138	392	894	11.3	3.41	93	.254	.304	-69	-39	106	50	49	.981	119	50	149	1.2	-4.5	.0	-.0	6.3
CIN	24	16	321	38	1490.1	1399	114	573	963	12.2	3.56	99	.256	.321	-96	-63	106	62	49	.978	144	79	144	-.2	-7.2	10.4	-.6	-.3
ATL	44	16	199	29	1474.2	1326	87	362	871	10.5	2.92	103	.241	.290	11	12	100	88	34	.980	125	68	139	.9	1.4	.7	.4	-3.3
PIT	42	19	244	30	1487.0	1322	73	485	897	11.2	2.74	107	.240	.304	.40	31	98	61	50	.979	139	62	162	.0	3.6	2.9	1.0	-8.5
PHI	42	12	227	27	1448.1	1416	91	421	935	11.7	3.36	89	.257	.313	-61	-57	101	56	56	.980	127	49	163	.7	-6.5	-2.6	-.5	4.0
LA	38	23	218	31	1448.2	1293	65	414	994	10.8	2.69	103	.241	.297	48	14	93	65	62	.977	144	60	144	-.3	1.6	-2.6	-.3	-3.4
NY	45	25	212	32	1483.1	1250	87	430	1014	10.5	2.72	111	.230	.290	43	48	101	71	49	.979	133	70	142	.4	5.5	-11.0	.0	-3.0
HOU	50	12	243	23	1446.2	1362	68	479	1021	11.7	3.26	91	.249	.311	-44	-49	99	108	28	.975	156	89	129	-1.0	-5.6	-3.2	-.8	1.7
TOT	471	185	2248	290	14681.0					11.7	3.26									.978	1389	646	1432					
										11.0	2.99		.243	.300						.978								

Batter-Fielder Wins	Batting Average	On-Base Percentage	Slugging Average	On-Base Plus Slugging	Adjusted OPS	Adjusted Batter Runs
H.Aaron-Atl 5.0	Rose-Cin 335	Rose-Cin 391	McCovey-SF 545	McCovey-SF 923	McCovey-SF 176	McCovey-SF 49.3
McCovey-SF 4.9	Alou-Pit 332	McCovey-SF 378	Allen-Phi 520	Allen-Phi 872	Allen-Phi 161	Wynn-Hou 41.4
Wynn-Hou 4.7	Alou-Atl 317	Wynn-Hou 376	Williams-Chi 500	Rose-Cin 861	Mays-SF 158	H.Aaron-Atl 39.7
Santo-Chi 4.4	A.Johnson-Cin 312	Staub-Hou 373	H.Aaron-Atl 498	Mays-SF 860	Wynn-Hou 158	Rose-Cin 39.5
Haller-LA 4.1	Flood-StL 301	Mays-SF 372	Mays-SF 488	H.Aaron-Atl 852	H.Aaron-Atl 154	Allen-Phi 38.2

Runs	Hits	Doubles	Triples	Home Runs	Total Bases	Runs Batted In
Beckert-Chi 98	Rose-Cin 210	Brock-StL 46	Brock-StL 14	McCovey-SF 36	Williams-Chi 321	McCovey-SF 105
Rose-Cin 94	Alou-Pit 210	Rose-Cin 42	Clemente-Pit 12	Allen-Phi 33	H.Aaron-Atl 302	Williams-Chi 98
Perez-Cin 93	Beckert-Chi 189	Bench-Cin 40	Davis-LA 10	Banks-Chi 32	Rose-Cin 294	Santo-Chi 98
Brock-StL 92	A.Johnson-Cin 188	Staub-Hou 37	Allen-Phi 9	Williams-Chi 30	Alou-Atl 290	Perez-Cin 92
Williams-Chi 91	Flood-StL 186	Alou-Atl 37	Williams-Chi 9	H.Aaron-Atl 29	McCovey-SF 285	Allen-Phi 90

Stolen Bases	Base Stealing Runs	Fielding Runs-Infield	Fielding Runs-Outfield	Wins	Winning Pct.	Complete Games
Brock-StL 62	Brock-StL 9.4	Kessinger-Chi 26.6	H.Aaron-Atl 11.9	Marichal-SF 26	Blass-Pit 750	Marichal-SF 30
Wills-Pit 52	Davis-LA 4.4	Alley-Pit 25.8	Wynn-Hou 10.6	Gibson-StL 22	Marichal-SF 743	Gibson-StL 28
Davis-LA 36	H.Aaron-Atl 4.4	Mazeroski-Pit 20.4	Flood-StL 9.1	Jenkins-Chi 20	Gibson-StL 710	Jenkins-Chi 20
H.Aaron-Atl 28	Wills-Pit 4.1	Santo-Chi 20.1	Clemente-Pit 7.4		Briles-StL 633	Perry-SF 19
Jones-NY 23	Taylor-Phi 3.1	Lanier-SF 16.7	Phillips-Chi 4.1			Koosman-NY 17

Strikeouts	Fewest BB/Game	Games	Saves	Base Runners/9	Adjusted Relief Runs	Relief Ranking
Gibson-StL 268	Hands-Chi 1.25	Abernathy-Cin 78	Regan-LA-Chi 25	Gibson-StL 7.89	Kline-Pit 15.3	Kline-Pit 23.0
Jenkins-Chi 260	Marichal-SF 1.27	Regan-LA-Chi 71	Carroll-Atl-Cin 17	Jarvis-Atl 8.93	Regan-LA-Chi 11.9	Regan-LA-Chi 18.5
Singer-LA 227	Seaver-NY 1.55	Carroll-Atl-Cin 68	Hoerner-StL 17	Seaver-NY 9.06	Abernathy-Cin 9.6	Linzy-SF 14.6
Marichal-SF 218	Pappas-Cin-Atl 1.57	Taylor-NY 58	Brewer-LA 14	Bolin-SF 9.07	Linzy-SF 7.8	Abernathy-Cin 13.0
Sadecki-SF 206	Niekro-Atl 1.58	Linzy-SF 57		Hands-Chi 9.15	Koonce-NY 7.2	Koonce-NY 8.6

Innings Pitched	Opponents' Avg.	Opponents' OBP	Earned Run Average	Adjusted ERA	Adjusted Starter Runs	Pitcher Wins
Marichal-SF 325.2	Gibson-StL 184	Gibson-StL 233	Gibson-StL 1.12	Gibson-StL 258	Gibson-StL 59.6	Gibson-StL 7.6
Jenkins-Chi 308.0	Bolin-SF 200	Jarvis-Atl 252	Bolin-SF 1.99	Bolin-SF 148	Seaver-NY 26.2	Seaver-NY 3.1
Gibson-StL 304.2	Veale-Pit 211	Bolin-SF 258	Veale-Pit 2.05	Koosman-NY 145	Koosman-NY 25.3	Koosman-NY 2.8
Perry-SF 290.2	Jarvis-Atl 214	Seaver-NY 261	Koosman-NY 2.08	Veale-Pit 142	Veale-Pit 23.6	Marichal-SF 2.5
Seaver-NY 278.0	Moose-Pit 218	Hands-Chi 265	Blass-Pit 2.12	Bolin-SF 138	Bolin-SF 20.2	Jenkins-Chi 2.5

No Hitting, Please

They called '68 the "Year of the Pitcher." And for good reason. Batting average fell to an all-time low, and slugging percentage was the lowest since 1919. Runs per game were just 3.43, the fewest in sixty years. It was really the Year of Bob Gibson. His 1.12 ERA is the best since 1914, and hasn't been matched. Only two pitchers have ever topped his 13 shutouts. Gibson was a unanimous Cy Young pick and won a close MVP vote.

Juan Marichal won 26 and threw 30 complete games, the most since 1952. Don Drysdale didn't allow an earned run for a record 58.2 consecutive innings. The Cubs didn't score in 48 innings; Fergie Jenkins lost 1-0 five times. Willie McCovey's 105 RBIs were the fewest for a league leader since 1920.

With the Cardinals dominating, the race was never close. The Giants were again bridesmaids, and the Cubs scraped into third. Cincinnati catcher Johnny Bench was Rookie of the Year, and New York improved 12 games due to an excellent young mound staff under new manager Gil Hodges. The difference from first to last was just 25 games, the fewest in a decade.

St. Louis magic ran out in the World Series as the Tigers, down three games to one, won it all. St. Louis scored just twice in the final two games at Busch Stadium. Cardinals owner Augie Busch, incensed, began disassembling his club.

The NL announced that new franchises in San Diego and Montreal would join the league in 1969. Not all went smoothly; veteran pitcher Larry Jackson retired after being selected by Montreal in the expansion draft. Bowie Kuhn was the new commissioner, combining a willingness to do the owners' bidding with the baseball knowledge lacking in predecessor William "Spike" Eckert. Kuhn inherited a troubled game. Attendance had dropped again in 1968, and the newly galvanized Players Association was making noises.

1968 American League

TEAM	W	L	T	PCT	GB	HW	HL	R	OR	PA	H	2B	3B	HR	BB	SO	HB	SH	AVG	OBP	SLG	OPS	AOPS	BR	ABR	PF	SB	CS	BSA	BSR
DET	103	59	2	.636		56	25	671	492	6179	1292	190	39	**185**	521	964	61	73	.235	.307	**.385**	692	113	**102**	84	103	26	32	45	-5
BAL	91	71	0	.562	12	47	33	579	497	6022	1187	**215**	28	133	570	1019	48	80	.225	.304	.352	656	105	45	46	100	78	32	**71**	6
CLE	86	75	1	.534	16.5	43	37	516	504	5988	1266	210	36	75	427	858	39	69	.234	.293	.327	620	96	-34	-25	98	115	61	65	4
BOS	86	76	0	.531	17	46	35	614	611	6036	1253	207	17	125	**582**	974	33	77	.236	**.313**	.352	665	102	67	31	106	76	62	55	-5
NY	83	79	2	.512	20	39	42	536	531	5992	1137	154	34	109	566	958	30	56	.214	.292	.318	610	94	-48	-31	97	90	50	64	2
OAK	82	80	1	.506	21	44	38	569	544	6026	**1300**	192	40	94	472	1022	35	78	**.240**	.304	.343	647	107	19	44	96	**147**	61	71	11
MIN	79	83	0	.488	24	41	40	562	546	5974	1274	207	**41**	105	445	966	49	69	.237	.299	.350	649	98	20	-10	106	98	54	64	3
CAL	67	95	0	.414	36	32	49	498	615	5942	1209	170	33	71	447	1080	40	75	.227	.291	.318	609	94	-53	-37	97	62	50	55	-4
CHI	67	95	0	.414	36	36	45	463	527	5965	1233	169	33	71	397	**840**	40	**90**	.228	.284	.311	595	86	-85	-91	101	90	50	64	0
WAS	65	96	0	.404	37.5	34	47	524	665	5971	1208	160	37	124	454	960	39	46	.224	.287	.336	623	98	-35	-17	97	29	19	60	0
TOT	812					418	391	5532		60095	12359	1874	338	1104	4881	9641	426	713	.230	.297	.339	637					811	471	63	14

TEAM	CG	SHO	GR	SV	IP	H	HR	BB	SO	BR/9	ERA	AERA	OAV	OOB	PR	APR	PF	OSB	OCS	FA	E	WPB	DP	FW	PW	BW	BSW	DIF
DET	59	19	238	29	1489.2	1180	129	486	1115	10.3	2.71	111	.217	.284	44	49	101	80	40	**.983**	105	50	133	2.0	5.6	**9.6**	-.7	5.4
BAL	53	16	234	31	1451.0	1111	101	502	1044	10.3	2.66	110	.212	.285	51	43	98	80	59	.981	120	77	131	1.0	4.9	5.3	.5	-1.8
CLE	48	**23**	222	32	1464.1	**1087**	98	540	**1157**	10.3	2.66	112	**.206**	.285	53	51	100	61	44	.979	128	92	147	.6	-3.1	3.6	-.7	4.7
BOS	55	17	225	31	1447.0	1303	115	523	972	11.7	3.33	95	.241	.312	-57	-27	106	104	42	.979	139	**34**	142	.0	2.3	-3.6	.0	3.2
NY	45	14	204	27	1467.1	1308	99	424	831	10.8	2.79	104	.240	.297	31	20	98	57	48	.979	145	75	136	-.4	-2.4	5.0	1.1	-2.3
OAK	45	18	252	29	1455.2	1220	124	505	997	10.9	2.94	96	.227	.295	6	-21	95	92	38	.973	145	61	117	-2.0	3.3	-1.1	.2	-2.4
MIN	46	14	229	29	1433.1	1224	**92**	414	996	10.5	2.89	107	.229	.288	13	29	104	78	36	.977	140	86	**156**	-.2	-9.6	-4.2	-.6	.7
CAL	29	11	320	31	1437.0	1234	131	519	869	11.2	3.43	85	.233	.303	-72	-84	98	84	56	.977	151	56	152	-.8	5.2	-10.4	.0	-8.0
CHI	20	11	**322**	**40**	1468.0	1290	97	451	834	11.1	2.75	110	.236	.301	38	45	102	88	55	.977	148	82	144	-.7	-13.5	-1.9	-.2	.8
WAS	26	11	296	28	1439.2	1402	118	517	826	12.3	3.64	80	.258	.325	-106	-118	98	86	54	.976								
TOT	426	154	2542	307	14553.0					10.9	2.98		.230	.297						.978	1373	677	1388					

Batter-Fielder Wins
Yastrzemski-Bos 6.3
Freehan-Det 5.2
F.Howard-Was 4.5
Campaneris-Oak 4.2
B.Robinson-Bal 3.3

Batting Average
Yastrzemski-Bos 301
Cater-Oak 290
Oliva-Min 289
Horton-Det 285
Uhlaender-Min 283

On-Base Percentage
Yastrzemski-Bos 426
F.Robinson-Bal 390
Mantle-NY 385
Monday-Oak 371
Andrews-Bos 368

Slugging Average
F.Howard-Was 552
Horton-Det 543
Harrelson-Bos 518
Yastrzemski-Bos 495
Oliva-Min 477

On-Base Plus Slugging
Yastrzemski-Bos 922
Horton-Det 895
F.Howard-Was 890
Harrelson-Bos 874
F.Robinson-Bal 834

Adjusted OPS
F.Howard-Was 173
Yastrzemski-Bos 169
Horton-Det 165
Harrelson-Bos 154
F.Robinson-Bal 153

Adjusted Batter Runs
Yastrzemski-Bos 53.1
F.Howard-Was 49.4
Horton-Det 39.1
Harrelson-Bos 34.8
F.Robinson-Bal 31.9

Runs
McAuliffe-Det 95
Yastrzemski-Bos 90
White-NY 89
Tovar-Min 89
Stanley-Det 88

Hits
Campaneris-Oak 177
Tovar-Min 167
F.Howard-Was 164
Aparicio-Chi 164
Yastrzemski-Bos 162

Doubles
Smith-Bos 37
B.Robinson-Bal 36
Yastrzemski-Bos 32
Tovar-Min 31

Triples
Fregosi-Cal 13
McCraw-Chi 12
Stroud-Was 10
McAuliffe-Det 10
Campaneris-Oak 9

Home Runs
F.Howard-Was 44
Horton-Det 36
Harrelson-Bos 35
Jackson-Oak 29

Total Bases
F.Howard-Was 330
Horton-Det 278
Harrelson-Bos 277
Yastrzemski-Bos 267
Northrup-Det 259

Runs Batted In
Harrelson-Bos 109
F.Howard-Was 106
Northrup-Det 90
Powell-Bal 85
Horton-Det 85

Stolen Bases
Campaneris-Oak 62
Cardenal-Cle 40
Tovar-Min 35
Buford-Bal 27
Foy-Bos 26

Base Stealing Runs
Campaneris-Oak 5.9
Tovar-Min 3.2
Foy-Bos 2.9
McCraw-Chi 2.7
Nelson-Cle 2.6

Fielding Runs-Infield
Clarke-NY 29.0
Aparicio-Chi 20.1
Belanger-Bal 19.3
Knoop-Cal 19.1
B.Robinson-Bal 18.6

Fielding Runs-Outfield
Yastrzemski-Bos 11.2
Unser-Was 10.0
Davalillo-Cle-Cal 6.6
Cardenal-Cle 6.5
Jackson-Oak 6.3

Wins
McLain-Det 31
McNally-Bal 22
Tiant-Cle 21
Stottlemyre-NY 21
Hardin-Bal 18

Winning Pct.
McLain-Det 838
Culp-Bos 727
Tiant-Cle 700
Ellsworth-Bos 696
McNally-Bal 688

Complete Games
McLain-Det 28
Tiant-Cle 19
Stottlemyre-NY 19
McNally-Bal 18
Hardin-Bal 16

Strikeouts
McDowell-Cle 283
McLain-Det 280
Tiant-Cle 264
Chance-Min 234
McNally-Bal 202

Fewest BB/Game
Peterson-NY 1.23
McLain-Det 1.69
Ellsworth-Bos 1.70
Kaat-Min 1.73
McNally-Bal 1.81

Games
Wood-Chi 88
Wilhelm-Chi 72
Locker-Chi 70
Perranoski-Min 66

Saves
Worthington-Min 18
Wood-Chi 16
Higgins-Was 13

Base Runners/9
McNally-Bal 7.91
Tiant-Cle 7.98
McLain-Det 8.30
Romo-Cle 8.32
Messersmith-Cal 8.85

Adjusted Relief Runs
Wood-Chi 20.0
Wilhelm-Chi 13.8
McMahon-Chi-Det 10.6
Locker-Chi 7.3

Relief Ranking
Wood-Chi 32.9
Romo-Cle 16.2
Wilhelm-Chi 14.5
Drabowsky-Bal 8.9
McMahon-Chi-Det 8.5

Innings Pitched
McLain-Det 336.0
Chance-Min 292.0
Stottlemyre-NY 278.2
McNally-Bal 273.0
McDowell-Cle 269.0

Opponents' Avg.
Tiant-Cle 168
McNally-Bal 182
McDowell-Cle 189
Siebert-Cle 198
McLain-Det 200

Opponents' OBP
McNally-Bal 232
Tiant-Cle 233
McLain-Det 243
Chance-Min 260
Nash-Oak 262

Earned Run Average
Tiant-Cle 1.60
McDowell-Cle 1.81
McNally-Bal 1.95
McLain-Det 1.96
John-Chi 1.98

Adjusted ERA
Tiant-Cle 185
McDowell-Cle 164
McLain-Det 154
John-Chi 153
McNally-Bal 150

Adjusted Starter Runs
Tiant-Cle 39.7
McLain-Det 36.3
McNally-Bal 30.9
McDowell-Cle 28.4
Bahnsen-NY 25.8

Pitcher Wins
Tiant-Cle 4.4
McLain-Det 4.4
McNally-Bal 4.3
Wood-Chi 3.8
McDowell-Cle 3.3

Burning Bright

The pennant-winning Tigers helped unite a riot-torn city, becoming the only AL team in the decade to draw more than two million fans. Denny McLain won 31 games, capturing the Cy Young and MVP trophies, and Detroit had the league's top attack—but that wasn't saying much.

The league batting average of .230 is the lowest ever recorded, and the 3.41 runs scored per game per team remains the fewest in AL history. As clubs tried to create runs by any means possible, stolen bases rose again by 19 percent. Cleveland's Luis Tiant allowed just 5.30 hits a game, a new record.

Chicago's Wilbur Wood pitched 88 games, another record, as his White Sox fell 22 games into eighth place. Gigantic Frank Howard won the home run title, but the Senators still finished last. Oakland improved 19½ games with a very young (and cheap) club. Catfish Hunter pitched the AL's first perfect game in the regular season since 1922.

For the World Series, Detroit manager Mayo Smith wanted shortstop Ray Oyler and his weak bat out of the lineup, so he shifted outfielder Mickey Stanley to short. The move allowed the Tigers to get Al Kaline into the lineup; the veteran hit .379 with 2 homers.

The Tigers trailed three games to one before capturing Game 5, behind Mickey Lolich; McLain won Game 6 in St. Louis, 13-1. Jim Northrup's three-run triple broke open a scoreless tie in the deciding contest, and Lolich won his third game of the Series, defeating Bob Gibson, 4-1.

Prior to the 1969 season, Mickey Mantle announced his retirement. Elston Howard and Roger Maris, already with other clubs, also hung up the spikes. The AL and NL announced expansion to 12 clubs each for 1969, with each loop split into East and West divisions and new League Championship Series to determine the pennant winners. And baseball felt obliged to correct the obvious pitching domination prior to the next season.

1967 National League

TEAM	W	L	T	PCT	GB	HW	HL	R	OR	PA	H	2B	3B	HR	BB	SO	HB	SH	AVG	OBP	SLG	OPS	AOPS	BR	ABR	PF	SB	CS	BSA	BSR
STL	101	60	0	.627		49	32	695	557	6152	1462	225	40	115	443	919	45	54	.263	.320	.379	699	108	53	62	99	102	54	65	4
SF	91	71	0	.562	10.5	51	31	652	551	6205	1354	201	39	140	520	978	42	92	.245	.313	.372	685	104	24	33	99	22	30	42	-6
CHI	87	74	1	.540	14	49	34	702	624	6148	1373	211	49	128	509	912	34	93	.251	.316	.378	694	100	45	16	105	63	50	56	-4
CIN	87	75	0	.537	14.5	49	32	604	563	6012	1366	251	54	109	372	969	31	56	.248	.297	.372	669	88	-20	-80	111	63		59	-4
PHI	82	80	0	.506	19.5	45	35	612	581	6096	1306	221	47	103	545	1033	27	90	.242	.313	.357	670	98	1	-5	101	92	63	59	-2
PIT	81	81	1	.500	20.5	49	32	679	693	6255	1585	193	62	91	387	914	36	80	.277	.324	.380	704	101	58	55	101	79	37	68	4
ATL	77	85	0	.475	24.5	48	33	631	640	6088	1307	191	29	158	512	947	33	57	.240	.307	.372	679	102	10	19	99	55	45	55	-4
LA	73	89	0	.451	28.5	42	39	519	595	6110	1285	203	38	82	485	881	43	65	.236	.301	.332	633	96	-74	-25	92	56	47	54	-4
HOU	69	93	0	.426	32.5	46	35	626	742	6177	1372	259	46	93	537	934	26	91	.249	.317	.364	681	106	24	47	97	88	38	70	6
NY	61	101	0	.377	40.5	36	42	498	672	5928	1288	178	23	83	362	981	37	68	.238	.288	.325	613	83	-121	-113	98	58	44	57	-3
TOT	810					464	345	6218		61171	13698	2133	427	1102	4672	9468	354	729	.249	.310	.363	673					694	470	60	-12

TEAM	CG	SHO	GR	SV	IP	H	HR	BB	SO	BR/9	ERA	AERA	OAV	OOB	PR	APR	PF	OSB	OCS	FA	E	WPB	DP	FW	PW	BW	BSW	DIF
STL	44	17	272	45	1465.0	1313	97	431	956	10.9	3.05	108	.239	.297	54	40	97	45	48	.978	140	48	127	.0	4.3	6.7	.6	8.9
SF	64	17	215	25	1474.1	1283	113	453	990	10.8	2.92	113	.234	.294	75	62	97	75	47	.979	134	66	149	.4	6.7	3.6	-.5	-.2
CHI	47	7	244	28	1457.0	1352	142	463	888	11.4	3.48	102	.246	.306	-17	9	105	57	38	.981	121	39	143	1.1	1.0	1.7	-.3	3.0
CIN	34	18	235	39	1468.0	1328	101	498	1065	11.5	3.05	123	.241	.306	54	103	111	81	44	.980	121	71	124	1.1	11.2	-8.7	-.0	2.5
PHI	46	17	214	23	1453.2	1372	86	403	967	11.2	3.10	110	.250	.304	44	49	101	63	41	.978	137	53	174	.2	5.3	-.5	-.3	-3.7
PIT	35	5	283	35	1458.1	1439	108	561	820	12.5	3.74	90	.261	.330	-59	-61	100	60	44	.978	141	55	186	.0	-6.6	6.0	.6	.0
ATL	35	5	276	32	1454.0	1377	118	449	862	11.6	3.47	96	.251	.310	-16	-25	98	86	54	.978	138	101	148	.2	-2.7	2.1	-.3	-3.2
LA	41	17	229	24	1473.0	1421	93	393	967	11.3	3.21	96	.254	.306	27	-20	92	58	48	.975	160	52	144	-1.1	-2.2	-2.7	-.3	-1.7
HOU	35	8	294	21	1445.2	1444	120	485	1060	12.3	4.03	82	.260	.322	-105	-117	98	82	48	.975	159	92	120	-1.0	-12.7	5.1	.8	-4.2
NY	36	10	277	19	1433.2	1369	124	536	893	12.1	3.73	91	.253	.321	-56	-54	100	87	58	.975	157	76	147	-.9	-5.8	-12.2	-.2	-.8
TOT	417	121	2539	291	14582.2					11.6	3.38		.249	.310						.978	1408	653	1462					

Batter-Fielder Wins
- Santo-Chi ... 7.7
- Aaron-Atl ... 5.4
- Clemente-Pit ... 5.1
- Allen-Phi ... 4.7
- Cepeda-StL ... 4.6

Batting Average
- Clemente-Pit ... .357
- Gonzalez-Phi ... .339
- Alou-Pit ... .338
- Flood-StL ... .335
- Staub-Hou ... .333

On-Base Percentage
- Allen-Phi ... .404
- Clemente-Pit ... .400
- Cepeda-StL ... .399
- Staub-Hou ... .398
- Gonzalez-Phi ... .396

Slugging Average
- Aaron-Atl ... .573
- Allen-Phi ... .566
- Clemente-Pit ... .554
- McCovey-SF ... .535
- Cepeda-StL ... .524

On-Base Plus Slugging
- Allen-Phi ... .970
- Clemente-Pit ... .954
- Aaron-Atl ... .943
- Cepeda-StL ... .923
- McCovey-SF ... .913

Adjusted OPS
- Allen-Phi ... 173
- Clemente-Pit ... 170
- Aaron-Atl ... 169
- Cepeda-StL ... 166
- McCovey-SF ... 162

Adjusted Batter Runs
- Aaron-Atl ... 53.1
- Cepeda-StL ... 51.5
- Cepeda-StL ... 50.7
- Allen-Phi ... 46.3
- Santo-Chi ... 43.6

Runs
- Brock-StL ... 113
- Aaron-Atl ... 113
- Santo-Chi ... 107
- Clemente-Pit ... 103
- Wynn-Hou ... 102

Hits
- Clemente-Pit ... 209
- Brock-StL ... 206
- Pinson-Cin ... 187
- Wills-Pit ... 186
- Alou-Pit ... 186

Doubles
- Staub-Hou ... 44
- Cepeda-StL ... 37
- Aaron-Atl ... 37

Triples
- Pinson-Cin ... 13
- Williams-Chi ... 12
- Brock-StL ... 12
- Morgan-Hou ... 11

Home Runs
- Aaron-Atl ... 39
- Wynn-Hou ... 37
- Santo-Chi ... 31
- McCovey-SF ... 31
- Hart-SF ... 29

Total Bases
- Aaron-Atl ... 344
- Brock-StL ... 325
- Clemente-Pit ... 324
- Williams-Chi ... 305
- Santo-Chi ... 300

Runs Batted In
- Cepeda-StL ... 111
- Clemente-Pit ... 110
- Aaron-Atl ... 109
- Wynn-Hou ... 107
- Perez-Cin ... 102

Stolen Bases
- Brock-StL ... 52
- Wills-Pit ... 29
- Morgan-Hou ... 29
- Pinson-Cin ... 26
- Phillips-Chi ... 24

Base Stealing Runs
- Brock-StL ... 5.1
- Morgan-Hou ... 4.6
- Pinson-Cin ... 2.9
- Wills-Pit ... 2.9
- Allen-Phi ... 2.7

Fielding Runs-Infield
- Santo-Chi ... 31.4
- Mazeroski-Pit ... 21.1
- Lanier-SF ... 20.2
- Wine-Phi ... 18.1
- Fuentes-SF ... 17.2

Fielding Runs-Outfield
- Gonzalez-Phi ... 8.0
- Phillips-Chi ... 7.4
- Aaron-Atl ... 6.1
- Flood-StL ... 4.8
- Clemente-Pit ... 4.7

Wins
- McCormick-SF ... 22
- Jenkins-Chi ... 20
- Osteen-LA ... 17
- Bunning-Phi ... 17

Winning Pct.
- Hughes-StL ... .727
- McCormick-SF ... .688
- Veale-Pit ... .667
- Jenkins-Chi ... .606
- Jarvis-Atl ... .600

Complete Games
- Jenkins-Chi ... 20
- Seaver-NY ... 18
- Perry-SF ... 18
- Marichal-SF ... 18

Strikeouts
- Bunning-Phi ... 253
- Jenkins-Chi ... 236
- Perry-SF ... 230
- Nolan-Cin ... 206
- Cuellar-Hou ... 203

Fewest BB/Game
- Pappas-Chi ... 1.57
- Osteen-LA ... 1.62
- Johnson-Atl ... 1.63
- Niekro-Chi ... 1.70
- L.Jackson-Phi ... 1.86

Games
- Perranoski-LA ... 70
- Abernathy-Cin ... 70
- Willis-StL ... 65
- Face-Pit ... 61

Saves
- Abernathy-Cin ... 28
- Linzy-SF ... 17
- Face-Pit ... 17
- Perranoski-LA ... 16
- Hoerner-StL ... 15

Base Runners/9
- Hughes-StL ... 8.78
- Abernathy-Cin ... 9.23
- Linzy-SF ... 9.50
- Farrell-Hou-Phi ... 9.64
- Lamabe-NY-StL ... 9.64

Adjusted Relief Runs
- Abernathy-Cin ... 25.6
- Linzy-SF ... 18.3
- McBean-Pit ... 12.6
- Nottebart-Cin ... 12.2
- Farrell-Hou-Phi ... 11.2

Relief Ranking
- Abernathy-Cin ... 34.7
- Linzy-SF ... 31.5
- Hall-Phi ... 19.8
- Farrell-Hou-Phi ... 18.4
- Face-Pit ... 15.3

Innings Pitched
- Bunning-Phi ... 302.1
- Perry-SF ... 293.0
- Jenkins-Chi ... 289.1
- Osteen-LA ... 288.1
- Drysdale-LA ... 282.0

Opponents' Avg.
- Hughes-StL ... .203
- Wilson-Hou ... .209
- Perry-SF ... .214
- Queen-Cin ... .215
- Bunning-Phi ... .217

Opponents' OBP
- Hughes-StL ... .251
- Bunning-Phi ... .271
- Queen-Cin ... .271
- Perry-SF ... .273
- Niekro-Atl ... .275

Earned Run Average
- Niekro-Atl ... 1.87
- Bunning-Phi ... 2.29
- Short-Phi ... 2.39
- Nolan-Cin ... 2.58
- Perry-SF ... 2.61

Adjusted ERA
- Niekro-Atl ... 178
- Bunning-Phi ... 149
- Nolan-Cin ... 145
- Short-Phi ... 142
- Queen-Cin ... 136

Adjusted Starter Runs
- Bunning-Phi ... 35.2
- Niekro-Atl ... 27.3
- Nolan-Cin ... 26.8
- Short-Phi ... 25.1
- Perry-SF ... 22.6

Pitcher Wins
- Bunning-Phi ... 3.9
- Abernathy-Cin ... 3.8
- Linzy-SF ... 3.5
- Niekro-Atl ... 3.0
- Jenkins-Chi ... 3.0

Gibson the Head Bird

St. Louis improved 18 games to win another flag despite losing ace Bob Gibson for much of the season to a broken leg. First sacker Orlando "El Toro" Cepeda, liberated from the Giants the previous year, was the league's unanimous MVP both for his hitting and his infectious charm. Tim McCarver, perhaps the game's top all-around receiver, finished second. The Cardinals were fast, strong defensively, deep in pitching, and blessed with racial harmony; they also benefited from an excellent outfield of Lou Brock, Curt Flood, and Roger Maris.

Cincinnati led the league through May and much of June, but injuries destroyed their chances. The Giants only began to hit late in the season. San Francisco was the NL's hottest club in the last month and finished second.

As pitcher Ferguson Jenkins enjoyed his first of six straight 20-win seasons, the Cubs—sparked by veterans Billy Williams and Ron Santo—improved 28½ games and leapt from last to third. Despite pitching in a good hitting park, Atlanta's Phil Niekro won the ERA crown.

The last-place Mets showed impressive arms, debuting Rookie of the Year Tom Seaver as well as 1968's runner-up, Jerry Koosman. Nolan Ryan, Tug McGraw, and Dick Selma quickly followed.

The 1967 season was first time that the leagues had separate Cy Young awards. The award had resided in southern California since 1962, thanks to Don Drysdale, Sandy Koufax, and Dean Chance; in 1967 it moved north up the freeway. San Francisco lefty Mike McCormick, the runaway winner, may be the least remembered Cy Young recipient ever. This was the last go-round for several key veterans of earlier seasons, including Lew Burdette, Dick Groat, Vern Law, and Curt Simmons.

The World Series was Bob Gibson's stage. Tossing complete-game victories in Games 1, 4, and 7, he allowed only 2 runs in 27 innings. Brock hit .414 and scored 8 runs. The dogged Red Sox came back to win Games 5 and 6, but Gibson himself homered in the 7-2 deciding game.

1967 American League

TEAM	W	L	T	PCT	GB	HW	HL	R	OR	PA	H	2B	3B	HR	BB	SO	HB	SH	AVG	OBP	SLG	OPS	AOPS	BR	ABR	PF	SB	CS	BSA	BSR
BOS	92	70	0	.568		49	32	**722**	614	6149	**1394**	216	39	**158**	522	1020	31	85	**.255**	.321	**.395**	716	109	**120**	66	108	68	59	54	-6
MIN	91	71	2	.562	1	52	29	671	590	6116	1309	**216**	48	131	512	976	46	66	.240	.309	.369	678	98	45	-4	108	55	37	60	-1
DET	91	71	1	.562	1	52	29	683	587	6200	1315	192	36	152	**626**	994	**51**	78	.243	**.325**	.376	701	**111**	103	**84**	103	37	21	64	-1
CHI	89	73	0	.549	3	49	33	531	**491**	6000	1209	181	34	89	480	**849**	38	67	.225	.291	.320	611	90	-82	-62	96	40	36	53	-4
CAL	84	77	0	.522	7.5	**53**	30	567	587	5902	1265	170	37	114	453	1021	31	52	.238	.301	.349	650	102	-15	7	96	40	36	53	-4
WAS	76	85	0	.472	15.5	40	40	550	637	6044	1211	168	25	115	472	1037	37	82	.235	.288	.326	614	91	-83	-62	96	53	37	59	-1
BAL	76	85	0	.472	15.5	35	42	654	592	6164	1312	215	44	138	531	1002	41	82	.240	.310	.372	682	109	56	61	99	54	37	59	-1
CLE	75	87	0	.463	17	36	45	559	613	6037	1282	213	35	131	413	984	50	85	.235	.293	.359	652	97	-15	-20	101	53	65	45	-11
NY	72	90	1	.444	20	43	38	522	621	6118	1225	166	17	100	532	1043	30	78	.225	.296	.317	613	90	-75	-55	96	63	37	63	1
KC	62	99	0	.385	29.5	37	44	533	660	5938	1244	212	**50**	69	452	1019	42	59	.233	.296	.330	626	94	-55	-37	97	**132**	59	**69**	**8**
TOT	810					446	362	5992		60668	12766	1949	365	1197	4993	9945	397	751	.236	.303	.351	654					679	470	59	-15

TEAM	CG	SHO	GR	SV	IP	H	HR	BB	SO	BR/9	ERA	AERA	OAV	OOB	PR	APR	PF	OSB	OCS	FA	E	WPB	DP	FW	PW	BW	BSW	DIF
BOS	41	9	254	44	1459.1	1307	142	477	1010	11.3	3.36	104	.239	.304	-21	19	108	63	38	.977	142	64	142	-.6	2.1	7.3	-.5	2.7
MIN	**58**	18	219	24	1461.0	1336	115	**396**	1089	10.9	3.14	110	.243	.296	15	49	107	70	48	.978	132	63	123	.1	5.4	-.4	.0	4.8
DET	46	17	254	40	1443.2	1230	151	472	1038	10.8	3.32	98	.230	.295	-14	-9	101	79	38	.978	132	63	126	.0	-1.0	**9.3**	.3	1.4
CHI	36	**24**	292	39	1490.1	**1197**	87	465	927	10.4	**2.45**	127	**.219**	.287	129	112	96	70	53	.979	138	84	149	-.3	**12.4**	-6.8	.0	2.8
CAL	19	14	301	**46**	1430.1	1246	118	525	892	11.4	3.19	98	.237	.308	6	-8	97	49	63	**.982**	111	74	135	**1.3**	-.9	.8	-.3	2.6
WAS	24	14	**330**	39	1473.1	1334	113	495	878	11.4	3.38	95	.242	.307	-25	37	98	57	46	.978	144	60	**167**	-.8	-4.1	-6.8	.0	7.1
BAL	29	17	248	36	1457.1	1218	116	566	1034	11.2	3.32	95	.228	.304	-15	-28	98	79	48	.980	124	76	144	.5	-3.1	6.7	-.0	-8.7
CLE	49	14	236	27	1477.2	1258	120	559	**1189**	11.3	3.25	101	.231	.305	-3	3	101	65	47	.981	116	93	138	1.0	.3	-2.2	-1.0	-4.1
NY	37	16	251	27	1480.2	1375	110	480	898	11.5	3.24	97	.249	.310	-2	-19	97	71	54	.976	154	**40**	144	-1.3	-2.1	-6.1	.3	.2
KC	26	10	265	34	1428.0	1265	125	558	990	11.7	3.68	87	.238	.313	-71	-80	99	76	36	.978	132	61	120	-.0	-8.8	-4.1	**1.0**	-6.6
TOT	365	153	2650	356	14601.2					11.2	3.23		.236	.303						.979	1325	678	1388					

Batter-Fielder Wins		Batting Average		On-Base Percentage		Slugging Average		On-Base Plus Slugging		Adjusted OPS		Adjusted Batter Runs	
Yastrzemski-Bos	.6.9	Yastrzemski-Bos	326	Yastrzemski-Bos	418	Yastrzemski-Bos	622	Yastrzemski-Bos	1040	Yastrzemski-Bos	189	Yastrzemski-Bos	67.2
B.Robinson-Bal	.5.3	F.Robinson-Bal	311	Kaline-Det	411	F.Robinson-Bal	576	F.Robinson-Bal	979	F.Robinson-Bal	189	F.Robinson-Bal	55.1
Kaline-Det	.5.1	Kaline-Det	308	Killebrew-Min	408	Killebrew-Min	558	Killebrew-Min	965	Kaline-Det	176	Killebrew-Min	54.5
F.Robinson-Bal	.4.3	Scott-Bos	303	F.Robinson-Bal	403	Kaline-Det	541	Kaline-Det	952	Killebrew-Min	170	Kaline-Det	47.4
Killebrew-Min	.4.2	Blair-Bal	293	Mantle-NY	391	Howard-Was	511	Mincher-Cal	854	Mincher-Cal	156	Mincher-Cal	35.6

Runs		Hits		Doubles		Triples		Home Runs		Total Bases		Runs Batted In	
Yastrzemski-Bos	112	Yastrzemski-Bos	189	Oliva-Min	34	Blair-Bal	12	Yastrzemski-Bos	44	Yastrzemski-Bos	360	Yastrzemski-Bos	121
Killebrew-Min	105	Tovar-Min	173	Tovar-Min	32	Buford-Chi	9	Killebrew-Min	44	Killebrew-Min	305	Killebrew-Min	113
Tovar-Min	98	Scott-Bos	171	Yastrzemski-Bos	31			Howard-Was	36	F.Robinson-Bal	276	F.Robinson-Bal	94
Kaline-Det	94	Fregosi-Cal	171	D.Johnson-Bal	30			F.Robinson-Bal	30	B.Robinson-Bal	265	Howard-Was	89
McAuliffe-Det	92	B.Robinson-Bal	164	Campaneris-KC	29					Howard-Was	265	Oliva-Min	83

Stolen Bases		Base Stealing Runs		Fielding Runs-Infield		Fielding Runs-Outfield		Wins		Winning Pct.		Complete Games	
Campaneris-KC	55	Campaneris-KC	6.5	B.Robinson-Bal	32.1	Blair-Bal	9.1	Wilson-Det	22	Horlen-Chi	731	Chance-Min	18
Buford-Chi	34	Clarke-NY	3.2	Clarke-NY	16.3	Monday-KC	8.4	Lonborg-Bos	22	Lonborg-Bos	710	Lonborg-Bos	15
Agee-Chi	28	Valentine-Was	2.7	Cullen-Was	14.6	Oliva-Min	7.6	Chance-Min	20	Wilson-Det	667	Hargan-Cle	15
McCraw-Chi	24	Agee-Chi	2.7	Oyler-Det	13.6	Hershberger-KC	7.5	Horlen-Chi	19	Sparma-Det	640		
Clarke-NY	21	Aparicio-Bal	2.2	McCraw-Chi	11.0	Kaline-Det	7.1	McLain-Det	17	Peters-Chi	593		

Strikeouts		Fewest BB/Game		Games		Saves		Base Runners/9		Adjusted Relief Runs		Relief Ranking	
Lonborg-Bos	246	Merritt-Min	1.19	Locker-Chi	77	Rojas-Cal	27	Horlen-Chi	8.72	Wilhelm-Chi	16.1	Wilhelm-Chi	22.4
McDowell-Cle	236	Kaat-Min	1.44	Rojas-Cal	72	Wyatt-Bos	20	Drabowsky-Bal	8.78	Drabowsky-Bal	15.7	Drabowsky-Bal	21.9
Chance-Min	220	Stange-Bos	1.59	Kelso-Cal	69	Locker-Chi	20	Hiller-Det	9.14	Locker-Chi	15.0	Locker-Chi	17.9
Tiant-Cle	219	Horlen-Chi	2.02	Womack-NY	65	Womack-NY	18	Merritt-Min	9.21	McMahon-Bos-Chi	14.2	Wyatt-Bos	17.3
Peters-Chi	215	Peterson-NY	2.13	McMahon-Bos-Chi	63	Worthington-Min	16	Watt-Bal	9.29	Watt-Bal	11.8	Gladding-Det	15.2

Innings Pitched		Opponents' Avg.		Opponents' OBP		Earned Run Average		Adjusted ERA		Adjusted Starter Runs		Pitcher Wins	
Chance-Min	283.2	Peters-Chi	199	Horlen-Chi	253	Horlen-Chi	2.06	Horlen-Chi	151	Horlen-Chi	33.5	**Horlen-Chi**	3.8
Lonborg-Bos	273.1	Boswell-Min	202	Merritt-Min	260	Peters-Chi	2.28	Siebert-Cle	137	Peters-Chi	24.1	**Peters-Chi**	3.6
Wilson-Det	264.0	Siebert-Cle	202	Siebert-Cle	266	Siebert-Cle	2.38	Merritt-Min	137	Merritt-Min	22.8	**Drabowsky-Bal**	2.8
Kaat-Min	263.1	Horlen-Chi	203	John-Chi	275	John-Chi	2.47	Peters-Chi	136	Chance-Min	17.8	**Wilhelm-Chi**	2.2
Peters-Chi	260.0	Downing-NY	217	Peters-Chi	276	Merritt-Min	2.53	Chance-Min	127	Siebert-Cle	16.9	**Siebert-Cle**	2.2

Boston's Summer of Love

In possibly the greatest and nuttiest pennant race of all time, four clubs converged in late July and bunched closer as the year went on. Chicago had excellent pitching and terrible hitting, even outside of cavernous Comiskey Park, but lacked a fourth starter. Boston featured a passel of young talent, led by Cy Young winner Jim Lonborg and slugger Carl Yastrzemski. Minnesota had Harmon Killebrew and Rookie of the Year Rod Carew, while Detroit's lineup sported four players with 20 or more homers. The Orioles slid to sixth as their young pitchers came up lame.

From early August until late September, the closely packed teams changed positions nearly hourly. The ongoing dramas and great performances added to the character of the race.

Chicago, in a position to win, dropped five straight to Kansas City and Washington in the last week to fall from contention. Minnesota came into the last two days of the season leading Boston and Detroit by 1 game. As the Tigers split two home doubleheaders with California, the Red Sox won their last two games at Fenway—over Minnesota. MVP Yastrzemski's hitting carried the day; rarely had one player so impacted a close pennant race. Yaz is the last player to date to collect a Triple Crown. Fittingly, AL attendance rose to an all-time high.

As the dissension-ridden A's sank to last, Charlie Finley finally swung a deal to move the franchise to Oakland, which gave the Angels a West Coast partner. Finley gave rookies Joe Rudi and Reggie Jackson a taste of major league baseball—Kansas City style; they hit .186 and .178 in their respective debuts.

The Red Sox magic faded in the World Series, as the Cardinals won in seven. It was the Junior Circuit's fifth Series defeat of the decade. Bob Gibson threw 3 complete-game wins for St. Louis, while Lonborg tossed a one-hitter in Game 2.

1966 National League

TEAM	W	L	T	PCT	GB	HW	HL	R	OR	PA	H	2B	3B	HR	BB	SO	HB	SH	AVG	OBP	SLG	OPS	AOPS	BR	ABR	PF	SB	CS	BSA	BSR
LA	95	67	0	.586		53	28	606	490	6066	1399	201	27	108	430	830	49	84	.256	.314	.362	676	102	-36	17	92	94	64	59	-2
SF	93	68	0	.578	1.5	47	34	675	626	6083	1373	195	31	181	414	860	32	70	.248	.303	.392	695	95	-16	-34	103	29	30	49	-4
PIT	92	70	0	.568	3	46	35	759	641	6229	1586	238	66	158	405	1011	35	73	.279	.329	.428	757	116	116	115	100	64	60	52	-7
PHI	87	75	0	.537	8	48	33	696	640	6256	1448	224	49	117	510	969	29	78	.258	.322	.378	700	101	13	12	100	56	42	57	-2
ATL	85	77	1	.525	10	43	38	782	683	6286	1476	220	32	207	512	913	40	72	.263	.326	.424	750	108	96	102	100	59	47	56	-3
STL	83	79	0	.512	12	43	38	571	577	5963	1377	196	61	108	345	977	35	59	.251	.298	.368	666	90	-70	-73	101	144	61	70	10
CIN	76	84	0	.475	18	46	33	692	702	6043	1434	232	33	149	394	877	20	69	.260	.309	.395	704	93	8	-45	109	70	50	58	-2
HOU	72	90	1	.444	23	45	36	612	695	6170	1405	203	35	112	491	885	34	97	.255	.318	.365	683	103	-18	29	93	90	47	66	3
NY	66	95	0	.410	28.5	32	49	587	761	5951	1286	187	35	98	446	992	33	63	.239	.301	.342	693	87	-100	-87	98	55	46	54	-4
CHI	59	103	0	.364	36	32	49	644	809	6213	1418	203	43	140	457	998	47	80	.254	.313	.380	693	97	-6	-14	101	76	47	62	0
TOT	809					435	373	6624		61260	14202	2099	412	1378	4404	9312	363	745	.256	.313	.384	697					737	494	60	-11

TEAM	CG	SHO	GR	SV	IP	H	HR	BB	SO	BR/9	ERA	AERA	OAV	OOB	PR	APR	PF	OSB	OCS	FA	E	WPB	DP	FW	PW	BW	BSW	DIF
LA	52	20	214	35	1458.0	1287	84	356	1084	10.3	2.62	126	.237	.286	159	119	91	54	42	.979	133	53	128	.9	12.5	1.8	-.0	-1.0
SF	52	14	250	27	1476.2	1370	140	359	973	10.7	3.24	113	.244	.292	61	69	102	84	43	.974	168	67	131	-1.2	7.2	-3.6	-.3	10.3
PIT	35	12	285	43	1463.1	1445	125	463	898	12.0	3.52	101	.261	.321	13	8	99	71	35	.978	141	58	215	.4	.8	12.1	-.6	-1.7
PHI	52	15	245	23	1459.2	1439	137	412	928	11.8	3.57	101	.258	.315	6	4	100	69	51	.982	113	60	147	2.0	.4	1.3	-.0	2.4
ATL	37	10	290	36	1469.1	1430	129	485	884	11.9	3.68	99	.257	.317	-12	-7	101	69	64	.976	154	110	139	-.3	-.7	10.1	-.2	-4.9
STL	47	19	261	32	1459.2	1345	130	448	892	11.3	3.11	115	.246	.306	80	77	100	55	49	.977	145	53	166	.2	8.1	-7.7	1.2	.2
CIN	28	10	270	35	1436.0	1408	153	490	1043	12.4	4.08	96	.258	.313	-76	-26	108	102	57	.980	122	65	133	1.4	-2.7	-4.7	-.0	2.2
HOU	34	13	261	26	1443.2	1468	130	391	929	11.8	3.76	91	.262	.313	-24	-57	95	70	44	.972	174	85	126	-1.4	-6.0	3.0	.4	-5.1
NY	37	9	288	22	1427.0	1497	166	521	773	12.9	4.17	87	.272	.337	-89	-84	101	85	51	.975	159	92	171	-.6	-8.8	-9.1	-.3	4.4
CHI	28	6	285	24	1458.0	1513	184	479	908	12.5	4.33	85	.268	.326	-118	-104	102	78	58	.974	166	58	132	-1.0	-10.9	-1.5	.1	-8.8
TOT	402	128	2649	303	14551.1					11.7	3.61		.256	.313						.977	1475	701	1488					

Batter-Fielder Wins
- Santo-Chi 7.6
- Allen-Phi 5.0
- Mazeroski-Pit 4.8
- Torre-Atl 4.5
- Mays-SF 3.9

Batting Average
- Alou-Pit .342
- Alou-Atl .327
- Carty-Atl .326
- Allen-Phi .317
- Clemente-Pit .317

On-Base Percentage
- Santo-Chi .412
- Morgan-Hou .410
- Allen-Phi .396
- McCovey-SF .391
- Carty-Atl .391

Slugging Average
- Allen-Phi .632
- McCovey-SF .586
- Stargell-Pit .581
- Torre-Atl .560
- Mays-SF .556

On-Base Plus Slugging
- Allen-Phi 1027
- McCovey-SF .977
- Stargell-Pit .962
- Santo-Chi .950
- Torre-Atl .943

Adjusted OPS
- Allen-Phi 181
- Stargell-Pit 164
- McCovey-SF 163
- Santo-Chi 161
- Torre-Atl 157

Adjusted Batter Runs
- Allen-Phi 57.2
- Santo-Chi 50.5
- McCovey-SF 44.9
- Stargell-Pit 42.4
- Torre-Atl 41.8

Runs
- Alou-Atl 122
- Aaron-Atl 117
- Allen-Phi 112
- Clemente-Pit 105
- Williams-Chi 100

Hits
- Alou-Atl 218
- Rose-Cin 205
- Clemente-Pit 202
- Beckert-Chi 188

Doubles
- Callison-Phi 40
- Rose-Cin 38
- Pinson-Cin 35
- Alou-Atl 32

Triples
- McCarver-StL 13
- Brock-StL 12
- Clemente-Pit 11

Home Runs
- Aaron-Atl 44
- Allen-Phi 40
- Mays-SF 37
- Torre-Atl 36
- McCovey-SF 36

Total Bases
- Alou-Atl 355
- Clemente-Pit 342
- Allen-Phi 331
- Aaron-Atl 325
- Mays-SF 307

Runs Batted In
- Aaron-Atl 127
- Clemente-Pit 119
- Allen-Phi 110
- White-Phi 103
- Mays-SF 103

Stolen Bases
- Brock-StL 74
- Jackson-Hou 49
- Wills-LA 38
- Phillips-Phi-Chi 32
- Harper-Cin 29

Base Stealing Runs
- Brock-StL 10.0
- Jackson-Hou 5.9
- Aaron-Atl 3.6
- Harper-Cin 2.9
- Phillips-Phi-Chi 1.8

Fielding Runs-Infield
- Mazeroski-Pit 41.3
- Santo-Chi 24.9
- Groat-StL 21.1
- Maxvill-StL 17.8
- Alley-Pit 14.9

Fielding Runs-Outfield
- Clemente-Pit 9.7
- Aaron-Atl 8.2
- Staub-Hou 7.7
- Phillips-Phi-Chi 7.1
- Shannon-StL 5.3

Wins
- Koufax-LA 27
- Marichal-SF 25
- Perry-SF 21
- Gibson-StL 21
- Short-Phi 20

Winning Pct.
- Marichal-SF .806
- Koufax-LA .750
- Perry-SF .724
- Short-Phi .667
- Maloney-Cin .667

Complete Games
- Koufax-LA 27
- Marichal-SF 25
- Gibson-StL 20
- Short-Phi 19
- Bunning-Phi 16

Strikeouts
- Koufax-LA 317
- Bunning-Phi 252
- Veale-Pit 229
- Gibson-StL 225
- Marichal-SF 222

Fewest BB/Game
- Marichal-SF 1.05
- Law-Pit 1.22
- Perry-SF 1.41
- Drysdale-LA 1.48
- Bunning-Phi 1.58

Games
- Carroll-Phi 73
- Mikkelsen-Pit 71
- Knowles-Phi 69
- Regan-LA 65
- McDaniel-SF 64

Saves
- Regan-LA 21
- McCool-Cin 18
- Face-Pit 18
- Raymond-Hou 16
- Linzy-SF 16

Base Runners/9
- Marichal-SF 7.88
- Regan-LA 8.41
- Jarvis-Atl 8.52
- Koufax-LA 8.86
- Gibson-StL 9.41

Adjusted Relief Runs
- Regan-LA 23.9
- Carroll-Atl 19.4
- Hoerner-StL 16.9
- McCool-Cin 15.1
- Woodeshick-StL 13.2

Relief Ranking
- Regan-LA 37.3
- McCool-Cin 26.4
- Carroll-Atl 21.5
- Hoerner-StL 18.5
- Linzy-SF 14.4

Innings Pitched
- Koufax-LA 323.0
- Bunning-Phi 314.0
- Marichal-SF 307.1
- Gibson-StL 280.1
- Drysdale-LA 273.2

Opponents' Avg.
- Marichal-SF .202
- Koufax-LA .205
- Gibson-StL .207
- Bolin-SF .211
- Maloney-Cin .214

Opponents' OBP
- Marichal-SF .230
- Koufax-LA .252
- Gibson-StL .265
- Bunning-Phi .268
- Cuellar-Hou .273

Earned Run Average
- Koufax-LA 1.73
- Cuellar-Hou 2.22
- Marichal-SF 2.23
- Bunning-Phi 2.41
- Gibson-StL 2.44

Adjusted ERA
- Koufax-LA 191
- Marichal-SF 165
- Cuellar-Hou 154
- Bunning-Phi 149
- Gibson-StL 147

Adjusted Starter Runs
- Koufax-LA 60.4
- Marichal-SF 49.1
- Bunning-Phi 42.4
- Gibson-StL 34.6
- Maloney-Cin 25.5

Pitcher Wins
- Koufax-LA 6.1
- Marichal-SF 5.8
- Gibson-StL 4.4
- Bunning-Phi 4.4
- Regan-LA 4.1

The Last Roundup

Prior to the season, Don Drysdale and Sandy Koufax staged a joint holdout. The Dodgers eventually paid each more than $100,000. Koufax won his third Cy Young and finished just behind Roberto Clemente in MVP voting. As Drysdale struggled, rookie Don Sutton provided a solid fourth starter.

Since winning the 1960 World Series, Pittsburgh had rebuilt with blacks and Latinos, becoming the game's colorblind franchise. The '66 Pirates took the league lead in August, with Los Angeles and San Francisco close behind. Matty Alou, Willie Stargell, and Clemente provided the firepower for the Bucs.

The Dodgers reeled off seven straight wins in mid-September to grab first place. Though the Giants, keyed by 20-game winners Juan Marichal and Gaylord Perry, surged in the final week, the Dodgers again took the flag on closing day. The Giants swept three from Pittsburgh to finish second. Any of the three teams could have won going into the last weekend.

Nolan Ryan made his major league debut with the Mets in 1966; he would later eclipse Koufax for most strikeouts in a season and Walter Johnson for most strikeouts ever. Veterans Robin Roberts, Frank Thomas, Del Crandall, and Joe Adcock ended their careers in '66. Rebuilding St. Louis opened up new Busch Stadium. The Cubs fell to last, but acquired Fergie Jenkins, Bill Hands, and Randy Hundley.

The league posted its highest average attendance until 1977. Eight NL teams surpassed one million. Interest in baseball history was galvanized by *The Glory of Their Times*, an essential book of interviews with players from the early twentieth century.

Los Angeles fell apart in the World Series, fielding poorly and scoring nothing in the final three games to suffer an unceremonious sweep at the hands of the Orioles. Following the season, Koufax retired due to chronic damage in his pitching elbow. Jim Gilliam also called it quits and Maury Wills and Tommy Davis were traded, bringing the golden era of Dodgers baseball—which began twenty years earlier in Brooklyn—to a climactic end.

1966 American League

TEAM	W	L	T	PCT	GB	HW	HL	R	OR	PA	H	2B	3B	HR	BB	SO	HB	SH	AVG	OBP	SLG	OPS	AOPS	BR	ABR	PF	SB	CS	BSA	BSR
BAL	97	63	0	.606	—	48	31	755	601	6199	1426	243	35	175	514	926	39	82	.258	.324	.409	733	118	118	130	98	55	43	56	-3
MIN	89	73	0	.549	9	49	32	663	581	6035	1341	219	33	144	513	844	39	49	.249	.316	.382	698	100	52	11	106	67	42	61	0
DET	88	74	0	.543	10	42	39	719	698	6195	1383	224	45	179	551	987	33	67	.251	.321	.406	727	111	105	88	102	41	34	55	-3
CHI	83	79	1	.512	15	45	36	574	517	6021	1235	193	40	87	476	872	44	109	.231	.297	.331	628	92	-84	-45	93	153	78	66	6
CLE	81	81	0	.500	17	41	40	574	586	6040	1300	156	25	155	450	914	27	56	.237	.297	.360	657	94	-41	-41	100	53	41	56	-3
CAL	80	82	0	.494	18	42	39	604*	643	6038	1244	179	54	122	525	1062	38	69	.232	.303	.354	657	98	-31	-14	97	80	54	60	-1
KC	74	86	0	.463	23	42	39	564	564	5873	1259	212	56	70	421	982	26	71	.236	.294	.337	631	90	-85	-68	97	132	50	73	12
WAS	71	88	0	.447	25.5	42	36	557	659	5905	1245	185	40	126	450	1069	20	84	.234	.295	.355	650	93	-52	-46	99	53	37	59	-1
BOS	72	90	0	.444	26	40	41	655	731	6175	1318	228	44	145	542	1020	32	65	.240	.310	.376	686	93	26	-36	110	35	24	59	-1
NY	70	89	1	.440	26.5	35	46	611	612	5936	1254	182	36	162	485	817	21	58	.235	.299	.374	673	103	-7	16	96	49	29	63	1
TOT	806					426	379	6276		60417	13005	2021	408	1365	4927	9493	319	710	.240	.306	.369	674				718	432	62	7

TEAM	CG	SHO	GR	SV	IP	H	HR	BB	SO	BR/9	ERA	AERA	OAV	OOB	PR	APR	PF	OSB	OCS	FA	E	WPB	DP	FW	PW	BW	BSW	DIF
BAL	23	13	253	51	1466.1	1267	127	514	1070	11.1	3.32	100	.233	.301	19	2	97	82	49	.981	115	76	142	1.3	.2	14.0	-.4	1.9
MIN	52	11	202	28	1438.2	1246	139	392	1015	10.4	3.13	115	.232	.286	48	71	105	72	42	.977	139	57	118	.0	7.6	1.2	-.0	-.8
DET	36	11	271	38	1454.1	1356	185	520	1026	11.9	3.85	90	.247	.315	-67	-59	101	57	33	.980	120	63	142	1.1	-6.3	9.5	-.4	3.2
CHI	38	22	239	34	1475.1	1229	101	403	896	10.2	2.68	118	.226	.282	123	86	92	81	41	.976	159	92	149	-1.1	9.2	-4.8	.6	-1.9
CLE	49	15	226	28	1467.1	1260	129	489	1111	10.9	3.23	107	.232	.297	34	35	100	49	44	.978	138	67	132	.0	3.8	-4.4	-.4	1.0
CAL	31	12	296	40	1457.1	1364	136	511	836	11.8	3.56	94	.251	.317	-21	-34	98	72	46	.979	136	65	186	.2	-3.7	-1.5	-.2	4.1
KC	19	11	306	47	1435.0	1281	106	630	854	12.2	3.56	96	.241	.323	-19	-25	99	82	43	.977	139	72	154	-.0	-2.7	-7.3	1.2	2.9
WAS	25	6	295	35	1419.0	1282	154	448	866	11.1	3.70	93	.242	.302	-42	-38	101	56	47	.977	142	57	139	-.3	-4.1	-4.9	-.2	1.0
BOS	32	10	311	31	1463.2	1402	164	577	977	12.4	3.92	97	.253	.325	-78	-16	100	114	49	.975	155	66	153	-.9	-1.7	-3.9	-.2	-2.3
NY	29	7	227	32	1415.2	1318	124	443	842	11.3	3.41	97	.248	.306	3	-15	97	53	38	.977	142	45	142	-.3	-1.6	1.7	.0	-9.4
TOT	334	118	2626	364	14492.2					11.3	3.44		.240	.306						.978	1385	660	1457					

Batter-Fielder Wins	Batting Average	On-Base Percentage	Slugging Average	On-Base Plus Slugging	Adjusted OPS	Adjusted Batter Runs
F.Robinson-Bal 6.3	F.Robinson-Bal 316	F.Robinson-Bal 410	F.Robinson-Bal 637	F.Robinson-Bal 1047	F.Robinson-Bal 200	F.Robinson-Bal 78.0
Fregosi-Cal.........4.4	Oliva-Min 307	Kaline-Det 392	Killebrew-Min 538	Killebrew-Min.........929	Kaline-Det 161	Killebrew-Min 44.2
Tresh-NY............4.2	Kaline-Det 288	Killebrew-Min 391	Kaline-Det 534	Kaline-Det 927	Powell-Bal 159	Kaline-Det 41.6
McAuliffe-Det.......3.8	Powell-Bal............287	McAuliffe-Det 373	Powell-Bal 532	Powell-Bal 903	Killebrew-Min 155	Powell-Bal............38.5
Kaline-Det 3.8	Killebrew-Min 281	Powell-Bal............372	McAuliffe-Det 509	McAuliffe-Det.........882	McAuliffe-Det.........148	Mantle-NY.............32.0

Runs	Hits	Doubles	Triples	Home Runs	Total Bases	Runs Batted In
F.Robinson-Bal 122	Oliva-Min 191	Yastrzemski-Bos 39	Knoop-Cal 11	F.Robinson-Bal 49	F.Robinson-Bal 367	F.Robinson-Bal 122
Oliva-Min 99	F.Robinson-Bal 182	B.Robinson-Bal 35	Campaneris-KC 10	Killebrew-Min 39	Oliva-Min 312	Killebrew-Min 110
Cash-Det 98	Aparicio-Bal.........182	F.Robinson-Bal 34	Brinkman-Was 9	Powell-Bal 34	Killebrew-Min 306	Powell-Bal 109
Agee-Chi 98	Agee-Chi 172	Oliva-Min 32		Cash-Det 32	Cash-Det 288	B.Robinson-Bal 100
	Cash-Det 168	Fregosi-Cal 32		Pepitone-NY 31	Agee-Chi 281	Horton-Det 100

Stolen Bases	Base Stealing Runs	Fielding Runs-Infield	Fielding Runs-Outfield	Wins	Winning Pct.	Complete Games
Campaneris-KC........52	Campaneris-KC 7.9	Knoop-Cal 21.8	Northrup-Det 10.1	Kaat-Min 25	Siebert-Cle 667	Kaat-Min 19
Buford-Chi............51	Buford-Chi 3.5	Boyer-NY 20.0	Yastrzemski-Bos.......9.7	McLain-Det 20	Kaat-Min 658	McLain-Det 14
Agee-Chi..............44	Fregosi-Cal 3.4	Fregosi-Cal 19.4	Hershberger-KC 9.4	Wilson-Bos-Det 18	Wilson-Bos-Det 621	Wilson-Bos-Det 12
Aparicio-Bal.........25	Tartabull-KC-Bos 2.8	Weis-Chi 12.8	Oliva-Min 8.8	Siebert-Cle 16	Palmer-Bal 600	Bell-Cle 12
Cardenal-Cal.........24	Salmon-Cle 1.9	Buford-Chi 10.6	Lock-Was 4.8	Palmer-Bal 15	McLain-Det 588	

Strikeouts	Fewest BB/Game	Games	Saves	Base Runners/9	Adjusted Relief Runs	Relief Ranking
McDowell-Cle 225	Kaat-Min 1.62	Fisher-Chi-Bal 67	Aker-KC 32	Wilhelm-Chi 7.52	Aker-KC 18.6	Aker-KC 28.2
Kaat-Min 205	Peterson-NY 1.67	Cox-Was 66	Kline-Was 23	Drabowsky-Bal 8.63	Wilhelm-Chi 13.2	S.Miller-Bal 20.1
Wilson-Bos-Det ..200	Grant-Min 1.77	Aker-KC 66	Sherry-Det 20	S.Miller-Bal 8.90	Worthington-Min 12.2	McMahon-Cle-Bos 17.5
Richert-Was 195	Peters-Chi 1.98	Worthington-Min 65	Fisher-Chi-Bal 19	Aker-KC 8.92	S.Miller-Bal 12.1	Worthington-Min 15.1
Bell-Cle 194	Hargan-Cle 2.11	Kline-Was 63	S.Miller-Bal 18	Peters-Chi 8.97	Lines-Was 11.1	Locker-Chi 13.8

Innings Pitched	Opponents' Avg.	Opponents' OBP	Earned Run Average	Adjusted ERA	Adjusted Starter Runs	Pitcher Wins
Kaat-Min 304.2	McDowell-Cle 188	Peters-Chi 260	Peters-Chi 1.98	Peters-Chi 160	Peters-Chi 28.9	Peters-Chi 4.0
McLain-Det 264.1	Boswell-Min 197	Richert-Was 270	Horlen-Chi 2.43	Perry-Min 142	Kaat-Min 24.9	Kaat-Min 3.6
Wilson-Bos-Det .264.0	Peters-Chi 212	Kaat-Min 270	Hargan-Cle 2.48	Hargan-Cle 138	Perry-Min 20.4	Wilson-Bos-Det 3.6
Chance-Cal 259.2	McLain-Det 214	Ortega-Was 274	Perry-Min 2.54	Kaat-Min 131	Horlen-Chi 20.2	Aker-KC 3.2
Bell-Cle.......254.1	Richert-Was 215	Siebert-Cle 276	John-Chi 2.62	Horlen-Chi 130	Hargan-Cle 19.9	Perry-Min 2.4

Rare Birds

Cleveland reeled off 10 wins to open the season, and led the league through May, but a poor attack proved their undoing. The Orioles, meanwhile, used a 21-6 run to zoom ahead and never looked back. MVP Frank Robinson, acquired the past winter from the Reds, collected the Triple Crown, and the Orioles got good performances from a young rotation; former "Baby Bird" Steve Barber was the old hand at 27. This was a team built for the long term; four position regulars were 24 or younger.

Minnesota, Detroit, and Chicago scrambled for the crumbs. The Twins came up second, with Oliva and Killebrew the big hitters. Detroit moved up with starters Denny McLain and Mickey Lolich, but saw managers Chuck Dressen and Bob Swift die during the same year; impressively, the Tigers still finished third with 88 wins. Fourth-place Chicago, playing in the league's worst run environment, had pitching but predictably feeble hitting.

Seventh-place Kansas City premiered Sal Bando and Rick Monday; Jack Aker saved 32 games to set a new mark. The ninth-place Red Sox decided to promote minor league skipper Dick Williams; they had already made George Scott and Joe Foy regulars with Mike Andrews and Reggie Smith en route. The Angels moved to a new park in Anaheim.

The American League was wide open; the Yankees had collapsed into the cellar. New York lost Bobby Richardson to retirement, with Roger Maris, Mickey Mantle, Whitey Ford, and Jim Bouton pulling up lame.

Emmett Ashford was the game's first black umpire, giving the AL a much-overdue chance to show some vision. By this time, Robinson, Oliva, Willie Horton, and Rookie of the Year Tommie Agee were among the game's biggest stars, and the AL's best teams had gotten the message on integration.

The Birds swept the Dodgers to collect their first-ever world title. Los Angeles didn't score after the third inning of Game 1. Frank Robinson smacked 2 homers, including a blast in the clincher that provided the margin of victory in Dave McNally's 1-0 shutout.

1965 National League

TEAM	W	L	T	PCT	GB	HW	HL	R	OR	PA	H	2B	3B	HR	BB	SO	HB	SH	AVG	OBP	SLG	OPS	AOPS	BR	ABR	PF	SB	CS	BSA	BSR
LA	97	65	0	.599		50	31	608	**521**	6107	1329	193	32	78	492	891	52	103	.245	.312	.335	647	95	-61	-19	93	**172**	77	69	**11**
SF	95	67	1	.586	2	**51**	30	682	593	6119	1384	169	43	159	476	**844**	31	80	.252	.313	.385	698	100	21	3	103	47	27	64	1
PIT	90	72	1	.556	7	49	32	675	580	6249	1506	217	57	111	419	1008	35	67	.265	.317	.382	699	102	25	22	101	51	38	57	-2
CIN	89	73	0	.549	8	49	32	**825**	704	6355	**1544**	268	**61**	183	538	1003	50	73	**.273**	**.339**	**.439**	778	118	192	136	107	82	40	67	4
MIL	86	76	0	.531	11	44	37	708	633	6077	1419	243	28	**196**	408	976	37	58	.256	.310	.416	726	109	69	65	101	64	37	63	1
PHI	85	76	1	.528	11.5	45	35	654	667	6172	1380	205	53	144	494	1091	46	75	.250	.313	.384	697	105	23	35	98	46	32	59	-1
STL	80	81	1	.497	16.5	42	39	707	674	6204	1415	234	46	109	477	882	35	72	.254	.314	.371	685	91	4	-53	109	100	52	66	4
CHI	72	90	2	.444	25	40	41	635	723	6205	1316	202	33	134	532	948	43	48	.238	.307	.358	665	92	-33	-48	102	65	47	58	-2
HOU	65	97	0	.401	32	36	45	569	711	6122	1299	188	42	97	502	877	46	57	.237	.305	.340	645	95	-74	-31	93	90	37	**71**	7
NY	50	112	2	.309	47	29	52	495	752	5976	1202	203	27	107	392	1129	39	76	.221	.277	.327	604	79	-166	-148	96	28	42	40	-9
TOT	813					435	374	6558		61586	13794	2122	422	1318	4730	9649	404	709	.249	.311	.374	685					745	429	63	14

TEAM	CG	SHO	GR	SV	IP	H	HR	BB	SO	BR/9	ERA	AERA	OAV	OOB	PR	APR	PF	OSB	OCS	FA	E	WPB	DP	FW	PW	BW	BSW	DIF
LA	**58**	**23**	202	34	1476.0	**1223**	127	425	1079	10.3	2.81	116	**.224**	**.283**	119	80	92	**53**	33	.979	134	**60**	135	.8	8.5	-2.0	**1.0**	7.7
SF	42	17	262	**42**	1465.1	1325	137	408	1060	10.9	3.20	112	.238	.293	55	64	102	65	30	.976	148	75	124	.0	6.8	.3	-.0	6.9
PIT	49	17	246	27	1479.0	1324	**89**	469	882	11.2	3.01	**117**	.241	.304	87	**83**	99	54	33	.977	152	65	**189**	-.1	**8.8**	2.3	-.4	-1.6
CIN	43	9	244	34	1457.1	1355	136	587	**1113**	12.3	3.88	96	.247	.322	-56	-21	106	91	46	**.981**	117	98	142	**1.8**	-2.2	**14.4**	.3	-6.2
MIL	43	4	266	38	1447.2	1336	123	541	966	11.8	3.52	100	.246	.316	3	1	100	84	58	.978	140	96	145	.5	.1	6.9	-.0	-2.4
PHI	50	18	246	21	1468.2	1426	116	466	1071	12.0	3.53	98	.256	.318	2	-12	98	74	54	.975	157	63	153	-.5	-1.3	3.7	-.3	2.8
STL	40	11	261	35	1461.1	1414	166	467	916	11.8	3.77	102	.255	.315	-37	11	109	80	35	.979	130	70	152	1.1	1.2	-5.6	.3	2.6
CHI	33	9	292	35	1472.0	1470	154	481	855	12.1	3.78	98	.260	.320	-39	-15	104	82	49	.974	171	65	166	-1.2	-1.6	-5.1	-.4	-.8
HOU	29	7	256	26	1461.0	1459	123	**388**	931	11.6	3.84	87	.260	.310	-49	-84	95	70	42	.974	166	78	130	-1.0	-8.9	-3.3	.6	-3.5
NY	29	11	**301**	14	1454.2	1462	147	498	776	12.4	4.06	87	.262	.326	-84	-86	100	92	49	.974	171	72	153	-1.2	-9.1	-15.6	-1.1	-4.0
TOT	416	126	2576	306	14643.0					11.6	3.54		.249	.311						.977	1486	742	1489					

Batter-Fielder Wins	
Mays-SF	6.9
Santo-Chi	6.2
Wynn-Hou	5.1
H.Aaron-Mil	4.8
Allen-Phi	4.2

Batting Average	
Clemente-Pit	.329
H.Aaron-Mil	.318
Mays-SF	.317
Williams-Chi	.315
Rose-Cin	.312

On-Base Percentage	
Mays-SF	.398
Robinson-Cin	.386
Rose-Cin	.382
McCovey-SF	.381
H.Aaron-Mil	.379

Slugging Average	
Mays-SF	.645
H.Aaron-Mil	.560
Williams-Chi	.552
Robinson-Cin	.540
McCovey-SF	.539

On-Base Plus Slugging	
Mays-SF	1043
H.Aaron-Mil	.938
Williams-Chi	.929
Robinson-Cin	.925
McCovey-SF	.920

Adjusted OPS	
Mays-SF	184
H.Aaron-Mil	161
Williams-Chi	155
McCovey-SF	152
Robinson-Cin	148

Adjusted Batter Runs	
Mays-SF	61.8
Williams-Chi	47.5
H.Aaron-Mil	47.1
Robinson-Cin	39.6
McCovey-SF	39.5

Runs	
Harper-Cin	126
Mays-SF	118
Rose-Cin	117
Williams-Chi	115

Hits	
Rose-Cin	209
Pinson-Cin	204
Williams-Chi	203
Clemente-Pit	194
Flood-StL	191

Doubles	
H.Aaron-Mil	40
Williams-Chi	39
Rose-Cin	35
Brock-StL	35
Pinson-Cin	34

Triples	
Callison-Phi	16
Clendenon-Pit	14
Clemente-Pit	14
Allen-Phi	14
Morgan-Hou	12

Home Runs	
Mays-SF	52
McCovey-SF	39
Williams-Chi	34
Santo-Chi	33
Robinson-Cin	33

Total Bases	
Mays-SF	360
Williams-Chi	356
Pinson-Cin	324
H.Aaron-Mil	319
Johnson-Cin	317

Runs Batted In	
Johnson-Cin	130
Robinson-Cin	113
Mays-SF	112
Williams-Chi	108
Stargell-Pit	107

Stolen Bases	
Wills-LA	94
Brock-StL	63
Wynn-Hou	43
Harper-Cin	35
W.Davis-LA	25

Base Stealing Runs	
Wills-LA	9.8
Wynn-Hou	8.1
Harper-Cin	5.6
Brock-StL	4.4
H.Aaron-Mil	3.9

Fielding Runs-Infield	
Mazeroski-Pit	25.9
Alley-Pit	23.8
Santo-Chi	22.0
Wills-LA	17.7
Wine-Phi	16.5

Fielding Runs-Outfield	
Callison-Phi	15.3
Mays-SF	9.6
Wynn-Hou	9.0
Clemente-Pit	6.8
H.Aaron-Mil	5.7

Wins	
Koufax-LA	26
Cloninger-Mil	24
Drysdale-LA	23
Marichal-SF	22
Ellis-Cin	22

Winning Pct.	
Koufax-LA	.765
Maloney-Cin	.690
Ellis-Cin	.688
Cloninger-Mil	.686
Bunning-Phi	.679

Complete Games	
Koufax-LA	27
Marichal-SF	24
Gibson-StL	20
Drysdale-LA	20
Cloninger-Mil	16

Strikeouts	
Koufax-LA	382
Veale-Pit	276
Gibson-StL	270
Bunning-Phi	268
Maloney-Cin	244

Fewest BB/Game	
Marichal-SF	1.40
Law-Pit	1.45
Bruce-Hou	1.49
Farrell-Hou	1.51
Johnson-Hou	1.87

Games	
Abernathy-Chi	84
Woodeshick-Hou-StL	78
McDaniel-Chi	71
Baldschun-Phi	65

Saves	
Abernathy-Chi	31
McCool-Cin	21
Linzy-SF	21

Base Runners	
Koufax-LA	7.83
Marichal-SF	8.35
Roberts-Hou	8.41
Law-Pit	9.11
O'Dell-Mil	9.62

Adjusted Relief Runs	
Linzy-SF	17.5
McBean-Pit	16.0
Abernathy-Chi	14.8
O'Dell-Mil	14.5
McDaniel-Chi	14.3

Relief Ranking	
Linzy-SF	33.3
O'Dell-Mil	24.0
Woodeshick-Hou-StL	21.8
McBean-Pit	20.9
Perranoski-LA	19.0

Innings Pitched	
Koufax-LA	335.2
Drysdale-LA	308.1
Gibson-StL	299.0
Short-Phi	297.1
Marichal-SF	295.1

Opponents' Avg.	
Koufax-LA	.179
Marichal-SF	.205
Maloney-Cin	.206
Bolin-SF	.214
Gibson-StL	.222

Opponents' OBP	
Koufax-LA	.227
Marichal-SF	.239
Law-Pit	.261
Drysdale-LA	.279
Bunning-Phi	.279

Earned Run Average	
Koufax-LA	2.04
Marichal-SF	2.13
Law-Pit	2.15
Maloney-Cin	2.54
Bunning-Phi	2.60

Adjusted ERA	
Koufax-LA	169
Law-Pit	163
Koufax-LA	160
Maloney-Cin	148
Shaw-SF	136

Adjusted Starter Runs	
Marichal-SF	48.0
Koufax-LA	47.6
Maloney-Cin	33.9
Law-Pit	30.9
Bunning-Phi	30.8

Pitcher Wins	
Marichal-SF	6.0
Koufax-LA	5.5
Maloney-Cin	4.6
Law-Pit	4.3
Drysdale-LA	4.2

Batting Around

The pennant race got ugly on August 22, when Giants pitcher Juan Marichal smashed Dodgers catcher John Roseboro in the head with a bat. The incident resulted in a fine and suspension for Marichal, and cemented tensions between the clubs.

San Francisco appeared to have the race in control, reeling off 14 straight wins in mid-September as Los Angeles foundered, but the Dodgers came back with 13 victories in a row, tying things up on September 26. While the Giants struggled over the last weekend, the Dodgers took the crown by winning three of four from Milwaukee, allowing only 3 runs in the series.

Cy Young winner Sandy Koufax outdid himself, fanning a record 382; he also pitched his fourth no-hitter—a perfect game—on September 9. When Tommy Davis broke an ankle, Rookie of the Year Jim Lefebvre and veteran outfielder Lou Johnson picked up the slack. Mays powered the Giants, winning his second MVP; he was the league's first 50-homer man since 1949, aside from Mays' own 1955 season. When Orlando Cepeda went down with knee troubles, Willie McCovey stepped in and hit 39 homers.

Chicago's Ted Abernathy pitched 85 times and notched 31 saves to set records. Cincinnati's hard-throwing Jim Maloney threw two extra-inning no-hitters, one of which he won. Warren Spahn, 44, retired with totals—notably 363 wins and 382 complete games—that would have been extraordinary even in the Dead Ball Era.

The Mets opened Shea Stadium in 1964, and this season Houston moved into the Astrodome. The first domed ballpark drew two million fans—and spawned millions of complaints about AstroTurf. Disappointed Phillies fans, meanwhile, began staying away; the club's attendance fell each year through 1969. The fifth-place Braves announced they would move to Atlanta for 1966.

A seven-game World Series against Minnesota should have been called The Sandy Koufax Show. After losing Game 2—he did not pitch in the opener in observance of Yom Kippur—Koufax shut out the Twins in Games 5 and 7. The final contest, a dominating 3-hitter pitched on just two days' rest, gave the Dodgers their third title in seven years.

1965 American League

TEAM	W	L	T	PCT	GB	HW	HL	R	OR	PA	H	2B	3B	HR	BB	SO	HB	SH	AVG	OBP	SLG	OPS	AOPS	BR	ABR	PF	SB	CS	BSA	BSR
MIN	102	60	0	.630		51	30	774	600	6213	1396	257	42	150	554	969	35	77	.254	.324	.399	723	107	87	56	104	92	33	74	9
CHI	95	67	0	.586	7	48	33	647	555	6217	1354	200	38	125	533	916	43	89	.246	.315	.364	679	105	1	43	94	50	33	60	-1
BAL	94	68	0	.580	8	46	33	641	578	6138	1299	227	38	125	529	907	28	95	.238	.307	.363	670	94	-20	-32	102	67	31	68	4
DET	89	73	0	.549	13	47	34	680	602	6064	1278	190	27	162	554	952	37	69	.238	.312	.374	686	100	1	4	101	57	41	58	-2
CLE	87	75	0	.537	15	52	30	663	613	6138	1367	198	21	156	663	857	33	90	.250	.315	.379	694	102	26	21	101	109	46	70	8
NY	77	85	0	.475	25	40	43	611	604	6081	1286	196	31	149	489	951	19	72	.235	.299	.364	663	95	-44	-40	99	35	20	64	1
CAL	75	87	0	.463	27	46	34	527	569	5956	1279	200	36	92	443	973	22	93	.239	.297	.341	638	89	-83	-70	98	107	57	65	4
WAS	70	92	0	.432	32	36	45	591	721	6078	1227	179	33	136	570	1125	34	63	.228	.304	.350	654	93	-48	-39	99	30	19	61	2
BOS	62	100	0	.383	40	34	47	669	791	6220	1378	244	40	165	607	964	30	57	.251	.327	.400	727	107	99	57	106	47	24	66	2
KC	59	103	0	.364	43	33	48	585	755	6058	1294	186	59	110	521	1020	35	74	.240	.309	.358	667	97	-28	-19	99				6
TOT	810					433	377	6388		61163	13158	2077	365	1370	5306	9634	316	779	.242	.311	.369	680					704	355	66	31

TEAM	CG	SHO	GR	SV	IP	H	HR	BB	SO	BR/9	ERA	AERA	OAV	OOB	PR	APR	PF	OSB	OCS	FA	E	WPB	DP	FW	PW	BW	BSW	DIF
MIN	32	12	299	45	1457.1	1278	166	503	934	11.2	3.14	113	.235	.301	52	66	103	53	34	.973	172	60	158	-2.3	7.0	6.0	.6	9.6
CHI	21	14	267	53	1481.2	1261	122	460	946	10.6	2.99	107	.231	.292	76	35	92	80	38	.980	127	108	156	.6	3.7	4.6	-.4	5.6
BAL	32	15	228	41	1477.2	1268	120	510	939	11.0	2.98	116	.233	.300	78	79	100	71	41	.980	126	48	152	.6	8.4	-3.4	.0	7.3
DET	45	14	240	31	1455.0	1283	137	509	1069	11.4	3.35	104	.237	.306	17	20	101	51	33	.981	116	71	126	1.3	2.1	.4	-.5	4.7
CLE	41	13	282	41	1458.1	1254	129	500	1156	11.0	3.30	106	.232	.298	26	30	101	51	40	.981	114	74	127	1.4	3.2	2.2	.5	-1.3
NY	41	11	252	31	1459.2	1337	126	511	1001	11.6	3.28	104	.245	.311	29	20	98	69	34	.978	137	59	166	-.0	2.1	-4.3	-.2	-1.6
CAL	39	14	236	33	1441.2	1259	91	563	847	11.5	3.17	107	.237	.312	46	37	98	57	29	.981	123	72	149	.8	3.9	-7.5	.0	-3.4
WAS	21	8	327	40	1435.2	1376	160	633	867	12.8	3.93	88	.254	.334	-75	-72	101	74	43	.977	143	70	148	-.4	-7.7	-4.2	-.3	1.6
BOS	33	9	268	25	1439.1	1443	158	543	993	12.6	4.24	88	.260	.327	-125	-76	108	101	36	.974	162	58	129	-1.6	-8.1	6.1	-.1	-15.2
KC	18	7	378	32	1433.0	1399	161	574	882	12.6	4.24	82	.256	.329	-124	-118	101	97	27	.977	139	87	142	-.2	-12.6	-2.0	.3	-7.5
TOT	323	117	2777	372	14539.1					11.6	3.46		.242	.311						.978	1359	707	1453					

Batter-Fielder Wins		Batting Average		On-Base Percentage		Slugging Average		On-Base Plus Slugging		Adjusted OPS		Adjusted Batter Runs	
Buford-Chi	5.3	Oliva-Min	.321	Yastrzemski-Bos	.395	Yastrzemski-Bos	.536	Yastrzemski-Bos	.932	Yastrzemski-Bos	154	Yastrzemski-Bos	38.1
Fregosi-Cal	3.7	Yastrzemski-Bos	.312	Colavito-Cle	.383	Conigliaro-Bos	.512	Cash-Det	.883	Cash-Det	147	Colavito-Cle	34.7
Yastrzemski-Bos	3.5	Davalillo-Cle	.301	Blefary-Bal	.381	Cash-Det	.512	Oliva-Min	.870	Wagner-Cle	143	Cash-Det	32.2
Knoop-Cal	3.5	Robinson-Bal	.297	Oliva-Min	.378	Wagner-Cle	.495	Wagner-Cle	.864	Oliva-Min	141	Oliva-Min	31.2
Versalles-Min	3.3	Wagner-Cle	.294	Mantilla-Bos	.374	Oliva-Min	.491	Colavito-Cle	.851	Colavito-Cle	140	Wagner-Cle	29.1

Runs		Hits		Doubles		Triples		Home Runs		Total Bases		Runs Batted In	
Versalles-Min	126	Oliva-Min	.185	Yastrzemski-Bos	.45	Versalles-Min	.12	Conigliaro-Bos	.32	Versalles-Min	.308	Colavito-Cle	.108
Oliva-Min	107	Versalles-Min	.182	Versalles-Min	.45	Campaneris-KC	.12	Cash-Det	.30	Tresh-NY	.287	Horton-Det	.104
Tresh-NY	94	Colavito-Cle	.170	Oliva-Min	.40	Aparicio-Bal	.10	Horton-Det	.29	Oliva-Min	.283	Oliva-Min	.98
Buford-Chi	93	Tresh-NY	.168	Tresh-NY	.29	W.Smith-Cal	.9	Wagner-Cle	.28	Colavito-Cle	.277	Mantilla-Bos	.92
Colavito-Cle	92	Fregosi-Cal	.167	Richardson-NY	.28						Conigliaro-Bos	.267	Whitfield-Cle	.90

Stolen Bases		Base Stealing Runs		Fielding Runs-Infield		Fielding Runs-Outfield		Wins		Winning Pct.		Complete Games	
Campaneris-KC	51	Campaneris-KC	4.6	Knoop-Cal	22.9	Conigliaro-Bos	9.0	Grant-Min	21	Grant-Min	.750	Stottlemyre-NY	18
Cardenal-Cal	37	Versalles-Min	4.2	Buford-Chi	21.5	Allison-Min	8.4	Stottlemyre-NY	20	McLain-Det	.727	McDowell-Cle	14
Versalles-Min	27	Davalillo-Cle	3.3	Boyer-NY	21.4	Davalillo-Cle	7.5	Kaat-Min	18	Stottlemyre-NY	.690	Grant-Min	14
Davalillo-Cle	26	Aparicio-Bal	3.3	Hansen-Chi	13.2	Hershberger-KC	5.3	McDowell-Cle	17	Fisher-Chi	.682	McLain-Det	13
Aparicio-Bal	26	Cardenal-Cal	2.9	Fregosi-Cal	9.6	Oliva-Min	3.0			Siebert-Cle	.667		

Strikeouts		Fewest BB/Game		Games		Saves		Base Runners/9		Adjusted Relief Runs		Relief Ranking	
McDowell-Cle	325	Terry-Cle	1.25	Fisher-Chi	82	Kline-Was	29	Wilhelm-Chi	7.63	Wilhelm-Chi	23.3	S.Miller-Bal	44.3
Lolich-Det	226	Monbouquette-Bos	1.57	Kline-Was	74	S.Miller-Bal	24	Fisher-Chi	8.87	S.Miller-Bal	22.4	B.Lee-Cal	29.3
McLain-Det	192	Horlen-Chi	1.60	B.Lee-Cal	69	Fisher-Chi	24	S.Miller-Bal	9.05	B.Lee-Cal	20.3	Wilhelm-Chi	26.7
Siebert-Cle	191	Ford-NY	1.84	Dickson-KC	68	B.Lee-Cal	23	Siebert-Cle	9.06	Fisher-Chi	15.2	Worthington-Min	22.7
Downing-NY	179	Grant-Min	2.03	S.Miller-Bal	67	Radatz-Bos	22	Hall-Bal	9.13	Hamilton-NY	12.5	Fisher-Chi	22.5

Innings Pitched		Opponents' Avg.		Opponents' OBP		Earned Run Average		Adjusted ERA		Adjusted Starter Runs		Pitcher Wins	
Stottlemyre-NY	291.0	McDowell-Cle	.185	Siebert-Cle	.259	McDowell-Cle	2.18	McDowell-Cle	160	McDowell-Cle	37.5	S.Miller-Bal	4.9
McDowell-Cle	273.0	Fisher-Chi	.205	Fisher-Chi	.259	Fisher-Chi	2.40	Siebert-Cle	143	Stottlemyre-NY	24.3	McDowell-Cle	3.8
Grant-Min	270.1	Siebert-Cle	.206	Terry-Cle	.268	Siebert-Cle	2.43	Perry-Min	135	Siebert-Cle	22.0	B.Lee-Cal	3.2
Kaat-Min	264.1	Brunet-Cal	.209	McLain-Det	.273	Brunet-Cal	2.56	Richert-Was	134	McLain-Det	20.1	Stottlemyre-NY	2.8
Newman-Cal	260.2	Richert-Was	.210	Horlen-Chi	.279	Richert-Was	2.60	Pappas-Bal	133	Richert-Was	19.0	Wilhelm-Chi	2.7

New Favorites

As scoring decreased, teams brought back "small-ball" strategy. Stolen bases increased 30 percent. Tellingly, however, the powerful Twins won the AL by 7 games, pulling away from Chicago and Baltimore in September. Minnesota had surprise MVP Zoilo Versalles, and four teammates connected for at least 20 home runs. In addition, the Twins posted the league's third-best ERA despite allowing the most homers in the majors.

The Yankees stumbled out of the gate and couldn't recover, finishing sixth—their worst placing since 1925—even as Mel Stottlemyre and Whitey Ford racked up 36 wins. Certainly the Yankees were unlucky. Tony Kubek was forced to retire due to a back problem, and injuries shelved Mickey Mantle, Roger Maris, and Elston Howard. But the team's reticence (some called it racism) to develop blacks and Latins had caught up.

Chicago's Eddie Fisher broke the mark for appearances with 82. Cleveland lefty "Sudden Sam" McDowell fanned 10.71

men per nine innings, a record that stood until 1984. Baltimore's Mark Belanger, Davey Johnson, and Jim Palmer made their major league debuts, as did Catfish Hunter of Kansas City and Roy White and Bobby Murcer of New York.

In the first amateur draft—designed to filter unsigned players through a system that would check ever-escalating bonuses—the Athletics made outfielder Rick Monday the initial pick. For an execrable last-place club, the A's made plenty of news. Satchel Paige, activated at age 58 to qualify for a pension, pitched 3 scoreless innings. Kansas City's 1965 attendance was the lowest of any franchise during the decade, and blowhard owner Charley Finley endlessly threatened to move the team.

A thrilling World Series went to the Dodgers, who shut out the Twins three times. Sandy Koufax allowed just 3 hits in winning the clincher at Metropolitan Stadium, the only game won by the visiting team.

1964 National League

TEAM	W	L	T	PCT	GB	HW	HL	R	OR	PA	H	2B	3B	HR	BB	SO	HB	SH	AVG	OBP	SLG	OPS	AOPS	BR	ABR	PF	SB	CS	BSA	BSR
STL	93	69	0	.574		48	33	715	652	6196	1531	240	53	109	427	925	18	94	.272	.324	.392	716	99	62	4	109	73	51	59	-2
PHI	92	70	0	.568	1	46	35	693	632	6116	1415	241	51	130	440	924	40	97	.258	.315	.391	706	106	42	51	99	30	35	46	-6
CIN	92	70	1	.568	1	47	34	660	566	6153	1383	220	38	130	457	974	33	65	.249	.308	.372	680	95	-10	-32	104	90	36	71	7
SF	90	72	0	.556	3	44	37	656	587	6194	1360	185	38	165	505	900	33	78	.246	.310	.382	692	99	15	1	102	64	35	65	2
MIL	88	74	0	.543	5	45	36	744	666	6206	1522	274	32	159	486	825	38	54	.272	.333	.418	751	117	138	133	101	53	41	56	-3
PIT	80	82	0	.494	13	42	39	663	636	6119	1469	225	54	121	408	970	24	87	.264	.315	.389	704	105	34	35	100	39	33	54	-3
LA	80	82	2	.494	13	41	40	614	572	6120	1375	180	39	79	438	893	19	120	.250	.305	.340	645	95	-73	-28	93	141	60	70	10
CHI	76	86	0	.469	17	40	41	649	724	6157	1391	239	50	145	499	1041	25	55	.251	.314	.390	704	101	39	12	104	70	49	59	-2
HOU	66	96	0	.407	27	41	40	495	628	5859	1214	162	41	70	381	872	49	87	.229	.285	.315	600	80	-163	-135	94	40	48	45	-8
NY	53	109	1	.327	40	33	48	569	776	6045	1372	195	31	103	353	932	48	52	.246	.296	.348	644	90	-87	-73	98	36	31	54	-3
TOT	812					427	383	6517		61165	14032	2161	427	1211	4394	9256	327	789	.254	.311	.374	685					636	419	60	-7

TEAM	CG	SHO	GR	SV	IP	H	HR	BB	SO	BR/9	ERA	AERA	OAV	OOB	PR	APR	PF	OSB	OCS	FA	E	WPB	DP	FW	PW	BW	BSW	DIF
STL	47	10	232	38	1445.1	1405	133	410	877	11.5	3.43	111	.255	.308	17	56	108	57	27	.973	172	49	147	-.7	5.9	.4	-.1	6.5
PHI	37	17	273	41	1461.0	1402	129	440	1009	11.7	3.36	103	.252	.312	28	17	98	58	45	.975	157	72	150	.0	1.8	5.4	-.6	4.3
CIN	54	14	203	35	1467.0	1306	112	436	1122	10.9	3.07	118	.238	.296	75	86	102	70	43	.979	130	69	137	1.6	9.1	-3.4	.8	2.9
SF	48	17	251	30	1476.1	1348	118	480	1023	11.4	3.19	112	.241	.304	57	61	101	70	36	.975	159	45	136	-.0	6.4	.1	.3	2.2
MIL	45	14	268	39	1434.2	1411	160	452	906	11.6	4.12	86	.257	.314	-92	-95	100	49	33	.977	143	87	139	.8	-10.0	14.0	-.2	2.4
PIT	42	14	274	29	1443.2	1429	92	476	951	12.1	3.52	100	.260	.320	2	-2	99	67	36	.972	177	74	179	-1.0	-.2	3.7	-.2	3.3
LA	47	19	213	27	1483.2	1289	88	458	1062	10.8	2.95	110	.232	.292	96	51	92	39	44	.973	170	65	126	-.5	5.4	-3.0	1.1	-4.0
CHI	58	11	255	19	1445.0	1510	144	423	737	12.1	4.08	91	.270	.321	-87	-56	105	52	51	.975	162	65	147	-.2	-5.9	1.3	-.1	-.0
HOU	30	9	248	31	1428.0	1421	105	353	852	11.4	3.41	100	.260	.306	20	1	97	95	38	.976	149	62	124	.5	-1.4	-14.3	-.6	-.6
NY	40	10	266	15	1438.2	1511	130	466	717	12.7	4.25	84	.272	.332	-115	-107	101	79	66	.974	167	85	154	-.4	-11.3	-7.7	-.2	-8.4
TOT	448	135	2483	304	14523.1					11.6	3.54		.254	.311						.975	1586	673	1439					

Batter-Fielder Wins		Batting Average		On-Base Percentage		Slugging Average		On-Base Plus Slugging		Adjusted OPS		Adjusted Batter Runs	
Santo-Chi	7.1	Clemente-Pit	.339	Santo-Chi	.398	Mays-SF	.607	Mays-SF	.990	Mays-SF	171	Mays-SF	54.2
Allen-Phi	5.9	Carty-Mil	.330	Robinson-Cin	.396	Santo-Chi	.564	Santo-Chi	.962	Allen-Phi	163	Allen-Phi	52.9
Mays-SF	5.8	Aaron-Mil	.328	Aaron-Mil	.393	Allen-Phi	.557	Robinson-Cin	.943	Santo-Chi	162	Santo-Chi	50.9
Menke-Mil	5.3	Torre-Mil	.321	Clemente-Pit	.388	Carty-Mil	.554	Carty-Mil	.942	Carty-Mil	162	Robinson-Cin	47.1
Robinson-Cin	4.5	Allen-Phi	.318	Carty-Mil	.388	Robinson-Cin	.548	Allen-Phi	.939	Robinson-Cin	158	Aaron-Mil	41.3

Runs		Hits		Doubles		Triples		Home Runs		Total Bases		Runs Batted In	
Allen-Phi	125	Flood-StL	211	Maye-Mil	44	Santo-Chi	13	Mays-SF	47	Allen-Phi	352	Boyer-StL	119
Mays-SF	121	Clemente-Pit	211	Clemente-Pit	40	Allen-Phi	13	Williams-Chi	33	Mays-SF	351	Santo-Chi	114
Brock-Chi-StL	111	Williams-Chi	201	Williams-Chi	39	Brock-Chi-StL	11	Hart-SF	31	Williams-Chi	343	Mays-SF	111
Robinson-Cin	103	Allen-Phi	201	Robinson-Cin	38	Pinson-Cin	11	Cepeda-SF	31	Santo-Chi	334	Torre-Mil	109
Aaron-Mil	103	Brock-Chi-StL	200	Allen-Phi	38			Callison-Phi	31	Callison-Phi	322	Callison-Phi	104

Stolen Bases		Base Stealing Runs		Fielding Runs-Infield		Fielding Runs-Outfield		Wins		Winning Pct.		Complete Games	
Wills-LA	53	Wills-LA	5.7	Mazeroski-Pit	34.7	W.Davis-LA	14.6	Jackson-Chi	24	Koufax-LA	.792	Marichal-SF	22
Brock-Chi-StL	43	W.Davis-LA	4.7	Santo-Chi	19.6	Callison-Phi	13.7	Marichal-SF	21	Marichal-SF	.724	Drysdale-LA	21
W.Davis-LA	42	Harper-Cin	4.2	Kasko-Cin	12.6	Aaron-Mil	9.9	Sadecki-StL	20	O'Toole-Cin	.708	Jackson-Chi	19
Harper-Cin	24	Aaron-Mil	3.4	Schofield-Pit	12.4	Altman-NY	9.7			Bunning-Phi	.704	Gibson-StL	17
Robinson-Cin	23	Robinson-Cin	3.3	Menke-Mil	11.8	T.Davis-LA	7.2			Jackson-Chi	.686	Ellsworth-Chi	16

Strikeouts		Fewest BB/Game		Games		Saves		Base Runners/9		Adjusted Relief Runs		Relief Ranking	
Veale-Pit	250	Bunning-Phi	1.46	B.Miller-LA	74	Woodeshick-Hou	23	Koufax-LA	8.35	McBean-Pit	15.4	McBean-Pit	25.5
Gibson-StL	245	Bruce-Hou	1.47	Perranoski-LA	72	McBean-Pit	22	Drysdale-LA	8.96	Ellis-Cin	14.5	Ellis-Cin	17.6
Drysdale-LA	237	Law-Pit	1.50	Baldschun-Phi	71	Baldschun-Phi	21	Short-Phi	9.34	McCool-Cin	11.7	McCool-Cin	15.0
Koufax-LA	223	Marichal-SF	1.74	Taylor-StL	63	McDaniel-Chi	15	Ellis-Cin	9.56	Roebuck-Phi	11.4	Roebuck-Phi	14.7
Bunning-Phi	219	Jackson-Chi	1.75	McDaniel-Chi	63			McCool-Cin	9.67	B.Miller-LA	9.5	B.Miller-LA	10.1

Innings Pitched		Opponents' Avg.		Opponents' OBP		Earned Run Average		Adjusted ERA		Adjusted Starter Runs		Pitcher Wins	
Drysdale-LA	321.1	Koufax-LA	191	Koufax-LA	240	Koufax-LA	1.74	Koufax-LA	187	Drysdale-LA	41.4	Drysdale-LA	5.0
Jackson-Chi	297.2	Drysdale-LA	207	Drysdale-LA	255	Drysdale-LA	2.18	Short-Phi	157	Koufax-LA	41.4	Koufax-LA	4.3
Gibson-StL	287.1	Veale-Pit	217	Short-Phi	266	Short-Phi	2.20	Drysdale-LA	148	Short-Phi	31.4	Short-Phi	3.6
Bunning-Phi	284.1	Short-Phi	217	Jackson-Chi	272	Marichal-SF	2.48	Marichal-SF	144	Marichal-SF	29.6	Marichal-SF	3.1
Veale-Pit	279.2	Bolin-SF	220	Marichal-SF	272	Bunning-Phi	2.63	O'Toole-Cin	136	Gibson-StL	26.6	McBean-Pit	2.9

A Philly Disappointment

The 1964 season has gone into legend as one of the NL's great races, but all the excitement came in the last two weeks. Boasting top rookie Richie Allen, outfielder Johnny Callison, and pitchers Jim Bunning and Chris Short, Philadelphia broke away from San Francisco in midsummer and led by 6½ on September 20. But with World Series tickets printed, Philadelphia dropped 10 straight, including three to hard-charging Cincinnati, winners of nine straight, and three to St. Louis, which had risen from the depths in August.

With the Giants awakening from their doldrums on the strength of Willie Mays, Juan Marichal, and rookie Japanese reliever Masanori Murakami, a four-way tie loomed in the last weekend. The Mets, of all teams, beat the Cardinals in the first two games of the season-ending series before St. Louis held on to take the finale. The Reds—aware that manager Fred Hutchinson was dying of cancer—lost to the Phillies. Philadelphia and Cincinnati both finished 1 game out.

Lou Brock, acquired midseason from the Cubs, ignited the Redbirds' attack. Ken Boyer was MVP, and Ray Sadecki and Bob Gibson combined for 39 wins. Veteran reliever Barney Schultz, like Pedro Ramos in the AL, was vital down the stretch. The Phillies seized up at the finish line as manager Gene Mauch relied almost solely on Bunning and Short.

Several longtime NL stars began their careers in 1964, including Phil Niekro, Tony Perez, and Larry Dierker. Duke Snider retired. Prior to the season, Cubs infielder Ken Hubbs was killed in a plane crash, and Colts reliever Jim Umbricht died of cancer.

The World Series went seven games. Both the Cardinals and Yankees blew leads, had exciting late-inning rallies, hit crucial home runs, and boasted great pitching performances. However, St. Louis' two wins at New York helped withstand Jim Bouton's two victories for the Yankees. Tim McCarver hit .478 and slugged a 10th inning homer to win Game 5. Gibson went all the way in Game 7 for a 7-5 win.

1964 American League

TEAM	W	L	T	PCT	GB	HW	HL	R	OR	PA	H	2B	3B	HR	BB	SO	HB	SH	AVG	OBP	SLG	OPS	AOPS	BR	ABR	PF	SB	CS	BSA	BSR
NY	99	63	2	.611		50	31	730	577	6358	1442	208	35	162	520	976	31	68	.253	.317	.387	704	100	12	1	102	54	18	75	6
CHI	98	64	0	.605	1	52	29	642	501	6246	1356	184	40	106	562	902	52	96	.247	.320	.353	673	97	-33	-15	97	75	39	66	3
BAL	97	65	1	.599	2	49	32	679	567	6143	1357	229	20	162	537	1019	27	69	.248	.316	.387	703	101	17	20	100	78	38	67	4
DET	85	77	1	.525	14	46	35	699	678	6183	1394	199	57	157	517	912	40	71	.253	.319	.395	714	102	33	23	102	60	27	69	4
LA	82	80	0	.506	17	45	36	544	551	5975	1297	186	27	102	472	920	26	78	.242	.304	.344	648	95	-91	-31	90	49	39	56	-3
MIN	79	83	1	.488	20	40	41	737	678	6318	1413	227	46	221	553	1019	44	74	.252	.322	.427	749	113	99	94	101	46	22	68	2
CLE	79	83	2	.488	20	41	40	689	693	6257	1386	208	22	164	500	1063	49	63	.247	.312	.380	692	99	-8	-3	99	79	51	61	0
BOS	72	90	0	.444	27	45	36	688	793	6106	1425	253	29	186	504	917	28	35	.258	.322	.416	738	106	79	45	105	18	16	53	-2
WAS	62	100	0	.383	37	31	50	578	733	6037	1246	199	28	125	514	1124	28	66	.231	.299	.348	647	86	-95	-92	100	47	30	61	0
KC	57	105	1	.352	42	26	55	621	836	6192	1321	216	29	166	548	1104	42	53	.239	.311	.379	690	95	-13	-32	103	34	20	63	0
TOT	814					425	385	6607		61815	13637	2109	333	1551	5227	9956	367	673	.247	.315	.382	696					540	300	64	14

TEAM	CG	SHO	GR	SV	IP	H	HR	BB	SO	BR/9	ERA	AERA	OAV	OOB	PR	APR	PF	OSB	OCS	FA	E	WPB	DP	FW	PW	BW	BSW	DIF
NY	46	18	215	45	1506.2	1312	129	504	989	11.0	3.15	115	.234	.299	79	78	100	33	25	.983	109	55	158	1.1	8.2	.1	.5	8.1
CHI	44	20	219	45	1467.2	1216	124	401	955	10.1	2.72	127	.226	.282	147	125	95	31	27	.981	122	84	164	.2	13.1	-1.6	.2	5.0
BAL	44	17	238	41	1458.2	1292	129	456	939	11.0	3.16	113	.239	.300	76	68	99	62	26	.985	95	51	159	1.9	7.2	2.1	.3	4.6
DET	35	11	248	35	1453.0	1343	164	536	993	12.0	3.84	95	.244	.316	-35	-29	101	25	31	.982	111	59	137	1.0	-3.0	2.4	.3	3.4
LA	30	28	285	41	1450.2	1273	100	530	965	11.5	2.91	113	.236	.309	115	67	91	52	37	.978	138	50	168	-.7	7.0	-3.3	-.5	-1.6
MIN	47	4	277	29	1477.2	1361	181	545	1099	11.8	3.58	100	.243	.312	8	1	99	51	35	.977	145	91	131	-1.1	.1	9.9	.0	-11.0
CLE	37	16	277	37	1487.2	1443	154	565	1162	12.3	3.75	96	.255	.324	-21	-25	99	61	31	.981	118	83	149	.6	-2.6	-.3	-.1	-2.7
BOS	21	9	252	38	1422.0	1464	186	571	1094	13.1	4.50	86	.266	.336	-138	-95	106	75	26	.977	138	61	123	-.7	-10.0	4.7	-.4	-4.5
WAS	27	5	291	26	1435.1	1417	172	505	794	12.2	3.98	93	.259	.322	-57	-44	102	54	36	.979	127	63	145	-.0	-4.6	-9.7	-.1	-4.5
KC	18	6	344	27	1455.2	1516	220	614	966	13.5	4.71	81	.269	.344	-175	-136	105	96	26	.975	158	73	152	-1.9	-14.3	-3.4	-.1	-4.3
TOT	349	134	2646	364	14615.0					11.8	3.63		.247	.315						.980	1261		670	1486				

Batter-Fielder Wins		Batting Average		On-Base Percentage		Slugging Average		On-Base Plus Slugging		Adjusted OPS		Adjusted Batter Runs	
Fregosi-LA	5.6	Oliva-Min	.323	Mantle-NY	.423	Powell-Bal	.606	Mantle-NY	1015	Mantle-NY	177	Mantle-NY	52.9
Hansen-Chi	4.7	B.Robinson-Bal	.317	Allison-Min	.404	Mantle-NY	.591	Powell-Bal	1005	Powell-Bal	176	Allison-Min	45.7
Powell-Bal	4.6	Howard-NY	.313	Powell-Bal	.399	Oliva-Min	.557	Allison-Min	.957	Allison-Min	163	Powell-Bal	45.5
Allison-Min	4.5	Mantle-NY	.303	Robinson-Chi	.388	Allison-Min	.553	Killebrew-Min	.924	Killebrew-Min	153	Oliva-Min	42.6
Howard-NY	4.2	Robinson-Chi	.301	Kaline-Det	.383	Killebrew-Min	.548	Oliva-Min	.916	Oliva-Min	150	Killebrew-Min	42.6

Runs		Hits		Doubles		Triples		Home Runs		Total Bases		Runs Batted In	
Oliva-Min	109	Oliva-Min	217	Oliva-Min	43	Versalles-Min	10	Killebrew-Min	49	Oliva-Min	374	B.Robinson-Bal	118
Howser-Cle	101	B.Robinson-Bal	194	Bressoud-Bos	41	Rollins-Min	10	Powell-Bal	39	B.Robinson-Bal	319	Stuart-Bos	114
Killebrew-Min	95	Richardson-NY	181	B.Robinson-Bal	35	Yastrzemski-Bos	9	Mantle-NY	35	Killebrew-Min	316	Mantle-NY	111
Wagner-Cle	94	Howard-NY	172	Versalles-Min	33	Oliva-Min	9	Colavito-KC	34	Colavito-KC	298	Killebrew-Min	111
Versalles-Min	94	Versalles-Min	171			Fregosi-LA	9	Stuart-Bos	33	Stuart-Bos	296	Colavito-KC	102

Stolen Bases		Base Stealing Runs		Fielding Runs-Infield		Fielding Runs-Outfield		Wins		Winning Pct.		Complete Games	
Aparicio-Bal	57	Aparicio-Bal	6.6	Knoop-LA	37.9	Yastrzemski-Bos	19.5	Peters-Chi	20	Bunker-Bal	.792	Chance-LA	15
Weis-Chi	22	Tresh-NY	2.9	Hansen-Chi	17.9	Brandt-Bal	12.5	Chance-LA	20	Ford-NY	.739	Pascual-Min	14
Davalillo-Cle	21	Weis-Chi	2.4	Green-KC	13.3	King-Was	9.8	Wickersham-Det	19	Peters-Chi	.714	Pappas-Bal	13
Howser-Cle	20	Wagner-Cle	2.4	Adair-Bal	13.1	Lock-Was	9.1	Pizarro-Chi	19	Pappas-Bal	.696	Osteen-Was	13
Hinton-Was	17	Howser-Cle	2.0	Fregosi-LA	9.8	Hinton-Was	6.9	Bunker-Bal	19	Chance-LA	.690	Kaat-Min	13

Strikeouts		Fewest BB/Game		Games		Saves		Base Runners/9		Adjusted Relief Runs		Relief Ranking	
Downing-NY	217	Monbouquette-Bos	1.54	Wyatt-KC	81	Radatz-Bos	29	Hall-Bal	7.60	B.Lee-LA	27.9	Radatz-Bos	46.7
Pascual-Min	213	Pappas-Bal	1.72	Radatz-Bos	79	Wilhelm-Chi	27	Horlen-Chi	8.59	Radatz-Bos	25.9	Wilhelm-Chi	39.6
Chance-LA	207	Newman-LA	1.85	Wilhelm-Chi	73	Miller-Bal	23	Wilhelm-Chi	8.63	Wilhelm-Chi	21.4	B.Lee-LA	27.9
Peters-Chi	205	Bouton-NY	1.99	McMahon-Cle	70	Wyatt-KC	20	Fisher-Chi	8.71	Stock-Bal-KC	19.4	Worthington-Min	27.5
Lolich-Det	192	Pizarro-Chi	2.07	Miller-Bal	66	B.Lee-LA	19	Chance-LA	9.12	Hall-Bal	17.5	Hall-Bal	20.7

Innings Pitched		Opponents' Avg.		Opponents' OBP		Earned Run Average		Adjusted ERA		Adjusted Starter Runs		Pitcher Wins	
Chance-LA	278.1	Horlen-Chi	.190	Horlen-Chi	.248	Chance-LA	1.65	Chance-LA	199	Chance-LA	57.7	Chance-LA	5.6
Peters-Chi	273.2	Chance-LA	.195	Chance-LA	.260	Horlen-Chi	1.88	Horlen-Chi	184	Ford-NY	38.8	Radatz-Bos	4.9
Bouton-NY	271.1	Bunker-Bal	.207	Pizarro-Chi	.267	Ford-NY	2.13	Ford-NY	170	Horlen-Chi	36.7	Wilhelm-Chi	4.2
Pascual-Min	267.1	Peters-Chi	.219	Bunker-Bal	.267	Peters-Chi	2.50	Peters-Chi	138	Peters-Chi	29.0	Horlen-Chi	4.0
Osteen-Was	257.0	Pizarro-Chi	.219	Bouton-NY	.272	Pizarro-Chi	2.56	Pizarro-Chi	135	Pizarro-Chi	24.3	Peters-Chi	3.9

Ragged End of the String

The Yankees struggled most of the way under new skipper Yogi Berra. Dissension racked the ranks in New York as the Orioles and White Sox ran the roost. On August 28 the Yankees were in third, 4½ games out. But a great September, which included 11 straight wins, propelled New York to the top. Baltimore and Chicago suffered key losses to second-division teams down the stretch.

Mickey Mantle and Roger Maris were great again for New York, and despite just three regular starters, the pitching was good enough. Veteran reliever Pedro Ramos was sterling in September.

The White Sox nearly pulled it out with a strong rotation and spectacular 40-year-old reliever Hoyt Wilhelm. Orioles third baseman Brooks Robinson dazzled with bat and glove to garner MVP honors. Baltimore also had Boog Powell, Luis Aparicio, and moundsmen Robin Roberts and Harvey Haddix.

The Twins fell to sixth, but Rookie of the Year Tony Oliva hit 32 homers, led the AL in runs, hits, and doubles, and won the batting title. Another rookie, 19-year-old Tony Conigliaro, hit 24 homers in only 111 games. Luis Tiant, Bert Campaneris, Mickey Lolich, Denny McLain, and Mel Stottlemyre also made impressive debuts.

Los Angeles' Dean Chance, pitching in spacious Chavez Ravine, won the Cy Young, leading the league in several key categories. In the bullpen, John Wyatt established a new major league best with 81 appearances for last-place Kansas City, and Boston's hard-throwing Dick Radatz had 29 saves. Six clubs had relief aces, the most to that point, and save totals were rising.

Once again, the Yankees looked human in the World Series, losing a seven-game tilt to the Cardinals. Nobody knew it at the time, but New York's long dynasty was over. Berra was canned after the Series—replaced by St. Louis manager Johnny Keane—Mantle's injuries had taken their toll, and several young players' careers quickly fell apart.

1963 National League

TEAM	W	L	T	PCT	GB	HW	HL	R	OR	PA	H	2B	3B	HR	BB	SO	HB	SH	AVG	OBP	SLG	OPS	AOPS	BR	ABR	PF	SB	CS	BSA	BSR
LA	99	63	1	.611	—	53	28	640	550	6045	1361	178	34	110	453	867	26	85	.251	.309	.357	666	106	-3	42	93	124	70	64	3
STL	93	69	0	.574	6	53	28	747	628	6283	1540	231	66	128	458	915	25	85	.271	.326	.403	729	107	119	55	109	77	42	65	2
SF	88	74	0	.543	11	50	31	725	641	6176	1442	206	35	197	441	889	45	72	.258	.316	.414	730	118	112	120	99	55	49	53	-5
PHI	87	75	0	.537	12	45	36	642	578	6092	1390	228	54	126	403	955	44	87	.252	.306	.381	687	105	28	36	99	56	39	59	-1
CIN	86	76	0	.531	13	46	35	648	594	6040	1333	225	44	122	474	960	47	62	.246	.310	.371	681	100	28	9	103	92	58	61	0
MIL	84	78	1	.519	15	45	36	677	603	6211	1345	204	39	139	525	954	43	82	.244	.312	.370	682	104	32	39	99	75	52	59	-2
CHI	82	80	0	.506	17	43	38	570	578	5987	1286	205	44	127	439	1049	36	64	.238	.297	.363	660	91	-21	-51	105	68	60	53	-6
PIT	74	88	0	.457	25	42	39	567	595	6110	1385	181	49	108	454	940	29	63	.250	.309	.359	668	98	-4	-8	101	57	41	58	-2
HOU	66	96	0	.407	33	44	37	464	640	5983	1184	170	39	62	456	938	30	86	.220	.283	.301	584	80	-161	-131	94	39	30	57	-2
NY	51	111	0	.315	48	34	47	501	774	5921	1168	156	35	96	457	1078	47	46	.219	.285	.315	600	78	-131	-138	102	41	52	44	-9
TOT	811					455	355	6181		60848	13434	1984	439	1215	4560	9545	372	732	.245	.306	.364	669					684	493	58	-22

TEAM	CG	SHO	GR	SV	IP	H	HR	BB	SO	BR/9	ERA	AERA	OAV	OOB	PR	APR	PF	OSB	OCS	FA	E	WPB	DP	FW	PW	BW	BSW	DIF
LA	51	24	209	29	1469.2	1329	111	402	1095	10.8	2.85	106	.239	.293	71	30	92	48	31	.975	159	60	129	-.0	3.3	4.6	.6	9.6
STL	49	17	243	32	1463.0	1329	124	463	978	11.3	3.32	107	.241	.303	-5	34	108	84	44	.976	147	69	136	.6	3.7	6.0	.5	1.3
SF	46	9	247	30	1469.0	1380	126	464	954	11.5	3.35	96	.246	.306	-9	-24	97	69	39	.975	156	53	113	.1	-2.6	13.0	-.3	-3.2
PHI	45	12	242	31	1457.1	1262	113	553	1052	11.4	3.09	105	.235	.309	32	24	98	79	61	.978	142	62	147	.9	2.6	3.9	.1	-1.6
CIN	55	22	182	36	1439.2	1307	117	425	1048	11.1	3.29	102	.242	.300	-1	8	102	69	46	.978	135	81	127	1.3	.9	1.0	.2	1.6
MIL	56	18	262	26	1471.2	1327	149	409	924	11.3	3.27	99	.241	.304	4	-8	98	62	45	.980	129	69	161	1.8	-.9	4.2	.0	-2.1
CHI	45	15	217	28	1457.0	1357	119	400	851	11.0	3.08	114	.249	.301	34	66	107	48	65	.976	155	62	172	.2	7.2	-5.5	-.4	-.4
PIT	34	16	292	33	1448.0	1350	99	457	900	11.5	3.10	107	.249	.311	31	33	100	82	53	.972	182	57	195	-1.4	3.6	-.9	.0	-8.3
HOU	36	16	232	20	1450.1	1341	95	378	937	10.9	3.44	92	.245	.295	-24	-48	96	82	49	.974	162	65	100	-.3	3.6	-14.2	.0	4.7
NY	42	5	233	12	1427.2	1452	162	529	806	12.8	4.12	85	.263	.330	-132	-95	106	61	60	.967	210	81	151	-3.1	-10.3	-15.0	-.7	-.9
TOT	459	154	2359	276	14553.1					11.4	3.29		.245	.306						.975	1577	659	1431					

Batter-Fielder Wins
Mays-SF 6.0 · Mazeroski-Pit 5.7 · H.Aaron-Mil 5.4 · Mathews-Mil 5.3 · Callison-Phi 4.2

Batting Average
T.Davis-LA .326 · Clemente-Pit .320 · Groat-StL .319 · H.Aaron-Mil .319 · Cepeda-SF .316

On-Base Percentage
Mathews-Mil .399 · H.Aaron-Mil .391 · Mays-SF .380 · Robinson-Cin .379 · Groat-StL .377

Slugging Average
H.Aaron-Mil .586 · Mays-SF .582 · McCovey-SF .566 · Cepeda-SF .563 · Pinson-Cin .514

On-Base Plus Slugging
H.Aaron-Mil .977 · Mays-SF .962 · Cepeda-SF .929 · McCovey-SF .915 · Pinson-Cin .861

Adjusted OPS
H.Aaron-Mil 180 · Mays-SF 176 · Cepeda-SF 166 · McCovey-SF 161 · Mathews-Mil 147

Adjusted Batter Runs
H.Aaron-Mil 65.6 · Mays-SF 58.1 · Cepeda-SF 47.5 · McCovey-SF 42.3 · Mathews-Mil 40.6

Runs
H.Aaron-Mil 121 · Mays-SF 115 · Flood-StL 112 · White-StL 106 · McCovey-SF 103

Hits
Pinson-Cin 204 · Groat-StL 201 · H.Aaron-Mil 201 · White-StL 200 · Flood-StL 200

Doubles
Groat-StL 43 · Pinson-Cin 37 · Williams-Chi 36 · Gonzalez-Phi 36 · Callison-Phi 36

Triples
Pinson-Cin 14 · Gonzalez-Phi 12 · Groat-StL 11 · Callison-Phi 11 · Brock-Chi 11

Home Runs
McCovey-SF 44 · H.Aaron-Mil 44 · Mays-SF 38 · Cepeda-SF 34 · Howard-LA 28

Total Bases
H.Aaron-Mil 370 · Mays-SF 347 · Pinson-Cin 335 · Cepeda-SF 326 · White-StL 323

Runs Batted In
H.Aaron-Mil 130 · Boyer-StL 111 · White-StL 109 · Pinson-Cin 106 · Mays-SF 103

Stolen Bases
Wills-LA 40 · H.Aaron-Mil 31 · Pinson-Cin 27 · Robinson-Cin 26 · W.Davis-LA 25

Base Stealing Runs
H.Aaron-Mil 5.1 · Pinson-Cin 3.1 · Gilliam-LA 2.4 · Maye-Mil 2.4 · Harper-Cin 2.3

Fielding Runs-Infield
Mazeroski-Pit 55.5 · Hubbs-Chi 19.3 · Schofield-Pit 16.7 · Mathews-Mil 14.1 · Wine-Phi 14.0

Fielding Runs-Outfield
Callison-Phi 19.0 · Brock-Chi 10.4 · W.Davis-LA 10.1 · Flood-StL 8.1 · Robinson-Cin 7.1

Wins
Marichal-SF 25 · Koufax-LA 25 · Spahn-Mil 23 · Maloney-Cin 23 · Ellsworth-Chi 22

Winning Pct.
Perranoski-LA .842 · Koufax-LA .833 · Spahn-Mil .767 · Maloney-Cin .767 · Marichal-SF .758

Complete Games
Spahn-Mil 22 · Koufax-LA 20 · Ellsworth-Chi 19 · Marichal-SF 18 · Drysdale-LA 17

Strikeouts
Koufax-LA 306 · Maloney-Cin 265 · Drysdale-LA 251 · Marichal-SF 248 · Gibson-StL 204

Fewest BB/Game
Friend-Pit 1.47 · Farrell-Hou 1.56 · Nuxhall-Cin 1.62 · Drysdale-LA 1.63 · Koufax-LA 1.68

Games
Perranoski-LA 69 · Baldschun-Phi 65 · Bearnarth-NY 58 · Sisk-Pit 57 · McDaniel-Chi 57

Saves
McDaniel-Chi 22 · Perranoski-LA 21 · Face-Pit 16 · Baldschun-Phi 16 · Henry-Cin 14

Base Runners/9
Koufax-LA 7.96 · Shantz-StL 8.39 · Umbricht-Hou 8.76 · Farrell-Hou 8.81 · Marichal-SF 9.02

Adjusted Relief Runs
Perranoski-LA 20.2 · Shantz-StL 17.6 · Klippstein-Phi 16.4 · Woodeshick-Hou 15.5 · Taylor-StL 15.8

Relief Ranking
Perranoski-LA 34.2 · Woodeshick-Hou 27.6 · Baldschun-Phi 18.3 · Klippstein-Phi 17.1 · Veale-Pit 15.8

Innings Pitched
Marichal-SF 321.1 · Drysdale-LA 315.1 · Koufax-LA 311.0 · Ellsworth-Chi 290.2 · Sanford-SF 284.1

Opponents' Avg.
Koufax-LA .189 · Maloney-Cin .202 · Culp-Phi .206 · Ellsworth-Chi .210 · Broglio-StL .216

Opponents' OBP
Koufax-LA .230 · Farrell-Hou .255 · Marichal-SF .255 · Ellsworth-Chi .262 · Friend-Pit .267

Earned Run Average
Koufax-LA 1.88 · Ellsworth-Chi 2.11 · Friend-Pit 2.34 · Marichal-SF 2.41 · Simmons-StL 2.48

Adjusted ERA
Ellsworth-Chi 167 · Koufax-LA 161 · Simmons-StL 143 · Friend-Pit 141 · Jackson-Chi 137

Adjusted Starter Runs
Koufax-LA 46.9 · Ellsworth-Chi 44.0 · Marichal-SF 28.6 · Friend-Pit 27.0 · Jackson-Chi 22.7

Pitcher Wins
Ellsworth-Chi 5.0 · Koufax-LA 4.1 · Perranoski-LA 3.9 · Woodeshick-Hou 3.2 · Jackson-Chi 3.1

Roger, Dodgers!

For the first several months, the Giants, Reds, Cardinals, and Dodgers jousted. Eventually, Los Angeles won 17 of 20 and made some space. But in late August, the Cardinals started their own streak, winning 19 of 20. This set up a crucial three-game set at St. Louis, which the Dodgers swept to end the race. St. Louis fans then had to deal with another disappointment as Stan Musial retired.

A healthy Sandy Koufax took the Cy Young and MVP, capitalizing on the newly enlarged strike zone and the comfortable dimensions of Chavez Ravine. The Dodgers, sixth in runs, were the NL's second-best offense on the road—better even than St. Louis, which led the league in scoring due to small Busch Stadium. While sore-legged Maury Wills' steals dropped to 40, Tommy Davis' batting title and Frank Howard's homers carried the day for the Dodgers.

The league batting average of .245 was the worst in fifty-four years, and the new hitting conditions sorted the haves from the have-nots. The last-place Mets' .219 average was the lowest of any team since 1908.

On September 10 Felipe, Matty, and Jesus Alou all played in the Giants' outfield. On September 27 Houston fielded an all-rookie lineup including Joe Morgan, Jimmy Wynn, and Jerry Grote. They sat another frosh, Rusty Staub, already the Colts' regular first baseman.

Milwaukee's Henry Aaron won his second of four home run titles. Cincinnati's scrappy second baseman Pete Rose was Rookie of the Year, and Gil Hodges retired to go into managing. Prior to the season, Rogers Hornsby, one of the game's greatest hitters, died.

Fittingly, the World Series was all pitching. Holding New York to a .171 average, the Dodgers pinned the Yankees with their first-ever four-game sweep. (The 1922 Giants also kept the Yankees from the win column, but that Series featured a tie). Koufax fanned 15 in Game 1 and captured the decisive fourth game as well.

1963 American League

TEAM	W	L	T	PCT	GB	HW	HL	R	OR	PA	H	2B	3B	HR	BB	SO	HB	SH	AVG	OBP	SLG	OPS	AOPS	BR	ABR	PF	SB	CS	BSA	BSR
NY	104	57	0	.646		58	22	714	547	6067	1387	197	35	188	434	808	31	66	.252	.309	.403	712	105	25	31	99	42	26	62	0
CHI	94	68	0	.580	10.5	49	33	683	544	6242	1379	208	40	114	571	896	40	79	.250	.323	.365	688	101	5	17	98	64	28	70	3
MIN	91	70	0	.565	13	48	33	767	602	6233	1408	223	35	225	547	912	41	84	.255	.325	.430	755	115	118	150	102	97	34	74	9
BAL	86	76	0	.531	18.5	48	33	644	621	6055	1359	207	32	146	469	940	28	73	.249	.310	.380	690	103	-7	18	96	73	32	70	5
DET	79	83	0	.488	25.5	47	34	700	703	6242	1388	195	36	148	592	908	38	64	.252	.327	.382	709	102	44	21	103	73	32	70	5
CLE	79	83	0	.488	25.5	41	40	635	702	6136	1314	214	29	169	469	1102	40	88	.239	.301	.381	682	97	-26	-20	99	59	36	62	0
BOS	76	85	0	.472	28	44	36	666	704	6145	1403	247	34	171	475	954	26	44	.252	.312	.400	712	102	33	12	103	27	16	63	1
KC	73	89	0	.451	31.5	36	45	615	704	6172	1356	225	38	95	529	829	25	77	.247	.313	.353	666	88	-40	-73	106	47	26	64	1
LA	70	91	0	.435	34	39	42	597	660	6127	1378	208	38	95	448	916	43	84	.250	.309	.354	663	97	-54	-16	94	43	30	59	-1
WAS	56	106	0	.346	48.5	31	49	578	812	6069	1237	190	35	138	497	963	30	57	.227	.293	.351	644	86	-98	-96	100	68	28	71	5
TOT	808					441	367	6599		61488	13609	2114	352	1489	5031	9228	342	716	.247	.312	.380	692					552	270	67	27

TEAM	CG	SHO	GR	SV	IP	H	HR	BB	SO	BR/9	ERA	AERA	OAV	OOB	PR	APR	PF	OSB	OCS	FA	E	WPB	DP	FW	PW	BW	BSW	DIF
NY	59	19	180	31	1449.0	1239	115	476	965	10.8	3.07	114	.232	.295	89	73	97	36	18	.982	110	42	162	1.4	7.7	3.3	-.3	11.5
CHI	49	21	211	39	1469.0	1311	100	440	932	10.9	2.97	118	.239	.297	107	90	97	51	32	.979	131	60	163	.3	9.5	1.8	.1	1.4
MIN	58	13	234	30	1446.1	1322	162	459	941	11.2	3.28	111	.242	.302	56	58	100	43	23	.976	144	70	140	-.5	6.1	10.8	-.0	-5.8
BAL	35	8	248	43	1452.0	1353	137	507	913	11.7	3.45	101	.248	.314	29	4	96	47	24	.984	99	42	157	2.1	.4	1.9	.7	-.0
DET	42	7	240	28	1456.1	1407	195	477	930	11.9	3.90	96	.253	.315	-44	-25	103	38	25	.982	113	63	124	1.3	-2.6	2.2	.2	-3.1
CLE	40	14	257	25	1469.0	1390	176	478	1018	11.6	3.79	95	.249	.309	-27	-28	100	51	34	.977	143	50	129	-.4	-2.9	-2.1	-.3	3.7
BOS	29	7	241	32	1449.2	1367	152	539	1009	12.0	3.97	95	.248	.316	-55	-29	104	62	17	.978	135	62	119	-.0	-3.0	1.3	-.3	-2.4
KC	35	11	247	29	1458.0	1417	156	540	887	12.4	3.92	100	.256	.324	-47	-3	108	96	26	.980	127	54	131	.5	-.3	-7.7	-.2	-.5
LA	30	13	315	31	1455.1	1317	120	578	889	12.0	3.52	97	.242	.312	17	-17	94	56	41	.974	163	66	155	-1.6	-1.8	-1.7	-.4	-5.0
WAS	29	8	276	25	1447.0	1486	176	537	744	12.8	4.42	84	.266	.331	-126	-111	102	73	28	.971	182	66	165	-2.6	-11.7	-10.1	.2	-.9
TOT	406	121	2449	313	14551.2					11.7	3.63		.247	.312						.978	1347	575	1445					

Batter-Fielder Wins	Batting Average	On-Base Percentage	Slugging Average	On-Base Plus Slugging	Adjusted OPS	Adjusted Batter Runs
Yastrzemski-Bos..4.2	Yastrzemski-Bos....321	Yastrzemski-Bos....418	Killebrew-Min....555	Allison-Min....911	Allison-Min....150	Yastrzemski-Bos....40.7
Battey-Min....4.0	Kaline-Det....312	Pearson-LA....402	Allison-Min....533	Killebrew-Min....904	Killebrew-Min....147	Allison-Min....37.7
Hansen-Chi....3.9	Rollins-Min....307	Cash-Det....386	Howard-NY....528	Yastrzemski-Bos....894	Yastrzemski-Bos....145	Killebrew-Min....32.2
Allison-Min....3.8	Pearson-LA....304	Allison-Min....378	Stuart-Bos....521	Kaline-Det....889	Kaline-Det....142	Kaline-Det....31.4
Howard-NY....3.4	Ward-Chi....295	Kaline-Det....375	Hall-Min....521	Howard-NY....869	Howard-NY....141	Pearson-LA....31.2

Runs	Hits	Doubles	Triples	Home Runs	Total Bases	Runs Batted In
Allison-Min....99	Yastrzemski-Bos....183	Yastrzemski-Bos....40	Versalles-Min....13	Killebrew-Min....45	Stuart-Bos....319	Stuart-Bos....118
Pearson-LA....92	Ward-Chi....177	Ward-Chi....34	Hinton-Was....12	Stuart-Bos....42	Ward-Chi....289	Kaline-Det....101
Yastrzemski-Bos....91	Pearson-LA....176	Torres-LA....32	Fregosi-LA....12	Allison-Min....35	Killebrew-Min....286	Killebrew-Min....96
Tresh-NY....91	Kaline-Det....172	Causey-KC....32	Cimoli-KC....11	Hall-Min....33	Kaline-Det....283	Colavito-Det....91
Colavito-Det....91	Fregosi-LA....170	Alvis-Cle....32		Howard-NY....28	Allison-Min....281	Allison-Min....91

Stolen Bases	Base Stealing Runs	Fielding Runs-Infield	Fielding Runs-Outfield	Wins	Winning Pct.	Complete Games
Aparicio-Bal....40	Aparicio-Bal....6.7	Hansen-Chi....27.5	Hall-Min....10.5	Ford-NY....24	Ford-NY....774	Terry-NY....18
Hinton-Was....25	Tartabull-KC....3.2	Boyer-NY....21.9	Yastrzemski-Bos....8.8	Pascual-Min....21	Bouton-NY....750	Pascual-Min....15
Wood-Det....18	Weis-Chi....3.0	Richardson-NY....12.9	Allison-Min....8.5	Bouton-NY....21	Radatz-Bos....714	Stigman-Min....15
Snyder-Bal....18	Richardson-NY....3.0	Causey-KC....11.6	Hinton-Was....6.9	Monbouquette-Bos....20	Peters-Chi....704	Herbert-Chi....14
Pearson-LA....17	Hinton-Was....2.3	Moran-LA....8.8	Clinton-Bos....6.7	Barber-Bal....20	Pascual-Min....700	Aguirre-Det....14

Strikeouts	Fewest BB/Game	Games	Saves	Base Runners/9	Adjusted Relief Runs	Relief Ranking
Pascual-Min....202	Donovan-Cle....1.22	S.Miller-Bal....71	S.Miller-Bal....27	Dailey-Min....8.20	Radatz-Bos....26.0	Radatz-Bos....48.1
Bunning-Det....196	Terry-NY....1.31	Radatz-Bos....66	Radatz-Bos....25	Hall-Bal....8.95	Dailey-Min....20.5	Dailey-Min....24.2
Stigman-Min....193	Herbert-Chi....1.40	Dailey-Min....66	Wyatt-KC....21	Fowler-LA....8.97	S.Miller-Bal....13.8	S.Miller-Bal....21.8
Peters-Chi....189	Monbouquette-Bos....1.42	Lamabe-Bos....65	Wilhelm-Chi....21	Wilhelm-Chi....9.24	Wilhelm-Chi....12.6	Wilhelm-Chi....15.2
Ford-NY....189	Roberts-Bal....1.43	Wyatt-KC....63	Dailey-Min....21	Cheney-Was....9.24	Fowler-LA....11.4	Fowler-LA....12.1

Innings Pitched	Opponents' Avg.	Opponents' OBP	Earned Run Average	Adjusted ERA	Adjusted Starter Runs	Pitcher Wins
Ford-NY....269.1	Downing-NY....184	Terry-NY....271	Peters-Chi....2.33	Peters-Chi....150	Peters-Chi....33.6	Radatz-Bos....5.0
Terry-NY....268.0	Morehead-Bos....211	Ramos-Cle....272	Pizarro-Chi....2.39	Pascual-Min....148	Pascual-Min....33.2	Peters-Chi....4.8
Monbouquette-Bos....266.2	Bouton-NY....212	Roberts-Bal....272	Pascual-Min....2.46	Pizarro-Chi....147	Bouton-NY....27.5	Pascual-Min....4.7
Barber-Bal....258.2	Drabowsky-KC....214	Downing-NY....277	Bouton-NY....2.53	Bouton-NY....139	Pizarro-Chi....25.2	Pizarro-Chi....3.9
Roberts-Bal....251.1	Peters-Chi....216	Peters-Chi....277	Downing-NY....2.56	Stange-Min....139	Ford-NY....22.3	Dailey-Min....2.9

Brother, Can You Spare a Bat?

Baseball authorities decided that the game had become too dependent on home runs. Therefore, to balance the game in favor of the pitcher, the strike zone was enlarged before the season and would now range from the top of the shoulders to the top of the knees. The result was an offensive disaster. Scoring fell to its lowest since 1946, and would continue to decline through 1968.

The odd thing? Home runs didn't decrease much. Strikeouts, however, shot up; the Indians set an all-time high for whiffs, and for the third straight year, a wild swinger broke the individual record. Chicago slugger Dave Nicholson's 175 strikeouts shattered the mark by 33.

Despite Nicholson's whiffs, the White Sox finished second on big seasons from rookies Gary Peters and Pete Ward. Minnesota, with a fearsome attack that topped the AL in homers both at home and on the road, led in scoring, but had very poor second-line pitching.

Early Wynn won his 300th career game, and then was immediately released by Cleveland, who also gave lefty Tommy John his first exposure to the majors. And in a year in which Harmon Killebrew won his third home run crown, Frank "Home Run" Baker, who had captured four such titles, died at 77.

Once again, the Yankees won, and easily. Excellent pitching and Elston Howard's MVP performance sprung the club from a tangle in June. They never looked back despite losing Mickey Mantle to injury. For the first time since 1951, the Yankees had two 20-game winners—Whitey Ford and Jim Bouton. But neither pitcher won in the World Series; in fact, no Yankee won. The Yankees, with six World Series sweeps to their credit, were themselves swept by the Dodgers. New York scored just 4 runs. Mantle batted just .133; Clete Boyer hit .077.

1962 National League

TEAM	W	L	T	PCT	GB	HW	HL	R	OR	PA	H	2B	3B	HR	BB	SO	HB	SH	AVG	OBP	SLG	OPS	AOPS	BR	ABR	PF	SB	CS	BSA	BSR
SF	103	62	0	.624		61	21	878	690	6277	1552	235	32	204	523	822	42	76	.278	.341	.441	782	118	126	141	98	73	50	59	-1
LA	102	63	0	.618	1	54	29	842	697	6362	1510	192	65	140	572	886	32	83	.268	.337	.400	737	111	39	90	94	198	43	82	29
CIN	98	64	0	.605	3.5	58	23	802	685	6273	1523	252	40	167	498	903	41	57	.270	.332	.417	749	104	57	32	103	66	39	63	1
PIT	93	68	0	.578	8	51	30	706	626	6035	1468	240	65	108	432	836	17	54	.268	.321	.394	715	98	-16	-17	100	50	39	56	-3
MIL	86	76	0	.531	15.5	49	32	730	665	6155	1376	204	38	181	581	975	34	47	.252	.326	.403	729	105	17	37	97	57	27	68	3
STL	84	78	1	.519	17.5	44	37	774	664	6307	1528	221	31	137	515	846	45	69	.271	.335	.394	729	93	23	-44	110	86	41	68	5
PHI	81	80	0	.503	20	46	34	705	759	6131	1410	199	39	142	531	923	53	83	.260	.330	.390	720	103	5	27	97	79	42	65	3
HOU	64	96	2	.400	36.5	32	48	592	717	6198	1370	170	47	105	493	806	35	78	.246	.310	.351	661	91	-120	-71	93	42	30	58	-1
CHI	59	103	0	.364	42.5	32	49	632	827	6173	1398	196	56	126	504	1044	39	54	.253	.317	.377	694	89	-55	-78	104	78	50	61	0
NY	40	120	1	.250	60.5	22	58	617	948	6242	1318	166	40	139	616	991	32	58	.240	.318	.361	679	88	-76	-86	102	59	48	55	-4
TOT	812					449	361	7278		62153	14453	2075	453	1449	5265	9032	373	656	.261	.327	.393	720				788	409	66	30

TEAM	CG	SHO	GR	SV	IP	H	HR	BB	SO	BR/9	ERA	AERA	OAV	OOB	PR	APR	PF	OSB	OCS	FA	E	WPB	DP	FW	PW	BW	BSW	DIF
SF	62	10	216	39	1461.2	1399	148	503	886	11.9	3.79	100	.251	.314	24	0	96	65	26	.977	142	47	153	1.0	.0	14.1	-.4	5.9
LA	44	8	249	46	1488.2	1386	115	588	1104	12.1	3.62	100	.245	.317	54	3	92	59	34	.970	193	71	144	-2.1	.3	9.0	2.6	9.7
CIN	51	13	222	35	1460.2	1397	149	567	964	12.4	3.75	107	.254	.327	31	43	102	75	36	.977	145	67	144	.6	4.3	3.2	-.2	9.1
PIT	40	13	263	41	1432.1	1433	118	466	897	12.1	3.37	117	.262	.320	90	89	100	86	31	.976	152	66	177	.2	8.9	-1.7	-.6	5.8
MIL	59	10	206	24	1434.2	1443	151	407	802	11.8	3.68	103	.262	.315	42	20	96	49	44	.980	124	50	154	1.9	2.0	3.7	.0	-2.6
STL	53	17	208	25	1463.1	1394	149	517	914	11.9	3.55	120	.252	.318	64	108	108	73	40	.979	132	76	170	1.5	10.8	-4.4	.2	-5.0
PHI	43	7	247	24	1469.1	1469	155	574	863	13.2	4.28	90	.268	.341	-53	-66	98	67	47	.977	138	89	167	1.0	-6.6	2.7	.0	3.4
HOU	34	9	264	19	1453.2	1446	113	471	1047	12.1	3.83	98	.259	.319	19	-15	97	119	43	.973	173	99	149	-1.0	-1.5	-7.1	-.4	-6.0
CHI	29	4	309	26	1438.1	1509	159	601	783	13.5	4.54	91	.272	.346	-95	-59	105	101	58	.977	146	99	171	.6	-5.9	-7.8	-.3	-8.6
NY	43	4	254	10	1430.0	1577	192	571	772	13.8	5.04	83	.281	.349	-175	-129	106	94	50	.967	210	97	167	-3.3	-12.9	-8.6	-.7	-14.5
TOT	458	95	2438	289	14490.0					12.5	3.94		.261	.327						.975	1555	761	1596					

Batter-Fielder Wins		Batting Average		On-Base Percentage		Slugging Average		On-Base Plus Slugging		Adjusted OPS		Adjusted Batter Runs	
Mays-SF	6.1	T.Davis-LA	.346	Robinson-Cin	.421	Robinson-Cin	.624	Robinson-Cin	1045	Robinson-Cin	172	Robinson-Cin	64.8
Robinson-Cin	5.7	Robinson-Cin	.342	Musial-StL	.416	H.Aaron-Mil	.618	H.Aaron-Mil	1008	H.Aaron-Mil	171	H.Aaron-Mil	58.3
H.Aaron-Mil	5.2	Musial-StL	.330	Skinner-Pit	.395	Mays-SF	.615	Mays-SF	.999	Mays-SF	167	Mays-SF	57.7
Mazeroski-Pit	4.7	White-StL	.324	Altman-Chi	.393	Howard-LA	.560	Musial-StL	.924	T.Davis-LA	151	T.Davis-LA	44.4
T.Davis-LA	3.8	H.Aaron-Mil	.323	H.Aaron-Mil	.390	T.Davis-LA	.535	T.Davis-LA	.910	Howard-LA	149	Mathews-Mil	31.6

Runs		Hits		Doubles		Triples		Home Runs		Total Bases		Runs Batted In	
Robinson-Cin	134	T.Davis-LA	230	Robinson-Cin	51	Wills-LA	10	Mays-SF	49	Mays-SF	382	T.Davis-LA	153
Wills-LA	130	Wills-LA	208	Mays-SF	36	Virdon-Pit	10	H.Aaron-Mil	45	Robinson-Cin	380	Mays-SF	141
Mays-SF	130	Robinson-Cin	208	Groat-Pit	34	W.Davis-LA	10	Robinson-Cin	39	H.Aaron-Mil	366	Robinson-Cin	136
H.Aaron-Mil	127	White-StL	199			Callison-Phi	10	Banks-Chi	37	T.Davis-LA	356	H.Aaron-Mil	128
T.Davis-LA	120	Groat-Pit	199					Cepeda-SF	35	Cepeda-SF	324	Howard-LA	119

Stolen Bases		Base Stealing Runs		Fielding Runs-Infield		Fielding Runs-Outfield		Wins		Winning Pct.		Complete Games	
Wills-LA	104	Wills-LA	18.3	Mazeroski-Pit	41.2	Callison-Phi	22.0	Drysdale-LA	25	Purkey-Cin	.821	Spahn-Mil	22
W.Davis-LA	32	W.Davis-LA	4.6	Lillis-Hou	16.2	Clemente-Pit	9.7	Sanford-SF	24	Sanford-SF	.774	O'Dell-SF	20
Pinson-Cin	26	Mays-SF	3.3	Groat-Pit	15.6	Mays-SF	6.5	Purkey-Cin	23	Drysdale-LA	.735	Mahaffey-Phi	20
Javier-StL	26	Pinson-Cin	2.9	McMillan-Mil	13.2	Flood-StL	6.2	Jay-Cin	21	Pierce-SF	.727	Drysdale-LA	19
Taylor-Phi	20	Javier-StL	2.6	Santo-Chi	12.9	W.Davis-LA	5.2			Shaw-Mil	.625		

Strikeouts		Fewest BB/Game		Games		Saves		Base Runners/9		Adjusted Relief Runs		Relief Ranking	
Drysdale-LA	232	Shaw-Mil	1.76	Perranoski-LA	70	Face-Pit	28	Face-Pit	9.20	Face-Pit	20.4	Face-Pit	40.9
Koufax-LA	216	Friend-Pit	1.82	Baldschun-Phi	67	Perranoski-LA	20	Umbricht-Hou	9.40	McMahon-Mil-Hou	19.5	Baldschun-Phi	21.1
Gibson-StL	208	Spahn-Mil	1.84	Roebuck-LA	64	Miller-SF	19	Koufax-LA	9.42	Shantz-Hou-StL	15.1	Shantz-Hou-StL	19.1
Farrell-Hou	203	Pierce-SF	1.94	Face-Pit	63	McDaniel-StL	14	Shantz-Hou-StL	9.88	Umbricht-Hou	12.8	Elston-StL	19.1
O'Dell-SF	195	Purkey-Cin	2.00	Olivo-Pit	62			Farrell-Hou	10.06	Baldschun-Phi	11.8		

Innings Pitched		Opponents' Avg.		Opponents' OBP		Earned Run Average		Adjusted ERA		Adjusted Starter Runs		Pitcher Wins	
Drysdale-LA	314.1	Koufax-LA	.197	Koufax-LA	.261	Koufax-LA	2.54	Gibson-StL	150	Purkey-Cin	34.7	Gibson-StL	4.7
Purkey-Cin	288.1	Gibson-StL	.204	Farrell-Hou	.279	Shaw-Mil	2.80	Purkey-Cin	143	Gibson-StL	34.5	Face-Pit	4.1
O'Dell-SF	280.2	Bennett-Phi	.224	Drysdale-LA	.282	Purkey-Cin	2.81	Koufax-LA	143	Broglio-StL	31.1	Spahn-Mil	3.5
Mahaffey-Phi	274.0	Drysdale-LA	.230	Pierce-SF	.283	Drysdale-LA	2.83	Broglio-StL	142	Friend-Pit	27.4	Drysdale-LA	3.3
Jay-Cin	273.0	Farrell-Hou	.233	Spahn-Mil	.284	Gibson-StL	2.85	Shaw-Mil	136	Drysdale-LA	27.1	Purkey-Cin	3.0

Shades of '51

The new ten-team National League had great teams, mediocre teams, and the Mets, perhaps the worst ever. Between first and last lay 60½ games, the largest gap in 27 years.

The Giants, Reds, and Dodgers battled at the top. Cincinnati hung close, but down the stretch the New York transplants provided the thrills.

Los Angeles, playing in new Chavez Ravine, saw attendance increase by 56 percent; solid pitching and expansive surroundings translated into the club's first 100-win season since 1953. Despite Maury Wills' record 104 steals and MVP award, Tommy Davis was the Dodgers' key. Don Drysdale took the Cy Young, while Sandy Koufax led in ERA. The two were 1-2 in strikeouts although Koufax missed two months with circulatory problems.

The Giants scored more runs than any team since 1953. Willie Mays, second in MVP voting, and Orlando Cepeda each drove in and scored more than 100. Meanwhile, 20-homer man Willie McCovey sat on the bench.

The Phillies improved nearly 30 games, and Pittsburgh debuted Willie Stargell and Bob Veale. Chicago's Ken Hubbs was Rookie of the Year—teammate Billy Williams had won the award the previous year. Richie Ashburn, the first batter in Mets history, retired rather than risk another 120-loss season.

While home runs rose to a record high, they decreased per game due to large new parks. Sparked by Wills, the stolen base made a comeback. Steals per game reached their highest level since the 1920s. League attendance rose annually through 1966; the Dodgers drew two million each year. In yet another honor, Jackie Robinson became the first African American Hall of Famer.

LA led by 4 games in mid-September. At that point, the Dodgers began losing, and despite playing .500 ball over the last two weeks, the Giants forced a tie. With their three-game playoff tied one game each, the Dodgers took a 4-2 lead to the top of the ninth in the third game. The Giants capitalized on walks and bobbles to win the game, and the pennant, 6-4. The World Series went to the Yankees in seven tight games.

1962 American League

TEAM	W	L	T	PCT	GB	HW	HL	R	OR	PA	H	2B	3B	HR	BB	SO	HB	SH	AVG	OBP	SLG	OPS	AOPS	BR	ABR	PF	SB	CS	BSA	BSR
NY	96	66	0	.593		50	30	817	680	6393	1509	240	29	199	584	842	32	79	.267	.337	.426	763	115	89	116	97	42	29	59	-1
MIN	91	71	1	.562	5	45	36	798	713	6362	1445	215	39	185	649	823	31	71	.260	.338	.412	750	104	68	39	104	33	20	62	0
LA	86	76	0	.531	10	40	41	718	706	6255	1377	232	35	137	602	917	29	82	.250	.325	.380	705	99	-22	1	97	46	27	63	1
DET	85	76	0	.528	10.5	49	33	758	692	6234	1352	191	36	209	651	894	33	56	.248	.330	.411	741	101	41	15	104	69	21	77	8
CHI	85	77	0	.525	11	43	38	707	658	6297	1415	250	56	92	620	674	41	82	.257	.334	.372	706	96	-11	-7	100	35	16	69	3
CLE	80	82	0	.494	16	43	38	682	745	6137	1341	202	22	180	502	939	54	52	.245	.312	.388	700	97	-48	-27	97	35	16	69	2
BAL	77	85	0	.475	19	44	38	652	680	6158	1363	225	34	156	516	931	32	75	.248	.314	.387	701	100	-43	2	94	45	32	58	-1
BOS	76	84	0	.475	19	39	40	707	756	6177	1429	257	53	146	525	923	27	59	.258	.324	.403	727	98	10	-12	103	39	33	54	-3
KC	72	90	0	.444	24	39	42	745	837	6302	1467	220	58	116	556	803	42	78	.263	.332	.386	718	95	2	-31	105	76	21	78	9
WAS	60	101	1	.373	35.5	27	53	599	716	6072	1370	206	38	132	466	789	15	71	.250	.308	.373	681	90	-85	-80	99	99	53	65	3
TOT	809					419	389	7183		62387	14068	2238	400	1552	5671	8535	336	705	.255	.325	.394	719				560	292	66	21

TEAM	CG	SHO	GR	SV	IP	H	HR	BB	SO	BR/9	ERA	AERA	OAV	OOB	PR	APR	PF	OSB	OCS	FA	E	WPB	DP	FW	PW	BW	BSW	DIF
NY	33	10	248	42	1470.1	1375	146	499	838	11.6	3.70	101	.247	.310	44	8	94	34	26	.979	131	34	151	.4	.8	11.7	-.3	2.5
MIN	53	11	241	27	1463.1	1400	166	493	948	11.9	3.89	105	.253	.317	13	30	103	41	31	.980	129	68	173	.5	3.0	3.9	-.2	2.8
LA	23	15	345	47	1466.0	1412	118	616	858	12.8	3.70	104	.253	.330	45	27	97	52	35	.973	175	55	153	-2.2	2.7	.1	-.1	4.5
DET	46	8	245	35	1443.2	1452	169	503	873	12.4	3.81	107	.259	.321	26	41	103	47	26	.974	156	45	114	-1.1	4.1	1.5	.6	-.6
CHI	50	13	265	28	1451.2	1380	123	537	821	12.0	3.73	105	.251	.317	38	29	98	72	24	.982	110	46	153	1.6	2.9	-.7	.0	.1
CLE	45	12	242	31	1441.0	1410	174	594	780	12.7	4.14	94	.258	.331	-27	-44	98	54	37	.978	139	43	168	-.1	-4.4	-2.7	-.1	6.2
BAL	32	8	253	33	1462.1	1373	147	549	898	12.0	3.69	100	.249	.318	45	1	93	80	37	.979	122	78	152	.9	.1	.2	-.3	-4.9
BOS	34	12	222	40	1437.2	1416	159	632	923	13.1	4.04	98	.258	.337	-40	-14	104	70	19	.979	131	60	152	.3	-1.4	-1.2	-.5	-1.1
KC	32	4	274	13	1434.0	1450	199	655	825	13.5	4.79	88	.263	.343	-131	-85	106	65	25	.979	132	88	131	.3	-8.5	-3.1	.7	1.7
WAS	38	11	266	13	1445.0	1400	151	593	771	12.5	4.04	100	.256	.328	-12	-1	102	45	32	.978	139	46	160	-.1	-.1	-8.0	.0	-12.3
TOT	386	104	2601	329	14515.0					12.4	3.97		.255	.325						.978	1364	563	1507					

Batter-Fielder Wins		Batting Average		On-Base Percentage		Slugging Average		On-Base Plus Slugging		Adjusted OPS		Adjusted Batter Runs	
Mantle-NY	5.0	Runnels-Bos	326	Mantle-NY	486	Mantle-NY	605	Mantle-NY	1091	Mantle-NY	198	Mantle-NY	62.9
Bressoud-Bos	3.7	Mantle-NY	321	Siebern-KC	412	Killebrew-Min	545	Killebrew-Min	912	Siebern-KC	138	Siebern-KC	36.5
Boyer-NY	3.6	Robinson-Chi	312	Cunningham-Chi	410	Colavito-Det	514	Siebern-KC	907	Killebrew-Min	137	Killebrew-Min	30.1
Colavito-Det	3.2	Hinton-Was	310	Runnels-Bos	408	Cash-Det	513	Cash-Det	894	Cash-Det	134	Colavito-Det	28.7
B.Robinson-Bal	3.1	Siebern-KC	308	Robinson-Chi	384	Allison-Min	511	Colavito-Det	885	Colavito-Det	132	Robinson-Chi	28.7

Runs		Hits		Doubles		Triples		Home Runs		Total Bases		Runs Batted In	
Pearson-LA	115	Richardson-NY	209	Robinson-Chi	45	Cimoli-KC	15	Killebrew-Min	48	Colavito-Det	309	Killebrew-Min	126
Siebern-KC	114	Lumpe-KC	193	Yastrzemski-Bos	43	Robinson-Chi	10	Cash-Det	39	B.Robinson-Bal	308	Siebern-KC	117
Allison-Min	102	B.Robinson-Bal	192	Bressoud-Bos	40	Lumpe-KC	10	Wagner-LA	37	Wagner-LA	306	Colavito-Det	112
Yastrzemski-Bos	99	Yastrzemski-Bos	191	Richardson-NY	38	Clinton-Bos	10	Colavito-Det	37	Yastrzemski-Bos	303	Robinson-Chi	109
Richardson-NY	99	Robinson-Chi	187							Killebrew-Min	301	Wagner-LA	107

Stolen Bases		Base Stealing Runs		Fielding Runs-Infield		Fielding Runs-Outfield		Wins		Winning Pct.		Complete Games	
Aparicio-Chi	31	Wood-Det	4.2	Versalles-Min	34.9	Colavito-Det	12.4	Terry-NY	23	Herbert-Chi	690	Pascual-Min	18
Hinton-Was	28	Howser-KC	3.5	Boyer-NY	34.3	DelGreco-KC	9.0	Pascual-Min	20	Ford-NY	680	Kaat-Min	16
Wood-Det	24	Charles-KC	3.0	Cottier-Was	23.7	Yastrzemski-Bos	8.4	Herbert-Chi	20	Donovan-Cle	667	Donovan-Cle	16
Charles-KC	20	Hinton-Was	2.7	Bressoud-Bos	22.7	Bruton-Det	8.0	Donovan-Cle	20	Aguirre-Det	667	Terry-NY	14
		Aparicio-Chi	2.6	Kindall-Cle	22.7	Green-Min	6.0	Bunning-Det	19	Terry-NY	657		

Strikeouts		Fewest BB/Game		Games		Saves		Base Runners/9		Adjusted Relief Runs		Relief Ranking	
Pascual-Min	206	Donovan-Cle	1.69	Radatz-Bos	62	Radatz-Bos	24	Hall-Bal	9.20	Radatz-Bos	26.4	Radatz-Bos	39.8
Bunning-Det	184	Terry-NY	1.72	Wyatt-KC	59	Bridges-NY	18	Terry-NY	9.55	Hall-Bal	21.4	Wilhelm-Bal	34.1
Terry-NY	176	Mossi-Det	1.80			Fox-Det	16	Aguirre-Det	9.67	Wilhelm-Bal	17.0	Hall-Bal	22.0
Pizarro-Chi	173	Roberts-Bal	1.93			Wilhelm-Bal	15	Wilhelm-Bal	9.77	Fox-Det	14.6	Fox-Det	18.0
Kaat-Min	173	Pascual-Min	2.06			Bell-Cle	12	Pena-KC	9.94	Fowler-LA	10.7	Fowler-LA	10.2

Innings Pitched		Opponents' Avg.		Opponents' OBP		Earned Run Average		Adjusted ERA		Adjusted Starter Runs		Pitcher Wins	
Terry-NY	298.2	Aguirre-Det	205	Aguirre-Det	267	Aguirre-Det	2.21	Aguirre-Det	184	Aguirre-Det	40.6	Radatz-Bos	3.9
Kaat-Min	269.0	Cheney-Was	213	Terry-NY	268	Roberts-Bal	2.78	Roberts-Bal	133	Ford-NY	27.3	Kaat-Min	3.8
Bunning-Det	258.0	Belinsky-LA	216	Pascual-Min	285	Ford-NY	2.90	Chance-LA	130	Kaat-Min	27.3	Pascual-Min	3.7
Pascual-Min	257.2	Terry-NY	231	Roberts-Bal	288	Chance-LA	2.96	Kaat-Min	130	Pascual-Min	24.4	Wilhelm-Bal	3.5
Ford-NY	257.2	Wilson-Bos	231	Fisher-Chi	291	Fisher-Chi	3.10	Ford-NY	129	Roberts-Bal	22.9	Aguirre-Det	3.4

Carrying the Mantle

The Indians led the AL at the start of July, but Cleveland soon dropped into the second division as the Yankees took over. Minnesota and Los Angeles hung around until September, although neither got close enough to scare New York. Mickey Mantle took home his third MVP trophy, even though he missed nearly 40 games with knee problems. The team's balanced attack led the AL in scoring. But New Yorkers again seemed blasé about success; with National League baseball back in the city, the Yankees' attendance dropped every year from 1962 through 1966.

The Twins finished second as Harmon Killebrew captured his first home run title (and set a new strikeout mark). All eight Minnesota regulars hit homers in double figures, and Camilo Pascual paced the AL in strikeouts, shutouts, and complete games. Outfielder Tony Oliva went 4-for-9 in his first big league action.

The surprising Angels ended up third. Moving from tiny Wrigley Field to huge Chavez Ravine, the Angels saw attendance increase 90 percent to break the million mark. Rookie pitcher Bo Belinsky took Tinseltown by storm, throwing a no-hitter and dating starlet Mamie Van Doren, though the nightlife led to a quick loss of effectiveness for the pitcher.

Boston's Pete Runnels won his second batting crown, but the Red Sox, beginning a fallow period, ended to eighth. The Orioles dropped to seventh as their young pitchers began to crumble under heavy workloads.

All seven games in the Yankees-Giants World Series were close. The big stars—Mantle, Maris, Mays, and McCovey—were non-factors. Unlikely heroes like Chuck Hiller, Bill Stafford, and Clete Boyer dominated the entertaining Series. With the Yankees up three games to two, California rain delayed the proceedings by three days. The Giants won Game 6, but Raph Terry shut out the Giants on 4 hits to win the decider, 1-0. The Series ended when second baseman Bobby Richardson caught McCovey's hard liner with the tying and winning runs in scoring position.

1961 National League

TEAM	W	L	T	PCT	GB	HW	HL	R	OR	PA	H	2B	3B	HR	BB	SO	HB	SH	AVG	OBP	SLG	OPS	AOPS	BR	ABR	PF	SB	CS	BSA	BSR
CIN	93	61	0	.604		47	30	710	**653**	5796	1414	**247**	35	158	423	761	29	50	.270	.325	.421	746	102	20	11	101	70	33	**68**	**4**
LA	89	65	0	.578	4	45	32	735	697	5940	1358	193	40	157	**596**	796	23	96	.262	**.338**	.405	743	95	30	-29	109	**86**	45	66	3
SF	85	69	1	.552	8	45	32	**773**	655	5887	1379	219	32	183	506	764	30	70	.264	.329	**.423**	752	108	**36**	64	96	79	54	59	-2
MIL	83	71	1	.539	10	45	32	712	656	5958	1365	199	34	**188**	534	880	34	62	.258	.328	.415	743	**109**	19	**66**	94	70	43	62	0
STL	80	74	1	.519	13	**48**	29	703	668	5944	1436	236	51	103	494	745	33	70	.271	.334	.393	727	89	-3	-66	110	46	28	62	0
PIT	75	79	0	.487	18	38	39	694	675	5867	**1448**	232	**57**	128	428	721	27	64	**.273**	.328	.410	738	101	7	5	100	26	30	46	-5
CHI	64	90	2	.416	29	40	37	689	800	6000	1364	238	51	176	539	1027	32	52	.255	.325	.410	743	101	17	8	101	35	25	58	-1
PHI	47	107	1	.305	46	22	55	584	796	5870	1265	185	50	103	475	928	**46**	**108**	.243	.310	.357	667	83	-126	-118	99	56	30	65	2
TOT	619					330	286	5600		47262	11029	1749	350	1196	3995	6622	254	572	.262	.327	.405	732				468	288	62	2

TEAM	CG	SHO	GR	SV	IP	H	HR	BB	SO	BR/9	ERA	AERA	OAV	OOB	PR	APR	PF	OSB	OCS	FA	E	WPB	DP	FW	PW	BW	BSW	DIF
CIN	46	**12**	210	**40**	1370.0	**1300**	147	500	829	12.0	3.78	107	.250	.318	38	42	101	68	34	.977	134	63	124	.7	4.2	1.1	**.4**	9.7
LA	40	10	239	35	1378.1	1346	167	544	**1105**	12.7	4.04	107	.256	.329	-2	43	108	53	32	.975	144	80	162	.1	4.3	-2.9	.3	10.2
SF	39	9	235	30	1388.0	1306	152	502	924	**11.9**	3.77	101	**.249**	**.316**	40	6	95	63	30	.977	133	43	126	.8	6.6	6.4	-.2	.5
MIL	**57**	8	194	16	1391.1	1357	153	493	652	12.1	3.89	96	.258	.322	21	-26	93	**42**	33	**.982**	**111**	41	152	**2.0**	-2.6	**6.5**	-.0	.0
STL	49	10	184	24	1368.2	1334	136	570	823	12.7	**3.74**	118	.256	.330	**44**	**92**	109	68	41	.972	166	61	165	-1.1	**9.1**	-6.5	-.0	1.5
PIT	34	9	236	29	1362.0	1442	**121**	**400**	759	12.3	3.92	102	.274	.326	17	10	99	44	25	.975	150	58	**187**	-.2	1.0	.5	-.5	-2.7
CHI	34	6	248	25	1385.0	1492	165	465	755	12.9	4.48	93	.277	.336	-70	-45	104	61	34	.970	183	85	175	-2.0	-4.5	.8	-.1	-7.2
PHI	29	9	**257**	13	1383.1	1452	155	521	775	13.1	4.61	88	.273	.340	-88	-81	101	69	**59**	.976	146	80	179	.0	-8.0	-11.7	.2	-10.5
TOT	328	73	1803	212	11026.2					12.5	4.03		.262	.327						.976	1167	511	1270					

Batter-Fielder Wins		**Batting Average**		**On-Base Percentage**		**Slugging Average**		**On-Base Plus Slugging**		**Adjusted OPS**		**Adjusted Batter Runs**	
Aaron-Mil	5.1	Clemente-Pit	.351	Moon-LA	.434	Robinson-Cin	.611	Robinson-Cin	1015	Aaron-Mil	165	Aaron-Mil	54.9
Robinson-Cin	5.1	Pinson-Cin	.343	Robinson-Cin	.404	Cepeda-SF	.609	Mays-SF	.977	Robinson-Cin	164	Robinson-Cin	51.9
Mays-SF	4.5	Boyer-StL	.329	Mathews-Mil	.402	Aaron-Mil	.594	Aaron-Mil	.974	Mays-SF	162	Mays-SF	51.8
Boyer-StL	4.1	Moon-LA	.328	Boyer-StL	.397	Mays-SF	.584	Cepeda-SF	.970	Cepeda-SF	158	Mathews-Mil	48.9
Mathews-Mil	4.1	Aaron-Mil	.327	Mays-SF	.393	Stuart-Pit	.581	Clemente-Pit	.949	Mathews-Mil	156	Cepeda-SF	45.4

Runs		**Hits**		**Doubles**		**Triples**		**Home Runs**		**Total Bases**		**Runs Batted In**	
Mays-SF	129	Pinson-Cin	208	Aaron-Mil	39	Altman-Chi	12	Cepeda-SF	46	Aaron-Mil	358	Cepeda-SF	142
Robinson-Cin	117	Clemente-Pit	201	Pinson-Cin	34	White-StL	11	Mays-SF	40	Cepeda-SF	356	Robinson-Cin	124
Aaron-Mil	115	Aaron-Mil	197	Santo-Chi	32	Callison-Phi	11	Robinson-Cin	37	Mays-SF	334	Mays-SF	123
Boyer-StL	109	Boyer-StL	194	Robinson-Cin	32	Boyer-StL	11	Stuart-Pit	35	Robinson-Cin	333	Aaron-Mil	120
		Cepeda-SF	182	Mays-SF	32			Adcock-Mil	35	Clemente-Pit	320	Stuart-Pit	117

Stolen Bases		**Base Stealing Runs**		**Fielding Runs-Infield**		**Fielding Runs-Outfield**		**Wins**		**Winning Pct.**		**Complete Games**	
Wills-LA	35	Robinson-Cin	3.8	Mazeroski-Pit	37.1	Clemente-Pit	9.4	Spahn-Mil	21	Podres-LA	.783	Spahn-Mil	21
Pinson-Cin	23	Wills-LA	2.5	Malkmus-Phi	24.2	Flood-StL	8.4	Jay-Cin	21	O'Toole-Cin	.679	Koufax-LA	15
Robinson-Cin	22	Maye-Mil	1.9	Banks-Chi	17.9	Pinson-Cin	7.5	O'Toole-Cin	19	Jay-Cin	.677	Jay-Cin	14
Aaron-Mil	21	Pinson-Cin	1.6	Boyer-StL	14.2	Robinson-Cin	5.8			Burdette-Mil	.621	Burdette-Mil	14
Mays-SF	18	Gonzalez-Phi	1.5	Gilliam-LA	13.7	Aaron-Mil	4.0			Spahn-Mil	.618		

Strikeouts		**Fewest BB/Game**		**Games**		**Saves**		**Base Runners/9**		**Adjusted Relief Runs**		**Relief Ranking**	
Koufax-LA	269	Burdette-Mil	1.09	Baldschun-Phi	65	Miller-SF	17	Miller-SF	9.81	Miller-SF	16.3	Miller-SF	28.0
Williams-LA	205	Friend-Pit	1.72	Miller-SF	63	Face-Pit	17	Face-Pit	10.27	Perranoski-LA	15.7	Perranoski-LA	20.9
Drysdale-LA	182	Purkey-Cin	1.86	Face-Pit	62	Henry-Cin	16	K.Johnson-Mil	10.30	Henry-Cin	9.6	Henry-Cin	15.1
O'Toole-Cin	178	Spahn-Mil	2.19	Elston-Chi	58	Brosnan-Cin	16	Sturdivant-Pit	10.40	McMahon-Mil	8.3	Schultz-Chi	13.8
Gibson-StL	166	Ellsworth-Chi	2.31	Anderson-Chi	57	L.Sherry-LA	15	Spahn-Mil	10.42	Brosnan-Cin	7.6	Henry-Cin	11.3

Innings Pitched		**Opponents' Avg.**		**Opponents' OBP**		**Earned Run Average**		**Adjusted ERA**		**Adjusted Starter Runs**		**Pitcher Wins**	
Burdette-Mil	272.1	Koufax-LA	.222	Spahn-Mil	.291	Spahn-Mil	3.02	Simmons-StL	141	O'Toole-Cin	25.8	Spahn-Mil	4.1
Spahn-Mil	262.2	Jay-Cin	.236	Koufax-LA	.295	O'Toole-Cin	3.10	Gibson-StL	136	Gibson-StL	24.3	Miller-SF	3.1
Cardwell-Chi	259.1	Sadecki-StL	.238	Burdette-Mil	.295	Simmons-StL	3.13	O'Toole-Cin	131	Spahn-Mil	22.8	Gibson-StL	2.9
Koufax-LA	255.2	Gibson-StL	.239	Purkey-Cin	.296	McCormick-SF	3.20	Spahn-Mil	124	Simmons-StL	21.0	O'Toole-Cin	2.6
O'Toole-Cin	252.2	O'Toole-Cin	.240	Jackson-StL	.301	Gibson-StL	3.24	Koufax-LA	123	Koufax-LA	19.9	Simmons-StL	2.5

Cincinnati Surprise

Cincinnati took the flag in one of the oddest seasons ever. The Reds were 17 games over .500 at home despite being outscored at Crosley Field. Cincinnati had the league's best pitching—as well as a more efficient offense—on the road. The club had Vada Pinson, the major league leader in hits, and MVP Frank Robinson, plus a few other decent regulars. Jerry Lynch enjoyed one of the all-time great seasons for a bench player, and five pitchers—three starters and two relievers—carried the load.

Second-place Los Angeles, mixing the unproven and the elderly, never capitalized despite the Reds' early-season sputtering. For the third straight year, however, Dodgers hurlers paced the NL in strikeouts.

The aging Pirates fell to eighth, although Roberto Clemente won his first of four batting titles. Chicago debuted Lou Brock and Kenny Hubbs on September 10. Neither would be around when the Cubs finally turned it around years later. Meanwhile, the Phillies lost 23 straight, falling far into the basement with the NL's worst record in a decade.

As runs per game rose to 4.52, the highest of the 1960s, complete games dropped to a new low; only Warren Spahn finished more than 15. Despite excellent seasons by Spahn and Hank Aaron, Milwaukee's classic era was over. Fans deserted the Braves; attendance plunged 26 percent, then 30 more in 1962. Attendance fell in every NL city except Cincinnati, so the league decided to pre-empt a proposed rival, the Continental League, by expanding to New York and Houston for 1962.

The Yankees blew apart the Reds, taking the World Series in five games. "Embarrassing, wasn't it?" wrote Cincy reliever Jim Brosnan the next year in a *Sports Illustrated* article. Just a few months after throwing out the first pitch at Game 3, former Reds outfielder Dummy Hoy died at age 99.

1961 American League

TEAM	W	L	T	PCT	GB	HW	HL	R	OR	PA	H	2B	3B	HR	BB	SO	HB	SH	AVG	OBP	SLG	OPS	AOPS	BR	ABR	PF	SB	CS	BSA	BSR
NY	109	53	1	.673		65	16	827	612	6239	1461	194	40	240	543	785	35	57	.263	.330	.442	772	118	79	124	95	28	18	61	0
DET	101	61	1	.623	8	50	31	841	671	6378	1481	215	53	180	673	867	38	64	.266	.347	.421	768	108	96	73	103	98	36	73	9
BAL	95	67	1	.586	14	48	33	691	588	6211	1393	227	36	149	581	902	23	78	.254	.326	.390	716	101	-16	10	97	39	30	57	-2
CHI	86	76	1	.531	23	53	28	765	726	6285	1475	216	46	138	550	612	57	71	.265	.335	.395	730	103	16	28	98	100	40	71	8
CLE	78	83	0	.484	30.5	40	41	737	752	6252	1493	257	39	150	492	720	28	73	.266	.326	.406	732	104	9	30	97	34	11	76	4
BOS	76	86	1	.469	33	50	31	729	792	6307	1401	251	37	112	647	847	29	81	.254	.334	.374	708	94	-19	-36	102	56	36	61	0
MIN	70	90	1	.438	38	36	44	707	778	6156	1353	215	40	167	597	840	33	67	.250	.326	.397	723	94	-5	-43	106	47	43	52	-5
LA	70	91	1	.435	38.5	46	36	744	784	6252	1331	218	22	189	681	1068	30	80	.245	.331	.398	729	91	15	-61	111	37	28	57	-2
WAS	61	100	1	.379	47.5	33	46	618	776	6062	1307	217	44	119	558	917	21	73	.244	.315	.367	682	89	-84	-74	99	81	47	63	1
KC	61	100	1	.379	47.5	33	47	683	863	6164	1342	216	47	90	580	772	25	89	.247	.320	.354	674	84	-91	-102	102	58	22	73	5
TOT	811					454	353	7342		62306	14037	2226	404	1534	5902	8330	319	733	.256	.329	.395	724					578	311	65	18

TEAM	CG	SHO	GR	SV	IP	H	HR	BB	SO	BR/9	ERA	AERA	OAV	OOB	PR	APR	PF	OSB	OCS	FA	E	WPB	DP	FW	PW	BW	BSW	DIF
NY	47	14	201	39	1451.0	1288	137	542	866	11.5	3.46	107	.239	.311	91	45	92	43	31	.980	124	46	180	1.6	4.5	12.3	-.2	9.8
DET	62	12	220	30	1459.1	1404	170	469	836	11.7	3.55	116	.252	.311	78	88	102	45	39	.976	146	42	147	.3	8.7	7.2	.7	3.0
BAL	54	21	168	33	1471.1	1226	109	617	926	11.5	3.22	120	.227	.308	132	108	96	52	31	.980	128	75	173	1.4	10.7	1.0	-.4	1.3
CHI	39	3	260	33	1448.2	1491	158	498	814	12.4	4.06	97	.268	.326	-5	-23	97	48	32	.980	128	35	138	1.4	-2.3	2.8	.6	2.5
CLE	35	12	228	23	1443.1	1426	178	599	801	12.8	4.15	95	.258	.331	-20	-34	98	53	38	.977	139	58	142	.6	-3.4	3.0	.2	-2.9
BOS	35	6	231	30	1442.2	1472	167	679	831	13.5	4.29	97	.266	.345	-43	-19	104	68	24	.977	144	55	170	.4	-1.9	-3.6	-.2	.2
MIN	49	14	217	23	1432.1	1415	163	570	914	12.8	4.28	99	.256	.329	-41	-6	105	56	24	.972	174	58	150	-1.4	-.6	-4.3	-.7	-3.0
LA	25	5	311	34	1438.0	1391	180	713	973	13.4	4.31	105	.254	.341	-46	28	112	78	32	.969	192	77	154	-2.4	2.8	-6.0	-.4	-4.4
WAS	39	8	220	21	1425.0	1405	131	586	666	12.8	4.23	96	.260	.333	-33	-34	100	83	34	.975	156	78	171	-.4	-3.4	-7.3	-.0	-8.3
KC	32	5	268	23	1415.0	1519	141	629	703	14.0	4.74	88	.275	.351	-113	-85	104	52	26	.972	175	75	160	-1.4	-8.4	-10.1	.3	.2
TOT	417	100	2324	289	14426.2					12.6	4.02		.256	.329						.976	1506	599	1585					

Batter-Fielder Wins
- Cash-Det 7.6
- Mantle-NY 7.5
- Gentile-Bal 5.5
- Colavito-Det 4.6
- Howard-NY 4.5

Batting Average
- Cash-Det 361
- Kaline-Det 324
- Piersall-Cle 322
- Mantle-NY 317
- Gentile-Bal 302

On-Base Percentage
- Cash-Det 487
- Mantle-NY 448
- Gentile-Bal 423
- Pearson-LA 420
- Killebrew-Min 405

Slugging Average
- Mantle-NY 687
- Cash-Det 662
- Gentile-Bal 646
- Maris-NY 620
- Killebrew-Min 606

On-Base Plus Slugging
- Cash-Det 1148
- Mantle-NY 1135
- Gentile-Bal 1069
- Maris-NY 1012
- Killebrew-Min 993

Adjusted OPS
- Mantle-NY 210
- Cash-Det 198
- Gentile-Bal 189
- Maris-NY 170
- Killebrew-Min 159

Adjusted Batter Runs
- Mantle-NY 85.6
- Cash-Det 83.0
- Gentile-Bal 65.4
- Maris-NY 56.8
- Colavito-Det 49.4

Runs
- Maris-NY 132
- Mantle-NY 132
- Colavito-Det 129
- Cash-Det 119
- Kaline-Det 116

Hits
- Cash-Det 193
- B.Robinson-Bal 192
- Kaline-Det 190
- Francona-Cle 178
- Richardson-NY 173

Doubles
- Wood-Det 41
- B.Robinson-Bal 38
- Kubek-NY 38
- Siebern-Cle 36
- Power-Cle 34

Triples
- Wood-Det 14
- Lumpe-KC 9
- Keough-Was 9

Home Runs
- Maris-NY 61
- Mantle-NY 54
- Killebrew-Min 46
- Gentile-Bal 46
- Colavito-Det 45

Total Bases
- Maris-NY 366
- Cash-Det 354
- Mantle-NY 353
- Colavito-Det 338
- Killebrew-Min 328

Runs Batted In
- Maris-NY 142
- Gentile-Bal 141
- Colavito-Det 140
- Cash-Det 132
- Mantle-NY 128

Stolen Bases
- Aparicio-Chi 53
- Howser-KC 37
- Wood-Det 30
- Hinton-Was 22
- Bruton-Det 22

Base Stealing Runs
- Aparicio-Chi 7.1
- Howser-KC 5.0
- Wood-Det 3.5
- Hinton-Was 3.1
- Bruton-Det 2.7

Fielding Runs-Infield
- Boyer-NY 28.5
- Lumpe-KC 21.2
- Kubek-NY 17.9
- Causey-KC 17.3
- Power-Cle 16.5

Fielding Runs-Outfield
- Kaline-Det 13.5
- Landis-Chi 7.8
- Piersall-Cle 7.6
- Colavito-Det 7.2
- Jensen-Bos 6.7

Wins
- Ford-NY 25
- Lary-Det 23
- Barber-Bal 18
- Bunning-Det 17
- Terry-NY 16

Winning Pct.
- Ford-NY 862
- Terry-NY 842
- Arroyo-NY 750
- Lary-Det 719

Complete Games
- Lary-Det 22
- Pascual-Min 15
- Barber-Bal 14

Strikeouts
- Pascual-Min 221
- Ford-NY 209
- Bunning-Det 194
- Pizarro-Chi 188
- McBride-LA 180

Fewest BB/Game
- Mossi-Det 1.76
- Brown-Bal 1.78
- Donovan-Was 1.87
- Terry-NY 2.01
- McClain-Was 2.04

Games
- Arroyo-NY 65
- Morgan-LA 59
- Lown-Chi 59
- Kunkel-KC 58
- Fornieles-Bos 57

Saves
- Arroyo-NY 29
- Wilhelm-Bal 18
- Fornieles-Bos 15
- Moore-Min 14
- Fox-Det 12

Base Runners/9
- Donovan-Was 9.39
- Morgan-LA 9.43
- Hall-Bal 9.71
- Terry-NY 9.80
- Fowler-LA 9.81

Adjusted Relief Runs
- Arroyo-NY 20.7
- Morgan-LA 18.1
- Wilhelm-Bal 18.0
- Fox-Det 16.2
- Hillman-Bos 12.4

Relief Ranking
- Arroyo-NY 41.5
- Wilhelm-Bal 30.3
- Fox-Det 25.4
- Morgan-LA 22.3
- Funk-Cle 16.2

Innings Pitched
- Ford-NY 283.0
- Lary-Det 275.1
- Bunning-Det 268.0
- Ramos-Min 264.1
- Pascual-Min 252.1

Opponents' Avg.
- Estrada-Bal 207
- Pappas-Bal 208
- Pascual-Min 217
- Barber-Bal 218
- Donovan-Was 224

Opponents' OBP
- Donovan-Was 267
- Terry-NY 275
- Bunning-Det 284
- Brown-Bal 284
- Lary-Det 290

Earned Run Average
- Donovan-Was 2.40
- Stafford-NY 2.68
- Mossi-Det 2.96
- Pappas-Bal 3.04
- Pizarro-Chi 3.05

Adjusted ERA
- Donovan-Was 167
- Stafford-NY 139
- Mossi-Det 139
- Archer-KC 131
- Schwall-Bos 129

Adjusted Starter Runs
- Hoeft-NY 28.2
- Mossi-Det 27.9
- Donovan-Was 26.9
- Bunning-Det 25.7
- Lary-Det 25.3

Pitcher Wins
- Arroyo-NY 4.4
- Lary-Det 3.3
- Donovan-Was 3.3
- Wilhelm-Bal 3.3
- Stafford-NY 2.8

As the Records Fall

Expansion to ten teams and 162 games meant more games, more traveling, and many new faces. Debuts included Carl Yastrzemski, who replaced Ted Williams in Boston; new Yankees Al Downing and Tom Tresh; Angels Dean Chance and Jim Fregosi; Cleveland's Sam McDowell; Detroit's Bill Freehan; and Baltimore's Boog Powell. By the mid-1960s, all had made significant contributions.

Playing more games, hitters clubbed 41 percent more homers—but home runs per contest also rose 8 percent, due largely to Los Angeles' tiny Wrigley Field, home to more than 3 homers *per game*. Expansion raised total attendance, but most teams' admissions declined; Chicago, Boston, Cleveland, and Baltimore experienced frightening decreases. One team that didn't draw, in 1961 or later, was the "new" Washington Senators, arguably the least successful franchise in league history.

Roger Maris and Mickey Mantle spent the summer chasing Babe Ruth's single-season homer record. Mantle dropped out due to injury, but Maris took it to the wire, clubbing No. 61 on closing day. Maris won his second straight MVP, but he lost a lot of hair in the grueling chase. The Yankees' 240 homers set an all-time record.

Detroit's rookie infielder Jake Wood broke the strikeout record; whiffs rose to 5.14 per game, a new high, and would keep rising. Yankee Luis Arroyo's 29 (unofficial) saves also established a new mark. The changes in baseball reflected strongly against the death of Dead Ball Era denizen Ty Cobb.

Detroit, flush with offense from Norm Cash, Al Kaline, and newly acquired Rocky Colavito, hung neck-and-neck with New York until early September. The Yankees simply out-clubbed them.

Under new manager Ralph Houk, the Bronx Bombers won a fairly easy five-game World Series from Cincinnati, blowing apart the Reds in the final two contests, 7-0, and 13-5. Whitey Ford broke Babe Ruth's mark for consecutive scoreless innings in Series play.

1960 National League

TEAM	W	L	T	PCT	GB	HW	HL	R	OR	PA	H	2B	3B	HR	BB	SO	HB	SH	AVG	OBP	SLG	OPS	AOPS	BR	ABR	PF	SB	CS	BSA	BSR
PIT	95	59	1	.617		52	25	734	593	6029	1493	236	56	120	486	747	20	69	.276	.335	.407	742	108	73	69	101	34	24	59	-1
MIL	88	66	0	.571	7	51	26	724	658	5868	1393	198	48	170	463	793	23	59	.265	.323	.417	740	117	58	116	93	69	37	65	2
STL	86	68	1	.558	9	51	26	639	616	5806	1317	213	48	138	501	792	31	52	.254	.321	.393	714	93	14	-38	109	48	35	58	-2
LA	82	72	0	.532	13	42	35	662	593	5935	1333	216	38	126	529	837	27	102	.255	.324	.383	707	93	7	-33	106	95	53	64	2
SF	79	75	2	.513	16	45	32	671	631	5923	1357	220	62	134	467	846	33	60	.255	.317	.393	710	106	-1	41	94	86	45	66	3
CIN	67	87	0	.435	28	37	40	640	692	5940	1324	230	40	140	512	858	34	60	.250	.318	.388	706	97	0	-11	102	73	37	66	3
CHI	60	94	2	.390	35	33	44	634	776	5960	1293	213	48	119	531	897	19	64	.243	.313	.369	682	93	-48	-41	99	51	34	60	-1
PHI	59	95	0	.383	36	31	46	546	691	5748	1235	196	44	99	448	1054	33	66	.239	.302	.351	653	84	-103	-104	100	45	48	48	-7
TOT	619					342	274	5250		47209	10745	1722	384	1042	3937	6824	220	532	.255	.319	.388	707					501	313	62	1

TEAM	CG	SHO	GR	SV	IP	H	HR	BB	SO	BR/9	ERA	AERA	OAV	OOB	PR	APR	PF	OSB	OCS	FA	E	WPB	DP	FW	PW	BW	BSW	DIF
PIT	47	11	205	33	1399.2	1363	105	386	811	11.3	3.49	107	.257	.307	42	41	100	44	32	.979	128	35	163	.7	4.2	7.1	-.1	6.1
MIL	55	13	182	28	1387.1	1327	130	518	807	12.2	3.76	91	.251	.320	0	-57	91	38	33	.976	141	57	137	-.0	-5.9	11.9	.2	4.8
STL	37	11	217	30	1371.0	1316	127	511	906	12.1	3.64	112	.253	.319	18	64	109	50	37	.976	141	48	152	.0	6.6	-3.9	-.2	6.5
LA	46	13	204	20	1398.0	1218	154	564	1122	11.7	3.40	117	.234	.311	56	84	106	42	34	.979	125	63	142	.9	8.6	-3.4	.2	-1.3
SF	55	16	214	26	1396.0	1288	107	512	897	11.8	3.44	101	.245	.313	50	6	93	77	20	.972	166	55	117	-1.3	.6	4.2	.3	-1.8
CIN	33	8	253	35	1390.1	1417	134	442	740	12.3	4.00	96	.267	.326	-37	-27	102	56	43	.979	125	43	155	.9	-2.8	-1.1	.3	-7.2
CHI	36	6	260	25	1402.2	1393	152	565	805	12.8	4.35	87	.260	.333	-92	-89	100	59	57	.977	143	54	133	-.0	-9.2	-4.2	-.1	-3.5
PHI	45	6	199	16	1375.1	1423	133	439	736	12.3	4.01	97	.270	.325	-38	-19	103	103	55	.974	155	53	129	-.8	-2.0	-10.7	-.7	-3.8
TOT	354	84	1734	213	11120.1					12.1	3.76		.255	.319						.977	1124	408	1128					

Batter-Fielder Wins		Batting Average		On-Base Percentage		Slugging Average		On-Base Plus Slugging		Adjusted OPS		Adjusted Batter Runs	
Banks-Chi	6.0	Groat-Pit	.325	Ashburn-Chi	.415	Robinson-Cin	.595	Robinson-Cin	1002	Mathews-Mil	170	Mathews-Mil	56.6
Mays-SF	5.0	Larker-LA	.323	Robinson-Cin	.407	Aaron-Mil	.566	Mathews-Mil	948	Robinson-Cin	169	Mays-SF	51.1
Robinson-Cin	4.6	Mays-SF	.319	Mathews-Mil	.397	Boyer-StL	.562	Mays-SF	936	Mays-SF	164	Robinson-Cin	47.7
Aaron-Mil	4.5	Clemente-Pit	.314	Moon-LA	.383	Mays-SF	.555	Boyer-StL	932	Aaron-Mil	161	Aaron-Mil	45.8
Boyer-StL	4.5	Boyer-StL	.304	Mays-SF	.381	Banks-Chi	.554	Aaron-Mil	919	Banks-Chi	145	Banks-Chi	36.3

Runs		Hits		Doubles		Triples		Home Runs		Total Bases		Runs Batted In	
Bruton-Mil	112	Mays-SF	190	Pinson-Cin	37	Bruton-Mil	13	Banks-Chi	41	Aaron-Mil	334	Aaron-Mil	126
Mathews-Mil	108	Pinson-Cin	187	Cepeda-SF	36	Pinson-Cin	12	Aaron-Mil	40	Banks-Chi	331	Mathews-Mil	124
Pinson-Cin	107	Groat-Pit	186	Skinner-Pit	33	Mays-SF	12	Mathews-Mil	39	Mays-SF	330	Banks-Chi	117
Mays-SF	107	Bruton-Mil	180	Robinson-Cin	33	Aaron-Mil	11	Boyer-StL	32	Boyer-StL	310	Mays-SF	103
Aaron-Mil	102	Clemente-Pit	179	Banks-Chi	32			Robinson-Cin	31	Pinson-Cin	308	Boyer-StL	97

Stolen Bases		Base Stealing Runs		Fielding Runs-Infield		Fielding Runs-Outfield		Wins		Winning Pct.		Complete Games	
Wills-LA	50	Wills-LA	6.8	Mazeroski-Pit	30.1	Walters-Phi	9.0	Spahn-Mil	21	Broglio-StL	.700	Spahn-Mil	18
Pinson-Cin	32	Pinson-Cin	2.8	Wills-LA	25.5	Virdon-Pit	4.8	Broglio-StL	21	Law-Pit	.690	Law-Pit	18
T.Taylor-Chi-Phi	26	Javier-StL	2.8	Javier-StL	16.9	Aaron-Mil	4.0	Law-Pit	20	Spahn-Mil	.677	Burdette-Mil	18
Mays-SF	25	Blasingame-SF	2.4	Boyer-StL	15.8	Mays-SF	3.9	Burdette-Mil	19	Buhl-Mil	.640	Hobbie-Chi	16
Bruton-Mil	22	Ashburn-Chi	2.1	Gilliam-LA	15.3	Kirkland-SF	2.4			Purkey-Cin	.607	Friend-Pit	16

Strikeouts		Fewest BB/Game		Games		Saves		Base Runners/9		Adjusted Relief Runs		Relief Ranking	
Drysdale-LA	246	Burdette-Mil	1.14	Face-Pit	68	McDaniel-StL	26	McDaniel-StL	8.51	McDaniel-StL	24.7	McDaniel-StL	42.9
Koufax-LA	197	Roberts-Phi	1.29	McDaniel-StL	65	Face-Pit	24	Brosnan-Cin	9.18	Brosnan-Cin	15.0	Face-Pit	21.6
S.Jones-SF	190	Law-Pit	1.33	Elston-Chi	60	Henry-Cin	17	Face-Pit	9.58	Roebuck-LA	14.0	Farrell-Phi	20.8
Broglio-StL	188	Friend-Pit	1.47	Farrell-Phi	59	Brosnan-Cin	12	Marichal-SF	9.63	Farrell-Phi	12.7	Brosnan-Cin	16.3
Friend-Pit	183	Haddix-Pit	1.98	Roebuck-LA	58			Drysdale-LA	9.90	Face-Pit	11.5	Roebuck-LA	14.0

Innings Pitched		Opponents' Avg.		Opponents' OBP		Earned Run Average		Adjusted ERA		Adjusted Starter Runs		Pitcher Wins	
Jackson-StL	282.0	Koufax-LA	.207	Drysdale-LA	.274	McCormick-SF	2.70	Broglio-StL	149	Drysdale-LA	32.9	McDaniel-StL	4.7
Friend-Pit	275.2	Williams-LA	.210	Friend-Pit	.280	Broglio-StL	2.74	Drysdale-LA	140	Broglio-StL	31.5	Broglio-StL	4.4
Burdette-Mil	275.2	Broglio-StL	.213	Williams-LA	.280	Drysdale-LA	2.84	Simmons-Phi-StL	134	McCormick-SF	24.9	Drysdale-LA	4.0
Law-Pit	271.2	Drysdale-LA	.215	Law-Pit	.286	Williams-LA	3.00	Williams-LA	133	Friend-Pit	24.6	McCormick-SF	3.0
Drysdale-LA	269.0	Buhl-Mil	.229	Burdette-Mil	.287	Friend-Pit	3.00	Podres-LA	129	Podres-LA	21.1	Face-Pit	2.6

The Wait Is Over

Pittsburgh took an early lead in the NL race, trying to win for the first time in 35 seasons. Milwaukee caught Pittsburgh in July, but then dropped 11 of 15. Victory was sweet for Pirates fans, not far removed from the horror of the early 1950s. Pittsburgh had it all: four quality starters, a bullpen ace, a solid everyday lineup, and a strong bench. Vernon Law won the Cy Young, while scrappy shortstop Dick Groat took MVP honors with equally fiery teammate Don Hoak second.

Milwaukee wasted Henry Aaron, Eddie Mathews, and Warren Spahn's great years; lousy middle-infield production doomed the Braves to second. The third-place Cardinals got nothing from their entire outfield, including 39-year-old Stan Musial. Fifth-place San Francisco moved into windy Candlestick Park, where Juan Marichal debuted July 19 with a one-hitter. Ron Santo joined the Cubs, but the Dodgers' Frank Howard was Rookie of the Year.

Gotham's NL glory days were quickly turning to memory; Alvin Dark, Carl Furillo, and Don Newcombe played their last games. Meanwhile, Dodgers hurler Sandy Koufax set a mark for strikeouts per game, then broke it in 1962. Bespectacled Reds reliever Jim Brosnan penned *The Long Season*, a diary of the 1959 campaign. Some dubbed Brosnan a "traitor" for discussing the goings-on of a major league clubhouse.

The Pirates certainly didn't *look* like a league champion in the three World Series games they lost to the Yankees: 16-3, 10-0, and 12-0. Pittsburgh captured three close ones, however. After taking a 4-0 lead in Game 7, the Pirates fell behind. Down 7-4 in the eighth, Hal Smith's homer put Pittsburgh ahead, 9-7. But the Yankees tied things in the ninth. The baseball season ended suddenly when Bill Mazeroski led off the home ninth with a home run. The last time the Pirates had won the World Series, in 1925, they counted two world championships to the Yankees' one; by the time Mazeroski touched home plate in the bedlam of Forbes Field, the tally was 19-3 in favor of New York—but the Bucs enjoyed their day.

1960 American League

TEAM	W	L	T	PCT	GB	HW	HL	R	OR	PA	H	2B	3B	HR	BB	SO	HB	SH	AVG	OBP	SLG	OPS	AOPS	BR	ABR	PF	SB	CS	BSA	BSR
NY	97	57	1	.630		55	22	746	627	5981	1377	215	40	193	537	818	28	81	.260	.329	.426	755	115	62	106	94	37	23	62	0
BAL	89	65	0	.578	8	44	33	682	606	5911	1307	206	33	123	596	801	36	72	.253	.332	.377	709	99	-7	2	99	37	24	61	0
CHI	87	67	0	.565	10	51	26	741	617	5966	1402	242	38	112	567	648	54	95	.270	.345	.396	741	107	60	67	99	122	48	72	10
CLE	76	78	0	.494	21	39	38	667	693	5921	1415	218	20	127	444	573	32	97	.267	.325	.388	713	101	-12	9	97	58	25	70	4
WAS	73	81	0	.474	24	32	45	672	696	6004	1283	205	43	147	584	883	48	86	.244	.324	.384	708	98	-19	-12	99	52	43	55	-4
DET	71	83	0	.461	26	40	37	633	644	5990	1243	188	34	150	636	728	33	85	.239	.324	.375	699	93	-32	-49	103	66	32	67	3
BOS	65	89	0	.422	32	36	41	658	775	5931	1359	234	32	124	570	798	25	70	.261	.333	.389	722	98	18	-5	104	34	28	55	-2
KC	58	96	1	.377	39	34	43	615	756	5858	1303	212	34	110	513	744	12	75	.249	.316	.366	682	89	-70	-74	101	16	11	59	0
TOT	617					331	285	5414		47562	10689	1720	274	1086	4447	5993	268	661	.255	.328	.388	716					422	234	64	11

TEAM	CG	SHO	GR	SV	IP	H	HR	BB	SO	BR/9	ERA	AERA	OAV	OOB	PR	APR	PF	OSB	OCS	FA	E	WPB	DP	FW	PW	BW	BSW	DIF
NY	38	16	263	42	1398.0	1225	123	609	712	12.0	3.52	102	.238	.320	55	11	93	43	30	.979	129	52	162	.2	1.1	10.7	-.1	8.1
BAL	48	11	177	22	1375.2	1222	117	552	785	11.8	3.52	108	.241	.317	54	45	98	54	23	.982	108	58	172	1.4	4.6	.2	-.1	6.0
CHI	42	11	254	26	1381.0	1338	127	533	695	12.3	3.60	105	.258	.326	41	28	98	41	31	.982	109	28	175	1.4	2.8	6.8	.9	-1.8
CLE	32	10	219	30	1382.1	1308	161	636	771	12.8	3.95	95	.252	.334	-12	-34	97	59	32	.978	128	51	165	.2	-3.4	.9	.3	1.1
WAS	34	10	258	35	1405.1	1392	130	538	775	12.6	3.77	103	.260	.329	16	18	100	40	40	.973	165	54	159	-2.1	1.8	-1.2	-.5	-1.9
DET	40	7	209	25	1405.2	1336	141	474	824	11.9	3.64	109	.251	.316	37	49	102	53	32	.977	138	50	138	-.5	5.0	-5.0	.2	-5.7
BOS	34	6	252	23	1361.0	1440	127	580	767	13.6	4.62	87	.273	.346	-113	-84	104	49	25	.976	141	67	156	-.6	-8.5	-.5	-.3	-2.0
KC	44	4	227	14	1374.0	1428	160	525	664	13.1	4.38	91	.271	.339	-77	-59	103	83	21	.979	127	54	149	.3	-6.0	-7.5	-.1	-5.7
TOT	312	75	1859	217	11083.0					12.5	3.87		.255	.328						.978	1045	414	1276					

Batter-Fielder Wins		Batting Average		On-Base Percentage		Slugging Average		On-Base Plus Slugging		Adjusted OPS		Adjusted Batter Runs	
Aparicio-Chi	3.9	Runnels-Bos	320	Yost-Det	414	Maris-NY	581	Mantle-NY	957	Mantle-NY	166	Mantle-NY	51.4
Maris-NY	3.7	Smith-Chi	315	Woodling-Bal	401	Mantle-NY	558	Maris-NY	952	Maris-NY	164	Maris-NY	42.4
Mantle-NY	3.6	Minoso-Chi	311	Runnels-Bos	401	Killebrew-Was	534	Sievers-Chi	930	Sievers-Chi	152	Williams-Bos	41.7
Runnels-Bos	3.5	Skowron-NY	309	Mantle-NY	399	Sievers-Chi	534	Killebrew-Was	909	Killebrew-Was	145	Sievers-Chi	34.1
Williams-Bos	3.4	Kuenn-Cle	308	Sievers-Chi	396	Skowron-NY	528	Skowron-NY	881	Skowron-NY	144	Skowron-NY	30.5

Runs		Hits		Doubles		Triples		Home Runs		Total Bases		Runs Batted In	
Mantle-NY	119	Minoso-Chi	184	Francona-Cle	36	Fox-Chi	10	Mantle-NY	40	Mantle-NY	294	Maris-NY	112
Maris-NY	98	Robinson-Bal	175	Skowron-NY	34	Robinson-Bal	9	Maris-NY	39	Maris-NY	290	Minoso-Chi	105
Minoso-Chi	89	Fox-Chi	175	Minoso-Chi	32			Lemon-Was	38	Skowron-NY	284	Wertz-Bos	103
Landis-Chi	89	Smith-Chi	169	Freese-Chi	32			Colavito-Det	35	Minoso-Chi	284	Lemon-Was	100
Sievers-Chi	87	Runnels-Bos	169					Killebrew-Was	31	Lemon-Was	268	Gentile-Bal	98

Stolen Bases		Base Stealing Runs		Fielding Runs-Infield		Fielding Runs-Outfield		Wins		Winning Pct.		Complete Games	
Aparicio-Chi	51	Aparicio-Chi	8.4	Aparicio-Chi	33.5	Piersall-Cle	8.6	Perry-Cle	18	Perry-Cle	643	Lary-Det	15
Landis-Chi	23	Landis-Chi	3.0	Boyer-NY	24.0	Tuttle-KC	8.4	Estrada-Bal	18	Ditmar-NY	625	Ramos-Was	14
Green-Was	21	Kaline-Det	2.8	Power-Cle	21.1	Allison-Was	4.8	B.Daley-KC	16	Estrada-Bal	621	Herbert-KC	14
Kaline-Det	19	Piersall-Cle	2.2	Fox-Chi	19.4	Stephens-Bos-Bal	4.5			Pappas-Bal	577	Wynn-Chi	13
Piersall-Cle	18	Mantle-NY	2.0	Robinson-Bal	16.8	Lopez-NY	3.5					B.Daley-KC	13

Strikeouts		Fewest BB/Game		Games		Saves		Base Runners/9		Adjusted Relief Runs		Relief Ranking	
Bunning-Det	201	Brown-Bal	1.25	Fornieles-Bos	70	Klippstein-Cle	14	Staley-Chi	9.52	Staley-Chi	15.4	Staley-Chi	28.2
Ramos-Was	160	Mossi-Det	1.82	Staley-Chi	64	Fornieles-Bos	14	Brown-Bal	10.08	Fornieles-Bos	15.2	Fornieles-Bos	23.1
Wynn-Chi	158	Hall-KC	1.88	Clevenger-Was	53	Moore-Chi-Was	13	Wilhelm-Bal	10.10	Sisler-Det	13.7	Sisler-Det	20.9
Lary-Det	149	Lary-Det	2.03	Moore-Chi-Was	51	B.Shantz-NY	11	Aguirre-Det	10.27	Aguirre-Det	12.7	Aguirre-Det	12.7
Estrada-Bal	144	Pierce-Chi	2.11	Kutyna-KC	51			Stafford-NY	10.35	Stobbs-Was	6.7	B.Shantz-NY	10.1

Innings Pitched		Opponents' Avg.		Opponents' OBP		Earned Run Average		Adjusted ERA		Adjusted Starter Runs		Pitcher Wins	
Lary-Det	274.1	Estrada-Bal	218	Brown-Bal	283	Baumann-Chi	2.67	Bunning-Det	142	Bunning-Det	30.6	Staley-Chi	3.2
Ramos-Was	274.0	Turley-NY	222	Bunning-Det	292	Bunning-Det	2.79	Baumann-Chi	141	Baumann-Chi	20.8	Fornieles-Bos	2.6
Perry-Cle	261.1	Barber-Bal	226	Mossi-Det	293	Brown-Bal	3.06	Brown-Bal	125	Herbert-KC	18.4	Bunning-Det	2.5
Herbert-KC	252.2	Ford-NY	235	Ford-NY	297	Ditmar-NY	3.06	Herbert-KC	121	Kralick-Was	16.8	Herbert-KC	2.3
Bunning-Det	252.0	Bunning-Det	236	Hall-KC	299	Ford-NY	3.08	Barber-Bal	118	Brown-Bal	13.4	Sisler-Det	2.2

Casey's Last Flag

The Yankees, eerily resembling the 1959 model, sleepwalked through much of the season, but eventually woke up; they overtook surprising Baltimore in September and brought it home by winning their final 15 contests. Right fielder Roger Maris won the MVP award for the Yankees, who set a league record with 193 homers. New York was the only AL club to draw more than one million fans each year of the decade. Once again, Casey Stengel manipulated a staff of largely undistinguished pitchers into a cohesive unit, and the starting lineup was successfully rebuilt.

Baltimore's "Baby Birds" staff, including four starting pitchers aged 21 or 22, propelled the Orioles from seventh place to second. Third-place Chicago reacquired Minnie Minoso, but had a poorly constructed offense and thin starting pitching. Washington, with young talent beginning to jell, rose from last to fifth, and announced plans to move to the Twin Cities for 1961. The AL scheduled a new expansion club for the capital, with another slated for Los Angeles; the move from eight to ten teams proved a seismic shift.

Owner Arnold Johnson of last-place Kansas City had, for years, been feeding talent to the Yankees—including Roger Maris—for very little in return. Johnson's death in 1960 ended that. Charlie Finley bought the club in 1961.

Boston's Ted Williams homered in his last at bat at Fenway to close out a spectacular career. The Yankees also lost Gil McDougald to the rocking chair, while two-time batting titlist Mickey Vernon hung 'em up to manage the new Senators.

Following the Yankees' disappointing World Series loss to the Pirates, New York management pulled what would later be called a "Steinbrenner" and sacked Stengel, the most successful manager in history. It was arguable that the game had passed The Old Professor by, but still. . . .

1959 National League

TEAM	W	L	T	PCT	GB	HW	HL	R	OR	PA	H	2B	3B	HR	BB	SO	HB	SH	AVG	OBP	SLG	OPS	AOPS	BR	ABR	PF	SB	CS	BSA	BSR
LA	88	68	0	.564		46	32	705	670	6033	1360	196	46	148	591	891	28	**100**	.257	.334	.396	730	94	16	-32	107	**84**	51	62	1
MIL	86	70	1	.551	2	**49**	29	724	623	6010	1426	216	36	**177**	488	765	27	31	.265	.326	.417	743	**114**	97	92		41	14	**75**	4
SF	83	71	0	.539	4	42	35	705	**613**	5890	1377	239	35	167	473	875	25	73	.261	.322	.414	736	104	17	33	98	81	34	70	**6**
PIT	78	76	1	.506	9	47	30	651	680	5952	1414	230	42	112	442	**715**	24	77	.263	.320	.384	704	95	-41	-35	99	32	26	55	-2
CIN	74	80	0	.481	13	43	34	**764**	738	5922	**1448**	**258**	34	161	490	763	32	53	**.274**	**.337**	**.427**	**764**	107	**80**	59	103	65	28	70	5
CHI	74	80	0	.481	13	38	39	673	688	5939	1321	209	44	163	498	**911**	**43**	62	.249	.317	.398	715	97	-24	-17	99	32	19	63	0
STL	71	83	0	.461	16	42	35	641	725	5907	1432	244	**49**	118	485	747	19	60	.269	.331	.400	731	95	14	-28	106	65	53	55	-4
PHI	64	90	1	.416	23	37	40	599	725	5735	1237	196	38	113	498	858	34	59	.242	.312	.362	674	85	-94	-103	102	39	46	46	-8
TOT	620					344	274	5462		47388	11015	1788	324	1159	3974	6525	232	548	.260	.325	.400	725					439	271	62	2

TEAM	CG	SHO	GR	SV	IP	H	HR	BB	SO	BR/9	ERA	AERA	OAV	OOB	PR	APR	PF	OSB	OCS	FA	E	WPB	DP	FW	PW	BW	BSW	DIF
LA	43	14	241	**26**	1411.2	1317	157	614	**1077**	12.6	3.79	**111**	.247	.329	24	64	107	24	32	**.981**	114	59	154	**1.5**	6.4	-3.2	.0	5.3
MIL	**69**	**18**	167	18	1400.2	1406	**128**	429	775	11.9	3.51	101	.260	.315	68	6	90	36	30	.979	127	**30**	138	.8	.6	**9.8**	.4	-3.5
SF	52	12	205	23	1376.1	**1279**	139	500	873	**11.8**	**3.47**	110	**.246**	**.314**	74	54	97	50	35	.974	152	36	118	-.8	5.4	3.3	**.6**	-2.6
PIT	48	7	225	17	1393.1	1432	134	**418**	730	12.1	3.90	99	.267	.320	7	-5	98	56	32	.975	154	53	**165**	-.8	-.5	-3.5	-.2	6.1
CIN	44	7	232	**26**	1357.1	1460	162	456	690	12.9	4.31	94	.275	.335	-55	-38	103	40	**39**	.978	126	35	157	.7	-3.8	5.9	.5	-6.3
CHI	30	11	**250**	25	1391.0	1337	152	519	765	12.2	4.01	98	.254	.321	-10	-10	100	**107**	28	.977	140	46	142	-.0	-1.0	-1.1	-.4	-.2
STL	36	8	231	21	1363.0	1427	137	564	846	13.3	4.34	98	.271	.341	-59	-14	107	53	28	.975	146	61	158	-.4	-1.4	-2.8	-.4	-.9
PHI	54	8	190	15	1354.0	1357	150	474	769	12.4	4.27	96	.261	.324	-49	-24	104	73	38	.973	154	53	132	-.8	-2.4	-10.4	-.8	1.4
TOT	376	85	1741	171	11047.1					12.4	3.95		.260	.325						.977	1113	373	1164					

Leader boxes

Batter-Fielder Wins
- Aaron-Mil 6.8
- Banks-Chi 6.2
- Mathews-Mil 6.0
- Mays-SF 4.1
- Boyer-StL 3.5

Batting Average
- Aaron-Mil .355
- Cunningham-StL .345
- Cepeda-SF .317
- Pinson-Cin .316
- Mays-SF .313

On-Base Percentage
- Cunningham-StL .453
- Aaron-Mil .401
- Moon-LA .394
- Robinson-Cin .391
- Mathews-Mil .390

Slugging Average
- Aaron-Mil .636
- Banks-Chi .596
- Mathews-Mil .593
- Robinson-Cin .583
- Mays-SF .583

On-Base Plus Slugging
- Aaron-Mil 1037
- Mathews-Mil .983
- Robinson-Cin .975
- Banks-Chi .970
- Mays-SF .964

Adjusted OPS
- Aaron-Mil 188
- Mathews-Mil 172
- Mays-SF 157
- Banks-Chi 156
- Robinson-Cin 152

Adjusted Batter Runs
- Aaron-Mil 77.3
- Mathews-Mil 59.6
- Mays-SF 46.9
- Banks-Chi 45.9
- Robinson-Cin 41.8

Runs
- Pinson-Cin 131
- Mays-SF 125
- Mathews-Mil 118
- Aaron-Mil 116
- Robinson-Cin 106

Hits
- Aaron-Mil 223
- Pinson-Cin 205
- Cepeda-SF 192
- Temple-Cin 186
- Mathews-Mil 182

Doubles
- Pinson-Cin 47
- Aaron-Mil 46
- Mays-SF 43
- Cimoli-StL 40

Triples
- Neal-LA 11
- Moon-LA 11
- White-StL 9
- Pinson-Cin 9
- Dark-Chi 9

Home Runs
- Mathews-Mil 46
- Banks-Chi 45
- Aaron-Mil 39
- Robinson-Cin 36
- Mays-SF 34

Total Bases
- Aaron-Mil 400
- Mathews-Mil 352
- Banks-Chi 351
- Mays-SF 335
- Pinson-Cin 330

Runs Batted In
- Banks-Chi 143
- Robinson-Cin 125
- Aaron-Mil 123
- Bell-Cin 115
- Mathews-Mil 114

Stolen Bases
- Mays-SF 27
- T.Taylor-Chi 23
- Gilliam-LA 23
- Cepeda-SF 23
- Pinson-Cin 21

Base Stealing Runs
- Mays-SF 4.5
- Pinson-Cin 2.5
- Temple-Cin 2.0
- T.Taylor-Chi 1.9
- Cepeda-SF 1.9

Fielding Runs-Infield
- Blasingame-StL 19.9
- Neal-LA 18.4
- Boyer-StL 12.7
- Kasko-Cin 10.2
- Adcock-Mil 9.8

Fielding Runs-Outfield
- Virdon-Pit 13.9
- H.Anderson-Phi 10.0
- Pinson-Cin 8.8
- Post-Phi 6.7
- Bell-Cin 3.7

Wins
- Spahn-Mil 21
- S.Jones-SF 21
- Antonelli-SF 21
- Buhl-Mil 19

Winning Pct.
- Face-Pit .947
- Law-Pit .667
- Antonelli-SF .655
- Buhl-Mil .625

Complete Games
- Spahn-Mil 21
- Law-Pit 20
- Burdette-Mil 20
- Roberts-Phi 19

Strikeouts
- Drysdale-LA 242
- S.Jones-SF 209
- Koufax-LA 173
- Antonelli-SF 165
- McCormick-SF 151

Fewest BB/Game
- Newcombe-Cin 1.09
- Burdette-Mil 1.18
- Roberts-Phi 1.22
- Purkey-Cin 1.78
- Law-Pit 1.79

Games
- Henry-Chi 65
- Elston-Chi 65
- McDaniel-StL 62
- McMahon-Mil 60
- Miller-SF 59

Saves
- McMahon-Mil 15
- McDaniel-StL 15
- Elston-Chi 13
- Henry-Chi 12

Base Runners/9
- Henry-Chi 9.25
- Haddix-Pit 9.63
- Craig-LA 9.90
- Newcombe-Cin 10.05
- Conley-Phi 10.15

Adjusted Relief Runs
- Henry-Chi 20.0
- Miller-SF 16.5
- Face-Pit 13.5
- McMahon-Mil 9.9
- Elston-Chi 6.8

Relief Ranking
- Face-Pit 27.0
- Henry-Chi 26.8
- Miller-SF 15.1
- Elston-Chi 13.3
- McMahon-Mil 12.9

Innings Pitched
- Spahn-Mil 292.0
- Burdette-Mil 289.2
- Antonelli-SF 282.0
- S.Jones-SF 270.2
- Drysdale-LA 270.2

Opponents' Avg.
- S.Jones-SF .228
- Haddix-Pit .228
- Antonelli-SF .233
- Drysdale-LA .233
- Conley-Phi .235

Opponents' OBP
- Haddix-Pit .271
- Newcombe-Cin .279
- Conley-Phi .280
- Law-Pit .281
- Antonelli-SF .285

Earned Run Average
- S.Jones-SF 2.83
- Miller-SF 2.84
- Buhl-Mil 2.86
- Spahn-Mil 2.96
- Law-Pit 2.98

Adjusted ERA
- Conley-Phi 137
- S.Jones-SF 135
- Miller-SF 134
- Law-Pit 130
- Jackson-StL 128

Adjusted Starter Runs
- Law-Pit 30.5
- S.Jones-SF 30.3
- Craig-LA 30.3
- Antonelli-SF 25.5
- Jackson-StL 25.1

Pitcher Wins
- S.Jones-SF 3.6
- Newcombe-Cin 3.6
- Spahn-Mil 3.4
- Law-Pit 3.1
- Drysdale-LA 2.9

The Sun-Kissed Dodgers

San Francisco, enjoying great years from Willie Mays and Orlando Cepeda, looked to have the race wrapped up in mid-August, but Los Angeles and underachieving Milwaukee caught fire around Labor Day. In mid-September the Dodgers came into San Francisco and swept three, and the Giants dropped like a stone. Milwaukee stayed hot, the Dodgers kept winning, and the season ended in a deadlock.

The resulting playoff was just as close. Underdog Los Angeles won two one-run games, the second in 12 innings, to take the pennant, effectively ending Milwaukee's run of success.

Don Drysdale, winning his first strikeout title, led Los Angeles' patchwork mound staff, and 26-year-old midseason call-up Maury Wills anchored an unspectacular infield. Milwaukee's Warren Spahn led the NL in wins for the sixth time, but Red Schoendienst's illness, and manager Fred Haney's use of weak-hitting first baseman Frank Torre, hamstrung a great attack.

An amazing rookie class sowed the seeds of success for many 1960s clubs. St. Louis debuted Bob Gibson and Tim McCarver, while the Phillies welcomed Chris Short. The Cubs brought up Billy Williams, while the Dodgers summoned Wills and Tommy Davis. San Francisco's Willie McCovey, the most impressive of all, won Rookie of the Year honors.

The Los Angeles Coliseum's ridiculous 252-foot left field fence led baseball to enact a rule that new ballparks must reach 325 feet at all fences and 400 to center. Still, the Dodgers were only fifth in home runs. Chicago's Ernie Banks won MVP honors again. Pittsburgh's Roy Face set an all-time winning percentage mark, while Cincinnati's Vada Pinson blossomed into a star.

Larry Sherry pitched just 14 times in relief (with 9 starts) during the regular season, but he was a bullpen wizard in the World Series. Sherry had 2 wins and 2 saves as Los Angeles wiped out the favored White Sox in six games. Second baseman Charlie Neal hit .370 with 2 homers and Gil Hodges batted .391.

1959 American League

TEAM	W	L	T	PCT	GB	HW	HL	R	OR	PA	H	2B	3B	HR	BB	SO	HB	SH	AVG	OBP	SLG	OPS	AOPS	BR	ABR	PF	SB	CS	BSA	BSR
CHI	94	60	2	.610		**47**	30	669	**588**	6054	1325	220	**46**	97	580	**634**	49	84	.250	.327	.364	691	96	-19	-10	99	**113**	53	68	6
CLE	89	65	0	.578	5	43	34	**745**	646	5860	1390	216	25	**167**	433	721	39	60	**.263**	.321	**.408**	729	109	31	59	96	33	36	48	-5
NY	79	75	1	.513	15	40	37	687	647	5980	**1397**	224	40	153	457	828	30	76	.260	.319	.402	721	107	16	41	97	45	22	67	2
DET	76	78	0	.494	18	41	36	713	732	5948	1346	196	30	160	580	737	44	73	.258	**.335**	.400	**735**	102	58	50	105	34	17	67	2
BOS	75	79	0	.487	19	43	34	726	696	5985	1335	**248**	28	125	**626**	810	23	65	.256	**.335**	.385	720	98	41	9	105	68	25	**73**	6
BAL	74	80	1	.481	20	38	39	551	621	5883	1240	182	23	109	536	690	20	**88**	.238	.310	.345	655	87	-98	-85	98	36	24	60	0
KC	66	88	0	.429	28	37	40	681	760	5885	1383	231	43	117	481	780	33	69	**.263**	.326	.390	716	100	16	4	102	34	24	59	-1
WAS	63	91	0	.409	31	34	43	619	701	5734	1205	173	32	163	517	881	26	64	.237	.308	.379	687	93	-45	-42	100	51	34	60	-1
TOT	618					323	293	5391		47329	10621	1690	267	1091	4210	6081	264	579	.253	.323	.384	707					414	235	64	9

TEAM	CG	SHO	GR	SV	IP	H	HR	BB	SO	BR/9	ERA	AERA	OAV	OOB	PR	APR	PF	OSB	OCS	FA	E	WPB	DP	FW	PW	BW	BSW	DIF
CHI	44	13	**242**	**36**	1425.1	1297	129	525	761	11.7	**3.29**	114	.242	**.311**	91	76	97	56	28	**.979**	130	**31**	141	.6	7.7	-1.0	.5	9.2
CLE	58	7	190	23	1383.2	**1230**	148	635	799	12.3	3.75	98	**.239**	.323	18	-10	95	60	30	.978	127	51	138	.7	-1.0	**6.0**	-.6	7.0
NY	38	**15**	222	28	1399.0	1281	120	594	**836**	12.2	3.60	101	.244	.322	40	7	94	42	32	.978	131	41	160	.5	.7	4.2	.0	-3.5
DET	53	9	197	24	1360.0	1327	177	**432**	829	11.9	4.20	97	.254	.315	-52	-20	105	45	32	.978	**124**	38	131	**.9**	-2.0	2.0	.0	-2.0
BOS	38	9	222	25	1364.0	1386	135	589	724	13.2	4.17	97	.266	.341	-47	-16	105	37	28	.978	131	51	**167**	.5	-1.6	.9	**.5**	-2.3
BAL	45	**15**	180	30	1400.1	1290	**111**	476	735	**11.5**	3.56	106	.246	**.311**	47	35	98	40	**43**	.976	146	85	156	-.4	3.5	-8.6	-.1	2.5
KC	44	8	241	21	1360.2	1452	148	492	703	13.2	4.35	98	.274	.338	-74	-51	104	49	20	.973	160	56	156	-1.2	-5.2	.4	-.2	-4.8
WAS	46	10	214	21	1360.0	1358	123	467	694	12.3	4.01	98	.259	.321	-23	-14	101	85	22	.973	162	56	140	-1.4	-1.4	-4.3	-.2	-6.7
TOT	366	86	1708	208	11053.0					12.3	3.86		.253	.323						.977	1111	409	1196					

Batter-Fielder Wins		Batting Average		On-Base Percentage		Slugging Average		On-Base Plus Slugging		Adjusted OPS		Adjusted Batter Runs	
Mantle-NY	3.6	Kuenn-Det	353	Yost-Det	435	Kaline-Det	530	Kaline-Det	940	Mantle-NY	152	Mantle-NY	40.7
Runnels-Bos	3.6	Kaline-Det	327	Runnels-Bos	415	Killebrew-Was	516	Killebrew-Was	904	Kaline-Det	149	Francona-Cle	40.3
Kaline-Det	3.3	Runnels-Bos	314	Kaline-Det	410	Mantle-NY	514	Kuenn-Det	903	Kuenn-Det	140	Kaline-Det	36.5
Francona-Cle	3.2	Fox-Chi	306	Kuenn-Det	402	Colavito-Cle	512	Yost-Det	871	Woodling-Bal	139	Yost-Det	33.8
Jensen-Bos	3.1	Minoso-Cle	302	Woodling-Bal	402	Lemon-Was	510	Killebrew-Was	870	Killebrew-Was	137	Kuenn-Det	31.8

Runs		Hits		Doubles		Triples		Home Runs		Total Bases		Runs Batted In	
Yost-Det	115	Kuenn-Det	198	Kuenn-Det	42	Allison-Was	9	Killebrew-Was	42	Colavito-Cle	301	Jensen-Bos	112
Mantle-NY	104	Fox-Chi	191	Malzone-Bos	34	McDougald-NY	8	Colavito-Cle	42	Killebrew-Was	282	Colavito-Cle	111
Power-Cle	102	Runnels-Bos	176	Fox-Chi	34			Lemon-Was	33	Kuenn-Det	281	Killebrew-Was	105
Jensen-Bos	101	Power-Cle	172	Williams-KC	33			Maxwell-Det	31	Mantle-NY	278	Lemon-Was	100
Kuenn-Det	99	Minoso-Cle	172	Runnels-Bos	33			Mantle-NY	31	Allison-Was	275	Maxwell-Det	95

Stolen Bases		Base Stealing Runs		Fielding Runs-Infield		Fielding Runs-Outfield		Wins		Winning Pct.		Complete Games	
Aparicio-Chi	56	Aparicio-Chi	7.8	Gardner-Bal	22.6	Tuttle-KC	9.2	Wynn-Chi	22	Shaw-Chi	750	Pascual-Was	17
Mantle-NY	21	Mantle-NY	3.6	Power-Cle	9.9	Minoso-Cle	9.2	McLish-Cle	19	McLish-Cle	704	Pappas-Bal	15
Landis-Chi	20	Jensen-Bos	2.7	Malzone-Bos	9.7	Jensen-Bos	8.4	Shaw-Chi	18	Wynn-Chi	688	Mossi-Det	15
Jensen-Bos	20	Malzone-Bos	1.3	McDougald-NY	9.0	Landis-Chi	6.7			Mossi-Det	654	Wynn-Chi	14
Allison-Was	13	Yost-Det	1.3	Runnels-Bos	6.3	Colavito-Cle	4.5					Bunning-Det	14

Strikeouts		Fewest BB/Game		Games		Saves		Base Runners/9		Adjusted Relief Runs		Relief Ranking	
Bunning-Det	201	Brown-Bal	1.76	Staley-Chi	67	Lown-Chi	15	Shantz-NY	9.22	Staley-Chi	17.2	Duren-NY	23.7
Pascual-Was	185	Lary-Det	1.86	Lown-Chi	60	Staley-Chi	14	Ditmar-NY	9.62	Duren-NY	16.2	Staley-Chi	22.0
Wynn-Chi	179	Garver-KC	1.88	Clevenger-Was	50	Loes-Bal	14	Pascual-Was	10.33	Shantz-NY	12.2	Lown-Chi	14.3
Score-Cle	147	Mossi-Det	1.93	Shaw-Chi	47	Duren-NY	14	Wilhelm-Bal	10.34	Lown-Chi	10.1	Shantz-NY	12.5
Wilhelm-Bal	139	Ramos-Was	2.00			Fornieles-Bos	11	O'Dell-Bal	10.43	Fornieles-Bos	9.3	Fornieles-Bos	11.0

Innings Pitched		Opponents' Avg.		Opponents' OBP		Earned Run Average		Adjusted ERA		Adjusted Starter Runs		Pitcher Wins	
Wynn-Chi	255.2	Score-Cle	210	Ditmar-NY	268	Wilhelm-Bal	2.19	Wilhelm-Bal	173	Wilhelm-Bal	39.8	**Pascual-Was**	4.7
Bunning-Det	249.2	Ditmar-NY	211	Pascual-Was	282	Pascual-Was	2.64	Pascual-Was	148	Pascual-Was	33.8	**Wilhelm-Bal**	3.7
Foytack-Det	240.1	Wynn-Chi	216	O'Dell-Bal	284	Shaw-Chi	2.69	Shaw-Chi	140	Shaw-Chi	30.7	**Shaw-Chi**	2.9
Pascual-Was	238.2	O'Dell-Bal	220	Mossi-Det	284	Ditmar-NY	2.90	Walker-Bal	130	Mossi-Det	19.5	**Daley-KC**	2.9
McLish-Cle	235.1	Wilhelm-Bal	224	Brown-Bal	289	Walker-Bal	2.92	O'Dell-Bal	129	O'Dell-Bal	18.7	**Perry-Cle**	2.7

Going to a Go-Go

All eight teams were bunched together until late June, when the White Sox and Indians forged ahead. Up by 1½ games on August 26, Chicago invaded Cleveland and took four straight, effectively ending the race. The "Go-Go" White Sox were called hitless, but outside cavernous Comiskey Park, Chicago had the league's third-best offense. Sherm Lollar's power, Luis Aparicio's defense and speed, and MVP Nellie Fox and Jim Landis' on-base ability supported a short pitching staff. Early Wynn won 22.

Despite Rocky Colavito's 42 homers, the Indians fell again. Cleveland hero Nap Lajoie died at 84, and former Indian Larry Doby ended his career as a part-timer in Chicago.

A slow start put the Yankees in seventh, and Casey Stengel's club never really came together. The pitching was mediocre; what worked with Tom Sturdivant and Bob Turley didn't with Duke Maas and Eli Grba. Mickey Mantle's slump and the aging of Hank Bauer and Yogi Berra contributed to New York's distant third-place finish. Perhaps as a result of New York's sputtering, AL attendance was its highest since 1949. Crowds increased in seven cities, doubling in Cleveland and nearly doing so in Chicago (now owned by Bill Veeck).

Even as steals rose to their highest level since the war, home runs increased as well; strikeouts rose for the sixth straight year to 4.92, a new high. Two pitchers who won 498 games between them—Jim Perry and Jim Kaat—debuted. The Red Sox became the last club to integrate, two years after Detroit had done so. The AL remained far behind the NL in employment of African Americans and dark-skinned Latinos, but would soon shorten the gap.

While the White Sox won Game 1 of the World Series, 11-0, they were outscored by the Dodgers the rest of the way, 21-12. Both teams batted .261, but Los Angeles won in six games. Chicago hasn't reached the Series since.

1958 National League

TEAM	W	L	T	PCT	GB	HW	HL	R	OR	PA	H	2B	3B	HR	BB	SO	HB	SH	AVG	OBP	SLG	OPS	AOPS	BR	ABR	PF	SB	CS	BSA	BSR
MIL	92	62	0	.597		48	29	675	541	5859	1388	221	21	167	478	646	36	79	.266	.329	.412	741	110	15	79	92	26	8	76	3
PIT	84	70	0	.545	8	49	28	662	607	5779	1386	229	68	134	396	753	28	68	.264	.317	.410	727	100	-24	-6	97	30	15	67	1
SF	80	74	0	.519	12	44	33	727	698	5996	1399	250	42	170	531	817	34	68	.263	.331	.422	753	106	40	57	98	64	29	69	4
CIN	76	78	0	.494	16	40	37	695	621	5980	1359	242	40	123	572	765	21	76	.258	.331	.389	720	91	-16	-50	105	61	38	62	0
STL	72	82	0	.468	20	39	40	619	704	5891	1371	216	39	111	533	637	20	44	.261	.329	.380	709	90	-37	-61	104	44	43	51	-5
CHI	72	82	0	.468	20	35	42	709	725	5902	1402	207	49	182	487	853	45	42	.265	.330	.426	756	107	38	50	98	39	23	63	1
LA	71	83	0	.461	21	39	38	668	761	5804	1297	166	50	172	495	850	25	68	.251	.317	.402	719	92	-37	-56	103	73	47	61	0
PHI	69	85	0	.448	23	35	42	664	762	6081	1424	238	56	124	573	871	38	70	.266	.339	.400	739	102	22	32	99	51	33	61	0
TOT	616					329	287	5419		47292	11026	1769	365	1183	4065	6192	247	515	.262	.328	.405	733				388	236	62	3

TEAM	CG	SHO	GR	SV	IP	H	HR	BB	SO	BR/9	ERA	AERA	OAV	OOB	PR	APR	PF	OSB	OCS	FA	E	WPB	DP	FW	PW	BW	BSW	DIF
MIL	72	16	149	17	1376.0	1261	125	426	773	11.2	3.21	110	.244	.303	113	53	89	41	34	.980	120	27	152	.8	5.3	8.0	.3	.6
PIT	43	10	222	41	1367.0	1344	123	470	679	12.1	3.56	109	.261	.323	59	47	98	45	36	.978	133	45	173	.1	4.7	-.6	.0	2.7
SF	38	7	255	25	1389.1	1400	166	512	775	12.6	3.98	96	.263	.330	-4	-26	97	41	37	.975	152	41	156	-.9	-2.6	5.7	.4	.4
CIN	50	7	219	20	1385.1	1422	148	419	705	12.1	3.73	111	.267	.322	34	61	105	37	28	.983	100	25	148	1.9	6.2	-5.0	-.0	-4.0
STL	45	6	240	25	1381.2	1398	158	567	822	13.1	4.12	100	.264	.338	-2	2	105	74	23	.974	153	48	163	-.9	-.2	-6.2	-.5	2.4
CHI	27	5	293	24	1361.0	1322	142	619	805	13.1	4.22	93	.254	.336	-40	-46	99	61	25	.975	150	48	161	-.8	-4.6	5.0	-.0	-4.7
LA	30	7	284	31	1368.1	1399	173	606	855	13.4	4.47	92	.267	.344	-79	-55	104	33	31	.975	146	76	198	-.6	-5.5	-5.6	-.0	5.8
PHI	51	6	221	15	1397.0	1480	148	446	778	12.5	4.32	92	.272	.326	-58	-56	100	56	22	.978	129	58	136	.3	-5.6	3.2	-.0	-5.9
TOT	356	64	1883	198	11025.2					12.5	3.95		.262	.328						.977	1083	368	1287					

Batter-Fielder Wins		Batting Average		On-Base Percentage		Slugging Average		On-Base Plus Slugging		Adjusted OPS		Adjusted Batter Runs	
Mays-SF	6.3	Ashburn-Phi	.350	Ashburn-Phi	.440	Banks-Chi	.614	Mays-SF	1002	Mays-SF	167	Mays-SF	59.2
Banks-Chi	5.9	Mays-SF	.347	Musial-StL	.423	Mays-SF	.583	Banks-Chi	.980	Banks-Chi	157	Aaron-Mil	48.4
Ashburn-Phi	4.5	Musial-StL	.337	Mays-SF	.419	Aaron-Mil	.546	Musial-StL	.950	Aaron-Mil	157	Banks-Chi	47.0
Boyer-StL	4.0	Aaron-Mil	.326	Temple-Cin	.405	Thomas-Pit	.528	Aaron-Mil	.931	Musial-StL	145	Ashburn-Phi	38.5
Aaron-Mil	3.6	Skinner-Pit	.321	Skinner-Pit	.387	Musial-StL	.528	H.Anderson-Phi	.897	H.Anderson-Phi	137	Musial-StL	34.7

Runs		Hits		Doubles		Triples		Home Runs		Total Bases		Runs Batted In	
Mays-SF	121	Ashburn-Phi	215	Cepeda-SF	38	Ashburn-Phi	13	Banks-Chi	47	Banks-Chi	379	Banks-Chi	129
Banks-Chi	119	Mays-SF	208	Groat-Pit	36	Virdon-Pit	11	Thomas-Pit	35	Mays-SF	350	Thomas-Pit	109
Aaron-Mil	109	Aaron-Mil	196	Musial-StL	35	Mays-SF	11	Robinson-Cin	31	Aaron-Mil	328	H.Anderson-Phi	97
Boyer-StL	101	Banks-Chi	193	H.Anderson-Phi	34	Banks-Chi	11	Mathews-Mil	31	Cepeda-SF	309	Mays-SF	96
Ashburn-Phi	98	Cepeda-SF	188	Aaron-Mil	34			Aaron-Mil	30	Thomas-Pit	297	Cepeda-SF	96

Stolen Bases		Base Stealing Runs		Fielding Runs-Infield		Fielding Runs-Outfield		Wins		Winning Pct.		Complete Games	
Mays-SF	31	Mays-SF	4.7	Zimmer-LA	24.1	Clemente-Pit	19.1	Spahn-Mil	22	Spahn-Mil	.667	Spahn-Mil	23
Ashburn-Phi	30	Blasingame-StL	2.7	Boyer-StL	24.1	Flood-StL	13.1	Friend-Pit	22	Burdette-Mil	.667	Roberts-Phi	21
T.Taylor-Chi	21	T.Taylor-Chi	2.5	Mazeroski-Pit	17.7	Ashburn-Phi	11.5	Burdette-Mil	20	Friend-Pit	.611	Burdette-Mil	19
Blasingame-StL	20	Ashburn-Phi	2.4	Logan-Mil	14.5	Mays-SF	7.0	Roberts-Phi	17	Purkey-Cin	.607	Purkey-Cin	17
Gilliam-LA	18	Zimmer-Mil	2.4	Neal-LA	13.3	Skinner-Pit	6.7	Purkey-Cin	17	Antonelli-SF	.552	Friend-Pit	16

Strikeouts		Fewest BB/Game		Games		Saves		Base Runners/9		Adjusted Relief Runs		Relief Ranking	
Jones-StL	225	Burdette-Mil	1.63	Elston-Chi	69	Face-Pit	20	Henry-Chi	8.96	Elston-Chi	11.4	Elston-Chi	20.6
Spahn-Mil	150	Roberts-Phi	1.70	Klippstein-Cin-LA	57	Labine-LA	14	Jay-Mil	9.68	Henry-Chi	10.6	Henry-Chi	12.3
Podres-LA	143	Law-Pit	1.73	Face-Pit	57	Farrell-Phi	11	Porterfield-Pit	10.06	Face-Pit	9.4	Face-Pit	12.1
Antonelli-SF	143	Purkey-Cin	1.76	Hobbie-Chi	55			Spahn-Mil	10.40	Schmidt-Cin	7.2	Farrell-Phi	11.0
Friend-Pit	135	Newcombe-LA-Cin	1.93					Miller-Mil	10.43	Porterfield-Pit	7.1	Porterfield-Pit	8.2

Innings Pitched		Opponents' Avg.		Opponents' OBP		Earned Run Average		Adjusted ERA		Adjusted Starter Runs		Pitcher Wins	
Spahn-Mil	290.0	Koufax-LA	.220	Miller-SF	.286	Miller-SF	2.47	Miller-SF	154	Jones-StL	30.7	Spahn-Mil	4.1
Burdette-Mil	275.1	Jones-StL	.223	Spahn-Mil	.287	Jones-StL	2.88	Jones-StL	143	Witt-Pit	26.8	Burdette-Mil	2.9
Friend-Pit	274.0	Miller-SF	.233	Roberts-Phi	.292	Burdette-Mil	2.91	Roberts-Phi	122	Miller-SF	26.7	Roberts-Phi	2.6
Roberts-Phi	269.2	Spahn-Mil	.237	Burdette-Mil	.300	Spahn-Mil	3.07	Brosnan-Chi-StL	121	Roberts-Phi	20.8	Witt-Pit	2.5
		Antonelli-SF	.239	Purkey-Cin	.304	Roberts-Phi	3.24	Burdette-Mil	121	Burdette-Mil	19.0	Jones-StL	2.5

Last of the Braves

Milwaukee spent the first half of the season underachieving, but turned on the burners in August and strolled to another relatively easy NL crown. Both Warren Spahn and Lew Burdette won 20 for the Braves, but most of the lineup slumped. The Giants and Dodgers, in their new California surroundings, had fallen into rebuilding mode. East Coast stalwarts Pee Wee Reese and Sal Maglie retired. San Francisco finished a surprising third despite playing youngsters, including Orlando Cepeda (a unanimous Rookie of the Year) and Felipe Alou.

Pittsburgh leapt from seventh to second, improving 22 games under manager Danny Murtaugh. While the team, featuring a cadre of players in their mid-20s, still had a few holes to fill, the Pirates had served notice that their days as a joke were through.

St. Louis' Sam Jones won his third strikeout crown, while Ernie Banks of the fifth-place Cubs took MVP honors. The Phillies, sparked by batting titlist Richie Ashburn, became the first last-place team to lead the NL in batting average; they also paced in hits, walks, and on-base percentage. Philadelphia pitchers, on the other hand, allowed the most runs and the highest opponent batting average in the league.

Unfortunately, the bloom was coming off the rose in Milwaukee, as attendance began to fall even as the Braves won their second straight league title. In fact, fans dropped the team like a hot potato; attendance fell by 11 percent or more every year until 1963. Once again, however, franchise shifting pumped league coffers as the Dodgers' and Giants' moves to the West Coast—and the surprising rise of the Pirates—lifted NL attendance 15 percent.

In retrospect, the World Series was the beginning of the end for the Braves in Milwaukee; up three games to one, and with the final two contests at County Stadium, the Braves lost three straight to the Yankees. This time, Burdette was racked. It was the franchise's last World Series appearance until 1991.

1958 American League

TEAM	W	L	T	PCT	GB	HW	HL	R	OR	PA	H	2B	3B	HR	BB	SO	HB	SH	AVG	OBP	SLG	OPS	AOPS	BR	ABR	PF	SB	CS	BSA	BSR
NY	92	62	1	.597		44	33	**759**	577	5971	**1418**	212	39	**164**	537	822	26	72	**.268**	.336	**.416**	752	**116**	89	117	96	48	32	60	-1
CHI	82	72	1	.532	10	47	30	634	615	5935	1348	191	42	101	518	669	49	72	.257	.327	.367	694	99	-14	-1	98	**101**	33	**75**	11
BOS	79	75	1	.513	13	**49**	28	697	691	5972	1335	**229**	30	155	**638**	820	27	60	.256	**.338**	.400	738	102	75	28	107	29	22	57	-1
CLE	77	76	0	.503	14.5	42	34	694	635	5840	1340	210	31	161	494	819	40	69	.258	.325	.403	728	108	39	56	98	50	49	51	-6
DET	77	77	0	.500	15	43	34	659	606	5805	1384	**229**	41	109	463	678	22	**75**	.266	.326	.389	715	95	21	-24	107	48	32	60	-1
BAL	74	79	1	.484	17.5	46	31	521	**575**	5720	1233	195	19	108	483	731	28	62	.241	.308	.350	658	91	-85	-55	95	33	35	49	-5
KC	73	81	2	.474	19	43	34	642	713	5845	1297	196	**50**	138	452	747	25	64	.247	.307	.381	688	92	-43	-54	102	22	36	38	-8
WAS	61	93	2	.396	31	33	44	553	747	5763	1240	161	38	121	477	751	35	57	.240	.307	.357	664	90	-82	-71	98	22	41	35	-10
TOT	619					347	268	5159		46851	10595	1623	290	1057	4062	6037	252	531	.254	.322	.383	705					353	280	56	-20

TEAM	CG	SHO	GR	SV	IP	H	HR	BB	SO	BR/9	ERA	AERA	OAV	OOB	PR	APR	PF	OSB	OCS	FA	E	WPB	DP	FW	PW	BW	BSW	DIF
NY	53	**21**	184	**33**	1379.0	**1201**	116	557	796	11.8	**3.22**	110	**.235**	.313	85	51	94	43	45	.978	128	**33**	182	-.1	5.3	**12.1**	.2	-2.4
CHI	55	15	204	25	1389.2	1296	152	515	751	11.8	3.61	101	.250	.317	25	5	97	37	34	.981	114	39	160	.7	.5	-.1	**1.4**	2.5
BOS	44	5	201	28	1380.0	1277	121	521	695	12.7	3.92	102	.264	.332	-23	13	106	36	38	.976	145	37	172	-1.1	1.3	2.9	.2	-1.3
CLE	51	2	221	19	1373.1	1283	123	**604**	766	12.5	3.73	98	.249	.328	6	-13	97	50	33	.974	152	68	171	-1.5	-1.3	5.8	-.4	-2.0
DET	**59**	8	220	19	1357.1	1294	133	437	**797**	11.8	3.59	**112**	.252	.314	26	**62**	107	40	32	**.982**	106	43	**140**	**1.1**	**6.4**	5.8	-.4	-5.2
BAL	55	15	183	28	1369.2	1277	**106**	**403**	749	**11.3**	3.40	106	.249	**.306**	57	32	95	**28**	25	.980	114	46	159	.6	3.3	-5.7	-.3	-.5
KC	42	9	**237**	25	1398.1	1405	150	467	721	12.2	4.15	94	.262	.323	-59	-36	104	39	34	.979	125	66	166	.1	-3.7	-5.6	-.6	5.8
WAS	28	6	222	28	1376.2	1443	156	558	762	13.3	4.53	84	.272	.341	-116	-108	101	80	39	.980	118	58	163	.5	-11.2	-7.3	-.8	2.8
TOT	387	81	1672	206	11024.0					12.2	3.77		.254	.322						.979	1002	390	1313					

Batter-Fielder Wins
Mantle-NY 6.0
Colavito-Cle 5.1
Cerv-KC 4.6
Runnels-Bos 3.7
Kaline-Det 3.7

Batting Average
Williams-Bos 328
Runnels-Bos 322
Kuenn-Det 319
Kaline-Det 313
Power-KC-Cle 312

On-Base Percentage
Williams-Bos 458
Mantle-NY 443
Runnels-Bos 416
Colavito-Cle 405
Jensen-Bos 396

Slugging Average
Colavito-Cle 620
Cerv-KC 592
Mantle-NY 592
Williams-Bos 584
Sievers-Was 544

On-Base Plus Slugging
Williams-Bos 1042
Mantle-NY 1035
Colavito-Cle 1024
Cerv-KC 963
Jensen-Bos 931

Adjusted OPS
Mantle-NY 189
Colavito-Cle 183
Williams-Bos 174
Cerv-KC 158
Sievers-Was 148

Adjusted Batter Runs
Mantle-NY 71.2
Colavito-Cle 57.1
Williams-Bos 48.3
Cerv-KC 38.7
Jensen-Bos 37.1

Runs
Mantle-NY 127
Runnels-Bos 103
Power-KC-Cle 98
Minoso-Cle 94
Cerv-KC 93

Hits
Fox-Chi 187
Malzone-Bos 185
Power-KC-Cle 184
Runnels-Bos 183
Kuenn-Det 179

Doubles
Kuenn-Det 39
Power-KC-Cle 37
Kaline-Det 34
Runnels-Bos 32
Jensen-Bos 31

Triples
Power-KC-Cle 10
Tuttle-KC 9
Lemon-Was 9
Aparicio-Chi 9
Harris-Det 8

Home Runs
Mantle-NY 42
Colavito-Cle 41
Sievers-Was 39
Cerv-KC 38
Jensen-Bos 35

Total Bases
Mantle-NY 307
Cerv-KC 305
Colavito-Cle 303
Sievers-Was 299
Jensen-Bos 293

Runs Batted In
Jensen-Bos 122
Colavito-Cle 113
Sievers-Was 108
Cerv-KC 104
Mantle-NY 97

Stolen Bases
Aparicio-Chi 29
Rivera-Chi 21
Landis-Chi 19
Mantle-NY 18
Minoso-Cle 14

Base Stealing Runs
Aparicio-Chi 4.3
Rivera-Chi 3.6
Mantle-NY 2.9
Wilson-Det 2.2

Fielding Runs-Infield
Kubek-NY 20.4
Malzone-Bos 16.6
Buddin-Bos 14.0
Aparicio-Chi 11.5
F.Bolling-Det 11.1

Fielding Runs-Outfield
Kaline-Det 19.8
Cerv-KC 14.8
Minoso-Cle 5.8
Kuenn-Det 3.5
Williams-Bal 2.9

Wins
Turley-NY 21
Pierce-Chi 17
McLish-Cle 16
Lary-Det 16

Winning Pct.
Turley-NY 750
McLish-Cle 667
Pierce-Chi 607
Portocarrero-Bal 577
Foytack-Det 536

Complete Games
Turley-NY 19
Pierce-Chi 19
Lary-Det 19
Harshman-Bal 17

Strikeouts
Wynn-Chi 179
Bunning-Det 177
Turley-NY 168
Harshman-Bal 161
Pascual-Was 146

Fewest BB/Game
Donovan-Chi 1.92
O'Dell-Bal 2.07
Sullivan-Bos 2.21
Lary-Det 2.35
Pierce-Chi 2.42

Games
Clevenger-Was 55
Tomanek-Cle-KC 54
Hyde-Was 53
Wall-Bos 52

Saves
Duren-NY 20
Hyde-Was 18
Kiely-Bos 12
Wall-Bos 10

Base Runners/9
Wilhelm-Cle-Bal 9.76
Ford-NY 9.81
Pierce-Chi 9.96
Portocarrero-Bal ...10.25
Hyde-Was 10.40

Adjusted Relief Runs
Hyde-Was 21.3
Duren-NY 13.5
Kiely-Bos 8.5
Wall-Bos 5.4
Daley-KC 4.4

Relief Ranking
Hyde-Was 32.6
Duren-NY 24.1
Kiely-Bos 9.5
Wall-Bos 8.3
Morgan-Det 4.5

Innings Pitched
Lary-Det 260.1
Ramos-Was 259.1
Donovan-Chi 248.0
Turley-NY 245.1
Pierce-Chi 245.0

Opponents' Avg.
Turley-NY 206
Bell-Chi 213
Ford-NY 217
Pierce-Chi 227
Grant-Cle 228

Opponents' OBP
Ford-NY 276
Pierce-Chi 279
O'Dell-Bal 284
Portocarrero-Bal 284
Harshman-Bal 292

Earned Run Average
Ford-NY 2.01
Pierce-Chi 2.68
Harshman-Bal 2.89
Lary-Det 2.90
O'Dell-Bal 2.97

Adjusted ERA
Ford-NY 176
Lary-Det 139
Pierce-Chi 136
Harshman-Bal 124
McLish-Cle 122

Adjusted Starter Runs
Ford-NY 37.4
Lary-Det 31.8
Pierce-Chi 25.8
Turley-NY 22.1
Wilhelm-Cle-Bal 18.1

Pitcher Wins
Ford-NY 3.9
Lary-Det 3.5
Hyde-Was 3.4
Harshman-Bal 3.3
Pierce-Chi 3.0

Yankees Take Rematch

The New York Yankees were again AL champs, this time with no challenges. As the Yankees started ferociously, the rest of the league was so bad that the Kansas City Athletics held second for nearly a month. New York drew well—with no National League competition for the first time—but few other teams boasted strong gates.

Those who went to games didn't see an overabundance of offense. Teams scored an average of just 4.17 times per game, the lowest total in a decade. Mickey Mantle led the AL in walks and runs and finished fourth in steals (the top three thieves were Chicagoans—only the White Sox used stolen bases as a weapon). Ted Williams hit .328 and won his final batting title at age 40.

Yankees righty Bob Turley won 21 games despite leading the AL with 128 walks, but Whitey Ford, just 14-7, was New York's top twirler, towering over the league with a 2.01 ERA. The second-place White Sox, just 82-72, rate as one of the worst-ever pre-expansion runners-up. The Yankees' poor late-season performance—they were barely .500 the last two months, and Hoyt Wilhelm no-hit them on September 20—foreshadowed New York's 1959 collapse.

Hall of Famer Tris Speaker and star outfielder Harry Heilmann died in 1958. Meanwhile, Norm Cash and Johnny Callison debuted with the White Sox. They soon departed for other teams, one reason why Chicago didn't win in the 1960s.

Down three games to one in the World Series, the Yankees appeared headed for a second straight Series loss to the Braves. But Turley shut out Milwaukee, 7-0 in Game 5; then, back in Wisconsin, the Yankees—using Turley in relief twice—took the final two contests. The inability to win just one more Series game was, in essence, the end of the Milwaukee Braves.

1957 National League

TEAM	W	L	T	PCT	GB	HW	HL	R	OR	PA	H	2B	3B	HR	BB	SO	HB	SH	AVG	OBP	SLG	OPS	AOPS	BR	ABR	PF	SB	CS	BSA	BSR
MIL	95	59	1	.617		45	32	772	613	6050	1469	221	62	199	461	729	30	64	.269	.327	.442	769	120	81	140	93	35	16	69	2
STL	87	67	0	.565	8	42	35	737	666	6082	1497	235	43	132	493	672	18	45	.274	.333	.405	738	102	37	23	102	58	44	57	-3
BRO	84	70	0	.545	11	43	34	690	591	5944	1325	188	38	147	550	848	33	78	.253	.325	.387	712	89	-11	-69	110	60	34	64	-1
CIN	80	74	0	.519	15	45	32	747	781	6104	1452	251	33	187	546	752	37	84	.269	.338	.432	770	105	102	50	107	51	36	59	-1
PHI	77	77	2	.500	18	38	39	623	656	5921	1311	213	44	117	534	758	45	52	.250	.322	.375	697	96	-38	-18	97	57	26	69	3
NY	69	85	0	.448	26	37	40	643	701	5892	1349	171	54	157	447	669	25	32	.252	.311	.393	704	94	-46	-44	100	64	38	63	1
PIT	62	92	1	.403	33	36	41	586	696	5942	1447	231	60	92	374	733	23	97	.260	.315	.384	699	96	-48	-29	97	46	35	57	-2
CHI	62	92	2	.403	33	31	46	628	722	5947	1312	223	31	147	461	989	26	58	.244	.305	.380	685	90	-77	-67	98	28	25	53	-3
TOT	619					317	299	5426		47882	11162	1733	365	1178	3866	6150	237	510	.260	.322	.400	722				399	254	61	-1

TEAM	CG	SHO	GR	SV	IP	H	HR	BB	SO	BR/9	ERA	AERA	OAV	OOB	PR	APR	PF	OSB	OCS	FA	E	WPB	DP	FW	PW	BW	BSW	DIF
MIL	60	9	183	24	1411.0	1347	124	570	693	12.3	3.47	101	.253	.325	64	5	90	57	37	.981	120	31	173	1.0	.5	14.2	.2	2.0
STL	46	11	229	29	1413.1	1385	140	506	778	12.2	3.78	105	.257	.322	16	29	102	45	29	.979	131	62	168	.4	2.9	2.3	-.3	4.6
BRO	44	18	204	29	1399.0	1285	144	456	891	11.4	3.35	124	.244	.305	82	118	107	37	31	.979	127	38	136	.6	12.0	-7.0	.1	1.3
CIN	40	5	279	29	1395.2	1486	179	429	707	12.7	4.62	89	.275	.331	-116	-75	106	44	26	.982	107	36	139	1.7	-7.6	5.1	-.0	4.0
PHI	54	9	209	23	1401.2	1363	139	412	858	11.5	3.79	100	.254	.307	13	1	98	71	24	.976	136	37	117	.2	.1	-1.8	.3	1.2
NY	35	9	270	20	1398.2	1436	150	471	701	12.5	4.01	98	.267	.327	-20	-12	101	37	30	.974	161	40	180	-1.3	-1.2	-4.5	.1	-1.1
PIT	47	9	264	15	1395.0	1463	158	421	663	12.3	3.88	98	.270	.323	0	-14	98	45	27	.972	170	40	143	-1.7	-1.4	-2.9	-.2	-8.7
CHI	30	5	263	26	1403.1	1397	144	601	859	13.0	4.13	94	.261	.336	-39	-41	100	63	50	.975	149	53	140	-.5	-4.2	-6.8	-.3	-3.2
TOT	356	75	1901	195	11217.2	1397	144	601	859	12.2	3.88		.260	.322						.977	1101	337	1196					

Batter-Fielder Wins
Mays-NY	5.6
Musial-StL	4.6
Aaron-Mil	4.3
Mathews-Mil	4.3
Banks-Chi	3.9

Batting Average
Musial-StL	351
Mays-NY	333
Robinson-Cin	322
Aaron-Mil	322
Groat-Pit	315

On-Base Percentage
Musial-StL	422
Mays-NY	407
Bouchee-Phi	394
Ashburn-Phi	390
Temple-Cin	387

Slugging Average
Mays-NY	626
Musial-StL	612
Aaron-Mil	600
Snider-Bro	587
Banks-Chi	579

On-Base Plus Slugging
Musial-StL	1034
Mays-NY	1033
Aaron-Mil	978
Snider-Bro	955
Banks-Chi	939

Adjusted OPS
Mays-NY	174
Musial-StL	172
Aaron-Mil	170
Mathews-Mil	157
Banks-Chi	150

Adjusted Batter Runs
Mays-NY	60.6
Aaron-Mil	58.1
Musial-StL	53.7
Mathews-Mil	47.9
Banks-Chi	41.4

Runs
Aaron-Mil	118
Banks-Chi	113
Mays-NY	112
Mathews-Mil	109
Blasingame-StL	108

Hits
Schoendienst-NY-Mil	200
Aaron-Mil	198
Robinson-Cin	197
Mays-NY	195
Ashburn-Phi	186

Doubles
Hoak-Cin	39
Musial-StL	38
Bouchee-Phi	35
Banks-Chi	34
Moryn-Chi	33

Triples
Mays-NY	20
Virdon-Pit	11
Mathews-Mil	9
Bruton-Mil	9

Home Runs
Aaron-Mil	44
Banks-Chi	43
Snider-Bro	40
Mays-NY	35
Mathews-Mil	32

Total Bases
Aaron-Mil	369
Mays-NY	366
Banks-Chi	344
Robinson-Cin	323
Mathews-Mil	309

Runs Batted In
Aaron-Mil	132
Ennis-StL	105
Musial-StL	102
Banks-Chi	102
Hodges-Bro	98

Stolen Bases
Mays-NY	38
Gilliam-Bro	26
Blasingame-StL	21
Temple-Cin	19
Fernandez-Phi	18

Base Stealing Runs
Temple-Cin	2.4
Gilliam-Bro	2.2
Fernandez-Phi	2.2
Mays-NY	1.7
Robinson-Cin	1.5

Fielding Runs-Infield
Logan-Mil	21.6
Blasingame-StL	19.8
O'Connell-Mil-NY	11.6
Spencer-NY	10.9
Schoendienst-Mil	8.7

Fielding Runs-Outfield
Ashburn-Phi	25.0
Robinson-Cin	11.5
Post-Cin	9.3
Thomas-Pit	8.0
Moryn-Chi	7.3

Wins
Spahn-Mil	21
Sanford-Phi	19
Buhl-Mil	18
Drysdale-Bro	17
Burdette-Mil	17

Winning Pct.
Buhl-Mil	720
Sanford-Phi	704
Spahn-Mil	656
Drysdale-Bro	654
Burdette-Mil	654

Complete Games
Spahn-Mil	18
Friend-Pit	17
Gomez-NY	16
Sanford-Phi	15

Strikeouts
Sanford-Phi	188
Drott-Chi	170
Drabowsky-Chi	170
Jones-StL	154
Drysdale-Bro	148

Fewest BB/Game
Newcombe-Bro	1.49
Roberts-Phi	1.55
Law-Pit	1.67
Purkey-Pit	1.90
Jeffcoat-Chi	2.00

Games
Lown-Chi	67
Face-Pit	59
Labine-Bro	58
Worthington-NY	55
Grissom-NY	55

Saves
Labine-Bro	17
Grissom-NY	14
Lown-Chi	12
Wilhelm-StL	11

Base Runners/9
Podres-Bro	9.78
Roberts-Phi	10.45
Newcombe-Bro	10.56
Spahn-Mil	10.66
V.McDaniel-StL	10.70

Adjusted Relief Runs
Roebuck-Bro	12.8
Farrell-Phi	11.4
Miller-Phi	8.6
Grissom-NY	8.0
Brosnan-StL	7.0

Relief Ranking
Farrell-Phi	17.8
Roebuck-Bro	14.4
Miller-Phi	10.9
Grissom-NY	10.0
Labine-Bro	8.3

Innings Pitched
Friend-Pit	277.0
Spahn-Mil	271.0
Burdette-Mil	256.2
Lawrence-Cin	250.1
Roberts-Phi	249.2

Opponents' Avg.
Sanford-Phi	221
Podres-Bro	230
Drott-Chi	234
Drysdale-Bro	236
Spahn-Mil	237

Opponents' OBP
Podres-Bro	273
Roberts-Phi	283
Newcombe-Bro	288
Law-Pit	290
Spahn-Mil	291

Earned Run Average
Podres-Bro	2.66
Drysdale-Bro	2.69
Spahn-Mil	2.69
Buhl-Mil	2.74
Law-Pit	2.87

Adjusted ERA
Podres-Bro	156
Drysdale-Bro	155
Law-Pit	132
Spahn-Mil	130
Buhl-Mil	128

Adjusted Starter Runs
Drysdale-Bro	33.3
Podres-Bro	31.2
Spahn-Mil	25.6
Buhl-Mil	18.9
Sanford-Phi	17.5

Pitcher Wins
Drysdale-Bro	4.1
Podres-Bro	3.4
Spahn-Mil	3.1
Newcombe-Bro	2.1
Farrell-Phi	1.9

On, Wisconsin!

All-Star ballot stuffing led Commissioner Ford Frick to override the election of eight Cincinnati players in the All-Star Game. He inserted Hank Aaron, Willie Mays, and Stan Musial into the lineup—the NL only had 4 hits and lost in Baltimore. Players, coaches, and managers were subsequently awarded the voting. Fans lost the franchise until 1970. Cincy All-Star shortstop Roy McMillan was a recipient of the inaugural Gold Glove, an award for fielders; Gil Hodges and Mays were the other NL choices. After just one player was honored at each position, the leagues awarded individual sets of winners in 1958.

The pennant chase was a quagmire, involving the Braves, Dodgers, Cardinals, Redlegs (it was the Communist-scared '50s), and Phillies. However, a 17-2 August spurt lifted the Braves up to stay. When the Cardinals threatened in September, Milwaukee won eight in a row to wrap things up. Unheralded rookie Bob "Hurricane" Hazle hit .403 in 41 games down the stretch, but a midseason deal to acquire second baseman Red Schoendienst really put the Braves over the top. Despite playing in a pitcher's park, Milwaukee led the NL in runs.

For just the second time since 1946, an NL team outside New York played in the World Series, and Milwaukee was fit for battle. Down two games to one, the Braves came back from a 5-4 deficit in the bottom of the 10th to win, 7-5, on a home run by Eddie Mathews. Milwaukee then took Game 5 behind Lew Burdette, 1-0. The Yanks won at home in Game 6, but Burdette, who had a 0.67 ERA in 27 innings, won for the third time to clinch. Aaron hit .393 with 3 homers.

Both the Dodgers and Giants departed for the West Coast following the 1957 season. Willie Mays said goodbye to New York by hitting 20 triples, a feat unmatched in the NL until 1996. Dodgers catcher Roy Campanella would never play in Los Angeles, however; in January 1958, he was paralyzed in a car accident.

1957 American League

TEAM	W	L	T	PCT	GB	HW	HL	R	OR	PA	H	2B	3B	HR	BB	SO	HB	SH	AVG	OBP	SLG	OPS	AOPS	BR	ABR	PF	SB	CS	BSA	BSR
NY	98	56	0	0.636		48	29	723	534	5993	1412	200	54	145	562	709	24	93	.268	.339	.409	748	112	75	87	98	49	38	56	-3
CHI	90	64	1	.584	8	45	32	707	566	6083	1369	208	41	106	633	745	68	75	.260	.345	.375	720	102	42	38	101	109	51	68	6
BOS	82	72	0	.532	16	44	33	721	668	5995	1380	231	32	153	624	739	25	41	.262	.341	.405	746	104	80	40	106	29	21	58	-5
DET	78	76	0	.506	20	45	32	614	614	6005	1376	224	37	116	504	643	27	96	.257	.323	.378	701	95	-18	-34	103	36	47	43	-9
BAL	76	76	2	.500	21	42	33	597	566	5966	1326	191	39	87	504	699	34	110	.252	.329	.382	711	101	11	18	99	40	47	46	-8
CLE	76	77	0	.497	21.5	40	37	682	722	5919	1304	199	26	140	591	786	26	78	.252	.329	.382	711	101	11	18	99	40	47	46	-8
KC	59	94	1	.386	38.5	37	40	563	710	5656	1262	195	40	166	364	760	24	62	.244	.295	.394	689	91	-64	-73	102	35	27	56	0
WAS	55	99	0	.357	43	28	49	603	808	5895	1274	215	38	111	527	733	46	50	.244	.316	.363	679	92	-55	-48	99	13	38	25	-10
TOT	616					329	285	5210		47512	10703	1663	307	1024	4309	5814	274	605	.255	.326	.382	708					368	304	55	-25

TEAM	CG	SHO	GR	SV	IP	H	HR	BB	SO	BR/9	ERA	AERA	OAV	OOB	PR	APR	PF	OSB	OCS	FA	E	WPB	DP	FW	PW	BW	BSW	DIF
NY	41	13	179	42	1395.1	1198	110	580	810	11.7	3.00	120	.234	.315	122	96	95	40	51	.980	123	39	183	.2	9.9	9.0	.0	1.8
CHI	59	16	200	27	1401.2	1305	124	470	665	11.6	3.35	112	.248	.311	69	62	99	38	31	.982	107	42	169	1.1	6.4	3.9	.9	.6
BOS	55	9	171	23	1376.2	1391	116	498	692	12.6	3.88	103	.264	.329	-14	16	105	34	31	.976	149	34	179	-1.2	1.7	4.1	.2	.2
DET	52	9	209	21	1417.2	1330	147	505	756	11.9	3.56	108	.250	.318	37	46	102	33	31	.980	121	31	151	.3	4.8	-3.5	-.6	.0
BAL	44	13	195	25	1408.0	1272	95	493	767	11.5	3.46	104	.243	.310	51	21	95	41	49	.981	112	43	159	.8	2.2	-3.0	.3	-.3
CLE	46	7	204	23	1380.2	1381	130	618	807	13.3	4.06	92	.261	.340	-42	-54	98	61	34	.974	153	60	154	-1.4	-5.6	1.9	-.5	5.1
KC	26	6	250	19	1369.2	1344	153	565	626	12.7	4.19	94	.260	.333	-61	-34	104	53	28	.979	125	67	162	.1	-3.5	-7.5	.1	-6.7
WAS	31	5	234	16	1377.0	1482	149	580	691	13.7	4.85	80	.278	.349	-162	-142	103	68	49	.979	128	44	159	-.0	-14.7	-5.0	-.7	-1.6
TOT	354	78	1642	196	11126.2					12.4	3.79		.255	.326						.979	1018	360	1316					

Batter-Fielder Wins
Mantle-NY ...8.2
Williams-Bos ...7.1
Fox-Chi ...6.1
McDougald-NY ...4.4
Sievers-Was ...3.9

Batting Average
Williams-Bos ...388
Mantle-NY ...365
Woodling-Cle ...321
Boyd-Bal ...318
Fox-Chi ...317

On-Base Percentage
Williams-Bos ...526
Mantle-NY ...512
Woodling-Cle ...408
Minoso-Chi ...408
Fox-Chi ...403

Slugging Average
Williams-Bos ...731
Mantle-NY ...665
Sievers-Was ...579
Woodling-Cle ...521
Wertz-Cle ...485

On-Base Plus Slugging
Williams-Bos ...1257
Mantle-NY ...1177
Sievers-Was ...967
Woodling-Cle ...929
Minoso-Chi ...862

Adjusted OPS
Williams-Bos ...227
Mantle-NY ...223
Sievers-Was ...163
Woodling-Cle ...155
Minoso-Chi ...136

Adjusted Batter Runs
Mantle-NY ...94.0
Williams-Bos ...84.3
Sievers-Was ...49.1
Woodling-Cle ...35.0
Minoso-Chi ...33.9

Runs
Mantle-NY ...121
Fox-Chi ...110
Piersall-Bos ...103
Sievers-Was ...99

Hits
Fox-Chi ...196
Malzone-Bos ...185
Minoso-Chi ...176
Mantle-NY ...173
Kuenn-Det ...173

Doubles
Minoso-Chi ...36
Gardner-Bal ...36
Malzone-Bos ...31
Kuenn-Det ...30

Triples
Simpson-KC-NY ...9
McDougald-NY ...9
Bauer-NY ...9
Fox-Chi ...8
Boyd-Bal ...8

Home Runs
Sievers-Was ...42
Williams-Bos ...38
Mantle-NY ...34
Wertz-Cle ...28
Zernial-KC ...27

Total Bases
Sievers-Was ...331
Mantle-NY ...315
Williams-Bos ...307
Kaline-Det ...276
Malzone-Bos ...271

Runs Batted In
Sievers-Was ...114
Wertz-Cle ...105
Minoso-Chi ...103
Malzone-Bos ...103
Jensen-Bos ...103

Stolen Bases
Aparicio-Chi ...28
Rivera-Chi ...18
Minoso-Chi ...18
Mantle-NY ...16

Base Stealing Runs
Aparicio-Chi ...3.4
Rivera-Chi ...3.3
Mantle-NY ...2.5
Landis-Chi ...1.7
Martin-NY-KC ...1.3

Fielding Runs-Infield
Fox-Chi ...25.0
Bridges-Was ...22.6
Malzone-Bos ...21.0
Klaus-Bos ...18.6
McDougald-NY ...16.9

Fielding Runs-Outfield
Maxwell-Det ...9.7
Colavito-Cle ...7.9
Woodling-Cle ...6.9
Maris-Cle ...6.7
Kaline-Det ...5.1

Wins
Pierce-Chi ...20
Bunning-Det ...20
Sturdivant-NY ...16
Donovan-Chi ...16
Brewer-Bos ...16

Winning Pct.
Sturdivant-NY ...727
Donovan-Chi ...727
Bunning-Det ...714
Wilson-Chi ...652
Pierce-Chi ...625

Complete Games
Pierce-Chi ...16
Donovan-Chi ...16
Brewer-Bos ...15

Strikeouts
Wynn-Cle ...184
Bunning-Det ...182
Johnson-Bal ...177
Pierce-Chi ...171
Turley-NY ...152

Fewest BB/Game
F.Sullivan-Bos ...1.80
Donovan-Chi ...1.84
Shantz-NY ...2.08
Loes-Bal ...2.14
Bunning-Det ...2.42

Games
Zuverink-Bal ...56
Hyde-Was ...52
Clevenger-Was ...52
Delock-Bos ...49
Trucks-KC ...48

Saves
Grim-NY ...19
Narleski-Cle ...16
Delock-Bos ...11
Zuverink-Bal ...9
Clevenger-Was ...8

Base Runners/9
O'Dell-Bal ...9.68
F.Sullivan-Bos ...9.76
Bunning-Det ...10.00
Brown-Bal ...10.26
Donovan-Chi ...10.44

Adjusted Relief Runs
Staley-Chi ...19.4
Zuverink-Bal ...13.1
Trucks-KC ...10.8
Grim-NY ...9.1
Lehman-Bal ...7.3

Relief Ranking
Zuverink-Bal ...19.1
Grim-NY ...18.2
Trucks-KC ...14.9
Staley-Chi ...12.9
Lehman-Bal ...12.1

Innings Pitched
Bunning-Det ...267.1
Wynn-Cle ...263.0
Pierce-Chi ...257.0
Johnson-Bal ...242.0
F.Sullivan-Bos ...240.2

Opponents' Avg.
Turley-NY ...194
Bunning-Det ...218
Foytack-Det ...226
F.Sullivan-Bos ...230
Sturdivant-NY ...232

Opponents' OBP
F.Sullivan-Bos ...273
Sturdivant-NY ...277
Pierce-Chi ...287
Johnson-Bal ...287
Donovan-Chi ...291

Earned Run Average
Shantz-NY ...2.45
Sturdivant-NY ...2.54
Bunning-Det ...2.69
Turley-NY ...2.71
F.Sullivan-Bos ...2.73

Adjusted ERA
Shantz-NY ...147
F.Sullivan-Bos ...146
Bunning-Det ...143
Sturdivant-NY ...141
Donovan-Chi ...135

Adjusted Starter Runs
F.Sullivan-Bos ...34.5
Bunning-Det ...32.5
Sturdivant-NY ...24.9
Donovan-Chi ...22.9
Shantz-NY ...21.3

Pitcher Wins
F.Sullivan-Bos ...3.5
Bunning-Det ...3.4
Shantz-NY ...2.7
Sturdivant-NY ...2.6
Donovan-Chi ...2.4

The Battle of Mickey and Teddy

The Yankees were again the class of the league. New York had 21-year-old Bobby Richardson at second and 20-year-old utility infielder Tony Kubek meshing with 41-year-old outfielder Enos Slaughter, the usual veterans like Yogi Berra and Hank Bauer, and a staff of reasonably talented arms. Mickey Mantle again was voted Most Valuable Player, hitting .365 with 146 walks, and three New York hurlers finished among the league's top five in ERA.

Al Lopez left Cleveland, where he had managed for six years, to take over the White Sox, who finished second after leading the league through June. Chicago became the first club since 1945 to steal more than 100 bases, more than doubling the number of steals of the runner-up (Orioles). Chicago's middle infield duo of Luis Aparicio (the league steals leader) and Nellie Fox (AL-high 196 hits) were turning heads. Meanwhile, the last-place Senators stole just 13 bases in 154 games, the fewest ever.

Ted Williams, 39, became the oldest player ever to win a batting crown; his .388 mark was the highest average in the game since his own .406 in '41. Just to make things a little sweeter, he kicked in 119 walks and 38 homers, but lost to Mantle in a much-disputed MVP vote. Boston finished a surprise third despite a mediocre—at best—pitching corps.

The Indians sank to sixth as their pitching fell apart, but the Tribe did install 22-year-old rookie Roger Maris in the outfield. The tragedy of the season involved Cleveland's Herb Score, who took a Gil McDougald line drive to his right eye on May 7. After a layoff, he returned, hurt his arm, and was never again effective.

A disappointing World Series loss to Milwaukee again showed that the Yankees were, indeed, human. Oddly, they outscored and outhit the Braves in the Series and had a better ERA, but the Braves came up in the clinches.

1956 National League

TEAM	W	L	T	PCT	GB	HW	HL	R	OR	PA	H	2B	3B	HR	BB	SO	HB	SH	AVG	OBP	SLG	OPS	AOPS	BR	ABR	PF	SB	CS	BSA	BSR
BRO	93	61	0	.604		52	25	720	601	5884	1315	212	36	179	649	738	17	86	.258	.342	.419	761	102	86	32	108	65	37	64	1
MIL	92	62	1	.597	1	47	29	709	569	5897	1350	212	54	177	486	714	20	142	.259	.323	.423	746	112	38	83	94	29	20	59	-1
CIN	91	63	1	.591	2	51	26	775	658	6003	1406	201	32	221	528	760	51	90	.266	.336	.441	777	107	105	58	106	45	22	67	2
STL	76	78	2	.494	17	43	34	678	698	5986	1443	234	49	124	503	622	33	41	.268	.333	.399	732	102	26	26	100	41	35	54	-3
PHI	71	83	0	.461	22	40	37	668	738	5910	1313	207	49	121	585	673	27	52	.252	.329	.381	710	99	-11	2	98	45	23	66	2
NY	67	87	0	.435	26	37	40	540	650	5709	1268	192	45	145	402	659	21	59	.244	.299	.382	681	89	-88	-84	99	67	34	66	3
PIT	66	88	3	.429	27	35	43	588	653	5757	1340	199	57	110	383	752	18	95	.257	.307	.380	687	92	-74	-61	98	24	33	42	-6
CHI	60	94	3	.390	33	39	38	597	708	5852	1281	202	50	142	446	776	13	87	.244	.302	.382	684	91	-82	-71	98	55	38	59	-1
TOT	621					344	272	5275		46998	10716	1659	372	1219	3982	5694	200	652	.256	.321	.401	722				371	242	61	-3

TEAM	CG	SHO	GR	SV	IP	H	HR	BB	SO	BR/9	ERA	AERA	OAV	OOB	PR	APR	PF	OSB	OCS	FA	E	WPB	DP	FW	PW	BW	BSW	DIF
BRO	46	12	201	30	1368.2	1251	171	441	772	11.3	3.57	111	.244	.305	31	57	105	32	27	.981	111	51	149	1.4	5.8	3.3	.1	5.3
MIL	64	12	177	27	1393.1	1295	133	467	639	11.5	3.11	111	.247	.309	102	59	92	33	30	.979	130	29	159	.3	6.0	8.5	-.0	.2
CIN	47	4	231	29	1389.0	1406	141	458	653	12.3	3.85	103	.265	.325	-12	19	106	50	31	.981	113	26	147	1.3	1.9	5.9	.2	4.5
STL	41	12	234	30	1388.2	1339	155	546	709	12.3	3.97	95	.257	.327	-30	-28	100	52	26	.978	134	53	157	.1	-2.9	2.7	-.3	-.7
PHI	57	4	212	15	1377.1	1407	172	437	750	12.2	4.20	89	.266	.323	-66	-74	99	63	23	.975	144	23	140	-.6	-7.6	.2	.2	1.7
NY	31	9	263	28	1378.0	1287	144	551	765	12.3	3.78	100	.250	.324	-1	1	100	35	30	.976	144	48	143	-.6	.1	-8.6	.3	-1.3
PIT	37	8	266	24	1376.1	1406	142	469	662	12.4	3.74	101	.267	.327	5	5	100	47	35	.973	162	54	140	-1.5	.5	-6.2	-.6	-3.2
CHI	37	6	220	17	1392.0	1325	161	613	744	12.7	3.96	95	.252	.332	-29	-29	100	59	40	.976	144	41	141	-.4	-3.0	-7.3	-.0	-6.3
TOT	360	67	1804	200	11063.1					12.1	3.77		.256	.321						.977	1082	325	1191					

Batter-Fielder Wins
Aaron-Mil 4.1
Mays-NY 4.1
McMillan-Cin 3.7
Musial-StL 3.6
Snider-Bro 3.2

Batting Average
Aaron-Mil 328
Virdon-StL-Pit 319
Clemente-Pit 311
Musial-StL 310
Boyer-StL 306

On-Base Percentage
Snider-Bro 399
Gilliam-Bro 399
Moon-StL 390
Musial-StL 386
Ashburn-Phi 384

Slugging Average
Snider-Bro 598
Adcock-Mil 597
Aaron-Mil 558
Robinson-Cin 558
Mays-NY 557

On-Base Plus Slugging
Snider-Bro 997
Robinson-Cin 936
Adcock-Mil 934
Mays-NY 926
Aaron-Mil 923

Adjusted OPS
Adcock-Mil 154
Aaron-Mil 154
Snider-Bro 152
Mays-NY 146
Mathews-Mil 146

Adjusted Batter Runs
Snider-Bro 43.3
Aaron-Mil 43.1
Mathews-Mil 37.4
Musial-StL 37.3
Mays-NY 37.0

Runs
Robinson-Cin.........122
Snider-Bro 112
Aaron-Mil 106
Mathews-Mil 103
Gilliam-Bro 102

Hits
Aaron-Mil 200
Ashburn-Phi 190
Virdon-StL-Pit 185
Musial-StL 184
Boyer-StL 182

Doubles
Aaron-Mil 34
Snider-Bro 33
Musial-StL 33
Lopata-Phi 33
Bell-Cin 31

Triples
Bruton-Mil 15
Aaron-Mil 14
Walls-Pit 11
Moon-StL 11
Virdon-StL-Pit 10

Home Runs
Snider-Bro 43
Robinson-Cin 38
Adcock-Mil 38
Mathews-Mil 37

Total Bases
Aaron-Mil 340
Snider-Bro 324
Mays-NY 322
Robinson-Cin 319
Musial-StL 310

Runs Batted In
Musial-StL 109
Adcock-Mil 103
Kluszewski-Cin 102
Snider-Bro 101
Boyer-StL 98

Stolen Bases
Mays-NY 40
Gilliam-Bro 21
White-NY 15
Temple-Cin 14
Reese-Bro 13

Base Stealing Runs
Mays-NY 5.3
Ashburn-Phi 1.9
Temple-Cin 1.7
Gilliam-Bro 1.5
Reese-Bro 1.5

Fielding Runs-Infield
McMillan-Cin 28.5
Robinson-Bro 19.0
Blasingame-StL 16.5
Baker-Chi 13.4
Gilliam-Bro 11.3

Fielding Runs-Outfield
Ashburn-Phi 18.7
King-Chi 11.9
Irvin-Chi 10.0
Moryn-Chi 6.4
Post-Cin 6.3

Wins
Newcombe-Bro 27
Spahn-Mil 20
Antonelli-NY 20

Winning Pct.
Newcombe-Bro......794
Buhl-Mil 692
Lawrence-Cin 655
Burdette-Mil 655
Spahn-Mil 645

Complete Games
Roberts-Phi 22
Spahn-Mil 20
Friend-Pit 19
Newcombe-Bro 18
Burdette-Mil 16

Strikeouts
Jones-Chi 176
Haddix-StL-Phi 170
Friend-Pit 166
Roberts-Phi 157
Mizell-StL 153

Fewest BB/Game
Roberts-Phi 1.21
Newcombe-Bro 1.54
Spahn-Mil 1.66
Fowler-Cin 1.77
Burdette-Mil 1.83

Games
Face-Phi 68
Wilhelm-NY 64
Freeman-Cin 64
Labine-Bro 62
Lown-Chi 61

Saves
Labine-Bro 19
Freeman-Cin 18
Lown-Chi 13
Jackson-StL 9
Bessent-Bro 9

Base Runners/9
Newcombe-Bro......9.00
Spahn-Mil 9.73
Acker-Cin 9.79
Grissom-NY 9.82
Maglie-Bro 9.94

Adjusted Relief Runs
Grissom-NY 20.2
Acker-Cin 14.8
Bessent-Bro 12.9
Labine-Bro 7.4
Freeman-Cin 7.4

Relief Ranking
Freeman-Cin 14.2
Bessent-Bro 13.5
Labine-Bro 12.0
Acker-Cin 11.5
Grissom-NY 10.1

Innings Pitched
Friend-Pit 314.1
Roberts-Phi 297.1
Spahn-Mil 281.1
Newcombe-Bro 268.0
Kline-Pit 264.0

Opponents' Avg.
Newcombe-Bro......221
Jones-Chi 221
Mizell-StL 222
Maglie-Bro 222
Craig-Bro 231

Opponents' OBP
Newcombe-Bro......257
Spahn-Mil 275
Rush-Chi 280
Maglie-Bro 281
Burdette-Mil 281

Earned Run Average
Burdette-Mil 2.70
Spahn-Mil 2.78
Antonelli-NY 2.86
Maglie-Bro 2.87
Newcombe-Bro 3.06

Adjusted ERA
Maglie-Bro 138
Antonelli-NY 132
Newcombe-Bro 130
Burdette-Mil 128
Spahn-Mil 124

Adjusted Starter Runs
Spahn-Mil 28.1
Antonelli-NY 26.1
Newcombe-Bro 25.7
Maglie-Bro 23.1
Burdette-Mil 23.0

Pitcher Wins
Newcombe-Bro......4.1
Spahn-Mil 3.7
Antonelli-NY 3.5
Burdette-Mil 2.6
Dickson-Phi-StL ..1.9

The Last of Flatbush

The Braves streaked to a big lead by Labor Day, but lost five straight to give hope to Brooklyn and Cincinnati (sparked by Rookie of the Year Frank Robinson). While Cincy dropped five straight, and couldn't recover, Brooklyn and Milwaukee juggled the lead until the last weekend. Brooklyn swept three from Pittsburgh at Ebbets Field while the Braves dropped two of three at St. Louis. Don Newcombe of the Dodgers was voted Most Valuable Player as well as winner of the first Cy Young Award, which was only given to one pitcher in the major leagues until 1967.

The Braves had blossoming star Hank Aaron as well as the league's best pitching. The Dodgers countered with Clem Labine, the NL's best reliever, and 19-year-old rookie Don Drysdale, who pitched well. Cincinnati's 3.85 ERA was middle of the pack, but the lineup's 221 homers set the all-time record.

Nineteen-year-old Bill Mazeroski took over at second base for the Pirates, who improved to seventh after four straight years in the basement. The Phillies moved in their center field fence, and Robin Roberts promptly served up 46 homers, setting a mark that lasted three decades.

After winning the first two World Series games, Brooklyn looked to rack up another championship. But it was not to be. Don Larsen's Game 5 perfecto, and a 9-0 Game 7 embarrassment at Ebbets, gave the Yankees yet another title.

The golden era for both New York teams was over. Ralph Branca and Monte Irvin played their final games, and when Walter O'Malley traded Jackie Robinson to the Giants following the Series, Robinson chose to retire. Brooklyn had the league's second-highest attendance in both 1955 and 1956, but the Giants' gate was dropping. The success of the Braves in Milwaukee, and problems getting new facilities built in New York, led O'Malley and Horace Stoneham to consider relocating.

En route to winter ball, Cardinals outfielder Charlie Peete—expected to contend for a starting job in 1957—was killed in an airplane crash.

1956 American League

TEAM	W	L	T	PCT	GB	HW	HL	R	OR	PA	H	2B	3B	HR	BB	SO	HB	SH	AVG	OBP	SLG	OPS	AOPS	BR	ABR	PF	SB	CS	BSA	BSR
NY	97	57	0	.630		49	28	857	631	6075	1433	193	55	190	615	755	30	82	.270	.347	.434	781	115	78	105	97	51	37	58	-2
CLE	88	66	1	.571	9	46	31	712	581	5988	1256	199	23	153	681	764	40	81	.244	.335	.381	716	92	-34	-49	102	40	32	56	-2
CHI	85	69	0	.552	12	46	31	776	634	6122	1412	218	43	128	619	660	75	86	.267	.349	.397	746	101	31	20	101	70	33	68	4
BOS	84	70	1	.545	13	43	34	780	751	6215	1473	261	45	139	727	687	25	68	.275	.362	.419	781	100	106	14	112	28	19	60	-2
DET	82	72	1	.532	15	37	40	789	699	6144	1494	209	50	150	644	618	28	58	.279	.356	.420	776	110	84	82	100	43	26	62	0
BAL	69	85	0	.448	28	41	36	571	705	5790	1242	198	34	91	563	725	22	84	.244	.320	.350	670	89	-125	-78	92	39	42	48	-6
WAS	59	95	1	.383	38	32	45	652	924	6043	1302	198	62	112	690	877	41	75	.250	.341	.377	718	95	-28	-27	100	37	34	52	-4
KC	52	102	0	.338	45	22	55	619	831	5860	1325	204	41	112	480	727	20	67	.252	.315	.370	685	86	-111	-113	100	40	30	57	-2
TOT	618					316	300	5756		48237	10937	1680	353	1075	5019	5813	281	601	.260	.341	.394	735					348	253	58	-12

TEAM	CG	SHO	GR	SV	IP	H	HR	BB	SO	BR/9	ERA	AERA	OAV	OOB	PR	APR	PF	OSB	OCS	FA	E	WPB	DP	FW	PW	BW	BSW	DIF
NY	50	10	181	35	1382.0	1285	114	652	732	12.9	3.63	107	.249	.335	82	40	93	34	32	.977	136	31	214	.6	3.9	10.3	-.0	5.3
CLE	67	17	182	24	1384.0	1233	116	564	845	11.9	3.32	127	.238	.314	129	134	101	51	23	.978	129	41	130	1.0	13.1	-4.8	-.0	1.7
CHI	65	11	196	13	1389.0	1351	118	524	722	12.3	3.73	110	.255	.324	67	59	99	28	21	.979	122	42	160	1.3	5.8	2.0	.5	-1.6
BOS	50	8	178	20	1398.0	1354	130	668	712	13.3	4.17	111	.254	.340	-1	64	111	39	29	.972	169	41	168	-1.2	6.3	1.4	.1	.4
DET	62	10	187	15	1379.0	1389	140	655	788	13.6	4.06	101	.264	.348	15	9	99	32	35	.976	140	40	151	.4	.9	8.0	.1	-4.5
BAL	38	10	231	24	1360.2	1362	99	547	715	12.8	4.20	93	.263	.334	-6	-45	94	58	33	.977	137	40	142	.5	-4.4	-7.6	-.4	4.0
WAS	36	1	244	18	1368.2	1539	171	730	663	15.1	5.33	81	.287	.373	-179	-147	104	55	40	.972	171	50	173	-1.3	-14.4	-2.6	-.2	.6
KC	30	3	251	18	1370.1	1424	187	679	636	14.1	4.86	89	.271	.357	-107	-78	104	51	40	.973	166	57	187	-1.1	-7.6	-11.1	-.0	-5.2
TOT	398	70	1650	167	11031.2					13.2	4.16		.260	.341						.975	1170	342	1325					

Batter-Fielder Wins		Batting Average		On-Base Percentage		Slugging Average		On-Base Plus Slugging		Adjusted OPS		Adjusted Batter Runs	
Mantle-NY	8.1	Mantle-NY	.353	Williams-Bos	.479	Mantle-NY	.705	Mantle-NY	1169	Mantle-NY	213	Mantle-NY	90.0
Berra-NY	4.3	Williams-Bos	.345	Mantle-NY	.464	Williams-Bos	.605	Williams-Bos	1084	Williams-Bos	164	Williams-Bos	43.6
Kaline-Det	3.9	Kuenn-Det	.332	Nieman-Chi-Bal	.436	Maxwell-Det	.534	Minoso-Chi	.950	Nieman-Chi-Bal	156	Minoso-Chi	42.5
McDougald-NY	3.5	Maxwell-Det	.326	Minoso-Chi	.425	Berra-NY	.534	Maxwell-Det	.948	Maxwell-Det	150	Maxwell-Det	40.0
Maxwell-Det	3.4	Nieman-Chi-Bal	.320	Maxwell-Det	.414	Kaline-Det	.530	Nieman-Chi-Bal	.931	Minoso-Chi	149	Maxwell-Det	37.5

Runs		Hits		Doubles		Triples		Home Runs		Total Bases		Runs Batted In	
Mantle-NY	132	Kuenn-Det	196	Piersall-Bos	40	Simpson-KC	11	Mantle-NY	52	Mantle-NY	376	Mantle-NY	130
Fox-Chi	109	Kaline-Det	194	Kuenn-Det	32	Minoso-Chi	11	Wertz-Cle	32	Kaline-Det	327	Kaline-Det	128
Minoso-Chi	106	Fox-Chi	192	Kaline-Det	32	Lemon-Was	11	Berra-NY	30	Jensen-Bos	287	Wertz-Cle	106
		Mantle-NY	188			Jensen-Bos	11	Sievers-Was	29	Minoso-Chi	286	Simpson-KC	105
		Jensen-Bos	182					Maxwell-Det	28			Berra-NY	105

Stolen Bases		Base Stealing Runs		Fielding Runs-Infield		Fielding Runs-Outfield		Wins		Winning Pct.		Complete Games	
Aparicio-Chi	21	Aparicio-Chi	3.2	McDougald-NY	8.8	Kaline-Det	12.2	Lary-Det	21	Ford-NY	.760	Pierce-Chi	21
Rivera-Chi	20	Avila-Cle	2.3	DeMaestri-KC	8.8	Piersall-Bos	7.3			Wynn-Cle	.690	Lemon-Cle	21
Avila-Cle	17	Mantle-NY	1.9	Yost-Was	8.3	Maxwell-Det	6.4			Score-Cle	.690	Lary-Det	20
Minoso-Chi	12	Jensen-Bos	1.4	Power-KC	7.8	Lemon-Was	4.2			Pierce-Chi	.690		
		Pilarcik-KC	1.3	Buddin-Bos	6.9	Stephens-Bos	3.5			Brewer-Bos	.679		

Strikeouts		Fewest BB/Game		Games		Saves		Base Runners/9		Adjusted Relief Runs		Relief Ranking	
Score-Cle	263	Stobbs-Was	2.03	Zuverink-Bal	62	Zuverink-Bal	16	Score-Cle	10.58	Narleski-Cle	17.7	Narleski-Cle	16.1
Pierce-Chi	192	Donovan-Chi	2.26	Crimian-KC	54	Mossi-Cle	11	Donovan-Chi	10.62	Grim-NY	9.3	Delock-Bos	11.1
Foytack-Det	184	Kucks-NY	2.89	Gorman-KC	52	Morgan-NY	11	Wynn-Cle	10.66	Byerly-Was	7.7	Mossi-Cle	9.4
Hoeft-Det	172	Wynn-Cle	2.95	Mossi-Cle	48	Shantz-KC	9	Brown-Bal	10.68	Delock-Bos	7.1	Byerly-Was	9.4
Lary-Det	165	Sturdivant-NY	2.96	Delock-Bos	48	Delock-Bos	9	Sturdivant-NY	10.80	Mossi-Cle	6.7	Grim-NY	9.3

Innings Pitched		Opponents' Avg.		Opponents' OBP		Earned Run Average		Adjusted ERA		Adjusted Starter Runs		Pitcher Wins	
Lary-Det	294.0	Score-Cle	.186	Donovan-Chi	.290	Ford-NY	2.47	Score-Cle	166	Wynn-Cle	46.3	Wynn-Cle	5.1
Wynn-Cle	277.2	Larsen-NY	.204	Score-Cle	.290	Score-Cle	2.53	Ford-NY	156	Score-Cle	44.9	Score-Cle	4.9
Pierce-Chi	276.1	Brewer-Bos	.220	Wynn-Cle	.291	Wynn-Cle	2.72	Wynn-Cle	154	Ford-NY	37.7	Lemon-Cle	4.6
Foytack-Det	256.0	Harshman-Chi	.221	Sturdivant-NY	.291	Lemon-Cle	3.03	Lemon-Cle	139	Lary-Det	31.7	Ford-NY	4.6
Lemon-Cle	255.1	Sturdivant-NY	.224	Ford-NY	.301	Harshman-Chi	3.10	Sullivan-Bos	135	Lemon-Cle	30.7	Brewer-Bos	3.9

His Favorite Year

Mickey Mantle had perhaps his greatest season, winning the Triple Crown and MVP honors, as the Yankees won another flag. Yogi Berra, Moose Skowron, and Gil McDougald contributed significantly on offense, and Whitey Ford captured the ERA title. These are the Yankees that people remember, with Mantle doing it all, Elston Howard and Joe Collins platooning, hard-nosed Hank Bauer in right field, Billy Martin at second, and otherwise undistinguished pitchers like Johnny Kucks, Don Larsen, and Tom Sturdivant enjoying their greatest moments.

The second-place Indians again had a trio of 20-game winners, but their offense had declined sharply. The race was never close. Third-place Chicago added shortstop Luis Aparicio, whose speed and defense garnered him Rookie of the Year honors.

For the first time, AL homers rose over 1,000; every team had a slow-footed slugger or two. Jim Lemon of the Senators whiffed 138 times to set a new record, while his teammate, Eddie Yost, collected 151 walks.

Orioles catcher Tom Gastall died September 20 in a private plane crash. Beloved A's owner-manager Connie Mack passed away at age 93; Mack's longtime lieutenant, Al Simmons, died three months later of a heart attack. Injured Al Rosen and aging Bob Feller retired from the Indians, and down the pennant stretch, the Yankees released Phil Rizzuto. The Scooter would start a forty-season run in the broadcast booth the following spring.

It didn't look like a great World Series for the Yankees, however, as they lost the first two at Ebbets Field. However, after New York tied things up with Ford and Sturdivant tossing complete-game victories, Don Larsen threw a perfect game at Brooklyn in Game 5, fanning Dale Mitchell for the last out. Clem Labine blanked the Yankees in Game 6, but Kucks breezed to a 9-0 win to give the Bronx its sixth championship in eight years. And after 13 "Subway Series" between New York's three teams since 1921—the Yankees winning 10 times—this would be the last of its kind until 2000.

1955 National League

TEAM	W	L	T	PCT	GB	HW	HL	R	OR	PA	H	2B	3B	HR	BB	SO	HB	SH	AVG	OBP	SLG	OPS	AOPS	BR	ABR	PF	SB	CS	BSA	BSR
BRO	98	55	1	.641		56	21	857	650	6037	1406	230	44	201	674	718	41	75	.271	.356	.448	804	115	147	124	103	79	56	59	-2
MIL	85	69	0	.552	13.5	46	31	743	668	5920	1377	219	55	182	504	735	28	72	.261	.326	.427	753	109	26	64	95	42	27	61	0
NY	80	74	0	.519	18.5	44	35	702	673	5940	1377	173	34	169	497	581	36	69	.260	.325	.402	727	97	-17	-18	100	38	22	63	1
PHI	77	77	0	.500	21.5	46	31	675	666	5864	1300	214	50	132	652	673	24	53	.255	.340	.395	735	102	16	29	98	44	32	58	-2
CIN	75	79	0	.487	23.5	46	31	761	684	5978	1424	216	28	181	556	657	33	76	.270	.341	.425	766	102	65	23	106	51	36	59	-1
CHI	72	81	1	.471	26	43	33	626	713	5766	1287	187	55	164	428	806	22	69	.247	.305	.398	703	90	-79	-77	100	37	35	51	-4
STL	68	86	0	.442	30.5	41	36	654	757	5855	1375	228	36	143	458	597	31	56	.261	.321	.400	721	95	-30	-29	100	64	59	52	-7
PIT	60	94	0	.390	38.5	36	39	560	767	5790	1262	210	60	91	471	652	21	93	.244	.308	.361	669	83	-129	-121	99	22	22	50	-3
TOT	616					358	257	5578		47150	10808	1677	362	1263	4240	5419	236	563	.259	.328	.407	735				377	289	57	-18

TEAM	CG	SHO	GR	SV	IP	H	HR	BB	SO	BR/9	ERA	AERA	OAV	OOB	PR	APR	PF	OSB	OCS	FA	E	WPB	DP	FW	PW	BW	BSW	DIF
BRO	46	11	209	37	1378.0	1296	168	483	773	11.7	3.68	110	.248	.313	54	58	101	36	24	.978	133	40	156	.5	5.8	12.3	.0	2.9
MIL	61	5	203	12	1383.0	1339	138	591	654	12.7	3.85	98	.256	.331	29	-15	93	38	45	.975	152	40	155	-1.5	6.4	.2		3.5
NY	52	6	246	14	1386.2	1347	155	560	721	12.7	3.77	107	.257	.332	41	39	100	42	37	.976	142	42	165	-.6	3.9	-1.8	.3	.6
PHI	58	11	193	21	1356.2	1291	161	477	657	11.9	3.93	101	.251	.315	17	6	98	43	29	.981	110	46	117	1.8	.6	2.9	.0	-5.3
CIN	38	12	245	22	1363.0	1373	161	443	576	12.1	3.95	107	.264	.322	13	41	105	37	28	.977	139	38	169	.2	4.1	2.3	.1	-8.6
CHI	47	10	209	23	1378.1	1306	153	601	686	12.6	4.17	98	.251	.330	-21	-13	101	73	42	.975	147	52	147	-.3	-1.3	-7.6	-.2	4.9
STL	42	10	209	15	1376.2	1376	185	549	730	12.9	4.56	89	.262	.334	-80	-76	101	42	35	.975	146	45	152	-.2	-7.5	-2.9	-.5	2.1
PIT	41	5	199	16	1362.0	1480	142	536	622	13.5	4.39	94	.281	.347	-54	-41	102	66	49	.972	166	49	175	-1.4	-4.1	-12.0	-.0	.5
TOT	385	70	1778	160	10984.1					12.5	4.04		.259	.328						.976	1135	352	1236					.5

Batter-Fielder Wins
- Mays-NY 6.8
- Banks-Chi 5.1
- Mathews-Mil 4.9
- Snider-Bro 4.5
- Musial-StL 4.5

Batting Average
- Ashburn-Phi .... .338
- Mays-NY .... .319
- Musial-StL .... .319
- Campanella-Bro .... .318
- Aaron-Mil .... .314

On-Base Percentage
- Ashburn-Phi .... .449
- Snider-Bro .... .418
- Mathews-Mil .... .413
- Musial-StL .... .408
- Mays-NY .... .400

Slugging Average
- Mays-NY .... .659
- Snider-Bro .... .628
- Mathews-Mil .... .601
- Banks-Chi .... .596
- Kluszewski-Cin .... .585

On-Base Plus Slugging
- Mays-NY 1059
- Snider-Bro 1046
- Mathews-Mil 1014
- Campanella-Bro .... .978
- Musial-StL .... .974

Adjusted OPS
- Mays-NY 176
- Mathews-Mil 175
- Snider-Bro 169
- Musial-StL 156
- Campanella-Bro 153

Adjusted Batter Runs
- Mays-NY 61.6
- Mathews-Mil 57.8
- Snider-Bro 57.0
- Musial-StL 47.7
- Ashburn-Phi 40.5

Runs
- Snider-Bro 126
- Mays-NY 123
- Post-Cin 116
- Kluszewski-Cin 116
- Gilliam-Bro 110

Hits
- Kluszewski-Cin 192
- Aaron-Mil 189
- Bell-Cin 188
- Post-Cin 186

Doubles
- Logan-Mil 37
- Aaron-Mil 37
- Snider-Bro 34
- Post-Cin 33
- Ashburn-Phi 32

Triples
- Mays-NY 13
- Long-Pit 13
- Bruton-Mil 12
- Clemente-Pit 11

Home Runs
- Mays-NY 51
- Kluszewski-Cin 47
- Banks-Chi 44
- Snider-Bro 42
- Mathews-Mil 41

Total Bases
- Mays-NY 382
- Kluszewski-Cin 358
- Banks-Chi 355
- Post-Cin 345
- Snider-Bro 338

Runs Batted In
- Snider-Bro 136
- Mays-NY 127
- Ennis-Phi 120
- Banks-Chi 117
- Kluszewski-Cin 113

Stolen Bases
- Bruton-Mil 25
- Mays-NY 24
- Boyer-StL 22
- Temple-Cin 19
- Gilliam-Bro 15

Base Stealing Runs
- Mays-NY 3.9
- Temple-Cin 2.8
- Bruton-Mil 1.7
- Robinson-Bro 1.6
- Blaylock-Phi 1.0

Fielding Runs-Infield
- McMillan-Cin 17.9
- Groat-Pit 16.7
- O'Connell-Mil 14.3
- Robinson-Bro 11.0
- Musial-StL 8.3

Fielding Runs-Outfield
- Mays-NY 11.7
- Clemente-Pit 10.8
- Bruton-Mil 8.7
- King-Chi 6.5
- Greengrass-Cin-Phi 5.8

Wins
- Roberts-Phi 23
- Newcombe-Bro 20
- Spahn-Mil 17
- Nuxhall-Cin 17

Winning Pct.
- Newcombe-Bro .... .800
- Roberts-Phi .... .622
- Nuxhall-Cin .... .586
- Spahn-Mil .... .548

Complete Games
- Roberts-Phi 26
- Newcombe-Bro 17
- Spahn-Mil 16

Strikeouts
- Jones-Chi 198
- Roberts-Phi 160
- Haddix-StL 150
- Newcombe-Bro 143
- Antonelli-NY 143

Fewest BB/Game
- Newcombe-Bro 1.46
- Roberts-Phi 1.56
- Hacker-Chi 1.82
- Friend-Pit 2.34
- Spahn-Mil 2.38

Games
- Labine-Bro 60
- Wilhelm-NY 59
- LaPalme-StL 56
- Grissom-NY 55
- Freeman-Cin 52

Saves
- Meyer-Phi 16
- Roebuck-Bro 12
- Labine-Bro 11
- Freeman-Cin 11
- Grissom-NY 8

Base Runners/9
- Rogovin-Phi 9.49
- Newcombe-Bro 10.05
- Crone-Mil 10.20
- Bessent-Bro 10.23
- Roberts-Phi 10.24

Adjusted Relief Runs
- Freeman-Cin 17.7
- Miller-Phi 16.3
- Labine-Bro 12.6
- Bessent-Bro 10.8
- LaPalme-StL 10.7

Relief Ranking
- Freeman-Cin 23.9
- Miller-Phi 20.0
- Labine-Bro 16.3
- Bessent-Bro 14.9
- Jeffcoat-Chi 11.8

Innings Pitched
- Roberts-Phi 305.0
- Nuxhall-Cin 257.0
- Spahn-Mil 245.2
- Jones-Chi 241.2
- Antonelli-NY 235.1

Opponents' Avg.
- Jones-Chi .... .206
- Buhl-Mil .... .227
- Rush-Chi .... .234
- Antonelli-NY .... .234
- Dickson-Phi .... .238

Opponents' OBP
- Newcombe-Bro .... .279
- Roberts-Phi .... .279
- Hacker-Chi .... .282
- Friend-Pit .... .291
- Rush-Chi .... .293

Earned Run Average
- Friend-Pit 2.83
- Newcombe-Bro 3.20
- Buhl-Mil 3.21
- Spahn-Mil 3.26
- Roberts-Phi 3.28

Adjusted ERA
- Friend-Pit 145
- Newcombe-Bro 127
- Nuxhall-Cin 122
- Roberts-Phi 121
- Antonelli-NY 121

Adjusted Starter Runs
- Friend-Pit 24.9
- Nuxhall-Cin 23.1
- Schmidt-StL 20.0
- Newcombe-Bro 19.2
- Roberts-Phi 18.4

Pitcher Wins
- Newcombe-Bro 4.0
- Roberts-Phi 3.4
- Nuxhall-Cin 2.8
- Friend-Pit 2.7
- Freeman-Cin 2.5

Is It Next Year Already?

There was no pennant race in 1955 as the Dodgers, 22-2 on May 10, cruised to an easy title over Milwaukee and New York. For the victorious Dodgers, Roy Campanella won his third MVP trophy, while 19-year-old lefty Sandy Koufax made his major league debut for his hometown team. Brooklyn's pitching was superb, especially considering the bandbox that was Ebbets Field.

The league saw another all-time high in homers in 1955; this was the only season until 1999 in which teams hit more than one per game. The uppercut era was in full "swing"—strikeouts rose and did so until 1960. Philadelphia's Robin Roberts illustrated the era: for the fourth straight year he led the NL in wins and also allowed a major league record 41 homers.

The Cardinals finished seventh but showcased promising youngsters Ken Boyer and Lindy McDaniel. Phil Cavaretta and Ralph Kiner ended their storied careers. Attendance fell for the seventh straight year in Pittsburgh, but the Pirates added rookie outfielder Roberto Clemente. And as a new icon came to Steeltown, a past one left: the beloved Honus Wagner died at age 81.

The 1955 World Series offered a surprise ending for people who had become accustomed to the Yankees-Dodgers plots of 1941, '47, '49, '52, and '53. It started familiarly with the Yankees winning the first two games at home, just as they had done when the teams last met. Brooklyn, though, came back to take the next three at home, blowing apart New York pitching. For Game 6 Dodgers manager Walter Alston used his sixth starting pitcher of the series, but Karl Spooner didn't finish the first as the Yankees won, 5-1.

The Dodgers, who had twice lost seventh games to the Yanks in the past, sent Johnny Podres against Whitey Ford in the finale. Gil Hodges drove in runs in the fourth and sixth, and Sandy Amoros' great running catch snuffed out a sixth-inning Yankees rally. Podres went all the way for the 2-0 win that finally brought "next year" to Flatbush.

1955 American League

TEAM	W	L	T	PCT	GB	HW	HL	R	OR	PA	H	2B	3B	HR	BB	SO	HB	SH	AVG	OBP	SLG	OPS	AOPS	BR	ABR	PF	SB	CS	BSA	BSR
NY	96	58	0	.623		52	25	762	569	5944	1342	179	55	175	609	658	46	79	.260	.340	.418	758	112	70	82	98	55	25	69	3
CLE	93	61	0	.604	3	49	28	698	601	6050	1325	195	31	148	723	715	35	87	.257	.349	.394	743	102	63	36	104	28	24	54	-2
CHI	91	63	1	.591	5	49	28	725	557	5999	1401	204	36	116	567	595	58	111	.268	.344	.388	732	100	32	12	103	69	45	61	0
BOS	84	70	0	.545	12	47	31	755	652	6131	1392	241	39	137	707	733	29	69	.264	.351	.402	753	100	83	18	109	43	17	72	4
DET	79	75	0	.513	17	46	31	775	658	6073	1407	211	38	130	641	583	21	71	.266	.345	.394	739	107	48	66	98	41	22	65	1
KC	63	91	1	.409	33	33	43	638	911	5916	1395	189	46	121	463	725	26	58	.261	.322	.382	704	94	-44	-51	101	22	36	38	-8
BAL	57	97	2	.370	39	30	47	540	754	5933	1263	177	39	54	560	742	19	70	.240	.314	.320	634	83	-162	-123	93	34	46	43	-6
WAS	53	101	0	.344	43	28	49	598	789	5833	1277	178	54	80	538	654	36	79	.248	.322	.351	673	92	-89	-56	95	25	32	44	-6
TOT	618					334	282	5491		47879	10802	1574	338	961	4808	5405	270	624	.258	.336	.381	717		317	247		56			-17

TEAM	CG	SHO	GR	SV	IP	H	HR	BB	SO	BR/9	ERA	AERA	OAV	OOB	PR	APR	PF	OSB	OCS	FA	E	WPB	DP	FW	PW	BW	BSW	DIF
NY	52	19	190	33	1372.1	1163	108	688	731	12.3	3.23	116	.232	.326	111	82	95	27	25	.978	128	31	180	.5	8.2	8.2	.5	1.6
CLE	45	15	215	36	1386.1	1285	111	558	877	12.1	3.39	118	.245	.319	88	92	101	36	28	.981	108	48	152	1.7	9.2	3.6	.0	1.5
CHI	55	20	202	23	1378.0	1301	111	497	720	11.9	3.37	117	.251	.329	90	89	100	30	23	.981	111	25	147	1.5	8.9	1.2	.1	2.2
BOS	44	9	187	34	1384.1	1333	128	582	674	12.7	3.72	115	.253	.329	37	81	104	47	34	.977	136	34	140	.0	8.1	1.8	.6	-3.5
DET	66	16	185	12	1380.1	1381	126	517	629	12.6	3.79	101	.261	.328	26	8	97	40	36	.976	139	38	159	-.2	.8	6.6	.3	-5.6
KC	29	9	255	23	1382.0	1486	175	707	572	14.6	5.35	78	.278	.363	-214	-172	105	36	23	.976	146	50	174	-.5	-17.2	-5.1	-.6	9.5
BAL	35	10	235	22	1388.2	1403	103	625	595	13.4	4.21	91	.266	.344	-39	-64	96	53	38	.972	167	64	159	-1.7	-6.4	-12.3	-.7	1.1
WAS	37	10	229	16	1354.2	1450	99	634	607	14.2	4.62	83	.279	.359	-100	-124	97	48	40	.974	154	45	170	-1.0	-12.4	-5.6	-.4	-4.5
TOT	363	108	1698	199	11026.2					13.0	3.96		.258	.336						.977	1089	335	1281					

Batter-Fielder Wins	Batting Average	On-Base Percentage	Slugging Average	On-Base Plus Slugging	Adjusted OPS	Adjusted Batter Runs
Mantle-NY 5.5	Kaline-Det 340	Mantle-NY 431	Mantle-NY 611	Mantle-NY 1042	Mantle-NY 181	Mantle-NY 62.2
Kaline-Det 4.9	Power-KC 319	Kaline-Det 421	Kaline-Det 546	Kaline-Det 967	Kaline-Det 163	Kaline-Det 53.6
Fox-Chi 4.4	Kell-Chi 312	Smith-Cle 407	Zernial-KC 508	Smith-Cle 880	Sievers-Was 136	Williams-Bos 52.2
Williams-Bos 4.3	Fox-Chi 311	Yost-Was 407	Doby-Cle 505	Doby-Cle 874	Vernon-Was 133	Smith-Cle 31.6
McDougald-NY 3.7	Kuenn-Det 306	Goodman-Bos 394	Power-KC 505	Power-KC 859	Smith-Cle 132	Vernon-Was 25.7

Runs	Hits	Doubles	Triples	Home Runs	Total Bases	Runs Batted In
Smith-Cle 123	Kaline-Det 200	Kuenn-Det 38	Mantle-NY 11	Mantle-NY 37	Kaline-Det 321	Jensen-Bos 116
Mantle-NY 121	Fox-Chi 198	Power-KC 34	Carey-NY 11	Zernial-KC 30	Mantle-NY 316	Boone-Det 116
Kaline-Det 121	Power-KC 190	Goodman-Bos 31	Power-KC 10	Williams-Bos 28	Power-KC 301	Berra-NY 108
Tuttle-Det 102	Kuenn-Det 190	White-Bos 30			Smith-Cle 287	Sievers-Was 106
Kuenn-Det 101	Smith-Cle 186	Finigan-KC 30			Jensen-Bos 275	Kaline-Det 102

Stolen Bases	Base Stealing Runs	Fielding Runs-Infield	Fielding Runs-Outfield	Wins	Winning Pct.	Complete Games
Rivera-Chi 25	Torgeson-Det 2.0	Fox-Chi 31.1	Rivera-Chi 11.4	F.Sullivan-Bos 18	Byrne-NY 762	Ford-NY 18
Minoso-Chi 19	Busby-Was-Chi 1.6	McDougald-NY 22.3	Minoso-Chi 5.6	Lemon-Cle 18	Ford-NY 720	Hoeft-Det 17
Jensen-Bos 16	Mantle-NY 1.4	Miranda-Bal 20.3	Zernial-KC 5.1	Ford-NY 18	Hoeft-Det 696	
Busby-Was-Chi 12	Minoso-Chi 1.4	Power-KC 14.2	Bauer-NY 5.1	Wynn-Cle 17	Lemon-Cle 643	
Smith-Cle 11	Klaus-Bos 1.3	Carey-NY 10.2	Tuttle-Det 4.8	Turley-NY 17	Donovan-Chi 625	

Strikeouts	Fewest BB/Game	Games	Saves	Base Runners/9	Adjusted Relief Runs	Relief Ranking
Score-Cle 245	Gromek-Cle 1.84	Narleski-Cle 60	Narleski-Cle 19	Kinder-Bos 9.85	Consuegra-Chi 17.5	Kinder-Bos 21.0
Turley-NY 210	Donovan-Chi 2.31	Mossi-Cle 57	Kinder-Bos 18	Consuegra-Chi 9.97	Kiely-Bos 14.1	Hurd-Bos 17.1
Pierce-Chi 157	Garcia-Cle 2.39	Gorman-KC 57	Gorman-KC 18	Pierce-Chi 10.02	Mossi-Cle 12.9	Consuegra-Chi 15.9
Ford-NY 137	Garver-Det 2.61	Dorish-Chi-Bal 48	Konstanty-NY 11	Ford-NY 10.71	Kinder-Bos 10.7	Konstanty-NY 13.7
Hoeft-Det 133	Porterfield-Was 2.73	Moore-Bal 46	Morgan-NY 10	Hoeft-Det 10.96	Dorish-Chi-Bal 10.1	Mossi-Cle 13.2

Innings Pitched	Opponents' Avg.	Opponents' OBP	Earned Run Average	Adjusted ERA	Adjusted Starter Runs	Pitcher Wins
F.Sullivan-Bos 260.0	Turley-NY 193	Pierce-Chi 277	Pierce-Chi 1.97	Pierce-Chi 201	Pierce-Chi 44.7	**Pierce-Chi** 5.3
Ford-NY 253.2	Score-Cle 194	Ford-NY 296	Ford-NY 2.63	Ford-NY 148	Ford-NY 34.4	**Ford-NY** 3.4
Turley-NY 246.2	Ford-NY 208	Hoeft-Det 296	Wynn-Cle 2.82	F.Sullivan-Bos 143	F.Sullivan-Bos 33.9	**F.Sullivan-Bos** 3.3
Wilson-Bal 235.1	Pierce-Chi 213	Wilson-Chi 297	Score-Cle 2.85	Wynn-Cle 142	Wynn-Cle 28.4	**Wynn-Cle** 3.3
Lary-Det 235.0	Harshman-Chi 224	Wynn-Cle 304	F.Sullivan-Bos 2.91	Score-Cle 140	Score-Cle 27.6	**Hoeft-Det** 2.7

Pinstripe Changes

Cleveland, the Yankees, the White Sox, and the Red Sox were bunched together by late August. The standings changed almost hourly from August 25 to September 5. Boston and Chicago dropped out after Labor Day, but the Indians got hot and the Yankees hung tough. With the race in hand, Cleveland promptly lost five straight, including three to fifth-place Detroit while the New York swept Boston, starting a nine-game winning streak. The Yankees clinched on September 23.

The Yankees again had spectacular pitching, with seven men making 10 or more starts. Mickey Mantle was the league's top hitter. Injuries and age began to erode Cleveland's lineup and pitching staff, and the club didn't recover. As Yogi Berra won his third MVP, his eventual successor, Elston Howard, was the Yankees' first African American player. Other rookies on the scene included Jim Bunning, Rocky Colavito, and 18-year-old Brooks Robinson. The most impressive freshman, Cleveland's fireballing Herb Score, set a record, fanning 9.70 hitters per game.

Boston first baseman Harry Agganis passed away on June 27 of a heart problem, sending the Hub into mourning. The great Cy Young, who threw the first pitch in the modern World Series as well as seemingly every other pitch from 1890–1911, died at 88. Three outstanding pitchers appeared in their final games: Hal Newhouser, Vic Raschi, and Johnny Sain.

Al Kaline of the Tigers became the youngest batting champion in history, while the sixth-place Athletics, in their first season in Kansas City, ranked second in attendance. Complete games fell by 100 to an all-time low, while saves rose to a new high; for the first time, the complete games leader, Whitey Ford, had fewer than 20.

Ford won Game 6 of the World Series with a nine-inning performance, but for the first time since 1942, the Yankees lost a Series. The Brooklyn Dodgers won their first title with a 2-0 Game 7 victory at Yankee Stadium.

1954 National League

TEAM	W	L	T	PCT	GB	HW	HL	R	OR	PA	H	2B	3B	HR	BB	SO	HB	SH	AVG	OBP	SLG	OPS	AOPS	BR	ABR	PF	SB	CS	BSA	BSR
NY	97	57	0	.630		53	23	732	550	5936	1386	194	42	186	522	561	33	84	.264	.332	.424	756	101	15	11	101	30	23	57	-1
BRO	92	62	0	.597	5	45	32	778	740	6058	1418	246	56	186	634	625	35	79	.270	.349	.444	793	109	103	78	103	46	39	54	-4
MIL	89	65	0	.578	8	43	34	670	556	5921	1395	217	41	139	471	619	35	110	.265	.327	.401	728	102	-34	12	94	54	31	64	1
PHI	75	79	0	.487	22	39	39	659	614	5937	1384	243	58	102	604	620	10	84	.267	.341	.395	736	98	0	1	100	30	27	53	-3
CIN	74	80	0	.481	23	41	36	729	763	5972	1369	221	46	147	557	645	29	101	.262	.333	.406	739	95	-8	-27	103	30	30	61	0
STL	72	82	0	.468	25	33	44	799	790	6127	1518	285	58	119	582	586	30	84	.281	.350	.421	771	106	69	63	101	63	46	58	-2
CHI	64	90	0	.416	33	40	37	700	766	5965	1412	229	45	159	478	693	32	56	.263	.325	.412	737	96	-22	-29	101	46	31	60	-1
PIT	53	101	0	.344	44	31	46	557	845	5836	1260	181	57	76	566	737	25	99	.248	.323	.350	673	82	-122	-113	99	21	13	62	0
TOT	616					325	291	5624		47752	11142	1816	403	1114	4414	5086	229	657	.265	.335	.407	742					337	240	58	-10

TEAM	CG	SHO	GR	SV	IP	H	HR	BB	SO	BR/9	ERA	AERA	OAV	OOB	PR	APR	PF	OSB	OCS	FA	E	WPB	DP	FW	PW	BW	BSW	DIF
NY	45	19	235	33	1390.0	1258	113	613	692	12.3	3.09	130	.243	.326	151	147	99	29	31	.975	154	38	172	-.5	14.6	1.1	.0	4.9
BRO	39	8	231	36	1393.2	1399	164	533	762	12.6	4.31	95	.261	.328	-36	-34	100	28	29	.978	129	32	138	.8	-3.4	7.7	-.3	10.1
MIL	63	13	193	21	1394.2	1296	106	553	698	12.1	3.19	117	.250	.323	137	91	92	42	32	.981	116	33	171	1.5	9.0	1.2	.2	.0
PHI	78	14	139	12	1365.1	1329	133	450	570	11.8	3.59	112	.256	.315	73	68	99	37	21	.975	145	29	133	-.0	-6.7	.0	-.2	-8.6
CIN	34	8	235	27	1367.1	1491	169	547	537	13.6	4.50	93	.282	.351	-65	-45	103	24	31	.977	137	33	194	.4	-4.5	-2.7	.1	3.6
STL	40	11	262	18	1390.1	1484	170	535	680	13.4	4.50	91	.275	.343	-66	-59	101	27	24	.976	146	43	178	-.0	-5.8	6.2	-.0	-5.2
CHI	41	6	210	19	1374.1	1375	131	619	622	13.2	4.51	93	.264	.340	-66	-45	103	71	31	.974	154	49	164	-.5	-4.5	-2.9	.0	-5.2
PIT	37	4	195	15	1346.0	1510	128	564	525	14.0	4.92	85	.287	.354	-127	-106	103	79	41	.971	173	46	136	-1.6	-10.5	-11.2	.1	-.9
TOT	377	83	1700	181	11021.2					12.9	4.07		.265	.335						.976	1154	303	1286					

Batter-Fielder Wins		Batting Average		On-Base Percentage		Slugging Average		On-Base Plus Slugging		Adjusted OPS		Adjusted Batter Runs	
Mays-NY	6.2	Mays-NY	.345	Ashburn-Phi	.441	Mays-NY	.667	Mays-NY	1078	Mathews-Mil	177	Snider-Bro	61.5
Mathews-Mil	5.4	Mueller-NY	.342	Musial-StL	.428	Snider-Bro	.647	Snider-Bro	1071	Mays-NY	176	Mays-NY	61.4
Musial-StL	4.7	Snider-Bro	.341	Snider-Bro	.423	Kluszewski-Cin	.642	Kluszewski-Cin	1049	Snider-Bro	170	Musial-StL	61.4
Schoendienst-StL	4.5	Musial-StL	.330	Mathews-Mil	.423	Musial-StL	.607	Musial-StL	1036	Musial-StL	166	Mathews-Mil	58.3
Snider-Bro	4.3	Kluszewski-Cin	.326	Mays-NY	.411	Mathews-Mil	.603	Mathews-Mil	1026	Kluszewski-Cin	165	Kluszewski-Cin	54.3

Runs		Hits		Doubles		Triples		Home Runs		Total Bases		Runs Batted In	
Snider-Bro	120	Mueller-NY	212	Musial-StL	41	Mays-NY	13	Kluszewski-Cin	49	Snider-Bro	378	Kluszewski-Cin	141
Musial-StL	120	Snider-Bro	199	Snider-Bro	39	Hamner-Phi	11	Hodges-Bro	42	Mays-NY	377	Snider-Bro	130
Mays-NY	119	Musial-StL	195	Repulski-StL	39	Snider-Bro	10	Sauer-Chi	41	Kluszewski-Cin	368	Hodges-Bro	130
Ashburn-Phi	111	Mays-NY	195	Hamner-Phi	39			Mays-NY	41	Musial-StL	359	Musial-StL	126
Gilliam-Bro	107	Moon-StL	193							Hodges-Bro	335	Ennis-Phi	119

Stolen Bases		Base Stealing Runs		Fielding Runs-Infield		Fielding Runs-Outfield		Wins		Winning Pct.		Complete Games	
Bruton-Mil	34	Bruton-Mil	2.9	Schoendienst-StL	27.7	Ashburn-Phi	13.2	Roberts-Phi	23	Antonelli-NY	.750	Roberts-Phi	29
Temple-Cin	21	Fondy-Chi	2.7	Grammas-StL	22.2	Mays-NY	9.5	Spahn-Mil	21	Lawrence-StL	.714	Spahn-Mil	23
Fondy-Chi	20	Temple-Cin	2.2	Logan-Mil	12.6	Thomas-Pit	7.2	Antonelli-NY	21	Gomez-NY	.654	Simmons-Phi	21
Moon-StL	18	Torgeson-Phi	1.2	Fondy-Chi	8.4	Furillo-Bro	4.0	Haddix-StL	18	Spahn-Mil	.636	Antonelli-NY	18
Ashburn-Phi	11	Mathews-Mil	1.1	Hodges-Bro	6.8	Gordon-Pit	3.1	Erskine-Bro	18	Roberts-Phi	.605		

Strikeouts		Fewest BB/Game		Games		Saves		Base Runners/9		Adjusted Relief Runs		Relief Ranking	
Roberts-Phi	185	Roberts-Phi	1.50	Hughes-Bro	60	Hughes-Bro	24	Roberts-Phi	9.36	Wilhelm-NY	23.2	Grissom-NY	36.8
Haddix-StL	184	Minner-Chi	2.06	Hetki-Pit	58	Smith-Cin	20	Johnson-Mil	10.15	Grissom-NY	23.0	Wilhelm-NY	33.3
Erskine-Bro	166	Hacker-Chi	2.10	Brazle-StL	58	Grissom-NY	19	Smith-Cin	10.22	Jolly-Mil	16.5	Jolly-Mil	26.0
Antonelli-NY	152	Burdette-Mil	2.34	Wilhelm-NY	57	Jolly-Mil	10	Poholsky-StL	10.61	Smith-Cin	12.4	Smith-Cin	24.8
Spahn-Mil	136	Meyer-Bro	2.45	Grissom-NY	56	Hetki-Pit	9	Antonelli-NY	10.72	Johnson-Mil	11.5	Hughes-Bro	14.2

Innings Pitched		Opponents' Avg.		Opponents' OBP		Earned Run Average		Adjusted ERA		Adjusted Starter Runs		Pitcher Wins	
Roberts-Phi	336.2	Antonelli-NY	.219	Roberts-Phi	.266	Antonelli-NY	2.30	Antonelli-NY	176	Antonelli-NY	49.5	Antonelli-NY	5.3
Spahn-Mil	283.1	Roberts-Phi	.231	Antonelli-NY	.292	Burdette-Mil	2.76	Simmons-Phi	144	Roberts-Phi	44.5	Roberts-Phi	4.3
Erskine-Bro	260.1	Simmons-Phi	.239	Hacker-Chi	.299	Simmons-Phi	2.81	Gomez-NY	140	Simmons-Phi	29.5	Grissom-NY	3.7
Haddix-StL	259.2	Littlefield-Pit	.239	Spahn-Mil	.300	Gomez-NY	2.88	Roberts-Phi	136	Gomez-NY	27.2	Wilhelm-NY	3.2
Antonelli-NY	258.2	Wehmeier-Cin-Phi	.239	Burdette-Mil	.300	Conley-Mil	2.96	Burdette-Mil	135	Burdette-Mil	25.6	Spahn-Mil	3.2

New York Life

Prior to the season, the Braves traded young hurler Johnny Antonelli to the Giants for outfielder Bobby Thomson. While Thomson broke his leg in spring training and played just 43 games, Antonelli broke out for New York, winning 21 and pacing the NL in ERA. With Willie Mays back from the army and winning MVP honors with his first great season, the Giants didn't miss Thomson. Pulling away from Brooklyn with superb pitching and the league's best home run offense, the Giants won their last pennant in New York. Thomson's injury did help Milwaukee, however. When the veteran went down, manager Charlie Grimm filled the gap with rookie Hank Aaron.

Attendance rose another 8 percent as the third-place Braves were the first NL team ever to draw two million. The game became a little less homespun in 1954, as players were no longer allowed to leave their gloves on the field. In addition, the use of relief pitching continued to gain steam as complete games fell sharply to an all-time low of 377.

After trading slugger Ralph Kiner, the Pirates removed the temporary fencing in left field, restoring Forbes Field to its larger dimensions. It didn't help the team, which again finished last, but Pittsburgh was beginning to rebuild.

In the World Series, the Giants blew away favored Cleveland in a four-game sweep. Three huge pinch hits by New York's Dusty Rhodes—one a three-run homer that won Game 1—provided the offensive difference. Willie Mays' catch of Vic Wertz' tremendous drive to center field in the opening game remains one of the great plays ever made in the postseason. The Giants effectively shut down the Indians' offense, allowing just 9 runs—and 4 of those runs came after New York had built a 7-0 lead in Game 4. The surprise win triggered a short period of NL dominance, as the Senior Circuit won five world titles in seven seasons.

1954 American League

TEAM	W	L	T	PCT	GB	HW	HL	R	OR	PA	H	2B	3B	HR	BB	SO	HB	SH	AVG	OBP	SLG	OPS	AOPS	BR	ABR	PF	SB	CS	BSA	BSR
CLE	111	43	2	.721		59	18	.746	504	6048	1368	188	39	156	637	668	23	107	.262	.341	.403	744	108	77	65	102	30	33	48	-5
NY	103	51	1	.669	8	54	23	805	.563	6027	1400	215	59	133	650	632	20	84	.268	.348	.408	756	118	103	131	97	34	41	45	-7
CHI	94	60	1	.610	17	45	32	711	521	5972	1382	203	47	94	604	536	51	96	.267	.347	.379	726	103	53	30	103	98	58	63	1
BOS	69	85	2	.448	42	38	39	700	728	6207	1436	244	41	123	654	660	23	78	.266	.345	.395	740	98	78	3	111	51	30	63	1
DET	68	86	1	.442	43	35	42	584	664	5865	1351	215	41	90	492	603	19	80	.258	.322	.367	689	97	-37	-25	98	48	44	52	-5
WAS	66	88	1	.429	45	37	41	632	680	6005	1292	188	69	81	610	719	27	77	.246	.325	.355	680	97	-47	-12	95	37	21	64	1
BAL	54	100	0	.351	57	32	45	483	668	5838	1309	195	49	52	468	634	21	99	.251	.313	.338	651	91	-107	-64	93	30	31	49	-4
PHI	51	103	2	.331	60	29	47	542	875	5823	1228	191	41	94	504	677	28	54	.236	.305	.342	647	83	-119	-121	100	30	29	51	-4
TOT	621					329	287	5203		47785	10766	1639	386	823	4619	5129	212	675	.257	.331	.373	704					358	287	56	-22

TEAM	CG	SHO	GR	SV	IP	H	HR	BB	SO	BR/9	ERA	AERA	OAV	OOB	PR	APR	PF	OSB	OCS	FA	E	WPB	DP	FW	PW	BW	BSW	DIM
CLE	77	12	160	36	1419.1	1220	89	486	678	10.9	2.78	132	.232	.297	148	142	99	43	35	.979	128	19	148	.7	14.7	6.7	-.2	12.1
NY	51	16	182	37	1379.1	1284	86	552	655	12.2	3.26	105	.251	.325	71	29	92	34	33	.979	126	27	198	.8	3.0	13.5	-.4	9.1
CHI	60	23	176	33	1383.0	1255	94	517	701	11.6	3.05	122	.244	.312	103	105	100	32	35	.982	108	27	149	1.8	10.8	3.1	.4	-8.2
BOS	41	10	224	22	1412.1	1434	118	612	707	13.3	4.01	102	.265	.341	-46	14	110	57	36	.972	176	37	163	-2.0	1.4	.3	.4	-5.6
DET	58	13	179	13	1383.0	1375	138	506	603	12.5	3.81	97	.261	.328	-13	-18	99	34	40	.978	129	19	131	.6	-1.9	-2.6	-.2	-4.9
WAS	69	10	158	7	1383.1	1396	79	573	562	13.0	3.84	93	.265	.338	-18	-46	96	51	29	.977	137	33	172	.2	-4.8	-1.2	-.4	-5.6
BAL	58	6	156	8	1373.1	1279	78	688	668	13.0	3.88	92	.250	.338	-24	-47	96	56	46	.975	147	32	152	-.4	-4.9	-6.6	-.1	-11.0
PHI	49	3	182	13	1371.1	1523	141	685	555	14.7	5.18	75	.285	.366	-222	-185	105	51	33	.972	169	52	163	-1.6	-19.1	-12.5	-.1	7.3
TOT	463	93	1417	169	11105.0					12.6	3.72		.257	.331						.977	1120	246	1276					

Batter-Fielder Wins		Batting Average		On-Base Percentage		Slugging Average		On-Base Plus Slugging		Adjusted OPS		Adjusted Batter Runs	
Williams-Bos	5.1	Avila-Cle	.341	Williams-Bos	.513	Minoso-Chi	.535	Williams-Bos	1148	Williams-Bos	193	Williams-Bos	60.7
Avila-Cle	4.8	Minoso-Chi	.320	Minoso-Chi	.411	Mantle-NY	.525	Minoso-Chi	.946	Mantle-NY	160	Mantle-NY	46.1
Berra-NY	4.4	Noren-NY	.319	Mantle-NY	.408	Rosen-Cle	.506	Mantle-NY	.933	Minoso-Chi	154	Minoso-Chi	43.3
Minoso-Chi	4.1	Fox-Chi	.319	Yost-Was	.405	Vernon-Was	.492	Rosen-Cle	.910	Rosen-Cle	148	Rosen-Cle	33.5
Mantle-NY	3.8	Berra-NY	.307	Rosen-Cle	.404	Berra-NY	.488	Avila-Cle	.880	Noren-NY	140	Avila-Cle	30.6

Runs		Hits		Doubles		Triples		Home Runs		Total Bases		Runs Batted In	
Mantle-NY	129	Kuenn-Det	201	Vernon-Was	33	Minoso-Chi	18	Doby-Cle	32	Minoso-Chi	304	Doby-Cle	126
Minoso-Chi	119	Fox-Chi	201	Smith-Cle	29	Runnels-Was	15	Williams-Bos	29	Vernon-Was	294	Berra-NY	125
Avila-Cle	112	Avila-Cle	189	Minoso-Chi	29	Vernon-Was	14	Mantle-NY	27	Mantle-NY	285	Jensen-Bos	117
Fox-Chi	111	Busby-Was	187			Mantle-NY	12	Jensen-Bos	25	Berra-NY	285	Minoso-Chi	116
Carrasquel-Chi	106	Minoso-Chi	182			Tuttle-Det	11			Doby-Cle	279		

Stolen Bases		Base Stealing Runs		Fielding Runs-Infield		Fielding Runs-Outfield		Wins		Winning Pct.		Complete Games	
Jensen-Bos	22	Busby-Was	3.0	Coleman-NY	14.6	Diering-Bal	9.8	Wynn-Cle	23	Consuegra-Chi	.842	Porterfield-Was	2
Rivera-Chi	18	Jacobs-Phi	2.7	Carrasquel-Chi	13.2	Power-Phi	8.0	Lemon-Cle	23	Grim-NY	.769	Lemon-Cle	2
Minoso-Chi	18	Jensen-Bos	2.4	Carey-NY	12.5	Kaline-Det	7.3	Grim-NY	20	Lemon-Cle	.767	Wynn-Cle	2
Jacobs-Phi	17	Cavarretta-Chi	.9	McDougald-NY	10.2	Sievers-Was	7.2	Trucks-Chi	19	Garcia-Cle	.704	Gromek-Det	1
Busby-Was	17	Michaels-Chi	.8	Terwilliger-Was	10.0	Renna-Phi	6.1	Garcia-Cle	19	Houtteman-Cle	.682		

Strikeouts		Fewest BB/Game		Games		Saves		Base Runners/9		Adjusted Relief Runs		Relief Ranking	
Turley-Bal	185	Lopat-NY	1.75	Dixon-Was-Phi	54	Sain-NY	22	Mossi-Cle	9.29	Mossi-Cle	18.6	Mossi-Cle	15.5
Wynn-Cle	155	Gromek-Det	2.03	Martin-Phi-Chi	48	Kinder-Bos	15	Sain-NY	9.47	Narleski-Cle	14.6	Narleski-Cle	13.2
Trucks-Chi	152	Garver-Det	2.27	Pascual-Was	48	Narleski-Cle	13	Dorish-Chi	9.74	Dorish-Chi	12.9	Dorish-Chi	11.9
Pierce-Chi	148	Garcia-Cle	2.47	Kinder-Bos	48			Garcia-Cle	10.19	Miller-Det	8.1	Kinder-Bos	10.5
Harshman-Chi	134	Zuverink-Det	2.75					Wynn-Cle	10.24	Kinder-Bos	6.4	Sain-NY	8.8

Innings Pitched		Opponents' Avg.		Opponents' OBP		Earned Run Average		Adjusted ERA		Adjusted Starter Runs		Pitcher Wins	
Wynn-Cle	270.2	Turley-Bal	.203	Garcia-Cle	.282	Garcia-Cle	2.64	Garcia-Cle	139	Garcia-Cle	31.0	Gromek-Det	3.5
Trucks-Chi	264.2	Wynn-Cle	.225	Wynn-Cle	.283	Lemon-Cle	2.72	Lemon-Cle	135	Trucks-Chi	29.6	Lemon-Cle	3.5
Garcia-Cle	258.2	Ford-NY	.227	Garver-Det	.286	Wynn-Cle	2.73	Wynn-Cle	135	Wynn-Cle	29.4	Wynn-Cle	3.5
Lemon-Cle	258.1	Trucks-Chi	.228	Gromek-Det	.294	Gromek-Det	2.74	Gromek-Det	135	Gromek-Det	28.0	Trucks-Chi	3.5
Gromek-Det	252.2	Garcia-Cle	.229	Trucks-Chi	.296	Trucks-Chi	2.79	Trucks-Chi	134	Lemon-Cle	25.4	Garcia-Cle	3.5

Tribal Gathering

The Indians, bridesmaids three straight times, stormed the altar in 1954. By July Cleveland, New York, and Chicago were the only three contenders. The Tribe would not be denied, pulling away in August and leaving two very good clubs in the dust. Cleveland allowed fewer runs than any full-season AL team since 1917. Featuring five top-flight right-handed starters, a lefty-righty relief duo, and a veteran southpaw middleman, the Indians had one of the greatest staffs ever. And the offense wasn't shoddy, featuring Al Rosen, Larry Doby, and batting champ Bobby Avila.

And Cleveland handily beat Casey Stengel's best team. The Yankees won 103 games and were the only major league team to score 800 runs, but they still lost by 8 games. Despite the Indians' victory, Yogi Berra won his second MVP award, and Mickey Mantle consolidated his position as the league's top center fielder.

The poor got poorer in 1954: there had not been a 60-game spread from first to last since 1939. Even in New York, winning was tired, as Yankees attendance declined each of the last

six years. The league champion Indians' attendance was just half of the club's 1948 total.

White Sox third baseman Cass Michaels' career was ended by a beanball that fractured his skull, while Johnny Pesky played out the string in Washington. Thirty-nine-year-old Allie Reynolds retired after another excellent season in New York. The sixth-place Senators called on two rookies who make considerable impact in the coming years: pitcher Camilo Pascual and infielder Harmon Killebrew. In their first season in Baltimore, the Orioles finished seventh. Following the season, the Mack family sold the last-place A's to Arnold Johnson, who moved the club to Kansas City.

While Cleveland set league records for victories and winning percentage, they crumbled in the World Series. The New York Giants ripped apart Tribe pitching and snuffed out their powerful offense, winning in four straight. It was the most shocking sweep since the 1914 "Miracle" Braves.

1953 National League

TEAM	W	L	T	PCT	GB	HW	HL	R	OR	PA	H	2B	3B	HR	BB	SO	HB	SH	AVG	OBP	SLG	OPS	AOPS	BR	ABR	PF	SB	CS	BSA	BSR
BRO	105	49	1	.682		60	17	955	689	6138	1529	274	59	208	655	686	35	75	.285	.366	.474	840	121	194	173	102	90	47	66	3
MIL	92	62	3	.597	13	45	31	738	589	5895	1422	227	52	156	439	637	27	80	.266	.325	.415	740	104	-24	23	94	46	27	63	1
STL	83	71	3	.539	22	48	30	768	713	6065	1474	281	56	140	574	617	39	55	.273	.347	.424	771	107	58	59	100	18	22	45	-4
PHI	83	71	2	.539	22	48	29	716	666	5916	1400	228	62	115	530	597	29	67	.265	.335	.396	731	97	-25	-21	99	42	21	67	2
NY	70	84	1	.455	35	38	39	768	747	5956	1452	195	45	176	499	608	28	67	.271	.336	.422	758	101	18	5	102	31	21	60	-1
CIN	68	86	1	.442	37	38	39	714	788	5912	1396	190	34	166	485	701	16	68	.261	.325	.403	728	94	-45	-50	101	25	20	56	-1
CHI	65	89	1	.422	40	43	34	633	835	5873	1372	204	57	137	514	746	14	73	.260	.328	.399	727	93	-43	-58	102	49	21	70	3
PIT	50	104	0	.325	55	26	51	622	887	5902	1297	178	49	99	524	715	36	89	.247	.319	.356	675	82	-133	-129	99	41	39	51	-5
TOT	622					346	270	5914		47657	11342	1777	414	1197	4220	5307	224	574	.266	.335	.411	747					342	218	61	-1

TEAM	CG	SHO	GR	SV	IP	H	HR	BB	SO	BR/9	ERA	AERA	OAV	OOB	PR	APR	PF	OSB	OCS	FA	E	WPB	DP	FW	PW	BW	BSW	DIF
BRO	51	11	212	29	1380.2	1337	169	509	817	12.1	4.10	104	.253	.320	29	25	99	22	25	.980	118	28	161	1.7	2.4	16.7	.3	7.0
MIL	72	14	159	15	1387.0	1282	107	539	738	12.0	3.30	119	.245	.318	153	105	92	48	33	.976	143	31	169	.4	10.1	2.2	.1	2.2
STL	51	11	234	36	1386.2	1406	139	533	732	12.9	4.23	101	.262	.333	9	5	99	53	29	.977	138	40	161	.7	.5	5.7	-.4	-.4
PHI	76	13	165	15	1369.2	1410	138	410	637	12.1	3.80	111	.265	.320	74	63	98	40	16	.975	147	33	161	.0	6.1	-2.0	.2	1.7
NY	46	10	217	20	1365.2	1403	146	610	647	13.4	4.25	101	.264	.343	5	6	100	33	30	.975	151	51	151	-.2	.6	.5	-.0	-7.8
CIN	47	7	202	15	1365.0	1484	179	488	506	13.2	4.64	94	.279	.343	-53	-42	102	35	18	.978	129	24	176	1.1	-4.0	-4.8	-.0	-1.1
CHI	38	3	238	22	1359.0	1491	151	554	623	13.8	4.79	93	.276	.347	-76	-49	104	47	34	.967	193	35	141	-2.5	-4.7	-5.6	.3	.5
PIT	49	4	211	10	1358.0	1529	168	577	607	14.1	5.22	86	.285	.356	-141	-108	104	64	33	.973	163	76	139	-.9	-10.4	-12.4	-.5	-2.8
TOT	430	73	1638	162	10971.2					12.9	4.29		.266	.335						.975	1182	318	1259	-.9	-10.4	-12.4	-.5	-2.8

Batter-Fielder Wins		Batting Average		On-Base Percentage		Slugging Average		On-Base Plus Slugging		Adjusted OPS		Adjusted Batter Runs	
Schoendienst-StL	6.5	Furillo-Bro	.344	Musial-StL	.437	Snider-Bro	.627	Snider-Bro	1046	Mathews-Mil	175	Musial-StL	65.6
Mathews-Mil	6.1	Schoendienst-StL	.342	Robinson-Bro	.425	Mathews-Mil	.627	Musial-StL	1046	Musial-StL	169	Mathews-Mil	65.3
Campanella-Bro	5.0	Musial-StL	.337	Snider-Bro	.419	Campanella-Bro	.611	Mathews-Mil	1033	Snider-Bro	165	Snider-Bro	57.8
Musial-StL	4.4	Snider-Bro	.336	Irvin-NY	.406	Musial-StL	.609	Campanella-Bro	1006	Campanella-Bro	154	Campanella-Bro	41.2
Snider-Bro	3.9	Mueller-NY	.333	Mathews-Mil	.406	Furillo-Bro	.580	Furillo-Bro	973	Furillo-Bro	146	Kluszewski-Cin	34.7

Runs		Hits		Doubles		Triples		Home Runs		Total Bases		Runs Batted In	
Snider-Bro	132	Ashburn-Phi	205	Musial-StL	53	Gilliam-Bro	17	Mathews-Mil	47	Snider-Bro	370	Campanella-Bro	142
Musial-StL	127	Musial-StL	200	Dark-NY	41	Bruton-Mil	14	Snider-Bro	42	Mathews-Mil	363	Mathews-Mil	135
Dark-NY	126	Snider-Bro	198	Snider-Bro	38	Hemus-StL	11	Campanella-Bro	41	Musial-StL	361	Snider-Bro	126
Gilliam-Bro	125	Dark-NY	194	Furillo-Bro	38	Fondy-Chi	11	Kluszewski-Cin	40	Kluszewski-Cin	325	Ennis-Phi	125
		Schoendienst-StL	193	Bell-Cin	37			Kiner-Pit-Chi	35	Bell-Cin	320	Hodges-Bro	122

Stolen Bases		Base Stealing Runs		Fielding Runs-Infield		Fielding Runs-Outfield		Wins		Winning Pct.		Complete Games	
Bruton-Mil	26	Reese-Bro	2.7	Schoendienst-StL	28.6	Ashburn-Phi	17.7	Spahn-Mil	23	Erskine-Bro	.769	Roberts-Phi	33
Reese-Bro	22	Robinson-Bro	2.3	Logan-Mil	20.8	Thomas-Pit	6.4	Roberts-Phi	23	Spahn-Mil	.767	Spahn-Mil	24
Gilliam-Bro	21	Bruton-Mil	1.9	Bridges-Cin	13.8	Marshall-Cin	4.9	Haddix-StL	20	Meyer-Bro	.750	Simmons-Phi	19
Robinson-Bro	17	Miksis-Chi	1.5	McMillan-Cin	10.0	Jeffcoat-Chi	4.7	Erskine-Bro	20	Burdette-Mil	.750	Haddix-StL	19
Snider-Bro	16	Torgeson-Phi	1.2	Bilko-StL	9.2	Bell-Cin	4.6	Staley-StL	18	Haddix-StL	.690	Erskine-Bro	16

Strikeouts		Fewest BB/Game		Games		Saves		Base Runners/9		Adjusted Relief Runs		Relief Ranking	
Roberts-Phi	198	Roberts-Phi	1.58	Wilhelm-NY	68	Brazle-StL	18	Spahn-Mil	9.55	Wilhelm-NY	18.3	Labine-Bro	26.8
Erskine-Bro	187	Raffensberger-Cin	1.71	Brazle-StL	60	Wilhelm-NY	15	Labine-Bro	9.95	Labine-Bro	17.5	Wilhelm-NY	21.3
Mizell-StL	173	Minner-Chi	1.79	Hetki-Pit	54	Hughes-Bro	9	Roberts-Phi	10.05	White-StL	11.5	White-StL	15.6
Haddix-StL	163	Staley-StL	2.11	Smith-Cin	50	Leonard-Chi	8	Milliken-Bro	10.40	Johnson-Mil	9.4	Hughes-Bro	8.8
Spahn-Mil	148	Hacker-Chi	2.19			Burdette-Mil	8	Haddix-StL	10.42	Hughes-Bro	9.0	Johnson-Mil	7.3

Innings Pitched		Opponents' Avg.		Opponents' OBP		Earned Run Average		Adjusted ERA		Adjusted Starter Runs		Pitcher Wins	
Roberts-Phi	346.2	Spahn-Mil	.217	Spahn-Mil	.270	Spahn-Mil	2.10	Spahn-Mil	187	Roberts-Phi	58.5	Spahn-Mil	7.0
Spahn-Mil	265.2	Gomez-NY	.218	Roberts-Phi	.276	Roberts-Phi	2.75	Roberts-Phi	153	Spahn-Mil	57.3	Roberts-Phi	6.4
Haddix-StL	253.0	Mizell-StL	.227	Haddix-StL	.287	Haddix-StL	3.06	Haddix-StL	139	Haddix-StL	32.6	Haddix-StL	4.5
Erskine-Bro	246.2	Erskine-Bro	.230	Hacker-Chi	.299	Antonelli-Mil	3.18	Simmons-Phi	131	Simmons-Phi	25.0	Labine-Bro	2.5
Simmons-Phi	238.0	Haddix-StL	.232	Simmons-Phi	.302	Simmons-Phi	3.21	Gomez-NY	126	Gomez-NY	20.3	Simmons-Phi	2.3

Brooklyn Blast

The Dodgers became the NL's first repeat champions since 1944, winning a race that wasn't close after mid-July. With MVP winner Roy Campanella and yet another African American Rookie of the Year in Jim Gilliam, Brooklyn easily outclassed the surprising Braves. The Dodgers were the league's last 100-game winner until 1962. Brooklyn again led the world in runs, in both home and road games, while Milwaukee sported the league's best pitching. The Dodgers dominated at Ebbets Field with a .779 winning percentage. No NL team had compiled a better home record since 1902.

Boston's move to Milwaukee, and the team's sudden rise to contention, juiced up NL attendance; the Braves drew league record crowds, causing ticket sales to increase 17 percent although attendance fell in five other cities. Turnout in Milwaukee, when compared to Boston in '52, was up an absurd 549 percent.

The Braves added two more impressive rookies to the mix, outfielder Bill Bruton and pitcher Bob Buhl, while the Cubs debuted Ernie Banks and last-place Pittsburgh introduced Elroy Face. The Cardinals began a dry spell, due to poor pitching, as several of their great 1940s stars—Harry Brecheen, Marty Marion, and Johnny Mize—played their last games, all for other clubs. The Pirates lost youngsters Vern Law and Dick Groat to military service, while the Giants did without Willie Mays and the Dodgers lost Don Newcombe, as the Korean conflict took its toll.

Runs per game rose to 4.75, the highest of the 1950s, as league batters yet again set an all-time record for home runs. The league ERA leapt more than a half a run, with only Warren Spahn and Robin Roberts finishing under the 3.00 mark, and bullpen use continued to increase.

The World Series was a high-scoring affair, with New York and Brooklyn combining for 17 homers in six games. Predictably, the Yankees came out on top.

1953 American League

TEAM	W	L	T	PCT	GB	HW	HL	R	OR	PA	H	2B	3B	HR	BB	SO	HB	SH	AVG	OBP	SLG	OPS	AOPS	BR	ABR	PF	SB	CS	BSA	BSR
NY	99	52	0	.656		50	27	801	547	5961	1420	226	52	139	656	644	34	77	.273	.359	.417	776	120	115	144	97	34	44	44	-8
CLE	92	62	1	.597	8.5	53	24	770	627	6019	1426	201	29	160	609	683	35	90	.270	.349	.410	759	114	77	98	97	33	29	53	-3
CHI	89	65	2	.578	11.5	41	36	716	592	5987	1345	226	53	74	601	530	54	120	.258	.341	.364	705	93	-17	-37	103	73	55	57	-3
BOS	84	69	0	.549	16	38	38	656	632	5879	1385	255	37	101	496	601	38	99	.264	.332	.384	716	94	-9	-43	105	33	45	42	3.9
WAS	76	76	0	.500	23.5	39	36	687	614	5858	1354	230	53	69	596	604	31	82	.263	.343	.368	711	100	-5	12	98	65	36	64	2
DET	60	94	4	.390	40.5	30	47	695	923	6152	1479	259	44	108	506	603	30	63	.266	.331	.387	718	100	-10	-1	99	30	35	46	-6
PHI	59	95	3	.383	41.5	27	50	632	799	6028	1398	205	38	116	498	602	24	51	.256	.321	.372	693	89	-64	-87	104	41	24	63	-8
STL	54	100	0	.351	46.5	23	54	555	778	5877	1310	214	25	112	507	644	17	89	.249	.317	.363	680	87	-85	-96	102	17	34	33	-8
TOT	618					301	312	5512		47761	11117	1816	331	879	4469	4911	263	671	.262	.337	.383	720					326	302	52	-34

TEAM	CG	SHO	GR	SV	IP	H	HR	BB	SO	BR/9	ERA	AERA	OAV	OOB	PR	APR	PF	OSB	OCS	FA	E	WPB	DP	FW	PW	BW	BSW	DIF
NY	50	18	176	39	1358.1	1286	94	500	604	12.1	3.20	115	.251	.321	120	80	92	33	31	.979	126	25	182	.3	8.0	14.4	-.4	1.1
CLE	81	11	135	15	1373.0	1311	92	519	586	12.1	3.64	103	.253	.325	53	17	94	46	30	.979	127	37	197	.4	1.7	9.8	.1	2.9
CHI	57	17	184	33	1403.2	1299	113	583	714	12.2	3.41	118	.246	.324	91	95	101	41	35	.980	125	41	144	.6	9.1	-3.7	.1	5.5
BOS	41	15	214	37	1373.0	1333	92	584	642	12.7	3.58	118	.254	.331	63	91	105	39	32	.975	148	36	173	-.9	9.1	-4.3	-.4	3.9
WAS	76	16	132	10	1344.2	1313	112	478	515	12.2	3.66	106	.258	.324	50	36	98	35	32	.979	120	28	173	.7	3.6	1.2	.6	-6.1
DET	50	2	218	16	1415.0	1633	154	585	645	14.4	5.25	77	.291	.363	-198	-183	102	55	47	.978	135	63	149	.1	-18.3	-.1	-.2	1.5
PHI	51	7	165	11	1409.0	1475	121	594	566	13.6	4.67	92	.271	.349	-106	-56	107	28	53	.977	137	66	161	-.0	-5.6	-8.7	.5	-4.2
STL	28	10	250	24	1383.2	1467	101	626	639	13.8	4.48	94	.273	.351	-74	-40	105	49	42	.974	152	41	165	-1.0	-4.0	-9.6	-.4	-8.0
TOT	434	96	1474	185	11060.1					12.9	3.99		.262	.337						.978	1070	337	1344					

Batter-Fielder Wins		Batting Average		On-Base Percentage		Slugging Average		On-Base Plus Slugging		Adjusted OPS		Adjusted Batter Runs	
Rosen-Cle	7.4	Vernon-Was	.337	Woodling-NY	.429	Rosen-Cle	.613	Rosen-Cle	1034	Rosen-Cle	181	Rosen-Cle	68.0
Berra-NY	3.8	Rosen-Cle	.336	Rosen-Cle	.422	Zernial-Phi	.559	Vernon-Was	.921	Vernon-Was	151	Vernon-Was	43.5
Boone-Cle-Det	3.6	Goodman-Bos	.313	Minoso-Chi	.410	Berra-NY	.523	Zernial-Phi	.914	Woodling-NY	147	Boone-Cle-Det	31.9
Strickland-Cle	3.3	Minoso-Chi	.313	Fain-Chi	.405	Boone-Cle-Det	.519	Boone-Cle-Det	.909	Boone-Cle-Det	146	Woodling-NY	31.7
Vernon-Was	3.0	Busby-Was	.312	Yost-Was	.403	Vernon-Was	.518	Woodling-NY	.898	Mantle-NY	145	Mantle-NY	31.4

Runs		Hits		Doubles		Triples		Home Runs		Total Bases		Runs Batted In	
Rosen-Cle	115	Kuenn-Det	209	Vernon-Was	43	Rivera-Chi	16	Rosen-Cle	43	Rosen-Cle	367	Rosen-Cle	145
Yost-Was	107	Vernon-Was	205	Kell-Bos	41	Vernon-Was	11	Zernial-Phi	42	Vernon-Was	315	Vernon-Was	115
Mantle-NY	105	Rosen-Cle	201	White-Bos	34	Piersall-Bos	9	Doby-Cle	29	Zernial-Phi	311	Boone-Cle-Det	114
Minoso-Chi	104	Philley-Phi	188	Kuenn-Det	33	Philley-Phi	9	Berra-NY	27	Philley-Phi	263	Zernial-Phi	108
Vernon-Was	101	Busby-Was	183	Goodman-Bos	33			Boone-Cle-Det	26	Berra-NY	263	Berra-NY	108

Stolen Bases		Base Stealing Runs		Fielding Runs-Infield		Fielding Runs-Outfield		Wins		Winning Pct.		Complete Games	
Minoso-Chi	25	Michaels-Phi	1.5	Strickland-Cle	21.0	Busby-Was	12.9	Porterfield-Was	22	Lopat-NY	.800	Porterfield-Was	24
Rivera-Chi	22	Coan-Was	1.5	Hunter-StL	13.9	Groth-StL	12.2	Parnell-Bos	21	Ford-NY	.750	B.Lemon-Cle	23
Jensen-Was	18	Jensen-Was	1.2	Dropo-Det	12.5	Piersall-Bos	10.9	B.Lemon-Cle	21	Parnell-Bos	.724	Garcia-Cle	21
Philley-Phi	13	Philley-Phi	1.1	Avila-Cle	12.5	Zernial-Phi	5.3	Trucks-StL-Chi	20	Porterfield-Was	.688	Pierce-Chi	19
Busby-Was	13	Zernial-Phi	.9	Rosen-Cle	9.4	Lund-Det	5.1					Trucks-StL-Chi	17

Strikeouts		Fewest BB/Game		Games		Saves		Base Runners/9		Adjusted Relief Runs		Relief Ranking	
Pierce-Chi	186	Lopat-NY	1.61	Kinder-Bos	69	Kinder-Bos	27	Raschi-NY	10.24	Kinder-Bos	24.7	Kinder-Bos	47.3
Trucks-StL-Chi	149	Sain-NY	2.14	Stuart-StL	60	Dorish-Chi	18	Lopat-NY	10.35	Dorish-Chi	11.0	Dorish-Chi	14.0
Wynn-Cle	138	A.Kellner-Phi	2.28	Martin-Phi	58	Reynolds-NY	13	Kinder-Bos	10.43	Paige-StL	8.7	Paige-StL	9.9
Parnell-Bos	136	Porterfield-Was	2.58	Paige-StL	57	Paige-StL	11	Keegan-Chi	10.49	Kuzava-NY	5.9	Kuzava-NY	6.9
Garcia-Cle	134	Hoeft-Det	2.64	Dorish-Chi	55	Sain-NY	9	Pierce-Chi	10.65	Bearden-Chi	4.4	Bearden-Chi	4.4

Innings Pitched		Opponents' Avg.		Opponents' OBP		Earned Run Average		Adjusted ERA		Adjusted Starter Runs		Pitcher Wins	
B.Lemon-Cle	286.2	Pierce-Chi	.218	Raschi-NY	.283	Lopat-NY	2.42	Lopat-NY	152	Pierce-Chi	37.8	Kinder-Bos	5.2
Garcia-Cle	271.2	McDermott-Bos	.224	Lopat-NY	.288	Pierce-Chi	2.72	Pierce-Chi	148	Trucks-StL-Chi	31.8	McDermott-Bos	4.1
Pierce-Chi	271.1	Raschi-NY	.224	Pierce-Chi	.292	Trucks-StL-Chi	2.93	McDermott-Bos	140	Parnell-Bos	27.8	Trucks-StL-Chi	3.6
Trucks-StL-Chi	264.1	Masterson-Was	.232	Masterson-Was	.304	Sain-NY	3.00	Trucks-StL-Chi	139	Lopat-NY	25.5	Pierce-Chi	3.5
Porterfield-Was	255.0	Trucks-StL-Chi	.238	Garcia-Cle	.307	Ford-NY	3.00	Parnell-Bos	137	McDermott-Bos	25.2	Porterfield-Was	3.3

Ho-Hum

The pennant race wasn't close in 1953, with the Yankees easily shaking off the Indians and White Sox to capture their 20th AL crown in 33 seasons. More than in previous years, the Yankees had a stable lineup, although per usual, manager Casey Stengel had six pitchers make at least 15 starts—one of whom was also his relief ace, Allie Reynolds. New York led the AL in runs and ERA by healthy margins.

Cleveland third baseman Al Rosen nearly won the Triple Crown, leading in the power categories and losing the batting championship to Washington's Mickey Vernon by less than a point. Rosen's MVP trophy didn't make up for another second-place finish, however.

Boston's Ellis Kinder racked up 27 saves (figured retroactively), tying Joe Page's record, helping his team finish fourth even with Ted Williams spending most of the season in the marines—Teddy Ballgame even survived his plane being shot down in Korea. Eighteen-year-old outfielder Al Kaline of sixth-place

Detroit made his debut, and to honor the Athletics' retired owner-manager, Shibe Park was renamed Connie Mack Stadium. The A's, however, tumbled to seventh and attendance fell by half. Overall, league attendance dropped for the fifth straight year as New York's victory routine proved tiresome. Football was already making huge inroads into the American postwar consciousness.

The St. Louis Browns' final season didn't pass without more weirdness. Alva "Bobo" Holloman pitched a no-hitter in his first major league start, May 6, but was subsequently shelled back to the minors. The AL forced Bill Veeck to sell the club, and the Browns moved to Baltimore.

The World Series went six games, with Stengel calling on five different starters. In an even more power-dominated Series than in 1952, the Yankees used big innings to win Games 1 and 5, then captured the deciding contest in the last of the ninth on Billy Martin's record-setting 12th hit. For the Yankees, it was their fifth straight world title.

1952 National League

TEAM	W	L	T	PCT	GB	HW	HL	R	OR	PA	H	2B	3B	HR	BB	SO	HB	SH	AVG	OBP	SLG	OPS	AOPS	BR	ABR	PF	SB	CS	BSA	BSR
BRO	96	57	2	.627	—	45	33	775	603	6068	1380	199	32	153	663	699	35	104	.262	.348	.399	747	113	111	103	101	90	49	65	3
NY	92	62	0	.597	4.5	50	27	722	639	5891	1337	186	56	151	536	672	38	88	.256	.329	.399	728	107	54	49	101	30	31	49	-4
STL	88	66	0	.571	8.5	48	29	677	630	5845	1386	247	54	97	537	479	43	65	.267	.340	.391	731	110	71	70	100	33	32	51	-4
PHI	87	67	0	.565	9.5	47	29	657	552	5875	1353	237	45	93	540	534	23	107	.260	.332	.376	708	104	28	35	99	60	41	59	-1
CHI	77	77	1	.500	19.5	42	35	628	631	5836	1408	223	45	107	422	712	21	63	.264	.321	.383	704	101	4	-4	101	50	40	56	-3
CIN	69	85	0	.448	27.5	38	39	615	659	5785	1303	212	45	104	480	709	18	53	.249	.314	.366	680	95	-37	-35	100	32	42	43	-8
BOS	64	89	2	.418	32	31	45	569	651	5828	1214	187	31	110	483	711	32	92	.233	.301	.343	644	88	-104	-85	97	58	34	63	1
PIT	42	112	1	.273	54.5	23	54	515	793	5775	1201	181	30	92	486	724	26	70	.231	.300	.331	631	79	-127	-140	103	43	41	51	-5
TOT	618					324	291	5158		46903	10582	1672	338	907	4147	5240	236	642	.253	.323	.374	697				396	310	56	-21

TEAM	CG	SHO	GR	SV	IP	H	HR	BB	SO	BR/9	ERA	AERA	OAV	OOB	PR	APR	PF	OSB	OCS	FA	E	WPB	DP	FW	PW	BW	BSW	DIF
BRO	45	11	196	24	1399.1	1295	121	544	773	12.0	3.53	103	.247	.321	31	17	98	29	38	.982	106	37	169	2.0	1.8	10.6	.6	4.5
NY	49	12	226	31	1371.0	1282	121	538	655	12.2	3.59	103	.248	.323	22	17	99	28	40	.974	158	37	175	-.8	5.1	-.1		3.0
STL	49	12	208	27	1361.1	1274	119	501	712	11.9	3.66	101	.247	.317	11	8	100	36	36	.977	141	31	159	.1	.8	7.2	-.1	3.0
PHI	80	17	142	16	1386.2	1306	96	373	609	11.0	3.07	119	.249	.301	102	92	98	50	34	.975	150	17	145	-.4	9.5	3.6	.2	-2.9
CHI	59	15	168	15	1386.1	1265	101	534	661	11.9	3.58	107	.240	.314	23	40	103	83	30	.976	146	65	123	-.1	4.1	-.4	-.0	-3.6
CIN	56	11	173	12	1363.1	1377	111	517	579	12.8	4.01	94	.267	.338	-43	-36	101	56	41	.982	107	24	145	1.9	-3.7	-3.6	-.6	-2.0
BOS	63	11	175	13	1396.0	1388	106	525	687	12.5	3.78	96	.259	.329	-7	-27	97	51	42	.975	154	45	143	-.5	-2.8	-8.8	.4	-.8
PIT	43	5	204	8	1363.2	1395	132	615	564	13.4	4.65	86	.265	.345	-139	-92	107	63	49	.970	182	34	167	-2.0	-9.5	-14.5	-.2	-8.8
TOT	444	94	1492	146	11027.2					12.2	3.73		.253	.323						.976	1144	290	1226					

Batter-Fielder Wins		Batting Average		On-Base Percentage		Slugging Average		On-Base Plus Slugging		Adjusted OPS		Adjusted Batter Runs	
Robinson-Bro	5.7	Musial-StL	336	Robinson-Bro	440	Musial-StL	538	Musial-StL	970	Musial-StL	167	Musial-StL	57.7
Schoendienst-StL	5.4	Baumholtz-Chi	325	Musial-StL	432	Sauer-Chi	531	Robinson-Bro	904	Robinson-Bro	149	Robinson-Bro	41.9
Musial-StL	4.2	Kluszewski-Cin	320	Hemus-StL	392	Kluszewski-Cin	509	Kluszewski-Cin	892	Kluszewski-Cin	146	Hodges-Bro	32.9
Hemus-StL	3.9	Robinson-Bro	308	Hodges-Bro	386	Kiner-Pit	500	Sauer-Chi	892	Gordon-Bos	144	Gordon-Bos	32.6
Sauer-Chi	3.1	Snider-Bro	303	Slaughter-StL	386	Hodges-Bro	500	Hodges-Bro	886	Sauer-Chi	143	Sauer-Chi	32.6

Runs		Hits		Doubles		Triples		Home Runs		Total Bases		Runs Batted In	
Musial-StL	105	Musial-StL	194	Musial-StL	42	Thomson-NY	14	Sauer-Chi	37	Musial-StL	311	Sauer-Chi	121
Hemus-StL	105	Schoendienst-StL	188	Schoendienst-StL	40	Slaughter-StL	12	Kiner-Pit	37	Sauer-Chi	301	Thomson-NY	108
Robinson-Bro	104	Adams-Cin	180	McMillan-Cin	32	Kluszewski-Cin	11	Hodges-Bro	32	Thomson-NY	293	Ennis-Phi	107
Lockman-NY	99	Dark-NY	177	Sauer-Chi	31	Ennis-Phi	10	Mathews-Bos	25	Ennis-Phi	281	Hodges-Bro	102
Reese-Bro	94	Lockman-NY	176	Ashburn-Phi	31			Gordon-Bos	25	Snider-Bro	264	Slaughter-StL	101

Stolen Bases		Base Stealing Runs		Fielding Runs-Infield		Fielding Runs-Outfield		Wins		Winning Pct.		Complete Games	
Reese-Bro	30	Reese-Bro	4.8	Schoendienst-StL	35.6	Sauer-Chi	10.3	Roberts-Phi	28	Wilhelm-NY	833	Roberts-Phi	30
Jethroe-Bos	28	Jethroe-Bos	3.0	Logan-Bos	12.5	Jeffcoat-Chi	10.0	Maglie-NY	18	Roberts-Phi	800	Dickson-Pit	21
Robinson-Bro	24	Robinson-Bro	2.8	McMillan-Cin	10.3	Ashburn-Phi	7.9	Staley-StL	17	Black-Bro	789	Spahn-Bos	19
Ashburn-Phi	16	Davis-Pit	1.3	Adams-Cin	7.0	Adcock-Cin	6.8	Rush-Chi	17	Maglie-NY	692	Raffensberger-Cin	18
		Ryan-Phi	1.1	Hemus-StL	5.0	Wyrostek-Cin-Phi	6.8	Raffensberger-Cin	17	Hacker-Chi	692	Rush-Chi	17

Strikeouts		Fewest BB/Game		Games		Saves		Base Runners/9		Adjusted Relief Runs		Relief Ranking	
Spahn-Bos	183	Roberts-Phi	1.23	Wilhelm-NY	71	Brazle-StL	16	Hacker-Chi	8.56	Black-Bro	22.9	Black-Bro	33.0
Rush-Chi	157	Hacker-Chi	1.51	Black-Bro	56	Black-Bro	15	Black-Bro	9.11	Wilhelm-NY	18.5	Wilhelm-NY	21.7
Roberts-Phi	148	Raffensberger-Cin	1.64	Yuhas-StL	54	Wilhelm-NY	11	Miller-StL	9.31	Leonard-Chi	12.3	Brazle-StL	20.7
Mizell-StL	146	Staley-StL	1.95	Smith-Cin	53	Leonard-Chi	11	Roberts-Phi	9.33	Brazle-StL	12.0	Yuhas-StL	15.0
Simmons-Phi	141	Drews-Phi	2.05	Main-Pit	48			Ramsdell-Chi	9.40	Yuhas-StL	10.7	Leonard-Chi	11.2

Innings Pitched		Opponents' Avg.		Opponents' OBP		Earned Run Average		Adjusted ERA		Adjusted Starter Runs		Pitcher Wins	
Roberts-Phi	330.0	Hacker-Chi	212	Hacker-Chi	247	Wilhelm-NY	2.43	Wilhelm-NY	152	Roberts-Phi	42.8	Roberts-Phi	4.6
Spahn-Bos	290.0	Rush-Chi	216	Roberts-Phi	263	Hacker-Chi	2.58	Hacker-Chi	149	Hacker-Chi	27.3	Rush-Chi	4.0
Dickson-Pit	277.2	Wilhelm-NY	220	Rush-Chi	282	Roberts-Phi	2.59	Rush-Chi	143	Raffensberger-Cin	25.6	Black-Bro	3.3
Rush-Chi	250.1	Erskine-Bro	220	Erskine-Bro	290	Loes-Bro	2.69	Roberts-Phi	141	Rush-Chi	25.5	Hacker-Chi	3.1
Raffensberger-Cin	247.0	Loes-Bro	224	Spahn-Bos	291	Rush-Chi	2.70	Loes-Bro	135	Drews-Phi	25.0	Drews-Phi	2.9

Dodgers Blue Again

The Dodgers were again the class of the league early on, but this time didn't crumble down the stretch. Only for a short time in mid-September, when the Dodgers slumped and the Giants turned on the heat, was the race close.

League batting average was just .253, the lowest between 1942 and 1963, and runs per game fell to 4.17, the fewest of the decade. NL home runs dipped below 1,000 for the first time since 1950, and for the last time to date. Strikeouts rose once more. Despite this, complete games dropped to a new low, and two 28-year-old freshman relievers were the league's sensations. Despite leading the NL in appearances, ERA, and winning percentage, the Giants' Hoyt Wilhelm lost Rookie of the Year balloting to Brooklyn's Joe Black.

Philadelphia's Robin Roberts won 28, the most by a Senior Circuit hurler since 1935, while Stan Musial took his third straight batting title for the third-place Cardinals. Pittsburgh did a full swan dive into the basement, posting the league's worst record since 1935 despite Ralph Kiner's seventh straight home run crown.

League attendance fell another 12.5 percent. Boston's gate dropped another 42 percent as the club announced its move to Milwaukee—the first major league franchise relocation since 1903. The Braves added to their growing arsenal with the debut of third baseman Eddie Mathews, who tied for fourth in the league in homers.

Recently retired Arky Vaughan, one of the greatest shortstops in baseball history, drowned in a fishing accident. And outfielder Pete Reiser, robbed of a potentially great career by catastrophic injuries, played his last game.

In the fourth all-New York World Series in five years, the Dodgers led the Yankees three games to two and had the final two games in Ebbets Field, but they couldn't close the deal despite Duke Snider's .345 average, 4 homers, and 8 RBIs. Brooklyn fans were starting to wonder if next year would ever come.

1952 American League

TEAM	W	L	T	PCT	GB	HW	HL	R	OR	PA	H	2B	3B	HR	BB	SO	HB	SH	AVG	OBP	SLG	OPS	AOPS	BR	ABR	PF	SB	CS	BSA	BSR
NY	95	59	0	.617		49	28	727	**557**	5990	**1411**	221	**56**	129	566	652	36	94	**.267**	.341	.403	744	121	89	136	94	52	42	55	-3
CLE	93	61	1	.604	2	49	28	**763**	606	6060	1399	211	49	**148**	626	749	20	84	.262	.342	**.404**	746	122	**95**	**147**	94	46	39	54	-4
CHI	81	73	2	.526	14	44	33	610	568	6036	1337	199	38	80	541	521	58	121	.252	.327	.348	675	93	-36	-41	101	**61**	38	**62**	0
PHI	79	75	1	.513	16	45	32	664	723	5975	1305	212	35	89	**683**	561	27	102	.253	**.343**	.359	702	96	29	-11	106	52	43	55	-4
WAS	78	76	3	.506	17	42	35	598	608	6046	1282	225	44	50	580	607	30	79	.239	.317	.326	643	88	16	-31	108	59	47	56	-3
BOS	76	78	0	.494	19	**50**	27	668	658	5885	1338	**233**	34	113	542	739	31	66	.255	.322	.356	705	96	-39	-56	103	30	34	47	-5
STL	64	90	1	.416	31	42	35	604	733	6001	1340	225	46	82	540	720	22	86	.250	.322	.356	678	92	-54	-59	101	27	38	42	-7
DET	50	104	2	.325	45	32	45	557	738	5914	1278	190	37	103	553	605	23	80	.243	.318	.352	670	92							
TOT	621					353	263	5191		47907	10690	1716	339	794	4631	5154	247	712	.253	.330	.365	695					375	318	54	-29

TEAM	CG	SHO	GR	SV	IP	H	HR	BB	SO	BR/9	ERA	AERA	OAV	OOB	PR	APR	PF	OSB	OCS	FA	E	WPB	DP	FW	PW	BW	BSW	DIF
NY	72	**21**	143	27	1381.0	**1240**	94	581	666	12.1	**3.14**	106	.243	.324	82	31	90	49	40	.979	127	21	**199**	.8	3.2	14.1	.0	-.2
CLE	**80**	19	143	18	1407.0	1278	94	556	671	11.9	3.32	101	.241	**.316**	55	4	91	50	40	.975	155	34	141	-.8	.4	**15.3**	-.0	1.2
CHI	53	15	**190**	28	1416.2	1251	86	578	**774**	11.7	3.25	112	**.238**	.316	66	**63**	99	63	34	**.980**	**123**	37	158	1.1	6.5	-4.3	**.4**	.2
PHI	73	11	137	15	1384.1	1402	113	562	562	12.4	4.15	95	.263	.333	-74	-28	108	37	**48**	.977	140	32	148	.0	-2.9	-1.1	-.0	6.0
WAS	75	10	137	15	1429.2	1405	**78**	577	574	12.7	3.37	105	.258	.332	48	30	97	42	31	.978	132	34	152	.6	3.1	-8.1	.2	5.2
BOS	53	7	176	24	1372.1	1332	107	623	624	13.1	3.80	104	.256	.340	-20	19	107	**35**	37	.976	145	37	181	-.3	2.0	-3.2	-.0	-.5
STL	48	**6**	181	18	1399.0	1388	111	598	581	13.0	4.12	95	.260	.339	-69	-30	107	51	47	.974	155	38	176	-.6	-3.1	-5.8	-.1	-3.1
DET	51	10	182	14	1388.1	1394	111	591	702	13.0	4.25	90	.262	.338	-89	-66	104	48	41	.975	152	.50	145	-.6	-6.8	-6.1	-.4	-13.1
TOT	505	99	1289	159	11178.1					12.5	3.67		.253	.330						.977	1129	283	1300					

Batter-Fielder Wins
Fain-Phi 4.5
Doby-Cle 4.4
Mantle-NY 3.9
Berra-NY 3.5
Goodman-Bos 3.4

Batting Average
Fain-Phi 327
Mitchell-Cle 323
Mantle-NY 311
Kell-Det-Bos 311
Woodling-NY 309

On-Base Percentage
Fain-Phi 438
Valo-Phi 432
Mantle-NY 394
Joost-Phi 388
Rosen-Cle 387

Slugging Average
Doby-Cle 541
Mantle-NY 530
Rosen-Cle 524
Easter-Cle 513
Wertz-Det-StL 506

On-Base Plus Slugging
Mantle-NY 924
Doby-Cle 924
Rosen-Cle 911
Wertz-Det-StL 887
Fain-Phi 867

Adjusted OPS
Doby-Cle 166
Mantle-NY 166
Rosen-Cle 162
Easter-Cle 144
Wertz-Det-StL 143

Adjusted Batter Runs
Mantle-NY 48.4
Rosen-Cle 47.1
Doby-Cle 45.8
Fain-Phi 32.5
Woodling-NY 28.7

Runs
Doby-Cle 104
Avila-Cle 102
Rosen-Cle 101
Berra-NY 97
Minoso-Chi 96

Hits
Fox-Chi 192
Avila-Cle 179
Robinson-Chi 176
Fain-Phi 176

Doubles
Fain-Phi 43
Mantle-NY 37
Vernon-Was 33
Robinson-Chi 33

Triples
Avila-Cle 11
Simpson-Cle 10
Rizzuto-NY 10
Fox-Chi 10

Home Runs
Doby-Cle 32
Easter-Cle 31
Berra-NY 30
Dropo-Bos-Det 29
Zernial-Phi 29

Total Bases
Rosen-Cle 297
Mantle-NY 291
Dropo-Bos-Det 282
Doby-Cle 281
Robinson-Chi 277

Runs Batted In
Rosen-Cle 105
Robinson-Chi 104
Doby-Cle 104
Zernial-Phi 100
Berra-NY 98

Stolen Bases
Minoso-Chi 22
Rivera-StL-Chi 21
Jensen-NY-Was 18
Rizzuto-NY 17
Throneberry-Bos 16

Base Stealing Runs
Jensen-NY-Was 1.9
Rizzuto-NY 1.6
Rivera-StL-Chi 1.5
Throneberry-Bos 1.1
Goodman-Bos 1.1

Fielding Runs-Infield
Goodman-Bos 23.0
Rizzuto-NY 21.4
Martin-NY 18.3
Fain-Phi 17.9
McDougald-NY 16.2

Fielding Runs-Outfield
Philley-Phi 6.9
Busby-Chi-Was 6.7
Woodling-NY 5.9
Rivera-StL-Chi 4.6
Jensen-NY-Was 2.3

Wins
Shantz-Phi 24
Wynn-Cle 23
Lemon-Cle 22
Garcia-Cle 22
Reynolds-NY 20

Winning Pct.
Shantz-Phi 774
Raschi-NY 727
Reynolds-NY 714
Lemon-Cle 667
Garcia-Cle 667

Complete Games
Lemon-Cle .....2?
Shantz-Phi .....2?
Reynolds-NY .....2?
Wynn-Cle .....1?
Garcia-Cle .....1?

Strikeouts
Reynolds-NY 160
Wynn-Cle 153
Shantz-Phi 152
Pierce-Chi 144
Garcia-Cle 143

Fewest BB/Game
Shantz-Phi 2.03
Pillette-StL 2.41
Marrero-Was 2.59
Houtteman-Det 2.65
Garcia-Cle 2.68

Games
Kennedy-Chi 47
Paige-StL 46
Garcia-Cle 46
Hooper-Phi 43

Saves
Dorish-Chi 11
Paige-StL 10
Sain-NY 7

Base Runners/9
Shantz-Phi 9.56
Dobson-Chi 10.05
Lemon-Cle 10.09
Gromek-Chi 10.20
Pierce-Chi 10.43

Adjusted Relief Runs
Dorish-Chi 11.9
Kennedy-Chi 5.5
Littlefield-Det-StL 3.6
Consuegra-Was 3.5
Newsom-Was-Phi 1.7

Relief Ranking
Dorish-Chi .....3.?
Kennedy-Chi .....3.?
Consuegra-Was .....3.?
Littlefield-Det-StL .....2.?
Newsom-Was-Phi .....2.?

Innings Pitched
Lemon-Cle 309.2
Garcia-Cle 292.1
Wynn-Cle 285.2
Shantz-Phi 279.2
Pierce-Chi 255.1

Opponents' Avg.
Lemon-Cle 208
Raschi-NY 216
Reynolds-NY 218
Dobson-Chi 222
Shantz-Phi 225

Opponents' OBP
Shantz-Phi 272
Lemon-Cle 279
Dobson-Chi 280
Pierce-Chi 289
Reynolds-NY 300

Earned Run Average
Reynolds-NY 2.06
Garcia-Cle 2.37
Shantz-Phi 2.48
Lemon-Cle 2.50
Dobson-Chi 2.51

Adjusted ERA
Reynolds-NY 161
Shantz-Phi 160
Dobson-Chi 145
Pierce-Chi 142
Garcia-Cle 141

Adjusted Starter Runs
Shantz-Phi 42.7
Reynolds-NY 35.3
Garcia-Cle 33.3
Pierce-Chi 33.0
Lemon-Cle 30.2

Pitcher Wins
Shantz-Phi .....5.?
Lemon-Cle .....4.?
Reynolds-NY .....4.?
Garcia-Cle .....3.?
Pierce-Chi .....3.?

By the Skin of Their Teeth

The Indians spent August and September shadowing the Yankees, and both clubs were 19-5 in the final month, with the Yankees only clinching in the final weekend. However, the Tribe's mediocre play in August had already doomed them. Once again, the Indians had a trio of 20-game winners, but Bob Feller began to show signs of wear. The Yankees had the better pitching despite the military-related absence of Whitey Ford and Tom Morgan; Allie Reynolds led the AL in ERA and strikeouts. Twenty-year-old Mickey Mantle became the club's offensive lynchpin.

Cleveland again had power to spare, with Larry Doby and Luke Easter finishing 1-2 in homers. The third-place White Sox didn't hit, but had speed and a fine bullpen. Ferris Fain won his second straight batting title, and his Athletics ended a surprising fourth.

For the third straight year, the Yankees lost an outfielder as Charlie Keller retired due to back problems. Boston player-manager Lou Boudreau also hung up his glove. Runs fell for the second year in a row, decreasing to just 4.18 per game, and the top five ERA qualifiers all had better averages than 1951's ERA champ.

Bob Neighbors, who had played for the 1939 Browns, went missing in action in Korea on August 8. Neighbors was the only major league player lost to the Korean War.

In a seesaw World Series dominated by home runs, the Dodgers had a three-games-to-two lead, but the Yankees worked their magic again, taking the final two games at Ebbets Field. Vic Raschi started and won Game 6 with relief help from Reynolds, and both came in to relieve the next day. Bob Kuzava saved the deciding game for the second straight season. The Yankees hit 10 homers in the Series: Johnny Mize slugged 3, Yogi Berra and Mantle added 2 apiece. Once again, Stengel's boys had scraped by.

1951 National League

TEAM	W	L	T	PCT	GB	HW	HL	R	OR	PA	H	2B	3B	HR	BB	SO	HB	SH	AVG	OBP	SLG	OPS	AOPS	BR	ABR	PF	SB	CS	BSA	BSR
NY	98	59	0	.624		50	28	781	641	6153	1396	201	53	179	671	624	40	82	.260	.347	.418	765	111	92	86	101	55	34	62	0
BRO	97	60	1	.618	1	49	29	855	672	6214	1511	249	37	184	603	649	44	75	.275	.352	.434	786	116	134	117	102	89	70	56	-5
STL	81	73	1	.526	15.5	44	34	683	671	6003	1404	230	57	95	569	492	31	86	.264	.339	.382	721	99	8	4	101	30	30	50	-4
BOS	76	78	1	.494	20.5	42	35	723	662	5968	1385	234	37	130	565	617	31	79	.262	.336	.394	730	111	22	76	93	80	34	70	6
PHI	73	81	0	.474	23.5	38	39	648	644	5961	1384	199	47	108	505	525	21	103	.260	.326	.375	701	96	-41	-31	99	63	28	69	4
CIN	68	86	1	.442	28.5	35	42	559	667	5775	1309	215	33	88	415	577	11	64	.248	.304	.351	655	81	-137	-145	102	44	40	52	-4
PIT	64	90	1	.416	32.5	32	45	689	845	5973	1372	218	56	137	557	615	22	76	.258	.331	.397	728	99	11	-9	103	29	27	52	-3
CHI	62	92	1	.403	34.5	32	45	614	750	5862	1327	200	47	103	477	647	22	56	.250	.315	.364	679	86	-89	-99	102	63	30	68	3
TOT	622					322	297	5552		47909	11088	1746	367	1024	4362	4746	222	621	.260	.331	.390	721					453	293	61	-3

TEAM	CG	SHO	GR	SV	IP	H	HR	BB	SO	BR/9	ERA	AERA	OAV	OOB	PR	APR	PF	OSB	OCS	FA	E	WPB	DP	FW	PW	BW	BSW	DIF
NY	64	9	189	18	1412.2	1334	148	482	625	11.7	3.48	113	.248	.313	75	69	99	41	40	.972	171	35	175	-1.0	6.9	8.6	.0	5.0
BRO	64	10	179	13	1423.1	1360	150	549	693	12.2	3.88	101	.253	.326	13	8	99	21	36	.979	129	39	192	1.3	.8	11.7	-.5	5.2
STL	58	9	183	23	1387.2	1391	119	568	546	12.8	3.95	100	.264	.338	1	2	100	49	30	.980	125	26	187	1.3	.2	.4	-.4	2.4
BOS	73	16	164	12	1389.0	1378	96	595	604	13.0	3.75	98	.259	.337	33	-12	93	67	47	.976	145	44	157	.3	-1.2	7.6	.6	-8.3
PHI	57	19	179	15	1384.2	1373	110	497	570	12.3	3.81	101	.258	.324	23	6	97	50	30	.977	138	46	146	.6	-3.1	.4	-.4	-2.5
CIN	55	14	204	23	1390.2	1357	119	490	584	12.3	3.70	110	.255	.323	40	56	103	75	29	.977	140	48	141	.5	5.6	-14.5	-.4	-.2
PIT	40	9	226	22	1380.1	1479	157	609	580	13.8	4.79	88	.274	.350	-128	-82	107	58	36	.972	170	36	178	-1.1	-8.2	-.9	-.3	-2.5
CHI	48	10	185	10	1385.2	1416	125	572	544	13.1	4.34	94	.265	.340	-58	-36	103	92	45	.971	181	60	161	-1.7	-3.6	-9.9	.3	-.1
TOT	459	96	1509	136	11154.0					12.6	3.96		.260	.331						.975	1199	334	1337					

Batter-Fielder Wins		Batting Average		On-Base Percentage		Slugging Average		On-Base Plus Slugging		Adjusted OPS		Adjusted Batter Runs	
Robinson-Bro	7.3	Musial-StL	355	Kiner-Pit	452	Kiner-Pit	627	Kiner-Pit	1079	Musial-StL	182	Musial-StL	70.1
Musial-StL	6.1	Ashburn-Phi	344	Musial-StL	449	Musial-StL	614	Musial-StL	1063	Kiner-Pit	182	Kiner-Pit	68.7
Campanella-Bro	5.9	Robinson-Bro	338	Robinson-Bro	415	Campanella-Bro	590	Campanella-Bro	983	Campanella-Bro	153	Robinson-Bro	44.7
Kiner-Pit	5.0	Campanella-Bro	325	Irvin-NY	415	Thomson-NY	562	Robinson-Bro	957	Robinson-Bro	153	Campanella-Bro	40.8
Ashburn-Phi	4.2	Irvin-NY	312	Stanky-NY	401	Hodges-Bro	527	Thomson-NY	947	Thomson-NY	150	Irvin-NY	39.9

Runs		Hits		Doubles		Triples		Home Runs		Total Bases		Runs Batted In	
Musial-StL	124	Ashburn-Phi	221	Dark-NY	41	Musial-StL	12	Kiner-Pit	42	Musial-StL	355	Irvin-NY	121
Kiner-Pit	124	Musial-StL	205	Kluszewski-Cin	35	Bell-Pit	12	Hodges-Bro	40	Kiner-Pit	333	Kiner-Pit	109
Hodges-Bro	118	Furillo-Bro	197	Robinson-Bro	33	Irvin-NY	11	Campanella-Bro	33	Hodges-Bro	307	Gordon-Bos	109
Dark-NY	114	Dark-NY	196	Campanella-Bro	33	Jethroe-Bos	10	Thomson-NY	32	Campanella-Bro	298	Musial-StL	108
Robinson-Bro	106	Robinson-Bro	185			Baumholtz-Chi	10	Musial-StL	32			Campanella-Bro	108

Stolen Bases		Base Stealing Runs		Fielding Runs-Infield		Fielding Runs-Outfield		Wins		Winning Pct.		Complete Games	
Jethroe-Bos	35	Jethroe-Bos	5.9	Robinson-Bro	19.1	Ashburn-Phi	21.4	Maglie-NY	23	Roe-Bro	880	Spahn-Bos	26
Ashburn-Phi	29	Ashburn-Phi	4.3	Schoendienst-StL	16.8	Furillo-Bro	12.4	Jansen-NY	23	Maglie-NY	793	Roberts-Phi	22
Robinson-Bro	25	Robinson-Bro	2.7	Hemus-StL	12.1	Sauer-Chi	8.4	Spahn-Bos	22	Newcombe-Bro	690	Maglie-NY	22
Torgeson-Bos	20	Jackson-Chi	2.0	Johnson-StL	9.6	Merriman-Cin	6.0	Roe-Bro	22	Jansen-NY	676	Roe-Bro	19
Reese-Bro	20	Irvin-NY	1.9	Strickland-Pit	8.6	Musial-StL	5.2	Roberts-Phi	21	Hearn-NY	654	Dickson-Pit	19

Strikeouts		Fewest BB/Game		Games		Saves		Base Runners/9		Adjusted Relief Runs		Relief Ranking	
Spahn-Bos	164	Raffensberger-Cin	1.38	Wilks-StL-Pit	65	Wilks-StL-Pit	13	Labine-Bro	9.92	Wilks-StL-Pit	13.8	Leonard-Chi	21.0
Newcombe-Bro	164	Jansen-NY	1.81	Werle-Pit	59	Smith-Cin	11	Raffensberger-Cin	9.99	Brazle-StL	13.8	Wilks-StL-Pit	13.9
Maglie-NY	146	Roberts-Phi	1.83	Konstanty-Phi	58	Konstanty-Phi	9	Roberts-Phi	10.03	Perkowski-Cin	11.9	Brazle-StL	10.2
Jansen-NY	145	Roe-Bro	2.24	Spencer-NY	57	Brazle-StL	7	Jansen-NY	10.11	Leonard-Chi	11.4	Smith-Cin	10.0
Rush-Chi	129	Sain-Bos	2.53	Brazle-StL	56			Maglie-NY	10.45	Kennedy-NY	10.6	Perkowski-Cin	9.7

Innings Pitched		Opponents' Avg.		Opponents' OBP		Earned Run Average		Adjusted ERA		Adjusted Starter Runs		Pitcher Wins	
Roberts-Phi	315.0	Maglie-NY	230	Roberts-Phi	278	Nichols-Bos	2.88	Maglie-NY	134	Maglie-NY	34.7	**Roberts-Phi**	3.8
Spahn-Bos	310.2	Newcombe-Bro	230	Jansen-NY	279	Maglie-NY	2.93	Roe-Bro	129	Jansen-NY	31.1	**Spahn-Bos**	3.6
Maglie-NY	298.0	Blackwell-Cin	233	Raffensberger-Cin	279	Spahn-Bos	2.98	Jansen-NY	129	Roberts-Phi	30.2	**Jansen-NY**	3.2
Dickson-Pit	288.2	Queen-Pit	233	Maglie-NY	289	Roberts-Phi	3.03	Nichols-Bos	127	Spahn-Bos	29.0	**Maglie-NY**	3.0
Jansen-NY	278.2	Branca-Bro	237	Newcombe-Bro	297	Jansen-NY	3.04	Roberts-Phi	127	Roe-Bro	27.6	**Blackwell-Cin**	2.5

Thomson's Blast Caps the Greatest Rally

The 1951 race looked like a cakewalk for Brooklyn; on August 12 the Dodgers led the slumping Giants by 13½ as Roy Campanella, Don Newcombe, Gil Hodges, Jackie Robinson, and Duke Snider were enjoying great seasons. At that point, however, the Giants, sparked by eventual Rookie of the Year Willie Mays and RBI champ Monte Irvin, won 16 straight to cut the lead to 5 games by Labor Day. Giants pitchers Larry Jansen and Sal Maglie were nearly unbeatable down the stretch.

On closing day, with both teams tied, New York won and Brooklyn managed a dramatic 14-inning victory at Philadelphia to force a best-of-three playoff. The teams split the first two, but the Dodgers jumped out in the third game and led, 4-1, in the last of the ninth. The Giants, though, rallied off Newcombe; with two on, two out, and the Dodgers up by two, Ralph Branca came in to face Bobby Thomson, who unloaded a three-run blast into the left field seats.

This, the first baseball game televised coast-to-coast, acquired a mythical quality over the years. Even in defeat, the Dodgers were honored; Campanella was voted MVP. What 1950s chauvinists don't admit is that fan interest sagged even during this great race; NL attendance dropped 13 percent. Boston's attendance fell by nearly half as rumors had the club moving to Milwaukee.

Commissioner Happy Chandler was forced out after trying to keep owners from signing high school players; Ford Frick, NL president, took the job and promised to keep out of the way. Warren Giles was voted the NL's new prexy.

Even though the charging Giants won two of the first three, the Yankees won the World Series in six. Bronx bats hammered Jansen and Maglie mercilessly. Irvin and Alvin Dark both batted over .400, but no other Giants regular even surpassed .240.

1951 American League

TEAM	W	L	T	PCT	GB	HW	HL	R	OR	PA	H	2B	3B	HR	BB	SO	HB	SH	AVG	OBP	SLG	OPS	AOPS	BR	ABR	PF	SB	CS	BSA	BSR
NY	98	56	0	.636		56	22	798	621	5927	1395	208	48	140	605	547	37	91	.269	.349	.408	757	113	61	90	96	78	39	67	4
CLE	93	61	1	.604	5	53	24	696	594	5946	1346	208	35	140	606	632	27	63	.256	.336	.389	725	106	-1	41	94	52	35	60	-1
BOS	87	67	0	.565	11	50	25	804	725	6211	1428	233	32	127	756	594	18	59	.266	.358	.392	756	98	67	-4	110	20	21	49	-3
CHI	81	73	1	.526	17	39	38	714	644	6128	1453	229	64	86	596	524	51	86	.265	.349	.385	734	105	22	38	98	99	70	59	-4
DET	73	81	0	.474	25	36	41	685	741	6008	1413	231	35	104	568	525	18	86	.265	.338	.380	718	99	-15	-18	100	37	34	52	-4
PHI	70	84	0	.455	28	38	41	736	745	6049	1381	262	43	102	677	565	34	61	.262	.349	.386	735	101	33	18	102	47	36	57	-2
WAS	62	92	0	.403	36	32	44	672	764	5979	1399	242	45	54	560	515	26	64	.263	.336	.355	691	93	-60	-48	98	45	38	54	-3
STL	52	102	0	.338	46	24	53	611	882	5848	1288	223	47	86	521	693	16	92	.247	.317	.357	674	84	-105	-122	103	35	38	48	-6
TOT	617					328	288	5716		48096	11103	1836	349	839	4889	4595	227	619	.262	.342	.381	723					413	311	57	-18

TEAM	CG	SHO	GR	SV	IP	H	HR	BB	SO	BR/9	ERA	AERA	OAV	OOB	PR	APR	PF	OSB	OCS	FA	E	WPB	DP	FW	PW	BW	BSW	DIF
NY	66	24	158	22	1367.0	1290	92	562	664	12.4	3.56	107	.250	.328	85	44	93	41	47	.975	144	28	190	.3	4.3	8.9	.6	6.9
CLE	76	10	135	19	1391.1	1287	85	577	642	12.2	3.38	112	.245	.323	114	68	92	54	36	.978	134	29	151	.9	6.7	4.0	.1	4.2
BOS	46	7	210	24	1399.0	1413	99	599	658	13.2	4.14	108	.264	.342	-2	46	108	47	27	.977	141	37	184	.5	4.5	-.4	-.0	5.5
CHI	74	11	150	14	1418.1	1353	109	549	572	12.2	3.50	115	.252	.323	97	86	98	57	25	.975	151	25	176	.0	8.5	3.7	-.0	-8.1
DET	51	8	195	17	1384.0	1385	103	602	597	13.2	4.29	97	.262	.342	-26	-18	101	71	43	.973	163	53	166	-.7	-1.8	-1.8	-.2	.4
PHI	52	7	157	22	1358.0	1421	109	677	437	13.4	4.47	96	.272	.347	-52	-27	104	34	46	.978	136	42	204	.8	-2.7	1.8	-.0	-6.9
WAS	58	6	160	13	1366.1	1429	110	630	475	13.7	4.49	91	.269	.348	-55	-59	99	52	36	.973	160	23	148	-.5	-5.8	-4.7	-.0	-3.9
STL	56	5	180	9	1370.1	1525	132	801	550	15.5	5.18	85	.282	.379	-160	-112	107	58	51	.971	172	41	179	-1.2	-11.0	-12.0	-.4	-.1
TOT	479	78	1345	140	11054.1					13.2	4.12		.262	.342						.975	1201	278	1398					

Batter-Fielder Wins		Batting Average		On-Base Percentage		Slugging Average		On-Base Plus Slugging		Adjusted OPS		Adjusted Batter Runs	
Fain-Phi	4.3	Fain-Phi	344	Williams-Bos	464	Williams-Bos	556	Williams-Bos	1019	Doby-Cle	163	Williams-Bos	52.1
Joost-Phi	4.3	Minoso-Cle-Chi	326	Fain-Phi	451	Doby-Cle	512	Doby-Cle	941	Williams-Bos	159	Doby-Cle	44.7
Williams-Bos	4.1	Kell-Det	319	Doby-Cle	428	Zernial-Chi-Phi	511	Minoso-Cle-Chi	922	Minoso-Cle-Chi	152	Minoso-Cle-Chi	41.5
Doby-Cle	3.8	Williams-Bos	318	Yost-Was	423	Wertz-Det	511	Fain-Phi	921	Fain-Phi	146	Yost-Was	34.5
Berra-NY	3.5	Fox-Chi	313	Minoso-Cle-Chi	422	Minoso-Cle-Chi	500	Wertz-Det	894	Wertz-Det	140	Fain-Phi	33.4

Runs		Hits		Doubles		Triples		Home Runs		Total Bases		Runs Batted In	
DiMaggio-Bos	113	Kell-Det	191	Minoso-Cle-Chi	36	Minoso-Cle-Chi	14	Zernial-Chi-Phi	33	Williams-Bos	295	Zernial-Chi-Phi	129
Minoso-Cle-Chi	112	Fox-Chi	189	Mele-Was	36	Coleman-StL-Chi	12	Williams-Bos	30	Zernial-Chi-Phi	292	Williams-Bos	126
Yost-Was	109	DiMaggio-Bos	189	Kell-Det	36	Fox-Chi	12	Robinson-Chi	29	Robinson-Chi	279	Robinson-Chi	117
Williams-Bos	109	Minoso-Cle-Chi	173			Young-StL	9			Berra-NY	269	Easter-Cle	103
Joost-Phi	107	Williams-Bos	169							DiMaggio-Bos	267	Rosen-Cle	102

Stolen Bases		Base Stealing Runs		Fielding Runs-Infield		Fielding Runs-Outfield		Wins		Winning Pct.		Complete Games	
Minoso-Cle-Chi	31	Minoso-Cle-Chi	3.3	Fain-Phi	16.2	Coan-Was	18.4	Feller-Cle	22	Feller-Cle	733	Garver-StL	24
Busby-Chi	26	Rizzuto-NY	2.9	Stephens-Bos	11.8	Noren-Was	12.3	Raschi-NY	21	Lopat-NY	700	Wynn-Cle	21
Rizzuto-NY	18	Busby-Chi	1.9	Carrasquel-Chi	11.6	Zernial-Chi-Phi	8.5	Lopat-NY	21	Reynolds-NY	680	Lopat-NY	20
		Carrasquel-Chi	1.7	Priddy-Det	11.3	Delsing-StL	7.7			Raschi-NY	677	Pierce-Chi	18
		McDougald-NY	1.3	Rizzuto-NY	11.2	Busby-Chi	6.7			Shantz-Phi	643		

Strikeouts		Fewest BB/Game		Games		Saves		Base Runners/9		Adjusted Relief Runs		Relief Ranking	
Raschi-NY	164	Hutchinson-Det	1.29	Kinder-Bos	63	Kinder-Bos	14	Aloma-Chi	10.13	Kinder-Bos	24.3	Kinder-Bos	28.4
Wynn-Cle	133	Lopat-NY	2.72	Brissie-Phi-Cle	56	Scheib-Phi	10	Zoldak-Phi	10.62	Aloma-Chi	18.5	Aloma-Chi	16.2
Lemon-Cle	132	Pierce-Chi	2.73	Garcia-Cle	47	Brissie-Phi-Cle	9	Lopat-NY	10.85	Masterson-Bos	7.2	Brissie-Phi-Cle	4.2
Gray-Det	131	Hooper-NY	2.90	Scheib-Phi	46	Reynolds-NY	7	Kinder-Bos	10.91	Brissie-Phi-Cle	5.2	Masterson-Bos	3.8
McDermott-Bos	127	Garcia-Cle	2.91			Garcia-Cle	6	Rogovin-Det-Chi	10.97	Ostrowski-NY	3.1	Ostrowski-NY	3.3

Innings Pitched		Opponents' Avg.		Opponents' OBP		Earned Run Average		Adjusted ERA		Adjusted Starter Runs		Pitcher Wins	
Wynn-Cle	274.1	Reynolds-NY	213	Lopat-NY	298	Rogovin-Det-Chi	2.78	Rogovin-Det-Chi	146	Rogovin-Det-Chi	29.7	Parnell-Bos	3.3
Lemon-Cle	263.1	Wynn-Cle	225	Rogovin-Det-Chi	301	Lopat-NY	2.91	Parnell-Bos	137	Pierce-Chi	28.0	Lopat-NY	3.3
Raschi-NY	258.1	McDermott-Bos	226	Wynn-Cle	301	Wynn-Cle	3.02	McDermott-Bos	133	Wynn-Cle	26.7	Pierce-Chi	3.1
Garcia-Cle	254.0	Rogovin-Det-Chi	235	Hutchinson-Det	302	Pierce-Chi	3.03	Pierce-Chi	133	Lopat-NY	26.2	Wynn-Cle	3.1
Feller-Cle	249.2	Lopat-NY	239	Reynolds-NY	304	Reynolds-NY	3.05	Lopat-NY	131	Parnell-Bos	23.7	Garver-StL	2.9

A Nation Turns Its Eyes From Joltin' Joe to The Mick

Perennial doormat Chicago jumped out in front and led the league during June. Outfielder Minnie Minoso helped manager Paul Richards turn the White Sox around. Chicago faded while the Yankees, Red Sox, and Indians took over. Cleveland and New York stayed neck-and-neck, with Boston close behind. On September 15-16, with the Indians up one game, New York took two from the Tribe at Yankee Stadium, starting Cleveland on a fatal slide.

Despite losing Whitey Ford to military service, New York pitchers led in shutouts and strikeouts, and catcher Yogi Berra was MVP. Casey Stengel continued his successful platoon system, supplementing what appeared to be an unprepossessing lineup. Bob Feller, Mike Garcia, and Early Wynn each won 20 for Cleveland, but three offensive dead spots negated Larry Doby and Al Rosen's hitting. Despite their big bats—Vern Stephens, Ted Williams, and Bobby Doerr (whose career was ended by knee problems)—the Red Sox didn't hit enough.

Bill Veeck, now owner of the St. Louis Browns, had to get creative to draw fans to his poor team. On August 19 he sent three-foot, seven-inch Eddie Gaedel to the plate as a pinch hitter. Five days later fans voted on in-game decisions with placards. The Browns drew 16 percent more fans than in 1950, but the club finished last both on the field and in attendance.

The Yankees took six games to win a defensive-oriented World Series from the Giants. The heroes were Eddie Lopat, who allowed 1 run in 18 innings, and four relievers who tossed 7.2 scoreless innings. Bob Kuzava saved decisive Game 6 for Vic Raschi.

After hitting .261 in the Series, 36-year-old Joe DiMaggio retired; injuries rendered him unable to play to his own standards. The Yankees had already broken in his successor, Mickey Mantle.

Hy Turkin and S.C. Thompson's Official Encyclopedia of Baseball, the first modern baseball reference, was published. In December "Shoeless" Joe Jackson, 62, became the first of the Black Sox to die.

1950 National League

TEAM	W	L	T	PCT	GB	HW	HL	R	OR	PA	H	2B	3B	HR	BB	SO	HB	SH	AVG	OBP	SLG	OPS	AOPS	BR	ABR	PF	SB	CS	BSA	BSR
PHI	91	63	3	.591		47	30	722	624	6051	1440	225	55	125	535	569	24	66	.265	.334	.396	730	100	-16	-4	98	33			
BRO	89	65	1	.578	2	48	30	847	724	6086	1461	247	46	194	607	632	27	88	.272	.349	.444	793	113	109	92	102	77			
NY	86	68	0	.558	5	44	32	735	643	5981	1352	204	50	133	627	629	41	75	.258	.342	.392	734	100	3	-1	101	42			
BOS	83	71	2	.539	8	46	31	785	736	6079	1411	246	36	148	615	616	27	74	.263	.342	.405	747	110	26	78	94	71			
STL	78	75	0	.510	12.5	47	29	693	670	5917	1353	255	50	102	606	604	23	73	.259	.339	.386	725	93	-12	-44	105	23			
CIN	66	87	0	.431	24.5	38	38	654	734	5845	1366	257	27	99	504	497	16	72	.260	.327	.376	703	91	-64	-66	100	37			
CHI	64	89	1	.418	26.5	35	42	643	772	5794	1298	224	47	161	479	767	31	54	.248	.315	.401	716	95	-56	-48	99	46			
PIT	57	96	1	.373	33.5	33	44	681	857	5976	1404	227	59	138	564	693	31	54	.264	.338	.406	744	99	11	-12	103	43			
TOT	618					338	276	5760		47729	11085	1885	370	1100	4537	5007	220	556	.261	.336	.401	737					372			

TEAM	CG	SHO	GR	SV	IP	H	HR	BB	SO	BR/9	ERA	AERA	OAV	OOB	PR	APR	PF	OSB	OCS	FA	E	WPB	DP	FW	PW	BW	BSW	DIF
PHI	57	13	167	27	1406.0	1324	122	530	620	12.0	3.50	116	.250	.320	101	88	98	47	29	.975	151	34	155	.1	8.6	-.4		5.7
BRO	62	10	195	21	1389.2	1397	163	591	772	13.0	4.28	96	.263	.339	-22	-29	99	33	38	.979	127	35	183	1.4	-2.8	9.0		4.5
NY	70	19	179	15	1375.0	1268	140	536	596	12.0	3.71	110	.246	.320	66	59	99	31	38	.977	137	37	181	.8	5.8	-.0		2.6
BOS	88	7	135	10	1385.1	1411	129	554	615	13.0	4.14	93	.263	.336	0	-48	93	53	44	.970	182	35	146	-1.7	-4.7	7.6		4.7
STL	57	10	185	14	1356.0	1398	119	535	603	13.0	3.97	108	.268	.339	26	47	104	37	30	.978	130	31	172	1.1	4.6	-4.3		.1
CIN	67	7	157	13	1357.2	1363	145	582	686	13.2	4.32	98	.259	.338	-26	-13	102	64	31	.976	140	49	132	.5	-1.3	-6.5		-3.3
CHI	55	9	199	19	1371.1	1452	130	593	559	13.6	4.28	98	.271	.347	-21	-11	101	70	42	.968	201	43	169	-2.8	-1.1	-4.7		-3.9
PIT	42	6	213	16	1368.2	1472	152	616	556	13.9	4.96	88	.275	.353	-124	-83	106	37	38	.977	136	39	165	.8	-8.1	-1.2		-11.0
TOT	498	81	1430	135	11009.2					13.0	4.14		.261	.336						.975	1204	303	1303					

Batter-Fielder Wins		Batting Average		On-Base Percentage		Slugging Average		On-Base Plus Slugging		Adjusted OPS		Adjusted Batter Runs	
Robinson-Bro	5.0	Musial-StL	.346	Stanky-NY	.460	Musial-StL	.596	Musial-StL	1034	Musial-StL	161	Musial-StL	52.7
Stanky-NY	4.6	Robinson-Bro	.328	Musial-StL	.437	Pafko-Chi	.591	Kiner-Pit	.998	Gordon-Bos	160	Kiner-Pit	45.4
Musial-StL	3.8	Snider-Bro	.321	Robinson-Bro	.423	Kiner-Pit	.590	Pafko-Chi	.989	Pafko-Chi	158	Gordon-Bos	43.8
Gordon-Bos	3.6	Ennis-Phi	.311	Glaviano-StL	.421	Gordon-Bos	.557	Gordon-Bos	.960	Kiner-Pit	154	Pafko-Chi	43.1
Seminick-Phi	3.6	Kluszewski-Cin	.307	Torgeson-Bos	.412	Snider-Bro	.553	Snider-Bro	.932	Elliott-Bos	143	Torgeson-Bos	40.7

Runs		Hits		Doubles		Triples		Home Runs		Total Bases		Runs Batted In	
Torgeson-Bos	120	Snider-Bro	199	Schoendienst-StL	43	Ashburn-Phi	14	Kiner-Pit	47	Snider-Bro	343	Ennis-Phi	126
Stanky-NY	115	Musial-StL	192	Musial-StL	41	Bell-Pit	11	Pafko-Chi	36	Musial-StL	331	Kiner-Pit	118
Kiner-Pit	112	Furillo-Bro	189	Robinson-Bro	39	Snider-Bro	10	Sauer-Chi	32	Ennis-Phi	328	Hodges-Bro	113
Snider-Bro	109	Ennis-Phi	185	Kluszewski-Cin	37	Smalley-Chi	9	Hodges-Bro	32	Kiner-Pit	323	Kluszewski-Cin	111
Musial-StL	105	Waitkus-Phi	182	Dark-NY	36	Schoendienst-StL	9			Pafko-Chi	304	Musial-StL	109

Stolen Bases		Base Stealing Runs		Fielding Runs-Infield		Fielding Runs-Outfield		Wins		Winning Pct.		Complete Games	
Jethroe-Bos	35			Smalley-Chi	19.6	Bell-Pit	4.5	Spahn-Bos	21	Maglie-NY	.818	Bickford-Bos	27
Reese-Bro	17			Cox-Bro	12.1	Lockman-NY	4.1	Sain-Bos	20	Konstanty-Phi	.696	Spahn-Bos	25
Snider-Bro	16			Schoendienst-StL	11.8	Marshall-Bos	3.6	Roberts-Phi	20	Simmons-Phi	.680	Sain-Bos	25
Torgeson-Bos	15			Robinson-Bro	9.6	Gordon-Bos	3.5			Roberts-Phi	.645	Roberts-Phi	21
Ashburn-Phi	14			Thompson-NY	8.2	Adcock-Cin	3.5					Jansen-NY	21

Strikeouts		Fewest BB/Game		Games		Saves		Base Runners/9		Adjusted Relief Runs		Relief Ranking	
Spahn-Bos	191	Raffensberger-Cin	1.51	Konstanty-Phi	74	Konstanty-Phi	22	Hearn-StL-NY	8.60	Konstanty-Phi	24.1	Konstanty-Phi	40.6
Blackwell-Cin	188	Jansen-NY	1.80	Dickson-Pit	51	Werle-Pit	8	Konstanty-Phi	9.36	Smith-Cin	4.0	Smith-Cin	3.9
Jansen-NY	161	Sain-Bos	2.26	Werle-Pit	48	Hogue-Bos	7	Jansen-NY	9.62	Kramer-NY	2.2	Kramer-NY	2.1
Simmons-Phi	146	Roberts-Phi	2.28	Maglie-NY	47	Branca-Bro	7	Roberts-Phi	10.68	Leonard-Chi	1.7	Leonard-Chi	1.5
Roberts-Phi	146	Roe-Bro	2.37	Brazle-StL	46			Church-Phi	10.71				

Innings Pitched		Opponents' Avg.		Opponents' OBP		Earned Run Average		Adjusted ERA		Adjusted Starter Runs		Pitcher Wins	
Bickford-Bos	311.2	Blackwell-Cin	.210	Jansen-NY	.271	Hearn-StL-NY	2.49	Maglie-NY	151	Roberts-Phi	37.7	Konstanty-Phi	3.8
Roberts-Phi	304.1	Simmons-Phi	.223	Roberts-Phi	.297	Maglie-NY	2.71	Blackwell-Cin	143	Jansen-NY	32.8	Blackwell-Cin	3.6
Spahn-Bos	293.0	Maglie-NY	.226	Brecheen-StL	.298	Blackwell-Cin	2.97	Lanier-StL	137	Blackwell-Cin	32.5	Jansen-NY	3.6
Sain-Bos	278.1	Spahn-Bos	.227	Spahn-Bos	.299	Jansen-NY	3.01	Jansen-NY	136	Maglie-NY	31.8	Roberts-Phi	3.2
Jansen-NY	275.0	Jansen-NY	.232	Blackwell-Cin	.301	Roberts-Phi	3.02	Roberts-Phi	134	Roe-Bro	24.5	Maglie-NY	3.1

Whizzing Into a Title

Prior to the season, the strike zone was shrunk to a range from the armpits to the top of knees. While league scoring rose 2.6 percent, which was predictable, strikeouts also increased by 10 percent—to an all-time NL high of 4.05 per game—which was not. Homers skyrocketed another 18 percent to 1,100, marking the first time either league had cracked four digits. Seven NL clubs cleared 100 long balls; the Reds hit 99.

Boston's farm system was producing players; Joe Adcock and Sam Jethroe made their debuts, and in 1951, Johnny Logan made his first appearance. Grover Cleveland Alexander, perhaps the NL's greatest right-hander ever, died destitute in a Nebraska rooming house at age 63. Meanwhile, two fine pitchers of the 1940s, Kirby Higbe and Bucky Walters, were finished.

The Phillies, nicknamed the "Whiz Kids" because of youngsters Robin Roberts, Curt Simmons, Granny Hamner, Willie Jones, and Richie Ashburn, emerged from the pack in July. However, a veteran—33-year-old reliever Jim Konstanty—was league MVP, appearing in relief a record 74 times and saving 22, an NL mark.

Philly was well in front until the fence-busting Dodgers, led by Duke Snider and Gil Hodges, made their move. Nine games down on September 18, the Dodgers won 13 of 15 while the Phils slumped. The lead was just one game with only one left to play—a showdown at Ebbets Field. But the Whiz Kids came through, defeating Brooklyn 4-1 on a Dick Sisler homer in the 10th. The heroics were through for the Phillies, however. The Yankees took them out in four straight in a competitive, but short, World Series.

For baseball, the postwar boom was over; for the third straight season, NL attendance dropped sharply. Owners in the minors and majors began worrying about television and the exodus to the suburbs.

1950 American League

TEAM	W	L	T	PCT	GB	HW	HL	R	OR	PA	H	2B	3B	HR	BB	SO	HB	SH	AVG	OBP	SLG	OPS	AOPS	BR	ABR	PF	SB	CS	BSA
NY	98	56	1	.636		53	24	914	691	6164	1511	234	70	159	687	463	31	85	.282	.367	.441	808	116	92	118	97	41	28	59
DET	95	59	3	.617	3	50	30	837	713	6232	1518	285	50	114	722	480	19	110	.282	.369	.417	786	104	65	38	103	23	40	37
BOS	94	60	0	.610	4	55	22	1027	804	6322	1665	287	61	161	719	582	25	62	.302	.385	.464	849	112	189	101	110	32	17	65
CLE	92	62	1	.597	6	49	28	806	654	6080	1417	222	46	164	693	624	38	86	.269	.358	.422	780	109	40	68	97	40	34	54
WAS	67	87	1	.435	31	35	42	690	813	6028	1365	190	53	76	671	606	32	74	.260	.347	.360	707	91	-96	-62	95	19	25	46
CHI	60	94	2	.390	38	35	42	625	749	5945	1368	172	47	93	551	566	28	106	.260	.333	.364	697	86	-131	-113	97	19	22	46
STL	58	96	0	.377	40	27	47	684	916	5970	1269	235	43	106	690	744	20	97	.246	.337	.370	707	84	-101	-125	104	39	40	49
PHI	52	102	0	.338	46	29	48	670	913	5993	1361	204	53	100	685	493	23	73	.261	.349	.378	727	94	-58	-44	98	42	25	63
TOT	620					333	283	6253		48734	11474	1829	423	973	5418	4558	216	693	.271	.356	.402	759				278	231	55	

TEAM	CG	SHO	GR	SV	IP	H	HR	BB	SO	BR/9	ERA	AERA	OAV	OOB	PR	APR	PF	OSB	OCS	FA	E	WPB	DP	FW	PW	BW	BSW	DI
NY	66	12	141	31	1372.2	1322	118	708	712	13.5	4.15	103	.255	.348	65	23	94	26	29	.980	119	27	188	1.3	2.2	11.0	.1	6.4
DET	72	9	153	20	1407.1	1444	141	553	576	13.0	4.12	114	.267	.339	71	86	102	26	26	.981	120	33	194	1.3	8.1	3.6	-.6	5.7
BOS	66	6	183	28	1362.1	1413	121	748	630	14.4	4.88	100	.270	.364	-46	2	107	31	22	.981	111	38	181	1.7	.2	9.5	.3	
CLE	69	11	184	16	1378.2	1289	120	647	674	12.8	3.75	115	.248	.333	126	94	95	24	36	.978	129	29	160	.7	8.8	6.4	-.0	
WAS	59	7	156	18	1364.2	1479	99	648	486	14.2	4.66	96	.278	.359	-12	-25	98	49	29	.972	167	37	181	-1.4	-2.3	-5.8	.2	
CHI	62	7	182	9	1365.2	1370	107	734	566	14.0	4.41	102	.263	.356	26	12	98	49	32	.977	140	36	181	.2	1.1	-10.6	-.1	
STL	56	7	188	14	1365.1	1629	129	651	448	15.2	5.20	95	.295	.372	-94	-35	108	36	38	.967	196	37	155	-3.1	-3.3	-11.7	-.2	
PHI	50	3	153	18	1346.1	1528	138	729	466	15.3	5.49	83	.287	.376	-136	-141	99	37	19	.974	155	49	208	-.8	-13.2	-4.1	.2	
TOT	500	62	1340	154	10963.0					14.0	4.58		.271	.356						.976	1137	286	1448					

Batter-Fielder Wins		Batting Average		On-Base Percentage		Slugging Average		On-Base Plus Slugging		Adjusted OPS		Adjusted Batter Runs	
Rizzuto-NY	4.0	Goodman-Bos	.354	Doby-Cle	.442	DiMaggio-NY	.585	Doby-Cle	.986	Doby-Cle	156	Doby-Cle	46
Rosen-Cle	4.0	Kell-Det	.340	Yost-Was	.440	Dropo-Bos	.583	DiMaggio-NY	.979	DiMaggio-NY	152	DiMaggio-NY	39
Berra-NY	3.8	DiMaggio-Bos	.328	Pesky-Bos	.437	Evers-Det	.551	Dropo-Bos	.961	Rosen-Cle	146	Rosen-Cle	39
Doby-Cle	3.2	Doby-Cle	.326	Fain-Phi	.430	Doby-Cle	.545	Evers-Det	.959	Evers-Det	139	Williams-Bos	34
Priddy-Det	3.2	Zarilla-Bos	.325	Goodman-Bos	.427	Rosen-Cle	.543	Rosen-Cle	.948	Berra-NY	136	Yost-Was	31

Runs		Hits		Doubles		Triples		Home Runs		Total Bases		Runs Batted In	
DiMaggio-Bos	131	Kell-Det	218	Kell-Det	56	Evers-Det	11	Rosen-Cle	37	Dropo-Bos	326	Stephens-Bos	14
Stephens-Bos	125	Rizzuto-NY	200	Wertz-Det	37	Doerr-Bos	11	Dropo-Bos	34	Stephens-Bos	321	Dropo-Bos	14
Rizzuto-NY	125	DiMaggio-Bos	193	Rizzuto-NY	36	DiMaggio-Bos	11	DiMaggio-NY	32	Berra-NY	318	Berra-NY	12
Berra-NY	116	Berra-NY	192	Evers-Det	35			Stephens-Bos	30	Kell-Det	310	Wertz-Det	12
		Stephens-Bos	185	Stephens-Bos	34			Zernial-Chi	29	DiMaggio-NY	307	DiMaggio-NY	12

Stolen Bases		Base Stealing Runs		Fielding Runs-Infield		Fielding Runs-Outfield		Wins		Winning Pct.		Complete Games	
DiMaggio-Bos	15	DiMaggio-Bos	1.9	Priddy-Det	27.9	Woodling-NY	12.4	B.Lemon-Cle	23	Raschi-NY	.724	B.Lemon-Cle	2
Valo-Phi	12	Vernon-Cle-Was	1.4	Pesky-Bos	16.4	Noren-Was	9.2	Raschi-NY	21	Wynn-Cle	.692	Garver-StL	2
Rizzuto-NY	12	Collins-NY	1.1	Carrasquel-Chi	10.7	Sievers-StL	7.3	Houtteman-Det	19	Lopat-NY	.692	Parnell-Bos	2
Coan-Was	10	Avila-Cle	1.1	Fain-Phi	10.7	Chapman-Phi	5.2			Hutchinson-Det	.680	Houtteman-Det	2
Lipon-Det	9	Jensen-NY	9	Doerr-Bos	9.4	Philley-Chi	4.6			B.Lemon-Cle	.676		

Strikeouts		Fewest BB/Game		Games		Saves		Base Runners/9		Adjusted Relief Runs		Relief Ranking	
B.Lemon-Cle	170	Hutchinson-Det	1.86	Harris-Was	53	Harris-Was	15	Gromek-Cle	10.56	Judson-Chi	7.8	Ferrick-StL-NY	10
Reynolds-NY	160	Lopat-NY	2.48	Kinder-Bos	48	Page-NY	13	Ford-NY	11.33	Aloma-Chi	5.7	Aloma-Chi	5
Raschi-NY	155	Overmire-StL	2.52	Ferrick-StL-NY	46	Ferrick-StL-NY	11	Ferrick-StL-NY	11.38	Ferrick-StL-NY	5.3	Flores-Cle	5
Wynn-Cle	143	Trout-Det	3.12	Judson-Chi	46	Kinder-Bos	9	Wynn-Cle	11.41	Flores-Cle	4.2	Benton-Cle	3
Feller-Cle	119	Houtteman-Det	3.24	Brissie-Phi	46	Brissie-Phi	8	Ostrowski-StL-NY	11.50	Benton-Cle	4.0	Judson-Chi	3

Innings Pitched		Opponents' Avg.		Opponents' OBP		Earned Run Average		Adjusted ERA		Adjusted Starter Runs		Pitcher Wins	
B.Lemon-Cle	288.0	Wynn-Cle	.212	Wynn-Cle	.305	Wynn-Cle	3.20	Garver-StL	146	Garver-StL	39.1	Garver-StL	
Houtteman-Det	274.2	Pierce-Chi	.228	Lopat-NY	.317	Garver-StL	3.39	Parnell-Bos	136	Houtteman-Det	37.5	Wynn-Cle	
Garver-StL	260.0	Reynolds-NY	.242	Houtteman-Det	.322	Feller-Cle	3.43	Wynn-Cle	135	Parnell-Bos	30.1	Houtteman-Det	3
Raschi-NY	256.2	Raschi-NY	.243	Feller-Cle	.325	Lopat-NY	3.47	Houtteman-Det	132	Wynn-Cle	27.6	B.Lemon-Cle	3
Parnell-Bos	249.0	Cain-Chi	.244	Raschi-NY	.327	Houtteman-Det	3.54	Feller-Cle	126	Feller-Cle	27.2	Parnell-Bos	3

Casey, Part II

A four-way race rolled into September with the clubs holding the exact positions in which they finished: New York, Detroit, Boston, and Cleveland. First, the seventh-place Browns knocked out the Indians, who then damaged the Red Sox and Tigers as the Yankees turned on the juice in the last week. While Yogi Berra and Joe DiMaggio enjoyed spectacular seasons for New York, shortstop Phil Rizzuto's surprise performance garnered him the MVP trophy.

Detroit used control pitching and on-base ability to finish just 3 games back. Cleveland led the league in ERA and homers, but Joe Gordon and Jim Hegan hit .235 and .219 in a league that batted .271.

The third-place Red Sox trampled their opponents at home, but were barely .500 on the road. Their offense scored a staggering 1,027 runs overall, by far highest in the AL, but ranked just fourth in scoring away from home. Mostly because Boston scored a ridiculous 8.16 runs per game at Fenway, league runs per contest jumped to 5.04, the most between 1939 and 199[4]. Homers also increased 27 percent to 973, another new record.

Whitey Ford successfully debuted for the Yankees whi[le] Tommy Henrich retired. Veteran middle infielders Gordon an[d] Luke Appling also called it quits, and Philadelphia manage[r] Connie Mack stepped down at age 87; he had managed th[e] Athletics for half a century.

Many AL teams were slow to sign blacks, and for sever[al] years the Junior Circuit developed few impressive youngsters. Th[e] top rookie of 1950 was 27-year-old first baseman Walt Drop[o].

The Yankees got a tougher bargain than they counted on i[n] the World Series against the Phillies, but swept anyway. The fir[st] three games were one-run affairs, and in Game 4 Ford led, 5-[ ] in the ninth until Philly scored twice. Allie Reynolds, the Gam[e] 2 winner, came in to save the day. New York held Philadelphia t[o] just 5 runs overall.

1949 National League

TEAM	W	L	T	PCT	GB	HW	HL	R	OR	PA	H	2B	3B	HR	BB	SO	HB	SH	AVG	OBP	SLG	OPS	AOPS	BR	ABR	PF	SB	CS	BSA	BSR
BRO	97	57	2	.630		48	29	879	651	6173	1477	236	47	152	638	570	33	102	.274	.354	.419	773	110	106	73	104	117			
STL	96	58	3	.623	1	51	26	766	616	6151	1513	281	54	102	569	482	25	94	.277	.348	.404	752	103	64	29	105	17			
PHI	81	73	0	.526	16	40	37	662	668	5935	1349	232	55	122	528	670	26	74	.254	.325	.388	713	100	-28	-9	97	27			
BOS	75	79	3	.487	22	43	34	706	719	6139	1376	246	33	103	684	656	23	96	.258	.345	.374	719	105	10	51	95	28			
NY	73	81	2	.474	24	43	34	736	693	6009	1383	203	52	147	613	523	24	64	.261	.340	.401	741	105	35	36	100	43			
PIT	71	83	0	.461	26	36	41	681	760	5870	1350	191	41	126	548	554	22	86	.259	.332	.384	716	96	-16	-33	103	48			
CIN	62	92	2	.403	35	35	42	627	770	5994	1423	264	35	86	429	559	20	76	.260	.316	.368	684	88	-84	-91	101	31			
CHI	61	93	0	.396	36	33	44	593	773	5723	1336	212	53	97	396	573	26	87	.256	.312	.373	685	91	-88	-72	97	53			
TOT	622					329	287	5650		47994	11207	1865	370	935	4405	4587	199	679	.262	.334	.389	723					364			

TEAM	CG	SHO	GR	SV	IP	H	HR	BB	SO	BR/9	ERA	AERA	OAV	OOB	PR	APR	PF	OSB	OCS	FA	E	WPB	DP	FW	PW	BW	BSW	DIF
BRO	62	15	193	17	1408.2	1306	132	582	743	12.2	3.80	108	.246	.324	37	46	102	25	31	.980	122	31	162	1.5	4.6	7.2		6.7
STL	64	13	187	19	1407.2	1356	87	507	606	12.1	3.44	121	.252	.319	94	110	103	40	25	.976	146	29	149	.3	10.9	2.9		5.0
PHI	58	12	190	15	1391.2	1389	104	502	495	12.4	3.89	101	.268	.335	23	9	98	56	39	.974	156	35	141	-.5	.9	-.9		4.5
BOS	68	12	159	11	1400.0	1466	110	520	589	12.9	3.99	95	.268	.334	8	-35	94	49	32	.976	148	30	144	.1	-3.5	5.1		-3.7
NY	68	10	186	9	1374.1	1328	132	544	516	12.4	3.82	104	.249	.321	33	25	99	50	26	.973	161	43	134	-.6	2.5	3.6		-9.4
PIT	53	9	179	15	1356.0	1452	142	535	556	13.4	4.57	92	.274	.344	-79	-53	106	35	38	.978	132	34	173	.9	-5.3	-3.3		1.7
CIN	55	10	210	6	1401.2	1423	124	640	538	13.4	4.34	96	.264	.345	-47	-24	104	41	39	.977	138	48	150	.6	-2.4	-9.0		-4.2
CHI	44	8	200	17	1357.2	1487	104	575	544	13.8	4.50	90	.279	.351	-70	-71	100	68	43	.970	186	56	160	-2.1	-7.0	-7.1		.3
TOT	472	89	1504	109	11097.2					12.8	4.04		.262	.334						.975	1189	306	1213					.3

Batter-Fielder Wins
Kiner-Pit 5.1
Musial-StL 5.1
Robinson-Bro 5.0
B.Elliott-Bos 4.0
Campanella-Bro ...3.1

Batting Average
Robinson-Bro 342
Musial-StL 338
Slaughter-StL 336
Furillo-Bro 322
Kiner-Pit 310

On-Base Percentage
Musial-StL 438
Robinson-Bro 432
Kiner-Pit 432
Slaughter-StL 418
Stanky-Bos 417

Slugging Average
Kiner-Pit 658
Musial-StL 624
Robinson-Bro 528
Ennis-Phi 525
Thomson-NY 518

On-Base Plus Slugging
Kiner-Pit 1089
Musial-StL 1062
Robinson-Bro 960
Slaughter-StL 929
Gordon-NY 909

Adjusted OPS
Kiner-Pit 183
Musial-StL 174
Robinson-Bro 150
Gordon-NY 142
Slaughter-StL 141

Adjusted Batter Runs
Kiner-Pit 67.0
Musial-StL 66.9
Robinson-Bro 45.7
Slaughter-StL 35.5
Gordon-NY 33.1

Runs
Reese-Bro 132
Musial-StL 128
Robinson-Bro 122
Kiner-Pit 116
Schoendienst-StL ..102

Hits
Musial-StL 207
Robinson-Bro 203
Thomson-NY 198
Slaughter-StL 191
Schoendienst-StL ...190

Doubles
Musial-StL 41
Ennis-Phi 39
Robinson-Bro 38
Hatton-Cin 38

Triples
Slaughter-StL 13
Musial-StL 13
Robinson-Bro 12
Ennis-Phi 11
Ashburn-Phi 11

Home Runs
Kiner-Pit 54
Musial-StL 36
Sauer-Cin-Chi 31
Thomson-NY 27
Gordon-NY 26

Total Bases
Musial-StL 382
Kiner-Pit 361
Thomson-NY 332
Ennis-Phi 320
Robinson-Bro 313

Runs Batted In
Kiner-Pit 127
Robinson-Bro 124
Musial-StL 123
Hodges-Bro 115
Ennis-Phi 110

Stolen Bases
Robinson-Bro 37
Reese-Bro 26

Base Stealing Runs

Fielding Runs-Infield
Schoendienst-StL ...27.5
Smalley-Chi 17.6
Marion-StL 12.4
Reich-Chi 12.2
B.Elliott-Bos 11.4

Fielding Runs-Outfield
Ashburn-Phi 10.4
Thomson-NY 7.6
Holmes-Bos 6.2
Diering-StL 6.2
Sauer-Cin-Chi 4.5

Wins
Spahn-Bos 21
Pollet-StL 20
Raffensberger-Cin ...18

Winning Pct.
Roe-Bro 714
Pollet-StL 690
Newcombe-Bro 680
Meyer-Phi 680
Munger-StL 652

Complete Games
Spahn-Bos 25
Raffensberger-Cin ...20
Newcombe-Bro 19
Pollet-StL 17
Jansen-NY 17

Strikeouts
Spahn-Bos 151
Newcombe-Bro 149
Jansen-NY 113
Roe-Bro 109
Branca-Bro 109

Fewest BB/Game
Koslo-NY 1.83
Roe-Bro 1.86
Werle-Pit 2.08
Jansen-NY 2.15
Leonard-Chi 2.15

Games
Wilks-StL 59
Konstanty-Phi 53
Palica-Bro 49
Banta-Bro 48
Muncrief-Pit-Chi 47

Saves
Wilks-StL 9
Potter-Bos 7
Konstanty-Phi 7
Staley-StL 6
Palica-Bro 6

Base Runners/9
Koslo-NY 10.02
Staley-StL 10.40
Roe-Bro 10.45
Bonham-Pit 10.52
Wilks-StL 10.88

Adjusted Relief Runs
Konstanty-Phi 8.1
Erautt-Cin 7.8
Wilks-StL 7.3
Hogue-Bos 5.1
Palica-Bro 5.0

Relief Ranking
Konstanty-Phi 11.8
Erautt-Cin 9.5
Palica-Bro 8.5
Wilks-StL 8.5
Hogue-Bos 3.0

Innings Pitched
Spahn-Bos 302.1
Raffensberger-Cin ...284.0
Jansen-NY 259.2
Heintzelman-Phi 250.0
Newcombe-Bro 244.1

Opponents' Avg.
Staley-StL 238
Koslo-NY 239
Kennedy-NY 242
Newcombe-Bro 243
Spahn-Bos 245

Opponents' OBP
Koslo-NY 278
Staley-StL 286
Pollet-StL 293
Spahn-Bos 299
Newcombe-Bro 301

Earned Run Average
Koslo-NY 2.50
Staley-StL 2.73
Pollet-StL 2.77
Roe-Bro 2.79
Heintzelman-Phi 3.02

Adjusted ERA
Koslo-NY 159
Staley-StL 152
Pollet-StL 150
Roe-Bro 147
Brazle-StL 131

Adjusted Starter Runs
Pollet-StL 35.2
Koslo-NY 34.5
Roe-Bro 31.9
Newcombe-Bro 27.3
Heintzelman-Phi 24.9

Pitcher Wins
Pollet-StL 4.2
Koslo-NY 4.1
Newcombe-Bro 2.9
Staley-StL 2.9
Roe-Bro 2.6

Jackie's Back

Some had labeled Jackie Robinson a one-year wonder after he slumped in 1948. But he had not yet begun to fight; his comeback season netted MVP honors and sparked the Dodgers in their thrilling pennant drive against the Cardinals.

Both contenders played in extreme hitters' parks. Brooklyn won with an overwhelming offense and mediocre hurling, while St. Louis had a spectacularly good staff and several weak hitters. The Cardinals were in the driver's seat, up 1½ games with one week left, but four straight losses doomed them to second place as the Dodgers capitalized. Once again, outfielders Stan Musial and Enos Slaughter had to carry the Cardinals attack. In a sign of what was to come, the Phillies improved by 15 games and leapt into to third place.

For the third straight season, the Dodgers debuted an impressive African American player as pitcher Don Newcombe won Rookie of the Year. Del Crandall and former Negro Leaguer Monte Irvin also made their first appearances in the majors, while it was the last year of service for Mort Cooper and Dixie Walker.

Ralph Kiner's 54 homers were the most in the majors since 1930, and NL home runs rose to 935, a new mark. For the first time, six clubs hit over 100 homers each. There was tragedy off the field. Pirates hurler Tiny Bonham died September 15 after an emergency appendectomy, and Phillies first baseman Eddie Waitkus was shot by a crazed admirer in a Chicago hotel room—he recovered to play six more years in the majors. In the face of a lawsuit that threatened baseball's reserve clause, Happy Chandler rescinded the ban on players who jumped to the Mexican League in 1946.

For the third time in the decade, the Yankees beat the Dodgers in the World Series, this time in five games. All were tight contests but the last, when the Brooklyn pitching collapsed.

1949 American League

TEAM	W	L	T	PCT	GB	HW	HL	R	OR	PA	H	2B	3B	HR	BB	SO	HB	SH	AVG	OBP	SLG	OPS	AOPS	BR	ABR	PF	SB	CS	BSA	BSR
NY	97	57	1	.630		54	23	829	637	6043	1396	215	60	115	731	539	32	84	.269	.362	.400	762	108	59	59	100	58	30	66	2
BOS	96	58	1	.623	1	61	16	896	667	6250	1500	272	36	131	835	510	17	78	.282	.381	.420	801	111	154	93	107	44	40	52	1
CLE	89	65	0	.578	8	49	28	675	574	5958	1358	194	58	112	601	534	23	113	.260	.339	.384	723	99	-35	-21	98	39	52	43	-10
DET	87	67	1	.565	10	50	27	751	655	6140	1405	215	51	88	751	502	23	107	.267	.361	.378	739	102	21	19	100	36	25	59	-1
PHI	81	73	0	.526	16	52	25	726	725	6048	1331	214	49	82	702	596	13	84	.257	.347	.347	694	93	-68	-46	97	62	55	53	-6
CHI	63	91	0	.409	34	32	45	648	737	6003	1340	207	66	43	702	700	21	83	.254	.339	.377	716	92	-41	-68	104	38	39	49	-5
STL	53	101	1	.344	44	36	41	667	913	5847	1301	213	30	117	631	493	25	63	.254	.338	.375	713	95	-48	-30	99	46	33	58	-1
WAS	50	104	0	.325	47	26	51	584	868	5912	1330	207	41	81	593	495	22	63	.254	.333	.356	689	90	-96	-82	98	43	25	55	-4
TOT	618					360	256	5776		48201	10961	1737	391	769	5627	4369	176	729	.263	.353	.379	732					366	299	55	-24

TEAM	CG	SHO	GR	SV	IP	H	HR	BB	SO	BR/9	ERA	AERA	OAV	OOB	PR	APR	PF	OSB	OCS	FA	E	WPB	DP	FW	PW	BW	BSW	DIF
NY	59	12	159	36	1371.1	1231	98	812	671	13.6	3.69	110	.242	.351	77	56	96	54	42	.977	138	40	195	.0	5.4	5.7	.5	8.3
BOS	84	16	120	16	1377.0	1375	82	661	598	13.5	3.97	110	.262	.347	34	57	104	35	28	.980	120	31	207	1.1	5.5	9.1	.4	2.9
CLE	65	10	168	19	1383.2	1275	82	611	594	12.4	3.36	119	.247	.329	129	103	95	32	37	.983	131	40	174	.4	5.9	1.8	-.7	2.5
DET	70	19	152	12	1393.2	1338	102	628	631	12.8	3.77	110	.254	.335	66	61	99	45	40	.976	140	43	217	-.1	-1.8	3.3	.2	2.5
PHI	85	9	107	11	1365.0	1359	105	758	490	14.1	4.23	97	.263	.360	-5	-19	98	46	40	.977	141	34	180	-.2	-1.8	-4.5	-.3	-7.2
CHI	57	10	174	17	1363.1	1362	108	693	502	13.7	4.30	97	.264	.353	-15	-19	99	51	38	.977	166	41	154	-1.6	-9.1	-6.6	-.2	-6.4
STL	43	3	231	16	1341.1	1583	113	685	432	15.4	5.21	87	.294	.377	-151	-94	108	47	38	.971	103	27	192	-.2	-1.8	-8.0	-.2	-8.2
WAS	44	9	206	9	1345.2	1438	79	779	451	15.0	5.10	84	.276	.373	-134	-124	101	56	39	.973	161	47	168	-1.4	-12.1	-8.0	.2	-5.7
TOT	507	88	1317	136	10941.0					13.8	4.20		.263	.353						.977	1100	303	1487					

Leaderboards

Batter-Fielder Wins: Williams-Bos 6.4, Doerr-Bos 5.1, Joost-Phi 5.1, Michaels-Chi 4.5, Stephens-Bos 3.9

Batting Average: Kell-Det .343, Dillinger-StL .324, Mitchell-Cle .317, Doerr-Bos .309

On-Base Percentage: Williams-Bos .490, Appling-Chi .439, Joost-Phi .429, Kell-Det .424, Michaels-Chi .417

Slugging Average: Williams-Bos .650, Stephens-Bos .539, Henrich-NY .526, Doerr-Bos .497, Berra-NY .480

On-Base Plus Slugging: Williams-Bos 1141, Henrich-NY .942, Stephens-Bos .930, Kell-Det .892, Doerr-Bos .890

Adjusted OPS: Williams-Bos 187, Henrich-NY 148, Joost-Phi 138, Kell-Det 136, Stephens-Bos 135

Adjusted Batter Runs: Williams-Bos 79.9, Joost-Phi 37.8, DiMaggio-Bos 32.1, Henrich-NY 30.6, Stephens-Bos 29.6

Runs: Williams-Bos 150, Joost-Phi 128, DiMaggio-Bos 126, Stephens-Bos 113, Pesky-Bos 111

Hits: Mitchell-Cle 203, Williams-Bos 194, DiMaggio-Bos 186, Wertz-Det 185, Pesky-Bos 185

Doubles: Williams-Bos 39, Kell-Det 38, DiMaggio-Bos 34, Zarilla-StL-Bos 33, Stephens-Bos 31

Triples: Mitchell-Cle 23, Dillinger-StL 13, Valo-Phi 12

Home Runs: Williams-Bos 43, Stephens-Bos 39

Total Bases: Williams-Bos 368, Stephens-Bos 329, Wertz-Det 283, Mitchell-Cle 274, Doerr-Bos 269

Runs Batted In: Williams-Bos 159, Stephens-Bos 159, Wertz-Det 133, Doerr-Bos 109, Chapman-Phi 108

Stolen Bases: Dillinger-StL 20, Rizzuto-NY 18, Valo-Phi 14, Philley-Chi 13

Base Stealing Runs: Rizzuto-NY 1.9, Philley-Chi 1.5, Tebbetts-Bos 1.4, Fain-Phi 1.4, Mapes-NY 1.3

Fielding Runs-Infield: Doerr-Bos 27.1, Pesky-Bos 18.9, Vernon-Cle 16.1, Michaels-Chi 15.0, Baker-Chi 11.0

Fielding Runs-Outfield: Valo-Phi 9.5, Evers-Det 8.0, Kokos-StL 7.4, Mapes-NY 6.4, DiMaggio-Bos 5.8

Wins: Parnell-Bos 25, Kinder-Bos 23, Lemon-Cle 22, Raschi-NY 21, Kellner-Phi 20

Winning Pct.: Kinder-Bos .793, Parnell-Bos .781, Reynolds-NY .739, Lemon-Cle .688

Complete Games: Parnell-Bos 27, Newhouser-Det 22, Lemon-Cle 22, Raschi-NY 21

Strikeouts: Trucks-Det 153, Newhouser-Det 144, Lemon-Cle 138, Kinder-Bos 138, Byrne-NY 129

Fewest BB/Game: Hutchinson-Det 2.48, Houtteman-Det 2.61, Lopat-NY 2.88, Garcia-Cle 3.07, Wynn-Cle 3.12

Games: Page-NY 60, Welteroth-Was 52, Ferrick-StL 50, Kennedy-StL 48, Surkont-Chi 44

Saves: Page-NY 27, Benton-Cle 10, Ferrick-StL 6, Paige-Cle 5

Base Runners/9: Hutchinson-Det 10.49, Trucks-Det 11.03, Garcia-Cle 11.07, Benton-Cle 11.14, Paige-Cle 11.28

Adjusted Relief Runs: Page-NY 22.7, Paige-Cle 10.3, Ferrick-StL 7.7, Papish-Cle 6.0, Starr-StL 2.2

Relief Ranking: Page-NY 41.9, Paige-Cle 13.7, Ferrick-StL 7.6, Papish-Cle 3.0, Starr-StL 1.9

Innings Pitched: Parnell-Bos 295.1, Newhouser-Det 292.0, Lemon-Cle 279.2, Trucks-Det 275.0, Raschi-NY 274.2

Opponents' Avg.: Byrne-NY .183, Lemon-Cle .211, Trucks-Det .211, Gray-Det .227, Pierce-Chi .228

Opponents' OBP: Hutchinson-Det .290, Trucks-Det .301, Garcia-Cle .308, Lemon-Cle .309, Gumpert-Chi .318

Earned Run Average: Garcia-Cle 2.36, Parnell-Bos 2.77, Trucks-Det 2.81, Hutchinson-Det 2.96, Lemon-Cle 2.99

Adjusted ERA: Garcia-Cle 169, Parnell-Bos 157, Trucks-Det 148, Hutchinson-Det 141, Lemon-Cle 133

Adjusted Starter Runs: Parnell-Bos 49.2, Trucks-Det 42.1, Lemon-Cle 33.8, Garcia-Cle 33.6, Benton-Cle 30.9

Pitcher Wins: Lemon-Cle 5.6, Parnell-Bos 5.2, Page-NY 4.0, Garcia-Cle 3.7, Trucks-Det 3.5

The First of Casey

While Cleveland stumbled early, Boston and New York put on a show. The oft-injured Yankees, with skipper Casey Stengel taking the helm, held a steady lead from July into late August, when the consistently improving Red Sox cut sagging New York's lead from 8 games to 1½ in a month.

New York hung on through September, then lost three straight at Boston with a week left. In the season's final series at New York, the Yankees, one game behind, won two pressure-packed games from the Red Sox to steal the crown from Boston skipper Joe McCarthy, who had enjoyed his share of New York glory.

Boston led the league in runs, thanks to Ted Williams, and got fine pitching from Mel Parnell and Ellis Kinder. Despite using a patchwork lineup, New York's offense was just fine; Joe DiMaggio was great when healthy and Yogi Berra developed into a terrific two-way player. Yankees pitching was deep and Joe Page's 27 saves set a new mark.

The White Sox brought in Comiskey Park's fences by 20 feet, and then returned them in early May. They finished sixth anyway. Third-place Cleveland debuted two more black players: Cuban outfielder Minnie Minoso and first baseman Luke Easter.

Baseball was now ruled by the slugging strategy of waiting for a good pitch and uppercutting it. In 1949, seven AL pitching staffs walked more hitters than they struck out. Behemoths Walt Dropo, Gus Zernial, and Roy Sievers debuted in '49, and similar lead-footed boppers ruled the game for much of the coming decade.

A strong Dodgers club was favored in the World Series, but Yankees pitching carried the day in a five-game victory. Joe Page again worked his magic in the late innings, and Allie Reynolds tossed 12.1 scoreless innings. This improbable season thus kicked off the next phase of Bronx Bombers' greatness.

1948 National League

TEAM	W	L	T	PCT	GB	HW	HL	R	OR	PA	H	2B	3B	HR	BB	SO	HB	SH	AVG	OBP	SLG	OPS	AOPS	BR	ABR	PF	SB	CS	BSA	BSR
BOS	91	62	1	.595		45	31	739	584	6125	1458	272	49	95	671	536	17	140	.275	.359	.399	758	114	101	115	98	43			
STL	85	69	1	.552	6.5	44	33	742	646	5994	1396	238	58	105	594	521	22	76	.263	.340	.389	729	98	31	-8	106	24			
BRO	84	70	1	.545	7.5	36	41	744	669	6047	1393	256	54	91	601	684	18	100	.261	.338	.381	719	98	15	-8	103	114			
PIT	83	71	2	.539	8.5	47	31	706	701	5943	1388	191	54	108	580	578	21	56	.263	.338	.380	718	99	7	-7	102	68			
NY	78	76	1	.506	13.5	37	40	780	703	5960	1352	210	49	164	599	648	19	65	.256	.334	.408	742	106	45	41	101	51			
PHI	66	88	1	.429	25.5	32	44	591	728	5830	1367	227	39	91	440	598	21	79	.259	.318	.368	686	94	-65	-54	98	68			
CIN	64	89	0	.418	27	32	45	588	751	5700	1266	221	37	104	478	586	16	79	.247	.313	.365	678	92	-77	-57	97	42			
CHI	64	90	1	.416	27.5	35	42	597	705	5894	1402	225	44	87	443	578	29	70	.262	.322	.369	691	97	-55	-29	96	39			
TOT	619					308	307	5487		47493	11022	1840	384	845	4406	4729	163	668	.261	.333	.383	716					449			

TEAM	CG	SHO	GR	SV	IP	H	HR	BB	SO	BR/9	ERA	AERA	OAV	OOB	PR	APR	PF	OSB	OCS	FA	E	WPB	DP	FW	PW	BW	BSW	DIF
BOS	70	10	167	17	1389.1	1354	93	430	579	11.6	3.37	114	.249	.306	89	73	97	63	35	.976	143	19	132	.7	7.3	11.5		-5.0
STL	60	13	205	18	1368.0	1392	103	476	625	12.4	3.91	105	.262	.324	7	27	103	20	33	.980	119	30	138	2.1	2.7	-.8		4.0
BRO	52	9	211	22	1392.2	1328	119	633	670	12.9	3.75	106	.253	.337	31	36	101	37	43	.973	161	49	151	-.2	3.6	-.8		4.4
PIT	65	5	166	19	1371.2	1373	120	564	543	12.9	4.15	98	.261	.335	-29	-12	103	53	49	.977	137	56	150	1.2	-1.2	-1.1		6.7
NY	54	15	230	21	1373.0	1425	122	556	527	13.2	3.93	100	.269	.342	4	0	100	49	25	.974	156	30	134	.1	.0	4.1		-3.2
PHI	61	6	162	15	1362.1	1385	95	556	550	13.0	4.08	97	.262	.335	-18	-20	100	86	46	.964	210	45	126	-2.8	-2.0	-5.4		-.8
CIN	40	8	211	20	1343.1	1410	104	572	599	13.4	4.47	87	.270	.344	-77	-86	99	80	26	.973	158	30	135	-.1	-8.6	-5.7		1.9
CHI	51	7	220	10	1355.1	1355	89	619	636	13.2	4.00	97	.261	.342	-7	-15	99	61	41	.972	172	38	152	-.7	-1.5	-2.9		1.9
TOT	453	73	1572	142	10955.2					12.8	3.95		.261	.333						.974	1256	297	1118					-7.9

Batter-Fielder Wins		Batting Average		On-Base Percentage		Slugging Average		On-Base Plus Slugging		Adjusted OPS		Adjusted Batter Runs	
Musial-StL	7.2	Musial-StL	376	Musial-StL	.450	Musial-StL	.702	Musial-StL	1152	Musial-StL	196	Musial-StL	82.1
Pafko-Chi	4.2	Ashburn-Phi	333	B.Elliott-Bos	.423	Mize-NY	.564	Mize-NY	.959	Mize-NY	156	Mize-NY	44.8
Mize-NY	4.2	Holmes-Bos	325	Ashburn-Phi	.410	Gordon-NY	.537	Gordon-NY	.927	Gordon-NY	148	B.Elliott-Bos	41.3
Gordon-NY	3.0	Dark-Bos	322	Slaughter-StL	.409	Kiner-Pit	.533	Kiner-Pit	.924	Kiner-Pit	145	Kiner-Pit	36.8
B.Elliott-Bos	2.9	Slaughter-StL	321	Mize-NY	.395	Ennis-Phi	.525	B.Elliott-Bos	.897	B.Elliott-Bos	145	Gordon-NY	35.1

Runs		Hits		Doubles		Triples		Home Runs		Total Bases		Runs Batted In	
Musial-StL	135	Musial-StL	230	Musial-StL	46	Musial-StL	18	Mize-NY	40	Musial-StL	429	Musial-StL	131
Lockman-NY	117	Holmes-Bos	190	Ennis-Phi	40	Hopp-Pit	12	Kiner-Pit	40	Mize-NY	316	Mize-NY	125
Mize-NY	110	Rojek-Pit	186	Dark-Bos	39	Slaughter-StL	11	Musial-StL	39	Ennis-Phi	309	Kiner-Pit	123
Robinson-Bro	108	Slaughter-StL	176	Robinson-Bro	38	Waitkus-Chi	10	Sauer-Cin	35	Kiner-Pit	296	Gordon-NY	107
Kiner-Pit	104	Dark-Bos	175	Holmes-Bos	35	Lockman-NY	10			Pafko-Chi	283	Pafko-Chi	101

Stolen Bases		Base Stealing Runs		Fielding Runs-Infield		Fielding Runs-Outfield		Wins		Winning Pct.		Complete Games	
Ashburn-Phi	32			Gustine-Pit	12.6	Ashburn-Phi	9.1	Sain-Bos	24	Brecheen-StL	741	Sain-Bos	28
Reese-Bro	25			Smalley-Chi	10.7	Furillo-Bro	7.2	Brecheen-StL	20	Jones-NY	667	Brecheen-StL	21
Rojek-Pit	24			Pafko-Chi	10.3	Hermanski-Bro	5.8	Schmitz-Chi	18	Sain-Bos	615	Schmitz-Chi	18
Robinson-Bro	22			Marion-StL	10.3	Sauer-Cin	4.4	Jansen-NY	18	Jansen-NY	600	Spahn-Bos	16
Torgeson-Bos	19			Waitkus-Chi	8.0	Jeffcoat-Chi	3.4	VanderMeer-Cin	17	Schmitz-Chi	581	Leonard-Phi	16

Strikeouts		Fewest BB/Game		Games		Saves		Base Runners/9		Adjusted Relief Runs		Relief Ranking	
Brecheen-StL	149	Roe-Bro	1.67	Gumbert-Cin	61	Potter-Bos	17	Wilks-StL	9.00	Wilks-StL	21.3	Wilks-StL	22.3
Barney-Bro	138	Jansen-NY	1.75	Wilks-StL	57	Wilks-StL	13	Brecheen-StL	9.41	Hansen-NY	10.2	Minner-Bro	9.6
Sain-Bos	137	Raffensberger-Cin	1.85	Higbe-Pit	56	Roe-Bro	10	Roe-Bro	9.68	Minner-Bro	9.2	Trinkle-NY	8.9
Jansen-NY	126	Brecheen-StL	1.89	Jones-NY	54	Trinkle-NY	7	Wilks-StL	10.47	Dobernic-Chi	8.1	Dobernic-Chi	7.9
Branca-Bro	122	Leonard-Phi	2.15	Dobernic-Chi	54	Behrman-Bro	7	Schmitz-Chi	10.60	Higbe-Pit	7.9	Higbe-Pit	7.9

Innings Pitched		Opponents' Avg.		Opponents' OBP		Earned Run Average		Adjusted ERA		Adjusted Starter Runs		Pitcher Wins	
Sain-Bos	314.2	Schmitz-Chi	215	Brecheen-StL	265	Brecheen-StL	2.24	Brecheen-StL	183	Brecheen-StL	46.9	Sain-Bos	5.3
Jansen-NY	277.0	Barney-Bro	217	Roe-Bro	271	Leonard-Phi	2.51	Leonard-Phi	157	Sain-Bos	43.0	Brecheen-StL	5.3
Spahn-Bos	257.0	Brecheen-StL	222	Schmitz-Chi	295	Sain-Bos	2.60	Roe-Bro	152	Leonard-Phi	31.4	Schmitz-Chi	3.8
Dickson-StL	252.1	Branca-Bro	232	Sain-Bos	296	Roe-Bro	2.63	Schmitz-Chi	148	Schmitz-Chi	30.5	Leonard-Phi	3.7
Barney-Bro	246.2	Roe-Bro	233	Raffensberger-Cin	296	Schmitz-Chi	2.64	Sain-Bos	147	Roe-Bro	26.5	Roe-Bro	2.6

Triumph of the Brave

Brooklyn general manager Branch Rickey was glad that things worked out with Jackie Robinson. For 1948 he imported catcher Roy Campanella from the Negro Leagues. But despite bringing in their left and center field fences, Dodgers hitters slumped, and the team fell to third. Manager Leo Durocher quit at midseason and took the helm of the hated Giants.

Stan Musial won his third batting title in six years, and led the NL in hits, runs, doubles, triples, and RBIs, while Harry Brecheen was arguably the league's top pitcher. However, teammate Murry Dickson gave up 39 homers, a new major league record, and the rest of the staff didn't give Brecheen much support; the Cardinals finished second.

The NL's class club was in Boston, which hadn't had a Senior Circuit champ since 1914. MVP Bob Elliott and a supporting cast including Alvin Dark, Tommy Holmes, and Jeff Heath, provided the hitting. Even with Johnny Sain and Warren Spahn combining to complete 44 games, the pitching was thin; the staff completed just 70, the lowest league-leading total to date.

And the Braves were no sure thing; on September 1, they were tied with Dodgers for the lead, with the Cardinals and surprising Pirates close behind. But a 14-of-15 streak, nine of them won by Spahn or Sain, put Boston ahead to stay.

Former stars Arky Vaughan and Joe Medwick retired, while Philadelphia's Richie Ashburn and Brooklyn's Carl Erskine made impressive major league debuts. And the Chicago Cubs fell into the cellar for first time since 1925, beginning a 20-year period of intense frustration.

Despite good pitching, the Braves couldn't do much in the World Series; five of the games were close, but aside from an 11-5 Game 5 blowout, Boston had no offense. Within just a few years, the Braves fell out of contention and attendance sagged, forcing a move to Milwaukee.

1948 American League

TEAM	W	L	T	PCT	GB	HW	HL	R	OR	PA	H	2B	3B	HR	BB	SO	HB	SH	AVG	OBP	SLG	OPS	AOPS	BR	ABR	PF	SB	CS	BSA	BSR
CLE	97	58	1	.626	—	48	30	840	568	6201	1534	242	54	155	646	575	24	85	.282	.360	.431	791	119	113	136	97	54	44	55	-4
BOS	96	59	0	.619	1	55	23	907	720	6284	1471	277	40	121	823	552	32	66	.274	.374	.409	783	109	124	82	105	38	17	69	2
NY	94	60	0	.610	2.5	50	27	857	633	6048	1480	251	75	139	623	478	23	78	.278	.356	.432	788	116	99	107	99	24	24	50	-2
PHI	84	70	0	.545	12.5	36	41	729	735	6049	1345	231	47	68	726	523	22	120	.260	.353	.362	715	96	-18	-19	100	40	32	56	-2
DET	78	76	0	.506	18.5	39	38	700	726	6063	1396	219	58	78	671	504	27	130	.267	.353	.375	728	96	-1	-20	103	22	32	41	-6
STL	59	94	2	.386	37	34	42	671	849	6013	1438	251	62	63	578	572	19	113	.271	.345	.378	723	96	-21	-39	103	63	44	59	-2
WAS	56	97	1	.366	40	29	48	578	796	5783	1245	203	75	31	568	572	20	84	.244	.322	.331	653	81	-156	-140	97	76	48	61	0
CHI	51	101	2	.336	44.5	27	48	559	814	5872	1303	172	39	55	595	528	12	73	.251	.329	.331	660	84	-138	-118	97	46	47	49	-21
TOT	618					318	297	5841		48313	11212	1846	450	710	5230	4304	179	749	.266	.349	.382	731				363	288	56	

TEAM	CG	SHO	GR	SV	IP	H	HR	BB	SO	BR/9	ERA	AERA	OAV	OOB	PR	APR	PF	OSB	OCS	FA	E	WPB	DP	FW	PW	BW	BSW	DIP
CLE	66	26	196	30	1409.1	1246	82	625	593	12.1	3.22	126	.239	.323	167	138	95	31	31	.982	114	24	183	1.4	13.4	13.2	-.1	-8.3
BOS	70	11	141	13	1379.1	1445	83	592	513	13.4	4.26	103	.270	.345	4	20	102	40	28	.981	116	31	174	1.2	1.9	7.9	.4	7.0
NY	62	16	162	24	1365.2	1289	94	641	654	12.9	3.75	109	.250	.336	82	53	95	49	40	.979	120	40	161	.9	5.1	10.4	-.0	.6
PHI	74	7	137	18	1368.2	1456	86	638	486	13.9	4.43	97	.275	.355	-21	-20	100	39	34	.981	155	44	143	-.9	3.2	-1.9	-.3	1.0
DET	60	5	187	22	1377.0	1367	92	589	678	12.9	4.15	105	.259	.335	21	33	102	49	28	.974	168	54	190	-1.6	-6.3	-3.8	.0	-5.9
STL	35	4	243	20	1373.1	1513	103	737	531	14.9	5.01	91	.281	.371	-109	-65	106	67	30	.972	154	31	144	-.9	-4.5	-13.6	.3	-1.8
WAS	42	4	201	22	1357.1	1439	81	734	446	14.6	4.65	93	.273	.364	-55	-46	101	35	59	.974	160	47	144	-1.2	-9.2	-11.4	-.3	-2.8
CHI	35	2	210	23	1345.2	1454	89	673	403	14.4	4.89	87	.280	.365	-90	-95	99	53	38	.974			176					
TOT	444	75	1477	172	10976.1					13.6	4.29		.266	.349						.977	1100	313	1351					

Batter-Fielder Wins
Boudreau-Cle 7.1
Williams-Bos 5.9
DiMaggio-NY 4.5
Priddy-StL 4.5
Doerr-Bos 3.7

Batting Average
Williams-Bos 369
Boudreau-Cle 355
Mitchell-Cle 336
Zarilla-StL 329
McCosky-Phi 326

On-Base Percentage
Williams-Bos 497
Boudreau-Cle 453
Appling-Chi 423
Goodman-Bos 414
Fain-Phi 412

Slugging Average
Williams-Bos 615
DiMaggio-NY 598
Henrich-NY 554
Boudreau-Cle 534
Keltner-Cle 522

On-Base Plus Slugging
Williams-Bos 1112
DiMaggio-NY 994
Boudreau-Cle 987
Henrich-NY 945
Keltner-Cle 917

Adjusted OPS
Williams-Bos 185
Boudreau-Cle 166
DiMaggio-NY 164
Henrich-NY 151
Keltner-Cle 146

Adjusted Batter Runs
Williams-Bos ....71.
Boudreau-Cle ....57.
DiMaggio-NY ....49.
Henrich-NY ....40.
Keltner-Cle ....36.

Runs
Henrich-NY 138
DiMaggio-Bos 127
Williams-Bos 124
Pesky-Bos 124
Boudreau-Cle 116

Hits
Dillinger-StL 207
Mitchell-Cle 204
Boudreau-Cle 199
DiMaggio-NY 190
Williams-Bos 188

Doubles
Williams-Bos 44
Henrich-NY 42
Majeski-Phi 41
Priddy-StL 40
DiMaggio-Bos 40

Triples
Henrich-NY 14
Stewart-NY-Was 13
Yost-Was 11
Mullin-Det 11
DiMaggio-NY 11

Home Runs
DiMaggio-NY 39
Gordon-Cle 32
Keltner-Cle 31
Stephens-Bos 29
Doerr-Bos 27

Total Bases
DiMaggio-NY 355
Henrich-NY 326
Williams-Bos 313
Stephens-Bos 299
Boudreau-Cle 299

Runs Batted In
DiMaggio-NY 15
Stephens-Bos 13
Williams-Bos 12
Gordon-Cle 12
Majeski-Phi 12

Stolen Bases
Dillinger-StL 28
Coan-Was 23
Vernon-Was 15
Mitchell-Cle 13

Base Stealing Runs
Dillinger-StL 2.3
Coan-Was 1.9
Robertson-Was 1.8
Tucker-Cle 1.7
DiMaggio-Bos 1.5

Fielding Runs-Infield
Priddy-StL 22.5
Pellagrini-StL 17.9
Michaels-Chi 16.3
Baker-Chi 15.8
Appling-Chi 13.4

Fielding Runs-Outfield
Coan-Was 11.9
Philley-Chi 9.6
DiMaggio-Bos 8.7
Hodgin-Chi 2.5
Henrich-NY 1.8

Wins
Newhouser-Det 21
Lemon-Cle 20
Bearden-Cle 20
Raschi-NY 19
Feller-Cle 19

Winning Pct.
Kramer-Bos 783
Bearden-Cle 741
Raschi-NY 704
Reynolds-NY 696

Complete Games
Lemon-Cle 1
Newhouser-Det 1
Raschi-NY 1
Feller-Cle 1

Strikeouts
Feller-Cle 164
Lemon-Cle 147
Newhouser-Det 143
Brissie-Phi 127
Raschi-NY 124

Fewest BB/Game
Hutchinson-Det ...1.95
Zoldak-StL-Cle ...2.42
Lopat-NY 2.62
Kramer-Bos 2.81
Houtteman-Det 2.85

Games
Page-NY 55
Widmar-StL 49
Biscan-StL 47
Thompson-Was 46

Saves
Christopher-Cle 17
Page-NY 16
Houtteman-Det 10
Ferrick-Was 10
Judson-Chi 8

Base Runners/9
Paige-Cle 10.40
Hutchinson-Det ...11.08
Lemon-Cle 11.12
Gumpert-NY-Chi ...11.18
Gromek-Cle 11.49

Adjusted Relief Runs
Klieman-Cle 13.6
Christopher-Cle 8.2
Thompson-Was 4.1
Widmar-StL 2.3
Ferrick-Was 2.2

Relief Ranking
Christopher-Cle 11
Klieman-Cle 9
Thompson-Was 4
Ferrick-Was 4
Widmar-StL 3

Innings Pitched
Lemon-Cle 293.2
Feller-Cle 280.1
Newhouser-Det 272.1
Dobson-Bos 245.1
Reynolds-NY 236.1

Opponents' Avg.
Shea-NY 208
Lemon-Cle 216
Bearden-Cle 229
Scarborough-Was 233
Trucks-Det 240

Opponents' OBP
Hutchinson-Det 297
Lemon-Cle 302
Scarborough-Was 307
Newhouser-Det 309
Raschi-NY 310

Earned Run Average
Bearden-Cle 2.43
Scarborough-Was 2.82
Lemon-Cle 2.82
Newhouser-Det 3.01
Parnell-Bos 3.14

Adjusted ERA
Bearden-Cle 167
Scarborough-Was 154
Newhouser-Det 145
Lemon-Cle 144
Parnell-Bos 140

Adjusted Starter Runs
Bearden-Cle 42.9
Lemon-Cle 42.5
Newhouser-Det 38.3
Scarborough-Was 28.8
Parnell-Bos 26.4

Pitcher Wins
Lemon-Cle 6
Bearden-Cle 5
Newhouser-Det 4
Scarborough-Was 3
Parnell-Bos 3

A Real Tribe

Bill Veeck was baseball's master showman, but he brought the crowds back to Cleveland not with stunts, but by building an integrated club that would contend for the next decade.

In early August the Indians, Red Sox, Yankees, and the surprising Athletics sat atop the AL in a virtual knot. While Philadelphia dropped out in early September, the other three teams kept winning, landing in a three-way tie September 23.

Cleveland attempted to pull away, but Boston knocked out New York October 2 and moved into a tie with the Indians, losers of two of three to Detroit, on the season's final day. In the league's first-ever playoff, the Indians invaded Fenway Park and whipped the Red Sox, 8-3, with rookie Gene Bearden winning his 20th.

The Indians, who had the league's best pitching and a strong offense, debuted two great pitchers: Negro Leagues legend Satchel Paige and Mike Garcia, the "Big Bear." Cleveland shortstop Lou Boudreau, nearing the end of his great playing career, was league MVP. Cleveland also set a new record b[y] drawing 2,620,627 fans. Boston's excellent attack couldn't quit[e] negate a mediocre pitching staff, while the Yankees didn't h[ave] enough and had a poor season from Joe Page. Both clubs se[t] new attendance marks for their parks as league attendance ros[e] another 17 percent to the highest total yet.

Babe Ruth's death from cancer on August 16 set Americ[a] into mourning. The Bambino was still a beloved hero and h[is] body was visited by more than 100,000 at Yankee Stadium.

The World Series pitted faux Native Americans fro[m] Cleveland and Boston. Despite Bob Feller's two losses, th[e] Indians won with fine pitching from Bob Lemon and Bearde[n]. While the Braves took Game 5, 11-5, they scored but six tim[es] in the other five contests. Larry Doby, at .318, was the hotte[st] Cleveland hitter.

1947 National League

TEAM	W	L	T	PCT	GB	HW	HL	R	OR	PA	H	2B	3B	HR	BB	SO	HB	SH	AVG	OBP	SLG	OPS	AOPS	BR	ABR	PF	SB	CS	BSA	BSR
BRO	94	60	1	.610		52	25	774	667	6125	1428	241	50	83	732	561	29	115	.272	.364	.384	748	102	67	38	104	88			
STL	89	65	2	.578	5	46	31	780	634	6131	1462	235	65	115	612	511	29	68	.270	.347	.401	748	101	41	9	104	28			
BOS	86	68	0	.558	8	50	27	701	626	5954	1444	265	42	85	558	500	14	129	.275	.346	.390	736	105	22	40	98	58			
NY	81	73	1	.526	13	45	31	830	761	5924	1446	220	48	221	494	568	23	64	.271	.335	.454	789	114	93	88	101	29			
CIN	73	81	0	.474	21	42	35	681	755	5954	1372	242	43	95	539	530	21	95	.259	.330	.375	705	95	-47	-42	99	46			
CHI	69	85	1	.448	25	36	43	569	722	5859	1373	231	48	71	471	578	19	64	.259	.321	.341	682	95	-95	-70	96	22			
PIT	62	92	2	.403	32	32	45	745	817	6008	1385	216	44	156	607	687	24	70	.261	.340	.406	746	102	31	11	103	30			
PHI	62	92	1	.403	32	38	38	589	687	5828	1354	210	52	60	464	594	26	82	.258	.321	.352	673	88	-112	-90	96	60			
TOT	620					341	275	5669		47783	11264	1860	392	886	4477	4529	185	687	.265	.338	.390	729					361			

TEAM	CG	SHO	GR	SV	IP	H	HR	BB	SO	BR/9	ERA	AERA	OAV	OOB	PR	APR	PF	OSB	OCS	FA	E	WPB	DP	FW	PW	BW	BSW	DIF
BRO	47	14	223	34	1375.0	1299	104	626	592	12.8	3.82	108	.251	.336	37	48	102	42	38	.978	129	47	169	.9	4.7	3.7		7.6
STL	65	12	187	20	1397.2	1417	106	495	642	12.4	3.53	117	.266	.330	83	92	102	39	27	.979	128	33	169	1.1	9.0	.9		1.0
BOS	74	14	167	13	1362.2	1342	93	453	494	11.9	3.62	108	.255	.316	67	43	96	52	37	.974	153	40	124	-.6	4.2	3.9		1.4
NY	58	6	212	14	1363.2	1428	122	590	553	13.4	4.44	92	.267	.342	-58	-56	100	29	27	.974	155	40	136	-.7	-5.5	8.7		1.5
CIN	54	13	190	13	1365.1	1442	102	589	633	13.5	4.41	93	.274	.349	-53	-46	101	45	41	.977	138	40	134	.3	-4.5	-4.1		4.3
CHI	46	8	216	15	1367.0	1449	106	618	571	13.7	4.04	98	.274	.353	4	-13	97	43	34	.975	150	40	159	-.4	-1.3	-6.9		.5
PIT	44	9	211	13	1374.0	1488	155	592	530	13.9	4.68	90	.278	.354	-95	-68	104	52	39	.975	149	47	131	-.2	-6.7	1.1		-9.2
PHI	70	8	161	14	1362.0	1399	98	513	514	12.8	3.96	101	.276	.346	15	8	99	59	38	.974	152	52	140	-.5	.8	-8.9		-6.5
TOT	458	84	1567	136	10967.1					13.1	4.06		.265	.338						.976	1154	303	1162					

Batter-Fielder Wins
- Kiner-Pit 5.3
- Mize-NY 5.0
- B.Elliott-Bos 3.8
- Walker-StL-Phi 3.8
- Marshall-NY 3.0

Batting Average
- Walker-StL-Phi 363
- B.Elliott-Bos 317
- Cavarretta-Chi 314
- Kiner-Pit 313
- Musial-StL 312

On-Base Percentage
- Galan-Cin 449
- Walker-StL-Phi 436
- Kurowski-StL 420
- Kiner-Pit 417
- Walker-Bro 415

Slugging Average
- Kiner-Pit 639
- Mize-NY 614
- W.Cooper-NY 586
- Kurowski-StL 544
- Marshall-NY 528

On-Base Plus Slugging
- Kiner-Pit 1055
- Mize-NY 998
- Kurowski-StL 964
- B.Elliott-Bos 927
- W.Cooper-NY 926

Adjusted OPS
- Kiner-Pit 172
- Mize-NY 160
- Walker-StL-Phi 150
- B.Elliott-Bos 148
- Kurowski-StL 148

Adjusted Batter Runs
- Kiner-Pit 58.3
- Mize-NY 48.0
- B.Elliott-Bos 40.9
- Walker-StL-Phi 38.9
- Kurowski-StL 37.9

Runs
- Mize-NY 137
- Robinson-Bro 125
- Kiner-Pit 118
- Musial-StL 113
- Kurowski-StL 108

Hits
- Holmes-Bos 191
- Walker-StL-Phi 186
- Musial-StL 183
- Gustine-Pit 183
- Baumholtz-Cin 182

Doubles
- Miller-Cin 38
- B.Elliott-Bos 35
- Ryan-Bos 33
- Holmes-Bos 33
- Baumholtz-Cin 32

Triples
- Walker-StL-Phi 16
- Slaughter-StL 13
- Musial-StL 13
- Schoendienst-StL 9
- Baumholtz-Cin 9

Home Runs
- Mize-NY 51
- Kiner-Pit 51
- Marshall-NY 36
- W.Cooper-NY 35
- Thomson-NY 29

Total Bases
- Kiner-Pit 361
- Mize-NY 360
- Marshall-NY 310
- W.Cooper-NY 302
- Musial-StL 296

Runs Batted In
- Mize-NY 138
- Kiner-Pit 127
- W.Cooper-NY 122
- B.Elliott-Bos 113
- Marshall-NY 107

Stolen Bases
- Robinson-Bro 29
- Reiser-Bro 14
- Walker-StL-Phi 13
- Hopp-Bos 13
- Torgeson-Bos 11

Base Stealing Runs

Fielding Runs-Infield
- Verban-Phi 17.5
- Gustine-Pit 16.4
- Marion-StL 15.6
- Kerr-NY 11.9
- Lowrey-Chi 10.2

Fielding Runs-Outfield
- Marshall-NY 9.4
- Kiner-Pit 8.4
- Holmes-Bos 5.5
- Ennis-Phi 4.2
- Walker-StL-Phi 4.2

Wins
- Blackwell-Cin 22
- Spahn-Bos 21
- Sain-Bos 21
- Jansen-NY 21
- Branca-Bro 21

Winning Pct.
- Jansen-NY 808
- Munger-StL 762
- Blackwell-Cin 733
- Hatten-Bro 680
- Spahn-Bos 677

Complete Games
- Blackwell-Cin 23
- Spahn-Bos 22
- Sain-Bos 22
- Jansen-NY 20
- Leonard-Phi 19

Strikeouts
- Blackwell-Cin 193
- Branca-Bro 148
- Leonard-Phi 132
- Spahn-Bos 123
- Munger-StL 123

Fewest BB/Game
- Jansen-NY 2.07
- Rowe-Phi 2.07
- Leonard-Phi 2.18
- Barrett-Bos 2.26
- Brazle-StL 2.57

Games
- Trinkle-NY 62
- Higbe-Bro-Pit 50
- Behrman-Bro-Pt-Bro 50
- Kush-Chi 47
- Dickson-StL 47

Saves
- Casey-Bro 18
- Trinkle-NY 10
- Gumbert-Cin 10
- Behrman-Bro-Pt-Bro 8

Base Runners/9
- Poat-NY 9.90
- Spahn-Bos 10.25
- Blackwell-Cin 10.75
- Leonard-Phi 10.84
- Jansen-NY 10.85

Adjusted Relief Runs
- Lanfranconi-Bos 7.4
- Kush-Chi 7.0
- Gumbert-Cin 3.1
- Casey-Bro 2.4
- Trinkle-NY 2.1

Relief Ranking
- Lanfranconi-Bos 8.6
- Kush-Chi 8.5
- Gumbert-Cin 6.1
- Casey-Bro 4.9
- Trinkle-NY 2.9

Innings Pitched
- Spahn-Bos 289.2
- Branca-Bro 280.0
- Blackwell-Cin 273.0
- Sain-Bos 266.0
- Jansen-NY 248.0

Opponents' Avg.
- Taylor-Bro 225
- Spahn-Bos 226
- Blackwell-Cin 234
- Branca-Bro 240
- Lombardi-Bro 241

Opponents' OBP
- Spahn-Bos 283
- Barrett-Bos 292
- Blackwell-Cin 304
- Leonard-Phi 306
- Jansen-NY 306

Earned Run Average
- Spahn-Bos 2.33
- Blackwell-Cin 2.47
- Branca-Bro 2.67
- Leonard-Phi 2.68
- Brazle-StL 2.84

Adjusted ERA
- Spahn-Bos 167
- Blackwell-Cin 166
- Branca-Bro 155
- Leonard-Phi 149
- Brazle-StL 146

Adjusted Starter Runs
- Spahn-Bos 51.9
- Blackwell-Cin 46.2
- Branca-Bro 42.6
- Leonard-Phi 32.6
- Jansen-NY 23.5

Pitcher Wins
- Spahn-Bos 5.3
- Blackwell-Cin 4.5
- Branca-Bro 4.2
- Leonard-Phi 3.9
- Brazle-StL 3.0

Hello to the Modern Era

Money, race, and television—they were the biggest issues of 1947, perhaps baseball's first true modern season. The Pirates, flush with money from new investor Bing Crosby, opened their wallets to lure Hank Greenberg east with an unprecedented $100,000 deal. The club shortened the left field fences to aid him (and Ralph Kiner), but Pittsburgh tied for last anyway.

On the other side of the pennant race were the Dodgers, who overtook the surprising Braves in midsummer and held off the Cardinals. Blessed with excellent pitching from 21-year old Ralph Branca and reliever Hugh Casey, Brooklyn had a lineup full of on-base machines and a 28-year-old rookie first baseman named Jackie Robinson.

Robinson, the majors' first twentieth-century African American, withstood heckling and threats to lead the Dodgers' efforts. His performance was spectacular enough to make him the first official Rookie of the Year. Several other future stars debuted, including Duke Snider, Ted Kluzewski, and Curt Simmons.

Former favorites Billy Herman, Ernie Lombardi, and Mel Ott ended their careers, and two stars from the first part of the century, Johnny Evers and Hal Chase, passed away. (Evers' double-play partner Joe Tinker died the next year.)

From 1947–49, six NL teams drew more than a million fans every year—everyone but Cincinnati and Philadelphia. Scoring rose 15 percent in 1947, with homers up 58 percent. Johnny Mize and Kiner became the first NLers with 50 homers since 1930. Cincinnati's Ewell "The Whip" Blackwell won 16 straight and nearly threw back-to-back no-hitters.

In the first televised World Series, and one of the most entertaining ever, the Yankees defeated the Dodgers in seven. Six of the games were nail-biters, and for the first time, any American with access to a TV could look in. And for that, and many other, reasons, the game was never the same.

1947 American League

TEAM	W	L	T	PCT	GB	HW	HL	R	OR	PA	H	2B	3B	HR	BB	SO	HB	SH	AVG	OBP	SLG	OPS	AOPS	BR	ABR	PF	SB	CS	BSA	BSR
NY	97	57	1	.630		55	22	794	568	6031	1439	230	72	115	610	581	27	86	.271	.349	.407	756	117	110	118	99	27	23	54	-2
DET	85	69	4	.552	12	46	31	714	642	6148	1363	234	42	103	762	565	13	97	.258	.353	.377	730	106	82	61	103	41	35	54	-3
BOS	83	71	3	.539	14	49	30	720	669	6099	1412	206	54	103	666	590	16	95	.265	.349	.382	731	102	72	21	107	29	25	54	-3
CLE	80	74	3	.519	17	38	39	687	588	5976	1392	234	51	112	502	609	14	93	.259	.324	.385	709	94	-23	-35	102	37	33	53	-3
PHI	78	76	2	.506	19	39	38	633	614	5971	1311	218	52	61	605	563	24	144	.252	.333	.349	682	94	8	26	97	91	57	61	0
CHI	70	84	1	.455	27	32	43	553	661	5837	1350	211	41	53	492	534	8	72	.256	.321	.342	663	84	-121	-107	97	53	51	51	-6
WAS	64	90	0	.416	33	36	41	496	675	5717	1234	186	48	42	525	664	15	76	.241	.314	.322	636	90	-57	-68	102	69	49	58	-2
STL	59	95	0	.383	38	29	48	564	744	5819	1238	189	52	90	583	527	15	56	.240	.319	.349	668	92	-71	-16	96	52	60	58	-10
TOT	623					324	292	5161		47598	10739	1708	412	679	4745	4633	132	719	.256	.333	.364	698					399	333	55	-29

TEAM	CG	SHO	GR	SV	IP	H	HR	BB	SO	BR/9	ERA	AERA	OAV	OOB	PR	APR	PF	OSB	OCS	FA	E	WPB	DP	FW	PW	BW	BSW	DIF
NY	73	14	140	21	1374.1	1221	95	628	691	12.2	3.39	104	.238	.323	48	23	95	61	32	.981	109	27	151	1.5	2.4	12.2	.2	3.7
DET	77	15	137	18	1398.2	1382	79	531	648	12.4	3.57	106	.258	.326	21	30	102	41	36	.977	137	47	172	-1.0	3.1	6.3	-.7	.2
BOS	64	13	184	19	1391.1	1383	84	575	586	12.8	3.81	102	.261	.335	-16	11	94	57	29	.983	104	36	178	1.9	.7	2.7	.2	-2.5
CLE	55	13	182	29	1402.1	1244	94	628	590	12.2	3.44	101	.240	.325	30	45	103	37	55	.976	143	19	161	-.4	4.7	-3.6	.0	-1.5
PHI	70	12	125	15	1391.1	1291	85	597	493	12.3	3.51	101	.247	.326	41	31	99	58	40	.975	155	35	180					
CHI	47	11	184	27	1391.1	1384	76	603	522	13.0	3.64	100	.261	.339	11	3	99	58	40	.975	155	48	142	-1.2	.3	-5.1	.4	-1.5
WAS	67	15	143	12	1362.0	1408	63	579	551	13.2	3.97	94	.267	.342	-40	-37	101	51	48	.976	143	23	151	-.5	-3.8	-11.1	-.2	2.7
STL	50	7	141	13	1365.0	1426	103	604	552	13.4	4.33	90	.272	.348	-94	-65	105	63	45	.977	134	28	169	.0	-6.7	-7.0	-.0	-4.4
TOT	503	100	1236	154	11076.0					12.7	3.71		.256	.333						.977	1080	263	1304					

Batter-Fielder Wins		Batting Average		On-Base Percentage		Slugging Average		On-Base Plus Slugging		Adjusted OPS		Adjusted Batter Runs	
Williams-Bos	7.2	Williams-Bos	.343	Williams-Bos	.499	Williams-Bos	.634	Williams-Bos	1133	Williams-Bos	199	Williams-Bos	82.7
Boudreau-Cle	5.3	McCosky-Phi	.328	Fain-Phi	.414	DiMaggio-NY	.522	DiMaggio-NY	.913	DiMaggio-NY	154	DiMaggio-NY	27.9
Cullenbine-Det	3.6	Pesky-Bos	.324	Cullenbine-Det	.401	Gordon-Cle	.496	Henrich-NY	.857	Henrich-NY	139	Henrich-NY	27.9
Doerr-Bos	3.3	Wright-Chi	.324	McCosky-Phi	.395	Henrich-NY	.485	Heath-StL	.850	Gordon-Cle	136	McQuinn-NY	25.0
Stephens-StL	3.1	Kell-Det	.320	McQuinn-NY	.395	Heath-StL	.485	Gordon-Cle	.842	Heath-StL	133	Fain-Phi	24.4

Runs		Hits		Doubles		Triples		Home Runs		Total Bases		Runs Batted In	
Williams-Bos	125	Pesky-Bos	207	Boudreau-Cle	45	Henrich-NY	13	Williams-Bos	32	Williams-Bos	335	Williams-Bos	114
Henrich-NY	109	Kell-Det	188	Williams-Bos	40	Vernon-Was	12	Gordon-Cle	29	Gordon-Cle	279	Henrich-NY	98
Pesky-Bos	106	Williams-Bos	181	Henrich-NY	35	Philley-Chi	11	Heath-StL	27	DiMaggio-NY	279	DiMaggio-NY	97
Stirnweiss-NY	102	McCosky-Phi	179	DiMaggio-NY	31			Cullenbine-Det	24	Henrich-NY	267	Jones-Chi-Bos	96
DiMaggio-NY	97							York-Chi-Bos	21	Pesky-Bos	250		

Stolen Bases		Base Stealing Runs		Fielding Runs-Infield		Fielding Runs-Outfield		Wins		Winning Pct.		Complete Games	
Dillinger-StL	34	Dillinger-StL	2.9	Doerr-Bos	25.2	DiMaggio-Bos	15.0	Feller-Cle	20	Reynolds-NY	.704	Newhouser-Det	24
Philley-Chi	21	Valo-Phi	1.4	Boudreau-Cle	18.8	Chapman-Phi	8.2	Reynolds-NY	19	Dobson-Bos	.692	Wynn-Was	22
Vernon-Was	12	Binks-Phi	1.1	Rizzuto-NY	17.7	Spence-Was	6.2	Marchildon-Phi	19	Marchildon-Phi	.679	Lopat-Chi	22
Pesky-Bos	12	Kolloway-Chi	1.0	Cullenbine-Det	17.5	Lindell-NY	5.6	Hutchinson-Det	18	Feller-Cle	.645	Marchildon-Phi	22
		Tucker-Chi	.8	Kell-Det	16.2	Henrich-NY	4.6	Dobson-Bos	18	Hutchinson-Det	.643	Feller-Cle	20

Strikeouts		Fewest BB/Game		Games		Saves		Base Runners/9		Adjusted Relief Runs		Relief Ranking	
Feller-Cle	196	Galehouse-StL-Bos	2.48	Klieman-Cle	58	Page-NY	17	Chandler-NY	9.91	Page-NY	18.1	Page-NY	30.
Newhouser-Det	176	Hutchinson-Det	2.50	Page-NY	56	Klieman-Cle	17	Feller-Cle	10.87	Christopher-Phi	7.7	Christopher-Phi	15.
Masterson-Was	135	Lopat-Chi	2.60	Johnson-Bos	45	Christopher-Phi	12	Dobson-Bos	10.90	Murphy-Bos	7.3	Klieman-Cle	7.
Reynolds-NY	129	Muncrief-StL	2.60	Savage-Phi	44	Ferrick-Was	9	Raschi-NY	11.01	Klieman-Cle	5.9	Ferrick-Was	5.
Marchildon-Phi	128	Dobson-Bos	2.87	Christopher-Phi	44			Shea-NY	11.08	Ferrick-Was	3.6	Murphy-Bos	3.

Innings Pitched		Opponents' Avg.		Opponents' OBP		Earned Run Average		Adjusted ERA		Adjusted Starter Runs		Pitcher Wins	
Feller-Cle	299.0	Shea-NY	.200	Dobson-Bos	.299	Haynes-Chi	2.42	Haynes-Chi	151	Feller-Cle	28.7	Newhouser-Det	3.
Newhouser-Det	285.0	Feller-Cle	.215	Feller-Cle	.300	Chandler-NY	2.46	Fowler-Phi	136	Newhouser-Det	28.0	Hutchinson-Det	3.
Marchildon-Phi	276.2	Marchildon-Phi	.224	Shea-NY	.303	Feller-Cle	2.68	Dobson-Bos	132	Lopat-Chi	26.0	Page-NY	3.
Masterson-Was	253.0	Reynolds-NY	.227	Hutchinson-Det	.304	Fowler-Phi	2.81	Newhouser-Det	131	Fowler-Phi	26.0	Feller-Cle	3.
Lopat-Chi	252.2	Embree-Cle	.233	Lopat-Chi	.307	Christopher-Phi	2.81	Feller-Cle	130	Dobson-Bos	23.1	Lopat-Chi	3.

It's . . . the Yankees

In April the Indians brought the power alleys at Municipal Stadium in by 70 feet, then a few weeks later shortened center field by 58. While this significantly increased home run production, the team made a much more important alteration July 5, when owner Bill Veeck made Larry Doby the league's first African American player. Cleveland also broke in rookie pitcher Bob Lemon, while infielder Nellie Fox began his career in Philadelphia. Red Ruffing, 43, retired with 273 wins, while catcher Al Lopez hung it up at 39.

The pennant race held few thrills. In late June New York emerged from a crowded field and pulled away. Under new manager Bucky Harris the Yankees led the league in runs and in fewest allowed. While few players had statistically impressive seasons, there were no weak spots. Joe Page, 29, became the league's dominant reliever. The second-place Tigers felt the loss of Hank Greenberg. Boston, with several offensive black holes, fell to third despite Ted Williams' Triple Crown. The Philadelphia A's improved by 29 games and had their first winning record since 1933.

The advance in glove technology, improvements in groundskeeping, and better defensive skill helped AL fielders, for the first time ever, complete more double plays than they made errors. Stolen bases, which had increased during World War II, dropped to the lowest level in league history—only to drop again in 1948.

Three of the seven games in an exciting Dodgers-Yankee World Series were one-run affairs. New York took the first two, then Brooklyn captured the following pair at Ebbets Field, including a thrilling Game 4 in which Yankees pitcher Bill Bevens lost his no-hitter, and the game, on Cookie Lavagetto's ninth-inning two-run pinch-double. After the well-matched clubs split the next two, the final contest took place at Yankee Stadium. Brooklyn's weary pitching staff couldn't hold off the Yankees, and Page saved the 5-2 win with five scoreless relief innings.

1946 National League

TEAM	W	L	T	PCT	GB	HW	HL	R	OR	PA	H	2B	3B	HR	BB	SO	HB	SH	AVG	OBP	SLG	OPS	AOPS	BR	ABR	PF	SB	CS	BSA	BSR
STL	98	58	0	.628		49	29	712	545	6020	1426	265	56	81	530	537	21	97	.265	.334	.381	715	105	56	28	104	58			
BRO	96	60	1	.615	2	56	22	701	570	6134	1376	233	66	55	691	575	17	141	.260	.348	.361	709	106	63	56	101	100			
CHI	82	71	2	.536	14.5	44	33	626	581	6024	1344	223	50	56	586	599	24	116	.254	.331	.346	677	100	-8	5	98	43			
BOS	81	72	1	.529	15.5	45	31	630	592	5940	1377	238	48	44	558	468	22	135	.264	.337	.353	690	101	18	11	101	60			
PHI	69	85	1	.448	28	41	36	560	705	5772	1351	209	40	80	417	590	19	103	.258	.315	.359	674	100	-32	-15	97	41			
CIN	67	87	2	.435	30	35	42	570	570	5934	1262	206	33	65	493	604	28	122	.239	.307	.327	634	88	-102	-82	96	82			
PIT	63	91	1	.409	34	37	40	552	668	5907	1300	202	52	60	592	555	15	101	.250	.328	.344	672	95	-19	-33	103	48			
NY	61	93	0	.396	36	38	39	612	685	5836	1326	176	37	121	532	546	27	86	.255	.328	.374	702	104	25	21	101	46			
TOT	621					345	272	4916		47567	10762	1752	382	562	4399	4474	173	901	.256	.329	.355	684								478

TEAM	CG	SHO	GR	SV	IP	H	HR	BB	SO	BR/9	ERA	AERA	OAV	OOB	PR	APR	PF	OSB	OCS	FA	E	WPB	DP	FW	PW	BW	BSW	DIF
STL	75	18	180	15	1397.0	1326	63	493	607	11.9	3.01	115	.254	.322	63	69	101	41	36	.980	124	29	167	2.1	7.3	3.0		7.6
BRO	52	14	223	28	1418.0	1280	58	671	647	12.5	3.08	111	.243	.331	58	53	99	37	60	.972	174	44	154	-.9	5.6	5.9		7.3
CHI	59	15	187	11	1393.0	1370	58	527	619	12.4	3.24	102	.256	.325	26	15	97	56	37	.976	146	28	119	.7	1.6	.5		2.7
BOS	74	10	167	12	1371.0	1291	76	478	566	11.7	3.35	102	.249	.314	10	13	101	74	39	.972	169	32	129	-.8	1.4	1.2		2.7
PHI	55	11	185	23	1369.0	1442	73	542	490	13.3	3.99	86	.273	.344	-88	-85	101	66	49	.975	148	44	144	.6	-9.0	-1.6		2.1
CIN	69	17	146	11	1413.1	1334	70	467	506	11.6	3.08	109	.252	.314	53	43	98	47	58	.975	155	17	192	.2	4.6	-8.7		-6.1
PIT	61	10	181	6	1370.0	1406	50	561	458	13.1	3.72	95	.269	.342	-46	-28	103	88	48	.970	184	28	127	-1.6	-3.0	-3.5		-5.9
NY	47	8	216	13	1353.1	1313	114	660	581	13.2	3.92	88	.256	.343	-76	-71	101	69	43	.973	159	38	121	-.2	-7.5	2.2		-10.5
TOT	492	103	1485	119	11084.2					12.5	3.41		.256	.329						.974	1259	260	1153					

Batter-Fielder Wins		Batting Average		On-Base Percentage		Slugging Average		On-Base Plus Slugging		Adjusted OPS		Adjusted Batter Runs	
Musial-StL	5.8	Musial-StL	365	Stanky-Bro	436	Musial-StL	587	Musial-StL	1021	Musial-StL	180	Musial-StL	66.0
Mize-NY	4.8	Hopp-Bos	333	Musial-StL	434	Ennis-Phi	485	Kurowski-StL	853	Ennis-Phi	144	Mize-NY	43.8
Cavarretta-Chi	3.0	Walker-Bro	319	Cavarretta-Chi	401	Slaughter-StL	465	Ennis-Phi	849	Cavarretta-Chi	140	Cavarretta-Chi	30.4
Stanky-Bro	2.9	Ennis-Phi	313	Herman-Bro-Bos	395	Kurowski-StL	462	Walker-Bro	839	Walker-Bro	136	Walker-Bro	28.2
Ennis-Phi	2.9	Holmes-Bos	310	Walker-Bro	391	Walker-Bro	448	Slaughter-StL	838	Kurowski-StL	136	Ennis-Phi	28.2

Runs		Hits		Doubles		Triples		Home Runs		Total Bases		Runs Batted In	
Musial-StL	124	Musial-StL	228	Musial-StL	50	Musial-StL	20	Kiner-Pit	23	Musial-StL	366	Slaughter-StL	130
Slaughter-StL	100	Walker-Bro	184	Holmes-Bos	35	Reese-Bro	10	Mize-NY	22	Slaughter-StL	283	Walker-Bro	116
Stanky-Bro	98	Slaughter-StL	183	Kurowski-StL	32	Cavarretta-Chi	10	Slaughter-StL	18	Ennis-Phi	262	Musial-StL	103
Schoendienst-StL	94	Holmes-Bos	176	Herman-Bro-Bos	31	Walker-Bro	9	Ennis-Phi	17	Walker-Bro	258	Kurowski-StL	89
Cavarretta-Chi	89	Schoendienst-StL	170									Holmes-Bos	241	Kiner-Pit	81

Stolen Bases		Base Stealing Runs		Fielding Runs-Infield		Fielding Runs-Outfield		Wins		Winning Pct.		Complete Games	
Reiser-Bro	34			Marion-StL	18.1	Ennis-Phi	10.1	Pollet-StL	21	Dickson-StL	714	Sain-Bos	24
Haas-Cin	22			Handley-Pit	12.0	Furillo-Bro	8.7	Sain-Bos	20	Higbe-Bro	680	Pollet-StL	22
Hopp-Bos	21			Gustine-Pit	7.8	Gilbert-Chi-Phi	6.0	Higbe-Bro	17	Pollet-StL	677	Koslo-NY	17
Adams-Cin	16			Kerr-NY	7.6	Holmes-Bos	5.4	Dickson-StL	15	Sain-Bos	588	Ostermueller-Pit	16
Walker-Bro	14			McCormick-Phi	4.8	Wyrostek-Phi	4.7	Brecheen-StL	15	Cooper-Bos	500	Cooper-Bos	15

Strikeouts		Fewest BB/Game		Games		Saves		Base Runners/9		Adjusted Relief Runs		Relief Ranking	
Schmitz-Chi	135	Cooper-Bos	1.76	Trinkle-NY	48	Raffensberger-Phi	6	Rowe-Phi	9.20	Casey-Bro	13.5	Casey-Bro	21.1
Higbe-Bro	134	Raffensberger-Phi	1.79	Dickson-StL	47	Pollet-StL	5	Cooper-Bos	9.95	Thompson-NY	11.6	Thompson-NY	18.4
Sain-Bos	129	Beggs-Cin	1.85	Behrman-Bro	47	Karl-Phi	5	Beggs-Cin	10.18	Malloy-Cin	3.5	Malloy-Cin	3.3
Koslo-NY	121	Heusser-Cin	2.09	Casey-Bro	46	Herring-Bro	5	Spahn-Bos	10.31	Budnick-NY	1.1	Wilks-StL	.7
Brecheen-StL	117	Strincevich-Pit	2.25			Casey-Bro	5	Sain-Bos	10.66	Wilks-StL	.9	Budnick-Bos	.6

Innings Pitched		Opponents' Avg.		Opponents' OBP		Earned Run Average		Adjusted ERA		Adjusted Starter Runs		Pitcher Wins	
Pollet-StL	266.0	Schmitz-Chi	221	Cooper-Bos	276	Pollet-StL	2.10	Pollet-StL	165	Pollet-StL	34.7	Sain-Bos	5.4
Koslo-NY	265.1	Kennedy-NY	224	Beggs-Cin	287	Sain-Bos	2.21	Sain-Bos	155	Sain-Bos	33.9	Pollet-StL	3.9
Sain-Bos	265.0	Blackwell-Cin	226	Sain-Bos	294	Beggs-Cin	2.32	Beggs-Cin	144	Brecheen-StL	25.2	Brecheen-StL	3.1
Brecheen-StL	231.1	Higbe-Bro	229	Dickson-StL	295	Blackwell-Cin	2.45	Brecheen-StL	139	Blackwell-Cin	19.9	Beggs-Cin	2.6
Schmitz-Chi	224.1	Sain-Bos	230	Pollet-StL	300	Brecheen-StL	2.49	Blackwell-Cin	136	Beggs-Cin	19.8	Ostermueller-Pit	2.5

Contract Jumping, Integration, and More!

The Dodgers and Cardinals, rejuvenated by players returning from the service, hung together at the top of the NL for the entire 1946 season, working in lockstep from July to the end. The teams matched win for win and ended the year in a tie—the first in major league history. Both teams blew chances to win outright in the final regular-season weekend. In a best-of-three playoff, the Cardinals got fine pitching from Howie Pollet, Murry Dickson, and Harry Brecheen to win the series in two.

Once again attendance reached an all-time NL record, increasing 69 percent. Five teams drew a million, an unprecedented total; the Dodgers set an all-time league record. Even with many veterans returning, several impressive youngsters debuted, including Carl Furillo, Ralph Kiner, Alvin Dark, and Bobby Thomson.

One of the year's odder stories involved the Mexican League, headed by entrepreneur Jorge Pasquel. Determined to make his league a serious player, he and his cohorts spent many thousands to lure away key players from the Cardinals, Dodgers, and Giants. New Commissioner Happy Chandler banned all jumpers from returning for five years, although this edict was softened when the Mexican League began to have problems paying its contracts.

The World Series was one of the best in history, with the Cardinals and Red Sox trading victories in the first six contests. In Game 7 Boston tied the score with 2 runs in the visiting eighth, but the Cardinals won in the bottom of the frame when Harry Walker's single scored the hustling Enos Slaughter from first. Brecheen had 3 wins, allowing just 1 earned run in 20 innings.

For all the exciting baseball played during the season, the most significant event of the year occurred out of the country. In Montreal, Dodgers farmhand Jackie Robinson became the first African American in professional ball in more than sixty years.

1946 American League

TEAM	W	L	T	PCT	GB	HW	HL	R	OR	PA	H	2B	3B	HR	BB	SO	HB	SH	AVG	OBP	SLG	OPS	AOPS	BR	ABR	PF	SB	CS	BSA	BSR
BOS	104	50	2	.675	–	61	16	792	594	6126	1441	268	50	109	687	661	15	106	.271	.356	.402	758	113	142	100	106	45	36	56	-3
DET	92	62	1	.597	12	48	30	704	567	6057	1373	212	41	108	622	616	13	80	.258	.337	.374	711	100	43	4	106	65	41	61	0
NY	87	67	0	.565	17	47	30	684	547	5879	1275	208	50	136	627	706	33	80	.248	.334	.387	721	107	56	47	101	48	35	58	-2
WAS	76	78	1	.494	28	38	38	608	706	5958	1388	260	63	60	511	641	24	86	.260	.327	.366	693	106	2	42	94	51	50	50	-6
CHI	74	80	1	.481	30	40	38	562	595	5911	1364	206	44	37	501	600	20	78	.245	.313	.333	656	94	-66	-44	96	78	64	55	-5
CLE	68	86	2	.442	36	36	41	537	638	5857	1285	233	56	79	506	697	13	96	.245	.313	.356	669	99	-50	-10	94	57	49	54	-5
STL	66	88	2	.429	38	35	41	621	710	5921	1350	220	46	84	465	713	16	67	.251	.313	.356	669	89	-55	-82	105	23	35	40	-7
PHI	49	105	1	.318	55	31	46	529	680	5796	1317	220	51	40	482	594	9	105	.253	.318	.338	656	91	-70	-67	99	39	30	57	-2
TOT	621					336	280	5037		47505	10793	1827	401	653	4401	5228	143	722	.256	.328	.364	692					406	340	54	-30

TEAM	CG	SHO	GR	SV	IP	H	HR	BB	SO	BR/9	ERA	AERA	OAV	OOB	PR	APR	PF	OSB	OCS	FA	E	WPB	DP	FW	PW	BW	BSW	DIF
BOS	79	15	151	20	1396.2	1359	89	501	667	12.1	3.38	108	.254	.319	19	42	105	39	28	.977	139	24	163	1.5	4.4	10.5	.0	10.6
DET	94	18	101	15	1402.0	1277	97	497	896	11.5	3.22	114	.241	.307	45	65	104	47	37	.974	155	35	138	.5	6.8	.4	.4	6.9
NY	68	17	152	17	1361.0	1232	66	552	653	11.9	3.13	110	.243	.319	56	49	99	42	49	.975	150	23	174	.7	5.1	4.9	-.2	-.9
WAS	71	8	157	10	1396.1	1459	81	547	537	13.1	3.74	89	.269	.339	-36	-64	96	55	46	.966	211	64	162	-2.8	-6.7	4.4	-.2	4.4
CHI	62	9	142	16	1392.1	1348	80	508	550	12.1	3.10	110	.255	.323	63	50	97	55	43	.972	175	49	170	-.7	5.2	-4.6	-.1	-2.8
CLE	63	16	170	13	1388.2	1282	84	649	789	12.6	3.62	91	.245	.331	-17	-51	94	42	42	.974	147	36	147	.3	-3.4	-8.6	-.3	1.0
STL	63	13	193	12	1382.1	1465	73	573	574	13.3	3.95	94	.272	.343	-69	-32	107	84	41	.974	159	46	157	-.2	-5.4	-7.0	.2	-15.5
PHI	61	10	145	5	1342.2	1371	83	577	562	13.2	3.90	91	.264	.340	-59	-52	101	42	54	.971	167	20	141					
TOT	561	106	1211	108	11062.0					12.5	3.50		.256	.328						.973	1303	297	1252					

Batter-Fielder Wins		Batting Average		On-Base Percentage		Slugging Average		On-Base Plus Slugging		Adjusted OPS		Adjusted Batter Runs	
Williams-Bos	8.1	Vernon-Was	.353	Williams-Bos	.497	Williams-Bos	.667	Williams-Bos	1164	Williams-Bos	211	Williams-Bos	88.?
Doerr-Bos	4.8	Williams-Bos	.342	Keller-NY	.405	Greenberg-Det	.604	Greenberg-Det	.977	Vernon-Was	163	Vernon-Was	48.?
Pesky-Bos	4.6	Pesky-Bos	.335	Vernon-Was	.403	Keller-NY	.533	Keller-NY	.938	Greenberg-Det	160	Keller-NY	45.?
Vernon-Was	4.3	Kell-Phi-Det	.322	Pesky-Bos	.401	DiMaggio-NY	.511	Vernon-Was	.910	Keller-NY	158	Greenberg-Det	40.?
Greenberg-Det	3.9	DiMaggio-Bos	.316	DiMaggio-NY	.393	Edwards-Cle	.509	DiMaggio-NY	.878	Edwards-Cle	151	Cullenbine-Det	

Runs		Hits		Doubles		Triples		Home Runs		Total Bases		Runs Batted In	
Williams-Bos	142	Pesky-Bos	208	Vernon-Was	51	Edwards-Cle	16	Greenberg-Det	44	Williams-Bos	343	Greenberg-Det	12?
Pesky-Bos	115	Vernon-Was	207	Spence-Was	50	Lewis-Was	13	Williams-Bos	38	Greenberg-Det	316	Williams-Bos	11?
Lake-Det	105	Appling-Chi	180	Pesky-Bos	43	Kell-Phi-Det	10	Keller-NY	30	Vernon-Was	298	York-Bos	11
Keller-NY	98	Williams-Bos	176	Williams-Bos	37	Spence-Was	10	Seerey-Cle	26	Spence-Was	287	Doerr-Bos	11
Doerr-Bos	95	Lewis-Was	170	Doerr-Bos	34	Keller-NY	10	DiMaggio-NY	25	Keller-NY	287	Keller-NY	10?

Stolen Bases		Base Stealing Runs		Fielding Runs-Infield		Fielding Runs-Outfield		Wins		Winning Pct.		Complete Games	
Case-Cle	28	Case-Cle	2.3	Doerr-Bos	27.3	Zarilla-StL	9.6	Newhouser-Det	26	Ferriss-Bos	.806	Feller-Bos	?2
Stirnweiss-NY	18	Stirnweiss-NY	1.9	Gordon-NY	18.1	Chapman-Phi	8.1	Feller-Cle	26	Newhouser-Det	.743	Newhouser-Det	2
Lake-Det	15	Dillinger-StL	1.4	Boudreau-Cle	17.2	Judnich-StL	5.3	Ferriss-Bos	25	Chandler-NY	.714	Ferriss-Bos	2
		Evers-Det	1.2	Rizzuto-NY	16.7	Lewis-Was	2.4	Hughson-Bos	20	Harris-Bos	.654	Trout-Det	2
		Wright-Chi	1.1	Pesky-Bos	12.3	Williams-Bos	2.4	Chandler-NY	20	Hughson-Bos	.645	Hughson-Bos	2

Strikeouts		Fewest BB/Game		Games		Saves		Base Runners/9		Adjusted Relief Runs		Relief Ranking	
Feller-Cle	348	Hughson-Bos	1.65	Feller-Cle	48	Klinger-Bos	9	Ruffing-NY	8.85	Caldwell-Chi	12.9	Caldwell-Chi	24.?
Newhouser-Det	275	Lopat-Chi	1.87	Savage-Phi	40	Caldwell-Chi	8	Caldwell-Chi	8.93	Klinger-Bos	8.3	Klinger-Bos	9
Hughson-Bos	172	Leonard-Was	2.00	Ferriss-Bos	40	Murphy-NY	7	Newhouser-Det	9.66	Kinder-StL	4.7	Lemon-Cle	3
Trucks-Det	161	Flores-Phi	2.21	Hughson-Bos	39	Ferrick-Cle-StL	6	Gumpert-NY	9.84	Lemon-StL	4.3	Kinder-StL	3
Trout-Det	151	Ferriss-Bos	2.33	Caldwell-Chi	39			Hughson-Bos	9.87				

Innings Pitched		Opponents' Avg.		Opponents' OBP		Earned Run Average		Adjusted ERA		Adjusted Starter Runs		Pitcher Wins	
Feller-Cle	371.1	Newhouser-Det	.201	Newhouser-Det	.269	Newhouser-Det	1.94	Newhouser-Det	189	Newhouser-Det	51.1	**Newhouser-Det**	?
Newhouser-Det	292.2	Feller-Cle	.208	Hughson-Bos	.274	Chandler-NY	2.10	Chandler-NY	164	Feller-Cle	50.1	**Feller-Cle**	5
Hughson-Bos	278.0	Chandler-NY	.218	Chandler-NY	.288	Feller-Cle	2.18	Trout-Det	156	Chandler-NY	38.5	**Trout-Det**	4
Trout-Det	276.1	Embree-Cle	.227	Lopat-Chi	.288	Bevens-NY	2.23	Bevens-NY	154	Trout-Det	37.0	**Chandler-NY**	4
Ferriss-Bos	274.0	Bevens-NY	.232	Feller-Cle	.291	Flores-Phi	2.32	Flores-Phi	153	Bevens-NY	33.6	**Bevens-NY**	3

Goodbye and Hello

Boston improved by 33 games, leaping from seventh to first. The core of the club—Ted Williams, Bobby Doerr, Johnny Pesky, Tex Hughson, Mickey Harris, and Dom DiMaggio—came home and made up for lost time. Despite two offensive dead spots, the Red Sox led the AL in runs by nearly 100, leaving second-place Detroit in the dust. Former contenders Washington, St. Louis, and Chicago all finished below .500.

With the boys back home, attendance shot up 72 percent to establish a new league record. This was the first time that the *average* AL team drew more than a million fans. In 1946 five clubs topped a million, and even St. Louis had its second-best attendance ever. The Yankees became the first club ever to draw two million customers. (New York's 1946 attendance was higher than the totals for the previous three seasons combined.)

Home runs increased by more than half, and continued to rise until 1950. Not coincidentally, strikeouts also reached a new high. Hal Newhouser, dispelling criticism that he was just a wartime star, set an AL mark with 8.46 whiffs per game. Two top catchers debuted in 1946, Sherm Lollar with the Indians and Yogi Berra, arguably the best in league history, with the Yankees. With Berra on the way, Bill Dickey retired. Ted Lyons, Chicago's 46-year-old "Sunday pitcher," retired following three years in the army—he went 1-4 but still had a 2.32 ERA.

Former Yankees star Tony Lazzeri died after falling down a flight of stairs, while Walter Johnson succumbed from a brain tumor. Manager Joe McCarthy departed the Yankees in midseason amid clashes with owner Larry MacPhail. And in another shocking departure, the Tigers waived Hank Greenberg, who wanted a $20,000 raise. Pittsburgh convinced Greenberg to play in 1947 by making him the game's first $100,000 player.

The World Series was a classic, with the St. Louis Cardinals winning in seven games. The final contest was a nail-biter all the way as the lead changed hands three times.

1945 National League

TEAM	W	L	T	PCT	GB	HW	HL	R	OR	PA	H	2B	3B	HR	BB	SO	HB	SH	AVG	OBP	SLG	OPS	AOPS	BR	ABR	PF	SB	CS	BSA	BSR
CHI	98	56	1	.636		49	26	735	532	6034	1465	229	52	57	554	462	32	150	.277	.349	.372	721	109	54	70	98	69			
STL	95	59	1	.617	3	48	29	756	582	6166	1498	256	44	64	515	488	26	138	.273	.338	.371	709	102	27	10	102	55			
BRO	87	67	1	.565	11	48	30	795	724	6183	1468	257	71	57	629	434	25	111	.271	.349	.376	725	109	69	75	99	77			
PIT	82	72	1	.532	16	45	34	753	686	6038	1425	259	56	72	590	480	17	88	.267	.342	.377	719	102	48	20	104	81			
NY	78	74	2	.513	19	47	30	668	701	5991	1439	175	35	114	501	457	40	100	.269	.336	.379	715	103	30	19	102	38			
BOS	67	85	2	.441	30	36	38	721	728	6078	1453	229	25	101	520	510	26	91	.267	.334	.374	708	102	21	17	101	82			
CIN	61	93	0	.396	37	36	41	536	694	5796	1317	221	26	56	392	532	26	95	.249	.304	.333	637	85	-124	-112	98	71			
PHI	46	108	0	.299	52	22	55	548	865	5738	1278	197	27	56	449	501	15	71	.246	.307	.326	633	84	-125	-110	97	54			
TOT	618					331	283	5512		48024	11343	1823	336	577	4150	3864	207	844	.265	.333	.364	696					527			

TEAM	CG	SHO	GR	SV	IP	H	HR	BB	SO	BR/9	ERA	AERA	OAV	OOB	PR	APR	PF	OSB	OCS	FA	E	WPB	DP	FW	PW	BW	BSW	DIF
CHI	86	15	135	14	1366.1	1301	57	385	541	11.3	2.98	123	.249	.304	125	106	96	43	33	.980	121	24	124	3.4	10.6	7.0		.0
STL	77	18	156	9	1408.2	1351	70	497	510	12.0	3.24	116	.253	.320	88	80	99	70	53	.977	137	24	150	2.4	8.0	1.0		6.6
BRO	61	7	163	18	1392.1	1357	74	586	557	12.8	3.70	101	.253	.331	15	7	99	60	36	.962	230	41	144	-3.2	.7	7.5		5.0
PIT	73	8	142	16	1387.1	1477	61	455	518	12.7	3.76	105	.272	.331	6	26	104	77	42	.971	178	24	141	-.0	2.6	2.0		.5
NY	53	13	179	21	1374.2	1401	85	528	529	12.8	4.04	96	.263	.332	-40	-22	103	43	42	.973	166	33	112	.6	-2.2	1.9		1.7
BOS	57	7	166	13	1391.2	1474	99	557	404	13.3	4.04	95	.272	.342	-37	-32	101	64	54	.969	193	25	160	-1.1	-3.2	1.7		-6.4
CIN	77	11	132	6	1365.2	1438	70	534	372	13.2	4.00	94	.271	.340	-31	-37	99	76	36	.976	146	31	138	1.8	-3.7	-11.2		-2.9
PHI	31	4	212	26	1352.2	1544	61	608	432	14.5	4.64	83	.285	.360	-126	-122	101	94	45	.962	234	50	150	-3.5	-12.2	-11.0		-4.2
TOT	515	83	1285	123	11039.1					12.8	3.80		.265	.333						.971	1405	252	1119					

Batter-Fielder Wins		Batting Average		On-Base Percentage		Slugging Average		On-Base Plus Slugging		Adjusted OPS		Adjusted Batter Runs	
Hack-Chi	5.3	Cavarretta-Chi	355	Cavarretta-Chi	449	Holmes-Bos	577	Holmes-Bos	997	Holmes-Bos	175	Holmes-Bos	63.9
Holmes-Bos	5.1	Holmes-Bos	352	Galan-Bro	423	Kurowski-StL	511	Cavarretta-Chi	949	Cavarretta-Chi	167	Cavarretta-Chi	50.2
Cavarretta-Chi	4.1	Rosen-Bro	325	Hack-Chi	420	Cavarretta-Chi	500	Ott-NY	910	Ott-NY	150	Galan-Bro	39.6
Stanky-Bro	3.7	Hack-Chi	323	Holmes-Bos	420	Ott-NY	499	Kurowski-StL	894	Kurowski-StL	144	Ott-NY	33.2
Lombardi-NY	2.8	Kurowski-StL	323	Stanky-Bro	417	Olmo-Bro	462	Galan-Bro	864	Galan-Bro	142	Hack-Chi	32.7

Runs		Hits		Doubles		Triples		Home Runs		Total Bases		Runs Batted In	
Stanky-Bro	128	Holmes-Bos	224	Holmes-Bos	47	Olmo-Bro	13	Holmes-Bos	28	Holmes-Bos	367	Walker-Bro	124
Rosen-Bro	126	Rosen-Bro	197	Walker-Bro	42	Pafko-Chi	12	Workman-Bos	25	Adams-Phi-StL	279	Holmes-Bos	117
Holmes-Bos	125	Hack-Chi	193	Galan-Bro	36	Rucker-NY	11	Adams-Phi-StL	22	Rosen-Bro	279	Pafko-Chi	110
Galan-Bro	114	Clay-Cin	184	Elliott-Pit	36	Rosen-Bro	11	Ott-NY	21	Walker-Bro	266	Olmo-Bro	110
Hack-Chi	110			Cavarretta-Chi	34	Cavarretta-Chi	10	Kurowski-StL	21	Kurowski-StL	261	Adams-Phi-StL	109

Stolen Bases		Base Stealing Runs		Fielding Runs-Infield		Fielding Runs-Outfield		Wins		Winning Pct.		Complete Games	
Schoendienst-StL	26			Kerr-NY	30.2	Gillenwater-Bos	17.0	Barrett-Bos-StL	23	Brecheen-StL	789	Barrett-Bos-StL	24
Barrett-Pit	25			Coscarart-Pit	21.2	Walker-Bro	9.6	Wyse-Chi	22	Burkhart-StL	692	Wyse-Chi	23
Clay-Cin	19			Hack-Chi	19.6	DiMaggio-Phi	9.0	Gregg-Bro	18	Wyse-Chi	688	Passeau-Chi	19
				Johnson-Cin	15.4	Russell-Pit	5.0	Burkhart-StL	18	Barrett-Bos-StL	657	Strincevich-Pit	18
				Mesner-Cin	15.0	Schoendienst-StL	4.7	Passeau-Chi	17	Passeau-Chi	654	Heusser-Cin	18

Strikeouts		Fewest BB/Game		Games		Saves		Base Runners/9		Adjusted Relief Runs		Relief Ranking	
Roe-Pit	148	Prim-Chi	1.25	Karl-Phi	67	Karl-Phi	15	Prim-Chi	9.04	Karl-Phi	14.5	Karl-Phi	14.3
Gregg-Bro	139	Barrett-Bos-StL	1.71	Adams-NY	65	Adams-NY	15	Beck-Cin-NY	10.00	Buker-Bro	4.2	Adams-NY	6.0
Voiselle-NY	115	Roe-Pit	1.76	Hutchings-Bos	57	Rescigno-Pit	9	Maglie-NY	10.25	Adams-NY	3.2	Buker-Bro	4.5
Mungo-NY	101	Wyse-Chi	1.78	Barrett-Bos-StL	45			Roe-Pit	10.53				
Hutchings-Bos	99	Strincevich-Pit	1.93	Fox-Cin	45			Passeau-Chi	10.55				

Innings Pitched		Opponents' Avg.		Opponents' OBP		Earned Run Average		Adjusted ERA		Adjusted Starter Runs		Pitcher Wins	
Barrett-Bos-StL	284.2	Prim-Chi	228	Prim-Chi	256	Borowy-Chi	2.13	Prim-Chi	152	Passeau-Chi	32.6	Passeau-Chi	3.9
Wyse-Chi	278.1	Gregg-Bro	232	Passeau-Chi	289	Prim-Chi	2.40	Brecheen-StL	149	Wyse-Chi	32.3	Wyse-Chi	3.3
Gregg-Bro	254.1	Brecheen-StL	238	Barrett-Bos-StL	295	Passeau-Chi	2.46	Passeau-Chi	149	Roe-Pit	31.7	Roe-Pit	3.2
Roe-Pit	235.0	Mungo-NY	238	Wyse-Chi	296	Brecheen-StL	2.52	Walters-Cin	140	Barrett-Bos-StL	24.6	Prim-Chi	2.9
Voiselle-NY	232.1	Passeau-Chi	238	Roe-Pit	296	Walters-Cin	2.68	Roe-Pit	137	Brecheen-StL	22.9	Walters-Cin	2.6

Chicago's Last Stand

With the war drawing to a merciful close, NL attendance rose 32 percent to its highest total since 1930. Many veterans, such as Paul Derringer, Leo Durocher, Lloyd Waner, and Lon Warneke, played their last innings in 1945, as did Dick Sipek, a deaf outfielder employed by the Reds.

The surprise team of the season was Chicago, which improved by 23 games. In early July the Cubs were stalled in fourth place, but Chicago then won 16 of 17 to pass the Dodgers for the league lead. Holding off a late St. Louis challenge, the Cubs won their last NL pennant of the century. Phil Cavaretta won the batting title and was named league MVP. Stan Hack, Andy Pafko and Bill Nicholson provided punch, but the team's real strength was pitching. Graybeards Ray Prim, Claude Passeau, and Paul Derringer combined for 46 wins, Hank Wyse was 22-10, and Hank Borowy—who came over from New York in an odd midseason waiver deal—went 11-2 with Chicago while leading the NL in ERA. Chicago's favorite patsies were the seventh-place Reds, who dropped 21 of 22 to the Cubs. Chicago was also very good at doubling up opponents, winning 20 doubleheaders.

While the Cardinals remained strong, they too were hit hard by the war; outfielders Danny Litwhiler and Stan Musial were finally inducted after several deferrals. Rookie Red Schoendienst filled in ably, pacing the NL in steals, but the missing big bats, and several pitching injuries, proved too much. Ace Adams of the Giants was again the league's top reliever. Boston's Tommy Holmes, whose 37-game hitting streak was the NL's longest since 1897, led the league in doubles, hits, and homers. The Phillies finished last for the eighth time in ten years, but their stock would soon rise.

A sloppy but entertaining World Series saw the Tigers walk away with the victory. Borowy, 2-2 in the Series, got the decision in each of the last three games; he won Game 6 for the Cubs in relief but was hit hard in Games 5 and 7.

1945 American League

TEAM	W	L	T	PCT	GB	HW	HL	R	OR	PA	H	2B	3B	HR	BB	SO	HB	SH	AVG	OBP	SLG	OPS	AOPS	BR	ABR	PF	SB	CS	BSA	BSR
DET	88	65	2	.575		50	26	633	565	5885	1345	227	47	77	517	533	9	102	.256	.324	.361	685	98	21	-16	106	60	54	53	-6
WAS	87	67	2	.565	1.5	46	31	622	562	6008	1375	197	63	27	545	489	23	114	.258	.330	.334	664	107	-9	47	92	110	65	63	1
STL	81	70	3	.536	6	47	27	597	548	5866	1302	215	37	63	500	555	15	124	.249	.316	.341	657	91	-29	-56	105	25	31	45	-1
NY	81	71	0	.533	6.5	48	28	676	606	5925	1343	189	61	93	618	567	36	95	.259	.343	.373	716	108	90	59	105	64	43	60	-1
CLE	73	72	2	.503	11	44	33	557	548	5536	1249	216	48	65	505	578	14	119	.255	.326	.359	685	109	24	50	96	19	31	38	-7
CHI	71	78	1	.477	15	44	29	596	633	5661	1330	204	55	22	470	467	14	100	.262	.326	.337	663	101	-14	2	97	78	54	59	-2
BOS	71	83	3	.461	17.5	42	35	599	674	6018	1393	225	44	50	541	534	23	87	.260	.330	.346	676	100	14	0	102	72	50	59	-2
PHI	52	98	3	.347	34.5	39	35	494	638	5861	1297	201	37	33	449	463	20	96	.245	.306	.316	622	86	-98	-96	100	25	45	36	-10
TOT	612					360	244	4774		46760	10634	1674	392	430	4145	4186	154	837	.255	.325	.346	671					453	373	55	-31

TEAM	CG	SHO	GR	SV	IP	H	HR	BB	SO	BR/9	ERA	AERA	OAV	OOB	PR	APR	PF	OSB	OCS	FA	E	WPB	DP	FW	PW	BW	BSW	DIF
DET	78	19	131	16	1393.2	1305	48	538	588	12.1	2.99	118	.250	.322	58	78	105	49	52	.975	158	40	173	.4	8.4	-1.7	-.2	4.7
WAS	82	19	110	11	1412.1	1307	42	440	550	11.2	2.92	106	.242	.301	69	30	92	45	33	.970	183	58	124	-1.0	3.2	5.0	.5	2.2
STL	91	10	110	8	1382.2	1307	59	506	570	11.8	3.14	112	.249	.316	34	55	105	60	36	.976	143	23	123	1.2	5.9	-6.0	-.1	4.6
NY	78	9	102	14	1355.0	1277	66	485	474	11.8	3.45	100	.250	.316	-13	1	103	74	53	.977	126	41	170	-.7	.1	6.3	.3	-1.0
CLE	76	14	116	12	1302.1	1269	39	501	497	12.4	3.31	98	.257	.328	8	-9	97	68	45	.977	126	41	149	1.7	-1.0	5.4	-.3	-5.3
CHI	84	13	86	13	1330.2	1400	63	448	486	12.7	3.69	90	.270	.332	-49	-56	99	35	50	.970	180	26	139	-1.1	-6.0	.2	.2	3.2
BOS	71	15	135	13	1390.2	1389	58	656	490	13.4	3.80	90	.264	.348	-67	-60	101	52	56	.973	169	48	198	-.1	-6.4	.0	.2	.3
PHI	65	11	120	8	1381.0	1380	55	571	531	12.9	3.62	95	.262	.337	-40	-29	102	70	48	.973	168	27	160	-.3	-3.1	-10.3	-.7	-8.7
TOT	625	110	910	95	10948.1					12.3	3.36		.255	.325						.973	1302	298	1236					

Batter-Fielder Wins
- Stirnweiss-NY 7.2
- Lake-Bos 6.5
- Mayo-Det 3.5
- Cullenbine-Cle-Det 3.1
- Boudreau-Cle 2.7

Batting Average
- Stirnweiss-NY 309
- Cuccinello-Chi 308
- Dickshot-Chi 302
- Estalella-Phi 299
- Myatt-Was 296

On-Base Percentage
- Lake-Bos 412
- Cullenbine-Cle-Det 402
- Estalella-Phi 399
- Grimes-NY 395
- Etten-NY 387

Slugging Average
- Stirnweiss-NY 476
- Stephens-StL 473
- Cullenbine-Cle-Det 444
- Etten-NY 437
- Estalella-Phi 435

On-Base Plus Slugging
- Stirnweiss-NY 862
- Cullenbine-Cle-Det 846
- Estalella-Phi 834
- Stephens-StL 825
- Etten-NY 824

Adjusted OPS
- Stirnweiss-NY 143
- Estalella-Phi 142
- Kuhel-Was 137
- Cullenbine-Cle-Det 137
- Lake-Bos 136

Adjusted Batter Runs
- Stirnweiss-NY 33.9
- Heath-Cle 33.0
- Cullenbine-Cle-Det 30.9
- Lake-Bos 28.6
- Kuhel-Was 27.5

Runs
- Stirnweiss-NY 107
- Stephens-StL 90
- Cullenbine-Cle-Det 83

Hits
- Stirnweiss-NY 195
- Moses-Chi 168
- Stephens-StL 165
- Hall-Phi 161
- Etten-NY 161

Doubles
- Moses-Chi 35
- Stirnweiss-NY 32
- Binks-Was 32
- McQuinn-StL 31

Triples
- Stirnweiss-NY 22
- Moses-Chi 15
- Kuhel-Was 13
- Dickshot-Chi 10
- Peck-Phi 9

Home Runs
- Stephens-StL 24
- Cullenbine-Cle-Det 18
- York-Det 18
- Etten-NY 18
- Heath-Cle 15

Total Bases
- Stirnweiss-NY 301
- Stephens-StL 270
- Etten-NY 247
- York-Det 246
- Moses-Chi 239

Runs Batted In
- Etten-NY 111
- Cullenbine-Cle-Det 93
- Stephens-StL 89
- York-Det 87
- Binks-Was 81

Stolen Bases
- Stirnweiss-NY 33
- Myatt-Was 30
- Case-Was 30
- Metkovich-Bos 19
- Dickshot-Chi 18

Base Stealing Runs
- Dickshot-Chi 2.9
- Myatt-Was 2.8
- Metkovich-Bos 2.1
- Stirnweiss-NY 1.3
- Crosetti-NY 1.2

Fielding Runs-Infield
- Stirnweiss-NY 25.2
- Lake-Bos 23.7
- Kell-Phi 21.8
- Mayo-Det 20.3
- Hall-Phi 20.1

Fielding Runs-Outfield
- Cullenbine-Cle-Det 9.1
- Case-Was 8.6
- Mackiewicz-Cle 7.3
- Byrnes-Was 6.5
- Moses-Chi 6.2

Wins
- Newhouser-Det 25
- Ferriss-Bos 21
- Wolff-Was 20
- Gromek-Cle 19

Winning Pct.
- Newhouser-Det 735
- Leonard-Was 708
- Gromek-Cle 679
- Ferriss-Bos 677
- Wolff-Was 667

Complete Games
- Newhouser-Det 29
- Ferriss-Bos 26
- Wolff-Was 21
- Potter-StL 21
- Gromek-Cle 21

Strikeouts
- Newhouser-Det 212
- Potter-StL 129
- Newsom-Phi 127
- Reynolds-Cle 112

Fewest BB/Game
- Bonham-NY 1.10
- Leonard-Was 1.46
- Wolff-Was 1.91
- Overmire-Det 2.33
- Gromek-Cle 2.37

Games
- Berry-Phi 52
- Reynolds-Cle 44
- Pieretti-Was 44
- Trout-Det 41
- Newhouser-Det 40

Saves
- Turner-NY 10
- Berry-Phi 5

Base Runners/9
- Wolff-Was 9.14
- Potter-StL 9.90
- Newhouser-Det 10.02
- Leonard-Was 10.21
- Bonham-NY 10.41

Adjusted Relief Runs
- Berry-Phi 15.0
- Holcombe-NY 7.4
- Barrett-Bos 6.9
- Zoldak-StL 1

Relief Ranking
- Berry-Phi 16.8
- Holcombe-NY 7.2
- Barrett-Bos 5.6
- Zoldak-StL ....

Innings Pitched
- Newhouser-Det 313.1
- Ferriss-Bos 264.2
- Newsom-Phi 257.1
- Potter-StL 255.1
- Gromek-Cle 251.0

Opponents' Avg.
- Newhouser-Det 211
- Wolff-Was 215
- Potter-StL 226
- Niggeling-Was 240
- Benton-Det 241

Opponents' OBP
- Wolff-Was 258
- Potter-StL 279
- Leonard-Was 279
- Newhouser-Det 281
- Bonham-NY 288

Earned Run Average
- Newhouser-Det 1.81
- Benton-Det 2.02
- Wolff-Was 2.12
- Leonard-Was 2.13
- Lee-Chi 2.44

Adjusted ERA
- Newhouser-Det 194
- Benton-Det 174
- Wolff-Was 146
- Leonard-Was 146
- Potter-StL 143

Adjusted Starter Runs
- Newhouser-Det 58.4
- Wolff-Was 31.3
- Potter-StL 30.4
- Benton-Det 24.4
- Leonard-Was 21.2

Pitcher Wins
- Newhouser-Det 7.8
- Potter-StL ....3.
- Wolff-Was 3.3
- Ferriss-Bos 3.6
- Gromek-Cle 2.6

End of the Patchwork Era

During the last and most depleted baseball season of the war years, the AL debuted a one-armed player (outfielder Pete Gray of St. Louis) and a one-legged player (pitcher Bert Shepard of Washington). And both their usually mediocre clubs were, again, in the pennant race. For the fifth straight season, home runs dropped. Only one player, Vern Stephens of the Browns, even hit 20, while the entire White Sox squad hit just 22—Chicago had slugged 25 in 1919.

The fourth-place Yankees again topped the AL in runs, with second baseman George "Snuffy" Stirnweiss beating up on substandard pitching. St. Louis had excellent hurling, but an even poorer attack than in 1944, and finished third. Second-place Washington boasted a speed-based offense and Roger Wolff, one of the most obscure 20-game winners of modern times.

Detroit's Hal Newhouser won his second straight MVP, this time with a 25-9 season that helped carry the Tigers over the top with the lowest winning percentage ever for an AL champ. Hank Greenberg, who returned at midseason from the military, hit a grand slam against St. Louis on September 30 to clinch the flag.

The World Series, an entertaining, sloppy, uneven affair featured the Tigers and the equally-not-great Cubs. (Asked for his pre-Series prediction, Chicago sportswriter Warren Brown opined, "I don't think either team can win it.") The clubs went to the brink, although the quality of play was far from solid. Game 6, a sloppy, 8-7, error-filled 12-inning affair won by Chicago on the brink of elimination, sapped their pitching; the Tigers won the final contest 9-3, behind Newhouser.

Harry O'Neill of the 1939 Athletics perished at Iwo Jima on March 6. He was the second and final big leaguer to die in World War II, but more than 50 American professional ballplayers were killed in the conflict.

1944 National League

TEAM	W	L	T	PCT	GB	HW	HL	R	OR	PA	H	2B	3B	HR	BB	SO	HB	SH	AVG	OBP	SLG	OPS	AOPS	BR	ABR	PF	SB	CS	BSA	BSR
STL	105	49	3	.682	—	54	22	772	490	6170	1507	274	59	100	544	473	27	124	.275	.344	.402	746	114	113	99	102	37			
PIT	90	63	5	.588	14.5	49	28	744	662	6099	1441	248	80	70	573	616	18	80	.265	.338	.379	717	104	58	29	104	87			
CIN	89	65	1	.578	16	45	33	573	537	5821	1340	229	31	51	423	391	27	100	.254	.313	.338	651	92	-74	-52	96	51			
CHI	75	79	3	.487	30	35	42	702	669	6108	1425	236	46	71	520	521	21	105	.261	.328	.360	688	101	-1	3	99	53			
NY	67	87	1	.435	38	39	36	682	773	5953	1398	191	47	93	512	480	20	115	.263	.331	.370	701	103	20	22	100	39			
BOS	65	89	1	.422	40	38	40	593	674	5868	1299	250	39	79	456	509	18	112	.246	.308	.353	661	88	-60	-83	104	37			
BRO	63	91	1	.409	42	37	39	690	832	6011	1450	255	51	56	486	451	14	118	.269	.331	.366	697	104	17	29	98	45			
PHI	61	92	1	.399	43.5	29	49	539	658	5911	1331	199	42	55	470	500	31	109	.251	.316	.336	652	92	-73	-53	97	32			
TOT	623					326	289	5295		47941	11191	1882	395	575	3984	3941	176	863	.261	.326	.363	689					381			

TEAM	CG	SHO	GR	SV	IP	H	HR	BB	SO	BR/9	ERA	AERA	OAV	OOB	PR	APR	PF	OSB	OCS	FA	E	WPB	DP	FW	PW	BW	BSW	DIF
STL	89	26	113	12	1427.0	1228	55	468	637	10.8	2.67	132	.233	.298	148	138	98	35	30	.982	112	22	162	3.7	14.2	10.2		-.0
PIT	77	10	140	19	1414.1	1466	65	435	452	12.2	3.44	108	.265	.321	27	43	103	43	35	.970	191	23	122	-1.1	4.4	3.0		7.2
CIN	93	17	96	12	1398.1	1292	60	390	369	10.9	2.97	117	.246	.300	99	83	97	31	19	.978	137	14	153	2.0	8.5	-5.3		6.8
CHI	70	11	156	13	1400.2	1484	75	458	545	12.5	3.59	98	.274	.331	4	-9	98	49	44	.970	186	35	151	-.8	-.9	.3		-.5
NY	47	4	200	21	1363.2	1413	116	587	499	13.4	4.29	85	.265	.342	-103	-93	102	45	35	.971	179	49	128	-.5	-9.5	2.3		-2.2
BOS	70	13	132	12	1388.1	1430	80	527	454	12.8	3.67	104	.267	.335	-9	21	106	76	41	.971	182	23	160	-.7	2.2	-8.5		-4.9
BRO	50	4	187	6	1367.2	1471	75	660	487	14.3	4.68	76	.274	.357	-162	-175	98	54	35	.966	197	48	112	-1.7	-18.0	3.0		2.6
PHI	66	11	155	6	1395.1	1407	49	459	496	12.2	3.64	99	.261	.321	-4	-4	100	48	33	.972	177	41	138	-.5	-.4	-5.4		-9.2
TOT	562	96	1179	108	11155.1					12.4	3.61		.261	.326						.972	1361	255	1126					

Batter-Fielder Wins		Batting Average		On-Base Percentage		Slugging Average		On-Base Plus Slugging		Adjusted OPS		Adjusted Batter Runs	
Musial-StL	5.5	Walker-Bro	.357	Musial-StL	.440	Musial-StL	.549	Musial-StL	.990	Musial-StL	174	Musial-StL	60.7
Walker-Bro	4.9	Musial-StL	.347	Walker-Bro	.434	Nicholson-Chi	.545	Ott-NY	.967	Walker-Bro	173	Walker-Bro	54.8
Galan-Bro	4.5	Medwick-NY	.337	Galan-Bro	.426	Ott-NY	.544	Walker-Bro	.963	Ott-NY	171	Galan-Bro	50.8
McCormick-Cin	3.8	Hopp-StL	.336	Ott-NY	.423	Walker-Bro	.529	Nicholson-Chi	.935	Nicholson-Chi	162	Nicholson-Chi	49.5
Nicholson-Chi	3.8	Cavarretta-Chi	.321	Hopp-StL	.404	Weintraub-NY	.524	Galan-Bro	.922	Galan-Bro	162	Ott-NY	41.7

Runs		Hits		Doubles		Triples		Home Runs		Total Bases		Runs Batted In	
Nicholson-Chi	116	Musial-StL	197	Musial-StL	51	Barrett-Pit	19	Nicholson-Chi	33	Nicholson-Chi	317	Nicholson-Chi	122
Musial-StL	112	Cavarretta-Chi	197	Galan-Bro	43	Elliott-Pit	16	Ott-NY	26	Musial-StL	312	Elliott-Pit	108
Russell-Pit	109	Holmes-Bos	195	Holmes-Bos	42	Cavarretta-Chi	15	Northey-Phi	22	Holmes-Bos	288	Northey-Phi	104
Hopp-StL	106	Walker-Bro	191			Russell-Pit	14	McCormick-Cin	20	Walker-Bro	283	Sanders-StL	102
Cavarretta-Chi	106	Russell-Pit	181			Musial-StL	14	Kurowski-StL	20	Northey-Phi	283	McCormick-Cin	102

Stolen Bases		Base Stealing Runs		Fielding Runs-Infield		Fielding Runs-Outfield		Wins		Winning Pct.		Complete Games	
Barrett-Pit	28			Kerr-NY	19.3	Pafko-Chi	10.2	Walters-Cin	23	Wilks-StL	.810	Tobin-Bos	28
Lupien-Phi	18			Williams-Cin	15.6	Russell-Pit	9.1	M.Cooper-StL	22	Brecheen-StL	.762	Walters-Cin	27
Hughes-Chi	16			Hughes-Chi	13.4	Medwick-NY	7.1	Voiselle-NY	21	M.Cooper-StL	.759	Voiselle-NY	25
Hopp-StL	15			Luby-NY	12.5	Olmo-Bro	5.2	Sewell-Pit	21	Walters-Cin	.742	Sewell-Pit	24
Kerr-NY	14			McCormick-Cin	12.3	Musial-StL	3.3	Tobin-Bos	18	Sewell-Pit	.636	M.Cooper-StL	22

Strikeouts		Fewest BB/Game		Games		Saves		Base Runners/9		Adjusted Relief Runs		Relief Ranking	
Voiselle-NY	161	Raffensberger-Phi	1.57	Adams-NY	65	Adams-NY	13	Wilks-StL	9.66	Karl-Phi	10.5	Karl-Phi	5.8
Lanier-StL	141	Strincevich-Pit	1.75	Webber-Bro	48	Schmidt-StL	5	Heusser-Cin	9.72	Donnelly-StL	9.9	Donnelly-StL	4.9
Javery-Bos	137	Davis-Bro	1.81	Rescigno-Pit	48	Rescigno-Pit	5	Karl-Phi	9.91				
Raffensberger-Phi	136	Shoun-Cin	1.87	Voiselle-NY	48	Davis-Bro	4	Munger-StL	10.04				
		Derringer-Chi	1.95	Tobin-Bos	43	Cuccurullo-Pit	4	DeLaCruz-Cin	10.16				

Innings Pitched		Opponents' Avg.		Opponents' OBP		Earned Run Average		Adjusted ERA		Adjusted Starter Runs		Pitcher Wins	
Voiselle-NY	312.2	Walters-Cin	.219	Wilks-StL	.275	Heusser-Cin	2.38	Heusser-Cin	146	Walters-Cin	34.0	Walters-Cin	4.7
Tobin-Bos	299.1	Wilks-StL	.227	Heusser-Cin	.275	Walters-Cin	2.40	Walters-Cin	145	M.Cooper-StL	33.1	Tobin-Bos	3.8
Sewell-Pit	286.0	Heusser-Cin	.231	Walters-Cin	.281	M.Cooper-StL	2.46	M.Cooper-StL	143	Munger-StL	29.1	M.Cooper-StL	3.7
Walters-Cin	285.0	Voiselle-NY	.232	DeLaCruz-Cin	.284	Wilks-StL	2.64	Wilks-StL	133	Wilks-StL	25.0	Munger-StL	3.4
Raffensberger-Phi	258.2	Lanier-StL	.234	Raffensberger-Phi	.285	Lanier-StL	2.65	Lanier-StL	133	Heusser-Cin	24.6	Heusser-Cin	3.1

Baby Face

The use of young players, by now a cliché of wartime baseball, reached a crest on June 10 when 15-year-old Joe Nuxhall pitched for the Cincinnati Reds. He remains the youngest big leaguer in history. Sixteen-year-old Tommy Brown played shortstop for the Dodgers, with 17-year-old Eddie Miksis filling in at both short and third. Eighteen-year-olds Cal McLish and Ralph Branca pitched for Brooklyn, who fell to seventh, crushed by wartime losses. The Phillies showcased infielders Putsy Caballero, 16, and Granny Hamner, 17, as well as hurler Rogers McKee, also 17. New York had two 19-year-old pitchers, and the Braves used two 17-year-olds.

Tellingly, the Cardinals, who became the first NL team to win 100 games three straight seasons, had no teenagers on their team. St. Louis was in control by May and coasted to another pennant. Outfielder Stan Musial and Johnny Hopp fattened up on wartime pitching, but the MVP went to their teammate, slick-fielding shortstop Marty Marion. Pittsburgh finished a surprising second; a patchwork pitching staff and a line-drive attack helped them finish just above Cincinnati, for whom hurler Bucky Walters had another dominating season.

In the game's only all-St. Louis World Series, the Cardinals snuffed out their crosstown rivals' attack, and the Browns committed 10 errors. The Cardinals came back from a two-games-to-one deficit to take the next three, allowing the Browns but 2 runs in the process. Four of the six games were decided by 1 or 2 runs, and excellent pitching—allowing the Browns just a .183 average—carried the day.

Judge Kenesaw Mountain Landis died on November 25 at age 78. The autocratic Commissioner served baseball for nearly a quarter-century, but with declining power; he could not stop the subjugation of the minors to the majors. But never again would the game be commanded by a strong, independent voice.

1944 American League

TEAM	W	L	T	PCT	GB	HW	HL	R	OR	PA	H	2B	3B	HR	BB	SO	HB	SH	AVG	OBP	SLG	OPS	AOPS	BR	ABR	PF	SB	CS	BSA	BSR
STL	89	65	0	.578		54	23	684	587	5928	1328	223	45	72	531	604	21	107	.252	.323	.352	675	94	-3	-37	106	44	33	57	-2
DET	88	66	2	.571	1	43	34	658	581	6011	1405	220	44	60	532	500	24	111	.263	.332	.354	686	97	22	-12	106	61	55	53	-6
NY	83	71	0	.539	6	47	31	674	617	5978	1410	216	74	96	523	627	22	102	.264	.333	.387	720	108	74	51	103	91	31	75	9
BOS	77	77	2	.500	12	47	30	739	676	6052	1456	277	56	69	522	505	20	110	.270	.336	.380	716	112	77	86	99	60	40	60	-1
PHI	72	82	1	.468	17	39	37	525	594	5873	1364	169	47	36	422	490	17	122	.257	.314	.327	641	90	-78	-70	99	42	32	57	-2
CLE	72	82	1	.468	17	39	38	643	677	6119	1458	270	50	70	512	593	19	107	.266	.331	.372	703	111	50	78	96	48	42	53	-2
CHI	71	83	0	.461	18	41	36	543	662	5819	1307	210	55	23	439	448	21	67	.247	.307	.320	627	86	-99	-92	99	66	47	58	-2
WAS	64	90	0	.416	25	40	37	592	664	5926	1386	186	42	33	470	477	29	108	.261	.324	.330	654	97	-43	-15	96	127	59	68	7
TOT	619					350	266	5058		47706	11114	1771	413	459	3951	4244	173	834	.260	.325	.353	678					539	339	61	0

TEAM	CG	SHO	GR	SV	IP	H	HR	BB	SO	BR/9	ERA	AERA	OAV	OOB	PR	APR	PF	OSB	OCS	FA	E	WPB	DP	FW	PW	BW	BSW	DIF
STL	71	16	127	17	1397.1	1392	58	469	581	12.1	3.17	114	.259	.320	41	63	105	76	31	.972	171	30	142	.5	6.6	-3.9	-.2	9.0
DET	87	20	119	8	1400.0	1373	39	452	568	11.9	3.09	116	.257	.318	54	72	104	37	60	.974	156	38	184	1.3	7.6	-1.3	-.6	5.8
NY	78	9	111	13	1390.1	1351	82	532	529	12.3	3.39	103	.257	.326	7	15	102	57	40	.972	171	40	154	.6	-6.9	9.0	-.1	-2.6
BOS	58	7	150	17	1394.1	1404	66	592	524	13.0	3.82	89	.263	.339	-60	-66	99	69	50	.972	176	42	127	.2	3.7	-7.4	-.2	-1.3
PHI	72	10	107	14	1397.1	1345	58	390	534	11.4	3.26	107	.252	.307	27	35	102	98	50	.971	183	40	192	.9	-6.1	8.2	-.4	-7.6
CLE	48	7	200	18	1419.1	1428	40	621	524	13.2	3.65	90	.265	.344	-35	-58	96	78	45	.974	165	44	154	-.2	-2.4	-9.7	-.2	6.5
CHI	64	5	112	17	1390.2	1411	68	420	481	12.0	3.58	96	.264	.320	-23	-23	100	56	40	.970	190	32	156	-2.3	-4.0	-1.6	.7	-5.9
WAS	83	13	110	11	1381.0	1410	48	475	503	12.4	3.49	93	.264	.327	-10	-38	95	68	35	.964	218	62	170					
TOT	561	87	1036	115	11170.1					12.3	3.43		.260	.325						.971	1430	328	1279					0

Batter-Fielder Wins		**Batting Average**		**On-Base Percentage**		**Slugging Average**		**On-Base Plus Slugging**		**Adjusted OPS**		**Adjusted Batter Runs**	
Boudreau-Cle	7.5	Boudreau-Cle	327	B.Johnson-Bos	431	Doerr-Bos	528	B.Johnson-Bos	959	B.Johnson-Bos	175	B.Johnson-Bos	56.6
Stirnweiss-NY	6.8	Doerr-Bos	325	Boudreau-Cle	406	B.Johnson-Bos	528	Doerr-Bos	927	Doerr-Bos	166	Spence-Was	44.0
Spence-Was	5.4	B.Johnson-Bos	324	Doerr-Bos	399	Lindell-NY	500	Spence-Was	877	Spence-Was	157	Doerr-Bos	39.9
B.Johnson-Bos	5.3	Stirnweiss-NY	319	Etten-NY	399	Spence-Was	486	Etten-NY	865	Boudreau-Cle	146	Boudreau-Cle	39.4
Doerr-Bos	5.1	Spence-Was	316	Byrnes-StL	396			Lindell-NY	851	Etten-NY	142	Etten-NY	34.8

Runs		**Hits**		**Doubles**		**Triples**		**Home Runs**		**Total Bases**		**Runs Batted In**	
Stirnweiss-NY	125	Stirnweiss-NY	205	Boudreau-Cle	45	Stirnweiss-NY	16	Etten-NY	22	Lindell-NY	297	Stephens-StL	109
B.Johnson-Bos	106	Boudreau-Cle	191	Keltner-Cle	41	Lindell-NY	16	Stephens-StL	20	Stirnweiss-NY	296	B.Johnson-Bos	106
Cullenbine-Cle	98	Spence-Was	187	B.Johnson-Bos	40	Gutteridge-StL	11	York-Det	18	Spence-Was	288	Lindell-NY	103
Doerr-Bos	95	Lindell-NY	178	Fox-Bos	37	Doerr-Bos	10	Spence-Was	18	B.Johnson-Bos	277	Spence-Was	100
Metkovich-Bos	94	Rocco-Cle	174	Stirnweiss-NY	35			Lindell-NY	18			York-Det	98

Stolen Bases		**Base Stealing Runs**		**Fielding Runs-Infield**		**Fielding Runs-Outfield**		**Wins**		**Winning Pct.**		**Complete Games**	
Stirnweiss-NY	55	Stirnweiss-NY	8.3	Mayo-Det	33.5	Spence-Was	15.4	Newhouser-Det	29	Hughson-Bos	783	Trout-Det	33
Case-Was	49	Case-Was	4.5	Boudreau-Cle	20.2	Tucker-Chi	10.8	Trout-Det	27	Newhouser-Det	763	Newhouser-Det	25
Myatt-Was	26	Myatt-Was	2.2	Stirnweiss-NY	18.0	B.Johnson-Bos	5.2	Potter-StL	19	Potter-StL	731		
Moses-Chi	21	Moses-Chi	2.2	Rocco-Cle	16.6	Garrison-Bos-Phi	4.9	Hughson-Bos	18	Trout-Det	659		
Gutteridge-StL	20	Gutteridge-StL	1.6	Hoover-Det	14.8	Lindell-NY	4.0			Borowy-NY	586		

Strikeouts		**Fewest BB/Game**		**Games**		**Saves**		**Base Runners/9**		**Adjusted Relief Runs**		**Relief Ranking**	
Newhouser-Det	187	Harris-Phi	1.34	Heving-Cle	63	Maltzberger-Chi	12	Berry-Phi	8.33	Berry-Phi	17.2	Berry-Phi	29.2
Trout-Det	144	Leonard-Was	1.45	Berry-Phi	53	Caster-StL	12	Hughson-Bos	9.52	Heving-Cle	13.5	Heving-Cle	13.7
Newsom-Phi	142	Bonham-NY	1.73	Trout-Det	49	Berry-Phi	12	Maltzberger-Chi	9.95	Maltzberger-Chi	6.8	Maltzberger-Chi	12.1
Kramer-StL	124	Gorsica-Det	1.78	Newhouser-Det	47	Heving-Cle	10	Trout-Det	10.24	Caster-StL	5.6	Caster-StL	9.3
Niggeling-Was	121	Hamlin-Phi	1.80	Klieman-Cle	47	Barrett-Bos	8	Leonard-Was	10.28				

Innings Pitched		**Opponents' Avg.**		**Opponents' OBP**		**Earned Run Average**		**Adjusted ERA**		**Adjusted Starter Runs**		**Pitcher Wins**	
Trout-Det	352.1	Gromek-Cle	219	Hughson-Bos	267	Trout-Det	2.12	Trout-Det	168	Trout-Det	53.1	Trout-Det	8.2
Newhouser-Det	312.1	Niggeling-Was	221	Leonard-Was	284	Newhouser-Det	2.22	Newhouser-Det	161	Newhouser-Det	44.7	Newhouser-Det	6.?
Newsom-Phi	265.0	Hughson-Bos	225	Trout-Det	284	Hughson-Bos	2.26	Hughson-Bos	151	Hughson-Bos	26.6	Kramer-StL	3.?
Kramer-StL	257.0	Newhouser-Det	230	Gromek-Cle	290	Niggeling-Was	2.32	Kramer-StL	145	Kramer-StL	26.6	Berry-Phi	3.?
Borowy-NY	252.2	Borowy-NY	236	Newhouser-Det	293	Kramer-StL	2.49	Niggeling-Was	141	Niggeling-Was	23.0	Hughson-Bos	3.?

Brownout

In a year that stretched baseball's ability to take itself seriously, a squad of especially unlikely heroes won the flag. The perpetually bad St. Louis Browns took advantage of a war-decimated league and climbed atop a four-team tangle by mid-August. Shortstop Vern Stephens was the club's only real threat at bat, but a veteran pitching staff, quality infield defense, and other teams' shortcomings kept the Brownies in the hunt.

At that point, the Red Sox dropped out. The Yankees got hot, but cooled off again, leaving the race to the Browns and Tigers. Detroit was fueled by Hal Newhouser and Dizzy Trout's pitching and outfielder Dick Wakefield's activation from the military rolls.

Both teams were on fire the last two weeks, but the Brownies came out on top, taking four straight from New York while the Tigers fell to Washington on the season's last day. This would be St. Louis' only AL crown, and the fact that it was accomplished by a collection of military-deferred 4-Fs, alcoholics, and graybeards is almost irrelevant.

The first big league player to die in World War II was 27-year-old Elmer Gedeon. A captain in the Army Air Corps, Gedeon's plane was shot down over France on April 20. He had played the outfield for the 1939 Senators.

During the 1940s, few teams altered their ballparks; due to the war, most construction was out. But this year, Detroit reconfigured its grounds, giving Tiger Stadium the dimensions it retained until closing in 1999. Total tickets sold skyrocketed 30 percent for the AL in 1944, and for the first time since 1925, the Browns didn't finish last in attendance. They came in fifth.

As if adhering to the demands of the war on travel, Sportsman's Park was the site for all six World Series games. The first all-St. Louis World Series was a much closer affair than anyone expected. The Browns actually went up two games to one before the deeper Cardinals took the next three.

1943 National League

TEAM	W	L	T	PCT	GB	HW	HL	R	OR	PA	H	2B	3B	HR	BB	SO	HB	SH	AVG	OBP	SLG	OPS	AOPS	BR	ABR	PF	SB	CS	BSA	BSR
STL	105	49	3	.682		58	21	679	475	6057	1515	259	72	70	428	438	19	172	.279	.333	.391	724	110	92	62	104	40			
CIN	87	67	1	.565	18	48	29	608	543	5910	1362	229	47	43	445	476	17	119	.256	.315	.340	655	96	-36	-28	99	49			
BRO	81	72	0	.529	23.5	46	31	716	675	6009	1444	263	35	39	580	422	21	99	.272	.346	.357	703	110	76	75	100	58			
PIT	80	74	3	.519	25	47	30	669	605	6030	1401	240	73	42	573	566	18	86	.262	.335	.357	692	103	46	24	103	64			
CHI	74	79	1	.484	30.5	36	38	632	599	5970	1380	207	56	52	574	522	21	96	.261	.336	.351	687	107	38	48	99	53			
BOS	68	85	0	.444	36.5	38	39	465	612	5780	1213	202	36	39	469	609	17	98	.233	.299	.309	608	82	-122	-115	99	56			
PHI	64	90	3	.416	41	33	43	571	676	5918	1321	186	36	66	499	556	21	101	.249	.316	.335	651	98	-39	-15	96	29			
NY	55	98	3	.359	49.5	34	43	558	713	5900	1309	153	33	81	480	470	23	107	.247	.313	.335	648	92	-52	-56	101	35			
TOT	621					340	274	4898		47574	10945	1739	388	432	4048	4059	157	878	.258	.324	.347	672					384			

TEAM	CG	SHO	GR	SV	IP	H	HR	BB	SO	BR/9	ERA	AERA	OAV	OOB	PR	APR	PF	OSB	OCS	FA	E	WPB	DP	FW	PW	BW	BSW	DIF
STL	94	21	104	15	1427.0	1246	33	477	639	11.0	2.57	131	.237	.303	129	127	99	30	34	.976	151	33	183	.9	13.6	6.6		6.9
CIN	78	18	119	17	1404.0	1299	38	579	498	12.1	3.13	106	.251	.328	39	28	98	41	50	.980	125	21	193	2.2	3.0	-3.0		7.8
BRO	50	13	182	22	1369.2	1326	59	637	588	13.1	3.88	86	.254	.338	-76	-80	99	46	39	.972	168	35	137	-.3	-8.5	8.0		5.4
PIT	74	11	157	12	1404.0	1424	44	422	396	11.9	3.08	113	.264	.319	47	58	103	33	44	.973	170	24	159	-.2	6.2	2.6		-5.5
CHI	67	13	160	14	1386.0	1379	53	394	513	11.6	3.31	101	.258	.311	11	4	99	37	19	.973	168	34	138	-.3	.4	5.1		-7.8
BOS	87	13	99	4	1397.2	1361	66	441	409	11.8	3.25	105	.255	.314	20	25	101	81	40	.972	176	18	139	-.8	2.7	-12.3		1.9
PHI	66	10	140	19	1392.2	1436	59	451	431	12.3	3.79	89	.267	.326	-62	-64	100	55	38	.969	189	39	143	-1.3	-6.8	-1.6		-3.3
NY	35	6	208	19	1394.2	1474	80	626	588	13.7	4.08	84	.272	.350	-108	-97	102	61	35	.973	166	43	140	-.0	-10.4	-6.0		-5.1
TOT	551	105	1169	117	11175.2					12.2	3.38		.258	.324						.974	1313	247	1232					

Batter-Fielder Wins		Batting Average		On-Base Percentage		Slugging Average		On-Base Plus Slugging		Adjusted OPS		Adjusted Batter Runs	
Musial-StL	5.7	Musial-StL	.357	Musial-StL	.425	Musial-StL	.562	Musial-StL	.988	Musial-StL	176	Musial-StL	60.7
Nicholson-Chi	4.5	Herman-Bro	.330	Galan-Bro	.412	Nicholson-Chi	.531	Nicholson-Chi	.917	Nicholson-Chi	166	Nicholson-Chi	50.1
Mueller-StL	3.8	W.Cooper-StL	.318	Herman-Bro	.398	W.Cooper-StL	.463	Elliott-Pit	.820	Tipton-Cin	138	Galan-Bro	29.9
Galan-Bro	3.6	Elliott-Pit	.315	Fletcher-Pit	.395	Elliott-Pit	.444	Tipton-Cin	.819	Galan-Bro	136	Herman-Bro	29.6
Witek-NY	3.2	Witek-NY	.314	Tipton-Cin	.395	Triplett-StL-Phi	.439	Galan-Bro	.818	Herman-Bro	135	Tipton-Cin	28.1

Runs		Hits		Doubles		Triples		Home Runs		Total Bases		Runs Batted In	
Vaughan-Bro	112	Musial-StL	220	Musial-StL	48	Musial-StL	20	Nicholson-Chi	29	Musial-StL	347	Nicholson-Chi	128
Musial-StL	108	Witek-NY	195	Herman-Bro	41	Klein-StL	14	Ott-NY	18	Nicholson-Chi	323	Elliott-Pit	101
Nicholson-Chi	95	Herman-Bro	193	DiMaggio-Pit	41	Lowrey-Chi	12	Northey-Phi	16	Elliott-Pit	258	Herman-Bro	100
Cavarretta-Chi	93	Nicholson-Chi	188	Vaughan-Bro	39	Elliott-Pit	12	Triplett-StL-Phi	15	Klein-StL	257	DiMaggio-Pit	88
Stanky-Chi	92	Vaughan-Bro	186	Holmes-Bos	33			DiMaggio-Pit	15				

Stolen Bases		Base Stealing Runs		Fielding Runs-Infield		Fielding Runs-Outfield		Wins		Winning Pct.		Complete Games	
Vaughan-Bro	20			Miller-Cin	23.8	DiMaggio-Pit	11.9	Sewell-Pit	21	M.Cooper-StL	.724	Sewell-Pit	25
Lowrey-Chi	13			Wietelmann-Bos	18.2	Litwhiler-Phi-StL	6.9	Riddle-Cin	21	Sewell-Pit	.700	Tobin-Bos	24
Workman-Bos	12			Marion-StL	16.2	Galan-Bro	6.4	M.Cooper-StL	21	Lanier-StL	.682	M.Cooper-StL	24
Russell-Pit	12			Witek-NY	15.3	Lowrey-Chi	5.7	Bithorn-Chi	18	Riddle-Cin	.656	Andrews-Bos	23
Gustine-Pit	12			Frey-Cin	12.9	Musial-StL	4.5	Javery-Bos	17	Bithorn-Chi	.600		

Strikeouts		Fewest BB/Game		Games		Saves		Base Runners/9		Adjusted Relief Runs		Relief Ranking	
VanderMeer-Cin	174	Rowe-Phi	1.31	Adams-NY	70	Webber-Bro	10	Pollet-StL	8,90	Beggs-Cin	10.6	Adams-NY	12.2
M.Cooper-StL	141	Wyse-Chi	1.96	Webber-Bro	54	Adams-NY	9	Wyatt-Bro	9.07	Adams-NY	9.4	Beggs-Cin	12.0
Javery-Bos	134	Derringer-Chi	2.02	Head-Bro	47	Shoun-Cin	7	Brecheen-StL	9.31	Prim-Chi	3.6	Prim-Chi	3.9
Lanier-StL	123	Davis-Bro	2.14	Shoun-Cin	45	Head-Bro	6	Gumbert-StL	9.95	Brandt-Pit	2.2	Brandt-Pit	1.7
Higbe-Bro	108	Wyatt-Bro	2.14	Mungo-NY	45	Beggs-Cin	6	Warneke-Chi	10.19				

Innings Pitched		Opponents' Avg.		Opponents' OBP		Earned Run Average		Adjusted ERA		Adjusted Starter Runs		Pitcher Wins	
Javery-Bos	303.0	Wyatt-Bro	.207	Wyatt-Bro	.255	Pollet-StL	1.75	Lanier-StL	177	M.Cooper-StL	32.9	Sewell-Pit	3.9
VanderMeer-Cin	289.0	VanderMeer-Cin	.224	Rowe-Phi	.279	Lanier-StL	1.90	M.Cooper-StL	146	Lanier-StL	30.8	M.Cooper-StL	3.3
Andrews-Bos	283.2	M.Cooper-StL	.226	M.Cooper-StL	.286	M.Cooper-StL	2.30	Sewell-Pit	137	Sewell-Pit	26.9	Rowe-Phi	3.3
M.Cooper-StL	274.0	Krist-StL	.233	Andrews-Bos	.291	Wyatt-Bro	2.49	Wyatt-Bro	135	Andrews-Bos	25.6	Andrews-Bos	3.2
Sewell-Pit	265.1	Barrett-Chi-Phi	.237	Bithorn-Chi	.294	Sewell-Pit	2.54	Butcher-Pit	134	Bithorn-Chi	23.2	Tobin-Bos	3.1

Life During Wartime

World War II was taking a bite out of baseball's economy. Attendance fell 13 percent further after dropping 9 percent in 1942. And it took a bite out of the ball, too—with cork and rubber unavailable to Spalding, the 1943 baseballs were made from a cork substitute called balata. The ball was deader than vaudeville, and public outcry soon forced the manufacture of a livelier spheroid.

Talent was draining from baseball as well. The Dodgers, losing Hugh Casey, Larry French, Pee Wee Reese, and Pete Reiser to military service, dropped to a distant third. The Reds sacrificed Ewell Blackwell to the war for three years; the Cubs lost Eddie Waitkus for four. Johnny Sain and Warren Spahn departed Boston from 1943–45, and the Giants lived without Johnny Mize for the same span.

St. Louis' excellent farm system produced Harry Brecheen, Lou Klein, and Al Brazle to supplement a club that lost Johnny Beazley, Frank Crespi, Terry Moore, and Enos Slaughter

for three seasons. Buoyed by big years from Stan Musial and Mort Cooper, the Cardinals ran away with the pennant. Only a late flurry by second-place Cincinnati cut St. Louis' winning margin under 20; this was the league's least competitive race in nearly forty years.

Breaking his own record for relief appearances, Ace Adams of the Giants became the first pitcher to appear in 70 games since 1883. The Phillies changed their name to the Blue Jays, but didn't get any better. In Brooklyn, 19-year-old first baseman Gil Hodges got his first major league at bats, while across town at the Polo Grounds, Carl Hubbell retired at 40 with arm problems. The Giants finished last.

Despite their great regular season, the Cardinals—perhaps challenged for competition—lost to the Yankees in a five-game World Series. The Cards, who batted just .224, actually outhit New York—only not when it counted. They scored 2 runs or less in all four losses.

1943 American League

TEAM	W	L	T	PCT	GB	HW	HL	R	OR	PA	H	2B	3B	HR	BB	SO	HB	SH	AVG	OBP	SLG	OPS	AOPS	BR	ABR	PF	SB	CS	BSA	BSR
NY	98	56	1	.636		54	23	669	542	6024	1350	218	59	100	624	562	25	93	.256	.337	.376	713	114	98	93	101	46	60	43	-9
WAS	84	69	0	.549	13.5	44	32	666	595	5965	1328	245	50	47	605	579	39	88	.254	.336	.347	683	110	49	74	96	142	55	72	12
CLE	82	71	0	.536	15.5	44	33	600	577	5968	1344	246	45	55	567	521	11	121	.255	.329	.350	679	112	35	76	94	47	58	45	-10
CHI	82	72	1	.532	16	40	36	573	594	5909	1297	193	46	33	561	581	22	72	.247	.322	.320	642	94	-34	-33	100	173	87	67	8
DET	78	76	1	.506	20	45	32	632	560	5983	1401	200	47	77	483	553	13	123	.261	.324	.359	683	98	29	-16	108	40	43	48	-6
STL	72	80	1	.474	25	44	33	596	604	5865	1269	229	36	78	569	646	15	106	.245	.322	.349	671	100	16	3	102	37	43	46	-2
BOS	68	84	3	.447	29	39	36	563	607	6010	1314	223	42	57	486	591	19	113	.244	.308	.332	640	92	-49	-58	102	86	61	59	-2
PHI	49	105	1	.318	49	27	51	497	717	5798	1219	174	44	26	430	465	29	95	.232	.294	.297	591	78	-143	-141	100	55	42	57	-3
TOT	617					337	276	4796		47522	10522	1728	369	473	4325	4498	173	811	.249	.322	.341	663					626	449	58	-19

TEAM	CG	SHO	GR	SV	IP	H	HR	BB	SO	BR/9	ERA	AERA	OAV	OOB	PR	APR	PF	OSB	OCS	FA	E	WPB	DP	FW	PW	BW	BSW	DIF
NY	83	14	98	13	1415.1	1229	60	489	653	11.0	2.93	110	.234	.301	58	47	98	48	50	.974	160	31	166	.2	5.1	10.1	-.9	6.5
WAS	61	16	134	21	1388.0	1293	48	540	495	12.0	3.18	101	.246	.318	17	3	97	59	51	.971	179	49	145	-1.0	.3	8.0	1.6	-1.4
CLE	64	14	158	20	1406.1	1234	52	606	585	11.9	3.15	99	.239	.322	23	-7	94	57	61	.975	157	13	183	.3	-.8	2.3	1.1	5.3
CHI	70	12	109	19	1400.1	1352	54	501	476	12.1	3.20	104	.255	.324	15	21	101	66	43	.973	166	35	167	-.0	2.3	-3.6	1.1	5.3
DET	67	18	130	20	1411.2	1226	51	549	706	11.4	3.00	117	.234	.308	46	76	101	84	80	.971	177	32	130	-.7	8.2	-1.7	-.4	-4.4
STL	64	10	130	14	1385.0	1397	74	488	572	12.4	3.41	97	.263	.327	-18	-13	101	124	54	.975	152	32	127	.6	-1.4	-.3	-.5	-3.0
BOS	62	13	140	16	1426.1	1369	61	615	513	12.6	3.45	96	.257	.335	-25	-22	101	80	55	.976	153	45	179	.6	-2.4	-6.3	.0	-.0
PHI	73	5	107	13	1394.0	1421	73	536	503	12.9	4.05	84	.265	.336	-117	-98	103	108	55	.973	162	43	148	.1	-10.6	-15.3	-.0	-2.2
TOT	544	102	1006	136	11227.0					12.0	3.30		.249	.322						.973	1306	280	1245					

Batter-Fielder Wins
- Boudreau-Cle 6.8
- Appling-Chi 6.3
- Gordon-NY 5.6
- York-Det 4.6
- Keller-NY 4.0

Batting Average
- Appling-Chi 328
- Wakefield-Det 316
- Hodgin-Chi 314
- Cramer-Det 300
- Case-Was 294

On-Base Percentage
- Appling-Chi 419
- Cullenbine-Cle 407
- Keller-NY 396
- Boudreau-Cle 388
- Curtright-Chi 382

Slugging Average
- York-Det 527
- Keller-NY 525
- Stephens-StL 482
- Heath-Cle 481
- Wakefield-Det 434

On-Base Plus Slugging
- Keller-NY 922
- Heath-Cle 893
- Cullenbine-Cle 850
- Stephens-StL 839
- Appling-Chi 825

Adjusted OPS
- Keller-NY 167
- Heath-Cle 157
- York-Det 148
- Cullenbine-Cle 146
- Appling-Chi 142

Adjusted Batter Runs
- Keller-NY 45.1
- Appling-Chi 36.7
- Cullenbine-Cle 34.4
- York-Det 33.3
- Heath-Cle 30.4

Runs
- Case-Was 102
- Keller-NY 97
- Wakefield-Det 91
- York-Det 90
- Vernon-Was 89

Hits
- Wakefield-Det 200
- Appling-Chi 192
- Cramer-Det 182
- Case-Was 180

Doubles
- Wakefield-Det 38
- Case-Was 36
- Gutteridge-StL 35
- Etten-NY 35

Triples
- Moses-Chi 12
- Lindell-NY 12
- York-Det 11
- Keller-NY 11
- Spence-Was 10

Home Runs
- York-Det 34
- Keller-NY 31
- Stephens-StL 22
- Heath-Cle 18

Total Bases
- York-Det 301
- Wakefield-Det 275
- Keller-NY 269
- Doerr-Bos 249
- Stephens-StL 247

Runs Batted In
- York-Det 118
- Etten-NY 107
- Johnson-NY 94
- Stephens-StL 91
- Spence-Was 88

Stolen Bases
- Case-Was 61
- Moses-Chi 56
- Tucker-Chi 29
- Appling-Chi 27
- Vernon-Was 24

Base Stealing Runs
- Case-Was 8.5
- Moses-Chi 7.4
- Appling-Chi 3.1
- Culberson-Bos 3.1
- Vernon-Was 2.5

Fielding Runs-Infield
- Boudreau-Cle 25.1
- Gordon-NY 24.7
- York-Det 18.6
- Clift-StL-Was 15.4
- Bloodworth-Det 15.4

Fielding Runs-Outfield
- Tucker-Chi 9.2
- Byrnes-StL 6.9
- Moses-Chi 6.6
- Johnson-Was 6.5
- Laabs-StL 4.6

Wins
- Trout-Det 20
- Chandler-NY 20
- Wynn-Was 18
- Smith-Cle 17
- Bagby-Cle 17

Winning Pct.
- Chandler-NY 833
- Smith-Cle 708
- Bonham-NY 652
- Trout-Det 625
- Grove-Chi 625

Complete Games
- Hughson-Bos 20
- Chandler-NY 20
- Wensloff-NY 18
- Trout-Det 18
- Grove-Chi 18

Strikeouts
- Reynolds-Cle 151
- Newhouser-Det 144
- Chandler-NY 134
- Bridges-Det 124
- Trucks-Det 118

Fewest BB/Game
- Leonard-Was 1.88
- Chandler-NY 1.92
- Bonham-NY 2.07
- Muncrief-StL 2.11
- Trucks-Det 2.31

Games
- Brown-Bos 49
- Trout-Det 44
- Wolff-Phi 41
- Ryba-Bos 40
- Carrasquel-Was 39

Saves
- Maltzberger-Chi 14
- Heving-Cle 9
- Brown-Bos 9
- Murphy-NY 8
- Caster-StL 8

Base Runners/9
- Chandler-NY 9.07
- Murphy-NY 9.79
- Trucks-Det 9.90
- Bonham-NY 9.97
- Wensloff-NY 10.07

Adjusted Relief Runs
- Brown-Bos 11.6
- Maltzberger-Chi 10.8
- Caster-StL 9.6
- Murphy-NY 5.6
- Heving-Cle 4.3

Relief Ranking
- Caster-StL 18.0
- Brown-Bos 15.9
- Maltzberger-Chi 14.3
- Murphy-NY 11.2
- Naymick-Cle 5.0

Innings Pitched
- Bagby-Cle 273.0
- Hughson-Bos 266.0
- Wynn-Was 256.2
- Chandler-NY 253.0
- Trout-Det 246.2

Opponents' Avg.
- Reynolds-Cle 202
- Niggeling-StL-Was 204
- Haefner-Was 208
- Chandler-NY 215
- Wensloff-NY 219

Opponents' OBP
- Chandler-NY 261
- Trucks-Det 276
- Wensloff-NY 282
- Bonham-NY 282
- Niggeling-StL-Was 282

Earned Run Average
- Chandler-NY 1.64
- Bonham-NY 2.27
- Haefner-Was 2.29
- Bridges-Det 2.39
- Trout-Det 2.48

Adjusted ERA
- Chandler-NY 197
- Bridges-Det 147
- Trout-Det 142
- Bonham-NY 141
- Haefner-Was 140

Adjusted Starter Runs
- Chandler-NY 42.1
- Bonham-NY 26.0
- Trout-Det 25.8
- Bridges-Det 23.9
- Hughson-Bos 19.6

Pitcher Wins
- Chandler-NY 5.3
- Trout-Det 4.1
- Bridges-Det 2.6
- Bonham-NY 2.5
- Caster-StL 2.0

Fathers Playing Catch with Sons

On September 6, 16-year-old Carl Scheib debuted as a pitcher for the Philadelphia A's. He became the youngest player in AL history, and joined others, like 20-year-olds Gene Woodling and George Kell, 18-year-old Vern Benson, and 17-year-old Cass Michaels in 1943's force-feeding derby.

In addition, several graybeards profited from the lack of available bodies. Forty-year-old Mike Ryba pitched 40 times for the Red Sox, who also used 41-year-old Al Simmons in the outfield. Joe Kuhel, Chicago's 37-year-old first baseman, batted .213 in 153 games. Johnny Niggeling, at 39, made 26 starts.

The Yankees won the pennant once more—but with Nick Etten at first base, outfielders Bud Matheny and Johnny Lindell replacing Joe DiMaggio and Tommy Henrich, and, again, a deep veteran pitching staff. Boston dropped into seventh and the Browns to sixth, leaving the Senators, Indians, and White Sox as the Yankees' closest pursuers.

For the third straight year, attendance declined, and average scoring fell for the fifth straight season to 3.89 runs per team—the fewest until 1966. As a result, speed became a factor. The Senators and White Sox both stole more bases than any AL club since 1923. Washington outfielder George Case's 61 steals were the highest individual total in more than a decade. The Yankees were the exception, with a major league-high 100 home runs.

Spud Chandler was a very good pitcher—but his 20-4 record and 1.64 ERA for the Yankees are reflective of the talent he was facing during the war years. Only three AL players hit 20 home runs in 1943. Yankees pitching was the World Series secret. St. Louis scored just 9 runs as New York won easily in five games. Chandler notched 2 complete-game victories, allowing just 1 earned run. Bill Dickey played in his last of eight Fall Classics and collected 4 RBIs.

1942 National League

TEAM	W	L	T	PCT	GB	HW	HL	R	OR	PA	H	2B	3B	HR	BB	SO	HB	SH	AVG	OBP	SLG	OPS	AOPS	BR	ABR	PF	SB	CS	BSA	BSR
STL	106	48	2	.688		60	17	755	480	6124	1454	282	69	60	551	507	22	130	.268	.338	.379	717	109	112	61	108	71			
BRO	104	50	1	.675	2	57	22	742	512	5990	1398	263	34	62	572	484	14	119	.265	.338	.362	700	110	85	74	102	81			
NY	85	67	2	.559	20	47	31	675	600	5879	1323	162	35	109	558	511	34	77	.254	.330	.361	691	108	58	55	101	39			
CIN	76	76	2	.500	29	38	39	527	545	5860	1216	198	39	66	483	549	15	94	.231	.299	.321	620	88	-83	-82	100	42			
PIT	66	81	4	.449	36.5	41	34	585	631	5754	1250	173	49	54	537	536	26	87	.245	.320	.330	650	95	-17	-31	103	41			
CHI	68	86	1	.442	38	36	41	591	665	5984	1360	224	41	75	504	607	19	104	.254	.321	.353	674	108	24	49	96	63			
BOS	59	89	2	.399	44	33	36	515	645	5661	1216	210	19	68	474	507	20	90	.240	.307	.329	636	94	-47	-36	98	49			
PHI	42	109	0	.278	62.5	23	51	394	706	5567	1174	168	37	44	392	488	16	99	.232	.289	.306	595	84	-130	-107	95	37			
TOT	613					335	271	4784		46819	10391	1680	323	538	4076	4189	174	800	.249	.318	.343	661					423			

TEAM	CG	SHO	GR	SV	IP	H	HR	BB	SO	BR/9	ERA	AERA	OAV	OOB	PR	APR	PF	OSB	OCS	FA	E	WPB	DP	FW	PW	BW	BSW	DIF
STL	70	18	149	15	1410.1	1192	49	473	651	10.7	2.55	134	.228	.294	120	133	103	33	56	.972	169	43	137	-.1	14.3	6.5		8.3
BRO	67	16	165	24	1398.2	1205	73	493	612	11.1	2.84	115	.231	.302	73	65	98	35	39	.977	138	19	150	1.7	7.0	7.9		10.4
NY	70	12	153	13	1370.0	1299	94	493	497	11.9	3.31	101	.250	.316	0	7	101	43	34	.977	138	29	128	1.6	.8	5.9		.7
CIN	80	12	115	8	1411.2	1213	47	526	616	11.2	2.82	117	.230	.302	78	74	99	57	45	.971	177	28	128	-.7	.8	-8.8		1.6
PIT	64	13	156	11	1351.1	1376	62	435	426	12.1	3.58	94	.262	.320	-41	-30	102	61	42	.969	184	29	128	-1.3	-3.2	-3.3		.4
CHI	71	10	150	14	1400.2	1447	70	507	527	12.8	3.60	89	.267	.334	-44	-65	97	48	48	.973	170	37	136	-.2	-7.0	5.3		-7.1
BOS	68	9	162	8	1334.0	1326	82	518	414	12.6	3.76	89	.260	.331	-66	-62	101	67	41	.976	142	40	138	1.1	-6.7	-3.9		-5.6
PHI	51	2	184	6	1341.0	1328	61	605	472	13.1	4.12	80	.260	.342	-120	-122	100	79	45	.968	194	36	147	-1.9	-13.1	-11.5		-7.0
TOT	541	92	1234	99	11017.2					11.9	3.31		.249	.318						.973	1312	261	1122					

Batter-Fielder Wins
- Nicholson-Chi 4.1
- **Ott-NY** 3.9
- **Slaughter-StL** 3.5
- **Reese-Bro** 3.3
- **Musial-StL** 3.2

Batting Average
- Lombardi-Bos 330
- Slaughter-StL 318
- Musial-StL 315
- Reiser-Bro 310
- Mize-NY 305

On-Base Percentage
- Fletcher-Pit 417
- Ott-NY 415
- Slaughter-StL 412
- Hack-Chi 402
- Musial-StL 397

Slugging Average
- Mize-NY 521
- Ott-NY 497
- Slaughter-StL 494
- Musial-StL 490
- Lombardi-Bos 482

On-Base Plus Slugging
- Ott-NY 912
- Slaughter-StL 906
- Mize-NY................901
- Musial-StL 888
- Nicholson-Chi 859

Adjusted OPS
- Ott-NY 165
- Mize-NY 161
- Nicholson-Chi 156
- Slaughter-StL 153
- Musial-StL 148

Adjusted Batter Runs
- Ott-NY 50.1
- Slaughter-StL 41.8
- Nicholson-Chi........41.8
- Mize-NY 40.5
- Hack-Chi 35.6

Runs
- Ott-NY....................118
- Slaughter-StL 100
- Mize-NY..................97
- Hack-Chi 91

Hits
- Slaughter-StL 188
- Nicholson-Chi 173
- Medwick-Bro 166
- Hack-Chi 166
- Elliott-Pit 166

Doubles
- Marion-StL.............38
- Medwick-Bro 37
- Hack-Chi 36
- Herman-Bro............34
- Reiser-Bro 33

Triples
- Slaughter-StL 17
- Nicholson-Chi 11
- Musial-StL 10
- Litwhiler-Phi 9

Home Runs
- Ott-NY 30
- Mize-NY 26
- Camilli-Bro...............26
- Nicholson-Chi 21
- West-Bos 16

Total Bases
- Slaughter-StL 292
- Mize-NY..................282
- Nicholson-Chi 280
- Ott-NY 273
- Camilli-Bro..............247

Runs Batted In
- Mize-NY 110
- Camilli-Bro...............109
- Slaughter-StL 98
- Medwick-Bro 96
- Ott-NY 93

Stolen Bases
- Reiser-Bro 20
- Reese-Bro 15
- Fernandez-Bos 15
- Merullo-Chi 14
- Hopp-StL 14

Base Stealing Runs

Fielding Runs-Infield
- May-Phi 19.1
- Reese-Bro 18.2
- Fletcher-Pit 11.1
- Glossop-Phi 10.4
- Bragan-Phi 8.9

Fielding Runs-Outfield
- DiMaggio-Pit 12.0
- Musial-StL 7.4
- Nicholson-Chi 6.9
- Barrett-Pit 5.5
- Holmes-Bos 5.2

Wins
- M.Cooper-StL 22
- Beazley-StL 21
- Wyatt-Bro 19
- Passeau-Chi 19
- VanderMeer-Cin 18

Winning Pct.
- French-Bro 789
- Beazley-StL 778
- M.Cooper-StL.........759
- Wyatt-Bro 731
- Davis-Bro 714

Complete Games
- Tobin-Bos 28
- Passeau-Chi 24
- M.Cooper-StL 22
- Walters-Cin 21
- VanderMeer-Cin 21

Strikeouts
- VanderMeer-Cin ...186
- M.Cooper-StL 152
- Higbe-Bro 115
- Walters-Cin 109
- Melton-Phi 107

Fewest BB/Game
- Warneke-StL-Chi ..1.79
- Lohrman-StL-NY ..1.85
- Hubbell-NY 1.94
- Derringer-Cin 2.11
- M.Cooper-StL 2.20

Games
- Adams-NY 61
- Casey-Bro 50
- Podgajny-Phi 43
- Beazley-StL 43

Saves
- Casey-Bro 13
- Adams-NY 11
- Beggs-Cin 8
- Sain-Bos 6
- Gumbert-StL 5

Base Runners/9
- M.Cooper-StL 9.04
- Shoun-StL-Cin 9.69
- Melton-NY 9.84
- Beggs-Cin 10.05
- Lohrman-StL-NY 10.07

Adjusted Relief Runs
- Adams-NY 14.0
- Casey-Bro 13.0
- Beggs-Cin 10.6
- Shoun-StL-Cin 8.6
- Webber-Bro 2.9

Relief Ranking
- Adams-NY 19.7
- Beggs-Cin 14.0
- Casey-Bro 12.8
- Shoun-StL-Cin 4.3
- Webber-Bro 2.7

Innings Pitched
- Tobin-Bos 287.2
- M.Cooper-StL 278.2
- Passeau-Chi..........278.1
- Starr-Cin 276.2
- Javery-Bos 261.0

Opponents' Avg.
- M.Cooper-StL 204
- VanderMeer-Cin 208
- Higbe-Bro 223
- Wyatt-Bro 225
- Starr-Cin 226

Opponents' OBP
- M.Cooper-StL 258
- Lohrman-StL-NY ...281
- Wyatt-Bro 286
- Warneke-StL-Chi ...286
- Davis-Bro 287

Earned Run Average
- M.Cooper-StL 1.78
- Beazley-StL 2.13
- Davis-Bro 2.36
- VanderMeer-Cin 2.43
- Lohrman-StL-NY ..2.48

Adjusted ERA
- M.Cooper-StL 193
- Beazley-StL 161
- Davis-Bro 138
- Lohrman-StL-NY 136
- VanderMeer-Cin 135

Adjusted Starter Runs
- M.Cooper-StL.........46.6
- Beazley-StL 27.6
- VanderMeer-Cin 24.6
- Starr-Cin 24.5
- French-Bro 22.0

Pitcher Wins
- **M.Cooper-StL** 4.7
- **Beazley-StL** 3.5
- **French-Bro** 3.3
- **VanderMeer-Cin** .3.1
- **Walters-Cin** 2.5

Where Did *You* Come From?

It looked like a cinch. On August 15 Brooklyn, starring 23-year-olds Pee Wee Reese and Pete Reiser, held a 9½ game lead over second-place St. Louis, which had played well all season but recently stumbled. But from that point, the Bums never knew what hit them. The Cardinals went 43-8 down the stretch, overtaking Brooklyn in mid-September. In winning 12 of their final 13, they held off the late-charging Dodgers. St. Louis pulled it off despite a starting infield with just 9 homers and only two pitchers with more than 13 wins. But they still led the league in runs and ERA.

For the third consecutive season, scoring dropped, this time to 3.90 runs per game. For the only time between 1918 and 1963, the league average sank below .250. As a result, the performances of Cardinals outfielders Enos Slaughter and Stan Musial look especially good. MVP Mort Cooper led the league in wins, shutouts, and ERA, and rookie Johnny Beazley won 21.

Relief pitching gained some definition in 1942 as Giants right-hander Ace Adams set a record with 61 bullpen appearances (he broke it the next year). While some teams continued to shuttle their best starters in and out of late-inning jobs, many clubs were already using a particular reliever in clutch situations.

Seeing their first action were two Braves pitchers who blossomed after the war: Warren Spahn and Johnny Sain. But 21-year-old Al Montgomery, Boston's backup catcher in 1941, was killed April 26 in a car wreck.

The World Series was highly anticipated; both the Cardinals and Yankees cleared 100 wins. But the classic went just five games; after losing the first contest, St. Louis took the next four to stun the New Yorkers. All five games were entertaining and close. Beazley twice fired complete-game victories, including the clincher.

1942 American League

TEAM	W	L	T	PCT	GB	HW	HL	R	OR	PA	H	2B	3B	HR	BB	SO	HB	SH	AVG	OBP	SLG	OPS	AOPS	BR	ABR	PF	SB	CS	BSA	BSR
NY	103	51	0	.669		58	19	801	507	6009	1429	223	57	108	591	556	29	84	.269	.346	.394	740	118	105	122	98	69	33	68	4
BOS	93	59	0	.612	9	53	24	761	594	5984	1451	244	55	103	591	508	22	123	.276	.352	.403	755	116	135	109	103	68	61	53	-6
STL	82	69	0	.543	19.5	40	37	730	637	5947	1354	239	62	98	609	607	13	96	.259	.338	.385	723	109	70	59	102	37	38	49	-5
CLE	75	79	2	.487	28	39	39	590	659	5931	1344	223	58	50	500	544	24	90	.253	.320	.345	665	100	-45	-7	94	69	74	48	-11
DET	73	81	2	.474	30	43	34	589	587	5928	1313	217	37	76	509	476	19	73	.246	.314	.344	658	85	-58	-103	108	39	40	49	-5
CHI	66	82	0	.446	34	35	35	538	609	5552	1215	214	36	25	497	427	16	90	.246	.316	.318	634	87	-87	-75	99	114	70	62	11
WAS	62	89	0	.411	39.5	35	42	653	817	5949	1364	224	49	40	581	536	19	54	.258	.333	.341	674	98	-14	-7	99	98	29	77	11
PHI	55	99	0	.357	48	25	51	549	801	5822	1315	213	46	33	440	490	23	74	.249	.309	.325	634	86	-104	-101	99	44	45	49	-6
TOT	611					328	281	5211		47122	10785	1797	400	533	4318	4144	165	684	.257	.329	.357	686					538	390	58	-18

TEAM	CG	SHO	GR	SV	IP	H	HR	BB	SO	BR/9	ERA	AERA	OAV	OOB	PR	APR	PF	OSB	OCS	FA	E	WPB	DP	FW	PW	BW	BSW	DIF
NY	88	18	89	17	1375.0	1259	71	431	558	11.2	2.91	118	.244	.304	115	87	94	37	50	.976	142	21	190	2.0	8.9	12.5	.6	1.9
BOS	84	11	108	17	1358.2	1260	65	553	500	12.1	3.44	108	.247	.322	32	42	102	62	48	.974	157	34	156	1.0	4.3	11.2	-.4	.9
STL	68	12	140	13	1363.0	1387	63	505	488	12.7	3.59	103	.262	.330	10	17	101	86	43	.972	167	51	143	.4	1.7	6.0	-.3	-1.4
CLE	61	12	162	11	1402.2	1353	61	560	448	12.4	3.59	96	.254	.327	10	-24	94	63	36	.974	163	24	175	1.0	-2.5	-.7	-.9	1.1
DET	65	12	126	14	1399.1	1321	60	598	671	12.5	3.13	126	.248	.326	82	118	108	71	56	.969	194	42	142	-.8	12.1	-10.6	-.3	-4.5
CHI	86	8	75	8	1314.1	1304	74	473	432	12.3	3.58	100	.258	.325	11	3	98	54	31	.970	173	43	144	-.1	.3	-7.7	.3	-.9
WAS	68	12	125	11	1346.2	1496	50	558	496	13.8	4.58	80	.279	.349	-139	-139	100	65	66	.962	222	41	133	-2.7	-14.2	-.7	1.4	2.7
PHI	67	5	114	9	1374.2	1404	89	639	546	13.5	4.45	85	.263	.344	-120	-99	103	96	60	.969	188	58	124	-.6	-10.1	-10.3	-.4	-.6
TOT	587	90	939	100	10934.1					12.6	3.66		.257	.329						.971	1406	314	1207					

Batter-Fielder Wins
Williams-Bos	8.5
Gordon-NY	5.8
Rizzuto-NY	4.6
Pesky-Bos	4.5
Keller-NY	4.2

Batting Average
Williams-Bos	.356
Pesky-Bos	.331
Spence-Was	.323
Gordon-NY	.322
Case-Was	.320

On-Base Percentage
Williams-Bos	.499
Keller-NY	.417
Judnich-StL	.413
Fleming-Cle	.412
Gordon-NY	.409

Slugging Average
Williams-Bos	.648
Keller-NY	.513
Judnich-StL	.499
DiMaggio-StL	.498
Laabs-StL	.498

On-Base Plus Slugging
Williams-Bos	1147
Keller-NY	.930
Judnich-StL	.912
Gordon-NY	.900
Laabs-StL	.878

Adjusted OPS
Williams-Bos	214
Keller-NY	164
Gordon-NY	156
Judnich-StL	153
DiMaggio-NY	148

Adjusted Batter Runs
Williams-Bos	89.9
Keller-NY	50.4
Gordon-NY	41.9
Fleming-Cle	40.1
DiMaggio-NY	36.6

Runs
Williams-Bos	141
DiMaggio-NY	123
DiMaggio-Bos	110
Clift-StL	108
Keller-NY	106

Hits
Pesky-Bos	205
Spence-Was	203
Williams-Bos	186
DiMaggio-NY	186
Keltner-Cle	179

Doubles
Kolloway-Chi	40
Clift-StL	39
Heath-Cle	37
DiMaggio-Bos	36

Triples
Spence-Was	15
Heath-Cle	13
DiMaggio-NY	13
McQuillen-StL	12

Home Runs
Williams-Bos	36
Laabs-StL	27
Keller-NY	26
York-Det	21
DiMaggio-NY	21

Total Bases
Williams-Bos	338
DiMaggio-NY	304
Keller-NY	279
Spence-Was	272
DiMaggio-Bos	272

Runs Batted In
Williams-Bos	137
DiMaggio-NY	114
Keller-NY	108
Gordon-NY	103
Doerr-Bos	102

Stolen Bases
Case-Was	44
Vernon-Was	25
Rizzuto-NY	22
Kuhel-Chi	22

Base Stealing Runs
Case-Was	7.6
Vernon-Was	3.4
Rizzuto-NY	2.7
Keller-NY	2.4
Appling-Chi	2.0

Fielding Runs-Infield
Rizzuto-NY	30.0
Pesky-Bos	19.6
York-Det	15.3
Doerr-Bos	12.0
Keltner-Cle	11.3

Fielding Runs-Outfield
DiMaggio-Bos	13.1
Moses-Chi	6.1
Johnson-Phi	5.4
Chartak-NY-Was-StL	5.4
Cullenbine-SL-W-NY	4.7

Wins
Hughson-Bos	22
Bonham-NY	21
Marchildon-Phi	17
Bagby-Cle	17
Chandler-NY	16

Winning Pct.
Bonham-NY	.808
Borowy-NY	.789
Hughson-Bos	.786
Chandler-NY	.762
Bagby-Cle	.654

Complete Games
Hughson-Bos	22
Bonham-NY	22
Lyons-Chi	20
Hudson-Was	19

Strikeouts
Newsom-Was	113
Hughson-Bos	113
Marchildon-Phi	110
Benton-Det	110
Niggeling-StL	107

Fewest BB/Game
Bonham-NY	.96
Lyons-Chi	1.30
Ruffing-NY	1.91
Breuer-NY	2.03
Bagby-Cle	2.13

Games
Haynes-Chi	40
Caster-StL	39

Saves
Murphy-NY	11
Haynes-Chi	6
Brown-Bos	6
Newhouser-Det	5
Caster-StL	5

Base Runners/9
Bonham-NY	8.92
Lyons-Chi	9.73
Ferrick-Cle	9.74
Butland-Bos	9.78
Ruffing-NY	10.55

Adjusted Relief Runs
Ferrick-Cle	14.5
Haynes-Chi	10.5
Caster-StL	7.5
Brown-Bos	1.7

Relief Ranking
Haynes-Chi	13.3
Caster-StL	9.5
Ferrick-Cle	9.2
Brown-Bos	3.3

Innings Pitched
Hughson-Bos	281.0
Bagby-Cle	270.2
Auker-StL	249.0
Marchildon-Phi	244.0
Hudson-Was	239.1

Opponents' Avg.
Newhouser-Det	.207
Niggeling-StL	.226
Dobson-Bos	.231
Trucks-Det	.231
Borowy-NY	.233

Opponents' OBP
Bonham-NY	.259
Lyons-Chi	.275
Ruffing-NY	.292
Breuer-NY	.295
Hughson-Bos	.296

Earned Run Average
Lyons-Chi	2.10
Bonham-NY	2.27
Chandler-NY	2.38
Newhouser-Det	2.45
Borowy-NY	2.52

Adjusted ERA
Lyons-Chi	172
Newhouser-Det	161
Bonham-NY	152
Chandler-NY	145
Trucks-Det	144

Adjusted Starter Runs
Hughson-Bos	35.0
Bonham-NY	31.3
Lyons-Chi	29.2
White-Det	24.9
Benton-Det	24.9

Pitcher Wins
Lyons-Chi	3.8
Hughson-Bos	3.7
Bonham-NY	3.0
Chandler-NY	3.0
Newhouser-Det	2.9

You're in the Army Now

At no point after mid-May was the pennant race close, as the Yankees buzzed their way to an even better record than in 1941. Joe McCarthy wielded deep pitching, with seven men starting 13 or more games, and a peerless outfield of Tommy Henrich, Joe DiMaggio, and Charlie Keller to lead in runs by 40 and ERA by 22 points.

The Red Sox, again a strong second, added another piece by promoting rookie shortstop Johnny Pesky, who hit .331. Ted Williams had another spectacular year, taking the Triple Crown, but the Bosox were weak at key positions, and their pitching wasn't up to standard. While the race featured little drama, the third-place team caused a buzz. The St. Louis Browns, 43-111 in 1939 and sixth the next two years, improved by 12½ games with a strong second half. Rookie shortstop Vern Stephens was a keeper. What the Browns showed most, though, was how World War II was affecting baseball.

When the war hit home in December 1941, the country needed healthy bodies. Therefore, many great players got the call; between 1943–45 Cleveland lost Bob Feller, Boston sacrificed Williams, Pesky, and Dom DiMaggio, and the Yankees lost Joe DiMaggio and Henrich. Detroit's Hank Greenberg, who joined the military before the U.S. was even in the war, played less than 100 games between 1941–45. Teammate Charlie Gehringer's career ended when he was called into service. Browns pitcher Elden Auker retired to devote time to a war job. Washington infielder Cecil Travis never recovered from his service. Johnny Sturm, the Yankees' first baseman in 1941, spent the next four years in the military and never returned to the majors. Two men who appeared briefly in the major leagues, Elmer Gedeon (Senators) and Harry O'Neill (Athletics), were killed in action.

Previously "good" teams were no longer a lock. Until the war was over, it was every club for itself. The Yankees' surprise five-game loss in the World Series to St. Louis showed that teams with good farm systems were in the best shape.

1941 National League

TEAM	W	L	T	PCT	GB	HW	HL	R	OR	PA	H	2B	3B	HR	BB	SO	HB	SH	AVG	OBP	SLG	OPS	AOPS	BR	ABR	PF	SB	CS	BSA	BSR
BRO	100	54	3	.649		52	25	800	581	6218	1494	286	69	101	600	535	27	106	.272	.347	.405	752	113	132	98	104	36			
STL	97	56	2	.634	2.5	53	24	734	589	6151	1482	254	56	70	540	543	28	126	.272	.340	.377	717	102	63	17	107	47			
CIN	88	66	0	.571	12	45	34	616	564	5819	1288	213	33	64	477	428	22	102	.247	.313	.337	650	89	-74	-76	100	68			
PIT	81	73	2	.526	19	45	32	690	643	5954	1417	233	65	56	547	516	15	95	.268	.338	.368	706	105	38	-41	100	59			
NY	74	79	3	.484	25.5	38	39	667	706	6018	1401	248	35	95	504	518	23	96	.260	.326	.371	697	101	16	3	102	36			
CHI	70	84	1	.455	30	38	39	666	670	5902	1323	239	25	99	559	670	14	99	.253	.327	.365	692	105	11	36	96	39			
BOS	62	92	2	.403	38	32	44	592	720	5968	1357	231	38	48	471	608	13	70	.251	.312	.334	646	92	-84	-59	96	61			
PHI	43	111	1	.279	57	23	52	501	793	5796	1277	188	38	64	451	596	22	90	.244	.307	.331	638	89	-101	-80	96	65			
TOT	622					326	289	5266		47826	11039	1892	359	597	4149	4414	164	784	.258	.326	.361	688					411			

TEAM	CG	SHO	GR	SV	IP	H	HR	BB	SO	BR/9	ERA	AERA	OAV	OOB	PR	APR	PF	OSB	OCS	FA	E	WPB	DP	FW	PW	BW	BSW	DIF
BRO	66	17	157	22	1421.0	1236	81	495	603	11.1	3.14	117	.233	.300	78	82	101	34	40	.974	162	29	125	.9	8.4	10.1		3.6
STL	64	15	171	20	1416.1	1289	85	502	659	11.5	3.19	118	.242	.310	70	87	104	42	48	.973	172	32	146	.2	8.9	1.7		9.6
CIN	89	19	112	10	1386.2	1300	61	510	627	11.9	3.17	114	.250	.319	72	67	99	64	46	.975	152	39	147	1.3	6.9	-7.8		10.7
PIT	71	8	150	12	1374.1	1392	66	492	410	12.4	3.48	104	.260	.323	23	19	99	47	42	.968	196	33	130	-1.1	2.0	4.2		-1.0
NY	55	12	175	18	1391.2	1455	90	539	566	13.0	3.94	94	.269	.337	-48	-38	102	46	41	.974	160	37	144	.9	-3.9	.3		.2
CHI	74	8	145	9	1364.2	1431	60	449	548	12.5	3.72	94	.267	.327	-13	-34	97	59	39	.970	180	30	139	-.3	-3.5	3.7		-6.9
BOS	62	10	176	9	1385.2	1440	75	554	446	13.2	3.95	90	.269	.341	-49	-59	98	53	47	.969	191	36	174	-.9	-6.1	-6.1		-2.0
PHI	35	4	201	9	1372.1	1499	79	606	552	14.0	4.50	82	.279	.355	-132	-119	102	66	52	.969	187	46	147	-.7	-12.2	-8.2		-12.9
TOT	516	93	1287	109	11112.2					12.4	3.63		.258	.326						.972	1400	282	1152					

Batter-Fielder Wins		Batting Average		On-Base Percentage		Slugging Average		On-Base Plus Slugging		Adjusted OPS		Adjusted Batter Runs	
Reiser-Bro	4.5	Reiser-Bro	343	Fletcher-Pit	421	Reiser-Bro	558	Reiser-Bro	964	Reiser-Bro	163	Camilli-Bro	46.5
Fletcher-Pit	3.6	Cooney-Bos	319	Hack-Chi	417	Camilli-Bro	556	Camilli-Bro	962	Camilli-Bro	162	Reiser-Bro	43.7
Camilli-Bro	3.3	Medwick-Bro	318	Camilli-Bro	407	Mize-StL	535	Mize-StL	941	Mize-StL	153	Fletcher-Pit	39.8
Hack-Chi	3.1	Hack-Chi	317	Reiser-Bro	406	Medwick-Bro	517	Ott-NY	898	Ott-NY	149	Hack-Chi	39.5
Ott-NY	3.0	Mize-StL	317	Mize-StL	406	Slaughter-StL	496	Slaughter-StL	886	Fletcher-Pit	148	Ott-NY	38.2

Runs		Hits		Doubles		Triples		Home Runs		Total Bases		Runs Batted In	
Reiser-Bro	117	Hack-Chi	186	Reiser-Bro	39	Reiser-Bro	17	Camilli-Bro	34	Reiser-Bro	299	Camilli-Bro	120
Hack-Chi	111	Reiser-Bro	184	Mize-StL	39	Fletcher-Pit	13	Ott-NY	27	Camilli-Bro	294	Young-NY	104
Medwick-Bro	100	Litwhiler-Phi	180	Rucker-NY	38	Hopp-StL	11	Nicholson-Chi	26	Medwick-Bro	278	Mize-StL	100
Rucker-NY	95	Rucker-NY	179	Dallessandro-Chi	36	Medwick-Bro	10	Young-NY	25	Litwhiler-Phi	275	DiMaggio-Pit	100
Fletcher-Pit	95	Medwick-Bro	171			Elliott-Pit	10	Dahlgren-Bos-Chi	23	Young-NY	265	Nicholson-Chi	98

Stolen Bases		Base Stealing Runs		Fielding Runs-Infield		Fielding Runs-Outfield		Wins		Winning Pct.		Complete Games	
Murtaugh-Phi	18			May-Phi	23.9	Litwhiler-Phi	13.3	Higbe-Bro	22	E.Riddle-Cin	826	Walters-Cin	27
Benjamin-Phi	17			Stringer-Chi	23.8	Walker-Bro	9.9	Wyatt-Bro	22	Higbe-Bro	710	Higbe-Bro	23
Handley-Pit	16			Miller-Bos	13.3	VanRobays-Pit	6.1	Walters-Cin	19	White-StL	708	Tobin-Bos	20
Frey-Cin	16			Werber-Cin	10.1	West-Bos	5.4	E.Riddle-Cin	19	Wyatt-Bro	688	Passeau-Chi	20
Hopp-StL	15			Fletcher-Pit	9.9	Moore-Bos	5.2			Warneke-StL	654		

Strikeouts		Fewest BB/Game		Games		Saves		Base Runners/9		Adjusted Relief Runs		Relief Ranking	
VanderMeer-Cin	202	Passeau-Chi	2.03	Higbe-Bro	48	Brown-NY	8	Wyatt-Bro	9.58	Pressnell-Chi	4.5	Pressnell-Chi	4.8
Wyatt-Bro	176	Derringer-Cin	2.13	Pearson-Phi	46	Crouch-Phi-StL	7	Davis-Bro	9.91	Brown-NY	2.9	Brown-NY	3.7
Walters-Cin	129	Lohrman-NY	2.26	Casey-Bro	45	Casey-Bro	7	E.Riddle-Cin	10.14	Crouch-Phi-StL	7	Crouch-Phi-StL	6
Higbe-Bro	121	Tobin-Bos	2.27	Hutchings-Bos	44	Pearson-Phi	6	White-StL	10.50				
M.Cooper-StL	118	Lee-Chi	2.31	Johnson-Bos	43			Pollet-StL	10.67				

Innings Pitched		Opponents' Avg.		Opponents' OBP		Earned Run Average		Adjusted ERA		Adjusted Starter Runs		Pitcher Wins	
Walters-Cin	302.0	Wyatt-Bro	212	Wyatt-Bro	270	E.Riddle-Cin	2.24	E.Riddle-Cin	160	Wyatt-Bro	41.6	Wyatt-Bro	5.3
Higbe-Bro	298.0	VanderMeer-Cin	214	E.Riddle-Cin	282	Wyatt-Bro	2.34	White-StL	157	E.Riddle-Cin	30.5	E.Riddle-Cin	3.5
Wyatt-Bro	288.1	White-StL	217	White-StL	287	White-StL	2.40	Wyatt-Bro	157	White-StL	28.1	Walters-Cin	3.3
Sewell-Pit	249.0	Higbe-Bro	220	Sewell-Pit	299	VanderMeer-Cin	2.82	VanderMeer-Cin	127	Walters-Cin	26.7	White-StL	3.0
Warneke-StL	246.0	E.Riddle-Cin	224	Tobin-Bos	300	Walters-Cin	2.83	Walters-Cin	127	VanderMeer-Cin	19.2	VanderMeer-Cin	2.1

Brooklyn Celebrates

The first thrilling Cardinals-Dodgers confrontation of the decade took place in 1941. From Opening Day, the two clubs clung to one another, soaring high above the rest of the league; defending champ Cincinnati never quite got it together, finishing third only with a late surge.

Joe Medwick's midseason trade from St. Louis to Brooklyn sparked controversy, and Ducky went on to finish third in the league in runs. As August rolled into September, the Redbirds and Bums stood in a flat-footed tie. A September 4 doubleheader loss at Chicago, however, started the Cardinals on a downswing from which they could not recover. Leo Durocher's Dodgers kept the pressure on down the stretch and on September 25 clinched Brooklyn's first flag since 1920.

Dodger hurlers Kirby Higbe and Whitlow Wyatt tied for the league lead in victories, and Pete Reiser played like the game's next big star. Meanwhile, the Dodgers became the first NL team since 1931 to draw a million fans, and, thanks to a series of beanball scares, they also were the first to don batting helmets.

St. Louis, weak offensively except for first sacker Johnny Mize, hung in the race on the wings of their deep pitching staff. Despite the pennant loss, a late-season .426 showing from 20-year-old rookie Stan Musial showed that the Cardinals had much to anticipate.

Catcher Gabby Hartnett ended his career for fifth-place New York. The floundering Braves, showing indecision typical of a loser, again fiddled with their field dimensions—as they would continue to do throughout the decade.

The World Series was painful for Dodgers fans. Just one strike away from a Series-tying win in Game 4, a wild pitch by Hugh Casey set off a Yankees rally that won that game and carried into the next. New York's 3-1 win the next day clinched the Series.

1941 American League

TEAM	W	L	T	PCT	GB	HW	HL	R	OR	PA	H	2B	3B	HR	BB	SO	HB	SH	AVG	OBP	SLG	OPS	AOPS	BR	ABR	PF	SB	CS	BSA	BSR
NY	101	53	2	.656		**51**	26	830	**631**	6137	1464	243	60	**151**	616	565	28	49	.269	.346	.419	765	111	64	75	99	51	33	61	0
BOS	84	70	1	.545	17	47	30	**865**	750	6177	**1517**	304	55	124	683	567	20	115	**.283**	**.366**	**.430**	796	115	**142**	121	102	67	51	57	-4
CHI	77	77	2	.500	24	38	39	638	649	6012	1376	245	47	47	510	476	24	74	.255	.322	.343	665	84	-130	-122	99	**91**	53	63	1
DET	75	79	1	.487	26	43	34	686	743	6077	1412	247	55	81	602	584	23	82	.263	.340	.375	715	87	-27	-92	110	43	28	61	0
CLE	75	79	1	.487	26	42	35	677	668	5914	1350	249	**84**	103	512	605	18	101	.256	.323	.393	716	101	-43	-8	95	63	47	57	-3
WAS	70	84	2	.455	31	40	37	728	798	6067	1502	257	80	52	470	488	14	62	.272	.331	.376	707	99	-58	-25	95	79	36	**69**	5
STL	70	84	3	.455	31	40	37	765	823	6285	1440	281	58	91	**775**	552	13	89	.266	.360	.390	750	103	61	35	103	50	39	56	-3
PHI	64	90	0	.416	37	36	41	713	840	5994	1431	240	69	85	574	588	8	76	.268	.340	.387	727	102	-9	9	98	27	36	43	-7
TOT	622					337	279	5902		48663	11492	2066	508	734	4742	4425	148	648	.266	.341	.389	730					471	323	59	-9

TEAM	CG	SHO	GR	SV	IP	H	HR	BB	SO	BR/9	ERA	AERA	OAV	OOB	PR	APR	PF	OSB	OCS	FA	E	WPB	DP	FW	PW	BW	BSW	DIF
NY	75	13	119	**26**	1396.1	**1309**	81	598	589	12.4	3.53	112	**.248**	.325	96	66	95	44	36	.973	165	35	**196**	.5	6.4	7.3	.1	9.7
BOS	70	8	137	11	1372.0	1453	88	611	574	13.7	4.19	100	.270	.347	-6	-3	101	54	34	.972	172	42	139	.0	-.3	**11.7**	-.2	-4.3
CHI	**106**	**14**	63	4	1416.0	1362	89	**521**	564	12.1	**3.52**	116	.252	**.320**	99	92	99	54	46	.971	180	50	145	-.3	**8.9**	-11.8	.2	3.0
DET	52	8	157	16	1381.2	1399	80	645	**697**	13.4	4.18	109	.260	.341	-4	52	110	69	46	.969	186	39	129	-.7	5.0	-8.9	.1	2.5
CLE	68	10	133	19	1377.0	1366	71	660	617	13.4	3.90	101	.259	.344	39	7	95	50	37	**.976**	142	34	158	**1.7**	.7	-.8	-.2	-3.4
WAS	69	8	140	7	1389.1	1524	**69**	603	544	13.9	4.35	93	.279	.353	-32	-49	98	59	**48**	.969	187	68	169	-.7	-4.7	-2.4	**.6**	.3
STL	65	7	**158**	10	1389.0	1563	120	549	454	13.8	4.72	91	.283	.350	-88	-62	104	64	38	.975	151	41	156	1.3	-6.0	3.4	-.2	-5.5
PHI	64	3	125	18	1365.1	1516	136	557	386	13.8	4.83	87	.279	.348	-104	-97	101	77	38	.967	200	69	150	-1.6	-9.4	.9	-.6	-2.3
TOT	569	71	1032	111	11086.2					13.3	4.15		.266	.341						.972	1383	378	1242					

Batter-Fielder Wins		Batting Average		On-Base Percentage		Slugging Average		On-Base Plus Slugging		Adjusted OPS		Adjusted Batter Runs	
Williams-Bos	8.5	Williams-Bos	.406	Williams-Bos	.553	Williams-Bos	.735	Williams-Bos	1287	Williams-Bos	232	Williams-Bos	101.7
DiMaggio-NY	6.6	Travis-Was	.359	Cullenbine-StL	.452	DiMaggio-NY	.643	DiMaggio-NY	1083	DiMaggio-NY	186	DiMaggio-NY	67.7
Travis-Was	5.1	DiMaggio-NY	.357	DiMaggio-NY	.440	Heath-Cle	.586	Keller-NY	.996	Heath-Cle	165	Heath-Cle	50.4
Keller-NY	4.0	Heath-Cle	.340	Keller-NY	.416	Keller-NY	.580	Heath-Cle	.982	Keller-NY	163	Keller-NY	48.0
S.Chapman-Phi	3.7	Siebert-Phi	.334	Foxx-Bos	.412	S.Chapman-Phi	.543	Travis-Was	.930	Travis-Was	152	Travis-Was	43.6

Runs		Hits		Doubles		Triples		Home Runs		Total Bases		Runs Batted In	
Williams-Bos	135	Travis-Was	218	Boudreau-Cle	45	Heath-Cle	20	Williams-Bos	37	DiMaggio-NY	348	DiMaggio-NY	125
DiMaggio-NY	122	Heath-Cle	199	DiMaggio-NY	43	Travis-Was	19	Keller-NY	33	Heath-Cle	343	Heath-Cle	123
DiMaggio-Bos	117	DiMaggio-NY	193	Judnich-StL	40	Keltner-Cle	13	Henrich-NY	31	Williams-Bos	335	Keller-NY	122
Clift-StL	108	Appling-Chi	186	Travis-Was	39			DiMaggio-NY	30	Travis-Was	316	Williams-Bos	120
		Williams-Bos	185	Kuhel-Chi	39			York-Det	27	S.Chapman-Phi	300	York-Det	111

Stolen Bases		Base Stealing Runs		Fielding Runs-Infield		Fielding Runs-Outfield		Wins		Winning Pct.		Complete Games	
Case-Was	33	Case-Was	4.1	Bloodworth-Was	27.2	Case-Was	11.7	Feller-Cle	25	Gomez-NY	.750	Lee-Chi	30
Kuhel-Chi	20	Kuhel-Chi	2.0	Keltner-Cle	20.3	S.Chapman-Phi	11.7	Lee-Chi	22	Ruffing-NY	.714	Feller-Cle	28
Heath-Cle	18	Kreevich-Chi	2.0	Rizzuto-NY	19.0	Lewis-Was	11.4	D.Newsome-Bos	19	Benton-Det	.714	Smith-Chi	19
Tabor-Bos	17	Rizzuto-NY	1.3	Boudreau-Cle	13.4	B.Johnson-Phi	8.7	Leonard-Was	18	Lee-Chi	.667	Lyons-Chi	19
Kreevich-Chi	17	Fox-Bos	1.3	Gordon-NY	8.6	Moses-Phi	7.8			Feller-Cle	.658	Leonard-Was	19

Strikeouts		Fewest BB/Game		Games		Saves		Base Runners/9		Adjusted Relief Runs		Relief Ranking	
Feller-Cle	260	Lyons-Chi	1.78	Feller-Cle	44	Murphy-NY	15	Humphries-Chi	10.55	Murphy-NY	17.5	Murphy-NY	30.1
Newsom-Det	175	Leonard-Was	1.90	Newsom-Det	43	Ferrick-Phi	7	Lee-Chi	10.61	Heving-Cle	13.2	Heving-Cle	13.9
Lee-Chi	130	Muncrief-StL	2.23	Brown-Cle	41	Benton-Det	7	Bonham-NY	10.66	Carrasquel-Was	6.6	Brown-Cle	5.2
Rigney-Chi	119	Ruffing-NY	2.62	Ryba-Bos	40	Ryba-Bos	6	Ruffing-NY	11.25	Brown-Cle	6.0	Carrasquel-Was	5.2
		Lee-Chi	2.76	Benton-Det	38			Benton-Det	11.30	Thomas-Det	3	Thomas-Det	1

Innings Pitched		Opponents' Avg.		Opponents' OBP		Earned Run Average		Adjusted ERA		Adjusted Starter Runs		Pitcher Wins	
Feller-Cle	343.0	Benton-Det	.221	Lee-Chi	.293	Lee-Chi	2.37	Lee-Chi	173	Lee-Chi	56.1	**Lee-Chi**	6.5
Lee-Chi	300.1	Feller-Cle	.226	Benton-Det	.302	Benton-Det	2.97	Benton-Det	153	Feller-Cle	34.3	Feller-Cle	3.4
Smith-Chi	263.1	Lee-Chi	.232	Ruffing-NY	.306	Wagner-Bos	3.07	Wagner-Bos	136	Smith-Chi	28.1	**Smith-Chi**	3.4
Leonard-Was	256.0	Donald-NY	.237	Chandler-NY	.307	Russo-NY	3.09	Smith-Chi	129	Benton-Det	24.1	**Murphy-NY**	2.9
Newsom-Det	250.1	Chandler-NY	.239	Lyons-Chi	.308	Feller-Cle	3.15	Harris-Chi	128	Wagner-Bos	22.3	**Benton-Det**	2.6

Joltin' Joe and Teddy Ballgame

The final year of normal baseball before America entered World War II was the stuff of legend, as immortals like Joe DiMaggio and Ted Williams grabbed the headlines and Mickey Owen grabbed the goat's horns. The Yankees returned to the top after a season in third place. Emerging from a five-team scramble in July, New York left everyone in the dust as they took league honors by 17 games.

The old Yankees were gone; in their place were a passel of new stars, including DiMaggio, Phil Rizzuto, Charlie Keller, Joe Gordon, and Tommy Henrich. DiMaggio hit .357 and enthralled the nation with his 56-game hitting streak. Keller batted .298 with 33 homers and 122 RBIs, and Johnny "Grandma" Murphy—one of the first true relief aces—saved 15 games.

Lacking a staff anchor, Joe McCarthy used seven starting pitchers at least 14 times, getting excellent performance from most of them. Both 32-year-old Lefty Gomez and Red Ruffing, 37, won 15. Finishing in second place were the Red Sox, who couldn't turn Williams' season (.406 average, 37 homers, 145 walks, and 135 runs—all of which led the AL) into a pennant because of mediocre pitching.

A few players left for the military during the season, most notably three-time home run champ Hank Greenberg. Fans were also busy in other matters. It was the first of three consecutive seasons of decreasing league attendance; NL attendance actually increased by 8 percent in 1941 before falling the next two years.

The Yankees won the World Series from the Dodgers in five games, four of which were decided by only one run. The one that wasn't (Game 4) featured a ninth-inning, four-run rally that began when Dodgers catcher Owen dropped a third strike that would have ended the game in favor of Brooklyn and tied the Series.

1940 National League

TEAM	W	L	T	PCT	GB	HW	HL	R	OR	PA	H	2B	3B	HR	BB	SO	HB	SH	AVG	OBP	SLG	OPS	AOPS	BR	ABR	PF	SB	CS	BSA	BSR
CIN	100	53	2	.654		**55**	21	707	**528**	5986	1427	264	38	89	453	503	36	**125**	.266	.327	.379	706	100	9	2	101	72			
BRO	88	65	3	.575	12	41	37	697	621	6089	1421	256	**70**	93	522	570	20	77	.260	.327	.383	710	96	15	-26	106	56			
STL	84	69	3	.549	16	41	36	747	699	6087	**1514**	266	61	**119**	479	610	21	88	.275	.336	**.411**	**747**	106	84	42	106	**97**			
PIT	78	76	2	.506	22.5	40	34	**809**	783	6115	1511	**276**	68	76	**553**	494	33	63	**.276**	**.346**	.394	740	**112**	87	93	99	69			
CHI	75	79	0	.487	25.5	40	37	681	636	5970	1441	272	48	86	482	566	29	70	.267	.331	.384	715	106	28	42	98	63			
NY	72	80	0	.474	27.5	33	43	663	659	5900	1423	201	46	91	453	**478**	**37**	86	.267	.329	.374	703	99	1	-4	101	45			
BOS	65	87	0	.428	34.5	35	40	623	745	5810	1366	219	50	59	402	581	17	62	.256	.311	.349	660	93	-86	-53	95	48			
PHI	50	103	0	.327	50	24	55	494	750	5673	1225	180	35	75	435	527	14	87	.238	.300	.331	631	83	-137	-116	96	25			
TOT	617					309	303	5421		47630	11328	1934	416	688	3779	4329	207	658	.264	.326	.376	702					475			

TEAM	CG	SHO	GR	SV	IP	H	HR	BB	SO	BR/9	ERA	AERA	OAV	OOB	PR	APR	PF	OSB	OCS	FA	E	WPB	DP	FW	PW	BW	BSW	DIF
CIN	**91**	10	106	11	1407.2	**1263**	73	445	557	11.0	3.05	124	.240	.302	125	117	98	51	29	.981	117	22	158	2.9	11.8	.2		8.6
BRO	65	**17**	169	14	1433.0	1366	101	393	**639**	11.2	3.50	114	.248	.302	56	76	104	52	**35**	.970	183	22	110	-.3	7.7	-2.6		6.8
STL	71	10	168	14	1396.0	1457	83	488	550	12.7	3.83	104	.266	.329	3	23	104	63	51	.971	174	45	134	.1	2.3	4.2		.8
PIT	49	8	**215**	**24**	1388.2	1569	72	492	491	13.6	4.36	87	.283	.345	-79	-86	99	80	**55**	.966	217	32	161	-2.0	-8.7	**9.4**		2.3
CHI	69	12	151	14	1392.0	1418	74	480	564	12.1	3.54	106	.262	.319	47	33	97	58	48	.968	199	**21**	143	-1.2	3.3	4.2		-8.4
NY	57	11	166	18	1360.1	1383	110	473	606	12.4	3.79	102	.262	.325	9	14	101	**44**	49	.977	139	36	132	1.6	1.4	-.4		-6.6
BOS	76	9	148	12	1359.0	1444	83	**573**	435	13.6	4.36	85	.274	.349	-77	-100	97	58	**61**	.970	184	31	**169**	-.6	-10.1	-5.4		5.1
PHI	66	5	133	8	1357.0	1429	92	475	485	12.8	4.40	89	.270	.333	-83	-74	101	69	43	.970	181	48	136	-.4	-7.5	-11.7		-6.9
TOT	544	82	1256	115	11093.2					12.4	3.85		.264	.326						.972	1394	257	1143					

Batter-Fielder Wins
Vaughan-Pit 5.1
Hack-Chi 4.5
Mize-StL 3.6
Miller-Bos 3.4
Danning-NY 3.1

Batting Average
Garms-Pit 355
Davis-Pit 326
Lombardi-Cin 319
Cooney-Bos 318
Hack-Chi 317

On-Base Percentage
Fletcher-Pit 418
Ott-NY 407
Mize-StL 404
Camilli-Bro 397
Hack-Chi 395

Slugging Average
Mize-StL 636
Nicholson-Chi 534
Camilli-Bro 529
DiMaggio-Cin-Pit ...519
Slaughter-StL 504

On-Base Plus Slugging
Mize-StL 1039
Camilli-Bro 926
Nicholson-Chi 899
Slaughter-StL 874
Ott-NY 864

Adjusted OPS
Mize-StL 173
Nicholson-Chi 148
Camilli-Bro 144
Gleeson-Chi 139
Fletcher-Pit 137

Adjusted Batter Runs
Mize-StL 56.9
Fletcher-Pit 33.9
Camilli-Bro 33.2
Ott-NY 32.2
Nicholson-Chi 30.9

Runs
Vaughan-Pit 113
Mize-StL 111
Werber-Cin 105
Frey-Cin 102
Hack-Chi 101

Hits
F.McCormick-Cin 191
Hack-Chi 191
Mize-StL 182
Vaughan-Pit 178
Medwick-StL-Bro 175

Doubles
F.McCormick-Cin 44
Vaughan-Pit 40
Gleeson-Chi 39
Hack-Chi 38
Walker-Bro 37

Triples
Vaughan-Pit 15
Ross-Bos 14
Slaughter-StL 13
Mize-StL 13
Camilli-Bro 13

Home Runs
Mize-StL 43
Nicholson-Chi 25
Rizzo-Pit-Cin-Phi 24
Camilli-Bro 23

Total Bases
Mize-StL 368
F.McCormick-Cin 298
Medwick-StL-Bro 280
Camilli-Bro 271
Vaughan-Pit 269

Runs Batted In
Mize-StL 137
F.McCormick-Cin 127
VanRobays-Pit 116
Fletcher-Pit 104
Young-NY 101

Stolen Bases
Frey-Cin 22
Hack-Chi 21
Moore-StL 18
Werber-Cin 16
Reese-Bro 15

Base Stealing Runs

Fielding Runs-Infield
Herman-Chi 20.3
Witek-NY 16.2
May-Phi 15.8
Frey-Cin 15.0
Miller-Bos 14.8

Fielding Runs-Outfield
Moore-StL 13.0
Moore-Bro-Bos 5.4
Ross-Bos 5.4
West-Bos 4.8
Slaughter-StL 4.5

Wins
Walters-Cin 22
Passeau-Chi 20
Derringer-Cin 20

Winning Pct.
Fitzsimmons-Bro ...889
Sewell-Pit 762
Walters-Cin 688
Thompson-Cin 640
Derringer-Cin 625

Complete Games
Walters-Cin 29
Derringer-Cin 26
Mulcahy-Phi 21
Passeau-Chi 20
Higbe-Phi 20

Strikeouts
Higbe-Phi 137
Wyatt-Bro 124
Passeau-Chi 124
Schumacher-NY 123

Fewest BB/Game
Derringer-Cin 1.46
Turner-Cin 1.54
Hamlin-Bro 1.68
Davis-StL-Bro 1.79
Warneke-StL 1.82

Games
Shoun-StL 54
Brown-NY 48
Passeau-Chi 46
Casey-Bro 44
Raffensberger-Chi ...44

Saves
Brown-NY 7
Derringer-Cin 7
Beggs-Cin 7
Shoun-StL 5
Passeau-Chi 5

Base Runners/9
Fitzsimmons-Bro ...9.78
Derringer-Cin 9.95
Walters-Cin 9.97
Pressnell-Bro 10.14
Passeau-Chi 10.33

Adjusted Relief Runs
Beggs-Cin 15.4
Russell-StL 6.8
Raffensberger-Chi ...3.1
Hutchings-Cin 2.8
Brown-NY 2.5

Relief Ranking
Beggs-Cin 30.3
Russell-StL 8.2
Raffensberger-Chi ...4.0
Pressnell-Bro 3.6
Brown-NY 3.1

Innings Pitched
Walters-Cin 305.0
Derringer-Cin 296.2
Higbe-Phi 283.0
Passeau-Chi 280.2
Mulcahy-Phi 280.0

Opponents' Avg.
Walters-Cin 220
Higbe-Phi 232
Thompson-Cin 233
Passeau-Chi 237
Casey-Bro 237

Opponents' OBP
Derringer-Cin 276
Passeau-Chi 278
Walters-Cin 283
Tamulis-Bro 288
Hamlin-Bro 292

Earned Run Average
Walters-Cin 2.48
Passeau-Chi 2.50
Sewell-Pit 2.80
Fitzsimmons-Bro ...2.81
Turner-Cin 2.89

Adjusted ERA
Walters-Cin 153
Passeau-Chi 150
Sewell-Pit 136
Turner-Cin 131
Hamlin-Bro 131

Adjusted Starter Runs
Walters-Cin 44.1
Passeau-Chi 37.1
Derringer-Cin 25.0
Sewell-Pit 20.5
Fitzsimmons-Bro ...18.7

Pitcher Wins
Passeau-Chi 5.1
Walters-Cin 4.7
Beggs-Cin 3.2
Olsen-Chi 2.5
Sewell-Pit 2.5

Reds Take It All

The dominant NL teams of the 1940s were St. Louis and Brooklyn. Listing the top debut players for the teams in 1940 tells why: The Cardinals brought up shortstop Marty Marion and pitchers Harry Brecheen and Walker Cooper, while the Dodgers summoned shortstop Pee Wee Reese and outfielder Pete Reiser.

While AL attendance rose, the NL's fell nearly 7 percent. To increase ticket sales, the Giants, Cardinals, and Pirates added lights to their parks, while the Braves changed their park's dimensions, moving in the foul lines and the center-field fences.

The Reds and Dodgers were the early leaders in the '40 race. In mid-July, once the surprising Giants fell from the race, Brooklyn began to slump. The Reds, meanwhile, took 19 of 21 to surge ahead. Brooklyn continued to stumble, and Cincinnati kept winning. The pitching-and-defense Reds set a new NL record with a .981 fielding percentage. Bucky Walters led the NL in wins, ERA, and innings, and was ably supported by Paul Derringer. Frank McCormick sparked a mediocre attack by topping the loop in hits and doubles.

There was one casualty. On August 2, following a tough loss, backup catcher Willard Hershberger took his life. By World Series time, everyday receiver Ernie Lombardi was too banged-up to play. Therefore, with Hershberger out of the picture, 40-year-old coach Jimmie Wilson was forced into action for six of the seven games. He hit .353.

The Tigers won their three games by an aggregate of 22-6, and led 1-0, 2-1, and 3-2 in games, but the Reds won the last two contests at home, clinching their first world championship since 1919. Derringer and Walters won all four games for Cincinnati. Detroit's Bobo Newsom won Game 5 three days after his father died, then fell 2-1 in a tension-filled finale.

1940 American League

TEAM	W	L	T	PCT	GB	HW	HL	R	OR	PA	H	2B	3B	HR	BB	SO	HB	SH	AVG	OBP	SLG	OPS	AOPS	BR	ABR	PF	SB	CS	BSA	BSR
DET	90	64	1	.584		50	29	888	717	6183	1549	312	65	134	664	556	24	77	.286	.366	.442	808	105	130	50	110	66	39	63	
CLE	89	65	1	.578	1	51	30	710	637	5957	1422	287	61	101	519	597	16	61	.265	.332	.398	730	98	-43	-22	97	53	36	60	-1
NY	88	66	1	.571	2	52	24	817	671	6046	1371	243	66	155	648	606	36	76	.259	.344	.418	762	107	25	58	96	59	36	62	0
CHI	82	72	1	.532	8	41	36	735	672	6002	1499	238	63	73	496	569	10	110	.278	.340	.387	727	93	-45	-54	101	52	60	46	-10
BOS	82	72	0	.532	8	45	34	872	825	6174	1566	301	80	145	590	597	12	91	.286	.356	.449	805	110	110	76	104	55	49	53	-5
STL	67	87	2	.435	23	37	39	757	882	6051	1423	278	58	118	556	642	16	63	.263	.333	.401	734	94	-35	-50	102	51	40	56	-3
WAS	64	90	0	.416	26	36	41	665	811	5912	1453	266	67	52	468	504	18	61	.271	.331	.374	705	95	-87	-41	94	94	40	70	7
PHI	54	100	0	.351	36	29	42	703	932	5948	1391	242	53	105	556	656	19	69	.262	.334	.387	721	95	-55	-40	98	48	33	59	-1
TOT	619					341	275	6147		48273	11674	2167	513	883	4497	4727	151	608	.271	.342	.407	750					478	333	59	-11

TEAM	CG	SHO	GR	SV	IP	H	HR	BB	SO	BR/9	ERA	AERA	OAV	OOB	PR	APR	PF	OSB	OCS	FA	E	WPB	DP	FW	PW	BW	BSW	DIF
DET	59	10	171	23	1375.1	1425	102	570	752	13.2	4.01	119	.266	.338	57	105	109	54	56	.968	194	33	116	-.7	9.9	4.7	.2	-1.2
CLE	72	13	151	22	1375.0	1328	86	512	686	12.2	3.63	116	.254	.324	115	93	96	42	47	.975	149	33	164	1.7	8.8	-2.1	.0	1.6
NY	76	10	125	14	1373.0	1389	119	511	559	12.6	3.89	104	.261	.328	76	24	92	43	43	.975	152	28	158	1.6	2.3	5.5	.1	1.2
CHI	83	10	91	18	1386.2	1335	111	480	574	11.9	3.74	118	.250	.313	99	105	101	55	32	.969	185	46	125	-.2	9.9	-5.1	-.8	1.2
BOS	51	4	178	16	1379.2	1568	124	625	613	14.5	4.89	92	.284	.359	-77	-58	103	64	32	.972	173	48	156	.4	-5.5	7.2	-.3	3.2
STL	64	4	180	9	1373.1	1592	113	646	439	14.8	5.12	89	.290	.367	-113	-79	105	63	33	.974	158	60	179	1.3	-7.5	-4.7	-.1	1.0
WAS	74	6	122	7	1350.0	1494	93	618	618	14.2	4.59	91	.281	.359	-31	-67	95	65	54	.968	194	70	166	-.7	-6.3	-3.9	.8	-2.9
PHI	72	4	117	12	1345.0	1543	135	534	488	14.0	5.22	85	.283	.348	-125	-114	101	92	36	.960	238	55	131	-3.1	-10.8	-3.8	.0	-5.4
TOT	551	61	1135	121	10958.0					13.4	4.38		.271	.342						.970	1443	373	1195					

Batter-Fielder Wins		Batting Average		On-Base Percentage		Slugging Average		On-Base Plus Slugging		Adjusted OPS		Adjusted Batter Runs	
DiMaggio-NY	4.5	DiMaggio-NY	.352	Williams-Bos	.442	Greenberg-Det	.670	Greenberg-Det	1103	DiMaggio-NY	176	Greenberg-Det	57.4
Greenberg-Det	4.5	Appling-Chi	.348	Greenberg-Det	.433	DiMaggio-NY	.626	DiMaggio-NY	1051	Greenberg-Det	166	DiMaggio-NY	56.3
Williams-Bos	4.0	Williams-Bos	.344	Gehringer-Det	.428	Williams-Bos	.594	Williams-Bos	1036	Williams-Bos	159	Williams-Bos	53.1
Gordon-NY	3.8	Radcliff-Stl	.342	DiMaggio-NY	.425	York-Det	.583	York-Det	993	Foxx-Bos	148	Foxx-Bos	39.2
Boudreau-Cle	3.5	Greenberg-Det	.340	Appling-Chi	.420	Foxx-Bos	.581	Foxx-Bos	993	Keller-NY	142	York-Det	37.3

Runs		Hits		Doubles		Triples		Home Runs		Total Bases		Runs Batted In	
Williams-Bos	134	Radcliff-Stl	200	Greenberg-Det	50	McCosky-Det	19	Greenberg-Det	41	Greenberg-Det	384	Greenberg-Det	150
Greenberg-Det	129	McCosky-Det	200	York-Det	46	Keller-NY	15	Foxx-Bos	36	York-Det	343	York-Det	134
McCosky-Det	123	Cramer-Bos	200	Boudreau-Cle	46	Finney-Bos	15	York-Det	33	Williams-Bos	333	DiMaggio-NY	133
Gordon-NY	112	Appling-Chi	197	Williams-Bos	43	Williams-Bos	14	Johnson-Phi	31	DiMaggio-NY	318	Foxx-Bos	119
Kuhel-Chi	111	Wright-Chi	196	Moses-Phi	41	Appling-Chi	13	DiMaggio-NY	31	Gordon-NY	315	Williams-Bos	113

Stolen Bases		Base Stealing Runs		Fielding Runs-Infield		Fielding Runs-Outfield		Wins		Winning Pct.		Complete Games	
Case-Was	35	Case-Was	4.2	Heffner-Stl	15.7	Kreevich-Chi	6.9	Feller-Cle	27	Rowe-Det	.842	Feller-Cle	31
Walker-Was	21	Walker-Was	3.2	Gordon-NY	13.8	Solters-Stl	6.2	Newsom-Det	21	Newsom-Det	.808	Lee-Chi	24
Gordon-NY	18	Gehringer-Det	2.2	Bloodworth-Was	13.7	Johnson-Phi	5.6	Milnar-Cle	18	Feller-Cle	.711	Leonard-Was	23
Lewis-Was	15	Bartell-Det	1.9	Doerr-Bos	13.4	DiMaggio-Bos	5.6	Hudson-Was	17	Smith-Cle	.682		
Kreevich-Chi	15	Rosar-NY	1.2	Bartell-Det	13.4	Moses-Phi	4.7			Milnar-Cle	.643		

Strikeouts		Fewest BB/Game		Games		Saves		Base Runners/9		Adjusted Relief Runs		Relief Ranking	
Feller-Cle	261	Lyons-Chi	1.79	Feller-Cle	43	Benton-Det	17	Bonham-NY	8.70	Eisenstat-Cle	10.6	Brown-Chi	10.3
Newsom-Det	164	Benton-Det	2.21	Benton-Det	42	Brown-Chi	10	Brown-Chi	10.34	Brown-Chi	6.0	Eisenstat-Cle	8.0
Rigney-Chi	141	Rowe-Det	2.29	Wilson-Bos	41	Murphy-NY	9	Murphy-NY	10.37	Trotter-Stl	4.4	Murphy-NY	7.5
Bridges-Det	133	Leonard-Was	2.43	Heusser-Phi	41			Rigney-Chi	10.65	Murphy-NY	3.7	Benton-Det	6.7
Chase-Was	129	Russo-NY	2.61	Dobson-Cle	40			Lyons-Chi	10.87	Benton-Det	3.3	Trotter-Stl	5.5

Innings Pitched		Opponents' Avg.		Opponents' OBP		Earned Run Average		Adjusted ERA		Adjusted Starter Runs		Pitcher Wins	
Feller-Cle	320.1	Feller-Cle	.210	Feller-Cle	.285	Feller-Cle	2.61	Newsom-Det	168	Feller-Cle	61.5	Feller-Cle	6.8
Leonard-Was	289.0	Smith-Chi	.228	Lyons-Chi	.287	Newsom-Det	2.83	Feller-Cle	161	Newsom-Det	47.0	Rigney-Chi	4.1
Rigney-Chi	280.2	Bridges-Det	.229	Rigney-Chi	.292	Rigney-Chi	3.11	Rigney-Chi	142	Rigney-Chi	38.9	Newsom-Det	3.9
Newsom-Det	264.0	Rigney-Chi	.230	Lee-Chi	.300	Smith-Chi	3.21	Bridges-Det	141	Bridges-Det	27.1	Rowe-Det	3.1
Auker-Stl	263.2	Newsom-Det	.238	Russo-NY	.303	Chase-Was	3.23	Smith-Chi	138	Rowe-Det	25.6	Bonham-NY	2.8

Tigers Fill Their Tank

The AL race of 1940 was made possible by a poor start from the usually dominant Yankees. Detroit and Cleveland made hay while New York struggled, and the Indians led into September. The Tribe—a league laughingstock due to a much-publicized player rebellion against autocratic manager Ossie Vitt—dropped five straight (three to the Tigers) while the Yankees won 19 of 23 to create a three-way tie on September 9. New York dropped out, but the Tigers and Indians clustered until Detroit took three of four from Cleveland in late September. In the clincher, unknown Floyd Giebell shut out Bob Feller and the Indians for his third (and last) major league victory.

Hank Greenberg led the AL in doubles, homers, and RBIs for overpowering Detroit, while 21-year-old Feller took the pitching Triple Crown. New York had deep pitching and power, but several regulars slumped. Fourth-place Boston made rookie Dom, the youngest DiMaggio, their center fielder.

Each AL team had an attendance bump, sending league sales to their highest total to date. The Tigers, the only AL team to top the million mark in the 1930s, became the only AL team to do so in the new decade until 1945, when they did it again. While homers rose to 883, a new league high that would last until 1950, runs per team fell to 4.97 per game—the top rate in what would be a pitching-friendly decade.

White Sox second baseman Jackie Hayes began to lose his sight, and was forced to retire midseason at age 33. Another veteran infielder, Billy Rogell, 35, finished his fourteen-season career but would live another 63 years.

The World Series was one of the best in years. The teams traded wins until the Reds pulled out Game 7. Detroit's Bobo Newsom, whose father died midway through the Series, was 2-1 with a 1.38 ERA.

1939 National League

TEAM	W	L	T	PCT	GB	HW	HL	R	OR	PA	H	2B	3B	HR	BB	SO	HB	SH	AVG	OBP	SLG	OPS	AOPS	BR	ABR	PF	SB	CS	BSA	BSR
CIN	97	57	2	.630		55	25	767	595	6106	1493	269	60	98	500	538	35	193	.278	.343	.405	748	106	52	48	101	46			
STL	92	61	2	.601	4.5	51	27	779	633	6116	1601	332	62	98	475	566	27	167	.294	.354	.432	786	110	127	79	106	44			
BRO	84	69	4	.549	12.5	51	27	708	645	6047	1420	265	57	78	564	639	26	107	.265	.338	.380	718	96	2	-22	104	59			
CHI	84	70	2	.545	13	44	34	724	678	5990	1407	263	62	62	491	553	34	140	.266	.336	.391	727	99	11	-1	102	61			
NY	77	74	0	.510	18.5	41	33	703	685	5767	1395	211	38	116	498	499	32	108	.272	.340	.396	736	103	27	22	101	26			
PIT	68	85	0	.444	28.5	35	42	666	721	5923	1453	261	60	63	477	420	21	156	.276	.338	.384	722	102	4	15	98	44			
BOS	63	88	1	.417	32.5	37	35	572	659	5795	1395	199	39	56	366	494	21	122	.264	.314	.348	662	91	-122	-80	93	41			
PHI	45	106	1	.298	50.5	29	44	553	856	5707	1341	232	40	49	421	486	9	144	.261	.318	.351	669	89	-100	-83	97	47			
TOT	616					343	267	5472		47451	11505	2032	418	649	3824	4195	205	1137	.272	.335	.386	721				368			

TEAM	CG	SHO	GR	SV	IP	H	HR	BB	SO	BR/9	ERA	AERA	OAV	OOB	PR	APR	PF	OSB	OCS	FA	E	WPB	DP	FW	PW	BW	BSW	DIF
CIN	86	13	143	9	1403.2	1340	81	499	637	12.0	3.27	117	.255	.322	101	89	98	42	43	.974	162	45	170	.6	8.9	4.8		5.7
STL	45	18	210	32	1384.2	1377	76	498	603	12.3	3.59	115	.260	.326	50	76	105	39	31	.971	177	43	140	-.2	7.6	7.9		.2
BRO	69	9	138	13	1410.1	1431	93	399	528	11.9	3.64	110	.263	.317	43	58	103	42	39	.972	176	30	157	-.0	5.8	-2.2		3.9
CHI	72	8	136	13	1392.1	1504	74	430	584	12.6	3.80	104	.276	.331	18	20	101	34	44	.970	186	33	126	-.6	2.0	-.1		5.7
NY	55	6	163	20	1319.0	1412	86	477	505	13.1	4.07	96	.275	.340	-22	-20	100	57	36	.975	153	40	151	.8	-2.0	2.2		.5
PIT	53	10	157	15	1354.0	1537	70	423	464	13.2	4.15	92	.287	.342	-36	-51	98	41	35	.972	168	26	153	.1	-5.1	1.5		-5.0
BOS	68	11	144	15	1358.1	1400	63	513	430	12.8	3.71	100	.271	.339	31	-3	94	32	41	.971	181	30	178	-.6	-.3	-8.0		-3.6
PHI	67	3	133	12	1326.2	1502	106	579	447	14.4	5.17	77	.289	.365	-185	-167	102	81	38	.970	171	47	136	-.0	-16.7	-8.3		-5.4
TOT	515	78	1224	129	10949.0					12.8	3.92		.272	.335						.972	1374	294	1211					

Batter-Fielder Wins	Batting Average	On-Base Percentage	Slugging Average	On-Base Plus Slugging	Adjusted OPS	Adjusted Batter Runs
Mize-StL 4.3	Mize-StL 349	Ott-NY 449	Mize-StL 626	Mize-StL 1070	Mize-StL 174	Mize-StL 61.8
Frey-Cin 4.0	McCormick-Cin 332	Mize-StL 444	Ott-NY 581	Ott-NY 1030	Ott-NY 173	Ott-NY 46.8
Vaughan-Pit 4.0	Medwick-StL 332	Camilli-Bro 409	Leiber-Chi 556	Camilli-Bro 933	Camilli-Bro 144	Camilli-Bro 38.5
Ott-NY 3.4	P.Waner-Pit 328	Goodman-Cin 401	Camilli-Bro 524	Goodman-Cin 916	Goodman-Cin 144	Goodman-Cin 29.9
Camilli-Bro 3.2	Arnovich-Phi 324	Arnovich-Phi 397	Goodman-Cin 515	Medwick-StL 886	West-Bos 139	Leiber-Chi 29.8

Runs	Hits	Doubles	Triples	Home Runs	Total Bases	Runs Batted In
Werber-Cin 115	McCormick-Cin 209	Slaughter-StL 52	Herman-Chi 18	Mize-StL 28	Mize-StL 353	McCormick-Cin 128
Hack-Chi 112	Medwick-StL 201	Medwick-StL 48	Goodman-Cin 16	Ott-NY 27	McCormick-Cin 312	Medwick-StL 117
Herman-Chi 111	Mize-StL 197	Mize-StL 44	Mize-StL 14	Camilli-Bro 26	Medwick-StL 307	Mize-StL 108
Camilli-Bro 105	Slaughter-StL 193	McCormick-Cin 41	Camilli-Bro 12	Leiber-Chi 24	Camilli-Bro 296	Camilli-Bro 104
	Brown-StL 192			Lombardi-Cin 20	Slaughter-StL 291	Leiber-Chi 88

Stolen Bases	Base Stealing Runs	Fielding Runs-Infield	Fielding Runs-Outfield	Wins	Winning Pct.	Complete Games
Handley-Pit 17		Jurges-NY 19.5	Arnovich-Phi 14.3	Walters-Cin 27	Derringer-Cin 781	Walters-Cin 31
Hack-Chi 17		Frey-Cin 14.1	Slaughter-StL 13.2	Derringer-Cin 25	Walters-Cin 711	Derringer-Cin 28
Werber-Cin 15		Vaughan-Pit 11.3	Moore-StL 7.6	Davis-StL 22	French-Chi 652	Lee-Chi 20
Lavagetto-Bro 14		Hassett-Bos 10.6	Goodman-Cin 6.6	Hamlin-Bro 20	Gumbert-NY 621	Hamlin-Bro 19
Hassett-Bos 13		May-Phi 9.9	Medwick-StL 4.8	Lee-Chi 19	Hamlin-Bro 606	Posedel-Bos 18

Strikeouts	Fewest BB/Game	Games	Saves	Base Runners/9	Adjusted Relief Runs	Relief Ranking
Passeau-Phi-Chi 137	Derringer-Cin 1.05	Shoun-StL 53	Shoun-StL 9	Hubbell-NY 10.29	Shoun-StL 3.2	J.Russell-Chi 2.2
Walters-Cin 137	Hubbell-NY 1.40	Sewell-Pit 52	Bowman-StL 9	Walters-Cin 10.30	J.Russell-Chi 2.1	Shoun-StL 1.7
Cooper-StL 130	Davis-StL 1.74	Bowman-StL 51	Davis-StL 7	Hamlin-Bro 10.31		
Derringer-Cin 128	Hamlin-Bro 1.80	Davis-StL 49	Brown-NY 7	Johnson-Phi 10.38		
Lee-Chi 105	Root-Chi 1.83	Brown-Pit 47	Brown-Pit 7	Wyatt-Bro 10.65		

Innings Pitched	Opponents' Avg.	Opponents' OBP	Earned Run Average	Adjusted ERA	Adjusted Starter Runs	Pitcher Wins
Walters-Cin 319.0	Walters-Cin 220	Hubbell-NY 280	Walters-Cin 2.29	Walters-Cin 168	Walters-Cin 54.4	Walters-Cin 8.2
Derringer-Cin 301.0	Bowman-StL 232	Hamlin-Bro 285	Bowman-StL 2.60	Bowman-StL 158	Derringer-Cin 30.5	Derringer-Cin 2.9
Lee-Chi 282.1	Hamlin-Bro 248	Walters-Cin 291	Hubbell-NY 2.75	Hubbell-NY 143	Bowman-StL 27.9	Davis-StL 2.8
Passeau-Phi-Chi 274.1	Hubbell-NY 249	Derringer-Cin 295	Casey-Bro 2.93	Casey-Bro 137	Casey-Bro 25.0	Bowman-StL 2.7
Hamlin-Bro 269.2	Moore-Cin 254	Bowman-StL 302	Derringer-Cin 2.93	Derringer-Cin 131	Thompson-Cin 21.9	Casey-Bro 2.7

Queen City Renaissance

Just 3½ games separated the eight teams in mid-May. From this point, however, the Cincinnati Reds asserted their dominance under second-year manager Bill McKechnie by winning 12 straight to leap to the top of the league. The Reds continued to lead the league, but slowed down, playing just .500 ball in August while the St. Louis Cardinals caught fire, taking 19 of 21 games. Responding to the challenge, Cincinnati recovered in September and clinched the pennant.

For the Reds, who captured their first flag since 1919, Bucky Walters (the league's MVP) and Paul Derringer combined for 52 victories; their progress made up for Johnny Vander Meer's slump. Bill Werber, purchased from the Athletics, proved an outstanding leadoff man, while first baseman Frank McCormick developed into a star. Cincinnati also enjoyed good defense. The pitching was efficient, and whenever runners got on, infielders Lonny Frey, Billy Myers, and Werber erased them; the Reds' 170 double plays were the third-highest total ever for an NL pennant winner.

Second-place St. Louis, playing in small Sportsman's Park, again had good offensive numbers. Their real strength, however, was the pitching of Curt Davis, Lon Warneke, and Mort Cooper. Slugger Johnny Mize didn't hurt; he won the first of his four home run crowns and his lone batting title in 1939.

Leo Durocher was hired to get the Brooklyn Dodgers out of the doldrums; this he did, moving the club from seventh to third and goosing the gate by 44 percent. Ebbets Field was also the site, on August 26, of the first-ever baseball telecast. The Dodgers had a decent enough offense, but a patchwork pitching staff provided the strength.

The Hall of Fame was dedicated in Cooperstown, New York. The opening lineup of inductees (alive and dead) elected since 1936 included National Leaguers Honus Wagner, Christy Mathewson, Grover Cleveland Alexander, Cy Young, John McGraw, Wee Willie Keeler, Buck Ewing, Al Spalding, Charley Radbourn, and Cap Anson. The World Series downstate was ho hum. The Yankees swept the Reds, who scored but 8 runs and only led for four innings of the entire series.

1939 American League

TEAM	W	L	T	PCT	GB	HW	HL	R	OR	PA	H	2B	3B	HR	BB	SO	HB	SH	AVG	OBP	SLG	OPS	AOPS	BR	ABR	PF	SB	CS	BSA	BSR
NY	106	45	1	.702		52	25	967	556	6129	1521	259	55	166	701	543	36	92	.287	.374	.451	825	119	137	152	98	72	37	66	3
BOS	89	62	1	.589	17	42	32	890	795	6054	1543	287	57	124	591	505	15	140	.291	.363	.436	799	106	81	49	104	42	44	49	-6
CLE	87	67	0	.565	20.5	44	33	797	700	6007	1490	291	79	85	557	574	14	120	.280	.350	.413	763	105	4	33	97	72	46	61	0
CHI	85	69	1	.552	22.5	50	27	755	737	6033	1451	220	56	64	579	502	21	146	.275	.349	.374	723	89	-64	-83	103	113	61	65	4
DET	81	73	1	.526	26.5	42	35	849	762	6108	1487	277	67	124	620	592	16	146	.279	.356	.426	782	99	45	-14	108	88	38	70	6
WAS	65	87	1	.428	41.5	37	39	702	797	6026	1483	249	79	44	547	460	11	134	.278	.346	.379	725	98	-65	-7	93	94	47	67	4
PHI	55	97	1	.362	51.5	28	48	711	1022	5965	1438	282	55	98	503	532	15	138	.271	.346	.400	736	96	-55	-39	98	60	34	64	1
STL	43	111	2	.279	64.5	18	59	733	1035	6133	1453	242	50	91	559	606	20	132	.268	.339	.381	720	88	-81	-96	102	48	38	56	-3
TOT	615					313	298	6404		48455	11866	2107	498	796	4657	4314	148	1056	.279	.352	.407	759				589	345	63	9

TEAM	CG	SHO	GR	SV	IP	H	HR	BB	SO	BR/9	ERA	AERA	OAV	OOB	PR	APR	PF	OSB	OCS	FA	E	WPB	DP	FW	PW	BW	BSW	DIF
NY	87	15	93	26	1348.2	1208	85	567	565	11.9	3.31	132	.241	.319	196	166	94	49	32	.978	126	29	159	2.9	15.3	14.0	.2	-1.9
BOS	52	4	187	20	1350.2	1533	77	543	539	14.0	4.56	104	.287	.355	9	25	102	85	43	.970	180	31	147	.0	2.3	4.5	-.7	7.2
CLE	69	10	142	13	1364.2	1394	75	602	614	13.3	4.08	108	.267	.344	81	51	95	67	43	.970	180	37	148	.2	-4.7	3.0	-.1	2.1
CHI	62	5	125	21	1377.0	1470	99	454	535	12.7	4.31	110	.275	.333	48	63	102	73	41	.972	167	35	140	1.0	5.8	-7.6	.3	8.6
DET	64	8	150	16	1367.1	1430	104	574	633	13.4	4.29	114	.268	.341	50	86	106	65	53	.967	198	47	146	-.6	-7.9	-1.3	.5	-2.4
WAS	72	4	122	10	1354.2	1420	75	602	521	13.6	4.60	94	.271	.348	2	-41	94	47	34	.966	205	70	167	-1.1	-3.8	-.6	.3	-5.7
PHI	50	6	155	12	1342.2	1687	148	579	397	15.3	5.79	81	.307	.375	-175	-159	102	103	43	.964	210	49	131	-1.4	-14.7	-3.6	.0	-1.4
STL	56	3	181	.3	1371.1	1724	133	739	516	16.4	6.01	81	.310	.393	-212	-166	105	100	56	.968	199	49	144	-.6	-15.3	-8.8	-.4	-8.8
TOT	512	55	1155	121	10877.0					13.8	4.62		.279	.352						.969	1465	347	1183					

Batter-Fielder Wins
DiMaggio-NY ...5.5
Foxx-Bos ...5.2
Johnson-Phi ...4.8
Dickey-NY ...4.5
Williams-Bos ...4.1

Batting Average
DiMaggio-NY ...381
Foxx-Bos ...360
Johnson-Phi ...338
Trosky-Cle ...335
Rolfe-NY ...329

On-Base Percentage
Foxx-Bos ...464
Selkirk-NY ...452
DiMaggio-NY ...448
Keller-NY ...447
Johnson-Phi ...440

Slugging Average
Foxx-Bos ...694
DiMaggio-NY ...671
Greenberg-Det ...622
Williams-Bos ...609
Trosky-Cle ...589

On-Base Plus Slugging
Foxx-Bos ...1158
DiMaggio-NY ...1119
Williams-Bos ...1045
Greenberg-Det ...1042
Trosky-Cle ...994

Adjusted OPS
DiMaggio-NY ...185
Foxx-Bos ...185
Williams-Bos ...158
Trosky-Cle ...157
Johnson-Phi ...156

Adjusted Batter Runs
Foxx-Bos ...62.0
DiMaggio-NY ...59.0
Williams-Bos ...52.7
Johnson-Phi ...49.4
Greenberg-Det ...40.1

Runs
Rolfe-NY ...139
Williams-Bos ...131
Foxx-Bos ...130
McCosky-Det ...120
Johnson-Phi ...115

Hits
Rolfe-NY ...213
McQuinn-StL ...195
Keltner-Cle ...191
McCosky-Det ...190
Williams-Bos ...185

Doubles
Rolfe-NY ...46
Williams-Bos ...44
Greenberg-Det ...42
McQuinn-StL ...37
Keltner-Cle ...35

Triples
Lewis-Was ...16
McCosky-Det ...14
McQuinn-StL ...13
Campbell-Cle ...13

Home Runs
Foxx-Bos ...35
Greenberg-Det ...33
Williams-Bos ...31
DiMaggio-NY ...30
Gordon-NY ...28

Total Bases
Williams-Bos ...344
Foxx-Bos ...324
Rolfe-NY ...321
McQuinn-StL ...318
Greenberg-Det ...311

Runs Batted In
Williams-Bos ...145
DiMaggio-NY ...126
Johnson-Phi ...114
Greenberg-Det ...112

Stolen Bases
Case-Was ...51
Kreevich-Chi ...23
Fox-Det ...23
McCosky-Det ...20

Base Stealing Runs
Case-Was ...5.3
McCosky-Det ...3.0
Kuhel-Chi ...2.2
Welaj-Was ...2.2
Chapman-Cle ...1.9

Fielding Runs-Infield
Doerr-Bos ...26.5
Clift-StL ...12.9
Trosky-Cle ...11.5
Lewis-Was ...10.9
Crosetti-NY ...9.8

Fielding Runs-Outfield
Johnson-Phi ...9.7
Kreevich-Chi ...9.5
Fox-Det ...8.4
Walker-Chi ...7.6
DiMaggio-NY ...4.5

Wins
Feller-Cle ...24
Ruffing-NY ...21
Newsom-StL-Det ...20
Leonard-Was ...20
Bridges-Det ...17

Winning Pct.
Grove-Bos ...789
Ruffing-NY ...750
Feller-Cle ...727
Leonard-Was ...714
Bridges-Det ...708

Complete Games
Newsom-StL-Det ...24
Feller-Cle ...24
Ruffing-NY ...22
Leonard-Was ...21
Grove-Bos ...17

Strikeouts
Feller-Cle ...246
Newsom-StL-Det ...192
Bridges-Det ...129
Rigney-Chi ...119
Chase-Was ...118

Fewest BB/Game
Lyons-Chi ...1.36
Leonard-Was ...1.97
Beckmann-Phi ...2.38
Lee-Chi ...2.68
Grove-Bos ...2.73

Games
Brown-Chi ...61
Dean-Phi ...54
Dickman-Bos ...48
Heving-Bos ...46

Saves
Murphy-NY ...19
Brown-Chi ...18
Heving-Bos ...7
Dean-Phi ...7
Appleton-Was ...6

Base Runners/9
Lyons-Chi ...9.85
Russo-NY ...9.93
Hildebrand-NY ...10.23
Ruffing-NY ...11.11
Leonard-Was ...11.26

Adjusted Relief Runs
Brown-Chi ...10.5
Heving-Bos ...6.1
Dickman-Bos ...1.5

Relief Ranking
Brown-Chi ...20.4
Heving-Bos ...8.1
Dickman-Bos ...1.5

Innings Pitched
Feller-Cle ...296.2
Newsom-StL-Det ...291.2
Leonard-Was ...269.1
Lee-Chi ...235.0
Ruffing-NY ...233.1

Opponents' Avg.
Feller-Cle ...210
Gomez-NY ...235
Hadley-NY ...237
Ruffing-NY ...240
Bridges-Det ...243

Opponents' OBP
Lyons-Chi ...276
Ruffing-NY ...301
Feller-Cle ...303
Bridges-Det ...304
Leonard-Was ...305

Earned Run Average
Grove-Bos ...2.54
Lyons-Chi ...2.76
Feller-Cle ...2.85
Ruffing-NY ...2.93
Hadley-NY ...2.98

Adjusted ERA
Grove-Bos ...186
Lyons-Chi ...171
Feller-Cle ...154
Ruffing-NY ...149
Hadley-NY ...146

Adjusted Starter Runs
Feller-Cle ...54.2
Grove-Bos ...45.2
Newsom-StL-Det ...42.2
Ruffing-NY ...37.8
Lyons-Chi ...31.7

Pitcher Wins
Feller-Cle ...6.0
Ruffing-NY ...4.8
Grove-Bos ...3.7
Lyons-Chi ...3.7
Newsom-StL-Det ...3.5

Williams Can't Unseat Yankees

An unparalleled rookie class graced the American League in 1939. Say hello to Ted Williams, Charlie Keller, Dizzy Trout, Mickey Vernon, Early Wynn, and Hal Newhouser, all of whom affected baseball in the 1940s and beyond. Let's focus on Williams, a lithe 20-year-old from San Diego. He was second in the league in doubles and walks, fifth in hits, and third in homers. The Red Sox ended up second, their best finish in two decades, on his hitting, that of Jimmie Foxx, and the ninth and final ERA crown won by ageless Lefty Grove.

But New York again rolled over the competition, leaving the Red Sox 17 games behind. It is a tribute to the Yankees that they kept winning even when Lou Gehrig was forced to retire due to a condition eventually defined as Amyotrophic Lateral Sclerosis. The disease would kill him in 1941, shortly before he would have turned 38. (Three other greats also left the active ranks in '39: Jimmy Dykes, Tony Lazzeri, and Heinie Manush.)

How did the Yanks do it? Balance, again, was the secret. All eight regulars hit at least 10 homers, and the Yankees led the league in runs, ERA, and saves. Keller, Joe DiMaggio, and George Selkirk comprised a top outfield, while manager Joe McCarthy gave seven pitchers at least 10 starts—and each won at least 10 games.

Another four-game World Series sweep, this one over Cincinnati, established the Yankees as perhaps the AL's greatest team to date. Bill Dickey, DiMaggio, and Keller did the damage as New York outscored the Reds 20-8. It was New York's eighth world championship since 1923, and even more dominating, it was their fifth sweep.

But even perfection becomes boring; attendance at Yankee Stadium dropped 11 percent. The Athletics, hoping to increase their gate, hosted the league's first night game on May 16. And while scoring dropped, the league's 512 complete games still ranked as the lowest total ever.

1938 National League

TEAM	W	L	T	PCT	GB	HW	HL	R	OR	PA	H	2B	3B	HR	BB	SO	HB	SH	AVG	OBP	SLG	OPS	AOPS	BR	ABR	PF	SB	CS	BSA	BSR
CHI	89	63	2	.586		44	33	713	597	5972	1435	242	70	65	522	476	29	88	.269	.338	.377	715	100	26	7	103	49			
PIT	86	64	2	.573	2	44	33	707	630	6007	1511	265	66	65	485	409	19	81	.279	.340	.388	728	106	49	44	101	47			
NY	83	67	2	.553	5	43	30	705	637	5841	1424	210	36	125	465	528	33	88	.271	.334	.396	730	106	45	39	101	31			
CIN	82	68	1	.547	6	43	34	723	634	5878	1495	251	57	110	366	518	32	89	.277	.327	.406	733	110	42	62	97	19			
BOS	77	75	1	.507	12	45	30	561	618	5775	1311	199	39	54	424	548	23	78	.250	.309	.333	642	91	-61	90	49			
STL	71	80	5	.470	17.5	36	41	725	722	6039	1542	288	74	91	412	492	16	83	.279	.331	.407	738	103	56	16	106	55			
BRO	69	80	2	.463	18.5	31	41	704	710	5853	1322	225	79	61	611	615	20	80	.257	.338	.367	705	98	14	-1	102	66			
PHI	45	105	1	.300	43	26	48	550	840	5713	1318	233	29	40	423	507	12	86	.254	.312	.333	645	85	-111	-95	97	38			
TOT	610					312	290	5388		47078	11358	1913	450	611	3708	4093	184	673	.267	.329	.376	705					354			

TEAM	CG	SHO	GR	SV	IP	H	HR	BB	SO	BR/9	ERA	AERA	OAV	OOB	PR	APR	PF	OSB	OCS	FA	E	WPB	DP	FW	PW	BW	BSW	DIF
CHI	67	16	148	18	1396.2	1414	71	454	583	12.1	3.37	113	.262	.322	64	66	101	40	30	.978	135	42	151	2.3	6.6	.7		3.4
PIT	57	8	144	15	1379.2	1406	71	432	557	12.2	3.46	109	.266	.324	49	50	100	44	45	.974	163	24	168	.5	5.0	4.4		1.1
NY	59	8	142	18	1349.0	1370	87	389	497	11.9	3.62	104	.261	.314	24	20	99	37	24	.973	168	20	147	.2	2.0	3.9		1.9
CIN	72	11	130	16	1362.0	1329	75	463	542	11.9	3.62	101	.254	.316	25	3	96	37	33	.971	172	39	133	-.1	.3	6.2		.6
BOS	83	15	109	12	1380.0	1375	66	465	413	12.2	3.40	101	.258	.322	58	3	91	27	42	.972	173	23	136	-.0	.3	-6.1		6.9
STL	58	10	179	16	1384.2	1482	77	474	534	12.8	3.84	103	.272	.333	-9	16	104	48	43	.967	199	36	145	-1.4	1.6	1.6		-6.3
BRO	56	12	155	14	1332.0	1464	88	446	469	13.1	4.07	96	.278	.338	-42	-25	103	47	31	.973	157	52	148	.8	-2.5	-.1		-3.6
PHI	68	3	140	6	1329.1	1516	76	582	492	14.4	4.93	79	.285	.358	-169	-151	103	74	35	.966	201	40	135	-1.8	-15.2	-9.6		-3.4
TOT	520	83	1147	115	10913.1					12.6	3.78		.267	.329						.972	1368	276	1163					

Batter-Fielder Wins
Ott-NY 6.4
Vaughan-Pit 6.4
Lombardi-Cin 4.1
Hack-Chi 4.0
Mize-StL 3.9

Batting Average
Lombardi-Cin 342
Mize-StL 337
McCormick-Cin 327
Medwick-StL 322
Vaughan-Pit 322

On-Base Percentage
Ott-NY 442
Vaughan-Pit 433
Mize-StL 422
Hack-Chi 411
Suhr-Pit 394

Slugging Average
Mize-StL 614
Ott-NY 583
Medwick-StL 536
Goodman-Cin 533
Lombardi-Cin 524

On-Base Plus Slugging
Mize-StL 1036
Ott-NY 1024
Lombardi-Cin 915
Medwick-StL 905
Goodman-Cin 901

Adjusted OPS
Ott-NY 178
Mize-StL 172
Lombardi-Cin 154
Goodman-Cin 149
Vaughan-Pit 140

Adjusted Batter Runs
Ott-NY 62.3
Mize-StL 53.0
Vaughan-Pit 37.6
Goodman-Cin 36.5
Lombardi-Cin 35.3

Runs
Ott-NY 116
Hack-Chi 109
Camilli-Bro 106
Goodman-Cin 103
Medwick-StL 100

Hits
McCormick-Cin 209
Hack-Chi 195
L.Waner-Pit 194
Medwick-StL 190
Mize-StL 179

Doubles
Medwick-StL 47
McCormick-Cin 40
Young-Pit 36
Martin-Phi 36

Triples
Mize-StL 16
Gutteridge-StL 15
Suhr-Pit 14
Riggs-Cin 13
Koy-Bro 13

Home Runs
Ott-NY 36
Goodman-Cin 30
Mize-StL 27
Camilli-Bro 24
Rizzo-Pit 23

Total Bases
Mize-StL 326
Medwick-StL 316
Ott-NY 307
Goodman-Cin 303
Rizzo-Pit 285

Runs Batted In
Medwick-StL 122
Ott-NY 116
Rizzo-Pit 111
McCormick-Cin 106
Mize-StL 102

Stolen Bases
Hack-Chi 16
Lavagetto-Bro 15
Koy-Bro 15
Vaughan-Pit 14
Gutteridge-StL 14

Base Stealing Runs

Fielding Runs-Infield
Bartell-NY 25.9
Young-Pit 25.1
Herman-Chi 21.5
Vaughan-Pit 16.7
Kampouris-Cin-NY 13.2

Fielding Runs-Outfield
Arnovich-Phi 17.4
DiMaggio-Bos 10.5
Rosen-Bro 9.1
Medwick-StL 8.0
Craft-Cin 7.1

Wins
Lee-Chi 22
Derringer-Cin 21
Bryant-Chi 19
Weiland-StL 16

Winning Pct.
Lee-Chi 710
Bryant-Chi 633
Brown-Pit 625
VanderMeer-Cin 600
Derringer-Cin 600

Complete Games
Derringer-Cin 26
Turner-Bos 22
Walters-Phi-Cin 20
MacFayden-Bos 19
Lee-Chi 19

Strikeouts
Bryant-Chi 135
Derringer-Cin 132
VanderMeer-Cin 125
Lee-Chi 121

Fewest BB/Game
Davis-StL 1.40
Derringer-Cin 1.44
Hubbell-NY 1.66
Root-Chi 1.68
Turner-Bos 1.81

Games
Coffman-NY 51
Brown-Pit 51
McGee-StL 47
Mulcahy-Phi 46

Saves
Coffman-NY 12
Root-Chi 8
Hamlin-Bro 6
Errickson-Bos 6

Base Runners/9
Dean-Chi 8.68
Brown-NY 9.40
Hubbell-NY 10.36
Johnson-Phi 10.63
Derringer-Cin 10.67

Adjusted Relief Runs
Brown-NY 17.6
Russell-Chi 5.6
Coffman-NY 3.7
Shoun-StL 7

Relief Ranking
Brown-NY 16.3
Coffman-NY 4.5
Russell-Chi 3.8
Shoun-StL 7

Innings Pitched
Derringer-Cin 307.0
Lee-Chi 291.0
Bryant-Chi 270.1
Turner-Bos 268.0
Mulcahy-Phi 267.1

Opponents' Avg.
VanderMeer-Cin 213
Bauers-StL 233
Bryant-Chi 235
MacFayden-Bos 247
Schumacher-NY 248

Opponents' OBP
Hubbell-NY 285
Derringer-Cin 291
Root-Chi 294
Lohrman-NY 294
Schumacher-NY 299

Earned Run Average
Lee-Chi 2.66
Root-Chi 2.86
Derringer-Cin 2.93
MacFayden-Bos 2.95
Klinger-Pit 2.99

Adjusted ERA
Lee-Chi 144
Root-Chi 134
Fitzsimmons-Bro 129
Klinger-Pit 127
Derringer-Cin 124

Adjusted Starter Runs
Lee-Chi 38.6
Derringer-Cin 27.8
Bryant-Chi 22.1
Fitzsimmons-Bro 18.0
Bauers-Pit 17.8

Pitcher Wins
Lee-Chi 4.1
Derringer-Cin 2.9
Bryant-Chi 2.6
Bauers-Pit 2.1
Fitzsimmons-Bro 1.8

Cubs Glow One Last Time

For all intents and purposes, 1938 looked like Pittsburgh's year. A 24-7 record in July allowed them to overtake the sliding Giants, and the Pirates led for all of August and most of September. Then the elements took over. A mid-September hurricane stopped play for four days and gave tired Chicago time to recover; the team reeled off seven straight wins to catch the stumbling Pirates, who had led by seven on Labor Day.

Chicago knocked Pittsburgh out with a three-game sweep September 27-29 at Wrigley Field. Player-manager Gabby Hartnett's dramatic "homer in the gloamin'," hit just before the umpires were set to call the game by darkness, provided the key hit in the second game. Pittsburgh had great relief pitching from Mace Brown, and a solid line-drive offense, but didn't have Chicago's rotation: Bill Lee of the Cubs led the NL in wins and ERA, while 19-game winner Clay Bryant had a superior season in an otherwise nondescript career.

Cincinnati leapt to fourth, raising attendance by 72 percent. Overpowering Johnny Vander Meer threw no-hitters in consecutive starts, while catcher Ernie Lombardi was MVP. Rebuilding St. Louis debuted future stars Mort Cooper and Enos Slaughter.

Stolen bases fell to just .29 per contest, the lowest total to that point in history. Vince DiMaggio again paced the league with 138 strikeouts, setting a record that lasted until 1956. Several teams altered their ballparks in 1938. The Cubs redesigned Wrigley Field, adding the bleachers still in use, while the Giants chopped 50 feet from center field with a temporary fence. The Phillies moved into Shibe Park, the Athletics' headquarters, on July 4; Shibe was much larger than the tiny Baker Bowl.

The Cubs had no more luck in the World Series than other NL teams of the period, losing to the Yankees in four. While 1938 was the Cubs' eleventh straight year among the NL's top three, it was also the *end* of the franchise as a consistent winner; Chicago did not contend again until 1945.

1938 American League

TEAM	W	L	T	PCT	GB	HW	HL	R	OR	PA	H	2B	3B	HR	BB	SO	HB	SH	AVG	OBP	SLG	OPS	AOPS	BR	ABR	PF	SB	CS	BSA	BSR
NY	99	53	5	.651		55	22	966	710	6259	1480	283	63	174	749	616	39	61	.274	.366	.446	812	111	81	86	100	91	28	76	10
BOS	88	61	1	.591	9.5	52	23	902	751	6004	1566	298	56	98	650	463	13	112	.299	.378	.434	812	105	91	51	105	55	51	52	-6
CLE	86	66	1	.566	13	46	30	847	782	6000	1506	300	89	113	550	605	16	78	.281	.350	.434	784	104	8	25	98	83	36	70	6
DET	84	70	1	.545	16	48	31	862	795	6060	1434	219	52	137	693	581	22	75	.272	.359	.411	770	94	-2	-46	106	76	41	65	2
WAS	75	76	1	.497	23.5	44	33	814	873	6158	1602	278	72	85	573	379	18	93	.293	.362	.416	778	108	11	74	93	65	37	64	1
CHI	65	83	1	.439	32	33	39	709	752	5805	1439	239	55	67	514	489	14	78	.277	.343	.383	726	86	-94	-110	102	56	39	59	-1
STL	55	97	4	.362	44	31	43	755	962	6049	1498	273	36	92	590	528	20	106	.281	.355	.397	752	95	-36	-34	100	51	40	56	-3
PHI	53	99	2	.349	46	28	47	726	956	5934	1410	243	62	98	605	590	22	78	.270	.348	.396	744	95	-58	-38	97	65	53	55	-4
TOT	613					337	268	6581		48269	11935	2133	485	864	4924	4251	164	681	.281	.358	.415	773					542	325	63	5

TEAM	CG	SHO	GR	SV	IP	H	HR	BB	SO	BR/9	ERA	AERA	OAV	OOB	PR	APR	PF	OSB	OCS	FA	E	WPB	DP	FW	PW	BW	BSW	DIF
NY	91	11	91	13	1382.0	1436	85	566	567	13.1	3.91	116	.268	.339	134	101	95	52	37	.973	169	39	177	.5	9.1	7.8	.8	4.8
BOS	67	10	147	15	1316.1	1472	102	528	484	13.8	4.46	111	.281	.349	48	67	103	63	35	.968	190	27	172	-1.1	6.1	4.6	-.6	4.6
CLE	68	5	145	17	1353.0	1416	100	681	717	14.1	4.60	101	.268	.355	29	7	97	82	49	.974	151	39	145	1.2	.6	2.3	.5	5.4
DET	75	3	134	11	1348.1	1532	110	608	435	14.4	4.79	104	.287	.361	1	31	104	48	35	.976	147	37	172	1.6	2.8	-4.2	.1	6.6
WAS	59	6	156	11	1360.1	1472	92	655	515	14.3	4.94	91	.276	.358	-22	-68	94	64	39	.970	180	60	179	-.5	-6.1	6.7	.0	-.6
CHI	83	5	84	9	1316.1	1449	101	550	432	13.8	4.36	112	.279	.350	62	76	102	57	42	.967	196	33	155	-1.6	6.9	-9.9	-.2	-4.2
STL	71	3	134	7	1344.2	1584	132	737	632	15.7	5.80	86	.295	.382	-151	-120	104	89	49	.965	145	37	163	1.8	-10.8	-3.1	-.3	-8.5
PHI	56	4	143	12	1324.0	1573	142	599	473	14.9	5.48	88	.292	.365	-101	-94	101	87	39	.965	206	43	119	-1.8	-8.5	-3.4	-.4	-8.9
TOT	570	47	1034	95	10745.0					14.3	4.79		.281	.358						.971	1384	315	1282					

Batter-Fielder Wins
Foxx-Bos 5.8
Clift-StL 5.3
Greenberg-Det 4.5
Cronin-Bos 4.4
Dickey-NY 4.1

Batting Average
Foxx-Bos .349
Heath-Cle .343
Chapman-Bos .340
Myer-Was .336
Travis-Was .335

On-Base Percentage
Foxx-Bos .462
Myer-Was .454
Greenberg-Det .438
Averill-Cle .429
Cronin-Bos .428

Slugging Average
Foxx-Bos .704
Greenberg-Det .683
Heath-Cle .602
DiMaggio-NY .581
York-Det .579

On-Base Plus Slugging
Foxx-Bos 1166
Greenberg-Det 1122
York-Det .995
Heath-Cle .985
Dickey-NY .981

Adjusted OPS
Foxx-Bos 180
Greenberg-Det 167
Heath-Cle 146
Dickey-NY 144
Clift-StL 143

Adjusted Batter Runs
Foxx-Bos 71.9
Greenberg-Det 58.3
Clift-StL 38.9
Johnson-Phi 36.0
Myer-Was 34.1

Runs
Greenberg-Det 144
Foxx-Bos 139
Gehringer-Det 133
Rolfe-NY 132
DiMaggio-NY 129

Hits
Vosmik-Bos 201
Cramer-Bos 198
Almada-Was-StL 197
Foxx-Bos 197
Rolfe-NY 196

Doubles
Cronin-Bos 51
McQuinn-StL 42
Trosky-Cle 40
Chapman-Bos 40
Vosmik-Bos 37

Triples
Heath-Cle 18
Averill-Cle 15
DiMaggio-NY 13

Home Runs
Greenberg-Det 58
Foxx-Bos 50
Clift-StL 34
York-Det 33
DiMaggio-NY 32

Total Bases
Foxx-Bos 398
Greenberg-Det 380
DiMaggio-NY 348
Johnson-Phi 311
Heath-Cle 302

Runs Batted In
Foxx-Bos 175
Greenberg-Det 146
DiMaggio-NY 140
York-Det 127
Clift-StL 118

Stolen Bases
Crosetti-NY 27
Lary-Cle 23
Werber-Phi 19
Lewis-Was 17
Fox-Det 16

Base Stealing Runs
Lary-Cle 3.0
Gehringer-Det 2.7
Rolfe-NY 2.5
Crosetti-NY 1.7
Moses-Phi 1.5

Fielding Runs-Infield
Gordon-NY 20.5
Crosetti-NY 18.4
Clift-StL 15.2
Rogell-Det 9.8
Doerr-Bos 9.0

Fielding Runs-Outfield
Johnson-Phi 9.6
Cramer-Bos 5.5
Chapman-Bos 5.4
Moses-Phi 4.3
Vosmik-Bos 3.5

Wins
Ruffing-NY 21
Newsom-StL 20
Gomez-NY 18
Harder-Cle 17
Feller-Cle 17

Winning Pct.
Ruffing-NY .750
Pearson-NY .696
Harder-Cle .630
Stratton-Chi .625
Feller-Cle .607

Complete Games
Newsom-StL 31
Ruffing-NY 22
Gomez-NY 20
Feller-Cle 20
Caster-Phi 20

Strikeouts
Feller-Cle 240
Newsom-StL 226
L.Mills-StL 134
Gomez-NY 129
Ruffing-NY 127

Fewest BB/Game
Leonard-Was 2.14
Harder-Cle 2.33
Lyons-Chi 2.40
Chandler-NY 2.46
Thomas-Phi 2.63

Games
Humphries-Cle 45
Newsom-StL 44
E.Smith-Phi 43
Bagby-Bos 43
Appleton-Was 43

Saves
Murphy-NY 11
McKain-Bos 6
Humphries-Cle 6
Potter-Phi 5
Appleton-Was 5

Base Runners/9
Leonard-Was 11.32
Eisenstat-Det 11.56
Harris-Bos 11.76
Ruffing-NY 11.94
Stratton-Chi 12.03

Adjusted Relief Runs
Murphy-NY 4.9
McKain-Bos 3.5

Relief Ranking
Murphy-NY 6.1
McKain-Bos 3.3

Innings Pitched
Newsom-StL 329.2
Caster-Phi 281.1
Feller-Cle 277.2
Ruffing-NY 247.1
Lee-Chi 245.1

Opponents' Avg.
Feller-Cle .220
Allen-Cle .246
Hadley-NY .254
Stratton-Chi .255
Rigney-Chi .256

Opponents' OBP
Leonard-Was .305
Stratton-Chi .315
Ruffing-NY .317
Harder-Cle .319
Grove-Bos .319

Earned Run Average
Grove-Bos 3.08
Ruffing-NY 3.31
Gomez-NY 3.35
Leonard-Was 3.43
Lee-Chi 3.49

Adjusted ERA
Grove-Bos 160
Lee-Chi 140
Rigney-Chi 138
Ruffing-NY 137
Gomez-NY 135

Adjusted Starter Runs
Ruffing-NY 37.1
Lee-Chi 33.0
Grove-Bos 32.5
Gomez-NY 31.0
Rigney-Chi 25.9

Pitcher Wins
Ruffing-NY 4.5
Gomez-NY 3.4
Gomez-NY 3.2
Grove-Bos 3.0
Leonard-Was 2.8

Crushing the Competition

While it was again a Yankees year, fans in Boston and Cleveland had plenty to cheer about. Both teams hung in with New York through late July, but couldn't compete with the Yankees' 48-13 record from July 1 through August 30. With the great all-around play of Joe DiMaggio, catcher Bill Dickey contributing another fine year at bat, and rookie Joe Gordon at second base, the Yankees were able to withstand the sudden decline of Lou Gehrig. Joe McCarthy began using Johnny Murphy in tough relief situations, which made the aging starting staff look even better.

Boston got great seasons from Jimmie Foxx and Joe Cronin, but a punchless outfield and thin pitching doomed the club. Cleveland's Bob Feller, a 19-year-old fireballer with a great fastball and a large ego, led the league in both walks and strikeouts. The Indians also gave 20-year-old infielder Lou Boudreau his first taste of the big leagues. St. Louis had one spectacular pitcher—30-year-old Bobo Newsom, who was 20-16 for the 55-97 Browns and led the league in starts and complete games. Two former star outfielders, Goose Goslin and Mule Haas, saw their careers grind to a halt with the clubs of their youth, Washington and Philadelphia, respectively.

While hitters set yet another new home run record, stolen bases continued to plummet; just two players swiped more than 20 sacks. However, the Yankees cornered the market in this field, as well, leading the loop in stolen bases as well as runs, home runs, and bases on balls.

When the New York met up with the Cubs in the World Series, nobody gave Chicago a chance. They were right. The Bombers' sweep was still impressive—the Yankees outscored the Cubs, 22-9, and put together late-inning rallies to break open close contests in Games 2 and 4.

1937 National League

TEAM	W	L	T	PCT	GB	HW	HL	R	OR	PA	H	2B	3B	HR	BB	SO	HB	SH	AVG	OBP	SLG	OPS	AOPS	BR	ABR	PF	SB	CS	BSA	BSR
NY	95	57	0	.625		50	25	732	602	5862	1484	251	41	111	412	492	31	90	.278	.334	.403	737	105	41	32	101	45			
CHI	93	61	0	.604	3	46	32	811	682	6028	1537	253	74	96	538	496	22	119	.287	.355	.416	771	111	118	85	104	71			
PIT	86	68	0	.558	10	46	32	704	647	5996	1550	223	86	47	463	480	11	89	.285	.343	.384	727	104	27	27	100	32			
STL	81	73	3	.526	15	45	33	789	733	5966	1543	264	67	94	385	569	16	89	.282	.331	.406	737	104	35	21	102	78			
BOS	79	73	0	.520	16	43	33	579	556	5740	1265	200	41	63	485	707	18	113	.247	.314	.339	653	91	-110	-54	91	45			
BRO	62	91	2	.405	33.5	36	39	616	772	5893	1401	258	53	37	469	583	20	109	.265	.327	.354	681	90	-55	-65	102	69			
PHI	61	92	2	.399	34.5	29	45	724	869	5993	1482	258	37	103	478	640	16	75	.273	.334	.391	725	95	24	-31	108	66			
CIN	56	98	1	.364	40	28	51	612	706	5763	1329	215	59	73	437	586	24	72	.254	.315	.360	675	94	-80	-49	95	53			
TOT	617					323	290	5567		47241	11591	1922	458	624	3667	4553	158	756	.272	.332	.382	714					459			

TEAM	CG	SHO	GR	SV	IP	H	HR	BB	SO	BR/9	ERA	AERA	OAV	OOB	PR	APR	PF	OSB	OCS	FA	E	WPB	DP	FW	PW	BW	BSW	DIF
NY	67	11	142	17	1361.0	1341	86	404	653	11.7	3.43	113	.258	.314	73	70	99	36	55	.974	159	35	143	.9	6.9	3.2		8.0
CHI	73	11	148	13	1381.1	1434	91	502	596	12.8	3.97	100	.267	.332	-10	0	102	47	50	.975	151	44	141	1.5	.0	8.4		6.1
PIT	67	12	149	17	1366.1	1398	71	428	643	12.2	3.56	108	.264	.321	53	46	99	47	50	.970	181	29	135	-.2	4.6	2.7		1.9
STL	81	10	141	4	1392.0	1546	95	448	571	13.0	3.98	100	.281	.337	-10	-1	102	62	51	.973	164	43	127	1.0	-.0	2.1		1.1
BOS	85	16	103	10	1359.1	1344	60	372	387	11.4	3.22	100	.259	.310	105	60	92	30	52	.975	157	14	128	1.0	6.0	-5.4		1.4
BRO	63	5	160	8	1362.2	1470	68	476	592	13.0	4.13	98	.274	.336	-33	-14	103	65	51	.964	217	42	127	-2.2	-1.4	-6.4		-4.5
PHI	59	6	178	15	1373.2	1629	115	501	529	14.2	5.05	86	.297	.359	-174	-103	111	42	41	.970	184	27	157	-.3	-10.2	-3.1		-1.9
CIN	64	10	162	18	1358.1	1428	38	533	581	13.1	3.94	95	.270	.339	-4	-33	95	78	48	.966	208	47	139	-1.6	-3.3	-4.9		-11.2
TOT	559	81	1183	102	10954.2					12.7	3.91		.272	.332						.971	1421	281	1097					

Batter-Fielder Wins		Batting Average		On-Base Percentage		Slugging Average		On-Base Plus Slugging		Adjusted OPS		Adjusted Batter Runs	
Bartell-NY	6.1	Medwick-StL	374	Camilli-Phi	446	Medwick-StL	641	Medwick-StL	1056	Medwick-StL	179	Medwick-StL	67.6
Medwick-StL	6.0	Mize-StL	364	Mize-StL	427	Mize-StL	595	Camilli-Phi	1034	Mize-StL	171	Mize-StL	56.2
Herman-Chi	4.9	Hartnett-Chi	354	Medwick-StL	414	Camilli-Phi	587	Mize-StL	1021	Camilli-Phi	165	Camilli-Phi	46.7
Camilli-Phi	3.8	P.Waner-Pit	354	P.Waner-Pit	413	Hartnett-Chi	548	Ott-NY	931	Ott-NY	149	Ott-NY	41.4
Ott-NY	3.5	Whitney-Phi	341	Ott-NY	408	Ott-NY	523	Herman-Chi	875	P.Waner-Pit	132	P.Waner-Pit	30.1

Runs		Hits		Doubles		Triples		Home Runs		Total Bases		Runs Batted In	
Medwick-StL	111	Medwick-StL	237	Medwick-StL	56	Vaughan-Pit	17	Ott-NY	31	Medwick-StL	406	Medwick-StL	154
Herman-Chi	106	P.Waner-Pit	219	Mize-StL	40	Suhr-Pit	14	Medwick-StL	31	Mize-StL	333	Demaree-Chi	115
Hack-Chi	106	Mize-StL	204	Bartell-NY	38	Handley-Pit	12	Camilli-Phi	27	Demaree-Chi	298	Mize-StL	113
Galan-Chi	104	Demaree-Chi	199	Phelps-Bro	37	Goodman-Cin	12	Mize-StL	25	Ott-NY	285	Suhr-Pit	97
Demaree-Chi	104	Herman-Chi	189	Moore-NY	37	Herman-Chi	11	Galan-Chi	18	Camilli-Phi	279	Ott-NY	95

Stolen Bases		Base Stealing Runs		Fielding Runs-Infield		Fielding Runs-Outfield		Wins		Winning Pct.		Complete Games	
Galan-Chi	23			Bartell-NY	35.5	Moore-Bos	11.2	Hubbell-NY	22	Hubbell-NY	733	Turner-Bos	24
Hack-Chi	16			Whitehead-NY	28.4	T.Moore-StL	7.7	Turner-Bos	20	Melton-NY	690	Fette-Bos	23
				Riggs-Cin	18.1	DiMaggio-Bos	7.5	Melton-NY	20	Fette-Bos	667	Weiland-StL	21
				Herman-Chi	15.4	Arnovich-Phi	6.8	Fette-Bos	20	Carleton-Chi	667		
				Young-Pit	13.0	Galan-Chi	5.4	Warneke-StL	18	Turner-Bos	645		

Strikeouts		Fewest BB/Game		Games		Saves		Base Runners/9		Adjusted Relief Runs		Relief Ranking	
Hubbell-NY	159	D.Dean-StL	1.51	Mulcahy-Phi	56	Melton-NY	7	Turner-Bos	9.82	Coffman-NY	5.6	Coffman-NY	7.4
Grissom-Cin	149	Root-Chi	1.61	Jorgens-Phi	52	Brown-Phi	7	Melton-NY	10.05				
Blanton-Pit	143	Hoyt-Pit-Bro	1.66			Grissom-Cin	6	Castleman-NY	10.16				
Melton-NY	142	Turner-Bos	1.82			Root-Chi	5	Root-Chi	10.53				
		Castleman-NY	1.85			Hollingsworth-Cin	5	Tobin-Pit	10.66				

Innings Pitched		Opponents' Avg.		Opponents' OBP		Earned Run Average		Adjusted ERA		Adjusted Starter Runs		Pitcher Wins	
Passeau-Phi	292.1	Mungo-Bro	229	Turner-Bos	274	Turner-Bos	2.38	Turner-Bos	150	Turner-Bos	36.2	Turner-Bos	4.8
Lee-Chi	272.1	Grissom-Cin	232	Melton-NY	280	Melton-NY	2.61	Melton-NY	149	Melton-NY	32.5	Melton-NY	3.4
Weiland-StL	264.1	Melton-NY	233	Castleman-NY	287	D.Dean-StL	2.69	D.Dean-StL	148	D.Dean-StL	25.4	D.Dean-StL	2.8
Hubbell-NY	261.2	Turner-Bos	235	Root-Chi	290	Bauers-Pit	2.88	Mungo-Bro	139	Fette-Bos	22.9	Fette-Bos	2.8
Fette-Bos	259.0	Carleton-Chi	236	D.Dean-StL	291	Fette-Bos	2.88	Bauers-Pit	134	Bauers-Pit	21.5	Mungo-Bro	2.8

Cardinals Sing Bye-Bye as Giants Tread

As the rest of the league floundered, the Cubs and Giants emerged in July. Chicago was up by 6½ as late as August 13, but the Cubs fell apart for the second straight year as the Giants shot to the top. New York won 37 of its final 51. Carl Hubbell was spectacular again, and unheralded Cliff Melton—who won 20 and saved 7—was even better, giving the Giants a devastating 1-2 lefty combo. Mel Ott led the league in homers and walks, while Chicago lacked anyone up to the level of New York's stars.

The already popular All-Star Game claimed its first serious casualty. Earl Averill's liner broke Dizzy Dean's big toe, causing the popular Cardinals hurler to alter his delivery, which in turn ruined his arm. With Dean's effectiveness curtailed, the Cardinals fell to fourth despite Joe Medwick's Triple Crown. Dean's injury marked the end of the first great St. Louis era. Five classic Cardinals ended their careers in 1937: Jim Bottomley, Frankie Frisch, Chick Hafey, Jesse Haines, and Rogers Hornsby. In addition, Pittsburgh's Pie Traynor, considered the league's finest third baseman until the 1960s, retired.

The Boston Braves, who had improved 41 games in two years, ended fifth as two 30-year old rookies, Lou Fette and Jim Turner, won 20 each (Turner also led the league in ERA). The Reds finished in the cellar for the last time until 1982. Strikeouts per game rose to 3.69, the highest level between 1916 and 1948. Oddly enough, league leader Hubbell whiffed just 159—the 1936 leader, Van Mungo, struck out 238—and Boston rookie Vince DiMaggio was the sole player to fan more than 100 times.

Once again, however, the Giants did nothing with the Yankees in the World Series, falling in five games, only one of which was close. The Giants did not hit a home run until the final game of the Series when Ott hit a two-run homer.

1937 American League

TEAM	W	L	T	PCT	GB	HW	HL	R	OR	PA	H	2B	3B	HR	BB	SO	HB	SH	AVG	OBP	SLG	OPS	AOPS	BR	ABR	PF	SB	CS	BSA	BSR
NY	102	52	3	.662		57	20	979	671	6291	1554	282	73	174	709	607	34	61	.283	.369	.456	825	113	113	107	101	60	36	63	1
DET	89	65	1	.578	13	49	28	935	841	6264	1611	309	62	150	656	711	22	70	.292	.370	.452	822	111	109	89	102	89	45	66	4
CHI	86	68	0	.558	16	47	30	780	730	5956	1478	280	76	67	549	447	19	111	.280	.350	.400	750	95	-39	-38	100	70	34	67	4
CLE	83	71	2	.539	19	50	28	817	768	6040	1499	304	76	103	570	551	21	96	.280	.352	.423	775	100	5	0	101	78	51	60	-1
BOS	80	72	2	.526	21	44	29	821	775	6084	1506	269	64	100	601	557	26	103	.281	.357	.411	768	96	-1	-31	104	79	61	56	-4
WAS	73	80	5	.477	28.5	43	35	757	841	6259	1559	245	84	47	591	503	23	67	.279	.351	.379	730	94	-79	-44	96	61	35	64	1
PHI	54	97	3	.358	46.5	27	50	699	854	5886	1398	278	60	94	583	557	5	70	.267	.341	.397	738	93	-64	-52	98	95	48	66	4
STL	46	108	2	.299	56	25	51	715	1023	6123	1573	327	44	71	514	510	14	85	.285	.348	.399	747	93	-45	-50	101	30	27	53	-3
TOT	622					342	271	6503		48903	12178	2294	539	806	4773	4443	164	663	.281	.355	.415	770					562	337	63	6

TEAM	CG	SHO	GR	SV	IP	H	HR	BB	SO	BR/9	ERA	AERA	OAV	OOB	PR	APR	PF	OSB	OCS	FA	E	WPB	DP	FW	PW	BW	BSW	DIF
NY	82	15	100	21	1396.0	1417	92	506	652	12.5	3.65	122	.261	.325	151	128	96	52	39	.972	170	23	134	.2	11.7	9.8	.0	3.2
DET	70	6	132	11	1378.0	1521	102	635	485	14.2	4.87	96	.279	.357	-38	-30	101	75	35	.976	147	43	149	1.4	-2.8	8.2	.3	4.9
CHI	70	15	108	21	1351.1	1435	115	532	533	13.2	4.17	110	.273	.341	68	65	100	59	43	.971	174	34	173	-.2	6.0	-3.5	.3	6.5
CLE	64	4	160	15	1364.2	1529	61	566	630	14.0	4.39	105	.285	.356	35	33	100	81	54	.974	159	26	153	.8	3.0	.0	-.2	2.4
BOS	74	6	132	14	1366.0	1518	92	597	682	14.0	4.48	106	.279	.352	21	39	103	62	32	.972	177	31	139	-.4	3.6	-2.8	-.4	4.1
WAS	75	5	122	14	1398.2	1498	96	671	524	14.1	4.58	97	.275	.357	7	-24	96	74	51	.972	170	36	181	.3	-2.2	-4.0	.0	2.5
PHI	65	6	143	9	1335.0	1490	105	613	469	14.3	4.85	97	.281	.358	-35	-20	102	75	38	.967	198	55	150	-1.7	-1.8	-4.8	.3	-13.5
STL	55	2	157	8	1363.0	1768	143	653	468	16.2	6.00	80	.315	.390	-209	-170	105	84	45	.972	173	42	166	-.0	-15.6	-4.6	-.3	-10.4
TOT	555	59	1054	113	10952.2					14.1	4.62		.281	.355						.972	1368	290	1245					

Batter-Fielder Wins		Batting Average		On-Base Percentage		Slugging Average		On-Base Plus Slugging		Adjusted OPS		Adjusted Batter Runs	
Clift-StL	7.4	Gehringer-Det	.371	Gehrig-NY	.473	DiMaggio-NY	.673	Gehrig-NY	1116	Gehrig-NY	177	Gehrig-NY	74.1
DiMaggio-NY	5.7	Gehrig-NY	.351	Gehringer-Det	.458	Greenberg-Det	.668	Greenberg-Det	1105	Greenberg-Det	171	Greenberg-Det	65.3
Dickey-NY	5.6	DiMaggio-NY	.346	Greenberg-Det	.436	York-Det	.651	DiMaggio-NY	1085	DiMaggio-NY	168	DiMaggio-NY	60.1
Greenberg-Det	5.1	Bonura-Chi	.345	Johnson-Phi	.425	Gehrig-NY	.643	Dickey-NY	.987	Johnson-Phi	147	Gehringer-Det	43.0
Gehrig-NY	4.8	Travis-Was	.344	Dickey-NY	.417	Bonura-Chi	.573	Bonura-Chi	.984	Bonura-Chi	146	Johnson-Phi	38.2

Runs		Hits		Doubles		Triples		Home Runs		Total Bases		Runs Batted In	
DiMaggio-NY	151	Bell-StL	218	Bell-StL	51	Walker-Chi	16	DiMaggio-NY	46	DiMaggio-NY	418	Greenberg-Det	183
Rolfe-NY	143	DiMaggio-NY	215	Greenberg-Det	49	Kreevich-Chi	16	Greenberg-Det	40	Greenberg-Det	397	DiMaggio-NY	167
Gehrig-NY	138	Walker-Det	213	Moses-Phi	48	Stone-Was	15	Gehrig-NY	37	Gehrig-NY	366	Gehrig-NY	159
Greenberg-Det	137	Lewis-Was	210	Vosmik-StL	47	DiMaggio-NY	15	Foxx-Bos	36	Moses-Phi	357	Dickey-NY	133
Gehringer-Det	133	Gehringer-Det	209	Lary-Cle	46	Greenberg-Det	14	York-Det	35	Trosky-Cle	329	Trosky-Cle	128

Stolen Bases		Base Stealing Runs		Fielding Runs-Infield		Fielding Runs-Outfield		Wins		Winning Pct.		Complete Games	
Chapman-Was-Bos	35	Chapman-Was-Bos	3.5	Clift-StL	41.3	Johnson-Phi	9.6	Gomez-NY	21	Allen-Cle	.938	W.Ferrell-Bos-Was	26
Werber-Phi	35	Werber-Phi	3.2	Hayes-Chi	23.4	West-StL	9.2	Ruffing-NY	20	Stratton-Chi	.750	Gomez-NY	25
Walker-Det	23	Walker-Det	2.6	Hale-Cle	22.4	Almada-Bos-Was	7.5	Lawson-Det	18	Ruffing-NY	.741	Ruffing-NY	22
		Hill-Was-Phi	2.6	Appling-Chi	16.7	Stone-Was	7.2	Grove-Bos	17	Lawson-Det	.720	Grove-Bos	21
		Kreevich-Chi	1.9	Foxx-Bos	11.4	Vosmik-StL	7.0	Auker-Det	17	Gomez-NY	.656	DeShong-Was	20

Strikeouts		Fewest BB/Game		Games		Saves		Base Runners/9		Adjusted Relief Runs		Relief Ranking	
Gomez-NY	194	Stratton-Chi	2.02	Brown-Chi	53	Brown-Chi	18	Stratton-Chi	9.89	Brown-Chi	12.0	Brown-Chi	20.0
Newsom-Was-Bos	166	Hudlin-Cle	2.20	Wilson-Bos	51	Murphy-NY	10	Gomez-NY	10.57	Fink-Phi	5.7	Murphy-NY	6.6
Grove-Bos	153	Marcum-Bos	2.30	Newsom-Was-Bos	41	Wilson-Bos	7	Ruffing-NY	10.92	Cohen-Was	5.1	Cohen-Was	5.8
Feller-Cle	150	Ruffing-NY	2.39	Kelley-Phi	41	Malone-NY	6	Chandler-NY	10.93	Murphy-NY	4.1	Fink-Phi	2.8
Bridges-Det	138	Lyons-Chi	2.39	Heving-Cle	40			Allen-Cle	11.55	Wyatt-Cle	2.9	Wyatt-Cle	1.8

Innings Pitched		Opponents' Avg.		Opponents' OBP		Earned Run Average		Adjusted ERA		Adjusted Starter Runs		Pitcher Wins	
W.Ferrell-Bos-Was	281.0	Gomez-NY	.223	Stratton-Chi	.280	Gomez-NY	2.33	Stratton-Chi	191	Gomez-NY	66.9	Gomez-NY	6.8
Gomez-NY	278.1	Stratton-Chi	.234	Gomez-NY	.287	Stratton-Chi	2.40	Gomez-NY	191	Grove-Bos	48.5	Stratton-Chi	4.3
Newsom-Was-Bos	275.1	Smith-Phi	.242	Ruffing-NY	.296	Allen-Cle	2.55	Allen-Cle	181	Ruffing-NY	43.2	Ruffing-NY	4.0
DeShong-Was	264.1	Allen-Cle	.244	Lee-Chi	.312	Ruffing-NY	2.98	Grove-Bos	157	Allen-Cle	40.3	Grove-Bos	3.9
Grove-Bos	262.0	Ruffing-NY	.247	Allen-Cle	.313	Grove-Bos	3.02	Ruffing-NY	149	Stratton-Chi	38.8	Allen-Cle	2.7

Goofy, Joe D., and Another Title

New York broke from the pack in June and coasted to another easy pennant. Despite excellent defense and the bats of Charlie Gehringer and Hank Greenberg, Detroit didn't have the firepower to contend with the Yankees. New York had the three top run scorers, three of the top four RBI men, and the league's best pitchers in Lefty Gomez and Red Ruffing. The multi-dimensional Joe DiMaggio had become the league's gem, and Lou Gehrig enjoyed his last great season. The Yankees also added two rookies, pitcher Spud Chandler and outfielder Tommy Henrich.

Attendance rose in every AL city but Boston; ironically, the Red Sox had their best year since 1918. Finishing 80-72, they added their first real homegrown star, second baseman Bobby Doerr. Detroit once again drew a million fans, and the league's overall turnstile clicks were the most in over a decade.

While overall runs fell by 500, AL hitters established another new record for homers. Hitters were both walking and striking out more than ever as the uppercut swing became better established. Cleveland's Johnny Allen set an all-time single-season record for winning percentage at .938, while the last-place Browns had a staff ERA over 6.00 for the second straight year. They'd once again reach that low in 1939.

The White Sox enlarged Comiskey Park, which significantly cut scoring, but Detroit shrunk its left field, which increased run production. Yankee Stadium's formerly cavernous center field was cut from 26 feet to a still huge 461 feet, and scoring there *increased* slightly.

The Yankees again wiped the floor with the Giants in the World Series. After three easy wins by the Yankees, the Giants staved off elimination in Game 4 behind Carl Hubbell, 7-2. Goofy Gomez shut down the Giants in Game 5 and also drove in the winning run.

1936 National League

TEAM	W	L	T	PCT	GB	HW	HL	R	OR	PA	H	2B	3B	HR	BB	SO	HB	SH	AVG	OBP	SLG	OPS	AOPS	BR	ABR	PF	SB	CS	BSA	BSR
NY	92	62	0	.597		52	26	742	621	6038	1529	237	48	97	431	452	35	123	.281	.337	.395	732	104	18	26	99	31			
STL	87	67	1	.565	5	43	33	795	794	6065	1554	332	60	88	442	577	15	71	.281	.336	.410	746	106	44	47	100	69			
CHI	87	67	0	.565	5	50	27	755	603	6069	1545	275	36	76	491	462	32	137	.286	.349	.392	741	104	48	31	102	68			
PIT	84	70	2	.545	8	46	30	804	718	6211	1596	283	80	60	517	502	26	82	.286	.349	.397	746	105	57	39	102	37			
CIN	74	80	0	.481	18	42	34	722	760	5904	1476	224	73	82	410	534	34	67	.274	.329	.388	717	106	-18	29	94	68			
BOS	71	83	3	.461	21	35	43	631	715	6041	1450	207	45	67	433	582	31	99	.265	.322	.356	678	94	-90	-46	94	23			
BRO	67	87	2	.435	25	37	40	662	752	6068	1518	263	43	33	390	458	25	79	.272	.323	.353	676	87	-93	-99	101	55			
PHI	54	100	0	.351	38	30	48	726	874	6040	1538	250	46	103	451	586	21	103	.281	.339	.401	740	95	32	-37	110	50			
TOT	620					335	281	5837		48436	12206	2071	431	606	3565	4203	219	761	.278	.335	.386	722					401			

TEAM	CG	SHO	GR	SV	IP	H	HR	BB	SO	BR/9	ERA	AERA	OAV	OOB	PR	APR	PF	OSB	OCS	FA	E	WPB	DP	FW	PW	BW	BSW	DIF
NY	60	12	148	22	1385.2	1458	75	401	500	12.2	3.46	113	.273	.327	86	69	97	40	48	.974	168	34	164	1.1	6.7	2.5		4.6
STL	65	5	166	24	1398.0	1610	89	434	559	13.4	4.47	88	.289	.344	-71	-85	98	41	39	.974	156	50	134	1.9	-8.3	4.6		11.9
CHI	77	18	139	10	1382.1	1413	77	434	597	12.2	3.54	113	.265	.324	74	69	99	39	46	.976	146	34	156	2.4	6.7	3.0		-2.1
PIT	67	5	137	12	1395.1	1475	74	379	559	12.1	3.89	104	.269	.319	20	25	101	68	44	.967	199	31	113	-.5	2.4	3.8		1.3
CIN	50	6	161	23	1367.1	1576	51	418	459	13.3	4.22	91	.287	.341	-31	-64	95	48	46	.969	191	46	150	-.2	-6.2	2.8		.6
BOS	61	7	134	13	1413.1	1566	69	451	421	13.0	3.94	97	.281	.337	12	-18	95	38	43	.971	189	26	175	.1	-1.8	-4.5		.1
BRO	59	7	169	18	1403.0	1466	84	528	651	13.0	3.98	104	.266	.333	5	21	103	76	47	.966	208	43	107	-1.0	2.0	-9.7		-1.4
PHI	51	7	169	14	1365.1	1630	87	515	454	14.4	4.64	98	.292	.356	-95	-15	113	51	33	.959	252	33	144	-3.7	-1.5	-3.6		-14.3
TOT	490	67	1223	136	11110.1					12.9	4.02		.278	.335						.969	1509	297	1143					

Batter-Fielder Wins		Batting Average		On-Base Percentage		Slugging Average		On-Base Plus Slugging		Adjusted OPS		Adjusted Batter Runs	
Bartell-NY	5.7	P.Waner-Pit	373	Vaughan-Pit	453	Ott-NY	588	Ott-NY	1036	Ott-NY	179	Ott-NY	65.1
Medwick-StL	5.2	Phelps-Bro	367	Ott-NY	448	Camilli-Phi	577	Camilli-Phi	1018	Medwick-StL	157	P.Waner-Pit	50.7
Herman-Chi	5.2	Medwick-StL	351	P.Waner-Pit	446	Mize-StL	577	P.Waner-Pit	965	Camilli-Phi	156	Medwick-StL	49.1
Ott-NY	4.8	Demaree-Chi	350	Camilli-Phi	441	Medwick-StL	577	Medwick-StL	964	P.Waner-Pit	156	Camilli-Phi	46.7
P.Waner-Pit	4.7	Vaughan-Pit	335	Suhr-Pit	410	P.Waner-Pit	520	Vaughan-Pit	927	Vaughan-Pit	146	Vaughan-Pit	45.7

Runs		Hits		Doubles		Triples		Home Runs		Total Bases		Runs Batted In	
Vaughan-Pit	122	Medwick-StL	223	Medwick-StL	64	Goodman-Cin	14	Ott-NY	33	Medwick-StL	367	Medwick-StL	138
P.Martin-StL	121	P.Waner-Pit	218	Herman-Chi	57	Medwick-StL	13	Camilli-Phi	28	Ott-NY	314	Ott-NY	135
Ott-NY	120	Demaree-Chi	212	P.Waner-Pit	53	Camilli-Phi	13	Klein-Chi-Phi	25	Klein-Chi-Phi	308	Suhr-Pit	118
Medwick-StL	115	Herman-Chi	211	Moore-StL	39			Berger-Bos	25	Camilli-Phi	306	Klein-Chi-Phi	104
Suhr-Pit	111	Moore-NY	205	Moore-Bos	38			Mize-StL	19	P.Waner-Pit	304		

Stolen Bases		Base Stealing Runs		Fielding Runs-Infield		Fielding Runs-Outfield		Wins		Winning Pct.		Complete Games	
P.Martin-StL	23			Bartell-NY	42.6	Medwick-StL	14.0	Hubbell-NY	26	Hubbell-NY	813	D.Dean-StL	28
S.Martin-StL	17			Whitehead-NY	32.1	Moore-Bos	13.1	D.Dean-StL	24	Lucas-Pit	789	Hubbell-NY	25
Hack-Chi	17			Kampouris-Cin	22.4	Moore-StL	13.0	Derringer-Cin	19	French-Chi	667	Mungo-Bro	22
Chiozza-Phi	17			Cuccinello-Bos	17.6	Cooney-Bro	8.5			D.Dean-StL	649	MacFayden-Bos	21
				Herman-Chi	17.0	Moore-NY	8.3			Lee-Chi	621	Lee-Chi	20

Strikeouts		Fewest BB/Game		Games		Saves		Base Runners/9		Adjusted Relief Runs		Relief Ranking	
Mungo-Bro	238	Lucas-Pit	1.33	Derringer-Cin	51	D.Dean-StL	11	Hubbell-NY	9.68	Johnson-Phi	4.6	Johnson-Phi	5.1
D.Dean-StL	195	Derringer-Cin	1.34	D.Dean-StL	51	Brennan-Cin	9	D.Dean-StL	10.46	Bryant-Chi	3.6	Bryant-Chi	1.8
Blanton-Pit	127	D.Dean-StL	1.51	Passeau-Phi	49	Smith-Bos	8	Lucas-Pit	10.61	Root-Chi	3	Root-Chi	3
Hubbell-NY	123	Hubbell-NY	1.69	Brown-Pit	47	Johnson-Phi	7	Hoyt-Pit	10.65				
Derringer-Cin	121	Gabler-NY	1.89			Coffman-NY	7	Blanton-Pit	11.19				

Innings Pitched		Opponents' Avg.		Opponents' OBP		Earned Run Average		Adjusted ERA		Adjusted Starter Runs		Pitcher Wins	
D.Dean-StL	315.0	Mungo-Bro	234	Hubbell-NY	276	Hubbell-NY	2.31	Hubbell-NY	169	Hubbell-NY	59.6	Hubbell-NY	6.2
Mungo-Bro	311.2	Hubbell-NY	236	D.Dean-StL	285	MacFayden-Bos	2.87	MacFayden-Bos	134	MacFayden-Bos	30.4	D.Dean-StL	3.0
Hubbell-NY	304.0	Lee-Chi	246	Lucas-Pit	287	Gabler-NY	3.12	Passeau-Phi	130	Mungo-Bro	27.6	MacFayden-Bos	2.8
Derringer-Cin	282.1	D.Dean-StL	253	Blanton-Pit	301	D.Dean-StL	3.17	Lucas-Pit	128	D.Dean-StL	26.9	Mungo-Bro	2.7
MacFayden-Bos	266.2	Blanton-Pit	257	Mungo-Bro	305	Lucas-Pit	3.18	Gabler-NY	125	Lee-Chi	19.3	Passeau-Phi	2.4

King Carl Reigns

After two years of late-season collapses, it was the Giants' turn to make a big run down the stretch. Tied for fourth place with a .500 record in mid-July, the Giants went on a 34-5 tear, moving from 10½ down to 3 up by the end of August. New York held on for dear life in September to claim the pennant.

The Giants rode to the flag on the left arm of King Carl Hubbell, who won his last 15 decisions, paced the league in ERA by more than half a run, and garnered league MVP honors. Seven Giants pitchers made 10 or more starts as manager Bill Terry searched for rotation depth. Shortstop Dick Bartell had a big year in the field and at bat, while Mel Ott led the league in homers for third of his six times. Three Giants of classic vintage—Travis Jackson, Freddie Lindstrom, and Terry—played in their last big league games.

While the second-place Cubs had excellent and very deep starting pitching, their attack was poor. Charlie Grimm ended his 20-year playing career as a player, but Jolly Cholly, the 1935 pennant still under his belt, remained as manager in his first of three stints at the helm of the Cubbies. Joe Medwick of the third-place Cardinals led the league in hits, RBIs, and doubles (64, a league record). St. Louis also benefited from the efforts of rookie first baseman Johnny Mize, who hit .329 with 19 homers.

While the Pirates had two great offensive players in Paul Waner, who won his third batting title, and shortstop Arky Vaughan, who paced the NL in on-base percentage for the third straight season. Mediocre pitching doomed the Bucs to fourth.

In the World Series, the thin Giants staff was battered around by the Yankees, who won in six games. Only Hubbell, 1-1 with a 2.25 ERA, escaped relatively unscathed.

1936 American League

TEAM	W	L	T	PCT	GB	HW	HL	R	OR	PA	H	2B	3B	HR	BB	SO	HB	SH	AVG	OBP	SLG	OPS	AOPS	BR	ABR	PF	SB	CS	BSA	BSR
NY	102	51	2	.667		56	21	1065	731	6391	1676	315	83	182	700	594	33	67	.300	.381	.483	864	124	164	203	97	77	40	66	3
DET	83	71	0	.539	19.5	44	33	921	871	6226	1638	326	55	94	640	462	34	88	.300	.377	.431	808	106	61	58	104	73	66	69	-1
CHI	81	70	2	.536	20	43	32	920	873	6283	1597	282	56	60	684	417	26	107	.292	.374	.397	771	94	-8	-39	104	66	29	69	4
WAS	82	71	0	.536	20	42	35	889	799	6094	1601	293	84	62	576	398	24	61	.295	.365	.414	779	105	-9	42	94	104	42	71	8
CLE	80	74	3	.519	22.5	49	30	921	862	6253	1715	357	82	123	514	470	16	77	.304	.364	.461	825	109	71	63	101	66	53	55	-4
BOS	74	80	1	.481	28.5	47	29	775	764	6098	1485	288	62	86	584	465	23	108	.276	.349	.400	749	86	-73	-116	106	55	44	56	-3
STL	57	95	3	.375	44.5	31	43	804	1064	6107	1502	299	66	79	625	627	19	72	.279	.356	.403	759	91	-51	-73	103	62	20	76	7
PHI	53	100	1	.346	49	31	46	714	1045	5990	1443	240	60	72	524	590	19	74	.269	.336	.376	712	84	-156	-142	98	59	43	58	-2
TOT	618					343	269	7009		49442	12657	2400	548	758	4847	4023	194	654	.289	.363	.421	784				562	320	64	12

TEAM	CG	SHO	GR	SV	IP	H	HR	BB	SO	BR/9	ERA	AERA	OAV	OOB	PR	APR	PF	OSB	OCS	FA	E	WPB	DP	FW	PW	BW	BSW	DIF
NY	77	6	119	21	1400.1	1474	84	663	624	13.8	4.17	112	.271	.351	135	81	92	47	43	.973	163	41	148	.8	7.2	17.9	.1	-.5
DET	76	13	127	13	1360.0	1568	100	562	526	14.2	5.00	99	.289	.358	6	-7	98	58	30	.975	153	49	159	1.3	-.6	5.1	-.2	.4
CHI	80	5	104	8	1365.0	1603	104	578	414	14.5	5.06	103	.293	.363	-4	20	103	58	46	.973	168	43	174	.4	1.8	-3.4	.2	6.6
WAS	78	8	112	14	1345.2	1484	73	588	462	14.0	4.58	104	.279	.353	68	31	95	73	47	.970	182	47	163	-.4	2.7	3.7	.6	-1.1
CLE	74	6	155	12	1389.1	1604	73	607	619	14.5	4.83	104	.289	.362	32	32	100	75	46	.971	178	59	154	.0	2.8	5.6	-.5	-5.0
BOS	78	11	143	9	1372.1	1501	78	552	584	13.6	4.39	121	.277	.346	99	134	106	81	44	.972	165	37	139	.7	11.8	-10.2	-.4	-4.9
STL	54	3	193	13	1348.1	1776	115	609	399	16.2	6.24	86	.314	.385	-180	-122	107	69	25	.969	188	53	143	-.6	-10.8	-6.4	.5	-1.6
PHI	68	3	130	12	1352.1	1645	131	696	405	15.7	6.08	84	.300	.381	-156	-144	101	101	39	.965	209	91	152	-1.9	-12.7	-12.5	-.3	3.9
TOT	585	55	1083	102	10933.1					14.6	5.04		.289	.363						.971	1406	420	1232					

Batter-Fielder Wins		Batting Average		On-Base Percentage		Slugging Average		On-Base Plus Slugging		Adjusted OPS		Adjusted Batter Runs	
Gehrig-NY	6.6	Appling-Chi	.388	Gehrig-NY	.478	Gehrig-NY	.696	Gehrig-NY	1174	Gehrig-NY	193	Gehrig-NY	90.9
Gehringer-Det	6.1	Averill-Cle	.378	Appling-Chi	.474	Trosky-Cle	.644	Foxx-Bos	1071	Averill-Cle	159	Averill-Cle	55.2
Appling-Chi	5.4	Dickey-NY	.362	Foxx-Bos	.440	Foxx-Bos	.631	Averill-Cle	1065	Foxx-Bos	153	Foxx-Bos	49.2
Dickey-NY	4.2	Gehringer-Det	.354	Averill-Cle	.438	Averill-Cle	.627	Trosky-Cle	1026	Trosky-Cle	148	Gehringer-Det	44.4
Averill-Cle	3.8	Gehrig-NY	.354	Gehringer-Det	.431	Dickey-NY	.617	Gehringer-Det	.987	Stone-Was	145	Trosky-Cle	40.9

Runs		Hits		Doubles		Triples		Home Runs		Total Bases		Runs Batted In	
Gehrig-NY	167	Averill-Cle	232	Gehringer-Det	60	Rolfe-NY	15	Gehrig-NY	49	Trosky-Cle	405	Trosky-Cle	162
Clift-StL	145	Gehringer-Det	227	Walker-Det	55	DiMaggio-NY	15	Trosky-Cle	42	Gehrig-NY	403	Gehrig-NY	152
Gehringer-Det	144	Trosky-Cle	216	Chapman-NY-Was	50	Averill-Cle	15	Foxx-Bos	41	Averill-Cle	385	Foxx-Bos	143
Crosetti-NY	137	Bell-StL	212	Hale-Cle	50	B.Johnson-Phi	14	DiMaggio-NY	29	Foxx-Bos	369	Bonura-Chi	138
Averill-Cle	136	Radcliff-Chi	207					Averill-Cle	28	DiMaggio-NY	367	Solters-StL	134

Stolen Bases		Base Stealing Runs		Fielding Runs-Infield		Fielding Runs-Outfield		Wins		Winning Pct.		Complete Games	
Lary-StL	37	Lary-StL	5.0	Hale-Cle	16.7	Solters-StL	12.5	Bridges-Det	23	Pearson-NY	.731	W.Ferrell-Bos	28
Powell-Was-NY	26	Hill-Was	2.4	Gehringer-Det	15.6	Cramer-Bos	11.4	Kennedy-Chi	21	Kennedy-Chi	.700	Bridges-Det	26
Werber-Bos	23	Powell-Was-NY	1.9	Appling-Chi	14.8	DiMaggio-NY	8.1	W.Ferrell-Bos	20	Bridges-Det	.676	Ruffing-NY	25
Chapman-NY-Was	20	Stone-Was	1.8	Hayes-Chi	13.4	West-StL	6.4	Allen-Cle	20	Allen-Cle	.667	Newsom-Was	24
Hughes-Cle	20	Sewell-Chi	1.7	Bonura-Chi	11.0	Stone-Was	5.8			Rowe-Det	.655	Grove-Bos	22

Strikeouts		Fewest BB/Game		Games		Saves		Base Runners/9		Adjusted Relief Runs		Relief Ranking	
Bridges-Det	175	Lyons-Chi	2.23	VanAtta-StL	52	Malone-NY	9	Grove-Bos	10.87	Brown-Chi	2.9	Brown-Chi	2.9
Allen-Cle	165	Grove-Bos	2.31	Knott-StL	47	Knott-StL	6	Walberg-Bos	12.11	Gumpert-Phi	.5	Gumpert-Phi	2
Newsom-Was	156	Rowe-Det	2.35			Murphy-NY	5	Rowe-Det	12.18				
Grove-Bos	130	Andrews-StL	2.35			Brown-Chi	5	Ruffing-NY	12.19				
Pearson-NY	118	Marcum-Bos	2.69			Hildebrand-Cle	4	Allen-Cle	12.30				

Innings Pitched		Opponents' Avg.		Opponents' OBP		Earned Run Average		Adjusted ERA		Adjusted Starter Runs		Pitcher Wins	
W.Ferrell-Bos	301.0	Pearson-NY	.233	Grove-Bos	.297	Grove-Bos	2.81	Grove-Bos	189	Grove-Bos	67.0	Grove-Bos	6.6
Bridges-Det	294.2	Grove-Bos	.246	Rowe-Det	.321	Allen-Cle	3.44	Allen-Cle	146	Allen-Cle	42.8	W.Ferrell-Bos	4.4
Newsom-Was	285.2	Gomez-NY	.254	Ruffing-NY	.323	Appleton-Was	3.53	Bridges-Det	137	Bridges-Det	42.8	Allen-Cle	4.3
Kennedy-Chi	274.1	Appleton-Was	.254	Appleton-Was	.324	Bridges-Det	3.60	Appleton-Was	135	W.Ferrell-Bos	35.7	Bridges-Det	4.2
Ruffing-NY	271.0	Bridges-Det	.255	Bridges-Det	.326	Pearson-NY	3.71	Kelley-Phi	132	Kelley-Phi	33.6	Ruffing-NY	3.9

The Dominators

The defending world champion Tigers stumbled out of the gate when first baseman Hank Greenberg broke his wrist in April and was lost for the year. The loss a few weeks later of catcher Mickey Cochrane to an emotional breakdown shot the club's chances.

That was enough to clear the way for the Yankees, who led the league in runs by 140 and fewest runs allowed by 33. Seven New Yorkers reached double figures in homers, while six hurlers won in double figures. After a brief challenge from Boston, which had imported stars like Jimmie Foxx and Joe Cronin, New York widened the gap and eventually won by 19½ games. The Red Sox were sixth.

League hitters continued their feast, setting new records for home runs and scoring. The 5.67 runs tallied by the average AL team has never been equaled, much less surpassed. For the first time, no club had an ERA under 4.00, and Lefty Grove—working in the unfriendly atmosphere of Fenway Park—was the only pitcher to record an ERA under 3.44. St. Louis and Philadelphia each posted ERAs over 6.00.

Fans saw the future of baseball as two of the greats in history, Joe DiMaggio and Bob Feller, debuted in 1936. DiMaggio, already famous for his exploits in the Pacific Coast League, hit .323 with 88 extra-base hits, tying for the lead in triples with Yankees teammate Red Rolfe. Feller, just 17, fanned 76 men in just 62 innings with Cleveland. Baseball began to officially celebrate its history in 1936, electing five players to the newly created Hall of Fame in Cooperstown, New York. Three of the five were AL stalwarts: Ty Cobb, Babe Ruth, and Walter Johnson.

The World Series went six games, with the Yankees defeating the Giants. Five of the games were close, but in the late innings, the Bronx Bombers and their unstoppable attack were able to salt things away.

1935 National League

TEAM	W	L	T	PCT	GB	HW	HL	R	OR	PA	H	2B	3B	HR	BB	SO	HB	SH	AVG	OBP	SLG	OPS	AOPS	BR	ABR	PF	SB	CS	BSA	BSR
CHI	100	54	0	.649		56	21	847	597	6133	1581	303	62	88	464	471	33	150	.288	.347	.414	761	110	86	81	101	66			
STL	96	58	0	.623	4	53	24	829	625	5977	1548	286	59	86	404	521	19	97	.284	.335	.405	740	101	35	6	104	71			
NY	91	62	3	.595	8.5	50	27	770	675	6163	1608	248	56	123	392	479	32	116	.286	.336	.416	752	110	53	68	98	32			
PIT	86	67	0	.562	13.5	46	31	743	647	5973	1543	255	90	66	457	437	24	77	.285	.343	.402	745	103	48	24	103	30			
BRO	70	83	1	.458	29.5	38	38	711	767	5937	1496	235	62	59	430	520	27	70	.277	.333	.376	709	99	-23	-7	98	60			
CIN	68	85	1	.444	31.5	41	35	646	772	5798	1403	244	68	73	392	547	30	80	.265	.319	.372	697	96	-53	-32	97	72			
PHI	64	89	3	.418	35.5	35	43	685	871	5944	1466	249	32	92	392	661	26	84	.269	.322	.378	700	85	-47	-109	110	52			
BOS	38	115	0	.248	61.5	25	50	575	852	5761	1396	233	33	75	353	436	19	80	.263	.311	.362	673	93	-99	-47	92	20			
TOT	617					344	269	5806		47686	12041	2053	462	662	3284	4072	210	754	.277	.331	.391	722					403			

TEAM	CG	SHO	GR	SV	IP	H	HR	BB	SO	BR/9	ERA	AERA	OAV	OOB	PR	APR	PF	OSB	OCS	FA	E	WPB	DP	FW	PW	BW	BSW	DIF
CHI	81	12	118	14	1394.1	1417	85	400	589	11.9	3.26	121	.263	.317	118	106	98	45	54	.970	186	45	163	.3	10.3	7.9		4.5
STL	73	10	139	18	1384.2	1445	68	377	602	12.0	3.52	116	.267	.318	76	87	102	43	12	.972	164	34	133	1.6	8.5	.6		8.4
NY	76	10	134	11	1403.2	1433	106	411	524	12.0	3.78	102	.262	.318	37	12	96	46	40	.972	174	46	129	1.1	1.2	6.6		5.6
PIT	76	15	118	11	1365.2	1428	63	312	549	11.6	3.42	120	.265	.307	91	101	102	64	41	.968	190	34	94	.0	9.8	2.3		-2.7
BRO	62	11	145	20	1358.0	1519	88	436	480	13.1	4.22	94	.281	.337	-31	-37	99	42	44	.969	188	49	146	.2	-3.6	-.7		-2.4
CIN	59	9	161	12	1356.0	1490	65	438	500	13.0	4.30	93	.278	.336	-43	-50	99	52	50	.966	204	40	139	-.7	-4.9	-3.1		-.2
PHI	53	8	202	15	1374.2	1652	106	505	475	14.4	4.76	95	.295	.358	-113	-31	113	50	34	.963	228	28	145	-2.0	-3.0	-10.6		3.1
BOS	54	6	136	5	1330.0	1645	81	404	355	14.0	4.93	77	.303	.354	-135	-180	94	61	33	.967	197	21	101	-.4	-17.5	-4.6		-16.0
TOT	534	81	1153	106	10967.0					12.7	4.02		.277	.331						.968	1531	297	1050					

Batter-Fielder Wins
Vaughan-Pit 6.6
Herman-Chi 5.2
Hartnett-Chi 4.7
Berger-Bos 4.4
Ott-NY 4.2

Batting Average
Vaughan-Pit 385
Medwick-StL 353
Hartnett-Chi 344
Lombardi-Cin 343
Herman-Chi 341

On-Base Percentage
Vaughan-Pit 491
Ott-NY 407
Hack-Chi 406
Galan-Chi 399
P.Waner-Pit 392

Slugging Average
Vaughan-Pit 607
Medwick-StL 576
Ott-NY 555
Berger-Bos 548
Hartnett-Chi 545

On-Base Plus Slugging
Vaughan-Pit 1098
Medwick-StL 962
Ott-NY 962
R.Collins-StL 915
Berger-Bos 903

Adjusted OPS
Vaughan-Pit 187
Ott-NY 159
Berger-Bos 151
Medwick-StL 149
Leiber-NY 143

Adjusted Batter Runs
Vaughan-Pit 69.2
Ott-NY 51.1
Medwick-StL 41.6
Berger-Bos 40.3
Leiber-NY 37.4

Runs
Galan-Chi 133
Medwick-StL 132
Martin-StL 121
Ott-NY 113
Herman-Chi 113

Hits
Herman-Chi 227
Medwick-StL 224

Doubles
Herman-Chi 57
Medwick-StL 46
Allen-Phi 46
Martin-StL 41
Galan-Chi 41

Triples
Goodman-Cin 18
L.Waner-Pit 14
Medwick-StL 13

Home Runs
Berger-Bos 34
Ott-NY 31
Camilli-Phi 25
Medwick-StL 23
R.Collins-StL 23

Total Bases
Medwick-StL 365
Ott-NY 329
Berger-Bos 323
Herman-Chi 317
Leiber-NY 314

Runs Batted In
Berger-Bos 130
Medwick-StL 126
R.Collins-StL 122
Ott-NY 114
Leiber-NY 107

Stolen Bases
Galan-Chi 22
Martin-StL 20
Bordagaray-Bro 18
Hack-Chi 14
Goodman-Cin 14

Base Stealing Runs

Fielding Runs-Infield
Jurges-Chi 24.9
Herman-Chi 16.0
Cuccinello-Bro 8.1
Riggs-Cin 8.1
Stripp-Bro 7.1

Fielding Runs-Outfield
Allen-Phi 12.7
Berger-Bos 9.2
T.Moore-StL 6.8
Lee-Bos 6.1
Goodman-Cin 5.1

Wins
Lee-Chi 28
Hubbell-NY 23
Derringer-Cin 22
Warneke-Chi 20
Lee-Chi 20

Winning Pct.
D.Dean-StL 769
Castleman-NY 714
D.Dean-StL 700
Schumacher-NY 679
Hubbell-NY 657

Complete Games
D.Dean-StL 29
Hubbell-NY 24
Blanton-Pit 23
Warneke-Chi 20
Derringer-Cin 20

Strikeouts
D.Dean-StL 190
Hubbell-NY 150
Mungo-Bro 143
P.Dean-StL 143
Blanton-Pit 142

Fewest BB/Game
Clark-Bro 1.22
Hubbell-NY 1.46
Hoyt-Pit 1.48
Derringer-Cin 1.59
Johnson-Phi 1.60

Games
Jorgens-Phi 53
D.Dean-StL 50
Bivin-Phi 47
Smith-Bos 46
P.Dean-StL 46

Saves
Leonard-Bro 8
Johnson-Phi 6
Hoyt-Pit 6

Base Runners/9
Blanton-Pit 9.80
Swift-Pit 10.21
Clark-Bro 10.61
Warneke-Chi 10.66
Schumacher-NY 10.66

Adjusted Relief Runs

Relief Ranking

Innings Pitched
D.Dean-StL 325.1
Hubbell-NY 302.2
Derringer-Cin 276.2
P.Dean-StL 269.2

Opponents' Avg.
Blanton-Pit 229
Schumacher-NY 238
Hollingsworth-Cin 243
Swift-Pit 247
P.Dean-StL 249

Opponents' OBP
Blanton-Pit 272
Swift-Pit 282
Clark-Bro 289
Schumacher-NY 292
P.Dean-StL 292

Earned Run Average
Blanton-Pit 2.58
Swift-Pit 2.70
Schumacher-NY 2.89
French-Chi 2.96
Lee-Chi 2.96

Adjusted ERA
Blanton-Pit 159
Swift-Pit 152
D.Dean-StL 135
Schumacher-NY 133
French-Chi 133

Adjusted Starter Runs
Blanton-Pit 41.3
D.Dean-StL 37.8
Swift-Pit 31.2
French-Chi 27.9
Schumacher-NY 27.5

Pitcher Wins
D.Dean-StL 4.5
Blanton-Pit 4.4
Swift-Pit 3.3
Warneke-Chi 3.3
Schumacher-NY 3.2

And There Was Light

Once again, the Giants started fast but flattened; by August, the dangerous Cardinals took over the league lead. But the Cubs had a surprise in store. In third place on Labor Day, Chicago captured 21 straight and won the pennant by besting Dizzy and Paul Dean in St. Louis September 25-26. Lon Warneke and Bill Lee won 20 apiece for Chicago, which led the league in both runs and ERA.

Other than Joe Medwick and Ripper Collins, St. Louis lacked offense, despite playing in a hitter's park. Chicago had a great defensive infield and topped the loop in walks and doubles. Third-place New York had Carl Hubbell and Mel Ott, but lacked depth. On the other side of the world, the Boston Braves were the NL's worst team ever, declining 40 games from their previous year's performance. Even a cameo by Babe Ruth couldn't save a team that posted just one good position player, outfielder Wally Berger.

The majors' first night game took place at Cincinnati on May 24. The Reds played 8 night games in 1935, and the excitement helped to raise team attendance 117 percent. Other clubs with poor gates noted Cincinnati's success and planned accordingly. League attendance rose 14 percent and would continue to increase throughout the decade.

Dodgers outfielder Len Koenecke, fifth in the NL in on-base percentage in 1934, had a mediocre season. On September 17 he became violent on a plane after being sent to the minors. When he assaulted a pilot, he was beaten to death with a fire extinguisher. Three longtime stars played their final games. Complications from a broken leg shut down shortstop Rabbit Maranville, while pitchers Dolf Luque and Dazzy Vance made their last appearances.

The Cubs outhomered the Tigers in the World Series, 5-1, but the 25 walks issued by Chicago made the difference in a tight six-game affair. Although Warneke won twice, the Cubs were left standing on the field—as they had been in 1929—to watch a foe celebrate a bottom-of-the-ninth clincher.

1935 American League

TEAM	W	L	T	PCT	GB	HW	HL	R	OR	PA	H	2B	3B	HR	SO	HB	SH	AVG	OBP	SLG	OPS	AOPS	BR	ABR	PF	SB	CS	BSA	BSR
DET	93	58	1	.616		53	25	919	665	6179	1573	301	83	106	627	456	19	110	.290	.366	.435	801	116	97	129	97	70	45	61	0
NY	89	60	0	.597	3	41	33	818	632	5917	1462	255	70	104	604	469	28	71	.280	.358	.416	774	111	42	89	94	68	46	60	-1
CLE	82	71	3	.536	12	48	29	776	739	6099	1573	324	77	93	460	567	17	88	.284	.341	.421	762	100	3	-11	102	63	54	54	-5
BOS	78	75	1	.510	16	41	37	718	732	6055	1458	281	63	69	609	470	21	137	.276	.353	.392	745	92	-9	-57	107	91	59	61	-1
CHI	74	78	1	.487	19.5	42	34	738	750	6025	1460	262	42	74	580	405	19	112	.275	.348	.382	730	92	-40	-58	103	46	28	62	0
WAS	67	86	1	.438	27	37	39	823	903	6299	1591	255	95	32	596	406	37	74	.285	.357	.381	738	99	-22	5	97	54	37	59	-1
STL	65	87	3	.428	28.5	31	44	718	930	6088	1446	291	51	73	593	561	14	116	.270	.344	.384	728	90	-47	-79	105	45	25	64	1
PHI	58	91	0	.389	34	30	42	710	869	5847	1470	243	44	112	475	602	17	86	.279	.341	.406	747	99	-25	-19	99	43	35	55	-3
TOT	611					323	283	6220		48509	12033	2212	525	663	4544	3936	172	794	.280	.351	.402	753				480	329	59	-10

TEAM	CG	SHO	GR	SV	IP	H	HR	BB	SO	BR/9	ERA	AERA	OAV	OOB	PR	APR	PF	OSB	OCS	FA	E	WPB	DP	FW	PW	BW	BSW	DIF
DET	87	16	95	11	1364.0	1440	78	522	584	13.1	3.82	109	.271	.339	96	57	94	44	41	.978	128	26	154	2.3	5.3	12.1	.1	-2.3
NY	76	12	120	13	1331.0	1276	91	516	594	12.2	3.60	112	.251	.321	126	72	91	44	35	.974	151	30	114	.8	6.7	8.3	.0	-1.4
CLE	67	12	138	21	1396.0	1527	68	457	498	12.9	4.15	108	.278	.335	47	54	101	54	37	.972	177	24	147	-.3	5.1	-1.0	-.4	2.1
BOS	82	6	138	11	1376.0	1520	67	520	470	13.5	4.05	117	.280	.346	62	100	107	49	55	.969	194	33	136	-1.4	9.4	-5.3	.0	-1.2
CHI	80	8	102	8	1360.2	1443	105	574	436	13.5	4.38	106	.272	.346	12	35	104	71	43	.976	146	44	133	1.3	3.3	-5.4	.1	-1.3
WAS	67	5	143	12	1378.2	1672	89	613	456	15.1	5.25	82	.302	.374	-122	-146	97	80	34	.972	171	44	186	-.0	-13.7	.5	.0	3.7
STL	42	4	219	15	1380.1	1667	92	641	435	15.2	5.26	91	.297	.371	-124	-67	108	54	35	.970	187	38	138	-.9	-6.3	-7.4	.2	3.4
PHI	58	7	148	10	1326.1	1486	73	704	469	15.0	5.12	89	.285	.372	-97	-83	102	84	49	.968	190	46	150	-1.4	-7.8	-1.8	-.2	-5.3
TOT	559	70	1103	101	10913.0					13.8	4.46		.280	.351						.972	1344	285	1158					

Batter-Fielder Wins	Batting Average	On-Base Percentage	Slugging Average	On-Base Plus Slugging	Adjusted OPS	Adjusted Batter Runs
Foxx-Phi 5.9	Myer-Was .349	Gehrig-NY .466	Foxx-Phi .636	Foxx-Phi 1096	Foxx-Phi 182	Gehrig-NY 71.7
Myer-Was 5.3	Vosmik-Cle .348	Foxx-Phi .461	Greenberg-Det .628	Gehrig-NY 1049	Gehrig-NY 180	Foxx-Phi 70.0
Gehrig-NY 5.3	Foxx-Phi .346	Cochrane-Det .452	Gehrig-NY .583	Greenberg-Det 1039	Greenberg-Det 171	Greenberg-Det 63.7
Appling-Chi 5.1	Cramer-Phi .332	Myer-Was .440	Vosmik-Cle .537	Vosmik-Cle .946	Vosmik-Cle 149	Myer-Was 41.8
Greenberg-Det 5.0	Gehringer-Det .330	Appling-Chi .437	Fox-Det .513	Gehringer-Det .911	Myer-Was 139	Gehringer-Det 36.8

Runs	Hits	Doubles	Triples	Home Runs	Total Bases	Runs Batted In
Gehrig-NY 125	Vosmik-Cle 216	Vosmik-Cle 47	Vosmik-Cle 20	Greenberg-Det 36	Greenberg-Det 389	Greenberg-Det 170
Gehringer-Det 123	Myer-Was 215	Greenberg-Det 46	Stone-Was 18	Foxx-Phi 36	Foxx-Phi 340	Gehrig-NY 119
Greenberg-Det 121	Cramer-Phi 214	Solters-Bos-StL 45	Greenberg-Det 16	Gehrig-NY 30	Vosmik-Cle 333	Foxx-Phi 115
Foxx-Phi 118	Greenberg-Det 203	Fox-Det 38	Cronin-Bos 14	Johnson-Phi 28	Solters-Bos-StL 314	Trosky-Cle 113
Chapman-NY 118		Chapman-NY 38	Averill-Cle 13	Trosky-Cle 26	Gehrig-NY 312	Solters-Bos-StL 112

Stolen Bases	Base Stealing Runs	Fielding Runs-Infield	Fielding Runs-Outfield	Saves	Wins	Winning Pct.	Complete Games
Werber-Was 29	Lary-Was-StL 4.8	Appling-Chi 24.9	Solters-Bos-StL 13.5	Knott-StL 7	W.Ferrell-Bos 25	Auker-Det .720	W.Ferrell-Bos 31
Lary-Was-StL 28	Werber-Bos 3.9	Travis-Was 19.2	Chapman-NY 13.4		Harder-Cle 22	Broaca-NY .682	Grove-Bos 23
Almada-Bos 20	Hughes-Cle 1.8	Melillo-StL-Bos 17.0	West-StL 11.4		Bridges-Det 21	Bridges-Det .677	Bridges-Det 23
White-Det 19	Solters-Bos-StL 1.7	Werber-Bos 13.6	Selkirk-NY 5.0		Grove-Bos 20	Harder-Cle .667	Rowe-Det 21
Chapman-NY 17		Berger-Cle 12.1	Johnson-Phi 4.1		Rowe-Det 19	Lyons-Chi .652	

Strikeouts	Fewest BB/Game	Games	Base Runners/9	Adjusted Relief Runs	Relief Ranking
Bridges-Det 163	Harder-Cle 1.66	VanAtta-NY-StL 58	Grove-Bos 11.11	L.Brown-Cle 13.7	L.Brown-Cle 16.2
Rowe-Det 140	Grove-Bos 2.14	Walkup-StL 55	Rowe-Det 11.17	Hogsett-Det 6.6	Hogsett-Det 8.2
Gomez-NY 138	Rowe-Det 2.22	Andrews-StL 50	Ruffing-NY 11.27	DeShong-NY 6.5	DeShong-NY 4.9
Grove-Bos 121	Andrews-StL 2.24	Thomas-StL 49	Allen-NY 11.37	Wilson-Bos 3.7	Wilson-Bos 3.8
Allen-NY 113	Hudlin-Cle 2.37	Knott-StL 48	Gomez-NY 11.38		

Innings Pitched	Opponents' Avg.	Opponents' OBP	Earned Run Average	Adjusted ERA	Adjusted Starter Runs	Pitcher Wins
W.Ferrell-Bos 322.1	Allen-NY .238	Rowe-Det .301	Grove-Bos 2.70	Grove-Bos 176	Grove-Bos 55.0	W.Ferrell-Bos 6.8
Harder-Cle 287.1	Ruffing-NY .239	Grove-Bos .302	Lyons-Chi 3.02	Lyons-Chi 153	W.Ferrell-Bos 41.2	Grove-Bos 5.5
Whitehill-Was 279.1	Gomez-NY .242	Ruffing-NY .303	Ruffing-NY 3.12	Harder-Cle 137	Harder-Cle 38.6	Ruffing-NY 4.2
Rowe-Det 275.2	Whitehead-Chi .250	Allen-NY .307	Gomez-NY 3.18	Andrews-StL 135	Lyons-Chi 29.9	Harder-Cle 4.1
Bridges-Det 274.1	Broaca-NY .254	Harder-Cle .307	Harder-Cle 3.29	W.Ferrell-Bos 135	Andrews-StL 28.3	Rowe-Det 3.2

Tigers Finally Destroy Prey

After a quick start by the White Sox, the AL race became a five-team mess in June. The Yankees tried to pull away, but a hot July propelled the Detroit Tigers into the lead. Detroit kept winning, and despite a late slump held off New York to win its second straight pennant. The Yankees had an excellent strikeout-oriented pitching staff, but couldn't score runs like the Tigers, who had offense from seven lineup spots and boasted four quality starting pitchers. The Tigers' success led to a financial windfall as they became the first AL club to draw one million fans since 1930.

Meanwhile, in St. Louis, the Browns drew just 80,000 fans. This horrible total is partially due to club's playing 19 home doubleheaders. Three times during the 1930s, however, the Brownies pulled in fewer than 100,000 fans for the season. The last team before the Browns to draw less than six figures was the 1917 Senators; when St. Louis drew 93,000 a year later, it marked the last time anyone has gone below six figures. Connie

Mack's Athletics, all their talent now distributed through the league, predictably drew 62 percent fewer fans than had come to witness the A's last pennant four years earlier. They would finish either last or seventh every year until 1943.

It was the end of an era as three glory-days Yankees retired. Babe Ruth played his last game not in the Bronx, but for the Boston Braves; center fielder Earle Combs' career was ended by a broken collarbone; and pitcher Sad Sam Jones was done at 43.

The six-game World Series featured three games decided by one-run, with Detroit winning two in its final turn. Game 6, played to 48,420 screaming fans in Detroit, climaxed with Goose Goslin's ninth-inning single scoring Mickey Cochrane for the Series-winning run. It was the Tigers' first world championship in their thirty-five-year history. Tommy Bridges won twice for Detroit, while unheralded outfielder Pete Fox batted .385.

1934 National League

TEAM	W	L	T	PCT	GB	HW	HL	R	OR	PA	H	2B	3B	HR	BB	SO	HB	SH	AVG	OBP	SLG	OPS	AOPS	BR	ABR	PF	SB	CS	BSA	BSR
STL	95	58	1	.621		48	29	**799**	656	5988	**1582**	294	75	104	392	535	18	76	**.288**	.337	**.425**	762	102	**63**	15	107	**69**			
NY	93	60	0	.608	2	**49**	26	760	**583**	5934	1485	240	41	**126**	406	526	24	**108**	.275	.329	.405	734	105	7	25	98	19			
CHI	86	65	1	.570	8	47	30	705	639	5841	1494	263	44	101	375	630	26	93	.279	.330	.402	732	103	5	20	98	59			
BOS	78	73	1	.517	16	40	35	683	714	5854	1460	233	44	83	375	440	28	81	.272	.323	.378	701	101	-54	-1	93	30			
PIT	74	76	1	.493	19.5	45	32	735	713	5878	1541	281	**77**	52	440	**398**	18	59	.287	.344	.398	742	102	34	17	102	44			
BRO	71	81	1	.467	23.5	43	33	748	795	6074	1526	284	52	79	**548**	555	22	77	.281	**.350**	.396	746	**112**	55	**97**	55	55			
PHI	56	93	0	.376	37	35	36	675	794	5724	1480	286	35	56	398	534	29	79	.284	.338	.384	722	87	0	-81	113	52			
CIN	52	99	1	.344	42	30	47	590	801	5785	1428	227	65	55	313	532	**33**	78	.266	.311	.364	675	88	-111	-97	98	34			
TOT	608					337	268	5695		47078	11996	2108	433	656	3247	4150	198	651	.279	.333	.394	727							362

TEAM	CG	SHO	GR	SV	IP	H	HR	BB	SO	BR/9	ERA	AERA	OAV	OOB	PR	APR	PF	OSB	OCS	FA	E	WPB	DP	FW	PW	BW	BSW	DIF
STL	**78**	**15**	146	16	1386.2	1463	77	411	**689**	12.4	3.69	115	.268	.323	58	79	104	41	**32**	.972	166	31	**141**	.3	7.7	1.5		9.0
NY	68	13	129	**30**	1370.0	**1384**	75	351	499	11.5	3.19	121	.260	.308	132	107	95	45	37	.972	179	46	**141**	-.5	10.4	2.4		4.2
CHI	73	11	129	9	1361.1	1432	80	417	633	12.3	3.76	103	.269	.325	46	19	95	37	48	**.977**	137	45	135	**1.9**	1.9	1.9		4.8
BOS	62	12	138	20	1359.2	1512	78	405	462	12.8	4.11	93	.279	.331	-7	-47	94	43	38	.972	169	19	120	.0	-4.6	-.0		7.2
PIT	63	8	159	8	1329.2	1523	78	354	487	12.9	4.20	98	.284	.332	-20	-13	101	66	-4	.975	145	22	118	1.4	-1.3	1.7		-2.8
BRO	66	6	166	12	1354.1	1540	81	475	520	13.6	4.48	87	.285	.346	-63	-91	96	47	36	.970	180	53	**141**	-.6	-8.9	9.4		-5.0
PHI	52	8	175	15	1297.0	1501	**126**	437	416	13.6	4.76	99	.288	.347	-101	-3	116	36	32	.966	197	28	140	-1.8	-.3	-7.9		-8.5
CIN	51	3	**182**	19	1347.2	1645	61	389	438	13.8	4.37	93	.299	.348	-46	-43	101	47	37	.970	181	35	136	-.7	-4.2	-9.4		-9.2
TOT	513	76	1224	129	10806.1					12.9	4.06		.279	.333						.972	1354	279	1072					

Batter-Fielder Wins	Batting Average	On-Base Percentage	Slugging Average	On-Base Plus Slugging	Adjusted OPS	Adjusted Batter Runs
Vaughan-Pit 5.5	P.Waner-Pit .362	Vaughan-Pit .431	Collins-StL .615	Collins-StL 1008	Ott-NY 170	Ott-NY 59.1
P.Waner-Pit 4.3	Terry-NY .354	P.Waner-Pit .429	Ott-NY .591	Ott-NY 1006	Collins-StL 155	P.Waner-Pit 47.3
Collins-StL 3.7	Cuyler-Chi .338	Ott-NY .415	DeLancey-StL .565	P.Waner-Pit .968	P.Waner-Pit 154	Collins-StL 45.7
Ott-NY 3.6	Vaughan-Pit .333	Terry-NY .414	Berger-Bos .546	Vaughan-Pit .942	Koenecke-Bro 152	Vaughan-Pit 43.1
Hartnett-Chi 3.5	Collins-StL .333	Koenecke-Bro .411	P.Waner-Pit .539	Koenecke-Bro .919	Berger-Bos 148	Berger-Bos 38.4

Runs	Hits	Doubles	Triples	Home Runs	Total Bases	Runs Batted In
P.Waner-Pit 122	P.Waner-Pit 217	Cuyler-Chi 42	Medwick-StL 18	Ott-NY 35	Collins-StL 369	Ott-NY 135
Ott-NY 119	Terry-NY 213	Allen-Phi 42	P.Waner-Pit 16	Collins-StL 35	Ott-NY 344	Collins-StL 128
Collins-StL 116	Collins-StL 200	Vaughan-Pit 41	Suhr-Pit 13	Berger-Bos 34	Berger-Bos 336	Berger-Bos 121
Vaughan-Pit 115	Medwick-StL 198	Medwick-StL 40	Collins-StL 12	Hartnett-Chi 22	Medwick-StL 328	Medwick-StL 106
Medwick-StL 110		Collins-StL 40		Klein-Chi 20	P.Waner-Pit 323	Suhr-Pit 103

Stolen Bases	Base Stealing Runs	Fielding Runs-Infield	Fielding Runs-Outfield	Wins	Winning Pct.	Complete Games
Martin-StL 23		Critz-NY 27.3	K.Davis-StL-Phi 13.7	D.Dean-StL 30	D.Dean-StL .811	Hubbell-NY 25
Cuyler-Chi 15		Bartell-Phi 18.4	Allen-Phi 10.6	Schumacher-NY 23	Hoyt-Pit .714	D.Dean-StL 24
Bartell-Phi 13		Ryan-NY 10.3	Boyle-Bro 8.6	Warneke-Chi 22	Schumacher-NY .697	Warneke-Chi 23
Taylor-Bro 12		Jackson-NY 9.6	J.Moore-Cin-Phi 7.8	Hubbell-NY 21	Warneke-Chi .688	Mungo-Bro 22
		Frey-Bro 9.5	Thompson-Bos 7.7		Frankhouse-Bos .654	Brandt-Bos 20

Strikeouts	Fewest BB/Game	Games	Saves	Base Runners/9	Adjusted Relief Runs	Relief Ranking
D.Dean-StL 195	Hubbell-NY 1.06	C.Davis-Phi 51	Hubbell-NY 8	Hubbell-NY 9.35	Haines-StL 6.3	Haines-StL 5.2
Mungo-Bro 184	Freitas-Cin 1.47	Hansen-Phi 50	Luque-NY 7	S.Johnson-Cin-Phi 10.00	Bell-NY 1.9	Bell-NY 2.6
P.Dean-StL 150	Frey-Cin 1.54	D.Dean-StL 50	D.Dean-StL 7	Warneke-Chi 10.53		
Warneke-Chi 143	Leonard-Bro 1.62	Hubbell-NY 49	Bell-NY 6	D.Dean-StL 10.66		
Derringer-Cin 122	Fitzsimmons-NY 1.74	French-Pit 49		Hoyt-Pit 10.81		

Innings Pitched	Opponents' Avg.	Opponents' OBP	Earned Run Average	Adjusted ERA	Adjusted Starter Runs	Pitcher Wins
Mungo-Bro 315.1	Parmelee-NY .238	Hubbell-NY .263	Hubbell-NY 2.30	Hubbell-NY 168	Hubbell-NY 55.5	**D.Dean-StL** 6.1
Hubbell-NY 313.0	Hubbell-NY .239	Warneke-Chi .287	D.Dean-StL 2.66	C.Davis-Phi 160	D.Dean-StL 50.6	**Hubbell-NY** 5.9
D.Dean-StL 311.2	D.Dean-StL .241	D.Dean-StL .289	Hoyt-Pit 2.93	D.Dean-StL 159	C.Davis-Phi 42.8	**C.Davis-Phi** 5.7
Schumacher-NY 297.0	Warneke-Chi .244	P.Dean-StL .292	C.Davis-Phi 2.95	Hoyt-Pit 141	Hoyt-Pit 23.3	**Schumacher-NY** 3.3
Warneke-Chi 291.1	P.Dean-StL .248	Hoyt-Pit .296	Fitzsimmons-NY 3.04	Walker-StL 135	Warneke-Chi 22.9	**Fitzsimmons-NY** 3.2

Dizzy, My Head Is Spinning

Dizzy Dean served notice of his greatness in 1934, becoming the last pitcher to win 30 games until 1968. With Dizzy and rookie brother Paul "Daffy" leading the mound staff, and an attack boasting Joe Medwick and Ripper Collins, St. Louis mounted a thrilling late-season comeback.

The Giants—sparked by Mel Ott and Carl Hubbell, who won 21 and saved 8—took the lead in June, but St. Louis won 33 of its last 45 while New York played .500 ball down the stretch. Dizzy clinched the pennant by shutting out Cincinnati on September 30.

It was a disappointing season for the Giants, who led by seven on September 5, but a great triumph for the "Gashouse Gang" Cardinals and their all-out style of play.

Third-place Chicago debuted Augie Galan, Bill Lee, and Phil Cavaretta, all of whom would contribute in 1935. The Reds finished last for the fourth straight year, but new owner Powel Crosley served notice that he would pay for quality players.

Two great New York managers died in 1933. John McGraw succumbed two years after leaving the Giants, while Little Napoleon's one-time pal and longtime adversary Wilbert Robinson passed on three years after departing Brooklyn.

Perhaps the top pitcher of 1934 was Philadelphia rookie Curt Davis, who led the league in appearances and went 19-17 with a seventh-place team playing in the tiny Baker Bowl. Scoring increased by 18 percent, making performances like Davis' less common; only four pitchers had sub-3.00 ERAs.

The World Series was wild and woolly, with a few routs and a few nail biters. In the seventh game, St. Louis blew out Elden Auker en route to an 11-0 shellacking of the Tigers. Pepper Martin, Collins, and Medwick each had 11 hits in the Series, while the Deans—as promised by Dizzy—earned all the wins. The Cardinals' victory was the Senior Circuit's final world title of the decade.

1934 American League

TEAM	W	L	T	PCT	GB	HW	HL	R	OR	PA	H	2B	3B	HR	BB	SO	HB	SH	AVG	OBP	SLG	OPS	AOPS	BR	ABR	PF	SB	CS	BSA	BSR
DET	101	53	0	.656		54	26	958	708	6239	1644	349	53	74	639	528	24	101	.300	.376	.424	800	113	119	117	100	125	55	69	8
NY	94	60	0	.610	7	53	24	842	669	6177	1494	226	61	135	700	597	20	89	.278	.364	.419	783	117	69	133	93	71	46	61	0
CLE	85	69	0	.552	16	47	31	814	763	6028	1550	340	46	100	526	433	19	87	.287	.353	.423	776	105	48	36	102	52	32	62	0
BOS	76	76	1	.500	24	42	35	820	775	6045	1465	287	70	51	610	535	11	85	.274	.350	.383	733	90	-27	-77	107	116	47	71	9
PHI	68	82	3	.453	31	34	40	764	838	5920	1491	236	50	144	491	584	13	99	.280	.343	.425	768	108	16	46	96	57	35	62	0
STL	67	85	2	.441	33	36	39	674	800	5922	1417	252	59	62	514	631	19	101	.268	.335	.373	708	82	-87	-140	108	43	31	58	-1
WAS	66	86	3	.434	34	34	40	729	806	6170	1512	278	70	51	570	447	21	131	.278	.348	.382	730	99	-36	-6	96	47	42	53	-2
CHI	53	99	1	.349	47	29	46	704	946	5994	1395	237	40	71	565	524	17	111	.263	.336	.363	699	84	-99	-119	103	36	27	57	-2
TOT	615					329	281	6305		48495	11968	2205	449	688	4615	4279	144	804	.279	.351	.399	750				547	315	63	10

TEAM	CG	SHO	GR	SV	IP	H	HR	BB	SO	BR/9	ERA	AERA	OAV	OOB	PR	APR	PF	OSB	OCS	FA	E	WPB	DP	FW	PW	BW	BSW	DIF
DET	74	13	128	14	1370.2	1467	86	488	640	12.9	4.06	108	.273	.335	67	52	98	43	44	.974	159	25	150	1.2	4.8	10.9	.6	6.5
NY	83	13	111	10	1382.2	1349	71	542	656	12.4	3.76	108	.254	.324	114	53	90	68	32	.973	157	22	151	1.3	4.9	12.4	-.1	-1.4
CLE	72	8	143	19	1367.0	1476	70	582	554	13.7	4.28	106	.275	.349	33	40	101	64	30	.972	172	49	164	.4	3.7	3.3	-.1	.6
BOS	68	9	138	9	1361.0	1527	70	543	538	13.8	4.32	111	.283	.351	27	68	107	61	30	.969	188	36	141	-.5	6.3	-7.2	.7	.6
PHI	68	8	144	8	1337.0	1429	84	693	480	14.4	5.01	87	.275	.363	-77	-97	97	80	41	.967	196	45	166	-1.0	-9.0	4.3	-.1	-1.2
STL	50	6	172	20	1350.0	1499	94	632	499	14.3	4.49	111	.283	.361	1	68	111	68	48	.969	187	37	160	-.4	6.3	-13.0	-.2	-1.7
WAS	61	4	163	12	1381.1	1622	74	503	412	13.9	4.68	92	.295	.355	-28	-57	96	49	42	.974	162	36	167	1.0	-5.3	-.6	-.5	-4.7
CHI	72	5	118	8	1355.0	1599	139	628	506	14.9	5.41	88	.292	.367	-137	-96	105	114	48	.966	207	60	126	-1.6	-8.9	-11.1	-.3	-1.1
TOT	548	66	1117	100	10904.2					13.8	4.50		.279	.351						.970	1428	310	1225				-.1	-1

Batter-Fielder Wins
Gehrig-NY 7.9
Foxx-Phi 6.1
Gehringer-Det 6.0
Averill-Cle 4.1
Werber-Bos 3.9

Batting Average
Gehrig-NY 363
Gehringer-Det.......356
Manush-Was 349
Simmons-Chi 344
Vosmik-Cle 341

On-Base Percentage
Gehrig-NY 465
Gehringer-Det.......450
Foxx-Phi 449
Cochrane-Det.........428
Myer-Was 419

Slugging Average
Gehrig-NY 706
Foxx-Phi 653
Greenberg-Det.......600
Trosky-Cle 598
Averill-Cle 569

On-Base Plus Slugging
Gehrig-NY 1172
Foxx-Phi 1102
Greenberg-Det 1005
Trosky-Cle 987
Averill-Cle 982

Adjusted OPS
Gehrig-NY 213
Foxx-Phi 188
Greenberg-Det 156
Trosky-Cle 149
Averill-Cle 149

Adjusted Batter Runs
Gehrig-NY 100.4
Foxx-Phi 73.4
Gehringer-Det........49.6
Greenberg-Det 48.7
Averill-Cle 45.5

Runs
Gehringer-Det 134
Werber-Bos 129
Gehrig-NY 128
Averill-Cle 128
Foxx-Phi 120

Hits
Gehringer-Det 214
Gehrig-NY 210
Trosky-Cle 206
Cramer-Phi 202
Greenberg-Det 201

Doubles
Greenberg-Det 63
Gehringer-Det 50
Averill-Cle 48
Trosky-Cle 45
Hale-Cle 44

Triples
Chapman-NY 13
Manush-Was 11

Home Runs
Gehrig-NY 49
Foxx-Phi 44
Trosky-Cle 35
Johnson-Phi 34
Averill-Cle 31

Total Bases
Gehrig-NY 409
Trosky-Cle 374
Greenberg-Det 356
Foxx-Phi 352
Averill-Cle 340

Runs Batted In
Gehrig-NY 165
Trosky-Cle 142
Greenberg-Det 139
Foxx-Phi 130
Gehringer-Det 127

Stolen Bases
Werber-Bos 40
White-Det 28
Chapman-NY 26
Fox-Det 25
Walker-Det 20

Base Stealing Runs
White-Det 4.1
Werber-Bos 3.5
Lazzeri-NY 2.1
Fox-Det 2.0
Rogell-Det 1.8

Fielding Runs-Infield
Hale-Cle 25.9
Werber-Bos 17.1
Melillo-StL 16.6
Warstler-Phi 15.8
Cronin-Was 13.4

Fielding Runs-Outfield
Johnson-Phi 8.6
Byrd-NY 6.1
Stone-Was 4.7
West-StL 4.6
Chapman-NY 4.1

Wins
Gomez-NY 26
Rowe-Det 24
Bridges-Det 22
Harder-Cle 20
Ruffing-NY 19

Winning Pct.
Gomez-NY 839
Rowe-Det 750
Marberry-Det 750
Auker-Det 682
Bridges-Det 667

Complete Games
Gomez-NY 25
Bridges-Det 23
Lyons-Chi 21
Rowe-Det 20

Strikeouts
Gomez-NY 158
Bridges-Det 151
Ruffing-NY 149
Rowe-Det 149
Pearson-Cle 140

Fewest BB/Game
W.Ferrell-Bos 2.44
Auker-Det 2.46
Blaeholder-StL 2.61
Rowe-Det 2.74
Weaver-Was 2.77

Games
Russell-Was 54
Newsom-StL 47
Rowe-Det 45
Knott-StL 45

Saves
Russell-Was 7
L.Brown-Cle 6
Newsom-StL 5

Base Runners/9
Gomez-NY 10.19
Rowe-Det 11.54
Bridges-Det 11.65
Murphy-NY 11.66
Harder-Cle 11.77

Adjusted Relief Runs
Pennock-Bos 8.9
McColl-Was 5.0
Bean-Cle 4.2
Wells-StL 1.2
Russell-Was 9

Relief Ranking
Pennock-Bos 4.5
Bean-Cle 4.5
McColl-Was 2.9
Wells-StL 8
Russell-Was 8

Innings Pitched
Gomez-NY 281.2
Bridges-Det 275.0
Rowe-Det 266.0
Newsom-StL...........262.1
Ruffing-NY 256.1

Opponents' Avg.
Gomez-NY 215
Ruffing-NY 236
Bridges-Det 241
Burke-Was 245
Benton-Phi 249

Opponents' OBP
Gomez-NY 282
Ruffing-NY 310
Rowe-Det 312
Bridges-Det 312
Harder-Cle 316

Earned Run Average
Gomez-NY 2.33
Harder-Cle 2.61
Murphy-NY 3.12
Burke-Was 3.21
Auker-Det 3.42

Adjusted ERA
Harder-Cle 174
Gomez-NY 174
Ostermueller-Bos 138
Burke-Was 134
W.Ferrell-Bos 132

Adjusted Starter Runs
Gomez-NY 59.3
Harder-Cle 50.1
Rowe-Det 31.5
Bridges-Det 27.7
Ostermueller-Bos ...26.5

Pitcher Wins
Harder-Cle 5.7
Gomez-NY 5.5
Rowe-Det 4.5
Newsom-StL.............2.8
W.Ferrell-Bos 2.8

Tigers Have AL by the Tail

For the first six weeks of the season, the Detroit Tigers, pennant-less since 1909, looked like nothing special. Then they began to win and shot up in the AL standings. By July, only the Yankees were a threat, and Detroit's 23-6 August put away the New Yorkers.

While the acquisitions of player-manager Mickey Cochrane and left fielder Goose Goslin helped push the Tigers over the hump, second baseman Charlie Gehringer and first baseman Hank Greenberg did most of the damage. Tommy Bridges won 16 straight games, and the pitching was deep if not spectacular. Second-place New York relied, uncharacteristically, on pitching rather than offense to contend. Lefty Gomez was now the league's top hurler and, aside from Triple Crown winner Lou Gehrig, the Yanks lacked big thumpers.

As the A's and Senators fell back into the second division, the Red Sox—last place finishers for most of the previous decade—bounded into fourth as new owner Tom Yawkey spent money on players like Billy Werber and Wes Ferrell. The pennant fever surrounding the Tigers and the increased interest in the Red Sox brought huge attendance gains as the overall league gate rose 29 percent.

Three ballparks were made smaller for the 1934 season. The Red Sox, who also replaced the wooden grandstands with concrete and steel, brought in the right-field fences at Fenway by 24 feet (after the fence had been pushed back a year earlier); the White Sox shrunk left and right field at Comiskey by 20 feet; and Detroit decreased left field at Briggs by 28 feet as AL ERA increased from 4.29 to 4.50.

The boisterous Cardinals bested the Tigers in a seven-game World Series, with the denouement an 11-0 debacle in Detroit. Angry fans threw so much debris at St. Louis left fielder Joe "Ducky" Medwick that he was removed from the game by Commissioner Landis for his own safety. The hometown crowd was mostly frustrated with their club, though, which couldn't win either of the final two games at home.

1933 National League

TEAM	W	L	T	PCT	GB	HW	HL	R	OR	PA	H	2B	3B	HR	BB	SO	HB	SH	AVG	OBP	SLG	OPS	AOPS	BR	ABR	PF	CS	BSA	BSR
NY	91	61	4	.599		48	27	636	515	5939	1437	204	41	82	377	477	15	86	.263	.312	.361	673	100	-16	-6	98	31		
PIT	87	67	0	.565	5	50	27	667	619	5962	1548	249	84	39	366	334	20	147	.285	.333	.383	716	111	70	71	100	34		
CHI	86	68	0	.558	6	56	23	646	536	5785	1422	256	51	72	392	475	30	108	.271	.325	.380	705	107	50	52	100	52		
BOS	83	71	2	.539	9	45	31	552	531	5728	1320	217	56	54	326	428	25	134	.252	.299	.345	644	98	-73	-26	92	25		
STL	82	71	1	.536	9.5	47	30	687	609	5911	1486	256	61	57	391	528	32	101	.276	.329	.378	707	103	55	22	105	99		
BRO	65	88	4	.425	26.5	36	41	617	695	5872	1413	224	51	62	397	453	18	90	.263	.316	.359	675	103	-8	19	96	82		
PHI	60	92	0	.395	31	32	40	607	760	5796	1439	240	41	60	381	479	29	125	.274	.326	.369	695	93	34	-39	113	55		
CIN	58	94	1	.382	33	37	42	496	643	5653	1267	208	37	34	349	354	33	115	.246	.298	.320	618	83	-111	-104	99	30		
TOT	618					351	261	4908		46646	11332	1854	422	460	2979	3528	202	906	.266	.317	.362	679					408		

TEAM	CG	SHO	GR	SV	IP	H	HR	BB	SO	BR/9	ERA	AERA	OAV	OOB	PR	APR	PF	OSB	OCS	FA	E	WPB	DP	FW	PW	BW	BSW	DIF
NY	75	23	126	15	1408.2	1280	61	400	555	10.9	2.71	118	.242	.299	98	81	96	53	45	.973	178	42	156	-.5	8.6	-.6		7.5
PIT	70	16	144	12	1373.1	1417	54	313	401	11.5	3.27	101	.264	.308	10	7	99	69	36	.972	166	24	133	.2	.7	7.5		1.6
CHI	95	16	97	9	1362.0	1316	51	413	488	11.6	2.93	112	.254	.312	62	53	98	35	43	.973	168	37	163	.0	5.6	5.5		-2.2
BOS	85	15	102	16	1403.0	1391	54	355	383	11.3	2.96	103	.261	.309	58	15	92	29	37	.978	138	20	148	2.1	1.6	-2.8		5.0
STL	73	11	128	16	1382.2	1391	55	452	635	12.1	3.37	103	.261	.321	-5	15	104	51	42	.973	162	37	119	.4	1.6	2.3		1.2
BRO	71	9	133	10	1386.1	1502	51	374	415	12.4	3.73	86	.275	.326	-60	-82	96	48	52	.971	177	38	120	-.3	-8.7	2.0		-4.5
PHI	52	10	170	13	1336.2	1563	87	410	341	13.6	4.34	88	.293	.348	-150	-69	114	66	45	.970	183	41	156	-1.1	-7.3	-4.1		-3.5
CIN	74	13	113	8	1352.0	1470	47	257	310	11.6	3.42	99	.279	.314	-13	-5	102	56	39	.971	177	37	139	-.6	-.5	-11.0		-5.8
TOT	595	113	1013	99	11004.2					11.9	3.34		.266	.317						.973	1349	276	1134					

Batter-Fielder Wins		Batting Average		On-Base Percentage		Slugging Average		On-Base Plus Slugging		Adjusted OPS		Adjusted Batter Runs	
Klein-Phi	5.6	Klein-Phi	368	Klein-Phi	422	Klein-Phi	602	Klein-Phi	1025	Berger-Bos	177	Klein-Phi	54.9
Berger-Bos	4.7	Davis-Phi	349	Davis-Phi	395	Berger-Bos	566	Berger-Bos	932	Klein-Phi	168	Berger-Bos	50.4
Vaughan-Pit	3.8	Stephenson-Chi	329	Vaughan-Pit	388	B.Herman-Chi	502	Davis-Phi	867	Vaughan-Pit	146	Vaughan-Pit	35.3
B.Herman-Chi	3.7	Piet-Pit	323	Martin-StL	387	Medwick-StL	497	Vaughan-Pit	866	B.Herman-Chi	142	Ott-NY	31.7
Critz-NY	3.1	Terry-NY	322	Terry-NY	375	Vaughan-Pit	478	B.Herman-Chi	855	Ott-NY	139	P.Waner-Pit	29.3

Runs		Hits		Doubles		Triples		Home Runs		Total Bases		Runs Batted In	
Martin-StL	122	Klein-Phi	223	Klein-Phi	44	Vaughan-Pit	19	Klein-Phi	28	Klein-Phi	365	Klein-Phi	120
P.Waner-Pit	101	Fullis-Phi	200	Medwick-StL	40	P.Waner-Pit	16	Berger-Bos	27	Berger-Bos	299	Berger-Bos	106
Klein-Phi	101	P.Waner-Pit	191	Lindstrom-Pit	39	Martin-StL	12	Ott-NY	23	Medwick-StL	296	Ott-NY	103
Ott-NY	98	Traynor-Pit	190	P.Waner-Pit	38	B.Herman-Chi	12	Medwick-StL	18	P.Waner-Pit	282	Medwick-StL	98
Medwick-StL	92	Martin-StL	189	Berger-Bos	37					Vaughan-Pit	274	Vaughan-Pit	97

Stolen Bases		Base Stealing Runs		Fielding Runs-Infield		Fielding Runs-Outfield		Wins		Winning Pct.		Complete Games	
Martin-StL	26			Critz-NY	45.0	Klein-Phi	8.1	Hubbell-NY	23	Cantwell-Bos	667	Warneke-Chi	26
Fullis-Phi	18			B.Herman-Chi	29.0	Medwick-StL	7.3	Dean-StL	20	Hubbell-NY	657	Dean-StL	26
Frisch-StL	18			Jurges-Chi	22.8	Lindstrom-Pit	6.3	Cantwell-Bos	20	Meine-Pit	652	Brandt-Bos	23
Klein-Phi	15			Ryan-NY	16.5	Hafey-Cin	6.2	Bush-Chi	20	Bush-Chi	625	Hubbell-NY	22
Orsatti-StL	14			Bartell-Phi	8.8	Rice-Cin	4.1	Schumacher-NY	19	Schumacher-NY	613		

Strikeouts		Fewest BB/Game		Games		Saves		Base Runners/9		Adjusted Relief Runs		Relief Ranking	
Dean-StL	199	Lucas-Cin	74	Dean-StL	48	Collins-Phi	6	Hubbell-NY	8.92	Bell-NY	13.3	Bell-NY	13.9
Hubbell-NY	156	Hubbell-NY	1.37	French-Pit	47	Hubbell-NY	5	Schumacher-NY	9.88	Luque-NY	5.7	Luque-NY	7.1
Carleton-StL	147	Swift-Pit	1.48	Liska-Phi	45	Harris-Pit	5	Betts-Bos	10.41				
Warneke-Chi	133	Hansen-Phi	1.60	Hubbell-NY	45	Betts-Bos	5	Bell-NY	10.42				
Parmelee-NY	132	French-Pit	1.70	Carleton-StL	44	Bell-NY	5	Swift-Pit	10.47				

Innings Pitched		Opponents' Avg.		Opponents' OBP		Earned Run Average		Adjusted ERA		Adjusted Starter Runs		Pitcher Wins	
Hubbell-NY	308.2	Schumacher-NY	214	Hubbell-NY	260	Hubbell-NY	1.66	Hubbell-NY	193	Hubbell-NY	55.3	Hubbell-NY	7.3
Dean-StL	293.0	Hubbell-NY	227	Schumacher-NY	280	Warneke-Chi	2.00	Warneke-Chi	163	Warneke-Chi	38.9	Warneke-Chi	5.8
French-Pit	291.1	Parmelee-NY	232	Swift-Pit	285	Schumacher-NY	2.16	Schumacher-NY	149	Schumacher-NY	33.3	Schumacher-NY	4.4
Brandt-Bos	287.2	Mungo-Bro	236	Betts-Bos	290	Brandt-Bos	2.60	Root-Chi	126	Brandt-Bos	21.1	Brandt-Bos	3.5
Warneke-Chi	287.1	Warneke-Chi	244	Cantwell-Bos	291	Root-Chi	2.60	French-Pit	122	French-Pit	20.7	Bush-Chi	2.0

Pitching Royalty and a Guy Named Mel

Three members of the Giants made the job easier for player-manager Bill Terry. Slugger Mel Ott led the league in walks and finished top five in runs, homers, and RBIs, while "King Carl" Hubbell and "Prince Hal" Schumacher were the pitching top twosome in the league. New York surged ahead in mid-June and never looked back, improving from seventh to win the flag.

Pittsburgh, Chicago, Boston (which set a new NL mark with a .978 fielding percentage), and St. Louis bunched together fighting for second. The Pirates were the eventual runners-up, finishing 5 games back.

Despite Chuck Klein winning the Triple Crown, the Phillies ended seventh. Philadelphia sold Klein to the Cubs for $125,000 after the season; they finished seventh again in 1934 and lost one more game than the previous year. Last-place Cincinnati was the final stop for two great pitchers. Eppa Rixey went 6-3 at age 42, while 23-year-vet Jack Quinn pitched his last game at the age of 50.

Due to the depression, major league teams cut their rosters to 23, and even Commissioner Landis took a pay cut. The average yearly salary for a major league player was $6,000. NL attendance fell another 18 percent in 1933, bringing league totals to their lowest since 1919. During the 1930s, the Cubs and Giants were the loop's only consistent draws. Both Chicago and New York had good ballparks, large populations, charismatic players, and were competitive most of the decade. In 1933 Cubs President William L. Veeck proposed a midseason slate of interleague games and a split season to spark more interest; he died a few months later.

Defeating the Washington Senators in five games, the Giants captured their first World Series since 1922. Hubbell pitched 20 innings without allowing an earned run, capturing Games 1 and 4. Ott's homer in the 10th-inning was the deciding blow in the final contest.

1933 American League

TEAM	W	L	T	PCT	GB	HW	HL	R	OR	PA	H	2B	3B	HR	BB	SO	HB	SH	AVG	OBP	SLG	OPS	AOPS	BR	ABR	PF	SB	CS	BSA	BSR
WAS	99	53	1	.651		46	30	850	**665**	6212	**1586**	281	**86**	60	539	395	21	**128**	**.287**	.353	.402	755	107	46	55	99	65	50	57	-4
NY	91	59	2	.607	7	51	23	**927**	768	6069	1495	241	75	**144**	**700**	506	17	78	.283	**.369**	**.440**	**809**	129	156	215	94	**76**	59	56	-4
PHI	79	72	1	.523	19.5	46	29	875	853	6051	1519	**297**	57	139	625	618	16	80	.285	.362	**.440**	802	118	140	131	101	34	34	50	-6
CLE	75	76	0	.497	23.5	45	32	654	669	5806	1366	218	77	50	448	426	17	101	.261	.321	.360	681	82	-109	-136	105	36	40	47	-6
DET	75	79	1	.487	25	43	35	722	733	6091	1479	283	78	57	475	523	21	93	.269	.342	.360	702	96	-51	-20	96	43	46	48	-7
CHI	67	83	1	.447	31	35	41	683	814	5991	1448	231	53	43	538	416	**27**	108	.272	.342	.360	702	96	-25	-18	99	58	37	**61**	0
BOS	63	86	0	.423	34.5	32	40	700	758	5857	1407	294	56	50	525	464	15	116	.271	.339	.377	716	97	-25	-18	99	68	50	58	0
STL	55	96	2	.364	43.5	30	46	669	820	5907	1337	244	64	64	520	556	15	87	.253	.322	.360	682	81	-104	-142	106	72	60	55	-5
TOT	608					328	276	6080		47984	11637	2089	546	607	4370	3904	149	791	.273	.342	.390	732					452	376	55	-32

TEAM	CG	SHO	GR	SV	IP	H	HR	BB	SO	BR/9	ERA	AERA	OAV	OOB	PR	APR	PF	OSB	OCS	FA	E	WPB	DP	FW	PW	BW	BSW	DIF
WAS	68	5	150	26	1389.2	1415	64	452	447	12.2	3.82	109	.263	.322	71	57	98	31	30	**.979**	131	22	149	2.6	5.4	5.2	.0	9.7
NY	70	8	123	22	1354.2	1426	66	612	**711**	13.6	4.36	89	.267	.344	-13	-80	91	35	39	.972	165	45	122	.4	-7.6	**20.4**	.0	2.8
PHI	69	6	142	14	1343.2	1523	77	644	423	14.6	4.81	89	.283	.361	-79	-78	100	67	38	.966	203	42	121	-1.9	-7.4	12.4	.0	.4
CLE	**74**	**12**	124	7	1350.0	**1382**	60	465	437	12.4	**3.71**	120	.264	.325	86	107	104	43	**65**	.974	156	**18**	127	.9	**10.1**	-12.9	-.2	1.5
DET	69	6	129	17	1398.0	1415	84	561	575	12.9	3.95	109	.263	.335	52	56	101	93	55	.971	178	21	**167**	-.2	5.3	-6.4	.0	-1.7
CHI	53	8	**167**	13	1371.1	1505	85	519	423	15.1	4.45	95	.277	.343	-26	-33	99	70	37	.970	186	41	143	-1.0	-3.1	-1.9	-.3	-1.7
BOS	60	4	146	14	1327.2	1396	75	591	467	13.6	4.35	101	.271	.348	-10	4	102	68	60	.966	204	22	133	-2.2	.4	-1.7	.4	-8.3
STL	55	7	147	10	1360.2	1574	96	531	426	14.0	4.82	97	.289	.354	-82	-23	109	45	52	.976	149	30	162	1.5	-2.2	-13.4	-.0	-6.3
TOT	518	56	1128	123	10895.2					13.3	4.28		.273	.342						.972	1372	241	1124					

Batter-Fielder Wins
Foxx-Phi ....6.9 · Ruth-NY ....4.7 · Gehrig-NY ....4.7 · Cochrane-Phi ....4.1 · Cronin-Was 3.9

Batting Average
Foxx-Phi ....356 · Manush-Was ....336 · Gehrig-NY ....334 · Simmons-Chi ....331 · Gehringer-Det 325

On-Base Percentage
Cochrane-Phi ....459 · Foxx-Phi ....449 · Bishop-Phi ....446 · Ruth-NY ....442 · Gehrig-NY 424

Slugging Average
Foxx-Phi ....703 · Gehrig-NY ....605 · Ruth-NY ....582 · Cochrane-Phi ....515 · Johnson-Phi 505

On-Base Plus Slugging
Foxx-Phi ....1153 · Gehrig-NY ....1030 · Ruth-NY ....1023 · Cochrane-Phi ....974 · Johnson-Phi 892

Adjusted OPS
Foxx-Phi ....199 · Gehrig-NY ....181 · Ruth-NY ....180 · Cochrane-Phi ....156 · Dickey-NY 138

Adjusted Batter Runs
Foxx-Phi ....82.4 · Gehrig-NY ....70.1 · Ruth-NY ....58.8 · Cochrane-Phi ....42.6 · Johnson-Phi 27.7

Runs
Gehrig-NY ....138 · Foxx-Phi ....125 · Manush-Was ....115 · Chapman-NY ....112 · Cramer-Phi 109

Hits
Manush-Was ....221 · Gehringer-Det ....204 · Foxx-Phi ....204 · Simmons-Chi ....200 · Gehrig-NY 198

Doubles
Cronin-Was ....45 · Johnson-Phi ....44 · Burns-StL ....43 · Rogell-Det ....42 · Gehringer-Det 42

Triples
Manush-Was ....17 · Combs-NY ....16 · Averill-Cle ....16 · Myer-Was ....15 · Reynolds-StL 14

Home Runs
Foxx-Phi ....48 · Ruth-NY ....34 · Gehrig-NY ....32 · Johnson-Phi ....21 · Lazzeri-NY 18

Total Bases
Foxx-Phi ....403 · Gehrig-NY ....359 · Manush-Was ....302 · Gehringer-Det ....294 · Simmons-Chi 291

Runs Batted In
Foxx-Phi ....163 · Gehrig-NY ....139 · Simmons-Chi ....119 · Cronin-Was ....118 · Kuhel-Was 107

Stolen Bases
Chapman-NY ....27 · Walker-Det ....26 · Swanson-Chi ....19 · Kuhel-Was 17

Base Stealing Runs
Walker-Det ....2.6 · Werber-NY-Bos ....1.5 · Kuhel-Was .....9 · Stumpf-Bos .....9 · Lazzeri-NY 9

Fielding Runs-Infield
Melillo-StL ....22.3 · Rogell-Det ....18.9 · Scharein-StL ....16.1 · Appling-Chi ....8.5 · Foxx-Phi 6.8

Fielding Runs-Outfield
Chapman-NY ....14.1 · Simmons-Chi ....9.4 · Schulte-Was ....7.6 · West-StL ....5.2 · Goslin-Was 4.6

Wins
Grove-Phi ....24 · Crowder-Was ....24 · Whitehill-Was 22

Winning Pct.
Grove-Phi ....750 · Whitehill-Was ....733 · Stewart-Was ....714 · Allen-NY 682

Complete Games
Grove-Phi ....21 · Whitehill-Was ....19 · Hadley-StL ....19 · Ruffing-NY 18

Strikeouts
Gomez-NY ....163 · Hadley-StL ....149 · Ruffing-NY ....122 · Bridges-Det ....120 · Allen-NY 119

Fewest BB/Game
Brown-Cle ....1.65 · Marberry-Det ....2.30 · Stewart-Was ....2.34 · Harder-Cle ....2.38 · Blaeholder-StL 2.43

Games
Crowder-Was ....52 · Russell-Was ....50 · Welch-Bos ....47 · Kline-Bos 46

Saves
Russell-Was ....13 · Hogsett-Det ....9 · Moore-NY ....8 · Heving-Chi ....6 · Grove-Phi 6

Base Runners/9
Heving-Chi ....10.83 · Russell-Was ....11.03 · Pearson-Cle ....11.04 · Marberry-Det ....11.10 · Stewart-Was 11.24

Adjusted Relief Runs
Russell-Was ....19.6 · Heving-Chi ....17.4 · Gray-StL ....7.3 · Faber-Chi ....7.2 · Burke-Was 5.5

Relief Ranking
Russell-Was ....30.3 · Heving-Chi ....17.9 · Gray-StL ....7.1 · Faber-Chi ....6.2 · Burke-Was 5.4

Innings Pitched
Hadley-StL ....316.2 · Crowder-Was ....299.1 · Grove-Phi ....275.1 · Whitehill-Was ....270.0 · Blaeholder-StL 255.2

Opponents' Avg.
Bridges-Det ....226 · Gomez-NY ....240 · Allen-NY ....242 · Weiland-Bos ....244 · Hildebrand-Cle 245

Opponents' OBP
Marberry-Det ....302 · Stewart-Was ....304 · Harder-Cle ....309 · Brown-Cle ....310 · Grove-Phi 316

Earned Run Average
Pearson-Cle ....2.33 · Harder-Cle ....2.95 · Bridges-Det ....3.09 · Gomez-NY ....3.18 · Grove-Phi 3.20

Adjusted ERA
Harder-Cle ....151 · Bridges-Det ....140 · Grove-Phi ....134 · Marberry-Det ....131 · Brown-Cle 130

Adjusted Starter Runs
Harder-Cle ....35.1 · Grove-Phi ....34.5 · Pearson-Cle ....29.5 · Marberry-Det ....29.5 · Bridges-Det 28.8

Pitcher Wins
Harder-Cle ....4.4 · **Bridges-Det** ....3.2 · **Pearson-Cle** ....3.1 · Grove-Phi ....3.1 · **Russell-Was** 3.1

Last Gasp for the Senators and A's

Following up on a strong finish in 1932, the Washington Senators moved ahead of the Yankees in June, withstood a challenge in late July, and then pulled away at the end. Player-manager Joe Cronin, just 26, keyed a line-drive power offense, three 30-something starters combined for 59 wins, and Jack Russell carried on the relief tradition of Firpo Marberry (departed to Detroit), winning 12 and being credited retroactively with 13 saves.

Prior to the season, Connie Mack looked at the finances and decided to tear apart his A's. After trading Al Simmons, Jimmy Dykes, and Mule Haas, the Athletics only finished third because of Jimmie Foxx (the Triple Crown winner), Lefty Grove, and Mickey Cochrane. After another attendance dip in '33, Mack finished the destruction by dealing Grove to Boston and Cochrane to Detroit. It was the finish of the Athletics as a competitive team in Philadelphia.

The Tigers spent 1933 in fifth place, breaking in two rookie pitchers who would soon be very important: Schoolboy Rowe and Elden Auker. Though the White Sox were a sixth-place crew, they remained in the news. Comiskey Park was the site of the first midsummer All-Star game. The AL won the game before a packed house, 4-2; Ruth christened the event with the first All-Star homer.

Red Faber, 44, the last active player from the 1919 White Sox and still a mainstay of the club, pitched in his last game. The same year, "Black Sox" manager Kid Gleason died, his heart still broken from the betrayal carried out by "his boys."

Although Lou Gehrig was outstanding, and Babe Ruth had his final big year, it was the Senators' grand finale. For 1920s holdovers Ossie Bluege, Sam Rice, and Goose Goslin (brought back for one year by owner Clark Griffith), it was their third flag in a decade—and the franchise's last in the capital. Washington's five-game World Series loss to the Giants was the end, rather than the beginning, of the excitement in D.C.

1932 National League

TEAM	W	L	T	PCT	GB	HW	HL	R	OR	PA	H	2B	3B	HR	BB	SO	HB	SH	AVG	OBP	SLG	OPS	AOPS	BR	ABR	PF	SB	CS	BSA	BSR
CHI	90	64	0	.584		53	24	720	633	6006	1519	296	60	69	398	514	28	118	.278	.330	.392	722	101	1	8	99	48			
PIT	86	68	0	.558	4	45	31	701	711	5906	1543	274	90	48	358	385	31	96	.285	.333	.395	728	103	7	20	98	71			
BRO	81	73	0	.526	9	44	34	752	747	5944	1538	296	59	110	388	574	24	99	.283	.334	.420	754	110	56	72	98	61			
PHI	78	76	0	.506	12	45	32	844	796	6108	1608	330	67	122	446	547	27	125	.292	.348	.442	790	105	136	44	112	71			
BOS	77	77	1	.500	13	44	33	649	655	5977	1460	262	53	63	347	496	19	105	.265	.311	.366	677	90	-96	-72	96	36			
STL	72	82	2	.468	18	42	35	684	717	5972	1467	307	51	76	420	514	25	69	.269	.324	.385	709	93	-24	-43	103	92			
NY	72	82	0	.468	18	37	40	755	706	5950	1527	263	54	116	348	391	23	49	.276	.322	.406	728	103	-1	14	98	31			
CIN	60	94	1	.390	30	33	44	575	715	5999	1429	265	68	47	436	436	20	100	.263	.320	.362	682	92	-78	-56	97	35			
TOT	618					343	273	5680		47862	12091	2293	502	651	3141	3857	197	761	.276	.328	.396	724					445			

TEAM	CG	SHO	GR	SV	IP	H	HR	BB	SO	BR/9	ERA	AERA	OAV	OOB	PR	APR	PF	OSB	OCS	FA	E	WPB	DP	FW	PW	BW	BSW	DIF
CHI	79	9	132	7	1401.0	1444	68	409	527	12.1	3.44	109	.264	.319	68	51	97	29	47	.973	173	43	146	.4	5.0	.8		6.8
PIT	71	12	126	12	1377.0	1472	86	338	377	11.9	3.75	102	.270	.314	20	11	98	63	30	.969	185	33	124	-.4	1.1	2.0		6.3
BRO	61	7	153	16	1379.2	1538	72	403	497	12.8	4.27	89	.282	.334	-60	-69	98	57	52	.971	183	31	169	-.3	-6.8	7.1		4.0
PHI	59	4	160	17	1384.0	1589	107	450	459	13.5	4.47	99	.287	.344	-91	-8	114	60	33	.968	194	23	133	-.9	-.8	4.4		-1.6
BOS	72	8	124	8	1414.0	1483	61	420	440	12.3	3.53	107	.272	.328	55	37	97	43	45	.976	152	22	145	1.7	3.7	-7.1		1.7
STL	70	13	139	9	1396.0	1533	76	455	681	13.0	3.97	98	.282	.340	-14	-5	101	68	63	.971	175	43	155	.4	-.5	-4.3		-.6
NY	57	3	156	16	1375.1	1533	112	387	506	12.7	3.83	97	.280	.330	8	-19	96	60	37	.969	191	33	143	-.7	-1.9	1.4		-3.8
CIN	83	6	112	6	1394.2	1505	69	276	359	11.6	3.79	102	.274	.311	14	10	99	65	43	.971	178	35	129	.1	1.0	-5.5		-12.6
TOT	552	62	1102	91	11121.2					12.5	3.88		.276	.328						.971	1431	263	1144					

Batter-Fielder Wins		Batting Average		On-Base Percentage		Slugging Average		On-Base Plus Slugging		Adjusted OPS		Adjusted Batter Runs	
Ott-NY	5.2	O'Doul-Bro	.368	Ott-NY	.424	Klein-Phi	.646	Klein-Phi	1050	Ott-NY	175	Ott-NY	64.0
Klein-Phi	4.9	Terry-NY	.350	O'Doul-Bro	.423	Ott-NY	.601	Ott-NY	1025	O'Doul-Bro	164	O'Doul-Bro	54.3
Terry-NY	4.8	Klein-Phi	.348	Hurst-Phi	.412	Terry-NY	.580	O'Doul-Bro	.978	Klein-Phi	158	Klein-Phi	52.8
Herman-Cin	4.5	P.Waner-Pit	.341	Klein-Phi	.404	O'Doul-Bro	.555	Terry-NY	.962	Terry-NY	158	Terry-NY	49.3
O'Doul-Bro	4.0	Hurst-Phi	.339	P.Waner-Pit	.397	Hurst-Phi	.547	Hurst-Phi	.959	Herman-Cin	152	Herman-Cin	41.9

Runs		Hits		Doubles		Triples		Home Runs		Total Bases		Runs Batted In	
Klein-Phi	152	Klein-Phi	226	P.Waner-Pit	62	Herman-Cin	19	Ott-NY	38	Klein-Phi	420	Hurst-Phi	143
Terry-NY	124	Terry-NY	225	Klein-Phi	50	Suhr-Pit	16	Klein-Phi	38	Terry-NY	373	Klein-Phi	137
O'Doul-Bro	120	O'Doul-Bro	219	Stephenson-Chi	49	Klein-Phi	15	Terry-NY	28	Ott-NY	340	Whitney-Phi	124
Ott-NY	119	P.Waner-Pit	215	Bartell-Phi	48			Hurst-Phi	24	O'Doul-Bro	330	Wilson-Bro	123
Bartell-Phi	118	Herman-Chi	206					Wilson-Bro	23	P.Waner-Pit	321	Ott-NY	123

Stolen Bases		Base Stealing Runs		Fielding Runs-Infield		Fielding Runs-Outfield		Wins		Winning Pct.		Complete Games	
Klein-Phi	20			Jurges-Chi	30.0	Herman-Cin	13.2	Warneke-Chi	22	Warneke-Chi	.786	Lucas-Cin	28
Piet-Pit	19			Cuccinello-Bro	20.8	Lee-Phi	9.2	Clark-Bro	20	Bush-Chi	.633	Warneke-Chi	25
Watkins-StL	18			Frisch-StL	15.8	L.Waner-Pit	9.0	Bush-Chi	19	Rhem-StL-Phi	.625	Hubbell-NY	22
Frisch-StL	18			Stripp-Bro	15.6	K.Davis-Phi	8.1			Clark-Bro	.625		
K.Davis-Phi	16			Terry-NY	15.1	Klein-Phi	6.7			Hubbell-NY	.621		

Strikeouts		Fewest BB/Game		Games		Saves		Base Runners/9		Adjusted Relief Runs		Relief Ranking	
Dean-StL	191	Swift-Pit	1.09	French-Pit	47	Quinn-Bro	8	Hubbell-NY	9.63	Quinn-Bro	5.3	Quinn-Bro	6.6
Hubbell-NY	137	Lucas-Cin	1.17	Dean-StL	46	Benge-Phi	6	Swift-Pit	9.78	Frankhouse-Bos	2	Frankhouse-Bos	2
Malone-Chi	120	Hubbell-NY	1.27	Carleton-StL	44	Luque-NY	5	Lucas-Cin	9.92				
Carleton-StL	113	Benton-Cin	1.35	Collins-Phi	43	Cantwell-Bos	5	Warneke-Chi	10.17				
Brown-Bos	110	Betts-Bos	1.42					Rixey-Cin	10.32				

Innings Pitched		Opponents' Avg.		Opponents' OBP		Earned Run Average		Adjusted ERA		Adjusted Starter Runs		Pitcher Wins	
Dean-StL	286.0	Swetonic-Pit	.221	Hubbell-NY	.268	Warneke-Chi	2.37	Warneke-Chi	159	Warneke-Chi	45.2	Hubbell-NY	4.7
Hubbell-NY	284.0	Warneke-Chi	.237	Swift-Pit	.272	Hubbell-NY	2.50	Hubbell-NY	148	Hubbell-NY	39.6	Lucas-Cin	4.4
Warneke-Chi	277.0	Hubbell-NY	.238	Lucas-Cin	.274	Betts-Bos	2.80	Swetonic-Pit	135	Lucas-Cin	26.4	Warneke-Chi	4.3
French-Pit	274.1	Brown-Bos	.238	Warneke-Chi	.283	Swetonic-Pit	2.82	Betts-Bos	134	Betts-Bos	23.3	Cantwell-Bos	2.6
Clark-Bro	273.0	Malone-Chi	.244	Swetonic-Pit	.286	Lucas-Cin	2.94	Lucas-Cin	131	Swetonic-Pit	20.8	Dean-StL	2.5

Managerial Ch-Ch-Ch-Ch-Changes

The Chicago Cubs led in the early going, but by August were in second and scuffling with brusque manager Rogers Hornsby. Charlie Grimm assumed the reins on August 7, and the Cubs reeled off a 14-game winning streak, rolling to the NL title. While the Cubs lacked a world-class offense, rookie Lon Warneke was arguably the league's top pitcher. Stan Hack began his long career as a part-time third baseman.

Home runs rose 30 percent, but overall scoring did not change significantly from 1931. Brooklyn's Ebbets Field was shrunk significantly in left and center fields, which increased runs, while the Pirates heightened Forbes Field's right-field wall, which had little effect.

The Pirates led the league for six weeks, but fell off the pace and finished second. Twenty-year-old rookie Arky Vaughan would become the team's best shortstop since Honus Wagner,

while Paul Waner took advantage of spacious Forbes Field to hit 62 doubles. Led by slugger Chuck Klein, the Phillies led the NL in scoring, finishing .500 for first time since 1917. Cardinals rookie Joe Medwick batted .349 in a late-season trial.

New York saw the end of an era as manager John McGraw, in ill health and feuding with his players, quit with the Giants in last. Despite a sixth-place finish in 1932, the team improved quickly under Bill Terry.

Parity ruled the day; the Cubs' 90 wins were the fewest for an NL flag winner since 1915, and the distance from first to seventh in the standings was just 18 games. The lack of overwhelming skill from the NL champs showed in the World Series as the Yankees swept Chicago. Although the pennant race was interesting, NL attendance dropped another 16 percent as the true level of the economic depression sank in.

1932 American League

TEAM	W	L	T	PCT	GB	HW	HL	R	OR	PA	H	2B	3B	HR	BB	SO	HB	SH	AVG	OBP	SLG	OPS	AOPS	BR	ABR	PF	SB	CS	BSA	BSR
NY	107	47	2	.695		62	15	**1002**	724	6346	1564	279	82	160	**766**	527	27	76	.286	**.376**	.454	**830**	128	**176**	232	95	77	66	54	-6
PHI	94	60	0	.610	13	51	26	981	752	6299	**1606**	303	52	**172**	647	630	21	94	**.290**	.366	**.457**	823	115	153	119	104	38	23	62	0
WAS	93	61	0	.604	14	51	26	840	716	6141	1565	303	**100**	61	505	442	26	95	.284	.347	.408	755	102	6	17	99	70	47	60	-7
CLE	87	65	1	.572	19	43	33	845	747	6121	1544	**310**	74	78	566	454	**33**	110	.285	.357	.413	770	99	46	-6	107	52	54	49	-7
DET	76	75	2	.503	29.5	42	34	799	787	5993	1479	291	80	80	486	523	13	85	.273	.335	.401	736	92	-37	-66	104	**103**	49	**68**	**6**
STL	63	91	0	.409	44	33	42	736	898	6065	1502	274	69	67	507	528	19	90	.276	.339	.388	727	89	-47	-88	106	89	58	61	-1
CHI	49	102	1	.325	56.5	28	49	667	897	5903	1426	274	56	36	459	**386**	19	89	.267	.327	.360	687	90	-124	-78	94	46	46	50	-6
BOS	43	111	0	.279	64	27	50	566	915	5856	1331	253	57	53	469	539	12	80	.251	.314	.351	665	80	-175	-158	97	69	62		-1
TOT	615					337	275	6436		48724	12017	2287	570	707	4405	4029	170	719	.277	.346	.404	750					544	405	57	-22

TEAM	CG	SHO	GR	SV	IP	H	HR	BB	SO	BR/9	ERA	AERA	OAV	OOB	PR	APR	PF	OSB	OCS	FA	E	WPB	DP	FW	PW	BW	BSW	DIF
NY	**96**	**11**	93	15	1408.0	1425	93	561	**780**	12.8	3.98	102	**.260**	.331	**78**	17	91	65	38	.969	188	37	124	.2	1.6	**21.5**	-.3	7.1
PHI	95	10	92	10	1386.0	1477	112	511	595	13.0	4.45	102	.271	.336	4	11	101	68	49	**.979**	**124**	36	142	**3.8**	1.0	11.0	.3	.9
WAS	66	10	139	**22**	1383.1	1463	73	526	437	13.0	4.16	104	.271	.337	49	25	96	**44**	48	**.979**	125	**23**	**157**	**3.8**	2.3	1.6	.2	8.2
CLE	94	6	92	8	1377.1	1506	70	**446**	439	**12.8**	4.12	**115**	.273	**.329**	55	**90**	106	57	41	.969	191	24	129	-.2	**8.3**	-.6	-.4	3.8
DET	67	9	120	17	1362.2	**1421**	89	592	521	13.5	4.30	109	.269	.346	27	58	105	67	51	.969	187	31	154	.0	-2.0	-6.1	-.4	-3.5
STL	63	8	150	11	1376.2	1592	103	574	496	14.3	5.01	97	.290	.359	-81	-22	108	61	53	.969	188	29	156	.0	-7.1	-7.2	.2	-7.7
CHI	50	2	166	12	1348.2	1551	88	580	379	14.4	4.82	90	.287	.359	-52	-77	97	76	**67**	.958	264	37	**170**	-4.6	-7.1	-7.2	.2	-7.7
BOS	42	3	**188**	7	1362.0	1574	79	612	365	14.6	5.02	90	.289	.364	-81	-79	100	106	58	.963	233	33	165	-2.6	-7.3	-14.6	-.3	-9.2
TOT	573	59	1040	102	11004.2					13.6	4.48		.277	.346						.969	1500	250	1197					

Leaders

Batter-Fielder Wins
Foxx-Phi 6.7 · Ruth-NY 6.5 · Gehrig-NY 5.1 · Cochrane-Phi 4.2 · Lazzeri-NY 3.9

Batting Average
Alexander-Det-Bos .367 · Foxx-Phi .364 · Gehrig-NY .349 · Manush-Was .342 · Ruth-NY .341

On-Base Percentage
Ruth-NY .489 · Foxx-Phi .469 · Gehrig-NY .451 · Bishop-Phi .412 · Cochrane-Phi .412

Slugging Average
Foxx-Phi .749 · Ruth-NY .661 · Gehrig-NY .621 · Averill-Cle .569 · Simmons-Phi .548

On-Base Plus Slugging
Foxx-Phi 1218 · Ruth-NY 1150 · Gehrig-NY 1072 · Averill-Cle .961 · Cochrane-Phi .921

Adjusted OPS
Ruth-NY 206 · Foxx-Phi 203 · Gehrig-NY 184 · Lazzeri-NY 140 · Averill-Cle 137

Adjusted Batter Runs
Foxx-Phi 91.5 · Ruth-NY 80.5 · Gehrig-NY 79.4 · Alexander-Det-Bos 34.5 · Averill-Cle 33.0

Runs
Foxx-Phi 151 · Simmons-Phi 144 · Combs-NY 143 · Gehrig-NY 138 · Manush-Was 121

Hits
Simmons-Phi 216 · Manush-Was 214 · Foxx-Phi 213 · Gehrig-NY 208 · Averill-Cle 198

Doubles
McNair-Phi 47 · Gehringer-Det 44 · Cronin-Was 43

Triples
Cronin-Was 18 · Myer-Was 16 · Lazzeri-NY 16 · Chapman-NY 15

Home Runs
Foxx-Phi 58 · Ruth-NY 41 · Simmons-Phi 35 · Gehrig-NY 34 · Averill-Cle 32

Total Bases
Foxx-Phi 438 · Gehrig-NY 370 · Simmons-Phi 367 · Averill-Cle 359 · Manush-Was 325

Runs Batted In
Foxx-Phi 169 · Simmons-Phi 151 · Gehrig-NY 151 · Ruth-NY 137 · Averill-Cle 124

Stolen Bases
Chapman-NY 38 · Walker-Det 30 · Johnson-Det-Bos 20 · Cissell-Chi-Cle 18

Base Stealing Runs
Walker-Det 4.5 · Johnson-Det-Bos 2.3 · Chapman-NY 2.1 · Blue-Chi 1.6 · Schuble-Det 1.3

Fielding Runs-Infield
Warstler-Bos 22.8 · Appling-Chi 14.8 · Rogell-Det 11.3 · Melillo-StL 11.3 · Kamm-Cle 9.3

Fielding Runs-Outfield
Vosmik-Cle 18.9 · West-Was 14.7 · Funk-Chi 5.5 · Goslin-StL 4.8 · Chapman-NY 4.1

Wins
Crowder-Was 26 · Grove-Phi 25 · Gomez-NY 24 · Ferrell-Cle 23 · Weaver-Was 22

Winning Pct.
Allen-NY .810 · Gomez-NY .774 · Ruffing-NY .720 · Grove-Phi .714 · Weaver-Was .688

Complete Games
Grove-Phi 27 · Ferrell-Cle 26 · Ruffing-NY 22

Strikeouts
Ruffing-NY 190 · Grove-Phi 188 · Gomez-NY 176 · Hadley-Chi-StL 145 · Pipgras-NY 111

Fewest BB/Game
Brown-Cle 1.71 · Crowder-Was 2.12 · Gray-StL 2.31 · Harder-Cle 2.40 · Grove-Phi 2.44

Games
Marberry-Was 54 · Gray-StL 52 · Crowder-Was 50

Saves
Marberry-Was 13 · Moore-Bos-NY 8 · Hogsett-Det 7 · Grove-Phi 7 · Faber-Chi 6

Base Runners/9
Grove-Phi 10.77 · Crowder-Was 10.90 · Allen-NY 11.39 · Ruffing-NY 11.71 · Sorrell-Det 12.06

Adjusted Relief Runs
Kimsey-StL-Chi 7.7 · Faber-Chi 4.5 · Krausse-Phi 0

Relief Ranking
Kimsey-StL-Chi 7.7 · Faber-Chi 5.6 · Krausse-Phi …

Innings Pitched
Crowder-Was 327.0 · Grove-Phi 291.2 · Ferrell-Cle 287.2 · Walberg-Phi 272.0 · Gomez-NY 265.1

Opponents' Avg.
Ruffing-NY .226 · Allen-NY .228 · Bridges-Det .233 · Grove-Phi .241 · Crowder-Was .252

Opponents' OBP
Grove-Phi .292 · Crowder-Was .295 · Allen-NY .306 · Ruffing-NY .311 · Brown-Cle .314

Earned Run Average
Grove-Phi 2.84 · Ruffing-NY 3.09 · Lyons-Chi 3.28 · Crowder-Was 3.33 · Bridges-Det 3.36

Adjusted ERA
Grove-Phi 159 · Bridges-Det 140 · Hogsett-Det 133 · Lyons-Chi 132 · Ruffing-NY 132

Adjusted Starter Runs
Grove-Phi 54.0 · Crowder-Was 36.9 · Ferrell-Cle 31.8 · Ruffing-NY 31.8 · Lyons-Chi 27.9

Pitcher Wins
Grove-Phi 5.9 · Ferrell-Cle 4.8 · Ruffing-NY 4.… · Crowder-Was 3.8 · Lyons-Chi 3.…

The Babe's Last Hurrah

While the AL's slugging torch passed from Babe Ruth to the younger Jimmie Foxx and Lou Gehrig, the Yankees were on the way up. Bill Dickey, Ben Chapman, and rookie shortstop Frankie Crosetti provided vital shots of youth, and New York no longer depended on one or two sluggers to carry the club.

The Athletics were strong hitters, but their pitching (besides Lefty Grove) was no longer the best in the league. As a result, the Yankees—with terrific mound work from Red Ruffing and Johnny Allen, as well as 24 wins from "Goofy" Gomez—won comfortably, giving skipper Joe McCarthy his first AL title.

A record 707 homers flew from AL parks in 1932, and for the first time since 1922, a non-Yankee (Foxx) captured the individual crown. The Red Sox scored the league's fewest runs, allowed the most, and absorbed 111 losses to finish last for the seventh time in eight years. Several canny trades soon lifted the club into the first division.

Attendance dropped another 19 percent, and the AL suf[fered] its worst full season totals since 1915. Chicago's pligh[t] during the 1930s was especially strange. Attendance for th[e] mostly moribund team ping-ponged each year: down 42 percent, up 71, down 41, up 98, down 6, up 33, down 42, and so on unti[l] 1939-40, when they had two straight years of growth. The Ind[ians], finishing fourth for the third of four straight years, opene[d] new Lakefront Stadium on July 31. The cavernous park, the firs[t] built with public money, was a failure from the start—it ha[d] been commissioned in the hopes of drawing the Olympics. Oddl[y] shaped League Park housed the Tribe's weekday games until 1946.

Ruth's last, and greatest, October show resulted in New York's third World Series sweep since 1927. The 37-year-old sta[r,] ripped mercilessly by Cubs bench jockeys, hit .333 with 2 homer[s] while Lou Gehrig batted .529 with 3 bombs. Ruth's "called shot" at Wrigley Field in Game 3 has passed into baseball lore.

1931 National League

TEAM	W	L	T	PCT	GB	HW	HL	R	OR	PA	H	2B	3B	HR	BB	SO	HB	SH	AVG	OBP	SLG	OPS	AOPS	BR	ABR	PF	SB	CS	BSA	BSR
STL	101	53	0	.656		54	24	815	614	5989	1554	353	74	60	432	475	32	90	.286	.342	.411	753	105	66	37	104	114			
NY	87	65	1	.572	13	50	27	768	599	5840	1554	251	64	101	383	395	26	59	.289	.340	.416	756	112	59	78	98	83			
CHI	84	70	2	.545	17	50	27	828	710	6178	1578	340	66	84	577	641	25	125	.289	.360	.422	782	115	138	124	102	49			
BRO	79	73	1	.520	21	46	29	681	673	5814	1464	240	77	71	409	512	27	69	.276	.331	.390	721	101	-7	-2	99	45			
PIT	75	79	1	.487	26	44	33	636	691	5999	1425	243	70	41	493	454	16	130	.266	.330	.360	690	93	-56	-49	99	59			
PHI	66	88	1	.429	35	40	36	684	828	5935	1502	299	52	81	437	492	23	100	.279	.336	.400	736	96	29	-24	108	42			
BOS	64	90	2	.416	37	36	41	533	680	5809	1367	221	59	34	368	430	22	123	.258	.309	.341	650	84	-142	-122	96	46			
CIN	58	96	0	.377	43	38	39	592	742	5861	1439	241	70	21	403	463	22	93	.269	.323	.352	675	94	-88	-50	94	24			
TOT	618					358	256	5537		47425	11883	2188	532	493	3502	3862	193	789	.277	.334	.387	721					462			

TEAM	CG	SHO	GR	SV	IP	H	HR	BB	SO	BR/9	ERA	AERA	OAV	OOB	PR	APR	PF	OSB	OCS	FA	E	WPB	DP	FW	PW	BW	BSW	DIF
STL	80	17	111	20	1384.2	1470	65	449	626	12.6	3.45	114	.273	.332	63	72	102	51	67	.974	160	41	169	1.0	7.2	3.7		12.2
NY	90	17	105	12	1360.2	1341	71	422	570	11.8	3.30	112	.255	.313	85	61	96	37	40	.974	159	28	126	1.0	6.1	7.8		-3.8
CHI	80	8	144	8	1385.2	1448	54	524	541	13.0	3.97	97	.268	.337	-17	-19	100	49	52	.973	169	38	141	.6	-1.9	12.3		-4.0
BRO	64	9	142	11	1356.0	1520	56	351	546	12.5	3.84	99	.283	.329	3	-5	99	57	46	.969	187	27	154	-.7	-.5	-.2		4.4
PIT	89	9	97	5	1390.0	1489	55	442	345	12.6	3.66	105	.274	.331	32	28	100	59	38	.968	194	30	167	-.9	2.8	-4.9		1.0
PHI	60	6	163	16	1360.1	1603	75	511	499	14.2	4.58	93	.293	.358	-108	-46	110	79	53	.966	210	38	149	-1.9	-4.6	-2.4		-2.2
BOS	78	12	122	9	1380.1	1465	66	406	419	12.3	3.90	97	.272	.325	-5	-18	98	57	42	.973	170	29	141	.5	-1.8	-12.1		.4
CIN	70	7	133	6	1345.0	1545	51	399	317	13.1	4.22	89	.294	.346	-53	-75	97	73	40	.973	165	23	194	.7	-7.5	-5.0		-7.3
TOT	611	85	1017	94	10962.2					12.8	3.86		.277	.334						.971	1414	254	1241					

Batter-Fielder Wins
- Terry-NY 3.7
- Berger-Bos 3.6
- Cuccinello-Cin ..3.5
- Ott-NY 3.4
- P.Waner-Pit 3.1

Batting Average
- Hafey-StL 349
- Terry-NY 349
- Bottomley-StL 348
- Klein-Phi 337
- O'Doul-Bro 336

On-Base Percentage
- Hafey-StL 404
- Cuyler-Chi 404
- P.Waner-Pit 404
- Grantham-Pit 400
- Klein-Phi 398

Slugging Average
- Klein-Phi 584
- Hornsby-Chi 574
- Hafey-StL 569
- Ott-NY 545
- Arlett-Phi 538

On-Base Plus Slugging
- Klein-Phi 982
- Hafey-StL 973
- Ott-NY 937
- Terry-NY 926
- Berger-Bos 892

Adjusted OPS
- Ott-NY 153
- Hafey-StL 153
- Terry-NY 150
- Klein-Phi 149
- Berger-Bos 143

Adjusted Batter Runs
- Terry-NY 42.0
- Klein-Phi 40.0
- Ott-NY 38.1
- Berger-Bos 36.7
- Hornsby-Chi 34.2

Runs
- Terry-NY 121
- Klein-Phi 121
- English-Chi 117
- Cuyler-Chi 110
- Ott-NY 104

Hits
- L.Waner-Pit 214
- Terry-NY 213
- English-Chi 202
- Cuyler-Chi 202
- Klein-Phi 200

Doubles
- Adams-StL 46
- Berger-Bos 44
- Terry-NY 43
- Herman-Bro 43
- Bartell-Phi 43

Triples
- Terry-NY 20
- Herman-Bro 16
- Traynor-Pit 15
- Bissonette-Bro ...14

Home Runs
- Klein-Phi 31
- Ott-NY 29
- Berger-Bos 19
- Herman-Bro 18
- Arlett-Phi 18

Total Bases
- Klein-Phi 347
- Ott-NY 323
- Herman-Bro 320
- Berger-Bos 316
- Cuyler-Chi 290

Runs Batted In
- Klein-Phi 121
- Ott-NY 115
- Terry-NY 112
- Traynor-Pit 103
- Herman-Bro 97

Stolen Bases
- Frisch-StL 28
- Herman-Bro 17
- Martin-StL 16
- Adams-StL 16
- Watkins-StL 15

Base Stealing Runs

Fielding Runs-Infield
- Hurst-Phi 11.4
- Frisch-StL 10.9
- Terry-NY 10.3
- Maguire-Bos 10.1
- Jackson-NY 9.7

Fielding Runs-Outfield
- P.Waner-Pit 13.8
- Crabtree-Cin 10.3
- L.Waner-Pit 10.1
- Berger-Bos 4.1
- Ott-NY 2.5

Wins
- Meine-Pit 19
- Hallahan-StL 19
- J.Elliott-Phi 19

Winning Pct.
- Derringer-StL 692
- Hallahan-StL 679
- Bush-Chi 667
- Grimes-StL 654

Complete Games
- Lucas-Cin 24
- Brandt-Bos 23
- Meine-Pit 22
- Hubbell-NY 21
- French-Pit 20

Strikeouts
- Hallahan-StL 159
- Hubbell-NY 155
- Vance-Bro 150
- Derringer-StL 134
- Root-Chi 131

Fewest BB/Game
- Johnson-StL 1.40
- Lucas-Cin 1.47
- Cantwell-Bos 1.96
- Clark-Bro 2.01
- Zachary-Bos 2.08

Games
- J.Elliott-Phi 52
- Johnson-Cin 42
- Collins-Phi 42

Saves
- Quinn-Bro 15
- Lindsey-StL 7
- J.Elliott-Phi 5
- Hallahan-StL 4
- Collins-Phi 4

Base Runners/9
- Hubbell-NY 10.23
- Walker-NY 10.49
- Johnson-StL 10.50
- Fitzsimmons-NY ...10.79
- Mooney-NY 11.05

Adjusted Relief Runs
- Lindsey-StL 7.2
- Quinn-Bro 5.8
- May-Chi 1.8

Relief Ranking
- Quinn-Bro 10.3
- Lindsey-StL 10.1
- May-Chi 2.1

Innings Pitched
- Meine-Pit 284.0
- French-Pit 275.2
- Johnson-Cin 262.1
- Fitzsimmons-NY ...253.2
- Root-Chi 251.0

Opponents' Avg.
- Hubbell-NY 227
- Walker-NY 231
- Brandt-Bos 244
- Fitzsimmons-NY ...251
- Root-Chi 252

Opponents' OBP
- Hubbell-NY 282
- Walker-NY 283
- Johnson-StL 286
- Fitzsimmons-NY ...296
- Cantwell-Bos 301

Earned Run Average
- Walker-NY 2.26
- Hubbell-NY 2.65
- Brandt-Bos 2.92
- Meine-Pit 2.98
- Johnson-StL 3.00

Adjusted ERA
- Walker-NY 164
- Hubbell-NY 139
- Benge-Phi 134
- Johnson-StL 131
- Brandt-Bos 130

Adjusted Starter Runs
- Walker-NY 37.3
- Hubbell-NY 29.9
- Benge-Phi 25.7
- Meine-Pit 25.0
- Brandt-Bos 23.8

Pitcher Wins
- Hubbell-NY 3.4
- Brandt-Bos 3.4
- Fitzsimmons-NY ...2.9
- Walker-NY 2.9
- Benge-Phi 2.9

Wild Horses

Several Senior Circuit clubs altered their ballparks in 1931, but this alone could not have been responsible for the spectacular decrease in offense. NL teams plated just 4.48 runs a game, the smallest output in more than a decade, with homers dropping a stunning 45 percent. The league also adopted a rule abolishing home runs on fair balls bouncing into the stands; they'd be doubles instead, as was already the law in the AL.

Into this new environment stepped the Cardinals, who led wire to wire. A tough, gritty team with homespun, rural players who liked to raise a ruckus on and off the diamond, St. Louis hit only 60 homers—fourth in the loop—but led in steals and finished second in runs. Hard-nosed competitors like Frankie Frisch, Pepper Martin, Ripper Collins, and Burleigh Grimes defined the club, and rookie Paul Derringer was 18-8 to give the team a strong second starter behind Wild Bill Hallahan.

The second-place Giants ended 13 out. The lack of a pennant race, and the fifth through eight place clubs each finishing between 26 and 43 games behind, factored in a frightening attendance drop of 15.6 percent, the biggest fall since 1918.

Along with Derringer, several key players debuted in 1931. Boston third baseman Bucky Walters eventually washed out as a hitter, then became the dominant NL right-hander of the early 1940s. Ernie Lombardi, who would later catch Walters (as well as Derringer) in Cincinnati, hit .297 for Brooklyn. Dixie Walker, later a favorite in Brooklyn, collected the first of his 2,064 hits. Wilbert Robinson finally stepped down in Brooklyn, allowing the team to change names, from Robins back to Dodgers, as well as managers; with a 1,399-1,398 career record, "Uncle Robbie" quit while he was ahead, barely.

St. Louis took home the NL's first World Series title since the Cards' win in 1926. Martin ran wild in the Series, hitting .500 and scoring 5 runs. This seven-game loss was it for Mack's club; after 1932, the Athletics never again contended in Philadelphia.

1931 American League

TEAM	W	L	T	PCT	GB	HW	HL	R	OR	PA	H	2B	3B	HR	BB	SO	HB	SH	AVG	OBP	SLG	OPS	AOPS	BR	ABR	PF	SB	CS	BSA	BSR
PHI	107	45	1	.704		60	15	858	626	6019	1544	311	64	118	528	543	35	79	.287	.355	.435	790	107	96	45	106	25	23	52	-3
NY	94	59	2	.614	13.5	51	25	1067	760	6471	1667	277	78	155	748	554	28	87	.297	.383	.457	840	135	222	285	94	138	68	67	7
WAS	92	62	2	.597	16	55	22	843	690	6183	1588	308	93	49	481	459	30	96	.285	.345	.400	745	100	6	2	101	72	64	53	-7
CLE	78	76	1	.506	30	45	31	885	833	6112	1612	321	62	71	488	580	12	91	.296	.363	.419	782	92	-41	-66	104	73	80	48	-12
STL	63	91	0	.409	45	39	38	721	870	5935	1455	287	69	76	405	565	12	68	.271	.333	.390	723	85	-155	-119	95	42	43	49	-6
BOS	62	90	1	.408	45	39	40	625	800	5864	1409	289	34	37	480	468	20	63	.262	.315	.349	664	87	-80	-103	103	117	75	61	-1
DET	61	93	0	.396	47	36	41	651	836	5993	1456	292	69	43	480	511	21	61	.268	.330	.371	701	86	-60	-80	94	94	39	71	7
CHI	56	97	3	.366	51.5	31	45	704	939	6099	1423	238	69	27	483	445	30	105	.260	.323	.343	666	86	-151	-111	94				
TOT	618					356	257	6354		48676	12154	2323	538	576	4168	4047	188	650	.278	.344	.396	740					624	452	58	-21

TEAM	CG	SHO	GR	SV	IP	H	HR	BB	SO	BR/9	ERA	AERA	OAV	OOB	PR	APR	PF	OSB	OCS	FA	E	WPB	DP	FW	PW	BW	BSW	DIF
PHI	97	12	82	16	1365.1	1342	73	457	574	11.9	3.47	130	.256	.316	138	152	103	66	51	.976	141	30	151	3.2	14.2	4.2	-.0	9.5
NY	78	4	132	17	1410.1	1461	67	543	686	12.9	4.20	94	.263	.332	28	-41	91	71	54	.972	169	24	131	1.7	-3.8	26.5	.9	-7.8
WAS	60	7	145	24	1394.1	1434	73	498	582	12.6	3.76	114	.264	.327	95	83	98	65	45	.976	142	28	148	3.3	7.7	.2	-.4	4.2
CLE	76	6	124	9	1354.2	1577	64	561	470	14.4	4.63	100	.286	.355	-38	-2	106	76	64	.963	232	30	143	-2.0	-.2	4.5	-.4	-.8
STL	65	4	129	10	1362.0	1623	84	448	436	13.8	4.76	97	.293	.348	-57	-17	106	69	51	.963	232	28	160	-2.1	-1.6	-6.1	-.9	-3.3
BOS	61	5	161	10	1366.2	1559	54	473	365	13.5	4.60	94	.285	.344	-33	-45	98	70	56	.970	188	28	127	-1.4	-4.2	-11.1	-.3	-5.1
DET	86	5	92	6	1384.1	1549	79	597	511	14.1	4.59	100	.282	.355	-32	-1	105	95	72	.964	220	33	139	-1.4	-.0	-9.6	.2	-5.1
CHI	54	6	170	10	1390.1	1613	82	588	421	14.5	5.04	85	.287	.358	-101	-125	97	112	59	.961	245	29	131	-2.7	-11.6	-10.3	.9	3.3
TOT	577	49	1035	102	11028.0					13.5	4.38		.278	.344						.968	1569	222	1130					

Batter-Fielder Wins
- **Ruth-NY** 8.1
- **Gehrig-NY** 6.0
- **Simmons-Phi** 4.6
- **Cochrane-Phi** 4.5
- **Cronin-Was** 4.5

Batting Average
- Simmons-Phi .390
- Ruth-NY .373
- Morgan-Cle .351
- Cochrane-Phi .349
- Gehrig-NY .341

On-Base Percentage
- Ruth-NY .495
- Morgan-Cle .451
- Gehrig-NY .446
- Simmons-Phi .444
- Blue-Chi .430

Slugging Average
- Ruth-NY .700
- Gehrig-NY .662
- Simmons-Phi .641
- Averill-Cle .576
- Foxx-Phi .567

On-Base Plus Slugging
- Ruth-NY 1.195
- Gehrig-NY 1.108
- Simmons-Phi 1.085
- Averill-Cle .979
- Cochrane-Phi .976

Adjusted OPS
- Ruth-NY 223
- Gehrig-NY 199
- Simmons-Phi 172
- Webb-Bos 151
- Goslin-StL 147

Adjusted Batter Runs
- Ruth-NY 104.4
- Gehrig-NY 91.0
- Simmons-Phi 52.4
- Webb-Bos 47.4
- Goslin-StL 41.

Runs
- Gehrig-NY 163
- Ruth-NY 149
- Averill-Cle 140
- Combs-NY 120
- Chapman-NY 120

Hits
- Gehrig-NY 211
- Averill-Cle 209
- Simmons-Phi 200
- Ruth-NY 199
- Webb-Bos 196

Doubles
- Webb-Bos 67
- Alexander-Det 47
- Kress-StL 46
- Cronin-Was 44

Triples
- Johnson-Det 19
- Gehrig-NY 15
- Blue-Chi 15
- Vosmik-Cle 14
- Reynolds-Chi 14

Home Runs
- Ruth-NY 46
- Gehrig-NY 46
- Averill-Cle 32
- Foxx-Phi 30
- Goslin-StL 24

Total Bases
- Gehrig-NY 410
- Ruth-NY 374
- Averill-Cle 361
- Simmons-Phi 329
- Goslin-StL 328

Runs Batted In
- Gehrig-NY 18
- Ruth-NY 16
- Averill-Cle 14
- Simmons-Phi 12
- Cronin-Was 12

Stolen Bases
- Chapman-NY 61
- Johnson-Det 33
- Burns-StL 19
- Lazzeri-NY 18
- Cissell-Chi 18

Base Stealing Runs
- Chapman-NY 5.4
- Cissell-Chi 1.9
- H.Walker-Det 1.9
- Blue-Chi 1.8
- Reynolds-Chi 1.6

Fielding Runs-Infield
- Melillo-StL 35.3
- Burns-StL 18.8
- Rhyne-Bos 18.0
- Hodapp-Cle 15.2
- McManus-Det-Bos 13.1

Fielding Runs-Outfield
- West-Was 13.6
- Johnson-Det 11.4
- Oliver-Bos 5.8
- Simmons-Phi 5.5
- Chapman-NY 5.3

Wins
- Grove-Phi 31
- Ferrell-Cle 22
- Gomez-NY 21
- Earnshaw-Phi 21
- Walberg-Phi 20

Winning Pct.
- Grove-Phi .886
- Marberry-Was .800
- Mahaffey-Phi .789
- Earnshaw-Phi .750
- Gomez-NY .700

Complete Games
- Grove-Phi 2
- Ferrell-Cle 2
- Earnshaw-Phi 2
- Whitehill-Det 2
- Stewart-StL 2

Strikeouts
- Grove-Phi 175
- Earnshaw-Phi 152
- Gomez-NY 150
- Ruffing-NY 132
- Hadley-Was 124

Fewest BB/Game
- Pennock-NY 1.43
- Gray-StL 1.88
- Grove-Phi 1.93
- Brown-Cle 2.12
- Blaeholder-StL 2.23

Games
- Hadley-Was 55
- Moore-Bos 53
- Caraway-Chi 51
- Frasier-Chi 46
- Fischer-Was 46

Saves
- Moore-Bos 10
- Hadley-Was 8
- Marberry-Was 7
- Kimsey-StL 7
- Earnshaw-Phi 6

Base Runners/9
- Grove-Phi 9.73
- Earnshaw-Phi 10.64
- Gomez-NY 10.93
- Coffman-StL 11.27
- Uhle-Det 11.33

Adjusted Relief Runs
- Kimsey-StL 7

Relief Ranking
- Kimsey-StL

Innings Pitched
- Walberg-Phi 291.0
- Grove-Phi 288.2
- Earnshaw-Phi 281.2
- Ferrell-Cle 276.1
- Whitehill-Det 271.1

Opponents' Avg.
- Hadley-Was .218
- Gomez-NY .226
- Grove-Phi .229
- Johnson-NY .234
- Earnshaw-Phi .236

Opponents' OBP
- Grove-Phi .271
- Earnshaw-Phi .288
- Gomez-NY .295
- Coffman-StL .298
- Uhle-Det .304

Earned Run Average
- Grove-Phi 2.06
- Gomez-NY 2.67
- Hadley-Was 3.06
- Brown-Was 3.20
- Marberry-Was 3.45

Adjusted ERA
- Grove-Phi 218
- Gomez-NY 149
- Hadley-Was 140
- Brown-Was 134
- Uhle-Det 131

Adjusted Starter Runs
- Grove-Phi 73.9
- Gomez-NY 36.5
- Walberg-Phi 28.2
- Earnshaw-Phi 27.8
- Brown-Was 27.2

Pitcher Wins
- **Grove-Phi** 8.
- **Ferrell-Cle** 5.
- **Gomez-NY** 3.
- **Earnshaw-Phi** 3.
- **Brown-Was** 3.

A Sticky End

There was little drama in the American League race, as Connie Mack's Athletics wiped up the competition. New York, with Joe McCarthy over to manage from the Cubs, finished 13½ games out despite a late charge. Led by Babe Ruth and Lou Gehrig again, the Yankees outscored their opponents at home and on the road. But New York's pitching wasn't nearly up to the Athletics' standards, and Mack's club had its own three-pronged attack of Jimmie Foxx, Al Simmons, and Mickey Cochrane. Philly also had 20-game winners Rube Walberg and George Earnshaw—and Lefty Grove, who set a major league mark for winning percentage and dominated other mound categories as well.

Homers fell 14 percent and overall scoring dropped 5 percent. Part of this change was due to park adjustments. The Tigers enlarged Navin Field's left field by 28 feet, and runs and homers fell dramatically. The Senators removed left-field seats at Griffith Stadium, relocating the wall to 407 feet, and scoring droppe[d] slightly. On the other hand, Boston brought in Fenway's right-field fence by 33 feet, and runs in their home games increased slightly though homers did not. (They moved the fence back in 1933.)

Reflecting the downfall of the running game, the 0.5 stolen bases per game was the *highest* rate of the decade. Boston's unheralded Earl Webb set an all-time mark with 67 doubles. And in a frightening development, AL attendance fell 17 percent in 1931, and the league had its lowest total since 1919.

White Sox owner Charles Comiskey died in October after his team pulled up last. The Old Roman had to be pleased to outlive AL founder and adversary Ban Johnson by eight months. In addition, October was the effective end of the Athletics dynasty, which began crumbling in a surprising seven-game World Series loss to St. Louis.

1930 National League

TEAM	W	L	T	PCT	GB	HW	HL	R	OR	PA	H	2B	3B	HR	BB	SO	HB	SH	AVG	OBP	SLG	OPS	AOPS	BR	ABR	PF	SB	CS	BSA	BSR
STL	92	62	0	.597		53	24	1004	784	6204	1732	373	89	104	479	496	28	185	.314	.372	.471	843	105	77	46	103	72			
CHI	90	64	2	.584	2	51	26	998	870	6354	1722	305	72	171	588	635	37	148	.309	.378	.481	859	111	113	106	101	70			
NY	87	67	0	.565	5	46	31	959	814	6161	1769	264	83	143	422	382	21	165	.319	.369	.473	842	110	63	83	98	59			
BRO	86	68	0	.558	6	49	28	871	738	6088	1654	303	73	122	481	541	27	147	.304	.364	.454	818	103	22	33	99	53			
PIT	80	74	0	.519	12	42	35	891	928	6058	1622	285	119	86	494	449	22	196	.303	.365	.449	814	101	12	9	100	76			
BOS	70	84	0	.455	22	39	38	693	835	5870	1503	246	78	66	332	397	28	154	.281	.326	.393	719	81	-192	-169	97	69			
CIN	59	95	0	.383	33	37	40	665	857	5880	1475	265	67	74	445	489	16	174	.281	.339	.400	739	87	-137	-100	95	48			
PHI	52	102	2	.338	40	35	42	944	1199	6288	1783	345	44	126	450	459	23	148	.315	.367	.458	825	97	42	-21	107	34			
TOT	618					352	264	7025		48903	13260	2386	625	892	3691	3848	202	1317	.303	.360	.448	808					481			

TEAM	CG	SHO	GR	SV	IP	H	HR	BB	SO	BR/9	ERA	AERA	OAV	OOB	PR	APR	PF	OSB	OCS	FA	E	WPB	DP	FW	PW	BW	BSW	DIF
STL	63	5	150	21	1380.2	1594	87	476	639	13.7	4.39	114	.293	.353	89	94	101	52	57	.970	183	53	176	.2	8.3	4.1		2.5
CHI	67	6	174	12	1403.2	1642	111	528	601	14.1	4.80	102	.294	.357	26	14	98	47	49	.973	170	41	167	1.0	1.2	9.4		1.4
NY	64	6	157	19	1363.1	1546	117	439	522	13.3	4.61	103	.290	.348	54	19	95	59	44	.974	164	26	144		1.7	7.3		-.3
BRO	74	13	138	15	1372.0	1480	115	394	526	12.4	4.03	122	.278	.330	144	136	99	59	46	.972	174	32	167	.7	12.0	2.9		-6.6
PIT	80	7	107	13	1361.1	1730	128	438	393	14.5	5.24	95	.313	.367	-41	-40	100	61	55	.965	216	33	164	-1.8	-3.5	.8		7.5
BOS	71	6	124	11	1361.0	1624	117	475	424	14.0	4.91	100	.302	.360	9	3	99	51	33	.971	178	26	164	.4	.3	-14.9		7.2
CIN	61	6	149	11	1335.0	1650	75	394	361	13.9	5.08	95	.310	.361	-15	-38	97	65	46	.973	161	42	164	1.4	-3.4	-8.8		-7.2
PHI	54	3	201	7	1372.2	1993	142	543	384	16.8	6.71	81	.346	.405	-266	-172	110	87	42	.962	239	34	169	-3.0	-15.2	-1.9		-5.0
TOT	534	52	1200	109	10949.2					14.1	4.97		.303	.360						.970	1485	287	1318					

Batter-Fielder Wins		Batting Average		On-Base Percentage		Slugging Average		On-Base Plus Slugging		Adjusted OPS		Adjusted Batter Runs	
Klein-Phi	5.7	Terry-NY	401	Ott-NY	458	Wilson-Chi	723	Wilson-Chi	1177	Wilson-Chi	177	Wilson-Chi	75.7
Terry-NY	5.6	Herman-Bro	393	Herman-Bro	455	Klein-Phi	687	Herman-Bro	1132	Herman-Bro	171	Herman-Bro	72.1
Lindstrom-NY	4.7	Klein-Phi	386	Wilson-Chi	454	Herman-Bro	678	Klein-Phi	1123	Terry-NY	159	Terry-NY	61.3
Wilson-Chi	4.7	O'Doul-Phi	383	O'Doul-Phi	453	Hafey-StL	652	Terry-NY	1071	Klein-Phi	155	Klein-Phi	57.7
Hartnett-Chi	4.1	Lindstrom-NY	379	Terry-NY	452	Hartnett-Chi	630	Hafey-StL	1059	Ott-NY	152	Ott-NY	50.2

Runs		Hits		Doubles		Triples		Home Runs		Total Bases		Runs Batted In	
Klein-Phi	158	Terry-NY	254	Klein-Phi	59	Comorosky-Pit	23	Wilson-Chi	56	Klein-Phi	445	Wilson-Chi	191
Cuyler-Chi	155	Klein-Phi	250	Cuyler-Chi	50	PWaner-Pit	18	Klein-Phi	40	Wilson-Chi	423	Klein-Phi	170
English-Chi	152	Herman-Bro	241	Herman-Bro	48	English-Chi	17	Berger-Bos	38	Herman-Bro	416	Cuyler-Chi	134
Wilson-Chi	146	Lindstrom-NY	231	Comorosky-Pit	47	Cuyler-Chi	17	Hartnett-Chi	37	Terry-NY	392	Herman-Bro	130
Herman-Bro	143	Cuyler-Chi	228	Frisch-StL	46	Terry-NY	15	Herman-Bro	35	Cuyler-Chi	351	Terry-NY	129

Stolen Bases		Base Stealing Runs		Fielding Runs-Infield		Fielding Runs-Outfield		Wins		Winning Pct.		Complete Games	
Cuyler-Chi	37			Frisch-StL	22.3	Klein-Phi	21.2	Malone-Chi	20	Fitzsimmons-NY	731	Malone-Chi	22
PWaner-Pit	18			Whitney-Phi	20.8	Heilmann-Cin	11.3	Kremer-Pit	20	Malone-Chi	690	Brame-Pit	22
Herman-Bro	18			Terry-NY	13.9	Welsh-Bos	7.0	Fitzsimmons-NY	19	Brame-Pit	680	French-Pit	21
				Durocher-Cin	11.3	Sothern-Phi-Pit	6.6			Kremer-Pit	625	Vance-Bro	20
				Gilbert-Bro	9.3	Bressler-Bro	6.1			Hallahan-StL	625	Seibold-Bos	20

Strikeouts		Fewest BB/Game		Games		Saves		Base Runners/9		Adjusted Relief Runs		Relief Ranking	
Hallahan-StL	177	Clark-Bro	1.71	Elliott-Phi	48	Bell-StL	8	Vance-Bro	10.47	Bell-StL	11.2	Lindsey-StL	8.4
Vance-Bro	173	Kolp-Cin	1.82	Collins-Phi	47	Heving-NY	6	Thurston-Bro	10.78	Lindsey-StL	7.5	Bell-StL	7.9
Malone-Chi	142	Johnson-StL	1.82	Malone-Chi	46	Clark-Bro	6	Clark-Bro	11.11				
Root-Chi	124	Lucas-Cin	1.88	Pruett-NY	45			Kolp-Cin	11.44				
Hubbell-NY	117	Vance-Bro	1.91	Malone-Chi	45			Fitzsimmons-NY	11.63				

Innings Pitched		Opponents' Avg.		Opponents' OBP		Earned Run Average		Adjusted ERA		Adjusted Starter Runs		Pitcher Wins	
Kremer-Pit	276.0	Vance-Bro	246	Vance-Bro	289	Vance-Bro	2.61	Vance-Bro	188	Vance-Bro	64.1	Vance-Bro	6.4
French-Pit	274.2	Hallahan-StL	260	Clark-Bro	306	Hubbell-NY	3.87	Elliott-Bro	124	Malone-Chi	26.1	Malone-Chi	2.6
Malone-Chi	271.2	Fitzsimmons-NY	266	Fitzsimmons-NY	314	Walker-NY	3.93	Malone-Chi	124	Hubbell-NY	24.8	Seibold-Bos	2.0
Vance-Bro	258.2	Walker-NY	268	Kolp-Cin	314	Malone-Chi	3.94	Grimes-Bos-StL	123	Elliott-Bro	23.4	Clark-Bro	2.0
Seibold-Bos	251.0	Malone-Chi	271	Hubbell-NY	327	Elliott-Bro	3.95	Hubbell-NY	122	Seibold-Bos	20.3	Root-Chi	1.9

Truly Offensive

If 1929 was a bad dream for pitchers, 1930 was hell. The league changed the ball, winding it tighter and reducing the size of the stitches, which impaired the pitcher's grip. The resulting league average rose to .303, the OPS .808, and runs per team per game to 5.68. None of these numbers have ever been topped.

For the Phillies, Chuck Klein scored 158 runs and hit .386 with 40 homers, and Lefty O'Doul scored 122 runs. The team hit .315 but finished last—with a 6.71 team ERA. Philadelphia's *average* game was a 7-6 loss. Even Grover Cleveland Alexander—back where he started—was finished after a short trial at age 43; his 9.14 ERA was almost equal to his ERAs added together with the Phils from 1913–17.

The true star of 1930 was Brooklyn's Dazzy Vance, whose 2.61 ERA led the league by more than a run; the league average was 4.98. Chicago's Hack Wilson was a slugging machine. His 56 homers survived as an NL record until 1998, and his RBI mark still stands—later research, in fact, resulted in his total *improving* to 191 almost seven decades after the fact.

St. Louis bounced back to top the league in runs, thanks to Jim Bottomley, Chick Hafey, Frankie Frisch, and an excellent bench. The Cardinals went 21-4 in September, passing the Cubs and the surprising Robins. Giants first baseman Bill Terry became the last NLer to hit over .400, but McGraw's men finished 5 games back.

Hall of Fame shortstop Dave Bancroft hung 'em up, as did Cy Williams, who hit 251 career homers. Cubs pitcher Hal Carlson died suddenly May 30 of a stomach hemorrhage, while rookie Lon Warneke of Chicago began his 192-win career. Dizzy Dean debuted with a 3-hitter for St. Louis on September 28.

Most believed that attendance would drop because of 1929's financial crash, but a 50 percent gain in Brooklyn helped overall attendance jump 10.6 percent. This unexpected leap was whistling in the dark—the bad times were about to begin.

1930 American League

TEAM	W	L	T	PCT	GB	HW	HL	R	OR	PA	H	2B	3B	HR	BB	SO	HB	SH	AVG	OBP	SLG	OPS	AOPS	BR	ABR	PF	SB	CS	BSA	BSR
PHI	102	52	0	.662		**58**	18	951	751	6158	1573	319	74	125	599	531	32	**182**	.294	.369	.452	821	108	106	66	104	48	33	59	-1
WAS	94	60	0	.610	8	56	21	892	**689**	6116	1620	300	98	57	537	438	38	171	.302	.369	.426	795	106	59	55	100	**101**	67	60	-1
NY	86	68	0	.558	16	47	29	**1062**	898	6272	**1683**	298	110	**152**	644	569	19	161	**.309**	**.384**	**.488**	872	131	208	259	96	91	60	60	-1
CLE	81	73	0	.526	21	44	33	890	915	6130	1654	**358**	59	72	490	461	26	175	.304	.364	.431	795	104	60	27	104	51	47	52	-5
DET	75	79	0	.487	27	45	33	783	833	5927	1504	298	90	82	461	508	25	144	.284	.344	.421	765	96	-19	-34	102	98	70	58	-3
STL	64	90	0	.416	38	38	40	751	886	5941	1415	289	67	75	497	550	15	151	.268	.333	.391	724	85	-96	-120	103	93	71	57	-4
CHI	62	92	0	.403	40	34	44	729	884	5995	1496	256	90	63	389	479	32	155	.276	.328	.391	719	89	-117	-92	97	74	40	**65**	2
BOS	52	102	0	.338	50	30	46	612	814	5807	1393	257	68	47	358	552	19	144	.264	.313	.365	678	79	-197	-172	96	42	35	55	-3
TOT	616					352	264	6670		48346	12338	2375	656	673	3975	4088	206	1283	.288	.351	.421	772				598	423	59	-16

TEAM	CG	SHO	GR	SV	IP	H	HR	BB	SO	BR/9	ERA	AERA	OAV	OOB	PR	APR	PF	OSB	OCS	FA	E	WPB	DP	FW	PW	BW	BSW	DIF
PHI	72	**8**	136	**21**	1371.0	1457	84	488	**672**	12.9	4.28	109	.274	.337	56	58	101	79	44	**.975**	145	36	121	3.0	5.2	6.0	.0	10.7
WAS	**78**	6	111	14	1369.0	**1367**	52	504	524	12.5	3.96	116	**.264**	.332	-36	-98	93	82	48	.965	207	50	132	-.7	-8.9	**23.4**	.0	-4.9
NY	65	7	**150**	15	1367.2	1566	93	524	572	13.9	4.88	88	.287	.352	-36	-9	104	92	51	.962	237	31	156	-2.5	-.8	2.4	-.3	5.2
CLE	68	5	139	14	1360.0	1663	85	528	442	14.6	4.88	99	.305	.368	-8	13	103	105	47	.962	192	44	156	.2	1.2	-3.1	-.0	.3
DET	68	4	137	17	1351.2	1507	86	570	574	14.0	4.70	102	.300	.359	-8	-29	105	59	**64**	.970	188	**14**	152	.4	-2.6	-10.9	-.2	.3
STL	68	5	122	10	1371.2	1639	124	449	470	13.9	5.07	96	.300	.356	-65	-29	105	59	61	.970	235	31	136	-2.4	-1.4	-8.3	**.4**	-3.3
CHI	63	2	146	10	1361.0	1629	74	**407**	471	13.6	4.71	98	.300	.352	-10	-15	99	78	61	.962	196	30	**161**	-.0	-1.1	-15.6	-.0	-8.2
BOS	**78**	4	92	5	1360.1	1515	75	488	356	13.4	4.68	98	.286	.348	-6	-12	99	**50**	55	.968	157	19	150					
TOT	560	41	1033	106	10912.1					13.6	4.65		.288	.351						.968	1557	255	1164					

Batter-Fielder Wins		Batting Average		On-Base Percentage		Slugging Average		On-Base Plus Slugging		Adjusted OPS		Adjusted Batter Runs	
Gehrig-NY	7.7	Simmons-Phi	381	Ruth-NY	493	Ruth-NY	732	Ruth-NY	1225	Ruth-NY	216	Ruth-NY	100.0
Ruth-NY	7.6	Gehrig-NY	379	Gehrig-NY	473	Gehrig-NY	721	Gehrig-NY	1194	Gehrig-NY	207	Gehrig-NY	98.5
Cronin-Was	6.9	Ruth-NY	359	Foxx-Phi	429	Simmons-Phi	708	Simmons-Phi	1130	Simmons-Phi	173	Simmons-Phi	58.1
Simmons-Phi	4.5	Reynolds-Chi	359	Bishop-Phi	426	Foxx-Phi	637	Foxx-Phi	1066	Foxx-Phi	159	Foxx-Phi	51.3
Cochrane-Phi	3.8	Cochrane-Phi	357	Combs-NY	424			Morgan-Cle	1014	Morgan-Cle	148	Morgan-Cle	42.3

Runs		Hits		Doubles		Triples		Home Runs		Total Bases		Runs Batted In	
Simmons-Phi	152	Hodapp-Cle	225	Hodapp-Cle	51	Combs-NY	22	Ruth-NY	49	Gehrig-NY	419	Gehrig-NY	174
Ruth-NY	150	Gehrig-NY	220	Manush-StL-Was	49	Reynolds-Chi	18	Gehrig-NY	41	Simmons-Phi	392	Simmons-Phi	165
Gehringer-Det	144	Simmons-Phi	211	Morgan-Cle	47	Gehrig-NY	17	Goslin-Was-StL	37	Ruth-NY	379	Foxx-Phi	156
Gehrig-NY	143	Rice-Was	207	Gehringer-Det	47	Simmons-Phi	16	Foxx-Phi	37	Foxx-Phi	358	Ruth-NY	153
Combs-NY	129	Morgan-Cle	204					Simmons-Phi	36			Goslin-Was-StL	138

Stolen Bases		Base Stealing Runs		Fielding Runs-Infield		Fielding Runs-Outfield		Wins		Winning Pct.		Complete Games	
McManus-Det	23	Lary-NY	2.4	Cronin-Was	26.5	Haas-Phi	7.4	Grove-Phi	28	Grove-Phi	848	Lyons-Chi	29
Gehringer-Det	19	McManus-Det	2.3	Melillo-StL	24.7	Oliver-Bos	6.0	Ferrell-Cle	25	Marberry-Was	750	Crowder-StL-Was	25
Goslin-Was-StL	17	Reynolds-Chi	2.1	Goldman-Cle	15.3	Johnson-Det	4.9	Lyons-Chi	22	Jones-Was	682	Ferrell-Cle	25
Johnson-Det	17	Simmons-Phi	1.3	Kamm-Chi	12.5	Goslin-Was-StL	4.5	Earnshaw-Phi	22	Ferrell-Cle	658	Stewart-StL	23
Cronin-Was	17	Dickey-NY	1.2	Hodapp-Cle	10.3	Harris-Chi-Was	4.1	Stewart-StL	20	Ruffing-Bos-NY	652	Grove-Phi	22

Strikeouts		Fewest BB/Game		Games		Saves		Base Runners/9		Adjusted Relief Runs		Relief Ranking	
Grove-Phi	209	Pennock-NY	1.15	Grove-Phi	50	Grove-Phi	9	Grove-Phi	10.45	Quinn-Phi	2.4	Quinn-Phi	4.2
Earnshaw-Phi	193	Lyons-Chi	1.72	Earnshaw-Phi	49	Braxton-Was-Chi	6	Burke-Was	11.38				
Hadley-Was	162	Grove-Phi	1.86	Pipgras-NY	44	Quinn-Phi	6	Stewart-StL	11.69				
Ferrell-Cle	143	Russell-Bos	2.08	Johnson-NY	44	Sullivan-Det	5	Rommel-Phi	11.74				
Ruffing-Bos-NY	131	Brown-Cle	2.15	Ferrell-Cle	43	McKain-Chi	5	Lyons-Chi	11.79				

Innings Pitched		Opponents' Avg.		Opponents' OBP		Earned Run Average		Adjusted ERA		Adjusted Starter Runs		Pitcher Wins	
Lyons-Chi	297.2	Lyons-Chi	247	Grove-Phi	288	Grove-Phi	2.54	Grove-Phi	184	Grove-Phi	65.8	**Grove-Phi**	6.9
Ferrell-Cle	296.2	Hadley-Was	247	Stewart-StL	315	Ferrell-Cle	3.31	Ferrell-Cle	146	Ferrell-Cle	45.9	**Ferrell-Cle**	5.9
Earnshaw-Phi	296.0	Crowder-StL-Was	259	Lyons-Chi	319	Stewart-StL	3.45	Stewart-StL	141	Stewart-StL	40.8	**Stewart-StL**	4.4
Grove-Phi	291.0	Collins-StL	259	Marberry-Was	321	Uhle-Det	3.65	Uhle-Det	131	Uhle-Det	31.3	**Lyons-Chi**	3.7
Crowder-StL-Was	279.2	Gaston-Bos	259	Crowder-StL-Was	321	Hadley-Was	3.73	Sorrell-Det	124	Crowder-StL-Was	29.6	**Uhle-Det**	3.4

Hitters Explode, but Pitching Carries the A's

Manager Walter Johnson's Senators, fifth in 1929, improved by 22 games and kept the race close until mid-July. Despite playing in a huge park, the Senators had good hitters like young shortstop Joe Cronin. But once again, the Athletics won by plenty.

Philadelphia enlarged Shibe Park in left and right field before the season, which helps explain how Lefty Grove's ERA declined from 2.81 to 2.54. But those changes don't explain how he dominated a league where offense increased by 8 percent. The incredible Grove was supported ably by George Earnshaw. Jimmie Foxx and Al Simmons provided the power, but the entire lineup added value.

The AL's 673 long balls set a new mark, while runs per team per game increased to 5.41, also an all-time record. Washington's 3.97 ERA was the highest to that point to lead the league. Foxx topped batters with 66 strikeouts, the lowest league-leading total for which figures are available. Despite becoming the first team in the twentieth century to top 1,000 runs, the Yankees floundered due to substandard pitching. Rookie Lefty Gomez and new acquisition Red Ruffing soon helped sort things out.

It was a tough time, though, at the box office. The Yankees were the last AL club to draw one million fans until 1935. The depression cut attendance nearly everywhere; despite the quality of the club, crowds fell each year from 1930–32 in Philadelphia. Hoping that fans would embrace hitting, speed and defense went out the window. This was the age of Smead Jolley, Zeke Bonura, and Buzz Arlett—sluggers whose modest hitting gifts are overstated by the offensive inflation of the era.

Grove and Earnshaw each won twice in the six-game World Series, allowing St. Louis just 7 runs in 5 starts between them. Only in Game 3 did anyone besides Grove or Earnshaw throw a pitch for the Athletics.

1929 National League

TEAM	W	L	T	PCT	GB	HW	HL	R	OR	PA	H	2B	3B	HR	BB	SO	HB	SH	AVG	OBP	SLG	OPS	AOPS	BR	ABR	PF	SB	CS	BSA	BSR
CHI	98	54	4	.645		52	25	982	758	6252	1655	310	46	139	589	567	29	163	.303	.373	.452	825	111	98	96	100	103			
PIT	88	65	1	.575	10.5	45	31	904	780	6198	1663	285	116	60	503	335	29	176	.303	.364	.430	794	101	25	5	102	94			
NY	84	67	1	.556	13.5	39	37	897	709	6060	1594	251	47	136	482	405	36	154	.296	.358	.436	794	103	18	21	100	85			
STL	78	74	2	.513	20	43	32	831	806	6030	1569	310	84	100	490	455	22	154	.293	.354	.438	792	101	13	5	101	72			
PHI	71	82	1	.464	27.5	39	37	897	1032	6216	1693	305	51	153	573	470	24	135	.309	.377	.467	844	108	130	70	107	59			
BRO	70	83	0	.458	28.5	42	35	755	888	5954	1535	232	69	99	504	454	22	155	.291	.355	.427	782	102	-1	16	98	80			
CIN	66	88	1	.429	33	38	39	686	760	5882	1478	258	79	34	412	347	26	175	.281	.336	.379	715	87	-137	-104	95	134			
BOS	56	98	0	.364	43	34	43	657	876	5923	1481	252	77	33	408	432	27	197	.280	.335	.375	710	85	-146	-118	96	65			
TOT	616					332	279	6609		48515	12668	2253	569	754	3961	3465	215	1309	.294	.357	.426	783					692			

TEAM	CG	SHO	GR	SV	IP	H	HR	BB	SO	BR/9	ERA	AERA	OAV	OOB	PR	APR	PF	OSB	OCS	FA	E	WPB	DP	FW	PW	BW	BSW	DIF
CHI	79	14	139	21	1398.2	1542	77	537	548	13.5	4.16	111	.284	.350	86	71	98	67	72	.975	154	36	169	1.4	6.5	8.7		5.4
PIT	79	5	134	13	1379.0	1530	96	439	409	13.0	4.36	109	.284	.340	54	61	101	87	67	.970	181	31	136	-.2	5.5	.5		5.7
NY	68	9	131	13	1372.0	1536	102	387	431	12.7	3.97	115	.287	.337	113	96	97	63	26	.975	158	24	163	.9	8.7	1.9		-3.1
STL	83	6	115	8	1359.2	1604	101	474	453	13.9	4.66	100	.297	.357	8	-1	99	76	63	.971	174	26	149	.2	-.0	.5		1.5
PHI	45	4	204	24	1348.0	1743	122	616	369	16.0	6.13	85	.319	.391	-212	-129	110	96	64	.969	191	30	153	-.8	-11.7	6.4		.7
BRO	59	8	173	16	1358.0	1553	92	549	549	14.2	4.92	94	.290	.360	-32	-49	98	146	65	.968	192	45	113	-.9	-4.5	1.5		-2.6
CIN	75	5	121	8	1369.1	1558	61	413	347	13.1	4.41	103	.292	.345	46	23	97	73	74	.974	162	19	148	.9	2.1	-9.5		-4.5
BOS	78	4	108	12	1352.2	1604	103	530	366	14.4	5.12	91	.302	.367	-62	-69	99	84	66	.967	204	32	146	-1.5	-6.3	-10.7		-2.5
TOT	566	56	1125	115	10937.1					13.8	4.71		.294	.357						.971	1416	243	1177					

Batter-Fielder Wins		Batting Average		On-Base Percentage		Slugging Average		On-Base Plus Slugging		Adjusted OPS		Adjusted Batter Runs	
Hornsby-Chi	6.8	O'Doul-Phi	.398	O'Doul-Phi	.465	Hornsby-Chi	.679	Hornsby-Chi	1139	Hornsby-Chi	178	Hornsby-Chi	75.7
Ott-NY	5.0	Herman-Bro	.381	Hornsby-Chi	.459	Klein-Phi	.657	O'Doul-Phi	1087	Ott-NY	166	Ott-NY	61.1
O'Doul-Phi	4.5	Hornsby-Chi	.380	Ott-NY	.449	Ott-NY	.635	Ott-NY	1084	Herman-Bro	160	O'Doul-Phi	59.1
Whitney-Phi	3.7	Terry-NY	.372	Stephenson-Phi	.445	Hafey-StL	.632	Klein-Phi	1065	O'Doul-Phi	157	Herman-Bro	53.1
Wilson-Chi	3.6	Stephenson-Chi	.362	Cuyler-Chi	.438	O'Doul-Phi	.622	Herman-Bro	1047	Wilson-Chi	155	Wilson-Chi	49.4

Runs		Hits		Doubles		Triples		Home Runs		Total Bases		Runs Batted In	
Hornsby-Chi	156	O'Doul-Phi	254	Frederick-Bro	52	L.Waner-Pit	20	Klein-Phi	43	Hornsby-Chi	409	Wilson-Chi	159
O'Doul-Phi	152	L.Waner-Pit	234	Hornsby-Chi	47	P.Waner-Pit	15	Ott-NY	42	Klein-Phi	405	Ott-NY	151
Ott-NY	138	Hornsby-Chi	229	Hafey-StL	47	Walker-Cin	15	Wilson-Chi	39	O'Doul-Phi	397	Hornsby-Chi	149
Wilson-Chi	135	Terry-NY	226	Klein-Phi	45	Whitney-Phi	14	Hornsby-Chi	39	Wilson-Chi	355	Klein-Phi	145
L.Waner-Pit	134	Klein-Phi	219	Kelly-Cin	45			O'Doul-Phi	32	Herman-Bro	348	Bottomley-StL	137

Stolen Bases		Base Stealing Runs		Fielding Runs-Infield		Fielding Runs-Outfield		Wins		Winning Pct.		Complete Games	
Cuyler-Chi	43			Whitney-Phi	23.4	Ott-NY	7.8	Malone-Chi	22	Root-Chi	.760	Lucas-Cin	28
Swanson-Cin	33			Maranville-Bos	21.4	L.Waner-Pit	7.2	Root-Chi	19	Bush-Chi	.720		
Frisch-StL	24			Jackson-NY	15.2	Orsatti-StL	6.9	Lucas-Cin	19	Grimes-Pit	.708		
Herman-Bro	21			English-Chi	14.0	Allen-Cin	4.6			Malone-Chi	.688		
Allen-Cin	21			Thompson-Phi	11.1	Richbourg-Bos	4.5			Kremer-Pit	.643		

Strikeouts		Fewest BB/Game		Games		Saves		Base Runners/9		Adjusted Relief Runs		Relief Ranking	
Malone-Chi	166	Vance-Bro	1.83	Bush-Chi	50	Morrison-Bro	8	Lucas-Cin	10.87	Hill-Pit-StL	5	Hill-Pit-StL	3
Clark-Bro	140	Lucas-Cin	1.93	Willoughby-Phi	49	Bush-Chi	8	Scott-NY	11.39				
Vance-Bro	126	Petty-Pit	2.05	Sweetland-Phi	43	Koupal-Bro-Phi	6	Hubbell-NY	11.62				
Root-Chi	124	Hubbell-NY	2.25	Root-Chi	43			Kremer-Pit	11.65				
Hubbell-NY	106	Clark-Bro	2.29	Collins-Phi	43			Petty-Pit	11.67				

Innings Pitched		Opponents' Avg.		Opponents' OBP		Earned Run Average		Adjusted ERA		Adjusted Starter Runs		Pitcher Wins	
Clark-Bro	279.0	Lucas-Cin	.257	Lucas-Cin	.297	Walker-NY	3.09	Grimes-Pit	152	Root-Chi	36.5	Lucas-Cin	4.3
Root-Chi	272.0	Johnson-StL	.265	Hubbell-NY	.313	Grimes-Pit	3.13	Walker-NY	148	Grimes-Pit	36.1	Grimes-Pit	4.0
Bush-Chi	270.2	Hubbell-NY	.265	Clark-Bro	.316	Root-Chi	3.47	Root-Chi	133	Malone-Chi	33.4	Malone-Chi	3.5
Lucas-Cin	270.0	Bush-Chi	.265	Vance-Bro	.316	Malone-Chi	3.57	Johnson-StL	129	Lucas-Cin	31.3	Root-Chi	2.7
Hubbell-NY	268.0	Grimes-Pit	.269	Petty-Pit	.317	Lucas-Cin	3.60	Malone-Chi	129	Walker-NY	30.5	Clark-Bro	2.7

Blowup

The big story was hitting, as teams scored an astounding 5.36 runs per game while league batters clubbed 754 home runs and hit .294—all historical highs. The Phillies' pitchers posted a ghastly 6.13 ERA, allowing more than 1,000 runs (the first time a team ever did this), but still finished fifth by clubbing 153 homers. Braves Field was shrunk 30 feet in center and 67 in right, but hitting increased just as much elsewhere. Raising the left-field wall at Baker Bowl to 12 feet didn't cut decrease extra-base hits.

The outmanned Reds tried the running game, swiping 134 bases, but still finished seventh. This year was the death knell for the steal; no NL club would steal even 100 sacks until 1941, and it would be 1962 before a team would best Cincinnati's total.

As the defending champion Cardinals slumped, and were forced to retool, the Cubs sailed into the breach, running away with the NL flag after overtaking the Pirates in July. In winning their first title since 1918, Chicago became the fourth team to take a chance on Rogers Hornsby in four years, and the star second sacker enjoyed his last great season.

Pitcher Bobo Newsom began his twenty-year, nine-team major league odyssey with the Robins/Dodgers. Pitching their last seasons were Carl Mays, 7-2 at 38 for the Giants, and Art Nehf, 8-5 for the Cubs at 37. It was also sayonara for Dead Ball Era standout Max Carey, 39, who led the NL in steals ten times.

Catcher Peck Lerian, following his second season as Phillies catcher, died October 22 after being hit by a car. George Stallings, superstitious skipper of the 1914 "Miracle Braves," died in Georgia. "Iron Man" Joe McGinnity, who had consecutive 30-wins seasons for the 1903–04 Giants, breathed his last in Brooklyn. Plenty of current pitchers wished they could do the same.

1929 American League

TEAM	W	L	T	PCT	GB	HW	HL	R	OR	PA	H	2B	3B	HR	BB	SO	HB	SH	AVG	OBP	SLG	OPS	AOPS	BR	ABR	PF	SB	CS	BSA	BSR
PHI	104	46	1	.693		57	16	901	615	5988	1539	288	76	122	543	440	28	213	.296	.365	.451	816	111	115	84	104	63	39	62	0
NY	88	66	0	.571	18	49	28	899	775	6103	1587	262	74	142	554	518	25	145	.295	.364	.450	814	123	111	174	93	52	50	51	-6
CLE	81	71	0	.533	24	44	32	717	736	5868	1525	294	79	62	453	363	26	202	.294	.354	.417	771	100	27	0	104	70	47	60	-1
STL	79	73	2	.520	26	41	36	733	713	5976	1426	277	64	46	589	431	22	191	.276	.352	.381	733	91	-31	-58	104	70	47	60	-1
WAS	71	81	1	.467	34	37	40	730	776	5995	1445	244	66	48	556	400	17	185	.276	.347	.375	722	90	-56	-61	101	89	63	59	-2
DET	70	84	1	.455	36	38	39	926	928	6253	1671	339	97	110	521	496	18	122	.299	.360	.453	813	114	112	108	100	95	75	56	-5
CHI	59	93	0	.388	46	35	41	627	792	5849	1406	240	74	37	425	436	22	154	.268	.325	.363	688	83	-138	-131	99	109	65	63	1
BOS	58	96	1	.377	48	32	45	605	803	5778	1377	285	69	28	413	494	28	177	.267	.325	.365	690	85	-131	-116	98	86	82	51	-10
TOT	613					333	277	6138		47810	11976	2229	599	595	4054	3578	186	1389	.284	.349	.407	757					639	508	56	-37

TEAM	CG	SHO	GR	SV	IP	H	HR	BB	SO	BR/9	ERA	AERA	OAV	OOB	PR	APR	PF	OSB	OCS	FA	E	WPB	DP	FW	PW	BW	BSW	DIF
PHI	70	9	126	24	1357.0	1371	73	487	573	12.4	3.44	123	.264	.329	121	119	100	89	44	.975	146	38	117	2.6	11.2	7.9	.4	6.8
NY	64	12	144	18	1366.2	1475	83	485	484	13.1	4.19	92	.278	.341	7	-57	91	78	54	.971	178	27	153	.8	-5.4	16.4	-.1	-.7
CLE	80	8	102	10	1352.0	1570	56	488	389	13.9	4.05	109	.295	.357	28	54	105	88	66	.968	198	24	162	-.6	5.1	.0	-.9	1.4
STL	83	15	117	10	1371.0	1469	100	462	415	12.8	4.08	108	.279	.340	25	49	104	59	61	.975	156	22	148	2.2	4.6	-5.5	.3	1.3
WAS	62	3	138	17	1354.2	1429	48	496	494	12.9	4.34	98	.276	.342	-15	-16	100	66	74	.968	195	38	156	-1.5	-5.8	.3	-.3	2.3
DET	82	5	139	9	1390.1	1641	73	646	467	15.0	4.96	86	.301	.377	-111	-104	101	110	61	.961	242	44	149	-3.0	-9.8	10.2	-.0	-4.3
CHI	78	5	100	7	1357.2	1481	84	505	328	13.4	4.41	97	.284	.351	-26	-22	101	75	61	.970	188	33	153	.0	-2.1	-12.4	.5	-3.2
BOS	84	9	105	5	1366.2	1537	78	496	416	13.6	4.43	96	.291	.355	-28	-25	101	74	77	.965	218	44	159	-1.6	-2.4	-10.9	-.5	-3.6
TOT	603	66	971	100	10916.0					13.4	4.24		.284	.349						.969	1521	270	1197					

Batter-Fielder Wins		Batting Average		On-Base Percentage		Slugging Average		On-Base Plus Slugging		Adjusted OPS		Adjusted Batter Runs	
Ruth-NY	5.4	Fonseca-Cle	.369	Foxx-Phi	.463	Ruth-NY	.697	Ruth-NY	1128	Ruth-NY	199	Ruth-NY	72.3
Lazzeri-NY	5.2	Simmons-Phi	.365	Gehrig-NY	.431	Simmons-Phi	.642	Foxx-Phi	1088	Foxx-Phi	171	Gehrig-NY	63.0
Simmons-Phi	5.1	Manush-StL	.355	Ruth-NY	.430	Foxx-Phi	.625	Gehrig-NY	1040	Gehrig-NY	170	Foxx-Phi	58.9
Gehrig-NY	4.5	Lazzeri-NY	.354	Lazzeri-NY	.429	Gehrig-NY	.584	Simmons-Phi	1015	Lazzeri-NY	164	Lazzeri-NY	53.7
Foxx-Phi	4.3	Foxx-Phi	.354	Fonseca-Cle	.427	Alexander-Det	.580	Lazzeri-NY	991	Simmons-Phi	158	Simmons-Phi	46.1

Runs		Hits		Doubles		Triples		Home Runs		Total Bases		Runs Batted In	
Gehringer-Det	131	Gehringer-Det	215	Manush-StL	.45	Gehringer-Det	.19	Ruth-NY	.46	Simmons-Phi	373	Simmons-Phi	157
Johnson-Det	128	Alexander-Det	215	Johnson-Det	.45	Scarritt-Bos	.17	Gehrig-NY	.35	Alexander-Det	363	Ruth-NY	154
Gehrig-NY	127	Simmons-Phi	212	Gehringer-Det	.45	B.Miller-Phi	.16	Simmons-Phi	.34	Ruth-NY	348	Alexander-Det	137
Foxx-Phi	123	Fonseca-Cle	209	Fonseca-Cle	.44			Foxx-Phi	.33	Gehringer-Det	337	Gehrig-NY	126
Ruth-NY	121	Manush-StL	204					Alexander-Det	.25			Heilmann-Det	120

Stolen Bases		Base Stealing Runs		Fielding Runs-Infield		Fielding Runs-Outfield		Wins		Winning Pct.		Complete Games	
Gehringer-Det	27	Gehringer-Det	2.4	Melillo-StL	20.4	Simmons-Phi	19.6	Earnshaw-Phi	24	Grove-Phi	.769	Thomas-Chi	24
Cissell-Chi	25	B.Miller-Phi	1.8	Durocher-NY	20.2	West-Was	13.2	Ferrell-Cle	21	Earnshaw-Phi	.750	Uhle-Det	23
Rothrock-Bos	24	Myer-Was	1.7	Kerr-Chi	17.1	B.Barrett-Chi-Bos	6.9	Grove-Phi	20	Ferrell-Cle	.677	Gray-StL	23
B.Miller-Phi	24	Goslin-Was	1.4	J.Sewell-Cle	14.4	Johnson-Det	6.3	Marberry-Was	19	Walberg-Phi	.621	Hudlin-Cle	22
Johnson-Det	20	Reynolds-Chi	1.0	McManus-Det	6.9	Schulte-StL	6.2			Marberry-Was	.613	Lyons-Chi	21

Strikeouts		Fewest BB/Game		Games		Saves		Base Runners/9		Adjusted Relief Runs		Relief Ranking	
Grove-Phi	170	Russell-Bos	1.58	Marberry-Was	49	Marberry-Was	11	Marberry-Was	11.07				
Earnshaw-Phi	149	Pennock-NY	1.60	Earnshaw-Phi	44	Moore-NY	8	Stewart-StL	11.43				
Pipgras-NY	125	Thomas-Chi	2.08	Gray-StL	43	Shores-Phi	7	Thomas-Chi	11.44				
Marberry-Was	121	Uhle-Det	2.10	Ferrell-Cle	43	Ferrell-Cle	5	Heimach-NY	11.56				
		Quinn-Phi	2.18					Grove-Phi	11.83				

Innings Pitched		Opponents' Avg.		Opponents' OBP		Earned Run Average		Adjusted ERA		Adjusted Starter Runs		Pitcher Wins	
Gray-StL	305.0	Earnshaw-Phi	.241	Marberry-Was	.308	Grove-Phi	2.81	Grove-Phi	150	Grove-Phi	42.6	**Marberry-Was**	4.0
Hudlin-Cle	280.1	Wells-NY	.248	Thomas-Chi	.310	Marberry-Was	3.06	Marberry-Was	139	Hudlin-Cle	34.2	**Grove-Phi**	3.6
Grove-Phi	275.1	Marberry-Was	.252	Grove-Phi	.316	Thomas-Chi	3.19	Thomas-Chi	134	Marberry-Was	33.3	**Hudlin-Cle**	3.5
Walberg-Phi	267.2	Walberg-Phi	.254	Hudlin-Cle	.318	Earnshaw-Phi	3.29	Earnshaw-Phi	133	Earnshaw-Phi	26.9	**Ferrell-Cle**	3.3
Crowder-StL	266.2	Grove-Phi	.262	Walberg-Phi	.320	Hudlin-Cle	3.34	Earnshaw-Phi	129	Gray-StL	23.9	**Thomas-Chi**	2.7

Mack Is Back

Babe Ruth led the league in homers again; Lou Gehrig hit .300 with 126 RBIs. But it was the Yankees' turn to be blown away. The Athletics pulled away in June and the race was never in doubt. Philadelphia had five players score 100 runs or more, and they scored just 2 runs more than New York for the season. The pitching was the difference. Lefty Grove, George Earnshaw, and Rube Walberg were Philadelphia's leading starters, and Connie Mack used relief pitchers efficiently.

Meanwhile, the Yankees dealt with the sudden death, due to blood poisoning, of manager Miller Huggins in late September. His passing effectively ended the first phase of the club's dynasty. The Indians improved 20 games and leapt to third, largely due to batting titlist Lew Fonseca and the heroics of rookie outfielder Earl Averill. Fifth-place Detroit had the loop's best offense and worst pitching, with only some of this attributable to their home field.

The game was changing—again. AL hitters set a new record with 595 homers, but 1929 was also the last year that batter strikeouts were fewer than three per game. From now on, there would be more whiffs as well as long balls.

The Athletics were distinct underdogs to the Cubs in the World Series. But Mack's surprising Game 1 starter—35-year-old Howard Ehmke, who appeared just 11 times all year—shut down Chicago, 3-1. The A's also won the next day. The Cubs captured Game 3 at Philadelphia, and led 8-0 in the seventh the next afternoon. But the Athletics exploded for a 10-run rally, ignited when Hack Wilson lost a flyball in the sun that scored three runs. The comeback, never equaled in Series history, turned the tide. Philadelphia rallied in the ninth inning of Game 5; Mule Haas' two-run shot tied things up. Al Simmons and Bing Miller doubled to give the Athletics their first title since 1913.

1928 National League

TEAM	W	L	T	PCT	GB	HW	HL	R	OR	PA	H	2B	3B	HR	BB	SO	HB	SH	AVG	OBP	SLG	OPS	AOPS	BR	ABR	PF	SB	CS	BSA	BSR
STL	95	59	0	.617		42	35	807	636	6144	1505	292	70	113	568	438	32	187	.281	.353	.425	778	108	77	63	102	82			
NY	93	61	1	.604	2	51	26	807	653	6103	1600	276	59	118	444	376	27	173	.293	.349	.430	779	110	69	66	100	62			
CHI	91	63	0	.591	4	52	25	714	615	6009	1460	251	64	92	508	517	31	210	.278	.345	.402	747	103	12	22	99	83			
PIT	85	67	1	.559	9	47	30	837	704	6037	1659	246	100	52	435	352	29	202	.309	.364	.421	785	108	86	55	104	64			
CIN	78	74	1	.513	16	44	33	648	686	5808	1449	229	67	32	386	330	26	212	.280	.333	.368	701	91	-80	-70	98	83			
BRO	77	76	2	.503	17.5	41	35	665	640	5992	1393	229	70	66	557	510	32	160	.266	.340	.374	714	94	-47	-37	99	81			
BOS	50	103	0	.327	44.5	25	51	631	878	5893	1439	241	41	52	447	377	27	191	.275	.335	.367	702	95	-70	-35	95	60			
PHI	43	109	0	.283	51	26	49	660	957	5917	1396	257	47	85	503	510	21	159	.267	.333	.382	715	90	-48	-70	103	53			
TOT	614					328	284	5769		47903	11901	2021	518	610	3848	3410	225	1494	.281	.344	.397	741					568			

TEAM	CG	SHO	GR	SV	IP	H	HR	BB	SO	BR/9	ERA	AERA	OAV	OOB	PR	APR	PF	OSB	OCS	FA	E	WPB	DP	FW	PW	BW	BSW	DIF
STL	83	4	119	21	1415.1	1470	86	399	422	12.1	3.38	118	.270	.323	97	98	100	55	53	.974	160	25	134	1.3	9.6	6.2		.9
NY	79	7	126	16	1394.0	1454	77	405	399	12.1	3.67	107	.273	.327	50	38	98	53	35	.972	178	29	175	.3	3.7	6.4		5.5
CHI	75	12	122	14	1380.2	1383	56	508	531	12.5	3.40	113	.267	.336	91	72	96	38	70	.975	156	26	176	1.6	7.0	2.1		3.3
PIT	82	8	112	11	1354.0	1422	66	446	385	12.6	3.95	103	.274	.335	7	16	102	88	55	.967	201	33	123	-1.3	1.6	5.4		3.3
CIN	68	11	120	11	1371.2	1516	58	410	355	12.7	3.94	100	.289	.342	8	2	99	67	61	.974	162	21	194	1.1	.2	-6.8		7.5
BRO	75	16	141	15	1396.0	1378	59	468	551	12.1	3.25	122	.261	.324	115	113	100	93	58	.965	217	18	113	-2.0	11.0	-3.6		-4.9
BOS	54	1	168	6	1360.0	1596	100	524	343	14.2	4.83	81	.298	.363	-127	-142	98	79	54	.969	193	36	141	-.7	-13.9	-3.4		-8.5
PHI	42	4	189	11	1346.2	1664	108	675	402	15.9	5.61	76	.315	.397	-242	-188	107	95	70	.971	181	29	171	-.0	-18.4	-6.8		-7.7
TOT	558	63	1097	105	11018.1					13.0	3.99		.281	.344						.971	1448	217	1227					

Batter-Fielder Wins		Batting Average		On-Base Percentage		Slugging Average		On-Base Plus Slugging		Adjusted OPS		Adjusted Batter Runs	
Hornsby-Bos	6.1	Hornsby-Bos	387	Hornsby-Bos	498	Hornsby-Bos	632	Hornsby-Bos	1130	Hornsby-Bos	204	Hornsby-Bos	83.4
Lindstrom-NY	4.9	P.Waner-Pit	370	P.Waner-Pit	446	Bottomley-StL	628	Bottomley-StL	1030	Bottomley-StL	163	Bottomley-StL	50.6
Hartnett-Chi	4.7	Lindstrom-NY	358	Grantham-Pit	408	Hafey-StL	604	Wilson-Chi	992	Wilson-Chi	159	P.Waner-Pit	49.4
Jackson-NY	4.2	Sisler-Bos	340	Stephenson-Chi	407	Wilson-Chi	588	P.Waner-Pit	992	Hafey-StL	152	Wilson-Chi	44.6
P.Waner-Pit	3.9	Herman-Bro	340	Wilson-Chi	404	P.Waner-Pit	547	Hafey-StL	990	P.Waner-Pit	152	Bissonette-Bro	38.2

Runs		Hits		Doubles		Triples		Home Runs		Total Bases		Runs Batted In	
P.Waner-Pit	142	Lindstrom-NY	231	P.Waner-Pit	50	Bottomley-StL	20	Wilson-Chi	31	Bottomley-StL	362	Bottomley-StL	136
Bottomley-StL	123	P.Waner-Pit	223	Hafey-StL	46	P.Waner-Pit	19	Bottomley-StL	31	Lindstrom-NY	330	Traynor-Pit	124
L.Waner-Pit	121	L.Waner-Pit	221	Hornsby-Bos	42	L.Waner-Pit	14	Hafey-StL	27	P.Waner-Pit	329	Wilson-Chi	120
Douthit-StL	111	Richburg-Bos	206	Bottomley-StL	42	Bressler-Bro	13	Bissonette-Bro	25	Bissonette-Bro	319	Hafey-StL	111
Frisch-StL	107	Traynor-Pit	192	Lindstrom-NY	39	Bissonette-Bro	13	Hornsby-Bos	21	Hafey-StL	314	Lindstrom-NY	107

Stolen Bases		Base Stealing Runs		Fielding Runs-Infield		Fielding Runs-Outfield		Wins		Winning Pct.		Complete Games	
Cuyler-Chi	37			Maguire-Chi	49.1	Douthit-StL	13.3	Grimes-Pit	25	Benton-NY	735	Grimes-Pit	28
Frisch-StL	29			Jackson-NY	28.0	Leach-Phi	5.6	Benton-NY	25	Haines-StL	714	Benton-NY	28
Walker-Cin	19			Lindstrom-NY	14.6	P.Waner-Pit	5.4	Vance-Bro	22	Bush-Chi	714	Vance-Bro	24
Thompson-Phi	19			Ford-Cin	14.5	Sothern-Phi	5.3	Sherdel-StL	21	Fitzsimmons-NY	690	Sherdel-StL	20
				Kelly-Cin	7.9	Richburg-Bos	3.8			Vance-Bro	688	Haines-StL	20

Strikeouts		Fewest BB/Game		Games		Saves		Base Runners/9		Adjusted Relief Runs		Relief Ranking	
Vance-Bro	200	Alexander-StL	1.37	Grimes-Pit	48	Sherdel-StL	5	Vance-Bro	9.79				
Malone-Chi	155	Sherdel-StL	2.03	Kolp-Cin	44	Haid-StL	5	Hubbell-NY	10.23				
Root-Chi	122	Benton-NY	2.06	Rixey-Cin	43	Carlson-Chi	4	Benton-NY	10.73				
Grimes-Pit	97	Rixey-Cin	2.07			Benton-NY	4	Grimes-Pit	10.81				
Benton-NY	90	Grimes-Pit	2.10					Lucas-Cin	11.08				

Innings Pitched		Opponents' Avg.		Opponents' OBP		Earned Run Average		Adjusted ERA		Adjusted Starter Runs		Pitcher Wins	
Grimes-Pit	330.2	Vance-Bro	221	Vance-Bro	277	Vance-Bro	2.09	Vance-Bro	191	Vance-Bro	60.5	Vance-Bro	7.2
Benton-NY	310.1	McWeeny-Bro	235	Grimes-Pit	297	Blake-Chi	2.47	Blake-Chi	156	Benton-NY	42.6	Grimes-Pit	4.9
Rixey-Cin	291.1	Malone-Chi	236	Benton-NY	300	Nehf-Chi	2.65	Clark-Bro	148	Blake-Chi	37.4	Benton-NY	4.1
Vance-Bro	280.1	Blake-Chi	240	Sherdel-StL	303	Clark-Bro	2.68	Nehf-Chi	145	Grimes-Pit	32.0	Blake-Chi	4.0
Fitzsimmons-NY	261.1	Root-Chi	242	Lucas-Cin	304	Benton-NY	2.73	Benton-NY	144	Sherdel-StL	30.9	Sherdel-StL	3.9

Holding Off the Giants

St. Louis, featuring an aging pitching staff and a veteran lineup, didn't lead the league in batting average, home runs, or ERA, but drew more walks than any other team and allowed fewer walks as well. First sacker Jim Bottomley was the club's best hitter, and 41-year-old Grover Cleveland Alexander finished 16-9. Moving ahead for good in early June, the Cardinals won the flag despite the dogged efforts of the Giants, who went 25-8 in September. John McGraw had found he could not get along with irascible Rogers Hornsby and dealt the him to seventh-place Boston in the off-season. As a result, New York's offense suffered. Hornsby, meanwhile, won his seventh (and last) batting title in near-obscurity for the pathetic Bees.

The Cubs continued to rise into contention, finishing just four games out as Hack Wilson hit 31 homers to tie Bottomley for the lead. The hard-drinking Wilson also fanned 94 times, a modern NL record. On the mound, Brooklyn's Dazzy Vance led the NL in strikeouts for the seventh (and last) time, but another outstanding pitcher debuted on July 26 when lefty Carl Hubbell pitched his first game for the Giants. Four days later, the Phillies gave slugging outfielder Chuck Klein his first major league action.

Six teams in the NL finished over .500, while Philadelphia and Boston—who desperately named Hornsby player-manager in midseason—ended a combined 95 games back. Large ticket sale drops in Boston, Philadelphia, and Pittsburgh, who dropped to fourth, led attendance to dip 8 percent.

Hitting was on the rise again as runs increased by 2.6 percent. Although league average fell a point, home runs skyrocketed by more than 25 percent and strikeouts decreased. Another indication of increased hitting? NL pitchers tossed just 558 complete games, by far the lowest total to date.

1928 American League

TEAM	W	L	T	PCT	GB	HW	HL	R	OR	PA	H	2B	3B	HR	BB	SO	HB	SH	AVG	OBP	SLG	OPS	AOPS	BR	ABR	PF	SB	CS	BSA	BSR
NY	101	53	0	.656		52	25	894	685	6070	**1578**	269	79	**133**	562	544	25	146	**.296**	.365	.450	815	124	147	**177**	97	51	52	50	-7
PHI	98	55	0	.641	2.5	52	25	829	**615**	5990	1540	**323**	75	89	533	442	31	200	.295	.363	.436	799	112	120	97	103	59	55	52	-6
STL	82	72	0	.532	19	44	33	772	742	6007	1431	276	76	63	548	**390**	28	**214**	.274	.346	.393	739	97	3	-19	103	99		5	99
WAS	75	79	1	.487	26	37	43	718	705	6009	1510	277	93	40	481	488	**31**	180	.284	.334	.358	692	88	-92	-83	99	**144**	88	62	1
CHI	72	82	1	.468	29	37	40	656	725	5907	1405	231	77	24	469	438	25	163	.279	.340	.401	741	99	-5	-16	102	113	79	59	-3
DET	68	86	0	.442	33	36	41	744	804	5949	1476	265	**97**	62	469	438	25	191	.285	.335	.382	717	93	-49	-56	101	50	52	49	-7
CLE	62	92	1	.403	39	29	48	674	830	5984	1535	299	61	34	377	426	30	191	.285	.319	.361	680	86	-119	-108	98	97	68	59	-2
BOS	57	96	1	.373	43.5	26	47	589	770	5754	1356	260	62	38	395	512	21	206	.264											
TOT	617					313	302	5876		47670	11831	2200	620	483	3834	3719	219	1500	.281	.344	.397	741					700	500	58	-21

TEAM	CG	SHO	GR	SV	IP	H	HR	BB	SO	BR/9	ERA	AERA	OAV	OOB	PR	APR	PF	OSB	OCS	FA	E	WPB	DP	FW	PW	BW	BSW	DIF
NY	82	13	112	21	1375.1	1466	59	452	487	12.7	3.74	101	.276	.335	46	3	93	102	64	.968	194	28	136	-.0	.3	**17.1**	-.4	7.1
PHI	81	**15**	103	16	1367.2	**1349**	66	**424**	607	11.8	**3.36**	119	.259	.318	103	98	99	83	45	.970	181	29	124	.6	**9.5**	9.4	-.3	5.9
STL	80	6	128	15	1374.1	1487	93	454	607	12.8	4.17	101	.282	.340	-20	3	104	98	51	.969	189	19	146	.2	.3	-1.8	.4	5.9
WAS	77	**15**	118	10	1384.0	1420	**40**	466	462	12.5	3.88	103	.272	.335	25	19	99	72	62	**.972**	178	30	146	**1.0**	1.8	.5	.4	-5.7
CHI	**88**	6	93	11	1378.0	1518	66	501	418	13.4	3.98	102	.287	.352	8	8	100	59	60	.970	186	27	149	.5	.8	-8.0	.4	1.4
DET	65	5	130	16	1372.0	1481	58	567	451	13.7	4.32	95	.281	.355	-42	-33	102	86	71	.965	218	31	140	-1.5	-3.2	-1.5	-.0	-2.8
CLE	71	4	122	15	1378.0	1615	52	511	416	14.2	4.47	93	.303	.369	-66	-51	103	90	72	.965	221	41	**187**	-1.6	-4.9	-5.4	-.4	-2.7
BOS	70	5	**131**	9	1352.0	1492	49	452	407	13.2	4.39	93	.288	.349	-53	-44	102	110	**77**	.971	178	18	139	.9	-4.3	-10.4	.0	-5.8
TOT	614	69	937	113	10981.1					13.0	4.04		.281	.344						.969	1545	223	1167					

Batter-Fielder Wins		On-Base Percentage		Home Runs		Adjusted OPS		Adjusted Batter Runs	
Ruth-NY	7.1								

Batter-Fielder Wins
Ruth-NY 7.1
Gehrig-NY 5.9
J.Sewell-Cle 5.3
Goslin-Was 4.9
Manush-StL 3.3

Batting Average
Goslin-Was 379
Manush-StL 378
Gehrig-NY 374
Simmons-Phi 351
Lazzeri-NY 332

On-Base Percentage
Gehrig-NY 467
Ruth-NY 463
Goslin-Was 442
Bishop-Phi 438
Manush-StL 414

Slugging Average
Ruth-NY 709
Gehrig-NY 648
Goslin-Was 614
Manush-StL 575
Simmons-Phi 558

On-Base Plus Slugging
Ruth-NY 1172
Gehrig-NY 1115
Goslin-Was 1056
Manush-StL 989
Simmons-Phi 954

Adjusted OPS
Ruth-NY 211
Gehrig-NY 196
Goslin-Was 176
Manush-StL 153
Simmons-Phi 144

Adjusted Batter Runs
Ruth-NY 92.1
Gehrig-NY 83.3
Goslin-Was 50.7
Manush-StL 46.3
Foxx-Phi 28.9

Runs
Ruth-NY 163
Gehrig-NY 139
Combs-NY 118
Blue-StL 116
Gehringer-Det 108

Hits
Manush-StL 241
Gehrig-NY 210
Rice-Was 202
Combs-NY 194
Gehringer-Det 193

Doubles
Manush-StL 47
Gehrig-NY 47
Meusel-NY 45
Schulte-StL 44
Lind-Cle 42

Triples
Combs-NY 21
Manush-StL 20
Gehringer-Det 16

Home Runs
Ruth-NY 54
Gehrig-NY 27
Goslin-Was 17
Hauser-Phi 16
Simmons-Phi 15

Total Bases
Ruth-NY 380
Manush-StL 367
Gehrig-NY 364
Combs-NY 290
Heilmann-Det 283

Runs Batted In
Ruth-NY 142
Gehrig-NY 142
Meusel-NY 113
Manush-StL 108

Stolen Bases
Myer-Bos 30
Mostil-Chi 23
Rice-Det 20
Cissell-Chi 18
Bluege-Was 18

Base Stealing Runs
Rice-Was 2.5
Goslin-Was 2.5
Reynolds-Chi 2.3
Judge-Was 2.1

Fielding Runs-Infield
Gerber-StL-Bos 25.7
J.Sewell-Cle 25.5
Regan-Bos 15.1
Tavener-Det 12.1
Bluege-Was 10.1

Fielding Runs-Outfield
Jamieson-Cle 15.9
Mostil-Chi 11.9
Schulte-StL 9.9
Goslin-Was 7.6
Taitt-Bos 6.0

Wins
Pipgras-NY 24
Grove-Phi 24
Hoyt-NY 23
Crowder-StL 21
Gray-StL 20

Winning Pct.
Crowder-StL 808
Hoyt-NY 767
Grove-Phi 750
Pennock-NY 739
Quinn-Phi 720

Complete Games
Ruffing-Bos 25
Thomas-Chi 24
Grove-Phi 24
Pipgras-NY 22

Strikeouts
Grove-Phi 183
Pipgras-NY 139
Thomas-Chi 129
Ruffing-Bos 118
Earnshaw-Phi 117

Fewest BB/Game
Rommel-Phi 1.35
Quinn-Phi 1.45
Pennock-NY 1.71
Braxton-Was 1.81
Russell-Bos 1.83

Games
Marberry-Was 48
Morris-Bos 47
Pipgras-NY 46
Rommel-Phi 43

Saves
Hoyt-NY 8
Hudlin-Cle 7
Lyons-Chi 6
Braxton-Was 6

Base Runners/9
Braxton-Was 9.32
Grove-Phi 10.08
Rommel-Phi 10.62
Pennock-NY 10.88
Heimach-NY 10.99

Adjusted Relief Runs

Relief Ranking

Innings Pitched
Pipgras-NY 300.2
Ruffing-Bos 289.1
Thomas-Chi 283.0
Hoyt-NY 273.0
Gray-StL 262.2

Opponents' Avg.
Braxton-Was 222
Grove-Phi 229
Earnshaw-Phi 240
Johnson-NY 250
Jones-Was 252

Opponents' OBP
Braxton-Was 267
Grove-Phi 277
Rommel-Phi 295
Pennock-NY 302
Thomas-Chi 310

Earned Run Average
Braxton-Was 2.51
Pennock-NY 2.56
Grove-Phi 2.58
Jones-Was 2.84
Quinn-Phi 2.90

Adjusted ERA
Braxton-Was 159
Grove-Phi 155
Pennock-NY 147
Jones-Was 141
Quinn-Phi 138

Adjusted Starter Runs
Grove-Phi 40.7
Braxton-Was 34.0
Thomas-Chi 30.7
Pennock-NY 30.6
Jones-Was 27.1

Pitcher Wins
Grove-Phi 4.7
Thomas-Chi 3.5
Jones-Was 3.2
Braxton-Was 3.2
Pennock-NY 3.1

Murderers' Row Survives A's, Kills Cards

Once again the Yankees enjoyed a great attack, leading the league both individually and collectively in nearly every offensive category. Lou Gehrig was now Babe Ruth's equal at bat, and the supporting cast continued to shine. Rookie catcher Bill Dickey made his first appearance and would soon join the fearsome lineup. While the Yankees' pitching was not nearly as strong as in the previous season, they were deep enough to withstand the loss (and, later that year, death from heart disease) of veteran righty Urban Shocker.

It wasn't easy, however. The Athletics were a worthy opponent, and after a late-season hot streak actually took a half-game lead over New York on September 8. The next day, more than 85,000 fans crammed into Yankee Stadium to see the two teams meet in a doubleheader; it was the most important regular-season matchup that baseball had seen in years, and the largest crowd to that point ever to watch a major league game. New York swept the twin bill, and despite a late flurry by Philadelphia, clinched the flag on September 28.

The Athletics, a fascinating mix of young and old, had seven Hall of Famers on the club. Lefty Grove had become the league's best pitcher, and he was well supported by 28-year-old rookie George Earnshaw, who held opponents to a .240 average. Earnshaw and Grove were 1-2 in the league in strikeouts per game, while teammates Eddie Rommel and Jack Quinn were the two stingiest in walks.

Offensively, the entire A's lineup contributed, and the bench sported a group of all-time greats. Three of them retired after the season: pitcher "Bullet Joe" Bush and two of the game's greatest center fielders, Ty Cobb and Tris Speaker. Forty-year-old Eddie Collins would hang around with Philadelphia until 1930.

But it was still the Yankees' show. Showing no signs of weakness, New York blew by the St. Louis Cardinals in four straight World Series games. Babe Ruth, who batted .625, and Gehrig, who hit .545, homered in the same game three times.

1927 National League

TEAM	W	L	T	PCT	GB	HW	HL	R	OR	PA	H	2B	3B	HR	BB	SO	HB	SH	AVG	OBP	SLG	OPS	AOPS	BR	ABR	PF	SB	CS	BSA	BSR
PIT	94	60	2	.610		48	31	817	659	6077	1648	258	78	54	437	355	29	214	.305	.361	.412	773	106	100	46	107	65			
STL	92	61	0	.601	1.5	55	25	754	665	5888	1450	264	79	84	484	511	26	171	.278	.343	.408	751	104	50	27	103	65			
NY	92	62	1	.597	2	49	25	817	720	6045	1594	251	62	109	461	462	32	180	.297	.356	.427	783	116	115	117	100	73			
CHI	85	68	0	.556	8.5	50	28	750	661	6018	1505	266	63	74	481	492	27	207	.284	.346	.400	746	106	47	45	100	65			
CIN	75	78	0	.490	18.5	45	35	643	653	5827	1439	222	77	29	402	332	21	219	.278	.332	.367	699	96	-49	-28	97	62			
BRO	65	88	1	.425	28.5	34	39	541	619	5752	1314	195	74	39	368	494	25	166	.253	.306	.342	648	79	-157	-159	100	106			
BOS	60	94	1	.390	34	32	41	651	771	5941	1498	216	61	37	346	363	28	197	.279	.326	.363	689	98	-76	-23	92	100			
PHI	51	103	1	.331	43	34	43	678	903	5956	1487	216	46	57	434	482	28	177	.280	.337	.370	707	94	-30	-39	101	68			
TOT	617					347	267	5651		47504	11935	1888	540	483	3413	3491	216	1531	.282	.339	.386	725					649			

TEAM	CG	SHO	GR	SV	IP	H	HR	BB	SO	BR/9	ERA	AERA	OAV	OOB	PR	APR	PF	OSB	OCS	FA	E	WPB	DP	FW	PW	BW	BSW	DIF
PIT	90	10	107	10	1385.0	1400	58	418	435	12.0	3.66	112	.267	.324	39	65	105	63	36	.969	187	32	130	.6	6.4	4.5		5.4
STL	89	14	110	11	1367.1	1416	72	363	394	11.8	3.57	110	.271	.320	52	56	101	85	64	.966	213	21	170	-1.0	5.5	2.7		5.4
NY	65	7	147	16	1381.2	1520	77	453	442	13.0	3.97	97	.283	.341	-8	-18	98	70	54	.969	195	34	160	.1	-1.8	11.5		8.3
CHI	75	11	114	5	1385.0	1439	50	514	465	12.9	3.65	106	.273	.342	40	32	99	52	58	.971	181	31	152	.8	3.2	4.4		5.1
CIN	87	12	93	12	1368.0	1472	36	316	407	11.9	3.54	107	.281	.325	57	38	97	100	31	.973	165	34	160	1.6	3.8	-2.8		.1
BRO	74	7	131	10	1375.1	1382	63	418	574	11.9	3.36	118	.265	.323	85	89	101	99	68	.963	229	25	117	-1.8	8.8	-15.7		-4.1
BOS	52	3	156	11	1390.0	1602	43	468	402	13.6	4.22	88	.296	.356	-48	-83	95	81	71	.963	231	40	130	-1.8	-8.2	-2.3		-4.7
PHI	81	5	112	6	1355.1	1710	84	462	377	14.7	5.36	77	.317	.374	-218	-177	106	99	42	.972	169	35	152	1.5	-17.5	-3.8		-6.2
TOT	613	69	970	81	11007.2					12.7	3.91		.282	.339						.969	1570	252	1171					

Batter-Fielder Wins
- Frisch-StL.....7.2
- Hornsby-NY.....6.8
- Jackson-NY.....5.4
- P.Waner-Pit.....3.9
- Dressen-Cin.....3.3

Batting Average
- P.Waner-Pit.....380
- Hornsby-NY.....361
- L.Waner-Pit.....355
- Stephenson-Chi.....344
- Traynor-Pit.....342

On-Base Percentage
- P.Waner-Pit.....448
- Hornsby-NY.....437
- Harper-NY.....435
- Stephenson-Chi.....415
- Harris-Pit.....402

Slugging Average
- Hafey-StL.....590
- Hornsby-NY.....586
- Wilson-Chi.....579
- P.Waner-Pit.....549
- Terry-NY.....529

On-Base Plus Slugging
- Hornsby-NY.....1035
- P.Waner-Pit.....986
- Wilson-Chi.....980
- Harper-NY.....930
- Terry-NY.....907

Adjusted OPS
- Hornsby-NY.....175
- Wilson-Chi.....159
- P.Waner-Pit.....152
- Harper-NY.....149
- Stephenson-Chi.....141

Adjusted Batter Runs
- Hornsby-NY.....64.1
- Wilson-Chi.....47.1
- Wilson-Chi.....46.1
- Harper-NY.....38.1
- Stephenson-Chi.....37.3

Runs
- L.Waner-Pit.....133
- Hornsby-NY.....133
- Wilson-Chi.....119
- P.Waner-Pit.....114
- Frisch-StL.....112

Hits
- P.Waner-Pit.....237
- L.Waner-Pit.....223
- Frisch-StL.....208
- Hornsby-NY.....205
- Stephenson-Chi.....199

Doubles
- Stephenson-Chi.....46
- P.Waner-Pit.....42
- Lindstrom-NY.....36
- Dressen-Bos.....36
- Brown-Bos.....35

Triples
- P.Waner-Pit.....18
- Bottomley-StL.....15
- Thompson-Phi.....14
- Terry-NY.....13
- Wilson-Chi.....12

Home Runs
- Wilson-Chi.....30
- Williams-Phi.....30
- Hornsby-NY.....26
- Terry-NY.....20
- Bottomley-StL.....19

Total Bases
- P.Waner-Pit.....342
- Hornsby-NY.....333
- Wilson-Chi.....319
- Terry-NY.....307
- Bottomley-StL.....292

Runs Batted In
- P.Waner-Pit.....131
- Hornsby-NY.....129
- Wilson-Chi.....125
- Bottomley-StL.....124
- Terry-NY.....121

Stolen Bases
- Frisch-StL.....48
- Carey-Bro.....32
- Hendrick-Bro.....29
- Adams-Chi.....26
- Richbourg-Bos.....24

Base Stealing Runs

Fielding Runs-Infield
- Frisch-StL.....49.3
- Jackson-NY.....26.3
- Friberg-Phi.....20.3
- Traynor-Pit.....14.3
- Cooney-Chi-Phi.....13.2

Fielding Runs-Outfield
- Leach-Phi.....16.3
- Statz-Bro.....9.9
- Welsh-Bos.....8.1
- P.Waner-Pit.....6.7
- Bressler-Cin.....5.2

Wins
- Root-Chi.....26
- Haines-StL.....24
- Hill-Pit.....22
- Alexander-StL.....21

Winning Pct.
- Benton-Bos-NY.....708
- Haines-StL.....706
- Kremer-Pit.....704
- Grimes-NY.....704
- Alexander-StL.....677

Complete Games
- Vance-Bro.....25
- Meadows-Pit.....25
- Haines-StL.....25
- Hill-Pit.....22
- Alexander-StL.....22

Strikeouts
- Vance-Bro.....184
- Root-Chi.....145
- May-Cin.....121
- Grimes-NY.....102
- Petty-Bro.....101

Fewest BB/Game
- Alexander-StL.....1.28
- Lucas-Cin.....1.46
- Donohue-Cin.....1.51
- Carlson-Phi-Chi.....1.63
- Henry-NY.....1.70

Games
- Scott-Phi.....48
- Root-Chi.....48
- Ehrhardt-Bro.....46
- Henry-NY.....45
- May-Cin.....44

Saves
- Sherdel-StL.....6
- Nehf-Cin-Chi.....5
- Mogridge-Bos.....5
- Henry-NY.....4

Base Runners/9
- Miljus-Pit.....9.40
- Alexander-StL.....10.07
- Lucas-Cin.....10.14
- Kremer-Pit.....10.27
- Vance-Bro.....10.44

Adjusted Relief Runs
- Clark-Bro.....13.2
- Ehrhardt-Bro.....4.0
- Cvengros-Pit.....3.6
- Morrison-Pit.....4

Relief Ranking
- Clark-Bro.....15.3
- Ehrhardt-Bro.....3.9
- Cvengros-Pit.....2.0
- Morrison-Pit.....4

Innings Pitched
- Root-Chi.....309.0
- Haines-StL.....300.2
- Meadows-Pit.....299.1
- Hill-Pit.....277.2
- Vance-Bro.....273.1

Opponents' Avg.
- Vance-Bro.....239
- Kremer-Pit.....244
- Haines-StL.....245
- Hill-Pit.....249
- Bush-Chi.....250

Opponents' OBP
- Alexander-StL.....286
- Lucas-Cin.....287
- Kremer-Pit.....289
- Vance-Bro.....291
- Petty-Bro.....293

Earned Run Average
- Kremer-Pit.....2.47
- Alexander-StL.....2.52
- Vance-Bro.....2.70
- Haines-StL.....2.72
- Petty-Bro.....2.98

Adjusted ERA
- Kremer-Pit.....166
- Alexander-StL.....157
- Vance-Bro.....147
- Haines-StL.....145
- Petty-Bro.....133

Adjusted Starter Runs
- Alexander-StL.....41.3
- Haines-StL.....39.4
- Kremer-Pit.....39.0
- Vance-Bro.....38.1
- Petty-Bro.....29.4

Pitcher Wins
- Alexander-StL.....5.0
- Kremer-Pit.....4.2
- Haines-StL.....4.1
- Vance-Bro.....3.9
- Lucas-Cin.....3.1

Raising the Skull and Crossbones

Once again, the Pittsburgh Pirates showed their facility in developing young players by debuting two more future stars: outfielder Lloyd Waner and shortstop Dick Bartell. Waner, and older brother Paul, would star in Pittsburgh for many years, but Bartell, sent to Philly in a poor 1930 trade, did most of his damage for other clubs. The great seasons of the Waners, and a big year from obscure pitcher Carmen Hill, propelled Pittsburgh to its second flag in three seasons.

The Cardinals finished 1½ games out after dealing productive but cranky Rogers Hornsby to the Giants for another second sacker, Frankie Frisch. While Frisch played well offensively and defensively for St. Louis, Mound City fans lambasted the deal. New York was third, 2 games back, with mediocre starting pitching and a power-based offense.

Several Senior Circuit veterans played their final seasons. First baseman Jacques Fournier was gone after 1,503 games, while 38-year-old Heinie Groh was released by the Pirates. Rifle-armed outfielder Irish Meusel's career careened to a premature end in Brooklyn, while future Hall of Famer Zach Wheat bowed out with a .324 season as a part-timer in Philadelphia. In addition, August "Garry" Herrmann, president of the Reds since 1902 and a kingpin of the National League, bowed out due to poor health that would lead to his death in 1931.

The Chicago Cubs, reconsidering an earlier promise to keep Wrigley Field single decked, decided to double-deck their park, and as a result became the first NL team to break the million mark in attendance. Their 1,159,168 turnstile clicks helped the entire league once again set a new high. The last-place Phillies, meanwhile, had to play at the Athletics' home, Shibe Park, for a few games after a section of Baker Bowl bleachers collapsed on May 14. Forbes Field took in a club-record 869,720, plus another 83,000 for the World Series, but on the field the Pirates were no match for the Yankees.

1927 American League

TEAM	W	L	T	PCT	GB	HW	HL	R	OR	PA	H	2B	3B	HR	BB	SO	HB	SH	AVG	OBP	SLG	OPS	AOPS	BR	ABR	PF	SB	CS	BSA	BSR
NY	110	44	1	.714		**57**	19	**975**	599	6207	**1644**	291	103	**158**	635	605	22	203	.307	.383	.489	872	135	236	268	97	90	64	58	-3
PHI	91	63	1	.591	19	50	27	841	726	6094	1606	281	70	56	551	**326**	30	217	.303	.372	.414	786	103	80	35	99	101	63	62	0
WAS	85	69	3	.552	25	51	28	782	730	6117	1549	268	87	29	498	359	31	199	.287	.351	.386	737	97	-27	-18	99	133	52	**72**	11
DET	82	71	3	.536	27.5	44	32	845	805	6112	1533	282	100	51	587	420	24	202	.289	.363	.409	772	105	46	35	101	89	75	54	-7
CHI	70	83	0	.458	39.5	38	37	662	708	5910	1433	285	61	36	493	389	26	**234**	.278	.344	.378	722	94	-53	-35	98	65	72	47	-11
CLE	66	87	0	.431	43.5	35	42	668	766	5843	1471	**321**	52	26	381	366	**48**	212	.283	.337	.379	718	90	-68	-73	101	90	66	58	2
STL	59	94	2	.386	50.5	38	38	**724**	904	5897	1440	262	59	55	443	420	43	191	.276	.338	.380	716	88	-69	-91	103	81	46	64	2
BOS	51	103	0	.331	59	29	49	597	856	5867	1348	271	78	28	430	456	39	191	.259	.320	.357	677	82	-152	-139	98	139	73		-5
TOT	619					342	272	6094		48047	12024	2261	610	439	4018	3341	263	1649	.285	.351	.399	751					788	511	61	

TEAM	CG	SHO	GR	SV	IP	H	HR	BB	SO	BR/9	ERA	AERA	OAV	OOB	PR	APR	PF	OSB	OCS	FA	E	WPB	DP	FW	PW	BW	BSW	DIF
NY	82	**11**	109	20	1389.2	**1403**	42	**409**	431	**11.9**	**3.20**	120	.267	.323	**145**	**107**	93	94	44	.969	195	22	123	.7	10.2	25.5	-.2	-3.1
PHI	65	8	160	**24**	1384.0	1467	65	442	**553**	12.6	3.97	107	.278	.338	26	44	103	**84**	47	.970	190	27	124	1.0	4.2	3.3	.5	5.4
WAS	62	10	**163**	23	1402.0	1434	53	491	497	12.6	3.97	102	.269	.335	26	14	98	86	55	.969	195	**18**	125	.8	1.3	-1.7	**1.1**	6.4
DET	75	5	131	17	1387.2	1542	52	577	421	14.0	4.14	102	.290	.364	0	9	102	100	62	**.971**	178	20	173	1.6	.9	3.3	.5	.7
CHI	**85**	10	95	8	1367.0	1467	55	440	365	12.7	3.91	103	.283	.342	34	20	98	86	68	.971	201	39	131	.2	-1.0	-6.9	-1.0	-6.0
CLE	72	5	132	8	1353.1	1542	37	508	366	13.9	4.27	98	.295	.361	-20	-11	102	86	91	.968	201	39	146	.2	-1.0	-6.9	-1.0	-1.7
STL	80	4	121	8	1353.1	1592	79	604	385	14.7	4.95	88	.304	.378	-122	-87	105	94	92	.960	248	48	166	-2.5	-8.3	-8.6	-.2	2.1
BOS	63	6	134	7	1366.1	1603	56	558	381	14.5	4.72	89	.305	.376	-88	-76	102	158	52	.964	228	34	167	-1.4	-7.2	-13.2	.3	-4.5
TOT	584	59	1045	115	11003.1					13.4	4.14		.285	.351						.967	1641	241	1155					

Batter-Fielder Wins
Ruth-NY 8.8
Gehrig-NY 8.4
Heilmann-Det 4.1
Lazzeri-NY 3.5
Simmons-Phi 3.3

Batting Average
Heilmann-Det .398
Simmons-Phi .392
Gehrig-NY .373
Fothergill-Det .359
Cobb-Phi .357

On-Base Percentage
Ruth-NY .486
Heilmann-Det .475
Gehrig-NY .474
Bishop-Phi .442
Cobb-Phi .440

Slugging Average
Ruth-NY .772
Gehrig-NY .765
Simmons-Phi .645
Heilmann-Det .616
Williams-StL .525

On-Base Plus Slugging
Ruth-NY 1.258
Gehrig-NY 1.240
Heilmann-Det 1.091
Fothergill-Det .929
Williams-StL .928

Adjusted OPS
Ruth-NY 229
Gehrig-NY 224
Heilmann-Det 179
Combs-NY 143
Fothergill-Det 138

Adjusted Batter Runs
Gehrig-NY 108.4
Ruth-NY 108.0
Heilmann-Det 62.6
Combs-NY 40.3
Simmons-Phi 39.3

Runs
Ruth-NY 158
Gehrig-NY 149
Combs-NY 137
Gehringer-Det 110
Heilmann-Det 106

Hits
Combs-NY 231
Gehrig-NY 218
Sisler-StL 201
Heilmann-Det 201
Goslin-Was 194

Doubles
Gehrig-NY 52
Burns-Cle 51
Heilmann-Det 50
J.Sewell-Cle 48
Meusel-NY 47

Triples
Combs-NY 23
Manush-Det 18
Gehrig-NY 18
Goslin-Was 15
Rice-Was 14

Home Runs
Ruth-NY 60
Gehrig-NY 47
Lazzeri-NY 18
Williams-StL 17
Simmons-Phi 15

Total Bases
Gehrig-NY 447
Ruth-NY 417
Combs-NY 331
Heilmann-Det 311
Goslin-Was 300

Runs Batted In
Gehrig-NY 175
Ruth-NY 164
Heilmann-Det 120
Goslin-Was 120
Fothergill-Det 114

Stolen Bases
Sisler-StL 27
Meusel-NY 24
Neun-Det 22
Lazzeri-NY 22
Cobb-Phi 22

Base Stealing Runs
Sisler-StL 3.5
Harris-Was 2.9
Goslin-Was 2.5
Neun-Det 2.4
Rice-Was 2.1

Fielding Runs-Infield
Gehringer-Det 17.1
Bluege-Was 14.8
Sisler-StL 12.1
Koenig-NY 12.1
O'Rourke-StL 11.2

Fielding Runs-Outfield
Falk-Chi 18.1
Rice-StL 10.9
Metzler-Chi 7.2
Barrett-Chi 6.9
Williams-StL 5.8

Wins
Lyons-Chi 22
Hoyt-NY 22
Grove-Phi 20

Winning Pct.
Hoyt-NY .759
Shocker-NY .750
Moore-NY .731
Pennock-NY .704
Lisenbee-Was .667

Complete Games
Lyons-Chi 30
Thomas-Chi 24
Hoyt-NY 23
Gaston-StL 21

Strikeouts
Grove-Phi 174
Walberg-Phi 136
Thomas-Chi 107
Lisenbee-Was 105
Braxton-Was 96

Fewest BB/Game
Quinn-Phi 1.65
Shocker-NY 1.85
Hoyt-NY 1.90
Braxton-Was 1.91
Lyons-Chi 1.96

Games
Braxton-Was 58
Marberry-Was 56
Grove-Phi 51
Moore-NY 50
Walberg-Phi 46

Saves
Moore-NY 13
Braxton-Was 13
Marberry-Was 9
Grove-Phi 9

Base Runners/9
Moore-NY 10.35
Braxton-Was 10.37
Lyons-Chi 10.47
Hoyt-NY 10.53
Thomas-Chi 10.71

Adjusted Relief Runs
Braxton-Was 18.7
Burke-Was 2.9
G.Smith-Det 2.7

Relief Ranking
Braxton-Was 24.1
G.Smith-Det 1.7
Burke-Was 1.4

Innings Pitched
Thomas-Chi 307.2
Lyons-Chi 307.2
Hudlin-Cle 264.2
Grove-Phi 262.1
Hoyt-NY 256.1

Opponents' Avg.
Moore-NY .234
Thomas-Chi .244
Hadley-Was .244
Lisenbee-Was .245
Braxton-Was .246

Opponents' OBP
Moore-NY .289
Braxton-Was .289
Lyons-Chi .292
Hoyt-NY .294
Thomas-Chi .303

Earned Run Average
Moore-NY 2.28
Hoyt-NY 2.63
Shocker-NY 2.84
Lyons-Chi 2.84
Hadley-Was 2.85

Adjusted ERA
Moore-NY 169
Hoyt-NY 146
Lyons-Chi 143
Hadley-Was 142
Braxton-Was 137

Adjusted Starter Runs
Thomas-Chi 42.0
Moore-NY 38.8
Lyons-Chi 38.2
Hoyt-NY 37.6
Hadley-Was 28.2

Pitcher Wins
Lyons-Chi 4.7
Moore-NY 4.5
Hoyt-NY 3.8
Thomas-Chi 3.8
Grove-Phi 3.0

Murder by Bat

Some felt that Babe Ruth's better days were behind him. But in 1927, he exploded again, tagging 60 home runs to set a mark that lasted until 1961. Lou Gehrig chipped in 175 RBIs, which still tops the AL list. Earle Combs led the league in hits and triples. The remainder of the offense assisted in the bludgeoning, and Murderer's Row outscored its closest rivals by 134. In addition, the Yankees pitching staff was the stingiest in the league by a margin of 109 runs. This dominating team was one of the best in baseball history.

Needless to say, the rest of the AL provided no challenge to the Yankees, whose 110 wins set a league record. Ruth and Gehrig, together, smacked 107 homers; Washington, Cleveland, Chicago, and Boston *combined* for only 119. The Red Sox, Ruth's former employer, finished 59 games behind, last for the third straight season.

As the Yankees eradicated the rest of the league, some of the great players of the pre-Ruth era called it quits. Walter Johnson pitched his last game at 39; first baseman Stuffy McInnis and shortstop Roger Peckinpaugh hung 'em up; and hurler Bob Shawkey, a consistent winner for New York even before the Babe's arrival, pitched his last game. On the horizon were the second-place Athletics, who continued to improve as Lefty Grove, Al Simmons, Mickey Cochrane, and Jimmie Foxx developed. But they were two years away.

The Pirates were a fine club, winning a tight NL race with solid hitting from the Waner brothers. But Pittsburgh was no match for the Yankees in the World Series, losing in four. While two games were decided by one run, the Bucs scored just 10 times in the Series; the Yankees tallied 23. Ruth batted .400 and hit the lone 2 homers of the Series.

1926 National League

TEAM	W	L	T	PCT	GB	HW	HL	R	OR	PA	H	2B	3B	HR	BB	SO	HB	SH	AVG	OBP	SLG	OPS	AOPS	BR	ABR	PF	SB	CS	BSA	BSR
STL	89	65	2	.578		47	30	**817**	678	6104	**1541**	259	82	**90**	478	518	33	212	.286	.348	**.415**	763	107	**77**	48	104	83			
CIN	87	67	3	.565	2	**53**	23	747	651	6047	**1541**	242	**120**	35	454	**333**	**34**	**239**	**.290**	**.349**	.400	749	**110**	49	**70**	97	51			
PIT	84	69	4	.549	4.5	49	28	769	689	5969	1514	243	106	44	434	350	33	190	.285		.396	739	99	25	-12	105	91			
CHI	82	72	1	.532	7	49	28	682	**602**	5902	1453	**291**	49	66	445	447	29	199	.278	.338	.390	728	100	12	4	101	85			
NY	74	77	0	.490	13.5	43	33	663	668	5667	1435	214	58	73	339	420	22	139	.278	.325	.384	709	97	-39	-31	99	**94**			
BRO	71	82	2	.464	17.5	38	38	623	705	5790	1348	246	62	40	475	464	27	158	.263	.328	.358	686	91	-63	-53	99	76			
BOS	66	86	1	.434	22	43	34	624	719	5870	1444	209	62	16	426	348	29	199	.277	.335	.350	685	99	-67	-5	91	81			
PHI	58	93	1	.384	29.5	33	42	687	900	5851	1479	244	50	75	422	479	22	153	.281	.337	.390	727	96	6	-28	105	47			
TOT	618					355	256	5612		47200	11755	1948	589	439	3473	3359	229	1489	.280	.338	.386	724					608			

TEAM	CG	SHO	GR	SV	IP	H	HR	BB	SO	BR/9	ERA	AERA	OAV	OOB	PR	APR	PF	OSB	OCS	FA	E	WPB	DP	FW	PW	BW	BSW	DIF
STL	**90**	10	118	6	1398.2	1423	76	397	365	11.8	3.67	106	**.269**	.322	24	35	102	60	**64**	.969	198	19	141	.3	3.5	4.7		3.5
CIN	88	**14**	107	8	1408.2	1449	40	**324**	424	**11.5**	3.42	108	.271	**.316**	64	44	97	76	43	.972	183	27	160	1.3	4.3	**6.9**		-2.6
PIT	83	12	131	**18**	1379.1	1422	50	455	387	12.5	3.67	107	.272	.334	24	41	103	63	44	.965	220	**18**	161	-.9	4.1	-1.2		5.5
CHI	77	13	114	14	1378.1	1407	**39**	486	508	12.6	**3.26**	**118**	.273	.340	87	89	101	42	68	**.974**	162	37	174	2.4	8.8	.4		5.5
NY	61	4	135	15	1341.2	**1370**	70	427	419	12.2	3.77	100	**.269**	.328	8	-3	98	84	54	.970	186	36	150	2.4	-.3	-3.1		-6.6
BRO	83	5	108	9	1361.2	1440	50	472	**517**	12.8	3.82	100	.273	.339	1	0	100	97	63	.963	229	34	95	.7	.0	-5.2		1.2
BOS	60	9	132	9	1365.1	1536	46	455	408	13.4	4.01	88	.294	.354	-28	-76	93	92	71	.967	208	42	150	-1.5	-7.5	-.5		1.3
PHI	68	5	**171**	5	1334.1	1699	68	454	331	14.7	5.03	82	.315	.371	-179	-123	108	94	56	.964	224	46	153	-1.5	-12.2	-2.8		-1.5
TOT	610	72	1016	84	10968.0					12.7	3.82		.280	.338						.968	1610	259	1184					-1.1

Batter-Fielder Wins
O'Farrell-StL ...3.2
Wilson-Chi ...2.8
Waner-Pit ...2.6
Bancroft-Bos ...2.6
Adams-Chi ...2.6

Batting Average
Hargrave-Cin ...353
Christensen-Cin ...350
Smith-Pit ...346
Williams-Phi ...345
Waner-Pit ...336

On-Base Percentage
Waner-Pit ...413
Blades-StL ...409
Wilson-Chi ...400
Grantham-Pit ...400
Bancroft-Bos ...399

Slugging Average
Williams-Phi ...568
Wilson-Chi ...539
Waner-Pit ...528
Hargrave-Cin ...525
L.Bell-StL ...518

On-Base Plus Slugging
Wilson-Chi ...944
Waner-Pit ...941
L.Bell-StL ...901
Grantham-Pit ...890
Herman-Bro ...875

Adjusted OPS
Wilson-Chi ...150
Waner-Pit ...144
Herman-Bro ...136
L.Bell-StL ...135
Grantham-Pit ...131

Adjusted Batter Runs
Wilson-Chi ...39.2
Waner-Pit ...34.0
L.Bell-StL ...27.6
Williams-Phi ...26.3
Herman-Bro ...24.3

Runs
Cuyler-Pit ...113
Waner-Pit ...101
Southworth-NY-StL ...99
Sand-Phi ...99

Hits
Brown-Bos ...201
Cuyler-Pit ...197
Adams-Chi ...193
L.Bell-StL ...189

Doubles
Bottomley-StL ...40
Roush-Cin ...37
Wilson-Chi ...36

Triples
Waner-Pit ...22
Walker-Cin ...20
Traynor-Pit ...17

Home Runs
Wilson-Chi ...21
Bottomley-StL ...19
Williams-Phi ...18
L.Bell-StL ...17
Southworth-NY-StL ...16

Total Bases
Bottomley-StL ...305
L.Bell-StL ...301
Wilson-Chi ...285
Waner-Pit ...283
Cuyler-Pit ...282

Runs Batted In
Bottomley-StL ...120
Wilson-Chi ...109
L.Bell-StL ...100
Southworth-NY-StL ...99
Pipp-Cin ...99

Stolen Bases
Cuyler-Pit ...35
Adams-Chi ...27
Frisch-NY ...23
Douthit-StL ...23
Youngs-NY ...21

Base Stealing Runs

Fielding Runs-Infield
Critz-Cin ...23.0
Friberg-Phi ...22.1
Adams-Chi ...20.1
Cooney-Chi ...17.8
Thevenow-StL ...16.2

Fielding Runs-Outfield
Heathcote-Chi ...8.5
Welsh-Bos ...8.2
Douthit-StL ...7.2
Cuyler-Pit ...6.7
Leach-Phi ...6.0

Wins
Rhem-StL ...20
Meadows-Pit ...20
Kremer-Pit ...20
Donohue-Cin ...20
Mays-Cin ...19

Winning Pct.
Kremer-Pit ...769
Rhem-StL ...741
Meadows-Pit ...690
Mays-Cin ...613
Donohue-Cin ...588

Complete Games
Mays-Cin ...24
Petty-Bro ...23
Root-Chi ...21
Rhem-StL ...20
Carlson-Phi ...20

Strikeouts
Vance-Bro ...140
Root-Chi ...127
May-Cin ...103
Benton-Bos ...103
Petty-Bro ...101

Fewest BB/Game
Donohue-Cin ...1.23
Alexander-Chi-StL ...1.39
Carlson-Phi ...1.58
Mays-Cin ...1.70
Lucas-Chi ...1.75

Games
Scott-NY ...50
Willoughby-Phi ...47
Donohue-Cin ...47
Ulrich-Phi ...45
May-Cin ...45

Saves
Davies-NY ...6
Scott-NY ...5
Kremer-Pit ...5
Ehrhardt-Bro ...4

Base Runners/9
Alexander-Chi-StL ...10.06
H.Bell-StL ...10.69
Petty-Bro ...10.71
Kremer-Pit ...10.74
Bush-Pit ...10.90

Adjusted Relief Runs
Hallahan-StL ...1.7

Relief Ranking
Hallahan-StL ...1.3

Innings Pitched
Donohue-Cin ...285.2
Mays-Cin ...281.0
Petty-Bro ...275.2
Root-Chi ...271.1
Carlson-Phi ...267.1

Opponents' Avg.
Petty-Bro ...240
Alexander-Chi-StL ...250
Rhem-StL ...250
Greenfield-NY ...251
Kremer-Pit ...252

Opponents' OBP
Alexander-Chi-StL ...281
Petty-Bro ...296
Kremer-Pit ...296
Donohue-Cin ...298
Rhem-StL ...305

Earned Run Average
Kremer-Pit ...2.61
Root-Chi ...2.82
Petty-Bro ...2.84
Bush-Chi ...2.86
Barnes-NY ...2.87

Adjusted ERA
Kremer-Pit ...151
Root-Chi ...136
Petty-Bro ...134
Bush-Chi ...134
Barnes-NY ...131

Adjusted Starter Runs
Kremer-Pit ...34.4
Root-Chi ...30.1
Petty-Bro ...25.2
Carlson-Phi ...24.9
Mays-Cin ...20.9

Pitcher Wins
Kremer-Pit ...3.9
Root-Chi ...3.1
Mays-Cin ...2.9
Carlson-Phi ...2.6
Petty-Bro ...2.4

Cardinals Nest at the Top

It had been a long upward crawl for the St. Louis Cardinals. Since joining the NL in 1892, the franchise had never won and rarely even contended. With slugging Rogers Hornsby taking the managerial reins, however, 1926 was different. St. Louis' powerful offense, led by Hornsby and Bottomley, bludgeoned its opponents into submission. Unheralded Les Bell (.325, 17 homers, 100 RBIs) turned in one of the best hitting performances by a third baseman to that time. Lowly Boston spiced things up by beating up on St. Louis in early September. The Braves in turn knocked Cincinnati, Chicago, and Pittsburgh out of the race.

Attendance again hit an all-time high. Since 1904, AL attendance had topped the NL's every season. But in 1926 the Senior Circuit outdrew its rival and would remain better attended for seven more seasons. Since five NL teams actually lost attendance in '26, the gains came from just three clubs: the Cardinals (60 percent increase), the Reds (69 percent), and the Cubs (70 percent).

Giants outfielder Ross Youngs came down with Bright's disease at midseason. He died in November 1927. However, 17-year-old Mel Ott moved in, hitting .383 in 35 games for the Giants. Two stellar Pittsburgh hurlers, Babe Adams and Wilbur Cooper, ended their careers with 416 combined victories. But the Bucs welcomed outfielder Paul Waner, who had a tremendous start to his Hall of Fame career. He led the NL in on-base percentage and went 6-for-6 against St. Louis on August 26.

The Cardinals-Yankees World Series was a thriller. Down three games to two in New York, St. Louis blew out the Bombers in Game 6 and held on for a thrilling Game 7 victory. Summoned in relief, Grover Cleveland Alexander quelled two New York rallies in the final contest after winning Games 2 and 6. Babe Ruth hit 4 homers, but he was thrown out stealing second to end the Series!

1926 American League

TEAM	W	L	T	PCT	GB	HW	HL	R	OR	PA	H	2B	3B	HR	BB	SO	HB	SH	AVG	OBP	SLG	OPS	AOPS	BR	ABR	PF	SB	CS	BSA	BSR
NY	91	63	1	.591		50	25	847	713	6104	1508	262	75	**121**	642	580	23	218	.289	**.369**	.437	806	119	124	**138**	98	79	62	56	-4
CLE	88	66	0	.571	3	49	31	738	612	6005	1529	**333**	49	27	455	332	35	222	.289	.349	.386	735	97	-13	-19	101	88	42	68	5
PHI	83	67	0	.553	6	44	27	677	**570**	5833	1359	259	65	61	523	369	**38**	195	**.292**	.364	.401	765	109	46	66	98	117	91	56	-6
WAS	81	69	2	.540	8	42	30	802	761	6011	1525	244	**97**	43	555	381	34	229	.289	.361	.390	751	106	29	58	96	**123**	78	61	0
CHI	81	72	2	.529	9.5	47	31	730	665	6039	**1547**	281	90	36	599	423	34	236	.291	.367	.398	765	105	53	58	101	88	71	55	-5
DET	79	75	3	.513	12	39	41	793	830	6184	1508	253	60	32	556	472	35	205	.276	.335	.394	729	92	-42	-73	105	64	66	49	-9
STL	62	92	1	.403	29	40	39	682	845	5936	1449	253	78	72	437	452	33	165	.256	.321	.343	664	82	-158	-140	97	52	48	52	-7
BOS	46	107	1	.301	44.5	25	51	562	835	5848	1325	249	54	32	465	454	25	239	.256	.321	.343	664					56	45		-3
TOT	616					336	275	5831		47960	11750	2195	568	424	4232	3463	257	1709	.281	.351	.392	743					667	503	57	-29

TEAM	CG	SHO	GR	SV	IP	H	HR	BB	SO	BR/9	ERA	AERA	OAV	OOB	PR	APR	PF	OSB	OCS	FA	E	WPB	DP	FW	PW	BW	BSW	DIF
NY	63	4	147	20	1372.1	1442	56	478	486	12.8	3.86	100	.274	.337	24	-1	96	95	67	.966	210	36	117	-1.1	-.0	**13.4**	-.0	1.9
CLE	**96**	**11**	81	4	1374.0	1412	49	**450**	381	12.5	3.40	119	.271	.334	94	100	101	**49**	41	.972	173	28	153	.9	**16.3**	-7.3	.0	-1.9
PHI	62	10	156	16	1346.0	**1362**	38	451	**571**	12.3	3.00	139	.268	.331	153	168	104	78	64	.972	171	35	131	.9	-7.2	6.4	-.2	6.8
WAS	65	5	143	**26**	1348.1	1489	45	566	418	14.0	4.34	89	.287	.361	-48	-74	96	80	59	**.973**	184	21	129	.2	1.6	5.6	.4	-4.7
CHI	85	**11**	100	12	1380.0	1426	47	506	458	12.7	3.74	103	.271	.336	43	17	96	59	59	.969	165	21	151	.0	-5.1	4.2	-.1	3.0
DET	57	10	164	18	1394.2	1570	58	555	469	14.0	4.41	92	.292	.363	-61	-53	101	100	70	.969	235	38	**167**	-2.6	-5.3	-7.1	-.5	.5
STL	64	5	139	9	1368.0	1549	86	654	337	14.7	4.66	92	.297	.379	-98	-55	107	67	**86**	.963	193	24	122					
BOS	53	6	163	5	1362.0	1520	45	546	336	13.9	4.72	86	.294	.365	-107	-99	101	139	59	.970	193	34	143	-.2	-9.6	-13.6	-.1	-7.1
TOT	545	62	1093	110	10945.1					13.3	4.02		.281	.351						.969	1524	237	1113					

Batter-Fielder Wins		Batting Average		On-Base Percentage		Slugging Average		On-Base Plus Slugging		Adjusted OPS		Adjusted Batter Runs	
Ruth-NY	8.5	Manush-Det	378	Ruth-NY	516	Ruth-NY	737	Ruth-NY	1253	Ruth-NY	228	Ruth-NY	102.8
Goslin-Was	4.6	Ruth-NY	372	Heilmann-Det	445	Simmons-Phi	564	Manush-Det	985	Goslin-Was	155	Gehrig-NY	47.5
Rigney-Bos	4.3	Fothergill-Det	367	Bishop-Phi	431	Manush-Det	564	Heilmann-Det	979	Gehrig-NY	154	Goslin-Was	45.0
Mostil-Chi	3.5	Heilmann-Det	367	Goslin-Was	425	Gehrig-NY	549	Gehrig-NY	969	Manush-Det	153	Heilmann-Det	41.8
J.Sewell-Cle	3.4	Burns-Cle	358	Manush-Det	421	Goslin-Was	542	Goslin-Was	967	Heilmann-Det	153	Manush-Det	37.3

Runs		Hits		Doubles		Triples		Home Runs		Total Bases		Runs Batted In	
Ruth-NY	139	Rice-Was	216	Burns-Cle	64	Gehrig-NY	20	Ruth-NY	47	Ruth-NY	365	Ruth-NY	146
Gehrig-NY	135	Burns-Cle	216	Simmons-Phi	53	Gehringer-Det	17	Simmons-Phi	19	Simmons-Phi	329	Lazzeri-NY	114
Mostil-Chi	120	Goslin-Was	201	Speaker-Cle	52	Lazzeri-NY	15	Lazzeri-NY	18	Gehrig-NY	314	Burns-Cle	114
Combs-NY	113	Simmons-Phi	199	Jacobson-StL-Bos	51	Goslin-Was	15	Williams-StL	17	Goslin-Was	308	Gehrig-NY	112
Goslin-Was	105	Mostil-Chi	197	Gehrig-NY	47			Goslin-Was	17	Burns-Cle	298	Simmons-Phi	109

Stolen Bases		Base Stealing Runs		Fielding Runs-Infield		Fielding Runs-Outfield		Wins		Winning Pct.		Complete Games	
Mostil-Chi	35	Mostil-Chi	2.8	Rigney-Bos	21.1	Goslin-Was	14.1	Uhle-Cle	27	Uhle-Cle	711	Uhle-Cle	32
Rice-Was	24	Hunnefield-Chi	2.1	Dykes-Phi	16.3	Rice-Was	9.4	Pennock-NY	23	Pennock-NY	676	Lyons-Chi	24
Hunnefield-Chi	24	McNeely-Was	1.9	Kamm-Chi	16.1	Falk-Chi	8.3	Shocker-NY	19	Shocker-NY	633	Johnson-Was	22
McNeely-Was	18	Simmons-Phi	1.4	Regan-Bos	15.7	Rice-StL	6.9	Lyons-Chi	18	Faber-Chi	625	Grove-Phi	20
J.Sewell-Cle	17	J.Sewell-Cle	1.3	McManus-StL	11.9	Mostil-Chi	6.7			Hoyt-NY	571	Pennock-NY	19

Strikeouts		Fewest BB/Game		Games		Saves		Base Runners/9		Adjusted Relief Runs		Relief Ranking	
Grove-Phi	194	Pennock-NY	1.45	Marberry-Was	64	Marberry-Was	22	Russell-Bos	10.93	Pate-Phi	19.6	Marberry-Was	21.2
Uhle-Cle	159	Smith-Cle	1.48	Pate-Phi	47	Dauss-Det	9	Pennock-NY	11.52	Marberry-Was	13.3	Pate-Phi	16.4
Thomas-Chi	127	Quinn-Phi	1.98	Grove-Phi	45	Pate-Phi	6	Rommel-Phi	11.55	Braxton-NY	7.6	Braxton-NY	6.6
Johnson-Was	125	Rommel-Phi	2.22	Thomas-Chi	44	Grove-Phi	6	Johnson-Was	11.64	Russell-Bos	7.6	Russell-Bos	3.8
Whitehill-Det	109	Wingfield-Bos	2.36			Jones-NY	5	Grove-Phi	11.65				

Innings Pitched		Opponents' Avg.		Opponents' OBP		Earned Run Average		Adjusted ERA		Adjusted Starter Runs		Pitcher Wins	
Uhle-Cle	318.1	Thomas-Chi	244	Pennock-NY	313	Grove-Phi	2.51	Grove-Phi	166	Uhle-Cle	44.6	**Uhle-Cle**	5.4
Lyons-Chi	283.2	Grove-Phi	244	Rommel-Phi	314	Uhle-Cle	2.83	Uhle-Cle	143	Grove-Phi	43.7	**Grove-Phi**	3.7
Pennock-NY	266.1	Lyons-Chi	252	Hoyt-NY	316	Lyons-Chi	3.01	Rommel-Phi	135	Lyons-Chi	28.8	**Lyons-Chi**	3.3
Johnson-Was	260.2	Uhle-Cle	253	Johnson-Was	317	Rommel-Phi	3.08	Buckeye-Cle	131	Rommel-Phi	27.1	**Walberg-Phi**	2.3
Shocker-NY	258.1	Levsen-Cle	261	Shocker-NY	318	Buckeye-Cle	3.10	Lyons-Chi	128	Walberg-Phi	19.3	**Rommel-Phi**	2.2

The Yankees Are Back

Due to the calamitous (at least for pitchers) rise in offense, the rules committee decided that any flyball over an outfield fence less than 250 feet from home was a ground-rule double. Three clubs also tried to curb production; St. Louis, a home run haven in '25, pushed out the fences by 10 feet. Boston enlarged Fenway Park's right field by 45 feet, and the White Sox grew center field by 30. Philadelphia, however, hoping to spur on their young power, shrunk Shibe Park to all fields. The Senators also chopped Griffith Stadium's left field by 66 feet. But the upshot to all these moves was a decline in scoring by nearly half a run and a loss of more than 100 homers.

Into this environment moved the Yankees, bolstered by the hitting of a healthy Babe Ruth, rookie infielder Tony Lazzeri, and 23-year-old Lou Gehrig, making his first appearance among the league leaders—although he actually hit more triples than homers. Miller Huggins' lineup destroyed the competition, but they just held off second-place Cleveland, whose first baseman George Burns rapped out a major league record 64 doubles.

The Indians and third-place Athletics played in inhospitable home run parks, and couldn't compete with New York's firepower, and their pitching wasn't good enough to overcome this. Washington fell to fourth as Walter Johnson finally went over the hill.

Shortstop Everett Scott retired with the record for most consecutive games played (1,307), and Hall of Fame hurler Eddie Plank died at age 50 of a stroke. Joe Cronin, later a standout with the Senators, debuted for the Pittsburgh Pirates—who soon gave up on him.

In addition to the Yankees' tough World Series loss to the Cardinals, 1926 was an ignominious year for the Junior Circuit in another way: the NL moved ahead in attendance for the first time since 1903. The Senior Circuit remained ahead until 1934.

1925 National League

TEAM	W	L	T	PCT	GB	HW	HL	R	OR	PA	H	2B	3B	HR	BB	SO	HB	SH	AVG	OBP	SLG	OPS	AOPS	BR	ABR	PF	SB	CS	BSA	BSR
PIT	95	58	0	.621		52	25	912	715	6036	1651	316	105	78	499	363	30	135	.307	.369	.449	818	108	120	62	107	159	63	72	13
NY	86	66	0	.566	8.5	47	29	736	702	5858	1507	239	61	114	411	494	25	95	.283	.337	.415	752	101	-28	3	96	79	65	55	-5
CIN	80	73	0	.523	15	44	32	690	643	5838	1490	221	90	44	409	327	23	173	.285	.339	.387	726	93	-71	-54	98	108	107	50	-14
STL	77	76	0	.503	18	48	28	828	764	5936	1592	292	80	109	446	414	27	134	.299	.356	.445	801	108	75	56	102	70	51	58	-2
BOS	70	83	0	.458	25	37	39	708	802	5945	1567	260	70	41	405	380	30	145	.292	.345	.390	735	102	-48	22	91	77	72	52	-8
PHI	68	85	0	.444	27	38	39	812	930	6035	1598	288	58	100	456	542	34	133	.295	.354	.425	779	96	39	-28	109	48	59	45	-10
BRO	68	85	0	.444	27	40	37	786	866	6045	1617	250	80	64	437	383	26	114	.296	.351	.406	757	102	-8	14	97	37	30	55	-2
CHI	68	86	0	.442	27.5	37	40	723	773	5933	1473	254	70	86	397	470	33	150	.275	.329	.397	726	89	-78	-88	102	94	70	57	-4
TOT	612					343	269	6195		47626	12495	2120	614	636	3460	3373	228	1079	.292	.348	.414	762					672	517	57	-33

TEAM	CG	SHO	GR	SV	IP	H	HR	BB	SO	BR/9	ERA	AERA	OAV	OOB	PR	APR	PF	OSB	OCS	FA	E	WPB	DP	FW	PW	BW	BSW	DIF
PIT	77	2	119	13	1354.2	1526	81	387	386	12.9	3.87	115	.287	.339	59	84	105	54	51	.964	224	36	171	-.9	7.9	5.8	1.6	4.1
NY	80	6	113	8	1354.0	1532	73	408	446	13.0	3.94	102	.289	.342	49	18	95	91	73	.968	199	20	129	.5	1.7	.3	-.0	7.6
CIN	92	11	103	12	1375.1	1447	35	324	437	11.8	3.38	121	.272	.317	135	115	96	107	52	.968	203	32	161	.3	10.8	-5.1	-.9	-1.6
STL	82	8	105	7	1335.2	1480	86	470	428	13.4	4.36	99	.283	.347	-14	-7	101	72	57	.966	204	25	156	.3	-.7	5.2	.2	-4.6
BOS	77	5	129	4	1366.2	1567	67	458	351	13.4	4.39	91	.291	.348	-19	-62	94	77	48	.964	221	29	145	-.7	-5.8	2.1	-.4	-1.7
PHI	69	8	151	9	1350.2	1753	117	444	371	14.8	5.02	95	.315	.368	-114	-34	112	89	54	.966	211	45	147	-1.1	-3.2	-2.6	-.5	-2.0
BRO	82	4	128	4	1350.2	1608	75	477	518	14.1	4.77	88	.301	.362	-76	-92	98	122	107	.966	210	50	130	-.0	-8.6	1.3	.2	-1.3
CHI	75	5	115	10	1370.0	1575	102	485	435	13.7	4.41	98	.292	.353	-21	-13	101	60	75	.969	198	21	161	.7	-1.2	-8.2	.0	-.3
TOT	634	49	963	67	10857.2					13.4	4.27		.292	.348						.966	1670	258	1200					-.3

Batter-Fielder Wins
Hornsby-StL 6.8
Fournier-Bro 4.2
Bancroft-Bos 3.9
Traynor-Pit 3.6
Cuyler-Pit 3.6

Batting Average
Hornsby-StL 403
Bottomley-StL 367
Wheat-Bro 359
Cuyler-Pit 357
Fournier-Bro 350

On-Base Percentage
Hornsby-StL 489
Fournier-Bro 446
Blades-StL 423
Cuyler-Pit 423
Carey-Pit 418

Slugging Average
Hornsby-StL 756
Cuyler-Pit 598
Wrightstone-Phi 591
Bottomley-StL 578
Fournier-Bro 569

On-Base Plus Slugging
Hornsby-StL 1245
Cuyler-Pit 1021
Fournier-Bro 1015
Bottomley-StL 992
Blades-StL 958

Adjusted OPS
Hornsby-StL 208
Fournier-Bro 162
Cuyler-Pit 148
Bottomley-StL 147
Wheat-Bro 143

Adjusted Batter Runs
Hornsby-StL 85.3
Fournier-Bro 53.9
Cuyler-Pit 44.1
Bottomley-StL 43.2
Wheat-Bro 38.8

Runs
Cuyler-Pit 144
Hornsby-StL 133
Wheat-Bro 125
Traynor-Pit 114
Blades-StL 112

Hits
Bottomley-StL 227
Wheat-Bro 221
Cuyler-Pit 220
Hornsby-StL 203
Stock-Bro 202

Doubles
Bottomley-StL 44
Cuyler-Pit 43
Wheat-Bro 42
Hornsby-StL 41
Burrus-Bos 41

Triples
Cuyler-Pit 26
Walker-Cin 16
Roush-Cin 16
Fournier-Bro 16

Home Runs
Hornsby-StL 39
Hartnett-Chi 24
Fournier-Bro 22
Meusel-NY 21
Bottomley-StL 21

Total Bases
Hornsby-StL 381
Cuyler-Pit 369
Bottomley-StL 358
Wheat-Bro 333
Fournier-Bro 310

Runs Batted In
Hornsby-StL 143
Fournier-Bro 130
Bottomley-StL 128
Wright-Pit 121
Barnhart-Pit 114

Stolen Bases
Carey-Pit 46
Cuyler-Pit 41
Adams-Chi 26
Roush-Cin 22
Frisch-NY 21

Base Stealing Runs
Carey-Pit 6.3
Cuyler-Pit 4.5
Smith-StL 3.7
Moore-Pit 1.7
Grantham-Pit 1.7

Fielding Runs-Infield
Adams-Chi 26.5
Traynor-Pit 23.3
Critz-Cin 19.7
Kelly-NY 18.3
Pinelli-Cin 17.0

Fielding Runs-Outfield
Felix-Bos 9.5
Blades-StL 9.3
Heathcote-Chi 8.3
Neis-Bos 7.1
Welsh-Bos 4.8

Wins
Vance-Bro 22
Rixey-Cin 21
Donohue-Cin 21
Meadows-Pit 19

Winning Pct.
Sherdel-StL 714
Vance-Bro 710
Aldridge-Pit 682
Kremer-Pit 680
Rixey-Cin 656

Complete Games
Donohue-Cin 27
Vance-Bro 26
Rixey-Cin 22
Luque-Cin 22
Ring-Phi 21

Strikeouts
Vance-Bro 221
Luque-Cin 140
Ring-Phi 93
Blake-Chi 93
Aldridge-Pit 88

Fewest BB/Game
Alexander-Chi 1.11
Donohue-Cin 1.47
Rixey-Cin 1.47
Cooney-Bos 1.83
Sherdel-StL 1.89

Games
Morrison-Pit 44
Donohue-Cin 42
Bush-Chi 42
Osborne-Bro 41
Kremer-Pit 40

Saves
Morrison-Pit 4
Bush-Chi 4

Base Runners/9
Fitzsimmons-NY 10.61
Luque-Cin 10.61
Donohue-Cin 10.79
Vance-Bro 10.96
Rixey-Cin 11.15

Adjusted Relief Runs
Huntzinger-NY 3.9

Relief Ranking
Huntzinger-NY 3.3

Innings Pitched
Donohue-Cin 301.0
Luque-Cin 291.0
Rixey-Cin 287.1
Ring-Phi 270.0
Vance-Bro 265.1

Opponents' Avg.
Luque-Cin 239
Benton-Bos 249
Vance-Bro 250
Donohue-Cin 268
Scott-NY 269

Opponents' OBP
Luque-Cin 291
Donohue-Cin 299
Vance-Bro 304
Rixey-Cin 307
Cooney-Bos 312

Earned Run Average
Luque-Cin 2.63
Rixey-Cin 2.88
Reinhart-StL 3.05
Donohue-Cin 3.08
Benton-Bos 3.09

Adjusted ERA
Luque-Cin 156
Rixey-Cin 143
Sherdel-StL 139
Donohue-Cin 133
Benton-Bos 130

Adjusted Starter Runs
Luque-Cin 48.3
Rixey-Cin 43.0
Donohue-Cin 38.3
Sherdel-StL 28.5
Scott-NY 25.5

Pitcher Wins
Luque-Cin 5.9
Donohue-Cin 4.6
Rixey-Cin 4.1
Scott-NY 3.5
Sherdel-StL 2.8

Fattening Up

NL hitters fattened up on Senior Circuit's hurlers in 1925. Each team averaged 5.06 runs per game, up 11 percent from '24. The biggest reason was the extra 137 home runs that NL batters slugged. The league ERA went up 40 points, and just two qualifying pitchers posted ERAs below 3.00.

The Pittsburgh Pirates shrunk right field at Forbes Field from 372 feet to just 300, which helped the Bucs score 188 more runs than in 1924, accounting for 40 percent of the league's increase. The cozier confines of Forbes Field did not harm Pittsburgh's crack staff at all; five Pirates had 15 or more victories. New York led the NL through June, but Pittsburgh—third-place finishers for the past three years—came on fast and took the lead for good in early July, eventually winning by 8½ games. Kiki Cuyler scored 144 runs and smacked 26 triples and Max Carey stole 46 bases. The Bucs had seven .300 hitters.

The second-place Giants led the league in homers, with Irish Meusel hitting 21 and George Kelly 20, but their lineup featured several offensive dead spots. Perhaps the top 1-2 punch in the league was St. Louis' Rogers Hornsby (league MVP and Triple Crown winner) and Jim Bottomley (the NL leader in hits and doubles), but the rest of the team was thin.

The Washington Senators took three of the first four games of the World Series, but the Bucs weren't done. Pittsburgh won Game 5 at Washington, 6-3, then came from behind to take the final two contests at Forbes Field. Down 7-6 in the eighth inning of Game 7, the Pirates scored three times off 37-year-old Walter Johnson to capture the Series. It would be the Bucs' last World Series appearance until 1960.

1925 American League

TEAM	W	L	T	PCT	GB	HW	HL	R	OR	PA	H	2B	3B	HR	BB	SO	HB	SH	AVG	OBP	SLG	OPS	AOPS	BR	ABR	PF	SB	CS	BSA	BSR
WAS	96	55	1	.636		53	22	829	670	5994	1577	251	71	56	533	427	47	208	.303	.373	.411	784	106	38	55	98	135	92	59	
PHI	88	64	1	.579	8.5	51	26	831	713	6071	1659	298	79	76	453	432	32	187	.307	.364	.434	798	101	53	0	107	67	60	53	-5
STL	82	71	1	.536	15	45	32	900	906	6110	1620	304	68	110	498	375	29	143	.298	.360	.439	799	103	53	11	105	85	78	52	
DET	81	73	2	.526	16.5	43	34	903	829	6264	1621	277	84	50	640	386	32	221	.302	.379	.413	792	109	64	78	99	97	63	61	
CHI	79	75	0	.513	18.5	44	33	811	770	6168	1482	299	59	38	662	405	51	231	.284	.370	.399	760	102	-2	43	95	131	87	60	
CLE	70	84	1	.455	27.5	37	39	782	817	6163	1613	285	58	52	520	379	27	180	.297	.361	.399	760	97	-12	-18	101	90	77	54	-1
NY	69	85	2	.448	28.5	42	36	706	774	6021	1471	247	74	110	470	482	24	174	.275	.336	.410	746	96	-65	-52	98	69	73	49	-1
BOS	47	105	0	.309	49.5	28	47	639	922	5845	1375	257	64	41	513	422	31	135	.266	.336	.364	700	83	-133	-132	100	42	56	43	-1
TOT	616					343	269	6401		48636	12418	2218	557	533	4289	3308	273	1479	.292	.360	.408	768					716	586	55	-4

TEAM	CG	SHO	GR	SV	IP	H	HR	BB	SO	BR/9	ERA	AERA	OAV	OOB	PR	APR	PF	OSB	OCS	FA	E	WPB	DP	FW	PW	BW	BSW	DI
WAS	69	10	145	21	1358.1	1434	49	543	463	13.3	3.70	114	.278	.351	105	82	96	74	64	.972	170	24	166	1.8	7.6	5.1	.4	5.
PHI	61	8	161	18	1381.2	1468	60	544	495	13.3	3.87	120	.276	.347	81	113	106	93	61	.966	211	41	148	-.6	10.5	.0	.0	2.
STL	67	7	160	10	1379.2	1588	99	675	419	15.0	4.92	95	.298	.380	-80	-37	106	103	94	.964	226	44	164	-1.4	-3.4	1.0	-.3	9.
DET	66	2	142	18	1383.2	1582	70	556	419	14.2	4.61	94	.296	.366	-32	-47	98	103	65	.972	173	34	143	1.9	-4.4	7.2	.5	-1.
CHI	71	12	129	13	1385.2	1579	69	489	374	13.6	4.29	97	.295	.356	17	-23	95	46	88	.968	200	26	162	.2	-2.1	4.0	.4	-.
CLE	93	6	103	-9	1372.1	1604	41	493	345	14.0	4.49	98	.296	.359	-15	-9	101	71	57	.974	210	26	146	-.4	-.8	-1.7	-.0	-4.
NY	80	8	123	13	1387.2	1560	78	505	492	13.6	4.33	98	.289	.353	10	-11	97	96	89	.974	160	32	150	2.7	-1.0	-4.8	-.4	-6.
BOS	68	6	128	6	1326.2	1615	67	510	310	14.7	4.97	92	.308	.374	-84	-60	103	130	68	.957	271	28	150	-4.2	-5.6	-12.2	-.4	-6.
TOT	575	59	1091	108	10975.2					14.0	4.39		.292	.360						.968	1621	255	1229					

Batter-Fielder Wins
- **Speaker-Cle** 4.3
- **J.Sewell-Cle** 3.9
- **Goslin-Was** 3.5
- **Cobb-Det** 3.5
- **Heilmann-Det** 3.4

Batting Average
- Heilmann-Det .393
- Speaker-Cle .389
- Simmons-Phi .387
- Cobb-Det .378
- Wingo-Det .370

On-Base Percentage
- Speaker-Cle .479
- Cobb-Det .468
- Collins-Chi .461
- Heilmann-Det .457
- Wingo-Det .456

Slugging Average
- Williams-StL .613
- Simmons-Phi .599
- Cobb-Det .598
- Speaker-Cle .578
- Heilmann-Det .569

On-Base Plus Slugging
- Cobb-Det 1066
- Speaker-Cle 1057
- Heilmann-Det 1026
- Simmons-Phi 1018
- Wingo-Det 983

Adjusted OPS
- Cobb-Det 171
- Speaker-Cle 166
- Heilmann-Det 161
- Wingo-Det 151
- Simmons-Phi 146

Adjusted Batter Runs
- Heilmann-Det 55.
- Cobb-Det 47.
- Speaker-Cle 47.
- Simmons-Phi 42.
- Wingo-Det 37.

Runs
- Mostil-Chi 135
- Simmons-Phi 122
- Combs-NY 117
- Goslin-Was 116
- Rice-Was 111

Hits
- Simmons-Phi 253
- Rice-Was 227
- Heilmann-Det 225
- Sisler-StL 224
- J.Sewell-Cle 204

Doubles
- McManus-StL 44
- Simmons-Phi 43
- Sheely-Chi 43
- Burns-Cle 41

Triples
- Goslin-Was 20
- Mostil-Chi 16
- Sisler-StL 15

Home Runs
- Meusel-NY 33
- Williams-StL 25
- Ruth-NY 25
- Simmons-Phi 24
- Gehrig-NY 20

Total Bases
- Simmons-Phi 392
- Meusel-NY 338
- Goslin-Was 329
- Heilmann-Det 326
- Sisler-StL 311

Runs Batted In
- Meusel-NY 13
- Heilmann-Det 13
- Simmons-Phi 12
- Goslin-Was 11
- Sheely-Chi 11

Stolen Bases
- Mostil-Chi 43
- Goslin-Was 27
- Rice-Was 26

Base Stealing Runs
- Goslin-Was 3.1
- Mostil-Chi 2.5
- Blue-Det 2.4
- Collins-Chi 2.1
- Haney-Det 2.1

Fielding Runs-Infield
- J.Sewell-Cle 15.8
- O'Rourke-Det 14.7
- Sisler-StL 10.4
- Wambsganss-Bos 8.4
- Davis-Chi 6.9

Fielding Runs-Outfield
- Goslin-Was 14.3
- Flagstead-Bos 14.0
- Wingo-Det 8.9
- Rice-Was 6.8
- Jamieson-Cle 5.0

Wins
- Rommel-Phi 21
- Lyons-Chi 21
- Johnson-Was 20
- Coveleski-Was 20
- Harriss-Phi 19

Winning Pct.
- Coveleski-Was .800
- Johnson-Was .741
- Ruether-Was .720
- Blankenship-Chi .680
- Rommel-Phi .677

Complete Games
- Smith-Cle 2
- Ehmke-Bos 2
- Pennock-NY 2
- Lyons-Chi 2
- Wingfield-Bos 1

Strikeouts
- Grove-Phi 116
- Johnson-Was 108
- Harriss-Phi 95
- Ehmke-Bos 95
- Jones-NY 92

Fewest BB/Game
- Smith-Cle 1.82
- Quinn-Bos-Phi 1.85
- Shocker-NY 2.14
- Faber-Chi 2.23
- Pennock-NY 2.31

Games
- Marberry-Was 55
- Walberg-Phi 53
- Vangilder-StL 52
- Rommel-Phi 52
- Pennock-NY 47

Saves
- Marberry-Was 15
- Doyle-Det 8
- Connally-Chi 8
- Walberg-Phi 7

Base Runners/9
- Pennock-NY 11.05
- Blankenship-Chi 11.13
- Coveleski-Was 11.39
- Gray-Phi 11.71
- Johnson-Was 11.87

Adjusted Relief Runs
- Marberry-Was 5.2
- Gregg-Was 9

Relief Ranking
- Marberry-Was 8
- Gregg-Was

Innings Pitched
- Pennock-NY 277.0
- Lyons-Chi 262.2
- Rommel-Phi 261.0
- Ehmke-Bos 260.2
- Wingfield-Bos 254.1

Opponents' Avg.
- Johnson-Was .250
- Blankenship-Chi .253
- Pennock-NY .254
- Coveleski-Was .255
- Gray-Phi .260

Opponents' OBP
- Pennock-NY .303
- Blankenship-Chi .308
- Coveleski-Was .312
- Johnson-Was .317
- Gray-Phi .319

Earned Run Average
- Coveleski-Was 2.84
- Pennock-NY 2.96
- Gray-Phi 3.03
- Johnson-Was 3.07
- Dauss-Det 3.16

Adjusted ERA
- Coveleski-Was 149
- Pennock-NY 144
- Gray-Phi 142
- Johnson-Was 138
- Blankenship-Chi 137

Adjusted Starter Runs
- Coveleski-Was 40.9
- Pennock-NY 36.3
- Blankenship-Chi 31.2
- Harriss-Phi 30.6
- Johnson-Was 30.1

Pitcher Wins
- **Johnson-Was** 3
- **Pennock-NY** 3
- **Harriss-Phi** 3
- **Rommel-Phi** 2
- **Coveleski-Was** 2

Walter's Disappointment

Has a team ever had a better set of players making their big league debuts than the 1925 A's? Both catcher Mickey Cochrane and pitcher Lefty Grove appeared for the first time on April 14, and first baseman Jimmie Foxx came up two weeks later. With Al Simmons rapping 253 hits in his sophomore season and Ed Rommel leading the league in wins for the second time, Philadelphia vaulted all the way to second.

But once again, it was Washington's year. The Senators broke away from the slumping Athletics in late August and won by 8½ games. A superannuated pitching staff featuring Walter Johnson and Stan Coveleski (aided by Firpo Marberry) was good enough, and outfielder Goose Goslin was spectacular.

The Yankees were no factor; Babe Ruth's wild nightlife shelved him. He collapsed during spring training from an intestinal problem; he missed seven weeks. When he returned, Ruth wasn't the same hitter—he was suspended in September. The undermanned Yanks finished seventh. Lou Gehrig did play his first full season.

The relative pitching calm of 1924 was replaced by stormy 1925 in which AL batters set a new homer record wit[h] 533—even with Ruth out of commission. The league batting an[d] slugging averages were also the highest ever. AL teams score[d] 5.20 runs per game, the most since 1901.

Former "Clean Sox" outfielders Nemo Leibold and Sha[n] Collins saw their final major league action, as did two othe[r] famous gardeners, Harry Hooper and Bobby Veach. In add[i]tion, Chief Bender, one of the great hurlers of the early cen[tury], pitched his last game.

The Senators went up three games to one on Pittsburgh i[n] the World Series, but couldn't close the deal. With the Series kno[t]ted, Johnson started Game 7; he completed the contest, althoug[h] he shouldn't have. He allowed all 9 runs (5 earned) and 15 hits i[n] a game in which the Senators led 6-4 through the sixth.

1924 National League

TEAM	W	L	T	PCT	GB	HW	HL	R	OR	PA	H	2B	3B	HR	BB	SO	HB	SH	AVG	OBP	SLG	OPS	AOPS	BR	ABR	PF	SB	CS	BSA	BSR
NY	93	60	1	.608		51	26	857	641	6067	1634	269	81	95	467	479	28	127	.300	.358	.432	790	120	127	151	97	82	53	61	-1
BRO	92	62	0	.597	1.5	46	31	717	679	5951	1534	227	54	72	447	357	22	143	.287	.345	.391	736	105	21	45	97	34	46	43	-9
PIT	90	63	0	.588	3	49	28	724	586	5833	1517	222	122	44	366	396	28	151	.287	.336	.400	736	100	7	-4	102	181	92	66	8
CIN	83	70	0	.542	10	43	33	649	579	5835	1539	236	111	36	349	334	26	159	.290	.337	.397	734	103	5	16	99	103	98	51	-12
CHI	81	72	1	.529	12	46	31	698	699	5796	1419	207	59	66	469	521	30	145	.290	.340	.378	718	96	-9	-15	101	137	149	48	-22
STL	65	89	0	.422	28.5	40	37	740	750	5909	1552	270	87	67	382	418	33	145	.290	.341	.411	752	108	43	57	98	86	86	50	-11
PHI	55	96	1	.364	37	26	49	676	849	5855	1459	256	56	94	382	452	36	131	.275	.328	.397	725	88	-10	-84	112	57	67	46	-11
BOS	53	100	1	.346	40	28	48	520	798	5767	1355	194	52	25	354	451	26	104	.256	.306	.327	633	77	-184	-162	96	74	68	52	-8
TOT	614					329	283	5581		47013	12009	1881	622	499	3216	3408	229	1123	.283	.337	.392	729					754	659	53	-65

TEAM	CG	SHO	GR	SV	IP	H	HR	BB	SO	BR/9	ERA	AERA	OAV	OOB	PR	APR	PF	OSB	OCS	FA	E	WPB	DP	FW	PW	BW	BSW	DIF
NY	71	4	148	21	1378.2	1464	77	392	406	12.2	3.62	101	.274	.326	38	7	95	96	74	.971	186	24	160	.4	.7	15.0	.7	-.3
BRO	97	10	84	5	1376.1	1432	58	403	638	12.2	3.64	103	.270	.326	35	17	97	108	95	.968	196	27	121	-.2	1.7	4.5	-.0	9.1
PIT	85	15	105	5	1382.0	1387	42	323	364	11.3	3.27	117	.267	.313	92	88	99	56	65	.971	183	31	161	.5	8.7	-.4	1.6	3.1
CIN	77	14	104	9	1378.0	1408	30	293	451	11.3	3.12	121	.267	.309	115	102	97	95	78	.966	217	23	142	-1.4	10.1	1.6	-.4	-3.4
CHI	85	4	107	6	1380.2	1459	89	438	416	12.5	3.83	102	.275	.333	6	11	101	76	80	.966	218	30	153	-1.4	1.1	-1.5	-1.4	7.7
STL	79	7	119	6	1364.2	1528	70	486	393	13.5	4.15	91	.290	.354	-43	-58	98	95	75	.969	188	32	162	.3	-5.8	5.7	-.3	-11.9
PHI	59	7	154	10	1354.1	1691	84	469	349	14.6	4.87	92	.314	.372	-151	-52	115	109	97	.972	175	43	168	.8	-5.2	-8.3	-.3	-7.6
BOS	66	10	123	4	1379.1	1607	49	402	364	13.3	4.46	86	.301	.353	-92	-101	99	119	95	.973	168	39	154	1.4	-10.0	-16.1	.0	1.2
TOT	619	71	944	66	10994.0					12.6	3.87		.283	.337						.970	1531	249	1221					

Batter-Fielder Wins		Batting Average		On-Base Percentage		Slugging Average		On-Base Plus Slugging		Adjusted OPS		Adjusted Batter Runs	
Hornsby-StL	9.3	Hornsby-StL	.424	Hornsby-StL	.507	Hornsby-StL	.696	Hornsby-StL	1203	Hornsby-StL	223	Hornsby-StL	99.4
Frisch-NY	6.0	Wheat-Bro	.375	Youngs-NY	.441	Williams-Phi	.552	Wheat-Bro	978	Fournier-Bro	165	Wheat-Bro	53.7
Fournier-Bro	4.9	Youngs-NY	.356	Fournier-Bro	.428	Wheat-Bro	.549	Fournier-Bro	965	Fournier-Bro	162	Fournier-Bro	53.7
Wheat-Bro	4.5	Cuyler-Pit	.354	Wheat-Bro	.428	Cuyler-Pit	.539	Youngs-NY	962	Youngs-NY	161	Youngs-NY	49.9
Youngs-NY	3.5	Roush-Cin	.348	Williams-Phi	.403	Fournier-Bro	.536	Williams-Phi	955	Cuyler-Pit	147	Kelly-NY	33.1

Runs		Hits		Doubles		Triples		Home Runs		Total Bases		Runs Batted In	
Hornsby-StL	121	Hornsby-StL	227	Hornsby-StL	43	Roush-Cin	21	Fournier-Bro	27	Hornsby-StL	373	Kelly-NY	136
Frisch-NY	121	Wheat-Bro	212	Wheat-Bro	41	Maranville-Pit	20	Hornsby-StL	25	Wheat-Bro	311	Fournier-Bro	116
Carey-Pit	113	Frisch-NY	198	Kelly-NY	37	Wright-Pit	18	Williams-Phi	24	Williams-Phi	308	Wright-Pit	111
Youngs-NY	112	High-Bro	191			Cuyler-Pit	16	Kelly-NY	21	Kelly-NY	303	Bottomley-StL	111
Williams-Phi	101	Fournier-Bro	188			Frisch-NY	15			Fournier-Bro	302	Meusel-NY	102

Stolen Bases		Base Stealing Runs		Fielding Runs-Infield		Fielding Runs-Outfield		Wins		Winning Pct.		Complete Games	
Carey-Pit	49	Carey-Pit	6.2	Frisch-NY	27.6	Smith-StL	8.8	Vance-Bro	28	Yde-Bro	842	Vance-Bro	30
Cuyler-Pit	32	Cuyler-Pit	3.2	Pinelli-Cin	24.3	Statz-Chi	8.8	Grimes-Bro	22	Vance-Bro	824	Grimes-Bro	30
Heathcote-Chi	26	Frisch-NY	1.7	Ford-Phi	8.9	Cunningham-Bos	5.3	Mays-Cin	20	Bentley-NY	762	Cooper-Pit	25
Traynor-Pit	24	Hartnett-Chi	1.5	Wright-Pit	8.7	Grigsby-Chi	4.5	Cooper-Pit	20	Mays-Cin	690	Barnes-Bos	21
Smith-StL	24	Freigau-StL	1.1	Groh-NY	7.4	Wheat-Bro	3.5	Kremer-Pit	18	Kremer-Pit	643	Aldridge-Chi	20

Strikeouts		Fewest BB/Game		Games		Saves		Base Runners/9		Adjusted Relief Runs		Relief Ranking	
Vance-Bro	262	Benton-Cin	1.33	Morrison-Pit	41	May-Cin	6	Vance-Bro	9.46	Jonnard-NY	10.8	Jonnard-NY	10.0
Grimes-Bro	135	Alexander-Chi	1.33	Kremer-Pit	41	Ryan-NY	5	Ehrhardt-Bro	9.57	May-Cin	9.1	May-Cin	6.2
Luque-Cin	86	Cooper-Pit	1.34	Keen-Chi	40	Jonnard-NY	5	Rixey-Cin	10.12	Stone-Pit	5.3	Stone-Pit	4.4
Morrison-Pit	85	Mays-Cin	1.43	Sheehan-Cin	39			Stone-Pit	10.13				
Kaufmann-Chi	79	Donohue-Cin	1.46					Jonnard-NY	10.64				

Innings Pitched		Opponents' Avg.		Opponents' OBP		Earned Run Average		Adjusted ERA		Adjusted Starter Runs		Pitcher Wins	
Grimes-Bro	310.2	Vance-Bro	.213	Vance-Bro	.269	Vance-Bro	2.16	Vance-Bro	173	Vance-Bro	56.6	Vance-Bro	5.9
Vance-Bro	308.1	Yde-Pit	.244	Rixey-Cin	.285	McQuillan-NY	2.69	Rixey-Cin	137	Rixey-Cin	28.5	Rixey-Cin	3.4
Cooper-Pit	268.2	Morrison-Pit	.245	Benton-Cin	.297	Rixey-Cin	2.76	McQuillan-NY	136	Yde-Pit	22.4	Mays-Cin	3.0
Barnes-Bos	267.2	Rixey-Cin	.248	Alexander-Chi	.299	Benton-Cin	2.77	Benton-Cin	136	Kremer-Pit	21.1	Cooper-Pit	2.7
Kremer-Pit	259.1	Doak-StL-Bro	.249	Nehf-NY	.301	Yde-Pit	2.83	Yde-Pit	136	McQuillan-NY	19.0	Yde-Pit	2.2

Big Mac's Last Stand

NL pitchers gained a foothold in 1924 as the league ERA fell to 3.87. Brooklyn's Dazzy Vance won his third straight strikeout title (as well as the win and ERA championships) as his whiffs rose from 197 to 262.

The Giants, gunning for their fourth straight flag, dominated early but blew a 10-game lead over Pittsburgh by sleepwalking through August. Brooklyn rode Vance's golden arm to 15 straight wins—including 11 games in eight days—to establish a three-way tangle.

By late September, the Giants, who led the league in nearly every offensive category, regained their momentum while Brooklyn and Pittsburgh knocked each other around. New York eventually won by 1½ over Brooklyn; Pittsburgh, again using a speed-oriented offense, finished 3 games back.

The race raised attendance in Brooklyn and Pittsburgh, and as result, NL tickets sold rose for the third straight year. Meanwhile, St. Louis saw a 19 percent decline even as Rogers Hornsby won his fifth batting title in a row—batting .424!—but his club ended sixth.

Two Hall of Famers debuted in 1924. Freddie Lindstrom was a utilityman for John McGraw's Giants, and Cardinals outfielder Chick Hafey got into 24 games down the stretch. Several prominent baseball figures died during the year. Candy Cummings, a 120-pound righty credited with inventing the curve in the 1860s, died at age 76. Pat Moran, 48, who guided the Phillies and the Reds to their first NL pennants, died from Bright's disease in spring training with Cincinnati. Hall of Famer Frank Chance died a year after managing the last-place Red Sox. Two notable active players also breathed their last. Third baseman Tony Boeckel of the Braves became the first player killed in a motor accident. Veteran first baseman Jake Daubert, Cincinnati's team captain who collected 2,326 hits, died October 9 following an appendectomy.

The Giants' loss in the World Series to Washington heralded the end of their dynasty. McGraw managed until 1932, but he never won another pennant.

1924 American League

TEAM	W	L	T	PCT	GB	HW	HL	R	OR	PA	H	2B	3B	HR	BB	SO	HB	SH	AVG	OBP	SLG	OPS	AOPS	BR	ABR	PF	SB	CS	BSA	BSR
WAS	92	62	2	.597		47	30	755	613	6098	1558	255	88	22	513	392	49	232	.294	.361	.387	748	101	-10	14	97	116	85	58	-4
NY	89	63	1	.586	2	45	32	798	667	5936	1516	248	86	98	478	420	29	189	.289	.352	.426	778	106	25	27	100	69	67	51	-8
DET	86	68	2	.558	6	45	33	849	796	6262	1604	315	76	35	607	400	41	225	.298	.373	.404	777	108	57	71	98	100	77	56	-7
STL	74	78	1	.487	17	41	36	769	807	5923	1543	266	62	67	465	349	32	190	.295	.356	.408	764	96	9	-35	106	85	85	50	-11
PHI	71	81	0	.467	20	36	39	685	778	5749	1459	251	59	41	374	484	35	156	.281	.334	.389	723	90	-80	-86	101	77	68	53	-7
CLE	67	86	0	.438	24.5	37	38	755	814	6031	1580	306	59	41	492	371	44	163	.296	.361	.399	760	100	11	1	101	85	57	60	-1
BOS	67	87	3	.435	25	41	36	735	806	6185	1481	302	63	30	603	417	47	195	.277	.356	.374	730	94	-39	-40	100	78	61	56	-4
CHI	66	87	1	.431	25.5	37	39	793	858	6125	1512	254	58	41	604	421	34	232	.288	.365	.382	747	101	-5	20	97	137	92	60	-2
TOT	617					329	283	6139		48309	12253	2197	551	397	4136	3254	311	1582	.290	.357	.397	754					747	592	56	-43

TEAM	CG	SHO	GR	SV	IP	H	HR	BB	SO	BR/9	ERA	AERA	OAV	OOB	PR	APR	PF	OSB	OCS	FA	E	WPB	DP	FW	PW	BW	BSW	DIF
WAS	74	13	128	25	1383.0	1329	34	505	469	12.2	3.34	121	.259	.330	136	112	95	62	55	.972	171	18	149	1.3	10.6	1.3	.1	1.6
NY	76	13	112	13	1359.1	1483	59	522	487	13.4	3.86	108	.284	.353	56	45	98	88	74	.974	156	55	131	2.0	4.2	2.5	-.2	4.4
DET	60	5	158	20	1394.2	1586	55	467	441	13.4	4.19	98	.293	.354	5	-12	97	101	77	.971	187	17	142	.4	-1.1	-.8	-.3	3.0
STL	66	11	176	7	1353.1	1511	68	517	386	13.8	4.57	98	.289	.358	-51	-9	107	100	82	.969	184	20	142	.3	-.8	-3.3	-.5	2.4
PHI	68	8	144	10	1345.0	1527	43	597	371	14.4	4.39	98	.292	.368	-24	-15	101	90	63	.971	180	31	157	.5	-1.4	-8.1	-.2	4.2
CLE	87	7	119	7	1349.0	1603	43	503	315	14.3	4.40	97	.300	.365	-25	-20	101	98	65	.967	205	43	130	-1.0	-1.9	.0	.4	-7.1
BOS	73	8	144	16	1391.1	1563	43	523	414	13.9	4.35	100	.290	.359	-19	2	103	100	82	.967	210	46	126	-1.0	.2	-3.8	.1	-5.5
CHI	76	1	118	11	1370.2	1635	52	512	360	14.3	4.74	87	.305	.368	-78	-98	97	108	94	.963	229	48	136	-2.4	-9.3	1.9	.3	-1.1
TOT	580	66	1099	109	10946.1					13.7	4.23		.290	.357						.969	1522	278	1113					

Batter-Fielder Wins		Batting Average		On-Base Percentage		Slugging Average		On-Base Plus Slugging		Adjusted OPS		Adjusted Batter Runs	
Ruth-NY	8.4	Ruth-NY	.378	Ruth-NY	.513	Ruth-NY	.739	Ruth-NY	1.252	Ruth-NY	.221	Ruth-NY	104.0
J.Sewell-Cle	4.5	Jamieson-Cle	.359	Collins-Chi	.441	Heilmann-Det	.533	Heilmann-Det	.961	Heilmann-Det	149	Heilmann-Det	43.5
Heilmann-Det	3.7	Falk-Chi	.352	Speaker-Cle	.432	Williams-StL	.533	Williams-StL	.958	Goslin-Was	145	Goslin-Was	39.2
Rigney-Det	3.5	Collins-Chi	.349	Heilmann-Det	.428	Jacobson-StL	.528	Speaker-Cle	.943	Speaker-Cle	141	Collins-Chi	34.9
Collins-Chi	3.0	Bassler-Det	.346	Sheely-Chi	.426	Myatt-Cle	.518	Goslin-Was	.937	Williams-StL	138	Speaker-Cle	32.2

Runs		Hits		Doubles		Triples		Home Runs		Total Bases		Runs Batted In	
Ruth-NY	143	Rice-Was	216	J.Sewell-Cle	45	Pipp-NY	19	Ruth-NY	46	Ruth-NY	391	Goslin-Was	129
Cobb-Det	115	Jamieson-Cle	213	Heilmann-Det	45	Goslin-Was	17	Hauser-Phi	27	Jacobson-StL	306	Ruth-NY	121
Collins-Chi	108	Cobb-Det	211	Wambsganss-Bos	41	Heilmann-Det	16	Jacobson-StL	19	Heilmann-Det	304	Meusel-NY	120
Hooper-Chi	107	Ruth-NY	200	Jacobson-StL	41	Rice-Was	14	Williams-StL	18	Goslin-Was	299	Hauser-Phi	115
Heilmann-Det	107	Goslin-Was	199	Meusel-NY	40	Jacobson-StL	12	Boone-Bos	13	Hauser-Phi	290		

Stolen Bases		Base Stealing Runs		Fielding Runs-Infield		Fielding Runs-Outfield		Wins		Winning Pct.		Complete Games	
Collins-Chi	42	Collins-Chi	3.3	J.Sewell-Cle	21.8	Hooper-Chi	10.4	Johnson-Was	23	Johnson-Was	.767	Thurston-Chi	28
Meusel-NY	26	Manush-Det	1.3	Lutzke-Cle	16.6	Jacobson-StL	9.9	Pennock-NY	21	Pennock-NY	.700	Ehmke-Bos	26
Rice-Was	24	Burns-Cle	1.3	Wambsganss-Bos	13.0	Falk-Chi	7.9	Thurston-Chi	20	Whitehill-Det	.654	Pennock-NY	25
Cobb-Det	23	Heilmann-Det	1.1	Peckinpaugh-Was	11.0	Mostil-Chi	6.6	Shaute-Cle	20	Zachary-Was	.625	Shaute-Cle	21
Jamieson-Cle	21			Scott-NY	10.3	Heilmann-Det	6.5	Ehmke-Bos	19			Rommel-Phi	21

Strikeouts		Fewest BB/Game		Games		Saves		Base Runners/9		Adjusted Relief Runs		Relief Ranking	
Johnson-Was	158	Smith-Cle	1.53	Marberry-Was	50	Marberry-Was	15	Johnson-Was	10.37	Speece-Was	4.0	Speece-Was	2.0
Ehmke-Bos	119	Thurston-Chi	1.86	Holloway-Det	49	Russell-Was	8	Collins-Det	11.08				
Shawkey-NY	114	Shocker-StL	1.90	Shaute-Cle	46	Quinn-Bos	7	Zachary-Was	11.28				
Pennock-NY	101	Pennock-NY	2.01	Hoyt-NY	46	Dauss-Det	6	Smith-Cle	11.48				
Shocker-StL	88	Quinn-Bos	2.05	Ehmke-Bos	45	Connally-Chi	6	Pennock-NY	11.54				

Innings Pitched		Opponents' Avg.		Opponents' OBP		Earned Run Average		Adjusted ERA		Adjusted Starter Runs		Pitcher Wins	
Ehmke-Bos	315.0	Johnson-Was	.224	Johnson-Was	.284	Johnson-Was	2.72	Baumgartner-Phi	149	Johnson-Was	43.8	Johnson-Was	4.9
Thurston-Chi	291.0	Collins-Det	.249	Collins-Det	.307	Zachary-Was	2.75	Johnson-Was	148	Pennock-NY	42.5	Pennock-NY	3.8
Pennock-NY	286.1	Marberry-Was	.262	Smith-Cle	.312	Pennock-NY	2.83	Pennock-NY	147	Ehmke-Bos	33.3	Zachary-Was	3.7
Shaute-Cle	283.0	Wingard-StL	.262	Pennock-NY	.314	Baumgartner-Phi	2.88	Zachary-Was	147	Smith-Cle	31.2	Ehmke-Bos	3.4
Rommel-Phi	278.0	Davis-StL	.263	Zachary-Was	.315	Smith-Cle	3.02	Smith-Cle	142	Zachary-Was	30.2	Bush-NY	3.2

First in War, First in Peace, First in Everything

Walter Johnson had pitched for a long time and never won a pennant. But in 1924, the Yankees were far from dominant, and the AL flag was ready for the picking. Washington, New York, and Detroit spent July and August twisted together. By September the Tigers had dropped out, and the Yankees chased the Senators to the end. Washington held on for its first flag thanks to the 36-year-old Johnson, the league's dominant hurler.

Playing in cavernous Griffith Stadium, the Senators lacked homers but hit plenty of triples, and Goose Goslin led the league in RBIs. Righty Firpo Marberry was credited (retroactively) with 15 saves and was the first reliever to lead the AL in appearances.

Homers declined to 397 as only nine players reached double figures. This was the final year in big-league history that either league hit fewer than 400. Fleet Walker, the first African American in the majors, died May 11, his legacy going unnoted

for decades. Three Hall of Famers reached the majors in 1924. Al Simmons debuted for Philadelphia; as he became a top slugger, the Athletics returned to contention. Red Ruffing, who would pitch until 1947, bowed for the Red Sox. Charlie Gehringer got into a few games in second base for Detroit.

The Senators and Giants produced a memorable World Series; each of the seven games was close, with four decided by one run. New York appeared to have Game 7 wrapped up until the Senators, down 3-1 in the bottom of the eighth, tied it when a grounder by player-manager Bucky Harris hopped over the head of Giants third baseman Freddie Lindstrom. With the game still knotted in the 12th, the Senators had Muddy Ruel on second and Johnson, on in relief since the ninth, on first. Rookie Earl McNeely's grounder bounced over Lindstrom's head. Washington had its first, and as it would happen, only world champion.

1923 National League

TEAM	W	L	T	PCT	GB	HW	HL	R	OR	PA	H	2B	3B	HR	BB	SO	HB	SH	AVG	OBP	SLG	OPS	AOPS	BR	ABR	PF	SB	CS	BSA	BSR
NY	95	58	0	.621		47	30	854	679	6083	1610	248	76	85	487	406	31	113	.295	.356	.415	771	110	73	84	99	106	70	60	-1
CIN	91	63	0	.591	4.5	46	32	708	629	5935	1506	237	95	45	439	367	33	185	.285	.344	.392	736	102	-2	13	98	96	105	48	-16
PIT	87	67	0	.565	8.5	47	30	786	696	5943	1592	224	111	49	407	362	28	103	.295	.347	.404	751	102	22	6	102	154	75	67	8
CHI	83	71	0	.539	12.5	46	31	756	704	5896	1516	243	52	90	455	485	31	151	.288	.348	.406	754	104	35	34	100	181	143	56	-10
STL	79	74	1	.516	16	42	35	746	732	6137	1582	274	76	63	438	446	38	135	.286	.343	.398	741	103	7	24	98	89	61	59	-2
BRO	76	78	1	.494	19.5	37	40	753	741	6082	1559	214	81	62	425	382	33	148	.285	.340	.387	727	100	-23	-2	97	71	50	59	-2
BOS	54	100	1	.351	41.5	22	55	636	798	5957	1455	213	58	32	429	404	31	168	.273	.331	.353	684	90	-100	-73	96	57	80	42	-15
PHI	50	104	1	.325	45.5	20	55	748	1008	6054	1528	259	39	112	414	556	39	110	.278	.333	.401	734	89	-12	-89	112	70	73	49	-10
TOT	617					307	308	5987		48087	12348	1912	588	538	3494	3408	264	1113	.286	.343	.395	737					824	657	56	-49

TEAM	CG	SHO	GR	SV	IP	H	HR	BB	SO	BR/9	ERA	AERA	OAV	OOB	PR	APR	PF	OSB	OCS	FA	E	WPB	DP	FW	PW	BW	BSW	DIF
NY	62	10	159	18	1378.0	1440	82	424	453	12.3	3.90	98	.271	.328	15	-14	96	63	69	.972	176	26	141	2.4	-1.3	8.1	.5	8.9
CIN	88	11	97	9	1391.1	1465	28	359	450	12.0	3.21	120	.273	.322	121	102	97	98	91	.969	202	31	144	.9	9.8	1.3	-1.0	3.0
PIT	92	5	99	9	1376.1	1513	53	402	414	12.7	3.87	103	.284	.337	19	19	100	78	70	.971	179	25	157	2.3	1.8	.6	1.4	4.0
CHI	80	8	107	11	1366.2	1539	86	435	408	12.4	3.82	105	.269	.329	27	25	100	80	69	.967	208	25	144	.5	2.4	3.3	-.4	.2
STL	77	9	126	7	1398.1	1539	70	456	398	13.1	3.87	101	.284	.344	20	5	98	111	71	.963	232	36	141	-.9	.5	2.3	.4	.2
BRO	94	8	92	5	1396.2	1503	55	476	548	13.0	3.74	103	.277	.340	39	21	97	131	103	.955	293	49	137	-4.4	2.0	-.2	.4	1.2
BOS	55	13	153	7	1392.2	1662	64	394	351	15.6	4.21	94	.302	.352	-34	-41	100	126	105	.964	230	32	157	-.7	-3.9	-7.0	-.9	-10.5
PHI	68	3	150	8	1376.1	1801	100	549	384	15.6	5.34	86	.322	.386	-205	-100	115	137	79	.966	217	60	172	.0	-9.6	-8.6	-.4	-8.5
TOT	616	67	983	74	11076.1					13.1	3.99		.286	.343						.966	1737	284	1193					

Batter-Fielder Wins		Batting Average		On-Base Percentage		Slugging Average		On-Base Plus Slugging		Adjusted OPS		Adjusted Batter Runs	
Fournier-Bro	4.2	Hornsby-StL	.384	Hornsby-StL	.459	Hornsby-StL	.627	Hornsby-StL	1086	Hornsby-StL	188	Hornsby-StL	55.7
O'Farrell-Chi	3.9	Wheat-Bro	.375	Bottomley-StL	.425	Fournier-Bro	.588	Fournier-Bro	.999	Fournier-Bro	165	Fournier-Bro	47.4
Hornsby-StL	3.8	Bottomley-StL	.371	Youngs-NY	.412	Williams-Phi	.576	Bottomley-StL	.960	Bottomley-StL	155	Bottomley-StL	42.1
Margrave-Chi	3.8	Fournier-Bro	.351	Fournier-Bro	.411	Barnhart-Pit	.563	Williams-Phi	.947	Roush-Cin	149	Roush-Cin	36.9
Traynor-Pit	3.6	Roush-Cin	.351	O'Farrell-Chi	.408	Bottomley-StL	.535	Roush-Cin	.938	Frisch-NY	133	Frisch-NY	30.0

Runs		Hits		Doubles		Triples		Home Runs		Total Bases		Runs Batted In	
Youngs-NY	121	Frisch-NY	223	Roush-Cin	41	Traynor-Pit	19	Williams-Phi	41	Frisch-NY	311	Meusel-NY	125
Carey-Pit	120	Statz-Chi	209	Tierney-Pit-Phi	36	Carey-Pit	19	Fournier-Bro	22	Williams-Phi	308	Williams-Phi	114
Frisch-NY	116	Traynor-Pit	208	Grantham-Chi	36	Roush-Cin	18	Miller-Chi	20	Fournier-Bro	303	Frisch-NY	111
Johnston-Bro	111	Johnston-Bro	203	Bottomley-StL	34	Southworth-Bos	16	Meusel-NY	19	Traynor-Pit	301	Kelly-NY	103
Statz-Chi	110	Youngs-NY	200					Hornsby-StL	17	Statz-Chi	288	Fournier-Bro	102

Stolen Bases		Base Stealing Runs		Fielding Runs-Infield		Fielding Runs-Outfield		Wins		Winning Pct.		Complete Games	
Carey-Pit	51	Carey-Pit	8.4	Tierney-Pit-Phi	15.1	Carey-Pit	12.1	Luque-Cin	27	Luque-Cin	.771	Grimes-Bro	33
Grantham-Chi	43	Smith-StL	3.2	Johnston-Bro	14.4	Statz-Chi	10.7	Morrison-Pit	25	Ryan-NY	.762	Luque-Cin	28
Smith-StL	32	Frisch-NY	2.2	Bancroft-NY	12.4	Bigbee-Pit	7.7	Alexander-Chi	22	Scott-NY	.696	Morrison-Pit	27
Heathcote-Chi	32	Rawlings-Pit	1.6	Smith-StL	11.6	Smith-StL	6.7	Grimes-Bro	21	Morrison-Pit	.658	Cooper-Pit	26
		Traynor-Pit	1.6	Maranville-Pit	10.9	Barnhart-Pit	5.9	Donohue-Cin	21	Alexander-Chi	.647	Alexander-Chi	26

Strikeouts		Fewest BB/Game		Games		Saves		Base Runners/9		Adjusted Relief Runs		Relief Ranking	
Alexander-Chi	197	Alexander-Chi	.89	Ryan-NY	45	Jonnard-NY	5	Alexander-Chi	9.97	Decatur-Bro	11.1	Decatur-Bro	6.9
Luque-Cin	151	B.Adams-Pit	1.42	Jonnard-NY	45	Ryan-NY	4	Luque-Cin	10.40	Jonnard-NY	3.6	Jonnard-NY	2.8
Grimes-Bro	119	Genewich-Bos	1.82	Oeschger-Bos	44			Cooney-Bos	10.74				
Morrison-Pit	114	Rixey-Cin	1.89	J.Barnes-NY-Bos	43			Ryan-NY	11.31				
Ring-Phi	112	Meadows-Phi-Pit	2.15	Genewich-Bos	43			Aldridge-Chi	11.49				

Innings Pitched		Opponents' Avg.		Opponents' OBP		Earned Run Average		Adjusted ERA		Adjusted Starter Runs		Pitcher Wins	
Grimes-Bro	327.0	Luque-Cin	.235	Alexander-Chi	.277	Luque-Cin	1.93	Luque-Cin	200	Luque-Cin	70.4	Luque-Cin	7.6
Luque-Cin	322.0	Vance-Bro	.250	Luque-Cin	.291	Rixey-Cin	2.80	Rixey-Cin	138	Rixey-Cin	36.7	Rixey-Cin	3.3
Rixey-Cin	309.0	Aldridge-Chi	.251	Aldridge-Chi	.307	Keen-Chi	3.00	Keen-Chi	133	Alexander-Chi	28.6	Alexander-Chi	3.1
Alexander-Chi	305.0	Morrison-Pit	.253	Ryan-NY	.308	Kaufmann-Chi	3.10	Kaufmann-Chi	129	Ring-Phi	25.0	Kaufmann-Chi	2.0
Ring-Phi	304.1	Osborne-Chi	.255	McQuillan-NY	.315	Haines-StL	3.11	Alexander-Chi	125	Keen-Chi	20.2	Cooper-Pit	1.8

Get Out of My Yard

Going wire-to-wire, the New York Giants won their third straight NL crown, beating back occasional challenges from the Reds and Pirates. The Giants again had the league's best offense and pitching in road games, and played well at home as well. They paced the NL in runs by a margin of 68.

As only the Polo Grounds—expanded to 54,000 capacity—made any alterations to its field dimensions, NL pitchers began to gain some control and runs per game decreased by 3 percent. The Cardinals, who fell 5 games in the standings despite the monster season of Rogers Hornsby, suffered a 37 percent attendance drop. Five NL clubs posted double-digit gains, and league turnstile clicks were up.

Cincinnati, on its last legs as a contender, fielded a team comprised mostly of players in their 30s. Pitcher Dolf Luque was the best in the league at 27-8. Two other Reds pitchers won 20 (Eppa Rixey and Pete Donahue), but their second-line pitching was very poor.

Veteran outfielder Burt Shotton, who twice led the AL in walks, played in his last game (for the Cardinals), but he would re-emerge some five years later as a manager with the moribund Phillies. Two future Hall of Famers joined the major league fraternity: Bill Terry and Hack Wilson.

New York featured productive performers at nearly every position, with two youngsters—24-year-old second baseman Frankie Frisch and 19-year-old shortstop Travis Jackson—providing special fire. Platoon outfielder Casey Stengel hit .339 and batted .417 with 2 homers in the World Series. The Yankees reveled in their new home, which opened in 1923 because the Giants asked them to vacate the Polo Grounds, and knocked off the Giants on their third try in the World Series.

1923 American League

TEAM	W	L	T	PCT	GB	HW	HL	R	OR	PA	H	2B	3B	HR	BB	SO	HB	SH	AVG	OBP	SLG	OPS	AOPS	BR	ABR	PF	SB	CS	BSA	BSR
NY	98	54	0	.645		46	30	823	622	6047	1554	231	79	105	521	516	34	145	.291	.357	.422	779	108	71	57	102	69	74	48	-11
DET	83	71	1	.539	16	45	32	831	741	6173	1579	270	69	41	596	385	55	256	.300	.377	.401	778	113	94	111	98	79	62	58	-3
CLE	82	71	0	.536	16.5	42	36	888	746	6171	1594	301	75	59	633	384	49	199	.301	.381	.420	801	117	141	143	100	102	68	60	-10
WAS	75	78	2	.490	23.5	43	34	720	747	6055	1436	224	93	26	532	448	47	232	.274	.346	.367	713	98	-49	-12	95	102	68	60	-1
STL	74	78	2	.487	24	40	36	688	720	5975	1489	248	62	82	442	423	26	209	.281	.339	.398	737	94	-17	-55	106	72	62	54	-5
PHI	69	83	1	.454	29	34	41	661	761	5853	1407	229	64	53	445	517	42	170	.271	.333	.370	703	89	-77	-85	101	72	62	54	-6
CHI	69	85	2	.448	30	30	45	692	741	6067	1463	254	57	42	532	458	40	249	.279	.350	.373	723	97	-25	-16	99	191	118	62	1
BOS	61	91	2	.401	37	37	40	584	809	5775	1354	253	54	34	391	480	42	161	.261	.318	.351	669	81	-144	-147	101	79	91	46	-14
TOT	616					317	294	5887		48116	11876	2010	553	442	4092	3611	335	1621	.262	.351	.388	739					743	608	55	-49

TEAM	CG	SHO	GR	SV	IP	H	HR	BB	SO	BR/9	ERA	AERA	OAV	OOB	PR	APR	PF	OSB	OCS	FA	E	WPB	DP	FW	PW	BW	BSW	DIF
NY	101	9	68	10	1380.2	1365	68	491	506	12.3	3.62	109	.263	.330	55	49	99	79	58	.977	144	53	131	3.3	4.7	5.5	-.5	8.9
DET	61	9	163	12	1373.2	1502	58	449	447	13.1	4.09	94	.283	.345	-16	-35	97	84	102	.968	200	30	103	.0	-3.4	10.7	.3	-1.7
CLE	77	10	143	11	1376.0	1517	36	465	407	13.2	3.91	101	.285	.346	11	4	100	79	43	.966	216	31	182	-.9	-3.1	-1.2	.5	3.2
WAS	71	8	130	16	1374.1	1527	56	563	474	14.0	3.98	95	.291	.364	0	-32	95	91	95	.966	177	23	145	1.4	3.4	-5.3	.1	-1.6
STL	83	10	126	10	1373.1	1430	59	528	488	13.2	3.93	106	.275	.348	9	35	105	99	79	.971	221	42	127	-1.4	.0	-8.2	.0	2.5
PHI	65	7	131	12	1364.2	1465	68	550	400	13.5	4.08	101	.280	.352	-15	1	103	91	75	.965	221	33	127	1.1	-1.3	-1.5	.7	-7.0
CHI	74	5	126	11	1397.0	1512	49	534	467	13.4	4.05	98	.283	.353	-10	-13	99	105	90	.971	184	33	138	1.1	-1.3	-1.5	.7	-7.0
BOS	77	3	115	11	1372.0	1534	48	520	412	13.9	4.20	98	.294	.366	-33	-15	103	115	89	.963	232	41	126	-2.0	-1.5	-14.2	-.8	3.4
TOT	609	61	1002	93	11011.2					13.3	3.98		.282	.351						.968	1600	281	1095					

Batter-Fielder Wins		Batting Average		On-Base Percentage		Slugging Average		On-Base Plus Slugging		Adjusted OPS		Adjusted Batter Runs	
Ruth-NY	10.1	Heilmann-Det	.403	Ruth-NY	.545	Ruth-NY	.764	Ruth-NY	1309	Ruth-NY	238	Ruth-NY	119.2
Speaker-Cle	6.5	Ruth-NY	.393	Heilmann-Det	.481	Heilmann-Det	.632	Heilmann-Det	1113	Heilmann-Det	195	Heilmann-Det	75.5
J.Sewell-Cle	6.2	Speaker-Cle	.380	Speaker-Cle	.469	Williams-StL	.623	Speaker-Cle	1079	Speaker-Cle	183	Speaker-Cle	74.1
Heilmann-Det	6.0	Collins-Chi	.360	J.Sewell-Cle	.456	Speaker-Cle	.610	Williams-StL	1062	Williams-StL	168	Williams-StL	54.7
Williams-StL	4.7	Williams-StL	.357	Collins-Chi	.455	Harris-Bos	.520	J.Sewell-Cle	935	J.Sewell-Cle	147	J.Sewell-Cle	44.9

Runs		Hits		Doubles		Triples		Home Runs		Total Bases		Runs Batted In	
Ruth-NY	151	Jamieson-Cle	222	Speaker-Cle	59	Rice-Was	18	Ruth-NY	41	Ruth-NY	399	Ruth-NY	131
Speaker-Cle	133	Speaker-Cle	218	Burns-Bos	47	Goslin-Was	18	Williams-StL	29	Speaker-Cle	350	Speaker-Cle	130
Jamieson-Cle	130	Heilmann-Det	211	Ruth-NY	45	Tobin-StL	15	Heilmann-Det	18	Williams-StL	346	Heilmann-Det	115
Heilmann-Det	121	Ruth-NY	205	Heilmann-Det	44	Mostil-Chi	15	Speaker-Cle	17	Heilmann-Det	331	J.Sewell-Cle	109
Rice-Was	117	Tobin-StL	202	J.Sewell-Cle	41			Hauser-Phi	17	Tobin-StL	303	Pipp-NY	108

Stolen Bases		Base Stealing Runs		Fielding Runs-Infield		Fielding Runs-Outfield		Wins		Winning Pct.		Complete Games	
Collins-Chi	48	Mostil-Chi	3.4	Peckinpaugh-Was	21.8	Mostil-Chi	16.0	Uhle-Cle	26	Pennock-NY	.760	Uhle-Cle	29
Mostil-Chi	41	Rice-Was	1.6	Harris-Was	18.6	Flagstead-Det-Bos	14.4	Jones-NY	21	Jones-NY	.724	Ehmke-Bos	28
Harris-Was	23	Barrett-Chi	1.6	Lutzke-Cle	16.0	Williams-StL	8.1	Dauss-Det	21	Hoyt-NY	.654	Shocker-StL	24
Rice-Was	20	Veach-Det	1.1	Ward-Was	9.5	Rice-Was	6.7	Shocker-StL	20	Shocker-StL	.625	Dauss-Det	22
				Judge-Was	8.3	Ruth-NY	6.4	Ehmke-Bos	20	Uhle-Cle	.619	Bush-NY	22

Strikeouts		Fewest BB/Game		Games		Saves		Base Runners/9		Adjusted Relief Runs		Relief Ranking	
Johnson-Was	130	Shocker-StL	1.59	Rommel-Phi	56	Russell-Was	9	Shocker-StL	11.16				
Shawkey-NY	125	Coveleski-Cle	1.66	Uhle-Cle	54	Quinn-Bos	7	Hoyt-NY	11.20				
Bush-NY	125	Thurston-StL-Chi	1.75	Russell-Was	52	Harriss-Phi	6	Pennock-NY	11.52				
Ehmke-Bos	121	Quinn-Bos	1.96	Cole-Det	52			Jones-NY	11.63				
		Dauss-Det	2.22	Dauss-Det	50			Coveleski-Cle	11.64				

Innings Pitched		Opponents' Avg.		Opponents' OBP		Earned Run Average		Adjusted ERA		Adjusted Starter Runs		Pitcher Wins	
Uhle-Cle	357.2	Shawkey-NY	.246	Shocker-StL	.306	Coveleski-Cle	2.76	Coveleski-Cle	143	Vangilder-StL	27.8	Uhle-Cle	3.4
Ehmke-Bos	316.2	Hoyt-NY	.253	Hoyt-NY	.307	Hoyt-NY	3.02	Vangilder-StL	136	Coveleski-Cle	26.2	Rommel-Phi	3.2
Dauss-Det	316.0	Jones-NY	.257	Faber-Chi	.311	Russell-Was	3.03	Hoyt-NY	131	Pennock-NY	24.6	Vangilder-StL	2.8
Rommel-Phi	297.2	Faber-Chi	.259	Jones-NY	.312	Vangilder-StL	3.06	Thurston-StL-Chi	127	Shocker-StL	24.1	Bush-NY	2.6
Vangilder-StL	282.1	Bush-NY	.260	Pennock-NY	.314	Mogridge-Was	3.11	Rommel-Phi	126	Rommel-Phi	23.7	Shocker-StL	2.6

The Year the Yankees Were Born

Kicked out of the Polo Grounds by the Giants the year before, the New York Yankees built their own park, Yankee Stadium, which quickly became a palace of American sport.

The Bronx Bombers put on a show for the million-plus fans that filled the park, running away with the pennant. Babe Ruth had another spectacular season, leading the loop in runs, homers, and RBIs—all while drawing 170 walks to set an AL record that still stands.

While the Yankees didn't score as many runs as the Tigers or Indians, they had much better pitching; New York's deep, if unspectacular, staff was the only one in the league with more strikeouts than walks, and easily led in complete games. New York used rookie Lou Gehrig in a few games, and Earle Combs came up the next year. Both were clearly part of the Yankees' future. The 1923 season also saw the debut of the first great relief pitcher in the game's history, Washington's Firpo Marberry. Ted

Lyons of Chicago began a playing career that would last—with three years as a Marine thrown in—until 1946.

The Tigers had a fine outfield. Harry Heilmann batted .403, and rookie Heinie Manush and 36-year-old Ty Cobb kicked in high averages, though Cobb continued to suffer from knee problems. For Cleveland, 35-year-old Tris Speaker set a new big-league record with 53 doubles and Charlie Jamieson notched 222 hits.

The Giants were again the Yankees' World Series opponents, and the NL won Game 1 on Casey Stengel's ninth-inning inside-the-park homer. But the story would end differently. The Yanks rebounded to win three times at their former home park. Trailing 4-1 at the Polo Grounds in Game 6, the Yankees put together a 5-run eighth to win the title. With another pennant, their first Series crown, a ballpark of their own, and the parts of a dynasty firmly coming into place, 1923 was the year the Yankees became the Yankees.

1922 National League

TEAM	W	L	T	PCT	GB	HW	HL	R	OR	PA	H	2B	3B	HR	BB	SO	HB	SH	AVG	OBP	SLG	OPS	AOPS	BR	ABR	PF	SB	CS	BSA	BSR
NY	93	61	2	.604		51	27	852	658	6109	1661	253	90	80	448	421	48	159	.305	.363	.428	791	109	79	72	101	116	83	58	-4
CIN	86	68	2	.558	7	48	29	766	677	5943	1561	226	99	45	436	381	36	189	.296	.353	.401	754	102	6	21	98	130	136	49	-19
STL	85	69	0	.552	8	42	35	863	819	6061	1634	280	88	107	447	425	28	161	.301	.357	.444	801	118	94	-137	95	73	63	54	-6
PIT	85	69	1	.552	8	45	33	865	736	6151	1698	239	110	52	423	326	32	175	.308	.360	.419	779	106	54	44	101	145	59	71	11
CHI	80	74	2	.519	13	39	37	771	808	6092	1564	248	71	42	525	447	27	205	.293	.359	.390	749	97	10	-5	102	97	108	47	-4
BRO	76	78	1	.494	17	44	34	743	754	5955	1569	235	76	56	339	318	25	178	.290	.335	.392	727	94	-60	-54	99	79	60	57	-4
PHI	57	96	1	.373	35.5	35	41	738	920	6088	1537	268	55	116	450	611	39	140	.282	.341	.415	756	92	1	-67	110	48	60	44	-10
BOS	53	100	1	.346	39.5	32	43	596	822	5750	1355	162	73	32	387	451	28	174	.263	.317	.341	658	78	-184	-158	96	67	65	51	-8
TOT	620					336	279	6194		48149	12579	1911	662	530	3455	3380	263	1381	.292	.348	.404	753				755	634	54	-56

TEAM	CG	SHO	GR	SV	IP	H	HR	BB	SO	BR/9	ERA	AERA	OAV	OOB	PR	APR	PF	OSB	OCS	FA	E	WPB	DP	FW	PW	BW	BSW	DIF
NY	76	7	135	15	1396.1	1454	71	393	388	12.0	3.45	116	.272	.324	100	85	98	70	58	.970	194	40	145	1.1	8.0	6.8	.3	-.2
CIN	88	8	93	3	1385.2	1481	49	326	357	11.9	3.53	113	.278	.322	87	71	97	77	69	.968	205	18	147	.4	6.7	2.0	-1.1	1.1
STL	60	8	172	12	1362.2	1609	61	447	465	13.9	4.44	87	.299	.358	-52	-93	94	90	83	.961	239	34	122	-2.0	-8.8	12.9	.0	5.8
PIT	88	15	114	7	1387.1	1613	52	358	490	13.0	3.98	102	.296	.343	18	14	99	92	64	.970	187	31	126	1.5	1.3	4.2	1.7	-.7
CHI	74	8	138	12	1397.2	1579	77	475	402	13.6	4.34	97	.292	.356	-38	-23	102	79	104	.968	204	35	154	.5	-2.2	-.5	-.9	6.0
BRO	82	12	115	8	1385.2	1574	74	490	499	13.6	4.05	100	.293	.356	6	2	99	128	82	.967	208	42	119	.1	.2	-5.1	.3	3.5
PHI	73	6	118	5	1372.0	1692	89	460	394	14.4	4.64	101	.307	.365	-82	6	114	123	76	.965	225	52	152	-1.1	.6	-6.3	-.3	-12.4
BOS	63	7	146	6	1348.0	1565	57	489	360	13.9	4.37	91	.298	.361	-41	-59	98	96	98	.965	215	34	121	-.4	-.6	-5.6	-14.9	-.0
TOT	604	71	1031	68	11035.1					13.3	4.10		.292	.348						.967	1677	286	1106					-2.5

Batter-Fielder Wins
Hornsby-StL 8.9
Bancroft-NY 4.9
O'Farrell-Chi 4.4
Carey-Pit 3.5
Grimes-Chi 3.2

Batting Average
Hornsby-StL 401
Grimes-Chi 354
Miller-Chi 352
Bigbee-Pit 350
Tierney-Pit 345

On-Base Percentage
Hornsby-StL 459
Grimes-Chi 442
O'Farrell-Chi 439
Carey-Pit 408
Bigbee-Pit 405

Slugging Average
Hornsby-StL 722
Grimes-Chi 572
Lee-Phi 540
Tierney-Pit 515
Williams-Phi 514

On-Base Plus Slugging
Hornsby-StL 1181
Grimes-Chi 1014
Williams-Phi 905
Miller-Chi 899
Walker-Phi 899

Adjusted OPS
Hornsby-StL 210
Grimes-Chi 157
Daubert-Cin 130
Wheat-Bro 129
Miller-Chi 128

Adjusted Batter Runs
Hornsby-StL 100.4
Grimes-Chi 46.8
Daubert-Cin 25.3
Wheat-Bro 25.2
Russell-Pit 23.4

Runs
Hornsby-StL 141
Carey-Pit 140
Smith-StL 117
Bancroft-NY 117
Maranville-Pit 115

Hits
Hornsby-StL 250
Bigbee-Pit 215
Bancroft-NY 209
Carey-Pit 207
Daubert-Cin 205

Doubles
Hornsby-StL 46
Grimes-Chi 45
Duncan-Cin 44
Bancroft-NY 41
Hollocher-Chi 37

Triples
Daubert-Cin 22
Meusel-NY 17
Maranville-Pit 15
Bigbee-Pit 15

Home Runs
Hornsby-StL 42
Williams-Phi 26
Lee-Phi 17
Kelly-NY 17

Total Bases
Hornsby-StL 450
Meusel-NY 314
Wheat-Bro 302
Williams-Phi 300
Daubert-Cin 300

Runs Batted In
Hornsby-StL 152
Meusel-NY 132
Wheat-Bro 112
Kelly-NY 107

Stolen Bases
Carey-Pit 51
Frisch-NY 31
Burns-Cin 30
Maranville-Pit 24
Bigbee-Pit 24

Base Stealing Runs
Carey-Pit 10.5
Traynor-Pit 2.7
Smith-StL 1.6
Bohne-Cin 1.5
T.Griffith-Bro 1.2

Fielding Runs-Infield
Parkinson-Phi 27.9
Bancroft-NY 22.1
Pinelli-Cin 21.9
Bohne-Cin 12.5
Kelly-NY 9.3

Fielding Runs-Outfield
Bigbee-Pit 13.7
Carey-Pit 9.9
Powell-Bos 6.0
Walker-Phi 4.5
Youngs-NY 2.6

Wins
Rixey-Cin 25
Cooper-Pit 23
Ruether-Bro 21
Pfeffer-StL 19
Nehf-NY 19

Winning Pct.
Donohue-Pit 667
Rixey-Cin 658
Couch-Cin 640
Ruether-Bro 636
Cooper-Pit 622

Complete Games
Cooper-Pit 27
Ruether-Bro 26
Rixey-Cin 26

Strikeouts
Vance-Bro 134
Cooper-Pit 129
Ring-Phi 116
Morrison-Pit 104
Grimes-Bro 99

Fewest BB/Game
Adams-Pit 79
Alexander-Chi 1.25
Rixey-Cin 1.29
Donohue-Cin 1.60
J.Barnes-NY 1.61

Games
North-StL 53
Sherdel-StL 47
Ryan-NY 46
Oeschger-Bos 46
Morrison-Pit 45

Saves
Jonnard-NY 5
North-StL 4

Base Runners/9
McNamara-Bos ..10.44
Douglas-NY 11.02
Adams-Pit 11.03
Rixey-Cin 11.09
Donohue-Cin 11.34

Adjusted Relief Runs
McNamara-Bos 11.8
Causey-NY 5.2
Jonnard-NY 3.9
Mamaux-Bro 2.6
Braxton-Bos 2.4

Relief Ranking
McNamara-Bos 10.5
Causey-NY 4.8
Jonnard-NY 3.0
Mamaux-Bro 1.5
Braxton-Bos 1.2

Innings Pitched
Rixey-Cin 313.1
Cooper-Pit 294.2
Morrison-Pit 286.1
Nehf-NY 268.1
Ruether-Bro 267.1

Opponents' Avg.
Douglas-NY 257
Luque-Cin 268
Ryan-NY 269
Osborne-Chi 271
Rixey-Cin 275

Opponents' OBP
Douglas-NY 302
Rixey-Cin 303
Adams-Pit 307
J.Barnes-NY 311
Donohue-Cin 312

Earned Run Average
Douglas-NY 2.63
Ryan-NY 3.01
Donohue-Cin 3.12
Cooper-Pit 3.18
Nehf-NY 3.29

Adjusted ERA
Douglas-NY 152
Weinert-Phi 137
Ryan-NY 133
Cooper-Pit 128
Donohue-Cin 128

Adjusted Starter Runs
Cooper-Pit 27.3
Douglas-NY 24.9
Donohue-Cin 21.6
Nehf-NY 21.1
Morrison-Pit 21.0

Pitcher Wins
Cooper-Pit 3.9
Meadows-Phi 2.6
Nehf-NY 2.5
Ruether-Bro 2.5
Ryan-NY 2.5

Polo Grounds Potency

Team runs per game rose to 5.00, more than an entire run higher than 1920 and the century's top total to date. The league pounded 530 homers, another all-time high; four-baggers had more than doubled in two years. Meanwhile, the stolen base was at its lowest ebb yet at .61 per game. More runs meant fewer pitchers racking up big totals; just three pitchers won 20, compared to seven in 1920.

John McGraw's Giants, first or second every year since 1917, took their second straight NL flag. Only for a few days did the Giants trail, and they won easily over second-place Cincinnati, which featured 25-game winner Eppa Rixey. Three Giants hurlers graced the top five in ERA, and the club featured seven .300-hitting regulars.

Rogers Hornsby enjoyed arguably his greatest season in 1922, batting .401 and taking the Triple Crown. However, his Cardinals, otherwise weak offensively, tied for third with Pittsburgh.

The Pirates topped the league in runs, bucking the trend by leading the loop in average and steals.

Three eventual Hall of Famers debuted. Cubs catcher Gabby Hartnett played the first of his 1,990 career games. Cardinals first baseman Jim Bottomley hit .325 after an August promotion. Finally, shortstop Travis Jackson began his fifteen-year career with a cameo appearance for the Giants. Two significant deaths bridged the old and the new. The great Cap Anson passed away at 70 on April 14. Meanwhile, 27-year-old Cardinals outfielder Austin McHenry, suffering from a brain tumor, died November 27.

The Giants again met—and vanquished—the Yankees at the Polo Grounds, making it 13 straight World Series games played at the same two-team venue. The Giants won in five (including one tie), allowing just 11 runs and batting .309. Nobody sensed that this would be the Giants' last world title for more than a decade.

1922 American League

TEAM	W	L	T	PCT	GB	HW	HL	R	OR	PA	H	2B	3B	HR	BB	SO	HB	SH	AVG	OBP	SLG	OPS	AOPS	BR	ABR	PF	SB	CS	BSA	BSR
NY	94	60	0	.610		50	27	758	618	6000	1504	220	75	95	497	532	40	218	.287	.353	.412	765	103	34	17	102	62	59	51	-7
STL	93	61	0	.604	1	54	23	867	643	6128	1693	291	94	98	473	381	36	203	.313	.372	.455	827	117	159	128	104	136	64		3
DET	79	75	1	.513	15	43	34	828	791	6170	1641	250	54	54	530	378	36	244	.306	.372	.415	787	115	94	122	97	78	62	56	0
CLE	78	76	1	.506	16	44	35	768	817	6095	1544	320	73	32	554	331	45	203	.292	.364	.398	762	104	49	43	101	90	58	61	0
CHI	77	77	1	.500	17	43	34	691	691	6023	1463	243	62	45	482	463	43	231	.278	.343	.373	716	92	-52	-49	100	109	84	56	-5
WAS	69	85	0	.448	25	40	39	650	706	5868	1395	229	76	45	458	442	57	152	.268	.334	.367	701	93	-86	-53	95	97	63	61	-1
PHI	65	89	1	.422	29	38	39	705	830	5854	1409	229	63	111	437	591	36	170	.263	.331	.402	733	94	-38	-55	103	60	69	47	-11
BOS	61	93	0	.396	33	31	42	598	769	5859	1392	250	55	45	366	455	44	161	.263	.316	.357	673	82	-151	-146	99	64	67	49	-9
TOT	618					343	273	5865		47997	12041	2032	585	525	3797	3573	337	1582	.285	.348	.398	746					696	538	56	-35

TEAM	CG	SHO	GR	SV	IP	H	HR	BB	SO	BR/9	ERA	AERA	OAV	OOB	PR	APR	PF	OSB	OCS	FA	E	WPB	DP	FW	PW	BW	BSW	DIF
NY	100	7	69	14	1393.2	1402	73	423	458	11.9	3.39	118	.268	.325	99	92	99	67	72	.975	157	37	124	2.0	8.9	1.7	-.3	4.6
STL	79	8	115	22	1392.0	1412	71	419	534	12.1	3.38	122	.268	.327	101	112	103	66	77	.968	201	24	158	-.5	10.9	12.4	.7	-7.5
DET	67	7	133	15	1391.0	1554	62	473	461	13.7	4.27	91	.288	.354	-37	-67	96	112	60	.970	191	29	133	.2	-6.5	11.8	-.0	-3.4
CLE	76	14	135	7	1383.2	1605	58	464	489	13.7	4.59	87	.296	.356	-85	-93	99	106	48	.968	202	48	147	-.5	-9.0	4.2	.4	5.9
CHI	86	13	99	8	1403.2	1472	57	529	484	13.0	3.94	103	.278	.346	15	15	101	75	76	.969	196	42	168	-.2	.6	-5.1	.3	-3.6
WAS	84	13	97	10	1362.1	1485	49	500	422	13.4	3.81	101	.286	.354	33	6	96	85	74	.969	155	19	143	2.2	1.5	-4.9	-.0	1.1
PHI	73	4	147	6	1362.1	1573	107	469	373	13.7	4.59	92	.297	.357	-85	-52	105	83	75	.966	215	38	118	-1.2	-5.0	-5.3	-.6	.2
BOS	71	10	130	6	1373.1	1508	48	503	359	13.5	4.30	95	.287	.354	-41	-31	102	102	56	.965	224	38	145	-1.8	-3.0	-14.2	-.4	3.4
TOT	636	76	925	88	11062.0					13.1	4.03		.285	.348						.969	1541	275	1136					

Batter-Fielder Wins
Sisler-StL 6.3
Speaker-Cle 5.1
Cobb-Det 4.2
Williams-StL 4.1
Ruth-NY 3.5

Batting Average
Sisler-StL .420
Cobb-Det .401
Speaker-Cle .378
Heilmann-Det .356
Miller-Phi .335

On-Base Percentage
Speaker-Cle .474
Sisler-StL .467
Cobb-Det .462
Ruth-NY .434
Heilmann-Det .432

Slugging Average
Ruth-NY .672
Williams-StL .627
Speaker-Cle .606
Heilmann-Det .598
Sisler-StL .594

On-Base Plus Slugging
Ruth-NY 1106
Speaker-Cle 1080
Sisler-StL 1061
Williams-StL 1040
Heilmann-Det 1030

Adjusted OPS
Ruth-NY 181
Speaker-Cle 178
Cobb-Det 172
Heilmann-Det 172
Sisler-StL 169

Adjusted Batter Runs
Sisler-StL 60.0
Cobb-Det 57.7
Speaker-Cle 54.6
Williams-StL 52.1
Ruth-NY 49.2

Runs
Sisler-StL 134
Blue-Det 131
Williams-StL 128
Tobin-StL 122

Hits
Sisler-StL 246
Cobb-Det 211
Tobin-StL 207
Veach-Det 202

Doubles
Speaker-Cle 48
Pratt-Bos 44
Sisler-StL 42
Cobb-Det 42

Triples
Sisler-StL 18
Jacobson-StL 16
Cobb-Det 16
Judge-Was 15
Mostil-Chi 14

Home Runs
Williams-StL 39
Walker-Phi 37
Ruth-NY 35
Miller-Phi 21
Heilmann-Det 21

Total Bases
Williams-StL 367
Sisler-StL 348
Walker-Phi 310
Cobb-Det 297
Tobin-StL 296

Runs Batted In
Williams-StL 155
Veach-Det 126
McManus-StL 109
Sisler-StL 105
Jacobson-StL 102

Stolen Bases
Sisler-StL 51
Williams-StL 37
Harris-Was 25
Johnson-Chi 21

Base Stealing Runs
Sisler-StL 4.6
Jacobson-StL 2.1
Evans-Cle 1.7
Harris-Was 1.7
Veach-Det 1.6

Fielding Runs-Infield
Harris-Was 31.2
Peckinpaugh-Was 18.3
Scott-NY 16.6
Sisler-StL 11.7
Jones-Det 10.1

Fielding Runs-Outfield
Veach-Det 9.7
Menosky-Bos 5.6
Miller-Phi 5.2
Hooper-Chi 4.8
Harris-Bos 4.0

Wins
Rommel-Phi 27
Bush-NY 26
Shocker-StL 24
Uhle-Cle 22
Faber-Chi 21

Winning Pct.
Bush-NY .788
Rommel-Phi .675
Shawkey-NY .625
Pillette-Det .613
Hoyt-NY .613

Complete Games
Faber-Chi 31
Shocker-StL 29
Uhle-Cle 23
Johnson-Was 23

Strikeouts
Shocker-StL 149
Faber-Chi 148
Shawkey-NY 130
Ehmke-Det 108
Johnson-Was 105

Fewest BB/Game
Shocker-StL 1.47
Vangilder-StL 1.76
Mays-NY 1.88
Kolp-StL 1.91
Hasty-Phi 1.92

Games
Rommel-Phi 51
Uhle-Cle 50
Shocker-StL 48
Harriss-Phi 47

Saves
Jones-NY 8
Pruett-StL 7
Wright-StL 5

Base Runners/9
Faber-Chi 10.82
Shocker-StL 11.02
Rommel-Phi 11.08
Vangilder-StL 11.09
Quinn-Bos 11.43

Adjusted Relief Runs
Murray-NY 1.2

Relief Ranking
Murray-NY 1.0

Innings Pitched
Faber-Chi 352.0
Shocker-StL 348.0
Shawkey-NY 299.2
Rommel-Phi 294.0
Uhle-Cle 287.1

Opponents' Avg.
Davis-NY .250
Bush-NY .252
Faber-Chi .252
Shawkey-NY .256
Pillette-Det .258

Opponents' OBP
Faber-Chi .299
Shocker-StL .304
Rommel-Phi .309
Vangilder-StL .310
Quinn-Bos .311

Earned Run Average
Faber-Chi 2.81
Pillette-Det 2.85
Shawkey-NY 2.91
Wright-StL 2.92
Shocker-StL 2.97

Adjusted ERA
Faber-Chi 144
Wright-StL 141
Shocker-StL 139
Shawkey-NY 137
Pillette-Det 136

Adjusted Starter Runs
Faber-Chi 46.6
Shocker-StL 43.8
Shawkey-NY 37.3
Pillette-Det 29.9
Rommel-Phi 29.9

Pitcher Wins
Shocker-StL 4.9
Faber-Chi 4.6
Vangilder-StL 3.8
Rommel-Phi 3.6
Shawkey-NY 3.3

Browns Come Close

Apparently deciding that if they couldn't beat 'em, they'd join 'em, the Athletics brought in the left-field fences at Shibe Park. As a result, Philadelphia hit the league' most homers in home games. Unfortunately, they also *allowed* the most, and finished seventh. These were hard years to be a Philadelphia baseball fan. The A's and Phillies both finished last in 1919, 1920, and 1921, and were seventh in 1922. Soon, Connie Mack's club would climb back to the top.

AL hitters pounded 525 homers, more than double the total of three years before. But this wasn't sloppy baseball; hitters still made contact (since 1918, no AL pitcher had notched 150 strike-outs). In addition, for the first time, the league's fielding percentage reached .970; it never again fell below .968. And as the 1910s faded into memory, so did two of the decade's standouts. Home Run Baker ended his career with the Yankees, and converted outfielder Smokey Joe Wood hit .297 in his final season for Cleveland.

The Yankees won the flag again. But one misconception about the Yankees teams of the 1920s is that they bludgeoned the opposition. It just isn't so; only twice in the '20s did they romp to the flag. In fact, in 1922, they almost lost—to the Browns. St. Louis was fueled by George Sisler, who set an AL record by hitting in 41 games. He also led the league in hits, runs, triples, while pounding out a .420 average (only surpassed in the AL by Nap Lajoie's .426 in 1901). The Browns scored 100 more runs than New York, had a better ERA, and stole more bases, but the Yankees moved ahead in August and eventually held on by 1 game.

The Yankees struggled without Babe Ruth and Bob Meusel, suspended a month for barnstorming. When the two returned, they carried the club's attack. They did little in October, though. The Yankees lost in five (four losses and one tie) to the pitching-rich Giants, who had served as their landlord at the Polo Grounds for a decade.

1921 National League

TEAM	W	L	T	PCT	GB	HW	HL	R	OR	PA	H	2B	3B	HR	BB	SO	HB	SH	AVG	OBP	SLG	OPS	AOPS	BR	ABR	PF	SB	CS	BSA	BSR
NY	94	59	0	.614		53	26	840	637	5946	1575	237	93	75	469	390	33	166	.298	**.359**	.421	780	112	97	95	100	**137**	114	55	-10
PIT	90	63	1	.588	4	45	31	692	**595**	5946	1533	231	**104**	37	341	371	23	203	.285	.330	.387	717	93	-40	-57	103	134	93	**59**	**-3**
STL	87	66	1	.569	7	48	29	809	681	5915	**1635**	**260**	88	83	382	452	29	195	**.308**	.358	**.437**	795	118	116	134	98	94	50		-12
BOS	79	74	0	.516	15	42	32	721	697	5982	1561	209	100	61	377	470	21	198	.290	.339	.400	739	107	3	45	95	94	100	48	-14
BRO	77	75	0	.507	16.5	41	37	667	681	5773	1476	209	85	59	325	400	21	164	.280	.325	.386	711	90	-54	-76	104	91	73	55	-6
CIN	70	83	0	.458	24	40	36	618	649	5727	1421	221	94	20	375	**308**	**45**	195	.278	.333	.370	703	96	-56	-26	95	117	120	49	-16
CHI	64	89	0	.418	30	32	44	668	773	5907	1553	234	56	37	343	374	35	**208**	.292	.339	.378	717	95	-29	-30	100	70	97	42	-19
PHI	51	103	0	.331	43.5	29	47	617	919	5760	1512	238	50	**88**	294	615	25	112	.284	.324	.397	721	89	-36	-84	108	66	80	45	-13
TOT	613					330	282	5632		46956	12266	1839	670	460	2906	3380	233	1441	.289	.338	.397	736					803	771	51	-93

TEAM	CG	SHO	GR	SV	IP	H	HR	BB	SO	BR/9	ERA	AERA	OAV	OOB	PR	APR	PF	OSB	OCS	FA	E	WPB	DP	FW	PW	BW	BSW	DIF
NY	71	9	127	**18**	1372.1	1497	79	**295**	357	11.9	3.55	103	.286	.326	34	17	97	80	94	.971	187	29	**155**	1.3	1.7	9.4	.2	5.0
PIT	**88**	10	91	10	1415.2	**1448**	37	322	**500**	11.5	3.17	**121**	.271	.316	96	103	101	73	87	.973	172	27	129	2.3	**10.2**	-5.6	.9	5.8
STL	70	10	**155**	16	1371.2	1486	61	399	464	12.6	3.62	101	.282	.337	24	5	97	104	94	.965	219	52	130	-.6	.5	**13.2**	-.0	-2.6
BOS	74	**11**	124	12	1385.0	1488	54	420	382	12.6	3.90	94	.280	.337	-18	-40	97	90	119	.969	199	**16**	122	.5	-3.9	4.4	-.2	1.7
BRO	82	8	106	12	1363.1	1556	46	361	471	12.9	3.70	105	.293	.342	13	27	103	117	94	.964	232	37	142	-1.5	2.7	-7.5	.6	6.8
CIN	83	7	95	9	1363.0	1500	**37**	305	408	12.0	3.46	103	.287	.328	48	17	95	87	78	.969	193	32	139	.9	1.7	-2.6	-.4	-6.1
CHI	73	7	120	7	1363.0	1605	67	409	441	13.6	4.39	87	.303	.357	-93	-87	101	107	103	**.974**	166	24	129	2.5	-8.6	-3.0	-.7	-2.8
PHI	82	5	107	8	1348.2	1665	79	371	333	13.8	4.48	94	.308	.356	-105	-35	112	145	102	.955	295	55	127	-5.2	-3.5	-8.3	-.1	-8.9
TOT	623	67	925	92	10982.2					12.6	3.78		.289	.338						.967	1663	272	1073					

Batter-Fielder Wins
Hornsby-StL 7.7
Bancroft-NY 5.3
Frisch-NY 4.5
Johnston-Bro
McHenry-StL 2.5

Batting Average
Hornsby-StL 397
Roush-Cin 352
McHenry-StL 350
Cruise-Bos 346
Fournier-StL 343

On-Base Percentage
Hornsby-StL 458
Youngs-NY 411
Fournier-StL 409
Grimes-Chi 406
Carey-Pit 395

Slugging Average
Hornsby-StL 639
McHenry-StL 531
Kelly-NY 528
Meusel-Phi-NY 515
Mann-StL 512

On-Base Plus Slugging
Hornsby-StL 1097
McHenry-StL 924
Fournier-StL 914
Meusel-Phi-NY 895
Kelly-NY 884

Adjusted OPS
Hornsby-StL 191
McHenry-StL 145
Fournier-StL 144
Kelly-NY 131
Youngs-NY 129

Adjusted Batter Runs
Hornsby-StL 79.2
Fournier-StL 37.6
McHenry-StL 36.8
Cruise-Bos 29.2
Roush-Cin 27.2

Runs
Hornsby-StL 131
Frisch-NY 121
Bancroft-NY 121
Powell-Bos 114
Burns-NY 111

Hits
Hornsby-StL 235
Frisch-NY 211
C.Bigbee-Pit 204
Johnston-Bro 203

Doubles
Hornsby-StL 44
Kelly-NY 42
Johnston-Bro 41
Grimes-Chi 38
McHenry-StL 37

Triples
Powell-Bos 18
Hornsby-StL 18
Grimm-Pit 17
Frisch-NY 17
C.Bigbee-Pit 17

Home Runs
Kelly-NY 23
Hornsby-StL 21
Williams-Phi 18
McHenry-StL 17
Fournier-StL 16

Total Bases
Hornsby-StL 378
Kelly-NY 310
McHenry-StL 305
Meusel-Phi-NY 302
Frisch-NY 300

Runs Batted In
Hornsby-StL 126
Kelly-NY 122
Youngs-NY 102
McHenry-StL 102
Frisch-NY 100

Stolen Bases
Frisch-NY 49
Carey-Pit 37
Johnston-Bro 28
Bohne-Cin 26
Maranville-Pit 25

Base Stealing Runs
Frisch-NY 6.2
Carey-Pit 3.9
Stock-StL 1.4
Cutshaw-Pit 1.3
Maranville-Pit 1.3

Fielding Runs-Infield
Lavan-StL 20.5
Bancroft-NY 19.1
Deal-Chi 12.8
Kelly-NY 11.7
Kilduff-Bro 11.5

Fielding Runs-Outfield
C.Bigbee-Pit 11.8
Williams-Phi 8.7
Griffith-Bro 7.1
McHenry-StL 5.2
Carey-Pit 5.1

Wins
Grimes-Bro 22
Cooper-Pit 22
Oeschger-Bos 20
Nehf-NY 20
Rixey-Cin 19

Winning Pct.
Doak-StL 714
Nehf-NY 667
Grimes-Bro 629
Barnes-NY 625
Toney-NY 621

Complete Games
Grimes-Bro 30
Cooper-Pit 29
Luque-Cin 25

Strikeouts
Grimes-Bro 136
Cooper-Pit 134
Luque-Cin 102
McQuillan-Bos 94

Fewest BB/Game
Adams-Pit 1.01
Alexander-Chi 1.18
Barnes-NY 1.53
Hubbell-Phi 1.55
Doak-StL 1.60

Games
Scott-Bos 47
Oeschger-Bos 46
McQuillan-Bos 45
Watson-Bos 44
Fillingim-Bos 44

Saves
North-StL 7
Barnes-NY 6
McQuillan-Bos 5

Base Runners/9
Adams-Pit 9.73
J.Morrison-Pit 10.31
Ryan-NY 10.57
Donohue-Cin 10.88
Glazner-Pit 10.92

Adjusted Relief Runs
North-StL 2.4

Relief Ranking
North-StL 2.4

Innings Pitched
Cooper-Pit 327.0
Luque-Cin 304.0
Grimes-Bro 302.1
Rixey-Cin 301.0
Oeschger-Bos 299.0

Opponents' Avg.
Glazner-Pit 250
Adams-Pit 251
Pertica-StL 267
Watson-Bos 270
Nehf-NY 271

Opponents' OBP
Adams-Pit 272
Glazner-Pit 306
Nehf-NY 311
Luque-Cin 312
Doak-StL 313

Earned Run Average
Doak-StL 2.59
Adams-Pit 2.64
Glazner-Pit 2.77
Rixey-Cin 2.78
Grimes-Bro 2.83

Adjusted ERA
Adams-Pit 145
Doak-StL 142
Glazner-Pit 138
Grimes-Bro 137
Mitchell-Bro 134

Adjusted Starter Runs
Grimes-Bro 32.8
Glazner-Pit 26.4
Rixey-Cin 22.6
Doak-StL 21.1
Adams-Pit 20.5

Pitcher Wins
Grimes-Bro 4.0
Adams-Pit 2.5
Rixey-Cin 2.2
Cooper-Pit 2.2
Mitchell-Bro 1.9

A Powerful Visitation

The home run made a splash in the NL in 1921. Four-baggers nearly doubled, from 261 to 460 as runs per team per game rose 16 percent to 4.59, the highest since 1912. Batters struck out less often, despite the rise of the homer, and stolen bases continued to fade. Prior to 1921, the Braves shortened their left-field fence by 25 feet. Cubs Park, Cincinnati's Redland Field, and St. Louis' Sportsman's Park were also shrunk, though Redland Field remained a home run desert.

The change to power baseball caused casualties. After fifteen years, outfielder Dode Paskert played his last game. Perhaps the quintessential Dead Ball Era player, Paskert's singles, walks, and steals were no longer in vogue. Meanwhile, future Hall of Famer Kiki Cuyler began his eighteen-year career, going 0-for-3 in his only appearance of the season for the Pirates.

Seeking their first flag in twelve years, Pittsburgh topped the league most of the season. The pitching, led by Wilbur Cooper and 39-year-old Babe Adams, was the league's best, and their offense rated well, even in cavernous Forbes Field. Down the stretch, though, John McGraw's Giants came up winners. First baseman George Kelly paced the NL with 23 homers, but New York did real damage by leading the loop in walks by a margin of nearly 100.

The Giants-Yankees World Series, the last best-of-nine affair, was classic. Each game was close into the late innings, with only two games settled by more than 2 runs. In the end, John McGraw's men were stronger as they gained their first world championship since 1905, in eight games.

1921 American League

TEAM	W	L	T	PCT	GB	HW	HL	R	OR	PA	H	2B	3B	HR	BB	SO	HB	SH	AVG	OBP	SLG	OPS	AOPS	BR	ABR	PF	SB	CS	BSA	BSR
NY	98	55	0	.641		53	25	948	708	6066	1576	285	87	134	588	569	40	189	.300	.375	.464	839	116	146	126	102	89	64	58	-3
CLE	94	60	0	.610	4.5	51	26	925	712	6275	1656	355	90	42	623	376	37	205	.304	.357	.425	782	98	24	-21	106	91	71	56	-5
STL	81	73	0	.526	17.5	43	34	835	845	6096	1655	246	106	67	413	407	36	205	.304	.357	.425	725	95	-83	-48	95	112	66	63	2
WAS	80	73	1	.523	18	46	30	704	738	6003	1468	240	96	42	462	472	59	188	.277	.342	.383	725	95	-83	-48	95	83	65	56	-4
BOS	75	79	0	.487	23.5	41	36	668	696	5851	1440	248	69	17	428	344	31	186	.277	.335	.361	696	84	-134	-117	97	95	89	52	-10
DET	71	82	1	.464	27	37	40	883	852	6302	1724	268	100	58	582	376	29	230	.316	.385	.433	818	115	121	130	99	94	93	50	-12
CHI	62	92	0	.403	36.5	37	40	683	858	5997	1509	242	82	35	445	474	37	186	.283	.343	.379	722	90	-88	-79	99	94	54	50	-4
PHI	53	100	2	.346	45	28	47	657	894	6067	1497	256	64	82	424	565	43	135	.274	.331	.389	720	88	-103	-106	101	69	56	55	-4
TOT	616					336	278	6303		48657	12525	2140	694	477	3965	3583	312	1551	.292	.357	.408	765					684	546	56	-41

TEAM	CG	SHO	GR	SV	IP	H	HR	BB	SO	BR/9	ERA	AERA	OAV	OOB	PR	APR	PF	OSB	OCS	FA	E	WPB	DP	FW	PW	BW	BSW	DIF
NY	92	8	96	15	1364.0	1461	51	470	481	13.1	3.82	111	.277	.342	70	63	99	82	61	.965	222	36	138	-.3	5.9	11.8	.2	3.9
CLE	81	11	114	14	1377.0	1534	43	431	475	13.0	3.90	109	.288	.344	58	55	100	96	52	.967	204	32	124	.8	5.1	10.0	.2	.8
STL	77	9	142	9	1379.0	1541	71	556	477	13.9	4.61	97	.288	.360	-51	-21	105	79	66	.964	235	36	153	-.9	2.2	-4.5	.7	6.1
WAS	80	10	108	10	1383.2	1568	51	442	452	13.3	3.97	104	.291	.349	47	23	96	59	67	.963	157	27	151	3.5	3.6	-10.9	.1	1.8
BOS	88	9	82	5	1364.1	1521	53	452	446	13.3	3.98	106	.291	.352	45	38	99	73	71	.975	157	27	151	3.5	3.6	-10.9	.1	1.8
DET	73	4	115	17	1386.1	1634	71	495	452	14.2	4.40	97	.297	.361	-18	-20	100	99	75	.963	232	34	107	-.8	-1.9	12.2	-.5	-14.6
CHI	84	7	106	9	1365.1	1603	52	549	392	14.4	4.94	86	.303	.372	-99	-109	99	98	79	.969	200	35	155	1.0	-10.2	-7.4	-.6	2.2
PHI	75	2	119	7	1400.1	1645	85	548	431	14.3	4.61	97	.300	.367	-52	-24	104	101	90	.958	274	48	144	-3.1	-2.2	-9.9	.1	-8.4
TOT	650	60	882	86	11020.0					13.7	4.28		.292	.357						.965	1748	272	1099					

Batter-Fielder Wins		Batting Average		On-Base Percentage		Slugging Average		On-Base Plus Slugging		Adjusted OPS		Adjusted Batter Runs	
Ruth-NY	9.4	Heilmann-Det	.394	Ruth-NY	.512	Ruth-NY	.846	Ruth-NY	1359	Ruth-NY	236	Ruth-NY	117.7
Cobb-Det	4.8	Cobb-Det	.389	Cobb-Det	.452	Heilmann-Det	.606	Heilmann-Det	1051	Heilmann-Det	167	Heilmann-Det	60.7
Collins-Chi	4.4	Ruth-NY	.378	Heilmann-Det	.444	Cobb-Det	.596	Cobb-Det	1048	Cobb-Det	167	Cobb-Det	52.2
Speaker-Cle	3.8	Sisler-StL	.371	Speaker-Cle	.439	Williams-StL	.561	Williams-StL	.990	Speaker-Cle	146	Speaker-Cle	38.5
Heilmann-Det	3.4	Speaker-Cle	.362	Williams-StL	.429	Sisler-StL	.560	Speaker-Cle	.977	Williams-StL	142	Williams-StL	36.3

Runs		Hits		Doubles		Triples		Home Runs		Total Bases		Runs Batted In	
Ruth-NY	177	Heilmann-Det	237	Speaker-Cle	52	Tobin-StL	18	Ruth-NY	59	Ruth-NY	457	Ruth-NY	171
Tobin-StL	132	Tobin-StL	236	Ruth-NY	44	Sisler-StL	18	Williams-StL	24	Heilmann-Det	365	Heilmann-Det	139
Peckinpaugh-NY	128	Sisler-StL	216	Veach-Det	43	Shanks-Was	18	Meusel-NY	24	Meusel-NY	334	Meusel-NY	135
Sisler-StL	125	Jacobson-StL	211	Heilmann-Det	43			T.Walker-Phi	23	Tobin-StL	327	Veach-Det	128
Cobb-Det	124	Veach-Det	207	Meusel-NY	40			Heilmann-Det	19	Sisler-StL	326	Gardner-Cle	120

Stolen Bases		Base Stealing Runs		Fielding Runs-Infield		Fielding Runs-Outfield		Wins		Winning Pct.		Complete Games	
Sisler-StL	35	Sisler-StL	3.8	Scott-Bos	41.2	Veach-Det	12.9	Shocker-StL	27	Mays-NY	.750	Faber-Chi	32
Harris-Was	29	Harris-Was	3.2	Collins-Chi	30.7	Speaker-Cle	9.2	Mays-NY	27	Shocker-StL	.692	Shocker-StL	30
Rice-Was	26	Judge-Was	2.5	Dykes-Phi	21.1	Cobb-Det	6.0	Faber-Chi	25	Bush-Bos	.640	Mays-NY	30
Johnson-Chi	22	Meusel-NY	1.6	Johnson-Chi	20.8	Rice-Was	5.9	Jones-Bos	23	Coveleski-Cle	.639	Coveleski-Cle	28
Cobb-Det	22	Rice-Was	1.5	Ward-NY	18.8	T.Walker-Phi	5.2	Coveleski-Cle	23	Faber-Chi	.625		

Strikeouts		Fewest BB/Game		Games		Saves		Base Runners/9		Adjusted Relief Runs		Relief Ranking	
Johnson-Was	143	Hasty-Phi	2.01	Mays-NY	49	Middleton-Det	7	Faber-Chi	10.53				
Shocker-StL	132	Mays-NY	2.03	Shocker-StL	47	Mays-NY	7	Morton-Cle	11.03				
Shawkey-NY	126	Mogridge-Was	2.06	Bayne-StL	47			Mays-NY	11.15				
Faber-Chi	124	Bagby-Cle	2.07	Rommel-Phi	46			Mogridge-Was	11.69				
Leonard-Det	120	Zachary-Was	2.12					Shocker-StL	12.04				

Innings Pitched		Opponents' Avg.		Opponents' OBP		Earned Run Average		Adjusted ERA		Adjusted Starter Runs		Pitcher Wins	
Mays-NY	336.2	Faber-Chi	.242	Faber-Chi	.297	Faber-Chi	2.48	Faber-Chi	171	Faber-Chi	64.1	Faber-Chi	6.8
Faber-Chi	330.2	Mays-NY	.257	Mays-NY	.303	Mogridge-Was	3.00	Mays-NY	139	Mays-NY	42.6	Mays-NY	5.4
Shocker-StL	326.2	Bush-Bos	.260	Mogridge-Was	.313	Mays-NY	3.05	Mogridge-Was	137	Mogridge-Was	35.8	Jones-Bos	4.3
Coveleski-Cle	315.0	Shawkey-NY	.263	Shocker-StL	.319	Hoyt-NY	3.09	Hoyt-NY	137	Hoyt-NY	35.3	Shocker-StL	4.2
Kerr-Chi	308.2	Johnson-Was	.263	Johnson-Was	.326	Jones-Bos	3.22	Jones-Bos	131	Jones-Bos	34.3	Hoyt-NY	3.3

The First of Many

Resurgent New York, riding a one-man power wave, engaged with Cleveland in one of the decade's best races. Neck-and-neck from mid-May onward, the teams counter-punched their way through mid-September. With the two clubs tied on September 23, the Indians started a four-game set at New York. After splitting the first two, the Yankees destroyed Cleveland, 21-7, on September 25, won again the next day, and never looked back. This was the first pennant ever for the Yankees.

Once again, Babe Ruth outhomered most AL clubs. Bob Meusel, Wally Pipp, and Roger Peckinpaugh supported The Bambino ably, as did a capable mound staff led by pariah Carl Mays. The game had changed almost overnight. Runs rose to 5.12 per team per game, and only Red Faber posted an ERA under 3.00. The overpowering force named Ruth set new major league marks for home runs and RBIs.

Stripped of talent by Judge Landis' lifetime suspensions, the White Sox fell to seventh. Due to the gambling scandal, the public lost confidence in baseball, especially in American League cities. Despite the excitement generated by Babe Ruth, attendance was down 9 percent in 1920; moreover, the perception of the AL as a "dirty league" helped the NL eventually surpass of the Junior Circuit in attendance as AL fans responded to the scandal by voting with their feet. AL attendance in 1930 was substantially less than the NL's, even though the AL had outdrawn the NL by 26 percent in 1920.

The Philadelphia A's expanded Shibe Park's right field by 40 feet in 1921, but that didn't stop the tide of home runs. New York, St. Louis, and Philadelphia were the league's big long-ball parks, but the Yankees led the loop in homers at home *and* on the road. In the crosstown World Series (the final best-of-nine classic), the Giants shut down the mighty Yankees, winning in eight.

1920 National League

TEAM	W	L	T	PCT	GB	HW	HL	R	OR	PA	H	2B	3B	HR	BB	SO	HB	SH	AVG	OBP	SLG	OPS	AOPS	BR	ABR	PF	SB	CS	BSA	BSR
BRO	93	61	1	.604		49	29	660	528	5966	1493	205	99	28	359	391	19	189	.277	.324	.367	691	100	17	-3	103	70	80	47	-13
NY	86	68	1	.558	7	45	35	682	543	5891	1427	210	76	46	432	545	26	124	.269	.327	.363	690	104	25	32	99	131	113	54	-11
CIN	82	71	1	.536	10.5	42	34	639	569	5799	1432	169	76	18	382	367	47	194	.277	.332	.349	681	102	10	19	99	158	128	55	-10
PIT	79	75	1	.513	14	42	35	530	552	5796	1342	162	90	16	374	405	29	174	.257	.310	.332	642	86	-71	-87	103	181	117	61	-1
STL	75	79	1	.487	18	38	38	675	682	6086	1589	238	96	32	373	484	26	192	.289	.337	.385	722	117	84	112	96	126	114	53	-12
CHI	75	79	0	.487	18	43	34	619	635	5811	1350	223	67	34	428	421	46	220	.264	.326	.354	680	98	11	-1	102	115	129	47	-20
BOS	62	90	1	.408	30	36	37	523	670	5802	1358	168	86	23	385	488	33	166	.260	.315	.339	654	97	-47	-22	96	88	98	47	-15
PHI	62	91	0	.405	30.5	32	45	565	714	5742	1385	229	54	64	283	531	36	159	.263	.305	.364	669	93	-28	-54	105	100	83	55	-7
TOT	617					327	287	4893		46893	11376	1604	644	261	3016	3632	262	1418	.270	.322	.357	679					969	862	53	-89

TEAM	CG	SHO	GR	SV	IP	H	HR	BB	SO	BR/9	ERA	AERA	OAV	OOB	PR	APR	PF	OSB	OCS	FA	E	WPB	DP	FW	PW	BW	BSW	DIF
BRO	89	17	93	10	1427.1	1381	25	327	553	10.9	2.62	122	.259	.304	81	89	102	132	99	.966	226	47	118	-.2	9.5	-.3	-.2	7.2
NY	86	18	103	9	1408.2	1379	44	297	380	10.8	2.80	107	.261	.303	51	32	96	95	89	.969	210	37	137	.8	3.4	3.4	.0	1.4
CIN	90	12	82	9	1391.2	1327	26	393	435	11.3	2.90	105	.256	.313	36	23	97	108	111	.968	200	32	125	1.3	2.5	2.0	.1	-.4
PIT	92	17	85	10	1415.1	1389	25	280	444	10.8	2.89	111	.261	.301	39	49	103	120	99	.971	186	37	119	2.2	5.2	-9.3	1.1	2.8
STL	72	9	135	12	1426.2	1488	30	479	529	12.8	3.43	87	.277	.343	-47	-75	95	141	97	.961	256	39	136	-2.0	-8.0	12.0	-.1	-3.9
CHI	95	13	93	9	1388.2	1459	37	382	508	12.1	3.27	98	.276	.328	-21	-10	102	115	97	.965	225	31	112	-1.2	-1.1	-.1	-1.0	.3
BOS	93	14	73	6	1386.1	1464	39	415	368	12.4	3.54	86	.280	.337	-62	-77	97	111	143	.964	239	32	125	-1.1	-8.2	-2.4	-.4	-1.9
PHI	77	8	102	11	1380.2	1480	35	444	419	12.8	3.63	94	.284	.345	-76	-32	109	147	107	.964	232	47	135	-.7	-3.4	-5.8	.4	-5.0
TOT	694	108	766	76	11225.1					11.7	3.13		.270	.322						.966	1774	302	1007					

Batter-Fielder Wins		Batting Average		On-Base Percentage		Slugging Average		On-Base Plus Slugging		Adjusted OPS		Adjusted Batter Runs	
Hornsby-StL	7.9	Hornsby-StL	.370	Hornsby-StL	.431	Hornsby-StL	.559	Hornsby-StL	.990	Hornsby-StL	190	Hornsby-StL	69.0
Bancroft-Phi-NY	5.6	Nicholson-Pit	.360	Youngs-NY	.427	Nicholson-Pit	.530	Youngs-NY	.904	Youngs-NY	161	Youngs-NY	49.2
Youngs-NY	4.1	Youngs-NY	.351	Roush-Cin	.386	Williams-Phi	.497	Williams-Phi	.861	Roush-Cin	142	Roush-Cin	30.7
Roush-Cin	3.1	Roush-Cin	.339	Wheat-Bro	.385	Youngs-NY	.477	Wheat-Bro	.848	Williams-Phi	139	Wheat-Bro	29.1
Williams-Phi	3.0	Wheat-Bro	.328	Groh-Cin	.375	Meusel-Phi	.473	Roush-Cin	.839	Wheat-Bro	138	Williams-Phi	28.4

Runs		Hits		Doubles		Triples		Home Runs		Total Bases		Runs Batted In	
Burns-NY	115	Hornsby-StL	218	Hornsby-StL	44	Myers-Bro	22	Williams-Phi	15	Hornsby-StL	329	Kelly-NY	94
Bancroft-Phi-NY	102	Youngs-NY	204	Bancroft-Phi-NY	36	Hornsby-StL	20	Meusel-Phi	14	Williams-Phi	293	Hornsby-StL	94
Daubert-Cin	97	Stock-StL	204	Williams-Phi	36	Roush-Cin	16	Kelly-NY	11	Youngs-NY	277	Roush-Cin	90
Hornsby-StL	96	Roush-Cin	196	Myers-Bro	36	Maranville-Bos	15	Robertson-Chi	10	Wheat-Bro	270	Duncan-Cin	83
Youngs-NY	92	Williams-Phi	192	Burns-NY	35	Bigbee-Pit	15	McHenry-StL	10	Myers-Bro	269	Myers-Bro	80

Stolen Bases		Base Stealing Runs		Fielding Runs-Infield		Fielding Runs-Outfield		Wins		Winning Pct.		Complete Games	
Carey-Pit	52	Carey-Pit	7.9	Bancroft-Phi-NY	36.8	Neale-Cin	12.0	Alexander-Chi	27	Grimes-Bro	676	Alexander-Chi	33
Roush-Cin	36	Frisch-NY	3.6	Terry-Chi	17.4	Burns-NY	10.9	Cooper-Pit	24	Alexander-Chi	659	Cooper-Pit	28
Frisch-NY	34	Neale-Cin	2.2	Maranville-Bos	15.3	Roush-Cin	10.2	Grimes-Bro	23	Toney-NY	656	Rixey-Phi	25
Bigbee-Pit	31	Bigbee-Pit	1.6	Fletcher-NY-Phi	14.4	Williams-Phi	10.2	Toney-NY	21	Pfeffer-Bro	640	Grimes-Bro	25
Neale-Cin	29	Gowdy-Bos	1.0	Deal-Chi	11.1	Heathcote-StL	9.8	Nehf-NY	21	Nehf-NY	636	Vaughn-Chi	24

Strikeouts		Fewest BB/Game		Games		Saves		Base Runners/9		Adjusted Relief Runs		Relief Ranking	
Alexander-Chi	173	Adams-Pit	.62	Haines-StL	47	Sherdel-StL	6	Adams-Pit	8.86				
Vaughn-Chi	131	Cooper-Pit	1.43	Douglas-NY	46	McQuillan-Bos	5	Alexander-Chi	10.03				
Grimes-Bro	131	Nehf-NY	1.44	Alexander-Chi	44	Alexander-Cin	5	Luque-Cin	10.05				
Haines-StL	120	Benton-NY	1.44	Scott-Bos	44	Hubbell-NY-Phi	4	J.Barnes-NY	10.12				
Schupp-StL	119	Marquard-Bro	1.66	Cooper-Pit	44	Mamaux-Bro	4	Grimes-Bro	10.14				

Innings Pitched		Opponents' Avg.		Opponents' OBP		Earned Run Average		Adjusted ERA		Adjusted Starter Runs		Pitcher Wins	
Alexander-Chi	363.1	Luque-Cin	225	Adams-Pit	259	Alexander-Chi	1.91	Alexander-Chi	168	Alexander-Chi	51.6	Alexander-Chi	6.9
Cooper-Pit	327.0	Grimes-Bro	238	Grimes-Bro	282	Adams-Pit	2.16	Adams-Pit	149	Grimes-Bro	30.1	Grimes-Bro	4.9
Grimes-Bro	303.2	Adams-Pit	244	Alexander-Chi	285	Grimes-Bro	2.22	Grimes-Bro	144	Adams-Pit	27.6	Smith-Bro	3.2
Haines-StL	301.2	Ponder-Pit	246	Luque-Cin	286	Cooper-Pit	2.39	Cooper-Pit	134	Cooper-Pit	26.1	Cooper-Pit	3.0
Vaughn-Chi	301.0	Ruether-Cin	247	Ponder-Pit	286	Ruether-Cin	2.47	Vaughn-Chi	126	Ruether-Cin	19.5	Vaughn-Chi	2.6

Runs, Hits, and Robins

Runs per game rose 8 percent in 1920, but home runs were not the culprit; the league leader, Cy Williams, hit just 15, and he played in Philadelphia, the league's one home run haven. Stolen bases, meanwhile, dropped to their lowest level yet. The decision by the rules committee to disallow scuffed baseballs was the biggest contributor to increased scoring.

On July 1 the Cardinals moved into Sportsman's Park, owned by the AL Browns. Sportsman's was smaller than Robison Field, a change that helped second sacker Rogers Hornsby compile huge numbers in the coming years. On September 15 third baseman Pie Traynor played the first of his 1,941 major league games—all in Pittsburgh flannels.

The post-war attendance boom continued as league attendance leapt 40 percent. The biggest off-field news of the year, the Black Sox scandal, broke in September after rumors had circulated for a year. While the probe focused on the AL, the Senior Circuit was hit as well. Before the 1921 season started, NL veterans Claude Hendrix, Buck Herzog, and Benny Kauff were banned from baseball due to gambling or racketeering. The scandal also tainted the Reds' 1919 world championship victory.

The lowly Brooklyn Robins—who had managed only three first-division finishes since 1903—found themselves in a surprising September tangle with the mighty Giants and Reds. As the other two clubs treaded water, Brooklyn won 16 of 18 to clinch the pennant. Outfielders Hy Myers (22 triples) and Zack Wheat were the chief offensive weapons, as spitballing Burleigh Grimes paced the league in ERA. The Robins led the NL in ERA though the staff was a patchwork job—manager Wilbert Robinson used six starting pitchers. The 1920 campaign was only temporary balm for Brooklyn fans; the club immediately returned to the NL's nether regions and would not win again until 1941.

1920 American League

TEAM	W	L	T	PCT	GB	HW	HL	R	OR	PA	H	2B	3B	HR	BB	SO	HB	SH	AVG	OBP	SLG	OPS	AOPS	BR	ABR	PF	SB	CS	BSA	BSR
CLE	98	56	0	.636		51	27	857	642	6064	1574	300	95	35	576	379	36	256	.303	.376	.417	793	113	130	104	103	73	93	44	-16
CHI	96	58	0	.623	2	52	25	794	665	6032	1574	263	37	37	471	355	38	195	.295	.357	.402	759	107	49	49	100	109	96	53	-10
NY	95	59	0	.617	3	49	28	838	629	5911	1448	268	71	115	539	626	22	174	.280	.350	.426	776	107	74	47	104	64	82	44	-15
STL	76	77	1	.497	21.5	40	38	797	766	6032	1651	279	83	50	427	339	39	208	.308	.363	.419	782	110	94	70	103	121	79	61	-1
BOS	72	81	1	.471	25.5	41	35	650	698	5997	1397	216	71	22	533	429	46	219	.269	.342	.350	692	93	-71	-41	96	98	111	47	-17
WAS	68	84	1	.447	29	37	38	723	802	5936	1526	233	81	36	433	543	53	199	.291	.351	.386	737	104	5	25	97	160	114	58	-5
DET	61	93	1	.396	37	32	46	652	833	5932	1408	228	72	30	479	391	19	219	.270	.334	.359	693	91	-82	-65	98	76	68	53	-7
PHI	48	106	2	.312	50	25	50	558	834	5823	1324	220	49	44	353	593	45	169	.252	.305	.338	643	74	-192	-197	101	50	67	43	-12
TOT	617					327	287	5869		47727	11902	2007	620	369	3811	3655	298	1639	.284	.347	.387	735					751	710	51	-83

TEAM	CG	SHO	GR	SV	IP	H	HR	BB	SO	BR/9	ERA	AERA	OAV	OOB	PR	APR	PF	OSB	OCS	FA	E	WPB	DP	FW	PW	BW	BSW	DIF
CLE	94	11	100	7	1377.0	1448	31	401	466	12.3	3.41	111	.276	.331	57	58	100	84	70	.971	184	31	124	2.1	5.6	10.1	-.5	3.7
CHI	109	9	66	10	1386.2	1467	45	405	438	12.3	3.59	105	.280	.335	31	24	99	61	82	.968	198	27	142	1.2	2.3	4.8	.0	10.7
NY	88	15	93	11	1368.0	1414	48	420	480	12.3	3.32	115	.270	.328	72	75	101	87	58	.969	194	31	129	1.4	7.3	4.6	-.4	5.2
STL	84	9	102	14	1378.2	1481	53	578	444	13.7	4.03	97	.283	.359	-38	-22	103	95	89	.963	233	23	119	-1.2	-1.2	6.8	.9	-4.8
BOS	92	11	76	6	1395.1	1481	39	461	481	12.7	3.82	95	.279	.339	-5	-31	96	123	83	.972	183	45	131	2.2	-3.0	-4.0	-.6	.9
WAS	81	10	102	10	1367.0	1521	51	520	418	13.7	4.17	89	.288	.357	-58	-71	98	91	99	.963	232	63	95	-1.3	-6.9	2.4	.5	-2.8
DET	74	9	122	7	1385.0	1487	46	561	483	13.7	4.04	92	.284	.359	-52	-58	107	96	133	.964	230	41	95	-.9	-5.0	-6.3	.3	-4.0
PHI	79	6	104	2	1380.1	1612	56	461	423	13.8	3.93	102	.302	.362	-21	11	106	104	133	.959	266	40	125	-3.3	1.1	-19.1	-.2	-7.5
TOT	701	80	765	67	11038.0					13.1	3.79		.284	.347						.966	1720	301	960					

Batter-Fielder Wins	Batting Average	On-Base Percentage	Slugging Average	On-Base Plus Slugging	Adjusted OPS	Adjusted Batter Runs
Ruth-NY 9.3	Sisler-StL .407	Ruth-NY .532	Ruth-NY .847	Ruth-NY 1379	Ruth-NY 252	Ruth-NY 110.5
Sisler-StL 7.9	Speaker-Cle .388	Speaker-Cle .483	Sisler-StL .632	Sisler-StL 1082	Sisler-StL 179	Sisler-StL 69.4
Speaker-Cle 5.4	Jackson-Chi .382	Sisler-StL .449	Jackson-Chi .589	Speaker-Cle 1045	Jackson-Chi 172	Speaker-Cle 63.9
E.Collins-Chi 5.4	Ruth-NY .376	Jackson-Chi .444	Speaker-Cle .562	Jackson-Chi 1033	Speaker-Cle 171	Jackson-Chi 59.0
Jackson-Chi 4.5	E.Collins-Chi .372	E.Collins-Chi .438	Felsch-Chi .540	E.Collins-Chi 932	E.Collins-Chi 146	E.Collins-Chi 43.1

Runs	Hits	Doubles	Triples	Home Runs	Total Bases	Runs Batted In
Ruth-NY 158	Sisler-StL 257	Speaker-Cle 50	Jackson-Chi 20	Ruth-NY 54	Sisler-StL 399	Ruth-NY 137
Speaker-Cle 137	E.Collins-Chi 224	Sisler-StL 49	Sisler-StL 18	Sisler-StL 19	Ruth-NY 388	Sisler-StL 122
Sisler-StL 137	Jackson-Chi 218	Jackson-Chi 42	Hooper-Bos 17	T.Walker-Phi 17	Jackson-Chi 336	Jacobson-StL 122
E.Collins-Chi 117	Jacobson-StL 216			Felsch-Chi 14	Speaker-Cle 310	Jackson-Chi 121
	Speaker-Cle 214				Jacobson-StL 305	Gardner-Cle 118

Stolen Bases	Base Stealing Runs	Fielding Runs-Infield	Fielding Runs-Outfield	Wins	Winning Pct.	Complete Games
Rice-Was 63	Rice-Was 3.4	Ward-NY 16.5	Rice-Was 17.0	Bagby-Cle 31	Bagby-Cle .721	Bagby-Cle 30
Sisler-StL 42	Sisler-StL 3.3	Dykes-Phi 15.4	Veach-Det 13.6	Mays-NY 26	Mays-NY .703	Faber-Chi 28
Roth-Was 24	E.Collins-Chi 1.6	Sisler-StL 15.1	Felsch-Chi 12.4	Coveleski-Cle 24	Kerr-Chi .700	Cicotte-Chi 28
Menosky-Bos 23	Williams-StL 1.2	Scott-Bos 14.1	Jacobson-StL 9.6	Faber-Chi 23	Cicotte-Chi .677	Mays-NY 26
Tobin-StL 21	Burns-Phi-Cle 1.1	Chapman-Cle 13.9	Speaker-Cle 6.0	Williams-Chi 22		Coveleski-Cle 26

Strikeouts	Fewest BB/Game	Games	Saves	Base Runners/9	Adjusted Relief Runs	Relief Ranking
Coveleski-Cle 133	Quinn-NY 1.71	Shocker-StL 48	Shocker-StL 5	Coveleski-Cle 10.09		
Williams-Chi 128	Coveleski-Cle 1.86	Ayers-Det 46	Kerr-Chi 5	Mails-Cle 10.23		
Shawkey-NY 126	Bagby-Cle 2.09	Mays-NY 45	Burwell-StL 4	W.Johnson-Was 10.46		
Faber-Chi 108	Cicotte-Chi 2.20	Kerr-Chi 45		Shocker-StL 10.92		
Shocker-StL 107	Perry-Phi 2.22	Zachary-Was 44		Rommel-Phi 10.99		

Innings Pitched	Opponents' Avg.	Opponents' OBP	Earned Run Average	Adjusted ERA	Adjusted Starter Runs	Pitcher Wins
Bagby-Cle 339.2	Coveleski-Cle .243	Coveleski-Cle .285	Shawkey-NY 2.45	Shawkey-NY 155	Coveleski-Cle 44.4	Coveleski-Cle 5.5
Faber-Chi 319.0	Collins-NY .247	Shocker-StL .305	Coveleski-Cle 2.49	Coveleski-Cle 153	Shawkey-NY 41.3	Bagby-Cle 4.7
Coveleski-Cle 315.0	Shawkey-NY .248	Shawkey-NY .308	Shocker-StL 2.71	Shocker-StL 144	Bagby-Cle 38.9	Shawkey-NY 4.6
Mays-NY 312.0	Shocker-StL .248	Quinn-NY .308	Rommel-Phi 2.85	Rommel-Phi 141	Shocker-StL 29.6	Shocker-StL 3.7
Cicotte-Chi 303.1	Ehmke-Det .253	Rommel-Phi .309	Bagby-Cle 2.89	Bagby-Cle 131	Mays-NY 28.0	Mays-NY 3.5

Scandal, Homers, and Clean Balls

Prior to the season, the major leagues decided that using discolored, lumpy baseballs could be dangerous for the players, offense, and attendance. The previous year's gains in runs per team per game continued, and the 1920 figure of 4.76 was the highest in eighteen years. The AL became the first league to draw five million fans, with the Yankees the first team to crack the million mark.

New rules preventing pitchers from defacing balls only increased the offense and excitement levels at the suddenly fuller parks. (Established spitball pitchers could continue their practice if they registered with the leagues.) St. Louis' George Sisler set an all-time record with 257 hits, and the 54 homers by new Yankee Babe Ruth made him a national hero.

The Indians, White Sox, and Yankees converged in June. Indians shortstop Ray Chapman was killed by an errant pitch thrown by Yankee Carl Mays on August 16, and for a time the Indians slumped. Cleveland, however, pulled shortstop Joe Sewell from the minors, and the Tribe regained its fire, winning seven straight while Chicago kayoed New York. The public outcry

following Chapman's death forced umpires to keep clean baseballs in play at all times, which further increased scoring.

On September 27, with Chicago a half-game back, eight White Sox players were indicted for fixing 1919's World Series. Owner Charles Comiskey, who had conspired to squelch the investigation, was forced to suspend the players. The decimated White Sox crumbled while Cleveland clinched. To restore public confidence in baseball, the newly appointed Commissioner Kenesaw Mountain Landis barred the eight Sox, and several other miscreants.

After falling behind two games to one in the best-of-nine World Series, the Indians won four straight from Brooklyn to clinch the title. In those four wins, Brooklyn scored just twice. In Game 5, Cleveland's Elmer Smith hit the first Series grand slam. Four innings later, a line drive at Indians second baseman Bill Wambsganss turned into the second unassisted triple play of the century.

1919 National League

TEAM	W	L	T	PCT	GB	HW	HL	R	OR	PA	H	2B	3B	HR	BB	SO	HB	SH	AVG	OBP	SLG	OPS	AOPS	BR	ABR	PF	SB	CS	BSA	BSR
CIN	96	44	0	.686		52	19	577	401	5214	1204	135	83	20	405	368	33	199	.263	.327	.342	669	110	42	57	97	143			
NY	87	53	0	.621	9	46	23	605	470	5157	1254	204	64	40	328	407	37	128	.269	.322	.366	688	113	67	73	99	157			
CHI	75	65	0	.536	21	40	31	454	407	5088	1174	166	58	21	298	359	42	167	.256	.308	.332	640	97	-14	-17	101	150			
PIT	71	68	0	.511	24.5	40	30	472	466	5050	1132	130	82	17	344	381	24	144	.249	.306	.325	631	92	-28	-45	104	196			
BRO	69	71	1	.493	27	36	33	525	513	5283	1272	167	66	25	258	405	28	153	.263	.304	.340	644	97	-15	-25	102	112			
BOS	57	82	1	.410	38.5	29	38	465	465	5299	1201	142	62	24	355	481	42	156	.253	.311	.326	635	100	-18	4	96	145			
STL	54	83	1	.394	40.5	34	35	463	552	5053	1175	163	52	18	304	418	18	143	.254	.305	.326	631	101	-28	2	94	148			
PHI	47	90	1	.343	47.5	26	44	510	699	5220	1191	208	50	42	323	469	28	123	.251	.303	.342	645	92	-5	-39	107	114			
TOT	558					303	253	4071		41364	9603	1315	517	207	2615	3288	252	1213	.258	.311	.337	648					1165			

TEAM	CG	SHO	GR	SV	IP	H	HR	BB	SO	BR/9	ERA	AERA	OAV	OOB	PR	APR	PF	OSB	OCS	FA	E	WPB	DP	FW	PW	BW	BSW	DIF
CIN	89	23	74	9	1274.0	1104	21	298	407	10.0	2.23	124	.239	.288	96	79	95	133	114	.974	151	28	98	2.7	8.8	6.3		8.2
NY	72	11	96	13	1256.0	1153	34	305	340	10.6	2.70	104	.247	.296	29	14	96	147	90	.964	216	27	96	-1.0	1.6	8.1		8.4
CHI	80	21	79	5	1265.0	1127	14	294	495	10.3	2.21	130	.242	.291	98	94	99	140	111	.969	185	26	87	.7	10.5	-1.9		-4.3
PIT	91	17	54	4	1249.0	1113	23	263	391	10.2	2.88	104	.244	.290	4	17	104	108	99	.970	165	24	89	1.8	1.9	-5.0		2.8
BRO	98	12	50	1	1281.0	1256	21	292	476	11.1	2.73	109	.262	.309	25	32	102	172	121	.963	219	39	84	-1.1	3.6	-2.8		-.6
BOS	79	5	74	9	1270.1	1313	29	337	374	11.8	3.17	90	.276	.327	-36	-46	98	147	133	.966	204	41	111	-.4	-5.1	.4		-7.5
STL	55	6	137	8	1217.1	1146	25	415	414	11.9	3.23	86	.256	.326	-44	-63	96	137	122	.963	214	50	112	-1.1	-7.0	.2		-6.6
PHI	93	6	57	2	1252.0	1391	40	408	397	13.3	4.14	78	.294	.356	-171	-116	111	181	135	.963	218	53	112	-1.3	-12.9	-4.3		-2.9
TOT	657	101	621	51	10064.2					11.2	2.91		.258	.311						.967	1572	288	789					

Batter-Fielder Wins
Hornsby-StL......5.1
Maranville-Bos...4.6
Stock-StL......4.4
Fletcher-NY......3.4
Groh-Cin......3.4

Batting Average
Roush-Cin......321
Hornsby-StL...318
Youngs-NY......311
Groh-Cin......310
Stock-StL......307

On-Base Percentage
Burns-NY......396
Groh-Cin......392
Hornsby-StL...384
Youngs-NY......384
Roush-Cin......380

Slugging Average
Myers-Bro......436
Doyle-NY......433
Groh-Cin......431
Roush-Cin......431
Hornsby-StL...430

On-Base Plus Slugging
Groh-Cin......823
Hornsby-StL...814
Roush-Cin......811
Burns-NY......801
Youngs-NY......799

Adjusted OPS
Hornsby-StL...154
Groh-Cin......151
Roush-Cin......147
Burns-NY......142
Youngs-NY......142

Adjusted Batter Runs
Hornsby-StL...34.1
Burns-NY......32.6
Groh-Cin......29.8
Cravath-Phi...29.4
Roush-Cin......29.2

Runs
Burns-NY......86
Groh-Cin......79
Daubert-Cin...79
Rath-Cin......77

Hits
Olson-Bro......164
Hornsby-StL...163
Roush-Cin......162
Burns-NY......162

Doubles
Youngs-NY......31
Luderus-Phi...30
Burns-NY......30
Kauff-NY......27
Meusel-Phi...26

Triples
Southworth-Pit...14
Myers-Bro......14

Home Runs
Cravath-Phi...12
Kauff-NY......10
Williams-Phi...9
Hornsby-StL...8
Doyle-NY......7

Total Bases
Myers-Bro......223
Hornsby-StL...220
Z.Wheat-Bro...219
Roush-Cin......217
Burns-NY......216

Runs Batted In
Myers-Bro......73
Roush-Cin......71
Hornsby-StL...71
Kauff-NY......67
Groh-Cin......63

Stolen Bases
Burns-NY......40
Cutshaw-Pit...36
Bigbee-Pit......31
Smith-StL......30

Base Stealing Runs

Fielding Runs-Infield
Maranville-Bos...26.3
Fletcher-NY......25.3
Stock-StL......19.4
Rath-Cin......12.9
Luderus-Phi...9.3

Fielding Runs-Outfield
Bigbee-Pit......14.5
Southworth-Pit...5.8
Roush-Cin......5.3
McHenry-StL...4.4
Myers-Bro......3.7

Wins
J.Barnes-NY......25
Vaughn-Chi......21
Sallee-Cin......21

Winning Pct.
Ruether-Cin......760
Sallee-Cin......750
J.Barnes-NY......735
Eller-Cin......679
Adams-Pit......630

Complete Games
Cooper-Pit......27
Pfeffer-Bro......26
Vaughn-Chi......25
Rudolph-Bos...24

Strikeouts
Vaughn-Chi......141
Eller-Cin......137
Alexander-Chi...121
Meadows-StL-Phi...116
Cooper-Pit......106

Fewest BB/Game
Adams-Pit......79
Sallee-Cin......79
J.Barnes-NY......1.07
Cadore-Bro......1.40
Alexander-Chi...1.46

Games
Tuero-StL......45
Meadows-StL-Phi...40
Vaughn-Chi......38
Eller-Cin......38
J.Barnes-NY......38

Saves
Tuero-StL......4

Base Runners/9
Adams-Pit......8.17
Alexander-Chi...8.35
J.Barnes-NY......9.13
Fisher-Cin......9.29
Miller-Pit......9.33

Adjusted Relief Runs

Relief Ranking

Innings Pitched
Vaughn-Chi......306.2
J.Barnes-NY......295.2
Cooper-Pit......286.2
Rudolph-Bos...273.2
Nehf-Bos-NY......270.2

Opponents' Avg.
Alexander-Chi...211
Adams-Pit......220
Ruether-Cin......223
Cooper-Pit......225
Nehf-Bos-NY......225

Opponents' OBP
Adams-Pit......241
Alexander-Chi...245
J.Barnes-NY......260
Fisher-Cin......271
Miller-Pit......272

Earned Run Average
Alexander-Chi...1.72
Vaughn-Chi......1.79
Ruether-Cin......1.82
Toney-NY......1.84
Adams-Pit......1.98

Adjusted ERA
Alexander-Chi...167
Vaughn-Chi......161
Ruether-Cin......152
Toney-NY......152
Adams-Pit......152

Adjusted Starter Runs
Vaughn-Chi......36.3
Alexander-Chi...33.5
Adams-Pit......29.7
Ruether-Cin......24.1
Sallee-Cin......20.2

Pitcher Wins
Alexander-Chi...4.6
Vaughn-Chi......4.3
Ruether-Cin......3.1
Adams-Pit......3.0
Sallee-Cin......2.5

The Reds Were Cheated, Too

With the war's end, attendance shot up 109 percent across the league, rising more than 90 percent in five cities. However, the NL continued to lag behind the AL in attendance, as it had throughout the decade. On the field, teams stole more than one base per game for the last time in NL history. The home run age would soon render the old rules obsolete.

With former Philadelphia skipper Pat Moran at the helm, the Cincinnati Reds used deep pitching and a speed-and-contact offense to coast to the NL flag, leaving John McGraw's Giants behind in August. Classic Dead Ball Era players like Edd Roush, Heinie Groh, and Morrie Rath fueled the attack, while former slugger Sherry Magee ended his career on the Cincinnati bench.

Second-place New York brought up another quality rookie, infielder Frankie Frisch, who soon became a star. McGraw's intellect was certainly in question when he decided to employ veteran game-fixer Hal Chase as his regular first baseman. Not only did the 36-year-old Chase provide below-average offense, he also used his influence to help fix games. For this, he was finally bounced from baseball after the season.

The Phillies, contenders two years before, tumbled into the basement after a series of ill-advised trades. Once a proud franchise, they would be laughingstocks for most of the next four decades.

Oddly enough, the two times in the decade that everyone felt the AL was a World Series cinch, the NL club pulled off an upset. This time, the Reds—who, few people seem to recall, actually had eight more regular-season wins than the White Sox—beat Chicago in eight games in the best-of-nine format. Unfortunately for the Reds, several White Sox weren't playing on the level, so their first world championship would be forever tainted despite their best efforts.

1919 American League

TEAM	W	L	T	PCT	GB	HW	HL	R	OR	PA	H	2B	3B	HR	BB	SO	HB	SH	AVG	OBP	SLG	OPS	AOPS	BR	ABR	PF	SB	CS	BSA	BSR
CHI	88	52	0	.629		48	22	667	534	5359	1343	218	70	25	427	358	34	223	.287	.351	.380	731	111	71	68	100	150			
CLE	84	55	0	.604	3.5	44	25	636	537	5322	1268	254	72	24	498	367	38	221	.278	.354	.381	735	107	83	45	106	117			
NY	80	59	2	.576	7.5	46	25	578	506	5358	1275	193	49	45	386	479	32	165	.267	.326	.356	682	96	-21	-25	101	101			
DET	80	60	0	.571	8	46	24	618	578	5328	1319	222	84	23	429	427	25	209	.283	.346	.381	727	113	61	76	98	121			
STL	67	72	1	.482	20.5	40	30	533	567	5299	1234	187	73	31	391	443	35	201	.264	.326	.355	681	95	-24	-37	103	74			
BOS	66	71	1	.482	20.5	35	30	564	552	5254	1188	181	49	33	471	411	45	190	.261	.336	.344	680	103	-9	25	94	108			
WAS	56	84	2	.400	32	32	40	533	570	5381	1238	177	63	24	416	511	40	168	.260	.325	.339	664	93	-49	-44	99	142			
PHI	36	104	0	.257	52	21	49	457	742	5230	1156	175	71	35	349	565	30	121	.244	.300	.334	634	82	-113	-118	101	103			
TOT	560					312	245	4586		42531	10021	1607	531	240	3367	3561	279	1498	.268	.333	.359	692					916			

TEAM	CG	SHO	GR	SV	IP	H	HR	BB	SO	BR/9	ERA	AERA	OAV	OOB	PR	APR	PF	OSB	OCS	FA	E	WPB	DP	FW	PW	BW	BSW	DIF
CHI	88	14	73	3	1265.2	1245	24	342	468	11.5	3.04	105	.262	.315	26	19	99	92	84	.969	176	15	116	1.6	2.0	7.1		7.2
CLE	79	10	93	10	1245.0	1242	19	362	432	11.8	2.94	114	.264	.321	39	51	104	81	75	.965	201	22	102	-.0	5.3	4.7		4.5
NY	85	14	90	7	1287.0	1143	47	433	500	11.3	2.82	113	.240	.309	58	54	99	111	88	.968	193	32	108	.7	5.7	-2.6		6.8
DET	85	10	74	4	1256.0	1254	35	436	428	12.4	3.30	97	.266	.333	-11	-14	99	128	76	.964	205	35	81	-.2	-1.5	8.0		3.7
STL	78	14	95	4	1256.0	1255	35	421	415	12.3	3.13	106	.263	.328	13	23	103	121	94	.963	215	35	98	-.8	2.4	-3.9		-.2
BOS	89	15	66	8	1224.1	1251	16	421	381	12.5	3.31	91	.275	.341	-12	-44	94	111	97	.975	140	56	118	3.8	-4.6	2.6		-4.3
WAS	68	13	97	10	1274.1	1237	20	451	536	12.2	3.01	106	.259	.328	30	28	99	120	104	.960	227	50	86	-1.4	2.9	-4.6		-10.9
PHI	72	1	89	3	1239.1	1371	44	503	417	13.8	4.26	80	.292	.364	-143	-111	106	144	118	.956	257	36	96	-3.5	-11.6	-12.4		-6.5
TOT	644	91	677	49	10047.2					12.2	3.22		.268	.333						.965	1614	281	805					

Batter-Fielder Wins	Batting Average	On-Base Percentage	Slugging Average	On-Base Plus Slugging	Adjusted OPS	Adjusted Batter Runs
Ruth-Bos ...7.3	Cobb-Det ...384	Ruth-Bos ...456	Ruth-Bos ...657	Ruth-Bos ...1114	Ruth-Bos ...224	Ruth-Bos ...76.3
Peckinpaugh-NY ..5.1	Veach-Det ...355	Cobb-Det ...429	Sisler-StL ...530	Cobb-Det ...944	Cobb-Det ...168	Cobb-Det ...44.7
Veach-Det ...4.5	Sisler-StL ...352	Jackson-Chi ...422	Veach-Det ...519	Jackson-Chi ...928	Veach-Det ...160	Jackson-Chi ...41.9
Sisler-StL ...4.4	Jackson-Chi ...351	Leibold-Chi ...404	Cobb-Det ...515	Sisler-StL ...921	Jackson-Chi ...159	Veach-Det ...40.9
Jackson-Chi ...3.3	Flagstead-Bos ...331	E.Collins-Chi ...400	Jackson-Chi ...506	Veach-Det ...916	Sisler-StL ...153	Sisler-StL ...33.3

Runs	Hits	Doubles	Triples	Home Runs	Total Bases	Runs Batted In
Ruth-Bos ...103	Veach-Det ...191	Veach-Det ...45	Veach-Det ...17	Ruth-Bos ...29	Ruth-Bos ...284	Ruth-Bos ...114
Sisler-StL ...96	Cobb-Det ...191	Speaker-Cle ...38	Sisler-StL ...15	T.Walker-Phi ...10	Veach-Det ...279	Veach-Det ...101
Cobb-Det ...92	Jackson-Chi ...181	Cobb-Det ...36	Heilmann-Det ...15	Sisler-StL ...10	Sisler-StL ...271	Jackson-Chi ...96
Weaver-Chi ...89	Sisler-StL ...180	O'Neill-Cle ...35	Jackson-Chi ...14	Baker-NY ...10	Jackson-Chi ...261	Heilmann-Det ...93
Peckinpaugh-NY ...89	Rice-Was ...179		Cobb-Det ...13	Smith-Cle ...9		Lewis-NY ...89

Stolen Bases	Base Stealing Runs	Fielding Runs-Infield	Fielding Runs-Outfield	Wins	Winning Pct.	Complete Games
E.Collins-Chi ...33		Peckinpaugh-NY ...25.5	Felsch-Chi ...17.4	Cicotte-Chi ...29	Cicotte-Chi ...806	Cicotte-Chi ...30
Sisler-StL ...28		Pratt-NY ...24.6	Speaker-Cle ...14.8	Coveleski-Cle ...24	Dauss-Det ...700	Williams-Chi ...27
Cobb-Det ...28		Vitt-Bos ...17.9	Ruth-Bos ...9.3	Williams-Chi ...23	Williams-Chi ...676	Johnson-Was ...27
Rice-Was ...26		Sisler-StL ...13.1	Veach-Det ...9.0	Dauss-Det ...21	Pennock-Bos ...667	Mays-Bos-NY ...26
		Wambsganss-Cle ...11.1	Leibold-Chi ...7.7		Coveleski-Cle ...667	Coveleski-Cle ...24

Strikeouts	Fewest BB/Game	Games	Saves	Base Runners/9	Adjusted Relief Runs	Relief Ranking
Johnson-Was ...147	Cicotte-Chi ...1.44	Shaw-Was ...45	Russell-NY-Bos ...5	Cicotte-Chi ...9.01	Phillips-Cle ...1.1	Phillips-Cle ...9
Shaw-Was ...128	Johnson-Was ...1.58	Russell-NY-Bos ...44	Shawkey-NY ...5	Johnson-Was ...9.08		
Williams-Chi ...125	Bagby-Cle ...1.64	Kinney-Phi ...43	Shaw-Was ...5	Williams-Chi ...10.12		
Shawkey-NY ...122	Williams-Chi ...1.76	Coveleski-Cle ...43	Coveleski-Cle ...4	Hoyt-Bos ...10.34		
Coveleski-Cle ...118	Coveleski-Cle ...1.89			Thormahlen-NY ...10.49		

Innings Pitched	Opponents' Avg.	Opponents' OBP	Earned Run Average	Adjusted ERA	Adjusted Starter Runs	Pitcher Wins
Shaw-Was ...306.2	Johnson-Was ...219	Johnson-Was ...259	Johnson-Was ...1.49	Johnson-Was ...215	Johnson-Was ...52.4	Johnson-Was ...6.7
Cicotte-Chi ...306.2	Cicotte-Chi ...228	Cicotte-Chi ...261	Cicotte-Chi ...1.82	Cicotte-Chi ...175	Cicotte-Chi ...47.2	Cicotte-Chi ...5.5
Williams-Chi ...297.0	Thormahlen-NY ...228	Williams-Chi ...289	Weilman-StL ...2.07	Weilman-StL ...160	Sothoron-StL ...26.7	Coveleski-Cle ...3.9
Johnson-Was ...290.1	Shawkey-NY ...231	Morton-Cle ...293	Mays-Bos-StL ...2.10	Sothoron-StL ...151	Coveleski-Cle ...26.2	Mays-Bos-NY ...3.1
Coveleski-Cle ...286.0	Mays-Bos-NY ...233	Quinn-NY ...295	Sothoron-StL ...2.20	Mays-Bos-NY ...147	Mays-Bos-NY ...25.5	Sothoron-StL ...2.5

Earthquake

With the war over, and the players back to their teams, baseball could resume as normal. Except nothing about 1919 was normal. First of all, the schedule was set at 140 games, with a nine-game World Series proposed to recoup lost gates. The extra games gave the gamblers infiltrating baseball more incentive to push their agenda, but nobody could see this at the time.

The season's biggest story was the way baseballs flew out of the parks. With Babe Ruth given a chance to play every day for Boston, the game changed entirely as he clouted an amazing 29 homers to set an all-time mark. Other players followed his example; four-baggers increased by 150 percent to 240, setting a new league record that would be broken each of the next three years.

This rise in long balls came with no appreciable rise in strikeouts, but stolen bases—the run-creating method of the scratch-out-a-run Dead Ball Era—fell to a new low. Old-school baseball men pointed out that Ruth's team finished 20½ games out, but part of the reason was because one of the league's best left-handers no longer took his regular turn in the Red Sox rotation. Boston's team ERA increased by a full run; the league ERA was up by half a run.

The peacetime economy and the excitement over Ruth's exploits caused attendance to rise in every AL city, increasing the league's turnstile clicks by 114 percent. Chicago and Detroit saw attendance increases of over 200 percent. While the White Sox had good battles from the Indians and Tigers, Chicago had the most talent in the league and pulled away, withstanding a late Cleveland charge to take the flag by 3½. An aggressive, intelligent bunch, the Sox could hit, run, field, and pitch like nobody's business.

Few knew that this White Sox team, which played so well together, was divided by class, temperament, and greed. Chicago's surprise World Series loss to Cincinnati raised red flags.

1918 National League

TEAM	W	L	T	PCT	GB	HW	HL	R	OR	PA	H	2B	3B	HR	BB	SO	HB	SH	AVG	OBP	SLG	OPS	AOPS	BR	ABR	PF	SB	CS	BSA	BSR
CHI	84	45	2	.651		49	25	538	393	4900	1147	164	53	21	358	343	27	190	.265	.325	.342	667	106	50	37	103	159			
NY	71	53	0	.573	10.5	35	21	480	415	4589	1081	150	53	13	271	365	33	121	.260	.310	.330	640	103	2	11	98	130			
CIN	68	60	1	.531	15.5	46	24	530	496	4762	1185	165	84	15	304	303	31	162	.278	.330	.366	696	120	86	96	98	128			
PIT	65	60	1	.520	17	42	28	466	412	4667	1016	107	72	15	371	285	25	180	.248	.315	.321	636	96	-1	-16	103	200			
BRO	57	69	0	.452	25.5	33	21	360	463	4578	1052	121	62	10	212	326	36	118	.250	.291	.315	606	90	-57	-55	100	113			
PHI	55	68	2	.447	26	27	29	430	507	4677	1022	158	28	25	346	400	20	119	.244	.305	.313	618	88	-25	-52	107	97			
BOS	53	71	0	.427	28.5	23	29	424	469	4691	1014	107	59	13	350	438	28	151	.244	.307	.307	614	97	-33	-14	96	83			
STL	51	78	2	.395	33	32	40	454	527	4863	1066	147	64	27	329	461	24	141	.244	.301	.325	626	99	-22	-6	97	119			
TOT	508					287	217	3682		37727	8583	1119	475	139	2541	2921	224	1182	.254	.311	.328	638					1029			

TEAM	CG	SHO	GR	SV	IP	H	HR	BB	SO	BR/9	ERA	AERA	OAV	OOB	PR	APR	PF	OSB	OCS	FA	E	WPB	DP	FW	PW	BW	BSW	DIF
CHI	92	23	52	8	1197.0	1050	13	296	472	10.3	2.18	128	.239	.291	77	80	101	121	100	.966	188	31	91	.5	8.9	4.1		5.9
NY	74	18	71	11	1111.2	1002	20	228	330	10.1	2.64	100	.243	.287	15	-1	95	131	63	.971	152	30	78	2.1	-.1	1.2		5.8
CIN	84	14	62	6	1142.1	1136	19	381	321	12.1	3.00	89	.268	.332	-30	-44	97	118	107	.964	192	30	127	.0	-4.9	10.7		-1.9
PIT	85	10	52	7	1140.1	1005	13	299	367	10.5	2.48	116	.243	.300	36	49	104	74	103	.966	179	19	108	.6	5.5	-1.8		-1.8
BRO	85	17	51	2	1131.1	1024	22	320	395	10.9	2.81	99	.248	.307	-6	-4	101	144	111	.963	193	50	74	-.3	-.4	-6.1		.9
PHI	78	10	61	6	1139.2	1086	22	369	312	11.7	3.15	95	.258	.323	-49	-19	109	133	99	.961	211	38	91	-1.5	-2.1	-5.8		3.0
BOS	96	13	31	0	1117.1	1111	14	277	340	11.4	2.90	93	.266	.316	-17	-28	97	144	101	.965	184	21	89	.0	-3.1	-1.6		-4.4
STL	72	3	79	5	1193.0	1148	16	352	361	11.6	2.96	91	.261	.321	-27	-34	98	164	119	.962	220	21	116	-1.5	-3.8	-.7		-7.5
TOT	666	108	459	45	9172.2					11.1	2.76		.254	.311						.965	1519	240	774					

Batter-Fielder Wins		Batting Average		On-Base Percentage		Slugging Average		On-Base Plus Slugging		Adjusted OPS		Adjusted Batter Runs	
Groh-Cin	4.1	Z.Wheat-Bro	335	Groh-Cin	395	Roush-Cin	455	Roush-Cin	823	Roush-Cin	153	Groh-Cin	29.5
Hornsby-StL	3.8	Roush-Cin	333	Hollocher-Chi	379	Daubert-Bro	416	Groh-Cin	791	Groh-Cin	144	Roush-Cin	25.5
Fletcher-NY	3.3	Groh-Cin	320	R.Smith-Bos	373	Hornsby-StL	416	Daubert-Bro	789	S.Magee-Cin	142	Hollocher-Chi	21.7
Fisher-StL	3.0	Hollocher-Chi	316	S.Magee-Cin	370	S.Magee-Cin	415	S.Magee-Cin	785	Daubert-Bro	141	S.Magee-Cin	20.2
R.Smith-Bos	2.9	Daubert-Bro	308	Z.Wheat-Bro	369	Wickland-Bos	398	Hollocher-Chi	775	Wickland-Bos	139	R.Smith-Bos	19.4

Runs		Hits		Doubles		Triples		Home Runs		Total Bases		Runs Batted In	
Groh-Cin	86	Hollocher-Chi	161	Groh-Cin	28	Daubert-Bro	15	Cravath-Phi	8	Hollocher-Chi	202	S.Magee-Cin	76
Burns-NY	80	Groh-Cin	158	Mann-Chi	27	Wickland-Bos	13	Williams-Phi	6	Roush-Cin	198	Cutshaw-Pit	68
Flack-Chi	74	Roush-Cin	145	Cravath-Phi	27	S.Magee-Cin	13	Cruise-StL	6	Groh-Cin	195	Luderus-Phi	67
Hollocher-Chi	72	Youngs-NY	143	Meusel-Phi	25	L.Magee-Cin	13			Mann-Chi	188	R.Smith-Bos	65
		Merkle-Chi	143	Merkle-Chi	25					Merkle-Chi	187	Merkle-Chi	65

Stolen Bases		Base Stealing Runs		Fielding Runs-Infield		Fielding Runs-Outfield		Wins		Winning Pct.		Complete Games	
Carey-Pit	58			Fletcher-NY	24.8	Carey-Pit	13.0	Vaughn-Chi	22	Hendrix-Chi	741	Nehf-Bos	28
Burns-NY	40			Bancroft-Phi	16.3	Burns-NY	9.2	Hendrix-Chi	20	Tyler-Chi	704	Vaughn-Chi	27
Hollocher-Chi	26			Blackburne-Cin	11.1	Myers-Bro	7.9	Tyler-Chi	19	Mayer-Phi-Pit	696	Cooper-Pit	26
Cutshaw-Pit	25			Doolan-Bro	9.5	Neale-Cin	6.8	Grimes-Bro	19	Vaughn-Chi	688	Tyler-Chi	22
Baird-StL	25			Hornsby-StL	9.4	Roush-Cin	5.0	Cooper-Pit	19	Grimes-Bro	679	Hendrix-Chi	21

Strikeouts		Fewest BB/Game		Games		Saves		Base Runners/9		Adjusted Relief Runs		Relief Ranking	
Vaughn-Chi	148	Sallee-NY	.82	Grimes-Bro	40	Toney-Cin-NY	3	Sallee-NY	9.14				
Cooper-Pit	117	Perritt-NY	1.47	Cooper-Pit	38	Oeschger-Phi	3	Vaughn-Chi	9.27				
Grimes-Bro	113	G.Smith-Cin-NY-Bro	1.50	Eller-Cin	37	Cooper-Pit	3	Harmon-Pit	9.62				
Tyler-Chi	102	Toney-Cin-NY	1.54			Anderson-NY	3	Grimes-Bro	9.67				
Nehf-Bos	96	Demaree-NY	1.58					Cooper-Pit	9.68				

Innings Pitched		Opponents' Avg.		Opponents' OBP		Earned Run Average		Adjusted ERA		Adjusted Starter Runs		Pitcher Wins	
Vaughn-Chi	290.1	Vaughn-Chi	208	Sallee-NY	259	Vaughn-Chi	1.74	Vaughn-Chi	161	Vaughn-Chi	34.0	Vaughn-Chi	4.5
Nehf-Bos	284.1	Grimes-Bro	216	Vaughn-Chi	266	Tyler-Chi	2.00	Tyler-Chi	139	Tyler-Chi	26.6	Tyler-Chi	3.2
Cooper-Pit	273.1	Cooper-Pit	223	Grimes-Bro	276	Cooper-Pit	2.11	Cooper-Pit	136	Cooper-Pit	21.6	Cooper-Pit	3.0
Grimes-Bro	270.0	Tyler-Chi	226	Perritt-NY	278	Douglas-Chi	2.13	Douglas-Chi	131	Grimes-Bro	15.6	Grimes-Bro	1.9
Tyler-Chi	269.1	Jacobs-Pit-Phi	233	Cooper-Pit	279	Grimes-Bro	2.13	Grimes-Bro	131	Hamilton-Pit	11.6	Hogg-Phi	1.8

The Abbreviated Race

World War I threatened to shut down the major leagues, and baseball saved face by agreeing to stop play on Labor Day. The loss of many regular players and pitchers to military jobs or combat assignments meant that expectations of who would win were completely thrown off.

The surprising Chicago Cubs, sparked by a big rookie season from infielder Charlie Hollocher, were up by 10½ games when the merry-go-round stopped. A good schedule, crammed with lots of early home games, helped; so did the great season of Jim "Hippo" Vaughn, the league's top pitcher.

The war, and its resultant drain on spectators and disposable income, brought league attendance down another 42 percent. Of course, there were fewer games, which decreased total tickets sold, but average attendance was down everywhere except Pittsburgh. For first time, batters' strikeouts declined to below three per game; they would remain less than three through 1929.

Part of the reason strikeouts were down? Grover Cleveland Alexander had entered the service. The war forced some teams to use very old and very young players. Pittsburgh brought back 40-year-old Tommy Leach as a utilityman; 38-year-old Mickey Doolan hit .179 as Brooklyn's second sacker. The last-place Cardinals, hit very hard by the war, used both 19-year-old Charlie Grimm and 44-year-old Bobby Wallace.

In the World Series, played by special government order, the Cubs and Red Sox nearly boycotted over their low shares, but finally took the field. Boston won in six games in the only World Series to end before the second week of September.

First baseman Jack Beckley, owner of 2,934 career hits for four NL clubs, died at age 51, but his death didn't merit quite the attention given Eddie Grant, the first player killed in World War I. The veteran infielder died in October in the Argonne Forest of France.

1918 American League

TEAM	W	L	T	PCT	GB	HW	HL	R	OR	PA	H	2B	3B	HR	BB	SO	HB	SH	AVG	OBP	SLG	OPS	AOPS	BR	ABR	PF	SB	CS	BSA	BSR
BOS	75	51	0	.595		49	21	474	380	4609	990	159	54	15	407	324	27	193	.249	.322	.327	649	103	7	15	98	110			
CLE	73	54	2	.575	2.5	38	22	504	447	4869	1084	176	67	9	491	386	42	170	.260	.344	.341	685	102	70	23	110	171			
WAS	72	56	2	.563	4	41	32	461	412	5017	1144	156	49	4	376	361	35	134	.256	.318	.315	633	98	-22	-14	98	137			
NY	60	63	3	.488	13.5	37	29	493	475	4785	1085	160	45	20	367	370	23	171	.257	.320	.330	650	99	2	-8	102	92			
STL	58	64	1	.475	15	23	30	426	448	4627	1040	152	40	5	397	340	35	176	.259	.331	.320	651	105	13	28	97	139			
CHI	57	67	0	.460	17	30	26	457	446	4698	1057	136	55	8	375	358	27	164	.256	.322	.321	643	103	-8	-11	101	119			
DET	55	71	2	.437	20	28	29	476	557	4879	1063	141	56	13	452	380	22	143	.249	.325	.318	643	103	-2	18	96	123			
PHI	52	76	2	.406	24	35	32	412	538	4777	1039	124	44	22	343	485	26	130	.243	.303	.308	611	88	-62	-66	101	83			
TOT	508					281	221	3703		38261	8502	1204	410	96	3208	3004	237	1281	.254	.323	.322	646					974			

TEAM	CG	SHO	GR	SV	IP	H	HR	BB	SO	BR/9	ERA	AERA	OAV	OOB	PR	APR	PF	OSB	OCS	FA	E	WPB	DP	FW	PW	BW	BSW	DIF
BOS	105	26	28	2	1120.0	931	9	380	392	10.8	2.31	116	.231	.302	58	49	97	112	92	.971	152	38	89	2.5	5.5	1.7		2.4
CLE	78	5	67	13	1161.0	1126	9	343	364	11.5	2.64	114	.262	.319	18	42	108	93	93	.962	207	24	82	-.7	4.7	2.6		2.9
WAS	75	19	74	8	1228.0	1021	10	395	505	10.6	2.14	127	.231	.298	86	81	98	126	101	.960	226	53	95	-1.8	9.0	-1.6		2.3
NY	59	8	88	13	1157.1	1103	25	463	370	12.5	3.00	94	.261	.340	-30	-23	102	106	92	.970	161	25	137	-2.6	-.9			.0
STL	67	8	79	8	1111.1	993	11	402	346	11.5	2.75	99	.246	.319	2	-2	99	140	96	.963	190	25	86	-.2	-.2	3.1		-5.7
CHI	76	9	68	8	1126.0	1092	9	300	349	11.3	2.73	100	.261	.314	5	-3	99	97	74	.967	169	24	98	1.2	-.3	-1.2		-4.7
DET	74	8	76	7	1160.2	1130	10	437	374	12.4	3.40	78	.263	.335	-81	-104	96	157	105	.960	212	33	77	-1.1	-11.6	2.0		2.7
PHI	80	13	67	9	1156.0	1106	13	486	277	12.7	3.22	91	.266	.348	-58	-37	106	146	124	.959	228	27	136	-1.9	-4.1	-7.4		1.4
TOT	614	96	547	68	9220.1					11.7	2.77		.254	.323						.964	1545	249	800					

Batter-Fielder Wins
- T.Cobb-Det 4.3
- Sisler-StL 4.0
- Burns-Phi 3.8
- Chapman-Cle 3.0
- Baker-NY 2.9

Batting Average
- T.Cobb-Det 382
- Burns-Phi 352
- Sisler-StL 341
- Speaker-Cle 318
- Baker-NY 306

On-Base Percentage
- T.Cobb-Det 440
- E.Collins-Chi 407
- Speaker-Cle 403
- Sisler-StL 400
- Hooper-Bos 391

Slugging Average
- Ruth-Bos 555
- T.Cobb-Det 515
- Burns-Phi 467
- Sisler-StL 440
- Speaker-Cle 435

On-Base Plus Slugging
- T.Cobb-Det 955
- Burns-Phi 857
- Sisler-StL 841
- Speaker-Cle 839
- Hooper-Bos 796

Adjusted OPS
- T.Cobb-Det 196
- Sisler-StL 159
- Burns-Phi 157
- Hooper-Bos 142
- Speaker-Cle 140

Adjusted Batter Runs
- T.Cobb-Det 47.7
- Ruth-Bos 37.5
- Burns-Phi 31.8
- Sisler-StL 31.5
- Hooper-Bos 27.3

Runs
- Chapman-Cle 84
- T.Cobb-Det 83
- Hooper-Bos 81
- Bush-Det 74
- Speaker-Cle 73

Hits
- Burns-Phi 178
- T.Cobb-Det 161
- Sisler-StL 154
- Baker-NY 154
- Speaker-Cle 150

Doubles
- Speaker-Cle 33
- Ruth-Bos 26
- Hooper-Bos 26
- Baker-NY 24

Triples
- T.Cobb-Det 14
- Veach-Det 13
- Hooper-Bos 13
- Roth-Cle 12

Home Runs
- Walker-Phi 11
- Ruth-Bos 11
- Burns-Phi 6
- Baker-NY 6

Total Bases
- Burns-Phi 236
- T.Cobb-Det 217
- Baker-NY 206
- Speaker-Cle 205
- Sisler-StL 199

Runs Batted In
- Veach-Det 78
- Burns-Phi 70
- Wood-Cle 66
- Ruth-Bos 66
- T.Cobb-Det 64

Stolen Bases
- Sisler-StL 45
- Roth-Cle 36
- Chapman-Cle 35
- T.Cobb-Det 34
- Speaker-Cle 27

Base Stealing Runs

Fielding Runs-Infield
- Peckinpaugh-NY ..22.1
- Scott-Bos 20.8
- Dugan-Phi 16.7
- Gedeon-StL 15.6
- Gardner-Phi 12.8

Fielding Runs-Outfield
- S.Collins-Chi 11.8
- Kopp-Phi 9.8
- Demmitt-StL 9.2
- Speaker-Cle 8.4
- Leibold-Chi 7.3

Wins
- Johnson-Was 23
- Coveleski-Cle 22
- Mays-Bos 21
- Perry-Phi 20
- Bagby-Cle 17

Winning Pct.
- Jones-Bos 762
- Johnson-Was 639
- Coveleski-Cle 629
- Mays-Bos 618
- Shaw-Was 571

Complete Games
- Perry-Phi 30
- Mays-Bos 30
- Johnson-Was 29
- Bush-Bos 26
- Coveleski-Cle 25

Strikeouts
- Johnson-Was 162
- Shaw-Was 129
- Bush-Bos 125
- Morton-Cle 123
- Mays-Bos 114

Fewest BB/Game
- Cicotte-Chi 1.35
- Mogridge-NY 1.62
- Benz-Chi 1.64
- Enzmann-Cle 1.91
- Johnson-Was 1.93

Games
- Mogridge-NY 45
- Bagby-Cle 45
- Perry-Phi 44
- Shaw-Was 41
- Ayers-Was 40

Saves
- Mogridge-NY 7
- Bagby-Cle 6
- Russell-NY 4
- Geary-Phi 4

Base Runners/9
- Johnson-Was 8.81
- Ruth-Bos 9.52
- Sothoron-StL 9.56
- Matteson-Was 9.71
- Wright-StL 9.86

Adjusted Relief Runs
- Houck-StL 3.2

Relief Ranking
- Houck-StL 2.6

Innings Pitched
- Perry-Phi 332.1
- Johnson-Was 326.0
- Coveleski-Cle 311.0
- Mays-Bos 293.1
- Bush-Bos 272.2

Opponents' Avg.
- Sothoron-StL 205
- Johnson-Was 210
- Harper-Was 212
- Ruth-Bos 214
- Mays-Bos 221

Opponents' OBP
- Johnson-Was 260
- Sothoron-StL 274
- Ruth-Bos 277
- Coveleski-Cle 279
- Mays-Bos 284

Earned Run Average
- Johnson-Was 1.27
- Coveleski-Cle 1.82
- Sothoron-StL 1.94
- Perry-Phi 1.98
- Bush-Bos 2.11

Adjusted ERA
- Johnson-Was 214
- Coveleski-Cle 164
- Perry-Phi 148
- Sothoron-StL 141
- Mogridge-NY 129

Adjusted Starter Runs
- Johnson-Was 51.4
- Coveleski-Cle 35.0
- Perry-Phi 32.5
- Harper-Was 17.3
- Sothoron-StL 16.9

Pitcher Wins
- Johnson-Was 7.6
- Coveleski-Cle 3.9
- Mays-Bos 3.7
- Perry-Phi 3.5
- Ruth-Bos 2.9

The Babe Does It All

Baseball's worst nightmare came true in 1918. Baseball had been declared a non-essential industry, forcing many players into military service or war-related jobs. The game shut down before it was forced to by the government. As a result, the Boston Red Sox were able to eke out a pennant when the abbreviated season ended on Labor Day. The defending champion White Sox lost Eddie Collins, Swede Risberg, Happy Felsch, Joe Jackson, Red Faber, and Lefty Williams; Chicago fell to sixth.

Boston had Carl Mays do the majority of heavy mound work, while Babe Ruth was 13-7 on the hill and hit .300 with 11 homers (tied for the league lead) in the outfield. Cleveland nearly scraped out a flag, but aside from Stan Coveleski, the pitching wasn't strong. Walter Johnson again was the league's top hurler, and the Senators were the only team with increased attendance.

This was a deadened form of baseball; homers fell to just .09 per game—only 1907 saw a lower percentage. Never again would a league hit fewer than the AL's 96 home runs. The average AL team tallied just 3.64 runs a game, the lowest production until 1968. The league's watered-down quality also meant parity. Last-place Philadelphia ended up just 24 out, a relative godsend for Connie Mack's sad crew. Eighteen-year-old Waite Hoyt debuted, and Smokey Joe Wood, forced to retire from the mound in 1915 because of a sore arm, resurrected his career as the right fielder for old pal Tris Speaker's Indians.

In a World Series held through special dispensation from the war department, the Red Sox won in six. Ruth and Mays each won twice as no team scored over 3 runs in a game. Boston took the Series despite being outscored (10-9), outhit (.210-.186), and outpitched (the Cubs' ERA was 1.04, Boston's 1.70). This bittersweet victory was one Boston would have to learn to savor. The club's fifth world championship in fifteen years would be their last of the century.

1917 National League

TEAM	W	L	T	PCT	GB	HW	HL	R	OR	PA	H	2B	3B	HR	BB	SO	HB	SH	AVG	OBP	SLG	OPS	AOPS	BR	ABR	PF	SB	CS	BSA	BSR
NY	98	56	4	.636		**50**	28	**635**	457	5787	1360	170	71	39	373	533	52	151	**.261**	**.317**	.343	660	113	50	70	97	**162**			
PHI	87	65	2	.572	10	46	29	578	500	5725	1262	**225**	60	38	**435**	533	20	186	.248	.310	.339	649	101	35	12	104	109			
STL	82	70	2	.539	15	38	38	531	567	5626	1271	159	93	26	359	652	24	160	.250	.303	.333	636	104	-1	14	97	159			
CIN	78	76	3	.506	20	39	38	601	611	5728	**1385**	196	**100**	26	312	477	34	131	**.264**	.309	**.354**	**663**	114	46	**72**	96	153			
CHI	74	80	3	.481	24	35	42	552	567	5775	1229	194	67	17	415	599	23	**202**	.239	.299	.313	612	86	-33	-71	108	127			
BOS	72	81	4	.471	25.5	35	42	536	552	5855	1280	169	75	22	427	587	45	182	.246	.309	.320	629	105	-2	32	94	155			
BRO	70	81	5	.464	26.5	36	38	511	559	5776	1299	159	78	25	334	527	29	162	.247	.296	.322	618	93	-35	-49	103	130			
PIT	51	103	3	.331	47	25	53	464	595	5788	1230	160	61	9	399	580	46	174	.238	.298	.298	596	86	-61	-76	103	150			
TOT	625					304	308	4408		46060	10316	1432	605	202	3054	4488	273	1348	.249	.305	.328	633					1145			

TEAM	CG	SHO	GR	SV	IP	H	HR	BB	SO	BR/9	ERA	AERA	OAV	OOB	PR	APR	PF	OSB	OCS	FA	E	WPB	DP	FW	PW	BW	BSW	DIF
NY	92	18	97	**14**	1426.2	**1221**	29	327	551	**9.9**	**2.27**	112	**.234**	**.283**	69	45	94	136	63	**.968**	208	31	122	**1.8**	5.1	7.9		6.2
PHI	102	**22**	65	5	1389.0	1258	25	**325**	616	10.5	2.46	**114**	.246	.295	38	**51**	104	125	**109**	.967	212	36	112	1.2	**5.8**	1.4		2.7
STL	66	16	**140**	10	1392.2	1257	29	421	502	11.1	3.03	89	.248	.311	-51	-55	99	**115**	124	.967	221	39	**153**	.6	-6.2	1.6		10.0
CIN	94	12	85	6	1397.1	1358	20	402	488	11.5	2.70	97	.260	.317	1	-15	97	159	116	.962	247	40	120	-.7	-1.7	**8.1**		-4.8
CHI	79	16	121	9	1404.0	1303	34	374	**654**	10.9	2.62	110	.253	.307	14	38	107	146	**127**	.959	267	63	121	-1.9	4.3	-8.0		2.6
BOS	**103**	21	81	3	1424.2	1309	19	371	593	10.8	2.77	92	.251	.304	-10	-40	94	126	116	.966	224	45	122	.7	-4.5	3.6		-4.3
BRO	99	8	81	9	1421.1	1288	32	405	582	11.0	2.78	100	.247	.307	-12	0	103	144	**106**	.962	245	40	102	-.7	.0	-5.5		.7
PIT	84	17	84	6	1417.2	1318	**14**	432	509	11.3	3.01	94	.253	.314	-48	-28	105	194	**129**	.961	251	43	119	-.9	-3.2	-8.6		-13.3
TOT	719	130	754	62	11273.1					10.9	2.70		.249	.305						.964	1875	337	971					

Batter-Fielder Wins	Batting Average	On-Base Percentage	Slugging Average	On-Base Plus Slugging	Adjusted OPS	Adjusted Batter Runs
Hornsby-StL..........7.8	Roush-Cin 341	Groh-Cin................385	Hornsby-StL 484	Hornsby-StL 868	Hornsby-StL 170	Hornsby-StL 42.4
Groh-Cin 5.8	Hornsby-StL 327	Hornsby-StL 385	Cravath-Phi 473	Cravath-Phi 842	Roush-Cin 162	Groh-Cin 39.7
Fletcher-NY 4.5	Z.Wheat-Bro...........312	Burns-NY 380	Roush-Cin 454	Roush-Cin 833	Cravath-Phi 151	Burns-NY 36.1
Bancroft-Phi 3.6	Kauff-NY 308	Roush-Cin 379	Z.Wheat-Bro...........423	Groh-Cin 796	Groh-Cin 150	Roush-Cin 35.7
Burns-NY 3.5	Groh-Cin 304	Kauff-NY 379	Burns-NY................412	Burns-NY..............792	Burns-NY 148	Cravath-Phi 31.8

Runs	Hits	Doubles	Triples	Home Runs	Total Bases	Runs Batted In
Burns-NY...............103	Groh-Cin 182	Groh-Cin................39	Hornsby-StL 17	Robertson-NY 12	Hornsby-StL 253	Zimmerman-NY.......102
Groh-Cin 91	Burns-NY................180	Merkle-Bro-Chi 31	Cravath-Phi 16	Cravath-Phi 12	Groh-Cin 246	Chase-Cin 86
Kauff-NY 89	Roush-Cin 178	Smith-Bos 31	Chase-Cin 15	Hornsby-StL 8	Burns-NY 246	Cravath-Phi 83
Hornsby-StL 86	Zimmerman-NY 174	Cravath-Phi 29	Roush-Cin 14		Cravath-Phi 238	Stengel-Bro 73
	Carey-Pit 174	Chase-Cin 28	Long-StL 14			Luderus-Phi.............72

Stolen Bases	Base Stealing Runs	Fielding Runs-Infield	Fielding Runs-Outfield	Wins	Winning Pct.	Complete Games
Carey-Pit 46		Bancroft-Phi 28.0	Carey-Pit 21.3	Alexander-Phi 30	Schupp-NY 750	Alexander-Phi 34
Burns-NY................40		Fletcher-NY 27.8	Stengel-Bro 11.3	Toney-Cin 24	Sallee-NY 720	Toney-Cin 31
Kauff-NY.................30		Hornsby-StL 19.0	Williams-Chi 10.8	Vaughn-Chi 23	Perritt-NY 708	Vaughn-Chi 27
Maranville-Bos.........27		Shean-Cin 17.4	King-Pit..................7.6	Schupp-NY 21	Alexander-Phi........698	Barnes-Bos 26
Baird-Pit-StL 26		Miller-StL 17.2	Griffith-Cin 7.0	Schneider-Cin 20	Nehf-Bos 680	Schupp-NY 25

Strikeouts	Fewest BB/Game	Games	Saves	Base Runners/9	Adjusted Relief Runs	Relief Ranking
Alexander-Phi 200	Alexander-Phi........1.30	Douglas-Chi 51	Sallee-NY 4	Anderson-NY 8.78		
Vaughn-Chi 195	Sallee-NY 1.42	Barnes-Bos 50		Schupp-NY...............9.13		
Douglas-Chi 151	Nehf-Bos 1.50	Schneider-Cin..........46		Alexander-Phi...........9.23		
Schupp-NY 147	Barnes-Bos 1.53	Alexander-Phi 45		Nehf-Bos 9.26		
Schneider-Cin 138	Douglas-Chi 1.53	Doak-StL 44		Bender-Phi...............9.32		

Innings Pitched	Opponents' Avg.	Opponents' OBP	Earned Run Average	Adjusted ERA	Adjusted Starter Runs	Pitcher Wins
Alexander-Phi.......388.0	Schupp-NY 209	Anderson-NY 255	Alexander-Phi.........1.83	Anderson-NY..........176	Alexander-Phi........39.3	**Alexander-Phi** 5.4
Toney-Cin 339.2	Anderson-NY 209	Schupp-NY............265	Anderson-NY 1.44	Alexander-Phi 153	Vaughn-Chi 25.3	**Vaughn-Chi**........3.4
Schneider-Cin........333.2	Nehf-Bos 231	Alexander-Phi 266	Perritt-NY...............1.88	Vaughn-Chi 144	Schupp-NY 21.5	**Schupp-NY**.........2.2
Cooper-Pit 297.2	Marquard-Bro 232	Nehf-Bos 268	Schupp-NY..............1.95	Perritt-NY...............135	Anderson-NY 18.1	**Rixey-Phi** 1.8
Vaughn-Chi 295.2	Pfeffer-Bro 234	Barnes-Bos 277	Vaughn-Chi 2.01	Schupp-NY.............130	Toney-Cin 16.7	**Cadore-Bro**..........1.7

Trouble Looming

The flag drive was never in doubt after June, as the Giants pulled away from the Phillies to win by 10 games. New York outfielder George Burns was the league's only 100-run man, and John McGraw used six quality starters. In Philadelphia, Grover Cleveland Alexander won 30 games for the third straight season, but his team didn't hit much.

Defending champion Brooklyn left the gate slowly and dropped all the way from first to seventh; their attack was too thin to help a decent pitching rotation. The Pirates dropped into the NL cellar for first time in the twentieth century, finishing 47 games from first place. Honus Wagner, a preseason holdout at 43, played his last season and hit just .265. St. Louis finished third, the franchise's best performance since joining the NL in 1892. Their top performer was infielder Rogers Hornsby. A 20-year-old outfielder named Ross Youngs debuted late in the year for the Giants. Room would be made for him in 1918.

In this, the twilight of the Dead Ball Era, even stolen bases fell to their lowest level yet as pitchers continued to deface, scuff, spit on, and otherwise render the baseball unhitable. No NL club had ever led the league with so few steals as New York's 162.

Following two years of gains, league attendance fell; only rejuvenated St. Louis reported an appreciable gain in tickets sold. For the Senior Circuit, at least, the hoped-for gains of the post-Federal League era had not yet materialized, and the coming conflict in Europe would take another bite out of baseball.

The phonograph record was a recent invention, and the World Series' platter was already skipping. Again the AL defeated the Senior Circuit's representative, with the White Sox putting lumps on the Giants' pitchers in a six-game set.

1917 American League

TEAM	W	L	T	PCT	GB	HW	HL	R	OR	PA	H	2B	3B	HR	BB	SO	HB	SH	AVG	OBP	SLG	OPS	AOPS	BR	ABR	PF	SB	CS	BSA	BSR
CHI	100	54	2	.649		**56**	21	**655**	463	5858	1281	152	18	**81**	522	479	**47**	232	.253	**.329**	.326	655	103	34	22	102	**219**			
BOS	90	62	5	.592	9	45	33	555	**455**	5858	1243	198	64	14	466	**473**	34	**310**	.246	.314	.319	633	100	-9	-3	99	105			
CLE	88	66	2	.571	12	43	34	584	543	5840	1224	**218**	64	13	**549**	596	35	262	.245	.324	.322	646	96	25	-16	107	210			
DET	78	75	1	.510	21.5	34	41	639	577	5814	**1317**	204	77	25	483	476	45	193	.259	.328	**.344**	672	111	62	65	100	163			
WAS	74	79	4	.484	25.5	42	36	544	566	5861	1238	173	70	4	500	574	43	176	.241	.313	.304	617	95	-35	-28	99	166			
NY	71	82	2	.464	28.5	35	40	524	558	5858	1226	172	52	27	496	535	38	188	.239	.310	.308	618	93	-34	-39	101	136			
STL	57	97	1	.370	43	31	46	510	687	5694	1250	183	63	15	405	540	31	167	.246	.305	.315	620	98	-40	-20	96	157			
PHI	55	98	1	.359	44.5	29	47	529	691	5780	1296	177	62	17	435	519	33	203	.254	.316	.323	639	101	-2	6	99	112			
TOT	622					315	298	4540		46563	10075	1477	533	133	3856	4192	306	1731	.248	.318	.320	638					1268			

TEAM	CG	SHO	GR	SV	IP	H	HR	BB	SO	BR/9	ERA	AERA	OAV	OOB	PR	APR	PF	OSB	OCS	FA	E	WPB	DP	FW	PW	BW	BSW	DIF
CHI	78	**22**	112	21	1424.1	1236	10	413	517	10.6	**2.16**	123	.238	.298	79	**76**	100	**108**	110	.967	204	**22**	117	2.3	**8.5**	2.4		9.8
BOS	**115**	15	51	7	1421.1	**1197**	12	413	509	**10.5**	2.20	117	**.231**	.295	73	62	97	138	**120**	**.972**	183	51	116	**3.9**	6.9	-.3		3.5
CLE	73	20	.129	**22**	1412.2	1270	17	438	451	11.1	2.52	112	.247	.310	22	45	106	144	131	.964	242	32	136	-.5	5.0	-1.8		8.3
DET	78	20	112	15	1396.1	1209	12	504	516	11.4	2.56	103	.240	.316	16	13	99	178	112	.964	234	39	95	-.1	1.4	**7.2**		-7.1
WAS	84	21	98	10	1413.0	1217	12	537	**637**	11.4	2.75	95	.239	.316	-14	-20	99	179	138	.961	251	64	127	-1.0	-2.2	-3.1		3.9
NY	87	10	93	6	1411.1	1280	28	427	571	11.1	2.66	101	.252	.314	0	3	101	124	131	.965	225	35	129	.6	.3	-4.3		-2.1
STL	66	12	**143**	12	1385.1	1320	19	537	429	12.3	3.20	81	.257	.332	-83	-99	98	188	130	.957	281	55	**139**	-3.4	-11.0	-2.2		-3.3
PHI	80	8	95	8	1365.2	1310	23	562	516	12.5	3.27	84	.261	.338	-92	-77	103	209	**151**	.961	251	54	106	-1.4	-8.6	.7		-12.3
TOT	661	128	833	101	11230.0					11.4	2.66		.248	.318						.964	1871	352	965					

Batter-Fielder Wins		Batting Average		On-Base Percentage		Slugging Average		On-Base Plus Slugging		Adjusted OPS		Adjusted Batter Runs	
Cobb-Det	7.4	Cobb-Det	383	Cobb-Det	444	Cobb-Det	570	Cobb-Det	1014	Cobb-Det	210	Cobb-Det	75.9
Chapman-Cle	5.8	Sisler-StL	353	Speaker-Cle	432	Speaker-Cle	486	Speaker-Cle	918	Speaker-Cle	168	Speaker-Cle	45.4
Sisler-StL	4.3	Speaker-Cle	352	Veach-Det	393	Veach-Det	457	Veach-Det	850	Sisler-StL	163	Veach-Det	41.2
Speaker-Cle	4.1	Veach-Det	319	Sisler-StL	390	Sisler-StL	453	Sisler-StL	843	Veach-Det	160	Sisler-StL	37.9
Veach-Det	4.0	Felsch-Chi	308	E.Collins-Chi	389	Jackson-Chi	429	Jackson-Chi	805	Jackson-Chi	142	Jackson-Chi	26.5

Runs		Hits		Doubles		Triples		Home Runs		Total Bases		Runs Batted In	
Bush-Det	112	Cobb-Det	225	Cobb-Det	44	Cobb-Det	24	Pipp-NY	9	Cobb-Det	335	Veach-Det	103
Cobb-Det	107	Sisler-StL	190	Speaker-Cle	42	Jackson-Chi	17	Veach-Det	8	Veach-Det	261	Felsch-Chi	102
Chapman-Cle	98	Speaker-Cle	184	Veach-Det	31	Judge-Was	15	Bodie-Phi	7	Speaker-Cle	254	Cobb-Det	102
Jackson-Chi	91	Veach-Det	182	Sisler-StL	30	Chapman-Cle	13			Sisler-StL	244	Heilmann-Det	86
E.Collins-Chi	91			Roth-Cle	30					Bodie-Phi	233	Jackson-Chi	75

Stolen Bases		Base Stealing Runs		Fielding Runs-Infield		Fielding Runs-Outfield		Wins		Winning Pct.		Complete Games	
Cobb-Det	55			Chapman-Cle	23.6	Felsch-Chi	14.6	Cicotte-Chi	28	Russell-Chi	750	Ruth-Bos	35
E.Collins-Chi	53			Pratt-StL	17.8	Menosky-Was	10.5	Ruth-Bos	24	Mays-Bos	710	Johnson-Was	33
Chapman-Cle	52			Wambsganss-Cle	14.8	Shanks-Was	8.4	Johnson-Was	23	Cicotte-Chi	700	Cicotte-Chi	29
Roth-Cle	51			Lavan-StL	12.8	Bodie-Phi	7.5	Bagby-Cle	23	Williams-Chi	680	Mays-Bos	27
Sisler-StL	37			Baker-NY	9.4	Jackson-Chi	5.5	Mays-Bos	22	Ruth-Bos	649		

Strikeouts		Fewest BB/Game		Games		Saves		Base Runners/9		Adjusted Relief Runs		Relief Ranking	
Johnson-Was	188	Russell-Chi	1.52	Danforth-Chi	50	Danforth-Chi	9	Cicotte-Chi	8.28				
Cicotte-Chi	150	Mogridge-NY	1.79	Cicotte-Chi	49	Bagby-Cle	7	Coveleski-Cle	8.96				
Leonard-Bos	144	Cicotte-Chi	1.82	Bagby-Cle	49	Boland-Det	6	Johnson-Was	9.11				
Coveleski-Cle	133	Johnson-Was	1.88	Sothoron-StL	48	Coumbe-Cle	5	Benz-Chi	9.60				
Ruth-Bos	128	Bagby-Cle	2.05					Russell-Chi	9.65				

Innings Pitched		Opponents' Avg.		Opponents' OBP		Earned Run Average		Adjusted ERA		Adjusted Starter Runs		Pitcher Wins	
Cicotte-Chi	346.2	Coveleski-Cle	194	Cicotte-Chi	248	Cicotte-Chi	1.53	Cicotte-Chi	173	Cicotte-Chi	44.8	**Cicotte-Chi**	5.7
Ruth-Bos	326.1	Cicotte-Chi	203	Coveleski-Cle	261	Mays-Bos	1.74	Coveleski-Cle	156	Coveleski-Cle	33.3	**Ruth-Bos**	4.9
Johnson-Was	326.0	Ruth-Bos	211	Johnson-Was	263	Coveleski-Cle	1.81	Mays-Bos	148	Bagby-Cle	30.2	**Mays-Bos**	4.0
Bagby-Cle	320.2	Johnson-Was	211	Russell-Chi	279	Faber-Chi	1.92	Bagby-Cle	142	Mays-Bos	24.7	**Bagby-Cle**	3.9
Coveleski-Cle	298.1	Mays-Bos	221	Mays-Bos	282	Russell-Chi	1.95	Faber-Chi	138	Ruth-Bos	22.2	**Coveleski-Cle**	3.2

White Sox Play Clean Ball

The waves of World War were causing the good ship baseball to list. America's economy sagged, and as a result, league attendance fell 17 percent. Speculation over an increased war effort led to cries of impending doom for baseball, which could lose much of its talent to conscription and military industry.

Despite a 1.79 ERA, 42-year-old Eddie Plank was 5-6 for seventh-place St. Louis, and his big-league career came to an end. Also finished at 36 was former White Sox ace "Big Ed" Walsh, whose arm was dead after leading the AL four times in a six-year span in innings pitched. No longer would pitchers be asked to shoulder the load that Walsh did in 1912, when he pitched 62 games and 393 innings (although that was actually a step back from his 464-inning, 40-win 1908 season).

Showing excellent all-around effort, Chicago pulled away from second-place Boston in September. The Red Sox were barely.500 down the stretch, while the White Sox came alive when they smelled the flag. Chicago won 100 games with an excellent attack, leading the league in runs scored, and 33-year-old spitballer Eddie Cicotte finally had his first 20-win season—28 to be precise.

Babe Ruth was 24-13 for the Bosox and hit .325, seeing extra duty as a pinch-hitter. The 1917 campaign was his final full season on the mound, as his bat would soon prove too hot to keep on the bench. Boston's attack was substandard; they didn't hit, draw walks, or steal bases.

The White Sox-Giants World Series started as a pitching paradise. Chicago allowed just 3 runs in winning the first pair at home. Back east, New York won the next two by shutouts. But Game 5 at Comiskey saw the Pale Hose outlast New York, 8-5, despite making 6 errors. Chicago then won the next game as the Giants made 3 miscues of their own. White Sox hurler Red Faber went 3-1 in 27 innings.

1916 National League

TEAM	W	L	T	PCT	GB	HW	HL	R	OR	PA	H	2B	3B	HR	BB	SO	HB	SH	AVG	OBP	SLG	OPS	AOPS	BR	ABR	PF	SB	CS	BSA	BSR
BRO	94	60	2	.610		50	27	585	471	5833	**1366**	195	80	28	355	550	41	203	.261	.313	.345	**658**	105	**46**	30	103	187			
PHI	91	62	1	.595	2.5	50	29	581	489	5597	1244	**223**	53	42	399	571	34	179	.250	.310	.341	651	102	39	19	104	149			
BOS	89	63	6	.586	4	41	31	542	**453**	5760	1181	166	73	22	**437**	646	46	202	.233	.299	.307	606	96	-38	-15	96	141			
NY	86	66	3	.566	7	47	30	**597**	504	5686	1305	188	74	42	356	558	44	134	.253	.307	.343	650	104	63	95		206			
CHI	67	86	3	.438	26.5	37	41	520	541	5778	1237	194	56	**46**	399	662	34	166	.239	.298	.325	623	88	-15	-66	111	133			
PIT	65	89	3	.422	29	37	40	484	586	5769	1246	147	**91**	20	372	618	50	166	.240	.298	.316	614	94	-36	-41	101	173			
STL	60	93	2	.392	33.5	36	40	476	629	5514	1223	195	74	25	335	651	33	116	.243	.295	.318	613	95	-38	-35	99	182			
CIN	60	93	2	.392	33.5	32	44	505	617	5783	1336	187	88	14	362	573	40	127	.254	.307	.331	638	105	11	25	98	157			
TOT	622					330	282	4290		45720	10138	1455	589	239	3015	4829	322	1293	.247	.303	.328	632					1328			

TEAM	CG	SHO	GR	SV	IP	H	HR	BB	SO	BR/9	ERA	AERA	OAV	OOB	PR	APR	PF	OSB	OCS	FA	E	WPB	DP	FW	PW	BW	BSW	DIF
BRO	96	22	92	9	1427.1	**1201**	24	372	634	10.2	2.12	**126**	.232	.289	78	**84**	102	162	119	.965	224	53	90	1.2	**9.6**	3.4		2.7
PHI	**97**	**25**	78	9	1382.1	1238	28	**295**	601	10.3	2.36	112	.244	.292	39	43	101	153	117	.963	234	60	119	.4	4.9	2.2		7.0
BOS	**97**	23	82	11	1415.2	1206	24	325	**644**	9.9	2.19	113	.235	**.285**	66	47	95	**100**	119	**.967**	212	40	124	2.1	5.4	-1.7		7.2
NY	88	22	103	12	1397.1	1267	41	310	638	10.4	2.60	93	.245	.293	2	-30	93	142	98	.966	217	55	108	1.5	-3.4	**7.2**		4.7
CHI	72	17	119	13	1416.2	1265	32	365	616	10.6	2.65	110	.244	.298	-6	35	111	177	134	.957	286	57	104	-2.6	4.0	-7.5		-3.4
PIT	88	11	102	7	1419.2	1277	24	443	596	11.1	2.76	97	.247	.311	-24	-14	103	192	142	.959	260	**40**	97	-.9	-1.6	-4.7		-4.8
STL	58	13	**127**	**15**	1355.0	1331	31	445	529	12.1	3.01	84	.253	.330	-80	-76	101	192	137	.957	278	51	124	-2.4	-8.7	-4.0		-1.4
CIN	86	7	98	6	1408.0	1356	35	461	569	11.9	3.10	84	.261	.326	-76	-82	99	210	**159**	.965	228	48	**126**	.9	-9.4	2.9		-10.9
TOT	682	140	801	82	11222.0					10.8	2.61		.247	.303						.963	1939	404	892					

Batter-Fielder Wins		Batting Average		On-Base Percentage		Slugging Average		On-Base Plus Slugging		Adjusted OPS		Adjusted Batter Runs	
Groh-Cin	4.8	Chase-Cin	339	Cravath-Phi	379	Z.Wheat-Bro	461	Williams-Chi	831	Chase-Cin	155	Z.Wheat-Bro	32.6
Fletcher-NY	4.7	Daubert-Bro	316	Hinchman-Pit	378	Chase-Cin	459	Z.Wheat-Bro	828	Hornsby-StL	150	Chase-Cin	32.3
Doyle-NY-Chi	3.8	Hinchman-Pit	315	Williams-Chi	372	Williams-Chi	459	Chase-Cin	822	Z.Wheat-Bro	149	Hinchman-Pit	29.9
Hornsby-StL	3.7	Hornsby-StL	313	Daubert-Bro	371	Hornsby-StL	444	Cravath-Phi	819	Cravath-Phi	146	Hornsby-StL	28.2
Z.Wheat-Bro	3.6	Z.Wheat-Bro	312	Groh-Cin	370	Cravath-Phi	440	Hornsby-StL	814	Hinchman-Pit	146	Cravath-Phi	26.8

Runs		Hits		Doubles		Triples		Home Runs		Total Bases		Runs Batted In	
Burns-NY	105	Chase-Cin	184	Niehoff-Phi	42	Hinchman-Pit	16	Williams-Chi	12	Z.Wheat-Bro	262	Zimmerman-Chi-NY	83
Carey-Pit	90	Robertson-NY	180	Z.Wheat-Bro	32	Roush-NY-Cin	15	Robertson-NY	12	Robertson-NY	250	Chase-Cin	82
Robertson-NY	88	Z.Wheat-Bro	177	Paskert-Phi	30	Kauff-NY	15	Cravath-Phi	11	Chase-Cin	249	Hinchman-Pit	76
Groh-Cin	85	Hinchman-Pit	175			Hornsby-StL	15	Z.Wheat-Bro	9	Hinchman-Pit	237	Kauff-NY	74
Paskert-Phi	82	Burns-NY	174					Kauff-NY	9	Burns-NY	229	Z.Wheat-Bro	73

Stolen Bases		Base Stealing Runs		Fielding Runs-Infield		Fielding Runs-Outfield		Wins		Winning Pct.		Complete Games	
Carey-Pit	63	Carey-Pit	7.2	Betzel-StL	29.4	Carey-Pit	21.9	Alexander-Phi	33	Hughes-Bos	842	Alexander-Phi	38
Kauff-NY	40	Bescher-StL	4.4	Bancroft-Phi	25.3	Snodgrass-Bos	8.9	Pfeffer-Bro	25	Alexander-Phi	733	Pfeffer-Bro	27
Bescher-StL	39	Daubert-Bro	2.2	Maranville-Bos	23.3	Neale-Cin	6.6	Rixey-Phi	22	Pfeffer-Bro	694	Rudolph-Bos	27
Burns-NY	37	Maranville-Bos	1.8	Fletcher-NY	21.6	Z.Wheat-Bro	6.2	Mamaux-Pit	21	Rixey-Phi	688	Mamaux-Pit	26
Herzog-Cin-NY	34	Chase-Cin	1.0	Doyle-NY-Chi	18.0	Stengel-Bro	4.8			Benton-NY	667	Demaree-Phi	25

Strikeouts		Fewest BB/Game		Games		Saves		Base Runners/9		Adjusted Relief Runs		Relief Ranking	
Alexander-Phi	167	Rudolph-Bos	1.10	Meadows-StL	51	Ames-StL	8	Schupp-NY	7.76				
Cheney-Bro	166	Alexander-Phi	1.16	Alexander-Phi	48	Packard-Chi	5	Rudolph-Bos	8.86				
Mamaux-Pit	163	Demaree-Phi	1.52	Mamaux-Pit	45	Marquard-Bro	5	Alexander-Phi	8.86				
Toney-Cin	146	Sallee-StL-NY	1.63	Ames-StL	45	Hughes-Bos	5	Prendergast-Chi	8.94				
Vaughn-Chi	144	Marquard-Bro	1.67					Marquard-Bro	9.09				

Innings Pitched		Opponents' Avg.		Opponents' OBP		Earned Run Average		Adjusted ERA		Adjusted Starter Runs		Pitcher Wins	
Alexander-Phi	389.0	Cheney-Bro	198	Rudolph-Bos	261	Alexander-Phi	1.55	Alexander-Phi	171	Alexander-Phi	47.0	**Alexander-Phi**	7.2
Pfeffer-Bro	328.2	Cooper-Pit	215	Alexander-Phi	262	Marquard-Bro	1.58	Marquard-Bro	169	Pfeffer-Bro	29.5	**Pfeffer-Bro**	4.1
Rudolph-Bos	312.0	Hughes-Bos	215	Marquard-Bro	267	Rixey-Phi	1.85	Cooper-Pit	144	Schupp-NY	23.7	**Rixey-Phi**	2.5
Mamaux-Pit	310.0	Ragan-Bos	218	Ragan-Bos	270	Cooper-Pit	1.87	Rixey-Phi	143	Marquard-Bro	23.1	**Tyler-Bos**	2.3
Toney-Cin	300.0	McConnell-Chi	223	McConnell-Chi	271	Pfeffer-Bro	1.92	Pfeffer-Bro	140	Rixey-Phi	21.0	**Cooper-Pit**	2.1

Ebbets Field's First Champeens

Offense continued its free fall as runs dropped for the fourth straight year. The average club tallied just 3.45 runs per game, the league's lowest total until 1968. The Federal League's demise meant fewer jobs for more players, and—as a result—lower salaries (and bigger profits) for the owners. The Cubs moved from West Side Grounds to Weeghman Park, and their attendance rose 109 percent.

Cy Williams led the NL in homers for first of four times, while the Pirates gave rookie Burleigh Grimes his first major league action; the right-hander lasted until 1934 and was the last to legally throw a spitball. The end of an era came on September 4, 1916: Three-Finger Brown, bowing out with the Cubs, and Christy Mathewson, now manager of Cincinnati, hooked up for their 25th and final duel. Matty's win gave each pitcher 12 wins against the other. It was the final big league game for both.

Grover Cleveland Alexander was the new breed. His 16 shutouts in '16 remain an all-time record and his 33 wins have not been matched since. "Alex" also paced the NL in strikeouts for the fourth time in five years. His 389 innings were 60 more than anyone else.

Alexander's Phillies opened September in a three-way race with Brooklyn and Boston. While the three clubs remained neck-and-neck into the last week, it was the Robins, so dubbed because of third-year manager Wilbert Robinson, who came out ahead. Philadelphia and Boston knocked each other out of the running. The late-charging Giants, who won a league-record 26 straight, fell just short in fourth.

This was big news for Brooklyn, which had spent most of the century as a league doormat. The Robins did it with balanced pitching and hitting. They had few stars (save Zack Wheat) but no weaknesses, and Jeff Pfeffer was arguably the league's second-best pitcher. In the World Series, however, the NL lost again as the Red Sox knocked out Brooklyn in five games.

1916 American League

TEAM	W	L	T	PCT	GB	HW	HL	R	OR	PA	H	2B	3B	HR	BB	SO	HB	SH	AVG	OBP	SLG	OPS	AOPS	BR	ABR	PF	SB	CS	BSA	BSR
BOS	91	63	2	.591		49	28	550	480	5758	1246	197	56	14	464	482	38	238	.248	.317	.318	635	97	-20	-22	100	129			
CHI	89	65	1	.578	2	49	28	601	497	5809	1277	194	100	17	447	591	60	221	.251	.319	.339	658	103	15	9	101	197			
DET	87	67	1	.565	4	49	28	670	595	5969	1371	202	96	17	545	529	29	202	.264	.337	.350	687	109	78	56	104	190			
NY	80	74	2	.519	11	46	31	577	561	5905	1277	194	59	35	516	632	36	155	.246	.318	.326	644	98	-4	-16	102	179			
STL	79	75	4	.513	12	45	32	588	545	5987	1262	181	50	14	626	638	42	164	.245	.307	.308	655	97	5	35	95	234			
CLE	77	77	3	.500	14	44	33	630	602	5853	1264	233	66	16	522	605	33	234	.250	.324	.331	655	97	21	-12	106	160			
WAS	76	77	6	.497	14.5	49	28	536	543	5864	1238	170	60	12	535	597	50	165	.242	.320	.306	626	95	-30	-24	99	185			
PHI	36	117	1	.235	54.5	23	53	447	776	5604	1212	169	65	19	406	631	30	158	.242	.303	.313	616	96	-65	-40	95	151			
TOT	625					354	261	4599		46749	10147	1540	552	144	4061	4705	318	1537	.248	.321	.324	645					1425			

TEAM	CG	SHO	GR	SV	IP	H	HR	BB	SO	BR/9	ERA	AERA	OAV	OOB	PR	APR	PF	OSB	OCS	FA	E	WPB	DP	FW	PW	BW	BSW	DIF
BOS	76	24	103	16	1410.2	1221	10	463	584	11.0	2.48	112	.239	.307	55	45	98	134	124	.972	183	40	108	3.0	5.0	-2.4		8.4
CHI	73	20	140	15	1412.1	1189	14	405	644	10.3	2.36	117	.236	.296	72	63	98	113	118	.968	205	28	134	1.5	7.0	1.0		2.5
DET	81	8	126	13	1410.0	1254	12	578	531	12.1	2.97	96	.248	.333	-23	-18	101	202	113	.968	211	50	110	1.1	-2.0	6.2		4.6
NY	84	12	102	17	1428.0	1249	37	476	616	11.2	2.77	104	.244	.314	8	17	102	135	160	.967	219	32	119	.7	1.9	-1.8		2.2
STL	74	9	141	13	1443.2	1292	15	478	505	11.3	2.58	106	.248	.316	39	27	97	210	114	.963	248	38	120	-.9	3.0	3.9		-3.9
CLE	65	9	140	16	1410.0	1383	16	467	537	12.0	2.90	103	.264	.328	-13	15	106	167	123	.965	232	58	130	.0	1.7	-1.3		-.3
WAS	85	11	107	7	1430.2	1271	14	490	706	11.3	2.67	104	.244	.314	25	18	99	178	125	.964	232	76	119	.2	2.0	-2.7		-.0
PHI	94	11	80	3	1343.2	1311	26	715	575	13.8	3.92	73	.267	.364	-163	-159	101	286	184	.951	314	70	126	-5.5	-17.6	-4.4		-13.0
TOT	632	104	939	100	11289.0					11.6	2.82		.248	.321						.965	1844	392	966					

Batter-Fielder Wins		Batting Average		On-Base Percentage		Slugging Average		On-Base Plus Slugging		Adjusted OPS		Adjusted Batter Runs	
Speaker-Cle	5.7	Speaker-Cle	386	Speaker-Cle	470	Speaker-Cle	502	Speaker-Cle	972	Speaker-Cle	181	Speaker-Cle	59.5
Cobb-Det	4.6	Cobb-Det	371	Cobb-Det	452	Jackson-Chi	495	Cobb-Det	944	Cobb-Det	177	Cobb-Det	54.6
Pratt-StL	4.0	Jackson-Chi	341	E.Collins-Chi	405	Cobb-Det	493	Jackson-Chi	888	Jackson-Chi	165	Jackson-Chi	44.0
Jackson-Chi	3.6	Strunk-Phi	316	Jackson-Chi	393	Veach-Det	433	Strunk-Phi	814	Strunk-Phi	152	Strunk-Phi	35.8
Shotton-StL	3.0	Gardner-Bos	308	Strunk-Phi	393	Baker-NY	428	E.Collins-Chi	802	E.Collins-Chi	139	E.Collins-Chi	29.0

Runs		Hits		Doubles		Triples		Home Runs		Total Bases		Runs Batted In	
Cobb-Det	113	Speaker-Cle	211	Speaker-Cle	41	Jackson-Chi	21	Pipp-NY	12	Jackson-Chi	293	Pratt-StL	103
Graney-Cle	106	Jackson-Chi	202	Graney-Cle	41	E.Collins-Chi	17	Baker-NY	10	Speaker-Cle	274	Pipp-NY	93
Speaker-Cle	102	Cobb-Det	201	Jackson-Chi	40	Witt-Phi	15	Schang-Phi	7	Cobb-Det	267	Veach-Det	91
Shotton-StL	97	Sisler-StL	177	Pratt-StL	35	Veach-Det	15	Felsch-Chi	7	Veach-Det	245	Speaker-Cle	79
Veach-Det	92	Shotton-StL	174	Veach-Det	33							Jackson-Chi	78

Stolen Bases		Base Stealing Runs		Fielding Runs-Infield		Fielding Runs-Outfield		Wins		Winning Pct.		Complete Games	
Cobb-Det	68	Cobb-Det	6.6	Lajoie-Was	26.7	Milan-Was	14.1	Johnson-Was	25	Cicotte-Chi	682	Johnson-Was	36
Marsans-StL	46	Hooper-Bos	2.1	Vitt-Det	26.3	Shanks-Was	13.5	Shawkey-NY	24	Ruth-Bos	657	Myers-Phi	31
Shotton-StL	41	Schalk-Chi	2.0	Lavan-StL	25.9	Shotton-StL	8.1	Ruth-Bos	23	Coveleski-Det	656	Bush-Phi	25
E.Collins-Chi	40	Roth-Cle	1.5	Pratt-StL	19.6	Speaker-Cle	5.6	Coveleski-Det	21	Faber-Chi	654	Ruth-Bos	23
Speaker-Cle	35	E.Collins-Chi	1.5	McBride-Was	13.6	Hooper-Bos	5.2	Dauss-Det	19	Shawkey-NY	632	Coveleski-Det	22

Strikeouts		Fewest BB/Game		Games		Saves		Base Runners/9		Adjusted Relief Runs		Relief Ranking	
Johnson-Was	228	Russell-Chi	1.43	Davenport-StL	59	Shawkey-NY	8	Russell-Chi	8.51				
Myers-Phi	182	Cullop-NY	1.72	Russell-Chi	56	Russell-NY	6	Benz-Chi	9.06				
Ruth-Bos	170	Coveleski-Det	1.75	Shawkey-NY	53	Leonard-Bos	6	Johnson-Was	9.28				
Bush-Phi	157	Shore-Bos	1.95	Gallia-Was	49	Cicotte-Chi	5	Shawkey-NY	9.47				
Harper-Was	149	Johnson-Was	2.00			Bagby-Cle	5	Coveleski-Det	9.77				

Innings Pitched		Opponents' Avg.		Opponents' OBP		Earned Run Average		Adjusted ERA		Adjusted Starter Runs		Pitcher Wins	
Johnson-Was	369.2	Ruth-Bos	201	Russell-Chi	254	Ruth-Bos	1.75	Ruth-Bos	158	Ruth-Bos	35.1	Ruth-Bos	5.7
Coveleski-Det	324.1	Shawkey-NY	209	Johnson-Was	270	Cicotte-Chi	1.78	Cicotte-Chi	155	Johnson-Was	34.9	Johnson-Was	5.2
Ruth-Bos	323.2	Cicotte-Chi	218	Shawkey-NY	273	Johnson-Was	1.90	Johnson-Was	147	Coveleski-Det	26.2	Shawkey-NY	3.4
Myers-Phi	315.0	Bush-Phi	219	Ruth-Bos	280	Coveleski-Det	1.97	Coveleski-Det	145	Shawkey-NY	23.6	Coveleski-Det	3.1
Davenport-StL	290.2	Johnson-Was	220	Coveleski-Det	282	Faber-Chi	2.02	Cullop-NY	141	Cicotte-Chi	18.3	Mays-Bos	2.8

Ruth Rises to the Occasion

Could Connie Mack's Athletics get worse? At 36-117, they set an AL record for losses and posted the worst team winning percentage of the twentieth century. Philadelphia dropped 20 in a row at one point. So many teams feasted on Philadelphia's misery that seventh-place Washington finished just one game under .500, and the Senators had even been in first place during May. Jack Nabors of the A's beat defending world champion Boston on May 22 for his first major league win; he lost his next 19 decisions and never won again. Nap Lajoie, 41, had an undignified finish to a great career, batting .246 for the pathetic A's.

On the other side of the pennant race, the Red Sox, White Sox, and Tigers clawed at each other into September. Despite trading Tris Speaker and Smokey Joe Wood to Cleveland in salary disputes, Boston held it together. While their attack was below par, Boston's five starters were extremely productive; Babe Ruth led the AL in ERA and shutouts.

Chicago had the better club on paper, featuring Eddie Collins and Joe Jackson, but lacked pitching depth (although Chisox righty Eddie Cicotte, at 15-7, led the loop in winning percentage and his 1.78 ERA was second). Detroit once again rode Ty Cobb's back into contention, as Sam Crawford began to slow up at age 36. Two future stars enjoyed excellent first full seasons. Stan Coveleski was 16-13 for Cleveland, while first baseman George Sisler won hearts in St. Louis. Both the Indians and Browns saw huge attendance gains as they began rebuilding. League attendance rose 42 percent.

Down the stretch, the Red Sox grabbed the flag with seven straight road victories against the White Sox, Tigers, and Indians. Boston was favored to win the World Series against Brooklyn, but after three one-run decisions—including a complete-game, 14-inning, 2-1 victory from Ruth in Game 2—the Red Sox barely led, two games to one. However, the Red Sox knocked out Rube Marquard and Jeff Pfeffer the next two games to repeat as champions.

1915 National League

TEAM	W	L	T	PCT	GB	HW	HL	R	OR	PA	H	2B	3B	HR	BB	SO	HB	SH	AVG	OBP	SLG	OPS	AOPS	BR	ABR	PF	SB	CS	BSA	BSR
PHI	90	62	1	.592		49	27	589	463	5591	1216	202	39	58	460	600	34	181	.247	.316	.340	656	104	35	29	101	121	113	52	-13
BOS	83	69	5	.546	7	49	27	582	545	5869	1219	231	57	17	549	620	56	194	.240	.321	.319	640	105	22	50	96	121	98	55	-8
BRO	80	72	2	.526	10	51	26	536	560	5635	1268	165	75	14	313	536	27	175	.248	.295	.317	612	89	-61	-70	102	131	126	51	-15
CHI	73	80	3	.477	17.5	42	34	570	620	5730	1246	212	66	53	393	639	41	182	.244	.303	.342	645	102	5	4	100	166	124	57	-7
PIT	73	81	2	.474	18	40	37	557	520	5743	1259	191	24	49	419	656	49	162	.246	.309	.334	643	102	7	15	99	182	111	62	1
STL	72	81	4	.471	18.5	42	36	590	601	5780	1297	159	92	20	457	658	42	175	.254	.320	.333	653	104	28	27	100	162	144	53	-15
CIN	71	83	6	.461	20	39	37	516	585	5836	1323	194	84	15	360	512	53	192	.253	.308	.331	639	98	-7	-17	102	156	142	52	-15
NY	69	83	3	.454	21	37	38	582	628	5703	1312	195	68	24	315	547	48	122	.251	.300	.329	629	103	-28	5	94	155	137	53	-14
TOT	624					349	262	4522		45887	10140	1555	572	225	3266	4728	350	1383	.248	.309	.331	640					1194	995	55	-86

TEAM	CG	SHO	GR	SV	IP	H	HR	BB	SO	BR/9	ERA	AERA	OAV	OOB	PR	APR	PF	OSB	OCS	FA	E	WPB	DP	FW	PW	BW	BSW	DIF
PHI	98	20	67	8	1374.1	1161	26	342	652	10.0	2.17	126	.234	.288	87	85	100	134	117	.966	216	33	99	.8	9.4	3.2	-.3	.8
BOS	95	17	78	13	1405.2	1257	23	366	630	10.7	2.57	100	.246	.302	27	1	94	110	124	.966	213	34	115	1.4	.1	5.6	.3	-.4
BRO	87	16	91	8	1389.2	1252	29	473	499	11.6	2.66	104	.245	.318	14	17	101	172	124	.963	238	49	96	-.5	1.9	-7.8	-.5	10.9
CHI	71	18	119	8	1399.0	1272	28	480	657	11.6	3.11	89	.247	.316	-57	-54	101	151	130	.958	268	58	94	-2.3	-6.0	.4	.4	4.0
PIT	91	18	91	11	1380.0	1229	21	384	544	10.8	2.60	105	.246	.304	23	19	99	164	126	.966	214	31	100	1.2	2.1	1.7	1.3	-10.3
STL	79	13	103	9	1400.2	1320	30	402	538	11.3	2.89	96	.256	.314	-22	-17	101	133	129	.964	235	34	109	-.0	-1.9	3.0	-.5	-5.1
CIN	80	19	113	12	1432.1	1304	28	497	572	11.6	2.84	101	.250	.321	-15	1	104	126	125	.966	222	36	148	1.1	.1	-1.9	-.5	-4.9
NY	78	15	105	9	1385.0	1350	40	325	637	11.2	3.11	82	.260	.308	-57	-92	93	167	120	.960	256	56	119	-1.6	-10.2	.6	-.4	4.7
TOT	679	136	767	78	11166.2					11.1	2.75		.248	.309						.964	1862	331	880					

Batter-Fielder Wins		Batting Average		On-Base Percentage		Slugging Average		On-Base Plus Slugging		Adjusted OPS		Adjusted Batter Runs	
Cravath-Phi	5.2	Doyle-NY	320	Cravath-Phi	393	Cravath-Phi	510	Cravath-Phi	902	Cravath-Phi	170	Cravath-Phi	47.3
Luderus-Phi	4.0	Luderus-Phi	315	Luderus-Phi	376	Luderus-Phi	457	Luderus-Phi	833	Doyle-NY	150	Doyle-NY	33.6
Herzog-Cin	4.0	Griffith-Cin	307	Daubert-Bro	369	Long-Stl	446	Hinchman-Pit	807	Luderus-Phi	150	Hinchman-Pit	31.6
Snyder-Stl	3.8	Hinchman-Pit	307	Hinchman-Pit	368	Saier-Chi	445	Doyle-NY	799	Hinchman-Pit	146	Luderus-Phi	30.7
Fletcher-NY	3.3	Daubert-Bro	301	Doyle-NY	358	Doyle-NY	442	Saier-Chi	795	Saier-Chi	140	Saier-Chi	24.7

Runs		Hits		Doubles		Triples		Home Runs		Total Bases		Runs Batted In	
Cravath-Phi	89	Doyle-NY	189	Doyle-NY	40	Long-Stl	25	Cravath-Phi	24	Cravath-Phi	266	Cravath-Phi	115
Doyle-NY	86	Griffith-Cin	179	Luderus-Phi	36	H.Wagner-Pit	17	Williams-Chi	13	Doyle-NY	261	Magee-Bos	87
Bancroft-Phi	85	Hinchman-Pit	177	Saier-Chi	35	Griffith-Cin	16	Schulte-Chi	12	Griffith-Cin	254	Griffith-Cin	85
Burns-NY	83	Groh-Cin	170	Smith-Bos	34	Hinchman-Pit	14	Saier-Chi	11	Hinchman-Pit	253	H.Wagner-Pit	78
O'Mara-Bro	77	Burns-NY	169	Magee-Bos	34	Burns-NY	14	Becker-Phi	11	H.Wagner-Pit	239	Hinchman-Pit	77

Stolen Bases		Base Stealing Runs		Fielding Runs-Infield		Fielding Runs-Outfield		Wins		Winning Pct.		Complete Games	
Carey-Pit	36	Saier-Chi	3.2	Fletcher-NY	34.8	Carey-Pit	11.1	Alexander-Phi	31	Alexander-Phi	756	Alexander-Phi	36
Herzog-Cin	35	Bresnahan-Chi	3.1	Herzog-Cin	30.3	Wilson-Stl	10.6	Rudolph-Bos	22	Toney-Cin	739	Rudolph-Bos	30
Saier-Chi	29	Baird-Pit	2.2	Maranville-Bos	20.0	Z.Wheat-Bro	9.1	Mayer-Phi	21	Mamaux-Pit	724	Pfeffer-Bro	26
Baird-Pit	29	Herzog-Cin	2.1	Cutshaw-Bro	13.8	Cravath-Phi	8.7	Mamaux-Pit	21	Vaughn-Chi	625	Harmon-Pit	25
Cutshaw-Bro	28	Carey-Pit	2.0	Groh-Cin	11.6	Magee-Bos	6.3	Vaughn-Chi	20	Coombs-Bro	600	Tesreau-NY	24

Strikeouts		Fewest BB/Game		Games		Saves		Base Runners/9		Adjusted Relief Runs		Relief Ranking	
Alexander-Phi	241	Mathewson-NY	.97	Hughes-Bos	50	Hughes-Bos	9	Alexander-Phi	7.82				
Tesreau-NY	176	Humphries-Chi	1.21	Dale-Cin	49	Benton-Cin-NY	5	Hughes-Bos	8.89				
Hughes-Bos	171	Adams-Pit	1.25	Alexander-Phi	49	Lavender-Chi	4	Tesreau-NY	9.26				
Mamaux-Pit	152	Alexander-Phi	1.53	Schneider-Cin	48	Cooper-Pit	4	Toney-Cin	9.54				
Vaughn-Chi	148	Rudolph-Bos	1.69	Sallee-Stl	46			Nehf-Bos	9.65				

Innings Pitched		Opponents' Avg.		Opponents' OBP		Earned Run Average		Adjusted ERA		Adjusted Starter Runs		Pitcher Wins	
Alexander-Phi	376.1	Alexander-Phi	191	Alexander-Phi	234	Alexander-Phi	1.22	Alexander-Phi	224	Alexander-Phi	58.3	Alexander-Phi	7.5
Rudolph-Bos	341.1	Toney-Cin	207	Hughes-Bos	265	Toney-Cin	1.58	Toney-Cin	181	Toney-Cin	32.1	Toney-Cin	3.0
Tesreau-NY	306.0	Mamaux-Pit	208	Tesreau-NY	269	Mamaux-Pit	2.04	Mamaux-Pit	134	Pfeffer-Bro	21.6	Pfeffer-Bro	2.9
Dale-Cin	296.2	Hughes-Bos	213	Toney-Cin	278	Pfeffer-Bro	2.10	Pfeffer-Bro	132	Mamaux-Pit	21.1	Mayer-Phi	2.5
Pfeffer-Bro	291.2	Tesreau-NY	215	Adams-Pit	280	Hughes-Bos	2.12	Hughes-Bos	122	Hughes-Bos	16.0	Mamaux-Pit	2.0

The Tightest Race Ever

On the field, the season was thrilling. Eddie Plank and Chief Bender escaped from Connie Mack after pitching the A's to the AL pennant a year earlier. Frank Allen of Pittsburgh pitched the first of four FL no-hitters. The Feds also outhomered the two established leagues in 1914–15, clubbing 545 as the NL hit 492 and the AL just 308. Dutch Zwilling, who would hit one career homer against non-FL pitching, smacked 29 in two years as the new league's home run king. Chicago, St. Louis, and Pittsburgh finished the year 1-2-3 as the Whales took the tightest race in major league history by exactly one percentage point; the Rebels were third by only .004.

Walter Johnson was the Whale that got away, even though Chicago Whales player-manager Joe Tinker signed Johnson to a three-year deal worth $58,500. Despite AL President Ban Johnson's assertion that The Big Train was "damaged goods," Washington owner Clark Griffith knew better. Aided by money from other AL clubs, he lured back his prized pitcher and later signed Johnson to a five-year, $80,000 contract, dimming the FL's long-term chances.

In January 1915 the FL sued the other two leagues for violating the Sherman Antitrust Act. They chose the U.S. District Court of Judge Kenesaw Mountain Landis, a noted trust-buster, as the venue. That proved to be as big a mistake as competing against two established leagues in a time of uncertainty because of the war in Europe. Landis, an ardent Cubs fan, effectively killed the Federal League by sitting on the case.

Absent a legal ruling, the competing leagues negotiated a complicated settlement that resulted in FL owners in St. Louis and Chicago buying the Browns and Cubs, bringing into the NL what would become Wrigley Field. The agreement paid off some—but not all—FL owners. FL players could return, but only eight former Feds later appeared in as many as 500 big league games.

1915 American League

TEAM	W	L	T	PCT	GB	HW	HL	R	OR	PA	H	2B	3B	HR	BB	SO	HB	SH	AVG	OBP	SLG	OPS	AOPS	BR	ABR	PF	SB	CS	BSA	BSR
BOS	101	50	4	.669		55	20	669	499	5865	1308	202	76	14	527	476	49	265	.260	.336	.339	675	110	48	69	97	118	117	50	-15
DET	100	54	2	.649	2.5	51	26	778	597	6046	1372	207	94	23	681	527	35	202	.268	.357	.358	715	114	135	98	105	241	146	62	2
CHI	93	61	1	.604	9.5	54	24	717	509	5838	1269	163	102	25	583	575	71	270	.258	.345	.348	693	110	82	62	103	233	183	56	-13
WAS	85	68	2	.556	17	50	29	569	491	5719	1225	152	79	12	458	541	45	187	.244	.312	.312	624	90	-55	-65	102	186	106	64	4
NY	69	83	2	.454	32.5	37	43	584	588	5765	1162	167	50	31	570	669	44	169	.233	.317	.305	622	91	-45	-44	100	198	133	60	-3
STL	63	91	5	.409	39.5	35	38	522	680	5800	1255	166	65	19	472	765	43	173	.246	.315	.315	630	98	-46	-23	96	202	160	56	-12
CLE	57	95	2	.375	44.5	27	50	539	670	5738	1210	169	79	20	490	681	37	177	.240	.312	.317	629	91	-46	-55	102	138	117	54	-11
PHI	43	109	2	.283	58.5	19	53	545	889	5708	1204	183	72	16	436	634	54	137	.237	.304	.311	615	92	-75	-56	97	127	69	59	-3
TOT	621					328	283	4923		46479	10005	1409	617	160	4217	4868	378	1580	.248	.325	.326	651					1443	1051	58	-50

TEAM	CG	SHO	GR	SV	IP	H	HR	BB	SO	BR/9	ERA	AERA	OAV	OOB	PR	APR	PF	OSB	OCS	FA	E	WPB	DP	FW	PW	BW	BSW	DIF
BOS	81	19	99	15	1397.0	1164	18	446	634	10.7	2.39	116	.231	.300	84	62	95	157	125	.964	226	51	95	2.5	6.6	7.3	-.9	10.1
DET	86	10	109	19	1413.1	1259	14	492	550	11.5	2.86	106	.243	.316	11	24	103	179	121	.961	258	62	107	.5	2.5	10.4	.9	8.7
CHI	91	16	91	9	1401.0	1242	14	350	635	10.4	2.43	122	.241	.294	78	83	101	101	100	.965	222	38	95	2.7	8.8	6.6	-.7	-1.4
WAS	87	21	99	13	1393.1	1161	12	455	715	10.7	2.31	129	.232	.302	97	101	101	156	123	.964	230	50	101	2.2	10.7	-6.9	1.1	1.4
NY	101	12	66	1	1382.2	1272	41	517	559	12.0	3.06	96	.254	.329	-20	-20	100	188	131	.966	217	38	118	2.9	-2.1	-4.7	.4	-3.5
STL	76	6	131	6	1403.0	1256	21	612	566	12.4	3.04	94	.249	.338	-17	-32	98	196	141	.949	336	69	144	-4.3	-3.4	-2.4	-.6	-3.2
CLE	62	11	138	10	1372.0	1287	18	518	610	12.0	3.13	97	.256	.329	-30	-13	104	170	135	.957	280	54	82	-1.2	-1.4	-5.8	-.5	-10.1
PHI	78	6	95	2	1348.1	1358	22	827	588	15.0	4.29	68	.278	.388	-204	-207	100	295	175	.947	338	85	118	-5.0	-22.0	-5.9	.4	-.4
TOT	662	101	828	75	11111.0					11.8	2.93		.248	.325						.959	2107	447	860					

Batter-Fielder Wins		Batting Average		On-Base Percentage		Slugging Average		On-Base Plus Slugging		Adjusted OPS		Adjusted Batter Runs	
E.Collins-Chi	6.6	Cobb-Det	.369	Cobb-Det	.486	Fournier-Chi	.491	Cobb-Det	.973	Cobb-Det	182	Cobb-Det	66.6
Cobb-Det	5.7	E.Collins-Chi	.332	E.Collins-Chi	.460	Cobb-Det	.487	Fournier-Chi	.920	Fournier-Chi	170	E.Collins-Chi	49.8
Speaker-Bos	3.6	Fournier-Chi	.322	Fournier-Chi	.429	Kavanagh-Det	.452	E.Collins-Chi	.896	E.Collins-Chi	163	Speaker-Bos	39.2
Fournier-Chi	3.6	Speaker-Bos	.322	Speaker-Bos	.416	J.Jackson-Cle-Chi	.445	J.Jackson-Cle-Chi	.830	Speaker-Bos	152	Fournier-Chi	38.4
Chapman-Cle	3.4	McInnis-Phi	.314	Shotton-StL	.409	Roth-Chi-Cle	.438	Speaker-Bos	.827	J.Jackson-Cle-Chi	145	Shotton-StL	32.3

Runs		Hits		Doubles		Triples		Home Runs		Total Bases		Runs Batted In	
Cobb-Det	144	Cobb-Det	208	Veach-Det	40	Crawford-Det	19	Roth-Chi-Cle	7	Cobb-Det	274	Veach-Det	112
E.Collins-Chi	118	Crawford-Det	183	Pratt-StL	31	Fournier-Chi	18	Oldring-Phi	6	Crawford-Det	264	Crawford-Det	112
Vitt-Det	116	Veach-Det	178	Lewis-Bos	31	Roth-Chi-Cle	17			Veach-Det	247	Cobb-Det	99
Speaker-Bos	108	Speaker-Bos	176	Crawford-Det	31	S.Collins-Chi	17			Pratt-StL	237	S.Collins-Chi	85
Chapman-Cle	101	Pratt-StL	175	Cobb-Det	31	Chapman-Cle	17			E.Collins-Chi	227	J.Jackson-Cle-Chi	81

Stolen Bases		Base Stealing Runs		Fielding Runs-Infield		Fielding Runs-Outfield		Wins		Winning Pct.		Complete Games	
Cobb-Det	96	Cobb-Det	7.8	Boone-NY	20.5	Strunk-Phi	11.1	Johnson-Was	27	Wood-Bos	.750	Johnson-Was	35
Maisel-NY	51	Maisel-NY	7.0	Lajoie-Phi	17.0	Hooper-Bos	8.7	Scott-Chi	24	Shore-Bos	.704	Caldwell-NY	31
E.Collins-Chi	46	Moeller-Was	3.5	Barry	16.0	T.Walker-StL	8.5	Faber-Chi	24	Foster-Bos	.704	Dauss-Det	27
Shotton-StL	43	Schang-Phi	2.9	Vitt-Det	12.9	Speaker-Bos	7.8	Dauss-Det	24	Ruth-Bos	.692	Scott-Chi	23
C.Milan-Was	40	Chapman-Cle	2.7	E.Collins-Chi	11.3	Shanks-Was	6.6	Coveleski-Det	22	Scott-Chi	.686	Dubuc-Det	22

Strikeouts		Fewest BB/Game		Games		Saves		Base Runners/9		Adjusted Relief Runs		Relief Ranking	
Johnson-Was	203	Johnson-Was	1.50	Faber-Chi	50	Mays-Bos	7	Johnson-Was	8.90				
Faber-Chi	182	Ayers-Was	1.62	Coveleski-Det	50			Morton-Cle	9.41				
Wyckoff-Phi	157	Benz-Chi	1.62	Scott-Chi	48			Wood-Bos	9.44				
Coveleski-Det	150	Russell-Chi	1.84	Jones-Cle	48			Ayers-Was	9.50				
Mitchell-Cle	149	Cicotte-Chi	1.93					Benz-Chi	9.63				

Innings Pitched		Opponents' Avg.		Opponents' OBP		Earned Run Average		Adjusted ERA		Adjusted Starter Runs		Pitcher Wins	
Johnson-Was	336.2	Leonard-Bos	.208	Johnson-Was	.260	Wood-Bos	1.49	Johnson-Was	191	Johnson-Was	51.1	Johnson-Was	7.4
Coveleski-Det	312.2	Ruth-Bos	.212	Morton-Cle	.268	Johnson-Was	1.55	Wood-Bos	186	Scott-Chi	27.6	Wood-Bos	3.9
Dauss-Det	309.2	Johnson-Was	.214	Wood-Bos	.275	Shore-Bos	1.64	Shore-Bos	169	Shore-Bos	27.2	Scott-Chi	2.9
Caldwell-NY	305.0	Morton-Cle	.216	Benz-Chi	.276	Scott-Chi	2.03	Scott-Chi	146	Morton-Cle	25.0	Foster-Bos	2.9
Faber-Chi	299.2	Wood-Bos	.216	Ayers-Was	.276	Fisher-NY	2.11	Morton-Cle	142	Wood-Bos	24.9	Ruth-Bos	2.8

Alexander the Greatest

With Grover Cleveland Alexander dominating on the hill, the Phillies found themselves in first place in mid-July. Withstanding challenges from Boston and Brooklyn down the stretch, Philadelphia won the pennant by 7 games. Playing in a great home run park, the Phillies again paced the league in long balls; Gavvy Cravath slugged an unheard-of 24. Amazingly, pitching half his games in the Baker Bowl, Alexander allowed just *three* taters in 376 innings and posted a 1.22 ERA, the best mark in the majors until 1968.

The level of parity between NL teams was even greater in 1915. Pitchers had made adjustments to the lively ball, and the NL's average continued its drop to .248, the lowest since 1909. Only 21 games separated Philadelphia from last-place New York. The Giants' ignominious tumble to the basement was hell on manager John McGraw and veteran pitcher Christy Mathewson; again Matty was the league's stingiest pitcher with walks, but an 8-14 record marked his last full season. Meanwhile, sixth-place St. Louis saw a flash of better times ahead with the debut of infielder Rogers Hornsby.

Overall league attendance rose 42 percent, with gains of over 100 percent in Brooklyn, Philadelphia, and—surprisingly—seventh-place Cincinnati. Defending world champion Boston finished second, but attendance began a four-year decline just as the club opened cavernous Braves Field (the center-field fence was 550 feet from home plate). Across town, the AL's Red Sox capped off a big year by edging the Phillies in a five-game World Series in which four of the games were settled by one run and the other by two.

Two teammates from the NL's first Chicago club died. Pitcher and sporting goods entrepreneur Al Spalding passed away in San Diego at age 65. Ross Barnes, the National League's inaugural batting champion in 1876, died in Chicago.

1915 Federal League

TEAM	W	L	T	PCT	GB	HW	HL	R	OR	PA	H	2B	3B	HR	BB	SO	HB	SH	AVG	OBP	SLG	OPS	AOPS	BR	ABR	PF	SB	CS	BSA	BSR
CHI	86	66	3	.566		44	32	640	538	5784	1320	185	77	50	444	590	30	177	.257	.320	.352	672	101	-113	-82	94	161			
STL	87	67	5	.565	0.5	43	34	634	527	5990	1344	199	81	23	576	502	36	233	.261	.340	.345	685	94	-71	-98	105	195			
PIT	86	67	3	.562	0.5	45	31	592	524	5728	1318	180	20	448	561	38	202	.262	.326	.341	667	94	-113	-109	99	224				
KC	81	72	0	.529	5.5	46	31	547	551	5551	1206	200	66	28	368	503	46	200	.244	.303	.329	632	87	-185	-168	96	144			
NEW	80	72	3	.526	6	40	39	585	562	5771	1283	210	80	17	438	550	36	200	.252	.315	.334	649	93	-151	-123	94	184			
BUF	74	78	1	.487	12	37	40	574	634	5620	1261	193	68	40	420	587	19	116	.249	.309	.338	647	85	-161	-170	102	184			
BRO	70	82	1	.461	16	34	40	647	673	5707	1348	205	75	36	473	654	47	152	.268	.336	.360	696	103	-57	-53	99	249			
BAL	47	107	0	.305	40	24	51	550	760	5744	1235	196	53	36	470	641	37	177	.244	.313	.325	638	82	-168	-181	103	128			
TOT	619					313	298	4769		45895	10315	1568	580	250	3637	4588	289	1457	.255	.320	.340	661					1469			

TEAM	CG	SHO	GR	SV	IP	H	HR	BB	SO	BR/9	ERA	AERA	OAV	OOB	PR	APR	PF	OSB	OCS	FA	E	WPB	DP	FW	PW	BW	BSW	DIF
CHI	97	21	68	10	1397.2	1232	34	402	576	10.7	2.64	95	.240	.299	14	-22	92	164	129	.964	233	50	102	.4	-2.4	-8.8		20.8
STL	94	24	88	9	1426.0	1267	22	396	698	10.7	2.73	105	.243	.300	-1	21	105	182	142	.967	212	47	111	2.0	2.3	-10.5		16.3
PIT	88	16	88	12	1382.1	1273	36	441	517	11.4	2.79	97	.253	.317	-10	-13	99	152	149	.971	182	40	98	3.5	-1.4	-11.7		19.1
KC	95	16	75	11	1359.0	1210	29	390	526	10.8	2.82	93	.242	.301	-14	-31	96	192	150	.962	246	53	96	-.5	-3.3	-18.1		26.5
NEW	100	16	76	7	1406.2	1308	15	453	581	11.6	2.60	98	.253	.319	19	-8	94	154	150	.963	239	39	124	.0	-.9	-13.2		18.0
BUF	79	14	97	11	1360.0	1271	35	553	594	12.3	3.38	83	.254	.331	-99	-86	103	234	166	.964	232	48	112	.3	-9.3	-18.3		25.3
BRO	78	10	99	16	1355.2	1299	27	536	467	12.3	3.37	81	.258	.332	-96	-98	100	211	148	.955	290	60	103	-3.1	-10.5	-5.7		13.4
BAL	85	5	92	7	1360.1	1455	52	466	570	13.0	3.96	72	.284	.349	-186	-157	105	180	147	.957	273	37	140	-2.0	-16.9	-19.5		8.4
TOT	716	122	683	83	11047.2					11.6	3.03		.255	.320						.963	1907	374	886					

Batter-Fielder Wins		Batting Average		On-Base Percentage		Slugging Average		On-Base Plus Slugging		Adjusted OPS		Adjusted Batter Runs	
Kauff-Bro	4.7	Kauff-Bro	.342	Kauff-Bro	.446	Kauff-Bro	.509	Kauff-Bro	.955	Kauff-Bro	.170	Kauff-Bro	43.0
Rariden-New	4.3	Fischer-Chi	.329	W.Miller-StL	.400	Konetchy-Pit	.483	Konetchy-Pit	.846	Konetchy-Pit	.138	Wilson-Chi	21.8
Wilson-Chi	2.6	Magee-Bro	.323	Borton-StL	.395	Chase-Buf	.471	Evans-Bro-Bal	.818	Zwilling-Chi	.135	Konetchy-Pit	17.9
Cooper-Bro	2.0	Konetchy-Pit	.314	Evans-Bro-Bal	.392	Fischer-Chi	.449	Zwilling-Chi	.808	Mann-Chi	.131	Zwilling-Chi	17.3
Louden-Buf	1.7	Flack-Chi	.314	Cooper-Bro	.388	Zwilling-Chi	.442	Mann-Chi	.795	Flack-Chi	.129	Evans-Bro-Bal	16.1

Runs		Hits		Doubles		Triples		Home Runs		Total Bases		Runs Batted In	
Borton-StL	97	Tobin-StL	184	Evans-Bro-Bal	34	Mann-Chi	19	Chase-Buf	17	Konetchy-Pit	278	Zwilling-Chi	94
Berghammer-Pit	96	Konetchy-Pit	181	Zwilling-Chi	32	Konetchy-Pit	18	Zwilling-Chi	13	Chase-Buf	267	Konetchy-Pit	93
Evans-Bro-Bal	94	Evans-Bro-Bal	171	Konetchy-Pit	31	Kelly-Pit	17	Kauff-Bro	12	Tobin-StL	254	Chase-Buf	89
Tobin-StL	92	Kauff-Bro	165	Chase-Buf	31	Gilmore-KC	15	Konetchy-Pit	10	Kauff-Bro	246	Kauff-Bro	83
Kauff-Bro	92	Chase-Buf	165					Walsh-Bal-StL	9	Zwilling-Chi	242	Borton-StL	83

Stolen Bases		Base Stealing Runs		Fielding Runs-Infield		Fielding Runs-Outfield		Wins		Winning Pct.		Complete Games	
Kauff-Bro	55			Doolan-Bal-Chi	31.0	Kelly-Pit	13.4	McConnell-Chi	25	McConnell-Chi	.714	Davenport-StL	30
Mowrey-Pit	40			Johnson-StL	16.4	Cooper-Bro	12.4	Allen-Pit	23	Brown-Chi	.680	Hendrix-Chi	26
Kelly-Pit	38			Louden-Buf	11.8	Kauff-Bro	11.2	Davenport-StL	22	Reulbach-New	.677	Schulz-Buf	25
Flack-Chi	37			Perring-KC	10.9	Mann-Chi	5.3	Cullop-KC	22	Cullop-KC	.667	Allen-Pit	24
Magee-Bro	34			Halt-Bro	5.9	Gilmore-KC	5.1			Plank-StL	.656		

Strikeouts		Fewest BB/Game		Games		Saves		Base Runners/9		Adjusted Relief Runs		Relief Ranking	
Davenport-StL	229	Plank-StL	1.81	Davenport-StL	55	Bedient-Buf	10	Plank-StL	9.02				
Schulz-Buf	160	Bender-Bal	1.87	Bedient-Buf	53	Barger-Pit	6	Davenport-StL	9.19				
McConnell-Chi	151	Hearn-Pit	1.90	Crandall-StL	51	Wiltse-Bro	5	Brown-Chi	9.90				
Plank-StL	147	Cullop-KC	1.99	Johnson-KC	46			Anderson-Buf	10.01				
		Quinn-Bal	2.07					Reulbach-New	10.17				

Innings Pitched		Opponents' Avg.		Opponents' OBP		Earned Run Average		Adjusted ERA		Adjusted Starter Runs		Pitcher Wins	
Davenport-StL	392.2	Davenport-StL	.215	Plank-StL	.262	Moseley-New	1.91	Plank-StL	138	Davenport-StL	28.3	Plank-StL	3.0
Crandall-StL	312.2	Plank-StL	.218	Davenport-StL	.268	Plank-StL	2.08	Moseley-New	134	Plank-StL	22.7	Crandall-StL	2.2
Schulz-Buf	309.2	Brown-Chi	.220	Brown-Chi	.279	Brown-Chi	2.09	Davenport-StL	131	Moseley-New	17.3	Brown-Chi	1.8
McConnell-Chi	303.0	Main-KC	.222	Anderson-Buf	.285	McConnell-Chi	2.20	Brown-Chi	120	Reulbach-New	12.2	McConnell-Chi	1.7
Cullop-KC	302.1	Anderson-Buf	.222	Reulbach-New	.287	Davenport-StL	2.20	Reulbach-New	115	Brown-Chi	10.7	Moseley-New	1.3

What Curse?

All season, the Red Sox and Tigers chased the flag together. For Boston, Smokey Joe Wood paced the league with a 1.49 ERA, while Babe Ruth was 18-6 and also hit .315. Peerless center fielder Tris Speaker served as the offense's one-man wrecking crew. Detroit's Sam Crawford, Bobby Veach, and Ty Cobb—who swiped 96 bases, establishing a big-league record that held until 1962—comprised the league's best outfield, an aggregation that helped make up for a very mediocre Tigers infield.

Chicago finished third, with newly acquired second baseman Eddie Collins enjoying another great season. His former team, the Athletics, declined an unprecedented 56 games from their 1914 performance, landing ignominiously in the AL basement. The club's attendance dropped 58 percent. While Mack divested himself of his talent, third sacker Frank Baker chose to hold out all year. Using a staggering 56 players in 1915, trying futilely to replace his formerly great team, Mack's club became the laughingstock of baseball and would finish last for the next *seven years*.

Walter Johnson's best efforts (he led the league in wins, strikeouts, and ERA) couldn't bring the Senators in above fourth, but Washington did give future Hall of Famer Sam Rice his first big-league action. Wally Pipp started his first season as New York's regular first baseman, a position he held for a decade until a headache forced him to sit out an afternoon in favor of Lou Gehrig.

The Red Sox held the cards in 1915. Rookie Carl Mays led the league with 7 saves, heading up a superb set of second-line pitchers who gave Boston much more mound depth that Detroit. The Tigers wound up 2½ games back despite winning 100 games. Boston took on the NL's surprise champions, the Phillies, in the World Series. After Philadelphia's opening victory, the Red Sox won four straight one-run contests, three times scoring the deciding run in the ninth inning. Harry Hooper hit .350 with 2 home runs for the Red Sox.

1914 Federal League

TEAM	W	L	T	PCT	GB	HW	HL	R	OR	PA	H	2B	3B	HR	BB	SO	HB	SH	AVG	OBP	SLG	OPS	AOPS	BR	ABR	PF	SB	CS	BSA	BSR
IND	88	65	4	.575		53	23	762	622	5907	1474	230	90	33	470	668	38	223	.285	.349	.383	732	95	-37	-97	111	273			
CHI	87	67	3	.565	1.5	41	34	621	517	5821	1314	227	55	52	520	645	41	162	.258	.331	.352	683	98	-123	-90	94	171			
BAL	84	70	6	.545	4.5	53	26	645	628	5831	1374	222	67	32	487	589	46	178	.268	.337	.357	694	92	-105	-121	103	152			
BUF	80	71	4	.530	7	47	29	620	602	5649	1264	177	74	37	430	761	23	132	.250	.311	.336	647	80	-207	-216	102	228			
BRO	77	77	3	.500	11.5	47	32	662	677	5805	1402	225	85	42	404	665	45	135	.269	.326	.368	694	96	-120	-116	99	220			
KC	67	84	3	.444	20	38	37	644	683	5712	1369	226	77	39	399	621	36	150	.267	.324	.364	688	97	-129	-107	96	171			
PIT	64	86	4	.427	22.5	37	37	605	698	5751	1339	180	90	65	410	575	34	188	.262	.321	.352	673	90	-159	-155	99	153			
STL	62	89	3	.411	25	31	44	565	697	5791	1254	193	65	26	503	662	34	176	.247	.319	.326	645	77	-200	-222	105	113			
TOT	624					347	262	5124		46267	10790	1680	598	295	3623	5186	302	1344	.263	.328	.355	682					1481			

TEAM	CG	SHO	GR	SV	IP	H	HR	BB	SO	BR/9	ERA	AERA	OAV	OOB	PR	APR	PF	OSB	OCS	FA	E	WPB	DP	FW	PW	BW	BSW	DIF
IND	104	15	67	9	1397.2	1352	29	476	664	12.1	3.06	102	.258	.325	-27	8	108	197	159	.956	289	45	113	-1.2	.8	-10.1		22.0
CHI	93	17	87	8	1420.1	1204	43	393	650	10.3	2.44	109	.233	.291	70	36	92	135	144	.962	249	41	114	1.1	3.7	-9.4		14.5
BAL	88	15	93	13	1392.0	1389	34	392	732	11.7	3.13	97	.268	.323	-15		105	175	144	.960	263	55	105	.6	-1.6	-12.6		20.6
BUF	89	15	91	16	1387.0	1249	45	505	662	11.7	3.16	94	.245	.318	-42	-31	103	154	149	.962	242	55	109	1.3	-3.2	-22.5		28.9
BRO	91	11	92	9	1385.1	1375	31	559	636	12.9	3.33	86	.264	.341	-69	-71	100	216	152	.956	283	49	120	-.9	-7.4	-12.1		20.3
KC	82	10	92	12	1361.0	1387	37	445	600	12.4	3.41	82	.268	.331	-79	-99	96	196	145	.957	279	61	135	-.9	-10.3	-11.1		13.8
PIT	97	9	71	6	1370.0	1416	38	444	510	12.4	3.56	80	.273	.333	-103	-107	99	182	151	.960	253	45	92	.6	-11.1	-16.1		15.7
STL	97	9	73	6	1367.2	1418	38	409	661	12.3	3.59	85	.267	.324	-107	-79	105	226	155	.957	273	59	94	-.6	-8.2	-23.1		18.4
TOT	741	101	666	79	11081.0					12.0	3.20		.263	.328						.959	2131	410	882					

Batter-Fielder Wins		Batting Average		On-Base Percentage		Slugging Average		On-Base Plus Slugging		Adjusted OPS		Adjusted Batter Runs	
Wilson-Chi	5.4	Kauff-Ind	.370	Kauff-Ind	.447	Evans-Bro	.556	Kauff-Ind	.981	Evans-Bro	165	Evans-Bro	39.0
Kenworthy-KC	5.1	Evans-Bro	.348	Evans-Bro	.416	Kauff-Ind	.534	Evans-Bro	.973	Kauff-Ind	150	Kauff-Ind	36.7
Kauff-Ind	3.7	Easterly-KC	.335	Lennox-Pit	.414	Kenworthy-KC	.525	Lennox-Pit	.907	Kenworthy-KC	148	Kenworthy-KC	25.7
Evans-Bro	3.3	Shaw-Bro	.324	Meyer-Bal	.395	Lennox-Pit	.493	Kenworthy-KC	.896	Lennox-Pit	148	Lennox-Pit	24.7
Doolan-Bal	1.7	Campbell-Ind	.318	Wilson-Chi	.394	Zwilling-Chi	.485	Wilson-Chi	.860	Wilson-Chi	142	Wilson-Chi	21.3

Runs		Hits		Doubles		Triples		Home Runs		Total Bases		Runs Batted In	
Kauff-Ind	120	Kauff-Ind	211	Kauff-Ind	44	Evans-Bro	15	Zwilling-Chi	16	Kauff-Ind	305	LaPorte-Ind	107
McKechnie-Ind	107	Zwilling-Chi	185	Evans-Bro	41	Esmond-Ind	15	Kenworthy-KC	15	Zwilling-Chi	287	Evans-Bro	96
Duncan-Bal	99	Evans-Bro	179	Kenworthy-KC	40	Kenworthy-KC	14	Hanford-Buf	12	Kenworthy-KC	286	Zwilling-Chi	95
Kenworthy-KC	93	Oakes-Pit	178	Zwilling-Chi	38			Evans-Bro	12	Evans-Bro	286	Kauff-Ind	95
Evans-Bro	93	Hanford-Buf	174							Hanford-Buf	264	Kenworthy-KC	91

Stolen Bases		Base Stealing Runs		Fielding Runs-Infield		Fielding Runs-Outfield		Wins		Winning Pct.		Complete Games	
Kauff-Ind	75			Doolan-Bal	34.1	Chadbourne-KC	9.2	Hendrix-Chi	29	Ford-Buf	.778	Hendrix-Chi	34
McKechnie-Ind	47			McKechnie-Ind	22.5	Kauff-Ind	8.5	Quinn-Bal	26	Hendrix-Chi	.744	Falkenberg-Ind	33
Myers-Bro	43			Kenworthy-KC	22.4	Hanford-Buf	6.9	Seaton-Bro	25	Quinn-Bal	.650	Moseley-Ind	29
Chadbourne-KC	42			Wisterzil-Bro	16.1	Tobin-StL	5.6	Falkenberg-Ind	25	Seaton-Bro	.641	Quinn-Bal	27
				Tinker-Chi	12.3	W.Miller-StL	4.7	Suggs-Bal	24	Suggs-Bal	.632		

Strikeouts		Fewest BB/Game		Games		Saves		Base Runners/9		Adjusted Relief Runs		Relief Ranking	
Falkenberg-Ind	236	Ford-Buf	1.49	Hendrix-Chi	49	Ford-Buf	6	Hendrix-Chi	8.55				
Moseley-Ind	205	Suggs-Bal	1.61	Falkenberg-Ind	49	Wilhelm-Bal	5	Ford-Buf	8.66				
Hendrix-Chi	189	Quinn-Bal	1.71	Wilhelm-Bal	47	Packard-KC	5	Johnson-Chi	9.07				
Seaton-Bro	172	Hendrix-Chi	1.91	Suggs-Bal	46	Hendrix-Chi	5	Falkenberg-Ind	10.16				
Groom-StL	167	Keupper-StL	2.07	Quinn-Bal	46			Fiske-Chi	10.32				

Innings Pitched		Opponents' Avg.		Opponents' OBP		Earned Run Average		Adjusted ERA		Adjusted Starter Runs		Pitcher Wins	
Falkenberg-Ind	377.1	Hendrix-Chi	.203	Hendrix-Chi	.251	Johnson-Chi	1.57	Ford-Buf	163	Hendrix-Chi	42.2	Hendrix-Chi	5.4
Hendrix-Chi	362.0	Krapp-Buf	.210	Ford-Buf	.254	Hendrix-Chi	1.69	Hendrix-Chi	157	Falkenberg-Ind	33.1	Falkenberg-Ind	3.2
Quinn-Bal	342.2	Ford-Buf	.214	Lange-Chi	.282	Ford-Buf	1.82	Falkenberg-Ind	141	Ford-Buf	30.1	Ford-Buf	2.7
Suggs-Bal	319.1	Lange-Chi	.224	Falkenberg-Ind	.284	Watson-Chi-StL	2.01	Watson-Chi-StL	137	Watson-Chi-StL	19.7	Quinn-Bal	2.5
Moseley-Ind	316.2	Watson-Chi-StL	.230	Anderson-Buf	.297	Falkenberg-Ind	2.22	Lange-Chi	119	Quinn-Bal	15.4	Suggs-Bal	1.7

A Federal Case

Chicago coal baron and machinery manufacturer Jim Gilmore, who had never even heard of the Federal League before August 1913, jumped in with both feet and took over the minor league's Chicago franchise late in the season. Gilmore then became league president and immediately escalated plans to become a major league, inducing well-to-do backers to support new franchises.

Robert B. Ward wanted to name his Brooklyn team the Tip-Tops, after his national bakery. Media outrage over such commercialism led to the alternate name Brookfeds. Restaurant chain owner Charles Weeghman took over the Chicago club, convinced by Gilmore it would take no more than $26,000. By the time new Weeghman Park opened in 1914, the franchise's backers had already spent $412,000.

Gilmore was better at landing big money than big players; Browns manager George Stovall was the first major league player to jump to the FL. The Feds also lured black sheep Hal Chase as well as Joe Tinker and Three Finger Brown, both past their prime.

From Terrapin Park in Baltimore, some of the 27,692 Opening Day patrons could see Oriole Park, where only 1,500 watched John McGraw's Giants play the International League Orioles in an exhibition game. Heavy FL-induced losses led Orioles owner Jack Dunn to offer Babe Ruth to Connie Mack; the A's said they couldn't afford Ruth, but new Red Sox owner Joe Lannin could. Dunn, who made $25,000 for selling Ruth and two others to Boston, moved his club to Richmond for 1915.

Good pitchers were rewarded with money, and victories. Ex-Pirates hurler Claude Hendrix won 29 and Jack Quinn, late of the Braves, won 26 in 1914. Chief Johnson, defying a permanent injunction to keep him from jumping from the Reds to the Feds, pitched through 1915 for Stovall's Kansas City Packers. Benny Kauff, whose major league experience consisted of 11 at bats with the Yankees in 1912, was an offensive force and led Indianapolis to the first FL pennant.

1914 National League

TEAM	W	L	T	PCT	GB	HW	HL	R	OR	PA	H	2B	3B	HR	BB	SO	HB	SH	AVG	OBP	SLG	OPS	AOPS	BR	ABR	PF	SB	CS	BSA	BSR
BOS	94	59	5	.614		51	25	657	548	5979	1307	213	60	35	502	617	50	221	.251	.323	.335	658	103	20	24	99	139			
NY	84	70	2	.545	10.5	43	36	672	576	5789	1363	222	59	30	447	479	57	139	.265	.330	.348	678	112	56	79	97	239			
STL	81	72	4	.529	13	42	34	558	540	5720	1249	203	65	33	445	618	42	187	.248	.314	.333	647	100	-7	0	99	204			
CHI	78	76	2	.506	16.5	46	30	605	638	5784	1229	199	74	42	501	577	42	191	.243	.317	.337	654	101	8	10	100	164			
BRO	75	79	0	.487	19.5	45	34	622	618	5751	1386	90	31	59	376	559	33	190	.269	.323	.355	678	106	39	25	102	173			
PHI	74	80	0	.481	20.5	48	30	651	687	5770	1345	211	52	62	472	570	27	161	.263	.329	.361	690	105	72	31	107	145			
PIT	69	85	4	.448	25.5	39	36	503	540	5753	1197	148	79	18	416	608	36	156	.233	.295	.303	598	88	-106	-84	96	147			
CIN	60	94	3	.390	34.5	34	42	530	651	5635	1178	142	64	16	441	627	54	149	.236	.305	.300	605	83	-81	-96	103	224			
TOT	625					348	267	4798		46181	10254	1510	543	267	3600	4655	341	1394	.251	.317	.334	651					1435			

TEAM	CG	SHO	GR	SV	IP	H	HR	BB	SO	BR/9	ERA	AERA	OAV	OOB	PR	APR	PF	OSB	OCS	FA	E	WPB	DP	FW	PW	BW	BSW	DIF
BOS	104	19	69	6	1421.0	1272	38	477	606	11.4	2.74	100	.249	.319	7	1	99	139	147	.963	246	54	143	1.8	.1	2.6		13.0
NY	88	20	89	9	1390.2	1298	47	367	563	11.0	2.94	90	.253	.306	-25	-49	95	129	121	.961	254	36	119	1.1	-5.3	8.5		2.7
STL	84	16	96	12	1424.2	1279	26	422	531	11.1	2.38	117	.250	.313	64	64	100	176	139	.964	239	36	109	2.2	6.9	.0		-4.6
CHI	70	14	110	11	1389.1	1169	37	528	651	11.2	2.71	103	.233	.311	12	9	100	201	145	.951	310	89	87	-2.7	1.0	1.1		1.7
BRO	80	11	99	11	1368.1	1282	36	466	605	11.8	2.82	101	.255	.323	-5	7	103	199	146	.961	248	42	112	1.2	.8	2.7		-6.7
PHI	85	14	98	7	1379.1	1403	46	452	650	12.4	3.06	96	.270	.335	-42	-20	105	241	170	.950	324	38	81	-3.9	-2.2	3.3		-.3
PIT	86	10	97	11	1405.0	1272	27	392	488	10.9	2.70	98	.249	.308	13	-10	95	170	133	.966	223	39	96	3.4	-1.1	-9.1		-1.2
CIN	74	15	106	15	1387.1	1259	30	489	607	11.7	2.94	100	.248	.320	-24	-3	105	180	146	.952	314	79	113	-2.9	-.3	-10.4		-3.5
TOT	671	119	764	82	11165.2					11.4	2.78		.251	.317						.958	2158	413	860					

Batter-Fielder Wins		Batting Average		On-Base Percentage		Slugging Average		On-Base Plus Slugging		Adjusted OPS		Adjusted Batter Runs	
Maranville-Bos	5.5	Daubert-Bro	.329	Stengel-Bro	.404	Magee-Phi	.509	Cravath-Phi	.901	Cravath-Phi	157	Burns-NY	39.3
Herzog-Cin	4.8	Becker-Phi	.325	Burns-NY	.403	Cravath-Phi	.499	Magee-Phi	.890	Magee-Phi	154	Cravath-Phi	37.5
Magee-Phi	4.2	Dalton-Bro	.319	Cravath-Phi	.402	Connolly-Bos	.494	Wheat-Bro	.830	Burns-NY	149	Magee-Phi	35.4
Wheat-Bro	3.8	Wheat-Bro	.319	Huggins-StL	.396	Wheat-Bro	.452	Stengel-Bro	.829	Stengel-Bro	143	Connolly-Bos	32.5
Smith-Bro-Bos	3.8	Stengel-Bro	.316	Dalton-Bro	.396	Becker-Phi	.446	Burns-NY	.820	Wheat-Bro	143	Wheat-Bro	27.7

Runs		Hits		Doubles		Triples		Home Runs		Total Bases		Runs Batted In	
Burns-NY	100	Magee-Phi	171	Magee-Phi	39	Carey-Pit	17	Cravath-Phi	19	Magee-Phi	277	Magee-Phi	103
Magee-Phi	96	Wheat-Bro	170	Zimmerman-Chi	36	Zimmerman-Chi	12	Saier-Chi	18	Cravath-Phi	249	Cravath-Phi	100
Daubert-Bro	89	Burns-NY	170	Burns-NY	35	Wilson-StL	12	Magee-Phi	15	Wheat-Bro	241	Wheat-Bro	89
Saier-Chi	87	Zimmerman-Chi	167	Connolly-Bos	28	Cutshaw-Bro	12	Luderus-Phi	12	Zimmerman-Chi	239	D.Miller-StL	88
Doyle-NY	87	Becker-Phi	167							Burns-NY	234	Zimmerman-Chi	87

Stolen Bases		Base Stealing Runs		Fielding Runs-Infield		Fielding Runs-Outfield		Wins		Winning Pct.		Complete Games	
Burns-NY	62			Maranville-Bos	49.8	Wheat-Bro	14.5	Alexander-Phi	27	James-Bos	.788	Alexander-Phi	32
Herzog-Cin	46			Herzog-Cin	33.4	Wilson-StL	12.1	Tesreau-NY	26	Doak-StL	.760	Rudolph-Bos	31
Dolan-StL	42			Cutshaw-Bro	27.6	Mann-Bos	9.5	Rudolph-Bos	26	Tesreau-NY	.722	James-Bos	30
Carey-Pit	38			Smith-Bro-Bos	18.3	Paskert-Phi	9.3	James-Bos	26	Rudolph-Bos	.722	Mathewson-NY	29
				Sweeney-Chi	15.8	Carey-Pit	6.7	Mathewson-NY	24	Pfeffer-Bro	.657	Pfeffer-Bro	27

Strikeouts		Fewest BB/Game		Games		Saves		Base Runners/9		Adjusted Relief Runs		Relief Ranking	
Alexander-Phi	214	Mathewson-NY	.66	Cheney-Chi	50	Sallee-StL	6	Rudolph-Bos	9.45				
Tesreau-NY	189	Adams-Pit	1.24	Mayer-Phi	48	Ames-Cin	6	Adams-Pit	9.51				
Vaughn-Chi	165	Marquard-NY	1.58	Ames-Cin	47	Cheney-Chi	5	Marnaux-Pit	9.57				
Cheney-Chi	157	Rudolph-Bos	1.63			Pfeffer-Bro	4	Mathewson-NY	9.78				
James-Bos	156	Alexander-Phi	1.93			McQuillan-Pit	4	Doak-StL	10.09				

Innings Pitched		Opponents' Avg.		Opponents' OBP		Earned Run Average		Adjusted ERA		Adjusted Starter Runs		Pitcher Wins	
Alexander-Phi	355.0	Tesreau-NY	.209	Adams-Pit	.276	Doak-StL	1.72	Doak-StL	162	James-Bos	31.0	James-Bos	3.6
Rudolph-Bos	336.1	Cheney-Chi	.215	Rudolph-Bos	.276	James-Bos	1.90	James-Bos	145	Pfeffer-Bro	30.4	Pfeffer-Bro	3.2
James-Bos	332.1	Doak-StL	.216	Mathewson-NY	.278	Pfeffer-Bro	1.97	Pfeffer-Bro	145	Doak-StL	27.2	Alexander-Phi	3.1
Tesreau-NY	322.1	Vaughn-Chi	.222	Alexander-Phi	.290	Vaughn-Chi	2.05	Vaughn-Chi	135	Sallee-StL	22.4	Sallee-StL	3.1
Mayer-Phi	321.0	Douglas-Cin	.223	Doak-StL	.290	Sallee-StL	2.10	Sallee-StL	133	Alexander-Phi	22.2	Doak-StL	2.6

Hub Miracle

In last place on July 18, the Boston Braves suddenly began to win. Taking 34 of their last 44, they not only caught and passed the New York Giants, but they blew away the league and took the flag by an amazing 10½ games. A three-man rotation carried the pitching load, and manager George Stallings made the most of a weak lineup by instituting a platoon system; this strategy was almost unknown at the time.

During the last month of the season, the Braves moved to Fenway Park due to suddenly huge crowds. Braves attendance had risen 72 percent in 1913, and went up another 84 percent in 1914; this led to the construction of massive Braves Field, which opened the following spring. Despite Boston's miracle victory, and the resulting excitement, overall league attendance fell a frightening 40 percent. Total turnstile clicks were under two million for the first time since 1902.

The birth of the Federal League led to player raids on the AL and NL. In the Senior Circuit, the lower talent level meant parity; the Braves' 94 wins were the lowest total for a flag winner in over a decade. But this didn't matter in October, as the heavily favored Philadelphia Athletics did a belly flop. Boston completed its ridiculous, unbelievable season with a four-game World Series sweep. It was the Senior Circuit's first Series win since 1909.

The Cubs' great 1900s infield was in the news in 1914. First baseman Frank Chance retired; second sacker Johnny Evers was the league MVP, hitting .279 with 87 walks for Boston; shortstop Joe Tinker managed the Federal League's Chicago club; and third baseman Harry Steinfeldt, out of the game since 1911, died at 36.

1914 American League

TEAM	W	L	T	PCT	GB	HW	HL	R	OR	PA	H	2B	3B	HR	BB	SO	HB	SH	AVG	OBP	SLG	OPS	AOPS	BR	ABR	PF	SB	CS	BSA	BSR
PHI	99	53	6	.651		51	24	749	529	5940	1392	165	80	29	545	517	52	217	.272	.348	.352	700	123	113	142	96	231	188	55	-15
BOS	91	62	6	.595	8.5	44	31	589	510	5816	1278	226	85	18	490	549	39	170	.250	.320	.338	658	105	28	28	100	177	176	50	-23
WAS	81	73	4	.526	19	40	33	572	519	5801	1245	176	81	18	470	640	46	177	.244	.313	.320	633	93	-19	-40	104	220	163	57	-9
DET	80	73	4	.523	19.5	42	35	615	618	5908	1318	195	84	25	557	537	44	205	.258	.336	.344	680	109	78	58	103	211	154	58	-7
STL	71	82	6	.464	28.5	42	36	523	615	5706	1241	185	75	17	423	863	35	147	.243	.306	.319	625	99	-40	-19	96	233	189	55	-15
NY	70	84	3	.455	30	36	40	537	550	5756	1144	149	52	12	577	711	47	140	.229	.315	.287	602	88	-59	-57	100	251	191	57	-16
CHI	70	84	3	.455	30	43	37	487	560	5698	1205	161	71	19	408	609	46	204	.239	.302	.311	613	92	-62	-55	99	167	152	52	-16
CLE	51	102	4	.333	48.5	32	47	538	709	5800	1262	178	70	10	450	685	39	154	.245	.310	.312	622	90	-40	-60	104	167	157	52	-18
TOT	631					330	283	4610		46425	10085	1435	598	148	3920	5111	348	1414	.248	.319	.323	642				1657	1370	55	-115

TEAM	CG	SHO	GR	SV	IP	H	HR	BB	SO	BR/9	ERA	AERA	OAV	OOB	PR	APR	PF	OSB	OCS	FA	E	WPB	DP	FW	PW	BW	BSW	DIF
PHI	89	24	95	16	1404.0	1264	18	521	720	11.6	2.78	94	.249	.322	-6	-29	95	228	176	.966	213	62	116	3.5	-3.2	15.7	-.0	7.1
BOS	88	24	92	7	1427.1	1207	18	393	602	10.3	2.36	114	.236	.295	59	51	98	172	156	.963	242	41	99	1.8	5.6	3.1	-1.0	4.9
WAS	75	25	120	19	1420.2	1170	20	520	784	11.0	2.54	111	.233	.311	31	40	103	196	166	.961	254	68	116	1.0	4.4	-4.4	.6	2.4
DET	81	14	117	11	1412.0	1285	17	498	567	11.8	2.86	98	.249	.322	-19	-10	103	230	171	.958	286	54	101	-1.1	-1.1	6.4	.8	-1.6
STL	81	15	113	9	1410.2	1309	20	540	553	12.1	2.85	95	.251	.327	-17	-23	99	212	171	.952	317	71	114	-2.7	-2.5	-2.1	-.0	2.0
NY	98	9	83	2	1397.1	1277	30	390	563	10.9	2.81	98	.250	.308	-12	-10	101	216	176	.963	238	52	93	1.9	-1.1	-6.3	.3	-1.7
CHI	74	17	124	11	1398.2	1207	15	401	660	10.5	2.48	108	.239	.298	40	31	98	164	164	.955	299	47	90	-1.9	3.4	-6.1	-.2	-2.3
CLE	69	9	129	2	1391.2	1365	10	666	688	13.4	3.21	90	.267	.357	-74	-53	105	233	190	.953	300	76	119	-1.9	-5.9	-6.6	-.4	-10.7
TOT	655	137	873	77	11262.1					11.5	2.73		.248	.319						.959	2149	471	848					

Batter-Fielder Wins		Batting Average		On-Base Percentage		Slugging Average		On-Base Plus Slugging		Adjusted OPS		Adjusted Batter Runs	
Speaker-Bos	7.3	Cobb-Det	.368	Collins-Phi	.452	Cobb-Det	.513	Speaker-Bos	.926	Collins-Phi	179	Speaker-Bos	57.6
Collins-Phi	6.9	Collins-Phi	.344	Speaker-Bos	.423	Speaker-Bos	.503	Collins-Phi	.904	Speaker-Bos	178	Collins-Phi	56.7
Bush-Det	5.1	Speaker-Bos	.338	Jackson-Cle	.399	Crawford-Det	.483	Crawford-Det	.871	Crawford-Det	157	Cobb-Det	40.7
Baker-Phi	5.0	Jackson-Cle	.338	Crawford-Det	.388	Jackson-Cle	.464	Jackson-Cle	.862	Baker-Phi	153	Crawford-Det	38.0
T.Walker-StL	4.2	Baker-Phi	.319	Baker-Phi	.380	Collins-Phi	.452	Baker-Phi	.822	Jackson-Cle	153	Baker-Phi	35.3

Runs		Hits		Doubles		Triples		Home Runs		Total Bases		Runs Batted In	
Collins-Phi	122	Speaker-Bos	193	Speaker-Bos	46	Crawford-Det	26	Baker-Phi	9	Speaker-Bos	287	Crawford-Det	104
Speaker-Bos	101	Crawford-Det	183	Lewis-Bos	37	Gardner-Bos	19	Crawford-Det	8	Crawford-Det	281	McInnis-Phi	95
Murphy-Phi	101	Baker-Phi	182	Pratt-StL	34	Speaker-Bos	18	T.Walker-StL	6	Baker-Phi	252	Speaker-Bos	90
Bush-Det	97	McInnis-Phi	181	Collins-Chi	34	T.Walker-StL	16	Fournier-Chi	6	Pratt-StL	240	Baker-Phi	89
		Collins-Phi	181	Leary-StL	28	Hooper-Bos	15			Collins-Phi	238	Collins-Phi	85

Stolen Bases		Base Stealing Runs		Fielding Runs-Infield		Fielding Runs-Outfield		Wins		Winning Pct.		Complete Games	
Maisel-NY	74	Maisel-NY	10.3	Bush-Det	31.8	Speaker-Bos	23.0	Johnson-Was	28	Bender-Phi	.850	Johnson-Was	33
Collins-Phi	58	Peckinpaugh-NY	2.4	Gandil-Was	23.3	T.Walker-StL	16.5	Coveleski-Det	22	Leonard-Bos	.792	Coveleski-Det	23
Speaker-Bos	42	Collins-Phi	2.3	Turner-Cle	22.3	Hooper-Bos	9.9	Collins-Bos	20	Plank-Phi	.682	Dauss-Det	22
Shotton-StL	40	Moriarty-Det	2.2	Boone-NY	17.7	Strunk-Phi	6.3	Leonard-Bos	19	Caldwell-NY	.667	Caldwell-NY	22
		Chapman-Cle	2.1	Moriarty-Det	15.8	Graney-Cle	5.0	Dauss-Det	19	Shawkey-Phi	.652		

Strikeouts		Fewest BB/Game		Games		Saves		Base Runners/9		Adjusted Relief Runs		Relief Ranking	
Johnson-Was	225	McHale-NY	1.55	Johnson-Was	51	Shaw-Was	4	Leonard-Bos	8.29				
Mitchell-Cle	179	Russell-Chi	1.77	Ayers-Was	49	Mitchell-StL	4	Caldwell-NY	8.79				
Leonard-Bos	176	Johnson-Was	1.79	Shaw-Was	48	Faber-Chi	4	Johnson-Was	9.01				
Shaw-Was	164	Warhop-NY	1.83	Benz-Chi	48	Bentley-Was	4	Shore-Bos	9.15				
Dauss-Det	150	Ayers-Was	1.83					Foster-Bos	9.48				

Innings Pitched		Opponents' Avg.		Opponents' OBP		Earned Run Average		Adjusted ERA		Adjusted Starter Runs		Pitcher Wins	
Johnson-Was	371.2	Leonard-Bos	.180	Leonard-Bos	.246	Leonard-Bos	.96	Leonard-Bos	279	Johnson-Was	45.3	Johnson-Was	7.2
Coveleski-Det	303.1	Caldwell-NY	.205	Caldwell-NY	.260	Foster-Bos	1.70	Johnson-Was	163	Leonard-Bos	43.3	Leonard-Bos	4.8
Hamilton-StL	302.1	Shaw-Was	.216	Johnson-Was	.265	Johnson-Was	1.72	Foster-Bos	158	Caldwell-NY	21.0	Caldwell-NY	3.0
Dauss-Det	302.0	Johnson-Was	.217	Foster-Bos	.274	Caldwell-NY	1.94	Caldwell-NY	142	Weilman-StL	20.6	Coveleski-Det	2.3
Weilman-StL	299.0	Foster-Bos	.218	Benz-Chi	.282	Shore-Bos	2.00	Cicotte-Chi	131	Foster-Bos	18.5	Cicotte-Chi	2.1

The End of an A's Era

Moundsmen came to terms with the cork-centered ball by developing techniques to increase movement on their pitches. As a result, in 1914 the AL's batting average dropped sharply for the third straight year to .248, where it would remain until 1918.

Only three players in the league scored 100 runs. Infielder Gus Williams of the Browns fanned 120 times to set new loop record. (His short career ended the next season.) Twenty-two-year-old southpaw Dutch Leonard of the Red Sox was spectacular, finishing 19-5 with an almost inconceivable 0.96 ERA, the best mark ever after the pitching mound was moved back to 60 feet, 6 inches.. The performance of Leonard, and the purchase from Baltimore of a young pitcher named George Ruth, helped the Red Sox improve to 91-62. Dominating Philadelphia remained out of reach, leading the league from June to the finish. Detroit debuted outfielder Harry Heilmann and improved to fourth, while the slumping Chisox got a good show from rookie hurler Red Faber.

Second baseman Eddie Collins of the Athletics led the AL in runs for the third straight season, cementing his reputation as one of baseball's smartest and most capable men. Once again, the entire A's infield was the class of the game, and seven of the eight regular position players hit at least .272. Seven Philadelphia pitchers had at least 10 wins.

Due to competition from the new Federal League, and a shrinking economy, AL attendance fell by nearly a quarter. Even in pennant-winning Philadelphia, without a Federal League competitor, crowds were down 39 percent. Perhaps the low attendance was a harbinger of doom. The heavily favored Athletics punted the World Series in four straight to the underdog Boston Braves. Conscious of his low box office receipts, and angry for his club's poor October play, the shrewd and thrifty Connie Mack chose to dismantle his dynasty.

1913 National League

TEAM	W	L	T	PCT	GB	HW	HL	R	OR	PA	H	2B	3B	HR	BB	SO	HB	SH	AVG	OBP	SLG	OPS	AOPS	BR	ABR	PF	SB	CS	BSA	BSR
NY	101	51	4	.664		54	23	684	515	5837	1427	226	70	31	444	501	63	112	.273	.338	.361	699	105	46	41	101	296	196	60	-3
PHI	88	63	8	.583	12.5	43	33	693	636	6001	1433	257	78	73	383	578	35	183	.265	.318	.382	700	102	31	4	104	156	122	56	-8
CHI	88	65	2	.575	13.5	51	25	720	630	5775	1289	195	96	59	554	634	41	158	.257	.335	.369	704	107	53	52	100	181	160	53	-16
PIT	78	71	6	.523	21.5	41	35	673	585	5830	1383	210	86	35	391	545	35	152	.263	.319	.356	675	103	-14	14	96	181	131	58	-6
BOS	69	82	3	.457	31.5	34	40	641	690	5845	1318	191	60	32	488	640	43	169	.256	.326	.335	661	93	-24	-36	102	177	153	54	-15
BRO	65	84	3	.436	34.5	29	47	595	613	5704	1394	193	86	39	361	555	31	147	.270	.321	.363	684	98	1	-16	103	188	150	56	-11
CIN	64	89	3	.418	37.5	32	44	607	717	5781	1339	170	96	27	458	579	29	162	.261	.325	.347	672	98	-13	-10	100	226	144	61	-1
STL	51	99	3	.340	49	25	48	528	755	5618	1229	152	72	15	451	573	44	156	.247	.316	.316	632	88	-80	-72	99	171	184	48	-27
TOT	620					309	295	5141		46391	10812	1594	644	311	3530	4605	321	1239	.262	.325	.354	679					1576	1240	56	-87

TEAM	CG	SHO	GR	SV	IP	H	HR	BB	SO	BR/9	ERA	AERA	OAV	OOB	PR	APR	PF	OSB	OCS	FA	E	WPB	DP	FW	PW	BW	BSW	DIF
NY	82	12	94	17	1422.0	1276	38	315	651	10.2	2.42	128	.243	.289	122	110	97	158	133	.961	254	34	107	-.6	11.4	4.3	.8	9.1
PHI	77	20	131	11	1455.1	1407	40	512	667	12.1	3.15	105	.261	.330	7	26	104	193	179	.968	214	42	112	2.2	2.7	.4	.3	6.9
CHI	89	12	90	15	1373.0	1330	39	478	556	12.1	3.13	101	.260	.328	10	5	99	176	169	.959	260	58	106	-1.1	.5	5.4	-.5	7.2
PIT	74	9	109	7	1400.0	1344	26	434	590	11.6	2.90	104	.260	.320	46	18	94	222	151	.964	226	42	94	1.1	1.9	1.5	.5	-1.4
BOS	105	13	64	3	1373.1	1343	38	419	597	11.8	3.19	103	.263	.324	1	11	103	195	151	.957	273	43	82	-2.0	1.1	-3.7	-.4	-1.4
BRO	71	9	104	7	1373.0	1287	33	439	548	11.6	3.13	105	.255	.321	11	22	103	197	146	.961	243	37	125	-.3	2.3	-1.7	.0	-9.8
CIN	71	10	113	10	1380.0	1398	40	456	522	12.4	3.46	94	.273	.338	-40	-35	101	185	146	.961	251	52	104	-.4	-3.6	-1.0	1.0	-8.4
STL	74	6	114	11	1351.2	1426	57	477	465	13.0	4.23	76	.280	.348	-156	-150	101	250	165	.965	219	39	113	1.3	-15.6	-7.5	-1.7	-.5
TOT	643	91	819	81	11128.1					11.9	3.20		.262	.325						.962	1940	347	843					

Batter-Fielder Wins		Batting Average		On-Base Percentage		Slugging Average		On-Base Plus Slugging		Adjusted OPS		Adjusted Batter Runs	
Tinker-Cin	3.8	Daubert-Bro	350	Huggins-StL	432	Cravath-Phi	568	Cravath-Phi	974	Cravath-Phi	169	Cravath-Phi	46.7
Evers-Chi	3.4	Cravath-Phi	341	Cravath-Phi	407	Becker-Cin-Phi	502	Zimmerman-Chi	868	Zimmerman-Chi	147	Viox-Pit	30.2
Zimmerman-Chi	3.3	Viox-Pit	317	Daubert-Bro	405	Zimmerman-Chi	490	Saier-Chi	850	Viox-Pit	142	Zimmerman-Chi	26.7
Cravath-Phi	3.0	Tinker-Cin	317	Viox-Pit	399	Saier-Chi	480	Magee-Phi	848	Saier-Chi	141	Saier-Chi	26.5
Meyers-NY	3.0	Becker-Cin-Phi	316	Leach-Chi	391	Magee-Phi	479	Daubert-Bro	829	Magee-Phi	135	Daubert-Bro	22.9

Runs		Hits		Doubles		Triples		Home Runs		Total Bases		Runs Batted In	
Leach-Chi	99	Cravath-Phi	179	Saier-Chi	40	Saier-Chi	21	Cravath-Phi	19	Cravath-Phi	298	Cravath-Phi	128
Carey-Pit	99	Daubert-Bro	178	Burns-NY	37	Miller-Pit	20	Luderus-Phi	18	Luderus-Phi	254	Zimmerman-Chi	95
Lobert-Phi	98	Burns-NY	173	Magee-Phi	36	Konetchy-StL	17	Saier-Chi	14	Saier-Chi	249	Saier-Chi	92
Saier-Chi	94	Lobert-Phi	172	Cravath-Phi	34	Wilson-Pit	14	Magee-Phi	11	Miller-Pit	243	Miller-Pit	90
Magee-Phi	92	Carey-Pit	172			Cravath-Phi	14	Wilson-Pit	10	Lobert-Phi	243	Luderus-Phi	86

Stolen Bases		Base Stealing Runs		Fielding Runs-Infield		Fielding Runs-Outfield		Wins		Winning Pct.		Complete Games	
Carey-Pit	61	Carey-Pit	7.5	Evers-Chi	27.7	Paskert-Phi	11.2	Seaton-Phi	27	Humphries-Chi	800	Tyler-Bos	28
Myers-Bos	57	Myers-Bos	6.2	Tinker-Cin	20.7	Carey-Pit	10.6	Mathewson-NY	25	Alexander-Phi	733	Mathewson-NY	25
Lobert-Phi	41	Marsans-Cin	4.3	Mowrey-StL	17.5	Murray-NY	8.9	Marquard-NY	23	Marquard-NY	697	Cheney-Chi	25
Burns-NY	40	Doyle-NY	3.5	Maranville-Bos	17.1	Magee-StL	8.7	Tesreau-NY	22	Mathewson-NY	694	Adams-Pit	24
Cutshaw-Bro	39	Cutshaw-Bro	2.6	Cutshaw-Bro	16.9	Wheat-Bro	7.9	Alexander-Phi	22	Seaton-Phi	692	Alexander-Phi	23

Strikeouts		Fewest BB/Game		Games		Saves		Base Runners/9		Adjusted Relief Runs		Relief Ranking	
Seaton-Phi	168	Mathewson-NY	62	Cheney-Chi	54	Cheney-Chi	11	Mathewson-NY	9.18	Crandall-NY	2.5	Crandall-NY	2.2
Tesreau-NY	167	Humphries-Chi	1.19	Seaton-Phi	52	Crandall-NY	6	Adams-Pit	9.18				
Alexander-Phi	159	Adams-Pit	1.41	Sallee-StL	50	Brown-Cin	6	Marquard-NY	9.38				
Marquard-NY	151	Marquard-NY	1.53	Alexander-Phi	47	Sallee-StL	5	Humphries-Chi	9.70				
Adams-Pit	144	Suggs-Cin	1.58	Camnitz-Pit-Phi	45			Demaree-NY	9.87				

Innings Pitched		Opponents' Avg.		Opponents' OBP		Earned Run Average		Adjusted ERA		Adjusted Starter Runs		Pitcher Wins	
Seaton-Phi	322.1	Tesreau-NY	220	Mathewson-NY	266	Mathewson-NY	2.06	Mathewson-NY	151	Mathewson-NY	36.8	Mathewson-NY	4.6
Adams-Pit	313.2	Seaton-Phi	226	Adams-Pit	267	Adams-Pit	2.15	Tesreau-NY	143	Adams-Pit	33.1	Adams-Pit	4.1
Alexander-Phi	306.1	Allen-Bro	231	Marquard-NY	273	Tesreau-NY	2.17	Demaree-NY	141	Tesreau-NY	27.8	Tesreau-NY	3.6
Mathewson-NY	306.0	Pierce-Chi	234	Humphries-Chi	277	Demaree-NY	2.21	Adams-Pit	140	Seaton-Phi	24.7	Cheney-Chi	2.6
Cheney-Chi	305.0	Tyler-Bos	235	Demaree-NY	286	Pierce-Chi	2.30	Brennan-Phi	139	Marquard-NY	23.0	Marquard-NY	2.4

Change of the Guard

The Phillies paced the loop through June, but the deeper Giants soon took over. Pitching again carried the day for New York, but they had a strong attack and the league's best manager, John McGraw. Despite New York's third straight pennant, and their fifth flag since 1904, it was a year of large-scale change in the Senior Circuit. The Phillies were a legitimate contender, riding the arm of Grover Cleveland Alexander and the bat of Gavvy Cravath, who led in homers with 19 (he learned to push the ball toward Baker Bowl's 272-foot right-field fence). In a decade that saw the Philadelphia's attendance wildly fluctuate each season, 1913 was a good year; fans came out in 80 percent greater numbers to greet the second-place club. On the other side of the state, though, Pittsburgh's attendance declined by 30 percent.

Brooklyn opened their new palace, Ebbets Field, and celebrated by beginning a steady improvement that would bring them the flag in 1916. Meanwhile, the Cubs began five years of misery by dumping several top players without talent ready to replace them. Owner Charlie Murphy caused so much bad PR for the franchise that in 1914 the Federal League was able to get a toehold, using Chicago as its bellwether.

The difference between athletics and baseball was clearly outlined in 1913. Debuting that year was Jim Thorpe, the world's greatest athlete; he could never hit the curve, however, and only exceeded 100 games played once in his six years in the majors. Edd Roush began a career that included three major leagues, two NL batting titles, and 2,376 hits. His only AL hit came with the 1913 White Sox.

Connie Mack's Athletics won the World Series against New York in five relatively easy games. It marked the third time since 1905 that the A's and Giants faced each other; the Mackmen took two of the matchups. It would be seventy-six years before they met again, when both teams resided in California's Bay Area.

1913 American League

TEAM	W	L	T	PCT	GB	HW	HL	R	OR	PA	H	2B	3B	HR	BB	SO	HB	SH	AVG	OBP	SLG	OPS	AOPS	BR	ABR	PF	SB	CS	BSA	BSF
PHI	96	57	0	.627		50	26	794	592	5817	1412	223	80	33	534	547	65	174	.280	.356	.375	731	124	140	157	98	221			
WAS	90	64	1	.584	6.5	42	35	596	562	5667	1281	156	81	19	440	595	42	111	.252	.317	.326	643	93	-38	-50	102	287			
CLE	86	66	3	.566	9.5	45	32	633	536	5712	1349	206	74	16	420	557	53	208	.268	.331	.348	679	102	31	13	103	191			
BOS	79	71	1	.527	15.5	41	34	631	610	5649	1334	220	101	17	467	534	39	174	.268	.336	.364	700	109	67	51	103	189			
CHI	78	74	1	.513	17.5	40	37	488	498	5452	1139	157	66	24	398	550	36	196	.236	.299	.311	610	86	-97	-92	99	156			
DET	66	87	0	.431	30	34	42	625	716	5760	1344	180	101	24	496	501	46	154	.265	.336	.355	691	111	54	64	99	218			
NY	57	94	2	.377	38	27	47	529	668	5611	1157	155	45	8	534	617	57	140	.237	.320	.292	612	85	-73	-75	100	203			
STL	57	96	2	.373	39	31	46	528	642	5667	1193	179	73	18	455	769	43	138	.237	.306	.312	618	90	-81	-66	97	209			
TOT	614					310	299	4824		45335	10209	1476	621	159	3744	4670	381	1295	.256	.325	.336	661					1674			

TEAM	CG	SHO	GR	SV	IP	H	HR	BB	SO	BR/9	ERA	AERA	OAV	OOB	PR	APR	PF	OSB	OCS	FA	E	WPB	DP	FW	PW	BW	BSW	DIF
PHI	69	17	124	22	1351.1	1200	24	532	630	11.8	3.19	87	.243	.321	-39	-69	94	188	162	.966	212	59	108	3.3	-7.3	16.7		6.9
WAS	78	23	120	20	1396.1	1177	35	465	758	11.0	2.73	108	.233	.306	31	34	101	177	156	.960	261	57	122	.4	3.6	-5.3		14.3
CLE	93	18	90	5	1386.2	1278	19	502	689	11.8	2.54	119	.251	.324	59	71	104	176	169	.962	242	56	124	1.6	7.6	1.4		-.5
BOS	83	12	95	10	1358.1	1323	6	442	710	11.9	2.94	100	.262	.325	-2	-3	100	229	169	.961	238	52	84	1.4	-.3	5.4		-2.5
CHI	84	17	98	8	1360.1	1190	10	438	602	11.0	2.33	125	.239	.305	91	89	100	166	144	.960	255	51	104	.5	9.5	-9.8		1.8
DET	90	4	87	7	1360.0	1359	13	504	468	12.6	3.38	86	.267	.339	-68	-71	100	256	177	.954	303	62	105	-2.5	-7.6	6.8		-7.2
NY	75	8	99	7	1344.0	1318	31	455	530	12.2	3.27	91	.262	.330	-51	-41	102	294	192	.954	293	56	94	-1.9	-4.4	-8.0		-4.2
STL	104	14	60	5	1382.1	1369	21	454	476	12.2	3.06	96	.269	.335	-20	-22	100	191	184	.954	301	45	125	-2.2	-2.3	-7.0		-7.9
TOT	676	113	773	84	10939.1					11.8	2.93		.256	.325						.959	2105	438	866					

Batter-Fielder Wins		Batting Average		On-Base Percentage		Slugging Average		On-Base Plus Slugging		Adjusted OPS		Adjusted Batter Runs	
Collins-Phi	7.0	Cobb-Det	.390	Cobb-Det	.467	Jackson-Cle	.551	Jackson-Cle	1011	Cobb-Det	196	Jackson-Cle	63.4
Baker-Phi	6.6	Jackson-Cle	.373	Jackson-Cle	.460	Cobb-Det	.535	Cobb-Det	1002	Jackson-Cle	190	Speaker-Bos	53.6
Speaker-Bos	6.5	Speaker-Bos	.363	Collins-Phi	.441	Speaker-Bos	.533	Speaker-Bos	.974	Speaker-Bos	180	Cobb-Det	53.5
Jackson-Cle	5.9	Collins-Phi	.345	Speaker-Bos	.441	Baker-Phi	.493	Baker-Phi	.906	Baker-Phi	168	Baker-Phi	49.9
Cobb-Det	4.6	Baker-Phi	.337	Baker-Phi	.413	Crawford-Det	.489	Collins-Phi	.894	Collins-Phi	165	Collins-Phi	49.1

Runs		Hits		Doubles		Triples		Home Runs		Total Bases		Runs Batted In	
Collins-Phi	125	Jackson-Cle	197	Jackson-Cle	39	Crawford-Det	23	Baker-Phi	12	Cobb-Det	298	Baker-Phi	117
Baker-Phi	116	Crawford-Det	193	Speaker-Bos	35	Speaker-Bos	22	Crawford-Det	9	Jackson-Cle	291	McInnis-Phi	90
Jackson-Cle	109	Baker-Phi	190	Baker-Phi	34	Jackson-Cle	17	Bodie-Chi	8	Baker-Phi	278	Lewis-Bos	90
Shotton-StL	105	Speaker-Bos	189	Crawford-Det	32	Williams-StL	16	Jackson-Cle	7	Speaker-Bos	277	Pratt-StL	87
E.Murphy-Phi	105	Collins-Phi	184			Cobb-Det	16			Collins-Phi	242	Barry-Phi	85

Stolen Bases		Base Stealing Runs		Fielding Runs-Infield		Fielding Runs-Outfield		Wins		Winning Pct.		Complete Games	
Milan-Was	75			Weaver-Chi	35.5	Speaker-Bos	18.6	Johnson-Was	36	Johnson-Was	.837	Johnson-Was	29
Moeller-Was	62			Collins-Phi	16.4	Lewis-Bos	11.2	Falkenberg-Cle	23	Bush-Phi	.714	Russell-Chi	29
Collins-Phi	55			Lajoie-Cle	14.5	Johnston-StL	9.8	Russell-Chi	22	Boehling-Was	.708	Scott-Chi	25
Cobb-Det	51			Turner-Cle	13.4	Hooper-Bos	7.7	Bender-Phi	21	Collins-Bos	.704		
Speaker-Bos	46			Baker-Phi	9.3	Shotton-StL	7.3			Falkenberg-Cle	.697		

Strikeouts		Fewest BB/Game		Games		Saves		Base Runners/9		Adjusted Relief Runs		Relief Ranking	
Johnson-Was	243	Johnson-Was	.99	Russell-Chi	52	Bender-Phi	13	Johnson-Was	7.26				
V.Gregg-Cle	166	Collins-Bos	1.35	Scott-Chi	48	Hughes-Was	6	Russell-Chi	9.55				
Falkenberg-Cle	166	Mitchell-StL	1.72	Johnson-Was	48	Bedient-Bos	5	Scott-Chi	10.00				
Scott-Chi	158	Plank-Phi	2.11	Bender-Phi	48			Cicotte-Chi	10.07				
Groom-Was	156	Weilman-StL	2.15	V.Gregg-Cle	44			Plank-Phi	10.13				

Innings Pitched		Opponents' Avg.		Opponents' OBP		Earned Run Average		Adjusted ERA		Adjusted Starter Runs		Pitcher Wins	
Johnson-Was	346.0	Johnson-Was	.190	Johnson-Was	.220	Johnson-Was	1.14	Johnson-Was	258	Johnson-Was	69.8	Johnson-Was	10.9
Russell-Chi	316.2	Mitchell-Cle	.202	Russell-Chi	.275	Cicotte-Chi	1.58	Cicotte-Chi	185	Russell-Chi	37.9	Russell-Chi	4.7
Scott-Chi	312.1	Engel-Was	.218	Cicotte-Chi	.283	Scott-Chi	1.90	Mitchell-Cle	159	Cicotte-Chi	36.4	Cicotte-Chi	4.1
V.Gregg-Cle	285.2	Russell-Chi	.220	Scott-Chi	.283	Russell-Chi	1.90	Scott-Chi	154	Scott-Chi	34.5	Scott-Chi	3.8
Falkenberg-Cle	276.0	Caldwell-NY	.221	Bender-Phi	.287	Mitchell-Cle	1.91	Russell-Chi	153	Falkenberg-Cle	27.0	Falkenberg-Cle	2.9

Chief Saves the Day

Prior to the season, another big-market AL club shifted its headquarters as New York moved into the Giants' home, the Polo Grounds. The dimensions were smaller than those of Hilltop Park, but the potential gate receipts were much higher.

After a year off, the Athletics won once more, withstanding an August challenge from eventual third-place finishers Cleveland, who had a big year from Joe Jackson. Washington's Walter Johnson won 14 games in a row, helping his Senators finish second again. However, Boston slipped to fourth as Smokey Joe Wood broke his arm.

Chief Bender was 21-10 for the Athletics, and also was credited many years later with 13 saves, which tied the retroactive all-time record. Frank Baker paced the AL in homers and RBIs, and the entire club led the league in hits, doubles, homers, slugging, walks, and, of course, runs. Four Philadelphians scored 100 runs or more; among the other seven clubs, only three players could boast such a feat. It was a year of yet more star debuts for the A's. Pitcher Bob Shawkey, who would go one to glory with the Yankees, was 6-5 for the Mackmen, and catcher Wally Schang played 79 games.

In an entertaining five-game World Series, the A's defeated New York. The Giants' only win came in Game 2, a 10-inning shutout by Christy Mathewson, who drove in the game-deciding run. Three of the Philadelphia wins were by two or fewer runs. Both Mathewson and Eddie Plank were superb, posting identical 0.95 ERAs. Bender won both his games. Joe Bush, winner of Game 3, was the only other A's pitcher used.

Former Cleveland Spiders outfielder Lou "Chief" Sockalexis, who lost his potentially great career to drinking, died at 42 on Christmas Eve. While his life ended sadly, he had a legacy: a few years later, the city's American League club would become known as the "Indians."

1912 National League

TEAM	W	L	T	PCT	GB	HW	HL	R	OR	PA	H	2B	3B	HR	BB	SO	HB	SH	AVG	OBP	SLG	OPS	AOPS	BR	ABR	PF	SB	CS	BSA	BSR
NY	103	48	3	.682		49	25	823	571	5802	1451	231	89	47	514	497	69	152	.286	.360	.395	755	110	92	69	103	319			
PIT	93	58	1	.616	10	44	31	751	565	5879	1493	222	129	39	420	514	26	181	.284	.340	.398	738	110	39	50	99	177			
CHI	91	59	2	.607	11.5	46	30	756	668	5830	1398	245	91	42	560	615	40	182	.277	.354	.386	740	109	65	68	100	164			
CIN	75	78	2	.490	29	45	32	656	722	5794	1310	183	89	21	479	492	25	175	.256	.323	.339	662	90	-93	-74	97	248			
PHI	73	79	0	.480	30.5	34	41	670	688	5754	1354	244	43	68	464	615	34	179	.267	.332	.367	699	91	-21	-63	107	159			
STL	63	90	0	.412	41	37	40	659	830	5813	1366	190	77	27	508	620	47	166	.268	.340	.352	692	97	-28	-11	98	193			
BRO	58	95	0	.379	46	33	43	651	744	5830	1377	220	73	32	490	584	40	159	.268	.336	.358	694	100	-27	1	96	179			
BOS	52	101	2	.340	52	31	47	693	871	6031	1465	227	68	35	454	690	48	168	.273	.335	.361	696	94	-27	-39	102	137			
TOT	613					319	289	5659		46733	11214	1762	684	286	3889	4627	329	1362	.272	.340	.369	710					1576			

TEAM	CG	SHO	GR	SV	IP	H	HR	BB	SO	BR/9	ERA	AERA	OAV	OOB	PR	APR	PF	OSB	OCS	FA	E	WPB	DP	FW	PW	BW	BSW	DIF
NY	93	8	76	16	1369.2	1352	35	338	652	11.3	2.58	130	.259	.307	124	120	99	141	113	.956	280	49	123	-2.1	11.8	6.8		11.0
PIT	94	18	76	7	1385.0	1268	28	497	664	11.8	2.85	114	.251	.324	84	63	96	154	137	.972	169	38	125	6.0	6.2	4.9		.4
CHI	80	15	104	9	1358.2	1307	33	493	554	12.2	3.42	97	.259	.331	-4	-20	98	153	150	.960	249	46	125	-.0	-2.0	6.7		11.3
CIN	86	13	89	10	1377.2	1455	28	452	561	12.9	3.42	98	.279	.344	-4	-14	99	202	153	.960	249	35	102	.4	-1.4	-7.3		6.8
PHI	81	10	99	9	1355.0	1381	43	515	616	12.9	3.25	111	.272	.344	23	50	106	221	173	.963	231	61	98	1.3	4.9	-6.2		-3.1
STL	61	6	134	12	1363.0	1466	31	560	487	13.7	3.85	89	.286	.361	-68	-63	101	266	188	.957	274	41	113	-1.8	-6.2	-1.1		-4.5
BRO	71	10	99	8	1357.0	1399	45	510	553	12.9	3.64	92	.273	.343	-37	-50	98	214	162	.959	255	36	96	-.3	-4.9	.0		-13.3
BOS	88	5	94	5	1390.2	1544	43	521	542	13.6	4.17	86	.291	.359	-119	-94	105	225	176	.954	297	69	129	-3.2	-9.2	-3.8		-8.2
TOT	654	85	771	76	10946.2					12.7	3.40		.272	.340						.960	2004	375	911					

Batter-Fielder Wins	Batting Average	On-Base Percentage	Slugging Average	On-Base Plus Slugging	Adjusted OPS	Adjusted Batter Runs
Wagner-Pit 5.9	Zimmerman-Chi 372	Evers-Chi 431	Zimmerman-Chi 571	Zimmerman-Chi 989	Zimmerman-Chi 170	Zimmerman-Chi ...51.1
Sweeney-Bos 5.6	Meyers-NY 358	Huggins-StL 422	Wilson-Pit 513	Wagner-Pit 891	Wagner-Pit 145	Wagner-Pit 34.0
Zimmerman-Chi ..5.3	Sweeney-Bos 344	Paskert-Phi 420	Wagner-Pit 496	Evers-Chi 873	Evers-Chi 139	Evers-Chi 30.1
Meyers-NY 4.0	Evers-Chi 341	Zimmerman-Chi 418	Meyers-NY 477	Doyle-NY 864	Wilson-Pit 134	Sweeney-Bos 29.5
Evers-Chi 3.7	Doyle-NY 330	Sweeney-Bos 416	Doyle-NY 471	Titus-Phi-Bos 862	Konetchy-StL 134	Meyers-NY 26.4

Runs	Hits	Doubles	Triples	Home Runs	Total Bases	Runs Batted In
Bescher-Cin...120	Zimmerman-Chi ...207	Zimmerman-Chi ...41	Wilson-Pit ...36	Zimmerman-Chi ...14	Zimmerman-Chi ...318	Wagner-Pit ...102
Carey-Pit ...114	Sweeney-Bos ...204	Paskert-Phi ...37	Wagner-Pit ...20	Schulte-Chi ...12	Wilson-Pit ...299	Sweeney-Bos ...100
Paskert-Phi ...102	Campbell-Bos ...185	Wagner-Pit ...35	Murray-NY ...20	Wilson-Pit ...11	Wagner-Pit ...277	Zimmerman-Chi ...99
Campbell-Bos ...102	Doyle-NY ...184	Miller-Pit ...33	Daubert-Bro ...16	Merkle-NY ...11	Sweeney-Bos ...264	Wilson-Pit ...95
	Wagner-Pit ...181	Doyle-NY ...33		Cravath-Phi ...11	Doyle-NY ...263	Murray-NY ...92

Stolen Bases	Base Stealing Runs	Fielding Runs-Infield	Fielding Runs-Outfield	Wins	Winning Pct.	Complete Games
Bescher-Cin...67		Tinker-Chi ...26.3	Sheckard-Chi ...9.3	Marquard-NY ...26	Hendrix-Pit ...727	Cheney-Chi ...28
Carey-Pit ...45		Sweeney-Bos ...26.0	Magee-StL ...5.9	Cheney-Chi ...26	Cheney-Chi ...722	Mathewson-NY ...27
Snodgrass-NY...43		Herzog-NY ...20.1	Cravath-Phi ...5.5	Hendrix-Pit ...24	Tesreau-NY ...708	Suggs-Cin ...25
Murray-NY ...38		Wagner-Pit ...17.1	Murray-NY ...5.3	Mathewson-NY ...23	Marquard-NY ...703	Hendrix-Pit ...25
		Fletcher-NY ...14.5	Miller-Bos-Phi ...4.3	Camnitz-Pit ...22	Richie-Chi ...667	Alexander-Phi ...25

Strikeouts	Fewest BB/Game	Games	Saves	Base Runners/9	Adjusted Relief Runs	Relief Ranking
Alexander-Phi ...195	Mathewson-NY ...99	Benton-Cin ...50	Sallee-StL ...6	Robinson-Pit ...9.57		
Hendrix-Pit ...176	Robinson-Pit ...1.54	Sallee-StL ...48	Mathewson-NY ...5	Mathewson-NY ...10.07		
Marquard-NY...175	Suggs-Cin ...1.66	Alexander-Phi ...46	Rucker-Bro ...4	Rucker-Bro ...10.49		
Benton-Cin ...162	Ames-NY ...1.76	Rucker-Bro ...45	Reulbach-Chi ...4	Tesreau-NY ...10.85		
Rucker-Bro ...151	Adams-Pit ...1.85	Seaton-Phi ...44		Adams-Pit ...10.94		

Innings Pitched	Opponents' Avg.	Opponents' OBP	Earned Run Average	Adjusted ERA	Adjusted Starter Runs	Pitcher Wins
Alexander-Phi...310.1	Tesreau-NY ...204	Mathewson-NY...281	Tesreau-NY ...1.96	Tesreau-NY ...172	Mathewson-NY ...43.1	Mathewson-NY ...5.3
Mathewson-NY...310.0	Cheney-Chi ...234	Robinson-Pit...284	Mathewson-NY ...2.12	Mathewson-NY ...159	Rucker-Bro ...37.3	Rucker-Bro...5.1
Cheney-Chi...303.1	Robinson-Pit ...237	Rucker-Bro...298	Rucker-Bro ...2.21	Rucker-Bro ...151	Tesreau-NY ...33.8	Hendrix-Pit...4.0
Suggs-Cin...303.0	Brown-Bos ...239	Tesreau-NY...298	Rixey-Phi ...2.26	Rixey-Phi ...145	Marquard-NY ...30.0	Marquard-NY...3.5
Benton-Cin...302.0	O'Toole-Pit ...241	Adams-Pit...303	Ames-NY ...2.46	Robinson-Pit ...144	Alexander-Phi...27.2	Alexander-Phi ...3.0

The Bats Take Over

Offense continued to increase in 1912 as runs scored reached 4.62 per game, the highest total in a decade. Honus Wagner led the league in RBIs at age 38, while Bob Bescher scored 120 runs and swiped 67 bases for the Reds. But the biggest numbers came from relative obscurities. Owen "Chief" Wilson, a 29-year-old Pittsburgh outfielder, rapped out an amazing 36 triples, the highest total before or since. Previously unheralded Cubs third baseman Heinie Zimmerman stomped the competition in batting average, slugging, hits, and doubles. Zimmerman's was one of the game's great fluke seasons.

There were pitchers of merit. Christy Mathewson, Rube Marquard, and rookie Jeff Tesreau combined to win 66 games for the Giants; Marquard's 19 wins in a row were the most in a season in the twentieth century and tied the all-time mark set by New York ace Tim Keefe in 1888. Two rookies made splashy entries in 1912: Eppa Rixey had 10 victories for Philadelphia, while Wilbur Cooper was a late-season sensation in Pittsburgh.

Two of the game's great personalities debuted, and one died. Casey Stengel started his career with Brooklyn, while Boston brought up 21-year-old shortstop Rabbit Maranville. Former Giants pitcher Bugs Raymond, who had partied his way out of the majors the year before, was beaten to death in September in an altercation during a semi-pro game.

The pennant race held little tension. The Giants won easily, capturing 16 straight at one point. The only early challenger, Cincinnati, dropped to fourth; their new digs, Redland Field, continuing a trend that saw five NL clubs open new parks during the decade. A lack of pennant-race excitement hurt attendance, which fell in six of eight cities and dropped by 15 percent. For the fifth consecutive year, New York, Pittsburgh, and Chicago ranked as the Senior Circuit's top clubs. However, the Giants again failed in the World Series, losing in five to Boston.

1912 American League

TEAM	W	L	T	PCT	GB	HW	HL	R	OR	PA	H	2B	3B	HR	BB	SO	HB	SH	AVG	OBP	SLG	OPS	AOPS	BR	ABR	PF	SB	CS	BSA	BSR
BOS	105	47	2	.691		57	20	799	544	5871	1404	269	84	29	565		45	190	.277	.355	.380	735	110	111	73	105	185			
WAS	91	61	2	.599	14	45	32	699	581	5729	1298	202	86	20	472		38	144	.256	.324	.341	665	94	-32	-36	101	273			
PHI	90	62	1	.592	15	45	31	779	658	5835	1442	204	108	22	485		38	201	.282	.349	.377	726	117	82	111	96	258			
CHI	78	76	4	.506	28	34	43	639	648	5867	1321	174	80	17	423		51	211	.255	.317	.329	646	93	-71	-50	97	213			
CLE	75	78	2	.490	30.5	41	35	677	681	5798	1403	219	77	12	407		51	208	.273	.333	.353	686	98	6	-15	103	194			
DET	69	84	1	.451	36.5	37	39	720	777	5882	1376	189	86	19	530		58	151	.268	.343	.349	692	106	27	51	97	277			
STL	53	101	3	.344	53	27	50	552	764	5710	1262	166	71	19	449		42	139	.248	.315	.320	635	90	-89	-67	96	176			
NY	50	102	1	.329	55	31	44	630	842	5772	1320	168	79	18	463		65	152	.259	.329	.334	663	90	-33	-70	106	247			
TOT	619					317	294	5495		46464	10826	1591	671	156	3794	5157	388	1396	.265	.333	.348	681					1823			

TEAM	CG	SHO	GR	SV	IP	H	HR	BB	SO	BR/9	ERA	AERA	OAV	OOB	PR	APR	PF	OSB	OCS	FA	E	WPB	DP	FW	PW	BW	BSW	DIF
BOS	108	18	59	6	1362.0	1243	18	385	712	11.0	2.76	124	.248	.306	88	101	103	202	163	.957	267	40	88	2.4	10.1	7.3		9.2
WAS	98	11	73	7	1376.2	1219	24	525	828	11.8	2.69	125	.242	.320	99	104	101	164	178	.954	297	70	92	.7	10.4	-3.6		7.6
PHI	95	11	81	9	1357.0	1273	12	518	601	12.3	3.32	93	.258	.336	2	-33	93	171	172	.959	263	55	115	2.5	-3.3	11.1		3.7
CHI	85	14	101	16	1413.0	1398	26	426	698	11.8	3.06	105	.264	.322	44	27	96	239	190	.956	291	50	102	1.5	2.7	-5.0		1.8
CLE	94	7	80	7	1352.2	1367	15	523	622	12.9	3.30	104	.272	.346	6	20	103	240	190	.954	287	65	124	1.4	2.0	-1.5		-3.4
DET	107	7	59	5	1367.1	1438	16	521	512	13.3	3.77	87	.277	.350	-66	-72	98	289	192	.950	338	83	91	-1.7	-7.2	5.1		-3.7
STL	85	8	89	5	1369.2	1433	17	442	547	12.7	3.71	90	.277	.341	-56	-55	100	271	193	.947	341	54	127	-1.6	-5.5	-6.7		-10.3
NY	105	5	60	3	1335.0	1448	28	436	637	13.0	4.13	88	.282	.344	-117	-66	108	248	186	.940	382	64	77	-4.4	-6.6	-7.0		-8.0
TOT	777	81	602	58	10933.1					12.3	3.34		.265	.333						.952	2466	481	816					

Batter-Fielder Wins		Batting Average		On-Base Percentage		Slugging Average		On-Base Plus Slugging		Adjusted OPS		Adjusted Batter Runs	
Speaker-Bos	7.2	Cobb-Det	.409	Speaker-Bos	.464	Cobb-Det	.584	Cobb-Det	1040	Cobb-Det	203	Cobb-Det	71.5
Jackson-Cle	7.1	Jackson-Cle	.395	Jackson-Cle	.458	Jackson-Cle	.579	Jackson-Cle	1036	Jackson-Cle	190	Speaker-Bos	68.2
Baker-Phi	6.5	Speaker-Bos	.383	Cobb-Det	.456	Speaker-Bos	.567	Speaker-Bos	1031	Speaker-Bos	185	Jackson-Cle	66.7
Collins-Phi	6.4	Lajoie-Cle	.368	Collins-Phi	.450	Baker-Phi	.541	Baker-Phi	945	Baker-Phi	176	Baker-Phi	54.4
Cobb-Det	5.6	Collins-Phi	.348	Lajoie-Cle	.414	Crawford-Det	.470	Collins-Phi	885	Collins-Phi	159	Collins-Phi	49.6

Runs		Hits		Doubles		Triples		Home Runs		Total Bases		Runs Batted In	
Collins-Phi	137	Jackson-Cle	226	Speaker-Bos	53	Jackson-Cle	26	Speaker-Bos	10	Jackson-Cle	331	Baker-Phi	130
Speaker-Bos	136	Cobb-Det	226	Jackson-Cle	44	Cobb-Det	23	Baker-Phi	10	Speaker-Bos	329	Lewis-Bos	109
Jackson-Cle	121	Speaker-Bos	222	Baker-Phi	40	Crawford-Det	21	Cobb-Det	7	Cobb-Det	323	Crawford-Det	109
Cobb-Det	120	Baker-Phi	200	Lewis-Bos	36	Baker-Phi	21			Baker-Phi	312	McInnis-Phi	101
Baker-Phi	116					Gardner-Bos	18			Crawford-Det	273		

Stolen Bases		Base Stealing Runs		Fielding Runs-Infield		Fielding Runs-Outfield		Wins		Winning Pct.		Complete Games	
Milan-Was	88			McBride-Was	27.8	Speaker-Bos	16.4	Wood-Bos	34	Wood-Bos	.872	Wood-Bos	35
Collins-Phi	63			Bush-Det	27.0	Jackson-Cle	13.9	Johnson-Was	33	Plank-Phi	.813	Johnson-Was	34
Cobb-Det	61			Louden-Det	17.6	Hogan-StL	9.9	Walsh-Chi	27	Johnson-Was	.733	Walsh-Chi	32
Speaker-Bos	52			Rath-Chi	16.2	Strunk-Phi	8.2	Plank-Phi	26	Bedient-Bos	.690	Ford-NY	30
Zeider-Chi	48			Collins-Phi	14.0	Milan-Was	6.8	Groom-Was	24	Coombs-Phi	.677		

Strikeouts		Fewest BB/Game		Games		Saves		Base Runners/9		Adjusted Relief Runs		Relief Ranking	
Johnson-Was	303	Bender-Phi	1.74	Walsh-Chi	62	Walsh-Chi	10	Johnson-Was	8.56				
Wood-Bos	258	Johnson-Was	1.85	Johnson-Was	50	Warhop-NY	3	Wood-Bos	9.44				
Walsh-Chi	254	Collins-Bos	1.90	Wood-Bos	43	Mogridge-Chi	3	Walsh-Chi	9.78				
Gregg-Cle	184	Powell-StL	1.99	Groom-Was	43	Lange-Chi	3	Bedient-Bos	10.29				
Groom-Was	179	Warhop-NY	2.06	Benz-Chi	42	Dubuc-Det	3	Collins-Bos	10.66				

Innings Pitched		Opponents' Avg.		Opponents' OBP		Earned Run Average		Adjusted ERA		Adjusted Starter Runs		Pitcher Wins	
Walsh-Chi	393.0	Johnson-Was	.196	Johnson-Was	.248	Johnson-Was	1.39	Johnson-Was	241	Johnson-Was	77.1	Johnson-Was	10.6
Johnson-Was	369.0	Wood-Bos	.216	Wood-Bos	.272	Wood-Bos	1.91	Wood-Bos	179	Wood-Bos	53.1	Wood-Bos	7.6
Wood-Bos	344.0	Walsh-Chi	.231	Walsh-Chi	.279	Walsh-Chi	2.15	Walsh-Chi	149	Walsh-Chi	49.0	Walsh-Chi	6.5
Groom-Was	316.0	Houck-Phi	.234	Bedient-Bos	.288	Plank-Phi	2.22	Plank-Phi	140	Gregg-Cle	27.5	Plank-Phi	3.2
Ford-NY	291.2	Dubuc-Det	.235	Collins-Bos	.297	Collins-Bos	2.53	Collins-Bos	135	Plank-Phi	24.9	Gregg-Cle	2.8

Glory on the Fens

It was quite a year in Boston. First, the Red Sox opened Fenway Park, a more intimate setting than cavernous Huntington Avenue Grounds. Second, pitcher Smokey Joe Wood finally got the support he needed to harness his dominating fastball. His heroics, and the spectacular play of Tris Speaker, propelled the Red Sox to the pennant. Wood's chief mound rival was Walter Johnson, who won 16 straight for surprising Washington. The two stars met September 5 in Boston, and Wood—also en route to winning 16 in a row—bested Johnson, 1-0.

A hitting slump dropped the Tigers to sixth, and the club fell lower in the public eye after striking in May to protest the suspension of Ty Cobb, who had severely beaten a heckler. With the club AWOL, a makeshift lineup of amateurs and Tigers coaches lost at Philadelphia, 24-2; Detroit ended the walkout the next day under pressure from AL President Ban Johnson. Rookie outfielder Bobby Veach would soon help the club regain its standing.

Earned runs for pitchers were first tabulated this year, but it would be until 1917 before ERA was an official statistic. Offensive players set two new league records: Joe Jackson of Cleveland hit 26 triples, while Washington's Clyde Milan swiped 88 bases. Buck Weaver and Ray Schalk made their debuts in Chicago, while Herb Pennock and Stan Coveleski pitched their first games, both for Philadelphia. Could Connie Mack pick 'em?

The Red Sox-New York Giants October matchup was the best World Series to date, going the full seven with a tie thrown in. Four one-run games kept fans on the edges of their seats. The Series ended with a thrilling duel between Christy Mathewson and Wood, on in relief of Hugh Bedient, went to the 10th before a wild series of plays gave the Red Sox a come-from-behind 3-2 win.

1911 National League

TEAM	W	L	T	PCT	GB	HW	HL	R	OR	PA	H	2B	3B	HR	BB	SO	HB	SH	AVG	OBP	SLG	OPS	AOPS	BR	ABR	PF	SB	CS	BSA	BSR
NY	99	54	1	.647		49	25	756	**542**	5781	1399	225	103	41	530	**506**	85	160	**.279**	**.358**	**.390**	748	113	111	87	103	**347**			
CHI	92	62	3	.597	7.5	49	32	**757**	607	5959	1335	218	101	54	585	617	42	**202**	.260	.341	.374	715	107	44	43	100	214			
PIT	85	69	1	.552	14.5	48	29	744	557	5907	1345	206	106	49	525	583	52	193	.262	.336	.372	708	101	27	1	104	160			
PHI	79	73	1	.520	19.5	42	34	658	669	5751	1307	214	56	**60**	490	588	31	186	.259	.328	.359	687	98	-10	-18	101	153			
STL	75	74	9	.503	22	36	38	671	745	5970	1295	199	86	26	**592**	650	65	181	.252	.337	.340	677	99	-17	2	97	175			
CIN	70	83	6	.458	29	38	42	682	706	6089	1379	180	105	21	578	594	35	185	.261	.337	.346	683	102	-13	13	96	289			
BRO	64	86	4	.427	33.5	31	42	539	659	5680	1198	151	71	28	425	683	39	157	.237	.301	.311	612	80	-157	-135	96	184			
BOS	44	107	5	.291	54	19	54	699	1021	6045	**1417**	**249**	54	37	554	577	31	152	.267	.340	.355	695	93	14	-40	108	169			
TOT	623					312	296	5506		47182	10675	1642	682	316	4279	4798	380	1416	.260	.335	.356	691					1691			

TEAM	CG	SHO	GR	SV	IP	H	HR	BB	SO	BR/9	ERA	AERA	OAV	OOB	PR	APR	PF	OSB	OCS	FA	E	WPB	DP	FW	PW	BW	BSW	DIF
NY	95	19	80	13	1368.0	1267	33	369	**771**	11.0	**2.69**	125	.246	.300	106	101	99	146	117	.959	256	41	86	.5	10.1	8.7		3.1
CHI	85	12	97	**16**	1411.0	1270	26	525	582	11.7	2.90	114	**.245**	.320	78	63	97	**133**	152	.960	260	46	114	.6	6.3	4.3		3.8
PIT	91	13	84	11	1380.1	**1249**	36	375	605	10.8	2.84	121	.248	.306	85	87	101	**185**	154	**.963**	232	43	**131**	2.1	8.7	.1		-2.9
PHI	90	**20**	78	10	1373.1	1285	43	598	697	12.7	3.30	104	.255	.340	14	19	101	243	179	.963	231	52	113	1.9	1.9	-1.8		1.0
STL	88	6	101	10	1402.1	1296	39	701	561	13.2	3.68	91	.254	.350	-46	-52	99	288	190	.960	261	51	106	.6	-5.2	.2		4.9
CIN	77	4	97	12	1425.0	1410	36	476	557	12.3	3.26	101	.265	.332	21	5	97	156	163	.955	295	38	108	-1.4	.5	1.3		-6.9
BRO	81	13	91	10	1371.2	1310	27	566	533	12.6	3.39	98	.263	.344	0	-13	98	256	195	.962	241	**25**	112	1.4	-1.3	-13.6		2.4
BOS	73	5	**115**	7	1374.0	1570	76	672	486	15.1	5.08	75	.296	.381	-258	-174	113	284	201	.947	347	55	110	-5.0	-17.5	-4.0		-5.0
TOT	680	92	743	89	11105.2					12.4	3.39		.260	.335						.958	2123	351	880					

Batter-Fielder Wins		Batting Average		On-Base Percentage		Slugging Average		On-Base Plus Slugging		Adjusted OPS		Adjusted Batter Runs	
Sheckard-Chi	4.1	Wagner-Pit	.334	Sheckard-Chi	.434	Schulte-Chi	.534	Wagner-Pit	.930	Schulte-Chi	156	Schulte-Chi	40.4
Wagner-Pit	4.1	Miller-Bos	.333	Wagner-Pit	.423	Doyle-NY	.527	Doyle-NY	.924	Wagner-Pit	154	Doyle-NY	35.4
Meyers-NY	3.3	Meyers-NY	.332	Bates-Cin	.415	Wagner-Pit	.507	Schulte-Chi	.918	Doyle-NY	153	Wagner-Pit	35.2
Sweeney-Bos	3.1	Clarke-Pit	.324	Sweeney-Bos	.404	Clarke-Pit	.492	Magee-Phi	.849	Magee-Phi	135	Sheckard-Chi	33.5
Tinker-Chi	2.9	Fletcher-NY	.319	Doyle-NY	.397	Magee-Phi	.483	Wilson-Pit	.826	Konetchy-StL	132	Bates-Cin	28.6

Runs		Hits		Doubles		Triples		Home Runs		Total Bases		Runs Batted In	
Sheckard-Chi	121	Miller-Bos	192	Konetchy-StL	38	Doyle-NY	25	Schulte-Chi	21	Schulte-Chi	308	Wilson-Pit	107
Huggins-StL	106	Hoblitzel-Cin	180	Miller-Bos	36	Mitchell-Cin	22	Luderus-Phi	16	Doyle-NY	277	Schulte-Chi	107
Bescher-Cin	106	Daubert-Bro	176	Wilson-Pit	34	Schulte-Chi	21	Magee-Phi	15	Luderus-Phi	260	Luderus-Phi	99
Schulte-Chi	105	Schulte-Chi	173	Herzog-Bos-NY	33	Zimmerman-Chi	17	Doyle-NY	13	Hoblitzel-Cin	258	Magee-Phi	94
Doyle-NY	102	Luderus-Phi	166	Sweeney-Bos	33	Byrne-Pit	17			Wilson-Pit	257		

Stolen Bases		Base Stealing Runs		Fielding Runs-Infield		Fielding Runs-Outfield		Wins		Winning Pct.		Complete Games	
Bescher-Cin	81			Tinker-Chi	21.6	Sheckard-Chi	14.8	Alexander-Phi	28	Marquard-NY	774	Alexander-Phi	31
Devore-NY	61			Doolan-Phi	17.0	Mitchell-Cin	8.6	Mathewson-NY	26	Crandall-NY	750	Mathewson-NY	29
Snodgrass-NY	51			Merkle-NY	15.5	Ingerton-Bos	8.2	Marquard-NY	24	Cole-Chi	720	Harmon-StL	28
Merkle-NY	49			Huggins-StL	11.4	Leach-Pit	7.8	Harmon-StL	23	Alexander-Phi	683	Leifield-Pit	26
				Sweeney-Bos	11.2	Carey-Pit	7.1			Mathewson-NY	667	Adams-Pit	24

Strikeouts		Fewest BB/Game		Games		Saves		Base Runners/9		Adjusted Relief Runs		Relief Ranking	
Marquard-NY	237	Mathewson-NY	1.11	Brown-Chi	53	Brown-Chi	13	Adams-Pit	9.30				
Alexander-Phi	227	Adams-Pit	1.29	Harmon-StL	51	Crandall-NY	5	Ames-NY	10.01				
Rucker-Bro	190	Steele-Pit-Bro	1.71	Rucker-Bro	48			Mathewson-NY	10.03				
Moore-Phi	174	Brown-Chi	1.83	Alexander-Phi	48			Steele-Pit-Bro	10.33				
Harmon-StL	144	Wiltse-NY	1.87					Alexander-Phi	10.35				

Innings Pitched		Opponents' Avg.		Opponents' OBP		Earned Run Average		Adjusted ERA		Adjusted Starter Runs		Pitcher Wins	
Alexander-Phi	367.0	Alexander-Phi	219	Adams-Pit	271	Mathewson-NY	1.99	Mathewson-NY	168	Mathewson-NY	42.4	**Mathewson-NY**	5.7
Harmon-StL	348.0	Marquard-NY	219	Ames-NY	277	Richie-Chi	2.31	Adams-Pit	147	Alexander-Phi	37.0	**Rucker-Bro**	3.9
Leifield-Pit	318.0	Ames-NY	223	Mathewson-NY	283	Adams-Pit	2.33	Richie-Chi	143	Adams-Pit	35.4	**Adams-Pit**	3.9
Rucker-Bro	315.2	Rucker-Bro	226	Wiltse-NY	292	Marquard-NY	2.50	Marquard-NY	134	Leifield-Pit	29.7	**Alexander-Phi**	3.7
Moore-Phi	308.1	Keefe-Cin	229	Alexander-Phi	293	Alexander-Phi	2.57	Alexander-Phi	133	Rucker-Bro	29.6	**Leifield-Pit**	3.4

A Time of Giants

The introduction in both leagues of a new cork-centered baseball led to an increase in scoring. NL runs rose 9.7 percent and homers ballooned to 316, a league record until 1921. However, stolen bases were also up, to 1.36 per game, the highest in NL history. Bob Bescher of the Reds set a league record with 81 steals, while Jimmy Sheckard of the Cubs established a mark with 147 walks, the Senior Circuit's highest until 1947, though bases on balls for hitters were not widely recognized.

New York's Christy Mathewson had another amazing season, while his chief mound rival, Chicago's Mordecai Brown, notched 13 saves, which also set a record. Philadelphia rookie Grover Cleveland Alexander enjoyed one of the more spectacular debuts in history. The righty was 28-13, leading the NL in wins, shutouts, innings, and opponents' average.

On the other side, the last-place Braves became the only NL team until1923 to allow more than 1,000 runs. In context, their staff rates as one of the worst of all time, posting a 5.09 ERA when the league ERA was 3.40, and leading in runs allowed by more than 250. Their hitters finished second in batting average and led in home runs, but it translated into 107 losses. Fans in the Hub showed an appropriate level of support; for the third straight year, attendance dropped more than 20 percent.

On June 28, the Giants moved into a new Polo Grounds, and experienced a huge gain in attendance. Gotham fans were rewarded in September when their club broke away from the Cubs to capture the flag. While much was made of New York's speed-based attack—they broke the league record with 347 swipes—the Giants won with the league's best pitching and hitters who led in batting average, on-base percentage, and slugging percentage. Unfortunately, the Giants didn't hit a lick in the World Series, losing to Philadelphia in five.

1911 American League

TEAM	W	L	T	PCT	GB	HW	HL	R	OR	PA	H	2B	3B	HR	BB	SO	HB	SH	AVG	OBP	SLG	OPS	AOPS	BR	ABR	PF	SB	CS	BSA	BSR
PHI	101	50	1	.669		54	20	861	602	5919	1540	237	93	35	424		65	231	.296	.357	.398	755	119	109	124	98	226			
DET	89	65	0	.578	13.5	51	25	831	777	5995	1544	230	96	30	471		49	181	.292	.355	.388	743	108	92	53	105	276			
CLE	80	73	3	.523	22	46	30	693	712	5885	1501	238	81	20	354		50	160	.282	.333	.369	702	101	1	-7	101	209			
CHI	77	74	3	.510	24	40	37	718	624	5850	1401	179	92	20	385		48	207	.269	.325	.350	675	97	-50	-28	97	201			
BOS	78	75	1	.510	24	39	37	680	643	5806	1379	203	66	35	506		74	212	.275	.350	.363	713	106	42	49	99	190			
NY	76	76	1	.500	25.5	36	40	684	723	5793	1374	190	96	25	493		64	184	.272	.344	.362	706	97	23	-21	107	269			
WAS	64	90	0	.416	38.5	39	38	624	765	5760	1308	159	54	16	466		80	149	.258	.330	.320	650	89	-75	-63	98	215			
STL	45	107	0	.296	56.5	25	53	567	812	5631	1192	187	63	17	460		34	141	.239	.307	.311	618	81	-143	-121	96	125			
TOT	614					330	280	5658		46639	11239	1623	641	198	3559	5093	464	1465	.273	.338	.358	696					1711			

TEAM	CG	SHO	GR	SV	IP	H	HR	BB	SO	BR/9	ERA	AERA	OAV	OOB	PR	APR	PF	OSB	OCS	FA	E	WPB	DP	FW	PW	BW	BSW	DIF
PHI	97	13	77	13	1375.2	1343	17	487	739	12.5	3.01	105	.264	.338	50	22	94	184	171	.964	225	48	100	4.9	2.2	12.2		6.3
DET	108	8	67	3	1387.2	1514	28	460	538	13.3	3.73	93	.283	.348	-60	-43	104	203	176	.951	318	55	78	-.9	-4.2	5.2		12.0
CLE	93	6	74	6	1390.2	1382	17	552	675	12.9	3.36	101	.267	.345	-3	7	102	246	193	.954	303	88	108	.3	.7	-.7		3.2
CHI	85	17	103	11	1386.1	1349	22	384	752	11.5	2.97	108	.255	.310	57	39	96	151	150	.961	252	60	98	3.4	3.8	-2.8		-2.9
BOS	87	10	85	8	1351.2	1309	21	473	711	12.2	2.74	119	.262	.332	89	80	98	219	177	.949	323	60	93	-1.4	7.9	4.8		-9.8
NY	90	5	79	3	1360.2	1404	26	406	667	12.3	3.54	101	.270	.329	-30	9	108	219	170	.949	328	53	99	-1.7	.9	-2.1		2.9
WAS	106	13	62	3	1353.1	1471	39	410	628	12.8	3.52	93	.277	.334	-27	-38	98	201	178	.953	305	96	90	-.0	-3.7	-6.2		-3.0
STL	92	8	80	1	1332.1	1465	28	463	383	13.4	3.86	87	.278	.342	-77	-73	101	291	186	.945	358	50	104	-3.8	-7.2	-11.9		-8.1
TOT	758	80	627	48	10938.1					12.6	3.34		.273	.338						.953	2412	510	770					

Batter-Fielder Wins		Batting Average		On-Base Percentage		Slugging Average		On-Base Plus Slugging		Adjusted OPS		Adjusted Batter Runs	
Cobb-Det	6.6	Cobb-Det	420	Jackson-Cle	468	Cobb-Det	621	Cobb-Det	1088	Cobb-Det	193	Cobb-Det	71.7
Jackson-Cle	6.5	Jackson-Cle	408	Cobb-Det	467	Jackson-Cle	590	Jackson-Cle	1058	Jackson-Cle	192	Jackson-Cle	71.5
Collins-Phi	4.6	Crawford-Det	378	Collins-Phi	451	Crawford-Det	526	Crawford-Det	964	Collins-Phi	163	Crawford-Det	47.0
Baker-Phi	3.5	Collins-Phi	365	Crawford-Det	438	Cree-NY	513	Collins-Phi	932	Crawford-Det	160	Collins-Phi	45.6
Gardner-Bos	3.3	Cree-NY	348	Speaker-Bos	418	Baker-Phi	508	Cree-NY	928	Speaker-Bos	158	Speaker-Bos	40.5

Runs		Hits		Doubles		Triples		Home Runs		Total Bases		Runs Batted In	
Cobb-Det	147	Cobb-Det	248	Cobb-Det	47	Cobb-Det	24	Baker-Phi	11	Cobb-Det	367	Cobb-Det	127
Jackson-Cle	126	Jackson-Cle	233	Jackson-Cle	45	Cree-NY	22	Speaker-Bos	8	Jackson-Cle	337	Crawford-Det	115
Bush-Det	126	Crawford-Det	217	Baker-Phi	42	Jackson-Cle	19	Cobb-Det	8	Crawford-Det	302	Baker-Phi	115
Milan-Was	109	Baker-Phi	198	Lord-Phi	37	Lord-Chi	18			Baker-Phi	301	Bodie-Chi	97
Crawford-Det	109	Milan-Was	194	LaPorte-StL	37	Wolter-NY	15			Cree-NY	267	Delahanty-Det	94

Stolen Bases		Base Stealing Runs		Fielding Runs-Infield		Fielding Runs-Outfield		Wins		Winning Pct.		Complete Games	
Cobb-Det	83			Tannehill-Chi	36.3	Hogan-Phi-StL	12.6	Coombs-Phi	28	Bender-Phi	773	Johnson-Was	36
Milan-Was	58			McBride-Was	27.4	Cobb-Det	6.7	Walsh-Chi	27	Gregg-Cle	767	Walsh-Chi	33
Cree-NY	48			Gardner-Bos	22.7	Milan-Was	6.6	Johnson-Was	25	Plank-Phi	742	Ford-NY	26
Callahan-Chi	45			Austin-StL	18.6	Hooper-Bos	5.8			Coombs-Phi	700	Coombs-Phi	26
Lord-Chi	43			Bush-Det	12.5	Jackson-Cle	5.3			Morgan-Phi	682		

Strikeouts		Fewest BB/Game		Games		Saves		Base Runners/9		Adjusted Relief Runs		Relief Ranking	
Walsh-Chi	255	White-Chi	1.47	Walsh-Chi	56	Walsh-Chi	4	Gregg-Cle	9.86				
Wood-Bos	231	Lake-StL	1.67	Coombs-Phi	47	Plank-Phi	4	Walsh-Chi	9.91				
Johnson-Was	207	Walsh-Chi	1.76	Wood-Bos	44	Hall-Bos	4	Wood-Bos	10.22				
Coombs-Phi	185	Warhop-NY	1.89	Caldwell-NY	41	Wood-Bos	3	Johnson-Was	10.33				
Ford-NY	158	Powell-StL	1.91			Bender-Phi	3	Ford-NY	10.59				

Innings Pitched		Opponents' Avg.		Opponents' OBP		Earned Run Average		Adjusted ERA		Adjusted Starter Runs		Pitcher Wins	
Walsh-Chi	368.2	Gregg-Cle	205	Walsh-Chi	280	Gregg-Cle	1.80	Gregg-Cle	189	Johnson-Was	43.1	Wood-Bos	5.7
Coombs-Phi	336.2	Wood-Bos	223	Johnson-Was	283	Johnson-Was	1.90	Johnson-Was	173	Gregg-Cle	42.8	Walsh-Chi	5.5
Johnson-Was	322.1	Krapp-Cle	232	Wood-Bos	284	Wood-Bos	2.02	Walsh-Chi	162	Walsh-Chi	42.1	Johnson-Was	5.4
Ford-NY	281.1	Ford-NY	237	Gregg-Cle	286	Plank-Phi	2.10	Ford-NY	158	Wood-Bos	33.7	Gregg-Cle	4.6
Wood-Bos	275.2	Johnson-Was	238	Ford-NY	291	Bender-Phi	2.16	Plank-Phi	150	Ford-NY	30.4	Plank-Phi	3.2

White Elephants on Parade

As the season opened, baseball fans were shocked by the death of Cleveland's mound ace, Addie Joss, from tuberculosis. The two-time league ERA leader died April 14, just two days after his 30th birthday. Cy Young threw his final pitch in the majors in 1911, going 7-9 for two clubs to raise his win total to 511.

The major leagues introduced a new cork-centered baseball, sending the previous rubber-centered ball to the trash bin. As a result, the league batting average rose 30 points. Home runs also increased and runs per game rose to 4.61, the highest total in a decade and the highest until 1920. Who better to benefit from this new ball than Ty Cobb, already the league's best player? The Georgia Peach set new AL marks in 1911 for hits, RBIs, runs, and total bases, and batted .420. Detroit started hot, leading by 9½

games in May, but from July through the end of the season played essentially .500 ball as the Athletics caught fire in August. Connie Mack's White Elephants pulled away and won by 13½ games.

Philadelphia's so-called "$100,000 Infield" of Stuffy McInnis, Eddie Collins, Jack Barry, and Frank Baker, showed good leather and fine stick, and the club's starting pitching was again excellent. The World Series went six games with the Athletics coming out on top for the second straight time. Baker hit two crucial long balls to gain the nickname "Home Run," and Chief Bender, Jack Coombs, and Eddie Plank bested the Giants. It was an exciting Series; the first five games were close, two of them extending into extra innings.

1910 National League

TEAM	W	L	T	PCT	GB	HW	HL	R	OR	PA	H	2B	3B	HR	BB	SO	HB	SH	AVG	OBP	SLG	OPS	AOPS	BR	ABR	PF	SB	CS	BSA	BSR
CHI	104	50	0	.675		58	19	712	499	5792	1333	219	84	34	542	501	39	234	.268	.344	.366	710	114	84	90	99	173			
NY	91	63	1	.591	13	52	26	715	567	5873	1391	204	83	31	562	489	57	193	.275	.354	.366	720	116	108	107	100	282			
PIT	86	67	1	.562	17.5	46	30	655	576	5794	1364	214	83	33	437	524	34	198	.266	.328	.360	688	100	30	-6	106	148			
PHI	78	75	4	.510	25.5	40	36	674	639	5925	1319	223	71	22	506	559	43	205	.255	.327	.338	665	97	-1	-21	103	199			
CIN	75	79	2	.487	29	39	37	620	684	5861	1326	150	79	23	529	515	29	182	.259	.332	.333	665	105	-3	26	96	310			
BRO	64	90	2	.416	40	39	39	497	623	5782	1174	166	73	25	434	706	40	183	.229	.294	.305	599	82	-136	-121	97	151			
STL	63	90	1	.412	40.5	35	41	639	718	5798	1217	167	70	15	655	581	78	153	.248	.345	.319	664	103	22	47	96	179			
BOS	53	100	4	.346	50.5	29	48	495	701	5710	1260	173	49	31	359	540	47	181	.246	.301	.317	618	81	-102	-124	105	152			
TOT	621					338	276	5007		46535	10384	1516	592	214	4024	4415	367	1529	.256	.328	.338	666					1594		

TEAM	CG	SHO	GR	SV	IP	H	HR	BB	SO	BR/9	ERA	AERA	OAV	OOB	PR	APR	PF	OSB	OCS	FA	E	WPB	DP	FW	PW	BW	BSW	DIF
CHI	100	25	74	13	1378.2	1171	18	474	609	11.0	2.51	115	.235	.307	79	57	95	145	148	.963	230	46	110	2.1	6.0	9.5		9.4
NY	96	9	80	10	1391.2	1290	30	397	717	11.2	2.68	110	.250	.308	54	45	98	192	153	.955	291	52	117	-1.7	4.7	11.3		-.3
PIT	73	13	100	12	1376.0	1254	20	392	479	11.1	2.83	109	.250	.311	29	37	102	168	145	.961	245	23	102	1.1	3.9	-.6		5.1
PHI	84	17	107	9	1411.1	1297	36	547	657	12.1	3.05	102	.253	.330	-5	9	103	213	163	.960	258	49	132	.6	.9	-2.2		2.1
CIN	86	16	88	11	1386.2	1334	27	528	497	12.5	3.08	94	.261	.338	-9	-30	96	153	145	.955	291	53	103	-1.6	-3.2	2.7		.0
BRO	103	15	65	5	1420.1	1331	17	545	555	12.1	3.07	99	.259	.335	-7	-9	100	215	188	.964	235	54	125	2.0	-.9	-12.7		-1.3
STL	81	4	96	14	1337.1	1396	30	541	466	13.3	3.78	79	.275	.350	-112	-122	98	264	138	.959	261	61	109	.0	-12.8	4.9		-5.6
BOS	72	12	107	9	1390.1	1328	36	599	531	12.8	3.22	103	.265	.349	-30	13	110	244	192	.954	305	57	137	-2.4	1.4	-13.1		-9.5
TOT	695	111	717	83	11092.1					12.0	3.02		.256	.328		13				.959	2116	395	935					

Batter-Fielder Wins		Batting Average		On-Base Percentage		Slugging Average		On-Base Plus Slugging		Adjusted OPS		Adjusted Batter Runs	
Konetchy-StL	3.9	Magee-Phi	331	Magee-Phi	445	Magee-Phi	507	Magee-Phi	952	Magee-Phi	172	Magee-Phi	52.7
Mowrey-StL	3.6	Campbell-Pit	326	Snodgrass-NY	440	Hofman-Chi	461	Snodgrass-NY	871	Snodgrass-NY	154	Hofman-Chi	33.3
Wagner-Pit	3.5	Hofman-Chi	325	Evers-Chi	413	Schulte-Chi	460	Hofman-Chi	867	Hofman-Chi	154	Snodgrass-NY	33.1
Magee-Phi	3.4	Snodgrass-NY	321	Hofman-Chi	406	Merkle-NY	441	Konetchy-StL	822	Konetchy-StL	145	Konetchy-StL	31.9
Hofman-Chi	2.8	Wagner-Pit	320	Huggins-StL	399	Campbell-Pit	436	Wagner-Pit	822	Schulte-Chi	137	Wagner-Pit	23.7

Runs		Hits		Doubles		Triples		Home Runs		Total Bases		Runs Batted In	
Magee-Phi	110	Wagner-Pit	178	Byrne-Pit	43	Mitchell-Cin	18	Schulte-Chi	10	Magee-Phi	263	Magee-Phi	123
Huggins-StL	101	Byrne-Pit	178	Magee-Phi	39	Magee-Phi	17	Beck-Bos	10	Schulte-Chi	257	Mitchell-Cin	88
Byrne-Pit	101	Wheat-Bro	172	Wheat-Bro	36	Konetchy-StL	16	Doyle-NY	8	Byrne-Pit	251	Murray-NY	87
Doyle-NY	97	Magee-Phi	172	Merkle-NY	35	Hofman-Chi	16	Daubert-Bro	8	Wheat-Bro	244	Hofman-Chi	86
Bescher-Cin	95	Hoblitzel-Cin	170	Wagner-Pit	34					Wagner-Pit	240	Wagner-Pit	81

Stolen Bases		Base Stealing Runs		Fielding Runs-Infield		Fielding Runs-Outfield		Wins		Winning Pct.		Complete Games	
Bescher-Cin	70			Shean-Bos	43.2	Paskert-Cin	9.6	Mathewson-NY	27	Cole-Chi	833	Rucker-Bro	27
Murray-NY	57			Doolan-Phi	17.8	Sheckard-Chi	8.1	Brown-Chi	25	Crandall-NY	810	Mathewson-NY	27
Paskert-Cin	51			Mowrey-StL	14.3	Collins-Bos	8.1	Moore-Phi	22	Mathewson-NY	750	Brown-Chi	27
Magee-Phi	49			Tinker-Chi	14.3	Murray-NY	5.9	Suggs-Cin	20	Adams-Pit	667	Bell-Bro	25
Devore-NY	43			Knabe-Phi	13.9	Bates-Phi	5.4	Cole-Chi	20	Brown-Chi	641	Barger-Bro	25

Strikeouts		Fewest BB/Game		Games		Saves		Base Runners/9		Adjusted Relief Runs		Relief Ranking	
Moore-Phi	185	Suggs-Cin	1.62	Mattern-Bos	51	Gaspar-Cin	7	Phillippe-Pit	9.10				
Mathewson-NY	184	Mathewson-NY	1.70	Gaspar-Cin	48	Brown-Chi	7	McQuillan-Phi	9.57				
Frock-Pit-Bos	171	Crandall-NY	1.86			Crandall-NY	5	Pfiester-Chi	9.78				
Drucke-NY	151	Brown-Chi	1.95			Richie-Bos-Chi	4	Brown-Chi	9.87				
Rucker-Bro	147	Wiltse-NY	1.99			Phillippe-Pit	4	Overall-Chi	10.02				

Innings Pitched		Opponents' Avg.		Opponents' OBP		Earned Run Average		Adjusted ERA		Adjusted Starter Runs		Pitcher Wins	
Rucker-Bro	320.1	Cole-Chi	211	Brown-Chi	277	McQuillan-Phi	1.60	Cole-Chi	159	Mathewson-NY	35.4	Mathewson-NY	5.3
Mathewson-NY	318.1	Drucke-NY	228	Mathewson-NY	286	Cole-Chi	1.80	Mathewson-NY	156	Cole-Chi	29.3	Brown-Chi	4.0
Bell-Bro	310.0	Moore-Phi	228	Crandall-NY	289	Brown-Chi	1.86	Brown-Chi	155	Brown-Chi	28.6	Cole-Chi	3.1
Mattern-Bos	305.0	Brown-Chi	232	Adams-Pit	291	Mathewson-NY	1.89	Adams-Pit	138	McQuillan-Phi	22.8	Moore-Phi	2.6
Brown-Chi	295.1	Scanlan-Bro	234	Bell-Bro	296	Ames-NY	2.22	Ames-NY	133	Moore-Phi	20.2	Suggs-Cin	2.4

End of an Era in Chicago

The rules committee made two codifications that seem oddly obvious: The batting order must be presented before the game and followed, and substitutions can only come when time was out. In addition, the passed ball and wild pitch were first defined.

Christy Mathewson and Three Finger Brown were again the league's top pitchers, maintaining their touch even as team runs per game topped 4.00 for first time in five years. NL batters clubbed 214 homers in 1910, the highest total since 1901. But another runaway by the Cubs dropped attendance 16 percent; attendance would not reach its 1908 level again until 1920.

Jake Daubert debuted as Brooklyn's everyday first baseman, and went on to a fifteen-year career and two batting titles. Catcher Hank Gowdy, who would spend his entire seventeen-year skein with the Giants and Braves, plus another season in France during World War I, played his first game in September 1910. Pirates outfielder Max Carey, who would lead the NL ten times in steals, made The Show at age 20.

Infielder Alan Storke, who split '09 between Pittsburgh and St. Louis, underwent a lung operation in March but died from complications. He was 26. Others playing their last games (but not dying) included Hall of Famer "Wee" Willie Keeler, Pirates hurler Sam Leever, and Vic Willis, who won 249 games in thirteen years.

For the fourth time in five years, the Cubs won more than 100 games, pulling from the pack in May and never looking back. Neither the Pirates, whose pitching staff had aged dangerously, or the rebuilding Giants were serious threats. However, John McGraw had restocked New York with some excellent young players. A loss to the Athletics in the World Series ended the Cubs' era of dominance; they would only win one more flag in the next two decades.

1910 American League

TEAM	W	L	T	PCT	GB	HW	HL	R	OR	PA	H	2B	3B	HR	BB	SO	HB	SH	AVG	OBP	SLG	OPS	AOPS	BR	ABR	PF	SB	CS	BSA	BSR
PHI	102	48	5	.680		57	19	674	442	5809	1373	191	105	19	409		47	199	.266	.326	.355	681	120	104	111	99	207			
NY	88	63	5	.583	14.5	49	25	626	557	5762	1254	164	75	20	464		71	176	.248	.320	.322	642	101	45	11	106	288			
DET	86	68	1	.558	18	46	31	679	584	5746	1317	190	72	28	459		51	197	.261	.329	.344	673	110	99	57	107	249			
BOS	81	72	5	.529	22.5	51	28	641	564	5917	1350	175	87	43	430		56	227	.259	.323	.351	674	114	94	78	102	194			
CLE	71	81	9	.467	32	39	36	548	657	5988	1316	188	64	9	366		37	190	.244	.296	.308	604	94	-39	-46	101	189			
CHI	68	85	3	.444	35.5	41	37	457	479	5661	1058	115	58	7	403		44	190	.211	.275	.261	536	76	-154	-136	96	183			
WAS	66	85	6	.437	36.5	38	35	501	551	5690	1175	145	47	9	449		82	170	.236	.309	.289	598	98	-30	-4	95	192			
STL	47	107	4	.305	57	26	51	451	743	5675	1105	131	60	12	415		36	147	.218	.281	.274	555	84	-120	-90	94	169			
TOT	628					347	262	4577		46248	9948	1299	568	147	3395	5278	424	1496	.243	.308	.313	621					1671			

TEAM	CG	SHO	GR	SV	IP	H	HR	BB	SO	BR/9	ERA	AERA	OAV	OOB	PR	APR	PF	OSB	OCS	FA	E	WPB	DP	FW	PW	BW	BSW	DIF
PHI	123	24	45	5	1421.2	1103	8	450	789	10.2	1.79	133	.221	.292	116	97	94	187	168	.965	230	49	117	3.9	10.8	12.3		.0
NY	110	14	57	8	1399.0	1238	16	364	654	10.7	2.61	102	.243	.300	-15	5	106	194	152	.956	286	48	95	.2	.6	1.2		10.5
DET	108	17	64	5	1380.1	1257	34	460	532	11.6	2.82	93	.248	.319	-47	-26	104	193	168	.956	288	48	79	-.0	-2.9	6.3		5.6
BOS	100	12	70	6	1430.0	1236	30	414	670	10.7	2.45	104	.235	.297	10	14	101	207	141	.954	309	52	80	-1.1	1.6	8.7		-4.6
CLE	92	13	82	3	1467.0	1392	10	488	617	11.9	2.88	90	.261	.330	-60	-49	103	259	190	.964	248	62	112	3.4	-5.4	-5.1		2.2
CHI	103	23	66	7	1421.0	1130	16	381	785	9.8	2.03	118	.222	.281	77	59	95	175	158	.954	314	48	100	-1.7	6.6	-15.1		1.8
WAS	119	19	43	3	1373.1	1215	19	375	674	10.8	2.46	101	.244	.304	8	5	99	201	170	.959	264	84	99	1.8	.6	-.4		-11.4
STL	101	9	72	3	1391.0	1356	14	532	557	12.6	3.09	80	.265	.341	-89	-97	98	252	196	.943	385	48	113	-6.3	-10.8	-10.0		-2.9
TOT	856	131	499	42	11283.1					11.0	2.52		.243	.308						.956	2324	439	795					

Batter-Fielder Wins		Batting Average		On-Base Percentage		Slugging Average		On-Base Plus Slugging		Adjusted OPS		Adjusted Batter Runs	
Lajoie-Cle	8.9	Cobb-Det	383	Cobb-Det	456	Cobb-Det	551	Cobb-Det	1008	Cobb-Det	202	Lajoie-Cle	69.3
Collins-Phi	7.0	Lajoie-Cle	384	Lajoie-Cle	445	Lajoie-Cle	514	Lajoie-Cle	960	Lajoie-Cle	198	Cobb-Det	61.5
Cobb-Det	6.3	Speaker-Bos	340	Speaker-Bos	404	Speaker-Bos	468	Speaker-Bos	873	Speaker-Bos	169	Speaker-Bos	42.5
Speaker-Bos	4.8	Collins-Phi	324	Collins-Phi	382	Murphy-Phi	436	Collins-Phi	800	Collins-Phi	152	Collins-Phi	33.9
McBride-Was	4.1	Knight-NY	312	Milan-Was	379	Oldring-Phi	430	Cree-NY	775	Murphy-Phi	143	Murphy-Phi	24.1

Runs		Hits		Doubles		Triples		Home Runs		Total Bases		Runs Batted In	
Cobb-Det	106	Lajoie-Cle	227	Lajoie-Cle	51	Crawford-Det	19	Stahl-Bos	10	Lajoie-Cle	304	Crawford-Det	120
Lajoie-Cle	94	Cobb-Det	194	Cobb-Det	35	Lord-Cle-Phi	18	Lewis-Bos	8	Cobb-Det	279	Cobb-Det	91
Speaker-Bos	92	Collins-Phi	188	Lewis-Bos	29	Murphy-Phi	18	Cobb-Det	8	Speaker-Bos	252	Collins-Phi	81
Bush-Det	90	Speaker-Bos	183	Murphy-Phi	28	Stahl-Bos	16	Speaker-Bos	7	Crawford-Det	249	Stahl-Bos	77
Milan-Was	89	Crawford-Det	170	Oldring-Phi	27	Cree-NY	16	Crawford-Det	5	Murphy-Phi	244	Lajoie-Cle	76

Stolen Bases		Base Stealing Runs		Fielding Runs-Infield		Fielding Runs-Outfield		Wins		Winning Pct.		Complete Games	
Collins-Phi	81			McBride-Was	32.8	Lewis-Bos	11.5	Coombs-Phi	31	Bender-Phi	821	Johnson-Was	38
Cobb-Det	65			Collins-Phi	29.8	Birmingham-Cle	10.3	Ford-NY	26	Ford-NY	813	Coombs-Phi	35
Zeider-Chi	49			Wallace-Stl	22.6	Hooper-Bos	8.8	Johnson-Was	25	Coombs-Phi	775	Walsh-Chi	33
Bush-Det	49			Lajoie-Cle	12.5	Speaker-Bos	8.6	Bender-Phi	23	Donovan-Det	708	Ford-NY	29
Milan-Was	44			Bush-Det	10.4	Milan-Was	7.6	Mullin-Det	21	Mullin-Det	636	Mullin-Det	27

Strikeouts		Fewest BB/Game		Games		Saves		Base Runners/9		Adjusted Relief Runs		Relief Ranking	
Johnson-Was	313	Walsh-Chi	1.49	Walsh-Chi	45	Walsh-Chi	5	Walsh-Chi	7.47				
Walsh-Chi	258	Young-Cle	1.49	Johnson-Was	45	Browning-Det	3	Ford-NY	8.17				
Coombs-Phi	224	Collins-Bos	1.51	Coombs-Phi	45			Johnson-Was	8.54				
Ford-NY	209	Bender-Phi	1.69	Scott-Chi	41			Bender-Phi	8.60				
Bender-Phi	155	Johnson-Was	1.85					Collins-Bos	9.09				

Innings Pitched		Opponents' Avg.		Opponents' OBP		Earned Run Average		Adjusted ERA		Adjusted Starter Runs		Pitcher Wins	
Johnson-Was	370.0	Walsh-Chi	187	Walsh-Chi	226	Walsh-Chi	1.27	Walsh-Chi	189	Coombs-Phi	46.6	Walsh-Chi	6.3
Walsh-Chi	369.2	Ford-NY	188	Ford-NY	245	Coombs-Phi	1.30	Johnson-Was	183	Walsh-Chi	45.5	Coombs-Phi	5.8
Coombs-Phi	353.0	Coombs-Phi	201	Bender-Phi	255	Johnson-Was	1.36	Coombs-Phi	182	Johnson-Was	43.4	Johnson-Was	5.5
Ford-NY	299.2	Johnson-Was	205	Johnson-Was	257	Morgan-Phi	1.55	Ford-NY	161	Ford-NY	33.9	Ford-NY	4.2
Morgan-Phi	290.2	Hall-Bos	207	Collins-Bos	264	Bender-Phi	1.58	Collins-Bos	158	Bender-Phi	25.2	Bender-Phi	4.1

Chalmers Promotion Sparks Chicanery and Controversy

The Indians began the season in brand-new League Park, while on July 1, the White Sox moved into Comiskey Park, the "Palace of Baseball." In two years, half of the league had built new concrete-and-steel parks; one more step towards the AL's consolidation of power. Despite this, attendance fell nearly 13 percent.

One of the biggest controversies of the era focused on the batting title, a battle between Cleveland's popular Nap Lajoie and Detroit's *unpopular* Ty Cobb. The Chalmers company promised a car to the batting titlist, and on the season's last day, the Browns had their third baseman play deep, allowing Lajoie to bunt for seven hits in a doubleheader and to finish at .384. Even so, Cobb won because of a clerical error that double-counted 2 of Cobb's hits, an error not corrected for 70 years. Chalmers awarded each man a car.

Connie Mack's Athletics pulled away from Detroit in early summer and coasted to the title. The Yankees moved from fifth to second with a speed-based attack and good pitching. The Tigers, disheartened by three straight World Series losses, ended third despite Cobb leading the league in runs, slugging, and on-base percentage, edging out Lajoie in those categories without any computation errors or uncontested bunts.

Two standouts played their last games. Outfielder Elmer Flick, a speed demon beset by injuries, was through at 34. Rube Waddell, the overpowering southpaw, could no longer get hitters out consistently, and was released by St. Louis. He would be dead within four years.

Setting an all-time AL record for team ERA at 1.74, Athletics pitchers—Jack Coombs and Chief Bender combined for 54 wins—did not allow a home run at Shibe Park *all season*. But they also had the league's best offense, as well as ERA, in road games. In the World Series, the Mackmen completely destroyed Chicago, mauling the Cubs for 35 runs in five games and allowing just 15.

1909 National League

TEAM	W	L	T	PCT	GB	HW	HL	R	OR	PA	H	2B	3B	HR	BB	SO	HB	SH	AVG	OBP	SLG	OPS	AOPS	BR	ABR	PF	SB	CS	BSA	BSR
PIT	110	42	2	.724		56	21	699	447	5855	1332	218	92	25	479		36	211	.260	.327	.353	680	109	102	50	108	185			
CHI	104	49	2	.680	6.5	47	29	635	390	5698	1227	203	60	20	420		31	248	.245	.308	.322	630	100	9	-4	102	187			
NY	92	61	5	.601	18.5	44	33	624	547	5951	1327	173	68	26	530		52	151	.254	.328	.329	657	109	71	61	102	240			
CIN	77	76	4	.503	33.5	39	38	606	599	5816	1273	159	72	22	478		38	212	.250	.319	.323	642	107	34	39	99	280			
PHI	74	79	1	.484	36.5	40	37	517	519	5696	1228	185	53	12	369		54	239	.244	.303	.309	612	95	-25	-29	101	185			
BRO	55	98	2	.359	55.5	34	45	444	627	5579	1157	176	59	16	330		20	173	.229	.279	.296	575	87	-100	-83	96	141			
STL	54	98	2	.355	56	26	48	583	731	5857	1242	148	56	15	568		62	119	.243	.326	.303	629	109	26	66	94	163			
BOS	45	108	2	.294	65.5	27	47	435	683	5636	1121	125	43	14	400		30	189	.223	.285	.274	559	76	-120	-139	105	135			
TOT	621					313	298	4543		46088	9907	1387	503	150	3574	4437	323	1542	.244	.310	.314	624					1516			

TEAM	CG	SHO	GR	SV	IP	H	HR	BB	SO	BR/9	ERA	AERA	OAV	OOB	PR	APR	PF	OSB	OCS	FA	E	WPB	DP	FW	PW	BW	BSW	DIF
PIT	93	21	82	11	1401.2	1174	12	320	490	9.9	2.07	131	.232	.284	81	95	105	129	143	.964	228	24	100	3.5	10.5	5.5		14.4
CHI	111	32	57	11	1399.1	1094	6	364	680	9.6	1.75	145	.215	.272	131	127	98	148	146	.962	244	37	95	2.6	14.1	-.4		11.2
NY	105	17	66	15	1440.2	1248	28	397	735	10.5	2.27	112	.238	.295	51	43	98	167	153	.954	307	55	99	-1.1	4.8	6.8		5.1
CIN	91	10	83	8	1407.0	1233	5	510	477	11.4	2.52	103	.240	.314	11	9	100	197	148	.952	309	56	120	-1.4	1.0	4.3		-3.5
PHI	89	17	84	6	1391.0	1190	23	472	612	11.0	2.44	106	.235	.304	23	20	100	184	153	.962	241	50	97	2.7	2.2	-3.2		-4.2
BRO	126	18	30	3	1384.1	1277	31	528	594	12.1	3.10	83	.256	.333	-79	-82	100	213	185	.955	282	34	86	.2	-9.1	-9.2		-3.4
STL	84	5	92	4	1379.2	1368	22	483	435	12.4	3.41	74	.263	.331	-126	-142	97	253	161	.950	322	61	90	-2.6	-15.7	7.3		-11.0
BOS	98	13	69	6	1370.2	1329	23	543	414	12.6	3.20	88	.263	.339	-93	-56	109	225	169	.948	342	67	101	-3.7	-6.2	-15.4		-6.1
TOT	797	133	563	64	11174.1					11.2	2.59		.244	.310						.956	2275	384	788					

Batter-Fielder Wins		Batting Average		On-Base Percentage		Slugging Average		On-Base Plus Slugging		Adjusted OPS		Adjusted Batter Runs	
Wagner-Pit	5.6	Wagner-Pit	339	Wagner-Pit	420	Wagner-Pit	489	Wagner-Pit	909	Wagner-Pit	168	Wagner-Pit	41.7
Gibson-Pit	3.7	Mitchell-Cin	310	Bridwell-NY	386	Mitchell-Cin	430	Mitchell-Cin	808	Mitchell-Cin	152	Konetchy-StL	31.0
Konetchy-StL	3.6	Hoblitzel-Cin	308	Clarke-Pit	384	Doyle-NY	419	Hoblitzel-Cin	782	Konetchy-StL	145	Mitchell-Cin	30.5
Devlin-NY	3.5	Doyle-NY	302	Mitchell-Cin	378	Hoblitzel-Cin	418	Doyle-NY	779	Hoblitzel-Cin	144	Doyle-NY	25.2
Mitchell-Cin	3.2	Bridwell-NY	294	Evers-Chi	369	McCormick-NY	402	Konetchy-StL	762	Doyle-NY	140	Hoblitzel-Cin	25.1

Runs		Hits		Doubles		Triples		Home Runs		Total Bases		Runs Batted In	
Leach-Pit	126	Doyle-NY	172	Wagner-Pit	39	Mitchell-Cin	17	Murray-NY	7	Wagner-Pit	242	Wagner-Pit	100
Clarke-Pit	97	Grant-Phi	170	Magee-Phi	33	Magee-Phi	14	Leach-Pit	6	Doyle-NY	239	Murray-NY	91
Byrne-StL-Pit	92	Wagner-Pit	168	D.Miller-Pit	31	Konetchy-StL	14	Doyle-NY	6	Konetchy-StL	228	D.Miller-Pit	87
Wagner-Pit	92	Konetchy-StL	165	Sheckard-Chi	29	D.Miller-Pit	13	Becker-Bos	6	Mitchell-Cin	225	Mitchell-Cin	86
		Burch-Bro	163	Leach-Pit	29			Wagner-Pit	5	D.Miller-Pit	222	Konetchy-StL	80

Stolen Bases		Base Stealing Runs		Fielding Runs-Infield		Fielding Runs-Outfield		Wins		Winning Pct.		Complete Games	
Bescher-Cin	54			Egan-Cin	23.7	Ellis-StL	12.9	M.Brown-Chi	27	Mathewson-NY	806	M.Brown-Chi	32
Murray-NY	48			Doolan-Phi	23.5	Clarke-Pit	7.3	Mathewson-NY	25	H.Camnitz-Pit	806	Bell-Bro	29
Egan-Cin	39			Tinker-Chi	18.3	Mitchell-Cin	5.3	H.Camnitz-Pit	25	M.Brown-Chi	750	Rucker-Bro	28
Magee-Phi	38			Devlin-NY	16.9	O'Hara-NY	4.2	Willis-Pit	22	Pfiester-Chi	739	Mathewson-NY	26
Burch-Bro	38			Byrne-StL-Pit	16.5	Bates-Bos-Phi	3.7			Leifield-Pit	704		

Strikeouts		Fewest BB/Game		Games		Saves		Base Runners/9		Adjusted Relief Runs		Relief Ranking	
Overall-Chi	205	Mathewson-NY	1.18	M.Brown-Chi	50	M.Brown-Chi	7	Mathewson-NY	7.45				
Rucker-Bro	201	M.Brown-Chi	1.39	Mattern-Bos	47	Crandall-NY	6	Adams-Pit	7.89				
Moore-Phi	173	Wiltse-NY	1.70	Gaspar-Cin	44			M.Brown-Chi	8.04				
M.Brown-Chi	172	Maddox-Pit	1.73	Beebe-StL	44			H.Camnitz-Pit	8.97				
Ames-NY	156	McQuillan-Phi	1.96					Curtis-Bos	9.22				

Innings Pitched		Opponents' Avg.		Opponents' OBP		Earned Run Average		Adjusted ERA		Adjusted Starter Runs		Pitcher Wins	
M.Brown-Chi	342.2	Overall-Chi	198	Mathewson-NY	228	Mathewson-NY	1.14	Mathewson-NY	223	M.Brown-Chi	45.2	Mathewson-NY	6.6
Mattern-Bos	316.1	Mathewson-NY	200	M.Brown-Chi	239	M.Brown-Chi	1.31	M.Brown-Chi	193	Mathewson-NY	42.2	M.Brown-Chi	5.3
Rucker-Bro	309.1	Fromme-Cin	201	Overall-Chi	262	Overall-Chi	1.42	Overall-Chi	178	Overall-Chi	35.5	Overall-Chi	5.2
Moore-Phi	299.2	M.Brown-Chi	202	H.Camnitz-Pit	267	H.Camnitz-Pit	1.62	H.Camnitz-Pit	167	H.Camnitz-Pit	31.3	H.Camnitz-Pit	3.5
Willis-Pit	289.2	Moore-Phi	210	McQuillan-Phi	271	Kroh-Chi	1.65	Reulbach-Chi	142	Reulbach-Chi	24.4	Fromme-Cin	3.2

The Great Cobb and Wagner Face Off

Offense increased slightly in the NL, due partly to park changes. On June 30, the Pirates opened Forbes Field, a slightly smaller field than their previous home, Exposition Park. Prior to the season, the Giants significantly reduced the size of center field at the Polo Grounds.

The NL's key rookie was 21-year-old Zack Wheat, who came up late in the season and joined Brooklyn's outfield. He remained with Brooklyn through 1926 before playing a final year with the Athletics while amassing 2,884 hits. John Clarkson, who three times led the NL in victories, died from pneumonia. His 49 wins in 1889, tops in the NL by 21 that year, remains the highest post-1885 total. Another who passed away was Herman Long, Boston's great shortstop of the 1890s, who died at 43 of consumption.

Pittsburgh, Chicago, and New York were again the class of the league. This time the Bucs emerged in May and floated away, finishing 6½ ahead of the Cubs, who themselves won 104 games. It was a return to glory for Honus Wagner, who won his fourth straight batting crown and led the NL in RBIs for the fourth time. Chicago again had the best pitching, but the Pirates sported the top four finishers in runs.

Then there was the league's doormat, the St. Louis Cardinals, who finished 50 or more games out of first for the fourth straight time. A somewhat respectable 43-57 on August 16, the Redbirds lost 15 straight down the stretch. As bad as the Cardinals were, Boston was even worse, ending up 65½ games out.

It was Babe Adams' turn to shine in the fall. The Pittsburgh righty, a fifth starter during the regular season, beat the Tigers three times in a World Series that went seven games. In the match-up of the game's two top stars, Wagner batted .333 with 6 RBIs, while Cobb hit .231 and scored just three times.

1909 American League

TEAM	W	L	T	PCT	GB	HW	HL	R	OR	PA	H	2B	3B	HR	BB	SO	HB	SH	AVG	OBP	SLG	OPS	AOPS	BR	ABR	PF	SB	CS	BSA	BSR
DET	98	54	6	.645		57	19	666	493	5763	1360	209	58	19	397		39	232	.267	.325	.342	667	113	102	75	104	280			
PHI	95	58	0	.621	3.5	49	27	605	411	5620	1257	186	88	21	403		64	247	.256	.321	.343	664	115	92	80	102	201			
BOS	88	63	1	.583	9.5	47	28	601	549	5575	1309	151	69	20	348		77	170	.263	.321	.333	654	112	73	60	102	215			
CHI	78	74	7	.513	20	42	34	492	464	5759	1109	145	56	4	441		57	243	.221	.291	.275	566	89	-72	-51	96	211			
NY	74	77	2	.490	23.5	41	35	589	587	5649	1234	143	61	16	407		63	198	.248	.313	.311	624	103	25	21	101	187			
CLE	71	82	2	.464	27.5	39	37	493	532	5536	1216	173	81	10	283		48	157	.241	.288	.313	601	92	-31	-50	104	173			
STL	61	89	4	.407	36	40	37	441	575	5487	1151	116	45	10	331		51	141	.232	.287	.279	566	91	-82	-48	93	136			
WAS	42	110	4	.276	56	27	48	380	656	5541	1113	149	41	9	321		42	195	.223	.276	.275	551	84	-109	-88	95	136			
TOT	620					342	265	4267		44930	9749	1272	499	109	2931	4918	441	1583	.244	.303	.309	612					1539			

TEAM	CG	SHO	GR	SV	IP	H	HR	BB	SO	BR/9	ERA	AERA	OAV	OOB	PR	APR	PF	OSB	OCS	FA	E	WPB	DP	FW	PW	BW	BSW	DIF
DET	117	17	50	12	1420.1	1254	16	359	528	10.6	2.26	111	.238	.293	33	39	102	190	155	.959	276	43	87	.4	4.4	8.5		8.7
PHI	110	27	61	3	1378.0	1069	9	386	728	9.9	1.93	124	.217	.282	82	74	97	152	162	.961	245	45	92	1.8	8.4	9.1		-.8
BOS	75	11	95	14	1360.1	1213	18	384	555	10.9	2.59	96	.243	.303	-19	-15	101	167	153	.955	292	52	95	-1.3	-1.7	6.8		8.7
CHI	115	26	49	4	1430.1	1182	8	340	669	9.9	2.05	114	.229	.283	67	47	95	210	158	.964	246	54	101	2.4	5.3	-5.8		.0
NY	94	18	64	8	1350.1	1223	21	422	597	11.4	2.65	95	.248	.316	-26	-21	102	207	156	.948	330	52	94	-3.6	-2.4	2.4		2.1
CLE	110	15	51	3	1361.0	1212	9	348	568	10.6	2.40	106	.250	.307	11	20	103	180	164	.957	278	65	110	-.0	2.3	-5.7		-2.0
STL	105	21	55	4	1354.2	1287	16	383	620	11.4	2.88	84	.261	.319	-61	-74	98	203	169	.958	267	51	107	.5	-8.4	-5.5		-.6
WAS	99	11	74	2	1374.2	1288	12	424	653	11.6	3.04	80	.248	.312	-87	-98	98	230	159	.957	280	72	100	-.0	-11.1	-10.0		-12.8
TOT	825	146	499	50	11029.2					10.8	2.47		.244	.303						.957	2214	434	786					

Batter-Fielder Wins
Cobb-Det 6.0
Collins-Phi 5.9
Lajoie-Cle 5.7
Speaker-Bos 4.6
Engle-NY 2.3

Batting Average
Cobb-Det 377
Collins-Phi 347
Lajoie-Cle 324
Lord-Bos 315
Crawford-Det 314

On-Base Percentage
Cobb-Det 431
Collins-Phi 416
Bush-Det 380
Lajoie-Cle 378
Stahl-Bos 377

Slugging Average
Cobb-Det 517
Crawford-Det 452
Collins-Phi 450
Baker-Phi 447
Speaker-Bos 443

On-Base Plus Slugging
Cobb-Det 947
Collins-Phi 866
Crawford-Det 817
Stahl-Bos 812
Lajoie-Cle 809

Adjusted OPS
Cobb-Det 190
Collins-Phi 170
Stahl-Bos 153
Crawford-Det 151
Speaker-Bos 151

Adjusted Batter Runs
Cobb-Det 59.2
Collins-Phi 48.1
Crawford-Det 33.2
Speaker-Bos 29.8
Stahl-Bos 27.2

Runs
Cobb-Det 116
Bush-Det 114
Collins-Phi 104
Lord-Bos 89
Crawford-Det 83

Hits
Cobb-Det 216
Collins-Phi 198
Crawford-Det 185
Speaker-Bos 168
Lord-Bos 168

Doubles
Crawford-Det 35
Lajoie-Cle 33
Cobb-Det 33
Collins-Phi 30
Murphy-Phi 28

Triples
Baker-Phi 19
Murphy-Phi 14
Crawford-Det 14

Home Runs
Cobb-Det 9
Speaker-Bos 7
Stahl-Bos 6
Crawford-Det 6
Murphy-Phi 5

Total Bases
Cobb-Det 296
Crawford-Det 266
Collins-Phi 257
Baker-Phi 242
Speaker-Bos 241

Runs Batted In
Cobb-Det 107
Crawford-Det 97
Baker-Phi 85
Speaker-Bos 77
Davis-Phi 75

Stolen Bases
Cobb-Det 76
Collins-Phi 63
Bush-Det 53
Lord-Bos 36
Dougherty-Chi 36

Base Stealing Runs

Fielding Runs-Infield
Lajoie-Cle 23.3
Parent-Chi 14.4
McBride-Was 13.0
Austin-NY 13.0
Wallace-StL 11.0

Fielding Runs-Outfield
Speaker-Bos 18.5
Engle-NY 14.9
Hartzell-StL 8.5
Milan-Was 4.7
Niles-Bos 2.3

Wins
Mullin-Det 29
Smith-Chi 25
Willett-Det 21

Winning Pct.
Mullin-Det 784
Krause-Phi 692
Bender-Phi 692
Summers-Det 679
Willett-Det 677

Complete Games
Smith-Chi 37
Young-Cle 30
Mullin-Det 29
Johnson-Was 27
Morgan-Bos-Phi 26

Strikeouts
Smith-Cle 177
Johnson-Was 164
Berger-Cle 162
Bender-Phi 161
Waddell-StL 141

Fewest BB/Game
Joss-Cle 1.15
White-Chi 1.57
Powell-StL 1.58
Bender-Phi 1.62
Summers-Det 1.66

Games
Smith-Chi 51
Arellanes-Bos 45
Groom-Was 44
Willett-Det 41

Saves
Arellanes-Bos 8
Powell-StL 3

Base Runners/9
Walsh-Chi 8.60
Joss-Cle 8.64
Smith-Chi 8.73
Bender-Phi 8.86
Krause-Phi 9.00

Adjusted Relief Runs

Relief Ranking

Innings Pitched
Smith-Cle 365.0
Mullin-Det 303.2
Johnson-Was 296.1
Young-Cle 294.1
Morgan-Bos-Phi 293.1

Opponents' Avg.
Morgan-Bos-Phi 202
Walsh-Chi 203
Krause-Phi 204
Cicotte-Bos 207
Wood-Bos 209

Opponents' OBP
Walsh-Chi 253
Bender-Phi 254
Joss-Cle 255
Smith-Chi 257
Krause-Phi 266

Earned Run Average
Krause-Phi 1.39
Walsh-Chi 1.41
Bender-Phi 1.66
Joss-Cle 1.71
Killian-Det 1.71

Adjusted ERA
Krause-Phi 172
Walsh-Chi 166
Joss-Cle 149
Killian-Det 147
Bender-Phi 145

Adjusted Starter Runs
Walsh-Chi 24.9
Morgan-Bos-Phi 24.3
Krause-Phi 23.3
Smith-Chi 22.9
Joss-Cle 20.9

Pitcher Wins
Walsh-Chi 4.1
Smith-Chi 4.1
Bender-Phi 2.7
Krause-Phi 2.7
Plank-Phi 2.6

Bengals Win Battle of Weak Bats

Detroit led the league almost the entire way as Cobb's Tigers captured their third straight AL pennant. Their challengers were the Athletics, led by second baseman Eddie Collins, and the Red Sox, led by center fielder Tris Speaker. Collins was an all-around standout, while Speaker set an AL mark with 35 outfield assists.

Chicago and Cleveland dropped from contention essentially because they couldn't score. Despite fielding just three quality offensive players—Ty Cobb, Donie Bush, and Sam Crawford—Detroit paced the AL in runs by more than 60. Cobb and Bush ranked first and second in runs, Cobb and Crawford first and second in RBIs. Cobb grabbed the Triple Crown and also led in on-base percentage, slugging, total bases, and steals. However, the Tigers magic wore off yet again in the World Series as Detroit fell to the Pirates.

Boston's Harry Hooper spent his rookie year as a part-time outfielder. Starting in 1910, he'd become a regular for sixteen years. Also for the Red Sox, star righty Jack Chesbro was done as a big leaguer at age 35. George Davis, a great shortstop of the nineteenth century, played his last game with the White Sox. Two active players died. Thirty-eight-year-old catcher Doc Powers passed away in April from complications of gangrene, while Jimmy Sebring, an outfielder who played one game for the Senators after five years in the NL, died in December from Bright's disease.

Two AL teams moved into shiny new digs. The Athletics built their revolutionary Shibe Park, which would serve them until they left the city in 1953, while the St. Louis Browns began playing in a new Sportsman's Park. The average AL team scored just 3.44 runs per game, the lowest mark until 1968; three starting pitchers had ERAs below 1.70. The fans apparently found the low-scoring style of play exciting enough, though, as attendance reached a pre-1920 peak.

1908 National League

TEAM	W	L	T	PCT	GB	HW	HL	R	OR	PA	H	2B	3B	HR	BB	SO	HB	SH	AVG	OBP	SLG	OPS	AOPS	BR	ABR	PF	SB	CS	BSA	BSR
CHI	99	55	4	.643		47	30	624	461	5813	1267	196	56	19	418		40	270	.249	.311	.321	632	105	53	29	104	212			
PIT	98	56	1	.636	1	42	35	585	468	5753	1263	162	98	25	420		40	184	.247	.309	.332	641	112	61	61	100	186			
NY	98	56	3	.636	1	52	25	651	455	5826	1339	182	43	20	494		76	250	.267	.342	.333	675	117	144	113	105	181			
PHI	83	71	1	.539	16	43	34	504	445	5612	1223	194	68	11	334		53	213	.244	.298	.316	614	100	13	-4	103	200			
CIN	73	81	1	.474	26	40	37	488	543	5511	1108	129	77	14	372		46	214	.227	.288	.294	582	95	-44	-31	97	196			
BOS	63	91	2	.409	36	35	42	537	622	5793	1228	137	43	17	414		54	194	.239	.303	.296	596	99	-12	-4	98	134			
BRO	53	101	0	.344	46	27	50	375	516	5415	1044	110	60	28	323		29	166	.213	.266	.277	543	82	-117	-102	96	113			
STL	49	105	0	.318	50	28	49	372	626	5450	1105	134	57	17	282		45	164	.223	.271	.283	554	87	-99	-79	95	150			
TOT	622					314	302	4136		45173	9577	1244	502	151	3057	4180	383	1655	.239	.299	.306	605					1372			

TEAM	CG	SHO	GR	SV	IP	H	HR	BB	SO	BR/9	ERA	AERA	OAV	OOB	PR	APR	PF	OSB	OCS	FA	E	WPB	DP	FW	PW	BW	BSW	DIF
CHI	108	29	60	12	1433.2	1137	20	437	668	10.1	2.14	109	.221	.287	33	30	100	158	156	.969	205	46	76	3.7	3.5	3.4		11.4
PIT	100	24	71	9	1402.1	1142	16	406	468	10.3	2.12	108	.223	.287	34	25	97	138	104	.964	226	27	74	1.9	2.9	7.1		9.1
NY	95	25	76	18	1411.0	1210	26	288	656	9.8	2.14	112	.232	.277	32	38	102	135	125	.962	250	41	79	.4	4.4	13.1		3.0
PHI	116	22	43	6	1393.0	1167	8	379	476	10.3	2.10	115	.234	.294	38	44	103	128	154	.963	238	45	75	1.0	5.1	-.5		.3
CIN	110	17	50	8	1384.0	1218	19	415	433	10.9	2.37	96	.243	.307	-4	-19	98	154	137	.959	255	40	72	-.2	-2.2	-3.6		2.0
BOS	92	14	77	1	1404.2	1262	24	423	461	11.2	2.79	86	.245	.310	-70	-66	102	199	152	.962	253	34	90	.0	-7.7	-.5		-6.0
BRO	118	20	43	4	1369.0	1165	17	444	535	11.0	2.47	94	.235	.306	-18	-24	99	203	162	.961	247	37	66	.3	-2.8	-11.9		-9.7
STL	97	13	72	4	1368.0	1217	16	430	528	11.1	2.64	89	.232	.296	-44	-51	100	257	173	.946	348	57	68	-6.8	-5.9	-9.2		-6.1
TOT	836	164	492	62	11165.2					10.6	2.35		.239	.299						.961	2022	327	.600					

Batter-Fielder Wins
- Wagner-Pit 6.9
- Tinker-Chi 4.5
- Dahlen-Bos 4.5
- Bresnahan-NY 3.8
- Ritchey-Bos 3.1

Batting Average
- Wagner-Pit 354
- Donlin-NY 334
- Doyle-NY 308
- Bransfield-Phi 304
- Evers-Chi 300

On-Base Percentage
- Wagner-Pit 415
- Evers-Chi 402
- Bresnahan-NY 401
- Titus-Phi 365
- Donlin-NY 364

Slugging Average
- Wagner-Pit 542
- Donlin-NY 452
- Magee-Phi 417
- Lobert-Cin 407
- Murray-StL 400

On-Base Plus Slugging
- Wagner-Pit 957
- Donlin-NY 816
- Evers-Chi 777
- Magee-Phi 776
- Bresnahan-NY 760

Adjusted OPS
- Wagner-Pit 205
- Donlin-NY 153
- Lobert-Cin 145
- Magee-Phi 143
- Evers-Chi 143

Adjusted Batter Runs
- Wagner-Pit 66.3
- Donlin-NY 32.0
- Lobert-Cin 26.5
- Bresnahan-NY 25.3
- Magee-Phi 25.3

Runs
- Tenney-NY 101
- Wagner-Pit 100
- Leach-Pit 93
- Evers-Chi 83
- Clarke-Pit 83

Hits
- Wagner-Pit 201
- Donlin-NY 198
- Murray-StL 167
- Lobert-Cin 167
- Bransfield-Phi 160

Doubles
- Wagner-Pit 39
- Magee-Phi 30
- Chance-Chi 27
- Knabe-Phi 26
- Donlin-NY 26

Triples
- Wagner-Pit 19
- Lobert-Cin 18
- Magee-Phi 16
- Leach-Pit 16

Home Runs
- Jordan-Bro 12
- Wagner-Pit 10
- Murray-StL 7
- Tinker-Chi 6
- Donlin-NY 6

Total Bases
- Wagner-Pit 308
- Donlin-NY 268
- Murray-StL 237
- Lobert-Cin 232
- Leach-Pit 222

Runs Batted In
- Wagner-Pit 109
- Donlin-NY 106
- Seymour-NY 92
- Bransfield-Phi 71
- Tinker-Chi 68

Stolen Bases
- Wagner-Pit 53
- Murray-StL 48
- Lobert-Cin 47
- Magee-Phi 40
- Evers-Chi 36

Base Stealing Runs

Fielding Runs-Infield
- Dahlen-Bos 37.5
- Tinker-Chi 26.4
- Ritchey-Bos 12.9
- Sweeney-Bos 12.2
- Devlin-NY 11.9

Fielding Runs-Outfield
- Clarke-Pit 10.2
- Burch-Bro 8.5
- Hummel-Bro 8.1
- Shaw-StL 7.3
- Seymour-NY 5.3

Wins
- Mathewson-NY 37
- Brown-Chi 29
- Reulbach-Chi 24

Winning Pct.
- Reulbach-Chi 774
- Mathewson-NY 771
- Brown-Chi 763
- Maddox-Pit 742
- Leever-Pit 682

Complete Games
- Mathewson-NY 34
- Wilhelm-Bro 33
- McQuillan-Phi 32
- Willis-Pit 30
- Rucker-Bro 30

Strikeouts
- Mathewson-NY 259
- Rucker-Bro 199
- Overall-Chi 167
- Raymond-StL 145
- Reulbach-Chi 133

Fewest BB/Game
- Mathewson-NY 97
- Brown-Chi 1.41
- Sparks-Phi 1.74
- Ewing-Cin 1.75
- Campbell-Cin 1.79

Games
- Mathewson-NY 56
- Raymond-StL 48
- McQuillan-Phi 48
- Reulbach-Chi 46

Saves
- McGinnity-NY 5
- Mathewson-NY 5
- Brown-Chi 5
- Overall-Chi 4
- Ewing-Cin 3

Base Runners/9
- Mathewson-NY 7.51
- Brown-Chi 7.72
- McQuillan-Phi 9.01
- Willis-Pit 9.28
- Ewing-Cin 9.47

Adjusted Relief Runs

Relief Ranking

Innings Pitched
- Mathewson-NY 390.2
- McQuillan-Phi 359.2
- Rucker-Bro 333.1
- Wilhelm-Bro 332.0
- Wiltse-NY 330.0

Opponents' Avg.
- Beebe-StL 193
- Brown-Chi 195
- Mathewson-NY 197
- McQuillan-Phi 207
- Raymond-StL 207

Opponents' OBP
- Mathewson-NY 222
- Brown-Chi 232
- Willis-Pit 262
- McQuillan-Phi 263
- Beebe-StL 267

Earned Run Average
- Mathewson-NY 1.43
- Brown-Chi 1.47
- McQuillan-Phi 1.53
- Camnitz-Pit 1.56
- Coakley-Cin-Chi 1.78

Adjusted ERA
- Mathewson-NY 168
- Brown-Chi 159
- McQuillan-Phi 158
- Camnitz-Pit 147
- Richie-Phi 132

Adjusted Starter Runs
- Mathewson-NY 40.8
- McQuillan-Phi 32.7
- Brown-Chi 32.0
- Reulbach-Chi 13.9
- Wilhelm-Bro 13.3

Pitcher Wins
- Mathewson-NY 6.5
- Brown-Chi 4.4
- McQuillan-Phi 3.8
- Reulbach-Chi 2.2
- Wiltse-NY 2.1

Merkle's Boner Leads to Thrilling Three-Way

By decree, pitchers were no longer allowed to rub dirt on the baseball to deface it. Despite this, scoring dropped to just 3.32 runs per team per game, the lowest since 1901. The league batting average of .239 was also the lowest ever. Rookie Gavvy Cravath, future home run king, hit just one in 94 games, while pitchers Hippo Vaughn and Rube Marquard also debuted. Marquard, who played in New York, is now in the Hall of Fame, but Vaughn was clearly greater. Two old Baltimore Orioles ended their big-league tenure: "Iron Man" Joe McGinnity's arm gave out, while outfielder Joe Kelley was finished at 37.

Despite poor hitting, the first great NL pennant race of the century boosted attendance 33 percent. The Giants were up by 4½ on September 18, but Philadelphia rookie left-hander Harry Coveleski beat New York thrice in the final week, drawing the race tighter. On a fateful September 23 in New York, the Giants scored in the ninth, apparently defeating Chicago, 2-1. While the "winning" run scored, however, Fred Merkle, who had been on first, failed to touch second base after the hit. Cubs infielder John Evers called for the ball; umpire Hank O'Day, who had ruled against the Cubs in a similar play weeks before, called Merkle out as fans poured onto the field. The game was later ruled a tie by NL President Harry Pulliam.

Chicago eliminated Pittsburgh on October 4, finishing the season knotted with the Giants. When the game was replayed on October 8, some 35,000 crazed fans at the Polo Grounds watched the Cubs defeat Christy Mathewson, 4-2. After this exhausting pennant race, Chicago's World Series win was almost anticlimactic. Ty Cobb hit .368, but Chicago took Detroit in five. Certainly, nobody at the time could have dreamed that this would be the mighty Cubs' last world championship of the century.

1908 American League

TEAM	W	L	T	PCT	GB	HW	HL	R	OR	PA	H	2B	3B	HR	BB	SO	HB	SH	AVG	OBP	SLG	OPS	AOPS	BR	ABR	PF	SB	CS	BSA	BSR
DET	90	63	1	.588		44	33	647	547	5668	1347	199	86	19	320		42	191	.263	.312	.347	659	115	103	77	104	165			
CLE	90	64	3	.584	0.5	51	26	569	459	5770	1221	188	58	18	364		55	243	.239	.297	.309	606	103	17	15	100	177			
CHI	88	64	4	.579	1.5	51	25	537	470	5788	1127	145	41	3	463		62	236	.224	.298	.271	569	91	-35	-27	98	209			
STL	83	69	4	.546	6.5	46	31	544	483	5726	1261	173	52	20	343		35	197	.245	.296	.310	606	102	14	11	101	126			
BOS	75	79	1	.487	15.5	37	40	564	513	5579	1239	117	88	14	289		69	173	.245	.296	.312	607	100	7	-8	103	156			
PHI	68	85	4	.444	22	46	30	486	562	5656	1131	183	50	21	368		37	186	.223	.281	.292	573	86	-43	-74	107	116			
WAS	67	85	3	.441	22.5	43	32	479	539	5648	1186	132	74	8	368		43	196	.235	.293	.296	589	106	-17	30	92	170			
NY	51	103	1	.331	39.5	30	47	460	713	5533	1190	142	50	13	288		45	153	.236	.283	.291	574	91	-46	-51	101	231			
TOT	622					348	264	4286		45368	9702	1279	499	116	2803	4930	388	1575	.239	.294	.304	598								1350

TEAM	CG	SHO	GR	SV	IP	H	HR	BB	SO	BR/9	ERA	AERA	OAV	OOB	PR	APR	PF	OSB	OCS	FA	E	WPB	DP	FW	PW	BW	BSW	DIF
DET	119	15	38	5	1374.1	1313	12	318	553	11.1	2.40	100	.255	.306	-3	2	101	176	147	.953	305	40	95	-2.1	.2	8.8		6.6
CLE	108	18	61	5	1424.1	1172	16	328	548	9.7	2.02	118	.229	.280	59	56	100	123	127	.962	257	46	95	1.6	6.4	1.7		3.3
CHI	107	23	62	10	1414.0	1165	11	284	623	9.4	2.22	104	.225	.269	26	14	97	149	127	.966	232	43	82	3.2	1.6	-3.1		10.3
STL	107	15	61	5	1397.0	1151	7	387	607	10.3	2.15	111	.230	.294	37	36	100	141	138	.964	237	45	97	2.7	4.1	1.3		-1.1
BOS	102	12	65	7	1380.1	1200	18	364	624	10.5	2.28	108	.238	.295	.17	26	103	167	155	.955	297	63	71	-1.4	3.0	-.9		-2.6
PHI	102	23	74	4	1400.1	1194	10	410	741	10.6	2.56	100	.235	.298	-27	-4	107	242	159	.957	272	60	68	.6	-.5	-8.4		-.2
WAS	106	15	60	7	1391.2	1236	16	348	649	10.5	2.34	97	.241	.294	7	-13	96	151	136	.958	275	63	89	.1	-1.5	3.4		-11.0
NY	90	11	75	3	1366.0	1293	26	458	585	12.0	3.16	78	.252	.322	-117	-102	104	201	140	.947	337	49	78	-4.1	-11.6	-5.8		-4.4
TOT	841	132	496	46	11148.0					10.5	2.39		.239	.294						.958	2212	409	675					

Batter-Fielder Wins		Batting Average		On-Base Percentage		Slugging Average		On-Base Plus Slugging		Adjusted OPS		Adjusted Batter Runs	
Lajoie-Cle	8.0	Cobb-Det	.324	Gessler-Bos	.394	Cobb-Det	.475	Cobb-Det	.842	Cobb-Det	166	Cobb-Det	40.0
McIntyre-Det	4.6	Crawford-Det	.311	McIntyre-Det	.392	Crawford-Det	.457	Gessler-Bos	.817	Gessler-Bos	161	Crawford-Det	34.7
Cobb-Det	4.1	Gessler-Bos	.308	Hemphill-NY	.374	Gessler-Bos	.423	Crawford-Det	.812	Crawford-Det	157	McIntyre-Det	33.4
McBride-Was	3.7	Hemphill-NY	.297	Hartsel-Phi	.371	Rossman-Det	.418	McIntyre-Det	.775	McIntyre-Det	146	Gessler-Bos	31.0
Wagner-Bos	3.2	McIntyre-Det	.295	Dougherty-Chi	.367	McIntyre-Det	.383	Rossman-Det	.748	Rossman-Det	137	Lajoie-Cle	24.3

Runs		Hits		Doubles		Triples		Home Runs		Total Bases		Runs Batted In	
McIntyre-Det	105	Cobb-Det	188	Cobb-Det	36	Cobb-Det	20	Crawford-Det	7	Cobb-Det	276	Cobb-Det	108
Crawford-Det	102	Crawford-Det	184	Rossman-Det	33	Stahl-NY-Bos	16	Hinchman-Cle	6	Crawford-Det	270	Crawford-Det	80
Schaefer-Det	96	McIntyre-Det	168	Crawford-Det	33	Crawford-Det	16	Niles-NY-Bos	5	Rossman-Det	219	Lajoie-Cle	74
Jones-Chi	92	Lajoie-Cle	168	Lajoie-Cle	32	Gessler-Bos	14	Stone-StL	5	McIntyre-Det	218	Ferris-StL	74
Stone-StL	89	Stone-StL	165	Stovall-Cle	29			Davis-Phi	5	Lajoie-Cle	218	Rossman-Det	71

Stolen Bases		Base Stealing Runs	Fielding Runs-Infield		Fielding Runs-Outfield		Wins		Winning Pct.		Complete Games	
Dougherty-Chi	47		Lajoie-Cle	46.8	McIntyre-Det	16.4	Walsh-Chi	40	Walsh-Chi	.727	Walsh-Chi	42
Hemphill-NY	42		McBride-Was	32.6	Murphy-Phi	5.3	Summers-Det	24	Donovan-Det	.720	Young-Bos	30
Schaefer-Det	40		Wagner-Bos	32.4	Hartzell-StL	5.0	Joss-Cle	24	Joss-Cle	.686	Joss-Cle	29
Cobb-Det	39		Tannehill-Chi	16.9	Milan-Was	4.7	Young-Bos	21	Summers-Det	.667	Howell-StL	26
J.Clarke-Cle	37		Wallace-StL	15.2	Stahl-NY-Bos	4.6	Waddell-StL	19	Young-Bos	.656	Mullin-Det	26

Strikeouts		Fewest BB/Game		Games		Saves		Base Runners/9		Adjusted Relief Runs	Relief Ranking
Walsh-Chi	269	Joss-Cle	.83	Walsh-Chi	66	Walsh-Chi	6	Joss-Cle	7.31		
Waddell-StL	232	Burns-Was	.99	Vickers-Phi	53	Hughes-Was	4	Steele-Bos	7.70		
Hughes-Was	165	Walsh-Chi	1.09	Chesbro-NY	45	Waddell-StL	3	Walsh-Chi	7.91		
Dygert-Phi	164	Young-Bos	1.11	Waddell-StL	43			Young-Bos	8.07		
Johnson-Was	160	Summers-Det	1.64	Hughes-Was	43			Burns-Was	8.62		

Innings Pitched		Opponents' Avg.		Opponents' OBP		Earned Run Average		Adjusted ERA		Adjusted Starter Runs		Pitcher Wins	
Walsh-Chi	464.0	Joss-Cle	.197	Joss-Cle	.218	Joss-Cle	1.16	Joss-Cle	205	Walsh-Chi	42.7	Walsh-Chi	6.8
Joss-Cle	325.0	Smith-Chi	.203	Walsh-Chi	.232	Young-Bos	1.26	Young-Bos	194	Joss-Cle	38.3	Joss-Cle	5.0
Howell-StL	324.1	Walsh-Chi	.203	Young-Bos	.240	Walsh-Chi	1.42	Walsh-Chi	163	Young-Bos	36.4	Young-Bos	4.1
Vickers-Phi	317.0	Johnson-Was	.211	Smith-Chi	.256	Summers-Det	1.64	Summers-Det	147	Johnson-Was	17.0	Rhoads-Cle	2.5
Summers-Det	301.0	Young-Bos	.213	Burns-Was	.257	Johnson-Was	1.65	Johnson-Was	138	Howell-StL	16.5	Howell-StL	2.2

Rained Out of a Flag

Once again, pitchers asserted themselves. The AL's .239 batting average was the league's lowest until 1967, and the league's .598 OPS is the lowest in the history of baseball. Four clubs *slugged* under .300. Boston enlarged the already huge Huntington Avenue Grounds, but run production at the park was barely affected. Their 18-year-old pitching phenom, "Smokey Joe" Wood, made a successful debut.

The aging A's began to rebuild, falling to sixth, but what an eye Connie Mack had for talent! Making their major league debuts for Philly in 1908 were outfielders Joe Jackson and Amos Strunk and infielders Jack Barry and Frank "Home Run" Baker. Three of them would shortly help the club become great again. However, Mack and Jackson never quite got along, and "Shoeless Joe" ended up in Cleveland.

Cleveland, Chicago, and Detroit remained in the pennant chase until the last day. While Detroit led big in midsummer, Cleveland won 16 of 18 to climb ahead in late September. On October 2 the Indians' Addie Joss—whose 1.16 ERA set a league record—tossed a perfect game at Chicago while White Sox hurler Ed Walsh struck out 15 and allowed just 1 run.

The Tigers put on a spurt, though, and won the crown on the last day of the season, October 5. "Wild Bill" Donovan shut out Chicago to clinch the flag by a half-game over the Indians because Detroit was not required to make up a rainout. The ensuing flap led the leagues to establish a new rule mandating that all rainouts and ties critical to a pennant race be replayed.

Once again, Detroit had a fearsome attack, featuring four of the league's five top sluggers and pacing the league in runs by 78. Nevertheless, for the second straight year, the Cubs easily whipped the Tigers in the Fall Classic. This time Detroit won one game and Ty Cobb scored three times.

1907 National League

TEAM	W	L	T	PCT	GB	HW	HL	R	OR	PA	H	2B	3B	HR	BB	SO	HB	SH	AVG	OBP	SLG	OPS	AOPS	BR	ABR	PF	SB	CS	BSA	BSR
CHI	107	45	3	.704		54	19	574	390	5570	1224	162	48	13	435		48	195	.250	.318	.311	629	98	28	-5	106	235			
PIT	91	63	3	.591	17	47	29	634	510	5650	1261	133	78	19	469		46	178	.254	.325	.324	649	109	61	53	101	264			
PHI	83	64	2	.565	21.5	45	30	514	476	5320	1113	162	65	12	424		41	130	.236	.304	.305	609	99	-9	-1	99	154			
NY	82	71	2	.536	25.5	45	30	574	510	5624	1222	160	63	48	516		69	165	.251	.331	.317	648	107	73	54	103	205			
BRO	65	83	5	.439	40	37	38	446	522	5468	1135	142	63	18	336		40	197	.232	.287	.298	585	98	-64	-25	92	121			
CIN	66	87	3	.431	41.5	43	36	526	519	5567	1226	126	90	15	372		34	195	.247	.304	.318	622	98	-1	-22	104	158			
BOS	58	90	4	.392	47	31	42	502	652	5623	1222	142	61	22	413		57	133	.243	.308	.309	617	100	2	4	100	120			
STL	52	101	2	.340	55.5	31	47	419	610	5518	1163	121	52	18	312		42	156	.232	.283	.288	571	88	-91	-76	97	125			
TOT	616					333	271	4189		44340	9566	1148	505	140	3277	4217	377	1349	.243	.308	.309	616					1382			

TEAM	CG	SHO	GR	SV	IP	H	HR	BB	SO	BR/9	ERA	AERA	OAV	OOB	PR	APR	PF	OSB	OCS	FA	E	WPB	DP	FW	PW	BW	BSW	DIF
CHI	114	32	45	8	1373.1	1054	11	402	586	9.8	1.73	144	.216	.281	112	114	101	148	132	.967	211	31	110	3.1	13.0	-.6		15.5
PIT	111	24	51	5	1363.0	1207	12	368	497	10.7	2.30	106	.241	.299	25	19	99	124	125	.959	256	41	75	.2	2.2	6.0		5.6
PHI	110	21	46	4	1299.1	1095	13	422	499	10.9	2.43	99	.233	.304	5	-3	98	136	139	.957	256	40	104	-.7	-.3	-.1		10.6
NY	109	22	63	13	1371.0	1219	24	369	655	10.7	2.45	101	.238	.294	2	1	100	135	121	.963	232	60	75	1.6	.1	6.1		-2.4
BRO	125	20	29	1	1356.1	1218	16	463	479	11.4	2.38	98	.249	.319	12	-9	95	208	152	.959	262	41	94	-.7	-1.0	-2.8		-4.5
CIN	118	10	39	2	1351.1	1223	16	444	481	11.5	2.41	107	.251	.322	8	24	105	173	150	.963	227	24	118	2.1	2.7	-2.5		-12.8
BOS	121	9	38	2	1338.2	1324	28	458	426	12.4	3.33	76	.268	.339	-129	-115	103	238	163	.961	249	51	128	.1	-13.1	.5		-3.5
STL	127	19	29	2	1365.2	1212	20	500	594	11.6	2.70	93	.243	.318	-35	-32	101	220	167	.948	340	74	105	-5.8	-3.6	-8.6		-6.5
TOT	935	157	340	37	10818.2					11.1	2.46		.243	.308						.960	2033	362	809					-6.5

Batter-Fielder Wins
Wagner-Pit ...6.7
Brain-Bos ...4.8
Magee-Phi ...4.5
Mitchell-Cin ...3.3
Beaumont-Bos ...3.0

Batting Average
Wagner-Pit ...350
Magee-Phi ...328
Beaumont-Bos ...322
Leach-Pit ...303
Seymour-NY ...294

On-Base Percentage
Wagner-Pit ...408
Magee-Phi ...396
Clarke-Pit ...383
Devlin-NY ...376
Thomas-Phi ...374

Slugging Average
Wagner-Pit ...513
Magee-Phi ...455
Lumley-Bro ...425
Beaumont-Bos ...424
Brain-Bos ...420

On-Base Plus Slugging
Wagner-Pit ...921
Magee-Phi ...852
Beaumont-Bos ...790
Clarke-Pit ...772
Leach-Pit ...756

Adjusted OPS
Wagner-Pit ...186
Magee-Phi ...169
Beaumont-Bos ...148
Lumley-Bro ...144
Jordan-Bro ...141

Adjusted Batter Runs
Wagner-Pit ...50.3
Magee-Phi ...40.7
Beaumont-Bos ...29.3
Jordan-Bro ...26.3
Clarke-Pit ...25.8

Runs
Shannon-NY ...104
Leach-Pit ...102
Wagner-Pit ...98
Clarke-Pit ...97
Tenney-Bos ...83

Hits
Beaumont-Bos ...187
Wagner-Pit ...180
Leach-Pit ...166
Magee-Phi ...165
Mitchell-Cin ...163

Doubles
Wagner-Pit ...38
Magee-Phi ...28
Steinfeldt-Chi ...25
Seymour-NY ...25
Brain-Bos ...24

Triples
Ganzel-Cin ...16
Alperman-Bro ...16
Wagner-Pit ...14
Beaumont-Bos ...14
Clarke-Pit ...13

Home Runs
Brain-Bos ...10
Lumley-Bro ...9
Murray-StL ...7
Wagner-Pit ...6
Browne-NY ...5

Total Bases
Wagner-Pit ...264
Beaumont-Bos ...246
Magee-Phi ...229
Leach-Pit ...221
Brain-Bos ...214

Runs Batted In
Magee-Phi ...85
Wagner-Pit ...82
Abbaticchio-Pit ...82
Seymour-NY ...75
Steinfeldt-Chi ...70

Stolen Bases
Wagner-Pit ...61
Magee-Phi ...46
Evers-Chi ...46
Leach-Pit ...43
Devlin-NY ...38

Base Stealing Runs

Fielding Runs-Infield
Evers-Chi ...27.1
Brain-Bos ...22.5
Byrne-StL ...20.6
Doolan-Phi ...14.8
Tinker-Chi ...13.4

Fielding Runs-Outfield
Mitchell-Cin ...25.1
Leach-Pit ...8.9
Clarke-Pit ...7.8
Magee-Phi ...7.8
Beaumont-Bos ...4.1

Wins
Mathewson-NY ...24
Overall-Chi ...23
Brown-Chi ...20
Sparks-Phi ...22
Willis-Pit ...21

Winning Pct.
Reulbach-Chi ...810
Brown-Chi ...769
Overall-Chi ...767
Sparks-Phi ...733
Lundgren-Chi ...720

Complete Games
McGlynn-StL ...33
Ewing-Cin ...32
Mathewson-NY ...31
Karger-StL ...29
Willis-Pit ...27

Strikeouts
Mathewson-NY ...178
Ewing-Cin ...147
Ames-NY ...146
Overall-Chi ...141
Beebe-StL ...141

Fewest BB/Game
Phillippe-Pit ...1.51
Mathewson-NY ...1.51
Brown-Chi ...1.55
McGinnity-NY ...1.68
Sparks-Phi ...1.73

Games
McGinnity-NY ...47
McGlynn-StL ...45
Mathewson-NY ...41
Ewing-Cin ...41

Saves
McGinnity-NY ...4
Overall-Chi ...3
Brown-Chi ...3

Base Runners/9
Mathewson-NY ...8.71
Brown-Chi ...8.73
Pfiester-Chi ...9.05
Overall-Chi ...9.42
Sparks-Phi ...9.48

Adjusted Relief Runs

Relief Ranking

Innings Pitched
McGlynn-StL ...352.1
Ewing-Cin ...332.2
Mathewson-NY ...315.0
Karger-StL ...314.0
McGinnity-NY ...310.1

Opponents' Avg.
Lundgren-Chi ...185
Pfiester-Chi ...207
Overall-Chi ...208
Camnitz-Pit ...211
Mathewson-NY ...212

Opponents' OBP
Mathewson-NY ...247
Brown-Chi ...262
Pfiester-Chi ...263
Overall-Chi ...268
Karger-StL ...270

Earned Run Average
Pfiester-Chi ...1.15
Lundgren-Chi ...1.17
Brown-Chi ...1.39
Leever-Pit ...1.66
Overall-Chi ...1.68

Adjusted ERA
Pfiester-Chi ...215
Lundgren-Chi ...212
Brown-Chi ...179
Ewing-Cin ...149
Overall-Chi ...148

Adjusted Starter Runs
Lundgren-Chi ...29.2
Brown-Chi ...28.8
Overall-Chi ...27.9
Ewing-Cin ...26.1
Pfiester-Chi ...20.5

Pitcher Wins
Overall-Chi ...3.9
Brown-Chi ...3.7
Lundgren-Chi ...3.5
Mathewson-NY ...2.7
Ewing-Cin ...2.6

Cubs are World Serious

Prior to the season, the rules committee voted that the strike zone should range from the knee to shoulder. With this on the books, runs continued to drop. The Cubs' 1.73 ERA set an all-time NL record.

Two soon-to-be-prominent New York Giants saw their first action in 1907. Second baseman "Laughing Larry" Doyle would play a dozen seasons for John McGraw, while first baseman Fred Merkle lasted sixteen years in the bigs despite being best remembered for a baserunning gaffe. Future batting star Heinie Zimmerman broke in with Chicago, while first baseman Ed Konetchy, a slick fielder who also collected 2,150 lifetime hits, came up at midseason to start for the Cardinals.

Appearing in their final games during 1907 were first baseman Jake Beckley (who collected 2,934 hits), veteran shortstop Tommy Corcoran (who played 21 seasons), third baseman Lave Cross (who played 21 seasons), and Bobby Lowe (Boston's regular second baseman for eleven years). Boston outfielder Cozy Dolan fell ill at spring training with pneumonia and typhoid fever and died on March 29.

After a great start, the Giants crumbled in May. John McGraw worked quickly to reconstruct his aging club, and New York would be back in 1908. As the Giants rebuilt, the Cubs again ran away and hid from the competition, winning the flag by 17 games over Pittsburgh.

The Cubs steamrolled the Tigers in October in five games (one was a tie). Chicago outscored Detroit 19-6 in the World Series, with Ty Cobb crossing the plate just once. This was the last Series until 1918 when at least one team didn't hit a home run.

Finally, in the year's biggest lie, the Mills Commission—appointed to investigate the beginnings of baseball—concluded with not one iota of reliable evidence that Civil War General Abner Doubleday invented the game in Cooperstown, New York, in 1839. Doubleday, who passed away in 1893, was too dead to be able to deny anything.

1907 American League

TEAM	W	L	T	PCT	GB	HW	HL	R	OR	PA	H	2B	3B	HR	BB	SO	HB	SH	AVG	OBP	SLG	OPS	AOPS	BR	ABR	PF	SB	CS	BSA	BSR
DET	92	58	3	.613		50	27	693	531	5721	1383	179	75	11	315		44	158	.266	.313	.335	648	108	62	40	104	196			
PHI	88	57	5	.607	1.5	50	20	584	511	5596	1276	220	44	22	384		27	175	.255	.311	.329	640	106	57	43	102	175			
CHI	87	64	6	.576	5.5	48	29	588	474	5720	1205	149	33	5	421		48	177	.238	.302	.283	585	95	-35	-16	97	175			
CLE	85	67	6	.559	8	46	31	531	525	5636	1221	182	68	11	335		56	177	.241	.295	.310	605	97	-12	-16	101	193			
NY	70	78	4	.473	21	33	40	605	667	5530	1288	150	67	15	304		53	129	.249	.299	.315	614	93	-1	-42	108	206			
STL	69	83	3	.454	24	36	40	541	555	5784	1324	154	63	10	370		39	151	.253	.308	.313	621	103	17	19	100	144			
BOS	59	90	6	.396	32.5	34	41	466	558	5721	1224	154	48	18	305		35	146	.234	.281	.292	573	89	-78	-74	99	125			
WAS	49	102	3	.325	43.5	27	47	506	693	5699	1243	134	57	12	390		60	137	.243	.304	.299	603	105	-10	37	92	223			
TOT	617					324	275	4514		45407	10134	1322	455	104	2824	4479	362	1254	.247	.302	.309	611					1399			

TEAM	CG	SHO	GR	SV	IP	H	HR	BB	SO	BR/9	ERA	AERA	OAV	OOB	PR	APR	PF	OSB	OCS	FA	E	WPB	DP	FW	PW	BW	BSW	DIF
DET	120	15	36	6	1370.2	1281	8	380	512	11.2	2.33	112	.251	.309	32	39	102	160	137	.959	260	46	79	1.0	4.3	4.4		7.3
PHI	106	27	65	6	1354.2	1106	13	378	789	10.3	2.35	111	.226	.290	29	37	102	181	149	.958	263	50	67	.4	4.1	4.7		6.3
CHI	112	17	53	9	1406.1	1279	13	305	604	10.3	2.22	108	.245	.290	50	28	94	153	130	.966	233	55	101	3.4	3.1	-1.8		6.8
CLE	127	20	36	5	1392.2	1253	8	362	513	10.8	2.26	111	.244	.300	43	36	99	174	115	.960	264	74	137	1.3	4.0	-1.8		5.5
NY	93	10	67	6	1333.2	1327	13	428	511	12.2	3.03	92	.262	.325	-73	-32	110	178	143	.947	334	52	79	-4.4	-3.5	-4.6		8.5
STL	129	15	28	9	1381.1	1254	17	352	463	10.8	2.61	96	.245	.300	-10	-16	99	198	145	.959	266	33	97	.8	-1.8	2.1		-8.1
BOS	100	17	70	7	1414.0	1222	22	337	517	10.2	2.45	105	.236	.288	14	18	101	160	155	.959	274	47	100	.2	2.0	-8.2		-9.5
WAS	106	12	57	5	1351.1	1383	10	344	570	11.8	3.11	78	.268	.320	-86	-111	95	195	137	.951	310	76	69	-2.4	-12.3	4.1		-15.9
TOT	893	133	412	53	11004.2					10.9	2.54		.247	.302						.958	2204	433	729					

Batter-Fielder Wins		Batting Average		On-Base Percentage		Slugging Average		On-Base Plus Slugging		Adjusted OPS		Adjusted Batter Runs	
Lajoie-Cle	7.0	Cobb-Det	.350	Hartsel-Phi	.405	Cobb-Det	.468	Cobb-Det	.848	Cobb-Det	164	Cobb-Det	40.4
Cobb-Det	4.9	Crawford-Det	.323	Stone-StL	.387	Crawford-Det	.460	Crawford-Det	.826	Crawford-Det	157	Stone-StL	35.5
Crawford-Det	3.9	Stone-StL	.320	Flick-Cle	.386	Flick-Cle	.412	Flick-Cle	.798	Flick-Cle	153	Crawford-Det	35.4
Flick-Cle	3.0	Flick-Cle	.302	Cobb-Det	.380	Stone-StL	.399	Stone-StL	.787	Stone-StL	151	Flick-Cle	34.6
Stone-StL	2.6	Nicholls-Phi	.302	Crawford-Det	.366	Davis-Phi	.395	Hartsel-Phi	.771	Hartsel-Phi	143	Hartsel-Phi	32.5

Runs		Hits		Doubles		Triples		Home Runs		Total Bases		Runs Batted In	
Crawford-Det	102	Cobb-Det	212	Davis-Phi	35	Flick-Cle	18	Davis-Phi	8	Cobb-Det	283	Cobb-Det	119
D.Jones-Det	101	Stone-StL	191	Crawford-Det	34	Crawford-Det	17	Seybold-Phi	5	Crawford-Det	268	Seybold-Phi	92
Cobb-Det	97	Crawford-Det	188	Lajoie-Cle	30	Cobb-Det	14	Hoffman-NY	5	Stone-StL	238	Davis-Phi	87
Hartsel-Phi	93	Ganley-Was	167	J.Collins-Bos-Phi	29	Unglaub-Bos	13	Cobb-Det	5	Davis-Phi	230	Crawford-Det	81
Hahn-Chi	87	Flick-Cle	166	Seybold-Phi	29					Flick-Cle	226	Wallace-StL	70

Stolen Bases		Base Stealing Runs		Fielding Runs-Infield		Fielding Runs-Outfield		Wins		Winning Pct.		Complete Games	
Cobb-Det	53			Lajoie-Cle	44.9	D.Jones-Det	12.8	White-Chi	27	Donovan-Det	.862	Walsh-Chi	37
Flick-Cle	41			Donahue-Chi	20.5	Birmingham-Cle	12.4	Joss-Cle	27	Dygert-Phi	.724	Mullin-Det	35
Conroy-NY	41			Elberfeld-NY	12.8	Cobb-Det	12.0	Killian-Det	25	Joss-Cle	.711	Joss-Cle	34
Ganley-Was	40			Isbell-Chi	8.1	Crawford-Det	7.0	Donovan-Det	25	Smith-Chi	.697	Young-Bos	33
Altizer-Was	38			Wallace-StL	7.9	Ganley-Was	6.6			White-Chi	.675	Plank-Phi	33

Strikeouts		Fewest BB/Game		Games		Saves		Base Runners/9		Adjusted Relief Runs		Relief Ranking	
Waddell-Phi	232	White-Chi	1.18	Walsh-Chi	56	Dinneen-Bos-StL	4	Young-Bos	9.02				
Walsh-Chi	206	Altrock-Chi	1.31	White-Chi	46	Walsh-Chi	4	Joss-Cle	9.04				
Plank-Phi	183	Young-Bos	1.34	Mullin-Det	46	Hughes-Was	4	Bender-Phi	9.11				
Dygert-Phi	151	Bender-Phi	1.40	Waddell-Phi	44			Winter-Bos	9.19				
Young-Bos	147	Joss-Cle	1.44					Walsh-Chi	9.29				

Innings Pitched		Opponents' Avg.		Opponents' OBP		Earned Run Average		Adjusted ERA		Adjusted Starter Runs		Pitcher Wins	
Walsh-Chi	422.1	Dygert-Phi	.214	Young-Bos	.263	Walsh-Chi	1.60	Walsh-Chi	150	Walsh-Chi	32.8	Walsh-Chi	4.6
Mullin-Det	357.1	Winter-Bos	.216	Joss-Cle	.264	Killian-Det	1.78	Killian-Det	146	Joss-Cle	26.7	Killian-Det	4.2
Plank-Phi	343.2	Walsh-Chi	.224	Bender-Phi	.265	Joss-Cle	1.83	Joss-Cle	136	Young-Bos	24.9	Joss-Cle	3.0
Young-Bos	343.1	Howell-StL	.225	Winter-Bos	.267	Howell-StL	1.93	Howell-StL	130	Killian-Det	24.7	Howell-StL	2.6
Joss-Cle	338.2	Donovan-Det	.226	Walsh-Chi	.269	Young-Bos	1.99	Young-Bos	129	Plank-Phi	17.1	Young-Bos	2.4

A Peach Takes Root in Motown

Four teams entered September within striking distance of the pennant. While Chicago and Cleveland played .500 ball during the last month and Philadelphia peaked early, Detroit finished the season on a high to take the crown. Rarely has one player made such a difference to an entire league as Ty Cobb did in 1907. In his first season of more than 100 games, Cobb won the first of his 12 batting titles and led in slugging, hits, total bases, RBIs, and steals. His outfield mates, Sam Crawford and Davy Jones, were first and second in runs (Cobb was third). The Tigers leapt from sixth to first, edging the Athletics by 1½ games. Just as importantly, Cobb's speed-based game would usher in a new era of "attack" baseball.

The blow of a bad year can be softened by the gain of a Hall of Famer. Boston playing manager Chick Stahl committed suicide in spring training, but the club gained freshman outfielder Tris Speaker. Washington finished last while summoning 19-year-old pitcher Walter Johnson. While the rookie finished 5-9, his ERA was a sparkling 1.87. The Senators, as well as the Tigers, experienced huge attendance gains, and total spectators for the league increased by 16 percent.

Once again, Topsy Hartsel and Harry Davis provided the Philadelphia offense, and the deep pitching was nearly good enough to overcome the fearsome Tigers attack. In the World Series, however, the Tigers were toothless, as the Cubs completely shut them down in five games, including one tie.

At this time, the strike zone was defined, rather vaguely, as reaching from the knees to the shoulders (no "top" or "bottom" of either to make the definition more precise). Strikeouts fell a bit as homers dropped nearly 25 percent. The AL also ruled in 1907 that anyone appearing as a pinch hitter, pinch runner, or defensive substitute would now receive credit for a game played.

1906 National League

TEAM	W	L	T	PCT	GB	HW	HL	R	OR	PA	H	2B	3B	HR	BB	SO	HB	SH	AVG	OBP	SLG	OPS	AOPS	BR	ABR	PF	SB	CS	BSA	BSR
CHI	116	36	3	.763		56	21	704	381	5742	1316	181	71	20	448		45	231	.262	.328	.339	667	109	85	49	106	283			
NY	96	56	1	.632	20	51	24	625	509	5556	1217	162	53	14	563		71	154	.255	.343	.320	663	112	96	82	102	288			
PIT	93	60	1	.608	23.5	49	27	623	470	5686	1313	164	67	12	424		42	190	.261	.324	.327	651	105	56	30	104	162			
PHI	71	82	1	.464	45.5	37	40	528	564	5524	1183	197	47	12	432		36	145	.241	.307	.307	614	98	-6	-7	100	180			
BRO	66	86	1	.434	50	31	44	496	625	5483	1156	141	68	25	388		36	162	.236	.297	.308	605	103	-33	10	92	176			
CIN	64	87	4	.424	51.5	36	40	533	582	5642	1198	140	71	16	395		58	164	.238	.301	.304	605	91	-30	-52	104	170			
STL	52	98	4	.347	63	28	48	470	607	5613	1195	137	69	9	361		38	139	.235	.291	.295	586	93	-70	-49	96	110			
BOS	49	102	1	.325	66.5	28	47	408	649	5452	1115	136	43	16	356		52	119	.226	.286	.281	567	85	-97	-85	97	93			
TOT	615					316	291	4387		44698	9693	1258	489	124	3367	4537	378	1304	.244	.310	.310	620					1462			

TEAM	CG	SHO	GR	SV	IP	H	HR	BB	SO	BR/9	ERA	AERA	OAV	OOB	PR	APR	PF	OSB	OCS	FA	E	WPB	DP	FW	PW	BW	BSW	DIF
CHI	125	30	33	10	1388.1	1018	12	446	702	9.8	1.75	150	.207	.280	135	135	100	107	143	.969	194	34	100	4.5	15.0	5.4		15.0
NY	105	19	55	18	1334.1	1207	12	394	639	11.0	2.49	105	.241	.300	20	15	99	144	154	.963	233	50	84	1.8	1.7	9.1		7.4
PIT	116	27	42	2	1358.0	1234	13	309	532	10.5	2.21	120	.245	.294	62	69	102	157	133	.964	228	52	109	2.2	7.7	3.3		3.3
PHI	108	21	52	5	1354.1	1201	18	436	500	11.3	2.58	101	.235	.304	7	0	99	203	119	.956	271	46	83	-.6	.0	-.8		-4.1
BRO	119	22	36	11	1348.2	1255	15	453	476	11.7	3.13	80	.249	.316	-76	-97	96	192	151	.955	283	34	73	-1.5	-10.8	1.1		1.2
CIN	126	12	31	5	1369.2	1248	14	470	567	11.6	2.69	102	.250	.320	-10	5	105	184	161	.959	262	55	97	.0	.6	-5.8		-6.4
STL	118	4	37	2	1354.0	1246	16	479	559	11.9	3.04	86	.246	.318	-63	-65	100	250	164	.957	272	75	92	-.7	-7.2	-5.4		-9.7
BOS	137	10	16	0	1334.1	1291	24	436	562	12.0	3.14	85	.261	.328	-76	-69	102	225	181	.947	337	49	102	-5.2	-7.7	-9.4		-4.2
TOT	954	145	302	53	10841.2					11.2	2.62		.244	.310						.959	2080	395	740					

Batter-Fielder Wins		Batting Average		On-Base Percentage		Slugging Average		On-Base Plus Slugging		Adjusted OPS		Adjusted Batter Runs	
Wagner-Pit	7.2	Wagner-Pit	.339	Bresnahan-NY	.419	Lumley-Bro	.477	Wagner-Pit	.875	Lumley-Bro	184	Lumley-Bro	45.3
Devlin-NY	6.6	Steinfeldt-Chi	.327	Chance-Chi	.419	Wagner-Pit	.459	Lumley-Bro	.864	Wagner-Pit	166	Wagner-Pit	42.2
Lumley-Bro	4.5	Lumley-Bro	.324	Wagner-Pit	.416	Strang-NY	.435	Chance-Chi	.849	Chance-Chi	156	Chance-Chi	35.0
Bresnahan-NY	4.2	Strang-NY	.319	Devlin-NY	.396	Steinfeldt-Chi	.430	Steinfeldt-Chi	.825	Jordan-Bro	153	Steinfeldt-Chi	31.5
Huggins-Cin	4.0	Chance-Chi	.319	Steinfeldt-Chi	.395	Chance-Chi	.430	Devlin-NY	.786	Steinfeldt-Chi	149	Devlin-NY	28.3

Runs		Hits		Doubles		Triples		Home Runs		Total Bases		Runs Batted In	
Wagner-Pit	103	Steinfeldt-Chi	176	Wagner-Pit	38	Schulte-Chi	13	Jordan-Bro	12	Wagner-Pit	237	Steinfeldt-Chi	83
Chance-Chi	103	Wagner-Pit	175	Magee-Phi	36	Clarke-Pit	13	Lumley-Bro	9	Steinfeldt-Chi	232	Nealon-Pit	83
Sheckard-Chi	90	Seymour-Cin-NY	165	Bransfield-Phi	28	Nealon-Pit	12	Seymour-Cin-NY	8	Lumley-Bro	231	Seymour-Cin-NY	80
Nealon-Pit	82	Magee-Phi	159	Steinfeldt-Chi	27	Lumley-Bro	12	Schulte-Chi	7	Magee-Phi	229	Jordan-Bro	78
		Huggins-Cin	159	Sheckard-Chi	27					Schulte-Chi	223		

Stolen Bases		Base Stealing Runs		Fielding Runs-Infield		Fielding Runs-Outfield		Wins		Winning Pct.		Complete Games	
Chance-Chi	57			Devlin-NY	28.8	Magee-Phi	11.9	McGinnity-NY	27	Reulbach-Chi	.826	Young-Bos	37
Magee-Phi	55			Brain-Bos	25.0	Maloney-Bro	9.1	Brown-Chi	26	Brown-Chi	.813	Pfeffer-Bos	33
Devlin-NY	54			Gilbert-NY	21.9	Thomas-Phi	8.4	Willis-Pit	23	Leever-Pit	.759		
Wagner-Pit	53			Huggins-Cin	21.9	Titus-Phi	6.8	Mathewson-NY	22	Lundgren-Chi	.739		
Evers-Chi	49			Wagner-Pit	20.0	Clarke-Pit	4.9	Leever-Pit	22	Pfiester-Chi	.714		

Strikeouts		Fewest BB/Game		Games		Saves		Base Runners/9		Adjusted Relief Runs		Relief Ranking	
Beebe-Chi-StL	171	Phillippe-Pit	1.07	McGinnity-NY	45	Ferguson-NY	7	Brown-Chi	8.53				
Pfeffer-Bos	158	Leever-Pit	1.66	Young-Bos	43	Wiltse-NY	6	Pfiester-Chi	8.94				
Ames-NY	156	Sparks-Phi	1.76	Sparks-Phi	42	Stricklett-Bro	5	Sparks-Phi	8.98				
Pfiester-Chi	153	Ewing-Cin	1.88	Duggleby-Phi	42			Reulbach-Chi	9.66				
		McGinnity-NY	1.88					Ewing-Cin	9.70				

Innings Pitched		Opponents' Avg.		Opponents' OBP		Earned Run Average		Adjusted ERA		Adjusted Starter Runs		Pitcher Wins	
Young-Bos	358.1	Reulbach-Chi	.175	Brown-Chi	.252	Brown-Chi	1.04	Brown-Chi	253	Brown-Chi	45.1	Brown-Chi	6.1
McGinnity-NY	339.2	Pfiester-Chi	.194	Sparks-Phi	.257	Pfiester-Chi	1.51	Pfiester-Chi	174	Willis-Pit	34.0	Willis-Pit	4.3
Willis-Pit	322.0	Brown-Chi	.202	Pfiester-Chi	.258	Reulbach-Chi	1.65	Reulbach-Chi	159	Pfiester-Chi	29.9	Reulbach-Chi	2.8
Sparks-Phi	316.2	Beebe-Chi-StL	.209	Phillippe-Pit	.276	Willis-Pit	1.73	Willis-Pit	154	Reulbach-Chi	25.6	Taylor-StL-Chi	2.8
Lindaman-Bos	307.1	Sparks-Phi	.211	Reulbach-Chi	.278	Leifield-Pit	1.87	Leifield-Pit	143	Taylor-StL-Chi	20.0	Weimer-Cin	2.8

A Chicago Revival

Staking their claim as the team of the decade, the Chicago Cubs walloped the rest of the league, going 116-36 to post the NL's best record ever while capturing the franchise's first flag since 1886. Chicago went 26-3 in August and easily held off a good New York team that won 96 games. Three Finger Brown had a 1.04 ERA, the best in modern NL history, and Ed Reulbach allowed just 5.33 hits per game, a record that would stand until 1968. The Cubs staff ERA was a spectacular 1.76.

The Cubs also had a productive offense headed by first baseman-manager Frank Chance and third sacker Harry Steinfeldt, one of baseball's first great offensive-minded third basemen. On the other hand, Boston (known as both the Doves and Beaneaters) lost 19 in a row and finished 66½ games out, an all-time National League record for team futility. The Cubs had seven players score more often than Boston's runs leader, Fred Tenney.

Pitcher Babe Adams made his debut with the Cardinals. Purchased by Pittsburgh the next year, Adams remained with the club until 1926 and won 194 games. Hugh Duffy, who batted .440 in 1894, saw his last at bat at age 39, and John McGraw ended his playing days to concentrate fully on managing from the dugout. Kid Nichols, a 361-game winner who starred for Boston from 1980-1901, and who was arguably the greatest pitcher of the nineteenth century, retired. Buck Ewing, a pre-eminent star of nineteenth century ball, died at age 47.

Offense again dropped significantly in 1906. Small-ball techniques like the sacrifice bunt and the steal were at their apex. The orthodox little man's game became relevant in October's intra-city World Series, where the "Hitless Wonder" White Sox pulled off a surprise upset of the Cubs.

1906 American League

TEAM	W	L	T	PCT	GB	HW	HL	R	OR	PA	H	2B	3B	HR	BB	SO	HB	SH	AVG	OBP	SLG	OPS	AOPS	BR	ABR	PF	SB	CS	BSA	BSR
CHI	93	58	3	.616		54	23	570	460	5654	1133	152	52	7	453		50	226	.230	.301	.286	587	91	-45	-31	97	216			
NY	90	61	4	.596	3	53	23	640	543	5661	1354	166	77	17	331		46	189	.266	.316	.339	655	101	57	-1	110	192			
CLE	89	64	4	.582	5	47	30	663	481	5987	1514	240	73	12	330		41	191	.279	.325	.357	682	121	114	124	99	203			
PHI	78	67	4	.538	12	48	23	561	539	5475	1206	213	49	32	385		43	164	.247	.308	.330	638	102	35	17	103	165			
STL	76	73	5	.510	16	40	34	560	499	5614	1244	145	60	20	366		47	171	.247	.304	.312	616	102	-7	18	96	221			
DET	71	78	2	.477	21	42	34	518	598	5474	1195	154	64	10	333		33	178	.242	.295	.306	601	91	-38	-51	103	206			
WAS	55	95	1	.367	37.5	33	41	519	665	5455	1180	144	65	26	306		49	144	.238	.289	.309	598	97	-46	-21	95	233			
BOS	49	105	1	.318	45.5	22	54	463	706	5645	1223	160	75	13	298		41	138	.237	.284	.304	588	89	-69	-68	100	99			
TOT	613					339	262	4494		44965	10049	1374	515	137	2802	4561	350	1401	.249	.303	.318	621					1535			

TEAM	CG	SHO	GR	SV	IP	H	HR	BB	SO	BR/9	ERA	AERA	OAV	OOB	PR	APR	PF	OSB	OCS	FA	E	WPB	DP	FW	PW	BW	BSW	DIF
CHI	117	32	43	4	1375.1	1212	11	255	543	9.8	2.13	119	.239	.280	85	66	94	133	133	.963	243	52	80	1.8	7.3	-3.4		11.8
NY	99	18	68	5	1357.2	1236	21	351	605	10.8	2.78	107	.246	.301	-13	25	110	184	144	.957	272	54	69	.1	2.7	-.1		11.7
CLE	133	27	27	4	1412.2	1197	16	365	530	10.3	2.09	125	.232	.289	94	87	97	170	140	.967	217	45	111	3.8	9.6	13.6		-14.5
PHI	107	19	51	4	1322.0	1135	9	425	749	11.0	2.60	105	.236	.305	13	16	101	192	159	.956	267	47	86	-.2	1.8	1.9		2.1
STL	133	17	21	5	1357.2	1132	14	314	558	10.0	2.23	116	.230	.284	70	56	96	211	151	.954	290	58	80	-1.1	6.2	2.0		-5.5
DET	128	7	25	4	1334.1	1398	14	389	469	12.4	3.06	90	.272	.330	-55	-42	103	171	161	.959	260	34	86	.4	-4.6	-5.6		6.3
WAS	115	13	47	1	1322.2	1331	15	451	558	12.4	3.25	81	.265	.331	-83	-93	98	229	161	.955	279	54	78	-.8	-10.2	-2.3		-6.7
BOS	124	6	35	6	1382.0	1360	37	285	549	11.0	3.41	81	.262	.306	-111	-103	102	245	182	.949	335	57	84	-3.9	-11.3	-7.5		-5.3
TOT	956	139	317	33	10864.1					11.0	2.69		.249	.303						.958	2163	401	674					

Batter-Fielder Wins		Batting Average		On-Base Percentage		Slugging Average		On-Base Plus Slugging		Adjusted OPS		Adjusted Batter Runs	
Lajoie-Cle	7.6	Stone-StL	.358	Stone-StL	.417	Stone-StL	.501	Stone-StL	.918	Stone-StL	195	Stone-StL	63.3
Stone-StL	5.9	Lajoie-Cle	.355	Lajoie-Cle	.392	Lajoie-Cle	.465	Lajoie-Cle	.857	Lajoie-Cle	170	Lajoie-Cle	48.2
Turner-Cle	4.2	Chase-NY	.323	Flick-Cle	.372	Davis-Phi	.459	Davis-Phi	.815	Flick-Cle	156	Flick-Cle	40.2
Davis-Phi	3.2	Congalton-Cle	.320	Hartsel-Phi	.363	Flick-Cle	.441	Flick-Cle	.813	Davis-Phi	150	Davis-Phi	32.1
Davis-Chi	3.2	Seybold-Phi	.316	Davis-Phi	.355	Hickman-Was	.421	Crawford-Det	.747	Hickman-Was	135	Seybold-Phi	20.0

Runs		Hits		Doubles		Triples		Home Runs		Total Bases		Runs Batted In	
Flick-Cle	98	Lajoie-Cle	214	Lajoie-Cle	48	Flick-Cle	22	Davis-Phi	12	Stone-StL	291	Davis-Phi	96
Keeler-NY	96	Stone-StL	208	Davis-Phi	42	Stone-StL	20	Hickman-Was	9	Lajoie-Cle	280	Lajoie-Cle	91
Hartsel-Phi	96	Flick-Cle	194	Flick-Cle	34	Crawford-Det	16	Stone-StL	6	Flick-Cle	275	Davis-Chi	80
Davis-Phi	94	Chase-NY	193	Murphy-Phi	28	Ferris-Bos	13	Seybold-Phi	5	Davis-Phi	253	Williams-NY	77
Stone-StL	91	Keeler-NY	180	Turner-Cle	27					Chase-NY	236	Chase-NY	76

Stolen Bases		Base Stealing Runs		Fielding Runs-Infield		Fielding Runs-Outfield		Wins		Winning Pct.		Complete Games	
Flick-Cle	39			Tannehill-Chi	32.4	Niles-StL	13.7	Orth-NY	27	Plank-Phi	.760	Orth-NY	36
Anderson-Was	39			Lajoie-Cle	21.3	McIntyre-Det	12.3	Chesbro-NY	23	White-Chi	.750	Mullin-Det	35
Isbell-Chi	37			Turner-Cle	18.6	Anderson-Was	6.6	Rhoads-Cle	22	Owen-Chi	.700	Hess-Cle	33
Altizer-Was	37			Schlafly-Was	16.2	Stahl-Bos	6.5	Owen-Chi	22	Rhoads-Cle	.688	Rhoads-Cle	31
Donahue-Chi	36			Williams-NY	13.9	Crawford-Det	5.2			Owen-Chi	.629		

Strikeouts		Fewest BB/Game		Games		Saves		Base Runners/9		Adjusted Relief Runs		Relief Ranking	
Waddell-Phi	196	Young-Bos	.78	Chesbro-NY	49	Hess-Cle	3	White-Chi	8.33				
Falkenberg-Was	178	Altrock-Chi	1.31	Orth-NY	45	Bender-Phi	3	Joss-Cle	8.49				
Walsh-Cle	171	Joss-Cle	1.37	Waddell-Phi	43			Patterson-Chi	8.87				
Hess-Cle	167	White-Chi	1.56	Hess-Cle	43			Walsh-Chi	9.05				
Bender-Phi	159	Jacobson-StL	1.57	Owen-Chi	42			Pelty-StL	9.18				

Innings Pitched		Opponents' Avg.		Opponents' OBP		Earned Run Average		Adjusted ERA		Adjusted Starter Runs		Pitcher Wins	
Orth-NY	338.2	Pelty-StL	.206	White-Chi	.249	White-Chi	1.52	White-Chi	167	Rhoads-Cle	28.5	White-Chi	3.9
Hess-Cle	333.2	White-Chi	.207	Joss-Cle	.252	Pelty-StL	1.59	Pelty-StL	163	Hess-Cle	28.3	Joss-Cle	3.5
Mullin-Det	330.0	Walsh-Chi	.217	Walsh-Chi	.265	Joss-Cle	1.72	Joss-Cle	152	White-Chi	28.3	Orth-NY	3.4
Chesbro-NY	325.0	Joss-Cle	.218	Pelty-StL	.267	Powell-StL	1.77	Powell-StL	146	Joss-Cle	28.1	Hess-Cle	3.3
Rhoads-Cle	315.0	Powell-StL	.223	Powell-StL	.275	Rhoads-Cle	1.80	Rhoads-Cle	145	Pelty-StL	26.9	Pelty-StL	2.9

Not Quite Hitless

As August began, six American League clubs boasted records over .500 (all but pathetic Washington and Boston, which had totally collapsed). When the dust cleared, it was the White Sox and the Highlanders jousting in the final weeks. While New York played middling ball down the stretch, the White Sox forged ahead and won by three games. Even with the good pennant race, attendance decreased for first time in the AL's short history.

The fourth-place Philadelphia Athletics debuted two future stars, pitcher Jack Coombs and second baseman Eddie Collins. And despite missing time to illness, sophomore outfielder Ty Cobb of Detroit showed that he would be a force to be reckoned with as he hit .316 in a league that batted just .249.

Although the White Sox were called "hitless wonders" while posting a .230 batting average (worst ever for a pennant winner), that appellation is truly a misnomer. The Chicago offense led the league in walks and actually ranked third in runs—second in scoring on the road. Spacious South Side Park kept their offense to just fifth in home contests, but it certainly helped their already excellent mound staff. Doc White paced the league in ERA, while Ed Walsh led in shutouts. Meanwhile, the second-place Yankees were outscored on the road but blew away their opposition at home.

When the World Series rolled around, it was a Second City delight—the Cubs had won 116 games during the regular season and were heavily favored against the White Sox. Nevertheless, the AL champs won two out of the first three, despite collecting just 9 hits in 27 innings off Cubs pitching.

After the Cubs' Three Finger Brown shut out the Sox on 2 hits to even the Series, the supposed "Hitless Wonders" opened up the baseball world's eyes by teeing off for 8-6 and 8-3 wins against Ed Reulbach and Brown to clinch the Series.

1905 National League

TEAM	W	L	T	PCT	GB	HW	HL	R	OR	PA	H	2B	3B	HR	BB	SO	HB	SH	AVG	OBP	SLG	OPS	AOPS	BR	ABR	PF	SB	CS	BSA	BSR
NY	105	48	2	.686		54	21	780	505	5839	1392	191	88	39	517		90	138	.273	.351	.368	719	119	148	132	102	291			
PIT	96	57	2	.627	9	49	28	692	570	5790	1385	190	91	22	382		36	159	.266	.320	.350	670	104	38	21	103	202			
CHI	92	61	2	.601	13	54	25	667	442	5810	1249	157	82	12	448		61	193	.245	.313	.314	627	90	-30	-53	104	267			
PHI	83	69	3	.546	21.5	39	36	708	603	5867	1362	187	82	16	406		44	174	.260	.318	.336	654	106	14	39	96	180			
CIN	79	74	2	.516	26	50	28	736	698	5865	1401	160	109	27	434		52	174	.269	.332	.354	686	101	73	3	111	181			
STL	58	96	0	.377	47.5	32	45	535	734	5609	1254	140	85	20	391		43	109	.248	.307	.321	628	97	-38	-19	97	162			
BOS	51	103	2	.331	54.5	29	46	468	733	5631	1217	148	52	17	302		54	85	.234	.284	.293	577	80	-137	-126	98	132			
BRO	48	104	3	.316	56.5	29	47	506	807	5604	1255	154	60	29	327		41	136	.246	.297	.317	614	97	-68	-23	93	186			
TOT	620					336	276	5092		46010	10515	1327	641	182	3207	4462	421	1168	.255	.315	.332	647					1601			

TEAM	CG	SHO	GR	SV	IP	H	HR	BB	SO	BR/9	ERA	AERA	OAV	OOB	PR	APR	PF	OSB	OCS	FA	E	WPB	DP	FW	PW	BW	BSW	DIF
NY	117	18	42	15	1370.0	1160	25	364	760	10.2	2.39	122	.229	.284	91	82	98	123	138	.960	258	82	93	2.3	8.5	13.7		4.0
PIT	113	12	47	6	1382.2	1270	12	389	512	11.2	2.86	104	.248	.308	20	16	100	164	152	.961	255	61	112	2.5	1.7	2.2		13.2
CHI	133	23	22	2	1407.1	1135	14	385	627	10.0	2.04	146	.224	.286	149	145	99	168	150	.962	248	45	99	2.9	15.1	-5.5		3.0
PHI	119	12	42	5	1398.2	1303	21	411	516	11.5	2.81	104	.252	.316	28	13	97	173	160	.957	275	40	99	1.2	1.4	4.1		.4
CIN	119	10	39	2	1365.2	1409	22	439	547	12.5	3.01	109	.272	.335	-3	38	110	203	176	.953	310	68	122	-1.0	3.9	.3		-.8
STL	135	10	19	2	1347.2	1431	28	367	411	12.3	3.59	83	.276	.329	-89	-93	99	238	161	.957	274	48	83	1.2	-9.7	-2.0		-8.5
BOS	139	14	18	0	1383.0	1390	36	433	533	12.1	3.52	88	.265	.326	-81	-66	103	278	191	.951	325	85	89	-1.8	-6.9	-13.1		-4.2
BRO	125	7	33	3	1347.0	1416	24	476	556	13.1	3.76	77	.274	.343	-114	-137	96	252	182	.937	408	40	101	-7.2	-14.2	-2.4		-4.2
TOT	1000	106	262	35	11002.0					11.6	2.99		.255	.315						.954	2353	469	798					

Batter-Fielder Wins	Batting Average	On-Base Percentage	Slugging Average	On-Base Plus Slugging	Adjusted OPS	Adjusted Batter Runs
Wagner-Pit ...7.5	Seymour-Cin ...377	Chance-Chi ...450	Seymour-Cin ...559	Seymour-Cin ...988	Seymour-Cin ...175	Seymour-Cin ...52.3
Seymour-Cin ...5.6	Wagner-Pit ...363	Seymour-Cin ...429	Wagner-Pit ...505	Wagner-Pit ...932	Wagner-Pit ...173	Wagner-Pit ...50.4
Huggins-Cin ...4.7	Donlin-NY ...356	Wagner-Pit ...427	Donlin-NY ...495	Donlin-NY ...908	Donlin-NY ...166	Donlin-NY ...49.3
Titus-Phi ...4.1	Beaumont-Pit ...328	Thomas-Phi ...417	Titus-Phi ...436	Chance-Chi ...883	Chance-Chi ...157	Titus-Phi ...40.4
Thomas-Phi ...4.1	Thomas-Phi ...317	Donlin-NY ...413	Grady-StL ...434	Titus-Phi ...834	Titus-Phi ...154	Chance-Chi ...34.8

Runs	Hits	Doubles	Triples	Home Runs	Total Bases	Runs Batted In
Donlin-NY ...124	Seymour-Cin ...219	Seymour-Cin ...40	Seymour-Cin ...21	Odwell-Cin ...9	Seymour-Cin ...325	Seymour-Cin ...121
Thomas-Phi ...118	Donlin-NY ...216	Titus-Phi ...36	Mertes-NY ...17	Seymour-Cin ...8	Donlin-NY ...300	Mertes-NY ...108
Huggins-Cin ...117	Wagner-Pit ...199	Wagner-Pit ...32	Magee-Phi ...17	Lumley-Bro ...7	Wagner-Pit ...277	Wagner-Pit ...101
Wagner-Pit ...114	Barry-Chi-Cin ...182	Donlin-NY ...31	Smoot-StL ...16	Donlin-NY ...7	Magee-Phi ...253	Magee-Phi ...98
	Magee-Phi ...180	Ritchey-Pit ...29	Donlin-NY ...16	Dahlen-NY ...7	Titus-Phi ...239	Titus-Phi ...89

Stolen Bases	Base Stealing Runs	Fielding Runs-Infield	Fielding Runs-Outfield	Wins	Winning Pct.	Complete Games
Maloney-Chi ...59		Huggins-Cin ...36.8	Sheckard-Bro ...16.6	Mathewson-NY ...31	Leever-NY ...800	Young-Bos ...41
Devlin-NY ...59		Tenney-Bos ...22.1	Thomas-Phi ...14.8	Pittinger-Phi ...23	Mathewson-NY ...775	Willis-Bos ...36
Wagner-Pit ...57		Gilbert-NY ...20.3	Seymour-Cin ...9.8	Ames-NY ...22	Ames-NY ...733	Fraser-Bos ...35
Mertes-NY ...52		Corcoran-Cin ...20.1	Magee-Phi ...9.7	McGinnity-NY ...21	Wiltse-NY ...714	Taylor-StL ...34
Magee-Phi ...48		Dahlen-NY ...19.8	Dunleavy-StL ...6.9		Lynch-Pit ...680	

Strikeouts	Fewest BB/Game	Games	Saves	Base Runners/9	Adjusted Relief Runs	Relief Ranking
Mathewson-NY ...206	Phillippe-Pit ...1.55	Pittinger-Phi ...46	Elliott-NY ...6	Mathewson-NY ...8.42		
Ames-NY ...198	Brown-Chi ...1.59	McGinnity-NY ...46	Wiltse-NY ...3	Reulbach-Chi ...9.23		
Overall-Cin ...173	Young-Bos ...1.69	Young-Bos ...43	McGinnity-NY ...3	Phillippe-Pit ...9.45		
Ewing-Cin ...164	Mathewson-NY ...1.70	Mathewson-NY ...43	Mathewson-NY ...3	Wicker-Chi ...9.46		
Young-Bos ...156	McGinnity-NY ...1.99	Overall-Cin ...42		Hillebrand-... ...9.49		

Innings Pitched	Opponents' Avg.	Opponents' OBP	Earned Run Average	Adjusted ERA	Adjusted Starter Runs	Pitcher Wins
Young-Bos ...378.0	Reulbach-Chi ...201	Mathewson-NY ...245	Mathewson-NY ...1.28	Mathewson-NY ...229	Mathewson-NY ...56.6	Mathewson-NY ...8.5
Willis-Bos ...342.0	Mathewson-NY ...205	Reulbach-Chi ...266	Reulbach-Chi ...1.42	Reulbach-Chi ...209	Reulbach-Chi ...48.0	Reulbach-Chi ...4.6
Mathewson-NY ...338.2	Wiltse-NY ...219	Brown-Chi ...271	Wicker-Chi ...2.02	Wicker-Chi ...147	Ewing-Cin ...26.9	Ewing-Cin ...2.9
Pittinger-Phi ...337.1	Lundgren-Chi ...220	Phillippe-Pit ...274	Briggs-Chi ...2.14	Briggs-Chi ...139	Wicker-Chi ...22.3	Weimer-Chi ...2.5
Fraser-Bos ...334.1	Wicker-Chi ...221	Wicker-Chi ...276	Brown-Chi ...2.17	Brown-Chi ...137	Phillippe-Pit ...22.1	Wiltse-NY ...2.3

Christy Blanks A's

Four-time batting champion Pete Browning died at 44 from complications of mastoiditis, a disease that plagued him throughout his career. Outfielder Jesse "The Crab" Burkett and first baseman Dirty Jack Doyle played their final major league games, bringing to an end two great careers as well as two great nicknames. More were coming.

The Mahatma entered the major leagues on June 16, as the St. Louis Browns inserted 24-year-old catcher Branch Rickey into a game. Rickey's tenure as a player was brief, but he remained a fixture in the game for sixty years. Two weeks after Rickey's debut, New York Giants outfielder Moonlight Graham played his only game; he would languish in obscurity until revived nearly eighty years later by author W.P. Kinsella.

The suddenly unstoppable Giants again blew away the league, pacing the field wire to wire and surviving their only challenge, a brief August initiative from the Pirates. The Cubs, however, won 17 of their last 20, forecasting their great 1906 performance to come.

The Giants boasted few offensive leaders, but their lineup did everything well. Using the stolen base, the base on balls, and even the home run, New York led the league in runs by more than 40. Pittsburgh finished second; Honus Wagner failed to lead the league in a major offensive category for the only time between 1900 and 1912, but he was still the league's best hitter. Christy Mathewson was its best pitcher. New York's star captured 31 victories to lead the league by a margin of eight. On the other side, Vic Willis of seventh-place Boston dropped 29, the highest total of the twentieth century.

While the AL champion Philadelphia Athletics were an excellent club, they were clearly no match for the Giants in the World Series. Philadelphia won Game 2 with a shutout, as were all five games. However, Mathewson threw three of New York's four whitewashes in one of the greatest performances in postseason history.

1905 American League

TEAM	W	L	T	PCT	GB	HW	HL	R	OR	PA	H	2B	3B	HR	BB	SO	HB	SH	AVG	OBP	SLG	OPS	AOPS	BR	ABR	PF	SB	CS	BSA	BSR
PHI	92	56	4	.622		**51**	22	**623**	488	5721	1310	**256**	51	24	376	644	34	165	**.255**	.310	.338	648	109	65	54	102	190			
CHI	92	60	6	.605	2	50	29	612	**451**	5852	1213	200	55	11	439	613	58	241	.237	.305	.304	609	103	3	28	96	194			
DET	79	74	1	.516	15.5	45	30	512	604	5566	1209	190	54	13	375	583	40	180	.243	.302	.311	613	99	1	-3	101	129			
BOS	78	74	1	.513	16	44	32	579	565	5711	1179	165	69	**29**	**486**	553	37	139	.234	.305	.311	616	100	13	7	101	131			
CLE	76	78	1	.494	19	41	36	564	587	5655	**1318**	211	**72**	18	286	712	55	148	**.255**	.301	.334	635	106	32	24	101	188			
NY	71	78	3	.477	21.5	40	35	586	621	5535	1228	163	61	23	360	**537**	**67**	151	.248	.307	.319	626	93	24	-35	111	**200**			
WAS	64	87	3	.424	29.5	33	42	559	623	5528	1121	193	68	22	298	824	54	161	.224	.274	.302	576	92	-72	-52	96	169			
STL	54	99	3	.353	40.5	34	42	512	608	5768	1205	153	49	16	362	639	52	150	.232	.288	.289	577	93	-66	-37	95	144			
TOT	617					338	268	4547		45336	9783	1531	479	156	2982	5105	397	1335	.241	.299	.314	613					1345			

TEAM	CG	SHO	GR	SV	IP	H	HR	BB	SO	BR/9	ERA	AERA	OAV	OOB	PR	APR	PF	OSB	OCS	FA	E	WPB	DP	FW	PW	BW	BSW	DIF
PHI	117	**19**	37	0	1383.1	**1137**	21	409	**895**	10.5	2.19	121	.227	.294	70	68	100	144	**124**	.957	265	61	64	.3	7.5	**5.9**		4.3
CHI	131	16	32	0	1427.0	1163	11	329	613	**9.6**	**1.99**	124	**.226**	**.277**	105	**78**	93	**132**	126	**.967**	218	58	**95**	4.1	8.6	3.1		.2
DET	124	17	31	1	1348.0	1226	11	474	578	11.7	2.83	96	.246	.318	-27	-18	103	232	142	.957	267	**38**	80	.4	-2.0	-.3		4.4
BOS	124	15	30	1	1356.1	1198	33	**292**	652	10.2	2.84	95	.238	.286	-29	-20	102	135	**132**	.953	296	51	75	-1.6	-2.2	.8		5.1
CLE	**140**	16	15	0	1363.1	1251	23	334	555	10.9	2.85	92	.245	.299	-30	-32	99	162	125	.963	233	56	84	2.8	-3.5	2.6		-2.9
NY	88	**19**	**76**	**4**	1353.2	1235	26	396	642	11.1	2.93	100	.246	.307	-42	-2	111	142	120	.952	293	69	88	-1.5	-.2	-3.8		2.1
WAS	118	12	40	1	1362.1	1250	12	385	539	11.2	2.87	92	.247	.308	-33	-36	100	168	150	.951	318	43	76	-3.0	-4.0	-5.7		1.1
STL	134	11	22	2	1384.2	1245	19	389	633	11.0	2.74	93	.243	.304	-14	-34	96	225	157	.955	296	61	78	-1.3	-3.7	-4.1		-13.4
TOT	976	125	283	9	10978.2					10.8	2.65		.241	.299						.957	2186	437	640					

Batter-Fielder Wins		Batting Average		On-Base Percentage		Slugging Average		On-Base Plus Slugging		Adjusted OPS		Adjusted Batter Runs	
Davis-Chi	4.4	Flick-Cle	308	Hartsel-Phi	409	Flick-Cle	462	Flick-Cle	845	Flick-Cle	165	Flick-Cle	37.7
Crawford-Det	4.2	Keeler-NY	302	Flick-Cle	383	Isbell-Chi	440	Crawford-Det	786	Crawford-Det	148	Hartsel-Phi	32.7
Wallace-StL	4.2	Bay-Cle	301	Keeler-NY	357	Crawford-Det	430	Stone-StL	756	Stone-StL	147	Stone-StL	32.0
Flick-Cle	3.3	Crawford-Det	297	Crawford-Det	357	Davis-Phi	422	Davis-Phi	756	Hartsel-Phi	138	Crawford-Det	31.4
Stone-StL	2.8	Isbell-Chi	296	Selbach-Bos	355	Stone-StL	410	Hartsel-Phi	755	Davis-Phi	137	Davis-Phi	25.1

Runs		Hits		Doubles		Triples		Home Runs		Total Bases		Runs Batted In	
Davis-Phi	93	Stone-StL	187	Davis-Phi	47	Flick-Cle	18	Davis-Phi	8	Stone-StL	259	Davis-Phi	83
Jones-Chi	91	Davis-Phi	173	Crawford-Det	38	Ferris-Bos	16	Stone-StL	7	Davis-Phi	256	L.Cross-Phi	77
Bay-Cle	90	Crawford-Det	171	Hickman-Det-Was	37	Turner-Cle	14			Crawford-Det	247	Donahue-Chi	76
Hartsel-Phi	88	Keeler-NY	169	Seybold-Phi	37	Stone-StL	13			Hickman-Det-Was	232	Crawford-Det	75
Keeler-NY	81	Bay-Cle	166			Burkett-Bos	13			Flick-Cle	231	Turner-Cle	72

Stolen Bases		Base Stealing Runs		Fielding Runs-Infield		Fielding Runs-Outfield		Wins		Winning Pct.		Complete Games	
Hoffman-Phi	46			Cassidy-Was	34.8	McIntyre-Det	17.8	Waddell-Phi	27	Waddell-Phi	730	Plank-Phi	35
Fultz-NY	44			Tannehill-Chi	25.3	Jones-Was	13.5	Plank-Phi	24	Tannehill-Bos	710	Mullin-Det	35
Stahl-Was	41			Wallace-StL	20.7	Crawford-Det	10.0	Killian-Det	23	Coakley-Phi	692	Howell-StL	35
Hartsel-Phi	37			Davis-Chi	16.4	Seybold-Phi	7.9	Altrock-Chi	23	Plank-Phi	667	Killian-Det	33
				Ferris-Bos	14.6	Jones-Chi	7.1	Tannehill-Bos	22	Altrock-Chi	657	Owen-Chi	32

Strikeouts		Fewest BB/Game		Games		Saves		Base Runners/9		Adjusted Relief Runs		Relief Ranking	
Waddell-Phi	287	Young-Bos	.84	Waddell-Phi	46	Buchanan-StL	2	Young-Bos	8.03				
Young-Bos	210	Joss-Cle	1.45	Mullin-Det	44			Griffith-NY	8.68				
Plank-Phi	210	Owen-Chi	1.51	Patten-Was	42			Patterson-Chi	9.03				
Howell-StL	198	Bernhard-Cle	1.76	Owen-Chi	42			Waddell-Phi	9.06				
Smith-Chi	171	Altrock-Chi	1.80					Owen-Chi	9.19				

Innings Pitched		Opponents' Avg.		Opponents' OBP		Earned Run Average		Adjusted ERA		Adjusted Starter Runs		Pitcher Wins	
Mullin-Det	347.2	Waddell-Phi	200	Young-Bos	241	Waddell-Phi	1.48	Waddell-Phi	179	Waddell-Phi	40.1	**Waddell-Phi**	4.5
Plank-Phi	346.2	Smith-Chi	208	Waddell-Phi	264	White-Chi	1.76	Young-Bos	147	Young-Bos	25.4	Howell-StL	3.6
Owen-Chi	334.0	Young-Bos	216	Owen-Chi	267	Young-Bos	1.82	Coakley-Phi	144	White-Chi	24.0	**White-Chi**	2.9
Waddell-Phi	328.2	Howell-StL	217	White-Chi	270	Coakley-Phi	1.84	White-Chi	140	Altrock-Chi	23.9	**Altrock-Chi**	2.7
Howell-StL	323.0	White-Chi	218	Joss-Cle	274	Altrock-Chi	1.88	Chesbro-NY	133	Plank-Phi	19.6	Young-Bos	2.7

Goose Eggs and Tough Guys

The Boston Americans and New York Highlanders sank from contention in 1905, falling to fourth and sixth places. After an early foray by Cleveland, the race settled into a battle between Philadelphia and Chicago. While both teams were hot down the stretch, the Athletics never trailed after early August.

The White Sox, finishing just 2 games out, were the first team since 1888 to post an ERA under 2.00. Of their six pitchers, the highest ERA belonged to Ed Walsh at 2.17. The White Sox hitters, an underrated bunch, were productive, with player-manager Fielder Jones scoring 91 runs—second in the league—despite hitting only .245.

Three influential players of great skill but questionable ethics made their debuts in 1905. On August 30, a Georgia freshman named Ty Cobb saw his first major league action for the Tigers. Two others with abundant talent but character even more dubious than that of Cobb made their first appearances: slick-fielding Hal Chase took over at first for New York, while 21-year-old pitcher Eddie Cicotte was 1-1 for Detroit. These two men would help to nearly destroy baseball in the next decade.

Enjoying another spectacular season in 1905, Philadelphia's Rube Waddell won the pitching "Triple Crown"; he also allowed just 6.33 hits per game, lowest in the AL until 1968. Eddie Plank, Andy Coakley, and Chief Bender rounded out one of the top rotations in history. However, the A's attack was equally strong: Topsy Hartsel led the league in walks for the second of five times, as first sacker Harry Davis provided the punch, pacing the AL in doubles, homers, RBIs, and runs. In a year where just three AL regulars hit over .300, Philadelphia—the league's best offense—scored 4.06 runs per game. However, the A's tallied just three in a five-game World Series loss to the Giants.

1904 National League

TEAM	W	L	T	PCT	GB	HW	HL	R	OR	PA	H	2B	3B	HR	BB	SO	HB	SH	AVG	OBP	SLG	OPS	AOPS	BR	ABR	PF	SB	CS	BSA	BSR
NY	106	47	5	.693		56	26	744	474	5829	1347	202	65	31	434		79	166	.262	.328	.344	672	109	92	62	104	283			
CHI	93	60	3	.608	13	49	27	597	517	5697	1294	157	62	22	298		48	141	.248	.295	.315	610	94	-41	-42	100	227			
CIN	88	65	4	.575	18	49	27	695	547	5814	1332	189	92	21	399		49	135	.255	.313	.338	651	98	42	-12	109	180			
PIT	87	66	3	.569	19	48	30	675	592	5722	1333	164	102	15	391		47	124	.258	.316	.338	654	105	46	29	103	178			
STL	75	79	1	.487	31.5	39	36	602	595	5622	1292	175	66	24	343		46	129	.253	.306	.327	633	106	7	36	96	199			
BRO	56	97	1	.366	50	31	44	497	614	5499	1142	159	53	15	411		42	129	.232	.297	.295	592	91	-56	-42	98	205			
BOS	55	98	2	.359	51	34	45	491	749	5594	1217	153	50	24	316		42	101	.237	.287	.300	587	90	-80	-61	96	143			
PHI	52	100	3	.342	53.5	28	43	571	784	5639	1268	170	54	23	377		40	119	.248	.305	.316	621	102	-10	12	96	159			
TOT	623					334	278	4872		45416	10225	1369	544	175	2969	4277	393	1044	.249	.306	.322	628					1574			

TEAM	CG	SHO	GR	SV	IP	H	HR	BB	SO	BR/9	ERA	AERA	OAV	OOB	PR	APR	PF	OSB	OCS	FA	E	WPB	DP	FW	PW	BW	BSW	DIF
NY	127	21	29	15	1396.2	1151	36	349	707	9.9	2.17	125	.222	.276	86	83	100	134	167	.956	294	43	93	2.3	8.8	6.6		11.9
CHI	139	18	17	6	1383.2	1150	16	402	618	10.3	2.30	115	.224	.285	65	55	97	160	164	.954	298	49	89	1.8	5.8	-4.4		13.3
CIN	142	12	15	2	1392.2	1256	13	343	502	10.7	2.34	125	.241	.295	60	82	107	192	176	.954	301	60	81	1.7	8.7	-1.3		2.4
PIT	133	15	25	1	1348.1	1273	13	379	455	11.4	2.89	95	.248	.306	-24	-24	100	187	160	.955	291	49	93	2.2	-2.5	3.1		7.7
STL	146	7	8	2	1368.0	1286	23	319	529	10.8	2.64	102	.239	.286	13	5	99	235	109	.952	307	42	83	1.1	.5	3.8		-7.4
BRO	135	12	20	2	1337.1	1281	27	414	453	11.8	2.70	101	.255	.319	4		100	193	180	.945	343	41	87	-1.4	.4	-4.4		-15.1
BOS	136	13	20	0	1348.1	1405	25	500	544	13.1	3.43	80	.272	.343	-105	-104	101	230	199	.945	353	77	91	-1.9	-11.0	-6.5		-2.2
PHI	131	10	25	2	1339.1	1418	22	425	469	12.9	3.39	79	.270	.332	-99	-112	98	243	183	.937	403	50	93	-5.1	-11.9	1.3		-8.3
TOT	1089	108	159	30	10914.1					11.3	2.73		.249	.306						.950	2590	411	710					

Batter-Fielder Wins		Batting Average		On-Base Percentage		Slugging Average		On-Base Plus Slugging		Adjusted OPS		Adjusted Batter Runs	
Wagner-Pit	5.3	Wagner-Pit	.349	Wagner-Pit	.423	Wagner-Pit	.520	Wagner-Pit	.944	Wagner-Pit	186	Wagner-Pit	51.7
Thomas-Phi	4.1	Donlin-Cin-NY	.329	Thomas-Phi	.416	Grady-StL	.474	Chance-Chi	.812	Chance-Chi	150	Thomas-Phi	32.5
Leach-Pit	4.0	Beckley-StL	.325	Chance-Chi	.382	Donlin-Cin-NY	.457	Seymour-Cin	.790	Beckley-StL	147	Beckley-StL	30.2
Chance-Chi	3.8	Grady-StL	.313	Huggins-Cin	.377	Seymour-Cin	.439	Beckley-StL	.778	Thomas-Phi	141	Chance-Chi	27.3
Dahlen-NY	3.2	Seymour-Cin	.313	Beckley-StL	.375	Chance-Chi	.430	Thomas-Phi	.761	Lumley-Bro	137	Grady-StL	25.7

Runs		Hits		Doubles		Triples		Home Runs		Total Bases		Runs Batted In	
Browne-NY	99	Beaumont-Pit	185	Wagner-Pit	44	Lumley-Bro	18	Lumley-Bro	9	Wagner-Pit	255	Dahlen-NY	80
Wagner-Pit	97	Beckley-StL	179	Mertes-NY	28	Wagner-Pit	14	Brain-StL	7	Lumley-Bro	247	Mertes-NY	78
Beaumont-Pit	97	Wagner-Pit	171	Delahanty-Bos	27	Tinker-Chi	13			Seymour-Cin	233	Lumley-Bro	78
Huggins-Cin	96	Browne-NY	169	Seymour-Cin	26	Seymour-Cin	13			Beaumont-Pit	230	Wagner-Pit	75
		Seymour-Cin	166	Dahlen-NY	26	Kelley-Cin	13			Beckley-StL	222	Corcoran-Cin	74

Stolen Bases		Base Stealing Runs		Fielding Runs-Infield		Fielding Runs-Outfield		Wins		Winning Pct.		Complete Games	
Wagner-Pit	53			Leach-Pit	35.8	Thomas-Phi	12.9	McGinnity-NY	35	McGinnity-NY	.814	Willis-Bos	39
Mertes-NY	47			Evers-Chi	28.2	Odwell-Cin	12.3	Mathewson-NY	33	Mathewson-NY	.733	Taylor-StL	39
Dahlen-NY	47			Dahlen-NY	25.0	Sheckard-Bro	10.5	Harper-Cin	23	Harper-Cin	.719	McGinnity-NY	38
McGann-NY	42			Tinker-Chi	15.6	Sebring-Pit-Cin	9.8	Taylor-NY	21	Flaherty-Pit	.679	Jones-Bro	38
Chance-Chi	42			Farrell-StL	14.5	Titus-Phi	9.7	Nichols-StL	21				

Strikeouts		Fewest BB/Game		Games		Saves		Base Runners/9		Adjusted Relief Runs		Relief Ranking	
Mathewson-NY	212	Hahn-Cin	1.06	McGinnity-NY	51	McGinnity-NY	5	Brown-Chi	8.94				
Willis-Bos	196	Phillippe-Pit	1.40	Mathewson-NY	48	Wiltse-NY	3	McGinnity-NY	8.96				
Weimer-Chi	177	Nichols-StL	1.42	Jones-Bro	46	Briggs-Chi	3	Robitaille-Pit	9.00				
Pittinger-Bos	146	Kellum-Cin	1.84	Willis-Bos	43	Ames-NY	3	Hahn-Cin	9.07				
McGinnity-NY	144	McFarland-StL	1.87	Fraser-Phi	42			Nichols-StL	9.17				

Innings Pitched		Opponents' Avg.		Opponents' OBP		Earned Run Average		Adjusted ERA		Adjusted Starter Runs		Pitcher Wins	
McGinnity-NY	408.0	Brown-Chi	.199	Brown-Chi	.253	McGinnity-NY	1.61	McGinnity-NY	169	McGinnity-NY	50.2	McGinnity-NY	5.4
Jones-Bro	377.0	Weimer-Chi	.204	Nichols-StL	.256	Garvin-Bro	1.68	Garvin-Bro	162	Hahn-Cin	27.2	Mathewson-NY	4.2
Mathewson-NY	367.2	McGinnity-NY	.206	McGinnity-NY	.256	Brown-Chi	1.86	Brown-Chi	142	Mathewson-NY	26.9	Hahn-Cin	3.2
Taylor-StL	352.0	Taylor-NY	.214	Hahn-Cin	.262	Weimer-Chi	1.91	Hahn-Cin	142	Nichols-StL	26.8	Weimer-Chi	2.8
Willis-Bos	350.0	Garvin-Bro	.218	Mathewson-NY	.270	Nichols-StL	2.02	Weimer-Chi	139	Weimer-Chi	25.9	Nichols-StL	2.8

Take a Giant Step

National League teams were first required to play a 154-game schedule in 1904, an arrangement that lasted for 58 years through 1961 (except for wartime changes). In addition, home teams were now required to provide more than one baseball for each game, and clubs had to wear different uniforms for home and road contests. Finally, outfield fences had to be at least 235 feet from home plate, and the distance from home plate to the backstop was first regulated.

The league's fielding average reached .950, and skyrocketed in the next two years. Oddly enough, shortstop Herman Long, a great defender in the nineteenth century, hung 'em up in 1904 at age 38. The Giants, meanwhile, brought back two popular 1880s stars for limited engagements. "Orator Jim" O'Rourke, who collected 2,304 hits in his 19-year career, was 1-for-4 in one game as a catcher at age 54, while 46-year-old outfielder Dan Brouthers, a five-time batting champ, went hitless in five tries.

Two star outfielders, neither of whom was born when Brouthers won his first home run title, debuted in 1904. Frank Schulte became a key component of the Cubs' success, while Philadelphia's Sherry Magee led the NL four times in RBIs.

Team runs decreased to 3.91 per game (batters clubbed more homers, but batting average fell 20 points to .249). George Browne of the Giants topped the NL with 99 runs; no league leader had fewer until 1915. The Giants won 18 straight at one point, moving into first for good in June. Skipper John McGraw had world-class pitching with Christy Mathewson, Iron Joe McGinnity, Dummy Taylor, and rookie Hooks Wiltse. Offensively, New York led in runs, hits, doubles, homers, and walks.

Nevertheless, the proud Giants refused to play a World Series. Calling the Junior Circuit "bush," McGraw and Giants owner John Brush invited a hailstorm of criticism as the Giants refused to accept the AL, and defending world champion Boston, as a peer.

1904 American League

TEAM	W	L	T	PCT	GB	HW	HL	R	OR	PA	H	2B	3B	HR	BB	SO	HB	SH	AVG	OBP	SLG	OPS	AOPS	BR	ABR	PF	SB	CS	BSA	BSR
BOS	95	59	3	.617		49	30	608	**466**	5784	1294	194	**105**	26	347	570	51	155	.247	.301	.340	641	102	41	9	106	101			
NY	92	59	4	.609	1.5	46	29	598	526	5724	**1354**	195	91	27	312	**548**	57	**197**	.242	.300	.316	616	104	6	29	96	**216**			
CHI	89	65	2	.578	6	**50**	27	600	482	5638	1217	193	68	14	**373**	586	41	164	.242	.298	.316	616	104	6	29	96	178			
CLE	86	65	3	.570	7.5	44	31	**647**	482	5669	1340	225	90	27	307	714	46	164	**.260**	**.308**	**.354**	662	116	80	86	99	137			
PHI	81	70	4	.536	12.5	47	31	557	503	5578	1266	197	77	31	313	605	40	137	.249	.298	.336	634	101	29	1	105	137			
STL	65	87	4	.428	29	32	43	481	604	5817	1266	153	53	10	332	609	56	138	.239	.291	.294	585	96	-53	-19	94	150			
DET	62	90	10	.408	32	34	40	505	627	5853	1231	154	69	11	344	635	34	154	.231	.282	.292	574	90	-77	-61	97	112			
WAS	38	113	6	.252	55.5	23	52	437	743	5606	1170	171	57	10	283	759	**59**	115	.227	.275	.288	563	84	-95	-88	98	150			
TOT	626					325	283	4433		45669	10138	1482	610	156	2611	5026	384	1195	.244	.295	.321	616					1207			

TEAM	CG	SHO	GR	SV	IP	H	HR	BB	SO	BR/9	ERA	AERA	OAV	OOB	PR	APR	PF	OSB	OCS	FA	E	WPB	DP	FW	PW	BW	BSW	DIF
BOS	148	21	9	1	1406.0	1208	31	**233**	612	9.4	2.12	126	.233	**.270**	75	**84**	103	118	**114**	.962	242	**41**	83	1.6	**9.4**	1.0		6.0
NY	123	15	**33**	1	1380.2	1180	29	311	684	10.0	2.57	106	.232	.282	4	21	104	161	**125**	.958	275	58	90	-.8	2.3	4.6		10.4
CHI	134	**26**	22	**3**	1380.0	1161	13	303	550	9.8	2.30	107	**.229**	.279	45	24	95	**112**	111	**.964**	**238**	57	95	**1.7**	2.7	3.2		4.4
CLE	141	20	15	0	1356.2	1273	**10**	285	627	10.6	2.22	114	.249	.294	56	48	98	121	110	.959	255	50	86	.4	5.4	**9.6**		-4.9
PHI	136	**26**	20	0	1361.1	**1149**	13	366	**887**	10.4	2.35	114	.230	.291	38	48	103	141	**104**	.959	250	44	78	-.2	-6.5	-2.1		-.8
STL	135	13	22	1	1410.0	1335	25	333	577	11.0	2.83	88	.251	.303	-36	-58	96	164	128	.960	267	44	78	-.2	-4.0	-6.8		-2.2
DET	143	15	21	0	1430.0	1345	16	433	556	11.6	2.77	92	.250	.314	-27	-36	98	188	**135**	.959	273	58	92	.0	-4.0	-6.8		-3.2
WAS	137	7	20	**3**	1359.2	1487	19	347	533	12.5	3.62	73	.279	.330	-155	-142	102	202	**139**	.951	314	52	**97**	-3.1	-15.9	-9.8		-8.6
TOT	1097	143	162	9	11084.1					10.7	2.60		.244	.295						.959	2114	404	688					

<table>
<tr><td colspan="2">Batter-Fielder Wins</td><td colspan="2">Batting Average</td><td colspan="2">On-Base Percentage</td><td colspan="2">Slugging Average</td><td colspan="2">On-Base Plus Slugging</td><td colspan="2">Adjusted OPS</td><td colspan="2">Adjusted Batter Runs</td></tr>
</table>

Batter-Fielder Wins
- **Lajoie-Cle** 7.4
- **Flick-Cle** 4.5
- **Bradley-Cle** 4.0
- **Murphy-Phi** 3.7
- **Davis-Chi** 3.7

Batting Average
- Lajoie-Cle 376
- Keeler-NY 343
- Davis-Phi 309
- Flick-Cle 306
- Bradley-Cle...........300

On-Base Percentage
- Lajoie-Cle 413
- Keeler-NY 390
- Flick-Cle 371
- Stahl-Bos 366
- Burkett-StL 363

Slugging Average
- Lajoie-Cle 546
- Davis-Phi 490
- Flick-Cle 449
- Murphy-Phi 440
- Hickman-Cle-Det ...437

On-Base Plus Slugging
- Lajoie-Cle 959
- Flick-Cle 820
- Keeler-NY 799
- Stahl-Bos 782
- Murphy-Phi 760

Adjusted OPS
- Lajoie-Cle 204
- Flick-Cle 160
- Keeler-NY 146
- Stahl-Bos 139
- Hickman-Cle-Det 137

Adjusted Batter Runs
- Lajoie-Cle ....64.
- Flick-Cle ....40.
- Keeler-NY ....28.
- Stahl-Bos ....27.
- Burkett-StL ....25.

Runs
- Dougherty-Bos-NY 113
- Flick-Cle 97
- Bradley-Cle 94
- Lajoie-Cle 92

Hits
- Lajoie-Cle 208
- Keeler-NY 186
- Bradley-Cle 183
- Dougherty-Bos-NY 181
- Flick-Cle 177

Doubles
- Lajoie-Cle 49
- Collins-Bos 33
- Bradley-Cle 32

Triples
- Stahl-Bos...............19
- Freeman-Bos............19
- Cassidy-Was 19
- Murphy-Phi 17
- Flick-Cle 17

Home Runs
- Davis-Phi................10
- Murphy-Phi 7
- Freeman-Bos.............7

Total Bases
- Lajoie-Cle 302
- Flick-Cle 260
- Bradley-Cle 249
- Freeman-Bos............246

Runs Batted In
- Lajoie-Cle 10:
- Freeman-Bos...........8-
- Bradley-Cle 8
- Anderson-NY..........8

Stolen Bases
- Flick-Cle 38
- Bay-Cle 38
- Heidrick-StL 35
- Davis-Chi..................32
- Conroy-NY................30

Base Stealing Runs

Fielding Runs-Infield
- Tannehill-Chi 27.3
- Davis-Chi 18.1
- Carr-Det-Chi 15.7
- Williams-NY 14.5
- Murphy-Phi............14.2

Fielding Runs-Outfield
- McIntyre-Det...........11.9
- Barrett-Det...............9.0
- Donovan-Was.............8.8
- Heidrick-StL 6.7
- Bay-Cle 6.3

Wins
- Chesbro-NY..............41
- Young-Bos................26
- Plank-Phi 26
- Waddell-Phi 25

Winning Pct.
- Chesbro-NY 774
- Tannehill-Bos 656
- Smith-Chi.................640
- Bernhard-Cle 639
- Dineen-Bos 622

Complete Games
- Chesbro-NY 4
- Mullin-Det 4
- Young-Bos.................4
- Waddell-Phi..............3
- Powell-NY 3

Strikeouts
- Waddell-Phi...........349
- Chesbro-NY 239
- Powell-NY 202
- Plank-Phi................201
- Young-Bos 200

Fewest BB/Game
- Young-Bos 69
- Tannehill-Bos 1.05
- Patterson-Chi 1.31
- Joss-Cle 1.40
- Altrock-Chi............1.41

Games
- Chesbro-NY 55
- Powell-NY 47
- Waddell-Phi 46
- Patten-Was 45
- Mullin-Det 45

Saves
- Patten-Was 3

Base Runners/9
- Young-Bos 8.53
- Chesbro-NY 8.57
- Owen-Chi 9.00
- Joss-Cle 9.22
- Dinneen-Bos 9.33

Adjusted Relief Runs

Relief Ranking

Innings Pitched
- Chesbro-NY 454.2
- Powell-NY..........390.1
- Waddell-Phi 383.0
- Mullin-Det 382.1
- Young-Bos 380.0

Opponents' Avg.
- Chesbro-NY 208
- Owen-Chi 214
- Smith-Chi 215
- Gibson-Bos 219
- Waddell-Phi 221

Opponents' OBP
- Young-Bos 251
- Chesbro-NY 252
- Owen-Chi 261
- Joss-Cle 266
- Dinneen-Bos 268

Earned Run Average
- Joss-Cle 1.59
- Waddell-Phi 1.62
- Hess-Cle 1.67
- White-Chi 1.78
- Chesbro-NY 1.82

Adjusted ERA
- Waddell-Phi 165
- Joss-Cle 159
- Chesbro-NY 149
- White-Chi 138
- Young-Bos 136

Adjusted Starter Runs
- Chesbro-NY 41.2
- Waddell-Phi 39.7
- Young-Bos 33.4
- Plank-Phi 23.4
- Joss-Cle 19.9

Pitcher Wins
- **Chesbro-NY**.............6:
- **Waddell-Phi** ....4.
- **Young-Bos** 3
- **Plank-Phi** 3
- **Owen-Chi** 3

Pilgrims' Progress

AL offense continued to plummet in 1904, as scoring decreased another 14 percent due to substantial drops in both homers (almost 30 percent) and steals (which fell to less than one per game for the only time until 1918). Concomitantly, strikeouts continued to increase as Rube Waddell broke his own record by fanning 349, a major league mark that would last until 1965. Another top hurler, Ed Walsh of the White Sox, debuted at 23; he would eventually win 195 games.

The "First in War, First in Peace, Last in the American League" Washington Senators moved into a new stadium. However, there was nothing to celebrate about the move, as the club's .252 winning percentage was the majors' worst until 1916. The Tigers played 162 games, 10 of them ties; outfielder Jimmy Barrett took part in *all* of them, setting a games-played record that stood until 1961 (when the AL expanded and increased the schedule from 154 to 162 games).

The young but successful American League posted anothe huge attendance increase. Chicago, New York, and Boston— the league's three top performers—enjoyed large crowds as th new league's first real pennant race set the sporting world abuzz

Jack Chesbro won 41 games, the most by anyone who playe after the nineteenth century, but "Happy Jack" would be remen bered more for a wild pitch that cost his team, the New York Higl landers, the pennant. New York and Boston, clinging together : the top of the standings for the final two months, met for a se: son-ending series at New York. With the Pilgrims up by 1½ an just two games remaining, Chesbro's ninth-inning wild pitc allowed the winning run—and resulted in a title—for Bosto Unfortunately, the obstinate New York Giants, perhaps afraid c losing, refused to agree to play in a World Series. This would b the only season without postseason baseball until 1994.

1903 National League

TEAM	W	L	T	PCT	GB	HW	HL	R	OR	PA	H	2B	3B	HR	BB	SO	HB	SH	AVG	OBP	SLG	OPS	AOPS	BR	ABR	PF	SB	CS	BSA	BSR
PIT	91	49	1	.650	—	46	24	793	613	5511	1429	208	110	34	364		50	109	.286	.341	.393	734	113	87	64	103	172			
NY	84	55	3	.604	6.5	41	27	729	567	5397	1290	181	49	20	379		92	185	.272	.338	.344	682	97	11	-13	104	264			
CHI	82	56	1	.594	8	45	28	695	599	5323	1300	191	62	9	422		50	118	.275	.340	.347	687	105	21	39	97	259			
CIN	74	65	2	.532	16.5	41	35	765	656	5379	1399	228	92	28	403		30	89	.288	.346	.390	736	104	97	20	111	151			
BRO	70	66	3	.515	19	40	33	667	682	5233	1201	177	56	15	522		53	124	.265	.348	.339	687	105	31	52	97	273			
BOS	58	80	2	.420	32	31	35	578	699	5240	1145	176	47	25	398		59	101	.245	.312	.318	630	90	-82	-58	96	159			
PHI	49	86	4	.363	39.5	25	33	617	738	5313	1283	186	62	12	338		39	155	.268	.322	.341	663	98	-34	-12	97	120			
STL	43	94	2	.314	46.5	22	45	505	795	5096	1176	138	65	8	277		34	96	.251	.297	.313	610	83	-130	-113	97	171			
TOT	560					291	260	5349		42492	10223	1485	543	151	3103	3767	407	977	.269	.331	.349	679					1569			

TEAM	CG	SHO	GR	SV	IP	H	HR	BB	SO	BR/9	ERA	AERA	OAV	OOB	PR	APR	PF	OSB	OCS	FA	E	WPB	DP	FW	PW	BW	BSW	DIF
PIT	117	16	26	5	1251.1	1215	9	384	454	11.8	2.91	111	.255	.316	48	44	99	151	143	.951	295	54	100	1.6	4.2	6.1		9.0
NY	115	8	29	8	1262.2	1257	20	371	628	11.9	2.95	113	.258	.316	43	54	102	163	155	.951	287	47	87	2.3	5.2	-1.2		8.3
CHI	117	6	24	6	1240.1	1182	14	354	451	11.4	2.77	113	.250	.307	67	48	96	161	156	.942	338	32	78	-1.6	4.6	3.7		6.3
CIN	126	11	16	1	1230.0	1277	14	378	480	12.6	3.07	116	.268	.331	26	60	109	166	150	.946	312	55	84	.4	5.8	1.9		-3.6
BRO	118	11	23	4	1221.1	1276	18	377	438	12.7	3.44	92	.275	.339	-25	-39	98	270	154	.951	284	46	98	2.0	-3.7	5.0		-1.3
BOS	125	8	15	1	1228.2	1310	30	460	516	13.4	3.34	96	.278	.348	-11	-21	98	206	184	.939	361	71	89	-3.0	-2.0	-5.6		-.4
PHI	126	5	13	3	1212.1	1347	21	425	381	13.6	3.96	82	.285	.352	-95	-97	100	235	169	.947	300	58	76	1.0	-9.3	-1.2		-9.0
STL	111	4	29	2	1212.1	1353	25	430	419	13.6	3.67	89	.284	.350	-55	-56	100	217	178	.940	354	51	111	-2.7	-5.4	-10.8		-6.6
TOT	955	69	175	30	9859.0					12.6	3.26		.269	.331						.946	2531	414	723					

Batter-Fielder Wins
- Sheckard-Bro 5.8
- Wagner-Pit 5.6
- Thomas-Phi 3.9
- Tenney-Bos 3.2
- Chance-Chi 3.1

Batting Average
- Wagner-Pit 355
- Clarke-Pit 351
- Donlin-Cin 351
- Bresnahan-NY 350
- Seymour-Cin 342

On-Base Percentage
- Thomas-Phi 453
- Bresnahan-NY 443
- Chance-Chi 439
- Sheckard-Bro 423
- Donlin-Cin 420

Slugging Average
- Clarke-Pit 532
- Wagner-Pit 518
- Donlin-Cin 516
- Bresnahan-NY 493
- Steinfeldt-Cin 481

On-Base Plus Slugging
- Clarke-Pit 946
- Donlin-Cin 936
- Bresnahan-NY 936
- Wagner-Pit 931
- Sheckard-Bro 899

Adjusted OPS
- Clarke-Pit 164
- Bresnahan-NY 161
- Sheckard-Bro 160
- Wagner-Pit 160
- Chance-Chi 155

Adjusted Batter Runs
- Sheckard-Bro 44.6
- Wagner-Pit 38.8
- Chance-Chi 37.9
- Bresnahan-NY 35.9
- Thomas-Phi 35.2

Runs
- Beaumont-Pit 137
- Donlin-Cin 110
- Browne-NY 105
- Slagle-Chi 104
- Farang-Bro 101

Hits
- Beaumont-Pit 209
- Seymour-Cin 191
- Browne-NY 185
- Wagner-Pit 182
- Donlin-Cin 174

Doubles
- Steinfeldt-Cin 32
- Mertes-NY 32
- Clarke-Pit 32

Triples
- Wagner-Pit 19
- Donlin-Cin 18
- Leach-Pit 17

Home Runs
- Sheckard-Bro 9

Total Bases
- Beaumont-Pit 272
- Seymour-Cin 267
- Wagner-Pit 265
- Donlin-Cin 256
- Sheckard-Bro 245

Runs Batted In
- Mertes-NY 104
- Wagner-Pit 101
- Doyle-Bro 91
- Leach-Pit 87
- Steinfeldt-Cin 83

Stolen Bases
- Sheckard-Bro 67
- Chance-Chi 67
- Wagner-Pit 46
- Farang-Bro 46
- Mertes-NY 45

Base Stealing Runs

Fielding Runs-Infield
- Farrell-StL 21.1
- Dahlen-Bro 19.3
- Wagner-Pit 17.9
- Ritchey-Pit 16.5
- Gremminger-Bos 16.3

Fielding Runs-Outfield
- Sheckard-Bro 25.2
- Thomas-Phi 12.0
- Mertes-NY 8.7
- Sebring-Pit 4.9
- Keister-Phi 4.8

Wins
- McGinnity-NY 31
- Mathewson-NY 30
- Phillippe-Pit 25
- Leever-Pit 25

Winning Pct.
- Leever-Pit 781
- Phillippe-Pit 735
- Weimer-Chi 714
- Mathewson-NY 714
- Wicker-StL-Chi 690

Complete Games
- McGinnity-NY 44
- Mathewson-NY 37
- Pittinger-Bos 35
- Hahn-Cin 34
- Taylor-Chi 33

Strikeouts
- Mathewson-NY 267
- McGinnity-NY 171
- Garvin-Bro 154
- Pittinger-Bos 140
- Weimer-Pit 128

Fewest BB/Game
- Phillippe-Pit 90
- Hahn-Cin 1.43
- Taylor-Chi 1.64
- McFarland-StL 1.89
- Leever-Pit 1.90

Games
- McGinnity-NY 55
- Mathewson-NY 45
- Pittinger-Bos 44
- Schmidt-Bro 40

Saves
- Miller-NY 3
- Lundgren-Chi 3

Base Runners/9
- Phillippe-Pit 9.39
- Taylor-Chi 9.77
- Leever-Pit 10.13
- Mathewson-NY 10.59
- Hahn-Cin 10.70

Adjusted Relief Runs

Relief Ranking

Innings Pitched
- McGinnity-NY 434.0
- Mathewson-NY 366.1
- Pittinger-Bos 351.2
- Jones-Bro 324.1
- Taylor-Chi 312.1

Opponents' Avg.
- Weimer-Chi 225
- Mathewson-NY 231
- Taylor-Chi 235
- McGinnity-NY 236
- Leever-Pit 238

Opponents' OBP
- Phillippe-Pit 263
- Taylor-Chi 273
- Leever-Pit 282
- Mathewson-NY 287
- McGinnity-NY 291

Earned Run Average
- Leever-Pit 2.06
- Mathewson-NY 2.26
- Weimer-Chi 2.30
- Phillippe-Pit 2.43
- McGinnity-NY 2.43

Adjusted ERA
- Leever-Pit 157
- Mathewson-NY 148
- Hahn-Cin 141
- McGinnity-NY 137
- Weimer-Chi 136

Adjusted Starter Runs
- McGinnity-NY 42.2
- Mathewson-NY 39.2
- Leever-Pit 37.5
- Hahn-Cin 32.4
- Weimer-Chi 27.7

Pitcher Wins
- Mathewson-NY 4.6
- McGinnity-NY 4.0
- Leever-Pit 3.4
- Hahn-Cin 3.1
- Phillippe-Pit 2.9

The Makings of a Struggle

Largely on the strength of Honus Wagner, who captured the first of his eight batting titles, the Pirates were the class of the Senior Circuit for the third straight year. The Bucs, whose pitching staff had nearly twice as many shutouts as home runs allowed, emerged from a tangle with the Cubs and Giants in June. Despite playing just 104 games, Pittsburgh player-manager Fred Clarke paced the league in doubles.

The Giants finished 47 games closer to first place than in 1902, edging out the much-improved Cubs for second place. New York's metamorphosis led to a 91 percent rise in crowds at the Polo Grounds in 1903 as league attendance jumped 42 percent.

Mordecai "Three-Finger Brown," a 27-year-old rookie righty with two fingers missing from his pitching hand, entered the league with St. Louis. The Cubs would acquire him over the winter, fortifying an already excellent pitching staff and setting up one of the great pitching rivalries: "Three Fingers" against "The Big Six," New York's Christy Mathewson. Matty, still just 23, struck out 267 batters, 96 more than his nearest rival.

One of the least remembered nineteenth-century stars, outfielder Jimmy Ryan, retired with 2,513 hits under his belt, most of them collected with Chicago. Another little-recalled veteran outfielder, George Van Haltren, called it quits at age 37 with 2,544 hits.

Following the two-year slump in offense, NL hitters got well and team runs boomed to 4.78 per contest. Homers were way up, and stolen bases rose to 1.40 per game, the highest in NL history. Also at a peak was the interest level in a postseason AL-NL series, as the AL and NL champions agreed to a best-of-nine competition. Before it started, the Pirates lost 16-game winner Ed Doheny to a mental breakdown. His loss, and an injury to Sam Leever, stretched the Bucs' pitching staff to its breaking point as Boston won the first modern World Series in eight games.

1903 American League

TEAM	W	L	T	PCT	GB	HW	HL	R	OR	PA	H	2B	3B	HR	BB	SO	HB	SH	AVG	OBP	SLG	OPS	AOPS	BR	ABR	PF	SB	CS	BSA	BSR
BOS	91	47	3	.659		49	20	708	504	5365	1336	222	113	48	262	561	36	148	.272	.313	.392	705	111	89	55	105	141			
PHI	75	60	2	.556	14.5	44	21	597	519	5074	1236	227	68	32	268	513	32	101	.264	.309	.363	672	102	39	13	105	157			
CLE	77	63	0	.550	15	49	25	639	579	5225	1265	231	95	31	259	595	40	153	.265	.308	.373	681	112	51	63	98	175			
NY	72	62	2	.537	17	41	26	579	573	5091	1136	193	62	18	332	465	65	129	.249	.309	.330	639	92	-3	-36	106	160			
DET	65	71	1	.478	25	37	28	567	539	5090	1229	162	91	12	292	526	46	170	.268	.318	.351	669	110	37	55	97	128			
STL	65	74	1	.468	26.5	38	32	500	525	5047	1133	166	68	12	271	539	26	111	.244	.290	.317	607	90	-68	-54	97	101			
CHI	60	77	1	.438	30.5	41	28	516	613	5175	1152	176	49	14	325	537	38	142	.247	.301	.314	615	94	-45	-21	96	180			
WAS	43	94	3	.314	47.5	29	40	437	691	4990	1066	172	72	17	257	463	39	81	.231	.277	.311	588	80	-100	-109	102	131			
TOT	554					328	220	4543		41057	9553	1549	618	184	2266	4199	322	1035	.255	.303	.344	648					1173			

TEAM	CG	SHO	GR	SV	IP	H	HR	BB	SO	BR/9	ERA	AERA	OAV	OOB	PR	APR	PF	OSB	OCS	FA	E	WPB	DP	FW	PW	BW	BSW	DIF
BOS	123	20	18	4	1255.0	1142	23	269	579	10.4	2.57	118	.242	.288	55	63	102	123	130	.959	239	44	86	2.3	6.5	5.7		7.5
PHI	112	10	28	1	1207.0	1124	20	315	728	11.3	2.98	103	.246	.305	-2	10	103	140	122	.960	217	58	66	3.2	1.0	1.3		1.9
CLE	125	20	15	0	1243.2	1161	16	271	521	10.6	2.73	105	.247	.293	32	18	96	135	120	.946	322	51	99	-3.2	1.9	6.5		1.8
NY	111	7	26	2	1201.1	1171	19	245	463	10.9	3.08	101	.255	.299	-16	5	105	133	89	.953	264	43	87	-.9	.5	-3.7		8.2
DET	123	15	15	2	1196.0	1169	19	336	554	11.5	2.75	106	.256	.310	28	21	98	185	126	.950	281	40	82	-.9	2.2	5.7		-10.0
STL	124	12	16	3	1222.1	1220	26	237	511	11.0	2.77	105	.260	.300	26	19	98	127	108	.953	268	34	94	.2	2.0	-5.6		-1.0
CHI	114	9	26	4	1235.0	1233	23	287	391	11.5	3.02	93	.260	.309	-8	-30	95	131	107	.949	297	52	85	-1.8	-3.1	-2.2		-1.4
WAS	122	6	18	3	1223.2	1333	38	306	452	12.4	3.82	82	.277	.325	-116	-89	106	199	127	.954	260	37	86	.8	-9.2	-11.3		-5.7
TOT	954	99	162	19	9784.0					11.2	2.96		.255	.303						.953	2148	359	685					

Batter-Fielder Wins		Batting Average		On-Base Percentage		Slugging Average		On-Base Plus Slugging		Adjusted OPS		Adjusted Batter Runs	
Lajoie-Cle	8.1	Lajoie-Cle	.344	Barrett-Det	.407	Lajoie-Cle	.518	Lajoie-Cle	.896	Lajoie-Cle	170	Lajoie-Cle	40.6
Bradley-Cle	4.8	Crawford-Det	.335	Hartsel-Phi	.391	Bradley-Cle	.496	Hartsel-Phi	.868	Crawford-Det	159	Crawford-Det	36.3
Crawford-Det	3.6	Dougherty-Bos	.331	Lajoie-Cle	.379	Freeman-Bos	.496	Crawford-Det	.855	Bradley-Cle	154	Barrett-Det	32.8
Barrett-Det	3.4	Barrett-Det	.315	Lush-Det	.379	Crawford-Det	.489	Bradley-Cle	.844	Hartsel-Phi	152	Bradley-Cle	32.5
Collins-Bos	2.9	Bradley-Cle	.313	Green-Chi	.375	Hartsel-Phi	.477	Freeman-Bos	.823	Green-Chi	146	Green-Chi	30.0

Runs		Hits		Doubles		Triples		Home Runs		Total Bases		Runs Batted In	
Dougherty-Bos	107	Dougherty-Bos	195	Seybold-Phi	45	Crawford-Det	25	Freeman-Bos	13	Freeman-Bos	281	Freeman-Bos	104
Bradley-Cle	101	Crawford-Det	184	Lajoie-Cle	41	Bradley-Cle	22	Hickman-Cle	12	Crawford-Det	269	Hickman-Cle	97
Keeler-NY	95	Parent-Bos	170	Freeman-Bos	39	Freeman-Bos	20	Ferris-Bos	9	Bradley-Cle	266	Lajoie-Cle	93
Barrett-Det	95	Bay-Cle	169	Bradley-Cle	36	Parent-Bos	17	Seybold-Phi	8	Lajoie-Cle	251	L.Cross-Phi	90
Bay-Cle	94	Bradley-Cle	168	Anderson-StL	34	Collins-Bos	17			Dougherty-Bos	250	Crawford-Det	89

Stolen Bases		Base Stealing Runs		Fielding Runs-Infield		Fielding Runs-Outfield		Wins		Winning Pct.		Complete Games	
Bay-Cle	45			Lajoie-Cle	39.1	Lush-Det	12.8	Young-Bos	28	Young-Bos	.757	Young-Bos	34
Pickering-Phi	40			Wallace-StL	18.4	Barrett-Det	6.7	Plank-Phi	23	Hughes-Bos	.741	Waddell-Phi	34
Holmes-Was-Chi	35			Williams-NY	15.5	Holmes-Was-Chi	6.4			Moore-Cle	.714	Donovan-Det	34
Dougherty-Bos	35			Ferris-Bos	14.3	Crawford-Det	5.2			Dinneen-Bos	.618		
Conroy-NY	33			Carr-Det	12.7	Robinson-Was	4.3			Plank-Phi	.590		

Strikeouts		Fewest BB/Game		Games		Saves		Base Runners/9		Adjusted Relief Runs		Relief Ranking	
Waddell-Phi	302	Young-Bos	.97	Plank-Phi	43	Young-Bos	2	Joss-Cle	8.82				
Donovan-Det	187	Bernhard-Cle	1.14	Mullin-Det	41	Powell-StL	2	Young-Bos	8.96				
Young-Bos	176	Donahue-StL-Cle	1.14	Young-Bos	40	Orth-Was	2	Bernhard-Cle	9.34				
Plank-Phi	176	Joss-Cle	1.17	Flaherty-Chi	40	Mullin-Det	2	Moore-Cle	9.56				
Mullin-Det	170	Tannehill-NY	1.28	Chesbro-NY	40	Dinneen-Bos	2	Dinneen-Bos	9.78				

Innings Pitched		Opponents' Avg.		Opponents' OBP		Earned Run Average		Adjusted ERA		Adjusted Starter Runs		Pitcher Wins	
Young-Bos	341.2	Moore-Cle	.217	Joss-Cle	.256	Moore-Cle	1.74	Moore-Cle	164	Young-Bos	34.0	Young-Bos	4.8
Plank-Phi	336.0	Donovan-Det	.220	Young-Bos	.259	Young-Bos	2.08	Young-Bos	146	Dinneen-Bos	27.8	Mullin-Det	3.5
Chesbro-NY	324.2	Joss-Cle	.223	Bernhard-Cle	.267	Bernhard-Cle	2.12	Bernhard-Cle	135	Moore-Cle	26.8	Donovan-Det	3.0
Waddell-Phi	324.0	Waddell-Phi	.229	Moore-Cle	.271	White-Chi	2.13	Dinneen-Bos	134	Donovan-Det	25.4	Dinneen-Bos	2.9
Mullin-Det	320.2	Dinneen-Bos	.230	Dinneen-Bos	.276	Joss-Cle	2.19	White-Chi	132	Waddell-Phi	23.2	White-Chi	2.8

Upstart Champions

Prior to the season, the NL weighed its options. After first proposing a merger with the AL, the Senior Circuit settled for a truce, and the two leagues agreed to respect each other's player contracts and to end their war. With the sale of the rubble of the Baltimore franchise to New York investors, the AL was now set with eight signature clubs, which remained in the same cities until 1953.

Two noteworthy players died. Tigers pitcher Win Mercer, apparently despondent at gambling losses, turned on the gas in a hotel room on January 13 and died at 28. He had recently been named Detroit's manager. In the year's oddest tragedy, slugging outfielder Ed Delahanty of Washington fell into the Niagara River on July 2 and was apparently swept over Niagara Falls to his death after being ejected from a train due to drunkenness. He was just 34.

On the field, the biggest story was the strikeout and the resulting huge 16 percent drop in scoring. The league's adoption of the foul-strike rule led, predictably, to K's rising by a whopping 58 percent. Rube Waddell of the Athletics shattered the big-league strikeout record by 63.

By the end of July, the AL race was essentially over. Boston, the league leader in runs and ERA, emerged from the pack and cruised to the pennant. Philadelphia's already good pitching was bolstered by rookie Chief Bender, but Boston had the league's best mound staff (ed by Cy Young) plus two first-rate hitters in Buck Freeman and Patsy Dougherty.

The first interleague championship since 1890 and the first modern World Series pitted the Boston Americans against NL champion Pittsburgh Pirates, with the newly "recognized" Junior Circuit winning the best-of-nine series, five games to three, after losing three of the first four games. Americans starter Bill Dinneen won thrice as Young took two more, besting the efforts of Pirates ace Deacon Phillippe, who pitched five complete games.

1902 National League

TEAM	W	L	T	PCT	GB	HW	HL	R	OR	PA	H	2B	3B	HR	BB	SO	HB	SH	AVG	OBP	SLG	OPS	AOPS	BR	ABR	PF	SB	CS	BSA	BSR
PIT	103	36	3	.741		56	15	775	440	5480	1410	189	95	18	372	446	64	118	.286	.344	.374	718	124	154	129	104	222			
BRO	75	63	3	.543	27.5	45	23	564	519	5344	1242	147	49	19	319	489	62	118	.256	.311	.319	630	99	-4	-8	101	145			
BOS	73	64	5	.533	29	42	27	572	516	5298	1178	142	39	14	398	481	43	131	.249	.313	.305	618	95	-13	-18	101	189			
CIN	70	70	1	.500	33.5	35	35	633	566	5342	1383	188	77	18	297	465	39	98	.282	.328	.362	690	109	96	38	110	131			
CHI	68	69	6	.496	34	31	38	544	505	5428	1224	133	40	6	358	572	44	156	.251	.308	.299	607	95	-37	-21	97	229			
STL	56	78	6	.418	44.5	28	38	517	695	5183	1226	116	37	10	273	438	52	107	.258	.306	.304	610	97	-39	-18	96	158			
PHI	56	81	1	.409	46	29	39	484	649	5125	1139	110	43	5	356	481	32	122	.247	.305	.293	598	90	-51	-51	100	108			
NY	48	88	5	.353	53.5	24	44	405	604	5034	1097	147	34	6	254	540	40	108	.237	.282	.287	569	81	-105	-101	99	187			
TOT	564					290	259	4494		42234	9899	1172	414	96	2627	3912	376	958	.259	.313	.318	631					1369			

TEAM	CG	SHO	GR	SV	IP	H	HR	BB	SO	BR/9	ERA	AERA	OAV	OOB	PR	APR	PF	OSB	OCS	FA	E	WPB	DP	FW	PW	BW	BSW	DIF
PIT	131	21	10	3	1264.2	1142	4	250	564	10.3	2.30	119	.241	.288	68	62	98	117	116	.958	247	39	87	3.4	6.5	13.6		10.0
BRO	131	14	10	3	1256.0	1113	10	363	536	10.8	2.69	103	.238	.298	12	9	99	217	142	.952	275	47	79	1.5	.9	-.8		4.4
BOS	124	14	18	4	1259.2	1233	16	372	523	11.8	2.61	108	.257	.316	24	29	102	156	134	.959	240	42	90	3.8	3.1	-1.9		-.5
CIN	130	9	13	1	1239.0	1228	15	352	430	11.9	2.67	112	.259	.318	15	41	108	143	141	.945	322	50	118	-1.4	4.3	4.0		-6.9
CHI	134	.17	9	2	1293.1	1244	7	281	447	10.9	2.19	123	.253	.300	85	75	97	158	138	.946	331	48	113	-1.7	7.9	-2.2		-4.5
STL	112	7	29	4	1227.2	1399	16	338	400	13.0	3.47	79	.287	.338	-95	-103	99	188	141	.944	336	35	107	-2.4	-10.9	-1.9		4.2
PHI	118	8	21	5	1211.0	1323	12	334	504	12.7	3.50	80	.278	.333	-97	-92	101	217	143	.946	305	47	81	-.8	-9.7	-5.4		3.3
NY	120	11	21	1	1242.1	1217	16	337	508	11.6	2.86	98	.257	.313	-11	-9	101	173	144	.943	337	60	107	-2.3	-.9	-10.7		-6.1
TOT	1000	101	131	21	9993.2					11.6	2.78		.259	.313						.949	2393	368	782					

Batter-Fielder Wins		Batting Average		On-Base Percentage		Slugging Average		On-Base Plus Slugging		Adjusted OPS		Adjusted Batter Runs	
Tenney-Bos	4.0	Beaumont-Pit	.357	R.Thomas-Phi	.414	Wagner-Pit	.463	Wagner-Pit	.857	Wagner-Pit	159	Wagner-Pit	37.1
Wagner-Pit	3.9	Crawford-Cin	.333	Tenney-Bos	.409	Crawford-Cin	.461	Clarke-Pit	.850	Clarke-Pit	157	Clarke-Pit	32.7
Leach-Pit	3.4	Keeler-Bro	.333	Beaumont-Pit	.404	Clarke-Pit	.449	Crawford-Cin	.848	Beaumont-Pit	148	Beaumont-Pit	31.3
Kling-Chi	2.7	Wagner-Pit	.330	Clarke-Pit	.401	Beckley-Cin	.427	Beaumont-Pit	.822	Crawford-Cin	147	Tenney-Bos	29.0
Farrell-StL	2.7	Beckley-Cin	.330	Wagner-Pit	.394	Leach-Pit	.426	Beckley-Cin	.804	Tenney-Bos	141	Crawford-Cin	28.9

Runs		Hits		Doubles		Triples		Home Runs		Total Bases		Runs Batted In	
Wagner-Pit	105	Beaumont-Pit	193	Wagner-Pit	30	Leach-Pit	22	Leach-Pit	6	Crawford-Cin	256	Wagner-Pit	91
Clarke-Pit	103	Keeler-Bro	186	Clarke-Pit	27	Crawford-Cin	22	Beckley-Cin	5	Wagner-Pit	247	Leach-Pit	85
Beaumont-Pit	100	Crawford-Cin	185	Cooley-Bos	26	Wagner-Pit	16	Sheckard-Bro	4	Beckley-Cin	227	Crawford-Cin	78
Leach-Pit	97	Wagner-Pit	176	Dahlen-Bro	25	Clarke-Pit	14	McCreery-Bro	4	Beaumont-Pit	226	Dahlen-Bro	74
Crawford-Cin	92	Beckley-Cin	175	Beckley-Cin	23	Gremminger-Bos	12			Leach-Pit	219		

Stolen Bases		Base Stealing Runs		Fielding Runs-Infield		Fielding Runs-Outfield		Wins		Winning Pct.		Complete Games	
Wagner-Pit	42			Farrell-StL	31.8	Donovan-StL	8.9	Chesbro-Pit	28	Chesbro-Pit	.824	Willis-Bos	45
Slagle-Chi	41			Steinfeldt-Cin	21.9	Lush-Bos	8.6	Willis-Bos	27	Doheny-Pit	.800	Pittinger-Bos	36
Donovan-StL	34			H.Long-Bos	19.8	Sheckard-Bro	8.5	Pittinger-Bos	27	Tannehill-Pit	.769	Hahn-Cin	35
Beaumont-Pit	33			Lowe-Chi	17.6	Dobbs-Cin-Chi	7.8	Taylor-Chi	23	Phillippe-Pit	.690	White-Phi	34
Smith-NY	32			Leach-Pit	12.4	Brodie-NY	7.3	Hahn-Cin	23	Leever-Pit	.682	Taylor-Chi	34

Strikeouts		Fewest BB/Game		Games		Saves		Base Runners/9		Adjusted Relief Runs		Relief Ranking	
Willis-Bos	225	Phillippe-Pit	.86	Willis-Bos	51	Willis-Bos	3	Taylor-Chi	8.90				
White-Phi	185	Tannehill-Pit	.97	Pittinger-Bos	46	M.O'Neill-StL	2	Tannehill-Pit	9.27				
Pittinger-Bos	174	Menefee-Chi	1.19	Yerkes-StL	39	Newton-Bro	2	McGinnity-NY	9.59				
Donovan-Bro	170	Taylor-Chi	1.21	Taylor-Chi	37	Leever-Pit	2	Hahn-Cin	9.70				
Mathewson-NY	164	Leever-Pit	1.26					Cronin-NY	9.71				

Innings Pitched		Opponents' Avg.		Opponents' OBP		Earned Run Average		Adjusted ERA		Adjusted Starter Runs		Pitcher Wins	
Willis-Bos	410.0	Newton-Bro	.217	Taylor-Chi	.258	Taylor-Chi	1.29	Taylor-Chi	209	Taylor-Chi	50.8	Taylor-Chi	6.1
Pittinger-Bos	389.1	McGinnity-NY	.219	Tannehill-Pit	.266	Hahn-Cin	1.77	Hahn-Cin	170	Hahn-Cin	40.6	Hahn-Cin	4.4
Taylor-Chi	333.2	Taylor-Chi	.224	McGinnity-NY	.273	Tannehill-Pit	1.95	Poole-Pit-Cin	142	Willis-Bos	27.9	Willis-Bos	2.8
Hahn-Cin	321.0	Donovan-Bro	.228	Hahn-Cin	.275	Lundgren-Chi	1.97	Tannehill-Pit	140	Chesbro-Pit	23.2	Tannehill-Pit	2.7
White-Phi	306.0	Chesbro-Pit	.229	Phillippe-Pit	.276	Phillippe-Pit	2.05	Lundgren-Chi	137	Phillippe-Pit	18.9	Phillips-Cin	2.6

Change is Gonna Come

By 1902 the old days were clearly gone. Jim "Pud" Galvin, a great nineteenth century hurler who once threw 72 complete games in a season, died at 46. Boston's Vic Willis topped the NL with 45 complete games as old-timers bemoaned pitchers' lack of stamina. Forty-year-old center fielder Dummy Hoy, who lived nearly sixty more years, played his final game.

The Reds opened The Palace of the Fans, which sported a 450-foot right-field line. Scoring decreased another 14 percent as foul bunts were also now counted as strikes. Homers dropped 58 percent as NL ERA dipped 51 points.

The already great Pirates further improved, taking the pennant by an amazing 27½ games. Leading from start to finish, Pittsburgh was 10 games up in mid-May. One of the dominant clubs of all time, the '02 Bucs led the league in runs by 142 and in runs allowed by 65. Competition would soon come from Chicago and New York as two pieces of a growing Cubs powerhouse, infielders Joe Tinker and Johnny Evers, debuted

in 1902. In New York, young right-hander Christy Mathewson had his second spectacular season for a terrible team, going 14-17 with 8 shutouts for the Giants.

The most significant news occurred with the AL's Baltimore Orioles. As a result of a complicated conspiracy that included John McGraw, Reds owner John Brush, and Giants owner Andrew Freedman, the Orioles were stripped of their best players by nefarious means. Several Orioles—John McGraw, Roger Bresnahan, and pitcher Joe McGinnity among them—ended up in New York. Others wound up in Cincinnati. Brush purchased the Giants after the season, reaping the benefits as the moribund franchise was transformed overnight into a contender. The story did not end perfectly for masterminds Brush and McGraw, though. Infuriated, AL President Ban Johnson engineered the sale of what was left of the Orioles to New York investors the following year, bringing major league competition into the NL's biggest market.

1902 American League

TEAM	W	L	T	PCT	GB	HW	HL	R	OR	PA	H	2B	3B	HR	BB	SO	HB	SH	AVG	OBP	SLG	OPS	AOPS	BR	ABR	PF	SB	CS	BSA	BSR
PHI	83	53	1	.610		56	17	775	636	5261	1369	235	67	38	343	293	38	118	.287	.340	.389	729	104	52	23	104	201			
STL	78	58	4	.574	5	49	21	619	607	5251	1254	208	61	29	373	327	38	104	.265	.323	.353	676	94	-37	-28	99	137			
BOS	77	60	1	.562	6.5	43	27	664	600	5292	1356	195	42	275	375	42	100	.278	.322	.383	705	98	-4	-22	103	132				
CHI	74	60	4	.552	8	48	19	675	602	5255	1248	170	50	14	411	381	36	154	.268	.332	.335	667	95	-43	-14	96	265			
CLE	69	67	1	.507	14	40	25	686	667	5303	1401	248	68	33	308	356	35	120	.289	.336	.389	725	111	43	73	96	140			
WAS	61	75	2	.449	22	40	28	707	790	5188	1338	261	66	47	329	296	44	81	.283	.335	.395	730	107	52	46	101	121			
DET	52	83	2	.385	30.5	35	33	566	657	5139	1167	141	55	22	359	287	53	83	.251	.312	.320	632	79	-112	-122	102	130			
BAL	50	88	3	.362	34	32	31	715	848	5348	1318	202	107	33	417	429	54	117	.277	.342	.385	727	103	50	19	104	189			
TOT	553					343	201	5407		42037	10451	1660	569	258	2815	2744	340	877	.275	.331	.369	700					1315			

TEAM	CG	SHO	GR	SV	IP	H	HR	BB	SO	BR/9	ERA	AERA	OAV	OOB	PR	APR	PF	OSB	OCS	FA	E	WPB	DP	FW	PW	BW	BSW	DIF
PHI	114	5	25	2	1216.1	1292	33	368	455	12.7	3.29	111	.273	.334	39	49	103	157	147	.953	270	41	75	1.4	4.6	2.2		6.8
STL	120	7	22	2	1244.0	1273	36	343	348	12.0	3.34	106	.266	.321	32	26	99	154	124	.953	274	45	122	1.5	2.5	-2.7		8.6
BOS	123	6	16	1	1238.0	1217	27	326	431	11.5	3.02	118	.258	.311	75	75	100	132	135	.955	263	40	101	2.0	7.1	-2.1		1.5
CHI	116	11	22	0	1221.2	1269	30	331	346	12.1	3.41	99	.269	.323	-22	-5	95	121	118	.955	257	54	125	2.3	-.5	-1.3		6.5
CLE	116	16	23	3	1204.1	1199	26	411	361	12.4	3.28	105	.260	.327	39	21	96	183	136	.950	287	66	96	.3	2.0	6.9		-8.3
WAS	130	2	8	0	1207.2	1403	56	312	341	13.2	4.36	85	.291	.341	-106	-85	104	173	128	.945	316	42	70	-1.3	-8.1	4.4		-2.0
DET	116	9	22	3	1190.2	1267	20	370	245	12.7	3.56	102	.274	.333	1	10	102	198	136	.943	332	44	111	-2.5	.9	-11.6		-2.4
BAL	119	3	22	1	1210.1	1531	30	354	258	14.3	4.33	87	.309	.360	-102	-73	106	197	119	.938	357	52	109	-3.5	-6.9	1.8		-10.4
TOT	954	59	160	12	9733.0					12.6	3.57		.275	.331						.949	2356	384	809					

Batter-Fielder Wins
Lajoie-Phi-Cle 5.6
Delahanty-Was 5.0
Bradley-Cle 4.8
Hickman-Bos-Cle 2.6
L.Cross-Phi 2.3

Batting Average
Delahanty-Was.......376
Lajoie-Phi-Cle........378
Hickman-Bos-Cle ...361
Dougherty-Bos 342
L.Cross-Phi 342

On-Base Percentage
Delahanty-Was.......453
Dougherty-Bos 407
Barrett-Det 397
Selbach-Bal 393
Jones-Chi 390

Slugging Average
Delahanty-Was.......590
Lajoie-Phi-Cle........565
Hickman-Bos-Cle...539
Bradley-Cle 515
Seybold-Phi 506

On-Base Plus Slugging
Delahanty-Was 1043
Hickman-Bos-Cle ..926
Bradley-Cle 890
Seybold-Phi 881
Williams-Bal 861

Adjusted OPS
Delahanty-Was 186
Hickman-Bos-Cle ..159
Bradley-Cle 151
Seybold-Phi 137
Freeman-Bos.........131

Adjusted Batter Runs
Delahanty-Was 57.7
Hickman-Bos-Cle ..39.4
Lajoie-Phi-Cle........37.3
Bradley-Cle...........35.8
Seybold-Phi 24.5

Runs
Hartsel-Phi 109
Fultz-Phi 109
Strang-Chi 108
Bradley-Cle 104
Delahanty-Was......103

Hits
Hickman-Bos-Cle ...193
L.Cross-Phi 191
Bradley-Cle 187
Delahanty-Was.......178
Freeman-Bos.........174

Doubles
Delahanty-Was.......43
Davis-Phi 43
L.Cross-Phi 39
Bradley-Cle 39
Freeman-Bos..........38

Triples
Williams-Bal 21
Freeman-Bos 19
Ferris-Bos 14
Delahanty-Was.......14
Hickman-Bos-Cle ...13

Home Runs
Seybold-Phi 16
Hickman-Bos-Cle 11
Freeman-Bos...........11
Bradley-Cle 11
Delahanty-Was 10

Total Bases
Hickman-Bos-Cle ..288
Freeman-Bos.........283
Bradley-Cle 283
Delahanty-Was 279
Seybold-Phi 264

Runs Batted In
Freeman-Bos 121
Hickman-Bos-Cle ...110
L.Cross-Phi 108
Seybold-Phi 97

Stolen Bases
Hartsel-Phi 47
Mertes-Chi 46
Fultz-Phi 44

Base Stealing Runs

Fielding Runs-Infield
Ferris-Bos 23.8
Padden-StL 12.3
Bradley-Cle...........12.0
Elberfeld-Det 11.6
M.Cross-Phi 9.3

Fielding Runs-Outfield
Selbach-Bal 10.4
Jones-Chi 9.8
Barrett-Det 5.7
Mertes-Chi 5.4
Burkett-StL 5.2

Wins
Young-Bos.............32
Waddell-Phi 24
Powell-StL 22
R.Donahue-StL 22
Dinneen-Bos 21

Winning Pct.
Bernhard-Phi-Cle ...783
Waddell-Phi 774
Young-Bos 744
R.Donahue-StL 667
Griffith-Chi 625

Complete Games
Young-Bos 41
Dinneen-Bos 39
Powell-StL 36
Orth-Was 36

Strikeouts
Waddell-Phi 210
Young-Bos.............160
Powell-StL 137
Dinneen-Bos 136
Plank-Phi...............107

Fewest BB/Game
Orth-Was 1.11
Young-Bos 1.24
Bernhard-Phi-Cle ..1.47
Siever-Det..............1.53
Plank-Phi 1.83

Games
Young-Bos.............45
Powell-StL 42
Dinneen-Bos 42
Wiltse-Phi-Bal 38
Orth-Was 38

Saves
Powell-StL 2

Base Runners/9
Bernhard-Phi-Cle ..8.68
Siever-Det...............9.56
Waddell-Phi 9.71
Young-Bos 9.73
Joss-Cle 10.46

Adjusted Relief Runs

Relief Ranking

Innings Pitched
Young-Bos.............384.2
Dinneen-Bos 371.1
Powell-StL 328.1
Orth-Was 324.0
R.Donahue-StL ..316.1

Opponents' Avg.
Bernhard-Phi-Cle ...216
Waddell-Phi 223
Joss-Cle 228
Siever-Det 237
Winter-Bos 238

Opponents' OBP
Bernhard-Phi-Cle ...254
Siever-Det 273
Waddell-Phi 276
Young-Bos 276
Joss-Cle 291

Earned Run Average
Siever-Det 1.91
Waddell-Phi 2.05
Bernhard-Phi-Cle ...2.15
Young-Bos 2.15
Garvin-Chi 2.21

Adjusted ERA
Siever-Det 191
Waddell-Phi 179
Young-Bos 166
Bernhard-Phi-Cle ...160
Garvin-Chi 153

Adjusted Starter Runs
Young-Bos 59.4
Waddell-Phi 48.3
Bernhard-Phi-Cle ...33.3
Dinneen-Bos..........33.1
Siever-Det..............29.4

Pitcher Wins
Young-Bos 6.0
Waddell-Phi 5.8
Bernhard-Phi-Cle...5.8
Dinneen-Bos 2.3
Plank-Phi 2.3

Growing Pains

Prior to 1902 the poorly attended and unsuccessful Milwaukee franchise shifted to St. Louis to become the Browns. The fledgling AL's other sticky spot was Baltimore, a franchise that was ultimately ripped apart by its manager, John McGraw, as part of his blood feud with AL President Ban Johnson. The Orioles finished last, despite topping the loop in on-base percentage and triples, losing their best players—as well as McGraw—to the NL. Orioles catcher Wilbert Robinson retired, later to manage in Brooklyn for 18 years.

Boston outfielder Patsy Dougherty hit .342 in his first season, and Cleveland hurler Addie Joss was equally impressive (17-13 with a league-best 5 shutouts) as a rookie. Joss, just 22, was an exception to the rule—few regulars or starting pitchers of the time were younger than 25.

The defending champion White Sox led in July by as much as 5½ games but fell apart in August as a four-team scramble developed. Out of the chaos came the Philadelphia Athletics, who pulled away from St. Louis and Boston in September. The Browns' surprising second-place finish was the only time the franchise ended above fourth place until 1921.

Philadelphia's league-best offense was powered by slugger Socks Seybold, on-base threat Topsy Hartsel, and third baseman Lave Cross, who batted in 108 runs without a single homer. Pitcher Rube Waddell, a man-child who wore out welcomes with the Pirates and the Cubs, found a home under Connie Mack's wing. He went 24-7, leading the AL in strikeouts.

Although runs fell by 8 percent, home runs skyrocketed to 258, the AL's highest total until 1920. Seybold's 16 taters were two more than hit by the entire White Sox team, and his total stood as the league record until Babe Ruth broke it in 1919. Cleveland and Philadelphia saw their attendance rise more than 100 percent as, overall, the league saw a healthy sales increase of 31 percent in its second campaign.

1901 National League

TEAM	W	L	T	PCT	GB	HW	HL	R	OR	PA	H	2B	3B	HR	BB	SO	HB	SH	AVG	OBP	SLG	OPS	AOPS	BR	ABR	PF	SB	CS	BSA	BSR
PIT	90	49	1	.647		45	24	776	534	5468	1407	182	92	29	386	493	52	117	.286	.345	.379	724	113	99	77	103	203			
PHI	83	57	0	.593	7.5	46	23	668	543	5411	1275	194	58	24	430	549	62	126	.266	.334	.346	680	101	33	20	102	199			
BRO	79	57	1	.581	9.5	43	25	744	600	5312	1399	206	93	32	312	449	41	80	.287	.335	.387	722	112	86	67	103	178			
STL	76	64	2	.543	14.5	40	31	792	689	5565	1430	187	94	39	314	540	90	122	.284	.337	.381	718	120	86	126	95	190			
BOS	69	69	2	.500	20.5	41	29	531	556	5218	1180	135	36	28	303	519	34	135	.249	.298	.310	608	75	-105	-149	109	158			
CHI	53	86	1	.381	37	30	39	578	699	5277	1250	153	61	18	314	532	52	67	.258	.310	.326	636	93	-58	-36	96	204			
NY	52	85	4	.380	37	30	38	544	755	5260	1225	167	46	19	303	575	45	73	.253	.303	.318	621	90	-83	-60	96	133			
CIN	52	87	3	.374	38	27	43	561	818	5392	1232	173	70	38	323	584	42	113	.251	.303	.338	641	97	-57	-15	93	137			
TOT	561					302	252	5194		42903	10398	1397	550	227	2685	4241	418	833	.267	.321	.348	669					1402			

TEAM	CG	SHO	GR	SV	IP	H	HR	BB	SO	BR/9	ERA	AERA	OAV	OOB	PR	APR	PF	OSB	OCS	FA	E	WPB	DP	FW	PW	BW	BSW	DIF
PIT	119	15	21	4	1244.2	1198	20	244	505	10.9	2.58	126	.252	.297	102	95	98	133	124	.950	287	44	97	1.2	9.3	7.5		2.4
PHI	125	15	16	2	1246.2	1221	19	259	480	11.0	2.87	119	.255	.300	63	71	102	173	135	.954	262	61	65	2.7	7.0	2.0		1.4
BRO	111	7	26	5	1213.2	1244	18	435	583	12.8	3.14	107	.264	.333	24	27	101	213	151	.950	281	59	99	1.2	2.6	6.6		.6
STL	118	5	29	5	1269.2	1333	39	332	445	12.3	3.68	86	.268	.321	-51	-74	96	186	146	.949	305	63	108	.4	-7.3	12.3		.5
BOS	128	11	13	0	1263.0	1196	29	349	558	11.3	2.90	125	.249	.305	59	91	109	139	128	.952	282	45	89	1.5	8.9	-14.6		4.2
CHI	131	2	9	0	1241.2	1348	27	324	586	12.5	3.33	97	.275	.327	-2	-14	98	189	143	.943	336	61	87	-1.8	-1.4	-3.5		-9.8
NY	118	11	24	1	1232.0	1389	24	377	542	13.4	3.87	85	.283	.342	-75	-79	99	205	154	.941	348	97	81	-2.3	-7.7	-5.9		-.5
CIN	126	4	18	0	1265.2	1469	51	365	542	13.5	4.17	77	.289	.345	-120	-143	96	166	143	.940	355	44	102	-2.6	-14.0	-1.5		.6
TOT	976	70	156	17	9977.0					12.2	3.32		.267	.321						.947	2456	474	728					.6

Batter-Fielder Wins
Burkett-StL 5.5
Wallace-StL 5.4
Davis-NY 4.6
Flick-Phi 4.5
Wagner-Pit 4.4

Batting Average
Burkett-StL 376
Delahanty-Phi 354
Sheckard-Bro 354
Wagner-Pit 353
Keeler-Bro 339

On-Base Percentage
Burkett-StL 440
Thomas-Phi 437
Delahanty-Phi.........427
Wagner-Pit 417
Hartsel-Chi 414

Slugging Average
Sheckard-Bro 534
Delahanty-Phi 528
Crawford-Cin 524
Burkett-StL 509
Flick-Phi 500

On-Base Plus Slugging
Delahanty-Phi 955
Burkett-StL 949
Sheckard-Bro 944
Wagner-Pit 911
Crawford-Cin 903

Adjusted OPS
Burkett-StL 184
Delahanty-Phi 173
Crawford-Cin 172
Sheckard-Bro 168
Hartsel-Chi 163

Adjusted Batter Runs
Burkett-StL 66.1
Delahanty-Phi........52.1
Hartsel-Chi............47.7
Sheckard-Bro.........46.7
Crawford-Cin.........44.0

Runs
Burkett-StL 142
Keeler-Bro 123
Beaumont-Pit 120
Clarke-Pit...............118
Sheckard-Bro 116

Hits
Burkett-StL 226
Keeler-Bro 202
Sheckard-Bro 196
Wagner-Pit 194
Delahanty-Phi 192

Doubles
Delahanty-Phi 38
Daly-Bro 38
Wagner-Pit 37
Beckley-Cin 36
Wallace-StL 34

Triples
Sheckard-Bro 19
Flick-Phi 17

Home Runs
Crawford-Cin 16
Sheckard-Bro 11
Burkett-StL 10

Total Bases
Burkett-StL 306
Sheckard-Bro 296
Delahanty-Phi 286
Wagner-Pit 271

Runs Batted In
Wagner-Pit 126
Delahanty-Phi 108
Sheckard-Bro 104
Crawford-Cin 104

Stolen Bases
Wagner-Pit 49
Hartsel-Chi 41
Strang-NY 40
Harley-Cin 37
Beaumont-Pit 36

Base Stealing Runs
Wallace-StL 27.2
Davis-NY 24.3
Dahlen-Bro 13.6
Daly-Bro 10.3
Leach-Pit 10.1

Fielding Runs-Infield
Flick-Phi 13.9
Sheckard-Bro 9.2
Green-Chi.................6.6
VanHaltren-NY 4.1
Nichols-StL...............4.0

Fielding Runs-Outfield

Wins
Donovan-Bro 25
Harper-StL 23
Phillippe-Pit 22
Hahn-Cin 22
Chesbro-Pit 21

Winning Pct.
Chesbro-Pit 677
Phillippe-Pit 647
Tannehill-Pit 643
Harper-StL 639
Kitson-Bro 633

Complete Games
Hahn-Cin 41
Taylor-NY 37
Mathewson-NY 36
Donovan-Bro 36

Strikeouts
Hahn-Cin 239
Donovan-Bro 226
Hughes-StL 225
Mathewson-NY 221
Waddell-Pit-Chi 172

Fewest BB/Game
Orth-Phi 1.02
Phillippe-Pit 1.16
Tannehill-Pit 1.28
Duggleby-Phi 1.30
Powell-StL 1.33

Games
Taylor-NY 45
Powell-StL 45
Donovan-Bro 45
Hahn-Cin 42
Mathewson-NY 40

Saves
Powell-StL 3
Donovan-Bro 3
Sudhoff-StL 2
Phillippe-Pit 2
Kitson-Bro 2

Base Runners/9
Orth-Phi 9.27
Phillippe-Pit 9.79
Tannehill-Pit 10.20
Chesbro-Pit 10.23
Willis-Bos 10.35

Adjusted Relief Runs

Relief Ranking

Innings Pitched
Hahn-Cin 375.1
Taylor-NY 353.1
Donovan-Bro 351.0
Powell-StL 338.1
Mathewson-NY 336.0

Opponents' Avg.
Townsend-Phi 223
Mathewson-NY.......230
Willis-Bos 231
Orth-Phi 237
Chesbro-Pit 241

Opponents' OBP
Orth-Phi 264
Phillippe-Pit 275
Tannehill-Pit 284
Chesbro-Pit 284
Willis-Bos 286

Earned Run Average
Tannehill-Pit 2.18
Phillippe-Pit 2.22
Orth-Phi 2.27
Willis-Bos 2.36
Chesbro-Pit 2.38

Adjusted ERA
Willis-Bos 153
Tannehill-Pit............150
Orth-Phi 150
Phillippe-Pit 147
Chesbro-Pit 137

Adjusted Starter Runs
Willis-Bos 38.5
Orth-Phi 33.1
Phillippe-Pit 33.0
Mathewson-NY 32.4
Chesbro-Pit 32.1

Pitcher Wins
Orth-Phi 4.4
Willis-Bos 4.2
Phillippe-Pit 4.1
Mathewson-NY 3.6
Tannehill-Pit 3.3

Impressive Instant

Declaring itself a major league, and announcing the fact by recruiting top stars from NL clubs, the American League—formerly a minor league known as the Western League—broke in with a bang. The Philadelphia Athletics lured second baseman Nap Lajoie from the crosstown NL club and were rewarded when Lajoie won the AL's Triple Crown, taking the batting title by nearly 100 points. Others, including the Baltimore Orioles and their hard-boiled player-manager John McGraw, weren't happy with the high salaries paid by the Athletics.

Lajoie alone couldn't carry his team to victory; the Athletics came in fourth. Boston's Cy Young was the league's top pitcher, finishing with an ERA 0.80 lower than his nearest rival, but Boston's fellow moundsmen weren't worthy. The Red Sox finished second behind the White Sox, who had the league's best offense. Chicago's hitters led the league in walks and steals; 39-year-old Dummy Hoy paced the AL with 86 bases on balls and tallied a third-best 113 runs.

The prowess of Hoy, the overwhelming dominance of Young and Lajoie, and other factors reveal that the American League was a bit behind the talent curve in 1901. Runs per game were at 5.35, the loop's highest total until 1930, and fielding average was just .938, a figure that the NL had passed back in 1897. In 1902, however, the talent began to even out as stubborn and penurious NL owners failed to match the salaries offered by their new rivals. The Junior Circuit could soon call itself a peer—maybe even superior.

Several youngsters made their first major league appearances in 1901 due to the AL's need for players. Future Tigers outfielders Davy Jones and Matty McIntyre debuted at age 21, while lefty Eddie Plank finally got a chance to shine with Philadelphia, going 17-13 as a 26-year-old rookie. He would win 309 more games in the majors before retiring, all but 42 with Philadelphia.

1901 American League

TEAM	W	L	T	PCT	GB	HW	HL	R	OR	PA	H	2B	3B	HR	BB	SO	HB	SH	AVG	OBP	SLG	OPS	AOPS	BR	ABR	PF	SB	CS	BSA	BSR
CHI	83	53	1	.610		49	21	819	631	5397	1303	173	89	32	475	337	62	135	.276	.350	.370	720	108	42	64	97	280			
BOS	79	57	2	.581	4	49	20	759	608	5349	1353	183	104	37	331	282	47	105	.278	.330	.381	711	104	6	20	98	157			
DET	74	61	1	.548	8.5	42	27	741	694	5245	1303	180	80	29	380	346	54	135	.279	.340	.370	710	98	16	-16	105	204			
PHI	74	62	1	.544	9	42	24	805	760	5320	1409	239	87	35	301	344	52	85	.289	.337	.395	732	103	45	12	104	173			
BAL	68	65	2	.511	13.5	40	25	760	750	5111	1348	179	111	24	369	377	52	101	.294	.353	.397	750	108	79	46	104	207			
WAS	61	72	5	.459	20.5	31	35	682	771	5259	1282	191	83	33	356	340	51	80	.269	.326	.364	690	97	-24	-13	99	127			
CLE	54	82	2	.397	29	28	39	666	831	5200	1311	197	68	12	243	326	48	76	.271	.313	.348	661	92	-83	-56	96	125			
MIL	48	89	2	.350	35.5	32	37	641	828	5288	1250	192	66	26	325	384	46	122	.261	.314	.345	659	91	-81	-47	95	176			
TOT	549					313	228	5873		42169	10559	1534	688	228	2780	2736	412	839	.277	.333	.371	704					1449			

TEAM	CG	SHO	GR	SV	IP	H	HR	BB	SO	BR/9	ERA	AERA	OAV	OOB	PR	APR	PF	OSB	OCS	FA	E	WPB	DP	FW	PW	BW	BSW	DIF
CHI	110	11	28	2	1218.1	1250	27	312	394	11.9	2.98	117	.263	.315	93	71	95	153	135	.941	345	55	100	.9	6.4	5.8		1.9
BOS	123	7	15	1	1217.0	1178	33	294	396	11.2	3.04	116	.251	.301	84	68	96	173	157	.943	337	35	104	1.6	6.1	1.8		1.5
DET	118	8	20	2	1188.2	1328	22	313	307	12.8	3.30	116	.280	.330	48	68	105	153	141	.930	410	38	127	-3.3	6.1	-1.4		5.1
PHI	124	6	14	1	1200.2	1346	20	374	350	13.3	4.00	94	.280	.339	-45	-31	103	187	148	.942	337	63	93	1.4	-2.8	1.1		6.3
BAL	115	4	21	3	1158.0	1313	21	344	271	13.3	3.73	104	.282	.338	-9	16	106	167	112	.926	401	49	76	-2.9	1.4	4.2		-1.2
WAS	118	8	20	2	1183.0	1396	43	308	308	13.3	4.00	89	.291	.339	-57	-58	100	170	134	.943	323	28	97	2.4	-5.2	-1.2		-1.5
CLE	122	7	19	4	1182.1	1365	22	464	334	14.5	4.12	86	.286	.358	-60	-78	97	199	152	.942	329	77	99	2.1	-7.0	-5.1		-4.0
MIL	107	3	34	3	1218.0	1383	32	395	376	13.6	4.06	89	.283	.344	-53	-65	98	247	171	.934	393	64	106	-1.8	-5.9	-4.2		-8.6
TOT	937	54	171	18	9566.0					13.0	3.66		.277	.333						.938	2875	409	802					

Batter-Fielder Wins		Batting Average		On-Base Percentage		Slugging Average		On-Base Plus Slugging		Adjusted OPS		Adjusted Batter Runs	
Lajoie-Phi	8.1	Lajoie-Phi	426	Lajoie-Phi	463	Lajoie-Phi	643	Lajoie-Phi	1106	Lajoie-Phi	196	Lajoie-Phi	69.2
Collins-Bos	4.2	Donlin-Bal	340	Jones-Chi	412	Freeman-Bos	520	Freeman-Bos	920	Freeman-Bos	157	Freeman-Bos	37.0
Elberfeld-Det	3.5	Freeman-Bos	339	Donlin-Bal	409	Seybold-Phi	503	Seybold-Phi	901	Seybold-Phi	142	Collins-Bos	31.2
Freeman-Bos	2.7	Seybold-Phi	334	Hoy-Chi	407	Williams-Bal	495	Donlin-Bal	883	Collins-Bos	142	McGraw-Bal	29.1
Anderson-Mil	2.5	Collins-Bos	332	Freeman-Bos	400	Collins-Bos	495	Williams-Bal	883	Donlin-Bal	138	Anderson-Mil	28.0

Runs		Hits		Doubles		Triples		Home Runs		Total Bases		Runs Batted In	
Lajoie-Phi	145	Lajoie-Phi	232	Lajoie-Phi	48	Williams-Bal	21	Lajoie-Phi	14	Lajoie-Phi	350	Lajoie-Phi	125
Jones-Chi	120	Anderson-Mil	190	Anderson-Mil	46	Keister-Bal	21	Freeman-Bos	12	Collins-Bos	279	Freeman-Bos	114
Williams-Bal	113	Collins-Bos	187	Collins-Bos	42	Mertes-Chi	17	Grady-Was	9	Anderson-Mil	274	Anderson-Mil	99
Hoy-Chi	112	Waldron-Mil-Was	186	Farrell-Was	32	Stahl-Bos	16			Freeman-Bos	255	Mertes-Chi	98
Barrett-Det	110	Dungan-Was	179			Collins-Bos	16			Williams-Bal	248	Williams-Bal	96

Stolen Bases		Base Stealing Runs		Fielding Runs-Infield		Fielding Runs-Outfield		Wins		Winning Pct.		Complete Games	
Isbell-Chi	52			Clingman-Was	22.1	Seymour-Bal	13.9	Young-Bos	33	Griffith-Chi	774	McGinnity-Bal	39
Mertes-Chi	46			Lajoie-Phi	22.0	Pickering-Cle	12.5	McGinnity-Bal	26	Young-Bos	767	Young-Bos	38
Seymour-Bal	38			Elberfeld-Det	19.4	Barrett-Det	11.4	Griffith-Chi	24	Callahan-Chi	652	Miller-Det	35
Jones-Chi	38			Conroy-Mil	16.9	Donlin-Bal	6.9	Miller-Det	23	Patten-Was	643	Fraser-Phi	35
				Collins-Bos	12.8	Farrell-Was	5.6	Fraser-Phi	22	Miller-Det	639	Carrick-Was	34

Strikeouts		Fewest BB/Game		Games		Saves		Base Runners/9		Adjusted Relief Runs		Relief Ranking	
Young-Bos	158	Young-Bos	.90	McGinnity-Bal	48	Hoffer-Cle	3	Young-Bos	8.92				
Patterson-Chi	127	Gear-Was	1.21	Dowling-Mil-Cle	43			Callahan-Chi	10.62				
Dowling-Mil-Cle	124	Lee-Was	1.55	Young-Bos	43			Griffith-Chi	11.10				
Garvin-Mil	122	Griffith-Chi	1.69	Carrick-Was	42			Lewis-Bos	11.32				
Fraser-Phi	110	Cronin-Det	1.72	Patterson-Chi	41			Winter-Bos	11.35				

Innings Pitched		Opponents' Avg.		Opponents' OBP		Earned Run Average		Adjusted ERA		Adjusted Starter Runs		Pitcher Wins	
McGinnity-Bal	382.0	Young-Bos	232	Young-Bos	256	Young-Bos	1.62	Young-Bos	217	Young-Bos	77.0	Young-Bos	7.9
Young-Bos	371.1	Callahan-Chi	239	Callahan-Chi	290	Callahan-Chi	2.42	Yeager-Det	147	Miller-Det	32.9	Griffith-Chi	4.2
Miller-Det	332.0	Moore-Cle	244	Griffith-Chi	300	Yeager-Det	2.61	Callahan-Chi	143	Griffith-Chi	28.6	Callahan-Chi	3.7
Fraser-Phi	331.0	Lewis-Bos	247	Lewis-Bos	304	Griffith-Chi	2.67	Griffith-Chi	130	Callahan-Chi	25.5	Miller-Det	3.3
Carrick-Was	324.0	Winter-Bos	252	Winter-Bos	304	Winter-Bos	2.80	Miller-Det	130	Yeager-Det	22.2	Yeager-Det	2.9

Contraction Leads to Competition as Scoring Drops

While the upstart AL's player raids damaged the Senior Circuit, the eight NL franchises were stable and remained in place until 1953. Their ballparks were not so durable. In-season fires damaged Cincinnati's League Park and St. Louis' Robison Field. Robison was repaired, but the Reds built a new ballpark—The Palace of the Fans—in the same location for 1902.

Contenders Brooklyn and Philadelphia were severely affected by the raiding: the Phillies lost Nap Lajoie, while Brooklyn did without Joe McGinnity and Lave Cross. Pittsburgh, though, came out relatively unscathed and passed New York in mid-June, cruising to the league crown. The Bucs had excellent pitching and a multidimensional offense. Future superstar Honus Wagner spent the year as a utility player yet still led the league in RBIs. In 1902, he'd take over fulltime at shortstop.

Two active players died in 1901. Tom O'Brien, Pittsburgh's first baseman in 1900, died February 4 from intestinal problems first suffered on a baseball trip to Cuba. Brooklyn pitcher Doc McJames, who lost the 1900 season to malaria, was 5-6 in 1901. Sent to South Carolina for rest, he fell from a moving carriage and died.

Two nineteenth century immortals ended their careers. "Sliding" Billy Hamilton, the previous century's top leadoff hitter, paced the NL four times in runs. Amos Rusie, a five-time strikeout champ who won 246 games from 1889–98, was traded at the end of 1900 to Cincinnati for young Christy Mathewson. Rusie's wing, however, was gone. During the season, two outstanding defensive catchers debuted. Pat Moran would later win a World Series as a manager, while Bill Bergen hit just .170 in his 947 big-league games.

NL teams scored only 4.63 runs per game, down more than 12 percent due to adoption of a rule counting foul balls as strikes. The league hit its most homers until 1911, with Sam Crawford's 16 the highest individual total for more than a decade.

1900 National League

TEAM	W	L	T	PCT	GB	HW	HL	R	OR	PA	H	2B	3B	HR	BB	SO	HB	SH	AVG	OBP	SLG	OPS	AOPS	BR	ABR	PF	SB	CS	BSA	BSR
BRO	82	54	6	.603	—	43	26	**816**	722	5440	1423	199	81	26	421	272	81	78	**.293**	**.359**	**.383**	**742**	104	**75**	29	106	**274**			
PIT	79	60	1	.568	4.5	42	28	733	**612**	5317	1312	185	**100**	26	327	321	63	110	.272	.327	.368	695	96	-27	-32	101	174			
PHI	75	63	3	.543	8	**45**	23	810	792	5594	**1439**	187	82	29	**440**	374	72	113	.290	.356	.378	734	**.109**	60	**67**	99	205			
BOS	66	72	4	.478	17	42	29	778	739	5499	1403	163	68	**48**	395	278	45	107	.283	.342	.373	715	92	15	-69	112	182			
STL	65	75	2	.464	19	40	31	744	748	5444	1420	141	81	36	406	318	**81**	80	.291	.356	.375	731	108	50	56	99	243			
CHI	65	75	2	.464	19	**45**	30	635	751	5445	1276	**202**	51	33	342	383	65	**130**	.260	.317	.342	659	90	-85	-60	96	189			
CIN	62	77	5	.446	21.5	27	34	703	745	5517	1335	178	83	33	333	408	50	108	.266	.318	.354	672	92	-73	-56	98	183			
NY	60	78	3	.435	23	38	31	713	823	5229	1317	177	61	23	369	343	56	80	.279	.338	.357	695	102	-15	19	95	236			
TOT	569					322	232	5932		43485	10925	1432	607	254	3034	2697	513	806	.279	.339	.366	705					1686			

TEAM	CG	SHO	GR	SV	IP	H	HR	BB	SO	BR/9	ERA	AERA	OAV	OOB	PR	APR	PF	OSB	OCS	FA	E	WPB	DP	FW	PW	BW	BSW	DIF
BRO	104	8	**40**	**4**	1225.2	1370	30	405	300	13.6	3.89	98	.282	.346	-27	-9	104	213	**156**	.948	303	**51**	102	2.6	-.8	2.7		9.6
PIT	114	11	30	1	1229.0	**1232**	24	**295**	415	**11.7**	**3.06**	119	**.261**	.313	**87**	**79**	98	166	151	.945	322	71	106	1.1	**7.2**	-2.9		4.1
PHI	116	7	28	3	1248.2	1506	29	402	284	14.2	4.12	88	.298	.357	-59	-73	98	272	**185**	.945	330	80	**125**	.8	-6.7	**6.1**		5.8
BOS	116	8	29	2	1240.1	1263	46	459	340	12.9	3.72	111	.264	.335	-4	49	112	213	165	**.953**	**273**	85	86	**4.4**	4.5	-6.3		-5.6
STL	117	**12**	26	0	1217.1	1373	37	299	325	12.7	3.75	97	.284	.331	-7	-17	98	216	167	.943	331	55	73	.8	-1.6	5.1		-9.4
CHI	**137**	9	9	1	1271.0	1375	**21**	324	357	12.6	3.23	112	.276	.330	66	53	98	234	**172**	.933	418	63	98	-3.9	4.8	-5.5		-.4
CIN	118	9	28	1	1274.2	1383	28	404	399	13.0	3.83	96	.276	.338	-20	-24	99	190	177	.945	341	77	120	.5	-2.2	-5.1		-.7
NY	113	4	31	0	1207.1	1423	26	442	277	14.6	3.96	91	.293	.363	-35	-49	98	182	177	.928	439	69	124	-6.0	-4.5	1.7		-.3
TOT	935	68	221	12	9914.0					13.2	3.69		.279	.339			98			.942	2757	551	834					

Batter-Fielder Wins
- Flick-Phi 4.5
- Lajoie-Phi 4.4
- Davis-NY 4.3
- Wagner-Pit 4.1
- Selbach-NY 3.7

Batting Average
- Wagner-Pit 381
- Flick-Phi 367
- Burkett-StL 363
- Keeler-Bro 362
- McGraw-StL 344

On-Base Percentage
- McGraw-StL 505
- Thomas-Phi 451
- Hamilton-Bos 449
- Flick-Phi 441
- Wagner-Pit 434

Slugging Average
- Wagner-Pit 573
- Flick-Phi 545
- Lajoie-Phi 510
- Kelley-Bro 485
- Hickman-NY 482

On-Base Plus Slugging
- Wagner-Pit 1007
- Flick-Phi 986
- McGraw-StL 921
- Burkett-StL 904
- Selbach-NY 885

Adjusted OPS
- Wagner-Pit 175
- Flick-Phi 172
- McGraw-StL 157
- Selbach-NY 151
- Burkett-StL 150

Adjusted Batter Runs
- Flick-Phi 55.6
- Wagner-Pit 53.3
- Selbach-NY 41.1
- Burkett-StL 39.3
- McGraw-StL 38.4

Runs
- Thomas-Phi 132
- Slagle-Phi 115
- VanHaltren-NY 114
- Barrett-Cin 114
- Wagner-Pit 107

Hits
- Keeler-Bro 204
- Burkett-StL 203
- Wagner-Pit 201
- Flick-Phi 200
- Beckley-Cin 190

Doubles
- Wagner-Pit 45
- Lajoie-Phi 33
- Flick-Phi 32
- Delahanty-Phi 32
- VanHaltren-NY 30

Triples
- Wagner-Pit 22
- Kelley-Bro 17
- Hickman-NY 17
- Stahl-Bos 16
- Flick-Phi 16

Home Runs
- Long-Bos 12
- Flick-Phi 11
- Donlin-StL 10
- Hickman-NY 9
- Sullivan-Bos 8

Total Bases
- Wagner-Pit 302
- Flick-Phi 297
- Burkett-StL 265
- Keeler-Bro 253
- Beckley-Cin 242

Runs Batted In
- Flick-Phi 110
- Delahanty-Phi 109
- Wagner-Pit 100
- Collins-StL 95
- Beckley-Cin 94

Stolen Bases
- VanHaltren-NY 45
- Donovan-StL 45
- Barrett-Cin 44
- Keeler-Bro 41

Base Stealing Runs

Fielding Runs-Infield
- Davis-NY 28.7
- Lajoie-Phi 22.4
- Dahlen-Bro 21.2
- Steinfeldt-Cin 16.1
- Childs-Chi 14.5

Fielding Runs-Outfield
- Selbach-NY 12.4
- VanHaltren-NY 8.5
- Keeler-Bro 5.7
- Burkett-StL 5.6
- Stahl-Bos 4.5

Wins
- McGinnity-Bro 28
- Tannehill-Pit 20
- Phillippe-Pit 20
- Kennedy-Bro 20
- Dinneen-Bos 20

Winning Pct.
- McGinnity-Bro 778
- Tannehill-Pit 769
- Fraser-Phi 625
- Phillippe-Pit 606
- Kennedy-Bro 606

Complete Games
- Hawley-NY 34
- Dinneen-Bos 33

Strikeouts
- Hahn-Cin 132
- Waddell-Pit 130
- Young-StL 115
- Garvin-Chi 107
- Dinneen-Bos 107

Fewest BB/Game
- Young-StL 1.01
- Phillippe-Pit 1.35
- Tannehill-Pit 1.65
- Griffith-Chi 1.85
- Leever-Pit 1.86

Games
- Carrick-NY 45
- McGinnity-Bro 44
- Scott-Cin 42
- Kennedy-Bro 42

Saves
- Kitson-Bro 4
- Bernhard-Phi 2

Base Runners/9
- Phillippe-Pit 10.42
- Waddell-Pit 10.52
- Young-StL 10.53
- Garvin-Chi 11.18
- Leever-Pit 11.30

Adjusted Relief Runs

Relief Ranking

Innings Pitched
- McGinnity-Bro 343.0
- Carrick-NY 341.2
- Hawley-NY 329.1
- Young-StL 321.1
- Dinneen-Bos 320.2

Opponents' Avg.
- Waddell-Pit 229
- Garvin-Chi 243
- Nichols-Bos 246
- Dinneen-Bos 250
- Phillippe-Pit 257

Opponents' OBP
- Phillippe-Pit 289
- Waddell-Pit 291
- Young-StL 291
- Garvin-Chi 304
- Leever-Pit 306

Earned Run Average
- Waddell-Pit 2.37
- Garvin-Chi 2.41
- Taylor-Chi 2.55
- Leever-Pit 2.71
- Sudhoff-StL 2.76

Adjusted ERA
- Waddell-Pit 153
- Garvin-Chi 149
- Taylor-Chi 141
- Nichols-Bos 134
- Leever-Pit 134

Adjusted Starter Runs
- Dinneen-Bos 31.8
- Garvin-Chi 28.0
- Young-StL 27.8
- Phillippe-Pit 25.7
- Leever-Pit 24.8

Pitcher Wins
- Dinneen-Bos 3.1
- Tannehill-Pit 2.7
- Young-StL 2.6
- Leever-Pit 2.5
- Garvin-Chi 2.4

The Last One-Horse Town

In January 1900 Boston Beaneaters catcher Marty Bergen, injured the previous season and possibly despondent over finances, killed himself and his entire family. The horrific crime was the beginning of the end of a once-great Boston franchise.

The new century saw a streamlined, eight-club NL, free of syndicate ownership and with no team finishing more than 23 games out of first place. The rules committee changed home plate from a 12-inch square to a five-sided shape 17 inches wide, largely for the benefit of umpires.

Brooklyn, now named the Superbas, won the flag again, leading the league in scoring and benefiting from the strong arm of former Oriole "Iron Man" Joe McGinnity, who led the league in wins, but also in walks and hit batsmen (40, the most ever). Second-place Pittsburgh, fortified with stars Honus Wagner, who won his first bat crown, Deacon Phillippe, Rube Waddell, and Fred Clarke from Louisville, made it a close race and positioned themselves as an up-and-coming club.

In the last postseason series between NL clubs until 1969, the Superbas took on the Pirates. Like the Temple Cup this trophy originated in Pittsburgh, and it was even less popular than the first try earlier in the decade. Brooklyn won three of four games from the Pirates for the *Chronicle-Telegraph* Cup. Only one crowd of more than 2,500 came out to see the series.

St. Louis, having changed its name to the Cardinals, purchased John McGraw and Wilbert Robinson, who again refused the call to join Brooklyn after the Orioles disbanded. McGraw once more led the league in on-base percentage, but the Cards ended tied for fifth. A young pitcher with last-place New York went 0-3, but this was just the start for Christy Mathewson.

It was also the beginning of the American League, formerly the minor Western League. President Ban Johnson declared the AL a major for 1900 and fielded eight clubs, one in Chicago and seven in former National League or American Association cities. The new loop counted George Stallings, Connie Mack, and Charlie Comiskey among its skippers, and would soon enter into a fierce battle for talent with the NL—and help save baseball in the process.

1899 National League

TEAM	W	L	T	PCT	GB	HW	HL	R	OR	PA	H	2B	3B	HR	BB	SO	HB	SH	AVG	OBP	SLG	OPS	AOPS	BR	ABR	PF	SB	CS	BSA	BSF
BRO	100	47	3	.680		60	16	892	658	5614	1436	178	97	27	477	263	125	75	.291	.368	.383	751	110	89	70	102	271			
BOS	95	57	1	.625	7.5	53	26	858	645	5897	1517	178	90	39	431	269	43	133	.287	.345	.377	722	94	20	-53	110	185			
PHI	94	58	2	.618	8.5	58	25	916	743	5986	1613	241	83	31	441	341	75	117	.301	.363	.395	758	118	100	134	97	212			
BAL	86	62	4	.581	14.5	51	24	827	691	5707	1509	204	71	17	418	383	122	94	.297	.365	.376	741	104	73	30	105	364			
STL	84	67	4	.556	18	50	33	819	739	5913	1514	172	88	47	468	262	33	108	.285	.347	.378	725	102	27	8	102	210			
CIN	83	67	7	.553	18.5	57	29	861	777	5946	1448	195	106	13	487	300	67	133	.275	.344	.360	704	96	-5	-19	102	228			
PIT	76	73	6	.510	25	49	34	841	771	6079	1582	196	121	29	386	346	63	144	.288	.342	.384	726	104	22	25	100	179			
CHI	75	73	4	.507	25.5	44	39	812	763	5766	1428	173	82	27	406	342	64	148	.277	.338	.359	697	99	-26	-5	97	247			
LOU	75	76	5	.497	27	33	28	833	782	6014	1491	195	70	40	437	379	78	163	.279	.343	.365	708	100	-1	1	100	234			
NY	60	90	3	.400	41.5	35	38	741	868	5621	1441	165	66	23	389	361	46	61	.281	.337	.353	690	98	-38	-11	97	235			
WAS	54	98	3	.355	48.5	35	43	743	983	5783	1429	162	87	47	350	341	87	90	.272	.328	.363	691	96	-48	-40	99	176			
CLE	20	134	0	.130	83.5	9	33	529	1252	5690	1333	142	50	12	289	280	65	57	.253	.299	.305	604	76	-213	-168	93	127			
TOT	923					534	368	9672		70016	17741	2201	1011	352	4979	3867	868	1323	.282	.343	.366	710					2668			

TEAM	CG	SHO	GR	SV	IP	H	HR	BB	SO	BR/9	ERA	AERA	OAV	OOB	PR	APR	PF	OSB	OCS	FA	E	WPB	DP	FW	PW	BW	BSW	DI
BRO	121	9	30	9	1269.1	1320	32	463	331	13.0	3.25	120	.268	.337	85	91	102	229	178	.948	314	52	125	2.9	8.2	6.3		9.0
BOS	138	13	17	4	1348.0	1273	44	432	385	11.8	3.26	127	.250	.317	87	123	108	193	169	.952	303	58	124	4.0	11.1	-4.8		8.7
PHI	129	15	26	2	1333.1	1398	17	370	281	12.5	3.47	106	.270	.329	56	31	96	206	178	.940	379	85	110	-.3	2.8	12.1		-2.4
BAL	132	9	20	5	1304.1	1403	13	349	294	12.6	3.31	119	.275	.330	78	90	103	176	127	.949	308	59	96	3.6	8.2	2.7		1.6
STL	134	7	23	1	1340.2	1476	41	321	331	12.4	3.36	118	.280	.328	73	88	103	180	173	.939	397	48	117	-1.2	8.0	.7		4.7
CIN	131	8	28	5	1373.0	1494	26	372	361	12.7	3.70	106	.278	.334	23	30	102	177	161	.947	341	43	113	2.3	2.7	-1.7		4.7
PIT	118	9	39	0	1373.0	1471	27	438	338	13.0	3.61	105	.274	.337	36	30	99	195	185	.945	363	53	100	.8	2.7	2.3		-4.
CHI	147	8	5	1	1331.1	1433	20	330	313	12.5	3.37	111	.275	.328	71	56	97	206	171	.935	428	33	145	-3.5	5.1	-.5		-.2
LOU	135	5	22	2	1360.1	1517	35	325	288	12.6	3.43	112	.282	.331	63	62	100	177	171	.939	399	30	103	-1.2	5.6	.0		-5.0
NY	139	4	14	0	1290.2	1463	19	630	402	15.3	4.27	88	.286	.375	-61	-80	97	249	192	.932	434	97	142	-3.7	-7.3	-1.0		-3.
WAS	131	3	28	0	1300.1	1649	35	422	328	14.9	4.93	79	.309	.368	-157	-147	102	288	197	.935	403	60	99	-1.6	-13.3	-3.6		-3.8
CLE	138	0	18	0	1264.0	1844	43	527	215	17.7	6.37	58	.340	.409	-354	-396	96	372	218	.937	388	66	121	-.8	-35.9	-15.2		-5.
TOT	1593	90	270	33	15888.1					13.4	3.85		.282	.343						.942	4457	684	1395					

Batter-Fielder Wins
- G.Davis-NY 6.1
- Delahanty-Phi 5.9
- McGraw-Bal 4.9
- Williams-Pit 4.7
- Wallace-StL 4.4

Batting Average
- Delahanty-Phi .... .410
- Burkett-StL .... .396
- McGraw-Bal .... .391
- Keeler-Bro .... .379
- Williams-Pit .... .354

On-Base Percentage
- McGraw-Bal .... .547
- Delahanty-Phi .... .464
- Burkett-StL .... .463
- Thomas-Phi .... .457
- Stahl-Bos .... .426

Slugging Average
- Delahanty-Phi .... .547
- Freeman-Was .... .563
- Williams-Pit .... .530
- Wagner-Lou .... .501
- Burkett-StL .... .500

On-Base Plus Slugging
- Delahanty-Phi 1046
- McGraw-Bal .... .994
- Burkett-StL .... .963
- Williams-Pit .... .946
- Freeman-Was .... .925

Adjusted OPS
- Delahanty-Phi 193
- McGraw-Bal 165
- Burkett-StL 160
- Williams-Pit 159
- Freeman-Was 154

Adjusted Batter Runs
- Delahanty-Phi .... 76.
- McGraw-Bal .... 52.
- Burkett-StL .... 49.
- Williams-Pit .... 48.
- Thomas-Phi .... 36.

Runs
- McGraw-Bal 140
- Keeler-Bro 140
- Thomas-Phi 137
- Delahanty-Phi 135
- Williams-Pit 126

Hits
- Delahanty-Phi 238
- Burkett-StL 221
- Williams-Pit 220
- Keeler-Bro 216
- Tenney-Bos 209

Doubles
- Delahanty-Phi 55
- Wagner-Lou 45
- Holmes-Bal 31
- Long-Bos 30
- Duffy-Bos 29

Triples
- Williams-Pit 27
- Freeman-Was 25
- Stahl-Bos 19
- Tenney-Bos 17
- McCarthy-Pit 17

Home Runs
- Freeman-Was 25
- Wallace-StL 12
- Williams-Pit 9
- Mertes-Chi 9
- Delahanty-Phi 9

Total Bases
- Delahanty-Phi 338
- Freeman-Was 331
- Williams-Pit 329
- Wagner-Lou 288
- Stahl-Bos 284

Runs Batted In
- Delahanty-Phi 13
- Freeman-Was 12
- Williams-Pit 11
- Wagner-Lou 10
- Wallace-StL 10

Stolen Bases
- Sheckard-Bal 77
- McGraw-Bal 73
- Heidrick-StL 55
- Holmes-Bal 50
- Clarke-Lou 49

Base Stealing Runs

Fielding Runs-Infield
- G.Davis-NY 46.3
- Cross-Cle-StL 35.6
- Wallace-StL 30.3
- Gleason-NY 28.6
- Collins-Bos 17.8

Fielding Runs-Outfield
- Sheckard-Bal 19.4
- Slagle-Was 18.2
- Selbach-Cin 10.9
- Kelley-Bro 9.8
- Lange-Chi 8.5

Wins
- McGinnity-Bal 28
- Hughes-Bro 28
- Willis-Bos 27
- Young-StL 26
- Tannehill-Pit 24

Winning Pct.
- Hughes-Bro .... .824
- Willis-Bos .... .771
- Hahn-Cin .... .742
- Donahue-Phi .... .724
- Kennedy-Bro .... .710

Complete Games
- Young-StL 4
- Powell-StL 4
- Carrick-NY 4
- Taylor-Chi 3
- McGinnity-Bal 3

Strikeouts
- Hahn-Cin 145
- Seymour-NY 142
- Leever-Pit 121
- Willis-Bos 120
- Doheny-NY 120

Fewest BB/Game
- Young-StL 1.07
- Cuppy-StL 1.36
- Tannehill-Pit 1.45
- Woods-Lou 1.79
- Kitson-Bal 1.79

Games
- Leever-Pit 51
- Powell-StL 48
- McGinnity-Bal 48
- Young-StL 44
- Carrick-NY 44

Saves
- Leever-Pit 3

Base Runners/9
- Young-StL 10.19
- Waddell-Lou 10.37
- Hahn-Cin 10.43
- Orth-Phi 10.64
- Nichols-Bos 10.85

Adjusted Relief Runs

Relief Ranking

Innings Pitched
- Leever-Pit 379.0
- Powell-StL 373.0
- Young-StL 369.1
- McGinnity-Bal 366.1
- Carrick-NY 361.2

Opponents' Avg.
- Willis-Bos .... .222
- Hughes-Bro .... .232
- Hahn-Cin .... .242
- Seymour-NY .... .245
- Leever-Pit .... .247

Opponents' OBP
- Young-StL .... .285
- Hahn-Cin .... .290
- Nichols-Bos .... .298
- Kitson-Bal .... .303
- Willis-Bos .... .304

Earned Run Average
- Orth-Phi 2.49
- Willis-Bos 2.50
- Young-StL 2.58
- Bernhard-Phi 2.65
- McGinnity-Bal 2.68

Adjusted ERA
- Willis-Bos 166
- Young-StL 154
- McGinnity-Bal 148
- Hahn-Cin 146
- Hughes-Bro 145

Adjusted Starter Runs
- Willis-Bos 58.2
- Young-StL 49.9
- McGinnity-Bal 48.2
- Kitson-Bal 41.9
- Hahn-Cin 41.1

Pitcher Wins
- Young-StL .... 5.
- Willis-Bos 4
- Hughes-Bro 4
- McGinnity-Bal 4
- Tannehill-Pit 4

Syndicate Bosses

It was a year destroyed by syndicate ownership. The Robison brothers, detested owners of the Cleveland Spiders, decided to also buy the St. Louis Browns, and siphoned off Cleveland players to contribute to the Browns' effort. Public anger at this sham forced the Spiders, already a traveling team for much of 1898, back to the road. The horrible club finished 84 games out and lost 134 times, both all-time lows. The 6,088 who paid to see the club in Cleveland (the average crowd was 145), was the smallest turnstile count in NL history. It was only right that the Browns finished fifth, although they were second in attendance.

Baltimore suffered through a similar debacle. Orioles stars Ned Hanlon, Willie Keeler, Hughie Jennings, and Joe Kelley were transferred to Brooklyn. John McGraw, however, stayed behind, and took over as player-manager. Wilbert Robinson, who happened to be Mugsy's partner in a Baltimore billiard parlor and bowling alley, also stayed put and batted .284 as the club's regular catcher. McGraw posted a .547 on-base percentage—the highest in the majors until 1941—for his beloved Orioles, who played surprisingly well.

The Bridegrooms used their mother lode to win the crown. Keeler tied for the league lead (with McGraw) in runs, and pitcher Jim Hughes paced in wins. It was a team effort—Hanlon's club had few weaknesses. Boston finished second as Vic Willis became arguably the league's top starter, and Ed Delahanty's bat crown and 55 doubles (the most until 1923) powered the third-place Phillies.

To eliminate unnecessary trickery, catchers were required to stay in their box when pitches were delivered. And from this point on all players' uniforms on the same team had to conform. Several big names debuted, including Joe McGinnity, Deacon Phillippe, Jack Chesbro, Turkey Mike Donlin, and Sam Crawford.

Realizing the inevitable—that twelve teams made no sense economically or otherwise—the NL contracted Louisville (owned by Barney Dreyfus, who also controlled Pittsburgh), Washington, Baltimore, and Cleveland for 1900. Such wisdom came too late, especially for the Spiders and their remaining fans. National League owners would reap the fruits of their poor stewardship of the game about a year later.

1898 National League

TEAM	W	L	T	PCT	GB	HW	HL	R	OR	PA	H	2B	3B	HR	BB	SO	HB	SH	AVG	OBP	SLG	OPS	AOPS	BR	ABR	PF	SB	CS	BSA	BSR
BOS	102	47	3	.685		62	15	872	614	5847	1531	190	55	53	405	303	32	134	.290	.344	.377	721	106	73	31	105	172			
BAL	96	53	5	.644	6	58	15	933	623	6000	1584	154	77	12	519	316	160	79	.302	.382	.368	750	118	160	143	102	250			
CIN	92	60	5	.605	11.5	58	28	831	740	5984	1448	207	101	19	455	300	59	136	.271	.335	.359	694	105	24	-28	107	165			
CHI	85	65	2	.567	17.5	58	31	828	679	5879	1431	175	84	18	476	394	71	113	.274	.343	.350	693	104	29	31	100	220			
CLE	81	68	7	.544	21	36	19	730	683	5962	1379	162	56	18	545	306	46	125	.263	.338	.325	663	96	-21	-10	99	93			
PHI	78	71	1	.523	24	49	31	823	784	5779	1431	238	81	33	472	382	69	120	.280	.348	.377	725	118	89	127	96	182			
NY	77	73	7	.513	25.5	45	28	837	800	5907	1422	190	86	34	428	372	69	61	.266	.328	.353	681	103	-5	20	97	214			
PIT	72	76	4	.486	29.5	39	35	634	694	5638	1313	140	88	14	336	343	74	141	.258	.313	.328	641	90	-83	-70	98	107			
LOU	70	81	3	.464	33	43	34	728	833	5775	1389	150	71	32	375	429	66	141	.267	.325	.342	667	97	-33	-22	99	235			
BRO	54	91	4	.372	46	30	41	638	811	5610	1314	156	66	17	328	314	65	91	.256	.309	.322	631	85	-101	-98	100	130			
WAS	51	101	3	.336	52.5	34	44	704	939	5785	1423	177	80	36	370	386	70	88	.271	.327	.355	682	100	-6	-4	100	197			
STL	39	111	4	.260	63.5	20	44	571	929	5798	1290	149	55	13	383	402	84	117	.247	.309	.305	614	78	-128	-142	102	104			
TOT	921					532	365	9129		69964	16955	2088	900	299	5092	4247	865	1346	.271	.334	.347	681					2069			

TEAM	CG	SHO	GR	SV	IP	H	HR	BB	SO	BR/9	ERA	AERA	OAV	OOB	PR	APR	PF	OSB	OCS	FA	E	WPB	DP	FW	PW	BW	BSW	DIF
BOS	127	9	26	8	1340.0	1186	37	470	432	11.6	2.98	124	.236	.310	93	103	102	149	125	.950	310	87	102	3.1	9.6	2.9		11.9
BAL	138	12	15	0	1323.0	1236	17	400	422	11.5	2.90	123	.246	.310	104	99	99	146	128	.947	326	65	105	2.5	9.3	13.4		-3.6
CIN	131	10	27	2	1385.1	1484	16	449	294	13.0	3.50	109	.272	.336	17	47	106	109	121	.950	325	44	128	2.9	4.4	-2.6		11.3
CHI	137	13	15	0	1342.2	1357	17	364	323	12.1	2.83	126	.261	.319	115	112	99	111	116	.936	412	51	149	-2.9	10.5	2.9		-.5
CLE	142	9	15	0	1334.0	1429	26	309	339	12.1	3.20	113	.272	.320	59	60	100	159	140	.952	301	46	95	4.2	5.6	-.9		-2.4
PHI	129	10	22	0	1288.1	1440	23	399	325	13.4	3.72	92	.281	.342	-17	-45	95	151	136	.937	379	54	102	-1.2	-4.2	11.9		-3.0
NY	141	9	15	1	1353.2	1359	21	587	558	13.5	3.44	101	.260	.344	25	5	96	188	156	.932	447	119	113	-4.2	.5	1.9		3.9
PIT	131	10	22	3	1323.2	1400	14	346	330	12.3	3.41	104	.270	.323	29	22	99	170	139	.946	340	42	105	1.4	2.1	-6.5		1.1
LOU	137	4	19	0	1334.0	1457	33	470	271	13.6	4.24	84	.276	.346	-95	-100	99	205	140	.939	382	54	114	-.8	-9.3	-2.1		6.7
BRO	134	1	17	0	1298.2	1446	34	476	294	13.7	4.01	89	.280	.348	-59	-64	99	184	140	.947	334	56	125	1.3	-6.0	-9.2		-4.6
WAS	129	0	27	1	1307.0	1577	29	450	371	14.5	4.52	81	.297	.360	-134	-125	102	256	161	.929	443	56	119	-4.2	-11.7	-.4		-8.7
STL	133	0	26	2	1324.1	1584	32	372	288	13.9	4.53	83	.295	.350	-137	-106	105	241	158	.939	388	56	97	-1.2	-9.9	-13.3		-11.6
TOT	1609	87	246	17	15954.2					12.9	3.60		.271	.334						.942	4387	730	1354					

Batter-Fielder Wins		Batting Average		On-Base Percentage		Slugging Average		On-Base Plus Slugging		Adjusted OPS		Adjusted Batter Runs	
Jennings-Bal	4.9	Keeler-Bal	385	Hamilton-Bos	480	Anderson-Br-Ws-Br	494	Hamilton-Bos	933	Hamilton-Bos	159	Delahanty-Phi	47.8
Dahlen-Chi	4.3	Hamilton-Bos	369	McGraw-Bal	475	Collins-Bos	479	Delahanty-Phi	880	Delahanty-Phi	159	McGraw-Bal	43.7
Davis-NY	4.0	McGraw-Bal	342	Jennings-Bal	454	Lajoie-Phi	461	Flick-Phi	878	Flick-Phi	158	Jennings-Bal	43.7
Delahanty-Phi	3.9	Smith-Cin	342	Flick-Phi	430	Delahanty-Phi	454	Jennings-Bal	876	Jennings-Bal	149	Flick-Phi	40.9
Collins-Bos	3.9	Burkett-Cle	341	Delahanty-Phi	426	Hamilton-Bos	453	McGraw-Bal	871	McGraw-Bal	149	Hamilton-Bos	39.2

Runs		Hits		Doubles		Triples		Home Runs		Total Bases		Runs Batted In	
McGraw-Bal	143	Keeler-Bal	216	Lajoie-Phi	43	Anderson-Br-Ws-Br	22	Collins-Bos	15	Collins-Bos	286	Lajoie-Phi	127
Jennings-Bal	135	Burkett-Cle	213	Delahanty-Phi	36	VanHaltren-NY	16	Wagner-Lou	10	Lajoie-Phi	280	Collins-Bos	111
VanHaltren-NY	129	VanHaltren-NY	204	Dahlen-Chi	35	Hoy-Lou	16	Joyce-NY	10	VanHaltren-NY	270	Kelley-Bal	110
Keeler-Bal	126	Lajoie-Phi	197	Collins-Bos	35			Anderson-Br-Ws-Br	9	Anderson-Br-Ws-Br	257	Duffy-Bos	108
Cooley-Phi	123			Anderson-Br-Ws-Br	33			McKean-Cle	9	Cooley-Phi	256	McGann-Bal	106

Stolen Bases		Base Stealing Runs		Fielding Runs-Infield		Fielding Runs-Outfield		Wins		Winning Pct.		Complete Games	
Delahanty-Phi	58			Davis-NY	29.5	Selbach-Was	19.4	Nichols-Bos	31	Lewis-Bos	765	Taylor-StL	42
Hamilton-Bos	54			Cross-StL	20.4	Harley-StL	8.3	Cunningham-Lou	28	Maul-Bal	741	Cunningham-Lou	41
DeMontreville-Bal	49			Dahlen-Chi	20.1	Anderson-Br-Ws-Br	7.4	McJames-Bal	27	Nichols-Bos	721	Young-Cle	40
Dexter-Lou	44			Wallace-Cle	18.3	Delahanty-Phi	7.0	Hawley-Cin	27	Hawley-Cin	711	Nichols-Bos	40
McGraw-Bal	43			Gleason-NY	17.6	F.Clarke-Lou	6.5	Lewis-Bos	26	Griffith-Chi	706	McJames-Bal	40

Strikeouts		Fewest BB/Game		Games		Saves		Base Runners/9		Adjusted Relief Runs		Relief Ranking	
Seymour-NY	239	Young-Cle	.98	Taylor-StL	50	Nichols-Bos	4	Nichols-Bos	9.63				
McJames-Bal	178	Dwyer-Cin	1.58	Nichols-Bos	50	Tannehill-Pit	2	Maul-Bal	9.76				
Willis-Bos	160	Cunningham-Lou	1.62	Young-Cle	46	Lewis-Bos	2	Young-Cle	10.41				
Nichols-Bos	138	Tannehill-Pit	1.74			Hickman-Bos	2	Griffith-Chi	10.75				
Piatt-Phi	121	Griffith-Chi	1.77			Dammann-Cin	2	McJames-Bal	10.88				

Innings Pitched		Opponents' Avg.		Opponents' OBP		Earned Run Average		Adjusted ERA		Adjusted Starter Runs		Pitcher Wins	
Taylor-StL	397.1	Nichols-Bos	221	Nichols-Bos	272	Griffith-Chi	1.88	Griffith-Chi	190	Griffith-Chi	63.3	Nichols-Bos	6.4
Nichols-Bos	388.0	Willis-Bos	229	Maul-Bal	275	Maul-Bal	2.10	Nichols-Bos	173	Nichols-Bos	62.5	Griffith-Chi	5.9
Young-Cle	377.2	Lewis-Bos	229	Young-Cle	288	Nichols-Bos	2.13	Maul-Bal	170	McJames-Bal	49.2	Maul-Bal	4.4
McJames-Bal	374.0	Maul-Bal	232	Griffith-Chi	294	McJames-Bal	2.36	McJames-Bal	151	Maul-Bal	42.2	Young-Cle	4.4
Cunningham-Lou	362.0	McJames-Bal	234	McJames-Bal	297	Callahan-Chi	2.46	Callahan-Chi	145	Young-Cle	40.4	McJames-Bal	4.3

Beans in My Ears

In another move geared to make the game cleaner and more orderly, the NL voted to allow two umpires to be assigned to cover any game. The league also instituted a rule to prevent balks and began approaching the modern standard of what constitutes a stolen base.

Pitching continued to have the upper hand, as scoring per team dipped to 4.96 runs per game, the lowest mark in a decade. Clark Griffith's 1.88 ERA for Chicago was the game's best since the 1880s. Griffith was a fine pitcher—although a better manager and executive in the next century—and his '98 performance was by far the best of his career.

Helping to spell ace Kid Nichols, rookie hurler Vic Willis won 25 for Boston. The Beaneaters took their second straight flag by holding off a great Baltimore club. Boston's Jimmy Collins, the finest defensive third baseman of his day, also led in homers, and Hugh Duffy and Billy Hamilton were outstanding.

The Orioles led the league in scoring, with John McGraw, Willie Keeler, Hugh Jennings, and Joe Kelley providing the punch.

A five-man pitching staff of obscurities and unexpected heroes kept Baltimore in the race until the end.

Giants outfielder George Van Haltren played 156 games, a mark that stood until 1904. Attendance fell, due in part to the Spanish-American War, and also because the twelve-team format hurt interest in many cities. Several clubs were so bad that their chances to win were finished by May. Crowds in Chicago rose dramatically as the Colts hosted more games than usual. The Cleveland Spiders, unpopular despite a winning record and the excellent pitching of Cy Young, were a traveling team much of the season.

Rookies included hurler Sam Leever, future Chicago standouts Harry Steinfeldt and Frank Chance, and two other up-and-comers, Elmer Flick and Tommy Leach. In his first full season, Honus Wagner led Louisville in homers and RBIs.

There was no Temple Cup in 1898—or ever again. Dwindling interest by fans and players alike led to the dissolution of the postseason series after four years.

1897 National League

TEAM	W	L	T	PCT	GB	HW	HL	R	OR	PA	H	2B	3B	HR	BB	SO	HB	SH	AVG	OBP	SLG	OPS	AOPS	BR	ABR	PF	SB	CS	BSA	BSF
BOS	93	39	3	.705		54	12	1025	665	5521	1574	230	83	45	423	262	47	114	.319	.378	.426	804	110	121	65	106	233			
BAL	90	40	6	.692	2	51	15	964	674	5496	1584	243	66	19	437	256	115	72	.325	.394	.414	808	119	145	145	100	401			
NY	83	48	7	.634	9.5	51	19	901	696	5395	1452	188	84	31	412	327	67	45	.298	.361	.390	751	106	22	46	97	332			
CIN	76	56	2	.576	17	49	18	763	705	5104	1311	219	69	22	380	218	65	135	.290	.353	.383	736	93	-2	-50	107	194			
CLE	69	62	1	.527	23.5	49	16	773	680	5175	1374	192	88	16	435	344	38	98	.298	.364	.389	753	99	27	-14	105	181			
WAS	61	71	3	.462	32	40	26	781	793	5141	1376	194	77	36	374	348	59	72	.297	.357	.395	752	104	19	23	100	208			
BRO	61	71	4	.462	32	38	29	802	845	5334	1343	202	72	24	351	255	58	115	.279	.336	.366	702	95	-74	-32	95	187			
PIT	60	71	4	.458	32.5	38	27	676	835	5114	1266	140	108	25	359	334	67	98	.276	.337	.370	707	95	-67	-39	96	170			
CHI	59	73	6	.447	34	36	30	832	894	5385	1356	189	97	38	430	317	49	103	.282	.347	.386	733	94	-17	-46	104	264			
PHI	55	77	2	.417	38	32	34	752	792	5294	1392	213	83	40	399	299	42	97	.293	.353	.398	751	106	14	36	97	163			
LOU	52	78	6	.400	40	34	31	675	869	5131	1209	161	70	40	375	460	68	101	.264	.328	.355	683	88	-102	-79	97	200			
STL	29	102	2	.221	63.5	18	41	592	1088	5183	1285	151	67	32	354	314	76	80	.275	.336	.357	693	89	-86	-72	98	172			
TOT	811					490	298	9536		63273	16522	2322	964	368	4729	3734	751	1130	.292	.354	.386	740					2705			

TEAM	CG	SHO	GR	SV	IP	H	HR	BB	SO	BR/9	ERA	AERA	OAV	OOB	PR	APR	PF	OSB	OCS	FA	E	WPB	DP	FW	PW	BW	BSW	DI
BOS	115	8	21	7	1194.1	1273	39	393	329	12.9	3.65	122	.271	.333	86	102	104	150	104	.951	272	56	80	3.9	8.7	5.6		8.
BAL	118	3	20	0	1197.2	1296	18	382	361	13.2	3.55	117	.274	.338	99	83	97	211	88	.951	277	67	110	3.7	7.1	12.4		1.8
NY	119	8	19	3	1196.1	1217	26	490	463	13.3	3.45	120	.262	.341	114	95	96	131	138	.930	399	89	109	-3.4	8.1	3.9		8.8
CIN	100	4	38	2	1156.2	1375	18	329	270	13.7	4.09	111	.294	.347	28	54	106	145	112	.948	273	30	100	3.6	4.6	-4.3		6.
CLE	111	6	20	0	1119.1	1297	32	289	277	13.1	3.95	114	.288	.337	44	63	104	194	118	.950	261	46	74	4.1	5.4	-1.2		-4.8
WAS	102	7	34	6	1148.0	1383	27	400	348	14.6	4.01	108	.296	.362	37	39	101	278	175	.933	369	68	103	-2.0	3.3	2.0		-8.
BRO	114	4	22	2	1194.2	1417	34	410	256	14.2	4.60	89	.293	.354	-40	-73	95	264	164	.936	364	50	99	-1.6	-6.3	-2.7		5.
PIT	112	2	24	2	1153.1	1397	22	398	342	13.9	4.67	89	.297	.350	-48	-69	97	274	116	.936	346	54	70	-.6	-5.9	-3.3		4.
CHI	131	2	7	1	1197.0	1485	30	433	361	14.9	4.53	98	.303	.367	-31	-12	104	261	146	.932	393	61	112	-3.0	-1.0	-3.9		1.
PHI	115	4	19	2	1155.1	1415	28	364	253	14.3	4.60	91	.300	.356	-39	-55	97	222	119	.944	296	58	72	2.3	-4.7	3.1		-11.
LOU	115	2	20	0	1155.0	1374	40	467	267	15.0	4.41	97	.294	.368	-14	-21	99	245	145	.930	399	44	87	-3.7	-1.8	-6.8		-8.
STL	110	1	25	1	1136.1	1594	54	454	207	16.8	6.17	71	.329	.394	-236	-221	102	330	154	.932	380	63	86	-3.0	-18.9	-6.2		-8.
TOT	1362	51	269	26	14004.0					14.1	4.30		.292	.354						.939	4029	733	1102					

Batter-Fielder Wins		Batting Average		On-Base Percentage		Slugging Average		On-Base Plus Slugging		Adjusted OPS		Adjusted Batter Runs	
Jennings-Bal	5.5	Keeler-Bal	.424	McGraw-Bal	.471	Lajoie-Phi	.569	Keeler-Bal	1003	F.Clarke-Lou	167	F.Clarke-Lou	54.
Davis-NY	5.1	F.Clarke-Lou	.390	Burkett-Cle	.468	Keeler-Bal	.539	F.Clarke-Lou	992	Keeler-Bal	164	Keeler-Bal	51.
F.Clarke-Lou	4.1	Burkett-Cle	.383	Keeler-Bal	.464	Delahanty-Phi	.538	Delahanty-Phi	.981	Delahanty-Phi	163	Delahanty-Phi	50.
Delahanty-Phi	4.0	Delahanty-Phi	.377	Jennings-Bal	.463	F.Clarke-Lou	.530	Lajoie-Phi	.960	Lajoie-Phi	156	Lajoie-Phi	39.
Keeler-Bal	3.7	Kelley-Bal	.362	F.Clarke-Lou	.461	Davis-NY	.509	Burkett-Cle	.944	Kelley-Bal	147	Kelley-Bal	38.

Runs		Hits		Doubles		Triples		Home Runs		Total Bases		Runs Batted In	
Hamilton-Bos	152	Keeler-Bal	239	Stenzel-Bal	.43	Davis-Pit	.28	Duffy-Bos	11	Lajoie-Phi	310	Davis-NY	13
Keeler-Bal	145	F.Clarke-Lou	205	Lajoie-Phi	.40	Lajoie-Phi	.23	Davis-NY	10	Keeler-Bal	304	Collins-Bos	13
Griffin-Bro	136	Delahanty-Phi	200	Delahanty-Phi	.40	Wallace-Cle	.21	Lajoie-Phi	9	Delahanty-Phi	285	Duffy-Bos	12
Jones-Bro	134	Burkett-Cle	198	Wallace-Cle	.33	Keeler-Bal	.19	Grady-Phi-StL	8	F.Clarke-Lou	279	Lajoie-Phi	12
Jennings-Bal	133	Lajoie-Phi	197	Ryan-Chi	.33			Beckley-NY-Cin	8			Kelley-Bal	11

Stolen Bases		Base Stealing Runs		Fielding Runs-Infield		Fielding Runs-Outfield		Wins		Winning Pct.		Complete Games	
Lange-Chi	73			Clingman-Lou	30.3	Selbach-Was	12.3	Nichols-Bos	31	Klobedanz-Bos	.788	Killen-Pit	3
Stenzel-Bal	69			Cross-StL	29.9	Delahanty-Phi	8.8	Rusie-NY	28	Nops-Bal	.769	Griffith-Chi	3
Hamilton-Bos	66			Jennings-Bal	23.0	Ryan-Chi	7.4	Klobedanz-Bos	26	Corbett-Bal	.750	Donahue-StL	3
Davis-NY	65			Davis-NY	19.9	VanHaltren-NY	6.7	Corbett-Bal	24	Nichols-Bos	.738	Nichols-Bos	3
Keeler-Bal	64			Werden-Lou	19.3	Hoy-Cin	5.1	Breitenstein-Cin	23	Rusie-NY	.737	Kennedy-Bro	3

Strikeouts		Fewest BB/Game		Games		Saves		Base Runners/9		Adjusted Relief Runs		Relief Ranking	
Seymour-NY	156	Young-Cle	1.31	Mercer-Was	47	Nichols-Bos	3	Nichols-Bos	10.59				
McJames-Was	156	Tannehill-Pit	1.52	Young-Cle	46	Mercer-Was	3	Rusie-NY	11.48				
Corbett-Bal	149	Nichols-Bos	1.66	Nichols-Bos	46			Amole-Bal	11.57				
Rusie-NY	135	Cuppy-Cle	1.70	Donahue-StL	46			Cuppy-Cle	11.80				
Nichols-Bos	127	Killen-Pit	2.03					Sullivan-Bos	12.03				

Innings Pitched		Opponents' Avg.		Opponents' OBP		Earned Run Average		Adjusted ERA		Adjusted Starter Runs		Pitcher Wins	
Nichols-Bos	368.0	Seymour-NY	.238	Nichols-Bos	.291	Rusie-NY	2.54	Nichols-Bos	169	Nichols-Bos	70.4	Nichols-Bos	6
Donahue-StL	348.0	Rusie-NY	.254	Rusie-NY	.308	Nichols-Bos	2.64	Rusie-NY	163	Rusie-NY	57.9	Rusie-NY	5
Griffith-Chi	343.2	Nichols-Bos	.255	Cuppy-Cle	.314	Nops-Bal	2.81	Nops-Bal	148	Mercer-Was	33.2	Mercer-Was	3
Kennedy-Bro	343.1	Hill-Lou	.268	Young-Cle	.318	Corbett-Bal	3.11	Powell-Cle	142	Breitenstein-Cin	31.4	Breitenstein-Cin	2
Mercer-Was	342.0	Corbett-Bal	.269	Nops-Bal	.319	Powell-Cle	3.16	Cuppy-Cle	140	Corbett-Bal	31.0	Seymour-NY	2

Clean Beaneaters

The league ruled before the season that pitchers could at no time intentionally deface the baseball, and that runners had to retouch bases when returning—ending the popular practice of simply cutting across the infield. These tactics were meant to clean up the game, but the best move toward making baseball more acceptable to the public was for "clean" teams to win.

This was accomplished when Frank Selee's Boston Beaneaters held off the Orioles to take the NL crown. Kid Nichols led the league in innings and wins, while Hugh Duffy, Fred Tenney, Jimmy Collins, and Billy Hamilton provided good defense as well as overpowering offensive punch—Boston was the last team to surpass 1,000 runs until 1930. Selee expertly combined youth and experience, and Beaneaters owner Arthur Soden challenged his club at midseason by forcing any player fined by an umpire to pay the tariff himself.

Baltimore didn't win despite runaway batting champ Willie Keeler's 44-game hitting streak and big years from Hughie Jennings and John McGraw. The Orioles had the last laugh, however, as they drubbed the Beantown nine in four of five high-scoring Temple Cup games. The Giants took third, with Amos Rusie returned from his holdout (other club owners, hip to Andrew Freedman's penury kicked in to raise Rusie's salary). Eleventh-place Louisville didn' have much, but they did have .390-hitting Fred Clarke and versatil rookie Honus Wagner. Other 1897 rookies included Roger Bresr ahan, Rube Waddell, and Jimmy Sheckard.

Prior to the season Brooklyn suffered the death of manage Dave Foutz, a 147-win pitcher and solid everyday hitter; he thre times led his league in games played. Under replacement skippe Billy Barnie, the Bridegrooms improved three spots, to seventh

The last original National Association player in the NL, Ch cago's Cap Anson, retired at age 45. Anson left the club at the cor clusion of a ten-year contract; Pop had been with the club fo nineteen seasons as manager, and twenty-two years as a player. Th sympathetic public dubbed the club the Orphans in his absence. H went to New York in 1898, but he lasted just two months at the heln

As the nineteenth century hurtled to its conclusion, sev eral other of the era's biggest stars, like Roger Connor, Buc Ewing, Silver King, Denny Lyons, and Fred Pfeffer took pa in their last major league action.

1896 National League

TEAM	W	L	T	PCT	GB	HW	HL	R	OR	PA	H	2B	3B	HR	BB	SO	HB	SH	AVG	OBP	SLG	OPS	AOPS	BR	ABR	PF	SB	CS	BSA	BSR
BAL	90	39	3	.698		49	16	995	662	5323	1548	207	100	23	386	201	120	98	.328	.393	.429	822	120	153	140	101	441			
CLE	80	48	7	.625	9.5	43	19	840	650	5435	1463	207	28	28	436	316	37	106	.301	.363	.391	754	97	29	-18	106	175			
CIN	77	50	1	.606	12	51	15	783	620	4911	1283	204	73	20	382	226	42	127	.294	.357	.388	745	95	9	-38	107	350			
BOS	74	57	1	.565	17	42	24	865	761	5306	1421	175	75	36	414	275	51	118	.301	.364	.393	757	98	29	-17	106	243			
CHI	71	57	4	.555	18.5	42	24	815	804	5118	1311	182	97	34	409	290	35	92	.286	.349	.390	739	95	-8	-37	104	332			
PIT	66	63	2	.512	24	35	31	787	741	5254	1371	169	94	27	387	286	58	108	.292	.353	.385	738	103	-9	25	96	217			
NY	64	67	2	.489	27	39	26	829	821	5225	1383	159	87	40	439	271	53	72	.297	.364	.394	758	107	31	56	97	274			
PHI	62	68	0	.477	28.5	38	29	890	891	5273	1382	234	84	49	438	297	60	95	.295	.363	.413	776	110	62	73	99	191			
WAS	58	73	2	.443	33	38	29	818	920	5315	1328	179	79	45	516	365	61	99	.286	.365	.388	753	103	32	32	100	258			
BRO	58	73	2	.443	33	35	28	692	764	5025	1292	174	87	28	344	269	39	94	.284	.340	.379	719	100	-47	-4	94	198			
STL	40	90	1	.308	50.5	27	34	593	929	4988	1162	134	78	37	332	300	35	101	.257	.313	.346	659	81	-154	-128	96	185			
LOU	38	93	3	.290	53	25	37	653	997	5057	1197	142	80	37	371	427	45	53	.261	.322	.351	673	85	-126	-101	96	195			
TOT	792					468	310	9560		62230	16141	2166	1006	404	4854	3523	636	1163	.290	.354	.387	742					3059			

TEAM	CG	SHO	GR	SV	IP	H	HR	BB	SO	BR/9	ERA	AERA	OAV	OOB	PR	APR	PF	OSB	OCS	FA	E	WPB	DP	FW	PW	BW	BSW	DIF
BAL	115	9	17	1	1168.1	1281	22	339	302	12.7	3.67	116	.277	.331	89	79	98	218	118	.945	296	58	114	2.7	6.7	11.9		4.3
CLE	113	9	24	5	1195.2	1363	27	280	336	12.6	3.46	131	.285	.329	119	136	104	183	133	.949	288	52	117	3.6	11.5	-1.5		2.4
CIN	105	12	26	4	1108.0	1240	27	310	219	13.0	3.67	125	.281	.335	85	108	106	167	114	.951	252	42	107	4.7	9.2	-3.2		2.9
BOS	110	6	24	3	1155.2	1254	57	397	277	13.1	3.78	120	.275	.337	75	93	104	228	175	.934	368	76	94	-1.7	7.9	-1.4		3.7
CHI	118	2	15	1	1161.1	1307	30	467	354	14.4	4.44	102	.282	.358	-11	11	104	271	146	.933	367	59	115	-1.6	.9	-3.1		10.8
PIT	108	8	26	1	1159.1	1286	18	439	362	13.9	4.30	97	.280	.351	7	-16	96	310	168	.941	317	68	103	1.2	-1.4	2.1		-.5
NY	104	1	30	2	1136.2	1303	33	403	312	14.0	4.54	-92	.286	.352	-24	-46	96	265	142	.933	365	93	90	-1.3	-3.9	4.8		-1.0
PHI	107	3	25	2	1117.0	1473	39	387	243	15.4	5.20	83	.316	.375	-104	-113	99	245	148	.941	313	48	112	1.3	-9.6	6.2		-.9
WAS	106	2	29	3	1136.2	1435	24	435	292	15.2	4.61	96	.306	.372	-32	-27	101	289	152	.927	398	79	99	-3.3	-2.3	2.7		-4.6
BRO	97	3	38	1	1144.0	1353	39	400	259	14.1	4.25	97	.292	.354	14	-18	95	248	140	.945	297	52	104	2.7	-1.5	-.3		-8.4
STL	115	1	18	1	1130.2	1448	40	456	279	15.5	5.33	82	.309	.376	-121	-125	100	303	192	.936	345	57	73	-.5	-10.6	-10.9		-3.1
LOU	108	1	29	4	1148.2	1398	48	541	288	15.9	5.12	84	.298	.381	-98	-103	99	332	182	.916	475	63	110	-7.8	-8.7	-8.6		-2.4
TOT	1306	57	301	28	13762.0					14.1	4.36		.290	.354						.938	4081	766	1238					

Batter-Fielder Wins
Jennings-Bal 6.7
Childs-Cle 6.3
Delahanty-Phi 6.0
Dahlen-Chi 5.5
Joyce-Was-NY 4.3

Batting Average
Burkett-Cle .410
Jennings-Bal .401
Delahanty-Phi .397
Keeler-Bal .386
Tiernan-NY .369

On-Base Percentage
Hamilton-Bos .478
Jennings-Bal .472
Delahanty-Phi .472
Joyce-Was-NY .470
Kelley-Bal .469

Slugging Average
Delahanty-Phi .631
Dahlen-Chi .553
McCreery-Lou .546
Kelley-Bal .543
Burkett-Cle .541

On-Base Plus Slugging
Delahanty-Phi 1103
Kelley-Bal 1013
Burkett-Cle 1002
Dahlen-Chi .990
Joyce-Was-NY .988

Adjusted OPS
Delahanty-Phi 192
Kelley-Bal 164
Joyce-Was-NY 162
Tiernan-NY 159
E.Smith-Pit 158

Adjusted Batter Runs
Delahanty-Phi 68.4
Kelley-Bal 53.7
Joyce-Was-NY 51.8
Tiernan-NY 48.5
Burkett-Cle 46.3

Runs
Burkett-Cle 160
Keeler-Bal 153
Hamilton-Bos 153
Kelley-Bal 148
Dahlen-Chi 137

Hits
Burkett-Cle 240
Keeler-Bal 210
Jennings-Bal 209
Delahanty-Phi 198
VanHaltren-NY 197

Doubles
Delahanty-Phi 44
Miller-Cin 38
Kelley-Bal 31
Dahlen-Chi 30

Triples
VanHaltren-NY 21
McCreery-Lou 21
Delahanty-Phi 19
Dahlen-Chi 19
Clarke-Lou 18

Home Runs
Joyce-Was-NY 13
Delahanty-Phi 13
Thompson-Phi 12
Connor-StL 11

Total Bases
Burkett-Cle 317
Delahanty-Phi 315
Kelley-Bal 282
VanHaltren-NY 272
Keeler-Bal 270

Runs Batted In
Delahanty-Phi 126
Jennings-Bal 121
Duffy-Bos 113
McKean-Cle 112

Stolen Bases
Kelley-Bal 87
Lange-Chi 84
Hamilton-Bos 83
Miller-Cin 76
Doyle-Bal 73

Base Stealing Runs

Fielding Runs-Infield
Childs-Cle 38.9
Jennings-Bal 31.2
Corcoran-Bro 25.9
Clingman-Lou 23.7
Dahlen-Chi 21.8

Fielding Runs-Outfield
Thompson-Phi 17.5
Delahanty-Phi 14.7
E.Smith-Pit 7.9
Selbach-Was 7.5
Parrott-StL 7.1

Wins
Nichols-Bos 30
Killen-Pit 30
Young-Cle 28
Meekin-NY 26

Winning Pct.
Hoffer-Bal .781
Hemming-Bal .714
Dwyer-Cin .686
Nichols-Bos .682
Griffith-Chi .676

Complete Games
Killen-Pit 44
Young-Cle 42
Mercer-Was 38

Strikeouts
Young-Cle 140
Hawley-Pit 137
Killen-Pit 134
Breitenstein-StL 114
Meekin-NY 110

Fewest BB/Game
Young-Cle 1.35
Clarke-NY 1.54
Dwyer-Cin 1.87
Cuppy-Cle 1.89
Griffith-Chi 1.98

Games
Killen-Pit 52
Young-Cle 51
Nichols-Bos 49
Hawley-Pit 49
Clarke-NY 48

Saves
Young-Cle 3
Hill-Lou 2
Fisher-Cin 2

Base Runners/9
Rhines-Cin 11.64
Cuppy-Cle 11.82
Klobedanz-Bos 11.94
Young-Cle 11.95
Nichols-Bos 11.97

Adjusted Relief Runs

Relief Ranking

Innings Pitched
Killen-Pit 432.1
Young-Cle 414.1
Hawley-Pit 378.0
Nichols-Bos 372.1
Mercer-Was 366.1

Opponents' Avg.
Rhines-Cin .238
Hawley-Pit .261
Sullivan-NY .261
Friend-Chi .264
Hoffer-Bal .264

Opponents' OBP
Rhines-Cin .311
Cuppy-Cle .314
Young-Cle .317
Nichols-Bos .317
Esper-Bal .319

Earned Run Average
Rhines-Cin 2.45
Nichols-Bos 2.83
Cuppy-Cle 3.12
Dwyer-Cin 3.15
Young-Cle 3.24

Adjusted ERA
Rhines-Cin 188
Nichols-Bos 160
Dwyer-Cin 146
Cuppy-Cle 146
Young-Cle 140

Adjusted Starter Runs
Nichols-Bos 59.4
Young-Cle 56.4
Cuppy-Cle 55.0
Dwyer-Cin 42.4
Hoffer-Bal 35.1

Pitcher Wins
Young-Cle 5.7
Cuppy-Cle 5.5
Nichols-Bos 5.4
Dwyer-Cin 4.4
Hoffer-Bal 3.9

Another Bird Victory

To aid the league's pitchers, the NL passed a rule allowing them to hide the baseball before or during their delivery. At least partially as a result, scoring decreased again, this time by half a run per game per team. The decrease in offense didn't stop everyone. Jesse Burkett's 240 hits set a mark that stood until 1911. Meanwhile, Hughie Jennings got hit by 51 pitches, an all-time high; he broke Curt Welch's 1891 record by 15. (Welch died in 1896, beset by the ravages of the bottle.)

The last player to hold out against wearing a fielder's glove, top shortstop Bid McPhee, finally gave in for 1896. The new innovation made him an even better shortstop. Meanwhile, two men who would go on to greater fame five years later, in the new American League, debuted: Fielder Jones, for Brooklyn, and Nap Lajoie, with Philadelphia.

Baltimore won its third straight league title. The club's offensive prowess put some distance between them and second-place Cleveland. Shortstop Jennings was an offensive and defensive force for the Orioles, and with the help of Willie Keeler, Joe Kelley, and Jack Doyle, the club batted .328, which was 27 points higher than the nearest rival. The Orioles scored 105 more runs and stole 91 more bases than anyone else. (Baltimore's 441 steals have never been surpassed, but there is a reason: through 1897 scorers also credited a stolen base if a runner advanced on a flyball or went two bases on a hit or infield out, as long as a palpable attempt was made to retire him.)

Cleveland again had Cy Young and Nig Cuppy on the hill, but the Spiders had little offense beyond the big three of Burkett, Ed McKean, and Cupid Childs. Surprising Cincinnati, under Buck Ewing, finished third, with Billy Rhines and Frank Dwyer finishing first and fourth in ERA. New York didn't contend, because mound mainstay Amos Rusie sat out the year rather than take a less-than-deserved pay cut.

The Orioles took revenge on Cleveland in their second Temple Cup match-up, sweeping them in four straight, with the *coup de grace* a 5-0 shutout in the finale. It was the only time that the first-place team in the regular season beat the second-place team in the four Temple Cup series.

Last-place Louisville increased its attendance by 30,000, but still drew barely 2,000 per game. The league's overall gate rose just 11,000, but the 2,900,973 tickets sold ranked as the highest total for any one league until 1904.

1895 National League

TEAM	W	L	T	PCT	GB	HW	HL	R	OR	PA	H	2B	3B	HR	BB	SO	HB	SH	AVG	OBP	SLG	OPS	AOPS	BR	ABR	PF	SB	CS	BSA	BSW
BAL	87	43	2	.669		54	12	1009	646	5311	1530	235	89	25	355	243	106	125	.324	.384	.427	811	110	94	68	103	310			
CLE	84	46	2	.646	3	47	13	921	725	5304	1433	194	69	29	476	365	49	87	.305	.375	.395	770	97	28	-22	106	188			
PHI	78	53	2	.595	9.5	51	21	1068	957	5689	1664	272	73	61	463	262	69	120	.330	.394	.450	844	122	167	163	100	276			
CHI	72	58	3	.554	15	43	26	866	854	5252	1401	171	85	55	422	344	42	80	.298	.361	.405	766	95	3	-50	107	260			
BRO	71	60	3	.542	16.5	43	22	879	838	5284	1346	191	78	41	397	319	63	67	.283	.346	.382	728	99	-64	6	92	184			
BOS	71	60	2	.542	16.5	48	19	911	829	5434	1377	198	57	54	505	239	52	127	.290	.364	.390	754	91	-3	-67	108	200			
PIT	71	61	3	.538	17	44	21	815	799	5226	1355	192	89	27	378	301	65	106	.290	.351	.386	737	99	-46	2	95	257			
CIN	66	64	2	.508	21	42	22	903	854	5190	1395	235	105	36	414	249	36	56	.298	.359	.416	775	99	18	-15	104	326			
NY	66	65	1	.504	21.5	40	27	852	834	5127	1324	191	90	32	454	292	30	38	.288	.355	.389	744	98	-30	-11	98	292			
WAS	43	85	5	.336	43	31	34	840	1052	5258	1326	209	101	55	522	403	52	69	.287	.366	.412	775	105	33	44	99	238			
STL	39	92	5	.298	48.5	25	41	752	1036	5296	1356	155	88	39	388	283	30	64	.282	.339	.375	714	89	-97	-86	99	208			
LOU	35	96	2	.267	52.5	19	38	698	1090	5205	1320	171	73	34	346	323	77	58	.279	.339	.368	707	92	-103	-51	94	156			
TOT	799					487	296	10514		63576	16827	2414	997	488	5120	3623	671	997	.296	.361	.400	761					2895			

TEAM	CG	SHO	GR	SV	IP	H	HR	BB	SO	BR/9	ERA	AERA	OAV	OOB	PR	APR	PF	OSB	OCS	FA	E	WPB	DP	FW	PW	BW	BSW	DI
BAL	104	10	30	4	1134.1	1216	31	430	244	13.4	3.80	125	.271	.340	123	119	100	155	149	.946	288	43	108	5.3	9.6	5.5		1.
CLE	109	6	25	3	1151.2	1284	34	350	330	13.0	3.92	127	.278	.334	110	130	104	207	130	.936	351	84	77	1.7	10.5	-1.8		8.
PHI	106	2	29	7	1161.0	1467	36	485	330	15.6	5.47	87	.304	.375	-89	-89	100	256	109	.933	369	68	93	.9	-7.2	13.2		5.
CHI	119	3	14	1	1150.2	1422	38	432	297	15.0	4.67	109	.300	.366	13	49	107	254	114	.928	401	72	113	-.9	4.0	-4.1		8.
BRO	104	5	29	6	1159.2	1366	42	397	218	14.0	4.93	89	.289	.350	-20	-75	92	188	143	.941	326	56	97	3.5	-6.1	-.5		7.
BOS	117	4	18	4	1185.1	1376	56	367	377	13.6	4.25	120	.287	.343	69	102	107	196	140	.935	365	76	106	1.1	8.3	-5.4		1.
PIT	107	4	29	6	1179.2	1279	19	500	383	14.2	4.10	110	.273	.353	89	55	94	230	144	.930	394	83	95	-.2	4.5	.2		
CIN	97	2	35	6	1147.1	1451	39	362	245	14.7	4.81	103	.304	.361	-5	-16	104	227	145	.931	377	54	112	.3	1.3	-1.2		
NY	115	6	18	1	1147.1	1359	34	415	409	14.3	4.51	103	.291	.354	33	16	97	247	157	.922	438	76	106	-3.1	1.3	-.9		2.
WAS	99	0	38	5	1111.1	1515	55	470	261	16.6	5.26	91	.321	.390	-60	-58	101	299	191	.917	450	81	97	-3.6	-4.7	3.6		-16.
STL	106	1	30	1	1161.1	1572	64	443	284	16.0	5.73	84	.319	.381	-123	-116	101	320	149	.913	383	45	94	.6	-9.4	-7.0		-10.
LOU	104	3	34	1	1117.1	1520	40	469	245	16.5	5.90	78	.320	.388	-139	-147	97	266	126	.913	477	-79	104	-5.2	-13.3	-4.1		
TOT	1287	46	329	45	13807.0					14.7	4.77		.296	.361						.930	4619	789	1202					

Leaderboards

Batter-Fielder Wins
Jennings-Bal 6.3
Thompson-Phi 5.0
Delahanty-Phi 4.6
Griffin-Bro 3.8
G.Davis-NY 3.2

Batting Average
Burkett-Cle 405
Delahanty-Phi 404
Clements-Phi 394
Thompson-Phi 392
Lange-Chi 389

On-Base Percentage
Delahanty-Phi 500
Hamilton-Phi 490
Burkett-Cle 482
McGraw-Bal 459
Lange-Chi 456

Slugging Average
Thompson-Phi 654
Delahanty-Phi 617
Clements-Phi 612
Lange-Chi 575
Kelley-Bal 546

On-Base Plus Slugging
Delahanty-Phi 1117
Thompson-Phi 1085
Lange-Chi 1032
Kelley-Bal 1003
Burkett-Cle 1001

Adjusted OPS
Delahanty-Phi 186
Thompson-Phi 177
Stenzel-Pit 160
Lange-Chi 155
Hamilton-Phi 154

Adjusted Batter Runs
Delahanty-Phi ....68.
Thompson-Phi ....56.
Hamilton-Phi 50
Stenzel-Pit 50
Burkett-Cle 44

Runs
Hamilton-Phi 166
Keeler-Bal 162
Jennings-Bal 159
Burkett-Cle 149
Delahanty-Phi 149

Hits
Burkett-Cle 225
Keeler-Bal 213
Thompson-Phi 211
Jennings-Bal 204
Hamilton-Phi 201

Doubles
Delahanty-Phi 49
Thompson-Phi 45
Jennings-Bal 41
Stenzel-Pit 38
Griffin-Bro 38

Triples
Selbach-Was 22
Tiernan-NY 21
Thompson-Phi 21
Cooley-StL 20

Home Runs
Thompson-Phi 18
Joyce-Was 17
Clements-Phi 13
Delahanty-Phi 11

Total Bases
Thompson-Phi 352
Delahanty-Phi 296
Burkett-Cle 288
McKean-Cle 284
Kelley-Bal 283

Runs Batted In
Thompson-Phi 16
Kelley-Bal 13
Brodie-Bal 13
Jennings-Bal 12
McKean-Cle 11

Stolen Bases
Hamilton-Phi 97
Lange-Chi 67
McGraw-Bal 61
Kelley-Bal 54

Base Stealing Runs

Fielding Runs-Infield
Jennings-Bal 37.4
Dahlen-Chi 34.7
Fuller-NY 33.1
Cross-Phi 32.4
Collins-Bos-Lou 19.3

Fielding Runs-Outfield
Selbach-Was 14.6
Clarke-Lou 13.2
Thompson-Phi 12.0
Griffin-Bro 11.8
Miller-Cin 10.4

Wins
Young-Cle 35
Hoffer-Bal 31
Hawley-Pit 31

Winning Pct.
Hoffer-Bal 838
Young-Cle 778
Rhines-Cin 655

Complete Games
Breitenstein-StL 4
Hawley-Pit 4
Nichols-Bos 4
Rusie-NY 4
Griffith-Chi 3

Strikeouts
Rusie-NY 201
Nichols-Bos 148
Hawley-Pit 142
Breitenstein-StL 131
Young-Cle 121

Fewest BB/Game
Young-Cle 1.83
Clarke-NY 1.92
Nichols-Bos 2.07
Staley-StL 2.21
Taylor-Phi 2.23

Games
Hawley-Pit 56
Breitenstein-StL 55
Rusie-NY 49
Nichols-Bos 48

Saves
Parrott-Cin 3
Nichols-Bos 3
Beam-Phi 3

Base Runners/9
McMahon-Bal 10.74
Young-Cle 10.86
Maul-Was 11.68
Nichols-Bos 12.19
Hawley-Pit 12.23

Adjusted Relief Runs

Relief Ranking

Innings Pitched
Hawley-Pit 444.1
Breitenstein-StL ..438.2
Rusie-NY 393.1
Nichols-Bos 390.2
Young-Cle 369.2

Opponents' Avg.
Foreman-Pit 245
Hoffer-Bal 246
Rusie-NY 252
Young-Cle 253
Maul-Was 257

Opponents' OBP
Young-Cle 294
Maul-Was 310
Nichols-Bos 319
Hawley-Pit 320
Cuppy-Cle 323

Earned Run Average
Maul-Was 2.45
McMahon-Bal 2.94
Hawley-Pit 3.18
Hoffer-Bal 3.21
Foreman-Pit 3.22

Adjusted ERA
Maul-Was 195
Young-Cle 153
Nichols-Bos 149
Hoffer-Bal 148
Hawley-Pit 142

Adjusted Starter Runs
Young-Cle 73.3
Nichols-Bos 67.4
Hawley-Pit 66.2
Hoffer-Bal 55.9
Cuppy-Cle 51.1

Pitcher Wins
Hawley-Pit 7
Young-Cle 6
Cuppy-Cle 5
Nichols-Bos 5
Hoffer-Bal 4

Refinement of the Formula

Pitchers got some relief in 1895, as scoring per game dipped nearly a run per team. The tight defense and strong teamwork of Baltimore led to as many imitators, as did their umpire-baiting and violence. For the first time the NL regulated the size and weight of fielders' gloves, except for those worn by catchers and first basemen. The league also inaugurated the infield fly rule to keep clubs from intentionally dropping popups. Those rules still couldn't keep the game from getting dirtier, though. The two most unscrupulous clubs, the Orioles and Cleveland Spiders, finished 1-2 in the league. Both clubs also had great talent, not just hardscrabble rowdies.

Despite injuries to many key players, the Orioles sported the best pitching (led by Bill Hoffer) and the second-most productive hitters; Willie Keeler and Hugh Jennings finished 2-3 in runs. Cleveland was carried by batting champ Jesse Burkett, shortstop Ed McKean, and hurlers Cy Young and Nig Cuppy. Spiders pitching overcame Baltimore bats to win the Temple Cup, 4 games to 1.

Boston fell to fifth but debuted future third base star Jimmy Collins, while shortstop Jack Glasscock, the 1890 bat-ting champ, tumbled out of the league at age 36. First baseman Harry Davis, who would later win four straight AL home run titles, also made his first appearance.

Nine teams finished over .500, with three former American Association members, who barely drew flies, bringing up the rear. Parity and a decent pennant race raised league attendance 16 percent, due to huge gains in Boston, Chicago, Cincinnati, and especially Philadelphia. The Phillies were the NL's biggest draw—becoming the first team to pass 400,000 fans—and once again featured the league's highest-scoring offense.

Several clubs had by now adopted the monikers by which we know still them, including the Cincinnati Reds, Pittsburgh Pirates, New York Giants, and Philadelphia Phillies—although the league still had its Boston Beaneaters, Chicago Colts, and Brooklyn Bridegrooms (or Superbas, take your pick). Two NL clubs also carried names that their AL successors would adopt, the Orioles and the St. Louis Browns.

1894 National League

AM	W	L	T	PCT	GB	HW	HL	R	OR	PA	H	2B	3B	HR	BB	SO	HB	SH	AVG	OBP	SLG	OPS	AOPS	BR	ABR	PF	SB	CS	BSA	BSR
AL	89	39	1	.695		52	15	1171	819	5564	1647	271	150	33	516	200	98	151	.343	.418	.483	901	116	174	124	104	324			
Y	88	44	7	.667	3	49	17	962	801	5480	1469	199	96	45	489	219	32	80	.301	.369	.409	778	92	-69	-63	99	326			
OS	83	49	1	.629	8	44	19	1220	1002	5657	1658	272	94	103	535	261	47	64	.331	.401	.484	885	109	138	54	108	241			
HI	71	57	4	.555	18	48	20	1179	995	5779	1780	259	137	40	508	254	60	122	.350	.415	.478	893	122	166	195	98	285			
RO	70	61	4	.534	20.5	42	24	1024	1020	5452	1514	231	130	42	467	295	34	100	.312	.376	.439	815	108	-3	71	93	282			
LE	68	61	1	.527	21.5	35	24	932	896	5336	1442	241	90	37	471	301	24	77	.303	.368	.414	782	89	-57	-91	104	220			
T	65	65	3	.500	25	46	28	965	981	5376	1465	223	125	48	444	210	69	163	.312	.379	.443	822	103	10	21	99	257			
HI	57	75	5	.432	34	35	30	1056	1080	5643	1574	268	87	65	507	306	38	76	.313	.381	.440	821	97	15	-40	106	332			
TL	56	76	1	.424	35	34	32	771	953	5204	1320	171	113	54	442	289	40	112	.286	.354	.408	762	87	-107	-107	100	190			
N	55	75	4	.423	35	38	28	936	1108	5375	1407	228	71	61	517	255	43	62	.296	.370	.412	782	89	-53	-83	103	223			
AS	45	87	0	.341	46	32	30	882	1122	5325	1317	218	118	59	617	375	71	56	.287	.381	.425	806	101	-6	24	97	249			
OU	36	94	1	.277	54	24	37	698	1019	5021	1216	173	89	42	355	368	54	93	.269	.330	.375	705	78	-207	-155	93	219			
OT	799					479	304	11796		65212	17809	2754	1300	629	5868	3333	610	1156	.309	.379	.435	814					3148			

AM	CG	SHO	GR	SV	IP	H	HR	BB	SO	BR/9	ERA	AERA	OAV	OOB	PR	APR	PF	OSB	OCS	FA	E	WPB	DP	FW	PW	BW	BSW	DIF
AL	97	1	36	11	1116.1	1371	31	472	275	15.2	5.00	109	.299	.371	41	56	103	202	115	.944	293	60	105	5.7	4.3	9.5		5.6
Y	113	5	30	5	1230.0	1310	37	546	403	13.8	3.82	138	.271	.349	206	197	99	256	187	.923	454	102	103	-1.8	15.1	-4.8		13.5
OS	108	3	25	2	1166.0	1529	89	441	262	15.3	5.41	105	.314	.372	-11	31	107	223	146	.925	415	76	120	-.6	2.4	4.1		11.1
HI	103	3	35	4	1151.2	1522	62	479	266	16.2	5.63	91	.315	.385	-38	-68	96	285	118	.934	351	82	114	2.9	-5.2	14.9		-5.6
RO	106	3	30	5	1171.1	1465	41	558	290	16.0	5.56	89	.303	.383	-30	-85	93	294	145	.928	393	103	85	1.0	-6.5	5.4		4.6
LE	106	6	28	2	1124.1	1390	54	435	254	14.9	4.97	110	.301	.366	45	60	103	161	150	.935	344	71	107	2.9	4.6	-7.0		3.0
T	106	2	31	0	1170.2	1563	39	466	308	15.9	5.62	93	.318	.381	-38	-52	98	261	158	.936	355	63	106	2.8	-4.0	1.6		-.4
HI	118	0	20	0	1163.0	1575	43	569	284	17.1	5.72	98	.321	.398	-51	-12	106	323	144	.918	458	68	115	-2.4	-.9	-3.1		-2.7
TL	114	2	24	0	1161.0	1418	48	500	319	15.2	5.29	102	.294	.371	5	15	102	257	173	.923	426	79	109	-1.2	1.1	-8.2		-1.7
N	112	4	22	3	1165.1	1615	85	500	223	16.8	5.99	92	.326	.394	-85	-57	104	273	155	.925	430	54	122	-1.3	-4.4	-6.4		2.0
AS	102	0	35	4	1107.0	1573	59	446	190	16.9	5.50	95	.331	.396	-23	-30	99	355	163	.908	499	82	81	-5.6	-2.3	1.8		-15.0
OU	114	2	17	1	1104.2	1478	41	486	259	16.4	5.50	93	.318	.387	-21	-52	96	258	187	.919	435	67	131	-2.1	-4.0	-11.9		-11.1
OT	1299	31	333	37	13831.1					15.8	5.33		.309	.379						.927	4853	907	1298					

Batter-Fielder Wins	Batting Average	On-Base Percentage	Slugging Average	On-Base Plus Slugging	Adjusted OPS	Adjusted Batter Runs
amilton-Phi 4.5	Duffy-Bos 440	Hamilton-Phi.......522	Thompson-Phi 696	Duffy-Bos 1196	Thompson-Phi 181	Hamilton-Phi.......65.9
uffy-Bos 4.5	Turner-Phi.........418	Kelley-Bal 502	Duffy-Bos 694	Thompson-Phi 1161	Joyce-Was 179	Duffy-Bos 63.8
ahlen-Chi 4.5	Thompson-Phi 415	Duffy-Bos 502	Joyce-Was 648	Joyce-Was 1143	Duffy-Bos 172	Thompson-Phi 56.6
yce-Was 4.3	E.Delahanty-Phi 404	Joyce-Was 496	Kelley-Bal 602	Kelley-Bal 1104	Kelley-Bal 158	Kelley-Bal 54.9
Delahanty-Phi ..4.2	Hamilton-Phi.......403	Childs-Cle 475	E.Delahanty-Phi 584	E.Delahanty-Phi 1059	E.Delahanty-Phi 158	Joyce-Was 52.4

Runs	Hits	Doubles	Triples	Home Runs	Total Bases	Runs Batted In
amilton-Phi 198	Duffy-Bos 237	Duffy-Bos 51	Reitz-Bal 31	Duffy-Bos 18	Duffy-Bos 374	Thompson-Phi 147
elley-Bal 165	Hamilton-Phi.......225	Kelley-Bal 48	Thompson-Phi 28	Lowe-Bos 17	Lowe-Bos 319	Duffy-Bos 145
eeler-Bal 165	Keeler-Bal 219	Wilmot-Chi.........45	Treadway-Bro 26	Joyce-Was 17	Thompson-Phi 314	E.Delahanty-Phi ...133
uffy-Bos 160	Lowe-Bos 212		Connor-NY-StL.......25	Dahlen-Chi 15	Kelley-Bal 305	Cross-Phi 132
we-Bos 158			Brouthers-Bal.......23		Keeler-Bal 305	Wilmot-Chi.........130

Stolen Bases	Base Stealing Runs	Fielding Runs-Infield	Fielding Runs-Outfield	Wins	Winning Pct.	Complete Games
amilton-Phi 100		Jennings-Bal.......33.0	Bannon-Bos 16.7	Rusie-NY.........36	Meekin-NY.........786	Breitenstein-StL.......46
cGraw-Bal 78		McPhee-Cin.........30.0	E.Delahanty-Phi 12.5	Meekin-NY.........33	McMahon-Bal 758	Rusie-NY 45
ilmot-Chi.........76		Dahlen-Chi.........25.7	McCarthy-Bos 9.4	Nichols-Bos.........32	Rusie-NY 735	Young-Cle 44
nge-Chi.........66		Cross-Phi.........25.0	Abbey-Was 7.7	Breitenstein-StL.......27	Nichols-Bos 711	Meekin-NY 41
Brown-Lou 66		Reitz-Bal.........20.5	Lange-Chi.........6.7			Nichols-Bos 40

Strikeouts	Fewest BB/Game	Games	Saves	Base Runners/9	Adjusted Relief Runs	Relief Ranking
usie-NY 195	Young-Cle 2.33	Breitenstein-StL.......56	Mullane-Bal-Cle.......4	Rusie-NY 12.79		
eitenstein-StL......140	Menefee-Lou-Pit.......2.48	Rusie-NY 54	Mercer-Was 3	Meekin-NY 12.94		
eekin-NY 137	Gleason-StL-Bal.......2.54	Meekin-NY 53	Hawke-Bal 3	Clarkson-Cle 13.08		
awley-StL 120	Staley-Bos 2.63	Hawley-StL 53		Young-Cle 13.19		
chols-Bos 113	Nichols-Bos 2.68	Young-Cle 52		Nichols-Bos 13.67		

Innings Pitched	Opponents' Avg.	Opponents' OBP	Earned Run Average	Adjusted ERA	Adjusted Starter Runs	Pitcher Wins
eitenstein-StL......447.1	Rusie-NY 250	Rusie-NY 331	Rusie-NY 2.78	Rusie-NY 189	Rusie-NY 118.0	Rusie-NY 10.2
usie-NY 444.0	Meekin-NY 256	Meekin-NY 333	Meekin-NY 3.70	Meekin-NY 142	Meekin-NY 80.9	Meekin-NY 6.2
eekin-NY 418.0	Stein-Bro 278	Clarkson-Cle 336	Mercer-Was 3.85	Young-Cle 139	Young-Cle 65.3	Young-Cle 5.0
ung-Cle 408.2	Breitenstein-StL......279	Young-Cle 338	Young-Cle 3.94	Mercer-Was 137	Mercer-Was 40.8	Mercer-Was 3.8
chols-Bos 407.0	Clarkson-Cle 285	Nichols-Bos 346	Taylor-Phi 4.08	McMahon-Bal 130	Nichols-Bos 38.8	Taylor-Phi 3.5

Bird-Brained Baseball

Offense continued to rise. The league average went to a stratospheric .309, and clubs scored 7.38 runs per game, a mark that has never been bettered. Philadelphia's Billy Hamilton scored the most runs in history—198—and his .522 on-base percentage set a new standard. Boston's Hugh Duffy hit .440, an all-time high, and his record .694 slugging percentage lasted until 1921. Heinie Reitz smacked 31 triples to tie Dave Orr's 1886 mark, and that record wasn't broken until 1912. Bobby Lowe of Boston became the first player in history to homer four times in one game. The 629 home runs hit during the season would not be surpassed until 1925.

The move toward increased offense came in spite of a rule change; as of 1894, foul bunts were counted as strikes. Meanwhile, pity the pitchers. St. Louis' Ted Breitenstein was tagged for 497 hits and 320 runs, figures of terror that no moundsman has been unlucky enough to match. (Breitenstein still managed to win 27 times.) New York's Amos Rusie was the only pitcher with an ERA under 3.00.

Fans responded to the offense—the NL set another attendance record—but the game was changing for the worse. Greedy owners paid lower salaries, and as payoffs got lower, competition got tougher. Rule-breaking, fistfights, and umpire intimidation (and sometimes outright assault) became the rule.

The kings of this new era were the 1894 champion Baltimore Orioles, who were not above tripping or spiking opponents or stomping on an umpire's toes. Manager Ned Hanlon brought together a talented, smart, and tough club, including Joe Kelley, Hughie Jennings, Willie Keeler, Reitz, and John McGraw; these players would do anything, legal or not, to win. And as the Birds succeeded, other clubs followed. New York was a close second, with an ERA that was a full run better than any other team, led by strikeout pitchers Rusie and Joe Meekin. Boston was third, leading the league with 1,220 runs, but the club's pitchers allowed more than 1,000. Despite scoring 209 fewer runs while finishing second behind Baltimore, New York blasted the Orioles in the inaugural Temple Cup match-up. The Giants won all four games, including a 16-3 massacre in the last game.

While alcohol-related disease killed Ed Williamson and King Kelly, other players ended their careers: Pete Browning, John Clarkson, Charlie Comiskey, and John Ward. Future stars Fred Clarke and Bobby Wallace debuted.

1893 National League

TEAM	W	L	T	PCT	GB	HW	HL	R	OR	PA	H	2B	3B	HR	BB	SO	HB	SH	AVG	OBP	SLG	OPS	AOPS	BR	ABR	PF	SB	CS	BSA	BSR
BOS	86	43	2	.667		49	15	1008	795	5285	1358	178	50	65	561	292	46		.290	.372	.391	763	99	58	-9	108	243			
PIT	81	48	2	.628	5	54	19	970	766	5433	1447	176	127	37	537	274	62		.299	.377	.411	788	116	94	114	98	210			
CLE	73	55	1	.570	12.5	47	22	976	839	5309	1425	222	98	32	532	229	30		.300	.374	.408	782	106	87	33	106	252			
PHI	72	57	4	.558	14	43	22	1011	841	5690	1553	246	90	80	468	335	71		.301	.368	.431	799	117	111	112	100	202			
NY	68	64	4	.515	19.5	49	20	941	845	5418	1424	182	101	61	504	281	56		.293	.366	.410	776	110	67	62	101	299			
CIN	65	63	3	.508	20.5	37	27	759	814	5196	1195	161	65	29	531	257	40		.259	.341	.341	682	84	-88	-106	102	238			
BRO	65	63	2	.508	20.5	43	24	775	845	5024	1200	173	83	45	473	296	40		.266	.341	.371	712	97	-47	-10	95	213			
BAL	60	70	0	.462	26.5	36	24	820	893	5260	1281	164	86	27	539	323	70		.275	.359	.365	724	95	-12	-25	102	233			
CHI	56	71	1	.441	29	38	34	829	874	5166	1299	186	93	32	466	261	36		.279	.349	.379	728	99	-21	-9	99	255			
STL	57	75	3	.432	30.5	40	30	745	829	5466	1288	152	98	10	524	251	63		.264	.343	.341	684	86	-92	-94	100	250			
LOU	50	75	1	.400	34	24	28	759	942	5105	1185	177	73	19	485	306	54		.260	.338	.343	681	92	-93	-30	92	203			
WAS	40	89	1	.310	46	21	27	722	1032	5328	1258	180	83	23	523	237	63		.265	.346	.353	699	92	-62	-40	97	154			
TOT	785					481	292	10315		63680	15913	2197	1047	460	6143	3342	639		.280	.356	.379	736					2752			

TEAM	CG	SHO	GR	SV	IP	H	HR	BB	SO	BR/9	ERA	AERA	OAV	OOB	PR	APR	PF	OSB	OCS	FA	E	WPB	DP	FW	PW	BW	BSW	DIF
BOS	114	2	20	2	1163.2	1314	66	402	253	13.6	4.43	111	.277	.339	30	60	106	176	91	.936	353	62	118	1.8	4.9	-.7		15.5
PIT	104	8	29	2	1167.0	1232	29	504	280	13.8	4.08	111	.263	.342	75	61	98	237	133	.938	347	77	112	2.1	5.0	9.3		.0
CLE	110	2	21	2	1140.1	1361	35	356	242	13.8	4.20	116	.288	.342	59	82	105	199	151	.929	395	98	92	-.9	6.7	2.7		.5
PHI	107	4	28	2	1189.0	1357	30	522	286	14.8	4.68	98	.279	.357	-2	-13	98	186	108	.944	318	60	121	4.1	9.2			-4.7
NY	111	6	26	4	1211.1	1271	36	581	395	14.2	4.29	108	.262	.347	49	48	100	238	174	.927	432	137	95	-1.8	3.9	5.1		-5.2
CIN	97	4	34	5	1172.0	1305	38	549	258	14.8	4.55	105	.274	.357	15	29	103	211	109	.943	321	89	138	3.6	2.4	-8.7		3.7
BRO	109	3	23	3	1154.0	1262	41	547	297	14.4	4.55	97	.270	.352	15	-17	95	233	118	.930	385	83	88	-.2	-1.4	-.8		3.4
BAL	104	1	26	2	1123.2	1325	29	534	275	15.2	4.97	95	.285	.364	-18	-29	102	248	100	.929	384	111	95	-.1	-2.4	-2.0		-.4
CHI	101	4	31	5	1117.1	1278	36	553	273	15.3	4.81	96	.279	.365	-18	-24	99	242	148	.922	421	79	92	-2.5	-.0	-.7		-2.3
STL	114	3	22	4	1207.0	1292	38	542	301	14.1	4.06	116	.266	.346	80	87	101	276	152	.930	398	107	110	-.0	7.1	-7.7		-8.3
LOU	113	4	13	1	1080.0	1431	38	479	190	16.3	5.90	74	.310	.380	-149	-194	94	206	138	.937	330	69	111	2.2	-15.9	-2.5		3.6
WAS	110	2	20	0	1139.0	1485	54	574	292	16.7	5.56	83	.306	.387	-114	-121	99	300	192	.912	497	85	96	-6.5	-9.9	-3.3		-4.8
TOT	1294	43	293	32	13864.1					14.7	4.66		.280	.356						.931	4581	1057	1268					

Batter-Fielder Wins
- Delahanty-Phi 5.4
- McPhee-Cin 3.6
- Childs-Cle 3.4
- Davis-NY 3.2
- Hamilton-Phi 3.0

Batting Average
- Thompson-Phi .370
- Hamilton-Phi .380
- Delahanty-Phi .368
- Duffy-Bos .363
- Davis-NY .355

On-Base Percentage
- Hamilton-Phi .490
- Childs-Cle .463
- Burkett-Cle .459
- McGraw-Bal .454
- Smith-Pit .435

Slugging Average
- Delahanty-Phi .583
- Davis-NY .554
- Thompson-Phi .530
- Smith-Pit .525
- Hamilton-Phi .524

On-Base Plus Slugging
- Hamilton-Phi 1014
- Delahanty-Phi 1007
- Davis-NY .964
- Smith-Pit .960
- Thompson-Phi .954

Adjusted OPS
- Hamilton-Phi 169
- Delahanty-Phi 166
- Smith-Pit 158
- Davis-NY 154
- Thompson-Phi 153

Adjusted Batter Runs
- Delahanty-Phi 53.1
- Smith-Pit 44.2
- Thompson-Phi 44.2
- Hamilton-Phi 41.4
- Davis-NY 38.0

Runs
- Long-Bos 149
- Duffy-Bos 147
- Delahanty-Phi 145
- Childs-Cle 145
- Burkett-Cle 145

Hits
- Thompson-Phi 222
- Delahanty-Phi 219
- Duffy-Bos 203
- Davis-NY 195
- Ward-NY 193

Doubles
- Thompson-Phi 37
- Delahanty-Phi 35
- Tebeau-Cle 32
- Beckley-Pit 32

Triples
- Werden-StL 29
- Davis-NY 27
- McKean-Cle 24
- Smith-Pit 23
- Beckley-Pit 19

Home Runs
- Delahanty-Phi 19
- Clements-Phi 17
- Tiernan-NY 14
- Lowe-Bos 14

Total Bases
- Delahanty-Phi 347
- Thompson-Phi 318
- Davis-NY 304
- Smith-Pit 272

Runs Batted In
- Delahanty-Phi 146
- McKean-Cle 133
- Thompson-Phi 126
- Nash-Bos 123
- Ewing-Cle 122

Stolen Bases
- T.Brown-Lou 66
- Dowd-StL 59
- Latham-Cin 57
- Burke-NY 54
- Brodie-StL-Bal 49

Base Stealing Runs

Fielding Runs-Infield
- McPhee-Cin 31.4
- G.Smith-Cin 16.4
- Long-Bos 15.8
- Wise-Was 15.5
- Allen-Phi 15.3

Fielding Runs-Outfield
- T.Brown-Lou 25.7
- Delahanty-Phi 23.7
- Treadway-Bal 7.8
- Griffin-Bro 7.3
- Radford-Was 6.5

Wins
- Killen-Pit 36
- Young-Cle 34
- Nichols-Bos 34
- Rusie-NY 33
- Kennedy-Bro 25

Winning Pct.
- Gastright-Pit-Bos .750
- Killen-Pit .720
- Nichols-Bos .708
- Young-Cle .680
- Staley-Bos .643

Complete Games
- Rusie-NY 50
- Nichols-Bos 43
- Young-Cle 42
- Kennedy-Bro 40

Strikeouts
- Rusie-NY 208
- Kennedy-Bro 107
- Young-Cle 102
- Breitenstein-StL 102
- Weyhing-Phi 101

Fewest BB/Game
- Young-Cle 2.19
- Nichols-Bos 2.50
- Cuppy-Cle 2.77
- Staley-Bos 2.77
- Stratton-Lou 2.86

Games
- Rusie-NY 56
- Killen-Pit 55
- Young-Cle 53
- Nichols-Bos 52
- Mullane-Cin-Bal 49

Saves
- Mullane-Cin-Bal 2
- Baldwin-Pit-NY 2
- Dwyer-Cin 2
- Donnelly-Chi 2
- Colcolough-Pit 2

Base Runners/9
- Young-Cle 11.82
- Nichols-Bos 11.84
- Killen-Pit 12.06
- Breitenstein-StL 12.30
- Stein-Bro 12.70

Adjusted Relief Runs

Relief Ranking

Innings Pitched
- Rusie-NY 482.0
- Nichols-Bos 425.0
- Young-Cle 422.2
- Killen-Pit 415.0

Opponents' Avg.
- Rusie-NY .240
- Breitenstein-StL .241
- Killen-Pit .246
- Kennedy-Bro .249
- Stein-Bro .250

Opponents' OBP
- Young-Cle .308
- Nichols-Bos .308
- Killen-Pit .312
- Breitenstein-StL .316
- Stein-Bro .323

Earned Run Average
- Breitenstein-StL 3.18
- Rusie-NY 3.23
- Young-Cle 3.36
- Ehret-Pit 3.44
- Clarkson-StL 3.48

Adjusted ERA
- Breitenstein-StL 149
- Young-Cle 145
- Rusie-NY 144
- Nichols-Bos 140
- Clarkson-StL 136

Adjusted Starter Runs
- Rusie-NY 74.0
- Young-Cle 73.8
- Breitenstein-StL 67.7
- Nichols-Bos 66.0
- Killen-Pit 45.5

Pitcher Wins
- Rusie-NY 6.8
- Young-Cle 6.5
- Breitenstein-StL 5.6
- Killen-Pit 5.5
- Nichols-Bos 5.5

Going Batty

League moguls decided to increase offense for 1893, and moved the mound 5 feet from the plate to its current distance of 60 feet, 6 inches. Pitchers were also now required to keep one foot on a rubber plate while delivering, effectively limiting them to just one stride. Some pitchers couldn't handle the new rules, including former mound stalwarts Gus Weyhing, Bill Hutchinson, and Silver King. On the other hand, Amos Rusie of New York made 52 starts, threw 482 innings, and walked 218 men. No hurler has matched these totals since.

Despite the league making flat-sided bats illegal, scoring duly increased 22 percent to 6.57 runs per game, a new high, with the loop average rising to an unprecedented .280. Five NL players scored 145 or more runs and two teams plated at least 1,000. St. Louis, which had the league's worst ERA in 1892 at 4.20, had the NL's best a year later at 4.06. (It translated into just one extra win for the Browns because of a mediocre offense.)

The Phillies, in a small park, were the league's top scoring club, and had the top three batting title contenders (Billy Hamilton, Sam Thompson, and Ed Delahanty). Philadelphia, though, finished a distant fourth because the team couldn't win on the road. Aside from the three big guns, the Phillies' offense was actually quite poor, and the team's pitching was below the necessary standard.

Although they lacked the big-name marquee stars of other clubs, Frank Selee's Boston Beaneaters took the prize, squeezing past Pittsburgh. Hugh Duffy, Bobby Lowe, and Herman Long provided offense and defense up the middle, and Kid Nichols adapted well to the new mound conditions. Three celebrated careers ended as Tim Keefe, King Kelly, and Curt Welch played their final games.

With more offense and a shorter schedule, fans had more interest in the league and attendance duly rose by 400,000, doubling in Chicago and New York. It marked the first time three teams attracted 300,000 fans, and the first time the league reached more than two million. There was no postseason tournament, however. With no rival league and no split schedule, the NL's moguls were at a loss for what to do after the end of the regular season. Thus, no postseason series was staged.

1892 National League

TEAM	W	L	T	PCT	GB	HW	HL	R	OR	PA	H	2B	3B	HR	BB	SO	HB	SH	AVG	OBP	SLG	OPS	AOPS	BR	ABR	PF	SB	CS	BSA	BSR
BOS	102	48	2	.680		54	21	862	649	5889	1325	203	51	34	526	492	62		.250	.325	.327	652	93	24	-43	109	338			
CLE	93	56	4	.624	8.5	54	24	855	613	6004	1376	196	96	26	552	538	40		.254	.328	.340	668	103	49	16	104	225			
BRO	95	59	4	.617	9	51	24	935	733	6168	1439	183	105	30	629	508	54		.262	.344	.350	694	119	111	147	96	409			
PHI	87	66	2	.569	16.5	55	26	860	690	5995	1420	225	95	50	528	515	54		.262	.334	.367	701	117	110	113	100	216			
CIN	82	68	5	.547	20	45	32	766	731	5890	1291	155	75	44	503	476	38		.241	.311	.323	634	98	-23	-12	99	270			
PIT	80	73	2	.523	23.5	52	34	802	796	5948	1288	143	108	38	435	453	44		.236	.297	.322	619	92	-65	-68	100	222			
CHI	70	76	1	.479	30	36	31	635	735	5526	1189	149	92	26	427	482	36		.235	.299	.316	615	90	-63	-70	101	233			
NY	71	80	2	.470	31.5	42	36	811	826	5835	1329	173	85	39	510	474	34		.251	.321	.338	659	106	26	39	98	301			
LOU	63	89	2	.414	40	37	31	649	804	5813	1209	133	61	18	433	508	46		.227	.290	.285	575	86	-138	-83	92	275			
WAS	58	93	2	.384	44.5	34	36	731	869	5772	1246	149	78	37	529	555	39		.239	.314	.319	633	99	-19	3	97	276			
STL	56	94	5	.373	46	37	36	703	922	5918	1188	138	45	45	607	492	52		.226	.312	.298	610	94	-53	-15	95	209			
BAL	46	101	5	.313	54.5	29	46	779	1020	5857	1343	160	111	30	499	480	62		.254	.325	.343	668	104	41	19	103	227			
TOT	921					526	377	9388		70615	15643	2007	1010	417	6178	5973	561		.245	.317	.328	644					3201			

TEAM	CG	SHO	GR	SV	IP	H	HR	BB	SO	BR/9	ERA	AERA	OAV	OOB	PR	APR	PF	OSB	OCS	FA	E	WPB	DP	FW	PW	BW	BSW	DIF
BOS	142	15	11	1	1336.0	1156	41	460	514	11.1	2.86	123	.224	.292	64	90	107	196	142	.929	454	106	128	.5	8.3	-4.0		22.2
CLE	140	11	12	2	1336.0	1178	28	413	472	10.9	2.41	140	.228	.289	130	139	103	205	131	.935	407	65	95	3.4	12.9	1.5		.8
BRO	132	12	26	5	1405.2	1285	26	600	597	12.4	3.25	97	.234	.315	6	-14	96	258	175	.940	398	130	98	4.8	-1.3	13.6		.9
PHI	131	10	24	5	1379.0	1309	24	492	511	12.1	2.93	111	.241	.310	54	48	99	207	108	.939	393	84	128	4.5	4.4	10.5		-9.0
CIN	130	8	25	2	1377.1	1327	39	535	437	12.5	3.17	103	.243	.317	18	15	99	233	119	.939	402	111	140	4.0	1.4	-1.1		2.7
PIT	130	3	22	1	1347.1	1300	28	537	455	12.7	3.10	106	.244	.320	28	27	100	240	201	.927	483	108	113	-.7	2.5	-6.3		8.0
CHI	133	6	13	1	1298.0	1269	35	424	518	12.0	3.16	105	.246	.308	18	22	101	247	152	.932	424	81	85	1.3	2.0	-6.5		.1
NY	139	5	13	1	1322.2	1165	32	635	650	12.6	3.29	98	.227	.318	-1	-12	98	371	223	.912	565	216	97	-5.8	-1.1	3.6		-1.2
LOU	147	9	7	0	1346.0	1358	24	447	430	12.3	3.34	92	.252	.313	-8	-44	93	297	164	.928	471	112	133	-.2	-4.1	-7.7		-1.1
WAS	129	5	26	3	1315.1	1293	40	556	479	13.1	3.46	94	.247	.327	-26	-32	99	386	178	.916	547	120	122	-4.8	-3.0	.3		-10.0
STL	139	4	22	1	1344.2	1466	47	543	478	13.8	4.20	76	.267	.339	-137	-156	97	287	138	.929	452	102	100	-1.1	-14.4	-1.4		-4.3
BAL	131	2	22	2	1298.2	1537	51	536	437	14.7	4.28	80	.284	.353	-144	-119	104	274	145	.910	584	115	100	-7.1	-11.0	1.8		-11.1
TOT	1623	90	223	24	16106.2					12.5	3.28		.245	.317						.928	5580	1350	1339					

Split Season: First-half Winner BOS (52-22); Second-half Winner CLE (53-23)

Batter-Fielder Wins		Batting Average		On-Base Percentage		Slugging Average		On-Base Plus Slugging		Adjusted OPS		Adjusted Batter Runs	
Brouthers-Bro	6.8	Brouthers-Bro	335	Childs-Cle	443	Delahanty-Phi	495	Brouthers-Bro	911	Brouthers-Bro	182	Brouthers-Bro	63.5
McPhee-Cin	4.7	Hamilton-Phi	330	Brouthers-Bro	432	Brouthers-Bro	480	Connor-Phi	883	Connor-Phi	167	Connor-Phi	53.4
Connor-Phi	4.2	Childs-Cle	317	Hamilton-Phi	423	Ewing-NY	473	Delahanty-Phi	855	Burns-Bro	162	Burns-Bro	42.3
Childs-Cle	3.9	Burns-Bro	315	Connor-Phi	420	Connor-Phi	463	Burns-Bro	849	Delahanty-Phi	158	Childs-Cle	41.2
Hamilton-Phi	3.7	Ewing-NY	310	Crooks-StL	400	Burns-Bro	454	Childs-Cle	841	Hamilton-Phi	152	Hamilton-Phi	40.4

Runs		Hits		Doubles		Triples		Home Runs		Total Bases		Runs Batted In	
Childs-Cle	136	Brouthers-Bro	197	Connor-Phi	37	Delahanty-Phi	21	Holliday-Cin	13	Brouthers-Bro	282	Brouthers-Bro	124
Hamilton-Phi	132	Thompson-Phi	186	Long-Bos	33	Virtue-Cle	20	Connor-Phi	12	Holliday-Cin	271	Thompson-Phi	104
Duffy-Bos	125	Duffy-Bos	184	Delahanty-Phi	30	Brouthers-Bro	20	Ryan-Chi	10	Thompson-Phi	263	Larkin-Was	96
Connor-Phi	123	Hamilton-Phi	183	Brouthers-Bro	30	Dahlen-Chi	19	Beckley-Pit	10	Connor-Phi	261	Burns-Bro	96
Brouthers-Bro	121	Long-Bos	181	Zimmer-Cle	29	Beckley-Pit	19	Thompson-Phi	9	Duffy-Bos	251	Beckley-Pit	96

Stolen Bases		Base Stealing Runs		Fielding Runs-Infield		Fielding Runs-Outfield		Wins		Winning Pct.		Complete Games	
Ward-Bro	88			D.Richardson-Was	44.8	Duffee-Was	17.7	Young-Cle	36	Young-Cle	750	Hutchison-Chi	67
Brown-Lou	78			Shindle-Bal	36.5	Brown-Lou	15.6	Hutchison-Chi	36	Terry-Bal-Pit	692	Rusie-NY	59
Latham-Cin	66			Bierbauer-Pit	29.1	Hamilton-Phi	12.3	Stivetts-Bos	35	Haddock-Bro	690	Nichols-Bos	49
Hoy-Was	60			Nash-Bos	25.1	Griffin-Bro	9.6	Nichols-Bos	35	Staley-Bos	688	Young-Cle	48
Dahlen-Chi	60			Smith-Cin	23.3	McAleer-Cle	8.5						

Strikeouts		Fewest BB/Game		Games		Saves		Base Runners/9		Adjusted Relief Runs		Relief Ranking	
Hutchison-Chi	314	Stratton-Lou	1.79	Hutchison-Chi	75	Weyhing-Phi	3	Young-Cle	9.77				
Rusie-NY	304	Dwyer-StL-Cin	1.98	Rusie-NY	65	Duryea-Cin-Was	2	Nichols-Bos	10.63				
Weyhing-Phi	202	Sanders-Lou	2.08	Killen-Was	60			Stratton-Lou	10.77				
Nichols-Bos	192	Young-Cle	2.34	Weyhing-Phi	59			Mullane-Cin	11.01				
Stein-Bro	190	Ehret-Pit	2.36	Baldwin-Pit	56			Duryea-Cin-Was	11.08				

Innings Pitched		Opponents' Avg.		Opponents' OBP		Earned Run Average		Adjusted ERA		Adjusted Starter Runs		Pitcher Wins	
Hutchison-Chi	622.0	Mullane-Cin	201	Young-Cle	266	Young-Cle	1.93	Young-Cle	176	Young-Cle	73.5	Young-Cle	6.4
Rusie-NY	541.0	Rusie-NY	202	Nichols-Bos	283	Keefe-Phi	2.36	J.Clarkson-Bos-Cle	139	Cuppy-Cle	36.7	Hutchison-Chi	4.0
Weyhing-Phi	469.2	Terry-Bal-Pit	205	Stratton-Lou	286	J.Clarkson-Bos-Cle	2.48	Keefe-Phi	138	J.Clarkson-Bos-Cle	35.7	Cuppy-Cle	3.7
Killen-Was	459.2	Young-Cle	211	Mullane-Cin	290	Cuppy-Cle	2.51	Cuppy-Cle	135	Hutchison-Chi	35.6	Stivetts-Bos	3.3
		Duryea-Cin-Was	212	Duryea-Cin-Was	291	Terry-Bal-Pit	2.57	Davies-Cle	131	Nichols-Bos	33.8	Nichols-Bos	3.3

Growing Overnight

The NL expanded to 12 teams by taking on former American Association franchises Baltimore, Louisville, St. Louis, and Washington. As the only "major league," League owners could now theoretically sit back, await the crowds, and print money. It didn't quite work out that way. First of all, the four "new" clubs were bad, already stripped of their best players. (Only St. Louis survived the century intact; Louisville merged with Pittsburgh in 1900.) In addition, the NL game soon became more violent and more crooked, partly due to syndicate ownership. teams, mostly terrible ones, went through multiple managers. In 1892 most NL clubs adopted old Association policies of Sunday ball, selling alcohol, and charging as little as 25 cents for admission. The league also expanded its schedule and played a "split season" in order to create a postseason tournament. Hitters could attempt to be hit by pitches, and any pitches striking the hand or forearm were ruled strikes. In addition, fair balls hit only 235 or fewer feet away were doubles.

Boston, a solid two-way squad, rode its pitching to squeeze by Brooklyn for the first-half title. The Cleveland Spiders, featuring suddenly dominant hurler Cy Young and on-base machine Cupid Childs, barely won the second half. Boston easily took the postseason series. Slugging Roger Connor of Philadelphia set an all-time mark by playing in 155 games. St. Louis infielder Jack Crooks established a record of 136 walks that lasted until 1911. Fittingly, Crooks was also a stolen base threat, even though his club's 209 steals represented the lowest figure in the league—200 fewer than NL-leader Brooklyn.

With no AA, there were fewer major league jobs (and lower salaries). Ending their big league tenures were Jim Galvin, George Gore, Ned Hanlon, Hardy Richardson, and Mickey Welch. Future star "Wee Willie" Keeler debuted in New York. The addition of the new teams swelled league attendance totals, though crowds dwindled in Chicago, Boston, New York, and Philadelphia. The split season may have had something to do with this.

1891 National League

TEAM	W	L	T	PCT	GB	HW	HL	R	OR	PA	H	2B	3B	HR	BB	SO	HB	SH	AVG	OBP	SLG	OPS	AOPS	BR	ABR	PF	SB	CS	BSA	BSR
BOS	87	51	2	.630		51	20	847	658	5571	1264	181	81	53	533	537	82		.255	.337	.356	693	97	54	-35	112	289			
CHI	82	53	2	.607	3.5	43	22	832	730	5449	1231	159	88	60	526	457	50		.253	.332	.358	690	107	40	41	100	238			
NY	71	61	4	.538	13	39	28	754	711	5307	1271	189	72	46	438	394	36		.263	.329	.360	689	111	34	68	96	224			
PHI	68	69	1	.496	18.5	35	34	756	773	5469	1244	180	51	21	482	412	58		.252	.326	.322	648	92	-25	-43	103	232			
CLE	65	74	2	.468	22.5	40	28	835	888	5639	1295	183	88	22	519	464	46		.255	.330	.339	669	97	7	-25	104	242			
BRO	61	76	0	.445	25.5	41	31	765	820	5249	1233	200	69	23	465	435	36		.260	.330	.345	675	103	18	23	99	337			
CIN	56	81	1	.409	30.5	26	41	646	790	5249	1158	148	90	40	414	439	44		.242	.308	.335	643	92	-53	-58	101	244			
PIT	55	80	2	.407	30.5	32	34	679	744	5271	1148	148	71	29	427	503	50		.239	.308	.318	626	90	-75	-58	98	205			
TOT	552					307	238	6114		43204	9844	1388	610	294	3804	3641	402		.252	.325	.342	667						2011		

TEAM	CG	SHO	GR	SV	IP	H	HR	BB	SO	BR/9	ERA	AERA	OAV	OOB	PR	APR	PF	OSB	OCS	FA	E	WPB	DP	FW	PW	BW	BSW	DIF
BOS	126	9	15	6	1241.2	1223	51	364	525	11.8	2.76	132	.248	.305	80	112	109	197	130	.938	358	79	96	4.7	10.0	-3.1		6.5
CHI	114	6	24	3	1220.2	1207	53	475	477	12.7	3.47	96	.249	.322	-17	-21	100	190	137	.932	397	126	119	1.5	-1.9	3.7		11.2
NY	117	11	21	2	1204.0	1098	26	593	651	13.1	2.99	107	.234	.327	47	29	96	306	174	.933	384	136	104	2.2	2.6	6.1		-5.8
PHI	105	3	34	5	1229.1	1279	30	507	342	13.4	3.73	91	.259	.333	-53	-46	102	275	128	.925	443	102	108	-1.3	-4.1	-3.8		8.8
CLE	118	1	25	3	1244.0	1371	24	476	400	13.7	3.50	99	.270	.337	-22	-6	103	279	203	.920	485	111	86	-3.5	-.5	-2.2		1.7
BRO	121	8	16	3	1204.2	1272	40	459	407	13.4	3.86	86	.261	.332	-68	-76	99	244	116	.924	432	95	73	-.8	-6.8	2.1		-2.0
CIN	125	6	13	1	1218.2	1234	40	465	393	13.0	3.55	95	.253	.326	-28	-25	101	279	134	.931	409	120	101	.9	-2.2	-5.2		-6.0
PIT	122	7	16	3	1197.2	1160	30	465	446	12.7	2.89	114	.245	.320	61	52	98	241	151	.917	475	119	76	-3.6	4.6	-5.2		-8.3
TOT	948	51	164	26	9760.2					13.0	3.34		.252	.325						.928	3383	888	763					

Batter-Fielder Wins
Hamilton-Phi 4.0
Richardson-NY 4.0
Latham-Cin 3.4
Tiernan-NY 3.0
Pfeffer-Chi 3.0

Batting Average
Hamilton-Phi...........340
Holliday-Cin 319
Browning-Pit-Cin ...317
Clements-Phi 310
Tiernan-NY 306

On-Base Percentage
Hamilton-Phi...........453
Connor-NY 399
Childs-Cle 395
Browning-Pit-Cin ...395
Tiernan-NY 388

Slugging Average
Stovey-Bos 498
Tiernan-NY 494
Holliday-Cin 473
Connor-NY 449
Ryan-Chi 434

On-Base Plus Slugging
Tiernan-NY 882
Hamilton-Phi 874
Stovey-Bos 871
Holliday-Cin 848
Connor-NY 848

Adjusted OPS
Tiernan-NY 163
Connor-NY 153
Hamilton-Phi 151
Holliday-Cin 145
Browning-Pit-Cin ...139

Adjusted Batter Runs
Tiernan-NY 44.0
Hamilton-Phi..........42.3
Connor-NY 36.6
Holliday-Cin 23.8
Browning-Pit-Cin ...23.0

Runs
Hamilton-Phi 141
Long-Bos 129
Childs-Cle 120
Latham-Cin 119
Stovey-Bos 118

Hits
Hamilton-Phi 179
McKean-Cle 170
Tiernan-NY 166
Davis-Cle 165
O'Rourke-NY 164

Doubles
Griffin-Bro 36
Davis-Cle 35
Stovey-Bos 31
Tiernan-NY 30

Triples
Stovey-Bos 20
Beckley-Pit 19
McPhee-Cin 16
Ryan-Chi 15
Virtue-Cle 14

Home Runs
Tiernan-NY 16
Stovey-Bos 16
Wilmot-Chi 11

Total Bases
Stovey-Bos 271
Tiernan-NY 268
Long-Bos 233
Davis-Cle 233
Beckley-Pit 232

Runs Batted In
Anson-Chi 120
Stovey-Bos 95
O'Rourke-NY 95
Nash-Bos 95
Connor-NY 94

Stolen Bases
Hamilton-Phi 111
Latham-Cin 87
Griffin-Bro 65
Long-Bos 60

Base Stealing Runs

Fielding Runs-Infield
Richardson-NY 44.6
Pfeffer-Chi 23.6
McPhee-Cin 23.5
Latham-Cin...........21.3
Long-Bos 15.0

Fielding Runs-Outfield
Griffin-Bro 20.0
Thompson-Phi 17.7
Brodie-Bos 7.8
Davis-Cle 7.8
Stovey-Bos 6.6

Wins
Hutchison-Chi 44
Rusie-NY 33
Clarkson-Bos 33
Young-Cle 30
Young-Cle 27

Winning Pct.
J.Ewing-NY 724
Hutchison-Chi 698
Staley-Pit-Bos.........649
Nichols-Bos 638
Clarkson-Bos 635

Complete Games
Hutchison-Chi 56
Rusie-NY 52
Baldwin-Pit 48
Clarkson-Bos..........47
Nichols-Bos 45

Strikeouts
Rusie-NY 337
Hutchison-Chi 261
Nichols-Bos 240
Baldwin-Pit 197
King-Pit 160

Fewest BB/Game
Nichols-Bos 2.18
Staley-Pit-Bos.........2.22
Galvin-Pit 2.26
Radbourn-Bos 2.56
Hutchison-Chi.........2.86

Games
Hutchison-Chi 66
Rusie-NY 61
Young-Cle 55
Clarkson-Bos 55

Saves
Nichols-Bos 3
Clarkson-Bos...........3
Young-Cle 2
Thornton-Phi 2

Base Runners/9
Staley-Pit-Bos........11.08
Hutchison-Chi.......11.12
Sharrott-NY 11.16
Nichols-Bos 11.28
J.Ewing-NY 11.80

Adjusted Relief Runs

Relief Ranking

Innings Pitched
Hutchison-Chi.....561.0
Rusie-NY 500.1
Clarkson-Bos 460.2
Baldwin-Pit 437.2
Mullane-Cin 426.1

Opponents' Avg.
Rusie-NY 207
Baldwin-Pit 228
J.Ewing-NY 228
Hutchison-Chi 233
Mullane-Cin 234

Opponents' OBP
Staley-Pit-Bos........292
Hutchison-Chi.......293
Nichols-Bos 296
J.Ewing-NY...........305
Clarkson-Bos 305

Earned Run Average
J.Ewing-NY 2.27
Nichols-Bos 2.39
Rusie-NY 2.55
Staley-Pit-Bos........2.58
Baldwin-Pit 2.76

Adjusted ERA
Nichols-Bos 153
J.Ewing-NY 141
Staley-Pit-Bos........138
Clarkson-Bos........131
Rusie-NY 125

Adjusted Starter Runs
Nichols-Bos 48.2
Clarkson-Bos........41.0
Rusie-NY 39.9
Staley-Pit-Bos........36.0
J.Ewing-NY...........29.8

Pitcher Wins
Nichols-Bos............4.5
Clarkson-Bos........4.4
Rusie-NY 3.9
Staley-Pit-Bos 3.3
J.Ewing-NY 2.5

Disassociation

Following the Players' League's dissolution, the AA coaxed the PL's Boston and Philadelphia franchises to join, despite the NL's best efforts to prevent this. As a result, the NL and AA engaged in cataclysmic season-long battles and machinations to destroy each other. There would be no final postseason meeting between the leagues on the field.

Boston was the AA's best club, featuring such stars as Hugh Duffy, Tom Brown, and batting champ Dan Brouthers. Pitchers George Haddock and Charlie Buffinton provided the league's top hill work and just held off St. Louis' strong team. With Charlie Comiskey back in the fold, the Browns—buoyed by Jack Stivetts' pitching, Dummy Hoy and Tommy McCarthy's on-base ability, and Denny Lyons' power—wound up second.

Three future stars debuted in the AA's final season: Clark Griffith, Hugh Jennings, and John McGraw. Veterans Paul Hines—who dated back to the National Association of 1872—and Abner Dalrymple ended their major league careers.

With the PL out of the way, AA attendance rose by more than 300,000, seeing gains in most league cities, but the NL outdrew the Association. Consistent financial woes from the league's worst clubs led league management to seek a truce.

Therefore, postseason meetings between NL and AA moguls ended the Association for good. Four of the league's clubs were absorbed into the National League: St. Louis, Baltimore, Washington, and Louisville. The remaining teams (Boston, Milwaukee—who had replaced defunct Cincinnati in August—Columbus, and Philadelphia, which had replaced the AA's original Philadelphia Athletics) were hung out to dry. The Beer and Whiskey League, as NL supporters had mockingly called the AA because three of the original owners were liquor and beer barons, survived a decade as a major league, drawing practically 10 million fans (outdrawing the NL over the same span).

Though the American Association was history, several of its tenets were adopted by the new 12-team NL-AA amalgam, including Sunday ball, alcohol sales, a permanent core of umpires, and the option to sell tickets cheaply. Unfortunately, the logistics of a 12-team league would pose plenty of problems for the National League in the years ahead.

1891 American Association

TEAM	W	L	T	PCT	GB	HW	HL	R	OR	PA	H	2B	3B	HR	BB	SO	HB	SH	AVG	OBP	SLG	OPS	AOPS	BR	ABR	PF	SB	CS	BSA	BSR
BOS	93	42	4	.689		51	17	**1028**	675	5606	**1341**	163	100	52	**651**	499	66		**.274**	**.367**	**.380**	747	121	129	144	99	447			
STL	85	51	3	.625	8.5	**52**	21	959	738	5640	1311	165	51	**57**	612	436	86		.265	.356	.354	710	94	66	-53	115	279			
MIL	21	15	0	.583	22.5	16	5	227	156	1407	332	58	15	13	107	114	29		.261	.333	.361	694	86	4	-32	120	47			
BAL	71	64	4	.526	22	44	24	850	798	5433	1217	142	99	30	551	553	**111**		.255	.346	.345	691	102	22	13	101	342			
PHI	73	66	4	.525	22	43	26	817	794	5560	1301	**182**	**123**	55	447	548	74		.258	.328	.376	704	106	20	17	100	149			
COL	61	76	1	.445	33	34	29	702	777	5263	1113	154	61	20	529	530	37		.237	.319	.308	627	89	-92	-50	94	280			
CIN	43	57	2	.430	32.5	24	20	549	**643**	4038	838	105	58	28	428	**385**	36		.234	.322	.320	642	81	-52	-95	108	164			
LOU	54	83	2	.394	40	39	32	698	873	5270	1229	127	68	17	438	465	68		.258	.329	.324	653	93	-54	-46	99	227			
WAS	44	91	4	.326	49	28	40	691	**1067**	5259	1183	147	84	19	468	485	76		.251	.328	.330	658	97	-44	-8	95	219			
TOT	557					331	214	6521		43476	9865	1243	659	291	4231	4015	583		.255	.338	.344	682					2154			

TEAM	CG	SHO	GR	SV	IP	H	HR	BB	SO	BR/9	ERA	AERA	OAV	OOB	PR	APR	PF	OSB	OCS	FA	E	WPB	DP	FW	PW	BW	BSW	DIF
BOS	108	**9**	34	7	1219.2	1158	42	497	524	**12.6**	**3.03**	115	.242	**.321**	92	64	94	**176**	**173**	.934	392	133	115	4.1	5.5	**12.4**		3.5
STL	101	8	**38**	**10**	1206.2	**1088**	50	571	**613**	12.9	3.23	**130**	**.233**	.325	64	**113**	113	230	134	.920	459	155	91	.1	**9.7**	-4.6		11.7
MIL	35	3	1	0	309.2	291	6	120	137	12.2	2.50	175	.241	.314	42	54	118	58	**30**	.922	116	23	20	.2	4.7	-2.8		.9
BAL	118	6	21	2	1217.0	1238	33	472	408	13.1	3.43	108	.255	.329	37	39	100	185	122	.915	503	123	103	-2.5	3.4	1.1		1.5
PHI	**135**	3	7	0	1233.2	1274	35	520	533	13.6	4.01	94	.258	.338	-42	-31	102	270	131	.933	389	129	109	**5.1**	-2.7	1.5		-.3
COL	118	6	21	0	1213.1	1141	**29**	588	502	13.5	3.75	92	.244	.336	-5	-44	93	364	172	**.935**	379	132	**126**	4.7	-3.8	-4.3		-4.1
CIN	86	2	18	1	902.0	921	20	446	331	14.2	3.43	119	.256	.347	28	59	110	231	163	.913	389	84	68	-3.0	5.1	-8.2		-.9
LOU	126	**9**	12	1	1210.0	1334	32	**451**	481	13.8	4.22	87	.271	.340	-69	-79	98	332	**202**	.922	454	168	112	.4	-6.8	-4.0		-4.1
WAS	123	2	17	2	1181.0	1420	44	566	486	15.9	4.83	77	.288	.374	-147	-145	101	308	184	.900	589	159	95	-7.6	-12.5	-.7		-2.7
TOT	950	48	169	23	9693.0					13.6	3.71		.255	.338						.922	3670	1106	839					

Batter-Fielder Wins
Farrell-Bos.....4.4
Brouthers-Bos.....3.5
Milligan-Phi.....3.2
Crooks-Col.....3.2
Duffy-Bos.....2.7

Batting Average
Brouthers-Bos 350
Duffy-Bos 336
O'Neill-StL 323
Brown-Bos 321
VanHaltren-Bal 318

On-Base Percentage
Brouthers-Bos 471
Lyons-StL 445
Hoy-StL 424
Seery-Cin 423
Duffy-Bos 408

Slugging Average
Brouthers-Bos 512
Milligan-Phi 505
Farrell-Bos 474
Brown-Bos 469
Cross-Phi 458

On-Base Plus Slugging
Brouthers-Bos 983
Milligan-Phi 903
Lyons-StL 900
Brown-Bos 865
Duffy-Bos 861

Adjusted OPS
Brouthers-Bos 184
Milligan-Phi 158
Brown-Bos 150
Duffy-Bos 149
Farrell-Bos 148

Adjusted Batter Runs
Brouthers-Bos 60.4
Brown-Bos 37.4
Duffy-Bos 34.4
Milligan-Phi 34.4
Joyce-Bos 29.0

Runs
Brown-Bos 177
VanHaltren-Bal 136
Hoy-StL 134
Duffy-Bos 134

Hits
Brown-Bos 189
VanHaltren-Bal 180
Duffy-Bos 180
McCarthy-StL 176
Brouthers-Bos 170

Doubles
Milligan-Phi 35
Brown-Bos 30
O'Neill-StL 28
Duffee-Col 28
Larkin-Phi 27

Triples
Brown-Bos 21
Brouthers-Bos 19
Canavan-Cin-Mil 18
Werden-Bal 18

Home Runs
Farrell-Bos 12
Milligan-Phi 11
Lyons-StL 11

Total Bases
Brown-Bos 276
VanHaltren-Bal 251
Brouthers-Bos 249
Duffy-Bos 243
Werden-Bal 234

Runs Batted In
Farrell-Bos 110
Duffy-Bos 110
Brouthers-Bos 109
Milligan-Phi 106
Werden-Bal 104

Stolen Bases
Brown-Bos 106
Duffy-Bos 85
VanHaltren-Bal 75
Hoy-StL 59
Radford-Bos 55

Base Stealing Runs

Fielding Runs-Infield
Stricker-Bos 23.6
Crooks-Col 18.2
Eagan-StL 17.9
Radford-Bos 17.3
Wheelock-Col 16.3

Fielding Runs-Outfield
Andrews-Cin 15.1
Weaver-Lou 13.8
Wood-Phi 9.9
Welch-Bal 7.0
Duffee-Col 6.3

Wins
McMahon-Bal 35
Haddock-Bos 34
Stivetts-StL 33
Weyhing-Phi 31
Buffinton-Bos 29

Winning Pct.
Buffinton-Bos 763
Haddock-Bos 756
Weyhing-Phi 608
Stivetts-StL 600
McMahon-Bal 593

Complete Games
McMahon-Bal 53
Weyhing-Phi 51
Knell-Col 47
Carsey-Was 46
Chamberlain-Phi 44

Strikeouts
Stivetts-StL 259
Knell-Col 228
Weyhing-Phi 219
McMahon-Bal 219
Chamberlain-Phi 204

Fewest BB/Game
Stratton-Lou 1.78
Sanders-Phi 2.30
McMahon-Bal 2.67
Ehret-Lou 2.85
Griffith-StL-Bos 2.90

Games
Stivetts-StL 64
McMahon-Bal 61
Knell-Col 58
Carsey-Was 54
Weyhing-Phi 52

Saves
Neale-StL 3
Griffith-StL-Bos 2
O'Brien-Bos 2
Daley-Bos 2

Base Runners/9
Buffinton-Bos 10.64
Haddock-Bos 11.40
Davies-Mil 11.65
McMahon-Bal 11.79
Killen-Mil 11.82

Adjusted Relief Runs

Relief Ranking

Innings Pitched
McMahon-Bal 503.0
Knell-Col 462.0
Weyhing-Phi 450.0
Stivetts-StL 440.0
Carsey-Was 415.0

Opponents' Avg.
Knell-Col 209
Stivetts-StL 215
Buffinton-Bos 219
Crane-Cin 225
Haddock-Bos 226

Opponents' OBP
Buffinton-Bos 285
Haddock-Bos 299
McMahon-Bal 306
Fitzgerald-Lou 316
Weyhing-Phi 317

Earned Run Average
Crane-Cin 2.45
Haddock-Bos 2.49
Buffinton-Bos 2.55
McMahon-Bal 2.81
Stivetts-StL 2.86

Adjusted ERA
Crane-Cin 167
Stivetts-StL 146
Haddock-Bos 140
Buffinton-Bos 136
Mains-Cin-Mil 134

Adjusted Starter Runs
Stivetts-StL 57.8
McMahon-Bal 54.0
Buffinton-Bos 45.3
Haddock-Bos 44.6
Crane-Cin 35.5

Pitcher Wins
Stivetts-StL 6.8
Haddock-Bos 5.3
McMahon-Bal 4.9
Buffinton-Bos 4.0
Crane-Cin 2.6

Winning the War

With the Players' League dissolved, the NL absorbed most of the players from the defunct loop's New York, Pittsburgh, Chicago, and Brooklyn clubs (including John Ward, who served as Brooklyn's player-manager). Boston claimed Harry Stovey from the Philadelphia AA team, citing a waiver error, and a committee ruled Boston did have such a right. The AA angrily responded by withdrawing from the National Agreement—the leagues were now officially at war. The AA's withdrawal from the agreement precluded even a financially rewarding postseason competition. The NL was happy with this decision, as it felt itself to be already winning the attendance war.

And this decision played itself out in the pennant race. Chicago led the NL hunt for most of the year, but an 18-game winning streak gave Boston the flag. Some sources now believe that Cap Anson's Chicago club, rumored despite the NL's objections to be willing to play AA champ Boston in a World Series, was jobbed out of the pennant by league-enforced umpire decisions.

Managed by Frank Selee, the Boston Beaneaters got power from Stovey, excellent all-around play from Herman Long, and top mound work from John Clarkson and Kid Nichols.

Chicago, despite big seasons from Anson, rookie Bill Dahlen, and Bill Hutchinson, settled for an angry second. Philadelphia had Billy Hamilton, probably the NL's top player, but the Phillies lacked other offense and finished fourth. Despite the returning talent (at a much lower cost) to the NL, future stars Joe Kelley and Dahlen debuted. Hoss Radbourn pitched his last major league ball for seventh-place Cincinnati.

Following the end of the controversial season, the NL absorbed four AA franchises, and until 1901 there would be but one major league. The decade-long Association war yielded far-reaching spoils. Four NL teams that still exist today—Pittsburgh Pirates, Cincinnati Reds, St. Louis Cardinals, and Los Angeles Dodgers—came from the American Association. Two others current NL teams originated from the National Association (Atlanta Braves and Chicago Cubs), seven more resulted from expansion since 1962, and an eighth originated in the American League. The Philadelphia Phillies and San Francisco Giants, organized in 1883, are the lone nineteenth century teams to play their first games as NL franchises and continue to do so.

1890 Players League

TEAM	W	L	T	PCT	GB	HW	HL	R	OR	PA	H	2B	3B	HR	BB	SO	HB	SH	AVG	OBP	SLG	OPS	AOPS	BR	ABR	PF	SB	CS	BSA	BS
BOS	81	48	1	.628		**48**	21	992	767	5321	1306	**223**	76	54	**652**	435	43		.282	**.376**	.398	**774**	105	**97**	34	107	**412**			
BRO	76	56	1	.576	6.5	46	19	964	893	5431	1352	186	93	34	502	369	42		.277	.349	.374	723	92	-14	-66	106	272			
NY	74	57	1	.565	8	47	19	**1018**	875	5430	**1393**	204	57	**66**	486	364	31		.284	.352	**.405**	757	98	39	-38	109	231			
CHI	75	62	1	.547	10	46	23	886	770	5503	1311	200	95	31	492	410	43		.264	.335	.361	696	87	-67	-101	104	276			
PHI	68	63	1	.519	14	35	30	941	855	5337	1350	187	**113**	49	431	**321**	51		.278	.343	.393	736	100	-2	-22	102	203			
PIT	60	68	0	.469	20.5	37	28	835	892	5200	1192	168	**113**	35	369	375	54		.260	.349	.369	718	106	-17	60	92	249			
CLE	55	75	1	.423	26.5	31	30	849	1027	5362	1370	213	94	27	509	345	49		**.285**	.360	.386	746	114	31	115	92	180			
BUF	36	96	2	.273	46.5	23	42	793	1199	5432	1249	180	64	20	541	367	**96**		.260	.347	.337	684	96	-66	11	92	160			
TOT	529					313	212	7278		43016	10523	1561	745	316	4182	2986	409		.274	.351	.378	729					1983			

TEAM	CG	SHO	GR	SV	IP	H	HR	BB	SO	BR/9	ERA	AERA	OAV	OOB	PR	APR	PF	OSB	OCS	FA	E	WPB	DP	FW	PW	BW	BSW	D
BOS	105	6	**26**	4	1137.1	1291	49	467	345	14.3	3.79	116	.274	.346	55	73	104	**143**	110	.918	460	97	109	1.7	5.8	2.7		6.
BRO	111	4	22	**7**	1184.0	1334	**26**	570	377	14.9	3.95	113	.273	.356	37	62	105	195	142	.909	531	110	114	-1.8	4.9	-5.3		12.
NY	111	3	23	6	1172.1	**1216**	37	569	449	14.1	4.17	109	.257	.343	8	44	107	254	**152**	**.921**	450	147	94	**2.8**	3.5	-3.0		5.
CHI	124	5	14	2	1219.1	1238	27	503	460	13.2	3.39	128	.252	.327	114	125	103	224	179	.918	492	**91**	107	1.6	**10.0**	-8.1		2.
PHI	118	4	14	2	1154.1	1292	33	495	361	14.4	4.05	105	.271	.347	22	27	101	258	151	.910	510	106	**118**	-.7	2.2	-1.8		2.
PIT	121	**7**	7	0	1116.2	1267	32	**334**	318	13.2	4.22	93	.274	.328	2	-43	92	231	**103**	.907	512	104	80	-1.7	-3.4	4.8		-3.
CLE	115	1	16	0	1143.2	1386	45	571	325	15.8	4.23	94	.287	.369	0	-35	94	361	**172**	.907	533	171	103	-2.3	-2.8	**9.2**		-14.
BUF	**125**	2	9	0	1141.0	1499	67	673	351	17.5	6.11	67	.304	.393	-239	-265	97	317	**160**	.914	491	141	116	.8	-21.1	.9		-10.
TOT	930	32	131	21	9268.2					14.7	4.23		.274	.351						.913	3979	967	841					

Batter-Fielder Wins	Batting Average	On-Base Percentage	Slugging Average	On-Base Plus Slugging	Adjusted OPS	Adjusted Batter Runs
Browning-Cle......4.9	Browning-Cle 373	Brouthers-Bos 466	Connor-NY 548	Connor-NY 998	Browning-Cle............175	Browning-Cle.........60.
Connor-NY 2.8	Orr-Bro 371	Browning-Cle 459	B.Ewing-NY 545	Browning-Cle...........976	Beckley-Pit..............156	Larkin-Cle.............42.
Radford-Cle 2.7	O'Rourke-NY 360	Connor-NY 450	Beckley-Pit...........535	Orr-Bro 948	Larkin-Cle...............153	Beckley-Pit...........39
Farrell-Chi 2.6	Connor-NY 349	Robinson-Pit...........434	Orr-Bro 534	Gore-NY 931	Connor-NY 152	Connor-NY 36
B.Ewing-NY 2.5	Ryan-Chi 340	Gore-NY 432	Browning-Cle 517	O'Rourke-NY 925	Orr-Bro 144	Brouthers-Bos.......32.

Runs	Hits	Doubles	Triples	Home Runs	Total Bases	Runs Batted In
Duffy-Chi 161	Duffy-Chi 191	Browning-Cle...........40	Visner-Pit 22	Connor-NY 14	Shindle-Phi 282	Richardson-Bos....14
Brown-Bos 146	Shindle-Phi 189	Beckley-Pit.............38	Beckley-Pit..............22	Richardson-Bos......13	Duffy-Chi 280	Orr-Bro 12
Stovey-Bos 142	Ward-Bro 188	O'Rourke-NY 37	Shindle-Phi 21	Stovey-Bos 12	Beckley-Pit 276	Beckley-Pit...........12
Ward-Bro 134	Browning-Cle...........184	Duffy-Chi 36	Fields-Pit 20	Shindle-Phi 10	Richardson-Bos......274	O'Rourke-NY 11
Connor-NY 133	Richardson-Bos......181	Brouthers-Bos 36	Joyce-Bro 18	Gore-NY 10	Connor-NY 265	Larkin-Cle.............11

Stolen Bases	Base Stealing Runs	Fielding Runs-Infield	Fielding Runs-Outfield	Wins	Winning Pct.	Complete Games
Stovey-Bos 97		Bierbauer-Bro 20.8	Wood-Phi 14.2	Baldwin-Chi 33	Daley-Bos...............720	Baldwin-Chi 5
Brown-Bos 79		Pfeffer-Chi 20.0	Griffin-Phi 13.1	Weyhing-Bro 30	Radbourn-Bos 692	King-Chi 4
Duffy-Chi...............78		Nash-Bos 18.5	Duffy-Chi 9.4	King-Chi 30	Knell-Phi 667	Staley-Pit 4
Hanlon-Pit 65		White-Buf 18.0	Seery-Bro 5.9	Radbourn-Bos 27	Gumbert-Bos 657	Gruber-Cle 3
Ward-Bro 63		Ward-Bro 16.8	Fields-Pit 5.5	Gumbert-Bos 23	Weyhing-Bro 652	Weyhing-Bro 3

Strikeouts	Fewest BB/Game	Games	Saves	Base Runners/9	Adjusted Relief Runs	Relief Ranking
Baldwin-Chi 206	Staley-Pit 1.72	Baldwin-Chi 58	Hemming-Cle-Bro 3	Staley-Pit 11.07		
King-Chi 185	Sanders-Phi 1.79	King-Chi 56	O'Day-NY 3	King-Chi 11.67		
Weyhing-Bro 177	Galvin-Pit 2.03	Weyhing-Bro 49		Radbourn-Bos 12.15		
Staley-Pit 145	Morris-Pit 2.18	Gruber-Cle 48		Keefe-NY 12.66		
J.Ewing-NY 145	Radbourn-Bos 2.62	Staley-Pit 46		Sanders-Phi 12.75		

Innings Pitched	Opponents' Avg.	Opponents' OBP	Earned Run Average	Adjusted ERA	Adjusted Starter Runs	Pitcher Wins
Baldwin-Chi 492.0	King-Chi 232	Staley-Pit 290	Staley-Pit 2.69	King-Chi 161	King-Chi 81.7	**King-Chi**.............6.
King-Chi 461.0	Crane-NY 245	King-Chi 301	Staley-Pit 3.23	Keefe-NY 134	Baldwin-Chi 48.7	**Baldwin-Chi** ....4.
Weyhing-Bro 390.0	Keefe-NY 246	Radbourn-Bos 310	Radbourn-Bos 3.31	Radbourn-Bos 133	Radbourn-Bos 45.5	**Radbourn-Bos** ...3.
Staley-Pit 387.2	Hemming-Cle-Bro .247	Keefe-NY 318	Baldwin-Chi 3.35	Baldwin-Chi 130	Weyhing-Bro 40.2	**Weyhing-Bro** 2
Gruber-Cle 383.1	Knell-Phi 250	Sanders-Phi 320	Keefe-NY 3.38	Weyhing-Bro 124	Staley-Pit 28.7	**Staley-Pit** ....2.

A Short-Lived Brotherhood

When John Ward and his associates broke away to form the Players' League, the magnates showed foresight. Their laudable and well-reasoned efforts to break the reserve clause, the use of two, rather than one, umpire to ensure fair play, and the decision to allow two free substitutes, rather than just one, foreshadowed future changes in the game. However, the league also used a substandard and much livelier ball, would not employ black players, did not sell alcohol in the parks, and refused to play ball on Sundays—ensuring that many working fans couldn't come to the games.

The Players' League went directly at the National League, setting up teams in seven NL cities—only Cincinnati was spared direct competition. Brooklyn and Philadelphia, also American Association cities, had three different major league teams simultaneously.

Hugh Duffy, formerly of the Chicago NL club, jumped to the PL's Chicago Pirates and led the new league in runs and hits. Pete Browning of Cleveland won his third big league batting title. Respected veterans like Ward, Ned Hanlon, Charlie Comiskey, and Buck Ewing served as PL managers.

But the league champ was Boston, featuring an all-time cast of characters: player-manager King Kelly, first baseman Dan Brou thers, slugging outfielders Hardy Richardson and outfielder Harr Stovey, plus 36-year-old pitcher Hoss Radbourn, enjoying his las hurrah despite a damaged wing. Brooklyn's club, Ward's Wonder finished second. Despite Duffy's exploits and the fine pitching o Mark Baldwin and Silver King, Chicago ended up fourth. Vetera shortstop Jack Rowe and 43-year-old infielder Deacon White pla yed their last seasons, for Buffalo. Former NL home run kin Ed Williamson also ended his career in the PL, falling prey to th alcoholism that would end his life four years later.

Despite being shut out of any postseason play, the PL finishe its first season as the people's choice, leading the three leagues i attendance. However, the costs of instituting a new league that pai players fairly proved daunting, and the league capitulated the following January. Some historians claim that the threat of th Players' League—coming at a cost of more than $250,000 for th National League—was the closest the NL ever came to toppling.

1890 National League

TEAM	W	L	T	PCT	GB	HW	HL	R	OR	PA	H	2B	3B	HR	BB	SO	HB	SH	AVG	OBP	SLG	OPS	AOPS	BR	ABR	PF	SB	CS	BSA	BSR
BRO	86	43	0	.667		58	16	884	620	4977	1166	184	75	43	517	361	41		.264	.346	.369	715	113	77	74	100	349			
CHI	84	53	2	.613	6	48	24	847	692	5453	1271	147	60	67	516	514	46		.260	.336	.356	692	102	37	5	104	329			
PHI	78	54	1	.591	9.5	54	22	823	707	5293	1267	220	78	23	522	403	64		.269	.350	.364	714	110	84	63	103	335			
CIN	77	55	2	.583	10.5	50	23	753	633	5128	1203	150	120	27	433	377	51		.259	.329	.360	689	106	20	24	100	312			
BOS	76	57	1	.571	12	43	23	763	593	5321	1220	175	62	31	530	515	69		.258	.342	.341	683	96	32	-27	108	285			
NY	63	68	4	.481	24	37	27	713	698	5232	1250	208	89	25	350	479	50		.259	.315	.354	669	99	-17	-18	100	289			
CLE	44	88	4	.333	43.5	30	37	630	832	5172	1073	132	59	21	497	474	42		.232	.312	.299	611	84	-98	-85	98	152			
PIT	23	113	2	.169	66.5	14	25	597	1235	5213	1088	160	43	20	408	458	66		.230	.300	.294	594	87	-134	-53	88	208			
TOT	539					334	197	6010		41789	9538	1376	586	257	3773	3581	429		.254	.329	.342	671					2259			

TEAM	CG	SHO	GR	SV	IP	H	HR	BB	SO	BR/9	ERA	AERA	OAV	OOB	PR	APR	PF	OSB	OCS	FA	E	WPB	DP	FW	PW	BW	BSW	DIF
BRO	115	6	14	2	1145.0	1102	27	401	403	12.2	3.06	112	.246	.315	64	49	96	304	118	.940	320	114	92	4.4	4.4	6.6		6.2
CHI	126	6	13	3	1237.1	1103	41	481	504	11.9	3.24	113	.234	.311	44	48	103	257	145	.940	344	138	89	4.8	4.3	.4		6.0
PHI	122	9	12	2	1194.2	1210	22	486	507	13.2	3.32	110	.255	.331	32	42	102	266	139	.929	398	102	122	.4	3.7	5.6		2.3
CIN	124	9	10	1	1190.2	1097	41	407	488	11.8	2.79	127	.238	.307	102	100	100	226	162	.932	382	116	106	1.5	8.9	2.1		-1.6
BOS	132	13	2	1	1187.0	1132	27	354	506	11.5	2.93	128	.245	.303	83	99	105	220	150	.935	359	94	77	2.9	8.8	-2.4		.2
NY	115	6	20	1	1177.0	1029	14	607	612	13.0	3.06	114	.230	.331	66	53	98	283	209	.922	440	164	104	-1.9	4.7	-1.6		-3.8
CLE	129	2	8	0	1184.1	1322	33	462	306	14.0	4.13	86	.275	.346	-75	-77	100	256	198	.929	405	108	108	.5	-6.8	-7.6		-8.1
PIT	119	3	20	0	1176.1	1520	52	573	381	16.6	5.97	55	.304	.384	-315	-379	92	447	200	.897	607	192	94	-11.6	-33.7	-4.7		5.0
TOT	982	54	99	10	9492.1					13.0	3.56		.254	.329						.928	3255	1028	792					

Batter-Fielder Wins		Batting Average		On-Base Percentage		Slugging Average		On-Base Plus Slugging		Adjusted OPS		Adjusted Batter Runs	
Glasscock-NY	4.8	Glasscock-NY	336	Anson-Chi	443	Tiernan-NY	495	Tiernan-NY	880	Tiernan-NY	156	Tiernan-NY	37.4
McPhee-Cin	3.9	Hamilton-Phi	325	Hamilton-Phi	430	Clements-Phi	472	Clements-Phi	864	Clements-Phi	148	Anson-Chi	33.9
Allen-Phi	3.2	Clements-Phi	315	Pinkney-Bro	411	Reilly-Cin	472	Anson-Chi	844	Pinkney-Bro	145	McKean-Cle	31.3
Clements-Phi	3.0	O'Brien-Bro	314	McKean-Cle	401	Burns-Bro	464	Pinkney-Bro	842	Glasscock-NY	143	Pinkney-Bro	31.1
Hamilton-Phi	2.6	Thompson-Phi	313	Glasscock-NY	395	Burkett-NY	461	Glasscock-NY	834	McKean-Cle	141	Hamilton-Phi	29.2

Runs		Hits		Doubles		Triples		Home Runs		Total Bases		Runs Batted In	
Collins-Bro	148	Thompson-Phi	172	Thompson-Phi	41	Reilly-Cin	26	Wilmot-Chi	13	Tiernan-NY	274	Burns-Bro	128
Carroll-Chi	134	Glasscock-NY	172	Glasscock-NY	32	McPhee-Cin	22	Tiernan-NY	13	Reilly-Cin	261	Anson-Chi	107
Hamilton-Phi	133	Tiernan-NY	168	Collins-Bro	32	Tiernan-NY	21	Burns-Bro	13	Thompson-Phi	243	Thompson-Phi	102
Tiernan-NY	132	Reilly-Cin	166	Myers-Phi	29	Beard-Cin	15	Long-Bos	8	Wilmot-Chi	239	Wilmot-Chi	99
McPhee-Cin	125	Carroll-Chi	166	O'Brien-Bro	28					Glasscock-NY	225	Foutz-Phi	98

Stolen Bases		Base Stealing Runs		Fielding Runs-Infield		Fielding Runs-Outfield		Wins		Winning Pct.		Complete Games	
Hamilton-Phi	102			Allen-Phi	32.3	Davis-Cle	12.3	Hutchison-Chi	42	Lovett-Bro	732	Hutchison-Chi	65
Collins-Bro	85			McPhee-Cin	26.4	Wilmot-Chi	10.9	Gleason-Phi	38	Gleason-Phi	691	Rusie-NY	56
Sunday-Pit-Phi	84			Glasscock-NY	23.3	Carroll-Chi	10.9	Lovett-Bro	30	Luby-Chi	690	Gleason-Phi	54
Wilmot-Chi	76			Smalley-NY	20.2	Sunday-Pit-Phi	10.3	Rusie-NY	29	Caruthers-Bro	676	Beatin-Cle	53
Tiernan-NY	56			Bassett-NY	18.7	Gilks-Cle	5.3	Rhines-Cin	28	Hutchison-Chi	627	Nichols-Bos	47

Strikeouts		Fewest BB/Game		Games		Saves		Base Runners/9		Adjusted Relief Runs		Relief Ranking	
Rusie-NY	341	Young-Cle	1.83	Hutchison-Chi	71	Rhines-Cin	2	Rhines-Cin	10.43				
Hutchison-Chi	289	Duryea-Cin	1.97	Rusie-NY	67	Nichols-Bos	2	Nichols-Bos	10.55				
Nichols-Bos	222	Getzien-Bos	2.11	Gleason-Phi	60	Foutz-Bro	2	Hutchison-Chi	10.70				
Gleason-Phi	222	Nichols-Bos	2.38	Beatin-Cle	54			Getzien-Bos	10.98				
Terry-Bro	185	Rhines-Cin	2.53	Nichols-Bos	48			Duryea-Cin	11.10				

Innings Pitched		Opponents' Avg.		Opponents' OBP		Earned Run Average		Adjusted ERA		Adjusted Starter Runs		Pitcher Wins	
Hutchison-Chi	603.0	Rusie-NY	212	Rhines-Cin	282	Rhines-Cin	1.95	Rhines-Cin	182	Rhines-Cin	67.5	Rhines-Cin	6.0
Rusie-NY	548.2	Mullane-Cin	221	Nichols-Bos	284	Nichols-Bos	2.23	Nichols-Bos	168	Nichols-Bos	63.5	Nichols-Bos	5.9
Gleason-Phi	506.0	Hutchison-Chi	221	Hutchison-Chi	287	Mullane-Cin	2.24	Mullane-Cin	159	Hutchison-Chi	51.3	Rusie-NY	5.9
Beatin-Cle	474.1	Rhines-Cin	221	Getzien-Bos	292	Rusie-NY	2.56	Gleason-Phi	139	Gleason-Phi	50.9	Hutchison-Chi	4.5
Nichols-Bos	424.0	Luby-Chi	222	Duryea-Cin	295	Gleason-Phi	2.56	Rusie-NY	137	Rusie-NY	50.0	Gleason-Phi	4.0

Ball of Confusion

The Players' League rocked the NL and AA in 1890, but the Senior Circuit had its own share of intrigue, snaring two more Association franchises, Brooklyn and Cincinnati. The two new teams helped the NL survive; Cincinnati led in the early going and Brooklyn ended up on top at the end.

The Bridegrooms won despite significant injuries. Right fielder Oyster Burns and second baseman Hub Collins were the key offensive contributors, and Bob Caruthers, Tom Lovett, and Adonis Terry provided strong pitching. Second-place Chicago was weak in spots, though 42-game winner Bill Hutchinson certainly helped. Third-place Philadelphia got excellent pitching from Kid Gleason and big hitting from Sam Thompson and new recruit Billy Hamilton. Cincinnati received excellent pitching from rookie Billy Rhines, the only pitcher in the three major leagues to have an ERA below 2.00 in 1890.

Amos Rusie of New York set a new major league record by walking 293 hitters and led the league in losses, but he also paced the NL in strikeouts. His Giants finished sixth even with batting champ Jack Glasscock. Last-place Pittsburgh was so awful that 21 different pitchers started games, none more than 21 times. Billy Gumbert led with 4 wins. The club averaged just over 400 fans per game and soon became a traveling team.

Though the NL and AA had outlawed the pitcher's practice of intentionally defacing the ball with dirt, dilution of talent among the leagues allowed NL pitchers to lower their collective ERA by half a point. The loss of manpower to the PL pushed a great crop of rookies to debut: George Davis, Jesse Burkett, Bobby Lowe, Kid Nichols, and Cy Young.

The postseason, originally expected to be a cakewalk for Brooklyn, instead ended with each team winning three times before rain and low attendance caused the rest of the games to be cancelled. In truth, fans would have been more interested in the World Series had the Players' League champion Boston Reds been involved. Unsurprisingly, given the PL's competition, NL attendance fell by nearly half.

1890 American Association

TEAM	W	L	T	PCT	GB	HW	HL	R	OR	PA	H	2B	3B	HR	BB	SO	HB	SH	AVG	OBP	SLG	OPS	AOPS	BR	ABR	PF	SB	CS	BSA	BSR
LOU	88	44	4	.667		57	13	819	588	5150	1310	156	65	15	410	460	53		.279	.344	.350	694	112	53	71	98	341			
COL	79	55	6	.590	10	47	22	831	617	5332	1225	159	77	16	545	557	46		.258	.341	.335	676	112	30	90	93	353			
STL	77	58	4	.570	12.5	45	25	870	736	5369	1308	178	73	48	474	490	95		.273	.350	.370	720	103	102	-8	114	307			
TOL	68	64	2	.515	20	40	27	739	689	5132	1152	152	152	24	486	558	71		.252	.333	.348	681	103	29	8	103	421			
ROC	63	63	7	.500	22	40	22	709	711	5056	1088	131	64	31	446	538	57		.239	.315	.316	631	98	-55	1	93	310			
BAL	15	19	4	.441	24	8	11	182	192	1366	278	34	16	2	125	152	28		.229	.316	.289	605	79	-24	-32	105	101			
SYR	55	72	1	.433	30.5	30	30	698	831	4961	1158	151	59	14	457	482	35		.259	.333	.329	662	112	1	85	90	292			
PHI	54	78	0	.409	34	36	36	702	945	5052	1057	181	51	24	475	540	87		.235	.320	.314	634	93	-37	-33	99	305			
BRO	26	72	2	.265	45	15	22	492	733	3834	769	116	47	13	328	456	31		.221	.294	.293	587	80	-99	-83	97	182			
TOT	540					318	208	6042		41252	9345	1258	560	187	3746	4233	503		.253	.330	.332	662					2612			

TEAM	CG	SHO	GR	SV	IP	H	HR	BB	SO	BR/9	ERA	AERA	OAV	OOB	PR	APR	PF	OSB	OCS	FA	E	WPB	DP	FW	PW	BW	BSW	DIF
LOU	114	13	20	7	1206.0	1120	18	293	587	10.9	2.57	149	.239	.291	173	171	100	247	198	.934	380	131	79	2.8	15.0	6.2		-2.1
COL	120	14	22	3	1214.2	976	20	471	624	11.2	2.99	120	.214	.297	118	87	93	321	205	.932	396	174	101	2.6	7.7	7.9		-6.2
STL	118	4	20	1	1195.1	1127	38	447	733	12.3	3.67	117	.242	.316	25	74	112	338	205	.916	478	158	93	-1.8	6.5	-.7		5.5
TOL	122	4	14	2	1159.1	1122	23	429	533	12.6	3.56	111	.247	.321	39	48	102	270	221	.925	419	173	75	.4	4.2	.7		-3.4
ROC	122	5	12	2	1161.2	1115	19	530	477	13.2	3.56	100	.246	.331	39	-2	92	284	184	.926	416	125	95	.4	-.2	.0		-.3
BAL	36	1	2	0	315.1	307	3	123	134	13.0	4.00	101	.248	.328	-5	2	105	75	59	.928	109	30	21	.6	.2	-2.8		.0
SYR	115	5	12	0	1089.2	1158	28	518	454	14.4	4.98	71	.265	.351	-135	-193	91	390	170	.925	391	142	90	.9	-17.0	7.5		.1
PHI	119	3	14	-2	1132.0	1405	17	514	461	15.8	5.22	74	.296	.373	-171	-170	100	379	169	.918	452	145	93	-1.6	-15.0	-2.9		7.5
BRO	96	0	4	0	879.0	1011	21	421	230	15.2	4.71	83	.281	.365	-83	-80	101	308	163	.909	404	121	92	-4.4	-7.0	-7.3		-4.3
TOT	962	49	120	17	9353.0					13.1	3.86		.253	.330						.923	3445	1199	739					

Batter-Fielder Wins		Batting Average		On-Base Percentage		Slugging Average		On-Base Plus Slugging		Adjusted OPS		Adjusted Batter Runs	
Childs-Syr	6.8	Wolf-Lou	363	Lyons-Phi	461	Lyons-Phi	531	Lyons-Phi	992	Lyons-Phi	193	Childs-Syr	61.0
Lyons-Phi	4.7	Lyons-Phi	354	Swartwood-Tol	444	Campau-Stl	513	Childs-Syr	915	Childs-Syr	189	Wolf-Lou	46.8
Swartwood-Tol	3.8	McCarthy-Stl	350	Childs-Syr	434	Childs-Syr	481	Wolf-Lou	900	Wolf-Lou	169	Johnson-Col	46.2
O'Connor-Col	3.7	Johnson-Col	346	McCarthy-Stl	430	Wolf-Lou	479	McCarthy-Stl	898	Johnson-Col	168	Lyons-Phi	43.9
Wolf-Lou	3.6	Childs-Syr	345	Wright-Syr	428	McCarthy-Stl	467	Swartwood-Tol	887	Swartwood-Tol	157	Swartwood-Tol	38.4

Runs		Hits		Doubles		Triples		Home Runs		Total Bases		Runs Batted In	
McTamany-Col	140	Wolf-Lou	197	Childs-Syr	33	Werden-Tol	20	Campau-Stl	9	Wolf-Lou	260	Johnson-Col	113
McCarthy-Stl	137	McCarthy-Stl	192	Wolf-Lou	29	Johnson-Col	18	Cartwright-Stl	8	McCarthy-Stl	256	Wolf-Lou	98
Fuller-Stl	118	Johnson-Col	186	Lyons-Phi	29	Alvord-Tol	16	Stivetts-Stl	7	Johnson-Col	248	Childs-Syr	89
Sneed-Tol-Col	117	Childs-Syr	170			Sneed-Tol-Col	15	Lyons-Phi	7	Childs-Syr	237	Knowles-Roc	84
Welch-Phi-Bal	116	Taylor-Lou	169							Werden-Tol	227	Shinnick-Lou	82

Stolen Bases		Base Stealing Runs		Fielding Runs-Infield		Fielding Runs-Outfield		Wins		Winning Pct.		Complete Games	
McCarthy-Stl	83			Gerhardt-Bro-Stl	38.2	Welch-Phi-Bal	11.9	McMahon-Phi-Bal	36	Stratton-Lou	708	McMahon-Phi-Bal	55
Scheffler-Roc	77			Reilly-Col	29.1	Lyons-Roc	10.9	Stratton-Lou	34	Chamberlain-Sl-Col	682	Barr-Roc	52
VanDyke-Tol	73			Tomney-Lou	15.0	Scheffler-Roc	8.1	Gastright-Col	30	Gastright-Col	682	Stratton-Lou	44
Welch-Phi-Bal	72			Childs-Syr	14.4	Duffee-Stl	7.0	Barr-Roc	28	Ehret-Lou	641	Healy-Tol	44
				Lehane-Col	9.9	Swartwood-Tol	6.5	Stivetts-Stl	27	McMahon-Phi-Bal	632		

Strikeouts		Fewest BB/Game		Games		Saves		Base Runners/9		Adjusted Relief Runs		Relief Ranking	
McMahon-Phi-Bal	291	Stratton-Lou	1.27	McMahon-Phi-Bal	60	Goodall-Col	4	Neale-Stl	9.39				
Stivetts-Stl	289	Ehret-Lou	1.98	Barr-Roc	57	Knauss-Col	2	Stratton-Lou	9.86				
Ramsey-Stl	257	Ramsey-Stl	2.63	Stivetts-Stl	54	Ehret-Lou	2	Gastright-Col	10.43				
Healy-Tol	225	Smith-Tol	2.83	Stratton-Lou	50			Knauss-Col	10.87				
Barr-Roc	209	McMahon-Phi-Bal	2.94	Gastright-Col	48			Healy-Tol	11.04				

Innings Pitched		Opponents' Avg.		Opponents' OBP		Earned Run Average		Adjusted ERA		Adjusted Starter Runs		Pitcher Wins	
McMahon-Phi-Bal	509.0	Knauss-Col	202	Stratton-Lou	270	Stratton-Lou	2.36	Stratton-Lou	163	Stratton-Lou	73.5	Stratton-Lou	8.9
Barr-Roc	493.1	Gastright-Col	208	Gastright-Col	282	Ehret-Lou	2.53	Ehret-Lou	152	Ehret-Lou	49.8	Healy-Tol	4.3
Stratton-Lou	431.0	Easton-Col	220	Knauss-Col	290	Knauss-Col	2.81	Healy-Tol	136	Healy-Tol	40.2	Stivetts-Stl	4.2
Stivetts-Stl	419.1	Chamberlain-Sl-Col	220	Healy-Tol	293	Chamberlain-Sl-Col	2.83	Meakim-Col	132	Stivetts-Stl	30.6	Ehret-Lou	4.1
Gastright-Col	401.1	Healy-Tol	221	Ehret-Lou	296	Healy-Tol	2.89	Chamberlain-Sl-Col	131	Gastright-Col	29.9	Gastright-Col	2.7

Barely There

Buffeted by defections and increased competition from the new Players' League, the AA struggled just to make it through 1890. Two top clubs, Brooklyn and Cincinnati, jumped to the NL, and Kansas City and Baltimore simply quit the league. New clubs in Toledo, Syracuse, and Rochester failed to garner much interest, and an expansion Brooklyn team lost its last 14 before disbanding in August. The Baltimore Orioles, who had deserted the American Association for the Atlantic Association, rejoined in order to help the AA finish the season.

Philadelphia ran out of money in August, and most of the club quit, forcing the recruitment of below-average substitutes. The dismal Athletics lost their final 22 games yet still had twice as many wins as miserable Brooklyn.

Many former Association players jumped to the NL and PL, including St. Louis' Charlie Comiskey, Arlie Latham, Tip O'Neill, and Silver King, Philadelphia slugger Harry Stovey, Kansas City shortstop Herman Long, and Louisville outfielder Pete Browning. The disemboweled Browns fell to third.

Perhaps the best indicator of the AA's quality is that the league champion, Louisville, had finished dead last the previous season with a .196 winning percentage and was the most games back of any team in league history. For 1890 the Colonels made few player changes and improved 67 games. Chicken Wolf, who had hit .300 just once in eight seasons, won the batting title at .363; pitcher Scott Stratton, 3-13 in 1889, went 34-14 and led the league in ERA. Columbus, leaping to second, couldn't provide enough of a challenge despite deep pitching and Jim McTamany's league-leading 140 runs.

Louisville was by far the league's top draw; St. Louis' attendance fell by 70,000, while Brooklyn's new club drew just 1,000 fans per game. Overall AA attendance sank to its lowest since its inaugural season in 1882. A postseason World Series between Louisville and turncoat Brooklyn was closer than expected, but rain postponed several contests. The games did not draw enough interest to continue play into November and the Series was called after six games.

1889 National League

TEAM	W	L	T	PCT	GB	HW	HL	R	OR	PA	H	2B	3B	HR	BB	SO	HB	SH	AVG	OBP	SLG	OPS	AOPS	BR	ABR	PF	SB	CS	BSA	BSR
NY	83	43	5	.659		47	15	935	708	5236	1319	208	77	52	538	386	27		.282	.360	.393	753	116	105	103	100	292			
BOS	83	45	5	.648	1	48	17	826	626	5140	1251	196	54	42	471	450	41		.270	.343	.363	706	97	22	-23	106	331			
CHI	67	65	4	.508	19	37	30	867	814	5397	1338	184	66	79	518	516	30		.276	.349	.390	739	107	76	34	105	243			
PHI	63	64	3	.496	20.5	43	24	742	748	5123	1248	215	52	44	393	353	35		.266	.357	.362	689	90	-17	-77	109	269			
PIT	61	71	2	.462	25	40	28	726	801	5212	1202	209	65	42	420	467	44		.253	.320	.351	671	103	-50	28	90	231			
CLE	61	72	3	.459	25.5	33	35	656	720	5140	1167	201	59	25	429	417	38		.250	.318	.319	637	85	-104	-91	98	237			
IND	59	75	1	.440	27	32	36	819	894	5300	1356	228	35	62	377	447	44		.278	.335	.377	712	102	24	9	102	252			
WAS	41	83	3	.331	41	24	29	632	892	4904	1105	151	57	25	466	456	43		.251	.329	.329	658	95	-56	-12	94	232			
TOT	531					304	214	6203		41452	9986	1522	465	371	3612	3492	302		.266	.335	.361	696					2087			

TEAM	CG	SHO	GR	SV	IP	H	HR	BB	SO	BR/9	ERA	AERA	OAV	OOB	PR	APR	PF	OSB	OCS	FA	E	WPB	DP	FW	PW	BW	BSW	DIF
NY	119	6	13	3	1150.0	1067	38	524	558	12.8	3.47	114	.240	.327	70	57	98	193		.919	437	102	90	-.3	4.9	8.9		6.5
BOS	121	10	12	5	1166.0	1152	41	413	497	12.4	3.36	124	.250	.318	86	102	104	186		.926	413	77	105	1.2	8.8	-2.0		10.9
CHI	123	6	13	2	1237.0	1313	71	408	434	12.8	3.73	112	.263	.324	41	62	104	301		.923	463	142	91	-.8	5.4	2.9		-6.5
PHI	106	4	27	2	1153.1	1288	33	428	443	13.6	4.00	109	.275	.339	3	39	108	229		.915	466	106	92	-2.0	3.4	-6.7		4.8
PIT	125	5	9	1	1130.2	1296	42	374	345	13.5	4.51	83	.272	.329	-60	-84	93	276		.931	385	140	94	2.8	-7.3	2.4		-3.0
CLE	132	6	5	1	1191.2	1182	36	519	435	13.2	3.66	110	.252	.332	48	47	100	271		.936	365	163	108	4.2	4.1	-7.9		-5.9
IND	109	3	29	2	1174.1	1365	36	420	408	14.0	4.85	86	.282	.345	-108	-85	104	297		.926	420	117	102	1.2	-7.4	.8		-2.6
WAS	113	1	16	0	1103.0	1261	37	527	388	14.9	4.68	85	.279	.360	-80	-92	98	334		.904	519	109	91	-5.2	-8.0	-1.0		-6.8
TOT	948	41	124	16	9306.0					13.4	4.02		.266	.335						.923	3468	956	773					

Batter-Fielder Wins		Batting Average		On-Base Percentage		Slugging Average		On-Base Plus Slugging		Adjusted OPS		Adjusted Batter Runs	
Glasscock-Ind	5.8	Brouthers-Bos	373	Carroll-Pit	486	Connor-NY	528	Carroll-Pit	970	Carroll-Pit	188	Carroll-Pit	49.6
Carroll-Pit	3.7	Glasscock-Ind	352	Brouthers-Bos	462	Ryan-Chi	516	Brouthers-Bos	969	Connor-NY	164	Tiernan-NY	46.9
Ewing-NY	3.7	Anson-Chi	342	Tiernan-NY	447	Brouthers-Bos	507	Connor-NY	955	Tiernan-NY	162	Connor-NY	46.1
Tiernan-NY	3.7	Tiernan-NY	335	Anson-Chi	440	Tiernan-NY	497	Tiernan-NY	944	Brouthers-Bos	160	Brouthers-Bos	42.4
Wilmot-Was	3.1	Carroll-Pit	330	Connor-NY	426	Thompson-Phi	492	Ryan-Chi	919	Ryan-Chi	147	Anson-Chi	36.5

Runs		Hits		Doubles		Triples		Home Runs		Total Bases		Runs Batted In	
Tiernan-NY	147	Glasscock-Ind	205	Kelly-Bos	41	Wilmot-Was	19	Thompson-Phi	20	Ryan-Chi	297	Connor-NY	130
Duffy-Chi	144	Ryan-Chi	187	Glasscock-Ind	40	Fogarty-Phi	17	Denny-Ind	18	Glasscock-Ind	272	Brouthers-Bos	118
Ryan-Chi	140	Duffy-Chi	182	Thompson-Phi	36	Connor-NY	17	Ryan-Chi	17	Thompson-Phi	262	Anson-Chi	117
Gore-NY	132	Brouthers-Bos	181	O'Rourke-NY	36	Tiernan-NY	14	Connor-NY	13	Connor-NY	262	Denny-Ind	112
Glasscock-Ind	128	Anson-Chi	177	Richardson-Ind	33	Ryan-Chi	14	Duffy-Chi	12	Duffy-Chi	253	Thompson-Phi	111

Stolen Bases		Base Stealing Runs		Fielding Runs-Infield		Fielding Runs-Outfield		Wins		Winning Pct.		Complete Games	
Fogarty-Phi	99			Glasscock-Ind	38.1	Fogarty-Phi	18.3	Clarkson-Bos	49	Clarkson-Bos	721	Clarkson-Bos	68
Kelly-Bos	68			Richardson-NY	14.9	Wilmot-Was	14.3	Keefe-NY	28	Staley-Pit	692	Staley-Pit	46
Brown-Bos	63			Denny-Ind	12.7	Ryan-Chi	8.5	Buffinton-Phi	28	Keefe-NY	683	Welch-NY	39
Ward-NY	62			Bassett-Ind	12.5	McGeachy-Ind	7.8	Welch-NY	27	Radbourn-Bos	645	O'Brien-Cle	39
Glasscock-Ind	57			Nash-Bos	11.4	McAleer-Cle	7.5	Galvin-Pit	23	Buffinton-Phi	636	Keefe-NY	39

Strikeouts		Fewest BB/Game		Games		Saves		Base Runners/9		Adjusted Relief Runs		Relief Ranking	
Clarkson-Bos	284	Galvin-Pit	2.06	Clarkson-Bos	73	Sowders-Bos-Pit	2	Clarkson-Bos	11.74				
Keefe-NY	225	Boyle-Ind	2.26	Staley-Pit	49	Welch-NY	2	Radbourn-Bos	11.76				
Staley-Pit	159	Radbourn-Bos	2.34	Keefe-NY	47	Bishop-Chi	2	Staley-Pit	11.94				
Buffinton-Phi	153	Dwyer-Chi	2.35	Buffinton-Phi	47			Welch-NY	11.98				
Getzien-Ind	139	Sanders-Phi	2.47	Boyle-Ind	46			Keefe-NY	12.07				

Innings Pitched		Opponents' Avg.		Opponents' OBP		Earned Run Average		Adjusted ERA		Adjusted Starter Runs		Pitcher Wins	
Clarkson-Bos	620.0	Keefe-NY	228	Clarkson-Bos	306	Clarkson-Bos	2.73	Clarkson-Bos	153	Clarkson-Bos	92.8	Clarkson-Bos	8.9
Staley-Pit	420.0	Welch-NY	234	Radbourn-Bos	306	Bakely-Cle	2.96	Bakely-Cle	136	Buffinton-Phi	44.6	Buffinton-Phi	4.0
Buffinton-Phi	380.0	Clarkson-Bos	243	Staley-Pit	309	Welch-NY	3.02	Buffinton-Phi	134	Welch-NY	40.8	Welch-NY	3.1
Boyle-Ind	378.2	Crane-NY	244	Welch-NY	310	Buffinton-Phi	3.24	Welch-NY	131	Bakely-Cle	29.5	Bakely-Cle	2.6
Welch-NY	375.0	Hutchison-Chi	245	Keefe-NY	311	Keefe-NY	3.36	Sanders-Phi	123	Keefe-NY	24.4	Sanders-Phi	2.4

Land of the Giants

The Detroit club left the NL, and Cleveland jumped from the American Association to fill the space. The new club finished sixth. The game itself underwent significant changes in 1889. First and forevermore, it now took four balls to draw a walk, which helped scoring increase by about 25 percent. In addition, the use of substitutes gained speed as teams were now allowed to change one player per game for any reason—not just injuries—at the end of any complete inning. Also, the owners' decision to institute a salary classification scheme infuriated players, who organized in secret.

New York won its second straight league title, edging out the Boston Beaneaters by 1 game. Tim Keefe's win on the season's last day clinched matters for the Giants, who sported the bats of Roger Connor, Mike Tiernan, and George Gore, and a great second starter in Mickey Welch. Boston contended largely on the arm of John Clarkson, who enjoyed one of the great ironman seasons by any pitcher. He led the league by huge margins in games, innings, wins, strikeouts, and ERA. His 68 complete games weren't quite a record, but no one has surpassed it since; the same can be said of his 49 wins, which still didn't match his career-high 53 victories in '85. Beaneaters teammate Dan Brouthers won his third batting title, but King Kelly, beginning to feel the effects of his dissipated lifestyle, fell off dramatically for Boston.

Future ace Amos Rusie debuted as a third starter for seventh-place Indianapolis. Sam Thompson led the league in homers and Jim Fogarty paced the NL in steals for Harry Wright's fourth-place Phillies.

The Giants took a hotly contested World Series from AA champ Brooklyn—New York's first "Subway Series," so to speak, even though the subway system did not open until 1904. The Bridegrooms, borrowing a tactic from AA St. Louis, won three times by stalling for darkness, but New York responded by outhitting Brooklyn, 102-67. Neither Keefe nor Welch had the strength to win a single contest—second-line hurlers Ed "Cannonball" Crane and Hank O'Day took over and saved the NL's bacon.

1889 American Association

TEAM	W	L	T	PCT	GB	HW	HL	R	OR	PA	H	2B	3B	HR	BB	SO	HB	SH	AVG	OBP	SLG	OPS	AOPS	BR	ABR	PF	SB	CS	BSA	BSR
BRO	93	44	3	.679		50	18	**995**	706	5414	1265	188	79	47	**550**	401	49		.263	.344	.364	708	106	44	41	100	389			
STL	90	45	6	.667	2	**51**	18	957	**680**	5487	1312	211	64	**58**	493	477	55		.266	.339	.370	709	94	41	-63	113	336			
PHI	75	58	5	.564	16	46	22	880	787	5464	**1339**	**239**	65	43	534	496	62		**.275**	**.354**	.377	731	**114**	**92**	**105**	99	252			
CIN	76	63	2	.547	18	47	26	897	769	5356	1307	197	**96**	52	452	511	60		.270	.340	**.382**	722	107	56	30	103	462			
BAL	70	65	4	.519	22	41	23	791	795	5256	1209	155	68	20	418	536	**82**		.254	.325	.328	653	88	-58	-71	102	311			
COL	60	78	2	.435	33.5	36	33	779	924	5365	1247	171	95	36	507	609	42		.259	.335	.356	691	106	7	52	95	304			
KC	55	82	2	.401	38	35	35	852	1031	5443	1256	162	76	18	430	626	66		.254	.322	.328	650	84	-68	-113	106	**472**			
LOU	27	111	2	.196	66.5	18	47	632	1091	5316	1249	170	75	22	320	521	41		.252	.303	.330	633	86	-114	-100	98	203			
TOT	559					324	222	6783		43101	10184	1493	618	296	3704	4177	457		.262	.333	.354	687					2729			

TEAM	CG	SHO	GR	SV	IP	H	HR	BB	SO	BR/9	ERA	AERA	OAV	OOB	PR	APR	PF	OSB	OCS	FA	E	WPB	DP	FW	PW	BW	BSW	DIF
BRO	120	**10**	20	1	1212.2	1205	33	**400**	471	12.2	3.61	103	.251	.315	31	15	97	361		**.928**	**421**	142	92	**4.6**	1.3	3.5		15.2
STL	121	7	20	4	1237.2	**1166**	39	413	**617**	11.9	3.00	141	.242	.309	116	152	110	326		.925	438	196	100	3.8	**12.9**	-5.3		11.2
PHI	**130**	9	8	1	1199.1	1199	35	509	479	13.4	3.53	107	.253	.335	42	34	98	**280**		.920	465	152	120	1.7	2.9	**8.9**		-5.0
CIN	114	3	**27**	**8**	1243.0	1270	35	475	562	13.0	3.50	111	.257	.328	47	53	102	294		.926	440	187	**121**	3.7	4.5	2.5		-4.2
BAL	128	**10**	12	1	1192.0	1168	**27**	424	540	12.6	3.56	111	.249	.322	38	48	103	305		.907	536	195	104	-2.1	4.1	-6.0		6.5
COL	114	9	**27**	4	1199.0	1274	33	551	610	14.1	4.39	82	.264	.346	-73	-110	94	431		.915	497	275	92	.3	-9.3	-4.4		-4.4
KC	128	0	11	2	1204.1	1373	51	457	447	14.1	4.36	97	.278	.347	-69	-15	110	363		.899	611	201	109	-6.3	-1.3	-9.6		3.6
LOU	127	2	.13	1	1226.1	1529	43	475	451	15.1	4.81	80	.297	.362	-132	-133	100	369		.906	584	234	117	-4.5	-11.3	-8.5		-17.7
TOT	982	50	138	22	9714.1					13.3	3.84		.262	.333						.916	3992	1582	855					

Batter-Fielder Wins		Batting Average		On-Base Percentage		Slugging Average		On-Base Plus Slugging		Adjusted OPS		Adjusted Batter Runs	
Stovey-Phi	5.0	Tucker-Bal	.372	Tucker-Bal	.450	Stovey-Phi	.525	Tucker-Bal	.934	Tucker-Bal	163	Tucker-Bal	46.3
Lyons-Phi	4.5	O'Neill-StL	.335	Larkin-Phi	.428	Holliday-Cin	.497	Stovey-Phi	.918	Stovey-Phi	162	Stovey-Phi	45.8
Bierbauer-Phi	4.3	Lyons-Phi	.329	Lyons-Phi	.426	Tucker-Bal	.484	O'Neill-StL	.897	Lyons-Phi	157	Lyons-Phi	43.3
Marr-Col	3.6	Orr-Col	.327	O'Neill-StL	.419	O'Neill-StL	.478	Lyons-Phi	.895	Larkin-Phi	145	Larkin-Phi	36.9
McPhee-Cin	3.6	Holliday-Cin	.321	Hamilton-KC	.413	Lyons-Phi	.469	Holliday-Cin	.869	Holliday-Cin	142	Marr-Col	35.2

Runs		Hits		Doubles		Triples		Home Runs		Total Bases		Runs Batted In	
Stovey-Phi	152	Tucker-Bal	196	Welch-Phi	39	Marr-Col	15	Stovey-Phi	19	Stovey-Phi	292	Stovey-Phi	119
Griffin-Bal	152	Orr-Col	183	Stovey-Phi	38	Griffin-Bal	14	Holliday-Cin	19	Holliday-Cin	280	Foutz-Bro	113
O'Brien-Bro	146	Holliday-Cin	181	Lyons-Phi	36	Beard-Cin	14	Duffee-StL	16	Tucker-Bal	255	O'Neill-StL	110
Hamilton-KC	144	O'Neill-StL	179	O'Neill-StL	33			Milligan-StL	12	O'Neill-StL	255	Bierbauer-Phi	105
Collins-Bro	139	Shindle-Bal	178	Long-KC	32					Orr-Col	250	Holliday-Cin	104

Stolen Bases		Base Stealing Runs		Fielding Runs-Infield		Fielding Runs-Outfield		Wins		Winning Pct.		Complete Games	
Hamilton-KC	111			McPhee-Cin	37.3	Stovey-Phi	17.7	Caruthers-Bro	40	Caruthers-Bro	.784	Kilroy-Bal	55
O'Brien-Bro	91			Bierbauer-Phi	36.4	Duffee-StL	15.7	King-StL	35	King-StL	.686	Baldwin-Col	54
Long-KC	89			Long-KC	31.2	McCarthy-StL	13.0	Duryea-Cin	32	Chamberlain-StL	.681	Weyhing-Phi	50
Nicol-Cin	80			Shindle-Bal	22.6	Hornung-Bal	12.3	Chamberlain-StL	32	Lovett-Bro	.630	King-StL	47
Latham-StL	69			Tomney-Lou	21.6	Sommer-Bal	9.1	Weyhing-Phi	30	Duryea-Cin	.627	Caruthers-Bro	46

Strikeouts		Fewest BB/Game		Games		Saves		Base Runners/9		Adjusted Relief Runs		Relief Ranking	
Baldwin-Col	368	Caruthers-Bro	2.10	Kilroy-Bal	63	Mullane-Cin	5	Stivetts-StL	10.61				
Kilroy-Bal	217	Conway-KC	2.42	Kilroy-Bal	59	Stivetts-StL	2	Caruthers-Bro	11.35				
Weyhing-Phi	213	King-StL	2.46	King-StL	56			Duryea-Cin	11.56				
Chamberlain-StL	202	Lovett-Bro	2.55	Caruthers-Bro	56			Foreman-Bal	11.76				
King-StL	188	Swartzel-KC	2.57	Weyhing-Phi	54			Conway-KC	11.77				

Innings Pitched		Opponents' Avg.		Opponents' OBP		Earned Run Average		Adjusted ERA		Adjusted Starter Runs		Pitcher Wins	
Baldwin-Col	513.2	Stivetts-StL	.212	Stivetts-StL	.285	Stivetts-StL	2.25	Stivetts-StL	187	Chamberlain-StL	56.0	**Duryea-Cin**	5.7
Kilroy-Bal	480.2	Weyhing-Phi	.223	Caruthers-Bro	.299	Duryea-Cin	2.56	Duryea-Cin	152	King-StL	51.7	**Kilroy-Bal**	5.7
King-StL	458.0	Terry-Bro	.228	Duryea-Cin	.303	Kilroy-Bal	2.85	Chamberlain-StL	142	Duryea-Cin	50.6	**Chamberlain-StL**	4.6
Weyhing-Phi	449.0	Foreman-Bal	.229	Foreman-Bal	.306	Weyhing-Phi	2.95	Kilroy-Bal	138	Kilroy-Bal	49.4	**Caruthers-Bro**	4.6
Caruthers-Bro	445.0	Baldwin-Col	.231	Conway-KC	.306	Chamberlain-StL	2.97	King-StL	134	Stivetts-StL	36.5	**King-StL**	4.4

Forfeiting a Title

Cleveland, a perennial doormat, left the league for the NL and was replaced by Columbus, which finished sixth. The big news in the AA was a dethroning of perennial champion St. Louis. The Browns' questionable on-field ethics, which included the tactic of stalling while ahead until darkness came and ended games, led to several forfeits. Brooklyn, white-hot down the stretch, grabbed the flag in the closest AA race since 1883.

The Bridegrooms led the league in runs despite lacking a single marquee star. Brooklyn moundsman Bob Caruthers paced the league in wins. St. Louis second baseman Yank Robinson broke his own record for walks and put together a .378 on-base percentage, but he hit just .208. Arlie Latham also disappointed at bat. Pitchers Silver King and Icebox Chamberlain were good, if unspectacular, though third arm Jack Stivetts paced the AA in ERA.

Once again, third-place Philadelphia had the AA's top power producer (this time Harry Stovey) as well as other bats in Curt Welch and Henry Larkin. Although the Athletics seem to have played in a good hitter's park, their offensive numbers, and their W-L record, were inadequate on the road.

With four balls once again required for a walk, Columbus pitcher Mark Baldwin set a record by passing 274 hitters. He also paced the league in games, strikeouts, and losses.

Baltimore improved 14 games, largely due to a great season from first baseman Tommy Tucker, who was the AA's surprise batting and on-base titlist in 1889. Seventh-place Kansas City installed rookie Herman Long at shortstop, and next to Billy Hamilton, Long was the team's best player. Meanwhile, last-place Louisville was almost unbelievably bad, finishing 66½ games out and running through four managers and five pitchers who made 18 or more starts.

League attendance rose by nearly 300,000, due to increases in Baltimore, Brooklyn, and Philadelphia. The Bridegrooms' tally of 353,690 was the highest attendance by any major league team to that point; it would not be surpassed for five years.

1888 National League

TEAM	W	L	T	PCT	GB	HW	HL	R	OR	PA	H	2B	3B	HR	BB	SO	HB	SH	AVG	OBP	SLG	OPS	AOPS	BR	ABR	PF	SB	CS	BSA	BSR
NY	84	47	7	.641		44	23	659	479	5046	1149	130	76	55	270	456	29		.242	.287	.336	623	105	18	26	99	314			
CHI	77	58	1	.570	9	43	27	734	659	4934	1201	147	95	77	290	563	28		.260	.308	.383	691	117	125	75	107	287			
PHI	69	61	2	.531	14.5	37	29	535	509	4847	1021	151	46	16	268	485	51		.225	.276	.290	566	82	-61	-89	105	246			
BOS	70	64	3	.522	15.5	36	30	669	619	5148	1183	167	89	56	282	524	32		.245	.291	.351	642	107	50	33	103	293			
DET	68	63	3	.519	16	40	26	721	629	5202	1275	177	72	51	307	396	46		.263	.313	.361	674	120	112	104	101	193			
PIT	66	68	5	.493	19.5	37	30	534	580	4953	1070	150	49	14	194	583	46		.227	.264	.289	553	90	-93	-44	91	287			
IND	50	85	1	.370	36	31	35	603	731	4902	1100	180	33	34	236	492	43		.238	.281	.313	594	93	-20	-31	102	350			
WAS	48	86	2	.358	37.5	26	38	482	731	4835	944	98	49	30	246	499	43		.208	.255	.271	526	78	-132	-99	93	331			
TOT	544					294	238	4937		39867	8943	1200	509	333	2093	3998	318		.239	.285	.325	609					2301			

TEAM	CG	SHO	GR	SV	IP	H	HR	BB	SO	BR/9	ERA	AERA	OAV	OOB	PR	APR	PF	OSB	OCS	FA	E	WPB	DP	FW	PW	BW	BSW	DIF
NY	133	20	4	1	1208.0	907	27	307	726	9.3	1.96	139	.199	.255	117	107	96			.924	432	193	76	1.2	10.5	2.6		4.2
CHI	123	13	12	1	1186.1	1139	63	308	588	11.4	2.96	102	.246	.301	-17	6	106			.927	417	186	112	1.7	.6	7.4		-.1
PHI	125	16	6	3	1167.0	1072	26	196	519	10.0	2.38	124	.236	.271	58	67	104			.923	424	128	70	.6	6.6	-8.8		5.6
BOS	134	7	3	0	1225.1	1104	36	269	484	10.2	2.61	110	.232	.280	30	30	101			.917	494	155	91	-2.2	3.0	3.2		-1.0
DET	130	10	4	1	1199.0	1115	44	183	522	10.0	2.74	101	.234	.266	12	2	98			.919	463	101	83	-1.1	.2	10.2		-6.8
PIT	135	13	3	0	1203.1	1190	23	223	367	10.8	2.67	98	.249	.287	22	-8	93			.927	416	141	88	2.3	-.8	-4.3		1.9
IND	132	6	5	0	1187.2	1260	64	308	388	12.2	3.81	77	.263	.313	-129	-113	104			.921	449	183	84	-.0	-11.1	-3.0		-3.3
WAS	133	6	3	0	1179.1	1157	50	298	406	11.5	3.54	78	.248	.300	-93	-110	97			.912	494	152	69	-2.4	-10.8	-9.7		4.0
TOT	1045	91	40	6	9556.0					10.7	2.83		.239	.285						.921	3589	1239	673					

Batter-Fielder Wins
Pfeffer-Chi 4.4
Nash-Bos 4.1
Ryan-Chi 3.8
Ewing-NY 3.8
Anson-Chi 3.8

Batting Average
Anson-Chi 344
Ryan-Chi 332
Kelly-Bos 318
Brouthers-Det 307
Ewing-NY 306

On-Base Percentage
Anson-Chi 400
Brouthers-Det 399
Connor-NY 389
Ryan-Chi 377
Hoy-Was 374

Slugging Average
Ryan-Chi 515
Anson-Chi 499
Connor-NY 480
Kelly-Bos 480
Johnston-Bos 472

On-Base Plus Slugging
Anson-Chi 899
Ryan-Chi 892
Connor-NY 869
Brouthers-Det 862
Kelly-Bos 848

Adjusted OPS
Connor-NY 178
Anson-Chi 172
Brouthers-Det 172
Ryan-Chi 170
Kelly-Bos 164

Adjusted Batter Runs
Brouthers-Det 47.2
Connor-NY 45.2
Ryan-Chi 42.1
Anson-Chi 41.5
Kelly-Bos 31.4

Runs
Brouthers-Det 118
Ryan-Chi 115
Johnston-Bos 102
Anson-Chi 101
Connor-NY 98

Hits
Ryan-Chi 182
Anson-Chi 177
Johnston-Bos 173
Brouthers-Det 160
White-Det 157

Doubles
Ryan-Chi 33
Brouthers-Det 33
Johnston-Bos 31
Denny-Ind 27
Hines-Ind 26

Triples
Johnston-Bos 18
Connor-NY 17
Nash-Bos 15
Ewing-NY 15

Home Runs
Ryan-Chi 16
Connor-NY 14
Johnston-Bos 12
Denny-Ind 12
Anson-Chi 12

Total Bases
Ryan-Chi 283
Johnston-Bos 276
Anson-Chi 257
Brouthers-Det 242
Connor-NY 231

Runs Batted In
Anson-Chi 84
Nash-Bos 75
Connor-NY 74
Williamson-Chi 73

Stolen Bases
Hoy-Was 82
Seery-Ind 80
Sunday-Pit 71
Pfeffer-Chi 64
Ryan-Chi 60

Base Stealing Runs

Fielding Runs-Infield
Pfeffer-Chi 37.7
Nash-Bos 18.3
Burns-Chi 17.4
Denny-Ind 15.8
Glasscock-Ind 13.9

Fielding Runs-Outfield
Sunday-Pit 15.1
Fogarty-Phi 14.1
Wilmot-Was 11.7
Seery-Ind 9.6
Hoy-Was 6.9

Wins
Keefe-NY 35
Clarkson-Bos 33
Conway-Det 30
Morris-Pit 29
Buffinton-Phi 28

Winning Pct.
Keefe-NY 745
Conway-Det 682
Sanders-Phi 655
Krock-Chi 641
Clarkson-Bos 623

Complete Games
Morris-Pit 54
Clarkson-Bos 53
Galvin-Pit 49
Keefe-NY 48
Welch-NY 47

Strikeouts
Keefe-NY 335
Clarkson-Bos 223
Getzien-Det 202
Buffinton-Phi 199
O'Day-Was 186

Fewest BB/Game
Sanders-Phi 1.08
Galvin-Pit 1.09
Krock-Chi 1.19
Getzien-Det 1.20
Madden-Bos 1.31

Games
Morris-Pit 55
Clarkson-Bos 54
Keefe-NY 51
Galvin-Pit 50
Welch-NY 47

Saves
Wood-Phi 2
VanHaltren-Chi 1
Tyng-Phi 1
Twitchell-Det 1
Crane-NY 1

Base Runners/9
Keefe-NY 8.68
Buffinton-Phi 8.70
Conway-Det 8.86
Sanders-Phi 9.02
Gruber-Det 9.04

Adjusted Relief Runs

Relief Ranking

Innings Pitched
Clarkson-Bos 483.1
Morris-Pit 480.0
Galvin-Pit 437.1
Keefe-NY 434.1
Welch-NY 425.1

Opponents' Avg.
Keefe-NY 196
Titcomb-NY 201
Welch-NY 207
Conway-Det 208
Buffinton-Phi 213

Opponents' OBP
Conway-Det 243
Keefe-NY 243
Buffinton-Phi 244
Gruber-Det 249
Titcomb-NY 253

Earned Run Average
Keefe-NY 1.74
Sanders-Phi 1.90
Buffinton-Phi 1.91
Welch-NY 1.93
Sowders-Bos 2.07

Adjusted ERA
Keefe-NY 156
Sanders-Phi 156
Buffinton-Phi 155
Welch-NY 141
Sowders-Bos 138

Adjusted Starter Runs
Keefe-NY 52.9
Buffinton-Phi 44.8
Welch-NY 41.9
Sanders-Phi 29.8
Krock-Chi 23.8

Pitcher Wins
Buffinton-Phi 5.1
Keefe-NY 4.7
Welch-NY 3.9
Conway-Det 3.9
Sanders-Phi 3.7

Casey Debuts in Mudville

The NL went back to the three-strikes-and-you're-out rule. The new ruling rule helped pitchers dominate. As the NL's batting average dropped by nearly 30 points, scoring fell dramatically in 1888. Whiffs skyrocketed and walks, which still took five balls, dipped.

In this pitcher's year, only Chicago's Jimmy Ryan slugged over .500, and last-place Washington had seven regulars bat .225 or worse. By 1888 nearly all catchers were using a mitt; the 1884 ruling allowing pitchers to throw overhand made the mitt a necessity. And as new ways came in, old ones went out: Ezra Sutton, 38, one of the last remaining active players from the 1871 National Association, retired.

Washington became the first team to do its spring training in Florida. The warm setting might have helped rookie outfielder Dummy Hoy loosen up—he led the NL in stolen bases. Other important first-year men included future Hall of Famers Hugh Duffy of Chicago, Pittsburgh first baseman Jake Beckley, and Philadelphia's Ed Delahanty. Also debuting in Philadelphia was pitcher Kid Gleason, who later became a solid second baseman but is remembered as the blameless manager of the 1919 Black Sox.

The debut with the most lasting impact, though, belonged to a fictional batsman. Ernest Lawrence Thayer's epic baseball poem "Casey at the Bat" was an immediate success, with actors all over the land performing dramatic readings and spreading Casey's name.

Cap Anson won his second batting title, and once again Chicago had the league's top attack. But thanks to pitching Triple Crown winner Tim Keefe and his second, Mickey Welch, New York's mound work was outstanding. Roger Connor and Buck Ewing provided the Giants with enough offense to win easily.

Keefe was dominating in the World Series as the Giants easily breezed by AA champ St. Louis in a 10-game set. The Giants won six of the first seven, defusing any tension that the final games might have otherwise had. Keefe threw 4 complete-game victories, allowing just 2 earned runs in 35 innings.

1888 American Association

TEAM	W	L	T	PCT	GB	HW	HL	R	OR	PA	H	2B	3B	HR	BB	SO	HB	SH	AVG	OBP	SLG	OPS	AOPS	BR	ABR	PF	SB	CS	BSA	BSR
STL	92	43	2	.681		60	21	789	501	5215	1189	149	47	36	410	521	50		.250	.316	.324	640	98	57	-20	111	468			
BRO	88	52	3	.629	6.5	53	20	758	584	5280	1177	172	70	25	353	439	56		.242	.300	.321	621	103	18	20	100	334			
PHI	81	52	10	.609	10	54	20	827	594	5208	1209	183	89	31	303	473	77		.250	.305	.344	649	113	60	66	99	434			
CIN	80	54	3	.597	11.5	56	25	745	628	5206	1161	132	82	32	345	555	60		.242	.301	.323	624	99	19	-18	105	469			
BAL	57	80	0	.416	36	30	26	653	779	5012	1068	162	70	19	298	479	58		.229	.284	.306	590	96	-37	-19	97	326			
CLE	50	82	3	.379	40.5	33	28	651	839	4997	1076	128	59	12	315	559	79		.234	.294	.295	589	96	-33	-13	97	353			
LOU	48	87	4	.356	44	27	29	689	870	5272	1177	183	67	14	322	604	69		.241	.297	.315	612	102	2	18	98	318			
KC	43	89	0	.326	47.5	23	34	579	896	4933	1000	142	61	19	288	604	57		.218	.273	.288	561	78	-85	-120	106	257			
TOT	548					336	203	5691		41123	9057	1251	545	188	2634	4234	506		.238	.297	.315	612					2959			

TEAM	CG	SHO	GR	SV	IP	H	HR	BB	SO	BR/9	ERA	AERA	OAV	OOB	PR	APR	PF	OSB	OCS	FA	E	WPB	DP	FW	PW	BW	BSW	DIF
STL	132	12	5	0	1212.2	939	19	225	517	9.1	2.09	156	.206	.254	130	147	107	254		.924	430	167	73	3.4	13.6	-1.8		9.3
BRO	138	9	5	0	1286.1	1059	15	285	577	9.7	2.33	128	.217	.266	104	94	97	345		.918	502	172	88	.6	8.7	1.8		6.9
PHI	133	13	3	0	1208.2	988	14	324	596	10.4	2.41	124	.216	.279	87	78	98	353		.919	475	267	73	.7	7.2	6.1		.5
CIN	132	10	5	2	1237.2	1103	19	310	539	10.8	2.73	116	.230	.288	46	58	104	289		.923	456	178	100	2.0	5.4	-1.7		7.3
BAL	130	3	9	0	1200.1	1162	23	419	525	12.5	3.78	79	.245	.318	-96	-111	97	434		.920	461	247	88	1.7	-10.3	-1.8		-1.2
CLE	131	6	4	1	1171.0	1235	38	389	500	12.9	3.72	83	.261	.324	-86	-82	101	388		.915	488	249	87	-.2	-7.6	-1.2		-7.0
LOU	133	6	6	0	1231.1	1265	28	281	599	11.7	3.25	95	.256	.304	-26	-24	100	384		.900	609	233	75	-6.2	-2.2	1.7		-12.7
KC	128	4	4	0	1157.2	1306	32	401	381	13.8	4.29	80	.275	.340	-159	-100	112	512		.914	507	222	95	-1.9	-9.2	-11.1		-.8
TOT	1057	63	41	3	9705.2					11.3	3.06		.238	.297					679	.917	3928	1735	679					

Batter-Fielder Wins	Batting Average	On-Base Percentage	Slugging Average	On-Base Plus Slugging	Adjusted OPS	Adjusted Batter Runs
Stovey-Phi ...3.5	O'Neill-StL ...335	Robinson-StL ...400	Reilly-Cin ...501	Reilly-Cin ...864	Reilly-Cin ...167	Stovey-Phi ...38.8
Collins-Lou-Bro ...3.2	Reilly-Cin ...321	O'Neill-StL ...390	Stovey-Phi ...460	O'Neill-StL ...836	Stovey-Phi ...165	Reilly-Cin ...36.0
McKean-Cle ...3.1	Browning-Lou ...313	Browning-Lou ...380	O'Neill-StL ...446	Stovey-Phi ...825	Browning-Lou ...164	Collins-Lou-Bro ...35.8
Davis-KC ...2.9	Collins-Lou-Bro ...307	Collins-Lou-Bro ...373	Browning-Lou ...436	Browning-Lou ...816	Collins-Lou-Bro ...158	Burns-Bal-Bro ...29.8
McPhee-Cin ...2.8	Orr-Bro ...305	Stovey-Phi ...365	Burns-Bal-Bro ...435	Collins-Lou-Bro ...796	Burns-Bal-Bro ...152	Browning-Lou ...29.0

Runs	Hits	Doubles	Triples	Home Runs	Total Bases	Runs Batted In
Pinkney-Bro ...134	O'Neill-StL ...177	Collins-Lou-Bro ...31	Stovey-Phi ...20	Reilly-Cin ...13	Reilly-Cin ...264	Reilly-Cin ...103
Collins-Lou-Bro ...133	Reilly-Cin ...169	Wolf-Lou ...28	Burns-Bal-Bro ...15	Stovey-Phi ...9	Stovey-Phi ...244	Larkin-Phi ...101
Stovey-Phi ...127	McKean-Cle ...164	Reilly-Cin ...28	McKean-Cle ...15	Larkin-Phi ...7	O'Neill-StL ...236	Foutz-Bro ...99
Welch-Phi ...125	Collins-Lou-Bro ...162	Larkin-Phi ...28	Reilly-Cin ...14		McKean-Cle ...233	O'Neill-StL ...98
Latham-StL ...119	Corkhill-Cin-Bro ...160		Foutz-Bro ...13		Burns-Bal-Bro ...230	Corkhill-Cin-Bro ...93

Stolen Bases	Base Stealing Runs	Fielding Runs-Infield	Fielding Runs-Outfield	Wins	Winning Pct.	Complete Games
Latham-StL ...109		Shindle-Bal ...38.1	McCarthy-StL ...25.5	King-StL ...45	Hudson-StL ...714	King-StL ...64
Nicol-Cin ...103		Davis-KC ...28.5	Lyons-StL ...6.2	Seward-Phi ...35	Chamberlain-Lou-SL .694	Bakely-Cle ...60
Welch-Phi ...95		Easterday-KC ...26.0	Collins-Lou-Bro ...6.1	Caruthers-Bro ...29	King-StL ...692	Seward-Phi ...57
McCarthy-StL ...93		McPhee-Cin ...25.5	Griffin-Bal ...4.9	Weyhing-Phi ...28	Caruthers-Bro ...659	Porter-KC ...53
Stovey-Phi ...87		Stricker-Cle ...23.1	Stovey-Phi ...3.3	Viau-Cin ...27	Viau-Cin ...659	Cunningham-Bal ...50

Strikeouts	Fewest BB/Game	Games	Saves	Base Runners/9	Adjusted Relief Runs	Relief Ranking
Seward-Phi ...272	King-StL ...1.17	King-StL ...66	Mullane-Cin ...1	King-StL ...8.33		
King-StL ...258	Caruthers-Bro ...1.22	Bakely-Cle ...61	Gilks-Cle ...1	Caruthers-Bro ...9.19		
Ramsey-Lou ...228	Hudson-StL ...1.59	Seward-Phi ...57		Seward-Phi ...9.32		
Bakely-Cle ...212	Ewing-Lou ...1.60	Porter-KC ...55		Foutz-Bro ...9.51		
Weyhing-Phi ...204	Hecker-Lou ...1.73	Cunningham-Bal ...51		Hughes-Bro ...9.55		

Innings Pitched	Opponents' Avg.	Opponents' OBP	Earned Run Average	Adjusted ERA	Adjusted Starter Runs	Pitcher Wins
King-StL ...584.2	Terry-Bro ...200	King-StL ...237	King-StL ...1.63	King-StL ...200	King-StL ...95.3	King-StL ...10.2
Bakely-Cle ...532.2	King-StL ...200	Caruthers-Bro ...255	Seward-Phi ...2.01	Seward-Phi ...148	Seward-Phi ...60.1	Seward-Phi ...5.1
Seward-Phi ...518.2	Seward-Phi ...201	Seward-Phi ...258	Terry-Bro ...2.03	Terry-Bro ...147	Hughes-Bro ...31.5	Caruthers-Bro ...3.7
Porter-KC ...474.0	Hughes-Bro ...206	Foutz-Bro ...262	Hughes-Bro ...2.13	Chamberlain-Lou-SL ...143	Weyhing-Phi ...30.2	Weyhing-Phi ...3.3
Cunningham-Bal 453.1	Chamberlain-Lou-SL .207	Hughes-Bro ...262	Chamberlain-Lou-SL 2.19	Hughes-Bro ...140	Caruthers-Bro ...28.2	Hudson-StL ...2.9

A Less Offensive League

Having lost the battle to the NL's Giants, the New York Metropolitans left the Association, replaced by Kansas City. The Blues duly finished last despite the debut of perhaps the greatest leadoff man of the century: "Sliding Billy" Hamilton. New rules, also adopted by the NL, increased strikeouts, chopped walks, and decreased scoring. Runs per team were down 1.5 per game in 1888 than the previous season. The top run-scoring team recorded 304 fewer runs than the in '87.

After dumping most of his high-salaried club over the winter, St. Louis owner Chris Von der Ahe was as surprised as anyone when his club took over the league lead in August and cruised to the title. Sporting the league's best pitching and second-best attack, the Browns were a complete club. Left fielder Tip O'Neill won his second straight batting title (although his average dropped an amazing 100 points), and unheralded Yank Robinson led the league in on-base percentage and garnered 116 bases on balls, the most walks in a season to that point. Arlie Latham, who paced in steals, was one of four Browns to score more than 100 runs. Silver King, given a bigger share of the load due to the sale of Dave Foutz and Bob Caruthers to Brooklyn, proved the league's top pitcher, posting the league's only ERA under 2.00.

George Pinkney of second-place Brooklyn played in 143 games, a new all-time record, and he led the league in runs. Foutz, when not pitching, was the right fielder for the Bridegrooms; his 99 RBIs were third-best in the league. Brooklyn didn't get much offense from anywhere else and couldn't hold the league lead.

Storm clouds were gathering. Perhaps aided by the decrease in hitting, league attendance dropped by more than 300,000 fans, and even in St. Louis, the crowds fell precipitously. For the first time AA attendance was significantly lower than that of the NL.

1887 National League

TEAM	W	L	T	PCT	GB	HW	HL	R	OR	PA	H	2B	3B	HR	BB	SO	HB	SH	AVG	OBP	SLG	OPS	AOPS	BR	ABR	PF	SB	CS	BSA	BSR
DET	79	45	3	.637		43	17	969	710	5079	1404	213	126	55	352	258	38		.299	.353	.434	787	117	133	98	104	267			
PHI	75	48	5	.610	3.5	38	23	901	702	5067	1269	213	89	47	385	346	52		.274	.337	.389	726	99	38	-10	106	355			
CHI	71	50	6	.587	6.5	44	18	813	716	4777	1177	178	98	80	407	400	20		.271	.336	.412	748	98	63	-32	113	382			
NY	68	55	6	.553	10.5	36	26	816	723	4924	1259	167	93	48	361	326	47		.279	.339	.389	728	111	36	76	95	415			
BOS	61	60	6	.504	16.5	38	21	834	792	4908	1255	185	94	53	340	392	37		.277	.333	.394	727	105	31	22	101	373			
PIT	55	69	1	.444	24	31	34	621	750	4771	1141	183	78	20	319	381	38		.258	.314	.349	663	95	-68	-14	93	221			
WAS	46	76	4	.377	32	27	33	601	825	4624	1039	149	63	47	269	339	41		.241	.292	.337	629	83	-128	-87	94	334			
IND	37	89	1	.294	43	24	39	628	965	4712	1080	162	70	33	300	379	44		.247	.302	.339	641	85	-105	-82	97	334			
TOT	508					281	211	6183		38862	9624	1450	711	383	2733	2821	317		.269	.326	.381	707					2681			

TEAM	CG	SHO	GR	SV	IP	H	HR	BB	SO	BR/9	ERA	AERA	OAV	OOB	PR	APR	PF	OSB	OCS	FA	E	WPB	DP	FW	PW	BW	BSW	DIF
DET	122	3	5	1	1116.1	1172	52	344	337	12.5	3.95	103	.264	.322	12	0	100			.925	394	95	92	3.3	.0	8.3		5.4
PHI	119	7	10	1	1132.2	1173	48	305	435	12.0	3.47	121	.259	.311	72	87	104			.912	471	152	76	-.4	7.4	-.8		7.4
CHI	117	4	12	3	1126.0	1156	55	338	510	12.4	3.46	129	.257	.317	73	110	110			.914	472	201	99	-.6	9.3	-2.7		4.5
NY	123	5	7	1	1111.2	1096	27	373	415	12.2	3.58	105	.250	.314	58	19	93			.920	431	196	83	1.8	1.6	6.4		-3.4
BOS	123	4	4	1	1100.2	1226	55	396	254	13.6	4.41	92	.273	.338	-44	-41	101			.905	522	154	94	-3.2	-3.5	1.9		5.3
PIT	123	4	2	0	1108.2	1287	39	246	248	12.7	4.12	93	.281	.322	-9	-40	94			.921	425	140	70	1.4	-3.4	-1.2		-3.8
WAS	124	3	2	0	1090.1	1216	47	299	396	12.9	4.19	95	.272	.323	-18	-26	99			.909	483	194	77	-1.4	-2.2	-7.4		-4.1
IND	118	4	10	1	1088.0	1289	60	431	245	14.6	5.24	79	.284	.352	-145	-135	102			.912	479	223	105	-1.0	-11.4	-6.9		-6.6
TOT	969	34	52	8	8874.1					12.8	4.05		.269	.326						.915	3677	1355	696					

Batter-Fielder Wins	Batting Average	On-Base Percentage	Slugging Average	On-Base Plus Slugging	Adjusted OPS	Adjusted Batter Runs
Ward-NY 4.3	Anson-Chi 347	Brouthers-Det 426	Thompson-Det 565	Brouthers-Det 988	Brouthers-Det 166	Brouthers-Det 46.3
Thompson-Det 4.2	Thompson-Det 372	Anson-Chi 422	Brouthers-Det 562	Thompson-Det 982	Connor-NY 164	Thompson-Det 44.6
Glasscock-Ind 4.0	Brouthers-Det 338	Thompson-Det 416	Connor-NY 541	Anson-Chi 939	Thompson-Det 164	Connor-NY 43.8
Denny-Ind 3.9	Ward-NY 338	Schomberg-Ind 397	Wise-Bos 522	Connor-NY 933	Carroll-Pit 154	Carroll-Pit 31.9
Richardson-Det 3.3	Wise-Bos 334	Kelly-Bos 393	Anson-Chi 517	Wise-Bos 913	Wise-Bos 150	Wise-Bos 30.6

Runs	Hits	Doubles	Triples	Home Runs	Total Bases	Runs Batted In
Brouthers-Det 153	Thompson-Det 203	Brouthers-Det 36	Thompson-Det 23	B.O'Brien-Was 19	Thompson-Det 308	Thompson-Det 166
Rowe-Det 135	Ward-NY 184	Kelly-Bos 34	Connor-NY 22	Connor-NY 17	Brouthers-Det 281	Connor-NY 104
Richardson-Det 131	Richardson-Det 178	Denny-Ind 34	Johnston-Bos 20	Pfeffer-Chi 16	Richardson-Det 263	Anson-Chi 102
Kelly-Bos 120	Rowe-Det 171	Anson-Chi 33	Brouthers-Det 20	Wood-Phi 14	Denny-Ind 256	Brouthers-Det 101
	Brouthers-Det 169		Wood-Phi 19		Connor-NY 255	Denny-Ind 97

Stolen Bases	Base Stealing Runs	Fielding Runs-Infield	Fielding Runs-Outfield	Wins	Winning Pct.	Complete Games
Ward-NY 111		Glasscock-Ind 38.7	Fogarty-Phi 30.1	Clarkson-Chi 38	Getzien-Det 690	Clarkson-Chi 56
Fogarty-Phi 102		Ward-NY 32.4	Johnston-Bos 22.5	Keefe-NY 35	Ferguson-Phi 688	Keefe-NY 54
Kelly-Bos 84		Pfeffer-Chi 22.9	Hornung-Bos 11.5	Getzien-Det 29	Casey-Phi 683	Radbourn-Bos 48
Hanlon-Det 69		Denny-Ind 21.8	Seery-Ind 6.8	Galvin-Pit 28	Keefe-NY 648	Galvin-Pit 47
Glasscock-Ind 62		Bassett-Ind 18.4	Thompson-Det 6.4	Casey-Phi 28	Clarkson-Chi 644	Whitney-Was 46

Strikeouts	Fewest BB/Game	Games	Saves	Base Runners/9	Adjusted Relief Runs	Relief Ranking
Clarkson-Chi 237	Whitney-Was .93	Clarkson-Chi 60	VanHaltren-NY 1	Keefe-NY 10.33		
Keefe-NY 189	Galvin-Pit 1.37	Keefe-NY 56	Twitchell-Det 1	Clarkson-Chi 10.55		
Baldwin-Chi 164	Ferguson-Phi 1.42	Radbourn-Bos 50	Tiernan-NY 1	Ferguson-Phi 10.75		
Buffinton-Phi 160	Clarkson-Chi 1.58	Galvin-Pit 47	Stemmeyer-Bos 1	Whitney-Was 10.85		
Whitney-Was 146	Boyle-Ind 1.89	Whitney-Was 47	Pettit-Chi 1	Welch-NY 11.32		
			Ferguson-Phi 1			
			Fass-Ind 1			
			Baldwin-Chi 1			

Innings Pitched	Opponents' Avg.	Opponents' OBP	Earned Run Average	Adjusted ERA	Adjusted Starter Runs	Pitcher Wins
Clarkson-Chi 523.0	Keefe-NY 230	Keefe-NY 276	Casey-Phi 2.86	Casey-Phi 147	Clarkson-Chi 76.4	Clarkson-Chi 7.5
Keefe-NY 476.2	Conway-Det 235	Clarkson-Chi 281	Conway-Det 2.90	Clarkson-Chi 145	Casey-Phi 56.6	Ferguson-Phi 4.7
Galvin-Pit 440.2	Casey-Phi 246	Whitney-Was 284	Ferguson-Phi 3.00	Ferguson-Phi 141	Ferguson-Phi 40.2	Keefe-NY 4.2
Radbourn-Bos 425.0	Clarkson-Chi 246	Ferguson-Phi 289	Clarkson-Chi 3.08	Conway-Det 140	Keefe-NY 39.2	Whitney-Was 3.9
Whitney-Was 404.2	Baldwin-Chi 248	Galvin-Pit 299	Keefe-NY 3.12	Baldwin-Chi 131	Baldwin-Chi 33.3	Casey-Phi 3.6

The Long October

Despite another National Agreement meeting in 1886, the gloves came off. For 1887 the NL lured over the AA's Pittsburgh franchise to replace bankrupt Kansas City. Both the NL and the AA used the same set of playing rules beginning in 1887, which at least helped in planning the World Series.

It was a year of rule changes. First of all, pitchers were prohibited from hiding the ball during their delivery or taking a running start before delivering. It once again took *four* strikes for a strikeout, while the number of balls needed for a walk was lowered to five.

Batters could no longer call for pitches in certain locations, and the strike zone was defined as ranging from the knee to the shoulder. For the first time NL batters hit by pitched balls were awarded first base—provided they at least tried to get out of the way.

For this year only, a walk truly was as good as a hit. Batters were given credits for hits if they drew bases on balls, leading to some stratospheric averages. Modern figures have Sam Thompson of pennant-winning Detroit taking the bat crown (after walks were removed from hit totals) and establishing a nineteenth century mark with 166 RBIs.

Thompson, Dan Brouthers, and Hardy Richardson supplied Detroit's offense, and the deep pitching staff did its best in what appears to have been a strong hitter's park. Second-place Philadelphia allowed the league's fewest runs.

Chicago owner Al Spalding jettisoned King Kelly, his most outspoken, and—not coincidentally—marketable talent. The outspoken, hard-drinking Kelly was sold to Boston for an unheard of $10,000. The White Stockings immediately slumped to third; Boston, with Kelly's 84 steals and 120 runs, did not budge from fifth. After the season, Spalding also dumped pitcher John Clarkson.

Detroit and AA champ St. Louis played a 15-game World Series, including stops at almost every major league city—one day the touring teams played a morning game in Washington and an afternoon tilt in Baltimore. Detroit won 10 to give the NL the crown. By the end of the interminable series, hardly anyone was watching.

1887 American Association

TEAM	W	L	T	PCT	GB	HW	HL	R	OR	PA	H	2B	3B	HR	BB	SO	HB	SH	AVG	OBP	SLG	OPS	AOPS	BR	ABR	PF	SB	CS	BSA	BSR
STL	95	40	3	.704		**58**	15	**1131**	761	5557	**1550**	261	78	**39**	442	340	67		.307	.371	.413	784	111	**157**	52	111	**581**			
CIN	81	54	1	.600	14	46	27	892	**745**	5235	1285	179	102	37	382	366	56		.268	.329	.371	700	97	-15	-35	102	527			
BAL	77	58	6	.570	18	42	21	975	861	5362	1337	202	100	31	**469**	334	68		.277	.349	.380	729	**114**	51	**110**	94	545			
LOU	76	60	3	.559	19.5	45	23	956	854	5392	1420	194	98	27	436	356	40		.289	.352	.385	737	107	60	41	102	466			
PHI	64	69	4	.481	30	41	27	893	890	5326	1370	231	84	29	321	388	51		.277	.327	.375	702	99	-13	-14	100	476			
BRO	60	74	4	.448	34.5	36	38	904	918	5420	1281	200	82	25	456	365	51		.261	.330	.350	680	92	-40	-50	101	409			
NY	44	89	5	.331	50	25	34	754	1093	5310	1197	193	66	21	439	463	50		.248	.318	.329	647	88	-98	-61	96	305			
CLE	39	92	2	.298	54	22	36	729	1112	5070	1170	178	77	14	375	463	46		.252	.314	.332	646	87	-101	-78	97	355			
TOT	550					315	221	7234		42672	10610	1638	687	223	3320	3075	429		.273	.336	.367	704					3664			

TEAM	CG	SHO	GR	SV	IP	H	HR	BB	SO	BR/9	ERA	AERA	OAV	OOB	PR	APR	PF	OSB	OCS	FA	E	WPB	DP	FW	PW	BW	BSW	DIF
STL	132	6	5	2	1199.1	1254	19	**323**	334	12.2	3.77	120	.258	**.311**	69	94	106	**335**		.916	**481**	171	86	**3.6**	7.6	4.2		12.1
CIN	129	**11**	6	1	1182.2	**1202**	28	396	330	12.6	**3.58**	121	**.257**	.322	**93**	**98**	101	358		.916	484	203	**106**	3.0	**7.9**	-2.8		5.4
BAL	132	8	**9**	0	1220.0	1288	**16**	418	470	13.0	3.87	106	.262	.326	58	31	95	482		.907	549	229	66	.8	2.5	**8.9**		-2.7
LOU	**133**	3	4	1	1205.2	1274	31	357	**544**	12.5	3.82	115	.260	.316	63	73	102	462		.903	574	221	83	-.9	5.9	3.3		-.3
PHI	131	5	6	1	1186.1	1227	29	433	417	13.1	4.59	93	.259	.331	-39	-41	100	476		.907	528	300	95	1.0	-3.3	-1.1		.9
BRO	132	3	6	**3**	1185.1	1348	27	454	332	14.0	4.47	96	.281	.348	-24	-24	100	520		.905	562	202	88	-.5	-1.9	-4.1		-.5
NY	132	1	**9**	0	1180.1	1545	39	406	316	15.3	5.28	80	.308	.365	-130	-139	99	508		.894	632	194	102	-4.0	-11.3	-4.9		-2.3
CLE	127	2	6	1	1136.0	1472	34	533	332	16.4	4.99	87	.308	.384	-88	-83	101	523		.898	576	245	97	-2.2	-6.7	-6.3		-11.3
TOT	1048	39	51	9	9495.2					13.6	4.29		.273	.336						.906	4386	1765	723					

Batter-Fielder Wins		Batting Average		On-Base Percentage		Slugging Average		On-Base Plus Slugging		Adjusted OPS		Adjusted Batter Runs	
O'Neill-StL	4.8	O'Neill-StL	435	O'Neill-StL	490	O'Neill-StL	691	O'Neill-StL	1180	O'Neill-StL	205	O'Neill-StL	70.6
Browning-Lou	3.8	Browning-Lou	402	Browning-Lou	464	Caruthers-StL	547	Browning-Lou	1011	Browning-Lou	178	Browning-Lou	58.5
Lyons-Phi	3.6	Orr-NY	368	Caruthers-StL	463	Browning-Lou	547	Caruthers-StL	1010	Burns-Bal	169	Burns-Bal	53.4
Burns-Bal	3.2	Lyons-Phi	367	Robinson-StL	445	Lyons-Phi	523	Lyons-Phi	943	Caruthers-StL	164	Lyons-Phi	47.8
McPhee-Cin	2.8	Caruthers-StL	357	Lyons-Phi	421	Burns-Bal	519	Burns-Bal	933	Lyons-Phi	162	Caruthers-StL	32.6

Runs		Hits		Doubles		Triples		Home Runs		Total Bases		Runs Batted In	
O'Neill-StL	167	O'Neill-StL	225	O'Neill-StL	52	Poorman-Phi	19	O'Neill-StL	14	O'Neill-StL	357	O'Neill-StL	123
Latham-StL	163	Browning-Lou	220	Lyons-Phi	43	O'Neill-StL	19	Reilly-Cin	10	Browning-Lou	299	Browning-Lou	118
Griffin-Bal	142	Lyons-Phi	209	Reilly-Cin	35	McPhee-Cin	19	Burns-Bal	9	Lyons-Phi	298	Davis-Bal	109
Poorman-Phi	140	Latham-StL	198	Latham-StL	35	Kerins-Lou	19			Burns-Bal	286	Welch-StL	108
Comiskey-StL	139	Burns-Bal	188	Browning-Lou	35	Davis-Bal	19			Reilly-Cin	263	Foutz-StL	108
						Burns-Bal	19						

Stolen Bases		Base Stealing Runs		Fielding Runs-Infield		Fielding Runs-Outfield		Wins		Winning Pct.		Complete Games	
Nicol-Cin	138			Smith-Bro	30.1	Welch-StL	17.2	Kilroy-Bal	46	Caruthers-StL	763	Kilroy-Bal	66
Latham-StL	129			McPhee-Cin	23.3	Corkhill-Cin	12.1	Ramsey-Lou	37	King-StL	727	Ramsey-Lou	61
Comiskey-StL	117			White-Lou	17.5	Wolf-Lou	8.8	Smith-Cin	34	Kilroy-Bal	708	Smith-Bal	54
Browning-Lou	103			Pinkney-Bro	14.8	D.O'Brien-NY	7.1	King-StL	32	Foutz-StL	676	Weyhing-Phi	52
McPhee-Cin	95			Stricker-Cle	11.1	Allen-Cle	6.2	Mullane-Cin	31	Smith-Cin	667	Seward-Phi	52

Strikeouts		Fewest BB/Game		Games		Saves		Base Runners/9		Adjusted Relief Runs		Relief Ranking	
Ramsey-Lou	355	Hecker-Lou	1.58	Kilroy-Bal	69	Terry-Bro	3	Smith-Cin	10.76				
Kilroy-Bal	217	Caruthers-StL	1.61	Ramsey-Lou	65			Caruthers-StL	10.93				
Smith-Bal	206	Lynch-NY	1.73	Smith-Bal	58			Kilroy-Bal	11.64				
Weyhing-Phi	193	Foutz-StL	2.39	Weyhing-Phi	55			Seward-Phi	11.65				
Smith-Cin	176	Kilroy-Bal	2.40	Seward-Phi	55			Ramsey-Lou	11.66				

Innings Pitched		Opponents' Avg.		Opponents' OBP		Earned Run Average		Adjusted ERA		Adjusted Starter Runs		Pitcher Wins	
Kilroy-Bal	589.1	Smith-Cin	230	Smith-Cin	286	Smith-Cin	2.94	Smith-Cin	148	Kilroy-Bal	71.6	**Kilroy-Bal**	7.2
Ramsey-Lou	561.0	Ramsey-Lou	242	Caruthers-StL	287	Kilroy-Bal	3.07	Caruthers-StL	137	Smith-Cin	71.0	**Smith-Cin**	6.3
Smith-Bal	491.1	Seward-Phi	244	Ramsey-Lou	299	Mullane-Cin	3.24	Mullane-Cin	134	Ramsey-Lou	57.8	**Caruthers-StL**	5.9
Seward-Phi	470.2	Caruthers-StL	247	Kilroy-Bal	306	Caruthers-StL	3.30	Kilroy-Bal	133	Mullane-Cin	51.1	**Mullane-Cin**	4.6
Weyhing-Phi	466.1	Kilroy-Bal	253	Foutz-StL	306	Ramsey-Lou	3.43	Ramsey-Lou	128	Caruthers-StL	45.5	**Ramsey-Lou**	3.7

Sitting in Coach

In agreeing to rewrite their rule book to match the NL's, owners of the American Association took a subordinate position. When the NL stole the AA's Pittsburgh franchise, it was war again. A Cleveland club was added to bring the Americans' total to eight teams.

Various rule changes served to elevate offense; the league's best pitching staff, second-place Cincinnati, had an ERA that would have ranked a poor fifth in the AA the previous season. The days of the one-pitcher team were long gone; all teams now had at least two pitchers (in Brooklyn's case, four) winning in double figures. To address charges that St. Louis' Arlie Latham was disgracing the game with his "coaching" routines, which involved running up and down the baselines shouting at the pitcher, coaches' boxes were installed. From this point, coaches were allowed only to address their own baserunners.

The loss of shouting privileges didn't seem to bother the Browns, who won again by a wide margin over Cincinnati. The Reds had one of the league's top hurlers, Elmer Smith, plus outfielder Hugh Nicol, who stole an all-time record 138 bases. But St. Louis was a juggernaut. The Browns plated a record 1,131 runs, and left fielder Tip O'Neill paced the league in nearly every significant offensive category. An unsung hero for the Browns? Bob Caruthers, who won 29 games on the hill and as a right fielder hit .357, fifth best in the AA.

While last-place Cleveland didn't have much talent, they could boast first baseman Jim Toy, the major leagues' first Native American player. Paul Radford of seventh-place New York became the first player in big league history to draw 100 walks in a season. Buoyed by gains in nearly every city, AA attendance rose to its all-time high, but the NL had caught up and passed its rival. The NL broke the one million mark for the first time and surpassed the AA's overall total for the first time since the Association's inaugural season in 1882.

1886 National League

TEAM	W	L	T	PCT	GB	HW	HL	R	OR	PA	H	2B	3B	HR	BB	SO	HB	SH	AVG	OBP	SLG	OPS	AOPS	BR	ABR	PF	SB	CS	BSA	BSR
CHI	90	34	2	.726		52	10	900	555	4838	1223	198	87	53	460	513			.279	.348	.401	749	116	180	69	115	213			
DET	87	36	3	.707	2.5	48	12	829	538	4875	1260	176	81	53	374	426			.280	.335	.390	725	122	137	108	104	194			
NY	75	44	5	.630	12.5	47	12	692	558	4535	1156	175	68	21	237	410			.269	.307	.356	663	106	29	22	101	155			
PHI	71	43	5	.623	14	45	14	621	498	4354	976	145	66	26	282	516			.240	.289	.327	616	91	-39	-44	101	226			
BOS	56	61	1	.479	30.5	32	25	657	661	4430	1085	151	59	24	250	537			.260	.301	.341	642	103	-1	16	97	156			
STL	43	79	4	.352	46	27	34	547	712	4485	1001	183	46	30	235	656			.236	.276	.321	597	92	-70	-31	94	156			
KC	30	91	5	.248	58.5	19	42	494	872	4505	967	177	48	19	269	608			.228	.274	.306	580	76	-91	-124	106	96			
WAS	28	92	5	.233	60	19	42	445	791	4347	856	135	51	23	265	582			.210	.258	.285	543	75	-145	-107	93	143			
TOT	495					289	191	5185		36369	8524	1340	506	249	2372	4248			.251	.300	.342	641					1339			

TEAM	CG	SHO	GR	SV	IP	H	HR	BB	SO	BR/9	ERA	AERA	OAV	OOB	PR	APR	PF	OSB	OCS	FA	E	WPB	DP	FW	PW	BW	BSW	DIF
CHI	116	8	10	3	1097.2	988	49	262	647	10.2	2.54	142	.232	.277	91	118	110			.912	475	197	82	-1.8	10.7	-6.3		12.8
DET	122	8	4	0	1103.2	995	20	270	592	10.3	2.85	116	.231	.276	53	55	101			.928	373	138	82	3.8	5.0	9.8		6.9
NY	119	3	5	1	1062.0	1029	23	280	588	11.1	2.86	111	.247	.294	50	39	97			.929	359	222	70	4.2	3.5	2.0		5.8
PHI	110	10	9	2	1045.2	923	29	264	540	10.2	2.45	134	.224	.271	97	95	100			.921	393	155	46	1.4	8.6	-4.0		8.0
BOS	116	3	2	0	1029.0	1049	33	298	511	11.8	3.24	99	.252	.302	5	-4	97			.905	465	217	63	-2.7	-.4	1.5		-.8
STL	118	6	8	0	1077.1	1050	34	392	501	12.0	3.24	99	.246	.309	6	-7	97			.914	452	293	92	-.5	-.6	-2.8		-14.0
KC	117	4	6	0	1066.2	1345	27	246	442	13.4	4.85	77	.295	.331	-185	-117	114			.910	482	230	79	-2.1	-10.6	-11.2		-6.5
WAS	115	4	7	0	1041.0	1147	34	379	500	13.2	4.30	75	.271	.331	-117	-132	98			.910	458	211	69	-1.0	-12.0	-9.7		-9.3
TOT	933	46	51	6	8523.0					11.5	3.29		.251	.300						.916	3457	1663	583					

Batter-Fielder Wins		Batting Average		On-Base Percentage		Slugging Average		On-Base Plus Slugging		Adjusted OPS		Adjusted Batter Runs	
Kelly-Chi	5.2	Kelly-Chi	388	Kelly-Chi	483	Brouthers-Det	581	Brouthers-Det	1026	Brouthers-Det	203	Brouthers-Det	62.6
Glasscock-StL	4.6	Anson-Chi	371	Brouthers-Det	445	Anson-Chi	544	Kelly-Chi	1018	Connor-NY	183	Kelly-Chi	48.1
Richardson-Det	4.5	Brouthers-Det	370	Gore-Chi	434	Connor-NY	540	Anson-Chi	977	Kelly-Chi	182	Connor-NY	47.6
Connor-NY	4.2	Connor-NY	355	Anson-Chi	433	Kelly-Chi	534	Connor-NY	945	Anson-Chi	170	Richardson-Det	43.4
Brouthers-Det	3.9	Richardson-Det	351	Connor-NY	405	Richardson-Det	504	Richardson-Det	906	Richardson-Det	168	Anson-Chi	41.9

Runs		Hits		Doubles		Triples		Home Runs		Total Bases		Runs Batted In	
Kelly-Chi	155	Richardson-Det	189	Brouthers-Det	40	Connor-NY	20	Brouthers-Det	11	Brouthers-Det	284	Anson-Chi	147
Gore-Chi	150	Anson-Chi	187	Anson-Chi	35	Wood-Phi	15	Brouthers-Det	11	Anson-Chi	274	Pfeffer-Chi	95
Brouthers-Det	139	Brouthers-Det	181	Kelly-Chi	32	Brouthers-Det	15	Anson-Chi	10	Richardson-Det	271	Thompson-Det	89
Richardson-Det	125	Kelly-Chi	175	Hines-Was	30	Thompson-Det	13	Hines-Was	9	Connor-NY	262	Rowe-Det	87
Anson-Chi	117	Connor-NY	172					Denny-StL	9	Kelly-Chi	241	Ward-NY	81

Stolen Bases		Base Stealing Runs		Fielding Runs-Infield		Fielding Runs-Outfield		Wins		Winning Pct.		Complete Games	
Andrews-Phi	56			Denny-StL	25.2	Johnston-Bos	13.5	Keefe-NY	42	Flynn-Chi	793	Keefe-NY	62
Kelly-Chi	53			Knowles-Was	21.3	Lillie-KC	10.6	Baldwin-Det	42	Ferguson-Phi	769	Radbourn-Bos	57
Hanlon-Det	50			Dunlap-StL-Det	17.4	Thompson-Det	8.2	Clarkson-Chi	36	Baldwin-Det	764	Welch-NY	56
Richardson-Det	42			Glasscock-StL	14.9	Richardson-Det	5.3	Welch-NY	33	McCormick-Chi	738	Baldwin-Det	55
Radford-KC	39			Burns-Chi	11.1	Hornung-Bos	5.1	McCormick-Chi	31	Getzien-Det	732	Clarkson-Chi	50

Strikeouts		Fewest BB/Game		Games		Saves		Base Runners/9		Adjusted Relief Runs		Relief Ranking	
Baldwin-Det	323	Whitney-KC	1.26	Keefe-NY	64	Ferguson-Phi	2	Baldwin-Det	8.70				
Clarkson-Chi	313	Ferguson-Phi	1.57	Welch-NY	59	Williamson-Chi	1	Ferguson-Phi	8.78				
Keefe-NY	297	Clarkson-Chi	1.66	Radbourn-Bos	58	Ryan-Chi	1	Flynn-Chi	9.46				
Welch-NY	272	Keefe-NY	1.72	Baldwin-Det	56	Flynn-Chi	1	Gilmore-Was	9.48				
Stemmeyer-Bos	239	Baldwin-Det	1.85	Clarkson-Chi	55	Devlin-NY	1	Clarkson-Chi	9.74				

Innings Pitched		Opponents' Avg.		Opponents' OBP		Earned Run Average		Adjusted ERA		Adjusted Starter Runs		Pitcher Wins	
Keefe-NY	535.0	Baldwin-Det	202	Baldwin-Det	243	Boyle-StL	1.76	Boyle-StL	182	Ferguson-Phi	59.3	**Ferguson-Phi**	6.5
Radbourn-Bos	509.1	Ferguson-Phi	210	Ferguson-Phi	244	Ferguson-Phi	1.98	Ferguson-Phi	166	Baldwin-Det	55.4	**Baldwin-Det**	5.7
Welch-NY	500.0	Flynn-Chi	210	Flynn-Chi	257	Baldwin-Det	2.24	Flynn-Chi	161	Clarkson-Chi	50.2	**Clarkson-Chi**	5.0
Baldwin-Det	487.0	Stemmeyer-Bos	218	Boyle-StL	261	Flynn-Chi	2.24	Clarkson-Chi	149	Keefe-NY	39.1	**McCormick-Chi**	3.8
Clarkson-Chi	466.2	Boyle-StL	220	Clarkson-Chi	264	Clarkson-Chi	2.41	Baldwin-Det	148	Casey-Phi	36.7	**Keefe-NY**	3.8

The Brotherhood of Man

When Providence and Buffalo folded following the 1885 season, the NL replaced them with Washington and Kansas City. They weren't inspired choices. The Kansas City Cowboys lasted one miserable year and the Washington Senators didn't see the next decade. The Senators, the first team to use that name, did provide 23-year-old catcher Connie Mack a start for his major league playing career. Finishing their careers, for the same poor club, were famous contract-jumper Davy Force and 43-year-old first baseman Joe Start, an original National Association player.

With salaries depressed by the end of the Union Association, the reserve clause in full effect, and owners ruling players with iron fists, New York Giants John Ward, Buck Ewing, and Tim Keefe were instrumental in establishing the Brotherhood of Professional Baseball Players, the game's first union.

The NL returned to the seven-ball walk, and also helped pitchers by allowing them to lift one foot when delivering the ball. This, and the lengthening of the pitcher's box, gave certain hard throwers an extra advantage, because they could get a running start to their delivery. While strikeouts increased, league ERA leapt by nearly half a run, mainly due to the incompetence of the expansion teams' pitching staffs.

The White Stockings won another close race, this one over Detroit. The Wolverines featured the bats of Dan Brouthers, Sam Thompson, and Hardy Richardson, as well as Lady Baldwin's pitching, but the club stalled in August. Cap Anson, King Kelly, and George Gore did the bat work for Chicago, while John Clarkson, Jim McCormick, and one-year wonder Jocko Flynn provided a top mound trio.

Kelly was one of the loop's dominant offensive performers, leading in runs, batting average, and on-base percentage. The charismatic, hard-living Kelly also finished second in the newly tabulated category of stolen bases, inspiring the popular song "Slide! Kelly! Slide!" However, Kelly and his Chicago teammates dropped a six-game World Series to the American Association champion St. Louis Browns.

1886 American Association

TEAM	W	L	T	PCT	GB	HW	HL	R	OR	PA	H	2B	3B	HR	BB	SO	HB	SH	AVG	OBP	SLG	OPS	AOPS	BR	ABR	PF	SB	CS	BSA	BSR
STL	93	46	0	.669		**52**	18	**944**	592	5461	**1365**	206	85	20	400	**425**	52		.273	.333	.360	693	116	117	75	105	336			
PIT	80	57	3	.584	12	46	29	810	647	5370	1171	186	**96**	16	**478**	713	38		.241	.314	.329	643	106	33	37	100	260			
BRO	76	61	4	.555	16	43	25	832	832	5504	1261	196	80	16	433	523	18		.250	.311	.330	641	103	24	16	101	248			
LOU	66	70	2	.485	25.5	37	30	833	805	5357	1294	182	88	20	410	558	26		.263	.323	.348	671	108	75	28	106	202			
CIN	65	73	3	.471	27.5	40	31	883	865	5354	1225	145	95	**45**	374	633	**65**		.249	.311	.345	656	106	42	16	103	185			
PHI	63	72	4	.467	28	37	32	772	942	5275	1142	192	82	21	378	697	41		.235	.296	.321	617	95	-20	-28	101	284			
NY	53	82	2	.393	38	30	33	628	766	5046	1047	108	72	18	330	578	33		.224	.279	.289	568	88	-106	-47	92	120			
BAL	48	83	8	.366	41	30	31	625	878	5054	945	124	51	8	379	603	36		.204	.269	.258	527	70	-165	-150	98	269			
TOT	557					315	229	6327		42421	9450	1339	649	164	3182	4730	309		.243	.305	.323	628					1904			

TEAM	CG	SHO	GR	SV	IP	H	HR	BB	SO	BR/9	ERA	AERA	OAV	OOB	PR	APR	PF	OSB	OCS	FA	E	WPB	DP	FW	PW	BW	BSW	DIF
STL	134	14	5	2	1229.1	**1087**	13	329	583	10.6	2.49	138	.227	.281	130	**128**	100	188		.915	494	**163**	96	3.3	**11.2**	6.6		2.4
PIT	137	**15**	3	1	1226.0	1130	**10**	299	515	10.7	2.83	120	.235	.285	84	76	98	**140**		**.917**	**487**	220	90	**3.9**	6.7	3.2		-2.3
BRO	**138**	6	3	0	1234.2	1202	17	464	540	12.4	3.42	102	.243	.312	3	8	101	229		.900	610	232	87	-2.2	.7	1.4		7.6
LOU	131	5	7	2	1209.2	1109	16	432	720	11.7	3.07	118	.230	.297	51	71	106	229		.901	593	289	89	-2.0	6.2	2.5		-8.7
CIN	129	3	**14**	0	1247.2	1267	25	481	495	13.0	4.18	84	.255	.327	-103	-92	102	224		.905	582	247	**122**	-.8	-8.1	1.4		3.4
PHI	134	4	6	0	1218.2	1309	35	388	513	13.0	3.97	88	.259	.319	-72	-65	102	303		.894	637	317	99	-4.0	-5.7	-2.5		7.7
NY	134	5	3	0	1186.1	1148	23	386	559	11.8	3.50	93	.243	.304	-8	-36	95	271		.907	544	262	81	.3	-3.2	-4.1		-7.6
BAL	134	5	7	0	1206.2	1197	25	403	**805**	12.3	4.08	84	.244	.308	-85	-91	99	319		.910	523	367	59	1.8	-8.0	-13.2		1.8
TOT	1071	57	48	5	9759.0					11.9	3.44		.243	.305						.906	4470	2097	723					

Batter-Fielder Wins	Batting Average	On-Base Percentage	Slugging Average	On-Base Plus Slugging	Adjusted OPS	Adjusted Batter Runs
McPhee-Cin....4.2	Hecker-Lou....341	Larkin-Phi....390	Orr-NY....527	Orr-NY....890	Orr-NY....193	Orr-NY....56.4
Orr-NY....3.8	Browning-Lou....340	Browning-Lou....389	Caruthers-StL....527	Larkin-Phi....839	Larkin-Phi....161	Larkin-Phi....41.1
Kerins-Lou....3.7	Orr-NY....338	O'Neill-StL....385	Larkin-Phi....450	Browning-Lou....830	Stovey-Phi....154	Caruthers-StL....37.8
Larkin-Phi....3.7	Caruthers-StL....334	Stovey-Phi....377	Hecker-Lou....446	O'Neill-StL....826	O'Neill-StL....151	O'Neill-StL....33.1
O'Neill-StL....3.2	O'Neill-StL....328	Swartwood-Bro....377	Browning-Lou....441	Stovey-Phi....817	Browning-Lou....151	Stovey-Phi....32.1

Runs	Hits	Doubles	Triples	Home Runs	Total Bases	Runs Batted In
Latham-StL....152	Hecker-Lou....193	Larkin-Phi....36	Orr-NY....31	McPhee-Cin....8	Orr-NY....301	O'Neill-StL....107
McPhee-Cin....139	O'Neill-StL....190	McClellan-Bro....33	Coleman-Phi-Pit....17	Stovey-Phi....7	O'Neill-StL....255	Corkhill-Cin....97
Larkin-Phi....133	Larkin-Phi....180	Welch-StL....31	Kuehne-Pit....17	Orr-NY....7	Larkin-Phi....254	Welch-StL....95
McClellan-Bro....131	Latham-StL....174	Barkley-Pit....31	Fennelly-Cin....17		Welch-StL....221	Orr-NY....91
Pinkney-Bro....119	Phillips-Bro....160	Browning-Lou....29	Larkin-Phi....16		McPhee-Cin....221	Reilly-Cin....79

Stolen Bases	Base Stealing Runs	Fielding Runs-Infield	Fielding Runs-Outfield	Wins	Winning Pct.	Complete Games
Stovey-Phi....68		McPhee-Cin....26.9	McTamany-Bro....11.3	Morris-Pit....41	Foutz-StL....719	Ramsey-Lou....66
Latham-StL....60		Hankinson-NY....26.8	Welch-StL....11.1	Foutz-StL....41	Caruthers-StL....682	Kilroy-Bal....65
Welch-StL....59		Smith-Pit....17.7	Wolf-Lou....9.3	Ramsey-Lou....38	Morris-Pit....672	Morris-Pit....63
Robinson-StL....51		White-StL....16.7	O'Neill-StL....7.7	Mullane-Cin....33	Hudson-StL....615	Mullane-Cin....55
McClellan-Bro....43		Smith-Bro....12.8	Sommer-Bal....7.2	Caruthers-StL....30	Atkinson-Phi....595	Foutz-StL....55

Strikeouts	Fewest BB/Game	Games	Saves	Base Runners/9	Adjusted Relief Runs	Relief Ranking
Kilroy-Bal....513	Galvin-Pit....1.55	Kilroy-Bal....68	Morris-Pit....1	Shaffer-NY....9.13		
Ramsey-Lou....499	Morris-Pit....1.91	Ramsey-Lou....67	Hudson-StL....1	Morris-Pit....9.40		
Morris-Pit....326	Caruthers-StL....2.00	Morris-Pit....64	Foutz-StL....1	Caruthers-StL....9.67		
Foutz-StL....283	McGinnis-StL-Bal....2.27	Mullane-Cin....63	Ely-Lou....1	Handiboe-Pit....10.03		
Mullane-Cin....250	Atkinson-Phi....2.29	Foutz-StL....59		Ramsey-Lou....10.18		

Innings Pitched	Opponents' Avg.	Opponents' OBP	Earned Run Average	Adjusted ERA	Adjusted Starter Runs	Pitcher Wins
Ramsey-Lou....588.2	Ramsey-Lou....198	Morris-Pit....258	Foutz-StL....2.11	Foutz-StL....163	Ramsey-Lou....77.3	**Foutz-StL**....7.6
Kilroy-Bal....583.0	Kilroy-Bal....210	Caruthers-StL....263	Caruthers-StL....2.32	Ramsey-Lou....148	Foutz-StL....71.4	**Caruthers-StL**....7.2
Morris-Pit....555.1	Morris-Pit....214	Ramsey-Lou....269	Ramsey-Lou....2.45	Caruthers-StL....148	Morris-Pit....61.6	**Ramsey-Lou**....6.7
Mullane-Cin....529.2	Foutz-StL....216	Foutz-StL....274	Morris-Pit....2.45	Morris-Pit....138	Caruthers-StL....50.8	**Morris-Pit**....4.8
Foutz-StL....504.0	Caruthers-StL....217	Kilroy-Bal....274	Galvin-Pit....2.67	Hecker-Lou....127	Galvin-Pit....31.2	**Hecker-Lou**....4.8

"The $15,000 Slide"

As the National League returned to the seven-ball walk, the AA reduced the free pass requirement to six. Walks nearly doubled. With the league also lengthening the pitching box and allowing hurlers to get running starts and deliver the ball with one foot off the ground, strikeouts soared as well.

The Baltimore Orioles finished last, but rookie pitcher Matt Kilroy set an all-time record by fanning 513 batters. Toad Ramsey of fourth-place Louisville came close to Kilroy, and his 499 is also second on the single-season list.

Rowdy, hard-bitten St. Louis cruised to an easy title. Pitchers Dave Foutz and Bob Caruthers won 71 games between themselves, better than all but two other teams. Arlie Latham scored 152 runs and was one of three Browns among the top four in stolen bases—an official statistic for the first time. Second-place Pittsburgh didn't have much offense, but pitchers Ed Morris and Jim Galvin carried the load.

The Browns took on the Chicago White Stockings in the World Series. Behind John Clarkson, Chicago won two of the first three at home. Then in St. Louis, the Browns whipped the White Stockings twice behind Foutz and third hurler Nat Hudson. Games 4 and 5 were plagued by charges that the White Stockings were "laying down" to extend the Series' gate receipts.

In Game 6, with the Browns up three games to two, the confident White Stockings had Clarkson on the hill and led 3-0 in the eighth. However, poor Chicago fielding and timely Browns hitting tied the game. St. Louis' Curt Welch and Foutz singled in the 10th, and then moved up a base on a sacrifice. On either a wild pitch or passed ball (sources differ), catcher King Kelly couldn't handle Clarkson's pitch and Welch scored the winning run. Some newspapers referred to Welch's plate-crossing as "The $15,000 Slide," referring to the Series' prize money, but it is still not certain whether Welch slid or scored standing up. Either way, the Association was vindicated yet again.

1885 National League

TEAM	W	L	T	PCT	GB	HW	HL	R	OR	PA	H	2B	3B	HR	BB	SO	HB	SH	AVG	OBP	SLG	OPS	AOPS	BR	ABR	PF	SB	CS	BSA	BSR
CHI	87	25	1	.777		42	14	834	470	4433	1079	184	75	54	340	429			.264	.320	.385	705	116	146	56	114				
NY	85	27	0	.759	2	45	10	691	370	4250	1085	150	82	16	221	312			.269	.307	.359	666	122	80	89	99				
PHI	56	54	1	.509	30	29	26	513	513	4113	891	156	35	20	220	401			.229	.270	.302	572	91	-44	-34	98				
PRO	53	57	0	.482	33	30	24	442	531	3992	820	114	30	6	265	430			.220	.272	.272	544	82	-74	-60	97				
BOS	46	66	1	.411	41	22	35	528	589	4140	915	144	53	22	190	522			.232	.267	.312	579	94	-42	-23	96				
DET	41	67	0	.380	44	29	23	514	582	3989	917	149	66	25	216	451			.243	.284	.337	621	105	17	16	100				
BUF	38	74	0	.339	49	19	38	495	761	4079	980	149	50	23	179	380			.251	.284	.333	617	100	10	-8	103				
STL	36	72	3	.333	49	23	33	390	593	3972	829	121	21	8	214	412			.221	.263	.270	533	81	-92	-62	94				
TOT	445					239	203	4407		32968	7516	1167	412	174	1845	3337			.241	.284	.322	606								

TEAM	CG	SHO	GR	SV	IP	H	HR	BB	SO	BR/9	ERA	AERA	OAV	OOB	PR	APR	PF	OSB	OCS	FA	E	WPB	DP	FW	PW	BW	BSW	DIF
CHI	108	14	5	4	1015.2	868	37	202	458	9.5	2.23	134	.221	.259	66	80	107			.903	496	133	80	-2.4	7.5	5.3		20.6
NY	109	16	3	1	994.0	758	11	265	516	9.3	1.72	155	.205	.258	121	112	95			.929	331	168	85	6.0	10.5	8.4		4.1
PHI	108	10	3	0	976.0	860	18	218	378	9.9	2.39	117	.224	.266	46	41	99			.905	447	167	66	-.3	3.9	-3.2		.6
PRO	108	8	3	0	960.2	912	18	235	371	10.7	2.71	99	.235	.278	12	-4	95			.903	459	165	70	-1.1	-.4	-5.6		5.1
BOS	111	10	2	0	981.0	1045	26	188	480	11.3	3.03	89	.261	.294	-23	-40	95			.901	478	184	79	-1.5	-3.8	-2.2		-2.6
DET	105	6	3	1	954.1	966	18	224	475	11.2	2.88	99	.249	.290	-6	-5	101			.901	462	115	61	-1.7	-.5	1.5		-12.4
BUF	107	4	5	1	956.0	1175	31	234	320	13.3	4.29	69	.289	.328	-157	-132	106			.901	464	196	65	-.9	-12.4	-.8		-3.9
STL	107	4	4	0	965.1	935	15	278	337	11.3	3.37	82	.245	.296	-59	-69	97			.916	398	178	67	2.3	-6.5	-5.8		-8.0
TOT	863	72	28	7	7803.0					10.8	2.82		.241	.284						.908	3535	1306	573					

Leaders

Batter-Fielder Wins
Connor-NY 4.3 · Dunlap-StL 4.1 · Glasscock-StL 3.5 · Bennett-Det 3.3 · Brouthers-Buf 3.1

Batting Average
Connor-NY .371 · Brouthers-Buf .359 · Dorgan-NY .326 · Richardson-Buf .319 · Gore-Chi .313

On-Base Percentage
Connor-NY .435 · Brouthers-Buf .408 · Gore-Chi .405 · Hanlon-NY .372 · Anson-Chi .357

Slugging Average
Brouthers-Buf .543 · Connor-NY .495 · Ewing-NY .471 · Anson-Chi .461 · Richardson-Buf .458

On-Base Plus Slugging
Brouthers-Buf .951 · Connor-NY .929 · Gore-Chi .858 · Anson-Chi .819 · Bennett-Det .812

Adjusted OPS
Connor-NY 203 · Brouthers-Buf 199 · Bennett-Det 161 · Ewing-NY 159 · O'Rourke-NY 158

Adjusted Batter Runs
Connor-NY 53.8 · Brouthers-Buf 44.4 · O'Rourke-NY 30.7 · Gore-Chi 28.0 · Bennett-Det 25.1

Runs
Kelly-Chi 124 · O'Rourke-NY 119 · Gore-Chi 115 · Dalrymple-Chi 109 · Connor-NY 102

Hits
Connor-NY 169 · Brouthers-Buf 146 · Anson-Chi 144 · Sutton-Bos 143 · O'Rourke-NY 143

Doubles
Anson-Chi 35 · Brouthers-Buf 32 · Rowe-Buf 28 · Dalrymple-Chi 27 · Mulvey-Phi 25

Triples
O'Rourke-NY 16 · Connor-NY 15 · Gore-Chi 13 · Bennett-Det 13

Home Runs
Dalrymple-Chi 11 · Kelly-Chi 9

Total Bases
Connor-NY 225 · Brouthers-Buf 221 · Dalrymple-Chi 219 · Anson-Chi 214 · O'Rourke-NY 211

Runs Batted In
Anson-Chi 108 · Kelly-Chi 75 · Pfeffer-Chi 73 · Burns-Chi 71

Stolen Bases

Base Stealing Runs

Fielding Runs-Infield
Dunlap-StL 26.5 · Pfeffer-Chi 22.3 · Glasscock-StL 21.1 · Williamson-Chi 9.1 · Gerhardt-NY 8.8

Fielding Runs-Outfield
Fogarty-Phi 19.5 · Manning-Bos-Det 7.1 · Kelly-Chi 6.1 · Radford-Pro 5.0 · Carroll-Pro 3.7

Wins
Clarkson-Chi 53 · Welch-NY 44 · Keefe-NY 32 · Radbourn-Pro 28

Winning Pct.
Welch-NY .800 · Clarkson-Chi .768 · McCormick-Pro-Chi .750 · Keefe-NY .711 · Radbourn-Pro .571

Complete Games
Clarkson-Chi 68 · Welch-NY 55 · Whitney-Bos 50

Strikeouts
Clarkson-Chi 308 · Welch-NY 258 · Buffinton-Bos 242 · Keefe-NY 227 · Whitney-Bos 200

Fewest BB/Game
Whitney-Bos .75 · Galvin-Buf 1.17 · Clarkson-Chi 1.40 · Baldwin-Det 1.41 · C.Sweeney-StL 1.64

Games
Clarkson-Chi 70 · Welch-NY 56 · Whitney-Bos 51 · Buffinton-Bos 51 · Daily-Phi 50

Saves
Williamson-Chi 2 · Pfeffer-Chi 2 · Welch-NY 1 · Galvin-Buf 1 · Baldwin-Det 1

Base Runners/9
Baldwin-Det 8.28 · Clarkson-Chi 8.58 · Keefe-NY 9.05 · Richardson-NY 9.12 · Welch-NY 9.20

Adjusted Relief Runs

Relief Ranking

Innings Pitched
Clarkson-Chi 623.0 · Welch-NY 492.0 · Radbourn-Pro 445.2 · Whitney-Bos 441.1 · Daily-Phi 440.0

Opponents' Avg.
Baldwin-Det .197 · Welch-NY .203 · Keefe-NY .203 · Clarkson-Chi .208 · Shaw-Pro .209

Opponents' OBP
Baldwin-Det .228 · Clarkson-Chi .239 · Shaw-Pro .254 · Keefe-NY .255 · Daily-Phi .256

Earned Run Average
Keefe-NY 1.58 · Welch-NY 1.66 · Clarkson-Chi 1.85 · Baldwin-Det 1.86 · Radbourn-Pro 2.20

Adjusted ERA
Keefe-NY 169 · Welch-NY 162 · Welch-NY 160 · Baldwin-Det 153 · Daily-Phi 126

Adjusted Starter Runs
Clarkson-Chi 70.8 · Welch-NY 59.7 · Keefe-NY 46.4 · Daily-Phi 28.8 · Ferguson-Phi 25.7

Pitcher Wins
Clarkson-Chi 7.3 · Welch-NY 6.0 · Keefe-NY 4.5 · Ferguson-Phi 4.3 · Radbourn-Pro 3.4

Back to Normal

The National League got sneaky, violating the National Agreement by adding the Union Association's St. Louis franchise (in place of Cleveland) to compete with the AA's popular Browns club. The AA laughed last, though, as the dreadful Maroons survived just two years in the NL and drew half the patrons of the Browns.

Syndicate ownership also reared its malformed head. The owner of both the AA and NL New York clubs transferred manager Jim Mutrie and top players Tim Keefe and Dude Esterbrook to the NL's Giants, ostensibly to field a better team for his 50-cent ticket prices. As a result, the Giants improved 23 games in the NL and the Mets fell 32 games in the AA standings.

For this season NL pitchers were constrained by an unusual rule—possibly instituted to balance their new permission to throw overhand—requiring moundsmen to keep both feet on the ground while delivering the ball. Catchers first wore chest protectors in 1885, and the new equipment allowed the receiver to play closer to the batter. Players were required to use round bats, though one section could be flat.

The NL also addressed Chicago infielder Ed Williamson's 27 homers in 1884, which doubled the previous mark. Since 25 of those homers were hit at a small home park, the NL ruled that, as had been common before 1884, fair balls clearing fences 210 feet or less from home plate were doubles.

The NL returned to its earlier form, with two outstanding contenders battling to the finish. New York had two spectacular hitters, Roger Connor and Buck Ewing, and strong pitching in Keefe and Mickey Welch, but couldn't quite match Chicago, who had ironman John Clarkson on the hill and powerful hitters at nearly every position. Unfortunately, the two best teams from the two biggest cities were followed by six also-rans; third-place Philadelphia finished 30 out. Sixth-place Detroit welcomed rookie outfielder Sam Thompson. Buffalo was seventh despite the best efforts of Dan Brouthers, Hardy Richardson, and pitcher Jim "Pud" Galvin. League attendance rose, led by increases in Chicago, New York, and Philadelphia.

1885 American Association

TEAM	W	L	T	PCT	GB	HW	HL	R	OR	PA	H	2B	3B	HR	BB	SO	HB	SH	AVG	OBP	SLG	OPS	AOPS	BR	ABR	PF	SB	CS	BSA	BSR
STL	79	33	0	.705		**44**	11	677	**461**	4255	979	132	57	17	234	**282**	49		.246	.297	.321	618	96	2	-25	105				
CIN	63	49	0	.563	16	35	21	642	575	4254	1046	108	77	26	153	420	**51**		.258	.294	.342	636	103	16	4	102				
PIT	56	55	0	.505	22.5	37	20	547	539	4208	955	123	79	5	189	537	44		.240	.282	.315	597	94	-34	-26	99				
PHI	55	57	1	.491	24	33	23	**764**	691	4410	**1099**	**169**	76	**30**	223	410	45		.265	.310	.365	675	111	80	39	106				
LOU	53	59	0	.473	26	37	19	564	598	4146	986	126	**83**	19	152	448	25		.248	.281	.336	617	99	-13	-12	100				
BRO	53	59	0	.473	26	36	22	624	650	4223	966	121	65	14	238	324	42		.245	.295	.319	614	97	-4	-8	101				
NY	44	64	0	.407	33	28	24	526	688	3983	921	123	57	21	217	428	35		.247	.295	.327	622	105	5	30	96				
BAL	41	68	1	.376	36.5	29	25	541	683	4141	837	124	59	17	**279**	529	42		.219	.280	.296	576	87	-51	-43	99				
TOT	445					279	165	4885		33620	7789	1026	553	149	1685	3378	333		.246	.292	.328	620								

TEAM	CG	SHO	GR	SV	IP	H	HR	BB	SO	BR/9	ERA	AERA	OAV	OOB	PR	APR	PF	OSB	OCS	FA	E	WPB	DP	FW	PW	BW	BSW	DIF
STL	111	11	1	0	1002.0	**879**	12	**168**	378	9.8	**2.44**	134	**.228**	.268	89	91	101			**.920**	**381**	190	64	3.0	8.2	-2.3		14.1
CIN	102	7	**10**	1	999.1	998	24	250	330	11.9	3.26	100	.253	.309	-2	-1	100			.911	423	**172**	86	.8	-.0	.4		5.9
PIT	104	8	7	0	1011.0	918	14	201	454	10.3	2.92	110	.232	.275	36	33	99			.912	422	213	77	.6	3.0	-2.3		-.8
PHI	105	5	8	0	1003.1	1038	**11**	212	**506**	11.6	3.23	106	.255	.299	2	21	106			.901	483	242	79	-2.2	1.9	**3.5**		-4.2
LOU	109	3	4	1	1002.0	927	13	217	462	10.6	2.68	120	.232	.278	63	61	99			.905	460	248	75	-1.1	5.5	-1.1		-6.3
BRO	110	3	2	1	991.2	955	27	211	436	10.8	3.46	95	.240	.283	-24	-18	102			.910	434	219	56	.2	-1.6	-.7		-.9
NY	103	2	6	0	937.0	1015	36	204	408	11.9	4.15	75	.262	.303	-94	-113	96			.901	452	202	62	-1.6	-10.2	2.7		-1.0
BAL	103	2	7	**4**	971.0	1059	12	222	395	12.3	3.90	83	.269	.316	-71	-70	100			.909	419	272	71	.6	-6.3	-3.9		-3.9
TOT	847	41	45	7	7917.1					11.1	3.24		.246	.292						.909	3474	1758	570					

Batter-Fielder Wins: Browning-Lou 4.2, G.Smith-Bro 3.9, Larkin-Phi 3.7, Jones-Cin 3.3, Nelson-NY 2.9

Batting Average: Browning-Lou .362, Orr-NY .342, Larkin-Phi .329, Jones-Cin .322, Stovey-Phi .315

On-Base Percentage: Browning-Lou .393, Larkin-Phi .373, Stovey-Phi .371, Brown-Phi .366, Phillips-Bro .364

Slugging Average: Orr-NY .543, Browning-Lou .530, Larkin-Phi .525, Stovey-Phi .488, Jones-Cin .462

On-Base Plus Slugging: Browning-Lou .923, Orr-NY .901, Larkin-Phi .899, Stovey-Phi .858, Jones-Cin .824

Adjusted OPS: Browning-Lou 190, Orr-NY 189, Larkin-Phi 171, Stovey-Phi 160, Jones-Cin 156

Adjusted Batter Runs: Browning-Lou 48.5, Orr-NY 42.4, Larkin-Phi 35.5, Stovey-Phi 32.4, Jones-Cin 29.2

Runs: Stovey-Phi 130, Larkin-Phi 114, Jones-Cin 108, Nelson-NY 98, Browning-Lou 98

Hits: Browning-Lou 174, Jones-Cin 157, Stovey-Phi 153, Orr-NY 152, Larkin-Phi 149

Doubles: Larkin-Phi 37, Browning-Lou 34, Orr-NY 29, Stovey-Phi 27

Triples: Orr-NY 21, Kuehne-Pit 19, Wolf-Lou 17, Jones-Cin 17, Fennelly-Cin 17

Home Runs: Orr-NY 13, Fennelly-Cin 10, Browning-Lou 9, Larkin-Phi 8, Orr-NY 6

Total Bases: Browning-Lou 255, Orr-NY 241, Larkin-Phi 238, Stovey-Phi 237, Jones-Cin 225

Runs Batted In: Fennelly-Cin 89, Larkin-Phi 88, Orr-NY 77, Stovey-Phi 75, Browning-Lou 73

Stolen Bases:

Base Stealing Runs:

Fielding Runs-Infield: G.Smith-Bro 40.3, Smith-Pit 28.7, Hankinson-NY 20.9, Houck-Phi 18.6, Nelson-NY 16.8

Fielding Runs-Outfield: Corkhill-Cin 15.9, Sommer-Bal 12.5, Welch-StL 12.0, Nicol-StL 11.4, Jones-Cin 11.2

Wins: Caruthers-StL 40, Morris-Pit 39, Porter-Bro 33, Foutz-StL 33

Winning Pct.: Caruthers-StL .755, Foutz-StL .702, Mathews-Phi .638, Morris-Pit .619, Porter-Bro .611

Complete Games: Morris-Pit 63, Henderson-Bal 59, Porter-Bro 53, Caruthers-StL 53, Hecker-Lou 51

Strikeouts: Morris-Pit 298, Mathews-Phi 286, Henderson-Bal 263, Hecker-Lou 209, Porter-Bro 197

Fewest BB/Game: Lynch-NY 1.00, Hecker-Lou 1.01, Caruthers-StL 1.06, Mathews-Phi 1.21, McGinnis-StL 1.53

Games: Morris-Pit 63, Henderson-Bal 61, Porter-Bro 54, Hecker-Lou 53, Caruthers-StL 53

Saves: Burns-Bal 3, Terry-Bro 1, Sommer-Bal 1, Reccius-Lou 1, Corkhill-Cin 1

Base Runners/9: Ramsey-Lou 8.32, Morris-Pit 8.89, Caruthers-StL 9.44, Hecker-Lou 9.86, McGinnis-StL 9.88

Adjusted Relief Runs:

Relief Ranking:

Innings Pitched: Morris-Pit 581.0, Henderson-Bal 539.1, Caruthers-StL 482.1, Porter-Bro 481.2, Hecker-Lou 480.0

Opponents' Avg.: Morris-Pit .208, Mays-Lou .219, Porter-Bro .223, McGinnis-StL .225, Foutz-StL .227

Opponents' OBP: Morris-Pit .247, Caruthers-StL .260, Hecker-Lou .265, Cushman-Phi-NY .266, Mathews-Phi .267

Earned Run Average: Caruthers-StL 2.07, Hecker-Lou 2.17, Morris-Pit 2.35, Mathews-Phi 2.43, Foutz-StL 2.63

Adjusted ERA: Caruthers-StL 158, Hecker-Lou 148, Mathews-Phi 141, Morris-Pit 137, Foutz-StL 124

Adjusted Starter Runs: Caruthers-StL 61.3, Morris-Pit 57.5, Hecker-Lou 51.4, Mathews-Phi 42.1, Foutz-StL 29.3

Pitcher Wins: Caruthers-StL 6.3, Hecker-Lou 6.0, Morris-Pit 4.7, Foutz-StL 3.5, Mathews-Phi 3.3

Gloves Off

With the Union Association dead, the two surviving leagues got dirty. The NL manipulated the rules and violated the National Agreement, then placated some aggrieved AA owners with cash payments, while the Association engaged in contract-breaking scams of its own. A midseason meeting resulted in the AA's sudden reversal on overhand pitching, which would now be permitted. This pushed the balance of power toward clubs with pitching and speed.

Therefore, the AA crowned a new champ: Charlie Comiskey's St. Louis Browns, a great defensive club sparked by aggressive baserunning and solid pitching. St. Louis moundsmen Bob Caruthers and Dave Foutz permitted the league's fewest hits, walks, and runs to breeze past Cincinnati by 16 games. Stripped by player transfers to the NL New York club, the defending champion Metropolitans sank to seventh.

The postseason "World Series" caused endless controversy and declared no champion. Game 1, in Chicago, was called by darkness shortly after the White Stockings tied the game in the eighth. The next contest in St. Louis was forfeited to the NL champion White Stockings when Comiskey pulled his team off the field in protest of a call. The Browns, however, won the next two in St. Louis. The teams then went to Pittsburgh for Game 5, which Chicago won, and Cincinnati the next day, resulting in another victory for the White Stockings by the same 9-2 score. The Browns won Game 7, also in Cincy, 13-4. The White Stockings ragged the umpiring, the games' locations, and the rules—all of which Chicago player-manager Cap Anson had agreed to beforehand.

Rival owners Chris Von der Ahe and Al Spalding benefited from the controversy—with no clear winner, the $1,000 purse was returned to them and never paid to the players. NL petulance provided a hearty laugh for AA supporters, but the ledgers supplied only indigestion. League attendance fell by 126,000, spiked by large dips in St. Louis and Baltimore.

1884 National League

TEAM	W	L	T	PCT	GB	HW	HL	R	OR	PA	H	2B	3B	HR	BB	SO	HB	SH	AVG	OBP	SLG	OPS	AOPS	BR	ABR	PF	SB	CS	BSA	BSR
PRO	84	28	2	.750		45	11	665	388	4393	987	153	43	21	300	469			.241	.293	.315	608	97	-16	-5	98				
BOS	73	38	5	.658	10.5	40	16	684	468	4396	1063	179	60	36	207	660			.254	.289	.351	640	105	18	21	100				
BUF	64	47	4	.577	19.5	37	18	700	626	4412	1099	163	69	39	215	458			.262	.298	.361	659	106	45	22	103				
NY	62	50	4	.554	22	34	22	693	623	4373	1053	149	68	22	249	492			.255	.298	.340	638	102	19	4	102				
CHI	62	50	1	.554	22	39	17	834	647	4446	1176	162	50	142	264	469			.281	.324	.446	770	133	203	139	108				
PHI	39	73	1	.348	45	19	37	549	824	4207	934	149	39	14	209	512			.234	.272	.301	573	88	-72	-45	95				
CLE	35	77	1	.313	49	22	34	458	716	4104	934	147	49	16	170	576			.237	.269	.312	581	83	-64	-82	103				
DET	28	84	2	.250	56	18	38	445	736	4177	825	114	47	31	207	699			.208	.247	.284	531	74	-134	-104	94				
TOT	457					254	193	5028		34508	8071	1216	425	321	1821	4335			.247	.287	.340	626								

TEAM	CG	SHO	GR	SV	IP	H	HR	BB	SO	BR/9	ERA	AERA	OAV	OOB	PR	APR	PF	OSB	OCS	FA	E	WPB	DP	FW	PW	BW	BSW	DIF
PRO	107	16	8	2	1036.1	825	26	172	639	8.7	1.61	177	.209	.242	158	150	96			.918	398	145	50	5.1	13.4	-.4		9.9
BOS	109	14	7	2	1037.0	932	30	135	742	9.3	2.47	117	.226	.250	58	51	97			.922	384	138	46	6.3	4.6	1.9		4.7
BUF	108	14	6	1	1001.0	1041	46	189	534	11.1	2.95	107	.254	.286	3	20	106			.905	462	167	71	1.9	1.8	2.0		2.8
NY	111	4	5	0	1014.0	1011	28	326	567	11.9	3.12	95	.245	.300	-16	-19	100			.895	514	200	69	-.6	-1.7	.4		8.0
CHI	106	9	9	0	997.1	1028	83	231	472	11.4	3.03	103	.250	.290	-6	10	105			.886	595	198	107	-5.6	.9	12.4		-1.7
PHI	106	3	7	1	981.0	1090	37	254	411	12.3	3.93	76	.261	.304	-103	-105	100			.888	536	326	67	-2.5	-9.4	-4.0		-1.1
CLE	107	7	6	0	994.2	1046	35	269	482	11.9	3.43	92	.256	.302	-50	-30	106			.897	512	230	75	-1.2	-2.7	-7.3		-9.8
DET	109	3	5	0	984.2	1097	36	245	488	12.3	3.38	86	.262	.302	-44	-55	97			.886	550	159	60	-3.0	-4.9	-9.3		-10.8
TOT	863	70	53	6	8046.0					11.1	2.98		.247	.287						.899	3951	1563	545					

Batter-Fielder Wins		Batting Average		On-Base Percentage		Slugging Average		On-Base Plus Slugging		Adjusted OPS		Adjusted Batter Runs	
Pfeffer-Chi	6.0	O'Rourke-Buf	347	Kelly-Chi	414	Brouthers-Buf	563	Brouthers-Buf	941	Brouthers-Buf	186	Kelly-Chi	40.9
Williamson-Chi	4.7	Kelly-Chi	354	Gore-Chi	404	Williamson-Buf	554	Kelly-Chi	938	Kelly-Chi	178	Brouthers-Buf	38.0
Kelly-Chi	3.3	Sutton-Bos	346	O'Rourke-Buf	392	Anson-Chi	543	Anson-Chi	916	Anson-Chi	170	Anson-Chi	36.8
Ewing-NY	3.1	Anson-Chi	335	Sutton-Bos	384	Kelly-Chi	524	Williamson-Chi	898	O'Rourke-Buf	167	O'Rourke-Buf	36.4
Sutton-Bos	2.8	Brouthers-Buf	327	Brouthers-Buf	378	Pfeffer-Chi	514	O'Rourke-Buf	872	Williamson-Chi	164	Sutton-Bos	34.7

Runs		Hits		Doubles		Triples		Home Runs		Total Bases		Runs Batted In	
Kelly-Chi	120	Sutton-Bos	162	Hines-Pro	36	Ewing-NY	20	Williamson-Chi	27	Dalrymple-Chi	263	Anson-Chi	102
O'Rourke-Buf	119	O'Rourke-Buf	162	O'Rourke-Buf	33	Brouthers-Buf	15	Pfeffer-Chi	25	Anson-Chi	258	Pfeffer-Chi	101
Hornung-Bos	119	Dalrymple-Chi	161	Anson-Chi	30	Rowe-Buf	14	Dalrymple-Chi	22	Pfeffer-Chi	240	Kelly-Chi	95
Dalrymple-Chi	111	Kelly-Chi	160	Manning-Phi	29	McKinnon-NY	13	Anson-Chi	21	Kelly-Chi	237	Williamson-Chi	84
Anson-Chi	108	Anson-Chi	159			Phillips-Cle	12	Brouthers-Buf	14	Williamson-Chi	231	Connor-NY	82

Stolen Bases		Base Stealing Runs		Fielding Runs-Infield		Fielding Runs-Outfield		Wins		Winning Pct.		Complete Games	
				Pfeffer-Chi	43.3	Lillie-Buf	15.8	Radbourn-Pro	59	Radbourn-Pro	831	Radbourn-Pro	73
				Williamson-Chi	21.7	Hanlon-Det	12.3	Buffinton-Bos	48	Buffinton-Bos	750	Galvin-Buf	71
				Mulvey-Phi	12.9	Evans-Cle	8.2	Galvin-Buf	46	Sweeney-Pro	680	Buffinton-Bos	63
				Ward-NY	10.6	Fogarty-Phi	6.9	Welch-NY	39	Galvin-Buf	676	Welch-NY	62
				Richardson-Buf	5.2	G.Wood-Det	4.0	L.Corcoran-Chi	35	Welch-NY	650	L.Corcoran-Chi	57

Strikeouts		Fewest BB/Game		Games		Saves		Base Runners/9		Adjusted Relief Runs		Relief Ranking	
Radbourn-Pro	441	Whitney-Bos	72	Radbourn-Pro	75	Morrill-Bos	2	Sweeney-Pro	7.41				
Buffinton-Bos	417	Galvin-Buf	89	Galvin-Buf	72	Sweeney-Pro	1	Whitney-Bos	8.01				
Galvin-Buf	369	Buffinton-Bos	1.17	Buffinton-Bos	67	Radbourn-Pro	1	Radbourn-Pro	8.30				
Welch-NY	345	Sweeney-Pro	1.18	Welch-NY	65	O'Rourke-Phi	1	Getzien-Det	8.74				
L.Corcoran-Chi	272	Coleman-Phi	1.28	L.Corcoran-Chi	60	Ferguson-Phi	1	Galvin-Buf	8.90				

Innings Pitched		Opponents' Avg.		Opponents' OBP		Earned Run Average		Adjusted ERA		Adjusted Starter Runs		Pitcher Wins	
Radbourn-Pro	678.2	Sweeney-Pro	187	Sweeney-Pro	215	Radbourn-Pro	1.38	Radbourn-Pro	206	Radbourn-Pro	116.2	Radbourn-Pro	10.7
Galvin-Buf	636.1	Getzien-Det	204	Whitney-Bos	223	Sweeney-Pro	1.55	Sweeney-Pro	184	Galvin-Buf	80.9	Galvin-Buf	6.3
Buffinton-Bos	587.0	Radbourn-Pro	205	Radbourn-Pro	234	Getzien-Det	1.95	Galvin-Buf	158	Buffinton-Bos	51.3	Buffinton-Bos	5.8
Welch-NY	557.1	Whitney-Bos	207	Getzien-Det	237	Galvin-Buf	1.99	Getzien-Det	148	Sweeney-Pro	35.7	Sweeney-Pro	4.4
L.Corcoran-Chi	516.2	Clarkson-Chi	208	Buffinton-Bos	244	Whitney-Bos	2.09	Clarkson-Chi	147	L.Corcoran-Chi	34.6	Whitney-Bos	3.6

Ride That Hoss

The National League expanded to 112 games, hoping to fight the new Union Association by garnering increased newspaper coverage. There were no franchise shifts. The league also first allowed its pitchers to throw overhand, although the Union and American Associations declined to make this change. Additionally, the NL cut the number of balls needed for a walk to six, while the other leagues held at seven.

The biggest story of the year was in Providence, which began the season with two star pitchers: Hoss Radbourn and Charlie Sweeney. When manager Frank Bancroft said that the two would share mound duties, an offended Radbourn loafed and earned a suspension.

Sweeney, receiving an offer from the wealthy St. Louis Union club, malingered and finagled a suspension as well. He then jumped to the outlaws, and Radbourn had the Grays where he wanted them. Radbourn pledged to pitch the rest of the season for Providence if the team would then allow him to depart via free agency. Radbourn went on to win 59 games, an all-time record. Unfortunately for Old Hoss, his arm was never quite the same, though he remained effective and had five 20-win seasons for Providence (he stayed through 1885) and Boston teams in two different leagues.

The '84 Grays had Paul Hines' big bat in center field, but offense wasn't their forte; four of the league's eight teams scored more runs. They still won by 10½ games, courtesy of Old Hoss. Providence then met American Association champs New York in a three-game tourney. Despite playing at New York's Polo Grounds and under Association rules, Radbourn won three straight—6-0, 3-1, and 11-2—to take what can legitimately be called the first World Series. The gate certainly wasn't great. Total attendance was less than 3,800, and just 300 people showed up for the inconsequential third game. Attendance for the whole NL season rose by just 5,000, despite the extra contests, and dropped precipitously in Detroit, Cleveland, and Chicago.

1884 American Association

TEAM	W	L	T	PCT	GB	HW	HL	R	OR	PA	H	2B	3B	HR	BB	SO	HB	SH	AVG	OBP	SLG	OPS	AOPS	BR	ABR	PF	SB	CS	BSA	BSR
NY	75	32	5	.701		42	9	734	423	4250	1052	155	64	22	203	315	35		.262	.304	.349	653	120	73	90	98				
COL	69	39	2	.639	6.5	38	16	585	459	4014	901	107	96	40	196	629	59		.240	.288	.351	639	121	45	98	92				
LOU	68	40	2	.630	7.5	41	14	573	425	4137	1004	152	69	17	146	408	34		.254	.286	.340	626	112	29	58	96				
STL	67	40	3	.626	8	38	14	658	539	4163	987	151	60	11	172	339	39		.250	.288	.327	615	100	18	-3	104				
CIN	68	41	3	.624	8	40	16	754	512	4296	1037	109	96	36	154	409	52		.254	.289	.354	643	108	49	19	105				
BAL	63	43	2	.594	11.5	42	18	636	515	4120	896	133	84	32	211	545	64		.233	.284	.336	620	101	26	3	104				
PHI	61	46	1	.570	14	38	16	700	546	4152	1057	167	100	26	153	434	40		.267	.301	.379	680	117	100	59	106				
TOL	46	58	6	.442	27.5	28	25	463	571	3895	859	153	48	8	157	545	26		.231	.268	.305	573	87	-36	-53	104				
BRO	40	64	5	.385	33.5	23	26	476	644	3958	845	112	47	16	179	417	16		.225	.263	.292	555	83	-61	-64	101				
RIC	12	30	4	.286	30.5	5	15	194	294	1546	326	40	33	7	53	282	24		.222	.261	.308	569	89	-19	-17	99				
PIT	30	78	2	.278	45.5	18	37	406	725	3873	777	105	50	2	143	411	41		.211	.248	.268	516	73	-110	-105	99				
IND	29	78	3	.271	46	17	39	462	755	3960	890	129	62	20	125	561	22		.233	.262	.315	577	93	-39	-25	97				
WAS	12	51	0	.190	41	10	20	248	481	2282	434	61	24	6	100	377	16		.200	.241	.259	500	75	-76	-44	88				
TOT	659					380	260	6889		48646	11065	1574	833	243	1992	5672	468		.240	.278	.326	604								

TEAM	CG	SHO	GR	SV	IP	H	HR	BB	SO	BR/9	ERA	AERA	OAV	OOB	PR	APR	PF	OSB	OCS	FA	E	WPB	DP	FW	PW	BW	BSW	DIF
NY	110	9	2	0	985.0	802	15	115	628	8.6	2.46	127	.209	.237	86	75	96			.907	441	137	42	2.3	6.9	8.2		4.1
COL	102	8	8	1	962.1	815	22	172	526	9.5	2.68	113	.217	.256	60	38	93			.908	433	191	74	2.3	3.5	9.0		.3
LOU	101	6	9	0	989.2	837	9	97	470	8.8	2.17	142	.216	.241	118	105	95			.912	426	190	84	2.6	9.6	5.3		-3.5
STL	99	8	11	0	987.0	881	16	172	477	10.0	2.67	122	.226	.266	63	63	100			.900	490	174	65	-.2	5.8	-.3		8.2
CIN	111	11	1	0	983.2	955	27	181	308	11.1	3.33	100	.243	.289	-10	-1	103			.909	430	164	82	2.8	-.0	1.7		9.0
BAL	105	8	3	1	955.2	869	16	219	635	10.5	2.71	128	.224	.271	56	74	107			.899	461	210	61	.7	6.8	.3		2.3
PHI	105	5	3	0	948.2	920	16	127	530	10.3	3.42	99	.237	.269	-18	-4	104			.901	457	199	63	.9	-.4	5.4		1.6
TOL	103	9	6	1	946.0	885	12	169	501	10.5	3.06	111	.233	.275	19	34	105			.900	469	294	67	.7	3.1	-4.8		-5.0
BRO	105	6	4	0	948.2	996	20	163	378	11.2	3.79	87	.254	.288	-58	-50	102			.889	520	266	68	-1.6	-4.6	-5.8		.0
RIC	45	1	0	0	370.1	402	14	52	167	11.4	4.52	73	.257	.288	-53	-49	102			.874	239	82	27	-1.5	-4.5	-1.6		-1.4
PIT	108	4	2	0	943.1	1059	25	216	338	12.7	4.35	76	.265	.312	-116	-109	102			.889	523	218	71	-1.6	-10.0	-9.6		-2.9
IND	107	2	3	0	937.2	1000	30	199	479	11.8	4.20	78	.254	.295	-100	-96	101			.889	515	250	45	-1.2	-8.8	-2.3		-12.2
WAS	62	3	1	0	543.2	644	21	110	235	12.8	4.01	76	.273	.311	-46	-64	93			.858	400	165	40	-5.3	-5.8	-4.0		-4.4
TOT	1263	80	53	3	11501.2					10.6	3.24		.240	.278						.897	5804	2540	789					

Batter-Fielder Wins		Batting Average		On-Base Percentage		Slugging Average		On-Base Plus Slugging		Adjusted OPS		Adjusted Batter Runs	
Barkley-Tol	4.8	Orr-NY	354	Jones-Cin	376	Reilly-Cin	551	Reilly-Cin	918	Orr-NY	195	Orr-NY	45.5
Fennelly-Was-Cin	4.2	Reilly-Cin	339	Nelson-NY	375	Stovey-Phi	545	Stovey-Phi	913	Reilly-Cin	186	Reilly-Cin	39.4
Smith-Col	4.1	Browning-Lou	336	Stovey-Phi	368	Orr-NY	539	Orr-NY	901	Fennelly-Was-Cin	186	Stovey-Phi	37.7
Latham-StL	4.1	Stovey-Phi	326	Fennelly-Was-Cin	367	Fennelly-Was-Cin	480	Fennelly-Was-Cin	847	Stovey-Phi	182	Browning-Lou	37.4
Esterbrook-NY	3.5	Lewis-StL	323	Reilly-Cin	366	Browning-Lou	472	Jones-Cin	846	Browning-Lou	176	Fennelly-Was-Cin	37.3

Runs		Hits		Doubles		Triples		Home Runs		Total Bases		Runs Batted In
Stovey-Phi	124	Orr-NY	162	Barkley-Tol	39	Stovey-Phi	23	Reilly-Cin	11	Reilly-Cin	247	
Jones-Cin	117	Browning-Lou	152	Browning-Lou	33	Reilly-Cin	19	Stovey-Phi	10	Orr-NY	247	
Latham-StL	115	Esterbrook-NY	150	Orr-NY	32	Mann-Col	18	Orr-NY	9	Stovey-Phi	244	
Reilly-Cin	114	Browning-Lou	150	Esterbrook-NY	29	Peltz-Ind	17	Mann-Col	7	Jones-Cin	222	
Nelson-NY	114	Jones-Cin	148	Lewis-StL	25	Jones-Cin	17	Jones-Cin	7	Browning-Lou	211	

Stolen Bases	Base Stealing Runs	Fielding Runs-Infield		Fielding Runs-Outfield		Wins		Winning Pct.		Complete Games	
		Latham-StL	37.2	Nicol-StL	18.4	Hecker-Lou	52	Morris-Col	723	Hecker-Lou	72
		Smith-Col	29.8	Welch-Tol	14.0	Lynch-NY	37	Hecker-Lou	722	Mullane-Tol	64
		Barkley-Tol	27.3	Knight-Phi	11.0	Keefe-NY	37	Foutz-StL	714	McKeon-Ind	59
		Gerhardt-Lou	22.5	Corkhill-Cin	10.3	Mullane-Tol	36	Lynch-NY	712	Keefe-NY	56
		Houck-Phi	22.0	Cline-Lou	6.1			Keefe-NY	685	Terry-Bro	54

Strikeouts		Fewest BB/Game		Games		Saves		Base Runners/9		Adjusted Relief Runs	Relief Ranking
Hecker-Lou	385	Driscoll-Lou	62	Hecker-Lou	75	O'Day-Tol	1	Hecker-Lou	8.02		
Henderson-Bal	346	Hecker-Lou	75	Mullane-Tol	67	Mountain-Col	1	Morris-Col	8.36		
Keefe-NY	334	Lynch-NY	76	McKeon-Ind	61	T.Burns-Bal	1	Lynch-NY	8.56		
Mullane-Tol	325	E.Dugan-Ric	81	Keefe-NY	58			Caruthers-StL	8.60		
McKeon-Ind	308	McGinnis-StL	89	Terry-Bro	56			Keefe-NY	8.68		

Innings Pitched		Opponents' Avg.		Opponents' OBP		Earned Run Average		Adjusted ERA		Adjusted Starter Runs		Pitcher Wins	
Hecker-Lou	670.2	Keefe-NY	204	Hecker-Lou	226	Hecker-Lou	1.80	Hecker-Lou	171	Hecker-Lou	103.0	Hecker-Lou	12.9
Mullane-Tol	567.0	Hecker-Lou	204	Morris-Col	234	Foutz-StL	2.18	Foutz-StL	149	Mullane-Tol	54.6	Mullane-Tol	7.1
McKeon-Ind	512.0	Morris-Col	204	Lynch-NY	236	Morris-Col	2.18	Morris-Col	139	Keefe-NY	46.2	Keefe-NY	5.5
Lynch-NY	496.0	Mountain-Col	209	Keefe-NY	239	Keefe-NY	2.25	Keefe-NY	138	Morris-Col	45.7	Morris-Col	4.5
Keefe-NY	483.0	Foutz-StL	212	Foutz-StL	255	Mountain-Col	2.45	Mullane-Tol	135	Henderson-Bal	36.7	Henderson-Bal	3.9

Mets Win New York's First Flag

While the National League believed it could live with the threat of the American Association, the threat from the new Union Association, whose owners did not respect the reserve clause, was another thing entirely. The NL supported Association expansion into four cities that the Unions might possibly inhabit: Brooklyn (which remains in the NL today as the Los Angeles Dodgers), Washington, Indianapolis, and Toledo.

While scrambling to keep their players from Union Association clutches, the AA debuted St. Louis pitchers Bob Caruthers and Dave Foutz , and Toledo outfielder Curt Welch and catcher Deacon McGuire. Brothers Moses and Welday Walker of Toledo became the first blacks ever to play major league baseball—and the last, thanks to various regressive thinkers, until 1947.

A five-team pennant race produced New York's first major league flag. Jim Mutrie's Metropolitans sported batting titlist Dave Orr and infielder Candy Nelson, whose 74 walks were *twice* the previous major league record. The Mets distributed the load equally on the mound. Tim Keefe and Jack Lynch each won 37 games, the first time in major league history two teammates

ranked so high in this category. Columbus and Louisville, with Guy Hecker winning 52 times, finished 2-3 in pitching. St. Louis finished fourth, but when Charlie Comiskey took over the reins late in the year, the team immediately sparked. Cincinnati had slugger John Reilly but little else.

Washington defaulted in August, replaced by Richmond, a club from the Eastern League. About the only positive thing Richmond brought was 19-year-old third baseman Billy Nash, who went on to a long NL career. Following the 1883 season, Richmond, Indianapolis, and Toledo were asked to leave the league, and Columbus merged with Pittsburgh.

Despite increasing the schedule to more than 100 games, and adding extra teams, AA attendance rose by just 75,000. Philadelphia's attendance, the league's best in 1883, dipped by around 60 percent, even though the city's Union club defaulted in early August. Crowds were smaller but there was still plenty of life in them. On August 13 Baltimore management surrounded its field with barbed wire the day after fans surged out of the stands and roughed up the umpire.

1884 Union Association

TEAM	W	L	T	PCT	GB	HW	HL	R	OR	PA	H	2B	3B	HR	BB	SO	HB	SH	AVG	OBP	SLG	OPS	AOPS	BR	ABR	PF	SB	CS	BSA	BSR
STL	94	19	1	.832		50	6	887	429	4466	1251	259	41	32	181	542			.292	.321	.394	715	113	-31	-55	104				
MIL	8	4	0	.667	35.5	8	4	53	34	415	88	25	0	0	20	70			.223	.260	.286	546	123	-26	5	55				
CIN	69	36	0	.657	21	35	17	703	466	3933	1027	118	63	26	147	482			.271	.298	.356	654	92	-119	-155	108				
BAL	58	47	1	.552	32	29	21	662	627	4027	952	150	26	17	144	652			.245	.272	.310	582	71	-219	-256	110				
BOS	58	51	2	.532	34	34	23	636	558	4068	928	168	32	19	128	787			.236	.260	.309	569	74	-245	-239	99				
CP	41	50	2	.451	42	21	18	438	482	3331	742	127	26	10	119	505			.231	.258	.296	554	70	-215	-212	99				
WAS	47	65	2	.420	46.5	36	27	572	679	4044	931	120	26	4	118	558			.237	.259	.284	543	68	-278	-266	97				
PHI	21	46	2	.313	50	13	21	414	545	2621	618	108	35	7	103	405			.245	.275	.324	599	89	-128	-105	92				
STP	2	6	1	.250	39.5	0	0	24	57	279	49	13	1	0	7	47			.180	.201	.235	436	61	-30	-19	55				
ALT	6	19	0	.240	44	6	12	90	216	921	223	30	6	2	22	130			.248	.266	.301	567	72	-56	-57	101				
KC	16	63	3	.203	61	11	23	311	618	2925	557	104	15	6	123	529			.199	.232	.253	485	55	-258	-230	87				
WIL	2	16	0	.111	44.5	1	6	35	114	543	91	8	8	2	22	123			.175	.208	.232	440	33	-58	-59	103				
TOT	428					244	178	4825		31573	7457	1230	279	125	1134	4830			.245	.272	.316	588								

TEAM	CG	SHO	GR	SV	IP	H	HR	BB	SO	BR/9	ERA	AERA	OAV	OOB	PR	APR	PF	OSB	OCS	FA	E	WPB	DP	FW	PW	BW	BSW	DIF
STL	104	8	9	6	993.0	838	9	110	550	8.6	1.96	122	.214	.235	53	47	98			.888	554	159	79	3.7	4.1	-4.8		34.5
MIL	12	3	0	0	104.0	49	1	13	139	5.4	2.25	59	.132	.161	2	-20	.55			.892	53	32	4	.6	-1.8	.4		2.7
CIN	95	11	8	1	914.1	831	17	90	503	9.1	2.38	107	.226	.245	5	16	105			.882	532	169	45	2.5	1.4	-13.6		26.1
BAL	92	4	14	0	946.2	1002	24	177	628	11.2	3.01	89	.254	.286	-61	-33	110			.872	616	259	53	-.8	-2.9	-22.4		31.6
BOS	100	5	9	1	953.1	885	17	110	753	9.4	2.70	88	.231	.252	-28	-36	98			.868	633	277	39	-.3	-3.2	-20.9		27.9
CP	86	6	6	0	803.2	743	12	137	679	9.9	2.72	89	.230	.261	-26	-27	100			.882	459	191	38	2.8	-2.4	-18.6		13.7
WAS	94	5	20	0	953.2	992	16	168	684	10.9	3.43	70	.251	.282	-105	-111	98			.869	625	284	55	.7	-9.7	-23.3		23.3
PHI	64	1	3	0	593.1	726	7	105	310	12.6	4.63	-50	.283	.311	-145	-161	95			.841	501	268	36	-5.2	-14.1	-9.2		16.0
STP	7	1	2	0	71.0	72	1	27	44	12.5	3.17	42	.248	.312	-6	-27	55			.872	47	12	6	.2	-2.4	-1.7		1.9
ALT	20	0	5	0	219.2	292	3	52	93	14.1	4.67	57	.300	.335	-55	-45	109			.862	156	63	4	-.6	-3.9	-5.0		3.1
KC	70	0	12	0	702.2	862	14	127	334	12.7	4.05	55	.283	.312	-126	-155	92			.861	520	209	51	-2.5	-13.6	-20.1		12.7
WIL	15	0	2	0	142.0	165	4	18	113	11.6	3.04	88	.273	.294	-10	-6	110			.860	104	62	10	-.1	-.5	-5.2		-1.2
TOT	759	44	90	8	7397.1					10.5	3.04		.245	.272						.872	4800	1985	420					

Batter-Fielder Wins		Batting Average		On-Base Percentage		Slugging Average		On-Base Plus Slugging		Adjusted OPS		Adjusted Batter Runs	
Dunlap-StL	7.1	Dunlap-StL	.412	Dunlap-StL	.448	Dunlap-StL	.621	Dunlap-StL	1069	Dunlap-StL	213	Dunlap-StL	50.1
Shafer-StL	1.9	Taylor-StL	.366	Shafer-StL	.398	Taylor-StL	.548	Shafer-StL	.899	Hoover-Phi	180	Shafer-StL	24.9
Hoover-Phi	1.7	Dickerson-StL	.365	Hoover-Phi	.390	Shafer-StL	.501	Hoover-Phi	.885	Shafer-StL	165	Hoover-Phi	19.4
Glasscock-Cin	1.4	Hoover-Phi	.364	Moore-Was	.363	Hoover-Phi	.495	Gleason-StL	.802	Moore-Was	140	Glasscock-Cin	13.6
Briody-Cin	1.1	Shafer-StL	.360	Gleason-StL	.361	Burns-Cin	.457	Moore-Was	.777	Gleason-StL	137	Taylor-StL	12.1

Runs		Hits		Doubles		Triples		Home Runs		Total Bases		Runs Batted In	
Dunlap-StL	160	Dunlap-StL	185	Shafer-StL	40	Burns-Cin	12	Dunlap-StL	13	Dunlap-StL	279		
Shafer-StL	130	Shafer-StL	168	Dunlap-StL	39	Rowe-StL	11	Crane-Bos	12	Shafer-StL	234		
Seery-Bal-KC	115	Moore-Was	155	Rowe-StL	32	Shafer-StL	10	Levis-Bal-Was	5	Rowe-StL	208		
Robinson-Bal	101	Seery-Bal-KC	146	O'Brien-Bos	31					Crane-Bos	193		
Rowe-StL	95	Rowe-StL	142	Gleason-StL	30					Seery-Bal-KC	192		

Stolen Bases		Base Stealing Runs		Fielding Runs-Infield		Fielding Runs-Outfield		Wins		Winning Pct.		Complete Games	
				Dunlap-StL	28.4	Wise-Was	8.3	B.Sweeney-Bal	40	McCormick-Cin	.875	B.Sweeney-Bal	58
				Evers-StL	14.5	Boyle-StL	5.3	Daily-CP-Was	28	Taylor-StL	.862	Daily-CP-Was	56
				Robinson-Bal	12.7	Harbridge-Cin	4.4	Taylor-StL	25	Boyle-StL	.833	Bakely-Phi-Wil-KC	43
				Hackett-Bos	11.6	Crane-Bos	4.1	Bradley-Cin	25	Sweeney-StL	.774	Bradley-Cin	36
				McCormick-Phi-Was	9.8	B.Sweeney-Bal	3.7	Sweeney-StL	24	B.Sweeney-Bal	.656	Shaw-Bos	35

Strikeouts		Fewest BB/Game		Games		Saves		Base Runners/9		Adjusted Relief Runs		Relief Ranking	
Daily-CP-Was	483	Sweeney-StL	.43	B.Sweeney-Bal	62	Taylor-StL	4	McCormick-Cin	7.07				
B.Sweeney-Bal	440	McCormick-Cin	.60	Daily-CP-Was	58	Sylvester-Cin	1	Sweeney-StL	7.31				
Shaw-Bos	309	Boyle-StL	.60	Wise-Was	50	Dunlap-StL	1	Shaw-Bos	7.53				
Wise-Was	268	Bradley-Cin	.61	Bakely-Phi-Wil-KC	46	Brown-Bos	1	Boyle-StL	7.68				
Burke-Bos	255	Murphy-Alt-StL	.62	Bradley-Cin	41	Werden-StL	1	Werden-StL	8.60				

Innings Pitched		Opponents' Avg.		Opponents' OBP		Earned Run Average		Adjusted ERA		Adjusted Starter Runs		Pitcher Wins	
B.Sweeney-Bal	538.0	McCormick-Cin	.188	McCormick-Cin	.202	McCormick-Cin	1.54	McCormick-Cin	165	McCormick-Cin	25.5	Taylor-StL	2.8
Daily-CP-Was	500.2	Shaw-Bos	.188	Sweeney-StL	.207	Taylor-StL	1.68	Taylor-StL	142	Taylor-StL	21.1	Sweeney-StL	2.1
Bakely-Phi-Wil-KC	394.2	Sweeney-StL	.197	Shaw-Bos	.212	Boyle-StL	1.74	Boyle-StL	137	Shaw-Bos	19.9	McCormick-Cin	1.9
Wise-Was	364.1	Boyle-StL	.202	Boyle-StL	.215	Shaw-Bos	1.77	Shaw-Bos	134	Sweeney-StL	16.4	Shaw-Bos	1.3
Bradley-Cin	342.0	Werden-StL	.205	Werden-StL	.235	Sweeney-StL	1.83	Sweeney-StL	130	Boyle-StL	9.5	Boyle-StL	.7

One-Shot Deal

The Union Association, set up ostensibly to challenge the reserve clause, sprang from the mind of St. Louis magnate Henry Lucas, who wanted to force his way into the big picture. It's no coincidence, then, that the St. Louis club was the class of the league, winning by 21 games. Several clubs, including Altoona, Philadelphia, and Chicago (which moved to Pittsburgh, *then* disbanded) weren't even around at the finish.

The Union owners went after low-level NL and AA players and the occasional regular, but almost immediately, contract-jumping and charges of game-throwing plagued the new league. Three good young players debuted in the Union Association before catching on elsewhere: shortstop Germany Smith and outfielders Tommy McCarthy and Oyster Burns. But the level of play was not high; journeyman pitcher Hugh "One Arm" Daily fanned 483 hitters, the third highest total ever. St. Louis' Fred Dunlap, the UA's star batter, hit .412 with 13 homers; he was a good hitter in the NL, but no superstar.

Much has been said about the league's thin qualifications as a major league. But the UA *operated* as a major league, raiding NL and AA rosters. It also played more games in 1884 than did clubs in any established minor league. The UA did, however, feature minor league teams. Wilmington, the champions of the Eastern League, jumped to the UA in August to replace Philadelphia. St. Paul joined the Union at the end of the Northwestern League season to finish out the season when Wilmington disbanded. The Milwaukee Grays, also of the Northwestern League, were the league's most successful replacement, going 8-4 in Pittsburgh's stead. Kansas City formed a team to replace Altoona, going 16-63. Only five teams were functioning at season's end.

The fragile league crumbled as soon as the NL accepted the St. Louis club for 1885 to provide competition for Chris Von der Ahe's successful AA franchise. Maroons dominated almost every UA statistical category and drew 116,000 of the league's 411,000 fans.

Vested-interest parties such as Al Spalding and Al Reach had nothing good to say about the Union Association. But many people hated the reserve clause, and it was only a few years until a more powerful league rose to combat it.

1883 National League

TEAM	W	L	T	PCT	GB	HW	HL	R	OR	PA	H	2B	3B	HR	BB	SO	HB	SH	AVG	OBP	SLG	OPS	AOPS	BR	ABR	PF	SB	CS	BSA	BSR
BOS	63	35	0	.643		41	8	669	456	3780	1010	209	86	34	123	423			.276	.300	.408	708	114	68	53	102				
CHI	59	39	0	.602	4	36	13	679	540	3787	1000	277	61	13	129	399			.273	.298	.393	691	104	55	7	108				
PRO	58	40	0	.592	5	34	15	636	436	3834	1001	189	59	21	149	309			.272	.300	.372	672	104	29	13	103				
CLE	55	42	3	.567	7.5	31	18	476	443	3596	852	184	38	8	139	374			.246	.276	.329	605	88	-52	-46	99				
BUF	52	45	1	.536	10.5	36	13	614	576	3876	1058	184	59	8	147	342			.284	.311	.371	682	108	44	30	102				
NY	46	50	2	.479	16	28	19	530	577	3651	900	139	69	24	127	297			.255	.281	.354	635	96	-23	-17	99				
DET	40	58	3	.408	23	23	26	524	650	3892	931	164	48	13	166	378			.250	.282	.330	612	93	-47	-21	95				
PHI	17	81	1	.173	46	9	40	437	887	3717	859	181	48	3	141	355			.240	.269	.320	589	90	-74	-27	91				
TOT	395					238	152	4565		30133	7611	1527	468	124	1121	2877			.262	.290	.360	650								

TEAM	CG	SHO	GR	SV	IP	H	HR	BB	SO	BR/9	ERA	AERA	OAV	OOB	PR	APR	PF	OSB	OCS	FA	E	WPB	DP	FW	PW	BW	BSW	DIF
BOS	89	6	9	3	860.0	853	11	90	538	9.9	2.55	121	.245	.264	56	53	99			.901	409	222	58	3.2	4.6	4.6		1.6
CHI	91	5	8	1	862.0	942	21	123	299	11.1	2.78	119	.260	.284	34	45	105			.879	543	137	76	-3.5	3.9	.6		8.9
PRO	88	4	10	1	871.0	827	12	111	376	9.7	2.37	130	.238	.262	74	69	98			.903	419	156	75	2.7	6.0	1.1		-.8
CLE	92	5	8	2	879.0	818	7	217	402	10.6	2.22	142	.237	.282	89	92	100			.909	389	135	69	4.6	8.0	-4.0		-2.1
BUF	90	5	9	2	859.1	971	12	101	362	11.2	3.32	96	.268	.288	-18	-9	101			.896	445	171	52	1.4	-.8	2.6		.3
NY	87	5	11	0	866.0	907	19	170	323	11.2	2.94	105	.253	.287	19	11	99			.889	468	181	52	.2	1.0	-1.5		-1.7
DET	89	5	12	2	894.1	1026	22	184	324	12.2	3.56	87	.270	.303	-42	-47	99			.893	470	132	77	.9	-4.1	-1.8		-3.9
PHI	91	3	9	0	864.2	1267	20	125	253	14.5	5.34	58	.318	.338	-212	-219	98			.858	639	179	62	-8.0	-19.1	-2.4		-2.5
TOT	717	38	76	11	6956.1					11.3	3.13		.262	.290						.891	3782	1313	521					

Batter-Fielder Wins		Batting Average		On-Base Percentage		Slugging Average		On-Base Plus Slugging		Adjusted OPS		Adjusted Batter Runs	
Farrell-Pro	3.5	Brouthers-Buf	.374	Brouthers-Buf	.397	Brouthers-Buf	.572	Brouthers-Buf	.969	Brouthers-Buf	186	Brouthers-Buf	42.7
Richardson-Buf	3.1	Connor-NY	.357	Connor-NY	.394	Morrill-Bos	.525	Connor-NY	.900	Connor-NY	173	Connor-NY	35.9
Brouthers-Buf	3.0	Gore-Chi	.334	Gore-Chi	.377	Connor-NY	.506	Morrill-Bos	.868	Morrill-Bos	155	Bennett-Det	26.3
Bennett-Det	3.0	Burdock-Bos	.330	Dunlap-Cle	.361	Sutton-Bos	.486	Gore-Chi	.849	Bennett-Det	155	Morrill-Bos	25.6
Dunlap-Cle	2.9	O'Rourke-Buf	.328	Burdock-Bos	.353	Ewing-NY	.481	Sutton-Bos	.836	Sutton-Bos	147	Dunlap-Cle	23.8

Runs		Hits		Doubles		Triples		Home Runs		Total Bases		Runs Batted In	
Hornung-Bos	107	Brouthers-Buf	159	Williamson-Chi	49	Brouthers-Buf	17	Ewing-NY	10	Brouthers-Buf	243	Brouthers-Buf	97
Gore-Chi	105	Connor-NY	146	Brouthers-Buf	41	Morrill-Bos	16	Hornung-Bos	8	Morrill-Bos	212	Burdock-Bos	88
O'Rourke-Buf	102	O'Rourke-Buf	143	Burns-Chi	37	Sutton-Bos	15	Denny-Pro	8	Connor-NY	207	Sutton-Bos	73
Sutton-Bos	101	Sutton-Bos	134	Anson-Chi	36	Connor-NY	15	Ward-NY	7	Sutton-Bos	201	Morrill-Bos	68
Hines-Pro	94	Wood-Det	133					Morrill-Bos	6	Hornung-Bos	199	Anson-Chi	68

Stolen Bases	Base Stealing Runs	Fielding Runs-Infield		Fielding Runs-Outfield		Wins		Winning Pct.		Complete Games	
		Farrell-Pro	24.7	Shafer-Buf	16.2	Radbourn-Pro	48	McCormick-Cle	.700	Galvin-Buf	72
		Williamson-Chi	17.7	Ward-NY	11.0	Galvin-Buf	46	Radbourn-Pro	.658	Radbourn-Pro	66
		Glasscock-Cle	17.7	Gore-Chi	8.5	Whitney-Bos	37	Buffinton-Bos	.641	Coleman-Phi	59
		Pfeffer-Chi	16.3	Kelly-Chi	8.3	Corcoran-Chi	34	Whitney-Bos	.638	Whitney-Bos	54
		Richardson-Chi	16.0	Manning-Phi	7.1	McCormick-Cle	28	Corcoran-Chi	.630	Corcoran-Chi	51

Strikeouts		Fewest BB/Game		Games		Saves		Base Runners/9		Adjusted Relief Runs	Relief Ranking
Whitney-Bos	345	Whitney-Bos	61	Radbourn-Pro	76	Wiedman-Det	2	Radbourn-Pro	8.81		
Radbourn-Pro	315	Galvin-Buf	69	Galvin-Buf	76	Whitney-Bos	2	Whitney-Bos	9.23		
Galvin-Buf	279	Radbourn-Pro	80	Coleman-Phi	65			Galvin-Buf	9.96		
Corcoran-Chi	216	Coleman-Phi	80	Whitney-Bos	62			McCormick-Cle	10.03		
Buffinton-Bos	188	Goldsmith-Chi	92	Corcoran-Chi	56			Ward-NY	10.04		

Innings Pitched		Opponents' Avg.		Opponents' OBP		Earned Run Average		Adjusted ERA		Adjusted Starter Runs		Pitcher Wins	
Galvin-Buf	656.1	Sawyer-Cle	.217	Radbourn-Pro	.244	McCormick-Cle	1.84	McCormick-Cle	171	Radbourn-Pro	73.5	Radbourn-Pro	8.3
Radbourn-Pro	632.1	Radbourn-Pro	.227	Whitney-Bos	.251	Radbourn-Pro	2.05	Radbourn-Pro	150	McCormick-Cle	47.4	Whitney-Bos	5.6
Coleman-Phi	538.1	McCormick-Cle	.233	Galvin-Buf	.265	Whitney-Bos	2.24	Whitney-Bos	138	Whitney-Bos	44.4	McCormick-Cle	4.8
Whitney-Bos	514.0	Sweeney-Pro	.237	Ward-NY	.267	Sawyer-Cle	2.36	Sawyer-Cle	133	Corcoran-Chi	36.8	Corcoran-Chi	3.2
Corcoran-Chi	473.2	Whitney-Bos	.238	McCormick-Cle	.268	Daily-Cle	2.42	Corcoran-Chi	132	Daily-Cle	34.0	Galvin-Buf	2.4

Tiny Steps

After a reasonably successful 1882 campaign, the NL awarded franchises to Philadelphia and New York, each competing with AA franchises in the same cities. Both NL teams survive to this day. Prior to 1883 New York had not had any major league team since 1876. A meeting between NL and AA delegates in New York resulted in a peace agreement between the two warring leagues. Each club would now be able to reserve 11 players, rather than 10, and league contracts would be respected.

Abraham Mills was voted the league's new president, to be replaced in 1885 by Nicholas Young. The NL rules committee stated that pitches must not be delivered above the line of the shoulder. Any exception to this would result in a base-advancing "balk." In addition, the league ruled once and for all that a foul must be caught on the fly to register as an out. The AA retained the one-bounce exception.

Chicago again finished just ahead of Providence, but a September rush by the surprising Boston Beaneaters shoved both clubs aside. Boston, with a slugging offense led by Joe Hornung and John Morrill, featured a terrific pitcher in Jim Whitney. Although the White Stockings still led the league in runs, King Kelly and Fred Pfeffer had poor seasons, and Fred Goldsmith lost some of his touch on the hill. Perhaps 1883's most interesting debut came in Chicago, where outfielder and future evangelist Billy Sunday showed off legs that moved almost as quickly as his mouth—Cap Anson signed the 20-year-old outfielder because he "ran like a scared deer."

With two new clubs in large cities, NL attendance increased, but lagged far behind that of the AA. More than twice as many fans came out to see the AA's Philadelphia franchise than to see any NL club. Philadelphia's NL entry, which used an unheard-of 29 players, was allowed to cut its admission to 25 cents to match the AA's price. The last-place club drew 75,000, but that was still just one quarter of the Athletics' business.

1883 American Association

TEAM	W	L	T	PCT	GB	HW	HL	R	OR	PA	H	2B	3B	HR	BB	SO	HB	SH	AVG	OBP	SLG	OPS	AOPS	BR	ABR	PF	SB	CS	BSA	BSR
PHI	66	32	0	.673		37	14	720	547	3912	974	149	50	20	200	268			.262	.300	.346	646	102	49	-4	109				
STL	65	33	0	.663	1	35	14	549	409	3619	891	118	46	7	124	240			.255	.280	.321	601	91	-13	-41	106				
CIN	61	37	0	.622	5	38	13	662	413	3808	961	122	74	34	139	261			.262	.289	.363	652	106	45	13	106				
NY	54	42	1	.563	11	29	17	498	405	3676	883	111	58	6	142	259			.250	.279	.319	598	91	-18	-40	104				
LOU	52	45	1	.536	13.5	29	18	564	562	3694	892	114	64	14	141	304			.251	.280	.331	611	107	-4	40	93				
COL	32	65	0	.330	33.5	18	29	476	659	3687	854	101	79	15	134	409			.240	.268	.326	594	102	-28	18	92				
PIT	31	67	0	.316	35	18	31	525	728	3771	892	120	58	13	164	345			.247	.280	.324	604	101	-10	14	96				
BAL	28	68	0	.292	37	18	31	471	742	3696	870	125	49	5	164	331			.246	.280	.314	594	91	-19	-35	103				
TOT	390					222	167	4465		29863	7217	960	478	114	1208	2417			.252	.282	.331	613								

TEAM	CG	SHO	GR	SV	IP	H	HR	BB	SO	BR/9	ERA	AERA	OAV	OOB	PR	APR	PF	OSB	OCS	FA	E	WPB	DP	FW	PW	BW	BSW	DIF
PHI	92	1	6	0	873.0	921	22	95	347	10.5	2.88	123	.254	.273	41	59	107			.865	584	168	40	-4.1	5.2	-.4		16.2
STL	93	9	5	1	879.1	729	7	150	325	9.0	2.23	156	.211	.244	104	115	106			.909	388	126	62	4.5	10.1	-3.6		5.0
CIN	96	8	2	0	866.2	766	17	168	215	9.7	2.26	143	.222	.258	100	95	98			.905	383	131	57	4.7	8.4	1.1		-2.2
NY	97	6	0	0	874.0	751	12	133	478	9.1	2.90	115	.218	.247	38	41	101			.905	391	117	45	4.1	3.6	-3.5		1.8
LOU	96	7	2	0	873.2	987	7	110	269	11.3	3.50	85	.267	.288	-20	-56	91			.886	478	156	67	.6	-4.9	3.5		4.3
COL	90	4	7	0	840.1	980	16	211	222	12.8	3.96	78	.274	.314	-62	-89	93			.874	535	170	69	-2.1	-7.8	1.6		-8.1
PIT	82	1	18	1	867.2	1140	21	151	271	13.4	4.62	70	.298	.325	-127	-135	99			.884	504	232	55	-.6	-11.9	1.2		-6.8
BAL	86	1	11	0	844.2	943	12	190	290	12.1	4.08	85	.265	.303	-74	-55	105			.855	624	277	44	-6.3	-4.8	-3.1		-5.8
TOT	732	37	51	2	6919.1					11.0	3.30		.252	.282						.885	3887	1377	439					

Batter-Fielder Wins		Batting Average		On-Base Percentage		Slugging Average		On-Base Plus Slugging		Adjusted OPS		Adjusted Batter Runs	
Richmond-Col	3.8	Swartwood-Pit	.357	Swartwood-Pit	.394	Stovey-Phi	.506	Swartwood-Pit	.869	Swartwood-Pit	186	Swartwood-Pit	40.9
Smith-Col	3.4	Browning-Lou	.338	Browning-Lou	.378	Reilly-Cin	.485	Stovey-Phi	.852	Browning-Lou	183	Browning-Lou	34.4
Swartwood-Pit	2.8	Clinton-Bal	.313	Moynahan-Phi	.360	Swartwood-Pit	.476	Browning-Lou	.842	Stovey-Phi	156	Stovey-Phi	25.4
Gerhardt-Lou	2.4	Rowe-Bal	.313	Clinton-Bal	.357	Jones-Cin	.471	Reilly-Cin	.810	Reilly-Cin	149	Reilly-Cin	21.1
Holbert-NY	2.2	Reilly-Cin	.311	Nelson-NY	.353	Browning-Lou	.464	Jones-Cin	.799	Jones-Cin	146	Jones-Cin	18.2

Runs		Hits		Doubles		Triples		Home Runs		Total Bases		Runs Batted In	
Stovey-Phi	110	Swartwood-Pit	147	Stovey-Phi	31	Smith-Col	17	Stovey-Phi	14	Stovey-Phi	213		
Reilly-Cin	103	Reilly-Cin	136	Swartwood-Pit	24	Reilly-Cin	14	Jones-Cin	10	Reilly-Cin	212		
Carpenter-Cin	99	Carpenter-Cin	130	Knight-Phi	23	Kuehne-Col	14	Reilly-Cin	9	Swartwood-Pit	196		
Knight-Phi	98	Stovey-Phi	128	Hayes-Pit	23	Mansell-Pit	13	Fulmer-Cin	5	Jones-Cin	184		
		Nelson-NY	127			Mann-Col	13	Brown-Cin	5	B.Gleason-StL	167		

Stolen Bases		Base Stealing Runs		Fielding Runs-Infield		Fielding Runs-Outfield		Wins		Winning Pct.		Complete Games	
				Battin-Pit	28.8	Wolf-Lou	16.2	White-Cin	43	Mullane-StL	.700	Keefe-NY	68
				Richmond-Col	26.9	Nicol-StL	11.3	Keefe-NY	41	Mathews-Phi	.698	White-Cin	64
				Latham-StL	21.3	Maskrey-Lou	9.9	Mullane-StL	35	Bradley-Phi	.696	Mountain-Col	57
				Smith-Col	19.5	Birchall-Phi	5.0	Mathews-Phi	30	White-Cin	.662	Hecker-Lou	51
				Gerhardt-Lou	18.4	Clinton-Bal	4.8			McGinnis-StL	.636	Mullane-StL	49

Strikeouts		Fewest BB/Game		Games		Saves		Base Runners/9		Adjusted Relief Runs		Relief Ranking	
Keefe-NY	359	Mathews-Phi	.73	Keefe-NY	68	Mullane-StL	1	Keefe-NY	8.67				
Mathews-Phi	203	Weaver-Lou	.79	White-Cin	65	Barr-Pit	1	Mullane-StL	8.71				
Mullane-StL	191	Lynch-NY	.88	Mountain-Col	59			Jones-Phi	8.86				
Hecker-Lou	164	Bradley-Phi	.92	Mullane-StL	53			White-Cin	9.00				
Mountain-Col	159	Driscoll-Pit	1.04	Hecker-Lou	53			McGinnis-StL	9.27				

Innings Pitched		Opponents' Avg.		Opponents' OBP		Earned Run Average		Adjusted ERA		Adjusted Starter Runs		Pitcher Wins	
Keefe-NY	619.0	Keefe-NY	.203	Keefe-NY	.237	White-Cin	2.09	Mullane-StL	159	White-Cin	74.8	White-Cin	6.9
White-Cin	577.0	Mullane-StL	.207	Mullane-StL	.238	Mullane-StL	2.19	White-Cin	155	Keefe-NY	60.8	Keefe-NY	6.0
Mountain-Col	503.0	White-Cin	.209	White-Cin	.244	Deagle-Cin	2.31	McGinnis-StL	149	Mullane-StL	59.6	Mullane-StL	5.5
Hecker-Lou	469.0	McGinnis-StL	.215	McGinnis-StL	.249	McGinnis-StL	2.33	Mathews-Phi	144	McGinnis-StL	49.3	McGinnis-StL	4.2
Mullane-StL	460.2	Deagle-Cin	.229	Bradley-Phi	.263	Keefe-NY	2.41	Deagle-Cin	140	Mathews-Phi	37.8	Mathews-Phi	2.8

Calm Before the Storm

After changing to the Reach baseball, the AA took the field for its second season with new clubs in New York City and Columbus, Ohio. The AA, like the NL, expanded its schedule to 98 games. Most clubs were going to larger rosters and deeper pitching staffs. The Athletics, Reds, and Baltimore used three pitchers for at least 16 starts, though New York (led by Tim Keefe, who completed all 68 of his starts) and Louisville made do with just two. Will White of Cincinnati was again the league's top hurler, but his club—despite leading the league in homers and batting average—was just 24-24 on the road, and finished third.

Philadelphia replaced first baseman Arlie Latham with Harry Stovey, and the new guy led the AA in runs, doubles, homers, and slugging. With fine pitching and an offense that led the league in walks and runs, the Athletics held off St. Louis by 1 game. The Browns, using fine pitching from Tony Mullane and solid defense, came close for garrulous owner Chris Von der Ahe and a fanatical fan base. The rough-and-tumble character of the team gained shape with the acquisition of Latham.

After eking out the league title, the Athletics were to meet the NL champion Boston Red Stockings in a postseason series, but suddenly reversed their decision after faring poorly in an October exhibition series against the NL's pathetic Philadelphia entry. Following this chain of events, the NL and AA met in New York that December and hammered out a "permanent" peace agreement with provisions for an annual postseason series between league champions.

The results of the AA's second season spoke loudly. The eight clubs combined to draw more than 1,000,000, with three clubs, (one of which was last-place Baltimore) pulling in more than 100,000 each. The entire NL drew just over 600,000—a nifty 35 percent increase—but not in the same league as the AA's 251 percent explosion.

1882 National League

TEAM	W	L	T	PCT	GB	HW	HL	R	OR	PA	H	2B	3B	HR	BB	SO	HB	SH	AVG	OBP	SLG	OPS	AOPS	BR	ABR	PF	SB	CS	BSA	BSR
CHI	55	29	0	.655		35	10	604	353	3367	892	209	54	15	142	262			.277	.307	.389	696	118	87	61	105				
PRO	52	32	0	.619	3	30	12	463	356	3206	776	121	53	11	102	255			.250	.274	.334	608	96	-17	-16	100				
BUF	45	39	0	.536	10	26	13	500	461	3244	858	146	47	18	116	228			.274	.300	.368	668	113	51	42	102				
BOS	45	39	1	.536	10	27	15	472	414	3252	823	114	50	15	134	244			.264	.294	.347	641	107	22	21	100				
CLE	42	40	2	.512	12	21	19	402	411	3131	716	139	40	20	122	261			.238	.268	.331	599	96	-23	-8	97				
DET	42	41	3	.506	12.5	24	18	407	488	3266	724	117	44	19	122	308			.230	.259	.314	573	84	-54	-53	100				
TRO	35	48	2	.422	19.5	22	20	430	522	3166	747	116	59	12	109	298			.244	.270	.333	603	99	-22	0	95				
WOR	18	66	0	.214	37	12	30	379	652	3097	689	109	57	16	113	303			.231	.259	.322	581	85	-45	-54	102				
TOT	338					197	137	3657		25729	6225	1071	404	126	960	2159			.251	.279	.342	622								

TEAM	CG	SHO	GR	SV	IP	H	HR	BB	SO	BR/9	ERA	AERA	OAV	OOB	PR	APR	PF	OSB	OCS	FA	E	WPB	DP	FW	PW	BW	BSW	DIF
CHI	83	7	1	0	763.2	667	13	102	279	9.1	2.22	129	.221	.246	57	52	99			.898	376	98	54	.1	4.7	5.5		2.6
PRO	80	10	4	1	752.0	690	12	87	273	9.3	2.27	123	.228	.250	51	48	97			.901	371	114	67	.4	4.4	-1.5		6.7
BUF	79	3	5	0	737.0	778	16	114	287	10.9	3.25	90	.254	.280	-30	-30	101			.910	315	136	42	3.3	-2.7	3.8		-1.4
BOS	81	4	4	0	749.0	738	10	77	352	9.8	2.80	102	.239	.258	7	4	99			.910	314	121	37	3.6	.4	1.9		-2.8
CLE	81	4	3	0	751.2	743	22	132	232	10.5	2.75	101	.249	.280	11	1	97			.905	358	163	71	1.1	.0	-.7		.6
DET	82	7	4	0	793.0	808	19	129	354	10.6	2.98	98	.248	.277	-9	-8	101			.893	396	88	44	-.4	-.7	-4.8		6.5
TRO	81	6	4	0	758.0	836	13	165	184	11.9	3.08	91	.267	.304	-16	-24	98			.887	432	106	70	-2.5	-2.2	.0		-1.8
WOR	75	0	9	0	738.1	964	21	151	195	13.6	3.75	82	.294	.325	-71	-51	107			.878	468	165	66	-4.6	-4.6	-4.9		-9.9
TOT	642	41	34	1	6042.2					10.7	2.88		.251	.279						.897	3030	991	451					

Batter-Fielder Wins		Batting Average		On-Base Percentage		Slugging Average		On-Base Plus Slugging		Adjusted OPS		Adjusted Batter Runs	
Glasscock-Cle	4.1	Brouthers-Buf	368	Brouthers-Buf	403	Brouthers-Buf	547	Brouthers-Buf	950	Brouthers-Buf	198	Brouthers-Buf	37.9
Brouthers-Buf	2.8	Anson-Chi	362	Anson-Chi	397	Connor-Tro	530	Anson-Chi	897	Connor-Tro	188	Connor-Tro	33.4
Dunlap-Cle	2.8	Connor-Tro	330	Whitney-Bos	382	Whitney-Bos	510	Whitney-Bos	892	Whitney-Bos	182	Anson-Chi	29.9
Bennett-Det	2.8	Start-Pro	329	Gore-Chi	369	Anson-Chi	500	Connor-Tro	884	Anson-Chi	177	Whitney-Bos	24.1
Williamson-Chi	2.6	Whitney-Bos	323	Connor-Tro	354	Hines-Pro	467	Hines-Pro	793	Hines-Pro	151	Hines-Pro	21.3

Runs		Hits		Doubles		Triples		Home Runs		Total Bases		Runs Batted In	
Gore-Chi	99	Brouthers-Buf	129	Kelly-Chi	37	Connor-Tro	18	Wood-Det	7	Brouthers-Buf	192	Anson-Chi	83
Dalrymple-Chi	96	Anson-Chi	126	Anson-Chi	29	Wood-Det	12	Muldoon-Cle	6	Connor-Tro	185	Brouthers-Buf	63
Stovey-Wor	90			Hines-Pro	28	Corey-Wor	12	Brouthers-Buf	6	Hines-Pro	177	Williamson-Chi	60
Kelly-Chi	81			Williamson-Chi	27					Anson-Chi	174	Richardson-Buf	57
Purcell-Buf	79			Glasscock-Cle	27					Dalrymple-Chi	167	Kelly-Chi	55

Stolen Bases		Base Stealing Runs		Fielding Runs-Infield		Fielding Runs-Outfield		Wins		Winning Pct.		Complete Games	
				Glasscock-Cle	24.2	Evans-Wor	14.6	McCormick-Cle	36	Corcoran-Chi	692	McCormick-Cle	50
				Richardson-Buf	19.3	Hornung-Bos	11.4	Radbourn-Pro	33	Radbourn-Pro	635	Radbourn-Pro	50
				Dunlap-Cle	17.9	Hanlon-Det	10.1	Goldsmith-Chi	28	Goldsmith-Chi	622	Galvin-Buf	48
				A.Irwin-Wor	16.7	Kelly-Chi	8.2	Galvin-Buf	28	Ward-Pro	594	Whitney-Bos	46
				Williamson-Chi	15.4	Stovey-Wor	3.2	Corcoran-Chi	27	Mathews-Bos	559	Goldsmith-Chi	45

Strikeouts		Fewest BB/Game		Games		Saves		Base Runners/9		Adjusted Relief Runs		Relief Ranking	
Radbourn-Pro	201	Mathews-Bos	69	McCormick-Cle	68	Ward-Pro	1	Corcoran-Chi	8.70				
McCormick-Cle	200	Galvin-Buf	81	Radbourn-Pro	54			Radbourn-Pro	9.14				
Derby-Det	182	Goldsmith-Chi	84	Galvin-Buf	52			Goldsmith-Chi	9.22				
Whitney-Bos	180	Wiedman-Det	85	Whitney-Bos	49			Wiedman-Det	9.42				
Corcoran-Chi	170	Whitney-Bos	88	Richmond-Wor	48			Mathews-Bos	9.47				

Innings Pitched		Opponents' Avg.		Opponents' OBP		Earned Run Average		Adjusted ERA		Adjusted Starter Runs		Pitcher Wins	
McCormick-Cle	595.2	Corcoran-Chi	200	Corcoran-Chi	234	Corcoran-Chi	1.95	Corcoran-Chi	147	Radbourn-Pro	34.7	Radbourn-Pro	3
Radbourn-Pro	466.0	Radbourn-Pro	226	Mathews-Bos	246	Radbourn-Pro	2.11	Radbourn-Pro	133	Corcoran-Chi	34.0	Corcoran-Chi	2.5
Galvin-Buf	445.1	Ward-Pro	232	Radbourn-Pro	247	McCormick-Cle	2.37	Goldsmith-Chi	117	McCormick-Cle	30.3	Whitney-Bos	2.8
Whitney-Bos	420.0	Mathews-Bos	232	Wiedman-Det	253	Goldsmith-Chi	2.42	McCormick-Cle	117	Goldsmith-Chi	23.2	McCormick-Cle	2.2
		Daily-Buf	234	Goldsmith-Chi	254	Keefe-Tro	2.49	Keefe-Tro	113	Wiedman-Det	18.3	Goldsmith-Chi	1.8

The War Is On

In 1882, for the first time, the NL had no franchise shifts or new clubs. However, the ground was still quaking under the Senior Circuit. On William Hulbert's death in April, the league elected Boston owner Arthur Soden as president. Soden took office just as the new American Association, formed the previous winter and setting up shop in six cities forsaken by the NL, prepared for play.

For the third straight season, Chicago defeated Providence to win the NL title, but this time by a small margin. The White Stockings again had a murderous attack, with George Gore, Abner Dalrymple, and King Kelly rating 1-2-4 in runs, and pitchers Fred Goldsmith and Larry Corcoran were every bit the equal of Providence's Hoss Radbourn and John Ward. Dan Brouthers of third-place Buffalo led the NL in batting average, slugging percentage, on-base percentage, total bases, and hits.

Even though 1882 saw the first padded glove (worn by Providence shortstop Art Irwin, and later popularized by teammate John Ward), the NL's fielding percentage decreased by nearly 10 points. Chicago was last NL pennant winner to have a fielding average below .900.

Six NL clubs finished over .500. Only Worcester was a disaster, compiling a .214 winning percentage. Worcester drew just 11,000 fans all year, and on September 28 the club drew the smallest crowd in major league history: 6, that's right, 6. Worcester, and seventh-place Troy, were bounced from the NL for 1883 as Soden and the other league owners awarded franchises to magnates in Philadelphia and New York.

After a late-season schedule change appeared to give Chicago an unfair advantage, the White Stockings and Grays met in a nine-game series to determine the league champ. Cap Anson's White Stockings appeared to tank the first three games to increase interest in the remaining six, and the series indeed lasted nine games, with the White Stockings triumphing. Prior to their ill-advised postseason skirmish with Providence, the White Stockings split a two-game series with Association champion Cincinnati. The relevant parties duly noted the interest in this matchup.

1882 American Association

TEAM	W	L	T	PCT	GB	HW	HL	R	OR	PA	H	2B	3B	HR	BB	SO	HB	SH	AVG	OBP	SLG	OPS	AOPS	BR	ABR	PF	SB	CS	BSA	BSR
CIN	55	25	0	.688		31	11	489	268	3109	795	95	47	5	102	204			.264	.289	.332	621	107	37	12	106				
PHI	41	34	0	.547	11.5	21	18	406	389	2832	660	89	21	5	125	164			.244	.277	.298	575	92	-3	-27	107				
LOU	42	38	0	.525	13	26	13	443	352	2934	728	110	28	9	128	193			.259	.292	.328	620	120	40	66	95				
PIT	39	39	1	.500	15	17	18	428	418	2994	730	110	59	18	90	183			.251	.274	.348	622	118	35	57	95				
STL	37	43	0	.463	18	24	20	399	496	2977	663	87	41	11	112	226			.231	.260	.302	562	90	-20	-35	104				
BAL	19	54	1	.260	32.5	9	25	273	515	2655	535	60	24	4	72	215			.207	.229	.254	483	72	-89	-66	92				
TOT	234					128	105	2438		17501	4111	551	220	52	629	1185			.244	.271	.312	582								

TEAM	CG	SHO	GR	SV	IP	H	HR	BB	SO	BR/9	ERA	AERA	OAV	OOB	PR	APR	PF	OSB	OCS	FA	E	WPB	DP	FW	PW	BW	BSW	DIF
CIN	77	11	3	0	721.1	609	7	125	165	9.2	1.65	160	.214	.247	83	80	98			.907	332	102	41	3.7	7.3	1.1		2.9
PHI	72	2	3	0	663.0	682	13	99	190	10.6	2.97	94	.249	.275	-21	-12	105			.895	361	119	36	1.2	-1.1	-2.5		5.9
LOU	73	6	7	0	693.1	637	6	112	240	9.7	2.03	122	.229	.259	51	37	92			.893	385	161	57	1.3	3.4	6.1		-8.7
PIT	77	2	2	0	696.2	694	4	82	252	10.0	2.79	93	.243	.264	-8	-15	97			.889	397	115	40	.5	-1.4	5.2		-4.3
STL	75	3	5	1	688.1	729	7	103	225	10.9	2.92	96	.254	.280	-18	-8	105			.875	446	205	41	-1.6	-.7	-3.2		2.5
BAL	64	1	12	0	646.1	760	15	108	113	12.1	3.88	71	.275	.302	-86	-80	102			.859	490	183	41	-5.0	-7.3	-6.1		.9
TOT	438	25	32	1	4109.0					10.4	2.68		.244	.271						.886	2411	885	256					

Batter-Fielder Wins	Batting Average	On-Base Percentage	Slugging Average	On-Base Plus Slugging	Adjusted OPS	Adjusted Batter Runs
Browning-Lou 4.6	Browning-Lou 378	Browning-Lou 430	Browning-Lou 510	Browning-Lou 940	Browning-Lou 228	Browning-Lou 40.9
Snyder-Cin 2.5	Carpenter-Cin 342	Swartwood-Pit 370	Swartwood-Pit 489	Swartwood-Pit 859	Swartwood-Pit 197	Swartwood-Pit 33.4
O'Brien-Phi 2.2	Swartwood-Pit 329	Carpenter-Cin 360	Taylor-Pit 452	Carpenter-Cin 782	Taylor-Pit 157	Carpenter-Cin 18.5
Swartwood-Pit 1.8	O'Brien-Phi 303	O'Brien-Phi 339	Mansell-Pit 438	O'Brien-Phi 758	Carpenter-Cin 154	Mansell-Pit 17.1
Mansell-Pit 1.6	Wolf-Lou 299	Sommer-Cin 333	Carpenter-Cin....422	Taylor-Pit 749	Mansell-Pit 150	Taylor-Pit 16.9

Runs	Hits	Doubles	Triples	Home Runs	Total Bases	Runs Batted In
Swartwood-Pit 86	Carpenter-Cin 120	Swartwood-Pit 18	Mansell-Pit 16	Walker-StL 7	Swartwood-Pit 159	
Sommer-Cin 82	Browning-Lou 109	Mansell-Pit 18	Taylor-Pit 13	Browning-Lou 5	Mansell-Pit 152	
Carpenter-Cin 78	Swartwood-Pit 107	Browning-Lou 17	Wheeler-Cin 11	Swartwood-Pit 4	Carpenter-Cin 148	
Browning-Lou 67	Sommer-Cin 102	Taylor-Pit 16	Swartwood-Pit 11		Browning-Lou 147	
Birchall-Phi 65	B.Gleason-StL 100	Cuthbert-StL 16	Wolf-Lou 8		Taylor-Pit 135	

Stolen Bases	Base Stealing Runs	Fielding Runs-Infield	Fielding Runs-Outfield	Wins	Winning Pct.	Complete Games
		Stricker-Phi 22.8	Walker-StL 5.7	White-Cin 40	White-Cin 769	White-Cin 52
		B.Gleason-StL 10.3	O'Brien-Phi 4.6	Mullane-Lou 30	Weaver-Phi 634	Mullane-Lou 51
		Browning-Lou 8.8	Sommer-Cin 3.4	Weaver-Phi 26	McGinnis-StL 581	McGinnis-StL 43
		Peters-Pit 5.7	Blakiston-Phi 3.2	McGinnis-StL 25	Mullane-Lou 556	Weaver-Phi 41
		Shetzline-Bal 4.1	Mansell-Pit 2.8	Salisbury-Pit 20	Salisbury-Pit 526	Salisbury-Pit 38

Strikeouts	Fewest BB/Game	Games	Saves	Base Runners/9	Adjusted Relief Runs	Relief Ranking
Mullane-Lou 170	Hecker-Lou 43	Mullane-Lou 55	Fusselback-StL 1	Hecker-Lou 6.92		
Salisbury-Pit 135	Driscoll-Pit 54	White-Cin 54		Dorr-StL 7.36		
McGinnis-StL 134	Weaver-Phi 85	McGinnis-StL 45		Driscoll-Pit 7.79		
White-Cin 122	Salisbury-Pit 99	Landis-Phi-Bal 44		McCormick-Cin....8.97		
Weaver-Phi 104	Landis-Phi-Bal 1.17	Weaver-Phi 42		White-Cin 9.04		

Innings Pitched	Opponents' Avg.	Opponents' OBP	Earned Run Average	Adjusted ERA	Adjusted Starter Runs	Pitcher Wins
White-Cin 480.0	Hecker-Lou 188	Hecker-Lou 199	Driscoll-Pit 1.21	Driscoll-Pit 216	White-Cin 60.3	White-Cin 6.7
Mullane-Lou 460.1	McCormick-Cin....206	Driscoll-Pit 218	Hecker-Lou 1.30	Hecker-Lou 191	Mullane-Lou 34.3	Mullane-Lou 5.0
McGinnis-StL 388.1	Driscoll-Pit 206	McCormick-Cin....243	McCormick-Cin 1.52	McCormick-Cin 174	Driscoll-Pit 26.6	Driscoll-Pit 2.1
Weaver-Phi 371.0	White-Cin 216	White-Cin 244	White-Cin 1.54	White-Cin 172	McCormick-Cin....24.9	McCormick-Cin 1.8
Landis-Phi-Bal 360.0	Geis-Bal 220	Salisbury-Pit 253	Mullane-Lou 1.88	Mullane-Lou 132	Hecker-Lou 11.1	Hecker-Lou 1.6

Association Baseball

The new American Association, in direct contrast to the NL, voted to allow Sunday ball and sale of alcohol at their parks, and allowed clubs to charge just a quarter for admission (the Senior Circuit's ticket prices were 50 cents). These attractions helped the new AA essentially match the NL in attendance for its premier season, even though the new league fielded just six clubs. Three original AA clubs—Cincinnati, Pittsburgh, and St. Louis—remain in operation today as National League franchises.

There were other differences between the leagues. The American Association did not fine pitchers who hit batters intentionally, but they did institute the practice of league-employed umpires, which the NL soon followed. Disdaining the NL's Spalding baseball, the AA used the Mahn ball.

Many of the new league's clubs had local flavors. The Cincinnati club had three regulars (Will White, Joe Sommer, and Hick Carpenter) who had played on the city's final NL entry back in 1880. Rather than go whole-hog to steal away "reserved" NL players, the AA instead used players who had enjoyed success in the minor leagues of the time or had previously washed out of the majors.

Nobody argued that the AA's talent was on an equal level to that of the major leagues, but several future stars got their start in the new loop. Among players making their major league debuts in the 1882 American Association were Louisville's Pete Browning (the league's top offensive player), St. Louis' Charlie Comiskey, and Bid McPhee of Cincinnati.

The Cincinnati Red Stockings ran away with the marbles, zooming out to a quick lead. The first-year league was fairly balanced, with four teams playing .500 ball or better, and St. Louis a respectable 18 games behind in fifth place; Baltimore was the league doormat. White was the AA's dominant pitcher, though he had competition from Tony Mullane of third-place Louisville. Hick Carpenter led the league in hits, while top defender McPhee anchored the infield.

1881 National League

TEAM	W	L	T	PCT	GB	HW	HL	R	OR	PA	H	2B	3B	HR	BB	SO	HB	SH	AVG	OBP	SLG	OPS	AOPS	BR	ABR	PF	SB	CS	BSA	BS
CHI	56	28	0	.667		32	10	550	380	3254	918	157	36	12	140	224			.295	.325	.380	705	119	88	63	105				
PRO	47	37	1	.560	9	23	20	447	426	3223	780	144	37	11	146	214			.253	.287	.335	622	100	-3	5	98				
BUF	45	38	0	.542	10.5	25	16	440	447	3127	797	157	50	12	108	270			.264	.289	.361	650	109	22	28	99				
DET	41	43	0	.488	15	23	19	440	429	3131	780	131	53	17	136	250			.260	.293	.357	650	103	21	4	104				
TRO	39	45	1	.464	17	24	18	399	427	3186	754	124	31	5	140	240			.248	.281	.314	595	86	-32	-52	105				
BOS	38	45	1	.458	17.5	20	22	347	410	3026	733	121	27	5	110	193			.251	.279	.317	596	94	-32	-14	95				
CLE	36	48	1	.429	20	20	22	392	414	3249	796	120	39	7	132	224			.255	.286	.326	612	100	-17	7	95				
WOR	32	50	1	.390	23	19	22	410	492	3214	781	114	31	7	121	169			.253	.281	.316	597	86	-32	-54	106				
TOT	336					185	149	3425		25410	6339	1068	304	76	1033	1784			.260	.290	.338	628								

TEAM	CG	SHO	GR	SV	IP	H	HR	BB	SO	BR/9	ERA	AERA	OAV	OOB	PR	APR	PF	OSB	OCS	FA	E	WPB	DP	FW	PW	BW	BSW	D
CHI	81	9	3	0	744.2	722	14	122	228	10.2	2.43	113	.243	.273	29	26	99			.916	309	105	54	2.1	2.4	5.9		3
PRO	76	7	9	0	757.2	756	5	138	264	10.6	2.40	111	.243	.275	32	22	96			.896	390	139	66	-2.0	2.1	.5		4
BUF	72	5	12	0	742.1	881	9	89	185	11.8	2.84	98	.281	.301	-5	-5	100			.892	408	150	48	-3.4	-.5	2.6		4
DET	83	10	1	0	744.2	785	8	137	265	11.1	2.65	110	.257	.289	11	21	105			.906	338	83	80	.5	2.0	.4		-3
TRO	85	8	0	0	771.0	805	11	161	207	11.3	2.96	99	.263	.299	-16	-2	106			.917	311	85	70	2.2	-.2	-4.9		
BOS	72	6	11	3	730.2	763	9	143	199	11.2	2.71	98	.258	.292	5	-4	96			.909	325	204	54	1.0	-.4	-1.3		-2
CLE	82	2	3	0	760.0	737	9	126	240	10.2	2.68	98	.244	.274	8	-5	94			.904	848	129	68	.2	-.5	.7		-6
WOR	80	5	3	0	737.1	882	11	120	196	12.2	3.54	85	.288	.315	-63	-39	109			.903	353	113	50	-.5	-3.6	-5.0		
TOT	631	52	42	3	5988.1					11.1	2.77		.260	.290						.905	2782	1008	490					

Batter-Fielder Wins		Batting Average		On-Base Percentage		Slugging Average		On-Base Plus Slugging		Adjusted OPS		Adjusted Batter Runs	
Anson-Chi	3.6	Anson-Chi	.399	Anson-Chi	.442	Brouthers-Buf	.541	Anson-Chi	.952	Anson-Chi	189	Anson-Chi	35
Dunlap-Cle	3.2	Powell-Det	.338	York-Pro	.362	Anson-Chi	.510	Brouthers-Buf	.902	Brouthers-Buf	182	Brouthers-Buf	25
Bennett-Det	3.2	Rowe-Buf	.333	Brouthers-Buf	.361	Rowe-Buf	.480	Bennett-Det	.819	Dunlap-Cle	159	Dunlap-Cle	24
Richardson-Buf	2.8	Start-Pro	.328	Dunlap-Cle	.358	Bennett-Det	.478	Dunlap-Cle	.802	York-Pro	150	York-Pro	19
Williamson-Chi	2.1	Dunlap-Cle	.325	Gore-Chi	.354	Dunlap-Cle	.444	York-Pro	.790	Bennett-Det	149	O'Rourke-Buf	16

Runs		Hits		Doubles		Triples		Home Runs		Total Bases		Runs Batted In	
Gore-Chi	86	Anson-Chi	137	Kelly-Chi	27	Rowe-Buf	11	Brouthers-Buf	8	Anson-Chi	175	Anson-Chi	
Kelly-Chi	84	Dalrymple-Chi	117	Hines-Pro	27	Phillips-Cle	10	Bennett-Det	7	Dunlap-Cle	156	Bennett-Det	
Dalrymple-Chi	72	Dickerson-Wor	116	Stovey-Wor	25			Farrell-Pro	5	Kelly-Chi	153	Kelly-Chi	
O'Rourke-Buf	71			Dunlap-Cle	25			Burns-Chi	4	Dalrymple-Chi	150		
Farrell-Pro	69			White-Buf	24					Dickerson-Wor	149		

Stolen Bases		Base Stealing Runs		Fielding Runs-Infield		Fielding Runs-Outfield		Wins		Winning Pct.		Complete Games	
				Force-Buf	24.5	Richardson-Buf	22.3	Whitney-Bos	31	Radbourn-Pro	.694	Whitney-Bos	
				Williamson-Chi	21.3	Hornung-Bos	11.8	Corcoran-Chi	31	Corcoran-Chi	.689	McCormick-Cle	
				Glasscock-Cle	9.4	Evans-Tro	11.4	Derby-Det	29	Goldsmith-Chi	.649	Derby-Det	
				Morrill-Bos	7.7	Dickerson-Wor	9.2	Galvin-Buf	28	Welch-Tro	.538	Richmond-Wor	
				Quest-Chi	7.6	Kelly-Chi	5.5	McCormick-Cle	26	Galvin-Buf	.538	Galvin-Buf	

Strikeouts		Fewest BB/Game		Games		Saves		Base Runners/9		Adjusted Relief Runs		Relief Ranking	
Derby-Det	212	Galvin-Buf	.87	Whitney-Bos	66	Mathews-Pro-Bos	2	Wiedman-Det	9.39				
McCormick-Cle	178	Wiedman-Det	.94	McCormick-Cle	59	Morrill-Bos	1	McCormick-Cle	9.72				
Whitney-Bos	162	Goldsmith-Chi	1.20	Galvin-Buf	56			Goldsmith-Chi	10.15				
Richmond-Wor	156	Richmond-Wor	1.32	Derby-Det	56			Radbourn-Pro	10.32				
Corcoran-Chi	150	McCormick-Cle	1.44	Richmond-Wor	53			Ward-Pro	10.34				

Innings Pitched		Opponents' Avg.		Opponents' OBP		Earned Run Average		Adjusted ERA		Adjusted Starter Runs		Pitcher Wins	
Whitney-Bos	552.1	Radbourn-Pro	.235	Wiedman-Det	.258	Wiedman-Det	1.80	Wiedman-Det	162	Derby-Det	33.7	Derby-Det	
McCormick-Cle	526.0	McCormick-Cle	.235	McCormick-Cle	.265	Ward-Pro	2.13	Derby-Det	132	Galvin-Buf	18.3	Whitney-Bos	
Derby-Det	494.2	Wiedman-Det	.238	Radbourn-Pro	.270	Derby-Det	2.20	Ward-Pro	125	Corcoran-Chi	15.8	Galvin-Buf	1
Galvin-Buf	474.0	Corcoran-Chi	.242	Goldsmith-Chi	.271	Corcoran-Chi	2.31	Corcoran-Chi	118	Ward-Pro	15.6	Ward-Pro	1
Richmond-Wor	462.1	Ward-Pro	.242	Ward-Pro	.271	Galvin-Buf	2.37	Galvin-Buf	117	Radbourn-Pro	14.2	Radbourn-Pro	1

The Last Solo Flight

The season's most significant change was the decision to move the pitcher's box back 5 feet to a distance of 50 feet from home plate. As a result of this change, league batting average rose 15 points, and scoring increased by nearly half a run. In addition, only seven balls were now required for a walk, and bases on balls shot up 40 percent. Oddly, although the number of strikes for a whiff was also reduced to the present-day three, strikeouts actually decreased.

Much to the delight of William Hulbert, Chicago won again, breaking the race open late in the summer. They led the league in runs and fewest allowed, also making the league's fewest errors. The White Stockings' dominant lineup, held over from 1880, included the top three in runs: George Gore, King Kelly, and Abner Dalrymple. Cap Anson's .399 average topped the loop by 61 points.

Detroit, replacing Cincinnati, finished a surprising fourth, largely due to catcher Charlie Bennett's power hitting. Meanwhile, outfielder Dan Brouthers broke through for Buffalo after tw[o] trials with Troy, helping the Bisons rise from seventh to thir[d]. Despite great pitching from John Ward and Hoss Radbour[n], Providence finished second because of several dead spots in th[e] lineup. Overall, the league was much stronger and more ba[l]anced; for once, each team was competitive.

With greater competition came bigger crowds, an[d] Detroit's admittance provided an unexpected attendance win[d]fall. Chicago still led the NL in spectators for the fifth time [in] six seasons. League attendance surpassed 300,000 for the fir[st] time, although Troy and Worcester lagged far behind the rest[.]

Big changes were on the horizon. Several large cities we[re] clamoring for big league ball, and in response, club owne[rs] from Philadelphia and Cincinnati founded the American As[s]ociation in fall 1881. Not around to deal with this new thre[at] was Hulbert, since 1876 the guiding force behind the Nation[al] League, who died in spring 1882.

1880 National League

TEAM	W	L	T	PCT	GB	HW	HL	R	OR	PA	H	2B	3B	HR	BB	SO	HB	SH	AVG	OBP	SLG	OPS	AOPS	BR	ABR	PF	SB	CS	BSA	BSR
CHI	67	17	2	.798		37	5	538	317	3239	876	164	39	4	104	217			.279	.303	.360	663	119	84	55	106				
PRO	52	32	3	.619	15	31	12	419	299	3285	793	114	34	8	89	186			.248	.268	.313	581	101	-6	8	97				
CLE	47	37	1	.560	20	23	19	387	337	3078	726	130	52	7	76	237			.242	.261	.327	588	102	-2	6	98				
TRO	41	42	0	.494	25.5	20	21	392	438	3127	755	114	37	5	120	260			.251	.280	.319	599	100	15	-5	105				
WOR	40	43	2	.482	26.5	24	17	412	370	3105	699	129	52	8	81	278			.231	.251	.316	567	86	-22	-52	109				
BOS	40	44	2	.476	27	25	17	416	456	3185	779	134	41	20	105	221			.253	.278	.343	621	115	35	50	97				
BUF	24	58	3	.293	42	13	29	331	502	3052	669	104	37	3	90	327			.226	.249	.289	538	82	-49	-55	102				
CIN	21	59	3	.263	44	14	25	296	472	2970	649	91	36	7	75	267			.224	.244	.288	532	82	-56	-52	99				
TOT	340					187	145	3191		25041	5946	980	328	62	740	1993			.245	.267	.320	587								

TEAM	CG	SHO	GR	SV	IP	H	HR	BB	SO	BR/9	ERA	AERA	OAV	OOB	PR	APR	PF	OSB	OCS	FA	E	WPB	DP	FW	PW	BW	BSW	DIF
CHI	80	8	8	3	775.0	622	8	129	367	8.7	1.93	126	.209	.242	38	42	102			.913	329	141	41	2.3	4.1	5.3		13.3
PRO	75	13	12	3	799.0	663	7	51	286	8.0	1.64	134	.215	.228	65	53	93			.910	357	99	53	1.1	5.2	.8		3.0
CLE	83	7	2	1	759.2	685	4	98	289	9.3	1.90	124	.228	.253	40	39	99			.910	330	117	52	2.0	3.8	.6		-1.4
TRO	81	4	2	0	738.0	760	8	112	169	10.6	2.74	92	.255	.282	-30	-17	106			.900	366	160	58	-.3	-1.7	-.5		2.0
WOR	68	7	18	5	762.2	709	13	97	297	9.5	2.27	115	.233	.257	9	26	109			.906	355	94	49	.7	2.5	-5.1		.3
BOS	70	4	17	0	744.2	840	2	86	187	11.2	3.08	74	.276	.296	-59	-70	96			.901	367	132	54	.3	-6.8	4.9		-.4
BUF	72	6	13	1	739.0	879	10	78	186	11.7	3.09	79	.279	.297	-59	-50	104			.891	408	185	55	-2.1	-4.9	-5.3		-4.7
CIN	79	3	4	0	713.1	785	10	88	208	11.0	2.44	102	.259	.280	-5	5	105			.877	437	119	49	-4.1	.5	-5.1		-10.4
TOT	608	52	76	13	6031.1					10.0	2.37		.245	.267						.901	2949	1047	411					

Batter-Fielder Wins	Batting Average	On-Base Percentage	Slugging Average	On-Base Plus Slugging	Adjusted OPS	Adjusted Batter Runs
Clapp-Cin ...3.2	Gore-Chi ...360	Gore-Chi ...399	Gore-Chi ...463	Gore-Chi ...862	Gore-Chi ...180	Gore-Chi ...27.3
Irwin-Wor ...3.2	Anson-Chi ...337	Anson-Chi ...362	Connor-Tro ...459	Connor-Tro ...816	Connor-Tro ...166	J.O'Rourke-Bos ...22.4
Dunlap-Cle ...2.6	Connor-Tro ...332	Connor-Tro ...357	Dalrymple-Chi ...458	Dalrymple-Chi ...793	Jones-Bos ...159	Connor-Tro ...22.2
Gore-Chi ...2.5	Dalrymple-Chi ...330	Dalrymple-Chi ...335	Stovey-Wor ...454	Anson-Chi ...781	J.O'Rourke-Bos ...158	Dalrymple-Chi ...20.4
Shafer-Cle ...2.3	Burns-Chi ...309	Burns-Chi ...333	J.O'Rourke-Bos ...441	J.O'Rourke-Bos ...756	Dalrymple-Chi ...156	Anson-Chi ...19.9

Runs	Hits	Doubles	Triples	Home Runs	Total Bases	Runs Batted In
Dalrymple-Chi ...91	Dalrymple-Chi ...126	Dunlap-Cle ...27	Stovey-Wor ...14	Stovey-Wor ...6	Dalrymple-Chi ...175	Anson-Chi ...74
Stovey-Wor ...76	Anson-Chi ...120	Dalrymple-Chi ...25	Dalrymple-Chi ...12	J.O'Rourke-Bos ...6	Stovey-Wor ...161	Kelly-Chi ...60
Kelly-Chi ...72	Gore-Chi ...116	Anson-Chi ...24	J.O'Rourke-Bos ...11	Jones-Bos ...5	J.O'Rourke-Bos ...160	Gore-Chi ...47
J.O'Rourke-Bos ...71	Hines-Pro ...115	Gore-Chi ...23	Hornung-Buf ...11	Dunlap-Cle ...4	Dunlap-Cle ...160	Connor-Tro ...47
Gore-Chi ...70	Connor-Tro ...113	J.O'Rourke-Bos ...22	Phillips-Cle ...10		Connor-Tro ...156	J.O'Rourke-Bos ...45

Stolen Bases	Base Stealing Runs	Fielding Runs-Infield	Fielding Runs-Outfield	Wins	Winning Pct.	Complete Games
		Irwin-Wor ...29.8	Shafer-Cle ...14.9	McCormick-Cle ...45	Goldsmith-Chi ...875	McCormick-Cle ...72
		Force-Buf ...26.4	Gillespie-Tro ...6.3	Corcoran-Chi ...43	Corcoran-Chi ...754	Welch-Tro ...64
		Bradley-Pro ...18.4	Bond-Bos ...4.8	Ward-Pro ...39	Ward-Pro ...619	Ward-Pro ...59
		Burdock-Bos ...15.1	J.O'Rourke-Bos ...4.0	Welch-Tro ...34	McCormick-Cle ...616	W.White-Cin ...58
		Williamson-Chi ...10.2	Dalrymple-Chi ...3.9	Richmond-Wor ...32	Welch-Tro ...531	

Strikeouts	Fewest BB/Game	Games	Saves	Base Runners/9	Adjusted Relief Runs	Relief Ranking
Corcoran-Chi ...268	Bradley-Pro ...28	Richmond-Wor ...74	Richmond-Wor ...3	Keefe-Tro ...7.20		
McCormick-Cle ...260	Galvin-Buf ...63	McCormick-Cle ...74	Corey-Wor ...2	Bradley-Pro ...7.53		
Richmond-Wor ...243	Ward-Pro ...68	Ward-Pro ...70	Corcoran-Chi ...2	Ward-Pro ...8.26		
Ward-Pro ...230	Wiedman-Buf ...71	Welch-Tro ...65	Bradley-Pro ...2	Corcoran-Chi ...8.44		
W.White-Cin ...161	Goldsmith-Chi ...77			Goldsmith-Chi ...8.86		

Innings Pitched	Opponents' Avg.	Opponents' OBP	Earned Run Average	Adjusted ERA	Adjusted Starter Runs	Pitcher Wins
McCormick-Cle ...657.2	Keefe-Tro ...178	Keefe-Tro ...212	Keefe-Tro ...86	Keefe-Tro ...294	McCormick-Cle ...39.5	McCormick-Cle ...4.2
Ward-Pro ...595.0	Corcoran-Chi ...199	Bradley-Pro ...217	Bradley-Pro ...1.38	Bradley-Pro ...160	Ward-Pro ...34.6	Ward-Pro ...3.5
Richmond-Wor ...590.2	Bradley-Pro ...210	Ward-Pro ...232	Ward-Pro ...1.74	Goldsmith-Chi ...138	Corcoran-Chi ...28.8	Corcoran-Chi ...2.9
Welch-Tro ...574.0	Ward-Pro ...217	Corcoran-Chi ...236	Goldsmith-Chi ...1.75	McCormick-Cle ...127	Richmond-Wor ...25.4	Bradley-Pro ...1.9
Corcoran-Chi ...536.1	Corey-Wor ...219	Corey-Wor ...239	McCormick-Cle ...1.85	Ward-Pro ...127	Bradley-Pro ...18.2	Keefe-Tro ...1.8

Bound for Good

Owners unilaterally instituted a reserve clause after the 1879 season, which allowed each team to protect five players from other offers. This tactic neutralized player mobility and put a drain on salaries. William Hulbert also shoehorned through a provision prohibiting alcohol sales on the grounds of any league club. While these two policies made sense, given Hulbert's love of high class and high profit, they eventually helped give birth to the American Association. Empowered, some owners began fining players for non-existent infractions and, in the case of Boston, blacklisted slugger Charlie Jones in a financial dispute.

Despite the league's machinations, five clubs finished under .500 and pennant-winner Chicago—the NL's only good draw —ran away from the competition. With an offense sporting Cap Anson, King Kelly, Abner Dalrymple, and George Gore, the team topped the league in runs by more than 100. Their pitching permitted the fewest hits, and rookie Larry Corcoran led in strikeouts. Chicago's defense committed 3.82 errors per game, the best in the NL.

Debut players included slugger Roger Connor (the pre-Ruth career home run record holder), pitchers Hoss Radbourn and Tim Keefe, who, as a rookie, set an all-time mark with an 0.86 ERA, outfielder Ned Hanlon, third baseman Arlie Latham, and catcher Buck Ewing, considered by many the greatest player of the nineteenth century.

The league ruled that fouls could be caught on one bounce for an out. In addition, it now took just eight balls for a walk. The league batting average dropped to .245, and scoring fell dramatically. On June 12 Worcester's Lee Richmond threw the first perfect game in major league annals; Providence's John Ward tossed the second just five days later. The NL would not attain perfection again until 1964.

After the season Hulbert marshaled a 7-1 vote to expel Cincinnati from the league. The club's owners, unable to compete financially otherwise, had rented their park to other local teams and allowed them to play on Sundays and sell beer.

1879 National League

TEAM	W	L	T	PCT	GB	HW	HL	R	OR	PA	H	2B	3B	HR	BB	SO	HB	SH	AVG	OBP	SLG	OPS	AOPS	BR	ABR	PF	SB	CS	BSA	BSR
PRO	59	25	1	.702		34	8	612	355	3483	1003	142	55	12	91	172			.296	.314	.381	695	134	111	121	98				
BOS	54	30	0	.643	5	29	13	562	348	3307	883	138	51	20	90	222			.274	.294	.368	662	118	69	58	102				
BUF	46	32	1	.590	10	23	16	394	365	2984	733	105	54	2	78	314			.252	.272	.328	600	98	-1	-11	102				
CHI	46	33	4	.582	10.5	29	13	437	411	3189	808	167	32	3	73	294			.259	.276	.336	612	98	18	-8	106				
CIN	43	37	1	.538	14	21	16	485	464	3151	813	127	53	8	66	207			.264	.279	.347	626	115	26	50	95				
CLE	27	55	0	.329	31	15	27	322	461	3024	666	116	29	4	37	214			.223	.232	.285	517	73	-83	-80	99				
SYR	22	48	1	.314	30	11	22	276	462	2639	592	61	19	5	28	238			.227	.235	.270	505	78	-85	-50	89				
TRO	19	56	2	.253	35.5	12	27	321	543	2886	673	102	24	4	45	182			.237	.249	.294	543	87	-54	-29	93				
TOT	321					174	142	3409		24663	6171	958	317	58	508	1843			.255	.271	.329	599								

TEAM	CG	SHO	GR	SV	IP	H	HR	BB	SO	BR/9	ERA	AERA	OAV	OOB	PR	APR	PF	OSB	OCS	FA	E	WPB	DP	FW	PW	BW	BSW	DIF
PRO	73	3	12	2	776.0	765	9	62	329	9.6	2.18	108	.243	.258	27	16	94			.902	382	128	41	1.8	1.5	11.2		2.6
BOS	79	13	5	0	753.0	757	9	46	230	9.6	2.19	114	.251	.262	26	25	100			.913	319	108	58	4.9	2.3	5.3		-.5
BUF	78	8	1	0	713.0	698	3	47	198	9.4	2.34	112	.242	.254	13	21	105			.906	331	99	62	2.9	1.9	-1.0		3.2
CHI	82	6	1	0	744.0	762	5	57	211	9.9	2.46	105	.244	.258	3	9	103			.878	450	166	48	-2.9	.4	4.6		.9
CIN	79	4	3	0	726.0	756	11	81	246	10.4	2.29	102	.248	.267	16	4	93			.889	406	178	42	-.3	-1.1	-7.4		-5.2
CLE	79	3	3	0	741.0	818	4	116	287	11.3	2.65	95	.265	.292	-12	-12	100			.873	398	150	37	-2.7	-5.7	-4.6		.0
SYR	64	5	7	0	649.0	775	4	52	132	11.5	3.19	74	.277	.290	-50	-62	95			.875	460	217	44	-4.4	-2.0	-2.7		-9.3
TRO	75	3	2	0	695.0	840	13	47	210	11.5	2.80	89	.275	.286	-23	-22	100				381	93	52					
TOT	609	45	34	2	5797.0					10.4	2.50		.255	.271						.892	3127	1139	384					

Batter-Fielder Wins
- Kelly-Cin 3.9
- Jones-Bos 3.6
- Williamson-Chi 3.3
- Hines-Pro 3.2
- Wright-Pro 2.9

Batting Average
- Anson-Chi .317
- Hines-Pro .357
- O'Rourke-Pro .348
- Kelly-Cin .348
- O'Rourke-Bos .341

On-Base Percentage
- O'Rourke-Pro .371
- Hines-Pro .369
- Jones-Bos .367
- Kelly-Cin .363
- O'Rourke-Bos .357

Slugging Average
- O'Rourke-Bos .521
- Jones-Bos .510
- Kelly-Cin .493
- Hines-Pro .482
- O'Rourke-Pro .459

On-Base Plus Slugging
- O'Rourke-Bos .877
- Jones-Bos .877
- Kelly-Cin .855
- Hines-Pro .851
- O'Rourke-Pro .829

Adjusted OPS
- Kelly-Cin 188
- Jones-Bos 182
- O'Rourke-Bos 181
- Hines-Pro 181
- O'Rourke-Pro 174

Adjusted Batter Runs
- Hines-Pro 34.
- Kelly-Cin 32.
- Jones-Bos 31.
- O'Rourke-Pro 28.
- O'Rourke-Bos 26.

Runs
- Jones-Bos 85
- Hines-Pro 81
- Wright-Pro 79
- Kelly-Cin 78
- Dickerson-Cin 73

Hits
- Hines-Pro 146
- O'Rourke-Pro 126
- Kelly-Cin 120
- Jones-Bos 112
- D.White-Cin 110

Doubles
- Eden-Cle 31
- York-Pro 25
- Hines-Pro 25
- Dalrymple-Chi 25
- Houck-Bos 24

Triples
- Dickerson-Cin 14
- Williamson-Chi 13
- Kelly-Cin 12
- O'Rourke-Bos 11

Home Runs
- Jones-Bos 9
- O'Rourke-Bos 6
- Brouthers-Tro 4
- Eden-Cle 3

Total Bases
- Hines-Pro 197
- Jones-Bos 181
- Kelly-Cin 170
- O'Rourke-Pro 166
- O'Rourke-Bos 165

Runs Batted In
- O'Rourke-Bos 6
- Jones-Bos 6
- Dickerson-Cin 5
- McVey-Cin 5

Stolen Bases

Base Stealing Runs

Fielding Runs-Infield
- Wright-Pro 19.6
- Williamson-Chi 18.9
- Fulmer-Buf 18.2
- Quest-Chi 16.0
- Hawkes-Tro 14.5

Fielding Runs-Outfield
- Shafer-Chi 19.2
- Evans-Tro 17.6
- M.Mansell-Syr 14.9
- Jones-Bos 13.0
- Hines-Pro 4.7

Wins
- Ward-Pro 47
- W.White-Cin 43
- Bond-Bos 43
- Galvin-Buf 37
- Larkin-Chi 31

Winning Pct.
- Ward-Pro .712
- Bond-Bos .694
- Hankinson-Chi .600
- W.White-Cin .581
- Galvin-Buf .578

Complete Games
- W.White-Cin 7
- Galvin-Buf 6
- McCormick-Cle 5
- Bond-Bos 5
- Ward-Pro 5

Strikeouts
- Ward-Pro 239
- W.White-Cin 232
- McCormick-Cle 197
- Bond-Bos 155
- Larkin-Chi 142

Fewest BB/Game
- Bond-Bos .39
- Galvin-Buf .47
- Bradley-Tro .48
- Larkin-Chi .53
- Ward-Pro .55

Games
- W.White-Cin 76
- Ward-Pro 70
- Galvin-Buf 66
- Bond-Bos 64
- McCormick-Cle 62

Saves
- Ward-Pro 1
- Mathews-Pro 1

Base Runners/9
- Goldsmith-Tro 8.86
- Bond-Bos 9.19
- Ward-Pro 9.31
- Galvin-Buf 9.35
- Larkin-Chi 9.54

Adjusted Relief Runs

Relief Ranking

Innings Pitched
- W.White-Cin 680.0
- Galvin-Buf 593.0
- Ward-Pro 587.0
- Bond-Bos 555.1
- McCormick-Cle 546.1

Opponents' Avg.
- McGunnigle-Buf .235
- W.White-Cin .238
- Ward-Pro .239
- Larkin-Chi .240
- Galvin-Buf .243

Opponents' OBP
- Larkin-Chi .250
- Ward-Pro .250
- Galvin-Buf .253
- W.White-Cin .256
- Bond-Bos .259

Earned Run Average
- Bond-Bos 1.96
- W.White-Cin 1.99
- Ward-Pro 2.15
- Salisbury-Tro 2.22
- Galvin-Buf 2.28

Adjusted ERA
- Bond-Bos 127
- W.White-Cin 117
- Galvin-Buf 115
- Salisbury-Tro 112
- Ward-Pro 110

Adjusted Starter Runs
- Bond-Bos 38.8
- W.White-Cin 22.1
- Galvin-Buf 20.5
- Ward-Pro 12.9
- Larkin-Chi 8.2

Pitcher Wins
- Bond-Bos 4.
- Ward-Pro 2.
- Galvin-Buf 2.
- McCormick-Cle
- Larkin-Chi

The Last Free Season

To increase revenues, the NL expanded its schedule to 84 games and brought in four new teams: Troy, Cleveland, and two top International Association clubs, Buffalo and Syracuse. Despite these changes, however, league attendance was only a little higher for eight teams than it was for six clubs in 1878. Syracuse and Troy were abject failures on the field and at the gate, while Cincinnati's attendance fell dramatically.

Chicago once again had first-rate talent, including Cap Anson and Ed Williamson, and a maniacal fan base, but their pennant hopes evaporated when player-manager Anson went down in midsummer with a liver infection. Hard-charging Providence held off a late Boston rally to claim their first flag. George Wright, in his only season as a manager, bested his brother Harry, whose Boston clubs had won six titles in the last seven years in both the NA and NL. (After a salary dispute with Providence, George would return to play sparingly for Harry's Red Stockings.) Paul Hines and Jim O'Rourke provided most of the big hits for the Grays, while John Ward topped the league in wins and strikeouts.

Ward spent the year tossing a Spalding baseball. Former star hurler Al Spalding had retired to sell sporting goods, and he used his ties to get his ball named the official spheroid for all NL contests. Spalding also remained part owner of the Chicago White Stockings. The league adopted several new rules. A foul, hitherto an out if caught on a bounce, now had to be caught on the fly. Rules governing batting orders were established, and pitchers found to be intentionally hitting batters were fined, although batters were not yet allowed to take first base.

Boston's John O'Rourke, brother of Jim, was the league's top rookie, leading in RBIs and slugging (both calculated retroactively). Another freshman, Buffalo third baseman Hardy Richardson, eventually was the bigger star. Cincinnati pitcher Will White set the all-time record with 680 innings pitched, completing each of his 75 starts.

Only Syracuse was judged unfit for the NL. Worcester joined for 1880, giving Massachusetts, New York, and Ohio two teams apiece. Hulbert and his fellow owners had a new surprise up their sleeves: the reserve clause.

1878 National League

AM	W	L	T	PCT	GB	HW	HL	R	OR	PA	H	2B	3B	HR	BB	SO	HB	SH	AVG	OBP	SLG	OPS	AOPS	BR	ABR	PF	SB	CS	BSA	BSR
OS	41	19	0	.683		23	7	298	241	2255	535	75	25	2	35	154			.241	.253	.300	553	79	-36	-55	108				
N	37	23	1	.617	4	25	8	333	281	2339	629	67	22	5	58	141			.276	.294	.331	625	120	20	55	91				
RO	33	27	2	.550	8	17	13	353	337	2348	604	107	30	8	50	218			.263	.279	.346	625	109	20	21	100				
HI	30	30	1	.500	11	17	18	371	331	2421	677	91	20	3	88	157			.290	.316	.350	666	115	58	34	107				
D	24	36	3	.400	17	10	17	293	328	2364	542	76	15	3	64	197			.236	.256	.286	542	95	-43	0	87				
L	15	45	1	.250	26	7	18	256	386	2281	552	65	20	2	69	214			.250	.272	.300	572	86	-19	-37	107				
OT	184					99	81	1904		14008	3539	481	132	23	364	1081			.259	.279	.319	598								

AM	CG	SHO	GR	SV	IP	H	HR	BB	SO	BR/9	ERA	AERA	OAV	OOB	PR	APR	PF	OSB	OCS	FA	E	WPB	DP	FW	PW	BW	BSW	DIF
OS	58	9	2	0	544.0	595	6	38	184	10.5	2.32	102	.272	.284	-1	2	102			.914	228	62	48	3.5	.2	-5.1		12.4
N	61	6	0	0	548.0	546	2	63	220	10.0	1.84	116	.248	.269	28	19	92			.900	269	99	37	1.5	1.8	5.1		-1.4
RO	59	6	4	0	556.0	609	5	86	173	11.3	2.38	93	.265	.291	-5	-12	96			.892	311	133	42	-.5	-1.1	2.0		2.7
HI	61	1	0	0	551.0	577	4	35	175	10.0	2.37	102	.253	.265	-4	3	105			.891	304	141	37	-.4	.3	3.2		-3.0
D	59	2	4	1	578.0	621	3	87	182	11.0	2.32	87	.262	.288	-1	-22	88			.898	290	95	37	.9	-2.1	.0		-4.8
L	54	1	7	0	547.0	589	3	55	147	10.6	2.60	101	.255	.272	-18	1	114			.866	376	149	32	-4.4	.0	-3.5		-7.2
OT	352	25	17	1	3324.0					10.6	2.30		.259	.279						.893	1778	679	233					

Batter-Fielder Wins	Batting Average	On-Base Percentage	Slugging Average	On-Base Plus Slugging	Adjusted OPS	Adjusted Batter Runs
?afer-Ind 3.3	Dalrymple-Mil 354	Ferguson-Chi 375	Hines-Pro 486	Hines-Pro 849	Shafer-Ind 196	Shafer-Ind.......29.3
?rguson-Chi ...2.8	Hines-Pro 358	Anson-Chi 372	York-Pro 465	Shafer-Ind 824	Hines-Pro 177	Hines-Pro 20.4
?rdock-Bos ...2.0	Ferguson-Chi 351	Shafer-Ind 369	Shafer-Ind 455	Start-Chi 794	Jones-Cin 163	Jones-Cin 17.5
?nes-Pro ...1.7	Start-Chi 351	Dalrymple-Mil 368	Brown-Pro 453	York-Pro 793	York-Pro 159	York-Pro 16.5
?nes-Cin ...1.7	Anson-Chi 341	Hines-Pro 363	Jones-Cin 441	Dalrymple-Mil 789	Brown-Pro 153	Clapp-Ind 15.6

Runs	Hits	Doubles	Triples	Home Runs	Total Bases	Runs Batted In
?gham-Pro 60	Start-Chi 100	Higham-Pro 22	York-Pro 10	Hines-Pro 4	York-Pro 125	Hines-Pro 50
?art-Chi 58	Dalrymple-Mil 96	Brown-Pro 21	O'Rourke-Bos 7	Jones-Cin 3	Start-Chi 125	Brown-Pro 43
?rk-Pro 56	Hines-Pro 92	York-Pro 19	Jones-Cin 7	McVey-Cin 2	Hines-Pro 125	Anson-Chi 40
?son-Cin 55	Ferguson-Chi 91	Shafer-Ind 19		McKelvy-Ind.......2	Shafer-Ind 121	Jones-Cin 39
?lrymple-Mil 52		O'Rourke-Bos 17			Higham-Pro 117	Ferguson-Chi.......39

Stolen Bases	Base Stealing Runs	Fielding Runs-Infield	Fielding Runs-Outfield	Wins	Winning Pct.	Complete Games
		Burdock-Bos.......21.2	Shafer-Ind.......7.6	Bond-Bos 40	Bond-Bos 678	Bond-Bos 57
		Hague-Pro 19.1	Cassidy-Chi 7.3	W.White-Cin 30	Ward-Pro 629	Larkin-Chi 56
		Ferguson-Chi 16.6	Dalrymple-Mil.......6.8	Larkin-Chi 29	W.White-Cin 588	W.White-Cin.......52
		Wright-Bos 10.3	Jones-Cin 4.4	Ward-Pro 22	Larkin-Chi 527	Weaver-Mil.......39
		Hankinson-Chi 7.9	Remsen-Chi 4.2	Nolan-Ind.......13		

Strikeouts	Fewest BB/Game	Games	Saves	Base Runners/9	Adjusted Relief Runs	Relief Ranking
?nd-Bos 182	Weaver-Mil 49	Bond-Bos 59	Healey-Pro-Ind 1	Weaver-Mil 9.21		
?White-Cin 169	Larkin-Chi.......55	Larkin-Chi 56		Ward-Pro 9.22		
?rkin-Chi 163	Bond-Bos.......56	W.White-Cin.......52		Larkin-Chi.......9.64		
?lan-Ind 125	Nichols-Pro.......73	Weaver-Mil.......45		Mitchell-Cin 9.79		
?ard-Pro 116	W.White-Cin 87	Nolan-Ind.......38		W.White-Cin 10.04		

Innings Pitched	Opponents' Avg.	Opponents' OBP	Earned Run Average	Adjusted ERA	Adjusted Starter Runs	Pitcher Wins
?nd-Bos.......532.2	Mitchell-Cin 223	Weaver-Mil 247	Ward-Pro 1.51	Ward-Pro 146	Weaver-Mil.......23.1	Ward-Pro 2.2
?rkin-Chi.......506.0	Ward-Pro 231	Ward-Pro 251	McCormick-Ind.......1.69	Weaver-Mil.......134	Ward-Pro 21.8	Weaver-Mil 2.1
?White-Cin.......468.0	Weaver-Mil 237	Larkin-Chi 257	W.White-Cin 1.79	McCormick-Ind 120	W.White-Cin 15.7	Larkin-Chi 1.9
?eaver-Mil.......383.0	Larkin-Chi.......246	Mitchell-Cin 265	Weaver-Mil 1.95	W.White-Cin.......119	Bond-Bos 13.8	Bond-Bos 9
?lan-Ind.......347.0	W.White-Cin 252	W.White-Cin 269	Bond-Bos 2.06	Bond-Bos 114	Larkin-Chi.......9.6	W.White-Cin 6

A Good Defense

With new franchises in Providence, Indianapolis, and Milwaukee, the six-team National League took on an increasingly Midwestern look. (Newly organized "minor" leagues, chiefly the International Association, had started up to fill the need for organized baseball in the East.) Beginning in 1878 clubs used turnstiles to figure attendance, and team captains mutually determined which team would hit first. Batting orders were also required to remain consistent during the game.

Fortified by free agents Cal McVey, who managed and played third base, and Deacon White, the Cincinnati Red Stockings rose from last to second. Pitcher Will White, Deacon's brother, was outstanding in his first full year, helping the club post the league's best ERA. Paul Hines of third-place Providence won the league's first Triple Crown, but abysmal second-line pitching and poor defense scuttled his club's chances.

Boston won the flag by 4 games under legendary skipper Harry Wright. The starting lineup played nearly every inning—the team's substitute, Harry Schaefer, appeared in only 2 games. Boston's pitcher, Tommy Bond, was the NL's workhorse. He pitched in all but 1 Red Stockings game and won 40 times, 10 more than runner-up White in Cincinnati. Outstanding fielding helped the Red Stockings survive their mediocre offense. The club's .914 fielding percentage was a new record, shattering the old mark by 10 points. At this point, only a few players used gloves—Boston simply had great fielders.

Some top players made their debuts in 1878, including Milwaukee's catcher Charlie Bennett and outfielder Abner Dalrymple, Cincinnati outfielder King Kelly, Indianapolis third baseman Ed Williamson, and Providence pitcher John Montgomery Ward, who led the league with a 1.51 ERA.

Perhaps the greatest achievement from 1878 was that the NL became the first league to complete its entire schedule. It did not mean that everyone would be back on the '79 schedule, though. Indianapolis and Milwaukee, which brought up the rear of the loop in wins and attendance, were both dropped from the league after the season. NL President William Hulbert was in dire straits; despite being a Midwest chauvinist, he was forced to reach back to the East for new clubs to invite to his party.

1877 National League

TEAM	W	L	T	PCT	GB	HW	HL	R	OR	PA	H	2B	3B	HR	BB	SO	HB	SH	AVG	OBP	SLG	OPS	AOPS	BR	ABR	PF
BOS	42	18	1	.700		27	5	419	263	2433	700	91	37	4	65	121			.296	.314	.370	684	114	49	35	104
LOU	35	25	1	.583	7	21	9	339	288	2413	659	75	36	9	58	140			.280	.297	.354	651	92	19	-37	118
HAR	31	27	2	.534	10	19	8	341	311	2388	637	63	31	4	30	97			.270	.279	.328	607	105	-18	22	89
STL	28	32	0	.467	14	20	10	284	318	2235	531	51	36	1	57	147			.244	.263	.302	565	84	-48	-32	95
CHI	26	33	1	.441	15.5	17	12	366	375	2330	633	79	30	0	57	111			.278	.296	.340	636	92	8	-29	112
CIN	15	42	1	.263	25.5	12	17	291	485	2213	545	72	34	6	78	110			.255	.282	.329	611	107	-10	29	89
TOT	180					116	61	2040		14012	3705	431	204	24	345	726			.271	.289	.338	627				

(columns SB CS BSA BSR shown in header with no values)

TEAM	CG	SHO	GR	SV	IP	H	HR	BB	SO	BR/9	ERA	AERA	OAV	OOB	PR	APR	PF	OSB	OCS	FA	E	WPB	DP	FW	PW	BW	BSW	DIF
BOS	61	7	0	0	548.0	557	5	38	177	9.8	2.15	130	.249	.261	40	40	100			.889	290	68	36	1.2	3.6	3.1		4.1
LOU	61	4	0	0	559.0	617	4	41	141	10.6	2.25	147	.270	.283	34	56	118			.904	267	80	37	2.4	5.0	-3.3		.9
HAR	59	4	1	0	544.0	572	2	56	99	10.4	2.32	105	.253	.271	30	8	87			.885	313	56	32	-.2	.7	2.0		-.5
STL	52	1	8	0	541.0	582	2	92	132	11.2	2.66	98	.262	.291	9	-4	93			.892	281	110	29	1.4	-.4	-2.9		-.2
CHI	45	3	16	3	534.0	630	7	58	92	11.6	3.37	88	.274	.292	-33	-22	106			.883	313	119	43	-.2	-2.0	-2.6		1.2
CIN	48	1	10	1	515.0	747	4	61	85	14.1	4.19	63	.318	.335	-79	-94	94			.851	394	128	33	-4.7	-8.4	2.6		-3.0
TOT	326	20	35	4	3241.0					11.2	2.81		.271	.289						.884	1858	561	210					

Batter-Fielder Wins
- Jones-Cin-Chi-Cin 2.6
- **D.White-Bos** 2.2
- **Peters-Chi** 2.0
- Gerhardt-Lou 1.7
- **Cassidy-Har** 1.6

Batting Average
- D.White-Bos 387
- Cassidy-Har 378
- McVey-Chi 368
- O'Rourke-Bos 362
- Anson-Chi 337

On-Base Percentage
- O'Rourke-Bos 407
- D.White-Bos 405
- McVey-Chi 387
- Cassidy-Har 386
- Anson-Chi 360

Slugging Average
- D.White-Bos 545
- Jones-Cin-Chi-Cin 471
- Cassidy-Har 458
- McVey-Chi 455
- O'Rourke-Bos 445

On-Base Plus Slugging
- D.White-Bos 950
- O'Rourke-Bos 852
- Cassidy-Har 844
- McVey-Chi 842
- Jones-Cin-Chi-Cin 824

Adjusted OPS
- D.White-Bos 190
- Cassidy-Har 184
- Jones-Cin-Chi-Cin 175
- O'Rourke-Bos 162
- Manning-Cin 157

Adjusted Batter Runs
- D.White-Bos 25.9
- Cassidy-Har 24.2
- Jones-Cin-Chi-Cin 21.7
- O'Rourke-Bos 19.6
- Manning-Cin 17.2

Runs
- O'Rourke-Bos 68
- G.Wright-Bos 58
- McVey-Chi 58
- Start-Har 55

Hits
- D.White-Bos 103
- McVey-Chi 98
- O'Rourke-Bos 96
- Cassidy-Har 95
- Start-Har 90

Doubles
- Anson-Chi 19
- York-Har 16
- Manning-Cin 16
- G.Wright-Bos 15
- Hall-Lou 15

Triples
- D.White-Bos 11
- Jones-Cin-Chi-Cin 10
- Hall-Lou 8
- Brown-Bos 8

Home Runs
- Pike-Cin 4
- Shafer-Lou 3
- Jones-Cin-Chi-Cin 2
- D.White-Bos 2
- Snyder-Lou 2

Total Bases
- D.White-Bos 145
- McVey-Chi 121
- O'Rourke-Bos 118
- Hall-Lou 118
- Cassidy-Har 115

Runs Batted In
- D.White-Bos 49
- Peters-Chi 41
- Sutton-Bos 39
- Jones-Cin-Chi-Cin 38
- York-Har 37

Stolen Bases

Base Stealing Runs

Fielding Runs-Infield
- Peters-Chi 20.0
- Gerhardt-Lou 18.6
- Ferguson-Har 17.3
- G.Wright-Bos 9.7
- Foley-Cin 6.7

Fielding Runs-Outfield
- Jones-Cin-Chi-Cin 12.8
- Shafer-Lou 12.7
- Crowley-Lou 7.5
- Addy-Cin 4.9
- Pike-Cin 2.5

Wins
- Bond-Bos 40
- Devlin-Lou 35
- Larkin-Har 29
- Nichols-StL 18
- Bradley-Chi 18

Winning Pct.
- Bond-Bos 702
- Devlin-Lou 583
- Larkin-Har 537
- Nichols-StL 439
- Bradley-Chi 439

Complete Games
- Devlin-Lou 61
- Bond-Bos 58
- Larkin-Har 55
- Nichols-StL 35
- Bradley-Chi 35

Strikeouts
- Bond-Bos 170
- Devlin-Lou 141
- Larkin-Har 96
- Nichols-StL 80
- Bradley-Chi 59

Fewest BB/Game
- Bond-Bos 62
- Devlin-Lou 66
- Cummings-Cin 75
- Bradley-Chi 89
- Larkin-Har 95

Games
- Devlin-Lou 61
- Bond-Bos 58
- Larkin-Har 56
- Bradley-Chi 50
- Nichols-StL 42

Saves
- McVey-Chi 2
- Spalding-Chi 1
- Manning-Cin 1

Base Runners/9
- Bond-Bos 9.78
- Larkin-Har 10.11
- Devlin-Lou 10.59
- Nichols-StL 11.03
- Bradley-Chi 11.22

Adjusted Relief Runs

Relief Ranking

Innings Pitched
- Devlin-Lou 559.0
- Bond-Bos 521.0
- Larkin-Har 501.0
- Bradley-Chi 394.0
- Nichols-StL 350.0

Opponents' Avg.
- Larkin-Har 245
- Bond-Bos 249
- Blong-StL 262
- Nichols-StL 263
- Bradley-Chi 269

Opponents' OBP
- Bond-Bos 261
- Larkin-Har 264
- Devlin-Lou 283
- Bradley-Chi 286
- Nichols-StL 289

Earned Run Average
- Bond-Bos 2.11
- Larkin-Har 2.14
- Devlin-Lou 2.25
- Nichols-StL 2.60
- Blong-StL 2.74

Adjusted ERA
- Devlin-Lou 147
- Bond-Bos 133
- Larkin-Har 114
- Nichols-StL 100
- Blong-StL 95

Adjusted Starter Runs
- Devlin-Lou 55.5
- Bond-Bos 39.8
- Larkin-Har 13.5
- Reis-Chi 7.8
- Nichols-StL 1.6

Pitcher Wins
- **Devlin-Lou** 5.0
- **Bond-Bos** 3.3
- **Larkin-Har** 1.6
- Reis-Chi 6

Ramblin' Gamblin' Man

Jim Devlin was one of the finest pitchers in baseball during the 1870s. His great mound work—and the bat of outfielder George Hall—led the Louisville Grays to a big lead in the 1877 NL race. But an inexplicable late-season slump gave Boston the crown. An investigation of the Grays' desultory stretch performance led William Hulbert to ban, for life, four Louisville players—Devlin, Hall, Bill Craver, and Al Nichols—for throwing games. The troubled Devlin died six years later, still begging for reinstatement.

Boston, under Harry Wright, won a tainted title but had the league's top hitters in Deacon White and Jim O'Rourke. Chicago fell to fifth, becoming the only big league team ever to go an entire season without a homer. St. Louis barely missed joining the White Stockings in ignominy, but the Brown Stockings were spared by Jim Battin's lone career NL long ball.

The catcher's mask was first worn this year, and Chicago's Al Spalding, losing his mound skill, began wearing a glove on his catching hand when he played first base. Spalding retired after a final game in 1878 to sell sporting goods. Candy Cummings, purported inventor of the curveball, threw his last major league pitch for Cincinnati. Cummings was a success in the National Association—winning at least 28 games each season—but he was a flop in the new circuit.

The modified strike zone had a "low" pitch ranging from belt to knee and a "high" pitch above the belt and up to the shoulder. Runs declined, although batting average and OPS rose. Strikeouts increased as well. Other rules changes included the abolition of the "fair-foul rule," which helped end Ross Barnes' career, and the placement of home plate in fair territory. In 1877 the home team was allowed to bat first, and no substitutions were allowed, except for injury, after the start of the second inning.

Following the traumatic season, Louisville—along with Hartford and St. Louis—dropped out of the league, which therefore had to scramble for new clubs prior to the 1878 season.

1876 National League

TEAM	W	L	T	PCT	GB	HW	HL	R	OR	PA	H	2B	3B	HR	BB	SO	HB	SH	AVG	OBP	SLG	OPS	AOPS	BR	ABR	PF	SB	CS	BSA	BSR
CHI	52	14	0	.788		25	6	624	257	2818	926	131	32	8	70	45			.337	.353	.417	770	140	164	102	112				
STL	45	19	0	.703	6	24	6	386	229	2537	642	73	27	2	59	63			.259	.276	.313	589	102	-7	14	95				
HAR	47	21	1	.691	6	23	9	429	261	2703	711	96	22	2	39	78			.267	.277	.322	599	92	2	-29	108				
BOS	39	31	0	.557	15	19	17	471	450	2780	723	96	24	9	58	98			.266	.281	.328	609	102	12	5	102				
LOU	30	36	3	.455	22	15	16	280	344	2594	641	68	14	6	24	98			.249	.256	.294	550	71	-43	-95	118				
NY	21	35	1	.375	26	13	20	260	412	2198	494	39	15	2	18	35			.227	.233	.261	494	75	-79	-42	87				
PHI	14	45	1	.237	34.5	10	24	378	534	2414	646	79	35	7	27	36			.271	.279	.342	621	108	15	18	99				
CIN	9	56	0	.138	42.5	6	24	238	579	2413	555	51	12	4	41	136			.234	.247	.271	518	86	-64	-14	86				
TOT	260					135	122	3066		20457	5338	633	181	40	336	589			.265	.277	.321	598								

TEAM	CG	SHO	GR	SV	IP	H	HR	BB	SO	BR/9	ERA	AERA	OAV	OOB	PR	APR	PF	OSB	OCS	FA	E	WPB	DP	FW	PW	BW	BSW	DIF
CHI	58	9	9	4	592.1	608	6	29	51	9.7	1.76	139	.247	.256	36	42	106			.899	282	34	33	6.0	3.7	9.0		.4
STL	63	16	1	0	577.0	472	3	39	103	8.0	1.22	175	.210	.224	70	64	93			.902	268	91	33	6.1	5.6	1.2		.0
HAR	69	11	0	0	624.0	570	2	27	114	8.6	1.67	142	.227	.235	44	47	103			.888	337	46	27	4.0	4.1	-2.5		7.4
BOS	49	3	21	7	632.0	732	7	104	77	11.9	2.51	90	.268	.295	-14	-18	98			.860	442	108	42	-1.1	-1.6	.4		6.3
LOU	67	5	2	0	643.0	605	3	38	125	9.0	1.69	160	.229	.240	44	62	118			.875	397	70	44	.9	5.5	-8.4		-1.0
NY	56	2	1	0	530.0	718	8	24	37	12.6	2.94	73	.302	.309	-37	-50	93			.825	473	40	18	-6.8	-4.4	-3.7		7.9
PHI	53	1	7	2	550.0	783	2	41	22	13.5	3.22	75	.310	.321	-56	-46	105			.839	456	143	32	-5.0	-4.0	1.6		-8.1
CIN	57	0	9	0	591.0	850	9	34	60	13.5	3.62	61	.313	.322	-86	-99	95			.841	469	109	45	-4.1	-8.7	-1.2		-9.5
TOT	472	47	50	13	4739.1					10.8	2.31		.265	.277						.866	3124	641	274					

Batter-Fielder Wins		Batting Average		On-Base Percentage		Slugging Average		On-Base Plus Slugging		Adjusted OPS		Adjusted Batter Runs	
Barnes-Chi	4.2	Barnes-Chi	.429	Barnes-Chi	.462	Barnes-Chi	.590	Barnes-Chi	1052	Barnes-Chi	222	Barnes-Chi	39.7
Anson-Chi	2.8	Hall-Phi	.366	Hall-Phi	.384	Hall-Phi	.545	Hall-Phi	.929	Hall-Phi	208	Hall-Phi	29.0
G.Wright-Bos	2.5	Anson-Chi	.356	Anson-Chi	.380	Pike-StL	.472	Anson-Chi	.830	Pike-StL	178	Pike-StL	23.5
Battin-StL	2.3	Peters-Chi	.351	White-Chi	.358	Anson-Chi	.450	Pike-StL	.813	Meyerle-Phi	165	Jones-Cin	20.6
Hall-Phi	2.0	McVey-Chi	.347	O'Rourke-Bos	.358	Meyerle-Phi	.449	Meyerle-Phi	.797	Jones-Cin	162	O'Rourke-Bos	18.8

Runs		Hits		Doubles		Triples		Home Runs		Total Bases		Runs Batted In	
Barnes-Chi	126	Barnes-Chi	138	Hines-Chi	21	Barnes-Chi	14	Hall-Phi	5	Barnes-Chi	190	White-Chi	60
G.Wright-Bos	72	Peters-Chi	111	Higham-Har	21	Hall-Phi	13	Jones-Cin	4	Hall-Phi	146	Hines-Chi	59
Peters-Chi	70	Anson-Chi	110	Barnes-Chi	21	Pike-StL	10			Anson-Chi	139	Barnes-Chi	59
White-Chi	66	McVey-Chi	107	Pike-StL	19	Meyerle-Phi	8			Hines-Chi	134	Anson-Chi	59
Burdock-Har	66	White-Chi	104									McVey-Chi	53

Stolen Bases		Base Stealing Runs		Fielding Runs-Infield		Fielding Runs-Outfield		Wins		Winning Pct.		Complete Games	
				Somerville-Lou	27.6	F.Treacey-NY	9.1	Spalding-Chi	47	Spalding-Chi	.797	Devlin-Lou	66
				Force-Phi-NY	19.8	Remsen-Har	7.0	Bradley-StL	45	Manning-Bos	.783	Bradley-StL	63
				Battin-StL	14.5	Pierson-Cin	4.5	Bond-Har	31	Bond-Har	.705	Mathews-NY	55
				G.Wright-Bos	14.1	Hines-Chi	4.4	Devlin-Lou	30	Bradley-StL	.703	Spalding-Chi	53
				Anson-Chi	13.7	Snyder-Cin	3.8	Mathews-NY	21	Cummings-Har	.667	Bond-Har	45

Strikeouts		Fewest BB/Game		Games		Saves		Base Runners/9		Adjusted Relief Runs		Relief Ranking	
Devlin-Lou	122	Zettlein-Phi	23	Devlin-Lou	68	Manning-Bos	5	Bradley-StL	7.98				
Bradley-StL	103	Fisher-Cin	24	Bradley-StL	64	Zettlein-Phi	2	Bond-Har	8.12				
Bond-Har	88	Bond-Har	29	Spalding-Chi	61	McVey-Chi	2	Devlin-Lou	8.73				
Spalding-Chi	39	Mathews-NY	42	Mathews-NY	56			Cummings-Har	9.54				
Mathews-NY	37	Williams-Cin	43	Bond-Har	45			Spalding-Chi	9.67				

Innings Pitched		Opponents' Avg.		Opponents' OBP		Earned Run Average		Adjusted ERA		Adjusted Starter Runs		Pitcher Wins	
Devlin-Lou	622.0	Bradley-StL	.211	Bradley-StL	.224	Bradley-StL	1.23	Bradley-StL	174	Devlin-Lou	67.5	Devlin-Lou	6.2
Bradley-StL	573.0	Bond-Har	.220	Bond-Har	.227	Devlin-Lou	1.56	Devlin-Lou	174	Bradley-StL	62.6	Bradley-StL	6.2
Spalding-Chi	528.2	Devlin-Lou	.224	Devlin-Lou	.235	Cummings-Har	1.67	Cummings-Har	142	Spalding-Chi	38.7	Spalding-Chi	4.3
Mathews-NY	516.0	Cummings-Har	.239	Cummings-Har	.251	Bond-Har	1.68	Bond-Har	141	Bond-Har	32.2	Bond-Har	3.1
Bond-Har	408.0	Spalding-Chi	.247	Spalding-Chi	.256	Spalding-Chi	1.75	Spalding-Chi	139	Cummings-Har	15.0	McVey-Chi	.7

Get This Party Started

William Hulbert, owner of Chicago's National Association club, created a new league with the power and profits resting with the owners, rather than players. The National League began play on April 22, Boston beating Philadelphia, 6-5, with Jim O'Rourke connecting for the first hit. Boston (Atlanta Braves) and Chicago (Cubs), both former NA clubs, continue NL affiliations to this day.

Since 1870s baseball was about action, batters called for pitches where they wanted them (high, low, or "fair"). Nine balls were required for a batter to earn a walk. Home plate was square, rather than five-sided, and catchers stood straight up. Nobody used gloves.

Four strikes were required for a strikeout; after two strikes, a hitter ignoring a good ball was given a warning. Though the pitcher's box was just 45 feet away, pitchers were still required to throw underhand or sidearm, and didn't get much speed on the ball. In addition, batted balls bouncing foul before crossing first or third base were counted as fair in 1876. Many, including batting champ Ross Barnes, specialized in such trick hits, and scoring was the highest until 1887 and strikeouts at an all-time nadir.

Barnes was the league's dominant player, scoring 54 more runs than his nearest rival, George Wright. Barnes' lone home run in 1876 was the NL's first long ball, although he also led the league in doubles and triples. His White Stockings teammates were a nineteenth century "Who's Who of Baseball": Cap Anson, Paul Hines, Cal McVey, Deacon White, and pitcher Al Spalding. Pitcher George Bradley of St. Louis threw the NL's first no-hitter and led in ERA; he was also one of a handful of pitchers to exceed a strikeout per game.

Chicago ran away with the championship and, not surprisingly, led in attendance, despite 50-cent admissions (double the old rate), no alcohol, and no Sunday games—Hulbert strategies, adopted league-wide, to attract classier fans. And only the White Stockings made a profit, due to a runaway pennant race. New York and Philadelphia, finishing sixth and seventh, didn't make their final westward road trips, and Hulbert expelled them from the NL. Hulbert made his point clearly: This was not the National Association.

1875 National Association

TEAM	W	L	T	PCT	GB	HW	HL	R	OR	PA	H'	2B	3B	HR	BB	SO	HB	SH	AVG	OBP	SLG	OPS	AOPS	BR	ABR	PF	SB	CS	BSA	BSR
BOS	71	8	3	.899		37	0	831	343	3548	1128	167	51	15	33	52			.321	.327	.410	737	153	195	169	104	93	37	72	8
HAR	54	28	4	.659	18.5	26	11	557	343	3390	871	92	35	2	34	64			.260	.267	.310	577	97	6	-20	105	65	33	66	3
ATH	53	20	4	.726	15	28	7	699	402	3288	941	124	57	7	38	55			.290	.298	.369	667	120	103	41	111	75	46	62	0
STL	39	29	2	.574	26.5	21	12	386	369	2706	643	85	29	0	32	102			.240	.249	.294	543	99	-23	17	91	108	36	75	11
PHI	37	31	2	.544	28.5	16	16	470	376	2742	683	67	27	5	21	58			.251	.257	.301	558	92	-13	-29	104	105	51	67	-4
MUT	30	38	3	.441	35.5	13	21	328	425	2704	633	82	21	7	19	47			.236	.241	.290	531	82	-35	-55	105	20	24	45	-4
CHI	30	37	2	.448	35	16	16	379	416	2706	699	83	16	0	21	65			.260	.266	.303	569	99	0	-4	101	69	50	58	-2
NH	7	40	0	.149	48	3	24	170	397	1728	373	41	13	2	14	62			.218	.224	.260	484	80	-49	-17	87	35	16	69	2
WAS	5	23	0	.179	40.5	2	10	107	338	1010	194	14	8	0	6	42			.193	.198	.223	421	50	-50	-46	96	23	7	77	3
RS	4	15	0	.211	37	3	11	60	161	700	137	20	1	0	12	45			.199	.213	.231	444	62	-28	-19	90	27	9	75	3
CEN	2	12	0	.143	36.5	0	7	70	138	540	125	22	3	0	10	25			.236	.250	.289	539	97	-5	2	92	4	0	0	1
ATL	2	42	0	.045	51.5	1	26	132	438	1570	304	33	6	2	8	36			.195	.199	.227	426	57	-75	-50	87	1	5	17	-2
WES	1	12	0	.077	37	1	7	45	88	450	81	9	6	0	1	22			.180	.182	.227	409	41	-25	-27	105	4	6	40	-1
TOT	345					167	168	4234		27082	6812	839	273	40	249	675			.254	.261	.310	571					629	320	66	26

TEAM	CG	SHO	GR	SV	IP	H	HR	BB	SO	BR/9	ERA	AERA	OAV	OOB	PR	APR	PF	OSB	OCS	FA	E	WPB	DP	FW	PW	BW	BSW	DIF
BOS	60	10	24	17	732.0	751	2	33	110	9.6	1.87	115	.248	.256	29	23	96			.870	483	113	56	4.3	2.0	14.4	.5	10.3
HAR	83	13	3	0	770.0	708	4	11	152	8.4	1.57	150	.228	.231	56	63	105			.881	438	98	47	7.8	5.4	-1.7	.0	1.5
ATH	75	6	2	0	687.0	776	4	39	45	10.7	2.40	100	.268	.278	-13	0	107			.876	419	83	51	5.7	.0	3.5	-.2	7.5
STL	67	5	3	1	630.0	636	3	21	71	9.4	2.10	96	.241	.247	9	-7	90			.869	425	94	36	3.0	-.6	1.5	.8	.4
PHI	64	5	6	0	628.0	652	6	30	42	9.8	2.12	107	.243	.251	7	11	102			.848	477	78	32	.5	.9	-2.5	.3	3.8
MUT	70	3	1	0	636.2	718	4	21	77	10.4	2.46	95	.258	.264	-17	-9	105			.838	526	100	30	-1.5	-.8	-4.7	-.5	3.5
CHI	65	7	4	0	625.0	649	0	26	55	9.7	1.63	139	.243	.250	42	44	102			.853	478	147	30	.1	3.8	-.3	-.3	-6.7
NH	40	0	8	0	425.0	501	5	21	54	11.1	2.65	78	.254	.262	-20	-29	93			.814	447	103	24	-5.7	-2.5	-1.5	-.0	-6.8
WAS	23	0	5	0	250.2	397	6	10	6	14.6	3.77	63	.311	.317	-43	-37	107			.791	285	69	8	-4.3	-3.2	-3.9	-.0	2.3
RS	16	2	3	0	171.0	209	0	3	21	11.2	2.63	83	.267	.269	-8	-9	98			.833	150	69	6	-.8	-1.6	.0		-2.3
CEN	14	0	0	0	126.0	169	0	5	6	12.4	2.71	80	.274	.280	-7	-8	98			.769	164	36	5	-3.2	-.7	.2	-.0	-1.2
ATL	31	0	14	0	396.0	535	6	17	16	12.5	3.16	66	.285	.291	-41	-51	94			.801	432	110	20	-6.0	-4.4	-4.3	-.3	-5.0
WES	13	0	0	0	113.0	111	0	12	20	9.8	1.83	133	.225	.243	5	7	110			.860	78	46	5	.6	.6	-2.3	-.3	-.3
TOT	621	51	73	18	6190.1					10.3	2.23		.254	.261						.849	4802	1146	350					

Batter-Fielder Wins		Batting Average		On-Base Percentage		Slugging Average		On-Base Plus Slugging		Adjusted OPS		Adjusted Batter Runs	
Barnes-Bos	4.2	White-Bos	.367	Barnes-Bos	.375	McVey-Bos	.517	McVey-Bos	.873	Pike-StL	210	Pike-StL	35.1
White-Bos	3.9	Barnes-Bos	.364	White-Bos	.372	Pike-StL	.494	Pike-StL	.846	McVey-Bos	193	McVey-Bos	34.8
McVey-Bos	3.7	McVey-Bos	.355	McVey-Bos	.356	Craver-Cen-Ath	.455	White-Bos	.824	White-Bos	178	Barnes-Bos	28.8
Pike-StL	2.8	Pike-StL	.346	Pike-StL	.352	White-Bos	.453	Barnes-Bos	.818	Barnes-Bos	177	White-Bos	27.8
G.Wright-Bos	2.1	G.Wright-Bos	.333	G.Wright-Bos	.337	Barnes-Bos	.443	Craver-Cen-Ath	.779	G.Wright-Bos	159	G.Wright-Bos	22.4

Runs		Hits		Doubles		Triples		Home Runs		Total Bases		Runs Batted In	
Barnes-Bos	115	Barnes-Bos	143	McVey-Bos	36	Craver-Cen-Ath	13	O'Rourke-Bos	6	McVey-Bos	201	McVey-Bos	87
G.Wright-Bos	106	McVey-Bos	138	White-Bos	23	Pike-StL	12	Start-Mut	4	G.Wright-Bos	176	Leonard-Bos	74
O'Rourke-Bos	97	G.Wright-Bos	136	Pike-StL	22	Hall-Ath	12	Hall-Ath	4	Barnes-Bos	168	O'Rourke-Bos	72
McVey-Bos	89	White-Bos	136	Force-Ath	22	McVey-Bos	9	Hallinan-Wes-Mut	3	White-Bos	168	Hall-Ath	62
Leonard-Bos	87	Leonard-Bos	127			Meyerle-Phi	8	McVey-Bos	3	Leonard-Bos	156	G.Wright-Bos	61

Stolen Bases		Base Stealing Runs		Fielding Runs-Infield		Fielding Runs-Outfield		Wins		Winning Pct.		Complete Games	
Murnane-Phi	30	Barnes-Bos	4.3	Barnes-Bos	23.0	Gedney-Mut	10.9	Spalding-Bos	54	Spalding-Bos	.915	Mathews-Mut	69
Barnes-Bos	29	Cuthbert-StL	3.6	Battin-StL	15.4	Anson-Ath	7.3	McBride-Ath	44	Manning-Bos	.889	McBride-Ath	59
Pike-StL	25	Murnane-Phi	3.5	Sutton-Ath	13.2	A.Allison-Was-Har	5.0	Cummings-Har	35	McBride-Ath	.759	Bradley-StL	52
Dehlman-StL	23	McGeary-Phi	2.8	Pearce-StL	11.3	York-Har	4.0	Bradley-StL	33	Cummings-Har	.745	Spalding-Bos	52
Burdock-Har	20	Battin-StL	2.3	Force-Ath	10.8	Eggler-Ath	3.8			Zettlein-Chi-Phi	.569	Zettlein-Chi-Phi	49

Strikeouts		Fewest BB/Game		Games		Saves		Base Runners/9		Adjusted Relief Runs		Relief Ranking	
Cummings-Har	82	Cummings-Har	.09	Spalding-Bos	72	Spalding-Bos	9	Borden-Phi	7.36				
Spalding-Bos	75	Blong-RS	.14	Mathews-Mut	70	Manning-Bos	6	Galvin-StL	7.84				
Mathews-Mut	75	Galvin-StL	.15	McBride-Ath	60	McVey-Bos	1	Bond-Har	7.90				
Bond-Har	70	Bond-Har	.18	Bradley-StL	60	Heifer-Bos	1	Cummings-Har	8.68				
Bradley-StL	60	Fisher-Phi	.23	Zettlein-Chi-Phi	52	Galvin-StL	1	Fisher-Phi	8.90				

Innings Pitched		Opponents' Avg.		Opponents' OBP		Earned Run Average		Adjusted ERA		Adjusted Starter Runs		Pitcher Wins	
Mathews-Mut	625.2	Borden-Phi	.181	Borden-Phi	.203	Galvin-StL	1.16	Galvin-StL	173	Cummings-Har	33.6	Spalding-Bos	4.4
Spalding-Bos	570.2	Galvin-StL	.209	Galvin-StL	.212	Bond-Har	1.41	Bond-Har	167	Spalding-Bos	33.2	Bond-Har	3.1
McBride-Ath	538.0	Bond-Har	.216	Bond-Har	.219	Borden-Phi	1.50	Borden-Phi	152	Bond-Har	32.7	Cummings-Har	2.7
Bradley-StL	535.2	Fisher-Phi	.229	Fisher-Phi	.233	Zettlein-Chi-Phi	1.59	Cummings-Har	146	Zettlein-Chi-Phi	23.7	Zettlein-Chi-Phi	1.4
Zettlein-Chi-Phi	463.1	Cummings-Har	.235	Cummings-Har	.236	Spalding-Bos	1.59	Zettlein-Chi-Phi	143	Fisher-Phi	13.5	Devlin-Chi	1.1

Windup

Why did the National Association last only five seasons? There were several factors, including gambling, revolving players, and the inability of most clubs to turn a profit. Many of these problems stemmed from the league's big issue—the lack of competition. Harry Wright's Boston Red Stockings won the final 24 games of 1875 after starting the year without a loss in their first 22. On the other end of the standings was Brooklyn, which finished with an unfathomable .045 winning percentage.

The coming and going of franchises severely hurt the league's credibility. Twenty-three different teams played in the NA over five seasons. Only the Red Stockings, Atlantics, and Mutuals were around for the whole show. Because the franchise fee was just $10, there were always teams seemingly guaranteed to fail.

Just seven of 13 teams finished the 1875 season. The Westerns of Keokuk, Iowa, played on a former cornfield bounded by a lake known to swallow up outfielders; it was no surprise that the Westerns disbanded after 13 games. The Washington Nationals, back in the league after a two-year absence, learned one afternoon in St. Louis that the team could not pay their players' way back home. The St. Louis Brown Stockings, who drew a league record 78,000 fans in their only season in the NA, covered their fares back to Washington.

While Boston killed competition in the league, it was the breaking up of that club by Chicago owner William Hulbert (even as the Red Stockings continued drubbing his team) that spelled doom for the NA. Hulbert induced Al Spalding, still under contract to Boston, to join his club. With Spalding's help, Hulbert signed three of Boston's best hitters—Cal McVey, Ross Barnes, and James "Deacon" White—while also luring Cap Anson from the Athletics.

Hulbert had undercut the NA's lax organization and, seeking greater professionalism and profit, made his own arrangements with the owners of other clubs that winter. Six cities that had fielded NA ballclubs in 1875 played ball in an eight-team confederation the next spring. This was the birth of the National League.

1874 National Association

TEAM	W	L	T	PCT	GB	HW	HL	R	OR	PA	H	2B	3B	HR	BB	SO	HB	SH	AVG	OBP	SLG	OPS	AOPS	BR	ABR	PF	SB	CS	BSA	BSR
BOS	52	18	1	.743		27	9	735	415	3163	977	121	61	17	34	28			.312	.320	.406	726	128	113	77	106	45	19	70	3
MUT	42	23	0	.646	7.5	27	8	501	377	2766	714	89	28	7	36	40			.262	.271	.322	593	90	-21	-35	103	36	4	90	7
ATH	33	22	0	.600	11.5	21	8	441	344	2283	647	83	18	6	24	51			.286	.294	.347	641	99	20	-14	109	36	14	72	3
PHI	29	29	0	.500	17	16	9	476	428	2463	677	78	50	2	28	33			.278	.286	.354	640	104	17	1	104	27	18	60	0
CHI	28	31	0	.475	18.5	18	10	418	480	2494	685	87	4	4	32	54			.278	.287	.322	609	97	-2	-6	101	32	12	73	3
ATL	22	33	1	.400	22.5	15	13	301	450	2200	498	45	8	1	31	51			.230	.240	.259	499	71	-85	-44	88	12	4	75	1
HAR	16	37	0	.302	27.5	13	17	371	371	2175	591	86	18	2	31	63			.276	.286	.335	621	97	6	-13	105	42	21	67	2
BAL	9	38	0	.191	31.5	7	13	227	505	1798	435	45	7	1	22	37			.245	.254	.280	534	75	-48	-46	99	12	5	71	1
TOT	232					144	87	3470		19342	5224	634	194	40	238	357			.273	.282	.333	616					242	97	71	19

TEAM	CG	SHO	GR	SV	IP	H	HR	BB	SO	BR/9	ERA	AERA	OAV	OOB	PR	APR	PF	OSB	OCS	FA	E	WPB	DP	FW	PW	BW	BSW	DIF
BOS	65	4	6	3	634.0	779	1	23	31	11.4	1.93	112	.274	.280	18	17	99			.850	489	50	53	4.5	1.3	6.0	.0	5.2
MUT	62	4	3	0	586.0	663	3	41	101	10.8	1.90	118	.261	.273	19	22	103			.847	438	91	22	4.6	1.7	-2.7	.4	5.6
ATH	55	0	0	0	487.0	514	6	32	37	10.1	1.64	141	.240	.251	30	34	106			.839	396	38	34	2.6	2.6	-1.1	.0	1.3
PHI	56	3	2	0	522.0	673	4	19	61	11.9	1.93	115	.278	.284	15	17	101			.809	518	32	38	-2.3	1.3	.0	-.2	1.1
CHI	58	3	1	0	533.2	684	7	45	26	12.3	2.65	84	.279	.292	-27	-24	102			.829	477	57	27	.2	-1.9	-.5	.0	.6
ATL	56	1	0	0	506.0	618	15	11	42	11.2	2.06	100	.266	.269	7	0	94			.822	500	79	15	-2.2	.0	-3.4	-.1	.3
HAR	45	0	8	0	481.0	653	1	28	39	12.7	2.53	91	.284	.293	-18	-11	105			.797	521	85	17	-4.5	-.9	-1.0	-.0	-4.1
BAL	42	0	6	0	420.0	640	3	39	20	14.5	3.13	71	.305	.318	-44	-41	102			.812	436	54	15	-2.7	-3.2	-3.6	-.1	-4.9
TOT	439	15	26	3	4169.2					11.8	2.19		.273	.282						.827	3775	486	221					

Batter-Fielder Wins	Batting Average	On-Base Percentage	Slugging Average	On-Base Plus Slugging	Adjusted OPS	Adjusted Batter Runs
Barnes-Bos 1.9	Meyerle-Chi 394	Meyerle-Chi 401	Pike-Har 504	Meyerle-Chi 889	Meyerle-Chi 182	Meyerle-Chi 22.9
Pike-Har 1.8	McVey-Bos 359	Pike-Har 368	Craver-Phi 498	Pike-Har 872	Pike-Har 168	McVey-Bos 20.3
McVey-Bos 1.7	Pike-Har 355	McMullin-Ath 366	Meyerle-Chi 488	Craver-Phi 851	Craver-Phi 164	Craver-Phi 17.6
Craver-Phi 1.5	Manning-Bal-Har ..346	McVey-Bos 360	McVey-Bos 481	McVey-Bos 842	McVey-Bos 158	Pike-Har 17.2
G.Wright-Bos ...1.5	McMullin-Ath 346	Barnes-Bos 360	G.Wright-Bos 476	G.Wright-Bos 816	G.Wright-Bos 150	G.Wright-Bos 14.7

Runs	Hits	Doubles	Triples	Home Runs	Total Bases	Runs Batted In
McVey-Bos 91	McVey-Bos 123	Pike-Har 22	G.Wright-Bos 15	O'Rourke-Bos 5	McVey-Bos 165	McVey-Bos 71
O'Rourke-Bos 82	Spalding-Bos 119	McVey-Bos 21	Craver-Phi 11	White-Bos 3	O'Rourke-Bos 150	O'Rourke-Bos 61
Spalding-Bos 80	White-Bos 106	Meyerle-Chi 19	Holdsworth-Phi 9	McVey-Bos 3	G.Wright-Bos 149	Craver-Phi 56
G.Wright-Bos 76	Leonard-Bos 106	Craver-Phi 19		Clapp-Ath 3	White-Bos 134	Spalding-Bos 54
White-Bos 75	O'Rourke-Bos 104	Leonard-Bos 18			Spalding-Bos 134	White-Bos 52

Stolen Bases	Base Stealing Runs	Fielding Runs-Infield	Fielding Runs-Outfield	Wins	Winning Pct.	Complete Games
Barlow-Har 17	Barlow-Har 2.3	White-Bal 27.3	Ryan-Bal..............13.1	Spalding-Bos 52	Spalding-Bos 765	Spalding-Bos 65
O'Rourke-Bos 11	Cuthbert-Chi 1.8	Barnes-Bos 18.8	York-Phi 7.7	Mathews-Mut 42	Mathews-Mut 656	Mathews-Mut 62
Leonard-Bos 11	O'Rourke-Bos 1.7	Burdock-Mut 10.1	Eggler-Phi 6.8	McBride-Ath 33	McBride-Ath 600	Zettlein-Chi 57
Craver-Phi 11	McGeary-Ath 1.5	Force-Chi 8.9	Hines-Chi 6.1	Cummings-Phi 28	Cummings-Phi 519	McBride-Ath 55
		Pearce-Atl 7.8	Hatfield-Mut 5.5	Zettlein-Chi 27	Zettlein-Chi 474	Bond-Atl 55

Strikeouts	Fewest BB/Game	Games	Saves	Base Runners/9	Adjusted Relief Runs	Relief Ranking
Mathews-Mut 101	Bond-Atl 14	Spalding-Bos 71	H.Wright-Bos 3	McBride-Ath 10.09		
Cummings-Phi........61	Spalding-Bos 28	Mathews-Mut 65		Mathews-Mut 10.79		
Bond-Atl 42	Cummings-Phi 34	Zettlein-Chi 57		Bond-Atl 11.12		
McBride-Ath 37	Fisher-Har 36	McBride-Ath 55		Spalding-Bos 11.28		
Spalding-Bos 31	McBride-Ath 59	Bond-Atl 55		Cummings-Phi 11.81		

Innings Pitched	Opponents' Avg.	Opponents' OBP	Earned Run Average	Adjusted ERA	Adjusted Starter Runs	Pitcher Wins
Spalding-Bos 617.1	McBride-Ath 240	McBride-Ath 251	McBride-Ath 1.64	McBride-Ath 141	McBride-Ath 34.3	Spalding-Bos 2.8
Mathews-Mut 578.0	Mathews-Mut 261	Bond-Atl 268	Mathews-Mut 1.90	Mathews-Mut 118	Mathews-Mut 21.7	McBride-Ath...........1.9
Zettlein-Chi........515.2	Bond-Atl 266	Mathews-Mut 273	Spalding-Bos 1.92	Cummings-Phi..........113	Spalding-Bos 16.9	Mathews-Mut.........1.5
Bond-Atl 497.0	Spalding-Bos 273	Spalding-Bos 278	Cummings-Phi..........1.96	Spalding-Bos 113	Cummings-Phi 15.9	Cummings-Phi..........7
McBride-Ath 487.0	Zettlein-Chi 273	Cummings-Phi 282	Bond-Atl 2.03	Bond-Atl 102	Fisher-Har 1.4	Bond-Atl 6

White Stockings to the Rescue, Sort Of

Gambling was officially made against the rules in 1874. Players were threatened with expulsion if they bet on games they were playing in—this at least made gambling more covert. Athletics outfielder John Radcliffe was expelled during the season for offering an umpire $175 to help Chicago win a game (he played 5 games in 1875 for the Centennials).

The batter's box was first introduced in 1874. Walks were awarded on three "wide balls" or nine balls too high or low. A proposal by Henry Chadwick for ten men and ten innings was defeated at the annual league meeting in Boston.

Chicago returned after two years, and, no coincidence, the NA finally surpassed its overall attendance mark set in 1871. The White Stockings outdrew the Red Stockings at the gate but could not compete with them on the diamond; in a 38-1 loss to the Mutuals in June, Chicago committed 36 errors.

In midseason, Boston and the Athletics set sail for Great Britain. Harry Wright planned this tour to his native country, sending Red Stockings star Al Spalding to England to make arrangements. Wright, a professional cricketer less than a decade earlier, was embarrassed that Spalding had led his hosts to believe the American ballplayers were also fine cricketers—they weren't. The tour lost $3,000.

That was about all the Red Stockings lost. Boston did not miss a beat after six weeks away: Cal McVey led an attack that featured teammates in the top five spots in runs, hits, and total bases. (Boston swept the top five in these categories again in 1875.) For good measure, Boston's "Orator" Jim O'Rourke led the NA in home runs in 1874–75.

Boston took the title by 7½ games over New York, but it was only that close because their 9-1 mark against the Lord Baltimores was thrown out when that club did not complete its schedule. Despite the return of the White Stockings, only one midseason team failure, steps to limit gambling, and international press (some of it good), the NA was at a critical juncture. The decision to allow six more teams for 1875 was the fuel that caused the league to explode.

1873 National Association

TEAM	W	L	T	PCT	GB	HW	HL	R	OR	PA	H	2B	3B	HR	BB	SO	HB	SH	AVG	OBP	SLG	OPS	AOPS	BR	ABR	PF	SB	CS	BSA	BSR
BOS	43	16	1	.729		24	8	739	460	2816	933	144	44	13	68	36			.340	.355	.438	793	128	129	74	108	145	48	75	15
PHI	36	17	0	.679	4	22	5	526	396	2388	645	83	20	8	62	41			.277	.296	.340	636	89	-18	-35	104	54	14	79	7
BAL	34	22	1	.607	7.5	19	6	644	451	2603	810	109	40	9	43	30			.316	.328	.401	729	121	59	62	100	28	13	68	2
MUT	29	24	0	.547	11	22	9	474	403	2254	622	51	36	5	43	22			.281	.295	.344	639	94	-20	-17	99	16	7	70	1
ATH	28	23	1	.549	11	21	6	474	403	2302	683	71	21	4	35	33			.301	.312	.356	668	95	6	-28	108	36	24	60	0
ATL	17	37	1	.315	23.5	14	14	366	549	2262	588	46	23	6	55	47			.262	.271	.315	586	80	-42	-33	97	11	8	58	0
WAS	8	31	0	.205	25	6	12	283	485	1580	408	40	19	2	20	36			.235	.243	.282	525	64	-42	-30	92	4	4	50	-1
RES	2	21	0	.087	23	0	8	98	299	878	204	25	8	0	9	30			.156	.156	.161	317	-5	-26	-21	77	0	0	0	0
MAR	0	6	0	.000	16.5	0	1	26	152	211	33	1	0	0	0	3														
TOT	199					128	69	3580		17294	4926	570	211	47	335	278			.290	.304	.357	661					314	131	71	23

TEAM	CG	SHO	GR	SV	IP	H	HR	BB	SO	BR/9	ERA	AERA	OAV	OOB	PR	APR	PF	OSB	OCS	FA	E	WPB	DP	FW	PW	BW	BSW	DIF
BOS	46	1	14	7	536.0	708	5	42	55	12.6	3.07	113	.288	.300	19	23	102			.836	472	99	54	.6	1.6	5.2	.9	5.2
PHI	50	0	3	0	481.0	628	3	44	29	12.6	2.92	118	.285	.299	26	28	101			.849	378	51	43	2.4	2.0	-2.5	.3	7.3
BAL	55	1	2	0	508.2	680	4	43	37	12.8	3.08	110	.285	.298	18	18	100			.862	345	53	32	5.6	1.3	4.4	-.0	-5.3
MUT	48	2	5	0	477.0	539	5	68	80	11.5	2.64	125	.255	.278	40	36	97			.840	390	84	30	1.4	1.8	-2.0	-.2	1.4
ATH	44	3	8	2	475.0	553	4	58	41	11.6	3.05	117	.257	.276	18	26	105			.817	515	53	34	-3.5	-4.1	.2	-.2	-2.4
ATL	52	1	3	0	500.0	737	8	43	16	14.0	4.14	77	.305	.317	-41	-58	93			.812	348	80	27	-1.7	-3.5	-2.3	-.2	-3.8
WAS	39	0	0	0	346.0	594	11	26	10	16.1	4.84	72	.337	.347	-55	-50	103			.789	244	22	14	-2.9	.4	-2.1	-.3	-4.6
RES	22	0	1	0	207.0	343	6	10	10	15.3	3.26	107	.312	.318	3	5	103			.761	74	5	0	-1.3	-2.0	-1.5	-.2	1.9
MAR	6	0	0	0	54.0	144	1	1	0	24.2	8.00	42	.393	.395	-28	-28	100											
TOT	362	8	36	9	3584.2					13.2	3.40		.290	.304						.830	3191	538	263					

Batter-Fielder Wins		Batting Average		On-Base Percentage		Slugging Average		On-Base Plus Slugging		Adjusted OPS		Adjusted Batter Runs	
Barnes-Bos	4.2	Barnes-Bos	.431	Barnes-Bos	.465	Barnes-Bos	.616	Barnes-Bos	1080	Barnes-Bos	200	Barnes-Bos	38.2
G.Wright-Bos	2.6	Anson-Ath	.398	Anson-Ath	.409	G.Wright-Bos	.511	G.Wright-Bos	914	McVey-Bal	159	G.Wright-Bos	19.6
Ferguson-Atl	1.6	White-Bos	.392	G.Wright-Bos	.404	White-Bos	.508	White-Bos	900	G.Wright-Bos	156	Pabor-Atl	17.3
White-Bos	1.4	G.Wright-Bos	.387	White-Bos	.392	McVey-Bal	.490	McVey-Bal	879	Pabor-Atl	153	White-Bos	16.7
Force-Bal	1.2	McVey-Bal	.380	McVey-Bal	.390	Meyerle-Phi	.479	Anson-Ath	.858	White-Bos	152	McVey-Bal	13.3

Runs		Hits		Doubles		Triples		Home Runs		Total Bases		Runs Batted In	
Barnes-Bos	125	Barnes-Bos	138	Barnes-Bos	31	Barnes-Bos	11	Pike-Bal	4	Barnes-Bos	197	White-Bos	7
G.Wright-Bos	99	G.Wright-Bos	125	O'Rourke-Bos	21	Mills-Bal	9	G.Wright-Bos	3	G.Wright-Bos	165	Spalding-Bos	7
Spalding-Bos	83	White-Bos	122	Mills-Bal	20	White-Bos	8	Meyerle-Phi	3	White-Bos	158	Leonard-Bos	6
Eggler-Mut	82	Spalding-Bos	106	Carey-Bal	18	Pike-Bal	8			Pike-Bal	133	Barnes-Bos	6
Leonard-Bos	81	Anson-Ath	101			Holdsworth-Mut	8					Meyerle-Phi	5

Stolen Bases		Base Stealing Runs		Fielding Runs-Infield		Fielding Runs-Outfield		Wins		Winning Pct.		Complete Games	
Barnes-Bos	43	Barnes-Bos	7.4	Ferguson-Atl	27.4	Gedney-Mut	14.2	Spalding-Bos	41	Spalding-Bos	.745	Britt-Atl	5
Leonard-Bos	27	White-Bos	3.1	G.Wright-Bos	19.9	York-Bal	11.2	Zettlein-Phi	36	Zettlein-Phi	.706	Zettlein-Phi	4
White-Bos	19	Leonard-Bos	2.8	Barnes-Bos	19.3	Bechtel-Phi	5.9	Mathews-Mut	29	Cummings-Bal	.667	Mathews-Mut	4
Schafer-Bos	14	Cuthbert-Phi	2.4	Fulmer-Phi	18.0	Fisher-Ath	5.8	Cummings-Bal	28	McBride-Ath	.558	Spalding-Bos	4
Cuthbert-Phi	14	Spalding-Bos	2.0	Beals-Was	9.0	Eggler-Mut	3.9	McBride-Ath	24	Mathews-Mut	.558	Cummings-Bal	4

Strikeouts		Fewest BB/Game		Games		Saves		Base Runners/9		Adjusted Relief Runs		Relief Ranking	
Mathews-Mut	79	H.Campbell-Res	.44	Spalding-Bos	60	H.Wright-Bos	4	Fisher-Ath	10.67				
Spalding-Bos	50	Stearns-Was	.51	Britt-Atl	54	Spalding-Bos	3	Mathews-Mut	11.19				
Cummings-Bal	34	Spalding-Bos	.65	Mathews-Mut	52	Fisher-Ath	2	McBride-Ath	11.76				
Zettlein-Phi	29	Brainard-Bal	.75	Zettlein-Phi	51			Cummings-Bal	11.97				
McBride-Ath	25	Britt-Atl		McBride-Ath	46			Spalding-Bos	12.30				

Innings Pitched		Opponents' Avg.		Opponents' OBP		Earned Run Average		Adjusted ERA		Adjusted Starter Runs		Pitcher Wins	
Spalding-Bos	496.2	Fisher-Ath	.231	Fisher-Ath	.250	Fisher-Ath	1.81	Fisher-Ath	197	Mathews-Mut	36.8	**Spalding-Bos**	3
Britt-Atl	480.2	Mathews-Mut	.251	Mathews-Mut	.274	Mathews-Mut	2.58	Mathews-Mut	128	Zettlein-Phi	30.1	**Mathews-Mut**	2
Zettlein-Phi	460.0	McBride-Ath	.262	McBride-Ath	.281	Cummings-Bal	2.80	Cummings-Bal	121	Cummings-Bal	28.4	**Cummings-Bal**	2
Mathews-Mut	443.0	Cummings-Bal	.274	Cummings-Bal	.287	Zettlein-Phi	2.86	Zettlein-Phi	121	Spalding-Bos	26.0	**Zettlein-Phi**	1
McBride-Ath	382.2	Zettlein-Phi	.284	Spalding-Bos	.296	H.Campbell-Res	2.95	H.Campbell-Res	119	McBride-Ath	15.0	**McBride-Ath**	1

Not Much of a Horse Race

Nine teams started 1873, but the Baltimore Marylands called it quits after going 0-6—the briefest of any team in the NA. The Resolutes of Elizabeth, New Jersey, stuck it out until August before quitting (although one of their two wins came against the powerhouse Red Stockings). League attendance was down 16 percent from 1871.

Lip Pike of the Lord Baltimores won his third successive home run crown in 1873. Although Pike homered just once more over the next two NA seasons, his 16 career long balls topped the circuit. Pike was also pretty fast, fast enough to beat a horse, outrunning a trotter in a 100-yard dash at Baltimore's Newington Park in August; "Clarence" had a 25-yard head start, but Pike took the race in 10 seconds flat.

Nearly 100 games into their existence, the Red Stockings were finally shut out. Unfazed, Boston marched to the pennant again, averaging almost 12 runs per game. The Red Stockings dominated every offensive category. Al Spalding not only won 41 times for Boston, he also drove in 71 runs in 60 games.

Cherokee Fisher had an interesting perspective on the NA. He pitched all five seasons in the league for a different team each year. In 1873, as an Athletic, he allowed the fewest runs per game for the second straight year, but he didn't pitch much because of the presence of veteran moundsman Dick McBride, the man who had finally shut out the mighty Red Stockings. Fisher played right field mostly and batted a career-best .262. The Athletics finished just 4 games behind Boston, the closest any NA team would ever get to the Red Stockings again.

Dick McBride managed every game the Athletics ever played as an NA club until October 9, 1875, when he had the rare distinction of being stripped of his job in the middle of a game against Boston. Following an on-field meeting by the club's board of directors, 23-year-old Adrian (not yet Cap) Anson made his managerial debut in the fifth inning.

1872 National Association

TEAM	W	L	T	PCT	GB	HW	HL	R	OR	PA	H	2B	3B	HR	BB	SO	HB	SH	AVG	OBP	SLG	OPS	AOPS	BR	ABR	PF	SB	CS	BSA	BSR
BOS	39	8	1	.830		20	1	521	236	2155	673	107	30	7	29	26			.317	.326	.405	731	120	62	36	105	48	14	77	6
BAL	35	19	4	.648	7.5	20	7	617	434	2600	753	106	31	14	29	28			.293	.301	.375	676	104	25	0	105	53	18	75	5
MUT	34	20	2	.630	8.5	20	8	523	362	2484	670	87	14	4	58	52			.276	.293	.329	622	99	-17	18	94	59	22	73	5
ATH	30	14	3	.682	7.5	22	4	539	349	2211	679	79	25	4	69	47			.317	.338	.383	721	124	60	58	100	58	31	65	2
TRO	15	10		.600	13	6	6	273	191	1108	330	58	8	5	9	14			.300	.306	.381	687	111	16	13	101	6	7	46	-1
ATL	9	28	0	.243	25	6	12	237	473	1476	377	35	10	1	19	25			.259	.268	.299	567	65	-40	-80	117	19	16	54	-1
CLE	6	16	0	.273	20.5	2	5	174	254	960	272	28	5	0	17	13			.288	.301	.329	630	102	-4	8	95	12	3	80	2
MAN	5	19	0	.208	22.5	4	7	220	348	1023	275	36	9	2	10	13			.271	.279	.331	610	94	-13	0	94	6	7	46	-1
ECK	3	26	0	.103	27	3	11	152	413	1090	248	29	9	0	18	40			.231	.244	.275	519	72	-47	-14	85	8	13	38	-3
OLY	2	7	0	.222	18	1	6	54	140	369	91	10	3	0	4	4			.249	.257	.293	550	75	-12	-8	95	0	3	0	-1
NAT	0	11	0	.000	21	0	7	80	190	452	99	6	1	0	1	3			.220	.221	.237	458	37	-30	-39	117	0	0	0	0
TOT	183					104	74	3390		15928	4467	581	145	37	263	265			.285	.297	.348	645					269	134	67	12

TEAM	CG	SHO	GR	SV	IP	H	HR	BB	SO	BR/9	ERA	AERA	OAV	OOB	PR	APR	PF	OSB	OCS	FA	E	WPB	DP	FW	PW	BW	BSW	DIF
BOS	41	4	7	4	430.1	443	0	27	29	9.8	1.86	197	.243	.254	86	86	100			.875	280	53	44	4.3	6.0	2.5	.3	2.3
BAL	48	1	10	1	516.0	573	3	63	77	11.1	2.90	127	.245	.265	43	45	101			.830	432	93	22	.4	3.1	.0	.3	4.2
MUT	54	1	2	1	512.0	622	2	33	46	11.5	3.02	112	.271	.282	36	22	93			.868	323	54	33	5.2	1.5	1.3	.3	-1.3
ATH	47	1	0	0	419.1	508	3	26	44	11.5	2.85	125	.265	.275	37	34	98			.858	298	28	20	3.0	2.4	4.0	.0	-1.5
TRO	17	2	8	1	225.0	277	2	10		11.5	2.60	140	.269	.276	26	26	100			.861	151	18	9	2.0	1.8	.9	-.1	-2.1
ATL	37	0	0	0	336.0	568	6	21	13	15.8	4.53	100	.326	.334	-33	0	124			.810	357	66	15	-4.0	-3.3	-5.6	-.1	.2
CLE	15	0	7	0	199.0	285	6	24	11	14.0	5.70	63	.290	.307	-45	-48	98			.816	184	53	17	-.9	-3.3	.6	-.0	-1.4
MAN	20	0	4	0	211.0	366	6	15	10	16.3	5.55	65	.326	.335	-44	-46	99			.804	231	18	11	-2.6	-3.2	.0	-.1	-1.1
ECK	28	0	1	0	259.1	484	7	36	13	18.0	5.55	61	.345	.361	-55	-66	93			.803	274	71	9	-2.8	-4.6	-1.0	-.3	-2.8
OLY	9	0	0	0	79.0	148	0	5	1	17.4	6.38	57	.333	.341	-24	-25	99			.786	96	30	7	-1.5	-1.7	-.6	-.1	1.4
NAT	11	0	0	0	99.0	193	2	3	2	17.8	6.18	75	.339	.343	-28	-13	127			.774	120	7	2	-1.9	-.9	-2.7	-.0	.1
TOT	327	11	39	7	3286.0					13.0	3.65		.285	.297						.837	2746	491	189					

Batter-Fielder Wins
Barnes-Bos 3.5
Eggler-Mut 2.2
G.Wright-Bos 2.2
Force-Tro-Bal 1.8
Ferguson-Atl 1.7

Batting Average
Barnes-Bos 430
Force-Tro-Bal 418
Anson-Ath 415
Hastings-Cle-Bal 362
McGeary-Ath 360

On-Base Percentage
Anson-Ath 455
Barnes-Bos 452
Force-Tro-Bal 423
Hastings-Cle-Bal 376
McGeary-Ath 366

Slugging Average
Barnes-Bos 583
Anson-Ath 525
Wood-Tro-Eck 500
Force-Tro-Bal 493
Meyerle-Ath 486

On-Base Plus Slugging
Barnes-Bos 1034
Anson-Ath 980
Force-Tro-Bal 916
Wood-Tro-Eck 833
G.Wright-Bos 816

Adjusted OPS
Barnes-Bos 205
Anson-Ath 200
Force-Tro-Bal 176
Wood-Tro-Eck 156
Meyerle-Ath 147

Adjusted Batter Runs
Barnes-Bos 28.0
Anson-Ath 25.8
Force-Tro-Bal 19.0
Eggler-Mut 16.8
Hatfield-Mut 14.7

Runs
Eggler-Mut 94
G.Wright-Bos 87
Cuthbert-Ath 83
Barnes-Bos 81
Hatfield-Mut 76

Hits
Barnes-Bos 99
Eggler-Mut 97
Force-Tro-Bal 94
Hatfield-Mut 93
Anson-Ath 90

Doubles
Barnes-Bos 28
Eggler-Mut 20
Hall-Bal 17
G.Wright-Bos 16

Triples
Gould-Bos 8
Anson-Ath 7
G.Wright-Bos 6
Hall-Bal 6

Home Runs
Pike-Bal 7
Gedney-Tro-Eck 3

Total Bases
Barnes-Bos 134
Pike-Bal 131
G.Wright-Bos 120
Eggler-Mut 117
Hall-Bal 116

Runs Batted In
Pike-Bal 60
Start-Mut 48
Fisler-Ath 48
Anson-Ath 48

Stolen Bases
Eggler-Mut 18
G.Wright-Bos 14
Cuthbert-Ath 14
McGeary-Ath 13

Base Stealing Runs
Barnes-Bos 1.9
Eggler-Mut 1.9
Pike-Bal 1.9
G.Wright-Bos 1.7
Cuthbert-Ath 1.7

Fielding Runs-Infield
Ferguson-Atl 34.5
Barnes-Bos 25.5
G.Wright-Bos 21.6
Fisler-Ath 7.3
Force-Tro-Bal 7.2

Fielding Runs-Outfield
Eggler-Mut 14.1
York-Bal 9.9
Reach-Ath 4.4
Meyerle-Ath 3.0
McMullin-Mut 2.9

Wins
Spalding-Bos 38
Cummings-Mut 33
McBride-Ath 30
Mathews-Bal 25
Zettlein-Tro-Eck 15

Winning Pct.
Spalding-Bos 826
McBride-Ath 682
Cummings-Mut 623
Mathews-Bal 581
Zettlein-Tro-Eck 484

Complete Games
Cummings-Mut 53
McBride-Ath 47
Spalding-Bos 41
Mathews-Bal 39
Britt-Atl 37

Strikeouts
Mathews-Bal 57
Cummings-Mut 45
McBride-Ath 44
Spalding-Bos 28
Zettlein-Tro-Eck 25

Fewest BB/Game
Stearns-Nat 27
Buttery-Man 46
Zettlein-Tro-Eck 48
Brainard-Oly-Man 52
McBride-Ath 56

Games
Cummings-Mut 55
Mathews-Bal 49
Spalding-Bos 48
McBride-Ath 47
Britt-Atl 37

Saves
H.Wright-Bos 4
Zettlein-Tro-Eck 1
McMullin-Mut 1
Fisher-Bal 1

Base Runners/9
Fisher-Bal 8.51
Spalding-Bos 9.87
Zettlein-Tro-Eck 11.19
McBride-Ath 11.46
Cummings-Mut 11.50

Adjusted Relief Runs
H.Wright-Bos 5.2

Relief Ranking
H.Wright-Bos 3.6

Innings Pitched
Cummings-Mut 497.0
McBride-Ath 419.1
Mathews-Bal 406.0
Spalding-Bos 404.2
Britt-Atl 336.0

Opponents' Avg.
Fisher-Bal 197
Spalding-Bos 244
Mathews-Bal 257
Zettlein-Tro-Eck 265
McBride-Ath 265

Opponents' OBP
Fisher-Bal 216
Spalding-Bos 255
Zettlein-Tro-Eck 273
McBride-Ath 275
Mathews-Bal 277

Earned Run Average
Fisher-Bal 1.80
Spalding-Bos 1.85
Zettlein-Tro-Eck 2.57
McBride-Ath 2.85
Cummings-Mut 3.01

Adjusted ERA
Fisher-Bal 205
Spalding-Bos 199
Zettlein-Tro-Eck 139
McBride-Ath 125
Mathews-Bal 115

Adjusted Starter Runs
Spalding-Bos 80.9
McBride-Ath 34.0
Zettlein-Tro-Eck 30.2
Mathews-Bal 26.0
Cummings-Mut 23.3

Pitcher Wins
Spalding-Bos 7.5
McBride-Ath 2.6
Zettlein-Tro-Eck 2.1
Fisher-Bal 1.2
Cummings-Mut 1.1

More Is Less

The NA increased to eleven teams in its second year, but several of the new clubs proved to be poor draws. Troy, Cleveland, the Brooklyn Eckfords, the Washington Olympics, and Mansfield of Middletown, Connecticut, wouldn't live to see 1873. Together they drew just 37,000; the six clubs that stuck it out had a combined attendance of 200,000. The Lord Baltimores, however, proved an inspired addition as they drew 40,500 fans and placed second to runaway winner Boston.

Harry Wright's Red Stockings were all business. In a league with questionable organization, officiating, and, in some cases, honesty of its participants, British-born Harry Wright was the pillar of class and professionalism. He had assembled the unbeatable Cincinnati Red Stockings of 1869, and he was hired to do the same thing in Boston in 1871. He brought several of his old Cincinnati players to Boston, including Cal McVey and Charlie Gould, but most important was Harry's brother, George. The Red Stockings finished 2 games back in 1871, but that failure would not happen again.

From 1872–75 Boston went 205-50 for an .804 winning percentage. Wright not only brought holdovers from Cincinnati, he also lured some of the best young talent to Boston. Al Spalding, who pitched in every one of Boston's games in 1872, and Ross Barnes, who averaged more than 2 hits per game during his NA career, both came from the Rockford club. Each was just 21.

Barnes and George Wright ranked 1-2 in runs, hits, doubles, total bases, and slugging. Defensively, second baseman Barnes and shortstop Wright were unmatched. Wright had superb hands and perfected the method of bending his elbows when catching the ball to cushion the shock. Barnes' .904 fielding average on the choppy NA fields was as impressive as his .430 batting average. Boston led the NA in double plays and fielding average as the Red Stockings lost just once in 21 tries at South End Grounds.

Baby-faced Candy Cummings, accused of signing contracts with three different teams before the season, dominated on the mound for the Mutuals. The reputed inventor of the curveball pitched in all but one of New York's games, completing 53. Cummings tossed more innings than every *team* except Baltimore.

1871 National Association

TEAM	W	L	T	PCT	GB	HW	HL	R	OR	PA	H	2B	3B	HR	BB	SO	HB	SH	AVG	OBP	SLG	OPS	AOPS	BR	ABR	PF	SB	CS	BSA	BSR
ATH	21	7	0	.750		12	3	376	266	1327	410	66	27	9	46	23			.320	.344	.435	779	125	39	43	99	56	12	82	8
BOS	20	10	1	.667	2	12	5	**401**	303	1432	426	70	37	3	60	19			.310	.339	.422	761	115	34	22	103	**73**	16	82	**10**
CHI	19	9	0	.679	2	**13**	3	302	**241**	1256	323	52	21	**10**	60	22			.287	.303	.350	653	97	-21	10	91	46	15	75	5
MUT	16	17	0	.485	7.5	12	7	302	313	1437	403	43	21	1	33	15			.277	.302	.369	671	98	-12	5	95	48	13	79	6
OLY	15	15	2	.500	7	8	5	310	303	1401	375	54	26	6	48	13			.308	.334	.417	751	114	25	20	101	62	24	72	5
TRO	13	15	1	.464	8	7	9	351	362	1297	384	51	34	6	49	19			.277	.292	.391	683	102	-10	6	95	18	8	69	1
CLE	10	19	0	.345	11.5	3	10	249	341	1212	328	35	**40**	7	26	25			.239	.271	.294	565	63	-34	-37	102	16	4	80	2
KEK	7	12	0	.368	9.5	5	4	137	243	779	178	19	8	2	33	9			.264	.291	.364	655	92	-16	-5	96	53	10	**84**	8
ROK	4	21	0	.160	15.5	3	4	231	287	1074	274	44	25	3	38	30														
TOT	127					75	50	2659		11215	3101	434	239	47	393	175			.287	.312	.384	695					441	123	78	54

TEAM	CG	SHO	GR	SV	IP	H	HR	BB	SO	BR/9	ERA	AERA	OAV	OOB	PR	APR	PF	OSB	OCS	FA	E	WPB	DP	FW	PW	BW	BSW	DIF
ATH	27	0	1	0	249.0	329	3	53	16	13.8	4.95	81	.284	.315	-20	-27	95			.845	194	28	13	1.1	-1.8	**2.8**	.1	4.7
BOS	22	**1**	**9**	**3**	276.0	367	2	42	23	13.3	3.55	117	.273	.296	20	19	99			.834	243	38	**24**	-.3	1.2	1.4	**.3**	2.3
CHI	25	0	3	1	251.0	**308**	6	28	22	**12.0**	**2.76**	**166**	**.264**	**.281**	41	47	109			.829	229	83	16	-.8	**3.1**	-2.2	.1	4.8
MUT	32	1	1	0	293.0	373	7	42	22	12.7	3.72	102	.271	.292	16	3	90			**.850**	218	49	20	**1.5**	-.4	.3	.0	-1.4
OLY	32	0	0	0	282.0	371	4	45	13	13.3	4.37	95	.281	.305	-5	-6	99			.845	198	96	22	1.3	-2.3	1.3	-.0	-1.2
TRO	28	0	1	0	250.0	431	4	75	14	18.2	5.51	76	.342	.378	-36	-36	100			.818	234	175	15	-.6	.0	.4	-.3	-3.9
CLE	23	0	6	0	254.0	346	13	53	**34**	14.1	4.11	100	.283	.312	3	0	98			.803	163	55	8	-.9	-.7	-2.4	-.3	1.7
KEK	19	1	0	0	169.0	261	5	21	17	15.0	5.17	88	.305	.322	-18	-10	108			.821	220	76	14	-1.5	-.4	-.3	.1	-6.4
ROK	23	1	2	0	226.0	315	3	34	16	13.9	4.30	95	.282	.303	-2	-6	97			.833	235	98	14					
TOT	231	4	23	4	2250.0					14.0	4.22		.287	.312						.833	1934	698	146					

Batter-Fielder Wins		Batting Average		On-Base Percentage		Slugging Average		On-Base Plus Slugging		Adjusted OPS		Adjusted Batter Runs	
Barnes-Bos	1.8	Meyerle-Ath	.492	Meyerle-Ath	.500	Meyerle-Ath	.700	Meyerle-Ath	1200	Meyerle-Ath	243	Meyerle-Ath	23.5
Wood-Chi	1.2	McVey-Chi	.431	G.Wright-Bos	.453	Pike-Tro	.654	G.Wright-Bos	1078	G.Wright-Bos	200	Wolters-Mut	17.2
Force-Oly	1.2	Barnes-Bos	.401	Barnes-Bos	.447	Bass-Cle	.640	Pike-Tro	1054	Pike-Tro	194	Barnes-Bos	17.1
Pike-Tro	1.1	King-Tro	.396	McVey-Bos	.435	Barnes-Bos	.580	Barnes-Bos	1027	Wolters-Mut	189	Pike-Tro	15.0
McVey-Bos	1.1	Wood-Chi	.378	Wood-Chi	.425	Treacey-Chi	.573	McVey-Bos	991	Barnes-Bos	186	McVey-Bos	14.0

Runs		Hits		Doubles		Triples		Home Runs		Total Bases		Runs Batted In	
Barnes-Bos	66	McVey-Bos	66	Anson-Rok	11	Bass-Cle	10	Treacey-Chi	4	Meyerle-Ath	91	Wolters-Mut	44
Birdsall-Bos	51	Meyerle-Ath	64			Wolters-Mut	9	Pike-Tro	4	Barnes-Bos	91	McVey-Bos	43
Radcliff-Ath	47	Barnes-Bos	63			Barnes-Bos	9	Meyerle-Ath	4	Pike-Tro	85	Meyerle-Ath	40
Cuthbert-Ath	47	Start-Mut	58			Pratt-Cle	8			McVey-Bos	85	Pike-Tro	39
Waterman-Oly	46	King-Tro	57							King-Tro	79		

Stolen Bases		Base Stealing Runs		Fielding Runs-Infield		Fielding Runs-Outfield		Wins		Winning Pct.		Complete Games	
McGeary-Tro	20	Wood-Chi	3.3	Force-Oly	17.8	Treacey-Chi	6.6	Spalding-Bos	19	McBride-Ath	.783	Wolters-Mut	31
Wood-Chi	18	McGeary-Tro	3.0	Barnes-Bos	12.3	Hall-Oly	5.5	Zettlein-Chi	18	Zettlein-Chi	.667	Brainard-Oly	30
Cuthbert-Ath	16	Cuthbert-Ath	2.8	Wood-Chi	8.3	Eggler-Mut	4.5	McBride-Ath	18	Spalding-Bos	.655	McMullin-Tro	28
Leonard-Oly	14	Mack-Rok	2.6	Pinkham-Tro	8.3	Cuthbert-Ath	3.3	Wolters-Mut	16	Wolters-Mut	.500	Zettlein-Chi	25
Eggler-Mut	14	Cone-Bos	2.3	Craver-Tro	6.4	King-Tro	3.0					McBride-Ath	25

Strikeouts		Fewest BB/Game		Games		Saves		Base Runners/9		Adjusted Relief Runs		Relief Ranking	
Pratt-Cle	34	Zettlein-Chi	.93	Wolters-Mut	32	H.Wright-Bos	3	Zettlein-Chi	12.08	Pinkham-Chi	1.8	Pinkham-Chi	2.0
Spalding-Bos	23	Mathews-Kek	1.12	Spalding-Bos	31	Pinkham-Chi	1	Wolters-Mut	12.21				
Zettlein-Chi	22	Wolters-Mut	1.24	Brainard-Oly	30			Spalding-Bos	12.98				
Wolters-Mut	22	Brainard-Oly	1.26	McMullin-Tro	29			McBride-Ath	13.18				
Mathews-Kek	17	Fisher-Rok	1.31					Brainard-Oly	13.57				

Innings Pitched		Opponents' Avg.		Opponents' OBP		Earned Run Average		Adjusted ERA		Adjusted Starter Runs		Pitcher Wins	
Wolters-Mut	283.0	Wolters-Mut	.263	Zettlein-Chi	.283	Zettlein-Chi	2.73	Zettlein-Chi	168	Zettlein-Chi	45.0	Zettlein-Chi	2.6
Brainard-Oly	264.0	Zettlein-Chi	.267	Wolters-Mut	.285	Spalding-Bos	3.36	Spalding-Bos	124	Spalding-Bos	22.3	Wolters-Mut	2.0
Spalding-Bos	257.1	Spalding-Bos	.268	Spalding-Bos	.290	Wolters-Mut	3.43	Wolters-Mut	110	Wolters-Mut	11.6	Spalding-Bos	1.6
McMullin-Tro	249.0	Pratt-Cle	.277	Fisher-Rok	.302	Pratt-Cle	3.77	Pratt-Cle	110	Pratt-Cle	7.2	Pratt-Cle	.8
Zettlein-Chi	240.2	McBride-Ath	.280	McBride-Ath	.307	Fisher-Rok	4.35	Fisher-Rok	94	Stearns-Oly	3.4	Stearns-Oly	.1

Up in Smoke

The Kekiongas of Fort Wayne won the first National Association game ever played as Bobby Mathews shut out Forest City of Cleveland, 2-0, on May 4, 1871. James "Deacon" White of Cleveland doubled for the first hit in the first professional baseball league. The Kekiongas lasted only 19 games into the season and drew just 3,500 fans. It was the start of a disaster-prone pattern that pervaded the NA's tenure: teams open with great fanfare, teams fare poorly, teams draw poorly, teams fold.

The NA had no set schedule, per se; clubs made their own arrangements. They were supposed to play five series of three games each, with the champion being declared based on winning percentage. Of course, not everyone played all the requisite series. Teams with little to gain and longer to travel didn't make every road trip—and the NA wasn't big on discipline for those who strayed. Clubs were often more interested in lucrative non-scheduled "exhibition games" than in fulfilling their league schedule. It was not uncommon for clubs to play twice as many nonleague contests as NA games.

The NA drew 266,500 in its inaugural season; the White Stockings' 69,000 led the circuit even though the Great Chicago Fire wiped out their ballpark and uniforms late in the season. The White Stockings (ancestors of today's Cubs) gamely continued their schedule on the road, wearing an odd assortment of uniforms and finishing a close second. Chicago did not return to the league for two seasons.

The Philadelphia Athletics won the first pennant, thanks in part to two forfeits by Rockford, which left the league after just one year. Rockford's 19-year-old third baseman, Cap Anson, would shift to the Athletics in 1872.

Philadelphia's Levi Meyerle, a notoriously horrendous fielder during a time of rough fields and rougher scorekeepers, began a long tradition of hapless defenders who played every day for a simple reason: they could hit. Numbers calculated years later confirmed eyewitness accounts: His 1871 fielding average was an incomprehensible .642, but he slugged .700 for his hometown Athletics. The brief NA season may have afforded Meyerle just 26 games, but his .492 batting average has never been approached by any batsman in the 132 years following.

BLACK BASEBALL AND THE NEGRO LEAGUES

As it flowed from its origin, part of the river of baseball history diverged at one point and formed a separate branch that paralleled the main stream for a half-century. Finally the waters were rejoined, making the river whole again.

During this separation, baseball was not complete. The majority of Americans went with the flow of the main stream, following its course intently, with only an occasional excursion to see the parallel branch.

Thus for a half-century, white Americans sat watching Major League Baseball, only vaguely aware of the shadowy world of black baseball that existed beyond the scope of their vision. To most white baseball observers, black ballplayers were as unreal as the shadows on Plato's wall. In this world of reflected images, there existed exceptionally talented players whose ability was unsurpassed anywhere.

Best known among these great black ballplayers in today's baseball world are Hall of Famers Satchel Paige and Josh Gibson. But as Satchel himself said, "There were many Satchels, many Joshs." And indeed there were. There in the shadows of black baseball were players who were yesteryear's equivalent of Hank Aaron, Willie Mays, Barry Bonds, Lou Brock, Bob Gibson, Reggie Jackson, Lee Smith, David Justice, Gary Sheffield, Cecil Fielder, Tony Gwynn, Ken Griffey Jr., Frank Thomas, Barry Larkin, Fred McGriff, Albert Belle, Ricky Henderson, Mo Vaughn, Derek Jeter, Andruw Jones, C.C. Sabathia, and so many others. The list is almost endless.

Try to imagine post-World War II baseball without its black stars. Visualize baseball today without black stars complementing the white stars. Obviously, all great black ballplayers were not born after 1947 when Jackie Robinson re-integrated Major League Baseball. They were always there, required by custom and circumstance to play in their separate leagues.

This period of separation is remote from the memory of the majority of the current populace. Today's younger generation, as well as most of the older generation now, do not fully understand the sociological factors which prohibited black and white baseball players from engaging in competition together. Consequently, they know and understand even less about the men who were destined to demonstrate their abilities to a comparatively small segment of American society. Just who were these men who displayed their talent in virtual obscurity?

During the half-century of dual baseball development, more than 4,000 men plied their trade in the arenas of black baseball, many of whom were of major league caliber. Many of these possessed sufficient skills to have been first-line players in the major leagues, and best of this group would have achieved stardom. Approximately two dozen of these stars shone with such magnificence as to have merited selection to the National Baseball Hall of Fame.

Extrapolating the past from the present, if the black leagues and the white leagues had been merged into a 30-team configuration, an average black team during this period of separation would have had 14 players on their roster who possessed major league talent. Seven of the first nine could have won starting positions in the major leagues, with the top three players being "stars." For any given year, two out of every three teams would have a player in their line-up with Hall of Fame qualifications. The better teams would have exceeded these parameters, while lesser teams would have failed to meet them.

Still, the greats, the near-greats, and the not-so-greats were there, unnoticed by the vast majority of America, until Jackie Robinson broke the color barrier in 1947 and finally opened the National Pastime to all men, regardless of the color of their skin.

What little exposure most white fans in larger cities got to the Negro Leagues came in the form of exhibition games against white major leaguers during barnstorming tours held during the off-season.

White major leaguers, looking to augment their baseball salaries, played exhibitions against black teams made up of the best Negro League players. That the black players not only held their own, but often beat the white teams, would hardly have been a surprise in a perfect world. Since that perfect world didn't exist, there was a lot on the line for the Negro Leaguers in those games. Buck O'Neil, black baseball's most famous spokesman, described the dynamics of these games in an interview with MLB.com:

"What a lot of people don't know is that we won a majority of those ballgames," O'Neil recalled. "Now that didn't mean we were better players than the Major Leaguers. We won the majority of the ballgames because the Major Leaguers were just making a payday. We wanted to prove to the world that they weren't superior because they were Major Leaguers and we weren't inferior because we played in the Negro Leagues. We stretched that single into a double, that double into a triple. We stole home. The Major Leaguers couldn't afford to twist an ankle or break a finger in an exhibition ballgame, but, honey, we went all out."

In smaller cities and towns, black teams would often play against factory-league teams or local semi-pro teams—many of which were good enough to be considered of minor league quality. These exhibitions would take place both during and after the regular season.

Baseball was originally a gentleman's game played by members of rival athletic clubs for recreation. In the aftermath of the Civil War, baseball enjoyed a great surge in interest, activity, and growth. Americans of all classes, creeds, and races joined in the game that quickly grew to become our National Pastime. Baseball was then an amateur sport: some black Americans played on all-black clubs, while others played on integrated teams.

However, black ballplayers were excluded from participation by the National Association of Base Ball Players on December 11, 1868 when the governing body voted unanimously to bar "any club which may be composed of one or more colored persons." This was the first appearance of an official color line in baseball.

When baseball openly admitted the professional status of top clubs in subsequent seasons, pro teams were not bound by the amateur association's ruling. Thus, during the nineteenth century, black ballplayers appeared on integrated teams and some black teams played in integrated leagues. Two brothers—Moses Fleetwood Walker and Welday Walker—even played in the major leagues in 1884 for Toledo of the American Association. Gradually, however, black players began to be excluded from the white leagues and, by the beginning of the new century, there were no black players in what was grandiloquently called Organized Baseball.

Nevertheless, black Americans continued to play baseball. By necessity they played on all-black teams and, eventually, formed all-black leagues. The first black professional team was the Cuban Giants in 1885, but black teams played as independent clubs until the first black league was organized in 1920. In the decade prior to the founding of the first black major league, many independent black clubs had developed impressive enough rosters to be considered of big-league quality. The critical change was the first great migration of African-Americans from the rural South to the industrial cities of the Northeast and Midwest during and after World War I. That massive social change ensured that there were large enough concentrations of black Americans to support organized leagues.

That year Rube Foster, considered the father of black baseball, founded the Negro National League. Three years later, in 1923, Ed Bolden formed the Eastern Colored League. These two leagues operated successfully for several years before they fell victim to financial difficulties. Three other black major leagues—the American Negro League (1929), the Negro Southern League (1932) and the East-West League (1932) operated for a single season but were not able to continue on a sound fiscal basis.

Many of the best players in the original Negro National League migrated to the Negro Southern League after the NNL's break-up; the NSL operated before and after 1932 as a minor league. And most of those players left the NSL after only one year to return to a newly reformed Negro National League, which began play in 1933. The Chicago American Giants played in both incarnations of the Negro National

League, as well as the NSL in 1932. The Indianapolis ABCs also played in the first NNL and the NSL

The new NNL and the Negro American League (chartered in 1937) both thrived until the color line was broken. During their existence, the Negro Leagues played eleven World Series (1924–27 and 1942–48) and created their own All-Star Game in 1933. The East-West Game became the biggest black sports attraction in the country.

The most famous of the Negro League clubs were the Homestead Grays and the Kansas City Monarchs, the latter ironically owned by a white businessman. Homestead, which featured such great players as Josh Gibson, Buck Leonard and Cool Papa Bell, won three Negro League World Series (1943, 1944, and 1948), and nine straight NNL pennants from 1937–45. That unparalleled streak included five years in which the Grays won both halves of a split season schedule. In three other years (1939, 1940, and 1942), the NNL did not play a split season, leaving 1941 as the only year in which Homestead failed to dominate the entire season—and in that year the Grays easily bested the New York Cubans in four games in the league's Championship Series.

Kansas City won the first Negro League World Series in 1924 over the Hilldale Daisies, and had many star players in its history, including Buck O'Neil. O'Neil, who would later go on to become the first black coach in the big leagues, signed future Hall of Famers Lou Brock and Ernie Banks while working for the Cubs as a scout. The Monarchs sent a host of players on to the big leagues, including Banks, Satchel Paige and Elston Howard, the first black to play for the legendary New York Yankees.

During most of the Negro Leagues existence, two leagues, one based in the east and one in the west, were dominant. The original Negro National League was comprised of teams from Pittsburgh west, while the Eastern Colored League, the NNL's main competition, featured teams based in eastern Pennsylvania, Baltimore, New York City, and New Jersey. From 1933 on, the new Negro National League became the predominant circuit in the eastern part of the country, while the Negro American League ruled the west.

That clear geographical division was one of the reasons why the East-West All-Star Game was so hotly contested by the players and so highly anticipated by the fans of black baseball. The game was held yearly in Chicago's Comiskey Park from 1933 to 1953, with additional East-West games played in the east in six years. Competition in these games was intense, and fan interest was always high, as the contests in the Windy City drew 30,000 or more people 11 times, including six crowds of more than 45,000. The paying customers got their money's worth as 19 of the 28 games were decided by four runs or less.

The Negro National League folded following the 1948 season and, although the Negro American League survived more than another decade and other black touring teams continued to play until the early 1960s, they were of greatly diminished quality after 1950 and certainly not of major league caliber after 1954. The demise of the Negro Leagues was inevitable as the best young black players were signed by Organized Baseball clubs.

The Negro Leagues would not have been able to survive even that long had racial prejudices not prevailed long after Jackie Robinson's big-league debut. Even after Robinson's immensely successful rookie season in 1947, many AL and NL clubs were hesitant to sign black players, having incorrectly assumed that Robinson's success with the Dodgers in 1947 was a fluke. It wasn't until after Robinson, and Larry Doby, the first black to play in the American League, equaled or bettered Robinson's rookie year in 1948 that other big-league clubs began to actively seek out black players.

Even so, many of the best Negro League players never got a shot in the big leagues, since most clubs wouldn't sign black players who were older than 28. There were some exceptions, Satchel Paige being the most famous; however, many other truly great ballplayers were denied entry into the majors, having been born a couple of years too early.

Josh Gibson, the greatest slugger in black baseball history, might have had a chance, like Paige, to play in the big leagues near the end of his career. Gibson led the NNL in home runs in 1945, hit .361 and slugged .958 in 1946, and had at least one

meeting with Washington Senators owner Clark Griffith about joining the perennial AL basement dwellers. However, the powerful home run hitter suffered a massive stroke and died in January 1947 when he was but thirty-five years old.

Despite the immediate success of black players in the majors, baseball wasn't fully integrated until well into the 1960s. In 1953, six years after Robinson debuted with Brooklyn, and the year he, Roy Campanella, and Jim Gilliam helped the Dodgers win their second straight pennant, only seven big-league clubs featured black players—not even half of the teams had the wisdom and the integrity to see what the future held.

For a half-century the best black players were not allowed to play on the same field with the best white players, and it was during this era of separation that two parallel baseball universes co-existed. The history of the white major leagues has been well chronicled, but only in recent years has the history of the black major leagues started to get the recognition that it deserves. The Negro Leagues showcased some of the greatest baseball talent of all-time, with a special essence that was all its own.

This section is designed to help preserve the fragmentary record of this segment of baseball history. It is respectfully dedicated to the men who played during this segregated era, so that they will be remembered as more than just a name in an obscure box score or as bits of dust caught in the cobwebs of the receding memory of old men.

Key to Negro League Section. James A. Riley, renowned black baseball historian and consultant to the Negro Leagues Baseball Museum, has selected the greatest black baseball and Negro League players of all-time. Players are grouped into five categories; rank numbers are deliberately not shown in order to avoid overemphasizing small differences between similar players in each group. An alphabetical index is included before the biographies to make it easier to find individual players.

Hall of Fame players are listed in the order of their induction in Cooperstown. In the four other groups, players are shown in order of merit. To show where players were throughout their careers, biographies include not only the Negro major league teams for which each star played, but also Negro minor league teams, Organized Baseball minor leagues, and overseas leagues. The teams that players are most commonly associated with are indicated by bold type.

Also included are synopses of top-level independent black baseball and Negro League seasons from 1910–1950, year-by-year standings, and results of any postseason intraleague championship series or interleague World Series. In the many years where some or all of the standings are unknown, the team that was declared the champion is listed first with other teams listed in alphabetical order. Ex Post Facto Most Valuable Player, Pitcher of the Year, and Rookie of the Year awards have been selected for the Negro major leagues from 1920–50, for the 1910–1919 period when there were four or more teams of big-league caliber, and during selected seasons when clubs that were major league caliber played independently in the east. During the non-league seasons the top performer is referred to as Player of the Year.

The All-Star Game list shows the results of every East-West All-Star Game played, including two games in 1938 that have rarely been mentioned. Most accounts of East-West games leave out several of the "second" games played; this is the first time a complete list has been published. There was only one year when an official MVP was selected for the East-West Game (1945). Therefore, we have chosen Ex Post Facto MVPs for all other East-West Games.

Finally, at the end of this section is a list of Negro League home ballparks, organized by city as in the major league Ballpark section of this encyclopedia. Negro League teams played thousands of games at neutral sites, in between official league games during the season as well as on off-season barnstorming tours. In fact, teams frequently played doubleheaders where the first game was an official league contest but the nightcap was just an exhibition—a distinction that was often conveniently ignored when promoting the games to draw a bigger crowd for the second game

NEGRO MAJOR LEAGUES

NNL Negro National League 1920–31
ECL Eastern Colored League 1923–28
NSL Negro Southern League 1932
ANL American Negro League 1929

EWL East-West League 1932
NNL Negro National League 1933–48
NAL Negro American League 1937–54
Ind. Independent Team of Major League Caliber

NEGRO MAJOR LEAGUE TEAMS AND BIG-LEAGUE CALIBER INDEPENDENT TEAMS

AC All Cubans (Touring) 1921 Ind.

Atl Atlanta Black Crackers 1938 NAL

Bac Bacharach Giants (Atlantic City NJ) 1923–28 ECL; 1929 ANL

Bal BS Baltimore Black Sox 1922 Ind.; 1923–28 ECL; 1929 ANL; 1930–31 Ind.; 1932 EWL; 1933–34 NNL

Bal EG Baltimore Elite Giants 1938–48 NNL; 1949–51 NAL

Bir Birmingham Black Barons 1924–25 NNL; 1927–30 NNL; 1932 NSL; 1937–38, 1940–54 NAL

Bow Bowser's ABCs (Indianapolis) 1916 Ind.

Bro E Brooklyn Eagles 1935 NNL

Bro RG Brooklyn Royal Giants 1905–14, 1916–22 Ind.; 1923–27 ECL; 1928–32 Ind.; 1933 NNL

Chi AG[1] Chicago American Giants 1920–31 NNL; 1932 NSL; 1933–35 NNL; 1936 Ind.; 1937–52 NAL

Chi CG Chicago Columbia Giants 1899–1900 Ind.

Chi G Chicago Giants 1920–21 NNL

Chi LG Chicago Leland Giants 1905–10 Ind.

Chi UG Chicago Union Giants 1901–04 Ind.

Chi U Chicago Unions 1888–1900 Ind.

Cin Bu Cincinnati Buckeyes 1942 NAL

Cin Cincinnati Tigers 1937 NAL

Cle Be Cleveland Bears 1939–40 NAL

Cle Br Cleveland Browns 1924 NNL

Cle Bu Cleveland Buckeyes 1943–48, 1950 NAL

Cle C Cleveland Cubs 1931 NNL

Cle E Cleveland Elites 1926 NNL

Cle G Cleveland Giants 1933 NNL

Cle H Cleveland Hornets 1927 NNL

Cle RS Cleveland Red Sox 1934 NNL

Cle S Cleveland Stars 1932 EWL

Cle TS Cleveland Tate Stars 1922 NNL

Cle T Cleveland Tigers 1928 NNL

Col BB Columbus Blue Birds 1933 NNL

Col B Columbus Buckeyes 1921 NNL

Col EG Columbus Elite Giants 1935 NNL

Cub HD[2] Cuban House of David (Touring) 1931–32 Ind.; 1932 EWL

Cub SE Cuban Stars [East] (Touring/New York) 1923–28 ECL; 1929 ANL

Cub SW[3] Cuban Stars [West] (Touring) 1920–30 NNL

Cub XG Cuban X-Giants (Touring/Philadelphia) 1897–1908 Ind.

Day Dayton Marcos [I] 1920 NNL; [II] 1926 NNL

Det S Detroit Stars [I] 1920–31 NNL; [II] 1933 NNL; [III] 1937 NAL

Det W Detroit Wolves 1932 EWL

Eth Ethiopian Clowns (Miami/Touring) 1940–42 Ind.

GCT GCT (Grand Central Terminal) Red Caps (New York City) 1918–19 Ind.

Har G Harrisburg Giants 1924–27 ECL

Har S Harlem Stars (New York City) 1931 Ind.

Hil Hilldale Daisies 1923–28 ECL; 1929 ANL; 1930–31 Ind.; 1932 EWL

Hom[4] Homestead Grays (Pittsburgh) 1929 ANL; 1930–31 Ind.; 1932 EWL; 1933–34 Ind.; 1935–48 NNL

Hou Houston Eagles 1949–50 NAL

Ind ABC Indianapolis ABCs [I] 1920–26 NNL; [II] 1931 NNL; 1932 NSL; [III] 1933 NNL; [IV] 1938–39 NAL

Ind A Indianapolis Athletics 1937 NAL

Ind Cl[5] Indianapolis Clowns 1943–54 NAL

Ind Cr Indianapolis Crawfords 1940 NAL

Jac Jacksonville Red Caps 1938, 1941–42 NAL

Jew Jewell's ABCs (Indianapolis) 1917 Ind.

KC Kansas City Monarchs 1920–31 NNL; 1932–36 Ind.; 1937–54 NAL

Lin Lincoln Giants (New York City) 1923–26 ECL; 1927 Ind.; 1928 ECL; 1929 ANL

Lou BCa Louisville Black Caps 1932 NSL

Lou BCo Louisville Black Colonels 1954 NAL

Lou Bu Louisville Buckeyes 1949 NAL

Lou WS Louisville White Sox 1931 NNL

Mem Memphis Red Sox 1924–25, 1927, 1929–30 NNL; 1932 NSL; 1937–54 NAL

Mil Milwaukee Bears 1923 NNL

Moh Mohawk Giants (Schenectady NY) 1913–15 Ind.

Mon M Monroe Monarchs 1932 NSL

Mon GS Montgomery Grey Sox 1932 NSL

Nas Nashville Elite Giants 1930 NNL; 1932 NSL; 1933–34 NNL

NO New Orleans Eagles 1951 NAL

NY BY[6] New York Black Yankees 1936–48 NNL

NY C New York Cubans 1935–36, 1939–48 NNL; 1949–50 NAL

NY LS New York Lincoln Stars 1914–16 Ind.

New B Newark Browns 1932 EWL

New D Newark Dodgers 1934–35 NNL

New E Newark Eagles 1936–48 NNL

New S Newark Stars 1926 ECL

Pen Penn (Pennsylvania) Red Caps of New York 1917–19 Ind.

PF Page Fence Giants (Adrian MI) 1894–98 Ind.

Phi BG Philadelphia Bacharach Giants 1934 NNL

Phi G Philadelphia Giants 1902–16 Ind.

Phi S Philadelphia Stars 1934–48 NNL; 1949–52 NAL

Phi T Philadelphia Tigers 1928 ECL

Pit C Pittsburgh Crawfords 1933–38 NNL

Pit K Pittsburgh Keystones 1922 NNL

Qua Quaker Giants (Philadelphia) 1909 Ind.

StL G St. Louis Giants 1920–21 NNL

StL S[7] St. Louis Stars [I] 1922–31 NNL; [II] 1937 NAL; [III] 1939 NAL; 1940 Ind.; 1941 NAL; 1943 NNL

Tol C Toledo Crawfords 1939 NAL

Tol T Toledo Tigers 1923 NNL

Was BS Washington Black Senators 1938 NNL

Was EG Washington Elite Giants 1936–37 NNL

Was Pi Washington Pilots 1932 EWL

Was Po Washington Potomacs 1924 ECL

Wil Wilmington Potomacs 1925 Ind.

Zul Zulu Cannibal Giants (Touring) 1934–37 Ind.

Notes
[1]played as Cole's American Giants, 1932–35
[2]also known as Cuban Stars when playing in 1932 EWL
[3]based in Cincinnati as Cincinnati Cuban Stars, 1921
[4]played home games in both Pittsburgh PA and Washington DC, 1937–48
[5]played selected home games in Cincinnati OH, 1943–45
[6]played home games in Rochester NY in 1948
[7]played selected home games in New Orleans LA in 1941 and Harrisburg PA in 1943

TOP 100 BLACK BASEBALL/NEGRO LEAGUE PLAYERS

Alpha List

Allen, Newt	HFC	12	Cooper, Andy	ATG	14	Grant, Leroy	LDC	1	McNair, Hurley	LDC	6	Shively, George	ATG	31
Bankhead, Sam	ATG	12	Crutchfield, Jimmie	ATG	27	Harris, Vic	ATG	8	Mendez, Jose	ATG	5	Smith, Chino	SBC	3
Barnhill, Dave	ATG	33	Dandridge, Ray	HOF	11	Hill, Pete	HFC	2	Monroe, Bill	ATG	10	Smith, Hilton	HOF	18
Beckwith, John	HFC	13	Davis, Piper	ATG	2	Holland, Bill	LDC	4	Moore, Dobie	SBC	4	Stearnes, Turkey	HOF	17
Bell, Cool Papa	HOF	5	Davis, Steel Arm	LDC	7	Hughes, Sammy T.	HFC	17	Oms, Alejandro	ATG	22	Strong, Ted	ATG	40
Bell, William Sr.	LDC	5	Day, Leon	HOF	12	Irvin, Monte	HOF	4	O'Neil, Buck	ATG	11	Suttles, Mule	HFC	7
Benjamin, Jerry	LDC	12	DeMoss, Bingo	HFC	15	Jenkins, Fats	ATG	15	Paige, Satchel	HOF	1	Taylor, Ben	HFC	11
Benson, Gene	ATG	25	Dihigo, Martin	HOF	9	Johnson, Heavy	ATG	44	Parnell, Roy	ATG	38	Thomas, Clint	ATG	7
Brewer, Chet	ATG	34	Dismukes, Dizzy	ATG	29	Johnson, Home Run	HFC	20	Petway, Bruce	ATG	16	Tiant, Luis	ATG	36
Brooks, Chester	ATG	21	Dixon, Rap	ATG	13	Johnson, Judy	HOF	6	Poles, Spot	HFC	10	Torriente, Cristobal	HFC	4
Brown, Barney	ATG	37	Donaldson, John	ATG	4	Jones, Slim	SBC	1	Radcliffe, Alex	ATG	3	Trent, Ted	ATG	30
Brown, Dave	SBC	2	Duncan, Frank	ATG	17	Kimbro, Henry	ATG	24	Radcliffe, Double Duty	ATG	1	Warfield, Frank	ATG	19
Brown, Larry	ATG	18	Duncan, Frank	LDC	11	Leonard, Buck	HOF	3	Redding, Dick	HFC	9	Wells, Willie	HOF	14
Brown, Ray	HFC	14	Earle, Frank	ATG	43	Lloyd, John Henry	HOF	3	Robinson, Neil	ATG	23	White, Chaney	ATG	26
Brown, Willard	HFC	8	Easterling, Howard	ATG	42	Lundy, Dick	HFC	3	Rogan, Bullet	HOF	16	Wickware, Frank	ATG	35
Byrd, Bill	HFC	19	Foster, Rube	HOF	10	Lyons, Jimmie	ATG	20	Rogers, Nat	LDC	9	Williams, Smokey Joe	HOF	15
Campanella, Roy	SBC	1	Foster, Willie	HOF	13	Mackey, Biz	HFC	1	Sampson, Tommy	ATG	441	Wilson, Artie	SBC	6
Cannady, Rev	LDC	2	Francis, Bill	LDC	10	Malarcher, Dave	ATG	47	Santop, Louis	HFC	6	Wilson, Jud	HFC	5
Carr, George	ATG	39	Gardner, Jelly	ATG	28	Marcelle, Oliver H.	HFC	18	Scales, George	ATG	9	Winters, Nip	ATG	6
Charleston, Oscar	HOF	7	Gibson, Josh	HOF	2	Mathis, Verdell	ATG	32	Seay, Dick	LDC	3	Wright, Bill	HFC	16

HOF: Hall of Famers   HFC: Hall of Fame-Caliber Careers   ATG: Other All-Time Greats   LDC: Long and Distinguished Careers   SBC: Short but Brilliant Careers

Hall of Famers

PAIGE, SATCHEL Robert LeRoy B7.7.1906 Mobile AL D6.8.1982 Kansas City MO BR/TR/6-4/180 d1927 HF 1971 ML 1948–49 1951–53 1965 P
Bir 1927–30 Bal BS 1930 Cle C 1931 **Pit C** 1931–37 KC 1935–36 [Dom 1937] Santo Domingo All-Stars 1937 New E 1938 [Mexico 1938] [Satchel Paige's All-Stars 1939]
KC 1939–48 NY BY 1943 Mem 1943 PhiS 1946 KC 1950 Phi S 1950 Chi AG 1951 KC 1955 [OB minors 1956–58 1961 1965–66]
The most famous and probably greatest Negro Leagues moundsman, the seemingly ageless Paige toiled for 25 years in baseball's Jim Crow era. Paige, a right-hander with great control of a humming fastball, curve, and change-up, was the model of a pitcher for many years—and not just for black fans.

GIBSON, JOSH Joshua B12.21.1911 Buena Vista GA D1.20.1947 Pittsburgh PA BR/TR/6-4/210 d1929 HF 1972 b-Jerry s-Josh Jr C, O, 3b, 1b
Hom 1929–31 Pit C 1932–36 [Dom 1937] **Hom** 1937–40 [Mexico 1940–41] **Hom** 1942–46
Legendary hitting feats and fine all-around defensive skills lend weight to the argument that Gibson was the greatest catcher ever, black or white. Gibson, anchor of the great Homestead Grays and Pittsburgh Crawfords clubs, stroked out at 36, still a remarkable hitter but no longer in shape to catch.

LEONARD, BUCK Walter Fenner B9.8.1907 Rocky Mount NC D11.27.1997 Rocky Mount NC BL/TL/5-10/185 d1933 HF 1972 1b, OF
Bro RG 1933 **Hom** 1934–50 [Mexico 1951 1955] [OB minors 1953]
A popular left-handed-batting first baseman who played 17 years for the Homestead Grays, Leonard hit for average and power, took walks, fielded his position as well as anyone in any league, and possessed smarts and character. He was a star south of the border as well as in the U.S.

IRVIN, MONTE Monford Merrill B2.25.1919 Halesburg AL d1937 HF1973 Col Lincoln Mil 1943–45 ML 1949–56 CF, SS, 3b
New E 1937–42 [Mexico 1942] **New E** 1945–48 [OB minors 1949–50, 1957]
A star with the Newark Eagles by age 21, Irvin had the speed and defensive ability to play center field and shortstop, and hit for power as well as average. Irvin played in several Negro All-Star games, won championships in Latin America, and had an excellent career in the majors.

BELL, COOL PAPA James Thomas B5.17.1903 Starkville MS D3.7.1991 St. Louis MO BB/TL/5-11/150 d1922 HF 1974 b-Fred CF, LF, 1b, P
StL S 1922–31 Det W 1932 KC 1932 **Hom** 1932 Pit C 1933–38 KC 1934 [Dom 1937] [Mexico 1938–41] Chi AG 1942 Mem 1942 **Hom** 1943–46
Speed was Bell's key marker, and he used it on the basepaths and in center field. Arguably the fastest player ever, the well-liked Bell didn't hit with power, but drove opponents to distraction anyway. He played for champions in St. Louis and Pittsburgh and also starred during his four years in Mexico.

JOHNSON, JUDY William Julius B10.26.1899 Snow Hill MD D6.15.1989 Wilmington DE BR/TR/5-11/150 d1918 HF 1974 3b, SS, M
Bac 1918 **Hil** 1921–29 Hom 1930 Hil 1931–32 Pit C 1932–36 Hom 1937
William Julius Johnson played a great third base, hit for high averages, and served as playing manager for the Homestead Grays and Hilldale Daisies. His career started during World War I and lasted through 1937, and Johnson would live another 50 years, some of which he spent as a big-league scout.

CHARLESTON, OSCAR Oscar McKinley "Charlie" B10.14.1896 Indianapolis IN D10.5.1954 Philadelphia PA BL/TL/6-0/190 d1915 HF 1976 CF, 1B, M
Ind ABC 1915–18 Lin S 1915–16 Bow ABC 1916 Chi AG 1919 **Ind ABC** 1920 StL G 1921 **Ind ABC** 1922–23 Har 1924–27 Hil 1928–29 Hom 1930–31 Pit C 1932–38
Tol C 1939 Ind C 1940 Phi S 1941 1942–44 1946–50
Was Charleston the greatest center fielder in baseball history? He could do it all in every facet of the game, and gained well-deserved comparisons to Ruth, Cobb, and Speaker. Winning titles in several different leagues, he played 27 years and was as famous in Latin America as in the U.S.

LLOYD, JOHN HENRY "Pop", "El Cuchara" B4.25.1884 Palatka FL D3.19.1964 Atlantic City NJ BL/TR/5-11/180 d1906 HF 1977 SS, 2b, 1b, C, M
Cub X 1906 Phi G 1907–09 Chi LG 1910 **Lin** 1911–15 Chi AG 1914–17 Lin S 1915 Bro RG 1918–20 Bac 1919 Col B 1921 Bac 1922 Hil 1923 Bac 1924–25 **Lin** 1926–30
Har S 1931 Bac 1931–32
A great shortstop comparable to Honus Wagner, Lloyd was the Dead Ball Era's top Negro Leaguer. He combined smarts and skills in every area of the game into a dominating package, slashing hits all over the field and fielding flawlessly. Babe Ruth once called Lloyd the greatest baseball player ever.

DIHIGO, MARTIN B5.25.1905 Matanzas, Cuba D5.22.1971 Cienfuegos, Cuba BR/TR/6-3/190 d1923 HF 1977 2b, OF, P, 1b, 3b, SS, C, M
Cub SE 1923–27 Hom 1928 Hil 1929–30 Cub SE 1930 Hil 1931 Bal BS 1931 [Venezuela 1933] NY C 1935–36 [Dom 1937] [Mexico 1940–44] NY C 1945
Dihigo could—and did—play every position on the diamond in his 22-year career, much of it spent in Mexico and his native Cuba. An all-around hitter with power and speed who also won over 200 games as a pitcher, Dihigo later served as minister of sports for Fidel Castro.

FOSTER, RUBE Andrew "Jock" B9.17.1879 Calvert TX D12.9.1930 Kankakee IL BR/TR/6-2/200 d1902 HF 1981 b-Willie P, 1b, OF, M
Chi UG 1902 Cub XG 1903 Phi G 1904–06 Chi LG 1907–10 **Chi AG** 1911–26
He was a great pitcher, but Foster is most lauded for his managing skill and founding of the Negro National League. Finished on the mound by the early 1910s, Foster excelled as manager of the Chicago American Giants. He later organized the NNL and ran the league until stepping down in 1926.

DANDRIDGE, RAY Raymond Emmitt "Dannie","Hooks","Squatty","Talua","Mamerto" B8.31.1913 Richmond VA D2.12.1994 Palm Bay FL d1933 HF 1987 BR/TR/5-7/170 3b,2b,SS
Det S 1933 Nas 1933 New D 1933–35 **New E** 1936–39 [Ven 1939] [Mex 1940–41] **New E** 1942 [Mex 1942–43] **New E** 1944 [Mex 1945–48] NY C 1949 [OB minors 1949–53]
Dandridge was really a shortstop playing third, as Willie Wells had short covered for Newark in the 1930s. In addition to being the greatest defensive player at the hot corner in Negro Leagues history, Dandridge was a fine spray hitter who made contact. He played several full seasons in Latin America.

DAY, LEON B10.30.1916 Alexandria VA D3.13.1995 Baltimore MD BR/TR/5-9/170 d1934 HF 1995 Mil 1944–45 P, 2b, OF
Bal BS 1934 Bro E 1935 **New E** 1936–39 [Ven 1940] [Mex 1940] **New E** 1941–43 1946 [Mex 1947–48] Bal EG 1949–50 [OB minors 1950–54]
With the Newark Eagles in the late 1930s and 1940s, Day was black baseball's best pitcher. He threw hard but also deceived hitters with movement and by changing speeds. He could hit, too, and was fast and agile enough to play other positions (center field and second base) when needed.

FOSTER, WILLIE William Hendrick "Bill" B6.12.1904 Calvert TX D9.16.1978 Lorman MS BB/TL/6.1/195 d1923 HF 1996 b-Rube Col Alcorn P, M
Mem 1923–24 Bir 1925 **Chi AG** 1923–30 Hom 1931 KC 1931 **Chi AG** 1932–35 Pit C 1936 **Chi AG** 1937 Mem 1938
This tall lefty pitched for the Chicago American Giants (for a time under his half-brother, Rube Foster) for more than a decade. An early proponent of the slider, he was fast with good control. Foster was also a member of the 1931 Homestead Grays, considered by many to be black baseball's greatest team.

WELLS, WILLIE James "The Devil","El Diablo" B8.10.1905 Austin TX D1.22.1989 Austin TX BR/TR/5-8/160 d1924 HF 1997 s-Willie Jr SS, 3b, 2b
StL S 1924–31 Det W 1932 Hom 1932 KC 1932 Chi AG 1933–34 KC 1934 Chi AG 1935 **New E** 1936–39 [Mex 1940–41] **New E** 1942 [Mex 1943–44] Chi AG 1944
Mem 1944 NY BY 1945–46 Bal EG 1946 Ind/Cin 1947 Mem 1948 [Can 1949–51] Bir 1954
Wells succeeded "Pop" Lloyd as the Negro Leagues' greatest shortstop. He won three titles with the St. Louis Stars, then contributed to other great teams (Homestead, Kansas City, Chicago, and Newark). While not blessed with a great throwing arm, Wells played excellent defense, hit the ball, worked hard, and knew the game.

WILLIAMS, SMOKEY JOE Joseph "Joe","Cyclone","Yank" B4.6.1886 Seguin TX D2.25.1951 New York NY BR/TR/6-4/190 d1911 HF 1999 P, M
Chi G 1910–11 **Lin** 1912–23 Moh 1913 Chi AG 1914 Bac 1916 Hil 1917 Bro RG 1924 **Hom** 1925–32 Det W 1932

The right-handed Williams was early black baseball's best pitcher, as famous in his time as Satchel Paige became. In early years, with the Lincoln Giants, "Cyclone" threw harder than anyone, and years later, with Homestead, won with smarts and command. Williams was especially good in competition against white major leaguers.

ROGAN, BULLET   Wilbur   B7.28.1889   Oklahoma City OK   D3.4.1967   Kansas City MO   BR/TR/5-7/180   d1920   HF 1998   P, OF, 1b, 2b, SS, M, U
KC 1920–38
Some feel that Rogan was the hardest thrower in black baseball. A star for nearly 20 years with the Kansas City Monarchs, the durable righty threw several pitches with great efficiency and also hit well enough to play the outfield. In addition, he served as player-manager for several years.

STEARNES, TURKEY   Norman Thomas   B5.8.1901   Nashville TN   D9.4.1979   Detroit MI   BL/TL/6.0/175   d1923   HF 2000   CF, LF, 1b
Det S 1923–30   Lin 1930   **Det S** 1931   KC 1931   Chi AG 1932–35   Det S 1933   KC 1934   Phi S 1936   Det S 1937   Chi AG 1938   KC 1938–41
Stearnes had the speed to lead off as well as the power to hit cleanup, and he did both during a 20-year career. The hard-nosed Stearnes, a lefty batter, was a fine center fielder; most of his fame came in Detroit, but he also starred for Chicago and Kansas City.

SMITH, HILTON   Lee   B2.27.1912   Giddings TX   D11.18.1983   Kansas City MO   BR/TR/6-2/180   d1932   HF 2001   Col Prairie View A&M   P, OF, 1b
Mon M 1932–35   **KC** 1936–48
Smith threw several pitches, the best a curve that nobody in black baseball (and maybe all baseball) could match. A 13-year star for Kansas City, he had as much talent as teammate Satchel Paige but never the acclaim. While not strong afield, Smith hit enough to play the outfield when needed.

Hall of Fame-Caliber Careers

MACKEY, BIZ   Raleigh   B7.27.1897   Eagle Pass TX   D9.22.1965   Los Angeles CA   BB/TR/6-0/200   d1920   C, SS, 3b, M
nd ABC 1920   Lin 1920   **Hil** 1923–31   Phi S 1933–35   Was D 1936–37   Bal EG 1938–39   New E 1939–41   1945–47   1950
No one played better defense behind the plate than Mackey, who was blessed with a great arm, agility, and strong baseball smarts (he later managed). In addition, he was a fearsome switch-hitter with some power. Mackey played organized black baseball from age 21 until he was past 50.

HILL, PETE   Joseph Preston   B10.12.1880   Pittsburgh PA   D11.26.1951   Buffalo NY   BL/TR/6-1/215   d1899   CF, LF, RF, 1b, 2b, M
Pit K 1899–1900   Cub XG 1901–02   **Phi G** 1903–07   Chi LG 1907–10   **Chi AG** 1911–18   Det S 1919–21   Mil 1923   Bal BS 1924–25
Black baseball's first great outfielder, and a great comparison for Ty Cobb, Hill starred for two decades after the turn of the century. Blessed with speed, the range to play center field, and a strong arm, Hill also drove pitchers crazy on the bases and hit for a high average.

LUNDY, DICK   Richard "King Richard"   B7.10.1898   Jacksonville FL   D1.5.1965   Jacksonville FL   BB/TR/5-11/180   d1916   SS, 3b, 2b, C, M
Bac 1916–18   Hil 1917–19   **Bac** 1920–28   Bal BS 1929–32   Phil S 1933   New D 1934–35   NY C 1935   New E 1936–37   Atl 1938   New E 1938–39
A decade-long star for the Bacharach Giants, Lundy was the Negro Leagues' top shortstop of the 1920s, during which he played on three pennant winners. A switch-hitter with pop who played gracefully and athletically in the field, "King Richard" was a natural leader and a successful playing manager.

TORRIENTE, CRISTOBAL   B11.16.1893   Cienfuegos, Cuba   D4.15.1938   New York NY   BL/TL/5-9/190   d1913   CF, LF, RF, P
Cub SW 1913–18   **Chi AG** 1918–25   KC 1926   Det S 1927–28
A Cuban-born center fielder with a power bat and excellent defensive skills, Torriente excelled for nearly a decade with Rube Foster's American Giants. He wasn't easy to manage—he loved the nightlife, had anger issues, and swung at bad balls—but Torriente was a "franchise player" for many great teams.

WILSON, JUD   Ernest Judson "Boojum"   B2.28.1899   Remington VA   D6.26.1963   Washington DC   BL/TR/5-8/185   d1922   Mil 1918   3b, 1b, 2b, SS, OF, M
Bal BS 1922–30   Hom 1931–32   Pit C 1932   **Phi S** 1933–39   Hom 1940–45
"Boojum" was one of the game's top batters in the 1930s, rapping out hit after hit for several great teams. Tough, pugnacious, and ill-tempered, Wilson argued constantly and was not strong defensively at any position (he played mostly at third) but was a truly fearsome hitter.

SANTOP, LOUIS   Louis Santop Loftin "Top", "Big Bertha"   B1.17.1890   Tyler TX   D1.6.1942   Philadelphia PA   BL/TR/6-4/240   d1909   Mil 1918–19   C, LF, RF, 1b, 3b, M
Phi G 1909–10   Lin 1911–14   Bro RG 1914   Chi AG 1915   NY LS 1915–16   Bro RG 1916–19   Hil 1917–26
The strong-armed, lefty-swinging catcher starred mostly for East Coast teams. Popular, well-paid, and genial, Santop showed an excellent power bat and was celebrated for his glove work. A key error in the 1924 Negro World Series, however, ushered in the decline phase of his great career.

SUTTLES, MULE   George   B3.31.1900   Brockton LA   D7.9.1966   Newark NJ   BR/TR/6-3/215   d1918   1b, LF, RF, M, U
Bir 1923–25   **StL S** 1926–1930   Bal BS 1930   StL S 1931   Det W 1932   Was Pi 1932   Chi AG 1933–35   **New E** 1936–39   Ind ABC 1939   **New E** 1940
NY BY 1941–42   New E 1942–44
While Suttles wasn't much in the field (first base and left field were his positions), he showed prodigious home run power and was particularly dangerous in All-Star competition. He may have struck out a little too often, but when he made contact, Suttles was unstoppable.

BROWN, WILLARD   Jesse "Home Run", "Esse Hombre", "Willie", "Sonny"   B6.26.1911   Shreveport LA   D8.8.1996   Houston TX   BR/TR/6-0/195   d1935   CF, LF, SS
KC 1935–40   [Mex 1940]   **KC** 1941–43   1946–51   Military 1944–45   ML 1947   [OB minors 1950 1953–56]
The top black power hitter of the 1940s, "Home Run" Brown had a huge strike zone but hit enough to play into his forties. Signed by the St. Louis Browns in 1947 at age 36, he hit the first home run ever by an AL black player, but questions lingered about his desire.

REDDING, DICK   Richard "Cannonball"   B1891   Atlanta   D1948   Islip NY   BR/TR/6-4/210   d1911   Mil 1918–19   P, OF, 1b, M
Phi G 1911   Lin 1911–14   Lin S 1915   Ind ABC 1915   **Lin** 1915–16   Bro RG 1916   Chi AG 1917–18   Bro RG 1918   Bac 1919–22   Bro RG 1923–32, 1938
"Cannonball Dick" pitched with blazing speed but also had a crazy-making "hesitation pitch" that froze batters who were waiting for yet another high, hard one. Durable, hard-working, and very successful, Redding was sought by many owners and changed teams often. In his latter years, he was a playing manager.

POLES, SPOT   Spottswood   B11.7.1889   Winchester VA   D9.12.1962   Harrisburg PA   BB/TR/5-7/165   d1909   Mil 1918   CF
Phi G 1909–10   Lin 1911–12   Bro RG 1912   Lin 1913–14   Lin S 1914–16   **Lin** 1917   Hil 1917   Bac 1919   Lin 1919   Hil 1920   Lin 1920–23
The early-century center fielder drove pitchers crazy with his speed, bunting ability, and confidence on the bases. A high-average leadoff hitter, Poles, one of black baseball's earliest stars, spent his entire career on the east coast. He was celebrated as one of the greatest athletes of his day.

TAYLOR, BEN   Benjamin   B7.1.1888   Anderson SC   D1.24.1953   Baltimore MD   BL/TL/6-1/190   d1910   b-C.I.   b-Jim   b-Johnny   1b, P, M, U
StL G 1911–12   Lin 1912   Chi AG 1913–14   **Ind ABC** 1914–18   Hil 1919   Bac 1919   **Ind ABC** 1920–22   Was Po 1923–24   Har 1925   Bal BS 1916–28   Bac 1929   Was Pi 1932
Pro E 1935   Was BS 1938   NY C 1940
Hitting for average and making good contact, fielding flawlessly at first base, and excelling at "inside baseball," Taylor did all the things a good Dead Ball Era player was asked to do. When the lively ball came around, Taylor's batting numbers improved. He also was a longtime manager and umpire.

ALLEN, NEWT   Newton Henry "Colt"   B5.19.1901   Austin TX   D6.11.1988   Cincinnati OH   BR/TR/5-8/160   d1922   2b, 3b, SS, OF, 1b, M
KC 1922–1931   StL S 1931   Det W 1932   Hom 1932   **KC** 1932–44   Ind C 1947
"Colt" ranks as one of the greatest second basemen in black baseball history. Fast, aggressive, and nimble in the field, Allen was also the prototypical #2 hole batter due to his bunting, dashing, and bat control skills. His smarts and all-around ability made Allen perhaps the ultimate Kansas City Monarchs player.

BECKWITH, JOHN   B6.20.1902   Louisville KY   D1.4.1956   New York NY   BR/TR/6-3/220   d1916   SS, 3b, C, OF, 1b, M
Chi UG 1916   Chi G 1916–23   Chi AG 1922–23   Hom 1924   Bal BS 1924–26   Har 1926–27   Hom 1928–29   Lin 29–30   Bal BS 1930–31   New B 1931–32   NY BY 1933–34
New D 1934   Hom 1935   Bro RG 1938
Despite a huge frame, Beckwith was agile enough to play any position, and in fact was a fine defensive shortstop. But defense was just a bonus—he had fantastic power, even though he was a rank pull hitter. Unfortunately, Beckwith also had a temper and didn't play "inside baseball."

BROWN, RAY   Raymond   B2.23.1908   Ashland Grove OH   D1965   Canada   BB/TR/6-1/195   d1930   P, OF, M
Day 1930   Ind ABC 1931   Det W 1932   **Hom** 1932–39   [Mex 1939]   **Hom** 1940–45   [Mex 1946–47]   **Hom** 1947–48   [Mex 1948–49]   [Can 1950–53]
A master of deception and movement, Brown had a full arsenal of pitches headed by a devastating curve. Brown, a star in Latin America and even Canada, sometimes played the outfield when he wasn't pitching. Many in the African-American press felt he would have been an ideal major-league pitcher.

DeMOSS, BINGO   Elwood   B9.5.1889   Topeka KS   D1.26.1965   Chicago IL   BR/TR/6-2/175   d1910   2b, SS, OF, M
Phi G 1913   Chi AG 1913   Ind ABC 1915–16   Bow ABC 1916   **Chi AG** 1917–25   Ind ABC 1926   Det S 1927–30   Cle 1933
DeMoss could do it all—run the bases, play sterling second base, hit for average and bunt, and outwit opponents. A perfect Dead Ball-Era player, he was highly celebrated and may be the greatest second sacker in the history of black baseball. DeMoss also spent nearly a decade as a manager.

WRIGHT, BILL   Burnis "Wild Bill"   B6.6.1914   Milan TN   D8.3.1996   Aguascalientes, Mexico   BB/TR/6-4/220   d1932   CF, RF, LF
Nas 1932–1934   Col EG 1935   Was EG 1936–37   **Bal EG** 1938–39   [Mex 1940–41]   Bal EG 1942   [Mex 1943–44]   **Bal EG** 1945   [Mex 1946–56]
A seven-time All-Star who could play both center field (excellent range) and right field (a strong arm), Wright was a capable #3 or #4 hitter with power and speed who rarely struck out. Wright started his career as a pitcher, but soon switched to the outfield. He won the 1943 Triple Crown in Mexico.

HUGHES, SAMMY T.   Samuel Thomas   B10.20.1910   Louisville TX   D8.9.1981   Los Angeles CA   BR/TR/6-3/190   d1931   Mil 1943–46   2b, SS
Lou WS 1929–31   Was Pi 1932   Nas 1933–34   Col EG 1935   Was EG 1936–37   **Bal EG** 1938–40   [Mex 1941]   Bal EG 1942, 1946

An excellent second baseman who saw his action before the Second World War, Hughes did everything well both offensively and defensively and had good speed, though he was not a home-run hitter. In 1946, his final season, he tutored Jim Gilliam to take over his position in Baltimore.

MARCELLE, OLIVER H. [Marcell] [Marcel] "Ghost" B6.24.1897 Thibedeaux LA D6.12.1949 Denver CO BR/TR/5-9/160 d1918 s-Everett 3b, SS
Bro RG 1918–19 Det S 1919 **Bac** 1920–22 Lin 1923–25 **Bac** 1925–28 Bal BS 1929 Bro RG 1930
Considered the best third baseman of the 1920s, Marcelle was a spectacular defender and a good enough hitter to bat second or third for many quality teams. "Ghost" had a temper and was easily riled, and lost part of his nose in a fight over a dice game.

BYRD, BILL William "Daddy" B7.15.1907 Canton GA D1.4.1991 Philadelphia PA BB/TR/6-1/210 d1932 P, 1b, OF
Col T 1932 Col BB 1933 Nas 1933 Cle RS 1934 Col EG 1935 Was EG 1936–37 **Bal EG** 1938–39 [Ven 1940] **Bal EG** 1941–50
"Daddy" Byrd was a beneficiary of the "grandfather" clause that allowed veteran pitchers to throw spitballs. He also used the knuckleball to great effect, and in his later years became a mentor to younger teammates. Byrd was slow afoot, but could hit and sometimes played first base and the outfield.

JOHNSON, HOME RUN Grant B1874 Findlay OH D1964 Buffalo NY BR/TR/5-10/170 d1895 SS, 2b, M
[OB minors 1894] PF 1895–98 Chi CG 1899 Chi U 1900 Cub XG 1903–04 Phi G 1905–06 Bro RG 1906–09 Chi L 1910 Chi G 1911 Lin 1911 Bro RG 1912
Lin 1912–13 Moh 1913 Lin S 1916
Black baseball's first great shortstop played with the best teams of his era, earning his nickname with power blasts as well as high averages. While not as slick defensively as others, he was solid with the glove. A stickler for conditioning, Johnson played until he was fifty-eight.

Other All Time Greats

RADCLIFFE, DOUBLE DUTY Theodore Roosevelt "Ted" B7.7.1902 Mobile AL BR/TR/5-10/190 d1928 b-Alex C, P, M
Det S 1928–29 StL S 1930 Det S 1931 Hom 1931 Pit C 1932 Col BB 1933 Cle B 1933 NY BY 1933 Hom 1933 Chi AG 1934 [Bismarck 1934–35] Bro E 1935 Hom 1936
Cin T 1936–37 Mem 1938–39 [Mex 1940] Chi AG 1941–43 Bir 1942–45 KC 1945 Bir 1946 Hom 1946 Lou B 1949 Chi AG 1949–50
As both a pitcher and catcher, "Duty" was a valuable member of the 1931 Homestead Grays, perhaps black baseball's greatest club. He had strong receiving skills and hit for power, and on the hill he mastered various quasi-legal deliveries. Radcliffe's colorful nature makes him a witty raconteur to this day.

DAVIS, PIPER Lorenzo B7.3.1917 Piper AL D5.21.1997 Birmingham AL BR/TR/6-3/186 d1942 2b, 1b, SS, M
Bir 1942–50 [OB minors 1950–58]
For nearly a decade, Davis was one of the game's top second basemen. Steady and dependable in the field, he turned the double play well and made solid contact at bat with some power. The Boston Red Sox made him their first black player, but Davis never made the majors.

RADCLIFFE, ALEX Alexander "Alec" B7.26.1905 Mobile AL D7.18.1983 Chicago IL BR/TR/6.0/205 d1932 b-"Double Duty" 3b, SS, OF
Chi AG 1932–35 NY C 1936 **Chi AG** 1936–39, 1941–42 Bir 1942 **Chi AG** 1943–44 Ind/Cin 1944–45 Mem 1946 **Chi AG** 1949
"Double Duty's" younger brother, a fearsome clutch hitter, might be the Negro Leagues' greatest All-Star performer, starring in 11 midsummer classics. Perhaps the NAL's best-ever third baseman, he was considered lazy by some observers but had a penchant to play his hardest for the biggest crowds.

DONALDSON, JOHN Wesley B2.20.1892 Glasgow MO D4.14.1970 Chicago IL BL/TL/6-0/185 d1913 Mil 1917 P, OF
[All Nations 1913–1917] Ind ABC 1918 Bro RG 1918 Lin 1918 Det S 1919 **KC** 1920–24 1933 1934
The best black left-handed pitcher of the 1910s, Donaldson threw a baffling curve; when his arm went bad, he relied on control and smarts to star for the Kansas City Monarchs. When not pitching, Donaldson filled in capably in the lineup, and transferred full-time to the outfield when his arm finally died.

MENDEZ, JOSE (Baez) "Joe", "The Black Diamond" B3.19.1887 Cardenas, Mantanzas, Cuba BR/TR/5-8/160 d1908 P, SS, 3b, 2b, OF, M
Bro RG 1908 Cub SW 1909–12 [All Nations 1912–17] Chi AG 1918 Det S 1919 KC 1920–26
"The Black Diamond" made his name both in Cuba and later in Kansas City for a blazing fastball, a good curve, an unmatched ability to change speeds, and a smooth, rapid delivery now called "quick-pitching." Mendez' fastball was so powerful that he once accidentally killed a teammate in practice.

WINTERS, NIP James H. Jr. "Jessee", "Nipper", "Jim" B4.29.1899 Washington DC D12.12.1971 Hockessin DE BL/TL/6-5/225 d1920 P, 1b, OF
Bal BS 1920 Bac 1921–22 **Hil** 1922–28 Hom 1928 Lin 1928–29 Bal BS 1929 New B 1931 Hil 1931 Bac 1931 Was Pi 1932 Bac 1932–33 Phi S 1933
Spending his entire career in the East, southpaw Winters threw a curveball that broke sharply (sometimes well out of the strike zone). A mighty carouser, Winters was devastating when on his game, and also hit well enough to occasionally play first base. He was very successful against major leaguers in exhibitions.

THOMAS, CLINT Clinton Cyrus "Hawk", "Buckeye" B11.25.1896 Greenup KY D12.2.1990 Charleston WV BR/TR/5-8/180 d1920 CF, RF, 2b
Bro RG 1920 Col B 1921 Det S 1922 **Hil** 1923–28 Bac 1928–29 Lin 1930 Har S 1931 Ind ABC 1932 **NY BY** 1932–35 New E 1936 **NY BY** 1937–38
Regarded as a complete player, "Hawk" flagged down everything hit to him in the outfield and hit for average and power. Popular with fans and teammates, Thomas was nicknamed "The Black DiMaggio" for his balance of skills. He once homered off Fidel Castro in an exhibition game in Cuba.

HARRIS, VIC Elander Victor B6.10.1905 Pensacola FL D2.23.1978 San Fernando CA BL/TR/5-10/168 d1923 Def 1943 LF, RF, CF, 1b
Cle TS 1923 Tol T 1923 Cle B 1924 Chi AG 1924–25 Hom 1925–31 Det W 1932 **Hom** 1932–33 Pit C 1934 **Hom** 1935–48 Bal EG 1949 Bir 1950
A lefty swinger who made solid contact and hit the ball all over the field, Harris played all three outfield positions with skill. Speedy and pugnacious, "Vicious Vic" ran the bases with abandon and never shied from a fight, but also was a steady and patient player-manager in his later years.

SCALES, GEORGE Walter "Tubby" B8.16.1900 Talladega AL D4.1976 Los Angeles CA BR/TR/5-11/195 2b, 3b, 1b, SS, OF, M
Pit K 1921 StL G 1921 Lin 1923–25 Hom 1925–26 New S 1926 Lin 1926–29 Hom 1929–31 NY BY 1932–34 Hom 1935 NY BY 1936 Bal EG 1938 NY BY 1939–40
Phi S 1940 Bal EG 1940–44 NY BY 1945 Bal EG 1946–48
"Tubby" lacked range at second base, but knew the hitters and used a very strong arm to turn the double play. He hit fifth for the 1931 Homestead Grays, supplying power and average, and continued to hit well into his forties. A real character, Scales was pugnacious and a tough manager.

MONROE, BILL William B1876 D3.16.1915 Chicago IL BR/TR d1896 2b, 3b, SS, 1b
Chi U 1896–1900 Cub XG 1900 Phi G 1903–06 Bro RG 1907 [Qua C 1908] Bro RG 1908–10 Chi AG 1911–13 Chi G 1913 Chi AG 1914
John McGraw said Monroe, whose career was only halted by death, was the greatest player ever. He could play any infield position with grace and style and had the skills to bat both leadoff and fourth. A handsome man, Monroe was the toast of black baseball audiences in Chicago and New York.

O'NEIL, BUCK John Jordan "Nancy" B11.13.1911 Carabelle FL BR/TR/6-2/190 d1937 Mil 1943–45 1b, M
Mem 1 **KC** 1938–43 1946–55
Famous for longevity, humor, and grace, O'Neil was also a fine player, especially in Kansas City. A slick-fielding first baseman who hit for high averages, O'Neil punched the ball the opposite way, making him a natural hit-and-run man. O'Neil later became the first black major league scout and signed Ernie Banks and Lou Brock to contracts for the Chicago Cubs.

BANKHEAD, SAM Samuel Howard B9.18.1905 Empire AL D7.24.1976 Pittsburgh PA BR/TR/5-8/175 d1830 b-Dan b-Fred b-Joe b-Garnett SS, CF, 2b, LF, RF, 3b
Bir 1929 Nas 1930 Bir 1931–32 Lou BC 1932 Nas 1932–34 KC 1934 Pit C 1935–36 [Dom 1937] Bir 1938 Pit C 1938 Tol C 1939 **Hom** 1939
[Mex 1940–41] **Hom** 1942–46 [Can 1951]
He had the range and arm to play both shortstop and center field, and would fill in wherever needed. The speedy Bankhead had some power but was more of a high-average hitter. While he starred in Cuba and against major-league players, Bankhead enjoyed his greatest fame in Pittsburgh.

DIXON, RAP Herbert Albert B9.2.1902 Kingston GA D7.20.1944 Detroit MI BR/TR/6-2/185 d1922 RF, CF, LF, M
Har 1922–23 Was Po 1924 Har 1924–27 Bal BS 1928–30 Chi AG 1930–31 Bal BS 1931 Hil 1931 Pit C 1932 Was Pi 1932 Phi S 1933 Bal BS 1934 Pit C 1934 Bro E 1935
NY 1935 Hom 1936 Pit C 1937
Famous for his disciplined batting approach, Dixon put the ball in play and racked up high averages and good power totals. He had the arm to play right field and the range to excel in center, and did both. Injuries and illness curtailed his career, and Dixon died young.

COOPER, ANDY Andrew L. "Lefty" B.4.4.1896 Waco TX D6.3.1841 Waco TX BR/TL/6-2/220 d1920 P, M
Det S 1920–27 **KC** 1928–30 **Det S** 1930 KC 1931–41
Using a solid repertoire, command, and smarts, Cooper remained an effective pitcher into his forties. He did all the things that make lefty pitchers helpful—he had a great pickoff move, changed speeds, and had a great screwball. Just prior to his premature death, Cooper was a successful manger for Kansas City.

JENKINS, FATS Clarence B1.19.1898 New York NY D12.6.1968 Philadelphia PA BL/TL/5-7/180 d1920 OF, M
Lin 1920 Bac 1922 Har G 1923–27 Lin 1928 Hil 1928 Bac 1928–29 Bal BS 1930 Lin 1930 Har S 1931 Pit C 1932 NY BY 1932–34 Bro E 1935 NY BY 1936–38 Pit C 1938
Tol C 1939 Bro RG 1939–40 NY BY 1940 Phi S 1940
A solid corner outfielder and leadoff man with speed, bat control, and smarts at bat and on the bases, Jenkins was also a superb basketball player as well as a famed musician who sang and played piano. A hustling player, Jenkins spent most of his career in New York.

PETWAY, BRUCE "Buddy" B1883 Nashville TN D7.4.1941 Chicago IL BB/TR/5-11/170 d1906 b-Howard C, 1b, OF, M
Cub XG 1906 Phi G 1907–09 Chi L 1910 **Chi AG** 1911–18 Det S 1919–25

he best defensive catcher in the game during black baseball's early years, the surprisingly lean and athletic Petway kept opposing runners close to the base but was an excellent asestealer himself. His bat skills and speed made him that unusual specimen—a catcher who sometimes batted leadoff.

DUNCAN, FRANK B2.14.1901 Kansas City MO D12.4.1973 Kansas City MO BR/TR/6-0/175 d1920 s-Frank III C, 1b, M
hi G 1920–21 **KC** 1921–31 NY BY 1931 Pit C 1932 Hom 1932 **KC** 1932–34 NY C 1935–37 **KC** 1937 Chi AG 1938 1940 **KC** 1941–47
a superb handler of pitchers who caught Paige, Rogan, Donaldson, and others for Kansas City, Duncan also had a strong arm and agility behind the plate. He was slow and only a nediocre hitter, but the very tough—almost mean—Duncan later served as a patient and effective manager.

BROWN, LARRY "Iron Man" B9.5.1905 Pratt City AL D4.7.1972 Memphis TN BB/TR/5-8/180 d1919 C, M
ir 1919 Ind ABC 1921–23 Pit K 1922 **Mem** 1923–25 Det S 1926 Chi AG 1927 **Mem** 1927–29 Chi AG 1929 Lin 1930 **Mem** 1931 Har S 1931 NY BY 1932 Chi AG 1932–35
hi S 1936–38 **Mem** 1938–40 Chi AG 1940 **Mem** 1941–48
Good enough to play on several championship clubs despite only an average bat, Brown was a fine defensive catcher. Although Brown was a heavy drinker, he gained the nickname ron Man" and played into his forties. He was tough on umpires but played the game hard.

WARFIELD, FRANK Francis Xavier "The Weasel" B1895 Indianapolis IN D7.24.1932 Pittsburgh PA BR/TR/5-7/160 d1915 2b, SS, 3b, OF, M
tL G 1914–15 Ind ABC 1915 StL G 1915–16 Bow ABC 1916 Ind ABC 1917–18 Day 1919 Det S 1919–21 KC 1921 Det S 1922 Hil 1923–28 Bal BS 1929–31 Was Pi 1932
a hustling middle infielder with fine leadoff skills and all the defensive tools (arm, range, hands, and an underhand "snap" throw), Warfield was a pariah with fellow players due to a violent nature that led to arguments. He carried a knife and bit off part of Oliver Marcelle's nose in a fight.

LYONS, JIMMIE B11.6.1892 Chicago IL D10.1963 Chicago IL BL/TR/5-8/175 d1910 LF, CF, RF, M
tL G 1910–11 Lin 1911 StL G 1912 Bro RG 1914 StL G 1915–16 Bow ABC 1916 Ind ABC 1916–17 StL G 1917 Chi G 1917 StL G 1919 Det S 1920 Bac 1920
hi AG 1921–23 Was Po 1924 Cle B 1924 Chi AG 1924–25 Lou BC 1932
yons' skill set was much valued in the early 20th century—he was one of the fastest players in baseball history and could bunt his way on base almost at will. Lyons was a star at mes, but lacked power and was not exceptional defensively, and suffered from injuries.

BROOKS, CHESTER "Irving","Beattie" B Nassau, Bahamas BR/TR d1918 CF, RF
ro RG 1918–33
ube Foster discovered him pitching in the late teens, but Brooks spent most of his career as a center fielder. He had the arm to play right field and enough power to hit fourth, but ayed his entire career with Brooklyn, who rarely contended for a championship.

OMS, ALEJANDRO "El Caballero","Walla Walla","Papa" B3.13.1895 Santa Clara, Cuba D11.9.1946 BL/TL/5-9/190 d1917 CF, LF, RF
ub SE 1917–1922–33 AC 1935
a showy player with a terrific power stroke, Oms was a key member of the Cuban Stars of the 1920s. He played a solid center field and could steal bases when needed. "El Caballero," who played for several championship clubs, was elected to the Cuban HOF.

ROBINSON, NEIL Cornelius Randall "Shadow" B7.7.1908 Grand Rapids MI D7.23.1983 Cincinnati OH BR/TR/5–11/182 d1934 CF, LF, RF, SS, 3b
om 1934 Cin T 1936–37 **Mem** 1938–52
a perennial All-Star, the popular Robinson (nicknamed "Shadow") was one of the game's top outfielders due to his fearsome power. While he was only average defensively, struck out so often, and struggled with the bottle, Robinson made undeniable offensive contributions in the NAL.

KIMBRO, HENRY Allen "Kimmie","Jimbo" B2.19.1912 Nashville TN D1.31.2001 Philadelphia PA BL/TR/5-8/175 d1937 CF, LF, M
as EG 1937 **Bal EG** 1938–1940 NYBY 1941 **Bal EG** 1942–51
n the field, Kimbro was nearly flawless, playing a solid center field with good range and doing it all at bat. The offensive leader boards perennially boasted his name in several ategories. Perhaps he was not more celebrated due to an aloof and brooding nature that invited little intimacy.

BENSON, GENE Eugene "Spider" B10.2.1913 Pittsburgh PA D4.6.1999 Philadelphia PA BL/TL/5-8/180 d1933 CF, LF
as EG 1936 Phi S 1937 Pit C 1938 Hom 1938 **Phi S** 1938–41 New E 1942 **Phi S** 1942–48
n unusual player, Benson was a left-handed batter who hit lefties better than righties. He used a slap approach but still generated good power. The Philly Star also was a fine utfielder with excellent range who made "circus" catches. Later he was a winter-ball roommate and counselor to Jackie Robinson.

WHITE, CHANEY S "Reindeer","Liz" B4.15.1894 Dallas TX D2.1.1967 Philadelphia PA BR/TL/5-10/195 d1919 OF
l 1919 Chi AG 1920 Hil 20–22 **Bac** 1923–24 Was Po 1924 Wil 1925 **Bac** 1925–28 Hil 1928 Hom 1930 Hil 1930–32 Bal BS 1932 Phi S 1933–35 NY C 1936
hite hit for high averages with moderate power. Fast and strong, he ran the bases with reckless abandon, which gave him the label of a "dirty" player. Off the field, he was well liked. espite his speed and good hands, White was best in left field because of a weak arm.

CRUTCHFIELD, JIMMIE John William B3.15.1910 Ardmore MO D3.31.1993 Chicago IL BL/TR/5-7/150 d1930 Mil 1943–44 CF, RF, LF
r 1930 Ind ABC 1931 Pit C 1931–33 Phi S 1933 **Pit C** 1934–36 New E 1937–38 Tol C 1939 Ind C 1940 Chi AG 1941–42 Cle Bu 1944 Chi AG 1944–45
mall in size but big in heart, Crutchfield was a team man all the way who played excellent "little ball." A superb outfielder, he was popular both for his defensive ability and entertaining unts. While not exactly a batting threat, he did hit for average and made other contributions.

GARDNER, JELLY Floyd B9.27.1895 Russellville AK D3.1.1977 Chicago IL BL/TR/5-7/160 d1919 RF, CF, LF, 1b
et S 1919 **Chi AG** 1920–1930 Lin G 1927 Hom 1928 Det S 1932 **Chi AG** 1933
n excellent outfielder blessed with speed, bunting skills, and a line-drive bat, Gardner also worked pitchers for walks, which made him a better leadoff man than some of his ontemporaries. Gardner did have trouble with breaking pitches, and was a carouser with a combative nature.

SMUKES, DIZZY William B3.15.1890 Birmingham AL D6.30.1961 Campbell OH BR/TR/6-0/180 d1910 Mil 1917–18 P, M
hi G 1912 Phi G 1913 Bro RG 1913–14 Lin S 1914 Ind ABC 1915–16 Chi AG 1916 Ind ABC 1917–18 Day 1918–19 Ind ABC 1920–21 Pit K 1921–23 Ind ABC 1923–24
r 1924 Mem 1925 StL S 1926–29 Chi AG 1930 Det W 1932 Col BB 1933–34 Chi AG 1935 StL S 1936–37 Bir 1938 Atl 1939 Hom 1940 KC 1941–42 Mem 1942 KC 1943–51
his college-educated, submarining hurler, who pitched with smarts and breaking stuff, is said to have tutored Carl Mays. He pitched for more than two decades and later served as a anager, Negro League club and league executive, and even as a major league scout.

TRENT, TED Theodore "Highpockets","Stringbean","Big Florida" B12.17.1903 Jacksonville FL D1.10.1944 Chicago IL BR/TR/6-3/185 d1927 P
tL S 1927–31 Was Pi 1932 Det W 1932 H om 1932 Bal BS 1932 KC 1932 NY BY 1933–34 Chi AG 1934–35 Chi AG 1936–39
he tall righty had his share of nicknames as well as strikeout stuff—a fastball, a variety of baffling curves, and a sharp slider. A great big-game pitcher, Trent was one of the best itchers in black baseball, but his career and life were shortened by a weak immune system brought about by the bottle.

SHIVELY, GEORGE Anner "Rabbit" B1893 Lebanon KY D6.7.1962 Bloomington IN BL/TR d1910 OF
d ABC 1914–15 Bow ABC 1916 Ind ABC 1916–18 Bac 1919–20 **Ind ABC** 1920–21 Bac 1921–22 Ind ABC 1923 Bro RG 1924 Was Po 1924 Bac 1924–25
he Rabbit" ran the bases at will and with great success. While Shively could run down fly balls, bunt for hits, and even show power on occasion, he was never one of the game's iggest stars in a time where these skills were almost a requirement to play.

MATHIS, VERDELL "Lefty" B11.18.1914 Crawfordsville AK D10.30.1998 Memphis TN BL/TL/5-11/150 d1940 P, OF, 1b
em 1940–50 Phi S 1943
he NAL's best lefty during the 1940s, Mathis' signature pitch was his curve, but he also threw hard and boasted a screwball and an excellent pickoff move. A big workload took its toll, owever—after World War II he underwent elbow surgery to remove bone chips and never again excelled.

BARNHILL, DAVE David "Impo","Skinny" B10.30.1914 Greenville NC D1.8.1983 Miami FL BB/TR/5-7/145 d1937 P
al 1937 Eth 1937–40 **NY C** 1941–49 [OB minors 1949–53]
e played four years with the Ethiopian Clowns, who were as much a comedy club as a competitive team, but Barnhill had a serious fastball. When he went to New York in 1941, kinny" immediately became a dominating strikeout pitcher. Barnhill also could help at bat and on the bases.

BREWER, CHET Chester Arthur B1.14.1907 Leavenworth KS D3.26.1990 Whittier CA BB/TR/6-4/187 d1925 P
C 1925–31 Was Pi 1932 **KC** 1932–35 [Bismarck 1935–36] NY C 1936 **KC** 1937 [Dom 1937] [Mex 1938–39] **KC** 1940–41 Phi S 1941 Cle Bu 1942–43 [Mex 1944]
hi AG 1946 Cle Bu 1946–48 [OB minors 1952]
hile Brewer was a finesse pitcher, using a screwball, slider, curve, or emery ball to get hitters out, he also would throw fastballs inside. He played all around the world, including in Asia, d was the first black American to play in Mexico. Brewer lived a full and fascinating life.

WICKWARE, FRANK "Smokey","Rawhide","The Red Ant","Smiley" B3.8.1888 Coffeeville KS D11.2.1967 Schenectady NY BR/TR d1910 Mil 1918–19 P
hi L 1909–10 Chi AG 1911–12 Bro RG 1912–13 Moh 1913–14 Lou WS 1914 Bro RG 1914 Chi AG 1914–16 Ind ABC 1916 Jew ABC 1917 Chi AG 1917–18 Det S 1919
n 1920 Chi AG 1920–21 [Can 1921] Lin 1925
fastballer with excellent mechanics and command, Wickware was, as one of the top pitchers of the teens, a tremendous gate attraction who—as was the practice—often jumped ntracts to get more money. Unfortunately, he was also a drinker, and his habits shortened his brilliant career.

TIANT, LUIS Eleuterio Sr. "Lefty","Sir","Skinny" B8.27.1906 Havana, Cuba D12.10.1976 Milton MA BL/TL/5-11/175 d1930 s-Luis P
ub SW 1930–32 Cub HD 1934 NY C 1935–36 1939–40 1943 1945–47

Using a herky-jerky motion, as his son would decades later, the elder Tiant had control of three power pitches (fastball, curve, slider) but his best pitch was a screwball. He worked with a junkballer's attitude and his mix of skills and approach served him well, especially in big games.

BROWN, BARNEY [Brownez] "Brinquitos" B10.23.1908 Hartsville SC D10.1.1985 Philadelphia PA BL/TL/5-9/165 d1931 Mil 1943 P, OF
Cub HD 1931–32 NY BY 1936–37 **Phi S** 1937 NY BY 1937–39 [Mex 1939–41] **Phi S** 1942–44 [Mex 1945] **Phi S** 1945–49 [Mex 1950–52] [OB minors 1952–53]
With good command and a screwball, Brown starred on the East Coast in the 30s and 40s, appearing in several All-Star contests. He also was a big winner in Puerto Rican winter ball. Brown was nearly as good at the plate as on the mound despite a small frame.

PARNELL, ROY "Red" B9.17.1905 Austin TX D6.1.1969 Terrell TX BR/TR/5-10/180 d1926 LF, RF, CF, 1b, P, M
Bir 1926–28 Mon M 1932 Nas 1934 Col EG 1935 **Phi S** 1936–43 [Dom 1937] NY BY 1937 Pit C 1946 Hou 1950
Unlike many Negro League stars, Parnell did not run particularly well or have a strong throwing arm. What he did was hit, both for average and power, and catch everything he reached in the outfield. Another drinking man, he batted #2 in the lineup for most of his long career.

CARR, GEORGE Henry "Tank" B1895 California D1.14.1948 Los Angeles CA BB/TR/6-2/230 d1917 1b, 3b, OF, 2b, C
KC 1920–22 Hil 1923–28 Lin 1928 **Bac** 1928–29 1933 Phi S 1933–34
A very productive hitter for power and high average in the 20s, Carr had some speed but was used almost exclusively at first base. He had a high arc, but Carr's career declined quickly because of a serious drinking problem and some resulting disciplinary issues.

STRONG, TED T.R. B1.2.1914 South Bend IL D3.1.1978 Chicago IL BB/TR/6-6/210 d1937 Mil 1943–45 RF, 1b, LF, SS, CF, 3b
Ind A 1937 Ind ABC 1938 KC 1937–39 [Mex 1940] KC 1941–42 1946–47 Ind C 1948 [OB minors 1950] Chi AG 1951
As his name suggests, Strong was a power hitter who disdained "little ball." A good right fielder with defensive tools, he won homer and RBI crowns, and hit for average, despite a free-swinging approach. Strong also played for the original Globetrotters basketball team. Drinking and womanizing shortened his career.

SAMPSON, TOMMY Thomas "Toots" B8.31.1912 Calhoun AL BR/TR/6-1/180 d1940 2b, 1b, OF, M
Bir 1940–47 Chi AG 1948 NY C 1949
"Toots" made four consecutive All-Star appearances at second base. Despite losing his right index finger in a coal mining accident, Sampson played strong defense and had fine bat control. He hit for average and stole bases, but a broken leg suffered in a 1944 car crash shortened his career.

EASTERLING, HOWARD B11.26.1911 Mount Olive MS D9.6.1993 Collins MS BB/TR/5-10,175 d1936 Mil 1944–45 3b, 2b, SS, OF
Cin T 1936–37 Chi AG 1938 Hom 1940–43 1946–47 NY C 1949 [Mex 1951–1952 1954]
Voted an All-Star both as a third baseman and shortstop, Easterling was a five-tool player who batted from both sides. Since he only started his organized black baseball career at 25, and he missed two years due to World War II, Easterling's star does not shine as bright as it might have.

EARLE, FRANK Charles [Frank] [Earl] [Charles Babcock] [Frank Peles] BR/TR d1906 LF, RF, CF, P, M
Bro RG 1909–14 StL G 1915 Lin 1915 Bro RG 1916–17 GCT 1918–19 Bac 1919 Pen 1919
The respected outfielder could run and hit, and was also the best pitcher on the 1909 championship Royal Giants club. An excellent table-setter, he spent most of his career in the East. Like many stars of his era, he is plagued by a lack of documentation of his greatness.

JOHNSON, HEAVY Oscar B11.2.1896 Atchison KS D1.1964 Cleveland OH BR/TR/6-0/250 d1922 OF, C, 2b
KC 1922–24 Bal BS 1925–26 Har 1927 Cle T 1928 Mem 1928–33
One of the heaviest players of his time, Johnson was a premier power producer who nonetheless played the outfield (though with little speed or grace) for quality teams. The oft-told stories of just-awoken Negro League players homering with fungo bats seems somehow more believable in Johnson's case.

Long and Distinguished Careers

GRANT, LEROY BR/TR/6-4/215 d1911 Mil1918–19 1b
Chi AG 1911 Lin 1912–15 Moh 1913 **Chi AG** 1916–25 Ind ABC 1923 Cle B 1924
The burly, plodding first sacker was slow and hit low in the order, but connected for big power, ran the bases intelligently, and usually played excellent defense. A key part of Rube Foster's American Giants dynasty, Grant also played with the New York Lincoln Giants early in his career.

CANNADY, REV Walter B3.6.1904 Lake City FL D12.3.1981 Ft. Myers FL BR/TR/6-0/180 d1921 2b, 3b, SS, OF, 1b, P, M
Col B 1921 Cle TS 1922 Hom 1923–24 Har 1925–27 Lin 1926–28 Hil 1928 Hom 1929 Lin 1930 Hil 1931 Pit C 1932 NYBY 1933–35 Pit C 1936 NYBY 1936–39 Bro RG 1940 Chi AG 1942 Ind/Cin 1943–44 Hom 1944 NY C 1945
A good hitter who excelled at pounding curve balls, Cannady had the defensive skills to man any infield spot, but played mostly at second base. He was mean, angry, and moody, not a favorite of other players, and never stayed in one place for very long.

SEAY, DICK Richard William B11.30.1904 West New York NY D4.6.1981 Jersey City NJ BR/TR/5-8/156 d1925 Mil 1943–45 2b, SS, 3b
Bro RG 1925 New S 1926 Bal BS 1926 Bro RG 1927–31 New B 1931 Bal BS 1932–33 Phi S 1933–36 Pit C 1935–36 NYBY 1936 New E 1937–40 NY BY 1941–42 1946–47
The slightly-built Seay, one of black baseball's all-time best defensive second basemen, played a key role for several championship teams. While a relatively weak hitter, Seay had the ability to bunt and hit-and-run, and his glove work was good enough to make up for his bat.

MALARCHER, DAVE David Julius "Gentleman Dave","Cap","Preacher" B10.18.1894 Whitehall LA D5.11.1982 Chicago IL BB/TR/5-7/148 d1916 Mil 1918–19 3b,2b,SS,RF,C,P,M
Ind ABC 1916–18 Det S 1919 **Chi AG** 1920–28 Chi AG 1931–35
Malarcher, an outstanding defensive third baseman, did everything well enough to help teams win but was not a world-class hitter. Most of his offensive value came from bunting, place-hitting, and speed. A clean-living man, Malarcher was an intelligent player who later managed.

BELL, WILLIAM Sr. B8.31.1897 Lavaca County TX D3.16.1969 El Campo TX BR/TR/5-11/185 d1923 s-William Jr. P, OF, M
KC 1923–30 Har S 1931 Det W 1932 Hom 1932 Pit C 1932–35 New D 1935 New E 1936–37 1948
A winning pitcher with good command of a fastball, curve, and change, Bell made a positive impact on several pennant races, especially in Kansas City. Bell hit well enough to play the outfield, taught younger pitchers, and always took the ball. After his playing career, he was a coach and manager.

McNAIR, HURLEY Alen "Mac","Bugger" B10.28.1888 Marshall TX D12.2.1948 Kansas City MO BB/TR/5-6/150 d1911 RF, LF, CF, P, U
Chi G 1911–12 Chi UG 1914 Chi AG 1915–16 Chi UG 1916 [All Nations 1917] Det S 1919 **KC** 1920–27 Det S 1928 KC 1934 Cin T 1937
A star outfielder for Kansas City, McNair was a patient hitter with power who could run and field. While he was haunted by a reputation for self-centeredness, McNair taught young players, including Willie Wells, then later umpired in the NAL—carrying a knife to emphasize his point.

HOLLAND, BILL Elvis William B2.2.1901 Indianapolis IN D New York NY BB/TR/5-9/180 d1920 P, M
Det S 1920–22 Chi AG 1921 Lin 1923–24 Bro RG 1925–27 Hil 1927 Lin 1927–30 Har S 1931 **NY BY** 1932–41 Phi S 1941
After an impressive first three years with Detroit, power pitcher Holland's career nosedived until his 1929 comeback. In 1930, he went 29-2 with the Lincoln Giants in their last season, becoming the first black player to pitch in Yankee Stadium and then the ace of Black Yankees staff in the 1930s.

ROGERS, NAT [Rodgers] William Nathaniel B6.7.1893 Spartanburg SC D12.1981 Memphis TN BL/TR/5-11/160 d1923 RF, LF, 1b
Bro RG 1923 Phi G 1924 Har 1924–25 **Mem** 1924–30 Chi AG 1927–28 Bir 1930 KC 1931 Chi AG 1931–34 Bro E 1935 Chi AG 1944
Hard-nosed and slightly built, Rogers was a powerful line-drive hitter as well as a good baserunner and bunter. His 31-game hitting streak propelled Chicago to a 1927 World Series victory; he also hit cleanup in 1932–33 for the pennant-winning American Giants. Defensively, Rogers was adequate with a plus arm.

DAVIS, STEEL ARM Walter C. B1902.Madison WI D1935 Chicago IL BL/TL/6-1/175 d1923 OF, 1b
Det S 1923 **Chi AG** 1924–30 Chi AG 1931–35 Nas 1934 Bro E 1935
A hot-tempered, hard-playing, high-average hitter with power, Davis' nickname derived from his career start as a pitcher. Because of his ability at the plate, however, he ended up as an All-Star outfielder and a middle-of-the-order hitter for the powerful American Giants. Davis was shot to death in a barroom brawl.

FRANCIS, BILL William "Billy","Brodie","Ducky" BR/TR/5-5/140 d1904 3b, SS, M
Phi G 1904–1910 Lin 1911–13 Moh 1913 Chi AG 1914–1919 Hil 1920–22 Bac 1923 Cle B 1924 Wil 1925 Chi AG 1925 Chi G 1925
Called one of the best black ballplayers of his era by legendary umpire Jocko Conlan, the stocky but speedy third sacker played on many great early teams. Soft hands and quick reflexes enabled him to play shallow at third; offensively he drew plenty of walks, and hit .396 in 1914.

DUNCAN, FRANK "Pete","Dunk" BL/TR d1909 LF, RF, CF, M
Phi G 1909 Chi L 1910 **Chi** AG 1911–18 Det S 1919 Chi G 1920 Tol T 1923 Mil 1923 Cle E 1926 Cle H 1927 Cle T 1928
Not to be confused with the catcher with the same name, he was an exceptional outfielder with Rube Foster's American Giants and a prototypical leadoff hitter, who dazzled opponents with his bunting, speed and basestealing ability. He hit a career-best .389 in 1910, and managed after his playing days finished.

BENJAMIN , JERRY Charles [Christopher] B11.9.1909 Montgomery AL D11.23.1974 Detroit MI BB/TR/5-9/165 d1932 CF
Mem 1932 Det S 1933 Bir 1934 Hom 1935–48 New E 1939 Tol C 1939 NY C 1948

An integral part of the Homestead Grays dynasty, Benjamin and Cool Papa Bell formed a fearsome pair of basestealers. A three-time East-West All-Star, he wowed home crowds with a .485 average (.392 overall) in 1943. Benjamin played for Toledo in 1939 using an alias in protest after being dealt to Newark.

Short but Brilliant Careers

CAMPANELLA, ROY "Campy" B11.19.1921 Philadelphia PA D6.26.1921 Woodland Hills CA BR/TR/5-9.5/195 d1937 HF1969 ML 1948–1957 C, 3b, OF
Bal EG 1937–42 [Mex 1943] **Bal EG** 1944–45 [OB minors 1946–48] [ML 1948–57]
A baseball prodigy who began his pro career at 15, playing only on the weekends, Campanella had a tryout with the Phillies scheduled as a teenager, until the club discovered his race. A career .353 hitter, most observers thought he should have jumped straight from black ball to the big leagues.

BROWN, DAVE David "Dave","Lefty" B1896 San Marcos TX D. Denver CO BL/TL/5-10/170 d1918 P
Chi AG 1918–22 Lin 1923–25
A dazzling pitcher in his prime, Brown used outstanding control of his fastball, curve and drop to go 29-6 combined in 1920–22. His career ended abruptly when he killed a man and fled New York to avoid arrest. Rumors had him playing as "Lefty Wilson" in the 1930s for Midwestern semipro teams.

SMITH, CHINO Charles "Charlie" B.1903 Greenwood SC D.1.16.1932 BL/TR/5-6/168 d1925 OF, 2b
Bro RG 1925–28 Lin 1929–30 Bro RG 1931
A line-drive power hitter, Smith was one of the best sluggers during his time. A lifetime .423 batter, Smith's top mark was .468 in 1931; he also led the ANL in batting and home runs in that league's only season. He died suddenly at age 29 after contracting yellow fever

MOORE, DOBIE Walter "Freckles","Scoops" B.2.27.1890 Rome GA D.4.1.1963 Detroit MI BR/TR/5-11/230 d1920 SS, OF
KC 1920–26
Recommended to Kansas City by Casey Stengel, Moore was outstanding at the plate and in the field. Offensively, he hit well over .300 after his first two seasons. As a shortstop, he displayed outstanding range and a powerful, accurate arm. A bullet wound broke two leg bones, ending his career.

JONES, SLIM Stuart B.5.6.1913 Baltimore MD D.12.1938 Baltimore MD BL/TL/6-6/185 d1932 P
Bal BS 1932–33 Phi S 1934–38
A towering presence on the mound, the fireballing Jones was an electrifying hurler. He was said to throw as hard as Lefty Grove, and dueled often with Satchel Paige, including a 10-inning dogfight in 1934, often considered the best Negro League game ever, stopped by darkness in a 1-1 tie.

WILSON, ARTIE Arthur Lee "Snoop" B10.28.1916 Springville AL BL/TR/5-10/160 d1944 ML 1951 SS
Bir 1944–48 [OB minors 1949–57 1962]
One of his league's top stolen base threats, Wilson used his opposite field approach at the plate to capture two NAL batting titles and two other second place finishes. He received but 22 at-bats in the major leagues, despite hitting .312 during the nine years he played in the Pacific Coast League.

BLACK BASEBALL/NEGRO LEAGUE SEASON SYNOPSES, 1910–1950

1910
Rube Foster's Chicago Leland Giants, featuring John Henry Lloyd, Pete Hill, Grant "Home Run" Johnson, and Bruce Petway, were black baseball's first "super team." Following their regular season, they traveled to Cuba where they played the best Cuban teams. When the touring Detroit Tigers (with Ty Cobb and Sam Crawford) and Philadelphia Athletics (with Eddie Plank and Chief Bender) arrived, the Cuban teams added Lloyd, Hill, Johnson, and Petway to their rosters to play against the white major leaguers.

1911
Rube Foster changed his team's name to the Chicago American Giants and continued their dominance in the West for the remainder of the decade. Jess McMahon, a white entrepreneur, formed the New York Lincoln Giants, and after enticing John Henry Lloyd to join his team, the Lincolns became the top club in the East.

1912
With John Henry Lloyd at the helm and joined in the lineup by slugger Louis Santop, speedster Spot Poles, and pitching greats Cyclone Joe Williams and Cannonball Dick Redding, the Lincoln Giants were again the top team in the East. Foster's American Giants continued as the top team in the West.

1913
The Chicago American Giants and the New York Lincoln Giants, who enjoyed their best season ever, remained the best teams in their regions. Cyclone Joe Williams defeated Grover Cleveland Alexander and the Philadelphia Phillies in a postseason exhibition game.

1914
Rube Foster lured John Henry Lloyd back to Chicago, and the American Giants fielded one of their strongest teams. In Lloyd's absence, the Brooklyn Royal Giants wrested the Eastern title from the Lincoln Giants.

1915
Parity was beginning to manifest itself in both the East and West. C. I. Taylor's Indianapolis ABCs waged a heated battle against Foster's American Giants for the Western title, while Jess McMahon left the Lincoln Giants to form a new franchise, the New York Lincoln Stars, and challenged his old team.

1916
Taylor's Indianapolis ABCs succeeded in their battle against Foster's American Giants to take the Western title, while the New York Lincoln Stars took the Eastern title.

1917
John Henry Lloyd returned to the Chicago American Giants and the Western championship returned with him. In the East the Lincoln Giants and Brooklyn Royal Giants were the top teams.

1918
John Henry Lloyd jumped back east again, this time to Nat Strong's Brooklyn Royal Giants. This gave the East three competitive teams, along with the Lincoln Giants and Hilldale, a new entry into the Eastern scene. The Chicago American Giants remained the top club in the West.

1919
Rube Foster's Chicago American Giants were challenged by the Detroit Stars under Foster's former star Pete Hill, who took the Stars helm as a player-manager. There was no dominant team in the East, with the Lincoln Giants, Bacharach Giants, and Hilldale all contending on relatively even terms.

1920
Rube Foster founded the first black league, the Negro National League, comprised of eight Midwestern teams. He also served as league president and, recognizing the need for a measure of parity, oversaw the transfer of players from stronger teams to weaker franchises. Despite losing players from his own team in this action, Foster's Chicago American Giants won the NNL's inaugural pennant to continue their dominance from the previous decade of independent blackball. The Detroit Stars and Kansas City Monarchs proved to be the other strong franchises.

1921
The NNL began the season with seven of the original teams and one replacement franchise. Rube Foster's Chicago American Giants, with what was called a "race horse" style

of play, nosed out the Kansas City Monarchs to repeat as champions. Key players were ace left-hander Dave Brown and Cristobal Torriente, who provided the power. Envisioning future eastward expansion, Foster played postseason series against two top eastern teams, Hilldale and the Bacharach Giants.

1922
Following the death of Indianapolis ABCs owner-manager C. I. Taylor, his brother Ben Taylor assumed the role of player-manager. Behind the hitting of Oscar Charleston, the team captured the Chicago American Giants, who captured their third straight NNL title. Chicago played a September series against the Bacharach Giants, a top eastern team, with the final game going 20 innings before Chicago eked out a 1-0 victory. Harold Treadwell went the entire distance in taking the loss, while Dave Brown pitched the last 14 innings to get the win.

1923
The big story of the year was the formation of the Eastern Colored League by Hilldale owner Ed Bolden, whose team won the inaugural pennant. Many NNL players jumped to eastern teams, including American Giants ace Dave Brown. His defection contributed to the Kansas City Monarchs' ending Chicago's skein of NNL titles. The nucleus of the NNL remained solid, though the raids on its teams created a war between the leagues that precluded a true Negro World Series being played.

1924
The ECL and NNL pennant races produced the same two winners as the previous season, but this year Hilldale and the Kansas City Monarchs faced each other in the first Negro World Series. The best five-of-nine series included a tie to make a total of ten games played in four different cities before the Monarchs emerged victorious. In the final game, Monarchs manager Jose Mendez, long past his prime as a player, fashioned a masterful three-hit shutout to seal the historic victory. His gem nullified the efforts of Nip Winters, who had posted three wins to get Hilldale to the final game.

1925
Hilldale won the ECL pennant, finishing ahead of a strong Harrisburg team. For the first time, the NNL featured a split-season format, with the winners of each half meeting in a playoff for the pennant. The Kansas City Monarchs defeated the St. Louis Stars in the first NNL Championship Series. For both champions, it was their third consecutive pennant and it set up a repeat of the inaugural Negro World Series. Rogan, who had won three games in the LCS, injured his knee and missed the Series, enabling Hilldale to win the rematch.

1926
Rube Foster became mentally incapacitated, so his protege Dave Malarcher took the helm to direct the Chicago American Giants to victory over the Kansas City Monarchs in the NNL's LCS. In a dramatic finish, needing wins in both ends of a doubleheader, Willie Foster pitched dual shutouts to beat Bullet Rogan twice and take the pennant. Meanwhile, player-manager Dick Lundy guided the Bacharach Giants to the ECL pennant, and the ensuing Negro World Series produced a historic event when the Bacharachs' Red Grier hurled the first Series no-hitter. Still, eleven games were required before a winner was determined. Foster again rose to the occasion with two wins, including a 1-0 victory in the final game.

1927
The Chicago American Giants swept the Birmingham Black Barons in four straight games to win the NNL's championship series. Birmingham rookie Satchel Paige pitched in two games without a decision. For the first time, the ECL also played a split-season schedule, but the Bacharachs won both halves to avoid a playoff. Chicago prevailed again in the Negro World Series rematch, as Willie Foster won twice, including in the final game. His one loss was also notable, as it came in a second World Series no-hitter. Luther Farrell's historic no-hit performance was less than masterful, as he was clinging to a 3-2 lead when darkness ended the game in the 7th inning.

1928
The St. Louis Stars battled the Chicago American Giants in the NNL's championship series, as Willie Wells' pair of homers in the final game of the best-of-nine series gave the Stars a hard-fought victory. There was no Negro World Series due to the demise of the ECL, whose decline had accelerated after Ed Bolden's nervous breakdown. After starting with a shaky five-team alignment, the ECL disbanded early in the season, although some teams continued to play as independent clubs.

1929

Owner Cum Posey's Homestead Grays, long an outstanding independent team that had eschewed league play, joined five teams from the nucleus of the ECL to form the American Negro League. However, the replacement eastern league would last only one season. The ANL and the established NNL both employed a split-season format; in each loop, strong teams won both halves. The Kansas City Monarchs were NNL champions, while the Baltimore Black Sox were ANL champions. No interleague postseason series was played, and there would be no more Negro World Series until 1942.

1930

The St. Louis Stars edged the Detroit Stars in seven games to win the NNL's LCS. With no league in the east, the Homestead Grays beat the New York Lincoln Giants in a ten-game challenge series for the Eastern Championship. In one of these games, Grays rookie Josh Gibson smashed a homer that almost went out of Yankee Stadium. The Grays played a night game under the portable lighting system of pioneering Kansas City Monarchs owner J. L. Wilkinson. The game featured a 12-inning, 1-0, duel between the Monarchs' Chet Brewer and the Grays' Smokey Joe Williams. Brewer allowed four hits and fanned 19, while Williams yielded only one hit and struck out 25 in taking the win. In December, legendary owner, promoter, and future Hall of Famer Rube Foster died in an asylum.

1931

The St. Louis Stars repeated as champions in the NNL's final season by taking both halves of the split season, as the NNL fell victim to the Great Depression after struggling for years. The Homestead Grays and Hilldale were the top eastern teams. The powerful 1931 Grays—featuring Hall of Fame sluggers Josh Gibson and Oscar Charleston, Hall of Fame pitchers Willie Foster and Smokey Joe Williams, as well as other greats like Jud "Boojum" Wilson and "Double Duty" Radcliffe—are considered to be one of black baseball's all-time greatest teams. With Foster winning three games, the Grays defeated the Kansa City Monarchs in what was falsely hyped as a championship series. Slugging outfielder Chino Smith's brief but brilliant career ended in the spring when he died of yellow fever at age 31.

1932

The 1932 season was one of depression-era chaos. Cum Posey's newly formed East-West League dissolved in midseason, with the Baltimore Black Sox in first place. Only the Negro Southern League, which had strengthened its rosters by adding players from the defunct NNL as well as assimilated select surviving franchises, completed the season. A longtime Negro minor league circuit, the NSL is considered to have been of big-league caliber for that one season. Willie Foster won the final two games as the Chicago American Giants edged the Nashville Elite Giants to win the NSL's seven-game League Championship Series.

1933

Pittsburgh Crawfords owner Gus Greenlee took two actions that gave impetus to black baseball's revival. First, he organized a new Negro National League and, although the first season was surrounded by controversy, he managed to salvage a viable league. The Chicago American Giants won the first half title. However, the second half schedule was not completed and discord intensified when Greenlee, who also served as league president, awarded his own team the championship. By contrast, Greenlee's promotion of the first East-West All-Star game proved an instant success, as Willie Foster pitched a complete game to give the West a victory in the inaugural contest. The annual Classic quickly became the most popular and prosperous black sporting event in the country.

1934

There were three strong teams in the NNL and, although the Pittsburgh Crawfords may have been the best, they were the team left out of the playoffs. The Philadelphia Stars edged the Chicago American Giants, four games to three, in the LCS, with ace left-hander Slim Jones pitching a 2-0 shutout in the final game. Jones and Satchel Paige were the two best pitchers in the league, and a highly publicized showdown between the pair at Yankee Stadium was ended by darkness after ten innings in a 1-1 deadlock—a game considered to be the greatest game ever played in Negro League history. At the prestigious annual semi-pro tournament sponsored by the *Denver Post*, an integrated House of David team led by Satchel Paige took the championship, besting the Kansas City Monarchs—the first all-black team to ever be allowed to compete in the tourney.

1935

The 1935 Pittsburgh Crawfords roster included no less than five future Hall of Famers (Satchel Paige, Josh Gibson, Oscar Charleston, Cool Papa Bell, and Judy Johnson) and are generally regarded as the greatest black team of all-time. Paige jumped the team to play with a semi-pro team in Bismarck, North Dakota, but Leroy Matlock filled the departed superstar pitcher's role and finished with a 17-0 mark. The Crawfords defeated the New York Cubans in a seven-game LCS by winning each of the last three games by one run. The 1935 West-East Classic produced the most exciting All-Star game ever, as the winner was not decided until the bottom of the 12th inning, when Mule Suttles smashed a three-run homer off Martin Dihigo to give the West an 11-8 victory.

1936

When the Chicago American Giants dropped out of the league and Tom Wilson moved his Elite Giants to Washington, the NNL became an entirely eastern league. The move must have agreed with the Elites, as they won the first half title, while the Pittsburgh Crawfords won the second half. The pennant race was interrupted when the NNL took an all-star team to the *Denver Post* Tournament, where their domination of the white opposition generated much greater awareness and recognition for the skill levels of black ballplayers. Hall of Famer Buck Leonard later said it was the best team he ever played on.

1937

The Negro American League was founded with teams from the Midwest and South. The Kansas City Monarchs defeated the Chicago American Giants in a championship series to win the first NAL pennant. In the east, Satchel Paige led a defection from the Crawfords to the Dominican Republic, which decimated Greenlee's team. NNL officials responded by banning the jumpers, except for Josh Gibson, who had received owner Cum Posey's permission. When he returned, Gibson teamed with Buck Leonard to power the Homestead Grays to their first of nine consecutive NNL pennants. Paige also returned after pitching Ciudad Trujillo to the championship, thumbing his nose at the Negro Leagues establishment and leading a barnstorming All-Star team of top black talent to the 1937 *Denver Post* tournament championship.

1938

The *New York Daily News* and the *Pittsburgh Courier*, a black newspaper, boldly published articles saying that the Giants and Pirates, respectively, would be guaranteed to win the NL pennant if they would sign selected star black players. Three Homestead Grays (Josh Gibson, Buck Leonard, and ace right-handed pitcher Ray Brown, who helped the Grays win another NNL pennant) were included on both lists. Southern teams prevailed in the NAL, as the Memphis Red Sox and the Atlanta Black Crackers won the two halves of the split season. They were recognized as co-champions when the LCS was cancelled after two games because of friction between the rival team officials.

1939

The Homestead Grays finished first in the NNL pennant race and, since there was no playoff, a postseason elimination tournament was held with the top four teams. The Grays beat the Philadelphia Stars and the Baltimore Elite Giants beat the Newark Eagles to advance to the final round, where the Elites upset the Grays to win the tournament trophy. In the NAL, the Kansas City Monarchs edged the St. Louis Stars in the LCS to begin a streak of four straight pennants.

1940

Mexican League officials lured many Negro League stars south of the border. Among the defectors were Josh Gibson, Ray Dandridge, Willie Wells, Leon Day, Cool Papa Bell, and Bill Wright. The loss of this top talent weakened the leagues considerably. In the absence of Gibson, Buck Leonard's bat and Ray Brown's pitching carried the Homestead Grays to a first place finish in the NNL pennant race. In the NAL, the Kansas City Monarchs edged the St. Louis Stars in the LCS to repeat as champions.

1941

Both Negro leagues were still suffering from talent depletion from the loss of so many players to Mexico. Monte Irvin had an outstanding year and was being touted by NNL owners as the player to break the color barrier in what was then arrogantly called "Organized Baseball." The Homestead Grays and the Kansas City Monarchs repeated as champions in their respective leagues. The Grays defeated the New York Cuban Stars in the split-season NNL's LCS, while the superlative pitching combination of Satchel Paige and Hilton Smith pitched the Monarchs to the NAL championship without a playoff.

1942

The onset of World War II and local draft boards contributed to a return of many players from Mexico. Josh Gibson's return reunited the "Thunder Twins," as he and Leonard were dubbed by the press. The Grays and Monarchs again won their league championships to establish themselves as the two dominant dynasties in the Negro Leagues. Finally, after a 15-year hiatus, there would be another Negro World Series. In the classic match-up of pitching versus power, the Monarchs swept the Series with Satchel Paige getting three wins and Hilton Smith one. Leon Day, the star of the East-West game, beat Satchel as a "ringer" in the Series, but the win was not allowed.

1943

World War II sent many African-American players into military service and the quality of the leagues suffered accordingly. The Kansas City Monarchs suffered more adversely than some teams, as their streak of four straight pennants was broken essentially by the draft. The Birmingham Black Barons defeated the Chicago American Giants in the LCS to win the NAL pennant. The Homestead Grays were less affected by the draft and fared better, winning the NNL's pennant and besting Birmingham in a hard-fought seven-game Negro World Series. Ray Brown and Johnny Wright won two games apiece, with Brown taking the final-game victory.

1944

Another war year saw a reprise for both the league champions and the Negro World Series. The Homestead Grays and Birmingham Black Barons each won both halves of their respective split schedules to create a rematch in the World Series. The outcome was the same, but this time around the Grays required only five games to defeat the Black Barons and win their second consecutive World Championship of black baseball.

1945

In the final year of World War II, the Homestead Grays won both halves of the NNL season to win their ninth straight pennant, while the Cleveland Buckeyes won both halves of the NAL split-season to win their first pennant. The veteran Grays were favored, but Manager Quincy Trouppe's upstart Cleveland club swept the Negro World Series in four games.

1946

With the end of World War II, soldiers traded their military uniforms for baseball uniforms and the leagues returned to their pre-war strength. Leon Day wasted no time and pitched an opening day no-hitter for the Newark Eagles. Monte Irvin and Larry Doby returned from the Army and Navy, respectively, and provided the firepower that elevated the Eagles to the top of the league, ending the long line of Grays NNL pennants. The Kansas City Monarchs' returning servicemen included Willard Brown, Buck O'Neil, and Joe Greene, and their presence in the lineup brought KC another NAL pennant. The Negro World Series was closely contested seven-game series, with Newark winning. No one foresaw it, but this was Josh Gibson's last season.

1947

The death knell for the Negro Leagues was sounded when Jackie Robinson put on a Brooklyn Dodgers uniform, but it took a couple of years before the full impact was felt. The NNL Newark started where it had left off, winning the first-half title before their momentum was stalled with the loss of Larry Doby to the major leagues. The New York Cubans captured the second-half title and were awarded the league pennant based on the total record for the season. The Cleveland Buckeyes won the NAL pennant but lost to the Cubans in the Negro World Series. The immortal Josh Gibson died tragically in January, going out as Jackie Robinson was finally smashing the racist barrier that had for so long excluded Gibson and other great black Americans from the white-owned National Pastime.

1948

After Jackie Robinson's successful rookie season, the press and fans virtually deserted the Negro Leagues. The handwriting was on the wall; only the foolish couldn't read it—integration had killed the Negro Leagues. Fittingly, the Homestead Grays were the last team to win a Negro World Series, defeating the Birmingham Black Barons. In symbolic contrast, future Hall of Famer Buck Leonard was the star for the Grays during the season, while teenaged Willie Mays made his debut with Birmingham to serve as a catalyst for their pennant race. The NNL folded after the season.

1949

The mounting financial losses that forced the collapse of the NNL were still a pressing reality, but the NAL absorbed four of the surviving franchises from their late "sister" league and began the season with two five-team divisions in anticipation of continuing the same general geographic structure that had existed since 1937. The Baltimore Elite Giants won both halves of the Eastern Division season and swept the Western Division second-half champion Chicago American Giants in four straight games to win the NAL pennant. However, more nails were being driven into the Negro Leagues' coffin. Reflecting the continuing decline of the talent on Negro League team rosters was the Kansas City Monarchs refusal to play Chicago for the Western Division title due to the loss of many of their best players to OB.

1950

After the success that Jackie Robinson and other pioneering black players had generated both on the field and at the box office, major league owners were inspired to accelerate their search for "another Robinson." Consequently, doors in Organized Baseball were now opening wide for young black players, and a mass exodus of African-American talent flowed into the major leagues in the 1950s—most into the National League. In 1950, the Indianapolis Clowns and Kansas City Monarchs won their divisional titles, but no League Championship Series was played.

Independent Award Winners (Pre-League Era)

1910

Player: Pete Hill
Pitcher: Frank Wickware
Rookie: Frank Wickware

1911

Player: John Henry Lloyd
Pitcher: Dick Redding
Rookie: Dick Redding

1912

Player: Louis Santop
Pitcher: Dick Redding
Rookie: Johnny Pugh

1913

Player: Joe Williams
Pitcher: Joe Williams
Rookie: Cristobal Torriente

1914

Player: John Henry Lloyd
Pitcher: Joe Williams
Rookie: George Shively

1915

Player: John Henry Lloyd
Pitcher: Dizzy Dismukes
Rookie: Oscar Charleston

1916

Player: John Henry Lloyd
Pitcher: John Donaldson
Rookie: Dick Lundy

1917

Player: Louis Santop
Pitcher: Tom Johnson
Rookie: Alejandro Oms

1918

Player: Oscar Charleston
Pitcher: Richard Whitworth
Rookie: Oliver Marcelle

1919

Player: Oscar Charleston
Pitcher: Joe Williams
Rookie: Dave Brown

1920

NNL

TEAM	W	L	PCT
Chi AG	32	13	.711
Det S	35	23	.603
KC	41	29	.586
Ind ABC	39	35	.527
StL G	25	32	.439
Cub SW	21	24	.467
Day	8	18	.308
Chi G	4	24	.143

MVP: Cristobal Torriente
Pitcher: Dave Brown
Rookie: Bullet Rogan

Eastern Independent Teams

Player: Chester Brooks
Pitcher: Dick Redding
Rookie: Fats Jenkins

1921

NNL

TEAM	W	L	PCT
Chi AG	41	21	.661
KC	50	31	.617
StL G	33	23	.589
Det S	30	27	.526
Ind ABC	30	29	.508
Col B	24	38	.387
Cub SW	23	39	.371
Chi G	10	32	.329

MVP: Oscar Charleston
Pitcher: Dave Brown
Rookie: Crush Holloway

Eastern Independent Teams

Player: Louis Santop
Pitcher: Joe Williams
Rookie: Nip Winters

1922

NNL

TEAM	W	L	PCT
Chi AG	36	23	.610
Ind ABC	46	33	.582
Det S	43	32	.573
KC	44	33	.571
StL S	23	23	.500
Pit K	16	21	.432
Cub SW	19	30	.388
Cle TS	17	29	.370

MVP: Cristobal Torriente
Pitcher: Dave Brown
Rookie: Heavy Johnson

Eastern Independent Teams

Player: John Henry Lloyd
Pitcher: Phil Cockrell
Rookie: Jud Wilson

1923

NNL

TEAM	W	L	PCT
KC	57	33	.633
Det S	40	27	.597
Chi AG	41	29	.586
Ind ABC	45	34	.570
Cub SW	27	31	.466
StL S	23	31	.426
Tol T†	11	15	.423
Mil‡	14	32	.304

†Folded July 15
‡Folded late in season

MVP: Bullet Rogan
Pitcher: Tom Williams
Rookie: Turkey Stearnes

ECL

TEAM	W	L	PCT
Hil	32	17	.673
Cub SE	23	17	.575
Bro RG	18	28	.500
Bac	19	23	.452
Lin	16	22	.421
Bal BS	19	30	.388

MVP: Biz Mackey
Pitcher: Nip Winters
Rookie: Rats Henderson

1924

NNL

TEAM	W	L	PCT
KC	55	22	.714
Chi AG	49	24	.671
Det S	37	27	.578
StL S	40	36	.526
Bir	32	37	.464
Mem†	29	37	.439
Cub SW	16	33	.327
Cle Br	15	34	.306

†started season as Indianapolis ABCs

MVP: Bullet Rogan
Pitcher: Bullet Rogan
Rookie: Willie Bobo

ECL

TEAM	W	L	PCT
Hil	47	22	.681
Bal BS	30	19	.612
Lin	31	25	.554
Bac	30	29	.508
Har	26	28	.481
Bro RG	16	25	.390
Was Po	21	37	.362
Cub SE	15	31	.326

MVP: Biz Mackey
Pitcher: Nip Winters
Rookie: Joe Strong

1925

NNL
First half

TEAM	W	L	PCT
KC	31	9	.775
StL S	31	14	.689
Det S	26	20	.565
Chi AG	26	22	.542
Cub SW	12	13	.480
Mem	18	24	.429
Ind ABC	13	24	.351
Bir	14	33	.298

Second half

TEAM	W	L	PCT
StL S	38	12	.760
KC	31	11	.738
Chi AG	28	18	.609
Det S	27	20	.574
Cub SW	10	12	.454
Bir	10	16	.384
Mem	12	24	.333
Ind ABC	4	33	.108

MVP: Bullet Rogan
Pitcher: Bullet Rogan
Rookie: Nelson Dean

ECL

TEAM	W	L	PCT
Hil	45	13	.775
Har	37	18	.673
Bal BS	31	19	.620
Bac	26	26	.500
Bro RG	13	20	.394
Cub SE	15	26	.366
Lin	7	39	.152

MVP: Oscar Charleston
Pitcher: Nip Winters
Rookie: Chino Smith

1926

NNL
First half

TEAM	W	L	PCT
KC	35	12	.745
Det S	33	17	.660
Chi AG	28	16	.636
StL S	29	18	.617
Ind ABC	28	18	.609
Cub SW	6	27	.182
Day	7	32	.179
Cle E	5	32	.135

Second Half

TEAM	W	L	PCT
Chi AG	29	7	.806
KC	21	7	.750
StL S	20	11	.645
Ind ABC	15	25	.375
Det S	13	23	.361
Cub SW	10	20	.333

MVP: Willie Foster
Pitcher: Willie Foster
Rookie: Hallie Harding

ECL

TEAM	W	L	PCT
Bac	34	20	.629
Har	25	17	.595
Hil	34	24	.586
Cub SE	28	21	.572
Lin	19	22	.463
Bal BS	18	29	.383
Bro RG	7	20	.260
New S†	1	10	.091

†Folded in mid-season

MVP: Dick Lundy
Pitcher: Rats Henderson
Rookie: Romando Garcia

1927

NNL
First half

TEAM	W	L	PCT
Chi AG	32	14	.696
KC	36	18	.667
StL S	32	19	.627
Det S	28	18	.609
Bir	23	29	.442
Mem	19	25	.432
Cub SW	15	23	.395
Cle H	10	37	.213

Second half

TEAM	W	L	PCT
Bir†			
Chi AG			
Cle H			
Cub SW			
Det S			
KC			
Mem			
StL S			

†Pennant winner; standings not published

MVP: Willie Wells
Pitcher: Willie Foster
Rookie: Red Parnell

ECL
First half

TEAM	W	L	PCT
Bac	29	17	.630
Bal BS	23	17	.575
Cub SE	24	19	.558
Har	25	20	.556
Hil	17	28	.378
Bro RG	10	21	.323

Second half

TEAM	W	L	PCT
Bac	25	18	.581
Har	16	12	.572
Hil	19	17	.528
Cub SE	9	13	.409
Bal BS	12	18	.400
Bro RG	5	10	.333

MVP: Jud Wilson
Pitcher: Rats Henderson
Rookie: Tetelo Vargas

1928

NNL

First half	Second half
StL S†	Chi AG†
Bir	Bir
Chi AG	Cub SW
Cub SW	Det S
Det S	StL S

†Pennant winners; standings not published

MVP: Mule Suttles
Pitcher: Ted Trent
Rookie: Double Duty Radcliffe

ECL†

TEAM	W	L	PCT
Bal BS	5	2	.714
Lin	3	2	.600
Cub SE	2	2	.500
Phi T	2	3	.400
Bac	2	5	.286

†League disbanded early in the season

Eastern Independent Teams

Player: Oscar Charleston
Pitcher: Laymon Yokely
Rookie: Ramon Bragana

1929

NNL
First half

TEAM	W	L	PCT
KC	28	11	.718
StL S	28	14	.667
Det S	24	16	.600
Bir	20	24	.454
Chi AG	22	29	.431
Mem	14	22	.389
Cub SW	6	14	.300

Second half

TEAM	W	L	PCT
KC	34	6	850
Chi AG	26	9	743
StL S	28	16	.636
Cub SW	12	12	.500
Det S	10	23	.303
Bir	9	27	.250
Mem	5	22	.185

MVP: Willie Wells
Pitcher: Chet Brewer
Rookie: Leroy Matlock

ANL
First half

TEAM	W	L	PCT
Bal BS	24	11	.686
Lin	22	11	.667
Hom	15	13	.536
Hil	15	20	.429
Bac	11	20	.355
Cub SE	6	16	.273

Second half

TEAM	W	L	PCT
Bal BS	25	10	.714
Hil	24	15	.615
Lin	18	15	.545
Hom	19	16	.543
Cub SE	9	23	.281
Bac	8	25	.242

MVP: Chino Smith
Pitcher: Connie Rector
Rookie: Buddy Burbage

1930

NNL
First half

TEAM	W	L	PCT
StL S	41	15	.732
KC	31	14	.689
Mem	20	17	.541
Bir	30	27	.526
Det S	26	26	.500
Cub SW	17	23	.425
Chi AG	24	39	.381
Nas	13	35	.271

Second half

TEAM	W	L	PCT
Det S	24	7	.774
StL S	22	7	.759
Chi AG	19	12	.613
KC	8	12	.400
Nas	7	12	.368
Cub SW	6	12	.333
Mem	7	14	.333
Bir	10	20	.333

MVP: Willie Wells
Pitcher: Eggie Hensley
Rookie: Jimmie Crutchfield

Eastern Independent Teams

Player: Chino Smith
Pitcher: Bill Holland
Rookie: Josh Gibson

1931

NNL

TEAM
StL S†
Chi AG
Cle C
Det S
Ind ABC
Lou WS
KC‡

†Won both halves; standings not published
‡KC re-joined league in 2nd half

MVP: Cool Papa Bell
Pitcher: Ted Trent
Rookie: Ray Brown

Eastern Independent Teams

Player: Josh Gibson
Pitcher: Willie Foster
Rookie: Chester Williams

1932

NSL
First half

TEAM	W	L	PCT
Chi AG	34	7	.829
Mon M	33	7	.825
Nas	24	13	.649
Mon GS	22	17	.564
Mem	22	22	.500
Lou BCa	13	17	.433
Ind ABC	14	19	.424

Second half

TEAM	W	L	PCT
Nas†	12	0	1.000
Chi AG			
Col T			
Ind ABC			
Mem			
Mon GS			
Mon M			

†leading the league when it folded in June

MVP: Turkey Stearnes
Pitcher: Willie Foster
Rookie: Alec Radcliffe

EWL

TEAM	W	L	PCT
Bal BS	20	9	.690
Det W†	20	6	.769
Hom	16	8	.667
Cub HD	12	15	.444
Was Pi	13	18	.419
Hil	10	17	.370
Cle S	8	16	.333
New B	3	14	.176

†Left league to merge with Homestead

MVP: Cool Papa Bell
Pitcher: Bert Hunter
Rookie: Cliff Allen

1933

NNL

First half

TEAM	W	L	PCT
Chi AG	21	7	.750
Pit C	20	8	.714
Bal BS	10	9	.526
Nas	12	13	.480
Det S	13	20	.394
Col BB	11	18	.379

Second half †

†schedule not completed

MVP: Josh Gibson
Pitcher: Willie Foster
Rookie: Ray Dandridge

1934

NNL

First half

TEAM	W	L	PCT
Chi AG	17	6	.739
Pit C	14	8	.636
Phi S	12	9	.571
New D	6	5	.545
Nas	9	11	.450
Cle RS	2	22	.083

Second half

TEAM	W	L	PCT
Phi S	11	4	.733
Nas	6	3	.667
Pit C	15	9	.625
Chi AG	11	9	.550
Cle RS	2	3	.400
New D	5	9	.357
Phi BG†	3	12	.200
Bal BS†	1	6	.143

†joined league in second half

MVP: Jud Wilson
Pitcher: Slim Jones
Rookie: Buck Leonard

1935

NNL

First half

TEAM	W	L	PCT
Pit C	26	6	.785
Col EG	17	11	.607
Hom	14	13	.519
Bro E	15	15	.500
Chi AG	14	16	.467
Phi S	14	17	.452
NY C	10	16	.385
New D	8	20	.286

Second half

TEAM	W	L	PCT
NY C	20	7	.741
Pit C	13	9	.591
Phi S	14	10	.583
Col EG	10	10	.500
Hom	9	10	.474
Bro E	13	16	.448
Chi AG	7	13	.350
New D	9	21	.300

MVP: Josh Gibson
Pitcher: Leroy Matlock
Rookie: Johnny Taylor

1936

NNL

First half

TEAM	W	L	PCT
Was EG	14	10	.583
Phi S	15	12	.556
Pit C	16	15	.516
New E	15	18	.455
NY C	9	11	.450
Hom	10	13	.435

Second half

TEAM	W	L	PCT
Pit C	20	9	.690
New E	15	11	.577
NY BY	8	7	.533
NY C	13	12	.520
Hom	12	14	.462
Phi S	10	18	.357
Was EG	7	14	.333

MVP: Josh Gibson
Pitcher: Satchel Paige
Rookie: Henry Spearman

1937

NNL

First half

TEAM	W	L	PCT
Hom	21	9	.700
New E	19	14	.576
Phi S	12	11	.522
Was EG	11	15	.423
Pit C	11	16	.407
NY BY	11	17	.393

Second half

TEAM	W	L	PCT
Hom†			
New E			
NY BY			
Phi S			
Pit C			
Was EG			

†overall winner; second half standings not published

MVP: Buck Leonard
Pitcher: Leon Day
Rookie: Henry Kimbro

NAL

First half

TEAM	W	L	PCT
KC	19	8	.704
Chi AG	18	8	.692
Cin	15	11	.577
Mem	13	13	.500
Det S	12	15	.444
Bir	10	17	.370
Ind A	9	18	.333
StL S	5	22	.185

Second half

TEAM	W	L	PCT
Chi AG†			
Bir			
Cin			
Det S			
Ind A			
KC			
Mem			
StL S			

†No standings published; played Kansas City in playoff

MVP: Newt Allen
Pitcher: Ted Trent
Rookie: Ted Strong

1938

NNL

First half

TEAM	W	L	PCT
Hom	26	6	.813
Phi S	20	11	.645
New E	11	11	.500
Pit C	14	14	.500
Bal EG	12	14	.462
NY BY	4	17	.190
Was BS	1	20	.048

Second half

TEAM	W	L	PCT
Hom†			
Phi S			
Pit C			
Bal EG			
New E			
NY BY			
Was BS‡			

†Records not available; teams listed in order of finish
‡Folded in second half

MVP: Josh Gibson
Pitcher: Ray Brown
Rookie: Jimmy Hill

NAL

First half

TEAM	W	L	PCT
Mem	21	4	.840
KC	19	5	.792
Ind ABC†	6	6	.500
Atl†	9	10	.474
Jac†	3	4	.429
Chi AG†	8	13	.381
Bir†	3	11	.214

†Last reported records; final results not available

Second half

TEAM	W	L	PCT
Atl	12	4	.750
Chi AG	17	7	.708
KC	13	10	.565
Ind ABC	8	13	.381
Mem	8	15	.348
Bir	5	12	.294

MVP: Neil Robinson
Pitcher: Hilton Smith
Rookie: Joe Greene

1939

NNL

TEAM	W	L	PCT
Hom	33	14	.702
New E	29	20	.592
Bal EG	25	21	.543
Phi S	31	32	.492
NY BY	15	21	.417
NY C	5	22	.185

MVP: Bill Wright
Pitcher: Bill Byrd
Rookie: Pedro Pages

NAL

First half

TEAM	W	L	PCT
KC	17	7	.708
Chi AG	17	11	.607
Mem	11	11	.500
Cle Be	9	9	.500
StL S	10	12	.455
Ind ABC†			

†left league shortly after start of season

Second half

TEAM	W	L	PCT
StL S†			
Chi AG			
Cle Be			
KC			
Mem			
Tol C			

†final standings not published; St. Louis played Kansas City in LCS

MVP: Turkey Stearnes
Pitcher: Hilton Smith
Rookie: Chin Green

1940

NNL

TEAM	W	L	PCT
Hom	28	13	.683
Bal EG	25	14	.641
New E	25	17	.595
NY C	12	19	.387
Phi S	16	31	.340
NY BY	10	22	.313

MVP: Buck Leonard
Pitcher: Ray Brown
Rookie: Frank Coimbre

NAL

First half

TEAM	W	L	PCT
KC	12	7	.632
Cle Be	10	10	.500
Mem	12	12	.500
Bir	9	9	.500
Chi AG	9	15	.429
Ind Cr	3	5	.375

Second half

TEAM	W	L	PCT
Bir†			
Chi AG			
Cle Be			
Ind Cr			
Mem			
KC			

†final standings not published; KC declared league champion

MVP: Buck O'Neil
Pitcher: Jack Matchett
Rookie: Tommy Sampson

1941

NNL

First half

TEAM	W	L	PCT
Hom	17	9	.654
New E	11	6	.647
Bal EG	13	10	.565
NY C	7	10	.412
Phi S	10	18	.357
NY BY	7	13	.350

Second half

TEAM	W	L	PCT
NY C	4	2	.667
New E	8	5	.615
Bal EG	8	5	.615
Hom	8	8	.500
NY BY	5	5	.500
Phi S	2	8	.200

MVP: Monte Irvin
Pitcher: Dave Barnhill
Rookie: Dave Barnhill

NAL

TEAM	W	L	PCT
Bir†			
Chi AG			
Jac			
KC			
Mem			
StL S			

†final standings not published

MVP: Ted Strong
Pitcher: Hilton Smith
Rookie: Gready McKinnis

1942

NNL

TEAM	W	L	PCT
Hom	21	11	.656
Bal EG	21	12	.636
New E	18	16	.529
Phi S	16	18	.471
NY C	8	14	.364
NY BY	7	20	.259

MVP: Josh Gibson
Pitcher: Leon Day
Rookie: Louis Louden

NAL

TEAM	W	L	PCT
KC†			
Bir			
Chi AG			
Cin Bu			
Jac			

†final standings not published

MVP: Willard Brown
Pitcher: Satchel Paige
Rookie: Bonnie Serrell

1943

NNL

First half

TEAM	W	L	PCT
Hom	17	4	.810
NY C	13	6	.684
StL S	5	4	.556
New E	9	10	.474
Phi S	11	16	.407
Bal EG	9	15	.375
NY BY	2	11	.154

Second half

TEAM	W	L	PCT
Hom	9	3	.750
New E	9	4	.692
NY C	4	3	.571
Bal EG	5	6	.455
Phi S	7	9	.438
NY BY	0	10	.000
StL S†			

†Suspended for second half by league

MVP: Josh Gibson
Pitcher: Johnny Wright
Rookie: Bill Cash

NAL

First half

TEAM	W	L	PCT
Bir†			
Chi AG			
Ind Cl			
Cle Bu			
KC			
Mem			

†first half winner; final standings not published

Second half

TEAM	W	L	PCT
Chi AG	13	5	.722
Bir	5	3	.625
Cle Bu	8	5	.615
KC	6	7	.462
Ind Cl	3	7	.300
Mem	4	11	.267

MVP: Piper Davis
Pitcher: John Markham
Rookie: Hank Thompson

1944

NNL

First half

TEAM	W	L	PCT
Hom	15	8	.652
New E	13	9	.591
NY C	12	10	.545
Bal EG	12	11	.522
Phi S	7	11	.389
NY BY	2	13	.133

Second half

TEAM	W	L	PCT
Hom	12	4	.750
Phi S	12	7	.632
Bal EG	12	9	.571
NY C	4	4	.500
New E	6	13	.316
NY BY	2	11	.154

MVP: Ray Dandridge
Pitcher: Ray Brown
Rookie: Frank Austin

NAL

First half

TEAM	W	L	PCT
Bir	24	9	.727
Ind Cl	18	13	.581
Cle Bu	20	20	.500
Mem	20	23	.465
KC	12	19	.387
Chi AG	10	20	.333

Second half

TEAM	W	L	PCT
Bir	24	13	.649
Ind Cl	22	18	.550
Chi AG	22	19	.537
Cle Bu	20	21	.488
Mem	24	28	.462
KC	11	23	.324

MVP: Artie Wilson
Pitcher: Gentry Jessup
Rookie: Artie Wilson

1945

NNL

First half

TEAM	W	L	PCT
Hom	18	7	.720
Phi S	14	9	.609
Bal EG	13	9	.591
New E	11	9	.550
NY C	3	11	.214
NY BY	2	16	.111

Second half

TEAM	W	L	PCT
Hom	14	6	.700
Bal EG	12	8	.600
New E	10	8	.556
Phi S	7	10	.412
NY BY	5	10	.333
NY C	3	9	.250

MVP: Josh Gibson
Pitcher: Roy Welmaker
Rookie: Garnet Blair

NAL

First half

TEAM	W	L	PCT
Cle Bu	31	9	.775
Bir	26	11	.703
KC	17	18	.486
Chi AG	17	24	.415
Ind Cl	15	26	.366
Mem	13	31	.295

Second half

TEAM	W	L	PCT
Cle Bu	22	7	.759
Chi AG	22	11	.667
KC	15	12	.556
Ind Cl	15	13	.536
Bir	13	19	.406
Mem	4	30	.118

MVP: Sam Jethroe
Pitcher: Willie Jefferson
Rookie: Jackie Robinson

1946

NNL

First half

TEAM	W	L	PCT
New E	25	9	.735
Phi S	17	12	.586
Hom	18	15	.545
NY C	13	13	.500
Bal EG	14	17	.451
NY BY	3	24	.111

Second half

TEAM	W	L	PCT
New E	22	7	.759
NY C	15	8	.652
Bal EG	14	14	.500
Hom	9	13	.409
Phi S	10	17	.370
NY BY	5	16	.238

MVP: Monte Irvin
Pitcher: Leon Day
Rookie: Junior Gilliam

NAL

First half

TEAM	W	L	PCT
KC	27	8	.771
Bir	22	15	.595
Cle Bu	14	17	.452
Ind Cl	15	19	.441
Mem	16	21	.432
Chi AG	14	28	.333

Second half

TEAM	W	L	PCT
KC†			
Bir			
Chi AG			
Cle Bu			
Ind Cl			
Mem			

†second half winner; final standings not published

TEAM	W	L	PCT
MVP: Willard Brown			
Pitcher: Dan Bankhead			
Rookie: Leon Kellman			

1947
NNL
First half

TEAM	W	L	PCT
New E	27	15	.643
NY C	20	12	.625
Bal EG	23	20	.535
Hom	19	20	.487
Phi S	13	16	.448
NY BY	6	25	.193

Second half

TEAM	W	L	PCT
NY C	22	6	.786
Bal EG	17	16	.526
Hom	13	14	.481
Phi S	13	15	.464
New E	19	22	.463
NY BY	4	15	.267

MVP: Luis Marquez
Pitcher: Luis Tiant
Rookie: Luke Easter

NAL

TEAM	W	L	PCT
Cle Bu	54	23	.701
KC	38	22	.633
Bir	35	27	.565
Mem	35	43	.449
Chi AG	27	51	.346
Ind Cl	22	45	.328

MVP: Sam Jethroe
Pitcher: Vibert Clarke
Rookie: John Ritchey

1948
NNL

TEAM	W	L	PCT
Hom†	38	20	.655
Bal EG‡	45	26	.634
New E	29	28	.509
Phi S	24	28	.462
NY C	16	26	.381
NY BY	8	32	.200

†First half winner
‡Second half winner

MVP: Buck Leonard
Pitcher: Max Manning
Rookie: Charles Gary

NAL
First half

TEAM	W	L	PCT
Bir	38	14	.731
Cle Bu	31	21	.596
KC	24	18	.571
Chi AG	20	31	.392
Ind Cl	20	33	.377
Mem	13	29	.310

Second half

TEAM	W	L	PCT
KC	19	7	.731
Bir	17	7	.708
Mem	20	15	.571
Ind Cl	7	13	.350
Cle Bu	10	21	.323
Chi AG	7	17	.292

MVP: Willard Brown
Pitcher: Lefty LaMarque
Rookie: Gene Baker

1949
NAL EASTERN DIVISION
First Half

TEAM	W	L	PCT
Bal EG	33	16	.673
NY C	17	15	.531
Ind Cl	22	30	.423
Phi S	17	24	.415
Lou Bu	12	39	.235

Second Half

TEAM	W	L	PCT
Bal EG	30	16	.652
NY C	9	5	.643
Phi S	11	11	.500
Ind Cl	22	22	.476
Lou Bu	7	26	.212

NAL WESTERN DIVISION
First Half

TEAM	W	L	PCT
KC	31	20	.608
Chi AG	32	23	.582
Bir	29	21	.580
Hou	19	21	.475
Mem	13	29	.310

Second Half

TEAM	W	L	PCT
Chi AG	19	12	.613
KC	23	17	.575
Hou	16	14	.533
Bir	18	21	.462
Mem	19	28	.404

MVP: Piper Davis
Pitcher: Bill Byrd

1950
NAL EASTERN DIVISION
First Half

TEAM	W	L	PCT
Ind Cl	29	17	.630
Bal EG	10	9	.526
NY C	12	13	.480
Phi S	10	21	.323
Cle Bu	3	37	.075

Second Half

TEAM	W	L	PCT
NY C	6	3	.667
Bal EG	14	11	.560
Ind Cl†	18	21	.462
Phi S	5	7	.417
Cle Bu‡	0	2	.000

†*Awarded second half title;*
league rule required minimum of
30 games per half to qualify for
the championship

‡*Dropped out of the league after*
July 6

NAL WESTERN DIVISION
First Half

TEAM	W	L	PCT
KC	30	11	.732
Bir	38	14	.731
Hou	18	21	.462
Mem	19	23	.452
Chi AG	13	16	.448

Second Half

TEAM	W	L	PCT
Mem	23	9	.719
KC	22	10	.688
Bir	14	11	.560
Hou	5	20	.200
Chi AG	2	15	.118

MVP: Sam Hairston
Pitcher: Bill Powell

1951
NAL EASTERN DIVISION
First Half

TEAM	W	L	PCT
Ind Cl	29	12	.707
Bir	15	21	.417
Phi S	12	17	.414
Bal EG	13	24	.351

Second Half

TEAM	W	L	PCT
Ind Cl	24	14	.632
Bal EG	15	12	.556
Phi S	6	11	.353
Bir	9	19	.321

NAL WESTERN DIVISION
First Half

TEAM	W	L	PCT
KC	28	15	.651
Chi AG	21	16	.568
Mem	13	17	.433
NO	17	26	.395

Second Half

TEAM	W	L	PCT
Chi AG	13	8	.619
NO	22	18	.550
KC	14	13	.519
Mem	9	17	.346

1952
NAL
First Half

TEAM	W	L	PCT
Ind Cl	26	14	.650
Bir	28	21	.571
Chi AG	16	16	.500
KC	12	12	.500
Mem	15	22	.405
Phi S	11	23	.324

Second Half

TEAM	W	L	PCT
Bir	21	15	.583
Ind Cl	18	16	.529
Chi AG	16	15	.516
KC	11	14	.440
Mem	14	18	.438
Phi S	11	15	.423

1953
NAL

TEAM	W	L	PCT
KC	56	21	.727
Bir	28	34	.452
Ind Cl	31	43	.419
Mem	20	37	.351

1954
NAL

TEAM	W	L	PCT
Ind Cl	43	22	.662
Mem	49	34	.590
Bir	41	38	.519
Det S	23	31	.426
Lou BCo	19	30	.388
KC	23	43	.348

All Star Games

Year/No.	Site	Players	Score (Innings)	Attendance	E-W Record	MVP (Team) [EPF]
1933	Comiskey Park	23	W 11, E 7	19,568	0-1	[Willie Foster (Chi AG)]
1934	Comiskey Park	26	E 1, W 0	30,000	1-1	[Satchel Paige (Pit C)]
1935	Comiskey Park	32	W 11, E 8 (11)	25,000	1-2	[Mule Suttles (Chi AG)]
1936	Comiskey Park	34	E 10, W 2	26,400	2-2	[Cool Papa Bell (Pit C)]
1937	Comiskey Park	28	E 7, W 2	25,000	3-2	[Bill Wright (Was EG) & Buck Leonard (Hom)]
1938 G1	Comiskey Park	25	W 5, E 4	30,000	3-3	[Neil Robinson (Mem)]
1938 G2	Penmar Park*	22	E 14, W 3	12,000	4-3	[Bill Wright (Bal EG)]
1938 G3	Polo Grounds*	23	E 5, W 4 (10)	15,000	5-3	[Bill Wright (Bal EG)]
1939 G1	Comiskey Park	27	W 4, E 2	40,000	5-4	[Dan Wilson (StL S) & Hilton Smith (KC)]
1939 G2	Yankee Stadium*	27	E 10, W 2	20,000	6-4	[Josh Gibson (Hom)]
1940	Comiskey Park	31	E 11, W 0	25,000	7-4	[Buck Leonard (Hom)]
1941	Comiskey Park	37	E 8, W 3	50,256	8-4	[Buck Leonard (Hom)]
1942 G1	Comiskey Park	32	E 5, W 2	45,179	9-4	[Leon Day (New E)]
1942 G2	Municipal Stadium·	29	E 9, W 2	10,791	10-4	[Willie Wells (New E)]
1943	Comiskey Park	31	W 2, E 1	51,723	10-5	[Satchel Paige (KC)]
1944	Comiskey Park	28	W 7, E 4	46,247	10-6	[Ted Radcliffe (Bir)]
1945	Comiskey Park	30	W 9, E 6	33,088	10-7	Roy Campanella (Bal EG)†
1946 G1	Griffith Stadium°	37	E 6, W 3	16,268	11-7	[Howard Easterling (Hom) & Bill Byrd (Bal EG)]
1946 G2	Comiskey Park	26	W 4, E 1	45,474	11-8	[Felix Evans (Mem)]
1947 G1	Comiskey Park	29	W 5, E 2	48,112	11-9	[Gentry Jessup (Chi AG)]
1947 G2	Polo Grounds*	32	W 8, E 2	38,402	11-10	[Artie Wilson (Bir)]
1948 G1	Comiskey Park	26	W 3, E 0	42,099	11-11	[Gentry Jessup (Chi AG) & Bob Boyd (Mem)]
1948 G2	Yankee Stadium*	31	E 6, W 1	17,928	12-11	[Luis Marquez (Hom) & Minnie Minoso (NY C)]
1949	Comiskey Park	30	E 4, W 0	31,097	13-11	[Bob Griffith (Phi S)]
1950	Comiskey Park	29	W 5, E 3	24,614	13-12	[Jesse Douglas (Chi AG)]
1951	Comiskey Park	27	E 3, W 1	21,312	14-12	[Norman Robinson (Bir)]
1952	Comiskey Park	25	W 7, E 3	18,279	14-13	[Hank Baylis (KC)]
1953	Comiskey Park	31	W 5, E 1	10,000	14-14	[John Jackson (KC)]

°Philadelphia   ·Cleveland   *Washington, DC   *New York City   †Only year when ASG MVP was chosen

NNL LCS

Year	Team Games Won	Game Scores
1925	Kansas City 4, St. Louis 3	8-6, 3-6, 2-3, 5-4, 1-2, 9-3, 4-0
1926	Chicago 5, Kansas City 4	3-4, 5-6, 0-5, 4-3, 5-11, 2-0, 4-3, 1-0, 5-0
1927	Chicago 4, Birmingham 1	5-0, 10-5, 5-6, 6-4, 6-2
1928	St. Louis 5, Chicago 4	3-7, 0-3, 6-4, 3-4, 3-5, 12-7, 7-9, 19-4, 9-2
1930	St. Louis 4, Detroit 3	5-4, 7-11, 7-2, 4-5, 5-7, 4-3, 13-7
1934	Philadelphia 4, Chicago 3	4-0, 0-3, 5-3, 1-2, 1-0, 4-1, 4-4, 2-0
1935	Pittsburgh 4, New York Cubans 3	2-6, 0-4, 3-0, 1-6, 3-2, 7-6, 8-7
1941	Homestead 4, New York Cubans 1	5-4, 6-0, 4-5, 20-0, 5-0
1948	Homestead 3, Baltimore 1	6-0, 5-3, 3-11, 9-0 (forfeit)

NNL Postseason Tournament 1939

Round	Team Games Won	Game Scores
1st	Homestead 3, Philadelphia 2	9-12, 15-9, 6-4, 3-5, 3-0
1st	Baltimore 3, Newark 1	6-8, 11-3, 7-3, 5-2
2nd	Baltimore 3, Homestead 1 (one tie)	1-2, 7-5, 1-1, 10-5, 2-0

NAL LCS

Year	Team Games Won	Game Scores
1937	Kansas City 4, Chicago 1	4-5, 8-7, 6-5, 2-2, 6-4, 2-1
1939	Kansas City 3, St. Louis 1	4-1, 6-5, 1-5, 7-0
1943	Birmingham 3, Chicago 2	2-3, 16-5, 4-5, 4-1, 1-0
1948	Birmingham 4, Kansas City 3	5-4, 6-5, 4-3, 1-3, 4-5, L, 5-1
1949	Baltimore 4, Chicago 0	

NSL LCS

Year	Team Games Won	Game Scores
1932	Chicago 4, Nashville 3	5-6, 3-4, 5-3, [W], [L], 10-5, 9-2

World Series

Year	Team (League) Games Won	Game Scores
1924	Kansas City (NNL) 5, Hilldale (ECL) 4	6-2, 0-11, 6-6, 3-4, 3-5, 6-5, 4-3, 3-2, 3-5, 5-0
1925	Hilldale (ECL) 5, Kansas City (NNL) 1	5-2, 3-5, 3-1, 7-3, 2-1, 5-2
1926	Chicago (NNL) 5, Bacharach (ECL) 3	3-3, 7-6, 0-10, 4-4, 5-7, 5-4, 0-3, 6-3, 13-0, 1-0
1927	Chicago (NNL) 5, Bacharach (ECL) 3	6-2, 11-1, 7-0, 9-1, 2-3, 1-1, 1-8, 5-6, 11-4

Year	Team (League) Games Won	Game Scores
1942	Kansas City (NAL) 4, Homestead (NNL) 0	8-0, 8-4, 9-3, 9-5
1943	Homestead (NNL) 4, Birmingham (NAL) 3	2-4, 4-3, 9-0, 10-11, 8-0, 0-1, 8-4
1944	Homestead (NNL) 4, Birmingham (NAL) 1	8-5, 6-1, 9-0, 0-6, 4-2
1945	Cleveland (NAL) 4, Homestead (NNL) 0	2-1, 4-2, 4-0, 5-0
1946	Newark (NNL) 4, Kansas City (NAL) 3	1-2, 7-4, 5-15, 8-1, 1-5, 9-7, 3-2
1947	NY Cubans (NNL) 4, Cleveland (NAL) 1	7-10, 6-0, 9-4, 9-2, 6-5
1948	Homestead (NNL) 4, Birmingham (NAL) 1	3-2, 5-3, 3-4, 14-1, 10-6

FIELDS OF SEGREGATED DREAMS

The tremendous amount of research done on the Negro Leagues in recent decades has dramatically increased knowledge of black and Latino ballplayers. Using Philip Lowry's *Green Cathedrals*, Michael Benson's *Ballparks of North America*, and other sources, we have collected information on the home parks for all big league-caliber Negro League teams from 1920–54.

Listed for each city are park names, years used by Negro League tenants, and any other available information such as capacity or outfield dimensions. Miscellaneous notes of interest are included for some parks. A dagger (†) indicates that the venue was the home park for a major league team; an asterisk (*) indicates that the park is still standing today. (See the Ballparks section of the encyclopedia for full explanation of capacity and dimensions data.)

Not included here are home parks for independent black baseball clubs of big-league caliber, parks used by touring teams, neutral fields where teams played when barnstorming, or parks that hosted All-Star contests or exhibitions with major leaguers. A list of such venues might well include almost every ballpark in the lower 48 states, Mexico, South America, and Canada.

During the peak years of the great Negro Leagues, only 11 U.S. cities had major-league teams (counting Brooklyn). Of those cities, all but one—Boston—also boasted at least one big league-caliber Negro League club. Way back in 1887, the National Colored Base Ball League, the first Negro League, did include a Boston club—the Resolutes—but the loop quickly crumbled. Aside from a couple of black semi-pro teams in the 1940s, Beantown was bereft of the glories of black baseball in the first half of the twentieth century.

While black ballplayers were prohibited by the game's racist white power structure from playing in "Organized Baseball," many major league teams had no compunctions about taking in the green dollars of black baseball fans. The White Sox, Indians, Yankees, Senators, Giants, Pirates, Reds, and Dodgers rented out their home parks to Negro League clubs at some point from 1920–50; the Cubs, Athletics, Browns, Tigers, and Phillies (before they moved to Connie Mack Stadium) did not. (The Cardinals were the tenants of the Browns; the Phillies were tenants of the A's from mid-1938 onward.) Because NL and AL clubs shared one field in St. Louis and Philadelphia, there were few open dates. In lily-white Boston, the last major league city to integrate, neither the Braves or Red Sox had to make such a choice.

Between the years of 1925 and 1945, only one new major league park opened: Municipal Stadium in Cleveland. Afterward, the Indians' old stomping grounds in League Park were given over to weekday AL games and Negro League contests. Even as a second-fiddle facility, that was a relatively good place to play. In many cities, black players had to play on badly maintained fields, many of them not even real ballparks.

Many Negro League games and exhibitions—featuring some of the greatest athletes ever to don a uniform—were held on fields laid out over horse-racing tracks, polo grounds, football fields, track-and-field layouts, or worse—in the case of New York City's 59th Street Stadium, a pitch of dirt under a bridge. Not that this took the zing out of black baseball. The modernist credo of "Clean living in difficult circumstances" could well have been applied to most of the hardy and oft-times heroic souls who played and watched Negro League baseball.

NEGRO LEAGUE HOME BALLPARKS BY CITY

PARK	YEARS	TENANTS	NOTES
ATLANTIC CITY, NJ			
Bacharach Park	1923–1928	ECL Bacharach Giants	*aka Bacharachs Athletic Park*
	1929	ANL Bacharach Giants	
ATLANTA			
Ponce de Leon Park	1938	NAL Black Crackers	Cap 15,000; Dim 365–525/448/?–324
BALTIMORE			
Maryland Baseball Park	1923–1928	ECL Black Sox	
	1929	ANL Black Sox	
Druid Hill	1925	ECL Black Sox	
Bugle Field	1932	EWL Black Sox	*aka Moore's Field*
	1933	NNL Black Sox	
Oriole Park V	1938–1944	NNL Elite Giants	Cap 14,000; Dim 305–?/412/?–310
Venable Stadium	1944–1948	NNL Elite Giants	Cap 58,917; Dim 291–?/?/?–291; Football stadium
	1949–1950	NAL Elite Giants	
Westport Park	1950–1951	NAL Elite Giants	
BIRMINGHAM, AL			
Rickwood Field	1924–1925, 1927–1930	NNL Black Barons	Cap 9,312 Dim 405–?/470/?–334
	1932	NSL Black Barons	
	1937–1938, 1940–1954	NAL Black Barons	
BROOKLYN			
Dexter Park	1923–1927	ECL Royal Giants	
Ebbets Field†	1935	NNL Eagles	Cap 28,000; Dim 356–365/399/352–318
CHICAGO			
South Side Park (III)	1920–1921	NNL Giants	Cap 15,000
	1920–1931	NNL American Giants	Cap 15,000
	1932	NSL American Giants	Cap 15,000
	1933–1935	NNL American Giants	Cap 15,000
	1937–1940	NAL American Giants	Cap 15,000
Leland Giants Field	1920s	NNL American Giants	
Asbury Ball Park	1920s	NNL American Giants	
67th and Langley Sts. Park	1920s	NNL American Giants	

PARK	YEARS	TENANTS	NOTES
37th and Butler Sts. Park	1920s	NNL American Giants	
Pyott's Park	1920s	NNL American Giants	Short LF porch
Normal Field	1920s	NNL American Giants	Football stadium
Soldier Field*	1920s	NNL American Giants	Football stadium
Comiskey Park (I)†	1941–1952	NAL American Giants	Cap 47,400; Dim 352–375/415/382–352; Lights 1939
CINCINNATI			
Redland Field	1920–1921	NNL Cuban Stars West	Cap 25,000; Dim 320–380/420/?–384
Northside Park	1921	NNL Cuban Stars West	
Crosley Field†	1937	NAL Tigers	Cap 33,000; Dim 339–380/407/?–377
	1942	NAL Buckeyes	Cap 33,000; Dim 328–380/387/?–342
	1943–1945	NAL Clowns	Cap 33,000; Dim 328–380/390/?–342
CLEVELAND			
Tate Park	1922	NNL Tate Stars	
	1924	NNL Browns	
	1926	NNL Elites	
Hooper Field	1927	NNL Hornets	
Cubs Stadium	1931	NNL Cubs	
	1932	EWL Stars	
Hardware Field	1931	NNL Cubs	
Luna Bowl	1928	NNL Tigers	Football stadium
	1933	NNL Giants	
	1934	NNL Red Sox	
League Park (II)†	1939–1940	NAL Bears	Cap 22,500; Dim 347–?/420/400–290
	1943–1948,	NAL Buckeyes	Cap 22,500; Dim 349–?/420/400–290
	1950		
COLUMBUS, OH			
Neil Park (II)	1921	NNL Buckeyes	
	1932	NSL Turfs	
Red Bird Stadium	1933	NNL Blue Birds	Dim 415–?/450/337–315
	1935	NNL Elite Giants	Dim 415–?/450/337–315
DAYTON, OH			
Ducks Park	1920, 1926	NNL Marcos	Cap 5,000; Dim 360–360/360/360–360

PARK	YEARS	TENANTS	NOTES
DETROIT			
Mack Park	1920–1929	NNL Stars	
Hamtramck Stadium	1930–1931,	NNL Stars	[Hamtramck]
	1933		Dim 315–?/?/?–407; Lights 1930
	1932	EWL Wolves	
Dequindre Park	1937	NAL Stars	
Briggs Stadium†*	1954	NAL Stars	Cap 54,000; Dim 340–365/440/370–325
HARRISBURG, PA			
West End Grounds	1924–1927	ECL Giants	
Island Stadium	1943	NNL Stars	Cap 3,700
HOUSTON			
Buff Stadium	1949–1950	NAL Eagles	Cap 14,000; Dim 345–?/440/?–325
INDIANAPOLIS			
ABCs Field	1920–1926	NNL ABCs [I]	aka Washington Park and Greenlawn Park
	1931	NNL ABCs [II]	
	1937	NAL Athletics	
	1939	NAL ABCs [IV]	
	1943–1954	NAL Clowns	
Perry Stadium/Victory Field	1932	NSL ABCs [II]	Cap 13,000; Dim 350–?/497/?–350
	1938	NAL ABCs [III]	Cap 13,254;
	1944	NAL Clowns	Dim 335–?/500/?–335
	1940	NAL Crawfords	
JACKSONVILLE, FL			
Red Cap Stadium	1938,	NAL Red Caps	Cap 4,564;
	1941–1942		Dim 350–?/400/?–309
KANSAS CITY			
Association Park (II)	1920–1922	NNL Monarchs	
Paradeway Park	1920s	NNL Monarchs	
Muehlebach Field	1923–1927,	NNL Monarchs	Cap 17,476;
	1929–1930		Dim 350–408/450/?–350; Lights 1929
	1937–1954	NAL Monarchs	Dim 350–408/432/?–350; Ruppert Stadium 1938–42; Blues Stadium 1943–54
LOUISVILLE			
Parkway Field	1931	NNL White Sox	Dim 329–512/467/?–345
	1932	NSL Black Caps	Dim 329–512/467/?–345
	1949	NAL Buckeyes	Dim 329–512/467/?–345
	1954	NAL Black Colonels	Cap 13,496
MEMPHIS			
Martin Park	1924–1925,	NNL Red Sox	
	1927,		
	1929–1930		
	1932	NSL Red Sox	
	1937–1954	NAL Red Sox	
MILWAUKEE			
Borchert Field	1923	NNL Bears	Cap 10,000; Dim 266–?/395/?–266
MONROE, LA			
Casino Park	1932	NSL Monarchs	Dim 360–?/450/?–330
MONTGOMERY, AL			
Cramton Bowl	1932	NSL Grey Sox	Cap 10,000; Dim 420–?/600/?–600; Football stadium
College Hill Park	1932	NSL Grey Sox	
NASHVILLE			
Wilson Park	1930	NNL Elite Giants	
	1932	NSL Elite Giants	
Sulphur Dell	1933–1934	NNL Elite Giants	Cap 7,000; Dim 334–?/421/?–262; Field full of inclines
NEWARK			
Newark Schools Stadium	1926	ECL Stars	Football stadium
Sprague Field	1932	EWL Browns	[Bloomfield NJ] aka General Electric Field
Meadowbrook Oval	1934–1935	NNL Dodgers	Dim 300–?/380/?–300
Ruppert Stadium	1936–1948	NNL Eagles	Cap 19,000; Dim 305–?/410/?–305
NEW ORLEANS			
Pelican Stadium	1941	NAL Stars (New Orleans/St. Louis)	Dim 427–?/405/?–418
	1951	NAL Eagles	

PARK	YEARS	TENANTS	NOTES
NEW YORK CITY			
Dyckman Oval	1923–1928	ECL Cuban Stars East	Lights 1930
	1923	ECL Bacharach Giants	
	1929	ANL Cuban Stars East	
	1932	EWL Cuban Stars East	
Catholic Protectory Oval	1923–1926,	ECL Lincoln Giants	
	1928		
	1935–1936	NNL Cubans	
Capital Texture	1929	ANL Lincoln Giants	aka Olympic Park
Hinchliffe Stadium	1936–1937,	NNL Black Yankees	Football stadium [Patterson, NJ]
	1939–1945		
Triborough Stadium	1938	NNL Black Yankees	Cap 21,141; Football stadium Underneath Queensboro Bridge
59th Street Stadium	1939	NNL Cubans	
Polo Grounds†	1940s	NNL Cubans	Cap 47,000; Dim 280–455/484/449–258; Lights 1940
Grove Street Oval	1940–1948	NNL Cubans	Dim 240–/360/–280
	1949–1950	NAL Cubans	
Yankee Stadium†*	1946–1947	NNL Black Yankees	Cap 70,000; Dim 301–457/461/407–296; Lights 1946
PHILADELPHIA			
Hilldale Park	1923–1927	ECL Hilldale	Dim 315–?/400/?–370 [Yeadon PA]
	1929	ANL Hilldale	Dim 315–?/400/?–370 [Yeadon PA]
	1932	EWL Hilldale	Dim 315–?/400/?–370 [Yeadon PA]
Passon Field	1934–1935	NNL Stars	
	1934	NNL Bacharach Giants	
Penncoyd Field	1928	ECL Tigers	
Penmar Park	1936–48	NNL Stars	330–?/410/?–310 Lights 1933
	1949–1952	NAL Stars	330–?/410/?–310
PITTSBURGH			
Ammon Field	1922	NNL Keystones	
Grays Field	1929	ANL Homestead Grays	
Gus Greenlee Field	1932	EWL Homestead Grays	
	1933–1938	NNL Crawfords	Lights 1933
	1935–1938	NNL Homestead Grays	
Point Stadium	1930s	NNL Homestead Grays	Dim 270–?/475/?–250 [Johnstown PA]
Cycler Park	1930s	NNL Homestead Grays	Dim 393–?/440/?–325 [McKeesport PA]
Page Park	1930s	NNL Homestead Grays	[Monessen PA]
Forbes Field†	1939–1948	NNL Homestead Grays	Cap 33,730; Dim 335–355/435/408–300; Lights 1940
ROCHESTER			
Red Wing Stadium	1948	NNL Black Yankees	
ST. LOUIS			
Giants Field	1920–1921	NNL Giants	
	1922	NNL Stars	
Stars Park	1922–1931	NNL Stars	Cap 10,000; Dim 250–?/422/?–?
Metropolitan Park	1937	NAL Stars	
South End Park	1939	NAL Stars	
Mounds Ballfield	1941	NAL Stars (New Orleans/St. Louis)	[Mounds IL]
TOLEDO, OH			
Swayne Field	1923	NNL Tigers	Cap 10,000; Dim 472–?/448/?–347
	1939	NAL Crawfords	Cap 12,500; Dim 472–?/448/?–347
WASHINGTON, DC			
Griffith Stadium†	1924	ECL Potomacs	Cap 32,000; Dim 424–391/421/378/326
	1932	EWL Pilots	Cap 32,000 Dim 407–391/421/378–320
	1936–1937	NNL Elite Giants	Cap 30,171; Dim 402–391/421/378–320
	1937–1948	NNL Homestead Grays	Cap 25,048; Dim 402–391/421/378–320
	1938	NNL Black Senators	Cap 30,171; Dim 402–391/421/378–320

MIDSUMMER CLASSICS: THE ALL-STAR GAMES

The All-Star Game was born in 1933, initially conceived as a one-time event to bring sports fans to Chicago's Century of Progress Exposition. Arch Ward, the sports editor of the Chicago Tribune, thought up the idea of "the game of the century." After experiencing opposition from Commissioner Landis as well as the two leagues, Ward ultimately convinced baseball's hierarchy, as well as sportswriters across the country, to make it happen.

The very first All-Star game was played at Comiskey Park—a coin-flip winner over Wrigley Field—on July 6, 1933 before 49,200 fans. The game featured a fairy-tale AL victory, sparked by a Babe Ruth home run that sent straw boaters flying in the grandstands. As remains the case today, each manager (John McGraw and Connie Mack in the first game) was the defending league champion's skipper.

The unexpected success of this special event persuaded everyone to make the game an annual affair, and only in 1945 has the summer not featured an All-Star Game; the game was cancelled due to wartime travel restrictions after attendance had dipped dramatically in previous two years. Baseball held two games each season from 1959–62, largely because players wanted the extra gate and television proceeds for their pension fund. The two-game format was never popular, and it was abolished when the owners agreed to a new formula for contributions to the players' pension fund.

The debate over who should elect or select the All-Star teams, over how to vote, and over whom to vote for has become an annual tradition. Over the years, the All-Star franchise has switched back and forth between fans, managers, and players. Initially, the manager of each team chose the entire squad, but fans were finally enfranchised in 1947.

The oft-told scandal surrounding the 1957 NL All-Star voting, in which Cincinnati fans stuffed ballot boxes with pre-printed votes for Reds players and elected their hometown heroes to seven of the eight starting spots, resulted in the fans being denied the vote from 1958 through 1969. During those seasons, players, managers, and coaches selected the All-Stars. Unfortunately, the lack of fan input at this critical time, when football, basketball, and hockey were making inroads into baseball's fan base, helped turn some interest away from baseball.

For the 1970 game, fans were again granted the privilege of picking the starting lineup. That same season, Pete Rose steamrolled over AL catcher Ray Fosse at home plate in the game's deciding play, providing a classic and enduring All-Star image.

Fans and pundits, meanwhile, have constantly debated about whether the most popular players—as opposed to simply the best players—should be voted onto the teams, as well as whether voting should be based on a player's current season performance or on his entire career. The fairly recent practice appointing of aging or recently retired stars as honorary captains for each team has somewhat addressed this issue.

Wall-to-wall national and regional television coverage of regular-season baseball in recent decades has made the All-Star Game less of a special event, as dramatically declining Nielsen ratings have shown. The advent of interleague play in 1997 has also clearly diminished interest in what was once "must-see" TV.

Nevertheless, Major League Baseball's annual Midsummer Classic is still by far the most popular all-star contest in American sports. Football's Pro Bowl is a thoroughly irrelevant post-Super-Bowl Hawaiian vacation; the NBA's All-Star game is little more than a shooting exhibition where style counts as much as the result; and the NHL's midseason game features almost no defensive play, leading to ridiculously high scores. While some purists decry the 2003 change that gave World Series home-field advantage to the All-Star Game-winning league, this decision at least puts something at stake besides league pride. In an era where interleague trades are commonplace through the end of July, where even the best players frequently change teams in the prime of their careers, and where distinctions between the so-called Senior Circuit and the Junior League have been substantially eroded, the All-Star Game is not nearly so special.

As the luster of the game itself has dulled, MLB has effectively increased interest in the event by turning it into a week-long fan festival that includes a very popular home run-hitting contest (started in 1985) and a "Futures Game" showcase of top minor league talent (first held in 1999). For a brief period in the 1980s, an old-timers' game was also part of the National Pastime's annual midsummer break.

The embarrassing 2002 incident in which both leagues ran out of pitchers at Miller Park, forcing Commissioner Selig to declare a tie game after 11 innings on his home turf, was another black eye for baseball. Media critics also have focused in recent years on the "must carry" rule mandating that at least one player from each big-league team be picked for the All-Star squad while more deserving candidates on other clubs are left home. Conversely, it is always an issue whenever an All-Star manager brings along six or seven of his own pitchers or reserve players at the expense of other players having better seasons.

It is a healthy indicator that MLB's All-Star Game continues to inspire spirited debate among baseball fans while no one cares much about such games in other major sports. It is also healthy that the patterns of success in the All-Star Game reflect the way that the game is played in general. The AL won 12 of the first 16 classics before the NL—bolstered by its far larger talent base of African-American players—reeled off a dominating 30-6-1 string starting in 1950.

In 1983, however, the AL clobbered the NL 13-3 at Comiskey Park in the 50th anniversary game as Fred Lynn slugged the first-ever All-Star Game grand slam. Since then, the Junior League has dominated the Midsummer Classic, party due to an edge in international scouting and partly due to the return to the traditionally AL power-based style of play in both leagues. The Americans have now won the last nine games as well as 17 of the last 23.

In recent years, the National Pastime has enjoyed some excellent Midsummer Classics, notably those in 1994, 1995, 1997, and 2003. Despite constant interest from baseball fans, however, the era of the All-Star Game as a major event in the country's cultural framework may be over. Several ideas have been proposed in recent years to reinvigorate the game, the most popular being a "U.S. versus the World" format where major league stars from Latin America and Asia would square off against American players, as in the Futures Game.

The All-Star Game table below shows the results of all 76 Midsummer Classics. The **Site** column shows the ballpark names as of the date of each game, so the first two games played at Tiger Stadium are properly shown as being played at Briggs Stadium. The **Rosters** column shows the size of each league's All-Star squad, not including players replaced due to injury. **Innings** are shown in the **Score** column only if the game went into extra innings or was shortened by rain. The **AL-NL Record** column shows the cumulative balance of power between the leagues (including ties starting with 1961's second game). **Ex Post Facto MVP** choices are shown in brackets prior to the inception of the official award in 1962; **MVPs** are italicized if they played for the losing league.

Year/No.	Host	Site	Rosters	Score (Innings)	Attendance	AL-NL Record	MVP/Team [Ex Post Facto]
1933	Chicago AL	Comiskey Park	18	AL 4, NL 2	49,200	1-0	[Lefty Gomez NY]
1934	New York NL	Polo Grounds	20	AL 9, NL 7	48,363	2-0	[Carl Hubbell NY]
1935	Cleveland AL	Lakefront Stadium	20	AL 4, NL 1	69,812	3-0	[Jimmie Foxx Phi]
1936	Boston NL	Braves Field	21	NL 4, AL 3	25,534	3-1	[Dizzy Dean StL]
1937	Washington AL	Griffith Stadium	23	AL 8, NL 3	31,391	4-1	[Lou Gehrig NY]
1938	Cincinnati NL	Crosley Field	23	NL 4, AL 1	27,607	4-2	[Johnny Vander Meer Cin]
1939	New York AL	Yankee Stadium	25	AL 3, NL 1	62,892	5-2	[Bob Feller Cle]
1940	St.Louis NL	Sportsman's Park	25	NL 4, AL 0	32,373	5-3	[Billy Herman Chi]
1941	Detroit AL	Briggs Stadium	25	AL 7, NL 5	54,674	6-3	[Ted Williams Bos]
1942	New York NL	Polo Grounds	25	AL 3, NL 1	33,694	7-3	[Spud Chandler NY]
1943	Philadelphia AL	Shibe Park	25	AL 5, NL 3	31,938	8-3	[Bobby Doerr Bos]
1944	Pittsburgh NL	Forbes Field	25	NL 7, AL 1	29,589	8-4	[Rip Sewell Pit]
1946	Boston AL	Fenway Park	25	AL 12, NL 0	34,906	9-4	[Ted Williams Bos]
1947	Chicago NL	Wrigley Field	25	AL 2, NL 1	41,123	10-4	[Hal Newhouser Det]
1948	St.Louis AL	Sportsman's Park	25	AL 5, NL 2	34,009	11-4	[Vic Raschi NY]
1949	Brooklyn NL	Ebbets Field	25	AL 11, NL 7	32,577	12-4	[Joe DiMaggio NY]
1950	Chicago AL	Comiskey Park	25	NL 4, AL 3 (14)	46,127	12-5	[Red Schoendienst StL]
1951	Detroit AL	Briggs Stadium	25	NL 8, AL 3	52,075	12-6	[Richie Ashburn Phi]
1952	Philadelphia NL	Shibe Park	25	NL 3, AL 2 (5)	32,785	12-7	[Hank Sauer Chi]
1953	Cincinnati NL	Crosley Field	25	NL 5, AL 1	30,846	12-8	[Enos Slaughter StL]
1954	Cleveland AL	Municipal Stadium	25	AL 11, NL 9	68,751	13-8	[Al Rosen Cle]
1955	Milwaukee NL	County Stadium	25	NL 6, AL 5 (12)	45,314	13-9	[Stan Musial StL]
1956	Washington AL	Griffith Stadium	25	NL 7, AL 3	28,843	13-10	[Willie Mays NY]
1957	St.Louis NL	Busch Stadium	25	AL 6, NL 5	30,693	14-10	[Jim Bunning Det]
1958	Baltimore AL	Memorial Stadium	25	AL 4, NL 3	48,829	15-10	[Billy O'Dell Bal]
1959 G1	Pittsburgh NL	Forbes Field	25	NL 5, AL 4	35,277	15-11	[Hank Aaron Mil]
1959 G2	Los Angeles NL	Memorial Coliseum	25	AL 5, NL 3	55,105	16-11	[Yogi Berra NY]
1960 G1	Kansas City AL	Municipal Stadium	25	NL 5, AL 3	30,619	16-12	[Ernie Banks Chi]
1960 G2	New York AL	Yankee Stadium	25	NL 6, AL 0	38,362	16-13	[Willie Mays SF]
1961 G1	San Francisco NL	Candlestick Park	25	NL 5, AL 4 (10)	44,115	16-14	[Roberto Clemente Pit]
1961 G2	Boston AL	Fenway Park	25	AL 1, NL 1	31,851	16-14-1	[No Selection]
1962 G1	Washington AL	District of Columbia Stadium	25	NL 3, AL 1	45,480	16-15-1	Maury Wills LA
1962 G2	Chicago NL	Wrigley Field	25	AL 9, NL 4	38,359	17-15-1	Leon Wagner LA
1963	Cleveland AL	Municipal Stadium	25	NL 5, AL 3	44,160	17-16-1	Willie Mays SF
1964	New York NL	Shea Stadium	25	NL 7, AL 4	50,850	17-17-1	Johnny Callison Phi
1965	Minnesota AL	Metropolitan Stadium	25	NL 6, AL 5	46,706	17-18-1	Juan Marichal SF
1966	St.Louis NL	Busch Memorial Stadium	25	NL 2, AL 1 (10)	49,936	17-19-1	Brooks Robinson Bal
1967	California AL	Anaheim Stadium	25	NL 2, AL 1 (15)	46,309	17-20-1	Tony Perez Cin
1968	Houston NL	Astrodome	25	NL 1, AL 0	48,321	17-21-1	Willie Mays SF
1969	Washington AL	Robert F. Kennedy Memorial Stadium	28	NL 9, AL 3	45,259	17-22-1	Willie McCovey SF
1970	Cincinnati NL	Riverfront Stadium	28	NL 5, AL 4 (12)	51,838	17-23-1	Carl Yastrzemski Bos
1971	Detroit AL	Tiger Stadium	28	AL 6, NL 4	53,559	18-23-1	Frank Robinson Bal
1972	Atlanta NL	Atlanta-Fulton County Stadium	28	NL 4, AL 3 (10)	53,107	18-24-1	Joe Morgan Cin
1973	Kansas City AL	Royals Stadium	28	NL 7, AL 1	40,849	18-25-1	Bobby Bonds SF
1974	Pittsburgh NL	Three Rivers Stadium	28	NL 7, AL 2	50,706	18-26-1	Steve Garvey LA
1975	Milwaukee AL	County Stadium	28	NL 6, AL 3	51,480	18-27-1	Bill Madlock Chi & Jon Matlack NY
1976	Philadelphia NL	Veterans Stadium	28	NL 7, AL 1	63,974	18-28-1	George Foster Cin
1977	New York AL	Yankee Stadium	28	NL 7, AL 5	56,683	18-29-1	Don Sutton LA
1978	San Diego NL	San Diego Stadium	28	NL 7, AL 3	51,549	18-30-1	Steve Garvey LA
1979	Seattle AL	Kingdome	28	NL 7, AL 6	58,905	18-31-1	Dave Parker Pit
1980	Los Angeles NL	Dodger Stadium	28	NL 4, AL 2	56,088	18-32-1	Ken Griffey Cin
1981	Cleveland AL	Cleveland Stadium	28	NL 5, AL 4	72,086	18-33-1	Gary Carter Mon
1982	Montreal NL	Olympic Stadium	28	NL 4, AL 1	59,057	18-34-1	Dave Concepcion Cin
1983	Chicago AL	Comiskey Park	28	AL 13, NL 3	43,801	19-34-1	Fred Lynn Cal
1984	San Francisco NL	Candlestick Park	28	NL 3, AL 1	57,756	19-35-1	Gary Carter Mon
1985	Minnesota AL	Metrodome	28	NL 6, AL 1	54,960	19-36-1	La Marr Hoyt SD
1986	Houston NL	Astrodome	28	AL 3, NL 2	45,774	20-36-1	Roger Clemens Bos
1987	Oakland AL	Oakland Coliseum	28	NL 2, AL 0 (12)	49,671	20-37-1	Tim Raines Mon
1988	Cincinnati NL	Riverfront Stadium	28	AL 2, NL 1	55,837	21-37-1	Terry Steinbach Oak
1989	California AL	Anaheim Stadium	28	AL 5, NL 3	64,036	22-37-1	Bo Jackson KC
1990	Chicago NL	Wrigley Field	28	AL 2, NL 0	39,071	23-37-1	Julio Franco Tex
1991	Toronto AL	SkyDome	28	AL 4, NL 2	52,383	24-37-1	Cal Ripken Bal
1992	San Diego NL	Jack Murphy Stadium	28	AL 13, NL 6	59,372	25-37-1	Ken Griffey Jr. Sea
1993	Baltimore AL	Oriole Park at Camden Yards	28	AL 9, NL 3	48,147	26-37-1	Kirby Puckett Min
1994	Pittsburgh NL	Three Rivers Stadium	28	NL 8, AL 7 (10)	59,568	26-38-1	Fred McGriff Atl
1995	Texas AL	The Ballpark in Arlington	28	NL 3, AL 2	50,920	26-39-1	Jeff Conine Fla
1996	Philadelphia NL	Veterans Stadium	28	NL 6, AL 0	62,670	26-40-1	Mike Piazza LA
1997	Cleveland AL	Jacobs Field	28	AL 3, NL 1	44,916	27-40-1	Sandy Alomar Jr. Cle
1998	Colorado NL	Coors Field	30	AL 13, NL 8	51,267	28-40-1	Roberto Alomar Bal
1999	Boston AL	Fenway Park	30	AL 4, NL 1	34,187	29-40-1	Pedro Martinez Bos
2000	Atlanta NL	Turner Field	30	AL 6, NL 3	51,323	30-40-1	Derek Jeter NY
2001	Seattle AL	SAFECO Field	30	AL 4, NL 1	47,364	31-40-1	Cal Ripken Bal
2002	Milwaukee NL	Miller Park	30	AL 7, NL 7 (11)	41,871	31-40-2	(No Selection)
2003	Chicago AL	U.S. Cellular Field	30	AL 7, NL 6	47,609	32-40-2	Garret Anderson Ana
2004	Houston NL	Minute Maid Park	30	AL 9, NL 4	41,886	33-40-2	Alfonso Soriano Tex
2005	Detroit	Comerica Park	30	AL 7, NL 5	41,617	34-40-2	Miguel Tejada Bal

OCTOBER CLASSICS: POSTSEASON SERIES AND PLAYOFFS

The 2004 postseason showed that, on its 101st anniversary, the World Series had come full circle since the Boston Americans (as the 2004 champion Red Sox were then called) had defeated the Pittsburgh Pirates in the 1903 Fall Classic. While the 1903 affair was certainly the first series of its kind, it was definitely not the first World Series.

Postseason play is almost as old as Organized Baseball itself. In the 1870s, National Association teams would play exhibition games against local teams after the regular season was over. The first series between two league champions occurred in 1882, when National League champion Chicago faced American Association champion St. Louis in two exhibition games. Starting in 1884, the regular-season winners of these two competing leagues officially met to determine the championship of professional baseball in the United States—and, thus, the world.

These nineteenth century championship series, often referred to today as "World Series" since they pitted two league winners against each other, were played in a variety of formats. The 1884 Series was a simple best-of-five arrangement; the 1885 and 1886 Series changed to a best out of seven games. The 1887 Series was stretched to an epic best-of-15 affair, with the NL Detroit Wolverines and the AA St. Louis Browns playing in ten different cities! Even *after* the Wolverines clinched the Series with their eighth win in the 11th game, the two teams still played out the final four games, largely to bring in gate receipts. The 1888 battle between the NL Giants and the AA Browns was downsized to a 10-game series played in four cities. The last year for this nineteenth century World Series was 1890, as the collapse of the American Association in 1891 left the National League as the only major league standing.

Without another league, the NL—conscious of the lucrative purses that could be generated by an end-of-year tournament—tried several different formats for postseason play. In 1892 the season was deliberately divided into two halves for the only time in big-league history, with the winner of the first half facing the second-half winner in an NL championship series. From 1894–97, the first place team in the NL faced the second place team in a postseason trophy series sponsored by wealthy sportsman William Temple. While the "Temple Cup" format did attract paying fans to the ballpark, it never generated that much excitement. (Not too surprising, as the first-place team had already shown itself superior during the regular season. Nevertheless, the second-place team did win three of the four Temple Cups.) After the demise of the Temple Cup, Pittsburgh's *Chronicle-Telegraph* newspaper sponsored a five-game match-up in 1900 between the second-place Pirates and the first-place Brooklyn Superbas.

In 1901 the American League emerged as an alternative major league. By outbidding the senior National League for most of the game's best players, ending the scourge of syndicate ownership, and putting a more refined game on the field, the AL quickly surpassed the NL in popularity. By 1903 the established league agreed to a ceasefire with its upstart rival. This agreement allowed the NL champion Pittsburgh Pirates to challenge AL champion Boston.

This first modern World Series was an enormous success in virtually every way, with Boston winning the series, five games to three. Baseball fans fully expected—but did not get—another World Series the next year. The 1903 arrangement was the result of a bilateral agreement between the two clubs involved, and was not officially sanctioned by either league. New York was the runaway NL winner in 1904, but Giants manager John McGraw—who disliked the AL and despised its president, Ban Johnson—had no intention of playing an AL team in the postseason.

Giants owner John Brush, who had problems of his own with the AL and with Ban Johnson, backed McGraw's stand in 1904. Then—perhaps bowing to public sentiment and perhaps lured by the financial possibilities—Brush changed his mind in the off-season and proposed an annual, officially sanctioned World Series, starting in 1905. The National Commission, which had

been formed to oversee the two leagues as a result of the 1903 ceasefire agreement, adopted most of Brush's suggestions. So the World Series became a permanent fixture of the National Pastime.

While the early World Series were marked with roughhouse play from even the game's biggest stars—the leagues truly didn't like each other back then—both sides on the field (and in the front offices) recognized the financial and public-relations value of the enterprise.

To be sure, the Fall Classic has provided more than its share of great moments. From Christy Mathewson's three shutouts to Willie Mays' amazing catch, from series-ending homers by Bill Mazeroski and Joe Carter to the memorable long balls of Carlton Fisk, Casey Stengel, and Reggie Jackson, individual efforts have brightened the Series stage. Classic World Series battles like 2002 have enthralled the American public as well as fans worldwide.

The World Series has run relatively smoothly since 1905, with few major crises affecting the Fall Classic. In 1918 the two leagues chose to shut down the season early during World War I, and the resulting Cubs-Red Sox World Series had only one travel day. Players nearly went on strike before Game Five to protect their already-meager postseason shares.

The next year, however, featured a far more serious scandal. The 1919 World Series, featuring the heavily favored Chicago White Sox and the Cincinnati Reds, ended in an upset as the Reds won the best-of-nine in eight contests. After a year full of rumors about game-fixing, late in the 1920 pennant race, the very core of the White Sox club was implicated in a plot to throw the previous year's series. The 1919 series had been expanded to a best-of-nine to bring in more profits for the owners, as the greed of the era manifested itself on all sides. Following the 1921 series, the Fall Classic was shrunk back to its current seven-game schedule.

The public shock and outcry over the White Sox' actions severely damaged the credibility of the World Series and of professional baseball itself. Only the harsh actions of new commissioner Judge Landis (who banned eight Chicago players from the game for life) and Babe Ruth's emergence as an international superstar kept the major leagues from falling from grace.

Even World War II couldn't cancel the World Series, though the level of play in 1944 and 1945 was predictably poor, with most big-leaguers off at war. Labor problems, though, knocked out the games in 1994, as the titanic dispute between owners and players resulted in a strike—the most disastrous in major league history. In September acting Commissioner Bud Selig did the unthinkable: he canceled the 1994 World Series, marking the first time in eighty-nine years that the Series had not been played. Baseball fans were more than angry—they were appalled and incredulous that the *World Series* wouldn't be played—a sad commentary on the times. Nevertheless, the Grand Old Game came back again in the late 1990s, revived by the great home run chase of 1998 and by some excellent postseason and World Series tussles.

Old-time fans remember the days when the World Series was the only time, besides the All-Star game, that the two leagues would meet. For more than sixty years after the modern World Series was founded, baseball's postseason stayed the course with little significant change. In the 1960s, however, baseball faced increasing competition from other sports, its own declining popularity, and the demands of expansion. The AL and NL separately expanded to ten teams in the early 1960 without changing the postseason.

As both leagues planned to go to 12 teams in 1969, MLB felt that the leagues could no longer maintain their traditional structures and keep most of the fans interested in the pennant races ("You can't sell a twelfth-place team," it was said, ignoring the fact that it wasn't possible to sell an eighth-place team before expansion, either.) Therefore, each league was split into East and West Divisions (though geography didn't always determine which division teams were placed in), and new League Championship Series were created to determine the pennant winners.

Initially, the LCS match-ups were best-of-five affairs; in 1985, MLB expanded the postseason to a best-of-seven format. The previous season, 1984, saw the Chicago Cubs attempting to reach the World Series for the first time in nearly forty years. The Cubbies fell short, however, losing the final three games on the road in San Diego. Had they played a seven-game set, the Cubs would have two more contests at Wrigley Field to play. In 1985, the Kansas City Royals, down 3-1 to the Toronto Blue Jays, took advantage of the new format, storming back to win the final three ALCS contests on the way to their only World Championship.

The other anomalous postseason in the twentieth century resulted from the 1981 strike and its ad hoc split season. First-half winners in each division faced second-half winners in best-of-five series in order to qualify for the LCS. The expanded format not only rewarded teams who played well before the work stoppage, but also created some extra revenue after the lost summer of the strike. And generated a lot of anguish in St. Louis and Cincinnati as the team with the best overall record in each NL division were shut out of postseason play.

The 1993 NL expansion gave each league 14 teams, with further expansion expected soon. A year later, therefore, baseball owners decided to add another postseason round, ushering in the era of Division Series. In 1994 MLB adopted a three-division structure out of which the division winners and one "Wild Card" team from each league would reach the postseason. This meant that a World Series champion would now have to win three short series: a best-of-five Division series, a best-of-seven League Championship Series, and the best-of-seven World Series. Since a wild card team has won the World Series in three out of the first nine years this system has been in place, it is clear that winning a regular-season title is no longer necessary.

While many traditionalists have been disappointed by the way the expanded postseason has reduced the importance of the regular season, MLB, the punditocracy, and most fans feel that the Wild Card has boosted interest in many cities late in the season. The remarkably tight 2003 NL Wild Card race—in which seven teams were competing well into the final month of the reason—added fuel to the discussion about expanding the postseason even further by adding more Wild Card berths.

While there is little question that a Wild Card race fueled interest in places like South Florida during 2003, the long-term damage to the pennant races and to the postseason is substantial, even though less clear. Division Series attendance has been mediocre at best in many places as fans wait to see if their team will survive the lightning round and play for the pennant. Even worse, the magnitude of baseball's showcase event, the World Series, has dimmed dramatically since the 1980s.

One thing that has not changed that much over the last 100 years of postseason history is the home-field advantage. The winning percentage for home teams has always hovered around 55 percent in the World Series, and even in the "old days" home games were not a walk in the park. In four of the first five Fall Classics, in fact, the visiting team won a majority of contests. The advantage hovers at 53–54 percent for the Division Series and LCS.

Among the Division Series, only one has featured a home-team sweep (1995 AL); in the LCS, every game has been won by the home team only three times (1982 AL, 1984 NL, and 2004 NL). Three World Series have been swept by the home teams: 1987, 1991, and 2001. Never in *any* postseason series— even a best-of-three—has the visiting team won every contest.

In 1998, the Division Series format was overhauled after complaints because the home-field advantage was being determined on a rotating basis rather than on the basis of the best record. After almost 30 years of LCS play, home-field advantage in the championship series was also now given to the team with the better record.

Furthermore, the format of the Division Series was changed from "2-3" format to "2-2-1" so that the team with the home-field advantage didn't have to play the first two games on the road.

Key to Postseason and Playoff Tables. The first World Series Most Valuable Player Award was created in 1949 by the New York chapter of the Baseball Writers Association of America in honor of Babe Ruth, who had died the previous year. In 1955 the editors of *SPORT* Magazine started choosing their own World Series MVP. That MVP Award often came with a Corvette, courtesy of General Motors' Chevrolet division.

Eventually, the winners of the *SPORT* award came to be determined by baseball writers and executives present at the World Series. Now MLB's official World Series MVP Award greatly overshadows the Babe Ruth Award, whose winner is generally not selected until several weeks after the Series ends. *SPORT*'s involvement with the World Series MVP Award ended with the magazine's demise in 2000. We have selected Ex Post Facto MVPs for all World Series prior to 1955 to honor the players who we think would have won the World Series MVP Award, had it existed. Selections in italics designate MVPs from losing teams. A single entry in the MVP column for the World Series means that the same player won both the SPORT/MLB award and the Babe Ruth Award.

MVPs for the League Championship Series have been awarded by the NL since 1977 and the AL since 1980. No MVP Award has been established for the more recent Division Series. We have made Ex Post Facto MVP picks for all Division Series and for the ALCS and NLCS played prior to the league awards.

The following tables show the results of all postseason series in baseball history, as well as the four NL playoff series and the six-single game playoffs. Prior to the advent of divisional play in 1969, NL first-place ties were broken by playing a three-game series, while the AL used a single-game playoff format. Since 1969 all ties for postseason qualification have been broken by one-game playoffs. MLB considers any playoff game or series that determines which club advances to the postseason to be part of the regular season.

Also note that game scores for each contest in every postseason series since 1884 are included. These scores appear in chronological order, with the scores given in reference to which team won the series. Therefore, "5-0"-indicates that the team that won the series won that game, while an "0-5" score means that the team that *lost* the series won that game.

National League Playoff Series

Year	Teams Games Won (Scores)
1946	St. Louis 2, Brooklyn 0 (4-2, 8-4)
1951	New York 2, Brooklyn 1 (3-1, 0-10, 5-4)
1959	Los Angeles 2, Milwaukee 0 (3-2, 6-5)
1962	San Francisco 2, Los Angeles 1 (8-0, 7-8, 6-4)

Single-Game Playoffs

Year	Title	Teams (Division) Score
1948	AL Pennant	Cleveland 8, Boston 3
1978	AL East Title	New York 5, Boston 4
1980	NL West Title	Houston 7, Los Angeles 1
1995	AL West Title	Seattle 9, California 1
1998	NL Wild Card	Chicago (C) 5, San Francisco (W) 3
1999	NL Wild Card	New York (E) 5, Cincinnati (C) 0

American League Division Series

Year	Team (Division) WC Games Won	Game Scores	[Ex Post Facto MVP]
1981	New York (E/1H) 3, Milwaukee (E/2H) 2	5-3,3-0,3-5,1-2,7-3	[Goose Gossage]
1981	Oakland (W/1H) 3, Kansas City (W/2H) 0	4-0,2-1,4-1	[Dwayne Murphy]
1995	Cleveland (C) 3, Boston (E) 0	5-4,4-0,8-2	[Eddie Murray]
1995	Seattle (W) 3, New York (E†) 2	6-9,5-7,7-4,11-8,6-5	[Edgar Martinez]
1996	Baltimore (E†) 3, Cleveland (C) 1	10-4,7-4,4-9,4-3	[Brady Anderson]
1996	New York (E) 3, Texas (W) 1	2-6,5-4,3-2,6-4	[Juan Gonzalez]
1997	Cleveland (C) 3, New York (E†) 2	6-8,7-5,1-6,3-2,4-3	[Mike Mussina]
1997	Baltimore (E) 3, Seattle (W) 1	9-3,9-3,2-4,3-1	[Omar Vizquel]
1998	New York (E) 3, Texas (W) 0	2-0,3-1,4-0	[Scott Brosius]
1998	Cleveland (C) 3, Boston (E†) 1	3-11,9-5,4-3,2-1	[Manny Ramirez]
1999	New York (E) 3, Texas (W) 0	8-0,3-1,3-0	[Bernie Williams]
1999	Boston (E†) 3, Cleveland (C) 2	2-3,1-11,9-3,23-7,12-8	[Pedro Martinez]
2000	New York (E) 3, Oakland (W) 2	3-5,4-0,4-2,1-11,7-5	[Mariano Rivera]
2000	Seattle (W†) 3, Chicago (C) 0	7-4,5-2,2-1	[Edgar Martinez]
2001	Seattle (W) 3, Cleveland (C) 2	7-4,1-0,6-2	[Edgar Martinez]
2001	New York (E) 3, Oakland (W†) 2	1-0,1-4,5-3,1-4,2-1	[Derek Jeter]
2002	Minnesota (C) 3, Oakland (W) 2	7-5,1-9,3-6,11-2,5-4	[A.J. Pierzynski]
2002	Anaheim (W†) 3, New York (E) 1	5-8,8-6,9-6,9-5	[Scott Spiezio]
2003	Boston (E†) 3, Oakland (W) 2	4-5,1-5,3-1,5-4,4-3	[Todd Walker]
2003	New York (E) 3, Minnesota (C) 1	1-3,4-1,3-1,8-1	[Derek Jeter]
2004	New York (E) 3, Minnesota (C) 1	0-2,7-6,8-4,6-5	[Alex Rodriguez]
2004	Boston (E†) 3, Anaheim (W) 0	9-3,8-3,8-6	[David Ortiz]
2005	Los Angeles (W) 3, New York (E) 2	2-4,5-3,11-7,2-3,5-3	[Bengie Molina]
2005	Chicago (C) 3, Boston (E†) 0	14-2,5-4,5-3	[A.J. Pierzynski]

National League Division Series

Year	Team (Division/WC) Games Won	Game Scores	[Ex Post Facto MVP]
1981	Montreal (E/2H) 3, Philadelphia (E/1H) 2	3-1,3-1,2-6,5-6,3-0	[Steve Rogers]
1981	Los Angeles (W/1H) 3, Houston (W/2H) 2	1-3,0-1,6-1,2-1,4-0	[Jerry Reuss]
1995	Atlanta (E) 3, Colorado (W†) 1	5-4,7-4,5-7,10-4	[Marquis Grissom]
1995	Cincinnati (C) 3, Los Angeles (W) 0	7-2,5-4,10-1	[Hal Morris]
1996	Atlanta (E) 3, Los Angeles (W†) 0	2-1,3-2,5-2	[Mark Wohlers]
1996	St. Louis (C) 3, San Diego (W) 0	3-1,5-4,7-5	[Brian Jordan]
1997	Florida (E†) 3, San Francisco (W) 0	2-1,7-6,6-2	[Gary Sheffield]
1997	Atlanta (E) 3, Houston (C) 0	2-1,13-3,4-1	[Chipper Jones]
1998	Atlanta (E) 3, Chicago (C†) 0	7-1,2-1,6-2	[Javy Lopez]
1998	San Diego (W) 3, Houston (C) 1	2-1,4-5,2-1,6-1	[Kevin Brown]
1999	New York (E†) 3, Arizona (W) 1	8-4,1-7,9-2,4-3	[Edgardo Alfonzo]
1999	Atlanta (W) 3, Houston (C) 1	1-6,5-1,5-3,7-5	[Brian Jordan]
2000	St. Louis (C) 3, Atlanta (E) 0	7-5,10-4,7-1	[Jim Edmonds]
2000	New York (E†) 3, San Francisco (W) 1	1-5,5-4,3-2,4-0	[Bobby Jones]
2001	Atlanta (E) 3, Houston (C) 0	0-5,5-1,2-17,6-2,3-1	[Chipper Jones]
2001	Arizona (W) 3, St. Louis (C†) 2	3-5,0-2,1-0,9-2,5-3	[Curt Schilling]
2002	St. Louis (C) 3, Arizona (W) 0	12-2,2-1,6-3	[Fernando Vina]
2002	San Francisco (W†) 3, Atlanta (E) 2	8-5,3-7,2-10,8-3,3-1	[Barry Bonds]
2003	Florida (E) 3, San Francisco (W†) 1	0-2,9-5,4-3,7-6	[Ivan Rodriguez]
2003	Chicago (C) 3, Atlanta (E) 2	4-2,3-5,3-1,4-6,5-1	[Kerry Wood]
2004	St. Louis (C) 3, Los Angeles (W) 1	8-3,8-3,0-4,6-2	[Edgar Renteria]
2004	Houston (C†) 3, Atlanta (E) 2	9-3,2-4,8-5,5-6,12-3	[Carlos Beltran]
2005	St. Louis (C) 3, San Diego (W) 0	8-5,6-2,7-4	[Reggie Sanders]
2005	Houston (C†) 3, Atlanta (E) 1	16-5,1-7,7-3,7-6	[Lance Berkman]

E: East Division; C: Central Division; W: West Division; †: Wild Card; 1H: First-half winner; 2H: Second-half winner

Nineteenth Century National League Championship Series

Year	Team Games Won	Game Scores	[Ex Post Facto MVP]
1892	Boston (1H) 5, Cleveland (2H) 0, 1 tie	0-0,4-3,3-2,4-0,12-7,8-3	[Hugh Duffy]
1894	New York (2) 4, Baltimore (1) 0	4-1,9-6,4-1,16-3	[Amos Rusie] Temple Cup
1895	Cleveland (2) 4, Baltimore (1) 1	5-4,7-2,7-1,0-5,5-2	[Cy Young] Temple Cup
1896	Baltimore (1) 4, Cleveland (2) 0	7-1,7-2,6-2,5-0	[Willie Keeler] Temple Cup
1897	Baltimore (2) 4, Boston (1) 1	12-13,13-11,8-3,12-11,9-3	[Jack Doyle] Temple Cup
1900	Brooklyn (1) 3, Pittsburgh (2) 1	5-2,4-2,0-10,6-1	[Joe McGinnity] *Chronicle-Telegraph* Cup

(1) Finished first in regular season; (2) Finished second in regular season; 1H: First-half winner; 2H: Second-half winner

American League Championship Series

Year	Team (Division/WC) Games Won	Game Scores	MVP [Ex Post Facto]
1969	Baltimore (E) 3, Minnesota (W) 0	4-3,1-0,11-2	[Dave McNally]
1970	Baltimore (E) 3, Minnesota (W) 0	10-6,11-3,6-1	[Boog Powell]
1971	Baltimore (E) 3, Oakland (W) 0	5-3,5-1,5-3	[Boog Powell]
1972	Oakland (W) 3, Detroit (E) 2	3-2,5-0,0-3,3-4,2-1	[Blue Moon Odom]
1973	Oakland (W) 3, Baltimore (E) 2	0-6,6-3,2-1,4-5,3-0	[Catfish Hunter]
1974	Oakland (W) 3, Baltimore (E) 1	3-6,5-0,1-0,2-1	[Sal Bando]
1975	Boston (E) 3, Oakland (W) 0	7-1,6-3,5-3	[Carl Yastrzemski]
1976	New York (E) 3, Kansas City (W) 2	4-1,3-7,5-3,4-7,7-6	[Chris Chambliss]
1977	New York (E) 3, Kansas City (W) 2	2-7,6-2,2-6,6-4,5-3	[Sparky Lyle]
1978	New York (E) 3, Kansas City (W) 1	7-1,4-10,6-5,2-1	[Reggie Jackson]
1979	Baltimore (E) 3, California (W) 1	6-3,9-8,3-4,8-0	[Eddie Murray]
1980	Kansas City (W) 3, New York (E) 0	7-2,3-2,4-2	Frank White
1981	New York (E) 3, Oakland (W) 0	3-1,13-3,4-0	Graig Nettles
1982	Milwaukee (E) 3, California (W) 2	3-8,2-4,5-3,9-5,4-3	Fred Lynn
1983	Baltimore (E) 3, Chicago (W) 1	1-2,4-0,11-1,3-0	Mike Boddicker
1984	Detroit (E) 3, Kansas City (W) 0	8-1,5-3,1-0	Kirk Gibson
1985	Kansas City (W) 4, Toronto (E) 3	1-6,5-6,6-5,1-3,2-0,5-3,6-2	George Brett
1986	Boston (E) 4, California (W) 3	1-8,9-2,3-5,3-4,7-6,10-4,8-1	Marty Barrett
1987	Minnesota (W) 4, Detroit (E) 1	8-5,6-3,6-7,5-3,9-5	Gary Gaetti
1988	Oakland (W) 4, Boston (E) 0	2-1,4-3,10-6,4-1	Dennis Eckersley
1989	Oakland (W) 4, Toronto (E) 1	7-3,6-3,3-7,6-5,4-3	Rickey Henderson
1990	Oakland (W) 4, Boston (E) 0	9-1,4-1,4-1,3-1	Dave Stewart
1991	Minnesota (W) 4, Toronto (E) 1	5-4,2-5,3-2,9-3,8-5	Kirby Puckett
1992	Toronto (E) 4, Oakland (W) 2	3-4,3-1,7-5,7-6,2-6,9-2	Roberto Alomar
1993	Toronto (E) 4, Chicago (W) 2	7-3,3-1,1-6,4-7,5-3,6-3	Dave Stewart
1995	Cleveland (C) 4, Seattle (W) 2	3-2,5-2,2-5,7-0,3-2,4-0	Orel Hershiser
1996	New York (E) 4, Baltimore (E†) 1	5-4,3-5,5-2,8-4,6-4	Bernie Williams
1997	Cleveland (C) 4, Baltimore (E) 2	0-3,5-4,2-1,8-7,2-4,1-0	Marquis Grissom
1998	New York (E) 4, Cleveland (C) 2	7-2,1-4,1-6,4-0,5-3,9-5	David Wells
1999	New York (E) 4, Boston (E†) 1	4-3,3-2,1-13,9-2,6-1	Orlando Hernandez
2000	New York (E) 4, Seattle (W) 2	6-2,6-5,2-8,10-6,7-0	David Justice
2001	New York (E) 4, Seattle (W) 1	2-0,1-8,5-1,11-4,3-2	Alfonso Soriano
2002	Anaheim (W†) 4, Minnesota (C) 1	1-2,6-3,2-1,7-1,13-5	Adam Kennedy
2003	New York (E) 4, Boston (E†) 3	2-5,6-2,4-3,2-3,4-2,6-9,6-5	Mariano Rivera
2004	Boston (E†) 4, New York (E) 3	7-10,1-3,8-19,6-4,5-4,4-2,10-3	David Ortiz
2005	Chicago (C) 4, Los Angeles (W) 1	2-3,2-1,5-2,8-2,6-3	Paul Konerko

National League Championship Series

Year	Team (Division/WC) Games Won	Game Scores	MVP [Ex Post Facto]
1969	New York (E) 3, Atlanta (W) 0	9-5,11-6,7-4	[Ken Boswell]
1970	Cincinnati (W) 3, Pittsburgh (E) 0	3-0,3-1,3-2	[Bobby Tolan]
1971	Pittsburgh (E) 3, San Francisco (W) 1	4-5,9-4,2-1,9-5	[Bob Robertson]
1972	Cincinnati (W) 3, Pittsburgh (E) 2	1-5,5-3,2-3,7-1,4-3	[Johnny Bench]
1973	New York (E) 3, Cincinnati (W) 2	1-2,5-0,9-2,1-2,7-2	[Rusty Staub]
1974	Los Angeles (W) 3, Pittsburgh (E) 1	3-0,5-2,0-7,12-1	[Don Sutton]
1975	Cincinnati (W) 3, Pittsburgh (E) 0	8-3,6-1,5-3	[Tony Perez]
1976	Cincinnati (W) 3, Philadelphia (E) 0	6-3,6-2,7-6	[Pete Rose]
1977	Los Angeles (W) 3, Philadelphia (E) 1	5-7,7-1,6-5,4-1	Dusty Baker
1978	Los Angeles (W) 3, Philadelphia (E) 1	9-5,4-0,4-9,4-3	Steve Garvey
1979	Pittsburgh (E) 3, Cincinnati (W) 0	5-2,3-2,7-1	Willie Stargell
1980	Philadelphia (E) 3, Houston (W) 2	3-1,4-7,0-1,5-3,8-7	Manny Trillo
1981	Los Angeles (W) 3, Montreal (E) 2	5-1,0-3,1-4,7-1,2-1	Burt Hooton
1982	St. Louis (E) 3, Atlanta (W) 0	7-0,4-3,6-2	Darrell Porter
1983	Philadelphia (E) 3, Los Angeles (W) 1	1-0,1-4,7-2,7-2	Gary Matthews
1984	San Diego (W) 3, Chicago (E) 2	0-13,2-4,7-1,7-5,6-3	Steve Garvey
1985	St. Louis (E) 4, Los Angeles (W) 2	1-4,2-8,4-2,12-2,3-2,7-5	Ozzie Smith
1986	New York (E) 4, Houston (W) 2	0-1,5-1,6-5,1-3,2-1,7-6	Mike Scott
1987	St. Louis (E) 4, San Francisco (W) 3	5-3,0-5,6-5,2-4,3-4,6-1,0-6	Jeffrey Leonard
1988	Los Angeles (W) 4, New York (E) 3	2-3,6-3,4-8,5-4,7-4,1-5,6-0	Orel Hershiser
1989	San Francisco (W) 4, Chicago (E) 1	11-3,5-9,5-4,6-4,3-2	Will Clark
1990	Cincinnati (W) 4, Pittsburgh (E) 2	3-4,2-1,6-3,5-3,2-3,2-1	Rob Dibble/Randy Myers
1991	Atlanta (W) 4, Pittsburgh (E) 3	1-5,1-0,10-3,2-3,0-1,1-0,4-0	Steve Avery
1992	Atlanta (W) 4, Pittsburgh (E) 3	5-1,13-5,2-3,6-4,1-7,4-13,3-2	John Smoltz
1993	Philadelphia (E) 4, Atlanta (W) 2	4-3,3-14,4-9,2-1,4-3,6-3	Curt Schilling
1995	Atlanta (E) 4, Cincinnati (C) 0	2-1,6-2,5-2,6-0	Mike Devereaux
1996	Atlanta (E) 4, St. Louis (C) 3	4-2,3-8,2-3,3-4,14-0,3-1,15-0	Javier Lopez
1997	Florida (E†) 4, Atlanta (E) 2	5-3,1-7,5-2,0-4,2-1,7-4	Livan Hernandez
1998	San Diego (W) 4, Atlanta (E) 2	3-2,3-0,4-1,3-8,6-7,5-0	Sterling Hitchcock
1999	Atlanta (E) 4, New York (E†) 2	4-2,4-3,1-0,2-3,3-4,10-9	Eddie Perez
2000	New York (E†) 4, St. Louis (C) 1	0-2,7-1,8-2,5-0,6-9,7	Mike Hampton
2001	Arizona (W) 4, Atlanta (E) 1	4-2,3-2,3-14,3-1,12-3	Craig Counsell
2002	San Francisco (W†) 4, St. Louis (C) 1	9-6,4-1,4-5,4-3,2-1	Benito Santiago
2003	Florida (E†) 4, Chicago (C) 3	9-8,3-12,4-5,3-8,4-0,8-3,9-6	Ivan Rodriguez
2004	St. Louis (C) 4, Houston (C†) 3	10-7,6-4,2-5,5-6,0-3,6-4,5-2	Albert Pujols
2005	Houston (C†) 4, St. Louis (C) 2	3-5,4-1, 4-3,2-1,4-5,5-1	Roy Oswalt

E: East Division; C: Central Division; W: West Division; †: Wild Card

Nineteenth Century World Series (American Association vs. National League)

Year	Teams (League) Games Won	Game Scores	MVP [Ex Post Facto]
1884	Providence (N) 3, New York (AA) 0	6-0,3-1,12-2	[Charles Radbourn]
1885	St. Louis (AA) 3, Chicago (N) 3, 1 tie	5-5,5-4,4-7,2-39,2-9,2-4,13	[Cap Anson]
1886	St. Louis (AA) 4, Chicago (N) 2	0-6,12-0,4-11,8-5,10-3,4-3	[Bob Caruthers]
1887	Detroit (N) 10, St. Louis (AA) 5	1-6,5-3,2-1,8-0,2-5,9-0,3-1,9-2,4-2,4-11,13-3,1-5,6-3,4-3,2-9	[Lady Baldwin]
1888	New York (N) 6, St. Louis (AA) 4	2-1,0-3,4-2,6-3,6-4,12-5,5-7,11-3,11-14,7-18	[Tim Keefe]
1889	New York (N) 6, Brooklyn (AA) 3	10-12,6-2,7-8,7-10,11-3,2-1,11-7,16-7,3-2	[John Ward]
1890	Brooklyn (N) 3, Louisville (AA) 3, 1 tie	9-0,5-3,7-7,4-5,7-2,8-9,2-6	[Red Ehret]

World Series

Year	Teams (League) Games Won	Game Scores	MVP [Ex Post Facto] Babe Ruth Award*
1903	Boston (A) 5, Pittsburgh (N) 3	3-7,3-0,2-4,4-5,11-2,6-3,7-3,3-0	[Bill Dineen]
1904	[No World Series held]		
1905	New York (N) 4, Philadelphia (A) 1	3-0,0-3,9-0,1-0,2-0	[Christy Mathewson]
1906	Chicago (A) 4, Chicago (N) 2	2-1,1-7,3-0,0-1,8-6,8-3	[George Davis]
1907	Chicago (N) 4, Detroit (A) 0, 1 tie	3-3,3-1,5-1,6-1,2-0	[Harry Steinfeldt]
1908	Chicago (A) 4, Detroit (A) 1	10-6,6-1,3-8,3-0,2-0	[Orval Overall]
1909	Pittsburgh (N) 4, Detroit (A) 3	4-1,2-7,8-6,0-5,8-4,4-5,8-0	[Babe Adams]
1910	Philadelphia (A) 4, Chicago (N) 1	4-1,9-3,12-5,3-4,7-2	[Jack Coombs]
1911	Philadelphia (A) 4, New York (N) 2	1-2,3-1,3-2,4-2,3-4,13-2	[Frank Baker]
1912	Boston (A) 4, New York (N) 3, 1 tie	4-3,6-6,1-2,3-1,2-1,2-5,4-11,3-2	[Joe Wood]
1913	Philadelphia (A) 4, New York (N) 1	6-4,0-3,8-2,6-5,3-1	[Frank Baker]
1914	Boston (N) 4, Philadelphia (A) 0	7-1,1-0,5-4,3-1	[Hank Gowdy]
1915	Boston (A) 4, Philadelphia (N) 1	1-3,2-1,2-1,2-1,5-4	[Harry Hooper]
1916	Boston (A) 4, Brooklyn (N) 1	6-5,2-1,3-4,6-2,4-1	[Ernie Shore]
1917	Chicago (A) 4, New York (N) 2	2-1,7-2,0-2,0-5,8-5,4-2	[Red Faber]
1918	Boston (A) 4, Chicago (N) 2	1-0,1-3,2-1,3-2,0-3,2-1	[Carl Mays]
1919	Cincinnati (N) 5, Chicago (A) 3	9-1,4-2,0-3,2-0,5-0,4-5,1-4,10-5	[Hod Eller]
1920	Cleveland (A) 5, Brooklyn (N) 2	3-1,0-3,1-2,5-1,8-1,1-0,3-0	[Stan Coveleski]
1921	New York (N) 5, New York (A) 3	0-3,0-3,13-5,4-2,1-3,8-5,2-1,1-0	[Waite Hoyt]
1922	New York (N) 4, New York (A) 0, 1 tie	3-2,3-3,3-0,4-3,5-3	[Irish Meusel]
1923	New York (A) 4, New York (N) 2	4-5,4-2,0-1,8-4,8-1,6-4	[Babe Ruth]
1924	Washington (A) 4, New York (N) 3	3-4,4-3,4-6,7-4,2-6,2-1,4-3	[Goose Goslin]
1925	Pittsburgh (N) 4, Washington (A) 3	1-4,3-2,3-4,0-4,6-3,3-2,9-7	[Max Carey]
1926	St.Louis (N) 4, New York (A) 3	1-2,6-2,4-0,5-10,2-3,10-2,3-2	[Grover Alexander]
1927	New York (A) 4, Pittsburgh (N) 0	5-4,6-2,8-1,4-3	[Babe Ruth]
1928	New York (A) 4, St.Louis (N) 0	4-1,9-3,7-3,7-3	[Lou Gehrig]
1929	Philadelphia (A) 4, Chicago (N) 1	3-1,9-3,1-3,10-8,3-2	[Jimmie Foxx]
1930	Philadelphia (A) 4, St.Louis (N) 2	5-2,6-1,0-5,1-3,2-0,7-1	[George Earnshaw]
1931	St.Louis (N) 4, Philadelphia (A) 3	2-6,2-0,5-2,0-3,5-1,1-8,4-2	[Pepper Martin]
1932	New York (A) 4, Chicago (N) 0	12-6,5-2,7-5,13-6	[Lou Gehrig]
1933	New York (N) 4, Washington (A) 1	4-2,6-1,0-4,2-1,4-3	[Carl Hubbell]
1934	St.Louis (N) 4, Detroit (A) 3	8-3,2-3,4-1,4-10,1-3,4-3,11-0	[Dizzy Dean]
1935	Detroit (A) 4, Chicago (N) 2	0-3,8-3,6-5,2-1,1-3,4-3	[Tommy Bridges]
1936	New York (A) 4, New York (N) 2	1-6,18-4,2-1,5-2,4-5,13-5	[Jake Powell]
1937	New York (A) 4, New York (N) 1	8-1,8-1,5-1,3-7,4-2	[Lefty Grove]
1938	New York (A) 4, Chicago (N) 0	3-1,6-3,5-2,8-3	[Joe Gordon]
1939	New York (A) 4, Cincinnati (N) 0	2-1,4-0,7-3,7-4	[Charlie Keller]
1940	Cincinnati (N) 4, Detroit (A) 3	2-7,5-3,4-7,5-2,0-8,4-0,2-1	[Jimmy Ripple]
1941	New York (A) 4, Brooklyn (N) 1	3-2,2-3,2-1,7-4,3-1	[Charlie Keller]
1942	St.Louis (N) 4, New York (A) 1	4-7,4-3,2-0,9-6,4-2	[Johnny Beazley]
1943	New York (A) 4, St.Louis (N) 1	4-2,3-4,6-2,2-1,2-0	[Spud Chandler]
1944	St.Louis (N) 4, St. Louis (A) 2	1-2,3-2,2-6,5-1,2-0,3-1	[Mort Cooper]
1945	Detroit (A) 4, Chicago (N) 3	0-9,4-1,0-3,4-1,8-4,7-8,9-3	[Hank Greenberg]
1946	St. Louis (N) 4, Boston (A) 3	2-3,3-0,0-4,12-3,3-6,4-1,4-3	[Harry Brecheen]
1947	New York (A) 4, Brooklyn (N) 3	5-3,10-3,8-9,2-3,2-1,6-8,5-2	[Johnny Lindell]
1948	Cleveland (A) 4, Boston (N) 2	0-1,4-1,2-0,2-1,5-11,4-3	[Bob Lemon]
1949	New York (A) 4, Brooklyn (N) 1	1-0,0-1,4-3,6-4,10-6	[Allie Reynolds] Joe Page*
1950	New York (A) 4, Philadelphia (N) 0	1-0,2-1,3-2,5-2	[Jerry Coleman]
1951	New York (A) 4, New York (N) 2	1-5,3-1,2-6,6-2,13-1,4-3	[Ed Lopat] Phil Rizzuto*
1952	New York (A) 4, Brooklyn (N) 3	2-4,7-1,3-5,2-0,5-6,3-2,4-2	[Mickey Mantle] Johnny Mize
1953	New York (A) 4, Brooklyn (N) 2	9-5,4-2,2-3,3-7,11-7,4-3	[Billy Martin]
1954	New York (N) 4, Cleveland (A) 0	5-2,3-1,6-2,7-4	[Dusty Rhodes]
1955	Brooklyn (A) 4, New York (A) 3	5-6,2-4,8-3,8-5,5-3,1-5,2-0	Johnny Podres
1956	New York (A) 4, Brooklyn (N) 3	3-6,8-13,5-3,6-2,2-0,0-1,9-0	Don Larsen
1957	Milwaukee (N) 4, New York (A) 3	1-3,4-2,3-12,7-5,1-0,2-3,5-0	Lew Burdette
1958	New York (A) 4, Milwaukee (N) 3	3-4,5-13,4-0,0-3,7-0,4-3,6-2	Bob Turley Elston Howard*
1959	Los Angeles (N) 4, Chicago (A) 2	0-11,4-3,3-1,5-4,0-1,9-3	Larry Sherry
1960	Pittsburgh (N) 4, New York (A) 3	6-4,3-16,0-10,3-2,5-2,0-12,10-9	Bobby Richardson Bill Mazeroski

Year	Teams (League) Games Won	Game Scores	MVP [Ex Post Facto] Babe Ruth Award*
1961	New York (A) 4, Cincinnati (N) 1	2-0,2-6,3-2,7-0,13-5	Whitey Ford
1962	New York (A) 4, San Francisco (N) 3	6-2,0-2,3-2,3-7,5-3,2-5,1-0	Ralph Terry
1963	Los Angeles (N) 4, New York (A) 0	5-2,4-1,1-0,2-1	Sandy Koufax
1964	St.Louis (N) 4, New York (A) 3	9-5,3-8,1-2,4-3,5-2,3-8,7-5	Bob Gibson
1965	Los Angeles (N) 4, Minnesota (A) 3	2-8,1-5,4-0,7-2,7-0,1-5,2-0	Sandy Koufax
1966	Baltimore (A) 4, Los Angeles (N) 0	5-2,6-0,1-0,1-0	Frank Robinson
1967	St. Louis (N) 4, Boston (A) 3	2-1,0-5,5-2,6-0,1-3,4-8,7-2	Bob Gibson Lou Brock*
1968	Detroit (A) 4, St.Louis (N) 3	0-4,8-1,3-7,1-10,5-3,13-1,4-1	Mickey Lolich
1969	New York (N) 4, Baltimore (A) 1	1-4,2-1,5-0,2-1,5-3	Donn Clendenon Al Weis*
1970	Baltimore (A) 4, Cincinnati (N) 1	4-3,6-5,9-3,5-6,9-3	Brooks Robinson
1971	Pittsburgh (N) 4, Baltimore (A) 3	3-5,3-11,5-1,4-3,4-0,2-3,2-1	Roberto Clemente
1972	Oakland (A) 4, Cincinnati (N)3	3-2,2-1,0-1,3-2,4-5,1-8,3-2	Gene Tenace
1973	Oakland (A) 4, New York (N) 3	2-1,7-10,3-2,1-6,0-2,3-1,5-2	Reggie Jackson Bert Campaneris*
1974	Oakland (A) 4, Los Angeles (N) 1	3-2,2-3,3-2,5-2,3-2	Rollie Fingers Dick Green*
1975	Cincinnati (N) 4, Boston (A) 3	0-6,3-2,6-5,4-5,6-2,6-7,4-3	Pete Rose Luis Tiant*
1976	Cincinnati (N) 4, New York (A) 0	5-1,4-3,6-2,7-2	Johnny Bench
1977	New York (A) 4, Los Angeles (N) 2	4-3,1-6,5-3,4-2,4-10,8-4	Reggie Jackson
1978	New York (A) 4, Los Angeles (N) 2	5-11,3-4,5-1,4-3,12-2,7-2	Bucky Dent
1979	Pittsburgh (N) 4, Baltimore (A) 3	4-5,3-2,4-8,6-9,7-1,4-0,4-1	Willie Stargell
1980	Philadelphia (N) 4, Kansas City (A) 2	7-6,6-4,3-4,3-5,4-3,4-1	Mike Schmidt Tug McGraw*
1981	Los Angeles (N) 4, New York (A) 2	3-5,0-3,5-4,8-7,2-1,9-2	Ron Cey Pedro Guerrero Steve Yeager Ron Cey*
1982	St. Louis (N) 4, Milwaukee (A) 3	0-10,5-4,6-2,5-7,4-6,13-1,6-3	Darrell Porter Bruce Sutter*
1983	Baltimore (A) 4, Philadelphia (N) 1	1-2,4-1,3-2,5-4,5-0	Rick Dempsey
1984	Detroit (A) 4, San Diego (N) 1	3-2,3-5,5-2,4-2,8-4	Alan Trammell Jack Morris*
1985	Kansas City (A) 4, St. Louis (N) 3	1-3,2-4,6-1,0-3,6-1,2-1,11-0	Bret Saberhagen
1986	New York (N) 4, Boston (A) 3	0-1,3-9,7-1,6-2,2-4,6-5,8-5	Ray Knight
1987	Minnesota (A) 4, St. Louis (N) 3	10-1,8-4,1-3,2-7,2-4,11-5,4-2	Frank Viola
1988	Los Angeles (N) 4, Oakland (A) 1	5-4,6-0,1-2,4-3,5-2	Orel Hershiser
1989	Oakland (A) 4, San Francisco (N) 0	5-0,5-1,13-7,9-6	Dave Stewart
1990	Cincinnati (N) 4, Oakland (A) 0	7-0,5-4,8-3,2-1	Jose Rijo Billy Hatcher*
1991	Minnesota (A) 4, Atlanta (N) 3	5-2,3-2,4-5,2-3,5-14,4-3,1-0	Jack Morris
1992	Toronto (A) 4, Atlanta (N) 2	1-3,5-4,3-2,2-1,2-7,4-3	Pat Borders Dave Winfield*
1993	Toronto (A) 4, Philadelphia (N) 2	8-5,4-6,10-3,15-14,0-2,8-6	Paul Molitor
1994	[World Series canceled]		
1995	Atlanta (N) 4, Cleveland (A) 2	3-2,4-3,6-7,5-2,4-5,1-0	Tom Glavine
1996	New York (A) 4, Atlanta (N) 2	1-12,0-4,5-2,8-6,1-0,3-2	John Wetteland Cecil Fielder*
1997	Florida (N) 4, Cleveland (A) 3	7-4,1-6,14-11,3-10,8-7,1-4,3-2	Livan Hernandez Moises Alou*
1998	New York (A) 4, San Diego (N) 0	9-6,9-3,5-4,3-0	Scott Brosius
1999	New York (A) 4, Atlanta (N) 0	4-1,7-2,6-5,4-1	Mariano Rivera
2000	New York (A) 4, New York (N) 1	4-3,6-5,2-4,3-2,4-2	Derek Jeter
2001	Arizona (N) 4, New York (A) 3	9-1,4-0,1-2,3-4,2-3,15-2,3-2	Randy Johnson Curt Schilling
2002	Anaheim (A) 4, San Francisco (N) 3	3-4,11-10,10-4,3-4,4-16,6-5,4-1	Troy Glaus
2003	Florida (N) 4, New York (A) 2	3-2,1-6,1-6,4-3,6-4,2-0	Josh Beckett
2004	Boston (A) 4, St. Louis (N) 0	11-9,6-2,4-1,3-0	Manny Ramirez Keith Foulke*
2005	Chicago (A) 4, Houston (N) 0	1-0,7-5,7-6,5-3	Jermaine Dye

THE GLORY OF THEIR TIMES: THE ALL-TIME LEADERS

The history of baseball is so appealing partly because it is possible to compare achievements from eras that are many years apart. While baseball has certainly evolved over time, it has not undergone radical changes that would make the sport unrecognizable. A fan from 1903 magically transported to a big-league game of today would not have a problem understanding what was happening on the field (though he might not be carrying a week's wages to pay for a hot dog).

The unchanging nature of the game is why the leaders section is often the first place a reader turns upon opening a book such as this. Most baseball statistics have maintained enough of their meaning over time so as to make comparisons between players of different eras possible, either directly or indirectly (by comparing to the league average). Only a few statistical categories have changed continually in one direction over baseball history. Those few include innings pitched, which has generally declined on a seasonal basis along with parallel statistics such as complete games; fielding average, which has risen due to improvements in gloves, better groundskeeping, and more lenient official scoring; and strikeouts, which have risen due to changes in the style of play. Most other statistics rise and fall with variances in the balance between offense and defense but haven't fundamentally changed over the years.

Some of the lists in this section are divided by time period in order to more clearly highlight the standout performers of each era. Eight significant eras in baseball history have been defined for this purpose—each is distinguished by major rules changes, by large changes in the number of leagues or teams, or by other important factors.

- The first era covers 1876–91, a period that started with the formation of the National League and ended with the collapse of the American Association;
- The next period, 1892–1900, marks the short period during which the National League stood unchallenged by any rival major league;
- The third era, 1901–20, covers the Dead Ball Era, World War I, the banning of the spitball, and the Black Sox scandal. It concludes as offensive levels start to jump (which came later in the NL than in the AL);
- The next period, 1921–42, takes the major leagues through the period in which offense dominated until World War II started to seriously deplete the majors;
- The fifth era, 1943–60, starts with the peak war years and continues through baseball's integration and the migration of the major leagues to the West Coast;
- The next period, 1961–72, is highlighted by the expansion of both leagues as well the change to division play, the expansion of the strike zone (and its subsequent reversion), and the resulting collapse of offense;
- The seventh era, 1973–1987, starts with the implementation of the designated hitter rule and includes the heyday of the multipurpose stadiums. This era is highlighted by the return of offense—as well as significantly higher attendance—to the game;
- The current era, which covers 1988 to the present, is marked by the explosion of home runs, the wave of retro ballparks, and a new period of expansion.

Players are only eligible to be listed in only one era each, even if their careers spanned several eras. They are placed in the era during which they played the most games or pitched the most innings. *However, their lifetime totals or averages are used to rank them in the era they played the most.*

A quick perusal of these leader lists will reveal the names of all of the National Pastime's immortals along with the all-time greats and numerous perennial all-stars. They recount the exploits of more than a few lucky players who happened to catch lightning in a bottle once or twice. The greatest players live on in the memories of most baseball fans; the lucky ones sometimes live on only in the pages of the record books. Regardless of the type of player, the vast majority of ballplayers who show up on these lists were truly the glory of their times.

The Glory of Their Times is one of the greatest baseball books ever published. In its pages, Lawrence Ritter captured the sweet essence of men in the twilight of their lives—men whose glory may have faded but whose memories have not. By recording the names of these all-time leaders, we hope to honor them as well as the game they played so well.

A few notes about some of the leader lists:

On-Base Percentage is calculated by the current official definition for every season since 1954. However, since a distinct sacrifice fly category was not kept before 1954, they are not included in the calculations for seasons before 1954, except for the years during which sacrifice flies were not counted as sacrifice hits. (1908–30 and 1939 were the other years when sac flies were awarded; in other years pre–1954, a sacrifice fly was counted as an at bat.)

Plate Appearances count every time a batter completes an at bat, including hits, outs, walks, sacrifices, hit-by-pitches, etc.

Strikeout Percentage divides strikeouts by at bats to indicate what percentage of the time a batter strikes out.

At Bats per Strikeout indicates how infrequently a batter strikes out.

Relative Batting Average is a player's batting average compared to the league's batting average (where the latter is 1.0).

Home Run Percentage divides home runs by at bats to show the percentage of times a batter hits a home run.

Runs/150 Games and **RBI/150 Games** show a player's typical production in a full season. While today the regular season lasts 162 games, for most of baseball history the regular season was 154 games or less.

Total Chances consist of assists plus putouts plus errors.

Relief Wins and **Relief Losses** include only decisions for pitchers who did not start the game.

Blown Saves and **Save Percentage** are available for 1969 to the present only.

The minimums for Single-Season leaders include:
- Starting Pitchers (for rate statistics): 1 inning pitched per scheduled game;
- Relief Pitchers (for rate statistics): 0.5 inning pitched per scheduled game;
- Pitcher Winning Percentage: 15 wins;
- Save Percentage: 20 saves;
- Batters (for rate statistics): 3.1 plate appearances per scheduled game;
- Pinch-Hit Batting Average: 30 at bats;
- Pitcher Batting Average: 20 hits;
- Stolen Base Percentage: 20 stolen bases;
- Fielding Statistics: 0.66 games played per scheduled game (exception: for outfielders with a 1.000 Fielding Average, a minimum of 250 total chances, and for pitchers with a 1.000 Fielding Average, a minimum of 50 total chances);
- Catcher Fielding Statistics: 0.5 games played per scheduled game.

The minimums for Career leaders include:
- Starting Pitchers (for rate statistics): 1,500 innings pitched;
- Relief Pitchers (for rate statistics): 750 innings pitched;
- Save Percentage: 50 Saves;
- Batters (for rate statistics): 1,000 games;
- Pinch-Hit Batting Average: 150 at bats;
- Pitcher Batting Average: 80 hits;
- Stolen Base Percentage: 100 stolen bases.

Games

1 Pete Rose 3562
2 Carl Yastrzemski 3308
3 Hank Aaron 3298
4 Rickey Henderson 3081
5 Ty Cobb 3034
6 Eddie Murray 3026
  Stan Musial 3026
8 Cal Ripken 3001
9 Willie Mays 2992
10 Dave Winfield 2973
11 Rusty Staub 2951
12 Brooks Robinson 2896
13 Robin Yount 2856
14 Al Kaline 2834
15 Rafael Palmeiro 2831
16 Harold Baines 2830
17 Eddie Collins 2826
18 Reggie Jackson 2820
19 Frank Robinson 2808
20 Honus Wagner 2794
21 Tris Speaker 2789
22 Tony Perez 2777
23 Barry Bonds 2730
  Mel Ott 2730
25 George Brett 2707
26 Graig Nettles 2700
27 Darrell Evans 2687
28 Paul Molitor 2683
29 Rabbit Maranville 2670
30 Joe Morgan 2649
31 Andre Dawson 2627
32 Lou Brock 2616
33 Dwight Evans 2606
34 Luis Aparicio 2599
35 Willie McCovey 2588
36 Ozzie Smith 2573
37 Craig Biggio 2564
38 Paul Waner 2549
39 Ernie Banks 2528
40 Bill Buckner 2517
  Sam Crawford 2517
42 Gary Gaetti 2507
43 Babe Ruth 2503
44 Tim Raines 2502
45 Carlton Fisk 2499
46 Dave Concepcion 2488
  Billy Williams 2488
48 Nap Lajoie 2480
49 Max Carey 2476
50 Rod Carew 2469
  Vada Pinson 2469
52 Dave Parker 2466
53 Fred McGriff 2460
54 Ted Simmons 2456
55 Bill Dahlen 2444
56 Ron Fairly 2442
57 Wade Boggs 2440
  Tony Gwynn 2440
59 Chili Davis 2436
60 Harmon Killebrew 2435
61 Roberto Clemente 2433
62 Willie Davis 2429
63 Luke Appling 2422
64 Zack Wheat 2410
65 Mickey Vernon 2409
66 Buddy Bell 2405
67 Sam Rice 2404
  Mike Schmidt 2404
69 Steve Finley 2401
  Mickey Mantle 2401
71 Eddie Mathews 2391
72 Lou Whitaker 2390
73 Jake Beckley 2389
74 Bobby Wallace 2383
75 Enos Slaughter 2380
76 Roberto Alomar 2379
77 Julio Franco 2377
78 George Davis 2372
79 Al Oliver 2368
80 Nellie Fox 2367
81 Willie Stargell 2360
82 Jose Cruz 2353
83 Brian Downing 2344
84 Steve Garvey 2332
85 Bert Campaneris 2328
86 Frank White 2324
87 Charlie Gehringer 2323
88 Jimmie Foxx 2317
89 B.J. Surhoff 2313
90 Frankie Frisch 2311
91 Harry Hooper 2309
92 Gary Carter 2296
93 Alan Trammell 2293
94 Don Baylor 2292
  Ted Williams 2292
96 Omar Vizquel 2290
97 Goose Goslin 2287
98 Jimmy Dykes 2282
99 Lave Cross 2278
100 Cap Anson 2277

Plate Appearances

1 Pete Rose 15861
2 Carl Yastrzemski 13991
3 Hank Aaron 13940
4 Rickey Henderson 13346
5 Ty Cobb 13068
6 Cal Ripken 12883
7 Eddie Murray 12817
8 Stan Musial 12712
9 Willie Mays 12493
10 Dave Winfield 12358
11 Robin Yount 12249
12 Paul Molitor 12160
13 Rafael Palmeiro 12046
14 Eddie Collins 12037
15 Tris Speaker 11988
16 Brooks Robinson 11782
17 Honus Wagner 11748
18 Frank Robinson 11743
19 George Brett 11624
20 Al Kaline 11597
21 Reggie Jackson 11416
22 Barry Bonds 11415
23 Craig Biggio 11341
24 Mel Ott 11337
25 Joe Morgan 11329
26 Rabbit Maranville 11256
27 Lou Brock 11235
28 Luis Aparicio 11230
29 Rusty Staub 11229
30 Harold Baines 11092
31 Tony Perez 10861
32 Ozzie Smith 10778
33 Max Carey 10770
34 Andre Dawson 10769
35 Paul Waner 10762
36 Wade Boggs 10740
37 Darrell Evans 10737
38 Babe Ruth 10617
39 Sam Crawford 10594
40 Dwight Evans 10569
41 Rod Carew 10550
42 Billy Williams 10519
43 Jake Beckley 10504
44 Nap Lajoie 10460
45 Bill Dahlen 10405
46 Vada Pinson 10403
47 Roberto Alomar 10400
48 Ernie Banks 10395
49 Tim Raines 10359
50 Nellie Fox 10349
51 Sam Rice 10246
52 Harry Hooper 10244
53 Luke Appling 10243
54 Charlie Gehringer 10237
55 Tony Gwynn 10232
56 Graig Nettles 10226
57 Roberto Clemente 10212
58 Dave Parker 10184
59 George Davis 10178
60 Fred McGriff 10174
61 Cap Anson 10123
62 Eddie Mathews 10101
63 Frankie Frisch 10100
64 Mike Schmidt 10062
65 Bill Buckner 10033
66 Buddy Bell 10009
67 Chili Davis 9996
  Zack Wheat 9996
69 Lou Whitaker 9967
70 Doc Cramer 9933
71 Mickey Mantle 9909
72 Steve Finley 9877
73 Carlton Fisk 9853
74 Fred Clarke 9838
75 Mickey Vernon 9834
76 Harmon Killebrew 9831
77 Willie Davis 9822
  Goose Goslin 9822
79 Gary Gaetti 9817
80 Ted Williams 9791
81 Al Oliver 9778
82 Lave Cross 9742
83 Richie Ashburn 9736
84 Willie McCovey 9686
85 Ted Simmons 9685
86 Jimmie Foxx 9670
87 Lou Gehrig 9660
88 Dave Concepcion 9640
89 Bert Campaneris 9625
90 Jesse Burkett 9620
91 Bobby Wallace 9612
92 Willie Keeler 9610
93 Omar Vizquel 9548
94 Brett Butler 9545
95 Al Simmons 9515
96 Rogers Hornsby 9475
97 Pee Wee Reese 9470
98 Steve Garvey 9466
99 Willie Randolph 9462
100 Julio Franco 9446

At Bats

1 Pete Rose 14053
2 Hank Aaron 12364
3 Carl Yastrzemski 11988
4 Cal Ripken 11551
5 Ty Cobb 11434
6 Eddie Murray 11336
7 Robin Yount 11008
8 Dave Winfield 11003
9 Stan Musial 10972
10 Rickey Henderson 10961
11 Willie Mays 10881
12 Paul Molitor 10835
13 Brooks Robinson 10654
14 Rafael Palmeiro 10472
15 Honus Wagner 10439
16 George Brett 10349
17 Lou Brock 10332
18 Luis Aparicio 10230
19 Tris Speaker 10195
20 Al Kaline 10116
21 Rabbit Maranville 10078
22 Frank Robinson 10006
23 Eddie Collins 9949
24 Andre Dawson 9927
25 Harold Baines 9908
26 Reggie Jackson 9864
27 Craig Biggio 9811
28 Tony Perez 9778
29 Rusty Staub 9720
30 Vada Pinson 9645
31 Nap Lajoie 9589
32 Sam Crawford 9570
33 Jake Beckley 9538
34 Paul Waner 9459
35 Mel Ott 9456
36 Roberto Clemente 9454
37 Ernie Banks 9421
38 Bill Buckner 9397
39 Ozzie Smith 9396
40 Max Carey 9363
41 Dave Parker 9358
42 Billy Williams 9350
43 Rod Carew 9315
44 Tony Gwynn 9288
45 Joe Morgan 9277
46 Sam Rice 9269
47 Nellie Fox 9232
48 Wade Boggs 9180
49 Willie Davis 9174
50 Barry Bonds 9140
  Doc Cramer 9140
52 Frankie Frisch 9112
53 Zack Wheat 9106
54 Cap Anson 9104
55 Lave Cross 9085
56 Roberto Alomar 9073
57 Al Oliver 9049
58 George Davis 9045
59 Bill Dahlen 9036
60 Dwight Evans 8996
61 Buddy Bell 8995
62 Graig Nettles 8986
63 Darrell Evans 8973
64 Gary Gaetti 8951
65 Steve Finley 8877
66 Tim Raines 8872
67 Charlie Gehringer 8860
68 Luke Appling 8856
69 Steve Garvey 8835
70 Tommy Corcoran 8812
71 Harry Hooper 8785
72 Al Simmons 8759
73 Fred McGriff 8757
74 Carlton Fisk 8756
75 Mickey Vernon 8731
76 Dave Concepcion 8723
77 Bert Campaneris 8684
78 Ted Simmons 8680
79 Chili Davis 8673
80 Goose Goslin 8656
81 Bobby Wallace 8618
82 Willie Keeler 8591
83 Fred Clarke 8584
84 Lou Whitaker 8570
85 Eddie Mathews 8537
86 Red Schoendienst 8479
87 Jesse Burkett 8426
88 Joe Carter 8422
  Julio Franco 8422
90 Larry Bowa 8418
91 Sammy Sosa 8401
92 Babe Ruth 8399
93 Omar Vizquel 8387
94 Ryne Sandberg 8385
95 Richie Ashburn 8365
96 Mike Schmidt 8352
97 Bid McPhee 8304
98 Alan Trammell 8288
99 Marquis Grissom 8275
100 George Sisler 8267

Runs

1 Rickey Henderson 2295
2 Ty Cobb 2246
3 Hank Aaron 2174
  Babe Ruth 2174
5 Pete Rose 2165
6 Barry Bonds 2078
7 Willie Mays 2062
8 Stan Musial 1949
9 Lou Gehrig 1888
10 Tris Speaker 1882
11 Mel Ott 1859
12 Frank Robinson 1829
13 Eddie Collins 1821
14 Carl Yastrzemski 1816
15 Ted Williams 1798
16 Paul Molitor 1782
17 Charlie Gehringer 1774
18 Jimmie Foxx 1751
19 Honus Wagner 1739
20 Cap Anson 1722
21 Jesse Burkett 1720
22 Willie Keeler 1719
23 Craig Biggio 1697
  Billy Hamilton 1697
25 Bid McPhee 1684
26 Mickey Mantle 1677
27 Dave Winfield 1669
28 Rafael Palmeiro 1663
29 Joe Morgan 1650
30 Cal Ripken 1647
31 Jimmy Ryan 1643
32 George Van Haltren 1642
33 Robin Yount 1632
34 Eddie Murray 1627
  Paul Waner 1627
36 Fred Clarke 1622
  Al Kaline 1622
38 Roger Connor 1620
39 Lou Brock 1610
40 Jake Beckley 1602
41 Ed Delahanty 1600
42 Bill Dahlen 1590
43 George Brett 1583
44 Rogers Hornsby 1579
45 Tim Raines 1571
46 Hugh Duffy 1554
47 Reggie Jackson 1551
48 Max Carey 1545
  George Davis 1545
50 Frankie Frisch 1532
51 Dan Brouthers 1523
  Tom Brown 1523
53 Jeff Bagwell 1517
54 Sam Rice 1514
55 Wade Boggs 1513
56 Eddie Mathews 1509
57 Roberto Alomar 1508
58 Al Simmons 1507
59 Mike Schmidt 1506
60 Nap Lajoie 1504
61 Harry Stovey 1492
62 Goose Goslin 1483
63 Arlie Latham 1481
64 Dwight Evans 1470
65 Herman Long 1456
66 Jim O'Rourke 1446
67 Harry Hooper 1429
  Dummy Hoy 1429
69 Rod Carew 1424
70 Sammy Sosa 1422
71 Joe Kelley 1421
72 Roberto Clemente 1416
73 Gary Sheffield 1411
74 John Ward 1410
  Billy Williams 1410
76 Mike Griffin 1406
77 Ken Griffey Jr. 1405
78 Sam Crawford 1391
79 Joe DiMaggio 1390
80 Lou Whitaker 1386
81 Tony Gwynn 1383
82 Andre Dawson 1373
83 Steve Finley 1368
84 Vada Pinson 1366
85 Kenny Lofton 1363
86 Brett Butler 1359
87 Doc Cramer 1357
  King Kelly 1357
89 Tommy Leach 1355
  Larry Walker 1355
91 Fred McGriff 1349
92 Darrell Evans 1344
93 Lave Cross 1338
  Pee Wee Reese 1338
95 Luis Aparicio 1335
96 Barry Larkin 1329
97 George Gore 1327
  Frank Thomas 1327
99 Richie Ashburn 1322
100 Patsy Donovan 1321

Runs by era

1988-2005
1 Rickey Henderson 2295
2 Barry Bonds 2078
3 Paul Molitor 1782
4 Craig Biggio 1697
5 Rafael Palmeiro 1663
6 Cal Ripken 1647
7 Tim Raines 1571
8 Jeff Bagwell 1517
9 Wade Boggs 1513
10 Roberto Alomar 1508

1973-1987
1 Pete Rose 2165
2 Dave Winfield 1669
3 Joe Morgan 1650
4 Robin Yount 1632
5 Eddie Murray 1627
6 George Brett 1583
7 Reggie Jackson 1551
8 Mike Schmidt 1506
9 Dwight Evans 1470
10 Rod Carew 1424

1961-1972
1 Hank Aaron 2174
2 Willie Mays 2062
3 Frank Robinson 1829
4 Carl Yastrzemski 1816
5 Al Kaline 1622
6 Lou Brock 1610
7 Roberto Clemente 1416
8 Billy Williams 1410
9 Vada Pinson 1366
10 Luis Aparicio 1335

1943-1960
1 Stan Musial 1949
2 Ted Williams 1798
3 Mickey Mantle 1677
4 Eddie Mathews 1509
5 Pee Wee Reese 1338
6 Richie Ashburn 1322
7 Nellie Fox 1279
8 Duke Snider 1259
9 Enos Slaughter 1247
10 Red Schoendienst 1223

1921-1942
1 Babe Ruth 2174
2 Lou Gehrig 1888
3 Mel Ott 1859
4 Charlie Gehringer 1774
5 Jimmie Foxx 1751
6 Paul Waner 1627
7 Rogers Hornsby 1579
8 Frankie Frisch 1532
9 Sam Rice 1514
10 Al Simmons 1507

1901-1920
1 Ty Cobb 2246
2 Tris Speaker 1882
3 Eddie Collins 1821
4 Honus Wagner 1739
5 Willie Keeler 1719
6 Fred Clarke 1622
7 Bill Dahlen 1590
8 Max Carey 1545
9 Nap Lajoie 1504
10 Harry Hooper 1429

1893-1900
1 Jesse Burkett 1720
2 Billy Hamilton 1697
3 Jimmy Ryan 1643
4 George Van Haltren 1642
5 Jake Beckley 1602
6 Ed Delahanty 1600
7 Hugh Duffy 1554
8 George Davis 1545
9 Herman Long 1456
10 Dummy Hoy 1429

1876-1892
1 Cap Anson 1722
2 Bid McPhee 1684
3 Roger Connor 1620
4 Dan Brouthers 1523
  Tom Brown 1523
6 Harry Stovey 1492
7 Arlie Latham 1481
8 Jim O'Rourke 1446
9 John Ward 1410
10 King Kelly 1357

Runs/150 Games by era

1988-2005

1	Alex Rodriguez	117.3
2	Barry Bonds	114.2
3	Derek Jeter	114.0
4	Rickey Henderson	111.7
5	Kenny Lofton	111.1
6	Todd Helton	108.4
7	Nomar Garciaparra	107.1
8	Jeff Bagwell	105.8
9	Manny Ramirez	104.8
10	Chuck Knoblauch	104.0

1973-1987

1	Bobby Bonds	102.1
2	Ron LeFlore	99.8
3	Mike Schmidt	94.0
4	Joe Morgan	93.4
5	Pete Rose	91.2
6	Kirk Gibson	90.4
7	Jim Rice	89.7
8	George Brett	87.7
9	Lou Whitaker	87.0
10	Rod Carew	86.5

1961-1972

1	Willie Mays	103.4
2	Hank Aaron	98.9
3	Frank Robinson	97.7
4	Dick Allen	94.3
5	Lou Brock	92.3
6	Roberto Clemente	87.3
7	Jimmy Wynn	86.3
8	Al Kaline	85.9
9	Billy Williams	85.0
10	Roger Maris	84.7

1943-1960

1	Ted Williams	117.7
2	Dom DiMaggio	112.2
3	Mickey Mantle	104.8
4	Jackie Robinson	102.8
5	Johnny Pesky	102.4
6	Ralph Kiner	98.9
7	Eddie Stanky	96.6
8	Stan Musial	96.6
9	Eddie Mathews	94.7
10	Larry Doby	93.9

1921-1942

1	Lou Gehrig	130.9
2	Babe Ruth	130.3
3	Earle Combs	122.3
4	Red Rolfe	120.3
5	Joe DiMaggio	120.1
6	Charlie Gehringer	114.6
7	Jimmie Foxx	113.4
8	Hank Greenberg	113.1
9	Earl Averill	110.0
10	Max Bishop	108.3

1901-1920

1	Willie Keeler	121.5
2	Ty Cobb	111.0
3	Fred Clarke	108.3
4	Roy Thomas	103.2
5	Tris Speaker	101.2
6	Fielder Jones	99.0
7	Donie Bush	98.7
8	Chick Stahl	98.7
9	Joe Jackson	98.3
10	Ginger Beaumont	97.9

1893-1900

1	Billy Hamilton	159.7
2	John McGraw	139.8
3	Mike Griffin	139.4
4	Hugh Duffy	134.1
5	Mike Tiernan	133.6
6	Ed Delahanty	130.6
7	Cupid Childs	125.0
8	Jesse Burkett	124.8
9	George Van Haltren	123.8
10	Jimmy Ryan	122.4

1876-1892

1	George Gore	151.9
2	Harry Stovey	150.6
3	King Kelly	139.9
4	Dan Brouthers	136.6
5	Arlie Latham	136.4
6	Sam Thompson	134.3
7	Buck Ewing	128.8
8	Tom Brown	127.8
9	Hardy Richardson	126.2
10	Tommy McCarthy	125.6

Hits

1	Pete Rose	4256
2	Ty Cobb	4189
3	Hank Aaron	3771
4	Stan Musial	3630
5	Tris Speaker	3514
6	Honus Wagner	3420
7	Carl Yastrzemski	3419
8	Paul Molitor	3319
9	Eddie Collins	3315
10	Willie Mays	3283
11	Eddie Murray	3255
12	Nap Lajoie	3242
13	Cal Ripken	3184
14	George Brett	3154
15	Paul Waner	3152
16	Robin Yount	3142
17	Tony Gwynn	3141
18	Dave Winfield	3110
19	Rickey Henderson	3055
20	Rod Carew	3053
21	Lou Brock	3023
22	**Rafael Palmeiro**	**3020**
23	Cap Anson	3012
24	Wade Boggs	3010
25	Al Kaline	3007
26	Roberto Clemente	3000
27	Sam Rice	2987
28	Sam Crawford	2961
29	Frank Robinson	2943
30	Jake Beckley	2934
31	Willie Keeler	2932
32	Rogers Hornsby	2930
33	Al Simmons	2927
34	Zack Wheat	2884
35	Frankie Frisch	2880
36	Mel Ott	2876
37	Babe Ruth	2873
38	Harold Baines	2866
39	Jesse Burkett	2850
40	Brooks Robinson	2848
41	Charlie Gehringer	2839
42	George Sisler	2812
43	**Craig Biggio**	**2795**
44	Andre Dawson	2774
45	Vada Pinson	2757
46	Luke Appling	2749
47	Al Oliver	2743
48	**Barry Bonds**	**2742**
49	Goose Goslin	2735
50	Tony Perez	2732
51	Roberto Alomar	2724
52	Lou Gehrig	2721
53	Rusty Staub	2716
54	Bill Buckner	2715
55	Dave Parker	2712
56	Billy Williams	2711
57	Doc Cramer	2705
58	Fred Clarke	2678
59	Luis Aparicio	2677
60	Max Carey	2665
	George Davis	2665
62	Nellie Fox	2663
63	Harry Heilmann	2660
64	Ted Williams	2654
65	Lave Cross	2651
66	Jimmie Foxx	2646
67	Rabbit Maranville	2605
	Tim Raines	2605
69	Steve Garvey	2599
70	Ed Delahanty	2597
71	Reggie Jackson	2584
72	Ernie Banks	2583
73	Richie Ashburn	2574
74	Willie Davis	2561
75	George Van Haltren	2544
76	Heinie Manush	2524
77	**Julio Franco**	**2521**
78	Joe Morgan	2517
79	Buddy Bell	2514
80	Jimmy Ryan	2513
81	Mickey Vernon	2495
82	Fred McGriff	2490
83	Ted Simmons	2472
84	Joe Medwick	2471
85	Roger Connor	2467
86	Harry Hooper	2466
87	Bill Dahlen	2461
88	Ozzie Smith	2460
89	Lloyd Waner	2459
90	Jim Rice	2452
91	Red Schoendienst	2449
92	Dwight Evans	2446
93	Mark Grace	2445
94	**Steve Finley**	**2426**
95	Pie Traynor	2416
96	Mickey Mantle	2415
97	Stuffy McInnis	2405
98	Ryne Sandberg	2386
99	Enos Slaughter	2383
100	Chili Davis	2380

Doubles

1	Tris Speaker	792
2	Pete Rose	746
3	Stan Musial	725
4	Ty Cobb	724
5	George Brett	665
6	Nap Lajoie	657
7	Carl Yastrzemski	646
8	Honus Wagner	643
9	Hank Aaron	624
10	Paul Molitor	605
	Paul Waner	605
12	**Craig Biggio**	**604**
13	Cal Ripken	603
14	**Rafael Palmeiro**	**585**
15	Robin Yount	583
16	Wade Boggs	578
17	Charlie Gehringer	574
18	**Barry Bonds**	**564**
19	Eddie Murray	560
20	Tony Gwynn	543
21	Harry Heilmann	542
22	Rogers Hornsby	541
23	Joe Medwick	540
	Dave Winfield	540
25	Al Simmons	539
26	Lou Gehrig	534
27	Cap Anson	529
	Al Oliver	529
29	Frank Robinson	528
30	Dave Parker	526
31	Ted Williams	525
32	Willie Mays	523
33	Ed Delahanty	522
34	Joe Cronin	515
35	Edgar Martinez	514
36	Mark Grace	511
37	Rickey Henderson	510
38	Babe Ruth	506
39	Tony Perez	505
40	Roberto Alomar	504
41	Andre Dawson	503
42	Goose Goslin	500
	John Olerud	500
44	Rusty Staub	499
45	Bill Buckner	498
	Al Kaline	498
	Sam Rice	498
48	**Luis Gonzalez**	**495**
49	Heinie Manush	491
50	Mickey Vernon	490
51	**Jeff Bagwell**	**488**
	Harold Baines	488
	Mel Ott	488
54	Lou Brock	486
	Billy Herman	486
56	Vada Pinson	485
57	Hal McRae	484
58	Dwight Evans	483
	Ted Simmons	483
60	Brooks Robinson	482
61	Zack Wheat	476
62	**Jeff Kent**	**474**
63	Jake Beckley	473
64	**Larry Walker**	**471**
65	Frankie Frisch	466
66	Jim Bottomley	465
67	Reggie Jackson	463
68	Dan Brouthers	460
69	Sam Crawford	458
	Jimmie Foxx	458
71	George Davis	453
	Jimmy Dykes	453
73	Paul O'Neill	451
	Jimmy Ryan	451
75	Joe Morgan	449
76	**Frank Thomas**	**447**
77	Rod Carew	445
	Ivan Rodriguez	**445**
79	George Burns	444
	Andres Galarraga	444
81	Gary Gaetti	443
82	Dick Bartell	442
	Don Mattingly	442
84	Roger Connor	441
	Barry Larkin	441
	Fred McGriff	441
87	Luke Appling	440
	Will Clark	440
	Roberto Clemente	440
	Steve Garvey	440
	B.J. Surhoff	**440**
92	Eddie Collins	438
93	Cesar Cedeno	436
	Joe Sewell	436
95	Wally Moses	435
96	Billy Williams	434
97	Joe Judge	433
98	Joe Carter	432
	Tim Wallach	432
100	Ken Griffey Jr.	430
	Tim Raines	430

Doubles by era

1988-2005

1	Paul Molitor	605
2	**Craig Biggio**	**604**
3	Cal Ripken	603
4	**Rafael Palmeiro**	**585**
5	Wade Boggs	578
6	**Barry Bonds**	**564**
7	Tony Gwynn	543
8	Edgar Martinez	514
9	Mark Grace	511
10	Rickey Henderson	510

1973-1987

1	Pete Rose	746
2	George Brett	665
3	Robin Yount	583
4	Eddie Murray	560
5	Dave Winfield	540
6	Al Oliver	529
7	Dave Parker	526
8	Tony Perez	505
9	Andre Dawson	503
10	Rusty Staub	499

1961-1972

1	Carl Yastrzemski	646
2	Hank Aaron	624
3	Frank Robinson	528
4	Willie Mays	523
5	Al Kaline	498
6	Lou Brock	486
7	Vada Pinson	485
8	Brooks Robinson	482
9	Roberto Clemente	440
10	Billy Williams	434

1943-1960

1	Stan Musial	725
2	Ted Williams	525
3	Mickey Vernon	490
4	Red Schoendienst	427
5	Enos Slaughter	413
6	Lou Boudreau	385
	George Kell	385
8	Bob Elliott	382
9	Bobby Doerr	381
10	Dixie Walker	376

1921-1942

1	Paul Waner	605
2	Charlie Gehringer	574
3	Harry Heilmann	542
4	Rogers Hornsby	541
5	Joe Medwick	540
6	Al Simmons	539
7	Lou Gehrig	534
8	Joe Cronin	515
9	Babe Ruth	506
10	Goose Goslin	500

1901-1920

1	Tris Speaker	792
2	Ty Cobb	724
3	Nap Lajoie	657
4	Honus Wagner	643
5	Zack Wheat	476
6	Sam Crawford	458
7	Eddie Collins	438
8	Sherry Magee	425
9	Max Carey	419
10	Bill Dahlen	413

1893-1900

1	Ed Delahanty	522
2	Jake Beckley	473
3	George Davis	453
4	Jimmy Ryan	451
5	Lave Cross	412
6	Joe Kelley	358
7	Herman Long	342
8	Hugh Duffy	325
9	Jesse Burkett	320
10	Jack Doyle	316

1876-1892

1	Cap Anson	529
2	Dan Brouthers	460
3	Roger Connor	441
4	Jim O'Rourke	414
5	Paul Hines	368
6	King Kelly	359
7	Harry Stovey	347
8	Sam Thompson	343
9	Jack Glasscock	313
10	Bid McPhee	303
	Hardy Richardson	303

Triples

1	Sam Crawford	309
2	Ty Cobb	295
3	Honus Wagner	252
4	Jake Beckley	244
5	Roger Connor	233
6	Tris Speaker	222
7	Fred Clarke	220
8	Dan Brouthers	205
9	Joe Kelley	194
10	Paul Waner	191
11	Bid McPhee	189
12	Eddie Collins	187
13	Ed Delahanty	186
14	Sam Rice	184
15	Jesse Burkett	182
	Ed Konetchy	182
	Edd Roush	182
18	Buck Ewing	178
19	Rabbit Maranville	177
	Stan Musial	177
21	Harry Stovey	174
22	Goose Goslin	173
23	Tommy Leach	172
	Zack Wheat	172
25	Rogers Hornsby	169
26	Joe Jackson	168
27	Roberto Clemente	166
	Sherry Magee	166
29	Jake Daubert	165
30	Elmer Flick	164
	George Sisler	164
	Pie Traynor	164
33	Bill Dahlen	163
	George Davis	163
	Lou Gehrig	163
	Nap Lajoie	163
37	Mike Tiernan	162
38	Sam Thompson	161
	George Van Haltren	161
40	Harry Hooper	160
	Heinie Manush	160
42	Max Carey	159
	Joe Judge	159
44	Ed McKean	158
45	Kiki Cuyler	157
	Jimmy Ryan	157
47	Tommy Corcoran	155
48	Earle Combs	154
49	Jim Bottomley	151
	Harry Heilmann	151
51	Kip Selbach	149
	Al Simmons	149
53	Wally Pipp	148
	Enos Slaughter	148
55	Bobby Veach	147
	Willie Wilson	147
57	Charlie Gehringer	146
58	Harry Davis	145
	Willie Keeler	145
60	Bobby Wallace	143
61	Lou Brock	141
62	Willie Mays	140
63	John Reilly	139
64	Tom Brown	138
	Willie Davis	138
	Frankie Frisch	138
	Jimmy Williams	138
68	George Brett	137
69	Lave Cross	136
	Babe Ruth	136
	Jimmy Sheckard	136
	Elmer Smith	136
73	Pete Rose	135
74	Shano Collins	133
75	Jim O'Rourke	132
	George Wood	132
77	Brett Butler	131
	Joe DiMaggio	131
	Buck Freeman	131
80	Buddy Myer	130
81	Tommy Burns	129
	Larry Gardner	129
83	Earl Averill	128
	Arky Vaughan	128
85	Vada Pinson	127
86	Hardy Richardson	126
	Robin Yount	126
88	Jimmie Foxx	125
89	John Anderson	124
	Cap Anson	124
	Hal Chase	124
	Frank Schulte	124
93	Larry Doyle	123
	Duke Farrell	123
95	Dummy Hoy	121
96	Fred Pfeffer	120
	Mickey Vernon	120
98	Hugh Duffy	119
99	Joe Cronin	118
	Chick Stahl	118
	Lloyd Waner	118

Triples by era

1988-2005
1 Brett Butler....131
2 Lance Johnson....117
3 Paul Molitor....114
4 Tim Raines....113
5 Steve Finley....112
6 Juan Samuel....102
7 Kenny Lofton....98
8 Willie McGee....94
9 Tony Fernandez....92
10 Andy Van Slyke....91

1973-1987
1 Willie Wilson....147
2 George Brett....137
3 Pete Rose....135
4 Robin Yount....126
5 Rod Carew....112
6 Garry Templeton....106
7 Larry Bowa....99
8 Andre Dawson....98
9 Joe Morgan....96
10 Jose Cruz....94

1961-1972
1 Roberto Clemente....166
2 Lou Brock....141
3 Willie Mays....140
4 Willie Davis....138
5 Vada Pinson....127
6 Hank Aaron....98
7 Luis Aparicio....92
8 Ernie Banks....90
9 Johnny Callison....89
10 Billy Williams....88

1943-1960
1 Stan Musial....177
2 Enos Slaughter....148
3 Mickey Vernon....120
4 Nellie Fox....112
5 Richie Ashburn....109
6 Bill Bruton....102
  Jeff Heath....102
8 Phil Cavarretta....99
9 Dixie Walker....96
10 Bob Elliott....94

1921-1942
1 Paul Waner....191
2 Sam Rice....184
3 Edd Roush....182
4 Rabbit Maranville....177
5 Goose Goslin....173
6 Rogers Hornsby....169
7 George Sisler....164
  Pie Traynor....164
9 Lou Gehrig....163
10 Heinie Manush....160

1901-1920
1 Sam Crawford....309
2 Ty Cobb....295
3 Honus Wagner....252
4 Tris Speaker....222
5 Fred Clarke....220
6 Eddie Collins....187
7 Ed Konetchy....182
8 Tommy Leach....172
  Zack Wheat....172
10 Joe Jackson....168

1893-1900
1 Jake Beckley....244
2 Joe Kelley....194
3 Ed Delahanty....186
4 Jesse Burkett....182
5 George Davis....163
6 Mike Tiernan....162
7 George Van Haltren....161
8 Ed McKean....158
9 Jimmy Ryan....157
10 Tommy Corcoran....155

1876-1892
1 Roger Connor....233
2 Dan Brouthers....205
3 Bid McPhee....189
4 Buck Ewing....178
5 Harry Stovey....174
6 Sam Thompson....161
7 John Reilly....139
8 Tom Brown....138
9 Jim O'Rourke....132
  George Wood....132

Home Runs

1 Hank Aaron....755
2 Babe Ruth....714
3 **Barry Bonds....708**
4 Willie Mays....660
5 **Sammy Sosa....588**
6 Frank Robinson....586
7 Mark McGwire....583
8 Harmon Killebrew....573
9 **Rafael Palmeiro....569**
10 Reggie Jackson....563
11 Mike Schmidt....548
12 **Ken Griffey Jr.....536**
  Mickey Mantle....536
14 Jimmie Foxx....534
15 Willie McCovey....521
  Ted Williams....521
17 Ernie Banks....512
  Eddie Mathews....512
19 Mel Ott....511
20 Eddie Murray....504
21 Lou Gehrig....493
  Fred McGriff....493
23 Stan Musial....475
  Willie Stargell....475
25 Dave Winfield....465
26 Jose Canseco....462
27 Carl Yastrzemski....452
28 **Jeff Bagwell....449**
  Gary Sheffield....449
30 **Frank Thomas....448**
31 Dave Kingman....442
32 Andre Dawson....438
33 **Manny Ramirez....435**
34 **Juan Gonzalez....434**
35 Cal Ripken....431
36 **Jim Thome....430**
37 **Alex Rodriguez....429**
38 Billy Williams....426
39 Darrell Evans....414
40 Duke Snider....407
41 Andres Galarraga....399
  Al Kaline....399
43 Dale Murphy....398
44 **Mike Piazza....397**
45 Joe Carter....396
46 Graig Nettles....390
47 Johnny Bench....389
48 Dwight Evans....385
49 Harold Baines....384
50 **Larry Walker....383**
51 Frank Howard....382
  Jim Rice....382
53 Albert Belle....381
54 Orlando Cepeda....379
  Tony Perez....379
56 Matt Williams....378
57 Norm Cash....377
58 Carlton Fisk....376
59 Rocky Colavito....374
60 Gil Hodges....370
61 **Carlos Delgado....369**
  Ralph Kiner....369
63 Joe DiMaggio....361
64 Gary Gaetti....360
65 Johnny Mize....359
66 Yogi Berra....358
67 Greg Vaughn....355
68 Lee May....354
69 Ellis Burks....352
70 Dick Allen....351
71 Chili Davis....350
72 George Foster....348
73 Ron Santo....342
74 Jack Clark....340
75 **Tino Martinez....339**
  Dave Parker....339
  Boog Powell....339
78 Don Baylor....338
79 Joe Adcock....336
80 Darryl Strawberry....335
81 Bobby Bonds....332
82 **Jim Edmonds....331**
  Hank Greenberg....331
  Chipper Jones....331
  Jeff Kent....331
86 Mo Vaughn....328
87 Willie Horton....325
88 Gary Carter....324
  Lance Parrish....324
90 Ron Gant....321
91 Cecil Fielder....319
92 Roy Sievers....318
93 George Brett....317
94 Ron Cey....316
  Luis Gonzalez....316
96 **Vinny Castilla....315**
97 Reggie Smith....314
98 **Jason Giambi....313**
99 Jay Buhner....310
100 Edgar Martinez....309

Home Runs by era

1988-2005
1 **Barry Bonds....708**
2 **Sammy Sosa....588**
3 Mark McGwire....583
4 **Rafael Palmeiro....569**
5 **Ken Griffey Jr.....536**
6 Fred McGriff....493
7 Jose Canseco....462
8 **Jeff Bagwell....449**
  Gary Sheffield....449
10 Frank Thomas....448

1973-1987
1 Reggie Jackson....563
2 Mike Schmidt....548
3 Eddie Murray....504
4 Dave Winfield....465
5 Dave Kingman....442
6 Andre Dawson....438
7 Darrell Evans....414
8 Dale Murphy....398
9 Graig Nettles....390
10 Johnny Bench....389

1961-1972
1 Hank Aaron....755
2 Willie Mays....660
3 Frank Robinson....586
4 Harmon Killebrew....573
5 Willie McCovey....521
6 Ernie Banks....512
7 Willie Stargell....475
8 Carl Yastrzemski....452
9 Billy Williams....426
10 Al Kaline....399

1943-1960
1 Mickey Mantle....536
2 Ted Williams....521
3 Eddie Mathews....512
4 Stan Musial....475
5 Duke Snider....407
6 Gil Hodges....370
7 Ralph Kiner....369
8 Yogi Berra....358
9 Joe Adcock....336
10 Roy Sievers....318

1921-1942
1 Babe Ruth....714
2 Jimmie Foxx....534
3 Mel Ott....511
4 Lou Gehrig....493
5 Joe DiMaggio....361
6 Johnny Mize....359
7 Hank Greenberg....331
8 Al Simmons....307
9 Rogers Hornsby....301
10 Chuck Klein....300

1901-1920
1 Zack Wheat....132
2 Gavy Cravath....119
3 Tilly Walker....118
4 Ty Cobb....117
  Tris Speaker....117
6 Honus Wagner....101
7 Sam Crawford....97
8 Frank Baker....96
9 Frank Schulte....92
10 Bill Dahlen....84
  Fred Luderus....84

1893-1900
1 Jimmy Ryan....118
2 Hugh Duffy....106
  Mike Tiernan....106
4 Ed Delahanty....101
5 Herman Long....91
6 Jake Beckley....87
7 Jesse Burkett....75
8 George Davis....73
9 Bobby Lowe....71
10 Bill Joyce....70

1876-1892
1 Roger Connor....138
2 Sam Thompson....126
3 Harry Stovey....122
4 Dan Brouthers....106
5 Cap Anson....97
6 Fred Pfeffer....94
7 Jack Clements....77
8 Jerry Denny....74
9 Buck Ewing....71
10 Hardy Richardson....70

Home Run Pct.

1 Mark McGwire....9.42
2 Babe Ruth....8.50
3 **Barry Bonds....7.75**
4 **Jim Thome....7.26**
5 **Manny Ramirez....7.10**
6 Ralph Kiner....7.09
7 Harmon Killebrew....7.03
8 **Sammy Sosa....7.00**
9 **Alex Rodriguez....6.92**
10 **Ken Griffey Jr.....6.81**
11 Ted Williams....6.76
12 **Carlos Delgado....6.67**
13 **Juan Gonzalez....6.62**
14 Dave Kingman....6.62
15 Mickey Mantle....6.62
16 Jimmie Foxx....6.57
17 Mike Schmidt....6.56
18 Jose Canseco....6.55
19 Albert Belle....6.51
20 **Frank Thomas....6.44**
21 **Mike Piazza....6.40**
22 Hank Greenberg....6.37
23 Willie McCovey....6.36
24 **Vladimir Guerrero....6.23**
25 Cecil Fielder....6.19
26 Jay Buhner....6.18
27 Darryl Strawberry....6.18
28 Lou Gehrig....6.16
29 Hank Aaron....6.11
30 Willie Mays....6.07
31 **Jason Giambi....6.05**
32 Hank Sauer....6.01
33 Eddie Mathews....6.00
34 Willie Stargell....5.99
35 **Jim Edmonds....5.96**
36 **Todd Helton....5.94**
37 Mo Vaughn....5.93
38 Rob Deer....5.93
39 Frank Howard....5.89
40 Frank Robinson....5.86
41 Greg Vaughn....5.82
42 Bob Horner....5.77
43 **Jeff Bagwell....5.76**
44 Roy Campanella....5.76
45 Rocky Colavito....5.75
46 Gus Zernial....5.74
47 Gorman Thomas....5.73
48 **Andruw Jones....5.71**
49 Reggie Jackson....5.71
50 Dick Stuart....5.70
51 **Gary Sheffield....5.69**
52 Duke Snider....5.68
53 Kevin Mitchell....5.66
54 Fred McGriff....5.63
55 Norm Cash....5.62
56 Dean Palmer....5.61
57 **Tony Clark....5.58**
58 Johnny Mize....5.57
59 **Larry Walker....5.55**
60 Dick Allen....5.54
61 **Chipper Jones....5.54**
62 **Jeromy Burnitz....5.54**
63 Ernie Banks....5.43
64 **Rafael Palmeiro....5.43**
65 David Justice....5.42
66 Mel Ott....5.40
67 Matt Williams....5.40
68 Roger Maris....5.39
69 Todd Hundley....5.36
70 **Matt Stairs....5.31**
71 Eric Davis....5.30
72 Joe DiMaggio....5.29
73 **Brian Giles....5.28**
74 Gil Hodges....5.26
75 **Paul Konerko....5.26**
76 Wally Post....5.24
77 Danny Tartabull....5.23
78 Mickey Tettleton....5.21
79 **Ryan Klesko....5.19**
80 Al Rosen....5.15
81 Hack Wilson....5.13
82 Glenn Davis....5.11
83 **Eric Chavez....5.10**
84 **Derrek Lee....5.09**
85 Bob Allison....5.09
86 Joe Adcock....5.09
87 Johnny Bench....5.08
88 Boog Powell....5.07
89 **Tim Salmon....5.07**
90 Jesse Barfield....5.06
91 **Javy Lopez....5.06**
92 Nate Colbert....5.06
93 **Scott Rolen....5.04**
94 Glenallen Hill....5.01
95 Dale Murphy....5.00
96 **Reggie Sanders....5.00**
97 Tony Batista....4.99
98 Charlie Keller....4.99
99 Roy Sievers....4.98
100 Ron Gant....4.98

Home Run Pct. by era

1988-2005
1 Mark McGwire....9.42
2 **Barry Bonds....7.75**
3 **Jim Thome....7.26**
4 **Manny Ramirez....7.10**
5 **Sammy Sosa....7.00**
6 **Alex Rodriguez....6.92**
7 **Ken Griffey Jr.....6.81**
8 **Carlos Delgado....6.67**
9 **Juan Gonzalez....6.62**
10 Jose Canseco....6.55

1973-1987
1 Dave Kingman....6.62
2 Mike Schmidt....6.56
3 Bob Horner....5.77
4 Gorman Thomas....5.73
5 Reggie Jackson....5.71
6 Johnny Bench....5.08
7 Jesse Barfield....5.06
8 Dale Murphy....5.00
9 Cliff Johnson....4.97
10 Jack Clark....4.97

1961-1972
1 Harmon Killebrew....7.03
2 Willie McCovey....6.36
3 Hank Aaron....6.11
4 Willie Mays....6.07
5 Willie Stargell....5.99
6 Frank Howard....5.89
7 Frank Robinson....5.86
8 Rocky Colavito....5.75
9 Dick Stuart....5.70
10 Norm Cash....5.62

1943-1960
1 Ralph Kiner....7.09
2 Ted Williams....6.76
3 Mickey Mantle....6.62
4 Hank Sauer....6.01
5 Eddie Mathews....6.00
6 Roy Campanella....5.76
7 Gus Zernial....5.74
8 Duke Snider....5.68
9 Gil Hodges....5.26
10 Wally Post....5.24

1921-1942
1 Babe Ruth....8.50
2 Jimmie Foxx....6.57
3 Hank Greenberg....6.37
4 Lou Gehrig....6.16
5 Johnny Mize....5.57
6 Mel Ott....5.40
7 Joe DiMaggio....5.29
8 Hack Wilson....5.13
9 Rudy York....4.70
10 Wally Berger....4.69

1901-1920
1 Gavy Cravath....3.01
2 Tilly Walker....2.33
3 Elmer Smith....2.19
4 Buck Freeman....1.95
5 Fred Luderus....1.73
6 Frank Baker....1.60
7 Charlie Hickman....1.48
8 Zack Wheat....1.45
9 Frank Schulte....1.41
10 Casey Stengel....1.40

1893-1900
1 Mike Tiernan....1.79
2 Hugh Duffy....1.50
3 Jimmy Ryan....1.44
4 Ed Delahanty....1.34
5 Herman Long....1.19
6 Bobby Lowe....1.00
7 Ed McKean....0.97
8 Joe Kelley....0.93
9 Duke Farrell....0.92
10 Jake Beckley....0.91

1876-1892
1 Sam Thompson....2.10
2 Harry Stovey....1.99
3 Jack Clements....1.79
4 Roger Connor....1.77
5 Dan Brouthers....1.58
6 Jerry Denny....1.50
7 John Reilly....1.47
8 Denny Lyons....1.44
9 Charlie Bennett....1.44
10 Fred Pfeffer....1.43

Extra Base Hits

1 Hank Aaron 1477
2 Stan Musial 1377
3 Babe Ruth 1356
4 Barry Bonds 1349
5 Willie Mays 1323
6 Rafael Palmeiro 1192
7 Lou Gehrig 1190
8 Frank Robinson 1186
9 Carl Yastrzemski 1157
10 Ty Cobb 1136
11 Tris Speaker 1131
12 George Brett 1119
13 Jimmie Foxx 1117
   Ted Williams 1117
15 Eddie Murray 1099
16 Dave Winfield 1093
17 Cal Ripken 1078
18 Reggie Jackson 1075
19 Mel Ott 1071
20 Pete Rose 1041
21 Andre Dawson 1039
22 Mike Schmidt 1015
23 Rogers Hornsby 1011
24 Ernie Banks 1009
25 Ken Griffey Jr. 1002
26 Honus Wagner 996
27 Al Simmons 995
28 Sammy Sosa 987
29 Al Kaline 972
30 Jeff Bagwell..................969
31 Tony Perez 963
32 Robin Yount 960
33 Fred McGriff 958
34 Paul Molitor 953
   Willie Stargell 953
36 Mickey Mantle 952
37 Billy Williams 948
38 Dwight Evans 941
39 Dave Parker 940
40 Eddie Mathews 938
41 Harold Baines 921
   Goose Goslin 921
43 Willie McCovey 920
44 Craig Biggio 916
   Larry Walker 916
46 Paul Waner 909
47 Frank Thomas 906
48 Charlie Gehringer 904
49 Nap Lajoie 902
50 Harmon Killebrew 887
51 Gary Sheffield.............886
52 Joe Carter 881
   Joe DiMaggio 881
54 Harry Heilmann 876
55 Andres Galarraga 875
56 Luis Gonzalez 874
57 Rickey Henderson 873
58 Vada Pinson 868
59 Sam Crawford 864
60 Manny Ramirez 861
61 Joe Medwick 858
62 Duke Snider 850
63 Juan Gonzalez 847
   Jeff Kent 847
65 Roberto Clemente 846
66 Carlton Fisk 844
67 Gary Gaetti 842
68 Mark McGwire 841
69 Edgar Martinez 838
   Rusty Staub 838
71 Jim Bottomley 835
72 Steve Finley 834
   Jim Rice 834
74 Al Oliver 825
75 Orlando Cepeda.............823
76 Brooks Robinson 818
77 Ellis Burks 817
78 Jose Canseco 816
79 Joe Morgan 813
80 Roger Connor 812
81 Ed Delahanty 809
   Johnny Mize 809
83 Jake Beckley 804
   Chili Davis 804
85 Joe Cronin 803
86 Roberto Alomar 794
   Johnny Bench 794
88 Alex Rodriguez 792
   Ruben Sierra 792
90 Albert Belle 791
91 Dale Murphy 787
92 Mickey Vernon 782
93 Hank Greenberg 781
94 Zack Wheat 780
95 Darrell Evans 779
   Bob Johnson 779
97 Ted Simmons 778
   Jim Thome 778
99 Lou Brock 776
100 Ron Santo 774

Total Bases

1 Hank Aaron 6856
2 Stan Musial 6134
3 Willie Mays 6066
4 Ty Cobb 5854
5 Babe Ruth 5793
6 Pete Rose 5752
7 Barry Bonds 5584
8 Carl Yastrzemski 5539
9 Eddie Murray 5397
10 Rafael Palmeiro 5388
11 Frank Robinson 5373
12 Dave Winfield 5221
13 Cal Ripken 5168
14 Tris Speaker 5101
15 Lou Gehrig 5060
16 George Brett 5044
17 Mel Ott 5041
18 Jimmie Foxx 4956
19 Ted Williams 4884
20 Honus Wagner 4870
21 Paul Molitor 4854
22 Al Kaline 4852
23 Reggie Jackson 4834
24 Andre Dawson 4787
25 Robin Yount 4730
26 Rogers Hornsby 4712
27 Ernie Banks 4706
28 Al Simmons 4685
29 Harold Baines 4604
30 Billy Williams 4599
31 Rickey Henderson 4588
32 Tony Perez 4532
33 Mickey Mantle 4511
   Sammy Sosa 4511
35 Roberto Clemente 4492
36 Paul Waner 4478
37 Nap Lajoie 4471
38 Fred McGriff 4458
39 Ken Griffey Jr. 4414
40 Dave Parker 4405
41 Mike Schmidt 4404
42 Eddie Mathews 4349
43 Sam Crawford 4328
44 Goose Goslin 4325
45 Craig Biggio 4283
46 Brooks Robinson 4270
47 Eddie Collins 4268
48 Vada Pinson 4264
49 Tony Gwynn 4259
50 Charlie Gehringer 4257
51 Lou Brock 4238
52 Dwight Evans 4230
53 Willie McCovey 4219
54 Jeff Bagwell..................4213
55 Willie Stargell 4190
56 Rusty Staub 4185
57 Jake Beckley 4156
58 Gary Sheffield.............4153
59 Harmon Killebrew 4143
60 Jim Rice 4129
61 Zack Wheat 4100
62 Al Oliver 4083
63 Cap Anson 4080
64 Wade Boggs 4064
65 Harry Heilmann 4053
66 Andres Galarraga 4038
67 Roberto Alomar 4018
68 Carlton Fisk 3999
69 Rod Carew 3998
70 Steve Finley 3966
71 Joe Morgan 3962
72 Orlando Cepeda.............3959
73 Sam Rice 3955
74 Frank Thomas 3949
75 Joe DiMaggio 3948
76 Steve Garvey 3941
77 Frankie Frisch 3937
78 Chili Davis 3914
79 Joe Carter 3910
80 Larry Walker 3904
81 Gary Gaetti 3881
82 George Sisler 3871
83 Darrell Evans 3866
84 Duke Snider 3865
85 Joe Medwick 3852
86 Bill Buckner 3833
87 Ed Delahanty 3794
88 Ted Simmons 3793
89 Roger Connor 3788
90 Ryne Sandberg 3787
91 Luis Gonzalez 3783
92 Graig Nettles 3779
   Ron Santo 3779
94 Willie Davis 3778
95 Tim Raines 3771
96 Jesse Burkett 3759
97 Mickey Vernon 3741
98 Jim Bottomley 3737
99 Dale Murphy 3733
100 Edgar Martinez 3718

Runs Batted In

1 Hank Aaron 2297
2 Babe Ruth 2213
3 Lou Gehrig 1995
4 Stan Musial 1951
5 Ty Cobb 1938
6 Jimmie Foxx 1922
7 Eddie Murray 1917
8 Willie Mays 1903
9 Cap Anson 1880
10 Mel Ott 1860
11 Barry Bonds 1853
12 Carl Yastrzemski 1844
13 Ted Williams 1839
14 Rafael Palmeiro 1835
15 Dave Winfield 1833
16 Al Simmons 1827
17 Frank Robinson 1812
18 Honus Wagner 1733
19 Reggie Jackson 1702
20 Cal Ripken 1695
21 Tony Perez 1652
22 Ernie Banks 1636
23 Harold Baines 1628
24 Goose Goslin 1609
25 Nap Lajoie 1599
26 George Brett 1595
   Mike Schmidt 1595
28 Andre Dawson 1591
29 Rogers Hornsby 1584
   Harmon Killebrew 1584
31 Al Kaline 1583
32 Jake Beckley 1578
33 Sammy Sosa 1575
34 Willie McCovey 1555
35 Fred McGriff 1550
36 Willie Stargell 1540
37 Harry Heilmann 1539
38 Joe DiMaggio 1537
39 Ken Griffey Jr. 1536
40 Jeff Bagwell..................1529
   Tris Speaker 1529
42 Sam Crawford 1525
43 Mickey Mantle 1509
44 Dave Parker 1493
45 Gary Sheffield.............1476
46 Billy Williams 1475
47 Ed Delahanty 1466
   Rusty Staub 1466
49 Frank Thomas 1465
50 Eddie Mathews 1453
51 Jim Rice 1451
52 Joe Carter 1445
53 George Davis 1440
54 Yogi Berra 1430
55 Charlie Gehringer 1427
56 Andres Galarraga 1425
57 Joe Cronin 1424
58 Jim Bottomley 1422
59 Mark McGwire 1414
   Manny Ramirez 1414
61 Jose Canseco 1407
62 Robin Yount 1406
63 Juan Gonzalez 1404
64 Ted Simmons 1389
65 Dwight Evans 1384
66 Joe Medwick 1383
67 Lave Cross 1378
68 Johnny Bench 1376
69 Chili Davis 1372
70 Orlando Cepeda.............1365
71 Brooks Robinson 1357
72 Darrell Evans 1354
73 Gary Gaetti 1341
74 Johnny Mize 1337
75 Duke Snider 1333
76 Ron Santo 1331
77 Carlton Fisk 1330
78 Al Oliver 1326
79 Roger Connor 1323
80 Ruben Sierra 1318
81 Graig Nettles 1314
   Pete Rose 1314
83 Jeff Kent 1312
84 Mickey Vernon 1311
   Larry Walker 1311
86 Paul Waner 1309
87 Steve Garvey 1308
88 Paul Molitor 1307
89 Roberto Clemente 1305
   Sam Thompson 1305
91 Enos Slaughter 1304
92 Hugh Duffy 1302
93 Eddie Collins 1300
94 Dan Brouthers 1296
95 Del Ennis 1284
96 Bob Johnson 1283
97 Don Baylor 1276
   Hank Greenberg 1276
99 Gil Hodges 1274
100 Pie Traynor 1273

Runs Batted In by era

1988-2005
1 Barry Bonds 1853
2 Rafael Palmeiro 1835
3 Cal Ripken 1695
4 Harold Baines 1628
5 Sammy Sosa 1575
6 Fred McGriff 1550
7 Ken Griffey Jr. 1536
8 Jeff Bagwell..................1529
9 Gary Sheffield.............1476
10 Frank Thomas 1465

1973-1987
1 Eddie Murray 1917
2 Dave Winfield 1833
3 Reggie Jackson 1702
4 Tony Perez 1652
5 George Brett 1595
   Mike Schmidt 1595
7 Andre Dawson 1591
8 Dave Parker 1493
9 Rusty Staub 1466
10 Jim Rice 1451

1961-1972
1 Hank Aaron 2297
2 Willie Mays 1903
3 Carl Yastrzemski 1844
4 Frank Robinson 1812
5 Ernie Banks 1636
6 Harmon Killebrew 1584
7 Al Kaline 1583
8 Willie McCovey 1555
9 Willie Stargell 1540
10 Billy Williams 1475

1943-1960
1 Stan Musial 1951
2 Ted Williams 1839
3 Mickey Mantle 1509
4 Eddie Mathews 1453
5 Yogi Berra 1430
6 Duke Snider 1333
7 Mickey Vernon 1311
8 Enos Slaughter 1304
9 Del Ennis.......................1284
10 Gil Hodges 1274

1921-1942
1 Babe Ruth 2213
2 Lou Gehrig 1995
3 Jimmie Foxx 1922
4 Mel Ott 1860
5 Al Simmons 1827
6 Goose Goslin 1609
7 Rogers Hornsby 1584
8 Harry Heilmann 1539
9 Joe DiMaggio 1537
10 Charlie Gehringer...........1427

1901-1920
1 Ty Cobb 1938
2 Honus Wagner 1733
3 Nap Lajoie 1599
4 Tris Speaker 1529
5 Sam Crawford 1525
6 Eddie Collins 1300
7 Zack Wheat 1248
8 Bill Dahlen 1234
9 Sherry Magee 1176
10 Bobby Veach 1166

1893-1900
1 Jake Beckley 1578
2 Ed Delahanty 1466
3 George Davis 1440
4 Lave Cross 1378
5 Hugh Duffy 1302
6 Joe Kelley 1194
7 Tommy Corcoran 1135
8 Ed McKean 1124
9 Jimmy Ryan 1093
10 Herman Long 1055

1876-1892
1 Cap Anson 1880
2 Roger Connor 1323
3 Sam Thompson 1305
4 Dan Brouthers 1296
5 Bid McPhee 1072
6 Fred Pfeffer 1021
7 Jim O'Rourke 1010
8 Billy Nash 979
9 King Kelly 950
10 Harry Stovey 908

RBI/150 Games by era

1988-2005
1 Manny Ramirez..........125.7
2 Juan Gonzalez 124.7
3 Albert Belle 120.8
4 Alex Rodriguez 115.5
5 Mark McGwire 113.2
6 Carlos Delgado 112.3
7 Frank Thomas 112.2
8 Jose Canseco 111.8
9 Ken Griffey Jr. 108.4
10 Vladimir Guerrero 107.9

1973-1987
1 Jim Rice 104.2
2 Bob Horner 100.7
3 Mike Schmidt 99.5
4 Johnny Bench 95.6
5 Eddie Murray 95.0
6 George Foster 94.0
7 Dave Kingman 93.5
8 Kent Hrbek 93.2
9 Greg Luzinski 92.9
10 Dave Winfield 92.5

1961-1972
1 Hank Aaron 104.5
2 Dick Stuart 100.2
3 Willie Stargell 97.9
4 Harmon Killebrew 97.6
5 Ernie Banks 97.1
6 Frank Robinson 96.8
7 Orlando Cepeda 96.4
8 Dick Allen 96.0
9 Willie Mays 95.4
10 Rocky Colavito 94.4

1943-1960
1 Ted Williams 120.4
2 Roy Campanella 105.7
3 Ralph Kiner 103.4
4 Al Rosen 103.0
5 Vern Stephens 102.4
6 Del Ennis 101.2
7 Yogi Berra 101.2
8 Bobby Doerr 100.3
9 Charlie Keller 97.4
10 Jackie Jensen 96.9

1921-1942
1 Lou Gehrig 138.3
2 Hank Greenberg 137.4
3 Joe DiMaggio 132.8
4 Babe Ruth 132.6
5 Jimmie Foxx 124.4
6 Al Simmons 123.7
7 Hack Wilson 118.3
8 Bob Meusel 113.8
9 Hal Trosky 112.7
10 Rudy York 107.8

1901-1920
1 Nap Lajoie 96.7
2 Bobby Veach 96.0
3 Ty Cobb 95.8
4 Buck Freeman 95.0
5 Frank Baker 94.0
6 Honus Wagner 93.0
7 Sam Mertes 90.9
8 Sam Crawford 90.9
9 John Anderson 89.7
10 Gavy Cravath 88.4

1893-1900
1 Ed Delahanty 119.7
2 Hugh Duffy 112.4
3 Ed McKean 101.9
4 Jake Beckley 99.1
5 Hughie Jennings 98.1
6 Joe Kelley 96.7
7 Patsy Tebeau 94.5
8 Steve Brodie 93.9
9 Jack Doyle 92.8
10 George Davis 91.1

1876-1892
1 Sam Thompson 138.8
2 Cap Anson 123.6
3 Dan Brouthers 116.2
4 Tip O'Neill 107.9
5 Henry Larkin 105.3
6 Tommy Burns 105.3
7 Denny Lyons 101.0
8 Buck Ewing 100.7
9 Roger Connor 99.3
10 Dave Foutz 99.0

Walks

1 Barry Bonds 2311
2 Rickey Henderson 2190
3 Babe Ruth 2062
4 Ted Williams 2021
5 Joe Morgan 1865
6 Carl Yastrzemski 1845
7 Mickey Mantle 1733
8 Mel Ott 1708
9 Eddie Yost 1614
10 Darrell Evans 1605
11 Stan Musial 1599
12 Pete Rose 1566
13 Harmon Killebrew 1559
14 Lou Gehrig 1508
15 Mike Schmidt 1507
16 Eddie Collins 1499
17 Frank Thomas 1466
18 Willie Mays 1464
19 Jimmie Foxx 1452
20 Eddie Mathews 1444
21 Frank Robinson 1420
22 Wade Boggs 1412
23 Hank Aaron 1402
24 Jeff Bagwell 1401
25 Dwight Evans 1391
26 Tris Speaker 1381
27 Reggie Jackson 1375
28 Rafael Palmeiro 1353
29 Willie McCovey 1345
30 Eddie Murray 1333
31 Tim Raines 1330
32 Tony Phillips 1319
33 Mark McGwire 1317
34 Fred McGriff 1305
35 Luke Appling 1302
36 Edgar Martinez 1283
37 Gary Sheffield 1280
38 Al Kaline 1277
39 John Olerud 1275
40 Ken Singleton 1263
41 Jack Clark 1262
42 Jim Thome 1257
43 Rusty Staub 1255
44 Ty Cobb 1249
45 Willie Randolph 1243
46 Jimmy Wynn 1224
47 Dave Winfield 1216
48 Pee Wee Reese 1210
49 Richie Ashburn 1198
50 Brian Downing 1197
   Lou Whitaker 1197
52 Chili Davis 1194
53 Billy Hamilton 1189
54 Charlie Gehringer 1186
55 Donie Bush 1158
56 Max Bishop 1156
57 Toby Harrah 1153
58 Harry Hooper 1136
59 Jimmy Sheckard 1135
60 Brett Butler 1129
   Cal Ripken 1129
62 Ron Santo 1108
63 Craig Biggio 1097
64 George Brett 1096
65 Paul Molitor 1094
66 Lu Blue 1092
   Stan Hack 1092
68 Paul Waner 1091
69 Graig Nettles 1088
70 Bobby Grich 1087
71 Mark Grace 1075
   Bob Johnson 1075
   Robin Ventura 1075
74 Ozzie Smith 1072
75 Harlond Clift 1070
   Keith Hernandez 1070
77 Bill Dahlen 1064
78 Harold Baines 1062
79 Joe Cronin 1059
80 Ron Fairly 1052
81 Billy Williams 1045
82 Norm Cash 1043
   Eddie Joost 1043
84 Roy Thomas 1042
85 Max Carey 1040
86 Ken Griffey Jr. 1038
   Rogers Hornsby 1038
88 Jim Gilliam 1036
   Bernie Williams 1036
90 Roberto Alomar 1032
91 Sal Bando 1031
92 Jesse Burkett 1029
93 Rod Carew 1018
   Enos Slaughter 1018
95 Ron Cey 1012
96 Ralph Kiner 1011
97 Chipper Jones 1009
98 Dummy Hoy 1006
99 Miller Huggins 1003
100 Roger Connor 1002

Walk Percentage (BB/PA)

1 Ted Williams 20.64
2 Max Bishop 20.00
3 Babe Ruth 19.42
4 Ferris Fain 18.43
5 Eddie Stanky 18.33
6 Barry Bonds 18.21
7 Roy Cullenbine 17.82
8 Gene Tenace 17.81
9 Eddie Yost 17.59
10 Mickey Mantle 17.49
11 Jim Thome 17.26
12 Mark McGwire 17.19
13 Frank Thomas 17.04
14 Charlie Keller 17.03
15 John McGraw 16.92
16 Mickey Tettleton 16.52
17 Joe Morgan 16.46
18 Rickey Henderson 16.41
19 Earl Torgeson 16.23
20 Bernie Carbo 16.20
21 Ralph Kiner 16.16
22 Brian Giles 15.94
23 Harmon Killebrew 15.86
24 Roy Thomas 15.85
25 Billy Hamilton 15.63
26 Lou Gehrig 15.61
27 Harlond Clift 15.52
28 Joe Ferguson 15.51
29 Bobby Abreu 15.47
30 Jason Giambi 15.47
31 Elmer Valo 15.47
32 Eddie Joost 15.38
33 Jack Clark 15.34
34 Jimmy Wynn 15.28
35 Lu Blue 15.15
36 Mel Ott 15.07
37 Jimmie Foxx 15.02
38 Mike Schmidt 14.98
39 Darrell Evans 14.95
40 Dolph Camilli 14.91
41 Jeff Bagwell 14.86
42 Edgar Martinez 14.79
43 Ken Singleton 14.76
44 Joe Cunningham 14.75
45 Miller Huggins 14.75
46 John Cangelosi 14.72
47 Cupid Childs 14.65
48 Elbie Fletcher 14.61
49 Darren Daulton 14.51
50 Tony Phillips 14.48
51 Merv Rettenmund 14.48
52 Dave Magadan 14.47
53 Topsy Hartsel 14.45
54 Mike Hargrove 14.42
55 Jason Thompson 14.35
56 Wayne Garrett 14.34
57 Eddie Mathews 14.30
58 Chipper Jones 14.28
59 Todd Helton 14.25
60 Dwayne Murphy 14.25
61 John Kruk 14.10
62 John Olerud 14.07
63 Augie Galan 13.98
64 Hank Greenberg 13.98
65 Gene Woodling 13.93
66 Andy Thornton 13.92
67 Willie McCovey 13.89
68 Tim Salmon 13.85
69 Larry Doby 13.82
70 Jorge Posada 13.82
71 Mickey Cochrane 13.81
72 Darrell Porter 13.77
73 Johnny Briggs 13.71
74 David Justice 13.68
75 Alvin Davis 13.67
76 John Mayberry 13.67
77 Gary Sheffield 13.63
78 Paul Radford 13.57
79 Billy North 13.57
80 Carlos Delgado 13.55
81 Steve Braun 13.48
82 Dave Hansen 13.48
83 Norm Siebern 13.44
84 Bob Allison 13.43
85 Al Rosen 13.42
86 Jay Buhner 13.36
87 Bob Johnson 13.36
88 Lee Mazzilli 13.29
89 Roger Bresnahan 13.29
90 Donie Bush 13.26
91 Bobby Grich 13.22
92 Wally Schang 13.22
93 Manny Ramirez 13.20
94 Mike Jorgensen 13.19
95 Carl Yastrzemski 13.19
96 Norm Cash 13.19
97 Rick Ferrell 13.16
98 Tommy Henrich 13.16
99 Dwight Evans 13.16
100 Toby Harrah 13.15

Strikeouts

1 Reggie Jackson 2597
2 Sammy Sosa 2194
3 Andres Galarraga 2003
4 Jose Canseco 1942
5 Willie Stargell 1936
6 Mike Schmidt 1883
7 Fred McGriff 1882
8 Tony Perez 1867
9 Dave Kingman 1816
10 Jim Thome 1762
11 Bobby Bonds 1757
12 Dale Murphy 1748
13 Lou Brock 1730
14 Mickey Mantle 1710
15 Harmon Killebrew 1699
16 Chili Davis 1698
17 Dwight Evans 1697
18 Rickey Henderson 1694
19 Dave Winfield 1686
20 Gary Gaetti 1602
21 Mark McGwire 1596
22 Lee May 1570
23 Jeff Bagwell 1558
24 Craig Biggio 1557
25 Dick Allen 1556
26 Ray Lankford 1550
   Willie McCovey 1550
28 Dave Parker 1537
29 Frank Robinson 1532
30 Lance Parrish 1527
31 Willie Mays 1526
   Devon White 1526
33 Eddie Murray 1516
34 Rick Monday 1513
   Reggie Sanders 1513
   Greg Vaughn 1513
37 Andre Dawson 1509
38 Tony Phillips 1499
39 Greg Luzinski 1495
40 Eddie Mathews 1487
41 Frank Howard 1460
42 Jay Bell 1443
43 Juan Samuel 1442
44 Harold Baines 1441
   Jack Clark 1441
46 Barry Bonds 1434
47 Mo Vaughn 1429
48 Jimmy Wynn 1427
49 Jim Rice 1423
50 George Foster 1419
51 George Scott 1418
52 Ken Griffey Jr. 1416
53 Jim Edmonds 1411
   Ron Gant 1411
55 Darrell Evans 1410
56 Rob Deer 1409
57 Jay Buhner 1406
58 Eric Davis 1398
59 Carl Yastrzemski 1393
60 Joe Carter 1387
61 Carlton Fisk 1386
62 Hank Aaron 1383
63 Travis Fryman 1369
64 Carlos Delgado 1363
   Matt Williams 1363
66 Danny Tartabull 1362
67 Larry Parrish 1359
68 Darryl Strawberry 1352
69 Jose Hernandez 1351
70 Robin Yount 1350
71 Manny Ramirez 1349
72 Rafael Palmeiro 1348
73 Ron Santo 1343
74 Ellis Burks 1340
   Jeff Kent 1340
76 Gorman Thomas 1339
77 Dean Palmer 1332
78 Babe Ruth 1330
79 Deron Johnson 1318
80 Cecil Fielder 1316
   Tim Salmon 1316
82 Willie Horton 1313
83 Jimmie Foxx 1311
84 Mickey Tettleton 1307
   Tim Wallach 1307
86 Cal Ripken 1305
87 Jeromy Burnitz 1302
88 Bret Boone 1295
89 Kirk Gibson 1285
90 Todd Zeile 1279
91 Johnny Bench 1278
   Bobby Grich 1278
93 Royce Clayton 1277
   Pete Incaviglia 1277
95 Juan Gonzalez 1273
96 Benito Santiago 1270
97 Julio Franco 1269
98 Claudell Washington 1266
99 Alex Rodriguez 1265
100 Ryne Sandberg 1260

At Bats per Strikeout

1 Joe Sewell 62.6
2 Lloyd Waner 44.9
3 Nellie Fox 42.7
4 Tommy Holmes 40.9
5 Andy High 33.8
6 Sam Rice 33.7
7 Frankie Frisch 33.5
8 Dale Mitchell 33.5
9 Johnny Cooney 31.5
10 Frank McCormick 30.3
11 Don Mueller 29.9
12 Billy Southworth 29.5
13 Rip Radcliff 28.9
14 Edd Roush 28.3
15 Pie Traynor 27.2
16 Doc Cramer 26.5
17 Carson Bigbee 26.0
18 Hank Severeid 25.5
19 George Sisler 25.3
20 Paul Waner 25.2
21 Sparky Adams 24.9
22 Lou Finney 24.9
23 Deacon White 24.8
24 Jack Rowe 24.8
25 Irish Meusel 24.6
26 Ezra Sutton 24.6
27 Red Schoendienst 24.5
28 Vic Power 24.5
29 Arky Vaughan 24.0
30 Felix Millan 23.9
31 Mickey Cochrane 23.8
32 Charlie Gehringer 23.8
33 John Ward 23.5
34 George Kell 23.4
35 George Cutshaw 23.2
36 Jack Tobin 23.1
37 Taffy Wright 23.1
38 Hughie Critz 23.1
39 Mark Koenig 22.5
40 Ernie Lombardi 22.3
41 Heinie Manush 22.2
42 Bobby Richardson 22.2
43 Jo-Jo Moore 22.0
44 Earl Sheely 21.8
45 Bill Dickey 21.8
46 Johnny Pesky 21.8
47 Rick Ferrell 21.8
48 Glenn Beckert 21.4
49 Tony Gwynn 21.4
50 Dick Siebert 21.2

Strikeout Percentage

1 Rob Deer 36.31
2 Jose Hernandez 30.25
3 Pete Incaviglia 30.17
4 Jim Thome 29.77
5 Gorman Thomas 28.63
6 Jay Buhner 28.05
7 Mickey Tettleton 27.82
8 Mike Cameron 27.67
9 Jose Canseco 27.52
10 Dave Kingman 27.20
11 Danny Tartabull 27.18
12 Dean Palmer 27.17
13 Cory Snyder 27.13
14 Ray Lankford 26.97
15 Gary Pettis 26.40
16 Nate Colbert 26.36
17 Reggie Jackson 26.33
18 Eric Davis 26.27
19 Todd Hundley 26.21
20 Sammy Sosa 26.12
21 Tony Clark 26.02
22 Charles Johnson 25.99
23 Jesse Barfield 25.93
24 Reggie Sanders 25.89
25 Mo Vaughn 25.83
26 Mark McGwire 25.80
27 Cecil Fielder 25.52
28 Jim Edmonds 25.39
29 John Vander Wal 25.37
30 Lee Stevens 24.97
31 Darryl Strawberry 24.95
32 Bobby Bonds 24.95
33 Greg Vaughn 24.79
34 Andres Galarraga 24.74
35 Paul Sorrento 24.74
36 Rick Monday 24.66
37 Carlos Delgado 24.65
38 Dick Allen 24.57
39 Jorge Posada 24.56
40 Donn Clendenon 24.53
41 Mack Jones 24.46
42 Willie Stargell 24.42
43 Derrek Lee 24.37
44 Jose Cruz 24.29
45 Jeromy Burnitz 24.12
46 Phil Nevin 24.08
47 Jose Valentin 23.95
48 Dick Stuart 23.94
49 Juan Samuel 23.71
50 Michael Tucker 23.49

Batting Average

1 Ty Cobb 366
2 Rogers Hornsby 358
3 Joe Jackson 356
4 Ed Delahanty 346
5 Tris Speaker 345
6 Billy Hamilton 344
7 Ted Williams 344
8 Dan Brouthers 342
9 Babe Ruth 342
10 Harry Heilmann 342
11 Pete Browning 341
12 Willie Keeler 341
13 Bill Terry 341
14 George Sisler 340
15 Lou Gehrig 340
16 Jesse Burkett 338
17 Tony Gwynn 338
18 Nap Lajoie 338
19 Todd Helton 337
20 Riggs Stephenson 336
21 Al Simmons 334
22 John McGraw 334
23 Paul Waner 333
24 Eddie Collins 333
25 Mike Donlin 333
26 Sam Thompson 331
27 Cap Anson 331
28 Stan Musial 331
29 Heinie Manush 330
30 Wade Boggs 328
31 Rod Carew 328
32 Honus Wagner 328
33 Tip O'Neill 326
34 Hugh Duffy 326
35 Bob Fothergill 325
36 Jimmie Foxx 325
37 Earle Combs 325
38 Joe DiMaggio 325
39 Babe Herman 324
40 Vladimir Guerrero 324
41 Joe Medwick 324
42 Edd Roush 323
43 Sam Rice 322
44 Ross Youngs 322
45 Kiki Cuyler 321
46 Charlie Gehringer 320
47 Chuck Klein 320
48 Nomar Garciaparra 320
49 Pie Traynor 320
50 Mickey Cochrane 320
51 Ken Williams 319
52 Kirby Puckett 318
53 Earl Averill 318
54 Arky Vaughan 318
55 Roberto Clemente 317
56 Chick Hafey 317
57 Joe Kelley 317
58 Zack Wheat 317
59 Roger Connor 316
60 Lloyd Waner 316
61 George Van Haltren 316
62 Frankie Frisch 316
63 Goose Goslin 316
64 Bibb Falk 314
65 Cecil Travis 314
66 Derek Jeter 314
67 Manny Ramirez 314
68 Hank Greenberg 313
69 Jack Fournier 313
70 Elmer Flick 313
71 Larry Walker 313
72 Bill Dickey 313
73 Dale Mitchell 312
74 Johnny Mize 312
75 Joe Sewell 312
76 Fred Clarke 312
77 Barney McCosky 312
78 Hughie Jennings 312
79 Edgar Martinez 312
80 Freddie Lindstrom 311
81 Bing Miller 311
82 Jackie Robinson 311
83 Baby Doll Jacobson 311
84 Taffy Wright 311
85 Rip Radcliff 311
86 Mike Piazza 311
87 Ginger Beaumont 311
88 Mike Tiernan 311
89 Luke Appling 310
90 Irish Meusel 310
91 Elmer Smith 310
92 Denny Lyons 310
93 Bobby Veach 310
94 Jim O'Rourke 310
95 Jim Bottomley 310
96 John Stone 310
97 Sam Crawford 309
98 Bob Meusel 309
99 Jack Tobin 309
100 Spud Davis 308

Batting Average by era

1988-2005
1 Tony Gwynn 338
2 Todd Helton...................337
3 Wade Boggs 328
4 Vladimir Guerrero 324
5 Nomar Garciaparra....320
6 Kirby Puckett 318
7 Derek Jeter 314
8 Manny Ramirez 314
9 Larry Walker 313
10 Edgar Martinez 312

1973-1987
1 Rod Carew 328
2 Ralph Garr 306
3 George Brett 305
4 Bill Madlock 305
5 Al Oliver 303
6 Pete Rose 303
7 Pedro Guerrero 300
8 Bake McBride 299
9 Cecil Cooper 298
10 Jim Rice 298

1961-1972
1 Roberto Clemente 317
2 Matty Alou 307
3 Hank Aaron 305
4 Tony Oliva 304
5 Manny Mota 304
6 Willie Mays 302
7 Rico Carty 299
8 Joe Torre 297
9 Al Kaline 297
10 Orlando Cepeda...........297

1943-1960
1 Ted Williams 344
2 Stan Musial 331
3 Dale Mitchell 312
4 Barney McCosky 312
5 Jackie Robinson 311
6 Richie Ashburn 308
7 Johnny Pesky 307
8 George Kell 306
9 Dixie Walker 306
10 Harvey Kuenn 303

1921-1942
1 Rogers Hornsby 358
2 Babe Ruth 342
3 Harry Heilmann 342
4 Bill Terry 341
5 George Sisler 340
6 Lou Gehrig 340
7 Riggs Stephenson........336
8 Al Simmons 334
9 Paul Waner 333
10 Heinie Manush 330

1901-1920
1 Ty Cobb.......................366
2 Joe Jackson 356
3 Tris Speaker 345
4 Willie Keeler 341
5 Nap Lajoie 338
6 Eddie Collins 333
7 Mike Donlin 333
8 Honus Wagner 328
9 Zack Wheat 317
10 Elmer Flick 313

1893-1900
1 Ed Delahanty 346
2 Billy Hamilton 344
3 Jesse Burkett 338
4 John McGraw 334
5 Hugh Duffy 326
6 Joe Kelley 317
7 George Van Haltren 316
8 Hughie Jennings 312
9 Mike Tiernan 311
10 Elmer Smith 310

1876-1892
1 Dan Brouthers..............342
2 Pete Browning 341
3 Sam Thompson 331
4 Cap Anson 331
5 Tip O'Neill 326
6 Roger Connor 316
7 Denny Lyons 310
8 Jim O'Rourke 310
9 King Kelly 308
10 Deacon White 303

On-Base Percentage

1 Ted Williams 482
2 Babe Ruth 474
3 John McGraw 466
4 Billy Hamilton 455
5 Lou Gehrig 447
6 **Barry Bonds** 442
7 Rogers Hornsby 434
8 Ty Cobb 433
   Todd Helton....................433
10 Jimmie Foxx 428
   Tris Speaker 428
12 **Frank Thomas** 427
13 Eddie Collins 424
   Ferris Fain 424
15 Max Bishop 423
   Dan Brouthers 423
   Joe Jackson 423
18 Mickey Mantle 421
19 Mickey Cochrane 419
20 Edgar Martinez 418
21 Stan Musial 417
22 Cupid Childs 416
23 Wade Boggs 415
   Jesse Burkett 415
25 Mel Ott 414
26 **Jason Giambi**..................413
   Brian Giles 413
   Roy Thomas 413
29 Hank Greenberg 412
30 **Bobby Abreu** 411
   Ed Delahanty 411
32 Harry Heilmann 410
   Charlie Keller 410
   Eddie Stanky 410
35 **Manny Ramirez**...............409
   Jackie Robinson 409
37 **Jeff Bagwell** 408
   Roy Cullenbine 408
   Jim Thome 408
40 Denny Lyons 407
   Riggs Stephenson 407
42 Arky Vaughan 406
43 Charlie Gehringer 404
   Paul Waner 404
45 Pete Browning 403
   Joe Cunningham 403
47 Lu Blue 402
   Joe Kelley 402
49 Rickey Henderson 401
   Chipper Jones................401
51 **Larry Walker** 400
52 Luke Appling 399
   Gary Sheffield................399
   Ross Youngs 399
55 Joe DiMaggio 398
   Ralph Kiner 398
   John Olerud 398
   Elmer Smith 398
   Elmer Valo 398
60 Earle Combs 397
   Roger Connor 397
   John Kruk 397
   Johnny Mize 397
64 Cap Anson 396
   Richie Ashburn 396
   Mike Hargrove 396
67 Earl Averill 395
   Hack Wilson 395
69 Frank Chance 394
   Stan Hack 394
   Mark Grace 394
   Johnny Pesky 394
   Eddie Yost 394
74 Rod Carew 393
   Carlos Delgado 393
   Bob Johnson 393
   Wally Schang 393
   Bill Terry 393
   Ken Williams 393
80 Jack Fournier 392
   George Grantham 392
   Joe Morgan 392
   Tip O'Neill 392
   Mike Tiernan 392
85 **Vladimir Guerrero** 391
   Hughie Jennings 391
   Joe Sewell 391
   Honus Wagner 391
89 Harlond Clift 390
   Joe Cronin 390
   Augie Galan 390
   Dave Magadan 390
93 Elmer Flick 389
   Minnie Minoso 389
   Buddy Myer 389
   Frank Robinson 389
97 Dolph Camilli 388
   Mike Griffin 388
   Tony Gwynn 388
   Willie Keeler 388
   Ken Singleton 388
   Gene Tenace 388

Slugging Average

1 Babe Ruth 690
2 Ted Williams 634
3 Lou Gehrig 632
4 **Barry Bonds** 611
5 Jimmie Foxx 609
6 **Todd Helton** 607
7 Hank Greenberg 605
8 **Manny Ramirez** 599
9 Mark McGwire 588
10 **Vladimir Guerrero** 587
11 Joe DiMaggio 579
12 **Alex Rodriguez** 577
13 Rogers Hornsby 577
14 **Frank Thomas** 568
15 **Larry Walker** 565
16 Albert Belle 564
17 **Jim Thome** 562
18 Johnny Mize 562
19 **Ken Griffey Jr.** 561
20 **Juan Gonzalez** 561
21 Stan Musial 559
22 **Carlos Delgado** 559
23 Willie Mays 557
24 Mickey Mantle 557
25 **Mike Piazza** 555
26 Hank Aaron 555
27 Ralph Kiner 548
28 Hack Wilson 545
29 **Nomar Garciaparra**........544
30 Chuck Klein 543
31 **Jim Edmonds** 543
32 **Brian Giles** 542
33 **Jeff Bagwell** 540
34 Duke Snider 540
35 **Jason Giambi** 539
36 **Chipper Jones** 538
37 Frank Robinson 537
38 **Sammy Sosa** 537
39 Al Simmons 535
40 Dick Allen 534
41 Earl Averill 534
42 Mel Ott 533
43 Babe Herman 532
44 Ken Williams 530
45 Willie Stargell 529
46 Mike Schmidt 527
47 **Gary Sheffield** 527
48 Chick Hafey 526
49 Mo Vaughn 523
50 Hal Trosky 522
51 Wally Berger 522
52 Harry Heilmann 520
53 Kevin Mitchell 520
54 Dan Brouthers 519
55 **Magglio Ordonez** 518
56 Charlie Keller 518
57 Joe Jackson 517
58 Edgar Martinez 515
59 Willie McCovey 515
60 Jose Canseco 515
61 **Rafael Palmeiro** 515
62 **Scott Rolen** 515
63 **Moises Alou** 513
64 Ty Cobb 512
65 **Bobby Abreu** 512
66 Ellis Burks 510
67 Eddie Mathews 509
68 Fred McGriff 509
69 Jeff Heath 509
70 Harmon Killebrew 509
71 **Ryan Klesko** 507
72 **Jeff Kent** 506
73 Bob Johnson 506
74 Bill Terry 506
75 Darryl Strawberry 505
76 Sam Thompson 505
77 Ed Delahanty 505
78 **Shawn Green** 505
79 Joe Medwick 505
80 **Andruw Jones**...............503
81 Jim Rice 502
82 **Derrek Lee** 501
83 Tris Speaker 500
84 David Justice 500
85 **Tim Salmon** 500
86 Jim Bottomley 500
87 **Mike Sweeney** 500
88 Goose Goslin 500
89 Roy Campanella 500
90 Ernie Banks 500
91 Orlando Cepeda 499
92 Bob Horner 499
93 Dante Bichette 499
94 Andres Galarraga 499
95 Frank Howard 499
96 **Javy Lopez** 498
97 Ted Kluszewski 498
98 Bob Meusel 497
99 Will Clark 497
100 Hank Sauer 496

On-Base plus Slugging

1 Babe Ruth 1164
2 Ted Williams 1116
3 Lou Gehrig 1079
4 **Barry Bonds** 1053
5 **Todd Helton** 1040
6 Jimmie Foxx 1037
7 Hank Greenberg 1017
8 Rogers Hornsby 1011
9 **Manny Ramirez** 1008
10 **Frank Thomas** 995
11 Mark McGwire 982
12 **Vladimir Guerrero** 978
13 Mickey Mantle 978
14 Joe DiMaggio 977
15 Stan Musial 976
16 **Jim Thome** 970
17 **Larry Walker** 965
18 **Alex Rodriguez** 962
19 Johnny Mize 959
20 **Brian Giles** 955
21 **Carlos Delgado** 952
22 **Jason Giambi** 952
23 **Jeff Bagwell** 948
24 Mel Ott 947
25 Ralph Kiner 946
26 Ty Cobb 945
27 Dan Brouthers 942
28 Willie Mays 941
29 Joe Jackson 940
   Hack Wilson 940
31 **Chipper Jones** 939
32 **Ken Griffey Jr.** 938
33 **Mike Piazza** 937
34 Albert Belle 933
   Edgar Martinez 933
36 Harry Heilmann 930
37 Hank Aaron 929
   Earl Averill 929
39 Charlie Keller 928
   Tris Speaker 928
41 **Jim Edmonds** 927
42 Frank Robinson 926
   Gary Sheffield............926
44 **Bobby Abreu** 923
45 Ken Williams 923
46 Chuck Klein 922
47 Duke Snider 920
48 Ed Delahanty 916
49 Al Simmons 915
50 Babe Herman 915
51 Dick Allen 912
52 **Nomar Garciaparra**....911
53 Mike Schmidt 907
54 Mo Vaughn 906
55 **Juan Gonzalez** 904
56 Bob Johnson 899
   Bill Terry 899
58 Chick Hafey 898
59 Mickey Cochrane 897
60 Hal Trosky 893
61 **Scott Rolen** 890
62 Willie McCovey 889
   Willie Stargell 889
   Sam Thompson 889
65 Billy Hamilton 887
66 Goose Goslin 887
67 Fred McGriff 886
   Tim Salmon 886
69 **Rafael Palmeiro** 886
70 Harmon Killebrew 885
   Eddie Mathews 885
72 Charlie Gehringer 884
73 Roger Connor 883
   Jackie Robinson 883
75 **Moises Alou** 882
   Magglio Ordonez 882
   Sammy Sosa 882
78 Wally Berger 881
   Will Clark 881
80 Dolph Camilli 880
   Kevin Mitchell 880
   Riggs Stephenson 880
83 Jeff Heath 879
   Al Rosen 879
85 David Justice 878
   Ryan Klesko 878
87 Paul Waner 877
88 Larry Doby 876
89 John McGraw 876
90 Jack Fournier 875
91 **Mike Sweeney** 874
92 Ellis Burks 873
   Tommy Henrich 873
94 Pete Browning 870
95 Jim Bottomley 869
96 Jose Canseco 868
   Bill Dickey 868
98 Joe Medwick 867
99 Rusty Greer 865
100 **Derrek Lee** 864
   Danny Tartabull 864
   Bernie Williams 864

Adjusted OPS

1 Babe Ruth 209
2 Ted Williams 186
3 **Barry Bonds** 183
4 Lou Gehrig 182
5 Rogers Hornsby 176
6 Mickey Mantle 173
7 Dan Brouthers 169
   Joe Jackson 169
9 Ty Cobb 167
10 Pete Browning 164
11 Mark McGwire 163
12 Jimmie Foxx 161
   Frank Thomas 161
14 Hank Greenberg 157
   Johnny Mize 157
   Stan Musial 157
17 Hank Aaron 156
   Dick Allen 156
   Joe DiMaggio 156
   Willie Mays 156
   Tris Speaker 156
22 Mel Ott 155
23 Roger Connor 154
   Manny Ramirez 154
25 Frank Robinson 153
26 Ed Delahanty 152
   Charlie Keller 152
28 **Vladimir Guerrero** 151
29 Nap Lajoie 150
   Honus Wagner 150
31 **Jeff Bagwell** 149
   Gavy Cravath 149
   Elmer Flick 149
   Mike Piazza 149
35 **Jason Giambi** 148
   Harry Heilmann 148
   Ralph Kiner 148
   Willie McCovey 148
39 Edgar Martinez 147
   Willie Stargell 147
   Jim Thome 147
42 **Brian Giles** 146
   Mike Schmidt 146
   Gary Sheffield 146
   Sam Thompson 146
46 Eddie Mathews 145
   Alex Rodriguez 145
   Hack Wilson 145
49 Albert Belle 144
   Ken Griffey Jr. 144
51 Sam Crawford 143
   Jack Fournier 143
   Frank Howard 143
54 Eddie Collins 142
   Carlos Delgado 142
   Mike Donlin 142
   Harmon Killebrew 142
   Henry Larkin 142
   Kevin Mitchell 142
60 **Bobby Abreu** 141
   Todd Helton 141
   Babe Herman 141
   Chipper Jones 141
   Harry Stovey 141
65 Wally Berger 140
   Jesse Burkett 140
   Jeff Heath 140
   Tip O'Neill 140
69 Cap Anson 139
   Billy Hamilton 139
   Reggie Jackson 139
   Bob Johnson 139
73 Norm Cash 138
   Pedro Guerrero 138
   Denny Lyons 138
   Al Rosen 138
   Duke Snider 138
   Darryl Strawberry 138
   Mike Tiernan 138
80 Jack Clark 137
   Will Clark 137
   Larry Doby 137
   Sherry Magee 137
   Gene Tenace 137
   Bill Terry 137
86 Frank Baker 136
   Jim Edmonds 136
   King Kelly 136
   Reggie Smith 136
   Arky Vaughan 136
   Larry Walker 136
   Ken Williams 136
93 Tommy Burns 135
   Frank Chance 135
   Chuck Klein 135
   John McGraw 135
97 George Brett 134
   Dolph Camilli 134
   George Gore 134
   Al Kaline 134
   John Kruk 134
   Boog Powell 134

Adjusted Batting Wins

1 Babe Ruth 135.3
2 Barry Bonds 122.6
3 Ty Cobb 103.4
4 Ted Williams 103.0
5 Hank Aaron 95.2
6 Lou Gehrig 93.7
7 Stan Musial 92.5
8 Mickey Mantle 89.4
9 Rogers Hornsby 87.6
10 Willie Mays 87.3
11 Tris Speaker 82.9
12 Frank Robinson 78.9
13 Mel Ott 78.2
14 Jimmie Foxx 70.0
15 Frank Thomas 67.6
16 Honus Wagner 66.0
17 Eddie Collins 64.4
18 Jeff Bagwell 61.8
19 Eddie Mathews 58.3
20 Mark McGwire 58.3
21 Nap Lajoie 57.9
22 Mike Schmidt 57.7
23 Willie McCovey 57.5
24 Gary Sheffield 56.6
25 Reggie Jackson 54.3
26 Edgar Martinez 54.2
27 Rickey Henderson 54.0
28 Dan Brouthers 53.4
29 Harry Heilmann 52.7
30 Carl Yastrzemski 52.3
31 Joe Morgan 52.1
32 Willie Stargell 52.1
33 Harmon Killebrew 51.3
34 Joe DiMaggio 50.2
35 George Brett 50.1
36 Dick Allen 49.9
37 Al Kaline 49.6
38 Johnny Mize 49.5
39 Sam Crawford 48.7
40 Ed Delahanty 48.5
41 Ken Griffey Jr. 48.4
42 Roger Connor 48.3
43 Manny Ramirez 48.1
44 Rafael Palmeiro 47.2
45 Eddie Murray 47.0
46 Paul Waner 46.6
47 Tony Gwynn 45.5
48 Wade Boggs 45.1
49 Joe Jackson 45.0
50 Dave Winfield 44.9
51 Jim Thome 44.4
52 Jesse Burkett 43.1
53 Fred McGriff 42.8
54 Rod Carew 42.8
55 Mike Piazza 42.3
56 Hank Greenberg 40.8
57 Jack Clark 40.3
58 Will Clark 40.2
59 Pete Rose 40.2
60 Jason Giambi 39.7
61 Billy Williams 39.6
62 Duke Snider 39.6
63 Cap Anson 39.6
64 Alex Rodriguez 38.8
65 Frank Howard 38.3
66 Ken Singleton 38.1
67 Norm Cash 37.8
68 Bob Johnson 37.7
69 Chipper Jones 37.6
70 John Olerud 37.4
71 Reggie Smith 37.0
72 Billy Hamilton 37.0
73 Roberto Clemente 37.0
74 Rusty Staub 36.8
75 Larry Walker 36.5
76 Ralph Kiner 36.5
77 Orlando Cepeda 35.9
78 Elmer Flick 35.9
79 Arky Vaughan 35.8
80 Sherry Magee 35.7
81 Fred Clarke 35.6
82 Albert Belle 35.4
83 Carlos Delgado 35.4
84 Dwight Evans 35.1
85 Zack Wheat 34.8
86 Brian Giles 34.6
87 Keith Hernandez 34.6
88 Paul Molitor 34.3
89 Pete Browning 34.0
90 Tim Raines 33.8
91 Boog Powell 33.7
92 Al Simmons 33.6
93 Vladimir Guerrero 33.5
94 Bill Terry 32.6
95 Sammy Sosa 32.5
96 Goose Goslin 32.4
97 Charlie Gehringer 32.0
98 Joe Medwick 32.0
99 Jimmy Wynn 31.7
100 Babe Herman 31.7

Adjusted Batting Wins

101 Joe Torre 31.6
102 Jim Edmonds 31.6
103 Jack Fournier 31.2
104 Minnie Minoso 30.7
105 Rocky Colavito 30.6
106 Jose Canseco 30.6
107 Bobby Abreu 30.5
108 Hack Wilson 30.4
109 Albert Pujols 30.3
110 Joe Kelley 30.3
111 Bernie Williams 30.0
112 Sam Thompson 29.9
113 Chuck Klein 29.9
114 Darryl Strawberry 29.8
115 Charlie Keller 29.3
116 Todd Helton 29.3
117 Pedro Guerrero 29.2
118 Ron Santo 29.0
119 Bobby Bonds 29.0
120 Brian Downing 28.9
121 Tony Perez 28.7
122 Larry Doby 28.7
123 Gene Tenace 28.7
124 Harold Baines 28.2
125 Johnny Bench 28.2
126 Greg Luzinski 28.1
127 Darrell Evans 28.0
128 Bobby Grich 28.0
129 Fred Lynn 27.9
130 Jim Rice 27.8
131 Earl Averill 27.7
132 Jake Beckley 27.6
133 Mike Tiernan 27.2
134 Willie Keeler 27.1
135 Dolph Camilli 26.9
136 Ernie Banks 26.9
137 Gavy Cravath 26.8
138 Don Mattingly 26.8
139 Wally Berger 26.6
140 Craig Biggio 26.6
141 Jeff Kent 26.6
142 Harry Stovey 26.5
143 Enos Slaughter 26.5
144 Frank Baker 26.4
145 Jim O'Rourke 26.3
146 Bob Watson 26.2
147 Bob Elliott 26.2
148 Juan Gonzalez 26.0
149 Jeff Heath 25.9
150 Chili Davis 25.9
151 Luis Gonzalez 25.8
152 Mark Grace 25.6
153 Bobby Bonilla 25.6
154 Tony Oliva 25.5
155 Tim Salmon 25.4
156 Rico Carty 25.4
157 Roy Thomas 25.4
158 Jimmy Sheckard 25.2
159 Moises Alou 25.2
160 Bill Nicholson 25.1
161 Stan Hack 25.1
162 Kiki Cuyler 25.1
163 Jose Cruz 25.0
164 Jackie Robinson 24.9
165 Al Oliver 24.9
166 Mo Vaughn 24.7
167 George Davis 24.6
168 Dave Parker 24.5
169 Ellis Burks 24.4
170 Ryan Klesko 24.4
171 George Sisler 24.3
172 Yogi Berra 24.3
173 Jim Bottomley 24.2
174 Cesar Cedeno 24.2
175 Kevin Mitchell 24.0
176 Bill Dickey 24.0
177 Edd Roush 23.8
178 Kent Hrbek 23.7
179 Danny Tartabull 23.7
180 Ken Williams 23.6
181 Ron Cey 23.5
182 George Foster 23.5
183 Gabby Hartnett 23.5
184 Bobby Veach 23.4
185 Bobby Murcer 23.4
186 David Justice 23.4
187 Mickey Cochrane 23.2
188 John McGraw 23.1
189 Lance Berkman 23.0
190 Paul O'Neill 23.0
191 Roy White 22.9
192 Lou Whitaker 22.8
193 Robin Yount 22.6
194 King Kelly 22.5
195 Sid Gordon 22.4
196 Paul Hines 22.4
197 Rick Monday 22.4
198 Hal McRae 22.4
199 Ted Simmons 22.4
200 Augie Galan 22.4

Pinch Hits

1 Lenny Harris 212
2 Manny Mota 150
3 Smoky Burgess 145
4 Greg Gross 143
5 Dave Hansen 139
6 Mark Sweeney 131
7 John Vander Wal 126
8 Jose Morales 123
9 Jerry Lynch 116
10 Red Lucas 114
11 Steve Braun 113
12 Terry Crowley 108
    Denny Walling 108
14 Gates Brown 107
15 Mike Lum 103
16 Jim Dwyer 102
17 Rusty Staub 100
18 Dave Clark 96
19 Larry Biittner 95
    Vic Davalillo 95
    Gerald Perry 95
22 Jerry Hairston 94
23 Dave Philley 93
    Joel Youngblood 93
25 Jay Johnstone 92
    Dave Magadan 92

Pinch Hit Average

(150 at-bats minimum)

1 Alex Arias 320
2 Tommy Davis 320
3 Frenchy Bordagaray ...312
4 Harold Baines 311
5 Greg Colbrunn 310
6 Frankie Baumholtz 307
7 Sid Bream 306
8 Mark Carreon 306
9 Red Schoendienst 303
10 Bob Fothergill 300
11 Dave Philley 299
12 Manny Mota 297
13 Ted Easterly 296
14 Harvey Hendrick 295
15 Larry Herndon 294
16 Rance Mulliniks 292
17 Julio Franco 292
18 Terry Puhl 289
19 Chip Hale 289
20 Manny Sanguillen 288
21 Todd Hollandsworth ...287
22 Midre Cummings 287
    Glenallen Hill 287
24 Carlos Baerga 286
25 Smoky Burgess 286

Pinch Hit Home Runs

1 Cliff Johnson 20
2 Jerry Lynch 18
    John Vander Wal 17
4 Gates Brown 16
    Smoky Burgess 16
    Willie McCovey 16
7 Dave Hansen 15
8 George Crowe 14
9 Glenallen Hill 13
    Mark Sweeney 13
11 Joe Adcock 12
    Bob Cerv 12
    Jose Morales 12
    Graig Nettles 12
15 Jeff Burroughs 11
    Jay Johnstone 11
    Candy Maldonado 11
    Orlando Merced 11
    Fred Whitfield 11
    Cy Williams 11
22 Mark Carreon 10
    Dave Clark 10
    Jim Dwyer 10
    Mike Lum 10
    Ken McMullen 10
    Don Mincher 10
    Wally Post 10
    Champ Summers 10
    Jerry Turner 10
    Gus Zernial 10

Stolen Bases

1 Rickey Henderson 1406
2 Lou Brock 938
3 Billy Hamilton 914
4 Ty Cobb 897
5 Tim Raines 808
6 Vince Coleman 752
7 Arlie Latham 742
8 Eddie Collins 741
9 Max Carey 738
10 Honus Wagner 723
11 Joe Morgan 689
12 Willie Wilson 668
13 Tom Brown 657
14 Bert Campaneris 649
15 Otis Nixon 620
16 George Davis 619
17 Dummy Hoy 596
18 Maury Wills 586
19 George Van Haltren 583
20 Ozzie Smith 580
21 Hugh Duffy 574
22 Bid McPhee 568
23 Kenny Lofton 567
24 Brett Butler 558
25 Davey Lopes 557
26 Cesar Cedeno 550
27 Bill Dahlen 548
28 John Ward 540
29 Herman Long 537
30 Patsy Donovan 518
    Jack Doyle 518
32 Fred Clarke 509
    Harry Stovey 509
34 Luis Aparicio 506
    Barry Bonds 506
36 Paul Molitor 504
37 Willie Keeler 495
    Clyde Milan 495
39 Omar Moreno 487
40 Roberto Alomar 474
41 Mike Griffin 473
42 Tommy McCarthy 468
43 Jimmy Sheckard 465
44 Delino DeShields 463
45 Bobby Bonds 461
46 Eric Young 457
47 Ed Delahanty 455
    Ron LeFlore 455
49 Curt Welch 453
50 Steve Sax 444
51 Joe Kelley 443
52 Sherry Magee 441
53 John McGraw 436
    Tris Speaker 436
55 Marquis Grissom 429
56 Bob Bescher 428
    Mike Tiernan 428
58 Frankie Frisch 419
    Jimmy Ryan 419
60 Charlie Comiskey 416
61 Tommy Harper 408
62 Craig Biggio 407
    Chuck Knoblauch 407
64 Donie Bush 406
65 Frank Chance 403
66 Bill Lange 400
67 Willie Davis 398
68 Sam Mertes 396
    Juan Samuel 396
70 Dave Collins 395
    Billy North 395
72 Jesse Burkett 389
73 Tommy Corcoran 387
74 Dan Daly 385
    Freddie Patek 385
76 George Burns 383
    Hugh Nicol 383
    Fred Pfeffer 383
    Walt Wilmot 383
80 Nap Lajoie 380
81 Barry Larkin 379
82 Harry Hooper 375
    George Sisler 375
84 Jack Glasscock 372
85 Lonnie Smith 370
86 Tom Goodwin 369
87 Tommy Dowd 368
    King Kelly 368
89 Sam Crawford 367
90 Hal Chase 363
91 Tony Womack 362
92 Tommy Leach 361
93 Hughie Jennings 359
    Fielder Jones 359
95 Buck Ewing 354
    Gary Pettis 354
97 Rod Carew 353
98 Willie McGee 352
    Tommy Tucker 352
100 Sam Rice 351

Stolen Base Average

1 Carlos Beltran 87.8
2 Pokey Reese 84.7
3 Tim Raines 84.7
4 Eric Davis 84.1
5 Henry Cotto 83.3
6 Willie Wilson 83.3
7 Tony Womack 83.2
8 Barry Larkin 83.1
9 Davey Lopes 83.0
10 Stan Javier 82.8
11 Doug Glanville 82.4
12 Carl Crawford 81.6
13 Julio Cruz 81.5
14 Brian Hunter 81.0
15 Joe Morgan 81.0
16 Vince Coleman 80.9
17 Rickey Henderson 80.8
18 Roberto Alomar 80.6
19 Andy Van Slyke 80.6
20 Alex Rodriguez 80.1
21 Mickey Mantle 80.1
22 Lenny Dykstra 79.8
23 Alfonso Soriano 79.7
24 Ozzie Smith 79.7
25 Enzo Hernandez 79.6
26 Gary Redus 79.5
27 Paul Molitor 79.4
28 Kenny Lofton 79.3
29 Mike Cameron 79.2
30 Derek Jeter 79.0
31 R. J. Reynolds 79.0
32 Johnny Damon 78.9
33 Luis Aparicio 78.8
34 Marquis Grissom 78.7
35 Orlando Cabrera 78.7
36 Damian Jackson 78.6
    Amos Otis 78.6
38 Kirk Gibson 78.5
39 Dave Roberts 78.2
40 Barry Bonds 78.2
41 Rafael Furcal 78.1
42 Jimmy Rollins 78.1
43 Alan Wiggins 78.1
44 Devon White 77.9
45 Tommy Harper 77.9
46 Rudy Law 77.8
47 Joe Carter 77.8
    Mike Felder 77.8
49 Chuck Knoblauch 77.7
50 Bob Dernier 77.6

Base Stealing Wins

1 Rickey Henderson 18.7
2 Tim Raines 12.7
3 Vince Coleman 10.6
4 Lou Brock 10.4
5 Willie Wilson 10.0
6 Joe Morgan 9.8
7 Davey Lopes 8.5
8 Ozzie Smith 7.9
9 Bert Campaneris 7.7
10 Otis Nixon 7.1
11 Kenny Lofton 7.0
12 Luis Aparicio 6.7
13 Paul Molitor 6.3
14 Roberto Alomar 6.2
15 Cesar Cedeno 6.1
16 Barry Bonds 6.1
17 Maury Wills 5.6
18 Barry Larkin 5.6
19 Eric Davis 5.4
20 Marquis Grissom 5.3
21 Tony Womack 5.3
22 Tommy Harper 5.2
23 Ron LeFlore 5.1
24 Delino DeShields 5.0
25 Julio Cruz 4.9
26 Craig Biggio 4.8
27 Chuck Knoblauch 4.6
28 Omar Moreno 4.5
29 Willie Davis 4.4
30 Amos Otis 4.4
31 Bobby Bonds 4.3
32 Gary Redus 4.3
33 Gary Pettis 4.2
34 Eric Young 4.2
35 Devon White 4.1
36 Freddie Patek 4.1
37 Ryne Sandberg 3.9
38 Dave Collins 3.9
39 Mookie Wilson 3.9
40 Willie Mays 3.9
41 George Case 3.9
42 Lenny Dykstra 3.8
43 Tom Goodwin 3.8
44 Juan Samuel 3.8
45 Steve Sax 3.7
46 Willie McGee 3.6
47 Stan Javier 3.6
48 Larry Bowa 3.5
49 Kirk Gibson 3.5
50 Brian Hunter 3.5

Pitcher Batting Average by era

1988-2005
1 Mike Hampton ... 242
2 Livan Hernandez ... 237
3 Javier Vazquez ... 214
4 Russ Ortiz ... 206
5 Woody Williams ... 206
6 Orel Hershiser ... 201
7 Mark Portugal ... 198
8 Doc Gooden ... 196
9 Jose Rijo ... 191
10 Tom Glavine ... 187

1973-1987
1 Ken Brett ... 262
2 Rick Rhoden ... 238
3 Don Robinson ... 231
4 Steve Renko ... 215
5 Bob Forsch ... 213
6 Jim Rooker ... 201
7 Steve Carlton ... 201
8 Fernando Valenzuela ... 200
9 Dave Roberts ... 194
10 Mike Krukow ... 193

1961-1972
1 Catfish Hunter ... 226
2 Gary Peters ... 222
3 Bob Gibson ... 206
4 Camilo Pascual ... 205
5 Juan Pizarro ... 202
6 Jim Maloney ... 201
7 Jim Perry ... 199
8 Rick Wise ... 195
9 Earl Wilson ... 195
10 Tony Cloninger ... 192

1943-1960
1 Fred Hutchinson ... 276
2 Don Newcombe ... 266
3 Mickey McDermott ... 250
   Carl Scheib ... 250
5 Tommy Byrne ... 246
6 Johnny Sain ... 245
7 Willard Nixon ... 242
8 Don Larsen ... 240
9 Bob Lemon ... 233
10 Murry Dickson ... 231

1921-1942
1 George Uhle ... 286
2 Wes Ferrell ... 284
3 Jack Scott ... 276
4 Sloppy Thurston ... 270
5 Red Ruffing ... 269
6 Carl Mays ... 268
7 Johnny Marcum ... 265
8 Dutch Ruether ... 264
9 Joe Shaute ... 260
10 Schoolboy Rowe ... 257

1901-1920
1 Babe Ruth ... 299
2 Doc Crandall ... 279
3 Al Orth ... 277
4 George Mullin ... 262
5 Jesse Tannehill ... 256
6 Joe Wood ... 241
7 Claude Hendrix ... 241
8 Ray Caldwell ... 241
9 Frank Kitson ... 240
10 Wilbur Cooper ... 239

1893-1900
1 Cy Seymour ... 280
2 Win Mercer ... 261
3 Brickyard Kennedy ... 261
4 Nixey Callahan ... 260
5 Jack Taylor ... 252
6 Al Maul ... 246
7 Jack Dunn ... 244
8 Jouett Meekin ... 243
9 Frank Killen ... 241
10 Pink Hawley ... 241

1876-1892
1 Guy Hecker ... 297
2 Jack Stivetts ... 295
3 Jim Devlin ... 293
4 Charlie Ferguson ... 288
5 Charlie Sweeney ... 284
6 Bob Caruthers ... 276
7 Ben Sanders ... 275
8 Scott Stratton ... 275
9 Ad Gumbert ... 274
10 Dave Foutz ... 262

Pitcher Batting Runs

1 Red Ruffing ... 143
2 Bob Caruthers ... 111
3 Wes Ferrell ... 100
4 Walter Johnson ... 99
5 Red Lucas ... 98
6 George Uhle ... 92
7 Guy Hecker ... 90
   Bob Lemon ... 90
9 Jim Whitney ... 89
10 Warren Spahn ... 88
11 George Mullin ... 87
12 Don Newcombe ... 79
13 Babe Ruth ... 78
14 Schoolboy Rowe ... 76
15 Early Wynn ... 72
16 Bob Gibson ... 65
   Jack Stivetts ... 65
18 Carl Mays ... 64
19 Al Orth ... 63
20 Don Drysdale ... 60
21 Christy Mathewson ... 59
22 Gary Peters ... 57
   Bucky Walters ... 57
   Earl Wilson ... 57
25 Doc Crandall ... 54
   Mike Hampton ... 54
   Jesse Tannehill ... 54
   Jim Tobin ... 54
29 Ad Gumbert ... 53
30 Burleigh Grimes ... 52
31 Claude Hendrix ... 50
   Tony Mullane ... 50
33 Joe Bush ... 49
   Charlie Ferguson ... 49
35 Steve Carlton ... 48
   Scott Stratton ... 48
37 Bob Forsch ... 47
38 Don Larsen ... 46
39 Dave Foutz ... 45
   Vern Law ... 45
   Dutch Ruether ... 45
   Adonis Terry ... 45
43 Frank Killen ... 44
   Rick Rhoden ... 44
   Jack Scott ... 44
46 Tommy Byrne ... 41
   Jim Kaat ... 41
48 Don Robinson ... 40
   Johnny Sain ... 40
50 Wilbur Cooper ... 39
   Livan Hernandez ... 39
   Fred Hutchinson ... 39
53 Claude Osteen ... 38
   Charley Radbourn ... 38
   Sloppy Thurston ... 38
56 Dolf Luque ... 37
   Doc White ... 37
58 Jack Coombs ... 36
   Mickey McDermott ... 36
60 Clark Griffith ... 35
   Harvey Haddix ... 35
   Win Mercer ... 35
   Frank Smith ... 35
64 Art Nehf ... 34
   Robin Roberts ... 34
   Jack Taylor ... 34
   Rick Wise ... 34
68 Chief Bender ... 33
   Erv Brame ... 33
   Catfish Hunter ... 33
   Ben Sanders ... 33
72 Ken Brett ... 32
   Hooks Dauss ... 32
   Tom Glavine ... 32
   Orel Hershiser ... 32
   Ted Lyons ... 32
   Al Maul ... 32
   Fernando Valenzuela ... 32
79 Ray Caldwell ... 31
   Dizzy Trout ... 31
   John Ward ... 31
   Joe Wood ... 31
83 Ed Brandt ... 30
   Lew Burdette ... 30
   Russ Ortiz ... 30
   Lefty Tyler ... 30
87 Doc Gooden ... 29
   Jack Harshman ... 29
   Ed Lopat ... 29
   Jouett Meekin ... 29
   Camilo Pascual ... 29
   Juan Pizarro ... 29
93 Jack Bentley ... 28
   Joe Nuxhall ... 28
   Urban Shocker ... 28
96 Charlie Buffinton ... 27
   Whitey Ford ... 27
   Brickyard Kennedy ... 27
   Frank Kitson ... 27
   Tom Seaver ... 27
   Bill Sherdel ... 27
   Lon Warneke ... 27

Games

First Base
1 Eddie Murray ... 2413
2 Jake Beckley ... 2380
3 Fred McGriff ... 2239
4 Mickey Vernon ... 2237
5 Mark Grace ... 2162
6 Rafael Palmeiro ... 2139
7 Lou Gehrig ... 2137
8 Charlie Grimm ... 2131
9 Jeff Bagwell ... 2111
10 Andres Galarraga ... 2106

Second Base
1 Eddie Collins ... 2650
2 Joe Morgan ... 2527
3 Roberto Alomar ... 2320
4 Lou Whitaker ... 2308
5 Nellie Fox ... 2295
6 Charlie Gehringer ... 2206
7 Willie Randolph ... 2152
8 Frank White ... 2150
9 Bid McPhee ... 2129
10 Bill Mazeroski ... 2094

Shortstop
1 Luis Aparicio ... 2581
2 Ozzie Smith ... 2511
3 Cal Ripken ... 2302
4 Omar Vizquel ... 2275
5 Larry Bowa ... 2222
6 Luke Appling ... 2218
7 Dave Concepcion ... 2178
8 Rabbit Maranville ... 2153
9 Alan Trammell ... 2139
10 Bill Dahlen ... 2133

Third Base
1 Brooks Robinson ... 2870
2 Graig Nettles ... 2412
3 Gary Gaetti ... 2282
4 Wade Boggs ... 2215
5 Mike Schmidt ... 2212
6 Buddy Bell ... 2183
7 Eddie Mathews ... 2181
8 Ron Santo ... 2130
9 Tim Wallach ... 2054
10 Eddie Yost ... 2008

Outfield
1 Ty Cobb ... 2934
2 Willie Mays ... 2842
3 Rickey Henderson ... 2826
4 Hank Aaron ... 2760
5 Tris Speaker ... 2698
6 Barry Bonds ... 2648
7 Lou Brock ... 2507
8 Al Kaline ... 2488
9 Dave Winfield ... 2469
10 Max Carey ... 2421
11 Vada Pinson ... 2403
12 Roberto Clemente ... 2370
13 Zack Wheat ... 2337
14 Steve Finley ... 2329
15 Tony Gwynn ... 2326
16 Willie Davis ... 2323
   Andre Dawson ... 2323
18 Mel Ott ... 2313
19 Sam Crawford ... 2299
20 Paul Waner ... 2288

Catcher
1 Carlton Fisk ... 2226
2 Bob Boone ... 2225
3 Gary Carter ... 2056
4 Tony Pena ... 1950
5 Jim Sundberg ... 1927
6 Al Lopez ... 1918
7 Benito Santiago ... 1917
8 Lance Parrish ... 1818
9 Ivan Rodriguez ... 1811
10 Rick Ferrell ... 1806

Pitcher
1 Jesse Orosco ... 1252
2 John Franco ... 1119
3 Dennis Eckersley ... 1071
4 Hoyt Wilhelm ... 1070
5 Dan Plesac ... 1064
6 Kent Tekulve ... 1050
7 Mike Stanton ... 1027
8 Lee Smith ... 1022
9 Mike Jackson ... 1005
10 Rich Gossage ... 1002

Fielding Average

First Base
1 Steve Garvey ... 996
2 Don Mattingly ... 996
3 Wes Parker ... 996
4 Todd Helton ... 996
5 J.T. Snow ... 996
6 David Segui ... 995
7 Lou Gehrig ... 995
8 Charlie Grimm ... 995
9 Jeff Bagwell ... 995
10 Sean Casey ... 995

Second Base
1 Ryne Sandberg ... 989
2 Tom Herr ... 989
3 Mickey Morandini ... 989
4 Jose Lind ... 988
5 Jody Reed ... 988
6 Bret Boone ... 986
7 Jim Gantner ... 985
8 Frank White ... 984
9 Bobby Grich ... 984
10 Roberto Alomar ... 984
11 Damion Easley ... 984

Shortstop
1 Omar Vizquel ... 984
2 Mike Bordick ... 982
3 Larry Bowa ... 980
4 Tony Fernandez ... 980
5 Cal Ripken ... 979
6 Ozzie Smith ... 978
7 Orlando Cabrera ... 978
8 Deivi Cruz ... 978
9 Neifi Perez ... 978
10 Alex Rodriguez ... 977

Third Base
1 Brooks Robinson ... 971
2 Ken Reitz ... 970
3 George Kell ... 969
4 Steve Buechele ... 968
5 Don Money ... 968
6 Don Wert ... 968
7 Willie Kamm ... 967
8 Heinie Groh ... 967
9 Scott Rolen ... 966
10 Jeff Cirillo ... 966

Outfield
1 Darryl Hamilton ... 995
2 Darren Lewis ... 994
3 Terry Puhl ... 993
4 Brett Butler ... 993
5 Pete Rose ... 991
6 Tom Goodwin ... 991
7 Amos Otis ... 991
8 Doug Glanville ... 991
9 Joe Rudi ... 991
10 Mickey Stanley ... 991
11 Robin Yount ... 990
12 Jim Piersall ... 990
13 Bernie Williams ... 990
14 Andruw Jones ... 990
15 Brian McRae ... 990
16 Jim Landis ... 989
17 Ken Berry ... 989
18 Otis Nixon ... 989
19 Johnny Damon ... 989
20 Brady Anderson ... 989

Catcher
1 Dan Wilson ... 995
2 Mike Matheny ... 994
3 Brad Ausmus ... 994
4 Charles Johnson ... 993
5 Darrin Fletcher ... 993
6 Bill Freehan ... 993
7 Brent Mayne ... 993
8 Elston Howard ... 993
9 Jim Sundberg ... 993
10 Javy Lopez ... 992

Pitcher
1 Don Mossi ... 990
2 Gary Nolan ... 990
3 Rick Rhoden ... 989
4 Lon Warneke ... 988
5 Jim Wilson ... 988
6 Kirk Rueter ... 988
7 Woodie Fryman ... 988
8 Brad Radke ... 986
9 Larry Gura ... 986
10 Grover Alexander ... 985

Total Chances/Game (Infield)

First Base
1 Tom Jones ... 11.38
2 George Stovall ... 11.30
3 George Kelly ... 11.09
4 Wally Pipp ... 11.05
5 Ed Konetchy ... 11.04
6 Candy LaChance ... 11.04
7 George Burns ... 10.92
8 Bill Terry ... 10.91
9 Cap Anson ... 10.85
10 Walter Holke ... 10.83
11 Bill Phillips ... 10.83
12 Fred Tenney ... 10.83
13 Hal Chase ... 10.82
14 Charlie Comiskey ... 10.82
15 Dan Brouthers ... 10.74
16 Roger Connor ... 10.74
17 Jake Beckley ... 10.73
18 Lu Blue ... 10.73
19 Stuffy McInnis ... 10.71
20 Fred Luderus ... 10.69
21 Fred Merkle ... 10.68
22 John Reilly ... 10.68
23 Kitty Bransfield ... 10.67
24 Dan McGann ... 10.65
25 Jack Doyle ... 10.63

Second Base
1 Fred Pfeffer ... 6.95
2 Bid McPhee ... 6.70
3 Cub Stricker ... 6.59
4 Lou Bierbauer ... 6.49
5 Cupid Childs ... 6.32
6 Ski Melillo ... 6.16
7 Hughie Critz ... 6.07
8 Frankie Frisch ... 6.05
9 Nap Lajoie ... 6.01
10 Bobby Lowe ... 6.01
11 Bucky Harris ... 6.00
12 Billy Herman ... 5.97
13 Jerry Priddy ... 5.93
14 Bobby Doerr ... 5.86
15 Kid Gleason ... 5.83
16 Hobe Ferris ... 5.82
17 Buddy Myer ... 5.79
18 Tony Cuccinello ... 5.78
19 Charlie Gehringer ... 5.78
20 Joe Quinn ... 5.78
21 Tom Daly ... 5.77
22 Bill Wambsganss ... 5.77
23 George Cutshaw ... 5.75
24 Bill Hallman ... 5.70
25 Bill Mazeroski ... 5.67

Shortstop
1 Herman Long ... 6.38
2 Dave Bancroft ... 6.33
3 Bill Dahlen ... 6.26
4 George Davis ... 6.22
5 Rabbit Maranville ... 6.10
6 Bobby Wallace ... 6.10
7 Tommy Corcoran ... 6.09
8 Monte Cross ... 6.06
9 Bones Ely ... 6.06
10 Honus Wagner ... 5.99
11 Germany Smith ... 5.98
12 Travis Jackson ... 5.96
13 Dick Bartell ... 5.92
14 Joe Tinker ... 5.88
15 Art Fletcher ... 5.87
16 Donie Bush ... 5.82
17 Mickey Doolan ... 5.81
18 Doc Lavan ... 5.81
19 Ivy Olson ... 5.81
20 Freddy Parent ... 5.77
21 George McBride ... 5.75
22 Jack Glasscock ... 5.71
23 Glenn Wright ... 5.69
24 Joe Sewell ... 5.64
25 Luke Appling ... 5.53

Third Base
1 Jerry Denny ... 4.21
2 Billy Shindle ... 4.15
3 Billy Nash ... 4.07
4 Arlie Latham ... 4.04
5 Denny Lyons ... 3.98
6 Jimmy Collins ... 3.89
7 Hick Carpenter ... 3.81
8 Jimmy Austin ... 3.74
9 Lave Cross ... 3.73
10 Frank Baker ... 3.64
11 Bill Bradley ... 3.63
12 Harry Steinfeldt ... 3.57
13 George Pinkney ... 3.56
14 Doc Casey ... 3.48
15 Art Devlin ... 3.48
16 Bobby Byrne ... 3.44
17 Harlond Clift ... 3.44
18 Red Smith ... 3.42
19 Billy Werber ... 3.42
20 Eddie Foster ... 3.41
21 Willie Kamm ... 3.40
22 Clete Boyer ... 3.38
23 Larry Gardner ... 3.32
24 Mike Mowrey ... 3.31
25 Pie Traynor ... 3.30

Assists (Infield)

First Base
1. Eddie Murray 1865
2. **Jeff Bagwell** 1704
3. Keith Hernandez 1682
4. Mark Grace 1665
5. **Rafael Palmeiro** 1587
6. George Sisler 1529
7. Wally Joyner 1470
8. Mickey Vernon 1448
9. Fred McGriff 1447
10. **John Olerud** 1418
11. Andres Galarraga 1376
12. Fred Tenney 1363
13. Eric Karros 1359
14. Bill Buckner 1351
     Chris Chambliss 1351
16. Norm Cash 1317
17. Jake Beckley 1316
18. Joe Judge 1301
19. Will Clark 1294
20. Ed Konetchy 1292
21. Gil Hodges 1281
22. Stuffy McInnis 1238
23. Jimmie Foxx 1222
     Willie McCovey 1222
25. Charlie Grimm 1214

Second Base
1. Eddie Collins 7630
2. Charlie Gehringer 7068
3. Joe Morgan 6967
4. Bid McPhee 6919
5. Bill Mazeroski 6685
6. Lou Whitaker 6653
7. Roberto Alomar 6524
8. Nellie Fox 6373
9. Ryne Sandberg 6363
10. Willie Randolph 6336
11. Nap Lajoie 6267
12. Frank White 6250
13. Frankie Frisch 6026
14. Bobby Doerr 5710
15. Billy Herman 5681
16. Bobby Grich 5381
17. Red Schoendienst 5243
18. Rogers Hornsby 5166
19. Hughie Critz 5138
20. Johnny Evers 5124
21. Fred Pfeffer 5108
22. Del Pratt 5075
23. **Craig Biggio** 4847
24. Steve Sax 4805
25. Kid Gleason 4776

Shortstop
1. Ozzie Smith 8375
2. Luis Aparicio 8016
3. Bill Dahlen 7505
4. Rabbit Maranville 7354
5. Luke Appling 7218
6. Tommy Corcoran 7110
7. Cal Ripken 6977
8. Larry Bowa 6857
9. Dave Concepcion 6594
10. Dave Bancroft 6561
11. **Omar Vizquel** 6534
12. Roger Peckinpaugh 6337
13. Bobby Wallace 6303
14. Don Kessinger 6212
15. Roy McMillan 6191
16. Alan Trammell 6172
17. Germany Smith 6166
18. Bert Campaneris 6160
19. Herman Long 6137
20. Donie Bush 6119
21. Garry Templeton 6041
     Honus Wagner 6041
23. Pee Wee Reese 5891
24. Barry Larkin 5858
25. Joe Tinker 5856

Third Base
1. Brooks Robinson 6205
2. Graig Nettles 5279
3. Mike Schmidt 5045
4. Buddy Bell 4925
5. Ron Santo 4581
6. Gary Gaetti 4531
7. Eddie Mathews 4322
8. Wade Boggs 4246
9. Aurelio Rodriguez 4150
10. Ron Cey 4018
11. Tim Wallach 3992
12. Terry Pendleton 3891
13. Sal Bando 3720
14. Lave Cross 3715
15. Jimmy Collins 3702
16. George Brett 3674
17. Eddie Yost 3659
18. Ken Boyer 3652
19. Robin Ventura 3552
20. Arlie Latham 3546
21. Pie Traynor 3521
22. Stan Hack 3494
23. Larry Gardner 3408
24. Matt Williams 3376
25. Willie Kamm 3345

Assists/Game (Infield)

First Base
1. Bill Buckner 0.87
2. **Todd Helton** 0.86
3. Ferris Fain 0.84
4. Keith Hernandez 0.84
5. Vic Power 0.83
6. **Jeff Bagwell** 0.81
7. Eric Karros 0.81
8. Mark Grace 0.78
9. Eddie Murray 0.78
10. Pete O'Brien 0.78
11. George Sisler 0.78
12. Wally Joyner 0.77
13. Rudy York 0.77
14. Fred Tenney 0.76
15. Mike Hargrove 0.75
16. **Derrek Lee** 0.75
17. **Rafael Palmeiro** 0.75
18. Dick Stuart 0.75
19. Willie Upshaw 0.74
20. Elbie Fletcher 0.71
21. George McQuinn 0.71
22. Bill Terry 0.71
23. Frank McCormick 0.70
24. **John Olerud** 0.70
25. George Stovall 0.70

Second Base
1. Hughie Critz 3.54
2. Frankie Frisch 3.42
3. Ski Melillo 3.38
4. Lou Bierbauer 3.35
5. Glenn Hubbard 3.34
6. Fred Pfeffer 3.33
7. Rogers Hornsby 3.31
8. Bid McPhee 3.25
9. Tony Cuccinello 3.23
10. Cupid Childs 3.22
11. Charlie Gehringer 3.21
12. Bill Mazeroski 3.20
13. Ryne Sandberg 3.19
14. Bobby Lowe 3.17
15. Max Bishop 3.14
16. Billy Herman 3.14
17. Hobe Ferris 3.10
18. Joe Gordon 3.10
19. Manny Trillo 3.10
20. Bobby Doerr 3.09
21. Nap Lajoie 3.08
22. Bucky Harris 3.07
23. Miller Huggins 3.07
24. Julio Cruz 3.06
25. Tony Lazzeri 3.06

Shortstop
1. Germany Smith 3.70
2. Art Fletcher 3.55
3. Bill Dahlen 3.52
4. Dave Bancroft 3.51
5. Bones Ely 3.50
6. Travis Jackson 3.50
7. George Davis 3.49
8. Jack Glasscock 3.46
9. Bobby Wallace 3.46
10. Tommy Corcoran 3.43
11. Herman Long 3.42
12. Rabbit Maranville 3.42
13. Freddy Parent 3.36
14. Joe Tinker 3.36
15. Ozzie Smith 3.34
16. Dick Bartell 3.33
17. Glenn Wright 3.31
18. Donie Bush 3.28
19. Luke Appling 3.26
20. Mickey Doolan 3.26
21. Rick Burleson 3.25
22. George McBride 3.25
23. Robin Yount 3.25
24. Joe Sewell 3.24
25. Billy Jurges 3.23
26. Doc Lavan 3.23
27. Eddie Miller 3.23

Third Base
1. Mike Schmidt 2.29
2. Billy Shindle 2.27
3. Buddy Bell 2.26
4. Arlie Latham 2.26
5. Clete Boyer 2.24
6. Jimmy Collins 2.20
7. Graig Nettles 2.19
8. George Brett 2.18
9. Terry Pendleton 2.18
10. Darrell Evans 2.17
11. Brooks Robinson 2.17
12. Lave Cross 2.16
13. Ron Santo 2.16
14. Doug Rader 2.15
15. Billy Nash 2.14
16. Bill Bradley 2.12
17. Billy Werber 2.12
18. Harland Clift 2.11
19. Jerry Denny 2.11
20. Frank Malzone 2.11
21. Aurelio Rodriguez 2.10
22. Doug DeCinces 2.09
23. Art Devlin 2.09
24. Ken McMullen 2.08
25. Jimmy Austin 2.07
26. **Scott Rolen** 2.07

Double Plays

First Base
1. Mickey Vernon 2044
2. Eddie Murray 2033
3. **Rafael Palmeiro** 1782
4. Fred McGriff 1775
5. Joe Kuhel 1769
6. Charlie Grimm 1733
7. Chris Chambliss 1687
8. Keith Hernandez 1654
9. Andres Galarraga 1648
10. **Jeff Bagwell** 1618

Second Base
1. Bill Mazeroski 1706
2. Nellie Fox 1619
3. Willie Randolph 1547
4. Lou Whitaker 1527
5. Bobby Doerr 1507
6. Joe Morgan 1505
7. Charlie Gehringer 1444
8. Roberto Alomar 1407
9. Frank White 1382
10. Red Schoendienst 1368

Shortstop
1. Ozzie Smith 1590
2. Cal Ripken 1565
3. Luis Aparicio 1553
4. **Omar Vizquel** 1480
5. Luke Appling 1424
6. Alan Trammell 1307
7. Roy McMillan 1304
8. Dave Concepcion 1290
9. Larry Bowa 1265
10. Pee Wee Reese 1246

Third Base
1. Brooks Robinson 618
2. Graig Nettles 470
3. Gary Gaetti 460
4. Mike Schmidt 450
5. Buddy Bell 430
6. Wade Boggs 423
7. Aurelio Rodriguez 408
8. Ron Santo 395
9. Eddie Mathews 369
10. Robin Ventura 359

Outfield
1. Tris Speaker 139
2. Ty Cobb 107
3. Max Carey 86
4. Tom Brown 85
5. Harry Hooper 81
6. Jimmy Sheckard 80
7. Mike Griffin 75
8. Dummy Hoy 72
9. Jimmy Ryan 71
10. Fielder Jones 70
11. Patsy Donovan 69
12. Sam Rice 67
13. George Van Haltren ... 64
14. Jesse Burkett 62
15. Sam Thompson 60
16. Willie Keeler 60
     Willie Mays 60
     Tommy McCarthy 60
     Mel Ott 60
20. Sam Crawford 59

Catcher
1. Ray Schalk 226
2. Steve O'Neill 193
3. Yogi Berra 175
4. Gabby Hartnett 163
5. Tony Pena 156
6. Bob Boone 154
7. Jimmie Wilson 153
8. Gary Carter 149
     Wally Schang 149
10. Carlton Fisk 147

Pitcher
1. Phil Niekro 83
2. Warren Spahn 82
3. **Greg Maddux** 80
4. Freddie Fitzsimmons ... 79
5. Bob Lemon 78
6. Bucky Walters 76
7. Burleigh Grimes 74
8. Walter Johnson 72
9. Tommy John 69
10. Jim Kaat 65

Putouts (Outfield)

Outfield
1. Willie Mays 7095
2. Tris Speaker 6788
3. Rickey Henderson 6468
4. Max Carey 6363
5. Ty Cobb 6361
6. Richie Ashburn 6089
7. Hank Aaron 5539
8. Willie Davis 5449
9. Doc Cramer 5412
10. Brett Butler 5296
11. **Barry Bonds** 5269
12. Andre Dawson 5158
13. Vada Pinson 5097
14. **Steve Finley** 5065
15. Willie Wilson 5060
16. Al Kaline 5035
17. Zack Wheat 4996
18. Chet Lemon 4993
19. Al Simmons 4988
20. Dave Winfield 4975
21. Amos Otis 4936
22. Paul Waner 4872
23. Lloyd Waner 4860
24. **Marquis Grissom** 4811
25. Fred Clarke 4795
26. Goose Goslin 4792
27. Sam Rice 4774
28. Devon White 4739
29. Roberto Clemente 4696
30. **Ken Griffey Jr.** 4569
31. Fred Lynn 4556
32. Edd Roush 4537
33. Joe DiMaggio 4516
34. Tony Gwynn 4512
35. Mel Ott 4511
36. Garry Maddox 4449
37. Babe Ruth 4444
38. Mickey Mantle 4438
39. Lou Brock 4394
40. Kirby Puckett 4392
41. Jose Cruz 4391
42. Dwight Evans 4371
43. **Sammy Sosa** 4369
44. Paul Blair 4343
45. **Bernie Williams** 4330
46. Sam McGee 4300
47. Willie McGee 4260
48. Jimmy Sheckard 4203
49. Tim Raines 4201
50. Cy Williams 4180
51. Ted Williams 4158
52. **Kenny Lofton** 4144
53. Cesar Cedeno 4131
54. Duke Snider 4099
55. Clyde Milan 4095
56. Reggie Jackson 4062
57. Dale Murphy 4053
58. Kiki Cuyler 4034
59. Curt Flood 4021
60. Bob Johnson 4003
61. Wally Moses 4000
62. Joe Medwick 3994
63. Harry Hooper 3981
64. Frank Robinson 3978
65. Earl Averill 3968
66. Dummy Hoy 3964
67. Jesse Burkett 3961
68. Carl Yastrzemski 3941
69. Enos Slaughter 3925
70. George Burns 3918
71. Jimmy Wynn 3912
72. Bill Bruton 3905
73. Dom DiMaggio 3859
74. Jim Piersall 3851
75. Heinie Manush 3841
76. Rick Manning 3831
77. George Foster 3809
78. Sherry Magee 3800
79. Dave Parker 3791
80. Bill Virdon 3777
81. Lloyd Moseby 3765
82. Bobby Veach 3754
83. George Hendrick 3751
84. Dode Paskert 3734
85. Stan Musial 3730
86. Paul O'Neill 3724
87. Brady Anderson 3713
88. Jimmy Ryan 3701
89. Reggie Smith 3676
90. Joe Carter 3669
91. Dusty Baker 3663
92. Gee Walker 3661
93. Bobby Bonds 3659
94. Tom Brown 3629
     Luis Gonzalez 3629
96. Sam Crawford 3626
97. Del Ennis 3621
98. Larry Doby 3616
99. Fielder Jones 3580
100. Sam Chapman 3579
     Dwayne Murphy 3579

Putouts/Game (Outfield)

Outfield
1. Taylor Douthit 3.01
2. Richie Ashburn 2.90
3. Dom DiMaggio 2.82
4. Dwayne Murphy 2.82
5. Mike Kreevich 2.81
6. Sam Chapman 2.74
7. Sam West 2.74
8. Fred Schulte 2.70
9. Lloyd Waner 2.68
10. **Mike Cameron** 2.67
11. Billy North 2.65
12. Garry Maddox 2.64
13. Max Carey 2.63
14. Joe DiMaggio 2.63
15. Vince DiMaggio 2.63
16. Terry Moore 2.63
17. Robin Yount 2.63
18. **Andruw Jones** 2.62
19. Gary Pettis 2.62
20. Chet Lemon 2.60
21. Kirby Puckett 2.59
22. Omar Moreno 2.58
23. Wally Berger 2.57
24. Jim Busby 2.57
25. Amos Otis 2.57
26. Lenny Dykstra 2.55
27. Rick Manning 2.55
28. Ruppert Jones 2.54
29. Devon White 2.54
30. Doc Cramer 2.53
31. Baby Doll Jacobson ... 2.53
32. Lance Johnson 2.53
33. Larry Doby 2.52
34. Mickey Rivers 2.52
35. Tris Speaker 2.52
36. **Bernie Williams** 2.52
37. Bill Bruton 2.51
38. Gorman Thomas 2.51
39. Earl Averill 2.50
40. Fred Lynn 2.50
41. Willie Mays 2.50
42. Willie Wilson 2.50
43. Earle Combs 2.49
44. **Jim Edmonds** 2.47
45. Lloyd Moseby 2.47
46. Brett Butler 2.46
47. Hy Myers 2.46
48. Edd Roush 2.46
49. Ethan Allen 2.45
50. **Kenny Lofton** 2.45
51. Bill Virdon 2.45
52. Mule Haas 2.44
53. Ron LeFlore 2.43
54. Jimmy McAleer 2.43
55. Mookie Wilson 2.43
56. **Ken Griffey Jr.** 2.42
57. Cesar Cedeno 2.41
58. Dave Henderson 2.41
59. Barney McCosky 2.41
60. Al Bumbry 2.40
61. Ira Flagstead 2.40
62. Mike Griffin 2.40
63. Jim Piersall 2.39
64. Tony Armas 2.37
65. George Case 2.37
66. Curt Flood 2.37
67. Tommy Leach 2.37
68. Bobby Thomson 2.37
69. **Johnny Damon** 2.36
70. Brian McRae 2.36
71. Willie Davis 2.35
72. **Marquis Grissom** 2.35
73. Ben Chapman 2.33
74. Hoot Evers 2.33
75. Al Simmons 2.33
76. Paul Blair 2.32
77. Mike Devereaux 2.32
78. Jim Landis 2.32
79. Tommy Holmes 2.30
80. Roy Thomas 2.30
81. Cy Williams 2.30
82. Rickey Henderson 2.29
83. Dode Paskert 2.29
84. Carl Reynolds 2.29
85. **Steve Finley** 2.28
86. Al Oliver 2.28
87. Ken Williams 2.28
88. **Garret Anderson** 2.27
89. Cliff Heathcote 2.27
90. Bob Johnson 2.27
91. Bill Tuttle 2.27
92. Gee Walker 2.27
93. Roberto Kelly 2.26
94. Carson Bigbee 2.24
95. Kiki Cuyler 2.24
96. Rick Miller 2.24
97. Wally Moses 2.24
98. Hack Wilson 2.24
99. Andre Dawson 2.23
100. **Doug Glanville** 2.23
101. Johnny Groth 2.23
102. **Ray Lankford** 2.23
103. Dave Philley 2.23
104. Andy Van Slyke 2.23
105. Gary Ward 2.23

Fielding Runs (by position)

First Base
1 Keith Hernandez 133
2 Fred Tenney 130
3 Vic Power 123
4 Bill Buckner 114
   Todd Helton...................114
6 Jeff Bagwell 95
7 George Sisler 93
8 Rafael Palmeiro 81
9 Darrell Evans 75
10 Sid Bream 73

Second Base
1 Bill Mazeroski 364
2 Nap Lajoie 341
3 Bid McPhee 283
4 Fred Pfeffer 240
5 Glenn Hubbard 213
6 Bobby Doerr 175
7 Manny Trillo 170
8 Bobby Knoop 169
9 Ski Melillo 149
10 Bobby Grich 139

Shortstop
1 Ozzie Smith 279
2 Bill Dahlen 273
3 Jack Glasscock 256
4 George Davis 182
5 Joe Tinker 181
6 Dave Bancroft 177
7 Neifi Perez 174
8 George McBride 171
9 Art Fletcher 170
10 Tim Foli 159

Third Base
1 Mike Schmidt 236
2 Buddy Bell 227
3 Clete Boyer 183
4 Ron Santo 162
5 Terry Pendleton 160
6 Lave Cross 136
7 Tim Wallach 134
8 Darrell Evans 132
9 Aurelio Rodriguez 129
10 Jimmy Collins 123
    Graig Nettles 123

Outfield
1 Tris Speaker 160
2 Max Carey 127
3 Richie Ashburn 121
4 Roberto Clemente 107
5 Jesse Barfield 101
6 Jimmy Sheckard 100
7 Jim Fogarty 97
8 Johnny Callison 93
9 Ed Delahanty 88
10 Rickey Henderson 84
11 Bob Johnson 83
12 Sam West 80
13 Andruw Jones 78
14 Curt Welch 76
15 Kip Selbach 71
    Carl Yastrzemski 71
17 Al Kaline 70
    Orator Shafer 70
19 Harry Hooper 69
20 Fred Clarke 66

Catcher
1 Ivan Rodriguez 181
2 Tony Pena 180
3 Chief Zimmer 164
4 Gary Carter 145
5 Pop Snyder 144
6 Lou Criger 137
7 Johnny Bench 128
8 Lance Parrish 123
9 Ray Schalk 122
10 Jim Sundberg 119

Pitcher
1 Greg Maddux 103
2 Ed Walsh 80
3 Carl Mays 72
4 Christy Mathewson 65
5 Kenny Rogers 64
6 Tommy John 62
7 Freddie Fitzsimmons 60
8 Bob Lemon 58
9 Burleigh Grimes 57
10 Harry Gumbert 50

Fielding Wins

1 Bill Mazeroski 36.4
2 Nap Lajoie 34.2
3 Bill Dahlen 29.2
4 Ozzie Smith 29.1
5 Bid McPhee 24.5
6 Mike Schmidt 24.4
7 Buddy Bell 23.4
8 Glenn Hubbard 22.1
9 George Davis 21.9
10 Jack Glasscock 21.8
11 Fred Pfeffer 21.4
12 Darrell Evans 21.2
13 Clete Boyer 20.4
14 Bobby Wallace 20.2
15 Neifi Perez 19.8
16 Joe Tinker 19.0
17 Tony Pena 18.2
18 George McBride 18.2
19 Dave Bancroft 18.1
20 Art Fletcher 18.0
21 Rey Sanchez 17.9
22 Ron Santo 17.6
23 Manny Trillo 17.5
24 Bobby Doerr 17.4
25 Tim Foli 17.4
26 Bobby Knoop 17.3
27 Mickey Doolan 17.2
28 Ivan Rodriguez 17.1
29 Dick Bartell 16.8
30 Terry Pendleton 16.3
31 Tris Speaker 16.1
32 Lee Tannehill 16.1
33 Gene Alley 14.9
34 Frank White 14.9
35 Lave Cross 14.6
36 Gary Carter 14.6
37 Ski Melillo 14.2
38 Chief Zimmer 14.2
39 Aurelio Rodriguez 14.1
40 Keith Hernandez 13.8
41 Tim Wallach 13.7
42 Lou Criger 13.5
43 Lou Boudreau 13.4
44 Red Schoendienst 13.4
45 Willie Randolph 13.3
46 Fred Tenney 13.3
47 Frankie Frisch 13.1
48 Joe Gerhardt 13.0
49 Max Carey 12.9
50 Pop Snyder 12.9
51 Vic Power 12.9
52 Billy Jurges 12.8
53 Rabbit Maranville 12.8
54 Graig Nettles 12.8
55 Rick Burleson 12.8
56 Bobby Grich 12.8
57 Hughie Jennings 12.8
58 Bobby Wine 12.7
59 Danny Richardson 12.4
60 Ray Schalk 12.3
61 Fred Dunlap 12.3
62 Jim Sundberg 12.2
63 Harold Reynolds 12.1
64 Hughie Critz 12.1
65 Mark Belanger 12.0
66 Jim Hegan 11.9
67 Richie Ashburn 11.9
68 Lance Parrish 11.8
69 Phil Rizzuto 11.7
70 Jimmy Collins 11.7
71 Germany Smith 11.7
72 Bill Holbert 11.6
73 Bill Buckner 11.5
74 Gary Gaetti 11.2
75 Everett Scott 11.1
76 Lou Bierbauer 11.0
77 John Ward 10.8
78 Scott Rolen 10.7
79 Todd Helton 10.7
80 Mike Scioscia 10.5
81 Julio Cruz 10.4
82 Roberto Clemente 10.3
83 Gabby Hartnett 10.3
84 Ron Hansen 10.2
85 Omar Vizquel 10.2
86 Hobe Ferris 10.2
87 Ryne Sandberg 10.2
88 Mike Benjamin 10.0
89 Brad Ausmus 10.0
90 Jesse Barfield 10.0
91 Brooks Robinson 10.0
92 Jody Reed 9.9
93 Roger Peckinpaugh 9.8
94 Don Kessinger 9.8
95 Carlton Fisk 9.7
96 Del Pratt 9.6
97 Rennie Stennett 9.6
98 Johnny Logan 9.5
99 Burgess Whitehead 9.4
100 Jerry Denny 9.4

Fielding Wins

101 Jeff Bagwell...................9.3
102 Placido Polanco..............9.1
103 George Sisler 9.1
104 Buddy Kerr 9.0
105 Hardy Richardson 9.0
106 Buck Ewing 9.0
107 Charlie Bennett 9.0
108 Miller Huggins 8.9
109 Joe Sewell 8.9
110 Jimmy Sheckard 8.8
111 Johnny Callison 8.8
112 Eddie Miller 8.7
113 Travis Jackson 8.7
114 Jack Wilson 8.7
115 Bill Killefer 8.6
116 Art Devlin 8.6
117 Buck Herzog 8.6
118 Gil McDougald 8.6
119 Pokey Reese 8.6
120 Matt Williams 8.6
121 Frank Malzone 8.5
122 Nolan Ventura 8.5
123 Honus Wagner 8.5
124 Dave Cash 8.5
125 Ted Sizemore 8.5
126 Davy Force 8.4
127 Thurman Munson 8.4
128 Johnny Bench 8.3
129 Carl Yastrzemski 8.3
130 Steve Yeager 8.3
131 Billy Shindle 8.2
132 Rickey Henderson 8.2
133 Jose Valentin 8.2
134 Wade Boggs 8.1
135 Cupid Childs 8.1
136 Dal Maxvill 8.1
137 Johnny Edwards 8.0
138 Hal Lanier 8.0
139 Luis Aparicio 8.0
140 Pinky May 8.0
141 Rick Dempsey 7.9
142 Bill Bergen 7.9
143 Rollie Hemsley 7.8
144 Charlie O'Brien 7.8
145 Scott Fletcher 7.8
146 John Valentin 7.8
147 Tommy Corcoran 7.7
148 Damian Miller 7.7
149 Rafael Palmeiro 7.7
150 Jerry Grote 7.6
151 John Farrell 7.6
152 Bob Johnson 7.5
153 Rocky Bridges 7.5
154 Babe Pinelli 7.5
155 Andruw Jones 7.5
156 Billy Rogell 7.4
157 Sid Bream 7.4
158 Doug Rader 7.4
159 Yogi Berra 7.4
160 Sam West 7.3
161 Miguel Tejada 7.3
162 Javy Lopez 7.3
163 Craig Counsell 7.3
164 Willie Kamm 7.3
165 Ernie Whitt 7.2
166 Billy Clingman 7.2
167 Jim Fogarty 7.2
168 Roy McMillan 7.2
169 Wid Conroy 7.2
170 Harlond Clift 7.1
171 Tommy Leach 7.1
172 Jerry Priddy 7.0
173 Nellie Fox 7.0
174 Bill Sweeney 7.0
175 Juan Uribe 6.9
176 Harry Hooper 6.9
177 Al Lopez 6.9
178 Al Kaline 6.9
179 Bill Terry 6.9
180 Muddy Ruel 6.9
181 Dick Groat 6.8
182 Mike Bordick 6.8
183 Bob Boone 6.8
184 Freddie Maguire 6.7
185 Alvaro Espinoza 6.7
186 Abraham Nunez 6.7
187 Eric Karros 6.7
188 Marty Marion 6.7
189 Jerry Royster 6.6
190 Kip Selbach 6.6
191 Eddie Murray 6.5
192 Pinky Whitney 6.5
193 Luke Appling 6.5
194 Rafael Furcal 6.5
195 Ken Boyer 6.5
196 Curt Welch 6.5
197 Dave Shean 6.5
198 Charlie Ganzel 6.4
199 Ed Konetchy 6.4
200 Garry Templeton 6.4

Batter-Fielder Wins by era

1988-2005
1 Barry Bonds 123.6
2 Rickey Henderson 72.1
3 Jeff Bagwell 54.0
4 Alex Rodriguez 51.5
5 Wade Boggs 51.0
6 Ken Griffey Jr. 48.5
   Frank Thomas 48.5
8 Edgar Martinez 45.1
9 Cal Ripken 44.1
10 Barry Larkin 42.9
11 Gary Sheffield 42.6
12 Mike Piazza 42.2
13 Ivan Rodriguez 40.0
14 Tim Raines 38.8
15 Tony Gwynn 38.5
16 Paul Molitor 37.8
17 Roberto Alomar 37.0
18 Ryne Sandberg 36.7
19 Jim Edmonds 36.6
20 Mark McGwire 36.0
21 Manny Ramirez 35.8
22 Craig Biggio 35.5
23 Jeff Kent 35.3
24 Rafael Palmeiro 34.9
25 Scott Rolen 33.6

1973-1987
1 Mike Schmidt 78.6
2 Joe Morgan 67.4
3 Bobby Grich 51.6
4 Ozzie Smith 45.7
5 George Brett 43.5
6 Johnny Bench 42.5
7 Darrell Evans 41.2
   Robin Yount 41.2
9 Rod Carew 40.3
10 Reggie Jackson 39.5
11 Gary Carter 39.2
12 Carlton Fisk 38.8
13 Willie Randolph 37.1
14 Eddie Murray 35.8
15 Lou Whitaker 35.6
16 Keith Hernandez 34.8
17 Reggie Smith 31.9
18 Alan Trammell 31.8
19 Dave Winfield 30.8
20 Jack Clark 29.6
21 Buddy Bell 28.7
22 Bobby Bonds 27.2
23 Gene Tenace 26.3
24 Thurman Munson 25.4
25 Dwight Evans 24.8

1961-1972
1 Willie Mays 84.6
2 Hank Aaron 81.3
3 Frank Robinson 64.7
4 Ron Santo 45.3
5 Al Kaline 43.2
6 Carl Yastrzemski 42.6
7 Dick Allen 39.2
8 Willie McCovey 39.0
9 Roberto Clemente 34.0
   Bill Mazeroski 34.0
11 Harmon Killebrew 32.5
12 Willie Stargell 30.8
13 Norm Cash 30.5
14 Jimmy Wynn 30.0
15 Ernie Banks 27.2
16 Jim Fregosi 25.5
17 Billy Williams 23.8
18 Rocky Colavito 22.6
   Frank Howard 22.6
20 Joe Torre 22.3
21 Tony Oliva 20.4
22 Ken Boyer 19.7
23 Orlando Cepeda 19.1
24 Gene Alley 18.8
25 Boog Powell 18.6

1943-1960
1 Ted Williams 87.0
2 Stan Musial 76.0
3 Mickey Mantle 72.5
4 Eddie Mathews 52.1
5 Lou Boudreau 43.6
6 Bobby Doerr 40.3
7 Yogi Berra 38.6
8 Jackie Robinson 34.3
9 Joe Gordon 28.8
10 Ralph Kiner 24.2
11 Roy Campanella 24.1
12 Duke Snider 23.0
13 Richie Ashburn 22.6
14 Charlie Keller 22.2
   Gil McDougald 22.2
16 Bob Elliott 21.4
17 Minnie Minoso 21.0
18 Vern Stephens 20.7
19 Eddie Stanky 20.1
20 Roy Cullenbine 18.8
   Ferris Fain 18.8
22 Phil Rizzuto 18.7
23 Larry Doby 18.1
24 Jeff Heath 17.2
   Bill Nicholson 17.2

Batter-Fielder Wins by era

1921-1942
1 Babe Ruth 112.6
2 Rogers Hornsby 86.0
3 Lou Gehrig 70.7
4 Mel Ott 60.7
5 Jimmie Foxx 58.4
6 Joe DiMaggio 45.8
7 Charlie Gehringer 45.1
8 Gabby Hartnett 44.3
9 Arky Vaughan 43.3
10 Luke Appling 42.4
11 Joe Cronin 39.6
12 Bill Dickey 38.5
13 Johnny Mize 37.7
14 Frankie Frisch 37.3
15 Dave Bancroft 36.2
16 Bob Johnson 35.3
17 Joe Sewell 35.2
18 Mickey Cochrane 34.7
19 Paul Waner 33.8
20 Harry Heilmann 33.2
21 Hank Greenberg 32.6
22 Billy Herman 31.6
23 Stan Hack 29.4
24 Dick Bartell 28.2
25 Bill Terry 26.7

1901-1920
1 Nap Lajoie 95.1
2 Ty Cobb 85.7
3 Tris Speaker 82.7
4 Honus Wagner 82.2
5 Eddie Collins 72.5
6 Bill Dahlen 48.5
7 Joe Jackson 38.3
8 Bobby Wallace 35.4
9 Frank Baker 33.7
10 Heinie Groh 30.4
11 Elmer Flick 29.7
12 Sam Crawford 29.3
13 Fred Clarke 27.9
14 Art Fletcher 27.2
15 Sherry Magee 26.2
16 Zack Wheat 24.1
17 Jimmy Collins 23.0
18 Fred Tenney 22.9
19 Roy Thomas 22.7
20 Frank Chance 22.6
21 Roger Bresnahan 22.5
   Del Pratt 22.5
23 Miller Huggins 22.3
24 Ed Konetchy 21.2
25 Jimmy Sheckard 20.7

1893-1900
1 George Davis 50.7
2 Ed Delahanty 43.1
3 Cupid Childs 30.4
4 Jesse Burkett 27.9
5 Billy Hamilton 27.3
6 Hughie Jennings 26.8
7 Jake Beckley 23.0
8 Chief Zimmer 20.7
9 Joe Kelley 20.6
10 John McGraw 19.5
11 Bill Joyce 19.3
12 Mike Griffin 18.3
13 Lave Cross 16.4
14 Mike Tiernan 14.4
15 Kip Selbach 13.8
16 Jimmy Ryan 12.8
17 Ed McFarland 10.3
18 George Van Haltren 10.2
19 Heinie Peitz 10.1
20 Jack Crooks 9.9
21 Duke Farrell 7.8
22 Bill Lange 7.8
   Elmer Smith 7.8
24 Mike Grady 7.7
25 Perry Werden 7.0

1876-1892
1 Roger Connor 43.4
2 Dan Brouthers 43.2
3 Bid McPhee 38.3
4 Jack Glasscock 36.6
5 Cap Anson 35.4
6 Sam Thompson 29.5
7 Buck Ewing 29.1
8 King Kelly 28.9
9 Fred Dunlap 28.1
10 Pete Browning 28.0
11 Hardy Richardson 26.7
12 Charlie Bennett 23.9
13 Harry Stovey 21.5
14 Fred Pfeffer 20.6
15 Denny Lyons 19.6
16 Charley Jones 19.4
17 Jim O'Rourke 16.0
18 Henry Larkin 15.2
19 Paul Hines 14.4
20 Dave Orr 13.8
21 Jocko Milligan 13.6
22 George Gore 13.5
23 Jack Clements 12.9
24 Fred Carroll 12.6
25 Orator Shafer 12.0

Batter-Fielder Wins

Rank	Player	Wins
1	Barry Bonds	123.6
2	Babe Ruth	112.0
3	Nap Lajoie	95.1
4	Ted Williams	87.0
5	Rogers Hornsby	86.0
6	Ty Cobb	85.7
7	Willie Mays	84.6
8	Tris Speaker	82.7
9	Honus Wagner	82.2
10	Hank Aaron	81.3
11	Mike Schmidt	78.6
12	Stan Musial	76.0
13	Eddie Collins	72.5
	Mickey Mantle	72.5
15	Rickey Henderson	72.1
16	Lou Gehrig	70.9
17	Joe Morgan	67.4
18	Frank Robinson	64.7
19	Mel Ott	60.7
20	Jimmie Foxx	58.3
21	Jeff Bagwell	54.0
22	Eddie Mathews	52.1
23	Bobby Grich	51.6
24	Alex Rodriguez	51.5
25	Wade Boggs	51.0
26	George Davis	50.7
27	Bill Dahlen	48.5
	Ken Griffey Jr.	48.5
	Frank Thomas	48.5
30	Joe DiMaggio	45.8
31	Ozzie Smith	45.7
32	Ron Santo	45.3
33	Charlie Gehringer	45.1
	Edgar Martinez	45.1
35	Gabby Hartnett	44.3
36	Cal Ripken	44.1
37	Lou Boudreau	43.6
38	George Brett	43.5
39	Roger Connor	43.4
40	Arky Vaughan	43.3
41	Dan Brouthers	43.2
	Al Kaline	43.2
43	Ed Delahanty	43.1
44	Barry Larkin	42.9
45	Gary Sheffield	42.6
	Carl Yastrzemski	42.6
47	Johnny Bench	42.5
48	Luke Appling	42.4
49	Mike Piazza	42.2
50	Darrell Evans	41.2
	Robin Yount	41.2
52	Rod Carew	40.3
	Bobby Doerr	40.3
54	Ivan Rodriguez	40.0
55	Joe Cronin	39.6
56	Reggie Jackson	39.5
57	Dick Allen	39.2
	Gary Carter	39.2
59	Willie McCovey	39.0
60	Carlton Fisk	38.8
	Tim Raines	38.8
62	Yogi Berra	38.6
63	Bill Dickey	38.5
	Tony Gwynn	38.5
65	Joe Jackson	38.3
	Bid McPhee	38.3
67	Paul Molitor	37.8
68	Johnny Mize	37.7
69	Frankie Frisch	37.3
70	Willie Randolph	37.1
71	Roberto Alomar	37.0
72	Ryne Sandberg	36.7
73	Jim Edmonds	36.6
	Jack Glasscock	36.6
75	Dave Bancroft	36.2
76	Mark McGwire	36.0
77	Eddie Murray	35.8
	Manny Ramirez	35.8
79	Bob Johnson	35.7
80	Lou Whitaker	35.6
81	Craig Biggio	35.5
82	Cap Anson	35.4
	Bobby Wallace	35.4
84	Jeff Kent	35.3
85	Joe Sewell	35.2
86	Rafael Palmeiro	34.9
87	Keith Hernandez	34.8
88	Mickey Cochrane	34.7
89	Jackie Robinson	34.3
90	Roberto Clemente	34.0
	Bill Mazeroski	34.0
92	Paul Waner	33.8
93	Frank Baker	33.7
94	Scott Rolen	33.6
95	Jim Thome	33.4
96	Harry Heilmann	33.2
97	Hank Greenberg	32.6
98	Harmon Killebrew	32.5
99	Reggie Smith	31.9
100	Alan Trammell	31.8

Batter-Fielder Wins

Rank	Player	Wins
101	Billy Herman	31.6
102	Larry Walker	31.3
103	Brian Giles	31.2
104	Willie Stargell	30.8
	Dave Winfield	30.8
106	Norm Cash	30.5
107	Cupid Childs	30.4
	Heinie Groh	30.4
109	Jimmy Wynn	30.0
110	Vladimir Guerrero	29.9
111	Elmer Flick	29.7
112	Albert Belle	29.6
	Jack Clark	29.6
114	Sam Thompson	29.5
115	Stan Hack	29.4
	Todd Helton	29.4
117	Sam Crawford	29.3
118	Buck Ewing	29.1
119	King Kelly	28.9
120	Joe Gordon	28.8
121	Buddy Bell	28.7
122	Dick Bartell	28.2
123	Fred Dunlap	28.1
124	Pete Browning	28.0
125	Jesse Burkett	27.9
	Fred Clarke	27.9
127	Billy Hamilton	27.3
128	Ernie Banks	27.2
	Bobby Bonds	27.2
	Art Fletcher	27.2
131	Hughie Jennings	26.8
132	Hardy Richardson	26.7
	Bill Terry	26.7
134	Albert Pujols	26.5
135	Harlond Clift	26.3
	Gene Tenace	26.3
137	Sherry Magee	26.2
138	Sammy Sosa	25.7
139	Joe Medwick	25.6
140	Jim Fregosi	25.5
141	Thurman Munson	25.4
	Robin Ventura	25.4
	Bernie Williams	25.4
144	Bobby Abreu	25.2
145	Will Clark	25.0
146	Nomar Garciaparra	24.9
147	Dwight Evans	24.8
	George Sisler	24.8
149	Jack Fournier	24.4
150	Ralph Kiner	24.2
151	Roy Campanella	24.1
	Zack Wheat	24.1
153	Charlie Bennett	23.9
	Chipper Jones	23.9
	Pete Rose	23.9
156	Billy Williams	23.8
157	Jose Canseco	23.7
	John Olerud	23.7
	Kirby Puckett	23.7
160	Miguel Tejada	23.6
161	Goose Goslin	23.3
162	Darryl Strawberry	23.1
163	Jake Beckley	23.0
	Jimmy Collins	23.0
	Lenny Dykstra	23.0
	Al Simmons	23.0
	Duke Snider	23.0
	Rusty Staub	23.0
169	Fred Tenney	22.9
170	Jason Giambi	22.8
	Javy Lopez	22.8
172	Fred McGriff	22.7
	Roy Thomas	22.7
174	Richie Ashburn	22.6
	Frank Chance	22.6
	Rocky Colavito	22.6
	Frank Howard	22.6
178	Roger Bresnahan	22.5
	Del Pratt	22.5
180	Cesar Cedeno	22.3
	Miller Huggins	22.3
	Joe Torre	22.3
183	Charlie Keller	22.2
	Gil McDougald	22.2
	Lance Parrish	22.2
186	Travis Jackson	22.0
187	Ted Simmons	21.7
188	Ken Caminiti	21.6
	Graig Nettles	21.6
190	Tony Fernandez	21.5
	Harry Stovey	21.5
192	Bob Elliott	21.4
193	Ron Cey	21.3
194	Jose Cruz	21.2
	Ed Konetchy	21.2
196	Chuck Klein	21.1
197	Wally Berger	21.0
	Minnie Minoso	21.0
	Tim Salmon	21.0
200	Darrell Porter	20.9

Batter-Fielder Wins

Rank	Player	Wins
201	Jimmy Sheckard	20.7
	Vern Stephens	20.7
	Chief Zimmer	20.7
204	Luis Gonzalez	20.6
	Joe Kelley	20.6
	Ernie Lombardi	20.6
	Kevin Mitchell	20.6
	Fred Pfeffer	20.6
209	Tony Oliva	20.4
	Wally Schang	20.4
	Ken Singleton	20.4
212	Eric Davis	20.3
	Brian Downing	20.3
214	Glenn Hubbard	20.2
215	Eddie Stanky	20.1
216	Carlos Delgado	20.0
	Art Devlin	20.0
218	Andruw Jones	19.8
	Jorge Posada	19.8
220	Ken Boyer	19.7
	Fred Lynn	19.7
	Matt Williams	19.7
223	Denny Lyons	19.6
224	John McGraw	19.5
	Joe Tinker	19.5
226	Toby Harrah	19.4
	Charley Jones	19.4
228	Bill Joyce	19.3
	Chet Lemon	19.3
	Tony Phillips	19.3
231	Orlando Cepeda	19.1
232	Gene Alley	18.8
	Roy Cullenbine	18.8
	Ferris Fain	18.8
235	Phil Rizzuto	18.7
236	Ray Lankford	18.6
	Boog Powell	18.6
	Jim Rice	18.6
239	George Foster	18.5
240	Gavy Cravath	18.4
	Juan Gonzalez	18.4
	Kenny Lofton	18.4
	Pie Traynor	18.4
244	Andre Dawson	18.3
	Mike Griffin	18.3
	Mike Scioscia	18.3
247	Bill Freehan	18.2
	Jason Kendall	18.2
	Hack Wilson	18.2
250	Rico Carty	18.1
	Larry Doby	18.1
252	Max Carey	18.0
	Pedro Guerrero	18.0
254	Dave Concepcion	17.9
	Bobby Veach	17.9
256	Tony Lazzeri	17.8
257	Lance Berkman	17.6
	John Valentin	17.6
259	Babe Herman	17.5
	Ken Williams	17.5
261	Earl Averill	17.3
262	Jeff Heath	17.2
	Chief Meyers	17.2
	Bill Nicholson	17.2
	Roy Smalley	17.2
266	Ellis Burks	17.1
267	Rick Burleson	17.0
	Andy Van Slyke	17.0
269	Bobby Knoop	16.7
270	Ray Chapman	16.6
271	Eric Chavez	16.5
	Johnny Logan	16.5
273	Lave Cross	16.4
274	Pee Wee Reese	16.3
275	Jay Bell	16.2
	Bobby Bonilla	16.2
	Al Rosen	16.2
278	Brett Butler	16.1
	Mike Hargrove	16.1
	Ray Schalk	16.1
281	Jim O'Rourke	16.0
282	Johnny Evers	15.9
	Don Mattingly	15.9
284	Dwayne Murphy	15.8
	Red Schoendienst	15.8
286	Ron Hansen	15.7
	David Justice	15.7
	Willie Kamm	15.7
	Paul O'Neill	15.7
290	Chili Davis	15.5
	Julio Franco	15.5
	Johnny Pesky	15.5
293	Rico Petrocelli	15.4
	Jimmy Williams	15.4
295	Augie Galan	15.3
	Roy White	15.3
297	Henry Larkin	15.2
298	Moises Alou	15.0
	Tommy Henrich	15.0
	Willie Keeler	15.0

Batter-Fielder Wins

Rank	Player	Wins
	Dave Parker	15.0
302	Doug DeCinces	14.9
303	Sid Gordon	14.8
	Derek Jeter	14.8
305	Hal McRae	14.7
306	Ben Chapman	14.5
	Enos Slaughter	14.5
308	Nellie Fox	14.4
	Paul Hines	14.4
	Johnny Kling	14.4
	Mike Tiernan	14.4
312	Buddy Myer	14.3
	Roger Peckinpaugh	14.3
	Brooks Robinson	14.3
315	Harold Baines	14.2
316	Jesse Barfield	14.1
	Davey Johnson	14.1
318	Bert Campaneris	14.0
	Kid Elberfeld	14.0
320	Gil Hodges	13.8
	Dave Orr	13.8
	Kip Selbach	13.8
323	John Titus	13.7
324	Lonny Frey	13.6
	Jocko Milligan	13.6
326	Kiki Cuyler	13.5
	George Gore	13.5
	Chick Hafey	13.5
	Red Smith	13.5
330	Dolph Camilli	13.4
331	Rudy York	13.3
332	Don Buford	13.2
	Hank Gowdy	13.2
	Danny Tartabull	13.2
	Robby Thompson	13.2
	Jose Valentin	13.2
337	Riggs Stephenson	13.1
338	Bob Allison	13.0
	Luis Aparicio	13.0
	Earl Battey	13.0
341	Jack Clements	12.9
	J.D. Drew	12.9
	Mark Grace	12.9
	Tom Haller	12.9
	Stan Spence	12.9
346	Cliff Floyd	12.8
	Greg Luzinski	12.8
	Tony Pena	12.8
	Jimmy Ryan	12.8
350	Ken Keltner	12.7
351	Fred Carroll	12.6
	Sherm Lollar	12.6
	Lefty O'Doul	12.6
	Roy Sievers	12.6
	Lonnie Smith	12.6
356	Davey Lopes	12.5
357	Rafael Furcal	12.4
	Dan McGann	12.4
	George Stone	12.4
360	Shawn Green	12.3
	Andy Thornton	12.3
	Bob Watson	12.3
363	Joe Harris	12.2
	Tommy Holmes	12.2
	Ichiro Suzuki	12.2
366	Kirk Gibson	12.1
	John Kruk	12.1
	Tim Wallach	12.1
369	Earle Combs	12.0
	Jim Gentile	12.0
	Harry Hooper	12.0
	Kent Hrbek	12.0
	Tommy Leach	12.0
	Amos Otis	12.0
	Orator Shafer	12.0
376	Lou Criger	11.9
	Gene Woodling	11.9
378	Oscar Gamble	11.8
379	Tony Cuccinello	11.7
	Darren Daulton	11.7
	Joe Ferguson	11.7
	Jerry Priddy	11.7
	Jim Sundberg	11.7
	Omar Vizquel	11.7
	Dixie Walker	11.7
386	Ryan Klesko	11.6
	Placido Polanco	11.6
	Heinie Zimmerman	11.6
389	Kal Daniels	11.5
	Rick Ferrell	11.5
	Melvin Mora	11.5
	Reggie Sanders	11.5
393	Walker Cooper	11.4
	Marcus Giles	11.4
395	Chris Hoiles	11.3
	Billy Nash	11.3
	Johnny Romano	11.3
	Deacon White	11.3
399	Don Baylor	11.2
	Ron Hunt	11.2

Batter-Fielder Wins

Rank	Player	Wins
	Ernie Whitt	11.2
	Ross Youngs	11.2
403	Tommy Burns	11.0
	Dave Cash	11.0
	Mike Donlin	11.0
	Dick McAuliffe	11.0
	Ed Swartwood	11.0
408	Max Bishop	10.9
	Bill Bradley	10.9
	Jake Daubert	10.9
	Harry Davis	10.9
	Benny Kauff	10.9
	Richie Zisk	10.9
414	Sixto Lezcano	10.8
	Jason Varitek	10.8
	Vic Wertz	10.8
417	Carlos Beltran	10.7
	Smoky Burgess	10.7
	Charlie Hickman	10.7
	Wally Joyner	10.7
	Kevin McReynolds	10.7
	Tip O'Neill	10.7
	Richie Sexson	10.7
424	Larry Doyle	10.6
	Buck Herzog	10.6
	Ed Williamson	10.6
427	Dick Groat	10.5
	Dale Murphy	10.5
	Bob Nieman	10.5
	Snuffy Stirnweiss	10.5
431	Derrek Lee	10.4
	Jody Reed	10.4
433	Mike Cameron	10.3
	Elston Howard	10.3
	Rabbit Maranville	10.3
	Ed McFarland	10.3
	Tony Perez	10.3
	Johnny Ray	10.3
	Andy Seminick	10.3
	Bump Wills	10.3
441	Pinky May	10.2
	Bob O'Farrell	10.2
	Cecil Travis	10.2
	George Van Haltren	10.2
	Jimmy Wolf	10.2
446	Johnny Callison	10.1
	Dom DiMaggio	10.1
	Magglio Ordonez	10.1
	Heinie Peitz	10.1
	Mike Sweeney	10.1
	Quilvio Veras	10.1
452	Chris Speier	10.0
453	Jack Crooks	9.9
	Solly Hemus	9.9
	Freddie Lindstrom	9.9
	Roger Maris	9.9
	Cy Seymour	9.9
	Mickey Tettleton	9.9
	Maury Wills	9.9
460	Adam Dunn	9.8
	Duke Farrell	9.8
	Don Money	9.8
463	Larry Hisle	9.7
	Geoff Jenkins	9.7
	Marty McManus	9.7
	Danny Murphy	9.7
	Doug Rader	9.7
	Edd Roush	9.7
	Billy Werber	9.7
470	Sal Bando	9.6
	Bernie Carbo	9.6
	Troy Glaus	9.6
473	Ken Griffey	9.5
	Bill Sweeney	9.5
	Garry Templeton	9.5
476	Donie Bush	9.4
	Topsy Hartsel	9.4
	Charlie Hollocher	9.4
	Kevin Seitzer	9.4
	Cy Williams	9.4
481	Von Hayes	9.3
	Billy Jurges	9.3
	Socks Seybold	9.3
484	Clete Boyer	9.2
	Alvin Davis	9.2
	Jackie Jensen	9.2
	Tim McCarver	9.2
	Frank White	9.2
489	Wes Westrum	9.1
490	Del Crandall	9.0
	Jerry Denny	9.0
	Damian Miller	9.0
	Freddie Patek	9.0
	Art Wilson	9.0
495	Larry Gardner	8.9
496	7 players tied	8.8

Wins

1 Cy Young....511
2 Walter Johnson....417
3 Grover Alexander....373
  Christy Mathewson....373
5 Warren Spahn....363
6 Jim Galvin....361
  Kid Nichols....361
8 Tim Keefe....342
9 Roger Clemens....341
10 Steve Carlton....329
11 John Clarkson....328
12 Eddie Plank....326
13 Nolan Ryan....324
  Don Sutton....324
15 Greg Maddux....318
  Phil Niekro....318
17 Gaylord Perry....314
18 Tom Seaver....311
19 Charley Radbourn....309
20 Mickey Welch....307
21 Lefty Grove....300
  Early Wynn....300
23 Tommy John....288
24 Bert Blyleven....287
25 Robin Roberts....286
26 Fergie Jenkins....284
  Tony Mullane....284
28 Jim Kaat....283
29 Tom Glavine....275
30 Red Ruffing....273
31 Burleigh Grimes....270
32 Jim Palmer....268
33 Bob Feller....266
  Eppa Rixey....266
35 Jim McCormick....265
36 Gus Weyhing....264
37 Randy Johnson....263
38 Ted Lyons....260
39 Red Faber....254
  Jack Morris....254
41 Carl Hubbell....253
42 Bob Gibson....251
43 Vic Willis....249
44 Jack Quinn....247
45 Joe McGinnity....246
  Amos Rusie....246
47 Dennis Martinez....245
  Jack Powell....245
49 Juan Marichal....243
50 Herb Pennock....241
51 Frank Tanana....240
52 Mordecai Brown....239
53 Clark Griffith....237
  Waite Hoyt....237
55 Whitey Ford....236
56 Charlie Buffinton....233
57 Sam Jones....229
  Luis Tiant....229
  Will White....229
60 George Mullin....228
61 David Wells....227
62 Jim Bunning....224
  Catfish Hunter....224
  Mike Mussina....224
65 Hooks Dauss....223
  Paul Derringer....223
  Mel Harder....223
68 Jerry Koosman....222
69 Joe Niekro....221
70 Jerry Reuss....220
71 Bob Caruthers....218
  Earl Whitehill....218
73 Freddie Fitzsimmons....217
  Mickey Lolich....217
75 Wilbur Cooper....216
  Charlie Hough....216
77 Stan Coveleski....215
  Jim Perry....215
79 Rick Reuschel....214
80 Chief Bender....212
81 Kevin Brown....211
  Bobo Newsom....211
  Billy Pierce....211
  Bob Welch....211
85 Jesse Haines....210
86 Vida Blue....209
  Eddie Cicotte....209
  Don Drysdale....209
  Milt Pappas....209
90 Carl Mays....208
91 Bob Lemon....207
  Hal Newhouser....207
93 Jamie Moyer....205
94 Orel Hershiser....204
  Al Orth....204
96 Lew Burdette....203
  Silver King....203
  Jack Stivetts....203
99 Rube Marquard....201
  Charlie Root....201

Losses

1 Cy Young....316
2 Jim Galvin....308
3 Nolan Ryan....292
4 Walter Johnson....279
5 Phil Niekro....274
6 Gaylord Perry....265
7 Don Sutton....256
8 Jack Powell....254
9 Eppa Rixey....251
10 Bert Blyleven....250
11 Robin Roberts....245
  Warren Spahn....245
13 Steve Carlton....244
  Early Wynn....244
15 Jim Kaat....237
16 Frank Tanana....236
17 Gus Weyhing....232
18 Tommy John....231
19 Bob Friend....230
  Ted Lyons....230
21 Fergie Jenkins....226
22 Tim Keefe....225
  Red Ruffing....225
24 Bobo Newsom....222
25 Tony Mullane....220
26 Jack Quinn....218
27 Sam Jones....217
28 Charlie Hough....216
29 Jim McCormick....214
30 Red Faber....213
31 Paul Derringer....212
  Chick Fraser....212
  Burleigh Grimes....212
34 Mickey Welch....210
35 Jerry Koosman....209
36 Grover Alexander....208
  Kid Nichols....208
38 Tom Seaver....205
  Vic Willis....205
40 Joe Niekro....204
  Jim Whitney....204
42 George Mullin....196
  Adonis Terry....196
44 Claude Osteen....195
45 Eddie Plank....194
  Charley Radbourn....194
47 Dennis Martinez....193
48 Mickey Lolich....191
  Rick Reuschel....191
  Jerry Reuss....191
  Tom Zachary....191
52 Greg Maddux....189
  Al Orth....189
54 Christy Mathewson....188
55 Mel Harder....186
  Mike Morgan....186
  Jack Morris....186
58 Earl Whitehill....185
59 Jim Bunning....184
  Joe Bush....184
  Tom Glavine....184
62 Larry Jackson....183
  Curt Simmons....183
64 Danny Darwin....182
  Hooks Dauss....182
  Waite Hoyt....182
67 Murry Dickson....181
  Dutch Leonard....181
  Rick Wise....181
70 Lee Meadows....180
71 Pink Hawley....179
  Dolf Luque....179
73 John Clarkson....178
  Wilbur Cooper....178
75 Bill Dinneen....177
  Rube Marquard....177
77 Mike Moore....176
78 Red Donahue....175
79 Doyle Alexander....174
  Bob Gibson....174
  Tom Hughes....174
  Jim Perry....174
  Amos Rusie....174
84 Chuck Finley....173
85 Roger Clemens....172
  Luis Tiant....172
87 Dennis Eckersley....171
  Larry French....171
89 Ted Breitenstein....170
  Camilo Pascual....170
91 Billy Pierce....169
92 Red Ames....167
  Jim Clancy....167
  Bert Cunningham....167
  Red Ehret....167
96 Don Drysdale....166
  Howard Ehmke....166
  Catfish Hunter....166
  George Uhle....166
  Will White....166

Winning Percentage

1 Pedro Martinez....701
2 Dave Foutz....690
3 Whitey Ford....690
4 Bob Caruthers....688
5 Lefty Grove....680
6 Vic Raschi....667
7 Larry Corcoran....665
8 Christy Mathewson....665
9 Roger Clemens....665
10 Sam Leever....660
11 Randy Johnson....659
12 Sal Maglie....657
13 Sandy Koufax....655
14 Johnny Allen....654
15 Andy Pettitte....654
16 Ron Guidry....651
17 Lefty Gomez....649
18 John Clarkson....648
19 Mordecai Brown....648
20 Dizzy Dean....644
21 Grover Alexander....642
22 Mike Mussina....638
23 Jim Palmer....638
24 Kid Nichols....634
25 Deacon Phillippe....634
26 Joe McGinnity....634
27 Doc Gooden....634
28 Ed Reulbach....632
29 Juan Marichal....631
30 Mort Cooper....631
31 Allie Reynolds....630
32 Bartolo Colon....629
33 Jesse Tannehill....627
34 Greg Maddux....627
  Ray Kremer....627
36 Firpo Marberry....627
37 Eddie Plank....627
38 Tommy Bond....627
39 Chief Bender....625
40 Don Newcombe....623
41 Nig Cuppy....623
42 Carl Mays....623
43 Addie Joss....623
44 Fred Goldsmith....622
45 Doc Crandall....622
46 Carl Hubbell....622
47 Bob Feller....621
48 Mel Parnell....621
49 John Tudor....619
50 Clark Griffith....619
51 Bob Lemon....618
52 Cy Young....618
53 Urban Shocker....615
54 Jeff Tesreau....615
55 Jim Maloney....615
56 Charley Radbourn....614
57 John Ward....614
58 Jimmy Key....614
59 David Wells....614
60 Lon Warneke....613
61 Gary Nolan....611
62 Schoolboy Rowe....610
63 Carl Erskine....610
64 Ed Walsh....607
65 Charlie Ferguson....607
66 Dave McNally....607
67 Hooks Wiltse....607
68 David Cone....606
69 Jack Stivetts....606
70 Ramon Martinez....605
71 Art Nehf....605
72 Charlie Buffinton....605
73 Orval Overall....603
74 Tim Keefe....603
75 Tom Seaver....603
76 Stan Coveleski....602
77 Preacher Roe....602
78 Wes Ferrell....601
79 J.R. Richard....601
80 Jack Chesbro....600
81 Walter Johnson....599
82 Tom Glavine....599
83 Herb Pennock....598
84 Freddie Fitzsimmons....598
85 Ed Lopat....597
86 Warren Spahn....597
87 Rip Sewell....596
88 Curt Schilling....594
89 Kevin Brown....594
90 Mike Garcia....594
91 Mickey Welch....594
92 Jack McDowell....593
93 Pat Malone....593
94 Alvin Crowder....592
95 John Candelaria....592
96 Kenny Rogers....592
97 Harry Brecheen....591
98 Bob Welch....591
99 Bob Gibson....591
100 Dutch Ruether....591

Games

1 Jesse Orosco....1252
2 John Franco....1119
3 Dennis Eckersley....1071
4 Hoyt Wilhelm....1070
5 Dan Plesac....1064
6 Kent Tekulve....1050
7 Mike Stanton....1027
8 Lee Smith....1022
9 Mike Jackson....1005
10 Rich Gossage....1002
11 Lindy McDaniel....987
12 Rollie Fingers....944
13 Gene Garber....931
14 Cy Young....906
15 Sparky Lyle....899
16 Jim Kaat....898
17 Mike Timlin....893
18 Roberto Hernandez....892
19 Jose Mesa....887
20 Paul Assenmacher....884
21 Jeff Reardon....880
22 Don McMahon....874
23 Phil Niekro....864
24 Charlie Hough....858
25 Roy Face....848
26 Doug Jones....846
27 Paul Quantrill....841
28 Steve Reed....833
29 Tug McGraw....824
30 Todd Jones....812
31 Nolan Ryan....807
32 Walter Johnson....802
33 Rick Honeycutt....797
34 Jeff Nelson....792
35 Buddy Groom....786
36 Gaylord Perry....777
37 Don Sutton....774
38 Mark Guthrie....765
  Darold Knowles....765
40 Tommy John....760
41 Trevor Hoffman....756
  Jack Quinn....756
43 Ron Reed....751
44 Tom Gordon....750
  Warren Spahn....750
46 Tom Burgmeier....745
  Gary Lavelle....745
48 Willie Hernandez....744
49 Steve Carlton....741
50 Eddie Guardado....738
51 Ron Perranoski....737
52 Ron Kline....736
53 Rick Aguilera....732
  Steve Bedrosian....732
55 Clay Carroll....731
56 Randy Myers....728
57 Mike Marshall....723
  Roger McDowell....723
59 Bob Wickman....721
60 Dave Righetti....718
61 Danny Darwin....716
62 Eric Plunk....714
63 Johnny Klippstein....711
64 Jeff Fassero....710
  Greg Minton....710
66 Rod Beck....704
  Stu Miller....704
68 Greg Harris....703
69 Joe Niekro....702
70 Bill Campbell....700
  Jeff Montgomery....700
72 Larry Andersen....699
73 Bob McClure....698
74 Jim Galvin....697
75 Grover Alexander....696
  Craig Lefferts....696
77 Bob Miller....694
78 Bert Blyleven....692
  Grant Jackson....692
  Dennis Martinez....692
  Eppa Rixey....692
82 Early Wynn....691
83 Eddie Fisher....690
84 Kenny Rogers....687
  David Weathers....687
86 Ted Abernathy....681
87 Terry Mulholland....680
88 Robin Roberts....676
89 Waite Hoyt....674
  Dan Quisenberry....674
91 Roger Clemens....672
92 Red Faber....669
93 Dave Giusti....668
94 Dennis Cook....665
95 Fergie Jenkins....664
  Greg Swindell....664
97 Bruce Sutter....661
98 Armando Benitez....658
99 Mariano Rivera....657
100 Steve Kline....656
  Tom Seaver....656

Games Started

1 Cy Young....815
2 Nolan Ryan....773
3 Don Sutton....756
4 Phil Niekro....716
5 Steve Carlton....709
6 Tommy John....700
7 Gaylord Perry....690
8 Bert Blyleven....685
9 Jim Galvin....681
10 Roger Clemens....671
11 Walter Johnson....666
12 Warren Spahn....665
13 Tom Seaver....647
14 Greg Maddux....639
15 Jim Kaat....625
16 Frank Tanana....616
17 Early Wynn....612
18 Robin Roberts....609
19 Tom Glavine....603
20 Grover Alexander....600
21 Fergie Jenkins....594
  Tim Keefe....594
23 Dennis Martinez....562
  Kid Nichols....562
25 Eppa Rixey....554
26 Christy Mathewson....552
27 Mickey Welch....549
28 Jerry Reuss....538
29 Red Ruffing....538
30 Eddie Plank....529
  Rick Reuschel....529
32 Jerry Koosman....527
  Jack Morris....527
34 Jim Palmer....521
35 Jim Bunning....519
36 John Clarkson....518
37 Jack Powell....516
38 Randy Johnson....513
39 Gus Weyhing....505
40 Tony Mullane....504
41 Charley Radbourn....502
42 Joe Niekro....500
43 Bob Friend....497
  Burleigh Grimes....497
45 Mickey Lolich....496
46 Claude Osteen....488
47 Sam Jones....487
48 Jim McCormick....485
  Jamie Moyer....485
50 Bob Feller....484
  Ted Lyons....484
  Luis Tiant....484
53 Red Faber....483
  Bobo Newsom....483
55 Bob Gibson....482
56 Kevin Brown....476
  Catfish Hunter....476
58 Vida Blue....473
  Earl Whitehill....473
60 Vic Willis....471
61 Chuck Finley....467
62 Orel Hershiser....466
63 Don Drysdale....465
  Milt Pappas....465
65 Doyle Alexander....464
66 Curt Simmons....462
  Bob Welch....462
68 Mike Torrez....458
69 Lefty Grove....457
  Juan Marichal....457
71 Rick Wise....455
72 Jim Perry....447
  David Wells....447
74 Paul Derringer....445
75 Mike Mussina....443
  Jack Quinn....443
77 Charlie Hough....440
  Mike Moore....440
79 Whitey Ford....438
80 Mel Harder....433
  Carl Hubbell....433
82 Billy Pierce....432
83 Larry Jackson....429
84 Mark Langston....428
  George Mullin....428
86 Amos Rusie....427
87 Freddie Fitzsimmons....425
  Waite Hoyt....425
89 Fernando Valenzuela....424
90 John Burkett....423
91 Bob Forsch....422
92 Frank Viola....420
93 David Cone....419
  Herb Pennock....419
95 Bob Knepper....413
96 Dave Stieb....412
97 Mike Morgan....411
98 Tom Candiotti....410
  Doc Gooden....410
  Ken Holtzman....410

Games Started by era

1988-2005
1 Roger Clemens 671
2 Greg Maddux 639
3 Tom Glavine 603
4 Randy Johnson 513
5 Jamie Moyer................485
6 Kevin Brown 476
7 Chuck Finley 467
8 Orel Hershiser 466
9 David Wells 447
10 Mike Mussina 443

1973-1987
1 Nolan Ryan 773
2 Don Sutton 756
3 Phil Niekro 716
4 Steve Carlton 709
5 Tommy John 700
6 Gaylord Perry 690
7 Bert Blyleven 685
8 Tom Seaver 647
9 Frank Tanana 616
10 Fergie Jenkins 594

1961-1972
1 Jim Kaat......................625
2 Jim Bunning 519
3 Mickey Lolich 496
4 Claude Osteen 488
5 Bob Gibson 482
6 Catfish Hunter 476
7 Don Drysdale 465
  Milt Pappas 465
9 Juan Marichal 457
10 Jim Perry 447

1943-1960
1 Warren Spahn 665
2 Early Wynn 612
3 Robin Roberts 609
4 Bob Friend 497
5 Bob Feller 484
6 Curt Simmons 462
7 Whitey Ford 438
8 Billy Pierce 432
9 Dutch Leonard 375
10 Hal Newhouser 374

1921-1942
1 Eppa Rixey 554
2 Red Ruffing 538
3 Burleigh Grimes 497
4 Sam Jones 487
5 Ted Lyons 484
6 Red Faber 483
  Bobo Newsom 483
8 Earl Whitehill 473
9 Lefty Grove 457
10 Paul Derringer 445

1901-1920
1 Cy Young.....................815
2 Walter Johnson 666
3 Grover Alexander 600
4 Christy Mathewson 552
5 Eddie Plank 529
6 Jack Powell 516
7 Vic Willis 471
8 George Mullin 428
9 Rube Marquard 407
10 Wilbur Cooper 406

1893-1900
1 Kid Nichols 562
2 Amos Rusie 427
3 Clark Griffith 372
4 Brickyard Kennedy 354
5 Pink Hawley 344
6 Ted Breitenstein 342
7 Frank Dwyer 318
8 Bert Cunningham 311
9 Red Ehret 309
10 Jouett Meekin 308

1876-1892
1 Jim Galvin 681
2 Tim Keefe 594
3 Mickey Welch 549
4 John Clarkson 518
5 Gus Weyhing 505
6 Tony Mullane 504
7 Charley Radbourn 502
8 Jim McCormick 485
9 Adonis Terry 406
10 Will White 401

Complete Games
1 Cy Young.....................749
2 Jim Galvin 639
3 Tim Keefe 554
4 Kid Nichols 532
5 Walter Johnson 531
6 Mickey Welch 525
7 Charley Radbourn 488
8 John Clarkson 485
9 Tony Mullane 468
10 Jim McCormick 466
11 Gus Weyhing 449
12 Grover Alexander 437
13 Christy Mathewson 435
14 Jack Powell 422
15 Eddie Plank 410
16 Will White 394
17 Amos Rusie 393
18 Vic Willis 388
19 Warren Spahn 382
20 Jim Whitney 377
21 Adonis Terry 367
22 Ted Lyons 356
23 George Mullin 353
24 Charlie Buffinton 351
25 Chick Fraser 342
26 Clark Griffith 337
27 Red Ruffing 335
28 Silver King 328
29 Al Orth.......................324
30 Bill Hutchison 321
31 Burleigh Grimes 314
  Joe McGinnity 314
33 Red Donahue 312
  Guy Hecker 312
35 Bill Dinneen 306
36 Robin Roberts 305
37 Gaylord Perry 303
38 Ted Breitenstein 301
39 Bob Caruthers 298
  Lefty Grove 298
41 Pink Hawley 297
  Ed Morris 297
43 Mark Baldwin 295
44 Tommy Bond 294
  Brickyard Kennedy 294
46 Eppa Rixey 290
  Early Wynn 290
48 Bill Donovan 289
  Bobby Mathews 289
50 Bert Cunningham 287
51 Wilbur Cooper 279
  Bob Feller 279
  Sadie McMahon 279
  Jack Taylor 279
55 Jack Stivetts 278
56 Charlie Getzien 277
57 Red Faber 273
58 Mordecai Brown 271
  Frank Dwyer 271
60 Jouett Meekin 270
61 Fergie Jenkins 267
62 Elton Chamberlain 264
  Matt Kilroy 264
  Jesse Tannehill 264
65 Doc White 262
66 Rube Waddell 261
67 Jack Chesbro 260
  Red Ehret 260
  Carl Hubbell 260
70 Larry Corcoran 256
71 Chief Bender 255
  Bob Gibson 255
73 Steve Carlton 254
74 Frank Killen 253
  Win Mercer 253
76 Paul Derringer 251
77 Sam Jones 250
  Ed Walsh 250
79 Eddie Cicotte 249
  Stump Wiedman 249
81 Herb Pennock 247
82 Bobo Newsom 246
83 George Bradley 245
  Hooks Dauss 245
  Phil Niekro 245
  John Ward 245
87 Harry Howell 244
  Juan Marichal 244
89 Jack Quinn 243
90 Bert Blyleven 242
  Deacon Phillippe 242
  Bucky Walters 242
93 Sam Leever 241
94 Kid Gleason 240
95 Addie Joss 234
96 George Uhle 232
97 Carl Mays 231
  Tom Seaver 231
  Harry Staley 231
100 Earl Moore 230

Complete Games by era

1988-2005
1 Roger Clemens 118
2 Greg Maddux 108
3 Randy Johnson 96
4 Curt Schilling 82
5 Mark Langston 81
6 Mike Moore 79
7 Bret Saberhagen 76
8 Frank Viola 74
9 Kevin Brown 72
  Tom Candiotti 68
  Doc Gooden 68
  Orel Hershiser 68

1973-1987
1 Gaylord Perry 303
2 Fergie Jenkins 267
3 Steve Carlton 254
4 Phil Niekro 245
5 Bert Blyleven 242
6 Tom Seaver 231
7 Nolan Ryan 222
8 Jim Palmer 211
9 Luis Tiant 187
10 Don Sutton 178

1961-1972
1 Bob Gibson 255
2 Juan Marichal 244
3 Mickey Lolich 195
4 Catfish Hunter 181
5 Jim Kaat.....................180
6 Mike Cuellar 172
7 Don Drysdale 167
8 Mel Stottlemyre 152
9 Jim Bunning 151
10 Larry Jackson 149

1943-1960
1 Warren Spahn 382
2 Robin Roberts 305
3 Early Wynn 290
4 Bob Feller 279
5 Hal Newhouser 212
6 Billy Pierce 193
7 Dutch Leonard 192
8 Bob Lemon 188
9 Ed Lopat 164
10 Bob Friend 163
  Curt Simmons 163

1921-1942
1 Ted Lyons 356
2 Red Ruffing 335
3 Burleigh Grimes 314
4 Lefty Grove 298
5 Eppa Rixey 290
6 Red Faber 273
7 Carl Hubbell 260
8 Paul Derringer 251
9 Sam Jones 250
10 Herb Pennock 247

1901-1920
1 Cy Young.....................749
2 Walter Johnson 531
3 Grover Alexander 437
4 Christy Mathewson 435
5 Jack Powell 422
6 Eddie Plank 410
7 Vic Willis 388
8 George Mullin 353
9 Chick Fraser 342
10 Al Orth.......................324

1893-1900
1 Kid Nichols 532
2 Amos Rusie 393
3 Clark Griffith 337
4 Ted Breitenstein 301
5 Pink Hawley 297
6 Brickyard Kennedy 294
7 Bert Cunningham 287
8 Frank Dwyer 271
9 Jouett Meekin 270
10 Red Ehret 260

1876-1892
1 Jim Galvin 639
2 Tim Keefe 554
3 Mickey Welch 525
4 Charley Radbourn 488
5 John Clarkson 485
6 Tony Mullane 468
7 Jim McCormick 466
8 Gus Weyhing 449
9 Will White 394
10 Jim Whitney 377

Shutouts
1 Walter Johnson 110
2 Grover Alexander 90
3 Christy Mathewson 79
4 Cy Young.....................76
5 Eddie Plank 69
6 Warren Spahn 63
7 Nolan Ryan 61
  Tom Seaver 61
9 Bert Blyleven 60
10 Don Sutton 58
11 Jim Galvin 57
  Ed Walsh 57
13 Bob Gibson 56
14 Mordecai Brown 55
  Steve Carlton 55
16 Jim Palmer 53
  Gaylord Perry 53
18 Juan Marichal 52
19 Rube Waddell 50
  Vic Willis 50
21 Don Drysdale 49
  Fergie Jenkins 49
  Luis Tiant 49
  Early Wynn 49
25 Kid Nichols 48
26 Roger Clemens 46
  Tommy John 46
  Jack Powell 46
29 Whitey Ford 45
  Addie Joss 45
  Phil Niekro 45
  Robin Roberts 45
  Red Ruffing 45
  Doc White 45
35 Babe Adams 44
  Bob Feller 44
37 Milt Pappas 43
38 Catfish Hunter 42
  Bucky Walters 42
40 Mickey Lolich 41
  Hippo Vaughn 41
  Mickey Welch 41
43 Chief Bender 40
  Jim Bunning 40
  Larry French 40
  Sandy Koufax 40
  Claude Osteen 40
  Ed Reulbach 40
  Mel Stottlemyre 40
50 Tim Keefe 39
  Sam Leever 39
  Jerry Reuss 39
53 Stan Coveleski 38
  Billy Pierce 38
  Nap Rucker 38
56 Vida Blue 37
  John Clarkson 37
  Larry Jackson 37
  Randy Johnson 37
  Eppa Rixey 37
  Steve Rogers 37
62 Mike Cuellar 36
  Bob Friend 36
  Carl Hubbell 36
  Sam Jones 36
  Camilo Pascual 36
  Allie Reynolds 36
  Curt Simmons 36
  Will White 36
70 Tommy Bond 35
  Joe Bush 35
  Jack Chesbro 35
  Eddie Cicotte 35
  Jack Coombs 35
  Wilbur Cooper 35
  Bill Donovan 35
  Burleigh Grimes 35
  Lefty Grove 35
  Greg Maddux 35
  George Mullin 35
  Herb Pennock 35
  Charley Radbourn 35
83 Bill Doak 34
  Earl Moore 34
  Frank Tanana 34
  Jesse Tannehill 34
87 Tommy Bridges 33
  Lew Burdette 33
  Dean Chance 33
  Mort Cooper 33
  Jerry Koosman 33
  Dutch Leonard 33
  Jim McCormick 33
  Dave McNally 33
  Hal Newhouser 33
  Bob Shawkey 33
  Virgil Trucks 33
98 Paul Derringer 32
  Lefty Leifield 32
  Joe McGinnity 32
  Jim Perry 32

Saves
1 Lee Smith....................478
2 Trevor Hoffman............436
3 John Franco 424
4 Dennis Eckersley 390
5 Mariano Rivera 379
6 Jeff Reardon 367
7 Randy Myers 347
8 Rollie Fingers 341
9 John Wetteland 330
10 Roberto Hernandez 324
  Troy Percival 324
12 Jose Mesa 319
13 Rick Aguilera 318
14 Robb Nen 314
15 Tom Henke 311
16 Rich Gossage 310
17 Jeff Montgomery 304
18 Doug Jones 303
19 Bruce Sutter 300
20 Rod Beck 286
21 Billy Wagner...............284
22 Armando Benitez 263
23 Todd Worrell 256
24 Dave Righetti 252
25 Dan Quisenberry 244
26 Sparky Lyle 238
27 Ugueth Urbina 237
28 Hoyt Wilhelm 227
29 Todd Jones................226
30 Gene Garber 218
31 Gregg Olson................217
32 Jason Isringhausen....216
  Dave Smith 216
34 Bob Wickman............214
35 Jeff Shaw 203
36 Bobby Thigpen 201
37 Roy Face 193
  Mike Henneman 193
39 Mitch Williams 192
40 Keith Foulke..............190
41 Mike Marshall 188
42 Jeff Russell 186
43 Steve Bedrosian 184
  Kent Tekulve 184
45 Danny Graves.............182
46 Tug McGraw 180
47 Ron Perranoski 179
48 Bryan Harvey 177
49 Jeff Brantley 172
  Lindy McDaniel 172
51 Eddie Guardado.........170
52 Billy Koch 163
53 Eric Gagne 160
54 Roger McDowell 159
55 Dan Plesac 158
56 Jay Howell 155
57 Stu Miller 154
  John Smoltz 154
59 Don McMahon 153
60 Greg Minton 150
61 Ted Abernathy 148
62 Willie Hernandez 147
63 Dave Giusti 145
64 Jesse Orosco 144
  Mike Williams 144
66 Clay Carroll 143
  Darold Knowles 143
68 Mike Jackson 142
69 Gary Lavelle 136
70 Jim Brewer 132
  Steve Farr 132
  Bob Stanley 132
73 Ron Davis 130
  Mike Timlin 130
75 Kazuhiro Sasaki 129
76 Terry Forster 127
77 Bill Campbell 126
  Dave LaRoche 126
  Mel Rojas 126
80 John Hiller 125
81 Jack Aker 123
82 Dick Radatz 122
83 Antonio Alfonseca.......121
  Duane Ward 121
85 Mark Wohlers 119
86 Ricky Bottalico 116
  Tom Gordon 116
88 Tippy Martinez 115
89 Francisco Cordero......111
  Frank Linzy 111
91 Jose Jimenez 110
  Al Worthington 110
93 Fred Gladding 109
94 Wayne Granger 108
  Ron Kline 108
96 Johnny Murphy 107
97 Bill Caudill 106
98 Braden Looper...........103
  Ron Reed 103
  John Wyatt 103

Saves by era

1988-2005
1 Trevor Hoffman............436
2 John Franco..............424
3 Mariano Rivera...........379
4 Randy Myers..............347
5 John Wetteland...........330
6 Roberto Hernandez........324
  Troy Percival............324
8 Jose Mesa................319
9 Rick Aguilera............318
10 Robb Nen................314

1973-1987
1 Lee Smith................478
2 Dennis Eckersley.........390
3 Jeff Reardon.............367
4 Rollie Fingers...........341
5 Rich Gossage.............310
6 Bruce Sutter.............300
7 Dave Righetti............252
8 Dan Quisenberry..........244
9 Sparky Lyle..............238
10 Gene Garber.............218

1961-1972
1 Ron Perranoski...........179
2 Lindy McDaniel...........172
3 Don McMahon..............153
4 Ted Abernathy............148
5 Dave Giusti..............145
6 Clay Carroll.............143
  Darold Knowles...........143
8 Jim Brewer...............132
9 Jack Aker................123
10 Dick Radatz.............122

1943-1960
1 Hoyt Wilhelm.............227
2 Roy Face.................193
3 Stu Miller...............154
4 Al Worthington...........110
5 Ron Kline................108
6 Ellis Kinder.............102
7 Clem Labine...............96
8 Bill Henry................90
9 Joe Page..................76
10 Jim Konstanty............74

1921-1942
1 Johnny Murphy............107
2 Firpo Marberry...........101
3 Al Benton.................66
4 Clint Brown...............64
5 Joe Heving................63
6 Jack Quinn................57
7 Hugh Casey................55
  Lefty Grove...............55
9 Waite Hoyt................52
10 Wilcy Moore..............49

1901-1920
1 Mordecai Brown............49
2 Allan Russell.............42
3 Hooks Dauss...............39
4 Red Ames..................36
  Slim Sallee...............36
6 Ed Walsh..................35
7 Chief Bender..............34
  Walter Johnson............34
9 Hooks Wiltse..............33
10 Grover Alexander.........32

1893-1900
1 Kid Nichols...............17
2 Win Mercer................10
3 Brickyard Kennedy..........9
  Jack Taylor................9
5 Clark Griffith.............8
6 Frank Dwyer................6
  George Hemming.............6
8 Nig Cuppy..................5
  Duke Esper.................5
  Amos Rusie.................5

1876-1892
1 Tony Mullane..............15
2 Kid Gleason................6
  Silver King................6
  Adonis Terry...............6
5 Mark Baldwin...............5
  John Clarkson..............5
  Jack Stivetts..............5
8 Charlie Ferguson...........4
  Frank Foreman..............4
  Dave Foutz.................4
  Bill Hutchison.............4
  Sadie McMahon..............4
  Hank O'Day.................4
  Billy Taylor...............4
  Mickey Welch...............4
  Gus Weyhing................4

Save percentage
1 Eric Gagne..............96.39
2 John Smoltz.............91.67
3 Trevor Hoffman..........89.53
4 Joe Nathan..............88.00
5 Mariano Rivera..........87.94
6 Billy Wagner............86.32
7 Jason Isringhausen......86.06
8 Armando Benitez.........85.95
9 Troy Percival...........85.94
10 Kazuhiro Sasaki........85.43
11 Robb Nen...............85.33
12 Jose Mesa..............85.29
13 Randy Myers............85.26
14 Mike Williams..........85.21
15 Tom Henke..............84.97
16 Chad Cordero...........84.93
17 Brad Lidge.............84.71
18 Bryan Harvey...........84.69
19 Dennis Eckersley.......84.60
20 Billy Koch.............84.46
21 Keith Foulke...........84.44
22 John Wetteland.........83.97
23 Rod Beck...............83.87
24 Ugueth Urbina..........83.16
25 Matt Mantei............83.04
26 Lee Smith..............82.27
27 Jose Jimenez...........82.09
28 Mark Wohlers...........82.07
29 Danny Graves...........81.98
30 Eddie Guardado.........81.73
31 Danys Baez.............80.95
32 Dan Kolb...............80.90
33 Kelvim Escobar.........80.82
34 John Franco............80.76
35 Dave Smith.............80.60
36 Jeff Russell...........80.52
37 Rick Aguilera..........80.51
38 Jeff Montgomery........80.42
39 Mike Henneman..........80.42
40 Dan Quisenberry........80.26
41 John Rocker............80.00
   Billy Taylor...........80.00
43 Jeff Shaw..............79.92
44 Francisco Cordero......79.86
45 Jorge Julio............79.81
46 Doug Jones.............79.74
47 Mike Schooler..........79.67
48 Alejandro Pena.........79.57
49 Gregg Olson............79.49
50 Bobby Thigpen..........79.45

Blown saves
1 Rich Gossage............112
2 Rollie Fingers..........109
3 Jeff Reardon............106
4 Lee Smith...............103
5 John Franco.............101
  Bruce Sutter............101
7 Roberto Hernandez........90
8 Sparky Lyle..............86
9 Gene Garber..............82
10 Kent Tekulve............81
11 Gary Lavelle............80
12 Rick Aguilera...........77
   Doug Jones..............77
14 Jesse Orosco............76
15 Mike Marshall...........74
   Jeff Montgomery.........74
   Dan Plesac.............74
   Dave Righetti..........74
19 Bill Campbell...........72
20 Dennis Eckersley........71
   Mike Timlin............71
   Todd Worrell...........71
23 John Wetteland..........63
24 Darold Knowles..........62
25 John Hiller.............60
   Todd Jones.............60
   Randy Myers............60
   Dan Quisenberry........60
29 Paul Assenmacher........59
   Mike Jackson...........59
31 Bob Wickman.............58
32 Steve Bedrosian.........57
33 Gregg Olson.............56
   Mitch Williams.........56
35 Rod Beck...............55
   Tom Henke..............55
   Roger McDowell.........55
   Jose Mesa..............55
   Bob Stanley............55
40 Greg Minton.............54
   Robb Nen...............54
42 Troy Percival...........53
43 Mariano Rivera..........52
   Dave Smith.............52
   Bobby Thigpen..........52
46 Trevor Hoffman..........51
   Jeff Shaw..............51
48 Tug McGraw..............50
   Mike Stanton...........50
50 Jay Howell.............49

Innings Pitched
1 Cy Young................7356.0
2 Jim Galvin..............5941.1
3 Walter Johnson..........5914.1
4 Phil Niekro.............5404.0
5 Nolan Ryan..............5386.0
6 Gaylord Perry...........5350.0
7 Don Sutton..............5282.1
8 Warren Spahn............5243.2
9 Steve Carlton...........5217.2
10 Grover Alexander.......5190.0
11 Kid Nichols............5067.1
12 Tim Keefe..............5049.2
13 Bert Blyleven..........4970.0
14 Mickey Welch...........4802.0
15 Christy Mathewson......4788.2
16 Tom Seaver.............4783.0
17 Tommy John.............4710.1
18 Roger Clemens..........4704.1
19 Robin Roberts..........4688.2
20 Early Wynn.............4564.0
21 John Clarkson..........4536.1
22 Tony Mullane...........4531.1
23 Jim Kaat...............4530.1
24 Charley Radbourn.......4527.1
25 Fergie Jenkins.........4500.2
26 Eddie Plank............4495.2
27 Eppa Rixey.............4494.2
28 Greg Maddux............4406.1
29 Jack Powell............4389.0
30 Red Ruffing............4344.0
31 Gus Weyhing............4337.0
32 Jim McCormick..........4275.2
33 Frank Tanana...........4188.1
34 Burleigh Grimes........4180.0
35 Ted Lyons..............4161.0
36 Red Faber..............4086.2
37 Dennis Martinez........3999.2
38 Vic Willis.............3996.0
39 Tom Glavine............3951.2
40 Jim Palmer.............3948.0
41 Lefty Grove............3940.2
42 Jack Quinn.............3920.1
43 Bob Gibson.............3884.1
44 Sam Jones..............3883.0
45 Jerry Koosman..........3839.1
46 Bob Feller.............3827.0
47 Jack Morris............3824.0
48 Charlie Hough..........3801.1
49 Amos Rusie.............3778.2
50 Waite Hoyt.............3762.1
51 Jim Bunning............3760.1
52 Bobo Newsom............3759.1
53 George Mullin..........3686.2
54 Jerry Reuss............3669.2
55 Paul Derringer.........3645.0
56 Mickey Lolich..........3638.1
57 Bob Friend.............3611.0
58 Randy Johnson..........3593.2
59 Carl Hubbell...........3590.1
60 Joe Niekro.............3584.1
61 Herb Pennock...........3571.2
62 Earl Whitehill.........3564.2
63 Rick Reuschel..........3548.1
64 Will White.............3542.2
65 Adonis Terry...........3514.1
66 Juan Marichal..........3507.0
67 Jim Whitney............3496.1
68 Luis Tiant.............3486.1
69 Wilbur Cooper..........3480.0
70 Claude Osteen..........3460.2
71 Catfish Hunter.........3449.1
72 Joe McGinnity..........3441.1
73 Don Drysdale...........3432.0
74 Mel Harder.............3426.1
75 Charlie Buffinton......3404.0
76 Hooks Dauss............3390.2
77 Clark Griffith.........3385.2
78 Doyle Alexander........3367.2
79 Chick Fraser...........3364.0
80 Al Orth................3354.2
81 Curt Simmons...........3348.1
82 Vida Blue..............3343.1
83 Rube Marquard..........3306.2
   Billy Pierce..........3306.2
85 Dennis Eckersley.......3285.2
   Jim Perry.............3285.2
87 Larry Jackson..........3262.2
88 Kevin Brown............3256.1
89 Eddie Cicotte..........3226.0
90 Freddie Fitzsimmons....3223.2
91 Dolf Luque.............3220.1
92 Dutch Leonard..........3218.1
93 Jesse Haines...........3208.2
94 David Wells............3206.1
95 Red Ames...............3198.0
96 Chuck Finley...........3197.1
   Charlie Root..........3197.1
98 Milt Pappas............3186.0
99 Silver King............3180.2
100 Mordecai Brown........3172.1

Innings Pitched by era

1988-2005
1 Roger Clemens...........4704.1
2 Greg Maddux.............4406.1
3 Tom Glavine.............3951.2
4 Randy Johnson...........3593.2
5 Kevin Brown.............3256.1
6 David Wells.............3206.1
7 Chuck Finley............3197.1
8 Jamie Moyer.............3139.2
9 Orel Hershiser..........3130.1
10 Danny Darwin...........3016.2

1973-1987
1 Phil Niekro.............5404.0
2 Nolan Ryan..............5386.0
3 Gaylord Perry...........5350.0
4 Don Sutton..............5282.1
5 Steve Carlton...........5217.2
6 Bert Blyleven...........4970.0
7 Tom Seaver..............4783.0
8 Tommy John..............4710.1
9 Fergie Jenkins..........4500.2
10 Frank Tanana...........4188.1

1961-1972
1 Jim Kaat................4530.1
2 Bob Gibson..............3884.1
3 Jim Bunning.............3760.1
4 Mickey Lolich...........3638.1
5 Juan Marichal...........3507.0
6 Claude Osteen...........3460.2
7 Catfish Hunter..........3449.1
8 Don Drysdale............3432.0
9 Jim Perry...............3285.2
10 Larry Jackson..........3262.2

1943-1960
1 Warren Spahn............5243.2
2 Robin Roberts...........4688.2
3 Early Wynn..............4564.0
4 Bob Feller..............3827.0
5 Bob Friend..............3611.0
6 Curt Simmons............3348.1
7 Billy Pierce............3306.2
8 Dutch Leonard...........3218.1
9 Whitey Ford.............3170.1
10 Lew Burdette...........3067.1

1921-1942
1 Eppa Rixey..............4494.2
2 Red Ruffing.............4344.0
3 Burleigh Grimes.........4180.0
4 Ted Lyons...............4161.0
5 Red Faber...............4086.2
6 Lefty Grove.............3940.2
7 Jack Quinn..............3920.1
8 Sam Jones...............3883.0
9 Waite Hoyt..............3762.1
10 Bobo Newsom............3759.1

1901-1920
1 Cy Young................7356.0
2 Walter Johnson..........5914.1
3 Grover Alexander........5190.0
4 Christy Mathewson.......4788.2
5 Eddie Plank.............4495.2
6 Jack Powell.............4389.0
7 Vic Willis..............3996.0
8 George Mullin...........3686.2
9 Wilbur Cooper...........3480.0
10 Joe McGinnity..........3441.1

1893-1900
1 Kid Nichols.............5067.1
2 Amos Rusie..............3778.2
3 Clark Griffith..........3385.2
4 Brickyard Kennedy.......3030.0
5 Pink Hawley.............3012.2
6 Ted Breitenstein........2973.1
7 Frank Dwyer.............2819.0
8 Red Ehret...............2754.1
9 Bert Cunningham.........2734.2
10 Jouett Meekin..........2605.1

1876-1892
1 Jim Galvin..............5941.1
2 Tim Keefe...............5049.2
3 Mickey Welch............4802.0
4 John Clarkson...........4536.1
5 Tony Mullane............4531.1
6 Charley Radbourn........4527.1
7 Gus Weyhing.............4337.0
8 Jim McCormick...........4275.2
9 Will White..............3542.2
10 Adonis Terry...........3514.1

Fewest Hits/Game
1 Nolan Ryan..............6.56
2 Sandy Koufax............6.79
3 Pedro Martinez..........6.82
4 Sid Fernandez...........6.85
5 J.R. Richard............6.88
6 Andy Messersmith........6.94
7 Hoyt Wilhelm............7.01
8 Sam McDowell............7.03
9 Randy Johnson...........7.06
10 Ed Walsh...............7.12
11 Bob Turley.............7.18
12 Orval Overall..........7.22
13 Jeff Tesreau...........7.24
14 Ed Reulbach............7.24
15 Mario Soto.............7.26
16 Addie Joss.............7.30
17 Jose DeLeon............7.38
18 Jim Maloney............7.39
19 Rich Gossage...........7.45
20 Tom Seaver.............7.47
21 Walter Johnson.........7.48
22 Rube Waddell...........7.48
23 Bob Gibson.............7.60
24 Don Wilson.............7.61
25 Jim Palmer.............7.63
26 Roger Clemens..........7.65
27 Larry Cheney...........7.68
28 Mordecai Brown.........7.68
29 Sam Jones..............7.68
30 Bob Feller.............7.69
31 Johnny Vander Meer.....7.69
32 Catfish Hunter.........7.72
33 Al Downing.............7.72
34 Jim Scott..............7.73
35 Charlie Hough..........7.77
36 David Cone.............7.77
37 Bobby Bolin............7.79
38 Stan Williams..........7.79
39 John Smoltz............7.79
40 Rollie Fingers.........7.80
41 Dean Chance............7.81
42 Frank Smith............7.82
43 Tug McGraw.............7.84
44 Barney Pelty...........7.85
45 Whitey Ford............7.85
46 Denny McLain...........7.85
47 Bob Veale..............7.87
48 Chief Bender...........7.89
49 George McQuillan.......7.89
50 Jack Coombs............7.89
51 Moe Drabowsky..........7.90
52 Tim Keefe..............7.91
53 Vida Blue..............7.91
54 Nap Rucker.............7.92
55 Allie Reynolds.........7.92
56 Eddie Plank............7.92
57 Christy Mathewson......7.93
58 Luis Tiant.............7.94
59 Rudy May...............7.94
60 Ray Culp...............7.95
61 Bill Donovan...........7.99
62 Howie Camnitz..........7.99
63 Don Sutton.............7.99
64 Juan Pizarro...........7.99
65 Dave Stieb.............7.99
66 Gary Bell..............8.01
67 Tom Gordon.............8.02
68 Earl Moore.............8.02
69 Hideo Nomo.............8.02
70 Sonny Siebert..........8.03
71 Ramon Martinez.........8.03
72 Lefty Tyler............8.03
73 Hal Newhouser..........8.04
74 Claude Hendrix.........8.06
75 Steve Carlton..........8.06
76 Hooks Wiltse...........8.06
77 Amos Rusie.............8.07
78 Willie Mitchell........8.07
79 Larry Corcoran.........8.08
80 Bill Singer............8.08
81 Bob Lemon..............8.08
82 Eddie Cicotte..........8.08
83 Mike Scott.............8.08
84 Don Drysdale...........8.09
85 Gary Nolan.............8.09
86 Stu Miller.............8.09
87 Juan Marichal..........8.09
88 Curt Schilling.........8.09
89 Al Leiter..............8.10
90 Doc White..............8.10
91 Virgil Trucks..........8.11
92 Hippo Vaughn...........8.11
93 Blue Moon Odom.........8.12
94 Kirby Higbe............8.13
95 Jim Shaw...............8.13
96 Jim Cuellar............8.13
97 Billy Pierce...........8.14
98 Mort Cooper............8.15
99 Red Ames...............8.15
100 Vic Willis............8.16

Fewest Hits/Game by era

1988-2005

1	Pedro Martinez	6.82
2	Sid Fernandez	6.85
3	Randy Johnson	7.06
4	Jose DeLeon	7.38
5	Roger Clemens	7.65
6	David Cone	7.77
7	John Smoltz	7.79
8	Tom Gordon	8.02
9	Hideo Nomo	8.02
10	Ramon Martinez	8.03

1973-1987

1	Nolan Ryan	6.56
2	J.R. Richard	6.88
3	Andy Messersmith	6.94
4	Mario Soto	7.26
5	Rich Gossage	7.45
6	Tom Seaver	7.47
7	Jim Palmer	7.63
8	Charlie Hough	7.77
9	Rollie Fingers	7.80
10	Tug McGraw	7.83

1961-1972

1	Sandy Koufax	6.79
2	Sam McDowell	7.03
3	Jim Maloney	7.39
4	Bob Gibson	7.60
5	Don Wilson	7.61
6	Catfish Hunter	7.72
7	Al Downing	7.72
8	Bobby Bolin	7.79
9	Stan Williams	7.79
10	Dean Chance	7.81

1943-1960

1	Hoyt Wilhelm	7.01
2	Bob Turley	7.18
3	Sam Jones	7.68
4	Bob Feller	7.69
5	Johnny Vander Meer	7.69
6	Whitey Ford	7.85
7	Allie Reynolds	7.92
8	Hal Newhouser	8.04
9	Bob Lemon	8.08
10	Stu Miller	8.09

1921-1942

1	Kirby Higbe	8.13
2	Mort Cooper	8.15
3	Lefty Gomez	8.23
4	Van Mungo	8.34
5	Tommy Bridges	8.52
6	Dazzy Vance	8.52
7	Johnny Allen	8.53
8	Whit Wyatt	8.61
9	Bucky Walters	8.67
10	Carl Hubbell	8.68

1901-1920

1	Ed Walsh	7.12
2	Orval Overall	7.22
3	Jeff Tesreau	7.24
4	Ed Reulbach	7.24
5	Addie Joss	7.30
6	Walter Johnson	7.48
7	Rube Waddell	7.48
8	Larry Cheney	7.68
9	Mordecai Brown	7.68
10	Jim Scott	7.73

1893-1900

1	Amos Rusie	8.07
2	Kid Nichols	8.75
3	Ed Stein	9.18
4	Billy Rhines	9.33
5	Ted Breitenstein	9.39
6	Brickyard Kennedy	9.75
7	Clark Griffith	9.76
8	Frank Killen	9.78
9	Jouett Meekin	9.80
10	Nixey Callahan	9.81

1876-1892

1	Tim Keefe	7.91
2	Larry Corcoran	8.08
3	Ed Morris	8.29
4	Dave Foutz	8.30
5	Toad Ramsey	8.32
6	Charlie Ferguson	8.33
7	Tony Mullane	8.33
8	John Ward	8.47
9	Bob Caruthers	8.52
10	John Clarkson	8.52

Fewest HR Allowed/Game by era

1988-2005

1	Zane Smith	0.57
2	Kevin Brown	0.57
3	Danny Jackson	0.58
4	Greg Maddux	0.61
5	Mark Gubicza	0.63
6	Bill Swift	0.65
7	Roger Clemens	0.66
8	Doc Gooden	0.67
9	Orel Hershiser	0.68
10	Tom Glavine	0.68

1973-1987

1	J.R. Richard	0.41
2	Steve Rogers	0.48
3	Mike LaCoss	0.51
4	Nolan Ryan	0.54
5	Steve Trout	0.54
6	Rick Reuschel	0.56
7	John Denny	0.57
8	Tommy John	0.58
9	Rich Gossage	0.59
10	Dock Ellis	0.59

1961-1972

1	Bob Veale	0.43
2	Dean Chance	0.51
3	Bill Singer	0.55
4	Steve Barber	0.56
5	Mel Stottlemyre	0.58
6	Bob Miller	0.59
7	Sam McDowell	0.59
8	Bob Gibson	0.60
9	Don Wilson	0.61
10	Blue Moon Odom	0.61

1943-1960

1	Max Lanier	0.36
2	Dizzy Trout	0.37
3	Hal Newhouser	0.41
4	Bill Wight	0.43
5	Johnny Vander Meer	0.43
6	Dutch Leonard	0.44
7	Allie Reynolds	0.48
8	Johnny Schmitz	0.48
9	Rip Sewell	0.49
10	Mike Garcia	0.50

1921-1942

1	Eppa Rixey	0.18
2	Stan Coveleski	0.19
3	Jakie May	0.20
4	Dutch Ruether	0.23
5	Jack Quinn	0.23
6	Lee Meadows	0.24
7	Red Faber	0.24
8	Sherry Smith	0.25
9	Al Hollingsworth	0.28
10	Pete Donohue	0.29

1901-1920

1	Ed Killian	0.05
2	Ed Walsh	0.07
3	Addie Joss	0.07
4	Willie Mitchell	0.08
5	Eddie Plank	0.08
6	Eddie Cicotte	0.09
7	Cy Falkenberg	0.09
8	Bill Donovan	0.09
9	Orval Overall	0.09
10	Harry Howell	0.09

1893-1900

1	Billy Rhines	0.12
2	Amos Rusie	0.18
3	Pink Hawley	0.18
4	Nixey Callahan	0.19
5	Frank Killen	0.20
6	Clark Griffith	0.20
7	Bert Cunningham	0.20
8	Red Ehret	0.21
9	Jouett Meekin	0.23
10	Win Mercer	0.23

1876-1892

1	Terry Larkin	0.07
2	John Ward	0.09
3	Tommy Bond	0.10
4	Jumbo McGinnis	0.12
5	Hardie Henderson	0.13
6	Tim Keefe	0.13
7	Ed Morris	0.14
8	Lee Richmond	0.15
9	Guy Hecker	0.15
10	George Bradley	0.16

Walks

1	Nolan Ryan	2795
2	Steve Carlton	1833
3	Phil Niekro	1809
4	Early Wynn	1775
5	Bob Feller	1764
6	Bobo Newsom	1732
7	Amos Rusie	1707
8	Charlie Hough	1665
9	Gus Weyhing	1570
10	Red Ruffing	1541
11	Roger Clemens	1520
12	Bump Hadley	1442
13	Warren Spahn	1434
14	Earl Whitehill	1431
15	Tony Mullane	1408
16	Sam Jones	1396
17	Jack Morris	1390
	Tom Seaver	1390
19	Gaylord Perry	1379
20	Bobby Witt	1375
21	Mike Torrez	1371
22	Walter Johnson	1363
23	Randy Johnson	1349
24	Don Sutton	1343
25	Chick Fraser	1338
26	Tom Glavine	1337
27	Bob Gibson	1336
28	Chuck Finley	1332
29	Bert Blyleven	1322
30	Sam McDowell	1312
31	Jim Palmer	1311
32	Mark Baldwin	1307
33	Adonis Terry	1298
34	Mickey Welch	1297
35	Burleigh Grimes	1295
36	Mark Langston	1289
37	Kid Nichols	1272
38	Joe Bush	1263
39	Joe Niekro	1262
40	Allie Reynolds	1261
41	Tommy John	1259
42	Frank Tanana	1255
43	Bob Lemon	1251
44	Hal Newhouser	1249
45	George Mullin	1238
46	Tim Keefe	1233
47	Cy Young	1217
48	Red Faber	1213
49	Vic Willis	1212
50	Ted Breitenstein	1207
51	Brickyard Kennedy	1203
52	Jerry Koosman	1198
53	Tommy Bridges	1192
54	John Clarkson	1191
55	Lefty Grove	1187
56	Vida Blue	1185
57	Billy Pierce	1178
58	Dennis Martinez	1165
59	Al Leiter	1163
60	Mike Moore	1156
61	Jack Stivetts	1155
62	Fernando Valenzuela	1151
63	David Cone	1137
64	Bill Hutchison	1132
	Johnny Vander Meer	1132
66	Jerry Reuss	1127
67	Ted Lyons	1121
	Bucky Walters	1121
69	Mel Harder	1118
70	Earl Moore	1108
71	Bob Buhl	1105
72	Luis Tiant	1104
73	Mickey Lolich	1099
74	Lefty Gomez	1095
75	Virgil Trucks	1088
76	Whitey Ford	1086
77	Jim Kaat	1083
78	Eppa Rixey	1082
79	Rick Sutcliffe	1081
80	Eddie Plank	1072
81	Camilo Pascual	1069
82	Bob Turley	1068
83	Hooks Dauss	1067
84	Elton Chamberlain	1065
85	Bert Cunningham	1064
86	Curt Simmons	1063
87	Bill Donovan	1059
88	Murry Dickson	1058
89	Jouett Meekin	1056
90	Vern Kennedy	1049
91	Dizzy Trout	1046
92	Howard Ehmke	1042
93	Wes Ferrell	1040
94	Tommy Byrne	1037
95	Red Ames	1034
	Dave Stewart	1034
	Dave Stieb	1034
	Bob Welch	1034
99	Rube Walberg	1031
100	Jack Powell	1021

Strikeouts

1	Nolan Ryan	5714
2	Roger Clemens	4502
3	Randy Johnson	4372
4	Steve Carlton	4136
5	Bert Blyleven	3701
6	Tom Seaver	3640
7	Don Sutton	3574
8	Gaylord Perry	3534
9	Walter Johnson	3509
10	Phil Niekro	3342
11	Fergie Jenkins	3192
12	Bob Gibson	3117
13	Greg Maddux	3052
14	Pedro Martinez	2861
15	Jim Bunning	2855
16	Mickey Lolich	2832
	Curt Schilling	2832
18	Cy Young	2803
19	Frank Tanana	2773
20	David Cone	2668
21	Chuck Finley	2610
22	Warren Spahn	2583
23	Bob Feller	2581
24	John Smoltz	2567
25	Tim Keefe	2564
26	Jerry Koosman	2556
27	Christy Mathewson	2507
28	Don Drysdale	2486
29	Jack Morris	2478
30	Mark Langston	2464
31	Jim Kaat	2461
32	Sam McDowell	2453
33	Luis Tiant	2416
34	Dennis Eckersley	2401
35	Mike Mussina	2400
36	Kevin Brown	2397
37	Sandy Koufax	2396
38	Charlie Hough	2362
39	Robin Roberts	2357
40	Tom Glavine	2350
41	Early Wynn	2334
42	Rube Waddell	2316
43	Juan Marichal	2303
44	Doc Gooden	2293
45	Lefty Grove	2266
46	Eddie Plank	2246
47	Tommy John	2245
48	Jim Palmer	2212
49	Grover Alexander	2198
50	Vida Blue	2175
51	Camilo Pascual	2167
52	Dennis Martinez	2149
53	Bobo Newsom	2082
54	David Wells	2081
55	Fernando Valenzuela	2074
56	Dazzy Vance	2045
57	Rick Reuschel	2015
58	Orel Hershiser	2014
59	Catfish Hunter	2012
60	Andy Benes	2000
61	Billy Pierce	1999
62	Kevin Appier	1994
63	Red Ruffing	1987
64	John Clarkson	1978
65	Al Leiter	1974
66	Bob Welch	1969
67	Whitey Ford	1956
68	Bobby Witt	1955
69	Amos Rusie	1950
70	Danny Darwin	1942
71	Hideo Nomo	1915
72	Jerry Reuss	1907
73	Jamie Moyer	1884
74	Kid Nichols	1881
75	Mickey Welch	1850
76	Frank Viola	1844
77	Charley Radbourn	1830
78	Tony Mullane	1803
79	Tom Gordon	1802
80	Jim Galvin	1799
81	Hal Newhouser	1796
82	Ron Guidry	1778
83	John Burkett	1766
84	Rudy May	1760
85	Kenny Rogers	1751
86	Joe Niekro	1747
87	Sid Fernandez	1743
88	Dave Stewart	1741
89	Ed Walsh	1736
90	Tom Candiotti	1735
91	Bob Friend	1734
92	Joe Coleman	1728
	Milt Pappas	1728
94	Kevin Gross	1727
95	Floyd Bannister	1723
96	Bret Saberhagen	1715
97	Chief Bender	1711
98	Larry Jackson	1709
99	Jim McCormick	1704
100	Bob Veale	1703

Strikeouts/Game

1	Randy Johnson	10.95
2	Pedro Martinez	10.25
3	Nolan Ryan	9.55
4	Sandy Koufax	9.28
5	Sam McDowell	8.86
6	Curt Schilling	8.77
7	Hideo Nomo	8.74
8	Roger Clemens	8.61
9	Sid Fernandez	8.40
10	J.R. Richard	8.37
11	David Cone	8.28
12	Tom Gordon	8.20
13	Jason Schmidt	8.01
14	Bob Veale	7.96
15	Chan Ho Park	7.89
16	John Smoltz	7.89
17	Jim Maloney	7.81
18	Javier Vazquez	7.77
19	Jose Rijo	7.69
20	Jose DeLeon	7.56
21	Mario Soto	7.54
22	Sam Jones	7.54
23	Mark Langston	7.49
24	Rich Gossage	7.47
25	Al Leiter	7.43
26	Kevin Millwood	7.39
27	Doc Gooden	7.37
28	Chuck Finley	7.35
29	Jeff Fassero	7.29
30	Bob Gibson	7.22
31	Andy Benes	7.18
32	Mike Mussina	7.17
33	Bobby Witt	7.14
34	Steve Carlton	7.13
35	Bartolo Colon	7.10
36	Dave Burba	7.08
37	Shane Reynolds	7.05
38	Rube Waddell	7.04
39	Mickey Lolich	7.01
40	Darryl Kile	6.93
41	Pedro Astacio	6.93
42	Kevin Appier	6.91
43	Rollie Fingers	6.87
44	Tom Seaver	6.85
45	Wilson Alvarez	6.85
46	Jim Bunning	6.83
47	Erik Hanson	6.80
48	Ramon Martinez	6.77
49	Denny Neagle	6.74
50	Juan Pizarro	6.73
51	Bobby Bolin	6.71
52	Bert Blyleven	6.70
53	Ron Guidry	6.69
54	Ray Culp	6.69
55	Stan Williams	6.66
56	Camilo Pascual	6.65
57	Bob Turley	6.65
58	Kevin Brown	6.62
59	Don Wilson	6.60
60	Tug McGraw	6.59
61	Dennis Eckersley	6.58
62	Denny Lemaster	6.57
63	Shawn Estes	6.56
64	Andy Messersmith	6.56
65	Andy Pettitte	6.54
66	Don Drysdale	6.52
67	Todd Stottlemyre	6.52
68	Al Downing	6.50
69	Floyd Bannister	6.49
70	Toad Ramsey	6.49
71	Jon Lieber	6.48
72	Diego Segui	6.46
73	Dean Chance	6.43
74	Hoyt Wilhelm	6.43
75	Mark Gardner	6.41
76	Alex Fernandez	6.40
77	Mike Scott	6.39
78	Fergie Jenkins	6.38
79	Moe Drabowsky	6.37
80	Fernando Valenzuela	6.37
81	Earl Wilson	6.37
82	Harvey Haddix	6.34
83	Sonny Siebert	6.32
84	Chris Short	6.31
85	Bruce Hurst	6.29
86	Pete Harnisch	6.28
87	Bill Singer	6.27
88	Kevin Gross	6.25
89	Woody Williams	6.25
90	Jack McDowell	6.25
91	Tim Wakefield	6.24
92	Luis Tiant	6.24
93	Greg Maddux	6.23
94	Turk Farrell	6.21
95	Greg Swindell	6.21
96	Frank Castillo	6.21
97	Dazzy Vance	6.20
98	Stu Miller	6.19
99	Clay Kirby	6.17
100	Gary Bell	6.15

Earned Run Average

1 Ed Walsh 1.82
2 Addie Joss 1.89
3 Mordecai Brown 2.06
4 John Ward 2.10
5 Christy Mathewson 2.13
6 Rube Waddell 2.16
7 Walter Johnson 2.17
8 Orval Overall 2.23
9 Tommy Bond 2.25
10 Ed Reulbach 2.28
   Will White 2.28
12 Jim Scott 2.30
13 Eddie Plank 2.35
14 Larry Corcoran 2.36
15 Eddie Cicotte 2.38
   Ed Killian 2.38
   George McQuillan 2.38
18 Doc White 2.39
19 Nap Rucker 2.42
20 Terry Larkin 2.43
   Jim McCormick 2.43
   Jeff Tesreau 2.43
23 Chief Bender 2.46
24 Sam Leever 2.47
   Lefty Leifield 2.47
   Hooks Wiltse 2.47
27 Bob Ewing 2.49
   Hippo Vaughn 2.49
29 George Bradley 2.50
30 Hoyt Wilhelm 2.52
31 Noodles Hahn 2.55
32 Grover Alexander 2.56
   Slim Sallee 2.56
34 Deacon Phillippe 2.59
   Frank Smith 2.59
36 Ed Siever 2.60
37 Bob Rhoads 2.61
38 Red Ames 2.63
   Tim Keefe 2.63
   Barney Pelty 2.63
   Vic Willis 2.63
   Cy Young 2.63
43 Claude Hendrix 2.65
   Jack Taylor 2.65
45 Joe McGinnity 2.66
   Dick Rudolph 2.66
47 Nick Altrock 2.67
   Charlie Ferguson 2.67
   Carl Weilman 2.67
50 Jack Chesbro 2.68
   Cy Falkenberg 2.68
   Charley Radbourn 2.68
53 Bill Donovan 2.69
   Fred Toney 2.69
55 Larry Cheney 2.70
56 Mickey Welch 2.71
57 Pedro Martinez 2.72
58 Fred Goldsmith 2.73
59 Harry Howell 2.74
60 Howie Camnitz 2.75
   Whitey Ford 2.75
   Dummy Taylor 2.75
63 Babe Adams 2.76
   Sandy Koufax 2.76
   Dutch Leonard 2.76
66 Jeff Pfeffer 2.77
67 Jack Coombs 2.78
   Earl Moore 2.78
69 Phil Douglas 2.80
   Jesse Tannehill 2.80
71 John Clarkson 2.81
72 Ray Fisher 2.82
   Ed Morris 2.82
   George Mullin 2.82
   Tully Sparks 2.82
76 Bob Caruthers 2.83
77 Dave Foutz 2.84
78 Andy Messersmith 2.86
   Jim Palmer 2.86
   Tom Seaver 2.86
81 Jim Galvin 2.87
   George Winter 2.87
83 Willie Mitchell 2.88
84 Wilbur Cooper 2.89
   Stan Coveleski 2.89
   Juan Marichal 2.89
87 Rollie Fingers 2.90
88 Bob Gibson 2.91
89 Harry Brecheen 2.92
   Dean Chance 2.92
   Doc Crandall 2.92
   Carl Mays 2.92
93 Dave Davenport 2.93
   Guy Hecker 2.93
95 Don Drysdale 2.95
   Jumbo McGinnis 2.95
   Lefty Tyler 2.95
98 Charlie Buffinton 2.96
   Kid Nichols 2.96
100 Mort Cooper 2.97
   Jack Powell 2.97
   Mel Stottlemyre 2.97
   Jim Whitney 2.97

Adjusted Earned Run Average

1 Pedro Martinez 166
2 Lefty Grove 148
3 Walter Johnson 147
4 Hoyt Wilhelm 146
5 Ed Walsh 145
6 Randy Johnson 144
7 Roger Clemens 143
8 Addie Joss 142
9 Kid Nichols 139
10 Greg Maddux 138
   Cy Young 138
12 Mordecai Brown 137
13 Christy Mathewson ...136
14 Grover Alexander 135
   Rube Waddell 135
16 John Clarkson 134
17 Harry Brecheen 133
   Whitey Ford 133
   Noodles Hahn 133
20 Sandy Koufax 131
21 Dizzy Dean 130
   Carl Hubbell 130
   Hal Newhouser 130
   Amos Rusie 130
25 Kevin Brown 128
   Curt Schilling 128
   Tom Seaver 128
29 Nig Cuppy 127
   Bob Gibson 127
   Sal Maglie 127
   John Smoltz 127
33 Tommy Bridges 126
   Rich Gossage 126
   Jim Palmer 126
   Bret Saberhagen 126
37 Lefty Gomez 125
   Tim Keefe 125
   Max Lanier 125
   Mike Mussina 125
   Mel Parnell 125
   John Tudor 125
   Dazzy Vance 125
44 Dave Foutz 124
   Urban Shocker 124
   Dizzy Trout 124
47 Bob Caruthers 123
   Eddie Cicotte 123
   Mort Cooper 123
   Larry Corcoran 123
   Sam Leever 123
   Orval Overall 123
   Dave Stieb 123
54 Kevin Appier 122
   Bob Feller 122
   Charlie Ferguson 122
   Jimmy Key 122
   Silver King 122
   Juan Marichal 122
   Eddie Plank 122
   Ed Reulbach 122
   Eddie Rommel 122
63 Don Drysdale 121
   Clark Griffith 121
   Andy Messersmith 121
   Jose Rijo 121
   Jack Stivetts 121
68 Tiny Bonham 120
   David Cone 120
   Rollie Fingers 120
   Tom Glavine 120
   Ron Guidry 120
   Joe McGinnity 120
   Andy Pettitte 120
   Deacon Phillippe 120
   Charley Radbourn 120
   Jim Scott 120
   Hippo Vaughn 120
   Will White 120
80 Dean Chance 119
   Red Faber 119
   Thornton Lee 119
   Bob Lemon 119
   Dutch Leonard 119
   Carl Mays 119
   Billy Pierce 119
   Nap Rucker 119
   Bobby Shantz 119
   Lon Warneke 119
90 Babe Adams 118
   Bert Blyleven 118
   Bartolo Colon 118
   Ted Lyons 118
   Sadie McMahon 118
   Tony Mullane 118
   Warren Spahn 118
   Bob Stanley 118
   John Ward 118
   Vic Willis 118
100 10 players tied 117

Adjusted ERA by era

1988-2005

1 Pedro Martinez 166
2 Randy Johnson 144
3 Roger Clemens 143
4 Greg Maddux 138
5 Kevin Brown 128
   Curt Schilling 128
7 John Smoltz 127
8 Bret Saberhagen 126
9 Mike Mussina 125
10 Kevin Appier 122
   Jimmy Key 122

1973-1987

1 Tom Seaver 128
2 Rich Gossage 126
   Jim Palmer 126
4 John Tudor 125
5 Dave Stieb 123
6 Andy Messersmith 121
7 Rollie Fingers 120
   Ron Guidry 120
9 Bert Blyleven 118
   Bob Stanley 118

1961-1972

1 Sandy Koufax 131
2 Bob Gibson 127
3 Juan Marichal 122
4 Don Drysdale 121
5 Dean Chance 119
6 Gary Nolan 116
7 Jim Maloney 115
8 Jim Bunning 114
   Bill Hands 114
10 Larry Jackson 113
   Sam McDowell 113
   Mel Stottlemyre 113
   Bob Veale 113

1943-1960

1 Hoyt Wilhelm 146
2 Harry Brecheen 133
   Whitey Ford 133
4 Hal Newhouser 130
5 Sal Maglie 127
6 Max Lanier 125
   Mel Parnell 125
8 Dizzy Trout 124
9 Bob Feller 122
10 Tiny Bonham 120

1921-1942

1 Lefty Grove 148
2 Dizzy Dean 130
   Carl Hubbell 130
4 Stan Coveleski 128
5 Tommy Bridges 126
6 Lefty Gomez 125
   Dazzy Vance 125
8 Urban Shocker 124
9 Mort Cooper 123
10 Eddie Rommel 122

1901-1920

1 Walter Johnson 147
2 Ed Walsh 145
3 Addie Joss 142
4 Cy Young 138
5 Mordecai Brown 137
6 Christy Mathewson ...136
7 Grover Alexander 135
   Rube Waddell 135
9 Noodles Hahn 133
10 Eddie Cicotte 123
   Sam Leever 123
   Orval Overall 123

1893-1900

1 Kid Nichols 139
2 Amos Rusie 130
3 Nig Cuppy 127
4 Clark Griffith 121
5 Frank Dwyer 115
6 Billy Rhines 114
7 Ted Breitenstein 109
   Nixey Callahan 109
   Frank Killen 109
10 Pink Hawley 107
   Win Mercer 107

1876-1892

1 John Clarkson 134
2 Tim Keefe 125
3 Dave Foutz 124
4 Bob Caruthers 123
   Larry Corcoran 123
6 Charlie Ferguson 122
   Silver King 122
8 Jack Stivetts 121
9 Charley Radbourn 120
   Will White 120

Opponent Batting Average

1 Nolan Ryan 204
2 Sandy Koufax 205
3 Pedro Martinez 208
4 Sid Fernandez 209
5 Andy Messersmith 212
   J.R. Richard 212
7 Randy Johnson 215
   Sam McDowell 215
9 Hoyt Wilhelm 216
10 Ed Walsh 218
11 Mario Soto 220
   Bob Turley 220
13 Addie Joss 223
   Orval Overall 223
   Jeff Tesreau 223
16 Jose DeLeon 224
   Jim Maloney 224
   Ed Reulbach 224
19 Larry Corcoran 226
   Tim Keefe 226
   Tom Seaver 226
22 Walter Johnson 227
23 Bob Gibson 228
   Rich Gossage 228
   Rube Waddell 228
   Don Wilson 228
27 Roger Clemens 229
28 Sam Jones 230
   Jim Palmer 230
30 Bobby Bolin 231
   Bob Feller 231
   Catfish Hunter 231
33 David Cone 232
   Al Downing 232
   Johnny Vander Meer .232
   Stan Williams 232
37 Mordecai Brown 233
   Charlie Ferguson 233
   Charlie Hough 233
   John Smoltz 233
41 Dean Chance 234
   Larry Cheney 234
   Denny McLain 234
   Toad Ramsey 234
   Amos Rusie 234
   John Ward 234
47 Ray Culp 235
   Rollie Fingers 235
   Whitey Ford 235
   Dave Foutz 235
   Ed Morris 235
   Tony Mullane 235
53 Moe Drabowsky 236
   Christy Mathewson ...236
   Don Sutton 236
   Luis Tiant 236
   Bob Veale 236
58 Vida Blue 237
   Juan Marichal 237
   Tug McGraw 237
   Juan Pizarro 237
   Frank Smith 237
63 Tom Gordon 238
   Rudy May 238
   Allie Reynolds 238
   Jim Scott 238
   Sonny Siebert 238
68 Gary Bell 239
   Chief Bender 239
   Bill Donovan 239
   Don Drysdale 239
   Ramon Martinez 239
   Hal Newhouser 239
   Gary Nolan 239
   Hideo Nomo 239
   Barney Pelty 239
   Eddie Plank 239
   Curt Schilling 239
   Dupee Shaw 239
   Dave Stieb 239
   Will White 239
82 Steve Carlton 240
   Bob Caruthers 240
   John Clarkson 240
   Mort Cooper 240
   Billy Pierce 240
   Mike Scott 240
   Bill Singer 240
   Virgil Trucks 240
90 Jack Coombs 241
   Kirby Higbe 241
   Bob Lemon 241
   George McQuillan 241
   Earl Moore 241
   Charley Radbourn 241
   Hooks Wiltse 241
97 10 players tied 242

Opponent On-Base Pct.

1 John Ward 254
2 Addie Joss 260
3 George Bradley 262
4 Terry Larkin 263
5 Larry Corcoran 264
   Ed Walsh 264
7 Tommy Bond 265
   Will White 265
9 Pedro Martinez 269
10 Charlie Ferguson 270
11 Christy Mathewson ..271
   Ed Morris 271
13 Jim McCormick 273
14 Fred Goldsmith 274
   Tim Keefe 274
   Sandy Koufax 274
   Jim Whitney 274
18 Juan Marichal 276
19 Mordecai Brown 277
   Charley Radbourn 277
21 Walter Johnson 278
   Dupee Shaw 278
23 Guy Hecker 280
   Jumbo McGinnis 280
25 Deacon Phillippe 281
   Tom Seaver 281
27 Babe Adams 282
   Jim Galvin 282
   Curt Schilling 283
30 Bob Caruthers 284
   Catfish Hunter 284
   Bobby Mathews 284
   Gary Nolan 284
34 Sid Fernandez 285
   Dave Foutz 285
   Don Sutton 285
37 Fergie Jenkins 286
   Andy Messersmith ...286
   Cy Young 286
40 Grover Alexander 287
   Rube Waddell 287
   Hoyt Wilhelm 287
43 Tiny Bonham 288
   Henry Boyle 288
   Noodles Hahn 288
   Jack Lynch 288
   Greg Maddux 288
   Bret Saberhagen 288
49 Dennis Eckersley 290
   Denny McLain 290
   Hooks Wiltse 290
52 Nick Altrock 291
   John Clarkson 291
   Carl Hubbell 291
   John Smoltz 291
56 Chief Bender 292
   Charlie Buffinton 292
   Rollie Fingers 292
   Ron Guidry 292
   Robin Roberts 292
   Mickey Welch 292
   Doc White 292
63 Don Drysdale 293
   Sam Leever 293
   Eddie Plank 293
66 Roger Clemens 294
   George McQuillan 294
   Mike Mussina 294
   Jim Palmer 294
   Mario Soto 294
   Ralph Terry 294
72 John Candelaria 295
   Randy Johnson 295
   Toad Ramsey 295
   Jeff Tesreau 295
76 Gaylord Perry 296
   Warren Spahn 296
78 Jim Bunning 297
   Jack Chesbro 297
   Eddie Cicotte 297
   Mike Cuellar 297
   Eddie Fisher 297
   Bob Gibson 297
   Don Mossi 297
   Mike Scott 297
   Frank Smith 297
   Jack Taylor 297
   Luis Tiant 297
   George Winter 297
90 Harry Brecheen 298
   Dizzy Dean 298
   Tony Mullane 298
   Don Newcombe 298
   Orval Overall 298
   Fritz Peterson 298
   Lee Richmond 298
   Dick Rudolph 298
98 Joe Horlen 299
   Ed Reulbach 299
   Slim Sallee 299
   John Tudor 299
   Don Wilson 299

Adjusted Pitching Wins

#	Player	
1	Cy Young	77.8
2	Walter Johnson	70.8
3	Roger Clemens	70.1
4	Lefty Grove	60.8
5	Greg Maddux	55.7
6	Kid Nichols	55.1
7	Grover Alexander	55.0
8	Randy Johnson	51.3
9	Pedro Martinez	50.8
10	Tom Seaver	46.8
11	Christy Mathewson	41.3
12	John Clarkson	39.6
13	Warren Spahn	38.2
14	Carl Hubbell	38.2
15	Bob Gibson	36.8
16	Jim Palmer	35.5
17	Whitey Ford	34.6
18	Bert Blyleven	34.2
19	Amos Rusie	33.9
20	Tim Keefe	33.1
21	Bob Feller	32.3
22	Gaylord Perry	32.3
23	Tom Glavine	32.0
24	Curt Schilling	31.6
25	Kevin Brown	31.3
26	Mike Mussina	30.1
27	Ed Walsh	30.0
28	Hal Newhouser	29.7
29	John Smoltz	29.3
30	Eddie Plank	29.1
31	Hoyt Wilhelm	28.8
32	Dazzy Vance	28.5
33	Charley Radbourn	27.8
34	Mordecai Brown	27.7
35	Steve Carlton	27.3
36	Ted Lyons	27.3
37	Phil Niekro	27.2
38	Robin Roberts	27.2
39	Stan Coveleski	27.0
40	Tommy Bridges	26.8
41	Fergie Jenkins	26.5
42	Bret Saberhagen	26.4
43	Sandy Koufax	25.9
44	Juan Marichal	25.8
45	Don Drysdale	25.2
46	Billy Pierce	24.6
47	Red Faber	24.6
48	Nolan Ryan	24.5
49	Rube Waddell	24.4
50	Eppa Rixey	23.7
51	Dave Stieb	23.7
52	Tony Mullane	23.5
53	Lefty Gomez	23.4
54	Clark Griffith	23.3
55	Urban Shocker	23.1
56	David Cone	23.0
57	Addie Joss	22.9
58	Kevin Appier	22.5
59	Silver King	22.3
60	Dennis Eckersley	21.9
61	Jimmy Key	21.6
62	Harry Brecheen	21.5
63	Eddie Cicotte	21.5
64	Vic Willis	21.4
65	Dizzy Trout	21.3
66	Jim Bunning	21.0
67	Dolf Luque	20.8
68	Joe McGinnity	20.7
69	Dutch Leonard	20.6
70	Eddie Rommel	20.5
71	Dizzy Dean	19.9
72	Bob Lemon	19.7
73	Carl Mays	19.6
74	Don Sutton	19.4
75	Bob Caruthers	19.4
76	Mariano Rivera	19.4
77	Luis Tiant	19.4
78	Jim McCormick	19.4
79	Chuck Finley	19.3
80	Red Ruffing	19.2
81	Mickey Welch	19.1
82	Nig Cuppy	19.1
83	Lon Warneke	19.0
84	Ron Guidry	19.0
85	Rick Reuschel	18.7
86	Tim Hudson	18.7
87	Noodles Hahn	18.1
88	Jack Stivetts	18.1
89	Babe Adams	17.9
90	Sam Leever	17.7
91	Virgil Trucks	17.6
92	Wes Ferrell	17.5
93	Waite Hoyt	17.5
94	Bucky Walters	17.2
95	Tommy John	17.1
96	Ed Reulbach	17.0
97	Will White	16.9
98	Sal Maglie	16.9
99	Wilbur Cooper	16.8
100	Steve Rogers	16.7

Relief Wins

1	Hoyt Wilhelm	124
2	Lindy McDaniel	119
3	Rich Gossage	115
4	Rollie Fingers	107
5	Sparky Lyle	99
6	Roy Face	96
7	Gene Garber	94
	Kent Tekulve	94
9	Mike Marshall	92
10	John Franco	90
	Don McMahon	90
12	Tug McGraw	89
13	Clay Carroll	88
14	Jesse Orosco	87
15	Pedro Borbon	85
	Bob Stanley	85
17	Bill Campbell	80
	Gary Lavelle	80
19	Tom Burgmeier	79
	Stu Miller	79
	Ron Perranoski	79
22	Johnny Murphy	73
	Jeff Reardon	73
24	John Hiller	72
25	Mark Clear	71
	Dick Hall	71
	Lee Smith	71
28	Willie Hernandez	70
	Roger McDowell	70
30	Bruce Sutter	68
31	Doug Jones	66
32	Steve Bedrosian	65
33	Al Hrabosky	64
34	Roberto Hernandez	63
	Darold Knowles	63
	Clem Labine	63
	Dave LaRoche	63
	Eric Plunk	63
39	Jim Brewer	62
	Turk Farrell	62
	Eddie Fisher	62
	Grant Jackson	62
	Paul Lindblad	62
	Frank Linzy	62
	Dan Plesac	62
	Mike Timlin	62
47	Paul Assenmacher	61
	Mike Jackson	61
49	Joe Heving	60
	Mike Stanton	60

Relief Losses

1	Gene Garber	108
2	Hoyt Wilhelm	103
3	Rollie Fingers	101
4	Mike Marshall	98
5	Kent Tekulve	90
6	Lindy McDaniel	88
7	John Franco	87
	Lee Smith	87
9	Rich Gossage	85
10	Roy Face	82
11	Doug Jones	78
	Jesse Orosco	78
13	Jeff Reardon	77
14	Sparky Lyle	76
15	Gary Lavelle	75
16	Ron Perranoski	74
17	Darold Knowles	71
	Bruce Sutter	71
19	Roger McDowell	69
	Tug McGraw	69
21	Stu Miller	67
	Dan Plesac	67
23	Clay Carroll	66
	Don McMahon	66
25	Bill Campbell	65
	Roberto Hernandez	65
27	Mike Jackson	63
28	Greg Minton	62
29	Steve Bedrosian	61
	Jose Mesa	61
	Bob Stanley	61
32	Mike Timlin	60
33	John Hiller	58
34	Frank Linzy	57
	Randy Myers	57
36	Mitch Williams	56
37	Willie Hernandez	55
38	Craig Lefferts	54
39	Pedro Borbon	53
	Tom Burgmeier	53
	Ron Davis	53
	Greg Harris	53
	Trevor Hoffman	53
	Dave Smith	53
	Mike Stanton	53
46	Rick Aguilera	52
	Jim Kern	52
	Randy Moffitt	52
	Dave Righetti	52
	Todd Worrell	52

Relief Games

#	Player	
1	Jesse Orosco	1248
2	John Franco	1119
3	Dan Plesac	1050
	Kent Tekulve	1050
5	Mike Stanton	1026
6	Hoyt Wilhelm	1018
7	Lee Smith	1016
8	Mike Jackson	998
9	Rich Gossage	965
10	Gene Garber	922
11	Lindy McDaniel	913
12	Rollie Fingers	907
13	Sparky Lyle	899
14	Roberto Hernandez	889
	Mike Timlin	889
16	Paul Assenmacher	883
17	Jeff Reardon	880
18	Don McMahon	872
19	Doug Jones	842
20	Steve Reed	833
21	Roy Face	821
22	Todd Jones	811
23	Jose Mesa	792
	Jeff Nelson	792
25	Tug McGraw	785
26	Paul Quantrill	777
27	Buddy Groom	771
28	Darold Knowles	757
29	Trevor Hoffman	756
30	Tom Burgmeier	742
	Gary Lavelle	742
32	Ron Perranoski	736
33	Willie Hernandez	733
34	Mark Guthrie	722
35	Roger McDowell	721
36	Randy Myers	716
37	Eddie Guardado	713
38	Dennis Eckersley	710
39	Rod Beck	704
40	Clay Carroll	703
	Greg Minton	703
42	Mike Marshall	699
	Jeff Montgomery	699
44	Larry Andersen	698
45	Bob Wickman	693
46	Bill Campbell	691
47	Steve Bedrosian	686
48	Dan Quisenberry	674
49	Eric Plunk	673
50	Bruce Sutter	661

Relief Innings Pitched

#	Player	
1	Hoyt Wilhelm	1871.0
2	Lindy McDaniel	1694.0
3	Rich Gossage	1556.2
4	Rollie Fingers	1500.1
5	Gene Garber	1452.2
6	Kent Tekulve	1436.2
7	Sparky Lyle	1390.1
8	Tug McGraw	1301.1
9	Don McMahon	1297.0
10	Pedro Borbon	1287.1
11	Jesse Orosco	1277.0
12	Mike Marshall	1259.1
13	Lee Smith	1252.1
14	Tom Burgmeier	1248.2
15	John Franco	1245.2
16	Roy Face	1212.1
17	Clay Carroll	1204.2
18	Eddie Fisher	1186.0
19	Bill Campbell	1177.1
20	Ron Perranoski	1170.2
21	Bob Stanley	1159.0
22	Mike Jackson	1154.2
23	Jeff Reardon	1132.1
24	Doug Jones	1097.1
25	Stu Miller	1094.2
26	Greg Minton	1087.1
27	Gary Lavelle	1077.2
28	Darold Knowles	1052.1
29	Paul Lindblad	1043.1
	Dan Quisenberry	1043.1
31	Bruce Sutter	1042.0
32	Johnny Klippstein	1040.2
33	Roger McDowell	1039.2
34	Mike Timlin	1016.2
35	Dan Plesac	1003.0
36	Willie Hernandez	994.1
37	Bob Miller	992.2
38	Larry Andersen	990.2
39	Mike Stanton	984.2
40	Dave LaRoche	976.0
41	Ted Abernathy	970.0
42	John Hiller	962.2
43	Roberto Hernandez	950.0
44	Steve Bedrosian	931.0
45	Greg Harris	922.1
46	Eric Plunk	920.0
47	Elias Sosa	905.0
48	Dale Murray	901.1
49	Todd Jones	900.2
50	Paul Quantrill	896.1

Adjusted Reliever Runs

#	Player	
1	Hoyt Wilhelm	252
2	Mariano Rivera	213
3	Rich Gossage	185
4	Dan Quisenberry	148
5	John Franco	145
6	Kent Tekulve	143
7	Lee Smith	138
8	John Wetteland	135
9	Billy Wagner	134
10	Roberto Hernandez	133
11	Tom Henke	132
12	Rollie Fingers	131
13	Trevor Hoffman	128
14	Mark Eichhorn	127
15	Keith Foulke	124
	Mike Jackson	124
	Jesse Orosco	124
18	Sparky Lyle	123
19	Doug Jones	121
20	Paul Quantrill	117
	Bob Stanley	117
22	Tug McGraw	116
23	Mike Timlin	115
24	Dennis Eckersley	112
	Bruce Sutter	112
26	Armando Benitez	111
	John Hiller	111
	Jeff Montgomery	111
29	Troy Percival	108
30	Lindy McDaniel	107
31	Mike Marshall	105
32	Bob Wickman	103
33	Tom Gordon	102
34	Robb Nen	100
	Steve Reed	100
36	Clay Carroll	99
37	Jeff Nelson	98
38	Gary Lavelle	97
39	Rick Aguilera	94
40	Ellis Kinder	93
41	Greg Harris	92
42	Gene Garber	88
	Ron Perranoski	88
44	Jeff Reardon	87
45	Tom Burgmeier	86
	Willie Hernandez	86
	Don McMahon	86
48	Stu Miller	85
49	Shigetoshi Hasegawa	84
	Eric Plunk	84

Relief Ranking

#	Player	
1	Mariano Rivera	379
2	Hoyt Wilhelm	366
3	Rich Gossage	318
4	John Franco	263
5	John Wetteland	251
6	Roberto Hernandez	249
7	Trevor Hoffman	244
8	Lee Smith	223
9	Dan Quisenberry	219
10	Rollie Fingers	218
11	Tom Henke	214
12	Billy Wagner	212
13	Robb Nen	205
	Kent Tekulve	205
15	Doug Jones	194
16	Sparky Lyle	190
17	Dennis Eckersley	189
18	Mike Marshall	187
19	Jesse Orosco	183
20	John Hiller	181
21	Rick Aguilera	178
22	Jeff Montgomery	175
	Bruce Sutter	175
24	Troy Percival	168
25	Tug McGraw	167
26	Armando Benitez	164
	Keith Foulke	164
28	Bob Stanley	158
29	Mike Timlin	155
30	Ellis Kinder	154
	Ron Perranoski	154
32	Bob Wickman	153
33	Tom Gordon	150
34	Mike Jackson	148
35	Gary Lavelle	147
36	Lindy McDaniel	145
37	Stu Miller	141
38	Mark Eichhorn	138
39	Roy Face	137
40	Gregg Olson	135
	Dan Plesac	135
	Jeff Reardon	135
43	Randy Myers	134
	Paul Quantrill	134
45	Mike Henneman	133
46	Gene Garber	129
	Dave Righetti	129
48	Clay Carroll	128
49	Jeff Shaw	126
	Ugueth Urbina	126

Pitcher Wins by era

1988-2005

#	Player	
1	Roger Clemens	70.4
2	Greg Maddux	63.9
3	Pedro Martinez	50.2
4	Randy Johnson	49.1
5	Tom Glavine	39.9
6	Mariano Rivera	36.6
7	John Smoltz	33.6
8	Kevin Brown	32.8
9	Mike Mussina	32.5
10	Curt Schilling	28.8

1973-1987

#	Player	
1	Tom Seaver	49.1
2	Jim Palmer	34.3
3	Steve Carlton	33.2
4	Gaylord Perry	32.8
5	Bert Blyleven	31.1
6	Fergie Jenkins	30.3
7	Dennis Eckersley	29.8
8	Rich Gossage	29.5
9	Phil Niekro	29.2
10	Dave Stieb	25.1

1961-1972

1	Bob Gibson	44.9
2	Don Drysdale	32.4
3	Juan Marichal	27.5
4	Sandy Koufax	22.3
5	Jim Bunning	16.4
6	Jim Kaat	16.1
	Mel Stottlemyre	16.1
8	Larry Jackson	16.0
9	Ron Perranoski	14.9
10	Wilbur Wood	14.8

1943-1960

1	Warren Spahn	51.4
2	Whitey Ford	37.2
	Hal Newhouser	37.2
4	Hoyt Wilhelm	37.1
5	Bob Lemon	34.2
6	Bob Feller	31.6
7	Robin Roberts	30.3
8	Dizzy Trout	29.7
9	Billy Pierce	25.6
10	Harry Brecheen	24.9

1921-1942

1	Lefty Grove	59.1
2	Carl Hubbell	40.2
3	Ted Lyons	33.5
4	Red Ruffing	31.4
5	Wes Ferrell	31.1
6	Dazzy Vance	29.2
7	Tommy Bridges	27.3
8	Urban Shocker	27.0
9	Bucky Walters	26.7
10	Dolf Luque	26.2

1901-1920

1	Walter Johnson	89.9
2	Cy Young	77.0
3	Grover Alexander	62.9
4	Christy Mathewson	56.3
5	Ed Walsh	37.7
6	Mordecai Brown	32.7
7	Carl Mays	31.7
8	Eddie Plank	30.3
9	Eddie Cicotte	24.3
10	Addie Joss	23.0

1893-1900

1	Kid Nichols	56.2
2	Amos Rusie	36.7
3	Clark Griffith	28.3
4	Nig Cuppy	20.4
5	Frank Dwyer	13.6
6	Ted Breitenstein	10.9
	Frank Killen	10.9
8	Nixey Callahan	9.3
9	Pink Hawley	8.3
10	Win Mercer	8.0

1876-1892

1	John Clarkson	42.5
2	Tim Keefe	35.6
3	Charley Radbourn	31.5
4	Tony Mullane	30.2
5	Bob Caruthers	30.0
6	Jack Stivetts	25.1
7	Silver King	23.0
8	Guy Hecker	22.5
9	Jim McCormick	21.1
10	Charlie Buffinton	19.6

Pitcher Wins

1 Walter Johnson 89.9
2 Cy Young 77.0
3 Roger Clemens 70.4
4 Greg Maddux 63.9
5 Grover Alexander 62.9
6 Lefty Grove 59.1
7 Christy Mathewson 56.3
8 Kid Nichols 56.2
9 Warren Spahn 51.4
10 Pedro Martinez 50.2
11 Randy Johnson 49.1
   Tom Seaver 49.1
13 Bob Gibson 44.9
14 John Clarkson 42.5
15 Carl Hubbell 40.2
16 Tom Glavine 39.9
17 Ed Walsh 37.7
18 Whitey Ford 37.2
   Hal Newhouser 37.2
20 Hoyt Wilhelm 37.1
21 Amos Rusie 36.7
22 Mariano Rivera 36.6
23 Tim Keefe 35.6
24 Jim Palmer 34.3
25 Bob Lemon 34.2
26 John Smoltz 33.6
27 Ted Lyons 33.5
28 Steve Carlton 33.2
29 Kevin Brown 32.8
   Gaylord Perry 32.8
31 Mordecai Brown 32.7
32 Mike Mussina 32.5
33 Don Drysdale 32.4
34 Carl Mays 31.7
35 Bob Feller 31.6
36 Charley Radbourn 31.5
37 Red Ruffing 31.4
38 Bert Blyleven 31.1
   Wes Ferrell 31.1
40 Fergie Jenkins 30.3
   Eddie Plank 30.3
   Robin Roberts 30.3
43 Tony Mullane 30.2
44 Bob Caruthers 30.0
45 Dennis Eckersley 29.8
46 Dizzy Trout 29.7
47 Rich Gossage 29.5
48 Phil Niekro 29.2
   Dazzy Vance 29.2
50 Curt Schilling 28.8
51 Clark Griffith 28.3
52 Bret Saberhagen 27.8
53 Juan Marichal 27.5
54 Tommy Bridges 27.3
55 Urban Shocker 27.0
56 Bucky Walters 26.7
57 Dolf Luque 26.2
58 Stan Coveleski 26.0
59 John Franco 25.8
60 Billy Pierce 25.6
61 Dave Stieb 25.1
   Jack Stivetts 25.1
63 Harry Brecheen 24.9
64 Eddie Cicotte 24.3
65 Eppa Rixey 24.2
66 Dan Quisenberry 23.6
67 Red Faber 23.3
   Trevor Hoffman 23.3
69 David Cone 23.1
70 Roberto Hernandez 23.0
   Addie Joss 23.0
   Silver King 23.0
   Eddie Rommel 23.0
74 Jimmy Key 22.8
75 Rollie Fingers 22.7
76 Lon Warneke 22.6
77 Guy Hecker 22.5
   Rick Reuschel 22.5
79 Lee Smith 22.4
80 Dizzy Dean 22.3
   Sandy Koufax 22.3
82 Dutch Leonard 22.2
   Rube Waddell 22.2
84 Tom Henke 21.5
   Red Lucas 21.5
   Nolan Ryan 21.5
   Luis Tiant 21.5
88 Billy Wagner 21.4
   Joe Wood 21.4
90 Jim McCormick 21.1
91 Kent Tekulve 20.9
92 John Hiller 20.7
   John Wetteland 20.7
94 Nig Cuppy 20.4
95 Jesse Tannehill 20.2
96 Lefty Gomez 20.1
   Tommy John 20.1
98 Vic Willis 20.0
99 Ron Guidry 19.9
100 Wilbur Cooper 19.7

Pitcher Wins

101 Kevin Appier 19.6
   Charlie Buffinton 19.6
103 Early Wynn 19.5
104 Jack Quinn 19.4
105 Chuck Finley 19.3
   Doug Jones 19.3
107 Mike Marshall 19.2
108 Spud Chandler 19.1
   Sparky Lyle 19.1
110 Freddie Fitzsimmons....19.0
111 Orel Hershiser 18.9
   Joe McGinnity 18.9
   Robb Nen 18.9
   Mickey Welch 18.9
115 Andy Pettitte 18.8
   Schoolboy Rowe 18.8
   Doc White 18.8
118 Bobby Shantz 18.7
119 Ed Lopat 18.6
   Don Newcombe 18.6
121 Burleigh Grimes 18.3
   Tim Hudson 18.3
   Jesse Orosco 18.3
124 Curt Davis 18.2
125 Bruce Sutter 17.9
126 Babe Adams 17.7
   Doc Gooden 17.7
128 Andy Messersmith 17.5
129 Ed Reulbach 17.3
130 Dave Foutz 17.2
   Jeff Montgomery 17.2
132 Noodles Hahn 17.0
   Mel Harder 17.0
   Babe Ruth 17.0
135 Rick Aguilera 16.8
   Larry French 16.8
   Don Sutton 16.8
   Virgil Trucks 16.8
139 Bob Shawkey 16.7
140 Jim Bunning 16.4
   Tom Gordon 16.4
142 Hippo Vaughn 16.3
143 John Candelaria 16.2
   Murry Dickson 16.2
145 Jim Kaat 16.1
   Sam Leever 16.1
   Mel Stottlemyre 16.1
   John Tudor 16.1
149 Larry Jackson 16.0
150 George Uhle 15.9
151 Armando Benitez 15.8
   Thornton Lee 15.8
153 Mike Garcia 15.7
   Waite Hoyt 15.7
   Max Lanier 15.7
   Jack Taylor 15.7
157 Roy Oswalt 15.6
   Deacon Phillippe 15.6
159 Mel Parnell 15.5
   Troy Percival 15.5
   Nap Rucker 15.5
162 Johnny Antonelli 15.4
   Keith Foulke 15.4
   Frank Viola 15.4
165 Stu Miller 15.3
166 Ned Garver 15.2
   Hal Schumacher 15.2
   Mike Timlin 15.2
169 Chief Bender 14.9
   Ellis Kinder 14.9
   Claude Passeau 14.9
   Ron Perranoski 14.9
173 Steve Rogers 14.8
   Bob Stanley 14.8
   Wilbur Wood 14.8
176 Jerry Koosman 14.6
   Randy Myers 14.6
178 Bartolo Colon 14.5
179 David Wells 14.4
   Barry Zito 14.4
181 Mort Cooper 14.3
   Charlie Ferguson 14.3
   Claude Hendrix 14.3
184 Mark Eichhorn 14.1
   Tug McGraw 14.1
186 Gregg Olson 14.0
187 Mike Jackson 13.9
188 Sal Maglie 13.8
   Dave Righetti 13.8
190 Fred Hutchinson 13.7
   Derek Lowe 13.7
   Firpo Marberry 13.7
   Jose Rijo 13.7
194 Frank Dwyer 13.6
   Jim Maloney 13.6
   Brad Radke 13.6
197 Jeff Reardon 13.5
   Kenny Rogers 13.5
   Charlie Root 13.5
200 Gary Lavelle 13.4

Pitcher Wins

   Claude Osteen 13.4
202 Roy Face 13.2
   Gene Garber 13.2
204 Mike Hampton 13.1
   Johan Santana 13.1
206 Sadie McMahon 13.0
   John Ward 13.0
208 Mark Buehrle 12.9
   Milt Pappas 12.9
210 Vida Blue 12.8
   Will White 12.8
   Bob Wickman 12.8
213 Lindy McDaniel 12.6
   Orval Overall 12.6
   Gary Peters 12.6
216 Larry Corcoran 12.5
   Willie Hernandez 12.5
   Harry Howell 12.5
219 Frank Lary 12.4
220 Howie Pollet 12.3
221 Steve Farr 12.2
   Jeff Pfeffer 12.2
   Jake Weimer 12.2
224 Mike Henneman 12.1
   Van Mungo 12.1
   Dan Plesac 12.1
   Ugueth Urbina 12.1
228 Frank Tanana 12.0
   Jim Whitney 12.0
230 Clay Carroll 11.9
   Alex Fernandez 11.9
   George Mullin 11.9
233 Charlie Hough 11.7
   Frank Linzy 11.7
235 Tom Burgmeier 11.5
   Bryan Harvey 11.5
237 Harvey Haddix 11.4
   Jon Matlack 11.4
   Dick Radatz 11.4
   Jim Tobin 11.4
241 Bill Hutchison 11.3
242 Jim Devlin 11.2
   Mark Langston 11.2
   Al Leiter 11.2
   Johnny Sain 11.2
246 Jim Perry 11.1
   Curt Simmons 11.1
248 Jack Chesbro 11.0
   Hooks Wiltse 11.0
250 Ted Breitenstein 10.9
   Frank Killen 10.9
   Don McMahon 10.9
253 Tiny Bonham 10.8
   Jeff Nelson 10.8
   Dave Smith 10.8
256 Ray Kremer 10.7
   Mark Mulder 10.7
258 Jim Brewer 10.6
   Roy Halladay 10.6
   Tom Zachary 10.6
261 Teddy Higuera 10.5
   Johnny Murphy 10.5
263 Eric Gagne 10.4
   Tex Hughson 10.4
265 Rod Beck 10.3
   Al Brazle 10.3
   Dennis Martinez 10.3
   Greg Minton 10.3
   Todd Worrell 10.3
270 Ewell Blackwell 10.2
   Dutch Ruether 10.2
   Slim Sallee 10.2
   Jeff Shaw 10.2
274 Jay Howell 10.1
   Lefty Leifield 10.1
276 Bob Ewing 10.0
   Jim Kern 10.0
278 Camilo Pascual 9.9
   Monte Pearson 9.9
280 Jim Galvin 9.8
   Jason Isringhausen ...9.8
   Jack McDowell 9.8
   Ed Morris 9.8
284 Elton Chamberlain 9.7
   Al Orth 9.7
   Fritz Ostermueller 9.7
   Sherry Smith 9.7
288 Francisco Cordero 9.6
   Joe Dobson 9.6
290 Jim Bagby 9.5
   Dean Chance 9.5
   Russ Ford 9.5
   Terry Forster 9.5
   Dutch Leonard 9.5
   Sam McDowell 9.5
   Bob Rush 9.5
   Carlos Zambrano 9.5
298 5 players tied 9.4

Player Overall Wins by era

1988-2005

1 Barry Bonds 123.6
2 Rickey Henderson 72.1
3 Roger Clemens 70.4
4 Greg Maddux 63.9
5 Jeff Bagwell 54.0
6 Alex Rodriguez 51.5
7 Wade Boggs 50.6
8 Pedro Martinez 50.2
9 Randy Johnson 49.1
10 Ken Griffey Jr. 48.5
   Frank Thomas 48.5
12 Edgar Martinez 45.1
13 Cal Ripken 44.1
14 Barry Larkin 42.9
15 Gary Sheffield 42.6
16 Mike Piazza 42.2
17 Ivan Rodriguez 40.0
18 Tom Glavine 39.9
19 Tim Raines 38.8
20 Tony Gwynn 38.5
21 Paul Molitor 37.8
22 Roberto Alomar 37.0
23 Ryne Sandberg 36.7
24 Mariano Rivera 36.6
   Jim Edmonds 36.6

1973-1987

1 Mike Schmidt 78.6
2 Joe Morgan 67.4
3 Bobby Grich 51.6
4 Tom Seaver 49.1
5 Ozzie Smith 45.7
6 George Brett 43.5
7 Johnny Bench 42.5
8 Darrell Evans 41.2
   Robin Yount 41.2
10 Rod Carew 40.3
11 Reggie Jackson 39.5
12 Gary Carter 39.2
13 Carlton Fisk 38.8
14 Willie Randolph 37.1
15 Eddie Murray 35.8
16 Lou Whitaker 35.6
17 Keith Hernandez 34.8
18 Jim Palmer 34.3
19 Steve Carlton 33.2
20 Gaylord Perry 32.8
21 Reggie Smith 31.9
22 Alan Trammell 31.8
23 Bert Blyleven 31.1
24 Dave Winfield 30.8
25 Fergie Jenkins 30.3

1961-1972

1 Willie Mays 84.6
2 Hank Aaron 81.3
3 Frank Robinson 64.7
4 Ron Santo 45.3
5 Bob Gibson 44.9
6 Al Kaline 43.2
7 Carl Yastrzemski 42.6
8 Dick Allen 39.2
9 Willie McCovey 39.0
10 Roberto Clemente 34.0
   Bill Mazeroski 34.0
12 Harmon Killebrew 32.5
13 Don Drysdale 32.4
14 Willie Stargell 30.8
15 Norm Cash 30.5
16 Jimmy Wynn 30.0
17 Juan Marichal 27.5
18 Ernie Banks 27.2
19 Jim Fregosi 25.5
20 Billy Williams 23.8
21 Rocky Colavito 22.7
22 Frank Howard 22.6
23 Sandy Koufax 22.3
   Joe Torre 22.3
25 Tony Oliva 20.4

1943-1960

1 Ted Williams 86.8
2 Stan Musial 76.0
3 Mickey Mantle 72.5
4 Eddie Mathews 52.1
5 Warren Spahn 51.4
6 Lou Boudreau 43.6
7 Bobby Doerr 40.3
8 Yogi Berra 38.6
9 Whitey Ford 37.2
   Hal Newhouser 37.2
11 Hoyt Wilhelm 37.1
12 Jackie Robinson 34.3
13 Bob Lemon 34.0
14 Bob Feller 31.6
15 Robin Roberts 30.3
16 Dizzy Trout 29.7
17 Joe Gordon 28.8
18 Billy Pierce 25.6
19 Harry Brecheen 24.9
20 Ralph Kiner 24.2
21 Roy Campanella 24.1
22 Duke Snider 23.0
23 Richie Ashburn 22.6
24 Dutch Leonard 22.2
   Charlie Keller 22.2
   Gil McDougald 22.2

Player Overall Wins by era

1921-1942

1 Babe Ruth 129.0
2 Rogers Hornsby 86.0
3 Lou Gehrig 70.9
4 Mel Ott 60.7
5 Lefty Grove 59.1
6 Jimmie Foxx 58.7
7 Joe DiMaggio 45.8
8 Charlie Gehringer 45.1
9 Gabby Hartnett 44.3
10 Arky Vaughan 43.3
11 Luke Appling 42.4
12 Carl Hubbell 40.2
13 Joe Cronin 39.6
14 Bill Dickey 38.5
15 Johnny Mize 37.7
16 Frankie Frisch 37.3
17 Dave Bancroft 36.2
18 Bob Johnson 35.7
19 Joe Sewell 35.2
20 Mickey Cochrane 34.7
21 Paul Waner 33.8
22 Ted Lyons 33.5
23 Harry Heilmann 33.2
24 Hank Greenberg 32.6
25 Billy Herman 31.6

1901-1920

1 Nap Lajoie 95.1
2 Walter Johnson 89.9
3 Ty Cobb 85.8
4 Tris Speaker 82.7
5 Honus Wagner 82.3
6 Cy Young 77.0
7 Eddie Collins 72.5
8 Grover Alexander 62.9
9 Christy Mathewson 56.3
10 Bill Dahlen 48.5
11 Bobby Wallace 38.4
12 Joe Jackson 38.3
13 Ed Walsh 37.7
14 Frank Baker 33.7
15 Mordecai Brown 32.7
16 Carl Mays 31.7
17 Heinie Groh 30.4
18 Eddie Plank 30.3
19 Elmer Flick 29.7
20 Sam Crawford 29.3
21 Fred Clarke 27.9
22 Art Fletcher 27.2
23 Sherry Magee 26.2
24 Eddie Cicotte 24.3
25 Zack Wheat 24.1

1893-1900

1 Kid Nichols 56.2
2 George Davis ....50.
3 Ed Delahanty ....43.
4 Amos Rusie 36.7
5 Cupid Childs 30.4
6 Clark Griffith ....28.
7 Billy Hamilton ....27.
8 Hughie Jennings ....26.
9 Jesse Burkett ....25.
10 Jake Beckley 22.6
11 Chief Zimmer ....20.
12 Joe Kelley ....20.
13 Nig Cuppy ....20.
14 John McGraw ....19.
15 Bill Joyce ....19.
16 Mike Griffin ....18.
17 Lave Cross ....16.
18 Elmer Smith ....14.
19 Kip Selbach ....13.
20 Frank Dwyer ....13.
21 Mike Tiernan ....13.
22 Jimmy Ryan ....13.
23 George Van Haltren ....11.
24 Ted Breitenstein ....10.
   Frank Killen ....10.

1876-1892

1 Roger Connor ....43.
2 John Clarkson ....42.
   Dan Brouthers ....42.
4 Bid McPhee ....38.
5 Jack Glasscock ....36.
6 Tim Keefe ....35.
7 Cap Anson 33
8 Bob Caruthers 33
   Bob Caruthers 33
10 Charley Radbourn 31
11 Tony Mullane 30
12 Sam Thompson 29
13 Buck Ewing 29
14 King Kelly 28
15 Fred Dunlap 28
16 Pete Browning 27
17 Hardy Richardson 26
18 Charlie Bennett 23
19 Jack Stivetts 23
20 Silver King 23
21 Guy Hecker 21
22 Harry Stovey 21
23 Jim McCormick 21
24 Fred Pfeffer 20
25 John Ward 20

Player	Wins	Player	Wins	Player	Wins	Player	Wins	Player	Wins
Hank Aaron	81.3	Nig Cuppy	20.4	Babe Herman	17.5	Chief Meyers	17.2	Cy Seymour	14.9
Bobby Abreu	**25.2**	Bill Dahlen	48.5	Billy Herman	31.6	Stu Miller	15.3	Bobby Shantz	18.7
Babe Adams	17.7	Curt Davis	18.2	**Roberto Hernandez**	**23.0**	Minnie Minoso	21.0	Bob Shawkey	16.7
Rick Aguilera	16.8	Chili Davis	15.4	Keith Hernandez	34.8	Kevin Mitchell	20.6	Jimmy Sheckard	20.7
Grover Alexander	62.9	Eric Davis	20.3	Orel Hershiser	18.9	Johnny Mize	37.7	**Gary Sheffield**	**42.6**
Dick Allen	39.2	George Davis	50.1	John Hiller	20.7	Paul Molitor	37.8	Urban Shocker	27.0
Gene Alley	18.8	Andre Dawson	18.3	Paul Hines	14.4	Jeff Montgomery	17.2	Al Simmons	23.0
Roberto Alomar	37.0	Dizzy Dean	22.3	**Trevor Hoffman**	**23.3**	Joe Morgan	67.4	Ted Simmons	21.7
Moises Alou	**15.0**	Doug DeCinces	14.9	Rogers Hornsby	86.0	Tony Mullane	30.0	Ken Singleton	20.4
Cap Anson	35.3	Ed Delahanty	43.1	Frank Howard	22.6	Thurman Munson	25.4	George Sisler	26.5
Johnny Antonelli	15.4	**Carlos Delgado**	**20.0**	Waite Hoyt	15.7	Dwayne Murphy	15.8	Enos Slaughter	14.5
Kevin Appier	19.6	Art Devlin	20.0	Glenn Hubbard	20.2	Eddie Murray	35.8	Roy Smalley	17.2
Luke Appling	42.4	Bill Dickey	38.5	Carl Hubbell	40.2	Stan Musial	76.0	Lee Smith	22.4
Richie Ashburn	22.6	Murry Dickson	16.2	**Tim Hudson**	**18.3**	**Mike Mussina**	**32.5**	Reggie Smith	31.9
Earl Averill	17.3	Joe DiMaggio	45.8	Miller Huggins	22.3	Buddy Myer	14.3	Ozzie Smith	45.7
Jeff Bagwell	**54.0**	Larry Doby	18.1	Larry Jackson	16.0	Randy Myers	14.6	**John Smoltz**	**33.6**
Harold Baines	14.2	Bobby Doerr	40.3	Joe Jackson	38.3	Robb Nen	18.9	Duke Snider	23.0
Frank Baker	33.7	Brian Downing	20.3	Reggie Jackson	39.5	Graig Nettles	21.6	**Sammy Sosa**	**25.7**
Dave Bancroft	36.2	Don Drysdale	32.4	Travis Jackson	22.0	Don Newcombe	18.6	Warren Spahn	51.4
Ernie Banks	27.2	Fred Dunlap	28.0	Fergie Jenkins	30.3	Hal Newhouser	37.2	Tris Speaker	82.7
Dick Bartell	28.2	Lenny Dykstra	23.0	Hughie Jennings	26.8	Kid Nichols	56.2	Eddie Stanky	20.1
Jake Beckley	22.6	Dennis Eckersley	29.8	**Derek Jeter**	**14.8**	Bill Nicholson	17.2	Bob Stanley	14.8
Buddy Bell	28.7	**Jim Edmonds**	**36.6**	Tommy John	20.1	Phil Niekro	29.2	Willie Stargell	30.8
Jay Bell	16.2	Bob Elliott	21.4	**Randy Johnson**	**49.1**	**John Olerud**	**23.7**	Rusty Staub	23.0
Albert Belle	29.6	Darrell Evans	41.2	Walter Johnson	89.9	Tony Oliva	20.4	Vern Stephens	20.7
Johnny Bench	42.5	Dwight Evans	24.8	Bob Johnson	35.7	Paul O'Neill	15.8	Dave Stieb	25.1
Chief Bender	14.9	Johnny Evers	15.9	Doug Jones	19.3	Jesse Orosco	18.3	Jack Stivetts	23.7
Armando Benitez	**15.8**	Buck Ewing	29.3	**Andruw Jones**	**19.8**	Jim O'Rourke	16.0	Mel Stottlemyre	16.1
Charlie Bennett	23.9	Red Faber	23.3	Charley Jones	19.4	**Roy Oswalt**	**15.6**	Harry Stovey	21.5
Wally Berger	21.0	Ferris Fain	18.8	**Chipper Jones**	**23.9**	Mel Ott	60.7	Darryl Strawberry	23.1
Lance Berkman	**17.6**	Bob Feller	31.6	Addie Joss	23.0	**Rafael Palmeiro**	**34.9**	Bruce Sutter	17.9
Yogi Berra	38.6	Charlie Ferguson	14.3	Bill Joyce	19.3	Jim Palmer	34.3	Don Sutton	16.8
Craig Biggio	**35.5**	Tony Fernandez	21.5	David Justice	15.7	Dave Parker	15.0	Jesse Tannehill	20.0
Bert Blyleven	31.1	Wes Ferrell	31.2	Jim Kaat	16.1	Mel Parnell	15.5	Jack Taylor	15.7
Wade Boggs	50.6	Rollie Fingers	22.7	Al Kaline	43.2	Lance Parrish	22.2	**Miguel Tejada**	**23.6**
Barry Bonds	**123.6**	Chuck Finley	19.3	Willie Kamm	15.7	Claude Passeau	14.9	Kent Tekulve	20.9
Bobby Bonds	27.2	Carlton Fisk	38.8	Tim Keefe	35.6	Roger Peckinpaugh	14.3	Gene Tenace	26.3
Bobby Bonilla	16.2	Freddie Fitzsimmons	19.0	Willie Keeler	15.0	**Troy Percival**	**15.5**	Fred Tenney	22.9
Lou Boudreau	43.6	Art Fletcher	27.2	Charlie Keller	22.2	Ron Perranoski	14.9	Bill Terry	26.7
Ken Boyer	19.7	Elmer Flick	29.7	Joe Kelley	20.6	Gaylord Perry	32.8	**Frank Thomas**	**48.5**
Harry Brecheen	24.9	Whitey Ford	37.2	King Kelly	28.4	Johnny Pesky	15.5	Roy Thomas	22.7
Roger Bresnahan	22.8	George Foster	18.5	**Jason Kendall**	**18.2**	Rico Petrocelli	15.4	**Jim Thome**	**33.4**
George Brett	43.5	**Keith Foulke**	**15.4**	**Jeff Kent**	**35.3**	**Andy Pettitte**	**18.8**	Sam Thompson	29.5
Tommy Bridges	27.3	Jack Fournier	24.4	Jimmy Key	22.8	Fred Pfeffer	20.8	Luis Tiant	21.5
Dan Brouthers	42.5	Nellie Fox	14.4	Harmon Killebrew	32.5	Deacon Phillippe	15.6	**Mike Timlin**	**15.2**
Kevin Brown	**32.8**	Jimmie Foxx	58.7	Ellis Kinder	14.9	Tony Phillips	19.3	Joe Tinker	19.5
Mordecai Brown	32.7	**John Franco**	**25.8**	Ralph Kiner	24.2	**Mike Piazza**	**42.2**	Joe Torre	22.3
Pete Browning	27.7	**Julio Franco**	**15.5**	Silver King	23.0	Billy Pierce	25.6	Alan Trammell	31.8
Charlie Buffinton	16.2	Bill Freehan	18.2	Chuck Klein	21.1	Eddie Plank	30.3	Pie Traynor	18.4
Jim Bunning	16.4	Jim Fregosi	25.5	Johnny Kling	14.4	Darrell Porter	20.9	Dizzy Trout	29.7
Jesse Burkett	25.9	Larry French	16.8	Bobby Knoop	16.7	**Jorge Posada**	**19.8**	Virgil Trucks	16.8
Ellis Burks	17.1	Frankie Frisch	37.3	Ed Konetchy	21.2	Boog Powell	18.6	John Tudor	16.1
Rick Burleson	17.0	Augie Galan	15.3	Jerry Koosman	14.6	Del Pratt	22.5	George Uhle	15.9
Brett Butler	16.1	Mike Garcia	15.7	Sandy Koufax	22.3	Kirby Puckett	23.7	John Valentin	17.6
Ken Caminiti	21.6	**Nomar Garciaparra**	**24.9**	Nap Lajoie	95.1	**Albert Pujols**	**26.5**	Dazzy Vance	29.2
Roy Campanella	24.1	Ned Garver	15.2	Max Lanier	15.7	Jack Quinn	19.4	Andy Van Slyke	17.0
John Candelaria	16.2	Lou Gehrig	70.9	Ray Lankford	18.6	Dan Quisenberry	23.6	Arky Vaughan	43.3
Jose Canseco	23.1	Charlie Gehringer	45.1	Barry Larkin	42.9	Charley Radbourn	31.5	Hippo Vaughn	16.3
Rod Carew	40.3	**Jason Giambi**	**22.8**	Henry Larkin	15.2	Tim Raines	38.8	Bobby Veach	17.9
Max Carey	18.0	Bob Gibson	44.9	Tony Lazzeri	17.8	**Manny Ramirez**	**35.8**	Robin Ventura	25.0
Steve Carlton	33.2	**Brian Giles**	**31.2**	Thornton Lee	15.8	Willie Randolph	37.1	Frank Viola	15.4
Gary Carter	39.2	Jack Glasscock	36.5	Sam Leever	16.1	Pee Wee Reese	16.3	Rube Waddell	22.2
Rico Carty	18.1	**Tom Glavine**	**39.9**	Bob Lemon	34.0	Ed Reulbach	17.3	**Billy Wagner**	**21.4**
Bob Caruthers	33.6	Lefty Gomez	20.1	Chet Lemon	19.3	Rick Reuschel	22.5	Honus Wagner	82.3
Norm Cash	30.5	**Juan Gonzalez**	**18.4**	Dutch Leonard	22.2	Jim Rice	18.6	**Larry Walker**	**31.3**
Cesar Cedeno	22.3	**Luis Gonzalez**	**20.6**	**Kenny Lofton**	**18.4**	Hardy Richardson	26.6	Bobby Wallace	38.4
Orlando Cepeda	19.1	Doc Gooden	17.7	Johnny Logan	16.5	Cal Ripken	44.1	Ed Walsh	37.7
Ron Cey	21.3	**Tom Gordon**	**16.4**	Ernie Lombardi	20.6	**Mariano Rivera**	**36.6**	Bucky Walters	24.8
Frank Chance	22.6	Joe Gordon	28.8	Ed Lopat	18.6	Eppa Rixey	24.2	Paul Waner	33.8
Spud Chandler	19.1	Sid Gordon	14.8	**Javy Lopez**	**22.8**	Phil Rizzuto	18.7	John Ward	20.7
Ray Chapman	16.6	Goose Goslin	23.3	Red Lucas	20.8	Robin Roberts	30.3	Lon Warneke	22.6
Ben Chapman	14.4	Rich Gossage	29.5	Dolf Luque	26.2	Brooks Robinson	14.3	Mickey Welch	18.9
Eric Chavez	**16.5**	Hank Greenberg	32.6	Sparky Lyle	19.1	Frank Robinson	64.7	**David Wells**	**14.4**
Cupid Childs	30.4	Bobby Grich	51.6	Fred Lynn	19.7	Jackie Robinson	34.3	John Wetteland	20.7
Eddie Cicotte	24.3	**Ken Griffey Jr.**	**48.5**	Ted Lyons	33.5	**Alex Rodriguez**	**51.5**	Zack Wheat	24.1
Jack Clark	29.6	Mike Griffin	18.3	Denny Lyons	19.6	**Ivan Rodriguez**	**40.0**	Lou Whitaker	35.6
Will Clark	25.0	Clark Griffith	28.3	**Greg Maddux**	**63.9**	Steve Rogers	14.8	Doc White	19.3
Fred Clarke	27.9	Burleigh Grimes	18.3	Sherry Magee	26.2	**Scott Rolen**	**33.6**	Roy White	15.3
John Clarkson	42.5	Heinie Groh	30.4	Mickey Mantle	72.5	Eddie Rommel	23.0	Hoyt Wilhelm	37.1
Roger Clemens	**70.4**	Lefty Grove	59.1	Juan Marichal	27.5	Pete Rose	23.9	**Bernie Williams**	**25.4**
Roberto Clemente	34.0	Pedro Guerrero	18.0	Mike Marshall	19.2	Al Rosen	16.2	Billy Williams	23.8
Harland Clift	26.3	**Vladimir Guerrero**	**29.9**	**Pedro Martinez**	**50.2**	Schoolboy Rowe	18.8	Jimmy Williams	15.4
Ty Cobb	85.8	Ron Guidry	19.9	Edgar Martinez	45.1	Nap Rucker	15.5	Ken Williams	17.5
Mickey Cochrane	34.7	Tony Gwynn	38.5	Eddie Mathews	52.1	Red Ruffing	31.2	Matt Williams	19.7
Rocky Colavito	22.7	Stan Hack	29.4	Christy Mathewson	56.3	Amos Rusie	36.7	Ted Williams	86.8
Eddie Collins	72.5	Noodles Hahn	17.0	Don Mattingly	15.9	Babe Ruth	129.0	Vic Willis	20.0
Jimmy Collins	23.0	Billy Hamilton	27.3	Carl Mays	31.7	Nolan Ryan	21.5	Hack Wilson	18.2
Bartolo Colon	**14.5**	Ron Hansen	15.7	Willie Mays	84.6	Bret Saberhagen	27.8	Dave Winfield	30.8
Dave Concepcion	18.0	Mel Harder	17.0	Bill Mazeroski	34.0	**Tim Salmon**	**21.0**	Joe Wood	22.1
David Cone	23.1	Mike Hargrove	16.1	Jim McCormick	21.1	Ryne Sandberg	36.7	Wilbur Wood	14.8
Roger Connor	43.4	Toby Harrah	19.4	Willie McCovey	39.0	Ron Santo	45.3	Early Wynn	19.5
Wilbur Cooper	19.7	Gabby Hartnett	44.3	Gil McDougald	22.2	Ray Schalk	16.1	Jimmy Wynn	30.0
Mort Cooper	14.3	Jeff Heath	17.2	Joe McGinnity	18.9	Wally Schang	20.4	Carl Yastrzemski	42.6
Stan Coveleski	26.0	Guy Hecker	21.9	John McGraw	19.5	**Curt Schilling**	**28.8**	Cy Young	77.0
Gavy Cravath	18.4	Harry Heilmann	33.2	Fred McGriff	22.7	Mike Schmidt	78.6	Robin Yount	41.2
Sam Crawford	29.3	**Todd Helton**	**29.4**	Mark McGwire	36.0	Red Schoendienst	15.8	Chief Zimmer	20.7
Joe Cronin	39.6	Rickey Henderson	72.1	Bid McPhee	38.3	Hal Schumacher	15.2	**Barry Zito**	**14.4**
Lave Cross	16.4	Claude Hendrix	14.3	Hal McRae	14.7	Mike Scioscia	18.3		
Jose Cruz	21.2	Tom Henke	21.5	Joe Medwick	25.6	Tom Seaver	49.1		
Roy Cullenbine	18.8	Tommy Henrich	15.0	Andy Messersmith	17.5	Joe Sewell	35.2		

Player Overall Wins

Rank	Player	Wins
1	Babe Ruth	129.0
2	Barry Bonds	123.6
3	Nap Lajoie	95.1
4	Walter Johnson	89.9
5	Ted Williams	86.8
6	Rogers Hornsby	86.0
7	Ty Cobb	85.8
8	Willie Mays	84.6
9	Tris Speaker	82.7
10	Honus Wagner	82.3
11	Hank Aaron	81.3
12	Mike Schmidt	78.6
13	Cy Young	77.0
14	Stan Musial	76.0
15	Eddie Collins	72.5
	Mickey Mantle	72.5
17	Rickey Henderson	72.1
18	Lou Gehrig	70.9
19	Roger Clemens	70.4
20	Joe Morgan	67.4
21	Frank Robinson	64.7
22	Greg Maddux	63.9
23	Grover Alexander	62.9
24	Mel Ott	60.7
25	Lefty Grove	59.1
26	Jimmie Foxx	58.7
27	Christy Mathewson	56.3
28	Kid Nichols	56.2
29	Jeff Bagwell	54.0
30	Eddie Mathews	52.1
31	Bobby Grich	51.6
32	Alex Rodriguez	51.5
33	Warren Spahn	51.4
34	Wade Boggs	50.6
35	Pedro Martinez	50.2
36	George Davis	50.1
37	Randy Johnson	49.1
	Tom Seaver	49.1
39	Bill Dahlen	48.5
	Ken Griffey Jr.	48.5
	Frank Thomas	48.5
42	Joe DiMaggio	45.8
43	Ozzie Smith	45.7
44	Ron Santo	45.3
45	Charlie Gehringer	45.1
	Edgar Martinez	45.1
47	Bob Gibson	44.9
48	Gabby Hartnett	44.3
49	Cal Ripken	44.1
50	Lou Boudreau	43.6
51	George Brett	43.5
52	Roger Connor	43.4
53	Arky Vaughan	43.3
54	Al Kaline	43.2
55	Ed Delahanty	43.1
56	Barry Larkin	42.9
57	Gary Sheffield	42.6
	Carl Yastrzemski	42.6
59	John Clarkson	42.5
	Johnny Bench	42.5
	Dan Brouthers	42.5
62	Luke Appling	42.4
63	Mike Piazza	42.2
64	Darrell Evans	41.2
	Robin Yount	41.2
66	Rod Carew	40.3
	Bobby Doerr	40.3
68	Carl Hubbell	40.2
69	Ivan Rodriguez	40.0
70	Tom Glavine	39.9
71	Joe Cronin	39.6
72	Reggie Jackson	39.5
73	Dick Allen	39.2
	Gary Carter	39.2
75	Willie McCovey	39.0
76	Carlton Fisk	38.8
	Tim Raines	38.8
78	Yogi Berra	38.6
79	Bill Dickey	38.5
	Tony Gwynn	38.5
81	Bobby Wallace	38.4
82	Joe Jackson	38.3
	Bid McPhee	38.3
84	Paul Molitor	37.8
85	Ed Walsh	37.7
	Johnny Mize	37.7
87	Frankie Frisch	37.3
88	Whitey Ford	37.2
	Hal Newhouser	37.2
90	Hoyt Wilhelm	37.1
	Willie Randolph	37.1
92	Roberto Alomar	37.0
93	Amos Rusie	36.7
	Ryne Sandberg	36.7
95	Mariano Rivera	36.6
	Jim Edmonds	36.6
97	Jack Glasscock	36.5
98	Dave Bancroft	36.2
99	Mark McGwire	36.0
100	Eddie Murray	35.8
	Manny Ramirez	35.8
102	Bob Johnson	35.7
103	Tim Keefe	35.6
	Lou Whitaker	35.6
105	Craig Biggio	35.5
106	Cap Anson	35.3
	Jeff Kent	35.3
108	Joe Sewell	35.2
109	Rafael Palmeiro	34.9
110	Keith Hernandez	34.8
111	Mickey Cochrane	34.7
112	Jim Palmer	34.3
	Jackie Robinson	34.3
114	Bob Lemon	34.0
	Roberto Clemente	34.0
	Bill Mazeroski	34.0
117	Paul Waner	33.8
118	Frank Baker	33.7
119	Bob Caruthers	33.6
	John Smoltz	33.6
	Scott Rolen	33.6
122	Ted Lyons	33.5
123	Jim Thome	33.4
124	Steve Carlton	33.2
	Harry Heilmann	33.2
126	Kevin Brown	32.8
	Gaylord Perry	32.8
128	Mordecai Brown	32.7
129	Hank Greenberg	32.6
130	Mike Mussina	32.5
	Harmon Killebrew	32.5
132	Don Drysdale	32.4
133	Reggie Smith	31.9
134	Alan Trammell	31.7
135	Carl Mays	31.7
136	Bob Feller	31.6
	Billy Herman	31.6
138	Charley Radbourn	31.5
139	Larry Walker	31.3
140	Wes Ferrell	31.2
	Red Ruffing	31.2
142	Brian Giles	31.2
143	Bert Blyleven	31.1
144	Willie Stargell	30.8
	Dave Winfield	30.8
146	Norm Cash	30.5
147	Cupid Childs	30.4
	Heinie Groh	30.4
149	Fergie Jenkins	30.3
	Eddie Plank	30.3
	Robin Roberts	30.3
152	Tony Mullane	30.0
	Jimmy Wynn	30.0
154	Vladimir Guerrero	29.9
155	Dennis Eckersley	29.8
156	Dizzy Trout	29.7
	Elmer Flick	29.7
158	Albert Belle	29.6
	Jack Clark	29.6
160	Rich Gossage	29.5
	Sam Thompson	29.5
162	Stan Hack	29.4
	Todd Helton	29.4
164	Sam Crawford	29.3
	Buck Ewing	29.3
166	Phil Niekro	29.2
	Dazzy Vance	29.2
168	Curt Schilling	28.8
	Joe Gordon	28.8
170	Buddy Bell	28.7
171	King Kelly	28.4
172	Clark Griffith	28.3
173	Dick Bartell	28.2
174	Fred Dunlap	28.0
175	Fred Clarke	27.9
176	Bret Saberhagen	27.8
177	Pete Browning	27.7
178	Juan Marichal	27.5
179	Tommy Bridges	27.3
	Billy Hamilton	27.3
181	Ernie Banks	27.2
	Bobby Bonds	27.2
	Art Fletcher	27.2
184	Urban Shocker	27.0
185	Hughie Jennings	26.8
186	Bill Terry	26.7
187	Hardy Richardson	26.6
188	Albert Pujols	26.5
	George Sisler	26.5
190	Harlond Clift	26.3
	Gene Tenace	26.3
192	Dolf Luque	26.2
	Sherry Magee	26.2
194	Stan Coveleski	26.0
195	Jesse Burkett	25.9
196	John Franco	25.8
197	Sammy Sosa	25.7
198	Billy Pierce	25.6
	Joe Medwick	25.6
200	Jim Fregosi	25.5
201	Thurman Munson	25.4
	Bernie Williams	25.4
203	Bobby Abreu	25.2
204	Dave Stieb	25.1
205	Will Clark	25.0
	Robin Ventura	25.0
207	Harry Brecheen	24.9
	Nomar Garciaparra	24.9
209	Bucky Walters	24.8
	Dwight Evans	24.8
211	Jack Fournier	24.4
212	Eddie Cicotte	24.3
213	Eppa Rixey	24.2
	Ralph Kiner	24.2
215	Roy Campanella	24.1
	Zack Wheat	24.1
217	Charlie Bennett	23.9
	Chipper Jones	23.9
	Pete Rose	23.9
220	Billy Williams	23.8
221	Jack Stivetts	23.7
	John Olerud	23.7
	Kirby Puckett	23.7
224	Dan Quisenberry	23.6
	Miguel Tejada	23.6
226	Red Faber	23.3
	Trevor Hoffman	23.3
	Goose Goslin	23.3
229	David Cone	23.1
	Jose Canseco	23.1
	Darryl Strawberry	23.1
232	Roberto Hernandez	23.0
	Addie Joss	23.0
	Silver King	23.0
	Eddie Rommel	23.0
	Jimmy Collins	23.0
	Lenny Dykstra	23.0
	Al Simmons	23.0
	Duke Snider	23.0
	Rusty Staub	23.0
241	Fred Tenney	22.9
242	Jimmy Key	22.8
	Roger Bresnahan	22.8
	Jason Giambi	22.8
	Javy Lopez	22.8
246	Rollie Fingers	22.7
	Rocky Colavito	22.7
	Fred McGriff	22.7
	Roy Thomas	22.7
250	Lon Warneke	22.6
	Richie Ashburn	22.6
	Jake Beckley	22.6
	Frank Chance	22.6
	Frank Howard	22.6
255	Rick Reuschel	22.5
	Del Pratt	22.5
257	Lee Smith	22.4
258	Dizzy Dean	22.3
	Sandy Koufax	22.3
	Cesar Cedeno	22.3
	Miller Huggins	22.3
	Joe Torre	22.3
263	Dutch Leonard	22.2
	Rube Waddell	22.2
	Charlie Keller	22.2
	Gil McDougald	22.2
	Lance Parrish	22.2
268	Joe Wood	22.1
269	Travis Jackson	22.0
270	Guy Hecker	21.9
271	Ted Simmons	21.7
272	Ken Caminiti	21.6
	Graig Nettles	21.6
274	Tom Henke	21.5
	Nolan Ryan	21.5
	Luis Tiant	21.5
	Tony Fernandez	21.5
	Harry Stovey	21.5
279	Billy Wagner	21.4
	Bob Elliott	21.4
281	Ron Cey	21.3
282	Jose Cruz	21.2
	Ed Konetchy	21.2
284	Jim McCormick	21.1
	Chuck Klein	21.1
286	Wally Berger	21.0
	Minnie Minoso	21.0
	Tim Salmon	21.0
289	Kent Tekulve	20.9
	Darrell Porter	20.9
291	Red Lucas	20.8
	Fred Pfeffer	20.8
293	John Hiller	20.7
	John Ward	20.7
	John Wetteland	20.7
	Jimmy Sheckard	20.7
	Vern Stephens	20.7
	Chief Zimmer	20.7
299	Luis Gonzalez	20.6
	Joe Kelley	20.6
	Ernie Lombardi	20.6
	Kevin Mitchell	20.6
303	Nig Cuppy	20.4
	Tony Oliva	20.4
	Wally Schang	20.4
	Ken Singleton	20.4
307	Eric Davis	20.3
	Brian Downing	20.3
309	Glenn Hubbard	20.2
310	Lefty Gomez	20.1
	Tommy John	20.1
	Eddie Stanky	20.1
313	Jesse Tannehill	20.0
	Vic Willis	20.0
	Carlos Delgado	20.0
	Art Devlin	20.0
317	Ron Guidry	19.9
318	Andruw Jones	19.8
	Jorge Posada	19.8
320	Wilbur Cooper	19.7
	Ken Boyer	19.7
	Fred Lynn	19.7
	Matt Williams	19.7
324	Kevin Appier	19.6
	Denny Lyons	19.6
326	Early Wynn	19.5
	John McGraw	19.5
	Joe Tinker	19.5
329	Jack Quinn	19.4
	Toby Harrah	19.4
	Charley Jones	19.4
332	Chuck Finley	19.3
	Doug Jones	19.3
	Doc White	19.3
	Bill Joyce	19.3
	Chet Lemon	19.3
	Tony Phillips	19.3
338	Mike Marshall	19.2
339	Spud Chandler	19.1
	Sparky Lyle	19.1
	Orlando Cepeda	19.1
342	Freddie Fitzsimmons	19.0
343	Orel Hershiser	18.9
	Joe McGinnity	18.9
	Robb Nen	18.9
	Mickey Welch	18.9
347	Andy Pettitte	18.8
	Schoolboy Rowe	18.8
	Gene Alley	18.8
	Roy Cullenbine	18.8
	Ferris Fain	18.8
352	Bobby Shantz	18.7
	Phil Rizzuto	18.7
354	Ed Lopat	18.6
	Don Newcombe	18.6
	Ray Lankford	18.6
	Boog Powell	18.6
	Jim Rice	18.6
359	George Foster	18.5
360	Gavy Cravath	18.4
	Juan Gonzalez	18.4
	Kenny Lofton	18.4
	Pie Traynor	18.4
364	Burleigh Grimes	18.3
	Tim Hudson	18.3
	Jesse Orosco	18.3
	Andre Dawson	18.3
	Mike Griffin	18.3
	Mike Scioscia	18.3
370	Curt Davis	18.2
	Bill Freehan	18.2
	Jason Kendall	18.2
	Hack Wilson	18.2
374	Rico Carty	18.1
	Larry Doby	18.1
376	Max Carey	18.0
	Dave Concepcion	18.0
	Pedro Guerrero	18.0
379	Bruce Sutter	17.9
	Bobby Veach	17.9
381	Tony Lazzeri	17.7
382	Babe Adams	17.7
	Doc Gooden	17.7
384	Lance Berkman	17.6
	John Valentin	17.6
386	Andy Messersmith	17.5
	Babe Herman	17.5
	Ken Williams	17.5
389	Ed Reulbach	17.3
	Earl Averill	17.3
391	Jeff Montgomery	17.2
	Jeff Heath	17.2
	Chief Meyers	17.2
	Bill Nicholson	17.2
	Roy Smalley	17.2
396	Ellis Burks	17.1
397	Noodles Hahn	17.0
	Mel Harder	17.0
	Rick Burleson	17.0
	Andy Van Slyke	17.0
401	Rick Aguilera	16.8
	Larry French	16.8
	Don Sutton	16.8
	Virgil Trucks	16.8
405	Bob Shawkey	16.7
	Bobby Knoop	16.7
407	Ray Chapman	16.6
408	Eric Chavez	16.5
	Johnny Logan	16.5
410	Jim Bunning	16.4
	Tom Gordon	16.4
	Lave Cross	16.4
413	Hippo Vaughn	16.3
	Pee Wee Reese	16.3
415	Charlie Buffinton	16.2
	John Candelaria	16.2
	Murry Dickson	16.2
	Jay Bell	16.2
	Bobby Bonilla	16.2
	Al Rosen	16.2
421	Jim Kaat	16.1
	Sam Leever	16.1
	Mel Stottlemyre	16.1
	John Tudor	16.1
	Brett Butler	16.1
	Mike Hargrove	16.1
	Ray Schalk	16.1
428	Larry Jackson	16.0
	Jim O'Rourke	16.0
430	George Uhle	15.9
	Johnny Evers	15.9
	Don Mattingly	15.9
433	Armando Benitez	15.8
	Thornton Lee	15.8
	Dwayne Murphy	15.8
	Paul O'Neill	15.8
	Red Schoendienst	15.8
438	Mike Garcia	15.7
	Waite Hoyt	15.7
	Max Lanier	15.7
	Jack Taylor	15.7
	Ron Hansen	15.7
	David Justice	15.7
	Willie Kamm	15.7
445	Roy Oswalt	15.6
	Deacon Phillippe	15.6
447	Mel Parnell	15.5
	Troy Percival	15.5
	Nap Rucker	15.5
	Julio Franco	15.5
452	Johnny Antonelli	15.4
	Keith Foulke	15.4
	Frank Viola	15.4
	Chili Davis	15.4
	Rico Petrocelli	15.4
	Jimmy Williams	15.4
458	Stu Miller	15.3
	Augie Galan	15.3
	Roy White	15.3
461	Ned Garver	15.2
	Hal Schumacher	15.2
	Mike Timlin	15.2
	Henry Larkin	15.2
465	Moises Alou	15.0
	Tommy Henrich	15.0
	Willie Keeler	15.0
	Dave Parker	15.0
469	Chief Bender	14.9
	Ellis Kinder	14.9
	Claude Passeau	14.9
	Ron Perranoski	14.9
	Doug DeCinces	14.9
	Cy Seymour	14.9
475	Steve Rogers	14.8
	Bob Stanley	14.8
	Wilbur Wood	14.8
	Sid Gordon	14.8
	Derek Jeter	14.8
480	Hal McRae	14.7
481	Jerry Koosman	14.6
	Randy Myers	14.6
483	Bartolo Colon	14.5
	Enos Slaughter	14.5
485	David Wells	14.4
	Barry Zito	14.4
	Ben Chapman	14.4
	Nellie Fox	14.4
	Paul Hines	14.4
	Johnny Kling	14.4
491	Mort Cooper	14.3
	Charlie Ferguson	14.3
	Claude Hendrix	14.3
	Buddy Myer	14.3
	Roger Peckinpaugh	14.3
	Brooks Robinson	14.3
497	Harold Baines	14.2
498	4 players tied	14.1

Plate Appearances

1 Lenny Dykstra, 1993 773
2 Pete Rose, 1974 770
3 Dave Cash, 1975 766
4 Pete Rose, 1975 764
5 Ichiro Suzuki, 2004......762
6 Maury Wills, 1962 759
  Pete Rose, 1976 759
8 Wade Boggs, 1985 758
9 Frankie Crosetti, 1938......757
  Pete Rose, 1965 757
  Omar Moreno, 1979 757
12 Dom DiMaggio, 1948 756
13 Woody English, 1930 755
14 Bobby Richardson, 1962....754
15 Taylor Douthit, 1928 752
  Pete Rose, 1973 752
  Mo Vaughn, 1996 752
  Derek Jeter, 2005 752
19 Paul Molitor, 1982 751
20 Paul Molitor, 1991 749
  Brady Anderson, 1992......749
  Craig Biggio, 1999 749
23 Taylor Douthit, 1930 748
  Augie Galan, 1935 748
  Derek Jeter, 1997 748
  Alex Rodriguez, 1998..748
  Juan Pierre, 2004 748
28 Rabbit Maranville, 1922......747
  Darin Erstad, 2000.......747
30 Matty Alou, 1969 746
  Jim Rice, 1978 746
  Juan Pierre, 2003 746
33 Dave Bancroft, 1922 745
  Lyn Lary, 1936 745
  Tommy Harper, 1965.......745
  Bobby Bonds, 1970.........745
  Dave Cash, 1974 745
  Omar Moreno, 1980 745
  Willie Wilson, 1980 745
40 Jo-Jo Moore, 1935 744
  Dwight Evans, 1985.........744
  Kirby Puckett, 1985 744
  Craig Biggio, 1997......744
44 Frankie Crosetti, 1939......743
  Pee Wee Reese, 1949......743
  Felix Millan, 1975 743
47 Charlie Jamieson, 1923......742
  Don Mattingly, 1986 742
  Wade Boggs, 1989 742
50 Kiki Cuyler, 1930 741
  Lyn Lary, 1937................741
  Ron LeFlore, 1978 741
  Johnny Damon, 2000 ..741
  Alfonso Soriano, 2002 ...741
55 Frankie Crosetti, 1936......740
  Red Rolfe, 1937 740
57 Curt Flood, 1964 739
  Sandy Alomar, 1971 739
  Derek Jeter, 1999 739
  Michael Young, 2004 ...739
  Ichiro Suzuki, 2005......739
62 Lou Gehrig, 1931 738
  Chuck Schilling, 1961 738
  Bobby Bonds, 1973........738
  Al Bumbry, 1980..............738
  Dwight Evans, 1984 738
  Brian Hunter, 1997 738
  Craig Biggio, 1998......738
  Ichiro Suzuki, 2001......738
70 Don Kessinger, 1969 737
  Juan Samuel, 1984 737
  Harold Reynolds, 1990......737
73 Brooks Robinson, 1961......736
  Kenny Lofton, 1996......736
75 Billy Herman, 1935 735
  Phil Rizzuto, 1950 735
  Dick Howser, 1964 735
  Sandy Alomar, 1970.........735
  Pete Rose, 1980 735
  Doug Glanville, 1998........735
  Vernon Wells, 2003......735
82 Eddie Yost, 1952.............734
  Sal Bando, 1969 734
  Rusty Staub, 1978...........734
  Nomar Garciaparra, 1997 ...734
  Rafael Furcal, 2003......734
  Alfonso Soriano, 2003......734
  Brian Roberts, 2004......734
89 Buddy Lewis, 1937...........733
  Darrell Evans, 1973 733
  Tony Phillips, 1992...........733
  Jose Reyes, 2005.........733
93 Max Carey, 1922..............732
  Eddie Lake, 1947 732
  Horace Clarke, 1970.........732
  Brett Butler, 1990............732
  Rafael Palmeiro, 1996......732
  Neifi Perez, 1999.........732
  Alex Rodriguez, 2001...732
  Jimmy Rollins, 2005...732
  Michael Young, 2005 ...732

At Bats

1 Willie Wilson, 1980 705
2 Ichiro Suzuki, 2004....704
3 Juan Samuel, 1984 701
4 Dave Cash, 1975 699
5 Matty Alou, 1969..............698
6 Woody Jensen, 1936 696
  Alfonso Soriano, 2002....696
  Jose Reyes, 2005.........696
9 Maury Wills, 1962 695
  Omar Moreno, 1979..........695
11 Bobby Richardson, 1962....692
  Ichiro Suzuki, 2001.....692
  Kirby Puckett, 1985..........691
14 Neifi Perez, 1999.........690
  Michael Young, 2004.....690
16 Lou Brock, 1967...............689
  Sandy Alomar, 1971..........689
18 Dave Cash, 1974 687
  Tony Fernandez, 1986......687
20 Horace Clarke, 1970..........686
  Alex Rodriguez, 1998......686
22 Nomar Garciaparra, 1997 ...684
23 Lance Johnson, 1996..........682
  Alfonso Soriano, 2003......682
25 Lloyd Waner, 1931............681
  Jo-Jo Moore, 1935 681
27 Pete Rose, 1973 680
  Frank Taveras, 1979.........680
  Kirby Puckett, 1986..........680
30 Harvey Kuenn, 1953..........679
  Curt Flood, 1964 679
  Bobby Richardson, 1964....679
  Ichiro Suzuki, 2003.....679
  Ichiro Suzuki, 2005.....679
35 Dick Groat, 1962..............678
  Doug Glanville, 1998.........678
  Vernon Wells, 2003......678
  Juan Pierre, 2004 678
39 Matty Alou, 1970..............677
  Jim Rice, 1978 677
  Don Mattingly, 1986 677
  Jimmy Rollins, 2005......677
42 Felix Millan, 1975 676
  Omar Moreno, 1980 676
  Darin Erstad, 2000......676
46 Rennie Stennett, 1974......673
  Bill Buckner, 1985...........673
  B.J. Surhoff, 1999.........673
49 Rabbit Maranville, 1922......672
  Tony Oliva, 1964 672
  Sandy Alomar, 1970.........672
  Garry Templeton, 1979......672
  Garret Anderson, 2001....672
54 Jack Tobin, 1921 671
  Marquis Grissom, 1996...671
56 Al Simmons, 1932.............670
  Pete Rose, 1965 670
  Buddy Bell, 1979.............670
  Cesar Izturis, 2004 670
60 Vada Pinson, 1965............669
  Larry Bowa, 1974 669
62 Buddy Lewis, 1937............668
  Brooks Robinson, 1961......668
  Ralph Garr, 1973.............668
  Juan Pierre, 2003 668
  Michael Young, 2005 ...668
67 Carl Furillo, 1951.............667
68 Billy Herman, 1935............666
  Zoilo Versalles, 1965.........666
  Felipe Alou, 1966 666
  Dave Cash, 1976 666
  Ron LeFlore, 1978 666
  Paul Molitor, 1982 666
  Michael Young, 2003 ...666
75 Tommy Davis, 1962 665
  Pete Rose, 1976 665
  Paul Molitor, 1991 665
78 Taylor Douthit, 1930..........664
  Bobby Richardson, 1965....664
  Don Kessinger, 1969.........664
  Lou Brock, 1970..............664
  Rafael Furcal, 2003......664
83 Jake Wood, 1961 663
  Bill Virdon, 1962..............663
  Bobby Bonds, 1970..........663
  Rick Burleson, 1977..........663
  Cal Ripken, 1983.............663
  Juan Samuel, 1985..........663
  Joe Carter, 1986.............663
  Carlos Beltran, 1999 663
91 Lloyd Waner, 1929............662
  Hughie Critz, 1930............662
  Richie Ashburn, 1949........662
  Granny Hamner, 1949........662
  Bobby Richardson, 1961....662
  Curt Flood, 1963 662
  Felipe Alou, 1968............662
  Pete Rose, 1975 662
  Kenny Lofton, 1996......662
  Dante Bichette, 1998 662
  Miguel Tejada, 2002 662

Runs

1 Billy Hamilton, 1894 198
2 Tom Brown, 1891 177
  Babe Ruth, 1921...............177
4 Tip O'Neill, 1887 167
  Lou Gehrig, 1936 167
6 Billy Hamilton, 1895 166
7 Willie Keeler, 1894............165
  Joe Kelley, 1894...............165
9 Arlie Latham, 1887............163
  Babe Ruth, 1928...............163
  Lou Gehrig, 1931 163
12 Willie Keeler, 1895...........162
13 Hugh Duffy, 1890.............161
14 Fred Dunlap, 1884 160
  Hugh Duffy, 1894.............160
  Jesse Burkett, 1896..........160
17 Hughie Jennings, 1895......159
18 Bobby Lowe, 1894............158
  Babe Ruth, 1920...............158
  Babe Ruth, 1927...............158
  Chuck Klein, 1930.............158
22 John McGraw, 1894 156
  Rogers Hornsby, 1929 156
24 King Kelly, 1886 155
  Kiki Cuyler, 1930 155
26 Dan Brouthers, 1887.........153
  Jesse Burkett, 1895..........153
  Billy Hamilton, 1896 153
  Willie Keeler, 1896 153
30 Arlie Latham, 1886...........152
  Mike Griffin, 1889.............152
  Harry Stovey, 1889...........152
  Billy Hamilton, 1897..........152
  Lefty O'Doul, 1929 152
  Woody English, 1930.........152
  Al Simmons, 1930.............152
  Chuck Klein, 1932.............152
  Jeff Bagwell, 2000 152
39 Babe Ruth, 1923..............151
  Jimmie Foxx, 1932............151
  Joe DiMaggio, 1937..........151
42 George Gore, 1886...........150
  Bill Dahlen, 1894.............150
  Jake Stenzel, 1894...........150
  Babe Ruth, 1930...............150
  Ted Williams, 1949...........150
47 Herman Long, 1893...........149
  Ed Delahanty, 1895..........149
  Lou Gehrig, 1927 149
  Babe Ruth, 1931...............149
51 Hub Collins, 1890.............148
  Ed Delahanty, 1894..........148
  Joe Kelley, 1895...............148
  Joe Kelley, 1896...............148
55 Mike Tiernan, 1889...........147
  Hugh Duffy, 1893.............147
  Patsy Donovan, 1894........147
  Ty Cobb, 1911................147
59 Darby O'Brien, 1889 146
  Tom Brown, 1890..............146
  Hack Wilson, 1930............146
  Rickey Henderson, 1985....146
  Craig Biggio, 1997......146
  Sammy Sosa, 2001 ...146
65 Jesse Burkett, 1893..........145
  Cupid Childs, 1893...........145
  Ed Delahanty, 1893..........145
  Willie Keeler, 1897 145
  Nap Lajoie, 1901.............145
  Harlond Clift, 1936...........145
71 Hugh Duffy, 1889 144
  Billy Hamilton, 1889 144
  Ty Cobb, 1915................144
  Kiki Cuyler, 1925 144
  Charlie Gehringer, 1930......144
  Al Simmons, 1932.............144
  Charlie Gehringer, 1936......144
  Hank Greenberg, 1938 144
79 Cupid Childs, 1894............143
  John McGraw, 1898 143
  Babe Ruth, 1924...............143
  Babe Herman, 1930...........143
  Lou Gehrig, 1930 143
  Earle Combs, 1932...........143
  Red Rolfe, 1937 143
  Lenny Dykstra, 1993.........143
  Larry Walker, 1997 143
  Jeff Bagwell, 1999 143
89 Mike Griffin, 1887.............142
  Harry Stovey, 1890...........142
  Jesse Burkett, 1901..........142
  Paul Waner, 1928.............142
  Ted Williams, 1946...........142
  Ellis Burks, 1996.............142
95 Billy Hamilton, 1891..........141
  Rogers Hornsby, 1922.......141
  Ted Williams, 1942...........141
  Alex Rodriguez, 1996...141
99 9 players tied 140

Runs by era

1988-2005

1 Jeff Bagwell, 2000 152
2 Craig Biggio, 1997.......146
  Sammy Sosa, 2001......146
4 Lenny Dykstra, 1993.......143
  Larry Walker, 1997 143
  Jeff Bagwell, 1999 143
7 Ellis Burks, 1996 142
8 Alex Rodriguez, 1996...141
9 Chuck Knoblauch, 1996....140
10 Roberto Alomar, 1999......138
  Todd Helton, 2000 138

1973-1987

1 Rickey Henderson, 1985...146
2 Paul Molitor, 1982 136
3 Willie Wilson, 1980 133
  Tim Raines, 1983............133
5 Bobby Bonds, 1973.........131
  Dale Murphy, 1983...........131
7 Pete Rose, 1976 130
  Rickey Henderson, 1986....130
9 Robin Yount, 1982............129
10 Rod Carew, 1977.............128

1961-1972

1 Billy Williams, 1970 137
2 Frank Robinson, 1962........134
  Bobby Bonds, 1970.........134
4 Mickey Mantle, 1961 132
  Roger Maris, 1961 132
6 Willie Mays, 1962 130
  Maury Wills, 1962 130
8 Willie Mays, 1961 129
  Rocky Colavito, 1961 129
10 Hank Aaron, 1962............127

1943-1960

1 Ted Williams, 1949..........150
2 Ted Williams, 1946..........142
3 Tommy Henrich, 1948.......138
4 Johnny Mize, 1947...........137
5 Stan Musial, 1948............135
6 Pee Wee Reese, 1949......132
  Duke Snider, 1953............132
  Mickey Mantle, 1956.........132
9 Dom DiMaggio, 1950.........131
  Vada Pinson, 1959...........131

1921-1942

1 Babe Ruth, 1921..............177
2 Lou Gehrig, 1936.............167
3 Babe Ruth, 1928..............163
  Lou Gehrig, 1931.............163
5 Babe Ruth, 1927..............158
  Chuck Klein, 1930............158
7 Rogers Hornsby, 1929.......156
8 Kiki Cuyler, 1930.............155
9 Lefty O'Doul, 1929...........152
  Woody English, 1930.........152
  Al Simmons, 1930.............152
  Chuck Klein, 1932.............152

1901-1920

1 Babe Ruth, 1920..............158
2 Ty Cobb, 1911................147
3 Nap Lajoie, 1901.............145
4 Ty Cobb, 1915................144
5 Jesse Burkett, 1901..........142
6 Ginger Beaumont, 1903.....137
  Eddie Collins, 1912...........137
  Tris Speaker, 1920...........137
  George Sisler, 1920...........137
10 Tris Speaker, 1912...........136

1893-1900

1 Billy Hamilton, 1894 198
2 Billy Hamilton, 1895 166
  Willie Keeler, 1894............165
  Joe Kelley, 1894...............165
5 Willie Keeler, 1895...........162
6 Hugh Duffy, 1894.............160
  Jesse Burkett, 1896..........160
8 Hughie Jennings, 1895......159
9 Bobby Lowe, 1894............158
10 John McGraw, 1894..........156

1876-1892

1 Tom Brown, 1891.............177
2 Tip O'Neill, 1887 167
3 Arlie Latham, 1887............163
4 Hugh Duffy, 1890.............161
5 Fred Dunlap, 1884...........160
6 King Kelly, 1886..............155
7 Dan Brouthers, 1887.........153
8 Arlie Latham, 1886...........152
  Mike Griffin, 1889.............152
  Harry Stovey, 1889...........152

Hits

1 Ichiro Suzuki, 2004......262
2 George Sisler, 1920 257
3 Lefty O'Doul, 1929 254
  Bill Terry, 1930 254
5 Al Simmons, 1925............253
6 Rogers Hornsby, 1922.......250
  Chuck Klein, 1930.............250
8 Ty Cobb, 1911................248
9 George Sisler, 1922 246
10 Ichiro Suzuki, 2001......242
11 Heinie Manush, 1928........241
  Babe Herman, 1930...........241
13 Jesse Burkett, 1896.........240
  Wade Boggs, 1985 240
  Darin Erstad, 2000......240
16 Willie Keeler, 1897...........239
  Rod Carew, 1977 239
18 Ed Delahanty, 1899..........238
  Don Mattingly, 1986 238
20 Hugh Duffy, 1894.............237
  Harry Heilmann, 1921.........237
  Paul Waner, 1927.............237
  Joe Medwick, 1937 237
24 Jack Tobin, 1921 236
25 Rogers Hornsby, 1921.......235
26 Lloyd Waner, 1929............234
  Kirby Puckett, 1988..........234
28 Joe Jackson, 1911............233
29 Nap Lajoie, 1901.............232
  Earl Averill, 1936.............232
31 Earle Combs, 1927...........231
  Freddie Lindstrom, 1928 231
  Freddie Lindstrom, 1930 231
  Matty Alou, 1969..............231
35 Stan Musial, 1948.............230
  Tommy Davis, 1962 230
  Joe Torre, 1971 230
  Pete Rose, 1973 230
  Willie Wilson, 1980 230
40 Rogers Hornsby, 1929 229
41 Kiki Cuyler, 1930 228
  Stan Musial, 1946............228
43 Nap Lajoie, 1910.............227
  Rogers Hornsby, 1924.......227
  Jim Bottomley, 1925.........227
  Sam Rice, 1925...............227
  Billy Herman, 1935...........227
  Charlie Gehringer, 1936......227
  Lance Johnson, 1996.........227
50 Jesse Burkett, 1901..........226
  Joe Jackson, 1912............226
  Bill Terry, 1929 226
  Chuck Klein, 1932.............226
55 Tip O'Neill, 1887 225
  Billy Hamilton, 1894..........225
  Jesse Burkett, 1895..........225
  Ty Cobb, 1917................225
  Harry Heilmann, 1925.........225
  Johnny Hodapp, 1930........225
  Bill Terry, 1932 225
  Paul Molitor, 1996 225
63 Eddie Collins, 1920...........224
  George Sisler, 1925 224
  Joe Medwick, 1935 224
  Tommy Holmes, 1945 224
67 Frankie Frisch, 1923 223
  Lloyd Waner, 1927 223
  Paul Waner, 1928.............223
  Chuck Klein, 1933.............223
  Joe Medwick, 1936 223
  Hank Aaron, 1959.............223
  Kirby Puckett, 1986..........223
74 Sam Thompson, 1893 222
  Tris Speaker, 1912...........222
  Charlie Jamieson, 1923......222
77 Jesse Burkett, 1899..........221
  Zack Wheat, 1925............221
  Lloyd Waner, 1928 221
  Heinie Manush, 1933.........221
  Richie Ashburn, 1951.........221
  Juan Pierre, 2004 221
  Michael Young, 2005 ...221
84 Pete Browning, 1887.........220
  Jimmy Williams, 1899 220
  Kiki Cuyler, 1925 220
  Lou Gehrig, 1930 220
  Stan Musial, 1943............220
  Tony Gwynn, 1997............220
90 Ed Delahanty, 1893..........219
  Willie Keeler, 1894............219
  Cy Seymour, 1905............219
  Chuck Klein, 1929.............219
  Lefty O'Doul, 1932...........219
  Paul Waner, 1937.............219
  Ralph Garr, 1971.............219
  Cecil Cooper, 1980...........219
  Dante Bichette, 1998 219
  Derek Jeter, 1999 219
100 12 players tied 218

Doubles

1 Earl Webb, 1931 67
2 George Burns, 1926 64
  Joe Medwick, 1936 64
4 Hank Greenberg, 1934 63
5 Paul Waner, 1932 62
6 Charlie Gehringer, 1936 ...60
7 Tris Speaker, 1923 59
  Chuck Klein, 1930 59
  Todd Helton, 2000 59
10 Billy Herman, 1935 57
   Billy Herman, 1936 57
   Carlos Delgado, 2000 ...57
13 Joe Medwick, 1937 56
   George Kell, 1950 56
   Craig Biggio, 1999 56
   Garret Anderson, 2002 ...56
   Nomar Garciaparra, 2002 ...56
18 Ed Delahanty, 1899 55
   Gee Walker, 1936 55
   Lance Berkman, 2001 55
21 Hal McRae, 1977 54
   John Olerud, 1993 54
   Alex Rodriguez, 1996 ...54
   Mark Grudzielanek, 1997 ...54
   Todd Helton, 2001 54
26 Tris Speaker, 1912 53
   Al Simmons, 1926 53
   Paul Waner, 1936 53
   Stan Musial, 1953 53
   Don Mattingly, 1986 53
   Jeff Cirillo, 2000 53
   Lyle Overbay, 2004 53
33 Tip O'Neill, 1887 52
   Tris Speaker, 1921 52
   Tris Speaker, 1926 52
   Lou Gehrig, 1927 52
   Johnny Frederick, 1929 ...52
   Enos Slaughter, 1939 52
   Albert Belle, 1995 52
   Edgar Martinez, 1995 52
   Edgar Martinez, 1996 52
42 Hugh Duffy, 1894 51
   Nap Lajoie, 1910 51
   Baby Doll Jacobson, 1926 ...51
   George Burns, 1927 51
   Johnny Hodapp, 1930 51
   Beau Bell, 1937 51
   Joe Cronin, 1938 51
   Stan Musial, 1944 51
   Mickey Vernon, 1946 51
   Frank Robinson, 1962 51
   Pete Rose, 1978 51
   Wade Boggs, 1989 51
   Mark Grace, 1995 51
   Craig Biggio, 1998 51
   Jose Vidro, 2000 51
   Nomar Garciaparra, 2000 ...51
   Alfonso Soriano, 2002 ...51
   Albert Pujols, 2003 51
   Albert Pujols, 2004 51
61 Tris Speaker, 1920 50
   Harry Heilmann, 1927 50
   Paul Waner, 1928 50
   Kiki Cuyler, 1930 50
   Chuck Klein, 1932 50
   Charlie Gehringer, 1934 ...50
   Odell Hale, 1936 50
   Ben Chapman, 1936 50
   Hank Greenberg, 1940 50
   Stan Musial, 1946 50
   Stan Spence, 1946 50
   Juan Gonzalez, 1998 50
   Bobby Abreu, 2002 50
   Brian Roberts, 2004 50
   Derrek Lee, 2005 50
   Miguel Tejada, 2005 50
77 Ed Williamson, 1883 49
   Ed Delahanty, 1895 49
   Nap Lajoie, 1904 49
   George Sisler, 1920 49
   Heinie Manush, 1930 49
   Riggs Stephenson, 1932 ...49
   Hank Greenberg, 1937 49
   Robin Yount, 1980 49
   Rafael Palmeiro, 1991 ...49
   Tony Gwynn, 1997 49
   Jeff Kent, 2001 49
   Marcus Giles, 2003 49
   Shawn Green, 2003 49
   Todd Helton, 2003 49
   Scott Rolen, 2003 49
   Garret Anderson, 2003 ...49
   Vernon Wells, 2003 49
   Todd Helton, 2004 49
95 19 players tied 48

Doubles by era

1988-2005
1 Todd Helton, 2000 59
2 Carlos Delgado, 2000 ...57
3 Craig Biggio, 1999 56
  Garret Anderson, 2002 ...56
  Nomar Garciaparra, 2002 ...56
6 Lance Berkman, 2001 55
7 John Olerud, 1993 54
  Alex Rodriguez, 1996 ...54
  Mark Grudzielanek, 1997 ...54
  Todd Helton, 2001 54

1973-1987
1 Hal McRae, 1977 54
2 Don Mattingly, 1986 53
3 Pete Rose, 1978 51
4 Robin Yount, 1980 49
5 Keith Hernandez, 1979 ...48
  Don Mattingly, 1985 48
7 Pete Rose, 1975 47
  Fred Lynn, 1975 47
  Cal Ripken, 1983 47
  Wade Boggs, 1986 47

1961-1972
1 Frank Robinson, 1962 51
2 Wes Parker, 1970 47
3 Lou Brock, 1968 46
4 Floyd Robinson, 1962 ...45
  Zoilo Versalles, 1965 ...45
  Carl Yastrzemski, 1965 ...45
7 Lee Maye, 1964 44
  Rusty Staub, 1967 44
9 Carl Yastrzemski, 1962 ...43
  Dick Groat, 1963 43
  Tony Oliva, 1964 43

1943-1960
1 George Kell, 1950 56
2 Stan Musial, 1953 53
3 Stan Musial, 1944 51
  Mickey Vernon, 1946 51
5 Stan Musial, 1946 50
  Stan Spence, 1946 50
7 Stan Musial, 1943 48
8 Tommy Holmes, 1945 47
  Vada Pinson, 1959 47
10 Stan Musial, 1948 46
   Hank Aaron, 1959 46

1921-1942
1 Earl Webb, 1931 67
2 George Burns, 1926 64
  Joe Medwick, 1936 64
4 Hank Greenberg, 1934 63
5 Paul Waner, 1932 62
6 Charlie Gehringer, 1936 ...60
7 Tris Speaker, 1923 59
  Chuck Klein, 1930 59
9 Billy Herman, 1935 57
  Billy Herman, 1936 57

1901-1920
1 Tris Speaker, 1912 53
2 Nap Lajoie, 1910 51
3 Tris Speaker, 1920 50
4 Nap Lajoie, 1904 49
  George Sisler, 1920 49
6 Nap Lajoie, 1901 48
  Nap Lajoie, 1906 48
8 Harry Davis, 1905 47
  Ty Cobb, 1911 47
10 John Anderson, 1901 46
   Tris Speaker, 1914 46

1893-1900
1 Ed Delahanty, 1899 55
2 Hugh Duffy, 1894 51
3 Ed Delahanty, 1895 49
4 Joe Kelley, 1894 48
5 Walt Wilmot, 1894 45
  Sam Thompson, 1895 45
  Honus Wagner, 1899 45
  Honus Wagner, 1900 45
9 Ed Delahanty, 1896 44
10 Jake Stenzel, 1897 43
   Nap Lajoie, 1898 43

1876-1892
1 Tip O'Neill, 1887 52
2 Ed Williamson, 1883 49
3 Denny Lyons, 1887 43
4 Dan Brouthers, 1883 41
  King Kelly, 1889 41
  Sam Thompson, 1890 41
7 Orator Shafer, 1884 40
  Dan Brouthers, 1886 40
  Jack Glasscock, 1889 ...40
  Pete Browning, 1890 40

Triples

1 Chief Wilson, 1912 36
2 Dave Orr, 1886 31
  Heinie Reitz, 1894 31
4 Perry Werden, 1893 29
5 Sam Thompson, 1894 28
  Harry Davis, 1897 28
7 George Davis, 1893 27
  Jimmy Williams, 1899 ...27
9 John Reilly, 1890 26
  George Treadway, 1894 ...26
  Joe Jackson, 1912 26
  Sam Crawford, 1914 26
  Kiki Cuyler, 1925 26
14 Roger Connor, 1894 25
   Buck Freeman, 1899 25
   Sam Crawford, 1903 25
   Larry Doyle, 1911 25
   Tom Long, 1915 25
19 Ed McKean, 1893 24
   Ty Cobb, 1911 24
   Ty Cobb, 1917 24
22 Harry Stovey, 1884 23
   Sam Thompson, 1887 23
   Elmer Smith, 1893 23
   Dan Brouthers, 1894 ...23
   Nap Lajoie, 1897 23
   Ty Cobb, 1912 23
   Sam Crawford, 1913 23
   Earle Combs, 1927 23
   Adam Comorosky, 1930 ...23
   Dale Mitchell, 1949 ...23
32 Roger Connor, 1887 22
   Bid McPhee, 1890 22
   Jake Beckley, 1890 22
   Joe Visner, 1890 22
   Willie Keeler, 1894 ...22
   Kip Selbach, 1895 22
   John Anderson, 1898 ...22
   Honus Wagner, 1900 22
   Tommy Leach, 1902 22
   Sam Crawford, 1902 22
   Bill Bradley, 1903 22
   Elmer Flick, 1906 22
   Mike Mitchell, 1911 ...22
   Birdie Cree, 1911 22
   Tris Speaker, 1913 22
   Hy Myers, 1920 22
   Jake Daubert, 1922 22
   Paul Waner, 1926 22
   Earle Combs, 1930 22
   Snuffy Stirnweiss, 1945 ...22
52 Dave Orr, 1885 21
   Mike Tiernan, 1890 21
   Billy Shindle, 1890 ...21
   Tom Brown, 1891 21
   Ed Delahanty, 1892 21
   Sam Thompson, 1895 21
   Mike Tiernan, 1895 21
   Tom McCreery, 1896 21
   George Van Haltren, 1896 ...21
   Bobby Wallace, 1897 ...21
   Jimmy Williams, 1901 ...21
   Bill Keister, 1901 21
   Jimmy Williams, 1902 ...21
   Cy Seymour, 1905 21
   Frank Schulte, 1911 ...21
   Frank Baker, 1912 21
   Sam Crawford, 1912 21
   Vic Saier, 1913 21
   Joe Jackson, 1916 21
   Edd Roush, 1924 21
   Earle Combs, 1928 21
   Willie Wilson, 1985 ...21
   Lance Johnson, 1996 ...21
75 37 players tied 20

Triples by era

1988-2005
1 Lance Johnson, 1996 21
2 Cristian Guzman, 2000 ...20
3 Carl Crawford, 2004 19
4 Tony Fernandez, 1990 ...17
  Chone Figgins, 2004 ...17
  Jose Reyes, 2005 17
7 Andy Van Slyke, 1988 ...15
  Ray Lankford, 1991 15
  Carl Crawford, 2005 ...15
10 9 players tied 14

1973-1987
1 Willie Wilson, 1985 21
2 George Brett, 1979 20
3 Garry Templeton, 1979 ...19
  Juan Samuel, 1984 19
  Ryne Sandberg, 1984 ...19
6 Garry Templeton, 1977 ...18
  Willie McGee, 1985 18
8 Ralph Garr, 1974 17
9 Rod Carew, 1977 16
  Paul Molitor, 1979 16

1961-1972
1 Johnny Callison, 1965 ...16
  Willie Davis, 1970 16
3 Gino Cimoli, 1962 15
4 Jake Wood, 1961 14
  Vada Pinson, 1963 14
  Dick Allen, 1965 14
  Roberto Clemente, 1965 ...14
  Donn Clendenon, 1965 ...14
  Lou Brock, 1968 14
  Don Kessinger, 1970 ...14

1943-1960
1 Dale Mitchell, 1949 23
2 Snuffy Stirnweiss, 1945 ...22
3 Stan Musial, 1943 20
  Stan Musial, 1946 20
  Willie Mays, 1957 20
6 Johnny Barrett, 1944 ...19
7 Stan Musial, 1948 18
  Minnie Minoso, 1954 ...18
9 Jim Gilliam, 1953 17
10 Bob Elliott, 1944 16
   Snuffy Stirnweiss, 1944 ...16
   Johnny Lindell, 1944 ...16
   Hank Edwards, 1946 16
   Harry Walker, 1947 16
   Jim Rivera, 1953 16

1921-1942
1 Kiki Cuyler, 1925 26
2 Earle Combs, 1927 23
  Adam Comorosky, 1930 ...23
4 Jake Daubert, 1922 22
  Paul Waner, 1926 22
  Earle Combs, 1930 22
7 Edd Roush, 1924 21
  Earle Combs, 1928 21
9 Rabbit Maranville, 1924 ...20
  Goose Goslin, 1925 20
  Curt Walker, 1926 20
  Lou Gehrig, 1926 20
  Jim Bottomley, 1928 ...20
  Heinie Manush, 1928 ...20
  Lloyd Waner, 1929 20
  Bill Terry, 1931 20
  Joe Vosmik, 1935 20
  Jeff Heath, 1941 20

1901-1920
1 Chief Wilson, 1912 36
2 Joe Jackson, 1912 26
  Sam Crawford, 1914 26
4 Sam Crawford, 1903 25
  Larry Doyle, 1911 25
  Tom Long, 1915 25
7 Ty Cobb, 1911 24
  Ty Cobb, 1917 24
9 Ty Cobb, 1912 23
  Sam Crawford, 1913 23

1893-1900
1 Heinie Reitz, 1894 31
2 Perry Werden, 1893 29
3 Sam Thompson, 1894 28
  Harry Davis, 1897 28
5 George Davis, 1893 27
  Jimmy Williams, 1899 ...27
7 George Treadway, 1894 ...26
8 Roger Connor, 1894 25
  Buck Freeman, 1899 25
10 Ed McKean, 1893 24

1876-1892
1 Dave Orr, 1886 31
2 John Reilly, 1890 26
3 Harry Stovey, 1884 23
  Sam Thompson, 1887 23
5 Roger Connor, 1887 22
  Bid McPhee, 1890 22
  Jake Beckley, 1890 22
  Joe Visner, 1890 22
9 Dave Orr, 1885 21
  Mike Tiernan, 1890 21
  Billy Shindle, 1890 ...21
  Tom Brown, 1891 21
  Ed Delahanty, 1892 21

Home Runs

1 Barry Bonds, 2001 73
2 Mark McGwire, 1998 70
3 Sammy Sosa, 1998 66
4 Mark McGwire, 1999 65
5 Sammy Sosa, 2001 64
6 Sammy Sosa, 1999 63
7 Roger Maris, 1961 61
8 Babe Ruth, 1927 60
9 Babe Ruth, 1921 59
10 Mark McGwire, 1997 58
   Jimmie Foxx, 1932 58
   Hank Greenberg, 1938 ...58
13 Luis Gonzalez, 2001 57
   Alex Rodriguez, 2002 ...57
15 Hack Wilson, 1930 56
   Ken Griffey Jr., 1997 ...56
   Ken Griffey Jr., 1998 ...56
18 Babe Ruth, 1920 54
   Babe Ruth, 1928 54
   Ralph Kiner, 1949 54
   Mickey Mantle, 1961 ...54
22 Mickey Mantle, 1956 ...52
   Willie Mays, 1965 52
   George Foster, 1977 ...52
   Mark McGwire, 1996 52
   Alex Rodriguez, 2001 ...52
   Jim Thome, 2002 52
28 Ralph Kiner, 1947 51
   Johnny Mize, 1947 51
   Willie Mays, 1955 51
   Cecil Fielder, 1990 ...51
   Andruw Jones, 2005 ...51
33 Jimmie Foxx, 1938 50
   Albert Belle, 1995 ...50
   Brady Anderson, 1996 ...50
   Greg Vaughn, 1998 50
   Sammy Sosa, 2000 50
38 Babe Ruth, 1930 49
   Lou Gehrig, 1934 49
   Lou Gehrig, 1936 49
   Ted Kluszewski, 1954 ...49
   Willie Mays, 1962 49
   Harmon Killebrew, 1964 ...49
   Frank Robinson, 1966 ...49
   Harmon Killebrew, 1969 ...49
   Andre Dawson, 1987 ...49
   Mark McGwire, 1987 ...49
   Ken Griffey Jr., 1996 ...49
   Larry Walker, 1997 ...49
   Albert Belle, 1998 ...49
   Barry Bonds, 2000 ...49
   Shawn Green, 2001 ...49
   Todd Helton, 2001 ...49
   Jim Thome, 2001 49
   Sammy Sosa, 2002 ...49
56 Jimmie Foxx, 1933 48
   Harmon Killebrew, 1962 ...48
   Frank Howard, 1969 ...48
   Willie Stargell, 1971 ...48
   Dave Kingman, 1979 ...48
   Mike Schmidt, 1980 ...48
   Albert Belle, 1996 ...48
   Ken Griffey Jr., 1999 ...48
   Adrian Beltre, 2004 ...48
   Alex Rodriguez, 2005 ...48
66 Babe Ruth, 1926 47
   Lou Gehrig, 1927 47
   Ralph Kiner, 1950 47
   Eddie Mathews, 1953 ...47
   Ted Kluszewski, 1955 ...47
   Ernie Banks, 1958 ...47
   Willie Mays, 1964 47
   Reggie Jackson, 1969 ...47
   Hank Aaron, 1971 47
   George Bell, 1987 ...47
   Kevin Mitchell, 1989 ...47
   Andres Galarraga, 1996 ...47
   Juan Gonzalez, 1996 ...47
   Rafael Palmeiro, 1999 ...47
   Jeff Bagwell, 2000 ...47
   Troy Glaus, 2000 ...47
   Rafael Palmeiro, 2001 ...47
   Jim Thome, 2003 ...47
   Alex Rodriguez, 2003 ...47
   David Ortiz, 2005 ...47
86 Babe Ruth, 1924 46
   Babe Ruth, 1929 46
   Babe Ruth, 1931 46
   Lou Gehrig, 1931 46
   Joe DiMaggio, 1937 ...46
   Eddie Mathews, 1959 ...46
   Orlando Cepeda, 1961 ...46
   Jim Gentile, 1961 ...46
   Harmon Killebrew, 1961 ...46
   Jim Rice, 1978 ...46
   Barry Bonds, 1993 ...46
   Juan Gonzalez, 1993 ...46
   Vinny Castilla, 1998 ...46
   Jose Canseco, 1998 ...46
   Barry Bonds, 2002 ...46
   Adam Dunn, 2004 ...46
   Albert Pujols, 2004 ...46
   Derrek Lee, 2005 46

Home Runs by era

1988-2005
1 Barry Bonds, 2001.........73
2 Mark McGwire, 1998.........70
3 Sammy Sosa, 1998......66
4 Mark McGwire, 1999.........65
5 Sammy Sosa, 2001......64
6 Sammy Sosa, 1999......63
7 Mark McGwire, 1997.........58
8 Luis Gonzalez, 2001 57
  Alex Rodriguez, 2002......57
10 Ken Griffey Jr., 1997.........56
  Ken Griffey Jr., 1998.........56

1973-1987
1 George Foster, 1977 52
2 Andre Dawson, 1987.........49
  Mark McGwire, 1987.........49
4 Dave Kingman, 1979 48
  Mike Schmidt, 1980.........48
6 George Bell, 1987.........47
7 Jim Rice, 1978.........46
8 Mike Schmidt, 1979.........45
  Gorman Thomas, 1979.........45
10 Willie Stargell, 1973.........44
  Dale Murphy, 1987.........44

1961-1972
1 Roger Maris, 1961 61
2 Mickey Mantle, 1961.........54
3 Willie Mays, 1965.........52
4 Willie Mays, 1962.........49
  Harmon Killebrew, 1964.....49
  Frank Robinson, 1966.........49
  Harmon Killebrew, 1969.....49
8 Harmon Killebrew, 1962.....48
  Frank Howard, 1969.........48
  Willie Stargell, 1971.........48

1943-1960
1 Ralph Kiner, 1949.........54
2 Mickey Mantle, 1956.........52
3 Ralph Kiner, 1947.........51
  Johnny Mize, 1947.........51
  Willie Mays, 1955.........51
6 Ted Kluszewski, 1954.........49
7 Ralph Kiner, 1950.........47
  Eddie Mathews, 1953.........47
  Ted Kluszewski, 1955.........47
  Ernie Banks, 1958.........47

1921-1942
1 Babe Ruth, 1927.........60
2 Babe Ruth, 1921.........59
3 Jimmie Foxx, 1932.........58
  Hank Greenberg, 1938 58
5 Hack Wilson, 1930.........56
6 Babe Ruth, 1928.........54
7 Jimmie Foxx, 1938.........50
8 Babe Ruth, 1930.........49
  Lou Gehrig, 1934.........49
  Lou Gehrig, 1936.........49

1901-1920
1 Babe Ruth, 1920.........54
2 Babe Ruth, 1919.........29
3 Gavy Cravath, 1915.........24
4 Frank Schulte, 1911.........21
5 Gavy Cravath, 1913.........19
  Gavy Cravath, 1914.........19
  George Sisler, 1920.........19
8 Fred Luderus, 1913.........18
  Vic Saier, 1914.........18
10 Hal Chase, 1915.........17
  Tilly Walker, 1920.........17

1893-1900
1 Buck Freeman, 1899.........25
2 Ed Delahanty, 1893.........19
3 Hugh Duffy, 1894.........18
  Sam Thompson, 1895 18
5 Jack Clements, 1893.........17
  Bill Joyce, 1894.........17
  Bobby Lowe, 1894.........17
  Bill Joyce, 1895.........17
9 Bill Dahlen, 1894.........15
  Jimmy Collins, 1898.........15

1876-1892
1 Ed Williamson, 1884 27
2 Fred Pfeffer, 1884.........25
3 Abner Dalrymple, 1884......22
4 Cap Anson, 1884.........21
5 Sam Thompson, 1889.........20
6 Billy O'Brien, 1887.........19
  Bug Holliday, 1889.........19
  Harry Stovey, 1889.........19
9 Jerry Denny, 1889.........18
10 Roger Connor, 1887.........17
  Jimmy Ryan, 1889.........17

Home Run Pct.

1 Barry Bonds, 2001.....15.34
2 Mark McGwire, 1998.....13.75
3 Mark McGwire, 1999.....12.48
4 Mark McGwire, 1996.....12.29
5 Barry Bonds, 2004.....12.06
6 Babe Ruth, 1920.....11.79
7 Barry Bonds, 2003.....11.54
8 Barry Bonds, 2002.....11.41
9 Babe Ruth, 1927.....11.11
10 Sammy Sosa, 2001.....11.09
11 Babe Ruth, 1921.....10.93
12 Jim Thome, 2002.....10.83
13 Mark McGwire, 1997.....10.74
14 Mickey Mantle, 1961.....10.51
15 Hank Greenberg, 1938 ...10.43
16 Roger Maris, 1961.....10.34
17 Sammy Sosa, 1998.....10.26
18 Barry Bonds, 2000.....10.21
19 Sammy Sosa, 1999.....10.08
20 Babe Ruth, 1928.....10.07
21 Jimmie Foxx, 1932.......9.91
22 Ralph Kiner, 1949.......9.84
23 Mickey Mantle, 1956.......9.76
24 Jeff Bagwell, 1994.......9.75
25 Kevin Mitchell, 1994.......9.68
26 Matt Williams, 1994.......9.66
27 Hack Wilson, 1930.......9.57
28 Frank Thomas, 1994.......9.52
29 Babe Ruth, 1926.......9.49
  Hank Aaron, 1971.......9.49
31 Jim Gentile, 1961.......9.47
32 Barry Bonds, 1994.......9.46
33 Babe Ruth, 1930.......9.46
34 Willie Stargell, 1971.......9.39
35 Luis Gonzalez, 2001.......9.36
36 Willie Mays, 1965.......9.32
37 Jim Thome, 2001.......9.32
38 Ken Griffey Jr., 1994.......9.24
39 Babe Ruth, 1929.......9.22
40 Ken Griffey Jr., 1997.......9.21
41 Boog Powell, 1964.......9.20
42 Willie McCovey, 1969.......9.16
43 Albert Belle, 1995.......9.16
44 Alex Rodriguez, 2002.......9.13
45 Ted Williams, 1957.......9.05
46 Ralph Kiner, 1947.......9.03
47 Dave Kingman, 1979.......9.02
48 Mark McGwire, 1992.......9.00
49 Ken Griffey Jr., 1996.......8.99
50 Babe Ruth, 1932.......8.97
51 Cecil Fielder, 1990.......8.90
52 Jimmie Foxx, 1938.......8.85
53 Ken Griffey Jr., 1998.......8.85
54 Harmon Killebrew, 1969.....8.83
55 Sammy Sosa, 2002.....8.81
56 Mark McGwire, 1987.......8.80
57 Willie Mays, 1955.......8.79
58 Mike Schmidt, 1980.......8.76
59 Mike Schmidt, 1981.......8.76
60 Harmon Killebrew, 1963.....8.74
  Albert Belle, 1994.......8.74
62 Greg Vaughn, 1998.......8.73
63 Jim Edmonds, 2003.....8.72
64 Johnny Mize, 1947.......8.70
  Andruw Jones, 2005 ..8.70
66 Babe Ruth, 1924.......8.70
  Harmon Killebrew, 1962.....8.70
68 Juan Gonzalez, 1996.....8.69
69 Manny Ramirez, 2000.....8.66
70 Kevin Mitchell, 1989.......8.66
71 Brady Anderson, 1996.......8.64
72 Larry Walker, 1997.....8.63
73 Babe Ruth, 1922.......8.62
74 Babe Ruth, 1931.......8.61
75 Ralph Kiner, 1950.......8.59
76 Gary Sheffield, 2000 ..8.58
77 Juan Gonzalez, 1993.....8.58
78 Reggie Jackson, 1969.......8.56
79 Ted Kluszewski, 1954.......8.55
80 Barry Bonds, 1993.....8.53
81 Jay Buhner, 1995.......8.51
82 Frank Robinson, 1966.......8.51
83 Harmon Killebrew, 1961.....8.50
84 Harmon Killebrew, 1964.....8.49
85 Lou Gehrig, 1934.......8.46
  Lou Gehrig, 1936.......8.46
87 George Foster, 1977.......8.46
88 Larry Walker, 1999.....8.45
89 Jim Edmonds, 2004.....8.43
90 Jason Giambi, 2000.....8.43
91 Willie Stargell, 1973.......8.43
  Manny Ramirez, 1999.....8.43
93 Hank Greenberg, 1946.......8.41
94 Eddie Mathews, 1954.......8.40
95 Gary Sheffield, 1994.....8.39
96 Rocky Colavito, 1958.......8.38
97 Jimmie Foxx, 1933.......8.38
98 Joe Adcock, 1956.......8.37
99 Alex Rodriguez, 1999.....8.37
100 Jack Clark, 1987.......8.35

Home Run Pct. by era

1988-2005
1 Barry Bonds, 2001.....15.34
2 Mark McGwire, 1998.....13.75
3 Mark McGwire, 1999.....12.48
4 Mark McGwire, 1996.....12.29
5 Barry Bonds, 2004.....12.06
6 Barry Bonds, 2003.....11.54
7 Barry Bonds, 2002.....11.41
8 Sammy Sosa, 2001.....11.09
9 Jim Thome, 2002.....10.83
10 Mark McGwire, 1997.....10.74

1973-1987
1 Dave Kingman, 1979.......9.02
2 Mark McGwire, 1987.......8.80
3 Mike Schmidt, 1980.......8.76
4 Mike Schmidt, 1981.......8.76
5 George Foster, 1977.......8.46
6 Willie Stargell, 1973.......8.43
7 Jack Clark, 1987.......8.35
8 Mike Schmidt, 1979.......8.32
9 Gorman Thomas, 1979.......8.08
10 Reggie Jackson, 1980.......7.98

1961-1972
1 Mickey Mantle, 1961.....10.51
2 Roger Maris, 1961.....10.34
3 Hank Aaron, 1971.......9.49
4 Jim Gentile, 1961.......9.47
5 Willie Stargell, 1971.......9.39
6 Willie Mays, 1965.......9.32
7 Boog Powell, 1964.......9.20
8 Willie McCovey, 1969.......9.16
9 Harmon Killebrew, 1969.....8.83
10 Harmon Killebrew, 1963...8.74

1943-1960
1 Ralph Kiner, 1949.......9.84
2 Mickey Mantle, 1956.......9.76
3 Ted Williams, 1957.......9.05
4 Ralph Kiner, 1947.......9.03
5 Willie Mays, 1955.......8.79
6 Johnny Mize, 1947.......8.70
7 Ralph Kiner, 1950.......8.59
8 Ted Kluszewski, 1954.......8.55
9 Hank Greenberg, 1946.......8.41
10 Eddie Mathews, 1954......8.40

1921-1942
1 Babe Ruth, 1927.....11.11
2 Babe Ruth, 1921.....10.93
3 Hank Greenberg, 1938 ...10.43
4 Babe Ruth, 1928.....10.07
5 Jimmie Foxx, 1932.......9.91
6 Hack Wilson, 1930.......9.57
7 Babe Ruth, 1926.......9.49
8 Babe Ruth, 1930.......9.46
9 Babe Ruth, 1929.......9.22
10 Babe Ruth, 1932.......8.97

1901-1920
1 Babe Ruth, 1920.....11.79
2 Babe Ruth, 1919.......6.71
3 Gavy Cravath, 1915.......4.60
4 Gavy Cravath, 1914.......3.81
5 Frank Schulte, 1911.......3.64
6 Gavy Cravath, 1913.......3.62
7 Sherry Magee, 1911.......3.37
8 Vic Saier, 1914.......3.35
9 Sam Crawford, 1901.......3.11
10 Socks Seybold, 1902.......3.07

1893-1900
1 Bill Joyce, 1894.......4.79
2 Jack Clements, 1893.......4.52
3 Buck Freeman, 1899.......4.25
4 Jim Canavan, 1894.......3.57
5 Bill Joyce, 1895.......3.55
6 Sam Thompson, 1895.......3.35
7 Hugh Duffy, 1894.......3.34
8 Ed Delahanty, 1893.......3.19
9 Bill Dahlen, 1894.......2.96
10 Sam Thompson, 1894.......2.88

1876-1892
1 Ed Williamson, 1884.......6.47
2 Fred Pfeffer, 1884.......5.35
3 Cap Anson, 1884.......4.42
4 Abner Dalrymple, 1884.......4.22
5 Billy O'Brien, 1887.......4.19
6 Sam Thompson, 1889.......3.75
7 Roger Connor, 1887.......3.61
8 Dan Brouthers, 1884.......3.52
9 Harry Stovey, 1889.......3.42
10 Bug Holliday, 1889.......3.37

Extra Base Hits

1 Babe Ruth, 1921.........119
2 Lou Gehrig, 1927.........117
3 Chuck Klein, 1930.........107
  Barry Bonds, 2001.........107
5 Todd Helton, 2001 105
6 Chuck Klein, 1932.........103
  Hank Greenberg, 1937 ...103
  Stan Musial, 1948.........103
  Albert Belle, 1995.........103
  Todd Helton, 2000 103
  Sammy Sosa, 2001.........103
12 Rogers Hornsby, 1922.........102
13 Lou Gehrig, 1930.........100
  Jimmie Foxx, 1932.........100
  Luis Gonzalez, 2001 100
16 Babe Ruth, 1920.........99
  Babe Ruth, 1923.........99
  Hank Greenberg, 1940 ...99
  Larry Walker, 1997 99
  Albert Belle, 1998.........99
  Carlos Delgado, 2000.......99
  Albert Pujols, 2004.........99
  Derrek Lee, 2005 99
24 Hank Greenberg, 1935 98
25 Babe Ruth, 1927.........97
  Hack Wilson, 1930.........97
  Joe Medwick, 1937.........97
  Juan Gonzalez, 1998.......97
29 Hank Greenberg, 1934 96
  Hal Trosky, 1936.........96
  Joe DiMaggio, 1937.........96
32 Lou Gehrig, 1934.........95
  Joe Medwick, 1936.........95
  Albert Pujols, 2003.........95
35 Rogers Hornsby, 1929.........94
  Chuck Klein, 1929.........94
  Babe Herman, 1930.........94
  Jimmie Foxx, 1933.........94
  Lance Berkman, 2001 94
40 Jim Bottomley, 1928.........93
  Al Simmons, 1930.........93
  Lou Gehrig, 1936.........93
  Ellis Burks, 1996.........93
  Ken Griffey Jr., 1997.........93
45 Babe Ruth, 1924.........92
  Lou Gehrig, 1931.........92
  Jimmie Foxx, 1938.........92
  Stan Musial, 1953.........92
  Hank Aaron, 1959.........92
  Frank Robinson, 1962.........92
  Brady Anderson, 1996.........92
  Ken Griffey Jr., 1998.........92
  Alfonso Soriano, 2002.......92
54 Babe Ruth, 1928.........91
  Alex Rodriguez, 1996.......91
  Mark McGwire, 1998.........91
  David Ortiz, 2004.........91
58 Rogers Hornsby, 1925.........90
  Stan Musial, 1949.........90
  Willie Mays, 1962.........90
  Willie Stargell, 1973.........90
62 Hal Trosky, 1934.........89
  Duke Snider, 1954.........89
  Andres Galarraga, 1996 ...89
  Albert Belle, 1996.........89
  Sammy Sosa, 1999.........89
  Richard Hidalgo, 2000.......89
  Sammy Sosa, 2000.........89
69 Joe DiMaggio, 1936.........88
  Barry Bonds, 1993.........88
  Barry Bonds, 1998.........88
  Albert Pujols, 2001.........88
  Garret Anderson, 2002.......88
  David Ortiz, 2005.........88
75 Tris Speaker, 1923.........87
  Kiki Cuyler, 1925.........87
  Lou Gehrig, 1928.........87
  Ripper Collins, 1934.........87
  Charlie Gehringer, 1936.......87
  Johnny Mize, 1940.........87
  Willie Mays, 1954.........87
  Robin Yount, 1982.........87
  Kevin Mitchell, 1989.........87
  Chipper Jones, 1999.........87
  Mark McGwire, 1999.........87
  Shawn Green, 1999.........87
  Frank Thomas, 2000.........87
  Jason Giambi, 2001.........87
  Alex Rodriguez, 2001.........87
  Todd Helton, 2003.........87
  Vernon Wells, 2003.........87
  Manny Ramirez, 2004.........87
  Mark Teixeira, 2005.........87
94 17 players tied 86

Total Bases

1 Babe Ruth, 1921.........457
2 Rogers Hornsby, 1922.........450
3 Lou Gehrig, 1927.........447
4 Chuck Klein, 1930.........445
5 Jimmie Foxx, 1932.........438
6 Stan Musial, 1948.........429
7 Sammy Sosa, 2001.........425
8 Hack Wilson, 1930.........423
9 Chuck Klein, 1932.........420
10 Lou Gehrig, 1930.........419
  Luis Gonzalez, 2001.........419
12 Joe DiMaggio, 1937.........418
13 Babe Ruth, 1927.........417
14 Babe Herman, 1930.........416
  Sammy Sosa, 1998.........416
16 Barry Bonds, 2001.........411
17 Lou Gehrig, 1931.........410
18 Rogers Hornsby, 1929.........409
  Lou Gehrig, 1934.........409
  Larry Walker, 1997.........409
21 Joe Medwick, 1937.........406
  Jim Rice, 1978.........406
23 Chuck Klein, 1929.........405
  Hal Trosky, 1936.........405
  Todd Helton, 2000 405
26 Jimmie Foxx, 1933.........403
  Lou Gehrig, 1936.........403
28 Todd Helton, 2001 402
29 Hank Aaron, 1959.........400
30 George Sisler, 1920.........399
  Babe Ruth, 1923.........399
  Albert Belle, 1998.........399
33 Jimmie Foxx, 1938.........398
34 Lefty O'Doul, 1929.........397
  Hank Greenberg, 1937 ...397
  Sammy Sosa, 1999.........397
37 Albert Pujols, 2003.........394
38 Ken Griffey Jr., 1997.........393
  Alex Rodriguez, 2001 .393
  Derrek Lee, 2005.........393
41 Al Simmons, 1925.........392
  Bill Terry, 1930.........392
  Al Simmons, 1930.........392
  Ellis Burks, 1996.........392
45 Babe Ruth, 1924.........391
46 Hank Greenberg, 1935 389
  Alex Rodriguez, 2002 ..389
  Albert Pujols, 2004.........389
49 Babe Ruth, 1920.........388
  George Foster, 1977 388
  Don Mattingly, 1986.........388
52 Ken Griffey Jr., 1998.........387
53 Earl Averill, 1936.........385
54 Hank Greenberg, 1940 ...384
  Alex Rodriguez, 1998 ..384
56 Mark McGwire, 1998.........383
  Sammy Sosa, 2000.........383
58 Stan Musial, 1949.........382
  Willie Mays, 1955.........382
  Willie Mays, 1962.........382
  Jim Rice, 1977.........382
  Juan Gonzalez, 1998......382
63 Rogers Hornsby, 1925.........381
  Alfonso Soriano, 2002.......381
65 Babe Ruth, 1928.........380
  Hank Greenberg, 1938 ...380
  Frank Robinson, 1962.........380
  Vinny Castilla, 1998 380
69 Babe Ruth, 1930.........379
  Ernie Banks, 1958.........379
  Alex Rodriguez, 1996 ..379
  Vladimir Guerrero, 2000...379
73 Rogers Hornsby, 1921 378
  Duke Snider, 1954.........378
  Carlos Delgado, 2000..378
76 Willie Mays, 1954.........377
  Albert Belle, 1995.........377
78 Mickey Mantle, 1956.........376
  Andres Galarraga, 1996 ...376
  Adrian Beltre, 2004 376
81 Albert Belle, 1996.........375
82 Hugh Duffy, 1894.........374
  Babe Ruth, 1931.........374
  Hal Trosky, 1934.........374
  Tony Oliva, 1964.........374
86 Rogers Hornsby, 1924.........373
  Al Simmons, 1929.........373
  Bill Terry, 1932.........373
  Billy Williams, 1970.........373
  Vernon Wells, 2003.....373
91 Lou Gehrig, 1932.........370
  Duke Snider, 1953.........370
  Hank Aaron, 1963.........370
  Don Mattingly, 1985.........370
  Mo Vaughn, 1996.........370
  Shawn Green, 2001.....370
  Mark Teixeira, 2005.....370
98 8 players tied 369

Runs Batted In

1 Hack Wilson, 1930 191
2 Lou Gehrig, 1931 184
3 Hank Greenberg, 1937 183
4 Lou Gehrig, 1927 175
Jimmie Foxx, 1938 175
6 Lou Gehrig, 1930 174
7 Babe Ruth, 1921 171
8 Chuck Klein, 1930............170
Hank Greenberg, 1935 170
10 Jimmie Foxx, 1932 169
11 Joe DiMaggio, 1937............167
12 Sam Thompson, 1887 166
13 Sam Thompson, 1895 165
Al Simmons, 1930............165
Lou Gehrig, 1934 165
Manny Ramirez, 1999..165
17 Babe Ruth, 1927............164
18 Babe Ruth, 1931............163
Jimmie Foxx, 1933............163
20 Hal Trosky, 1936............162
21 **Sammy Sosa, 2001......160**
22 Hack Wilson, 1929............159
Lou Gehrig, 1937............159
Ted Williams, 1949............159
Vern Stephens, 1949............159
26 **Sammy Sosa, 1998......158**
27 Al Simmons, 1929............157
Juan Gonzalez, 1998...157
29 Jimmie Foxx, 1930............156
30 Ken Williams, 1922............155
Joe DiMaggio, 1948............155
32 Babe Ruth, 1929............154
Joe Medwick, 1937............154
34 Babe Ruth, 1930............153
Tommy Davis, 1962............153
36 Rogers Hornsby, 1922............152
Lou Gehrig, 1936............152
Albert Belle, 1998............152
39 Mel Ott, 1929............151
Lou Gehrig, 1932............151
Al Simmons, 1932............151
42 Hank Greenberg, 1940....150
Andres Galarraga, 1996....150
Miguel Tejada, 2004 150
45 Rogers Hornsby, 1929....149
George Foster, 1977....149
47 Johnny Bench, 1970............148
Albert Belle, 1996............148
Rafael Palmeiro, 1999 148
David Ortiz, 2005.........148
51 Cap Anson, 1886............147
Sam Thompson, 1894............147
Ken Griffey Jr., 1997......147
Mark McGwire, 1998......147
Mark McGwire, 1999......147
Todd Helton, 2000......147
57 Hardy Richardson, 1890....146
Ed Delahanty, 1893............146
Babe Ruth, 1926............146
Hank Greenberg, 1938............146
Ken Griffey Jr., 1998......146
Todd Helton, 2001......146
63 Hugh Duffy, 1894............145
Chuck Klein, 1929............145
Ted Williams, 1939............145
Al Rosen, 1953............145
Don Mattingly, 1985............145
Manny Ramirez, 1998..145
Edgar Martinez, 2000............145
Carlos Delgado, 2003..145
71 Walt Dropo, 1950............144
Vern Stephens, 1950............144
Juan Gonzalez, 1996...144
Vinny Castilla, 1998...144
Mike Sweeney, 2000...144
Manny Ramirez, 2005...144
Mark Teixeira, 2005...144
78 Rogers Hornsby, 1925...143
Earl Averill, 1931............143
Don Hurst, 1932............143
Jimmie Foxx, 1936............143
Ernie Banks, 1959............143
Mo Vaughn, 1996............143
Frank Thomas, 2000...143
85 Lou Gehrig, 1928............142
Babe Ruth, 1928............142
Hal Trosky, 1934............142
Roy Campanella, 1953...142
Orlando Cepeda, 1961...142
Roger Maris, 1961............142
Rafael Palmeiro, 1996...142
Matt Williams, 1999............142
Luis Gonzalez, 2001....142
Alex Rodriguez, 2002...142
95 Ted Kluszewski, 1954...141
Jim Gentile, 1961............141
Willie Mays, 1962............141
Dante Bichette, 1996............141
Tino Martinez, 1997...141
Sammy Sosa, 1999......141
Bret Boone, 2001.........141
Preston Wilson, 2003 ..141

Runs Batted In by era

1988-2005
1 **Manny Ramirez, 1999..165**
2 **Sammy Sosa, 2001......160**
3 **Sammy Sosa, 1998......158**
4 **Juan Gonzalez, 1998...157**
5 Albert Belle, 1998 152
6 Andres Galarraga, 1996...150
Miguel Tejada, 2004 150
8 Albert Belle, 1996............148
Rafael Palmeiro, 1999 148
David Ortiz, 2005.........148

1973-1987
1 George Foster, 1977 149
2 Don Mattingly, 1985............145
3 Jim Rice, 1978............139
Don Baylor, 1979............139
5 Andre Dawson, 1987............137
6 George Bell, 1987............134
7 Hal McRae, 1982............133
8 Greg Luzinski, 1977............130
Jim Rice, 1979............130
10 Johnny Bench, 1974............129

1961-1972
1 Tommy Davis, 1962............153
2 Johnny Bench, 1970 148
3 Orlando Cepeda, 1961............142
Roger Maris, 1961............142
5 Jim Gentile, 1961............141
Willie Mays, 1962............141
7 Rocky Colavito, 1961............140
Harmon Killebrew, 1969...140
9 Joe Torre, 1971............137
10 Frank Robinson, 1962............136

1943-1960
1 Ted Williams, 1949............159
Vern Stephens, 1949............159
3 Joe DiMaggio, 1948............155
4 Al Rosen, 1953............145
5 Walt Dropo, 1950............144
Vern Stephens, 1950............144
7 Ernie Banks, 1959............143
8 Roy Campanella, 1953 142
9 Ted Kluszewski, 1954 141
10 Johnny Mize, 1947............138

1921-1942
1 Hack Wilson, 1930............191
2 Lou Gehrig, 1931............184
3 Hank Greenberg, 1937............183
4 Lou Gehrig, 1927............175
Jimmie Foxx, 1938............175
6 Lou Gehrig, 1930............174
7 Babe Ruth, 1921............171
8 Chuck Klein, 1930............170
Hank Greenberg, 1935 170
10 Jimmie Foxx, 1932............169

1901-1920
1 Babe Ruth, 1920............137
2 Frank Baker, 1912............130
3 Gavy Cravath, 1913............128
4 Ty Cobb, 1911............127
5 Honus Wagner, 1901............126
6 Nap Lajoie, 1901............125
7 Sherry Magee, 1910............123
8 George Sisler, 1920............122
Baby Doll Jacobson, 1920 ...122
10 Buck Freeman, 1902............121
Cy Seymour, 1905............121
Joe Jackson, 1920............121

1893-1900
1 Sam Thompson, 1895 165
2 Sam Thompson, 1894............147
3 Ed Delahanty, 1893............146
4 Hugh Duffy, 1894............145
5 Ed Delahanty, 1899............137
6 George Davis, 1897............135
7 Steve Brodie, 1895............134
Joe Kelley, 1895............134
9 Ed McKean, 1893............133
Ed Delahanty, 1894............133

1876-1892
1 Sam Thompson, 1887 166
2 Cap Anson, 1886............147
3 Hardy Richardson, 1890...146
4 Roger Connor, 1889............130
5 Tommy Burns, 1890............128
6 Dave Orr, 1890............124
Dan Brouthers, 1892............124
8 Tip O'Neill, 1887............123
9 Jake Beckley, 1890............120
Cap Anson, 1891............120

Walks

1 **Barry Bonds, 2004........232**
2 **Barry Bonds, 2002......198**
3 **Barry Bonds, 2001......177**
4 Babe Ruth, 1923............170
5 Ted Williams, 1947............162
Ted Williams, 1949............162
Mark McGwire, 1998............162
8 Ted Williams, 1946............156
9 Eddie Yost, 1956............151
Barry Bonds, 1996............151
11 Babe Ruth, 1920............150
12 Eddie Joost, 1949............149
Jeff Bagwell, 1999............149
14 Eddie Stanky, 1945............148
Jimmy Wynn, 1969............148
Barry Bonds, 2003............148
17 Jimmy Sheckard, 1911 147
Ted Williams, 1941............147
19 Mickey Mantle, 1957............146
20 Babe Ruth, 1921............145
Ted Williams, 1942............145
Harmon Killebrew, 1969...145
24 Babe Ruth, 1926............144
Eddie Stanky, 1950............144
Ted Williams, 1951............144
27 Babe Ruth, 1924............142
Gary Sheffield, 1996............142
29 Eddie Yost, 1950............141
30 **Frank Thomas, 1991....138**
31 Babe Ruth, 1927............137
Babe Ruth, 1928............137
Eddie Stanky, 1946............137
Roy Cullenbine, 1947............137
Ralph Kiner, 1951............137
Willie McCovey, 1970............137
Jason Giambi, 2000......137
38 Jack Crooks, 1892............136
Babe Ruth, 1930............136
Ferris Fain, 1949............136
Ted Williams, 1954............136
Jack Clark, 1987............136
Frank Thomas, 1995......136
44 Eddie Yost, 1959............135
Jeff Bagwell, 1996............135
Brian Giles, 2002............135
47 Ferris Fain, 1950............133
Mark McGwire, 1999............133
49 Lou Gehrig, 1935............132
Frank Howard, 1970............132
Joe Morgan, 1975............132
Jack Clark, 1989............132
Tony Phillips, 1993............132
54 Bob Elliott, 1948............131
Eddie Yost, 1954............131
Harmon Killebrew, 1967...131
57 Babe Ruth, 1932............130
Lou Gehrig, 1936............130
Barry Bonds, 1998............130
60 Eddie Yost, 1952............129
Mickey Mantle, 1958............129
Lenny Dykstra, 1993............129
Jason Giambi, 2001......129
Jason Giambi, 2003......129
65 Billy Hamilton, 1894............128
Max Bishop, 1929............128
Max Bishop, 1930............128
Babe Ruth, 1931............128
Harmon Killebrew, 1970...128
Carl Yastrzemski, 1970...128
Mike Schmidt, 1983............128
Adam Dunn, 2002......128
73 Lu Blue, 1931............127
Lou Gehrig, 1937............127
Eddie Stanky, 1951............127
Jimmy Wynn, 1976............127
Barry Bonds, 1992............127
Jeff Bagwell, 1997............127
Jim Thome, 1999............127
Bobby Abreu, 2004............127
Lance Berkman, 2004............127
Todd Helton, 2004............127
83 Lu Blue, 1929............126
Ted Williams, 1948............126
Eddie Yost, 1951............126
Mickey Mantle, 1961............126
Darrell Evans, 1974............126
Rickey Henderson, 1989...126
Barry Bonds, 1993............126
Chipper Jones, 1999............126
91 Richie Ashburn, 1954............125
Eddie Yost, 1960............125
Gene Tenace, 1977............125
Wade Boggs, 1988............125
Rickey Henderson, 1996...125
Tony Phillips, 1996............125
John Olerud, 1999............125
98 John McGraw, 1899............124
Norm Cash, 1961............124
Eddie Mathews, 1963............124
Darrell Evans, 1973............124

Walk Percentage (BB/PA)

1 **Barry Bonds, 2004....37.60**
2 **Barry Bonds, 2002....32.35**
3 **Barry Bonds, 2003....26.91**
4 **Barry Bonds, 2001....26.66**
5 Ted Williams, 1954....25.86
6 Jack Clark, 1987....24.37
7 Babe Ruth, 1920....24.35
8 Babe Ruth, 1923....24.32
9 Mickey Mantle, 1962....24.30
10 Ted Williams, 1941....24.26
11 Mark McGwire, 1998....23.79
12 Mickey Mantle, 1957....23.43
13 Ted Williams, 1947....23.38
14 Jack Crooks, 1892....23.33
15 Ted Williams, 1946....23.21
16 John McGraw, 1899....23.01
17 Jimmy Wynn, 1969....22.66
18 Roy Cullenbine, 1947....22.57
19 **Barry Bonds, 1996....22.37**
20 Jack Clark, 1989....22.26
21 Ted Williams, 1949....22.19
22 Babe Ruth, 1926....22.09
23 Eddie Yost, 1956....22.08
24 Babe Ruth, 1932....22.07
25 Max Bishop, 1926....21.93
26 Eddie Joost, 1949....21.85
27 Mickey Tettleton, 1994....21.85
28 Ted Williams, 1957....21.79
29 Max Bishop, 1930....21.77
30 Jimmy Wynn, 1976....21.75
31 Toby Harrah, 1985....21.69
32 Ted Williams, 1942....21.61
33 Gene Tenace, 1977....21.51
34 Willie McCovey, 1970....21.47
35 Max Bishop, 1927....21.47
36 Eddie Stanky, 1946....21.34
37 Ted Williams, 1951....21.33
38 Mark McGwire, 1996....21.17
39 **Frank Thomas, 1994....21.08**
40 Max Bishop, 1932....21.07
41 **Frank Thomas, 1995....21.02**
42 **Barry Bonds, 1997....21.01**
43 Max Bishop, 1933....20.99
44 **Gary Sheffield, 1996....20.97**
45 **Brian Giles, 2002....20.96**
46 Jack Crooks, 1893....20.93
47 Babe Ruth, 1921....20.92
48 Jimmy Sheckard, 1911 ...20.88
49 Willie Mays, 1971....20.86
50 Babe Ruth, 1924....20.85
51 Eddie Stanky, 1950....20.84
52 Jimmy Wynn, 1975....20.79
53 **Gary Sheffield, 1997....20.79**
54 Max Bishop, 1929....20.78
55 Rickey Henderson, 1996...20.76
56 **Barry Bonds, 1992....20.75**
57 Joe Morgan, 1975....20.66
58 **Jason Giambi, 2000....20.63**
59 Yank Robinson, 1889....20.49
60 Harmon Killebrew, 1969...20.45
61 Ralph Kiner, 1951....20.45
62 **Jeff Bagwell, 1999....20.44**
63 Elmer Valo, 1952....20.40
64 Hank Greenberg, 1947 ..20.39
65 Eddie Stanky, 1945....20.39
66 Ted Williams, 1956....20.28
67 Ferris Fain, 1949....20.24
68 Ferris Fain, 1950....20.21
69 **Jim Thome, 1999....20.19**
70 Mark McGwire, 1999....20.12
71 Babe Ruth, 1930....20.12
72 Babe Ruth, 1928....20.03
73 Eddie Yost, 1959....20.00
74 **Jim Thome, 2002....19.90**
75 Yank Robinson, 1888....19.90
76 Babe Ruth, 1927....19.83
77 Babe Ruth, 1933....19.83
78 **Jason Giambi, 2005..19.82**
79 Ted Williams, 1948....19.75
80 Mickey Mantle, 1958....19.72
81 **Frank Thomas, 1991....19.71**
82 Bill Joyce, 1890....19.71
83 Mel Ott, 1943....19.71
84 Cupid Childs, 1893....19.70
85 Mel Ott, 1939....19.69
86 Rickey Henderson, 1993...19.67
87 Eddie Yost, 1960....19.65
88 Lou Gehrig, 1935....19.64
89 Gene Tenace, 1978....19.61
90 Danny Tartabull, 1992...19.58
91 Mickey Tettleton, 1995...19.56
92 Mickey Cochrane, 1933...19.56
93 Luke Appling, 1949....19.55
94 John McGraw, 1897....19.53
95 Mickey Mantle, 1954....19.50
96 Eddie Stanky, 1951....19.45
97 Johnny Evers, 1910....19.42
98 Willie McCovey, 1969....19.42
99 Bob Elliott, 1948....19.41
100 Edgar Martinez, 1996 ....19.40

Strikeouts

1 **Adam Dunn, 2004......195**
2 Bobby Bonds, 1970............189
3 **Jose Hernandez, 2002......188**
4 Bobby Bonds, 1969............187
Preston Wilson, 2000 ..187
6 Rob Deer, 1987............186
7 Pete Incaviglia, 1986............185
Jose Hernandez, 2001......185
Jim Thome, 2001......185
10 Cecil Fielder, 1990............182
Jim Thome, 2003......182
12 Mo Vaughn, 2000............181
13 Mike Schmidt, 1975............180
14 Rob Deer, 1986............179
15 **Richie Sexson, 2001....178**
16 **Jose Hernandez, 2003......177**
Mark Bellhorn, 2004......177
18 **Mike Cameron, 2002......176**
19 Dave Nicholson, 1963............175
Gorman Thomas, 1979............175
Jose Canseco, 1986............175
Rob Deer, 1991............175
Jay Buhner, 1997............175
24 **Sammy Sosa, 1997......174**
25 Jim Presley, 1986............172
Bo Jackson, 1989............172
27 Reggie Jackson, 1968............171
Sammy Sosa, 1998......171
Sammy Sosa, 1999......171
Jim Thome, 1999......171
Jim Thome, 2000......171
32 Gorman Thomas, 1980............170
Adam Dunn, 2002......170
34 Andres Galarraga, 1990 ...169
Rob Deer, 1993............169
Craig Wilson, 2004......169
37 Juan Samuel, 1984............168
Pete Incaviglia, 1987............168
Sammy Sosa, 2000......168
Corey Patterson, 2004......168
Adam Dunn, 2005......168
42 Jim Edmonds, 2000............167
Richie Sexson, 2005....167
44 Gary Alexander, 1978............166
Steve Balboni, 1985............166
Cory Snyder, 1987............166
47 **Derrek Lee, 2002......166**
Troy Glaus, 2000......166
50 Butch Hobson, 1977............162
Juan Samuel, 1987............162
Ron Gant, 1997............162
Pat Burrell, 2001......162
54 Dick Allen, 1968............161
Reggie Jackson, 1971............161
Brad Wilkerson, 2002..161
57 Mickey Tettleton, 1990............160
Henry Rodriguez, 1996...160
Pat Burrell, 2005......160
60 Mark McGwire, 1997............159
Richie Sexson, 2000......159
Jay Buhner, 1996............159
Jose Canseco, 1998............159
Ben Grieve, 2001 159
65 Bo Jackson, 1987............158
Andres Galarraga, 1989 ...158
Rob Deer, 1989............158
Jose Canseco, 1990............158
Melvin Nieves, 1996............158
Jeromy Burnitz, 1998...158
Troy Glaus, 2001......158
72 Danny Tartabull, 1986............157
Jose Canseco, 1987............157
Jim Presley, 1987............157
Andres Galarraga, 1986...157
Melvin Nieves, 1997............157
Lee Stevens, 2001............157
Alfonso Soriano, 2002 ...157
79 Tommie Agee, 1970............156
Dave Kingman, 1982............156
Reggie Jackson, 1982............156
Tony Armas, 1984............156
Danny Tartabull, 1993............156
Preston Wilson, 1999 ...156
85 Frank Howard, 1967............155
Jeff Burroughs, 1975............155
Mark McGwire, 1998............155
Mike Cameron, 2001...155
Brad Wilkerson, 2003...155
90 Willie Stargell, 1971............154
Larry Parrish, 1987............154
Dean Palmer, 1992............154
Dean Palmer, 1993............154
Mo Vaughn, 1996............154
Mo Vaughn, 1997............154
96 Dave Kingman, 1975............153
Andres Galarraga, 1988...153
Rob Deer, 1988............153
Pete Incaviglia, 1988............153
Dean Palmer, 1993............153
Sammy Sosa, 2001......153
Pat Burrell, 2002............153

Strikeout Percentage

1988-2005
1. Rob Deer, 1991 ....39.06
2. Rob Deer, 1993 ....36.27
3. Mickey Tettleton, 1990 ....36.04
4. **Jose Hernandez, 2002 ....35.81**
5. Benji Gil, 1995 ....35.42
6. **Jim Thome, 2001 ....35.17**
7. **Jim Thome, 1999 ....34.62**
8. **Adam Dunn, 2004 ....34.33**
9. **Jose Hernandez, 2001 ....34.13**
10. **Jose Hernandez, 2003 ....34.10**

1973-1987
1. Rob Deer, 1987 ....39.24
2. Rob Deer, 1986 ....38.41
3. Pete Incaviglia, 1986 ....34.26
4. Gary Alexander, 1978 ....33.33
5. Jack Clark, 1987 ....33.17
6. Pete Incaviglia, 1987 ....33.01
7. Mike Schmidt, 1975 ....32.03
8. Gorman Thomas, 1979 ....31.42
9. Danny Tartabull, 1986 ....30.72
10. Dave Kingman, 1975 ....30.48

1961-1972
1. Dave Nicholson, 1963 ....38.98
2. Dick Allen, 1969 ....32.88
3. Reggie Jackson, 1970 ....31.69
4. Larry Hisle, 1969 ....31.54
5. Reggie Jackson, 1968 ....30.92
6. Dick Allen, 1968 ....30.90
7. Willie Stargell, 1971 ....30.14
8. Bobby Bonds, 1969 ....30.06
9. Frank Howard, 1967 ....29.87
10. Rick Monday, 1968 ....29.67

1943-1960
1. Pancho Herrera, 1960 ....26.56
2. Jim Lemon, 1956 ....25.65
3. Dick Stuart, 1960 ....24.43
4. Frank Howard, 1960 ....24.11
5. Harmon Killebrew, 1960 ....23.98
6. Jim Lemon, 1958 ....23.95
7. Mickey Mantle, 1960 ....23.72
8. Larry Doby, 1953 ....23.59
9. Pat Seerey, 1945 ....23.43
10. Mickey Mantle, 1959 ....23.29

1921-1942
1. Vince DiMaggio, 1938 ....24.81
2. Vince DiMaggio, 1937 ....22.52
3. Chet Ross, 1940 ....22.32
4. Dolph Camilli, 1941 ....21.74
5. Joe Orengo, 1940 ....21.69
6. Jimmie Foxx, 1941 ....21.15
7. Boze Berger, 1935 ....21.04
8. Jimmie Foxx, 1936 ....20.34
9. Dolph Camilli, 1938 ....19.84
10. Babe Ruth, 1922 ....19.70

1901-1920
1. Gus Williams, 1914 ....24.05
2. Grover Gilmore, 1914 ....20.38
3. Gavy Cravath, 1916 ....19.87
4. Ed McDonald, 1912 ....19.83
5. Art Wilson, 1914 ....18.18
6. Gavy Cravath, 1912 ....17.66
7. Cozy Dolan, 1914 ....17.58
8. Max Carey, 1911 ....17.56
9. Danny Moeller, 1913 ....17.49
10. Babe Ruth, 1920 ....17.47

1893-1900
1. Billy Lush, 1896 ....13.92
2. Tom Daly, 1893 ....13.83
3. Tom Brown, 1894 ....13.68
4. Tom McCreery, 1896 ....13.15
5. Tom Brown, 1895 ....12.27
6. Billy Clingman, 1896 ....12.06
7. Tom Brown, 1893 ....11.91
8. Bill Joyce, 1895 ....11.69
9. Tom Daly, 1895 ....11.30
10. Tom Brown, 1896 ....11.26

1876-1892
1. Frank Meinke, 1884 ....26.10
2. Jim Galvin, 1883 ....24.53
3. Sam Wise, 1884 ....24.41
4. Jim Galvin, 1879 ....21.13
5. Charlie Bastian, 1885 ....21.08
6. Will White, 1878 ....20.81
7. Silver Flint, 1883 ....20.78
8. John Morrill, 1884 ....19.86
9. John Morrill, 1885 ....19.80
10. Charlie Bastian, 1886 ....19.57

Batting Average

1. Hugh Duffy, 1894 440
2. Tip O'Neill, 1887 435
3. Ross Barnes, 1876 429
4. Nap Lajoie, 1901 426
5. Willie Keeler, 1897 424
6. Rogers Hornsby, 1924 424
7. George Sisler, 1922 420
8. Ty Cobb, 1911 420
9. Sam Thompson, 1894 415
10. Fred Dunlap, 1884 412
11. Ed Delahanty, 1899 410
12. Jesse Burkett, 1896 410
13. Ty Cobb, 1912 409
14. Joe Jackson, 1911 408
15. George Sisler, 1920 407
16. Ted Williams, 1941 406
17. Jesse Burkett, 1895 405
18. Ed Delahanty, 1895 404
19. Ed Delahanty, 1894 404
20. Billy Hamilton, 1894 403
21. Rogers Hornsby, 1925 403
22. Harry Heilmann, 1923 403
23. Pete Browning, 1887 402
24. Rogers Hornsby, 1922 401
25. Bill Terry, 1930 401
26. Hughie Jennings, 1896 401
27. Ty Cobb, 1922 401
28. Cap Anson, 1881 399
29. Lefty O'Doul, 1929 398
30. Harry Heilmann, 1927 398
31. Rogers Hornsby, 1921 397
32. Ed Delahanty, 1896 397
33. Jesse Burkett, 1899 396
34. Joe Jackson, 1912 395
35. Tony Gwynn, 1994 394
36. Harry Heilmann, 1921 394
37. Harry Heilmann, 1925 393
38. Babe Ruth, 1923 393
39. Babe Herman, 1930 393
40. Joe Kelley, 1894 393
41. Sam Thompson, 1895 392
42. John McGraw, 1899 391
43. Ty Cobb, 1913 390
44. Al Simmons, 1931 390
45. George Brett, 1980 390
46. Fred Clarke, 1897 390
47. Tris Speaker, 1925 389
48. Bill Lange, 1895 389
49. Billy Hamilton, 1895 389
50. Ty Cobb, 1921 389
51. Ted Williams, 1957 388
52. King Kelly, 1886 388
53. Rod Carew, 1977 388
54. Luke Appling, 1936 388
55. Tris Speaker, 1920 388
56. Lave Cross, 1894 387
57. Deacon White, 1877 387
58. Al Simmons, 1925 387
59. Rogers Hornsby, 1928 387
60. Tris Speaker, 1916 386
61. Willie Keeler, 1896 386
62. Chuck Klein, 1930 386
63. Hughie Jennings, 1895 386
64. Willie Keeler, 1898 385
65. Arky Vaughan, 1935 385
66. Rogers Hornsby, 1923 384
67. Ty Cobb, 1919 384
68. Nap Lajoie, 1910 384
69. Ty Cobb, 1917 383
70. Jesse Burkett, 1897 383
71. Tris Speaker, 1912 383
72. Ty Cobb, 1917 383
73. Lefty O'Doul, 1930 383
74. Joe Jackson, 1920 382
75. Ty Cobb, 1918 382
76. Honus Wagner, 1900 381
77. Babe Herman, 1929 381
78. Joe DiMaggio, 1939 381
79. Al Simmons, 1930 381
80. Paul Waner, 1927 380
81. Rogers Hornsby, 1929 380
82. Billy Hamilton, 1893 380
83. Tris Speaker, 1923 380
84. Goose Goslin, 1928 379
85. Freddie Lindstrom, 1930 379
86. **Larry Walker, 1999 ....379**
87. Willie Keeler, 1899 379
88. Lou Gehrig, 1930 379
89. John Cassidy, 1877 378
90. Pete Browning, 1882 378
91. Ty Cobb, 1925 378
92. Babe Ruth, 1924 378
93. Sam Crawford, 1911 378
94. Tris Speaker, 1922 378
95. Earl Averill, 1936 378
96. Babe Ruth, 1921 378
97. Heinie Manush, 1928 378
98. Heinie Manush, 1926 378
99. Ed Delahanty, 1897 377
100. Willie Keeler, 1895 377

Batting Average by era

1988-2005
1. Tony Gwynn, 1994 394
2. **Larry Walker, 1999 ....379**
3. **Todd Helton, 2000 ....372**
4. **Nomar Garciaparra, 2000 ...372**
5. **Ichiro Suzuki, 2004 ....372**
6. Tony Gwynn, 1997 372
7. Andres Galarraga, 1993 370
8. **Barry Bonds, 2002 ....370**
9. Tony Gwynn, 1995 368
10. **Jeff Bagwell, 1994 ....368**

1973-1987
1. George Brett, 1980 390
2. Rod Carew, 1977 388
3. Tony Gwynn, 1987 370
4. Wade Boggs, 1985 368
5. Rod Carew, 1974 364
6. Wade Boggs, 1987 363
7. Wade Boggs, 1983 361
8. Rod Carew, 1975 359
9. Wade Boggs, 1986 357
10. Bill Madlock, 1975 354

1961-1972
1. Rico Carty, 1970 366
2. Joe Torre, 1971 363
3. Norm Cash, 1961 361
4. Roberto Clemente, 1967 ...357
5. Roberto Clemente, 1961 ...351
6. Pete Rose, 1969 348
7. Tommy Davis, 1962 346
8. Roberto Clemente, 1969 ...345
9. Ralph Garr, 1971 343
10. Vada Pinson, 1961 343

1943-1960
1. Ted Williams, 1957 388
2. Stan Musial, 1948 376
3. Ted Williams, 1948 369
4. Stan Musial, 1946 365
5. Mickey Mantle, 1957 365
6. Harry Walker, 1947 363
7. Dixie Walker, 1944 357
8. Stan Musial, 1943 357
9. Phil Cavarretta, 1945 355
10. Lou Boudreau, 1948 355

1921-1942
1. Rogers Hornsby, 1924 424
2. George Sisler, 1922 420
3. Ted Williams, 1941 406
4. Rogers Hornsby, 1925 403
5. Harry Heilmann, 1923 403
6. Rogers Hornsby, 1922 401
7. Bill Terry, 1930 401
8. Ty Cobb, 1922 401
9. Lefty O'Doul, 1929 398
10. Harry Heilmann, 1927 398

1901-1920
1. Nap Lajoie, 1901 426
2. Ty Cobb, 1911 420
3. Ty Cobb, 1912 409
4. Joe Jackson, 1911 408
5. George Sisler, 1920 407
6. Joe Jackson, 1912 395
7. Ty Cobb, 1913 390
8. Tris Speaker, 1920 388
9. Tris Speaker, 1916 386
10. Ty Cobb, 1919 384

1893-1900
1. Hugh Duffy, 1894 440
2. Willie Keeler, 1897 424
3. Sam Thompson, 1894 415
4. Ed Delahanty, 1899 410
5. Jesse Burkett, 1896 410
6. Jesse Burkett, 1895 405
7. Ed Delahanty, 1895 404
8. Ed Delahanty, 1894 404
9. Billy Hamilton, 1894 403
10. Hughie Jennings, 1896 401

1876-1892
1. Tip O'Neill, 1887 435
2. Ross Barnes, 1876 429
3. Fred Dunlap, 1884 412
4. Pete Browning, 1887 402
5. Cap Anson, 1881 399
6. King Kelly, 1886 388
7. Deacon White, 1877 387
8. John Cassidy, 1877 378
9. Pete Browning, 1882 378
10. Dan Brouthers, 1883 374

Relative Batting Average

1. Ross Barnes, 1876 ....1.608
2. Tip O'Neill, 1887 ....1.564
3. Nap Lajoie, 1910 ....1.537
4. Ty Cobb, 1910 ....1.534
5. Pete Browning, 1882 ....1.526
6. Cap Anson, 1881 ....1.512
7. King Kelly, 1886 ....1.508
8. Roger Connor, 1885 ....1.506
9. Tris Speaker, 1916 ....1.506
10. Ty Cobb, 1917 ....1.501
11. Ty Cobb, 1912 ....1.501
12. Nap Lajoie, 1901 ....1.501
13. Nap Lajoie, 1904 ....1.499
14. Ty Cobb, 1911 ....1.493
15. Ty Cobb, 1909 ....1.492
16. Rod Carew, 1977 ....1.476
17. Ty Cobb, 1913 ....1.475
18. Ted Williams, 1941 ....1.472
19. Ty Cobb, 1918 ....1.469
20. George Gore, 1880 ....1.462
21. Rogers Hornsby, 1924 ....1.461
22. Rod Carew, 1977 ....1.458
23. **Barry Bonds, 2002 ....1.457**
24. Dan Brouthers, 1885 ....1.455
25. Joe Jackson, 1911 ....1.452
26. Joe Jackson, 1912 ....1.451
27. Dan Brouthers, 1882 ....1.449
28. Dave Orr, 1884 ....1.448
29. George Brett, 1980 ....1.448
30. Ty Cobb, 1915 ....1.448
31. Pete Browning, 1887 ....1.446
32. Ty Cobb, 1916 ....1.445
33. Cap Anson, 1886 ....1.442
34. Pete Browning, 1885 ....1.439
35. Dan Brouthers, 1886 ....1.439
36. Tony Gwynn, 1994 ....1.436
37. Honus Wagner, 1908 ....1.434
38. George Sisler, 1922 ....1.433
39. Cap Anson, 1882 ....1.428
40. Cy Seymour, 1905 ....1.425
41. Willie Keeler, 1897 ....1.423
42. Ed Delahanty, 1899 ....1.414
43. Wade Boggs, 1988 ....1.413
44. King Kelly, 1884 ....1.411
45. Joe Jackson, 1913 ....1.411
46. Rod Carew, 1974 ....1.408
47. Wade Boggs, 1985 ....1.407
48. Tris Speaker, 1912 ....1.406
49. Deacon White, 1877 ....1.405
50. Dan Brouthers, 1883 ....1.402
51. Jimmy Wolf, 1890 ....1.401
52. George Stone, 1906 ....1.400
53. Stan Musial, 1948 ....1.400
54. Cap Anson, 1888 ....1.399
55. George Sisler, 1920 ....1.398
56. Joe Torre, 1971 ....1.397
57. Hugh Duffy, 1894 ....1.393
58. Stan Musial, 1946 ....1.393
59. Ed Swartwood, 1883 ....1.392
60. Ty Cobb, 1919 ....1.392
61. Rod Carew, 1975 ....1.391
62. Tommy Tucker, 1889 ....1.391
63. Nap Lajoie, 1906 ....1.390
64. John Reilly, 1884 ....1.390
65. Harry Heilmann, 1923 ....1.389
66. Mickey Mantle, 1957 ....1.388
67. Willie Keeler, 1898 ....1.387
68. Honus Wagner, 1907 ....1.387
69. Roberto Clemente, 1967 ....1.385
70. George Sisler, 1917 ....1.383
71. Jim O'Rourke, 1884 ....1.383
72. Pete Browning, 1886 ....1.382
73. Tris Speaker, 1917 ....1.380
74. Ezra Sutton, 1884 ....1.380
75. Ty Cobb, 1907 ....1.379
76. Hick Carpenter, 1882 ....1.379
77. Roger Connor, 1886 ....1.378
78. Jesse Burkett, 1896 ....1.378
79. Paul Hines, 1879 ....1.377
80. Tony Gwynn, 1997 ....1.374
81. **Ichiro Suzuki, 2004 ..1.375**
82. **Larry Walker, 1999 ...1.375**
83. Pete Browning, 1884 ....1.374
84. Tris Speaker, 1913 ....1.374
85. Tony Gwynn, 1997 ....1.374
86. Kirby Puckett, 1988 ....1.374
87. John Cassidy, 1877 ....1.373
88. Eddie Collins, 1909 ....1.373
89. Honus Wagner, 1905 ....1.372
90. Dave Orr, 1886 ....1.372
91. Rico Carty, 1970 ....1.372
92. George Hall, 1876 ....1.372
93. Tip O'Neill, 1888 ....1.370
94. Wade Boggs, 1987 ....1.370
95. Ty Cobb, 1922 ....1.370
96. Dan Brouthers, 1889 ....1.370
97. Cap Anson, 1880 ....1.368
98. Norm Cash, 1961 ....1.368
99. Jesse Burkett, 1899 ....1.367
100. Andres Galarraga, 1993 ....1.366

On-Base Percentage

1. **Barry Bonds, 2004 ....609**
2. **Barry Bonds, 2002 ....582**
3. Ted Williams, 1941 553
4. John McGraw, 1899 547
5. Babe Ruth, 1923 545
6. Babe Ruth, 1920 532
7. **Barry Bonds, 2003 ....529**
8. Ted Williams, 1957 526
9. Billy Hamilton, 1894 522
10. Babe Ruth, 1926 516
11. **Barry Bonds, 2001 ....515**
12. Ted Williams, 1954 513
13. Babe Ruth, 1924 513
14. Babe Ruth, 1921 512
15. Mickey Mantle, 1957 512
16. Rogers Hornsby, 1924 507
17. John McGraw, 1900 505
18. Joe Kelley, 1894 502
19. Hugh Duffy, 1894 502
20. Ed Delahanty, 1895 500
21. Ted Williams, 1942 499
22. Ted Williams, 1947 499
23. Rogers Hornsby, 1928 498
24. Ted Williams, 1946 497
25. Ted Williams, 1948 497
26. Bill Joyce, 1894 496
27. Babe Ruth, 1931 495
28. Babe Ruth, 1930 493
29. Arky Vaughan, 1935 491
30. Ted Williams, 1949 490
31. Billy Hamilton, 1895 490
32. Billy Hamilton, 1893 490
33. Tip O'Neill, 1887 490
34. Rogers Hornsby, 1925 489
    Babe Ruth, 1932 489
36. **Frank Thomas, 1994 ....487**
37. Norm Cash, 1961 487
38. Ty Cobb, 1915 486
39. Mickey Mantle, 1962 486
40. Babe Ruth, 1927 486
41. Tris Speaker, 1920 483
42. King Kelly, 1886 483
43. Jesse Burkett, 1895 482
44. Harry Heilmann, 1923 481
45. Billy Hamilton, 1898 480
46. Tris Speaker, 1925 479
    Ted Williams, 1956 479
48. Edgar Martinez, 1995 478
49. Billy Hamilton, 1896 478
50. Lou Gehrig, 1934 478
51. **Jason Giambi, 2001 ....477**
52. **Jason Giambi, 2000 ....476**
53. Wade Boggs, 1988 476
54. Cupid Childs, 1894 475
55. John McGraw, 1898 475
56. Ed Delahanty, 1894 475
57. Harry Heilmann, 1927 475
58. Tris Speaker, 1922 474
59. Lou Gehrig, 1927 474
60. Luke Appling, 1936 474
61. Lou Gehrig, 1930 473
62. Lou Gehrig, 1937 473
63. **John Olerud, 1993 ....473**
64. Hughie Jennings, 1896 472
65. Ed Delahanty, 1896 472
66. John McGraw, 1897 471
67. Dan Brouthers, 1891 471
68. Tris Speaker, 1916 470
69. Bill Joyce, 1896 470
70. Mark McGwire, 1998 470
71. **Carlos Delgado, 2000 ....470**
72. Joe Kelley, 1896 469
73. Tris Speaker, 1923 469
74. Jimmie Foxx, 1932 469
75. **Todd Helton, 2004 ....469**
76. Jesse Burkett, 1897 468
77. Ty Cobb, 1925 468
78. Joe Jackson, 1911 468
79. Lou Gehrig, 1928 467
80. Ty Cobb, 1913 467
81. Mark McGwire, 1996 467
82. George Sisler, 1922 467
83. Cupid Childs, 1896 467
84. Ty Cobb, 1911 467
85. Joe Morgan, 1975 466
86. Dan Brouthers, 1890 466
87. Lou Gehrig, 1935 466
88. **Gary Sheffield, 1996 ...465**
89. Lou Gehrig, 1934 465
90. Lefty O'Doul, 1929 465
91. Mike Griffin, 1894 465
92. Sam Thompson, 1894 465
93. Jimmie Foxx, 1939 464
94. Tris Speaker, 1912 464
95. Ed Delahanty, 1899 464
96. Pete Browning, 1887 464
97. Mickey Mantle, 1956 464
98. Edgar Martinez, 1995 464
99. Ted Williams, 1951 464
100. Willie Keeler, 1897 464

Slugging Average

1 Barry Bonds, 2001 863
2 Babe Ruth, 1920 847
3 Babe Ruth, 1921 846
4 Barry Bonds, 2004 812
5 Barry Bonds, 2002 799
6 Babe Ruth, 1927 772
7 Lou Gehrig, 1927 765
8 Babe Ruth, 1923 764
9 Rogers Hornsby, 1925 756
10 Mark McGwire, 1998 752
11 Jeff Bagwell, 1994 750
12 Jimmie Foxx, 1932 749
   Barry Bonds, 2003 749
14 Babe Ruth, 1924 739
15 Babe Ruth, 1926 737
16 Sammy Sosa, 2001 737
17 Ted Williams, 1941 735
18 Babe Ruth, 1930 732
19 Ted Williams, 1957 731
20 Mark McGwire, 1996 730
21 Frank Thomas, 1994 729
22 Hack Wilson, 1930 723
23 Rogers Hornsby, 1922 722
24 Lou Gehrig, 1930 721
25 Larry Walker, 1997 720
26 Albert Belle, 1994 714
27 Larry Walker, 1999 710
28 Babe Ruth, 1928 709
29 Al Simmons, 1930 708
30 Lou Gehrig, 1934 706
31 Mickey Mantle, 1956 705
32 Jimmie Foxx, 1938 704
33 Jimmie Foxx, 1933 703
34 Stan Musial, 1948 702
35 Babe Ruth, 1931 700
36 Todd Helton, 2000 698
37 Babe Ruth, 1929 697
38 Manny Ramirez, 2000 697
39 Mark McGwire, 1999 697
40 Sam Thompson, 1894 696
41 Lou Gehrig, 1936 696
42 Rogers Hornsby, 1924 696
43 Hugh Duffy, 1894 694
44 Jimmie Foxx, 1939 694
45 Tip O'Neill, 1887 691
46 Albert Belle, 1995 690
47 Luis Gonzalez, 2001 688
48 Barry Bonds, 2000 688
49 Mickey Mantle, 1961 687
50 Chuck Klein, 1930 687
51 Todd Helton, 2001 685
52 Hank Greenberg, 1938 683
53 Kevin Mitchell, 1994 681
54 Rogers Hornsby, 1929 679
55 Babe Herman, 1930 678
56 Barry Bonds, 1993 677
57 Jim Thome, 2002 677
58 Ken Griffey Jr., 1994 674
59 Joe DiMaggio, 1937 673
60 Babe Ruth, 1922 672
61 Joe DiMaggio, 1939 671
62 Hank Greenberg, 1940 670
63 Hank Aaron, 1971 669
64 Hank Greenberg, 1937 668
65 Ted Williams, 1946 667
66 Willie Mays, 1954 667
67 Albert Pujols, 2003 667
68 Mickey Mantle, 1957 665
69 Carlos Delgado, 2000 664
70 Vladimir Guerrero, 2000 664
71 George Brett, 1980 664
72 Manny Ramirez, 1999 663
73 Lou Gehrig, 1931 662
74 Larry Walker, 2001 662
75 Norm Cash, 1961 662
76 Derrek Lee, 2005 662
77 Babe Ruth, 1932 661
78 Jason Giambi, 2001 660
79 Willie Mays, 1955 659
80 Ralph Kiner, 1949 658
81 Chuck Klein, 1929 657
82 Babe Ruth, 1919 657
83 Albert Pujols, 2004 657
84 Willie McCovey, 1969 656
85 Albert Belle, 1998 655
86 Sam Thompson, 1895 654
87 Jimmie Foxx, 1934 653
88 Chick Hafey, 1930 652
89 Ted Williams, 1949 650
90 Bill Joyce, 1894 648
91 Lou Gehrig, 1928 648
92 Ted Williams, 1942 648
93 Duke Snider, 1954 647
94 Barry Bonds, 1994 647
   Jason Giambi, 2000 647
96 Sammy Sosa, 1998 647
97 Manny Ramirez, 2002 647
98 Ken Griffey Jr., 1997 646
99 Mark McGwire, 1997 646
100 Chuck Klein, 1932 646

On-Base plus Slugging

1 Barry Bonds, 2004 1422
2 Barry Bonds, 2002 1381
3 Babe Ruth, 1920 1379
4 Barry Bonds, 2001 1379
5 Babe Ruth, 1921 1359
6 Babe Ruth, 1923 1309
7 Ted Williams, 1941 1287
8 Barry Bonds, 2003 1278
9 Babe Ruth, 1927 1258
10 Ted Williams, 1957 1257
11 Babe Ruth, 1926 1253
12 Babe Ruth, 1924 1252
13 Rogers Hornsby, 1925 1245
14 Lou Gehrig, 1927 1240
15 Babe Ruth, 1930 1225
16 Mark McGwire, 1998 1222
17 Jimmie Foxx, 1932 1218
18 Frank Thomas, 1994 ..1217
19 Rogers Hornsby, 1924 1203
20 Jeff Bagwell, 1994 1201
21 Mark McGwire, 1996 1198
22 Hugh Duffy, 1894 1196
23 Babe Ruth, 1931 1195
24 Lou Gehrig, 1930 1194
25 Rogers Hornsby, 1922 1181
26 Tip O'Neill, 1887 1180
27 Hack Wilson, 1930 1177
28 Mickey Mantle, 1957 1177
29 Sammy Sosa, 2001 1174
30 Lou Gehrig, 1936 1174
31 Babe Ruth, 1928 1172
32 Larry Walker, 1997 1172
33 Lou Gehrig, 1934 1172
34 Mickey Mantle, 1956 1169
35 Larry Walker, 1999 1168
36 Jimmie Foxx, 1938 1166
37 Ted Williams, 1946 1164
38 Todd Helton, 2000 1162
39 Sam Thompson, 1894 1161
40 Jimmie Foxx, 1939 1158
41 Manny Ramirez, 2000 1154
42 Jimmie Foxx, 1933 1153
43 Stan Musial, 1948 1152
44 Albert Belle, 1994 1152
45 Babe Ruth, 1932 1150
46 Norm Cash, 1961 1148
47 Ted Williams, 1954 1148
48 Ted Williams, 1942 1147
49 Bill Joyce, 1894 1143
50 Ted Williams, 1949 1141
51 Rogers Hornsby, 1929 1139
52 Jason Giambi, 2001 ..1137
53 Barry Bonds, 1993 1136
54 Mickey Mantle, 1961 1135
55 Carlos Delgado, 2000 1134
56 Ted Williams, 1947 1133
57 Babe Herman, 1930 1132
58 Al Simmons, 1930 1130
59 Rogers Hornsby, 1928 1130
60 Babe Ruth, 1929 1128
61 Barry Bonds, 2000 1127
62 Chuck Klein, 1930 1123
63 Jason Giambi, 2000 1123
64 Jim Thome, 2002 1122
65 Hank Greenberg, 1938 1122
66 Mark McGwire, 1999 1120
67 Joe DiMaggio, 1939 1119
68 George Brett, 1980 1118
69 Ed Delahanty, 1895 1117
70 Luis Gonzalez, 2001 1117
71 Todd Helton, 2001 1116
72 Lou Gehrig, 1937 1116
73 Lou Gehrig, 1928 1115
74 Babe Ruth, 1919 1114
75 Harry Heilmann, 1923 1113
76 Ted Williams, 1941 1112
77 Larry Walker, 2001 1111
78 Kevin Mitchell, 1994 1110
79 Willie McCovey, 1969 1108
80 Lou Gehrig, 1931 1108
81 Edgar Martinez, 1995 1107
82 Nap Lajoie, 1901 1106
83 Babe Ruth, 1922 1106
84 Albert Pujols, 2003 1106
85 Manny Ramirez, 1999 1105
86 Hank Greenberg, 1937 1105
87 Joe Kelley, 1894 1104
88 Hank Greenberg, 1940 1103
89 Ed Delahanty, 1896 1103
90 Jimmie Foxx, 1934 1102
91 Arky Vaughan, 1935 1098
92 Rogers Hornsby, 1921 1097
93 Manny Ramirez, 2002 1097
94 Jimmie Foxx, 1935 1096
95 Albert Belle, 1995 1091
96 Mickey Mantle, 1962 1091
97 Harry Heilmann, 1927 1091
98 Gary Sheffield, 1996 1090
99 Ralph Kiner, 1949 1089
100 Todd Helton, 2004 1088

Adjusted OPS

1 Barry Bonds, 2002 274
2 Barry Bonds, 2001 263
3 Barry Bonds, 2004 255
4 Babe Ruth, 1920 252
5 Babe Ruth, 1923 238
6 Babe Ruth, 1921 236
7 Ted Williams, 1941 232
8 Babe Ruth, 1927 229
9 Pete Browning, 1882 229
10 Babe Ruth, 1926 228
11 Ted Williams, 1957 227
12 Barry Bonds, 2003 226
13 Lou Gehrig, 1927 224
14 Babe Ruth, 1919 224
15 Babe Ruth, 1931 223
16 Mickey Mantle, 1957 223
17 Rogers Hornsby, 1924 222
18 Ross Barnes, 1876 222
19 Babe Ruth, 1924 221
20 Jeff Bagwell, 1994 219
21 Mark McGwire, 1998 217
22 Babe Ruth, 1930 216
23 Ted Williams, 1942 214
24 Lou Gehrig, 1934 213
25 Mickey Mantle, 1956 213
26 Frank Thomas, 1994 212
27 Willie McCovey, 1969 211
28 Ted Williams, 1946 211
29 Babe Ruth, 1928 211
30 Mickey Mantle, 1961 210
31 Rogers Hornsby, 1922 210
32 Ty Cobb, 1917 210
33 George Hall, 1876 208
34 Rogers Hornsby, 1925 208
35 Barry Bonds, 1993 207
36 Lou Gehrig, 1930 207
37 Babe Ruth, 1932 206
38 Tip O'Neill, 1887 205
39 Sammy Sosa, 2001 205
40 Honus Wagner, 1908 205
41 Rogers Hornsby, 1928 204
42 Sammy Sosa, 2001 204
43 Nap Lajoie, 1904 204
44 Ty Cobb, 1912 203
45 Jimmie Foxx, 1932 203
46 Roger Connor, 1885 203
47 Dan Brouthers, 1886 203
48 Ty Cobb, 1910 202
49 George Brett, 1980 201
50 Frank Robinson, 1966 200
51 Jimmie Foxx, 1933 199
52 Mark McGwire, 1996 199
53 Ted Williams, 1947 199
54 Lou Gehrig, 1931 199
55 Dan Brouthers, 1885 199
56 Babe Ruth, 1929 199
57 Norm Cash, 1961 198
58 Mickey Mantle, 1962 198
59 Dick Allen, 1972 198
60 Dan Brouthers, 1882 198
61 Nap Lajoie, 1910 198
62 Ed Swartwood, 1882 197
63 Lou Gehrig, 1928 197
64 Stan Musial, 1948 196
65 Jason Giambi, 2001 196
66 Ty Cobb, 1918 196
67 Ty Cobb, 1913 196
68 Nap Lajoie, 1901 196
69 Orator Shafer, 1878 196
70 George Stone, 1906 195
71 Harry Heilmann, 1923 195
72 Dave Orr, 1884 195
73 Kevin Mitchell, 1989 194
74 Dave Orr, 1886 193
75 Mike Schmidt, 1981 193
76 Lou Gehrig, 1936 193
77 Barry Bonds, 2000 193
78 Ed Delahanty, 1899 193
79 Ty Cobb, 1911 193
80 Ted Williams, 1954 193
81 Joe Jackson, 1911 192
82 Ed Delahanty, 1896 192
83 Rogers Hornsby, 1921 191
84 Ty Cobb, 1909 190
85 Gary Sheffield, 1996 190
86 Jim Thome, 2002 190
87 Joe Jackson, 1913 190
88 Pete Browning, 1885 190
89 Deacon White, 1877 190
90 Joe Jackson, 1912 190
91 Rogers Hornsby, 1920 190
92 Hank Aaron, 1971 190
93 Albert Belle, 1994 190
94 Dave Orr, 1885 189
95 Jim Gentile, 1961 189
96 Cupid Childs, 1890 189
97 Carl Yastrzemski, 1967 189
98 Ty Cobb, 1910 189
99 Frank Robinson, 1967 189
100 Cap Anson, 1881 189

Adjusted Batting Wins

1 Barry Bonds, 2001 ....12.4
2 Barry Bonds, 2002 ....12.0
3 Barry Bonds, 2004 ....11.2
4 Babe Ruth, 1923 ....11.1
5 Babe Ruth, 1921 ....10.6
6 Babe Ruth, 1920 ....10.2
7 Lou Gehrig, 1927 ....10.0
8 Babe Ruth, 1927 ....9.9
9 Babe Ruth, 1926 ....9.6
10 Ted Williams, 1941 ....9.5
11 Babe Ruth, 1924 ....9.5
12 Rogers Hornsby, 1924 ....9.5
13 Babe Ruth, 1931 ....9.4
14 Mickey Mantle, 1957 ....9.4
15 Mark McGwire, 1998 ....9.2
16 Rogers Hornsby, 1922 ....9.1
17 Lou Gehrig, 1934 ....9.0
18 Ted Williams, 1942 ....8.9
19 Ted Williams, 1946 ....8.9
20 Sammy Sosa, 2001 ....8.9
21 Babe Ruth, 1930 ....8.8
22 Barry Bonds, 1993 ....8.7
23 Lou Gehrig, 1930 ....8.7
24 Babe Ruth, 1928 ....8.6
25 Mickey Mantle, 1956 ....8.5
26 Ted Williams, 1957 ....8.4
27 Ted Williams, 1947 ....8.3
28 Barry Bonds, 2003 ....8.3
29 Mickey Mantle, 1961 ....8.3
30 Lou Gehrig, 1931 ....8.2
31 Jimmie Foxx, 1932 ....8.2
32 Ty Cobb, 1917 ....8.2
33 Willie McCovey, 1969 ....8.1
34 Frank Robinson, 1966 ....8.1
35 Norm Cash, 1961 ....8.0
36 Stan Musial, 1948 ....8.0
37 Rogers Hornsby, 1928 ....7.9
38 Lou Gehrig, 1936 ....7.8
39 Jason Giambi, 2001 ....7.8
40 Barry Bonds, 1992 ....7.8
41 Lou Gehrig, 1928 ....7.8
42 Rogers Hornsby, 1925 ....7.7
43 Babe Ruth, 1919 ....7.7
44 Rogers Hornsby, 1921 ....7.6
45 Ted Williams, 1949 ....7.6
46 Jimmie Foxx, 1933 ....7.6
47 Hank Aaron, 1959 ....7.5
48 Jeff Bagwell, 1996 ....7.5
49 Gary Sheffield, 1996 ....7.5
50 Albert Pujols, 2003 ....7.5
51 Nap Lajoie, 1910 ....7.4
52 Honus Wagner, 1908 ....7.4
53 Babe Ruth, 1932 ....7.3
54 Carl Yastrzemski, 1967 ....7.2
55 Rogers Hornsby, 1920 ....7.2
56 Dick Allen, 1972 ....7.2
57 Harry Heilmann, 1923 ....7.2
58 Barry Bonds, 1996 ....7.2
59 Mickey Mantle, 1958 ....7.1
60 Reggie Jackson, 1969 ....7.1
61 Lou Gehrig, 1932 ....7.1
62 John Olerud, 1993 ....7.1
63 Barry Bonds, 1998 ....7.1
64 Mike Piazza, 1997 ....7.0
65 Ty Cobb, 1912 ....7.0
66 Hank Aaron, 1963 ....7.0
67 Tris Speaker, 1923 ....7.0
68 Kevin Mitchell, 1989 ....7.0
69 Nap Lajoie, 1904 ....6.9
70 Jeff Bagwell, 1994 ....6.9
71 Frank Thomas, 1991 ....6.9
72 Ty Cobb, 1915 ....6.9
73 Carlos Delgado, 2000 ....6.9
74 Jason Giambi, 2000 ....6.9
75 Ty Cobb, 1911 ....6.9
76 Stan Musial, 1951 ....6.8
77 Stan Musial, 1946 ....6.8
78 Joe Jackson, 1911 ....6.8
79 Rogers Hornsby, 1929 ....6.8
80 Ralph Kiner, 1951 ....6.8
81 George Stone, 1906 ....6.7
82 Ed Delahanty, 1899 ....6.7
83 Frank Thomas, 1994 ....6.7
84 Barry Bonds, 2000 ....6.7
85 Ted Williams, 1948 ....6.7
86 Rod Carew, 1977 ....6.7
87 Frank Thomas, 1997 ....6.7
88 Edgar Martinez, 1995 ....6.7
89 Frank Howard, 1969 ....6.7
90 Al Rosen, 1953 ....6.6
91 Lou Gehrig, 1937 ....6.6
92 Tris Speaker, 1912 ....6.6
93 Jimmie Foxx, 1934 ....6.6
94 Babe Ruth, 1929 ....6.6
95 Lou Gehrig, 1935 ....6.6
96 Joe Medwick, 1937 ....6.6
97 Carl Yastrzemski, 1970 ....6.6
98 Ty Cobb, 1910 ....6.6
99 Hack Wilson, 1930 ....6.6
100 Frank Thomas, 1992 ....6.6

Pinch Hits

1 John Vander Wal, 1995 28
2 Lenny Harris, 1999 26
3 Jose Morales, 1976 25
4 Dave Philley, 1961 24
  Vic Davalillo, 1970 24
  Rusty Staub, 1983 24
  Gerald Perry, 1993 24
8 Greg Norton, 2003 23
9 Sam Leslie, 1932 22
  Peanuts Lowrey, 1953 22
  Red Schoendienst, 1962 22
  Wallace Johnson, 1988 22
  Mark Sweeney, 1997 22
  Lenny Harris, 2002 22
15 Doc Miller, 1913 21
  Smoky Burgess, 1966 21
  Merv Rettenmund, 1977 21
18 Ed Coleman, 1936 20
  Frenchy Bordagaray, 1938 20
  Joe Frazier, 1954 20
  Smoky Burgess, 1965 20
  Ken Boswell, 1976 20
  Jerry Turner, 1978 20
  Thad Bosley, 1985 20
  Chris Chambliss, 1986 20
  Dave Clark, 1997 20
  Jacob Cruz, 2005 20

Pinch Hit Average
(30 at-bats minimum)

1 Ed Kranepool, 1974 486
2 Smead Jolley, 1931 467
3 Frenchy Bordagaray, 1938 465
4 Rick Miller, 1983 457
5 Bill Spiers, 1997 455
  Jorge Piedra, 2005 455
7 Jose Pagan, 1969 452
8 Elmer Valo, 1955 452
  Mark Johnson, 1996 452
10 Gates Brown, 1968 450
11 Ted Easterly, 1912 433
  Milt Thompson, 1985 433
  Randy Bush, 1986 433
14 Joe Cronin, 1943 429
  Don Dillard, 1961 429
16 Candy Maldonado, 1986 429
17 Richie Ashburn, 1962 418
  Dick Williams, 1962 418
19 Merritt Ranew, 1963 418
  Carl Taylor, 1969 418
21 Kurt Bevacqua, 1983 41
22 Jerry Turner, 1978 40
23 Bob Bowman, 1958 40
  Chico Walker, 1991 40
  Sid Bream, 1994 40

Pinch Hit Home Runs

1 Dave Hansen, 2000 ....
  Craig Wilson, 2001 ....
3 Johnny Frederick, 1932 ....
4 Joe Cronin, 1943 ....
  Butch Nieman, 1945 ....
  Gene Freese, 1959 ....
  Jerry Lynch, 1961 ....
  Cliff Johnson, 1974 ....
  Lee Lacy, 1978 ....
  Jerry Turner, 1978 ....
  Billy Ashley, 1996 ....
  David Dellucci, 2001 ....
  Erubiel Durazo, 2001 ....
  Mark Sweeney, 2004 ....
15 Ernie Lombardi, 1946 ....
  Del Wilber, 1953 ....
  Bill Taylor, 1955 ....
  Bob Thurman, 1957 ....
  Rip Repulski, 1958 ....
  George Crowe, 1959 ....
  George Crowe, 1960 ....
  Johnny Blanchard, 1961 ....
  Carl Sawatski, 1961 ....
  Jerry Lynch, 1963 ....
  Don Mincher, 1964 ....
  Hal Breeden, 1973 ....
  Mike Ivie, 1978 ....
  Del Unser, 1979 ....
  Jeff Burroughs, 1982 ....
  Danny Heep, 1983 ....
  Candy Maldonado, 1986 ....
  Mark Carreon, 1989 ....
  Tommy Gregg, 1990 ....
  Ernest Riles, 1990 ....
  Howard Johnson, 1994 ....
  John Vander Wal, 1995 ....
  Jack Howell, 1996 ....
  Mark Johnson, 1996 ....
  Bob Hamelin, 1998 ....
  Angelo Echevarria, 1999 ....
  Bubba Trammell, 2000 ....
  Orlando Merced, 2001 ....
  Greg Norton, 2003 ....
  Matthew LeCroy, 2004 ....

Stolen Bases

1 Hugh Nicol, 1887 138
2 Rickey Henderson, 1982...130
3 Arlie Latham, 1887.........129
4 Lou Brock, 1974............118
5 Charlie Comiskey, 1887 ...117
6 John Ward, 1887............111
   Billy Hamilton, 1889.......111
   Billy Hamilton, 1891.......111
9 Vince Coleman, 1985.......110
10 Arlie Latham, 1888........109
   Vince Coleman, 1987.......109
12 Rickey Henderson, 1983...108
   Vince Coleman, 1986.......107
14 Tom Brown, 1891...........106
15 Maury Wills, 1962.........104
16 Pete Browning, 1887.......103
   Hugh Nicol, 1888..........103
18 Jim Fogarty, 1887.........102
   Billy Hamilton, 1890......102
20 Billy Hamilton, 1894......100
   Rickey Henderson, 1980...100
22 Jim Fogarty, 1889..........99
23 Harry Stovey, 1890.........97
   Billy Hamilton, 1895.......97
   Ron LeFlore, 1980..........97
26 Ty Cobb, 1915.............96
   Omar Moreno, 1980.........96
28 Bid McPhee, 1887...........95
   Curt Welch, 1888...........95
30 Mike Griffin, 1887..........94
   Maury Wills, 1965..........94
32 Tommy McCarthy, 1888 93
   Rickey Henderson, 1988...93
34 Darby O'Brien, 1889........91
35 Tim Raines, 1983...........90
36 Curt Welch, 1887...........89
   Herman Long, 1889..........89
38 Tom Poorman, 1887..........88
   Blondie Purcell, 1887.......88
   John Ward, 1892............88
   Clyde Milan, 1912...........88
42 Harry Stovey, 1888..........87
   Arlie Latham, 1891..........87
   Joe Kelley, 1896............87
   Rickey Henderson, 1986...87
46 Cub Stricker, 1887..........86
47 Tommy Tucker, 1887.........85
   Hub Collins, 1890..........85
   Hugh Duffy, 1891...........85
50 King Kelly, 1887............84
   Chippy McGarr, 1887........84
   Billy Sunday, 1890.........84
   Bill Lange, 1896............84
54 Tommy McCarthy, 1890 83
   Billy Hamilton, 1896........83
   Ty Cobb, 1911.............83
   Willie Wilson, 1979.........83
58 Dummy Hoy, 1888...........82
   John Reilly, 1888...........82
60 Eddie Collins, 1910..........81
   Bob Bescher, 1911..........81
   Vince Coleman, 1988........81
63 Emmett Seery, 1888.........80
   Hugh Nicol, 1889...........80
   Rickey Henderson, 1985...80
   Eric Davis, 1986...........80
67 Tom Brown, 1890...........79
   Dave Collins, 1980.........79
   Willie Wilson, 1980.........79
70 Hugh Duffy, 1890...........78
   Tom Brown, 1892...........78
   John McGraw, 1894.........78
   Ron LeFlore, 1979.........78
   Tim Raines, 1982...........78
   Marquis Grissom, 1992 78
76 Ted Scheffler, 1887.........77
   Jimmy Sheckard, 1899 77
   Davey Lopes, 1975.........77
   Omar Moreno, 1979.........77
   Rudy Law, 1983............77
   Rickey Henderson, 1989...77
   Vince Coleman, 1990.......77
83 Ed McKean, 1887...........76
   Walt Wilmot, 1890..........76
   Walt Wilmot, 1894..........76
   Dusty Miller, 1896..........76
   Ty Cobb, 1909.............76
   Marquis Grissom, 1991 76
89 Yank Robinson, 1887........75
   George Van Haltren, 1891...75
   Clyde Milan, 1913..........75
   Benny Kauff, 1914..........75
   Billy North, 1976..........75
   Tim Raines, 1984..........75
   Kenny Lofton, 1996 75
96 Frank Fennelly, 1887........74
   Harry Stovey, 1887.........74
   Fritz Maisel, 1914.........74
   Lou Brock, 1966...........74
   Brian Hunter, 1997.........74

Stolen Base Average

1 Kevin McReynolds, 1988 ....100.0
   Paul Molitor, 1994 ....100.0
3 Brady Anderson, 1994 ......96.9
   Carlos Beltran, 2001 ..96.9
5 Max Carey, 1922 ....96.2
6 **Ken Griffey Jr., 1980 ......95.8**
7 **Jason Bay, 2005 ....95.5**
8 Stan Javier, 1988 ....95.2
9 Doug Glanville, 1999........94.4
10 Amos Otis, 1970 ....94.3
11 Jack Perconte, 1985 ......93.9
12 **Alfonso Soriano, 2005 .....93.8**
13 **Carlos Beltran, 2004 ...93.3**
14 Miguel Dilone, 1984 ....93.1
   Bob Dernier, 1986 ....93.1
16 Kirk Gibson, 1990 ....92.9
   Barry Larkin, 1994 ....92.9
18 **Dave Roberts, 2004 ...92.7**
19 **Rafael Furcal, 2003 ...92.6**
20 Don Baylor, 1972 ....92.3
   Oddibe McDowell, 1987...92.3
   Orlando Cabrera, 2003 ...92.3
23 Davey Lopes, 1985 ....92.2
24 Eric Davis, 1988 ....92.1
25 Delino DeShields, 2001 ..92.0
   Henry Cotto, 1992.........92.0
   Mike Cameron, 1997 ...92.0
28 Bobby Bonds, 1969.........91.8
   Davey Lopes, 1978 ....91.8
30 Davey Lopes, 1979.........91.7
   Marquis Grissom, 1990 ...91.7
32 Jimmy Wynn, 1965 ....91.5
33 Larry Bowa, 1977 ....91.4
   Derek Jeter, 2002 ......91.4
35 Ryne Sandberg, 1987 ......91.3
   Alan Trammell, 1987 ......91.3
   Rich Amaral, 1995 ....91.3
   Orlando Cabrera, 2005 ...91.3
39 Jerry Mumphrey, 1980 .....91.2
40 Tom Herr, 1985 ....91.2
41 **Carlos Beltran, 2003 ..91.1**
42 Barry Larkin, 1995 ....91.1
43 Jack Smith, 1925 ....90.9
   Davey Lopes, 1981 ....90.9
   Tim Raines, 1987 ....90.9
   Bip Roberts, 1995 ....90.9
   Roberto Alomar, 1995 .....90.9
   Chris Singleton, 2002 ...90.9
   Lew Ford, 2004 ....90.9
50 2 players tied 90.7

Base Stealing Wins

1 Vince Coleman, 1986.......2.0
2 Maury Wills, 1962 ....1.8
3 Rickey Henderson, 1983...1.7
4 Vince Coleman, 1985.......1.6
5 Vince Coleman, 1987.......1.6
6 Rickey Henderson, 1988...1.6
7 Ron LeFlore, 1980 ....1.6
8 Tim Raines, 1983..........1.5
9 Lou Brock, 1974...........1.5
10 Eric Davis, 1986..........1.4
11 Willie Wilson, 1980.......1.4
12 Rickey Henderson, 1982...1.4
13 Willie Wilson, 1979.......1.4
14 Rickey Henderson, 1985...1.4
15 **Marquis Grissom, 1992 ....1.4**
16 Tim Raines, 1984..........1.3
17 Davey Lopes, 1975.........1.3
18 Rudy Law, 1983............1.3
19 Rickey Henderson, 1980...1.3
20 Tim Raines, 1985..........1.3
21 Tim Raines, 1986..........1.3
22 Rickey Henderson, 1986...1.3
23 Tim Raines, 1981..........1.3
24 Tim Raines, 1982..........1.2
25 Rickey Henderson, 1989...1.2
26 Ron LeFlore, 1979 ....1.2
27 Vince Coleman, 1989.......1.2
28 Bert Campaneris, 1969.....1.1
29 Joe Morgan, 1975 ....1.1
30 Fritz Maisel, 1914.........1.1
31 Vince Coleman, 1990.......1.1
32 **Marquis Grissom, 1991 ....1.1**
33 Juan Samuel, 1984 ....1.1
34 Davey Lopes, 1976 ....1.1
35 **Tony Womack, 1999 ...1.1**
36 Lou Brock, 1968...........1.1
37 **Scott Podsednik, 2004...1.1**
38 Mickey Rivers, 1975.......1.1
39 Rickey Henderson, 1990...1.1
40 **Tony Womack, 1997 ...1.1**
41 Dave Collins, 1980 ....1.1
42 **Kenny Lofton, 1992 ....1.0**
43 Lou Brock, 1966...........1.0
44 Alan Wiggins, 1983 ....1.0
45 Maury Wills, 1965 ....1.0
46 Joe Morgan, 1976 ....1.0
47 Tommy Harper, 1969 ......1.0
48 Willie Wilson, 1979 ....1.0
49 Jerry Mumphrey, 1980 .....1.0
50 Omar Moreno, 1980 ....1.0

Pitcher Batting Average by era

1988-2005

1 Orel Hershiser, 1993 356
2 **Mike Hampton, 2002 ...344**
3 **Mike Hampton, 1999 ...311**
4 **Jason Marquis, 2005 ...310**
5 Fernando Valenzuela, 1990 ...304
6 **Carlos Zambrano, 2005 ....300**
7 **Livan Hernandez, 2001 ...296**
8 **Jason Marquis, 2004 ...292**
9 **Mike Hampton, 2001 ...291**
10 Tom Glavine, 1996 289

1973-1987

1 Rick Rhoden, 1984 333
2 Ken Brett, 1974 310
3 Bob Forsch, 1975...........308
   Rick Rhoden, 1976.........308
5 Jim Rooker, 1974 305
6 Rick Mahler, 1984 296
7 Bob Forsch, 1980...........295
8 Tom Griffin, 1974 294
9 Steve Carlton, 1978 291
10 Don Robinson, 1982........282

1961-1972

1 Catfish Hunter, 1971 350
2 Curt Simmons, 1961 303
3 Bob Gibson, 1970...........303
4 Don Drysdale, 1965 300
5 Claude Osteen, 1972 273
6 Gary Peters, 1971 271
7 Rick Wise, 1969 270
8 Camilo Pascual, 1962 268
9 Blue Moon Odom, 1969...266
   Sonny Siebert, 1971 266

1943-1960

1 Don Newcombe, 1955 359
2 Gene Bearden, 1952 354
3 Johnny Sain, 1947 346
4 Warren Spahn, 1958 333
5 Fritz Ostermueller, 1946 ...328
6 Fred Hutchinson, 1950......326
7 Oscar Judd, 1946...........316
8 Fred Hutchinson, 1946......315
9 Rip Sewell, 1945 313
   Tom Sturdivant, 1956......313

1921-1942

1 Walter Johnson, 1925 433
2 Jack Bentley, 1923 427
3 Curt Davis, 1939 381
4 Red Ruffing, 1930..........374
5 George Uhle, 1923..........361
6 Erv Brame, 1930...........353
7 Dutch Ruether, 1921 351
8 Wes Ferrell, 1935..........347
9 Wilbur Cooper, 1924 346
   Dolf Luque, 1926 346

1901-1920

1 Snake Wiltse, 1901 373
2 Doc Crandall, 1910 342
3 Bill Phillips, 1902..........342
4 Nixey Callahan, 1901.......331
5 Babe Ruth, 1917...........325
6 Frank Foreman, 1901.......325
   George Mullin, 1902........325
8 Al Orth, 1907 324
9 Claude Hendrix, 1912.......322
10 Cy Young, 1903 321

1893-1900

1 Ad Gumbert, 1895 361
2 Ted Breitenstein, 1899......352
3 Kid Gleason, 1894 349
4 Adonis Terry, 1894 347
5 Jack Stivetts, 1896.........347
6 Tom Parrott, 1895..........343
7 Jack Taylor, 1899 338
8 Jesse Tannehill, 1900 335
9 Al Orth, 1897 329
10 Jack Stivetts, 1894........328

1876-1892

1 Billy Taylor, 1884 366
2 Guy Hecker, 1886 341
3 Charlie Ferguson, 1887 337
4 Bob Caruthers, 1886.......334
5 Scott Stratton, 1890 315
6 Jim Whitney, 1882.........323
7 Charlie Sweeney, 1884 316
8 Jim Devlin, 1876 315
9 Ed Crane, 1890...........315
   Curry Foley, 1879.........315

Pitcher Batting Runs

1 Guy Hecker, 1884 ....27.5
2 Bob Caruthers, 1886.......23.4
3 Jim Whitney, 1882..........22.2
4 Don Drysdale, 1965 ....21.6
5 Wes Ferrell, 1935..........20.2
6 Don Newcombe, 1955 ......19.6
7 Guy Hecker, 1886 ....18.4
8 Jim Whitney, 1883.........17.7
9 Schoolboy Rowe, 1943 ....17.7
10 Warren Spahn, 1958.......17.4
11 Charlie Ferguson, 1885 ...17.1
12 Wes Ferrell, 1931.........16.9
13 Babe Ruth, 1917..........16.5
14 Scott Stratton, 1890.......16.4
15 George Uhle, 1923.........16.4
16 Red Ruffing, 1930..........16.4
17 Walter Johnson, 1925......16.2
18 Tony Mullane, 1884........16.2
19 Bob Lemon, 1950..........16.1
20 Bob Caruthers, 1889.......15.7
21 Bob Caruthers, 1887.......15.7
22 Red Lucas, 1930...........15.4
23 Bob Lemon, 1949..........15.0
24 Jack Bentley, 1923.........15.0
25 Babe Ruth, 1915..........15.0
26 John Ward, 1879..........15.0
27 Claude Hendrix, 1912.......14.8
28 Don Newcombe, 1959 ....14.7
29 Red Ruffing, 1936.........14.3
30 Jim Tobin, 1942...........14.3
31 Red Lucas, 1932...........14.2
32 Frank Killen, 1893.........14.2
33 Robin Roberts, 1955........13.9
34 Jack Stivetts, 1892.........13.8
35 Pink Hawley, 1895..........13.7
36 Scott Stratton, 1888.......13.4
37 Pete Conway, 1888.........13.4
38 Charlie Ferguson, 1887 ...13.3
39 Red Ruffing, 1932.........13.2
40 Jack Coombs, 1911.........13.1
41 Clark Griffith, 1901.........13.1
42 Jack Stivetts, 1890.........13.1
43 Joe Bush, 1924............13.1
44 Babe Ruth, 1916..........13.0
45 Adonis Terry, 1890.........13.0
46 Schoolboy Rowe, 1935.....12.9
47 Bob Lemon, 1948..........12.9
48 Red Ruffing, 1935.........12.9
49 Elam Vangilder, 1922.......12.9
50 Dave Foutz, 1887..........12.9
51 Terry Larkin, 1878.........12.8
52 Red Lucas, 1933...........12.7
53 Bucky Walters, 1939.......12.7
54 Red Ruffing, 1928.........12.4
55 Catfish Hunter, 1971.......12.3
56 Ad Gumbert, 1891.........12.2
57 Johnny Sain, 1947.........12.0
58 Joe Bowman, 1939.........12.0
59 Jouett Meekin, 1896.......11.8
60 Doc Crandall, 1915.........11.8
61 Babe Ruth, 1918..........11.8
62 Jim Whitney, 1887.........11.7
63 Bob Gibson, 1970..........11.7
64 Cy Young, 1903...........11.7
65 George Mullin, 1904........11.7
66 Curt Davis, 1939..........11.6
67 Red Lucas, 1931...........11.6
68 Jim Whitney, 1881.........11.5
69 Charley Radbourn, 1883..11.5
70 Tim Keefe, 1884...........11.4
71 Wes Ferrell, 1936.........11.3
72 Red Lucas, 1929...........11.3
73 Billy Taylor, 1884.........11.3
74 Erv Brame, 1929...........11.3
75 Dizzy Trout, 1944..........11.3
76 Adonis Terry, 1889.........11.2
77 Schoolboy Rowe, 1934 ....11.2
78 Frank Foreman, 1891.......11.2
79 Dutch Ruether, 1921 ......11.2
80 Jack Stivetts, 1896.........11.1
81 Charlie Ferguson, 1886 ...11.1
82 Ad Gumbert, 1895.........11.1
83 Guy Hecker, 1883.........11.0
84 Red Ruffing, 1941.........10.9
85 Bob Caruthers, 1891.......10.9
86 Jack Scott, 1921...........10.9
87 Charlie Buffinton, 1884 ....10.8
88 Ben Sanders, 1892.........10.8
89 Blue Moon Odom, 1969...10.8
90 Guy Hecker, 1887.........10.8
91 Scott Stratton, 1892.......10.8
92 Carl Mays, 1921...........10.7
93 Erv Brame, 1930...........10.7
94 Dave Ferriss, 1945.........10.6
95 Tony Mullane, 1882........10.5
96 **Mike Hampton, 1999 ...10.5**
97 Ken Brett, 1974...........10.5
98 Claude Hendrix, 1915......10.5
99 Al Maul, 1893.............10.5
100 George Van Haltren, 1888 ...10.4

Fielding Average

First Base

1 Steve Garvey, 1984.........1.000
2 Stuffy McInnis, 1921........999
3 Frank McCormick, 1946......999
4 David Segui, 1998...........999
5 **J.T. Snow, 1998...........999**
6 Steve Garvey, 1981..........999
7 Jim Spencer, 1973..........999
8 Wes Parker, 1968...........999

Second Base

1 **Bret Boone, 1997..........997**
2 Bobby Grich, 1985..........997
3 Jose Oquendo, 1990.........996
4 Ryne Sandberg, 1991........995
5 Jody Reed, 1994............995
6 Rob Wilfong, 1980..........995
7 **Placido Polanco, 2004.......995**
8 Bobby Grich, 1973..........995
9 Marcos Scutaro, 2004.......995
10 Frank White, 1988..........994

Shortstop

1 Mike Bordick, 2002..........998
2 Cal Ripken, 1990...........996
3 **Omar Vizquel, 2000.....995**
4 **Rey Sanchez, 2000.....994**
5 Rey Ordonez, 1999..........994
6 **Omar Vizquel, 1998.....993**
7 Tony Fernandez, 1989.......992
8 Larry Bowa, 1979..........991
9 Ed Brinkman, 1972..........990
10 Cal Ripken, 1989..........990

Third Base

1 Tony Fernandez, 1994 991
2 Steve Buechele, 1991.......991
3 Don Money, 1974...........989
4 Hank Majeski, 1947.........988
5 Aurelio Rodriguez, 1978......987
6 **Vinny Castilla, 2004.....987**
7 Willie Kamm, 1933..........984
8 Gary Gaetti, 1998..........983
9 **Mike Lowell, 2005.........983**
10 George Kell, 1946..........983

Outfield (250 chances accepted)

1 Danny Litwhiler, 1942 ......1.000
   Tony Gonzalez, 1962......1.000
   Rocky Colavito, 1965 .....1.000
   Curt Flood, 1966..........1.000
   Mickey Stanley, 1968 .....1.000
   Mickey Stanley, 1970 .....1.000
   Roy White, 1971 ....1.000
   Ken Berry, 1972 ....1.000
   Carl Yastrzemski, 1977 ...1.000
   Terry Puhl, 1979 ....1.000
   Brian Downing, 1982.......1.000
   Brian Downing, 1984.......1.000
   Brett Butler, 1991 ....1.000
   Darryl Hamilton, 1992......1.000
   Brett Butler, 1993 ....1.000
   Darren Lewis, 1993.........1.000
   Lance Johnson, 1994.......1.000
   Stan Javier, 1995 ....1.000
   Darryl Hamilton, 1996......1.000
   Paul O'Neill, 1996 ....1.000
   Darryl Hamilton, 1999......1.000
   B.J. Surhoff, 1999......1.000
   Eric Owens, 2000..........1.000
   Bernie Williams, 2000 ...1.000
   Luis Gonzalez, 2001 ....1.000
   Dave Roberts, 2002..1.000
   Juan Encarnacion, 2003..1.000
   Carlos Lee, 2004 ......1.000
   Shawn Green, 2005...1.000
   Vernon Wells, 2005...1.000

Catcher

1 Spud Davis, 1939...........1.000
   Buddy Rosar, 1946.........1.000
   Lou Berberet, 1957.........1.000
   Pete Daley, 1957 ....1.000
   Yogi Berra, 1958 ....1.000
   Rick Cerone, 1988 ....1.000
   Charles Johnson, 1997 ...1.000
   Chris Hoiles, 1997..........1.000
   Mike Matheny, 2003 ......1.000

Pitcher (90 chances accepted)

1 Kid Nichols, 1896...........1.000
   Frank Owen, 1904..........1.000
   Mordecai Brown, 1908......1.000
   Grover Alexander, 1913 .....1.000
   Walter Johnson, 1913 ....1.000
   Eppa Rixey, 1917 ....1.000
   Walter Johnson, 1917 .....1.000
   Grover Alexander, 1919 .....1.000
   Jesse Barnes, 1921........1.000
   Hal Schumacher, 1935......1.000
   Larry Jackson, 1964........1.000
   Randy Jones, 1976.........1.000
   Greg Maddux, 1990 ..1.000

Total Chances/Game (Infield)

First Base
1 Joe Gerhardt, 1876....13.28
2 Jiggs Donahue, 1907....12.73
3 Oscar Walker, 1879....12.60
4 Joe Start, 1878....12.54
5 Tim Murnane, 1878....12.52
6 Joe Start, 1879....12.49
7 Jake Goodman, 1878....12.45
8 Herman Dehlan, 1876....12.36
9 Phil Todt, 1926....12.36
10 Joe Start, 1877....12.35
11 George Burns, 1914....12.32
12 George Stovall, 1908....12.20
13 Stuffy McInnis, 1918....12.19
14 Juice Latham, 1877....12.19
15 Bill Phillips, 1888....12.12
16 Joe Start, 1880....12.11
17 Tom Jones, 1905....12.09
18 George Kelly, 1920....12.08
19 Gene Paulette, 1918....12.08
20 George Stovall, 1907....12.08
21 Hal Chase, 1919....12.07
22 Cap Anson, 1885....12.04
23 Bill Everitt, 1899....12.01
24 Charlie Comiskey, 1883....11.96
25 Jiggs Donahue, 1905....11.95

Second Base
1 Thorny Hawkes, 1879....8.44
2 Chick Fulmer, 1879....8.34
3 Jack Burdock, 1878....8.30
4 Ed Somerville, 1876....8.28
5 Joe Gerhardt, 1877....8.12
6 Fred Pfeffer, 1884....8.08
7 Jack Burdock, 1879....7.88
8 Joe Quest, 1878....7.81
9 Pop Smith, 1885....7.74
10 Joe Quest, 1879....7.73
11 Jack Farrell, 1879....7.67
12 Pop Smith, 1883....7.66
13 Joe Gerhardt, 1883....7.65
14 Hardy Richardson, 1883....7.62
15 Jack Burdock, 1880....7.59
16 Bid McPhee, 1886....7.56
17 Bid McPhee, 1884....7.54
18 Fred Pfeffer, 1883....7.53
19 Cub Stricker, 1882....7.53
20 Jack Burdock, 1877....7.53
21 Joe Gerhardt, 1884....7.51
22 Fred Dunlap, 1882....7.48
23 George Wright, 1877....7.47
24 Hardy Richardson, 1882....7.45
25 Ben Ferguson, 1880....7.40

Shortstop
1 Herman Long, 1889....7.27
2 Hughie Jennings, 1895....7.16
3 Dave Bancroft, 1918....7.14
4 Phil Tomney, 1889....7.12
5 George Davis, 1899....7.10
6 Hughie Jennings, 1896....7.07
7 Hughie Jennings, 1897....7.03
8 Bobby Wallace, 1901....6.97
9 Monte Cross, 1897....6.97
10 Bill Dahlen, 1895....6.93
11 Gene DeMontreville, 1897....6.91
12 Rabbit Maranville, 1919....6.89
13 Bill Dahlen, 1893....6.82
George Davis, 1898....6.82
15 Herman Long, 1893....6.81
16 Bob Allen, 1890....6.81
17 Hughie Jennings, 1894....6.79
18 George Davis, 1900....6.77
19 Kid Elberfeld, 1901....6.77
20 Honus Wagner, 1903....6.76
21 Herman Long, 1896....6.74
22 Bill Dahlen, 1898....6.73
23 Monte Cross, 1898....6.73
24 Bill Dahlen, 1900....6.71
25 Rabbit Maranville, 1914....6.71
Dave Bancroft, 1922....6.71

Third Base
1 Al Nichols, 1876....5.81
2 Bob Ferguson, 1877....5.61
3 Jumbo Davis, 1888....5.13
4 Cap Anson, 1876....5.03
5 George Bradley, 1880....4.93
6 Billy Shindle, 1892....4.93
7 Jack Gleason, 1882....4.90
8 Bill Bradley, 1900....4.87
9 Will Foley, 1879....4.79
10 Levi Meyerle, 1876....4.78
11 Joe Battin, 1876....4.76
12 Harry Schafer, 1876....4.73
13 Jerry Denny, 1882....4.73
14 Patsy Tebeau, 1890....4.69
15 Joe Battin, 1883....4.68
16 Arlie Latham, 1884....4.67
17 Frank Hankinson, 1878....4.65
18 Ed Williamson, 1883....4.64
19 Billy Shindle, 1889....4.61
20 Arlie Latham, 1891....4.61
21 Billy Shindle, 1891....4.59
22 Hick Carpenter, 1880....4.58
23 Charlie Reilly, 1890....4.58
24 Jerry Denny, 1881....4.55
25 Hick Carpenter, 1882....4.55

Assists (Infield)

First Base
1 Bill Buckner, 1985....184
2 Mark Grace, 1990....180
3 Mark Grace, 1991....167
4 Sid Bream, 1986....166
5 Bill Buckner, 1983....161
6 Bill Buckner, 1982....159
7 Bill Buckner, 1980....157
8 Todd Helton, 2003....156
9 Mickey Vernon, 1949....155
10 Fred Tenney, 1905....152
Eddie Murray, 1985....152
12 Ferris Fain, 1952....150
13 Rudy York, 1943....149
Keith Hernandez, 1986....149
Keith Hernandez, 1987....149
Todd Helton, 2000....149
17 Keith Hernandez, 1983....147
Eric Karros, 1993....147
Rafael Palmeiro, 1993....147
Jeff King, 1997....147
21 Rudy York, 1942....146
Keith Hernandez, 1979....146
Pete O'Brien, 1987....146
Todd Helton, 1998....146
25 Vic Power, 1960....145
Eddie Murray, 1987....145
Wally Joyner, 1993....145

Second Base
1 Frankie Frisch, 1927....641
2 Hughie Critz, 1926....588
3 Rogers Hornsby, 1927....582
4 Ski Melillo, 1930....572
5 Ryne Sandberg, 1983....571
6 Rabbit Maranville, 1924....568
7 Frank Parkinson, 1922....562
8 Tony Cuccinello, 1936....559
9 Johnny Hodapp, 1930....557
10 Lou Bierbauer, 1892....555
11 Pep Young, 1938....554
12 Burgess Whitehead, 1936....552
13 Sparky Adams, 1925....551
14 Ryne Sandberg, 1984....550
15 Rogers Hornsby, 1929....547
16 Hod Ford, 1924....543
Ski Melillo, 1931....543
Bill Mazeroski, 1964....543
19 Hughie Critz, 1925....542
Charlie Gehringer, 1933....542
Woody Williams, 1944....542
Jerry Priddy, 1950....542
23 Hughie Critz, 1933....541
24 Glenn Hubbard, 1985....539
Ryne Sandberg, 1992....539

Shortstop
1 Ozzie Smith, 1980....621
2 Glenn Wright, 1924....601
3 Dave Bancroft, 1920....598
4 Tommy Thevenow, 1926....597
5 Ivan DeJesus, 1977....595
6 Cal Ripken, 1984....583
7 Whitey Wietelmann, 1943....581
8 Dave Bancroft, 1922....579
9 Rabbit Maranville, 1914....574
10 Don Kessinger, 1968....573
11 Roy Smalley, 1979....572
12 Terry Turner, 1906....570
Joe Tinker, 1908....570
Leo Cardenas, 1969....570
Ozzie Guillen, 1988....570
16 Heinie Wagner, 1908....569
Ed Brinkman, 1970....569
18 George McBride, 1908....568
19 Donie Bush, 1909....567
20 Art Fletcher, 1917....565
21 Luis Aparicio, 1969....563
22 Germany Smith, 1892....561
Tommy Corcoran, 1898....561
24 Larry Bowa, 1971....560
Bill Russell, 1973....560

Third Base
1 Graig Nettles, 1971....412
2 Graig Nettles, 1973....410
Brooks Robinson, 1974....410
4 Harlond Clift, 1937....405
Brooks Robinson, 1967....405
6 Mike Schmidt, 1974....404
7 Doug DeCinces, 1982....399
8 Clete Boyer, 1962....396
Mike Schmidt, 1977....396
Buddy Bell, 1982....396
11 Ron Santo, 1967....393
12 Terry Pendleton, 1989....392
13 Ron Santo, 1966....391
14 Aurelio Rodriguez, 1974....389
Vinny Castilla, 1996....389
16 Ossie Vitt, 1916....385
17 Graig Nettles, 1976....383
Buddy Bell, 1983....383
Tim Wallach, 1985....383
20 Billy Shindle, 1892....382
21 Darrell Evans, 1975....381
22 Graig Nettles, 1975....379
23 Frank Malzone, 1958....378
Ron Santo, 1968....378
Brandon Inge, 2005....378

Assists/Game (Infield)

First Base
1 Mark Grace, 1990....1.18
2 Bill Buckner, 1986....1.14
3 Bill Buckner, 1985....1.14
4 Jeff Bagwell, 1995....1.13
5 Bill Buckner, 1983....1.12
6 Jeff Bagwell, 1994....1.10
7 Sid Bream, 1986....1.08
8 Eric Karros, 1994....1.08
9 Cecil Fielder, 1994....1.06
10 Ferris Fain, 1951....1.05
11 Mark Grace, 1991....1.04
12 Ferris Fain, 1952....1.04
13 Wally Joyner, 1993....1.04
14 Fred Tenney, 1905....1.03
15 Keith Hernandez, 1983....1.02
16 Bob Robertson, 1971....1.02
17 Sid Bream, 1988....1.01
18 Mickey Vernon, 1949....1.01
19 Darrell Evans, 1985....1.01
20 Roy Cullenbine, 1947....1.01
21 Vic Power, 1961....1.01
22 Keith Hernandez, 1986....1.00
Todd Helton, 1998....1.00
24 Bill Buckner, 1982....0.99
25 Eddie Murray, 1985....0.99

Second Base
1 Joe Gerhardt, 1877....4.28
2 Frankie Frisch, 1927....4.19
3 Thorny Hawkes, 1879....4.13
4 Hughie Critz, 1933....4.07
5 Frank Parkinson, 1922....4.04
6 Joe Quest, 1879....3.99
7 Chick Fulmer, 1879....3.96
8 Ed Somerville, 1876....3.92
9 Ski Melillo, 1930....3.86
10 Glenn Hubbard, 1985....3.85
11 Frankie Frisch, 1930....3.85
12 Jack Farrell, 1883....3.84
13 Sparky Adams, 1925....3.83
14 Freddie Maguire, 1928....3.80
15 Hughie Critz, 1926....3.79
16 Fred Pfeffer, 1884....3.77
17 Hughie Critz, 1925....3.76
18 Danny Richardson, 1891....3.76
19 John Kerr, 1929....3.76
20 Frankie Frisch, 1924....3.76
21 Rogers Hornsby, 1927....3.75
22 Hod Ford, 1924....3.74
23 Hardy Richardson, 1883....3.74
24 Rabbit Maranville, 1924....3.74
25 Charley Bassett, 1887....3.73

Shortstop
1 Germany Smith, 1885....4.21
2 Arthur Irwin, 1880....4.13
3 Art Fletcher, 1919....4.10
4 Bill Dahlen, 1895....4.09
5 Phil Tomney, 1889....4.05
6 Bobby Wallace, 1901....4.04
7 Jack Glasscock, 1887....4.04
8 Germany Smith, 1892....4.04
9 Henry Easterday, 1888....3.99
10 Dave Bancroft, 1922....3.99
11 Rogers Hornsby, 1918....3.98
12 Robin Yount, 1981....3.98
13 Germany Smith, 1894....3.98
14 Bob Ferguson, 1878....3.96
15 Shorty Fuller, 1895....3.96
16 George Davis, 1900....3.95
17 Ozzie Smith, 1980....3.93
18 Glenn Wright, 1924....3.93
19 Garry Templeton, 1980....3.92
20 Monte Cross, 1897....3.91
21 Art Fletcher, 1918....3.90
22 Hughie Jennings, 1894....3.90
23 Sadie Houck, 1885....3.89
24 Bill Dahlen, 1900....3.89
25 Davy Force, 1876....3.89

Third Base
1 Jumbo Davis, 1888....2.96
2 Buddy Bell, 1981....2.93
3 George Bradley, 1880....2.89
4 Bill Hague, 1878....2.85
5 Billy Shindle, 1892....2.85
6 Bob Ferguson, 1877....2.77
7 Ed Williamson, 1879....2.76
8 Arlie Latham, 1884....2.75
9 Bill Bradley, 1900....2.75
10 Arlie Latham, 1891....2.74
11 Buddy Bell, 1982....2.73
12 Brooks Robinson, 1974....2.68
13 Aaron Ward, 1920....2.66
14 Mike Schmidt, 1977....2.66
15 Joe Battin, 1883....2.63
16 Harlond Clift, 1937....2.61
17 Arlie Latham, 1883....2.61
18 Graig Nettles, 1973....2.61
19 Doug DeCinces, 1982....2.61
20 Graig Nettles, 1971....2.61
21 Billy Nash, 1892....2.60
22 Ed Williamson, 1883....2.60
23 Charlie Reilly, 1890....2.58
24 Ron Santo, 1966....2.57
25 Brooks Robinson, 1967....2.56

Double Plays

First Base
1 Ferris Fain, 1949....194
2 Ferris Fain, 1950....192
3 Donn Clendenon, 1966....182
4 Andres Galarraga, 1997....176
5 Ron Jackson, 1979....175
Albert Pujols, 2005....175
7 Gil Hodges, 1951....171
8 Mickey Vernon, 1949....168
9 Ted Kluszewski, 1954....166
Carlos Delgado, 2001....166

Second Base
1 Bill Mazeroski, 1966....161
2 Jerry Priddy, 1950....150
3 Bill Mazeroski, 1961....144
4 Nellie Fox, 1957....141
Dave Cash, 1974....141
6 Buddy Myer, 1935....138
Bill Mazeroski, 1962....138
Carlos Baerga, 1992....138
9 Jerry Coleman, 1950....137
Jackie Robinson, 1951....137
Red Schoendienst, 1954....137

Shortstop
1 Rick Burleson, 1980....147
2 Roy Smalley, 1979....144
3 Bobby Wine, 1970....137
4 Lou Boudreau, 1944....134
5 Spike Owen, 1986....133
6 Mike Bordick, 1999....132
7 Rafael Ramirez, 1982....130
8 Roy McMillan, 1954....129
Jack Wilson, 2004....129
10 Hod Ford, 1928....128
Vern Stephens, 1949....128
Gene Alley, 1966....128

Third Base
1 Graig Nettles, 1971....54
2 Harlond Clift, 1937....50
3 Johnny Pesky, 1949....48
Paul Molitor, 1982....48
5 Sammy Hale, 1927....46
Clete Boyer, 1965....46
Gary Gaetti, 1983....46
8 Eddie Yost, 1950....45
Frank Malzone, 1961....45
Darrell Evans, 1974....45
Jeff Cirillo, 1998....45

Outfield
1 Happy Felsch, 1919....15
2 Jimmy Sheckard, 1899....14
3 Tom Brown, 1893....13
4 Tom Brown, 1886....12
Tommy McCarthy, 1888....12
Jimmy Bannon, 1894....12
Mike Griffin, 1895....12
Danny Green, 1899....12
Cy Seymour, 1905....12
Ginger Beaumont, 1907....12
Ty Cobb, 1907....12
Tris Speaker, 1909....12
Jimmy Sheckard, 1911....12
Tris Speaker, 1914....12
Mel Ott, 1929....12
16 Sam Thompson, 1886....11
Tommy McCarthy, 1889....11
Billy Sunday, 1890....11
Sam Thompson, 1896....11
Bill Lange, 1899....11
Fielder Jones, 1902....11
Jimmy Sebring, 1903....11
Phil Geier, 1904....11
Ben Koehler, 1905....11
Burt Shotton, 1913....11
Chief Wilson, 1914....11

Catcher
1 Steve O'Neill, 1916....36
2 Frankie Hayes, 1945....29
3 Ray Schalk, 1916....25
Yogi Berra, 1951....25
5 Jack Lapp, 1915....23
Muddy Ruel, 1924....23
Tom Haller, 1966....23
8 Steve O'Neill, 1914....22
Bob O'Farrell, 1922....22
10 Gabby Hartnett, 1927....21
Wes Westrum, 1950....21

Pitcher
1 Bob Lemon, 1953....15
2 Eddie Rommel, 1924....12
Curt Davis, 1934....12
Randy Jones, 1976....12
5 Scott Perry, 1919....11
Tom Rogers, 1919....11
Art Nehf, 1920....11
Burleigh Grimes, 1925....11
Gene Bearden, 1948....11
Kirk Rueter, 2001....11

Putouts (Outfield)

Outfield
1 Taylor Douthit, 1928....547
2 Richie Ashburn, 1951....538
3 Richie Ashburn, 1949....514
4 Chet Lemon, 1977....512
5 Dwayne Murphy, 1980....507
6 Dom DiMaggio, 1948....503
Richie Ashburn, 1956....503
8 Richie Ashburn, 1957....502
9 Richie Ashburn, 1953....496
10 Richie Ashburn, 1958....495
11 Andruw Jones, 1999....492
12 Jim Busby, 1954....491
13 Omar Moreno, 1979....490
14 Baby Doll Jacobson, 1924....488
Bobby Thomson, 1949....488
Al Bumbry, 1980....488
17 Mike Cameron, 2003....485
18 Lloyd Waner, 1931....484
19 Richie Ashburn, 1954....483
20 Jim Busby, 1953....482
Willie Wilson, 1980....482
22 Omar Moreno, 1980....479
23 Tom Oliver, 1930....477
24 Dwayne Murphy, 1984....474
25 Lloyd Moseby, 1984....473
26 Jim Busby, 1952....472
27 Rick Manning, 1973....471
28 Lenny Dykstra, 1993....469
29 Johnny Lindell, 1944....468
30 Rick Bosetti, 1979....466
31 Ruppert Jones, 1977....465
Kirby Puckett, 1985....465
33 Ken Henderson, 1974....462
Gary Pettis, 1986....462
35 Andruw Jones, 2001....461
36 George Wright, 1983....460
Torii Hunter, 2001....460
38 Wally Berger, 1931....457
39 Wally Berger, 1931....457
Vince DiMaggio, 1943....457
41 Jim Piersall, 1956....455
Gorman Thomas, 1980....455
43 Sam Rice, 1920....454
44 Ruppert Jones, 1979....453
45 Dwayne Murphy, 1982....452
Darin Erstad, 2002....452
47 Carden Gillenwater, 1945....451
48 Max Carey, 1923....450
Lloyd Waner, 1929....450
Sam West, 1932....450
Sam Chapman, 1949....450
Kirby Puckett, 1988....450
53 Max Carey, 1922....449
Eddie Brown, 1925....449
Sam West, 1935....449
Buster Adams, 1944....449
57 Willie Mays, 1954....448
Brett Butler, 1984....448
59 Al Simmons, 1925....447
Gus Bell, 1953....447
Paul Blair, 1974....447
62 Johnny Mostil, 1925....446
Dain Clay, 1945....446
Cesar Cedeno, 1974....446
65 Garry Maddox, 1978....444
Joe Carter, 1988....444
Robin Yount, 1988....444
68 Doc Cramer, 1936....443
Devon White, 1992....443
70 Taylor Douthit, 1929....442
Sam West, 1936....442
Dave Philley, 1952....442
Bill Tuttle, 1955....442
74 Joe DiMaggio, 1948....441
Garry Maddox, 1976....441
76 Max Carey, 1917....440
Happy Felsch, 1917....440
Taylor Douthit, 1926....440
Johnny Mostil, 1926....440
Ron LeFlore, 1978....440
81 Dom DiMaggio, 1942....439
Gorman Thomas, 1983....439
Rickey Henderson, 1985....439
Lenny Dykstra, 1990....439
Devon White, 1991....439
86 Jigger Statz, 1923....438
Kirby Puckett, 1984....438
Kirby Puckett, 1989....438
Ray Lankford, 1992....438
Andruw Jones, 2000....438
91 Billy North, 1974....43
Brett Butler, 1985....43
Rocco Baldelli, 2003....43
94 Harry Craft, 1938....43
Darrin Jackson, 1992....43
96 Gorman Thomas, 1979....43
Andre Dawson, 1983....43
98 Stan Spence, 1944....43
Brett Butler, 1986....43
100 Tom Oliver, 1931....43
Fred Schulte, 1933....43
Garry Maddox, 1979....43
Lance Johnson, 1992....43

Putouts/Game (Outfield)

Outfield

1 Taylor Douthit, 1928 ....3.55
2 Fred Treacey, 1876 ....3.54
3 Richie Ashburn, 1951 ......3.49
4 Thurman Tucker, 1944 ....3.45
5 Chet Lemon, 1977 ....3.44
6 Kirby Puckett, 1984 ....3.42
7 Richie Ashburn, 1949 ......3.34
8 Irv Noren, 1951 ....3.33
9 Sam West, 1935 ....3.33
10 Mike Cameron, 2003 ..3.30
11 Jim Busby, 1952 ....3.28
12 Richie Ashburn, 1956 ....3.27
13 Richie Ashburn, 1958 ....3.26
14 Lloyd Waner, 1932 ....3.25
15 Dom DiMaggio, 1948 .....3.25
16 Carden Gillenwater, 1945..3.22
17 Richie Ashburn, 1957 ....3.22
18 Jim Busby, 1953 ....3.21
19 Baby Doll Jacobson, 1924 ..3.21
20 Dwayne Murphy, 1980 ...3.21
21 Taylor Douthit, 1926 ......3.19
22 Richie Ashburn, 1953 ....3.18
23 Andre Dawson, 1981 ......3.17
24 Taylor Douthit, 1927 ......3.17
25 Jim Busby, 1954 ....3.17
26 Billy North, 1974 ....3.17
27 Sam West, 1931 ....3.16
28 Lloyd Waner, 1932 ....3.16
29 Darin Erstad, 2002 .....3.16
30 Richie Ashburn, 1954 ....3.16
31 Sam West, 1932 ....3.15
32 Terry Moore, 1936 ....3.14
33 Johnny Lindell, 1944 ......3.14
34 Devon White, 1988 ....3.14
35 Torii Hunter, 2001 .....3.13
36 Bobby Thomson, 1949 ...3.13
37 Sam Chapman, 1948 ......3.12
38 Rickey Henderson, 1985..3.11
39 Fred Schulte, 1929 ....3.11
40 Billy North, 1973 ....3.11
41 Max Carey, 1921 ....3.10
42 Dwayne Murphy, 1984 ...3.10
43 Tom Oliver, 1930 ....3.10
44 Garry Maddox, 1979.......3.09
45 Kiddo Davis, 1932 ....3.09
46 Rick Bosetti, 1978...........3.09
47 Dom DiMaggio, 1947 ......3.08
48 Lance Johnson, 1994 ......3.08
49 Dwayne Murphy, 1981 ...3.08
50 Dwayne Murphy, 1982 ...3.07
51 Wally Berger, 1935 ....3.07
52 Ruppert Jones, 1978 ......3.07
53 Garry Maddox, 1976 ......3.06
54 Sam Chapman, 1950 ......3.06
55 Rickey Henderson, 1981..3.06
56 Redleg Snyder, 1876......3.05
57 Al Bumbry, 1980 ....3.05
   Chet Lemon, 1984 ....3.05
59 Jim Rivera, 1952 ....3.05
60 Fred Schulte, 1933 ....3.05
61 Mike Mansell, 1879 ....3.04
62 Billy North, 1975 ....3.04
63 Jigger Statz, 1927 ....3.04
64 Andruw Jones, 1999 ..3.04
65 Lloyd Moseby, 1984 ......3.03
66 Willie Wilson, 1980 ....3.03
67 Amos Otis, 1981 ....3.03
68 Terry Moore, 1935..........3.03
69 Omar Moreno, 1979 ....3.02
70 Thurman Tucker, 1943 ...3.02
71 Gary Pettis, 1986 ....3.02
72 Gary Pettis, 1985 ....3.02
73 Mike Kreevich, 1939 ......3.01
74 Johnny Groth, 1953 ....3.01
75 Johnny Mostil, 1928 ....3.01
76 Kiddo Davis, 1934 ....3.00
   Ruppert Jones, 1977 ......3.00
   Otis Nixon, 1992 ....3.00
Bernie Williams, 1995 ....3.00
80 Johnny Mostil, 1926 ....2.99
81 Mickey Rivers, 1976........2.99
82 Willie Wilson, 1984 ....2.99
83 Sam Chapman, 1939 ......2.99
84 Jimmy Welsh, 1930.........2.99
85 Sam West, 1936 ....2.99
86 Wally Judnich, 1946........2.99
87 Taylor Douthit, 1931 ....2.98
88 Freddie Lindstrom, 1933 ..2.98
89 Mike Kreevich, 1938 ....2.98
90 Rick Miller, 1979 ....2.98
Mike Cameron, 1997 ..2.98
92 Rick Manning, 1983 ....2.98
93 Lloyd Waner, 1929 ....2.98
94 Ira Flagstead, 1925 ....2.98
95 Dave Philley, 1948..........2.98
96 Buster Adams, 1944 ....2.97
97 Mike Kreevich, 1940 ....2.97
98 Amos Otis, 1974 ....2.97
99 Eric Davis, 1987.............2.97
100 Sam Rice, 1920 ....2.97

Fielding Runs

First Base

1 Bill Buckner, 1985 25
2 Mark Grace, 1990 25
3 Chick Gandil, 1914 23
4 Fred Tenney, 1905..............22
5 Bill Buckner, 1983 22
6 Sid Bream, 1986..................21
7 Jeff King, 1997 21
8 Jiggs Donahue, 1907...........20
9 Jake Beckley, 1892 20
10 Vic Power, 1960 20

Second Base

1 Glenn Hubbard, 1985 60
2 Bill Mazeroski, 1963.............55
3 Frankie Frisch, 1927 49
4 Freddie Maguire, 1928.........49
5 Nap Lajoie, 1908.................45
6 Hughie Critz, 1933 45
7 Orlando Hudson, 2003 45
8 Ryne Sandberg, 1983 44
9 Danny Richardson, 1891 43
10 Fred Pfeffer, 1884 43

Shortstop

1 Rabbit Maranville, 1914.........50
2 George Davis, 1899..............46
3 Ivan DeJesus, 1977 45
4 Dick Bartell, 1936 43
5 Everett Scott, 1921 41
6 Ozzie Guillen, 1988 41
7 Germany Smith, 1885...........40
8 Freddie Patek, 1973 40
9 Cal Ripken, 1984 39
10 Jack Glasscock, 1887 39

Third Base

1 Graig Nettles, 1971 46
2 Harlond Clift, 1937 41
3 Billy Shindle, 1892 40
4 Buddy Bell, 1982 38
5 Billy Shindle, 1888 38
6 Arlie Latham, 1884 37
7 Tommy Leach, 1904 36
8 Tim Wallach, 1985 36
9 Lave Cross, 1899 36
10 Terry Pendleton, 1989 35

Outfield

1 Jim Fogarty, 1887 30
2 Tom Brown, 1893 26
3 Tommy McCarthy, 1888 26
4 Jimmy Sheckard, 1903 25
5 Mike Mitchell, 1907..............25
6 Richie Ashburn, 1957 25
7 Ed Delahanty, 1893 24
8 Dave Parker, 1977 23
9 Chet Lemon, 1977 23
10 Tris Speaker, 1914 23
11 Dick Johnston, 1887 23
12 Hardy Richardson, 1881 22
13 Johnny Callison, 1962..........22
14 Max Carey, 1916 22
15 Richie Ashburn, 1951 21
16 Max Carey, 1917 21
17 Chuck Klein, 1930...............21
18 Andruw Jones, 1998 20
19 Mike Griffin, 1891 20
20 Al Kaline, 1958...................20

Catcher

1 Bill Holbert, 1883 34
2 Jim Sundberg, 1977 32
3 John Warner, 1897 32
4 Paul LoDuca, 2003 31
5 Damian Miller, 2001..........29
6 Tom Daly, 1887 28
7 Duke Farrell, 1894 27
8 John Kerins, 1886 27
9 Morgan Murphy, 1891..........27
10 Chief Zimmer, 1894 27

Pitcher

1 Ed Walsh, 1907 21
2 Harry Howell, 1905..............17
3 Ed Walsh, 1911..................14
4 Ed Walsh, 1908...................13
5 Will White, 1882 12
6 John Clarkson, 1889 11
7 Tony Mullane, 1882 10
8 Sadie McMahon, 1890..........10
9 Carl Mays, 1926 10
10 Ed Walsh, 1910.................10

Fielding Wins

1 Glenn Hubbard, 1985 ....6.3
2 Bill Mazeroski, 1963............6.1
3 Rabbit Maranville, 1914........5.4
4 Nap Lajoie, 1908................5.3
5 Graig Nettles, 1971 ....4.9
6 Nap Lajoie, 1907................4.9
7 Freddie Maguire, 1928.........4.8
8 Frankie Frisch, 1927 ....4.8
9 Hughie Critz, 1933 ....4.8
10 Ryne Sandberg, 1983.........4.7
11 Ivan DeJesus, 1977 ....4.6
12 Dave Shean, 1910 ....4.6
13 Bill Dahlen, 1908................4.3
14 Bill Mazeroski, 1966...........4.3
15 Freddie Patek, 1972 ....4.3
16 Orlando Hudson, 2003.....4.3
17 Danny Richardson, 1892 ....4.2
18 Ozzie Guillen, 1988 ....4.2
19 George Davis, 1899 ....4.2
20 Dick Bartell, 1936 ....4.1
21 Glenn Hubbard, 1986 ....4.1
22 Bill Mazeroski, 1962...........4.1
23 Ozzie Smith, 1980 ....4.1
24 Freddie Patek, 1973 ....4.1
25 Bobby Knoop, 1964............4.0
26 Danny Richardson, 1891 ....4.0
27 Nap Lajoie, 1903................4.0
28 Dave Bancroft, 1920 ....3.9
29 Cal Ripken, 1984 ....3.9
30 Everett Scott, 1921 ....3.9
31 Art Fletcher, 1915...............3.9
32 Joe Cassidy, 1905..............3.9
33 Fred Pfeffer, 1884 ....3.8
34 Miller Huggins, 1905...........3.8
35 Rey Sanchez, 2001 ....3.8
36 Buck Weaver, 1913 ....3.8
37 Tommy Leach, 1904............3.8
38 Tim Wallach, 1985 ....3.8
39 Harlond Clift, 1937 ....3.8
40 Garry Templeton, 1980 ....3.7
41 Ozzie Smith, 1982 ....3.7
42 Buddy Bell, 1982 ....3.7
43 Terry Pendleton, 1989.........3.7
44 George McBride, 1908.........3.7
45 Bill Mazeroski, 1961...........3.7
46 Heinie Wagner, 1908...........3.7
47 Fred Pfeffer, 1888 ....3.7
48 Bill Mazeroski, 1964...........3.7
49 Red Schoendienst, 1952.....3.7
50 Tim Foli, 1974 ....3.7
51 George McBride, 1910..........3.6
52 Germany Smith, 1885...........3.6
53 Lee Tannehill, 1906.............3.6
54 Buck Herzog, 1914 ....3.6
55 Lee Tannehill, 1911.............3.6
56 Mickey Doolan, 1914 ....3.6
57 Buddy Bell, 1981................3.6
58 Spike Owen, 1986..............3.6
59 Eddie Mayo, 1944 ....3.5
60 Billy Shindle, 1888 ....3.5
61 Zoilo Versalles, 1962...........3.5
62 Brooks Robinson, 1967........3.5
63 Donie Bush, 1914 ....3.5
64 Dick Bartell, 1937 ....3.5
65 Neifi Perez, 2000 ....3.5
66 Garry Templeton, 1978 ....3.5
67 Clete Boyer, 1962...............3.4
68 Bobby Knoop, 1969.............3.4
69 Luis Aparicio, 1969 ....3.4
70 Luis Aparicio, 1960 ....3.4
71 Mickey Doolan, 1915...........3.4
72 Billy Shindle, 1892 ....3.4
73 Joe Gerhardt, 1890.............3.4
74 Horace Clarke, 1968...........3.4
75 Buck Herzog, 1915 ....3.4
76 John Farrell, 1902...............3.4
77 Bruno Betzel, 1916 ....3.4
78 Ron Santo, 1967 ....3.3
79 Graig Nettles, 1973............3.3
80 Arlie Latham, 1884..............3.3
81 Mike Benjamin, 1999 ....3.3
82 Ozzie Smith, 1984 ....3.3
83 Vinny Castilla, 1996 ......3.3
84 Ski Melillo, 1931.................3.3
85 Ed Brinkman, 1970 ....3.3
86 David Eckstein, 2005 ...3.3
87 Jack Glasscock, 1889.........3.3
88 Cupid Childs, 1896..............3.3
89 Jack Glasscock, 1887.........3.3
90 Eddie Collins, 1910.............3.3
91 Mike Bordick, 1999.............3.3
92 Darrell Evans, 1975 ....3.3
93 Lave Cross, 1899...............3.2
94 Jim Sundberg, 1977............3.2
95 Alex Gonzalez, 2001.....3.2
96 Dave Cash, 1974 ....3.2
97 Paul LoDuca, 2003 ....3.2
98 Roy Smalley, 1979 ....3.2
99 Ozzie Smith, 1978 ....3.2
100 Dave Bancroft, 1917 ....3.2

Batter-Fielder Wins

1 Barry Bonds, 2001......11.7
2 Barry Bonds, 2002......11.5
3 Barry Bonds, 2004......10.6
4 Babe Ruth, 1923 ....10.1
5 Babe Ruth, 1921...............9.4
   Cal Ripken, 1984 ....9.4
7 Babe Ruth, 1920...............9.3
   Rogers Hornsby, 1924 ......9.3
9 Nap Lajoie, 1910...............8.9
   Rogers Hornsby, 1922 ......8.9
11 Babe Ruth, 1927 ....8.8
12 Sammy Sosa, 2001.......8.6
13 Babe Ruth, 1926 ....8.5
   Ted Williams, 1941 ....8.5
   Ted Williams, 1942 ....8.5
   Cal Ripken, 1991 ....8.5
17 Babe Ruth, 1924..............8.4
   Lou Gehrig, 1927 ....8.4
19 Mickey Mantle, 1957 ....8.2
Craig Biggio, 1997 ....8.2
Barry Bonds, 2003........8.2
22 Nap Lajoie, 1901 ....8.1
   Nap Lajoie, 1903...............8.1
   Babe Ruth, 1931...............8.1
   Ted Williams, 1946............8.1
   Mickey Mantle, 1956 ....8.1
   Joe Morgan, 1975 ....8.1
28 Nap Lajoie, 1908...............8.0
Barry Bonds, 1993........8.0
30 Rogers Hornsby, 1920 ......7.9
   George Sisler, 1920 ....7.9
   Lou Gehrig, 1934 ....7.9
Barry Bonds, 1992........7.9
34 Rogers Hornsby, 1917 ......7.8
35 Rogers Hornsby, 1921 ......7.7
   Lou Gehrig, 1930 ....7.7
   Ron Santo, 1967 ....7.7
   Rickey Henderson, 1990....7.7
Jeff Bagwell, 1994 ....7.7
Mike Piazza, 1997 ....7.7
41 Nap Lajoie, 1906...............7.6
   Babe Ruth, 1930...............7.6
   Norm Cash, 1961...............7.6
   Ron Santo, 1966 ....7.6
   Rico Petrocelli, 1969..........7.6
Barry Bonds, 1996........7.6
47 Honus Wagner, 1905 ....7.5
   Lou Boudreau, 1944 ....7.5
   Mickey Mantle, 1961..........7.5
50 Nap Lajoie, 1904...............7.4
   Ty Cobb, 1917..................7.4
   Harlond Clift, 1937 ....7.4
   Al Rosen, 1953 ....7.4
   Joe Morgan, 1973 ....7.4
   Ken Caminiti, 1996.............7.4
Alex Rodriguez, 2002 ...7.4
57 Tris Speaker, 1914............7.3
   Babe Ruth, 1919...............7.3
   Jackie Robinson, 1951.......7.3
   Mike Schmidt, 1974 ....7.3
61 Honus Wagner, 1906 ....7.2
   Tris Speaker, 1912 ....7.2
   Frankie Frisch, 1927 ....7.2
   Snuffy Stirnweiss, 1945 .....7.2
   Ted Williams, 1947............7.2
   Stan Musial, 1948.............7.2
67 Fred Dunlap, 1884 ....7.1
   Joe Jackson, 1912.............7.1
   Babe Ruth, 1928...............7.1
   Lou Boudreau, 1948 ....7.1
   Ted Williams, 1957............7.1
   Ron Santo, 1964 ....7.1
   Mike Schmidt, 1981...........7.1
   Robin Yount, 1982.............7.1
Jeff Bagwell, 1996 ......7.1
   Mark McGwire, 1998..........7.1
Albert Pujols, 2003........7.1
78 Nap Lajoie, 1907...............7.0
   Eddie Collins, 1910............7.0
   Eddie Collins, 1913............7.0
   Joe Morgan, 1974 ....7.0
   Cal Ripken, 1983 ....7.0
83 Honus Wagner, 1908 ....6.9
   Eddie Collins, 1914............6.9
   Joe Cronin, 1930...............6.9
   Jimmie Foxx, 1933 ....6.9
   Willie Mays, 1965..............6.9
   Carl Yastrzemski, 1967......6.9
   Rod Carew, 1974 ....6.9
   Toby Harrah, 1975 ....6.9
   Rickey Henderson, 1985....6.9
Alex Rodriguez, 2001 ...6.9
93 Cupid Childs, 1890.............6.8
   Dan Brouthers, 1892..........6.8
   Rogers Hornsby, 1925 ....6.8
   Rogers Hornsby, 1927 ....6.8
   Rogers Hornsby, 1929 ....6.8
   Lou Boudreau, 1943 ....6.8
   Snuffy Stirnweiss, 1944 .....6.8
   Willie Mays, 1955..............6.8

Batter-Fielder Wins

   Hank Aaron, 1959 ....6.8
   Mike Schmidt, 1980 ....6.8
Barry Bonds, 2000........6.8
104 Hughie Jennings, 1896 .....6.7
   Honus Wagner, 1907 ....6.7
   Jimmie Foxx, 1932 ....6.7
   Rod Carew, 1975 ....6.7
   Joe Morgan, 1976 ....6.7
   Gary Carter, 1982 ....6.7
Alex Rodriguez, 2003 ...6.7
111 Art Devlin, 1906...............6.6
   Ty Cobb, 1911..................6.6
   Frank Baker, 1913.............6.6
   Eddie Collins, 1915............6.6
   Arky Vaughan, 1935 ....6.6
   Lou Gehrig, 1936...............6.6
   Joe DiMaggio, 1941...........6.6
   Ryne Sandberg, 1984.........6.6
   George Brett, 1985............6.6
Barry Bonds, 1998........6.6
Alex Rodriguez, 2000 ...6.6
Miguel Tejada, 2004......6.6
123 Joe Jackson, 1911...........6.5
   Frank Baker, 1912.............6.5
   Tris Speaker, 1913 ....6.5
   Tris Speaker, 1923 ....6.5
   Babe Ruth, 1932...............6.5
   Eddie Lake, 1945..............6.5
   Red Schoendienst, 1953.....6.5
   Willie McCovey, 1969.........6.5
   Willie McCovey, 1970.........6.5
   Johnny Bench, 1972 ....6.5
   Bobby Grich, 1973 ....6.5
   Rod Carew, 1977 ....6.5
   George Brett, 1980............6.5
   Wade Boggs, 1987 ....6.5
137 Eddie Collins, 1912...........6.4
   Mel Ott, 1938 ....6.4
   Arky Vaughan, 1938 ....6.4
   Ted Williams, 1949............6.4
   Mike Schmidt, 1977 ....6.4
   Mike Schmidt, 1983 ....6.4
   Wade Boggs, 1988 ....6.4
Barry Bonds, 1990........6.4
Jeff Kent, 2000 ....6.4
Scott Rolen, 2004 ....6.4
147 Hughie Jennings, 1895 .....6.3
   Cupid Childs, 1896.............6.3
   Ty Cobb, 1910..................6.3
   George Sisler, 1922 ....6.3
   Luke Appling, 1943 ....6.3
   Willie Mays, 1958..............6.3
   Frank Robinson, 1966.........6.3
   Carl Yastrzemski, 1968......6.3
   Reggie Jackson, 1969........6.3
   Darrell Evans, 1973 ....6.3
   Mike Schmidt, 1982 ....6.3
Jason Giambi, 2001........6.3
Derrek Lee, 2005 ....6.3
160 Joe Sewell, 1923.............6.2
   Willie Mays, 1954..............6.2
   Ernie Banks, 1959 ....6.2
   Ron Santo, 1965 ....6.2
   Dickie Thon, 1983.............6.2
   Kevin Mitchell, 1989..........6.2
   Barry Larkin, 1991.............6.2
Barry Bonds, 1997........6.2
Todd Helton, 2004..........6.2
169 George Davis, 1899..........6.1
   Rogers Hornsby, 1928........6.1
   Jimmie Foxx, 1934............6.1
   Charlie Gehringer, 1936 ......6.1
   Dick Bartell, 1937 ....6.1
   Stan Musial, 1951.............6.1
   Eddie Mathews, 1953.........6.1
   Nellie Fox, 1957 ....6.1
   Willie Mays, 1962..............6.1
   Alan Trammell, 1987...........6.1
179 Fred Pfeffer, 1884 ....6.0
   Ed Delahanty, 1896............6.0
   Ty Cobb, 1909..................6.0
   Harry Heilmann, 1923..........6.0
   Frankie Frisch, 1924 ....6.0
   Lou Gehrig, 1931...............6.0
   Charlie Gehringer, 1934 ......6.0
   Joe Medwick, 1937 ....6.0
   Mickey Mantle, 1958 ....6.0
   Eddie Mathews, 1959.........6.0
   Ernie Banks, 1960 ....6.0
   Willie Mays, 1963..............6.0
   Bobby Grich, 1974 ....6.0
Gary Sheffield, 1992 ....6.0
   Barry Larkin, 1996.............6.0
   Roberto Alomar, 1999.........6.0
Jeff Bagwell, 1997 ....6.0
Ken Griffey Jr., 1997.....6.0
Mike Piazza, 1998.........6.0
198 19 players tied 5.9

Wins

1 Charley Radbourn, 1884....59
2 John Clarkson, 1885....53
3 Guy Hecker, 1884....52
4 John Clarkson, 1889....49
5 Charley Radbourn, 1883....48
  Charlie Buffinton, 1884....48
7 Al Spalding, 1876....47
  John Ward, 1879....47
9 Jim Galvin, 1883....46
  Jim Galvin, 1884....46
  Matt Kilroy, 1887....46
12 George Bradley, 1876....45
  Jim McCormick, 1880....45
  Silver King, 1888....45
15 Mickey Welch, 1885....44
  Bill Hutchison, 1891....44
17 Billy Taylor, 1884....43
  Tommy Bond, 1879....43
  Will White, 1879....43
  Larry Corcoran, 1880....43
  Will White, 1883....43
22 Lady Baldwin, 1886....42
  Tim Keefe, 1886....42
  Bill Hutchison, 1890....42
25 Charlie Sweeney, 1884....41
  Tim Keefe, 1883....41
  Dave Foutz, 1886....41
  Ed Morris, 1886....41
  Jack Chesbro, 1904....41
30 Jim McCormick, 1884....40
  Tommy Bond, 1877....40
  Tommy Bond, 1878....40
  Will White, 1882....40
  Bill Sweeney, 1884....40
  Bob Caruthers, 1885....40
  Bob Caruthers, 1889....40
  Ed Walsh, 1908....40
38 John Ward, 1880....39
  Mickey Welch, 1884....39
  Ed Morris, 1885....39
41 Toad Ramsey, 1886....38
  John Clarkson, 1887....38
  Kid Gleason, 1890....38
44 Jim Galvin, 1879....37
  Jim Whitney, 1883....37
  Tim Keefe, 1884....37
  Jack Lynch, 1884....37
  Toad Ramsey, 1887....37
  Christy Mathewson, 1908....37
50 Jim McCormick, 1882....36
  Tony Mullane, 1884....36
  John Clarkson, 1886....36
  Sadie McMahon, 1890....36
  Bill Hutchison, 1892....36
  Cy Young, 1892....36
  Frank Killen, 1893....36
  Amos Rusie, 1894....36
  Walter Johnson, 1913....36
59 Jim Devlin, 1877....35
  Tony Mullane, 1883....35
  Larry Corcoran, 1884....35
  Tim Keefe, 1887....35
  Tim Keefe, 1888....35
  Ed Seward, 1888....35
  Silver King, 1889....35
  Sadie McMahon, 1891....35
  Kid Nichols, 1892....35
  Jack Stivetts, 1892....35
  Cy Young, 1895....35
  Joe McGinnity, 1904....35
71 Mickey Welch, 1880....34
  Larry Corcoran, 1883....34
  Ed Morris, 1884....34
  Will White, 1884....34
  Elmer Smith, 1887....34
  Scott Stratton, 1890....34
  George Haddock, 1891....34
  Kid Nichols, 1893....34
  Cy Young, 1893....34
  Joe Wood, 1912....34
81 Charley Radbourn, 1882....33
  Dave Foutz, 1885....33
  Henry Porter, 1885....33
  Mickey Welch, 1886....33
  Tony Mullane, 1886....33
  John Clarkson, 1888....33
  Mark Baldwin, 1890....33
  John Clarkson, 1891....33
  Amos Rusie, 1891....33
  Jack Stivetts, 1891....33
  Amos Rusie, 1893....33
  Jouett Meekin, 1894....33
  Cy Young, 1901....33
  Christy Mathewson, 1904....33
  Walter Johnson, 1912....33
  Grover Alexander, 1916....33
97 10 players tied....32

Wins by era

1988-2005

1 Bob Welch, 1990....27
2 Frank Viola, 1988....24
  John Smoltz, 1996....24
  Randy Johnson, 2002....24
5 Orel Hershiser, 1988....23
  Danny Jackson, 1988....23
  Bret Saberhagen, 1989....23
  Pedro Martinez, 1999....23
  Curt Schilling, 2002....23
  Barry Zito, 2002....23

1973-1987

1 Catfish Hunter, 1974....25
  Fergie Jenkins, 1974....25
  Ron Guidry, 1978....25
  Steve Stone, 1980....25
5 Ron Bryant, 1973....24
  Wilbur Wood, 1973....24
  Steve Carlton, 1980....24
  La Marr Hoyt, 1983....24
  Doc Gooden, 1985....24
  Roger Clemens, 1986....24

1961-1972

1 Denny McLain, 1968....31
2 Sandy Koufax, 1966....27
  Steve Carlton, 1972....27
4 Sandy Koufax, 1965....26
  Juan Marichal, 1968....26
6 Whitey Ford, 1961....25
  Don Drysdale, 1962....25
  Sandy Koufax, 1963....25
  Juan Marichal, 1963....25
  Juan Marichal, 1966....25
  Jim Kaat, 1966....25
  Tom Seaver, 1969....25
  Mickey Lolich, 1971....25

1943-1960

1 Hal Newhouser, 1944....29
2 Robin Roberts, 1952....28
3 Dizzy Trout, 1944....27
  Don Newcombe, 1956....27
5 Hal Newhouser, 1946....26
  Bob Feller, 1946....26
7 Hal Newhouser, 1945....25
  Dave Ferriss, 1946....25
  Mel Parnell, 1949....25
10 Johnny Sain, 1948....24
  Bobby Shantz, 1952....24

1921-1942

1 Lefty Grove, 1931....31
2 Dizzy Dean, 1934....30
3 Dazzy Vance, 1924....28
  Lefty Grove, 1930....28
  Dizzy Dean, 1935....28
6 Carl Mays, 1921....27
  Urban Shocker, 1921....27
  Eddie Rommel, 1922....27
  Dolf Luque, 1923....27
  George Uhle, 1926....27
  Bucky Walters, 1939....27
  Bob Feller, 1940....27

1901-1920

1 Jack Chesbro, 1904....41
2 Ed Walsh, 1908....40
3 Christy Mathewson, 1908....37
4 Walter Johnson, 1913....36
5 Joe McGinnity, 1904....35
6 Joe Wood, 1912....34
7 Cy Young, 1901....33
  Christy Mathewson, 1904....33
  Walter Johnson, 1912....33
  Grover Alexander, 1916....33

1893-1900

1 Frank Killen, 1893....36
  Amos Rusie, 1894....36
3 Cy Young, 1895....35
4 Kid Nichols, 1893....34
  Cy Young, 1893....34
6 Amos Rusie, 1893....33
  Jouett Meekin, 1894....33
8 Kid Nichols, 1894....32
9 Pink Hawley, 1895....31
  Bill Hoffer, 1895....31
  Kid Nichols, 1897....31
  Kid Nichols, 1898....31

1876-1892

1 Charley Radbourn, 1884....59
2 John Clarkson, 1885....53
3 Guy Hecker, 1884....52
4 John Clarkson, 1889....49
5 Charley Radbourn, 1883....48
  Charlie Buffinton, 1884....48
7 Al Spalding, 1876....47
  John Ward, 1879....47
9 Jim Galvin, 1883....46
  Jim Galvin, 1884....46
  Matt Kilroy, 1887....46

Losses

1 John Coleman, 1883....48
2 Will White, 1880....42
3 Larry McKeon, 1884....41
4 George Bradley, 1879....40
  Jim McCormick, 1879....40
6 Henry Porter, 1888....37
  Kid Carsey, 1891....37
  George Cobb, 1892....37
9 Stump Wiedman, 1886....36
  Bill Hutchison, 1892....36
11 Jim Devlin, 1876....35
  Jim Galvin, 1880....35
  Fleury Sullivan, 1884....35
  Adonis Terry, 1884....35
  Hardie Henderson, 1885....35
  Red Donahue, 1897....35
17 Bobby Mathews, 1876....34
  Bob Barr, 1884....34
  Matt Kilroy, 1886....34
  Al Mays, 1887....34
  Mark Baldwin, 1889....34
  Amos Rusie, 1890....34
23 Hardie Henderson, 1883....33
  Dupee Shaw, 1884....33
  Harry McCormick, 1879....33
  Jim Whitney, 1881....33
  Lee Richmond, 1882....33
  Frank Mountain, 1883....33
  Jersey Bakely, 1888....33
30 Lee Richmond, 1880....32
  John Harkins, 1884....32
  Jim Whitney, 1885....32
  Jim Whitney, 1886....32
34 Sam Weaver, 1878....31
  Will White, 1879....31
  Charley Radbourn, 1886....31
  Dupee Shaw, 1886....31
  Billy Crowell, 1887....31
  Amos Rusie, 1892....31
40 Mickey Welch, 1880....30
  Jim McCormick, 1881....30
  Jim McCormick, 1882....30
  Jersey Bakely, 1884....30
  Jack Lynch, 1886....30
  Phenomenal Smith, 1887....30
  Toad Ramsey, 1888....30
  John Ewing, 1889....30
  Ed Beatin, 1890....30
  Ted Breitenstein, 1895....30
  Jim Hughey, 1899....30
51 Tommy Bond, 1880....29
  Doc Landis, 1882....29
  Jim Galvin, 1883....29
  John Healy, 1887....29
  Hank O'Day, 1888....29
  Bert Cunningham, 1888....29
  Red Ehret, 1889....29
  Silver King, 1891....29
  Bill Hart, 1896....29
  Jack Taylor, 1898....29
  Vic Willis, 1905....29
62 Jim McCormick, 1880....28
  Hank O'Day, 1884....28
  Hugh Daily, 1884....28
  Gus Weyhing, 1887....28
  Mark Baldwin, 1891....28
  Duke Esper, 1893....28
  Bill Hill, 1896....28
69 Jim Galvin, 1879....27
  Tim Keefe, 1881....27
  Tim Keefe, 1883....27
  Charlie Buffinton, 1885....27
  Al Mays, 1886....27
  Tony Mullane, 1886....27
  Toad Ramsey, 1886....27
  Toad Ramsey, 1887....27
  Park Swartzel, 1889....27
  Phil Knell, 1891....27
  Mark Baldwin, 1892....27
  Pink Hawley, 1894....27
  Chick Fraser, 1896....27
  Bill Hart, 1897....27
  Willie Sudhoff, 1898....27
  Bill Carrick, 1899....27
  Dummy Taylor, 1901....27
  George Bell, 1910....27
  Paul Derringer, 1933....27
88 20 players tied....26

Winning Percentage

1 Roy Face, 1959....947
2 Johnny Allen, 1937....938
3 Greg Maddux, 1995....905
4 Randy Johnson, 1995..900
5 Ron Guidry, 1978....893
6 Freddie Fitzsimmons, 1940....889
7 Lefty Grove, 1931....886
8 Bob Stanley, 1978....882
9 Preacher Roe, 1951....880
10 Fred Goldsmith, 1880....875
11 Joe Wood, 1912....872
12 David Cone, 1988....870
  Roger Clemens, 2001..870
14 Orel Hershiser, 1985....864
15 Bill Donovan, 1907....862
  Whitey Ford, 1961....862
17 Doc Gooden, 1985....857
  Roger Clemens, 1986..857
19 Pedro Martinez, 1999..852
20 Chief Bender, 1914....850
  John Smoltz, 1998....850
22 Lefty Grove, 1930....848
23 Mike Hampton, 1999...846
24 Tom Hughes, 1916....842
  Emil Yde, 1924....842
  Schoolboy Rowe, 1940....842
  Sandy Consuegra, 1954....842
  Ralph Terry, 1961....842
  Ron Perranoski, 1963....842
30 Lefty Gomez, 1934....839
31 Bill Hoffer, 1895....838
  Denny McLain, 1968....838
33 Walter Johnson, 1913....837
34 Henry Boyle, 1884....833
  King Cole, 1910....833
  Spud Chandler, 1943....833
  Hoyt Wilhelm, 1952....833
  Sandy Koufax, 1963....833
  Randy Johnson, 1997..833
  Pedro Martinez, 2002..833
41 Charley Radbourn, 1884..831
42 Randy Johnson, 2002..828
43 Ed Reulbach, 1906....826
  Elmer Riddle, 1941....826
  Greg Maddux, 1997....826
46 Jay Hughes, 1899....824
  Jack Chesbro, 1902....824
  Dazzy Vance, 1924....824
49 Chief Bender, 1910....821
  Bob Purkey, 1962....821
  Barry Zito, 2002....821
52 Sal Maglie, 1950....818
  Bob Welch, 1990....818
  Mark Portugal, 1993....818
  David Wells, 1998....818
  Roger Clemens, 2004....818
57 Joe McGinnity, 1904....814
58 Mordecai Brown, 1906....813
  Russ Ford, 1910....813
  Eddie Plank, 1913....813
  Carl Hubbell, 1936....813
62 Dizzy Dean, 1934....811
63 Ed Reulbach, 1907....810
  Doc Crandall, 1910....810
  Johnny Allen, 1932....810
  Ted Wilks, 1944....810
  Phil Niekro, 1982....810
  Jimmy Key, 1994....810
  Paul Abbott, 2001....810
70 Alvin Crowder, 1928....808
  Bobo Newsom, 1940....808
  Tiny Bonham, 1942....808
  Larry Jansen, 1947....808
  Dave McNally, 1971....808
  Catfish Hunter, 1973....808
  Chris Carpenter, 2005....808
77 Christy Mathewson, 1909....806
  Howie Camnitz, 1909....806
  Dave Ferriss, 1946....806
  Juan Marichal, 1966....806
81 Eddie Cicotte, 1919....806
82 Mickey Welch, 1885....800
  Ed Doheny, 1902....800
  Sam Leever, 1905....800
  Bert Humphries, 1913....800
  Stan Coveleski, 1925....800
  Firpo Marberry, 1931....800
  Robin Roberts, 1952....800
  Ed Lopat, 1953....800
  Don Newcombe, 1955....800
  Jim Palmer, 1969....800
  John Candelaria, 1977....800
  Larry Gura, 1978....800
  Tommy Greene, 1993....800
  Denny Neagle, 1997....800
96 Al Spalding, 1876....797
97 Don Newcombe, 1956....794
98 Jocko Flynn, 1886....793
  Ellis Kinder, 1949....793
  Sal Maglie, 1951....793
  Bret Saberhagen, 1989....793

Games

1 Mike Marshall, 1974....106
2 Kent Tekulve, 1979....94
3 Mike Marshall, 1973....92
4 Kent Tekulve, 1978....91
5 Wayne Granger, 1969....90
  Mike Marshall, 1979....90
  Kent Tekulve, 1987....90
8 Mark Eichhorn, 1987....89
  Julian Tavarez, 1997....89
  Steve Kline, 2001....89
  Paul Quantrill, 2003....89
  Jim Brower, 2004....89
13 Wilbur Wood, 1968....88
  Mike Myers, 1997....88
  Sean Runyan, 1998....88
16 Rob Murphy, 1987....87
17 Paul Quantrill, 2002....86
  Oscar Villarreal, 2003....86
  Ray King, 2004....86
  Paul Quantrill, 2004....86
  Scott Eyre, 2005....86
22 Kent Tekulve, 1982....85
  Frank Williams, 1987....85
  Mitch Williams, 1987....85
25 Ted Abernathy, 1965....84
  Enrique Romo, 1979....84
  Dick Tidrow, 1978....84
  Dan Quisenberry, 1985....84
  Stan Belinda, 1997....84
  Graeme Lloyd, 2001....84
  Billy Koch, 2002....84
  Rheal Cormier, 2004....84
  Chris Reitsma, 2004....84
  Salomon Torres, 2004....84
35 Ken Sanders, 1971....83
  Craig Lefferts, 1986....83
  Eddie Guardado, 1996...83
  Mike Myers, 1996....83
  Steve Kline, 2000....83
  Kelly Wunsch, 2000....83
  Octavio Dotel, 2002....83
  Scott Eyre, 2004....83
  Mike Stanton, 2004....83
44 Eddie Fisher, 1965....82
  Bill Campbell, 1983....82
  Juan Agosto, 1990....82
  Paul Quantrill, 1998....82
  Steve Kline, 1999....82
  Jeff Fassero, 2001....82
  Ray King, 2001....82
51 Ugueth Urbina, 2005....81
  John Wyatt, 1964....81
  Dale Murray, 1976....81
  Jeff Robinson, 1987....81
  Duane Ward, 1991....81
  Joe Boever, 1992....81
  Kenny Rogers, 1992....81
  Mike Jackson, 1993....81
  Brad Clontz, 1996....81
  Mike Stanton, 1996....81
  Rod Beck, 1998....81
  Greg Swindell, 1998....81
  J.C. Romero, 2002....81
  Luis Ayala, 2004....81
  Mike Timlin, 2005....81
66 Mudcat Grant, 1970....80
  Pedro Borbon, 1973....80
  Willie Hernandez, 1984....80
  Mitch Williams, 1986....80
  Doug Jones, 1992....80
  Greg Harris, 1993....80
  Turk Wendell, 1999....80
  Felix Rodriguez, 2001....80
  David Weathers, 2001...80
  Paul Quantrill, 2001....80
  Tim Worrell, 2002....80
  Ray King, 2003....80
  Tom Martin, 2003....80
  Brad Lidge, 2004....80
  Tom Gordon, 2004....80
  Scott Schoeneweis, 2005...80
82 Scott Sauerbeck, 2003....79
  Ron Villone, 2005....79
  Dick Radatz, 1964....79
  Duane Ward, 1992....79
  Bob Patterson, 1996....79
  Eddie Guardado, 1998...79
  Scott Sullivan, 1999....79
  Anthony Telford, 1999....79
  Scott Sullivan, 2000....79
  Robb Nen, 2001....79
  Scott Sullivan, 2001....79
  Todd Jones, 2002....79
  Mike Stanton, 2002....79
  Trever Miller, 2003....79
  Antonio Alfonseca, 2004....79
  Gary Majewski, 2005....79
  Duaner Sanchez, 2005....79
  Tom Gordon, 2005....79
  Bob Howry, 2005....79

Games by era

1988-2005
1 Julian Tavarez, 1997 89
  Steve Kline, 2001.........89
  Paul Quantrill, 2003......89
  Jim Brower, 2004 89
5 Mike Myers, 1997..........88
  Sean Runyan, 1998.........88
7 Paul Quantrill, 2002......86
  Oscar Villarreal, 2003....86
  Ray King, 2004 86
  Paul Quantrill, 2004......86
  Scott Eyre, 2005..........86

1973-1987
1 Mike Marshall, 1974.......106
2 Kent Tekulve, 1979........94
3 Mike Marshall, 1973.......92
4 Kent Tekulve, 1978........91
5 Mike Marshall, 1979.......90
  Kent Tekulve, 1987........90
7 Mark Eichhorn, 1987.......89
8 Rob Murphy, 1987..........87
9 Kent Tekulve, 1982........85
  Frank Williams, 1987......85
  Mitch Williams, 1987......85

1961-1972
1 Wayne Granger, 1969.......90
2 Wilbur Wood, 1968.........88
3 Ted Abernathy, 1965.......84
4 Ken Sanders, 1971.........83
5 Eddie Fisher, 1965........82
6 John Wyatt, 1964..........81
7 Mudcat Grant, 1970........80
8 Dick Radatz, 1964.........79
9 Hal Woodeshick, 1965......78
  Ted Abernathy, 1968.......78

1943-1960
1 Jim Konstanty, 1950.......74
2 Hoyt Wilhelm, 1952........71
3 Ace Adams, 1943...........70
  Mike Fornieles, 1960......70
5 Ellis Kinder, 1953........69
  Don Elston, 1958..........69
7 Hoyt Wilhelm, 1953........68
  Roy Face, 1956............68
  Roy Face, 1960............68
10 Andy Karl, 1945..........67
  Turk Lown, 1957...........67
  Gerry Staley, 1959........67

1921-1942
1 Firpo Marberry, 1926......64
2 Clint Brown, 1939.........61
  Ace Adams, 1942...........61
4 Garland Braxton, 1927.....58
  Russ Van Atta, 1935.......58
6 Eddie Rommel, 1923........56
  Firpo Marberry, 1927......56
  Hugh Mulcahy, 1937........56
9 Firpo Marberry, 1925......55
  Bump Hadley, 1931.........55
  Jim Walkup, 1935..........55

1901-1920
1 Ed Walsh, 1908............66
2 Ed Walsh, 1912............62
3 Dave Davenport, 1916......59
4 Ed Walsh, 1907............56
  Christy Mathewson, 1908...56
  Ed Walsh, 1911............56
  Reb Russell, 1916.........56
8 Joe McGinnity, 1903.......55
  Jack Chesbro, 1904........55
  Dave Davenport, 1915......55

1893-1900
1 Amos Rusie, 1893..........56
  Ted Breitenstein, 1894....56
  Pink Hawley, 1895.........56
4 Frank Killen, 1893........55
  Ted Breitenstein, 1895....55
6 Amos Rusie, 1894..........54
7 Cy Young, 1893............53
  Pink Hawley, 1894.........53
  Jouett Meekin, 1894.......53
10 Kid Nichols, 1893........52
  Cy Young, 1894............52
  Frank Killen, 1896........52

1876-1892
1 Will White, 1879..........76
  Jim Galvin, 1883..........76
  Charley Radbourn, 1883....76
4 Charley Radbourn, 1884....75
  Guy Hecker, 1884..........75
  Bill Hutchison, 1892......75
7 Jim McCormick, 1880.......74
  Lee Richmond, 1880........74
9 John Clarkson, 1889.......73
10 Jim Galvin, 1884.........72

Games Started by era

1988-2005
1 Dave Stewart, 1988........37
  Tom Browning, 1989........37
  Greg Maddux, 1991.........37
4 Frank Viola, 1989.........36
  Tom Browning, 1988........36
  Rick Reuschel, 1988.......36
  Bob Welch, 1988...........36
  Jose DeLeon, 1989.........36
  Mark Gubicza, 1989........36
  Bob Milacki, 1989.........36
  Dave Stewart, 1989........36
  Jack Morris, 1990.........36
  Dave Stewart, 1990........36
  Tom Browning, 1991........36
  Charlie Leibrandt, 1991...36
  John Smoltz, 1991.........36
  Mike Moore, 1992..........36
  Rick Sutcliffe, 1992......36
  Tom Glavine, 1993.........36
  Greg Maddux, 1993.........36
  Jose Rijo, 1993...........36
  Cal Eldred, 1993..........36
  Mike Moore, 1993..........36
  Tom Glavine, 1996.........36
  Mike Mussina, 1996........36
  Scott Erickson, 1998......36
  Tom Glavine, 2002.........36
  Greg Maddux, 2003.........36
  Roy Halladay, 2003........36

1973-1987
1 Wilbur Wood, 1973.........48
2 Phil Niekro, 1979.........44
3 Wilbur Wood, 1975.........43
  Phil Niekro, 1977.........43
5 Stan Bahnsen, 1973........42
  Mickey Lolich, 1973.......42
  Wilbur Wood, 1974.........42
  Phil Niekro, 1978.........42
9 8 players tied...........41

1961-1972
1 Wilbur Wood, 1972.........49
2 Mickey Lolich, 1971.......45
3 Don Drysdale, 1963........42
  Jack Sanford, 1963........42
  Don Drysdale, 1965........42
  Jim Kaat, 1965............42
  Fergie Jenkins, 1969......42
  Wilbur Wood, 1971.........42
9 14 players tied..........41

1943-1960
1 Bob Feller, 1946..........42
  Bob Friend, 1956..........42
3 Bill Voiselle, 1944.......41
  Robin Roberts, 1953.......41
5 Dizzy Trout, 1944.........40
6 Johnny Sain, 1948.........39
  Robin Roberts, 1950.......39
  Warren Spahn, 1950........39
  Vern Bickford, 1950.......39
  Robin Roberts, 1951.......39
  Ron Kline, 1956...........39
  Lew Burdette, 1959........39

1921-1942
1 George Uhle, 1923.........44
2 Stan Coveleski, 1921......40
  George Uhle, 1922.........40
  George Caster, 1938.......40
  Bobo Newsom, 1938.........40
  Bob Feller, 1941..........40
7 Red Faber, 1921...........39
  Hooks Dauss, 1923.........39
  Howard Ehmke, 1923........39
  Watty Clark, 1929.........39
  George Earnshaw, 1930.....39
  Alvin Crowder, 1932.......39
  Kirby Higbe, 1941.........39

1901-1920
1 Jack Chesbro, 1904........51
2 Ed Walsh, 1908............49
3 Joe McGinnity, 1903.......48
4 Vic Willis, 1902..........46
  Christy Mathewson, 1904...46
  Rube Waddell, 1904........46
  Ed Walsh, 1907............46
  Dave Davenport, 1915......46
9 2 players tied...........45

1893-1900
1 Amos Rusie, 1893..........52
2 Ted Breitenstein, 1895....51
3 Ted Breitenstein, 1894....50
  Amos Rusie, 1894..........50
  Pink Hawley, 1895.........50
  Frank Killen, 1896........50
7 Jouett Meekin, 1894.......49
8 Frank Killen, 1893........48
9 3 players tied...........47

1876-1892
1 Will White, 1879..........75
  Jim Galvin, 1883..........75
3 Jim McCormick, 1880.......74
4 Charley Radbourn, 1884....73
  Guy Hecker, 1884..........73
6 Jim Galvin, 1884..........72
  John Clarkson, 1889.......72
8 John Clarkson, 1885.......70
  Bill Hutchison, 1892......70
10 Matt Kilroy, 1887........69

Complete Games

1 Will White, 1879..........75
2 Charley Radbourn, 1884....73
3 Jim McCormick, 1880.......72
  Jim Galvin, 1883..........72
  Guy Hecker, 1884..........72
6 Jim Galvin, 1884..........71
7 Tim Keefe, 1883...........68
  John Clarkson, 1885.......68
  John Clarkson, 1889.......68
10 Bill Hutchison, 1892.....67
11 Jim Devlin, 1876.........66
  Charley Radbourn, 1883....66
  Matt Kilroy, 1886.........66
  Toad Ramsey, 1886.........66
  Matt Kilroy, 1887.........66
16 Jim Galvin, 1879.........65
  Jim McCormick, 1882.......65
  Bill Hutchison, 1890......65
19 Mickey Welch, 1880.......64
  Will White, 1883..........64
  Tony Mullane, 1884........64
  Silver King, 1888.........64
23 Jim McCormick, 1884......63
  George Bradley, 1876......63
  Charlie Buffinton, 1884...63
  Ed Morris, 1885...........63
  Ed Morris, 1886...........63
28 Mickey Welch, 1884.......62
  Tim Keefe, 1886...........62
30 Jim Devlin, 1877.........61
  Toad Ramsey, 1887.........61
32 Dupee Shaw, 1884.........60
  Jersey Bakely, 1888.......60
34 Billy Taylor, 1884.......59
  Tommy Bond, 1879..........59
  Jim McCormick, 1879.......59
  John Ward, 1880...........59
  John Coleman, 1883........59
  Larry McKeon, 1884........59
  Hardie Henderson, 1885....59
  Amos Rusie, 1892..........59
42 Tommy Bond, 1877.........58
  John Ward, 1879...........58
  Will White, 1880..........58
  Bill Sweeney, 1884........58
46 Tommy Bond, 1878.........57
  Terry Larkin, 1879........57
  Larry Corcoran, 1880......57
  Lee Richmond, 1880........57
  Jim McCormick, 1881.......57
  Jim Whitney, 1881.........57
  Frank Mountain, 1883......57
  Larry Corcoran, 1884......57
  Charley Radbourn, 1886....57
  Ed Seward, 1888...........57
56 Terry Larkin, 1878.......56
  Tim Keefe, 1884...........56
  Hugh Daily, 1884..........56
  Mickey Welch, 1886........56
  John Clarkson, 1887.......56
  Amos Rusie, 1890..........56
  Bill Hutchison, 1891......56
63 Bobby Mathews, 1876......55
  Terry Larkin, 1877........55
  George Derby, 1881........55
  Mickey Welch, 1885........55
  Lady Baldwin, 1886........55
  Dave Foutz, 1886..........55
  Tony Mullane, 1886........55
  Matt Kilroy, 1889.........55
  Sadie McMahon, 1890.......55
72 Jim Whitney, 1883........54
  Adonis Terry, 1884........54
  Tim Keefe, 1887...........54
  Phenomenal Smith, 1887 ...54
  Ed Morris, 1888...........54
  Mark Baldwin, 1889........54
  Kid Gleason, 1890.........54
79 Charlie Sweeney, 1884....53
  Al Spalding, 1876.........53
  George Bradley, 1879......53
  Jack Lynch, 1884..........53
  Bob Caruthers, 1885.......53
  Henry Porter, 1885........53
  Gus Weyhing, 1887.........53
  John Clarkson, 1888.......53
  Henry Porter, 1888........53
  Ed Beatin, 1890...........53
  Mark Baldwin, 1890........53
  Sadie McMahon, 1891.......53
91 Will White, 1878.........52
  Will White, 1882..........52
  Will White, 1884..........52
  Ed Seward, 1887...........52
  Bob Barr, 1890............52
  Amos Rusie, 1891..........52
97 Tony Mullane, 1882.......51
  Larry Corcoran, 1883......51
  Guy Hecker, 1883..........51
  Fleury Sullivan, 1884.....51
  Guy Hecker, 1885..........51
  Gus Weyhing, 1891.........51

Complete Games by era

1988-2005
1 Orel Hershiser, 1988......15
  Danny Jackson, 1988.......15
  Jack McDowell, 1991.......15
  Curt Schilling, 1998......15
5 Roger Clemens, 1988.......14
  Dave Stewart, 1988........14
7 Eric Show, 1988...........13
  Bobby Witt, 1988..........13
  Roger Clemens, 1991.......13
  Jack McDowell, 1992.......13
  Chuck Finley, 1993........13
  Pedro Martinez, 1997 13

1973-1987
1 Catfish Hunter, 1975......30
2 Gaylord Perry, 1973.......29
  Fergie Jenkins, 1974......29
4 Gaylord Perry, 1973.......28
  Rick Langford, 1980.......28
6 Mickey Lolich, 1974.......27
7 Nolan Ryan, 1973..........26
  Nolan Ryan, 1974..........26
9 Bert Blyleven, 1973.......25
  Luis Tiant, 1974..........25
  Jim Palmer, 1975..........25
  Gaylord Perry, 1975.......25
  Randy Jones, 1976.........25

1961-1972
1 Juan Marichal, 1968.......30
  Fergie Jenkins, 1971......30
  Steve Carlton, 1972.......30
4 Mickey Lolich, 1971.......29
  Gaylord Perry, 1972.......29
6 Bob Gibson, 1968..........28
  Denny McLain, 1968........28
  Bob Gibson, 1969..........28
9 Sandy Koufax, 1965........27
  Sandy Koufax, 1966........27
  Juan Marichal, 1969.......27

1943-1960
1 Bob Feller, 1946..........36
2 Dizzy Trout, 1944.........33
  Robin Roberts, 1953.......33
4 Robin Roberts, 1952.......30
5 Hal Newhouser, 1945.......29
  Hal Newhouser, 1946.......29
  Robin Roberts, 1954.......29
8 Jim Tobin, 1944...........28
  Johnny Sain, 1948.........28
  Bob Lemon, 1952...........28

1921-1942
1 Burleigh Grimes, 1923.....33
2 Red Faber, 1921...........32
  George Uhle, 1926.........32
4 Red Faber, 1922...........31
  Wes Ferrell, 1935.........31
  Bobo Newsom, 1938.........31
  Bucky Walters, 1939.......31
  Bob Feller, 1940..........31
9 Burleigh Grimes, 1921.....30
  Carl Mays, 1921...........30
  Urban Shocker, 1921.......30
  Dazzy Vance, 1924.........30
  Burleigh Grimes, 1924.....30
  Ted Lyons, 1927...........30
  Thornton Lee, 1941........30

1901-1920
1 Jack Chesbro, 1904........48
2 Vic Willis, 1902..........45
3 Joe McGinnity, 1903.......44
4 George Mullin, 1904.......42
  Ed Walsh, 1908............42
6 Noodles Hahn, 1901........41
  Cy Young, 1902............41
  Irv Young, 1905...........41
9 Cy Young, 1904............40
10 Joe McGinnity, 1901......39
  Bill Dinneen, 1902........39
  Vic Willis, 1904..........39
  Jack Taylor, 1904.........39
  Rube Waddell, 1904........39

1893-1900
1 Amos Rusie, 1893..........50
2 Ted Breitenstein, 1895....47
3 Ted Breitenstein, 1894....46
4 Amos Rusie, 1894..........45
5 Cy Young, 1894............44
  Pink Hawley, 1895.........44
  Frank Killen, 1896........44
8 Kid Nichols, 1893.........43
  Kid Nichols, 1895.........43
10 Cy Young, 1893...........42
  Amos Rusie, 1895..........42
  Cy Young, 1896............42
  Jack Taylor, 1898.........42

1876-1892
1 Will White, 1879..........75
2 Charley Radbourn, 1884....73
3 Jim McCormick, 1880.......72
  Jim Galvin, 1883..........72
  Guy Hecker, 1884..........72
6 Jim Galvin, 1884..........71
7 Tim Keefe, 1883...........68
  John Clarkson, 1885.......68
  John Clarkson, 1889.......68
10 Bill Hutchison, 1892.....67

Shutouts

1 George Bradley, 1876......16
  Grover Alexander, 1916....16
3 Jack Coombs, 1910.........13
  Bob Gibson, 1968..........13
5 Jim Galvin, 1884..........12
  Ed Morris, 1886...........12
  Grover Alexander, 1915....12
8 Tommy Bond, 1879..........11
  Charley Radbourn, 1884....11
  Dave Foutz, 1886..........11
  Christy Mathewson, 1908...11
  Ed Walsh, 1908............11
  Walter Johnson, 1913......11
  Sandy Koufax, 1963........11
  Dean Chance, 1964.........11
16 Jim McCormick, 1884......10
  John Clarkson, 1885.......10
  Cy Young, 1904............10
  Ed Walsh, 1906............10
  Joe Wood, 1912............10
  Dave Davenport, 1915......10
  Carl Hubbell, 1933........10
  Mort Cooper, 1942.........10
  Bob Feller, 1946..........10
  Bob Lemon, 1948...........10
  Juan Marichal, 1965.......10
  Jim Palmer, 1975..........10
  John Tudor, 1985..........10
29 Tommy Bond, 1878.........9
  George Derby, 1881........9
  Cy Young, 1892............9
  Joe McGinnity, 1904.......9
  Mordecai Brown, 1906......9
  Addie Joss, 1906..........9
  Mordecai Brown, 1908......9
  Addie Joss, 1908..........9
  Orval Overall, 1909.......9
  Grover Alexander, 1913....9
  Walter Johnson, 1914......9
  Cy Falkenberg, 1914.......9
  Babe Ruth, 1916...........9
  Stan Coveleski, 1917......9
  Grover Alexander, 1919....9
  Bill Lee, 1938............9
  Bob Porterfield, 1953.....9
  Luis Tiant, 1968..........9
  Denny McLain, 1969........9
  Don Sutton, 1972..........9
  Nolan Ryan, 1972..........9
  Bert Blyleven, 1973.......9
  Ron Guidry, 1978..........9
52 Al Spalding, 1876........8
  John Ward, 1880...........8
  Will White, 1882..........8
  Charlie Buffinton, 1884...8
  Tim Keefe, 1888...........8
  Ben Sanders, 1888.........8
  John Clarkson, 1889.......8
  Jack Taylor, 1902.........8
  Christy Mathewson, 1902...8
  Jack Chesbro, 1902........8
  Rube Waddell, 1904........8
  Christy Mathewson, 1905...8
  Ed Killian, 1905..........8
  Lefty Leifield, 1906......8
  Rube Waddell, 1906........8
  Orval Overall, 1907.......8
  Christy Mathewson, 1907...8
  Eddie Plank, 1907.........8
  Mordecai Brown, 1909......8
  Christy Mathewson, 1909...8
  Ed Walsh, 1909............8
  Russ Ford, 1910...........8
  Walter Johnson, 1910......8
  Reb Russell, 1913.........8
  Jeff Tesreau, 1914........8
  Al Mamaux, 1915...........8
  Jeff Tesreau, 1915........8
  Joe Bush, 1916............8
  Grover Alexander, 1917....8
  Jim Bagby, 1917...........8
  Walter Johnson, 1917......8
  Hippo Vaughn, 1918........8
  Walter Johnson, 1918......8
  Carl Mays, 1918...........8
  Babe Adams, 1920..........8
  Hal Newhouser, 1945.......8
  Steve Barber, 1961........8
  Camilo Pascual, 1961......8
  Whitey Ford, 1964.........8
  Sandy Koufax, 1965........8
  Don Drysdale, 1968........8
  Juan Marichal, 1969.......8
  Vida Blue, 1971...........8
  Steve Carlton, 1972.......8
  Wilbur Wood, 1972.........8
  Fernando Valenzuela, 1981.8
  Doc Gooden, 1985..........8
  Orel Hershiser, 1988......8
  Roger Clemens, 1988.......8
  Tim Belcher, 1989.........8

Saves

1 Bobby Thigpen, 1990........57
2 John Smoltz, 2002.........55
  Eric Gagne, 2003.........55
4 Randy Myers, 1993........53
  Trevor Hoffman, 1998......53
  Mariano Rivera, 2004......53
7 Eric Gagne, 2002.........52
8 Dennis Eckersley, 1992....51
  Rod Beck, 1998...........51
10 Mariano Rivera, 2001.....50
11 Francisco Cordero, 2004.....49
12 Dennis Eckersley, 1990....48
  Rod Beck, 1993...........48
  Jeff Shaw, 1998..........48
15 Lee Smith, 1991.........47
  Armando Benitez, 2004.....47
  Jason Isringhausen, 2004.....47
  Chad Cordero, 2005......47
19 Lee Smith, 1993.........46
  Dave Righetti, 1986......46
  Bryan Harvey, 1991.......46
  Jose Mesa, 1995..........46
  Tom Gordon, 1998.........46
  Mike Williams, 2002......46
25 Dan Quisenberry, 1983....45
  Bruce Sutter, 1984.......45
  Dennis Eckersley, 1988....45
  Bryan Harvey, 1993.......45
  Jeff Montgomery, 1993.....45
  Duane Ward, 1993.........45
  Randy Myers, 1997........45
  Mariano Rivera, 1999.....45
  Antonio Alfonseca, 2000....45
  Robb Nen, 2001...........45
  Kazuhiro Sasaki, 2001....45
  Jose Mesa, 2002..........45
  Eddie Guardado, 2002.....45
  John Smoltz, 2003........45
  Eric Gagne, 2004.........45
  Francisco Rodriguez, 2005.....45
  Bob Wickman, 2005.......45
42 Dan Quisenberry, 1984....44
  Mark Davis, 1989.........44
  Jeff Brantley, 1996......44
  Todd Worrell, 1996.......44
  Billy Koch, 2002.........44
  Billy Wagner, 2003.......44
  John Smoltz, 2004........44
  Joe Nathan, 2004.........44
50 Doug Jones, 1990........43
  Dennis Eckersley, 1991....43
  Lee Smith, 1992..........43
  John Wetteland, 1993.....43
  Mitch Williams, 1993.....43
  John Wetteland, 1996.....43
  Mariano Rivera, 1997.....43
  Roberto Hernandez, 1999....43
  John Wetteland, 1999.....43
  Trevor Hoffman, 2000.....43
  Armando Benitez, 2001....43
  Trevor Hoffman, 2001.....43
  Jeff Shaw, 2001..........43
  Robb Nen, 2002...........43
  Keith Foulke, 2003.......43
  Jose Mesa, 2004..........43
  Trevor Hoffman, 2005.....43
  Joe Nathan, 2005.........43
  Mariano Rivera, 2005.....43
69 Jeff Reardon, 1988......42
  Rick Aguilera, 1991......42
  Trevor Hoffman, 1996.....42
  Jeff Shaw, 1997..........42
  Troy Percival, 1998......42
  John Wetteland, 1998.....42
  Todd Jones, 2000.........42
  Derek Lowe, 2000.........42
  Jose Mesa, 2001..........42
  Keith Foulke, 2001.......42
  Brad Lidge, 2005.........42
80 Jeff Reardon, 1985......41
  Rick Aguilera, 1992......41
  Ugueth Urbina, 1999......41
  Armando Benitez, 2000....41
  Robb Nen, 2000...........41
  Jose Jimenez, 2002.......41
  Eddie Guardado, 2003.....41
  Danny Graves, 2004.......41
  Trevor Hoffman, 2004.....41
  Danys Baez, 2005.........41
90 Steve Bedrosian, 1987....40
  Jeff Reardon, 1991.......40
  Tom Henke, 1993..........40
  Robb Nen, 1998...........40
  Mike Jackson, 1998.......40
  Trevor Hoffman, 1999.....40
  Troy Percival, 2002......40
  Ugueth Urbina, 2002......40
  Mariano Rivera, 2003.....40
  Todd Jones, 2005.........40
100 11 players tied.......39

Saves by era

1988-2005
1 Bobby Thigpen, 1990........57
2 John Smoltz, 2002.........55
  Eric Gagne, 2003.........55
4 Randy Myers, 1993........53
  Trevor Hoffman, 1998......53
  Mariano Rivera, 2004......53
7 Eric Gagne, 2002.........52
8 Dennis Eckersley, 1992....51
  Rod Beck, 1998...........51
10 Mariano Rivera, 2001.....50

1973-1987
1 Dave Righetti, 1986.........46
2 Dan Quisenberry, 1983.....45
  Bruce Sutter, 1984.......45
4 Dan Quisenberry, 1984.....44
5 Jeff Reardon, 1985.......41
6 Steve Bedrosian, 1987....40
7 John Hiller, 1973........38
8 Rollie Fingers, 1978.....37
  Bruce Sutter, 1979.......37
  Dan Quisenberry, 1985....37

1961-1972
1 Clay Carroll, 1972........37
2 Wayne Granger, 1970......35
  Sparky Lyle, 1972........35
4 Ron Perranoski, 1970.....34
5 Jack Aker, 1966..........32
6 Ted Abernathy, 1965......31
  Ron Perranoski, 1969.....31
  Ken Sanders, 1971........31
9 Dave Giusti, 1971........30
10 Luis Arroyo, 1961.......29
  Dick Radatz, 1964........29
  Ron Kline, 1965..........29
  Fred Gladding, 1969......29
  Lindy McDaniel, 1970.....29
  Terry Forster, 1972......29

1943-1960
1 Joe Page, 1949...........27
  Ellis Kinder, 1953.......27
3 Lindy McDaniel, 1960.....26
4 Jim Hughes, 1954.........24
  Roy Face, 1960...........24
6 Jim Konstanty, 1950......22
  Johnny Sain, 1954........22
8 Frank Smith, 1954........20
  Roy Face, 1958...........20
  Ryne Duren, 1958.........20

1921-1942
1 Firpo Marberry, 1926......22
2 Johnny Murphy, 1939......19
3 Clint Brown, 1937........18
  Clint Brown, 1939........18
5 Al Benton, 1940..........17
6 Firpo Marberry, 1924.....15
  Firpo Marberry, 1925.....15
  Jack Quinn, 1931.........15
  Johnny Murphy, 1941......15
10 Wilcy Moore, 1927.......13
  Garland Braxton, 1927....13
  Firpo Marberry, 1932.....13
  Jack Russell, 1933.......13
  Hugh Casey, 1942.........13

1901-1920
1 Mordecai Brown, 1911......13
  Chief Bender, 1913.......13
3 Larry Cheney, 1913.......11
4 Ed Walsh, 1912...........10
  Hugh Bedient, 1915.......10
6 Tom Hughes, 1915.........9
  Dave Danforth, 1917......9
8 Frank Arellanes, 1909....8
  Red Ames, 1916...........8
  Bob Shawkey, 1916........8

1893-1900
1 Tony Mullane, 1894........4
  Kid Nichols, 1898........4
  Frank Kitson, 1900.......4
4 Bill Hawke, 1894.........3
  Win Mercer, 1894.........3
  Kid Nichols, 1895........3
  Tom Parrott, 1895........3
  Cy Young, 1896...........3
  Win Mercer, 1897.........3
  Kid Nichols, 1897........3
  Sam Leever, 1899.........3

1876-1892
1 Jack Manning, 1876........5
  Tony Mullane, 1889.......5
3 Billy Taylor, 1884.......4
  Herb Goodall, 1890.......4
5 Lee Richmond, 1880.......3
  Tommy Burns, 1885........3
  Adonis Terry, 1887.......3
  Bill Sowders, 1889.......3
  Hank O'Day, 1890.........3
  George Hemming, 1890.....3
  John Clarkson, 1891......3
  Kid Nichols, 1891........3
  Joe Neale, 1891..........3
  Gus Weyhing, 1892........3

Save percentage

1 Rod Beck, 1994...........100.0
  Eric Gagne, 2003.......100.0
3 Trevor Hoffman, 1998.....98.1
4 Tom Gordon, 1998.........97.9
5 Randy Myers, 1997........97.8
6 Willie Hernandez, 1984....97.0
7 Mudcat Grant, 1970.......96.0
  Dennis Eckersley, 1990....96.0
9 Jose Mesa, 1995..........95.8
10 Eric Gagne, 2004........95.7
11 Ken Tatum, 1969.........95.7
12 Billy Wagner, 2001......95.1
13 Tom Henke, 1995.........94.7
  Doug Jones, 1997.........94.7
15 Dennis Eckersley, 1992....94.4
16 Ryan Dempster, 2005......94.3
17 Billy Wagner, 2003.......93.6
  Joe Nathan, 2004.........93.6
19 Armando Benitez, 2001....93.5
  Trevor Hoffman, 2001.....93.5
  Trevor Hoffman, 2005.....93.5
22 Keith Foulke, 2001.......93.3
23 John Smoltz, 2002........93.2
24 Doug Jones, 1994........93.1
25 Trevor Hoffman, 1999......93.0
26 Mariano Rivera, 2004......93.0
27 John Franco, 1988........92.9
  Billy Wagner, 1999.......92.9
  Troy Percival, 2001......92.9
  Eric Gagne, 2002.........92.9
31 Trevor Hoffman, 2002......92.7
  Billy Wagner, 2005.......92.7
33 Clay Carroll, 1972.......92.5
  Kazuhiro Sasaki, 2000....92.5
35 Tom Burgmeier, 1980......92.3
  Dave Righetti, 1990......92.3
  Rod Beck, 1993...........92.3
  Troy Percival, 1996......92.3
39 Armando Benitez, 2004......92.2
40 Mike Williams, 2002......92.0
41 Tom Henke, 1992.........91.9
42 Bryan Harvey, 1993.......91.8
  Mariano Rivera, 1999......91.8
  Antonio Alfonseca, 2000....91.8
  John Smoltz, 2003........91.8
46 Rick Camp, 1980.........91.7
  Dan Quisenberry, 1980....91.7
  Mark Davis, 1989.........91.7
  Matt Anderson, 2001......91.7
50 3 players tied........91.5

Blown saves

1 Rollie Fingers, 1976......14
  Bruce Sutter, 1978.......14
  Bob Stanley, 1983........14
  Ron Davis, 1984..........14
5 John Hiller, 1976........13
  Rich Gossage, 1983.......13
  Jeff Reardon, 1986.......13
  Dan Plesac, 1987.........13
  Dave Righetti, 1987......13
10 Mike Marshall, 1973.....12
  Mike Marshall, 1974......12
  Enrique Romo, 1978.......12
  Bruce Sutter, 1985.......12
  Dan Quisenberry, 1985....12
  Matt Young, 1986.........12
  Lee Smith, 1987..........12
  Duane Ward, 1989.........12
  Mark Leiter, 1998........12
19 Ron Perranoski, 1969.....11
  Dick Selma, 1970.........11
  Darold Knowles, 1970.....11
  Ron Perranoski, 1970.....11
  Rollie Fingers, 1977.....11
  Bill Campbell, 1977......11
  Bill Campbell, 1978......11
  Kent Tekulve, 1980.......11
  Ed Farmer, 1980..........11
  Joey McLaughlin, 1983......11
  Rich Gossage, 1984.......11
  Rich Gossage, 1986.......11
  Greg Harris, 1986........11
  Lance McCullers, 1987......11
  Tim Burke, 1989..........11
  Mitch Williams, 1989.....11
  Jeff Reardon, 1989.......11
  Greg McMichael, 1997.....11
  Norm Charlton, 1997......11
  Scott Radinsky, 1998.....11
  Rick Aguilera, 1998......11
40 50 players tied.......10

Innings Pitched

1 Will White, 1879.........680.0
2 Charley Radbourn, 1884....678.2
3 Guy Hecker, 1884.........670.2
4 Jim McCormick, 1880......657.2
5 Jim Galvin, 1883.........656.1
6 Jim Galvin, 1884.........636.1
7 Charley Radbourn, 1883....632.1
8 John Clarkson, 1885......623.0
9 Jim Devlin, 1876.........622.0
  Bill Hutchison, 1892.....622.0
11 John Clarkson, 1889......620.0
12 Tim Keefe, 1883.........619.0
13 Bill Hutchison, 1890....603.0
14 Jim McCormick, 1882......595.2
15 John Ward, 1882.........595.0
16 Jim Galvin, 1879........593.0
17 Lee Richmond, 1880......590.2
18 Matt Kilroy, 1887.......589.1
19 Toad Ramsey, 1886.......588.2
20 John Ward, 1879.........587.0
  Charlie Buffinton, 1884....587.0
22 Silver King, 1888.......584.2
23 Matt Kilroy, 1886.......583.0
24 Ed Morris, 1885.........581.0
25 Will White, 1883........577.0
26 Mickey Welch, 1880......574.0
27 George Bradley, 1876....573.0
28 Jim McCormick, 1884......569.0
29 Tony Mullane, 1884......567.0
30 Toad Ramsey, 1887.......561.0
  Bill Hutchison, 1891.....561.0
32 Jim Devlin, 1877........559.0
33 Mickey Welch, 1884......557.1
34 Tommy Bond, 1879........555.1
  Ed Morris, 1886..........555.1
36 Jim Whitney, 1881.......552.1
37 Amos Rusie, 1890........548.2
38 Jim McCormick, 1879......546.1
39 Dupee Shaw, 1884........543.1
40 Amos Rusie, 1892........541.0
41 Hardie Henderson, 1885....539.1
42 John Coleman, 1883......538.1
43 Bill Sweeney, 1884......538.0
44 Larry Corcoran, 1880....536.1
45 Tim Keefe, 1886.........535.0
46 Tommy Bond, 1878........532.2
  Jersey Bakely, 1888......532.2
48 Tony Mullane, 1883......529.2
49 Al Spalding, 1876.......528.2
50 Jim McCormick, 1881......526.0
51 Billy Taylor, 1884......523.0
  John Clarkson, 1887......523.0
53 Tommy Bond, 1877........521.0
54 Ed Seward, 1888.........518.2
55 Will White, 1880........517.1
56 Larry Corcoran, 1884....516.2
57 Bobby Mathews, 1876......516.0
58 Jim Whitney, 1883.......514.0
59 Mark Baldwin, 1889......513.2
60 Terry Larkin, 1879......513.1
61 Larry McKeon, 1884......512.0
62 Charley Radbourn, 1886....509.1
63 Sadie McMahon, 1890.....509.0
64 Terry Larkin, 1878......506.0
  Kid Gleason, 1890........506.0
66 Dave Foutz, 1886........504.0
67 Frank Mountain, 1883....503.0
  Sadie McMahon, 1891......503.0
69 Terry Larkin, 1877......501.0
70 Hugh Daily, 1884........500.2
71 Amos Rusie, 1891........500.1
72 Mickey Welch, 1886......500.0
73 Jack Lynch, 1884........496.0
74 George Derby, 1881......494.2
75 Bob Barr, 1890..........493.1
76 Tommy Bond, 1880........493.0
77 Charlie Sweeney, 1884....492.0
  Mickey Welch, 1885.......492.0
  Mark Baldwin, 1890.......492.0
80 Phenomenal Smith, 1887....491.1
81 George Bradley, 1879....487.0
  Lady Baldwin, 1886.......487.0
83 John Clarkson, 1888.....483.1
84 Tim Keefe, 1884.........483.0
85 Bob Caruthers, 1885.....482.1
86 Amos Rusie, 1893........482.0
87 Henry Porter, 1885......481.2
88 Matt Kilroy, 1889.......480.2
89 Will White, 1882........480.0
  Guy Hecker, 1885.........480.0
  Ed Morris, 1888..........480.0
92 Tim Keefe, 1887.........476.2
93 Adonis Terry, 1884......476.0
94 Ed Beatin, 1890.........474.1
95 Jim Galvin, 1881........474.0
  Henry Porter, 1888.......474.0
97 Larry Corcoran, 1883....473.2
98 Ed Seward, 1887.........470.2
99 Gus Weyhing, 1892.......469.2
100 Guy Hecker, 1883.......469.0

Innings Pitched by era

1988-2005
1 Dave Stewart, 1988........275.2
2 Randy Johnson, 1999.....271.2
3 Roger Clemens, 1991.....271.1
4 Mark Gubicza, 1988......269.2
5 Curt Schilling, 1998....268.2
6 Greg Maddux, 1992.......268.0
7 Orel Hershiser, 1988....267.0
  Dave Stewart, 1990.......267.0
  Greg Maddux, 1993.......267.0
10 Roy Halladay, 2003......266.0

1973-1987
1 Wilbur Wood, 1973.........359.1
2 Gaylord Perry, 1973.....344.0
3 Phil Niekro, 1979.......342.0
4 Phil Niekro, 1978.......334.1
5 Nolan Ryan, 1974........332.2
6 Phil Niekro, 1977.......330.1
7 Fergie Jenkins, 1974....328.1
8 Catfish Hunter, 1975....328.0
9 Nolan Ryan, 1973........326.0
10 Bert Blyleven, 1973.....325.0

1961-1972
1 Wilbur Wood, 1972.........376.2
2 Mickey Lolich, 1971.....376.0
3 Steve Carlton, 1972.....346.1
4 Gaylord Perry, 1972.....342.2
5 Denny McLain, 1968......336.0
6 Sandy Koufax, 1965......335.2
7 Wilbur Wood, 1971.......334.0
8 Gaylord Perry, 1970.....328.2
9 Mickey Lolich, 1972.....327.1
10 Juan Marichal, 1968.....325.2

1943-1960
1 Bob Feller, 1946.........371.1
2 Dizzy Trout, 1944.......352.1
3 Robin Roberts, 1953.....346.2
4 Robin Roberts, 1954.....336.2
5 Robin Roberts, 1952.....330.0
6 Robin Roberts, 1951.....315.0
7 Johnny Sain, 1948.......314.2
8 Bob Friend, 1956........314.1
9 Hal Newhouser, 1945.....313.1
10 Bill Voiselle, 1944.....312.2

1921-1942
1 George Uhle, 1923.........357.2
2 Red Faber, 1922.........352.0
3 Urban Shocker, 1922.....348.0
4 Bob Feller, 1941........343.0
5 Carl Mays, 1921.........336.2
6 Red Faber, 1921.........330.2
  Burleigh Grimes, 1928....330.2
8 Bobo Newsom, 1938.......329.2
9 Wilbur Cooper, 1921.....327.0
  Burleigh Grimes, 1923....327.0
  Alvin Crowder, 1932......327.0

1901-1920
1 Ed Walsh, 1908...........464.0
2 Jack Chesbro, 1904......454.2
3 Joe McGinnity, 1903.....434.0
4 Ed Walsh, 1907..........422.1
5 Vic Willis, 1902........410.0
6 Joe McGinnity, 1904.....408.0
7 Ed Walsh, 1912..........393.0
8 Dave Davenport, 1915....392.2
9 Christy Mathewson, 1908....390.2
10 Jack Powell, 1904.......390.1

1893-1900
1 Amos Rusie, 1893.........482.0
2 Ted Breitenstein, 1894....447.1
3 Pink Hawley, 1895.......444.1
4 Amos Rusie, 1894........444.0
5 Ted Breitenstein, 1895....438.2
6 Frank Killen, 1896......432.1
7 Kid Nichols, 1893.......425.0
8 Cy Young, 1893..........422.2
9 Jouett Meekin, 1894.....418.0
10 Frank Killen, 1893......415.0

1876-1892
1 Will White, 1879.........680.0
2 Charley Radbourn, 1884....678.2
3 Guy Hecker, 1884........670.2
4 Jim McCormick, 1880......657.2
5 Jim Galvin, 1883........656.1
6 Jim Galvin, 1884........636.1
7 Charley Radbourn, 1883....632.0
8 John Clarkson, 1885.....623.0
9 Jim Devlin, 1876........622.0
  Bill Hutchison, 1892.....622.0

Fewest Hits/Game

1 Nolan Ryan, 1972....5.26
2 Luis Tiant, 1968....5.30
3 Nolan Ryan, 1991....5.31
4 **Pedro Martinez, 2000....5.31**
5 Ed Reulbach, 1906....5.33
6 Dutch Leonard, 1914....5.57
7 Carl Lundgren, 1907....5.65
8 Sid Fernandez, 1985....5.71
9 Tommy Byrne, 1949....5.74
10 Dave McNally, 1968....5.77
11 Sandy Koufax, 1965....5.79
12 Russ Ford, 1910....5.83
13 Tim Keefe, 1880....5.83
14 **Hideo Nomo, 1995....5.83**
15 Al Downing, 1963....5.84
16 Herb Score, 1956....5.85
17 Bob Gibson, 1968....5.85
18 Sam McDowell, 1965....5.87
19 Ed Walsh, 1910....5.89
20 **Pedro Martinez, 1997....5.89**
21 Mike Scott, 1986....5.95
22 Mario Soto, 1980....5.96
23 Floyd Youmans, 1986....5.96
24 Nolan Ryan, 1977....5.96
25 Nolan Ryan, 1974....5.98
26 Nolan Ryan, 1981....5.98
27 Nolan Ryan, 1986....6.02
28 Sam McDowell, 1966....6.02
29 Vida Blue, 1971....6.03
30 Walter Johnson, 1913....6.03
31 Nolan Ryan, 1990....6.04
32 Grover Alexander, 1915....6.05
33 Sam McDowell, 1968....6.06
34 Joe Horlen, 1964....6.07
35 Andy Messersmith, 1969....6.08
36 Nolan Ryan, 1989....6.09
37 Stan Coveleski, 1917....6.09
38 Catfish Hunter, 1972....6.09
39 Nolan Ryan, 1976....6.11
40 Sid Fernandez, 1988....6.11
41 Bob Turley, 1957....6.12
42 Bob Turley, 1955....6.13
43 Don Sutton, 1972....6.14
44 Nolan Ryan, 1983....6.14
45 Ron Guidry, 1978....6.15
46 **Johan Santana, 2004....6.16**
47 Mordecai Brown, 1908....6.17
48 Sandy Koufax, 1963....6.19
49 **Randy Johnson, 1997....6.21**
50 Jack Pfiester, 1906....6.21
51 Sandy Koufax, 1964....6.22
52 Roger Nelson, 1972....6.23
53 Herb Score, 1955....6.26
54 Cy Morgan, 1909....6.26
55 Dean Chance, 1964....6.27
56 Christy Mathewson, 1909....6.28
   J.R. Richard, 1978....6.28
58 Art Fromme, 1909....6.28
59 **Greg Maddux, 1995....6.31**
60 Walter Johnson, 1912....6.32
61 **Kerry Wood, 1998....6.32**
62 Jack Coombs, 1910....6.32
63 Rube Waddell, 1905....6.33
64 Vean Gregg, 1911....6.33
65 Jeff Robinson, 1988....6.33
66 Larry Cheney, 1916....6.33
67 Sonny Siebert, 1968....6.33
68 Allie Reynolds, 1943....6.34
69 Roger Clemens, 1986....6.34
70 Willie Mitchell, 1913....6.35
71 Jose DeLeon, 1989....6.36
72 Pascual Perez, 1988....6.37
73 Walter Johnson, 1910....6.37
74 Dave Boswell, 1966....6.38
75 Harry Krause, 1909....6.38
76 Dutch Leonard, 1915....6.38
77 Eddie Cicotte, 1917....6.39
78 Wayne Simpson, 1970....6.39
79 **Al Leiter, 1996....6.39**
80 Babe Ruth, 1916....6.40
81 Spec Shea, 1947....6.40
82 Jim Bibby, 1973....6.42
83 Ed Reulbach, 1905....6.42
84 Gaylord Perry, 1974....6.42
85 Eddie Fisher, 1965....6.42
86 Addie Joss, 1908....6.42
87 Mordecai Brown, 1906....6.43
88 **Roger Clemens, 2005....6.43**
89 Luis Tiant, 1972....6.44
90 Frank Smith, 1908....6.44
91 Doc Gooden, 1985....6.44
92 Orval Overall, 1909....6.44
93 Sid Fernandez, 1989....6.44
94 Denny McLain, 1968....6.46
95 Mordecai Brown, 1909....6.46
96 Ray Caldwell, 1914....6.46
97 Fred Toney, 1915....6.47
98 Gary Peters, 1967....6.47
99 Christy Mathewson, 1908....6.47
100 Bob Turley, 1954....6.48

Fewest Hits/Game by era

1988-2005
1 Nolan Ryan, 1991....5.31
2 **Pedro Martinez, 2000....5.31**
3 **Hideo Nomo, 1995....5.83**
4 **Pedro Martinez, 1997....5.89**
5 Nolan Ryan, 1990....6.04
6 Nolan Ryan, 1989....6.09
7 Sid Fernandez, 1988....6.11
8 **Johan Santana, 2004....6.16**
9 Randy Johnson, 1997....6.21
10 **Greg Maddux, 1995....6.31**

1973-1987
1 Sid Fernandez, 1985....5.71
2 Mike Scott, 1986....5.95
3 Mario Soto, 1980....5.96
4 Floyd Youmans, 1986....5.96
5 Nolan Ryan, 1977....5.96
6 Nolan Ryan, 1974....5.98
7 Nolan Ryan, 1981....5.98
8 Nolan Ryan, 1986....6.02
9 Nolan Ryan, 1976....6.11
10 Nolan Ryan, 1983....6.14

1961-1972
1 Nolan Ryan, 1972....5.26
2 Luis Tiant, 1968....5.30
3 Dave McNally, 1968....5.77
4 Sandy Koufax, 1965....5.79
5 Al Downing, 1963....5.84
6 Bob Gibson, 1968....5.85
7 Sam McDowell, 1965....5.87
8 Sam McDowell, 1966....6.02
9 Vida Blue, 1971....6.03
10 Sam McDowell, 1968....6.06

1943-1960
1 Tommy Byrne, 1949....5.74
2 Herb Score, 1956....5.85
3 Bob Turley, 1957....6.12
4 Bob Turley, 1955....6.13
5 Herb Score, 1955....6.26
6 Allie Reynolds, 1943....6.34
7 Spec Shea, 1947....6.40
8 Bob Turley, 1954....6.48
9 Sam Jones, 1955....6.52
10 Bob Turley, 1958....6.53

1921-1942
1 Mort Cooper, 1942....6.69
2 Hal Newhouser, 1942....6.71
3 Johnny Vander Meer, 1941....6.84
4 Bob Feller, 1940....6.88
5 Bob Feller, 1939....6.89
6 Hal Schumacher, 1933....6.92
7 Johnny Vander Meer, 1942....6.93
8 Dazzy Vance, 1924....6.95
9 Whit Wyatt, 1941....6.96
10 Bucky Walters, 1939....7.05

1901-1920
1 Ed Reulbach, 1906....5.33
2 Dutch Leonard, 1914....5.57
3 Carl Lundgren, 1907....5.65
4 Russ Ford, 1910....5.83
5 Ed Walsh, 1910....5.89
6 Walter Johnson, 1913....6.03
7 Grover Alexander, 1915....6.05
8 Stan Coveleski, 1917....6.09
9 Mordecai Brown, 1908....6.17
10 Jack Pfiester, 1906....6.21

1893-1900
1 Vic Willis, 1899....7.28
2 Kid Nichols, 1898....7.33
3 Rube Waddell, 1900....7.59
4 Vic Willis, 1898....7.64
5 Ted Lewis, 1898....7.67
6 Jay Hughes, 1899....7.71
7 Al Maul, 1898....7.77
8 Doc McJames, 1898....7.87
9 Cy Seymour, 1898....7.90
10 Jay Hughes, 1898....8.02

1876-1892
1 Tim Keefe, 1880....5.83
2 Guy Hecker, 1882....6.49
3 Tim Keefe, 1888....6.57
4 Charlie Sweeney, 1884....6.59
5 Adonis Terry, 1888....6.69
6 Silver King, 1888....6.70
7 Frank Knauss, 1890....6.73
8 Ed Seward, 1888....6.73
9 Tim Keefe, 1885....6.75
10 Tony Mullane, 1892....6.77

Fewest HR Allowed/Game by era

1988-2005
1 **Greg Maddux, 1994....0.18**
2 Joe Magrane, 1989....0.19
3 **Greg Maddux, 1992....0.24**
4 **Tom Glavine, 1992....0.24**
5 Bob Walk, 1988....0.25
6 **Andy Pettitte, 1997....0.26**
7 Danny Jackson, 1992....0.27
8 **Roger Clemens, 1990....0.28**
9 **Kevin Brown, 1998....0.28**
   Bob Ojeda, 1988....0.28

1973-1987
1 Nolan Ryan, 1981....0.12
2 Reggie Cleveland, 1976....0.16
3 Bill Gullickson, 1981....0.17
4 Ron Reed, 1975....0.18
5 Burt Hooton, 1981....0.19
6 Lary Sorensen, 1978....0.19
7 Randy Jones, 1978....0.21
8 Bruce Berenyi, 1981....0.21
9 Ken Brett, 1976....0.22
10 Al Fitzmorris, 1976....0.22

1961-1972
1 Bob Veale, 1965....0.17
2 Bill Singer, 1967....0.22
3 Claude Osteen, 1966....0.22
4 Dean Chance, 1964....0.23
5 Bob Veale, 1964....0.26
6 Tommie Sisk, 1967....0.26
   Don Sutton, 1968....0.26
8 Bob Moose, 1968....0.26
9 Andy Messersmith, 1972....0.27
10 Sam McDowell, 1965....0.30

1943-1960
1 Ewell Blackwell, 1946....0.05
2 Rube Melton, 1944....0.05
3 Stubby Overmire, 1944....0.09
4 Eddie Smith, 1943....0.10
5 Jack Kramer, 1944....0.11
6 Allie Reynolds, 1944....0.11
7 Marino Pieretti, 1945....0.12
8 Oscar Judd, 1943....0.12
9 Max Lanier, 1943....0.13
10 Early Wynn, 1944....0.13

1921-1942
1 Allen Sothoron, 1921....0.00
2 Slim Harriss, 1926....0.00
3 Eppa Rixey, 1921....0.03
4 Sam Jones, 1921....0.03
5 Stan Coveleski, 1926....0.04
6 Babe Adams, 1922....0.05
7 Dolf Luque, 1923....0.06
8 George Mogridge, 1924....0.08
9 Herb Pennock, 1928....0.09
10 Eppa Rixey, 1923....0.09

1901-1920
1 Walter Johnson, 1916....0.00
2 Jack Coombs, 1910....0.00
3 Ed Killian, 1904....0.00
4 Babe Ruth, 1916....0.00
5 Vic Willis, 1906....0.00
6 Rube Vickers, 1908....0.00
7 Ed Killian, 1905....0.00
8 Jake Weimer, 1906....0.00
9 Frank Smith, 1905....0.00
10 Cy Morgan, 1910....0.00

1893-1900
1 Billy Rhines, 1898....0.00
2 Brownie Foreman, 1895....0.00
3 Clark Griffith, 1898....0.03
4 Bill Hoffer, 1896....0.03
5 Chick Fraser, 1899....0.03
6 Jerry Nops, 1899....0.03
7 Ed Doheny, 1899....0.04
8 Harry Howell, 1899....0.04
9 Ned Garvin, 1899....0.05
10 Pink Hawley, 1896....0.05

1876-1892
1 Jersey Bakely, 1884....0.00
2 Lon Knight, 1876....0.00
3 Frank Hankinson, 1879....0.00
4 Candy Cummings, 1876....0.00
5 Denny Driscoll, 1882....0.00
6 Joe Blong, 1877....0.00
7 Ren Deagle, 1883....0.00
8 Bobby Mathews, 1877....0.00
   John Kirby, 1885....0.00
10 John Fox, 1881....0.00

Walks

1 Amos Rusie, 1890....289
2 Mark Baldwin, 1889....274
3 Amos Rusie, 1892....270
4 Amos Rusie, 1891....262
5 Mark Baldwin, 1890....249
6 Jack Stivetts, 1891....232
7 Mark Baldwin, 1891....227
8 Phil Knell, 1891....226
9 Bob Barr, 1890....219
10 Amos Rusie, 1893....218
11 Cy Seymour, 1898....213
12 Gus Weyhing, 1889....212
13 Ed Crane, 1890....208
   Bob Feller, 1938....208
15 Toad Ramsey, 1886....207
16 Elton Chamberlain, 1891....206
17 Mike Morrison, 1887....205
18 Henry Gruber, 1890....204
   Nolan Ryan, 1977....204
20 Ed Crane, 1891....203
   John Clarkson, 1889....203
22 Nolan Ryan, 1974....202
23 Bert Cunningham, 1890....201
24 Amos Rusie, 1894....200
25 Bill Hutchison, 1890....199
26 Mark Baldwin, 1892....194
   Bob Feller, 1941....194
28 Bobo Newsom, 1938....192
29 Ted Breitenstein, 1894....191
30 Bill Hutchison, 1892....190
31 Ed Crane, 1892....189
   Tony Mullane, 1893....189
33 Tony Mullane, 1891....187
   Kid Gleason, 1893....187
35 Ed Beatin, 1890....186
36 Sam Jones, 1955....185
37 Tom Vickery, 1890....184
38 Nolan Ryan, 1976....183
39 Matt Kilroy, 1886....182
   Frank Killen, 1892....182
   Ted Breitenstein, 1895....182
42 Willie McGill, 1893....181
   Bob Harmon, 1911....181
   Bob Turley, 1954....181
45 Jack Stivetts, 1890....179
   Gus Weyhing, 1890....179
   Tommy Byrne, 1949....179
48 Bill Hutchison, 1891....178
49 Bob Turley, 1955....177
50 Phenomenal Smith, 1887....176
   Jouett Meekin, 1894....176
52 George Hemming, 1893....175
53 Silver King, 1892....171
   Jack Stivetts, 1891....171
   Bump Hadley, 1932....171
56 Elton Chamberlain, 1892....170
   Ed Stein, 1894....170
   Cy Seymour, 1899....170
59 Gus Weyhing, 1892....168
   Brickyard Kennedy, 1893....168
   Cy Seymour, 1897....168
   Elmer Myers, 1916....168
63 Toad Ramsey, 1887....167
   Gus Weyhing, 1887....167
   Darby O'Brien, 1889....167
   Kid Gleason, 1890....167
   Bill Daley, 1890....167
   Bobo Newsom, 1937....167
69 Tony Mullane, 1886....166
   Sadie McMahon, 1890....166
   Phil Knell, 1890....166
   Chick Fraser, 1896....166
73 Elton Chamberlain, 1889....165
   Dan Casey, 1890....165
   Kid Gleason, 1890....165
   Weldon Wyckoff, 1915....165
77 Earl Moore, 1911....164
   Phil Niekro, 1977....164
79 Mickey Welch, 1886....163
   Silver King, 1890....163
   Willie McGill, 1891....163
   George Haddock, 1892....163
83 Johnny Vander Meer, 1943....162
   Nolan Ryan, 1973....162
85 Hank O'Day, 1890....161
   John Sowders, 1890....161
   Kid Carsey, 1891....161
   Gus Weyhing, 1891....161
89 Tommy Byrne, 1950....160
90 George Hemming, 1894....159
   Amos Rusie, 1895....159
   Marty O'Toole, 1912....159
93 Ed Doheny, 1899....158
   Joe Coleman, 1974....158
95 Matt Kilroy, 1887....157
   Bert Cunningham, 1888....157
   Pink Hawley, 1896....157
   Grover Lowdermilk, 1915....157
   Nolan Ryan, 1972....157
100 Ted Breitenstein, 1893....156
   Duke Esper, 1893....156
   Bill Hutchison, 1893....156
   Sadie McMahon, 1893....156

Strikeouts

1 Matt Kilroy, 1886....513
2 Toad Ramsey, 1886....499
3 Hugh Daily, 1884....483
4 Dupee Shaw, 1884....451
5 Charley Radbourn, 1884....441
6 Charlie Buffinton, 1884....417
7 Guy Hecker, 1884....385
8 Nolan Ryan, 1973....383
9 Sandy Koufax, 1965....382
10 Bill Sweeney, 1884....374
11 **Randy Johnson, 2001....372**
12 Jim Galvin, 1884....369
13 Mark Baldwin, 1889....368
14 Nolan Ryan, 1974....367
15 **Randy Johnson, 1999....364**
16 Tim Keefe, 1883....359
17 Toad Ramsey, 1887....355
18 Rube Waddell, 1904....349
19 Bob Feller, 1946....348
20 **Randy Johnson, 2000....347**
21 Hardie Henderson, 1884....346
22 Jim Whitney, 1883....345
   Mickey Welch, 1884....345
24 Jim McCormick, 1884....343
25 Amos Rusie, 1890....341
   Nolan Ryan, 1977....341
27 Charlie Sweeney, 1884....337
   Amos Rusie, 1891....337
29 Tim Keefe, 1888....335
30 Tim Keefe, 1884....334
   Randy Johnson, 2002....334
32 **Randy Johnson, 1998....329**
   Nolan Ryan, 1972....329
34 Nolan Ryan, 1976....327
35 Ed Morris, 1886....326
36 Tony Mullane, 1884....325
   Sam McDowell, 1965....325
38 Lady Baldwin, 1886....323
39 **Curt Schilling, 1997....319**
40 Sandy Koufax, 1966....317
41 **Curt Schilling, 2002....316**
42 Charley Radbourn, 1883....315
43 Bill Hutchison, 1892....314
44 John Clarkson, 1886....313
   Walter Johnson, 1910....313
   J.R. Richard, 1979....313
   Pedro Martinez, 1999....313
48 Steve Carlton, 1972....310
49 Larry McKeon, 1884....308
   John Clarkson, 1885....308
   Mickey Lolich, 1971....308
   Randy Johnson, 1993....308
53 Sandy Koufax, 1963....306
   Mike Scott, 1986....306
55 **Pedro Martinez, 1997....305**
56 Amos Rusie, 1892....304
   Sam McDowell, 1970....304
58 Walter Johnson, 1912....303
   J.R. Richard, 1978....303
60 Ed Morris, 1884....302
   Rube Waddell, 1903....302
62 Vida Blue, 1971....301
   Nolan Ryan, 1989....301
64 **Curt Schilling, 1998....300**
65 Ed Morris, 1885....298
66 Tim Keefe, 1886....297
67 **Randy Johnson, 1995....294**
68 **Curt Schilling, 2001....293**
69 Jack Lynch, 1884....292
   Roger Clemens, 1997....292
71 Sadie McMahon, 1890....291
   Roger Clemens, 1988....291
   Randy Johnson, 1997....291
74 **Randy Johnson, 2004....290**
75 Bill Hutchison, 1890....289
   Jack Stivetts, 1890....289
   Tom Seaver, 1971....289
78 Rube Waddell, 1905....287
79 Bobby Mathews, 1884....286
   Bobby Mathews, 1885....286
   Steve Carlton, 1980....286
   Steve Carlton, 1982....286
83 Billy Taylor, 1884....284
   John Clarkson, 1889....284
   Pedro Martinez, 2000....284
86 Dave Foutz, 1886....283
   Sam McDowell, 1968....283
   Tom Seaver, 1970....283
89 Denny McLain, 1968....280
90 Jim Galvin, 1883....279
   Sam McDowell, 1969....279
92 Bob Veale, 1965....276
   Doc Gooden, 1984....276
   John Smoltz, 1996....276
95 Hal Newhouser, 1946....275
   Steve Carlton, 1983....275
97 Bob Gibson, 1970....274
   Fergie Jenkins, 1970....274
   Mario Soto, 1982....274
100 Fergie Jenkins, 1969....273

Strikeouts/Game

1 Randy Johnson, 2001 .....13.41
2 Pedro Martinez, 1999 .....13.20
3 Kerry Wood, 1998 .....12.58
4 Randy Johnson, 2000 .....12.56
5 Randy Johnson, 1995 .....12.35
6 Randy Johnson, 1997 .....12.30
7 Randy Johnson, 1998 .....12.12
8 Randy Johnson, 1999 .....12.06
9 Pedro Martinez, 2000 .....11.78
10 Randy Johnson, 2002 .....11.56
11 Nolan Ryan, 1987 .....11.48
12 Doc Gooden, 1984 .....11.39
13 Pedro Martinez, 1997 .....11.37
14 Kerry Wood, 2003 .....11.35
15 Nolan Ryan, 1989 .....11.32
16 Curt Schilling, 1997 .....11.29
17 Kerry Wood, 2001 .....11.20
18 Hideo Nomo, 1995 .....11.10
19 Oliver Perez, 2004 .....10.97
20 Curt Schilling, 2002 .....10.97
21 Randy Johnson, 1993 .....10.86
22 Pedro Martinez, 2002 .....10.79
23 Sam McDowell, 1965 .....10.71
24 Randy Johnson, 1994 .....10.67
25 Randy Johnson, 2004 .....10.62
26 Nolan Ryan, 1973 .....10.57
27 Nolan Ryan, 1991 .....10.56
28 Sandy Koufax, 1962 .....10.55
29 Johan Santana, 2004 .....10.46
30 Mark Prior, 2003 .....10.43
31 Nolan Ryan, 1972 .....10.43
32 Sam McDowell, 1966 .....10.42
33 Roger Clemens, 1998 .....10.39
34 Curt Schilling, 2003 .....10.39
35 Nolan Ryan, 1976 .....10.35
36 Randy Johnson, 1992 .....10.31
37 Curt Schilling, 2001 .....10.27
38 Nolan Ryan, 1977 .....10.26
39 David Cone, 1997 .....10.25
40 Sandy Koufax, 1965 .....10.24
41 Nolan Ryan, 1990 .....10.24
42 Randy Johnson, 1991 .....10.19
43 Mark Prior, 2005 .....10.15
44 Bartolo Colon, 2000 .....10.15
45 Sandy Koufax, 1960 .....10.13
46 Hideo Nomo, 1997 .....10.11
47 Curt Schilling, 1998 .....10.05
48 Jason Schmidt, 2004 .....10.04
49 Ben Sheets, 2004 .....10.03
50 Mike Scott, 1986 .....10.00
51 Hideo Nomo, 2001 .....10.00
52 Rick Ankiel, 2000 .....9.98
53 Nolan Ryan, 1978 .....9.97
54 Roger Clemens, 1997 .....9.95
55 Pedro Martinez, 2003 .....9.93
56 Nolan Ryan, 1974 .....9.93
57 Roger Clemens, 1988 .....9.92
58 David Cone, 1990 .....9.91
59 J.R. Richard, 1978 .....9.90
60 Andy Benes, 1994 .....9.87
61 Nolan Ryan, 1986 .....9.81
62 John Smoltz, 1996 .....9.79
63 Herb Score, 1955 .....9.70
64 Pedro Martinez, 1998 .....9.67
65 Nolan Ryan, 1984 .....9.65
66 J.R. Richard, 1979 .....9.64
67 Roger Clemens, 2002 .....9.60
68 Jake Peavy, 2005 .....9.58
69 Mario Soto, 1982 .....9.57
70 Tom Griffin, 1969 .....9.56
71 Roger Clemens, 1996 .....9.53
72 Jim Maloney, 1963 .....9.53
73 Jason Schmidt, 2002 .....9.52
74 Sid Fernandez, 1985 .....9.51
75 Herb Score, 1956 .....9.49
76 Sandy Koufax, 1961 .....9.47
77 Sam McDowell, 1968 .....9.47
78 Matt Clement, 2004 .....9.45
79 Matt Clement, 2002 .....9.44
80 Pedro Martinez, 2004 .....9.41
81 David Cone, 1992 .....9.41
82 Frank Tanana, 1975 .....9.41
83 Javier Vazquez, 2003 .....9.40
84 Don Wilson, 1969 .....9.40
85 Jake Peavy, 2004 .....9.36
86 Bob Veale, 1965 .....9.34
87 Nolan Ryan, 1988 .....9.33
88 David Cone, 1991 .....9.32
89 John Smoltz, 1998 .....9.29
90 Johan Santana, 2005 .....9.25
91 Luis Tiant, 1967 .....9.22
92 Hideo Nomo, 1996 .....9.22
93 Pedro Martinez, 1996 .....9.22
94 Brandon Duckworth, 2002 .....9.22
95 Mark Langston, 1986 .....9.21
96 Luis Tiant, 1968 .....9.20
97 Dave Boswell, 1966 .....9.19
98 Sam McDowell, 1964 .....9.19
99 Roger Clemens, 2004 .....9.15
100 Kerry Wood, 2002 .....9.14

Earned Run Average

1 Tim Keefe, 1880 .....0.86
2 Dutch Leonard, 1914 .....0.96
3 Mordecai Brown, 1906 .....1.04
4 Bob Gibson, 1968 .....1.12
5 Christy Mathewson, 1909 .....1.14
6 Walter Johnson, 1913 .....1.14
7 Jack Pfiester, 1907 .....1.15
8 Addie Joss, 1908 .....1.16
9 Carl Lundgren, 1907 .....1.17
10 Denny Driscoll, 1882 .....1.21
11 Grover Alexander, 1915 .....1.22
12 George Bradley, 1876 .....1.23
13 Cy Young, 1908 .....1.26
14 Ed Walsh, 1910 .....1.27
15 Walter Johnson, 1918 .....1.27
16 Christy Mathewson, 1905 .....1.28
17 Jack Taylor, 1902 .....1.29
18 Guy Hecker, 1882 .....1.30
19 Jack Coombs, 1910 .....1.30
20 Mordecai Brown, 1909 .....1.31
21 Walter Johnson, 1910 .....1.36
22 George Bradley, 1880 .....1.38
23 Charley Radbourn, 1884 .....1.38
24 Walter Johnson, 1912 .....1.39
25 Mordecai Brown, 1907 .....1.39
26 Harry Krause, 1909 .....1.39
27 Ed Walsh, 1909 .....1.41
28 Ed Walsh, 1908 .....1.42
29 Ed Reulbach, 1905 .....1.42
30 Orval Overall, 1909 .....1.42
31 Christy Mathewson, 1908 .....1.43
32 Fred Anderson, 1917 .....1.44
33 Mordecai Brown, 1908 .....1.47
34 Rube Waddell, 1905 .....1.48
35 Joe Wood, 1915 .....1.49
36 Walter Johnson, 1919 .....1.49
37 Jack Pfiester, 1906 .....1.51
38 John Ward, 1878 .....1.51
39 Harry McCormick, 1882 .....1.52
40 Doc White, 1906 .....1.52
41 George McQuillan, 1908 .....1.53
42 Doc Gooden, 1985 .....1.53
43 Eddie Cicotte, 1917 .....1.53
44 Will White, 1882 .....1.54
45 Cy Morgan, 1910 .....1.55
46 Grover Alexander, 1916 .....1.55
47 Walter Johnson, 1915 .....1.55
48 Howie Camnitz, 1908 .....1.56
49 Greg Maddux, 1994 .....1.56
50 Jim Devlin, 1876 .....1.56
51 Tim Keefe, 1885 .....1.58
52 Fred Toney, 1915 .....1.58
53 Eddie Cicotte, 1913 .....1.58
54 Rube Marquard, 1916 .....1.58
55 Chief Bender, 1910 .....1.58
56 Barney Pelty, 1906 .....1.59
57 Addie Joss, 1904 .....1.59
58 Ed Walsh, 1907 .....1.60
59 Luis Tiant, 1968 .....1.60
60 Joe McGinnity, 1904 .....1.61
61 Ray Collins, 1910 .....1.62
62 Rube Waddell, 1904 .....1.62
63 Howie Camnitz, 1909 .....1.62
64 Cy Young, 1901 .....1.62
65 Silver King, 1888 .....1.63
66 Spud Chandler, 1943 .....1.64
67 Ernie Shore, 1915 .....1.64
68 Ed Summers, 1908 .....1.64
69 Dean Chance, 1964 .....1.65
70 Walter Johnson, 1908 .....1.65
71 Ed Reulbach, 1906 .....1.65
72 Russ Ford, 1910 .....1.65
73 Chief Bender, 1909 .....1.66
74 Sam Leever, 1907 .....1.66
75 Carl Hubbell, 1933 .....1.66
76 Mickey Welch, 1885 .....1.66
77 Candy Cummings, 1876 .....1.67
78 Tommy Bond, 1876 .....1.68
79 Orval Overall, 1907 .....1.68
80 Ed Reulbach, 1907 .....1.69
81 Claude Hendrix, 1914 .....1.69
82 Nolan Ryan, 1981 .....1.69
83 Jim McCormick, 1878 .....1.69
84 Joe Wood, 1910 .....1.69
85 Rube Foster, 1914 .....1.70
86 Charlie Sweeney, 1884 .....1.70
   Bill Burns, 1908 .....1.70
89 Addie Joss, 1909 .....1.71
90 Ed Killian, 1909 .....1.71
91 Walter Johnson, 1914 .....1.72
92 Ned Garvin, 1904 .....1.72
93 Doc White, 1909 .....1.72
94 Bill Doak, 1914 .....1.72
95 Addie Joss, 1906 .....1.72
   Grover Alexander, 1919 .....1.72
97 Sandy Koufax, 1966 .....1.73
98 Bob Ewing, 1907 .....1.73
99 Vic Willis, 1906 .....1.73
100 Sandy Koufax, 1964 .....1.74

Earned Run Average by era

1988-2005

1 Greg Maddux, 1994 .....1.56
2 Greg Maddux, 1995 .....1.63
3 Pedro Martinez, 2000 .....1.74
4 Roger Clemens, 2005 .....1.87
5 Kevin Brown, 1996 .....1.89
6 Pedro Martinez, 1997 .....1.90
7 Roger Clemens, 1990 .....1.93
8 Roger Clemens, 1997 .....2.05
9 Pedro Martinez, 1999 .....2.07
10 Bill Swift, 1992 .....2.08

1973-1987

1 Doc Gooden, 1985 .....1.53
2 Nolan Ryan, 1981 .....1.69
3 Ron Guidry, 1978 .....1.74
4 John Tudor, 1985 .....1.93
5 Orel Hershiser, 1985 .....2.03
6 Tom Seaver, 1973 .....2.08
7 Jim Palmer, 1975 .....2.09
8 Bob Knepper, 1981 .....2.18
9 Don Sutton, 1980 .....2.20
10 Mike Scott, 1986 .....2.22

1961-1972

1 Bob Gibson, 1968 .....1.12
2 Luis Tiant, 1968 .....1.60
3 Dean Chance, 1964 .....1.65
4 Sandy Koufax, 1966 .....1.73
5 Sandy Koufax, 1964 .....1.74
6 Tom Seaver, 1971 .....1.76
7 Sam McDowell, 1968 .....1.81
8 Vida Blue, 1971 .....1.82
9 Phil Niekro, 1967 .....1.87
10 Joe Horlen, 1964 .....1.88

1943-1960

1 Spud Chandler, 1943 .....1.64
2 Hal Newhouser, 1945 .....1.81
3 Max Lanier, 1943 .....1.90
4 Hal Newhouser, 1946 .....1.94
5 Billy Pierce, 1955 .....1.97
6 Whitey Ford, 1958 .....2.01
7 Al Benton, 1945 .....2.02
8 Allie Reynolds, 1952 .....2.06
9 Howie Pollet, 1946 .....2.10
10 Spud Chandler, 1946 .....2.10

1921-1942

1 Carl Hubbell, 1933 .....1.66
2 Mort Cooper, 1942 .....1.78
3 Dolf Luque, 1923 .....1.93
4 Lon Warneke, 1933 .....2.00
5 Lefty Grove, 1931 .....2.06
6 Dazzy Vance, 1928 .....2.09
7 Ted Lyons, 1942 .....2.10
8 Johnny Beazley, 1942 .....2.13
9 Hal Schumacher, 1933 .....2.16
10 Dazzy Vance, 1924 .....2.16

1901-1920

1 Dutch Leonard, 1914 .....0.96
2 Mordecai Brown, 1906 .....1.04
3 Christy Mathewson, 1909 .....1.14
4 Walter Johnson, 1913 .....1.14
5 Jack Pfiester, 1907 .....1.15
6 Addie Joss, 1908 .....1.16
7 Carl Lundgren, 1907 .....1.17
8 Grover Alexander, 1915 .....1.22
9 Cy Young, 1908 .....1.26
10 Ed Walsh, 1910 .....1.27

1893-1900

1 Clark Griffith, 1898 .....1.88
2 Al Maul, 1898 .....2.10
3 Kid Nichols, 1898 .....2.13
4 Doc McJames, 1898 .....2.36
5 Rube Waddell, 1900 .....2.37
6 Ned Garvin, 1900 .....2.41
7 Al Maul, 1895 .....2.45
   Billy Rhines, 1896 .....2.45
9 Nixey Callahan, 1898 .....2.46
10 Vic Willis, 1899 .....2.50

1876-1892

1 Tim Keefe, 1880 .....0.86
2 Denny Driscoll, 1882 .....1.21
3 George Bradley, 1876 .....1.23
4 Guy Hecker, 1882 .....1.30
5 George Bradley, 1880 .....1.38
6 Charley Radbourn, 1884 .....1.38
7 John Ward, 1878 .....1.51
8 Harry McCormick, 1882 .....1.52
9 Will White, 1882 .....1.54
10 Jim Devlin, 1876 .....1.56

Adjusted Earned Run Average

1 Tim Keefe, 1880 294
2 Pedro Martinez, 2000 288
3 Dutch Leonard, 1914 280
4 Greg Maddux, 1994 277
5 Greg Maddux, 1995 265
6 Walter Johnson, 1913 258
7 Bob Gibson, 1968 258
8 Mordecai Brown, 1906 254
9 Pedro Martinez, 1999 241
10 Walter Johnson, 1912 240
11 Christy Mathewson, 1905 230
12 Doc Gooden, 1985 229
13 Grover Alexander, 1915 225
14 Roger Clemens, 1997 224
15 Roger Clemens, 2005 224
16 Christy Mathewson, 1909 223
17 Pedro Martinez, 1997 220
18 Lefty Grove, 1931 218
19 Kevin Brown, 1996 218
20 Cy Young, 1901 217
21 Jack Pfiester, 1907 216
22 Denny Driscoll, 1882 216
23 Walter Johnson, 1919 216
24 Walter Johnson, 1918 215
25 Carl Lundgren, 1907 213
26 Roger Clemens, 1990 212
27 Pedro Martinez, 2003 210
28 Ed Reulbach, 1905 210
29 Ron Guidry, 1978 210
30 Jack Taylor, 1902 209
31 Charley Radbourn, 1884 206
32 Addie Joss, 1908 206
33 Billy Pierce, 1955 201
34 Dolf Luque, 1923 200
35 Silver King, 1888 200
36 Dean Chance, 1964 199
37 Randy Johnson, 1997 199
38 Pedro Martinez, 2002 198
39 Spud Chandler, 1943 197
40 Al Maul, 1895 196
41 Tom Seaver, 1971 195
42 Cy Young, 1908 195
43 Hal Newhouser, 1945 194
44 Nolan Ryan, 1981 194
45 Mordecai Brown, 1909 193
46 Randy Johnson, 2002 193
47 Carl Hubbell, 1933 193
48 Mort Cooper, 1942 193
49 Randy Johnson, 1995 193
50 Walter Johnson, 1915 191
51 Monty Stratton, 1937 191
52 Guy Hecker, 1882 191
53 Lefty Gomez, 1937 191
54 Sandy Koufax, 1966 191
55 Ed Siever, 1902 191
56 Clark Griffith, 1898 191
57 Dazzy Vance, 1928 191
58 Greg Maddux, 1997 191
59 Amos Rusie, 1894 189
60 Lefty Grove, 1936 189
61 Vean Gregg, 1911 189
62 Ed Walsh, 1910 189
63 Hal Newhouser, 1946 189
64 Dazzy Vance, 1930 188
65 Billy Rhines, 1896 188
66 Jack Stivetts, 1889 188
67 Greg Maddux, 1998 187
68 Joe Wood, 1915 187
69 Warren Spahn, 1953 187
70 Sandy Koufax, 1964 187
71 Randy Johnson, 2001 186
72 Wilbur Wood, 1971 186
73 Randy Johnson, 1999 186
74 Lefty Grove, 1939 185
75 Eddie Cicotte, 1913 185
76 Luis Tiant, 1968 185
77 John Tudor, 1985 185
78 Lefty Grove, 1930 184
79 Hank Aguirre, 1962 184
80 Joe Horlen, 1964 184
81 Vida Blue, 1971 183
82 Walter Johnson, 1910 183
83 Harry Brecheen, 1948 183
84 Henry Boyle, 1886 183
85 Steve Carlton, 1972 183
86 Billy Rhines, 1890 183
87 Jack Coombs, 1910 182
88 Jason Schmidt, 2003 182
89 Fred Toney, 1915 182
90 Randy Johnson, 2000 181
91 Johnny Allen, 1937 180
92 Kevin Appier, 1993 180
93 Rube Waddell, 1905 180
94 Mordecai Brown, 1907 179
95 Bret Saberhagen, 1989 179
96 Mark Prior, 2003 179
97 Orval Overall, 1909 179
98 Rube Waddell, 1902 179
99 Joe Wood, 1912 178
100 Phil Niekro, 1967 178

Adjusted Earned Run Average

101 Johan Santana, 2004 178
102 Max Lanier, 1943 177
103 Roger Clemens, 1994 177
104 Roger Clemens, 1992 177
105 Fred Anderson, 1917 177
106 Roger Clemens, 1998 176
107 Cy Young, 1892 176
108 Johnny Antonelli, 1954 176
109 Andy Pettitte, 2005 176
110 Whitey Ford, 1958 176
111 Lefty Grove, 1935 176
112 Tom Seaver, 1973 176
113 Randy Johnson, 2004 175
114 Jack Pfiester, 1906 175
115 Eddie Cicotte, 1919 175
116 Mel Harder, 1934 174
117 Lefty Gomez, 1934 174
118 Harry McCormick, 1882 174
119 Al Benton, 1945 174
120 George Bradley, 1876 174
121 Jim Devlin, 1876 174
122 Eddie Cicotte, 1917 174
123 Jeff D'Amico, 2000 174
124 Jake Peavy, 2004 174
125 Dazzy Vance, 1924 173
126 Derek Lowe, 2002 173
127 Kid Nichols, 1898 173
128 Thornton Lee, 1941 173
129 Walter Johnson, 1911 173
130 Hoyt Wilhelm, 1959 173
131 Orel Hershiser, 1985 173
132 Kevin Brown, 2003 173
133 Harry Krause, 1909 172
134 Jeff Tesreau, 1912 172
135 Kevin Brown, 2000 172
136 John Candelaria, 1977 172
137 Will White, 1882 172
138 Ted Lyons, 1942 172
139 Greg Maddux, 1993 172
140 Guy Hecker, 1884 172
141 Juan Guzman, 1996 171
142 Ted Lyons, 1939 171
143 Grover Alexander, 1916 171
144 David Cone, 1994 171
145 Dave Stieb, 1985 171
146 Red Faber, 1921 171
147 Jim McCormick, 1883 171
148 Gaylord Perry, 1972 170
149 Al Maul, 1898 170
150 Tim Hudson, 2003 170
151 Rube Marquard, 1916 170
152 Whitey Ford, 1964 170
153 Jim Palmer, 1975 170
154 Noodles Hahn, 1902 170
155 Luis Tiant, 1972 170
156 Tim Keefe, 1885 169
157 Roger Clemens, 1986 169
158 Mike Garcia, 1949 169
159 Ernie Shore, 1915 169
160 Joe McGinnity, 1904 169
161 Steve Ontiveros, 1994 169
162 Christy Mathewson, 1908 169
163 Kid Nichols, 1897 169
164 Wilcy Moore, 1927 169
165 Christy Mathewson, 1911 169
166 Danny Darwin, 1990 169
167 Juan Marichal, 1965 169
168 Carl Hubbell, 1936 169
169 Kid Nichols, 1890 169
170 Tom Glavine, 1998 168
171 Dizzy Trout, 1944 168
172 Carl Hubbell, 1934 168
173 Grover Alexander, 1920 168
174 Bobo Newsom, 1940 168
175 Howie Camnitz, 1909 168
176 Bucky Walters, 1939 168
177 Doc White, 1906 167
178 Rick Honeycutt, 1983 167
179 Grover Alexander, 1919 167
180 Dick Donovan, 1961 167
181 Juan Marichal, 1969 167
182 Allan Anderson, 1988 167
183 Ed Crane, 1891 167
184 Warren Spahn, 1947 167
185 Gene Bearden, 1948 167
186 Al Leiter, 1998 167
187 Kevin Brown, 1998 167
188 Vic Willis, 1899 167
189 Dick Ellsworth, 1963 167
190 Kevin Millwood, 1999 167
191 Buzz Capra, 1974 166
192 Ray Kremer, 1927 166
193 Herb Score, 1956 166
194 Ed Walsh, 1909 166
195 Bill Bernhard, 1902 166
196 Greg Maddux, 1992 166
197 Charlie Ferguson, 1886 166
198 Cy Young, 1902 166
199 Tom Seaver, 1969 166
200 Lefty Grove, 1926 166

Opponent Batting Average

1 Pedro Martinez, 2000 ..167
2 Luis Tiant, 1968 ...168
3 Nolan Ryan, 1972 ...171
4 Nolan Ryan, 1991 ...172
5 Ed Reulbach, 1906 ...175
6 Tim Keefe, 1880 ...178
7 Sandy Koufax, 1965 ...179
8 Dutch Leonard, 1914 ...180
9 Sid Fernandez, 1985 ...181
10 Hideo Nomo, 1995 ...182
11 Dave McNally, 1968 ...182
12 Tommy Byrne, 1949 ...183
13 Pedro Martinez, 1997 ...184
14 Al Downing, 1963 ...184
15 Bob Gibson, 1968 ...184
16 Sam McDowell, 1965 ...185
17 Carl Lundgren, 1907 ...185
18 Herb Score, 1956 ...185
19 Mike Scott, 1986 ...186
20 Nolan Ryan, 1989 ...187
21 Ed Walsh, 1910 ...187
22 Mario Soto, 1980 ...187
23 Nolan Ryan, 1981 ...188
24 Russ Ford, 1910 ...188
25 Nolan Ryan, 1986 ...188
26 Nolan Ryan, 1990 ...188
27 Floyd Youmans, 1986 ...188
28 Sam McDowell, 1966 ...188
29 Guy Hecker, 1882 ...188
30 Sandy Koufax, 1963 ...189
31 Sam McDowell, 1968 ...189
32 Don Sutton, 1972 ...189
33 Catfish Hunter, 1972 ...189
34 Vida Blue, 1971 ...189
35 Walter Johnson, 1913 ...190
36 Nolan Ryan, 1974 ...190
37 Joe Messersmith, 1969 ...190
38 Joe Horlen, 1964 ...190
39 Sid Fernandez, 1988 ...191
40 Grover Alexander, 1915 ...191
41 Sandy Koufax, 1964 ...191
42 Johan Santana, 2004 ...192
43 Bob Turley, 1955 ...193
44 Nolan Ryan, 1977 ...193
45 Fred Beebe, 1908 ...193
46 Charlie Sweeney, 1884 ...193
47 Ron Guidry, 1978 ...193
48 Stan Coveleski, 1917 ...194
49 Bob Turley, 1957 ...194
50 Randy Johnson, 1997 ...194
51 Herb Score, 1955 ...194
52 Jack Pfiester, 1906 ...194
53 Mordecai Brown, 1908 ...195
54 Nolan Ryan, 1976 ...195
55 Nolan Ryan, 1983 ...195
56 Dean Chance, 1964 ...195
57 Roger Clemens, 1986 ...195
58 Tim Keefe, 1888 ...196
59 Kerry Wood, 1998 ...196
60 Walter Johnson, 1912 ...196
61 Roger Nelson, 1972 ...196
62 J.R. Richard, 1978 ...196
63 Pascual Perez, 1988 ...196
64 Greg Maddux, 1995 ...197
65 Jeff Robinson, 1988 ...197
66 Lady Baldwin, 1885 ...197
67 Jose DeLeon, 1989 ...197
68 Dave Boswell, 1966 ...197
69 Sandy Koufax, 1962 ...197
70 Randy Johnson, 2004 ...197
71 Addie Joss, 1908 ...197
72 Christy Mathewson, 1908 ...197
73 Roger Clemens, 1998 ...197
74 Sonny Siebert, 1968 ...198
75 Sid Fernandez, 1989 ...198
76 Toad Ramsey, 1886 ...198
77 Larry Cheney, 1916 ...198
78 Wayne Simpson, 1970 ...198
79 Pedro Martinez, 2002 ...198
80 Roger Clemens, 2005 ...198
81 Orval Overall, 1909 ...198
82 Gary Peters, 1967 ...199
83 Larry Corcoran, 1880 ...199
84 Adonis Terry, 1888 ...199
85 Nolan Ryan, 1987 ...199
86 Mordecai Brown, 1904 ...199
87 Silver King, 1888 ...200
88 Christy Mathewson, 1909 ...200
89 Rube Waddell, 1905 ...200
90 Denny McLain, 1968 ...200
91 Larry Corcoran, 1882 ...200
92 Bobby Bolin, 1968 ...200
    Jim Palmer, 1969 ...200
    Sid Fernandez, 1990 ...200
95 Jason Schmidt, 2003 ...200
96 Spec Shea, 1947 ...200
97 Ed Seward, 1888 ...200
98 Tony Mullane, 1892 ...201
99 Art Fromme, 1909 ...201
100 Babe Ruth, 1916 ...201

Opponent On-Base Pct.

1 Guy Hecker, 1882 ...199
2 Charlie Sweeney, 1884 ...211
3 Tim Keefe, 1880 ...212
4 Pedro Martinez, 2000 ...214
5 Henry Boyle, 1884 ...215
6 George Bradley, 1880 ...217
7 Denny Driscoll, 1882 ...218
8 Addie Joss, 1908 ...218
9 Walter Johnson, 1913 ...220
10 Christy Mathewson, 1908 ...222
11 Jim Whitney, 1884 ...223
12 George Bradley, 1876 ...224
13 Greg Maddux, 1995 ...225
14 Guy Hecker, 1884 ...226
15 Ed Walsh, 1910 ...226
16 Tommy Bond, 1876 ...227
17 Lady Baldwin, 1885 ...228
18 Sandy Koufax, 1965 ...228
19 Christy Mathewson, 1909 ...228
20 Sandy Koufax, 1963 ...230
21 Juan Marichal, 1966 ...230
22 John Ward, 1880 ...232
23 Mordecai Brown, 1908 ...232
24 Ed Walsh, 1908 ...232
25 Luis Tiant, 1968 ...233
26 Bob Gibson, 1968 ...233
27 Grover Alexander, 1915 ...234
28 Dave McNally, 1968 ...234
29 Larry Corcoran, 1882 ...234
30 Charley Radbourn, 1884 ...234
31 Ed Morris, 1884 ...234
32 Perry Werden, 1884 ...235
33 Jim Devlin, 1876 ...235
34 Jack Lynch, 1884 ...236
35 Larry Corcoran, 1880 ...236
36 Roger Nelson, 1972 ...236
37 Silver King, 1888 ...237
38 Charlie Getzien, 1887 ...237
39 Tim Keefe, 1883 ...237
40 Tony Mullane, 1885 ...238
41 John Clarkson, 1885 ...239
42 Tim Keefe, 1884 ...239
43 Mordecai Brown, 1909 ...239
44 Fred Corey, 1880 ...239
45 Juan Marichal, 1965 ...240
46 Cy Young, 1908 ...240
47 Don Sutton, 1972 ...240
48 Cy Young, 1905 ...241
49 Babe Adams, 1919 ...241
50 Sandy Koufax, 1964 ...241
51 Catfish Hunter, 1972 ...242
52 Randy Johnson, 2004 ...243
53 Pete Conway, 1888 ...243
54 Harry McCormick, 1882 ...243
55 Denny McLain, 1968 ...243
56 Tim Keefe, 1888 ...243
57 Lady Baldwin, 1886 ...243
58 Mike Scott, 1986 ...244
59 Charley Radbourn, 1883 ...244
60 Will White, 1883 ...244
61 Charlie Ferguson, 1886 ...244
62 Charlie Buffinton, 1888 ...244
63 Will White, 1882 ...244
64 Charlie Buffinton, 1884 ...244
65 Russ Ford, 1910 ...245
66 Grover Alexander, 1919 ...245
67 Christy Mathewson, 1905 ...245
68 Greg Maddux, 1994 ...245
69 Dutch Leonard, 1914 ...246
70 Bobby Mathews, 1882 ...246
71 Jim Galvin, 1884 ...246
72 Sam Weaver, 1878 ...247
73 Charley Radbourn, 1882 ...247
74 Charlie Gagus, 1884 ...247
75 Christy Mathewson, 1907 ...247
76 Warren Hacker, 1952 ...247
77 Jim McCormick, 1880 ...247
78 Ed Morris, 1885 ...247
79 Fred Goldsmith, 1880 ...247
80 Dupee Shaw, 1884 ...247
81 Eddie Cicotte, 1917 ...248
82 Walter Johnson, 1912 ...248
83 Doc White, 1906 ...249
84 John Clarkson, 1884 ...249
85 Jumbo McGinnis, 1883 ...249
86 John Tudor, 1985 ...249
87 Pedro Martinez, 1999 ...249
88 Henry Gruber, 1888 ...249
89 Hugh Daily, 1884 ...250
90 Ron Guidry, 1978 ...250
91 Joe Horlen, 1964 ...250
92 Pedro Martinez, 1997 ...250
93 Terry Larkin, 1879 ...250
94 Johan Santana, 2004 ...250
95 John Ward, 1879 ...250
96 John Ward, 1878 ...251
97 Johan Santana, 2005 ...251
98 Billy Taylor, 1884 ...251
99 Jason Schmidt, 2003 ...251
100 Candy Cummings, 1876 ...251

Relief Wins

1 Roy Face, 1959 ...18
2 John Hiller, 1974 ...17
    Bill Campbell, 1976 ...17
4 Jim Konstanty, 1950 ...16
    Ron Perranoski, 1963 ...16
    Dick Radatz, 1964 ...16
    Tom Johnson, 1977 ...16
8 Mace Brown, 1938 ...15
    Hoyt Wilhelm, 1952 ...15
    Luis Arroyo, 1961 ...15
    Dick Radatz, 1963 ...15
    Eddie Fisher, 1965 ...15
    Mike Marshall, 1974 ...15
    Dale Murray, 1975 ...15
15 Joe Page, 1947 ...14
    Joe Black, 1952 ...14
    Hersh Freeman, 1956 ...14
    Stu Miller, 1961 ...14
    Stu Miller, 1965 ...14
    Phil Regan, 1966 ...14
    Frank Linzy, 1969 ...14
    Mike Marshall, 1972 ...14
    Mike Marshall, 1973 ...14
    Ron Davis, 1979 ...14
    Mark Clear, 1982 ...14
    Jim Slaton, 1983 ...14
    Roger McDowell, 1986 ...14
    Mark Eichhorn, 1986 ...14
29 Dick Tidrow, 1979 ...13
    Wilcy Moore, 1927 ...13
    Earl Caldwell, 1946 ...13
    Clyde Shoun, 1943 ...13
    Joe Page, 1949 ...13
    Clyde King, 1951 ...13
    Lindy McDaniel, 1959 ...13
    Larry Sherry, 1960 ...13
    Gerry Staley, 1960 ...13
    Lindy McDaniel, 1963 ...13
    Al Hrabosky, 1975 ...13
    Rollie Fingers, 1976 ...13
    Bill Campbell, 1977 ...13
    Sparky Lyle, 1977 ...13
    Gary Lavelle, 1978 ...13
    Bob Stanley, 1978 ...13
    Ron Reed, 1979 ...13
    Jim Kern, 1979 ...13
    Aurelio Lopez, 1980 ...13
    Jesse Orosco, 1983 ...13
    Rich Gossage, 1983 ...13
50 34 players tied ...12

Relief Losses

1 Gene Garber, 1979 ...16
2 Darold Knowles, 1970 ...14
    John Hiller, 1974 ...14
    Mike Marshall, 1975 ...14
    Mike Marshall, 1979 ...14
6 Wilbur Wood, 1970 ...13
    Rollie Fingers, 1978 ...13
    Skip Lockwood, 1978 ...13
9 Roy Face, 1956 ...12
    Roy Face, 1961 ...12
    Ken Sanders, 1971 ...12
    Mike Marshall, 1974 ...12
    Gene Garber, 1975 ...12
    Jim Willoughby, 1976 ...12
    Charlie Hough, 1977 ...12
    Mike Marshall, 1978 ...12
    Kent Tekulve, 1980 ...12
    Ken Howell, 1986 ...12
    Roger Mason, 1993 ...12
    Luis Ayala, 2004 ...12
21 Nels Potter, 1949 ...11
    Frank Funk, 1961 ...11
    Dick Radatz, 1965 ...11
    Frank Linzy, 1966 ...11
    Wilbur Wood, 1968 ...11
    Wilbur Wood, 1969 ...11
    Mike Marshall, 1973 ...11
    Rollie Fingers, 1976 ...11
    Rich Gossage, 1978 ...11
    Dave Heaverlo, 1979 ...11
    Mark Clear, 1980 ...11
    Greg Minton, 1983 ...11
    Ron Davis, 1985 ...11
    Mark Davis, 1985 ...11
    Joe Boever, 1989 ...11
    Jose Paniagua, 1999 ...11
    Scot Shields, 2005 ...11
38 49 players tied ...10

Relief Games

1 Mike Marshall, 1974 ...106
2 Kent Tekulve, 1979 ...94
3 Mike Marshall, 1973 ...92
4 Kent Tekulve, 1978 ...91
5 Wayne Granger, 1969 ...90
    Kent Tekulve, 1987 ...90
7 Mike Marshall, 1979 ...89
    Mark Eichhorn, 1987 ...89
    Julian Tavarez, 1997 ...89
    Steve Kline, 2001 ...89
    Paul Quantrill, 2003 ...89
    Jim Brower, 2004 ...89
13 Mike Myers, 1997 ...88
    Sean Runyan, 1998 ...88
15 Rob Murphy, 1987 ...87
16 Wilbur Wood, 1968 ...86
    Paul Quantrill, 2002 ...86
    Ray King, 2004 ...86
    Paul Quantrill, 2004 ...86
    Scott Eyre, 2005 ...86
21 Kent Tekulve, 1982 ...85
    Frank Williams, 1987 ...85
    Oscar Villarreal, 2003 ...85
24 Ted Abernathy, 1965 ...84
    Enrique Romo, 1979 ...84
    Dick Tidrow, 1980 ...84
    Dan Quisenberry, 1985 ...84
    Mitch Williams, 1987 ...84
    Stan Belinda, 1997 ...84
    Graeme Lloyd, 2001 ...84
    Billy Koch, 2002 ...84
    Rheal Cormier, 2004 ...84
    Chris Reitsma, 2004 ...84
    Salomon Torres, 2004 ...84
35 Ken Sanders, 1971 ...83
    Craig Lefferts, 1986 ...83
    Eddie Guardado, 1996 ...83
    Mike Myers, 1996 ...83
    Steve Kline, 2000 ...83
    Kelly Wunsch, 2000 ...83
    Octavio Dotel, 2002 ...83
    Scott Eyre, 2004 ...83
    Mike Stanton, 2004 ...83
44 Eddie Fisher, 1965 ...82
    Bill Campbell, 1983 ...82
    Juan Agosto, 1990 ...82
    Paul Quantrill, 1998 ...82
    Steve Kline, 1999 ...82
    Jeff Fassero, 2001 ...82
    Ray King, 2001 ...82

Relief Innings Pitched

1 Mike Marshall, 1974 ...208.1
2 Mike Marshall, 1973 ...179.0
3 Bob Stanley, 1982 ...168.1
4 Bill Campbell, 1976 ...167.2
5 Andy Karl, 1945 ...166.2
6 Eddie Fisher, 1965 ...165.1
7 Hoyt Wilhelm, 1952 ...159.1
8 Dick Radatz, 1964 ...157.0
    Mark Eichhorn, 1986 ...157.0
10 Jim Konstanty, 1950 ...152.0
11 John Hiller, 1974 ...150.0
12 Tom Johnson, 1977 ...146.2
13 Garland Braxton, 1927 ...146.0
14 Bob Stanley, 1983 ...145.1
15 Hoyt Wilhelm, 1953 ...145.0
    Wilbur Wood, 1968 ...145.0
17 Allan Russell, 1923 ...144.2
    Wayne Granger, 1969 ...144.2
19 Steve Foucault, 1974 ...144.1
20 Hoyt Wilhelm, 1965 ...144.0
21 Jim Kern, 1979 ...143.0
22 Charlie Hough, 1976 ...142.2
23 Rich Gossage, 1975 ...141.2
24 Mike Marshall, 1979 ...140.2
25 Sammy Stewart, 1983 ...140.1
    Willie Hernandez, 1984 ...140.1
27 Bill Campbell, 1977 ...140.0
28 Jack Lamabe, 1963 ...139.2
29 Pedro Borbon, 1974 ...139.0
    Dan Quisenberry, 1983 ...139.0
31 Lindy McDaniel, 1973 ...138.1
32 Aurelio Lopez, 1984 ...137.2
33 Clay Carroll, 1966 ...137.1
34 Sparky Lyle, 1977 ...137.0
    Tom Hume, 1980 ...137.0
36 Dan Quisenberry, 1982 ...136.2
37 Ted Abernathy, 1965 ...136.1
    Ken Sanders, 1971 ...136.1
    Doug Corbett, 1980 ...136.1
40 Mudcat Grant, 1970 ...135.1
    Joe Page, 1949 ...135.1
    Ted Abernathy, 1968 ...135.1
    Kent Tekulve, 1978 ...135.1
44 Clay Carroll, 1968 ...135.0
45 Phil Regan, 1968 ...134.2
    Rollie Fingers, 1976 ...134.2
47 Bill Henry, 1959 ...134.1
    Dick Selma, 1970 ...134.1
    Rich Gossage, 1978 ...134.1
    Kent Tekulve, 1979 ...134.1

Adjusted Reliever Runs

1 Mark Eichhorn, 1986 ...44.0
2 Jim Kern, 1979 ...39.0
3 John Hiller, 1973 ...35.0
    Doug Corbett, 1980 ...35.0
    Mariano Rivera, 1996 ...35.0
6 Rich Gossage, 1977 ...34.0
    Willie Hernandez, 1984 ...34.0
8 Dan Tavarez, 1983 ...33.0
9 Keith Foulke, 1999 ...32.0
10 Rich Gossage, 1975 ...31.0
    Bruce Sutter, 1977 ...31.0
12 Lindy McDaniel, 1960 ...29.8
13 Mudcat Grant, 1970 ...28.0
    Sid Monge, 1979 ...28.0
    Tim Burke, 1987 ...28.0
    Derek Lowe, 1999 ...28.0
    Eric Gagne, 2003 ...28.0
18 Wilcy Moore, 1927 ...27.3
19 Ellis Kinder, 1951 ...27.1
20 Aurelio Lopez, 1979 ...27.0
    Roberto Hernandez, 1996 ...27.0
    Guillermo Mota, 2003 ...27.0
23 Bob Lee, 1964 ...26.8
24 Mike Marshall, 1979 ...26.7
25 Dick Radatz, 1962 ...26.0
    Dick Radatz, 1963 ...26.0
    Dick Radatz, 1964 ...26.0
    Ted Abernathy, 1967 ...26.0
    Sparky Lyle, 1977 ...26.0
    Bruce Sutter, 1984 ...26.0
    Jeff Montgomery, 1989 ...26.0
    Jeff Zimmerman, 1999 ...26.0
    Gabe White, 2000 ...26.0
    Octavio Dotel, 2002 ...26.0
    Damaso Marte, 2003 ...26.0
    Brad Lidge, 2004 ...26.0
37 Ellis Kinder, 1953 ...25.0
    Bob James, 1985 ...25.0
    Dan Quisenberry, 1985 ...25.0
    Dennis Eckersley, 1990 ...25.0
    John Wetteland, 1993 ...25.0
    Jose Mesa, 1995 ...25.0
    Billy Wagner, 1999 ...25.0
    Derek Lowe, 2000 ...25.0
    Billy Wagner, 2003 ...25.0
    Shigetoshi Hasegawa, 2003 ...25.0
47 19 players tied ...24.0

Relief Ranking

1 Jim Kern, 1979 ...62.0
2 John Hiller, 1973 ...61.5
3 Rich Gossage, 1977 ...59.6
4 Mark Eichhorn, 1986 ...55.9
5 Roberto Hernandez, 1996 ...54.0
6 Mike Marshall, 1979 ...53.3
7 Lindy McDaniel, 1960 ...52.8
8 Sid Monge, 1979 ...51.5
9 John Wetteland, 1993 ...50.0
10 Eric Gagne, 2003 ...48.6
11 Dick Radatz, 1963 ...48.2
12 Robb Nen, 1998 ...48.0
    Mariano Rivera, 2005 ...48.0
14 Ellis Kinder, 1953 ...47.8
15 Donnie Moore, 1985 ...47.6
16 Mariano Rivera, 2004 ...47.4
17 Keith Foulke, 2003 ...47.3
18 Dick Radatz, 1964 ...46.9
19 Rich Gossage, 1975 ...46.3
20 Jesse Orosco, 1983 ...46.1
21 Doug Jones, 1997 ...46.0
    Ugueth Urbina, 1998 ...46.0
    Mariano Rivera, 1999 ...46.0
24 Doug Corbett, 1980 ...45.5
25 Bob James, 1985 ...44.9
26 Dennis Eckersley, 1990 ...44.6
27 Bruce Sutter, 1984 ...44.2
28 Mike Marshall, 1972 ...44.0
    Jeff Montgomery, 1993 ...44.0
    Scott Williamson, 1999 ...44.0
31 Tom Murphy, 1974 ...43.9
32 Trevor Hoffman, 1998 ...43.9
33 Jose Mesa, 1995 ...43.6
34 Dan Quisenberry, 1985 ...43.6
35 Stu Miller, 1965 ...43.5
36 Mariano Rivera, 2003 ...43.0
37 Joe Page, 1949 ...42.4
38 Rollie Fingers, 1981 ...42.2
39 Bill Campbell, 1977 ...42.1
40 Dan Spillner, 1982 ...42.0
41 Luis Arroyo, 1961 ...42.0
    Bill Caudill, 1984 ...42.0
    Dave Righetti, 1986 ...42.0
    Mariano Rivera, 1997 ...42.0
    Danny Graves, 2000 ...42.0
    Robb Nen, 2000 ...42.0
    Keith Foulke, 2001 ...42.0
    Francisco Cordero, 2004 ...42.0
49 Sparky Lyle, 1977 ...41.8
50 Willie Hernandez, 1984 ...41.6

Adjusted Pitching Wins

1 Charley Radbourn, 1884..10.5
2 Amos Rusie, 1894 ....9.7
3 Guy Hecker, 1884 ....9.7
4 Silver King, 1888.............9.4
5 Walter Johnson, 1912 ....9.4
6 Walter Johnson, 1913 ....9.3
7 Lefty Grove, 1931............8.6
8 John Clarkson, 1889 ....8.5
9 Pedro Martinez, 2000 ...8.2
10 Pedro Martinez, 1999 ...7.9
11 Cy Young, 1901 ....7.9
12 Roger Clemens, 1997 ...7.7
13 Dolf Luque, 1923 ....7.3
14 Jim Galvin, 1884 ....7.3
15 Bob Gibson, 1968 ....7.3
16 Red Faber, 1921 ....7.1
17 Toad Ramsey, 1886 ....7.1
18 Will White, 1883 ....7.0
19 Lefty Gomez, 1937 ....7.0
20 Charley Radbourn, 1883....7.0
21 Grover Alexander, 1915 ....7.0
22 Cy Young, 1892 ....7.0
23 John Clarkson, 1885 ....7.0
24 Silver King, 1890 ....7.0
25 Christy Mathewson, 1905....7.0
26 Scott Stratton, 1890 ....7.0
27 Sandy Koufax, 1966 ....7.0
28 Lefty Grove, 1930............6.9
29 Steve Carlton, 1972 ....6.9
30 Cy Young, 1895 ....6.9
31 John Clarkson, 1887 ....6.9
32 Dazzy Vance, 1930 ....6.9
33 Cy Young, 1893 ....6.9
34 Doc Gooden, 1985............6.8
35 Hal Newhouser, 1945........6.8
36 Bob Feller, 1940 ....6.8
37 Lefty Grove, 1936............6.8
38 Dave Foutz, 1886 ....6.7
39 Dazzy Vance, 1928 ....6.7
40 Kid Nichols, 1897 ....6.7
41 Kevin Brown, 1996 ....6.7
42 Carl Hubbell, 1933 ....6.7
43 Billy Rhines, 1890 ....6.5
44 Gaylord Perry, 1972 ....6.5
45 Amos Rusie, 1893 ....6.5
46 Greg Maddux, 1994 ......6.5
47 Dean Chance, 1964 ....6.4
48 Walter Johnson, 1915 ....6.4
49 Walter Johnson, 1918 ....6.4
50 Ron Guidry, 1978 ....6.4
51 Walter Johnson, 1919 ....6.4
52 Hal Newhouser, 1946........6.4
53 Kid Nichols, 1898 ....6.3
54 Greg Maddux, 1995 ......6.3
55 Grover Alexander, 1920 ....6.3
56 Bucky Walters, 1939 ....6.3
57 Robin Roberts, 1953 ....6.3
58 Warren Spahn, 1953 ....6.3
59 Dizzy Trout, 1944 ....6.3
60 Elmer Smith, 1887 ....6.2
61 Tom Seaver, 1971 ....6.2
62 Dazzy Vance, 1924 ....6.2
63 Carl Hubbell, 1936 ....6.2
64 Wilbur Wood, 1971 ....6.1
65 Roger Clemens, 1990 ...6.1
66 Grover Alexander, 1916 ....6.1
67 Randy Johnson, 2002....6.1
68 Cy Young, 1902 ....6.0
69 Clark Griffith, 1898..........6.0
70 Pink Hawley, 1895............6.0
71 Mickey Welch, 1885 ....6.0
72 Lefty Grove, 1932............6.0
73 Matt Kilroy, 1887 ....6.0
74 Ted Breitenstein, 1893 ......6.0
75 Derek Lowe, 2002 ...6.0
76 Jouett Meekin, 1894.........6.0
77 Pedro Martinez, 1997 ...6.0
78 Lefty Grove, 1935............5.9
79 Lefty Gomez, 1934 ....5.9
80 Walter Johnson, 1914 ....5.9
81 Thornton Lee, 1941 ....5.9
82 Juan Marichal, 1965.........5.9
83 Vida Blue, 1971...............5.9
84 Dizzy Dean, 1934 ....5.9
85 Jack Stivetts, 1891 ....5.9
86 Joe Wood, 1912 ....5.9
87 Mordecai Brown, 1906.......5.8
88 George Bradley, 1876........5.8
89 Randy Johnson, 2001....5.8
90 Kid Nichols, 1893 ....5.8
91 Kid Nichols, 1890 ....5.8
92 Jim Devlin, 1876 ....5.8
93 Jack Coombs, 1910 ....5.8
94 Carl Hubbell, 1934 ....5.7
95 Mel Harder, 1934.............5.7
96 Bob Caruthers, 1885.........5.7
97 Bob Feller, 1946 ....5.7
98 Christy Mathewson, 1908....5.7
99 Eddie Cicotte, 1917..........5.7
100 Will White, 1882.............5.7

Pitcher Wins

1 Guy Hecker, 1884 ....12.9
2 Walter Johnson, 1913 ......10.9
3 Charley Radbourn, 1884..10.7
4 Walter Johnson, 1912 ......10.6
5 Silver King, 1888.............10.2
   Amos Rusie, 1894 ....10.2
7 John Clarkson, 1889 ....8.9
   Scott Stratton, 1890 ....8.9
9 Christy Mathewson, 1905....8.5
10 Pedro Martinez, 2000 ...8.4
11 Charley Radbourn, 1883....8.3
12 Lefty Grove, 1931............8.2
   Bucky Walters, 1939 ....8.2
   Dizzy Trout, 1944 ....8.2
15 Pedro Martinez, 1999 ...8.1
16 Cy Young, 1901 ....7.9
   Roger Clemens, 1997 ...7.9
18 Dave Foutz, 1886 ....7.6
   Joe Wood, 1912 ....7.6
   Walter Johnson, 1918 ....7.6
   Dolf Luque, 1923 ....7.6
   Hal Newhouser, 1945.........7.6
   Bob Gibson, 1968 ....7.6
   Doc Gooden, 1985.............7.6
25 John Clarkson, 1887 ....7.5
   Grover Alexander, 1915 .....7.5
27 Pink Hawley, 1895............7.4
   Walter Johnson, 1915 ....7.4
   Steve Carlton, 1972 ....7.4
30 John Clarkson, 1885 ....7.3
   Carl Hubbell, 1933 ....7.3
32 Bob Caruthers, 1886.........7.2
   Matt Kilroy, 1887 ....7.2
   Walter Johnson, 1914 ....7.2
   Grover Alexander, 1916 ....7.2
   Dazzy Vance, 1928 ....7.2
37 Tony Mullane, 1884..........7.1
38 Warren Spahn, 1953 ....6.9
39 Will White, 1883 ....6.9
   Cy Young, 1895 ....6.9
   Kid Nichols, 1897 ....6.9
   Grover Alexander, 1920 ....6.9
   Lefty Grove, 1930............6.9
   Kevin Brown, 1996 ....6.9
45 Jack Stivetts, 1891 ....6.8
   Amos Rusie, 1893 ....6.8
   Ed Walsh, 1908...............6.8
   Red Faber, 1921 ....6.8
   Wes Ferrell, 1935.............6.8
   Lefty Gomez, 1937 ....6.8
   Bob Feller, 1940 ....6.8
   Gaylord Perry, 1972 ....6.8
   Greg Maddux, 1994 ......6.8
54 Will White, 1882 ....6.7
   Toad Ramsey, 1886 ....6.7
   Walter Johnson, 1919 ....6.7
   Tom Seaver, 1971 ....6.7
   John Hiller, 1973 ....6.7
59 Silver King, 1890 ....6.6
   Christy Mathewson, 1909....6.6
   Lefty Grove, 1936............6.6
   Bob Lemon, 1948 ....6.6
63 Charlie Sweeney, 1884 ....6.5
   Charlie Ferguson, 1886 ....6.5
   Cy Young, 1893 ....6.5
   Christy Mathewson, 1908....6.5
   Ed Walsh, 1912...............6.5
   Thornton Lee, 1941 ....6.5
   Greg Maddux, 1995 ......6.5
70 Cy Young, 1892 ....6.4
   Kid Nichols, 1898 ....6.4
   Dazzy Vance, 1930 ....6.4
   Hal Newhouser, 1946.........6.4
   Robin Roberts, 1953 ....6.4
   Rich Gossage, 1977 ....6.4
   Ron Guidry, 1978 ....6.4
   Greg Maddux, 1998 ......6.4
78 Jim Galvin, 1884 ....6.3
   Bob Caruthers, 1885.........6.3
   Elmer Smith, 1887 ....6.3
   Ed Walsh, 1910...............6.3
   Bob Gibson, 1969 ....6.3
   Jim Kern, 1979 ....6.3
84 George Bradley, 1876........6.2
   Jim Devlin, 1876 ....6.2
   Jouett Meekin, 1894.........6.2
   Carl Hubbell, 1936 ....6.2
   Roger Clemens, 1990 ...6.2
   Derek Lowe, 2002 ...6.2
90 Jack Taylor, 1902 ....6.1
   Jack Chesbro, 1904 ....6.1
   Mordecai Brown, 1906.......6.1
   Dizzy Dean, 1934 ....6.1
   Hal Newhouser, 1944.........6.1
   Sandy Koufax, 1966 ....6.1
96 Tim Keefe, 1884 ....6.0
   Mickey Welch, 1885 ....6.0
   Guy Hecker, 1885 ....6.0
   Billy Rhines, 1890 ....6.0
   Cy Young, 1902 ....6.0

Pitcher Wins

Bob Feller, 1939 ....6.0
Juan Marichal, 1965...........6.0
Greg Maddux, 1992 ......6.0
104 Bob Caruthers, 1887.........5.9
   Kid Nichols, 1890 ....5.9
   Amos Rusie, 1890 ....5.9
   Amos Rusie, 1897 ....5.9
   Clark Griffith, 1898...........5.9
   Dazzy Vance, 1924 ....5.9
   Dolf Luque, 1925 ....5.9
   Wes Ferrell, 1930.............5.9
   Lefty Grove, 1932............5.9
   Carl Hubbell, 1934 ....5.9
114 Charlie Buffinton, 1884 ....5.8
   Rube Waddell, 1902 ....5.8
   Jack Coombs, 1910 ....5.8
   Lon Warneke, 1933...........5.8
   Mark Eichhorn, 1986 ....5.8
   Pedro Martinez, 1997 ...5.8
   Dontrelle Willis, 2005..........5.8
122 Lady Baldwin, 1886...........5.7
   Jesse Duryea, 1889 ....5.7
   Matt Kilroy, 1889 ....5.7
   Cy Young, 1896 ....5.7
   Christy Mathewson, 1911....5.7
   Joe Wood, 1911 ....5.7
   Babe Ruth, 1916 ....5.7
   Eddie Cicotte, 1917...........5.7
   Curt Davis, 1934 ....5.7
   Mel Harder, 1934..............5.7
   Wilbur Wood, 1971 ....5.7
   Jim Palmer, 1975 ....5.7
   Randy Johnson, 2002....5.7
   Roger Clemens, 2005....5.7
136 Jim Whitney, 1883...........5.6
   Ted Breitenstein, 1893 ......5.6
   Bob Lemon, 1949 ....5.6
   Dean Chance, 1964 ....5.6
   Fergie Jenkins, 1971 ....5.6
   John Tudor, 1985..............5.6
   Randy Johnson, 1997....5.6
   Tom Glavine, 1998........5.6
   Johan Santana, 2004 ...5.6
145 Tony Mullane, 1883 ....5.5
   Tim Keefe, 1884 ....5.5
   Frank Killen, 1893 ....5.5
   Kid Nichols, 1893 ....5.5
   Nig Cuppy, 1896..............5.5
   Walter Johnson, 1910 ....5.5
   Ed Walsh, 1911...............5.5
   Eddie Cicotte, 1919...........5.5
   Stan Coveleski, 1920 ....5.5
   Lefty Gomez, 1934 ....5.5
   Lefty Grove, 1935.............5.5
   Gene Bearden, 1948 ....5.5
   Sandy Koufax, 1965...........5.5
   Tom Seaver, 1973 ....5.5
   Steve Carlton, 1977 ....5.5
   Esteban Loaiza, 2003....5.5
161 Kid Nichols, 1896 ....5.4
   Joe McGinnity, 1904.........5.4
   Walter Johnson, 1911 ....5.4
   Claude Hendrix, 1914 ....5.4
   Grover Alexander, 1917 ....5.4
   Carl Mays, 1921 ....5.4
   George Uhle, 1926............5.4
   Johnny Sain, 1946 ....5.4
   Bob Feller, 1946 ....5.4
   Mike Marshall, 1979 ....5.4
   Randy Johnson, 2001....5.4
172 Billy Taylor, 1884 ....5.3
   George Haddock, 1891.......5.3
   Mordecai Brown, 1909.......5.3
   Christy Mathewson, 1910....5.3
   Christy Mathewson, 1912....5.3
   Whit Wyatt, 1941..............5.3
   Spud Chandler, 1943 ....5.3
   Warren Spahn, 1947..........5.3
   Harry Brecheen, 1948 ....5.3
   Johnny Sain, 1948 ....5.3
   Johnny Antonelli, 1954.......5.3
   Billy Pierce, 1955 ....5.3
   Tom Seaver, 1969 ....5.3
   Vida Blue, 1971...............5.3
   Bert Blyleven, 1973...........5.3
   Rick Reuschel, 1977..........5.3
   Bret Saberhagen, 1989......5.3
   Roger Clemens, 1992....5.3
   Greg Maddux, 1993 ......5.3
   Greg Maddux, 1997 ......5.3
   Mike Hampton, 1999 ....5.3
   Randy Johnson, 2004....5.3
194 13 players tied 5.2

Pitcher Wins by era

1988-2005

1 Pedro Martinez, 2000 ...8.4
2 Pedro Martinez, 1999 ...8.1
3 Roger Clemens, 1997 ...7.9
4 Kevin Brown, 1996 ....6.9
5 Greg Maddux, 1994 ......6.8
6 Greg Maddux, 1995 ......6.5
7 Greg Maddux, 1998 ......6.4
8 Roger Clemens, 1990 ...6.2
   Derek Lowe, 2002 ....6.2
10 Greg Maddux, 1992 ......6.0

1973-1987

1 Doc Gooden, 1985.........7.6
2 John Hiller, 1973 ....6.7
3 Rich Gossage, 1977 ....6.4
   Ron Guidry, 1978 ....6.4
5 Jim Kern, 1979 ....6.3
6 Mark Eichhorn, 1986 ......5.8
7 Jim Palmer, 1975 ....5.7
8 John Tudor, 1985...........5.6
9 Tom Seaver, 1973 ....5.5
   Steve Carlton, 1977 ....5.5

1961-1972

1 Bob Gibson, 1968 ....7.6
2 Steve Carlton, 1972 ....7.4
3 Gaylord Perry, 1972 ....6.8
4 Tom Seaver, 1971 ....6.7
5 Bob Gibson, 1969 ....6.3
6 Sandy Koufax, 1966 ....6.1
7 Juan Marichal, 1965........6.0
8 Juan Marichal, 1966........5.8
9 Wilbur Wood, 1971 ....5.7
10 Dean Chance, 1964 ....5.6
   Fergie Jenkins, 1971 ....5.6

1943-1960

1 Dizzy Trout, 1944 ....8.2
2 Hal Newhouser, 1945.......7.6
3 Warren Spahn, 1953 ....7.0
4 Bob Lemon, 1948 ....6.6
5 Hal Newhouser, 1946.......6.4
   Robin Roberts, 1953 ....6.4
7 Hal Newhouser, 1944.......6.1
8 Bob Lemon, 1949 ....5.6
9 Gene Bearden, 1948 ....5.5
10 Johnny Sain, 1946 ....5.4
   Bob Feller, 1946 ....5.4

1921-1942

1 Lefty Grove, 1931...........8.2
   Bucky Walters, 1939 ....8.2
3 Dolf Luque, 1923 ....7.6
4 Carl Hubbell, 1933 ....7.3
5 Dazzy Vance, 1928 ....7.2
6 Lefty Grove, 1930...........6.9
7 Red Faber, 1921 ....6.8
   Wes Ferrell, 1935...........6.8
   Lefty Gomez, 1937 ....6.8
   Bob Feller, 1940 ....6.8

1901-1920

1 Walter Johnson, 1913 ....10.9
2 Walter Johnson, 1912 ....10.6
3 Christy Mathewson, 1905....8.5
4 Cy Young, 1901 ....7.9
5 Joe Wood, 1912 ....7.6
   Walter Johnson, 1918 ......7.6
7 Grover Alexander, 1915 ...7.5
8 Walter Johnson, 1915 .....7.4
9 Walter Johnson, 1914 .....7.2
   Grover Alexander, 1916 ...7.2

1893-1900

1 Amos Rusie, 1894 ....10.2
2 Pink Hawley, 1895...........7.4
3 Cy Young, 1895 ....6.9
   Kid Nichols, 1897 ....6.9
5 Amos Rusie, 1893 ....6.8
6 Cy Young, 1893 ....6.5
7 Kid Nichols, 1898 ....6.4
8 Jouett Meekin, 1894........6.2
9 Amos Rusie, 1897 ....5.9
   Clark Griffith, 1898..........5.9

1876-1892

1 Guy Hecker, 1884 ....12.9
2 Charley Radbourn, 1884..10.7
3 Silver King, 1888............10.2
4 John Clarkson, 1889 ....8.9
   Scott Stratton, 1890 ....8.9
6 Charley Radbourn, 1883....8.3
7 Dave Foutz, 1886 ....7.6
8 John Clarkson, 1887 ....7.5
9 John Clarkson, 1885 ....7.3
10 Bob Caruthers, 1886........7.2
   Matt Kilroy, 1887 ....7.2

Player Overall Wins alpha

Hank Aaron, 1959 ....6.8
Grover Alexander, 1915 ......7.5
Grover Alexander, 1916 ......7.2
Grover Alexander, 1920 ......6.9
Roberto Alomar, 1996 ....6.0
Luke Appling, 1943 ....6.3
Jeff Bagwell, 1994 ....7.7
Jeff Bagwell, 1996 ....7.1
Jeff Bagwell, 1997 ....7.0
Frank Baker, 1912 ....6.5
Frank Baker, 1913 ....6.6
Ernie Banks, 1959 ....6.6
Ernie Banks, 1960 ....6.6
Dick Bartell, 1937 ....6.5
Johnny Bench, 1972 ....6.5
Craig Biggio, 1997 ....8.2
Wade Boggs, 1987 ....6.5
Wade Boggs, 1988 ....6.5
Barry Bonds, 1990 ....6.6
Barry Bonds, 1992 ....7.9
Barry Bonds, 1993 ....8.0
Barry Bonds, 1996 ....7.1
Barry Bonds, 1997 ....6.5
Barry Bonds, 1998 ....6.6
Barry Bonds, 2000 ....6.6
Barry Bonds, 2001 ....11.7
Barry Bonds, 2002 ....11.8
Barry Bonds, 2003 ....8.5
Barry Bonds, 2004 ....10.6
Lou Boudreau, 1943 ....6.6
Lou Boudreau, 1944 ....7.0
Lou Boudreau, 1948 ....6.9
George Bradley, 1876 ....6.5
George Brett, 1980 ....6.5
George Brett, 1985 ....6.6
Dan Brouthers, 1892 ....6.6
Mordecai Brown, 1906.........6.1
Kevin Brown, 1996 ....6.9
Ken Caminiti, 1996 ....7.4
Rod Carew, 1974 ....6.6
Rod Carew, 1975 ....7.0
Rod Carew, 1977 ....7.6
Steve Carlton, 1972 ....7.4
Gary Carter, 1982 ....6.5
Bob Caruthers, 1885...........6.3
Bob Caruthers, 1886...........7.2
Norm Cash, 1961 ....7.3
Jack Chesbro, 1904 ....6.1
Cupid Childs, 1890.............6.6
Cupid Childs, 1896.............6.6
John Clarkson, 1885 ....7.3
John Clarkson, 1887 ....7.5
John Clarkson, 1889 ....8.9
Roger Clemens, 1990 ...6.2
Roger Clemens, 1997 ...7.9
Harlond Clift, 1937 ....7.0
Ty Cobb, 1909..................7.0
Ty Cobb, 1910..................7.0
Ty Cobb, 1911..................7.0
Ty Cobb, 1917..................7.0
Eddie Collins, 1910 ....6.5
Eddie Collins, 1912 ....6.6
Eddie Collins, 1913 ....6.6
Eddie Collins, 1914 ....6.5
Eddie Collins, 1915 ....6.5
Joe Cronin, 1930................6.6
George Davis, 1899 ....6.6
Dizzy Dean, 1934 ....6.1
Ed Delahanty, 1896............6.6
Jim Devlin, 1876 ....5.8
Art Devlin, 1906................6.5
Joe DiMaggio, 1941 ....6.5
Fred Dunlap, 1884 ....6.5
Darrell Evans, 1973 ....6.5
Red Faber, 1921 ....7.1
Bob Feller, 1939 ....6.0
Bob Feller, 1940 ....6.8
Charlie Ferguson, 1886 ....6.5
Wes Ferrell, 1935..............6.8
Dave Foutz, 1886 ....6.7
Nellie Fox, 1957 ....6.5
Jimmie Foxx, 1932 ....6.6
Jimmie Foxx, 1933 ....6.6
Jimmie Foxx, 1934 ....6.6
Frankie Frisch, 1924 ....6.6
Frankie Frisch, 1927 ....6.6
Jim Galvin, 1884 ....7.3
Lou Gehrig, 1927 ....6.6
Lou Gehrig, 1930 ....6.6
Lou Gehrig, 1931 ....6.6
Lou Gehrig, 1934 ....6.6
Lou Gehrig, 1936 ....6.6
Charlie Gehringer, 1934 ....6.6
Charlie Gehringer, 1936 ....6.6
Jason Giambi, 2001.........6.5
Bob Gibson, 1968 ....7.3
Bob Gibson, 1969 ....6.3
Lefty Gomez, 1937 ....7.0
Doc Gooden, 1985.............6.8
Rich Gossage, 1977 ....6.4

Player Overall Wins alpha

Bobby Grich, 1974 ....6.0
Bobby Grich, 1975 ....6.5
Ken Griffey Jr., 1997 ....6.0
Lefty Grove, 1930 ....6.9
Lefty Grove, 1931 ....8.2
Lefty Grove, 1936 ....6.6
Ron Guidry, 1978 ....6.4
Toby Harrah, 1975 ....6.9
Pink Hawley, 1895 ....7.4
Guy Hecker, 1884 ....12.9
Guy Hecker, 1885 ....6.0
Harry Heilmann, 1923 ....6.0
Todd Helton, 2004 ....6.2
Rickey Henderson, 1985...6.9
Rickey Henderson, 1990...7.7
John Hiller, 1973 ....6.7
Rogers Hornsby, 1917 ....7.8
Rogers Hornsby, 1920 ....7.9
Rogers Hornsby, 1921 ....7.7
Rogers Hornsby, 1922 ....8.9
Rogers Hornsby, 1924 ....9.3
Rogers Hornsby, 1925 ....6.8
Rogers Hornsby, 1927 ....6.8
Rogers Hornsby, 1928 ....6.1
Rogers Hornsby, 1929 ....6.8
Carl Hubbell, 1933 ....7.3
Carl Hubbell, 1936 ....6.2
Joe Jackson, 1911 ....6.5
Joe Jackson, 1912 ....7.1
Reggie Jackson, 1969 ....6.3
Hughie Jennings, 1895 ....6.3
Hughie Jennings, 1896 ....6.7
Walter Johnson, 1912 ......10.6
Walter Johnson, 1913 ......10.9
Walter Johnson, 1914 ....7.2
Walter Johnson, 1915 ....7.4
Walter Johnson, 1918 ....7.6
Walter Johnson, 1919 ....6.7
Tim Keefe, 1883 ....6.0
Jeff Kent, 2000 ....6.4
Jim Kern, 1979 ....6.3
Matt Kilroy, 1887 ....7.2
Silver King, 1888 ....10.2
Silver King, 1890 ....6.6
Sandy Koufax, 1966 ....6.1
Nap Lajoie, 1901 ....8.1
Nap Lajoie, 1903 ....8.1
Nap Lajoie, 1904 ....7.4
Nap Lajoie, 1906 ....7.6
Nap Lajoie, 1907 ....7.0
Nap Lajoie, 1908 ....8.0
Nap Lajoie, 1910 ....8.9
Eddie Lake, 1945 ....6.5
Barry Larkin, 1991 ....6.2
Barry Larkin, 1996 ....6.0
Thornton Lee, 1941 ....6.5
Derek Lee, 2005 ....6.3
Bob Lemon, 1948 ....6.6
Derek Lowe, 2002 ....6.2
Dolf Luque, 1923 ....7.6
Greg Maddux, 1992 ......6.0
Greg Maddux, 1994 ......6.8
Greg Maddux, 1995 ......6.5
Greg Maddux, 1998 ......6.4
Mickey Mantle, 1956 ....8.1
Mickey Mantle, 1957 ....8.2
Mickey Mantle, 1958 ....6.0
Mickey Mantle, 1961 ....7.5
Juan Marichal, 1965 ....6.0
Pedro Martinez, 1999 ....8.1
Pedro Martinez, 2000 ....8.4
Eddie Mathews, 1953 ....6.1
Eddie Mathews, 1959 ....6.1
Christy Mathewson, 1905...8.5
Christy Mathewson, 1908...6.5
Christy Mathewson, 1909...6.6
Willie Mays, 1954 ....6.2
Willie Mays, 1955 ....6.8
Willie Mays, 1958 ....6.3
Willie Mays, 1962 ....6.1
Willie Mays, 1963 ....6.0
Willie Mays, 1965 ....6.9
Willie McCovey, 1969 ....6.5
Willie McCovey, 1970 ....6.5
Mark McGwire, 1998 ....7.1
Joe Medwick, 1937 ....6.0
Jouett Meekin, 1894 ....6.2
Kevin Mitchell, 1989 ....6.2
Joe Morgan, 1973 ....7.4
Joe Morgan, 1974 ....7.0
Joe Morgan, 1975 ....8.1
Joe Morgan, 1976 ....6.7
Tony Mullane, 1884 ....7.1
Stan Musial, 1948 ....7.2
Stan Musial, 1951 ....6.1
Hal Newhouser, 1944 ....6.1
Hal Newhouser, 1945 ....7.6
Hal Newhouser, 1946 ....6.4
Kid Nichols, 1897 ....6.9
Kid Nichols, 1898 ....6.4

Player Overall Wins alpha

Mel Ott, 1938 ....6.4
Gaylord Perry, 1972 ....6.8
Rico Petrocelli, 1969 ....7.6
Fred Pfeffer, 1884 ....6.0
Mike Piazza, 1997 ....7.7
Mike Piazza, 1998 ....6.0
Albert Pujols, 2003 ....7.1
Charley Radbourn, 1883...8.3
Charley Radbourn, 1884...10.7
Toad Ramsey, 1886 ....6.7
Billy Rhines, 1890 ....6.0
Cal Ripken, 1983 ....7.0
Cal Ripken, 1984 ....9.4
Cal Ripken, 1991 ....8.5
Robin Roberts, 1953 ....6.4
Jackie Robinson, 1951...7.3
Frank Robinson, 1966 ....6.3
Alex Rodriguez, 2000 ....6.6
Alex Rodriguez, 2001 ....6.9
Alex Rodriguez, 2002 ....7.4
Alex Rodriguez, 2003 ....6.7
Scott Rolen, 2004 ....6.4
Al Rosen, 1953 ....7.4
Amos Rusie, 1893 ....6.8
Amos Rusie, 1894 ....10.2
Babe Ruth, 1919 ....7.3
Babe Ruth, 1920 ....9.3
Babe Ruth, 1921 ....9.4
Babe Ruth, 1923 ....10.1
Babe Ruth, 1924 ....8.4
Babe Ruth, 1926 ....8.5
Babe Ruth, 1927 ....8.8
Babe Ruth, 1928 ....7.1
Babe Ruth, 1930 ....7.6
Babe Ruth, 1931 ....8.1
Babe Ruth, 1932 ....6.5
Ryne Sandberg, 1984 ....6.6
Ron Santo, 1964 ....7.1
Ron Santo, 1965 ....6.2
Ron Santo, 1966 ....7.6
Ron Santo, 1967 ....7.7
Mike Schmidt, 1974 ....7.3
Mike Schmidt, 1977 ....6.4
Mike Schmidt, 1980 ....6.8
Mike Schmidt, 1981 ....7.1
Mike Schmidt, 1982 ....6.3
Mike Schmidt, 1983 ....6.4
Red Schoendienst, 1953...6.5
Tom Seaver, 1971 ....6.7
Joe Sewell, 1923 ....6.2
Gary Sheffield, 1992 ....6.0
George Sisler, 1920 ....7.9
George Sisler, 1922 ....6.3
Elmer Smith, 1887 ....6.3
Sammy Sosa, 2001 ....8.6
Warren Spahn, 1953 ....7.0
Tris Speaker, 1912 ....7.2
Tris Speaker, 1913 ....6.5
Tris Speaker, 1914 ....7.3
Tris Speaker, 1923 ....6.5
Snuffy Stirnweiss, 1944 ....6.8
Snuffy Stirnweiss, 1945 ....7.2
Jack Stivetts, 1891 ....6.8
Scott Stratton, 1890 ....8.9
Charlie Sweeney, 1884 ....6.5
Jack Taylor, 1902 ....6.1
Miguel Tejada, 2004 ....6.6
Dickie Thon, 1983 ....6.2
Alan Trammell, 1987 ....6.1
Dizzy Trout, 1944 ....8.2
Dazzy Vance, 1928 ....7.2
Dazzy Vance, 1930 ....6.4
Arky Vaughan, 1935 ....6.6
Arky Vaughan, 1938 ....6.4
Honus Wagner, 1905 ....7.5
Honus Wagner, 1906 ....7.2
Honus Wagner, 1907 ....6.7
Honus Wagner, 1908 ....6.9
Ed Walsh, 1908 ....6.8
Ed Walsh, 1910 ....6.3
Ed Walsh, 1912 ....6.5
Bucky Walters, 1939 ....8.2
Mickey Welch, 1885 ....6.0
Will White, 1882 ....6.7
Will White, 1883 ....6.9
Ted Williams, 1941 ....8.5
Ted Williams, 1942 ....8.5
Ted Williams, 1946 ....8.1
Ted Williams, 1947 ....7.2
Ted Williams, 1949 ....6.4
Ted Williams, 1957 ....7.1
Joe Wood, 1912 ....7.6
Carl Yastrzemski, 1967 ....6.9
Carl Yastrzemski, 1968 ....6.3
Cy Young, 1892 ....6.4
Cy Young, 1893 ....6.5
Cy Young, 1895 ....6.9
Cy Young, 1901 ....7.9
Cy Young, 1902 ....6.0
Robin Yount, 1982 ....7.1

Player Overall Wins

1 Guy Hecker, 1884 ....12.9
2 Barry Bonds, 2001.....11.7
3 Barry Bonds, 2002.....11.5
4 Walter Johnson, 1913 ....10.9
5 Charley Radbourn, 1884...10.7
6 Walter Johnson, 1912 ....10.6
Barry Bonds, 2004 ....10.6
8 Silver King, 1888 ....10.2
Amos Rusie, 1894 ....10.2
10 Babe Ruth, 1923 ....10.1
11 Babe Ruth, 1921 ....9.4
Cal Ripken, 1984 ....9.4
13 Babe Ruth, 1920 ....9.3
Rogers Hornsby, 1924 ....9.3
15 John Clarkson, 1889 ....8.9
Scott Stratton, 1890 ....8.9
Nap Lajoie, 1910 ....8.9
Rogers Hornsby, 1922 ....8.9
19 Babe Ruth, 1927 ....8.8
20 Sammy Sosa, 2001 ....8.6
21 Christy Mathewson, 1905...8.5
Babe Ruth, 1926 ....8.5
Ted Williams, 1941 ....8.5
Ted Williams, 1942 ....8.5
Cal Ripken, 1991 ....8.5
26 Pedro Martinez, 2000 ...8.4
Babe Ruth, 1924 ....8.4
Lou Gehrig, 1927 ....8.4
29 Charley Radbourn, 1883...8.3
30 Lefty Grove, 1931 ....8.2
Bucky Walters, 1939 ....8.2
Dizzy Trout, 1944 ....8.2
Mickey Mantle, 1957 ....8.2
Craig Biggio, 1997 ....8.2
Barry Bonds, 2003 ....8.2
36 Pedro Martinez, 1999 ....8.1
Nap Lajoie, 1901 ....8.1
Nap Lajoie, 1903 ....8.1
Babe Ruth, 1931 ....8.1
Ted Williams, 1946 ....8.1
Mickey Mantle, 1956 ....8.1
Joe Morgan, 1975 ....8.1
43 Nap Lajoie, 1908 ....8.0
Barry Bonds, 1993 ....8.0
45 Cy Young, 1901 ....7.9
Roger Clemens, 1997 ...7.9
Rogers Hornsby, 1920 ....7.9
George Sisler, 1920 ....7.9
Lou Gehrig, 1934 ....7.9
Barry Bonds, 1992 ....7.9
51 Rogers Hornsby, 1917 ....7.8
52 Rogers Hornsby, 1921 ....7.7
Lou Gehrig, 1930 ....7.7
Ron Santo, 1967 ....7.7
Rickey Henderson, 1990...7.7
Jeff Bagwell, 1994 ....7.7
Mike Piazza, 1997 ....7.7
58 Dave Foutz, 1886 ....7.6
Joe Wood, 1912 ....7.6
Walter Johnson, 1918 ....7.6
Dolf Luque, 1923 ....7.6
Hal Newhouser, 1945 ....7.6
Bob Gibson, 1968 ....7.6
Doc Gooden, 1985 ....7.6
Nap Lajoie, 1906 ....7.6
Babe Ruth, 1930 ....7.6
Norm Cash, 1961 ....7.6
Ron Santo, 1966 ....7.6
Rico Petrocelli, 1969 ....7.6
Barry Bonds, 1996........7.6
71 John Clarkson, 1887 ....7.5
Grover Alexander, 1915 ....7.5
Honus Wagner, 1905 ....7.5
Lou Boudreau, 1944 ....7.5
Mickey Mantle, 1961 ....7.5
76 Pink Hawley, 1895 ....7.4
Walter Johnson, 1915 ....7.4
Steve Carlton, 1972 ....7.4
Nap Lajoie, 1904 ....7.4
Ty Cobb, 1917 ....7.4
Harlond Clift, 1937 ....7.4
Al Rosen, 1953 ....7.4
Joe Morgan, 1973 ....7.4
Ken Caminiti, 1996 ....7.4
Alex Rodriguez, 2002 ...7.4
86 John Clarkson, 1885 ....7.3
Carl Hubbell, 1933 ....7.3
Tris Speaker, 1914 ....7.3
Babe Ruth, 1919 ....7.3
Jackie Robinson, 1951 ....7.3
Mike Schmidt, 1974 ....7.3
92 Bob Caruthers, 1886 ....7.2
Matt Kilroy, 1887 ....7.2
Walter Johnson, 1914 ....7.2
Grover Alexander, 1916 ....7.2
Dazzy Vance, 1928 ....7.2
Honus Wagner, 1906 ....7.2
Tris Speaker, 1912 ....7.2
Frankie Frisch, 1927 ....7.2
Snuffy Stirnweiss, 1945 ....7.2

Player Overall Wins

Ted Williams, 1947 ....7.2
Stan Musial, 1948 ....7.2
103 Tony Mullane, 1884 ....7.1
Fred Dunlap, 1884 ....7.1
Joe Jackson, 1912 ....7.1
Babe Ruth, 1928 ....7.1
Lou Boudreau, 1948 ....7.1
Ted Williams, 1957 ....7.1
Ron Santo, 1964 ....7.1
Mike Schmidt, 1981 ....7.1
Robin Yount, 1982 ....7.1
Jeff Bagwell, 1996 ....7.1
Mark McGwire, 1998 ....7.1
Albert Pujols, 2003 ....7.1
115 Warren Spahn, 1953 ....7.0
Nap Lajoie, 1907 ....7.0
Eddie Collins, 1910 ....7.0
Eddie Collins, 1913 ....7.0
Joe Morgan, 1974 ....7.0
Cal Ripken, 1983 ....7.0
121 Will White, 1883 ....6.9
Cy Young, 1895 ....6.9
Kid Nichols, 1897 ....6.9
Grover Alexander, 1920 ....6.9
Lefty Grove, 1930 ....6.9
Kevin Brown, 1996 ....6.9
Honus Wagner, 1908 ....6.9
Eddie Collins, 1914 ....6.9
Joe Cronin, 1930 ....6.9
Jimmie Foxx, 1933 ....6.9
Willie Mays, 1965 ....6.9
Carl Yastrzemski, 1967 ....6.9
Rod Carew, 1974 ....6.9
Toby Harrah, 1975 ....6.9
Rickey Henderson, 1985...6.9
Alex Rodriguez, 2001 ...6.9
137 Jack Stivetts, 1891 ....6.8
Amos Rusie, 1893 ....6.8
Ed Walsh, 1908 ....6.8
Red Faber, 1921 ....6.8
Wes Ferrell, 1935 ....6.8
Lefty Gomez, 1937 ....6.8
Bob Feller, 1940 ....6.8
Gaylord Perry, 1972 ....6.8
Greg Maddux, 1994 ......6.8
Cupid Childs, 1890 ....6.8
Dan Brouthers, 1892 ....6.8
Rogers Hornsby, 1925 ....6.8
Rogers Hornsby, 1927 ....6.8
Rogers Hornsby, 1929 ....6.8
Lou Boudreau, 1943 ....6.8
Snuffy Stirnweiss, 1944 ....6.8
Willie Mays, 1955 ....6.8
Hank Aaron, 1959 ....6.8
Mike Schmidt, 1980 ....6.8
Barry Bonds, 2000 ....6.8
157 Will White, 1882 ....6.7
Toad Ramsey, 1886 ....6.7
Walter Johnson, 1919 ....6.7
Tom Seaver, 1971 ....6.7
John Hiller, 1973 ....6.7
Hughie Jennings, 1896 ....6.7
Honus Wagner, 1907 ....6.7
Jimmie Foxx, 1932 ....6.7
Rod Carew, 1975 ....6.7
Joe Morgan, 1976 ....6.7
Gary Carter, 1982 ....6.7
Alex Rodriguez, 2003 ...6.7
169 Silver King, 1890 ....6.6
Christy Mathewson, 1909...6.6
Lefty Grove, 1936 ....6.6
Bob Lemon, 1948 ....6.6
Art Devlin, 1906 ....6.6
Ty Cobb, 1911 ....6.6
Frank Baker, 1913 ....6.6
Eddie Collins, 1915 ....6.6
Arky Vaughan, 1935 ....6.6
Lou Gehrig, 1936 ....6.6
Joe DiMaggio, 1941 ....6.6
Ryne Sandberg, 1984 ....6.6
George Brett, 1985 ....6.6
Barry Bonds, 1998........6.6
Alex Rodriguez, 2000 ...6.6
Miguel Tejada, 2004 ....6.6
185 Charlie Sweeney, 1884 ....6.5
Charlie Ferguson, 1886 ....6.5
Cy Young, 1893 ....6.5
Christy Mathewson, 1908...6.5
Ed Walsh, 1912 ....6.5
Thornton Lee, 1941 ....6.5
Greg Maddux, 1995 ......6.5
Joe Jackson, 1911 ....6.5
Frank Baker, 1912 ....6.5
Tris Speaker, 1913 ....6.5
Tris Speaker, 1923 ....6.5
Babe Ruth, 1932 ....6.5
Eddie Lake, 1945 ....6.5
Red Schoendienst, 1953 ....6.5
Willie McCovey, 1969 ....6.5
Willie McCovey, 1970 ....6.5

Player Overall Wins

Johnny Bench, 1972 ....6.5
Bobby Grich, 1975 ....6.5
Rod Carew, 1977 ....6.5
George Brett, 1980 ....6.5
Wade Boggs, 1987 ....6.5
206 Cy Young, 1892 ....6.4
Kid Nichols, 1898 ....6.4
Dazzy Vance, 1930 ....6.4
Hal Newhouser, 1946 ....6.4
Robin Roberts, 1953 ....6.4
Rich Gossage, 1977 ....6.4
Ron Guidry, 1978 ....6.4
Greg Maddux, 1998 ....6.4
Eddie Collins, 1912 ....6.4
Mel Ott, 1938 ....6.4
Arky Vaughan, 1938 ....6.4
Ted Williams, 1949 ....6.4
Mike Schmidt, 1977 ....6.4
Mike Schmidt, 1983 ....6.4
Wade Boggs, 1988 ....6.4
Barry Bonds, 1990 ....6.4
Jeff Kent, 2000 ....6.4
Scott Rolen, 2004 ....6.4
224 Jim Galvin, 1884 ....6.3
Bob Caruthers, 1885 ....6.3
Elmer Smith, 1887 ....6.3
Ed Walsh, 1910 ....6.3
Bob Gibson, 1969 ....6.3
Jim Kern, 1979 ....6.3
Hughie Jennings, 1895 ....6.3
Cupid Childs, 1896 ....6.3
Ty Cobb, 1910 ....6.3
George Sisler, 1922 ....6.3
Luke Appling, 1943 ....6.3
Willie Mays, 1958 ....6.3
Frank Robinson, 1966 ....6.3
Carl Yastrzemski, 1968 ....6.3
Reggie Jackson, 1969 ....6.3
Darrell Evans, 1973 ....6.3
Mike Schmidt, 1982 ....6.3
Jason Giambi, 2001 ....6.3
Derek Lee, 2005 ....6.3
243 George Bradley, 1876 ....6.2
Jim Devlin, 1876 ....6.2
Jouett Meekin, 1894 ....6.2
Carl Hubbell, 1936 ....6.2
Roger Clemens, 1990 ...6.2
Derek Lowe, 2002 ....6.2
Joe Sewell, 1923 ....6.2
Willie Mays, 1954 ....6.2
Ernie Banks, 1959 ....6.2
Ron Santo, 1965 ....6.2
Dickie Thon, 1983 ....6.2
Kevin Mitchell, 1989 ....6.2
Barry Larkin, 1991 ....6.2
Barry Bonds, 1997........6.2
Todd Helton, 2004 ....6.2
258 Jack Taylor, 1902 ....6.1
Jack Chesbro, 1904 ....6.1
Mordecai Brown, 1906 ....6.1
Dizzy Dean, 1934 ....6.1
Hal Newhouser, 1944 ....6.1
Sandy Koufax, 1966 ....6.1
George Davis, 1899 ....6.1
Rogers Hornsby, 1928 ....6.1
Jimmie Foxx, 1934 ....6.1
Charlie Gehringer, 1936 ....6.1
Dick Bartell, 1937 ....6.1
Stan Musial, 1951 ....6.1
Eddie Mathews, 1953 ....6.1
Nellie Fox, 1957 ....6.1
Willie Mays, 1962 ....6.1
Alan Trammell, 1987 ....6.1
274 Tim Keefe, 1883 ....6.0
Mickey Welch, 1885 ....6.0
Guy Hecker, 1885 ....6.0
Billy Rhines, 1890 ....6.0
Cy Young, 1902 ....6.0
Bob Feller, 1939 ....6.0
Juan Marichal, 1965 ....6.0
Greg Maddux, 1992 ......6.0
Fred Pfeffer, 1884 ....6.0
Ed Delahanty, 1896 ....6.0
Ty Cobb, 1909 ....6.0
Harry Heilmann, 1923 ....6.0
Frankie Frisch, 1924 ....6.0
Lou Gehrig, 1931 ....6.0
Charlie Gehringer, 1934 ....6.0
Joe Medwick, 1937 ....6.0
Mickey Mantle, 1958 ....6.0
Eddie Mathews, 1959 ....6.0
Ernie Banks, 1960 ....6.0
Willie Mays, 1963 ....6.0
Bobby Grich, 1974 ....6.0
Gary Sheffield, 1992 ....6.0
Barry Larkin, 1996 ....6.0
Roberto Alomar, 2000 ....6.0
Jeff Bagwell, 1997 ....6.0
Ken Griffey Jr., 1997 ....6.0
Mike Piazza, 1998..........6.0

THE NATURALS: THE HALL OF FAME

While lesser sports have copied the National Baseball Hall of Fame and Museum, no other athletic Hall of Fame commands nearly so much respect, interest, or passion. In a cynical modern era when very few athletic heroes are idolized, those fortunate few inducted into Cooperstown have achieved a kind of immortality. Many of these bronze demigods were *naturals* in the true sense of the word, whether they triumphed over their demons like Robert Redford in Barry Levinson's 1984 film *The Natural*—or whether they succumbed like Roy Hobbs in Bernard Malamud's classic novella on which the movie was based.

In 1934 in the middle of the Great Depression, Alexander Cleland, a civic leader in Cooperstown, New York, came up with an idea to boost tourism in his small city: He decided that Cooperstown could benefit from building a baseball museum. Cooperstown was (and still is) an out-of-the-way place. However, the town was home to a rich foundation—Cleland's employer, the Clark Foundation—that would support these types of projects, and it was also the supposed birthplace of baseball. Even then, many people realized that Abner Doubleday most certainly did *not* invent baseball in Cooperstown, and that neither the famous general nor the picturesque town had even played a role in the development of baseball. Nonetheless, creation myths are very powerful, and Cooperstown has been able to take great advantage of its part in this fictional tale.

Once Cooperstown officials were convinced of the wisdom of building a baseball museum, they contacted Major League Baseball. Coincidentally, NL President Ford Frick had come up with an idea of his own that would enhance any baseball museum: a Hall of Fame. Frick had recently visited the Hall of Fame for Great Americans at New York University and been inspired to do something similar for baseball's legendary stars.

While the phrase "Hall of Fame" was well known at the time, it was almost always used as a metaphor. Today there are more Halls of Fame in the United States than anyone has the patience to count—there's even a Shuffleboard Hall of Fame in Texas—but the Hall for Great Americans was the first of its kind when it opened in 1900. The Baseball Hall of Fame would be the first such institution devoted to a sport. So Cooperstown leaders and baseball officials reached an agreement to build the National Baseball Hall of Fame and Museum in upstate New York.

Though the museum would not be ready to open until 1939, the process of electing players to the Hall began in 1936. Two groups were formed to elect players—a large group of more than 200 writers from the Baseball Writers Association of America and a 78-member Old-Timers Committee. While the Old-Timers Committee was formed specifically to evaluate long-retired players, the two sets of voters were given almost no further guidance on whom to elect. Several active players received significant support from the BBWAA, while other players received votes from both the writers and the Old Timers. A 75-percent vote of either group was needed to earn induction in the Hall. In the end, the writers selected five of the all-time greats: Ty Cobb, Babe Ruth, Honus Wagner Christy Mathewson, and Walter Johnson. A divided and confused Old-Timers Committee elected no one.

The BBWAA would hold three more elections before the official opening of the Hall of Fame, electing Nap Lajoie, Tris Speaker, and Cy Young in 1937, Grover Cleveland Alexander in 1938, and George Sisler, Eddie Collins, and Willie Keeler in 1939. Afterward, the BBWAA held a vote only once every three years. The organization went back to having an annual election in 1946, then reduced the frequency of their balloting to every two years after 1956. Finally, the BBWAA permanently returned to an annual election in 1966. In 1954, it was decided that all future candidates would not appear on the BBWAA ballot until five years after retirement. After Roberto Clemente's death in 1972, the rules were modified so that any player who died before eligibility could be considered by the writers only six months later.

After the failure of the Old-Timers Committee to elect anyone in 1936, a smaller Centennial Commission was formed to elect executives, managers, and other pioneers. This commission elected Morgan B. Bulkeley, Ban Johnson, Connie Mack, John McGraw, and George Wright in 1937, and added Alexander Cartwright (though not Abner Doubleday) and Henry Chadwick in 1938. The idea of an Old-Timers Committee was revived in 1939, electing various players and officials in 1939, 1944, 1945, 1946, and 1949. The committee's election of 21 players and executives in 1945 and 1946 started a long tradition of questionable choices, which didn't stop the formation of a permanent Veterans Committee in 1953. The Veterans Committee continued to elect managers and executives—as well as players that the writers had passed over—until it was disbanded after 2001.

While the Veterans Committee certainly made some worthy selections, its voting process was politicized from the start: The number of friends or teammates a player under consideration had on the committee was often the best indicator of whether he would be elected. Separate committees for the Negro Leagues and for the nineteenth century did a much better job dealing with leagues and eras of which previous voters showed little knowledge. However, even the Negro Leagues Committee was criticized for relying too much on the opinion of one man, Buck O'Neil.

A new Veterans Committee (which includes all living Hall of Famers and all living recipients of either the Frick or the Spink awards) has now been assembled to consider players every two years; the group also votes on umpires, managers, and executives every four years. No one came remotely close to winning induction into the Hall in the new committee's voting in 2003 and 2005. Unless the rules or composition of the committee is changed, it seems unlikely that it will elect many candidates since Hall of Famers usually want the Hall to be more exclusive after they've been elected. In a group far too big for the kind of personal politicking that was so effective on the old Veterans Committee, it will probably be very hard to reach consensus. In 2005, a new 12-member committee of Negro League historians was appointed to vote in February 2006 on a pre-selected group of 30 Negro League players and 9 pre-Negro League pioneers. Candidates receiving 75 percent of that vote will be inducted into the Hall in summer 2006 along with Bruce Sutter.

What follows is a listing of every member of the Hall of Fame. Also listed are those not in the Hall of Fame who have ever received a vote (not including 2006), plus the leading vote getters each year. The first and last years of everyone's **Career** is shown, regardless of whether their seasons were consecutive. Voting totals include the candidate's first-year percentage of votes (**1st Yr/Pct**) and the final year totals (**Last Yr/Pct**) through 2005, as well as the year the player received his highest vote total and the percentage of that vote he received (**Max Yr/Pct**). (Hall of Fame election results for 2006 were announced as this edition went to press; therefore, only the voting for new HOF member Bruce Sutter is reflected in this section.) For Hall of Fame members, their actual **Votes** received are also shown alongside the number of votes **Needed** to be elected. The Year-by-Year section includes the totals of all candidates who received at least 25 percent of the BBWAA votes in a given year; also provided are the number of votes (which fluctuate each year) required to gain induction.

Hall of Famers and other candidates are listed by their primary position (**Pos**); non-players are listed as executives (*Exe*), managers (*Mgr*), pioneers (*Pio*), or umpires (*Ump*). Special elections and abbreviations include *1936V* (for Veterans Election) and *1946N* (for Nominating Ballot, where no one was to be elected). The Negro Leagues Committee is represented by an *N*, while *C* stands for Centennial, *V* for Veterans, and *S* for Special. An *R* after a year indicates a run-off election, held after no one was elected on the regular ballot. A maximum of one player could be elected in the three run-off elections, even if more than one received 75 percent of the run-off vote.

MEMBERS OF THE HALL OF FAME

MEMBER	CAREER	POS	ELECTED	MAX YR	PCT	VOTES	NEEDED	1ST YR	PCT	VOTES	NEEDED	LAST YR	PCT	VOTES	NEEDED
Hank Aaron	1954–1976	RF	1982	1982	97.8	406	312								
Grover Alexander	1911–1930	P	1938	1938	80.9	212	197	1936	24.3	55	170	1938	80.9	212	197
Walter Alston	1954–1976	Mgr	1983V												
Sparky Anderson	1970–1995	Mgr	2000V												
Cap Anson	1871–1897	1B	1939O	1936O	51.3	40	59								
Luis Aparicio	1956–1973	SS	1984	1984	84.6	341	303	1979	27.8	120	324	1984	84.6	341	303
Luke Appling	1930–1950	SS	1964	1964R	83.6	189	170	1953	0.8	2	198	1964R	83.6	189	170
Richie Ashburn	1948–1962	CF	1995V	1978	41.7	158	285	1968	2.1	6	213	1982	30.4	126	312
Earl Averill	1929–1941	CF	1975V	1958	5.3	14	200	1949	0.7	1	115	1962	1.9	3	120
Frank Baker	1908–1922	3B	1955V	1947	30.4	49	121	1936	0.4	1	170	1951	3.5	8	170
Dave Bancroft	1915–1930	SS	1971V	1958	16.2	43	200	1937	1.5	3	151	1960	11.2	30	202
Ernie Banks	1953–1971	1B	1977	1977	83.8	321	288								
Al Barlick	1940–1971	Ump	1989V												
Ed Barrow	1903–1947	Exe	1953V												
Jake Beckley	1888–1907	1B	1971V	1936V	1.3	1	59	1936V	1.3	1	59	1942	0.4	1	175
Cool Papa Bell	1922–1946	CF	1974N												
Johnny Bench	1967–1983	C	1989	1989	96.4	431	336								
Chief Bender	1903–1917	P	1953V	1947	44.7	72	121	1936	0.9	2	170	1953	39.4	104	198
Yogi Berra	1946–1965	C	1972	1972	85.6	339	297	1971	67.2	242	270	1972	85.6	339	297
Wade Boggs	1982–1999	3B	2005	2005	91.9	474	387								
Jim Bottomley	1922–1937	1B	1974V	1960	33.1	89	202	1948	3.3	4	91	1962	12.5	20	120
Lou Boudreau	1938–1952	SS	1970	1970	77.3	232	225	1956	1.0	2	145	1970	77.3	232	225
Roger Bresnahan	1897–1915	C	1945O	1945	53.8	133	186	1936	20.8	47	170	1945	53.8	133	186
George Brett	1973–1993	3B	1999	1999	98.2	488	373								
Lou Brock	1961–1979	LF	1985	1985	79.7	315	297								
Dan Brouthers	1879–1896	1B	1945O	1936V	2.6	2	59								
Mordecai Brown	1903–1916	P	1949O	1946N	27.7	56	152	1936	2.7	6	170	1946	18.3	48	198
Morgan Bulkeley	1876–1876	Exe	1937C												
Jim Bunning	1955–1971	P	1996V	1988	74.2	317	321	1977	38.1	146	288	1991	63.7	282	333
Jesse Burkett	1890–1905	LF	1946O	1942	1.7	4	175	1936V	1.3	1	59	1946N	1.0	2	152
Roy Campanella	1948–1957	C	1969	1969	79.4	270	255	1964	57.2	115	151	1969	79.4	270	255
Rod Carew	1967–1985	1B	1991	1991	90.5	401	333								
Max Carey	1910–1929	CF	1961V	1958	51.1	136	200	1937	3.0	6	151	1958	51.1	136	200
Steve Carlton	1965–1988	P	1994	1994	95.8	436	342								
Gary Carter	1974–1992	C	2003	2003	78.0	387	372	1998	42.3	200	355	2003	78.0	387	372
Alexander Cartwright	1845–1848	Pio	1938C												
Orlando Cepeda	1958–1974	1B	1999V	1994	73.6	335	342	1980	12.5	48	289	1994	73.6	335	342
Henry Chadwick	1858–1908	Pio	1938C												
Frank Chance	1898–1914	1B	1946O	1945	72.5	179	186	1936	2.2	5	170	1946	57.0	150	198
Happy Chandler	1945–1951	Exe	1982V												
Oscar Charleston	1915–1940	CF	1976N												
Jack Chesbro	1899–1909	P	1946O	1939	2.2	6	206	1937	0.5	1	151	1946N	0.5	1	152
Nestor Chylak	1954–1978	Ump	1999V												
Fred Clarke	1894–1915	LF	1945O	1942	24.9	58	175	1936V	11.5	9	59	1945	21.5	53	186
John Clarkson	1882–1894	P	1963V	1936V	6.4	5	59	1936V	6.4	5	59	1946N	0.5	1	152
Roberto Clemente	1955–1972	RF	1973S												
Ty Cobb	1905–1928	CF	1936	1936	98.2	222	170								
Mickey Cochrane	1925–1937	C	1947	1947	79.5	128	121	1936	35.4	80	170	1947	79.5	128	121
Eddie Collins	1906–1930	2B	1939	1939	77.7	213	206	1936	26.5	60	170	1939	77.7	213	206
Jimmy Collins	1895–1908	3B	1945O	1945	49.0	121	186	1936V	10.3	8	59	1945	49.0	121	186
Earle Combs	1924–1935	CF	1970V	1960	16.0	43	202	1937	2.0	4	151	1962	3.8	6	120
Charlie Comiskey	1882–1894	Exe	1939O	1936V	7.7	6	59								
Jocko Conlan	1941–1964	Ump	1974V												
Tommy Connolly	1898–1931	Ump	1953V												
Roger Connor	1880–1897	1B	1976V												
Stan Coveleski	1912–1928	P	1969V	1958	12.8	34	200	1938	0.4	1	197	1958	12.8	34	200
Sam Crawford	1899–1917	RF	1957V	1946N	4.5	9	152	1936	0.4	1	170	1946N	4.5	9	152
Joe Cronin	1926–1945	SS	1956	1956	78.8	152	145	1947	3.7	6	121	1956	78.8	152	145
Candy Cummings	1872–1877	Pio	1939O												
Kiki Cuyler	1921–1938	RF	1968V	1958	33.8	90	200	1948	2.5	3	91	1962	19.4	31	120
Ray Dandridge	1933–1949	3B	1987V												
George Davis	1890–1909	SS	1998V												
Leon Day	1934–1950	P	1995V												
Dizzy Dean	1930–1940	P	1953	1953	79.2	209	198	1936	0.4	1	170	1953	79.2	209	198
Ed Delahanty	1888–1903	LF	1945O	1939	52.9	145	206	1936V	28.2	22	59	1945	44.9	111	186
Bill Dickey	1928–1946	C	1954	1954	80.2	202	189	1945	6.9	17	186	1954	80.2	202	189
Martin Dihigo	1923–1945	2B	1977N												
Joe DiMaggio	1936–1951	CF	1955	1955	88.8	223	189	1945	0.4	1	186	1955	88.8	223	189
Larry Doby	1947–1959	CF	1998V	1967	3.4	10	219	1966	2.3	7	227	1967R	0.3	1	230
Bobby Doerr	1937–1951	2B	1986V	1970	25.0	75	225	1953	0.8	2	198	1971	21.7	78	270
Don Drysdale	1956–1969	P	1984	1984	78.4	316	303	1975	21.0	76	272	1984	78.4	316	303
Hugh Duffy	1888–1906	CF	1945O	1942	33.0	77	175	1936V	5.1	4	59	1945	25.9	64	186
Leo Durocher	1939–1973	Mgr	1994V	1958	10.5	28	200	1948	0.8	1	91	1964R	0.9	2	170
Dennis Eckersley	1975–1998	P	2004	2004	83.2	421	380								
Billy Evans	1906–1927	Ump	1973V												
Johnny Evers	1902–1929	2B	1946O	1946N	64.4	130	152	1936	2.7	6	170	1946	41.8	110	198
Buck Ewing	1880–1897	C	1939O	1936V	51.3	40	59	1936V	51.3	40	59	1939	0.7	2	206
Red Faber	1914–1933	P	1964V	1960	30.9	83	202	1937	1.5	3	151	1962	18.8	30	120
Bob Feller	1936–1956	P	1962	1962	93.8	150	120								
Rick Ferrell	1929–1947	C	1984V	1956	0.5	1	145	1956	0.5	1	145	1960	0.4	1	202
Rollie Fingers	1968–1985	P	1992	1992	81.2	349	323	1991	65.7	291	333	1992	81.2	349	323
Carlton Fisk	1969–1993	C	2000	2000	79.6	397	375	1999	66.4	330	373	2000	79.6	397	375
Elmer Flick	1898–1910	RF	1963V	1938	0.4	1	197								
Whitey Ford	1950–1967	P	1974	1974	77.8	284	274	1973	67.1	255	285	1974	77.8	284	274
Bill Foster	1923–1937	P	1996V												
Rube Foster	1902–1926	Mgr	1981V												
Nellie Fox	1947–1965	2B	1997V	1985	74.7	295	297	1971	10.8	39	270	1985	74.7	295	297
Jimmie Foxx	1925–1945	1B	1951	1951	79.2	179	170	1936	9.3	21	170	1951	79.2	179	170
Ford Frick	1934–1965	Exe	1970V												
Frankie Frisch	1919–1937	2B	1947	1947	84.5	136	121	1936	6.2	14	170	1947	84.5	136	121
Pud Galvin	1875–1892	P	1965V												
Lou Gehrig	1923–1939	1B	1939S	1936	22.6	51	170								
Charlie Gehringer	1924–1942	2B	1949	1949R	85.0	159	141	1936	0.4	1	170	1949R	85.0	159	141
Josh Gibson	1930–1946	C	1972N												
Bob Gibson	1959–1975	P	1981	1981	84.0	337	301								
Warren Giles	1946–1969	Exe	1979V												
Lefty Gomez	1930–1943	P	1972V	1956	46.1	89	145	1945	2.8	7	186	1962	12.5	20	120
Goose Goslin	1921–1938	LF	1968V	1956	13.5	26	145	1948	0.8	1	91	1962	8.8	14	120
Hank Greenberg	1930–1947	1B	1956	1956	85.0	164	145	1945	1.2	3	186	1956	85.0	164	145
Clark Griffith	1891–1907	Exe	1946O	1945	43.7	108	186	1937	2.0	4	151	1946	31.2	82	198
Burleigh Grimes	1916–1934	P	1964V	1960	34.2	92	202	1937	0.5	1	151	1962	26.9	43	120
Lefty Grove	1925–1941	P	1947	1947	76.4	123	121	1936	5.3	12	170	1947	76.4	123	121

MEMBER	CAREER	POS	ELECTED	MAX YR	PCT	VOTES	NEEDED	1ST YR	PCT	VOTES	NEEDED	LAST YR	PCT	VOTES	NEEDED
Chick Hafey	1924–1937	LF	1971V	1960	10.8	29	202	1948	0.8	1	91	1962	4.4	7	120
Jesse Haines	1918–1937	P	1970V	1958	8.3	22	200	1939	0.4	1	206	1962	1.9	3	120
Billy Hamilton	1888–1901	CF	1961V	1936V	2.6	2	59	1936V	2.6	2	59	1942	0.4	1	175
Ned Hanlon	1889–1907	Mgr	1996V												
Will Harridge	1931–1959	Exe	1972V												
Bucky Harris	1924–1956	Mgr	1975V	1958	16.9	45	200	1938	0.4	1	197	1960	11.5	31	202
Gabby Hartnett	1922–1941	C	1955	1955	77.7	195	189	1936	0.4	1	170	1955	77.7	195	189
Harry Heilmann	1914–1932	RF	1952	1952	86.8	203	176	1937	5.0	10	151	1952	86.8	203	176
Billy Herman	1931–1947	2B	1975V	1967	20.2	59	219	1948	0.8	1	91	1967R	4.6	14	230
Harry Hooper	1909–1925	RF	1971V	1937	3.0	6	151	1937	3.0	6	151	1951	1.3	3	170
Rogers Hornsby	1915–1937	2B	1942	1942	78.1	182	175	1936	46.5	105	170	1942	78.1	182	175
Waite Hoyt	1918–1938	P	1969V	1956	19.2	37	145	1939	0.4	1	206	1962	11.3	18	120
Cal Hubbard	1936–1951	Ump	1976V												
Carl Hubbell	1928–1943	P	1947	1947	87.0	140	121	1945	9.7	24	186	1947	87.0	140	121
Miller Huggins	1913–1929	Mgr	1964V	1946N	63.9	129	152	1937	2.5	5	151	1950	1.2	2	126
William Hulbert	1877–1882	Exe	1995V												
Catfish Hunter	1965–1979	P	1987	1987	76.3	315	310	1985	53.7	212	297	1987	76.3	315	310
Monte Irvin	1939–1956	LF	1973N												
Reggie Jackson	1967–1987	LF	1993	1993	93.6	396	318								
Travis Jackson	1922–1936	SS	1982V	1956	7.3	14	145	1948	4.1	5	91	1962	0.6	1	120
Fergie Jenkins	1965–1983	P	1991	1991	75.4	334	333	1989	52.3	234	336	1991	75.4	334	333
Hughie Jennings	1891–1903	SS	1945O	1945	37.2	92	186	1936V	14.1	11	59	1945	37.2	92	186
Ban Johnson	1901–1927	Exe	1937C												
Judy Johnson	1921–1938	3B	1975N												
Walter Johnson	1907–1927	P	1936	1936	83.6	189	170								
Addie Joss	1902–1910	P	1978V	1942	14.2	33	175	1937	5.5	11	151	1960	0.4	1	202
Al Kaline	1953–1974	RF	1980	1980	88.3	340	289								
Tim Keefe	1880–1893	P	1964V	1936V	0.4	1	59								
Willie Keeler	1892–1910	RF	1939	1939	75.5	207	206	1936V	42.3	33	59	1939	75.5	207	206
George Kell	1943–1957	3B	1983V	1977	36.8	141	288	1964	16.4	33	151	1977	36.8	141	288
Joe Kelley	1891–1908	LF	1971V	1942	0.4	1	175	1939	0.4	1	206	1942	0.4	1	175
George Kelly	1915–1932	1B	1973V	1960	1.9	5	202	1947	0.6	1	121	1962	0.6	1	120
King Kelly	1878–1893	C	1945O	1936V	19.2	15	59								
Harmon Killebrew	1954–1975	1B	1984	1984	83.1	335	303	1981	59.6	239	301	1984	83.1	335	303
Ralph Kiner	1946–1955	LF	1975	1975	75.4	273	272	1962	3.1	5	120	1975	75.4	273	272
Chuck Klein	1928–1944	RF	1980V	1964	27.9	56	151	1948	2.5	3	91	1964R	8.0	18	170
Bill Klem	1905–1941	Ump	1953V												
Sandy Koufax	1955–1966	P	1972	1972	86.9	344	297								
Nap Lajoie	1896–1916	2B	1937	1937	83.6	168	151	1936V	2.6	2	59	1937	83.6	168	151
Judge Landis	1920–1944	Exe	1944O												
Tom Lasorda	1976–1996	Mgr	1997V												
Tony Lazzeri	1926–1939	2B	1991V	1956	33.2	64	145	1945	0.4	1	186	1962	5.0	8	120
Bob Lemon	1941–1958	P	1976	1976	78.6	305	291	1964	11.9	24	151	1976	78.6	305	291
Buck Leonard	1933–1950	1B	1972N												
Freddie Lindstrom	1924–1936	3B	1976V	1962	4.4	7	120	1949	0.7	1	115	1962	4.4	7	120
John Henry Lloyd	1905–1931	SS	1977N												
Ernie Lombardi	1931–1947	C	1986V	1964	16.4	33	151	1950	1.8	3	126	1967R	8.2	25	230
Al Lopez	1928–1947	Mgr	1977V	1967	39.0	114	219	1949	0.7	1	115	1967R	16.3	50	230
Ted Lyons	1923–1946	P	1955	1955	86.5	217	189	1945	1.6	4	186	1955	86.5	217	189
Connie Mack	1894–1950	Mgr	1937C	1936	0.4	1	170								
Larry MacPhail	1934–1947	Exe	1978V												
Lee MacPhail	1941–1985	Exe	1998V												
Mickey Mantle	1951–1968	CF	1974	1974	88.2	322	274								
Heinie Manush	1923–1939	LF	1964V	1962	9.4	15	120	1948	0.8	1	91	1962	9.4	15	120
Rabbit Maranville	1912–1935	SS	1954	1954	82.9	209	189	1937	12.4	25	151	1954	82.9	209	189
Juan Marichal	1960–1975	P	1983	1983	83.7	313	281	1981	58.1	233	301	1983	83.7	313	281
Rube Marquard	1908–1925	P	1971V	1955	13.9	35	189	1936	0.4	1	170	1955	13.9	35	189
Eddie Mathews	1952–1968	3B	1978	1978	79.4	301	285	1974	32.3	118	274	1978	79.4	301	285
Christy Mathewson	1900–1916	P	1936	1936	90.7	205	170								
Willie Mays	1951–1973	CF	1979	1979	94.7	409	324								
Bill Mazeroski	1956–1972	2B	2001V	1992	42.3	182	323	1978	6.1	23	285	1992	42.3	182	323
Joe McCarthy	1926–1950	Mgr	1957V	1947	1.2	2	121	1939	1.1	3	206	1958	0.8	2	200
Tommy McCarthy	1884–1896	RF	1946O	1936V	1.3	1	59								
Willie McCovey	1959–1980	1B	1986	1986	81.4	346	319								
Joe McGinnity	1899–1908	P	1946O	1946N	26.2	53	152	1937	6.0	12	151	1946	17.9	47	198
Bill McGowan	1925–1954	Ump	1992V												
John McGraw	1891–1906	Mgr	1937C	1936V	21.8	17	59	1936V	21.8	17	59	1937	17.4	35	151
Bill McKechnie	1922–1946	Mgr	1962V	1951	3.5	8	170	1945	0.8	2	186	1951	3.5	8	170
Bid McPhee	1882–1899	2B	2000V												
Joe Medwick	1932–1948	LF	1968	1968	84.8	240	213	1948	0.8	1	91	1968	84.8	240	213
Johnny Mize	1936–1953	1B	1981V	1971	43.6	157	270	1960	16.7	45	202	1973	41.3	157	285
Paul Molitor	1978–1998	DH	2004	2004	85.2	431	380								
Joe Morgan	1963–1984	2B	1990	1990	81.8	363	333								
Eddie Murray	1977–1997	1B	2003	2003	85.3	423	372								
Stan Musial	1941–1963	LF	1969	1969	93.2	317	255								
Hal Newhouser	1939–1955	P	1992V	1975	42.8	155	272	1962	2.5	4	120	1975	42.8	155	272
Kid Nichols	1890–1906	P	1949O	1936V	3.8	3	59	1936V	3.8	3	59	1946N	0.5	1	152
Phil Niekro	1964–1987	P	1997	1997	80.3	380	355	1993	65.7	278	318	1997	80.3	380	355
Jim O'Rourke	1872–1893	LF	1945O												
Mel Ott	1926–1947	RF	1951	1951	87.2	197	170	1949	61.4	94	115	1951	87.2	197	170
Satchel Paige	1927–1953	P	1971N	1951	0.4	1	170								
Jim Palmer	1965–1984	P	1990	1990	92.6	411	333								
Herb Pennock	1912–1934	P	1948	1948	77.7	94	91	1937	7.5	15	151	1948	77.7	94	91
Tony Perez	1964–1986	1B	2000	2000	77.2	385	375	1992	50.0	215	323	2000	77.2	385	375
Gaylord Perry	1962–1983	P	1991	1991	77.2	342	333	1989	68.0	304	336	1991	77.2	342	333
Eddie Plank	1901–1917	P	1946O	1942	27.0	63	175	1937	11.4	23	151	1946N	16.8	34	152
Kirby Puckett	1984–1995	CF	2001	2001	82.1	423	387								
Charley Radbourn	1880–1891	P	1939O	1936V	20.5	16	59								
Pee Wee Reese	1940–1958	SS	1984V	1976	47.9	186	291	1964	36.3	73	151	1978	44.6	169	285
Sam Rice	1915–1934	RF	1963V	1960	53.2	143	202	1938	0.4	1	197	1962	50.6	81	120
Branch Rickey	1913–1965	Exe	1967V	1942	1.3	3	175	1942	1.3	3	175	1945	0.8	2	186
Eppa Rixey	1912–1933	P	1963V	1960	52.8	142	202	1937	0.5	1	151	1962	30.6	49	120
Phil Rizzuto	1941–1956	SS	1994V	1976	38.4	149	291	1956	0.5	1	145	1976	38.4	149	291
Robin Roberts	1948–1966	P	1976	1976	86.9	337	291	1973	56.1	213	285	1976	86.9	337	291
Brooks Robinson	1955–1977	3B	1983	1983	92.0	344	281								
Frank Robinson	1956–1976	RF	1982	1982	89.2	370	312								
Jackie Robinson	1947–1956	2B	1962	1962	77.5	124	120								
Wilbert Robinson	1886–1902	Mgr	1945O	1942	38.2	89	175	1936V	7.7	6	59	1945	32.8	81	186
Bullet Joe Rogan	1920–1938	P	1998V												
Edd Roush	1913–1931	CF	1962V	1960	54.3	146	202	1936	0.9	2	170	1960	54.3	146	202
Red Ruffing	1924–1947	P	1967	1967R	86.9	266	230	1948	3.3	4	91	1967R	86.9	266	230
Amos Rusie	1889–1901	P	1977V	1936V	15.4	12	59	1936V	15.4	12	59	1945	0.4	1	186
Babe Ruth	1914–1935	RF	1936	1936	95.1	215	170								
Nolan Ryan	1966–1993	P	1999	1999	98.8	491	373								

MEMBER	CAREER	POS	ELECTED	MAX YR	PCT	VOTES	NEEDED	1ST YR	PCT	VOTES	NEEDED	LAST YR	PCT	VOTES	NEEDED
Ryne Sandberg	1981–1997	2B	2005	2005	76.2	393	387	2003	49.2	244	372	2005	76.2	393	387
Ray Schalk	1912–1929	C	1955V	1955	45.0	113	189	1936	1.8	4	170	1955	45.0	113	189
Mike Schmidt	1972–1989	3B	1995	1995	96.5	444	345								
Red Schoendienst	1945–1963	2B	1989V	1980	42.6	164	289	1969	19.1	65	255	1983	39.0	146	281
Tom Seaver	1967–1986	P	1992	1992	98.8	425	323								
Frank Selee	1890–1905	Mgr	1999V												
Joe Sewell	1920–1933	SS	1977V	1960	8.6	23	202	1937	0.5	1	151	1960	8.6	23	202
Al Simmons	1924–1944	LF	1953	1953	75.4	199	198	1936	1.8	4	170	1953	75.4	199	198
George Sisler	1915–1930	1B	1939	1939	85.8	235	206	1936	34.1	77	170	1939	85.8	235	206
Enos Slaughter	1938–1959	RF	1985V	1978	68.9	261	285	1966	33.1	100	227	1979	68.8	297	324
Hilton Smith	1933–1948	P	2001V												
Ozzie Smith	1978–1996	SS	2002	2002	91.7	433	354								
Duke Snider	1947–1964	CF	1980	1980	86.5	333	289	1970	17.0	51	225	1980	86.5	333	289
Warren Spahn	1942–1965	P	1973	1973	83.2	316	285								
Al Spalding	1871–1878	Pio	1939O	1936V	5.1	4	59								
Tris Speaker	1907–1928	CF	1937	1937	82.1	165	151	1936	58.8	133	170	1937	82.1	165	151
Willie Stargell	1962–1982	LF	1988	1988	82.4	352	321								
Turkey Stearnes	1923–1940	CF	2000V												
Casey Stengel	1934–1965	Mgr	1966V	1953	23.1	61	198	1938	0.8	2	197	1953	23.1	61	198
Bruce Sutter	1976–1988	P	2006	2006	76.9	400	390	1994	24.0	109	342	2006	76.9	400	390
Don Sutton	1966–1988	P	1998	1998	81.6	386	355	1994	56.9	259	342	1998	81.6	386	355
Bill Terry	1923–1936	1B	1954	1954	77.4	195	189	1936	4.0	9	170	1954	77.4	195	189
Sam Thompson	1885–1898	RF	1974V												
Joe Tinker	1902–1916	SS	1946O	1946N	27.2	55	152	1937	7.5	15	151	1946	17.1	45	198
Pie Traynor	1920–1937	3B	1948	1948	76.9	93	91	1936	7.1	16	170	1948	76.9	93	91
Dazzy Vance	1915–1935	P	1955	1955	81.7	205	189	1936	0.4	1	170	1955	81.7	205	189
Arky Vaughan	1932–1948	SS	1985V	1968	29.0	82	213	1953	0.4	1	198	1968	29.0	82	213
Bill Veeck	1933–1980	Exe	1991V												
Rube Waddell	1897–1910	P	1946O	1939	65.3	179	206	1936	14.6	33	170	1946	33.1	87	198
Honus Wagner	1897–1917	SS	1936	1936	95.1	215	170	1936V	6.4	5	59	1936	95.1	215	170
Bobby Wallace	1894–1918	SS	1953V	1938	2.7	7	197	1936V	1.3	1	59	1945	1.2	3	186
Ed Walsh	1904–1917	P	1946O	1946N	56.9	115	152	1936	8.8	20	170	1946	40.3	106	198
Lloyd Waner	1927–1945	CF	1967V	1964	23.4	47	151	1949	2.0	3	115	1964R	5.3	12	170
Paul Waner	1926–1945	RF	1952	1952	83.3	195	176	1946N	2.0	4	152	1952	83.3	195	176
John Ward	1878–1894	SS	1964V	1936V	3.8	3	59								
Earl Weaver	1968–1986	Mgr	1996V												
George Weiss	1932–1971	Exe	1971V												
Mickey Welch	1880–1892	P	1973V												
Willie Wells	1924–1948	SS	1997V												
Zack Wheat	1909–1927	LF	1959V	1947	23.0	37	121	1937	2.5	5	151	1956	13.5	26	145
Hoyt Wilhelm	1952–1972	P	1985	1985	83.8	331	297	1978	41.7	158	285	1985	83.8	331	297
Billy Williams	1959–1976	LF	1987	1987	85.7	354	310	1982	23.4	97	312	1987	85.7	354	310
Joe Williams	1910–1932	P	1999V												
Ted Williams	1939–1960	LF	1966	1966	93.4	282	227								
Vic Willis	1898–1910	P	1995V												
Hack Wilson	1923–1934	CF	1979V	1956	38.3	74	145	1937	0.5	1	151	1962	24.4	39	120
Dave Winfield	1973–1995	RF	2001	2001	84.5	435	387								
George Wright	1871–1882	Pio	1937C	1936V	7.7	6	59								
Harry Wright	1871–1893	Pio	1953V												
Early Wynn	1939–1963	P	1972	1972	76.0	301	297	1969	27.9	95	255	1972	76.0	301	297
Tom Yawkey	1933–1976	Exe	1980V												
Carl Yastrzemski	1961–1983	LF	1989	1989	94.6	423	336								
Cy Young	1890–1911	P	1937	1937	76.1	153	151	1936V	41.0	32	59	1937	76.1	153	151
Ross Youngs	1917–1926	RF	1972V	1947	22.4	36	121	1936	4.4	10	170	1956	9.8	19	145
Robin Yount	1974–1993	SS	1999	1999	77.5	385	373								

NON-HALL OF FAMERS WHO HAVE RECEIVED VOTES

Through 2005 election; does not include 2006 Hall of Fame election results.

CANDIDATE	CAREER	POS	MAX YR (PCT)	1ST YR (PCT)	LAST YR (PCT)	CANDIDATE	CAREER	POS	MAX YR (PCT)	1ST YR (PCT)	LAST YR (PCT)
Jim Abbott	1989–1999	P	2005 (2.5)			Vida Blue	1969–1986	P	1993 (8.7)	1992 (5.3)	1995 (5.7)
Babe Adams	1906–1926	P	1947 (13.7)	1937 (4.0)	1955 (9.6)	Ossie Bluege	1922–1939	3B	1948 (1.7)	1948 (1.7)	1960 (1.1)
Sparky Adams	1922–1934	2B	1958 (0.4)	1958 (0.4)	1960 (0.4)	Bert Blyleven	1970–1992	P	2005 (40.9)	1998 (17.5)	2005 (40.9)
Bobby Adams	1946–1959	2B	1966 (0.3)			Ping Bodie	1911–1921	CF	1937 (1.0)	1937 (1.0)	1949 (0.7)
Dick Allen	1963–1977	1B	1996 (18.9)	1983 (3.7)	1997 (16.7)	Joe Boley	1927–1932	SS	1942 (0.4)		
Johnny Allen	1932–1944	P	1955 (0.4)			Tommy Bond	1874–1884	P	1936V (1.3)		
Doug Allison	1871–1883	C	1936V (1.3)			Bobby Bonds	1968–1981	RF	1993 (10.6)	1987 (5.8)	1997 (4.2)
Felipe Alou	1958–1974	RF	1980 (0.8)			Bob Boone	1972–1990	C	1996 (7.7)	1996 (7.7)	2000 (4.2)
Jesus Alou	1963–1979	LF	1985 (0.3)			Jim Bouton	1962–1970	P	1984 (0.7)		
Matty Alou	1960–1974	CF	1980 (1.3)			Larry Bowa	1970–1985	SS	1991 (2.5)		
Nick Altrock	1898–1909	P	1958 (7.5)	1937 (1.5)	1960 (6.7)	Clete Boyer	1955–1971	3B	1979 (0.7)	1978 (0.3)	1979 (0.7)
Jimmy Archer	1904–1918	C	1937 (3.0)	1937 (3.0)	1939 (1.1)	Ken Boyer	1955–1969	3B	1988 (25.5)	1975 (2.5)	1994 (11.9)
Jimmy Austin	1909–1922	3B	1958 (0.4)			Bill Bradley	1899–1915	3B	1937 (2.5)	1936 (0.4)	1946N (0.5)
Bob Bailey	1962–1978	3B	1984 (0.2)			Harry Brecheen	1940–1953	P	1960 (2.6)	1960 (2.6)	1973 (0.8)
Dusty Baker	1968–1986	LF	1992 (0.9)			Ted Breitenstein	1891–1901	P	1937 (0.5)		
Sal Bando	1966–1981	3B	1987 (0.7)			Jim Brewer	1960–1976	P	1982 (0.5)		
Ross Barnes	1871–1881	2B	1936V (3.8)			Tommy Bridges	1930–1946	P	1964 (7.5)	1956 (1.6)	1966 (5.3)
Jack Barry	1908–1919	SS	1938 (1.1)	1938 (1.1)	1939 (0.4)	Gates Brown	1963–1975	LF	1981 (0.2)		
Dick Bartell	1927–1946	SS	1948 (0.8)	1948 (0.8)	1960 (0.4)	Tom Browning	1984–1995	P	2001 (0.2)		
Joe Battin	1871–1890	3B	1936V (1.3)			Bill Bruton	1953–1964	CF	1971 (0.3)		
Don Baylor	1970–1988	DH	1994 (2.6)	1994 (2.6)	1995 (2.6)	Bill Buckner	1969–1990	1B	1996 (2.1)		
Hank Bauer	1948–1961	RF	1967 (7.9)	1967 (7.9)	1967R (2.9)	Lew Burdette	1950–1967	P	1984 (24.1)	1973 (3.2)	1987 (23.2)
Ginger Beaumont	1899–1910	CF	1946N (0.5)	1938 (0.4)	1946N (0.5)	Smoky Burgess	1949–1967	C	1974 (0.5)	1973 (0.3)	1974 (0.5)
Glenn Beckert	1965–1975	2B	1981 (0.2)			George J. Burns	1911–1925	LF	1937 (1.5)	1937 (1.5)	1950 (1.2)
Steve Bedrosian	1981–1995	P	2001 (0.2)			Jeff Burroughs	1970–1985	RF	1991 (0.2)		
Mark Belanger	1965–1982	SS	1988 (3.7)			Guy Bush	1923–1945	P	1956 (1.0)		
Buddy Bell	1972–1989	3B	1995 (1.7)			Joe Bush	1912–1928	P	1958 (1.9)		
George Bell	1981–1993	LF	1999 (1.2)			Donie Bush	1908–1923	SS	1946N (1.0)	1937 (0.5)	1953 (0.4)
Charlie Bennett	1878–1893	C	1936V (3.8)			Brett Butler	1981–1997	CF	2003 (0.4)		
Larry Benton	1923–1935	P	1958 (0.4)			Leon Cadore	1915–1924	P	1948 (0.8)		
Moe Berg	1923–1939	C	1960 (1.9)	1958 (1.1)	1960 (1.9)	Johnny Callison	1958–1973	RF	1979 (0.2)		
Marty Bergen	1896–1899	C	1937 (1.0)	1937 (1.0)	1939 (0.4)	Dolf Camilli	1933–1945	1B	1958 (1.5)	1948 (0.8)	1960 (1.1)
Wally Berger	1930–1940	CF	1958 (0.8)	1956 (0.5)	1958 (0.8)	Howie Camnitz	1904–1915	P	1945 (0.4)		
Charlie Berry	1925–1938	C	1958 (1.1)	1955 (0.4)	1958 (1.1)	Bert Campaneris	1964–1983	SS	1989 (3.1)		
Jim Bibby	1972–1984	P	1990 (0.2)			Bill Campbell	1973–1987	P	1993 (0.2)		
Carson Bigbee	1916–1926	LF	1948 (0.8)			John Candelaria	1975–1993	P	1999 (0.2)		
Jack Billingham	1968–1980	P	1986 (0.2)			Tom Candiotti	1983–1999	P	2005 (0.4)		
Max Bishop	1924–1935	2B	1960 (1.9)	1955 (0.4)	1960 (1.9)	Jose Cardenal	1963–1980	CF	1986 (0.2)		
Ewell Blackwell	1942–1955	P	1970 (4.7)	1968 (1.8)	1970 (4.7)	Leo Cardenas	1960–1975	SS	1981 (0.2)	1981 (0.2)	1982 (0.2)
Ray Blades	1922–1932	LF	1958 (0.4)	1958 (0.4)	1960 (0.4)	Chico Carrasquel	1950–1959	SS	1966 (0.3)		
Paul Blair	1964–1980	CF	1986 (1.9)			Bill Carrigan	1913–1929	Mgr	1937 (2.5)	1937 (2.5)	1945 (1.2)
Steve Blass	1964–1974	P	1980 (0.5)			Clay Carroll	1964–1978	P	1984 (0.2)		
Lu Blue	1921–1933	1B	1954 (0.4)			Joe Carter	1983–1998	LF	2004 (3.8)		

CANDIDATE	CAREER	POS	MAX YR (PCT)	1ST YR (PCT)	LAST YR (PCT)
Rico Carty	1963–1979	LF	1985 (0.3)		
George Case	1937–1947	LF	1964 (1.0)	1958 (0.4)	1964 (1.0)
Dave Cash	1969–1980	2B	1986 (0.5)		
Norm Cash	1958–1974	1B	1980 (1.6)		
Phil Cavaretta	1934–1955	1B	1975 (35.6)	1962 (1.3)	1975 (35.6)
Cesar Cedeno	1970–1986	CF	1992 (0.5)		
Ron Cey	1971–1987	3B	1993 (1.9)		
Spud Chandler	1937–1947	P	1964 (3.0)	1950 (1.2)	1964 (3.0)
Ben Chapman	1930–1946	CF	1949 (0.7)	1949 (0.7)	1952 (0.4)
Ray Chapman	1912–1920	SS	1938 (0.4)		
Sam Chapman	1938–1951	CF	1958 (0.4)		
Hal Chase	1905–1919	1B	1937 (9.0)	1936 (4.9)	1937 (9.0)
Bill Cissell	1938–1938	2B	1937 (0.5)		
Jack Clark	1975–1992	RF	1998 (1.5)		
Watty Clark	1924–1937	P	1958 (0.4)		
Andy Coakley	1902–1911	P	1938 (0.4)		
Rocky Colavito	1955–1968	RF	1974 (0.5)	1974 (0.5)	1975 (0.3)
Vince Coleman	1985–1997	LF	2003 (0.6)		
Shano Collins	1910–1925	RF	1937 (0.5)		
Dave Concepcion	1970–1988	SS	1998 (16.9)	1994 (6.8)	2005 (10.7)
Wid Conroy	1901–1911	3B	1945 (0.4)		
Jack Coombs	1906–1920	P	1948 (1.7)	1937 (1.0)	1951 (0.4)
Mort Cooper	1938–1949	P	1958 (1.1)	1956 (1.0)	1969 (0.9)
Walker Cooper	1940–1957	C	1976 (14.4)	1968 (2.8)	1977 (11.7)
Wilbur Cooper	1912–1926	P	1955 (4.4)	1938 (0.4)	1955 (4.4)
Clint Courtney	1951–1961	C	1967 (0.3)		
Billy Cox	1941–1955	3B	1962 (0.6)		
Doc Cramer	1929–1948	CF	1964 (6.0)	1956 (2.1)	1964 (6.0)
Del Crandall	1949–1966	C	1976 (3.9)	1976 (3.9)	1979 (2.1)
Doc Crandall	1908–1918	P	1938 (0.4)		
Gavvy Cravath	1908–1920	Exe	1947 (1.2)	1937 (1.0)	1947 (1.2)
Lou Criger	1896–1912	C	1937 (8.0)	1936V (1.3)	1946N (3.0)
Hughie Critz	1924–1935	2B	1956 (1.0)		
Frank Crosetti	1932–1948	SS	1968 (5.3)	1950 (0.6)	1968 (5.3)
Lave Cross	1887–1907	3B	1942 (0.4)	1939 (0.4)	1942 (0.4)
Al Crowder	1926–1936	P	1958 (0.4)	1958 (0.4)	1960 (0.4)
Walt Cruise	1914–1924	LF	1938 (0.4)		
Jose Cruz	1970–1988	LF	1994 (0.4)		
Tony Cuccinello	1930–1945	2B	1958 (1.1)	1956 (0.5)	1958 (1.1)
Bill Dahlen	1891–1911	SS	1936V (1.3)	1936V (1.3)	1938 (0.4)
Harry Danning	1933–1942	C	1958 (0.4)	1958 (0.4)	1960 (0.4)
Alvin Dark	1946–1960	SS	1979 (18.5)	1966 (5.6)	1980 (11.2)
Ron Darling	1983–1995	P	2001 (0.2)		
Jake Daubert	1910–1924	1B	1937 (1.0)	1936 (0.4)	1955 (0.4)
Darren Daulton	1983–1997	C	2003 (0.2)		
Chili Davis	1981–1999	CF	2005 (0.6)		
Curt Davis	1934–1946	P	1958 (0.4)		
Harry Davis	1895–1917	1B	1946N (1.0)	1945 (0.4)	1946N (1.0)
Mark Davis	1980–1997	P	2003 (0.2)		
Tommy Davis	1959–1976	LF	1982 (1.2)		
Spud Davis	1928–1945	C	1948 (0.8)	1948 (0.8)	1949 (0.7)
Andre Dawson	1976–1996	RF	2005 (52.3)	2002 (45.3)	2005 (52.3)
Doug DeCinces	1973–1987	3B	1993 (0.5)		
Rick Dempsey	1969–1992	C	1998 (0.2)		
Jerry Denny	1881–1894	3B	1936V (7.7)		
Bucky Dent	1973–1984	SS	1990 (0.7)		
Paul Derringer	1931–1945	P	1956 (6.2)	1948 (0.8)	1960 (3.0)
Jim Deshaies	1984–1995	P	2001 (0.2)		
Dom DiMaggio	1940–1953	CF	1973 (11.3)	1960 (1.5)	1973 (11.3)
Bill Dinneen	1898–1909	P	1939 (2.6)	1938 (1.5)	1946N (0.5)
Bill Doak	1912–1929	P	1958 (1.1)		
Mike Donlin	1899–1914	RF	1937 (3.0)	1937 (3.0)	1945 (0.4)
Bill Donovan	1898–1918	P	1946N (2.0)	1937 (1.5)	1946N (2.0)
Red Dooin	1902–1916	C	1937 (0.5)	1937 (0.5)	1938 (0.4)
Brian Downing	1973–1992	LF	1998 (0.4)		
Jack Doyle	1889–1905	1B	1936V (1.3)		
Larry Doyle	1907–1920	2B	1938 (1.5)	1937 (1.0)	1939 (0.4)
Doug Drabek	1986–1998	P	2004 (0.4)		
Walt Dropo	1949–1961	1B	1967 (0.3)		
Joe Dugan	1917–1931	3B	1960 (3.0)	1937 (0.5)	1960 (3.0)
Fred Dunlap	1880–1891	2B	1936V (2.6)		
Jack Dunn	1907–1928	Exe	1946N (0.5)	1942 (0.4)	1946N (0.5)
Eddie Dyer	1946–1950	Mgr	1947 (0.6)		
Jimmy Dykes	1918–1939	3B	1960 (10.0)	1948 (4.1)	1962 (3.8)
Lenny Dykstra	1985–1996	CF	2002 (0.2)		
George Earnshaw	1928–1936	P	1948 (2.5)	1948 (2.5)	1956 (1.6)
Hank Edwards	1941–1953	RF	1960 (0.7)		
Howard Ehmke	1915–1930	P	1960 (4.5)	1938 (0.4)	1960 (4.5)
Jim Eisenreich	1982–1998	RF	2004 (0.6)		
Kid Elberfeld	1898–1914	SS	1945 (0.8)	1936 (0.4)	1945 (0.8)
Jumbo Elliott	1923–1934	P	1958 (0.4)		
Bob Elliott	1939–1953	3B	1964 (2.0)	1960 (0.7)	1964 (2.0)
Dock Ellis	1968–1979	P	1985 (0.3)		
Del Ennis	1946–1959	RF	1966 (1.0)	1966 (1.0)	1967 (0.7)
Jewel Ens	1929–1931	Mgr	1950 (0.6)		
Carl Erskine	1948–1959	P	1968 (3.2)	1966 (2.0)	1974 (3.0)
Darrell Evans	1969–1989	3B	1995 (1.7)		
Dwight Evans	1972–1991	RF	1998 (10.4)	1997 (5.9)	1999 (3.6)
Elroy Face	1953–1969	P	1987 (18.9)	1976 (5.9)	1990 (11.3)
Ron Fairly	1959–1978	1B	1985 (0.8)		
Cy Falkenberg	1903–1917	P	1937 (0.5)		
Sid Fernandez	1983–1997	P	2003 (0.4)		
Wes Ferrell	1927–1941	P	1956 (3.6)	1948 (0.8)	1962 (0.6)
Cecil Fielder	1985–1998	1B	2004 (0.2)		
Fred Fitzsimmons	1925–1943	P	1958 (6.0)	1948 (1.7)	1962 (0.6)
Mike Flanagan	1975–1992	P	1998 (0.4)		
Art Fletcher	1909–1922	SS	1948 (2.5)	1937 (1.0)	1951 (1.8)
Curt Flood	1956–1971	CF	1996 (15.1)	1977 (4.2)	1996 (15.1)
Lew Fonseca	1921–1933	1B	1950 (1.2)	1948 (1.2)	1960 (1.1)
Bob Forsch	1974–1989	P	1995 (0.4)		
Eddie Foster	1910–1923	2B	1938 (0.8)		
George Foster	1969–1986	LF	1993 (6.9)	1992 (5.6)	1995 (4.1)
Chick Fraser	1896–1909	P	1939 (0.4)		
Bill Freehan	1961–1976	C	1982 (0.5)		
Jim Fregosi	1961–1978	SS	1984 (1.0)		
Carl Furillo	1946–1960	RF	1971 (1.4)	1966 (0.7)	1972 (0.5)
Augie Galan	1934–1949	LF	1970 (1.0)	1968 (0.7)	1970 (1.0)
Phil Garner	1973–1988	2B	1994 (0.4)		
Ned Garver	1948–1961	P	1967 (0.3)		
Steve Garvey	1969–1987	1B	1995 (42.6)	1993 (41.6)	2005 (20.5)
Charlie Gelbert	1929–1940	SS	1949 (1.3)	1947 (0.6)	1951 (0.4)
Kirk Gibson	1979–1995	LF	2001 (2.5)		
Dave Giusti	1962–1977	P	1983 (0.3)		
Jack Glasscock	1879–1895	SS	1936V (2.6)		
Kid Gleason	1888–1912	2B	1937 (0.5)	1937 (0.5)	1945 (0.4)
Mike Gonzales	1912–1932	C	1958 (1.1)	1950 (0.6)	1960 (0.7)
Joe Gordon	1938–1950	2B	1969 (28.5)	1945 (0.4)	1970 (26.3)
Rich Gossage	1972–1994	P	2005 (55.2)	2000 (33.3)	2005 (55.2)
Hank Gowdy	1910–1930	C	1955 (35.9)	1937 (1.0)	1960 (14.1)
Eddie Grant	1905–1915	2B	1942 (1.3)	1938 (0.4)	1946N (0.5)
George Grantham	1922–1934	2B	1958 (0.4)		
Mike Greenwell	1985–1996	LF	2002 (0.4)		
Bobby Grich	1970–1986	2B	1992 (2.6)		
Ken Griffey Sr.	1973–1991	RF	1997 (4.7)		
Charlie Grimm	1916–1936	1B	1958 (9.8)	1939 (0.4)	1962 (1.3)
Marv Grissom	1946–1959	P	1966 (0.7)		
Dick Groat	1952–1967	SS	1973 (1.8)	1973 (1.8)	1978 (0.8)
Heinie Groh	1912–1927	3B	1955 (2.0)	1937 (0.5)	1960 (0.4)
Steve Gromek	1941–1957	P	1964 (0.5)		
Orval Grove	1940–1949	P	1960 (2.6)	1958 (1.9)	1960 (2.6)
Pedro Guerrero	1978–1992	LF	1998 (1.3)		
Ron Guidry	1975–1988	P	2000 (8.8)	1994 (5.3)	2002 (4.9)
Bill Gullickson	1979–1994	P	2000 (0.2)		
Frank Gustine	1939–1950	3B	1958 (1.1)		
Mule Haas	1925–1938	CF	1956 (0.5)	1955 (0.4)	1960 (0.4)
Stan Hack	1932–1947	3B	1950 (4.8)	1948 (1.7)	1960 (2.2)
Harvey Haddix	1952–1965	P	1985 (3.8)	1971 (2.8)	1985 (3.8)
Noodles Hahn	1899–1906	P	1939 (0.4)		
Bill Hallahan	1925–1938	P	1948 (0.8)	1948 (0.8)	1960 (0.7)
Mel Harder	1928–1947	P	1964 (25.4)	1949 (2.6)	1967R (4.6)
Bubbles Hargrave	1913–1930	C	1947 (0.6)	1947 (0.6)	1960 (0.4)
Mike Hargrove	1974–1985	1B	1991 (0.2)		
Toby Harrah	1969–1986	3B	1992 (0.2)		
Bud Harrelson	1965–1980	SS	1986 (0.2)		
Grady Hatton	1946–1960	3B	1966 (1.3)	1966 (1.3)	1967 (0.3)
Jim Hearn	1947–1959	P	1967 (0.3)	1966 (0.3)	1967 (0.3)
Richie Hebner	1968–1985	3B	1991 (0.2)		
Jim Hegan	1941–1960	C	1966 (1.7)	1966 (1.7)	1967 (0.7)
Tommy Helms	1964–1977	2B	1983 (0.3)		
Solly Hemus	1949–1959	SS	1966 (0.3)		
Dave Henderson	1981–1994	CF	2000 (0.4)		
Tom Henke	1982–1995	P	2001 (1.2)		
Tommy Henrich	1937–1950	RF	1970 (20.7)	1952 (1.7)	1970 (20.7)
Babe Herman	1926–1937	RF	1956 (5.7)	1942 (0.4)	1960 (2.6)
Keith Hernandez	1974–1990	1B	1998 (10.8)	1996 (5.1)	2004 (4.3)
Willie Hernandez	1977–1989	P	1995 (0.4)		
Buck Herzog	1908–1920	2B	1938 (0.4)		
Jim Hickman	1962–1974	CF	1980 (0.3)		
Mike Higgins	1930–1946	3B	1958 (2.3)	1950 (1.2)	1960 (1.1)
John Hiller	1965–1980	P	1986 (2.6)		
Bill Hinchman	1905–1920	RF	1937 (0.5)		
Gil Hodges	1943–1963	1B	1983 (63.4)	1969 (24.1)	1983 (63.4)
Tommy Holmes	1942–1952	RF	1958 (0.8)	1958 (0.8)	1960 (0.7)
Ken Holtzman	1965–1979	P	1986 (1.2)	1985 (1.0)	1986 (1.2)
Rick Honeycutt	1977–1997	P	2003 (0.4)		
Burt Hooton	1971–1985	P	1991 (0.2)		
Willie Horton	1963–1980	LF	1986 (0.9)		
Charlie Hough	1970–1994	P	2000 (0.8)		
Art Houtteman	1945–1957	P	1964 (1.0)		
Elston Howard	1955–1968	C	1981 (20.7)	1974 (5.2)	1988 (12.4)
Frank Howard	1958–1973	LF	1979 (1.4)		
Al Hrabosky	1970–1982	P	1988 (0.2)		
Kent Hrbek	1981–1994	1B	2000 (1.0)		
Bruce Hurst	1980–1994	P	2000 (0.2)		
Fred Hutchinson	1939–1953	P	1964 (5.0)	1962 (0.6)	1964 (5.0)
Charlie Irwin	1893–1902	3B	1938 (0.4)	1938 (0.4)	1939 (0.4)
Joe Jackson	1908–1920	LF	1946N (1.0)	1936 (0.9)	1946N (1.0)
Sonny Jackson	1963–1974	SS	1980 (0.3)		
Jackie Jensen	1950–1961	RF	1968 (1.1)	1967 (1.0)	1972 (0.3)
Tommy John	1963–1989	P	2001 (28.3)	1995 (21.3)	2005 (23.8)
Bob Johnson	1933–1945	LF	1948 (0.8)	1948 (0.8)	1956 (0.5)
Dave Johnson	1965–1978	2B	1984 (0.7)		
Fielder Jones	1896–1908	CF	1946N (0.5)		
Sam P. Jones	1914–1935	P	1956 (0.5)	1939 (0.4)	1956 (0.5)
Tim Jordan	1901–1910	1B	1951 (0.4)		
Mike Jorgensen	1968–1985	1B	1991 (0.2)		
Joe Judge	1915–1934	1B	1960 (5.6)	1937 (0.5)	1960 (5.6)
Billy Jurges	1931–1947	SS	1949 (1.3)	1949 (1.3)	1958 (0.4)
Jim Kaat	1959–1983	P	1993 (29.6)	1989 (19.5)	2003 (26.2)
Willie Kamm	1923–1935	3B	1958 (1.1)	1958 (1.1)	1960 (1.0)
Charlie Keller	1939–1952	LF	1972 (6.1)	1953 (0.4)	1972 (6.1)
Ken Keltner	1937–1955	3B	1958 (0.4)	1958 (0.4)	1960 (0.4)
Terry Kennedy	1978–1991	C	1997 (0.2)		
Dickie Kerr	1919–1925	P	1955 (10.0)	1937 (0.5)	1955 (10.0)
Don Kessinger	1964–1979	SS	1985 (0.5)		
Jimmy Key	1984–1998	P	2004 (0.6)		
Daryl Kile	1991–2002	P	2003 (1.4)		
Bill Killefer	1909–1921	C	1946N (0.5)		
Matt Kilroy	1886–1898	P	1936V (1.3)		
Ellis Kinder	1946–1957	P	1964 (1.5)		
Dave Kingman	1971–1986	LF	1992 (0.7)		
Johnny Kling	1900–1913	C	1937 (10.0)	1936 (3.5)	1953 (0.4)
Ted Kluszewski	1947–1961	1B	1977 (14.4)	1967 (3.1)	1981 (14.0)
Otto Knabe	1905–1916	2B	1946N (0.5)	1939 (0.4)	1946N (0.5)
Ray Knight	1974–1988	3B	1994 (0.2)		
Jerry Koosman	1967–1985	P	1991 (0.9)		
Ray Kremer	1924–1933	P	1948 (0.8)	1948 (0.8)	1958 (0.8)
Red Kress	1927–1940	SS	1960 (1.1)	1958 (1.1)	1960 (1.1)

CANDIDATE	CAREER	POS	MAX YR (PCT)	1ST YR (PCT)	LAST YR (PCT)
John Kruk	1986–1995	1B	2001 (0.2)		
Mike Krukow	1976–1989	P	1995 (0.2)		
Harvey Kuenn	1952–1966	SS	1988 (39.3)	1977 (14.9)	1991 (22.6)
Joe Kuhel	1930–1947	1B	1956 (0.5)		
Bob Kuzava	1946–1957	P	1964 (0.5)		
Bill Lange	1893–1899	CF	1936V (7.7)	1936V (7.7)	1953 (0.4)
Hal Lanier	1964–1973	SS	1979 (0.2)		
Carney Lansford	1978–1992	3B	1998 (0.6)		
Don Larsen	1953–1967	P	1979 (12.3)	1974 (7.9)	1988 (7.3)
Arlie Latham	1880–1899	3B	1936V (1.3)	1936V (1.3)	1942 (0.4)
Cookie Lavagetto	1934–1947	3B	1958 (1.5)	1958 (1.5)	1960 (0.7)
Vern Law	1950–1967	P	1973 (2.4)	1973 (2.4)	1979 (2.1)
Fred Leach	1923–1932	LF	1958 (0.8)	1958 (0.8)	1960 (0.4)
Tommy Leach	1898–1918	CF	1937 (0.5)	1937 (0.5)	1939 (0.4)
Bill Lee	1969–1982	P	1988 (0.7)		
Sam Leever	1898–1910	P	1937 (0.5)		
Chet Lemon	1975–1990	CF	1996 (0.2)		
Dennis Leonard	1974–1986	P	1992 (0.2)		
Emil Leonard	1933–1953	P	1968 (1.8)	1960 (0.7)	1973 (1.6)
Duffy Lewis	1910–1921	LF	1955 (13.5)	1937 (1.5)	1955 (13.5)
Hans Lobert	1903–1917	3B	1937 (1.0)	1937 (1.0)	1960 (0.4)
Whitey Lockman	1945–1960	1B	1966 (1.3)		
Mickey Lolich	1963–1979	P	1988 (25.5)	1985 (19.7)	1999 (5.2)
Jim Lonborg	1965–1979	P	1985 (0.8)	1985 (0.8)	1986 (0.7)
Herman Long	1889–1904	SS	1936V (20.5)	1936V (20.5)	1946N (0.5)
Ed Lopat	1944–1955	P	1971 (1.1)	1968 (0.7)	1972 (0.5)
Davey Lopes	1972–1987	2B	1993 (0.5)		
Bobby Lowe	1890–1907	2B	1936V (2.6)	1936V (2.6)	1945 (0.8)
John Lowenstein	1970–1985	LF	1991 (0.2)		
Red Lucas	1923–1938	P	1949 (1.3)	1949 (1.3)	1958 (0.4)
Dolph Luque	1919–1935	P	1958 (5.6)	1937 (0.5)	1960 (1.5)
Greg Luzinski	1970–1984	LF	1990 (0.2)		
Fred Lynn	1974–1990	CF	1996 (5.5)	1996 (5.5)	1997 (4.7)
Bill Madlock	1973–1987	3B	1993 (4.5)		
Sherry Magee	1904–1919	LF	1937 (1.0)	1937 (1.0)	1951 (0.9)
Sal Maglie	1945–1958	P	1964 (6.5)	1964 (6.5)	1968 (3.9)
Jim Maloney	1960–1971	P	1978 (0.5)	1978 (0.5)	1979 (0.5)
Gus Mancuso	1928–1945	C	1958 (0.4)		
Firpo Marberry	1923–1936	P	1958 (1.9)	1938 (0.4)	1962 (1.3)
Marty Marion	1940–1953	SS	1970 (40.0)	1956 (0.5)	1973 (33.4)
Roger Maris	1957–1968	RF	1988 (43.1)	1974 (21.4)	1988 (43.1)
Mike Marshall	1967–1981	P	1987 (1.5)		
Billy Martin	1950–1961	2B	1967 (0.3)		
Pepper Martin	1928–1944	CF	1958 (17.3)	1942 (0.9)	1964R (2.2)
Morrie Martin	1949–1959	P	1966 (0.7)		
Dennis Martinez	1976–1998	P	2004 (3.2)		
Don Mattingly	1982–1995	1B	2001 (28.2)	2001 (28.2)	2005 (11.4)
Lee May	1965–1982	1B	1988 (0.5)		
Carl Mays	1915–1929	P	1958 (2.3)		
Jim McAleer	1889–1902	CF	1936V (1.3)		
Tim McCarver	1959–1980	C	1986 (3.8)		
Frank McCormick	1934–1948	1B	1964 (3.0)	1956 (1.6)	1968 (1.1)
Lindy McDaniel	1955–1975	P	1982 (0.7)	1981 (0.2)	1982 (0.7)
Gil McDougald	1951–1960	2B	1966 (1.7)	1966 (1.7)	1974 (0.8)
Jack McDowell	1987–1999	P	2005 (0.8)		
Willie McGee	1982–1999	CF	2005 (5.0)		
Tug McGraw	1965–1984	P	1990 (1.4)		
Stuffy McInnis	1909–1927	1B	1949 (5.2)	1937 (0.5)	1951 (1.3)
Denny McLain	1963–1972	P	1979 (0.7)	1978 (0.3)	1985 (0.5)
Larry McLean	1901–1915	C	1937 (0.5)		
Don McMahon	1957–1974	P	1980 (0.3)		
Marty McManus	1920–1934	2B	1958 (0.8)	1958 (0.8)	1960 (0.7)
Roy McMillan	1951–1966	SS	1972 (2.3)	1972 (2.3)	1974 (1.1)
Dave McNally	1962–1975	P	1986 (2.8)	1981 (1.2)	1986 (2.8)
Cal McVey	1871–1879	1B	1936V (1.3)		
Lee Meadows	1915–1929	P	1958 (0.8)		
Andy Messersmith	1968–1979	P	1985 (0.8)	1985 (0.8)	1986 (0.7)
Bob Meusel	1920–1930	LF	1948 (5.0)	1937 (0.5)	1960 (3.7)
Eddie Miksis	1944–1958	2B	1964 (0.5)		
Clyde Milan	1907–1922	CF	1955 (2.4)	1938 (0.4)	1955 (2.4)
Felix Millan	1966–1977	2B	1983 (0.3)		
Bing Miller	1921–1936	RF	1960 (2.2)	1958 (0.4)	1960 (2.2)
Dots Miller	1909–1921	1B	1948 (0.8)		
Hack Miller	1916–1925	LF	1937 (0.5)		
Minnie Minoso	1949–1964	LF	1988 (21.1)	1969 (1.8)	1999 (14.7)
Kevin Mitchell	1984–1998	LF	2004 (0.4)		
Rick Monday	1966–1984	CF	1990 (0.5)		
Don Money	1968–1983	3B	1989 (0.2)		
Jeff Montgomery	1987–1999	P	2005 (0.4)		
Wally Moon	1954–1965	LF	1971 (0.6)		
Jo-Jo Moore	1930–1941	LF	1950 (0.6)		
Terry Moore	1935–1948	CF	1968 (11.7)	1950 (0.6)	1968 (11.7)
Pat Moran	1901–1914	C	1937 (0.5)	1937 (0.5)	1945 (0.4)
Jack Morris	1977–1994	P	2005 (33.3)	2000 (22.2)	2005 (33.3)
Wally Moses	1935–1951	RF	1971 (1.9)	1958 (0.4)	1971 (1.9)
Johnny Mostil	1918–1929	CF	1956 (0.5)	1956 (0.5)	1958 (0.4)
Manny Mota	1962–1982	LF	1988 (4.2)	1988 (4.2)	1989 (2.0)
Hugh Mulcahy	1935–1947	P	1948 (0.8)		
Van Mungo	1931–1945	P	1948 (0.8)	1945 (0.4)	1960 (0.7)
Thurman Munson	1969–1979	C	1981 (15.5)	1981 (15.5)	1995 (6.5)
Bobby Murcer	1965–1983	RF	1989 (0.7)		
Dale Murphy	1976–1993	CF	2000 (23.2)	1999 (19.3)	2005 (10.5)
Danny Murphy	1900–1915	2B	1937 (0.5)	1937 (0.5)	1945 (0.4)
Red Murray	1906–1917	RF	1937 (0.5)	1937 (0.5)	1938 (0.4)
Buddy Myer	1925–1941	2B	1949 (0.7)		
Randy Myers	1985–1998	P	2004 (0.2)		
Art Nehf	1915–1929	P	1958 (4.9)	1937 (1.5)	1958 (4.9)
Graig Nettles	1967–1988	3B	1994 (8.4)	1994 (8.4)	1997 (4.7)
Don Newcombe	1949–1960	P	1980 (15.3)	1966 (2.3)	1980 (15.3)
Bobo Newsom	1929–1953	P	1969 (9.4)	1960 (2.2)	1973 (8.7)
Bill Nicholson	1936–1953	RF	1960 (0.4)		
Joe Niekro	1967–1988	P	1994 (1.3)		
Ron Northey	1942–1957	RF	1964 (0.5)		
Jim Northrup	1964–1975	RF	1981 (0.2)		
Lefty O'Doul	1919–1934	LF	1960 (16.7)	1948 (3.3)	1962 (8.1)
Joe Oeschger	1914–1925	P	1948 (0.8)		
Bob O'Farrell	1915–1935	C	1950 (2.4)	1950 (2.4)	1960 (1.1)
Charlie O'Leary	1904–1913	SS	1953 (0.4)	1953 (0.4)	1960 (0.4)
Tony Oliva	1962–1976	RF	1988 (47.3)	1982 (15.2)	1996 (36.2)
Al Oliver	1968–1985	CF	1991 (4.3)		
Steve O'Neill	1911–1928	C	1953 (4.9)	1948 (1.7)	1958 (3.8)
Claude Osteen	1957–1975	P	1981 (0.5)		
Charlie Pabor	1871–1875	LF	1936V (1.3)		
Andy Pafko	1943–1959	CF	1966 (0.7)	1966 (0.7)	1967 (0.3)
Milt Pappas	1957–1973	P	1979 (1.2)		
Dave Parker	1973–1991	RF	1998 (24.5)	1997 (17.5)	2005 (12.6)
Lance Parrish	1977–1995	C	2001 (1.7)		
Larry Parrish	1974–1988	3B	1994 (0.4)		
Camilo Pascual	1954–1971	P	1977 (0.8)	1977 (0.8)	1978 (0.3)
Dode Paskert	1907–1921	CF	1937 (0.5)		
Monte Pearson	1932–1941	P	1958 (0.4)		
Roger Peckinpaugh	1910–1927	SS	1937 (1.5)	1937 (1.5)	1955 (0.4)
Heinie Peitz	1893–1906	C	1939 (0.4)		
Tony Pena	1980–1997	C	2003 (0.4)		
Terry Pendleton	1984–1998	3B	2004 (0.2)		
Hub Perdue	1911–1915	P	1938 (0.4)	1938 (0.4)	1939 (0.4)
Cy Perkins	1915–1931	C	1958 (0.8)		
Ron Perranoski	1961–1973	P	1979 (1.4)		
Jim Perry	1959–1975	P	1983 (1.9)	1981 (1.5)	1983 (1.9)
Johnny Pesky	1942–1954	SS	1960 (0.4)		
Rico Petrocelli	1963–1976	SS	1982 (0.7)		
Deacon Phillippe	1899–1911	P	1945 (0.8)	1939 (0.4)	1946N (0.5)
Tony Phillips	1982–1999	LF	2005 (0.2)		
Billy Pierce	1945–1964	P	1971 (1.9)	1970 (1.7)	1974 (1.1)
Lip Pike	1871–1881	CF	1936V (1.3)		
Lou Piniella	1964–1984	LF	1990 (0.5)		
Vada Pinson	1958–1975	CF	1988 (15.7)	1981 (4.5)	1996 (10.9)
Wally Pipp	1913–1928	1B	1958 (0.4)		
Johnny Podres	1953–1969	P	1975 (0.8)	1975 (0.8)	1977 (0.8)
Bob Porterfield	1948–1959	P	1966 (0.3)		
Boog Powell	1961–1977	1B	1983 (1.3)		
Vic Power	1954–1965	1B	1972 (0.8)	1971 (0.6)	1972 (0.8)
Herb Pruett	1922–1932	P	1949 (0.7)	1949 (0.7)	1953 (0.4)
Terry Puhl	1977–1991	RF	1997 (0.2)		
Jack Quinn	1909–1933	P	1958 (3.4)	1948 (1.7)	1960 (0.7)
Dan Quisenberry	1979–1990	P	1996 (3.8)		
Willie Randolph	1975–1992	2B	1998 (1.1)		
Vic Raschi	1946–1955	P	1975 (10.2)	1962 (0.6)	1975 (10.2)
Bugs Raymond	1904–1911	P	1937 (0.5)		
Jeff Reardon	1979–1994	P	2000 (4.8)		
Pete Reiser	1940–1952	CF	1960 (3.0)	1958 (2.3)	1960 (3.0)
Jack Remsen	1872–1884	CF	1936V (1.3)		
Jerry Remy	1975–1984	2B	1990 (0.2)		
Rick Reuschel	1972–1991	P	1997 (0.4)		
Jerry Reuss	1969–1990	P	1996 (0.4)		
Allie Reynolds	1942–1954	P	1968 (33.6)	1956 (0.5)	1974 (27.7)
Del Rice	1945–1961	C	1966 (0.7)		
Jim Rice	1974–1989	LF	2005 (59.5)	1995 (29.8)	2005 (59.5)
J. R. Richard	1971–1980	P	1986 (1.6)		
Hardy Richardson	1879–1892	2B	1936V (1.3)		
Bobby Richardson	1955–1966	2B	1972 (2.0)	1972 (2.0)	1974 (1.4)
Dave Righetti	1979–1995	P	2001 (0.4)		
Jose Rijo	1984–1995	P	2001 (0.2)		
Jimmy Ring	1917–1928	P	1949 (0.7)		
Claude Ritchey	1897–1909	2B	1945 (0.4)		
Mickey Rivers	1970–1984	CF	1990 (0.5)		
Dave Robertson	1912–1922	RF	1953 (0.4)		
Preacher Roe	1938–1954	P	1971 (0.8)	1960 (0.4)	1972 (0.5)
Red Rolfe	1931–1942	3B	1958 (4.9)	1950 (4.2)	1962 (0.6)
Eddie Rommel	1920–1932	P	1960 (4.5)	1948 (2.5)	1960 (4.5)
Charlie Root	1923–1941	P	1948 (2.5)	1945 (0.4)	1960 (0.7)
Pete Rose	1963–1986	RF	1992 (9.5)	1992 (9.5)	2000 (3.4)
Schoolboy Rowe	1933–1949	P	1969 (5.0)	1958 (4.5)	1969 (5.0)
Nap Rucker	1907–1916	P	1942 (6.4)	1936 (0.4)	1946N (6.4)
Dick Rudolph	1910–1923	P	1937 (0.5)	1937 (0.5)	1951 (0.4)
Muddy Ruel	1915–1934	C	1956 (8.3)	1946N (0.5)	1960 (3.3)
Bill Russell	1969–1986	SS	1992 (0.7)		
Ray Sadecki	1960–1977	P	1983 (0.5)		
Johnny Sain	1942–1955	P	1975 (34.0)	1962 (0.6)	1975 (34.0)
Juan Samuel	1983–1998	2B	2004 (0.4)		
Manny Sanguillen	1967–1980	C	1986 (0.5)		
Ron Santo	1960–1974	3B	1998 (43.1)	1980 (3.9)	1998 (43.1)
Hank Sauer	1941–1959	LF	1966 (1.3)		
Steve Sax	1981–1994	2B	2000 (0.4)		
Al Schacht	1919–1921	P	1951 (1.8)	1939 (0.4)	1956 (0.5)
Germany Schaefer	1901–1918	2B	1942 (0.4)	1942 (0.4)	1953 (0.4)
Wally Schang	1913–1931	C	1960 (4.1)	1948 (0.8)	1960 (4.1)
Ossie Schreck	1897–1908	C	1937 (1.0)	1937 (1.0)	1939 (0.7)
Frank Schulte	1904–1918	RF	1937 (0.5)		
Hal Schumacher	1931–1946	P	1964 (5.0)	1948 (0.8)	1964 (5.0)
Everett Scott	1914–1926	SS	1955 (3.2)	1937 (1.0)	1956 (0.5)
George Scott	1969–1979	1B	1986 (0.2)		
Jack Scott	1916–1929	P	1958 (0.4)		
Mike Scott	1979–1991	P	1997 (0.4)		
George Selkirk	1934–1942	LF	1951 (0.9)	1948 (0.8)	1953 (0.4)
Hank Severeid	1911–1926	C	1948 (0.8)		
Luke Sewell	1921–1942	C	1958 (1.1)	1948 (0.8)	1962 (0.6)
Rip Sewell	1932–1949	P	1962 (0.6)	1958 (0.4)	1964 (0.5)
Cy Seymour	1896–1913	CF	1945 (0.4)		
Bobby Shantz	1949–1964	P	1970 (2.3)	1970 (2.3)	1974 (0.8)
Jim Sheckard	1897–1913	LF	1946N (0.5)	1938 (0.4)	1946N (0.5)
Bill Sherdel	1918–1932	P	1948 (0.8)	1948 (0.8)	1960 (0.7)
Urban Shocker	1916–1928	P	1958 (1.5)	1938 (0.4)	1958 (1.5)
Chris Short	1959–1973	P	1979 (0.2)		
Sonny Siebert	1964–1975	P	1981 (0.2)		
Roy Sievers	1949–1965	1B	1971 (1.1)	1971 (1.1)	1972 (0.8)
Curt Simmons	1947–1967	P	1973 (1.3)	1973 (1.3)	1974 (0.8)

CANDIDATE	CAREER	POS	MAX YR (PCT)	1ST YR (PCT)	LAST YR (PCT)
Ted Simmons	1968–1988	C	1994 (3.7)		
Sibby Sisti	1939–1954	2B	1960 (0.4)		
Roy Smalley	1948–1958	SS	1964 (0.5)		
Earl Smith	1919–1930	C	1948 (0.8)	1948 (0.8)	1956 (0.5)
Lee Smith	1980–1997	P	2003 (42.3)	2003 (42.3)	2005 (38.8)
Lonnie Smith	1978–1994	LF	2000 (0.2)		
Reggie Smith	1966–1982	RF	1988 (0.7)		
Sherry Smith	1911–1927	P	1948 (0.8)		
Billy Southworth	1940–1951	Mgr	1958 (6.8)	1945 (0.4)	1958 (6.8)
Tully Sparks	1897–1910	P	1946N (0.5)		
Chris Speier	1971–1989	SS	1995 (0.2)		
Jake Stahl	1903–1913	1B	1938 (0.4)	1938 (0.4)	1939 (0.4)
Eddie Stanky	1943–1953	2B	1960 (1.1)		
Mickey Stanley	1964–1978	CF	1984 (0.5)		
Rusty Staub	1963–1985	RF	1994 (7.9)	1991 (6.3)	1997 (3.8)
Terry Steinbach	1986–1999	C	2005 (0.2)		
Harry Steinfeldt	1898–1911	3B	1937 (0.5)	1937 (0.5)	1942 (0.4)
Riggs Stephenson	1921–1934	LF	1960 (1.5)	1956 (1.0)	1962 (0.6)
Dave Stewart	1978–1995	P	2001 (7.4)	2001 (7.4)	2002 (4.9)
Dave Stieb	1979–1998	P	2004 (1.4)		
Mel Stottlemyre	1964–1974	P	1980 (0.8)		
Harry Stovey	1880–1893	1B	1936V (7.7)		
Darryl Strawberry	1983–1999	RF	2005 (1.2)		
Gabby Street	1904–1912	C	1937 (0.5)	1937 (0.5)	1953 (0.4)
Gus Suhr	1930–1940	1B	1956 (0.5)	1956 (0.5)	1960 (0.4)
Clyde Sukeforth	1926–1934	C	1958 (0.4)		
Billy Sullivan	1899–1916	C	1937 (0.5)	1937 (0.5)	1946N (0.5)
Jim Sundberg	1974–1989	C	1995 (0.2)		
Rick Sutcliffe	1976–1994	P	2000 (1.8)		
Bill Sweeney	1907–1914	2B	1945 (0.4)		
Jess Tannehill	1894–1911	P	1946N (0.5)		
Danny Tartabull	1984–1997	RF	2003 (0.2)		
Birdie Tebbetts	1936–1952	C	1958 (3.0)	1958 (3.0)	1960 (0.4)
Kent Tekulve	1974–1989	P	1995 (1.3)		
Gary Templeton	1976–1991	SS	1997 (0.4)		
Gene Tenace	1969–1983	C	1989 (0.2)		
Fred Tenney	1894–1911	1B	1938 (3.1)	1936V (1.3)	1946N (0.5)
Tommy Thevenow	1924–1938	SS	1950 (1.2)		
Ira Thomas	1906–1915	C	1938 (0.4)		
Bobby Thomson	1946–1960	CF	1968 (4.6)	1966 (4.0)	1979 (2.5)
Andre Thornton	1973–1987	DH	1993 (0.5)		
Luis Tiant	1964–1982	P	1988 (30.9)	1988 (30.9)	2002 (18.0)
Jim Tobin	1914–1927	RF	1956 (1.0)		
Fred Toney	1911–1923	P	1949 (0.7)		
Earl Torgeson	1947–1961	1B	1967 (0.7)		
Joe Torre	1960–1977	C	1997 (22.2)	1983 (5.3)	1997 (22.2)
Mike Torrez	1967–1984	P	1990 (0.2)		
Alan Trammell	1977–1996	SS	2005 (16.9)	2002 (15.7)	2005 (16.9)
Dizzy Trout	1939–1952	P	1964 (0.5)		
Virgil Trucks	1941–1958	P	1964 (2.0)		
John Tudor	1979–1990	P	1996 (0.4)		
Jim Turner	1937–1945	P	1956 (0.5)		
Terry Turner	1901–1919	SS	1947 (1.2)		
George Uhle	1919–1936	P	1958 (1.5)	1956 (0.5)	1960 (1.5)
Ellis Valentine	1975–1985	RF	1991 (0.2)		
Fernando Valenzuela	1980–1997	P	2003 (6.3)	2003 (6.3)	2004 (3.8)
Elmer Valo	1940–1961	RF	1967 (0.7)		
Johnny Vander Meer	1937–1951	P	1967 (29.8)	1945 (0.4)	1971 (27.2)
George Van Haltren	1887–1903	CF	1936V (1.3)		
Bobby Veach	1912–1925	LF	1937 (0.5)		
Mickey Vernon	1939–1960	1B	1980 (24.9)	1966 (6.6)	1980 (24.9)
Frank Viola	1982–1996	P	2002 (0.4)		
Bill Virdon	1955–1968	CF	1974 (0.8)	1974 (0.8)	1975 (0.3)
Rube Walberg	1923–1937	P	1958 (0.4)	1958 (0.4)	1960 (0.4)
Dixie Walker	1931–1949	RF	1964 (3.0)	1962 (0.6)	1969 (2.6)
Harry Walker	1940–1951	CF	1958 (0.4)		
Tim Wallach	1980–1996	3B	2002 (0.2)		
Bucky Walters	1931–1950	P	1968 (23.7)	1950 (2.4)	1970 (9.7)
Bill Wambsganss	1914–1926	2B	1955 (2.0)	1942 (0.4)	1956 (0.5)
Lon Warneke	1930–1945	P	1964 (6.5)	1949 (1.3)	1964 (6.5)
Bob Watson	1966–1984	1B	1990 (0.7)		
Bob Welch	1978–1994	P	2000 (0.2)		
Billy Werber	1930–1942	3B	1958 (1.1)	1949 (0.7)	1958 (1.1)
Vic Wertz	1947–1963	RF	1975 (1.4)	1970 (0.7)	1978 (1.1)
Sam West	1927–1942	CF	1948 (0.8)		
Wes Westrum	1947–1957	C	1964 (1.0)		
Lou Whitaker	1977–1995	2B	2001 (2.9)		
Deacon White	1871–1890	3B	1936V (1.3)		
Frank White	1973–1990	2B	1996 (3.8)		
Will White	1877–1886	P	1975 (1.9)	1975 (1.9)	1977 (1.0)
Burgess Whitehead	1933–1946	2B	1956 (0.5)		
Earl Whitehill	1923–1939	P	1960 (1.1)	1956 (1.1)	1960 (1.1)
Fred Williams	1912–1930	CF	1956 (5.7)	1938 (0.4)	1960 (4.1)
Ken Williams	1915–1929	LF	1956 (0.5)	1956 (0.5)	1958 (0.4)
Ned Williamson	1878–1890	3B	1936V (2.6)		
Maury Wills	1959–1972	SS	1981 (40.6)	1978 (30.3)	1992 (25.6)
Jimmie Wilson	1923–1940	C	1956 (8.8)	1948 (6.6)	1962 (2.5)
Jim Wilson	1945–1958	P	1964 (1.0)		
Willie Wilson	1976–1994	CF	2000 (2.0)		
Whitey Witt	1916–1926	CF	1949 (0.7)		
Joe Wood	1908–1922	P	1947 (18.0)	1937 (6.5)	1951 (2.2)
Wilbur Wood	1961–1978	P	1988 (7.0)	1984 (3.5)	1989 (3.1)
Glenn Wright	1924–1935	SS	1960 (6.7)	1948 (1.7)	1962 (0.6)
Whit Wyatt	1929–1945	P	1958 (0.4)		
Steve Yeager	1972–1986	C	1992 (0.5)		
Steve Yerkes	1909–1916	2B	1945 (0.4)		
Rudy York	1934–1948	1B	1964 (5.0)	1962 (0.6)	1964 (5.0)
Pep Young	1933–1945	2B	1958 (0.4)		
Tom Zachary	1918–1936	P	1958 (0.4)	1958 (0.4)	1960 (0.4)
Chief Zimmer	1884–1903	C	1938 (0.4)		

TOP VOTE-GETTERS BY YEAR

1936 Veterans
Needed to Elect: 59
Cap Anson 40
Buck Ewing 40
Willie Keeler 33
Cy Young 32
Ed Delahanty 22

1936
Needed to Elect: 170
Ty Cobb 222
Babe Ruth 215
Honus Wagner 215
Christy Mathewson 205
Walter Johnson 189
Nap Lajoie 146
Tris Speaker 133
Cy Young 111
Rogers Hornsby 105
Mickey Cochrane 80
George Sisler 77
Eddie Collins 60
Jimmy Collins 58

1937
Needed to Elect: 151
Nap Lajoie 168
Tris Speaker 165
Cy Young 153
Pete Alexander 125
Eddie Collins 115
Willie Keeler 115
George Sisler 106
Ed Delahanty 70
Rube Waddell 67
Jimmy Collins 66
Ed Walsh 56
Rogers Hornsby 53

1938
Needed to Elect: 197
Pete Alexander 212
George Sisler 179
Willie Keeler 177
Eddie Collins 175
Rube Waddell 148
Frank Chance 133

Ed Delahanty 132
Ed Walsh 110
Johnny Evers 91
Jimmy Collins 79
Rabbit Maranville 73
Roger Bresnahan 67

1939
Needed to Elect: 206
George Sisler 235
Eddie Collins 213
Willie Keeler 207
Rube Waddell 179
Rogers Hornsby 176
Frank Chance 158
Ed Delahanty 145
Ed Walsh 132
Johnny Evers 107
Miller Huggins 97
Rabbit Maranville 82
Jimmy Collins 72

1942
Needed to Elect: 175
Rogers Hornsby 182
Frank Chance 136
Rube Waddell 126
Ed Walsh 113
Miller Huggins 111
Ed Delahanty 104
Johnny Evers 91
Wilbert Robinson 89
Mickey Cochrane 88
Frankie Frisch 84
Hugh Duffy 77
Herb Pennock 72
Clark Griffith 71
Jimmy Collins 68
Rabbit Maranville 66
Hughie Jennings 64
Mordecai Brown 63
Eddie Plank 63
Joe McGinnity 59
Fred Clarke 58

1945
Needed to Elect: 185
Frank Chance 179
Rube Waddell 154
Ed Walsh 137
Johnny Evers 134
Roger Bresnahan 133
Miller Huggins 133
Mickey Cochrane 125
Jimmy Collins 121
Ed Delahanty 111
Clark Griffith 108
Frankie Frisch 101
Hughie Jennings 92
Wilbert Robinson 81
Pie Traynor 81
Hugh Duffy 64

1946 Nominating
Total Voting: 202
Frank Chance 144
Johnny Evers 130
Miller Huggins 129
Rube Waddell 122
Ed Walsh 115
Frankie Frisch 104
Carl Hubbell 101
Mickey Cochrane 80
Clark Griffith 73
Lefty Grove 71
Pie Traynor 65

1946
Needed to Elect: 197
Frank Chance 150
Johnny Evers 110
Miller Huggins 106
Ed Walsh 106
Rube Waddell 87
Clark Griffith 82
Carl Hubbell 75
Frankie Frisch 67

1947
Needed to Elect: 121
Carl Hubbell 140
Frankie Frisch 136

Mickey Cochrane 128
Lefty Grove 123
Pie Traynor 119
Charlie Gehringer 105
Rabbit Maranville 91
Dizzy Dean 88
Herb Pennock 86
Chief Bender 72
Harry Heilmann 65
Ray Schalk 50
Dazzy Vance 50
Frank Baker 49
Bill Terry 46

1948
Needed to Elect: 91
Herb Pennock 94
Pie Traynor 93
Al Simmons 60
Charlie Gehringer 52
Bill Terry 52
Paul Waner 51
Jimmie Foxx 50
Dizzy Dean 40
Harry Heilmann 40
Bill Dickey 39
Rabbit Maranville 38
Gabby Hartnett 33

1949
Needed to Elect: 115
Charlie Gehringer 102
Mel Ott 94
Al Simmons 89
Dizzy Dean 88
Jimmie Foxx 85
Bill Terry 81
Paul Waner 73
Hank Greenberg 67
Bill Dickey 65
Harry Heilmann 59
Rabbit Maranville 58

1949 Run Off
Needed to Elect: 140
One Player Maximum
Charlie Gehringer 159

Mel Ott 128
Jimmie Foxx 89
Dizzy Dean 81
Al Simmons 76
Paul Waner 63
Harry Heilmann 52
Bill Terry 48

1950
Needed to Elect: 125
Mel Ott 115
Bill Terry 105
Jimmie Foxx 103
Paul Waner 95
Al Simmons 90
Harry Heilmann 87
Dizzy Dean 85
Bill Dickey 78
Rabbit Maranville 64
Hank Greenberg 64
Gabby Hartnett 54
Dazzy Vance 52
Ted Lyons 42

1951
Needed to Elect: 170
Mel Ott 197
Jimmie Foxx 179
Paul Waner 162
Harry Heilmann 153
Bill Terry 148
Dizzy Dean 145
Bill Dickey 118
Al Simmons 116
Rabbit Maranville 110
Ted Lyons 71
Dazzy Vance 70
Hank Greenberg 67
Gabby Hartnett 57

1952
Needed to Elect: 176
Harry Heilmann 203
Paul Waner 195
Bill Terry 155
Dizzy Dean 152
Al Simmons 141

Bill Dickey 139
Rabbit Maranville 133
Dazzy Vance 105
Ted Lyons 101
Gabby Hartnett 77
Hank Greenberg 75
Chief Bender 70

1953
Needed to Elect: 198
Dizzy Dean 209
Al Simmons 199
Bill Terry 191
Bill Dickey 179
Rabbit Maranville 164
Dazzy Vance 156
Ted Lyons 139
Joe DiMaggio 117
Chief Bender 104
Gabby Hartnett 104
Hank Greenberg 8
Joe Cronin 6

1954
Needed to Elect: 189
Rabbit Maranville 20
Bill Dickey 20
Bill Terry 19
Joe DiMaggio 17
Ted Lyons 17
Dazzy Vance 15
Gabby Hartnett 15
Hank Greenberg 9
Joe Cronin 8

1955
Needed to Elect: 188
Joe DiMaggio 22
Ted Lyons 20
Dazzy Vance 20
Gabby Hartnett 19
Hank Greenberg 13
Joe Cronin 13
Max Carey 1
Ray Schalk 11
Edd Roush 9
Hank Gowdy 9

ck Wilson................81
y Gomez................71
y Lazzeri................66

...56
ded to Elect: 145
nk Greenberg........164
Cronin................152
d Ruffing................97
d Roush................91
ty Gomez................89
ck Wilson................74
x Carey................65
y Lazzeri................64
i Cuyler................55
nk Gowdy................49

58
eded to Elect: 200
x Carey................136
d Roush................112
d Ruffing................99
ck Wilson................94
i Cuyler................90
m Rice................90
ny Lazzeri................80
ty Gomez................76
rleigh Grimes........71
d Faber................68

60
eded to Elect: 202
d Roush................146
m Rice................143
pa Rixey................142
rleigh Grimes........92
n Bottomley........89
d Ruffing................86
d Faber................83
ke Appling................72
i Cuyler................72
ck Wilson................72

62
eded to Elect: 120
b Feller................150
ckie Robinson........124
m Rice................81
d Ruffing................72
pa Rixey................49
ke Appling................48
l Rizzuto................44
rleigh Grimes........43

964
eded to Elect: 151
ke Appling................142
d Ruffing................141
by Campanella........115
e Medwick................108
ee Wee Reese........73
u Boudreau................68
Lopez................57
uck Klein................56
hnny Mize................54
el Harder................51
hnny Vander Meer....51
arty Marion................50

964 Run Off
eeded to Elect: 170
ne Player Maximum
ke Appling................189
d Ruffing................184
by Campanella........138
e Medwick................130

966
eeded to Elect: 227
d Williams................282
d Ruffing................208
oy Campanella........197
e Medwick................187
u Boudreau................115
Lopez................109
nos Slaughter........100
ee Wee Reese........95
arty Marion................86
hnny Mize................81

967
eded to Elect: 219
e Medwick................212
ed Ruffing................212
oy Campanella........204
ou Boudreau................143
alph Kiner................124
nos Slaughter........123
Lopez................114
arty Marion................90
hnny Mize................89
ee Wee Reese........89
hnny Vander Meer....87
llie Reynolds................77

967 Run Off
Needed to Elect: 230
ne Player Maximum

Red Ruffing................266
Joe Medwick................248
Roy Campanella................170

1968
Needed to Elect: 212
Joe Medwick................240
Roy Campanella................205
Lou Boudreau................146
Enos Slaughter................129
Ralph Kiner................118
Johnny Mize................103
Allie Reynolds................95
Marty Marion................89
Arky Vaughan................82
Pee Wee Reese................81
Johnny Vander Meer................79
Joe Gordon................77
Phil Rizzuto................74

1969
Needed to Elect: 255
Stan Musial................317
Roy Campanella................270
Lou Boudreau................218
Ralph Kiner................137
Enos Slaughter................128
Johnny Mize................116
Marty Marion................112
Allie Reynolds................98
Joe Gordon................97
Johnny Vander Meer....95
Early Wynn................95
Pee Wee Reese................89

1970
Needed to Elect: 225
Lou Boudreau................232
Ralph Kiner................167
Gil Hodges................145
Early Wynn................140
Enos Slaughter................133
Johnny Mize................126
Marty Marion................120
Pee Wee Reese................97
Red Schoendienst................97
George Kell................90
Allie Reynolds................89
Johnny Vander Meer....88
Hal Newhouser................80
Joe Gordon................79
Phil Rizzuto................79
Bobby Doerr................75

1971
Needed to Elect: 270
Yogi Berra................242
Early Wynn................240
Ralph Kiner................212
Gil Hodges................180
Enos Slaughter................165
Johnny Mize................157
Pee Wee Reese................127
Marty Marion................123
Red Schoendienst................123
Allie Reynolds................110
George Kell................105
Johnny Vander Meer....98
Hal Newhouser................94
Phil Rizzuto................92
Bob Lemon................90

1972
Needed to Elect: 297
Sandy Koufax................344
Yogi Berra................339
Early Wynn................301
Ralph Kiner................235
Gil Hodges................161
Johnny Mize................157
Enos Slaughter................149
Pee Wee Reese................129
Marty Marion................120
Bob Lemon................117
George Kell................115
Allie Reynolds................105
Red Schoendienst................104
Phil Rizzuto................103

1973
Needed to Elect: 285
Warren Spahn................316
Whitey Ford................255
Ralph Kiner................235
Gil Hodges................218
Robin Roberts................213
Bob Lemon................177
Johnny Mize................157
Enos Slaughter................145
Marty Marion................127
Pee Wee Reese................126
George Kell................114
Phil Rizzuto................111
Duke Snider................101
Red Schoendienst........96

1974
Needed to Elect: 274
Mickey Mantle................322
Whitey Ford................284
Robin Roberts................224
Ralph Kiner................215
Gil Hodges................198
Bob Lemon................190
Enos Slaughter................145
Pee Wee Reese................141
Eddie Mathews................118
Phil Rizzuto................111
Duke Snider................111
Red Schoendienst................110
Allie Reynolds................101
George Kell................94

1975
Needed to Elect: 272
Ralph Kiner................273
Robin Roberts................263
Bob Lemon................233
Gil Hodges................188
Enos Slaughter................177
Hal Newhouser................155
Pee Wee Reese................154
Eddie Mathews................148
Phil Cavarretta................129
Duke Snider................129
Johnny Sain................123
Phil Rizzuto................117
George Kell................114
Red Schoendienst................94

1976
Needed to Elect: 291
Robin Roberts................337
Bob Lemon................305
Gil Hodges................233
Enos Slaughter................197
Eddie Mathews................189
Pee Wee Reese................186
Nellie Fox................174
Duke Snider................159
Phil Rizzuto................149
George Kell................129
Red Schoendienst................129
Don Drysdale................114

1977
Needed to Elect: 287
Ernie Banks................321
Eddie Mathews................239
Gil Hodges................224
Enos Slaughter................222
Duke Snider................212
Don Drysdale................197
Pee Wee Reese................163
Nellie Fox................152
Jim Bunning................146
George Kell................141
Richie Ashburn................139
Red Schoendienst................105

1978
Needed to Elect: 284
Eddie Mathews................301
Enos Slaughter................261
Duke Snider................254
Gil Hodges................226
Don Drysdale................219
Jim Bunning................181
Pee Wee Reese................169
Richie Ashburn................158
Hoyt Wilhelm................158
Nellie Fox................149
Red Schoendienst................130
Maury Wills................115

1979
Needed to Elect: 324
Willie Mays................409
Duke Snider................308
Enos Slaughter................297
Gil Hodges................242
Don Drysdale................233
Nellie Fox................174
Hoyt Wilhelm................168
Maury Wills................166
Red Schoendienst................159
Jim Bunning................147
Richie Ashburn................130
Roger Maris................127
Luis Aparicio................120

1980
Needed to Elect: 289
Al Kaline................340
Duke Snider................333
Don Drysdale................238
Gil Hodges................230
Hoyt Wilhelm................209
Jim Bunning................177
Red Schoendienst................164
Nellie Fox................161
Maury Wills................146
Richie Ashburn................134
Luis Aparicio................124

Roger Maris................111
Mickey Vernon................96

1981
Needed to Elect: 301
Bob Gibson................337
Don Drysdale................243
Gil Hodges................241
Harmon Killebrew................239
Hoyt Wilhelm................238
Juan Marichal................233
Nellie Fox................168
Red Schoendienst................166
Jim Bunning................164
Maury Wills................163
Richie Ashburn................142

1982
Needed to Elect: 311
Hank Aaron................406
Frank Robinson................370
Juan Marichal................305
Harmon Killebrew................246
Hoyt Wilhelm................236
Don Drysdale................233
Gil Hodges................205
Luis Aparicio................174
Jim Bunning................138
Red Schoendienst................135
Nellie Fox................127
Richie Ashburn................126

1983
Needed to Elect: 281
Brooks Robinson................344
Juan Marichal................313
Harmon Killebrew................269
Luis Aparicio................252
Hoyt Wilhelm................243
Don Drysdale................242
Gil Hodges................237
Nellie Fox................173
Billy Williams................153
Red Schoendienst................146
Jim Bunning................138

1984
Needed to Elect: 302
Luis Aparicio................341
Harmon Killebrew................335
Don Drysdale................316
Hoyt Wilhelm................290
Nellie Fox................246
Billy Williams................202
Jim Bunning................201
Orlando Cepeda................124
Tony Oliva................124
Roger Maris................107
Harvey Kuenn................106
Maury Wills................104

1985
Needed to Elect: 296
Hoyt Wilhelm................331
Lou Brock................315
Nellie Fox................295
Billy Williams................252
Jim Bunning................214
Catfish Hunter................212
Roger Maris................128
Harvey Kuenn................125
Orlando Cepeda................114
Tony Oliva................114

1986
Needed to Elect: 319
Willie McCovey................346
Billy Williams................315
Catfish Hunter................289
Jim Bunning................279
Roger Maris................177
Tony Oliva................154
Orlando Cepeda................152
Harvey Kuenn................144
Maury Wills................124

1987
Needed to Elect: 310
Billy Williams................354
Catfish Hunter................315
Jim Bunning................289
Orlando Cepeda................179
Roger Maris................176
Tony Oliva................160
Harvey Kuenn................144
Bill Mazeroski................125
Maury Wills................113

1988
Needed to Elect: 320
Willie Stargell................352
Jim Bunning................317
Tony Oliva................202
Orlando Cepeda................199
Roger Maris................184
Harvey Kuenn................168
Bill Mazeroski................143
Luis Tiant................132
Maury Wills................127

Ken Boyer................109
Mickey Lolich................109
Ron Santo................108

1989
Needed to Elect: 335
Johnny Bench................431
Carl Yastrzemski................423
Gaylord Perry................304
Jim Bunning................283
Fergie Jenkins................234
Orlando Cepeda................176
Tony Oliva................135
Bill Mazeroski................134
Harvey Kuenn................115

1990
Needed to Elect: 333
Jim Palmer................411
Joe Morgan................363
Gaylord Perry................320
Fergie Jenkins................296
Jim Bunning................257
Orlando Cepeda................211
Tony Oliva................142
Bill Mazeroski................131

1991
Needed to Elect: 332
Rod Carew................401
Gaylord Perry................342
Fergie Jenkins................334
Rollie Fingers................291
Jim Bunning................282
Orlando Cepeda................192
Tony Oliva................160
Bill Mazeroski................142
Ron Santo................116

1992
Needed to Elect: 323
Tom Seaver................425
Rollie Fingers................349
Orlando Cepeda................246
Tony Perez................215
Bill Mazeroski................182
Tony Oliva................175
Ron Santo................136
Jim Kaat................114
Maury Wills................110

1993
Needed to Elect: 317
Reggie Jackson................396
Phil Niekro................278
Orlando Cepeda................252
Tony Perez................233
Steve Garvey................176
Tony Oliva................157
Ron Santo................155
Jim Kaat................125

1994
Needed to Elect: 341
Steve Carlton................436
Orlando Cepeda................335
Phil Niekro................273
Tony Perez................263
Don Sutton................259
Steve Garvey................166
Tony Oliva................158
Ron Santo................150

1995
Needed to Elect: 345
Mike Schmidt................444
Phil Niekro................286
Don Sutton................264
Tony Perez................259
Steve Garvey................196
Tony Oliva................149
Ron Santo................139
Jim Rice................137
Bruce Sutter................137

1996
Needed to Elect: 353
Phil Niekro................321
Tony Perez................309
Don Sutton................300
Steve Garvey................175
Ron Santo................174
Tony Oliva................170
Jim Rice................166
Bruce Sutter................137

1997
Needed to Elect: 355
Phil Niekro................380
Don Sutton................346
Tony Perez................312
Ron Santo................186
Jim Rice................178
Steve Garvey................167
Bruce Sutter................130

1998
Needed to Elect: 355
Don Sutton................386
Tony Perez................321

Ron Santo................204
Jim Rice................203
Gary Carter................200
Steve Garvey................195
Bruce Sutter................147
Tommy John................129
Jim Kaat................129

1999
Needed to Elect: 373
Nolan Ryan................491
George Brett................488
Robin Yount................385
Carlton Fisk................330
Tony Perez................302
Gary Carter................168
Steve Garvey................150
Jim Rice................146

2000
Needed to Elect: 374
Carlton Fisk................397
Tony Perez................385
Jim Rice................257
Gary Carter................248
Bruce Sutter................192
Goose Gossage................166
Steve Garvey................160
Tommy John................135
Jim Kaat................125

2001
Needed to Elect: 386
Dave Winfield................435
Kirby Puckett................423
Gary Carter................334
Jim Rice................298
Bruce Sutter................245
Goose Gossage................228
Steve Garvey................176
Tommy John................146
Don Mattingly................145
Jim Kaat................139

2002
Needed to Elect: 354
Ozzie Smith................433
Gary Carter................343
Jim Rice................260
Bruce Sutter................238
Andre Dawson................214
Goose Gossage................203
Steve Garvey................134
Tommy John................127
Bert Blyleven................124

2003
Needed to Elect: 372
Eddie Murray................423
Gary Carter................387
Bruce Sutter................266
Jim Rice................259
Andre Dawson................248
Ryne Sandberg................244
Lee Smith................210
Goose Gossage................209
Bert Blyleven................145
Steve Garvey................138
Jim Kaat................130

2004
Needed to Elect: 380
Paul Molitor................431
Dennis Eckersley................421
Ryne Sandberg................309
Bruce Sutter................301
Jim Rice................276
Andre Dawson................253
Rich Gossage................206
Lee Smith................185
Bert Blyleven................179
Jack Morris................133

2005
Needed to Elect: 387
Wade Boggs................474
Ryne Sandberg................393
Bruce Sutter................344
Jim Rice................307
Rich Gossage................285
Andre Dawson................270
Bert Blyleven................211
Lee Smith................200
Jack Morris................172

2006
Needed to Elect: 390
Bruce Sutter................400
Jim Rice................337
Rich Gossage................336
Andre Dawson................317
Bert Blyleven................277
Lee Smith................234
Jack Morris................214
Tommy John................154
Steve Garvey................135

BIOGRAPHICAL INFORMATION FOR OTHER HALL OF FAMERS
(i.e., those who were not major league players or managers or Negro League players)

AL BARLICK Albert Joseph B4.2.1915 Springfield IL D12.27.1995 Springfield IL 5-6/195 HF 1989
Umpire, National League, 1940–71

MORGAN BULKELEY Morgan B12.26.1837 East Haddam CT D11.6.1922 Hartford CT HF 1937 Col Yale; Trinity College
Organizer and President, National League, 1876

ALEXANDER CARTWRIGHT Alexander Joy Jr. B4.17.1820 New York NY D7.12.1892 Honolulu HI HF 1939
One of the Fathers of Baseball; Organizer, Secretary, and Vice President of Knickerbocker Base Ball Club, 1845

HENRY CHADWICK Henry B10.5.1824 Exeter, England D4.29.1908 Brooklyn NY HF 1938
One of the Fathers of Baseball; Sportwriter for *New York Clipper*, *New York Herald*, and *Brooklyn Daily Eagle*, 1858–1908; Chairman of Rules Committee, National Association of Base Ball Players; Editor, *The Spalding Guide*, 1881–1908

ALBERT "HAPPY" CHANDLER Albert B. B7.14.1898 Corydon KY D6.15.1991 Versailles KY HF 1982
Commissioner of Baseball, 1945–51

NESTOR CHYLAK Nestor B5.11.1922 Oliphant PA D2.17.1982 Dunmore PA 6-0/200 HF 1999
Umpire, American League, 1954–78; Asst. Supervisor of Umpires, American League, 1978–84

TOMMY CONNOLLY Thomas Francis B12.31.1870 Manchester, England D4.28.1961 Natick MA 5-7/170 HF 1953
Umpire, National League, 1898–1900; Umpire; American League, 1901–31; Umpire-in-Chief, American League, 1931–54

BILLY EVANS William G. B2.10.1884 Chicago IL D1.23.1956 Miami FL 5-11.5/225 HF 1973
Umpire, American League, 1906–27; GM, Cle A, 1928–35; Farm Director, Bos A, 1936–40; GM, Det A, 1947–51

FORD FRICK Ford B12.19.1894 Wawaka IN D4.8.1978 Bronxville NY HF 1970
PR Director, National League, 1934; President, National League, 1934–51; Proposed founding of National Baseball Hall of Fame and Museum, 1939; Commissioner of Baseball, 1951–65

WARREN GILES Warren B5.28.1896 Tiskilwa IL D2.7.1979 Cincinnati OH HF 1979
GM, Cin N, 1936–51; President, National League, 1951–69

WILL HARRIDGE William B10.16.1883 Chicago IL D4.9.1971 Evanston IL HF 1972
President, American League, 1931–58; Chairman, American League, 1958–71

CAL HUBBARD Robert Calvin B10.31.1900 Keytesville MO D10.17.1977 St. Petersburg FL 6-2.5/265 HF 1976 Col Centenary; Geneva
Umpire, American League, 1936–51; Asst. Supervisor of Umpires, American League, 1952–54; Supervisor of Umpires, American League, 1954–70

WILLIAM HULBERT William A. B10.23.1832 Burlington Flats NY D4.10.1882 Chicago IL HF 1995 Col Beloit
Owner, Chi NA, 1875; Owner, Chi N, 1876–82; Founder, National League, 1876; President, National League, 1877–82

BAN JOHNSON Byron Bancroft B1.5.1864 Norwalk OH D3.28.1931 St. Louis MO HF 1937 Col Marietta; Cincinnati Law School
President, Western League, 1894–99; President, (minor league) American League, 1900; Founder/Organizer, American League 1901; President, American League, 1901–27; Member, National Commission, 1903–20

BILL KLEM William J. B2.22.1874 Rochester NY D9.1.1951 Miami FL 5-7.5/157 HF 1953
Umpire, National League, 1905–40; Chief of Umpires, National League, 1941–51

KENESAW MOUNTAIN LANDIS Kenesaw Mountain B11.20.1866 Millville OH D11.25.1944 Chicago IL 5-6/135 HF 1945 Col YMCA Law School of Cincinnati; Union Law School
Commissioner of Baseball, 1920–44

LARRY MacPHAIL Leland Stanford B2.3.1890 Cass City MI D10.1.1975 Miami FL HF 1978 s-Lee Col Beloit; Michigan; George Washington
GM, Cin N, 1935; GM, Bro N, 1938–45; GM, NY A, 1946–47

LEE MacPHAIL Leland Stanford Jr. B10.25.1917 Nashville TN HF 1998 f-Larry
GM, Bal A, 1958–66; GM, NY A, 1966–73; President, American League, 1974–84

BILL McGOWAN William A. B1.18.1896 Wilmington DE D12.9.1954 Silver Spring MD 5-9/178 HF 1992
Umpire, American League, 1925–54

BILL VEECK William Louis Jr. B2.9.1914 Chicago IL D1.2.1986 Chicago IL HF 1991 Col Kenyon
Owner, Cle A, 1946–49; Owner, Stl A, 1951–53; Owner, Chi A, 1959–61, 1975–80

GEORGE WEISS George B6.23.1895 New Haven CT D8.13.1972 Greenwich CT HF 1971
Owner, New Haven EL, 1920–29; Owner, Bal IL, 1929–32; Farm Director, NY A, 1932–47; GM, NY A, 1948–60; President and GM, NY N, 1961–66; Director, NY N, 1966–71

TOM YAWKEY Thomas Austin B2.21.1903 Detroit MI D7.9.1976 Boston MA HF 1980
Owner, Bos A, 1933–76; Vice President, American League, 1956–73

THE BOYS OF SUMMER: AWARDS AND OTHER HONORS

Roger Kahn's 1971 masterwork about baseball and life struck a deep chord with Americans. As a result, the term *Boys of Summer* established itself forever in the popular lexicon. Merely playing in the big leagues, even for a moment, is certainly a tremendous accomplishment. However, the boys of our fondest summer memories are typically the stars whose ability, skill, and determination make them rise above the ordinary and place them ahead of their peers. Recognition by others in their field usually follows.

Most of this encyclopedia—indeed, most of any baseball encyclopedia—is filled with statistics. This section, however, is different: It records what the people who have watched baseball for a living thought about the players who produced the statistics. Who was the most valuable player? The *best* player? The best pitcher? The most impressive rookie? Which managers did the best job? Who were the best minor league prospects? Which players were leaders in their communities?

If you look carefully at the players who won the major awards, you'll also see signs of how the game has evolved. Different eras have brought different skills to the forefront, and the weight that the voters have given the various aspects of baseball has changed significantly over time. The major awards shown in this section represent the collective opinions of writers, editors, managers, coaches, and ballplayers over the past century, from the Chalmers Award in 1911 to last year's Rookie of the Year Award. Unanimous selections for all awards are indicated by asterisks.

Lists of "Ex Post Facto" awards for Most Valuable Player, Cy Young, and Rookie of the Year are also presented. Going back in time, we have chosen the players that we think would have won the major awards if they had been given out then (or if the awards had been given out in both leagues). Note that these Ex Post Facto awards do not necessarily represent who we think *should* have won. Instead, we have tried to apply the standards of times past and, based on what the writers historically valued, we have chosen who we think *would have won* had the writers of the time been given the opportunity to vote.

MOST VALUABLE PLAYER AWARD

The most important award in baseball is undoubtedly the Most Valuable Player Award. No other annual sports award generates as much debate as much as the AL and NL MVPs. Furthermore, no other award in American sports has as long and controversial a history.

The first incarnation of the MVP award was the Chalmers Award, named after Hugh Chalmers, an automobile manufacturer who decided in 1910 that it would be great publicity to give one of his company's automobiles to the player with the highest batting average in each league at the season's end. Unfortunately for the sponsor, the AL batting race that year ended in a white-hot controversy as the St. Louis Browns allowed Nap Lajoie to lay down 7 bunt hits on the last day of the season to give him an edge over the widely disliked Ty Cobb. AL President Ban Johnson ruled that a recalculation showed that Cobb had won the race anyway, and Chalmers ended up awarding cars to both Lajoie and Cobb.

To avoid this type of embarrassment, Chalmers decided in 1911 to change the rules of the contest, constituting a committee of baseball writers to determine—following the season—the "most important and useful player to his club and to the league." This was clearly the first Most Valuable Player Award. However, the Chalmers Award did not prove to be the hoped-for marketing bonanza, and the award was discontinued after 1914.

In 1922 the American League created a new award to honor "the baseball player who is of greatest all-around service to his club." Regrettably, the league saddled the new award with several rules that led to widespread dissatisfaction. Voters were required to select one (and only one) player from each team and were not allowed to vote for player-managers. Moreover, previous award winners were disqualified from consideration. Flawed from its inception, the award was dropped in 1929. The National League, which had in 1924 instituted its own contest (without the controversial restrictions), again followed the AL's lead and eliminated its award in 1930.

After a brief interregnum the Baseball Writers Association of America created the modern MVP award in 1931, adopting the same system that the NL had used for its abandoned MVP award. One writer in each league city was asked to fill out a ten-place ballot; ten points was awarded to the recipient of a first-place vote, nine points for a second-place vote, and so on, with one point awarded for a tenth place vote. In 1938 the BBWAA began polling three writers in each league city and raised the number of points for first-place votes to fourteen. The only significant change in the MVP balloting since then has been the reduction of writers polled to two per league city in 1961.

Despite continuing debate, the BBWAA has never spelled out the definition of the Most Valuable Player. Is the MVP simply the *best* player? Should candidates on pennant winners get special consideration? Must the MVP play on a contending team? Should starting pitchers qualify for the honor despite not participating in the great majority of their team's games? What about relief pitchers? Can any player be "most valuable" if his team finishes last?

While there have never been official answers to these questions, it is clear that the voting patterns of the BBWAA have changed over time. In the 1950s, for example, MVP voting favored "up the middle" players: center fielders, middle infielders, and catchers. Players like Nellie Fox (who won the 1959 AL MVP) and Dick Groat (1960 NL MVP) would not be serious candidates for the award today; in the last twenty-five years, writers have valued sluggers with high RBI totals (e.g., Juan Gonzalez and Jeff Kent) more highly than any other type of player. It is difficult to tell whether these voting patterns will persist; the argument over whether Alex Rodriguez of the last-place Rangers deserved the 2003 AL MVP is a perfect example of the utter lack of definition for the award.

Award voting, especially MVP balloting, frequently seems to stir up more controversy than it used to. Voters in the last twenty years have made some very debatable selections, including some outright mistakes, but it's wise to recall that their counterparts in earlier times were perfectly capable of picking less-than-qualified winners. Glamour statistics, mostly RBIs, have always tended to help players that are having otherwise modest seasons win prestigious trophies. Jackie Jensen, Hank Sauer, Frank McCormick, and Jeff Burroughs—MVP winners all—are good examples. Furthermore, decent but otherwise unspectacular players having that one "career year" (e.g., Zoilo Versalles, Bobby Shantz, and Bob Elliott) have copped awards despite clearly superior competition. Compared to some of the stranger BBWAA decisions of earlier times, the record-setting seventh MVP and Cy Young Awards given to Barry Bonds and Roger Clemens in 2004 seem like no-brainers.

Chalmers Award

	American League		National League
1911	Ty Cobb*, Det	1911	Frank Schulte, Chi
1912	Tris Speaker, Bos	1912	Larry Doyle, NY
1913	Walter Johnson, Was	1913	Jake Daubert, Bro
1914	Eddie Collins, Phi	1914	Johnny Evers, Bos
1922	George Sisler, StL		
1923	Babe Ruth*, NY		
1924	Walter Johnson, Was	1924	Dazzy Vance, Bro
1925	Roger Peckinpaugh, Was	1925	Rogers Hornsby, StL
1926	George Burns, Cle	1926	Bob O'Farrell, StL
1927	Lou Gehrig, NY	1927	Paul Waner, Pit
1928	Mickey Cochrane, Phi	1928	Jim Bottomley, StL
		1929	Rogers Hornsby, Chi

BBWAA AL & NL MVP Awards

	American League		National League
1931	Lefty Grove, Phi	1931	Frankie Frisch, StL
1932	Jimmie Foxx, Phi	1932	Chuck Klein, Phi

American League	National League
1933 Jimmie Foxx, Phi	1933 Carl Hubbell, NY
1934 Mickey Cochrane, Det	1934 Dizzy Dean, StL
1935 Hank Greenberg*, Det	1935 Gabby Hartnett, Chi
1936 Lou Gehrig, NY	1936 Carl Hubbell*, NY
1937 Charlie Gehringer, Det	1937 Joe Medwick, StL
1938 Jimmie Foxx, Bos	1938 Ernie Lombardi, Cin
1939 Joe DiMaggio, NY	1939 Bucky Walters, Cin
1940 Hank Greenberg, Det	1940 Frank McCormick, Cin
1941 Joe DiMaggio, NY	1941 Dolph Camilli, Bro
1942 Joe Gordon, NY	1942 Mort Cooper, StL
1943 Spud Chandler, NY	1943 Stan Musial, StL
1944 Hal Newhouser, Det	1944 Marty Marion, StL
1945 Hal Newhouser, Det	1945 Phil Cavarretta, Chi
1946 Ted Williams, Bos	1946 Stan Musial, StL
1947 Joe DiMaggio, NY	1947 Bob Elliott, Bos
1948 Lou Boudreau, Cle	1948 Stan Musial, StL
1949 Ted Williams, Bos	1949 Jackie Robinson, Bro
1950 Phil Rizzuto, NY	1950 Jim Konstanty, Phi
1951 Yogi Berra, NY	1951 Roy Campanella, Bro
1952 Bobby Shantz, Phi	1952 Hank Sauer, Chi
1953 Al Rosen*, Cle	1953 Roy Campanella, Bro
1954 Yogi Berra, NY	1954 Willie Mays, NY
1955 Yogi Berra, NY	1955 Roy Campanella, Bro
1956 Mickey Mantle*, NY	1956 Don Newcombe, Bro
1957 Mickey Mantle, NY	1957 Hank Aaron, Mil
1958 Jackie Jensen, Bos	1958 Ernie Banks, Chi
1959 Nellie Fox, Chi	1959 Ernie Banks, Chi
1960 Roger Maris, NY	1960 Dick Groat, Pit
1961 Roger Maris, NY	1961 Frank Robinson*, Cin
1962 Mickey Mantle, NY	1962 Maury Wills, LA
1963 Elston Howard, NY	1963 Sandy Koufax, LA
1964 Brooks Robinson, Bal	1964 Ken Boyer, StL
1965 Zoilo Versalles, Min	1965 Willie Mays, SF
1966 Frank Robinson*, Bal	1966 Roberto Clemente, Pit
1967 Carl Yastrzemski, Bos	1967 Orlando Cepeda*, StL
1968 Denny McLain*, Det	1968 Bob Gibson, StL
1969 Harmon Killebrew, Min	1969 Willie McCovey, SF
1970 Boog Powell, Bal	1970 Johnny Bench, Cin
1971 Vida Blue, Oak	1971 Joe Torre, StL
1972 Dick Allen, Chi	1972 Johnny Bench, Cin
1973 Reggie Jackson*, Oak	1973 Pete Rose, Cin
1974 Jeff Burroughs, Tex	1974 Steve Garvey, LA
1975 Fred Lynn, Bos	1975 Joe Morgan, Cin
1976 Thurman Munson, NY	1976 Joe Morgan, Cin
1977 Rod Carew, Min	1977 George Foster, Cin
1978 Jim Rice, Bos	1978 Dave Parker, Pit
1979 Don Baylor, Cal	1979 Keith Hernandez, StL
	(tie) Willie Stargell, Pit
1980 George Brett, KC	1980 Mike Schmidt*, Phi
1981 Rollie Fingers, Mil	1981 Mike Schmidt, Phi
1982 Robin Yount, Mil	1982 Dale Murphy, Atl
1983 Cal Ripken, Bal	1983 Dale Murphy, Atl
1984 Willie Hernandez, Det	1984 Ryne Sandberg, Chi
1985 Don Mattingly, NY	1985 Willie McGee, StL
1986 Roger Clemens, Bos	1986 Mike Schmidt, Phi
1987 George Bell, Tor	1987 Andre Dawson, Chi
1988 Jose Canseco*, Oak	1988 Kirk Gibson, LA
1989 Robin Yount, Mil	1989 Kevin Mitchell, SF
1990 Rickey Henderson, Oak	1990 Barry Bonds, Pit
1991 Cal Ripken, Bal	1991 Terry Pendleton, Atl
1992 Dennis Eckersley, Oak	1992 Barry Bonds, Pit
1993 Frank Thomas*, Chi	1993 Barry Bonds, SF
1994 Frank Thomas, Chi	1994 Jeff Bagwell*, Hou
1995 Mo Vaughn, Bos	1995 Barry Larkin, Cin
1996 Juan Gonzalez, Tex	1996 Ken Caminiti*, SD
1997 Ken Griffey Jr.*, Sea	1997 Larry Walker, Col
1998 Juan Gonzalez, Tex	1998 Sammy Sosa, Chi
1999 Ivan Rodriguez, Tex	1999 Chipper Jones, Atl
2000 Jason Giambi, Oak	2000 Jeff Kent, SF
2001 Ichiro Suzuki, Sea	2001 Barry Bonds, SF
2002 Miguel Tejada, Oak	2002 Barry Bonds, SF
2003 Alex Rodriguez, Tex	2003 Barry Bonds, SF
2004 Vladimir Guerrero, Ana	2004 Barry Bonds, SF
2005 Alex Rodriguez, NY	2005 Albert Pujols, StL

National League	American League
1903 Honus Wagner, Pit	1901 Nap Lajoie, Phi
1904 Joe McGinnity, NY	1902 Cy Young, Bos
1905 Christy Mathewson, NY	1903 Nap Lajoie, Cle
1906 Frank Chance, Chi	1904 Jack Chesbro, NY
1907 Honus Wagner, Pit	1905 Rube Waddell, Phi
1908 Christy Mathewson, NY	1906 Nap Lajoie, Cle
1909 Honus Wagner, Pit	1907 Ty Cobb, Det
1910 Sherry Magee, Phi	1908 Ed Walsh, Chi
[1911–14 See Chalmers Awards]	1909 Ty Cobb, Det
1915 Grover Alexander, Phi	1910 Jack Coombs, Phi
1916 Grover Alexander, Phi	[1911–14 See Chalmers Awards]
1917 Grover Alexander, Phi	1915 Ty Cobb, Det
1918 Hippo Vaughn, Chi	1916 Ty Cobb, Det
1919 Edd Roush, Cin	1917 Eddie Cicotte, Chi
1920 Rogers Hornsby, StL	1918 Babe Ruth, Bos
1921 Rogers Hornsby, StL	1919 Eddie Cicotte, Chi
1922 Rogers Hornsby, StL	1920 Babe Ruth, NY
1923 Dolf Luque, Cin	1921 Babe Ruth, NY
[1924–29 See NL Awards]	[1922–28 See AL Awards]
1930 Hack Wilson, Chi	1929 Lew Fonseca, Cle
	1930 Joe Cronin, Was

BBWAA CY YOUNG AWARD

In 1956 the BBWAA, prodded by Commissioner Ford Frick, created the Cy Young Award in order to annually honor the best pitcher in the major leagues. The award was named after Cy Young, the all-time leader in pitching wins (and losses), who had died in 1955. The impetus for the award's creation was the lack of support pitchers had been receiving in MVP balloting. Ironically, the creation of the Cy Young would further reduce that support. In 1967 voters began selecting one Cy Young winner in each league. In 1970 a three-place ballot replaced the original one-place ballot.

There's no debating the goal of the Cy Young Award; voters do not give extra credit to pitchers on contenders, and you'll rarely hear talk about a pitcher's leadership skills from the electorate. However, there has been one major change over the last forty years in the voting pattern—the rise in the status of relief pitchers. No relief pitcher had ever appeared in the Cy Young results until Lindy McDaniel in 1960. It would not be until 1974 that a relief pitcher, in this case Mike Marshall, would capture a Cy Young Award. No reliever has yet won one unanimously, though Eric Gagne came within two first-place votes of doing so in 2003. Some baseball writers have argued that it would be more appropriate for relievers to compete against everyday players in the MVP race rather than against starting pitchers for the Cy Young.

Cy Young Award

1956	Don Newcombe, Bro NL	1961	Whitey Ford, NY AL
1957	Warren Spahn, Mil NL	1962	Don Drysdale, LA NL
1958	Bob Turley, NY AL	1963	Sandy Koufax*, LA NL
1959	Early Wynn, Chi AL	1964	Dean Chance, LA AL
1960	Vern Law, Pit NL	1965	Sandy Koufax*, LA NL
		1966	Sandy Koufax*, LA NL

AL & NL Cy Young Awards

	AL	NL
1967	Jim Lonborg, Bos	Mike McCormick, SF
1968	Denny McLain*, Det	Bob Gibson*, StL
1969	Mike Cuellar, Bal	Tom Seaver, NY
(tie)	Denny McLain, Det	
1970	Jim Perry, Min	Bob Gibson, StL
1971	Vida Blue, Oak	Fergie Jenkins, Chi
1972	Gaylord Perry, Cle	Steve Carlton*, Phi
1973	Jim Palmer, Bal	Tom Seaver, NY
1974	Catfish Hunter, Oak	Mike Marshall, LA
1975	Jim Palmer, Bal	Tom Seaver, NY
1976	Jim Palmer, Bal	Randy Jones, SD
1977	Sparky Lyle, NY	Steve Carlton, Phi
1978	Ron Guidry*, NY	Gaylord Perry, SD
1979	Mike Flanagan, Bal	Bruce Sutter, Chi
1980	Steve Stone, Bal	Steve Carlton, Phi
1981	Rollie Fingers, Mil	Fernando Valenzuela, LA
1982	Pete Vuckovich, Mil	Steve Carlton, Phi
1983	La Marr Hoyt, Chi	John Denny, Phi
1984	Willie Hernandez, Det	Rick Sutcliffe*, Chi
1985	Bret Saberhagen, KC	Dwight Gooden*, NY
1986	Roger Clemens*, Bos	Mike Scott, Hou
1987	Roger Clemens, Bos	Steve Bedrosian, Phi
1988	Frank Viola, Min	Orel Hershiser*, LA
1989	Bret Saberhagen, KC	Mark Davis, SD
1990	Bob Welch, Oak	Doug Drabek, Pit
1991	Roger Clemens, Bos	Tom Glavine, Atl
1992	Dennis Eckersley, Oak	Greg Maddux, Chi
1993	Jack McDowell, Chi	Greg Maddux, Atl
1994	David Cone, KC	Greg Maddux*, Atl
1995	Randy Johnson, Sea	Greg Maddux*, Atl
1996	Pat Hentgen, Tor	John Smoltz, Atl
1997	Roger Clemens, Tor	Pedro Martinez*, Mon
1998	Roger Clemens*, Tor	Tom Glavine, Atl

Ex Post Facto MVP Award

National Association

1871	Levi Meyerle, Ath
1872	Ross Barnes, Bos
1873	Ross Barnes, Bos
1874	Cal McVey, Bos
1875	Cal McVey, Bos

American Association

1882	Hick Carpenter, Cin
1883	Harry Stovey, Phi
1884	Guy Hecker, Lou
1885	Bob Caruthers, StL
1886	Bob Caruthers, StL
1887	Tip O'Neill, StL
1888	Silver King, StL
1889	Harry Stovey, Phi
1890	Jimmy Wolf, Lou
1891	Dan Brouthers, Bos

Union Association

1884	Fred Dunlap, StL

Players League

1890	Hardy Richardson, Bos

Federal League

1914	Benny Kauff, Ind
1915	Ed Konetchy, Pit

National League

1876	Ross Barnes, Chi
1877	Deacon White, Bos
1878	Paul Hines, Pro
1879	Paul Hines, Pro
1880	George Gore, Chi
1881	Cap Anson, Chi
1882	Cap Anson, Chi
1883	Jim Whitney, Bos
1884	Charley Radbourn, Pro
1885	John Clarkson, Chi
1886	King Kelly, Chi
1887	Sam Thompson, Det
1888	Buck Ewing, NY
1889	John Clarkson, Bos
1890	Jack Glasscock, NY
1891	Billy Hamilton, Phi
1892	Dan Brouthers, Bro
1893	Ed Delahanty, Phi
1894	Hugh Duffy, Bos
1895	Hughie Jennings, Bal
1896	Hughie Jennings, Bal
1897	Willie Keeler, Bal
1898	Jimmy Collins, Bos
1899	Ed Delahanty, Phi
1900	Honus Wagner, Pit
1901	Honus Wagner, Pit
1902	Honus Wagner, Pit

	AL	NL
1999	Pedro Martinez*, Bos	Randy Johnson, Ari
2000	Pedro Martinez*, Bos	Randy Johnson, Ari
2001	Roger Clemens, NY	Randy Johnson, Ari
2002	Barry Zito, Oak	Randy Johnson*, Ari
2003	Roy Halladay, Tor	Eric Gagne, LA
2004	Johan Santana*, Min	Roger Clemens, Hou
2005	Bartolo Colon, Chi	Chris Carpenter, StL

Ex Post Facto Cy Young Awards

National Association

1871	George Zettlein, Chi
1872	Al Spalding, Bos
1873	Al Spalding, Bos
1874	Al Spalding, Bos
1875	Al Spalding, Bos

American Association

1882	Will White, Cin
1883	Will White, Cin
1884	Guy Hecker, Lou
1885	Bob Caruthers, StL
1886	Dave Foutz, StL
1887	Matt Kilroy, Bal
1888	Silver King, StL
1889	Bob Caruthers, Bro
1890	Scott Stratton, Lou
1891	George Haddock, Bos

Union Association

1884	Bill Sweeney, Bal

Players League

1890	Silver King, Chi

Federal League

1914	Claude Hendrix, Chi
1915	George McConnell, Chi

National League

1876	George Bradley, StL
1877	Tommy Bond, Bos
1878	Tommy Bond, Bos
1879	Tommy Bond, Bos
1880	Larry Corcoran, Chi
1881	Larry Corcoran, Chi
1882	Charley Radbourn, Pro
1883	Charley Radbourn, Pro
1884	Charley Radbourn, Pro
1885	John Clarkson, Chi
1886	Lady Baldwin, Det
1887	John Clarkson, Chi
1888	Tim Keefe, NY
1889	John Clarkson, Bos
1890	Bill Hutchison, Chi
1891	Bill Hutchison, Chi
1892	Cy Young, Cle
1893	Amos Rusie, NY
1894	Amos Rusie, NY
1895	Cy Young, Cle
1896	Kid Nichols, Bos
1897	Kid Nichols, Bos
1898	Kid Nichols, Bos
1899	Vic Willis, Bos
1900	Joe McGinnity, Bro
1901	Deacon Phillippe, Pit
1902	Jack Chesbro, Pit
1903	Christy Mathewson, NY
1904	Joe McGinnity, NY
1905	Christy Mathewson, NY
1906	Mordecai Brown, Chi
1907	Orval Overall, Chi
1908	Christy Mathewson, NY
1909	Mordecai Brown, Chi
1910	Christy Mathewson, NY
1911	Christy Mathewson, NY
1912	Rube Marquard, NY
1913	Christy Mathewson, NY
1914	Bill James, Bos
1915	Grover Alexander, Phi
1916	Grover Alexander, Phi
1917	Grover Alexander, Phi
1918	Hippo Vaughn, Chi
1919	Hippo Vaughn, Chi
1920	Pete Alexander, Chi
1921	Burleigh Grimes, Bro
1922	Wilbur Cooper, Pit
1923	Dolf Luque, Cin
1924	Dazzy Vance, Bro
1925	Dazzy Vance, Bro
1926	Ray Kremer, Pit
1927	Charles Root, Chi
1928	Burleigh Grimes, Pit
1929	Burleigh Grimes, Pit
1930	Pat Malone, Chi
1931	Ed Brandt, Bos
1932	Lou Warneke, Chi
1933	Carl Hubbell, NY
1934	Dizzy Dean, StL
1935	Dizzy Dean, StL

National League

1936	Carl Hubbell, NY
1937	Carl Hubbell, NY
1938	Bill Lee, Chi
1939	Bucky Walters, Cin
1940	Bucky Walters, Cin
1941	Whit Wyatt, Bro
1942	Mort Cooper, StL
1943	Mort Cooper, StL
1944	Bucky Walters, Cin
1945	Red Barrett, Bos-StL
1946	Howie Pollet, StL
1947	Ewell Blackwell, Cin
1948	Johnny Sain, Bos
1949	Warren Spahn, Bos
1950	Jim Konstanty, Phi
1951	Sal Maglie, NY
1952	Robin Roberts, Phi
1953	Warren Spahn, Mil
1954	Johnny Antonelli, NY
1955	Robin Roberts, Phi
1958	Warren Spahn, Mil
1959	Sam Jones, SF
1961	Warren Spahn, Mil
1964	Sandy Koufax, LA

American League

1901	Cy Young, Bos
1902	Cy Young, Bos
1903	Cy Young, Bos
1904	Jack Chesbro, NY
1905	Rube Waddell, Phi
1906	Al Orth, NY
1907	Bill Donovan, Det
1908	Ed Walsh, Chi
1909	George Mullin, Det
1910	Jack Coombs, Phi
1911	Walter Johnson, Was
1912	Walter Johnson, Was
1913	Walter Johnson, Was
1914	Walter Johnson, Was
1915	Walter Johnson, Was
1916	Babe Ruth, Bos
1917	Eddie Cicotte, Chi
1918	Walter Johnson, Was
1919	Eddie Cicotte, Chi
1920	Jim Bagby, Cle
1921	Red Faber, Chi
1922	Eddie Rommel, Phi
1923	George Uhle, Cle
1924	Walter Johnson, Was
1925	Stan Coveleski, Was
1926	George Uhle, Cle
1927	Waite Hoyt, NY
1928	Lefty Grove, Phi
1929	Lefty Grove, Phi
1930	Lefty Grove, Phi
1931	Lefty Grove, Phi
1932	Lefty Grove, Phi
1933	Lefty Grove, Phi
1934	Lefty Gomez, NY
1935	Wes Ferrell, Bos
1936	Tommy Bridges, Det
1937	Lefty Gomez, NY
1938	Red Ruffing, NY
1939	Bob Feller, Cle
1940	Bob Feller, Cle
1941	Bob Feller, Cle
1942	Tex Hughson, Bos
1943	Spud Chandler, NY
1944	Hal Newhouser, Det
1945	Hal Newhouser, Det
1946	Hal Newhouser, Det
1947	Bob Feller, Cle
1948	Bob Lemon, Cle
1949	Mel Parnell, Bos
1950	Bob Lemon, Cle
1951	Ed Lopat, NY
1952	Bobby Shantz, Phi
1953	Billy Pierce, Chi
1954	Bob Lemon, Cle
1955	Whitey Ford, NY
1956	Billy Pierce, Chi
1957	Jim Bunning, Det
1960	Chuck Estrada, Bal
1962	Dick Donovan, Cle
1963	Whitey Ford, NY
1965	Mudcat Grant, Min
1966	Jim Kaat, Min

BBWAA Rookie of the Year Award

Inspired by its Chicago branch, which had been honoring top rookies since 1940, the Baseball Writers Association of America took the Rookie of the Year awards national starting in 1947. After honoring only one rookie in 1947 and 1948, the BBWAA started giving the award to a rookie in each league in 1949. In the early days of the award, there was significant confusion over which players qualified as rookies. The first set of standards dealing with this was established in 1957. The current standards, which say that any player who has accumulated more than 130 at bats, 50 innings, or a certain amount of time on the major league roster is no longer a rookie, took effect in 1971. Writers used a one-place ballot for most the award's history until 1980, when voters shifted over to a three-place ballot.

Though there's no longer any debate over which players are technically rookies, there is discussion as to whether certain players should be *considered* rookies. Hideki Matsui lost the 2003 AL Rookie of the Year Award because two voters purposely left him off their ballots as a result of his Japanese pro experience. Ironically, the first BBWAA Rookie of the Year Award winner, Jackie Robinson, and many of the other players who won the award in its first decade of existence, came from the high-level Negro Leagues and thus had a similar baseball background to the Japanese players of today who are competing for MLB's rookie awards.

A more general issue is whether voters should favor younger rookies who show greater potential over older rookies who perform better in their first years but have much lower ceilings. With more Japanese players entering the majors, this issue will remain a hot topic, but it appears unlikely that the rules will be altered anytime soon.

Rookie of the Year Award

1947	Jackie Robinson, Bro NL
1948	Alvin Dark, Bos NL

AL Rookie of the Year Award		NL Rookie of the Year Award	
1949	Roy Sievers, StL	1949	Don Newcombe, Bro
1950	Walt Dropo, Bos	1950	Sam Jethroe, Bos
1951	Gil McDougald, NY	1951	Willie Mays, NY
1952	Harry Byrd, Phi	1952	Joe Black, Bro
1953	Harvey Kuenn, Det	1953	Jim Gilliam, Bro
1954	Bob Grim, NY	1954	Wally Moon, StL
1955	Herb Score, Cle	1955	Bill Virdon, StL
1956	Luis Aparicio, Chi	1956	Frank Robinson*, Cin
1957	Tony Kubek*, NY	1957	Jack Sanford, Phi
1958	Albie Pearson, Was	1958	Orlando Cepeda*, SF
1959	Bob Allison, Was	1959	Willie McCovey*, SF
1960	Ron Hansen, Bal	1960	Frank Howard, LA
1961	Don Schwall, Bos	1961	Billy Williams, Chi
1962	Tom Tresh, NY	1962	Ken Hubbs, Chi
1963	Gary Peters, Chi	1963	Pete Rose, Cin
1964	Tony Oliva, Min	1964	Richie Allen, Phi
1965	Curt Blefary, Bal	1965	Jim Lefebvre, LA
1966	Tommie Agee, Chi	1966	Tommy Helms, Cin
1967	Rod Carew, Min	1967	Tom Seaver, NY
1968	Stan Bahnsen, NY	1968	Johnny Bench, Cin
1969	Lou Piniella, KC	1969	Ted Sizemore, LA
1970	Thurman Munson, NY	1970	Carl Morton, Mon
1971	Chris Chambliss, Cle	1971	Earl Williams, Atl
1972	Carlton Fisk, Bos	1972	Jon Matlack, NY
1973	Al Bumbry, Bal	1973	Gary Matthews, SF
1974	Mike Hargrove, Tex	1974	Bake McBride, StL
1975	Fred Lynn*, Bos	1975	John Montefusco, SF
1976	Mark Fidrych, Det	1976	Pat Zachary, Cin
		(tie)	Butch Metzger, SD
1977	Eddie Murray, Bal	1977	Andre Dawson, Mon
1978	Lou Whitaker, Det	1978	Bob Horner, Atl
1979	Alfredo Griffin, Tor	1979	Rick Sutcliffe, LA
(tie)	John Castino, Min		
1980	Joe Charboneau, Cle	1980	Steve Howe, LA
1981	Dave Righetti, NY	1981	Fernando Valenzuela, LA
1982	Cal Ripken, Bal	1982	Steve Sax, LA
1983	Ron Kittle, Chi	1983	Darryl Strawberry, NY
1984	Alvin Davis, Sea	1984	Dwight Gooden, NY
1985	Ozzie Guillen, Chi	1985	Vince Coleman*, StL
1986	Jose Canseco, Oak	1986	Todd Worrell, StL
1987	Mark McGwire*, Oak	1987	Benito Santiago*, SD
1988	Walt Weiss, Oak	1988	Chris Sabo, Cin
1989	Gregg Olson, Bal	1989	Jerome Walton, Chi
1990	Sandy Alomar Jr.*, Cle	1990	David Justice, Atl
1991	Chuck Knoblauch, Min	1991	Jeff Bagwell, Hou
1992	Pat Listach, Mil	1992	Eric Karros, LA
1993	Tim Salmon*, Cal	1993	Mike Piazza*, LA
1994	Bob Hamelin, KC	1994	Raul Mondesi*, LA
1995	Marty Cordova, Min	1995	Hideo Nomo, LA
1996	Derek Jeter*, NY	1996	Todd Hollandsworth, LA
1997	Nomar Garciaparra, Bos	1997	Scott Rolen*, Phi
1998	Ben Grieve, Oak	1998	Kerry Wood, Chi
1999	Carlos Beltran, KC	1999	Scott Williamson, Cin
2000	Kazuhiro Sasaki, Sea	2000	Rafael Furcal, Atl
2001	Ichiro Suzuki, Sea	2001	Albert Pujols*, StL
2002	Eric Hinske, Tor	2002	Jason Jennings, Col
2003	Angel Berroa, KC	2003	Dontrelle Willis, Fla
2004	Bobby Crosby, Oak	2004	Jason Bay, Pit
2005	Huston Street, Oak	2005	Ryan Howard, Phi

Ex Post Facto Rookie of the Year Award

National Association

1872	Candy Cummings, Mut
1873	Paul Hines, Was
1874	Tommy Bond, Atl
1875	George Bradley, StL

American Association

1882	Pete Browning, Lou
1883	Arlie Latham, StL
1884	Dave Orr, NY
1885	Norm Baker, Lou
1886	Matt Kilroy, Bal
1887	Mike Griffin, Bal
1888	Mickey Hughes, Bro
1889	Jesse Duryea, Cin
1890	Cupid Childs, Syr
1891	Willard Mains, Cin

Union Association

1884	Harry Moore, Was

Players League

1890	Phil Knell, Phi

Federal League

1914	Benny Kauff, Ind
1915	Jim Kelly, Pit

National League

1876	Charley Jones, Cin
1877	Terry Larkin, Har
1878	Abner Dalrymple, Mil
1879	John O'Rourke, Bos
1880	Roger Connor, Tro
1881	Jim Whitney, Bos
1882	Mike Muldoon, Cle
1883	Charlie Buffinton, Bos
1884	John Clarkson, Chi
1885	Ed Daily, Phi
1886	Jocko Flynn, Chi
1887	Mark Baldwin, Chi
1888	Ben Sanders, Phi
1889	Patsy Tebeau, Cle
1890	Billy Rhines, Cin
1891	Bill Dahlen, Chi
1892	Nig Cuppy, Cle
1893	Heinie Reitz, Bal
1894	Win Mercer, Was
1895	Bill Hoffer, Bal
1896	Gene DeMontreville, Was
1897	Chick Stahl, Bos
1898	Elmer Flick, Phi
1899	Jimmy Williams, Pit
1900	Jimmy Barrett, Cin
1901	Christy Mathewson, NY
1902	Homer Smoot, StL
1903	Jake Weimer, Chi
1904	Harry Lumley, Bro

National League

1905	George Stone, StL
1906	Jack Pfiester, Chi
1907	Nap Rucker, Bro
1908	George McQuillan, Phi
1909	Harry Gaspar, Cin
1910	King Cole, Chi
1911	Grover Alexander, Phi
1912	Larry Cheney, Chi
1913	Jim Viox, Pit
1914	Jeff Pfeffer, Bro
1915	Tom Long, StL
1916	Rogers Hornsby, StL
1917	Leon Cadore, Bro
1918	Charlie Hollocher, Chi
1919	Oscar Tuero, StL
1920	Pat Duncan, Cin
1921	Ray Grimes, Chi
1922	Hack Miller, Chi
1923	George Grantham, Chi
1924	Kiki Cuyler, Pit
1925	Jimmy Welsh, Bos
1926	Paul Waner, Pit
1927	Lloyd Waner, Pit
1928	Del Bissonette, Bro
1929	Johnny Frederick, Bro
1930	Wally Berger, Bos
1931	Paul Derringer, StL
1932	Dizzy Dean, StL
1933	Frank Demaree, Chi
1934	Curt Davis, Phi
1935	Cy Blanton, Pit
1936	Johnny Mize, StL
1937	Cliff Melton, NY
1938	Johnny Rizzo, Pit
1939	Bob Bowman, StL
1940	Babe Young, NY
1941	Elmer Riddle, Cin
1942	Johnny Beazley, StL
1943	Lou Klein, StL
1944	Bill Voiselle, NY
1945	Ken Burkhart, StL
1946	Del Ennis, Phi

American League

1901	Socks Seybold, Phi
1902	Addie Joss, Cle
1903	Chief Bender, Phi
1904	Fred Glade, StL
1905	George Stone, StL
1906	Claude Rossman, Cle
1907	Glenn Liebhardt, Cle
1908	Ed Summers, Det
1909	Frank Baker, Phi
1910	Russ Ford, NY
1911	Vean Gregg, Cle
1912	Del Pratt, StL

American League

1913	Reb Russell, Chi
1914	George Burns, Det
1915	Babe Ruth, Bos
1916	Jim Bagby, Cle
1917	Joe Harris, Cle
1918	Scott Perry, Phi
1919	Dickie Kerr, Chi
1920	Bob Meusel, NY
1921	Joe Sewell, Cle
1922	Herman Pillette, Det
1923	Homer Summa, Cle
1924	Ike Boone, Bos
1925	Earle Combs, NY
1926	Tony Lazzeri, NY
1927	Wilcy Moore, NY
1928	Ed Morris, Bos
1929	Dale Alexander, Det
1930	Smead Jolley, Chi
1931	Joe Vosmik, Cle

American League

1932	Johnny Allen, NY
1933	Bob Johnson, Phi
1934	Hal Trosky, Cle
1935	Jake Powell, Was
1936	Joe DiMaggio, NY
1937	Rudy York, Det
1938	Ken Keltner, Cle
1939	Ted Williams, Bos
1940	Walt Judnich, StL
1941	Phil Rizzuto, NY
1942	Johnny Pesky, Bos
1943	Billy Johnson, NY
1944	Joe Berry, Phi
1945	Dave Ferriss, Bos
1946	Hoot Evers, Det
1947	Spec Shea, NY
1948	Gene Bearden, Cle

BBWAA Manager of the Year Award

The Baseball Writers Association of America was a late-comer to honoring the major leagues' best managers, but today the trophy given to the BBWAA's Manager of the Year is the most prestigious of its kind. Voting is done with the same three-place ballot that the BBWAA uses for the Cy Young and Rookie of the Year.

	AL	NL
1983	Tony La Russa, Chi	Tommy Lasorda, LA
1984	Sparky Anderson, Det	Jim Frey, Chi
1985	Bobby Cox, Tor	Whitey Herzog, StL
1986	John McNamara, Bos	Hal Lanier, Hou
1987	Sparky Anderson, Det	Buck Rodgers, Mon
1988	Tony La Russa, Oak	Tommy Lasorda, La
1989	Frank Robinson, Bal	Don Zimmer, Chi
1990	Jeff Torborg, Chi	Jim Leyland, Pit
1991	Tom Kelly, Min	Bobby Cox, Atl
1992	Tony La Russa, Oak	Jim Leyland, Pit
1993	Gene Lamont, Chi	Dusty Baker, SF
1994	Buck Showalter, NY	Felipe Alou, Mon
1995	Lou Piniella, Sea	Don Baylor, Col
1996	Johnny Oates, Tex	Bruce Bochy, SD
(tie)	Joe Torre, NY	

	AL	NL
1997	Davey Johnson, Bal	Dusty Baker, SF
1998	Joe Torre, NY	Larry Dierker, Hou
1999	Jimy Williams, Bos	Jack McKeon, Cin
2000	Jerry Manuel, Chi	Dusty Baker, SF
2001	Lou Piniella, Sea	Larry Bowa, Phi
2002	Mike Scioscia, Ana	Tony La Russa, StL
2003	Tony Pena, KC	Jack McKeon, Fla
2004	Buck Showalter, Tex	Bobby Cox, Atl
2005	Ozzie Guillen, Chi	Bobby Cox, Atl

The Sporting News Player and Pitcher of the Year Awards

The Sporting News was once known as "Baseball's Bible." (Some especially avid baseball fans referred to the Bible as "*The Sporting News* of religion.") That reputation endowed *The Sporting News*' awards with a great deal of prestige. Many fans held the newspaper's selections in equal or even higher regard than the choices made by the BBWAA. That time is long gone, but *The Sporting News* still gives out more baseball awards than any other organization, and the long tradition of these awards gives them unmatched historical value.

The Sporting News started its tradition of awards in 1929 after the American League abandoned choosing a Most Valuable Player. Over the following twenty years, *The Sporting News* alternated between competing with the BBWAA's MVP awards and endorsing them. In 1948, *The Sporting News* started annually selecting Players and Pitchers of the Year in each league as well as continuing their Major League Player of the Year, which had been selected annually since 1935. In 1992, *The Sporting News* decided to drop its AL and NL Player of the Year Awards in order to focus exclusively on its Major League Player of the Year Award, which would heretofore be selected by big league players. The remaining *Sporting News* awards are still selected by the magazine's editors.

	AL PLAYER	AL PITCHER	NL PLAYER	NL PITCHER	ML PLAYER
1929	Al Simmons, Phi				
1930	Joe Cronin, Was		Bill Terry, NY		
1931	Lou Gehrig, NY		Chuck Klein, Phi		
1932	Jimmie Foxx, Phi		Chuck Klein, Phi		
1933	Jimmie Foxx, Phi			Carl Hubbell, NY	
1934	Lou Gehrig, NY			Dizzy Dean, StL	
1935	Hank Greenberg, Det		Arky Vaughan, Pit		
1936	Lou Gehrig, NY			Carl Hubbell, NY	Carl Hubbell, NY
1937	Charlie Gehringer, Det	Johnny Allen, Cle	Joe Medwick, StL		Johnny Allen, Cle
1938	Jimmie Foxx, Bos		Ernie Lombardi, Cin	Johnny Vander Meer, Cin	Johnny Vander Meer, Cin
1939	Joe DiMaggio, NY			Bucky Walters, Cin	Joe DiMaggio, NY
1940	Hank Greenberg, Det	Bob Feller, Cle	Frank McCormick, Cin		Bob Feller, Cle
1941	Joe DiMaggio, NY		Dolf Camilli, Bro		Ted Williams, Bos
1942	Joe Gordon, NY			Mort Cooper, StL	Ted Williams, Bos
1943		Spud Chandler, NY	Stan Musial, StL		Spud Chandler, NY
1944	Bobby Doerr, Bos	Hal Newhouser, Det	Marty Marion, StL	Bill Voiselle, NY	Marty Marion, StL
1945	Eddie Mayo, Det	Hal Newhouser, Det	Tommy Holmes, Bos	Hank Borowy, Chi	Hal Newhouser, Det
1946			Stan Musial, StL		Stan Musial, StL
1947	Ted Williams, Bos				Ted Williams, Bos
1948	Lou Boudreau, Cle	Bob Lemon, Cle	Stan Musial, StL	Johnny Sain, Bos	Lou Boudreau, Cle
1949	Ted Williams, Bos	Ellis Kinder, Bos	Enos Slaughter, StL	Howie Pollet, StL	Ted Williams, Bos
1950	Phil Rizzuto, NY	Bob Lemon, Cle	Ralph Kiner, Pit	Jim Konstanty, Phi	Phil Rizzuto, NY
1951	Ferris Fain, Phi	Bob Feller, Cle	Stan Musial, StL	Preacher Roe, Bro	Stan Musial, StL
1952	Luke Easter, Cle	Bobby Shantz, Phi	Hank Sauer, Chi	Robin Roberts, Phi	Robin Roberts, Phi
1953	Al Rosen, Cle	Bob Porterfield, Was	Roy Campanella, Bro	Warren Spahn, Mil	Al Rosen, Cle

	AL PLAYER	AL PITCHER	NL PLAYER	NL PITCHER	ML PLAYER
1954	Bobby Avila, Cle	Bob Lemon, Cle	Willie Mays, NY	John Antonelli, NY	Willie Mays, NY
1955	Al Kaline, Det	Whitey Ford, NY	Duke Snider, Bro	Robin Roberts, Phi	Duke Snider, Bro
1956	Mickey Mantle, NY	Billy Pierce, Chi	Hank Aaron, Mil	Don Newcombe, Bro	Mickey Mantle, NY
1957	Ted Williams, Bos	Billy Pierce, Chi	Stan Musial, StL	Warren Spahn, Mil	Ted Williams, Bos
1958	Jackie Jensen, Bos	Bob Turley, NY	Ernie Banks, Chi	Warren Spahn, Mil	Bob Turley, NY
1959	Nellie Fox, Chi	Early Wynn, Chi	Ernie Banks, Chi	Sam Jones, SF	Early Wynn, Chi
1960	Roger Maris, NY	Chuck Estrada, Bal	Dick Groat, Pit	Vern Law, Pit	Bill Mazeroski, Pit
1961	Roger Maris, NY	Whitey Ford, NY	Frank Robinson, Cin	Warren Spahn, Mil	Roger Maris, NY
1962	Mickey Mantle, NY	Dick Donovan, Cle	Maury Wills, LA	Don Drysdale, LA	Don Drysdale, LA
1963	Al Kaline, Det	Whitey Ford, NY	Hank Aaron, Mil	Sandy Koufax, LA	Sandy Koufax, LA
1964	Brooks Robinson, Bal	Dean Chance, LA	Ken Boyer, StL	Sandy Koufax, LA	Ken Boyer, StL
1965	Tony Oliva, Min	Mudcat Grant, Min	Willie Mays, SF	Sandy Koufax, LA	Sandy Koufax, LA
1966	Frank Robinson, Bal	Jim Kaat, Min	Roberto Clemente, Pit	Sandy Koufax, LA	Frank Robinson, Bal
1967	Carl Yastrzemski, Bos	Jim Lonborg, Bos	Orlando Cepeda, StL	Mike McCormick, SF	Carl Yastrzemski, Bos
1968	Ken Harrelson, Bos	Denny McLain, Det	Pete Rose, Cin	Bob Gibson, StL	Denny McLain, Det
1969	Harmon Killebrew, Min	Denny McLain, Det	Willie McCovey, SF	Tom Seaver, NY	Willie McCovey, SF
1970	Harmon Killebrew, Min	Sam McDowell, Cle	Johnny Bench, Cin	Bob Gibson, StL	Johnny Bench, Cin
1971	Tony Oliva, Min	Vida Blue, Oak	Joe Torre, StL	Fergie Jenkins, Chi	Joe Torre, StL
1972	Dick Allen, Chi	Wilbur Wood, Chi	Billy Williams, Chi	Steve Carlton, Phi	Billy Williams, Chi
1973	Reggie Jackson, Oak	Jim Palmer, Bal	Bobby Bonds, SF	Ron Bryant, SF	Reggie Jackson, Oak
1974	Jeff Burroughs, Tex	Catfish Hunter, Oak	Lou Brock, StL	Mike Marshall, LA	Lou Brock, StL
1975	Fred Lynn, Bos	Jim Palmer, Bal	Joe Morgan, Cin	Tom Seaver, NY	Joe Morgan, Cin
1976	Thurman Munson, NY	Jim Palmer, Bal	George Foster, Cin	Randy Jones, SD	Joe Morgan, Cin
1977	Rod Carew, Min	Nolan Ryan, Cal	George Foster, Cin	Steve Carlton, Phi	Rod Carew, Min
1978	Jim Rice, Bos	Ron Guidry, NY	Dave Parker, Pit	Vida Blue, SF	Ron Guidry, NY
1979	Don Baylor, Cal	Mike Flanagan, Bal	Keith Hernandez, StL	Joe Niekro, Hou	Willie Stargell, Pit
1980	George Brett, KC	Steve Stone, Bal	Mike Schmidt, Phi	Steve Carlton, Phi	George Brett, KC
1981	Tony Armas, Oak	Jack Morris, Det	Andre Dawson, Mon	Fernando Valenzuela, LA	Fernando Valenzuela, LA
1982	Robin Yount, Mil	Dave Stieb, Tor	Dale Murphy, Atl	Steve Carlton, Phi	Robin Yount, Mil
1983	Cal Ripken, Bal	La Marr Hoyt, Chi	Dale Murphy, Atl	John Denny, Phi	Cal Ripken, Bal
1984	Don Mattingly, NY	Willie Hernandez, Det	Ryne Sandberg, Chi	Rick Sutcliffe, Chi	Ryne Sandberg, Chi
1985	Don Mattingly, NY	Bret Saberhagen, KC	Willie McGee, StL	Dwight Gooden, NY	Don Mattingly, NY
1986	Don Mattingly, NY	Roger Clemens, Bos	Mike Schmidt, Phi	Mike Scott, Hou	Roger Clemens, Bos
1987	George Bell, Tor	Jimmy Key, Tor	Andre Dawson, Chi	Rick Sutcliffe, Chi	George Bell, Tor
1988	Jose Canseco, Oak	Frank Viola, Min	Andy Van Slyke, Pit	Orel Hershiser, LA	Orel Hershiser, LA
1989	Ruben Sierra, Tex	Bret Saberhagen, KC	Kevin Mitchell, SF	Mark Davis, SD	Kevin Mitchell, SF
1990	Cecil Fielder, Det	Bob Welch, Oak	Barry Bonds, Pit	Doug Drabek, Pit	Barry Bonds, Pit
1991	Cal Ripken, Bal	Roger Clemens, Bos	Barry Bonds, Pit	Tom Glavine, Atl	Cal Ripken, Bal
1992		Dennis Eckersley, Oak		Greg Maddux, Chi	Gary Sheffield, SD
1993		Jack McDowell, Chi		Greg Maddux, Atl	Frank Thomas, Chi
1994		Jimmy Key, NY		Greg Maddux, Atl	Jeff Bagwell, Hou
1995		Randy Johnson, Sea		Greg Maddux, Atl	Albert Belle, Cle
1996		Pat Hentgen, Tor		John Smoltz, Atl	Alex Rodriguez, Sea
1997		Roger Clemens, Tor		Pedro Martinez, Mon	Ken Griffey Jr., Sea
1998		Roger Clemens, Tor		Kevin Brown, SD	Sammy Sosa, Chi
1999		Pedro Martinez, Bos		Mike Hampton, Hou	Rafael Palmeiro, Tex
2000		Pedro Martinez, Bos		Tom Glavine, Atl	Carlos Delgado, Tor
2001		Roger Clemens, NY		Curt Schilling, Ari	Barry Bonds, SF
2002		Barry Zito, Oak		Curt Schilling, Ari	Alex Rodriguez, Tex
2003		Roy Halladay, Oak		Eric Gagne, LA	Albert Pujols, StL
2004		Johan Santana, Min		Jason Schmidt, SF	Barry Bonds, SF
2005		Bartolo Colon, Cle		Chris Carpenter, StL	Andruw Jones, Atl

The Sporting News Rookie Player and Pitcher of the Year Awards

The Sporting News started selecting a Rookie of the Year in 1946, and moved tentatively to selecting one player from each league in 1949. It selected a separate Rookie Pitcher of the Year in 1957, one in each league in 1958 and 1961, and no pitchers at all in 1959, 1960, and 1962. Finally, in 1963, *The Sporting News* settled on annually picking both a Rookie Player of the Year and a Rookie Pitcher of the Year from each league. In 2004, however, *The Sporting News* eliminated its Rookie Pitcher of the Year awards. (The top rookie—if a pitcher—is listed under the pitcher heading before 1957 and after 2003 but, in those cases, the pitcher is simply *The Sporting News* Rookie of the Year for his league.)

	AL PLAYER	AL PITCHER	NL PLAYER	NL PITCHER
1946			Del Ennis, Phi	
1947			Jackie Robinson, Bro	
1948			Richie Ashburn, Phi	
1949	Roy Sievers, StL			Don Newcombe, Bro
1950		Whitey Ford, NY		
1951	Minnie Minoso, Chi		Willie Mays, NY	
1952	Clint Courtney, StL			Joe Black, Bro
1953	Harvey Kuenn, Det		Junior Gilliam, Bro	
1954		Bob Grim, NY	Wally Moon, StL	
1955		Herb Score, Cle	Bill Virdon, StL	
1956	Luis Aparicio, Chi		Frank Robinson, Cin	
1957	Tony Kubek, NY		Ed Bouchee, Phi	Jack Sanford, Phi
1958	Albie Pearson, Was	Ryne Duren, NY	Orlando Cepeda, SF	Carlton Willey, Mil
1959	Bob Allison, Was		Willie McCovey, SF	
1960	Ron Hansen, Bal		Frank Howard, LA	
1961	Dick Howser, KC	Don Schwall, Bos	Billy Williams, Chi	Ken Hunt, Cin
1962	Tom Tresh, NY		Ken Hubbs, Chi	
1963	Pete Ward, Chi	Gary Peters, Chi	Pete Rose, Cin	Ray Culp, Phi
1964	Tony Oliva, Min	Wally Bunker, Bal	Richie Allen, Phi	Billy McCool, Cin
1965	Curt Blefary, Bal	Marcelino Lopez, Cal	Joe Morgan, Hou	Frank Linzy, SF
1966	Tommie Agee, Chi	Jim Nash, KC	Tommy Helms, Cin	Don Sutton, La
1967	Rod Carew, Min	Tom Phoebus, Bal	Lee May, Cin	Dick Hughes, StL
1968	Del Unser, Was	Stan Bahnsen, NY	Johnny Bench, Cin	Jerry Koosman, NY
1969	Carlos May, Chi	Mike Nagy, Bos	Coco Laboy, Mon	Tom Griffin, Hou
1970	Roy Foster, Cle	Bert Blyleven, Min	Bernie Carbo, Cin	Carl Morton, Mon
1971	Chris Chambliss, Cle	Bill Parsons, Mil	Earl Williams, Atl	Reggie Cleveland, StL
1972	Carlton Fisk, Bos	Dick Tidrow, Cle	Dave Rader, SF	Jon Matlack, NY
1973	Al Bumbry, Bal	Steve Busby, KC	Gary Matthews, SF	Steve Rogers, Mon
1974	Mike Hargrove, Tex	Frank Tanana, Cal	Greg Gross, Hou	John D'Acquisto, SF
1975	Fred Lynn, Bos	Dennis Eckersley, Cle	Gary Carter, Mon	John Montefusco, SF
1976	Butch Wynegar, Min	Mark Fidrych, Det	Larry Herndon, SF	Butch Metzger, SD
1977	Mitchell Page, Oak	Dave Rozema, Det	Andre Dawson, Mon	Bob Owchinko, SD
1978	Paul Molitor, Mil	Rich Gale, KC	Bob Horner, Atl	Don Robinson, Pit
1979	Pat Putnam, Tex	Mark Clear, Cal	Jeff Leonard, Hou	Rick Sutcliffe, LA
1980	Joe Charboneau, Cle	Britt Burns, Chi	Lonnie Smith, Phi	Bill Gullickson, Mon
1981	Rich Gedman, Bos	Dave Righetti, NY	Tim Raines, Mon	Fernando Valenzuela, LA
1982	Cal Ripken, Bal	Ed Vande Berg, Sea	Johnny Ray, Pit	Steve Bedrosian, Atl
1983	Ron Kittle, Chi	Mike Boddicker, Bal	Darryl Strawberry, NY	Craig McMurtry, Atl

	AL PLAYER	AL PITCHER	NL PLAYER	NL PITCHER
1984	Alvin Davis, Sea	Mark Langston, Sea	Juan Samuel, Phi	Dwight Gooden, NY
1985	Ozzie Guillen, Chi	Ted Higuera, Mil	Vince Coleman, StL	Tom Browning, Cin
1986	Jose Canseco, Oak	Mark Eichhorn, Tor	Robby Thompson, SF	Todd Worrell, StL
1987	Mark McGwire, Oak	Mike Henneman, Det	Benito Santiago, SD	Mike Dunne, Pit
1988	Walt Weiss, Oak	Bryan Harvey, Cal	Mark Grace, Chi	Tim Belcher, LA
1989	Craig Worthington, Bal	Tom Gordon, KC	Jerome Walton, Chi	Andy Benes, SD
1990	Sandy Alomar Jr., Cle	Kevin Appier, KC	Dave Justice, Atl	Mike Harkey, Chi
1991	Chuck Knoblauch, Min	Juan Guzman, Tor	Jeff Bagwell, Hou	Al Osuna, Hou
1992	Pat Listach, Mil	Cal Eldred, Mil	Eric Karros, LA	Tim Wakefield, Pit
1993	Tim Salmon, Cal	Aaron Sele, Bos	Mike Piazza, LA	Kirk Rueter, Mon
1994	Bob Hamelin, KC	Brian Anderson, Cal	Raul Mondesi, LA	Steve Trachsel, Chi
1995	Garret Anderson, Cal	Julian Tavarez, Cle	Chipper Jones, Atl	Hideo Nomo, LA
1996	Derek Jeter, NY	James Baldwin, Chi	Jason Kendall, Pit	Alan Benes, StL
1997	Nomar Garciaparra, Bos	Jason Dickson, Ana	Scott Rolen, Phi	Matt Morris, StL
1998	Ben Grieve, Oak	Rolando Arrojo, TB	Todd Helton, Col	Kerry Wood, Chi
1999	Carlos Beltran, KC	Tim Hudson, Oak	Preston Wilson, Fla	Scott Williamson, Cin
2000	Mark Quinn, KC	Kazuhiro Sasaki, Sea	Rafael Furcal, Atl	Rick Ankiel, StL
2001	Ichiro Suzuki, Sea	C.C. Sabathia, Cle	Albert Pujols, StL	Roy Oswalt, Hou
2002	Eric Hinske, Tor	Rodrigo Lopez, Bal	Brad Wilkerson, Mon	Jason Jennings, Col
2003	Jody Gerut, Cle	Rafael Soriano, Sea	Scott Podsednik, Mil	Dontrelle Willis, Fla
2004	Bobby Crosby, Oak		Jason Bay, Pit	
2005		Huston Street, Oak	Willy Tavares, Hou	

The Sporting News Manager of the Year Award

The Sporting News has honored a Manager of the Year since 1936, forty-six years before the BBWAA first gave a comparable award. In response to the BBWAA's selection of a Manager of the Year for each major league, The Sporting News started doing the same in 1986.

1936	Joe McCarthy, NY AL	1961	Ralph Houk, NY AL
1937	Bill McKechnie, Bos NL	1962	Bill Rigney, LA AL
1938	Joe McCarthy, NY AL	1963	Walt Alston, LA NL
1939	Leo Durocher, Bro NL	1964	Johnny Keane, StL NL
1940	Bill McKechnie, Cin NL	1965	Sam Mele, Min AL
1941	Billy Southworth, StL NL	1966	Hank Bauer, Bal AL
1942	Billy Southworth, StL NL	1967	Dick Williams, Bos AL
1943	Joe McCarthy, NY AL	1968	Mayo Smith, Det AL
1944	Luke Sewell, StL AL	1969	Gil Hodges, NY NL
1945	Ossie Bluege, Was AL	1970	Danny Murtaugh, Pit NL
1946	Eddie Dyer, StL NL	1971	Charlie Fox, SF NL
1947	Bucky Harris, NY AL	1972	Chuck Tanner, Chi AL
1948	Billy Meyer, Pit NL	1973	Gene Mauch, Mon NL
1949	Casey Stengel, NY AL	1974	Bill Virdon, NY AL
1950	Red Rolfe, Det AL	1975	Darrell Johnson, Bos AL
1951	Leo Durocher, NY NL	1976	Danny Ozark, Phi NL
1952	Eddie Stanky, StL NL	1977	Earl Weaver, Bal AL
1953	Casey Stengel, NY AL	1978	George Bamberger, Mil AL
1954	Leo Durocher, NY NL	1979	Earl Weaver, Bal AL
1955	Walt Alston, Bro NL	1980	Bill Virdon, Hou NL
1956	Birdie Tebbetts, Cin NL	1981	Billy Martin, Oak AL
1957	Fred Hutchinson, StL NL	1982	Whitey Herzog, StL NL
1958	Casey Stengel, NY AL	1983	Tony La Russa, Chi AL
1959	Walt Alston, LA NL	1984	Jim Frey, Chi NL
1960	Danny Murtaugh, Pit NL	1985	Bobby Cox, Tor AL

	AL	NL
1986	John McNamara, Bos	Hal Lanier, Hou
1987	Sparky Anderson, Det	Buck Rodgers, Mon
1988	Tony La Russa, Oak	Jim Leyland, Pit
1989	Frank Robinson, Bal	Don Zimmer, Chi
1990	Jeff Torborg, Chi	Jim Leyland, Pit
1991	Tom Kelly, Min	Bobby Cox, Atl
1992	Tony La Russa, Oak	Jim Leyland, Pit
1993	Johnny Oates, Bal	Bobby Cox, Atl
1994	Buck Showalter, NY	Felipe Alou, Mon
1995	Mike Hargrove, Cle	Don Baylor, Col
1996	Johnny Oates, Tex	Bruce Bochy, SD
1997	Davey Johnson, Bal	Dusty Baker, SF
1998	Joe Torre, NY	Bruce Bochy, SD
1999	Jimy Williams, Bos	Bobby Cox, Atl
2000	Jerry Manuel, Chi	Dusty Baker, SF
2001	Lou Piniella, Sea	Larry Bowa, Phi
2002	Mike Scioscia, Ana	Bobby Cox, Atl
2003	Tony Peña, KC	Bobby Cox, Atl
2004	Ron Gardenhire, Min	Bobby Cox, Atl
(tie)	Buck Showalter, Tex	
2005	Ozzie Guillen, StL	Bobby Cox, Atl

The Sporting News Comeback Player of the Year Award

Other organizations have selected Comeback Player of the Year awards, but only The Sporting News version has stood the test of time. No one has ever really defined a "comeback" for the purposes of this award, but it's safe to say that no other award for on-field achievement in baseball honors players with a higher average age.

	AL	NL
1965	Norm Cash, Det	Vern Law, Pit
1966	Boog Powell, Bal	Phil Regan, LA
1967	Dean Chance, Min	Mike McCormick, SF
1968	Ken Harrelson, Bos	Alex Johnson, Cin
1969	Tony Conigliaro, Bos	Tommie Agee, NY
1970	Clyde Wright, Cal	Jim Hickman, Chi
1971	Norm Cash, Det	Al Downing, LA
1972	Luis Tiant, Bos	Bobby Tolan, Cin
1973	John Hiller, Det	Davey Johnson, Atl
1974	Ferguson Jenkins, Tex	Jimmy Wynn, LA

	AL	NL
1975	Boog Powell, Cle	Randy Jones, SD
1976	Dock Ellis, NY	Tommy John, LA
1977	Eric Soderholm, Chi	Willie McCovey, SF
1978	Mike Caldwell, Mil	Willie Stargell, Pit
1979	Willie Horton, Sea	Lou Brock, StL
1980	Matt Keough, Oak	Jerry Reuss, LA
1981	Richie Zisk, Sea	Bob Knepper, Hou
1982	Andre Thornton, Cle	Joe Morgan, SF
1983	Alan Trammell, Det	John Denny, Phi
1984	Dave Kingman, Oak	Joaquin Andujar, StL
1985	Gorman Thomas, Sea	Rick Reuschel, Pit
1986	John Candelaria, Cal	Ray Knight, NY
1987	Bret Saberhagen, KC	Rick Sutcliffe, Chi
1988	Storm Davis, Oak	Tim Leary, LA
1989	Bert Blyleven, Cal	Lonnie Smith, Atl
1990	Dave Winfield, Cal	John Tudor, StL
1991	Jose Guzman, Tex	Terry Pendleton, Atl
1992	Rick Sutcliffe, Bal	Gary Sheffield, SD
1993	Bo Jackson, Chi	Andres Galarraga, Col
1994	Jose Canseco, Tex	Tim Wallach, LA
1995	Tim Wakefield, Bos	Ron Gant, Cin
1996	Kevin Elster, Tex	Eric Davis, Cin
1997	David Justice, Cle	Darren Daulton, Phi-Fla
1998	Bret Saberhagen, Bos	Greg Vaughn, SD
1999	John Jaha, Oak	Rickey Henderson, NY
2000	Frank Thomas, Chi	Andres Galarraga, Atl
2001	Ruben Sierra, Tex	Matt Morris, StL
2002	Tim Salmon, Phi	Mike Lieberthal, Phi
2003	Gil Meche, Sea	Javy Lopez, Atl
2004	Paul Konerko, Chi	Chris Carpenter, SL
2005	Jason Giambi, NY	Ken Griffey Jr., Cin

The Sporting News Fireman/Reliever of the Year Award

No comparison of baseball teams these days is complete without a discussion about relief pitchers, especially closers. Many baseball fans today view closers as one of their team's most valuable commodities, and blown leads by relievers earn the ire of baseball fans unlike any other failure in the game. Contrast that to the first half of the twentieth century, when relief pitchers were an anonymous and unappreciated lot. When The Sporting News created their Fireman of the Year award in 1960, no reliever had ever received a Cy Young vote, and only one, Hoyt Wilhelm in 1952, had ever finished in the top ten in MVP voting. The Fireman award winner was originally selected based on a strict statistical formula, devised by Jerome Holtzman, which added relief wins and saves. Today, the award winner (called Reliever of the Year as of 2001) is chosen by the magazine's editors.

	AL	NL
1960	Mike Fornieles, Bos	Lindy McDaniel, StL
1961	Luis Arroyo, NY	Stu Miller, SF
1962	Dick Radatz, Bos	Roy Face, Pit
1963	Stu Miller, Bal	Lindy McDaniel, Chi
1964	Dick Radatz, Bos	Al McBean, Pit
1965	Eddie Fisher, Chi	Ted Abernathy, Chi
1966	Jack Aker, KC	Phil Regan, LA
1967	Minnie Rojas, Cal	Ted Abernathy, Cin
1968	Wilbur Wood, Chi	Phil Regan, Chi
1969	Ron Perranoski, Min	Wayne Granger, Cin
1970	Ron Perranoski, Min	Wayne Granger, Cin
1971	Ken Sanders, Mil	Dave Giusti, Pit
1972	Sparky Lyle, NY	Clay Carroll, Cin
1973	John Hiller, Det	Mike Marshall, Mon
1974	Terry Forster, Chi	Mike Marshall, LA
1975	Rich Gossage, Chi	Al Hrabosky, StL
1976	Bill Campbell, Min	Rawly Eastwick, Cin
1977	Bill Campbell, Bos	Rollie Fingers, SD
1978	Rich Gossage, NY	Rollie Fingers, SD
1979	Jim Kern, Tex	Bruce Sutter, Chi
(tie)	Mike Marshall, Min	

	AL	NL
1980	Dan Quisenberry, KC	Rollie Fingers, SD
(tie)		Tom Hume, Cin
1981	Rollie Fingers, Mil	Bruce Sutter, StL
1982	Dan Quisenberry, KC	Bruce Sutter, StL
1983	Dan Quisenberry, KC	Al Holland, Phi
(tie)		Lee Smith, Chi
1984	Dan Quisenberry, KC	Bruce Sutter, StL
1985	Dan Quisenberry, KC	Jeff Reardon, Mon
1986	Dave Righetti, NY	Todd Worrell, StL
1987	Jeff Reardon, Min	Steve Bedrosian, Phi
(tie)	Dave Righetti, NY	
1988	Dennis Eckersley, Oak	John Franco, Cin
1989	Jeff Russell, Tex	Mark Davis, SD
1990	Bobby Thigpen, Chi	John Franco, NY
1991	Dennis Eckersley, Oak	Lee Smith, StL
(tie)	Bryan Harvey, Cal	
1992	Dennis Eckersley, Oak	Doug Jones, Hou
(tie)		Lee Smith, StL
1993	Jeff Montgomery, KC	Randy Myers, Chi
1994	Lee Smith, Bal	John Franco, NY
1995	Jose Mesa, Cle	Randy Myers, Chi
1996	John Wetteland, NY	Trevor Hoffman, SD
1997	Mariano Rivera, NY	Jeff Shaw, Cin
1998	Tom Gordon, Bos	Trevor Hoffman, SD
1999	Mariano Rivera, NY	Ugueth Urbina, Mon
2000	Todd Jones, Det	Antonio Alfonseca, Fla
2001	Mariano Rivera, NY	Armando Benitez, NY
(tie)		Robb Nen, SF
2002	Billy Koch, Oak	John Smoltz, Atl
2003	Keith Foulke, Oak	Eric Gagne, LA
2004	Mariano Rivera, NY	Eric Gagne, LA
2005	Mariano Rivera, NY	Chad Cordero, Was
(tie)	Joe Nathan, Min	

The Sporting News Major League Executive of the Year Award

Nearly all baseball awards honor on-field performance, but there may be no one more responsible for a team's on-field performance than its top executive. This *Sporting News* award has long honored the men behind the scenes who build baseball teams. While many of today's fans are familiar with their team's top front office personnel, this was not the case when the award was created. The most frequent recipient of this award was George Weiss, who was selected four times while running the Yankees during their most successful dynasty from the late 1940s to the early 1960s.

1936	Branch Rickey, StL NL	1971	Cedric Tallis, KC AL
1937	Ed Barrow, NY AL	1972	Roland Hemond, Chi AL
1938	Warren Giles, Cin NL	1973	Bob Howsam, Cin NL
1939	Larry MacPhail, Bro NL	1974	Gabe Paul, NY AL
1940	Walter Briggs Sr., Det AL	1975	Dick O'Connell, Bos AL
1941	Ed Barrow, NY AL	1976	Joe Burke, KC AL
1942	Branch Rickey, StL NL	1977	Bill Veeck, Chi AL
1943	Calvin Griffith, Was AL	1978	Spec Richardson, SF NL
1944	William DeWitt, StL AL	1979	Hank Peters, Bal AL
1945	Phil Wrigley, Chi NL	1980	Tal Smith, Hou NL
1946	Tom Yawkey, Bos AL	1981	John McHale, Mon NL
1947	Branch Rickey, Bro NL	1982	Harry Dalton, Mil AL
1948	Bill Veeck, Cle AL	1983	Hank Peters, Bal AL
1949	Bob Carpenter, Phi NL	1984	Dallas Green, Chi NL
1950	George Weiss, NY AL	1985	John Schuerholz, KC AL
1951	George Weiss, NY AL	1986	Frank Cashen, NY NL
1952	George Weiss, NY AL	1987	Al Rosen, SF NL
1953	Lou Perini, Mil NL	1988	Fred Claire, LA NL
1954	Horace Stoneham, NY NL	1989	Roland Hemond, Bal AL
1955	Walter O'Malley, Bro NL	1990	Bob Quinn, Cin NL
1956	Gabe Paul, Cin NL	1991	Andy MacPhail, Min AL
1957	Frank Lane, StL NL	1992	Dan Duquette, Mon NL
1958	Joe Brown, Pit NL	1993	Lee Thomas, Phi NL
1959	Buzzie Bavasi, LA NL	1994	John Hart, Cle NL
1960	George Weiss, NY AL	1995	John Hart, Cle NL
1961	Dan Topping, NY AL	1996	Doug Melvin, Tex AL
1962	Fred Haney, LA AL	1997	Cam Bonifay, Pit NL
1963	Bing Devine, StL NL	1998	Gerry Hunsicker, Hou NL
1964	Bing Devine, StL NL	1999	Billy Beane, Oak AL
1965	Calvin Griffith, Min AL	2000	Walt Jocketty, StL NL
1966	Lee MacPhail, MLB	2001	Pat Gillick, Sea AL
1967	Dick O'Connell, Bos AL	2002	Terry Ryan, Min AL
1968	Jim Campbell, Det AL	2003	Brian Sabean, SF NL
1969	Johnny Murphy, NY NL	2004	Walt Jocketty, StL NL
1970	Harry Dalton, Bal AL	2005	Mark Shapiro, Cle AL

Rolaids Relief Man of the Year Award

The owners of Rolaids® antacids created this award for relief pitchers in order to impress upon potential customers that Rolaids® did indeed "spell relief" for heartburn and indigestion. This marketing effort proved enormously successful, raising the profile of both the antacid and the pitchers. The winners of the award have always been determined by a statistical formula, which originally took into account saves, wins, and losses, and later included blown saves as well as tough saves. Rolaids® has expanded this promotional award throughout the minor leagues.

	AL	NL
1976	Bill Campbell, Min	Rawly Eastwick, Cin
1977	Bill Campbell, Bos	Rollie Fingers, SD

	AL	NL
1978	Rich Gossage, NY	Rollie Fingers, SD
1979	Jim Kern, Tex	Bruce Sutter, Chi
1980	Dan Quisenberry, KC	Rollie Fingers, SD
1981	Rollie Fingers, Mil	Bruce Sutter, StL
1982	Dan Quisenberry, KC	Bruce Sutter, StL
1983	Dan Quisenberry, KC	Al Holland, Phi
1984	Dan Quisenberry, KC	Bruce Sutter, StL
1985	Dan Quisenberry, KC	Jeff Reardon, Mon
1986	Dave Righetti, NY	Todd Worrell, StL
1987	Dave Righetti, NY	Steve Bedrosian, Phi
1988	Dennis Eckersley, Oak	John Franco, Cin
1989	Jeff Russell, Tex	Mark Davis, SD
1990	Bobby Thigpen, Chi	John Franco, NY
1991	Bryan Harvey, Cal	Lee Smith, StL
1992	Dennis Eckersley, Oak	Lee Smith, StL
1993	Jeff Montgomery, KC	Randy Myers, Chi
1994	Lee Smith, Bal	Rod Beck, SF
1995	Jose Mesa, Cle	Tom Henke, StL
1996	John Wetteland, NY	Jeff Brantley, Cin
1997	Randy Myers, Bal	Jeff Shaw, Cin
1998	Tom Gordon, Bos	Trevor Hoffman, SD
1999	Mariano Rivera, NY	Billy Wagner, Hou
2000	Todd Jones, Det	Antonio Alfonseca, Fla
2001	Mariano Rivera, NY	Armando Benitez, NY
2002	Billy Koch, Oak	John Smoltz, Atl
2003	Keith Foulke, Oak	Eric Gagne, LA
2004	Mariano Rivera, NY	Eric Gagne, LA
2005	Mariano Rivera, NY	Chad Cordero, Was

GOLD GLOVE AWARDS

MLB Gold Gloves

Defense is the most difficult skill in baseball to judge by sight alone. The way a player looks when he makes plays is often misleading, because positioning is very important and poor defenders can make easy plays look hard. Defense is also the hardest act in baseball to statistically measure. The Gold Glove Awards were created to systematically use subjective analysis to bring recognition to the best fielders at each position.

Rawlings, the manufacturer of the great majority of big leaguers' gloves at the time, teamed up in 1957 to present the Gold Gloves to *The Sporting News* All-Fielding Team. The awards were given to one player at each position in the major leagues, as selected by a panel of sportswriters. In 1958 voting was handed over to major league players and gold gloves were awarded for each position in each league. In 1961 voters were told to simply select three outfielders, regardless of whether they were left fielders, center fielders, or right fielders (which remains the practice today). In 1966 major league managers and coaches took over the voting.

Knowledgeable baseball observers are skeptical about the results of Gold Glove voting, largely because so many players win year after year. Many great defensive players earn their first Gold Gloves several years after they have established their defensive prowess, then keep winning Gold Gloves even after their defensive decline has become obvious. Some players seem to be given this defensive award partly for their offense, while weak hitters with great gloves are frequently ignored. The award's most recent controversy occurred when the AL's 1999 first base Gold Glove was awarded to designated hitter Rafael Palmeiro, who played first base in only 28 games that year.

1957 Gold Gloves

P	Bobby Shantz, NY AL
C	Sherm Lollar, Chi AL
1B	Gil Hodges, Bro NL
2B	Nellie Fox, Chi AL
3B	Frank Malzone, Bos AL
SS	Roy McMillan, Cin NL
LF	Minnie Minoso, Chi AL
CF	Willie Mays, NY NL
RF	Al Kaline, Det AL

AL Gold Gloves		NL Gold Gloves	
1958	**AL**		**NL**
P	Bobby Shantz, NY	P	Harvey Haddix, Cin
C	Sherm Lollar, Chi	C	Del Crandall, Mil
1B	Vic Power, KC-Cle	1B	Gil Hodges, LA
2B	Frank Bolling, Det	2B	Bill Mazeroski, Pit
3B	Frank Malzone, Bos	3B	Ken Boyer, StL
SS	Luis Aparicio, Chi	SS	Roy McMillan, Cin
LF	Norm Siebern, NY	LF	Frank Robinson, Cin
CF	Jim Piersall, Bos	CF	Willie Mays, SF
RF	Al Kaline, Det	RF	Hank Aaron, Mil
1959	**AL**		**NL**
P	Bobby Shantz, NY	P	Harvey Haddix, Pit
C	Sherm Lollar, Chi	C	Del Crandall, Mil

1959

	AL		NL
1B	Vic Power, Cle	1B	Gil Hodges, LA
2B	Nellie Fox, Chi	2B	Charlie Neal, LA
3B	Frank Malzone, Bos	3B	Ken Boyer, StL
SS	Luis Aparicio, Chi	SS	Roy McMillan, Cin
LF	Minnie Minoso, Cle	LF	Jackie Brandt, SF
CF	Al Kaline, Det	CF	Willie Mays, SF
RF	Jackie Jensen, Bos	RF	Hank Aaron, Mil

1960

	AL		NL
P	Bobby Shantz, NY	P	Harvey Haddix, Pit
C	Earl Battey, Was	C	Del Crandall, Mil
1B	Vic Power, Cle	1B	Bill White, StL
2B	Nellie Fox, Chi	2B	Bill Mazeroski, Pit
3B	Brooks Robinson, Bal	3B	Ken Boyer, StL
SS	Luis Aparicio, Chi	SS	Ernie Banks, Chi
LF	Minnie Minoso, Chi	LF	Wally Moon, LA
CF	Jim Landis, Chi	CF	Willie Mays, SF
RF	Roger Maris, NY	RF	Hank Aaron, Mil

1961

	AL		NL
P	Frank Lary, Det	P	Bobby Shantz, Pit
C	Earl Battey, Min	C	Johnny Roseboro, LA
1B	Vic Power, Cle	1B	Bill White, StL
2B	Bobby Richardson, NY	2B	Bill Mazeroski, Pit
3B	Brooks Robinson, Bal	3B	Ken Boyer, StL
SS	Luis Aparicio, Chi	SS	Maury Wills, LA
OF	Jim Piersall, Cle	OF	Willie Mays, SF
OF	Jim Landis, Chi	OF	Roberto Clemente, Pit
OF	Al Kaline, Det	OF	Vada Pinson, Cin

1962

	AL		NL
P	Jim Kaat, Min	P	Bobby Shantz, Hou-StL
C	Earl Battey, Min	C	Del Crandall, Mil
1B	Vic Power, Min	1B	Bill White, StL
2B	Bobby Richardson, NY	2B	Ken Hubbs, Chi
3B	Brooks Robinson, Bal	3B	Jim Davenport, SF
SS	Luis Aparicio, Chi	SS	Maury Wills, LA
OF	Mickey Mantle, NY	OF	Willie Mays, SF
OF	Jim Landis, Chi	OF	Roberto Clemente, Pit
OF	Al Kaline, Det	OF	Bill Virdon, Pit

1963

	AL		NL
P	Jim Kaat, Min	P	Bobby Shantz, StL
C	Elston Howard, NY	C	Johnny Edwards, Cin
1B	Vic Power, Min	1B	Bill White, StL
2B	Bobby Richardson, NY	2B	Bill Mazeroski, Pit
3B	Brooks Robinson, Bal	3B	Ken Boyer, StL
SS	Zoilo Versalles, Min	SS	Bobby Wine, Phi
OF	Carl Yastrzemski, Bos	OF	Willie Mays, SF
OF	Jim Landis, Chi	OF	Curt Flood, StL
OF	Al Kaline, Det	OF	Roberto Clemente, Pit

1964

	AL		NL
P	Jim Kaat, Min	P	Bobby Shantz, StL-Chi-Phi
C	Elston Howard, NY	C	Johnny Edwards, Cin
1B	Vic Power, Min-LA	1B	Bill White, StL
2B	Bobby Richardson, NY	2B	Bill Mazeroski, Pit
3B	Brooks Robinson, Bal	3B	Ron Santo, Chi
SS	Luis Aparicio, Bal	SS	Ruben Amaro, Phi
OF	Vic Davalillo, Cle	OF	Willie Mays, SF
OF	Jim Landis, Chi	OF	Curt Flood, StL
OF	Al Kaline, Det	OF	Roberto Clemente, Pit

1965

	AL		NL
P	Jim Kaat, Min	P	Bob Gibson, StL
C	Bill Freehan, Det	C	Joe Torre, Mil
1B	Joe Pepitone, NY	1B	Bill White, StL
2B	Bobby Richardson, NY	2B	Bill Mazeroski, Pit
3B	Brooks Robinson, Bal	3B	Ron Santo, Chi
SS	Zoilo Versalles, Min	SS	Leo Cardenas, Cin
OF	Al Kaline, Det	OF	Roberto Clemente, Pit
OF	Carl Yastrzemski, Bos	OF	Willie Mays, SF
OF	Tom Tresh, NY	OF	Curt Flood, StL

1966

	AL		NL
P	Jim Kaat, Min	P	Bob Gibson, StL
C	Bill Freehan, Det	C	John Roseboro, LA
1B	Joe Pepitone, NY	1B	Bill White, Phi
2B	Bobby Knoop, Cal	2B	Bill Mazeroski, Pit
3B	Brooks Robinson, Bal	3B	Ron Santo, Chi
SS	Luis Aparicio, Bal	SS	Gene Alley, Pit
OF	Al Kaline, Det	OF	Curt Flood, StL
OF	Tommie Agee, Chi	OF	Roberto Clemente, Pit
OF	Tony Oliva, Min	OF	Willie Mays, SF

1967

	AL		NL
P	Jim Kaat, Min	P	Bob Gibson, StL
C	Bill Freehan, Det	C	Randy Hundley, Chi
1B	George Scott, Bos	1B	Wes Parker, LA
2B	Bobby Knoop, Cal	2B	Bill Mazeroski, Pit
3B	Brooks Robinson, Bal	3B	Ron Santo, Chi
SS	Jim Fregosi, Cal	SS	Gene Alley, Pit
OF	Paul Blair, Bal	OF	Curt Flood, StL
OF	Al Kaline, Det	OF	Roberto Clemente, Pit
OF	Carl Yastrzemski, Bos	OF	Willie Mays, SF

1968

	AL		NL
P	Jim Kaat, Min	P	Bob Gibson, StL
C	Bill Freehan, Det	C	Johnny Bench, Cin
1B	George Scott, Bos	1B	Wes Parker, LA
2B	Bobby Knoop, Cal	2B	Glenn Beckert, Chi
3B	Brooks Robinson, Bal	3B	Ron Santo, Chi
SS	Luis Aparicio, Chi	SS	Dal Maxvill, StL
OF	Mickey Stanley, Det	OF	Curt Flood, StL
OF	Reggie Smith, Bos	OF	Roberto Clemente, Pit
OF	Carl Yastrzemski, Bos	OF	Willie Mays, SF

1969

	AL		NL
P	Jim Kaat, Min	P	Bob Gibson, StL
C	Bill Freehan, Det	C	Johnny Bench, Cin
1B	Joe Pepitone, NY	1B	Wes Parker, LA
2B	Davey Johnson, Bal	2B	Felix Millan, Atl
3B	Brooks Robinson, Bal	3B	Clete Boyer, Atl
SS	Mark Belanger, Bal	SS	Don Kessinger, Chi
OF	Carl Yastrzemski, Bos	OF	Curt Flood, StL
OF	Paul Blair, Bal	OF	Roberto Clemente, Pit
OF	Mickey Stanley, Det	OF	Pete Rose, Cin

1970

	AL		NL
P	Jim Kaat, Min	P	Bob Gibson, StL
C	Ray Fosse, Cle	C	Johnny Bench, Cin
1B	Jim Spencer, Cal	1B	Wes Parker, LA
2B	Davey Johnson, Bal	2B	Tommy Helms, Cin
3B	Brooks Robinson, Bal	3B	Doug Rader, Hou
SS	Luis Aparicio, Chi	SS	Don Kessinger, Chi
OF	Paul Blair, Bal	OF	Tommie Agee, NY
OF	Mickey Stanley, Det	OF	Roberto Clemente, Pit
OF	Ken Berry, Chi	OF	Pete Rose, Cin

1971

	AL		NL
P	Jim Kaat, Min	P	Bob Gibson, StL
C	Ray Fosse, Cle	C	Johnny Bench, Cin
1B	George Scott, Bos	1B	Wes Parker, LA
2B	Davey Johnson, Bal	2B	Tommy Helms, Cin
3B	Brooks Robinson, Bal	3B	Doug Rader, Hou
SS	Mark Belanger, Bal	SS	Bud Harrelson, NY
OF	Amos Otis, KC	OF	Roberto Clemente, Pit
OF	Carl Yastrzemski, Bos	OF	Bobby Bonds, SF
OF	Paul Blair, Bal	OF	Willie Davis, LA

1972

	AL		NL
P	Jim Kaat, Min	P	Bob Gibson, StL
C	Carlton Fisk, Bos	C	Johnny Bench, Cin
1B	George Scott, Mil	1B	Wes Parker, LA
2B	Doug Griffin, Bos	2B	Felix Millan, Atl
3B	Brooks Robinson, Bal	3B	Doug Rader, Hou
SS	Ed Brinkman, Det	SS	Larry Bowa, Phi
OF	Bobby Murcer, NY	OF	Roberto Clemente, Pit
OF	Paul Blair, Bal	OF	Cesar Cedeno, Hou
OF	Ken Berry, Cal	OF	Willie Davis, LA

1973

	AL		NL
P	Jim Kaat, Min-Chi	P	Bob Gibson, StL
C	Thurman Munson, NY	C	Johnny Bench, Cin
1B	George Scott, Mil	1B	Mike Jorgensen, Mon
2B	Bobby Grich, Bal	2B	Joe Morgan, Cin
3B	Brooks Robinson, Bal	3B	Doug Rader, Hou
SS	Mark Belanger, Bal	SS	Roger Metzger, Hou
OF	Paul Blair, Bal	OF	Willie Davis, LA
OF	Amos Otis, KC	OF	Cesar Cedeno, Hou
OF	Mickey Stanley, Det	OF	Bobby Bonds, SF

1974

	AL		NL
P	Jim Kaat, Chi	P	Andy Messersmith, LA
C	Thurman Munson, NY	C	Johnny Bench, Cin
1B	George Scott, Mil	1B	Steve Garvey, LA
2B	Bobby Grich, Bal	2B	Joe Morgan, Cin
3B	Brooks Robinson, Bal	3B	Doug Rader, Hou
SS	Mark Belanger, Bal	SS	Dave Concepcion, Cin
OF	Paul Blair, Bal	OF	Cesar Geronimo, Cin
OF	Joe Rudi, Oak	OF	Cesar Cedeno, Hou
OF	Amos Otis, KC	OF	Bobby Bonds, SF

1975

	AL		NL
P	Jim Kaat, Chi	P	Andy Messersmith, LA
C	Thurman Munson, NY	C	Johnny Bench, Cin
1B	George Scott, Mil	1B	Steve Garvey, LA
2B	Bobby Grich, Bal	2B	Joe Morgan, Cin
3B	Brooks Robinson, Bal	3B	Ken Reitz, StL
SS	Mark Belanger, Bal	SS	Dave Concepcion, Cin
OF	Paul Blair, Bal	OF	Garry Maddox, SF-Phi
OF	Joe Rudi, Oak	OF	Cesar Geronimo, Cin
OF	Fred Lynn, Bos	OF	Cesar Cedeno, Hou

1976

	AL		NL
P	Jim Palmer, Bal	P	Jim Kaat, Phi
C	Jim Sundberg, Tex	C	Johnny Bench, Cin
1B	George Scott, Mil	1B	Steve Garvey, LA
2B	Bobby Grich, Bal	2B	Joe Morgan, Cin
3B	Aurelio Rodriguez, Det	3B	Mike Schmidt, Phi
SS	Mark Belanger, Bal	SS	Dave Concepcion, Cin
OF	Rick Manning, Cle	OF	Cesar Cedeno, Hou
OF	Dwight Evans, Bos	OF	Garry Maddox, Phi
OF	Joe Rudi, Oak	OF	Cesar Geronimo, Cin

1977

	AL		NL
P	Jim Palmer, Bal	P	Jim Kaat, Phi
C	Jim Sundberg, Tex	C	Johnny Bench, Cin
1B	Jim Spencer, Chi	1B	Steve Garvey, LA
2B	Frank White, KC	2B	Joe Morgan, Cin
3B	Graig Nettles, NY	3B	Mike Schmidt, Phi
SS	Mark Belanger, Bal	SS	Dave Concepcion, Cin
OF	Al Cowens, KC	OF	Cesar Geronimo, Cin
OF	Carl Yastrzemski, Bos	OF	Dave Parker, Pit
OF	Juan Beniquez, Tex	OF	Garry Maddox, Phi

1978

	AL		NL
P	Jim Palmer, Bal	P	Phil Niekro, Atl
C	Jim Sundberg, Tex	C	Bob Boone, Phi
1B	Chris Chambliss, NY	1B	Keith Hernandez, StL
2B	Frank White, KC	2B	Davey Lopes, LA
3B	Graig Nettles, NY	3B	Mike Schmidt, Phi
SS	Mark Belanger, Bal	SS	Larry Bowa, Phi
OF	Rick Miller, Cal	OF	Garry Maddox, Phi
OF	Fred Lynn, Bos	OF	Ellis Valentine, Mon
OF	Dwight Evans, Bos	OF	Dave Parker, Pit

1979

Pos	AL	NL
P	Jim Palmer, Bal	Phil Niekro, Atl
C	Jim Sundberg, Tex	Bob Boone, Phi
1B	Cecil Cooper, Mil	Keith Hernandez, StL
2B	Frank White, KC	Manny Trillo, Phi
3B	Buddy Bell, Tex	Mike Schmidt, Phi
SS	Rick Burleson, Bos	Dave Concepcion, Cin
OF	Fred Lynn, Bos	Dave Parker, Pit
OF	Sixto Lezcano, Mil	Garry Maddox, Phi
OF	Dwight Evans, Bos	Dave Winfield, SD

1980

Pos	AL	NL
P	Mike Norris, Oak	Phil Niekro, Atl
C	Jim Sundberg, Tex	Gary Carter, Mon
1B	Cecil Cooper, Mil	Keith Hernandez, StL
2B	Frank White, KC	Doug Flynn, NY
3B	Buddy Bell, Tex	Mike Schmidt, Phi
SS	Alan Trammell, Det	Ozzie Smith, SD
OF	Dwayne Murphy, Oak	Garry Maddox, Phi
OF	Fred Lynn, Bos	Dave Winfield, SD
OF	Willie Wilson, KC	Andre Dawson, Mon

1981

Pos	AL	NL
P	Mike Norris, Oak	Steve Carlton, Phi
C	Jim Sundberg, Tex	Gary Carter, Mon
1B	Mike Squires, Chi	Keith Hernandez, StL
2B	Frank White, KC	Manny Trillo, Phi
3B	Buddy Bell, Tex	Mike Schmidt, Phi
SS	Alan Trammell, Det	Ozzie Smith, SD
OF	Dwayne Murphy, Oak	Dusty Baker, LA
OF	Rickey Henderson, Oak	Garry Maddox, Phi
OF	Dwight Evans, Bos	Andre Dawson, Mon

1982

Pos	AL	NL
P	Ron Guidry, NY	Phil Niekro, Atl
C	Bob Boone, Cal	Gary Carter, Mon
1B	Eddie Murray, Bal	Keith Hernandez, StL
2B	Frank White, KC	Manny Trillo, Phi
3B	Buddy Bell, Tex	Mike Schmidt, Phi
SS	Robin Yount, Mil	Ozzie Smith, StL
OF	Dwayne Murphy, Oak	Andre Dawson, Mon
OF	Dwight Evans, Bos	Dale Murphy, Atl
OF	Dave Winfield, NY	Garry Maddox, Phi

1983

Pos	AL	NL
P	Ron Guidry, NY	Phil Niekro, Atl
C	Lance Parrish, Det	Tony Peña, Pit
1B	Eddie Murray, Bal	Keith Hernandez, StL-NY
2B	Lou Whitaker, Det	Ryne Sandberg, Chi
3B	Buddy Bell, Tex	Mike Schmidt, Phi
SS	Alan Trammell, Det	Ozzie Smith, StL
OF	Dwayne Murphy, Oak	Dale Murphy, Atl
OF	Dave Winfield, NY	Willie McGee, StL
OF	Dwight Evans, Bos	Andre Dawson, Mon

1984

Pos	AL	NL
P	Ron Guidry, NY	Joaquin Andujar, StL
C	Lance Parrish, Det	Tony Peña, Pit
1B	Eddie Murray, Bal	Keith Hernandez, NY
2B	Lou Whitaker, Det	Ryne Sandberg, Chi
3B	Buddy Bell, Tex	Mike Schmidt, Phi
SS	Alan Trammell, Det	Ozzie Smith, StL
OF	Dwight Evans, Bos	Dale Murphy, Atl
OF	Dwayne Murphy, Oak	Bob Dernier, Chi
OF	Dave Winfield, NY	Andre Dawson, Mon

1985

Pos	AL	NL
P	Ron Guidry, NY	Rick Reuschel, Pit
C	Lance Parrish, Det	Tony Peña, Pit
1B	Don Mattingly, NY	Keith Hernandez, NY
2B	Lou Whitaker, Det	Ryne Sandberg, Chi
3B	George Brett, KC	Tim Wallach, Mon
SS	Alfredo Griffin, Oak	Ozzie Smith, StL
OF	Dave Winfield, NY	Dale Murphy, Atl
OF	Dwight Evans, Bos	Willie McGee, StL
OF	Gary Pettis, Cal	Andre Dawson, Mon
OF	Dwayne Murphy, Oak	

1986

Pos	AL	NL
P	Ron Guidry, NY	Fernando Valenzuela, LA
C	Bob Boone, Cal	Jody Davis, Chi
1B	Don Mattingly, NY	Keith Hernandez, NY
2B	Frank White, KC	Ryne Sandberg, Chi
3B	Gary Gaetti, Min	Mike Schmidt, Phi
SS	Tony Fernandez, Tor	Ozzie Smith, StL
OF	Kirby Puckett, Min	Dale Murphy, Atl
OF	Jesse Barfield, Tor	Willie McGee, StL
OF	Gary Pettis, Cal	Tony Gwynn, SD

1987

Pos	AL	NL
P	Mark Langston, Sea	Rick Reuschel, Pit-SF
C	Bob Boone, Cal	Mike LaValliere, Pit
1B	Don Mattingly, NY	Keith Hernandez, NY
2B	Frank White, KC	Ryne Sandberg, Chi
3B	Gary Gaetti, Min	Terry Pendleton, StL
SS	Tony Fernandez, Tor	Ozzie Smith, StL
OF	Dave Winfield, NY	Andre Dawson, Chi
OF	Jesse Barfield, Tor	Eric Davis, Cin
OF	Kirby Puckett, Min	Tony Gwynn, SD

1988

Pos	AL	NL
P	Mark Langston, Sea	Orel Hershiser, LA
C	Bob Boone, Cal	Benito Santiago, SD
1B	Don Mattingly, NY	Keith Hernandez, NY
2B	Harold Reynolds, Sea	Ryne Sandberg, Chi
3B	Gary Gaetti, Min	Tim Wallach, Mon
SS	Tony Fernandez, Tor	Ozzie Smith, StL
OF	Gary Pettis, Det	Andre Dawson, Chi
OF	Devon White, Cal	Andy Van Slyke, Pit
OF	Kirby Puckett, Min	Eric Davis, Cin

1989

Pos	AL	NL
P	Bret Saberhagen, KC	Ron Darling, NY
C	Bob Boone, KC	Benito Santiago, SD
1B	Don Mattingly, NY	Andres Galarraga, Mon
2B	Harold Reynolds, Sea	Ryne Sandberg, Chi
3B	Gary Gaetti, Min	Terry Pendleton, StL
SS	Tony Fernandez, Tor	Ozzie Smith, StL
OF	Kirby Puckett, Min	Tony Gwynn, SD
OF	Gary Pettis, Det	Andy Van Slyke, Pit
OF	Devon White, Cal	Eric Davis, Cin

1990

Pos	AL	NL
P	Mike Boddicker, Bos	Greg Maddux, Chi
C	Sandy Alomar Jr., Cle	Benito Santiago, SD
1B	Mark McGwire, Oak	Andres Galarraga, Mon
2B	Harold Reynolds, Sea	Ryne Sandberg, Chi
3B	Kelly Gruber, Tor	Tim Wallach, Mon
SS	Ozzie Guillen, Chi	Ozzie Smith, StL
OF	Gary Pettis, Tex	Tony Gwynn, SD
OF	Ken Griffey Jr., Sea	Andy Van Slyke, Pit
OF	Ellis Burks, Bos	Barry Bonds, Pit

1991

Pos	AL	NL
P	Mark Langston, Cal	Greg Maddux, Chi
C	Tony Pena, Bos	Tom Pagnozzi, StL
1B	Don Mattingly, NY	Will Clark, SF
2B	Roberto Alomar, Tor	Ryne Sandberg, Chi
3B	Robin Ventura, Chi	Matt Williams, SF
SS	Cal Ripken, Bal	Ozzie Smith, StL
OF	Devon White, Tor	Barry Bonds, Pit
OF	Ken Griffey Jr., Sea	Tony Gwynn, SD
OF	Kirby Puckett, Min	Andy Van Slyke, Pit

1992

Pos	AL	NL
P	Mark Langston, Cal	Greg Maddux, Chi
C	Ivan Rodriguez, Tex	Tom Pagnozzi, StL
1B	Don Mattingly, NY	Mark Grace, Chi
2B	Roberto Alomar, Tor	Jose Lind, Pit
3B	Robin Ventura, Chi	Terry Pendleton, Atl
SS	Cal Ripken, Bal	Ozzie Smith, StL
OF	Devon White, Tor	Andy Van Slyke, Pit
OF	Ken Griffey Jr., Sea	Barry Bonds, Pit
OF	Kirby Puckett, Min	Larry Walker, Mon

1993

Pos	AL	NL
P	Mark Langston, Cal	Greg Maddux, Atl
C	Ivan Rodriguez, Tex	Kirt Manwaring, SF
1B	Don Mattingly, NY	Mark Grace, Chi
2B	Roberto Alomar, Tor	Robby Thompson, SF
3B	Robin Ventura, Chi	Matt Williams, SF
SS	Omar Vizquel, Sea	Jay Bell, Pit
OF	Kenny Lofton, Cle	Barry Bonds, SF
OF	Devon White, Tor	Larry Walker, Mon
OF	Ken Griffey Jr., Sea	Marquis Grissom, Mon

1994

Pos	AL	NL
P	Mark Langston, Cal	Greg Maddux, Atl
C	Ivan Rodriguez, Tex	Tom Pagnozzi, StL
1B	Don Mattingly, NY	Jeff Bagwell, Hou
2B	Roberto Alomar, Tor	Craig Biggio, Hou
3B	Wade Boggs, NY	Matt Williams, SF
SS	Omar Vizquel, Cle	Barry Larkin, Cin
OF	Kenny Lofton, Cle	Marquis Grissom, Mon
OF	Ken Griffey Jr., Sea	Barry Bonds, SF
OF	Devon White, Tor	Darren Lewis, SF

1995

Pos	AL	NL
P	Mark Langston, Cal	Greg Maddux, Atl
C	Ivan Rodriguez, Tex	Charles Johnson, Fla
1B	J.T. Snow, Cal	Mark Grace, Chi
2B	Roberto Alomar, Tor	Craig Biggio, Hou
3B	Wade Boggs, NY	Ken Caminiti, SD
SS	Omar Vizquel, Cle	Barry Larkin, Cin
OF	Kenny Lofton, Cle	Marquis Grissom, Atl
OF	Ken Griffey Jr., Sea	Steve Finley, SD
OF	Devon White, Tor	Raul Mondesi, LA

1996

Pos	AL	NL
P	Mike Mussina, Bal	Greg Maddux, Atl
C	Ivan Rodriguez, Tex	Charles Johnson, Fla
1B	J.T. Snow, Cal	Mark Grace, Chi
2B	Roberto Alomar, Bal	Craig Biggio, Hou
3B	Robin Ventura, Chi	Ken Caminiti, SD
SS	Omar Vizquel, Cle	Barry Larkin, Cin
OF	Ken Griffey Jr., Sea	Marquis Grissom, Atl
OF	Jay Buhner, Sea	Steve Finley, SD
OF	Kenny Lofton, Cle	Barry Bonds, SF

1997

Pos	AL	NL
P	Mike Mussina, Bal	Greg Maddux, Atl
C	Ivan Rodriguez, Tex	Charles Johnson, Fla
1B	Rafael Palmeiro, Bal	J.T. Snow, SF
2B	Chuck Knoblauch, Min	Craig Biggio, Hou
3B	Matt Williams, Cle	Ken Caminiti, SD
SS	Omar Vizquel, Cle	Rey Ordoñez, NY
OF	Ken Griffey Jr., Sea	Raul Mondesi, LA
OF	Bernie Williams, NY	Larry Walker, Col
OF	Jim Edmonds, Ana	Barry Bonds, SF

1998

Pos	AL	NL
P	Mike Mussina, Bal	Greg Maddux, Atl
C	Ivan Rodriguez, Tex	Charles Johnson, Fla-LA
1B	Rafael Palmeiro, Bal	J.T. Snow, SF
2B	Roberto Alomar, Bal	Bret Boone, Cin
3B	Robin Ventura, Chi	Scott Rolen, Phi
SS	Omar Vizquel, Cle	Rey Ordoñez, NY
OF	Ken Griffey Jr., Sea	Larry Walker, Col
OF	Bernie Williams, NY	Barry Bonds, SF
OF	Jim Edmonds, Ana	Andruw Jones, Atl

1999	AL		NL
P	Mike Mussina, Bal	P	Greg Maddux, Atl
C	Ivan Rodriguez, Tex	C	Mike Lieberthal, Phi
1B	Rafael Palmeiro, Tex	1B	J.T. Snow, SF
2B	Roberto Alomar, Cle	2B	Pokey Reese, Cin
3B	Scott Brosius, NY	3B	Robin Ventura, NY
SS	Omar Vizquel, Cle	SS	Rey Ordoñez, NY
OF	Ken Griffey Jr., Sea	OF	Larry Walker, Col
OF	Shawn Green, Tor	OF	Andruw Jones, Atl
OF	Bernie Williams, NY	OF	Steve Finley, Ari

2000	AL		NL
P	Kenny Rogers, Tex	P	Greg Maddux, Atl
C	Ivan Rodriguez, Tex	C	Mike Matheny, StL
1B	John Olerud, Sea	1B	J.T. Snow, SF
2B	Roberto Alomar, Cle	2B	Pokey Reese, Cin
3B	Travis Fryman, Cle	3B	Scott Rolen, Phi
SS	Omar Vizquel, Cle	SS	Neifi Perez, Col
OF	Darin Erstad, Ana	OF	Andruw Jones, Atl
OF	Bernie Williams, NY	OF	Steve Finley, Ari
OF	Jermaine Dye, KC	OF	Jim Edmonds, StL

2001	AL		NL
P	Mike Mussina, NY	P	Greg Maddux, Atl
C	Ivan Rodriguez, Tex	C	Brad Ausmus, Hou
1B	Doug Mientkiewicz, Min	1B	Todd Helton, Col
2B	Roberto Alomar, Cle	2B	Fernando Viña, StL
3B	Eric Chavez, Oak	3B	Scott Rolen, Phi
SS	Omar Vizquel, Cle	SS	Orlando Cabrera, Mon
OF	Mike Cameron, Sea	OF	Andruw Jones, Atl
OF	Ichiro Suzuki, Sea	OF	Jim Edmonds, StL
OF	Torii Hunter, Min	OF	Larry Walker, Col

2002	AL		NL
P	Kenny Rogers, Tex	P	Greg Maddux, Atl
C	Bengie Molina, Ana	C	Brad Ausmus, Hou
1B	John Olerud, Sea	1B	Todd Helton, Col
2B	Bret Boone, Sea	2B	Fernando Viña, StL
3B	Eric Chavez, Oak	3B	Scott Rolen, Phi-StL
SS	Alex Rodriguez, Tex	SS	Edgar Renteria, StL
OF	Torii Hunter, Min	OF	Andruw Jones, Atl
OF	Darin Erstad, Ana	OF	Larry Walker, Col
OF	Ichiro Suzuki, Sea	OF	Jim Edmonds, StL

2003	AL		NL
P	Mike Mussina, NY	P	Mike Hampton, Atl
C	Bengie Molina, Ana	C	Mike Matheny, StL
1B	John Olerud, Sea	1B	Derrek Lee, Fla
2B	Bret Boone, Sea	2B	Luis Castillo, Fla
3B	Eric Chavez, Oak	3B	Scott Rolen, StL
SS	Alex Rodriguez, Tex	SS	Edgar Renteria, StL
OF	Mike Cameron, Sea	OF	Jim Edmonds, StL
OF	Torii Hunter, Min	OF	Andruw Jones, Atl
OF	Ichiro Suzuki, Sea	OF	Jose Cruz Jr., SF

2004	AL		NL
P	Kenny Rogers, Tex	P	Greg Maddux, Chi
C	Ivan Rodriguez, Det	C	Mike Matheny, SL
1B	Darin Erstad, Ana	1B	Todd Helton, Col
2B	Bret Boone, Sea	2B	Luis Castillo, Fla
3B	Eric Chavez, Oak	3B	Scott Rolen, SL
SS	Derek Jeter, NY	SS	Cesar Izturis, LA
OF	Vernon Wells, Tor	OF	Jim Edmonds, SL
OF	Ichiro Suzuki, Sea	OF	Steve Finley, Ari-LA
OF	Torii Hunter, Min	OF	Andruw Jones, Atl

2005	AL		NL
P	Kenny Rogers, Tex	P	Greg Maddux, Chi
C	Jason Varitek, Bos	C	Mike Matheny, SF
1B	Mark Teixeira, Tex	1B	Derrek Lee, Chi
2B	Orlando Hudson, Tor	2B	Luis Castillo, Fla
3B	Eric Chavez, Oak	3B	Mike Lowell, Fla
SS	Derek Jeter, NY	SS	Omar Vizquel, SF
OF	Ichiro Suzuki, Sea	OF	Jim Edmonds, StL
OF	Vernon Wells, Tor	OF	Andruw Jones, Atl
OF	Torii Hunter, Min	OF	Bob Abreu, Phi

Baseball America Minor League Player of the Year Award

When *The Sporting News* sharply reduced its coverage of baseball—especially minor league baseball—in the early 1980s, a new publication called *Baseball America* stepped into the breach. In its two decades-plus of regular publication, *Baseball America* has emerged as an authority on the minor leagues and on minor league prospects. Each year, this award honors the best performing prospect, ignoring older players who succeed in the minors as a result of many more years of experience.

1981	Mike Marshall, 1B (Dodgers)	1994	Derek Jeter, SS (Yankees)
1982	Ron Kittle, OF (White Sox)	1995	Andruw Jones, OF (Braves)
1983	Dwight Gooden, RHP (Mets)	1996	Andruw Jones, OF (Braves)
1984	Mike Bielecki, RHP (Pirates)	1997	Paul Konerko, 1B (Dodgers)
1985	Jose Canseco, OF (Athletics)	1998	Eric Chavez, 3B (Athletics)
1986	Gregg Jefferies, SS (Mets)	1999	Rick Ankiel, LHP (Cardinals)
1987	Gregg Jefferies, SS (Mets)	2000	Jon Rauch, RHP (White Sox)
1988	Tom Gordon, RHP (Royals)	2001	Josh Beckett, RHP (Marlins)
1989	Sandy Alomar Jr., C (Padres)	2002	Rocco Baldelli, OF (Devil Rays)
1990	Frank Thomas, 1B (White Sox)	2003	Joe Mauer, C (Twins)
1991	Derek Bell, of (Blue Jays)	2004	Jeff Francis, LHP (Rockies)
1992	Tim Salmon, OF (Angels)	2005	Delmon Young, OF (Devil Rays)
1993	Manny Ramirez, OF (Indians)		

Baseball America Organization of the Year Award

Baseball America has helped emphasize the importance of building major league teams through their minor league systems by annually awarding this honor to organizations that have assembled a deep talent pool at every level and shown the ability to further develop that talent.

1982	Oakland Athletics	AL	1994	Kansas City Royals	AL
1983	New York Mets	NL	1995	New York Mets	NL
1984	New York Mets	NL	1996	Atlanta Braves	NL
1985	Milwaukee Brewers	AL	1997	Detroit Tigers	AL
1986	Milwaukee Brewers	AL	1998	New York Yankees	AL
1987	Milwaukee Brewers	AL	1999	Oakland Athletics	AL
1988	Montreal Expos	NL	2000	Chicago White Sox	AL
1989	Texas Rangers	AL	2001	Houston Astros	NL
1990	Montreal Expos	NL	2002	Minnesota Twins	AL
1991	Atlanta Braves	NL	2003	Florida Marlins	NL
1992	Cleveland Indians	AL	2004	Minnesota Twins	AL
1993	Toronto Blue Jays	AL	2005	Atlanta Braves	NL

The Roberto Clemente Award

Created in 1971 by Commissioner Bowie Kuhn, this was originally known as the Commissioner's Award. The award was renamed after Roberto Clemente, the much beloved right fielder from Puerto Rico, died in a plane crash while on a humanitarian mission to assist earthquake victims in Nicaragua on New Year's Day, 1973. This trophy is given annually to the player who best combines good play on the field with strong work in his community.

1971	Willie Mays, SF NL		1989	Gary Carter, NY NL
1972	Brooks Robinson, Bal AL		1990	Dave Stewart, Oak AL
1973	Al Kaline, Det AL		1991	Harold Reynolds, Sea AL
1974	Willie Stargell, Pit NL		1992	Cal Ripken, Bal AL
1975	Lou Brock, StL NL		1993	Barry Larkin, Cin NL
1976	Pete Rose, Cin NL		1994	Dave Winfield, Min AL
1977	Rod Carew, Min AL		1995	Ozzie Smith, StL NL
1978	Greg Luzinski, Phi AL		1996	Kirby Puckett, Min AL
1979	Andy Thornton, Cle AL		1997	Eric Davis, Bal AL
1980	Phil Niekro, Atl NL		1998	Sammy Sosa, Chi NL
1981	Steve Garvey, LA NL		1999	Tony Gwynn, SD NL
1982	Ken Singleton, Bal AL		2000	Al Leiter, NY NL
1983	Cecil Cooper, Mil AL		2001	Curt Schilling, Ari NL
1984	Ron Guidry, NY AL		2002	Jim Thome, Cle AL
1985	Don Baylor, NY AL		2003	Jamie Moyer, Sea AL
1986	Garry Maddox, Phi NL		2004	Edgar Martinez, Sea AL
1987	Rick Sutcliffe, Chi NL		2005	John Smoltz, Atl NL
1988	Dale Murphy, Atl NL			

The Fred Hutchinson Memorial Award

This award was created in 1965 to honor Fred Hutchinson, a highly-respected major league manager and former player who had died the previous year from cancer. Given annually to the major league player with the high character and strong level of competitiveness that Hutchinson was known for, the award honors those who have overcome physical adversity and shown strong commitments to their family and community.

1965	Mickey Mantle, NY AL		1986	Dennis Leonard, KC AL
1966	Sandy Koufax, LA NL		1987	Paul Molitor, Mil AL
1967	Carl Yastrzemski, Bos NL		1988	Ron Oester, Cin NL
1968	Pete Rose, Cin NL		1989	Dave Dravecky, SF NL
1969	Al Kaline, Det AL		1990	Sid Bream, Pit NL
1970	Tony Conigliaro, Bos AL		1991	Bill Wegman, Mil AL
1971	Joe Torre, StL NL		1992	Carney Lansford, Oak AL
1972	Bobby Tolan, Cin NL		1993	John Olerud, Tor AL
1973	John Hiller, Det AL		1994	Andre Dawson, Bos AL
1974	Danny Thompson, Min AL		1995	Jim Abbott, Cal AL
1975	Gary Nolan, Cin NL		1996	Omar Vizquel, Cle AL
1976	Tommy John, LA NL		1997	Eric Davis, Bal AL
1977	Willie McCovey, SF NL		1998	David Cone, NY AL
1978	Willie Stargell, Pit NL		1999	Sean Casey, Cin NL
1979	Lou Brock, StL NL		2000	Jason Giambi, Oak AL
1980	George Brett, KC AL		2001	Curt Schilling, Ari NL
1981	Johnny Bench, Cin NL		2002	Tim Salmon, Cal AL
1982	Andre Thornton, Cle AL		2003	Jamie Moyer, Sea AL
1983	Ray Knight, Hou NL		2004	Trevor Hoffman SD NL
1984	Don Robinson, Pit NL		2005	Craig Biggio, Hou NL
1985	Rick Reuschel, Chi NL			

The Lou Gehrig Memorial Award

The Lou Gehrig Memorial Award was established in 1955 by Phi Delta Theta, Gehrig's college fraternity. It is given annually to a player who gives back to his community and strongly exemplifies the integrity, spirit, and giving nature that Gehrig possessed. The award is announced each spring for the previous year.

1955	Alvin Dark, NY NL		1965	Vern Law, Pit NL
1956	Pee Wee Reese, Bro NL		1966	Brooks Robinson, Bal AL
1957	Stan Musial, StL NL		1967	Ernie Banks, Chi NL
1958	Gil McDougald, NY AL		1968	Al Kaline, Det AL
1959	Gil Hodges, LA NL		1969	Pete Rose, Cin NL
1960	Dick Groat, Pit NL		1970	Hank Aaron, Atl NL
1961	Warren Spahn, Mil NL		1971	Harmon Killebrew, Min AL
1962	Robin Roberts, Bal AL		1972	Wes Parker, LA NL
1963	Bobby Richardson, NY AL		1973	Ron Santo, Chi NL
1964	Ken Boyer, StL NL		1974	Willie Stargell, Pit NL

1975	Johnny Bench, Cin NL	1990	Glenn Davis, Hou NL
1976	Don Sutton, LA NL	1991	Kent Hrbek, Min AL
1977	Lou Brock, StL NL	1992	Cal Ripken, Bal AL
1978	Don Kessinger, Chi AL	1993	Don Mattingly, NY AL
1979	Phil Niekro, Atl NL	1994	Barry Larkin, Cin NL
1980	Tony Perez, Bos AL	1995	Curt Schilling, Phi NL
1981	Tommy John, NY AL	1996	Brett Butler, LA NL
1982	Ron Cey, LA NL	1997	Paul Molitor, Min AL
1983	Mike Schmidt, Phi NL	1998	Tony Gwynn, SD NL
1984	Steve Garvey, SD NL	1999	Mark McGwire, StL NL
1985	Dale Murphy, Atl NL	2000	Todd Stottlemyre, Ari NL
1986	George Brett, KC AL	2001	John Franco, NY NL
1987	Rick Sutcliffe, Chi NL	2002	Danny Graves, Cin NL
1988	Buddy Bell, Cin NL	2003	Jamie Moyer, Sea AL
1989	Ozzie Smith, StL NL	2004	Jim Thome, Phi NL

The J.G. Taylor Spink Award

The J.G. Taylor Spink Award, given annually (and sometimes posthumously) to a sportswriter for "meritorious contributions to baseball writing," is named after the founder and longtime editor of *The Sporting News,* who was the first recipient. Each winner is presented with the award at the annual Hall of Fame induction ceremony (though they are not inducted into the Hall themselves) and is permanently recognized in the "Scribes & Mikemen" exhibit in Cooperstown. In several seasons, more than one writer has been so honored. They are listed along with the city where they worked.

1962	J.G. Taylor Spink, St Louis	1973	Warren Brown, Chicago
1963	Ring Lardner, New York		John Drebinger, New York
1964	Hugh Fullerton, New York		John F. Kieran, New York
1965	Charles Dryden, Chicago	1974	John Carmichael, Chicago
1966	Grantland Rice, New York		James Isaminger, Philadelphia
1967	Damon Runyon, New York	1975	Tom Meany, New York
1968	Harry G. Salsinger, Detroit		Shirley Povich, Washington DC
1969	Sid Mercer, New York	1976	Harold Kaese, Boston
1970	Heywood C. Broun, New York		Red Smith, New York
1971	Frank Graham, New York	1977	Gordon Cobbledick, Cleveland
1972	Dan Daniel, New York		Edgar Munzel, Chicago
	Fred Lieb, New York	1978	Tim Murnane, Boston
	J. Roy Stockton, St Louis		Dick Young, New York

1979	Bob Broeg, St Louis	1991	Ritter Collett, Dayton
	Tommy Holmes, Brooklyn	1992	Leonard Koppett, New York
1980	Joe Reichler, New York		Bus Saidt, Philadelphia
	Milton Richman, New York	1993	Wendell Smith, Pittsburgh
1981	Allen Lewis, Philadelphia	1994	(no selection)
	Bob Addie, Washington DC	1995	Joseph Durso, New York
1982	Si Burick, Dayton	1996	Charley Feeney, New York
1983	Ken Smith, New York	1997	Sam Lacy, Washington DC
1984	Joe McGuff, Kansas City	1998	Bob Stevens, San Francisco
1985	Earl Lawson, Cincinnati	1999	Hal Lebovitz, Cleveland
1986	Jack Lang, Brooklyn	2000	Ross Newhan, Los Angeles
1987	Jim Murray, Los Angeles	2001	Joe Falls, Detroit
1988	Bob Hunter, Los Angeles	2002	Hal McCoy, Cincinnati
	Ray Kelly, Philadelphia	2003	Murray Chass, New York
1989	Jerome Holtzman, Chicago	2004	Peter Gammons, Boston
1990	Phil Collier, San Diego	2005	Tracy Ringolsby, Denver

The Ford C. Frick Award

This award, named after the former broadcaster and commissioner Ford C. Frick, is presented annually to a baseball voice in recognition of "excellence in baseball broadcasting." The Frick Award, clearly modeled after the Spink Award, was first presented in 1978 to the two best known pioneers of baseball broadcasting, Mel Allen and Red Barber, and has been awarded to one announcer every year since. As in the case of the Spink Award, the winner is honored at the Hall of Fame induction ceremony, and recognized by a permanent exhibit, but is not himself an inductee.

1978	Mel Allen, Red Barber	1992	Milo Hamilton
1979	Bob Elson	1993	Chuck Thompson
1980	Russ Hodges	1994	Bob Murphy
1981	Ernie Harwell	1995	Bob Wolff
1982	Vin Scully	1996	Herb Carneal
1983	Jack Brickhouse	1997	Jimmy Dudley
1984	Curt Gowdy	1998	Jaime Jarrin
1985	Buck Canel	1999	Arch McDonald
1986	Bob Prince	2000	Marty Brennaman
1987	Jack Buck	2001	Rafael "Felo" Ramirez
1988	Lindsey Nelson	2002	Harry Kalas
1989	Harry Caray	2003	Bob Uecker
1990	By Saam	2004	Lon Simmons
1991	Joe Garagiola	2005	Jerry Coleman

RETIRED UNIFORM NUMBERS

It took a long time for uniform numbers to catch on in baseball after they were first promoted in the 1880s. In 1883 the Cincinnati Red Stockings tried to convince their players to wear numbers on their sleeves, but the players rejected the notion. It wasn't until 1916 that another team, the Cleveland Indians, tried again, but the idea did not stick. However, the pressure on baseball teams to use numbers grew since many football and basketball teams were already using them. In 1929 the Indians tried again, successfully. The New York Yankees soon followed suit and, by 1932, all teams had put numbers on at least their road uniforms. The Philadelphia Athletics were the last team to add numbers to their jerseys.

The first number to be retired was "the luckiest man of the face of the earth," Lou Gehrig, whose No. 4 was retired by the Yankees on July 4, 1939. The second number to be retired was Carl Hubbell's No. 11 by the New York Giants. Babe Ruth's No. 3 was retired in 1948. The Yankees retired No. 8 in honor of two players: Hall of Fame catchers, Bill Dickey and Yogi Berra. Montreal retired No. 10 to honor both Andre Dawson and Rusty Staub.

Retiring numbers has become much more popular during the last two decades, though teams vary widely on what makes a player's number worthy of being retired. The Seattle Mariners, Arizona Diamondbacks, Colorado Rockies, and Toronto Blue Jays have not retired any uniform numbers, and the Marlins have not retired the number of any player. Some teams have now gone so far to "retire" numbers for players or managers who never wore a number on their back.

The Detroit Tigers, after years of pressure to retire the numbers of Hall of Famers Hank Greenberg and Charlie Gehringer, retired Al Kaline's No. 6 in 1980. Greenberg and Gerhinger's numbers followed three years later on the same day. The reason that the team held out for so long? Because Ty Cobb—"The Greatest Tiger of Them All"—never wore a number that could be retired.

In 1997 Major League Baseball retired former Brooklyn Dodger Jackie Robinson's No. 42 on behalf of all teams, though players who were wearing the number at that time—most of whom who took the number to honor Robinson in the first place—have been allowed to keep wearing the number until retirement.

Three teams have even retired numbers in honor of off-the-field personnel. The Florida Marlins only retired number (No. 5) was retired in honor of former team president Carl Barger, who helped bring the Marlins into existence but died before the franchise its first game. The St. Louis Cardinals and Anaheim Angels have both retired numbers as tributes to former longtime owners: the Cardinals No. 85 was retired in honor of August Busch, and the Angels No. 26 was retired in honor of Gene Autry.

Only three franchises that have relocated have retired the numbers of any players that are strongly identified with their former cities. The Giants actually distinguish between the retired numbers of five New York Giants and the four San Francisco Giants whose numbers they have also retired (including Willie Mays, who played for the Giants in both New York and San Francisco). The Dodgers have retired the numbers of four players who made their greatest contributions in Brooklyn. The Atlanta Braves have retired the number of Warren Spahn, who played his whole, 21-year career in Boston and Milwaukee.

Other franchises, however, such as the Baltimore Orioles and Minnesota Twins, have ignored their previous identities and not retired any numbers that were worn before the teams moved to their current location. On the other hand, the new Washington Nationals do remember their past as the Montreal Expos and acknowledge the retired numbers of Gary Carter, Andre Dawson, Tim Raines, and Rusty Staub.

Atlanta/Milwaukee/Boston (NL)

Dale Murphy	3
Warren Spahn	21
Phil Niekro	35
Eddie Mathews	41
Hank Aaron	44

Baltimore (AL)

Earl Weaver (Manager)	4
Brooks Robinson	5
Cal Ripken	8
Frank Robinson	20
Jim Palmer	22
Eddie Murray	33

Boston (AL)

Bobby Doerr	1
Joe Cronin	4
Carl Yastrzemski	8
Ted Williams	9
Carlton Fisk	27

Chicago (AL)

Nellie Fox	2
Harold Baines	3
Luke Appling	4
Minnie Minoso	9
Luis Aparicio	11
Ted Lyons	16
Billy Pierce	19
Carlton Fisk	72

Chicago (NL)

Ron Santo	10
Ernie Banks	14
Ryne Sandberg	23
Billy Williams	26

Cincinnati (NL)

Fred Hutchinson (Manager)	1
Johnny Bench	5
Joe Morgan	8
Sparky Anderson (Manager)	10
Ted Kluszewski	18
Frank Robinson	20
Tony Perez	24

Cleveland (AL)

Earl Averill	3
Lou Boudreau	5
Larry Doby	14
Mel Harder	18
Bob Feller	19
Bob Lemon	21

Detroit (AL)

Charlie Gehringer	2
Hank Greenberg	5
Al Kaline	6
Hal Newhouser	16
Willie Horton	23
Ty Cobb	—
Ernie Harwell (Broadcaster)	—

Florida (NL)

Carl Barger (Executive)	5

Houston (NL)

Jimmy Wynn	24
Jose Cruz	25
Jim Umbricht	32
Mike Scott	33
Nolan Ryan	34
Don Wilson	40
Larry Dierker	49

Kansas City (AL)

George Brett	5
Dick Howser (Manager)	10
Frank White	20

Los Angeles/Anaheim/California (AL)

Jim Fregosi	11
Gene Autry (Owner)	26
Rod Carew	29
Nolan Ryan	30
Jimmie Reese (Coach)	50

Los Angeles/Brooklyn (NL)

Pee Wee Reese	1
Tommy Lasorda (Manager)	2
Duke Snider	4
Jim Gilliam	19
Don Sutton	20
Walt Alston (Manager)	24
Sandy Koufax	32
Roy Campanella	39
Jackie Robinson	42
Don Drysdale	53

Milwaukee (AL-NL)

Paul Molitor	4
Robin Yount	19

Minnesota/Washington (AL)

Rollie Fingers	34
Hank Aaron	44

Minnesota/Washington (AL)

Harmon Killebrew	3
Tony Oliva	6
Kent Hrbek	14
Rod Carew	29
Kirby Puckett	34

New York (AL)

Billy Martin (Manager)	1
Babe Ruth	3
Lou Gehrig	4
Joe DiMaggio	5
Mickey Mantle	7
Bill Dickey	8
Yogi Berra	8
Roger Maris	9
Phil Rizzuto	10
Thurman Munson	15
Whitey Ford	16
Don Mattingly	23
Elston Howard	32
Casey Stengel (Manager)	37
Reggie Jackson	44
Ron Guidry	49

New York (NL)

Gil Hodges (Manager)	14
Casey Stengel (Manager)	37
Tom Seaver	41

Oakland (AL)

Reggie Jackson	9
Catfish Hunter	27
Dennis Eckersley	34
Rollie Fingers	34

Philadelphia (NL)

Richie Ashburn	1
Jim Bunning	14
Mike Schmidt	20
Steve Carlton	32
Robin Roberts	36
Chuck Klein	—
Grover Alexander	—

Pittsburgh (NL)

Billy Meyer (Manager)	1
Ralph Kiner	4

Pittsburgh (NL) *(continued)*

Willie Stargell	8
Bill Mazeroski	9
Pie Traynor	20
Roberto Clemente	21
Honus Wagner	33
Danny Murtaugh (Manager)	40

San Diego (NL)

Steve Garvey	6
Tony Gwynn	19
Dave Winfield	31
Randy Jones	35

San Francisco/New York (NL)

Bill Terry	3
Mel Ott	4
Carl Hubbell	11
Willie Mays	24
Juan Marichal	27
Orlando Cepeda	30
Gaylord Perry	36
Willie McCovey	44
Christy Mathewson	—
John McGraw (Manager)	—

St. Louis (NL)

Ozzie Smith	1
Red Schoendienst	2
Stan Musial	6
Enos Slaughter	9
Ken Boyer	14
Dizzy Dean	17
Lou Brock	20
Bob Gibson	45
August Busch (Owner)	85
Rogers Hornsby	—

Tampa Bay (AL)

Wade Boggs	12

Texas (AL)

Nolan Ryan	34
Johnny Oates (Manager)	26

Washington/Montreal (NL)

Gary Carter	8
Andre Dawson	10
Rusty Staub	10
Tim Raines	30

GREAT PERFORMANCES

This section details some of the greatest individual performances in baseball history, including 2004's record-setting feats: Barry Bonds' .609 On-Base Percentage, 232 Walks, and 120 Intentional Walks; Ichiro's 262 hits; and Eric Gagne's 84 consecutive Saves.

Joe DiMaggio's 56-game hitting streak is one of the most revered records in baseball; no player has ever come remotely close to breaking it. Since DiMaggio set the record, only three players have accomplished a 36-game hitting streak or better. The late Stephen Jay Gould wrote that DiMaggio's hitting streak is the "most extraordinary thing that ever happened in American sports" because it totally defied the laws of probability.

DiMaggio didn't accomplish the streak without some controversy. There certainly were some questionable calls that enabled the streak to continue, but the streak lasted until DiMaggio was finally shut down on July 17, 1941 in Cleveland. The Yankees won, 4-3, but DiMaggio grounded out in each of his 3 at bats. In his final chance to extend the streak in eighth inning, Indians pitcher Jim Bagby induced DiMaggio to hit into a double play. DiMaggio's record may never be broken, but that hasn't prevented baseball fans from getting excited every time a player makes any kind of run at his record. Even a 20-game hitting streak quickens the pulses of the media and generates detailed coverage.

Most Consecutive Games Batted Safely, Season

Games	Player, Team	Year	Games	Player, Team	Year
56	Joe DiMaggio, NY AL	1941	31	Ed Delahanty, Phi NL	1899
44	Willie Keeler, Bal NL	1897	31	Nap Lajoie, Cle AL	1906
44	Pete Rose, Cin NL	1978	31	Sam Rice, Was AL	1924
42	Bill Dahlen, Chi NL	1894	31	Willie Davis, LA NL	1969
41	George Sisler, StL AL	1922	31	Rico Carty, Atl NL	1970
40	Ty Cobb, Det AL	1911	31	Ken Landreaux, Min AL	1980
39	Paul Molitor, Mil AL	1987	31	Vladimir Guerrero, Mon NL	1999
37	Tommy Holmes, Bos NL	1945	30	Cal McVey, Chi NL	1876
36	Jimmy Rollins, Phi NL	2005	30	Elmer Smith, Cin NL	1898
35	Fred Clarke, Lou NL	1895	30	Tris Speaker, Bos AL	1912
35	Ty Cobb, Det AL	1917	30	Goose Goslin, Det AL	1934
35	Luis Castillo, Fla NL	2002	30	Stan Musial, StL NL	1950
34	George Sisler, StL AL	1925	30	Ron LeFlore, Det AL	1976
34	George McQuinn, StL AL	1938	30	George Brett, KC AL	1980
34	Dom DiMaggio, Bos AL	1949	30	Jerome Walton, Chi NL	1989
34	Benito Santiago, SD NL	1987	30	Sandy Alomar Jr., Cle AL	1997
33	Hal Chase, NY AL	1907	30	Nomar Garciaparra, Bos AL	1997
33	George Davis, NY NL	1893	30	Eric Davis, Bal AL	1998
33	Rogers Hornsby, StL NL	1922	30	Luis Gonzalez, Ari NL	1999
33	Heinie Manush, Was AL	1933	30	Albert Pujols, StL NL	2003

DiMaggio's 56-game Hitting Streak

Joltin' Joe's legendary hitting streak caused a national sensation, became a song, made him a celebrity, and overshadowed a superior overall season by Ted Williams. Below (sans melody) is how The Yankee Clipper did it. Numbers in parentheses refer to hits off each pitcher on a given date.

Date	Opposing Pitcher, Team	AB	H	2B	3B	HR
May 15	Eddie Smith, Chi	4	1	0	0	0
May 16	Thornton Lee, Chi	4	2	0	1	1
May 17	Johnny Rigney, Chi	3	1	0	0	0
May 18	Bob Harris (2),					
	Johnny Niggeling (1), StL	3	3	1	0	0
May 19	Denny Galehouse, StL	3	1	1	0	0
May 20	Eldon Auker, StL	5	1	0	0	0
May 21	Schoolboy Rowe (1),					
	Al Benton (1), Det	5	2	0	0	0
May 22	Archie McKain, Det	4	1	0	0	0
May 23	Dick Newsome, Bos	5	1	0	0	0
May 24	Earl Johnson, Bos	4	1	0	0	0
May 25	Lefty Grove, Bos	4	1	0	0	0
May 27	Ken Chase (1),					
	Red Anderson (2),					
	Alex Carrasquel (1), Was	5	4	0	0	1
May 28	Sid Hudson, Was	4	1	0	1	0
May 29	Steve Sundra, Was	3	1	0	0	0
May 30G1	Earl Johnson, Bos	2	1	0	0	0
May 30G2	Mickey Harris, Bos	3	1	1	0	0
June 1G1	Al Milnar, Cle	4	1	0	0	0
June 1G2	Mel Harder, Cle	4	1	0	0	0
June 2	Bob Feller, Cle	4	2	1	0	0
June 3	Dizzy Trout, Det	4	1	0	0	1
June 5	Hal Newhouser, Det	5	1	0	1	0
June 7	Bob Muncrief (1),					
	Johnny Allen (1),					
	George Caster (1), StL	5	3	0	0	0
June 8G1	Eldon Auker, StL	4	2	0	0	2
June 8G2	George Caster (1),					
	Jack Kramer (1), StL	4	2	1	0	1
June 10	Johnny Rigney, Chi	5	1	0	0	0
June 12	Thornton Lee, Chi	4	2	0	0	1
June 14	Bob Feller, Cle	2	1	1	0	0

DiMaggio's 56-game Hitting Streak continued

Date	Opposing Pitcher, Team	AB	H	2B	3B	HR
June 15	Jim Bagby Jr., Cle	3	1	0	0	1
June 16	Al Milnar, Cle	5	1	1	0	0
June 17	Johnny Rigney, Chi	4	1	0	0	0
June 18	Thornton Lee, Chi	3	1	0	0	0
June 19	Eddie Smith (1),					
	Buck Ross (1), Chi	3	3	0	0	1
June 20	Bobo Newsom (2),					
	Archie McKain (2), Det	5	4	1	0	0
June 21	Dizzy Trout, Det	4	1	0	0	0
June 22	Hal Newhouser (1),					
	Bobo Newsom (1) Det	5	2	1	0	1
June 24	Bob Muncrief, StL	4	1	0	0	0
June 25	Denny Galehouse, StL	4	1	0	0	1
June 26	Eldon Auker, StL	4	1	0	0	0
June 27	Chubby Dean, Phi	3	2	0	0	1
June 28	Johnny Babich (1),					
	Lum Harris (1), Phi	5	2	1	0	0
June 29G1	Emil "Dutch" Leonard, Was	4	1	1	0	0
June 29G2	Red Anderson, Was	5	1	0	0	0
July 1G1	Mickey Harris (1),					
	Mike Ryba (1), Bos	4	2	0	0	0
July 1G2	Jack Wilson, Bos	3	1	0	0	0
July 2	Dick Newsome, Bos	5	1	0	0	1
July 5	Phil Marchildon, Phi	4	1	0	0	1
July 6G1	Johnny Babich (1),					
	Bump Hadley (3), Phi	5	4	1	0	0
July 6G2	Jack Knott, Phi	4	2	0	1	0
July 10	Johnny Niggeling, StL	2	1	0	0	0
July 11	Bob Harris (3),					
	Jack Kramer (1), StL	5	4	0	0	1
July 12	Eldon Auker (1),					
	Bob Muncrief (1), StL	5	2	1	0	0
July 13G1	Ted Lyons (2),					
	Jack Hallett (1), Chi	4	3	0	0	0
July 13G2	Thornton Lee, Chi	4	1	0	0	0
July 14	Johnny Rigney, Chi	3	1	0	0	0
July 15	Eddie Smith, Chi	4	2	1	0	0
July 16	Al Milnar (2),					
	Joe Krakauskas (1), Cle	4	3	1	0	0
Totals (56 games)		223	91	16	4	15

Consecutive Games On-Base Streak

Even when DiMaggio's great hitting steak was finally stopped by the Indians, he managed to extend another streak with a walk, eventually reaching base in 74 consecutive games that year. At the time, that was a record. Ted Williams, however, broke that mark eight years later when he reached base an incredible 84 games in a row. These records were unknown at the time, but researcher Herman Krabbenhoft has recently documented the history of on-base streaks. In 2003 Barry Bonds tied the NL all-time mark by getting on base in 58 consecutive games. Here is a list of all on-base streaks that have lasted at least 50 games.

Player, Team	Year	Games	Player, Team	Year	Games
Ted Williams, Bos AL	1949	84	Derek Jeter, NY AL	1999	53
Joe DiMaggio, NY AL	1941	74	Alex Rodriguez, NY AL	2004	53
Ted Williams, Bos AL	1941	69	Mel Amada, StL AL	1938	52
Ted Williams, Bos AL	1948	65	Ty Cobb, Det AL	1914	52
Bill Joyce, Bos AL	1891	64	Lou Gehrig, NY AL	1934	52
Barry Bonds, SF NL	2003	58	Greg Gross, Hou NL	1975	52
Duke Snider, Bro NL	1954	58	Denny Lyons, Phi AA	1887	52
Wade Boggs, Bos AL	1985	57	Tony Phillips, Det AL	1993	52
Cupid Childs, Cle NL	1892	57	Gary Sheffield, Atl NL	2002	52
George Kell, Det AL	1950	57	Tris Speaker, Cle AL	1920	52
Ed Delahanty, Phi NL	1896	56	Frank Thomas, Chi AL	1996	52
Bill Joyce, WAS NL-NY NL	1896	56	Jack Tobin, StL AL	1922	52
Ryan Klesko, SD NL	2002	56	Jimmy Wynn, Hou NL	1969	52
Arky Vaughn, Pit NL	1936	56	George Brett, KC AL	1980	51
Ty Cobb, Det AL	1915	56	Joe DiMaggio, NY AL	1937	51
Billy Hamilton, Bos NL	1896	55	Joe Kelley, Bal NL	1896	51
Stan Musial, StL NL	1943	55	Babe Ruth, NY AL	1923	51
Jim Thome, Cle AL	2002	55	Ken Williams, StL AL	1923	51
Ray Blades, StL NL	1925	54	Vince Coleman, StL	1987	51
Bill Joyce, Was NL	1894	54	Tris Speaker, Cle AL	1926	50
Luke Appling, Chi AL	1936	53	Lou Whitaker, Det	1991	50
Shawn Green, LA NL	2000	53			

Ichiro's 262-Hit Season

On Friday, October 1, 2004, Seattle's Ichiro Suzuki smacked a ground ball up the middle and broke a record that had stood for 84 years. Ichiro's 258th hit surpassed St. Louis Browns great George Sisler's 1920 record of 257 hits in a single season. While 257 never had the ring of 60 or 714 or 4192 and has never been one of baseball's magic numbers, the record's longevity speaks for itself.

Sisler clearly had a better year in 1920 than Ichiro did in 2004, posting a batting average of .404 with an on-base percentage of .449 and a slugging percentage of .632, in contrast to Ichiro's .372 batting average, .414 on-base percentage, and

.455 slugging percentage. Sisler knocked out 1.67 hits per game, playing in all 154 of the Browns games; Ichiro rapped 1.63 hits per game while playing in all but one of the Mariners 162 games. On the other hand, Ichiro did break the record while playing half his games in the best pitchers' park in the league in 2004, while Sisler had the benefit of a favorable environment for hitters at his home park in 1920. In fact, Ichiro hit .405 on the road in breaking the record in 2004, becoming the first hitter to hit .400 on the road in a season since Lou Boudreau in 1948, while Sisler hit .473 at home and .341 on the road in 1920. And there's no doubt that Ichiro faced far tougher pitching than Sisler ever did, and no one had even come close to challenging Sisler's mark since 1930. Ichiro's month-by-month hit totals and batting average are shown below (IS) alongside Sisler's 1920 (GS).

Month	IS H	AVG	GS H	AVG	Month	IS H	AVG	GS H	AVG
April	26	.255	12	.333	August	56	.463	42	.400
May	50	.400	39	.355	September	44	.373	57	.442
Jun	29	.274	60	.526	October	6	.429	7	.500
July	51	.432	40	.325	Total	262	.372	257	.407

Consecutive Games Played

It was only twenty years ago that most people considered Lou Gehrig's consecutive games played record to be unbreakable. Then ironman Cal Ripken came along and eventually surpassed Gehrig's record by a wide margin. Even Ripken's record is breakable, but it will take a unique combination of fortitude and luck to surpass it. Miguel Tejada, another shortstop, holds the longest consecutive games played streak of any active player, with 918 consecutive games at the end of 2005. Tejada would need to play every game of the next ten seasons and 95 games of the season after that to break Cal Ripken's record.

Player	Games	Years	Player	Games	Years
Cal Ripken	2,632	1982–98	Miguel Tejeda	918	2000–present
Lou Gehrig	2,130	1925–39	Stan Musial	895	1952–57
Everett Scott	1,307	1916–25	Eddie Yost	829	1949–55
Steve Garvey	1,207	1975–83	Gus Suhr	822	1931–37
Billy Williams	1,117	1963–70	Nellie Fox	798	1955–60
Joe Sewell	1,103	1922–30			

Four-Homer Games

Only fifteen players have hit 4 home runs in a game, and only twelve of those players did it in a regulation nine-inning game. Some great players are on the list, but there are also a few surprises: Mark Whiten, who hit only 105 home runs in his career, and Pat Seerey, who hit only 85 home runs. Carlos Delgado slugged his way onto this short list during the last week of the 2003 season.

Player, Team	Date
Bobby Lowe, Bos NL	May 30, 1894
Ed Delahanty, Phi NL	July 13, 1896
Lou Gehrig, NY AL	June 3, 1932
Chuck Klein, Phi NL	July 10, 1936 (10 inn)
Pat Seerey, Chi AL	July 18, 1948 G1 (11 inn)
Gil Hodges, Bro NL	Aug. 31, 1950
Joe Adcock, Mil NL	July 31, 1954
Rocky Colavito, Cle AL	June 10, 1959
Willie Mays, SF NL	Apr. 30, 1961
Mike Schmidt, Phi NL	Apr. 17, 1976 (10 inn)
Bob Horner, Atl NL	July 6, 1986
Mark Whiten, StL NL	Sept. 7, 1993 G2
Mike Cameron, Sea AL	May 2, 2002
Shawn Green, LA NL	May 23, 2002
Carlos Delgado, Tor AL	Sept. 25, 2003

Career Grand Slam Home Run Leaders

The grand slam is not just another home run; it has an identity of its own as the rarest type of home run. A grand slam usually changes the very complexion of a game since a team that's already ahead usually has an impenetrable lead once a grand slam is hit, and a team that is behind can use a grand slam to suddenly make the game competitive again. A grand slam is by far the biggest single scoring event in any major pro sport.

Baseball fans might reasonably expect the career grand slams leaders list to look similar to the all-time home run leader list, but there are significant differences. Lou Gehrig has four more grand slams than any other player in baseball history, despite not being among the top twenty in career home

runs. Some of the top home run hitters of all-time, including Barry Bonds, Frank Robinson and Sammy Sosa, have hit less than half as many grand slams as Gehrig. And several players who didn't even reach the 300-career home run mark are among the leaders in grand slams.

Player	Career GS	Player	Career GS	Player	Career GS
Lou Gehrig	23	Babe Ruth	16	Jeff Kent	13
Manny Ramirez	20	Ken Griffey Jr.	14	Ralph Kiner	13
Eddie Murray	19	Gil Hodges	14	Ernie Banks	12
Willie McCovey	18	Mark McGwire	14	Don Baylor	12
Robin Ventura	18	Mike Piazza	14	Rogers Hornsby	12
Jimmie Foxx	17	Harold Baines	13	Rafael Palmeiro	12
Ted Williams	17	Albert Belle	13	Joe Rudi	12
Hank Aaron	16	Joe DiMaggio	13	Matt Williams	12
Dave Kingman	16	George Foster	13	Rudy York	12

The Single-Season Home Run Record

Widespread perception to the contrary, the major league single-season home run record has actually changed quite often over the course of baseball history. Despite all the hoopla over Mark McGwire setting the home run record in 1998, he held the mark for the shortest length of time of any individual since the 1880s.

Year	Player, Team	HR	Year	Player, Team	HR
1876	George Hall, Phi NL	5	1921	Babe Ruth, NY AL	59
1879	Charley Jones, Bos NL	9	1927	Babe Ruth, NY AL	60
1883	Buck Ewing, NY NL	10	1961	Roger Maris, NY AL	61
1884	Ed Williamson, Chi NL	27	1998	Mark McGwire, StL NL	70
1919	Babe Ruth, Bos AL	29	2001	Barry Bonds, SF NL	73
1920	Babe Ruth, NY AL	54			

The Home Run Records of Bonds, McGwire, Maris, and Ruth

Three years after Mark McGwire and Sammy Sosa electrified the world with their great home run chase in 1998, Barry Bonds shattered the highest-profile record in sports with his 73 home runs. Babe Ruth made the home run baseball's dominant offensive stratagem in 1920 by hitting an unheard of 54 round-trippers, and The Bambino's 60 home runs in 1927 invested a unique magic in that mark.

The lists below detail the all-time home run record seasons since 1927. "Gm" indicates the team game number in which the home run was hit. Left-handed pitchers are asterisked. Pitchers who allowed multiple home runs in a game are listed only once. Daggers after the opposing teams indicate road games.

Bonds played in 153 of the Giants 162 games in 2001. McGwire played in 155 of the Cardinals 163 games in 1998. Maris played in 161 of the Yankees 163 games in 1961. Ruth played in 151 of the Yankees 155 games in 1927.

Bonds' 73 Home Runs (2001)

HR (Gm)	Date	Off (Pitcher/Team)	HR (Gm)	Date	Off (Pitcher/Team)
1 (1)	Apr. 2	Woody Williams SD	37 (70)	June 19	Adam Eaton SD
2 (9)	Apr. 12	Adam Eaton SD	38 (71)	June 20	Rodney Myers SD
3 (10)	Apr. 13	Jamey Wright Mil	39 (74)	June 23	Darryl Kile StL
4 (11)	Apr. 14	Jimmy Haynes Mil	40 (89)	July 12	Paul Abbott Sea
5 (12)	Apr. 15	David Weathers Mil	41 (95)	July 18	Mike Hampton* Col
6 (13)	Apr. 17	Terry Adams LA	42 (95)	July 18	
7 (14)	Apr. 18	Chan Ho Park LA	43 (103)	July 26	Curt Schilling Ari
8 (16)	Apr. 20	Jimmy Haynes Mil	44 (103)	July 26	
9 (19)	Apr. 24	Jim Brower Cin	45 (104)	July 27	Brian Anderson* Ari
10 (21)	Apr. 26	Scott Sullivan Cin	46 (108)	Aug. 1	Joe Beimel* Pit
11 (24)	Apr. 29	Manny Aybar Chi	47 (111)	Aug. 4	Nelson Figueroa Phi
12 (26)	May 2	Todd Ritchie Pit	48 (115)	Aug. 7	Danny Graves Cin
13 (27)	May 3	Jimmy Anderson* Pit	49 (115)	Aug. 9	Scott Winchester Cin
14 (28)	May 4	Bruce Chen* Phi	50 (117)	Aug. 11	Joe Borowski Chi
15 (35)	May 11	Steve Trachsel NY	51 (119)	Aug. 14	Ricky Bones Fla
16 (40)	May 17	Chuck Smith Fla	52 (121)	Aug. 16	A.J. Burnett Fla
17 (41)	May 18	Mike Remlinger* Atl	53 (121)	Aug. 16	Vic Darensbourg* Fla
18 (42)	May 19	Odalis Perez* Atl	54 (123)	Aug. 18	Jason Marquis Atl
19 (42)	May 19	Jose Cabrera Atl	55 (127)	Aug. 23	Graeme Lloyd* Mon
20 (42)	May 19	Jason Marquis Atl	56 (135)	Aug. 27	Kevin Appier NY
21 (43)	May 20	John Burkett Atl	57 (135)	Aug. 31	John Thomson Col
22 (43)	May 20	Mike Remlinger* Atl	58 (138)	Sept. 3	Jason Jennings Col
23 (44)	May 21	Curt Schilling Ari	59 (141)	Sept. 4	Miguel Batista Ari
24 (45)	May 22	Russ Springer Ari	60 (141)	Sept. 6	Albie Lopez Ari
25 (47)	May 24	John Thomson Col	61 (144)	Sept. 9	Scott Elarton Col
26 (50)	May 27	Denny Neagle* Col	62 (144)	Sept. 9	
27 (53)	May 30	Robert Ellis Ari	63 (144)	Sept. 9	Todd Belitz* Col
28 (53)	May 30		64 (147)	Sept. 20	Wade Miller Hou
29 (54)	June 1	Shawn Chacon Col	65 (150)	Sept. 23	Jason Middlebrook SD
30 (57)	June 4	Bobby J. Jones SD	66 (150)	Sept. 23	
31 (58)	June 5	Wascar Serrano SD	67 (151)	Sept. 24	James Baldwin LA
32 (60)	June 7	Brian Lawrence SD	68 (154)	Sept. 28	Jason Middlebrook SD
33 (64)	June 12	Pat Rapp Ana	69 (155)	Sept. 29	Chuck McElroy* SD
34 (66)	June 14	Lou Pote Ana	70 (159)	Oct. 4	Wilfredo Rodriguez* Hou
35 (67)	June 15	Mark Mulder* Oak	71 (160)	Oct. 5	Chan Ho Park LA
36 (67)	June 15		72 (160)	Oct. 5	
			73 (162)	Oct. 7	Dennis Springer LA

McGwire's 70 Home Runs (1998)

HR (Gm)	Date	Off (Pitcher/Team)	HR (Gm)	Date	Off (Pitcher/Team)
1 (1)	Mar. 31	Ramon Martinez LA	36 (79)	June 27	Mike Trombley Min
2 (2)	Apr. 2	Frank Lankford LA	37 (81)	June 30	Glendon Rusch* KC
3 (3)	Apr. 3	Mark Langston* SD	38 (89)	July 11	Billy Wagner* Hou
4 (4)	Apr. 4	Don Wengert SD	39 (90)	July 12	Sean Bergman Hou
5 (13)	Apr. 14	Jeff Suppan Ari	40 (90)	July 12	Scott Elarton Hou
6 (13)	Apr. 14		41 (95)	July 17	Brian Bohanon* LA
7 (13)	Apr. 14	Barry Manuel Ari	42 (95)	July 17	Antonio Osuna LA
8 (15)	Apr. 17	Matt Whiteside Phi	43 (98)	July 20	Brian Boehringer SD
9 (19)	Apr. 21	Trey Moore* Mon	44 (104)	July 26	John Thomson Col
10 (23)	Apr. 25	Jerry Spradlin Phi	45 (105)	July 28	Mike Myers* Mil
11 (27)	Apr. 30	Marc Pisciotta Chi	46 (115)	Aug. 8	Mark Clark Chi
12 (28)	May 1	Rod Beck Chi	47 (118)	Aug. 11	Bobby Jones NY
13 (34)	May 8	Rick Reed NY	48 (124)	Aug. 19	Matt Karchner Chi
14 (36)	May 12	Paul Wagner Mil	49 (124)	Aug. 19	Terry Mulholland* Chi
15 (38)	May 14	Kevin Millwood Atl	50 (125)	Aug. 20	Willie Blair NY
16 (40)	May 16	Livan Hernandez Fla	51 (126)	Aug. 20	Rick Reed NY
17 (42)	May 18	Jesus Sanchez* Fla	52 (129)	Aug. 22	Francisco Cordova Pit
18 (43)	May 19	Tyler Green Phi	53 (130)	Aug. 23	Ricardo Rincon* Pit
19 (43)	May 19		54 (133)	Aug. 26	Justin Speier Fla
20 (43)	May 19	Wayne Gomes Phi	55 (137)	Aug. 30	Dennis Martinez Atl
21 (46)	May 22	Mark Gardner SF	56 (139)	Sept. 1	Livan Hernandez Fla
22 (47)	May 23	Rich Rodriguez* SF	57 (139)	Sept. 1	Donn Pall Fla
23 (47)	May 23	John Johnstone SF	58 (140)	Sept. 2	Brian Edmondson Fla
24 (48)	May 25	Robb Nen SF	59 (140)	Sept. 2	Rob Stanifer Fla
25 (49)	May 25	John Thomson Col	60 (142)	Sept. 5	Dennis Reyes* Cin
26 (52)	May 29	Dan Miceli SD	61 (144)	Sept. 7	Mike Morgan Chi
27 (53)	May 30	Andy Ashby SD	62 (145)	Sept. 8	Steve Trachsel Chi
28 (59)	June 5	Orel Hershiser SF	63 (152)	Sept. 15	Jason Christiansen* Pit
29 (62)	June 8	Jason Bere Chi AL	64 (155)	Sept. 18	Rafael Roque* Mil
30 (64)	June 10	Jim Parque* Chi AL	65 (157)	Sept. 20	Scott Karl* Mil
31 (65)	June 12	Andy Benes Ari	66 (161)	Sept. 25	Shayne Bennett Mon
32 (69)	June 17	Jose Lima Hou	67 (162)	Sept. 26	Dustin Hermanson Mon
33 (70)	June 18	Shane Reynolds Hou	68 (162)	Sept. 26	Kirk Bullinger Mon
34 (76)	June 24	Jaret Wright Cle	69 (163)	Sept. 27	Mike Thurman Mon
35 (77)	June 25	Dave Burba Cle	70 (163)	Sept. 27	Carl Pavano Mon

Maris' 61 Home Runs (1961)

HR (Gm)	Date	Off (Pitcher/Team)	HR (Gm)	Date	Off (Pitcher/Team)
1 (11)	Apr. 26	Paul Foytack Det	32 (78)	July 5	Frank Funk Cle
2 (17)	May 3	Pedro Ramos Min	33 (82)	July 9	Bill Monbouquette Bos
3 (20)	May 6	Eli Grba LA	34 (84)	July 13	Early Wynn Chi
4 (29)	May 17	Pete Burnside* Was	35 (86)	July 15	Ray Herbert Chi
5 (30)	May 19	Jim Perry Cle	36 (92)	July 21	Bill Monbouquette Bos
6 (31)	May 20	Gary Bell Cle	37 (95)	July 25	Frank Baumann* Chi
7 (32)	May 21	Chuck Estrada Bal	38 (95)	July 25	Don Larsen Chi
8 (35)	May 24	Gene Conley Bos	39 (96)	July 25	Russ Kemmerer Chi
9 (38)	May 28	Cal McLish Chi	40 (96)	July 25	Warren Hacker Chi
10 (40)	May 30	Gene Conley Bos	41 (106)	Aug. 4	Camilo Pascual Min
11 (40)	May 30	Mike Fornieles Bos	42 (114)	Aug. 11	Pete Burnside Was
12 (41)	May 31	Billy Muffett Bos	43 (115)	Aug. 12	Dick Donovan Was
13 (43)	June 2	Cal McLish Chi	44 (116)	Aug. 13	Bennie Daniels Was
14 (44)	June 3	Bob Shaw Chi	45 (117)	Aug. 13	Marty Kutyna Was
15 (45)	June 4	Russ Kemmerer Chi	46 (118)	Aug. 15	Juan Pizarro* Chi
16 (48)	June 6	Ed Palmquist Min	47 (119)	Aug. 16	Billy Pierce* Chi
17 (49)	June 7	Pedro Ramos Min	48 (119)	Aug. 16	
18 (52)	June 9	Ray Herbert KC	49 (124)	Aug. 20	Jim Perry Cle
19 (55)	June 11	Eli Grba LA	50 (125)	Aug. 22	Ken McBride LA
20 (55)	June 11	Johnny James LA	51 (129)	Aug. 26	Jerry Walker KC
21 (57)	June 13	Jim Perry Cle	52 (135)	Sept. 2	Frank Lary Det
22 (58)	June 14	Gary Bell Cle	53 (135)	Sept. 2	Hank Aguirre* Det
23 (61)	June 17	Don Mossi* Det	54 (140)	Sept. 6	Tom Cheney Was
24 (62)	June 18	Jerry Casale Det	55 (141)	Sept. 7	Dick Stigman* Cle
25 (63)	June 19	Jim Archer* KC	56 (143)	Sept. 9	Mudcat Grant Cle
26 (64)	June 20	Joe Nuxhall* KC	57 (151)	Sept. 16	Frank Lary Det
27 (66)	June 22	Norm Bass KC	58 (152)	Sept. 17	Terry Fox Det
28 (74)	July 1	Dave Sisler Was	59 (155)	Sept. 20	Milt Pappas Bal
29 (75)	July 2	Pete Burnside* Was	60 (159)	Sept. 26	Jack Fisher Bal
30 (75)	July 2	Johnny Klippstein* Was	61 (163)	Oct. 1	Tracy Stallard Bos
31 (77)	July 4	Frank Lary Det			

Ruth's 60 Home Runs (1927)

HR (Gm)	Date	Off (Pitcher/Team)	HR (Gm)	Date	Off (Pitcher/Team)
1 (4)	Apr. 15	Howard Ehmke Phi	31 (94)	July 24	Tommy Thomas Chi
2 (11)	Apr. 23	Rube Walberg* Phi	32 (95)	July 26	Milt Gaston StL
3 (12)	Apr. 24	Sloppy Thurston Was	33 (95)	July 26	
4 (14)	Apr. 29	Slim Harriss Bos	34 (98)	July 28	Lefty Stewart* StL
5 (16)	May 1	Jack Quinn Phi	35 (106)	Aug. 5	George S. Smith Det
6 (16)	May 1	Rube Walberg* Phi	36 (110)	Aug. 10	Tom Zachary* Was
7 (24)	May 10	Milt Gaston StL	37 (114)	Aug. 16	Tommy Thomas Chi
8 (25)	May 11	Ernie Nevers StL	38 (115)	Aug. 17	Sarge Connally Chi
9 (29)	May 17	Rip Collins Det	39 (118)	Aug. 20	Jake Miller* Cle
10 (33)	May 22	Ben Karr Cle	40 (120)	Aug. 22	Joe Shaute* Cle
11 (34)	May 23	Sloppy Thurston Was	41 (124)	Aug. 27	Ernie Nevers StL
12 (37)	May 28	Sloppy Thurston Was	42 (125)	Aug. 28	Ernie Wingard* StL
13 (39)	May 29	Danny MacFayden Bos	43 (127)	Aug. 31	Tony Welzer Bos
14 (40)	May 30	Rube Walberg* Phi	44 (128)	Sept. 2	Rube Walberg* Phi
15 (42)	May 31	Jack Quinn Phi	45 (132)	Sept. 6	Tony Welzer Bos
16 (43)	May 31	Howard Ehmke Phi	46 (132)	Sept. 6	
17 (47)	June 5	Earl Whitehill* Det	47 (133)	Sept. 6	Jack Russell Bos
18 (48)	June 7	Tommy Thomas Chi	48 (134)	Sept. 7	Danny MacFayden Bos
19 (52)	June 11	Garland Buckeye* Cle	49 (134)	Sept. 7	Slim Harriss Bos
20 (52)	June 11		50 (138)	Sept. 11	Milt Gaston Bos
21 (53)	June 12	George Uhle Cle	51 (139)	Sept. 13	Willis Hudlin Cle
22 (55)	June 16	Tom Zachary* StL	52 (140)	Sept. 13	Joe Shaute* Cle
23 (60)	June 22	Hal Wiltse* Bos	53 (143)	Sept. 16	Ted Blankenship Chi
24 (60)	June 22		54 (147)	Sept. 18	Ted Lyons Chi
25 (70)	June 30	Slim Harriss Bos	55 (148)	Sept. 21	Sam Gibson Det
26 (73)	July 3	Hod Lisenbee Was	56 (149)	Sept. 22	Ken Holloway Det
27 (78)	July 8	Don Hankins Det	57 (152)	Sept. 27	Lefty Grove* Phi
28 (79)	July 9	Ken Holloway Det	58 (153)	Sept. 29	Hod Lisenbee Was
29 (79)	July 9		59 (153)	Sept. 29	Paul Hopkins Was
30 (83)	July 12	Joe Shaute* Cle	60 (154)	Sept. 30	Tom Zachary* Was

On-Base Percentage, Walks, and Intentional Walks

Despite Barry Bonds' assaults on the single season and career home run records, Bonds' most valuable achievements have come by way of his ability to get on base. Bonds' extraordinary strike zone judgment and plate discipline—combined with his opponents' sometimes irrational fear of his batting prowess—has enabled Bonds to obliterate all the major previous single-season records for walks and on-base percentage. Not once, but twice: first in 2002, then again in 2004.

Since 1893, when the distance from the pitching rubber to the plate was first set at its present length of sixty feet, six inches, the single-season walk and on-base percentage records have each been held by only four players.

The single-season record for intentional walks has changed more frequently since intentional walks became an official statistic in 1955, indicating changes in managerial tactics as well as the unique intimidation factor of Barry Bonds.

On-Base Percentage

Year	Player	Avg
1893	Billy Hamilton Phi NL	.490
1894	Billy Hamilton Phi NL	.522
1899	John McGraw Bal NL	.547
1941	Ted Williams Bos AL	.553
2002	Barry Bonds SF NL	.582
2004	Barry Bonds SF NL	.609

Walks

Year	Player	BB
1893	Jack Crooks StL NL	121
1911	Jimmy Sheckard Chi NL	147
1920	Babe Ruth NY AL	150
1923	Babe Ruth NY AL	170
2002	Barry Bonds SF NL	198
2004	Barry Bonds SF NL	232

Intentional Walks

Year	Player	IBB
1955	Ted Kluszewski Cin NL	25
1956	Duke Snider Bro NL	26
1957	Ted Williams Bos AL	33
1969	Willie McCovey SF NL	45
2002	Barry Bonds SF NL	68
2004	Barry Bonds SF NL	120

Most Consecutive Hits

The ability to get 9 or more consecutive hits is not the sign of a great hitter; however, it is the sign of a good hitter who has gotten very lucky. Here is a list of those players who qualified as both skilled and fortunate.

No.	Player, Team	Year(s)	No.	Player, Team	Year(s)
12	Pinky Higgins, Bos AL	1938	9	Sam Rice, Was AL	1925
12	Walt Dropo, Det AL	1952	9	Taylor Douthit, StL NL	1926
11	Tris Speaker, Cle AL	1920	9	Babe Herman, Bro NL	1926
11	Johnny Pesky, Bos AL	1946	9	Hal Trosky, Cle AL	1936
11	Bernie Williams, NY AL	2002	9	Ted Williams, Bos AL	1939
10	Jake Stenzel, Pit NL	1893	9	Billy Jurges, NY NL	1941
10	Ed Delahanty, Phi NL	1897	9	Terry Moore, StL NL	1947
10	Jake Gettman, Was NL	1897	9	Dick Sisler, Phi NL	1950
10	Nap Lajoie, Phi AL	1901	9	Eddie Waitkus, Phi NL	1950
10	Ed Konetchy, Bro NL	1919	9	Dave Philley, Phi NL	1958–59
10	George Sisler, StL AL	1921	9	Felipe Alou, SF NL	1962
10	Harry Heilmann, Det AL	1922	9	Willie Stargell, Pit NL	1966
10	Kiki Cuyler, Pit NL	1925	9	Tony Oliva, Min AL	1967
10	Harry McCurdy, Chi AL	1926	9	Rennie Stennett, Pit NL	1975
10	Chick Hafey, StL NL	1929	9	Ron Cey, LA NL	1977
10	Joe Medwick, StL NL	1936	9	Jorge Orta, Cle NL	1980
10	Rip Radcliff, Chi AL	1938	9	Mickey Hatcher, Min AL	1985
10	Buddy Hassett, Bos NL	1940	9	Andres Galarraga, Col NL	1993
10	Woody Williams, Cin NL	1943	9	Sammy Sosa, Chi NL	1993
10	Ken Singleton, Bal NL	1981	9	Lance Johnson, Chi AL	1995
10	Bip Roberts, Cin NL	1992	9	Jose Vizcaino, NY NL	1996
10	Frank Thomas, Chi AL	1997	9	Barry Bonds, SF NL	1998
10	Joe Randa, KC AL	1999	9	John Olerud, NY NL	1998
10	Frank Catalanotto, Tex AL	2000	9	Todd Walker, Min AL	1998
9	George Van Haltren, Bal AA	1891	9	Charles Johnson, Bal AL	1999
9	Joe Kelley, Bal NL	1894	9	Jim Edmonds, StL NL	2000
9	Roger Connor, SL NL	1895	9	Ben Molina, Ana AL	2001
9	Joe Kelley, Bal NL	1898	9	Dmitri Young, Cin NL	2001
9	Doc Johnston, Cle AL	1919	9	Manny Ramirez, Bos AL	2002
9	Bobby Veach, Det AL	1921	9	Marcus Giles, Atl NL	2003
9	Rogers Hornsby, StL NL	1924	9	Raul Ibanez, Sea AL	2004
9	Ty Cobb, Det AL	1925			

Triple Crown Batters

It's been thirty-nine years since someone last won the Triple Crown, and an incredible sixty-nine years since a NL player has won one. With today's significantly stronger and larger talent base, it's much harder for an individual player to lead the league in all three glamorous offensive categories in a single year. The Triple Crown's three categories ensure that only a multidimensional hitter can win it, not just a home run hitter or a singles hitter with a very high average. Every twentieth-century Triple Crown winner is in the Hall of Fame.

Player, Team	Year	AVG	HR	RBI
Tip O'Neill, StL AA	1887	.435	14	123
Nap Lajoie, Phi AL	1901	.426	14	125
Ty Cobb, Det AL	1909	.377	9	115
Rogers Hornsby, StL NL	1922	.401	42	152
Rogers Hornsby, StL NL	1925	.403	39	143
Jimmie Foxx, Phi AL	1933	.356	48	163
Chuck Klein, Phi NL	1933	.368	28	120

Triple Crown Batters continued

Player, Team	Year	AVG	HR	RBI
Lou Gehrig, NY AL	1934	.363	49	165
Joe Medwick, StL NL	1937	.374	31	154
Ted Williams, Bos AL	1942	.356	48	163
Ted Williams, Bos AL	1947	.343	32	114
Mickey Mantle, NY AL	1956	.353	52	130
Frank Robinson, Bal AL	1966	.316	49	122
Carl Yastrzemski, Bos AL	1967	.325	44	121

Triple Crown Pitchers

Pitchers have won their Triple Crown more than twice as often as their batting counterparts, yet it remains an achievement that garners much less attention than its batting counterpart. The pitchers who win have to be dominating hurlers who receive solid run support from their offenses, but the skills required to win all three categories tend to work with each other, not against each other. Twenty-five of the 28 pitching Triple Crowns achieved since 1900 have been won by Hall of Famers or by recent pitchers seemingly assured of future Hall of Fame status.

Year	Player, Team	Wins	ERA	SO
1877	Tommy Bond, Bos NL	40	2.11	170
1884	Guy Hecker, Lou AA	52	1.80	385
1884	Charley Radbourn, Pro NL	59	1.38	441
1888	Tim Keefe, NY NL	35	1.74	335
1889	John Clarkson, Bos NL	49	2.73	284
1894	Amos Rusie, NY NL	36	2.78	195
1901	Cy Young, Bos NL	33	1.62	158
1905	Rube Waddell, Phi, AL	27	1.48	287
1905	Christy Mathewson, NY NL	31	1.28	206
1913	Walter Johnson, Was AL	36	1.14	243
1915	Grover Alexander, Phi NL	31	1.22	241
1916	Grover Alexander, Phi NL	33	1.55	167
1917	Grover Alexander, Phi, NL	30	1.83	200
1918	Hippo Vaughn, Chi NL	22	1.74	148
1918	Walter Johnson, Was AL	23	1.27	162
1920	Grover Alexander, Chi NL	27	1.91	173
1924	Walter Johnson, Was	23	2.72	158
1924	Dazzy Vance, Bro NL	28	2.16	262
1930	Lefty Grove, Phi AL	28	2.54	209
1931	Lefty Grove, Phi AL	31	2.06	175
1934	Lefty Gomez, NY AL	26	2.33	158
1937	Lefty Gomez, NY AL	21	2.33	194
1939	Bucky Walters, Cin NL	27	2.29	137
1940	Bob Feller, Cle AL	27	2.61	261
1945	Hal Newhouser, Det AL	25	1.81	212
1963	Sandy Koufax, LA NL	25	1.88	306
1965	Sandy Koufax, LA NL	26	2.04	382
1966	Sandy Koufax, LA NL	27	1.73	317
1972	Steve Carlton, Phi NL	27	1.97	310
1985	Dwight Gooden, NY NL	24	1.53	268
1997	Roger Clemens, Tor AL	21	2.05	292
1998	Roger Clemens, Tor AL	20	2.65	271
1999	Pedro Martinez Bos AL	23	2.07	313
2002	Randy Johnson, Ari NL	24	2.32	334

Most Strikeouts in a Game

When a pitcher strikes out at least 18 batters in a nine-inning game, he's almost certainly a dominating pitcher. If he's not yet a great pitcher, he probably will be one someday if he can refine his control. Pitching a game of this type is far more rare than a no-hitter, and it may be more of an achievement. Of the pitchers who have fanned 18 or more in a nine-inning game, only Randy Johnson failed to complete the game, pitching 9 of 11 innings in 2001 when he registered 20 K's. Tom Seaver struck out 10 in a row (a record in itself) on the way to his 19-strikeout game in 1970.

Not more than 9 innings pitched

Pitcher, Team	Date	No.
Roger Clemens, Bos AL	Apr. 29, 1986	20
Roger Clemens, Bos AL	Sept. 18, 1996	20
Kerry Wood, Chi NL	May 6, 1998	20
Randy Johnson, Ari NL	May 8, 2001	20
Charlie Sweeney, Pro NL	June 7, 1884	19
Hugh Daily, Chi UA	July 7, 1884	19
Steve Carlton, StL NL	Sept. 15, 1969	19
Tom Seaver, NY NL	Apr. 22, 1970	19
Nolan Ryan, Cal AL	Aug. 12, 1974	19
David Cone, NY NL	Oct. 6, 1991	19
Randy Johnson, Sea AL	June 24, 1997	19
Randy Johnson, Sea AL	Aug. 8, 1997	19
Dupee Shaw, Bos UA	July 19, 1884	18
Henry Porter, Mil UA	Oct. 3, 1884	18
Bob Feller, Cle AL	Oct. 2, 1938 G1	18
Sandy Koufax, LA NL	Aug. 31, 1959	18
Sandy Koufax, LA NL	Apr. 24, 1962	18
Don Wilson, Hou NL	July 14, 1968	18
Nolan Ryan, Cal AL	Sept. 10, 1976	18
Ron Guidry, NY AL	June 17, 1978	18
Bill Gullickson, Mon NL	Sept. 10, 1980	18
Ramon Martinez, LA NL	June 4, 1990	18

Not more than 9 innings pitched continued

Randy Johnson, Sea AL	Sept. 27, 1992	18
Roger Clemens, Tor AL	Aug. 25, 1998	18
Ben Sheets, Mil NL	May 16, 2004	18

More than 9 innings pitched

Pitcher, Team	Date	No.	
Tom Cheney, Was AL	Sept. 12, 1962	21	16 innings
Luis Tiant, Cle AL	July 3, 1968	19	10 innings
Nolan Ryan, Cal AL	June 14, 1974	19	12 innings
Nolan Ryan, Cal AL	Aug. 20, 1974	19	11 innings
Nolan Ryan, Cal AL	June 8, 1977	19	10 innings
Jim Whitney, Bos NL	June 14, 1884	18	15 innings
Jack Coombs, Phi AL	Sept. 1, 1906	18	24 innings
Warren Spahn, Bos NL	June 14, 1952	18	15 innings
Jim Maloney, Cin NL	June 14, 1965	18	11 innings
Chris Short, Cin NL	Oct. 2, 1965	18	15 IP of 18

Most Consecutive Save Opportunities Converted

Since the save rule first became an official part of baseball in 1969, both the definition of a save and the usage patterns of relievers have changed drastically. When Ken Tatum became the first pitcher to convert at least 15 straight save opportunities in a row in 1969 and 1970, 65 percent of his saves required more than one inning pitched. During Eric Gagne's streak of 84 straight save opportunities converted in 2002–04, however, he had to get more than three outs less than 25 percent of the time. Also, unlike Tatum, he was never called upon to make an appearance of more than 2 innings for any reason. So it would be unfair to say that the streaks listed below are strictly comparable. Nevertheless, the list does illustrate many of the greatest relief pitching streaks of the last 37 years —as well as the evolution of the closer's role.

Year(s)	Pitcher	SV	Year(s)	Pitcher	SV
1969–70	Ken Tatum, Cal AL	17	1991–92	Dennis Eckersley Oak AL	40
1969–70	Mudcat Grant, SL NL–Oak AL	22	1993–95	Rod Beck SF NL	40
1972	Clay Carroll Cin NL	23	1997–98	Trevor Hoffman SD NL	41
1972–73	John Hiller Det AL	24	1998–99	Tom Gordon Bos AL	54
1980	Rich Gossage NY AL	25	2002–04	Eric Gagne LA NL	84
1984	Willie Hernandez Det AL	32			

Gagne's 84-Save Streak

Eric Gagne didn't just break the old consecutive saves record with his 2002–04 streak; he shattered it. Earlier record holders often had the advantage of having an easier road than their predecessors as a result of the evolving role of the closer. Gagne, however, had no such advantage over Tom Gordon, the previous record holder, yet he still managed to exceed the old record by 55 percent. (Note: Runs and earned runs are combined since Gagne never allowed an unearned run during the streak.)

Year/Date	Opponent	Score	IP	R/ER	Year/Date	Opponent	Score	IP	R/ER
Aug. 28, 2002	Ari NL	1-0	1.0	0	July 27, 2003	Ari NL	1-0	1.1	0
Sept. 1, 2002	Hou NL	2-1	1.0	0	Aug. 5, 2003	Cin NL	5-2	1.0	0
Sept. 3, 2002	Ari NL	3-2	1.1	1	Aug. 6, 2003	Cin NL	2-1	1.0	0
Sept. 6, 2002	Hou NL	3-2	1.0	0	Aug. 7, 2003	Cin NL	4-3	1.0	0
Sept. 16, 2002	SF NL	7-6	1.2	0	Aug. 8, 2003	Chi NL	3-1	1.0	0
Sept. 21, 2002	SD NL	5-3	1.0	0	Aug. 14, 2003	Fla NL	6-4	1.0	0
Sept. 22, 2002	SD NL	4-3	1.0	0	Aug. 17, 2003	Chi NL	3-0	1.0	0
Sept. 26, 2002	SD NL	6-5	1.0	0	Aug. 21, 2003	Mon NL	2-1	1.0	0
April 8, 2003	Ari NL	5-3	1.0	0	Aug. 22, 2003	NY NL	2-1	1.0	0
April 9, 2003	Ari NL	5-2	1.0	0	Aug. 28, 2003	Hou NL	6-3	1.1	0
April 16, 2003	SD NL	3-0	1.0	0	Aug. 29, 2003	Col NY	6-4	1.0	0
April 17, 2003	SD NL	4-3	1.0	0	Aug. 31, 2003	Col NY	3-0	1.0	0
April 22, 2003	Cin NL	2-1	1.0	0	Sept. 2, 2003	Hou NL	4-1	1.1	0
April 25, 2003	Pit NL	5-2	1.0	0	Sept. 5, 2003	Col NY	8-7	1.0	0
April 26, 2003	Pit NL	4-3	1.0	0	Sept. 7, 2003	Col NY	6-2	1.0	0
April 30, 2003	Phi NL	4-0	0.1	0	Sept. 9, 2003	Ari NL	4-1	1.0	0
May 3, 2003	Pit NL	4-1	1.0	0	Sept. 14, 2003	SD NL	5-2	1.1	0
May 4, 2003	Pit NL	3-2	1.0	1	Sept. 18, 2003	Ari NL	2-0	2.0	0
May 7, 2003	NY NL	2-1	1.0	0	Sept. 21, 2003	SF NL	7-5	1.1	0
May 11, 2003	Mon NL	4-3	1.1	0	Sept. 23, 2003	SD NL	2-1	1.0	0
May 16, 2003	Fla NL	2-1	1.0	0	Sept. 24, 2003	SD NL	2-1	1.0	0
May 17, 2003	Fla NL	4-1	1.0	0	April 10, 2004	Col NL	7-4	1.0	0
May 18, 2003	Fla NL	2-1	1.0	0	April 15, 2004	SD NL	7-5	1.1	0
May 20, 2003	Col NL	3-1	1.0	0	April 16, 2004	SF NL	3-2	1.0	2
May 21, 2003	Col NL	3-2	1.0	0	April 17, 2004	SF NL	5-4	1.0	1
May 22, 2003	Col NL	4-3	1.0	0	April 18, 2004	SF NL	7-6	1.0	0
May 31, 2003	Mil NL	3-0	1.0	0	April 28, 2004	NY NL	3-2	1.1	0
June 5, 2003	KC AL	5-2	1.0	0	May 1, 2004	Mon NL	5-4	1.0	0
June 6, 2003	Chi AL	2-1	1.0	0	May 4, 2004	Fla NL	4-3	1.0	0
June 10, 2003	Det AL	3-1	1.0	0	May 6, 2004	Fla NL	9-4	0.1	0
June 11, 2003	Det AL	3-1	1.0	0	May 8, 2004	Pit NL	4-3	1.0	0
June 12, 2003	Det AL	3-2	1.0	0	May 25, 2004	Mil NL	5-3	1.0	0
June 13, 2003	Cle AL	4-3	1.0	0	May 30, 2004	Ari NL	3-0	1.0	0
June 15, 2003	Cle AL	4-3	1.0	0	June 2, 2004	Mil NL	5-2	1.1	1
June 17, 2003	SF NL	4-1	1.0	0	June 15, 2004	Bal AL	5-1	0.2	0
June 20, 2003	Ana AL	5-2	1.0	0	June 16, 2004	Bal AL	6-3	1.1	0
June 21, 2003	Ana AL	4-2	1.0	1	June 17, 2004	Bal AL	4-3	1.0	0
July 5, 2003	Ari NL	2-0	1.0	0	June 18, 2004	NY AL	6-3	1.0	0
July 9, 2003	SL NL	6-5	1.1	0	June 20, 2004	NY AL	5-4	1.1	1
July 17, 2003	SL NL	6-3	0.1	0	June 29, 2004	SF NL	2-1	1.0	0
July 18, 2003	SL NL	8-5	1.0	0	July 1, 2004	SF NL	5-4	1.0	0
July 22, 2003	Col NL	5-2	1.0	0	July 3, 2004	Ana AL	8-5	1.0	0

Consecutive Scoreless Inning Streaks

Orel Hershiser was the biggest baseball story of the year in 1988, even before he earned MVP awards in the NLCS and World Series. He broke Don Drysdale's record of 58.2 consecutive scoreless innings, hurling 10 shutout innings in his final start of the season to do it. It's a feat unlikely to be matched in the near future. Virtually all of the top streaks listed below were achieved in low-scoring environments, quite the opposite of the current state of baseball.

Year	Dates	Pitcher, Team	IP
1988	Aug. 30–Sept. 28	Orel Hershiser, LA NL	59.0
1968	May 14–June 8	Don Drysdale, LA NL	58.2
1913	Apr. 10–June 14	Walter Johnson, Was AL	55.2
1910	Sept. 5–Sept. 25	Jack Coombs, Phi AL	53.0
1968	June 2–June 26	Bob Gibson, Stl NL	47.0
1933	July 13–Aug. 1	Carl Hubbell, NY NL	45.1
1950	Aug. 16–Sept. 13	Sal Maglie, NY NL	45.0
1904	Sept. 12–Sept. 30	Doc White, Chi AL	45.0
1904	Apr. 25–May 17	Cy Young, Bos AL	45.0
1908	Sept. 17–Oct. 3	Ed Reulbach, Chi NL	44.0
1905	Aug. 22–Sept. 5	Rube Waddell, Phi AL	43.2
1914	May 1–May 26	Rube Foster, Bos AL	42.0
1902	June 26–July 16	Jack Chesbro, Pit NL	41.0
1911	Sept. 7–Sept. 24	Grover Alexander, Phi NL	41.0
1917	Sept. 13–Oct. 4	Art Nehf, Bos NL	41.0
1968	Apr. 28–May 17	Luis Tiant, Cle AL	41.0
1918	May 7–May 26	Walter Johnson, Was AL	40.0
1967	Aug. 28–Sept. 10	Gaylord Perry, SF NL	40.0
1972	Aug. 19–Sept. 8	Luis Tiant, Bos AL	40.0

Multiple No-Hitters

Lots of mediocre pitchers have pitched a no-hitter, but throwing 2 no-hitters is a different story—that can't happen just by luck. Below is a list of all the pitchers who have thrown at least two no-hitters. Following this distinguished list are lists of perfect games, no-hitters, and unofficial no-hitters.

Some no-hitters came with their own unique twist. Hugh Daily's no-hitter in September 1883 was the first no-hitter ever thrown by a one-handed pitcher; Jim Abbott duplicated the feat 110 years later. Johnny Vander Meer's no-hitter on June 15, 1938 marked the only time a major leaguer has thrown no-hitters in consecutive starts. The only Opening Day no-hitter was thrown by Bob Feller on Apr. 16, 1940. The only postseason no-hitter was a perfect game pitched by Don Larsen during the World Series on October 8, 1956. Mike Scott pitched the only no-hitter to clinch a title—the 1986 NL Western Division championship—on September 25, 1986.

Perhaps the oddest no-hitter ever came on June 23, 1917 when Ernie Shore pitched one in relief. Shore rang up 27 outs by retiring 26 hitters in a row after Babe Ruth walked the first batter and argued himself out of the game; that runner was subsequently thrown out stealing. The most recent non-perfect no-hitter also deserves notice, because it required a record six pitchers: the starter, Roy Oswalt, had to be pulled after the first inning due to injury, and the Astros ran out five relief pitchers over the next eight innings on June 11, 2003.

Notes. Perfect games are listed separately from no-hitters. Italics indicate that it was the pitcher's first major league start. G1 and G2 denote first and second games of doubleheaders. Extra-inning games are noted in parentheses. CD means game was called on account of darkness. WS indicates World Series game. Finally, Loss means that the pitcher who threw the no-hitter also lost the game.

Pitchers with More Than One No-Hitter

Nolan Ryan	7	Jim Galvin	2	Dutch Leonard	2	Don Wilson	2
Sandy Koufax	4	Al Atkinson	2	Johnny Vander Meer	2	Ken Holtzman	2
Larry Corcoran	3	Adonis Terry	2	Allie Reynolds	2	Bill Stoneman	2
Cy Young	3	Ted Breitenstein	2	Virgil Trucks	2	Steve Busby	2
Bob Feller	3	Frank Smith	2	Carl Erskine	2	Bob Forsch	2
Jim Maloney	3	Addie Joss	2	Warren Spahn	2	Hideo Nomo	2
Christy Mathewson	2	Tom L. Hughes	2	Jim Bunning	2	Randy Johnson	2

Perfect Games

Pitcher	Opponents	Score	Date
Lee Richmond	Wor vs. Cle NL	1-0	June 12, 1880
John M. Ward	Pro vs. Buf NL	5-0	June 17, 1880
Cy Young	Bos vs. Phi AL	3-0	May 5, 1904
Addie Joss	Cle vs. Chi AL	1-0	Oct. 2, 1908
Charlie Robertson	Chi at Det AL	2-0	Apr. 30, 1922
Jim Bunning	Phi at NY NL	6-0	June 21, 1964 G1
Don Larsen	NY AL vs. Bro NL	2-0	Oct. 8, 1956 WS

Perfect Games continued

Pitcher	Opponents	Score	Date
Sandy Koufax	LA vs. Chi NL	1-0	Sept. 9, 1965
Catfish Hunter	Oak vs. Min AL	4-0	May 8, 1968
Len Barker	Cle vs. Tor AL	3-0	May 15, 1981
Mike Witt	Cal at Tex AL	1-0	Sept. 30, 1984
Tom Browning	Cin vs. LA NL	1-0	Sept. 16, 1988
Dennis Martinez	Mon at LA NL	2-0	July 28, 1991
Kenny Rogers	Tex vs. Cal AL	4-0	July 28, 1994
David Wells	NY vs. Min AL	4-0	May 17, 1998
David Cone	NY AL vs. Mon NL	6-0	July 18, 1999
Randy Johnson	Ari vs. Atl NL	2-0	May 18, 2004

No-Hit Games, Nine or More Innings

Pitcher	Opponents	Score	Date
Joe Borden	Phi vs. Chi NA	4-0	July 28, 1875
George Bradley	StL vs. Har NL	2-0	July 15, 1876
Larry Corcoran	Chi vs. Bos NL	6-0	Aug. 19, 1880
Jim Galvin	Buf at Wor NL	1-0	Aug. 20, 1880
Tony Mullane	Lou at Cin AA	2-0	Sept. 11, 1882
Guy Hecker	Lou at Pit AA	3-1	Sept. 19, 1882
Larry Corcoran	Chi vs. Wor NL	5-0	Sept. 20, 1882
Charley Radbourn	Pro at Cle NL	8-0	July 25, 1883
Hugh Daily	Cle at Phi NL	1-0	Sept. 13, 1883
Al Atkisson	Phi vs. Pit AA	10-1	May 24, 1884
Ed Morris	Col at Pit AA	5-0	May 29, 1884
Frank Mountain	Col at Was AA	12-0	June 5, 1884
Larry Corcoran	Chi vs. Pro NL	6-0	June 27, 1884
Jim Galvin	Buf at Det NL	18-0	Aug. 4, 1884
Dick Burns	Cin at KC UA	3-1	Aug. 26, 1884
Ed Cushman	Mil vs. Was UA	5-0	Sept. 28, 1884
Sam Kimber	Bro vs. Tol AA	0-0	Oct. 4, 1884 CD (10 inn)
John Clarkson	Chi at Pro NL	4-0	July 27, 1885
Charlie Ferguson	Phi vs. Pro NL	1-0	Aug. 29, 1885
Al Atkisson	Phi vs. NY AA	3-2	May 1, 1886
Adonis Terry	Bro vs. StL AA	1-0	July 24, 1886
Matt Kilroy	Bal at Pit AA	6-0	Oct. 6, 1886
Adonis Terry	Bro vs. Lou AA	4-0	May 27, 1888
Henry Porter	KC at Bal AA	4-0	June 6, 1888
Ed Seward	Phi vs. Cin AA	12-2	July 26, 1888
Gus Weyhing	Phi vs. KC AA	4-0	July 31, 1888
Cannonball Titcomb	Roc vs. Syr AA	7-0	Sept. 15, 1890
Tom Lovett	Bro vs. NY NL	4-0	June 22, 1891
Amos Rusie	NY vs. Bro NL	6-0	July 31, 1891
Ted Breitenstein	*StL vs. Lou AA*	8-0	Oct. 4, 1891 G1
Jack Stivetts	Bos vs. Bro NL	11-0	Aug. 6, 1892
Ben Sanders	Lou vs. Bal NL	6-2	Aug. 22, 1892
Bumpus Jones	*Cin vs. Pit NL*	7-1	Oct. 15, 1892
Bill Hawke	Bal vs. Was NL	5-0	Aug. 16, 1893
Cy Young	Cle vs. Cin NL	6-0	Sept. 18, 1897 G1
Ted Breitenstein	Cin vs. Pit NL	11-0	Apr. 22, 1898
Jim Hughes	Bal vs. Bos NL	8-0	Apr. 22, 1898
Red Donahue	Phi vs. Bos NL	5-0	July 8, 1898
Walter Thornton	Chi vs. Bro NL	2-0	Aug. 21, 1898 G2
Deacon Phillippe	Lou vs. NY NL	7-0	May 25, 1899
Noodles Hahn	Cin vs. Phi NL	4-0	July 12, 1900
Christy Mathewson	NY at StL NL	5-0	July 15, 1901
Nixey Callahan	Chi vs. Det AL	3-0	Sept. 20, 1902 G1
Chick Fraser	Phi at Chi NL	10-0	Sept. 18, 1903 G2
Jesse Tannehill	Bos at Chi AL	6-0	Aug. 17, 1904
Christy Mathewson	NY at Chi NL	1-0	June 13, 1905
Weldon Henley	Phi at StL AL	6-0	July 22, 1905 G1
Frank Smith	Chi at Det AL	15-0	Sept. 6, 1905 G2
Bill Dinneen	Bos vs. Chi AL	2-0	Sept. 27 1905 G1
Johnny Lush	Phi at Bro NL	6-0	May 1, 1906
Mal Eason	Bro at StL NL	2-0	July 20, 1906
Frank (Jeff) Pfeffer	Bos vs. Cin NL	6-0	May 8, 1907
Nick Maddox	Pit vs. Bro NL	2-1	Sept. 20, 1907
Cy Young	Bos at NY AL	8-0	June 30, 1908
Hooks Wiltse	NY vs. Phi NL	1-0	July 4, 1908 G1 (10 inn)
Nap Rucker	Bro vs. Bos NL	6-0	Sept. 5, 1908 G2
Dusty Rhoads	Cle vs. Bos AL	2-1	Sept. 18, 1908
Frank Smith	Chi vs. Phi AL	1-0	Sept. 20, 1908
Addie Joss	Cle at Chi AL	1-0	Apr. 20, 1910
Chief Bender	Phi vs. Cle AL	4-0	May 12, 1910
Joe Wood	Bos vs. StL AL	5-0	July 29, 1911 G2
Ed Walsh	Chi vs. Bos AL	5-0	Aug. 27, 1911
George Mullin	Det vs. StL AL	7-0	July 4, 1912 G2
Earl Hamilton	StL at Det AL	5-1	Aug. 30, 1912
Jeff Tesreau	NY at Phi NL	3-0	Sept. 6, 1912 G1
Joe Benz	Chi vs. Cle AL	6-1	May 31, 1914
George Davis	Bos vs. Phi NL	7-0	Sept. 9, 1914 G2
Ed Lafitte	Bro vs. KC FL	6-2	Sept. 19, 1914 G1
Rube Marquard	NY vs. Bro NL	2-0	Apr. 15, 1915
Frank Allen	Pit at StL FL	2-0	Apr. 24, 1915
Claude Hendrix	Chi at Pit FL	10-0	May 15, 1915
Alex Main	KC at Buf FL	5-0	Aug. 16, 1915
Jimmy Lavender	Chi at NY NL	2-0	Aug. 31, 1915 G1
Dave Davenport	StL vs. Chi FL	3-0	Sept. 7, 1915 G1
Tom L. Hughes	Bos vs. Pit NL	2-0	June 16, 1916
Rube Foster	Bos vs. NY AL	2-0	June 21, 1916
Joe Bush	Phi vs. Cle AL	5-0	Aug. 26, 1916
Dutch Leonard	Bos vs. StL AL	4-0	Aug. 30, 1916
Eddie Cicotte	Chi at StL AL	11-0	Apr. 14, 1917
George Mogridge	NY at Bos AL	2-1	Apr. 24, 1917
Fred Toney	Cin at Chi NL	1-0	May 2, 1917 (10 inn)
Ernie Koob	StL vs. Chi AL	1-0	May 5, 1917
Bob Groom	StL vs. Chi AL	3-0	May 6, 1917 G2
Ernie Shore	Bos vs. Was AL	4-0	June 23, 1917 G1
Dutch Leonard	Bos at Det AL	5-0	June 3, 1918
Hod Eller	Cin vs. StL NL	6-0	May 11, 1919
Ray Caldwell	Cle at NY AL	3-0	Sept. 10, 1919 G1
Walter Johnson	Was at Bos AL	1-0	July 1, 1920

No-Hit Games, Nine or More Innings continued

Pitcher	Opponents	Score	Date
Jesse Barnes	NY vs. Phi NL	6-0	May 7, 1922
Sam Jones	NY at Phi AL	2-0	Sept. 4, 1923
Howard Ehmke	Bos at Phi AL	4-0	Sept. 7, 1923
Jesse Haines	StL vs. Bos NL	5-0	July 17, 1924
Dazzy Vance	Bro vs. Phi NL	10-1	Sept. 13, 1925 G1
Ted Lyons	Chi at Bos AL	6-0	Aug. 21, 1926
Carl Hubbell	NY vs. Pit NL	11-0	May 8, 1929
Wes Ferrell	Cle vs. StL AL	9-0	Apr. 29, 1931
Bobby Burke	Was vs. Bos AL	5-0	Aug. 8, 1931
Paul Dean	StL at Bro NL	3-0	Sept. 21, 1934 G2
Vern Kennedy	Chi vs. Cle AL	5-0	Aug. 31, 1935
Bill Dietrich	Chi vs. StL AL	8-0	June 1, 1937
Johnny Vander Meer	Cin vs. Bos NL	3-0	June 11, 1938
Johnny Vander Meer	Cin at Bro NL	6-0	June 15, 1938
Monte Pearson	NY vs. Cle AL	13-0	Aug. 27, 1938 G2
Bob Feller	Cle at Chi AL	1-0	Apr. 16, 1940 OD
Tex Carleton	Bro at Cin NL	3-0	Apr. 30, 1940
Lon Warneke	StL at Cin NL	2-0	Aug. 30, 1941
Jim Tobin	Bos vs. Bro NL	2-0	Apr. 27, 1944
Clyde Shoun	Cin vs. Bos NL	1-0	May 15, 1944
Dick Fowler	Phi vs. StL AL	1-0	Sept. 9, 1945 G2
Ed Head	Bro vs. Bos NL	5-0	Apr. 23, 1946
Bob Feller	Cle at NY AL	1-0	Apr. 30, 1946
Ewell Blackwell	Cin vs. Bos NL	6-0	June 18, 1947
Don Black	Cle vs. Phi AL	3-0	July 10, 1947 G1
Bill McCahan	Phi vs. Was AL	3-0	Sept. 3, 1947
Bob Lemon	Cle at Det AL	2-0	June 30, 1948
Rex Barney	Bro at NY NL	2-0	Sept. 9, 1948
Vern Bickford	Bos vs. Bro NL	7-0	Aug. 11, 1950
Cliff Chambers	Pit at Bos NL	3-0	May 6, 1951 G2
Bob Feller	Cle vs. Det AL	2-1	July 1, 1951 G1
Allie Reynolds	NY at Cle AL	1-0	July 12, 1951
Allie Reynolds	NY vs. Bos AL	8-0	Sept. 28, 1951 G1
Virgil Trucks	Det vs. Was AL	1-0	May 15, 1952
Carl Erskine	Bro vs. Chi NL	5-0	June 19, 1952
Virgil Trucks	Det at NY AL	1-0	Aug. 25, 1952
Bobo Holloman	*StL. vs. Phi AL*	*6-0*	*May 6, 1953*
Jim Wilson	Mil vs. Phi NL	2-0	June 12, 1954
Sam Jones	Chi vs. Pit NL	4-0	May 12, 1955
Carl Erskine	Bro vs. NY NL	3-0	May 12, 1956
Mel Parnell	Bos vs. Chi AL	4-0	July 14, 1956
Sal Maglie	Bro vs. Phi NL	5-0	Sept. 25, 1956
Bob Keegan	Chi vs. Was AL	6-0	Aug. 20, 1957 G2
Jim Bunning	Det at Bos AL	3-0	July 20, 1958 G1
Hoyt Wilhelm	Bal vs. NY AL	1-0	Sept. 20, 1958
Don Cardwell	Chi vs. StL NL	4-0	May 15, 1960 G2
Lew Burdette	Mil vs. Phi NL	1-0	Aug. 18, 1960
Warren Spahn	Mil vs. Phi NL	4-0	Sept. 16, 1960
Warren Spahn	Mil vs. SF NL	1-0	Apr. 28, 1961
Bo Belinsky	LA vs. Bal AL	2-0	May 5, 1962
Earl Wilson	Bos vs. LA AL	2-0	June 26, 1962
Sandy Koufax	LA vs. NY NL	5-0	June 30, 1962
Bill Monbouquette	Bos at Chi AL	1-0	Aug. 1, 1962
Jack Kralick	Min vs. KC AL	1-0	Aug. 26, 1962
Sandy Koufax	LA vs. SF NL	8-0	May 11, 1963
Don Nottebart	Hou vs. Phi NL	4-1	May 17, 1963
Juan Marichal	SF vs. Hou NL	1-0	June 15, 1963
Ken T. Johnson	Hou vs. Cin NL	0-1	Apr. 23, 1964 Loss
Sandy Koufax	LA at Phi NL	3-0	June 4, 1964
Jim Maloney	Cin at Chi NL	1-0	Aug. 19, 1965 G1 (10 inn)
Dave Morehead	Bos vs. Cle AL	2-0	Sept. 16, 1965
Sonny Siebert	Cle vs. Was AL	2-0	June 10, 1966
Steve D. Barber (8.2 IP) &			
Stu Miller (0.1 IP)	Bal vs. Det AL	1-2	Apr. 30, 1967 G1 Loss
Don Wilson	Hou vs. Atl NL	2-0	June 18, 1967
Dean Chance	Min at Cle AL	2-1	Aug. 25, 1967 G2
Joe Horlen	Chi vs. Det AL	6-0	Sept. 10, 1967 G1
Tom Phoebus	Bal vs. Bos AL	6-0	Apr. 27, 1968
George Culver	Cin at Phi NL	6-1	July 29, 1968 G2
Gaylord Perry	SF vs. StL NL	1-0	Sept. 17, 1968
Ray Washburn	StL at SF NL	2-0	Sept. 18, 1968
Bill Stoneman	Mon at Phi NL	7-0	Apr. 17, 1969
Jim Maloney	Cin vs. Hou NL	10-0	Apr. 30, 1969
Don Wilson	Hou at Cin NL	4-0	May 1, 1969
Jim Palmer	Bal vs. Oak AL	8-0	Aug. 13, 1969
Ken Holtzman	Chi vs. Atl NL	3-0	Aug. 19, 1969
Bob Moose	Pit at NY NL	4-0	Sept. 20, 1969
Dock Ellis	Pit at SD NL	2-0	June 12, 1970 G1
Clyde Wright	Cal vs. Oak AL	4-0	July 3, 1970
Bill Singer	LA vs. Phi NL	5-0	July 20, 1970
Vida Blue	Oak vs. Min AL	6-0	Sept. 21, 1970
Ken Holtzman	Chi at Cin NL	1-0	June 3, 1971
Rick Wise	Phi at Cin NL	4-0	June 23, 1971
Bob Gibson	StL at Pit NL	11-0	Aug. 14, 1971
Burt Hooton	Chi vs. Phi NL	4-0	Apr. 16, 1972
Milt Pappas	Chi vs. SD NL	8-0	Sept. 2, 1972
Bill Stoneman	Mon vs. NY NL	7-0	Oct. 2, 1972 G1
Steve Busby	KC at Det AL	3-0	Apr. 16, 1973
Nolan Ryan	Cal at KC AL	3-0	May 15, 1973
Nolan Ryan	Cal at Det AL	6-0	July 15, 1973
Jim Bibby	Tex at Oak AL	6-0	July 30, 1973
Phil Niekro	Atl vs. SD NL	9-0	Aug. 5, 1973
Steve Busby	KC at Mil AL	2-0	June 19, 1974
Dick Bosman	Cle vs. Oak AL	4-0	July 19, 1974
Nolan Ryan	Cal vs. Min AL	4-0	Sept. 28, 1974
Nolan Ryan	Cal vs. Bal AL	1-0	June 1, 1975
Ed Halicki	SF vs. NY NL	6-0	Aug. 24, 1975 G2
Vida Blue (5 IP),			
Glenn Abbott (1 IP),			
Paul Lindblad (1 IP) &			
Rollie Fingers (2 IP)	Oak vs. Cal AL	5-0	Sept. 28, 1975
Larry Dierker	Hou vs. Mon NL	6-0	July 9, 1976

No-Hit Games, Nine or More Innings continued

Pitcher	Opponents	Score	Date
Blue Moon Odom (5 IP) &			
Francisco Barrios (4 IP)	Chi at Oak AL	2-1	July 28, 1976
John Candelaria	Pit vs. LA NL	2-0	Aug. 9, 1976
John Montefusco	SF at Atl NL	9-0	Sept. 29, 1976
Jim Colborn	KC vs. Tex AL	6-0	May 14, 1977
Dennis Eckersley	Cle vs. Cal AL	1-0	May 30, 1977
Bert Blyleven	Tex at Cal AL	6-0	Sept. 22, 1977
Bob Forsch	StL vs. Phi NL	5-0	Apr. 16, 1978
Tom Seaver	Cin vs. StL NL	4-0	June 16, 1978
Ken Forsch	Hou vs. Atl NL	6-0	Apr. 7, 1979
Jerry Reuss	LA at SF NL	8-0	June 27, 1980
Charlie Lea	Mon vs. SF NL	4-0	May 10, 1981 G2
Nolan Ryan	Hou vs. LA NL	5-0	Sept. 26, 1981
Dave Righetti	NY vs. Bos AL	4-0	July 4, 1983
Bob Forsch	StL vs. Mon NL	3-0	Sept. 26, 1983
Mike Warren	Oak vs. Chi AL	3-0	Sept. 29, 1983
Jack Morris	Det at Chi AL	4-0	Apr. 7, 1984
Joe Cowley	Chi at Cal AL	7-1	Sept. 19, 1986
Mike Scott	Hou vs. SF NL	2-0	Sept. 25, 1986
Juan Nieves	Mil at Bal AL	7-0	Apr. 15, 1987
Mark Langston (7 IP) &			
Mike Witt (2 IP)	Cal vs. Sea AL	1-0	Apr. 11, 1990
Randy Johnson	Sea vs. Det AL	2-0	June 2, 1990
Nolan Ryan	Tex at Oak AL	5-0	June 11, 1990
Dave Stewart	Oak at Tor AL	5-0	June 29, 1990
Fernando Valenzuela	LA vs. StL NL	6-0	June 29, 1990
Terry Mulholland	Phi vs. SF NL	6-0	Aug. 15, 1990
Dave Stieb	Tor at Cle AL	3-0	Sept. 2, 1990
Nolan Ryan	Tex vs. Tor AL	3-0	May 1, 1991
Tommy Greene	Phi at Mon NL	2-0	May 23, 1991
Bob Milacki (6 IP),			
Mike Flanagan (1 IP),			
Mark Williamson (1 IP) &			
Gregg Olson (1 IP)	Bal at Oak AL	2-0	July 13, 1991
Wilson Alvarez	Chi at Bal AL	7-0	Aug. 11, 1991
Bret Saberhagen	KC vs. Chi AL	7-0	Aug. 26, 1991
Kent Mercker (6 IP),			
Mark Wohlers (2 IP) &			
Alejandro Pena (1 IP)	Atl at SD NL	1-0	Sept. 11, 1991
Kevin Gross	LA vs. SF NL	2-0	Aug. 17, 1992
Chris Bosio	Sea vs. Bos AL	7-0	Apr. 22, 1993
Jim Abbott	NY vs. Cle AL	4-0	Sept. 4, 1993
Darryl Kile	Hou vs. NY NL	7-1	Sept. 8, 1993
Kent Mercker	Atl at LA NL	6-0	Apr. 8, 1994
Scott Erickson	Min vs. Mil AL	6-0	Apr. 27, 1994
Ramon Martinez	LA vs. Fla NL	7-0	July 14, 1995
Al Leiter	Fla vs. Col NL	11-0	May 11, 1996
Dwight Gooden	NY vs. Sea AL	2-0	May 14, 1996
Hideo Nomo	LA at Col NL	9-0	Sept. 17, 1996
Kevin Brown	Fla at SF NL	9-0	June 10, 1997
Francisco Cordova (9 IP) &			
Ricardo Rincon (1 IP)	Pit vs. Hou NL	3-0	July 12, 1997
Jose Jimenez	StL at Ari NL	1-0	June 25, 1999
Eric Milton	Min vs. Ana AL	7-0	Sept. 11, 1999
Hideo Nomo	Bos at Bal AL	3-0	Apr. 4, 2001
A.J. Burnett	Fla at SD NL	3-0	May 12, 2001
Bud Smith	StL at SD NL	4-0	Sept. 3, 2001
Derek Lowe	Bos vs. TB AL	10-0	Apr. 27, 2002
Kevin Millwood	Phi vs. SF NL	1-0	Apr. 27, 2003
Roy Oswalt (1 IP),			
Peter Munro (2.2 IP),			
Kirk Saarloos (1.1 IP),			
Brad Lidge (2 IP),			
Octavio Dotel (1 IP) &			
Billy Wagner (1 IP)	Hou NL at NY AL	8-0	June 11, 2003

No-Hit Games, Less Than 9 Innings Pitched

Sometimes even the best days end too soon. Many no-hit bids have been spoiled by rain, by darkness, by having to catch a train, or simply by prior agreement. Three times a pitcher has held the home club hitless for 8 innings, only to not pitch the ninth because his team lost and the game was over. One much luckier pitcher actually allowed a hit in a short no-hit game, but showers washed that blemish away when in 1959 Mike McCormick allowed a hit in the sixth before rain caused the game to revert to 5 innings. Bold signifies an abbreviated perfect game.

Pitcher	Innings	Reason	Matchup	Score	Date
Larry McKeon	6	rain	Ind at Cin AA	0-0	May 6, 1884
Charlie Gagus	8	darkness	Was vs. Wil UA	12-1	Aug. 21, 1884
Charlie Getzien	6	rain	Det vs. Phi NL	1-0	Oct. 1, 1884
Charlie Sweeney	(2 IP)				
& Henry Boyle	(3 IP)				
	5	rain	StL vs. StP UA	0-1	Oct. 5, 1884
Dupee Shaw	5	agreement	Pro at Buf NL	4-0	Oct. 7, 1885 G1
George Van Haltren	6	rain	Chi vs. Pit NL	1-0	June 21, 1888
Ed Crane	7	darkness	NY vs. Was NL	3-0	Sept. 27, 1888
Matt Kilroy	7	darkness	Bal vs. StL AA	0-0	July 29, 1889 G2
Silver King	8	road loss	Chi vs. Bro PL	0-1	June 21, 1890 Loss
George Nicol	7	darkness	StL vs. Phi AA	21-2	Sept. 23, 1890
Hank Gastright	8	darkness	Col vs. Tol AA	6-0	Oct. 12, 1890
Jack Stivetts	5	Bos. train	Bos at Was NL	4-0	Oct. 15, 1892 G2
Elton Chamberlain	7	darkness	Cin vs. Bos NL	6-0	Sept. 23, 1893 G2
Ed Stein	6	rain	Bro vs. Chi NL	6-0	June 2, 1894
Red Ames	5	darkness	NY at StL NL	5-0	Sept. 14, 1903 G2
Rube Waddell	5	rain	Phi vs. StL AL	2-0	Aug. 15, 1905
Jake Weimer	7	agreement	Cin vs. Bro NL	1-0	Aug. 24, 1906 G2
Stoney McGlynn	7	agreement	StL at Bro NL	1-1	Sept. 24, 1906 G2

No-Hit Games, Less Than 9 Innings Pitched continued

Pitcher	Innings	Reason	Matchup	Score	Date
Lefty Leifield	6	darkness	Pit at Phi NL	8-0	Sept. 26, 1906 G2
Ed Walsh	5	rain	Chi vs. NY AL	8-1	May 26, 1907
Ed Karger	**7**	**agreement**	**StL vs. Bos NL**	**4-0**	**Aug. 11, 1907 G2**
Howie Camnitz	5	agreement	Pit at NY NL	1-0	Aug. 23, 1907 G2
Rube Vickers	**5**	**darkness**	**Phi at Was AL**	**4-0**	**Oct. 5, 1907 G2**
Johnny Lush	6	rain	StL at Bro NL	2-0	Aug. 6, 1908
King Cole	7	Chi. train	Chi at StL NL	4-0	July 31, 1910 G2
Jay Cashion	6	Cle. train	Was vs. Cle AL	2-0	Aug. 20, 1912 G2
Walter Johnson	7	rain	Was vs. StL AL	2-0	Aug. 25, 1924
Fred Frankhouse	7.2	rain	Bro vs. Cin NL	5-0	Aug. 27, 1937
John Whitehead	6	rain	StL vs. Det NL	4-0	Aug. 5, 1940 G2
Jim Tobin	5	darkness	Bos vs. Phi NL	7-0	June 22, 1944 G2
Mike McCormick	5	rain	SF at Phi NL	3-0	June 12, 1959
Sam Jones	7	rain	SF at StL NL	4-0	Sept. 26, 1959
Dean Chance	**5**	**rain**	**Min vs. Bos AL**	**2-0**	**Aug. 6, 1967**
David Palmer	**5**	**rain**	**Mon at StL NL**	**4-0**	**Apr. 21, 1984 G2**
Pascual Perez	5	rain	Mon at Phi NL	1-0	Sept. 24, 1988
Andy Hawkins	8	road loss	NY at Chi AL	0-4	July 1, 1990 Loss
Melido Perez	6	rain	Chi at NY AL	8-0	July 12, 1990
Matt Young	8	road loss	Bos at Cle AL	1-2	Apr. 12, 1992 G1 Loss

No-Hitters Broken Up in Extra Innings

Sometimes even the best days can be spoiled by bad luck or by a lack of support. Harvey Haddix's famous 1959 perfect game remains the benchmark for magnificent failure, but many other pitchers have had their no-hit efforts torpedoed after the regulation 9 innings.

Pitcher	Opponents	Score	Date	Comment
Earl Moore	Cle vs. Chi AL	2-4	May 9, 1901	Lost on 2 hits in 10th
Bob Wicker	Chi at NY NL	1-0	June 11, 1904	Won in 12 inn. after 1st hit in 10th
Harry McIntyre	Bro vs. Pit NL	0-1	Aug. 1, 1906	Lost on 4 hits in 13 inn. after 1st hit in 11th
Red Ames	NY vs. Bro NL	0-3	Apr. 15, 1909	Lost on 7 hits in 13 inn. after 1st hit in 10th
Tom L. Hughes	NY vs. Cle AL	0-5	Aug. 30, 1910 G2	Lost on 7 hits in 11 inn. after 1st hit in 10th
Jim Scott	Chi at Was AL	0-1	May 14, 1914	Lost on 2 hits in 10th
Hippo Vaughn	Chi vs. Cin NL	0-1	May 2, 1917	Lost on 2 hits in 10th; Fred Toney pitched no-hitter in this game
Bobo Newsom	StL vs. Bos AL	1-2	Sept. 18, 1934	Lost on 1 hit in 10th
Johnny Klippstein (7 IP), Hershell Freeman (1 IP) & Joe Black (3 IP)	Cin at Mil NL	1-2	May 26, 1956	Lost on 3 hits in 11 inn. after 1st hit in 10th
Harvey Haddix	Pit at Mil NL	0-1	May 26, 1959	Lost on hit in 13th after 12 perfect innings
Jim Maloney	Cin vs. NY NL	0-1	June 14, 1965	Lost on 2 hits in 11th
Mark Gardner	Mon at LA NL	0-1	July 26, 1991	9 IP lost on 2 hits in 10th; relieved by Jeff Fassero, who allowed 1 hit
Pedro J. Martinez (9 IP) & Mel Rojas (1 IP)	Mon at SD NL	1-0	June 3, 1995	Martinez pitched 9 perfect innings but allowed hit in 10th; Rojas finished game

FIELDS OF DREAMS: BIG LEAGUE BALLPARKS

After the success of Phil Alden Robinson's 1989 movie *Field of Dreams*—based upon W.P. Kinsella's terrific novel *Shoeless Joe*—the phrase has become a staple of American vocabulary. Baseball parks are truly fields of dreams, both for those who play there as well as those who root from the stands. They are idiosyncratic, individual, and—when designed and built with care—as much a part of urban life as commercial buildings or government offices. Other sports have their stadiums, but only baseball has *ballparks*, a felicitous marriage of two of the most joyous words in the English language.

Since the 1870s, the parks that baseball has been played in have evolved as much as the game itself. Ballparks have always been constructed using the latest technology available, whether they were the wood parks of the game's early days, the concrete-and-steel edifices of the early 1900s, the enormous superstadiums of the 1960s and 1970s, or today's fashionable steel-and-brick retro designs. Many ballparks have been built on a tight budget, from the quickly constructed skeletons of the 1880s to some of the latest retro parks.

Ballparks didn't start out by simply providing cheap seats for the regular guys. Contrary to what many might think, private boxes—constructed to separate the rich from the rest of the crowd—existed almost from the inception of the first ballpark as the moneyed sat apart from their lower-class brethren. Al Spalding, owner of the Chicago White Stockings, had a private telephone line run into his owner's box at Lakefront Park in the 1880s so he could conduct business during the games. At the same time, St. Louis' American Association ballpark had a special seating pavilion devoted just to high society.

There's no such discrimination in this section of the encyclopedia, where low-grade facilities in out-of-the-way cities like Altoona in 1884 rub shoulders with the splendor of modern meccas like Oriole Park at Camden Yards in Baltimore. Each facility served, however briefly, as a venue for big league games and qualifies, therefore, as a major league ballpark. Some parks served as home fields for several teams and will, therefore, have two or more entries.

On the following pages you will see an entry with details of every park that has hosted a major league game since 1871. The section is organized by major league city, with each park in the city shown chronologically by opening year from 1871 to the present. Ballparks are listed under their current (or their last) name, with any earlier (official) names noted in italics. Common nicknames for ballparks are in quotes. Current major league ballparks are shown in bold.

The **Open** column shows the first and last years that a park was used for major league games. Current parks will have only an opening year. Parks that are no longer used by a major league team but which are still standing (e.g., Tiger Stadium) are indicated with an asterisk.

All clubs that called a park home for even one game are included in the **Tenants** column. Current (or last) team names are used for all entries; so the NL Dodgers are called the Dodgers in all entries, even if they were known as the Robins or Superbas at the time. Short-lived St. Paul in the Union Association never played any home games and therefore, has no listing. League abbreviations are the same as in the player registers.

Capacity lists each park's current or final seating capacity along with its initial seating capacity (when known) in parentheses. There were no recorded capacities or dimensions for most nineteenth century ballparks, and such details for early twentieth century parks are frequently lacking.

The next two columns give details on each ballpark's configuration showing its most important **Dimensions**. The **Current/Final** dimensions for parks are listed in the fifth column. Each park's **Original** dimensions, if known, are listed in the sixth column. From left to right, the dimensions shown are left

field foul line (**LF**), left-center field (**LCF**), center field (**CF**), right-center field (**RCF**), and right field foul line (**RF**). LF-LCF and RF-RCF are separated by hyphens; CF is delimited by slashes. If the deepest part of the ballpark was *not* straightaway center field, the deepest dimension (if known) is shown in the **Notes** column. Question marks indicate unknown dimensions.

Despite the painstaking research done by Philip Lowry, Michael Benson, Michael Gershman, Larry Ritter, and others, there is still much that we do not know about the parks of the nineteenth century. This is, in part, because no one kept careful records of such things. However, another reason is that, back in the very "old days," baseball fields often did not even *have* dimensions as such—they were essentially big pastures with the playing diamonds laid out on them.

Some of the earliest parks lacked grandstands as well; those that did have grandstands lacked bleachers until the twentieth century. Overflow crowds were typically accommodated by allowing them to stand in foul territory or in fair territory behind the outfielders—in many pictures from the 1890s, horse-drawn carriages, holding fans, still ringed the outfield.

It is very interesting to note how dimensions have changed over the years. In days of yore, ballparks were built on whatever convenient piece of land could hold them, thus rendering most parks asymmetrical. For instance, New York's Polo Grounds, through its demise in 1962, had foul lines of less than 300 feet and a center field fence more than 200 feet deeper. To mitigate somewhat the effects of extremely short fences, the leagues drew up ground rules to eliminate cheap home runs. Finally, in the 1950s, the major leagues instituted minimum outfield fence distances for newly built parks.

From the mid-1960s through the 1980s, new park design involved symmetrical dimensions designed to accommodate football fields. These uniform venues seemed to reflect clean-lined, suburban spaciousness rather than the intimate urban settings of classic ballparks. The paradigm shift caused by the opening of Camden Yards has convinced teams that fans want odd dimensions and asymmetrical features as well as intimate spaces and comfortable seats and amenities. So these retro ballparks are deliberately asymmetrical, though this is now being done mostly for aesthetic reasons.

The **Notes** column includes miscellaneous information about artificial turf; domes or retractable roofs; and when lights were installed (if the park didn't have lights when it opened). No ballpark that closed before 1935 ever had lights; every ballpark built afterward always had lights. A *p* next to a year indicates the information applied for only part of that year.

Finally, if a team played a "home" game in a park that was not located in its hometown, the location of that park is shown in square brackets. In the 1800s, clubs often played official league games at neutral sites, either to benefit from a larger gate or to squeeze in a game—and, thus, a gate—on long road trips.

The last page of the Ballparks section has a list of all spring training sites for AL, NL, and Federal League clubs since 1901. The sites are shown chronologically by franchise, so the original Washington Senators spring training sites from 1901–60 are under Minnesota, and the expansion Senators spring bases from 1961–71 are under Texas.

A few teams will have two spring sites listed for some years. This is either because they trained at one city before moving to another city to play most or all of their home exhibition games, or because split their spring camps into two locations. Neutral sites (where teams sometimes play a game or two on the way home from spring training) are not shown.

In a few rare cases, teams play no or very few home spring games—the Mariners played all of their spring games in other teams' parks in Arizona in 1993 while their new ballpark in Peoria was being built.

CITY/PARK	OPEN	TENANTS	CAPACITY	DIMENSIONS LF–LCF/CF/RCF–RF Current/Final	Original	NOTES
ALTOONA, PA						
Columbia Park	1884	UA Mountain Cities				
ANAHEIM/LOS ANGELES [CALIFORNIA 1966–96]						
Angel Stadium of Anaheim	**1966–**	**AL Angels**	**45,030** (43,204)	**330–387/400/370–330**	333–?/406/?–333	*Anaheim Stadium 1966–97; Edison International Field of Anaheim 1998–03 "The Big A"; rebuilt 1997–98*
ARLINGTON [TEXAS]						
Arlington Stadium	1972–1993	AL Rangers	43,521 (35,185)	330–380/400/380–330		OF configuration different 1974–80
Ameriquest Field in Arlington	**1994–**	**AL Rangers**	**49,115** (49,292)	**332–390/400/381–325**		*The Ballpark in Arlington 1994–2004*
ATLANTA						
Atlanta-Fulton County Stadium	1966–1996	NL Braves	52,769 (50,893)	330–385/402/385–330	325–385/402/385–325	
Turner Field	**1997–**	**NL Braves**	**50,096** (50,528)	**335–380/401/390–330**		Built for 1996 Olympics; rebuilt for MLB
BALTIMORE						
Newington Park	1872–1874	NA Lord Baltimores				
	1873	NA Maryland				
	1882	AA Orioles				
Oriole Park (I)	1883–1889	AA Orioles				
Oriole Park (II)	1890–1891	AA Orioles			300–?/?/?–350	
Belair Lot	1884	UA Monumentals				
Monumental Park	1884	UA Monumentals				Selected dates
Oriole Park (III)	1891	AA Orioles	11,000 (30,000)	300–?/?/?–350		
	1892–1899	NL Orioles				
Oriole Park (IV)	1901–1902	AL Orioles	16,000	300–?/450/?–335		
Terrapin Park	1914–1915	FL Terrapins	53,371 (47,855)	309–385/405/385–309	309–446/445/446–309	
Memorial Stadium	1954–1991	AL Orioles				
Oriole Park at Camden Yards	**1992–**	**AL Orioles**	**48,286** (48,041)	**333–410/400/373–318**		
BOSTON						
South End Grounds (I)	1871–1875	NA Red Stockings				Became NL Braves
	1876–1887	NL Braves				
Hampden Park Race Track	1873	NA Red Stockings				[Springfield MA] 2 games
Dartmouth Grounds	1884	UA Unions				
South End Grounds (II)	1888–1894	NL Braves	6,800			
Congress Street Grounds	1890	PL Red Stockings		250–?/?/?–?		
	1891	AA Red Stockings				
	1894	NL Braves				
South End Grounds (III)	1894–1914	NL Braves		250–450/440/?–255		
Huntington Avenue Grounds	1901–1911	AL Red Sox	9,000	350–440/635/?–320	350–440/530/?–280	RCF 420; lights 1947; Day capacity 34,679
Fenway Park	**1912–**	**AL Red Sox**	**35,095** (35,000)	**310–379/390/380–302**	321–?/488/?–314	28 Sept. games & World Series, 1914
	1914–1915	NL Braves				RCF 390 (550); lights 1946
Braves Field	1915–1952	NL Braves	37,106 (40,000)	337–355/370/355–318	402–403/440/402–402	World Series only
	1915–1916	AL Red Sox				Sundays
	1929–1932	AL Red Sox				
BROOKLYN						
Capitoline Grounds	1872	NA Atlantics				
Union Grounds	1872	NA Eckfords	1,500	500–500/500/500–350		
	1873–1875	NA Atlantics				
Washington Park (I)	1884–1889	AA Atlantics	2,000			14 Sunday games
Ridgewood Park	1886–1889	AA Atlantics				29 games
	1890	AA Gladiators				
Washington Park (II)	1889	AA Atlantics	3,000			
	1890	NL Dodgers				
Long Island Grounds	1890	AA Gladiators				[Maspeth NY] 2 games
Eastern Park	1890	PL Ward's Wonders				
	1891–1897	NL Dodgers				
Washington Park (III)	1898–1912	NL Dodgers		376–444/425/300–302	335–500/445/300–215	Rebuilt 1914 for Federal League
	1914–1915	FL Tip-Tops	18,800	300–?/400/?–275		[West New York NJ] 3 games
West NY Field Club Grounds	1898	NL Dodgers				Lights 1938
Ebbets Field	1913–1957	NL Dodgers	31,902 (18,000)	348–351/393/352–297	419–?/450/?–301	[Jersey City NJ] 14 games total
Roosevelt Stadium	1956–1957	NL Dodgers	24,500 (24,167)	330–397/411/397–330		
BUFFALO						
Riverside Grounds	1879–1883	NL Bisons			210–420/410/420–210	
Olympic Park (I)	1884–1885	NL Bisons				[Elmira NY] 1 game
Maple Avenue Driving Park	1885	NL Bisons				
Olympic Park (II)	1890	PL Bisons				*aka Federal League Park*
Federal Field	1914–1915	FL Blues	20,000	290–?/400/?–300		
CHICAGO						
Union Base–Ball Grounds	1871	NA White Stockings	7,000			Became NL Cubs; *aka Lake Park*
23rd Street Grounds	1874–1875	NA White Stockings				
	1876–1877	NL Cubs				
Lake Front Park (I)	1878–1882	NL Cubs				
Lake Front Park (II)	1883–1884	NL Cubs	5,000	180–280/300/252–196	186–280/300/252–196	
South Side Park (I)	1884	UA Browns				[Baltimore MD] 1 game
Belair Lot	1884	UA Browns			216–?/?/?–216	Mondays/Wednesdays/Fridays 1891
West Side Park	1885–1891	NL Cubs				
South Side Park (II)	1890	PL Pirates				Tuesdays/Thursdays/Saturdays 1891
	1891–1893	NL Cubs				
West Side Grounds	1893–1915	NL Cubs	16,000 (12,500)	340–441/560/435–316		
South Side Park (III)	1901–1910	AL White Sox	15,000			Lights 1939; turf IF/grass OF 1969–75
Comiskey Park (I)	1910–1990	AL White Sox	43,951 (28,800)	347–382/409/382–347	363–382/420/382–363	*White Sox Park 1967–75*
Wrigley Field	1914–1915	FL Whales	**39,538** (18,000)	**355–368/400/368–353**	310–?/400/?–350	Lights 1988; *Weeghman Park 1914–18, Cubs Park 1919–25*
	1916–	**NL Cubs**				
Milwaukee County Stadium	1968–1969	AL White Sox	53,192 (35,911)	315–392/402/392–315	320–397/404/397–320	[Milwaukee WI] 20 games total
U.S. Cellular Field	**1991–**	**AL White Sox**	**40,615** (44,702)	**330–377/400/372–335**	347–383/400/383–347	*Comiskey Park (II) 1991–2002 "New Comiskey"*
Tokyo Dome*	2000	NL Cubs	55,000	318–360/400/360–318		[Japan] Dome; turf; 1 game
CINCINNATI						
Avenue Grounds	1876–1879	NL Reds				
Bank St. Grounds	1880	NL Reds				
	1882–1883	AA Red Stockings				
	1884	UA Outlaw Reds				
League Park (I)	1884–1889	AA Red Stockings				
	1890–1893	NL Reds				[Pendleton Park OH]
Pendleton Park	1891	AA Kelly's Killers		253–?/?/?–?		
League Park (II)	1894–1901	NL Reds	6,000	?–?/?/?–450		
Palace of the Fans	1902–1911	NL Reds			360–380/420/?–385	Lights 1935; *Redland Field 1912–33;*
Crosley Field	1912–1970	NL Reds	29,603 (23,500)	328–380/387/383–366		replica built in Blue Ash OH

CITY/PARK	OPEN	TENANTS	CAPACITY	DIMENSIONS LF–LCF/CF/RCF–RF Current/Final	Original	NOTES
Cinergy Field	1970–2002	NL Reds	40,007 (50,000)	325–370/393/374–325	330–375/404/375–330	Turf 1970–2000; *Riverfront Stadium 1970–96*
Great American Ball Park	**2003–**	**NL Reds**	**42,271** (42,059)	**328–379/404/370–325**		LF–CF seats demolished after 2000
CLEVELAND						
National Association Grounds	1871–1872	NA Forest City				
Lincoln Park Grounds	1871	NA Forest City				
National League Park (I)	1879–1884	NL Blues				[Cincinnati OH] 1 date
National League Park (II)	1887–1888	AA Blues			410–?/420/?–410	
	1889–1890	NL Spiders			410–?/420/?–410	
Geauga Lake Baseball Grounds	1888	AA Blues				[Geauga Lake OH] 3 games
Beyerle's Park	1888	AA Blues				[Newburgh OH] 1 date
Brotherhood Park	1890	PL Infants				
Indianapolis Park	1890	NL Spiders				[Indianapolis IN] a few dates
League Park (I)	1891–1899	NL Spiders	9,000		?–?/?/?–290	
	1901–1909	AL Indians				
Euclid Beach Park	1898	NL Spiders				[Collinwood OH] selected dates
Ontario Beach Grounds	1898	NL Spiders				[Charlotte NY] 1 date
League Park (II)	1910–1946	AL Indians	21,000	375–415/420/400–290	385–505/420/400–290	Selected dates 1932–46
Mahaffey Park	1902–1903	AL Indians			324–?/382/?–302	[Canton OH] 3 dates
Cleveland Stadium	1932–1993	AL Indians	74,483 (78,000)	320–375/404/370–320	320–435/470/435–320	Lights 1939; selected dates 1932–46; *Lakefront Stadium 1932–37; Cleveland Public Municipal Stadium 1938; Municipal Stadium 1939–64*
Jacobs Field	**1994–**	**AL Indians**	**43,405** (42,865)	**325–370/405/375–325**		"The Jake"
COLUMBUS, OH						
Recreation Park (I)	1883–1884	AA Buckeyes				
Recreation Park (II)	1889–1891	AA Solons			?–?/?/?–400	
DENVER [COLORADO]						
Mile High Stadium	1993–1994	NL Rockies	76,100	333–366/423/400–370	335–375/423/400–370	
Coors Field	**1995–**	**NL Rockies**	**50,449** (50,000)	**347–390/415/375–350**		RCF 424
DETROIT						
Recreation Park	1881–1888	NL Wolverines				
Bennett Park	1901–1911	AL Tigers	14,000 (6,000)			
Burns Park	1901–1902	AL Tigers	8,000 (5,500)			23 Sunday games
Tiger Stadium*	1912–1999	AL Tigers	46,846 (23,000)	340–365/440/370–325	345–?/467/?–370	Lights 1948; *Navin Field 1912–33; Briggs Stadium 1934–60*
Comerica Park	**2000–**	**AL Tigers**	**41,070** (40,120)	**345–370/420/365–330**	345–395/420/365–330	
ELIZABETH, NJ						
Waverly Fairgrounds	1873	NA Resolutes				[Waverly NJ]
FORT WAYNE, IN						
Hamilton Field	1871	NA Kekiongas				
HARTFORD						
Hartford Ball Club Grounds	1874–1875	NA Dark Blues				
South End Grounds	1874	NA Dark Blues				
Hartford Ball Club Grounds	1876	NL Dark Blues				[Boston MA] 1 date
Union Grounds	1877	NL Dark Blues		?–500/500/500–?		[Brooklyn NY]
HOUSTON						
Colt Stadium	1962–1964	NL Colt .45s	33,010 (32,601)	360–395/420/395–360		RCF & LCF 427; Most of ballpark moved to Torreon, Mexico, in 1969
Astrodome*	1965–1999	NL Astros	54,370 (46,217)	325–375/400/375–325	340–375/406/375–340	Dome; turf (turf IF/grass OF 1966p)
Minute Maid Park	**2000–**	**NL Astros**	**40,950** (42,180)	**315–362/435/373–326**		Retractable roof; RCF 436; *Enron Field 2000–01, Astros Field 2002*
INDIANAPOLIS						
South Street Park	1878	NL Blues				
Seventh St. Park (I)	1884	AA Hoosiers				
Bruce Grounds	1884	AA Hoosiers				
Seventh St. Park (II)	1887	NL Hoosiers				11 Sunday games
Seventh St. Park (III)	1888–1889	NL Hoosiers			286–?/?/?–261	
Hoosier Park	1914	FL Hoosiers	20,000	375–?/400/?–310		*aka Greenlawn Park/Federal League Park*
KANSAS CITY						
Athletic Park	1884	UA Cowboys				
Association Park	1886	NL Cowboys				
	1888	AA Cowboys				
Gordon & Koppel Field	1914–1915	FL Packers	12,000			
Municipal Stadium	1955–1967	AL Athletics	35,561 (30,296)	369–408/421/382–338	312–382/430/382–347	
	1969–1972	AL Royals				
Kauffman Stadium	**1973–**	**AL Royals**	**40,785** (40,613)	**330/385–410–385/330**	330–375/405/375–330	Turf 1973–94; *Royals Stadium 1973–93p*
KEOKUK, IA						
Perry Park	1875	NA Westerns				
LOS ANGELES [incl. CALIFORNIA 1965] (also see Anaheim)						
Memorial Coliseum*	1958–1961	NL Dodgers	94,600 (93,000)	252–417/420/380–300	250–425/425/440–301	
Wrigley Field	1961	AL Angels	20,457	340–345/412/345–339		
Dodger Stadium	**1962–**	**NL Dodgers**	**56,000**	**330–385/395/385–330**	330–380/410/380–330	
	1962–1965	AL Angels				*Chavez Ravine Stadium 1962–65 (Angels games only); LA Angels changed name to California in 1965 before move to Anaheim*
LOUISVILLE						
Louisville Baseball Park	1876–1877	NL Grays				
Eclipse Park (I)	1882–1891	AA Colonels (1885)		360–405/495/360–320		
	1892–1893	NL Colonels				
Eclipse Park (II)	1893–1899	NL Colonels				
MIAMI [FLORIDA]						
Dolphins Stadium	**1993–**	**NL Marlins**	**36,331** (43,909)	**330–385/404/385–345**	335–380/410/380–345	RCF 434; postseason cap. 65,000+; *Joe Robbie Stadium 1993–96; Pro Player Stadium 1997–2004*
MIDDLETOWN, CT						
Mansfield Club Grounds	1872	NA Mansfields				
Hartford Trotting Park	1872	NA Mansfields				[Hartford CT] 3 games
MILWAUKEE						
Milwaukee Base–Ball Grounds	1878	NL Grays				
Wright Street Grounds	1884	UA Brewers				
Borchert Field	1891	AA Brewers	10,000		266–?/395/?–266	
Athletic Park	1891	AA Brewers			275–?/?/?–250	[Minneapolis MN] 1 date

CITY/PARK	OPEN	TENANTS	CAPACITY	DIMENSIONS LF–LCF/CF/RCF–RF Current/Final	Original	NOTES
						aka Milwaukee Park
Lloyd Street Grounds	1901	AL Brewers				
Milwaukee County Stadium	1953–1965	NL Braves	53,192 (35,911)	315–392/402/392–315	320–397/404/397–320	
	1968–1969	AL White Sox				20 games total
	1970–1997	AL Brewers				
	1998–2000	NL Brewers				
Miller Park	**2001–**	**NL Brewers**	**41,900** (42,500)	**344–371/400/374–345**		Retractable roof
MINNEAPOLIS [MINNESOTA]						
Metropolitan Stadium	1961–81	AL Twins	45,919 (30,022)	343–406/402/410–330	329–402/412/402–329	[Bloomington MN]
Hubert H. Humphrey Metrodome	**1982–**	**AL Twins**	**45,423** (54,711)	**343–385/408/367–327**		Dome; turf; *"The Homerdome"*
MONTREAL						
Parc Jarry	1969–1976	NL Expos	28,456 (28,000)	340–368/420/368–340	340–368/415/368–340	*Jarry Park*
Stade Olympique	1977–2004	NL Expos	46,338 (58,838)	325–375/404/375–325		Turf; built for 1976 Olympics; *Olympic Stadium; "The Big O"*; Open-air 1977–86; fixed roof 1987–88; retractable roof 1989–91p; fixed roof p1991–98p; no roof 1998p; fixed roof 1999–2004
Estadio Hiram Bithorn	2003–2004	NL Expos	19,000 (20,000)	325/375–404/375/325	315–340/399/340–315	*Hiram Bithorn Stadium* [San Juan PR] turf; Power alleys listed 360', actually 340'; 22 games each season in 2003–04
NEWARK						
Harrison Park	1915	FL Peppers	21,000	375–?/450/?–375		*aka Peppers Park*
NEW HAVEN, CT						
Howard Avenue Grounds	1875	NA Elm Citys				*aka Brewster Park*
Adelaide Avenue Grounds	1875	NA Elm Citys				[Providence RI] 1 date
NEW YORK						
Union Grounds	1871–1875	NA Mutuals	1,500	500–500/500/500–350		[Brooklyn NY]
	1876	NL Mutuals				
Polo Grounds (I)	1883–1888	NL Giants				
	1884–1885	AA Metropolitans				
Polo Grounds (II)	1883	AA Metropolitans				33 games
Metropolitan Park	1884	AA Metropolitans				[St. George NY]
St. George Cricket Grounds	1886–1887	AA Metropolitans	4,100			[Weehawken NJ] 1 date
Monitor Park	1887	AA Metropolitans				
Polo Grounds (III)	1889–1890	NL Giants		?–?/360/?–?		[Jersey City NJ] 2 games
Oakdale Park	1889	NL Giants				
Polo Grounds (IV)	1890	PL Giants	16,000	277–?/500/?–258	335–?/500/?–335	*Brotherhood Park 1890*
	1891–1911	NL Giants				[West New York NJ] selected dates
West N.Y. Field Club Grounds	1899	NL Giants				
Hilltop Park	1903–1912	AL Yankees	15,000	365–?/542/?–400		
	1911	NL Giants				28 games
Polo Grounds (V)	1911–1957	NL Giants	56,000 (16,000)	279–455/483/449–258	277–?/433/?–257	Lights 1940
	1913–1922	AL Yankees				
	1962–1963	NL Mets				
Yankee Stadium	**1923–**	**AL Yankees**	**57,478** (58,000)	**318–399/408/385–314**	281–395/490/429–295	LCF 411; lights 1946; rebuilt 1974–75 *"The House That Ruth Built"*
Shea Stadium	**1964–**	**NL Mets**	**57,369** (55,000)	**338–378/410/378–338**	341–371/410/371–341	
	1974–75; 1998	AL Yankees				1 game in 1998
Tokyo Dome*	2000	NL Mets	55,000	318–360/400/360–318		[Japan] Dome; turf; 1 game
	2004	AL Yankees				1 game
OAKLAND						
McAfee Coliseum	**1968–**	**AL Athletics**	**34,179** (50,000)	**330–388/400/388–330**	330–378/410/378–330	Postseason cap. 50,000+; *Oakland–Alameda County Coliseum 1968–98 Network Associates Coliseum 1999–2004*
Cashman Field*	1996	AL Athletics	9,370	328–364/433/364–328		[Las Vegas NV] 6 games
PHILADELPHIA						
Jefferson Street Grounds	1871–1875	NA Athletics		?–?/500/?–?		First press box installed here
	1873–1875	NA White Stockings				
	1876	NL Athletics				
	1883–1890	AA Athletics				*aka Athletic Park*
Fairview Park Fairgrounds	1875	NA Athletics				[Dover DE] 1 date
Centennial Park	1875	NA Centennials				*aka Centennial Grounds*
Star Baseball Park	1875	NA White Stockings				[Covington KY] 1 date
Ludlow Baseball Park	1875	NA White Stockings				[Ludlow KY] 1 date
Oakdale Park	1882	AA Athletics				
Recreation Park	1883–1886	NL Phillies				
Keystone Park	1884	UA Keystones				
Philadelphia Baseball Grounds	1887–1894	NL Phillies	15,000	500–?/?/?–310		[Gloucester City NJ] 30 Sunday games
Gloucester Point Grounds	1888–1890	AA Athletics				One week
University of Pennsylvania Athletic Field	1894	NL Phillies				
Forepaugh Park	1890	PL Quakers		345–?/450/?–380		
	1891	AA Athletics				
Columbia Park	1901–1908	AL Athletics	13,600 (9,500)			16 games
	1903	NL Phillies				*National League Park 1895-1913*
Baker Bowl	1895–1938	NL Phillies	18,800 (18,000)	342–359/408/300–281	?–?/408/300–?	Huntingdon Street Grounds
Connie Mack Stadium	1909–1954	AL Athletics	33,608 (20,000)	334–387/410/390–329	360–393/515/393–360	*Shibe Park 1909–52*; lights 1939
	1938–1970	NL Phillies				
Veterans Stadium	1971–2003	NL Phillies	61,831 (56,371)	330–371/408/371–330		Turf
Citizens Bank Park	**2004–**	**NL Phillies**	**43,304** (43,500)	**329–374/401/369–330**	329–369/401/369–330	LCF 409; LF power alley actually 359, 2004p
PHOENIX [ARIZONA]						
Chase Field	**1998–**	**NL Diamondbacks**	**49,033** (48,500)	**330–376/407/376–334**		*"The BOB"*; retractable roof; RCF 412 *Bank One Ballpark 1998–2005*
PITTSBURGH						
Exposition Park (I)	1882–1883	AA Alleghenys				
	1884	UA Stogies				
Exposition Park (II)	1883	AA Alleghenys				
Recreation Park	1884–1886	AA Alleghenys	17,000			
	1887–1890	NL Pirates	17,000			
Exposition Park (III)	1890	PL Burghers		400–?/450/?–400		
	1891–1909	NL Pirates				
	1914–1915	FL Rebels	16,000			[Canton OH] 1 date
Mahaffey Park	1890	NL Pirates		324–?/382/?–302		[Wheeling WV] 1 date
Island Grounds	1890	NL Pirates				
Forbes Field	1909–1970	NL Pirates	35,000 (28,000)	365–406/435/408–300	360–419/447/410–376	LCF 457 (462); lights 1940
Three Rivers Stadium	1970–2000	NL Pirates	47,687 (49,023)	335–375/400/375–335	340–385/410/385–340	Turf
PNC Park	**2001–**	**NL Pirates**	**38,496**	**325–389/399/375–320**		LCF 410
PROVIDENCE, RI						
Messer Street Grounds	1878	NL Grays				[Pittsburgh PA] selected dates
Union Park	1878	NL Grays	2,500			

CITY/PARK	OPEN	TENANTS	CAPACITY	DIMENSIONS LF–LCF/CF/RCF–RF Current/Final	Original	NOTES
RICHMOND, VA						
Virginia Baseball Park	1884	AA Virginians				
ROCHESTER, NY						
Culver Field (I)	1890	AA Broncos				
Windsor Beach	1890	AA Broncos				[Irondequoit NY] 6 games
ROCKFORD, IL						
Agricultural Society Fairgrounds	1871	NA Forest City	500			
ST. LOUIS						
Red Stocking Base-Ball Park	1875	NA Red Stockings				
Grand Avenue Park	1875	NA Brown Stockings				
	1876–1877	NL Brown Stockings	3,000			
Union Grounds	1884	UA Maroons	10,000	285–?/?/?–285		
	1885–1886	NL Maroons				
Seventh Street Park (I)	1885	NL Maroons				
Sportsman's Park (I)	1882–1891	AA Cardinals	12,000 (6,000)	350–400/460/330–285		[Indianapolis IN] selected dates
	1892	NL Cardinals				
Robison Field	1893–1920	NL Cardinals	21,000 (10,000)	380–400/435/320–?	470–520/500/330–290	aka League Park
Athletic Park	1901	NL Cardinals				1 game
Sportsman's Park (II)	1902–1908	AL Browns	18,000			
Busch Stadium (I)	1909–1953	AL Browns	30,500 (17,600)	351–379/420/354–3109	368–379/?/?–335	Lights 1940
	1920–1966	NL Cardinals				Sportsman's Park (III) 1909–53
Handlan's Park	1914–1915	FL Terriers	15,000 (12,000)	325–?/375/?–300		aka Steininger Field
Busch Stadium (II)	1966–2005	NL Cardinals	50,345 (49,275)	330–372/402/372–330	330–386/414/386–330	Busch Memorial Stadium 1966–83; turf 1970–95
Busch Stadium (III)	**2006–**	**NL Cardinals**	**46,000**	**336–390/400/390–335**		
ST. PETERSBURG [TAMPA BAY]						
Tropicana Field	**1998–**	**AL Devil Rays**	**41,315 (45,200)**	**315–370/404/370–322**	315–370/410/370–322	Dome; turf; LCF 410 (417)
Tokyo Dome*	2004	AL Devil Rays	55,000	318–360/400/360–318		[Japan] Dome; turf; 1 game
SAN DIEGO						
Qualcomm Stadium*	1969–2003	NL Padres	63,890 (50,000)	327–370/405/370–330	330–370/420/370–330	San Diego Stadium 1969–80; San Diego/ Jack Murphy Stadium 1981–97
Estadio Monterrey*	1996	NL Padres	25,644	325–?/405/?–325		Monterrey Stadium [Mexico] 3 games
	1999	NL Padres				1 game
Aloha Stadium*	1997	NL Padres	50,000	325–375/420/375–325		[Honolulu HI] 3 games; turf
Petco Park	**2004–**	**NL Padres**	**46,000**	**334–367/396/387–322**		RCF 400
SAN FRANCISCO						
Seals Stadium	1958–1959	NL Giants	22,900	361–364/400/397–350	365–375/410/397–355	
3Com Park at Candlestick Point*	1960–1999	NL Giants	63,000 (42,500)	335–365/400/365–328	330–365/410/375–330	Candlestick Park 1960–95
SBC Park	**2000–**	**NL Giants**	**41,584 (40,800)**	**339–364/399/421–309**	335–364/404/420–307	Turf IF/grass OF 1971; turf 1972–78 Pacific Bell Park 2000–03
SEATTLE						
Sick's Stadium	1969	AL Pilots	25,420 (18,000)	305–345/402/345–305		
Kingdome	1977–1999	AL Mariners	59,084 (59,059)	331–389/405/380–312	315–375/405/365–315	Dome; turf
Safeco Field	**1999–**	**AL Mariners**	**47,447 (47,116)**	**331–390/405/387–327**		Retractable roof
SYRACUSE, NY						
Star Park (I)	1879	NL Stars				
Star Park (II)	1890	AA Stars				
Iron Pier	1890	AA Stars				
Three Rivers Park	1890	AA Stars				1 game scheduled; forfeited [Three Rivers, NY] 5 games
TOLEDO, OH						
League Park	1884	AA Blue Stockings				
Tri-State Fair Grounds	1884	AA Blue Stockings				
Speranza Park	1890	AA Maumees				
TORONTO						
Exhibition Stadium	1977–1989	AL Blue Jays	43,737 (38,522)	330–375/400/375–330		Turf
Rogers Centre	**1989–**	**AL Blue Jays**	**50,516**	**328–375/400/375–328**	330–375/400/375–330	Retractable roof; turf SkyDome 1989–2004
Estadio Hiram Bithorn*	2001	AL Blue Jays	20,000	315–340/398/340–313		Hiram Bithorn Stadium; turf; 1 game Power alleys listed 360', actually 340'
TROY, NY						
Haymakers' Grounds	1871–1872	NA Haymakers				
	1880–1881	NL Trojans				
Hampden Park Race Track	1872	NA Haymakers				[Springfield MA] 1 date
Putnam Grounds	1879	NL Trojans				
Riverside Park	1880–1882	NL Trojans				[Albany NY] selected dates
Troy Ball Club Grounds	1882	NL Trojans				[Watervliet NY]
WASHINGTON, DC						
Olympic Grounds	1871–1872	NA Olympics				
	1873	NA Nationals				
	1875	NA Nationals				
Madison Avenue Grounds	1871	NA Olympics				
Lincoln Park Grounds	1871	NA Olympics				[Baltimore MD] 1 date
White Lot	1871–1872	NA Olympics				[Cincinnati OH] 2 games
Maryland Avenue Park	1871–1872	NA Olympics				Selected dates
Nationals Grounds	1872	NA Nationals				Selected dates
Newington Park	1875	NA Nationals				
Virginia State Agricultural Society	1875	NA Nationals				[Baltimore MD] 2 games
Athletic Park	1884	AA Nationals				[Richmond VA] selected dates
Capitol Grounds	1884	UA Nationals	6,000			
Swampoodle Grounds	1886–1889	NL Senators	6,000			
Boundary Field	1891	AA Statesmen	6,500			
	1892–1899	NL Senators				
American League Park (I)	1901–1903	AL Senators	(6,000)		200–?/?/?–?	
American League Park (II)	1904–1910	AL Senators				
Griffith Stadium	1911–1960	AL Senators (I)	28,669 (12,000)	388–372/408/373–320	407–391/421/378–328	League Park 1911–19; LCF 426; lights 1941
	1961	AL Senators (II)				
Robert F. Kennedy Memorial Stadium	1962–71	AL Senators (II)	42,250 (42,000)	336–380/410/380–336	335–385/410/385–335	District of Columbia Stadium 1962–68
	2005–	**NL Nationals**				
WILMINGTON, DE						
Union Street Park	1884	UA Quicksteps				
WORCESTER, MA						
Agricultural County Fair Grounds	1880–1882	NL Brown Stockings				

SPRING TRAINING SITES (SINCE 1901)

AMERICAN LEAGUE

Anaheim/Los Angeles
(incl. California, 1966–96)

1993–	Tempe AZ
1984–92	Mesa AZ
	Palm Springs CA
1982–83	Casa Grande AZ
	Palm Springs CA
1980–81	Palm Springs CA
1966–79	Holtville CA
	Palm Springs CA

Los Angeles 1961–64
California 1965

1961–65	Palm Springs CA

Baltimore

1996–	Ft. Lauderdale FL
1992–95	Sarasota FL
	St. Petersburg FL
1991	Sarasota FL
1989–90	Sarasota FL
	Miami FL
1959–88	Miami FL
1956–58	Scottsdale AZ
1955	Daytona Beach FL
1954	Yuma AZ

St. Louis

1953	San Bernardino CA
1949–52	Burbank CA
1948	San Bernardino CA
1947	Miami FL
1946	Anaheim CA
1943–45	Cape Girardeau MO
1942	Deland FL
1937–41	San Antonio TX
1928–36	West Palm Beach FL
1925–27	Tarpon Springs FL
1922–24	Mobile AL
1921	Bogalusa AL
1920	Taylor AL
1919	San Antonio TX
1918	Shreveport LA
1916–17	Palestine TX
1915	Houston TX
1914	St. Petersburg FL
1913	Waco TX
1912	Montgomery AL
1911	Hot Springs AR
1909–10	Houston TX
1908	Shreveport LA
1907	San Antonio TX
1905–06	Dallas TX
1904	Corsicana TX
1903	Baton Rouge LA
1902	French Lick IN
1901	St. Louis MO

Boston

1993–	Ft. Myers FL
1966–92	Winter Haven FL
1959–65	Scottsdale AZ
1946–58	Sarasota FL
1945	Pleasantville NJ
1944	Baltimore MD
1943	Medford MA
1933–42	Sarasota FL
1932	Savannah GA
1930–31	Pensacola FL
1928–29	Bradenton FL
1925–27	New Orleans LA
1924	San Antonio TX
1920–23	Hot Springs AR
1919	Tampa FL
1912–18	Hot Springs AR
1911	Redondo Beach CA
1909–10	Hot Springs AR
1907–08	Little Rock AR
1903–06	Macon GA
1902	Augusta GA
1901	Charlottesville VA

Chicago

1998–	Tucson AZ
1960–97	Sarasota FL
1954–59	Tampa FL
1953	El Centro CA
1952	Pasadena CA
	El Centro CA
1951	Pasadena CA
	Palm Springs CA
1946–50	Pasadena CA
1945	Terre Haute IN
1943–44	French Lick IN
1933–42	Pasadena CA
1930–32	San Antonio TX
1929	Dallas TX
1925–28	Shreveport LA
1924	Winter Haven FL
1922–23	Seguin TX
1921	Waxahachie TX
1920	Waco TX
1916–19	Mineral Wells TX
1913–15	Paso Robles CA
1912	Waco TX
1911	Mineral Wells TX
1909–10	San Francisco CA

1908	Los Angeles CA
1907	Mexico City, Mexico
1905–06	New Orleans LA
1904	Marlin TX
1903	Mobile AL
1901–02	Excelsior Springs MO

Cleveland

1993–	Winter Haven FL
1947–92	Tucson AZ
1946	Clearwater FL
1943–45	Lafayette IN
1940–42	Ft. Myers FL
1928–39	New Orleans LA
1923–27	Lakeland FL
1921–22	Dallas TX
1916–20	New Orleans LA
1915	San Antonio TX
1914	Athens GA
1913	Pensacola FL
1912	New Orleans LA
1910–11	Alexandria LA
1907–09	Macon GA
1905–06	New Orleans LA
1904	San Antonio TX
1902–03	New Orleans LA
1901	Cleveland OH

Detroit

1946–	Lakeland FL
1943–45	Evansville IN
1934–42	Lakeland FL
1933	San Antonio TX
1932	Palo Alto CA
1931	Sacramento CA
1930	Tampa FL
1929	Phoenix AZ
1927–28	San Antonio TX
1922–26	Augusta GA
1921	San Antonio TX
1919–20	Macon GA
1916–18	Waxahachie TX
1913–15	Gulfport MS
1911–12	Monroe LA
1909–10	San Antonio TX
1908	Hot Springs AR
	Little Rock AR
1905–07	Augusta GA
1903–04	Shreveport LA
1902	Ypsilanti MI
1901	Detroit MI

Kansas City

2003–	Surprise AZ
1988–2002	Davenport FL
1969–87	Ft. Myers FL

Minnesota

1991–	Ft. Myers FL
1961–90	Orlando FL

Washington

1946–60	Orlando FL
1943–45	College Park MD
1936–42	Orlando FL
1930–35	Biloxi MS
1920–29	Tampa FL
1918–19	Augusta GA
1917	Atlanta GA
1912–16	Charlottesville VA
1911	Atlanta GA
1910	Norfolk VA
1907–09	Galveston TX
1906	Charlottesville VA
1905	Hampton VA
1902–04	Washington DC
1901	Phoebus VA

New York

1996–	Tampa FL
1962–95	Ft. Lauderdale FL
1952–61	St. Petersburg FL
1951	Phoenix AZ
1946–50	St. Petersburg FL
1944–45	Atlantic City NJ
1943	Asbury Park NJ
1925–42	St. Petersburg FL
1922–24	New Orleans LA
1921	Shreveport LA
1919–20	Jacksonville FL
1916–18	Macon GA
1915	Savannah GA
1914	Houston TX
1913	Hamilton, Bermuda
1912	Atlanta GA
1910–11	Athens GA
1909	Macon GA
1907–08	Atlanta GA
1906	Birmingham AL
1905	Montgomery AL
1903–04	Atlanta GA
1902	Savannah GA
1901	Baltimore MD

Oakland

1982–	Phoenix AZ
1979–81	Scottsdale AZ
1969–78	Mesa AZ
1968	Bradenton FL

Kansas City

1963–67	Bradenton FL
1955–62	West Palm Beach FL

Philadelphia

1946–54	West Palm Beach FL
1944–45	Frederick MD
1943	Wilmington DE
1940–42	Anaheim CA
1938–39	Lake Charles LA
1937	Mexico City, Mexico
1925–36	Ft. Myers FL
1923–24	Montgomery AL
1922	Eagle Pass TX
1920–21	Lake Charles LA
1919	Philadelphia PA
1914–18	Jacksonville FL
1912–13	San Antonio TX
1911	Savannah GA
1910	Atlanta GA
1908–09	New Orleans LA
1907	Dallas TX
1906	Montgomery AL
1905	Shreveport LA
1904	Spartanburg SC
1903	Jacksonville FL
1902	Charlotte NC
1901	Philadelphia PA

Seattle

1993–	Peoria AZ
1977–92	Tempe AZ

Tampa Bay

1998–	St. Petersburg FL

Texas

2003–	Surprise AZ
1987–2002	Port Charlotte FL
1972–86	Pompano Beach FL
	[Washington]
1961–71	Pompano Beach FL

Toronto

1977–	Dunedin FL

FEDERAL LEAGUE

Baltimore

1915	Fayetteville NC
1914	Southern Pines NC

Brooklyn

1915	Browns Wells MS
1914	Columbia SC

Buffalo

1915	Athens GA
1914	Danville VA

Chicago

1914–15	Shreveport LA

Indianapolis/Newark

1914	Wichita Falls TX
1915	Valdosta GA

Kansas City

1915	Wichita Falls TX
1914	Marshall TX

Pittsburgh

1915	Augusta GA
1914	Lynchburg VA

St. Louis

1915	Havana, Cuba
1914	Monroe LA

NATIONAL LEAGUE

Arizona

1998–	Tucson AZ

Atlanta

1998–	Kissimmee FL
1966–97	West Palm Beach FL

Milwaukee

1963–65	West Palm Beach FL
1953–62	Bradenton FL

Boston

1948–52	Bradenton FL
1946–47	Ft. Lauderdale FL
1945	Washington DC
1943–44	Wallingford CT
1942	Sanford FL
1941	San Antonio TX
1938–40	Bradenton FL
1922–37	St. Petersburg FL
1921	Galveston TX
1919–20	Columbus GA
1916–18	Miami FL
1914–15	Macon GA
1913	Athens GA
1908–12	Augusta GA
1907	Thomasville GA
1906	Jacksonville FL
1905	Charleston SC
1902–04	Thomasville GA
1901	Norfolk VA

Chicago

1979–	Mesa AZ
1967–78	Scottsdale AZ
1966	Long Beach CA
1952–65	Mesa AZ
1946–51	Catalina Island CA
1942–45	French Lick IN
1921–41	Catalina Island CA
1917–20	Pasadena CA
1913–16	Tampa FL
1912	New Orleans LA
1910–11	West Baden IN
	New Orleans LA
1909	West Baden IN
	Hot Springs AR
	Shreveport LA
1908	West Baden IN
	Vicksburg MS
1907	West Baden IN
	New Orleans LA
1906	West Baden IN
	Champaign IL
	Vicksburg MS
1905	Santa Monica CA
1903–04	Los Angeles CA
1901–02	Champaign IL

Cincinnati

1998–	Sarasota FL
1988–97	Plant City FL
1946–87	Tampa FL
1943–45	Bloomington IN
1931–42	Tampa FL
1923–30	Orlando FL
1922	Mineral Wells TX
1921	Cisco TX
1920	Miami FL
1919	Waxahachie TX
1918	Montgomery AL
1916–17	Shreveport LA
1914–15	Alexandria LA
1913	Mobile AL
1912	Columbus GA
1910–11	Hot Springs AR
1909	Atlanta GA
1908	St. Augustine FL
1907	Marlin TX
1906	San Antonio TX
1905	Jacksonville FL
1904	Dallas TX
1903	Augusta GA
1901–02	Cincinnati OH

Colorado

1993–	Tucson AZ

Florida

2003–	Jupiter FL
1994–2002	Viera FL
1993	Cocoa FL

Houston

1985–	Kissimmee FL
1964–84	Cocoa FL
1962–63	Apache Junction AZ

Los Angeles

1958–	Vero Beach FL

Brooklyn

1949–57	Vero Beach FL
1948	Vero Beach FL
	Ciudad Trujillo, D.R.
1947	Havana, Cuba
1946	Daytona Beach FL
1943–45	Bear Mountain NY
1941–42	Havana, Cuba
1936–40	Clearwater FL
1934–35	Orlando FL
1933	Miami FL
1923–32	Clearwater FL
1922	Jacksonville FL
1921	New Orleans LA
1919–20	Jacksonville FL
1917–18	Hot Springs AR
1915–16	Daytona Beach FL
1913–14	Augusta GA
1910–12	Hot Springs AR
1907–09	Jacksonville FL
1902–06	Columbia SC
1901	Charlotte NC

Milwaukee (AL 1969–96)

1998–	Maryvale AZ
1986–97	Chandler AZ
1973–85	Sun City AZ
1970–72	Tempe AZ

Seattle

1969	Tempe AZ

Montreal

2003–	Viera FL
1998–2002	Jupiter FL
1981–97	West Palm Beach FL
1973–80	Daytona Beach FL
1969–72	West Palm Beach FL

New York

1988–	Port St. Lucie FL
1962–87	St. Petersburg FL

Philadelphia

1947–	Clearwater FL
1946	Miami Beach FL
1944–45	Wilmington DE
1943	Hershey PA
1940–42	Miami Beach FL
1939	New Braunfels TX
1938	Biloxi MS
1928–37	Winter Haven FL
1925–27	Bradenton FL
1922–24	Leesburg FL
1921	Gainesville FL
1920	Birmingham AL
1919	Charlotte NC
1915–18	St. Petersburg FL
1914	Wilmington NC
1913	Southern Pines NC
1912	Hot Springs AR
1911	Southern Pines NC
1909–10	Southern Pines NC
1906–08	Savannah GA
1905	Augusta GA
1904	Savannah GA
1903	Richmond VA
1902	Washington DC
1901	Philadelphia PA

Pittsburgh

1969–	Bradenton FL
1955–68	Ft. Myers FL
1954	Ft. Pierce FL
1953	Havana, Cuba
1949–52	San Bernardino CA
1948	Hollywood CA
1947	Miami Beach FL
1946	San Bernardino CA
1943–45	Muncie IN
1937–42	San Bernardino CA
1936	San Antonio TX
1935	San Bernardino CA
1924–34	Paso Robles CA
1920–23	Hot Springs AR
1919	Birmingham AL
1918	Jacksonville FL
1915–17	Dawson Springs KY
	Hot Springs AR
1901–14	Hot Springs AR

St. Louis

1998–	Jupiter FL
1946–97	St. Petersburg FL
1943–45	Cairo IL
1938–42	St. Petersburg FL
1937	Daytona Beach FL
1930–36	Bradenton FL
1927–29	Avon Park FL
1926	San Antonio TX
1925	Stockton CA
1923–24	Bradenton FL
1921–22	Orange TX
1920	Brownsville TX
1919	St. Louis MO
1918	San Antonio TX
1915–17	Hot Wells TX
1914	St. Augustine FL
1913	Columbus GA
1912	Jackson MS
1911	West Baden IN
1909–10	Little Rock AR
1906–08	Houston TX
1905	Marlin TX
1904	Houston TX
1903	Dallas TX
1901–02	St. Louis MO

San Diego

1994–	Peoria AZ
1969–93	Yuma AZ

San Francisco

1982–	Scottsdale AZ
1958–81	Phoenix AZ

New York

1952–57	Phoenix AZ
1951	St. Petersburg FL
1947–50	Phoenix AZ
1946	Miami FL
1943–45	Lakewood NJ
1941–42	Miami FL
1940	Winter Haven FL
1938–39	Baton Rouge LA
1937	Havana, Cuba
1936	Pensacola FL
1934–35	Miami Beach FL
1932–33	Los Angeles CA
1929–31	San Antonio TX
1928	Augusta GA
1924–27	Sarasota FL
1920–23	San Antonio TX
1919	Gainesville FL
1908–18	Marlin TX
1907	Los Angeles CA
1906	Memphis TN
1903–05	Savannah GA
1901–02	New York NY

THE GLOBAL GAME: INTERNATIONAL AND AMATEUR BASEBALL

While America's national game doesn't have the far-reaching popularity of soccer, baseball is played enthusiastically all around the world. Outside of the United States, baseball remains most popular in the Caribbean and in East Asia, but the game is continuing to spread. Over 100 countries participate in Little League Baseball worldwide. Twelve countries participated in the European Baseball Championships in 2003, and Australia, Korea, and Taiwan continue to produce major league prospects.

In 1992 baseball finally became an Olympic sport. However, baseball's future in international competition is very much in doubt, since the International Olympic Committee voted in 2005 to eliminate baseball from the 2012 Paris Olympics. Meanwhile, MLB and the International Baseball Federation are planning to hold the first World Baseball Classic in March 2006, with 16 teams from 14 countries (plus Puerto Rico and Taiwan) scheduled to compete.

In the United States, there may be fewer kids playing stickball on the streets or pick-up games on small-town sandlots than in years past, but youth baseball organizations are prospering. The number of leagues available for various age groups and talent levels is staggering, and college baseball is also thriving as never before.

BASEBALL IN LATIN AMERICA

The passion much of Latin America has for baseball is no secret in the United States. Baseball has a longer tradition in the Caribbean than anywhere else except for the U.S. In the Dominican Republic, Cuba, Venezuela, and Puerto Rico, baseball is still the king of all sports, and it has been so for a very long time.

The first place that the American National Pastime landed in the Caribbean was Cuba, where American sailors and local workers were reportedly playing as early as 1866. Cuba had its first real team two years later and a professional league began competition in 1878, only two years after the National League's debut. Until the political upheavals of the late 1950s, Cuba was a baseball hub, attracting players from many other countries and sending many of its own to the major leagues and Negro Leagues. Cuba was also baseball's ambassador to the rest of the Caribbean. By the end of the nineteenth century, baseball was a fixture in every country in the area. U.S. military activity around the turn of the century helped push baseball further along in many of these places.

In the 1930s and 1940s the Caribbean winter leagues were attracting many major leaguers and Negro Leaguers in need of supplemental incomes. Following World War II, some rich owners in the Mexican League even raided the major leagues by signing more than twenty American players, though the threat from south of the border was short-lived.

After the color line was broken in the majors in 1947 and the crisis over the Mexican League raids had passed, Organized Baseball established official ties with most of the Caribbean leagues. The Caribbean Series began in that period, bringing together the winners of the winter leagues from Cuba, Panama, Puerto Rico, and Venezuela for an annual tournament. Cuba's 1959 revolution disrupted not only the Serie del Caribe, which took a hiatus from 1961–69, but all of baseball. While newly communist Cuba continued to field strong amateur teams, most of the connections between the island and the rest of the baseball world were severed by the revolution. Therefore, the nexus of Latin American baseball moved to the Dominican Republic.

In recent years the importance of the winter leagues has faded. With the astronomical leaps in major league salaries, few ballplayers need to supplement their income. Moreover, big league teams want to keep their investments safe and often discourage veteran players from playing winter ball and risking injury. These days most of the major leaguers who play winter ball are either local heroes or are playing to develop a new skill or increase their marketability as free agents. This trend has not, however, diminished the level of popularity of baseball in these countries or the skill level of their players, as 30 percent of today's major leaguers are Latinos, more than double the percentage of fifteen years ago.

While the winter leagues may no longer attract as many baseball stars or baseball fans, the leagues themselves are still mostly successful (though the 2002–03 Venezuelan season was cancelled as a result of domestic unrest). The Caribbean Series was revived in 1970, with Mexico and the Dominican Republic replacing Panama and Cuba. It has been played every year since then, with the exception of 1981. In 2003–04 Major League Baseball arranged for the Montreal Expos to play part of their home schedule in Puerto Rico, and both San Juan and Monterrey, Mexico bid for the Expos before the team moved to Washington DC. The Mexican League, the only significant summer league in the region, still attracts many former major leaguers, though it continues to struggle for financial security.

Baseball faces many more challenges in the Caribbean than it did a century ago, but it still remains the favorite pastime of many Latin nations.

Caribbean Series (Serie Del Caribe) Results

Yr (Series)	Winning Tm, Country	Host	Yr (Series)	Winning Tm, Country	Host
1949 (I)	Almendares, Cuba	Cuba	1982 (XXIV)	Caracas, Venez.	Mex.
1950 (II)	Carta Vieja, Pan.	P.R.	1983 (XXV)	Arecibo, P.R.	Venez.
1951 (III)	Santurce, P.R.	Venez.	1984 (XXVI)	Zulia, Venez.	P.R.
1952 (IV)	La Habana, Cuba	Pan.	1985 (XXVII)	Licey, D.R.	Mex.
1953 (V)	Santurce, P.R.	Cuba	1986 (XXVIII)	Mexicali, Mex.	Venez.
1954 (VI)	Caguas, P.R.	P.R.	1987 (XXIX)	Caguas, Venez.	Mex.
1955 (VII)	Santurce, P.R.	Venez.	1988 (XXX)	Escogido, D.R.	D.R.
1956 (VIII)	Cienfuegos, Cuba	Pan.	1989 (XXXI)	Zulia, Venez.	Mex.
1957 (IX)	Marianao, Cuba	Cuba	1990 (XXXII)	Escogido, D.R.	U.S.
1958 (X)	Marianao, Cuba	P.R.	1991 (XXXIII)	Licey, D.R.	U.S.
1959 (XI)	Almendares, Cuba	Venez.	1992 (XXXIV)	Mayaguez, P.R.	Mex.
1960 (XII)	Cienfuegos, Cuba	Pan.	1993 (XXXV)	Mayaguez, P.R.	Mex.
1970 (XIII)	Magallanes, Venez.	Venez.	1994 (XXXVI)	Licey, D.R.	Mex.
1971 (XIV)	Licey, D.R.	P.R.	1995 (XXXVII)	San Juan, P.R.	P.R.
1972 (XV)	Ponce, P.R.	D.R.	1996 (XXXVIII)	Culiacan, D.R.	D.R.
1973 (XVI)	Licey, D.R.	Venez.	1997 (XXXIX)	Aguilas, D.R.	Mex.
1974 (XVII)	Caguas, P.R.	Mex.	1998 (XL)	Aguilas, D.R.	Venez.
1975 (XVIII)	Bayamon, P.R.	P.R.	1999 (XLI)	Licey, D.R.	P.R.
1976 (XIX)	Hermosillo, Mex.	D.R.	2000 (XLII)	Santurce, P.R.	D.R.
1977 (XX)	Licey, D.R.	Venez.	2001 (XLIII)	Aguilas, D.R.	Mex.
1978 (XXI)	Mayaguez, P.R.	Mex.	2002 (XLIV)	Culiacan, D.R.	Venez.
1979 (XXII)	Magallanes, Venez.	P.R.	2003 (XLV)	Aguilas, D.R.	P.R.
1980 (XXIII)	Licey, D.R.	D.R.	2004 (XLVI)	Licey, D.R.	D.R.
			2005 (XLVII)	Mazatlan, Mex.	Mex.

Cuban Professional Baseball League Champions

Season	Team	Season	Team	Season	Team
1878–79	Habana	1910	Almendares	1937–38	Santa Clara
1879–80	Habana	1910–11	Almendares	1938–39	Santa Clara
1880–81	Habana &	1912	Habana	1939–40	Almendares
	Fe (disputed)	1913	Fe	1940–41	Habana
1882–83	Habana	1913–14	Almendares	1941–42	Almendares
1885	Habana	1914–15	Habana	1942–43	Almendares
1885–86	Habana	1915–16	Almendares	1943–44	Habana
1886–87	Habana	1917	Orientals	1944–45	Almendares
1887–88	Fe	1918–19	Habana	1945–46	Cienfuegos
1888–89	Habana	1919–20	Almendares	1946–47	Habana
1889–90	Habana	1920–21	Habana	1947–48	Habana
1890–91	Fe	1921	Habana	1948–49	Almendares
1891–92	Habana	1922–23	Marianao	1949–50	Almendares
1892–93	Matanza	1923–24	Santa Clara	1950–51	Habana
1893–94	Almendares	1924–25	Almendares	1951–52	Habana
1898–99	Habanista	1925–26	Almendares	1952–53	Habana
1900	San Francisco	1926–27	Habana	1953–54	Almendares
1901	Habana	1927–28	Habana	1954–55	Almendares
1902	Habana	1928–29	Habana	1955–56	Cienfuegos
1903	Habana	1929–30	Cienfuegos	1956–57	Marianao
1904	Habana	1931–32	Almendares	1957–58	Marianao
1905	Almendares	1932–33	Almendares	1958–59	Almendares
1906	Fe	1934–35	Almendares	1959–60	Cienfuegos
1907	Almendares		& Habana (tie)	1960–61	Cienfuegos
1908	Almendares	1935–36	Santa Clara		
1908–09	Habana	1936–37	Marianao		

Cuban Baseball Federation Champions

Year	Team	Year	Team	Year	Team
1967	Orientales	1980	Santiago de Cuba	1993	Villa Clara
1968	Habana	1981	Vegueros	1994	Villa Clara
1969	Azucareros	1982	Vegueros	1995	Villa Clara
1970	Henequeneros	1983	Villa Clara	1996	Villa Clara
1971	Azucareros	1984	Citricultores	1997	Pinar del Rio
1972	Azucareros	1985	Vegueros	1998	Pinar del Rio
1973	Industriales	1986	Industriales	1999	Santiago de Cuba
1974	Habana	1987	Vegueros	2000	Santiago de Cuba
1975	Agricultores	1988	Vegueros	2001	Santiago de Cuba
1976	Ganaderos	1989	Santiago de Cuba	2002	Holguin
1977	Citricultores	1990	Henequeneros	2003	Industriales
1978	Vegueros	1991	Henequeneros	2004	Industriales
1979	Sancti Spiritus	1992	Industriales	2005	Santiago de Cuba

Latin American Winter Leagues

Season	Puerto Rican	Venezuelan	Dominican Republic	Mexican Pacific
1940–41	Caguas			
1941–42	Ponce			
1942–43	Ponce			
1943–44	Ponce			

Latin American Winter Leagues continued

Season	Puerto Rican	Venezuelan	Dominican Republic	Mexican Pacific
1944–45	Ponce			
1945–46	San Juan	Vargas		
1946–47	Ponce	Vargas		
1947–48	Caguas	Caracas		
1948–49	Mayaguez	Caracas		
1949–50	Caguas			
1950–51	Santurce	Magallanes		
1951–52	San Juan	Magallanes	Licey (1951)	
1952–53	Santurce	Caracas	Aguilas (1952)	
1953–54	Caguas	Caracas	Licey (1953)	
1954–55	Santurce	Occidente	Estrellas Orientales (1954)	
1955–56	Caguas	Magallanes	Escogido	
1956–57	Mayaguez	Valencia	Escogido	
1957–58	Caguas	Caracas	Escogido	
1958–59	Santurce	Valencia	Licey	Guaymas
1959–60	Caguas	Valencia	Escogido	Guaymas
1960–61	San Juan	Valencia	Escogido	Hermosillo
1961–62	Santurce	Caracas		Hermosillo
1962–63	Mayaguez	Valencia		Guaymas
1963–64	San Juan	Caracas	Licey	Hermosillo
1964–65	Santurce	La Guaira	Aguilas	Guaymas
1965–66	Mayaguez	La Guaira		Obregon
1966–67	Santurce	Caracas	Aguilas	Culiacan
1967–68	Caguas	Caracas	Estrellas Orientales	Guaymas
1968–69	Ponce	La Guaira	Escogido	Los Mochis
1969–70	Ponce	Magallanes	Licey	Culiacan
1970–71	Santurce		Licey	Hermosillo
1971–72	Ponce	Aragua	Aguilas	Guasave
1972–73	Santurce	Caracas	Licey	Obregon
1973–74	Caguas		Licey	Mazatlan
1974–75	Bayamon	Aragua	Aguilas	Hermosillo
1975–76	Bayamon	Aragua	Aguilas	Hermosillo
1976–77	Caguas	Magallanes	Licey	Mazatlan
1977–78	Mayaguez	Caracas	Aguilas	Culiacan
1978–79	Caguas	Magallanes	Aguilas	Navojoa
1979–80	Bayamon	Caracas	Licey	Hermosillo
1980–81	Caguas	Caracas	Escogido	Obregon
1981–82	Ponce	Caracas	Escogido	Hermosillo
1982–83	Arecibo	La Guaira	Licey	Culiacan
1983–84	Mayaguez	Zulia	Licey	Los Mochis
1984–85	San Juan	La Guaira	Licey	Culiacan
1985–86	Mayaguez	La Guaira	Aguilas	Mexicali
1986–87	Caguas	Caracas	Aguilas	Mazatlan
1987–88	Mayaguez	Caracas	Escogido	Tijuana
1988–89	Mayaguez	Zulia	Licey	Mexicali
1989–90	San Juan	Caracas	Escogido	Hermosillo
1990–91	Santurce	Lara	Licey	Tijuana
1991–92	Mayaguez	Zulia	Escogido	Hermosillo
1992–93	Santurce	Zulia	Aguilas	Mazatlan
1993–94	San Juan	Magallanes	Licey	Hermosillo
1994–95	San Juan	Caracas	Azucueros	Hermosillo
1995–96	Arecibo	Magallanes	Aguilas	Culiacan
1996–97	Mayaguez	Magallanes	Aguilas	Culiacan
1997–98	Mayaguez	Lara	Aguilas	Mazatlan
1998–99	Mayaguez	Lara	Licey	Mexicali
1999–00	Santurce	Zulia	Aguilas	Navojoa
2000–01	Caguas	Lara	Aguilas	Hermosillo
2001–02	Bayamon	Magallanes	Licey	Culiacan
2002–03	Mayaguez		Aguilas	Los Mochis
2003–04	Ponce	Aragua	Licey	Culiacan
2004–05	Mayaguez	Aragua	Aguilas	Mazatlan

Mexican League Champions

Year	Team	Year	Team
1925	Puebla 74th Regiment	1963	Puebla Parrots
1926	Jalapa Ocampo	1964	Mexico City Red Devils
1927	Mexico City Police Station	1965	Mexico City Tigers
1928	Mexico City Police	1966	Mexico City Tigers
1929	Mexico City Adams Chiclets	1967	Jalisco Charros
1930	Comintra Tigers	1968	Mexico City Red Devils
1931	Mexico City Traffic	1969	Reynosa Broncos
1932	Mexico City Public Works	1970	Veracruz Eagle
1933	Comintra Tigers	1971	Jalisco Charros
1934	Mexico City Mercy Hill	1972	Cordoba Coffee Growers
1935	Mexico City Agrarians	1973	Mexico City Red Devils
1936	Mexico City Agrarians	1974	Mexico City Red Devils
1937	Veracruz Eagle	1975	Tampico Lightermen
1938	Veracruz Eagle	1976	Mexico City Red Devils
1939	Cordoba Coffee Growers	1977	New Laredo Owls
1940	Veracruz Blues	1978	Aguascalientes Railroadmen
1941	Veracruz Blues	1979	Puebla Angels
1942	Torreon (Union Laguna) Cotton Dealers	1980	Puebla Angels
1943	Monterrey Sultans	1981	Mexico City Red Devils
1944	Veracruz Blues	1982	Ciudad Juarez Indians
1945	Tampico Lightermen	1983	Campeche Pirates
1946	Tampico Lightermen	1984	Yucatan Lions
1947	Monterrey Sultans	1985	Mexico City Red Devils
1948	Monterrey Sultans	1986	Puebla Angels
1949	Monterrey Sultans	1987	Mexico City Red Devils
1950	Torreon (Union Laguna) Cotton Dealers	1988	Mexico City Red Devils
1951	Veracruz Blues	1989	Laredo Owls
1952	Veracruz Eagle	1990	Leon Braves
1953	Nuevo Laredo Owls	1991	Monterrey Sultans
1954	Nuevo Laredo Owls	1992	Mexico City Tigers
1955	Mexico City Tigers	1993	Tabasco Olmecs
1956	Mexico City Red Devils	1994	Mexico City Red Devils
1957	Yucatan Lions	1995	Monterrey Sultans
1958	New Laredo Owls	1996	Monterrey Sultans
1959	Poza Rica Oilers	1997	Mexico City Tigers
1960	Mexico City Tigers	1998	Oaxaca Warriors
1961	Veracruz Eagles	1999	Mexico City Red Devils
1962	Monterrey Sultans	2000	Mexico City Tigers

Mexican League Champions continued

Year	Team	Year	Team
2001	Mexico City Tigers	2004	Campeche Pirates
2002	Mexico City Red Devils	2005	Mexico City Tigers
2003	Mexico City Red Devils		

Note: Mexican League championship series were played in 1949–51, 1966, 1970–79, and 1981–present. Prior to 1970, the first-half winner played the second-half winner. Since 1970 the league has been divided into divisions. In 1980, Puebla had the best record in a strike-shortened season.

THE OLYMPICS

Baseball appeared as a demonstration sport in six different Olympics (1912, 1936, 1956, 1964, 1984, and 1988) before being accepted as a medal sport. Its future in the Olympics, however, is not assured. Despite the lifting of the ban on professional players before the 2000 Olympics in Sydney, Australia, Major League Baseball has shown no interest in interrupting its regular season to let the best players in the world participate in Olympic competition. Consequently, the International Olympic Committee has voted to drop baseball from the Olympics after the 2008 Olympic Games in Beijing, China.

The International Baseball Federation is working to reverse that decision and return baseball to the Olympics in future competitions. Nevertheless, Major League Baseball's blase attitude towards the Olympics and USA Baseball's failure to earn its way to the 2004 Olympics (the national team lost to Mexico in the qualifying tournament) has lengthened the odds against the IBF succeeding.

Olympic Medal Winners

Year	Host City (Country)	Gold	Silver	Bronze
1992	Barcelona (Spain)	Cuba	Chinese Taipei	Japan
1996	Atlanta (U.S.)	Cuba	Japan	United States
2000	Sydney (Australia)	United States	Cuba	South Korea
2004	Athens (Greece)	Cuba	Australia	Japan

Note: Japan won the virtual gold medal when baseball was a demonstration sport in 1984 the United States won the demonstration competition in 1988.

THE PAN AMERICAN GAMES

The Pan American Games were originally proposed in the 1930s. The first games were scheduled for 1942, but World War II and its aftermath delayed the initial games until 1951. The games have since been held every four years as scheduled and have steadily grown in size: more than 5,000 athletes from 42 countries participated in the most recent competition in the Dominican Republic.

The Pan American Sports Organization runs the games, which follow the same rules and eligibility requirements as the Olympics. The competition includes every sport featured in the Summer Olympics, although it is not limited to those sports. Thus, the National Pastime of the United States and several Latin American countries has been a major part of the Pan American Games since their inception.

Over the history of the games, the United States and Cuba have both won 12 medals in baseball, though Cuba has won 1 gold medals while the United States has won only one. While professional athletes are now permitted to participate in the Pan Am Games, it seems unlikely that major league players will be featured in the competition in the near future because of the calendar conflict with MLB's regular season.

Year	Host City (Country)	Gold	Silver	Bronze
1951	Buenos Aires (Argentina)	Cuba	United States	Mexico
1955	Mexico City	Dominican Rep.	United States	Venezuela
1959	Chicago (U.S.)	Venezuela	Puerto Rico	United States
1963	Sao Paulo (Brazil)	Cuba	United States	Mexico
1967	Winnipeg (Canada)	United States	Cuba	Puerto Rico
1971	Cali (Colombia)	Cuba	United States	Colombia
1975	Mexico City	Cuba	United States	Venezuela
1979	San Juan (Puerto Rico)	Cuba	Dominican Rep.	Puerto Rico
1983	Caracas (Venezuela)	Cuba	Nicaragua	United States
1987	Indianapolis (U.S.)	Cuba	United States	Puerto Rico
1991	Havana (Cuba)	Cuba	Puerto Rico	United States
1995	Mar del Plata (Argentina)	Cuba	Nicaragua	Puerto Rico
1999	Winnipeg	Cuba	United States	Canada
2003	Santo Domingo (D.R.)	Cuba	United States	Mexico

BASEBALL IN JAPAN

Japanese baseball and American baseball have moved much closer during the last decade. Stars such as Hide Nomo, Kazuhiro Sasaki, Ichiro Suzuki, and Hideki Mats have successfully moved from Japan to America, as have lesser players in non-starring roles. Players with experience in the United States, such as Roberto Petagine, still cross the Pacific in the other direction seeking greater opportunity. American fans who know little about Japanese baseball are now almost forced to pay some attention.

Baseball has been played in Japan since the nineteenth century, first in 1873 at Tokyo University under the tutelage of an American professor. After the turn of the century, baseball became extremely popular in both high school and college. American baseball players started touring Japan after 1910, and the efforts of a man named Herbert Hunter helped school thousands of Japanese boys in the fundamentals of the game. An All-Star tour in 1934, featuring Babe Ruth, Lou Gehrig, Jimmy Foxx, Al Simmons and Lefty Gomez, left the greatest impression. The first professional Japanese team was the group organized to play these All-Stars. That team would become known as the Tokyo Giants, and by 1936 six other teams would join the Giants in the new Japanese Professional Baseball League.

World War II disrupted the new league, but the American occupying force brought the game back in 1946. In 1950 Japanese professional baseball added seven new teams and split into two leagues, the Central and the Pacific. Professional baseball grew in popularity over the next several decades, with television giving it a big boost. The Giants dominated Japanese baseball during this period, winning far more Japan Series (and fans) than any other team. Baseball remains Japan's most popular sport, though there are serious concerns about what the continuing loss of much of its star talent to the United States will mean for the Japanese game in the future.

Japan Professional Baseball League Champions

Year	Team	Year	Team
1937	Spring: Tokyo Giants	1942	Tokyo Giants
	Fall: Osaka Tigers	1943	Tokyo Giants
1938	Spring: Osaka Tigers	1944	Hanshin
	Fall: Tokyo Giants	1946	Kinki Greatring
1939	Tokyo Giants	1947	Osaka Tigers
1940	Tokyo Giants	1948	Nankai Hawks
1941	Tokyo Giants	1949	Yomiuri Giants

Japan Series Champions

Year	Central League Winner	Pacific League Winner	Series Result
1950	Shochiku Robins	Mainichi Orions	Orions, 4-2
1951	Yomiuri Giants	Nankai Hawks	Giants, 4-1
1952	Yomiuri Giants	Nankai Hawks	Giants, 4-2
1953	Yomiuri Giants	Nankai Hawks	Giants, 4-2-1
1954	Chunichi Dragons	Nishitetsu Lions	Dragons, 4-3
1955	Yomiuri Giants	Nankai Hawks	Giants, 4-3
1956	Yomiuri Giants	Nishitetsu Lions	Lions, 4-2
1957	Yomiuri Giants	Nishitetsu Lions	Lions, 4-0-1
1958	Yomiuri Giants	Nishitetsu Lions	Lions, 4-3
1959	Yomiuri Giants	Nankai Hawks	Hawks, 4-0
1960	Taiyo Whales	Daimai Orions	Whales, 4-0
1961	Yomiuri Giants	Nankai Hawks	Giants, 4-2
1962	Hanshin Tigers	Toei Flyers	Flyers, 4-2-1
1963	Yomiuri Giants	Nishitetsu Lions	Giants, 4-3
1964	Hanshin Tigers	Nankai Hawks	Hawks, 4-3
1965	Yomiuri Giants	Nankai Hawks	Giants, 4-1
1966	Yomiuri Giants	Nankai Hawks	Giants, 4-2
1967	Yomiuri Giants	Hankyu Braves	Giants, 4-2
1968	Yomiuri Giants	Hankyu Braves	Giants, 4-2
1969	Yomiuri Giants	Hankyu Braves	Giants, 4-2
1970	Yomiuri Giants	Lotte Orions	Giants, 4-1
1971	Yomiuri Giants	Hankyu Braves	Giants, 4-1
1972	Yomiuri Giants	Hankyu Braves	Giants, 4-1
1973	Yomiuri Giants	Nankai Hawks	Giants, 4-1
1974	Chunichi Dragons	Lotte Orions	Orions, 4-2
1975	Hiroshima Carp	Hankyu Braves	Braves, 4-0-2
1976	Yomiuri Giants	Hankyu Braves	Braves, 4-3
1977	Yomiuri Giants	Hankyu Braves	Braves, 4-1
1978	Yakult Swallows	Hankyu Braves	Swallows, 4-3
1979	Hiroshima Carp	Kintetsu Buffaloes	Carp, 4-3
1980	Hiroshima Carp	Kintetsu Buffaloes	Carp, 4-3
1981	Yomiuri Giants	Nippon Ham Fighters	Giants, 4-2
1982	Chunichi Dragons	Seibu Lions	Lions, 4-2
1983	Yomiuri Giants	Seibu Lions	Lions, 4-3
1984	Hiroshima Carp	Hankyu Braves	Carp, 4-3
1985	Hanshin Tigers	Seibu Lions	Tigers, 4-2
1986	Hiroshima Carp	Seibu Lions	Lions, 4-3-1
1987	Yomiuri Giants	Seibu Lions	Lions, 4-2
1988	Chunichi Dragons	Seibu Lions	Lions, 4-1
1989	Yomiuri Giants	Kintetsu Buffaloes	Giants, 4-3
1990	Yomiuri Giants	Seibu Lions	Lions, 4-0
1991	Hiroshima Carp	Seibu Lions	Lions, 4-3
1992	Yakult Swallows	Seibu Lions	Lions, 4-3
1993	Yakult Swallows	Seibu Lions	Swallows, 4-3
1994	Yomiuri Giants	Seibu Lions	Giants, 4-2
1995	Yakult Swallows	Orix BlueWave	Swallows, 4-3
1996	Yomiuri Giants	Orix BlueWave	BlueWave, 4-1

Japan Series Champions continued

Year	Central League Winner	Pacific League Winner	Series Result
1997	Yakult Swallows	Seibu Lions	Swallows, 4-1
1998	Yokohama BayStars	Seibu Lions	Bay Stars, 4-2
1999	Chunichi Dragons	Fukuoka Daiei Hawks	Hawks, 4-1
2000	Yomiuri Giants	Fukuoka Daiei Hawks	Giants, 4-2
2001	Yakult Swallows	Kintetsu Buffaloes	Swallows, 4-1
2002	Yomiuri Giants	Seibu Lions	Giants, 4-0
2003	Hanshin Tigers	Fukuoka Daiei Hawks	Hawks, 4-3
2004	Chunichi Dragons	Seibu Lions	Lions, 4-3
2005	Hanshin Tigers	Chiba Lotte Marines	Marines, 4-0

TAIWAN

Japanese occupying forces introduced baseball to Taiwan in 1905. The Taiwanese picked up the game in the 1920s and even provided Japan with a few professional players before World War II. Baseball grew in Taiwan after the war, though primarily on the amateur level. The nation became a juggernaut in Little League competition and also had significant success in other international competitions.

It wasn't until 1990 that the country's first professional baseball league, the Chinese Professional Baseball League, was organized. The league was successful almost immediately, but a huge gambling operation that was fixing CPBL games came to light in 1996, greatly damaging the loop's credibility. A second baseball league, the Taiwan Major League, emerged in 1997 and further weakened the CPBL. The two leagues finally merged in 2003, and that fall came more good news when the national team upset South Korea to qualify for the Olympics. Baseball is arguably the most popular sport in Taiwan, so the CPBL could have a bright future if it can avoid repeating its past problems.

Chinese Professional Baseball League Champions

Year	Team	Year	Team
1989	Weichuan Dragons	1998	Weichuan Dragons
1990	President Lions	1999	President Lions
1991	Brother Elephants	2000	Sinon Bulls
1992	Brother Elephants	2001	Brother Elephants
1993	Brother Elephants	2002	Brother Elephants
1994	President Lions	2003	Brother Elephants
1995	President Lions	2004	Sinon Bulls
1996	Weichuan Dragons	2005	Sinon Bulls
1997	Weichuan Dragons		

Taiwan Major League Champions

Year	Team	Year	Team
1997	Chia-Nan Braves	2000	Taipei Suns
1998	Taipei Suns	2001	Taichung Robots
1999	Taichung Robots	2002	Taichung Robots

SOUTH KOREA

In 1905 an American missionary introduced baseball to Korea, but it wasn't until 1982 that the government of South Korea decided to instigate the creation of a professional league. The newly formed Korean Baseball Organization proved to be a success, but its progress was halted in the mid-1990s by the country's financial crisis. More recently, Korean baseball has lost a number of talented players to the major leagues. In response the KBO began allowing teams to sign non-Koreans in 1998. The league still faces many challenges, including fallout from the recent failure of the South Korean national team to qualify for the 2004 Olympics.

Korean Series Champions

Year	Team	Year	Team	Year	Team
1982	OB Bears	1990	LG Twins	1998	Hyundai Unicorns
1983	Haitai Tigers	1991	Haitai Tigers	1999	Hyundai Unicorns
1984	Lotte Giants	1992	Lotte Giants	2000	Hyundai Unicorns
1985	Samsung Lions	1993	Haitai Tigers	2001	Doosan Bears
1986	Haitai Tigers	1994	LG Twins	2002	Samsung Lions
1987	Haitai Tigers	1995	OB Bears	2003	Hyundai Unicorns
1988	Haitai Tigers	1996	Haitai Tigers	2004	Hyundai Unicorns
1989	Haitai Tigers	1997	Haitai Tigers	2005	Samsung Lions

KONAMI CUP ASIA SERIES

On November 13, 2005, the Chiba Lotte Marines emerged as the winners of the inaugural Konami Cup, a contest between Japan, Taiwan, South Korea, and China to determine an East Asian baseball champion. The initial tournament featured competition between the 2005 winners of the Japan Series, Korean Series, and Chinese Baseball Championship Series along with a team of all-stars from mainland China. The four-day event consisted of three days of round-robin combination (with two games played each day) along with a championship game on the last night featuring the two best teams from the first three days. Though the idea for the competition came from South Korea and Taiwan, the inaugural edition of the Cup was held in Japan, where all games were played in the Tokyo Dome. Prize money of 100 million yen was awarded to the participating teams, with half of that going to the Cup winner. The series finale drew a crowd of 37,000 and attracted 15 percent of the television audience in Japan, so the initial Konami Cup was considered a success and a second series is planned for 2006.

Year	Champion (W-L)	Runner-Up (W-L)	Score	MVP	Location
2005	Chiba Lotte Marines (4-0)	Samsung Lions (2-2)	5-3	Benny Agbayani (CLM)	Tokyo Dome

AUSTRALIA

According to legend, the first baseball game in Australia was played by American visitors in the 1850s. Australians first participated in a baseball game in 1879 when a local cricket team played a visiting minstrel group from the United States. Most Australians remained ignorant about baseball until A.G. Spalding and his Chicago White Stockings team came to Australia in late 1888 to promote the sport throughout the country. Spalding's tour was very successful and planted the game "down under" permanently.

In 1934, three Australian states sent their teams to Adelaide to compete for the first Claxton Shield. All of Australia's mainland states were participating in the competition by 1939 and, following World War II, the Shield competition would be held annually until 1989.

Controversy ended the Claxton Shield and left an opening in the Australia baseball world, which was quickly filled by Australia's first professional league, the Australian Baseball League. Unfortunately, the league proved to have a lot more talent on the field than off it. By 1998 it was clear that the ABL was in terrible financial trouble. Former ABL player (and major league All-Star) David Nilsson purchased the ABL's assets and tried to build a better league, the International Baseball League of Australia, out of the ABL's ashes. The new league was a disaster, though, and barely made it through one season before collapsing.

Australia today continues to do without a national baseball competition. However, baseball is still very popular on the local level and the country continues to produce talent capable of playing at a very high level. It is certainly possible that a new national league will rise again during the next decade, perhaps with the aid of Major League Baseball.

Australian Baseball League Champions

Season	Team	Season	Team
1989–90	Waverly	1995–96	Sydney Blues
1990–91	Perth	1996–97	Perth
1991–92	Gold Coast	1997–98	Melbourne Reds
1992–93	Melbourne	1998–99	Gold Coast
1993–94	Brisbane	1999–00	Western Heelers
1994–95	Waverly		

COLLEGE BASEBALL

The first college baseball game was played on July 1, 1859 in Pittsfield, Massachusetts between Amherst and Williams. Amherst won the game by the incredible score of 73-32. Baseball fans watching a videotape of such a game would recognize the sport's similarities to baseball, but they would also find the play proceeding very differently, especially due to the shorter distances between the bases and between the mound and the batter's box. Baseball's rules had not been standardized in 1859; by the time the first professional league emerged 12 years later, the game more closely resembled that of today.

Since 1871, when the National Association began play, college has served as a feeder system to the professional leagues. Its significance as a factor in the development of major league players has waxed and waned, depending on the importance placed by society on attending college as well as the scope of minor league baseball and the influence of international scouting. For much of professional baseball's early history, some of the nation's most talented college athletes chose a different career path than that of a pro ballplayer. As a result, the top

college teams of the late 1800s and early 1900s were far clo to a major league talent level than college teams are today.

Despite talented players, early college baseball drew lit attention from baseball fans. The major universities of t Northeast and Midwest played the best college ball, but th also suffered from the worst weather. After World War II, ho ever, the NCAA created the College World Series, an event th slowly but surely increased the overall popularity of colle baseball. The first two College World Series were held Kalamazoo, Michigan in 1947–48. In 1949 the tourname moved to Omaha, Nebraska, where it has remained ever sin

The biggest difference between college baseball and maj league baseball may be the aluminum bat, introduced in 19 by the NCAA at the same it adopted the DH rule. Aluminu bats changed the college game dramatically. The high scoring games attracted more fans and fewer broken bats ma it cheaper to run a college baseball program. Metal bats al made for a much rougher transition for hitters going from c lege to the minor leagues. The latter problem has led to the fo mation of summer prospect leagues, where top college baseb players around the continent use wooden bats. The most fa ous such loop is the Cape Cod League.

Since ESPN began broadcasting the College World Seri in 1989, the popularity of college baseball has grown ev further, especially in those climates hospitable to the game in la winter. After many years in which Southwestern teams domina ed the CWS, teams from the South and Southeast captured t majority of championships in the 1990s. The lists below conta the results of every College World Series played, as well as t championship series played NAIA college teams, plus the Mc Outstanding Player selections for the various series.

At the end of the collegiate championships are the winne of the two most prestigious awards for college ballplayers: t Golden Spikes Award and the *Baseball America*'s Colle Player of the Year award.

USA Baseball, the national governing body for the spo and the organization responsible for putting together t national baseball teams representing the USA, was created an act of Congress in 1978. It selects the best amateur baseba player in the country, who receives the Golden Spikes Awar The award does not necessarily have to go to a college baseba player, but it always has so far. *Baseball America* has chosen i highly regarded College Player of the Year every year since t newspaper's inception in 1981. Not surprisingly, the two awar often go the same player.

NCAA Division I College World Series

Year	Winner	Runner-up	Scr	Year	Winner	Runner-up	Scr
1947	California*	Yale	8-7	1977	Arizona St.	South Carolina	2-
1948	USC	Yale	9-2	1978	USC*	Arizona St.	10
1949	Texas*	Wake Forest	10-3	1979	Cal St.-Fullerton	Arkansas	2-
1950	Texas	Washington St.	3-0	1980	Arizona	Hawaii	5-
1951	Oklahoma*	Tennessee	3-2	1981	Arizona St.	Oklahoma St.	7-
1952	Holy Cross	Missouri	8-4	1982	Miami*	Wichita St.	9-
1953	Michigan	Texas	7-5	1983	Texas*	Alabama	4-
1954	Missouri	Rollins	4-1	1984	Cal St.-Fullerton	Texas	3-
1955	Wake Forest	Western Michigan	7-6	1985	Miami	Texas	10
1956	Minnesota	Arizona	12-1	1986	Arizona	Florida St.	10
1957	California*	Penn St.	1-0	1987	Stanford	Oklahoma St.	9-
1958	USC	Missouri	8-7	1988	Stanford	Arizona St.	9-
1959	Oklahoma St	Arizona	5-3	1989	Wichita St.	Texas	5-
1960	Minnesota	USC	2-1	1990	Georgia	Oklahoma St.	2-
1961	USC*	Oklahoma St.	1-0	1991	Louisiana St.*	Wichita St.	6-
1962	Michigan	Santa Clara	5-4	1992	Pepperdine*	Cal St.-Fullerton	3-
1963	USC	Arizona	5-2	1993	Louisiana St.	Wichita St.	8-
1964	Minnesota	Missouri	5-1	1994	Oklahoma*	Georgia Tech	13
1965	Arizona St.	Ohio St.	2-1	1995	Cal St.-Fullerton*	USC	11
1966	Ohio St.	Oklahoma St.	8-2	1996	Louisiana St.*	Miami	9-
1967	Arizona St.	Houston	11-2	1997	Louisiana St.*	Alabama	13
1968	USC*	Southern Illinois	4-3	1998	USC	Arizona St.	2-
1969	Arizona St.	Tulsa	10-1	1999	Miami*	Florida St.	6-8
1970	USC	Florida St.	2-1	2000	Louisiana St.*	Stanford	6-4
1971	USC	Southern Illinois	7-2	2001	Miami*	Stanford	12
1972	USC	Arizona St.	1-0	2002	Texas*	South Carolina	12
1973	USC*	Arizona St.	4-3	2003	Rice	Stanford	14
1974	USC	Miami	7-3	2004	Cal St.-Fullerton	Texas	3-2
1975	Texas	South Carolina	5-1	2005	Texas	Florida	6-2
1976	Arizona	Eastern Michigan	7-1				

*Undefeated in World Series play

Division I Most Outstanding Player

Year	Player	School	Year	Player	School
1949	Charles Teague 2B	Wake Forest	1978	Rod Boxberger P	USC
1950	Ray Van Cleef CF	Rutgers	1979	Tony Hudson P	Cal St.-Fullerton
1951	Sidney Hatfield P-1B	Tennessee	1980	Terry Francona LF	Arizona
1952	James O'Neill P	Holy Cross	1981	Stan Holmes LF	Arizona St.
1953	J.L. Smith P	Texas	1982	Dan Smith P	Miami
1954	Tom Yewcic C	Michigan	1983	Calvin Schiraldi P	Texas
1955	Tom Borland P	Oklahoma St.	1984	John Fishel LF	Cal St.-Fullerton
1956	Jerry Thomas P	Minnesota	1985	Greg Ellena DH	Miami
1957	Cal Emery P-1B	Penn St.	1986	Mike Senne LF	Arizona
1958	Bill Thom P	USC	1987	Paul Carey RF	Stanford
1959	Jim Dobson 3B	Oklahoma St.	1988	Lee Pleme P	Stanford
1960	John Erickson 2B	Minnesota	1989	Greg Brummett P	Wichita St.
1961	Littleton Fowler P	Oklahoma St.	1990	Mike Rehban P	Georgia
1962	Bob Garibaldi P	Santa Clara	1991	Gary Hymel C	Louisiana St.
1963	Bud Hollowell c	USC	1992	Phil Nevin 3B	Cal St.-Fullerton
1964	Joe Ferris P	Maine	1993	Todd Walker 2B	Louisiana St.
1965	Sal Bando 3B	Arizona St.	1994	Chip Glass OF	Oklahoma
1966	Steve Arlin P	Ohio St.	1995	Mark Kotsay OF-P	Cal St.-Fullerton
1967	Ron Davini C	Arizona St.	1996	Pat Burrell 3B	Miami
1968	Bill Seinsoth 1B	USC	1997	Brandon Larson SS	Louisiana St.
1969	John Dolinsek lf	Arizona State	1998	Jason Lane P-DH	USC
1970	Gene Ammann P	Florida St.	1999	Marshall McDougall 2B	Florida St.
1971	Jerry Tabb 1B	Tulsa	2000	Trey Hodges P	Louisiana St.
1972	Russ McQueen P	USC	2001	Charlton Jimerson CF	Miami
1973	Dave Winfield P-OF	Minnesota	2002	Huston Street P	Texas
1974	George Milke P	USC	2003	John Hudgins P	Stanford
1975	M. Reichenbach 1B	Texas	2004	Jason Windsor P	Cal St.-Fullerton
1976	Steve Powers P-DH	Arizona	2005	David Maroul 3B	Texas
1977	Bob Horner 3B	Arizona St.			

NCAA Division II College World Series

Year	Winner	Runner-Up	Score
1968	Chapman*	Delta St.	11-0
1969	Illinois St.*	Southwest Missouri	12-0
1970	Cal St.-Northridge	Nicholls St.	2-1
1971	Florida Southern	Central Michigan	4-0
1972	Florida Southern	Cal St.-Northridge	5-1
1973	California-Irvine*	Ithaca	9-6
1974	California-Irvine	New Orleans	14-0
1975	Florida Southern	Marietta	10-7
1976	Cal Poly-Pomona	So. Illinois-Edwardsville	17-3
1977	California-Riverside	Eckerd	4-1
1978	Florida Southern	Delta St.	7-2
1979	Valdosta St.	Florida Southern	3-2
1980	Cal Poly-Pomona	New Haven	13-6
1981	Florida Southern*	Eastern Illinois	9-0
1982	California-Riverside*	Florida Southern	10-1
1983	Cal Poly-Pomona	Jacksonville St.	9-7
1984	Cal St.-Northridge	Florida Southern	10-5
1985	Florida Southern*	Cal Poly-Pomona	15-5
1986	Troy St.	Columbus St.	5-0
1987	Troy St.*	Tampa	7-5
1988	Florida Southern*	Cal St.-Sacramento	5-4
1989	Cal Poly-San Luis Obispo	New Haven	9-5
1990	Jacksonville St.	Cal St.-Northridge	12-8
1991	Jacksonville St.	Missouri Southern	20-4
1992	Tampa	Mansfield	7-5
1993	Tampa*	Cal Poly-San Luis Obispo	14-9
1994	Central Missouri	Florida Southern	14-9
1995	Florida Southern*	Georgia College	15-0
1996	Kennesaw St.*	St. Joseph's (IN)	4-0
1997	Cal St.-Chico*	Central Oklahoma	13-12
1998	Tampa*	Kennesaw St.	6-1
1999	Cal St.-Chico	Kennesaw St.	11-5
2000	Southeastern Oklahoma	Fort Hays St.	7-2
2001	St. Mary's (TX)	Central Missouri	11-3
2002	Columbus St.	Cal St.-Chico	5-3
2003	Central Missouri*	Tampa	11-4
2004	Delta St.	Grand Valley St.	12-8
2005	Florida Southern	North Florida	12-9

*Undefeated in World Series play
*Participation vacated by the NCAA Committee on Infractions

Division II Most Outstanding Player

Year	Winner	School	Year	Winner	School
1968	Tony Spono OF	Chapman	1986	Wendell Stephens 3B	Troy St.
1969	Tom Klein 1B	Illinois St.	1987	Jude Rinaldi 1B	Troy St.
1970	Chuck Stone OF	Cal St.-Northridge	1988	Chris Leach P	Florida Southern
1971	Greg Pryor 2B	Florida Southern	1989	Steve DiBartolomeo P	New Haven
	Kevin Bryant 3B	Florida Southern	1990	Tim Van Egmond P	Jacksonville St.
1972	Jay Smith P	Florida Southern	1991	Tim Van Egmond P	Jacksonville St.
1973	Terry Stupy C	California Irvine	1992	Joe Urso 2B	Tampa
1974	Jeff Malinoff 1B	California Irvine	1993	David Dion OF	Tampa
1975	Joe Yazombek C	Marietta	1994	James Vida 1B	Florida Southern
1976	Ken Hellyer OF	Cal Poly-Pomona	1995	Brett Tomko P	Florida Southern
1977	Joe Lefebvre OF-P	Eckerd	1996	Chris Halliday C	Kennesaw St.
	Steve Glaum P	California Riverside	1997	Angel Diaz C	Tampa
1978	Ricky Perkins 3B	Delta St.	1998	Ronnie Merrill SS	Tampa
1979	Frank DeGennaro OF	Valdosta St.	1999	John-Eric Hernandez P	Cal St.-Chico
1980	Brian Zell OF	Cal Poly-Pomona	2000	Aaron Thompson P	Southeastern Oklahoma
1981	Joe Sickles OF	Florida Southern	2001	Jesse Guttierez 1B	St. Mary's (TX)
1982	Joe Sickles OF	Florida Southern	2002	Brian Baker P	Columbus St.
1983	Larry Beardman OF	Cal Poly-Pomona	2003	Jay Hyland OF	Tampa
1984	Perry Husband 2B	Cal St.-Northridge	2004	Bert Pickard 1B	Delta St.
1985	Tom Temrowski 1B	Florida Southern	2005	Kyle DeYoung P	Florida Southern

NCAA Division III College World Series

Year	Winner	Runner-Up	Score
1976	Cal St.-Stanislaus	Ithaca	13-6
1977	Cal St.-Stanislaus	Brandeis	8-5
1978	Rowan	Marietta	5-3
1979	Rowan	Cal St.-Stanislaus	3-0
1980	Ithaca	Marietta	12-5
1981	Marietta	Ithaca	13-12
1982	Eastern Connecticut	Cal St.-Stanislaus	11-6
1983	Marietta	Otterbein	36-8
1984	Ramapo	Marietta	5-4
1985	Wisconsin-Oshkosh	Marietta	11-6
1986	Marietta	Ithaca	11-6
1987	Montclair St.	Wisconsin-Oshkosh	13-12
1988	Ithaca	Wisconsin-Oshkosh	7-5
1989	N.C. Wesleyan	Cal St.-Stanislaus	8-7
1990	Eastern Connecticut	Aurora (IL)	8-1
1991	Southern Maine	Trenton St.	9-0
1992	William Paterson	California Lutheran	3-1
1993	Montclair St.	Wisconsin-Oshkosh	3-1
1994	Wisconsin-Oshkosh	Wesleyan (CT)	6-2
1995	La Verne	Methodist (NC)	5-3
1996	William Patterson	California Lutheran	6-5
1997	Southern Maine	Wooster	15-1
1998	Eastern Connecticut	Montclair St.	16-1
1999	N.C. Wesleyan	St. Thomas (MN)	1-0
2000	Montclair St.	St. Thomas (MN)	6-2
2001	St. Thomas (MN)	Marietta	8-4
2002	Eastern Connecticut	Marietta	8-0
2003	Chapman	Christopher Newport	15-7
2004	George Fox	Eastern Connecticut	6-3
2005	Wis.-Whitewater	Cortland St.	11-4

Division III Most Outstanding Player

Year	Winner	School	Year	Winner	School
1976	Dan Boer 1B	Cal St.-Stanislaus	1991	Gary Williamson OF	Southern Maine
1977	Rusty Kuntz OF	Cal St.-Stanislaus	1992	Ralph Perdomo 1B	William Patterson
1978	Bob Pfeffer P	Rowan	1993	Drew Yocum P	Montclair St.
1979	Tap Upshur 2B	Rowan	1994	Tim Jorgensen SS	Wis.-Oshkosh
1980	John Nicolo SS	Ithaca	1995	Jeff Polinsky 3B	La Verne
1981	John Schaly 2B	Marietta	1996	Mark deMenna OF	William Patterson
1982	Jeff Biobaum P	Cal St.-Stanislaus	1997	Jason Jensen P	Southern Maine
1983	Jim Pancher 2B	Marietta	1998	Chris D'Amato 2B	Eastern Connecticut
1984	Derek Bastinck C	Ramapo	1999	Barry Blake SS	Wesleyan (CT)
1985	Terry Jorgensen LF	Wisconsin-Oshkosh	2000	Corey Hamman P	Montclair St.
1986	Mike Brandis 3B	Marietta	2001	Brad Bonine CF	St. Thomas (MN)
1987	John Deutsch RF	Montclair St.	2002	John Kubachka 1B	Eastern Connecticut
1988	Joe Sottolano P	Ithaca	2003	Alex Taylor 2B	Chapman
1989	James Anderson 1B	N.C. Wesleyan	2004	Scott Hyde P	George Fox
1990	Brian Mercado DH	Eastern Connecticut	2005	Kevin Tomasiewicz P	Wis.-Whitewater

NAIA World Series

Year	Champion	Runner-Up	Score (Inn.)
1957	Sul Ross St. (TX)	Rollins (FL)	8-7
1958	San Diego St. (CA)	Southwestern Oklahoma	23-9
1959	Southern-Baton Rouge (LA)	Nebraska-Omaha	10-2
1960	Whitworth (WA)	Georgia Southern	4-0
1961	East Carolina (NC)	Sacramento St. (CA)	13-7
1962	Georgia Southern	Portland St. (OR)	2-1
1963	Sam Houston St. (TX)	Grambling (LA)	2-1
1964	West Liberty St. (WV)	Grambling (LA)	3-2
1965	Carson-Newman (TN)	Nebraska-Omaha	3-2
1966	Linfield (OR)	Lewis (IL)	15-4
1967	New Mexico Highlands	Glassboro St. (NJ)	6-1
1968	William Jewell (MO)	Georgia Southern	4-3 (13)
1969	William Carey (MS)	La Verne (CA)	5-3
1970	Eastern Michigan	Northeastern Louisiana	1-0
1971	Linfield (OR)	David Lipscomb (TN)	9-8 (10)
1972	La Verne (CA)	David Lipscomb (TN)	4-1
1973	U.S. International (CA)	Eastern Connecticut	7-2
1974	Lewis (IL)	Sam Houston St. (TX)	3-2
1975	Lewis (IL)	Sam Houston St. (TX)	2-1
1976	Lewis (IL)	Lewis-Clark St. (ID)	16-8
1977	David Lipscomb (TN)	Southeastern Oklahoma	2-1
1978	Emporia St. (KS)	Missouri Southern	8-6
1979	David Lipscomb (TN)	High Point (NC)	5-4
1980	Grand Canyon (AZ)	Lewis (IL)	5-4 (10)
1981	Grand Canyon (AZ)	Winthrop (SC)	11-4
1982	Grand Canyon (AZ)	Lewis-Clark St. (ID)	10-6
1983	Lubbock Christian (TX)	Lewis-Clark St. (ID)	12-9
1984	Lewis-Clark St. (ID)	Azusa Pacific (CA)	15-2
1985	Lewis-Clark St. (ID)	Dallas Baptist (TX)	10-6
1986	Grand Canyon (AZ)	Lewis-Clark St. (ID)	6-5 (10)
1987	Lewis-Clark St. (ID)	Emporia St. (KS)	11-4
1988	Lewis-Clark St. (ID)	Grand Canyon (AZ)	9-3
1989	Lewis-Clark St. (ID)	St. Francis (IL)	5-2
1990	Lewis-Clark St. (ID)	Auburn-Montgomery (AL)	9-4
1991	Lewis-Clark St. (ID)	Oral Roberts (OK)	7-0
1992	Lewis-Clark St. (ID)	Mary Hardin-Baylor (TX)	14-4
1993	St. Francis (IL)	Southeastern Oklahoma	4-2
1994	Kennesaw St. (GA)	Southeastern Oklahoma	2-0
1995	Bellevue (NE)	Cumberland (TN)	8-5
1996	Lewis-Clark St. (ID)	St. Ambrose (IA)	9-0
1997	Brewton-Parker (GA)	Bellevue (NE)	8-4
1998	Albertson (ID)	Indiana Tech	6-3
1999	Lewis-Clark St. (ID)	Albertson (ID)	7-2
2000	Lewis-Clark St. (ID)	Dallas Baptist (TX)	10-1
2001	Birmingham-Southern (AL)	Lewis-Clark St. (ID)	8-3
2002	Lewis-Clark St. (ID)	Oklahoma City	12-8
2003	Lewis-Clark St. (ID)	Oklahoma City	7-5
2004	Cumberland (TN)	Oklahoma City	10-3
2005	Oklahoma City	Embry-Riddle (FL)	8-1

USA Baseball Golden Spikes Award Winner

Year	Winner	School	Year	Winner	School
1978	Bob Horner 3B	Arizona St.	1981	Mike Fuentes OF	Florida St.
1979	Tim Wallach 1B	Cal St.-Fullerton	1982	Augie Schmidt SS	New Orleans
1980	Terry Francona OF	Arizona	1983	Dave Magadan 1B	Alabama

Year	Winner	School	Year	Winner	School
1984	Oddibe McDowell OF	Arizona St.	1995	Mark Kotsay OF-P	Cal St.-Fullerton
1985	Will Clark 1B	Mississippi St.	1996	Travis Lee 1B	San Diego St.
1986	Mike Loynd P	Florida St.	1997	J.D. Drew OF	Florida St.
1987	Jim Abbott P	Michigan	1998	Pat Burrell 3B	Miami
1988	Robin Ventura 3B	Oklahoma St.	1999	Jason Jennings DH-P	Baylor
1989	Ben McDonald P	Louisiana St.	2000	Kip Bouknight P	South Carolina
1990	Alex Fernandez P	Miami-Dade South	2001	Mark Prior P	USC
1991	Mike Kelly OF	Arizona St.	2002	Khalil Greene SS	Clemson
1992	Phil Nevin 3B	Cal St.-Fullerton	2003	Rickie Weeks 2B	Southern
1993	Darren Dreifort P-DH	Wichita St.	2004	Jered Weaver P	Long Beach St.
1994	Jason Varitek C	Georgia Tech	2005	Alex Gordon 3B	Nebraska

Baseball America College Player of the Year

Year	Player Position	School	Year	Player Position	School
1981	Mike Sodders 3B	Arizona St.	1994	Jason Varitek C	Georgia Tech
1982	Jeff Ledbetter OF-P	Florida St.	1995	Todd Helton 1B-P	Tennessee
1983	Dave Magadan 1B	Alabama	1996	Kris Benson P	Clemson
1984	Oddibe McDowell OF	Arizona St.	1997	J.D. Drew OF	Florida
1985	Pete Incaviglia OF	Oklahoma St.	1998	Jeff Austin P	Stanford
1986	Casey Close OF	Michigan	1999	Jason Jennings DH-P	Baylor
1987	Robin Ventura 3B	Oklahoma St.	2000	Mark Teixeira 3B	Georgia Tech
1988	John Olerud 1B-P	Washington St.	2001	Mark Prior P	USC
1989	Ben McDonald P	Louisiana St.	2002	Khalil Greene SS	Clemson
1990	Mike Kelly OF	Arizona St.	2003	Richie Weeks 2B	Southern
1991	David McCarty 1B	Stanford	2004	Jered Weaver P	Long Beach St.
1992	Phil Nevin 3B	Cal St.-Fullerton	2005	Alex Gordon 3B	Nebraska
1993	Brooks Kieschnick DH-P	Texas			

LITTLE LEAGUE BASEBALL

Little League Baseball is a worldwide phenomenon these days, bringing in teams from almost every corner of the globe. But when Carl Stotz founded the organization in 1939, it started with three teams playing in a vacant lot in Williamsport, Pennsylvania.

Stotz' organization created what is now known as the Little League World Series in 1947; it was then called the National Little League Tournament. Even that name was a wild overstatement, as it was only in that year that the organization moved into a second state, New Jersey.

Today, Little League Baseball enrolls over three million young baseball players from more than one hundred countries into its programs, and its World Series draws the greatest teams of 11- and 12-year-olds on the planet to a state-of-the-art Williamsport facility. The title game of the Little League World Series now draws much higher television ratings nationally than any MLB Game of the Week.

It's important to note, however, that Little League is not the *only* major youth baseball organization in the United States, and that it is not even the most popular youth baseball organization in all age groups. Babe Ruth League baseball—founded in Hamilton Township, New Jersey in 1951—has over 800,000 players in the United States, primarily in the 13-to-15-year-old age group. American Legion Baseball is the most important youth baseball organization for 16- through 18-year-olds. Other important youth baseball organizations include Pony Baseball/Softball (which has about 400,000 players around the world), Dixie Youth Baseball (nearly 500,000 players in the southeastern United States), and Hap Dumont Baseball. MLB has sponsored its own very successful RBI program—Reviving Baseball in Inner Cities—for the past 17 years.

And there are also various youth baseball organizations, such as the American Athletic Union, the United States Specialty Sports Association, the National Amateur Baseball Federation, the American Amateur Baseball Congress, the Continental Amateur Baseball Association, and the United States Amateur Baseball Federation, which focus on organizing competition and tournaments among travel teams. These are becoming more popular in almost every participatory sport due to the higher rate of specialization among young athletes. Travel teams almost always require a far greater commitment and a higher level of talent from their participants than recreational leagues do. A few of these leagues, such as the NABF and AABC, also organize adult leagues and tournaments.

Little League World Series

Year	Winner	Runner-Up	Score (Inn.)
1947	Williamsport PA	Lock Haven PA	16-7
1948	Lock Haven PA	St. Petersburg FL	6-5
1949	Hammonton NJ	Pensacola FL	5-0
1950	Houston TX	Bridgeport CT	2-1
1951	Stamford CT	Austin TX	3-0

Year	Winner	Runner-Up	Score (Inn.)
1952	Norwalk CT	Monongahela PA	4-3
1953	Birmingham AL	Schenectady NY	1-0
1954	Schenectady NY	Colton CA	7-5
1955	Morrisville PA	Delaware Township NJ	4-3
1956	Roswell NM	Delaware Township NJ	3-1
1957	Monterrey, Mexico	La Mesa CA	4-0
1958	Monterrey, Mexico	Kankakee IL	10-1
1959	Hamtramck MI	Auburn CA	12-0
1960	Levittown PA	Fort Worth TX	5-0
1961	El Cajon CA	El Campo TX	4-2
1962	San Jose CA	Kankakee IL	3-0
1963	Granada Hills CA	Stratford CT	2-1
1964	Staten Island NY	Monterrey, Mexico	4-0
1965	Windsor Locks CT	Stoney Creek ON, Canada	3-1
1966	Houston TX	West New York NJ	8-2
1967	West Tokyo, Japan	Chicago IL	4-1
1968	Wakayama, Japan	Richmond VA	1-0
1969	Taiwan	Santa Clara CA	5-0
1970	Wayne NJ	Campbell CA	2-0
1971	Taiwan	Gary IN	12-3
1972	Taiwan	Hammond IN	6-0
1973	Taiwan	Tucson AZ	12-0
1974	Taiwan	Red Bluff CA	12-1
1975	Lakewood NJ	Tampa Bay FL	4-3
1976	Tokyo	Campbell CA	10-3
1977	Taiwan	El Cajon CA	7-2
1978	Taiwan	Danville CA	11-1
1979	Taiwan	Campbell CA	2-1
1980	Taiwan	Tampa Bay FL	4-3
1981	Taiwan	Tampa Bay FL	4-2
1982	Kirkland WA	Chai-Yi-Hsien, Taiwan	6-0
1983	Marietta GA	Barahona, D.R.	3-1
1984	Seoul, South Korea	Altamonte Springs FL	6-2
1985	Seoul, South Korea	Mexicali, Mexico	7-1
1986	Taiwan	Tucson AZ	12-0
1987	Taiwan	Irvine CA	21-1
1988	Taiwan	Pearl City HI	10-0
1989	Trumbull CT	Taiwan	5-2
1990	Taiwan	Shippensburg PA	9-0
1991	Taiwan	Danville CA	11-0
1992	Long Beach CA	Philippines	6-0 (forfeit)
1993	Long Beach CA	Panama	3-2
1994	Venezuela	Northridge CA	4-3
1995	Taiwan	Spring TX	17-3
1996	Taiwan	Cranston RI	13-3 (5)
1997	Guadalupe, Mexico	Mission Viejo CA	5-4
1998	Toms River NJ	Kashima, Japan	12-9
1999	Osaka, Japan	Phenix City AL	5-0
2000	Maracaibo, Venez.	Bellaire TX	3-2
2001	Tokyo Kitasuna	Apopka FL	2-1
2002	Louisville KY	Sendai, Japan	1-0
2003	Tokyo Musashi-Fuchu	Boynton Beach FL	10-1
2004	Willemstad, Curacao	Thousand Oaks CA	5-2
2005	Ewa Beach HI	Willemstad, Curacao	7-6

RBI

RBI–Reviving Baseball in Inner Cities–was the brainchil of John Young, a former major league player and scout. Youn had noticed a decrease in the number of skilled ballplayers com ing from inner-city neighborhoods as early as the late 1970s, an he decided to try to reverse that trend. After studying the issu Young realized that there was a significant drop in participatio around age 13, so he set out to establish a new comprehensiv youth baseball program for 13- to 16-year-olds in his old neigh borhood in South Central Los Angeles. Young's aims for th program were twofold: to develop the kids' baseball skills as we as to provide local youth with a constructive activity that woul challenge them and keep them safe. Young also worked to mak RBI a well-rounded program, instituting academic incentive and training participants for life as well as baseball.

The program proved to be extremely successful in attract ing participants and, with the support of Major Leagu Baseball, RBI quickly spread across the nation. By 1994, RB had spread to 28 American cities and, in the years since, ove 200 cities around the world have participated in the program Major League Baseball officially took over RBI administratio in 1991 and, in 1993, the first RBI World Series was held in S Louis. RBI expanded in the 1990s to include a Senior Divisio for older boys as well as a softball division for girls. In 1997 RBI merged with the youth baseball and softball programs c the Boys & Girls Clubs of America. There is no question tha RBI is a successful and worthwhile program for most of th 120,000 youngsters who have participated over the years. Mor than 150 RBI participants have been drafted by major leagu teams, including 3 in the first round. Unfortunately, the overal problem that John Young spotted over 25 years ago has defi nitely not been solved, and today there are even fewer players—

especially African-Americans—coming into professional baseball from inner-city communities.

RBI World Series Champions

Year	Host City (Team)	Boys Jr. Champion	Boys Sr. Champion	Girls Champion
1993	St. Louis (Cardinals)	Atlanta	Atlanta	
1994	Anaheim (Angels)	Puerto Rico	Puerto Rico	
1995	Philadelphia (Phillies)	Atlanta	Los Angeles	Newark
1996	Cleveland (Indians)	Puerto Rico	Puerto Rico	Puerto Rico
1997	Denver (Rockies)	Miami	Puerto Rico	St. Petersburg
1998	Kissimmee (Braves)	Puerto Rico	Atlanta	Denver
1999	Kissimmee (Braves)	Puerto Rico	Puerto Rico	Miami
2000	Kissimmee (Braves)	Los Angeles	Los Angeles	Los Angeles
2001	Kissimmee (Braves)	Los Angeles	Tampa	Atlanta
2002	Chicago (White Sox)	Atlanta	Los Angeles	Atlanta
2003	Houston (Astros)	Los Angeles	Los Angeles	Atlanta
2004	Detroit (Tigers)	Puerto Rico	Miami	Atlanta
2005	Pittsburgh (Pirates)	Los Angeles	Los Angeles	Atlanta

AMERICAN LEGION BASEBALL

American Legion Baseball is the oldest and largest baseball organization for older teenagers in the United States. Founded in 1925 by World War I veterans in an effort to give back to the community and provide a way for young people to stay in shape, over ten million teenagers have participated since. Today, over 100,000 players between the ages of 15 and 19 participate annually in Legion ball. Over 5,400 teams, spread over all 50 states and Puerto Rico, are sponsored by American Legion posts or non-profit outside sponsors. Fully 55 percent of big-league ballplayers, as well as 80 percent of college players, have seen action in American Legion ball, and 46 members of the Baseball Hall of Fame played on American Legion teams.

American Legion Baseball has long maintained strong ties with Major League Baseball. The winners of the American Legion World Series are honored each fall with a plaque from the Commissioner of Major League Baseball at the World Series The American Legion Player of the Year is honored each year with a plaque at the annual Baseball Hall of Fame induction ceremony in Cooperstown, New York. In the 1960s, MLB even briefly held a separate draft for American Legion ballplayers.

American Legion Baseball National Championship

Year	Winner (Post No.)	Runner-Up	Site
1926	Yonkers NY #321	Pocatello ID	Philadelphia PA
1927	[No national tournament held]		
1928	Oakland CA #5	Worcester MA	Chicago IL
1929	Buffalo NY #721	New Orleans LA	Louisville KY
1930	Baltimore MD #81	New Orleans LA #125	Memphis TN
1931	Chicago IL #493	Columbia SC #6	Houston TX
1932	New Orleans LA #132	Springfield MA #21	Manchester NH
1933	Chicago IL #467	Trenton NJ	New Orleans LA
1934	Cumberland MD #13	New Orleans LA	Chicago IL
1935	Gastonia NC #23	Sacramento CA #391	Gastonia NC
1936	Spartanburg SC #28	Los Angeles CA	Spartanburg SC
1937	East Lynn MA #291	New Orleans LA	New Orleans LA
1938	San Diego CA #6	Spartanburg SC #28	Spartanburg SC
1939	Omaha NE #1	Berwyn IL	Omaha NE
1940	Albermarle NC #76	San Diego CA #6	Albermarle NC
1941	San Diego CA #6	Berwyn IL	San Diego CA
1942	Los Angeles CA #357	Manchester NH	Manchester NH
1943	Richfield MN #435	Springfield OH	Miles City MT
1944	Cincinnati OH #50	Albermarle NC	Minneapolis MN
1945	Shelby NC #82	Trenton NJ	Charlotte NC
1946	New Orleans LA #125	Trenton NJ	Charleston SC
1947	Cincinnati OH #50	Little Rock AR #1	Los Angeles CA
1948	Trenton NJ #93	Jacksonville FL #9	Indianapolis IN
1949	Oakland CA #337	Cincinnati OH #507	Omaha NE
1950	Oakland CA #337	St. Louis MO #245	Omaha NE
1951	Los Angeles CA #716	White Plains NY #135	Detroit MI
1952	Cincinnati OH #50	San Diego CA #364	Denver CO
1953	Yakima WA #36	Winnetka IL #10	Miami FL
1954	San Diego CA #492	Gastonia NC #23	Yakima WA
1955	Cincinnati OH #216	Washington DC #31	St. Paul MN
1956	St. Louis MO #245	New Orleans LA #345	Bismarck ND
1957	Cincinnati OH #50	Portland OR #102	Billings MT
1958	Cincinnati OH #50	Everett MA #176	Colorado Springs CO
1959	Detroit MI #187	Hampton VA #48	Hastings NE
1960	New Orleans LA #125	Billings MT #4	Hastings NE
1961	Phoenix AZ #1	Cincinnati OH #554	Hastings NE
1962	St. Louis MO #299	Honolulu HI #11	Bismarck ND
1963	Long Beach CA #27	Memphis TN #1	Keene NH
1964	Upland CA #73	Charlotte NC #9	Little Rock AR
1965	Charlotte NC #9	Omaha NE #1	Aberdeen SD
1966	Oakland CA #337	Tuscaloosa AL #34	Orangeburg SC
1967	Tuscaloosa CA #34	Northbrook IL #791	Memphis TN
1968	Memphis TN #1	Klamath Falls OR #8	Manchester NH

Year	Winner (Post No.)	Runner-Up	Site
1969	Portland OR #105	Towson MD #22	Hastings NE
1970	West Covina CA #790	Levittown PA	Klamath Falls OH
1971	West Covina CA #790	Cedar Rapids IA #5	Tucson AZ
1972	Ballwin MO #611	Memphis TN #1	Memphis TN
1973	Rio Piedras PR #146	Memphis TN #1	Lewiston ID
1974	Rio Piedras PR #146	Lake Oswego OR #92	Roseburg OR
1975	Yakima WA #36	Cedar Rapids IA #5	Rapid City SD
1976	Santa Monica CA #123	Des Plaines IL #36	Manchester NH
1977	South Bend IN #50	Hattiesburg MS #78	Manchester NH
1978	Hialeah FL #32	E. Springfield MA	Yakima WA
1979	Yakima WA #36	Barrington RI #8	Greenville MS
1980	Honolulu HI*	Boyertown PA #471	Ely MN
1981	West Tampa FL #248	Richmond VA #361	Sumter SC
1982	Boyertown PA #471	Lafayette CA #517	Boyertown PA
1983	Edina MN #471	Boyertown PA #471	Fargo ND
1984	Guaynabo PR #134	Brooklawn NJ #72	New Orleans LA
1985	Midlothian VA #186	Sacramento CA*	Kokomo IN
1986	Jensen Beach FL #126	Las Vegas NV #8	Rapid City SD
1987	Boyertown PA #471	Vancouver WA #176	Stevens Point WI
1988	Cincinnati OH #507	Boyertown PA #471	Middletown CT
1989	Woodland Hills CA #826	Rio Piedras PR #134	Millington TN
1990	Mayo MD #226	Bayamon PR #148	Corvallis OR
1991	Brooklawn NJ #72	Newark OH #85	Boyertown PA
1992	Newbury Park CA*	Arlington Heights #208	Fargo ND
1993	Rapid City SD #22	Las Vegas NV #8	Roseburg OR
1994	Miami FL #346	Chino CA #299	Boyertown PA
1995	Aiea HI*	Bellevue WA*	Fargo ND
1996	Yardley PA #317	Gonzalez LA #81	Roseburg OR
1997	Sanford FL #53	Medford OR #15	Rapid City SD
1998	Edwardsville IL #199	Cherryville NC #100	Las Vegas NV
1999	New Brighton MN #513	Kennewick WA #34	Middletown CT
2000	Danville CA #246	Paducah KY #17	Alton IL
2001	Brooklawn NJ #72	Lewiston ID #13	Yakima WA
2002	West Point MS #212	Excelsior MN #259	Danville VA
2003	Rochester MN #92	Cherryville NC #100	Bartlesville OK
2004	Portland ME*	Kennewick WA #32	Corvallis OR
2005	Enid OK #4	Twin Cities WA #34	Rapid City SD

* outside sponsorship

George W. Rulon American Legion Player Of The Year

Year	Winner Position	City
1949	Ray Herrara SS	Oakland CA
1950	J. W. Porter C	Oakland CA
1951	Grover Jones Jr. C	White Plains NY
1952	Russell Nixon C	Cincinnati OH
1953	Charles Lindstrom P	Winnetka IL
1954	Billy Capps 3B	San Diego CA
1955	Frank Birri 3B	Cincinnati OH
1956	Jim Harwell P	New Orleans LA
1957	Fred Fox 3B	Cincinnati OH
1958	Kiebler James P-SS	Greenwood SC
1959	Fred Bowen SS	Detroit MI
1960	Richard R. Roniger P	New Orleans LA
1961	James J. Gerber SS	Cincinnati OH
1962	William D. Matan Jr. C	St. Louis MO
1963	Richard Allen Dash 2B	Long Beach CA
1964	Roland G. Fingers P-OF	Upland CA
1965	Kenneth J. Fila P	Omaha NE
1966	William C. Parker Jr. OF	Tuscaloosa AL
1967	Ray Lynn Larson C	Northbrook IL
1968	Donald Hardy Castle P-OF	Memphis TN
1969	John David Adeimy SS	West Palm Beach FL
1970	Carroll Wayne Watts SS	Tulsa OK
1971	Randolph Gregory Haas OF	West Covina CA
1972	Michael Charles Murphy P-OF	Ballwin MO
1973	Thomas Steven Ashford SS	Memphis TN
1974	Edwin C. Lopez OF	Rio Piedras PR
1975	David Delmar Edler P-OF	Yakima WA
1976	Gustavo Martin Malespin OF	Metairie LA
1977	William Floyd Schell SS	South Bend IN
1978	Ross Jones 1B	Hialeah FL
1979	Patrick Scott Allen 2B	Yakima WA
1980	Tomas Gil OF	Hialeah FL
1981	David Joseph Magadan 3B-P	West Tampa FL
1982	Ivan S. Snyder OF-P	Boyertown PA
1983	Michael Holloran C	Edina MN
1984	Jorge Robles SS	Guaynabo PR
1985	Tris Lipscomb P-2B	Midlothian VA
1986	Joe Grahe P	Jensen Beach FL
1987	Wilbur Stout C	Boyertown PA
1988	Mike Kessler 1B-P	Cincinnati OH
1989	Del Marine C	Woodland Hills CA
1990	Mark Foster P-OF	Mayo MD
1991	Ryan Beeney SS	Newark OH
1992	David Lamb SS	Newbury Park CA
1993	Ben Thomas 1B-P	Rapid City SD
1994	Fernando Rodriguez P	Miami FL
1995	Jason Adaro P-C-OF	Aiea HI
1996	Christian Bourgeois 1B	Gonzales LA
1997	Nate Philo OF	Medford OR
1998	Chad Opel SS	Edwardsville IL
1999	Jeremy S. Roberts OF	Rison AR
2000	Josh Zender P	Deming WA
2001	Jay Threet P-1B	Adrian MI
2002	Ty Henkaline P	Sidney OH
2003	Jared Willis 2-B	Logan WV
2004	Nolan Gallagher P	Red Lodge MT
2005	Fernando Irizarry	Montero PR

At Bats: The definition of at bat has varied over the years, primarily due to the changing definitions of events that constitute plate appearances that are not at bats, such as sacrifice hits and sacrifice flies.

Average Value: Virtually every analytical statistic in this encyclopedia uses league average as a baseline. The use of this baseline, which is set to equal either 0 or 100, depending on the statistic, makes the quality of a player's performance—whether a player is above average, average, or below average—immediately obvious most of the time. Above-average players are needed to win pennants. Average and below-average players who are better than a typical replacement make only minor contributions toward a winning season.

Average is not the only reasonable baseline, of course—there is no "right" baseline, though there are more useful and less useful baselines. Some analysts use "replacement level" as their baseline. That baseline is hard to define, but there are circumstances where it may be more useful than the average baseline. Different tasks require different tools and, thus, different baselines. The primary advantage of an average baseline is that it clearly shows how the performance of players translates into wins and losses on the field. All teams start the season 0–0; only better-than-average players enable a team to rise above .500.

Bases on Balls: Permanently established at the count of 4 balls in 1889. The number had come down one at a time since 1874, when 9 balls were required to reach first base.

Basestealing Runs: The formula for calculating BSR is $(.22*SB) - (.38*CS)$. SB stands for stolen bases, CS is for caught stealing, and * signifies multiplication.

Basestealing Wins: Divide basestealing runs by runs per win, which in this case equals 10 times the square root of runs per inning.

Batter-Fielder Wins: The sum of a player's batting wins, basestealing wins, and fielding wins.

Batting Runs: The formula for calculating batting runs is $.33*(BB+HBP)$ plus $.47*H$ plus $.38*2B$ plus $.55*3B$ plus $.93*HR–ABF*(AB-H)$.

ABF, known as the league batting factor, makes the value of an average batter equal 0. ABF is computed with the following formula (all statistics in the equation are league statistics):

$$\frac{.33*(BB+HBP) + .47*H + .38*2B + .55*3B + .93*HR}{(AB - LGF*H)}.$$

LGF, the league factor, adjusts for the quality of league play, and equals 1 except for the Union Association (1884), for which it equals 0.8, and the Federal League (1914–15), for which it equals 0.9.

Adjusted batting runs, which appear in the batting register, are calculated with the following formula: (BR – (batters' park factor – 1)*RPA*PA/batters' park factor). RPA is the number of runs per plate appearance in the league.

Batting Wins: This is calculated by dividing adjusted batting runs by runs per win. In this case, runs per win equals 10 times the square root of (runs per inning + player adjusted batting runs/games/9).

Blown Saves: Save opportunities not converted because the relief pitcher allowed the tying or go-ahead run to score. Only calculated since 1969.

Caught Stealing: The data is available for 1914, 1915, and from 1920 onward for the AL; and for 1913, 1915, 1920–1925, and from 1951 onward in the NL. Caught Stealing totals are also available for 1916 for all players who stole at least 20 bases.

Differential: This measures the difference between the won-lost record a team was *projected* to achieve (based on its batting, pitching, fielding, and basestealing), and the record that the team *actually* attained. If a team was projected to finish 89–73 (that is, +8) but actually concluded the season at 85–77 (that is, +4), the team's differential would be –4.

Earned Run Average: The number of earned runs allowed per 9 innings pitched. It is calculated by multiplying earned runs by 9 and dividing by innings pitched. Adjusted ERA is calculated by dividing league ERA by the pitcher (or team) ERA and then multiplying by the pitchers' park factor. Note that a small number of runs can be earned runs for the pitcher but unearned runs for the team.

ERA has been kept officially since 1912 in the NL and 1913 in the AL. Before then, Information Concepts Inc. researchers calculated earned runs from game accounts. Some earned run data include estimates, although in every case, at least half the earned runs for a team were known from game accounts. This was for 1881–86 (all leagues) and 1887 and 1890 in the American Association. Earned run data in box scores and the official guides in the nineteenth century were not used. Bases on balls were usually considered errors in those years and, in fact, the fielding stats often gave pitchers assists on strikeouts and errors on walks. Such assists and errors have been removed from the fielding averages in this book.

Fielding Runs: Fielding runs are based on the player's fielding statistics at each position compared to the league average for the number of innings played. The number of innings played was obtained from play-by-play data for 1969 onward. For most years before 1969, innings are estimated from defensive and offensive data for all players on the team. Comparing the formulas for estimated defensive innings to actual defensive innings taken from 1969–2003 play-by-play data showed an average difference of 12 for infielders and 19 for outfielders for players with 1,000 or more innings.

The basic formula is:

PFR/(PO–SO for team)–LFR/(PO–SO for league)*Player Innings.

PFR is the player fielding rate, while LFR is the league fielding rate.

The ratings used as fielding rates vary by position as follows

1B	$.2*(2*A – E)$
P, 2B, SS, 3B	$.2*(PO + 2*A – E + DP)$
OF	$.2*(PO + 4*A – E + DP)$
C	$.2*(PO – SO + .4*(A – CS) – E + DP + PB/2)$

A stands for assists, PO for putouts, E for errors, SO for strikeouts, DP is for double plays, and PB for passed balls. Strikeouts are subtracted because a team that strikes out a lot of batters will have many fewer chances to create outs from balls put into play. When calculating a pitchers' fielding, his actual strikeout total is used; for other fielders, the team average strikeout total is used.

Two more factors are used to adjust for the amount of left-handed and right-handed pitching on a team and for the number of double play opportunities. Teams with more left-handed pitching tend to face more right-handed batters as a result of platooning, and this effect in turn alters the distribution of balls hit into play. A careful historical study of this factor showed that its effect was non-existent before 1910, then slowly grew until 1970, when it hit a similar level to today.

Right-handed batters shift the distribution of ground balls over from the right side of the infield to the left side while shifting flyballs and popups from the left side of the field to the right side. Second basemen also gain more putouts with a right-handed hitter at the plate since they are more likely to be covering second base.

To adjust the number of expected league average putouts and assists for each player, the relevant statistic is multiplied by this equation:

$$(1 + ADJ*YF*DLHP).$$

ADJ is the adjustment figure appropriate for the position (1B, 2B, 3B, SS, LF, or RF) and statistic (putouts or assists). The chart below supplies the appropriate figure.

ADJ	PO	A
1B	n/a	−.40
2B	.23	−.27
SS	−.10	.14
3B	−.22	.34
LF	−.16	n/a
RF	.09	n/a

YF is the year factor, necessary because this factor steadily increased in importance from 1910 to 1970. Before 1910 the YF is 0, so no adjustment is necessary. The adjustment can be calculated for each year from 1910 through 1970 by subtracting 1910 from the year in question and then dividing by 60. After 1970 the YF is always 1.

DLHP is the difference in the percentage of left-handed pitching from the league average.

So if a second baseman was on a team with 10 percent more innings by left-handed pitchers than average in 1960, his adjustment is:

Assists = (1 − .27 x (1960-1910)/60 x .10) = .9775
Putouts = (1 + .23 x (1960-1910)/60 x .10) = 1.0192.

If the league average second baseman in 1960 finished the season with 400 assists and 200 putouts, the expected league average would be adjusted to 391 and 204.

Pitchers have a further correction, since left-handed pitchers have fewer putouts as a result of facing fewer left-handed batters. Up until 1910 left- and right-handed pitcher putouts were about equal, declining to about 62 percent for left-handers in 1970 before leveling off. Thus, a separate expected putout rate is calculated for each type of pitcher based on the year and the number of left-handed innings.

Double play opportunities were estimated from hits, bases on balls, hit-by-pitches, and home runs allowed, plus errors committed. (On average, 57.5 percent of errors result in a runner reaching base; the other errors just allow existing baserunners to take extra bases.) Using a multiplier for homers to account for double play opportunities lost did not improve the estimate in years where there are actual data; the average error in these years was around 2 percent. The formula for calculating double play opportunities is:

.662*(H − HR + BB + HB + .575*E).

Individual double plays were divided by the team double play opportunities divided by the league average double play opportunities.

For catchers, there is an additional defensive calculation made to rate them on other defensive aspects. The formula for that calculation is:

(−.22*SB) + (CSF*CS) + .1*APR*IP/TIP.

APR is the catcher's team's adjusted pitching runs; IP is the catcher's innings pitched to; TIP is team innings pitched; and CSF is the caught stealing factor that ensures that the average value of a catcher defensively stays at 0. The formula to calculate CSF is:

22*(LSB − TSB) divided by (LCS − TCS).

Also, since artificial turf results in about a 5 percent higher stolen base success rate, a small adjustment is made to the results of players and teams from the turf era. The size of the adjustment depends on the exact split of games between ballparks with turf in the basepaths and those with dirt basepaths. Most ballparks with turf fields have turf basepaths with dirt only in the sliding cutouts around the bases. However, a few ballparks, especially in the early years of artificial turf, have had all-dirt basepaths with turf fields.

Fielding Wins: Divide fielding runs by runs per win, which in this case equals 10 times the square root of runs per inning.

Games Behind: This is the number of games one team is behind another team in the standing, almost always measured from first place. If a team's record stands at 78–71 and the first-place team's record is 82–68, then the former team is 3½ games behind the first-place team.

Grounded into Double Play: This became an official statistic in 1933 in the NL and in 1939 in the AL.

Hit-by-Pitch: The rule awarding first base to batters hit by a pitch was instituted in 1884 by the American Association and in 1887 by the National League.

Innings Pitched: Fractions of innings pitched in a season have only been officially counted since 1982. Prior to that, both leagues rounded off fractional innings. This encyclopedia has full innings pitched (i.e., not rounded off) for all major league seasons.

Normalizing: Baseball statistics tell us very little without context. A .450 slugging average in Dodger Stadium in 1965 means something very different than a .450 slugging average in Coors Field in 2003—the former is an impressive performance while the latter is sub-par. Many of the statistics in this encyclopedia are normalized using league average as a baseline, enabling readers to see whether a player is better than or worse than his average peer as well as to what extent he is better or worse. By putting different seasons played in different circumstances on the same scale, normalization makes it much easier to compare seasons. Some statistics in this encyclopedia are further normalized to account for the home parks of players since some ballparks are far more conducive to scoring than others. As a result, both the ease of producing a run and the value of a run can vary significantly from ballpark to ballpark, even in the same season. Normalizing a statistic for ballpark effects ensures that players can be compared on a level playing field.

On-Base Percentage: Declared an official statistic in 1984, OBP is defined as (hits plus bases on balls plus hit-by-pitches) divided by (at bats plus bases on balls plus hit-by-pitches plus sacrifice flies). This encyclopedia uses the current definition back to 1954, when sacrifice fly data became permanently available. Previous to 1954, sacrifice flies were either counted as outs or were included with sacrifice hits (1908–30 and 1939) and, therefore, cannot be used.

On-Base plus Slugging: Often referred to as OPS, this statistic, which was introduced by Pete Palmer and John Thorn in *The Hidden Game of Baseball* in 1984, has exploded in popularity the past few years. This encyclopedia does not feature a separate column for the basic version of OPS in the batter register since it is very easy to calculate—simply adds on-base percentage and slugging average—and the two columns are adjacent. Adjusted OPS (which has its own column) then normalizes OPS for the league and the player's home park(s), then converts it to a scale in which 100 is league average. The exact calculation is ((player OBP/league OBP) plus (player slugging/league slugging) − 1) divided by batters' park factor. When calculating adjusted OPS for non-pitchers, league average statistics do not include pitcher batting. For consistency in historical comparisons, the definition of on-base percentage used in adjusted OPS does not use sacrifice flies in the denominator.

Opponents' Batting Average: Figures are based on estimated at bats from 1901–07 in the AL; from 1889–1902 in the NL; in 1882–83 and 1888–91 in the American Association; in 1884 in the Union Association; and in 1890 in the Player's League.

Opponents' Caught Stealing: Exact totals for 1969 to the present came from play-by-play records. Estimated totals for catchers came from team totals found in league records from 1920–68 for the AL and from 1920–25 and from 1951–68 for the NL. For most other years since 1890, team totals were estimated from other team data and catcher totals were estimated from the team estimates. Some years from 1912–19 have only runner caught stealing data, some have team caught stealing, and some have individual catcher caught stealing.

Opponents' On-Base Percentage: Based on the official definition of OBP since 1954. The definition used in previous years depends on the available data (as with the OBP definition above).

Opponents' Stolen Bases: Exact totals for 1969 to the present came from play-by-play records. Estimated totals for catchers came from team totals found in league records for 1890–1968 (except for the 1890 NL data, which came from box scores).

Park Factor: This measure of how the team's home park affects hitters and pitchers is used to adjust the team's performance in a way that takes into account the context of the team's home park. Separate park factors are used for batting and pitching in order to adjust for the fact that pitchers and hitters never get to face their own teammates.

Pitching Runs: This measure of how many runs a pitcher prevented compared to the average pitcher is calculated with this formula:

$$LERA * IP/9 - ER + URF.$$

LERA is the league ERA and ER stands for earned runs. URF is the unearned run factor that accounts for the unearned runs the pitcher is responsible for and is calculated by multiplying (0.5) times (ER – R*TER/TR).

Adjusted pitching runs is calculated the same as pitching runs above, except that LERA* PPF is used instead of plain LERA—that is, the league ERA is multiplied by the pitcher park factor. Then the result of the entire calculation is divided by the pitcher park factor. Thus the formula is (PPF*LERA*IP/9 – ER + URF)/PPF.

Pitcher Batting: This measure of a pitcher's offensive performance is calculated the same way as adjusted batting runs; the difference is that a pitcher is compared to the average-hitting pitcher, not the average hitter. If a pitcher spent time at other defensive positions, his offense will be divided proportionately based on how much he played each position; only the appropriate fraction will count for pitcher batting.

Pitcher Wins: The total number of wins a pitcher is worth to his team compared to the average pitcher (including pitching, fielding, batting, and basestealing). It is calculated by multiplying adjusted pitcher runs by XMULR (see below), adding the pitcher's non-pitching contributions, and then dividing by runs per win.

In order to properly credit relief pitchers for the extra or lesser value of their innings pitched, a factor is used when converting adjusted pitching runs to pitching wins. The formula for that multiplier (XMULR) is:

$$9*(W + L + SV/XSV)/IP.$$

XSV is calculated by dividing league saves by league wins and multiplying by 10. XSV cannot be less than 4, so any result lower than 4 is set at 4. The multiplier cannot not be less than 0.5 or more than 2, so any result not in that range is considered to be either 0.5 or 2, depending on whether it was above or below the range.

Pitching Wins: The wins a pitcher achieves by his pitching is calculated by dividing adjusted pitching runs by runs per win. In this case, the formula for runs per win is 10 times the square root of (RPI – APR/G/9). Thus, if a pitcher reduces the number of runs scored by the opponent in his games, the value of each run is increased by a reduction in the runs per win figure. Pitchers, especially starting pitchers, have a much stronger effect on runs per win because their effect on scoring is spread out over fewer games.

Positional Adjustment: Baseball fans know not to expect a shortstop to hit like a first baseman, exceptions like Alex Rodriguez notwithstanding. Second basemen who slug .370 can usually hold on to their starting spot, but first basemen who slug .370 are likely to be benched or dropped off the roster. That's because it's fairly easy to find an acceptable defensive first baseman that can hit with power, while players who can handle second base defensively and hit with power are usually scarce. In order to account for the ability of players to handle the most valuable positions defensively, the offense of these players is compared to their peers at the same position. This approach accounts for the differing value major league teams place on fielding ability at each position and also makes it simple to adjust for the changing demands of a position. For example, higher defensive expectations for third basemen a century ago made it significantly harder to find a third baseman with a good bat back then than today. Whether that was because teams demanded a higher level of defense from third basemen then, or because there are more good defensive third basemen these days who can hit is irrelevant. We don't have to know the answer to that question to account for the decreasing scarcity of good-hitting third basemen by using a smaller positional adjustment.

POWR (Player Overall Win Rating): POWR, featured in the All-Time Leaders section, adds the batting wins, fielding wins, basestealing wins, and pitching wins of every player to rate his overall value compared to an average player.

Range: This category is calculated different ways for different positions. For infielders, range is based on assists per inning. For outfielders, range is based on putouts per inning. For catchers, the statistic in the range column is based on stolen bases allowed per inning. Outfielders are rated for their (weighted) play at all outfield positions, while infielders are only rated for their play at their primary position. The data is then adjusted in comparison to the league average, with 100 equaling league average. *Higher is always better.* All statistics are adjusted for context, including the number of balls put into play and the distribution of balls in play. The adjustments for each statistic are detailed in the fielding runs entry. Innings played data are calculated from play-by-play accounts from 1969 onward; it is estimated prior to 1969.

Relative Batting Average: A normalized translation of batting average. The formula is player average divided by league average.

Runs Batted In: RBIs have been recognized as an official statistic since 1920. Runs driven in by a force double play were no longer counted as RBIs after 1938.

Relief Ranking: Generated by multiplying the XMULR factor (described in the pitcher wins entry) by adjusted pitcher runs. Since innings pitched in relief is not historically available, relief pitchers are classified as those pitchers who average less than 3 innings per appearance.

Run Support: Basic run support is calculated by adding up all the runs scored in a pitcher's starts and then dividing that total by his games started. The support figures presented in the pitcher register have been normalized for the context of the offensive level of the league and the player's home park(s), then converted to a scale in which 100 is league average. A run support figure of 90 would indicate that pitcher had 10 percent less runs scored in his starts than average; a figure of 110 would indicated 10 percent above-average. The formula to produce the adjusted run support is (pitcher run support) divided by (league average run support) divided by (batters' park factor) times 100.

Run support stats have been published widely since 1990, usually counting all appearances for a pitcher and normalizing the runs scored by his team while he was in the game to 9 innings pitched. While this stat is useful, it is not calculable pre-1969.

Furthermore, it is not a substitute for calculating run support for starting pitchers, since runs scored after a pitcher leaves the game materially affect a pitcher's record. If a starter leaves the game in the seventh inning with his team trailing 5–1, then his team scores 6 times in the eighth to take the lead, he avoids being tagged with the loss and clearly benefits from runs scored after he had left the game.

Runs Per Win: The number of runs needed, on average, to gain an additional win in the standings. Historically, about 10 runs have equaled a win. The value of runs per win is used in several entries in this glossary to translate runs into wins. Individual players, especially starting pitchers, can have a significant effect on the number of runs that it takes to achieve a win in their own games, so the runs per win calculation often takes into account the performance level of the individual or team being evaluated.

Sacrifice Fly: First recognized as a distinct statistical category in 1954. Previous to 1975, only fair fly balls which drove in runners were counted in this category. From 1908–1930 and again in 1939, sacrifice flies were counted as sacrifice hits. In all other seasons before 1954, sacrifice flies are indistinguishable from other at bats.

Save: Recognized as an official statistic in 1969, saves were at first awarded to any relief pitcher that finished pitching a victory and was not credited with the win. In 1973 requirements were significantly tightened so that saves were only awarded if the pitcher either entered the game with the potential tying run on base or at the plate or pitched at least 3 effective innings while preserving the lead. In 1975 the rule was set to where it stands today: In order to earn a save, a reliever must finish off a victory without ever giving up the lead after entering the game with a lead of no more than 3 runs and pitching at least an inning, or he can earn a save by finishing a victory without giving up the lead after entering the game with the tying run on base, at the plate, or on deck. Saves may also be earned by pitching effectively for at least the last 3 innings of a victory, without getting credit for the win. The original 1969 rule has been used in awarding saves prior to 1969.

Save Opportunities and Save Percentage: Save Opportunities are defined as Saves plus Blown Saves—a narrow definition that makes Save Percentage useful only when comparing closers to each other. Save Percentage is calculated by dividing Saves by Save Opportunities. Blown Saves are defined by Rolaids, which has given the Rolaids Relief Man Award annually since 1976. By virtue of the prestige that this award has accrued, Rolaids effectively controls the definition of the Blown Save since it is not an official statistic.

Though setup pitchers and middle relievers get charged with Blown Saves when they blow a lead in a save situation, they don't get many saves because they are almost always replaced by their team's closer before the game ends. The effect, therefore, is that setup and middle relievers rarely show a high Save Percentage: they get nicked for the negative stat when they fail to protect a lead, but they rarely get a chance to earn the positive stat when they protect a lead.

The unofficial "Hold" statistic that gained currency in the 1990s was an attempt to address that gap. Unfortunately, neither of the two versions of the "Hold" stat solve the problem. The earlier version doesn't even require a relief pitcher to retire a hitter to get credit for a "Hold"—if a reliever comes into the game with a 1-run lead and no one on base, then walks the bases loaded before being yanked, he can get a "Hold" despite his miserable performance. The later version of the "Hold," promulgated by Stats, Inc., and still used today, requires a relief pitcher to pitch at least ⅓ of an inning to gain a "Hold." Better. That's better, but still not nearly good enough.

The reason that the "Hold" doesn't work as a fair evaluation of middle and setup relievers is that it requires a pitcher to enter the game in a save situation before he can earn a "Hold." Yet the role of middle and setup relief necessarily involves entering many games in which the score is tied or their team is down by 1–2 runs. Sure, they have the opportunity to earn a Win in those situations. However, if they pitch a scoreless inning or two and leave with the game still tied or their club behind, they earn *nada*. All of which means that a meaningful measure to evaluate the performance of middle and setup relievers has yet to be devised.

Stolen Bases: Stolen bases were always a part of the game, but they were not officially tabulated from 1876–85. This statistic is available for all seasons in all leagues from 1886 onward. National Association stolen bases were obtained from box scores, which did not always report them, so 1871–75 data is incomplete.

The exact scoring definition of a stolen base was changed repeatedly before 1955, when most of the current rules regarding stolen bases were put into place. Before 1898, stolen bases were sometimes awarded for taking extra bases on hits and outs, so the data in this earlier period is not strictly comparable to later data.

Strikeouts: Available for batters in all years except for the 1882–88 and 1890 American Association, the 1884 Union Association, from 1897–1909 in the NL, and from 1901–12 in the AL. There is no missing data for pitchers' strikeouts. As in the case of bases on balls and stolen bases, there were some very different rules governing strikeouts in the nineteenth century, making comparisons across time rather tricky.

Throwing: This new category is calculated in different ways for different positions. For infielders, the throwing column shows their double plays per inning. For outfielders, throwing is based on assists per inning. For catchers, throwing is based on caught stealing rates per inning. The data is then adjusted in comparison to league average, with 100 equaling league average. All statistics are adjusted for context by various methods; the adjustments for each statistic are detailed in the fielding runs entry. Innings played data was calculated from play-by-play accounts from 1969 to the present; it is estimated for previous seasons. Outfielders are rated for their play at all outfield positions, while infielders are only rated for their play at their primary position.